Gary Pratico, Th.D.
Gordon-Conwell Theological Seminary

Richard L. Pratt, Jr., Th.D.
Reformed Theological Seminary

Elmer Smick, Ph.D. (deceased)
Reformed Theological Seminary

Marion Ann Taylor, Ph.D.
Wycliffe College

Willem A. VanGemeren, Ph.D.
Trinity Evangelical Divinity School

J. Robert Vannoy, Th.D.
Biblical Theological Seminary

Bruce Waltke, Th.D., Ph.D.
Regent College

Barry Webb, Ph.D.
Moore Theological College

Gordon Wenham, Ph.D.
Cheltenham and Gloucester College of Higher Education

John Woodhouse, Ph.D.
Moore Theological College

New Testament Contributors

Knox Chamblin, Th.D.
Reformed Theological Seminary

Karl J. Cooper, Th.M.
Providence, RI

Sinclair B. Ferguson, Ph.D.
Westminster Theological Seminary

T. David Gordon, Ph.D.
Gordon-Conwell Theological Seminary

Wayne Grudem, Ph.D.
Trinity Evangelical Divinity School

Charles Hill, Ph.D.
Reformed Theological Seminary

Kenneth J. Howell, Ph.D.
Reformed Theological Seminary

Dennis Ireland, Ph.D.
Reformed Theological Seminary

Dennis Johnson, Ph.D.
Westminster Theological Seminary in California

Peter Jones, Ph.D.
Westminster Theological Seminary in California

Reggie M. Kidd, Ph.D.
Reformed Theological Seminary

Simon J. Kistemaker, Th.D.
Reformed Theological Seminary

W. Harold Mare, Ph.D.
Covenant Theological Seminary

Dan McCartney, Ph.D.
Westminster Theological Seminary

Leon Morris, Ph.D. (emeritus)
Ridley College

Vern S. Poythress, D.Th.
Westminster Theological Seminary

Moisés Silva, Ph.D.
Westminster Theological Seminary

R. C. Sproul, Drs.
Ligonier Ministries

Frank Thielman, Ph.D.
The Beeson Divinity School

Joseph Trafton, Ph.D.
Western Kentucky University

Explanation of
Features
Included in this Edition

The Reformation Study Bible includes a number of valuable features to encourage the reading and study of the Bible. A brief description is provided below explaining the purpose and use of *The Reformation Study Bible* features.

CENTER-COLUMN CROSS-REFERENCE SYSTEM

The Reformation Study Bible includes one of the the most extensive and useful cross-reference systems available. The English Standard Version cross-reference system is based on a comprehensive system developed more than a hundred years ago by a team of Bible scholars from Oxford and Cambridge Universities. As far as possible this system also included the cross-references used in the original King James Version of 1611. The resulting cross-reference system was first used in the English Revised Version (RV) and his been highly regarded around the world for its effectiveness in showing the internal interrelationship of the text thorughout the Bible.

The cross-reference system as it appears in the ESV Classic Reference Edition has been adapted as needed from the RV system for use with the ESV text. In some cases, therefore, the specific wording of the reference passage may differ, although the underlying meaning and relationship to the referenced text is normally the same.

Because the ESV is an essentially literal, word-for-word translation, the ESV is especially suited for cross-reference study of key words and concepts throughout the Bible.

Using the ESV Cross-Reference System

An *alphabetical* superscript, *preceding* a word or phrase, is used to indicate each word or phrase that is cross-referenced. *Numerical* superscripts, however, which *follow* words or phrases, refer to footnotes at the bottom of the page. See, for example, the word "[p]sound[7]" in Titus 2:1, where the letter superscript "p" preceding the word refers to the cross-reference, while the number superscript "7" refers to the footnote at the bottom of the page.

Types of Cross-References

The ESV cross-reference system includes several types of cross-references, as illustrated here from Romans 3:3-4. These include:

(1) *References to Specific Word or Phrases.* References to *words and phrases* within the same chapter appear as, e.g., "ver. 7"; within the same book, as, e.g., "ch. 9:6"; in other books of the Bible, as, e.g., "Heb. 4:2."

(2) *Comparative References.* These references direct the reader to passages with the *same theme* and are indicated by square brackets, e.g., "[ch. 9:6; 2 Tim. 2:13]." In this example the theme of God's faithfulness as found in Romans 3:3 is cross-referenced with the same theme found later in Romans 9:6 and in 2 Timothy 2:13.

Romans 3:3-4

3 [z]ch. 10:16 Heb. 4:2 [a][ch. 9:6; 2 Tim. 2:13]
4 [b]see Jn. 8:26 [c]Ps. 62:9; 116:11 [ver. 7] [d]Cited from Ps. 51:4 (Gk.) [e][Job 9:32]

3 [z]What if some were unfaithful? [a]Does their faithlessness nullify the faithfulness of God? **4** By no means! [b]Let God be true though [c]every one were a liar, as it is written,

[d]"That you may be justified in your words,
and prevail when you are judged."

(3) *Less Direct References.* These references generally provide additional information or insight about a specific theme and are introduced with the word "See," e.g., "See Jn. 8:26." In this example the reader is directed to John 8:26, where God is presented as a trustworthy judge, thereby illustrating the theme of God's faithfulness as taught in Romans 3:4.

(4) *Quoted References.* These references indicate the source for verses or phrases quoted from other places in the Bible, e.g., "Cited from Ps. 51:4." (In this example the reference includes the abbreviation

THE REFORMATION STUDY BIBLE

R. C. SPROUL
GENERAL EDITOR

KEITH MATHISON
ASSOCIATE EDITOR

ENGLISH STANDARD VERSION

CONTAINING THE
OLD AND NEW TESTAMENTS

LIGONIER MINISTRIES
ORLANDO FLORIDA

Published by: Ligonier Ministries
400 Technology Park
Lake Mary, FL 32746
USA

Produced and
distributed by: Presbyterian and Reformed Publishing Company
P.O. Box 817
Phillipsburg, NJ 08865
USA

ISBN: 0-87552-643-8 (hardcover edition)
0-87552-786-8 (leather edition: black)
0-87552-787-6 (leather edition: burgundy)

Acknowledgments: "Providence": quotation from L. Berkhof, *Systematic Theology*, 2d rev. ed. (Grand Rapids: Wm. B. Eerdmans Publishing Co., 1941), p. 168. "One and Three: The Trinity": quotation from Benjamin Breckinridge Warfield, *Biblical and Theological Studies*, edited by Samuel G. Craig (Philadelphia: Presbyterian and Reformed Publishing Company, 1968), p. 36.

Library of Congress Catalog Control Number: 2004112397

Printed in the United States of America.

Table of Contents

The Old Testament

The New Testament

Introduction

The Reformation Study Bible

R. C. Sproul

The Bible is a *book*. It may be called a collection of books compiled together into one majestic volume. As a book it is designed to be read. In this respect it is like all other books. But the Bible is not like any other book. It is the Book of Books. We customarily call this book the *Holy* Bible. Its holiness is found in its "otherness." It is a sacred book because it transcends and stands apart from, above, every other book. It is holy because its ultimate Author is holy. It is holy because its message is holy. It is holy because its content is designed to make us holy.

The Bible is an *inspired* book, that is, "breathed out" by God. Inspiration reaches far beyond the scope of the inspiration of human artists as commonly understood. The Bible offers more than brilliant insight, more than human sagacity. It is called "inspired" not because of its supernatural mode of *transmission* via human authors, but because of its *origin*. It is not merely a book *about* God; it is a book *from* God. Therefore the church confesses its trust and confidence that the Bible is the *vox Dei*, the veritable "voice of God."

The Bible is a *normative* book. The church has declared that the Bible is the "Norm of norms, and without norm." A norm is a standard, a measuring rod by which things are judged. We may use many lesser standards to regulate our lives, but all such regulations must be subordinate to Scripture. To be the "Norm of norms" is to be the superlative norm, the standard by which all other norms are measured. The Bible is not simply "first among equals"—it has no parity with other standards. As Jesus is exalted to be Lord of lords and King of kings, so we submit to His Word as the Norm of norms, the standard of truth and the one rule for the people of God.

God is the Lord of heaven and earth, and He alone is able to impose absolute obligation upon His creatures. He does this through the written word. The reformers of the sixteenth century recognized this unique authority of the Bible, expressing it in the watchword *Sola Scriptura*, "the Scripture alone." The reformers did not despise other authorities, or deny the value of tradition and the creeds, but they distinguished the singular authority of the Bible, "the only infallible rule of faith and practice."

God calls every Christian to pursue righteousness. Our trust is to be childlike, but our understanding must be mature. Such trust and understanding require study of God's word. The authentic disciple meditates on it day and night, continuing and remaining in it. Our goal is more than knowledge; it is wisdom and the fruit of inward and outward obedience.

The Reformation Study Bible is so called because it stands in the Reformed tradition of the original Geneva Bible of the sixteenth century. In modern Geneva, Switzerland, a memorial wall has been built and dedicated to the sixteenth century Reformation. This Reformation Monument is adorned with statues of the great leaders, Calvin, Beza, Farel, and Knox. Surrounding these figures is the phrase, *Post Tenebras Lux*—"After darkness, light."

The light of the Reformation was the light of the Bible. Luther translated the Latin Bible that could be read only by professionals into everyday German that could be read by the people. In England, Wycliffe and then William Tyndale had translated the Bible into English. Yet there was substantial opposition to these efforts. Tyndale was burned at the stake in 1536. During the reign of Mary Tudor (1553-1558) the Reformation was suppressed. The Roman Catholic mass had to be celebrated, services could not be conducted in

English, and priests were forbidden to marry. Two hundred eighty-eight persons were burned, including the Archbishop of Canterbury, Thomas Cranmer.

These persecutions drove exiles from Britain to Europe. The most capable scholars among them came to Geneva, Switzerland. There they undertook the task of preparing a new translation of the Bible in English. The Geneva Bible was published in 1560, carefully designed to be accurate and understandable. It was the first English Bible to use verse divisions, as "most profitable for memory" and for finding and comparing other passages. It was provided with marginal notes based on Reformed principles.

The Geneva Bible dominated the English-speaking world for a hundred years. It was the Bible used by Shakespeare. The King James Bible was published in 1611 but did not supplant the Geneva Bible until fifty years later. The Pilgrims and Puritans carried the Geneva Bible to the shores of the New World. American colonists were reared on the Geneva Bible. They read it, studied it, and sought to live by its light.

Since that time a multitude of English translations and study Bibles have appeared. *The Reformation Study Bible* contains a modern restatement of Reformation truth in its comments and theological notes. Its purpose is to present the light of the Reformation afresh.

The Reformed accept the Christian faith as expressed in the ecumenical creeds and believed by Christians everywhere. The distinctive ideas of the Reformed are the result of accepting the Bible as the supreme authority for faith and practice. The words of the Bible are true and its message is powerful. It conveys the infallible promise of God, its Author, that it will not return to Him empty, but will certainly accomplish His intended purpose.

Contributors

The production of *The Reformation Study Bible* has involved the joint efforts of the contributors and editors. The process has been similar to that of Bible translation in which each person has a creative function.

The Old and New Testament contributors wrote introductions, outlines, and annotations for specific books of the Bible. The annotations in particular were edited and revised at length by the editorial staff. The contributors then responded concerning all editorial changes and revisions. Thus, the final form of the study material represents the combined work of contributors and editors. The result is the most comprehensive set of helps in study Bible format for Christians interested in the Reformed tradition.

General Editor
R. C. Sproul, Drs., Ph.D.
Ligonier Ministries

Associate Editor
Keith A. Mathison, Ph.D.
Ligonier Ministries

Old Testament Editor
Bruce Waltke, Th.D., Ph.D.
Regent College

New Testament Editor
Moisés Silva, Ph.D.
Westminster Theological Seminary

Associate Editors
James Boice, D.Th. (deceased)
Tenth Presbyterian Church

Edmund Clowney, S.T.M., D.D.
Westminster Theological Seminary

Roger Nicole, Ph.D.
Reformed Theological Seminary

J. I. Packer, D.Phil.
Regent College

Assistant Editors
William B. Evans, Ph.D. (cand.)
Erskine College

John Mason, Ph.D. (cand.)
Nashville Presbytery
Presbyterian Church in America

Old Testament Contributors

Carl E. Armerding, Ph.D.
Schloss Mittersill Study Centre

Raymond Dillard, Ph.D. (deceased)
Westminster Theological Seminary

William Dumbrell, Ph.D.
Moore Theological College

Mark Futato, Ph.D.
Westminster Theological Seminary in California

Graeme Goldsworthy, Ph.D.
Moore Theological College

J. Alan Groves, Ph.D.
Westminster Theological Seminary

R. Laird Harris, Ph.D. (emeritus)
Covenant Theological Seminary

Kenneth J. Howell, Ph.D.
Reformed Theological Seminary

M. M. Kline, Ph.D. (cand.)
Gordon-Conwell Theological Seminary

Gary Knoppers, Ph.D.
Penn State University

Donald Leggett, Ph.D.
Ontario Theological Seminary

V. Philips Long, Ph.D.
Covenant Theological Seminary

Tremper Longman III, Ph.D.
Westminster Theological Seminary

J. Gordon McConville, Ph.D.
Wycliffe Hall, Oxford

Allan A. MacRae, Ph.D. (emeritus)
Biblical Theological Seminary

Jeffrey Niehaus, Ph.D.
Gordon-Conwell Theological Seminary

Dirk H. Odendaal, Ph.D. (deceased)
University of Stellenbosch

Raymond C. Ortlund, Jr., Ph.D.
Trinity Evangelical Divinity School

"Gk.," indicating that in this specific case the source of the quote is the Septuagint, the Greek translation of the Old Testament, which was often used by the New Testament writers instead of the original Hebrew Old Testament.)

FOOTNOTES

Several kinds of footnotes related to the ESV text are provided throughout the ESV Bible to assist the reader. These footnotes appear at the bottom of the right-hand column and are indicated in the ESV text by a superscript *number* that *follows* the word or phrase to which the footnote applies (e.g., "Isaac[2]"). Superscript *letters* that *precede* a word (e.g., "[c]Isaac") are used to indicate cross-references (see cross-reference explanation above).

The footnotes included in the ESV Bible are an integral part of the text and provide important information concerning the understanding and translation of the text. The footnotes fall mainly into four categories, as illustrated in the examples below.

Types of Footnotes

(1) *Alternative Translations*. Footnotes of this kind provide alternative translations for specific words or phrases when there is a strong possibility that such words or phrases could be translated in another way, such as: "Or *keep awake*" (see Matt. 26:38); and "Or *down payment*" (see Eph. 1:14). In such cases, the translation deemed to have the stronger support is in the text while other possible renderings are given in the note.

(2) *Explanation of Greek and Hebrew Terms*. Notes of this kind relate primarily to the meaning of specific Greek or Hebrew terms, as illustrated by the following examples:

(a) Notes about the meaning of names in the original languages, such as: "*Isaac* means *he laughs*" (see Gen. 17:19); and "*Simeon* sounds like the Hebrew for *heard*" (see Gen. 29:33).

(b) Notes that give the literal translation of a Greek or Hebrew word or phrase deemed too awkward to be used in the English text, such as: "Greek *girding up the loins of your mind*" (see 1 Pet. 1:13).

(c) Notes indicating that absolute certainty of the meaning of a word or phrase is not possible given our best understanding of the original language (e.g., Hebrew words occurring so infrequently in the Old Testament that their meaning cannot be determined with certainty). Such words are identified with a note stating that "The meaning of the Hebrew is uncertain" (see, e.g., Josh. 17:11).

(d) Notes that indicate the specialized use of a Greek word, such as: "brothers," translating the Greek word *adelphoi* (see, e.g., the extended note on Rom. 1:13, corresponding to the first occurrence of *adelphoi* in any New Testament book, and the abbreviated note, e.g., on Rom. 7:1, corresponding to subsequent occurrences of *adelphoi* in any New Testament book); and "sons," translating the Greek word *huioi* (see, e.g., Rom. 8:14). See also the discussion of *adelphoi* and *huioi* in the preface.

(3) *Other Explanatory Notes*. Footnotes of this kind provide clarifying information as illustrated by the following examples:

(a) Notes clarifying additional meanings that may not otherwise be apparent in the text, such as: "*Leprosy* was a term for several skin diseases; see Leviticus 13."

(b) Notes clarifying important grammatical points that would not otherwise be apparent in English, such as: "In Hebrew *you* is plural in verses 1-5" (see Gen. 3:1).

(c) Notes clarifying when the referent for a pronoun has been supplied in the English text, such as: "Greek *he*" (see, e.g., Mark 1:43).

(d) Notes giving English equivalents for weights, measures, and monetary values.

(4) *Technical Translation Notes*. Footnotes of this kind indicate how decisions have been made in the translation of difficult Hebrew and Greek passages. Such notes occasionally include technical terms. For an explanation of these terms the reader is referred to standard Bible study reference works. See further the section in the preface on "Textual Basis" for an explanation of the original-language texts used in the translation of the ESV Bible and how the translation of difficult passages has been resolved.

Preface
to the
English Standard Version

The Bible

"This Book [is] the most valuable thing that this world affords. Here is Wisdom; this is the royal Law; these are the lively Oracles of God." With these words the Moderator of the Church of Scotland hands a Bible to the new monarch in Britain's coronation service. These words echo the King James Bible translators, who wrote in 1611: "God's sacred Word . . . is that inestimable treasure that excelleth all the riches of the earth." This assessment of the Bible is the motivating force behind the publication of the English Standard Version.

Translation Legacy

The English Standard Version (ESV) stands in the classic mainstream of English Bible translations over the past half-millennium. The fountainhead of that stream was William Tyndale's New Testament of 1526; marking its course were the King James Version of 1611 (KJV), the English Revised Version of 1885 (RV), the American Standard Version of 1901 (ASV), and the Revised Standard Version of 1952 and 1971 (RSV). In that stream, faithfulness to the text and vigorous pursuit of accuracy were combined with simplicity, beauty, and dignity of expression. Our goal has been to carry forward this legacy for a new century.

To this end each word and phrase in the ESV has been carefully weighed against the original Hebrew, Aramaic, and Greek, to ensure the fullest accuracy and clarity and to avoid under-translating or overlooking any nuance of the original text. The words and phrases themselves grow out of the Tyndale-King James legacy, and most recently out of the RSV, with the 1971 RSV text providing the starting point for our work. Archaic language has been brought to current usage and significant corrections have been made in the translation of key texts. But throughout, our goal has been to retain the depth of meaning and enduring language that have made their indelible mark on the English-speaking world and have defined the life and doctrine of the church over the last four centuries.

Translation Philosophy

The ESV is an "essentially literal" translation that seeks as far as possible to capture the precise wording of the original text and the personal style of each Bible writer. As such, its emphasis is on "word-for-word" correspondence, at the same time taking into account differences of grammar, syntax, and idiom between current literary English and the original languages. Thus it seeks to be transparent to the original text, letting the reader see as directly as possible the structure and meaning of the original.

In contrast to the ESV, some Bible versions have followed a "thought-for-thought" rather than "word-for-word" translation philosophy, emphasizing "dynamic equivalence" rather than the "essentially literal" meaning of the original. A "thought-for-thought" translation is of necessity more inclined to reflect the interpretive opinions of the translator and the influences of contemporary culture.

Every translation is at many points a trade-off between literal precision and readability, between "formal equivalence" in expression and "functional equivalence" in communication, and the ESV is no exception. Within this framework we have sought to be "as literal as possible" while maintaining clarity of expression and literary excellence. Therefore, to the extent that plain English permits and the meaning in each case allows, we have sought to use the same English word for important recurring words in the original; and, as far as grammar and syntax allow, we have rendered Old Testament passages cited in the New in ways that show their correspondence. Thus in each of these areas, as well as throughout the Bible as a whole, we have sought to capture the echoes and overtones of meaning that are so abundantly present in the original texts.

As an essentially literal translation, then, the ESV seeks to carry over every possible nuance of meaning in the original words of Scripture into our own language. As such, it is ideally suited for in-depth study of the Bible. Indeed, with its emphasis on literary excellence, the ESV is equally suited for public reading and preaching, for private reading and reflection, for both academic and devotional study, and for Scripture memorization.

Translation Style

The ESV also carries forward classic translation principles in its literary style. Accordingly it retains theological terminology—words such as grace, faith, justification, sanctification, redemption, regeneration, reconciliation, propitiation—because of their central importance for Christian doctrine and also because the underlying Greek words were already becoming key words and technical terms in New Testament times.

The ESV lets the stylistic variety of the biblical writers fully express itself—from the exalted prose that opens Genesis, to the flowing narratives of the historical books, to the rich metaphors and dramatic imagery of the poetic books, to the ringing rhetorical indictments in the prophetic books, to the smooth elegance of Luke, to the profound simplicities of John, and the closely-reasoned logic of Paul.

In punctuating, paragraphing, dividing long sentences, and rendering connectives, the ESV follows the path that seems to make the ongoing flow of thought clearest in English. The biblical languages regularly connect sentences by frequent repetition of words such as "and," "but," and "for," in a way that goes beyond the conventions of literary English. Effective translation, however, requires that these links in the original be reproduced so that the flow of the argument will be transparent to the reader. We have therefore normally translated these connectives, though occasionally we have varied the rendering by using alternatives (such as "also," "however," "now," "so," "then," or "thus") when they better capture the sense in specific instances.

In the area of gender language, the goal of the ESV is to render literally what is in the original. For example, "anyone" replaces "any man" where there is no word corresponding to "man" in the original languages, and "people" rather than "men" is regularly used where the original languages refer to both men and women. But the words "man" and "men" are retained where a male meaning component is part of the original Greek or Hebrew. Similarly, the English word "brothers" (translating the Greek word *adelphoi*) is retained as an important familial form of address between fellow-Jews and fellow-Christians in the first century. A recurring note is included to indicate that the term "brothers" (*adelphoi*) was often used in Greek to refer to both men and women, and to indicate the specific instances in the text where this is the case. In addition, the English word "sons" (translating the Greek word *huioi*) is retained in specific instances because of its meaning as a legal term in the adoption and inheritance laws of first-century Rome. As used by the apostle Paul, this term refers to the status of all Christians, both men and women, who, having been adopted into God's family, now enjoy all the privileges, obligations, and inheritance rights of God's children.

The inclusive use of the generic "he" has also regularly been retained, because this is consistent with similar usage in the original languages and because an essentially literal translation would be impossible without it. Similarly, where God and man are compared or contrasted in the original, the ESV retains the generic use of "man" as the clearest way to express the contrast within the framework of essentially literal translation.

In each case the objective has been transparency to the original text, allowing the reader to understand the original on its own terms rather than on the terms of our present-day culture.

Textual Basis

The ESV is based on the Masoretic text of the Hebrew Bible as found in *Biblia Hebraica Stuttgartensia* (2nd ed., 1983), and on the Greek text in the 1993 editions of the *Greek New Testament* (4th corrected ed.), published by the United Bible Societies (UBS), and *Novum Testamentum Graece* (27th ed.), edited by Nestle and Aland. The currently renewed respect among Old Testament scholars for the Masoretic text is reflected in the ESV's attempt, wherever possible, to translate difficult Hebrew passages as they stand in the Masoretic text rather than resorting to emendations or to finding an alternative reading in the ancient versions. In exceptional, difficult cases, the Dead Sea Scrolls, the Septuagint, the Samaritan Pentateuch, the Syriac Peshitta, the Latin Vulgate, and other sources were consulted to shed possible light on the text, or, if necessary, to support a divergence from the Masoretic text. Similarly, in a few difficult cases in the New Testament, the ESV has followed a Greek text different from the text given preference in the UBS/Nestle-Aland 27th edition. In this regard the footnotes that accompany the ESV text are an integral part of the ESV translation, informing the reader of textual variations and difficulties and showing how these have been resolved by the ESV translation team. In addition to this, the footnotes indicate significant alternative readings and occasionally provide an explanation for technical terms or for a difficult reading in the text. Throughout, the translation team has benefited greatly from the massive textual resources that have become readily available recently, from new insights into biblical laws and culture, and from current advances in Hebrew and Greek lexicography and grammatical understanding.

Publishing Team

The ESV publishing team includes more than a hundred people. The fourteen-member Translation Oversight Committee has benefited from the work of fifty biblical experts serving as Translation Review Scholars and from the comments of the more than fifty members of the Advisory Council, all of which has been carried out under the auspices of the Good News Publishers Board of Directors. This hundred-member team, which shares a common commitment to the truth of God's Word and to historic Christian orthodoxy, is international in scope and includes leaders in many denominations.

To God's Honor and Praise

We know that no Bible translation is perfect or final; but we also know that God uses imperfect and inadequate things to his honor and praise. So to our triune God and to his people we offer what we have done, with our prayers that it may prove useful, with gratitude for much help given, and with ongoing wonder that our God should ever have entrusted to us so momentous a task.

Soli Deo Gloria!—To God alone be the glory!

*The Translation Oversight Committee**

*A complete list of the Translation Oversight Committee, the Translation Review Scholars, and the Advisory Council, is available upon request from Crossway Bibles, a division of Good News Publishers.

Theological Notes

In-Text Maps

Charts

Books of the Old and New Testaments

The Old Testament

The New Testament

THE OLD TESTAMENT

INTRODUCTION TO THE

Pentateuch

The first five books of the Bible (Genesis, Exodus, Leviticus, Numbers, Deuteronomy), commonly called "the Law" or "the Pentateuch" (Greek *pentateuchos*, "five volume [book]"), are the first and most important section of the Old Testament in both Jewish and Christian Bibles. The threefold division of the Hebrew Bible into Law, Prophets, and Writings can be traced as far back as the New Testament (Luke 24:44) and the prologue to Sirach (c. 180 B.C.). The arrangement of the Old Testament in Christian Bibles, based on the Greek Old Testament (the Septuagint; c. 150 B.C.), also gives the Pentateuch such primacy.

AUTHOR AND DATE

References to the Pentateuch by such terms as "the Book of Moses" (Neh. 13:1; 2 Chr. 25:4), "the Book of the Law of Moses" (Neh. 8:1), "the Law of the LORD" (1 Chr. 16:40; Ezra 7:10), and "the Book of the Law of God" (Neh. 8:18) are largely restricted to writings following the Babylonian exile of the Jews in the sixth century B.C. It is uncertain whether references to "the law" in earlier books refer to the Pentateuch or to parts of it (e.g., Josh. 1:8; 8:34; 2 Kin. 14:6; 22:8). The New Testament uses similar designations for the Pentateuch (Matt. 12:5; Mark 12:26; Luke 16:16; John 7:19; Gal. 3:10). These various headings underscore the Mosaic authorship of the Pentateuch and its binding authority. That is, Israel's divine King caused His commands to be written down through Moses (c. 1400 B.C.).

Besides these titles indicating Moses' authorship, Jesus said, "Moses . . . wrote of Me" (John 5:46), and He explained to His disciples on the road to Emmaus what the Scriptures said about Him "beginning with Moses" (Luke 24:27). The Pentateuch itself tells of Moses' decisive contribution to it: he wrote the great legal code, the Book of the Covenant (Ex. 24:3–7), and the exposition of the law recorded in Deuteronomy (Deut. 31:24–26).

During the past two centuries, however, most scholars who do not accept the Bible's own witness about its authorship have held that it was composed by editors in the period following the Babylonian exile of the sixth century B.C. Such scholars maintain that the editors creatively pieced together at least four earlier literary documents. The theory is based on the following observations: the distribution of divine names, especially "Elohim" and "Yahweh"; variations of vocabulary, such as the different Hebrew words for "maidservant"; similar stories (e.g., Gen. 12:10–20; 20:1–19; 26:1–11); the repetition of laws, such as those for the Passover (Ex. 12:1–20, 21–23; Deut. 16:1–8); and supposedly varying theologies. They regard the Pentateuch as a composite of works by the "Yahwist," the "Elohist," the "Deuteronomist," and the "Priestly" writer. The corresponding documents, conventionally abbreviated "J," "E," "D," and "P," are assigned approximate dates of 950, 850, 600, and 500 B.C.

More recently the consensus of the scholars following this view has been significantly modified. On the basis of literary forms and archaeological evidence it has become clear that the alleged documents contain older material, some of which might even go back to Moses. Today it is thought that the writers of "J," "E," "D," and "P" were themselves editors who collected and arranged earlier materials. The goals and methods that led to the original specification of diverse sources for the Pentateuch have been subject to continuing discussion. At the same time, there is increasing admiration for the unified structure of the Pentateuch.

In conformity with known practices in the ancient Near East, Moses probably used literary sources. Sometimes these are clearly identified (e.g., Gen. 5:1; Num. 21:14); in other places they may be inferred by distinctive literary styles (cf. Gen. 1:1–2:3 and Gen. 2:4–25). Then too, prophets of later times who succeeded Moses in mediating God's authoritative word (cf. Deut. 18:15–20) kept the text up-to-date linguistically and historically, adding some material such as Gen. 36:31 and Moses' obituary (Deut. 34:1–12).

UNITY

The Pentateuch is both a composite document of individual books and also a seamless narrative of a complete story from creation to the death of Moses. Both aspects are important.

In the first place, each of the books holds its own interest and unity. Genesis reveals its literary structure by repeating ten times the formula, "these are the generations of" what follows. Exodus reveals itself to be a unity in a number of ways. For example, the law promulgated in chs. 19–40 is based on the narrative of Israel's exodus from Egypt (chs. 1–18; Ex. 19:3–6). Without the narrative, the law has no historical foundation. God confirmed His call to Moses by leading the nation out of Egypt back to Mount Horeb, the mountain where Moses was commissioned in the first place (Ex. 3:1, 12). Leviticus is a liturgical manual for priests. Numbers recounts Israel's march from the wilderness of Sinai to Canaan. As the Exodus from Egypt memorialized by the Passover prefigures the salvation of the new Israel from sin through the sacrifice of Christ, so the history in Numbers dramatizes the spiritual march of all God's children through a wilderness on their way to the Promised Land, warning them not to lose faith. Finally, Deuteronomy records Moses' exposition of the law he received at Mount Sinai.

At the same time, the five books of the Pentateuch are linked together as a continuous narrative. Exodus continues the story begun in Genesis of the Israelites who had gone to Egypt (Gen. 46:26, 27; Ex. 1:1). Moses fulfills Joseph's deathbed oath to carry up his bones out of Egypt (Gen. 50:25; Ex. 13:19). Leviticus 1–9 explains the rituals of the tabernacle, as a kind of supplement to the instructions for building it found in Ex. 25–40. Leviticus also shows how the service for ordaining priests, outlined in Exodus 29, was carried out. Numbers shares many connections with Exodus and Leviticus; large portions of all three books take place in the wilderness of Sinai and share similar ceremonial regulations and concerns. In his first address in Deuteronomy, Moses summarizes Israel's history from Sinai to Moab as recorded in Numbers. In his second address he makes frequent allusions to Exodus, repeating with slight modification the Ten Commandments and Israel's response to them (Ex. 20 and Deut. 5).

THEME

The Pentateuch is a mixture of history and law. These are not unrelated: the narrative history explains the laws. For example, the law about circumcision is given in the narrative about God's covenant with Abraham and Sarah (Gen. 17:9–14), and breaking the Sabbath is made a capital offense in the story about gathering sticks on the Sabbath (Num. 15:32–36). But as noted above, the Pentateuch's main interest is God's covenant with Abraham, Isaac, and Jacob, His deliverance of their descendants from Egypt, and their obligation to keep the laws of God given to them in the Sinai wilderness.

God's purpose in bringing Israel out of Egypt is that they would worship Him, and become a holy nation for Him. Through them, His blessing would reach all the nations of the world. According to Galatians, this gracious promise announced to Abraham is the same gospel preached by Jesus Christ and realized through His death and resurrection (Gal. 3:8, 14). The enduring power of the Pentateuch is not a mystery, but a consequence of its inspiration by the Spirit of God.

THE FIRST BOOK OF MOSES CALLED

Genesis

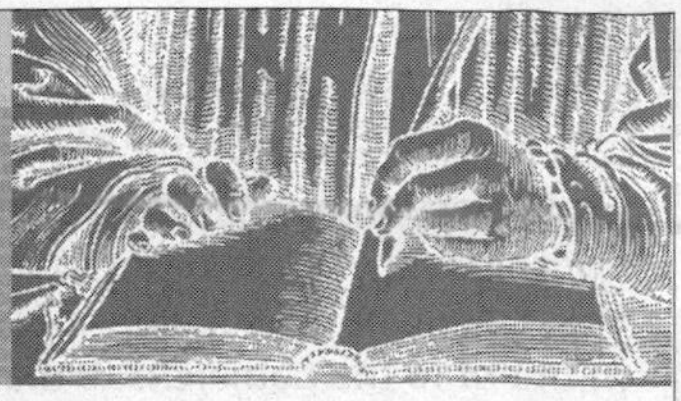

AUTHOR

Because this anonymous book is part of the unified Pentateuch, establishing its authorship and date cannot be separated from the composition of that "Five-Volumed Book" ("Introduction to the Pentateuch"). Evidence relating to Genesis itself, however, suggests that, like the remainder of the Pentateuch, Moses gave the book its essential substance and later editors supplemented it, all by the Holy Spirit's inspiration.

It would be arbitrary to exclude Genesis from the New Testament testimony that Moses (fifteenth century B.C.) authored the Pentateuch. More specifically, our Lord said that "Moses gave you circumcision" (John 7:22; Acts 15:1), which is uniquely given in Gen. 17. It is not surprising that the founder of Israel's theocracy gave this masterful foundation to the Law. Its historical narrative furnished the theological and ethical underpinnings of the Torah: Israel's unique covenantal relationship with God (Deut. 9:5) and its singular laws (e.g., the Sabbath, 7:2 note). Moreover, since creation myths are basic to pagan religions, it is natural that Moses would have included a creation account opposing the pagan myths. This account is, in addition, foundational to the Law Moses mediated (1:1–2:3 notes).

This Bible's own witness to Moses' authorship is supported by extrabiblical data. The first eleven chapters of Genesis share many parallels and conscious dissimilarities with ancient Near Eastern myths that preceded the time of Moses and were known to him (Mesopotamian creation accounts such as the *Enuma Elish* and flood accounts such as those included in the *Atrahasis Epic* and the eleventh tablet of the *Gilgamesh Epic*). Names and customs in the narratives about the patriarchs (chs. 12–50) accurately reflect their era, suggesting an early author with reliable documents. The Ebla texts (twenty-fourth century B.C.) mention Ebrium, possibly the Eber of Gen. 10:21, and the Mari texts (eighteenth century B.C.) attest to names such as "Abraham," "Jacob," and "Amorite." The practice of granting a birthright (i.e., additional privileges to the eldest son, 25:5–6, 32–34; 39:3–4; 43:33; 49:3) was widespread in the ancient Near East, and the sale of an inheritance (25:29–34) is documented at different periods in this area. The adoption of one's own slave (15:1–3) is found in a Larsa letter from Old Babylonia, and the adoption of Ephraim and Manasseh by their grandfather (48:5) may be compared with a similar adoption of a grandson at Ugarit (fourteenth century B.C.). The gift of a female slave as part of a dowry and her presentation to her husband by an infertile wife (16:1–6; 30:1–3 and notes) are attested in the laws of Hammurabi (c. 1750 B.C.). These and similar facts corroborate the historical reliability of the narrative.

DATE AND OCCASION

Given the biblical and extrabiblical evidence linking Genesis and its contents to Moses and his era, we may reasonably conclude that the book dates from the fifteenth century B.C. Certainly, for example, since David (c. 1000 B.C.) set the creation account of Gen. 1 to music (Ps. 8), a date of composition in the second millennium is indicated for Gen. 1. Readers should be aware, however, that, although occasionally words known only from the middle of the second millennium appear in the text, the grammar of the Pentateuch was updated at some point, as were some place-names (14:14 note). Also, the list of kings in 36:31–43 was apparently added after the time of Saul.

Like its authorship and date, the purpose of Genesis cannot be considered apart from its place within the Pentateuch as a whole ("Introduction to the Pentateuch"). The Pentateuch is a unique combination of history and law, a history that explains the origins of its laws. For example, the narratives in Genesis explain the rite of circumcision (17:9–14), the prohibition against eating the sciatic tendon (32:32), and Sabbath observance (2:2, 3). More importantly, its narrative recounts God's election of Israel to a unique covenant relationship with Him, in order to bless a fallen world. That covenant relationship consists of God's commitment to the patriarchs to make of their elect offspring a great nation and the chosen nation's commitment to obey Him and so to become a light to the Gentiles. Genesis recounts the origins of this redemptive nation, reaching back to the beginnings of mankind and the world and of the conflict between the kingdom of God and the kingdom of Satan in which the nation was to play a crucial role.

The Hebrew title, following the ancient custom of naming books by their first word(s), is *bereshith*, "in the beginning." The Greek title, based on the book's content, is *genesis*, "origin." Both titles are appropriate since the book is about the origin of history.

INTERPRETIVE DIFFICULTIES

The tension between Genesis and modern science about the origins of the universe and of living species is largely resolved when it is recognized that they are speaking from different perspectives. Genesis is concerned about who created and why, not about how and when. Science cannot answer the former questions, and Genesis is largely mute about the latter (1:2, 5, 6, 11 and notes).

For the past century scholars holding to the "documentary hypothesis" have contended that Genesis is composed of conflicting documents: *J* (for Jahweh/Yahweh, "the LORD"), *E* (for Elohim, "God"), *D* (for Deuteronomist), and *P* (for Priestly writer). While this scheme is still widely accepted, few believe any longer that these documents can be used to reconstruct a history of Israel's religion because all the alleged documents contain what are thought to be "early" and "late" materials. In other words, the alleged four documents actually share elements and characteristics that were supposed to belong in only one of these hypothetical sources (e.g., *J* contains material that would be expected to occur only in *E*). To be sure, documents were composed in the ancient Near East by combining earlier written sources, but Moses himself probably used them (5:1 note). Moreover, many scholars today question the criteria used for identifying these alleged sources and emphasize instead the unity of the text as we have it. For example, the Flood story, once thought to be a classic example of the documentary hypothesis, is now conceded to have remarkable integrity (6:9–9:29 note). See "Introduction to the Pentateuch."

CHARACTERISTICS AND THEMES

A study of the literary structure of Genesis discloses the following highlights. After the prologue Genesis is divided into ten parts marked out by the formula: "These are the generations of." This heading is followed by a genealogy of the person named or by stories involving his notable descendants. The first three accounts pertain to the pre-Flood world and the last seven to the post-Flood period. Accounts one through three and four through six parallel one another: (a) stories about the developments of mankind universally at the creation and at the re-creation after the Flood (accounts one and four respectively); (b) the genealogy of the redemptive lines through Seth and Shem (accounts two and five); and (c) the stories of the epochal covenant transactions with Noah and Abraham (accounts three and six). The final two pairs of accounts expand the Abrahamic line, contrasting his rejected offspring, Ishmael and Esau (accounts seven and nine), with stories about the elect, Isaac and Jacob respectively (accounts eight and ten).

The key to the stories is often given in an opening revelation: e.g., the promise to Abraham (12:1–3), the prenatal sign of the rivalry between Jacob and Esau (25:22, 23), and Joseph's dreams (37:1–11). A transitional section is found at the end of the accounts (e.g., 4:25, 26; 6:1–8; 9:18–29; 11:10–26; Outline).

The closing section of the last account contains strong links with Exodus, concluding with an oath Joseph elicited from his brothers to take his embalmed body with them when God came to their aid and returned them to Canaan (50:24, 25; Ex. 13:19).

The book's focus on the origins of Israel unfolds against a backdrop of matters affecting the world. Moses tells us that prior to God's election of the patriarchs, the fathers of Israel (chs.

12–50), mankind asserted its independence from God by striving to know good and evil apart from God and in defiance of His command (chs. 2; 3). Humans proved their depravity by token religion, fratricide, and unrestrained vengeance (Cain, ch. 4); by tyranny, harems, and thinking evil continually (the pre-Flood kings, 6:1–8); and by erecting an anti-kingdom against God (Nimrod and the infamous tower, 10:8–12; 11:1–9 note). God's verdict about mankind stands: "the intention of man's heart is evil from his youth" (8:21).

Just as miraculously and surely as God sovereignly transformed the dark, empty void at earth's origin (1:2) into a glorious habitat for mankind and brought it to rest (1:3–2:3), so also God sovereignly elected His covenant people in Christ to conquer Satan (3:15) and to bless the depraved world (12:1–3). Unconditionally He elected the patriarchs, Abraham, Isaac, and Jacob, promising to make of their elect descendants the nation destined to bless the earth, a promise entailing an eternal seed, land, and king (12:1–3, 7; 13:14–17; 17:1–8; 26:2–6; 28:10–15). Before Jacob was born and had done either good or evil, God chose Jacob, not Esau, his older twin brother (25:21–23). He chose Jacob, even though he cheated his brother, deceived his father, and blasphemed God (ch. 27). God even used Judah's scandalous wrongs against Tamar, and her daring ruse as well, to advance the messianic line (ch. 38). The heavenly King displayed His glorious rule by miraculously preserving the matriarchs in pagan harems (12:10–20; ch. 20) and opening their barren wombs (17:15–22; 18:1–15; 21:1–7; 25:21; 29:31; 30:22). He overrode man's ways and customs by time and again choosing the younger, not the older, to inherit the blessing (25:23 note). Blatant prophecies and subtle types are sterling witnesses that God directs history. For example, Noah prophesied Shem's subjugation of Canaan (9:24–26), and the greater Exodus led by Moses was prefigured when God delivered Abraham and Sarah from the oppression of Egypt with wealth (12:10–20 note).

God inclined the heart of His elect to trust His promises and to obey His commands. Against all hope, Abraham counted on God to give him an innumerable offspring, and the lawgiver says that God credited that as righteousness (15:6). Confident of God's sure promises, Abraham gave up his rights to the land (ch. 13); and Jacob, renamed "Israel" and clinging only to God (ch. 22), symbolically gave back the birthright to Esau (ch. 33). At the beginning of the Joseph story, Judah sold Joseph as a slave (37:26, 27), but at its end the former slave trader was willing to become a slave in the place of his brother (44:33, 34). Secure in the truth that God's gracious design had brought good out of sins as heinous as murder and slave trading, Joseph forgave his brothers without recrimination (45:4–8; 50:24).

What was begun in Genesis is fulfilled in Christ. The genealogy begun in ch. 5, and advanced in ch. 11, is completed with the birth of Jesus Christ (Matt. 1; Luke 3:23–27). He is the ultimate offspring promised to Abraham (12:1–3; Gal. 3:16). The elect are blessed in Him because He alone, by His active and passive obedience, satisfied the law's demands and died in their stead. All who are baptized into Christ and united with Him by faith are Abraham's descendants (Gal. 3:26–29). The bold prophecies and subtle types in Genesis show that God is writing a history leading to a rest in Christ. On the threshold of biblical prophecy Noah predicted that the Japhethites would find salvation through the Semites, a prophecy fulfilled in the New Testament (9:27 and note), and God Himself proclaimed that the woman's offspring would destroy Satan (3:15). That offspring is Christ and His church (Rom. 16:20). The gift of the bride to Adam prefigures the gift of the church to Christ (2:18–25; Eph. 5:22–32); Melchizedek's priesthood is like the Son of God's (14:18–20; Heb. 7); and as Israel redeemed out of bondage in Egypt found rest, resources, and refuge in the Promised Land, the church redeemed out of the cursed world finds that life in Christ (13:15 note). The paradise lost by the first Adam is restored by the Last Adam. This marvelously unified sacred history certifies that the focus of Genesis is Christ.

OUTLINE OF GENESIS

I. Prologue: Creation of Heaven and Earth (1:1–2:3)

II. Account of Heavens and Earth (2:4–4:26)

- A. *Adam and Eve on Probation in Paradise (2:4–25)*
- B. *The Fall and Its Consequences (ch. 3)*
- C. *Escalation of Sin in the Line of Cain (4:1–24)*
- D. *A Godly Remnant (4:25, 26)*

III. Account of Adam (5:1–6:8)

- A. *The Covenant Line of Seth (ch. 5)*
- B. *Escalation of Sin Before the Flood (6:1–8)*

IV. Account of Noah (6:9–9:29)

- A. *Preparation for the Flood (6:9–7:10)*
- B. *The Flood and Salvation (7:11–8:19)*
- C. *God's Covenant Not to Destroy the Earth (8:20–9:17)*
- D. *Prophecies About Noah's Sons (9:18–29)*

V. Account of Shem, Ham, and Japheth (10:1–11:9)

- A. *Table of Nations (ch. 10)*
- B. *Escalation of Evil in Babylon (11:1–9)*

VI. Account of Shem (11:10–26)

VII. Account of Terah (11:27–25:11)

- A. *Genealogy (11:27–32)*
- B. *The Abrahamic Covenant: His Land and People (12:1–22:19)*
  1. Migration to the Promised Land (12:1–9)
  2. Deliverance from Egypt (12:10–20)
  3. Lot's Separation from the Land (ch. 13)
  4. Victory over the Eastern Kings (ch. 14)
  5. God's Covenant Ratified (ch. 15)
  6. Hagar and Ishmael Rejected (ch. 16)
  7. God's Covenant Confirmed (ch. 17)
  8. Sarah to Have a Son (18:1–15)
  9. Lot's Rescue from Sodom (18:16–19:38)
  10. Protection from the Philistines (ch. 20)
  11. Birth of Isaac and Blessing in the Land (ch. 21)
  12. God's Oath to Bless the World Through Abraham's Offspring (22:1–19)
- C. *Transition to Isaac (22:20–25:11)*
  1. Rebekah's Family Background (22:20–24)
  2. Death of Sarah (ch. 23)
  3. Isaac's Marriage to Rebekah (ch. 24)
  4. Isaac the Sole Heir (25:1–6)
  5. Death of Abraham (25:7–11)

VIII. Account of Ishmael (25:12–18)

IX. Account of Isaac (25:19–35:29)

- A. *Rivalry in the Family (25:19–34)*
- B. *Covenant Blessings on Isaac (ch. 26)*
- C. *Jacob's Theft of Esau's Blessing (27:1–40)*
- D. *Covenant Blessings on Jacob and His Exile (27:41–32:32)*
  1. Jacob Sent to Laban (27:41–28:9)
  2. Encounter with the Angel at Bethel (28:10–22)
  3. Conflict with Laban (29:1–30)
  4. Birth of Tribal Fathers (29:31–30:24)
  5. Jacob's Prosperity and Flight from Laban (30:25–31:55)
  6. Encounter with Angels at Mahanaim and Peniel (ch. 32)
- E. *Esau's Reconciliation with Jacob (33:1–17)*
- F. *Transition to Jacob: Itinerary and Deaths from Shechem to Mamre (33:18–35:29)*

X. Account of Esau (36:1–37:1)

XI. Account of Jacob (37:2–50:26)

- A. *Joseph's Dream of Rulership (37:2–11)*
- B. *The Sins of Jacob's Family (37:12–38:30)*
- C. *Joseph's Rise to Rulership over Egypt (chs. 39–41)*
- D. *Joseph's Ruse and the Reconciliation of the Covenant Family (chs. 42–45)*
- E. *Transition to Exodus (chs. 46–50)*
  1. Migration to Egypt (46:1–27)
  2. Preservation in Goshen (46:28–47:31)
  3. Jacob's Blessings on the Twelve Tribes (48:1–49:28)
  4. Jacob's Death and Burial in Canaan (49:29–50:14)
  5. Joseph's Death in Egypt with the Promise of Canaan (50:15–26)

The Beginning of Creation

1 In the [a]beginning, God created the
heavens and the earth. 2 The earth was
[b]without form and void, and darkness was
over the face of the deep. And the Spirit of
God was hovering over the face of the
waters.

The Six Days of Creation

3 And God said, [c]"Let there be light," and
there was light. 4 And God saw that the light
was good. And God separated the light from
the darkness. 5 God called the light Day, and
the darkness he called Night. And there was
evening and there was morning, the first
day.

6 And God said, [d]"Let there be an
expanse[1] in the midst of the waters, and let
it separate the waters from the waters."

[1] Or *a canopy*; also verses 7, 8, 14, 15, 17, 20

Chapter 1
1 [a]Job 38:4-7; Ps. 33:6; 136:5; Isai. 42:5; 45:18; John 1:1-3; Acts 14:15; 17:24; Col. 1:16, 17; Heb. 1:10; 11:3; Rev. 4:11
2 [b]Jer. 4:23
3 [c]2 Cor. 4:6
6 [d]Job 37:18; Ps. 136:5; Jer. 10:12; 51:15

1:1–2:25 See "God the Creator" at Ps. 148:5.

1:1–2:3 This account of creation lays the foundation of Israel's world view about God, human beings, creation, and the laws that pertain to mankind (e.g., to worship no other gods, to keep the Sabbath, and to take no innocent life).

1:1 In the beginning, God. The Hebrew word for "God," the first subject of Genesis and the Bible, is plural to denote His majesty. There is no other god (Deut. 4:39; Is. 40:21, 28; 43:10; John 1:1; Col. 1:17). He is truth, the basis for all sound knowledge (John 14:6). God is personal; He speaks and acts.

created. This translates a Hebrew word reserved for God's creative activity alone. Linguistically possible, though less likely, is the translation "When God began to create the heavens and the earth, the earth was without form and void." God's creative activity was not merely the ordering of preexistent matter (like an artisan fashioning a product), however, for other passages clearly teach that the universe was created *ex nihilo* (i.e., out of nothing, John 1:3; Heb. 11:3; 2 Pet. 3:5) and that only God is eternal and transcendent (e.g., Ps. 102:25–27; Prov. 8:22–31). Not even the darkness exists apart from God's creative word (Is. 45:7). While the narrative here is fully consistent with the doctrine of creation *ex nihilo*, the emphasis falls on God's progressive ordering of a formless and empty world (v. 2 note).

the heavens and the earth. This compound of opposites signifies the organized universe.

1:2 The earth . . . deep. The primordial earth is lightless and landless. Neither the origins of darkness and the abyss nor the origin of Satan (3:1–6) is explained in Genesis. Their beginnings are a mystery, but only God is eternal (Ps. 90:2; Prov. 8:22–31). In the new heaven and new earth there will be no sea or darkness (Rev. 21:1, 25).

earth was without form and void. This description signifies the as yet unordered or unfilled creation. Some view it as a negative threat of chaos that is overcome by God's creative power.

Some suggest that vv. 1 and 2 refer to two separate creative acts separated by a span of time. They argue that the initial creation fell into a desolate condition (perhaps because of the fall of Satan), and that the Hebrew word here translated "was" should be rendered "became." This view is very doubtful, however, because the proposed translation "became" is unlikely in this context, and because the description "without form and void" refers more naturally to a creation yet to be formed and filled, rather than to one that had fallen into disrepair.

Spirit of God. God's Spirit gives life to all; when He withdraws His Spirit, life ceases. He continues to give life and to withdraw life (Job 33:4; Ps. 104:30; Eccl. 12:7; Luke 23:46). The Spirit also builds "temples": the cosmos (Ps. 104:1–4); the tabernacle (Ex. 28:3; 35:31); Christ (Luke 1:35; cf. John 2:19); the church (1 Cor. 3:16; Eph. 2:22). See "The Holy Spirit" at John 14:26.

hovering over the . . . waters. Hovering eagle-like over the primordial abyss, the almighty Spirit makes the earth into a habitation for human beings.

1:3–31 The creation progresses over two triads of days looking back respectively to "without form and void" of v. 2:

Day 1—Light (v. 3)
 Day 4—Luminaries (v. 14)
Day 2—Sky/water (v. 6)
 Day 5—Fish/fowl (v. 21)
Day 3—Land, vegetation (vv. 9–11)
 Day 6—Animals and humans (vv. 24–30)

In the first triad God gives the earth form by separating the light of day from the darkness of night, the sea below from the clouds above, and the dry land with vegetation from the sea; in the second He fills these realms. Each triad, moving from sky to earth, progresses from a single creative act (vv. 3–5, 14–19) to one creative act with two aspects (vv. 6–8, 20–23), to two separate creative acts, each culminating in the earth bringing forth (vv. 9–13, 24–31). The pattern of each day is similar: an announcement ("God said"); a command ("let there be"); a report ("and it was so"); an evaluation ("it was good"); and a chronological framework (e.g., "the first day").

1:3 God said. God's free act of creation through the divine Word (Ps. 33:6, 9; cf. John 1:1, 3) signifies that the universe is not an emanation or part of the divine being, thus ruling out all forms of pantheism. Though creation is not part of God's being, all creation is utterly dependent on God for its existence, for He creates and sustains all that is by the power of His own being.

Let there be. God's will is irresistible. It is carried out by divine imperative.

1:4 light. God is the ultimate source of the daylight that alternates with darkness; the sun is later introduced as the immediate cause (vv. 14–18; v. 5 and note). Light symbolizes life and blessing (Ps. 4:7; 56:13; Is. 9:2; John 1:4, 5).

good. Brought within God's constraints, even the darkness and watery deep (vv. 2, 10) are now "good," serving God's benevolent purposes (Ps. 104:19–26). The creation bears witness to God's handiwork (Ps. 19:1–6).

separated. The Hebrew here is also translated "set apart." Separation is fundamental both to creation and to Israel's existence (3:15; 4:1–17; 12:1; Lev. 20:24, 25; Num. 8:14).

1:5 called. God shows He is ruler of the cosmos by naming its spheres (17:5; cf. Num. 32:38; 2 Kin. 23:34; 24:17). By His creative commands and designations, God gave existence and meaning to everything according to His eternal counsel. For God Himself there are no mysteries, and all creation has coherence and meaning within His will. For man, the beginning of wisdom is the fear of the all-wise God (Prov. 1:7).

first day. This presentation of the creation week enables God's covenant people to imitate the Creator in their weekly pattern of work and rest (Ex. 20:11; 31:13, 17).

Reformed scholars have proposed several interpretations of the creative "day." Some view these as literal, sequential, 24-hour days. This interpretation usually entails the view that the earth is relatively "young" (c. 10,000 years old or less). Other scholars, noting that the Hebrew word for "day" (*yom*) can refer to periods of time (e.g., 2:4), have proposed the "day-age theory," that the creative "days" refer to extended ages or epochs of time. Still others suggest that literal, 24-hour days are intended, but that these days were separated by extended periods of time. Finally, some scholars argue that the "days" of creation constitute a literary framework (vv. 3–31 note) designed to teach that God alone is the creator of an orderly universe, and to call upon human beings made in the image of the creator God to reflect God's creative activity in their own pattern of labor (2:2; Ex. 31:17). This "framework hypothesis" views the days of creation as God's gracious accommodation to the limitations of human knowledge—an expression of the infinite Creator's work in terms understandable to finite and frail human beings. This last group of scholars observes that the universe gives the appearance of great antiquity, that the phrase "morning and evening" seems inconsistent with the "day-age" theory, and that the notion of intervening ages between isolated 24-hour days is not apparent from the text.

1:6–8 During the second and third creative days, the watery deep is structured into a benevolent system of rain clouds, springs, and rivers.

1:6 expanse. Describing the sky in terms of how it appears from the

7 And God made the expanse and [e]separated
the waters that were under the expanse from
the waters that were [f]above the expanse.
And it was so. 8 And God called the expanse
Heaven.[1] And there was evening and there
was morning, the second day.
9 And God said, [g]"Let the waters under
the heavens be gathered together into one
place, and let the dry land appear." And it
was so. 10 God called the dry land Earth,[2]
and the waters that were gathered together
he called Seas. And God saw that it was
good.
11 And God said, [h]"Let the earth sprout
vegetation, plants[3] yielding seed, and fruit
trees bearing fruit in which is their seed,
each according to its kind, on the earth."
And it was so. 12 The earth brought forth
vegetation, plants yielding seed according
to their own kinds, and trees bearing fruit
in which is their seed, each according to its
kind. And God saw that it was good. 13 And
there was evening and there was morning,
the third day.
14 And God said, "Let there be lights in
the expanse of the heavens to separate the
day from the night. And let them be for
[i]signs and for [j]seasons,[4] and for days and
years, 15 and let them be lights in the expanse of the heavens to give light upon the
earth." And it was so. 16 And God [k]made[5]
the two great lights—the greater light to
rule the day and the lesser light to rule the
night—and the stars. 17 And God set them
in the expanse of the heavens to give light
on the earth, 18 to [l]rule over the day and
over the night, and to separate the light
from the darkness. And God saw that it
was good. 19 And there was evening and
there was morning, the fourth day.
20 And God said, "Let the waters swarm
with swarms of living creatures, and let
birds[6] fly above the earth across the
expanse of the heavens." 21 So [m]God created the great sea creatures and every living
creature that moves, with which the waters
swarm, according to their kinds, and every
winged bird according to its kind. And God
saw that it was good. 22 And God blessed
them, saying, [n]"Be fruitful and multiply
and fill the waters in the seas, and let birds
multiply on the earth." 23 And there was
evening and there was morning, the fifth
day.
24 And God said, "Let the earth bring
forth living creatures according to their
kinds—livestock and creeping things and
beasts of the earth according to their
kinds." And it was so. 25 And God made the
beasts of the earth according to their kinds
and the livestock according to their kinds,
and everything that creeps on the ground
according to its kind. And God saw that it
was good.
26 Then God said, [o]"Let us make man[7] in
our image, [p]after our likeness. And [q]let them

7 [e]Prov. 8:27-29 [f]Ps. 148:4
9 [g]Job 38:8-11; Ps. 33:7; 136:6; Jer. 5:22; 2 Pet. 3:5
11 [h]Ps. 104:14
14 [i]Jer. 10:2; Ezek. 32:7, 8; Joel 2:30, 31; 3:15; Matt. 24:29; Luke 21:25 [j]Ps. 104:19
16 [k]Deut. 4:19; Ps. 136:7-9
18 [l]Jer. 31:35
21 [m]Ps. 104:25, 26
22 [n]ch. 8:17; 9:1
26 [o]ch. 3:22; 11:7; Isai. 6:8 [p]ch. 5:1; 9:6; 1 Cor. 11:7; Eph. 4:24; Col. 3:10; James 3:9 [q]ch. 9:2; Ps. 8:6-8; James 3:7

[1] Or *Sky*; also verses 9, 14, 15, 17, 20, 26, 28, 30; 2:1 [2] Or *Land*; also verses 11, 12, 22, 24, 25, 26, 28, 30; 2:1 [3] Or *small plants*; also verses 12, 29 [4] Or *appointed times* [5] Or *fashioned* [6] Or *flying things*; see Leviticus 11:19-20 [7] The Hebrew word for *man* (*adam*) is the generic term for mankind and becomes the proper name *Adam*

earth, the Hebrew suggests something flat and hard (Job 37:18; Is. 40:22). In vv. 6–8 it refers ambiguously to the atmosphere or sky (or both). Here it separates rain clouds from rivers and seas.

1:10 Earth. The word connotes that which is benevolently ordered by God's sovereignty in the interests of human life and security (Ps. 24:1, 2; cf. Prov. 2:21, 22).

1:11 according to its kind. There are no species of life apart from God's design and creative acts. He intended the vegetation to serve as food for higher forms of life (vv. 29, 30).

1:14 in . . . the heavens. The description is phenomenological (i.e., as things appear to the eye).

1:16 two great lights. The sun and moon, principal deities in ancient Near Eastern pagan pantheons, are not even named, effectively demoting them and emphasizing that they serve mankind according to God's design.

rule. The moving forms of the second triad of days seem to rule over the spheres that house and shelter them (1:3–31 note): the luminaries over the day and night (Ps. 136:7–9), the birds and fish over the sky and sea respectively, and the animals over the land and its vegetation with man over both.

the stars. Pagans often credited the stars (which were numbered among their gods) with controlling human destiny. Here they are mentioned almost in passing.

1:21 created. See v. 1.

great sea creatures. In Old Testament poetry these are the dreaded sea-dragons associated with ancient mythology, thought by pagans to rival the creating gods (Ps. 74:13; Is. 27:1; 51:9; Jer. 51:34). By adapting and modifying this pagan imagery, the Hebrew writers subverted the pagan theology—the goodness of creation and the subservience of the aquatic animals is stressed.

1:22 Be fruitful and multiply. This entails the notion of multiplication so as to rule (cf. v. 28). The birds and fish rule their realms through multiplication. The Lord Jesus blessed His disciples to multiply spiritually (Matt. 28:18–20; Luke 24:50, 51).

1:24 livestock . . . beasts of the earth. The contrast between wild and domesticated animals differentiates carnivores from cattle (the Hebrew here for "beasts of the earth" is the same as that in Job 5:22; Ps. 79:2; Ezek. 29:5; 32:4; 34:28).

1:26 Let us . . . our . . . our. The use of the plural here is variously interpreted. Some view this as an indication of plurality within the divine unity, hinting at the later New Testament revelation of the one God as Father, Son, and Spirit. Others explain this usage grammatically—either as a plural of majesty (cf. v. 1 note) or as a deliberative plural (in which God directs the statement to Himself). Finally, some argue that God and His heavenly angelic court are in view (Is. 6:8 note).

have dominion over the fish of the sea and over the birds of the heavens and over the livestock and over all the earth and over every creeping thing that creeps on the earth."

27 So God created man in his own image,
in the image of God he created him;
[r] male and female he created them.

28 And God blessed them. And God said to them, [s] "Be fruitful and multiply and fill the earth and subdue it and have dominion over the fish of the sea and over the birds of the heavens and over every living thing that moves on the earth."
29 And God said, "Behold, I have given you every plant yielding seed that is on the face of all the earth, and every tree with seed in its fruit. [t] You shall have them for food.
30 And [u] to every beast of the earth and to every bird of the heavens and to everything that creeps on the earth, everything that has the breath of life, I have given every green plant for food." And it was so.
31 [v] And God saw everything that he had made, and behold, it was very good. And there was evening and there was morning, the sixth day.

27 [r] ch. 2:18, 21-23; 5:2; Mal. 2:15; Matt. 19:4; Mark 10:6
28 [s] ch. 9:1, 7
29 [t] ch. 9:3; Ps. 104:14, 15; 145:15, 16
30 [u] Ps. 147:9
31 [v] Eccles. 7:29; 1 Tim. 4:4

The Image of God

Scripture teaches (Gen. 1:26, 27, echoed in 5:1; 9:6; 1 Cor. 11:7; James 3:9) that God made man and woman in His own image, so that human beings are like God as no other earthly creatures are. The special dignity of being human is that as men and women we may reflect and reproduce at our own creaturely level the holy ways of God. Human beings were made for this purpose, and in one sense we are truly human to the extent that we fulfill it.

The scope of God's image in humanity is not specified in Gen. 1:26, 27, but the context of the passage helps to define it. Genesis 1:1–25 sets forth God as personal, rational (having intelligence and will), creative, ruling over the world He has made, and morally admirable (in that all He creates is good). Plainly, God's image will reflect these qualities. Verses 28–30 show God blessing the newly created humans and setting them to rule creation as His representatives and deputies. The human capacity for communication and relationship with both God and other humans appears as a further facet of the image.

God's image in humanity at creation, then, consisted in: (a) existence as a "soul" or "spirit" (Gen. 2:7), that is, as personal and self-conscious, with a God-like capacity for knowledge, thought, and action; (b) being morally upright, a quality lost at the Fall but now being progressively restored in Christ (Eph. 4:24; Col. 3:10); (c) dominion over the environment; (d) the human body as the means through which we experience reality, express ourselves, and exercise dominion; and (e) the God-given capacity for eternal life.

The Fall diminished God's image, not only in Adam and Eve, but in all their descendants, the whole human race. We retain the image structurally, in the sense that we remain human beings, but not functionally, for we are now slaves to sin, unable to use our powers to mirror God's holiness. Regeneration begins the process of restoring God's moral image in our lives. But not until we are fully sanctified and glorified shall we reflect God perfectly in thought and action as we were made to do and as the incarnate Son of God in His humanity actually did (John 4:34; 5:30; 6:38; 8:29, 46).

image . . . likeness. Humans in their whole being—body and soul—adequately and faithfully represent God (Ps. 94:10), possess life from Him and therefore potential intimacy with Him (2:7 and note), and serve on earth as His administrators (Ps. 8). The image is passed on to every human, giving each person dignity (5:3; 9:6; Prov. 22:2 and notes).

Medieval theologians strongly distinguished "image" and "likeness," with "image" viewed as a reference to natural reason, and "likeness" as a reference to the original righteousness lost in the Fall. More recent scholarship notes that the two Hebrew terms are used synonymously in Scripture (v. 27; 5:1, 3; 9:6).

have dominion. God gave humans the cultural mandate to rule the creation as benevolent kings (9:2; Ps. 8:5–8; Heb. 2:5–9). Natural man can rule the animal (v. 28) and plant (v. 29) kingdoms, but he cannot rule the heavenly powers, especially Satan (ch. 3; Eph. 6:10–12). Only the Last Adam, the very image of God's Person (Col. 1:15; Heb. 1:3) and those united with Him can do that (3:15; Matt. 4:1–11; Col. 3:10).

1:27 See theological note "The Image of God."

created. See note on v. 1. These apparently poetic lines (the verb "create" is used three times) celebrate the creation of man.

male and female. See "Body and Soul, Male and Female" at 2:7.

1:28 blessed. See v. 22; 9:1 and notes. The genealogies of chs. 5; 9; 11; 25; 36; and 46 bear witness to the fulfillment of this blessing.

have dominion . . . earth. Under divine blessing, humans accomplish the cultural mandate (v. 26 and note) by naming the creation (v. 5; 2:19, 20). This activity expresses their bearing the image of the Creator-King. Fallen man, however, distorts this activity into self-deification and abuse of the creation.

1:29 plant . . . tree. In Mesopotamian myths man was created to provide the gods with food; here God creates food for man. The human and animal (v. 30) diets were originally vegetarian, a situation altered after the Flood (9:3 note).

The Seventh Day, God Rests

2 Thus the heavens and the earth were
finished, and [w]all the host of them.
2 And [x]on the seventh day God finished his
work that he had done, and he rested on
the seventh day from all his work that he
had done. 3 So God blessed the seventh day
and made it holy, because on it God rested
from all his work that he had done in creation.

Chapter 2
1 [w]Deut. 4:19; Ps. 33:6
2 [x]Ex. 20:8-11; 31:17; Deut. 5:12-14; Heb. 4:4
4 [y]ch.1:1

The Creation of Man and Woman

4 [y]These are the generations
of the heavens and the earth when
they were created,
in the day that the LORD God made
the earth and the heavens.

Body and Soul, Male and Female

Each human being in this world consists of a material body animated by an immaterial personal self. Scripture calls this self a "soul" or "spirit." "Soul" emphasizes the distinctness of a person's conscious selfhood; "spirit" carries the nuances of the self's derivation from God, dependence on Him, and distinctness from the body as such.

Biblical usage leads us to say that we have and are both souls and spirits, but it is a mistake to think that soul and spirit are two different things; a "trichotomous" view of man as body, soul, and spirit is incorrect. The common idea that the soul is an organ of this-worldly awareness only, while the spirit is a distinct organ of communion with God, brought to life in regeneration, is out of step with biblical teaching. Moreover, such a view leads to a crippling anti-intellectualism whereby spiritual insight and theological reflection are separated to the impoverishment of both—theology being regarded as "soulish" and unspiritual, while spiritual perception is viewed as unrelated to the work of teaching and learning God's revealed truth.

The embodiment of the soul is integral to God's design for humanity. Through the body we experience our environment, enjoy and control things around us, and relate to other people. There was nothing evil or corruptible about the body as God first made it. If sin had not occurred, the physical aging and decline that leads to death as we know it would have been no part of human experience (Gen. 2:17; 3:19, 22; Rom. 5:12). Now, however, all people are corrupt throughout their psycho-physical being, as the disordered desires of mind and body, warring against each other as well as against the rules of wisdom and righteousness, clearly show.

At death the soul leaves the body behind, but this is not the happy release that Greek philosophers and some cults have imagined. The Christian hope is not redemption *from* the body but redemption *of* the body. We look forward to having a part of Christ's resurrection in and through the resurrection of our bodies. Though the exact composition of our future glorified bodies is presently unknown, we know that there will be a continuity with our present bodies (1 Cor. 15:35–49; Phil. 3:20, 21; Col. 3:4).

The two genders, male and female, belong to the creation pattern. Men and women are equally image-bearers of God (Gen. 1:27), and their dignity is equal in consequence. The complementary nature of the genders is meant to lead to enriching cooperation (see Gen. 2:18–23), not only in marriage, procreation, and family life, but in life's wider activities also. Perception of the difference between a person of the other gender and oneself is meant to be a school for learning the practice and joy of appreciation, openness, honor, service, and fidelity.

2:1 The concluding summary statement underscores that the Creator perfectly executed His will (v. 31).

2:2 God finished . . . he rested. The creation cycle was completed on the sixth day and God rested on the seventh, providing man with a model for the cycle of labor and rest. No mention is made of "evening and morning," perhaps because the Sabbath ordinance continues and man is exhorted to participate in it (Ex. 31:17), and to look forward to the eternal redemptive sabbath rest (Heb. 4:3–10).

2:3 made it holy. The seventh day is the first thing in the Torah to which God imparts His holiness and so sets apart to Himself (Ex. 20:11). It summons mankind to imitate the pattern of the King and so to confess God's lordship and their consecration to Him. This sign of a covenant with God (Ex. 31:13, 17) and type of Christ (Col. 2:16, 17) gives promise of divine rest both now and forever (Matt. 11:28).

2:4–4:26 Moses' narration moves from the prologue concerning the creation of heaven and earth to the account (2:4 note and text note) of heaven and earth. Moses treats the creation and probation of Adam and Eve in Paradise (2:4–25), their fall into sin and its consequences (ch. 3), the escalation of sin in the ungodly line of Cain (4:1–24), and the preservation of a godly remnant in the line of Seth (4:25, 26).

2:4–3:24 This story presents the fall of Adam and Eve from innocence into sin. Though historical persons (1 Chr. 1:1; Matt. 19:5; Luke 3:23–38; Rom. 5:12–14; 1 Cor. 15:45), Adam and Eve also represent every man and woman (2:24; 3:16–19; Matt. 19:4–6). The chief actor throughout is God: He forms the man (v. 7; Job 10:8–12), plants the garden (Ps. 87:1; Matt. 16:18), sovereignly places man in it (v. 15; Eph. 1:3–14), orders his life (vv. 16, 17; Ps. 31:15), gives him his wife (vv. 18–25; Matt. 19:6), judges the first parents for their sin, and restores them (ch. 3; Heb. 9:27, 28).

2:4 the generations of. This Hebrew word (*toledoth*), sometimes rendered "the history of" or "the genealogy of," introduces major new developments in the Genesis narrative (5:1; 6:9; 10:1; 11:10, 27; 25:12, 19; 36:1, 9; 37:2). The "generations of the heavens and the earth" pertains to what follows—to what the universe generated—rather than to the preceding account of the generation or creation of the earth.

5 When no [z]bush of the field[1] was yet in
the land[2] and no small plant of the field
had yet sprung up—for the LORD God had
not caused it to rain on the land, and
there was no man [a]to work the ground,
6 and a mist[3] was going up from the land
and was watering the whole face of the
ground— 7 then the LORD God formed the
man of [b]dust from the ground and
[c]breathed into his [d]nostrils the breath of
life, and [e]the man became a living creature. 8 And the LORD God planted a [f]gar-
den in Eden, in the east, and there he put
the man whom he had formed. 9 And out
of the ground the LORD God made to
spring up every tree that is pleasant to the
sight and good for food. [g]The tree of life
was in the midst of the garden, [h]and the
tree of the knowledge of good and evil.

10 A river flowed out of Eden to water the
garden, and there it divided and became
four rivers. 11 The name of the first is the
Pishon. It is the one that flowed around the
whole land of [i]Havilah, where there is gold.
12 And the gold of that land is good; bdellium and onyx stone are there. 13 The name
of the second river is the Gihon. It is the
one that flowed around the whole land of
Cush. 14 And the name of the third river is
the [j]Tigris, which flows east of Assyria. And
the fourth river is the Euphrates.

15 The LORD God took the man [k]and put
him in the garden of Eden to work it and
keep it. 16 And the LORD God commanded
the man, saying, "You may surely eat of
every tree of the garden, 17 but of the tree of
the knowledge of good and evil [l]you shall

5 [z][ch. 1:11, 12] [a]ch. 3:23
7 [b]ch. 3:19, 23; 18:27; Ps. 103:14; Eccles.12:7; 1 Cor. 15:47 [c]ch. 7:22; Job 33:4; Isai. 2:22 [d]Job 27:3 [e]Cited 1 Cor. 15:45
8 [f]ver. 15; ch. 13:10; Isai. 51:3; Ezek. 28:13; 31:8; Joel 2:3
9 [g]ch. 3:22; Rev. 2:7; 22:2, 14 [h]ver. 17
11 [i]ch. 10:7, 29; 25:18; 1 Sam. 15:7
14 [j]Dan. 10:4
15 [k]ver.8
17 [l]ch. 3:1-3, 11, 17

1 Or *open country* 2 Or *earth;* also verse 6 3 Or *spring*

LORD God. Normally these names for God are isolated: "God" to represent Him as sovereign Creator of all, and "LORD" to signify His unique covenant commitment to Israel (Ex. 3:14, 15). Here they are combined to stress that the Creator is also Israel's covenant God.

2:5 no bush . . . no small plant of the field. Inedible growth, such as thorns (3:18) and cultivated grains (3:17), respectively. Because of the crucial role played by the garden, trees, and the cursed ground, this introduction to the Fall narrative focuses on plants, not animals.

2:7 See theological note "Body and Soul, Male and Female."

formed. This figure from pottery making represents God's activity in shaping each person (Job 10:8–12).

man . . . from the ground. The wordplay in Hebrew, "man" (Hebrew *'adam*) and "ground" (Hebrew *'adamah*), shows man's close connection with the ground (2:5, 15; 3:19), and underlies Paul's later teaching that the first Adam was fashioned in a natural body for an earthly existence. The heavenly Son of Man (Dan. 7:13) shared in this earthly state in order to secure for fallen man a spiritual body of imperishable glory in the resurrection of the redeemed (1 Cor. 15:42–49).

breathed. This figure represents the Spirit's creative activity (Ps. 104:30; Ezek. 37:1–10, 14).

living creature. The Hebrew here does not say "a living being became man"—man is not formed from preexistent life. Man is differentiated from the animals by bearing the image of God (1:26 and notes), and he shows his authority over the animals by naming them (vv. 19, 20).

2:8–17 The account of man's probation begins with his creation (v. 7). The stage for this drama was the paradisal Garden of Eden (vv. 8–14), while the plot consisted of the events during that probation that tested man's obedience to the covenant obligation (vv. 15–17). In this covenant arrangement God graciously offers life to humankind, but He demands obedience to His command. The first Adam, representing all mankind, failed to obey and brought death upon all. The active obedience of the Last Adam, Christ, representing the elect, satisfies God's demands and earns for them eternal life (Rom. 5:12–19; 1 Cor. 15:45–49).

2:8–14 The Creator, by providing man with every blessing, pressed upon him the claims of God's love and made his rebellion inexcusable (Rom. 1:20). Mankind was meant for fellowship with God in the garden; his expulsion from that paradise is unnatural.

2:8 garden. A sanctuary where God invites humanity to enjoy fellowship and peace with Him. Cherubim protect the garden's sanctity (3:24 and note; Ex. 26:1; 2 Chr. 3:7) so that sin and death will be excluded (3:23; Rev. 21:8). Faith and obedience are prerequisites for living in this place of special communion with God.

in the east. In biblical times the east, where the sun rises, represented life and light (3:24 note).

Eden. The origin of the term "Eden" is disputed; it may derive from an Accadian term meaning "plain" or "prairie," or from the Hebrew term meaning "pleasure" or "delight" (from which the association of Eden with the term "paradise" derives). Eden was apparently the region in which the garden was located (v. 10). The mention of Assyria and the Tigris and Euphrates rivers (v. 14 and text note) indicates a location east of Palestine in Mesopotamia.

2:9 every tree . . . food. Life in the garden is represented as a banquet table.

tree of life. This tree represents life in its highest potency—eternal life. It is available only to those who reenter the garden through the Second Adam (3:22; Rev. 22:14). The New Testament counterpart of this tree's life-giving fruit is found in partaking of the life-giving Christ (John 6:53–56).

tree of the knowledge of good and evil. Good and evil, a compound of opposites like heaven and earth (1:1), is a figure for potentially unlimited knowledge. It is a good tree (3:22), but man must not seize it. The illicit taking of this fruit involved the assertion of human autonomy, the attempt to know all apart from God. Man must live by faith in God's word and not by a professed self-sufficiency of knowledge (Deut. 8:3; Ezek. 28:6, 15–17). The law makes wise the simple (Ps. 19:7–9).

2:10 A river. The location of this river is now unknown. The Tigris and Euphrates do not have a single source, but some translate this verse as indicating a river formed by the confluence of four rivers (rather than branching into four).

This river reminds us of the spring of living water, the spiritual source of life, that issues from the throne of the living God (Ps. 36:8; Jer. 17:13; Ezek. 47:1–12; Rev. 22:1). Jesus also used the symbol of "living water" in describing the blessings of salvation (John 4:14; 7:37–39).

2:11–13 The identity of the Pishon and Gihon rivers is uncertain.

2:11 Havilah. Probably located in Arabia (10:7, 29; 25:18; 1 Sam. 15:7).

2:15 work it and keep it. Man was to find fulfillment, not in idleness, but in a life of rewarding labor in obedience to God's command. The Hebrew behind the latter term (translated "guard" in 3:24) also entails the notion of protecting it against enemies.

2:16 commanded. God's first words to man assume his ability to choose and his moral capacity and responsibility.

2:17 you shall not eat. This unique exclusion, an exception to man's dominion over the creation (1:29), confronted him with the Creator's rule over him.

not eat, for in the day that you eat[1] of it you
[m]shall surely die."
18 Then the LORD God said, "It is not
good that the man should be alone; [n]I will
make him a helper fit for[2] him." 19 [o]So out
of the ground the LORD God formed[3] every
beast of the field and every bird of the
heavens and [p]brought them to the man to
see what he would call them. And whatever the man called every living creature,
that was its name. 20 The man gave names
to all livestock and to the birds of the
heavens and to every beast of the field. But
for Adam[4] there was not found a helper fit
for him. 21 So the LORD God caused a [q]deep
sleep to fall upon the man, and while he
slept took one of his ribs and closed up its
place with flesh. 22 And the rib that the
LORD God had taken from the man he
made[5] into a woman and brought her to
the man. 23 Then the man said,

"This at last is [r]bone of my bones
and flesh of my flesh;
she shall be called Woman,
because she was [s]taken out of
Man."[6]

24 [t]Therefore a man shall leave his father
and his mother and hold fast to his wife,
and they shall become one flesh. 25 And the
man and his wife were both naked and
were not ashamed.

The Fall

3 Now [u]the serpent was more crafty than
any other beast of the field that the
LORD God had made.
He said to the woman, "Did God actually say, 'You[7] shall not eat of any tree in the
garden'?" 2 And the woman said to the serpent, "We may eat of the fruit of the trees
in the garden, 3 but God said, [v]'You shall
not eat of the fruit of the tree that is in the
midst of the garden, neither shall you touch
it, lest you die.'" 4 [w]But the serpent said to

17 [m]Rom. 6:23; James 1:15
18 [n]1 Cor. 11:9; 1 Tim. 2:13
19 [o]ch. 1:20, 24 [p]Ps. 8:6
21 [q]ch. 15:12; 1 Sam. 26:12
23 [r]ch. 29:14; Judg. 9:2; 2 Sam. 5:1; 19:13; [Eph. 5:28-30]
[s]1 Cor. 11:8
24 [t]Cited Matt. 19:5; Mark 10:7; 1 Cor. 6:16; Eph. 5:31; [Ps. 45:10; 1 Cor 7:10, 11]
Chapter 3
1 [u]Matt. 10:16; 2 Cor. 11:3; Rev. 12:9; 20:2
3 [v]ch. 2:17
4 [w]ver. 13; John 8:44; [2 Cor. 11:3]

[1] Or *when you eat* [2] Or *corresponding to*; also verse 20 [3] Or *had formed* [4] Or *the man* [5] Hebrew *built* [6] The Hebrew words for *woman* (*ishshah*) and *man* (*ish*) sound alike [7] In Hebrew *you* is plural in verses 1-5

2:18–25 The gift of the first bride presents marriage before the Fall, and so provides the foundation for the laws against adultery (Ex. 20:14; Heb. 13:4), a model for marriage, the basis for government in the home and church (1 Cor. 11:3–12; 1 Tim. 2:12, 13), as well as a type of Christ's relationship to His church (Eph. 5:22–32). The focus in 1:26, 27 is on their sexuality as male and female; here, their social relationship as husband and wife. See "Body and Soul, Male and Female" at 2:7.

2:18 not good. See 1:4 and note. Man needs companionship on earth. In the Old Testament the most holy person, the high priest, marries (Lev. 21:13), and the Nazirite, uniquely set apart to God, is not celibate (Num. 6:1–4). Abstention from lawful marriage is never commanded in Scripture (cf. 1 Tim. 4:3), although some are given the gift of celibacy for service (1 Cor. 7:7).

helper. Man was first formed, giving him social priority, and the woman was later given to him as a helper (1 Cor. 11:3–12; 1 Tim. 2:10). The word "helper" entails his inadequacy, not her inferiority, for elsewhere it is often used of God.

fit for him. The expression assumes a complementary relationship; what he lacked she supplied and vice versa. Both share the image of God (1:26, 27).

2:19, 20 Adam is being prepared for God's gift of Eve by becoming aware of his loneliness and lack of companionship.

2:19 called. See 1:5 and note. The image-bearer now carries out the cultural mandate (1:26 and note). The place of humans is a little lower than heavenly beings and higher than the animals (Ps. 8:5).

2:20–25 See "Marriage and Divorce"at Mal. 2:16.

2:21 one of his ribs. Or, "from his side." The woman derives from the man, giving him priority within the institution of marriage (1 Cor. 11:3, 8) and pointing to the harmony and intimacy that should characterize the marriage relationship (v. 22; Eph. 5:28).

2:23 This . . . Man. Man's first poem, his only recorded statement prior to the Fall, celebrates his wife's kinship and companionship with him.

called. His twofold naming of her entails his authority in the home (3:20; cf. Num. 30:6–8). In ancient times the authority to name implied authority to govern (v. 19; 1:5 and notes).

2:24 leave. At marriage a man's priorities change. Obligations to his wife take precedence.

hold fast to. This is the language of covenant commitment. Humans are never more like the covenant-keeping God than when they pledge themselves in covenant to one another. Marriage pictures God's relationship to His people (Hos. 2:14–23; Eph. 5:22–32).

one flesh. A phrase pointing to the profound solidarity of the marriage relationship. The singular and total commitment involved implies that God intended marriage to be monogamous.

2:25 not ashamed. This statement does not idealize nudity, but shows why humans must wear clothes. With the Fall came a tragic loss of innocence (together with the resulting shame). When people's minds are enlightened by the gospel, they understand their moral frailty and practice customs of dress that shield them against sexual temptation.

3:1–24 The guardians of the sanctuary (2:15 note) are now tested for fidelity to their King. The test is administered under a covenant of works: obedience entitles them to life with God; disobedience brings death. Their failure points to their need for justification and sanctification through Christ's fulfillment of the covenant of grace.

3:1 the serpent. In the biblical world snakes were variously symbolic of life, wisdom, and chaos; the god of chaos is sometimes likened to a serpent (Job 26:12, 13; Is. 27:1). This serpent is an incarnation of Satan, the Adversary. See v. 15 note; "Satan" at Job 1:6.

more crafty. Satan's choice of embodiment was a fitting instrument for his own malevolent brilliance (cf. 2 Cor. 11:13–15). His words must be carefully scrutinized. He can only be withstood with the help of God's splendid armor (Matt. 4:1–11; Eph. 6:10–20).

woman. Satan subverts the marriage institution by bypassing the man, tempting the woman to usurp his authority (1 Tim. 2:12, 14). Nevertheless, the husband is held accountable for obeying her (vv. 9, 17).

3:2–5 The serpent tempts Eve by: emphasizing God's prohibition, not His provision; reducing God's command to a question; casting doubt upon God's sincerity and defaming His motives; and denying the truthfulness of His threat. The woman gradually yields to Satan's denials and half-truths by disparaging her privileges in adding to the prohibition ("neither shall you touch it," v. 3), and minimizing the threat (v. 6).

the woman, "You will not surely die. 5For
God knows that when you eat of it your
eyes will be opened, and you will be like
God, knowing good and evil." 6So when the
woman saw that the tree was good for food,
and that it was a delight to the eyes, and
that the tree was to be desired to make one
wise,[1] she took of its fruit [x]and ate, and she
also gave some to her husband who was
with her, [y]and he ate. 7[z]Then the eyes of
both were opened, [a]and they knew that
they were naked. And they sewed fig leaves
together and made themselves loincloths.

6 [x]1 Tim. 2:14 [y]ver. 12, 17; Hos. 6:7
7 [z]ver. 5 [a]ch. 2:25

[1] Or *to give insight*

The Fall

In Romans, Paul affirms that all mankind is naturally under the guilt and power of sin, the reign of death, and the inescapable wrath of God (Rom. 1:18, 19; 3:9, 19; 5:17, 21). He traces this back to the sin of the one man Adam, whom he describes as our common ancestor (Acts 17:26; Rom. 5:12–14; cf. 1 Cor. 15:22). Paul as an apostle has given this authoritative interpretation of the history recorded in Gen. 3, where we find the account of the Fall, the original human lapse from God and godliness into sin and lostness. The main points in that history, as seen through the lens of Paul's interpretation, are:

1. God made the first man the representative for all his posterity, just as He was to make Jesus Christ the representative for all God's elect (Rom. 5:15–19; cf. 8:29, 30; 9:22–26). In each case the representative involved those whom he represented in the fruits of his personal action, whether it was for their wealth or their woe. This divinely chosen arrangement, whereby Adam determined the destiny of his descendants, has been called the "covenant of works," though this precise phrase does not occur in Scripture.

2. God placed Adam in a state of happiness and promised permanently to establish him and his posterity in it if he showed fidelity by obeying God's command not to eat from a tree described as "the tree of the knowledge of good and evil" (Gen. 2:17). Apparently the issue was whether Adam would let God determine what was good and bad, or would seek to decide that for himself, in disregard of what God had said.

3. Adam, led by Eve who was herself led by the serpent (Satan in disguise, 2 Cor. 11:3, 14; Rev. 12:9), defied God by eating the forbidden fruit. As a result, first of all, the anti-God, self-aggrandizing mindset expressed in Adam's sin became part of him, and of the moral nature that he passed on to his descendants (Gen. 6:5; Rom. 3:9–20). Second, Adam and Eve were gripped by a sense of pollution and guilt that made them ashamed and fearful before God—with good reason. Third, they were cursed with expectations of pain and death, and expelled from Eden. At the same time, however, God began to show them saving mercy. He made them garments to cover their nakedness, and He promised that the woman's Seed would one day break the serpent's head. This promise foreshadowed Christ.

Though the story is recounted in a somewhat figurative style, Genesis asks us to read it as history. In Genesis, Adam is linked to the patriarchs and through them to the rest of the human race by genealogy (chs. 5; 10; 11), making him as much a part of history as Abraham, Isaac, and Jacob. All the book's main characters after Adam, except Joseph, are clearly shown to be sinners in one way or another, and the death of Joseph, like the death of almost everyone else in the story, is carefully recorded (Gen. 50:22–26). Paul's statement, "in Adam all die" (1 Cor. 15:22), only makes explicit what Genesis already clearly implies.

It may fairly be claimed that the Fall narrative alone gives any convincing explanation of the perversity of human nature. Pascal said that the doctrine of original sin seems an offense to reason, but once accepted it makes total sense of the human condition. He was right; and the same thing may and should be said of the Fall narrative itself.

3:5 good and evil. See 2:9 and note.

3:6 Sin is essentially man's failure to trust in God, an act or state of unbelief, an assertion of autonomy (2:9 note). True religion consists of communion with God based on trust and issuing into obedience (John 14:15). See theological note "The Fall."

tree . . . wise. Her decision was based on practical values, aesthetic appreciation, and intellectual gratification.

took of its fruit. By this act she sealed an alliance with the prince of death and darkness. God's loving election and plan of redemption are her only hope (v. 15 and notes).

he ate. Man becomes a rebel: surrounded with sufficient motives to trust and obey God, he chooses disobedience against God (6:5; 8:21). Salvation depends entirely upon the Lord, not the rebel. By God's appointment Adam represented the race as its federal head and brought death upon all (Rom. 5:12–19). He also represents, as a model and prototype, mankind's hostility against God (2:4–3:24 note).

3:7–11 Their spiritual death (2:17 and note) is shown by their alienation from one another, symbolized by the sewing of fig leaves together for clothing, and separation from God, signified by their hiding among the trees.

3:7 naked. Nakedness in the Old Testament suggests weakness, need, and humiliation (Deut. 28:48; Job 1:21; Is. 58:7). The Hebrew word for "naked" sounds like the Hebrew for "crafty" in 3:1. The intimacy of marriage is shattered (cf. 2:21, 24 and notes); trust is replaced by distrust. The first experience of guilt was expressed in terms of an awareness of nakedness. Redemption is linked to God's providing a covering for human sin (v. 21 and notes; cf. Ex. 25:17 note).

8 And they heard the sound of the LORD
God walking in the garden in the cool of
the day, and the man and his wife [b]hid
themselves from the presence of the LORD
God among the trees of the garden. 9 But
the LORD God called to the man and said to
him, "Where are you?"[1] 10 And he said, "I
heard the sound of you in the garden, and
I was afraid, [c]because I was naked, and I
hid myself." 11 He said, "Who told you that
you were naked? Have you eaten of the tree
of which I commanded you not to eat?"
12 The man said, [d]"The woman whom you
gave to be with me, she gave me fruit of the
tree, and I ate." 13 Then the LORD God said
to the woman, "What is this that you have
done?" The woman said, [e]"The serpent
deceived me, and I ate."

14 The LORD God said to the serpent,

"Because you have done this,
cursed are you above all livestock
and above all beasts of the field;
on your belly you shall go,
and [f]dust you shall eat
all the days of your life.

15 I will put enmity between you and
the woman,
and between your offspring[2] and
[g]her offspring;
[h]he shall bruise your head,
and you shall bruise his heel."

16 To the woman he said,

"I will surely multiply your pain in
childbearing;
[i]in pain you shall bring forth
children.
[j]Your desire shall be for[3] your husband,
and he shall [k]rule over you."

17 And to Adam he said,

"Because you have listened to the
voice of your wife
and have eaten of the tree
[l]of which I commanded you,
'You shall not eat of it,'
[m]cursed is the ground because of you;
[n]in pain you shall eat of it all the
days of your life;

8 [b][Ps. 139:1-12; Jer. 23:23, 24] 10 [c]ver. 7; ch. 2:25 12 [d]ch. 2:18; Job 31:33 13 [e]ver. 4; 2 Cor. 11:3; 1 Tim. 2:14 14 [f]Isai. 65:25; Mic. 7:17 15 [g]Isai. 7:14; Mic. 5:3; Matt. 1:23, 25; Luke 1:34, 35; Gal. 4:4; 1 Tim. 2:15 [h]Rom. 16:20; Heb. 2:14; Rev. 20:1-3, 10 16 [i][John 16:21] [j]ch. 4:7; S. of S. 7:10 [k]1 Cor. 11:3; 14:34; Eph. 5:22-24; Col. 3:18; 1 Tim. 2:11, 12; Tit. 2:5; 1 Pet. 3:1, 5, 6 17 [l]ch. 2:17 [m]ch. 5:29; [Rom. 8:20-22] [n]Eccles. 2:22, 23

[1] In Hebrew *you* is singular in verses 9 and 11 [2] Hebrew *seed*; so throughout Genesis [3] Or *against*

3:8 hid themselves. Their consciences condemning them, they shrank from the intimacy with God they formerly enjoyed in the garden (Rom. 2:12–16). Their expulsion from it matches their attitudes and actions.

3:9 Where. Though omniscient, God accommodates His speech to human limitations. Here the question induces them to come to Him (cf. 4:9; 11:5).

3:10 I heard the sound of you. Ironically, the word translated "heard" is also a Hebrew idiom for "obeyed"—precisely what Adam did not do.

3:11 Who. See note 11:5. The questions (v. 13) prod them to confess their guilt. God asks Satan no questions, simply consigning him to judgment (v. 14).

3:12, 13 They show their allegiance to Satan by distorting the truth, accusing one another, and ultimately accusing God (cf. James 1:13). Their efforts to conceal their sin only expose it.

3:13 deceived. This word underlies Paul's teaching in 1 Tim. 2:12, 14.

3:14–20 God's weighty judgments against Satan (vv. 14–15), the woman (v. 16), and the man (vv. 17–19) nevertheless include the promise of salvation for God's people (v. 15).

3:14, 15 The language has a double reference, referring both to the serpent and Satan.

3:14 cursed. Cursed, the opposite of blessed (1:22 and note), denotes a breaking of the serpent's powers.

dust you shall eat all the days. Dust is the symbol of abject humiliation (Ps. 44:25; 72:9), an indignity lasting forever. Satan's final defeat under the heel of the Messiah (v. 15) is delayed so that God's program of redemption through the promised Seed of the woman may be accomplished.

3:15 I will put enmity. God graciously converts the depraved woman's affections from Satan to Himself.

your offspring and her offspring. Humanity is now divided into two communities: the redeemed, who love God, and the reprobate, who love self (John 8:33, 44; 1 John 3:8). The division finds immediate expression in the hostility of Cain against Abel (ch. 4). This prophecy finds ultimate fulfillment in the triumph of the Second Adam, and the community united with Him, over the forces of sin, death, and the devil (Dan. 7:13, 14; Rom. 5:12–19; 16:20; 1 Cor. 15:45–49; Heb. 2:14, 15).

bruise . . . bruise. Before His glorious victory, the woman's Seed must suffer to win the new community from the serpent's dominion (Is. 53:12; Luke 24:26, 46; 2 Cor. 1:5–7; Col. 1:24; 1 Pet. 1:11).

head . . . heel. The suffering Christ is victorious. He has already won the victory at the Cross by providing an atonement for the saints (Col. 2:13–15) and will consummate it at His Second Coming (2 Thess. 1:5–10).

3:16–19 The woman is frustrated in her natural relationships within the home: painful labor in bearing children and subordination toward her husband. The man is frustrated in his activity to provide food. Each experiences pain by these reversals.

3:16 pain . . . bring forth children. Pain is experienced even at a point of great fulfillment for the woman. Nevertheless, in her role of bearing and raising children of promise in Jesus Christ, the woman is privileged to participate in God's plan to create a people for Himself (v. 15; cf. 1 Tim. 2:15).

desire. The phrase "he shall rule over you" and the parallel wording in 4:7 suggests that her desire is to dominate. The marriage ordinance continues, but is frustrated by the battle of the sexes.

rule over you. The harmony, intimacy, and complementarity of the pre-Fall marriage relationship (2:21–24 and notes) are corrupted by sin, and marred by domination and enforced submission. The restoration of these relationships takes place through new life in Christ (Eph. 5:22–33).

3:17 ground. Man's natural relationship to the ground, to rule over it, is reversed; instead of submitting to him, it resists and eventually swallows him (2:7 and note). The earth, frustrated by the Creator's assignment to disharmony, longs for restoration (Rom. 8:20–22).

in pain. Labor itself is a blessing because man's work reflects the activity of the working God (2:2 note). But the object of man's labor, the ground, is cursed and becomes a source of frustration.

18 thorns and thistles it shall bring forth
for you;
and you shall eat the plants of the
field.
19 By the sweat of your face
you shall eat bread,
till you return to the ground,
for out of it you were taken;
[o] for you are dust,
and [p] to dust you shall return."

20 The man called his wife's name Eve,[1]
because she was the mother of all living.
21 And the LORD God made for Adam and
for his wife garments of skins and clothed
them.
22 Then the LORD God said, [q] "Behold, the
man has become like one of us in knowing
good and evil. Now, lest he reach out his
hand [r] and take also of the tree of life and
eat, and live forever—" 23 therefore the LORD
God sent him out from the garden of Eden
[s] to work the ground from which he was
taken. 24 He drove out the man, and at the
east of the garden of Eden he placed the
[t] cherubim and a flaming sword that turned
every way to guard the way to the tree of life.

Cain and Abel

4 Now Adam knew Eve his wife, and she
conceived and bore Cain, saying, "I have
gotten[2] a man with the help of the LORD."
2 And again, she bore his brother Abel. Now
Abel was a keeper of sheep, and Cain a
worker of the ground. 3 In the course of time
Cain brought to the LORD an offering of [u] the
fruit of the ground, 4 and Abel also brought
of [v] the firstborn of his flock and of their fat
portions. And the LORD [w] had regard for Abel
and his offering, 5 but [x] for Cain and his offering he had no regard. So Cain was very
angry, and his face fell. 6 The LORD said to
Cain, "Why are you angry, and why has
your face fallen? 7 [y] If you do well, will you
not be accepted?[3] And if you do not do well,
sin is crouching at the door. [z] Its desire is
for[4] you, but you must rule over it."

19 [o] ch. 2:7; Ps. 103:14 [p] Job 34:15; Ps. 104:29; Eccles. 3:20; 12:7; Rom. 5:12
22 [q] ver. 5 [r] ch. 2:9
23 [s] ch. 2:5
24 [t] Ps. 18:10; 104:4; Heb. 1:7; [Ex. 25:18-22; Ezek. 28:11-16]
Chapter 4
3 [u] Lev. 2:12; Num. 18:12
4 [v] Ex. 13:12; Num. 18:17; Prov. 3:9 [w] Heb. 11:4
5 [x] [Prov. 21:27]
7 [y] Eccles. 8:12, 13; Isai. 3:10, 11; Rom. 2:6-11 [z] ch. 3:16

[1] *Eve* sounds like the Hebrew for *life-giver* and resembles the word for *living* [2] *Cain* sounds like the Hebrew for *gotten* [3] Hebrew *will there not be a lifting up* [of your face]? [4] Or *against*

3:19 you are dust. Man's earthly body makes physical death possible.

to dust you shall return. Physical death is both a judgment and a blessing. It renders all activity vain, but delivers the redeemed from earthly frustration and opens the way to an eternal salvation that outlasts the grave (Ps. 73:24; Prov. 14:32).

3:20 called. See 1:5; 2:23 and notes.

mother of all living. Adam's choice of the name Eve demonstrates his faith in God's promise that the woman would bear children, including the Seed who would defeat Satan.

3:21 garments of skins. God's durable "tunics" contrast with the inadequate attempt by Adam and Eve to cover their shame (3:7). His provision also entailed killing an animal, perhaps suggesting a sacrifice for sin (3:7 note; Lev. 17:11).

3:22 us. See note 1:26.

live forever. Adam and Eve are protected from an eternal bondage to sin and misery that would result if they ate of the tree of life (v. 19 note).

3:23 sent him out. God cleanses His temple-garden (2:8 note; cf. Luke 10:18; John 2:12–17; Rev. 21:27).

3:24 east. See 2:8 and note. Israel's tabernacle and temple, like the medieval cathedrals, faced toward the east.

cherubim. These heavenly beings protect God's holiness, prohibiting sinners' access to Him (Ex. 25:18; 2 Chr. 3:7).

to guard. The coming heavenly Adam, who bears the curse of toil, sweat, thorns, conflict, death on a tree, and descent into dust, will regain the garden, tearing apart the veil of the temple on which the cherubim were sewn (2:8 and note; Ex. 26:1; Matt. 27:51; Heb. 6:19; 9:3; Rev. 22:1–3, 14). The flaming sword is the first weapon of government or law-enforcement.

4:1–26 The prophesied hostility between the offspring of the serpent and the offspring of the woman (cf. 3:15) takes shape immediately in the hostility of ungodly Cain against godly Abel (vv. 1–16), and in the contrast of Cain's ungodly offspring versus the godly line of Seth (4:17–5:32). There is a horrendous escalation of sin from Cain to Lamech.

4:1–16 The focus is on Cain, the archetype of Satan's followers. Cain displays his kinship with the devil by his hostility against God and his murder of a good man (v. 8; Matt. 23:35; Heb. 11:4), together with his lies (v. 9; John 8:44; 1 John 3:12).

4:1 Adam knew Eve. The Hebrew word for "know" is used to denote the sexual intimacy of the marriage relationship.

a man with the help of the LORD. Humans, both originally (1:26, 27) and presently, owe their existence to God. Woman originally came from the man, now man comes forth from the woman. The sexes are dependent on one another, and both are dependent on God (1 Cor. 11:8–12).

4:2 Abel. The name means "breath," "vapor," or "nothing" with the connotation of "perishable," a somber prophecy of what follows.

sheep . . . ground. In spite of Adam's Fall, humans still carry out the cultural mandate to manage the earth's resources (1:26, 28).

4:4, 5 offering. The Hebrew here is the common word for "tribute," the gift of an inferior to a superior (1 Sam. 10:27; 1 Kin. 4:21). Each brother brought a gift appropriate to his vocation (cf. Gen. 32:13–21).

4:4 firstborn. As the Author and Owner of life, God was entitled to the first share produced by plants (firstfruits, Deut. 26:1–11) and by animals and man (firstborn, Ex. 13:2, 12; 34:19), and to the best of what a worshiper had to offer (fat, Lev. 3:14–16). Abel brought both the first and the best; Cain brought neither. Many also point out that Abel brought a blood sacrifice, while Cain did not.

the LORD had regard. God sees the heart (cf. 1 Sam. 16:7).

Abel and his offering. The worshiper and his offering are inseparable: by faith Abel was commended as a righteous man when God spoke well of his offerings; without faith neither Cain nor his offerings were pleasing to God (Heb. 11:4, 6).

4:5 Cain was very angry. Cain's failure in worship, and his subsequent angry response, were basic to his unethical behavior. The elect and nonelect are differentiated by their basic attitudes toward God.

4:6 Why. God's question introduces the admonition in v. 7 (3:9 note).

4:7 crouching at the door. The Hebrew suggests a threatening demon

8 Cain spoke to Abel his brother.[1] And
when they were in the field, Cain rose up
against his brother Abel and [a]killed him.
9 Then the LORD said to Cain, "Where is
Abel your brother?" He said, [b]"I do not
know; am I my brother's keeper?" 10 And
the LORD said, "What have you done? The
voice of your brother's blood [c]is crying to
me from the ground. 11 And now [d]you are
cursed from the ground, which has
opened its mouth to receive your brother's blood from your hand. 12 When you
work the ground, it shall no longer yield
to you its strength. You shall be a fugitive
and a wanderer on the earth." 13 Cain said
to the LORD, "My [e]punishment is greater
than I can bear.[2] 14 Behold, [f]you have driv-
en me today away from the ground, and
[g]from your face I shall be hidden. I shall
be a fugitive and a wanderer on the earth,
[h]and whoever finds me will kill me."
15 Then the LORD said to him, "Not so! If
anyone kills Cain, vengeance shall be
taken on him [i]sevenfold." And the LORD
[j]put a mark on Cain, lest any who found
him should attack him. 16 Then Cain went
away from the presence of the LORD and

8 [a]Matt. 23:35; Heb. 12:24; 1 John 3:12; Jude 11
9 [b]John 8:44
10 [c]Heb. 12:24; [Rev. 6:10]
11 [d]Deut. 27:24; [Num. 35:33]
13 [e]ch. 19:15
14 [f]Job 15:20-24 [g]2 Kin. 24:20; Ps. 51:11; 143:7; Jer. 52:3 [h]ch. 9:6; Num. 35:19
15 [i]Ps. 79:12 [j][Ezek. 9:4, 6; Rev. 14:9, 11]

settled in the land of Nod,[3] east of Eden.
17 Cain knew his wife, and she conceived
and bore Enoch. When he built a city, he
called the name of the city after the name of
his son, Enoch. 18 To Enoch was born Irad,
and Irad fathered Mehujael, and Mehujael
fathered Methushael, and Methushael
fathered Lamech. 19 And Lamech took two
wives. The name of the one was Adah, and
the name of the other Zillah. 20 Adah bore
Jabal; he was the father of those who dwell
in tents and have livestock. 21 His brother's
name was Jubal; he was the father of all
those who play the lyre and pipe. 22 Zillah
also bore Tubal-cain; he was the forger of all
instruments of bronze and iron. The sister
of Tubal-cain was Naamah.
23 Lamech said to his wives:

"Adah and Zillah, hear my voice;
you wives of Lamech, listen to
what I say:
I have killed a man for
wounding me,
a young man for striking me.

[1] Hebrew; Samaritan, Septuagint, Syriac, Vulgate add *Let us go out to the field* [2] Or *My guilt is too great to bear* [3] *Nod* means *wandering*

crouching outside the door of a house. Perhaps there is also an allusion to the serpent lying in wait to strike the heel (3:15; cf. 1 Pet. 5:8).

desire. See note 3:16.

rule over it. Knowing Cain's heart, God warns him not to submit to the murderous temptation of the devil (cf. 1 John 3:12). Although unregenerate humans can rule over the ground and flocks, they cannot finally master sin (1:26 note; Ps. 53:3; Rom. 8:7).

4:8 spoke to Abel. Ignoring God and His warning, Cain's subsequent actions reveal his answer. Abel is mentioned only for his birth, offering, and death.

killed him. The fracturing of family ties by sin, begun in ch. 3, quickly reaches the extreme of murder. Seeking autonomy from God like his parents (3:6 note), Cain usurps divine sovereignty over life.

4:9 Where is Abel. See note 11:5.

am I my brother's keeper. The sarcastic hypocrite had already killed his brother.

4:10–14 Cain the murderer, alienated both from the ground and from society, has no rest.

4:10 What have you done. The question registers God's outrage.

crying. Whereas Abel's blood cried out for vengeance (Is. 26:21; Matt. 23:35; Rev. 6:10), Christ's blood cries out for forgiveness (Heb. 12:24).

4:11 cursed. God's curse now links Cain with Satan (3:14; 1 John 3:12). His time of grace ended, he is consigned to judgment (Heb. 9:27; 10:27). Whereas in 3:17–19 the ground is cursed so as not to yield its produce without frustrating labor, now Cain is cursed to become a fugitive without a permanent place and security.

4:13 greater than I can bear. Cain responds with self-pity instead of repenting for his sin against God and man. He fears physical and social exposure but not the God who made him.

4:14 whoever finds me. The story up to now has focused on Cain, not on Adam's other descendants (v. 17; 5:4). Ironically, after murdering his brother, Cain now fears vengeance from his own family (cf. Num. 35:19).

kill me. Cain anticipates the violent behavior of his descendants (6:5, 11).

4:15 mark. This may have been a protective tattoo identifying Cain as one under God's protection.

4:17–24 The ambivalence of godless human culture is portrayed by advances in civilization, including the first city, with a parallel increase in violence.

4:17, 18 Cain . . . Enoch . . . Irad . . . Mehujael . . . Methushael . . . Lamech. The names are similar to those in ch. 5, not because they represent variations of the same source, but to parallel and contrast the two offspring of Adam. The seventh from Adam through Cain and Seth, respectively the ungodly Lamech (vv. 19–24) and the godly Enoch (5:24), stand in sharp contrast to one another. The former inflicted death; the latter did not die.

4:17 knew his wife . . . bore Enoch. See note on v. 1. In God's common grace, family life is enjoyed by unbelievers as well as by believers.

he built a city. In seeking the security of a city, it appears that sinful Cain both defied the divine judgment that he should be a vagabond (v. 12) and showed his lack of faith in the protection provided by God's mark (v. 15). The earthly city provides both civilization and protection, but culminates in the building of a city that challenges God's supremacy (11:4). The faithful by contrast look for a heavenly city (Phil. 3:20; Col. 3:1–4; Heb. 11:10, 16; 12:22; 13:14).

4:19–24 Lamech. Lamech represents both a progressive hardening in sin—polygamy (cf. 2:24; Matt. 19:5, 6) and a grossly unjust vendetta—and the extension of the cultural mandate from animal husbandry (v. 20) to the arts (v. 21) and sciences (v. 22). Lamech expresses, indeed celebrates, his deepening depravity by his song (vv. 23, 24).

4:19 two wives. Bigamy is an abuse of the marriage institution that God intended to be monogamous (2:24 note).

24 [k] If Cain's revenge is sevenfold,
then Lamech's is seventy-
sevenfold."

25 And Adam knew his wife again, and
she bore a son and called his name Seth,
for she said, "God has appointed[1] for me
another offspring instead of Abel, for Cain
killed him." 26 To [l] Seth also a son was born,
and he called his name [m] Enosh. At that
time people began [n] to call upon the name
of the LORD.

Adam's Descendants to Noah

5 This is the book of the generations of
Adam. When God created man, [o] he
made him in the likeness of God. 2 Male and
female he created them, and he blessed them
and named them Man[2] when they were created. 3 When Adam had lived 130 years, he
fathered a son in his own likeness, after his
image, and [p] named him Seth. 4 [q] The days of
Adam after he fathered Seth were 800 years;
and he had other sons and daughters. 5 Thus
all the days that Adam lived were 930 years,
[r] and he died.
6 When Seth had lived 105 years, [s] he
fathered Enosh. 7 Seth lived after he fathered
Enosh 807 years and had other sons and
daughters. 8 Thus all the days of Seth were
912 years, and he died.
9 When Enosh had lived 90 years, he
fathered Kenan. 10 Enosh lived after he
fathered Kenan 815 years and had other
sons and daughters. 11 Thus all the days of
Enosh were 905 years, and he died.
12 When Kenan had lived 70 years, he
fathered Mahalalel. 13 Kenan lived after he
fathered Mahalalel 840 years and had other
sons and daughters. 14 Thus all the days of
Kenan were 910 years, and he died.
15 When Mahalalel had lived 65 years, he
fathered Jared. 16 Mahalalel lived after he
fathered Jared 830 years and had other
sons and daughters. 17 Thus all the days of
Mahalalel were 895 years, and he died.
18 When Jared had lived 162 years he
fathered [t] Enoch. 19 Jared lived after he
fathered Enoch 800 years and had other
sons and daughters. 20 Thus all the days of
Jared were 962 years, and he died.
21 When Enoch had lived 65 years, he

24 [k] ver. 15
26 [l] 1 Chr. 1:1; Luke 3:38 [m] ch. 5:6 [n] Ps. 116:17; Zeph. 3:9; Zech. 13:9
Chapter 5
1 [o] See ch. 1:26, 27
3 [p] ch. 4:25
4 [q] For ver. 4-32, see 1 Chr. 1:1-4; Luke 3:36-38
5 [r] ch. 3:19
6 [s] ch. 4:26
18 [t] Jude 14

1 *Seth* sounds like the Hebrew for *he appointed* 2 Hebrew *adam*

4:24 seventy-sevenfold. Cain's violence and vindictiveness are greatly magnified in his descendant. The depth of Lamech's depravity is evident in his arrogant assurance and self-reliance (in contrast to Cain's fear, v. 14).

4:25, 26 This episode provides a transition between the two accounts begun in 2:4 and 5:1 (cf. 6:1–8; 9:18–29).

4:25 knew his wife. See note on v. 1. The comparison and contrast with vv. 1, 17 signal the transition to the line of the godly offspring predicted in 3:15.

Seth. His name, derived from the Hebrew verb translated "appointed" (text note), expresses Eve's faith that God would continue the covenant family in spite of death (3:15; cf. 3:20 note).

4:26 call upon the name of the LORD. The covenant family, making its petition and praise in the name of the Lord, glorifies God, not man (cf. vv. 23, 24).

5:1–6:8 In this account of Adam's genealogy, Moses focuses on the covenant line of Seth (ch. 5) and then summarizes the escalation of sin on the earth before the Flood (6:1–8).

5:1–3 The godly line of Seth, in contrast with that of Cain (4:17–24), is begun by linking it with the original creation: vv. 1–2 summarize 1:1–2:3, especially 1:27, 28. Verse 3b echoes both 1:27, 28 and 4:25 (11:10–26). God's intention for creation will be realized through Seth, not Cain.

5:1 This is the book of the generations. A new section of the Book of Genesis begins (2:4 note). The mention of a "book" or "document" indicates that the author used sources (11:10–26).

5:2 blessed. The creation blessing is reiterated (1:28; 9:1 note).

named. See 1:5 and note.

5:3–32 These verses contain ten paragraphs, each written in the same form, with one paragraph for each generation in Adam's line through Seth. There are some similarities, as well as significant differences, between this material and the Sumerian King List (written c. 2000 B.C.), which mentions eight antediluvian (pre-Flood) kings who reigned for exceptionally long periods (up to 72,000 years). Following the Sumerian flood account (cf. chs. 6–9), there is another list of shorter-lived postdiluvians (cf. ch. 11).

More significant are the formal similarities and material differences between this Sethite genealogy and the Cainite genealogy in ch. 4. Both are initially linear, focusing on one individual in each generation, and both conclude by dividing the line among three sons (4:20–22; 5:32; the same is true in 11:10–26). But the central themes of these genealogies contrast sharply. Cain's line dies in the Flood; Seth's lives through it. Whereas the former presents the curse-laden line of Cain that concludes with murderer begetting murderer (4:17–24), the latter links the founder of humanity, Adam, with its re-founder, Noah (4:25, 26 note). The Enoch and Lamech in Seth's line cannot be confused with the first and last descendants bearing these names in Cain's line. Enoch, the seventh in the line of Seth, "walked with God" and "God took him" (v. 24); and the Sethite Lamech names his son Noah, hoping the Lord will "bring us relief" (cf. v. 29).

Because the Hebrew word translated "fathered" often means "became the ancestor of," and because some of the numbers appear to be symbolic, many scholars argue that there are gaps in these genealogies, and that they therefore cannot be used to compute a precise chronology. The significant seventh generation of each genealogy marks a high point—the height of wickedness in the Cainite Lamech (4:18–24), and the height of godliness in the Sethite Enoch (vv. 18–24; cf. vv. 21–24 note). The figure of ten generations from Seth to Noah (vv. 3–32) matches the ten generations from Shem to Abram in 11:10–26 (this latter genealogy appears to contain gaps, 11:10–26 note; cf. Matt. 1:17 note). Also, the ages of some antediluvians may be symbolic, and are perhaps related to astronomical periods known to the ancient Near Eastern peoples (e.g., the three hundred sixty-five years of Enoch's life, vv. 21–24 note).

5:5 he died. See 3:19 and notes. Through Adam's transgression death had come upon all (Rom. 5:12–14). On the other hand, in spite of this judgment God's grace preserves the messianic line (3:15 and note) even while sin abounds in the earth (4:17–24).

5:21–24 The number seven (or multiples of it) is often significant in biblical genealogies (5:3–32 note; Matt. 1:17 note; Jude 14).

fathered Methuselah. 22 Enoch [u]walked
with God[1] after he fathered Methuselah
300 years and had other sons and daughters. 23 Thus all the days of Enoch were 365
years. 24 Enoch [u]walked with God, and he
was not,[2] [v]for God took him.
25 When Methuselah had lived 187 years,
he fathered Lamech. 26 Methuselah lived
after he fathered Lamech 782 years and
had other sons and daughters. 27 Thus all
the days of Methuselah were 969 years,
and he died.
28 When Lamech had lived 182 years, he
fathered a son 29 and called his name Noah,
saying, "Out of the ground [w]that the LORD
has cursed this one shall bring us relief[3]
from our work and from the painful toil of
our hands." 30 Lamech lived after he
fathered Noah 595 years and had other
sons and daughters. 31 Thus all the days of
Lamech were 777 years, and he died.
32 After Noah was 500 years old, Noah
fathered [x]Shem, Ham, and [y]Japheth.

Increasing Corruption on Earth

6 When man began to multiply on the
face of the land and daughters were
born to them, 2 the sons of God saw that the
daughters of man were attractive. And they

22 [u]ver. 24; ch. 6:9; [Mic. 6:8; Mal. 2:6]
24 [u][See ver. 22 above] [v]Heb. 11:5; [2 Kin. 2:11]
29 [w]ch. 3:17
32 [x]ch. 6:10 [y]ch. 10:21

[1] Septuagint *pleased God* [2] Septuagint *was not found* [3] *Noah* sounds like the Hebrew for *rest*

5:22 walked with God. The expression, repeated twice (here and v. 24), signifies intimate fellowship (3:8; 6:9), including special revelation.

5:23 365 years. Perhaps a symbolic number corresponding to the days of the solar year and signifying a life of special privilege. Although longevity is often a sign of divine blessing and favor (Ps. 91:16), the blessed Enoch's relatively short life span, especially compared to his son Methuselah, shows that being in God's presence is an even greater privilege (John 17:24).

5:24 was not, for God took him. Of all recorded Old Testament saints, only Enoch and Elijah did not experience physical death (2 Kin. 2:1–12; Heb. 11:5).

5:29 this one shall bring us relief. Whereas the Cainite Lamech sought to redress wrong through revenge (4:24), the Sethite Lamech looked in hope to the Lord to provide the seed through whom would come deliverance from the curse.

5:32 500. See 6:3 and note.

Shem, Ham, and Japheth. See 9:18 where their story is resumed.

6:1–8 This section, by the mention of Noah (5:32; 6:8, 9), signals the transition from the godly line of Seth to the flood story (6:9–9:17) and recalls the ominous situation at the end of the Cainite lineage (4:17–24).

6:2 sons of God. These have been identified as Sethites (the traditional Christian interpretation), as angels (the earliest Jewish interpretation; cf. Job 1:6), and as royal tyrannical successors to Lamech who gathered harems (proposed by rabbis of the second-century A.D.). All three interpretations can be defended linguistically. On the surface, the first interpretation best fits the immediate preceding context (a contrast of the curse-laden line of

Ages of the Patriarchs (5:5)

In the genealogy of Gen. 5 the patriarchs who lived before the Flood had an average life span of about 900 years. This contrasts with the genealogy of Gen. 11:10–26 where the ages of post-Flood patriarchs dropped rapidly and gradually leveled off.

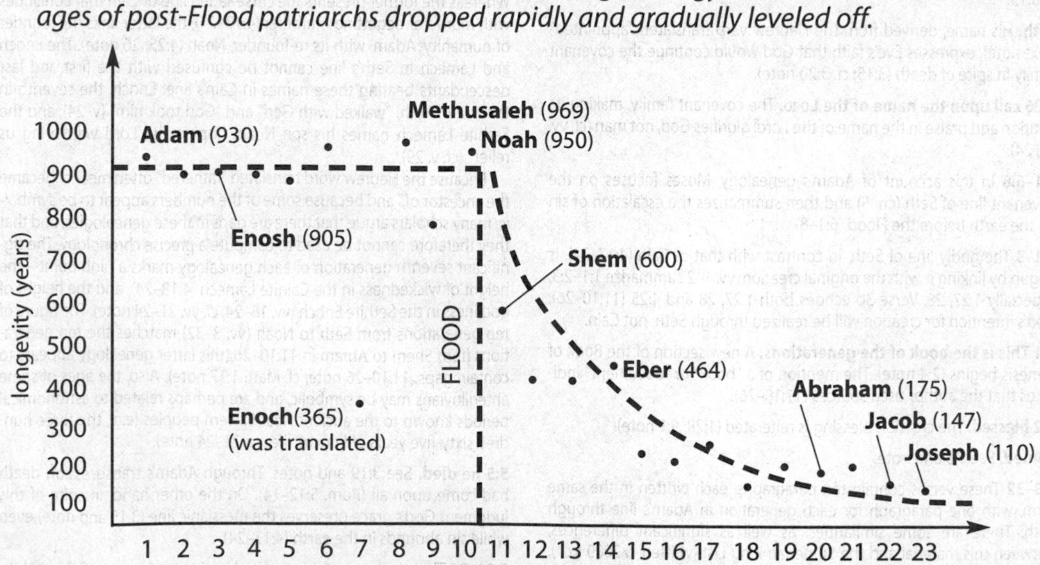

took as their wives any they chose. **3**Then
the LORD said, [z]"My Spirit shall not abide
in[1] man forever, [a]for he is flesh: his days
shall be 120 years." **4**The Nephilim[2] were
on the earth in those days, and also afterward, when the sons of God came in to the
daughters of man and they bore children to
them. These were the mighty men who
were of old, the men of renown.
5[b]The LORD saw that the wickedness of
man was great in the earth, and that every
[c]intention of the thoughts of his heart was
only evil continually. **6**And [d]the LORD was
sorry that he had made man on the earth,
and it [e]grieved him to his heart. **7**So the LORD
said, "I will blot out man whom I have created from the face of the land, man and animals
and creeping things and birds of the heavens,
for I am sorry that I have made them." **8**But
Noah [f]found favor in the eyes of the LORD.

Noah and the Flood

9These are the generations of Noah.
[g]Noah was a righteous man, [h]blameless in
his generation. Noah [i]walked with God.
10And Noah had three sons, Shem, Ham,
and Japheth.
11Now the earth was corrupt in God's
sight, and the earth was filled with violence.
12And God [j]saw the earth, and behold, it
was corrupt, [k]for all flesh had corrupted
their way on the earth. **13**And God said to
Noah, [l]"I have determined to make an end
of all flesh,[3] for the earth is filled with

Chapter 6
3 [z]1 Pet. 3:19, 20; [Neh. 9:30; Gal. 5:16, 17] [a]Ps. 78:39
5 [b]Ps. 14:2, 3 [c]ch. 8:21; Job 14:4; 15:14; Ps. 51:5; Jer. 17:9; Matt. 15:19; Rom. 3:23
6 [d]1 Sam. 15:11; 2 Sam. 24:16; Joel 2:13; [Num. 23:19; 1 Sam 15:29] [e]Isai. 63:10; Eph. 4:30
8 [f]ch. 19:19; Ex. 33:12, 13, 16, 17
9 [g]ch. 7:1; Ezek. 14:14, 20; 2 Pet. 2:5 [h]Job 1:1, 8; Luke 1:6 [i]ch. 5:22, 24; [Heb. 11:7]
12 [j]Ps. 14:2, 3; 53:2, 3 [k]Job 22:15-17
13 [l]Ezek. 7:2, 3, 6

1 Or *My Spirit shall not contend with* 2 Or *giants* 3 Hebrew *The end of all flesh has come before me*

Cain with the godly line of Seth), but it fails to explain adequately how "daughters of man" refers specifically to Cainite women. The second view has ancient support, but seems to contradict Jesus' statement that angels do not marry (Mark 12:25) and does not explain why the focus is on mortals (v. 3) and the judgment on them (vv. 5–7). The third interpretation best explains the phrase "any they chose" (12:10–20; 20:1; 1 Sam. 11) but lacks as much ancient support. The best solution is probably a combination of the last two. These human offspring are also the spiritual offspring of Satan (3:15), empowered by demons (cf. Deut. 32:17).

saw . . . attractive . . . took. The Hebrew term here translated "attractive" is often rendered "good." Their sin repeats the pattern ("saw . . . good . . . took") of the original sin in 3:6.

6:3 My Spirit. See note 1:2.

abide in. The Hebrew word is difficult to translate. Some scholars relate it to a term meaning "rule" or "judge," while ancient translators understood it to mean "remain" or "contend" (text note). Either way, the sentence points to the withdrawal of God's life-giving Spirit (1:2 note).

120 years. Probably the span of time between this proclamation and the Flood (5:32; 7:6). It may refer to an individual's life span, but that interpretation seems contradicted by the age of the postdiluvians who at first lived much longer (Gen. 11) and then much less (Ps. 90:10).

6:4 Nephilim. See text note. These giant-like "mighty men," the offspring of the demonic tyrants (v. 2 note), filled the earth with violence (v. 11; Num. 13:32). The Hebrew root means "to fall," and may suggest their fate (Ezek. 32:20–28).

and also afterward. This parenthetical remark reminds the book's original audience that the same kind of horrible people existed after the Flood (Num. 13:32).

mighty men. The Hebrew here is also used for Nimrod and his bestial kingdom (10:8–11).

6:5 every intention . . . of his heart. A vivid portrayal of the depth and comprehensiveness of human depravity (cf. 8:21).

6:6 was sorry. Here a reference to a change of attitudes and actions. There is no contradiction between this verse and passages teaching the changelessness (immutability) of God (Mal. 3:6; James 1:17) and that God does not change His mind (Num. 23:19; 1 Sam. 15:29; Ps. 33:11; Is. 46:10). Remembering that this description is anthropopathic (God is depicted in terms of the human experience of knowledge and emotion), we must also recognize that the immutable and sovereign God deals appropriately with changes in human behavior. When they sin or repent of sin, He "changes His mind" with regard to the blessing or punishment appropriate to the situation (Ex. 32:12, 14; 1 Sam. 15:11; 2 Sam. 24:16; Jer. 18:11; Amos 7:3, 6)—all in accordance with His sovereign and eternal purposes. Because God is changeless in His being, and eternally loyal to His covenant promises, we can have firm confidence in Him who is "the same yesterday and today and forever" (Heb. 13:8 and note).

grieved him to his heart. The Hebrew here means "indignant rage" (cf. 34:7). Christ's sacrifice pacifies God's bitter indignation against sin (8:21).

6:7 I will blot out. In this story the first created order is destroyed by a flood and the second inaugurated, a scenario constituting a prophetic model of the present order to be destroyed by fire and replaced by the third and perfect one (2 Pet. 3:3–13). Jesus also uses this model as a type of the Day of the Lord (Matt. 24:37–39).

animals . . . heavens. As the ground endured the consequences of its rulers' sin, so also must the animals.

6:8 But Noah. See Rom. 11:3–6.

found favor. God's "grace" is always His unmerited favor, and Noah's integrity could not earn God's acceptance (Rom. 3:10–12). God saved Noah, as He saves us, as an unconditional gift, which Christ would later purchase with His own blood. Even so, Noah seems to be a type of Christ: just as Noah represented his family, so Christ represents the whole family of God.

6:9–9:29 Although stories of a great flood are found in many cultures all over the world, none are so strikingly similar to this account as those of ancient Mesopotamia (e.g., the Gilgamesh Epic and the Atrahasis Epic). There are crucial differences, however. In the Mesopotamian tales, the petty pagan gods bring about a flood to control overpopulation or to quiet the annoying noise of people, and once it comes they are frightened by it. In contrast, the true God sovereignly brings the Flood because of man's wickedness, and in response to Noah's sacrifices He pledges never again to destroy the earth. See note 6:22.

6:9–22 This section depicts the covenant relationship: Noah was righteous (v. 9), obeying God's commands, and God confirmed the covenant with him to preserve creation (v. 18). Corresponding to the creation account of ch. 1, God's commands (vv. 13–21) are followed by obedience (v. 22).

6:9 These are the generations of. See note 2:4.

righteous. The word presupposes a covenant in which those who are joined to the Lord by faith (15:6) follow His moral standards. These standards were revealed to Noah in conscience (3:8 and note) and special revelation (5:22 note).

blameless. Not that Noah never sinned (cf. 9:20–23), but that his devotion to God and His commandments was unchallenged (cf. 2 Sam. 22:24).

walked with God. See note 5:22.

violence through them. Behold, I will
destroy them with the earth. **14**Make yourself an ark of gopher wood.[1] Make rooms in
the ark, and cover it inside and out with
pitch. **15**This is how you are to make it: the
length of the ark 300 cubits,[2] its breadth 50
cubits, and its height 30 cubits. **16**Make a
roof[3] for the ark, and finish it to a cubit
above, and set the door of the ark in its side.
Make it with lower, second, and third decks.
17[m]For behold, I will bring a flood of waters
upon the earth to destroy all flesh in which
is the breath of life under heaven.
Everything that is on the earth shall die.
18But [n]I will establish my covenant with you,
and you shall come into the ark, you, your
sons, your wife, and your sons' wives with
you. **19**And of every living thing of all flesh,
you shall bring two of every sort into the ark
to keep them alive with you. They shall be
male and female. **20**Of the birds according to
their kinds, and of the animals according to
their kinds, of every creeping thing of the
ground, according to its kind, two of every
sort shall come in to you to keep them alive.
21Also take with you every sort of food that
is eaten, and store it up. It shall serve as
food for you and for them." **22**[o]Noah did
this; he did all that God commanded him.

7 Then the LORD said to Noah, [p]"Go into
the ark, you and all your household, for
I have seen that [q]you are righteous before
me in this generation. **2**Take with you seven
pairs of all [r]clean animals,[4] the male and his
mate, and a pair of the animals that are not
clean, the male and his mate, **3**and seven
pairs[5] of the birds of the heavens also, male
and female, to keep their offspring alive on
the face of all the earth. **4**For in seven days
[s]I will send rain on the earth forty days and
forty nights, [t]and every living thing[6] that I
have made I will blot out from the face of
the ground." **5**[u]And Noah did all that the
LORD had commanded him.
6Noah was six hundred years old when

17 [m]ch. 7:4; 2 Pet. 2:5
18 [n]ch. 9:9, 11
22 [o]Heb. 11:7; [Ex. 40:16]
Chapter 7
1 [p]Matt. 24:38, 39; Luke 17:26, 27; Heb. 11:7; 1 Pet. 3:20; 2 Pet. 2:5 [q]ch. 6:9
2 [r]ch. 8:20; [Lev. ch. 11]
4 [s]ver. 12, 17; [Job 37:11-13] [t]ch 6:17
5 [u]ch. 6:22

[1] An unknown kind of tree; transliterated from Hebrew [2] A *cubit* was about 18 inches or 45 centimeters [3] Or *skylight* [4] Or *seven of each kind of clean animal* [5] Or *seven of each kind* [6] Hebrew *all existence*; also verse 23

6:13 destroy. The same Hebrew word lies behind "corrupt" and "corrupted" in vv. 11, 12. The punishment matches the crime: as man ruined the good earth, so God will ruin the earth against man.

6:14 ark . . . pitch. The same Hebrew terms are used in Ex. 2:3 for the ark (of bulrushes) that protected Moses, whom God also used to bring forth a new humanity from a world under judgment.

6:15 This is how. The LORD uniquely specified the design for the building of the ark, the Exodus tabernacle, and Solomon's temple. The ark preserved Noah's covenant family through chaotic water; the latter structures would sustain the later covenant people among the chaotic nations.

300 cubits . . . 30 cubits. See text note. The dimensions (450 by 75 by 45 feet) indicate a stable and seaworthy vessel similar in size to a modern battleship. By contrast the ark in the Babylonian Gilgamesh Epic, though pitched within and without, is an unstable 180-foot cube, about four times larger in volume than Noah's ark (7:4 and note).

6:17 I will bring a flood of waters. God sovereignly rules over the Flood (Ps. 29:10).

earth . . . all flesh. A worldwide flood seems to be in view (7:19–23; 8:21; 9:11,15; 2 Pet. 3:5–7). But comprehensive language can also be used for limited situations (Dan. 2:38; 4:22; 5:19).

6:18–21 God preserved His creation in miniature: humans (v. 18), animals (v. 20), food (v. 21). In that some of every sort were preserved, God's work here was a type of Christ's work of definite redemption (e.g., Rev. 5:9, where Christ is said to have purchased not all, but some from "every tribe and language and people and nation").

6:18 establish my covenant. The first occurrence in Genesis of the Hebrew term for "covenant" (*berith*), though the concept itself and related terms are present earlier. See notes 2:4; 2:8–17; 2:24; 3:1–24. The Hebrew here denotes not the initiation of a completely new covenant, but the confirmation to Noah of a covenant already in existence. Noah's salvation from the waters of the Flood is an example of God's covenant grace and mercy. See "God's Covenant of Grace" at 12:1.

your sons . . . with you. This refrain (7:7, 13; 8:16, 18; cf. 7:1) emphasizes that God preserves humanity in its basic family structure and that God often deals savingly with the entire family unit, including the children. Here physical salvation is secured in the midst of floodwater, a type of Christian baptism (1 Pet. 3:20, 21).

6:20 shall come in to you. God's power can be discerned in the animals' coming to Noah.

6:22 The ancient Mesopotamian flood stories focused on human heroes or mighty men such as Utnapishtim, the only survivor of the flood in the Gilgamesh Epic (6:9–9:29 note). By contrast, the Genesis account focuses on God and mentions only Noah's obedience (7:5, 9, 16).

7:1–10 See note 6:9–9:29. The gathering and preservation of this remnant is a prototype of God's salvation of His elect in the Day of the Lord (Matt. 3:12; 24:31; 2 Thess. 2:1). This remnant from the Flood, however, will prove itself a mixture of elect and non-elect (9:20–27 and notes).

7:1 all your household. See note 6:18.

righteous. See notes 6:9.

7:2, 3 These precise directives clarify, rather than contradict, those of 6:19, 20.

7:2 seven. The additional clean animals were needed for sacrificial purposes (8:20) and for food (9:3).

all . . . animals. See 6:19, 20 and note.

clean. Noah would have known of the distinction between clean and unclean through special revelation (5:22 note). Fundamental institutions of the Law—the Sabbath (2:1–3), the ideal sanctuary (2:8 note), and sacrifice (3:21; 4:3–5)—reach back to the pre-Flood creation order; others, such as tithing (14:20) and circumcision (17:9–14), to at least the time of the patriarchs. Earth's future depended on these sacrificial animals (8:20–22 and notes; Lev. 11:1–47 note).

7:4 in seven days. A hundred and twenty years were needed to build the ark (6:3 and note) and one week to fill it. A Babylonian flood account imagines seven days to build a ship much bigger than Noah's and a flood lasting seven days (6:15 note).

forty. Forty is a conventional number for a long time and signals the introduction of a new age: by Noah, Moses (Ex. 24:18); Elijah (1 Kin. 19:8); Christ (Acts 1:3). The forty days are part of the 150 total days (8:4).

7:5 commanded. See note 6:22.

7:6 six hundred. See 6:3 and note. The precise day is given in v. 11.

7:7 sons. See 6:18 and note.

the flood of waters came upon the earth.
7 And Noah and his sons and his wife and
his sons' wives with him went into the ark
to escape the waters of the flood. 8 Of clean
animals, and of animals that are not clean,
and of birds, and of everything that creeps
on the ground, 9 two and two, male and
female, went into the ark with Noah, as
God had commanded Noah. 10 And after
seven days the waters of the flood came
upon the earth.

11 In the six hundredth year of Noah's
life, in the second month, on the seventeenth day of the month, on that day all the
[v]fountains of the great deep burst forth,
and [w]the windows of the heavens were
opened. 12 And rain fell upon the earth forty
days and forty nights. 13 On the very same
day Noah and his sons, Shem and Ham
and Japheth, and Noah's wife and the three
wives of his sons with them entered the
ark, 14 they and every beast, according to its
kind, and all the livestock according to
their kinds, and every creeping thing that
creeps on the earth, according to its kind,
and every bird, according to its kind, every
winged creature. 15 They [x]went into the ark
with Noah, two and two of all flesh in
which there was the breath of life. 16 And
those that entered, male and female of all
flesh, went in [y]as God had commanded
him. And the LORD shut him in.

17 The flood [z]continued forty days on the
earth. The waters increased and bore up
the ark, and it rose high above the earth.
18 The waters prevailed and increased greatly on the earth, and the ark floated on the
face of the waters. 19 And the waters prevailed so mightily on the earth that all the
high mountains under the whole heaven
were covered. 20 The waters prevailed above
the mountains, covering them fifteen
cubits[1] deep. 21 And [a]all flesh died that
moved on the earth, birds, livestock,
beasts, all swarming creatures that swarm
on the earth, and all mankind. 22 Everything
on the dry land [b]in whose nostrils was the
breath of life died. 23 He blotted out every
living thing that was on the face of the
ground, man and animals and creeping
things and birds of the heavens. They were
blotted out from the earth. Only [c]Noah was
left, and those who were with him in the
ark. 24 And the waters prevailed on the
earth 150 days.

The Flood Subsides

8 But God [d]remembered Noah and all
the beasts and all the livestock that
were with him in the ark. And [e]God made
a wind blow over the earth, and the waters
subsided. 2 [f]The fountains of the deep and
[f]the windows of the heavens were closed,

11 [v]ch. 8:2; Prov. 8:28; [Amos 9:6] [w]ch. 8:2; 2 Kin. 7:19; Isai. 24:18; Mal. 3:10; [Ps. 78:23] **15** [x]ch. 6:20 **16** [y]ver. 2, 3 **17** [z]ver. 4, 12 **21** [a]ver. 4; ch. 6:13, 17; 2 Pet. 3:6 **22** [b]ch. 2:7 **23** [c]2 Pet. 2:5 **Chapter 8** **1** [d]ch. 19:29; 30:22; Ex. 2:24; 1 Sam. 1:19 [e]Ex. 14:21 **2** [f]ch. 7:11

1 A *cubit* was about 18 inches or 45 centimeters

7:9 went. See note 6:20.

7:10 waters . . . came upon the earth. See note 6:17.

7:11 fountains . . . windows. Poetic expressions for the unrestrained release of water (Ps. 78:23; Is. 24:18; Amos 8:4; Mal. 3:10). The earth is being returned to its primordial condition by the release of the bounded waters above and by the upsurge of the subterranean waters (1:2, 6–9; 8:2–5 note).

deep. See note 1:2.

7:13–16 See note 6:18–20. The full roll call, with the phrase "according to its kind," echoes the creation account (e.g., 1:21, 24, 25).

7:13 On the very same day. This phrase suggests a memorable occasion (17:23, 26; Ex. 12:41, 51; Deut. 32:48).

7:16 the LORD shut. God's works of grace are both sovereign and particular. In a Babylonian flood account the hero shuts the door; God is the chief actor throughout the biblical account. In shutting the door, God also distinguishes between the righteous and the wicked (6:18–20 note). Elsewhere in Scripture doors provide safety for God's people in times of judgment. Behind closed doors while God rained judgment on the wicked, Lot (19:10), Israel (Ex. 12:23), and Rahab (Josh. 2:19) found safety. Jesus uses this symbol of separation in describing the safety of the righteous in the day of the Lord's coming (Matt. 25:10–13).

7:17–24 In this climactic section the churning waters multiply and triumph, destroying the creation. Contrast this scene with the blessing of 1:22.

7:17 forty. See note on v. 4.

7:18 prevailed. The Hebrew word, repeated in vv. 19, 20, is a military term for triumph in battle.

7:20 fifteen cubits deep. The mountains were submerged to a depth of fifteen cubits (22.5 feet), a depth sufficient to keep the ark from grounding.

7:21 The creatures are listed in the order of their creation (1:20–25).

all flesh died. See note 6:17.

7:23 Only Noah . . . in the ark. See note 6:18. The Flood was God's means for punishing the old world and purifying humanity for the new one.

8:1–12:9 The account of post-Flood history mirrors the pre-Flood period: the creation out of dark waters (1:1–2:3; cf. 8:1–9:16), the depraved condition of the human founders, Adam and Noah (3:1–14; cf. 9:18–23); the division of the founder's sons into elect and reprobate lines (ch. 4; cf. 9:24–27); the tyrannical non-elect building a city and making a name for themselves, Cain and Nimrod (4:17–24; cf. 10:8–12; 11:1–9); the preservation of a godly line (5:1–32; cf. 11:10–26) and of a faithful agent of blessing in the fallen world (6:1–9; cf. 11:27–12:9). The parallel judgment on the reprobate (6:9–7:24) will come with the fiery judgment and the introduction of the new heavens and the new earth (2 Pet. 3:13–17; Rev. 21:1).

8:1 God remembered Noah. The Hebrew expression indicates action based on a previous commitment (9:15; 19:29; 30:22; Ex. 2:24; 6:5; Luke 1:72,73), not merely mental recall.

wind. The Hebrew word here is the same one for "Spirit" in 1:2, recalling the original creation account and introducing God's first re-creative act renewing the earth out of the waters (8:1–12:9 note). Successive

the rain from the heavens was restrained,
3 and the waters receded from the earth
continually. At the end [g]of 150 days the
waters had abated, 4 and in the seventh
month, on the seventeenth day of the
month, the ark came to rest on the mountains of [h]Ararat. 5 And the waters continued
to abate until the tenth month; in the tenth
month, on the first day of the month, the
tops of the mountains were seen.
6 At the end of forty days Noah opened
the window of the ark that he had made
7 and sent forth a raven. It went to and fro
until the waters were dried up from the
earth. 8 Then he sent forth a dove from him,
to see if the waters had subsided from the
face of the ground. 9 But the dove found no
place to set her foot, and she returned to
him to the ark, for the waters were still on
the face of the whole earth. So he put out
his hand and took her and brought her into
the ark with him. 10 He waited another
seven days, and again he sent forth the
dove out of the ark. 11 And the dove came
back to him in the evening, and behold, in
her mouth was a freshly plucked olive leaf.
So Noah knew that the waters had subsided from the earth. 12 Then he waited
another seven days and sent forth the dove,
and she did not return to him anymore.
13 In the six hundred and first year, in the
first month, the first day of the month, the
waters were dried from off the earth. And
Noah removed the covering of the ark and
looked, and behold, the face of the ground
was dry. 14 In the second month, on the
twenty-seventh day of the month, the earth
had dried out. 15 Then God said to Noah,
16 "Go out from the ark, [i]you and your wife,
and your sons and your sons' wives with
you. 17 Bring out with you every living thing
that is with you of all flesh—birds and animals and every creeping thing that creeps
on the earth—that they may swarm on the
earth, and [j]be fruitful and multiply on the
earth." 18 So Noah went out, and his sons
and his wife and his sons' wives with him.
19 Every beast, every creeping thing, and
every bird, everything that moves on the
earth, went out by families from the ark.

God's Covenant with Noah

20 Then Noah built an altar to the LORD
and took some of every clean animal and
some of every clean bird and offered burnt
offerings on the altar. 21 And when the LORD
smelled [k]the pleasing aroma, the LORD said
in his heart, "I will never again [l]curse[1] the
ground because of man, for [m]the intention
of man's heart is evil from his youth.
[n]Neither will I ever again strike down every
living creature as I have done. 22 [o]While the
earth remains, seedtime and harvest, cold
and heat, summer and winter, [p]day and
night, shall not cease."

[1] Or *dishonor*

3 [g]ch. 7:24
4 [h]2 Kin. 19:37; Isai. 37:38; Jer. 51:27

16 [i]ch. 7:13
17 [j]ch. 1:22, 28; 9:1
21 [k]Ex. 29:18, 25, 41; Lev. 1:9, 13, 17; See Ezek. 16:19; 20:41; 2 Cor. 2:15; Eph. 5:2; Phil. 4:18 [l]ch. 3:17; 6:17 [m]ch. 6:5; Ps. 58:3; Rom. 1:21; [Matt. 15:19] [n]ch. 9:11, 15; Isai. 54:9
22 [o]Jer. 5:24 [p]Jer. 33:20, 25

re-creative acts mirroring the original creation follow: the gathering of the waters (vv. 2–5; cf. 1:6–9), the placing of birds in the heavens (vv. 6–12; cf. 1:20–23), the establishment of dry ground (v. 13; cf. 1:9–12), the emergence of animals and humans upon the earth to multiply (vv. 16–19; cf. 1:24–27), and the divine blessing (9:1–3; cf. 1:28–30).

8:4 mountains of Ararat. In the area of ancient Urartu (2 Kin. 19:37), now part of northeastern Turkey and Armenia.

8:6 forty. See note 7:4.

8:16 Go out. Since the Flood was a type of Christian baptism (1 Pet. 3:20, 21), the coming of Noah and his family out of the ark may be thought of as their emerging out of the waters of death into a new life (cf. John 5:28, 29; 11:43; Rom. 6:3–6). They prefigure the new humanity who prevail over evil (Rev. 21:7).

your sons. See 6:18 and note.

8:18 So Noah went out. See note 6:22.

8:20–9:17 The Noahic covenant is established. Although Noah was already in covenant relationship with God (6:18 note), the Lord graciously promises with a solemn covenant oath never again to destroy the earth by flood. As with other biblical covenants, the covenant promise (8:21, 22; 9:11) is accompanied by covenant mandates or stipulations (9:1–7) and the giving of a covenant sign (9:12–17).

8:20 altar . . . burnt offerings. Significantly, Noah's first act after emerging from the ark was to worship God. Though mentioned here for the first time, these aspects of the sacrificial system are presupposed (7:2 note). The burnt offering signified dedication to God and propitiation for sin (v. 21 note; Lev. 1:4; 6:8–13).

clean. See note 7:2.

8:21 pleasing. A play on words results from the similarity between this Hebrew word and Noah's name. This reference to the divine sense of smell anthropomorphically portrays the pleasure God takes in the worship of His people (Ezek. 20:41; Eph. 5:2; cf. 2 Cor. 2:15, 16). As a propitiatory sacrifice, Noah's burnt offering soothed God's indignation against sin (6:6) and prefigured the death of Christ (Is. 53:10). Pleased with the sacrifice of His servant Noah (cf. 4:4), God resolves never again to send a flood (cf. 6:6 note).

curse the ground. God is not lifting the curse of 3:17 but promising not to destroy the earth again by flood (9:11).

for the intention . . . evil. The gracious character of the Noahic covenant is underscored by the divine promise, despite the continuing presence of human sin deserving judgment, never again to send a deluge. Such grace also underlies God's preservation of Israel (Ex. 33:3; 34:9).

Neither will I ever again strike. God's grace toward Noah is extended to mankind in general (6:8; 9:12).

8:22 While the earth remains. This qualifies "neither will I ever again" in v. 21. God will preserve the earth until the final judgment (2 Pet. 3:7,13); the earthly order will not end prematurely.

9 And God blessed Noah and his sons and said to them, [q]"Be fruitful and multiply and fill the earth. 2 [r]The fear of you and the dread of you shall be upon every beast of the earth and upon every bird of the heavens, upon everything that creeps on the ground and all the fish of the sea. Into your hand they are delivered. 3 [s]Every moving thing that lives shall be food for you. And [t]as I gave you the green plants, I give you everything. 4 But you shall not eat flesh with its [u]life, that is, its blood. 5 And for your lifeblood I will require a reckoning: [v]from every beast I will require it and [w]from man. From his fellow man I will require a reckoning for the life of man.

6 [x]"Whoever sheds the blood of man,
by man shall his blood be shed,
[y]for God made man in his own image.

7 And you,[1] be fruitful and multiply, teem on the earth and multiply in it."

8 Then God said to Noah and to his sons with him, 9 "Behold, [z]I establish my covenant with you and your offspring after you, 10 and with every living creature that is with you, the birds, the livestock, and every beast of the earth with you, as many as came out of the ark; it is for every beast of the earth. 11 [a]I establish my covenant with you, that never again shall all flesh be cut off by the waters of the flood, and never again shall there be a flood to destroy the earth." 12 And God said, [b]"This is the sign of the covenant that I make between me and you and every living creature that is with you, for all future generations: 13 I have set [c]my bow in the cloud, and it shall be a sign of the covenant between me and the earth. 14 When I bring clouds over the earth and the bow is seen in the clouds, 15 [d]I will remember my covenant that is between me and you and every living creature of all flesh. And the waters shall never again become a flood to destroy all flesh. 16 When the bow is in the clouds, I will see it and remember [e]the everlasting covenant between God and every living creature of all flesh that is on the earth." 17 God said to Noah, "This is the sign of the covenant that I have established between me and all flesh that is on the earth."

Noah's Descendants

18 The sons of Noah who went forth from the ark were [f]Shem, Ham, and Japheth. (Ham was the father of Canaan.) 19 These three were the sons of Noah, and [g]from these the people of the whole earth were dispersed.[2]

Chapter 9
1 [q]ch. 1:22, 28; 8:17
2 [r][Ps. 8:6-8; James 3:7]
3 [s]Deut. 12:15; 1 Tim. 4:3, 4 [t]ch. 1:29
4 [u]Lev. 17:10, 11, 14; Deut. 12:16, 23; 1 Sam. 14:33; Acts 15:20, 29
5 [v]Ex. 21:28 [w]ch. 4:10, 11
6 [x]Ex. 21:12, 14; Lev. 24:17; Num. 35:31, 33; [Matt. 26:52; Rev. 13:10] [y]ch. 1:27; 5:1; James 3:9
9 [z]ch. 6:18; 8:22
11 [a]Isai. 54:9, 10
12 [b]ch. 17:11
13 [c]Ezek. 1:28; [Rev. 4:3; 10:1]
15 [d][Lev. 26:42, 45; 1 Kin. 8:23; Ezek. 16:60]
16 [e]ch. 17:7, 13, 19
18 [f]ch. 5:32; 10:1
19 [g]ch. 10:32

[1] In Hebrew *you* is plural [2] Or *from these the whole earth was populated*

9:1 blessed. The third time God blessed humans (1:28; 5:2) and commanded them to be fruitful (1:28; 8:17). God's blessing on Noah, to be fruitful and have dominion, constitutes the climactic act in God's renewal of creation (8:1 note).

9:2 fear of you. The reference to "fear" underscores the changes from the pre-Fall situation, where man was vegetarian (v. 3 note). Now human dominion over creation includes the exploitation of the animal kingdom for food.

9:3 Every moving thing . . . everything. The human diet is expanded to include meat (1:29 note), though the consumption of carrion (Lev. 11:40; Deut. 14:21) and blood (v. 4; Lev. 17:10) is forbidden. Rather than initiating the practice of meat-eating, this divine injunction may simply permit what sinful humanity had earlier practiced. No distinction is made between clean and unclean, a situation restored under the new covenant (Mark 7:19; Acts 10:9–16; 1 Tim. 4:3–5).

9:4 not eat . . . blood. This law points to the symbolic connection between blood and life, a concept also basic to the sacrificial system (Lev. 17:11) and the atoning work of Christ (Heb. 9:14, 22). See Lev. 3:17; 7:27; 19:26; Deut. 12:16; 1 Sam. 14:32–34.

9:5 I will require . . . require . . . require. This threefold usage of the same Hebrew verb underscores the principle—human life in the image of God (v. 6) is so valuable that God demands as compensation nothing less than the life of the murderer. Ultimately, the Lord is the Vindicator of life (Ps. 9:12; 2 Kin. 9:26). Murder burdens the guilty with its pollution (Num. 35:33; Ps. 106:38) and is expiated by the death of the murderer (v. 6; 1 Kin. 2:31, 32) or through atonement when the murderer is unknown (Deut. 21:7–9). If these measures were not used, it brought the Lord's judgment on the land (2 Sam. 21; Deut. 19:13; 1 Kin. 2:9, 31–33).

from every beast. See Ex. 21:28, 29.

9:6 by man. See v. 5; 4:16 and notes. God's endowment of humans with this judicial authority shows they stand in God's stead as rulers (1:26), and lays the foundation for government by the state (Rom. 13:1–7).

image. Though distorted by sin, the image of God continues in man (1:26 and note; 8:21). This explains why homicidal blood, in contrast to animal blood, must be compensated for. See "The Image of God" at 1:27.

9:9 I establish my covenant. See notes 6:9–22; 8:20–9:17. God's promise to preserve the earth (8:20–22) is now confirmed by a covenant (cf. 12:1–3; ch. 15). In 6:18 the covenant relationship was exclusively with Noah (6:18 note); now it is extended to his descendants and to all creation (v. 12). See "God's Covenant of Grace" at 12:1.

In a sense, God mediated His mercy through Noah for the created order, and later through Moses for Israel. So Noah and Moses were subordinate types of the true Mediator to come, Jesus Christ (Heb. 3:1–6).

9:12 sign. Biblical covenants are usually certified by visual symbols; these include circumcision for the Abrahamic covenant (17:11), the Sabbath for the Mosaic (Ex. 31:13, 17), and the Lord's Supper for the new covenant (Luke 22:20). The Davidic covenant required none since David's offspring were its visible token (2 Sam. 7:11–16). Often these signs were already in existence (e.g., the Sabbath and circumcision), but were given new significance.

9:15 remember. See 8:1 and note.

9:16 everlasting. See note 8:22.

9:18–29 This transitional section links the Noahic covenant with the Table of Nations in ch. 10 by focusing on Noah's three sons (Introduction: Characteristics and Themes).

20 Noah began to be a man of the soil, and
he planted a vineyard.[1] 21 He drank of the
wine and became drunk and lay uncovered
in his tent. 22 And Ham, the father of
Canaan, saw the nakedness of his father
and told his two brothers outside. 23 Then
Shem and Japheth took a garment, laid it
on both their shoulders, and walked backward and covered the nakedness of their
father. Their faces were turned backward,
and they did not see their father's nakedness. 24 When Noah awoke from his wine
[h] and knew what his youngest son had done
to him, 25 he said,

[i] "Cursed be Canaan;
[j] a servant of servants shall he be to
his brothers."

26 He also said,

"Blessed be the LORD, the God of Shem;
and let Canaan be his servant.
27 May God enlarge Japheth,[2]
and let him dwell in the tents of
Shem,
and let Canaan be his servant."

28 After the flood Noah lived 350 years.
29 All the days of Noah were 950 years, and
he died.

Nations Descended from Noah

10 These are the generations of the sons
of Noah, Shem, Ham, and Japheth.
Sons were born to them after the flood.
2 [k] The sons of Japheth: Gomer, Magog,
Madai, Javan, Tubal, Meshech, and Tiras.
3 The sons of Gomer: Ashkenaz, Riphath,

24 [h] [Hab. 2:15]
25 [i] Deut. 27:16 [j] Josh. 9:23; Judg. 1:28; 1 Kin. 9:20, 21

Chapter 10
2 [k] For ver. 1-5, see 1 Chr. 1:5-7; Ezek. 38:1-6

1 Or *Noah, a man of the soil, was the first to plant a vineyard* 2 *Japheth* sounds like the Hebrew for *enlarge*

9:21 drank of the wine. Scripture both looks favorably on wine (Num. 15:5–10; Deut. 14:26; Ps. 104:15; John 2:1–11) and soberly warns of its dangers (Is. 5:22; Prov. 21:17; 23:20, 21, 29–35; Is. 28:7), particularly the moral laxity exemplified by self-exposure (Lam. 4:21; Hab. 2:15). Nazirites (Num. 6:3, 4), officiating priests (Lev. 10:9), and rulers making decisions (Prov. 31:4, 5) were to abstain from it.

became drunk. Just as Adam, the original head of the human race, sinned through eating (3:6), so Noah, the head of the human race after the Flood, sinned through drinking. The striking parallels between Adam and Noah (8:1 note), and the contrast between saintly Noah before the Flood (6:8, 9) and the drunken sinner after it, direct the reader to God, not man, for salvation.

lay uncovered. Self-exposure is both publicly demeaning (2 Sam. 6:16) and incompatible with living in God's presence (Ex. 20:26; cf. Deut. 23:12–14).

9:22 saw the nakedness of his father. Gazing at another's nakedness, either in lust or scorn, is morally wrong. See notes 2:25; 3:7. Ham's scornful leering at the father whom he should have revered was particularly reprehensible (Ex. 21:15, 17; Deut. 21:18–21; Mark 7:10).

told. If it is wrong to publicize another's sin (Prov. 10:12b; 17:9), how much more a father's. The story further condemns the failure to respect one's parents.

9:24–27 This division of humanity parallels ch. 4 (8:1–12:9 note).

9:25 Cursed. The Canaanites succeed the Cainites as the curse-laden people (4:11 and note).

Canaan. Since the curses and blessings on the three sons had their descendants in view, it is not strange that the curse was on his son, not on Ham himself (vv. 18, 22), especially since God had already blessed Ham (9:1). As Ham, the youngest son of Noah, wronged his father, so the curse will fall on Ham's youngest son (v. 24), who shares his moral decadence (Lev. 18:3; Deut. 9:3). Nevertheless, Ham's descendants include, in addition to the Canaanites, the names of Israel's most dreaded enemies: Egypt, Philistia, Assyria, and Babylon (10:6–13).

servant of servants. Noah prophetically alludes to the coming subjugation of Canaan's offspring by the offspring of Shem (e.g., Israel) and Japheth (the Sea Peoples, 10:2–5) on the other. Because this curse of servitude falls upon Canaan, a Caucasian, there is no basis for the racist view that African peoples are cursed.

9:26 Blessed . . . God of Shem. With this doxological blessing Noah acknowledges God as the Author of life and extends the blessing to Shem (1:22 and note; 14:19). The line of messianic promise is now narrowed to Shem's offspring (cf. 3:15; 4:26 and notes), and it will be further specified in Genesis as through Abraham (12:1–3), Isaac (21:8–12), Jacob (25:23; 27:28, 29), and Judah (49:10). With the coming of the Messiah and the new covenant, the covenant promise is extended to all who believe (Acts 10:34, 35; Gal. 3:29).

9:27 dwell in the tents. Perhaps a reference to tribal conquests or to the future victories of Greece and Rome. Alternatively, Japheth may be a guest, drawn to Shem and to God—a promise finding final fulfillment in the New Testament (10:5 note; Acts 14:27; Eph. 2:11–22; 3:6).

9:28, 29 The genealogy begun in 5:32 is now completed according to the pattern of ch. 5.

10:1–11:9 The "account" or "generations" of Noah's family (2:4 note) consists of the Table of Nations (ch. 10) and the Tower of Babel narrative (11:1–9). Chronologically, the Tower of Babel precedes the Table of Nations, for the table presupposes the confusion of languages (10:5, 17, 20, 31). Two different yet complementary perspectives are present within this account: the Table of Nations presents the nations as of one blood, multiplying under God's blessing (9:1), while the Tower of Babel narrative presents the nations as confused due to divine judgment (11:1–9).

10:1–32 The tripartite arrangement of the Table of Nations (vv. 2–5, 6–20, 21–31) reflects the threefold division of humanity. Seventy (representing a large and complete number, cf. Judg. 8:30; 2 Kin. 10:1) nations are given: fourteen from Japheth, thirty from Ham, and twenty-six from Shem. The Japhethites migrated westward, the Hamites, south by southwest, and the Semites, south by southeast.

This selective list is not always racial; "sons of" or "fathered" may refer to political, geographical, social, or linguistic relationships (4:20, 21; 10:31). Some names are personal (e.g., Japheth, Nimrod); others are placenames (e.g., Sidon, Sheba) or names of peoples (e.g., Ludim, Caphtorim). Some belong to more than one family because of early mixtures.

10:1 These are the generations. See note 2:4.

10:2 Gomer. The Cimmerians, a nomadic people to the north of the Black Sea. They later migrated into Asia Minor. See Ezek. 38:6.

Magog. See Ezek. 38:2; 39:6; its identity is disputed.

Madai. The Medes. See 2 Kin. 17:6; Jer. 51:11; Dan. 5:28.

Javan. The Greeks.

Tubal, Meshech. Located in central and eastern Asia Minor.

Tiras. One of the Sea Peoples from the region of the Aegean Sea. Perhaps to be identified as the Etruscans, who eventually settled in Italy.

10:3 Ashkenaz. Probably the Scythians, later derided by the Greeks as uncivilized (Col. 3:11 note).

Riphath. Located in Asia Minor.

and Togarmah. 4 The sons of Javan: Elishah, [l]Tarshish, [m]Kittim, and Dodanim.
5 From these [n]the coastland peoples spread
in their lands, each with his own language,
by their clans, in their nations.
6 [o]The sons of Ham: Cush, Egypt, Put,
and Canaan. 7 The sons of Cush: Seba,
Havilah, Sabtah, Raamah, and Sabteca. The
sons of Raamah: Sheba and Dedan. 8 Cush
fathered Nimrod; he was the first on earth
to be a mighty man.[1] 9 He was a mighty
hunter before the LORD. Therefore it is said,
"Like Nimrod a mighty hunter before the
LORD." 10 The beginning of his kingdom
was [p]Babel, Erech, Accad, and Calneh, in
[q]the land of Shinar. 11 From that land he
went into Assyria and built Nineveh,

4 [l]Ps. 72:10; Ezek. 38:13 [m]Num. 24:24; Isai. 23:1, 12; Dan. 11:30
5 [n]Isai. 11:11; Jer. 2:10; 25:22; Ezek. 27:6; Zeph. 2:11
6 [o]For ver. 6-8, see 1 Chr. 1:8-10
10 [p]ch. 11:9 [q]ch. 11:2

[1] *Or he began to be a mighty man on the earth*

Togarmah. Possibly the area west of the upper Euphrates.

10:4 Elishah. Often identified as part of Cyprus (cf. Ezek. 27:7).

Tarshish. Usually identified with Tartessus in southern Spain.

Kittim. Inhabitants of Cyprus.

Dodanim. Possibly north of Tyre. If "Rodanim" is preferred, the reference is probably to the Greek island of Rhodes.

10:5 coastland peoples. The Hebrew here is rendered "coastlands" in Is. 41:5; 42:4. Isaiah, perhaps reaching back to Gen. 9:27 and 10:2, presents them as coming to salvation in the messianic age (9:27 note).

each . . . language. An anticipation of 11:1–9.

10:6–20 The Egyptians, Babylonians, and Canaanites, Israel's most bitter and influential neighbors, are mentioned in this list (9:25 note).

10:6 Cush. The area south of Egypt.

Put. Traditionally identified as Libya.

10:7 sons of Cush. These nations were probably all located in Arabia.

Havilah. Probably in Arabia. Its relation to the locations mentioned in v. 29 and 2:11 is uncertain.

10:8–12 This break in the genealogy is of prime importance to Israel's history: it explains the racial and spiritual origins of Assyria and Babylon who later conquered them.

10:8 Nimrod. His name means "we shall rebel"; later Jewish tradition identifies him as the builder of the Tower of Babel (11:1–9). This hunter and warrior is an archetype of Mesopotamian ideals of kingship.

he was the first. This and similar phrases are used to mark important historical developments (4:26; 6:1; 9:20; 11:6).

mighty man. This title may link him with the tyrants in 6:4.

10:10 beginning of his kingdom. See note 8:1–12:9. Nimrod, the prototypical city and kingdom builder, marks the beginning of man's post-Flood quest for domination and autonomy over and against God (4:17 note; 11:4–6).

Babel. The Babylonians, infamous destroyers of Judah.

Erech. One of the oldest known cities, Erech (or Uruk; modern Warka) was an important city on the Euphrates River. Inhabitants of this area were later deported to Samaria by the Assyrians (Ezra 4:9, 10).

Accad. Though the home of the famous King Sargon of Accad (c. 2350–2295 B.C.), it has not been located.

Calneh. Not the Calneh of Amos 6:2; this site has not been identified.

Shinar. The region of Babylonia.

10:11 Assyria. One of the cruelest nations of ancient history, Assyria was the infamous destroyer of Israel's northern kingdom (cf. Mic. 5:5, 6).

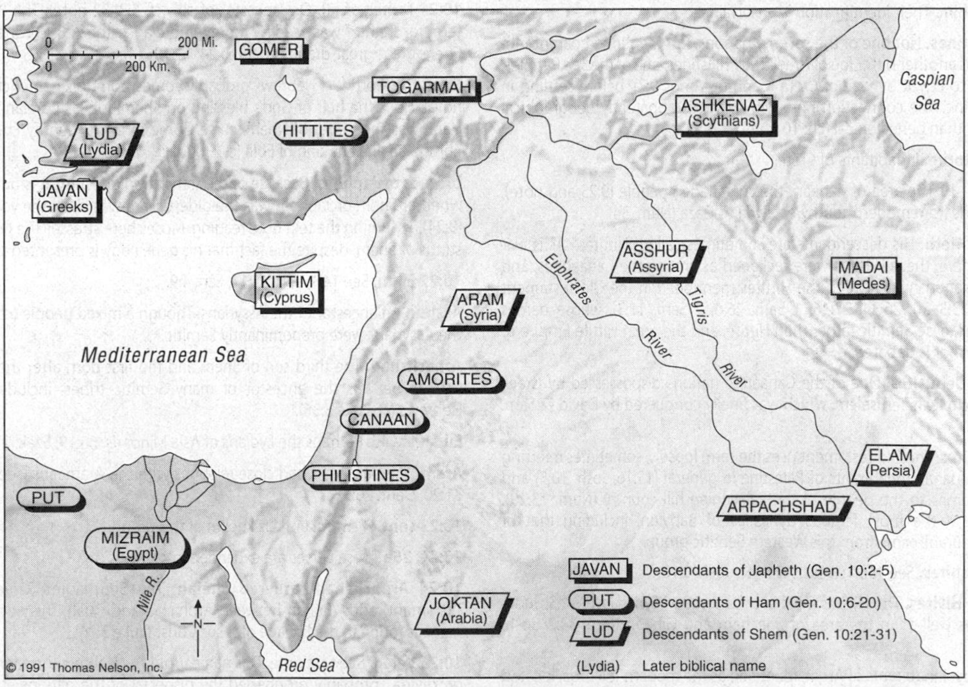

The Nations of Genesis 10

Rehoboth-Ir, Calah, and 12 Resen between
Nineveh and Calah; that is the great city.
13 [r]Egypt fathered Ludim, Anamim, Lehabim, Naphtuhim, 14 Pathrusim, Casluhim
(from whom[1] the Philistines came), and
[s]Caphtorim.
15 [t]Canaan fathered Sidon his firstborn
and Heth, 16 and the Jebusites, the Amorites, the Girgashites, 17 the Hivites, the
Arkites, the Sinites, 18 the Arvadites, the
Zemarites, and the Hamathites. Afterward
the clans of the Canaanites dispersed.
19 And the territory of the Canaanites
extended from Sidon in the direction of
Gerar as far as Gaza, and in the direction of
Sodom, Gomorrah, Admah, and Zeboiim,
as far as Lasha. 20 These are the sons of
Ham, by their clans, their languages, their
lands, and their nations.
21 To Shem also, the father of all the children of Eber, the elder brother of Japheth,
children were born. 22 The [u]sons of Shem:
Elam, Asshur, Arpachshad, Lud, and Aram.
23 The sons of Aram: Uz, Hul, Gether, and
Mash. 24 Arpachshad fathered [v]Shelah; and
Shelah fathered Eber. 25 [w]To Eber were born
two sons: the name of the one was Peleg,[2]
for in his days the earth was divided, and
his brother's name was Joktan. 26 Joktan
fathered Almodad, Sheleph, Hazarmaveth, Jerah, 27 Hadoram, Uzal, Diklah,

13 [r]For ver. 13-18, see 1 Chr. 1:11-16
14 [s]Deut. 2:23; Jer. 47:4; Amos 9:7
15 [t][ch. 15:18-21]
22 [u]For ver. 22-29, see 1 Chr. 1:17-25
24 [v]ch. 11:12; Luke 3:35, 36
25 [w]1 Chr. 1:19

[1] Or *from where* [2] *Peleg* means *division*

Calah. Located on the site of the modern Nimrud, where the Tigris and Zab rivers meet.

10:12 Resen. The location is uncertain.

the great city. Probably Nineveh (Jon. 3:2, 3).

10:13 Egypt. The infamous place of Israel's slavery.

Ludim. The Ludim probably lived near Egypt. See v. 22.

Anamim. These descendants of Egypt have not been precisely identified.

Lehabim. Generally regarded as variant of "Lubim," the Libyans.

Naphtuhim. Probably inhabitants of the Nile Delta region of Lower Egypt.

10:14 Pathrusim. Inhabitants of Pathros in Upper or southern Egypt.

Casluhim. Their identification is uncertain.

Philistines. Not one of the seventy nations, but mentioned parenthetically as another bitter foe of Israel. The Philistines, one of the Sea Peoples, came to Egypt by way of Crete (Caphtor, Amos 9:7), before settling in Palestine. The connection here with Egypt is apparently geographical rather than genealogical (ch. 10 note).

Caphtorim. Inhabitants of Crete.

10:15–19 The area of Canaan, the curse-laden people (9:25 and note), extends from modern southwest Syria to Gaza (Num. 34).

10:15 Heth. His descendants are sometimes called "Hittites." As is evident here, these Hittites were reckoned as among the Canaanites, and the relationship between the Hittites mentioned in the Old Testament (e.g., 23:3–20; 26:34; 27:46; 1 Sam. 26:6; 2 Sam. 11:3), whose names appear to be Semitic rather than Hittite, and the great Hittite Empire of Asia Minor is debated.

10:16 Jebusites. One of the Canaanite nations dispossessed by Israel. Their city was Jerusalem, which was finally conquered by David (2 Sam. 5:6–9).

Amorites. The Old Testament uses the term loosely, sometimes referring to the pagan inhabitants of Palestine in general (15:16; Josh. 10:5) and sometimes to the people of the Palestinian hill country (Num. 13:29). Some of the most famous dynasties of Babylon, including that of Hammurabi, came from this Western Semitic group.

Girgashites. See 15:21; Deut. 7:1 note; Josh. 3:10.

10:17 Hivites. The Hivites lived in Lebanon and Syria (Josh. 11:3; Judg. 3:3), as well as in the area of Shechem and Gibeon (Gen. 34:2; Josh. 9:1, 7).

Arkites. Inhabitants of Arqat, identified as the modern Tell Arqa, located twelve miles northeast of Tripoli.

Sinites. Inhabitants of a Phoenician coastal town near Arqa.

10:18 Arvadites. This group lived on an island now called Ruad, fifty miles north of Byblos (Gebal).

Zemarites. This group has not been identified.

Hamathites. Inhabitants of the city of Hamath (modern Hama), located on the Orontes River (Num. 34:8; Josh. 13:5; 2 Sam. 8:9, 10).

dispersed. See note 10:1–11:9.

10:19 Gerar. Modern Tell Abu Hureira, eleven miles southeast of Gaza. See chs. 20; 21; 26.

Sodom . . . Zeboiim. See chs. 13; 14; 18; 19.

Lasha. Its identity is uncertain.

10:21–31 The elect line of Shem is presented last (9:26 note) and overlaps with the more specific lineage of the elect Eber (v. 21) in 11:10–26.

10:21 father of all. Or, "ancestor of all" (cf. 5:3–32 note). The Hebrew term for "father" was used for more remote ancestors (28:13). Shem was Eber's great-great-grandfather (10:24; 11:10–14).

Eber. The word for "Hebrew" probably comes from this name (cf. 14:13 note). He is the heir of God's blessing on Shem, just as Canaan, son of Ham, was the target of Noah's curse. Some scholars identify Eber with Ebrum, an ancient king of Ebla (c. 2300 B.C.).

brother of Japheth. Because of the translation difficulty, it is uncertain whether Shem or Japheth was the oldest. Ham was likely the youngest (9:24). Assuming the text note reading, Moses here stresses the firstborn status of Shem, despite the fact that his genealogy is presented last.

10:22 Elam. See 14:1, 9; Is. 11:11; Ezra 4:9.

Asshur. An ancestor of the Assyrians. Though a mixed people (cf. v. 11), the Assyrians were predominantly Semitic.

Arpachshad. The third son of Shem and the first born after the Flood (11:10), he was the ancestor of many Semitic tribes, including the Hebrews (cf. Luke 3:36).

Lud. Cf. v. 13. Perhaps the Lydians of Asia Minor (Is. 66:19; Ezek. 27:10).

Aram. The patriarchs had close relations with the Arameans (see 25:20; 31:20; Deut. 26:5).

10:23 sons of Aram. Little is known of this group.

10:24, 25a These verses are expanded in 11:12–17.

10:24 Arpachshad fathered Shelah. The Septuagint (Greek Old Testament) adds Cainan between Arphaxad and Salah; this additional name is found in the lineage of Jesus Christ (Luke 3:36).

10:25 Peleg. See text note. This name, from the Hebrew term for "split" or "divide," probably prophesied the dispersal of the nations at Babel. See Ps. 55:9, where the same Hebrew term is employed in the phrase "divide their tongues."

28 Obal, Abimael, Sheba, 29 [x]Ophir, Havilah,
and Jobab; all these were the sons of
Joktan. 30 The territory in which they lived
extended from Mesha in the direction of
Sephar to the hill country of the east.
31 These are the sons of Shem, by their
clans, their languages, their lands, and
their nations.
32 These are the clans of the sons of
Noah, according to their genealogies, in
their nations, [y]and from these the nations
spread abroad on the earth after the flood.

The Tower of Babel

11 Now the whole earth had one language and the same words. 2 And as
people migrated from the east, they found
a plain in [z]the land of Shinar and settled
there. 3 And they said to one another,
"Come, let us make bricks, and burn them
thoroughly." And they had brick for stone,
[a]and bitumen for mortar. 4 Then they said,
"Come, let us build ourselves a city and a
tower [b]with its top in the heavens, and let
us make a name for ourselves, lest we be
dispersed over the face of the whole earth."
5 And [c]the LORD came down to see the city
and the tower, which the children of man
had built. 6 And the LORD said, "Behold,
they are one people, and they have all one
language, and this is only the beginning of
what they will do. And nothing that they
propose to do will now be impossible for
them. 7 Come, [d]let us go down and there
confuse their language, so that they may
not understand one another's speech." 8 So
[e]the LORD dispersed them from there over
the face of all the earth, and they left off
building the city. 9 Therefore its name was
called [f]Babel, because there the LORD confused[1] the language of all the earth. And
from there the LORD dispersed them over
the face of all the earth.

Shem's Descendants

10 [g]These are the generations of Shem.
When Shem was 100 years old, he fathered
Arpachshad two years after the flood.
11 And Shem lived after he fathered
Arpachshad 500 years and had other sons
and daughters.
12 When Arpachshad had lived 35 years,
he fathered Shelah. 13 And Arpachshad
lived after he fathered Shelah 403 years
and had other sons and daughters.
14 When Shelah had lived 30 years, he
fathered Eber. 15 And Shelah lived after he

29 [x]1 Kin. 9:28; 10:11
32 [y]ver. 1; ch. 9:19
Chapter 11
2 [z]ch. 10:10; 14:1, 9; Isai. 11:11; Dan. 1:2; Zech. 5:11
3 [a]ch. 14:10; Ex. 2:3
4 [b]Deut. 1:28
5 [c]ch. 18:21
7 [d]ch. 1:26; [Ps. 2:4]
8 [e]ch. 10:25, 32; Luke 1:51
9 [f]ch. 10:10
10 [g][ch. 10:22]; For ver. 10-26, see 1 Chr. 1:17-27

1 *Babel* sounds like the Hebrew for *confused*

10:29 Ophir. A region, perhaps in Arabia, known for its pure gold (1 Kin. 9:28; Job 22:24).

Havilah. See note on v. 7.

10:30 from Mesha . . . Sephar. Though these locations are unidentified, the names of the sons of Joktan point to a location in southern Arabia.

11:1–9 See note 10:1–11:9. Some scholars identify the tower in this narrative as the three-hundred-foot high temple ziggurat of Marduk at Babylon. The same arrogant pride that inspired rebellious Eve and Adam to rival God's knowledge (3:5) and the ungodly Cain to build his city (4:17), now inspired "the whole earth" (v. 4). The mention of "Shinar" (v. 2; cf. 10:10) and "Babel" (v. 9; cf. 10:10) recall Nimrod's rebellious kingdom (10:8–12 and notes).

11:1 whole earth. See note 10:1–11:9.

11:4 city. See notes 4:17; 8:1–12:9; and 10:10.

tower . . . in the heavens. This description suggests a monumental effort motivated by pride (cf. Is. 2:15–17). Human beings—this time in a titanic attempt at corporate self-assertion—again sacrilegiously challenge God (3:6 note).

make a name for ourselves. Since "name" connotes fame and progeny, these city builders were attempting to find significance and immortality in their own achievements. But only God gives an everlasting name (12:2) to those who magnify His name (4:26; 12:8; Is. 63:12,14).

lest we be dispersed. Like Cain in their isolation from God, these proud sinners feared dislocation, and perhaps one another as well (4:14). Also like Cain, they found their solution in an abiding city rivaling God—a strategy that involved disobeying God's command to "fill the earth" (9:1).

11:5 the LORD came down to see. Divine investigation prior to judgment is frequently depicted in Genesis (3:11–13; 4:9, 10; 18:21). Rather than conflict with the doctrine of divine omniscience (cf. 6:6 note), this anthropomorphic description of God's activity serves to emphasize that divine judgment is always according to truth. The Mesopotamian ziggurat towers were built as descending stairways for the gods. But God comes down in judgment on this tower of human pride.

11:6 the beginning of what they will do. See note 10:8.

11:7 let us go down. See note 1:26.

11:8 dispersed. Ironically, instead of attaining significance and immortality they achieved alienation and dispersal. Expulsion was the earlier fate of Adam and Eve (3:23) and of Cain (4:12). This judgment was also an act of grace; in isolation the peoples were more likely to turn to God (12:3; Acts 17:26, 27).

11:9 Babel. An ironic etymology derived from the Hebrew word meaning "confuse." To the Babylonians, Babel meant "gate of god."

11:10–26 See note 5:3–32. This genealogy of the elect, like 5:3–32, is first linear and at the end segmented into three sons (8:1 note). It overlaps with 10:21–31 and forms a transition from primeval history to the account of Abraham (Introduction: Characteristics and Themes).

As is common in ancient genealogies, it is apparent that this genealogy contains gaps. If it were precisely sequential, the events of chs. 9–11 would cover less than three centuries, all of Abraham's ancestors would have been still living when he was born, and Shem would outlive Abraham by fourteen years. The purpose of this genealogy is to record the advances of the messianic line (Introduction: Date and Occasion).

11:10 These are the generations of. See note 2:4.

11:12 In the Sumerian flood story the ages of the kings also are reduced after the flood (5:3–32 note).

11:14 Eber. See note 10:21.

fathered Eber 403 years and had other sons
and daughters.
16 When Eber had lived 34 years, he
fathered Peleg. 17 And Eber lived after he
fathered Peleg 430 years and had other
sons and daughters.
18 When Peleg had lived 30 years, he
fathered Reu. 19 And Peleg lived after he
fathered Reu 209 years and had other sons
and daughters.
20 When Reu had lived 32 years, he
fathered Serug. 21 And Reu lived after he
fathered Serug 207 years and had other
sons and daughters.
22 When Serug had lived 30 years, he
fathered Nahor. 23 And Serug lived after he
fathered Nahor 200 years and had other
sons and daughters.
24 When [h]Nahor had lived 29 years, he
fathered Terah. 25 And Nahor lived after he
fathered Terah 119 years and had other
sons and daughters.
26 When [h]Terah had lived 70 years, he
fathered Abram, Nahor, and Haran.

Terah's Descendants

27 Now these are the generations of Terah.
Terah fathered Abram, Nahor, and Haran;
and Haran fathered Lot. 28 Haran died in the
presence of his father Terah in the land of his
kindred, in Ur of the Chaldeans. 29 And
Abram and Nahor took wives. The name of
Abram's wife was [i]Sarai, and the name of
Nahor's wife, [j]Milcah, the daughter of Haran
the father of Milcah and Iscah. 30 Now Sarai
was barren; she had no child.
31 Terah [k]took Abram his son and Lot the
son of Haran, his grandson, and Sarai his
daughter-in-law, his son Abram's wife, and
they went forth together [l]from Ur of the
Chaldeans to go into the land of Canaan,
but when they came to Haran, they settled
there. 32 The days of Terah were 205 years,
and Terah died in Haran.

24 [h]Josh. 24:2
26 [h][See ver. 24 above]
29 [i]ch. 17:15 [j]ch. 22:20
31 [k]ch. 12:1 [l]ch. 15:7; Josh. 24:2; Neh. 9:7; Acts 7:2, 4

11:16 Peleg. See note 10:25.

11:26 Abram. See notes 17:5.

11:27–32 This introduction to the Abraham story identifies the main characters in Abraham's life: father, brother, wife, sister-in-law, and nephew.

11:27 these are the generations of Terah. See note 2:4. Terah, the father of the principal figure, Abraham, gives his name to the family history, since the family involved in this story descends from him (Introduction: Characteristics and Themes). After this introduction he is not mentioned again, probably because he did not share Abraham's faith. The family may have been involved in moon worship, since Ur and Haran were important centers for worship of the Mesopotamian moon gods Nanna and Sin.

Nahor. See 22:20–24.

11:28 Haran died. Haran's premature death explains the fate of his children in this closely knit family. Abraham adopted Lot, Haran's son (v. 31; 12:4), and Nahor married Milcah, Haran's daughter.

Ur of the Chaldeans. Probably the important city in southern Mesopotamia on the Euphrates River (flourished c. 3000–1900 B.C.), though some scholars suggest that Urfa (Edessa) in northern Mesopotamia may be intended. Because the Chaldeans did not reach southern Mesopotamia until after the time of Moses (and almost a millennium after Abraham), this description of Ur may represent an updating of the text after the time of Moses (Introduction: Date and Occasion).

11:29 Sarai. She was the daughter of Terah by a different mother than Abraham's (20:2). The prohibition against such a marriage was unknown in patriarchal times (cf. Lev. 18:9; 20:17; Deut. 27:22).

Nahor's wife . . . daughter of Haran. The later Mosaic law did not prohibit marriage to one's niece.

11:30 barren. This mention of childlessness anticipates the miraculous provision of offspring to continue the covenant line of promise (18:1–15; 21:1–12).

11:32 205 years. If Abram was born when Terah was seventy years old (v. 26) and if Abram departed Haran when he was seventy-five years old (12:4) after the death of his father Terah (Acts 7:4), Terah would have been only 145 years old at his death. Several possible solutions to this apparent difficulty have been advanced. Some suggest that Stephen in Acts 7:4 relies on a different Hebrew textual tradition (the Samaritan Pentateuch text of this passage reads "145 years"). Others propose that the Hebrew word rendered "fathered" in v. 26 means "began to father" and that Abram was not the firstborn.

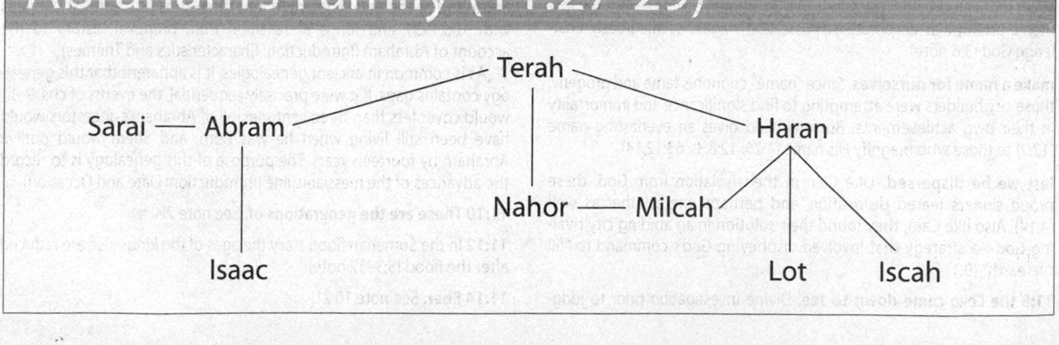

The Call of Abram

12 Now [m] the LORD said[1] to Abram, "Go
from your country and your kindred
and your father's house to the land that I
will show you. **2** [n] And I will make of you a
great nation, and I will bless you and make
your name great, so that you will be a
blessing. **3** [o] I will bless those who bless you,
and him who dishonors you I will curse,
and [p] in you all the families of the earth
shall be blessed."[2]

Chapter 12
1 [m] Acts 7:3; Heb. 11:8
2 [n] ch. 17:6; 18:18; [Gal. 3:14]
3 [o] ch. 27:29; Num. 24:9
[p] ch. 18:18; 22:18; 26:4; 28:14; Jer. 4:2; Acts 3:25; Gal. 3:16; Cited Gal. 3:8

[1] Or *had said* [2] Or *by you all the families of the earth shall bless themselves*

12:1–22:19 God's division of the world into nations (11:1–9) provided a backdrop against which Moses now begins to display God's distinguishing grace in election. With Abram commences the story of God's creation of Israel, a story in which He will reveal His freedom in being merciful to Israel, His holiness in judging them, His faithfulness in restoring them, and His absolute sovereignty over human history. Abram's story begins with his departure from a city of man (Ur) in search of the city "whose designer and builder is God" (Heb. 11:10).

12:1–9 Abraham's call as an agent of redemptive grace parallels Noah's as the mediator of a covenant to all creation (8:1–12:9 note). The form of God's call to Abraham also resembles His pattern in creation (1:3–31 note): announcement, command (v. 1), and report (vv. 4–9), but the pattern is broken by the divine promise (vv. 2–3), highlighting Abraham's faith and believing obedience (vv. 4–9; cf. 22:1–19; Rom. 4:3; Heb. 11:8–12).

12:1–3 The covenant structure is apparent (17:2 note). God sovereignly obligated Himself to Abraham (vv. 2, 3) while assigning him a task (v. 1). God's commands were fulfilled through Abraham's obedient faith in God's promise (6:9–22 note).

These verses mark a pivotal point in Genesis and in the history of redemption as God begins to establish a covenant people for Himself. The progress of God's redemptive plan is evident in His setting Abraham apart (v. 1) and making Israel into a great nation (v. 2; 46:3). It climaxes in Jesus Christ, the true Seed of Abraham (Gal. 3:16), who brings salvation to the world (v. 3). The call to Abraham is passed on to the next two patriarchs, Isaac (26:2–4) and Jacob (28:14). The nation will be formed from Jacob's twelve sons (ch. 49). See theological note "God's Covenant of Grace" on next page.

12:1 said. The call came to Abraham in Ur before his father died, not in Haran (15:7).

the land. The scope of this land grant will be progressively defined (12:7; 13:14–17; 15:18–21).

12:2 bless. Crucial elements of divine blessing and promise in Genesis—fruitfulness and dominion—are evident here and are further spelled out in 22:17 (9:1 note).

make your name great. What the city builders at Babel sought in their own strength (11:4 note), God gave in sovereign grace. Subsequent history confirmed God's promise—the great names of Abraham and David (2 Sam. 7:9) prefigured that of Jesus Christ (Phil. 2:9–11).

you will be a blessing. This last occurrence of the verb "to bless" is an imperative. Abraham will not only be blessed, but is to be a blessing to others (v. 3).

12:3 bless those . . . him . . . I will curse. The extent of God's merciful and gracious intention is indicated in the Hebrew by a switch from the plural object of blessing to the singular object of cursing. Many are to receive God's blessing through the Seed of Abraham (18:18; Gal. 3:8; Rev. 7:9, 10).

those who bless. Those who acknowledge Abraham and his offspring as God's agent of blessing.

him who dishonors you I will curse. The Hebrew words here translated "dishonors" and "curse" differ: the second means "to disdain"; the first often has the sense of "to weaken" (3:14). God will be an effective adversary of those who curse Abraham and his seed.

in you. In Jesus Christ, the Seed of Abraham (Gal. 3:16), and in the spiritual Israel of all ages united with Him (Gal. 3:29; Phil. 3:3 note), rather than in unbelieving ethnic Israel (John 8:39; Rom. 9:6–8).

shall be blessed. Some have argued that the Hebrew verb should be translated reflexively: "shall bless themselves" (i.e., will desire the blessing of Abraham). While grammatically possible, this proposed reading hardly does justice to the context of this divine promise, and the passive translation here ("be blessed") presents no real linguistic difficulties. In addition, the Septuagint (Greek Old Testament) rendered it as passive. We are fully justified in viewing this promise as a reference to God's plan for the salvation of the world.

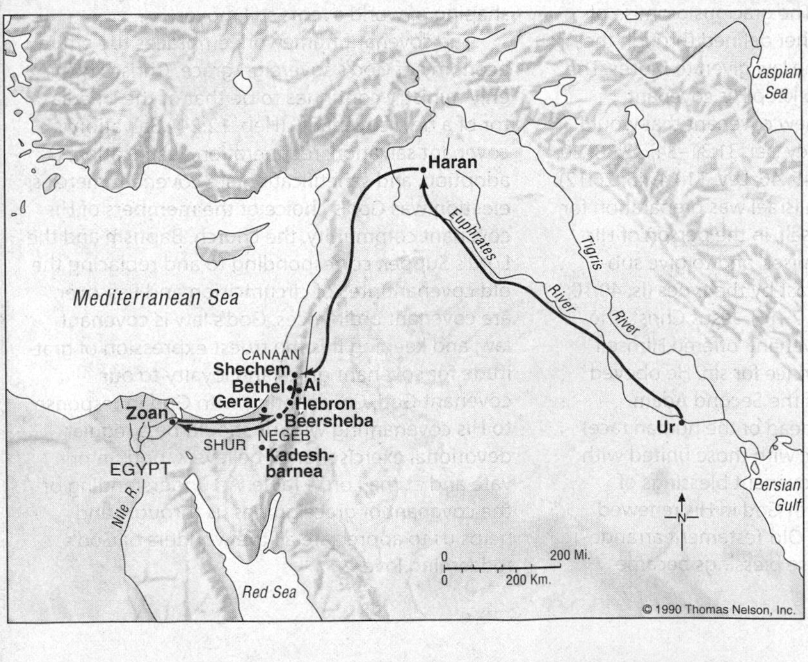

Abraham's Journey of Faith. Abraham's 1,500-mile journey was fueled by faith. "And he went out, not knowing where he was going. By faith he went to live in the land of promise, as in a foreign land, . . . For he was looking forward to the city that has foundations, whose designer and builder is God" (Heb. 11:8-10).

God's Covenant of Grace

Covenants in Scripture are solemn agreements, negotiated or unilaterally imposed, that bind the parties to each other in permanent defined relationships, with specific promises, claims, and obligations on both sides (e.g., the marriage covenant, Mal. 2:14).

When God makes a covenant with His creatures, He alone establishes its terms, as His covenant with Noah and every living creature shows (Gen. 9:9). When Adam and Eve failed to obey the terms of the covenant of works (see Gen. 3:6 and theological note "The Fall"), God did not destroy them, but revealed His covenant of grace by promising a Savior (Gen. 3:15). God's covenant rests on His promise, as is clear from His covenant with Abraham. He called Abraham to go to the land that He would give him, and promised to bless him and all the families of the earth through him (Gen. 12:1–3). Abraham heeded God's call because he believed God's promise; it was his faith in the promise that was credited to him for righteousness (Gen. 15:6; Rom. 4:18–22). God's covenant with Israel at Sinai is in the form of the ancient Near Eastern suzerainty treaties. These are covenants imposed unilaterally by a powerful king on a vassal king and a servant people.

Although the covenant at Sinai required obedience to God's laws under the threat of His curse, it was a continuation of the covenant of grace (Ex. 3:15; Deut. 7:7, 8; 9:5, 6). God gave the commandments to a people He had already redeemed and claimed (Ex. 19:4; 20:2). The gracious promise of God's covenant was further defined through the types and shadows of the law given to Moses. The failure of the Israelites to keep His covenant showed the need for a new covenant that would bestow the power to obey (Jer. 31:31–34; 32:38–40; cf. Gen. 17:7; Ex. 6:7; 29:45, 46; Lev. 11:44, 45; 26:12).

God's covenant with Israel was preparation for the coming of God Himself, in the person of His Son, to fulfill all His promises, and to give substance to the shadows cast by the types (Is. 40:10; Mal. 3:1; John 1:14; Heb. 7–10). Jesus Christ, the Mediator of the new covenant, offered Himself as the true and final sacrifice for sin. He obeyed the law perfectly, and as the Second Adam (second representative head of the human race) He became the inheritor, with those united with Him by faith, of all the covenant blessings of peace and fellowship with God in His renewed creation. The temporary Old Testament arrangements for imparting those blessings became obsolete when what they anticipated was realized.

As Heb. 7–10 explains, through Christ God inaugurated a better version of His one eternal covenant with sinners (Heb. 13:20)—a better covenant with better promises (Heb. 8:6), based on a better sacrifice (Heb. 9:23) offered by a better high priest in a better sanctuary (Heb. 7:26–8:6, 11, 13, 14). This better covenant guarantees a better hope than had ever been made explicit by the former version of the covenant—glory with God in "a better country, that is, a heavenly one" (Heb. 11:16; cf. v. 40).

The fulfillment of the old covenant in Christ opens the door of faith to the Gentiles. The "offspring of Abraham," the community with which the covenant was made, was redefined in Christ—the final and definitive offspring of Abraham (Gal. 3:16). Gentiles and Jews who are united to Christ by faith become Abraham's offspring in Him (Gal. 3:26–29), while no one outside of Christ can be in a saving covenant relationship with God (Rom. 4:9–17; 11:13–24).

The goal of God's covenantal dealings is, as it has always been, the gathering and sanctifying of the covenant people "from every nation, from all tribes and peoples and languages" (Rev. 7:9), who will one day inhabit the New Jerusalem in a renewed world order (Rev. 21:1, 2). Here the covenant relationship will find its fullest expression—"they will be his people, and God himself will be with them as their God" (Rev. 21:3; cf. Gen. 17:7 note; Ex. 29:45, 46). Towards this goal God's shaping of world events still moves.

The covenant framework embraces the entire economy of God's sovereign grace. Christ's heavenly ministry continues to be that of the "mediator of a new covenant" (Heb. 12:24). Salvation is covenant salvation: regeneration, justification, adoption, and sanctification are covenant mercies; election was God's choice of the members of His covenant community, the church. Baptism and the Lord's Supper, corresponding to and replacing the old covenant rites of circumcision and Passover, are covenant ordinances. God's law is covenant law, and keeping it is the truest expression of gratitude for covenant grace and loyalty to our covenant God. Covenanting with God in response to His covenanting with us should be a regular devotional exercise for all believers, both in private and at the Lord's Table. An understanding of the covenant of grace guides us through, and helps us to appreciate all the wonders of God's redeeming love.

4 So Abram went, as the LORD had told
him, and Lot went with him. Abram was
seventy-five years old when he departed
from [q]Haran. 5 And Abram took Sarai his
wife, and Lot his brother's son, and all
their possessions that they had gathered,
and the people that they had acquired in
Haran, and they set out to go to the land
of Canaan. When they came to the land of
Canaan, 6 Abram [r]passed through the land
to the place at Shechem, to [s]the oak[1] of
[t]Moreh. At that time [u]the Canaanites were
in the land. 7 Then the LORD appeared to
Abram and said, [v]"To your offspring I will
give this land." So he built there an altar
to the LORD, who had appeared to him.
8 From there he moved to the hill country
on the east of [w]Bethel and pitched his tent,
with Bethel on the west and Ai on the east.
And there he built an altar to the LORD and
called upon the name of the LORD. 9 And
Abram journeyed on, still going toward the
Negeb.

Abram and Sarai in Egypt

10 Now [x]there was a famine in the land. So
Abram went down to Egypt to sojourn
there, for the famine was severe in the land.
11 When he was about to enter Egypt, he said
to Sarai his wife, "I know that you are a
woman beautiful in appearance, 12 and when
the Egyptians see you, they will say, 'This is
his wife.' Then they [y]will kill me, but they
will let you live. 13 Say you are my sister, that
it may go well with me because of you, and
that my life may be spared for your sake."
14 When Abram entered Egypt, the Egyptians
saw that the woman was very beautiful.
15 And when the princes of Pharaoh saw her,
they praised her to Pharaoh. And the
woman was taken into Pharaoh's house.
16 And for her sake he dealt well with Abram;
and he had sheep, oxen, male donkeys,
male servants, female servants, female donkeys, and camels.
17 But the LORD [z]afflicted Pharaoh and his
house with great plagues because of Sarai,
Abram's wife. 18 So Pharaoh called Abram
and said, "What is this you have done to
me? Why did you not tell me that she was
your wife? 19 Why did you say, 'She is my
sister,' so that I took her for my wife? Now
then, here is your wife; take her, and go."
20 And Pharaoh gave men orders concerning him, and they sent him away with his
wife and all that he had.

Abram and Lot Separate

13 So Abram went up from Egypt, he
and his wife and all that he had, and
Lot with him, [a]into the Negeb.
2 [b]Now Abram was very rich in livestock,
in silver, and in gold. 3 And he journeyed

4 [q]ch. 11:31
6 [r][Heb. 11:9] [s]ch. 13:18 [t]Deut. 11:30; Judg. 7:1 [u]ch. 13:7
7 [v]ch. 13:15; 17:8; Ex. 33:1; Ps. 105:9-12; [Num. 32:11]
8 [w]ch. 28:19
10 [x]ch. 26:1; 43:1
12 [y]See ch. 20:1-18; 26:6-11
17 [z]1 Chr. 16:21; Ps. 105:14
Chapter 13
1 [a]ch. 12:9
2 [b]ch. 24:35; [Ps. 112:1-3; Prov. 10:22]

[1] Or *terebinth*

12:4 seventy-five. See note 11:32.

12:6 Shechem. See 33:18–34:31; 48:22; 50:25 and notes.

oak of Moreh. A tree whose greater height made it a preferred place of worship (13:18; 18:1; 21:33). Although pagans worshiped fertility deities under such trees, Abraham, who looked for a heavenly city (Heb. 11:10), worshiped only the true God (v. 8). The name "Moreh" means "teacher." This was probably a pagan site for oracles; the Lord sanctified it by appearing to Abraham (v. 7).

the Canaanites . . . in the land. Two obstacles stood in the way of God's promise: Sarah's barrenness (11:30) and the Canaanites who prevented him from settling in the land.

12:7 appeared. The sojourning patriarchs were prophets (15:1, 4; 17:1; 18:1; 20:7; 26:2, 24; 28:10–15; 31:3; 35:9; 48:3; cf. Ps. 105:12–15).

offspring. Grammatically, the Hebrew for "offspring" is a collective singular noun. Paul declares that it pertains uniquely to Jesus Christ (Gal. 3:16) and to all those who share Abraham's faith in God (Rom. 4:16, 23–24; Gal. 3:26–29).

built there an altar. By this act the father of the new nation consecrates the Promised Land to God (Ex. 20:24; Josh. 22:19). See v. 8; 13:18; 22:9; 26:25; 35:7.

12:8 called upon the name of the LORD. See 4:26 and note.

12:9 the Negeb. The desert region southwest of the Dead Sea. Covering an area of about 4,500 square miles, its rainfall is too low to sustain cultivated grain.

12:10–20 The matriarch Sarah is also endangered in chs. 20 and 26. Abraham's exodus from Egypt typifies the nation's later exodus: God sent a famine (v. 10; 47:4), the Egyptians afflicted them (vv. 12–15; Ex. 1:11–14); God plagued the Egyptians (v. 17; Ex. 8–11); the Egyptians let them go with great wealth (vv. 16, 20; Ex. 12:33–36); they return to the land by stages through the wilderness (13:3; Ex. 17:1); and finally arrive back in the land where they worship the Lord (13:3; Ex. 15:17). See Ps. 105:14, 15; 1 Cor. 10:1–4.

12:12 Egyptians . . . will kill me. Although hospitality to strangers was a duty in the ancient Near East (18:2–5; Deut. 10:18, 19), strangers were vulnerable (cf. 19:3–11). Abraham was not necessarily selling Sarah's honor to save himself, for this ruse had been planned long before (20:13), perhaps to stall for time in dangerous circumstances (cf. 24:55; 34:13–17).

12:13 sister. See note 11:29.

12:15 was taken. The Hebrew here does not necessarily imply sexual intercourse (cf. 20:2, 4, 6); the text does not add "and humiliated her" (34:2) or "and went in to her" (38:2).

13:1–18 Lot's separation from Abraham alienated him from blessing. He turned his back on his uncle and ignored the dangers of Sodom. But "even as he thought he was living in heaven, he had already sunk almost into hell" (Calvin, *Commentary* on Gen. 13:10). In contrast to Lot, Abraham trusted God and by faith inherited "all the land . . . forever" (v. 15) and "offspring as the dust" (v. 16).

13:2 rich. The Hebrew word here is translated "severe" in 12:10, inviting a contrast in Abraham's situation before and after he went to Egypt (12:10–20 note).

on from the Negeb as far as Bethel to the
place where his tent had been at the
beginning, between Bethel and Ai, 4 to
[c]the place where he had made an altar at
the first. And there Abram called upon the
name of the LORD. 5 And Lot, who went
with Abram, also had flocks and herds
and tents, 6 so that [d]the land could not
support both of them dwelling together;
for their possessions were so great that
they could not dwell together, 7 [e]and there
was strife between the herdsmen of
Abram's livestock and the herdsmen of
Lot's livestock. At that time [f]the Canaanites and the Perizzites were dwelling in
the land.
8 Then Abram said to Lot, [g]"Let there be
no strife between you and me, and
between your herdsmen and my herdsmen, [h]for we are kinsmen.[1] 9 [i]Is not the
whole land before you? Separate yourself
from me. If you take the left hand, then I
will go to the right, or if you take the right
hand, then I will go to the left." 10 And Lot
lifted up his eyes and saw that the [j]Jordan
Valley was well watered everywhere like
[k]the garden of the LORD, like the land of
Egypt, in the direction of [l]Zoar. (This was
before the LORD [m]destroyed Sodom and
Gomorrah.) 11 So Lot chose for himself all
the Jordan Valley, and Lot journeyed east.
Thus they separated from each other.
12 Abram settled in the land of Canaan,
while Lot settled among the cities of the
valley and moved his tent as far as Sodom.
13 Now the men of Sodom [n]were wicked,
great sinners against the LORD.
14 The LORD said to Abram, after Lot had
separated from him, "Lift up your eyes and
look from the place where you are, [o]north-
ward and southward and eastward and
westward, 15 for all the land that you see I
will give [p]to you and [q]to your offspring forever. 16 [r]I will make your offspring as the
dust of the earth, so that if one can count
the dust of the earth, your offspring also
can be counted. 17 Arise, walk through the
length and the breadth of the land, for I
will give it to you." 18 So Abram moved his
tent and came and [s]settled by the [t]oaks[2] of
Mamre, which [u]are at Hebron, and there he
built an altar to the LORD.

Abram Rescues Lot

14 In the days of Amraphel king of
[v]Shinar, Arioch king of Ellasar,
Chedorlaomer king of [w]Elam, and Tidal king

4 [c]ch. 12:7, 8
6 [d]ch. 36:6, 7
7 [e]ch. 26:20 [f]ch. 12:6
8 [g][1 Cor. 6, 7] [h][Acts 7:26]
9 [i]ch. 20:15; 34:10
10 [j]ch. 19:17, 25, 28; Deut. 34:3; 1 Kin. 7:46; [Matt. 3:5] [k]ch. 2:8; Isai. 51:3; Ezek. 28:13; Joel 2:3 [l]ch. 14:2, 8; 19:22 [m]ch. 19:24, 25
13 [n]ch. 18:20; Ezek. 16:49; 2 Pet. 2:7, 8
14 [o]ch. 28:14
15 [p]ch. 17:8; 28:13; 35:12; Acts 7:5 [q]ch. 12:7; 15:18; 24:7; 26:4; Deut. 34:4; 2 Chr. 20:7
16 [r]ch. 22:17; 28:14; 32:12; Num. 23:10; [1 Kin. 3:8]; See ch. 15:5
18 [s]ch. 14:13 [t]ch. 12:6 [u]ch. 35:27
Chapter 14
1 [v]ch. 10:10; 11:2 [w]ch. 10:22; Isai. 11:11; Acts 2:9

1 Hebrew *we are men, brothers* 2 Or *terebinths*

13:6 possessions were so great. Paradoxically, God's blessing, not famine, provoked the problem (v. 10 note).

13:8–17 Lot and Abraham are compared and contrasted: both looked around (vv. 10, 14), were offered land (vv. 9, 15–17), and traveled to their allotted portion (vv. 11–12, 18). But Lot, who chose by sight, will escape twice by the skin of his teeth (14:12, 16; 19:1–29), while by faith Abraham will be enriched forever.

13:9 If you . . . then I. Faith in God's sovereignty gave Abraham the freedom to be generous (cf. 14:19, 20). His generosity typified that of Israel to Moab and Ammon, Lot's descendants (Deut. 2:8–19). God applauds generosity and peacemakers (Lev. 19:18; Ps. 133; Matt. 5:43–48; James 3:17, 18).

13:10 Jordan Valley. The edge of the Promised Land or just beyond it (Num. 34:2–12); this area is contrasted with Canaan in v. 12.

like the garden of the LORD. Man's environment is not the cause of sin—human depravity is. In the ideal environment of Eden sin originated, and sin now abounded in this rich territory (v. 13; 18:16–19:29).

13:12 moved his tent. See note 14:12.

13:14 look . . . westward. The Lord invited Moses to a similar panoramic overview of the land (Deut. 34:1–4). In each case, the invitation was given to confirm the promise to one who himself would not participate in dispossessing the Canaanites.

13:15 land . . . forever. See 12:1 and note. The promises of land were fulfilled several times but never consummated. God fulfilled the promise through Joshua (Josh. 21:43–45), but not completely (Josh. 13:1–7); even more so through David and Solomon (1 Kin. 4:20–25; Neh. 9:8), but still not completely (Ps. 95:11; Heb. 4:6–8; 11:39, 40). As Israel's Exodus from Egypt through the Passover (Ex. 12:1) is a type of the church's exodus from the condemned world through Christ (1 Cor. 5:7; 10:1–4), so also old Israel's life in the land is a type of New Israel's life in Christ. Both are a gift (15:7, 18; Deut. 1:8; Rom. 6:23), and are received by faith (Num. 14:26–44; Josh. 7 and John 3:16). Both uniquely possess the blessed presence, life, and rest of God (Ex. 23:20–31; Deut. 11:12; 12:9,10; 28:1–14; John 1:51; 14:9; Matt. 11:28), and demand persevering faith (Deut. 28:15–19; Heb. 6). The land promises are consummated forever in the new heaven and new earth (Heb. 11:39, 40; Rev. 21:1–22:6).

13:16 as the dust. See 32:12. The promise of offspring also finds fulfillment in old Israel (Num. 23:10; 1 Kin. 4:20; 2 Chr. 1:9) and consummation in the New Israel, composed of Jew and Gentile (12:3 and note; Rom. 4:16–18; Gal. 3:29; Rev. 7:9).

13:17 Arise, walk. According to ancient custom, a property transfer was finalized by the new owner's visit to the tract. God commands Abraham to lay symbolic claim to the Promised Land (12:7 and note; Josh. 1:3; 18:4; 24:3).

13:18 oaks. See note 12:6.

Mamre. An Amorite who sought security in an alliance with Abraham (14:13). He will be blessed through Abraham (14:24).

built an altar. See 12:7 and note.

14:1–24 Abraham displayed obedient faith by risking war to deliver his nephew, Lot. His victory is astonishing since the plundering confederacy of five kings had just conquered many Canaanites and a confederacy of five Dead Sea kings. See note on v. 4.

14:1, 2 None of these kings has been definitely identified in extrabiblical sources. One comes from Elam (part of modern Iran), one from Babylon (part of modern Iraq), and two probably from the region of modern Turkey.

14:1 Shinar. See note 10:10.

of Goiim, 2 these kings made war with [x]Bera
king of Sodom, Birsha king of Gomorrah,
Shinab king of [y]Admah, Shemeber king of
[y]Zeboiim, and the king of Bela (that is, Zoar).
3 And all these joined forces in the Valley of
Siddim ([z]that is, the Salt Sea). 4 Twelve years
they had served Chedorlaomer, but in the
thirteenth year they rebelled. 5 In the fourteenth year Chedorlaomer and the kings
who were with him came and defeated the
[a]Rephaim in [b]Ashteroth-karnaim, the [c]Zuzim
in Ham, the [d]Emim in Shaveh-kiriathaim,
6 and the [e]Horites in their hill country of Seir
as far as [f]El-paran on the border of the
wilderness. 7 Then they turned back and
came to En-mishpat (that is, [g]Kadesh) and
defeated all the country of the Amalekites,
and also the Amorites who were dwelling [h]in
Hazazon-tamar.

8 Then the king of Sodom, the king of
Gomorrah, the king of Admah, the king of
Zeboiim, and the king of Bela (that is, Zoar)
went out, and they joined battle in the
Valley of Siddim 9 with Chedorlaomer king
of Elam, Tidal king of Goiim, Amraphel
king of Shinar, and Arioch king of Ellasar,
four kings against five. 10 Now the Valley of
Siddim was full of [i]bitumen pits, and as the
kings of Sodom and Gomorrah fled, some
fell into them, and the rest fled [j]to the hill
country. 11 So the enemy took [k]all the possessions of Sodom and Gomorrah, and all
their provisions, and went their way.
12 They also took Lot, [l]the son of Abram's
brother, [m]who was dwelling in Sodom, and
his possessions, and went their way.

13 Then one who had escaped came and
told Abram the Hebrew, [n]who was living by
the [o]oaks[1] of Mamre the Amorite, brother
of Eshcol and of Aner. These were allies of
Abram. 14 When Abram heard that his kinsman had been taken captive, he led forth
his trained men, [p]born in his house, 318 of
them, and went in pursuit as far as [q]Dan.
15 And he divided his forces against them by
night, he and his servants, and defeated
them and pursued them to Hobah, north
of Damascus. 16 Then he brought back all
the possessions, and also brought back his
kinsman Lot [r]with his possessions, and the
women and the people.

Abram Blessed by Melchizedek

17 After his return from the defeat of
Chedorlaomer and the kings who were
with him, the king of Sodom went out to
meet him at the Valley of Shaveh (that is,
the [s]King's Valley). 18 And [t]Melchizedek
king of Salem brought out bread and wine.
(He was [u]priest of [v]God Most High.) 19 And
he blessed him and said,

> [w]"Blessed be Abram by God Most
> High,
> [x]Possessor[2] of heaven and earth;

2 [x]ver. 8; ch. 13:10; 19:22 [y]Deut. 29:23
3 [z]Num. 34:12; Deut. 3:17; Josh. 3:16
5 [a]ch. 15:20; Deut. 2:11; 3:11 [b]Deut. 1:4 [c][Deut. 2:20] [d]Deut. 2:10, 11
6 [e]Deut. 2:12, 22 [f][ch. 21:21; Num. 12:16; 13:3]
7 [g]ch. 16:14; 20:1; Num. 13:26 [h]2 Chr. 20:2
10 [i]ch. 11:3; Ex. 2:3 [j]ch. 19:17, 30
11 [k]ver. 16, 21
12 [l]ch. 12:5 [m]ch. 13:12
13 [n]ch. 13:18 [o]ch. 12:6
14 [p]ch. 15:3; 17:12, 13, 23, 27; Eccles. 2:7 [q]Judg. 18:29
16 [r]ver. 11, 12
17 [s]2 Sam. 18:18
18 [t]Heb. 7:1 [u]Ps. 110:4; Heb. 5:6, 10; 7:1, 11, 17 [v]Ps. 57:2; Acts 16:17
19 [w]Heb. 7:6, 7 [x]Matt. 11:25

1 Or *terebinths* 2 Or *Creator*; also verse 22

14:4 they had served. They were subject as vassals to the king of Elam with the obligation to pay tribute.

14:5 Rephaim . . . Zuzim . . . Emim. See note Deut. 2:10–12. Zuzim is probably an alternate term for the Zamzummim (Deut. 2:20). The mention of these defeated giants further emphasizes the impressiveness of Abraham's victory.

14:6 Horites. See note Deut. 2:10–12.

14:12 dwelling in Sodom. Note the progressive identification of Lot with Sodom: camping near it (13:12), living in it, and residing as a respected citizen in it (19:1, 6; cf. Ps. 1:1).

14:13 the Hebrew. Probably an ethnic identification designating Abraham as a descendant of Eber (10:21 note). However, some contend that the term derives from *habiru*, a disparaging word used to designate a widely dispersed social class of semi-nomads in the ancient Near East of the second millennium B.C.

oaks of Mamre. See note 12:6.

Amorite. Sometimes a blanket term for the earlier inhabitants of Palestine (48:22; Deut. 1:44; Josh. 2:10). Mamre the Amorite, an ally of Abraham who accompanied him in battle, found blessing through his identification with Abraham (v. 24; 12:3).

14:14 kinsman. The term explains the character of Abraham's action: the godly display of loving loyalty toward his brethren.

trained men. Servants trained in the use of weapons. A fighting force of three hundred men was a sizable army in Abraham's time.

Dan. This place-name was updated from Laish after the time of Moses (Introduction: Date and Occasion; Judg. 18:29).

14:18 Melchizedek. Lit. "king of righteousness." The Hebrew word *melech* means "king," and *zedek* means "righteousness." See Introduction: Characteristics and Themes; Heb. 7:1–3 and notes.

king of Salem . . . priest of God. The introduction of Melchizedek emphasizes that he was a king as well as a priest. As such he is a type of Christ, who is our Prophet, Priest, and King. Salem was apparently an ancient name for Jerusalem (Ps. 76:2).

bread and wine. The combination means a full dinner, a banquet.

14:19 blessed him. That Melchizedek blessed Abraham is understood by the author of Hebrews to indicate that Melchizedek was greater than Abraham (Heb. 7:7).

God Most High. Hebrew *El Elyon*. El, the supreme god in the Canaanite pantheon at the time of Abraham, had similar titles (e.g., *El Olam*, "Everlasting God"). The patriarchs used these titles for the LORD, the true God, Creator of heaven and earth. Abraham interpreted Melchizedek's praise in this way, repeating the same titles but adding the covenantal divine name LORD (Yahweh) in v. 22. Though a Canaanite, Melchizedek had come to know the true God—a pagan priest could not meaningfully have "blessed" Abraham, nor would Abraham, who was consecrating the land to the LORD (12:7 note), have given "a tithe" to the priest of the depraved Canaanite god El.

20 and blessed be God Most High,
who has delivered your enemies
into your hand!"

And Abram gave him [y]a tenth of everything. 21 And the king of Sodom said to
Abram, "Give me the persons, but take the
goods for yourself." 22 But Abram said to
the king of Sodom, [z]"I have lifted my
hand[1] to the LORD, God Most High,
Possessor of heaven and earth, 23 that [a]I
would not take a thread or a sandal strap or
anything that is yours, lest you should say,
'I have made Abram rich.' 24 I will take
nothing but what the young men have
eaten, and the share of the men who went
with me. Let [b]Aner, Eshcol, and Mamre
take their share."

God's Covenant with Abram

15 After these things the word of the
LORD came to Abram in a vision:
[c]"Fear not, Abram, I am [d]your shield; your
reward shall be very great." 2 But Abram
said, "O Lord GOD, what will you give me,
for I continue[2] childless, and the heir of my
house is Eliezer of Damascus?" 3 And
Abram said, "Behold, you have given me
no offspring, and [e]a member of my household will be my heir." 4 And behold, the
word of the LORD came to him: "This man
shall not be your heir; [f]your very own son[3]
shall be your heir." 5 And he brought him
outside and said, "Look toward heaven,
and [g]number the stars, if you are able to
number them." Then he said to him, [h]"So
shall your offspring be." 6 And [i]he believed
the LORD, and [j]he counted it to him as
righteousness.

7 And he said to him, "I am the LORD who
[k]brought you out from Ur of the Chaldeans
[l]to give you this land to possess." 8 But he
said, "O Lord GOD, [m]how am I to know
that I shall possess it?" 9 He said to him,
"Bring me a heifer three years old, a female
goat three years old, a ram three years old,
a turtledove, and a young pigeon." 10 And
he brought him all these, [n]cut them in half,
and laid each half over against the other.
But [o]he did not cut the birds in half. 11 And
when birds of prey came down on the carcasses, Abram drove them away.

20 [y]Heb. 7:4; [ch. 28:22] **22** [z]Ex. 6:8; Num. 14:30; Deut. 32:40; Ezek. 20:5, 6, 15, 23, 28; Dan. 12:7; Rev. 10:5, 6 **23** [a][Esth. 9:15, 16] **24** [b]ver. 13 **Chapter 15** **1** [c]ch. 26:24; Dan. 10:12; Luke 1:13, 30 [d]Ps. 3:3; 18:2; 84:11; 119:114 **3** [e]ch. 14:14 **4** [f]ch. 17:16 **5** [g]Ps. 147:4 [h]ch. 22:17; 26:4; Ex. 32:13; Deut. 1:10; 10:22; 1 Chr. 27:23; Heb. 11:12; Cited Rom. 4:18 **6** [i]Rom. 4:9, 22; Gal. 3:6; James 2:23 [j]Cited Rom. 4:3; [Ps. 106:31] **7** [k]ch. 11:31; 12:1; Neh. 9:7, 8; Acts 7:2-4 [l]Ps. 105:42, 44 **8** [m][Judg. 6:17; 2 Kin. 20:8; Ps. 86:17; Isai. 7:11-13; Luke 1:18] **10** [n]Jer. 34:18, 19 [o]Lev. 1:17

1 Or *I have taken a solemn oath* 2 Or *I shall die* 3 Hebrew *what will come out of your own loins*

14:20 tenth. The practice of paying a tenth to a king or to a god was widespread in the ancient Near East, and predates the Mosaic law (28:22; Lev. 27:30–33; Num. 18:21–32). Abraham's gift to Melchizedek was probably not the payment of the "king's tithe" (cf. 1 Sam. 8:15, 17), but rather was an offering that reflected Abraham's regard for Melchizedek as a priest of the true God.

everything. The booty.

14:22 LORD. See note on v. 19.

14:23 I would not take . . . yours. In contrast to his dealings with Melchizedek, from whom he accepted bread and wine (v. 18) and to whom he gave a tithe (v. 20), Abraham wanted nothing to do with the wicked king of Sodom.

14:24 of the men . . . with me. The spoil was their rightful share. This disposition of the goods emphasizes Abraham's fairness and generosity.

15:1–19 After Abraham's expression of faith in God's reward (14:22, 23), God certified His promise of offspring (vv. 1–6) and land (12:7 and note) by making a covenant (Neh. 9:8). The two night scenes (vv. 5, 17) parallel each other: the Lord promises a reward (vv. 1, 7); Abraham questions the sovereign Lord about the inheritance (vv. 2–3, 8); and the Lord responds with a visual act (vv. 4–5, 9–21). Abraham's faith was accounted to him as righteousness (v. 6).

15:1 word of the LORD came. This phrase typically introduces a revelation to a prophet (12:7 note; 20:7; Jer. 18:1; Ezek. 6:1; Hos. 1:1).

vision. Visions were an ancient mode of revelation (Num. 12:6), and often occurred at night (v. 5; 1 Sam. 3:1–3; Job 33:14–16).

reward. See note 14:23.

15:2, 3 God's people would not come by natural generation. As Adam and Noah were founders of the fallen race, Abraham was the father of the new race, symbolically raised from the dead (17:5).

15:2 continue childless. This Hebrew metaphor may mean either "to live childless" or "to die childless." Abraham was perplexed, perhaps in part because childlessness was seen as a sign of divine judgment (Lev. 20:20, 21; 1 Sam. 1:11; Jer. 22:30).

15:3 a member of my household . . . heir. The practice of a childless couple adopting a slave as heir is attested in the Nuzi texts (c. 1500 B.C.), a collection of over four thousand clay tablets found near Kirkuk in modern Iraq.

15:5 offspring. See 12:7; 13:16 and notes.

15:6 This verse provides the early core doctrine of justification by faith, not by works (Gal. 3:6–14). Abraham believed the promise of the birth of an heir from the dead (Rom. 4:17–21; Heb. 11:11, 12), and God counted Abraham to be righteous, to be meeting His covenant demand. Abraham's justification by faith is a model of our faith in the resurrection of Jesus Christ, God's sacrifice for sin, and God's crediting His righteousness to us by faith (Rom. 4:22–25).

believed. Abraham is father of all who believe (Rom. 4:11), and all who believe are children of Abraham (Gal. 3:7).

righteousness. See 6:9 and note; Heb. 11:6–12.

15:7 I am the LORD who brought you out. A portent of God's self-identification after the Exodus (Ex. 20:2).

land. See note 13:15.

15:8 how am I to know. His request for a sign is motivated by faith (v. 6; cf. Is. 7:10–14).

15:9 heifer . . . pigeon. All the species that were suitable for sacrifice.

15:11 birds of prey. Symbolic of the unclean nations seeking to destroy the descendants of Abraham.

drove them away. Abraham symbolically defends his promised inheritance against foreign attackers.

12 As the sun was going down, a [p]deep
sleep fell on Abram. And behold, dreadful
and great darkness fell upon him. 13 Then
the LORD said to Abram, "Know for certain
[q]that your offspring will be sojourners in a
land that is not theirs and will be servants
there, and [r]they will be afflicted for [s]four
hundred years. 14 But [t]I will bring judgment
on the nation that they serve, and afterward [u]they shall come out with great possessions. 15 As for yourself, you shall go to
your fathers in peace; [v]you shall be buried
in a good old age. 16 And they shall come
back here in the fourth generation, for [w]the
iniquity of the Amorites [x]is not yet complete."

17 When the sun had gone down and it
was dark, behold, a smoking fire pot and a
flaming torch passed between these
pieces. 18 On that day the LORD made a
covenant with Abram, saying, [y]"To your
offspring I give[1] this land, from [z]the river
of Egypt to the great river, the river
Euphrates, 19 the land of the Kenites, the
Kenizzites, the Kadmonites, 20 the Hittites,
the Perizzites, the Rephaim, 21 the Amorites, the Canaanites, the Girgashites and
the Jebusites."

12 [p]ch. 2:21
13 [q]Acts 7:6, 7 [r]Ex. 1:11, 12; 3:7 [s]Acts 7:6; [Ex. 12:40, 41; Gal. 3:17]
14 [t]Ex. 6:6 [u]Ex. 12:36; Ps. 105:37
15 [v]ch. 25:8
16 [w]1 Kin. 21:26; Amos 2:9 [x][Dan. 8:23; Matt. 23:32; 1 Thess. 2:16]
18 [y]ch. 12:7; 13:15; 24:7; 26:4; Num. 34:2; Deut. 34:4; Neh. 9:8 [z]Ex. 23:31; Deut. 1:7; Josh. 1:4

Chapter 16
1 [a]ch. 15:2, 3 [b]ch. 21:9; Gal. 4:24
3 [c]ch. 12:5
4 [d][1 Sam. 1:6, 7]
5 [e]ch. 31:53; 1 Sam. 24:12

Sarai and Hagar

16 [a]Now Sarai, Abram's wife, had borne
him no children. She had a female
Egyptian servant whose name was [b]Hagar.
2 And Sarai said to Abram, "Behold now, the
LORD has prevented me from bearing children. Go in to my servant; it may be that I
shall obtain children[2] by her." And Abram
listened to the voice of Sarai. 3 So, after
Abram [c]had lived ten years in the land of
Canaan, Sarai, Abram's wife, took Hagar
the Egyptian, her servant, and gave her to
Abram her husband as a wife. 4 And he went
in to Hagar, and she conceived. And when
she saw that she had conceived, [d]she
looked with contempt on her mistress.[3]
5 And Sarai said to Abram, "May the wrong
done to me be on you! I gave my servant to
your embrace, and when she saw that she
had conceived, she looked on me with contempt. May [e]the LORD judge between you
and me!" 6 But Abram said to Sarai,
"Behold, your servant is in your power; do
to her as you please." Then Sarai dealt
harshly with her, and she fled from her.

7 The angel of the LORD found her by a

[1] Or *have given* [2] Hebrew *be built up*, which sounds like the Hebrew for *children* [3] Hebrew *her mistress was dishonorable in her eyes*; similarly in verse 5

15:12–14 Israel must inherit Canaan through God's supernatural act of redemption from slavery.

15:13 four hundred years. A round number for the period spent in Egypt (cf. Ex. 12:40, 41).

15:15 good old age. See 25:8.

15:16 Amorites. See note 14:13.

15:17 smoking fire pot and a flaming torch. Symbols of God's presence with Israel on their way to the Promised Land (Ex. 13:21; 19:18; 20:18).

passed between these pieces. As other ancient Near Eastern texts and Jer. 34:18 indicate, by passing between the torn animals (signifying the punishment due those who break the covenant) God invokes a self-maledictory oath or curse upon Himself should He fail to keep His covenant. Because He can swear by no higher authority, God swears by Himself to keep the covenantal terms. See 22:16, 17; Heb. 6:13 note.

15:18 covenant. God's covenant with Abraham closely parallels ancient Near Eastern royal land grants made by kings to loyal servants and their descendants in perpetuity.

from the river . . . Euphrates. Delineation of borders was an important part of the ancient royal land grants.

river of Egypt. It is debated whether the brook of Egypt, the Wadi el Arish in northeastern Sinai (Num. 34:5), or the eastern branch of the Nile delta is in view. See 1 Kin. 4:21.

15:19–21 In addition to its geographical boundaries the land is defined by its occupants. See 10:15–18.

16:1–15 In her impatience, Sarah tried to fulfill the divine promise through her own initiative by means of her maidservant, Hagar. The immediate result is strife in the home, and its long-term consequence is the mixed blessing of numerous progeny who will inherit Hagar's defiant spirit (v. 12). This natural generation did not bring peace; only the greater Seed of Abraham (Gal. 3:16), the Son of the God of peace, can do that.

16:1 servant. The Hebrew term denotes a personal servant of the wife, not a slave girl (cf. 21:10 note). Her relationship to Sarah resembled Eliezer's to Abraham (15:2).

16:2 obtain children by her. In this custom, attested so far in the Code of Hammurabi and in texts from Nuzi and Nimrud, the authority over the children resulting from this union belonged to the chief wife, not the slave-wife (Introduction: Author).

16:3 ten years. See 12:4.

16:4 looked with contempt. The Hebrew word here is translated "curse" in 12:3 (12:3 note; cf. Prov. 30:23). Because she treated Sarah with disdain, Hagar was alienated from the family of blessing.

16:5 May the wrong done to me be on you. Sarah lays responsibility for the situation upon Abraham. Only he has the judicial authority to effect a change and up to now has not acted to protect their marriage.

May the LORD judge. She appeals to a still higher court (31:53; Ex. 5:21; 1 Sam. 24:12, 15).

16:6 as you please. According to the Code of Hammurabi, the despised mistress in this situation could not sell her maidservant, but she could mark her with the slave mark and count her among the slaves.

dealt harshly . . . fled. The intractable Ishmael is the unruly son of a mother who chose the freedom of the wilderness over submitting to the yoke of her mistress (v. 9).

16:7 angel of the LORD. The identity of the angel of the Lord is debated. According to some, although the "angel of the Lord" sometimes may be distinguished from God (e.g., 21:17; 2 Sam. 24:16; 2 Kin. 19:35), in other instances the angel of the Lord appears to be a theophany, a visual manifestation of God Himself (e.g., 18:1–33; 22:11–18; 32:24–30; Ex. 3:2–6).

spring of water in the wilderness, the
spring on the way to [f]Shur. 8 And he said,
"Hagar, servant of Sarai, where have you
come from and where are you going?" She
said, "I am fleeing from my mistress Sarai."
9 The angel of the LORD said to her, "Return
to your mistress and submit to her." 10 The
angel of the LORD also said to her, [g]"I will
surely multiply your offspring so that they
cannot be numbered for multitude." 11 And
the angel of the LORD said to her,

"Behold, you are pregnant
and shall bear a son.
You shall call his name Ishmael,[1]
[h]because the LORD has listened to
your affliction.
12 He shall be [i]a wild donkey of a man,
his hand against everyone
and everyone's hand against him,
and he shall dwell [j]over against all
his kinsmen."

13 So she called the name of the LORD who
spoke to her, "You are a God of seeing,"[2]
for she said, [k]"Truly here I have seen him
who looks after me."[3] 14 Therefore the well
was called [l]Beer-lahai-roi;[4] it lies between
[m]Kadesh and Bered.

15 And Hagar bore Abram a son, and Abram
called the name of his son, whom Hagar
bore, Ishmael. 16 Abram was eighty-six years
old when Hagar bore Ishmael to Abram.

Abraham and the Covenant of Circumcision

17 When Abram was ninety-nine years
old the LORD appeared to Abram
and said to him, "I am God Almighty;[5]
walk before me, and be [n]blameless, 2 that I
may make my covenant between me and
you, and [o]may multiply you greatly."
3 Then Abram [p]fell on his face. And God
said to him, 4 "Behold, my covenant is with
you, and you shall be [q]the father of a multitude of nations. 5 No longer shall your
name be called Abram,[6] but [r]your name
shall be Abraham,[7] [s]for I have made you
the father of a multitude of nations. 6 I will
make you exceedingly fruitful, and I will
make [t]you into nations, and [u]kings shall
come from you. 7 And I will [v]establish my
covenant between me and you and your
offspring after you throughout their generations for an everlasting covenant, [w]to be

1 *Ishmael* means *God hears* 2 Or *You are a God who sees me* 3 Hebrew *Have I really seen him here who sees me?* or *Would I have looked here for the one who sees me?* 4 *Beer-lahai-roi* means *the well of the Living One who sees me* 5 Hebrew *El Shaddai* 6 *Abram* means *exalted father* 7 *Abraham* means *father of a multitude*

7 [f]ch. 25:18; Ex. 15:22
10 [g]ch. 17:20; 21:18; See ch. 25:12-18
11 [h][ch. 29:32]
12 [i]Job 39:5-8; [ch. 21:20] [j]ch. 25:18
13 [k][ch. 32:30; Ex. 19:21; 33:20; Judg. 13:22]
14 [l]ch. 24:62; 25:11 [m]ch. 14:7; 20:1; Num. 13:26

Chapter 17
1 [n]ch. 6:9; Deut. 18:13; Job 1:1; Ps. 119:1; Matt. 5:48
2 [o]ch. 12:2; 13:16; 22:17
3 [p]ver. 17
4 [q]Rom. 4:11, 12, 16
5 [r]Neh. 9:7 [s]Cited Rom. 4:17
6 [t]ch. 35:11 [u]ver. 16
7 [v]Gal. 3:17 [w]Heb. 11:16; [ch. 26:24; 28:13]

Others, however, note that "angel" means "messenger." They argue that as secular messengers are fully equated with their senders (Judg. 11:13; 2 Sam. 3:12, 13; 1 Kin. 20:2–4), so God's angel is identified with Him (see also Gen. 21:17; 31:11; Ex. 14:9; 23:20; 32:34).

Shur. The name means "wall," a reference to the Egyptian border forts. Hagar apparently fled toward her home in Egypt (cf. v. 1).

16:8 where. See notes 3:9 and 11:5.

16:10 multiply your offspring. Abraham fathers many descendants, both elect (13:16 note) and non-elect. It is not the mere natural children who finally inherit the promise (Rom. 9:8). Even the physical offspring of Abraham may persecute the sons of promise (21:9; Gal. 4:29, 30).

16:12 against everyone. The fierce, aggressive ways of the Ishmaelites will leave a legacy of conflict.

16:13 You are a God of seeing. This divine name is not attested elsewhere. It expresses the deep significance to Hagar of God's gracious revelation to her. Even while she was lost in the wilderness, God had seen her and revealed Himself to her.

16:14 it lies between Kadesh and Bered. Today the site is uncertain.

16:15 a son. The genealogy is given in 25:12–18.

17:1 God Almighty. See text note. This divine name may signify God's universal dominion. It occurs frequently in Job, and in the patriarchal narratives, often when the covenant promise of progeny is stressed (28:3; 35:11; 43:14; 48:3; 49:25).

walk before me, and be blameless. These phrases denote the service due a king. Even Israel's kings were commanded to "walk before" their greater Sovereign, the Lord Himself (1 Kin. 9:4; 2 Kin. 20:3). The covenantal arrangement again surfaces: God's gracious promises call for the obedient response of Abraham.

17:2 my covenant. The covenant relationship between God and Abraham includes both promises obligating God to Abraham (vv. 4–8, 16), and commands obligating Abraham and Sarah to God ("As for you," vv. 9–15). This pattern of mutual obligation is not a relationship of equal parties (as in a human contract), however, for God sovereignly bestows the covenant, gives the grace of faith and obedience to man, and graciously provides the remedy for human disobedience (28:20 note). The history of the covenant in the Old Testament is largely one of human failure fully to obey the covenantal requirements. Nevertheless, the gracious covenant God remains faithful to His promises, even when human beings are faithless (v. 7 note; Lev. 26:44, 45; Deut. 4:30, 31; 2 Tim. 2:13 and note).

17:5 Abram . . . Abraham. Abram, an ancient West Semitic name, means "exalted father," perhaps originally a reference to Abraham's father Terah. "Abraham" sounds like a Hebrew expression meaning "father of a multitude of nations." His old name spoke of his aristocratic ancestry; the new speaks of his many offspring.

your name shall be. The name changes of the patriarch and matriarch show they are under God's rule (1:5 note) and are called to a new destiny and mission.

father of a multitude of nations. Abraham was the physical father of many nations—ethnic Israel through the promised son Isaac, Ishmaelites (v. 20; 21:13; 25:12–18), Edomites (25:23; 36:1–43), and his descendants through Keturah (25:1–4). But this promise finds final fulfillment in the multitude from every tribe, language, and nation who share the faith of Abraham and are baptized into Jesus Christ (Rom. 4:16, 17; 15:8–12; Gal. 3:29; Rev. 7:9).

17:7 your offspring. The descendants of Abraham through the child of promise, Isaac (Rom. 4:19; 9:6–9). Gentile believers participate in this covenant promise through spiritual incorporation into Israel (Eph. 2:11–13; 1 Pet. 2:10 note) by union with Christ, the great offspring of Abraham (Gal. 3:16, 26–29).

everlasting. The unilateral and gracious nature of God's covenant with Abraham is underscored by its *eternal* character (v. 2 note). God's

God to you and to your offspring after you.
8 And [x]I will give to you and to your offspring after you the land of your sojournings, all the land of Canaan, for an everlast-

8 [x]ch. 12:7; 13:15; Ps. 105:11

[y]Ex. 6:7; Lev. 26:12

ing possession, and [y]I will be their God."
9 And God said to Abraham, "As for you,
you shall keep my covenant, you and
your offspring after you throughout their

Infant Baptism

Baptizing the infant children of believers (sometimes called "paedobaptism"), in the belief that this accords with God's revealed will, has been the historic practice of most churches. However, the worldwide Baptist community, which includes distinguished Reformed thinkers, disputes this practice.

Baptists insist that membership in local congregations is only for those who have publicly professed a personal faith. The argument often includes the claim that Christ instituted baptism primarily as a public profession of faith, and that this profession is part of the definition of baptism, with the result that infant baptism is not really baptism at all. On this ground Baptist churches rebaptize persons baptized in infancy who have come to faith—from the Baptist standpoint they have never been baptized. Historic Reformed theology contests the view that only adult, believer's baptism is true baptism, and it rejects the exclusion of believers' children from the visible community of faith. These differences regarding the nature of the visible church form the background for all discussions of infant baptism.

The practice of infant baptism is neither prescribed nor forbidden in the New Testament, nor is it explicitly illustrated (though some argue that the New Testament practice of household baptisms probably included infants and small children). Rather, the scriptural case for baptizing believers' infants rests on the parallel between Old Testament circumcision and New Testament baptism as signs and seals of the covenant of grace (Gen. 17:11; Rom. 4:11; Col. 2:11, 12), and on the claim that the principle of family solidarity in the covenant community (the church, as it is now called) was not affected by the transition from the "old" to the "new" form of God's covenant brought about by the coming of Christ. Infant children of believers have the status of covenant children and therefore should be baptized, just as Jewish male infants had previously been circumcised. The Old Testament precedent requires it and there are no divine instructions explicitly revoking this principle.

Further evidence that the principle of family solidarity continues in the New Testament period is found in 1 Cor. 7:14, where Paul notes that even the children of but one Christian parent are relationally and covenantally "holy" (that is, set apart to God together with the one Christian parent). So the principle of parent-child solidarity still stands, as Peter also indicated in his Pentecost sermon (Acts 2:39). And if infants are deemed members of the visible covenant community with their parent, it is fitting to give them the sign of covenant status and of their place in the covenant community; in fact, it would be unfitting for the church to withhold it. This fitness is demonstrated in that when circumcision was the sign of covenant status and community inclusion, God commanded it to be done (Gen. 17:9–14).

Against these arguments, Baptists allege that first, circumcision was primarily a sign of Jewish ethnic identity, so the parallel between it and Christian baptism is mistaken; second, that under the new covenant the requirement of personal faith before baptism is absolute; and third, that practices not explicitly recognized and approved in Scripture must not be brought into church life.

Certainly, all adult church members must profess faith personally before the church. Communions that baptize infants provide for this in confirmation or the equivalent. The Christian nurture of Baptist and paedobaptist children will be similar: They will be dedicated to God in infancy, either by baptism or by a rite of dedication; they will be brought up to live for the Lord and led to the point of publicly professing faith, in confirmation or baptism. After this they will enjoy full communicant status. The ongoing debate is not about nurture, but about God's way of defining the church.

It is sometimes said that infant baptism leads to a false presumption that the rite by itself guarantees the child's salvation. In the absence of biblical instruction on its meaning, this unfortunate misconception is possible. But it should be remembered that such a misunderstanding is equally possible in the case of adult, believer's baptism. See the warning in "Baptism" at Rom. 6:3.

covenant endures forever because He does not change and Jesus Christ fulfills every condition (2 Cor. 1:20; Eph. 2:12, 13).

to be God to you. Although there is a legal dimension to the covenant (v. 2 note), God's covenant relationship with His people is first and foremost one of divine-human communion and fellowship (Ex. 6:7; Deut. 29:13). God graciously dwells with His people, and they gratefully respond in faith, love, and obedience.

17:8 land of Canaan . . . everlasting possession. See 13:15 and note.

generations. 10 This is my covenant, which
you shall keep, between me and you and
your offspring after you: Every male among
you shall be circumcised. 11 You shall be
circumcised in the flesh of your foreskins,
and it shall be a [z]sign of the covenant
between me and you. 12 He who is [a]eight
days old among you shall be circumcised.
Every male throughout your generations,
whether born in your house or [b]bought
with your money from any foreigner who is
not of your offspring, 13 both he who is
born in your house and he who is bought
with your money, shall surely be circumcised. So shall my covenant be in your flesh
an everlasting covenant. 14 Any uncircumcised male who is not circumcised in the
flesh of his foreskin shall be cut off from
his people; he has broken my covenant."

Isaac's Birth Promised

15 And God said to Abraham, "As for
Sarai your wife, you shall not call her name
Sarai, but Sarah[1] shall be her name. 16 I will
bless her, and moreover, I will [c]give[2] you a
son by her. I will bless her, and [d]she shall
become nations; kings of peoples shall
come from her." 17 Then Abraham [e]fell on
his face [f]and laughed and said to himself,
"Shall a child be born to a man who is a
hundred years old? Shall Sarah, who is
ninety years old, bear a child?" 18 And
Abraham said to God, "Oh that Ishmael
might live before you!" 19 God said, "No,
but [g]Sarah your wife shall bear you a son,
and you shall call his name [h]Isaac.[3] I will
establish my covenant with him as an everlasting covenant for his offspring after him.
20 As for Ishmael, I have heard you; behold,
I have blessed him and will make him fruitful and [i]multiply him greatly. He [j]shall
father twelve princes, and [k]I will make him
into a great nation. 21 But [l]I will establish
my covenant with Isaac, [m]whom Sarah
shall bear to you at this time next year."
22 When he had finished talking with
him, [n]God went up from Abraham. 23 Then
Abraham took Ishmael his son and all
those born in his house or bought with his
money, every male among the men of
Abraham's house, and he circumcised the
flesh of their foreskins that very day, as
God had said to him. 24 Abraham was
ninety-nine years old when he was circumcised in the flesh of his foreskin. 25 And
Ishmael his son was thirteen years old
when he was circumcised in the flesh of his
foreskin. 26 That very day Abraham and his
son Ishmael were circumcised. 27 And all
the men of his house, those born in the
house and those bought with money from
a foreigner, were circumcised with him.

18 And the LORD appeared to him by
the [o]oaks[4] of Mamre, as he sat at the
door of his tent in the heat of the day. 2 He
lifted up his eyes and looked, and behold,

11 [z]Acts 7:8; Rom. 4:11
12 [a]Lev. 12:3; Luke 1:59; 2:21; Phil. 3:5 [b][Ex. 12:48, 49]
16 [c]ch. 18:10 [d]ch. 35:11
17 [e]ver. 3 [f]ch. 21:6; Rom. 4:19; [John 8:56]
19 [g]ch. 18:10; 21:2; Gal. 4:23, 28 [h]ch. 21:3
20 [i]ch. 16:10 [j]See ch. 25:12-16 [k]ch. 21:13, 18
21 [l]ch. 26:2-5 [m]ch. 21:2
22 [n]ch. 35:13
Chapter 18
1 [o]ch. 13:18; 14:13

[1] *Sarai* and *Sarah* mean *princess* [2] Hebrew *have given* [3] *Isaac* means *he laughs* [4] Or *terebinths*

17:10 circumcised. By this ritual the organ of procreation was consecrated to God (cf. Lev. 19:23). More importantly, God wanted the heart and ear consecrated to Him (Deut. 10:16; 30:6; Jer. 4:4; 6:10; Ezek. 44:7, 9). Mere circumcision in the flesh is inadequate to please God (17:11–14 notes; Jer. 9:25, 26).

17:11 sign of the covenant. See note 9:12.

17:12 eight days old. See Luke 1:59; 2:21; Phil. 3:5. Some ancient Near Eastern cultures circumcised their children at puberty as a rite of passage from childhood to manhood. God employed the sign for infants to show that the children of believing parents are "holy" (they are separated from the profane world and belong to the covenant community, Rom. 11:16; 1 Cor. 7:14). God continues to use the family institution (Acts 16:31). The initiation rite into the covenant community today is baptism. In Christ there is no longer male or female, Jew or Gentile, so all may come (Gal. 3:26–29; Col. 2:11, 12). See theological note "Infant Baptism" on page 37.

17:13 born . . . bought. The covenant promises were extended to all within the household of faith. Even in the Old Testament, the scope of the covenant community was not exclusively determined by ancestry—a foreshadowing of the expansion of the covenant to a multitude from every tribe and nation. See notes on vv. 6, 7.

in your flesh an everlasting covenant. See note on v. 7. The covenant of grace between God and His people is indeed an eternal covenant, although the mode of administration changes with the transition from Israel to the church (e.g., circumcision is replaced by baptism, v. 12 note). See "The Sacraments" at Matt. 28:19.

17:15 Sarai . . . Sarah. See text note. Both names seem to be variants meaning "princess." Her birth name probably looked back on her noble descent, whereas her covenant name looks ahead to her noble descendants (v. 5 and note).

17:16 bless. See note 12:2.

17:17 laughed. See note 21:3.

17:20 twelve princes. See 25:12–16.

17:21 with Isaac. By His own sovereign counsel the Lord elected Isaac, not Ishmael (Introduction: Date and Occasion). Isaac's miraculous birth signifies that the people of God result, not from mere natural generation, but from the promise and the supernatural grace of the Holy Spirit (Rom. 4:17; Gal. 4:21–31).

17:23 that very day. Abraham demonstrated his faith in God's gracious covenant by his obedience (v. 1 note; Rom. 4:9–12).

18:1 appeared. See note 12:7.

oaks of Mamre. See note 12:6.

heat of the day. The time when travelers seek shade and rest.

18:2 three men. The Lord and two angels (vv. 1, 13; 19:1). The New Testament admonition to show hospitality in Heb. 13:2 is based on the incidents in chs. 18 and 19.

three men were standing in front of him.
[p]When he saw them, he ran from the tent
door to meet them and bowed himself to
the earth **3**and said, "O Lord,[1] if I have
found favor in your sight, do not pass by
your servant. **4**Let a [q]little water be brought,
and wash your feet, and rest yourselves
under the tree, **5**while I bring a morsel of
bread, that [r]you may refresh yourselves,
and after that you may pass on—[s]since you
have come to your servant." So they said,
"Do as you have said." **6**And Abraham went
quickly into the tent to Sarah and said,
"Quick! Three seahs[2] of fine flour! Knead it,
and make cakes." **7**And Abraham ran to the
herd and took a calf, tender and good, and
gave it to a young man, who prepared it
quickly. **8**Then he took curds and milk and
the calf that he had prepared, and set it
before them. And he stood by them under
the tree while they ate.
9They said to him, "Where is Sarah your
wife?" And he said, "She is [t]in the tent."
10The LORD said, "I will surely return to you
[u]about this time next year, and [v]Sarah your
wife shall have a son." And Sarah was listening at the tent door behind him. **11**Now
[w]Abraham and Sarah were old, advanced in
years. The way of women had ceased to be
with Sarah. **12**[x]So Sarah laughed to herself,
saying, [y]"After I am worn out, and [z]my lord
is old, shall I have pleasure?" **13**The LORD
said to Abraham, "Why did Sarah laugh
and say, 'Shall I indeed bear a child, now
that I am old?' **14**[a]Is anything too hard[3] for
the LORD? [b]At the appointed time I will
return to you about this time next year, and
Sarah shall have a son." **15**But Sarah denied
it,[4] saying, "I did not laugh," for she was
afraid. He said, "No, but you did laugh."
16Then the men set out from there, and
they looked down toward Sodom. And
Abraham went with them to set them on
their way. **17**The LORD said, [c]"Shall I hide
from Abraham what I am about to do,
18seeing that Abraham shall surely become
a great and mighty nation, and all the
nations of the earth shall be [d]blessed in
him? **19**For I have [e]chosen[5] him, that he
may command his children and his household after him to keep the way of the LORD
by doing righteousness and justice, so that
the LORD may bring to Abraham what he
has promised him." **20**Then the LORD said,
"Because [f]the outcry against Sodom and
Gomorrah is great and their sin is very
grave, **21**[g]I will go down to see whether they
have done altogether[6] according to the outcry that has come to me. And if not, [h]I will
know."

Abraham Intercedes for Sodom

22[i]So the men turned from there and
went toward Sodom, but Abraham [j]still
stood before the LORD. **23**Then Abraham
drew near and said, [k]"Will you indeed

2 [p]ch. 19:1; [Heb. 13:2]
4 [q]ch. 19:2; 24:32; 43:24; [Luke 7:44; John 13:14]
5 [r]Judg. 19:5; [Ps. 104:15] [s]ch. 19:8; 33:10
9 [t]ch. 24:67
10 [u]ver. 14; 2 Kin. 4:16 [v]ch. 17:19, 21; 21:2; Cited Rom. 9:9
11 [w]ch. 17:17; Rom. 4:19; Heb. 11:11, 12
12 [x][ch. 17:17] [y][Luke 1:18] [z]1 Pet. 3:6
14 [a]Job 42:2; Zech. 8:6; Matt. 19:26; Luke 1:37 [b]ver. 10
17 [c][Ps. 25:14; Amos 3:7; John 15:15]
18 [d]ch. 12:3; 22:18; 26:4; Acts 3:25; Gal. 3:8
19 [e][Amos 3:2]
20 [f]ch. 4:10; 19:13; [Isai. 3:9; James 5:4]
21 [g]ch. 11:5, 7; Ex. 3:8 [h]Josh. 22:22
22 [i]ver. 16; ch. 19:1 [j]ver. 1; [Ps. 106:23; Jer. 18:20]
23 [k]ch. 20:4; Num. 16:22; 2 Sam. 24:17

[1] Or *My lord* [2] A *seah* was about 7 quarts or 7.3 liters [3] Or *wonderful*
[4] Or *acted falsely* [5] Hebrew *known* [6] Or *they deserve destruction;* Hebrew *they have made a complete end*

ran. Observing the ancient Near Eastern custom of hospitality, Abraham typifies the gracious host and is completely at the service of his guests. His behavior contrasts with the immorality of the Sodomites (19:4, 5).

18:3 O Lord. This Hebrew term unequivocally refers to God.

18:9 Where. See notes 3:9 and 11:5.

18:10 Sarah . . . son. See 11:30; 15:2–4; 16:11; 17:15, 16; Rom. 9:9.

18:11 The way of women had ceased to be. Lit. "Sarah no longer experienced the cycle of women." Her body was no longer able to conceive (Heb. 11:11, 12; Rom. 4:19).

18:14 too hard. Despite her initial skepticism, Sarah too came to believe the promise (Heb. 11:11), and joined her husband in faith (Rom. 4:13–25).

18:15 you did laugh. See note 21:3.

18:16–33 The Lord's promise of a miraculous offspring anticipated that Abraham would become a great and powerful nation to bless the earth. Such a nation had to learn justice, beginning with its father, Abraham (vv. 17–19). The Lord demonstrated His justice to Abraham in the judgment upon the wicked cities of Sodom and Gomorrah (vv. 20–33). God investigated the accusations thoroughly (vv. 20–21; 11:5 note); even if there had been ten righteous people He would have spared the cities (v. 32).

18:17 Shall I hide. See note 12:7. God so esteemed His servants, the prophets, that He revealed His plans to them (20:7; Amos 3:7; cf. John 15:15). As a prophet, Abraham also interceded (cf. Jer. 15:1; 27:18).

18:19 I have chosen him, that he may. The Hebrew word translated "chosen" here means "chosen in love." The purpose of God's sovereign and gracious election is that His people might be holy and righteous in His sight (Eph. 1:4).

that the LORD . . . what he has promised. Those promises claimed by Abraham in faith must be claimed by his descendants as well. Their hope in God's covenant will be demonstrated by their covenant obedience. God's plan will be realized through the covenant faithfulness of His people (22:18; 26:4, 5). See note 17:2.

18:20 outcry. All cries of wrongdoing come to the attention of the "Judge of all the earth" (v. 25; cf. 4:10). Despite the mercy shown to Sodom through Abraham (ch. 14), Sodom had not repented of its sin.

their sin. The sinfulness of Sodom was both proverbial and extensive (13:13; Jer. 23:14). It involved extreme displays of sexual depravity (particularly homosexuality, 19:5; Jude 7), arrogance and abuse of the poor (Ezek. 16:49, 50), and a failure to show hospitality (19:8).

18:21 go down to see. See note 11:5.

18:23 Will you indeed sweep away the righteous. Clearly, no one would escape the massive destruction intended for the cities, so

sweep away the righteous with the
wicked? 24 Suppose there are fifty righteous within the city. Will you then sweep
away the place and not spare it for the
fifty righteous who are in it? 25 Far be it
from you to do such a thing, to put the
righteous to death with the wicked, [l]so
that the righteous fare as the wicked! Far
be that from you! [m]Shall not the Judge of
all the earth do what is just?” 26 And the
LORD said, [n]“If I find at Sodom fifty righteous in the city, I will spare the whole
place for their sake.”
27 Abraham answered and said, [o]“Behold, I have undertaken to speak to the
Lord, I who am but dust and ashes.
28 Suppose five of the fifty righteous are
lacking. Will you destroy the whole city for
lack of five?” And he said, “I will not
destroy it if I find forty-five there.” 29 Again
he spoke to him and said, “Suppose forty
are found there.” He answered, “For the
sake of forty I will not do it.” 30 Then he
said, “Oh let not the Lord be angry, and I
will speak. Suppose thirty are found
there.” He answered, “I will not do it, if
I find thirty there.” 31 He said, “Behold, I
have undertaken to speak to the Lord.
Suppose twenty are found there.” He
answered, “For the sake of twenty I will
not destroy it.” 32 Then he said, [p]“Oh let
not the Lord be angry, and I will speak
again but this once. Suppose ten are found
there.” He answered, “For the sake of ten
I will not destroy it.” 33 And the LORD went
his way, when he had finished speaking to
Abraham, and Abraham returned to his
place.

God Rescues Lot

19 The [q]two angels came to Sodom in
the evening, and Lot was sitting in
the gate of Sodom. When Lot saw them, he
rose to meet them and bowed himself with
his face to the earth 2 and said, “My lords,
[r]please turn aside to your servant’s house
and spend the night [s]and wash your feet.
Then you may rise up early and go on your
way.” They said, [t]“No; we will spend the
night in the town square.” 3 But he pressed
them strongly; so they turned aside to him
and entered his house. And he made them
a feast and baked unleavened bread, and
they ate.
4 But before they lay down, the men of
the city, the men of Sodom, both young
and old, all the people to the last man, surrounded the house. 5 [u]And they called to
Lot, “Where are the men who came to you
tonight? [v]Bring them out to us, that we
[w]may know them.” 6 Lot went out to the
men at the entrance, shut the door after
him, 7 and said, “I beg you, my brothers, do
not act so wickedly. 8 [x]Behold, I have two
daughters who have not known any man.
Let me bring them out to you, and do to
them as you please. Only do nothing to
these men, for they have come under the
shelter of my roof.” 9 But they said, “Stand
back!” And they said, “This fellow [y]came to
sojourn, and [z]he has become the judge!
Now we will deal worse with you than with
them.” Then they pressed hard against the
man Lot, and drew near to break the door
down. 10 But the men reached out their
hands and brought Lot into the house with
them and shut the door. 11 And they struck

25 [l][Job 8:20] [m]Deut. 32:4; Job 8:3; 34:10; Rom. 3:5, 6
26 [n]Jer. 5:1; Ezek. 22:30; [Isai. 65:8]
27 [o][Luke 18:1]
32 [p]Judg. 6:39

Chapter 19
1 [q]ch. 18:22
2 [r]Heb. 13:2; [Judg. 4:18] [s]See ch. 18:4 [t][Luke 24:28]
5 [u]Isai. 3:9; [ch. 13:13] [v]Judg. 19:22 [w]Rom. 1:24, 27; Jude 7
8 [x][Judg. 19:24]
9 [y]ch. 13:12 [z]Ex. 2:14

Abraham petitions God on behalf of the righteous who might reside there. The series of questions and answers that follow serve to establish beyond doubt the justice of God’s judgment.

18:32 ten. God’s mercy is evident in His willingness to spare the sinful majority for the sake of even ten righteous. Fewer than ten could be saved individually, as happens in ch. 19. In cases of special punishment inflicted upon cities and nations, righteous individuals were sometimes singled out for preservation (Josh. 6:25; cf. Ezek. 14:14, 16, 18, 20). See “The Spiritual Nature of God”at Is. 66:1.

19:1–29 Just as God had rescued righteous Noah from the sinful pre-Flood world (chs. 6–8), so also He rescues Lot from Sodom. Ultimately, Lot was saved because of God’s mercy to him (v. 16) and because of God’s covenantal commitment to Abraham (v. 29). The destruction of Sodom becomes a paradigm of God’s judgment on sin (Is. 1:9, 10; Ezek. 16:46–49; Amos 4:11; Rom. 9:29; 2 Pet. 2:5, 6).

19:1–11 See the similar episode recorded in Judg. 19:15–25.

19:1 two angels. See note 18:2 and “Angels” at Zech. 1:9. The two angels continue on to Sodom, but the Lord Himself does not appear after 18:33; He will rain down the judgment from heaven (v. 24).

sitting in the gate. See 14:12 and note. That Lot was sitting in the city gate indicates his status as a respected member of the community. Legal matters were decided at the city gate by community elders such as Lot (Deut. 21:18–21; Amos 5:15).

bowed himself. Throughout the story Lot demonstrated his righteousness by his hospitality to strangers (18:2 and notes; cf. 2 Pet. 2:6, 7).

19:4 young and old . . . to the last man. These details are necessary to show that everyone destroyed was wicked (18:23 note). See also 6:5; 8:21; Rom. 1:26–32.

19:7 so wickedly. The character of Lot’s appeal demonstrates his righteousness (2 Pet. 2:6, 7).

19:8 See notes 18:2 and 19:1. As one bound by the ancient Near Eastern code of hospitality, which required the protection of guests, Lot was willing to risk danger to his own family rather than allow harm to come to his guests.

19:10 shut the door. See note 7:16.

with [a]blindness the men who were at the
entrance of the house, both small and
great, so that they wore themselves out
groping for the door.
12 Then the men said to Lot, "Have you
anyone else here? Sons-in-law, sons,
daughters, or anyone you have in the city,
[b]bring them out of the place. 13 For we are
about to destroy this place, [c]because the
outcry against its people has become great
before the LORD, and the LORD has sent us
to destroy it." 14 So Lot went out and said to
his sons-in-law, who were to marry his
daughters, [d]"Up! Get out of this place, for
the LORD is about to destroy the city." But
he seemed to his sons-in-law to be jesting.
15 As morning dawned, the angels urged
Lot, saying, "Up! Take your wife and your
two daughters who are here, lest you be
swept away in the punishment of the city."
16 But he lingered. So the men seized him
and his wife and his two daughters by the
hand, [e]the LORD being merciful to him, and
they brought him out and set him outside
the city. 17 And as they brought them out,
one said, "Escape for your life. [f]Do not
look back or stop anywhere in the [g]valley.
Escape to the hills, lest you be swept
away." 18 And Lot said to them, "Oh, no,
my lords. 19 Behold, your servant has found
favor in your sight, and you have shown me
great kindness in saving my life. But I cannot escape to the hills, lest the disaster
overtake me and I die. 20 Behold, this city is
near enough to flee to, and it is a little one.
Let me escape there—is it not a little
one?—and my life will be saved!" 21 He said
to him, "Behold, I grant you this favor also,
that I will not overthrow the city of which
you have spoken. 22 Escape there quickly,
for I can do nothing till you arrive there."
Therefore the name of the city was called
[h]Zoar.[1]

11 [a][2 Kin. 6:18; Acts 13:11]
12 [b]2 Pet. 2:7, 9; [Rev. 18:4, 5]
13 [c]ch. 18:20
14 [d]Num. 16:21, 26, 45; Jer. 51:6
16 [e][Ps. 34:22]
17 [f]ver. 26; [Matt. 24:16-18] [g]ch. 13:10

God Destroys Sodom

23 The sun had risen on the earth when
Lot came to Zoar. 24 Then [i]the LORD rained
on Sodom and Gomorrah sulfur and fire
from the LORD out of heaven. 25 And he
overthrew those cities, and all the valley,
and all the inhabitants of the cities, and
what grew on the ground. 26 But Lot's wife,
behind him, looked back, and she became
[j]a pillar of salt.
27 And Abraham went early in the morning to the place where he had [k]stood before
the LORD. 28 And he looked down toward
Sodom and Gomorrah and toward all the
land of the valley, and he looked and,
behold, the smoke of the land went up like
the smoke of a furnace.
29 So it was that, when God destroyed the
cities of the valley, God [l]remembered
Abraham and sent Lot out of the midst of
the overthrow when he overthrew the cities
in which Lot had lived.

Lot and His Daughters

30 Now Lot went up out of Zoar and
[m]lived in the hills with his two daughters,
for he was afraid to live in Zoar. So he lived
in a cave with his two daughters. 31 And the
firstborn said to the younger, "Our father is
old, and there is not a man on earth to
come in to us after the manner of all the
earth. 32 Come, let us make our father drink

22 [h]ch. 14:2
24 [i]Deut. 29:23; Jer. 20:16; 50:40; Lam. 4:6; Amos 4:11; Zeph. 2:9; Luke 17:29; 2 Pet. 2:6
26 [j]Luke 17:32
27 [k]ch. 18:22
29 [l]See ch. 8:1
30 [m]ver. 17, 19

[1] *Zoar* means *little*

19:15 wife . . . daughters. The family is saved from the city's destruction as a unit, but this family, like Noah's, will prove to be a mixture of those who persevere (Lot) and those who do not (Lot's wife and daughters, vv. 26, 30–38).

19:16 he lingered. Lot's status in the city was probably due to his great wealth (13:6) and to his uncle Abraham's rescue of the city (ch. 14). Now, having to flee with virtually nothing from the comforts of the city (vv. 18–21), Lot hesitates.

19:24 the LORD rained . . . sulfur and fire. A detailed explanation of the inferno that engulfed the cities remains difficult; the Bible is concerned with the final divine Cause, rather than secondary causes. Deposits of sulfur are found near the Dead Sea. Some suggest that an earthquake caused a mixture of sulfur, asphalt (also abundant in this area, 14:10), and gasses from the earth to ignite (cf. Is. 34:9, 10).

19:26 Lot's wife . . . looked back. Lot's wife is a sobering lesson against vacillation when God's judgment is at hand (Luke 17:28–37).

19:29 remembered. See note 8:1. Twice Lot was saved because of faithful Abraham (14:1–16; 19:1–29).

19:30–38 The desperate act by Lot's daughters to preserve seed from their drunken father brings to a conclusion the tragic account of Lot that began with his separation from Abraham in 13:11. In spite of Lot's affiliation with Sodom and the unbelief of his family, the Lord protected his lineage and land because of his faith and his relationship to Abraham (Deut. 2:16–19).

19:30 afraid to live in Zoar. See note on v. 16. Ironically, while Lot had sought to live in Zoar because of his fear of the mountains (v. 19), he now lives in the mountains for fear of Zoar. Note the contrast with Lot's prosperity and prospect in 13:1–13.

19:31 old. He was too old to remarry and unlikely to father further descendants.

19:32 drink wine . . . lie with him. See note 9:21. The daughters' initiative contrasts with Lot, who apparently had made no effort to find spouses for his daughters. Their sexual immorality anticipates their descendants' seduction of Israel's men (Num. 25).

wine, and we will lie with him, that we may
preserve offspring from our father." 33 So
they made their father drink wine that
night. And the firstborn went in and lay
with her father. He did not know when she
lay down or when she arose.
34 The next day, the firstborn said to the
younger, "Behold, I lay last night with my
father. Let us make him drink wine tonight
also. Then you go in and lie with him, that
we may preserve offspring from our father."
35 So they made their father drink wine that
night also. And the younger arose and lay
with him, and he did not know when she
lay down or when she arose. 36 Thus both
the daughters of Lot became pregnant by
their father. 37 The firstborn bore a son and
called his name Moab.[1] [n]He is the father of
the Moabites to this day. 38 The younger
also bore a son and called his name Ben-
ammi.[2] [o]He is the father of the Ammonites
to this day.

Abraham and Abimelech

20 From there Abraham journeyed
toward the territory of the Negeb and
lived between [p]Kadesh and Shur; and he
[q]sojourned in [r]Gerar. 2 And Abraham said of
Sarah his wife, [s]"She is my sister." And
Abimelech king of Gerar sent and took
Sarah. 3 [t]But God came to Abimelech [u]in a
dream by night and said to him, "Behold,
you are a dead man because of the woman
whom you have taken, for she is a man's
wife." 4 Now Abimelech had not approached
her. So he said, [v]"Lord, will you kill an innocent people? 5 Did he not himself say to me,
'She is my sister'? And she herself said, 'He
is my brother.' In the integrity of my heart
and the innocence of my hands I have done
this." 6 Then God said to him in the dream,
"Yes, I know that you have done this in the
integrity of your heart, and it was I who
kept you from sinning [w]against me.
Therefore I did not let you touch her. 7 Now
then, return the man's wife, [x]for he is a
prophet, so that he will pray for you, and
you shall live. But if you do not return her,
know that you shall surely die, you, [y]and all
who are yours."
8 So Abimelech rose early in the morning
and called all his servants and told them all
these things. And the men were very much
afraid. 9 Then Abimelech called Abraham
and said to him, "What have you done to
us? And how have I sinned against you,
that you have brought on me and my kingdom a great sin? You have done to me
things that ought not to be done." 10 And
Abimelech said to Abraham, "What did
you see, that you did this thing?" 11 Abraham said, "I did it because I thought,
[z]There is no fear of God at all in this place,
and [a]they will kill me because of my wife.
12 Besides, [b]she is indeed my sister, the
daughter of my father though not the
daughter of my mother, and she became
my wife. 13 And when [c]God caused me to
wander from my father's house, I said to
her, 'This is the kindness you must do me:

[1] *Moab* sounds like the Hebrew for *from father* [2] *Ben-ammi* means *son of my people*

37 [n]Deut. 2:9
38 [o]Deut. 2:19
Chapter 20
1 [p]ch. 16:7, 14 [q]ch. 26:3 [r]ch. 26:6
2 [s]See ch. 12:13-20; 26:7-11
3 [t]Ps. 105:14 [u]Job 33:15, 16; Matt. 1:20; 2:12
4 [v]ch. 13:23; [1 Chr. 21:17]
6 [w]ch. 39:9; Ps. 51:4
7 [x]1 Sam. 7:5; Job 42:8 [y][Num. 16:32, 33]
11 [z]Prov. 16:6 [a]ch. 12:12; 26:7
12 [b][ch. 11:29]
13 [c]ch. 12:1

19:37, 38 This genealogical conclusion (vv. 37, 38) begins the story of the bitter animosity of Moab and Ammon against Israel (Num. 23–25; 2 Kin. 3). The Moabites and Ammonites were rejected by God, not because of their questionable lineage, but because they mistreated Israel (Deut. 23:3–6; Neh. 13:1, 2). Ruth, an ancestor of Jesus Christ, was a Moabite (Ruth 4:18–22; Matt. 1:5), but through her faith she was eventually counted in the tribe of Judah.

20:1–18 Again Abraham fails to trust God for protection, and resorts instead to deception (cf. 12:10–20). Despite Abraham's failure, God preserves the covenant line of promise, just as He had in Egypt.

20:1 the Negeb. See note 12:9.

20:2 my sister. See v. 11 and note on 11:29.

Abimelech. Lit. "my father is king" or "father of a king." This Abimelech was probably the father or grandfather of the Abimelech encountered by Isaac (26:1). A ruler of Tyre (c. 1375 B.C.) had this name, which may have been a royal title (Ps. 34; cf. 1 Sam. 27:2).

sent and took Sarah. See 12:15 and note. On the brink of Isaac's conception (18:10–14; 21:1, 2), the program of redemption through the seed of Abraham was placed in jeopardy. Salvation finally depends on the faithful Lord, not on unfaithful humans, and here God protected the purity of Sarah (vv. 4, 6).

20:3 in a dream. God often communicated with His people through dreams in the Old Testament (28:12; 37:5–9; Num. 12:6). Sometimes such dreams were given to those outside the covenant community (31:24; 40:5; 41:1; Num. 22:9, 20; Dan. 2:1–45).

20:4 will you kill an innocent people. See 18:23, 32 and notes.

20:5 integrity of my heart. God judges people without the written law by their consciences (3:8; 6:9; Rom. 2:14 and notes).

20:7 prophet. The first use of this term in the Bible. Abraham was a man of God who received revelations and interceded for others (12:7; 15:1; 18:17 and notes).

20:9 great sin. Adultery was considered a great sin by the peoples of the ancient Near East. Many ancient law codes, including that of Hammurabi, contained provisions for dealing with adultery (cf. 26:10; 39:9). See note Ex. 20:14.

20:11 fear of God. Though this term often denotes the proper worship, reverence, and obedience of the true God (e.g., 22:12), here (and in 42:18) the expression probably means adherence (out of fear of divine judgment) to moral standards known through conscience.

20:12 my sister. See notes 11:29 and 12:12.

at every place to which we come, [d]say of me, He is my brother.'" **14** Then Abimelech [e]took sheep and oxen, and male servants and female servants, and gave them to Abraham, and returned Sarah his wife to him. **15** And Abimelech said, "Behold, [f]my land is before you; dwell where it pleases you." **16** To Sarah he said, "Behold, I have given [g]your brother a thousand pieces of silver. It is [h]a sign of your innocence in the eyes of all[1] who are with you, and before everyone you are vindicated." **17** Then [i]Abraham prayed to God, and God healed Abimelech, and also healed his wife and female slaves so that they bore children. **18** For the LORD [j]had closed all the wombs of the house of Abimelech because of Sarah, Abraham's wife.

The Birth of Isaac

21 The LORD [k]visited Sarah as he had said, and the LORD did to Sarah [l]as he had promised. **2** And Sarah [m]conceived and bore Abraham a son in his old age [n]at the time of which God had spoken to him. **3** Abraham called the name of his son who was born to him, whom Sarah bore him, [o]Isaac.[2] **4** And Abraham [p]circumcised his son Isaac when he was eight days old, [q]as God had commanded him. **5** [r]Abraham was a hundred years old when his son Isaac was born to him. **6** And Sarah said, [s]"God has made laughter for me; everyone who hears will laugh over me." **7** And she said, "Who would have said to Abraham that Sarah would nurse children? [t]Yet I have borne him a son in his old age."

God Protects Hagar and Ishmael

8 And the child grew and was weaned. And Abraham made a great feast on the day that Isaac was weaned. **9** But Sarah [u]saw the son of Hagar the Egyptian, whom she had borne to Abraham, [v]laughing.[3] **10** So she said to Abraham, [w]"Cast out this slave woman with her son, for the son of this slave woman shall not be heir with my son Isaac." **11** And the thing was very displeasing to Abraham on account of his son. **12** But God said to Abraham, "Be not displeased because of the boy and because of your slave woman. Whatever Sarah says to you, do as she tells you, for [x]through Isaac shall your offspring be named. **13** And I will make [y]a nation of the son of the slave woman also, because he is your offspring." **14** So Abraham rose early in the morning and took bread and a skin of water and

13 [d]ch. 12:13
14 [e]ch. 12:16
15 [f]ch. 13:9; 34:10
16 [g][ver. 5] [h][ch. 24:65]
17 [i][James 5:16]
18 [j][ch. 12:17]
Chapter 21
1 [k]1 Sam. 2:21 [l]ch. 17:19; 18:10, 14
2 [m]Heb. 11:11; [Gal. 4:22] [n]ch. 17:21
3 [o]ch. 17:19
4 [p]Acts 7:8 [q]ch. 17:10, 12
5 [r]ch. 17:1, 17; Rom. 4:19
6 [s][Isai. 54:1; Gal. 4:27]
7 [t]ch. 18:11, 12
9 [u]ch. 16:1, 15 [v][Gal. 4:29]
10 [w]Cited Gal. 4:30
12 [x]Cited Rom. 9:7; Heb. 11:18
13 [y]ver. 18; ch. 16:10; 17:20

1 Hebrew *It is a covering of eyes for all* 2 *Isaac* means *he laughs*
3 Possibly *laughing in mockery*

20:14–16 Abimelech gave gifts to Abraham (vv. 14, 15) and Sarah (v. 16) to honor God and their special relationship to Him, not to compensate for his guilt (v. 16 note; cf. 12:19, 20). God not only delivered His chosen servants out of dreadful peril but rewarded them with unexpected riches.

20:16 given your brother. Social convention demanded that the gift to Sarah be given through the male head of the family.

a thousand pieces of silver. A very large amount.

before everyone you are vindicated. Abimelech was guiltless and under no obligation to Abraham and Sarah (v. 6). Out of regard for the God of Abraham, however, Abimelech seeks to restore the honor that Sarah may have lost in the eyes of others.

20:17 Abraham prayed to God. See note on v. 7.

21:1–7 The report of Isaac's birth concludes the story of Sarah's barrenness begun in 11:27–32. The covenantal arrangement is underscored: God keeps His promise to give Abraham a son by Sarah (vv. 1–2; 17:1–6, 15–16; 18:1–15), and Abraham responds in obedience by naming him Isaac (v. 3; 17:19) and circumcising him (vv. 4, 5; 17:9–14), while Sarah responds with praise (vv. 6, 7).

21:1 visited. See 50:24 and note for this same expression of God's gracious intervention.

21:2 in his old age at the time. See 17:17, 24; 18:11–14. Abraham's greater Offspring also came at the appointed time (Gal. 4:4).

21:3 Isaac. See text note. Both Abraham and Sarah at first laughed in disbelief (17:17; 18:12), but when Isaac was born Sarah laughed for joy at the supernatural work of grace (v. 6).

21:4 circumcised. See note 17:12.

21:6 will laugh. See note on v. 3.

21:8–11 The expulsion of Hagar and Ishmael removed any threat to Isaac's inheritance. The accounts of the birth of Isaac and the removal of Ishmael are linked by another reference to laughter, Ishmael's "scoffing" at Isaac (v. 9 text note).

21:8 weaned. This rite of passage from the dangerous stage of infancy to childhood occurred at about three years of age. Here the occasion is celebrated by a feast.

21:9 Sarah saw. From her experience with Hagar (ch. 16) Sarah perceived the significance of Ishmael's disdain for Isaac and his threat to her son's inheritance.

laughing. The Hebrew root means "to laugh," but the form here signifies "to laugh at" or "make sport of" (text note). The son of the slave woman persecuted the son of the free (Gal. 4:29).

21:10 Cast out. So as to disinherit (cf. 25:5, 6).

slave woman. The Hebrew word here differs from the one translated "servant" in 16:1 (16:1 note). In her anger Sarah stresses Hagar's servile status—an indication of the animosity between these two rivals.

21:11 displeasing. As a father, Abraham felt genuine love and affection for Ishmael (17:18). In addition, there may have been customs prohibiting the expulsion of Hagar and her son (16:6 note).

21:12 your offspring be named. God's promises will reach their fulfillment through the miraculous offspring, Isaac, not through the natural (Rom. 9:7, 8). See note 17:7.

21:13 nation. See v. 18. Because of God's great love for Abraham, even his natural children were blessed on earth, though they were not part of the line of covenant promise (17:6 and note).

gave it to Hagar, putting it on her shoulder,
along with the child, and sent her away.
And she departed and wandered in the
wilderness of [z]Beersheba.
15 When the water in the skin was gone,
she put the child under one of the bushes.
16 Then she went and sat down opposite
him a good way off, about the distance of a
bowshot, for she said, "Let me not look on
the death of the child." And as she sat
opposite him, she lifted up her voice and
wept. 17 And God heard the voice of the boy,
and the angel of God called to Hagar from
heaven and said to her, "What troubles
you, Hagar? Fear not, for God has heard the
voice of the boy where he is. 18 Up! Lift up
the boy, and hold him fast with your hand,
for I will make him into a great nation."
19 Then [a]God opened her eyes, and she saw
a well of water. And she went and filled the
skin with water and gave the boy a drink.
20 And God was with the boy, and he grew
up. He lived in the wilderness [b]and became
an expert with the bow. 21 He lived in the
wilderness of Paran, and his mother took a
wife for him from the land of Egypt.

A Treaty with Abimelech

22 At that time [c]Abimelech and Phicol the
commander of his army said to Abraham,
[d]"God is with you in all that you do. 23 Now
therefore swear to me here by God that you
will not deal falsely with me or with my
descendants or with my posterity, but [e]as I
have dealt kindly with you, so you will deal
with me and with the land where you have
sojourned." 24 And Abraham said, "I will
swear."
25 When Abraham reproved Abimelech
about a well of water that Abimelech's servants [f]had seized, 26 Abimelech said, "I do
not know who has done this thing; you did
not tell me, and I have not heard of it until
today." 27 So Abraham took sheep and oxen
and gave them to Abimelech, and the two
men [g]made a covenant. 28 Abraham set
seven ewe lambs of the flock apart. 29 And
Abimelech said to Abraham, "What is the
meaning of these seven ewe lambs that you
have set apart?" 30 He said, "These seven
ewe lambs you will take from my hand,
that this[1] may be a witness for me that I
dug this well." 31 Therefore [h]that place was
called Beersheba,[2] because there both of
them swore an oath. 32 So they made a
covenant at Beersheba. Then Abimelech
and Phicol the commander of his army rose
up and returned to the land of the
Philistines. 33 Abraham planted a tamarisk
tree in Beersheba and [i]called there on the
name of the LORD, [j]the Everlasting God.
34 And Abraham sojourned many days in
the land of the Philistines.

The Sacrifice of Isaac

22 After these things [k]God tested
Abraham and said to him,
"Abraham!" And he said, "Here am I." 2 He
said, "Take your son, your only son Isaac,

[1] Or *you* [2] *Beersheba* means *well of seven* or *well of the oath*

14 [z]ver. 31
19 [a]Num. 22:31; 2 Kin. 6:17, 18, 20; [Luke 24:16, 31]
20 [b]ch. 16:12
22 [c]ch. 20:2; [ch. 26:1, 26] [d][ch. 26:28]
23 [e]ch. 20:14
25 [f][ch. 26:15, 18, 20-22]
27 [g]ch. 26:31
31 [h]ch. 26:33
33 [i]ch. 4:26; 12:8 [j]Isai. 40:28; [Ps. 90:2]
Chapter 22
1 [k]1 Cor. 10:13; Heb. 11:17; James 1:12, 13; 1 Pet. 1:6, 7

21:21 wilderness of Paran. A region in the east-central portion of the Sinai peninsula. Ishmael's departure from the covenant family seals his destiny; he will not inherit the divine promises of offspring and land.

Egypt. See 16:1.

21:22–34 Through divine blessing, Abraham and his household had become a formidable presence in the land (14:13; 23:6). That a Philistine king and his commander would seek a permanent non-aggression pact with Abraham and his descendants provides concrete evidence of God's rich covenant blessing on Abraham.

21:22 Abimelech. See note 20:2. Abraham's first encounter with Abimelech pertained to seed (ch. 20); this one, to land.

Phichol. Probably a title, rather than a personal name, for the Philistine army commander (26:26).

21:23 by God. The oaths were in God's name (vv. 31, 33; Deut. 6:13 note).

my posterity. While this treaty was intended to endure, tensions surfaced as early as the next generation (26:23–31).

21:30 seven ewe lambs . . . my hand. By accepting the gift, Abimelech was obliged to acknowledge Abraham's right to the well. The covenant had to be ratified by witnesses and oaths (v. 31).

21:31 swore. A verbal agreement to the covenant terms was not enough (v. 23). It had to be ratified by an oath (v. 31).

21:33 tamarisk tree. The planting of this small tree in the Negev probably served as a landmark of God's grace, a pledge that Abraham would stay in the land, and perhaps as a symbol of God's shading presence.

Everlasting God. Hebrew *El Olam.* See note 14:19.

21:34 sojourned. The Hebrew term here may be translated "sojourn" or "stay for a while." It denotes a resident alien (Ex. 6:4 text note; Heb. 11:9, 13).

22:1–19 Having already graciously committed Himself to Abraham, God tested Abraham's obedience. In his obedience, Abraham displayed his full commitment to the Lord, symbolically receiving Isaac, the child of promise, back from death (vv. 1–12). God's provision of the ram typifies the sacrifice of Jesus Christ, who died instead of the elect so that they would live (vv. 13–14). In taking an oath to bless Abraham and all nations through him, God guaranteed the promise to Abraham's offspring (vv. 15–19). See note Heb. 11:17–19.

22:1 tested. God tests His saints to prove the quality of their faith and obedience, often through adversity or hardship (Ex. 20:20; Deut. 8:2; 2 Chr. 32:31). The Hebrew here does not mean "enticed to do wrong." People, however, must not put God to the test (Ex. 17:2, 7; Deut. 6:16).

Here am I. So also Moses (Ex. 3:4), Samuel (1 Sam. 3:4), and Isaiah (Is. 6:8). See also Christ's own words to the same effect (Heb. 10:7; cf. Ps. 40:7, 8).

22:2 your only son . . . whom you love. Isaac is the beloved son, the

whom you love, and go to [l]the land of
Moriah, and offer him there as a burnt
offering on one of the mountains of which
I shall tell you." 3 So Abraham rose early in
the morning, saddled his donkey, and took
two of his young men with him, and his
son Isaac. And he cut the wood for the
burnt offering and arose and went to
the place of which God had told him. 4 On
the third day Abraham lifted up his eyes
and saw the place from afar. 5 Then
Abraham said to his young men, "Stay here
with the donkey; I and the boy[1] will go
over there and worship and come again to
you." 6 And Abraham took the wood of the
burnt offering and [m]laid it on Isaac his son.
And he took in his hand the fire and the
knife. So they went both of them together.
7 And Isaac said to his father Abraham, "My
father!" And he said, "Here am I, my son."
He said, "Behold, the fire and the wood,
but where is the lamb for a burnt offering?"
8 Abraham said, [n]"God will provide for
himself the lamb for a burnt offering, my
son." So they went both of them together.
9 When they came to the place of which
God had told him, Abraham built the altar
there and laid the wood in order and
bound Isaac his son and [o]laid him on the
altar, on top of the wood. 10 Then Abraham
reached out his hand and took the knife to
slaughter his son. 11 But the angel of the
LORD called to him from heaven and said,
"Abraham, Abraham!" And he said, "Here
am I." 12 He said, [p]"Do not lay your hand
on the boy or do anything to him, for [q]now
I know that you fear God, seeing you have
not withheld your son, your only son, from
me." 13 And Abraham lifted up his eyes and
looked, and behold, behind him was a
ram, caught in a thicket by his horns. And
Abraham went and took the ram and
offered it up as a burnt offering instead of
his son. 14 So Abraham called the name of
that place, [r]"The LORD will provide";[2] as it
is said to this day, "On the mount of the
LORD it shall be provided."[3]

15 And the angel of the LORD called to
Abraham a second time from heaven
16 and said, [s]"By myself I have sworn,
declares the LORD, because you have done
this and have not withheld your son, your
only son, 17 I will surely bless you, and I
will surely multiply your offspring [t]as the
stars of heaven and [u]as the sand that is on
the seashore. And your offspring shall
possess [v]the gate of his[4] enemies, 18 and
[w]in your offspring shall all the nations of
the earth be blessed, [x]because you have
obeyed my voice." 19 So Abraham returned
to his young men, and they arose and went
together to [y]Beersheba. And Abraham lived
at [y]Beersheba.

20 Now after these things it was told to
Abraham, "Behold, [z]Milcah also has borne
children to your brother Nahor: 21 [a]Uz his

2 [l]2 Chr. 3:1
6 [m][John 19:17]
8 [n][John 1:29, 36; 1 Pet. 1:19; Rev. 5:12]
9 [o]Heb. 11:17; James 2:21
12 [p][Mic. 6:7, 8] [q][ch. 26:5]
14 [r]ver. 8
16 [s]Ps. 105:9; Luke 1:73; Heb. 6:13
17 [t]Jer. 33:22; See ch. 15:5 [u]See ch. 13:16 [v]ch. 24:60; Ps. 127:5
18 [w]ch. 12:3; 18:18; 26:4; Gal. 3:8; Cited Acts 3:25 [x]ver. 3; ch. 26:5
19 [y]ch. 21:31
20 [z]ch. 11:29
21 [a]Job 1:1

[1] Or *young man*; also verse 12 [2] Or *will see* [3] Or *he will be seen* [4] Or *their*

only son of the promise (25:1–18 note). Ishmael had been disinherited and sent away (21:10, 14), leaving Isaac as Abraham's only son. These terms are applied to Christ in the New Testament (Matt. 3:17; 17:5; John 3:16; Eph. 1:6; 2 Pet. 1:17).

land of Moriah. Later the site of Israel's temple in Jerusalem (2 Chr. 3:1).

offer him. This command is perplexing at first. Without knowing what God really had in mind (cf. Ex. 13:11–13; 22:29; 34:19, 20), the command seems to contradict the sixth commandment (Ex. 20:13). As the narrative unfolds, however, it is evident that the test was whether Abraham would proceed with the preparations for sacrifice while holding steadfastly to the promise of 21:12, "through Isaac shall your offspring be named." Abraham knew that God was obliged to keep His promise, and he knew that a dead Isaac could not continue the covenant line. Heb. 11:19 unveils Abraham's secret: he concluded "that God was able even to raise him from the dead."

burnt offering. See note 8:20.

22:3 early in the morning. Another example of Abraham's prompt obedience (17:23 and note).

22:8 provide . . . the lamb. A type of Jesus Christ (John 1:29, 36).

22:11 angel of the LORD. See note 16:7.

22:12 you have not withheld. Abraham's faith was confirmed by his obedience (Gal. 5:6; Heb. 11:17; James 2:21 note).

22:13 instead of his son. The substitutionary purpose of the sacrifice is evident, and points forward to the sacrifice of Christ who died in our stead (Mark 10:45; Rom. 8:32; 2 Cor. 5:21; Titus 2:14).

22:14 The LORD will provide. The Hebrew word here translated "provide" means "see," or "see to it" (used in vv. 4, 8, 13, 14). The name by which Abraham commemorates the event shows that he perceives God's revelation of His saving purpose.

22:16 By myself I have sworn. God reinforces the surety of His infallible promise by an oath (15:8–21; 22:17; cf. Heb. 6:13–18). While sinful and fallible human beings swear by an authority higher than themselves, God, the supreme Being and Authority, swears by Himself (Heb. 6:13 note).

not withheld . . . your only son. Abraham's action points forward to God's provision of "his only Son" as the final sacrifice for sin (John 3:16; Rom. 8:32).

22:18 because you have obeyed my voice. See notes 17:2 and 18:19.

22:20–25:11 This final section of the account of Terah provides a transition from the patriarchal headship of Abraham to that of Isaac (2:4 note; Introduction: Outline). It narrates Sarah's death (ch. 23), Isaac's marriage to Rebekah (ch. 24), the dismissal of Abraham's other children, leaving Isaac as the sole heir (25:1–6), and Abraham's death (25:7–11).

22:20–24 The twelve children of Nahor (eight by the wife and four from the concubine) parallel the twelve tribes of Israel (30:1–24; 35:16–18; 49:28).

firstborn, [b]Buz his brother, Kemuel the
father of Aram, 22 Chesed, Hazo, Pildash,
Jidlaph, and Bethuel." 23 ([c]Bethuel fathered
Rebekah.) These eight Milcah bore to
Nahor, Abraham's brother. 24 Moreover, his
concubine, whose name was Reumah, bore
Tebah, Gaham, Tahash, and Maacah.

Sarah's Death and Burial

23 Sarah lived 127 years; these were
the years of the life of Sarah. 2 And
Sarah died at [d]Kiriath-arba (that is,
[e]Hebron) in the land of Canaan, and
Abraham went in to mourn for Sarah and
to weep for her. 3 And Abraham rose up
from before his dead and said to the
Hittites,[1] 4 [f]"I am a sojourner and foreigner
among you; [g]give me property among you
for a burying place, that I may bury my
dead out of my sight." 5 The Hittites
answered Abraham, 6 "Hear us, my lord;
you are a prince of God[2] among us. Bury
your dead in the choicest of our tombs.
None of us will withhold from you his
tomb to hinder you from burying your
dead." 7 Abraham rose and bowed to the
Hittites, the people of the land. 8 And he
said to them, "If you are willing that I
should bury my dead out of my sight, hear
me and entreat for me Ephron the son of
Zohar, 9 that he may give me the cave of
Machpelah, which he owns; it is at the end
of his field. For the full price let him give it
to me in your presence as property for a
burying place."
10 Now Ephron was sitting among the
Hittites, and Ephron the Hittite answered
Abraham in the hearing of the Hittites, of
all who [h]went in at the gate of his city,
11 "No, my lord, hear me: I give you the
field, and I give you the cave that is in it. In
the sight of the sons of my people I give it

21 [b]Jer. 25:23
23 [c]ch. 24:15
Chapter 23
2 [d]ch. 35:27; Josh. 14:15; Judg. 1:10 [e]ver. 19
4 [f]ch. 17:8; 1 Chr. 29:15; Ps. 105:12; Heb. 11:9, 13 [g]Acts 7:5
10 [h]ch. 34:20, 24; Ruth 4:1

[1] Hebrew *sons of Heth*; also verses 5, 7, 10, 16, 18, 20 [2] Or *a mighty prince*

22:23 Rebekah. Isaac's future wife is introduced (ch. 24). Her father Bethuel was the son of Milcah, the daughter of Haran and wife of Nahor, Abraham's brothers (11:28 note).

23:3–18 The extensive description of the negotiation and sale of the cave demonstrates that Abraham secured an impeccable legal claim to the field in Machpelah. Anticipating the greater fulfillment of the land grant promise (13:15 note), Abraham now became legal heir to a small plot in the Promised Land.

23:4 a sojourner and foreigner. Though Abraham lived in the Promised Land as a sojourner (21:34 note; Heb. 11:9, 13), he demonstrated his faith in the covenant promises by buying his first piece of property in the Promised Land—a cave to serve as a burial site.

23:6 a prince of God. Or, "a mighty prince" (text note). Though some suggest that this was merely respectful flattery, it is likely that the citizens of Hebron had discerned God's blessing on Abraham (cf. 21:22).

23:10 gate. Legal transactions took place at the gates of ancient Near Eastern cities (19:1 note; Ruth 4:1, 2).

23:11 I give. As the excessive price requested (v. 15 note) and Abraham's offer of money (v. 13) indicate, Ephron's offer to give the cave and field was part of the Near Eastern bargaining ritual. The seeming generosity of the offer was probably intended either to obligate Abraham to respond with a gift of even greater value (if accepted) or to discourage Abraham from lengthy negotiation over the price.

The Abrahamic Covenant (22:15-18)

Genesis 12:1–3	God initiated His covenant with Abram when he was living in Ur of the Chaldeans, promising a land, descendants and blessing.
Genesis 12:4, 5	Abram went with his family to Haran, lived there for a time, and left at the age of 75.
Genesis 13:14–17	After Lot separated from Abram, God again promised the land to him and his descendants.
Genesis 15:1–21	This covenant was ratified when God passed between the sacrificial animals Abram laid before God.
Genesis 17:1–27	When Abram was 99, God renewed His covenant, changing Abram's name to Abraham ("father of a Multitude"). Sign of the covenant: circumcision.
Genesis 22:15–18	Confirmation of the covenant because of Abraham's obedience.

The Abrahamic covenant was foundational to other covenants:

- The promise of kingly descendants in the Davidic covenant (2 Sam. 7:12–16)
- The promise of blessing in the "old" and "new" covenants (Ex. 19:3–6; Jer. 31:31–40)

to you. Bury your dead." 12 Then Abraham
bowed down before the people of the land.
13 And he said to Ephron in the hearing of
the people of the land, "But if you will,
hear me: I give the price of the field. Accept
it from me, that I may bury my dead there."
14 Ephron answered Abraham, 15 "My lord,
listen to me: a piece of land worth four
hundred [i]shekels[1] of silver, what is that
between you and me? Bury your dead."
16 Abraham listened to Ephron, and
Abraham [j]weighed out for Ephron the silver that he had named in the hearing of the
Hittites, four hundred shekels of silver,
according to the weights current among
the merchants.
17 So [k]the field of Ephron in Machpelah,
which was to the east of Mamre, the field
with the cave that was in it and all the trees
that were in the field, throughout its whole
area, was made over 18 to Abraham as a possession in the presence of the Hittites,
before all who went in at the gate of his
city. 19 After this, Abraham buried Sarah his
wife in the cave of the field of Machpelah
east of Mamre (that is, Hebron) in the land
of Canaan. 20 The field and the cave that is
in it [l]were made over to Abraham as property for a burying place by the Hittites.

Isaac and Rebekah

24 Now Abraham was old, well advanced in years. And the LORD [m]had
blessed Abraham in all things. 2 And Abraham said to his servant, [n]the oldest of his
household, who had charge of all that he
had, [o]"Put your hand under my thigh, 3 that
I may make you swear by the LORD, the God
of heaven and God of the earth, that [p]you
will not take a wife for my son from the
daughters of the Canaanites, among whom I
dwell, 4 [q]but will go to my country and to my
kindred, and take a wife for my son Isaac."
5 The servant said to him, "Perhaps the
woman may not be willing to follow me to
this land. Must I then take your son back to
the land from which you came?" 6 Abraham
said to him, "See to it that you do not take
my son back there. 7 The LORD, the God of
heaven, [r]who took me from my father's
house and from the land of my kindred, and
who spoke to me and swore to me, [s]'To your
offspring I will give this land,' [t]he will send
his angel before you, and you shall take a
wife for my son from there. 8 But if the
woman is not willing to follow you, then
[u]you will be free from this oath of mine; only
you must not take my son back there." 9 So
the servant [v]put his hand under the thigh of
Abraham his master and swore to him concerning this matter.
10 Then the servant took ten of his master's camels and departed, taking all sorts of
choice gifts from his master; and he arose
and went to [w]Mesopotamia[2] to the city of
Nahor. 11 And he made the camels kneel
down outside the city by the well of water
at the time of evening, the time when
[x]women go out to draw water. 12 And he
said, "O LORD, [y]God of my master Abraham, [z]please grant me success today and
show steadfast love to my master Abraham.
13 Behold, [a]I am standing by the spring of
water, and the daughters of the men of
the city are coming out to draw water. 14 Let
the young woman to whom I shall say,
'Please let down your jar that I may drink,'
and who shall say, 'Drink, and I will water

15 [i]Ex. 30:13; Ezek. 45:12
16 [j]1 Chr. 21:25; Jer. 32:9; Zech. 11:12
17 [k]ch. 25:9; 49:29-32; 50:13
20 [l][Ruth 4:7-10; Jer. 32:10-14]
Chapter 24
1 [m]ver. 35; ch. 13:2
2 [n][ch. 15:2] [o]ver. 9; ch. 47:29
3 [p]ch. 26:34, 35; 27:46; Deut. 7:3; [2 Cor. 6:14]
4 [q][ch. 28:2]
7 [r]ch. 12:1 [s]See ch. 12:7 [t]Ex. 23:20, 23; 33:2; [Heb. 1:14]
8 [u]See Josh. 2:17-20
9 [v]ver. 2
10 [w]Deut. 23:4; Judg. 3:8
11 [x]1 Sam. 9:11; John 4:7
12 [y]ver. 27, 42, 48 [z]ch. 27:20
13 [a]ver. 43

[1] A *shekel* was about 2/5 ounce or 11 grams [2] Hebrew *Aram-naharaim*

23:15 four hundred shekels. A high price, especially when compared with the field that Jeremiah bought for seventeen shekels (Jer. 32:9) and with the hill of Samaria that Omri purchased for two talents of silver (six thousand shekels, 1 Kin. 16:24).

23:16 Abraham weighed out. Abraham was willing to pay an excessive price in return for an unimpeachable sale.

23:19 buried . . . in the cave. In faithful expectation that God would fulfill the covenant promise of land (13:15 and note), Abraham sought to anchor his descendants in the Promised Land (24:6–9; 25:9; 49:30; 50:13).

24:1–9 See "Honest Speech, Oaths, and Vows" at Neh. 5:12.

24:2 oldest. Abraham assigned this important mission only to his most trusted manager, perhaps Eliezer of Damascus (15:2, 3).

Put your hand under my thigh. The loins were viewed as the source of vital and procreative power (Deut. 33:11; Job 40:16; Heb. 7:10). Such an oath was inviolable, even after the death of the one to whom it was sworn (47:29–31).

24:3 the LORD . . . of the earth. See 14:22.

not . . . from the daughters of the Canaanites. Abraham sets an example for his descendants to secure wives from the blessed Semites, not the cursed Canaanites (9:24–27; Deut. 7:1–4).

24:6 do not take my son back there. See note 23:19.

24:7 I will give . . . he will send. Claiming God's covenant promise (12:7), Abraham looks forward to God's continuing guidance and provision. Abraham had learned from his experience with Hagar not to trust the flesh to secure the promise but to rely on God's supernatural provision (ch. 16).

24:12 O LORD, God. The meeting of Abraham's servant and Rebekah was framed in prayer (vv. 26, 27).

steadfast love. The Hebrew word *ḥesed* means loyalty to a covenant relationship (Ex. 15:13 note).

your camels'—let her be the one whom you
have appointed for your servant Isaac. [b]By
this[1] I shall know that you have shown
steadfast love to my master."
15 Before he had finished speaking,
behold, Rebekah, who was born to Bethuel
the son of [c]Milcah, the wife of Nahor,
Abraham's brother, came out with her
water jar on her shoulder. 16 The young
woman [d]was very attractive in appearance, a
maiden[2] whom no man had known. She
went down to the spring and filled her jar
and came up. 17 Then the servant ran to
meet her and said, "Please give me a little
water to drink from your jar." 18 She said,
"Drink, my lord." And she quickly let down
her jar upon her hand and gave him a drink.
19 When she had finished giving him a drink,
she said, "I will draw water for your camels
also, until they have finished drinking." 20 So
she quickly emptied her jar into the trough
and ran again to the well to draw water, and
she drew for all his camels. 21 The man gazed
at her in silence to learn whether the LORD
had prospered his journey or not.
22 When the camels had finished drinking, the man took a gold ring weighing a
half shekel,[3] and two bracelets for her arms
weighing ten gold shekels, 23 and said,
"Please tell me whose daughter you are. Is
there room in your father's house for us to
spend the night?" 24 She said to him, [e]"I am
the daughter of Bethuel the son of Milcah,
whom she bore to Nahor." 25 She added,
"We have plenty of both straw and fodder,
and room to spend the night." 26 [f]The man
bowed his head and worshiped the LORD
27 and said, "Blessed be the LORD, [g]the God
of my master Abraham, who has not forsaken [h]his steadfast love and his faithfulness toward my master. As for me, the
LORD [i]has led me in the way to the house
of my master's kinsmen." 28 Then the
young woman ran and told her mother's
household about these things.
29 Rebekah had a brother whose name
was [j]Laban. Laban ran out toward the man,
to the spring. 30 As soon as he saw the ring
and the bracelets on his sister's arms, and
heard the words of Rebekah his sister,
"Thus the man spoke to me," he went to
the man. And behold, he was standing by
the camels at the spring. 31 He said, "Come
in, [k]O blessed of the LORD. Why do you
stand outside? For I have prepared the
house and a place for the camels." 32 So the
man came to the house and unharnessed
the camels, and gave [l]straw and fodder to
the camels, and there was [m]water to wash
his feet and the feet of the men who were
with him. 33 Then food was set before him
to eat. But he said, "I will not eat until I
have said what I have to say." He said,
"Speak on."
34 So he said, "I am Abraham's servant.
35 The LORD [n]has greatly blessed my master, and he has become great. He has
given him flocks and herds, silver and
gold, male servants and female servants,
camels and donkeys. 36 And Sarah my
master's wife [o]bore a son to my master
when she was old, and [p]to him he has
given all that he has. 37 [q]My master made
me swear, saying, 'You shall not take a
wife for my son from the daughters of the
Canaanites, in whose land I dwell, 38 but
you shall go to my father's house and to
my clan and take a wife for my son.' 39 I
said to my master, 'Perhaps the woman
will not follow me.' 40 But he said to me,
'The LORD, [r]before whom I have walked,
will send his angel with you and [s]prosper
your way. You shall take a wife for my son
from my clan and from my father's house.
41 Then you will be free from my oath,
when you come to my clan. And if they
will not give her to you, you will be free
from my oath.'
42 "I came today to the spring and said,
[t]'O LORD, the God of my master Abraham,

14 [b]See ch. 15:8
15 [c]ch. 11:29; 22:23
16 [d]ch. 26:7
24 [e]ver. 15; ch. 22:23
26 [f]ver. 48, 52; Ex. 4:31
27 [g]ver. 12, 42, 48 [h]ch. 32:10; Ps. 98:3 [i]ver. 48
29 [j]ch. 25:20; 28:2; 29:5
31 [k][ch. 26:29; Judg. 17:2; Ruth 3:10]
32 [l]ch. 43:24; Judg. 19:21 [m]See ch. 18:4
35 [n]ver. 1
36 [o]ch. 21:2 [p]ch. 25:5
37 [q]ver. 3-8
40 [r]ch. 17:1 [s]ver. 21
42 [t]ver. 12, 27

[1] Or *By her* [2] Or *a woman of marriageable age* [3] A *shekel* was about 2/5 ounce or 11 grams

24:14 By this I shall know. A request for a sign was appropriate in connection with the servant's mission to advance the messianic line (cf. Is. 7:10–14).

24:15 Rebekah. See note 22:23.

24:16 a maiden whom no man had known. Her virginity was important to ensure that the offspring would be Isaac's.

24:27 the LORD has led me. God guides His saints through providential acts (cf. 50:20). Later in the Pentateuch the expression is used for God's special guidance of His people through the wilderness to the Promised Land (Ex. 13:17, 21; 15:13).

24:29 Laban. Laban took responsibility for the family, probably because Bethuel was incapacitated (v. 50 and note).

24:33 not eat until I have said. The servant recounts the story (vv. 34–48) in detail so that Rebekah and her family will acknowledge the hand of the Lord (v. 50).

24:36 he has given all that he has. An important detail, considering Abraham's considerable wealth (cf. 25:5, 6).

if now you [s]are prospering the way that I go, **43** behold, I am standing [u]by the spring of water. Let the virgin who comes out to draw water, to whom I shall say, "Please give me a little water from your jar to drink," **44** [v]and who will say to me, "Drink, and I will draw for your camels also," let her be the woman whom the LORD has appointed for my master's son.'

45 "Before I had finished [w]speaking in my heart, behold, Rebekah came out with her water jar on her shoulder, and she went down to the spring and drew water. I said to her, 'Please let me drink.' **46** She quickly let down her jar from her shoulder and said, 'Drink, and I will give your camels drink also.' So I drank, and she gave the camels drink also. **47** Then I asked her, 'Whose daughter are you?' She said, 'The daughter of Bethuel, Nahor's son, whom Milcah bore to him.' [x]So I put the ring on her nose and the bracelets on her arms. **48** [y]Then I bowed my head and worshiped the LORD and blessed the LORD, [t]the God of my master Abraham, who had led me by the right way[1] to take [z]the daughter of my master's kinsman for his son. **49** Now then, if you are going to [a]show steadfast love and faithfulness to my master, tell me; and if not, tell me, that I may turn to the right hand or to the left."

50 Then Laban and Bethuel answered and said, "The thing has come from the LORD; we cannot [b]speak to you bad or good. **51** Behold, Rebekah is before you; take her and go, and let her be the wife of your master's son, [c]as the LORD has spoken."

52 When Abraham's servant heard their words, [y]he bowed himself to the earth before the LORD. **53** And the servant brought out jewelry of silver and of gold, and garments, and gave them to Rebekah. He also gave to her brother and to her mother costly ornaments. **54** And he and the men who were with him ate and drank, and they spent the night there. When they arose in the morning, he said, [d]"Send me away to my master." **55** Her brother and her mother said, "Let the young woman remain with us a while, at least ten days; after that she may go." **56** But he said to them, "Do not delay me, since the LORD has prospered my way. Send me away that I may go to my master." **57** They said, "Let us call the young woman and ask her." **58** And they called Rebekah and said to her, "Will you go with this man?" She said, "I will go." **59** So they sent away Rebekah their sister and [e]her nurse, and Abraham's servant and his men. **60** And they blessed Rebekah and said to her,

"Our sister, may you [f]become
thousands of ten thousands,
and [g]may your offspring possess
the gate of those who hate them!"

61 Then Rebekah and her young women arose and rode on the camels and followed the man. Thus the servant took Rebekah and went his way.

62 Now Isaac had returned from [h]Beer-lahai-roi and was dwelling in the Negeb. **63** And Isaac went out [i]to meditate in the field toward evening. And he lifted up his eyes and saw, and behold, there were camels coming. **64** And Rebekah lifted up her eyes, and when she saw Isaac, she dismounted from the camel **65** and said to the servant, "Who is that man, walking in the field to meet us?" The servant said, "It is my master." So she took her veil and covered herself. **66** And the servant told Isaac all the things that he had done. **67** Then Isaac brought her into the tent of Sarah his mother and took Rebekah, and she became his wife, and he loved her. So Isaac was [j]comforted after his mother's [k]death.

[1] Or *faithfully*

42 [s][See ver. 40 above]
43 [u]ver. 13
44 [v]ver. 14, 18
45 [w]1 Sam. 1:13
47 [x][Ezek. 16:11, 12]
48 [y]ver. 26, 52 [t][See ver. 42 above] [z][ch. 22:23]
49 [a]ch. 47:29; Josh. 2:14
50 [b]ch. 31:24; 2 Sam. 13:22
51 [c]See ver. 13-15, 42-46
52 [y][See ver. 48 above]
54 [d]ver. 56, 59
59 [e]ch. 35:8
60 [f]ch. 17:16 [g]ch. 22:17
62 [h]ch. 16:14; 25:11
63 [i]Ps. 77:12; 143:5
67 [j]ch. 37:35; 38:12 [k]ch. 23:2

24:50 Laban and Bethuel. The irregular sequence of mentioning the son before the father suggests that Bethuel was incapacitated. In v. 55 only the brother and mother are mentioned (cf. v. 28).

The thing has come from the LORD. They acknowledged God's providence in the matter.

24:60 thousands of ten thousands . . . possess the gate. See 13:16; 15:5; 22:17.

24:64, 65 Rebekah dismounted as a sign of respect for her new husband (cf. 1 Sam. 25:23). The customary bridal veil shielded the bride's face from the husband until the consummation of the marriage (cf. Song 4:1).

24:66 told Isaac. Abraham lived another 35 years after Isaac's marriage (21:5; 25:7, 9, 20). As the attention shifts to Isaac, the narrative omits the servant's report to Abraham and goes directly to the future patriarch.

24:67 brought . . . took . . . loved her. God granted complete success to the journey. In obedience to God both Isaac and Rebekah found fulfillment.

the tent of Sarah. Rebekah replaced Sarah as matriarch of the family.

Abraham's Death and His Descendants

25 Abraham took another wife, whose
name was Keturah. 2 [l]She bore him
Zimran, Jokshan, Medan, Midian, Ishbak,
and Shuah. 3 Jokshan fathered Sheba and
Dedan. The sons of Dedan were Asshurim,
Letushim, and Leummim. 4 The sons of
Midian were Ephah, Epher, Hanoch,
Abida, and Eldaah. All these were the children of Keturah. 5 [m]Abraham gave all he
had to Isaac. 6 But to the sons of his concubines Abraham gave gifts, and while he was
still living he [n]sent them away from his son
Isaac, eastward [o]to the east country.
7 These are the days of the years of
Abraham's life, 175 years. 8 Abraham
[p]breathed his last and [q]died in a good old
age, an old man and full of years, and was
gathered to his people. 9 Isaac and Ishmael
[r]his sons buried him in the cave of
Machpelah, in the field of Ephron the son
of Zohar the Hittite, east of Mamre, 10 the
field [s]that Abraham purchased from the
Hittites. [t]There Abraham was buried, with
Sarah his wife. 11 After the death of Abraham, God blessed Isaac his son. And Isaac
settled at [u]Beer-lahai-roi.
12 These are the generations of Ishmael,
Abraham's son, [v]whom Hagar the Egyptian, Sarah's servant, bore to Abraham.
13 [w]These are the names of the sons of
Ishmael, named in the order of their birth:
[x]Nebaioth, the firstborn of Ishmael; and
[x]Kedar, Adbeel, Mibsam, 14 Mishma,
Dumah, Massa, 15 Hadad, [y]Tema, [z]Jetur,
[z]Naphish, and Kedemah. 16 These are the
sons of Ishmael and these are their names,
by their villages and by their encampments, [a]twelve princes according to their
tribes. 17 (These are the years of the life of
Ishmael: 137 years. He [b]breathed his last
and died, and was gathered to his people.)
18 [c]They settled from Havilah to [d]Shur,
which is opposite Egypt in the direction of
Assyria. He settled[1] over against all his
kinsmen.

The Birth of Esau and Jacob

19 These are the generations of Isaac,
Abraham's son: [e]Abraham fathered Isaac,
20 and Isaac was forty years old when he
took Rebekah to be his wife, [f]the daughter
of Bethuel the Aramean of [g]Paddan-aram,
[h]the sister of Laban the Aramean. 21 And
Isaac prayed to the LORD for his wife,

Chapter 25
2 [l]1 Chr. 1:32, 33
5 [m]ch. 24:36
6 [n]ch. 21:14 [o][Judg. 6:3]
8 [p]ver. 17; ch. 35:29; 49:33 [q]ch. 15:15
9 [r]ch. 35:29
10 [s]ch. 23:16; 50:13 [t]ch. 49:30, 31
11 [u]ch. 16:14; 24:62
12 [v]ch. 16:15
13 [w]1 Chr. 1:29-31 [x]Isai. 60:7
14 [y]Job 6:19; Isai. 21:14 [z]1 Chr. 5:19
16 [a]ch. 17:20
17 [b]ver. 8
18 [c]1 Sam. 15:7 [d]ch. 16:7; 20:1; Ex. 15:22
19 [e]Matt.1:2
20 [f]ch. 22:23 [g]See ch. 28:2 [h]ch. 24:29

[1] Hebrew *fell*

25:1–18 The genealogies that precede (vv. 1–4) and follow (vv. 12–18) the account of Abraham's death (vv. 7–11) are of Abraham's natural sons. They highlight that the offspring through Sarah is miraculous, that Abraham's many natural offspring in no way disadvantage Isaac's inheritance in the land (vv. 5–6), and that the elect one has a blood relation, but not a spiritual bond, with the natural offspring. Isaac was Abraham's "only son" of promise (22:2 and note).

25:1 took another wife. Keturah was a concubine (v. 6; 1 Chr. 1:32). No attempt is made to date this secondary offspring of Abraham.

25:2–4 Some of these names are associated with Syria and Arabia.

25:5 gave all he had to Isaac. See 24:36. Abraham dispossessed his children by Keturah as he had dispossessed Ishmael, the son of Hagar (21:10 and note).

25:6 while he was still living. Abraham himself legally secured Isaac's inheritance in the land.

25:8 died. Abraham died in faith, seeing the promises afar off (Heb. 11:13–16).

in a good old age. In fulfillment of the divine promise in 15:15.

was gathered to his people. A Hebrew idiom meaning that the deceased had entered the realm of death to join his ancestors (v. 17; 35:29; 49:29, 33; Deut. 32:50).

25:9 in the cave. See ch. 23; 35:27–29; 49:29–32.

25:12–18 The genealogy of Ishmael demonstrates God's faithfulness in keeping His promise to Abraham (17:20).

25:12 These are the generations. See note 2:4.

25:13–15 Some of these names are Arabic, and others are attested in extrabiblical texts as northwest Arabian tribes.

25:16 twelve princes. See 17:20.

25:18 settled over against all his kinsmen. The Hebrew of this phrase is difficult to render. It could also mean that he died in the presence of all his brethren.

25:19–35:29 The account of Isaac is one of conflict between Isaac and Rebekah (v. 28; ch. 27), Jacob and Esau (25:19–34; chs. 27; 32; 33), Jacob and Laban (chs. 29–31), Leah and Rachel (29:31–30:24), and finally and decisively between Jacob and the Angel of the Lord (32:22–32; cf. 16:7 note). At the story's core is the promise to Abraham (24:7), passed on to Isaac and Jacob (28:3, 4, 13–15; 35:11–12). The promise is elaborated to include God's protective presence (28:15; 31:42; 32:9, 12; 35:3). Overarching the entire story is God's sovereign good pleasure (Rom. 9:10–12). He opened Rebekah's barren womb, established the supremacy of Jacob over Esau, contravened human customs regarding firstborn rights, and overrode Isaac's patriarchal authority, Laban's social position, and Esau's military might.

25:19–26 The struggle for supremacy between Jacob and Esau in the womb and the Lord's sovereign choice of Jacob form a fitting introduction to this account and sets its tone (Introduction: Characteristics and Themes).

25:19 the generations of Isaac. Or, "the account of Isaac" (2:4 note). This account (25:19–35:29) covers the period from Isaac's marriage to his death. Much of the story, however, features Jacob (Introduction: Outline). After Isaac tries to thwart God's blessing on Jacob (ch. 27), he is not heard from again until his death (35:27–29).

25:20 Paddan-aram. The region surrounding the city of Haran in northern Mesopotamia (24:10; 28:2).

25:21 prayed . . . barren. The next generation also had to learn that the seed of promise is a gift of God's grace (11:30; 17:15, 16; 18:1–15; 21:1–7), and sovereignly chosen by Him (v. 23). Both Isaac's wife and offspring were secured through prayer (24:12).

because she was barren. And [i]the LORD
granted his prayer, and Rebekah his wife
conceived. 22 The children struggled together within her, and she said, "If it is thus,
why is this happening to me?"[1] So she
went [j]to inquire of the LORD. 23 And the
LORD said to her,

[k]"Two nations are in your womb,
and two peoples from within you[2]
shall be divided;
[l]the one shall be stronger than the
other,
[m]the older shall serve the younger."

24 When her days to give birth were completed, behold, there were twins in her
womb. 25 The first came out red, [n]all his
body like a hairy cloak, so they called his
name Esau. 26 Afterward his brother came
out with [o]his hand holding Esau's heel, so
[p]his name was called Jacob.[3] Isaac was
sixty years old when she bore them.
27 When the boys grew up, Esau was [q]a
skillful hunter, a man of the field, while
Jacob was a quiet man, [r]dwelling in tents.
28 Isaac loved Esau because [s]he ate of his
game, but Rebekah loved Jacob.

Esau Sells His Birthright

29 Once when Jacob was cooking stew,
Esau came in from the field, and he was
exhausted. 30 And Esau said to Jacob, "Let
me eat some of that red stew, for I am
exhausted!" (Therefore his name was
called Edom.[4]) 31 Jacob said, "Sell me your
birthright now." 32 Esau said, "I am about
to die; of what use is a birthright to me?"
33 Jacob said, "Swear to me now." So he
swore to him and [t]sold his birthright to
Jacob. 34 Then Jacob gave Esau bread and
lentil stew, and he ate and drank and rose
and went his way. Thus Esau despised his
birthright.

God's Promise to Isaac

26 Now there was a famine in the land,
besides [u]the former famine that was
in the days of Abraham. And Isaac went to
Gerar to [v]Abimelech king of the [w]Philistines.
2 And the LORD appeared to him and said,
"Do not go down to Egypt; dwell [x]in the
land of which I shall tell you. 3 [y]Sojourn in
this land, and [z]I will be with you and will
bless you, for [a]to you and to your offspring

21 [i]2 Sam. 21:14; 24:25; 1 Chr. 5:20; 2 Chr. 33:13; Ezra 8:23
22 [j][1 Sam. 9:9]
23 [k]ch. 17:16; 24:60 [l][2 Sam. 8:14]; See Obad. 18-21 [m]ch. 27:29, 40; Cited Rom. 9:12
25 [n]ch. 27:11, 16, 23
26 [o]Hos. 12:3 [p]ch. 27:36
27 [q]ch. 27:3, 5 [r]Heb. 11:9
28 [s]ch. 27:4, 7, 9
33 [t]Heb. 12:16
Chapter 26
1 [u]ch. 12:10 [v]ch. 20:2 [w]ch. 21:34
2 [x]ch. 12:1
3 [y]ch. 20:1; Heb. 11:9 [z]ch. 28:15 [a]See ch. 13:15

1 Or *why do I live?* 2 Or *from birth* 3 *Jacob* means *He takes by the heel,* or *He cheats* 4 *Edom* sounds like the Hebrew for *red*

25:23 the LORD said. God often displayed His sovereign control through prophecies given on the threshold of new historical eras: Adam and Eve (3:15); Noah's descendants (9:25–27); Abraham (12:1–3); Jacob and Esau (27:27–29, 39, 40); and Joseph and his brothers (37:1–11). See Introduction: Characteristics and Themes.

older shall serve the younger. Jacob owed his supremacy to sovereign election, not natural rights (cf. Deut. 21:15–17). The prophecy found fulfillment as Esau's descendants, the Edomites, were often subjugated by Israel, and at last were included in the Jewish state during the intertestamental period (1 Sam. 14:47; 2 Sam. 8:13, 14; 2 Kin. 14:7).

God's choice of Jacob (the younger) over Esau (the older) is a paradigmatic example of divine sovereign election (Rom. 9:9–13, 18–23). God deals justly with all, but He has mercy on some (Matt. 20:1–16).

25:25 hairy. The Hebrew word sounds like "Seir," where Esau later lived (36:8).

25:26 Jacob. See text note. Though destined to supplant his brother, Jacob tarnished his name to mean "deceitful" through cunning efforts to gain his brother's privilege (25:29–34; 27:1–40).

25:27–34 Esau was a profane, rough-and-ready man of the field who shortsightedly gratified his appetite and despised the family's future inheritance. Despite his dishonesty, Jacob had farsightedness to value the inheritance.

25:27 quiet. The Hebrew here suggests a civilized man.

25:28 Isaac loved . . . Rebekah loved. Parental favoritism further set the family at loggerheads. God's sovereign choice had to prevail over Isaac's appetite (27:18–27), for Isaac had the legal authority to pass on the family's inheritance and blessing (24:36; 25:5).

25:30 Let me eat. The Hebrew indicates the impulsive and hurried request of one who lived for the moment. Esau's impulsiveness is further revealed in v. 32.

that red stew. Lit. "the red stuff, that red stuff." Esau's clumsy repetition of the Hebrew word for "red" (*'adom*) recalls v. 25, and explains the name by which his descendants were known (Hebrew *'edom*).

25:31 Sell me. Jacob took advantage of his brother's weakness. His behavior contrasts sharply with Abraham's treatment of Lot (13:8, 9) and will be corrected (33:1–17).

birthright. The firstborn had the right to be the principal heir of the family's fortunes (27:33; Deut. 21:17; 1 Chr. 5:1, 2). In the covenant family, this fortune included the substance of the Abrahamic blessing of offspring and land (12:2, 3, 7).

25:34 ate and drank and rose and went his way. The staccato style of the Hebrew narrative implies that Esau himself was as crude and unreflective as his speech.

despised his birthright. By despising his birthright, Esau held God's promises in contempt (Heb. 12:16, 17).

26:1–33 After the introduction to the account of Isaac (25:19–34), Isaac is linked with the covenant promises (ch. 26). There are two revelations of covenantal promises (vv. 2–6, 24). Also, the extensive parallels between Isaac's experience in ch. 26 and Abraham's in chs. 12; 13; 20; 21—famine (v. 1; cf. 12:10), deception involving the marital status of the matriarch (v. 7; cf. 12:13; 20:2), material prosperity (vv. 13, 14; cf. 12:16; 13:6), conflict over land (vv. 20, 21; cf. 13:7), and the covenant with the Philistines at Beersheba (vv. 26–33; cf. 21:22–34)—are included to show that Isaac was indeed the recipient of the covenant promises made to Abraham. Although they remained sojourners (v. 3 note), the patriarchs had a foretaste of life in the land.

26:2–6 The form and content of the Lord's command and promise to Isaac, and Isaac's obedience, are linked with Abraham (12:1–4 and notes).

26:3 Sojourn in this land. The Hebrew word translated "sojourn" indicates a resident alien (21:34 note; Heb. 11:9, 13). Isaac is to remain there as a "stranger" who does not yet have the land in possession.

bless. See note 12:2.

I will give all these lands, and I will establish
[b]the oath that I swore to Abraham your
father. 4 [c]I will multiply your offspring as the
stars of heaven and will give to your offspring all these lands. And [d]in your offspring
all the nations of the earth shall be blessed,
5 because [e]Abraham obeyed my voice and
kept my charge, my commandments, my
statutes, and my laws."

Isaac and Abimelech

6 So Isaac settled in Gerar. 7 When the men
of the place asked him about his wife, [f]he
said, "She is my sister," for [g]he feared to say,
"My wife," thinking, "lest the men of the
place should kill me because of Rebekah,"
because [h]she was attractive in appearance.
8 When he had been there a long time,
Abimelech king of the Philistines looked out
of a window and saw Isaac laughing with[1]
Rebekah his wife. 9 So Abimelech called
Isaac and said, "Behold, she is your wife.
How then could you say, 'She is my sister'?"
Isaac said to him, "Because I thought, 'Lest
I die because of her.'" 10 Abimelech said,
"What is this you have done to us? One of
the people might easily have lain with your
wife, and [i]you would have brought guilt
upon us." 11 So Abimelech warned all the
people, saying, "Whoever touches this man
or his wife shall surely be put to death."
12 And Isaac sowed in that land and reaped
in the same year a hundredfold. The LORD
[j]blessed him, 13 and the man became rich,
and gained more and more until he became
very wealthy. 14 He had possessions of flocks
and herds and many servants, so that the
Philistines [k]envied him. 15 (Now the Philistines had stopped and filled with earth all
the wells [l]that his father's servants had dug
in the days of Abraham his father.) 16 And
Abimelech said to Isaac, "Go away from us,
for you are much mightier than we."
17 So Isaac departed from there and
encamped in the valley of Gerar and settled
there. 18 And Isaac dug again the wells of
water that had been dug in the days of
Abraham his father, which the Philistines
had stopped after the death of Abraham.
And [m]he gave them the names that his father
had given them. 19 But when Isaac's servants
dug in the valley and found there a well of
spring water, 20 the herdsmen of Gerar [n]quar-
reled with Isaac's herdsmen, saying, "The
water is ours." So he called the name of the
well Esek,[2] because they contended with
him. 21 Then they dug another well, and they
quarreled over that also, so he called its
name Sitnah.[3] 22 And he moved from there
and dug another well, and they did not quarrel over it. So he called its name Rehoboth,[4]
saying, "For now the LORD has made room
for us, and we shall be fruitful in the land."
23 From there he went up to Beersheba.

3 [b][Mic. 7:20]; See ch. 22:16-18
4 [c]Cited Ex. 32:13; See ch. 15:5 [d]See ch. 12:3
5 [e]ch. 22:18
7 [f]ch. 12:13; 20:2, 13 [g][Prov. 29:25] [h]ch. 24:16
10 [i]ch. 20:9
12 [j]ver. 3; ch. 24:1, 35
14 [k][Eccles. 4:4]
15 [l]ch. 21:30
18 [m]ch. 21:31
20 [n]ch. 21:25

1 Hebrew may suggest an intimate relationship 2 *Esek* means *contention* 3 *Sitnah* means *enmity* 4 *Rehoboth* means *broad places*, or *room*

give all these lands. See note 13:15.

establish the oath. See 15:18; 17:21; and especially 22:16–18 and notes. The promise to Abraham is secure, but Isaac's participation in the covenant blessings requires his obedience.

26:4 stars of heaven. See 15:5.

offspring. See notes 12:3, 7.

26:5 because. See 22:18; notes on 17:2; 18:19.

my charge, my commandments, my statutes . . . laws. Abraham's obedience is described in terms that recall Israel's requirement to keep the law of Moses (cf. Deut. 11:1). Abraham is a type of Christ, who by His obedience fulfilled the righteous requirements of the law and secured its blessings for His seed (Matt. 5:17, 18).

26:6 So Isaac settled. Like his father Abraham, Isaac responds obediently to God's promise (12:4; 17:23; 22:3 and notes).

26:7–11 This narrative of deception and peril to Rebekah closely parallels those involving Sarah (12:10–20; ch. 20), but the significant differences in the accounts indicate that they are not merely the same event retold. Though father and son made the same mistake, they are protected.

26:7 sister. See 12:13; 20:2.

26:8 looked out of a window. Whereas Abraham was spared by a special revelation to Abimelech (20:3), Isaac is spared by providence.

laughing with. The Hebrew here means "play" and is from the same Hebrew root as the name Isaac.

26:9 Abimelech. See note 20:2.

26:10 brought guilt. See note 20:9.

26:12 sowed. Isaac became more stationary than his nomadic father. His success depended on rain from heaven.

hundredfold. His obedience during the famine was rewarded (vv. 2–6). God's blessing is as evident upon Isaac, the chosen successor to God's promises, as upon his father Abraham (21:22).

26:15 Philistines had stopped . . . wells. With Abraham gone, the Philistines effectively negated their non-aggression pact (21:22–34 note). They had no genuine faith in Abraham's God.

26:16 much mightier than we. See 21:22, 23; Ex. 1:9.

26:17–22 The wealthy Isaac retreated from the fertile land into the Valley of Gerar, depending on wells originally dug by Abraham (v. 18). None of the patriarchs rashly risked war for the Promised Land. They trusted God to give their descendants the land at the right time (15:13, 14). The names of the wells commemorate God's provision and protection.

26:21 Sitnah. See text note. This word is from the same Hebrew root as the name "Satan."

26:22 the LORD has made room for us. God's protection of Isaac during this rivalry over wells recalls His reward to Abraham during the controversy with Lot (13:6–18).

26:23 Beersheba. The site of the original non-aggression pact with the Philistines (21:32).

24 And the LORD appeared to him the same
night and said, [o]"I am the God of Abraham
your father. [p]Fear not, for [q]I am with you
and will bless you and multiply your offspring for my servant Abraham's sake."
25 So he [r]built an altar there and called
upon the name of the LORD and pitched his
tent there. And there Isaac's servants dug a
well.
26 When Abimelech went to him from
Gerar with Ahuzzath his adviser and
[s]Phicol the commander of his army, 27 Isaac
said to them, "Why have you come to me,
seeing that you hate me and [t]have sent me
away from you?" 28 They said, "We see
plainly that the LORD has been with you. So
we said, let there be a sworn pact between
us, between you and us, and let us make a
covenant with you, 29 that you will do us no
harm, just as we have not touched you and
have done to you nothing but good and
have sent you away in peace. [u]You are now
the blessed of the LORD." 30 So he made
them a feast, and they ate and drank. 31 In
the morning they rose early and [v]ex-
changed oaths. And Isaac sent them on
their way, and they departed from him in
peace. 32 That same day Isaac's servants
came and told him about the well that they
had dug and said to him, "We have found
water." 33 He called it Shibah;[1] therefore the
name of the city is [w]Beersheba to this day.
34 When Esau was forty years old, he took
[x]Judith the daughter of Beeri the Hittite to
be his wife, and Basemath the daughter of
Elon the Hittite, 35 and [y]they made life bitter[2] for Isaac and Rebekah.

Isaac Blesses Jacob

27 When Isaac was old and [z]his eyes
were dim so that he could not see, he
called Esau his older son and said to him,
"My son"; and he answered, "Here I am."
2 He said, "Behold, I am old; I do not know
the day of my death. 3 [a]Now then, take your
weapons, your quiver and your bow, and go
out to the field and hunt game for me, 4 and
prepare for me delicious food, such as I love,
and bring it to me so that I may eat, that my
soul [b]may bless you before I die."
5 Now Rebekah was listening when Isaac
spoke to his son Esau. So when Esau went
to the field to hunt for game and bring it,
6 Rebekah said to her son Jacob, "I heard
your father speak to your brother Esau,
7 'Bring me game and prepare for me delicious food, that I may eat it and bless you
before the LORD before I die.' 8 Now therefore, my son, [c]obey my voice as I command

24 [o]ch. 17:7; 24:12; 28:13; Ex. 3:6 [p]ch. 15:1; See Ps. 27:1-3 [q]ch. 28:15; 31:3; [ch. 21:22, 23]
25 [r]ch. 12:7; 13:18
26 [s]ch. 21:22
27 [t]ver. 16
29 [u]ch. 24:31
31 [v]ch. 21:31
33 [w]ch. 21:31; 22:19
34 [x][ch. 28:9; 36:2, 3]
35 [y]ch. 27:46
Chapter 27
1 [z]ch. 48:10; 1 Sam. 3:2
3 [a]ch. 25:27, 28
4 [b]ver. 10:25; ch. 48:9, 15; 49:28; Deut. 33:1
8 [c]ver. 13

1 *Shibah* sounds like the Hebrew for *oath* 2 Hebrew *they were bitterness of spirit*

26:24 The form and content of God's blessing to Isaac again underscores the theme of continuity with the Abrahamic covenant promises (vv. 2–5; 15:1; 17:7).

26:25 built an altar. Like his father, Isaac built an altar in response to God's revelation (12:7, 8).

26:26 Abimelech. See note 20:2.

Phichol. See note 21:22.

26:28 We see plainly . . . LORD has been with you. Their statement bore unintended witness to the Lord's promise in vv. 3–4 (21:22; cf. 1 Kin. 10:9).

a sworn pact . . . a covenant. See 21:23 and notes.

26:33 name of the city is Beersheba. The Lord's protection of Abraham at Beersheba is now extended to Isaac (21:32).

26:34–27:46 The theme of family conflict, between the parents and between the twins, now becomes full-blown in pursuit of the patriarch's blessing. Isaac depended on his fallible senses rather than divine guidance (27:4; cf. 25:23), and Rebekah used deception (27:6–17). Esau broke his oath (27:5 note) and Jacob blasphemously lied (27:19, 20). Though the blessing is passed on according to God's good pleasure, the divine verdict on their actions is pronounced in the disastrous consequences: Esau resolved to murder Jacob (27:41; cf. 4:8) and Jacob fled the land. Rebekah died without memorial (35:8 and note), and Isaac lived on without significance (35:28 and note).

Implicit here is a contrast between Abraham, who in faith provided for Isaac's future according to God's elective purposes (ch. 24), and Isaac, who seems to have made no attempt to find suitable wives for his sons (cf. 24:2–4), and who tried to thwart the divine election (27:1–4; cf. 25:23).

26:34, 35 The story of the stolen blessing is framed by references to Esau's marriage to Hittite women, and his parents' resulting displeasure (27:46). Profane Esau showed his disregard for the covenant blessings by marrying daughters of the land (24:3–4; 31:50 and notes). By intermarrying with the Canaanites, and so vexing his parents (27:46), he effectively sealed himself off from the sacred inheritance (21:21; 25:6).

26:34 Hittite. See note 10:15.

27:4 delicious food, such as I love. Isaac's sensuality was at the root of this conflict (vv. 18–27 note; 25:27, 28).

27:5–17 Rebekah is the chief figure here. Though her method was deplorable (cf. 2 Cor. 4:2), her spiritual values were sound (25:23; 26:35; 27:46).

27:5 Rebekah was listening. Isaac neither provided spiritual leadership in the home nor listened to his wife's counsel—factors that strongly contributed to his family difficulties. Isaac's behavior contrasts with that of Abraham (21:8–14).

Esau went. Though birthright and blessing were not identical, they were related because both pertained to the inheritance. Esau reneged on the oath he had made with Jacob (24:33), but the original act of unbelief in selling his inheritance was decisive (Heb. 12:16, 17).

27:7 bless you. In patriarchal times, a solemn family blessing was given at departures (24:60; 28:1–5) or when death was imminent. It could be given to only one person and could not be altered. The patriarchal blessings of Abraham, Isaac, and Jacob had spiritual significance because the Lord used the social customs of those times to communicate His sovereign purposes. While God initially mediated His covenant blessing through the patriarchs, after the Mosaic law was given, God's blessing was mediated to all His people through the priest (Num. 6:22–27).

you. **9** Go to the flock and bring me two
good young goats, so that I may prepare
from them delicious food for your father,
such as he loves. **10** And you shall bring it to
your father to eat, [d]so that he may bless
you before he dies." **11** But Jacob said to
Rebekah his mother, "Behold, [e]my brother
Esau is a hairy man, and I am a smooth
man. **12** Perhaps my father [f]will feel me, and
I shall seem to be mocking him and bring
[g]a curse upon myself and not a blessing."
13 His mother said to him, [h]"Let your curse
be on me, my son; only obey my voice, and
go, bring them to me."
14 So he went and took them and brought
them to his mother, and his mother prepared delicious food, such as his father
loved. **15** Then Rebekah took the [i]best garments of Esau her older son, which were
with her in the house, and put them on
Jacob her younger son. **16** And the skins of
the young goats she put on his hands and
on the smooth part of his neck. **17** And she
put the delicious food and the bread,
which she had prepared, into the hand of
her son Jacob.
18 So he went in to his father and said,
"My father." And he said, "Here I am. Who
are you, my son?" **19** Jacob said to his father,
"I am Esau your firstborn. I have done as
you told me; now sit up and eat of my
game, that your soul may bless me." **20** But
Isaac said to his son, "How is it that you
have found it so quickly, my son?" He
answered, "Because the LORD your God
granted me success." **21** Then Isaac said to
Jacob, "Please come near, that I [j]may feel
you, my son, to know whether you are really my son Esau or not." **22** So Jacob went
near to Isaac his father, who felt him and
said, "The voice is Jacob's voice, but the
hands are the hands of Esau." **23** And he did
not recognize him, because [k]his hands
were hairy like his brother Esau's hands.
[l]So he blessed him. **24** He said, "Are you
really my son Esau?" He answered, "I am."
25 Then he said, "Bring it near to me, [m]that
I may eat of my son's game and bless you."
So he brought it near to him, and he ate;
and he brought him wine, and he drank.
26 Then his father Isaac said to him,
"Come near and kiss me, my son." **27** So he
came near and kissed him. And Isaac
smelled the smell of his garments [l]and
blessed him and said,

"See, [n]the smell of my son
is as the smell of a field that the
LORD has blessed!
28 May God give you of [o]the dew of
heaven
and of the fatness of the earth
and [p]plenty of grain and wine.
29 Let peoples serve you,
and nations [q]bow down to you.
[r]Be lord over your brothers,
and may your mother's sons bow
down to you.
[s]Cursed be everyone who curses you,
and blessed be everyone who
blesses you!"

30 As soon as Isaac had finished blessing
Jacob, when Jacob had scarcely gone out
from the presence of Isaac his father, Esau
his brother came in from his hunting. **31** He
also prepared delicious food and brought it
to his father. And he said to his father, "Let
my father arise and eat of his son's game,
that you may bless me." **32** His father Isaac
said to him, "Who are you?" He answered,
"I am your son, your firstborn, Esau."
33 Then Isaac trembled very violently and
said, "Who was it then that hunted game
and brought it to me, and I ate it all before
you came, and I have blessed him? Yes,
and he shall be blessed." **34** As soon as Esau
heard the words of his father, [t]he cried out
with an exceedingly great and bitter cry

10 [d]ver. 4
11 [e]ch. 25:25
12 [f]ver. 21, 22
[g][Deut. 27:18]
13 [h][1 Sam. 25:24; 2 Sam. 14:9; Matt. 27:25]
15 [i]ver. 27
21 [j]ver. 12
23 [k]ver. 16
[l]Heb. 11:20
25 [m]ver. 10
27 [l][See ver. 23 above]
[n][Hos. 14:6]
28 [o]Deut. 33:13; Zech. 8:12; [ch. 49:25; 2 Sam. 1:21] [p]Deut. 7:13; 33:28; Joel 2:19
29 [q][ch. 49:8] [r][2 Sam. 8:14] [s]ch. 12:3; Num. 24:9
34 [t]Heb. 12:17

27:11, 12 Jacob had no qualms about the morality of the plan, only about its feasibility.

27:15 garments. Jacob too was later deceived by clothing (37:31–33).

27:18–27 Isaac failed because he depended on his fallible senses—touch (v. 22), taste (v. 25), and smell (v. 27)—rather than upon spiritual understanding (v. 4 note; cf. 13:8–17 note).

27:20 the LORD your God. Jacob compounded his guilt by taking the Lord's name in vain (Ex. 20:7 note). Here Jacob regards the Lord as the God of his father. Later the Lord will reveal Himself as the God of Jacob (28:13–15, 20–22; 33:20 text note).

27:26 kiss. This physical contact was part of the blessing ritual (48:1 note).

27:28, 29 What Isaac perceived through the sense of smell (v. 27) gave form to the blessing, which pertained to the land's fertility (v. 28), and to dominion (v. 29). The blessing's similarity to the prenatal oracle (25:23) points to the Lord's sovereign rule of history.

27:28 dew . . . fatness . . . plenty. These terms anticipate the blessing on the nation of Israel when settled in the Promised Land (Deut. 7:13; 33:28).

27:29 Cursed be everyone who curses. See 12:3.

27:34 great and bitter cry. See Heb. 12:16, 17 and notes.

and said to his father, "Bless me, even me
also, O my father!" 35 But he said, "Your
brother came deceitfully, and he has taken
away your blessing." 36 Esau said, [u]"Is he
not rightly named Jacob?[1] For he has
cheated me these two times. [v]He took away
my birthright, and behold, now he has
taken away my blessing." Then he said,
"Have you not reserved a blessing for me?"
37 Isaac answered and said to Esau,
"Behold, [w]I have made him lord over you,
and all his brothers I have given to him for
servants, and [x]with grain and wine I have
sustained him. What then can I do for you,
my son?" 38 Esau said to his father, "Have
you but one blessing, my father? Bless me,
even me also, O my father." And [t]Esau lifted up his voice and wept.
39 Then Isaac his father answered and
said to him:

"Behold, [y]away from[2] the fatness of
the earth shall your dwelling be,
and away from[3] the dew of heaven
on high.
40 By your sword you shall live,
and you [z]shall serve your brother;
but when you grow restless
[a]you shall break his yoke from your
neck."

41 Now Esau [b]hated Jacob because of the
blessing with which his father had blessed
him, and Esau said to himself, [c]"The days
of mourning for my father are approaching;
[d]then I will kill my brother Jacob." 42 But
the words of Esau her older son were told
to Rebekah. So she sent and called Jacob
her younger son and said to him, "Behold,
your brother Esau comforts himself about
you by planning to kill you. 43 Now therefore, my son, obey my voice. Arise, flee to
Laban my brother in Haran 44 and stay with
him a while, until your brother's fury turns
away— 45 until your brother's anger turns
away from you, and he forgets what you
have done to him. Then I will send and
bring you from there. Why should I be
bereft of you both in one day?"
46 Then Rebekah said to Isaac, [e]"I loathe
my life because of the Hittite women.[4] [f]If
Jacob marries one of the Hittite women like
these, one of the women of the land, what
good will my life be to me?"

Jacob Sent to Laban

28 Then Isaac called Jacob [g]and
blessed him and directed him,
[f]"You must not take a wife from the
Canaanite women. 2 [h]Arise, go to Paddan-
aram to the house of [i]Bethuel your mother's father, and take as your wife from there
one of the daughters of Laban your mother's brother. 3 [j]God Almighty[5] bless you
and make you fruitful and multiply you,
that you may become a company of peoples. 4 May he give [k]the blessing of Abraham to you and to your offspring with you,
that you may take possession of [l]the land
of your sojournings that God gave to Abraham!" 5 Thus Isaac sent Jacob away. And he
went to Paddan-aram, to Laban, the son of
Bethuel the Aramean, the brother of
Rebekah, Jacob's and Esau's mother.

36 [u]ch. 25:26 [v]ch. 25:33
37 [w]ver. 29 [2 Sam. 8:14] [x]ver. 28
38 [t][See ver. 34 above]
39 [y]ver. 28; ch. 36:6, 7
40 [z]ch. 25:23; [2 Sam. 8:14]; See Obad. 18-21 [a][2 Kin. 8:20-22]
41 [b][ch. 37:4] [c]ch. 50:3, 4, 10 [d][Amos 1:11; Obad. 10]
46 [e]ch. 26:34, 35; 28:8 [f]ch. 24:3
Chapter 28
1 [g]ver. 6 [f][See ch. 27:46 above]
2 [h]Hos. 12:12 [i]ch. 22:23
3 [j]See ch. 17:1
4 [k]See ch. 12:2, 3 [l]ch. 17:8; 36:7; 37:1

[1] *Jacob* means *He takes by the heel*, or *He cheats* [2] Or *Behold, of* [3] Or *and of* [4] Hebrew *daughters of Heth* [5] Hebrew *El Shaddai*

27:36 Jacob. See text note; note on 25:26.

27:37 What then can I do for you. Though Isaac knew God had elected Jacob, he had intended to give everything to Esau (26:34–27:46 note).

27:39 from the fatness . . . from the dew. The Hebrew wording is similar to Jacob's blessing, but with a very different meaning. While God was to give to Jacob "of the dew" and "of the fatness" (v. 28), Esau was to dwell "from" (lit. "away from") "the fatness of the earth" and away from "the dew of heaven." This blessing found fulfillment as Esau's descendants, the Edomites, settled in the arid region south of the Dead Sea. Esau inherited an anti-blessing: he was denied the earth's fertility and dominion over his brother (cf. vv. 28, 29).

27:40 break his yoke. See note 25:23. From time to time Edom was able to break free of Israelite domination (2 Kin. 8:20–22). In addition, Herod the Great was a descendant of Esau.

27:45 I will send. Jacob was to be absent for twenty years (31:38); Rebekah never saw her son again (35:8 note).

bereft of you both in one day. Both would be lost if Jacob was killed by his brother Esau, and Esau then by an avenger of blood (9:6; Num. 35:19–21).

27:46 This transitional verse provides a conclusion to 26:34–27:46 (26:34, 35 note) and an introduction to 27:46–28:9.

Rebekah said. As Sarah took initiative to provide for Isaac (21:10), here Rebekah acted for Jacob.

the Hittite women. See 26:34 and note on 10:15.

28:1, 2 The negative and positive commands correspond to those of Abraham (24:3–4).

28:1 blessed. See note 27:7. The first blessing (27:27–29) determined the patriarchal succession; this one explicitly linked Jacob with the blessings of the Abrahamic covenant (17:1–8).

28:2 Paddan-aram. See note 25:20.

28:3 God Almighty. See note 17:1.

a company of peoples. See 17:5 and note; 35:11.

28:4 take possession. The Hebrew verb here can mean "taking possession by force," perhaps anticipating the concept of holy war against the Canaanites (15:16; Ex. 23:22–33).

Esau Marries an Ishmaelite

6 Now Esau saw that Isaac had blessed
Jacob and sent him away to Paddan-aram
to take a wife from there, and that as he
blessed him he directed him, "You must
not take a wife from the Canaanite
women," 7 and that Jacob had obeyed his
father and his mother and gone to Paddan-
aram. 8 So when Esau saw [m] that the Canaanite women did not please Isaac his
father, 9 Esau went to Ishmael and took as
his wife, besides the wives he had, [n] Mahalath the daughter of Ishmael, Abraham's
son, the sister of [o] Nebaioth.

Jacob's Dream

10 Jacob left [p] Beersheba and went toward
[q] Haran. 11 And he came to a certain place
and stayed there that night, because the
sun had set. Taking one of the stones of the
place, he put it under his head and lay
down in that place to sleep. 12 And he
[r] dreamed, and behold, there was a ladder[1]
set up on the earth, and the top of it
reached to heaven. And behold, [s] the angels
of God were ascending and descending on
it! 13 And behold, [t] the LORD stood above it[2]
and said, [u] "I am the LORD, the God of
Abraham your father and the God of Isaac.
[v] The land on which you lie I will give to you
and to your offspring. 14 Your offspring shall
be like [w] the dust of the earth, and you shall
spread abroad to the west and to the east
and to the north and to the south, and in
you and [x] your offspring shall all the families
of the earth be blessed. 15 Behold, [y] I am with
you and will keep you wherever you go, and
[z] will bring you back to this land. For I will
[a] not leave you until I have done what I have
promised you." 16 Then Jacob awoke from
his sleep and said, "Surely the LORD is [b] in
this place, and I did not know it." 17 And he
was afraid and said, "How awesome is this
place! This is none other than the house of
God, and this is the gate of heaven."
18 So early in the morning Jacob took the
stone that he had put under his head and
set it up [c] for a pillar [d] and poured oil on the
top of it. 19 He called the name of that place
[e] Bethel,[3] but the name of the city was Luz
at the first. 20 Then Jacob [f] made a vow, saying, "If God will be with me and will keep
me in this way that I go, and will give me
bread to eat and clothing to wear, 21 [g] so that
I come again to my father's house in peace,
[h] then the LORD shall be my God, 22 and this
stone, which I have set up for a pillar, [i] shall
be God's house. And [j] of all that you give me
I will give a full tenth to you."

8 [m] ch. 24:3; 26:35
9 [n] [ch. 36:3] [o] ch. 25:13; 36:3
10 [p] ch. 21:31; 26:33 [q] [Acts 7:2]
12 [r] [Num. 12:6; Job 33:15, 16] [s] [John 1:51]
13 [t] [ch. 35:1; 48:3] [u] ch. 26:24 [v] ch. 35:12; See ch. 13:14-16
14 [w] See ch. 13:16 [x] See ch. 12:3
15 [y] ch. 26:24; 31:3 [z] ch. 35:6 [a] 1 Kin. 8:57
16 [b] Ex. 3:5; Josh. 5:15
18 [c] ch. 31:13, 45; 35:14; [1 Sam. 7:12; 2 Sam. 18:18] [d] [Lev. 8:10, 11; Num. 7:1]
19 [e] ch. 35:7; Judg. 1:23, 26
20 [f] ch. 31:13
21 [g] [Judg. 11:31; 2 Sam. 15:7-9] [h] Deut. 26:17
22 [i] ch. 35:7, 14 [j] ch. 14:20; Lev. 27:30-33

[1] Or *a flight of steps* [2] Or *beside him* [3] *Bethel* means *the house of God*

28:6–9 Acting out of rivalry with his brother (v. 6) and a desire to please his father (v. 8), Esau sought another wife from among his relatives, the family of Ishmael (v. 9). Even in this effort Esau lacked spiritual perception, for Ishmael was the rejected natural offspring of Abraham (17:18–21; 21:12, 13).

28:10–22 The Lord appeared to Jacob and gave him promises at critical points in his life: during his flight to Paddan-aram (28:10–22), on his return to confront Esau (32:1, 2, 22–32), and when Jacob faced threats from Laban's sons (31:1–3) and the Canaanites (35:1–15).

28:11 under his head. The Hebrew term here is translated "at his head" in 1 Sam. 26:7. Instead of serving as a pillow, the rock may have protected his head.

28:12 a ladder. Probably a vast stone ramp with steps. The phrase "top of it reached to heaven" recalls the description of the tower of Babel (11:4). Jacob may have seen a ziggurat. See notes 11:1–9 and 11:5.

earth . . . heaven . . . ascending and descending. Jacob's dream of a meeting place between heaven and earth points forward to Jesus Christ, the God-Man who reunites heaven and earth (John 1:51 and note). Through Christ, the only "mediator between God and men" (1 Tim. 2:5), we have access to the Father (Eph. 2:18).

angels of God. See "Angels"at Zech. 1:9.

28:13 the LORD stood above it. Or, "the LORD stood beside him." If this second reading is preferred (note Jacob's response in v. 16: "Surely the LORD is in this place"), then God came down the stairway. He did not stand above the stairway, but over a sleeping Jacob.

I am the LORD. See note 27:20.

land on which you lie. God's promise was adapted to the immediate situation.

offspring. The Hebrew term here may be translated "seed" or "descendants" (12:7 note). The language of vv. 13–15 vividly recalls God's promises to Abraham (cf. 12:3; 13:14–16).

28:14 blessed. See note 12:3; 18:18; 22:18.

28:15 I am with you. See 26:3; Ex. 3:12; Ps. 23; 46; Heb. 13:5. The promises of this verse pertained to Jacob's own lifetime.

wherever you go. In contrast to pagan deities, whose powers were thought to be tied to particular localities.

until I have done. The Hebrew here signifies only that the promise will be completed, not that it will be changed after its fulfillment.

28:17 he was afraid. Worshipful fear in God's presence is appropriate (Ex. 3:6; 19:16; Ps. 2:11).

28:18 a pillar. A witness and monument drawing attention to the importance of the place (cf. 31:45–59).

poured oil. An act of consecration (35:14; Ex. 40:9; 2 Sam. 1:21).

28:20–22 The longest vow recorded in the Old Testament.

28:20 If God will be with me. Jacob's reaction contrasts strikingly with Abraham's (15:6). Though Jacob's journey of faith had begun, he still had far to go. Note that God's unconditional promises of vv. 13–15 are here transformed into a conditional bargain: if God does His part then Jacob will acknowledge Him as God (v. 21). God had sovereignly chosen Jacob in the womb (25:23 and note), and now He graciously bestows the patriarchal promise quite apart from Jacob's faith; that too must be the gift of God (17:2 note).

28:22 give a full tenth. See note 14:20.

Jacob Marries Leah and Rachel

29 Then Jacob went on his journey and came to [k]the land of the people of the east. 2 As he looked, he saw a well in the field, and behold, three flocks of sheep lying beside it, for out of that well the flocks were watered. The stone on the well's mouth was large, 3 and when all the flocks were gathered there, the shepherds would roll the stone from the mouth of the well and water the sheep, and put the stone back in its place over the mouth of the well.

4 Jacob said to them, "My brothers, where do you come from?" They said, [l]"We are from Haran." 5 He said to them, "Do you know Laban the son of Nahor?" They said, "We know him." 6 He said to them, "Is it well with him?" They said, "It is well; and see, Rachel his daughter is coming with the sheep!" 7 He said, "Behold, it is still high day; it is not time for the livestock to be gathered together. Water the sheep and go, pasture them." 8 But they said, "We cannot until all the flocks are gathered together and the stone is rolled from the mouth of the well; then we water the sheep."

9 While he was still speaking with them, [m]Rachel came with her father's sheep, for she was a shepherdess. 10 Now as soon as Jacob saw Rachel the daughter of Laban his mother's brother, and the sheep of Laban his mother's brother, Jacob came near and rolled the stone from the well's mouth and watered the flock of Laban his mother's brother. 11 Then Jacob kissed Rachel and wept aloud. 12 And Jacob told Rachel that he was [n]her father's kinsman, and that he was Rebekah's son, [o]and she ran and told her father.

13 As soon as Laban heard the news about Jacob, his sister's son, [o]he ran to meet him and embraced him and kissed him and brought him to his house. Jacob told Laban all these things, 14 and Laban said to him, [p]"Surely you are my bone and my flesh!" And he stayed with him a month.

15 Then Laban said to Jacob, "Because you are my kinsman, should you therefore serve me for nothing? Tell me, what shall your wages be?" 16 Now Laban had two daughters. The name of the older was Leah, and the name of the younger was Rachel. 17 Leah's eyes were weak,[1] but Rachel was beautiful in form and appearance. 18 Jacob loved Rachel. And he said, [q]"I will serve you seven years for your younger daughter Rachel." 19 Laban said, "It is better that I give her to you than that I should give her to any other man; stay with me." 20 So Jacob [q]served seven years for Rachel, and they seemed to him but a few days because of the love he had for her.

21 Then Jacob said to Laban, "Give me my wife that I may go in to her, for my time is completed." 22 So Laban gathered together all the people of the place and [r]made a feast. 23 But in the evening he took his daughter Leah and brought her to Jacob, and he went in to her. 24 (Laban gave[2] [s]his female servant Zilpah to his daughter Leah to be her servant.) 25 And in the morning, behold, it was Leah! And Jacob said to Laban, "What is this you have done to me? Did I not serve with you for Rachel? Why then have you deceived me?" 26 Laban said, "It is not so done in our country, to give the younger before the firstborn. 27 [t]Complete the week of this one, and we will give you the other also in return for

Chapter 29
1 [k]Num. 23:7; Judg. 6:3
4 [l]ch. 27:43
9 [m]Ex. 2:16, 17
12 [n]ch. 13:8; 14:14, 16 [o][ch. 24:28, 29]
13 [o][See ver. 12 above]
14 [p]ch. 2:23; 37:27; Judg. 9:2; 2 Sam. 5:1; 19:12, 13; 1 Chr. 11:1
18 [q]ch. 30:26; 31:41; [Hos. 12:12]
20 [q][See ver. 18 above]
22 [r]Judg. 14:10; [John 2:1, 2]
24 [s]See ch. 30:9-12
27 [t][Judg. 14:12]

1 Or *soft* 2 Or *had given;* also verse 29

29:1–30 Jacob experienced the blessings of divine providence in meeting Rachel (vv. 1–14), and in a bitter irony the deceiver became the deceived (vv. 15–29). Behind the two scenes the gracious and just hand of the sovereign God, who works all things according to His own purpose and who promised to be with Jacob (28:15), can be discerned.

29:2 well. The similarity of this meeting at the well with the meeting in 24:11–33 suggests the benevolence of divine providence, but also highlights the contrast between the prayerful servant and the prayerless patriarch.

29:4 My brothers. The greeting was a gesture of goodwill.

29:10 rolled the stone. The stone was large (v. 2). Earlier the gold jewelry of Abraham's servant had attracted Laban's attention (24:30); now Jacob's feat of strength impressed him with the kind of service Jacob could render.

29:11 kissed. A customary greeting among relatives (v. 14; 31:55).

29:16 Leah . . . Rachel. The name Rachel means "ewe," while Leah perhaps means "wild cow" or "wild ox."

29:23 evening. As Jacob took advantage of his father's blindness to deceive him, so Laban used the cover of night to outwit Jacob.

he took his daughter Leah. The custom of veiling the bride (24:64, 65 note) and of marrying off the elder daughter first (v. 26) served Laban's selfish intentions. He shamelessly used his unloved daughter and introduced a source of continuing discord into Jacob's family (30:1, 2; 31:15). Laban's daughters were not deceived by his unscrupulous behavior (31:14–16).

29:25 deceived me. See 27:35.

29:26 the younger before the firstborn. This statement underscores the irony of Jacob's situation. Jacob had stolen the blessing customarily reserved for the firstborn (ch. 27), and here Laban deceives Jacob in order to uphold a similar custom.

29:27 Complete the week. The week of bridal feasting. The extended feast (v. 22) celebrated Laban's cleverness and Jacob's humiliation, turning what should have been a joyous occasion into a bad joke.

serving me another seven years." 28 Jacob did so, and completed her week. Then Laban gave him his daughter Rachel to be his wife. 29 (Laban gave [u]his female servant Bilhah to his daughter Rachel to be her servant.) 30 So Jacob went in to Rachel also, and he loved Rachel more than Leah, and served Laban [v]for another seven years.

Jacob's Children

31 When the LORD saw that Leah was [w]hated, [x]he opened her womb, but Rachel was barren. 32 And Leah conceived and bore a son, and she called his name Reuben,[1] for she said, "Because the LORD [y]has looked upon my affliction; for now my husband will love me." 33 She conceived again and bore a son, and said, "Because the LORD has heard that I am hated, he has given me this son also." And she called his name Simeon.[2] 34 Again she conceived and bore a son, and said, "Now this time my husband will be [z]attached to me, because I have borne him three sons." Therefore his name was called Levi.[3] 35 And she conceived again and bore a son, and said, "This time I will praise the LORD." Therefore she called his name [a]Judah.[4] Then she ceased bearing.

30 When Rachel saw that [b]she bore Jacob no children, she envied her sister. She said to Jacob, "Give me children, or I shall die!" 2 Jacob's anger was kindled against Rachel, and he said, "Am I in the place of God, [c]who has withheld from you the fruit of the womb?" 3 Then she said, "Here is my servant [d]Bilhah; go in to her, so that she may give birth [e]on my behalf,[5] that even I may have children[6] through her." 4 So she gave him her servant Bilhah as a wife, and Jacob went in to her. 5 And Bilhah conceived and bore Jacob a son. 6 Then Rachel said, "God has [f]judged me, and has also heard my voice and given me a son." Therefore she called his name Dan.[7] 7 Rachel's servant Bilhah conceived again and bore Jacob a second son. 8 Then Rachel said, "With mighty wrestlings[8] I have wrestled with my sister and have prevailed." So she called his name [g]Naphtali.[9]

9 When Leah saw that she had ceased bearing children, she took her servant Zilpah and [h]gave her to Jacob as a wife. 10 Then Leah's servant Zilpah bore Jacob a son. 11 And Leah said, [i]"Good fortune has come!" so she called his name [i]Gad.[10] 12 Leah's servant Zilpah bore Jacob a second son. 13 And Leah said, "Happy am I! For women [j]have called me happy." So she called his name Asher.[11]

14 In the days of wheat harvest Reuben went and found [k]mandrakes in the field and brought them to his mother Leah. Then Rachel said to Leah, "Please give me some of your son's mandrakes." 15 But she said to her, "Is it a small matter that you have taken away my husband? Would you take away my son's mandrakes also?" Rachel said, "Then he may lie with you tonight in exchange for your son's mandrakes." 16 When Jacob came from the field in the evening, Leah went out to meet him and said, "You must come in to me, for I have hired you with my son's mandrakes." So he lay with her that night. 17 And God listened to Leah, and she conceived and bore Jacob a fifth son. 18 Leah said, "God has given me my wages because I gave my servant to my husband." So she called his name Issachar.[12]

29 [u]See ch. 30:3-7
30 [v]ver. 20; ch. 31:41
31 [w]Deut. 21:15 [x][ch. 30:22]
32 [y]ch. 31:42; Ex. 3:7; 4:31; Deut. 26:7
34 [z][Num. 18:2, 4]
35 [a]Matt. 1:2; [ch. 49:8]
Chapter 30
1 [b]ch. 29:31
2 [c][ch. 16:2; 1 Sam. 1:5]
3 [d]ch. 29:29 [e]ch. 50:23
6 [f][ch. 49:16]
8 [g][Matt. 4:13]
9 [h]ver. 4; ch. 29:24
11 [i][ch. 49:19]
13 [j][Luke 1:48]
14 [k]S. of S. 7:13

[1] *Reuben* means *See, a son* [2] *Simeon* sounds like the Hebrew for *heard* [3] *Levi* sounds like the Hebrew for *attached* [4] *Judah* sounds like the Hebrew for *praise* [5] Hebrew *on my knees* [6] Hebrew *be built up*, which sounds like the Hebrew for *children* [7] *Dan* sounds like the Hebrew for *judged* [8] Hebrew *With wrestlings of God* [9] *Naphtali* sounds like the Hebrew for *wrestling* [10] *Gad* sounds like the Hebrew for *good fortune* [11] *Asher* sounds like the Hebrew for *happy* [12] *Issachar* sounds like the Hebrew for *wages*, or *hire*

29:31–30:24 God blessed Jacob with twelve sons in spite of his prayerlessness and the rivalry of Rachel and Leah, who competed for his affections by bearing him sons (25:19–35:29 note). The names the mother's gave these children reflect this struggle and also their recognition of God's assistance to them in their unloved or childless states. God graciously built up Israel by championing the needy (e.g., Hannah in 1 Sam. 1), but the spiritual failures of Jacob's family later resulted in rivalries among Israelite tribes.

29:31–35 God graciously gave Leah, the unloved wife, half of Jacob's sons, including the priestly line of Levi (v. 34) and the messianic line of Judah (v. 35; 49:10). The first and last of the children born in Paddan-aram are given by the Lord to compensate disgraced wives, first Leah (v. 32), and then Rachel (30:23, 24).

29:31 opened. See 16:2; 20:17, 18.

barren. See 25:21.

29:35 Judah. The name means "praised," here of the Lord, and in 49:8 of Judah himself.

30:1 or I shall die. A hyperbolic expression of her extreme distress (25:32; 27:46). Ironically, she later died in childbirth (35:16–18).

30:2 Am I in the place of God. Jacob's angry retort contrasts sharply with the fervent prayer of Isaac for his childless wife (25:21).

30:3 Here is . . . Bilhah. See 16:1, 2 and notes.

on my behalf. Literally, "on my knees." The knee was symbolic of parental care (50:23; Job 3:12). According to ancient Near Eastern custom, the delivery of the concubine's child upon the knees of the wife symbolized the adoption of the child by the wife.

30:14 mandrakes. Sometimes called "love apples," the roots of the mandrake plant were considered an aphrodisiac by the ancients, and used to promote sexual activity and conception (cf. Song 7:13).

19 And Leah conceived again, and she
bore Jacob a sixth son. 20 Then Leah said,
"God has endowed me with a good endowment; now my husband will honor me,
because I have borne him six sons." So she
called his name [l]Zebulun.[1] 21 Afterward she
bore a daughter and called her name Dinah.
22 Then God [m]remembered Rachel, and
God listened to her and [n]opened her
womb. 23 She conceived and bore a son and
said, "God has taken away [o]my reproach."
24 And she called his name Joseph,[2] saying,
[p]"May the LORD add to me another son!"

Jacob's Prosperity

25 As soon as Rachel had borne Joseph,
Jacob said to Laban, "Send me away, that I
may go to my own home and country.
26 Give me my wives and my children [q]for
whom I have served you, that I may go, for
you know the service that I have given
you." 27 But Laban said to him, "If I have
found favor in your sight, I have learned by
divination that[3] the LORD has blessed me
because of you. 28 [r]Name your wages, and I
will give it." 29 Jacob said to him, [s]"You
yourself know how I have served you, and
how your livestock has fared with me.
30 For you had little before I came, [t]and it
has increased abundantly, and the LORD
has blessed you wherever I turned. But
now when shall I [u]provide for my own
household also?" 31 He said, "What shall I
give you?" Jacob said, "You shall not give
me anything. If you will do this for me, I
will again pasture your flock and keep it:
32 let me pass through all your flock today,
removing from it every speckled and spotted sheep and every black lamb, and the
spotted and speckled among the goats, and
[v]they shall be my wages. 33 So my honesty
will answer for me later, when you come to
look into my wages with you. Every one
that is not speckled and spotted among the
goats and black among the lambs, if found
with me, shall be counted stolen." 34 Laban
said, "Good! Let it be as you have said."
35 But that day Laban removed the male
goats that were striped and spotted, and all
the female goats that were speckled and
spotted, every one that had white on it,
and every lamb that was black, and put
them in charge of his sons. 36 And he set a
distance of three days' journey between
himself and Jacob, and Jacob pastured the
rest of Laban's flock.
37 Then [w]Jacob took fresh sticks of poplar
and almond and plane trees, and peeled
white streaks in them, exposing the white
of the sticks. 38 He set the sticks that he had
peeled in front of the flocks in the troughs,
that is, the [x]watering places, where the
flocks came to drink. And since they bred
when they came to drink, 39 the flocks bred
in front of the sticks and so the flocks
brought forth striped, speckled, and spotted. 40 And Jacob separated the lambs and
set the faces of the flocks toward the
striped and all the black in the flock of
Laban. He put his own droves apart and
did not put them with Laban's flock.

20 [l][Matt. 4:13]
22 [m]See ch. 8:1 [n]ch. 29:31; [Ps. 127:3]
23 [o]Luke 1:25; [Isai. 4:1; 1 Sam. 1:6]
24 [p]ch. 35:17
26 [q]ch. 29:20, 30
28 [r]ch. 29:15
29 [s]ch. 31:6, 38-40
30 [t]ver. 43 [u][1 Tim. 5:8]
32 [v]ch. 31:8
37 [w]See ch. 31:8-12
38 [x][Ex. 2:16]

1 *Zebulun* sounds like the Hebrew for *honor* 2 *Joseph* means *May he add,* and sounds like the Hebrew for *taken away* 3 Or *have become rich and*

30:20 endowment. A dowry.

30:21 Dinah. Dinah is the only daughter of Jacob whose name is given (cf. 46:7) because she figures prominently in ch. 34.

30:22 Then God remembered. See note 8:1. This verse is the climax of 29:31–30:24. Rachel credited the birth of Joseph, not to the aphrodisiac (v. 14 note), but to God (v. 23).

30:25–43 God sovereignly blessed Jacob's flocks at Laban's expense in spite of the inexcusable cunning of both men. Jacob appears to outwit Laban, repaying Laban's trickery, but he obtained his family and wealth entirely by God's grace (29:31–30:24; 31:9).

30:27 If I have found favor. A formula of courtesy in negotiations.

learned by divination. Many ancient extrabiblical texts from Mesopotamia pertain to the practice of occult divination, something forbidden in Israel (Deut. 18:10, 14). Noting Jacob's good fortune, the pagan Laban had attempted to discover the reason through divination (31:19 and note).

blessed me because of you. Once again, those outside the covenant are blessed through their association with the patriarchs (12:2, 3; 13:5, 6; 14:13 and note).

30:28 Name your wages. The opportunistic Laban wanted to manipulate the Lord through Jacob to serve his own greed. Thus he hoped to receive God's blessing.

30:31–34 In the ancient Near East, most lambs were white and most goats black or dark brown. Thinking the agreement posed little risk to himself, Laban eagerly granted Jacob's request for the unusually colored animals (v. 34). Jacob's proposal depended upon the faulty notion that vivid visual impressions during the act of reproduction determined the traits of the offspring. He thought that placing alternating colors in front of mating animals would result in unusually colored offspring (vv. 37, 38, 41, 42). Even though Jacob's scheming would deny God His rightful praise, God's intention to bless Jacob was not thwarted (31:11, 12).

30:35 that day Laban removed. The unscrupulous Laban immediately cheated. According to the agreement the unusually colored animals should have been Jacob's starting flock (v. 32). Jacob began with none of these, a fact highlighting the supernatural blessing on him.

30:39 flocks brought forth. Jacob's success was due to God's grace (31:9–12), not to his ill-founded theory of animal husbandry.

41 Whenever the stronger of the flock were
breeding, Jacob would lay the sticks in the
troughs before the eyes of the flock, that
they might breed among the sticks, 42 but
for the feebler of the flock he would not lay
them there. So the feebler would be
Laban's, and the stronger Jacob's. 43 Thus
the man [y]increased greatly and [z]had large
flocks, female servants and male servants,
and camels and donkeys.

Jacob Flees from Laban

31 Now Jacob heard that the sons of
Laban were saying, "Jacob has taken
all that was our father's, and from what
was our father's he has gained all this
wealth." 2 And Jacob saw [a]that Laban did
not regard him with favor as before. 3 Then
the LORD said to Jacob, [b]"Return to the
land of your fathers and to your kindred,
and I will be with you."

4 So Jacob sent and called Rachel and
Leah into the field where his flock was
5 and said to them, [c]"I see that your father
does not regard me with favor as he did
before. But the God of my father [d]has been
with me. 6 [e]You know that I have served
your father with all my strength, 7 yet your
father has cheated me and changed my
wages [f]ten times. But God did not permit
him to harm me. 8 If he said, [g]'The spotted
shall be your wages,' then all the flock bore
spotted; and if he said, 'The striped shall
be your wages,' then all the flock bore
striped. 9 Thus God has [h]taken away the
livestock of your father and given them to
me. 10 In the breeding season of the flock I
lifted up my eyes and saw in a dream that
the goats that mated with the flock were
striped, spotted, and mottled. 11 Then the
angel of God said to me in the dream,
'Jacob,' and I said, 'Here I am!' 12 And he
said, 'Lift up your eyes and see, all the
goats that mate with the flock are striped,
spotted, and mottled, for [i]I have seen all
that Laban is doing to you. 13 I am the God
of Bethel, [j]where you anointed a pillar and
made a vow to me. Now [k]arise, go out from
this land and return to the land of your
kindred.'" 14 Then Rachel and Leah
answered and said to him, "Is there [l]any
portion or inheritance left to us in our
father's house? 15 Are we not regarded by
him as foreigners? For [m]he has sold us, and
he has indeed devoured our money. 16 All
the wealth that God has taken away from
our father belongs to us and to our children. Now then, whatever God has said to
you, do."

17 So Jacob arose and set his sons and his
wives on camels. 18 He drove away all his
livestock, all his property that he had
gained, the livestock in his possession that
he had acquired in [n]Paddan-aram, to go to
the land of Canaan to his father Isaac.
19 Laban had gone to shear his sheep, and
Rachel stole her father's [o]household gods.
20 And Jacob tricked[1] Laban the Aramean,
by not telling him that he intended to flee.

[1] Hebrew *stole the heart of*; also verses 26, 27

43 [y]ver. 30 [z]ch. 24:35; 26:13, 14
Chapter 31
2 [a]ch. 4:5
3 [b]ver. 13; ch. 28:15; 32:9
5 [c]ver. 2 [d]ver. 3
6 [e]ver. 38-40; ch. 30:29
7 [f]ver. 41; [Num. 14:22; Neh. 4:12; Job 19:3; Zech. 8:23]
8 [g]ch. 30:32
9 [h]ver. 1
12 [i][Ex. 3:7]
13 [j]See ch. 28:18-22 [k]ver. 3; ch. 32:9
14 [l][2 Sam. 20:1; 1 Kin. 12:16]
15 [m]ch. 30:26; See ch. 29:15-20, 27
18 [n]ch. 25:20; 28:2, 6, 7
19 [o]ver. 30, 34; [Judg. 17:5; 1 Sam. 15:23; 19:13; Ezek. 21:21; Hos. 3:4; Zech. 10:2]

30:43 increased greatly. God did abundantly more than Jacob had asked (28:20).

31:1–55 In fulfillment of His promise in 28:15, the Lord led a chastened Jacob back to the Promised Land with great wealth at Laban's expense, and over Laban's opposition (v. 42). God remained faithful to His promises despite Jacob's scheming and the pagan idolatry in his household (v. 19 and note; 28:20 note).

31:3 Return to the land. Jacob's departure with his sons from Paddan-aram foreshadows the later Exodus of the twelve tribes of Israel from Egypt: they go in response to God's call to worship in the land of Canaan (vv. 3, 13; cf. Ex. 3:13–18); they spoil the enemy of his wealth (v. 9; cf. Ex. 12:35, 36); they are pursued by superior forces and delivered by divine intervention (vv. 21–42; cf. Ex. 14:5–31). These Old Testament examples in turn point forward to the pilgrimage of the New Israel, the church (1 Cor. 10:1–4).

I will be with you. See 28:15 and notes.

31:4 So Jacob sent and called. Jacob finally began to respond to God in prompt obedience (cf. 12:4; 17:23; 22:3).

31:5 God of my father has been with me. Acknowledging the Lord's faithfulness, Jacob was ready to pay his vow (v. 13; 28:20–22 and notes).

31:6 with all my strength. See note 29:10.

31:7 ten times. The number ten signified completeness; Jacob here is perhaps deploring the magnitude of Laban's dishonesty.

God did not permit him. In spite of his own schemes, Jacob recognized that the Lord had blessed him.

31:8 spotted . . . striped. See note 30:31–34.

31:9 Thus God has taken away. Through his dishonest behavior toward Jacob, Laban subjected himself to covenantal curses (12:3; 27:29).

31:11 angel of God. See note 16:7.

31:14–16 In bitterness against their dishonest father (vv. 14–15) and in recognition of God's providence (v. 16), Leah and Rachel decided to follow Jacob.

31:15 he has sold us. They resented their "bought marriages." The price paid was Jacob's labor (29:18, 27).

devoured our money. This phrase occurs in similar social contexts in Mesopotamian texts from Nuzi (c. 1500 B.C.). Legally, at least part of the compensation received by a father in return for giving his daughter in marriage was to be given to the daughter.

31:18 Paddan-aram. See note 25:20.

31:19 household gods. Small household gods, or *teraphim* were thought to provide protection and were used in divination (30:27 note; Ezek. 21:21; Zech. 10:2). Unlike Sarah and Rebekah, Rachel had not given up her pagan idols or ethics (vv. 34, 35; 35:2).

21 He fled with all that he had and arose and
crossed the [p]Euphrates, and [q]set his face
toward the hill country of Gilead.
22 When it was told Laban on the third
day that Jacob had fled, 23 he took his kinsmen with him and pursued him for seven
days and followed close after him into the
hill country of Gilead. 24 But God came to
Laban the Aramean [r]in a dream by night
and said to him, "Be careful not to say anything to Jacob, [s]either good or bad."
25 And Laban overtook Jacob. Now Jacob
had pitched his tent in the hill country,
and Laban with his kinsmen pitched tents
in the hill country of Gilead. 26 And Laban
said to Jacob, "What have you done, that
you have [t]tricked me and driven away my
daughters like captives of the sword?
27 Why did you flee secretly [t]and trick me,
and did not tell me, so that I might have
sent you away with mirth and songs, with
tambourine and lyre? 28 And why did you
not permit me [u]to kiss my sons and my
daughters farewell? Now you have done
foolishly. 29 It is [v]in my power to do you
harm. But the [w]God of your[1] father spoke
to me last night, saying, 'Be careful not to
say anything to Jacob, [x]either good or bad.'
30 And now you have gone away because
you longed greatly for your father's house,
but why did you [y]steal my gods?" 31 Jacob
answered and said to Laban, "Because I
was afraid, for I thought that you would
take your daughters from me by force.
32 [z]Anyone with whom you find your gods
shall not live. In the presence of our kinsmen point out what I have that is yours,
and take it." Now Jacob did not know that
Rachel had stolen them.
33 So Laban went into Jacob's tent and into
Leah's tent and into the tent of the two
female servants, but he did not find them.
And he went out of Leah's tent and entered
Rachel's. 34 Now Rachel had taken the household gods and put them in the camel's
saddle and sat on them. Laban felt all about
the tent, but did not find them. 35 And she
said to her father, "Let not my lord be angry
that I cannot [a]rise before you, for the way of
women is upon me." So he searched but
did not find the household gods.
36 Then Jacob became angry and berated
Laban. Jacob said to Laban, "What is my
offense? What is my sin, that you have
hotly pursued me? 37 For you have felt
through all my goods; what have you
found of all your household goods? Set it
here before my kinsmen and [b]your kinsmen, that they may decide between us two.
38 These twenty years I have been with you.
Your ewes and your female goats have not
miscarried, and I have not eaten the rams
of your flocks. 39 What was torn by wild
beasts I did not bring to you. I bore the loss
of it myself. [c]From my hand you required
it, whether stolen by day or stolen by night.
40 There I was: by day the heat consumed
me, and the cold by night, and my sleep
fled from my eyes. 41 These twenty years I
have been in your house. [d]I served you
fourteen years for your two daughters, and
six years for your flock, and [e]you have
changed my wages ten times. 42 [f]If the God
of my father, the God of Abraham and the
[g]Fear of Isaac, had not been on my side,
surely now you would have sent me away
empty-handed. [h]God saw my affliction and
the labor of my hands and [i]rebuked you
last night."
43 Then Laban answered and said to
Jacob, "The daughters are my daughters,
the children are my children, the flocks
are my flocks, and all that you see is mine.

[1] The Hebrew for *your* is plural here

21 [p]Ex. 23:31; Ps. 72:8 [q]2 Kin. 12:17; Luke 9:51
24 [r]See ch. 20:3 [s]ch. 24:50; Num. 24:13; 2 Sam. 13:22
26 [t]ver. 20
27 [t][See ver. 26 above]
28 [u]ver. 55; Ruth 1:9, 14; 1 Kin. 19:20; Acts 20:37
29 [v]Deut. 28:32; Neh. 5:5 (Heb.); Prov. 3:27; Mic. 2:1 [w]ver. 42, 53; ch. 28:13 [x]ver. 24
30 [y]ver. 19; Judg. 18:24
32 [z][ch. 44:9]
35 [a][Lev. 19:32]
37 [b]ver. 54
39 [c][Ex. 22:12]
41 [d]ch. 29:27, 28 [e]ver. 7
42 [f]Ps. 124:1, 2 [g]ver. 53 [h]See ch. 29:32 [i]ver. 29

31:23 his kinsmen. Laban had military superiority (v. 29).

31:24 God came. God sovereignly protected Jacob as He had Abraham (12:17; 20:3) and Isaac (26:8 and note).

31:27 mirth . . . lyre. Again Laban appealed to custom (cf. 29:26), this time complaining that the conventional departure ritual had not been followed (cf. 24:60).

31:29 It is in my power to . . . harm. See v. 23 and note.

31:34 Rachel . . . sat on them. The narrative ridicules the false gods—here the powerless idols were sat on by a menstruating woman (v. 35 note; Lev. 15:19–24).

felt all about. Trusting in their senses, neither Isaac nor Laban discovered the truth (27:18–27 note).

31:35 the way of women. The time of her menstrual period. The Mosaic law later specified that women were ceremonially unclean at this time (Lev. 15:19–24). As in ch. 27, the younger child deceived the father.

31:39 I bore the loss. According to ancient laws specifying the responsibilities of shepherds, such as those in the Code of Hammurabi (c. 1750 B.C.), Jacob should not have been liable for the loss.

31:42 If the God . . . on my side. See 28:15, 20 and notes.

the Fear of Isaac. Or, "the Awesome One of Isaac." See v. 53 and note.

sent me away empty-handed. An allusion to one of Laban's more conspicuous faults—his failure to pay workers their just wages (29:25; 31:7, 41).

31:43 all that you see is mine. Laban's claim shows that Jacob's fears had been justified (v. 31).

But what can I do this day for these my
daughters or for their children whom they
have borne? 44 Come now, [j]let us make a
covenant, you and I. [k]And let it be a witness between you and me." 45 So Jacob
[l]took a stone and set it up as a pillar.
46 And Jacob said to his kinsmen, "Gather
stones." And they took stones and made a
heap, and they ate there by the heap.
47 Laban called it Jegar-sahadutha,[1] but
Jacob called it Galeed.[2] 48 Laban said,
[m]"This heap is a witness between you and
me today." Therefore he named it Galeed,
49 [n]and Mizpah,[3] for he said, "The LORD
watch between you and me, when we are
out of one another's sight. 50 If you
oppress my daughters, or if you take wives
besides my daughters, although no one is
with us, see, [o]God is witness between you
and me."
51 Then Laban said to Jacob, "See this
heap and the pillar, which I have set
between you and me. 52 [p]This heap is a witness, and the pillar is a witness, that I will
not pass over this heap to you, and you will
not pass over this heap and this pillar to
me, to do harm. 53 The God of Abraham and
the God of Nahor, the God of their father,
judge between us." So Jacob swore by the
[q]Fear of his father Isaac, 54 and Jacob offered
a sacrifice in the hill country and called [r]his
kinsmen to eat bread. They ate bread and
spent the night in the hill country.
55 [4] Early in the morning Laban arose and
kissed [s]his grandchildren and his daughters and blessed them. Then Laban departed and returned home.

Jacob Fears Esau

32 Jacob went on his way, and the
angels of God met him. 2 And when
Jacob saw them he said, "This is God's
[t]camp!" So he called the name of that place
[u]Mahanaim.[5]
3 And Jacob sent[6] messengers before him
to Esau his brother in the land of [v]Seir, the
country of Edom, 4 instructing them, "Thus
you shall say to my lord Esau: Thus says
your servant Jacob, 'I have sojourned with
Laban and stayed until now. 5 I have oxen,
donkeys, flocks, male servants, and female
servants. I have sent to tell my lord, in
order that [w]I may find favor in your sight.'"
6 And the messengers returned to Jacob,
saying, "We came to your brother Esau,
and [x]he is coming to meet you, and there
are four hundred men with him." 7 Then
Jacob was [y]greatly afraid and distressed. He
divided the people who were with him, and
the flocks and herds and camels, into two
camps, 8 thinking, "If Esau comes to the
one camp and attacks it, then the camp
that is left will escape."
9 And Jacob said, [z]"O God of my father
Abraham and God of my father Isaac, O
LORD who [a]said to me, 'Return to your
country and to your kindred, that I may do
you good,' 10 [b]I am not worthy of the least

44 [j]ch. 26:28 [k]Josh. 24:27
45 [l]ch. 28:18
48 [m]ver. 44
49 [n]Judg. 11:29, 34
50 [o]Judg. 11:10; 1 Sam. 12:5; Jer. 42:5; Mic. 1:2; [Job 16:19]
52 [p]ver. 43, 44
53 [q]ver. 42
54 [r]ver. 37
55 [s]ver. 28, 43

Chapter 32
2 [t][Josh. 5:14; Luke 2:13] [u]Josh. 21:38; 2 Sam. 2:8; 17:24, 27; 1 Kin. 2:8
3 [v]ch. 36:8, 9; Deut. 2:5; Josh. 24:4
5 [w]ch. 33:8, 15
6 [x]ch. 33:1
7 [y]ch. 35:3
9 [z]ch. 28:13; 31:42, 53 [a]ch. 31:3, 13
10 [b][2 Sam. 7:18]

1 Aramaic *the heap of witness* 2 Hebrew *the heap of witness* 3 *Mizpah* means *watchpost* 4 Genesis 32:1 in Hebrew 5 *Mahanaim* means *two camps* 6 Or *had sent*

31:44 make a covenant. This covenant, or "treaty," was like the nonaggression treaties Abraham and Isaac made with the Philistines (21:27; 26:28), but unlike the covenant God made with Abraham (15:8).

31:50 wives besides my daughters. Terah's family valued the family structure, in contrast to the Canaanites (24:3, 4; 26:34, 35; 27:46; 28:9 and notes). This prohibition was found commonly in marriage contracts from the ancient Near East.

31:52 a witness. It was assumed that the terms of the treaty would be passed on faithfully through generations.

31:53 The God of Abraham . . . Nahor . . . father. The pagan Laban apparently regarded the God of Abraham as one of the gods of his family. Terah, the father of Abraham and Nahor, had probably been a moon-worshiper in Ur (11:27 note; Josh. 24:14).

Fear of his father Isaac. Not equating the God of Abraham with the God of Nahor, Jacob swore by the "Fear of his father Isaac" (v. 42 note), another name for the God of Abraham.

31:55 blessed. See 24:60; 27:7; 28:1 and notes.

32:1 angels of God. Jacob again encountered the angels of God whom he met at Bethel (28:12). These angelic encounters upon leaving and returning to the Promised Land frame Jacob's experiences with Laban (28:10–22 note) and attest to God's promise to be with and protect Jacob wherever he went (28:15). Faithful to His promise, God had been with Jacob—not only protecting him, but also remaking his character. The formerly prayerless and ambitiously deceptive Jacob was now a humble man of prayer (vv. 9–12).

32:2 Mahanaim. See text note. Jacob may have had in mind both his camp and God's camp, a heavenly shield and escort. As Bethel was the house of God and the gate of heaven (28:17), Mahanaim was God's camp on earth. Mahanaim later served as a capital for Saul's son Ishbosheth (2 Sam. 2:8) and as a refuge for David during Absalom's rebellion (2 Sam. 17:24). Mahanaim was situated east of the Jordan River near the River Jabbok, but its precise location is uncertain.

32:3 Seir. See 25:25 and note.

32:4, 5 Jacob's humble manner of address toward his brother and former rival suggests that his character change was real (v. 1 note). Like Abraham with Lot (13:8, 9), Jacob did not insist on his covenantal privileges but left the matter in God's hands.

32:6 four hundred men. Jacob had reason to fear (14:14; 27:40, 41), yet he had survived Laban's stronger forces with God's help (31:29 and note).

32:9 Jacob said. Jacob's first recorded prayer (vv. 9–12) stands between the two presents to Esau (vv. 3–8, 13–21). This structure suggests that he trusted God to prosper his two gifts.

32:10 I am not worthy. A spiritual transformation had taken place in Jacob: he submitted to Esau and recognized his unworthiness before God.

of all the deeds of steadfast love and all the
faithfulness that you have shown to your
servant, for with only my staff I crossed this
Jordan, and now I have become two
camps. 11 Please deliver me from the hand
of my brother, from the hand of Esau, for [c]I
fear him, that he may come and attack me,
the mothers with the children. 12 But [d]you
said, 'I will surely do you good, and make
your offspring as the sand of the sea, which
cannot be numbered for multitude.'"
13 So he stayed there that night, and from
what he had with him he took [e]a present
for his brother Esau, 14 two hundred female
goats and twenty male goats, two hundred
ewes and twenty rams, 15 thirty milking
camels and their calves, forty cows and ten
bulls, twenty female donkeys and ten male
donkeys. 16 These he handed over to his
servants, every drove by itself, and said to
his servants, "Pass on ahead of me and put
a space between drove and drove." 17 He
instructed the first, "When Esau my brother meets you and asks you, 'To whom do
you belong? Where are you going? And
whose are these ahead of you?' 18 then you
shall say, 'They belong to your servant
Jacob. They are a present sent to my lord
Esau. And moreover, he is behind us.'"
19 He likewise instructed the second and
the third and all who followed the droves,
"You shall say the same thing to Esau when
you find him, 20 and you shall say,
'Moreover, your servant Jacob is behind
us.'" For he thought, "I may appease him[1]
with the present that goes ahead of me,
and afterward I shall see his face. Perhaps
he will accept me."[2] 21 So the present
passed on ahead of him, and he himself
stayed that night in the camp.

11 [c][Prov. 18:19]
12 [d]ch. 28:13-15
13 [e]ch. 43:11; [Prov. 17:8; 18:16; 19:6; 21:14]

Jacob Wrestles with God

22 The same night he arose and took his
two wives, his two female servants, and his
eleven children, and crossed the ford of the
[f]Jabbok. 23 He took them and sent them
across the stream, and everything else that
he had. 24 And Jacob was left alone. And [g]a
man wrestled with him until the breaking
of the day. 25 When the man saw that he
did not prevail against Jacob, he touched
his hip socket, and Jacob's hip was put out
of joint as he wrestled with him. 26 Then he
said, "Let me go, for the day has broken."
But Jacob said, [h]"I will not let you go
unless you bless me." 27 And he said to
him, "What is your name?" And he said,
"Jacob." 28 Then he said, [i]"Your name shall
no longer be called Jacob, but Israel,[3] for
[j]you have striven with God and [k]with men,
and have prevailed." 29 Then Jacob asked
him, "Please tell me your name." But he
said, [l]"Why is it that you ask my name?"
And there he blessed him. 30 So Jacob called
the name of the place Peniel,[4] saying, "For
[m]I have seen God face to face, and yet my
life has been delivered." 31 The sun rose

22 [f]Deut. 2:37; 3:16; Josh. 12:2
24 [g]Hos. 12:3, 4
26 [h][Luke 18:1]; See Matt. 15:21-28
28 [i]ch. 35:10; 2 Kin. 17:34 [j]Hos. 12:3, 4 [k]ch. 33:4
29 [l]Judg. 13:18
30 [m]ch. 16:13; Ex. 24:10, 11; Deut. 5:24; Judg. 6:22; 13:22; [Ex. 33:20; Isai. 6:5]

1 Hebrew *appease his face* 2 Hebrew *he will lift my face* 3 *Israel* means *He strives with God*, or *God strives* 4 *Peniel* means *the face of God*

steadfast love . . . faithfulness. Words often used to describe God's loyalty to His covenant promises (24:27; Ex. 15:13 note; Ps. 40:11; 61:7). Jacob now identified himself fully with God's covenant to Abraham and Isaac, and his faith rested firmly on God's covenant promises.

32:12 make your offspring as the sand. In faith Jacob applied to himself the language of the covenantal promise to Abraham (22:17; cf. 28:14).

32:13 a present. The Hebrew here connotes tribute, a gift expressing loyalty to a superior. See notes 33:3, 4 and 33:11.

32:14, 15 Five hundred fifty animals was an extravagant gift.

32:20 appease him. Lit. "cover his face," an expression meaning the covering over of guilt. Jacob was painfully aware that he had sinned against his brother.

32:22–32 In wrestling with Jacob, God appeared in human form and deprived Jacob of his natural strength, but Jacob emerged the victor by clinging to God for blessing.

32:24 a man wrestled with him. This mysterious Man was a theophany, a visible (and in this case tangible) manifestation of the God who is intrinsically invisible, the Angel of the Lord (16:7 note; Hos. 12:4). The Lord unexpectedly initiated the match.

32:25 he did not prevail. Though Jacob was apparently a man of considerable strength (29:2, 10), the Angel of the Lord accommodated His strength to Jacob's.

touched. God dislocated Jacob's hip, the wrestler's pivot of strength (v. 31). Having previously depended upon his wits and strength, Jacob's natural powers were now crippled. Every step he would take in the future would remind him of his dependence upon divine grace.

32:27 What is your name. See note 3:9.

32:28 Your name. See note 17:6.

Israel. See text note. The new name indicates that the elect patriarch had matured in his faith.

striven with God. The "man" is implicitly identified as God Himself (v. 30).

32:29 Why is it that you ask. In ancient times, a name was thought to express essential nature as well as identity. The divine name partakes of the sacredness of God's being (Judg. 13:18), and was to be reverenced (Ex. 20:7). The pagans believed that knowing the name of a god imparted ability to invoke that deity's power. Here, however, the divine name is withheld (cf. 28:13; Hos. 12:5), showing that the Lord's revelation of His name is a gracious act of divine initiative, not a response to human effort to invoke and control God.

32:30 Peniel. See text note. Peniel was located on the River Jabbok near the modern Tulul edh-Dhahab. The town was destroyed by Gideon (Judg. 8:8) and later fortified by Jeroboam I (1 Kin. 12:25).

delivered. Jacob's preservation during his "face-to-face" meeting with the almighty God confirmed his preservation during his imminent encounter with Esau, a mere human being (cf. v. 11).

upon him as he passed [n]Penuel, limping because of his hip. **32** Therefore to this day the people of Israel do not eat the sinew of the thigh that is on the hip socket, because he touched the socket of Jacob's hip on the sinew of the thigh.

Jacob Meets Esau

33 And Jacob lifted up his eyes and looked, and behold, [o]Esau was coming, and four hundred men with him. So he divided the children among Leah and Rachel and the two female servants. **2** And he put the servants with their children in front, then Leah with her children, and Rachel and Joseph last of all. **3** He himself went on before them, [p]bowing himself to the ground seven times, until he came near to his brother.

4 [q]But Esau ran to meet him and embraced him [r]and fell on his neck and kissed him, and they wept. **5** And when Esau lifted up his eyes and saw the women and children, he said, "Who are these with you?" Jacob said, [s]"The children whom God has graciously given your servant." **6** Then the servants drew near, they and their children, and bowed down. **7** Leah likewise and her children drew near and bowed down. And last Joseph and Rachel drew near, and they bowed down. **8** Esau said, "What do you mean by [t]all this company[1] that I met?" Jacob answered, [u]"To find favor in the sight of my lord." **9** But Esau said, "I have enough, my brother; keep what you have for yourself." **10** Jacob said, "No, please, if I have found favor in your sight, then accept my present from my hand. [v]For I have seen your face, which is like seeing the face of God, and you have accepted me. **11** Please accept my [w]blessing that is brought to you, because God has dealt graciously with me, and because I have enough." Thus he [x]urged him, and he took it.

12 Then Esau said, "Let us journey on our way, and I will go ahead of[2] you." **13** But Jacob said to him, "My lord knows that the children are frail, and that the nursing flocks and herds are a care to me. If they are driven hard for one day, all the flocks will die. **14** Let my lord pass on ahead of his servant, and I will lead on slowly, at the pace of the livestock that are ahead of me and at the pace of the children, until I come to my lord [y]in Seir."

31 [n]Judg. 8:8, 17; 1 Kin. 12:25
Chapter 33
1 [o]ch. 32:6
3 [p]ch. 18:2; 42:6; 43:26
4 [q]ch. 32:28 [r]ch. 45:14
5 [s]ch. 48:9; Ps. 127:3; Isai. 8:18
8 [t]ch. 32:16 [u]ver. 15; ch. 32:5
10 [v]ch. 18:5; 19:8
11 [w]2 Kin. 5:15 [x][2 Sam. 13:25, 27; 2 Kin. 5:23]
14 [y]ch. 32:3

[1] Hebrew *camp* [2] Or *along with*

32:32 to this day. The restriction against eating the sciatic tendon, mentioned elsewhere only in extrabiblical Jewish literature, commemorated this foundational event in the nation's history.

33:1 four hundred men. See note 32:6.

33:3, 4 Jacob greeted Esau as a vassal greets his patron in the ceremony of a royal court, with the deference appropriate to a superior—note the sevenfold obeisance (common practice in ancient Near Eastern court protocol, v. 3), the submissive address of a "servant" (v. 5) to his "lord" (vv. 8, 13), and the presentation of gifts of homage (vv. 10, 11). In contrast, Esau greeted Jacob as one brother greets another after a long separation (vv. 4, 9).

33:5 graciously given. As Jacob remembered his troubled history, he confessed God's unmerited kindness in giving him children (29:31–30:24) and prosperity (30:25–31:55).

33:10 present. See 32:13 and note.

like seeing the face of God. As at Peniel, when Jacob saw God's face by theophany and his life was graciously spared (32:30), so also now he saw the dreaded face of Esau and was graciously received.

33:11 my blessing. Jacob's statement recalls his earlier theft of the paternal blessing in ch. 27. Jacob here offered recompense out of the many blessings God had given him.

urged . . . took. The reconciliation was sealed by accepting the gift.

33:14 until I come to . . . Seir. Given his intention to travel to Succoth (v. 17), Jacob may have been speaking deceptively, but more probably Esau knew that this was Jacob's polite way of not contradicting him (cf. 23:11 note). Though reconciled, the brothers would live apart.

Jacob Returns to Canaan. After 20 years in Paddan-aram, located in Northern Mesopotamia, Jacob returned to Canaan. He met the angels of God at Mahanaim. At Peniel he wrestled with a messenger of the Lord and prevailed.

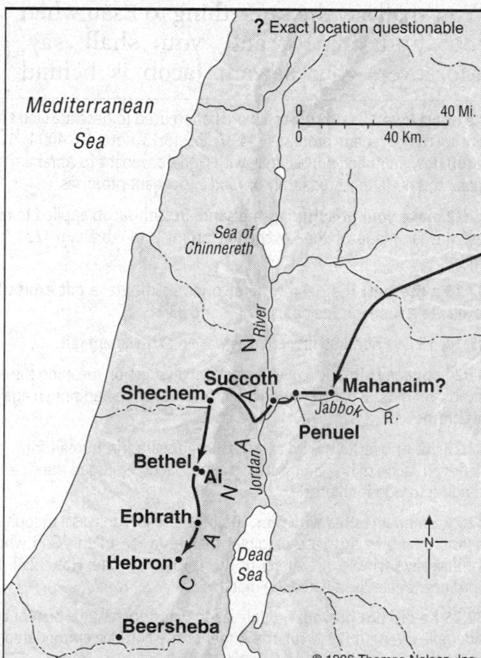

[15]So Esau said, "Let me leave with you some of the people who are with me." But he said, "What need is there? [z]Let me find favor in the sight of my lord." [16]So Esau returned that day on his way to [a]Seir. [17]But Jacob journeyed to [b]Succoth, and built himself a house and made booths for his livestock. Therefore the name of the place is called Succoth.[1]

[18]And Jacob came safely[2] to the city of [c]Shechem, which is in the land of Canaan, on his way from Paddan-aram, and he camped before the city. [19]And from the sons of [d]Hamor, Shechem's father, [e]he bought for a hundred pieces of money[3] the piece of land on which he had pitched his tent. [20]There he erected an altar and called it El-Elohe-Israel.[4]

The Defiling of Dinah

34 Now [f]Dinah the daughter of Leah, whom she had borne to Jacob, went out to see the women of the land. [2]And when Shechem the son of [g]Hamor the Hivite, the prince of the land, saw her, he seized her and lay with her and humiliated her. [3]And his soul was drawn to Dinah the daughter of Jacob. He loved the young woman and spoke tenderly to her. [4]So Shechem [h]spoke to his father Hamor, saying, "Get me this girl for my wife."

[5]Now Jacob heard that he had defiled his daughter Dinah. But his sons were with his livestock in the field, so Jacob held his peace until they came. [6]And Hamor the father of Shechem went out to Jacob to speak with him. [7]The sons of Jacob had come in from the field as soon as they heard of it, and the men were indignant and [i]very angry, because he [j]had done an outrageous thing in Israel by lying with Jacob's daughter, [k]for such a thing must not be done.

[8]But Hamor spoke with them, saying, "The soul of my son Shechem longs for your[5] daughter. Please give her to him to be his wife. [9]Make marriages with us. Give your daughters to us, and take our daughters for yourselves. [10]You shall dwell with us, and [l]the land shall be open to you. Dwell and [m]trade in it, and [n]get property in it." [11]Shechem also said to her father and to her brothers, [o]"Let me find favor in your eyes, and whatever you say to me I will give. [12]Ask me for as great a [p]bride price[6] and gift as you will, and I will give whatever you say to me. Only give me the young woman to be my wife."

[13]The sons of Jacob answered Shechem and his father Hamor deceitfully, because he had defiled their sister Dinah. [14]They said to them, "We cannot do this thing, to give our sister to one who is uncircumcised, for [q]that would be a disgrace to us. [15]Only on this condition will we agree with you—that you will become as we are by every male among you being circumcised. [16]Then we will give our daughters to you, and we will take your daughters to ourselves, and we will dwell with you and become one people. [17]But if you will not listen to us and be circumcised, then we will take our daughter, and we will be gone."

[18]Their words pleased Hamor and Hamor's son Shechem. [19]And the young man did not delay to do the thing, because

15 [z]ver. 8; ch. 34:11; 47:25; Ruth 2:13
16 [a]ch. 32:3
17 [b]Josh. 13:27; Judg. 8:5; Ps. 60:6
18 [c]Josh. 24:1; Judg. 9:1; Ps. 60:6; Acts 7:16
19 [d]Acts 7:16 [e]Josh. 24:32; John 4:5
Chapter 34
1 [f]ch. 30:21
2 [g]Acts 7:16
4 [h][Judg. 14:2]
7 [i]ch. 49:7 [j]Josh. 7:15; Judg. 20:6 [k]ver. 31; ch. 20:9; 2 Sam. 13:12
10 [l]ch. 13:9; 20:15 [m]ver. 21; ch. 42:34 [n]ch. 47:27
11 [o]See ch. 33:15
12 [p]Ex. 22:16, 17; 1 Sam. 18:25; [Deut. 22:29]
14 [q]Josh. 5:9

1 *Succoth* means *booths* 2 Or *peacefully* 3 Hebrew *a hundred qesitah*; a unit of money of unknown value 4 *El-Elohe-Israel* means *God, the God of Israel* 5 The Hebrew for *your* is plural here 6 Or *engagement present*

33:18–35:29 This final section of "the account of Isaac" (Introduction: Outline), like the closing section in "the account of Abraham" (22:20–25:11), records the transition of patriarchies. It is structured according to Jacob's itinerary back in the land, featuring deaths at various sites (which mark the passage of Isaac's generation), and important episodes in the "account" such as the sins of Reuben, Simeon, and Levi.

33:20 There he erected an altar. Jacob built his altar at Shechem where Abraham built his first altar in the Promised Land (see 12:6, 7). See also 28:20–22.

34:1–31 The threat to the covenant community at Shechem was severe. Hamor's proposal would have meant the assimilation of Jacob's family into the surrounding peoples (vv. 8–10; Num. 25:1–3 note).

The transition from Jacob's act of worship (33:20) to the depraved behavior of ch. 34 is striking. Instead of residing at Shechem (33:18, 19), perhaps Jacob should have fulfilled his vow at Bethel (28:22; 31:13; 35:1). There is no mention of God in this chapter and no separation from idolatry (35:1–5), a sad commentary on Jacob's spiritual leadership (35:4 note).

34:2 Hivite. See 9:25; 10:15, 17 and notes.

saw . . . seized . . . humiliated. This was forcible rape; Dinah did not consent. The Hebrew word translated "humiliated" is rendered "violated" in 2 Sam. 13:12, 14, 22, 32. The sequence "saw . . . seized" recalls 3:6 and 6:2.

34:7 in Israel. The nation of Israel. This description assumes the later development of the nation from the sons of Israel (cf. 49:28).

34:9 Make marriages. See note on ch. 34.

34:12 bride price. This was not the dowry given by the bride's family to the groom, but rather a reciprocal gift given by the groom to the bride's father (24:53; 1 Sam. 18:25).

34:13 sons of Jacob answered . . . deceitfully. Jacob reaped the whirlwind; his sons copied his deception (27:35, 36), but killing was their goal.

34:15 every male . . . circumcised. Jacob's sons sacrilegiously emptied the holy covenant sign of its religious significance (17:10, 11 and notes) and abused it for the purpose of inflicting vengeance.

he delighted in Jacob's daughter. Now [r]he
was the most honored of all his father's
house. 20 So Hamor and his son Shechem
[s]came to the gate of their city and spoke to
the men of their city, saying, 21 "These men
are at peace with us; let them dwell in the
land and [t]trade in it, for behold, the land is
large enough for them. Let us take their
daughters as wives, and let us give them our
daughters. 22 Only on this condition will the
men agree to dwell with us to become one
people—when every male among us is circumcised as they are circumcised. 23 Will
not their livestock, their property and all
their beasts be ours? Only let us agree with
them, and they will dwell with us." 24 And
all who went out of the gate of his city listened to Hamor and his son Shechem, and
every male was circumcised, all who [u]went
out of the gate of his city.
25 On the third day, when they were sore,
two of the sons of Jacob, [v]Simeon and Levi,
[w]Dinah's brothers, took their swords and
came against the city while it felt secure
and killed all the males. 26 They killed
Hamor and his son Shechem with the
sword and took Dinah out of Shechem's
house and went away. 27 The sons of Jacob
came upon the slain and plundered the
city, because they had defiled their sister.
28 They took their flocks and their herds,
their donkeys, and whatever was in the city
and in the field. 29 All their wealth, all their
little ones and their wives, all that was in
the houses, they captured and plundered.
30 Then Jacob said to Simeon and Levi,
[x]"You have brought trouble on me [y]by
making me stink to the inhabitants of the
land, [z]the Canaanites and the Perizzites.
[a]My numbers are few, and if they gather
themselves against me and attack me, I
shall be destroyed, both I and my household." 31 But they said, "Should he treat our
sister like a prostitute?"

God Blesses and Renames Jacob

35 God said to Jacob, "Arise, go up to
[b]Bethel and dwell there. Make an
altar there to the God who appeared to you
[c]when you fled from your brother Esau."
2 So Jacob said to his [d]household and to all
who were with him, "Put away [e]the foreign
gods that are among you and [f]purify yourselves and change your garments. 3 Then let
us arise and go up to Bethel, so that I may
make there an altar to the God [g]who
answers me in the day of my distress and
[h]has been with me wherever I have gone."
4 So they gave to Jacob all the foreign gods
that they had, and the rings that were in
their ears. Jacob hid them under [i]the terebinth tree that was near Shechem.
5 And as they journeyed, a terror from God
fell upon the cities that were around them,
so that they did not pursue the sons of Jacob.
6 And Jacob came to [j]Luz (that is, Bethel),
which is in the land of Canaan, he and all the
people who were with him, 7 and there he
built an altar and called the place El-bethel,[1]
because [k]there God had revealed himself
to him when he fled from his brother.

[1] *El-bethel* means *God of Bethel*

19 [r][1 Chr. 4:9]
20 [s]See Ruth 4:1
21 [t]ver. 10; ch. 42:34
24 [u][ch. 23:10]
25 [v]See ch. 49:5-7 [w]ch. 29:33, 34; 30:21
30 [x]Josh. 7:25 [y]Ex. 5:21; 1 Sam. 13:4; 27:12; 2 Sam. 10:6; 16:21; 1 Chr. 19:6 (Heb.) [z]ch. 13:7; 15:20, 21 [a]1 Chr. 16:19; Ps. 105:12
Chapter 35
1 [b]ch. 28:19 [c]ch. 27:43
2 [d]ch. 18:19; Josh. 24:15 [e][ch. 31:19; Josh. 24:23; 1 Sam. 7:3] [f]Ex. 19:10
3 [g]ch. 32:7, 24 [h]ch. 28:20; 31:3
4 [i]Josh. 24:26; Judg. 9:6
6 [j]ch. 28:19
7 [k]ver. 1

34:20 gate. See note 23:10.

34:24 all . . . listened to Hamor. The Shechemites probably neither knew nor cared about the religious significance of the rite; they agreed only to advance their own interests (v. 23).

34:25 killed all the males. Under the Mosaic law, Shechem's sin against Dinah would not have earned such excessive punishment (Deut. 22:28, 29). The action of Simeon and Levi prematurely (and illegitimately) anticipated the holy war that Israel was to wage against the inhabitants of the land (15:16; Ex. 23:27–31; Deut. 20:16–20).

34:27 plundered. By their unbridled, faithless, and rash revenge Simeon and Levi lost leadership and land in Israel (49:5–7).

34:30 I shall be destroyed. Jacob here displayed fear, not obedient faith (cf. 35:5).

35:1–29 Jacob's journey through time, as indicated by births (vv. 16–18), deaths (vv. 8, 19, 20), and genealogies (vv. 23–26), and through space, as indicated by itineraries (vv. 6, 16, 21, 27), is brought to completion because God was with him (v. 3). He returns to pay his vow at Bethel (vv. 1–8), is confirmed as the successor to God's Abrahamic promises (vv. 9–15), sees the twelve tribes of Israel safely settled in the Promised Land (vv. 16–26), and is reunited with his father and brother (vv. 27–29).

35:1 go up to Bethel. Jacob had a vow to fulfill (28:20–22; 34:1–31 note). God's revelation at Bethel (vv. 9–13) reiterates the covenant promises to Abraham, who himself had earlier worshiped at Bethel (12:8; 13:3, 4).

35:2 Put away. Repentance involves renouncing whatever hinders or tarnishes the worship and service of God. The covenant's primary requirement is exclusive allegiance to the Lord (Ex. 20:3–5; Josh. 24:14; Judg. 10:16).

foreign gods. See note 31:19; Josh. 24:23.

35:4 they gave to Jacob. Jacob recovered his spiritual leadership of the family (30:2 note; 34:1–31 note).

rings . . . ears. These were amulets associated with pagan worship (cf. v. 2).

terebinth tree . . . near Shechem. Probably the sacred tree associated with Abraham (12:6 and note).

35:5 terror from God. God's protection of Jacob's family by divinely induced panic (cf. Ex. 23:27; Josh. 2:9) was necessary because their reputation had changed from that of peaceful shepherds (34:21) to rapacious warriors (34:30).

35:7 built an altar. Jacob finally fulfilled his vow to the Lord (28:20–22).

8 And [l]Deborah, Rebekah's nurse, died, and
she was buried under an oak below Bethel.
So he called its name Allon-bacuth.[1]
9 God appeared[2] to Jacob again, when he
came from Paddan-aram, and blessed him.
10 And God said to him, "Your name is Jacob;
[m]no longer shall your name be called Jacob,
but [n]Israel shall be your name." So he called
his name Israel. 11 And God said to him, [o]"I
am God Almighty:[3] be [p]fruitful and multiply.
[q]A nation and a company of nations shall
come from you, and kings shall come from
your own body.[4] 12 [r]The land that I gave to
Abraham and Isaac I will give to you, and I
will give the land to your offspring after you."
13 Then God [s]went up from him in the place
where he had spoken with him. 14 And Jacob
[t]set up a pillar in the place where he had spoken with him, a pillar of stone. He poured
out a drink offering on it and poured oil on
it. 15 So Jacob called the name of the place
where God had spoken with him [u]Bethel.

The Deaths of Rachel and Isaac

16 Then they journeyed from Bethel.
When they were still some distance[5] from
Ephrath, Rachel went into labor, and she
had hard labor. 17 And when her labor was
at its hardest, the midwife said to her, "Do
not fear, for [v]you have another son." 18 And
as her soul was departing (for she was
dying), she called his name Ben-oni;[6] [w]but
his father called him Benjamin.[7] 19 So
[x]Rachel died, and she was buried on the
way to [y]Ephrath (that is, Bethlehem), 20 and
Jacob set up a pillar over her tomb. It is
[z]the pillar of Rachel's tomb, which is there
to this day. 21 Israel journeyed on and
pitched his tent beyond the tower of Eder.
22 While Israel lived in that land, Reuben
went and [a]lay with Bilhah his father's concubine. And Israel heard of it.
Now the sons of Jacob were twelve.
23 The sons of Leah: [b]Reuben (Jacob's firstborn), Simeon, Levi, Judah, Issachar, and
Zebulun. 24 The sons of Rachel: Joseph and
Benjamin. 25 The sons of Bilhah, Rachel's
servant: Dan and Naphtali. 26 The sons of
Zilpah, Leah's servant: Gad and Asher.
These were the sons of Jacob who were
born to him in Paddan-aram.
27 And Jacob came to his father Isaac at
[c]Mamre, or [d]Kiriath-arba (that is, Hebron),
where Abraham and Isaac had sojourned.
28 Now the days of Isaac were 180 years.
29 And Isaac breathed his last, and he died
[e]and was gathered to his people, old and
full of days. And [f]his sons Esau and Jacob
buried him.

Esau's Descendants

36 These are the generations of Esau
(that is, [g]Edom). 2 Esau [h]took his

8 [l]ch. 24:59
10 [m][ch. 17:5, 15] [n]ch. 32:28
11 [o]See ch. 17:1 [p]ch. 28:3; 48:4 [q]ch. 17:5, 6, 16; 26:4
12 [r]ch. 12:7; 13:15; 17:8; 26:3; 28:13
13 [s]ch. 17:22
14 [t]ch. 28:18; 31:45
15 [u]ch. 28:19
17 [v]ch. 30:24
18 [w][Luke 1:59, 60]
19 [x]ch. 48:7 [y]Ruth 1:2; 4:11; Mic. 5:2; Matt. 2:6, 16-18 [z]1 Sam. 10:2; [2 Sam. 18:18]
22 [a]ch. 49:4; 1 Chr. 5:1; [2 Sam. 16:22; 20:3; 1 Cor. 5:1]
23 [b]For ver. 23-26, see ch. 46:8-27; Ex. 1:2-4
27 [c]ch. 13:18; 23:19 [d]ch. 23:2; Josh. 14:15; 15:13
29 [e]ch. 15:15; 25:8 [f]ch. 25:9; 49:31
Chapter 36
1 [g]ch. 25:30
2 [h]ch. 26:34

[1] *Allon-bacuth* means *oak of weeping* [2] Or *had appeared* [3] Hebrew *El Shaddai* [4] Hebrew *from your loins* [5] Or *about two hours' distance* [6] *Ben-oni* could mean *son of my sorrow*, or *son of my strength* [7] *Benjamin* means *son of the right hand*

By such altar building, the patriarchal family acknowledged the covenant promises and consecrated the Promised Land. Regular worship was crucial if they were to maintain their religious separation from the surrounding Canaanites (ch. 34; Num. 25:1–3 and notes). See 12:7 and note; 13:18; 22:9; 33:20.

35:8 Rebekah's nurse. Scripture memorializes the death of the aged, faithful nurse of Rebekah, rather than the matriarch herself, probably because of Rebekah's deception (ch. 27).

35:9–15 God's revelation to Jacob after his return from Paddan-aram to Bethel confirmed the earlier promises of 28:13, 14. Using language that closely parallels the Abrahamic promises of nations, royalty, and land (17:5–8), God confirms His promises to Israel, the transformed Jacob (32:28), and indirectly to his twelve sons.

35:9 Paddan-aram. See note 25:20.

35:11 be fruitful. God's gracious blessing on all mankind (1:28; 9:1, 7) was focused particularly on the covenant community (28:3; cf. 47:27; Ex. 1:7).

35:12 land . . . offspring. See notes 12:7; 13:15.

35:13 God went up from him. This recalls Jacob's first meeting with the Lord at Bethel (28:13 note).

35:16–20 Near Ephrath, Rachel died giving birth to Jacob's twelfth son (30:1 note). The birth of Benjamin completed the patriarchal roster of the twelve tribes of Israel.

35:17 another son. Rachel's prayer was answered (30:24).

35:18 Ben-oni. See text note. Rachel's weeping for her child portended an anguished future for the nation (Jer. 31:15–17; Matt. 2:17, 18).

Benjamin. See text note. The Hebrew word *yamin* can refer both to the right hand and to the south (the Hebrews often described directions in terms of a person facing the east—the right hand thus pointed to the south). Jacob's other sons were born in Padan Aram, northeast of Canaan.

35:22 Reuben . . . lay with Bilhah. To gratify his lusts and perhaps to certify his leadership as firstborn over the next generation (cf. 2 Sam. 16:15–23; 1 Kin. 2:22). For his sin Reuben was deprived of his status as firstborn (48:1 note) and of his leadership (49:3, 4; Deut. 22:30), which Judah, Leah's fourth son, would assume instead (49:8–10).

35:26 sons . . . born . . . in Paddan-aram. Benjamin was not actually born in Paddan-aram, but after the return to Canaan (vv. 16–18). The statement must be taken as an informal review of the sons born to Jacob during this general period of his sojourn in Paddan-aram and the immediate aftermath (46:8–27 note). This association of the twelve sons with Paddan-aram perhaps underscores the similarities of Jacob's "exodus" from Paddan-aram and the Exodus of the twelve tribes from Egypt (31:3 note).

35:27–29 Isaac again appears in the narrative (28:5). His journey ended with a full length of years, but God passed him by after he tried to thwart God's purpose in the blessing (25:19 note).

36:1 generations. With this genealogy, or account, of Esau, a new section of Genesis begins (2:4 note).

Esau (that is, Edom). "Edom," derived from the Hebrew word for "red," was another name for Esau (25:25; 25:30 and note). The term was also appro-

wives from the Canaanites: Adah the
daughter of Elon the Hittite, [i]Oholibamah
the daughter of Anah the daughter[1] of
Zibeon the Hivite, 3 and [j]Basemath, Ishmael's daughter, the sister of Nebaioth.
4 And Adah bore to Esau, [k]Eliphaz; Basemath bore Reuel; 5 and Oholibamah bore
Jeush, Jalam, and Korah. These are the
sons of Esau who were born to him in the
land of Canaan.

6 Then Esau took his wives, his sons, his
daughters, and all the members of his
household, his livestock, all his beasts, and
all his property that he had acquired in the
land of Canaan. He went into a land away
from his brother Jacob. 7 [l]For their possessions were too great for them to dwell
together. [m]The land of their sojournings
could not support them because of their
livestock. 8 So Esau settled in [n]the hill
country of Seir. ([o]Esau is Edom.)

9 These are the generations of Esau the
father of [p]the Edomites in the hill country
of Seir. 10 These are the names of Esau's
sons: [q]Eliphaz the son of Adah the wife of
Esau, Reuel the son of Basemath the wife of
Esau. 11 The sons of Eliphaz were Teman,
Omar, Zepho, Gatam, and Kenaz. 12 (Timna
was a concubine of Eliphaz, Esau's son;
she bore [r]Amalek to Eliphaz.) These are the
sons of Adah, Esau's wife. 13 These are the
sons of Reuel: Nahath, Zerah, Shammah,
and Mizzah. These are the sons of Basemath, Esau's wife. 14 These are the sons of
[s]Oholibamah the daughter of Anah the
daughter of Zibeon, Esau's wife: she bore
to Esau Jeush, Jalam, and Korah.

15 These are [t]the chiefs of the sons of
Esau. [u]The sons of Eliphaz the firstborn of
Esau: the chiefs Teman, Omar, Zepho,
Kenaz, 16 Korah, Gatam, and Amalek; these
are the chiefs of Eliphaz in the land of
Edom; these are the sons of Adah. 17 These
are the sons of [v]Reuel, Esau's son: the
chiefs Nahath, Zerah, Shammah, and Mizzah; these are the chiefs of Reuel in the
land of Edom; these are the sons of Basemath, Esau's wife. 18 These are the sons of
[w]Oholibamah, Esau's wife: the chiefs
Jeush, Jalam, and Korah; these are the
chiefs born of Oholibamah the daughter of
Anah, Esau's wife. 19 These are the sons of
Esau ([x]that is, Edom), and these are their
chiefs.

20 [y]These are the sons of [z]Seir the Horite,
the inhabitants of the land: Lotan, Shobal,
Zibeon, Anah, 21 Dishon, Ezer, and Dishan;
these are the chiefs of the Horites, the sons
of Seir in the land of Edom. 22 The sons of
Lotan were Hori and Hemam; and Lotan's
sister was Timna. 23 These are the sons of
Shobal: Alvan, Manahath, Ebal, Shepho,
and Onam. 24 These are the sons of Zibeon:
Aiah and Anah; he is the Anah who found
the hot springs in the wilderness, as he
pastured the donkeys of Zibeon his father.
25 These are the children of Anah: Dishon
and [a]Oholibamah the daughter of Anah.
26 These are the sons of Dishon: Hemdan,
Eshban, Ithran, and Cheran. 27 These are
the sons of Ezer: Bilhan, Zaavan, and Akan.
28 These are the sons of Dishan: Uz and
Aran. 29 These are the chiefs of the Horites:
the [b]chiefs Lotan, Shobal, Zibeon, Anah,
30 Dishon, Ezer, and Dishan; these are the
chiefs of the Horites, chief by chief in the
land of Seir.

31 [c]These are the kings who reigned in the
land of Edom, before any king reigned over
the Israelites. 32 Bela the son of Beor
reigned in Edom, the name of his city being
Dinhabah. 33 Bela died, and Jobab the son
of Zerah of Bozrah reigned in his place.
34 Jobab died, and Husham of the land of
the Temanites reigned in his place.

2 [i]ver. 14, 18, 25
3 [j][ch. 28:9]
4 [k]ver. 10; 1 Chr. 1:35
7 [l]ch. 13:6 [m]ch. 17:8; 23:4; 28:4; 37:1; Heb. 11:9
8 [n]See ch. 32:3 [o]ver. 1, 19
9 [p]ver. 43
10 [q]ver. 4
12 [r]Num. 24:20; 1 Sam. 15:2, 3
14 [s]ver. 2
15 [t]Ex. 15:15 [u]ver. 11, 12
17 [v]ver. 13
18 [w]ver. 14
19 [x]ver. 1, 8
20 [y]For ver. 20-28, see 1 Chr. 1:38-42 [z]ch. 14:6; Deut. 2:12, 22
25 [a]ver. 2
29 [b]ver. 20
31 [c]For ver, 31-43, see 1 Chr. 1:43-54

1 Hebrew; Samaritan, Septuagint, Syriac *son*; also verse 14

priate for the land of Edom, with its red sandstone formations and soil.

36:2–8 This genealogy focuses on Esau's Canaanite wives and the children born in Canaan prior to his migration to Mount Seir.

36:2 took his wives. See 26:34; 27:46 and notes.

Canaanites. See 9:25; 10:15–19. The word broadly covers the tribes in the land.

Adah. The names of Esau's wives here differ from those in 26:34; 28:9. The use of alternate names may account for some of the variation.

36:6 went into a land. Jacob's return to Mamre clinched Esau's decision to move permanently to Edom. Separated in spirit, Jacob and Esau were to be separated by geography as well (cf. 33:14 note).

36:9–14 This genealogy focuses on Esau's twelve sons (vv. 2–8), not counting Amalek, the son of Eliphaz's concubine, Timna (v. 12).

36:15–19 This list shows the transition of Esau's descendants from a family to a tribal structure.

36:20–30 This genealogy presents the aboriginal inhabitants of Mount Seir whom the sons of Esau destroyed (Deut. 2:22) and, in other cases, married (vv. 22, 25).

36:31–39 The list shows Edom's transition from tribal structure to designated kingship.

36:31 before any king reigned over the Israelites. See Introduction: Date and Occasion.

35 Husham died, and Hadad the son of Bedad, who defeated Midian in the country of Moab, reigned in his place, the name of his city being Avith. 36 Hadad died, and Samlah of Masrekah reigned in his place. 37 Samlah died, and Shaul of [d]Rehoboth on the Euphrates[1] reigned in his place. 38 Shaul died, and Baal-hanan the son of Achbor reigned in his place. 39 Baal-hanan the son of Achbor died, and Hadar reigned in his place, the name of his city being Pau; his wife's name was Mehetabel, the daughter of Matred, daughter of Mezahab.

40 These are the names of the chiefs of Esau, according to their clans and their dwelling places, by their names: the chiefs Timna, Alvah, Jetheth, 41 Oholibamah, Elah, [e]Pinon, 42 Kenaz, Teman, Mibzar, 43 Magdiel, and Iram; these are the chiefs of Edom (that is, Esau, the father of [f]Edom), according to their dwelling places in the land of their possession.

Joseph's Dreams

37 Jacob lived in [g]the land of his father's sojournings, in the land of Canaan.

2 These are the generations of Jacob.

Joseph, being seventeen years old, was pasturing the flock with his brothers. He was a boy with the sons of Bilhah and Zilpah, his father's wives. And Joseph brought [h]a bad report of them to their father. 3 Now Israel loved Joseph more than any other of his sons, because he was [i]the son of his old age. And he made him [j]a robe of many colors.[2] 4 But when his brothers saw that their father loved him more than all his brothers, they hated him and could not speak peacefully to him.

5 Now Joseph had a dream, and when he told it to his brothers they hated him even more. 6 He said to them, "Hear this dream that I have dreamed: 7 Behold, we were binding sheaves in the field, and behold, [k]my sheaf arose and stood upright. And behold, your sheaves gathered around it and [l]bowed down to my sheaf." 8 His brothers said to him, "Are you indeed to reign over us? Or are you indeed to rule over us?" So they hated him even more for his dreams and for his words.

9 Then he dreamed another dream and told it to his brothers and said, "Behold, I have dreamed another dream. Behold, the sun, the moon, and eleven stars were bowing down to me." 10 But when he told it to his father and to his brothers, his father rebuked him and said to him, "What is this dream that you have dreamed? Shall I and [m]your mother and your brothers indeed come [n]to bow ourselves to the ground before you?" 11 And [o]his brothers were jealous of him, [p]but his father kept the saying in mind.

37 [d][ch. 26:22]
41 [e][Num. 33:42]
43 [f]ver. 9
Chapter 37
1 [g]See ch. 36:7
2 [h][1 Sam. 2:23, 24]
3 [i]ch. 44:20 [j]ver. 23, 32
7 [k]ch. 42:6, 9 [l]ch. 43:23; 44:14
10 [m][ch. 35:18] [n]ver. 7, 9
11 [o]Acts 7:9 [p][Luke 2:19, 51]

1 Hebrew *the River* 2 See Septuagint, Vulgate; or (with Syriac) *a robe with long sleeves*. The meaning of the Hebrew is uncertain; also verses 23, 32

37:2–50:26 The final section of Genesis, "the generations of Jacob," begins. It starts on a negative note with the shattering of the covenant family's peace (ch. 37) and their intermarriage with the Canaanites (ch. 38), but concludes with the family's reconciliation and preservation in Egypt.

Just as Jacob figured prominently in the "account of Isaac," so also does Joseph in the "generations of Jacob." God used Joseph, the rejected, godly brother, to save and reconcile the covenant family (45:5–8; 50:24). Though the striking parallels are not developed in the New Testament, the Christian church has traditionally viewed Joseph as a type of Christ. Godly Joseph, beloved by his father (37:3; cf. Mark 1:11), was sent to his brothers, but was then sold for twenty pieces of silver (37:28; cf. Matt. 26:15). After suffering persecution and temptation (37:18–36; 39:7–20; cf. Matt. 4:1–11), righteous Joseph was exalted as lord over his brothers (37:5–11; 41:37–45; 42:6; cf. Phil. 2:9, 10).

37:2 the generations of Jacob. See note 2:4.

sons of Bilhah and Zilpah. Dan, Naphtali, Gad, and Asher (30:4–13).

37:3 loved. Parental favoritism again promoted family discord, deception, and the disappearance of the preferred son, but God graciously used it to achieve His good purpose (cf. 25:28).

old age. See 30:22–24.

robe of many colors. A sign of Joseph's preferential status (cf. 2 Sam. 13:18), and a galling reminder to Joseph's brothers of their father's favoritism. The exact nature of the coat is uncertain. The rendering "of many colors" reflects the Septuagint (Greek Old Testament) translation. Some suggest that the Hebrew means a "long coat with sleeves."

37:4 could not speak peacefully to him. Or, "could not greet him with peace." The greeting, or salutation, was a crucial element of ancient etiquette (cf. 1 Sam. 25:6). Such a failure to extend the greeting indicated the depth of their animosity.

37:5 dream. As in certain other Genesis narratives, the key to the Joseph story is given in an opening revelation (cf. 12:1–3; 25:22, 23). This prophetic dream shows that God's sovereign purpose lay behind all the events of the narrative (45:5–8). See note 20:3.

37:7 bowed down. See 42:6; 43:26; 44:14.

37:8 reign. Their rhetorical question was later answered when Joseph came to rule "over all the land of Egypt" (41:43) and then over the covenant family living in Egypt. Joseph's status as head of the covenant family was confirmed when he received "the birthright" from his father Jacob (1 Chr. 5:2; cf. Deut. 33:16).

37:9 another dream. The reiteration of the theme in Joseph's second dream, like the similar repetition in Pharaoh's dreams (41:1–7), shows that the matter was determined by God and would quickly come to pass (41:32).

37:10 mother. Probably a reference to Joseph's stepmother Leah; his mother Rachel had earlier died in childbirth (35:16–20).

37:11 kept the saying in mind. This statement perhaps anticipates Jacob's later decision to give Joseph the birthright and double portion (v. 8 note; 48:5, 6).

Joseph Sold by His Brothers

12 Now his brothers went to pasture their
father's flock near [q]Shechem. 13 And Israel
said to Joseph, "Are not your brothers pasturing the flock at Shechem? Come, I will
send you to them." And he said to him,
"Here I am." 14 So he said to him, "Go now,
see if it is well with your brothers and with
the flock, and bring me word." So he sent
him from the Valley of [r]Hebron, and he
came to Shechem. 15 And a man found him
wandering in the fields. And the man asked
him, "What are you seeking?" 16 "I am seeking my brothers," he said. "Tell me, please,
where they are pasturing the flock." 17 And
the man said, "They have gone away, for I
heard them say, 'Let us go to [s]Dothan.'" So
Joseph went after his brothers and found
them at [s]Dothan.
18 They saw him from afar, and before he
came near to them [t]they conspired against
him to kill him. 19 They said to one another, "Here comes this dreamer. 20 Come
now, [u]let us kill him and throw him into
one of the pits.[1] Then we will say that a
fierce animal has devoured him, and we
will see what will become of his dreams."
21 But when [v]Reuben heard it, he rescued
him out of their hands, saying, "Let us not
take his life." 22 And Reuben said to them,
"Shed no blood; cast him into this pit here
in the wilderness, but do not lay a hand on
him"—[w]that he might rescue him out of
their hand to restore him to his father. 23 So
when Joseph came to his brothers, they
stripped him of his robe, [x]the robe of many
colors that he wore. 24 And they took him
and [y]cast him into a pit. The pit was
empty; there was no water in it.
25 Then they sat down to eat. And looking
up they saw a [z]caravan of [a]Ishmaelites
coming from Gilead, with their camels
bearing [b]gum, balm, and myrrh, on their
way to carry it down to Egypt. 26 Then
Judah said to his brothers, "What profit is
it [c]if we kill our brother and conceal his
blood? 27 Come, let us sell him to the
Ishmaelites, and [d]let not our hand be upon
him, for he is our brother, our own flesh."
And his brothers listened to him. 28 Then
[e]Midianite traders passed by. And they
drew Joseph up and lifted him out of the
pit, and [f]sold him to the Ishmaelites for
twenty shekels[2] of silver. They took Joseph
to Egypt.
29 When Reuben returned to the pit and
saw that Joseph was not in the pit, he [g]tore
his clothes 30 and returned to his brothers
and said, "The boy [h]is gone, and I, where
shall I go?" 31 Then they took [i]Joseph's robe

12 [q]See ch. 33:18
14 [r]ch. 13:18; 35:27
17 [s]2 Kin. 6:13
18 [t][Ps. 37:12, 32]
20 [u]ver. 26
21 [v]ch. 42:22
22 [w]ver. 29, 30
23 [x]ver. 3
24 [y][Jer. 38:6; Lam. 3:53]
25 [z]Job 6:19; Isai. 21:13 [a][ver. 28, 36; ch. 39:1] [b]ch. 43:11; Jer. 8:22; 46:11
26 [c]ver. 20
27 [d][1 Sam. 18:17]
28 [e]ver. 36; Judg. 8:22, 24 [f]ch. 45:4; Ps. 105:17; Acts 7:9
29 [g]ch. 44:13; Num. 14:6; 2 Sam. 1:11; 3:31; Job 1:20
30 [h]ch. 42:13, 32, 36; 44:31; Jer. 31:15; Lam. 5:7
31 [i]ver. 23

[1] Or *cisterns*; also verses 22, 24 [2] A *shekel* was about 2/5 ounce or 11 grams

37:15 wandering in the fields. Because of this divinely ordained delay the Ishmaelites arrived at just the right time (vv. 21–28).

37:21 Reuben . . . rescued him. As the eldest brother (29:32), Reuben assumed leadership in Jacob's absence and was responsible for the safety of his brothers (vv. 29, 30).

37:25 they sat down to eat. The brothers later acknowledged the heartlessness of their behavior (42:21).

Ishmaelites. These traders are also identified as Midianites (v. 28). Both groups were descended from Abraham and had no doubt intermarried (25:2, 12).

37:27 sell him. Note the later prohibition in the Mosaic law against kidnapping (Ex. 21:16; Deut. 24:7).

37:28 twenty shekels. See Lev. 27:5.

37:30 where shall I go. Under such circumstances, Reuben dreaded returning to his father, to whom he must give an account (v. 21 note).

37:31–33 Note the irony of these verses. Having deceived his father Isaac with goat skins (27:9) and with Esau's clothing (27:27), Jacob here is deceived by goat's blood on his son's clothes.

Joseph Becomes a Slave in Egypt. Joseph followed his shepherd brothers from Hebron to Dothan, where they sold him to a caravan of Ishmaelites en route to Egypt.

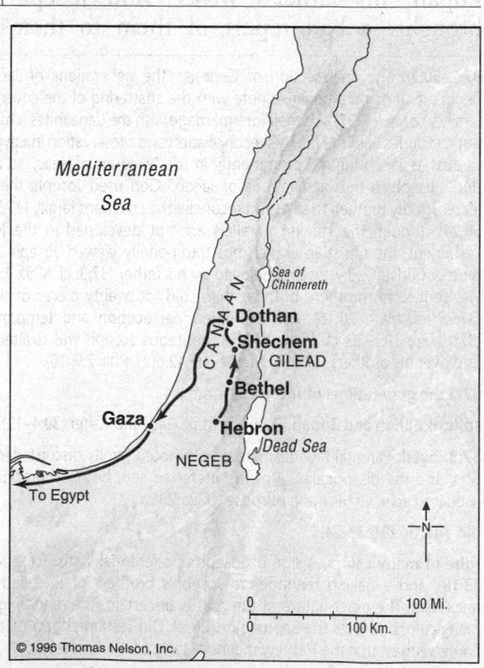

and slaughtered a goat and dipped the robe
in the blood. 32 And they sent the robe of
many colors and brought it to their father
and said, "This we have found; please identify whether it is your son's robe or not."
33 And he identified it and said, "It is my
son's robe. [j]A fierce animal has devoured
him. Joseph is without doubt torn to
pieces." 34 Then Jacob tore his garments
and put sackcloth on his loins and
mourned for his son many days. 35 All his
sons and all his daughters [k]rose up to comfort him, but he refused to be comforted
and said, "No, [l]I shall go down to Sheol to
my son, mourning." Thus his father wept
for him. 36 Meanwhile [m]the Midianites had
sold him in Egypt to Potiphar, an officer of
Pharaoh, [n]the captain of the guard.

Judah and Tamar

38 It happened at that time that Judah
went down from his brothers and
[o]turned aside to a certain [p]Adullamite,
whose name was Hirah. 2 There Judah saw
the daughter of a certain Canaanite whose
name was [q]Shua. He took her and went in
to her, 3 and she conceived and bore a son,
and he called his name [r]Er. 4 She conceived
again and bore a son, and she called his
name [r]Onan. 5 Yet again she bore a son,
and she called his name [r]Shelah. Judah[1]
was in Chezib when she bore him.
6 And Judah took a wife for Er his firstborn, and her name was Tamar. 7 But Er,
Judah's firstborn, [s]was wicked in the sight
of the LORD, and the LORD put him to
death. 8 Then Judah said to Onan, "Go in
to [t]your brother's wife and [u]perform the
duty of a brother-in-law to her, and raise
up offspring for your brother." 9 But Onan
knew that the offspring would not be his.
So whenever he went in to his brother's
wife he would waste the semen on the
ground, so as not to give offspring to his
brother. 10 And what he did was wicked in
the sight of the LORD, and he put him to
death also. 11 Then Judah said to Tamar his
daughter-in-law, [v]"Remain a widow in your
father's house, till Shelah my son grows
up"—for he feared that he would die, like
his brothers. So Tamar went and remained
[w]in her father's house.
12 In course of time the wife of Judah,
Shua's daughter, died. When Judah [x]was
comforted, he went up to [y]Timnah to his
sheepshearers, he and his friend Hirah the
Adullamite. 13 And when Tamar was told,
"Your father-in-law is going up to Timnah
to shear his sheep," 14 she took off her
widow's garments [z]and covered herself
with a veil, wrapping herself up, and sat at
the entrance to [a]Enaim, which is on the
road to Timnah. For she saw that Shelah
was grown up, [b]and she had not been given
to him in marriage. 15 When Judah saw her,
he thought she was a prostitute, for she
had covered her face. 16 He turned to her at
the roadside and said, "Come, let me come
in to you," for he did not know that she
was his daughter-in-law. She said, "What
will you give me, that you may come in to
me?" 17 He answered, "I will send you a

33 [j]ver. 20; ch. 44:28
34 [k][2 Sam. 12:17] [l]ch. 42:38; 44:29, 31
36 [m]ver. 28; [ver. 25; ch. 39:1] [n]ch. 40:3, 4; 41:10, 12
Chapter 38
1 [o]ver. 16; ch. 19:3; 2 Kin. 4:8 [p]1 Sam. 22:1; 2 Sam. 23:13; 1 Chr. 11:15; Mic. 1:15
2 [q][1 Chr. 2:3]
3 [r]ch. 46:12; Num. 26:19, 20
4 [r][See ver. 3 above]
5 [r][See ver. 3 above]
7 [s]1 Chr. 2:3
8 [t]Matt. 22:24; Mark 12:19; Luke 20:28; See Deut. 25:5-10 [u]See Deut. 25:5
11 [v][Ruth 1:12, 13] [w]Lev. 22:13
12 [x]ch. 24:67; 37:35; 2 Sam. 13:39 [y]Judg. 14:1
14 [z][ver. 19; ch. 24:65] [a]ver. 21 [b]ver. 26

1 Hebrew *He*

37:36 Potiphar. This Egyptian name means, "he whom [the sun god] Ra has given."

38:1–30 The shattered covenant family began to intermarry with the cursed Canaanites and risked the loss of their distinctive identity (34:1–31 note). God met this threat by sending Joseph ahead of them into Egypt where they were to be segregated (43:32; 46:34). There He preserved them until they had become a great nation and the iniquity of the Amorite was full (15:13–16). That the bizarre episode of Judah and Tamar should contribute to the genealogy of Jesus Christ is a vivid demonstration of God's grace (Matt. 1:3–16 note).

38:1 Judah went down. From Hebron in the hill country to the lowlands (35:27). The family further degenerates by disloyalty.

Adullamite. An inhabitant of the royal Canaanite city of Adullam (Josh. 12:15).

38:2 Canaanite. See 9:25, 26 and notes.

took her. See 24:3; 26:34, 35 and notes.

38:5 Chezib. A town near Adullam (v. 1 note). The mention of this Canaanite town, the name of which means "deceptive," underscores the theme of deception in the story of Jacob and his family.

38:8 raise up offspring for your brother. The first reference in Scripture to the widespread ancient custom of levirate marriage, whereby the brother of a deceased man (who lacked a heir) was expected to marry the widow. The offspring were considered children and heirs of the deceased. See note Deut. 25:5.

38:9 so as not to give offspring to his brother. Because the deceased Er was the firstborn, his heir would have inherited his position of family leadership and double portion (37:11 note). Desiring the place of first-born for himself, second-born Onan (v. 4) had intercourse with Tamar but prevented conception of a child. In so doing he was unfair to both his deceased brother and Tamar.

38:11 for he feared. Failing to perceive God's judgment on his folly and on his wicked sons, Judah superstitiously regarded Tamar as a wife who brings misfortune. Because Judah was not about to risk the life of his third son, Tamar's future (which depended on having offspring) was bleak.

38:13 to shear his sheep. Judah departed with his Canaanite friend Hirah (v. 1) to attend the sheep-shearing, an event marked by a great feast. This provided Tamar with an opportunity to effect her plan.

38:14 garments. Once again clothing plays a part in deception (37:31–33 note).

young goat from the flock." And she said,
"If you give me a pledge, until you send
it—" 18 He said, "What pledge shall I give
you?" She replied, [c]"Your signet and your
cord and your staff that is in your hand."
So he gave them to her and went in to her,
and she conceived by him. 19 Then she
arose and went away, and taking off [d]her
veil she put on the garments of her widowhood.
20 When Judah sent the young goat by his
friend the Adullamite to take back the
pledge from the woman's hand, he did not
find her. 21 And he asked the men of the
place, "Where is the cult prostitute[1] who
was at [e]Enaim at the roadside?" And they
said, "No cult prostitute has been here."
22 So he returned to Judah and said, "I have
not found her. Also, the men of the place
said, 'No cult prostitute has been here.'"
23 And Judah replied, "Let her keep the
things as her own, or we shall be laughed
at. You see, I sent this young goat, and you
did not find her."
24 About three months later Judah was
told, "Tamar your daughter-in-law [f]has been
immoral.[2] Moreover, she is pregnant by
immorality."[3] And Judah said, "Bring her
out, and [g]let her be burned." 25 As she was
being brought out, she sent word to her
father-in-law, "By the man to whom these
belong, I am pregnant." And she said,
"Please identify whose these are, [h]the signet
and the cord and the staff." 26 Then Judah
identified them and said, [i]"She is more righteous than I, since [j]I did not give her to my
son Shelah." And he did not know her again.
27 When the time of her labor came, there
were twins in her womb. 28 And when she
was in labor, one put out a hand, and the
midwife took and tied a scarlet thread on
his hand, saying, "This one came out first."
29 But as he drew back his hand, behold, his
brother came out. And she said, "What a
breach you have made for yourself!"
Therefore his name was called [k]Perez.[4]
30 Afterward his brother came out with the
scarlet thread on his hand, and his name
was called [k]Zerah.

Joseph and Potiphar's Wife

39 Now Joseph had been brought
down to Egypt, and [l]Potiphar, an
officer of Pharaoh, the captain of the guard,
an Egyptian, [m]had bought him from the
[n]Ishmaelites who had brought him down
there. 2 [o]The LORD was with Joseph, and he
became a successful man, and he was in
the house of his Egyptian master. 3 His
master saw that the LORD was with him and
that the LORD [p]caused all that he did to
succeed in his hands. 4 So Joseph [q]found
favor in his sight and attended him, and he
made him overseer of his house [r]and put
him in charge of all that he had. 5 From the
time that he made him overseer in his
house and over all that he had the LORD
blessed the Egyptian's house [s]for Joseph's
sake; the blessing of the LORD was on all
that he had, in house and field. 6 So he left

[1] Hebrew *sacred woman;* a woman who served a pagan deity by prostitution; also verse 22 [2] Or *has committed prostitution* [3] Or *by prostitution* [4] *Perez* means *a breach*

18 [c]ver. 25
19 [d]ver. 14
21 [e]ver. 14
24 [f]Judg. 19:2 [g]Lev. 21:9; [Deut. 22:21; John 8:5]
25 [h]ver. 18
26 [i]1 Sam. 24:17 [j]ver. 14
29 [k]ch. 46:12; Num. 26:20; 1 Chr. 2:4; Matt. 1:3
30 [k][See ver. 29 above]
Chapter 39
1 [l]ch. 37:36 [m]ch. 37:28 [n]ch. 37:25
2 [o]ver. 21; Acts 7:9; [ch. 21:22; 26:24, 28; 28:15; 1 Sam. 16:18; 18:14, 28]
3 [p]2 Chr. 26:5; Ps. 1:3
4 [q]ver. 21; ch. 19:19; 33:10 [r]ver. 8
5 [s][ch. 30:27]

38:18 Your signet and your cord. A cylinder seal, worn on a cord around the neck, was the insignia of a prominent man. He signed contracts by rolling the seal over the clay on which the contract was etched.

38:21 prostitute. Out of deference to Judah, his friend here used a more respectable term meaning "shrine prostitute" (a different Hebrew word is translated "prostitue" in v. 15). Cultic prostitution was integral to the Canaanite fertility religions, and was later a persistent snare to Israel (Deut. 23:17; 1 Kin. 14:24 text note; 2 Kin. 23:7 text note).

38:24 burned. A punishment later codified in the Mosaic law for a priest's daughter who prostituted herself (Lev. 21:9; cf. Deut. 22:21).

38:26 more righteous than I. Though she played on Judah's vice, Tamar was commended for her daring ruse to redress Judah's wrong and build up her family. Thus she became a heroine in Israel (Ruth 4:12).

did not know her again. To do so would have made him guilty of incest.

38:27–30 Another notable birth of twins where the identity of the firstborn is crucial to the story (cf. 25:21–34). Having identified one child as the firstborn with a thread, the midwife is surprised when the other twin is born first.

38:29 Perez. Named for the circumstance of his unusual birth (text note), Perez becomes part of the messianic line (Ruth 4:18–22; Matt. 1:1–6; Luke 3:33).

39:1–23 The narrative returns to Joseph in Egypt, where he survives a succession of injustices and is advanced because "the LORD was with him" (vv. 2, 23). God orchestrates an astonishing chain of events that move unerringly to save His people (Ps. 105:16–22). Joseph's initial privilege in Potiphar's house (vv. 2–6; cf. 47:6), his affliction and imprisonment (v. 20; cf. Ex. 1:8–14), and his deliverance (v. 21; 41:37–45; cf. Ex. 3:21; 12:31–42) prefigure the later experience of Israel as a whole in Egypt. See note 37:2–50:26.

39:1 Potiphar. See note 37:36.

Ishmaelites. See note 37:25.

39:2 The LORD was with Joseph. This repeated formula provides the theological theme of the story (vv. 3, 21, 23), and the link between Joseph and the patriarchs (28:15; cf. Acts 7:9). God's beneficent presence was experienced even in slavery, outside the land of blessing.

39:5 the LORD blessed the Egyptian's house. Once again the elect line is a means of blessing to those outside the covenant (12:3 note; 14:13, 24 and notes).

39:6 the food he ate. Probably a figure of speech for his private affairs.

all that he had in Joseph's charge, and
because of him he had no concern about
anything but the food he ate.
Now Joseph was [t]handsome in form and
appearance. 7 And after a time his master's
wife cast her eyes on Joseph and said, "Lie
with me." 8 But he refused and said to his
master's wife, "Behold, because of me my
master has no concern about anything in
the house, and [u]he has put everything that
he has in my charge. 9 He is not greater in
this house than I am, nor has he kept back
anything from me except yourself, because
you are his wife. How then can I do this
great wickedness and [v]sin against God?"
10 And as she spoke to Joseph day after day,
he [w]would not listen to her, to lie beside
her or to be with her.
11 But one day, when he went into the
house to do his work and none of the men
of the house was there in the house, 12 [x]she
caught him by his garment, saying, "Lie
with me." But he left his garment in her
hand and fled and got out of the house.
13 And as soon as she saw that he had left
his garment in her hand and had fled out
of the house, 14 she called to the men of
her household and said to them, "See, he
has brought among us a Hebrew to laugh
at us. He came in to me to lie with me, and
I cried out with a loud voice. 15 And as
soon as he heard that I lifted up my voice
and cried out, he left his garment beside
me and fled and got out of the house."
16 Then she laid up his garment by her
until his master came home, 17 and she
told him the same story, saying, "The
Hebrew servant, whom you have brought
among us, came in to me to laugh at me.
18 But as soon as I lifted up my voice and
cried, he left his garment beside me and
fled out of the house."
19 As soon as his master heard the words
that his wife spoke to him, "This is the way
your servant treated me," his anger was
kindled. 20 And Joseph's master took him
and [y]put him into the [z]prison, the place
where the king's prisoners were confined,
and he was there in prison. 21 But [a]the LORD
was with Joseph and showed him steadfast
love [b]and gave him favor in the sight of the
keeper of the prison. 22 And the keeper of
the prison [c]put Joseph in charge of all the
prisoners who were in the prison.
Whatever was done there, he was the one
who did it. 23 The keeper of the prison paid
no attention to anything that was in
Joseph's charge, because [d]the LORD was
with him. And whatever he did, the LORD
made it succeed.

Joseph Interprets Two Prisoners' Dreams

40 Some time after this, the [e]cupbearer
of the king of Egypt and his baker
committed an offense against their lord the
king of Egypt. 2 And Pharaoh was angry
with his two officers, the chief cupbearer
and the chief baker, 3 [f]and he put them in
custody in the house of the captain of the
guard, in the prison where Joseph was confined. 4 The captain of the guard appointed
Joseph to be with them, and he attended
them. They continued for some time in
custody.
5 And one night they both dreamed—the
cupbearer and the baker of the king of
Egypt, who were confined in the prison—
each his own dream, and each dream with
its own interpretation. 6 When Joseph came
to them in the morning, he saw that they
were troubled. 7 So he asked Pharaoh's officers who were with him in custody in his
master's house, [g]"Why are your faces
downcast today?" 8 They said to him, [h]"We
have had dreams, and there is no one to
interpret them." And Joseph said to them,
[i]"Do not interpretations belong to God?
Please tell them to me."

6 [t][ch. 29:17; 1 Sam. 16:12] **8** [u]ver. 4 **9** [v]2 Sam. 12:13; Ps. 51:4 **10** [w][Prov. 1:10] **12** [x][Prov. 7:13, 18]

20 [y]Ps. 105:18 [z]ch. 40:3, 5; [ch. 40:15; 41:14] **21** [a]ver. 2; Acts 7:9, 10 [b]Ex. 3:21; 11:3; 12:36 **22** [c]ch. 40:4 **23** [d]ver. 2, 3
Chapter 40
1 [e]Neh. 1:11 **3** [f][ch. 39:20] **7** [g][Neh. 2:2] **8** [h]ch. 41:15 [i]ch. 41:16; Dan. 2:28, 47

39:9 sin against God. Adultery was considered a great sin in the ancient Near East (20:9 and note), but Joseph was particularly conscious that he lived in the presence of God (cf. 2 Sam. 12:13; Ps. 51:4).

39:14 a Hebrew. See note 14:13; 41:12; 43:32.

39:19, 20 Though Potiphar's anger may have initially been directed at Joseph, his subsequent action indicates that he doubted his wife's accusation. Attempted rape of the master's wife by a slave would probably have earned a death sentence, but Joseph's punishment (confinement with the king's prisoners) was relatively mild.

39:21 gave him favor. God similarly commended the Israelites to the Egyptians before the Exodus (Ex. 3:21; 11:3; 12:36).

40:3 custody. They were awaiting Pharaoh's sentence.

40:8 dreams. See notes 20:3 and 37:9. The three sets of dreams, to Joseph (37:5–11), to the cupbearer and baker (ch. 40), and to Pharaoh (ch. 41), show God's sovereign control (41:28).

no one to interpret. Dreams were valued in the ancient Near East as a means of discerning the future; professional dream interpreters were often employed by royal courts.

interpretations belong to God. Joseph corrects the pagan beliefs of the Egyptian prisoners by acknowledging that God alone is the source of reliable interpretation, and that He bestows the gift of interpretation as He pleases (41:16; Dan. 2:24–49).

tell them to me. Joseph recognized himself as a prophet (37:5–11).

9 So the chief cupbearer told his dream to
Joseph and said to him, "In my dream
there was a vine before me, 10 and on the
vine there were three branches. As soon as
it budded, its blossoms shot forth, and the
clusters ripened into grapes. 11 Pharaoh's
cup was in my hand, and I took the grapes
and pressed them into Pharaoh's cup and
placed the cup in Pharaoh's hand." 12 Then
Joseph said to him, [j]"This is its interpretation: [k]the three branches are three days.
13 In three days Pharaoh will [l]lift up your
head and restore you to your office, and
you shall place Pharaoh's cup in his hand
as formerly, when you were his cupbearer.
14 Only remember me, when it is well with
you, and please do me the kindness to
mention me to Pharaoh, and so get me out
of this house. 15 For [m]I was indeed stolen
out of the land of the Hebrews, and [n]here
also I have done nothing that they should
put me into the pit."

16 When the chief baker saw that the
interpretation was favorable, he said to
Joseph, "I also had a dream: there were
three cake baskets on my head, 17 and in
the uppermost basket there were all sorts
of baked food for Pharaoh, but the birds
were eating it out of the basket on my
head." 18 And Joseph answered and said,
[o]"This is its interpretation: the three baskets are three days. 19 [p]In three days
Pharaoh will lift up your head—from
you!—and [q]hang you on a tree. And the
birds will eat the flesh from you."

20 On the third day, which was Pharaoh's
[r]birthday, he made a feast for all his servants and [s]lifted up the head of the chief
cupbearer and the head of the chief baker
among his servants. 21 [t]He restored the
chief cupbearer to his position, and [u]he
placed the cup in Pharaoh's hand. 22 But he
[v]hanged the chief baker, as Joseph had
interpreted to them. 23 Yet the chief cupbearer did not remember Joseph, but forgot
him.

Joseph Interprets Pharaoh's Dreams

41 After two whole years, Pharaoh
dreamed that he was standing by the
Nile, 2 and behold, there came up out of
the Nile seven cows attractive and plump,
and they fed in the reed grass. 3 And
behold, seven other cows, ugly and thin,
came up out of the Nile after them, and
stood by the other cows on the bank of the
Nile. 4 And the ugly, thin cows ate up the
seven attractive, plump cows. And Pharaoh
awoke. 5 And he fell asleep and dreamed a
second time. And behold, seven ears of
grain, plump and good, were growing on
one stalk. 6 And behold, after them sprouted seven ears, thin and [w]blighted by the
east wind. 7 And the thin ears swallowed up
the seven plump, full ears. And Pharaoh
awoke, and behold, it was a dream. 8 So in
the morning [x]his spirit was troubled, and
he sent and called for all the [y]magicians of
Egypt and all its wise men. Pharaoh told
them his dreams, but there was none who
could interpret them to Pharaoh.

9 Then the chief cupbearer said to
Pharaoh, "I remember my offenses today.
10 When Pharaoh was [z]angry with his servants [a]and put me and the chief baker in
custody in the house of the captain of the
guard, 11 [b]we dreamed on the same night,
he and I, each having a dream with its own

12 [j]ver. 18; ch. 41:12; [Dan. 2:36] [k][ch. 41:26, 27]
13 [l]2 Kin. 25:27; Jer. 52:31; [ver. 19, 20, 22; Ps. 3:3]
15 [m]ch. 37:28 [n]ch. 39:20
18 [o]See ver. 12
19 [p]ver. 13 [q]ver. 22
20 [r]Matt. 14:6; Mark 6:21 [s]ver. 13, 19
21 [t]ver. 13 [u]Neh. 2:1
22 [v]ver. 19
Chapter 41
6 [w][Ezek. 17:10; 19:12]; Hos. 13:15
8 [x]Ps. 77:4; Dan. 2:1, 3 [y]ver. 24; Ex. 7:11, 22; [Dan. 1:20; 2:2; 4:7; Matt. 2:1]
10 [z]ch. 40:2, 3 [a][ch. 39:20]
11 [b]ch. 40:5

40:13 lift up your head. A Hebrew idiom often meaning "restore to honor" or "release" (2 Kin. 25:27; Ps. 24:7). Here it may refer more particularly to a ritual audience with Pharaoh in which the servant is singled out for special attention (v. 20). Note the pun in v. 19, where a slight variation in the Hebrew gives the meaning "lift off your head" (perhaps a reference to execution by decapitation).

40:15 the pit. An exaggerated description reflecting the frustrated prisoner's point of view. Joseph's place of confinement with the king's prisoners was not excessively miserable (39:19–23 and notes).

40:16 on my head. Ancient Egyptian art portrayed a baker carrying a basket on his head.

40:20 lifted up the head. See note on v. 13.

40:22 he hanged the chief baker. Not a reference to hanging as a method of execution, but to the public display of the corpse after death (v. 13 note; Deut. 21:22 note).

41:1–57 God exalted faithful Joseph over all Egypt by giving him supernatural wisdom: the ability to interpret dreams (v. 16) and skill in political economy and statesmanship (vv. 33, 38). Joseph prefigured Moses at the founding of Israel, and Daniel at the end of Israel's monarchy. All three were oppressed captives who came to power in a hostile land by pitting God's wisdom against the wise of this world, displaying the superiority of God's wisdom and His rule over the nations. They prefigure Jesus Christ, the incarnate Wisdom of God (1 Cor. 1:30; Col. 2:3), who was raised from the dead to rule the world (1 Cor. 1:18–2:16; Rev. 12:1–5).

41:1 dreamed. People of the ancient Near East typically viewed kings as chosen representatives of the gods. Royal dreams were seen as particularly significant (40:8 and notes).

the Nile. The source of Egypt's fertility.

41:8 magicians. Like many other ancient rulers, the Egyptian pharaohs retained sorcerers, dream interpreters, and wise men (40:8 note; Ex. 7:11; Dan. 2:2) for counsel in important matters.

none who could interpret. See 40:8 and note.

interpretation. 12 A young Hebrew was
there with us, a servant of the captain of
the guard. When we told him, [c]he interpreted our dreams to us, giving an interpretation to each man according to his
dream. 13 And [d]as he interpreted to us, so it
came about. I was restored to my office,
and the baker was hanged."
14 [e]Then Pharaoh sent and called Joseph,
and they [f]quickly brought him [g]out of the
pit. And when he had shaved himself and
changed his clothes, he came in before
Pharaoh. 15 And Pharaoh said to Joseph, "I
have had a dream, and there is no one who
can interpret it. [h]I have heard it said of you
that when you hear a dream you can interpret it." 16 Joseph answered Pharaoh, [i]"It is
not in me; [j]God will give Pharaoh a favorable answer."[1] 17 Then Pharaoh said to
Joseph, "Behold, [k]in my dream I was
standing on the banks of the Nile. 18 Seven
cows, plump and attractive, came up out
of the Nile and fed in the reed grass.
19 Seven other cows came up after them,
poor and very ugly and thin, such as I had
never seen in all the land of Egypt. 20 And
the thin, ugly cows ate up the first seven
plump cows, 21 but when they had eaten
them no one would have known that
they had eaten them, for they were still as
ugly as at the beginning. Then I awoke.
22 I also saw in my dream seven ears growing on one stalk, full and good. 23 Seven
ears, withered, thin, and blighted by the
east wind, sprouted after them, 24 and
the thin ears swallowed up the seven
good ears. And [l]I told it to the magicians,
but there was no one who could explain it
to me."
25 Then Joseph said to Pharaoh, "The
dreams of Pharaoh are one; [m]God has
revealed to Pharaoh what he is about to
do. 26 The seven good cows are seven years,
and the seven good ears are seven years;
the dreams are one. 27 The seven lean and
ugly cows that came up after them are
seven years, and the seven empty ears
blighted by the east wind are also [n]seven
years of famine. 28 It is as I told Pharaoh;
[o]God has shown to Pharaoh what he is
about to do. 29 There will come [p]seven
years of great plenty throughout all the
land of Egypt, 30 but after them there will
arise [q]seven years of famine, and all the
plenty will be forgotten in the land of
Egypt. [r]The famine will consume the
land, 31 and the plenty will be unknown in
the land by reason of the famine that will
follow, for it will be very severe. 32 And the
doubling of Pharaoh's dream means that
the [s]thing is fixed by God, and God will
shortly bring it about. 33 Now therefore let
Pharaoh select a discerning and wise
man, and set him over the land of Egypt.
34 Let Pharaoh proceed to appoint overseers over the land and take one-fifth of
the produce of the land[2] of Egypt during
the seven plentiful years. 35 And [t]let them
gather all the food of these good years
that are coming and store up grain under
the authority of Pharaoh for food in the
cities, and let them keep it. 36 That food
shall be a reserve for the land against the
seven years of famine that are to occur in
the land of Egypt, so that the land may
not perish through the famine."

Joseph Rises to Power

37 This proposal pleased Pharaoh and all
his servants. 38 And Pharaoh said to his servants, "Can we find a man like this, [u]in
whom is the Spirit of God?"[3] 39 Then
Pharaoh said to Joseph, "Since God has
shown you all this, there is none so discerning and wise as you are. 40 [v]You shall be
over my house, and all my people shall
order themselves as you command.[4] Only

12 [c]See ch. 40:12-19
13 [d]ch. 40:21, 22
14 [e]Ps. 105:20 [f][Dan. 2:25] [g][1 Sam. 2:8; Ps. 113:7, 8]
15 [h]ver. 12; Dan. 5:16
16 [i]Dan. 2:30 [j]ch. 40:8; Dan. 2:22, 28, 47
17 [k]See ver. 1-7
24 [l]ver. 8; [Dan. 4:7]
25 [m][Dan. 2:28, 29, 45; Rev. 4:1]
27 [n][2 Kin. 8:1]
28 [o]ver. 25
29 [p]ver. 47
30 [q]ver. 54; ch. 45:6 [r]ch. 47:13
32 [s]Num. 23:19; Isai. 14:24; 46:10, 11
35 [t]ver. 48
38 [u]Num. 27:18; Dan. 4:8, 18; 5:11, 14
40 [v]Ps. 105:21; Acts 7:10

1 Or (compare Samaritan, Septuagint) *Without God it is not possible to give Pharaoh an answer about his welfare* 2 Or *over the land and organize the land* 3 Or *of the gods* 4 Hebrew *and according to your command all my people shall kiss the ground*

41:12 Hebrew. See 14:13 and note; 39:14; 43:32.

41:14 shaved . . . and changed his clothes. Unlike most ancient Near Eastern men (including the Hebrews), Egyptians were normally clean shaven. It would have been inappropriate for Joseph to appear before the king in prison rags (cf. 2 Kin. 25:29).

41:16 It is not in me; God will give. See note 40:8; cf. 2 Cor. 3:5.

41:25 God has revealed to Pharaoh. Both the dream and its interpretation were from God (40:8 and note). Joseph was inspired by God; he did not act as a magician. Neither Pharaoh nor his officials were in control; God and His servant were in charge, as they would be centuries later in the time of Moses (Ex. 7:1–5).

41:32 the doubling of Pharaoh's dream. See note 37:9.

41:38 Spirit of God. Joseph pointed to God's action in giving the dream (v. 16), and Pharaoh acknowledged God's power at work in Joseph (41:1–57 note).

41:39 none so discerning and wise as you. Joseph had just defeated Egypt's best wise men (cf. Ex. 8:18; Dan. 2:10, 27, 28).

as regards the throne will I be greater than
you." 41 And Pharaoh said to Joseph, "See,
[w]I have set you over all the land of Egypt."
42 Then Pharaoh [x]took his signet ring from
his hand and put it on Joseph's hand, and
[y]clothed him in garments of fine linen [z]and
put a gold chain about his neck. 43 And he
made him ride in his second chariot. [a]And
they called out before him, "Bow the
knee!"[1] Thus he set him [b]over all the land
of Egypt. 44 Moreover, Pharaoh said to
Joseph, "I am Pharaoh, and [c]without your
consent no one shall lift up hand or foot in
all the land of Egypt." 45 And Pharaoh
called Joseph's name Zaphenath-paneah.
And he gave him in marriage Asenath, the
daughter of Potiphera priest of On. So
Joseph went out over the land of Egypt.
46 Joseph was thirty years old when he
[d]entered the service of Pharaoh king of
Egypt. And Joseph went out from the presence of Pharaoh and went through all the
land of Egypt. 47 During the seven plentiful
years the earth produced abundantly,
48 and he gathered up all the food of these
seven years, which occurred in the land of
Egypt, and put the food in the cities. He
put in every city the food from the fields
around it. 49 And Joseph stored up grain in
great abundance, [e]like the sand of the sea,
until he ceased to measure it, for it could
not be measured.
50 Before the year of famine came, [f]two
sons were born to Joseph. Asenath, the
daughter of Potiphera priest of On, bore
them to him. 51 Joseph called the name of the
firstborn Manasseh. "For," he said, "God has
made me forget all my hardship and all my
father's house."[2] 52 The name of the second
he called Ephraim, "For God has [g]made me
fruitful in the land of my affliction."[3]
53 The seven years of plenty that occurred
in the land of Egypt came to an end, 54 and
[h]the seven years of famine began to come,
[i]as Joseph had said. There was famine in all
lands, but in all the land of Egypt there was
bread. 55 When all the land of Egypt was
famished, the people cried to Pharaoh for
bread. Pharaoh said to all the Egyptians,
"Go to Joseph. What he says to you, do."
56 So when the famine had spread over all
the land, Joseph opened all the storehouses[4] and [j]sold to the Egyptians, for the
famine was severe in the land of Egypt.
57 Moreover, all the earth came to Egypt to
Joseph to buy grain, because the famine
was severe [k]over all the earth.

Joseph's Brothers Go to Egypt

42 When [l]Jacob learned that there was
grain for sale in Egypt, he said to his
sons, "Why do you look at one another?"
2 And he said, "Behold, I have heard that
there is grain for sale in Egypt. Go down
and buy grain for us there, that we may
[m]live and not die." 3 So ten of Joseph's
brothers went down to buy grain in Egypt.
4 But Jacob did not send Benjamin,
[n]Joseph's brother, with his brothers, for
[o]he feared that harm might happen to him.
5 Thus the sons of Israel came to buy
among the others who came, for the famine
was in the land of Canaan.

41 [w]ch. 42:6
42 [x]Esth. 3:10; 8:2, 8, 10 [y][Esth. 8:15] [z]Ezek. 16:11; [Dan. 5:7, 29]
43 [a][Esth. 6:9] [b]ver. 40; ch. 42:6; 45:8, 9, 26
44 [c][Ps. 105:21, 22]
46 [d]1 Sam. 16:21; 1 Kin. 12:6, 8; Dan. 1:19
49 [e]ch. 22:17; Judg. 7:12; 1 Sam. 13:5; Ps. 78:27
50 [f]ch. 46:20; 48:5
52 [g][ch. 49:22; Hos. 13:15]
54 [h]Ps. 105:16; Acts 7:11 [i]ver. 30
56 [j]ch. 42:6; [ch. 47:14, 20, 24]
57 [k]ver. 54, 56
Chapter 42
1 [l]Acts 7:12
2 [m]ch. 43:8
4 [n]ch. 35:13 [o]ver. 38

[1] *Abrek*, probably an Egyptian word, similar in sound to the Hebrew word meaning *to kneel* [2] *Manasseh* sounds like the Hebrew for *making to forget* [3] *Ephraim* sounds like the Hebrew for *making fruitful* [4] Hebrew *all that was in them*

41:41–46 Joseph's installation as viceroy over Egypt consisted of a public act of installation (vv. 41–44), the conferring of a new name (v. 45), and the elevation to nobility by marriage (v. 46).

41:41 set you over all the land. Joseph, who had been faithful in little (39:4, 22), was put in charge of much (cf. Luke 16:10; 19:17).

41:45 Zaphenath-paneah. Joseph's role in Egypt was like that of Daniel in Babylon: both accepted pagan names without embracing pagan religion (Dan. 1:7).

Asenath. Her name means "belongs to [the goddess] Neit."

Potiphera. Probably a variant spelling of Potiphar (37:36 note).

On. Called Heliopolis in Greek, this city was a center for the worship of the sun god Ra (Jer. 43:13 text note); its high priest was one of the most prominent in ancient Egypt.

41:46 thirty years. Joseph had risen from slavery to become the king's second-in-command in a mere thirteen years (37:2).

41:51, 52 See text notes. As the names of his sons indicate, Joseph was ever mindful of God's hand upon him. The first commemorates God's preservation through great hardship (v. 51), the second memorializes the divine favor with echoes of the Abrahamic blessing (v. 52; cf. 17:6, 20; 28:3; 48:4; cf. Ps. 105:23, 24).

41:57 all the earth. The temporal salvation (from starvation) of the known world depended on one descendant of the patriarchs (12:3; 39:5 and notes). In mediating this blessing, Joseph prefigures the work of Christ (1 John 2:2). See note 37:2–50:26.

42:1–38 Joseph used the providential famine and his authority to help reconcile the shattered family. By confronting them with life and death (vv. 18, 20) he awakened their consciences to confess their guilt (vv. 21–24) and to protect Benjamin from harm (v. 37; 43:8, 9; 44:18–34). See note on chs. 43–45.

42:1 grain for sale in Egypt. See 12:10; 26:1, 2.

42:4 did not send Benjamin. Joseph's full brother had taken his place in his father's affections (37:3 and notes). The brothers' treatment of him and of their father would indicate whether there had been a spiritual change in them.

6 Now Joseph was governor [p]over the land. He was the one who sold to all the people of the land. And Joseph's brothers came and [q]bowed themselves before him with their faces to the ground. 7 Joseph saw his brothers and recognized them, but he treated them like strangers and [r]spoke roughly to them. "Where do you come from?" he said. They said, "From the land of Canaan, to buy food." 8 And Joseph recognized his brothers, but they did not recognize him. 9 And Joseph [s]remembered the dreams that he had dreamed of them. [t]And he said to them, "You are spies; you have come to see the nakedness of the land." 10 They said to him, "No, my lord, your servants have come to buy food. 11 We are all sons of one man. We are honest men. Your servants have never been spies."

12 He said to them, "No, it is the nakedness of the land that you have come to see." 13 And they said, "We, your servants, are twelve brothers, the sons of one man in the land of Canaan, and behold, the youngest is this day with our father, and one [u]is no more." 14 But Joseph said to them, "It is as I said to you. You are spies. 15 By this you shall be tested: by the life of Pharaoh, you shall not go from this place unless your youngest brother comes here. 16 Send one of you, and let him bring your brother, while you remain confined, that your words may be tested, whether there is truth in you. Or else, by the life of Pharaoh, surely you are spies." 17 And he put them all together in custody for three days.

18 On the third day Joseph said to them, "Do this and you will live, [v]for I fear God: 19 if you are honest men, let one of your brothers remain confined where you are in custody, and let the rest go and carry [w]grain for the famine of your households, 20 and [x]bring your youngest brother to me. So your words will be verified, and you shall not die." And they did so. 21 Then they said to one another, [y]"In truth we are guilty concerning our brother, in that we saw the distress of his soul, when he begged us and we did not listen. That is why this distress has come upon us." 22 And Reuben answered them, [z]"Did I not tell you not to sin against the boy? But you did not listen. So now [a]there comes a reckoning for his blood." 23 They did not know that Joseph understood them, for there was an interpreter between them. 24 Then he turned away from them and [b]wept. And he returned to them and spoke to them. And he took Simeon from them and bound him before their eyes. 25 [c]And Joseph gave orders to fill their bags with grain, and to replace every man's money in his sack, and to give them provisions for the journey. This was done for them.

26 Then they loaded their donkeys with their grain and departed. 27 And as [d]one of them opened his sack to give his donkey fodder at [e]the lodging place, he saw his money in the mouth of his sack. 28 He said to his brothers, "My money has been put back; here it is in the mouth of my sack!" At this their hearts failed them, and they turned trembling to one another, saying, "What is this that God has done to us?"

29 When they came to Jacob their father in the land of Canaan, they told him all

6 [p]ch. 41:41 [q]ch. 37:7, 9, 10
7 [r]ver. 30
9 [s]ch. 37:5, 9 [t]ver. 7, 30
13 [u]ver. 32; See ch. 37:30
18 [v]Lev. 25:43; Neh. 5:15
19 [w]ver. 33
20 [x]ver. 34; ch. 43:5; 44:23
21 [y][Job 36:8, 9]; See ch. 37:23-28
22 [z]ch. 37:21 [a]ch. 9:5; 2 Chr. 24:22; [1 Kin. 2:32; Ps. 9:12; Luke 11:50, 51]
24 [b]ch. 43:30
25 [c]ch. 44:1
27 [d]ver. 35; ch. 43:21 [e]Ex. 4:24; Jer. 9:2

42:6 bowed. To preserve their lives they unwittingly fulfilled Joseph's dream (37:5 and note).

42:7 like strangers . . . spoke roughly. As the rest of the narrative shows, Joseph was acting to ascertain his brothers' attitudes and to heal the breach between him and his brothers. A quick pardon would not have led to true repentance and spiritual healing within the family.

42:8 they did not recognize him. Joseph had grown from a boy of seventeen to a man of almost forty (41:46, 47, 54; 45:6 note). He had the appearance of an august Egyptian official (41:14, 41–43) and used an interpreter (v. 23).

42:11 sons of one man. They were a family unit, not spies of a nation bent on war (cf. Num. 13:2).

42:12 you have come to see. This interrogation, with its repeated accusations (cf. v. 9), was necessary for the ruse and to extract information out of them so that Joseph could take his next step (43:7).

42:13 they said. The brothers no doubt thought the added details strengthened their credibility.

42:15 by the life of Pharaoh. The ancients swore solemn oaths by the life of the king or name of a deity (2 Sam. 15:21; Deut. 6:13 note).

42:18–20 Joseph's presentation of a choice—life or death—had the desired effect (v. 21).

42:18 I fear God. Joseph assured the brothers that he would deal honestly with them (20:11 note).

42:21 In truth we are guilty. Though falsely accused of spying, they saw the Egyptian as the tool of God's higher justice, matching their punishment with their real crime against Joseph.

we did not listen. Their consciences awakened, the brothers' heartless behavior came back to haunt them (37:25 and note).

42:24 he . . . wept. With their confession of guilt, reconciliation was possible.

42:28 God has done. The first explicit mention of God by the brothers; they saw the hand of God at work behind their frightful circumstances (vv. 21, 22).

that had happened to them, saying, 30 "The
man, the lord of the land, [f]spoke roughly to
us and took us to be spies of the land.
31 But we said to him, 'We are honest men;
we have never been spies. 32 We are twelve
brothers, sons of our father. One [g]is no
more, and the youngest is this day with our
father in the land of Canaan.' 33 Then the
man, the lord of the land, said to us, [h]'By
this I shall know that you are honest men:
leave one of your brothers with me, and
take [i]grain for the famine of your households, and go your way. 34 Bring your
youngest brother to me. Then I shall know
that you are not spies but honest men, and
I will deliver your brother to you, and you
shall [j]trade in the land.'"

35 [k]As they emptied their sacks, behold,
every man's bundle of money was in his
sack. And when they and their father saw
their bundles of money, they were afraid.
36 And Jacob their father said to them, "You
have [l]bereaved me of my children: Joseph
is no more, and Simeon is no more, and
now you would take Benjamin. All this has
come against me." 37 Then Reuben said to
his father, "Kill [m]my two sons if I do not
bring him back to you. Put him in my
hands, and I will bring him back to you."
38 But he said, "My son shall not go down
with you, for [n]his brother is dead, and he is
the only one left. [o]If harm should happen
to him on the journey that you are to make,
[p]you would bring down my gray hairs with
sorrow to Sheol."

Joseph's Brothers Return to Egypt

43 Now the famine was [q]severe in the
land. 2 And when they had eaten
the grain that they had brought from
Egypt, their father said to them, "Go
again, buy us a little food." 3 But Judah
said to him, "The man solemnly warned
us, saying, 'You shall not see my face
unless your [r]brother is with you.' 4 If you
will send our brother with us, we will go
down and buy you food. 5 But if you will
not send him, we will not go down, for
the man said to us, 'You shall not see my
face, unless your brother is with you.'"
6 Israel said, "Why did you treat me so
badly as to tell the man that you had
another brother?" 7 They replied, "The
man questioned us carefully about ourselves and our kindred, saying, 'Is your
father still alive? Do you have another
brother?' What we told him was in answer
to these questions. Could we in any way
know that he would say, 'Bring your
brother down'?" 8 And Judah said to Israel
his father, "Send the boy with me, and we
will arise and go, that we may [s]live and
not die, both we and you and also our little ones. 9 I will be a pledge of his safety.
From my hand you shall require him. [t]If I
do not bring him back to you and set him
before you, then let me bear the blame
forever. 10 If we had not delayed, we would
now have returned twice."

11 Then their father Israel said to them,
"If it must be so, then do this: take some of
the choice fruits of the land in your bags,
and carry a present down to the man, a little [u]balm and a little honey, gum, myrrh,
pistachio nuts, and almonds. 12 Take double the money with you. Carry back with
you the money [v]that was returned in the
mouth of your sacks. Perhaps it was an
oversight. 13 Take also your brother, and
arise, go again to the man. 14 May [w]God
Almighty[1] [x]grant you mercy before the
man, and may he send back your other
brother and Benjamin. And as for me, [y]if
I am bereaved of my children, I am bereaved."

[1] Hebrew *El Shaddai*

30 [f]ver. 7, 9
32 [g]ver. 13
33 [h]ver. 15, 19, 20 [i]ver. 19
34 [j]ch. 34:10, 21
35 [k]ver. 27; ch. 43:21
36 [l]ch. 43:14
37 [m][ch. 46:9]
38 [n]ver. 13, 32, 36; ch. 37:33; 44:28 [o]ver. 4; ch. 44:29 [p]ch. 37:35; 44:31
Chapter 43
1 [q]ch. 41:54, 57
3 [r]ch. 42:20; 44:23
8 [s]ch. 42:2
9 [t]ch. 42:37; 44:32
11 [u]See ch. 37:25
12 [v]ch. 42:25, 27, 35
14 [w]See ch. 17:1 [x][Neh. 1:11] [y]ch. 42:36

42:34 you shall trade in the land. In order not to distress their aged father further, they changed Joseph's threat of death (vv. 18, 20) to a promise of economic opportunity.

42:37 Kill my two sons. Jacob did not accept Reuben's ill-considered proposal. Only the threat of starvation coupled with Judah's assurances would change his mind (43:1–14).

43:1–45:28 Joseph's ruse had already begun to move his brothers from indifference to integrity and loyalty toward one another (42:21, 22). This change is further manifested in Judah's offer of himself as surety (43:9) and in his offer to sacrifice himself in Benjamin's stead (44:33). Finally, Joseph makes himself known to his brothers and, seeing their sins in the light of God's purpose, he forgives them (ch. 45).

43:1–34 Through Joseph, the merciful (v. 14), providing (v. 23), and gracious (v. 29) God of the fathers begins to bring peace to the shattered family (vv. 23, 26–28). See note on ch. 42.

43:3 Judah. Another brother had to step forward after Jacob's definitive refusal to Reuben (42:37, 38; cf. 49:3, 4). With his leadership rebuffed, Reuben is henceforth eclipsed by Joseph (who assumes the firstborn's privileges, 37:8 note) and by Judah (who here takes Reuben's place of responsibility for the eleven brothers and whose royal tribe was to produce the Messiah, vv. 8, 9; 49:10).

43:8 live and not die. A reference to the severe famine (v. 1) that also recalls Joseph's threat (42:18–20, 34 and note).

43:11 a present. See note 32:13.

43:14 God Almighty. See note 17:1.

15 So the men took this present, and they
took double the money with them, and
Benjamin. They arose and went down to
Egypt and stood before Joseph.
16 When Joseph saw Benjamin with
them, he said to the [z]steward of his house,
"Bring the men into the house, and slaughter an animal and make ready, for the men
are to dine with me at noon." 17 The man
did as Joseph told him and brought the
men to Joseph's house. 18 And the men
were afraid because they were brought to
Joseph's house, and they said, "It is
because of the money, which was replaced
in our sacks the first time, that we are
brought in, so that he may assault us and
fall upon us to make us servants and seize
our donkeys." 19 So they went up to the
steward of Joseph's house and spoke with
him at the door of the house, 20 and said,
[a]"Oh, my lord, [b]we came down the first
time to buy food. 21 And [c]when we came to
the lodging place we opened our sacks,
and there was each man's money in the
mouth of his sack, our money in full
weight. So we have brought it again with
us, 22 and we have brought other money
down with us to buy food. We do not
know who put our money in our sacks."
23 He replied, "Peace to you, do not be
afraid. Your God and the God of your
father has put treasure in your sacks for
you. I received your money." Then he
brought Simeon out to them. 24 And when
the man had brought the men into
Joseph's house and [d]given them water, and
they had washed their feet, and when he
had given their donkeys fodder, 25 they prepared [e]the present for Joseph's coming at
noon, for they heard that they should eat
bread there.
26 When Joseph came home, they brought
into the house to him the present that they
had with them and [f]bowed down to him to
the ground. 27 And he inquired about their
welfare and said, "Is your father well, the
old man [g]of whom you spoke? Is he still
alive?" 28 They said, "Your servant our
father is well; he is still alive." And they
[h]bowed their heads and prostrated themselves. 29 And he lifted up his eyes and saw
his brother Benjamin, [i]his mother's son,
and said, "Is this your youngest brother,
[g]of whom you spoke to me? God be gracious to you, my son!" 30 Then Joseph hurried out, for [j]his compassion grew warm for
his brother, and he sought a place to weep.
And he entered his chamber and [k]wept
there. 31 Then he washed his face and came
out. And [l]controlling himself he said,
"Serve the food." 32 They served him by
himself, and them by themselves, and the
Egyptians who ate with him by themselves,
because the Egyptians could not eat with
the Hebrews, for that is [m]an abomination
to the Egyptians. 33 And they sat before
him, the firstborn according to his
birthright and the youngest according to
his youth. And the men looked at one
another in amazement. 34 [n]Portions were
taken to them from Joseph's table, but
Benjamin's portion was [o]five times as
much as any of theirs. And they drank and
were merry[1] with him.

Joseph Tests His Brothers

44 Then he commanded [p]the steward
of his house, [q]"Fill the men's sacks
with food, as much as they can carry, and
put each man's money in the mouth of his
sack, 2 and put my cup, the silver cup, in
the mouth of the sack of the youngest, with
his money for the grain." And he did as
Joseph told him.

16 [z]ver. 19; ch. 44:1, 4; [ch. 24:2; 39:4]
20 [a]ch. 44:18 [b]ch. 42:3, 10
21 [c]ch. 42:27
24 [d]See ch. 18:4
25 [e]ver. 11
26 [f]ch. 42:6; See ch. 37:5-11
27 [g]ch. 42:11, 13
28 [h]ver. 26
29 [i]ch. 35:18 [g][See ver. 27 above]
30 [j]1 Kin. 3:26; [Jer. 31:20] 30 [k]ch. 42:24
31 [l]ch. 45:1
32 [m]ch. 46:34; Ex. 8:26
34 [n][2 Sam. 11:8] [o][ch. 45:22]
Chapter 44
1 [p]ver. 4; See ch. 43:16 [q]ch. 42:25

1 Hebrew *and became intoxicated*

43:26 bowed down. See 37:5–11. At their first meeting they bowed in submission (42:6); here they bowed in homage with tribute in hand (v. 28; cf. Matt. 2:11).

43:29 God be gracious. Joseph reserved a special greeting for his beloved full-brother Benjamin (cf. Num. 6:25; Rom. 1:7).

43:32 Hebrews. See 14:13 and note; 39:14; 41:12.

an abomination to the Egyptians. As Palestinian shepherds, the Hebrews followed different dietary practices and slaughtered for food animals that were sacred to the Egyptians (46:34 and note). Such customs served the divine purpose by isolating the Israelites in the land of Goshen and preventing their assimilation into the pagan Egyptian culture (38:1–30 note).

43:33 amazement. The assigned seating of the brothers (in order of their birth) understandably amazed them.

43:34 Benjamin's . . . five times as much. This display of favoritism toward Benjamin (v. 29 note; cf. 37:3–11) was designed to test the brothers for jealousy. Their behavior ("they drank and were merry") indicated that their change of heart was real.

44:2 put my cup. Joseph was putting the brothers to the final test of family fidelity.

sack of the youngest. The original crime pertained to Joseph, Rachel's son and Jacob's favorite, and the brothers selling him into slavery in Egypt. To test the brothers, Joseph brilliantly created a situation where Rachel's other son (and Jacob's favorite), Benjamin, was also threatened with slavery in Egypt.

3 As soon as the morning was light, the
men were sent away with their donkeys.
4 They had gone only a short distance from
the city. Now Joseph said to his [r]steward,
"Up, follow after the men, and when you
overtake them, say to them, 'Why have you
repaid evil for good?[1] 5 Is it not from this
that my lord drinks, and [s]by this that he
practices divination? You have done evil in
doing this.'"
6 When he overtook them, he spoke to
them these words. 7 They said to him,
"Why does my lord speak such words as
these? Far be it from your servants to do
such a thing! 8 Behold, [t]the money that we
found in the mouths of our sacks we
brought back to you from the land of
Canaan. How then could we steal silver or
gold from your lord's house? 9 [u]Whichever
of your servants is found with it shall die,
and we also will be [v]my lord's servants."
10 He said, "Let it be as you say: he who is
found with it shall be my servant, and the
rest of you shall be innocent." 11 Then each
man quickly lowered his sack to the
ground, and each man opened his sack.
12 And he searched, beginning with the eldest and ending with the youngest. And
the cup was found in Benjamin's sack.
13 Then they [w]tore their clothes, and every
man loaded his donkey, and they returned
to the city.
14 When Judah and his brothers came to
Joseph's house, he was still there. They
[x]fell before him to the ground. 15 Joseph
said to them, "What deed is this that you
have done? Do you not know that a man
like me [y]can indeed practice divination?"
16 And Judah said, "What shall we say to
my lord? What shall we speak? Or how can
we clear ourselves? God has found out [z]the
guilt of your servants; behold, we are [a]my
lord's servants, both we and he also in
whose hand the cup has been found."

4 [r]ver. 1
5 [s]ver. 15; ch. 30:27; [2 Kin. 21:6; 2 Chr. 33:6]
8 [t]ch. 43:21
9 [u][ch. 31:32] [v]ver. 16
13 [w]ch. 37:29
14 [x]ch. 37:7, 9, 10; 42:6; 43:26, 28
15 [y]ver. 5
16 [z]ch. 37:18; [Num. 32:23] [a]ver. 9
18 [b]ch. 43:20 [c]Ex. 32:22 [d]ch. 41:40
20 [e]ver. 30; [ch. 43:8] [f][ch. 37:3]
21 [g]ch. 42:15, 20; 43:3, 5
22 [h][ver. 31]
23 [i]ch. 43:3
25 [j]ch. 43:2
27 [k]ch. 46:19
28 [l]ch. 37:33
29 [m]ch. 42:36, 38 [n]ch. 42:4, 38

17 But he said, "Far be it from me that I
should do so! Only the man in whose hand
the cup was found shall be my servant. But
as for you, go up in peace to your father."
18 Then Judah went up to him and said,
[b]"O my lord, please let your servant speak
a word in my lord's ears, and [c]let not your
anger burn against your servant, for [d]you
are like Pharaoh himself. 19 My lord asked
his servants, saying, 'Have you a father, or
a brother?' 20 And we said to my lord, 'We
have a father, an old man, [e]and a young
brother, [f]the child of his old age. His brother is dead, and he alone is left of his mother's children, and his father loves him.'
21 Then you said to your servants, [g]'Bring
him down to me, that I may set my eyes on
him.' 22 We said to my lord, 'The boy cannot leave his father, for if he should leave
his father, [h]his father would die.' 23 Then
you said to your servants, [i]'Unless your
youngest brother comes down with you,
you shall not see my face again.'
24 "When we went back to your servant
my father, we told him the words of my
lord. 25 And when [j]our father said, 'Go
again, buy us a little food,' 26 we said, 'We
cannot go down. If our youngest brother
goes with us, then we will go down. For we
cannot see the man's face unless our
youngest brother is with us.' 27 Then your
servant my father said to us, 'You know
that my wife bore me [k]two sons. 28 One left
me, and I said, [l]Surely he has been torn to
pieces, and I have never seen him since.
29 If you [m]take this one also from me, [n]and
harm happens to him, you will bring down
my gray hairs in evil to Sheol.'
30 "Now therefore, as soon as I come to
your servant my father, and the boy is not
with us, then, as his life is bound up in the
boy's life, 31 as soon as he sees that the boy
is not with us, he will die, and your servants

[1] Septuagint (compare Vulgate) adds *Why have you stolen my silver cup?*

44:5 practices divination. Hydromancy, a form of ancient Near Eastern divination, made use of vessels of water. Objects or liquids put in the water generated patterns that were thought to reveal the future. This description and Joseph's statement in v. 15 do not indicate that he actually practiced pagan divination; this description was necessary to the ruse and identified the silver cup as a treasured possession (cf. 42:7, 12). Joseph received revelation from God alone (40:8 and note; 41:16).

44:10 shall be my servant. Joseph's modification of the brothers' offer (v. 9) was necessary: he was testing their attitude toward making Benjamin a slave (v. 17 and note).

44:13 they tore their clothes. This display of extreme distress demonstrated their affection for both father and brother.

44:14 fell before him. Now they bowed before Joseph asking for mercy (43:26 note).

44:15 divination. See note on v. 5.

44:16 found out the guilt of your servants. Judah saw the impending penalty as punishment for their treatment of Joseph (42:21 and note).

44:17 man . . . shall be my servant. The stage for the great test was set (v. 2 note). Would they show compassion on their father and loyalty to Joseph's brother?

44:18 Judah. Representing the brothers (43:3 note).

will bring down the gray hairs of your servant our father with sorrow to Sheol. 32 For
your servant became a pledge of safety for
the boy to my father, saying, [o]'If I do not
bring him back to you, then I shall bear the
blame before my father all my life.' 33 Now
therefore, please let your servant remain
instead of the boy as a servant to my lord,
and let the boy go back with his brothers.
34 For how can I go back to my father if the
boy is not with me? I fear to see the evil
that would find my father."

Joseph Provides for His Brothers and Family

45 Then Joseph could not [p]control
himself before all those who stood
by him. He cried, "Make everyone go out
from me." So no one stayed with him when
Joseph made himself known to his brothers. 2 And he wept aloud, so that the
Egyptians heard it, and the household of
Pharaoh heard it. 3 And Joseph said to his
brothers, [q]"I am Joseph! Is my father still
alive?" But his brothers could not answer
him, for they were dismayed at his presence.
4 So Joseph said to his brothers, "Come
near to me, please." And they came near.
And he said, "I am your brother, Joseph,
[r]whom you sold into Egypt. 5 And now do
not be distressed or angry with yourselves
because you sold me here, [s]for God sent
me before you to preserve life. 6 For the
famine has been in the land these two
years, and there are [t]yet five years in
which there will be neither [u]plowing nor
harvest. 7 And God sent me before you to
preserve for you a remnant on earth, and
to keep alive for you many survivors. 8 So
it was not you who sent me here, but
God. He has made me a father to Pharaoh,
and lord of all his house and [v]ruler over
all the land of Egypt. 9 Hurry and go up to
my father and say to him, 'Thus says your
son Joseph, God has made me lord of all
Egypt. Come down to me; do not tarry.
10 [w]You shall dwell in the land of Goshen,
and you shall be near me, you and your
children and your children's children, and
your flocks, your herds, and all that you
have. 11 [x]There I will provide for you, for
there are yet five years of famine to come,
so that you and your household, and all
that you have, do not come to poverty.'
12 And now your eyes see, and the eyes of
my brother Benjamin see, that it is [y]my
mouth that speaks to you. 13 You must tell
my father of all my honor in Egypt, and of
all that you have seen. Hurry and [z]bring
my father down here." 14 Then he fell
upon his brother Benjamin's neck and
wept, and Benjamin wept upon his neck.
15 And he kissed all his brothers and wept
upon them. After that his brothers talked
with him.
16 When the report was heard in
Pharaoh's house, "Joseph's brothers have
come," it pleased Pharaoh and his servants. 17 And Pharaoh said to Joseph, "Say
to your brothers, 'Do this: load your beasts
and go back to the land of Canaan, 18 and
take your father and your households, and
come to me, and [a]I will give you the best of
the land of Egypt, and you shall eat the fat
of the land.' 19 And you, Joseph, are commanded to say, 'Do this: take [b]wagons
from the land of Egypt for your little ones
and for your wives, and bring your father,

32 [o]ch. 43:9
Chapter 45
1 [p]ch. 43:31; [Esth. 5:10]
3 [q]Acts 7:13
4 [r]ch. 37:28
5 [s]ch. 50:20; Ps. 105:16, 17
6 [t]ch. 41:30 [u]Ex. 34:21; Deut. 21:4; 1 Sam. 8:12; [Isai. 30:24]
8 [v]ver. 26; ch. 41:43
10 [w]ch. 46:34; 47:1, 4, 6, 27; 50:8; Ex. 8:22; [ch. 47:11; Josh. 10:41]
11 [x]ch. 47:12; 50:21
12 [y][ch. 42:23]
13 [z]Acts 7:14
18 [a]ch. 47:6
19 [b]ch. 46:5

44:33 instead of the boy. Here is a Judah very different from the one who sold his brother into slavery (37:26, 27). Judah's self-sacrificing love prefigures the vicarious atonement of Christ who by His voluntary suffering healed the breach between God and humans.

44:34 see the evil. See 37:34, 35.

45:1–28 In this narrative of forgiveness and reconciliation, Joseph presents a model of submission to God's eternal and benevolent purpose (vv. 5–8). All the evil done to him by his brothers was only part of God's secret plan designed for the good, not only of Joseph, but of his wicked brothers as well. We learn that "all things work together" to accomplish God's excellent purpose (Rom. 8:28), not only for us who presently "love God," but for the "great multitude" that will comprise the everlasting city (Rev. 7:9).

45:5–8 These verses, with Joseph's repeated affirmation "God sent me" (vv. 5, 7, 8), form the theological heart of the Joseph narrative (cf. 50:19–21; Acts 7:9–14). God oversees the course of human action to achieve His good and set purpose (Acts 2:23; 4:28).

45:5 do not . . . angry with yourselves. Joseph directed their gaze away from their sins to God's grace (50:19).

45:6 these two years. Joseph was thirty-nine years old at this time (41:46; 42:8 note).

45:7 remnant. Joseph's use of this term indicates his strong faith, tested by hard experience, in the faithfulness of God to His covenant promises. Out of this small endangered group a great nation would be built (12:1–3; 17:7). The prophets would later use this term in affirming that even in trying circumstances God would always preserve a people for Himself (Is. 10:20; 37:30–32; Mic. 2:12, 13).

45:8 it was not you . . . but God. Without excusing their sin, for which repentance was necessary (42:4 note), Joseph encourages the now contrite sinners to rejoice in God's sovereign and gracious overruling of their evil intentions.

45:10 land of Goshen. A region in northeastern Egypt near the Wadi Tumilat in the Nile Delta. This fertile region provided ample grazing for their flocks (v. 18; 47:4, 6).

and come. 20 Have no concern for[1] your
goods, for the best of all the land of Egypt
is yours.'"
21 The sons of Israel did so: and Joseph
gave them [b]wagons, according to the command of Pharaoh, and gave them provisions for the journey. 22 To each and all of
them he gave [c]a change of clothes, but to
Benjamin he gave three hundred shekels[2]
of silver and [d]five changes of clothes. 23 To
his father he sent as follows: ten donkeys
loaded with the good things of Egypt, and
ten female donkeys loaded with grain,
bread, and provision for his father on the
journey. 24 Then he sent his brothers away,
and as they departed, he said to them,
[e]"Do not quarrel on the way."
25 So they went up out of Egypt and came
to the land of Canaan to their father Jacob.
26 And they told him, "Joseph is still alive,
and he is ruler over all the land of Egypt."
And his heart became numb, for he did not
believe them. 27 But when they told him all
the words of Joseph, which he had said to
them, and when he saw [f]the wagons that
Joseph had sent to carry him, the spirit of
their father Jacob revived. 28 And Israel said,
"It is enough; Joseph my son is still alive. I
will go and see him before I die."

Joseph Brings His Family to Egypt

46 So Israel took his journey with all
that he had and came to [g]Beer-
sheba, and offered sacrifices [h]to the God
of his father Isaac. 2 And God spoke to
Israel [i]in visions of the night and said,
"Jacob, Jacob." And he said, "Here am I."
3 Then he said, "I am God, [j]the God of your
father. Do not be afraid to go down to
Egypt, for there I will [k]make you into a
great nation. 4 I myself will go down with
you to Egypt, and I will also [l]bring you up
again, and [m]Joseph's hand shall close your
eyes."
5 Then Jacob set out from Beersheba. The
sons of Israel carried Jacob their father,
their little ones, and their wives, in the wagons [n]that Pharaoh had sent to carry him.
6 They also took their livestock and their
goods, which they had gained in the land of
Canaan, and [o]came into Egypt, Jacob and
all his offspring with him, 7 his sons, and his
sons' sons with him, his daughters, and his
sons' daughters. All his offspring he
brought with him into Egypt.
8 [p]Now [q]these are the names of the
descendants of Israel, who came into Egypt,
Jacob and his sons. [r]Reuben, Jacob's firstborn, 9 and the sons of Reuben: Hanoch,
Pallu, Hezron, and Carmi. 10 The sons of
Simeon: Jemuel, Jamin, Ohad, Jachin,
Zohar, and Shaul, the son of a Canaanite
woman. 11 The sons of [s]Levi: Gershon,
Kohath, and Merari. 12 The sons of [t]Judah:
Er, Onan, Shelah, Perez, and Zerah (but
[u]Er and Onan died in the land of Canaan);
and the sons of [v]Perez were Hezron and
Hamul. 13 [w]The sons of Issachar: Tola,
Puvah, Yob, and Shimron. 14 The sons of
Zebulun: Sered, Elon, and Jahleel. 15 These
are the sons of Leah, [x]whom she bore to
Jacob in Paddan-aram, together with his

21 [b][See ver. 19 above] **22** [c][2 Kin. 5:5, 22, 23] [d][ch. 43:34] **24** [e][ch. 42:22] **27** [f]ver. 19, 21; ch. 46:5
Chapter 46
1 [g]ch. 21:31, 33; 26:33; 28:10 [h]ch. 26:24, 25; 28:13; 31:42 **2** [i]ch. 15:1; Job 33:14, 15
3 [j]ch. 28:13 [k]ch. 35:11; [ch. 12:2; Ex. 1:7, 9; Deut. 26:5] **4** [l]ch. 15:16; 28:15; 48:21; 50:24; Ex. 3:8 [m]ch. 50:1 **5** [n]ch. 45:19, 21, 27 **6** [o]Josh. 24:4; Ps. 105:23; Isai. 52:4; Acts 7:14, 15 **8** [p]For ver. 8-11, see Ex. 6:14-16 [q]Ex. 1:1-5 [r]Num. 26:5; 1 Chr. 5:1-3 **11** [s]1 Chr. 6:1 **12** [t]1 Chr. 2:3; 4:21 [u]ch. 38:3, 7, 10 [v]ch. 38:29; 1 Chr. 2:5 **13** [w]1 Chr. 7:1 **15** [x]See ch. 29:32-35; 30:1-21

1 Hebrew *Let your eye not pity* 2 A *shekel* was about 2/5 ounce or 11 grams

45:22 a change of clothes. In striking contrast to when the brothers stripped Joseph of his tunic (37:23).

45:24 Do not quarrel. The brothers were not to quarrel among one another, particularly over responsibility for their crime against Joseph, and how to explain it to their father.

46:1–50:26 This closing section of the "generations of Jacob" (37:2) provides a transition to the Book of Exodus (Introduction: Characteristics and Themes).

46:1 offered sacrifices. Beersheba was the place of worship for Abraham (21:32, 33), Isaac (26:23–25), and Jacob (28:10–15).

46:2 God spoke. Once again, upon Jacob's departure from the Promised Land, God repeated His promise to be with him and to bring the people back (28:15).

visions of the night. The patriarchs functioned from time to time as prophets (12:7; 15:1; 18:17; 20:7 and notes). No visions to Jacob's twelve sons regarding the covenant promises of seed and land are recorded.

46:3 I am . . . the God. God repeated His assuring promises to Isaac (26:24) and Jacob (28:13–15).

I will make you into a great nation. An elaboration of the covenant promise to Abraham (12:2; 15:13, 14; 18:18; cf. Ex. 1:7).

46:4 Joseph's hand shall close your eyes. A word of comfort for the aged Jacob; he would die peacefully in Joseph's presence (50:1; cf. 15:15).

46:8–27 This catalog of sons closes the patriarchal period in Canaan and forms a transition to the Exodus from Egypt (Ex. 1:1–7). The list includes the sons and grandsons of Jacob (some of whom were born in Egypt) through his various wives and concubines, although his daughters, except for Dinah (v. 15) and Serah (v. 17), are omitted. Thus the list is designed to culminate in the significant number seventy (v. 27 note) to show both God's blessing on the family and to anticipate their further expansion into a great nation.

46:8 who came into Egypt. This list includes the sons of Benjamin, who were probably born in Egypt (vv. 21, 27), just as the catalog of those born in Paddan-aram (35:23–26) included Benjamin, who was obviously born in Canaan (35:26 note). The offspring were viewed as present in their parents (cf. Heb. 7:9, 10).

46:10 Ohad. Perhaps an inadvertent scribal addition, this name is omitted in Num. 26:12 and 1 Chr. 4:24.

46:15 Paddan-aram. See note 25:20.

daughter Dinah; altogether his sons and his daughters numbered thirty-three.

16 The sons of Gad: Ziphion, Haggi, Shuni, Ezbon, Eri, Arodi, and Areli. 17 [y]The sons of Asher: Imnah, Ishvah, Ishvi, Beriah, with Serah their sister. And the sons of Beriah: Heber and Malchiel. 18 [z]These are the sons of Zilpah, [a]whom Laban gave to Leah his daughter; and these she bore to Jacob—sixteen persons.

19 The sons of Rachel, Jacob's wife: Joseph and Benjamin. 20 And [b]to Joseph in the land of Egypt were born Manasseh and Ephraim, whom Asenath, the daughter of Potiphera the priest of [c]On, bore to him. 21 And [d]the sons of Benjamin: Bela, Becher, Ashbel, Gera, Naaman, Ehi, Rosh, Muppim, Huppim, and Ard. 22 These are the sons of Rachel, who were born to Jacob—fourteen persons in all.

23 The sons of Dan: Hushim. 24 [e]The sons of Naphtali: Jahzeel, Guni, Jezer, and Shillem. 25 [f]These are the sons of Bilhah, [g]whom Laban gave to Rachel his daughter, and these she bore to Jacob—seven persons in all.

26 All the persons belonging to Jacob who came into Egypt, who were his own descendants, not including Jacob's sons' wives, were sixty-six persons in all. 27 And the sons of Joseph, who were born to him in Egypt, were two. [h]All the persons of the house of Jacob who came into Egypt were seventy.

Jacob and Joseph Reunited

28 He had sent Judah ahead of him to Joseph to show the way before him in Goshen, and they came [i]into the land of Goshen. 29 Then Joseph prepared his chariot and went up to meet Israel his father in Goshen. He presented himself to him and [j]fell on his neck and wept on his neck a good while. 30 Israel said to Joseph, [k]"Now let me die, since I have seen your face and know that you are still alive." 31 Joseph said to his brothers and to his father's household, [l]"I will go up and tell Pharaoh and will say to him, 'My brothers and my father's household, who were in the land of Canaan, have come to me. 32 [m]And the men are shepherds, for they have been keepers of livestock, and they have brought their flocks and their herds and all that they have.' 33 When Pharaoh calls you and says, [m]'What is your occupation?' 34 you shall say, [m]'Your servants have been keepers of livestock [n]from our youth even until now, both we and our fathers,' in order that you may dwell [o]in the land of Goshen, for every shepherd is [p]an abomination to the Egyptians."

Jacob's Family Settles in Goshen

47 So Joseph [q]went in and told Pharaoh, "My father and my brothers, with their flocks and herds and all that they possess, have come from the land of Canaan. They are now in [r]the land of Goshen." 2 And from among his brothers he took five men and [s]presented them to Pharaoh. 3 Pharaoh said to his brothers, [t]"What is your occupation?" And they said to Pharaoh, [u]"Your servants are shepherds, as our fathers were." 4 They said to Pharaoh, [v]"We have come to sojourn in the

17 [y]1 Chr. 7:30
18 [z]See ch. 30:10-13 [a]ch. 29:24
19 [b]ch. 41:50-52 [c]ch. 41:45
21 [d]See Num. 26:38-40; 1 Chr. 7:6-12; 8:1
24 [e]1 Chr. 7:13
25 [f]See ch. 30:5-8 [g]ch. 29:29
27 [h]Ex. 1:5; Deut. 10:22; [Acts 7:14]
28 [i]See ch. 45:10
29 [j][ch. 45:14]
30 [k][Luke 2:29, 30]
31 [l]ch. 47:1
32 [m]ch. 47:3
33 [m][See ver. 32 above]
34 [m][See ver. 32 above] [n]ch. 37:12 [o]ver. 28 [p]ch. 43:32; Ex. 8:26
Chapter 47
1 [q]ch. 46:31 [r]See ch. 45:10
2 [s]Acts 7:13
3 [t]ch. 46:33 [u]ch. 46:32, 34
4 [v]ch. 15:13; Deut. 26:5

thirty-three. The total of Jacob and his offspring through Leah—six sons, twenty-five grandsons, two great-grandsons, and daughter Dinah—comes to thirty-five. The figure thirty-three may reflect the omission of Er and Onan (v. 12), or perhaps of Ohad (v. 10 note) and Jacob.

46:26 sixty-six. The total of thirty-three (v. 15 and note), sixteen (v. 18), fourteen (v. 22), and seven (v. 25) comes to seventy. The figure of sixty-six persons probably reflects the omission of Er and Onan (v. 12) and Ephraim and Manasseh (vv. 20, 27).

46:27 seventy. The covenant family is represented by the symbolic number seventy (vv. 8–27 note), signifying a large and complete number (cf. ch. 10 note; Ex. 24:1; Ps. 90:10). In this group of seventy, the emerging nation of Israel was comprehended.

The Septuagint (Greek Old Testament) adds five sons and grandsons of Manasseh and Ephraim at v. 20 and gives a total of seventy-five, a reading followed by Stephen in Acts 7:14. Such variations occasionally occur in the Greek Old Testament, and we don't always have the information necessary to explain them.

46:28–47:31 Through Joseph's wisdom God preserved Israel in Goshen, both physically, by providing food and land (45:10 note), and spiritually, by providing for their isolation from the pagan Egyptians until the Exodus (43:32; Num. 25:1–3 and notes). Under Jacob's blessing on Pharaoh (47:7, 10; cf. 12:2) and Pharaoh's honoring of Israel (45:17–20; 47:6; cf. 12:3) everyone prospered: Pharaoh gained control of all the property and people in Egypt (47:19–21), the Egyptians hailed Joseph as a savior (47:25), and Israel prospered even more than the Egyptians (47:27; Ex. 1:7). This mutual blessing and prosperity contrasts with the situation four hundred years later when another pharaoh cursed Israel and was cursed (Ex. 1:8–14).

46:32 shepherds. Their identity as shepherds would assure Pharaoh that they entertained no social or political ambitions under their brother's auspices, and would help insulate them from intermarriage with the pagan Egyptians (v. 34; 43:32 and notes). The latter threat increased when they possessed property in Egypt (v. 11).

46:34 every shepherd is an abomination. The Egyptians too kept animals (47:6; Ex. 9:3, 4); this probably refers to foreign shepherds (43:32 note).

land, for there is no pasture for your servants' flocks, for the famine is severe in the
land of Canaan. And now, please let your
servants dwell [w]in the land of Goshen."
5 Then Pharaoh said to Joseph, "Your father
and your brothers have come to you. 6 The
land of Egypt is before you. Settle your
father and your brothers [x]in the best of the
land. [y]Let them settle in the land of
Goshen, and if you know any [z]able men
among them, put them in charge of my
livestock."

7 Then Joseph brought in Jacob his father
and stood him before Pharaoh, [a]and Jacob
blessed Pharaoh. 8 And Pharaoh said to
Jacob, "How many are the days of the years
of your life?" 9 And Jacob said to Pharaoh,
"The days of the years of my [b]sojourning
are 130 years. [c]Few and evil have been the
days of the years of my life, and [d]they have
not attained to the days of the years of the
life of my fathers in the days of their [b]so-
journing." 10 And Jacob [e]blessed Pharaoh
and went out from the presence of Pharaoh. 11 Then Joseph settled his father and
his brothers and gave them a possession in
the land of Egypt, in the best of the land, in
the land of [f]Rameses, [g]as Pharaoh had
commanded. 12 And Joseph [h]provided his
father, his brothers, and all his father's
household with food, according to the
number of their dependents.

Joseph and the Famine

13 Now there was no food in all the land,
for the famine was very severe, so that the
land of Egypt and the land of Canaan languished by reason of the famine. 14 [i]And
Joseph gathered up all the money that was
found in the land of Egypt and in the land
of Canaan, in exchange for the grain that
they bought. And Joseph brought the
money into Pharaoh's house. 15 And when
the money was all spent in the land of
Egypt and in the land of Canaan, all the
Egyptians came to Joseph and said, "Give
us food. [j]Why should we die before your
eyes? For our money is gone." 16 And
Joseph answered, "Give your livestock,
and I will give you food in exchange for
your livestock, if your money is gone."
17 So they brought their livestock to
Joseph, and Joseph gave them food in
exchange for the horses, the flocks, the
herds, and the donkeys. He supplied
them with food in exchange for all their
livestock that year. 18 And when that year
was ended, they came to him the following year and said to him, "We will not
hide from my lord that our money is all
spent. The herds of livestock are my
lord's. There is nothing left in the sight of
my lord but our bodies and our land.
19 Why should we die before your eyes,
both we and our land? [k]Buy us and our
land for food, and we with our land will
be servants to Pharaoh. And give us seed
that we may live and not die, and that the
land may not be desolate."

20 So Joseph bought all the land of Egypt
for Pharaoh, for all the Egyptians sold their
fields, because the famine was severe on
them. The land became Pharaoh's. 21 As for
the people, he made servants of them[1]
from one end of Egypt to the other. 22 [l]Only
the land of the priests he did not buy, for
the priests had a fixed allowance from
Pharaoh and lived on the allowance that
Pharaoh gave them; therefore they did not
sell their land.

23 Then Joseph said to the people,
"Behold, I have this day bought you and
your land for Pharaoh. Now here is seed for
you, and you shall sow the land. 24 And at
the harvests you shall give a [m]fifth to

4 [w]ch. 46:34
6 [x]ch. 45:18 [y]ver. 4 [z]Ex. 18:21, 25
7 [a]ver. 10
9 [b]1 Chr. 29:15; Ps. 39:12; 119:19, 54; Heb. 11:9, 13 [c]Job 14:1; [Ps. 39:4, 5; James 4:14] [d]ch. 11:32; 25:7; 35:28
10 [e]ver. 7
11 [f]Ex. 1:11; 12:37; [ch. 45:10] [g]ver. 6
12 [h]ch. 45:11; 50:21
14 [i]ch. 41:56
15 [j]ver. 19
19 [k][Neh. 5:2, 3]
22 [l][Ezra 7:24]
24 [m]ch. 41:34

1 Samaritan, Septuagint, Vulgate; Hebrew *he removed them to the cities*

47:7–10 In this remarkable audience with mighty Pharaoh—the greater typically blesses the lesser (14:19 and note)—the aged shepherd patriarch demonstrated his dignity. His blessing was fulfilled in vv. 13–25.

47:9 sojourning. The Hebrew term denotes a temporary abode, the condition of a resident alien. Jacob described his own life, and that of his fathers, as a sojourn (21:34; 24:3; 26:3 and notes). Though awaiting the fulfillment of the divine covenant promise of land, their hope extended beyond Canaan to a heavenly and eternal country, to a "city . . . whose designer and builder is God" (Heb. 11:10). See notes 13:15 and Heb. 11:8–10.

Few and evil. Jacob did not glory in the number of his years. Though blessed by God and a blessing to others, he had his share of human failings and afflictions.

47:11 land of Rameses. Assuming an early date for the Exodus from Egypt (Introduction to Exodus: Interpretive Difficulties), this designation of the land of Goshen, after Pharaoh Rameses II (c. 1304–1236 B.C.), indicates that the place-name was updated after the time of Moses (14:14 note; Introduction: Date and Occasion).

47:13–26 Joseph brought all the money, land, and people under Pharaoh in exchange for food, and preserved the Egyptians.

47:21 made servants of them. The Hebrew is uncertain. This reading describes the result of Joseph's policies—servitude for the people. The people, however, viewed Joseph not as a tyrant but as a savior (v. 25; cf. 45:7).

Pharaoh, and four fifths shall be your own,
as seed for the field and as food for yourselves and your households, and as food
for your little ones." 25 And they said, "You
have saved our lives; [n]may it please my
lord, we will be servants to Pharaoh." 26 So
Joseph made it a statute concerning the
land of Egypt, and it stands to this day,
that Pharaoh should have the fifth; [o]the
land of the priests alone did not become
Pharaoh's.
27 Thus Israel settled in the land of Egypt,
[p]in the land of Goshen. [q]And they gained
possessions in it, and were fruitful and
multiplied greatly. 28 And Jacob lived in the
land of Egypt seventeen years. [r]So the days
of Jacob, the years of his life, were 147
years.
29 And [s]when the time drew near that
Israel must die, he called his son Joseph
and said to him, "If now [t]I have found
favor in your sight, [u]put your hand under
my thigh and [v]promise to deal kindly and
truly with me. [w]Do not bury me in Egypt,
30 but let me lie with my fathers. Carry me
out of Egypt and [x]bury me in their burying
place." He answered, "I will do as you have
said." 31 And he said, "Swear to me"; and
he swore to him. Then [y]Israel bowed himself upon the head of his bed. [1]

25 [n]See ch. 33:15
26 [o]ver. 22
27 [p]See ch. 45:10 [q]ch. 46:3
28 [r][ver. 9]
29 [s]Deut. 31:14; 1 Kin. 2:1 [t]See ch. 33:15 [u]ch. 24:2 [v]ch. 24:49 [w][ch. 50:25]
30 [x]ch. 49:29; 50:5, 13
31 [y]ch. 48:2; 1 Kin. 1:47; [Heb. 11:21]

Chapter 48
3 [z]See ch. 17:1 [a]ch. 28:13, 19; 35:6, 9
4 [b]ch. 17:8
5 [c]ch. 41:50-52; 46:20 [d]Josh. 13:7; 14:4; 17:17
7 [e]See ch. 35:9-19

Jacob Blesses Ephraim and Manasseh

48 After this, Joseph was told, "Behold,
your father is ill." So he took with
him his two sons, Manasseh and Ephraim.
2 And it was told to Jacob, "Your son Joseph
has come to you." Then Israel summoned
his strength and sat up in bed. 3 And Jacob
said to Joseph, [z]"God Almighty[2] appeared
to me at [a]Luz in the land of Canaan and
blessed me, 4 and said to me, 'Behold, I will
make you fruitful and multiply you, and I
will make of you a company of peoples and
will give this land to your offspring after you
[b]for an everlasting possession.' 5 And now
your [c]two sons, who were born to you in the
land of Egypt before I came to you in Egypt,
[d]are mine; Ephraim and Manasseh shall be
mine, as Reuben and Simeon are. 6 And the
children that you fathered after them shall
be yours. They shall be called by the name
of their brothers in their inheritance. 7 As for
me, when I came from Paddan, to my sorrow [e]Rachel died in the land of Canaan on
the way, when there was still some distance[3]
to go to Ephrath, and I buried her there on
the way to Ephrath (that is, Bethlehem)."
8 When Israel saw Joseph's sons, he said,
"Who are these?" 9 Joseph said to his father,

[1] Hebrew; Septuagint *staff* [2] Hebrew *El Shaddai* [3] Or *about two hours' distance*

47:27–31 Having witnessed God's faithfulness, by faith Jacob looked beyond his death in Egypt to his burial in the Promised Land.

47:27 gained possessions . . . multiplied greatly. In fulfillment of the divine promise (46:3 and notes). The independence and prosperity of the Israelites contrasts with the fate of the Egyptians (vv. 13–26 note). This description also provides a link with Ex. 1:7.

47:29 Joseph. Jacob later repeated the command to all his sons in 49:29–32, but Joseph was in charge (48:1 note).

put your hand under my thigh. See note 24:2.

47:30 in their burying place. By faith Israel saw his destiny in the Promised Land, not in an embalmed body in the best land of Egypt (v. 11; 50:2).

47:31 Swear to me. Jacob asked that Joseph confirm his promise (v. 30) with a solemn oath. Likewise, God underscores the surety of His gracious covenant promise with an oath (15:8–21; 22:17; Heb. 6:13, 14 note). For Joseph's fulfillment of his oath see 50:1–14.

bowed himself. An expression of reverent thanksgiving to God that his last wish would be fulfilled (cf. 1 Kin. 1:47, 48).

48:1 Manasseh and Ephraim. Joseph received the rights of firstborn and the double portion through Jacob's adoption and elevation of his two sons to the status of founding fathers among Israel's twelve tribes (37:8; 43:3; 1 Chr. 5:2 and notes). The adoption ritual included Jacob's statements of authority (vv. 3, 4) and intent to adopt Ephraim and Manasseh (vv. 5–7), legal gestures (vv. 8–12), and words of blessing (vv. 15–16). An ancient text from the city of Ugarit (Ras Shamra) describes a similar adoption of a grandson (c. 1500 B.C.).

48:3 God Almighty. See note 17:1.

appeared . . . blessed me. God's direct revelation of the covenant blessing to Jacob empowered him to legitimate Joseph's two sons as numbered among the twelve (v. 5) and to bless the twelve tribes (48:5–49:28). This preference for Joseph, giving him the double portion, reasserted God's sovereign prerogative to do as He pleased with Israel (Introduction: Characteristics and Themes).

at Luz. See 28:19.

48:4 fruitful . . . company . . . land. Jacob briefly summarizes the content of the covenant promises to the patriarchs (12:1–3, 7; 13:14–17; 15:12–21; 17:4–8; 22:15–18; 28:3, 4, 13–15).

48:5 Ephraim and Manasseh. The younger (Ephraim) is again preferred before the older (vv. 17–20; 25:23 and note).

Reuben and Simeon. The first two sons of Leah are mentioned because they are bypassed to give the double portion to Joseph, Rachel's firstborn. Reuben lost his rights as firstborn because he defiled his father's marriage bed (35:22; 43:3 note; 49:3, 4).

48:6 shall be yours . . . name of their brothers. Joseph's other sons were not adopted by Jacob, but would be embraced within the clans of Ephraim and Manasseh. These younger sons of Joseph are probably included in Num. 26:28–37; 1 Chr. 7:14–29.

48:7 Paddan. See note 25:20.

Rachel. Though Leah was buried in the family grave (49:31; cf. 35:16–20), Rachel is honored and memorialized in the double portion given her firstborn.

48:8 Who are these. Identification of the beneficiaries was part of the blessing ritual (v. 1 note). The nearly sightless Jacob (cf. 27:1) carefully identified the recipients of the irrevocable blessing (27:7 note).

[f]"They are my sons, whom God has given
me here." And he said, "Bring them to me,
please, that [g]I may bless them." **10** Now [h]the
eyes of Israel were dim with age, so that he
could not see. So Joseph brought them near
him, [i]and he kissed them and embraced
them. **11** And Israel said to Joseph, [j]"I never
expected to see your face; and behold, God
has let me see your offspring also." **12** Then
Joseph removed them from his knees, and
he bowed himself with his face to the earth.
13 And Joseph took them both, Ephraim in
his right hand toward Israel's left hand, and
Manasseh in his left hand toward Israel's
right hand, and brought them near him.
14 [k]And Israel stretched out his right hand
and laid it on the head of Ephraim, who
was the younger, and his left hand on the
head of Manasseh, [l]crossing his hands (for
Manasseh was the firstborn). **15** And he
blessed Joseph and said,

"The God [m]before whom my fathers
Abraham and Isaac walked,
the God who has been my shepherd
all my life long to this day,
16 [n]the angel who has [o]redeemed me
from all evil, bless the boys;
and in them let [p]my name be
carried on, and the name of
my fathers Abraham and Isaac;
and let them [q]grow into a multitude[1]
in the midst of the earth."

17 When Joseph saw that his father [r]laid
his right hand on the head of Ephraim, it
displeased him, and he took his father's
hand to move it from Ephraim's head to
Manasseh's head. **18** And Joseph said to his
father, "Not this way, my father; since this
one is the firstborn, put your right hand on
his head." **19** But his father refused and
said, [r]"I know, my son, I know. He also
shall become a people, and he also shall be
great. Nevertheless, [s]his younger brother
shall be greater than he, and his offspring
shall become a multitude[2] of nations." **20** So
he blessed them that day, saying,

"By you Israel will pronounce
blessings, saying,
[t]'God make you as Ephraim and
as Manasseh.'"

Thus he put Ephraim before Manasseh.
21 Then Israel said to Joseph, "Behold, I am
about to die, but [u]God will be with you and
will bring you again to the land of your
fathers. **22** Moreover, I have given to [v]you
rather than to your brothers one mountain
slope[3] that I took from the hand of the
Amorites with my sword and with my bow."

Jacob Blesses His Sons

49 [w]Then Jacob called his sons and
said, "Gather yourselves together,
that I may tell you what shall happen to
you [x]in days to come.

[1] Or *let them be like fish for multitude* [2] Hebrew *fullness* [3] Or *one portion of the land*; Hebrew *shekem*, which sounds like the town and district called *Shechem*

9 [f][ch. 33:5] [g]ch. 49:25, 26; Heb. 11:21; [ch. 27:4] **10** [h][ch. 27:1] [i]ch. 27:27 **11** [j][ch. 37:33; 45:26] **14** [k]ver. 17 [l]ver. 19 **15** [m]ch. 17:1; 24:40 **16** [n]ch. 28:15; 31:11, 13, 24; Ex. 23:20 [o]Isai. 44:22, 23; 49:7; 63:9; [2 Sam. 4:9; Ps. 34:22; 121:7] [p]Amos 9:12; Acts 15:17 [q][Num. 26:34, 37] **17** [r]ver. 14
19 [r][See ver. 17 above] [s]Num. 1:33, 35; 2:19, 21; Deut. 33:17 **20** [t][Ruth 4:11, 12] **21** [u]ch. 46:4; 50:24 **22** [v]Josh. 24:32; John 4:5
Chapter 49
1 [w]For ver. 1-27, see Deut. 33:6-25 [x]Num. 24:14; Deut. 4:30; 31:29; Isai. 2:2; Jer. 23:20; Dan. 2:28; 10:14; Hos. 3:5

48:9 whom God has given. Joseph, who shared his father's faith, gave the same answer as Jacob gave Esau to a similar question (33:5; cf. 41:51, 52 and note).

48:10 kissed them and embraced them. Part of the blessing ritual (27:26 and note).

48:11–16 In the blessing, Jacob's perspective shifts from thanksgiving for God's covenant faithfulness and miraculous provision (v. 15) to anticipation of God's faithfulness and blessing on future generations (v. 16).

48:12 Joseph . . . bowed. The one second only to Pharaoh (41:40) humbled himself before the patriarch who mediated God's promises.

from his knees. In the ancient Near East, the knee was symbolic of parental care and, by extension, of adoption (30:3 note).

48:14 right hand. In the ancient Near East oral statements were accompanied by the correct placement of the right hand, an action that functioned as a legal safeguard. This is also the first instance in Scripture where a blessing is accompanied by the laying on of hands (cf. Ps. 139:5; Matt. 19:13–15).

48:15 he blessed Joseph. Joseph was represented in his two sons. Joseph was later blessed without distinguishing his two sons (49:22–26). See note 27:7.

before whom my fathers . . . walked. See note 17:1.

48:16 the angel. See note 16:7; 28:12; 31:11; 32:1, 22–32.

48:17–20 An explanatory notice appended here to the ritual so as not to interrupt the narrative (v. 1 note).

younger brother shall be greater. Against social convention, the younger is blessed, as in the divine choices of Isaac over Ishmael (17:18, 19), Jacob over Esau (25:23), and Joseph over Reuben (v. 1 note). God's sovereign choice overrode the natural ways of men (cf. Is. 55:8, 9).

48:20 Ephraim before Manasseh. Jacob's prophetic blessing was fulfilled after the Exodus as Ephraim became the dominant Israelite tribe in the northern part of the Promised Land (Deut. 33:17 note).

48:22 given to you . . . mountain slope. The Hebrew word translated "mountain slope" (*shechem*) often means "shoulder" or "ridge", and is identical to the place-name "Shechem" (33:19). Some see here a reference to the double portion in the Promised Land that Joseph received through Ephraim and Manasseh (v. 1 note). Others infer that Jacob bequeathed the area of Shechem, where Jacob purchased a tract of land (33:18, 19) and which his sons later conquered (34:25–31), to Joseph's descendants (Josh. 24:32).

49:1–28 The blessings of the inspired patriarch prophesied the fate of the twelve tribes descended from his sons, mostly by means of wordplays on their names or comparisons to animals. The names and actions (good or bad) of the twelve sons portended the destiny of the tribe. These prophetic blessings at the end of the patriarchal era are arranged according to the mothers—Leah's six sons (vv. 3–15), the handmaids' four (vv. 16–21); and Rachel's two (vv. 22–27)—and exhibit God's sovereignty over the nation. They will be expanded in the parallel "Moses' final blessing" (Deut. 33), given on the threshold of Israel's conquest of the land.

49:1 days to come. Jacob's prophecies embrace the entire history of Israel

2 "Assemble and listen, O sons of
Jacob,
listen to Israel your father.

3 "Reuben, you are [y]my firstborn,
my might, and the [z]firstfruits of my
strength,
preeminent in dignity and
preeminent in power.
4 Unstable as water, you shall not have
preeminence,
because you [a]went up to your
father's bed;
then you defiled it—he went up to
my couch!

5 [b]"Simeon and Levi are brothers;
weapons [c]of violence are their
swords.
6 Let my soul come not into their
council;
[d]O my glory, [e]be not joined to their
company.
For in their anger they killed men,
and in their willfulness they
[f]hamstrung oxen.
7 Cursed be their anger, for it is fierce,
and their wrath, for it is cruel!
I will [g]divide them in Jacob
and scatter them in Israel.

8 "Judah, [h]your brothers shall praise you;
[i]your hand shall be on the neck of
your enemies;
[j]your father's sons shall bow down
before you.
9 Judah is [k]a lion's cub;
from the prey, my son, you have
gone up.
[l]He stooped down; he crouched as a
lion
and as a lioness; who dares rouse
him?
10 The [m]scepter shall not depart from
Judah,
nor the ruler's staff [n]from between
his feet,
until tribute comes to him;[1]
and to him shall be the obedience
of the peoples.
11 Binding his foal to the vine
and his donkey's colt to the choice
vine,
he has washed his garments in wine
and his vesture in the blood of
grapes.
12 His [o]eyes are darker than wine,
and his teeth whiter than milk.

13 [p]"Zebulun shall dwell at the [q]shore of
the sea;
he shall become a haven for ships,
and his border shall be at Sidon.

14 "Issachar is a strong donkey,
crouching between [r]the
sheepfolds.[2]

3 [y]ch. 29:32 [z]Deut. 21:17
4 [a]ch. 35:22; 1 Chr. 5:1
5 [b]ch. 29:33, 34 [c]ch. 34:25, 26
6 [d][Ps. 16:9; 57:8] [e][Ps. 26:9] [f]Josh. 11:6, 9; 2 Sam. 8:4
7 [g]See Num. 3:5-13; Josh. 19:1-9; 1 Chr. 4:24-39
8 [h]ch. 29:35; [ch. 27:29] [i][Job 16:12] [j]1 Chr. 5:2
9 [k]Rev. 5:5; [Deut. 33:22; Hos. 5:14] [l][Num. 23:24; 24:9]
10 [m]Num. 24:17; Zech. 10:11
10 [n]Deut. 28:57
12 [o]Prov. 23:29
13 [p][Deut. 33:18, 19]; Josh. 19:10, 11 [q][Deut. 1:7; Josh. 9:1; Judg. 5:17]
14 [r]Judg. 5:16; [1 Chr. 12:32]

1 By a slight revocalization; a slight emendation yields (compare Septuagint, Syriac, Targum) *until he comes to whom it belongs*; Hebrew *until Shiloh comes*, or *until he comes to Shiloh* 2 *Or between its saddlebags*

from the conquest and distribution of the land to the reign of the Messiah, Jesus Christ (v. 10 and note). See Num. 24:14; Deut. 31:28, 29; Is. 2:2.

49:3–7 The prophecies about Leah's first three sons, Reuben, Simeon and Levi, pronounce punishment for crimes and do not use animal comparisons. The sins of the fathers are visited upon the children (Ex. 20:5).

49:3 Reuben. See 29:32; 35:22 and note. A son's inheritance in the ancient Near East could not be altered by a father's arbitrary decision, but such changes could be made after serious sexual offenses by the son against the family.

49:4 Unstable. Reuben's behavior was reckless and destructive. The Hebrew here connotes pride and presumption (cf. Judg. 9:4; 1 Chr. 5:1, 2).

49:5 Simeon and Levi. See 29:33, 34; 34:25 and note.

49:7 divide . . . scatter. Sharing an inclination toward destructive anger and cruelty, Simeon and Levi posed a threat to peace (34:25–31). After the Exodus from Egypt, the tribe of Simeon declined in importance and was not mentioned in Moses' blessing (Deut. 33). Simeon received no separate inheritance in the Promised Land, but was allotted cities within the inheritance of Judah (Josh. 19:1–9). Similarly, the priestly tribe of Levi was allotted cities throughout the land (Josh. 21:1–42).

49:8 Judah. See 29:35; 43:3 and notes.

your father's sons shall bow. The tribes bowed down to Judah's descendant David because of his heroic deeds (2 Sam. 5:1–3).

49:9 lion's cub. Signifying strength, courage, and boldness (Judg. 14:18; Prov. 28:1), the lion was an apt symbol of the warrior kings of Judah's Davidic line—a royal line culminating in the conquering Messiah, Jesus Christ (Rev. 5:5).

49:10 scepter shall not depart. A prophecy further elaborated and confirmed by the Davidic covenant (2 Sam. 7:16).

until tribute comes to him. Lit. "Until Shiloh comes." The precise meaning of this phrase is debated. Some understand "Shiloh" as a place-name ("until Judah's leadership comes to Shiloh," cf. Josh. 18:1) or as a reference to tribute ("until tribute is brought to Judah"). Others see this as a reference to a coming Judahite ruler: "until he comes to whom it belongs" (cf. Ezek. 21:27) or "until Shiloh [possibly a messianic term] comes." The subsequent mention of dominion over "people" (or "peoples," the Hebrew noun is plural) points to the final realization of this prophecy in the universal messianic reign of Christ (1 Cor. 15:24–28; Rev. 5:5). God's plan for mankind to rule and have dominion (1:26–28) is concentrated in Him.

49:11, 12 The blessedness of the messianic ruler is represented by wine (a symbol of prosperity, 27:28) and by his beauty (Ps. 45:2–9).

49:11 donkey's colt. See Zech. 9:9; Matt. 21:7.

49:13 Zebulun. See 30:20; Deut. 33:19, 20; Josh. 19:10–16.

49:14 Issachar. See 30:18.

15 He saw that a resting place was good,
and that the land was pleasant,
so he bowed his shoulder to bear,
and [s]became a servant at forced
labor.

16 [t]"Dan shall [u]judge his people
as one of the tribes of Israel.
17 Dan [v]shall be a serpent in the way,
a viper by the path,
that bites the horse's heels
so that his rider falls backward.
18 I [w]wait for your salvation, O LORD.

19 [x]"Raiders shall raid [y]Gad,[1]
but he shall raid at their heels.

20 [z]"Asher's food shall be rich,
and he shall yield royal delicacies.

21 [a]"Naphtali is a doe let loose
that bears beautiful fawns.[2]

22 "Joseph is [b]a fruitful bough,
a fruitful bough by a spring;
his branches run over the wall.[3]
23 The archers [c]bitterly attacked him,
shot at him, and harassed him
severely,
24 yet [d]his bow remained unmoved;
his arms[4] were made agile
by the hands of the [e]Mighty One of
Jacob
(from there is [f]the Shepherd,[5] [g]the
Stone of Israel),
25 [h]by the God of your father who will
help you,
by [i]the Almighty[6] [j]who will bless
you
with blessings of heaven above,
blessings of the deep that crouches
beneath,
blessings of the breasts and of the
womb.
26 The blessings of your father
are mighty beyond the blessings of
my parents,
up to the bounties [k]of the
everlasting hills.[7]
May they be [l]on the head of Joseph,
and on the brow of him who was
set apart from his brothers.

27 [m]"Benjamin is a ravenous wolf,
in the morning devouring the prey
and at evening [n]dividing the spoil."

Jacob's Death and Burial

28 All these are the twelve tribes of Israel. This is what their father said to them as he blessed them, blessing each with the blessing suitable to him. 29 Then he commanded them and said to them, "I am to be [o]gathered to my people; [p]bury me with my fathers [q]in the cave that is in the field of Ephron the Hittite, 30 in the cave that is in the field at Machpelah, to the east of Mamre, in the land of Canaan, [r]which

15 [s]Josh. 16:10
16 [t][Deut. 33:22] [u]ch. 30:6
17 [v]Judg. 18:27
18 [w]Ps. 25:5; 119:166, 174; Isai. 25:9; Mic. 7:7; [Luke 2:25]
19 [x][Deut. 33:20] [y]See 1 Chr. 5:18-22
20 [z][Deut. 33:24]
21 [a][Deut. 33:23]
22 [b]ch. 41:52; Josh. 17:14, 18
23 [c][ch. 37:24, 28; 39:20]
24 [d]Job 29:20 [e]Ps. 132:2, 5; Isai. 1:24 [f]Ps. 23:1; 80:1 [g]Isai. 28:16; Eph. 2:20; 1 Pet. 2:4; [Deut. 32:4]
25 [h]ch. 35:3; 50:17
[i]ch. 17:1; 35:11 [j]Deut. 33:13
26 [k]Deut. 33:15; Hab. 3:6 [l]Deut. 33:16
27 [m][Judg. 20:21, 25; Ezek. 22:27] [n]Zech. 14:1; [Ezek. 39:10]
29 [o]ver. 33; ch. 25:8 [p]ch. 47:30 [q]ch. 50:13; [ch. 23:9]
30 [r]See ch. 23:16-18

1 *Gad* sounds like the Hebrew for *raiders* and *raid* 2 Or *he gives beautiful words, or that bears fawns of the fold* 3 Or *Joseph is a wild donkey, a wild donkey beside a spring, his wild colts beside the wall* 4 Hebrew *the arms of his hands* 5 Or *by the name of the Shepherd* 6 Hebrew *Shaddai* 7 A slight emendation yields (compare Septuagint) *the blessings of the eternal mountains, the bounties of the everlasting hills*

49:15 a servant. Failing to drive the Canaanites out of its territory, the tribe of Issachar was apparently willing to trade its liberty for forced labor (cf. Judg. 1:28, 30). Issachar threw off the Canaanite yoke under the leadership of Deborah and Barak (Judg. 5:15).

49:16 judge his people. Or, provide justice for them. See 30:6.

49:17 a serpent. Though small, Dan was dangerous and struck unexpectedly to overthrow larger foes (Judg. 18). The Danite Samson single-handedly struck the Philistines (Judg. 13–16).

49:18 A brief prayer stands in the middle of the oracles.

49:19 Gad. This verse consists of a play on words (four of the six Hebrew words sound like "Gad") pointing to the constant danger to Gad from its southern and eastern neighbors (Ammon and Moab).

49:20 food . . . delicacies. A reference to its fertile land (Deut. 33:24; Josh. 19:24–31). See 30:13.

49:21 Naphtali. See 30:8; Josh. 19:32–38.

49:22 Joseph. See 30:24; 48:15–20.

fruitful. Barren Rachel would produce the most fruitful tribe (30:2, 22; 41:52).

run over the wall. The children of Joseph later sought to increase their territory (Josh. 17:14–18).

49:24, 25 Note the striking multiplication of divine names.

49:24 Stone. Israel's sure defense (Deut. 32:4 note).

49:25 Almighty. See note 17:1.

bless. The Hebrew root for "bless" is used six times in this verse. These blessings were fertility of land fed by water from heaven above and earth below (1:6–8 and note) and fertility of body (1:22; cf. Num. 24:5–7). Blessings given mankind at creation were concentrated on Joseph.

49:26 set apart. See note Deut. 33:16.

49:27 Benjamin . . . wolf. See 35:18. This tribe was later to have a fierce reputation (Judg. 20:14–25).

49:29–50:26 Believing in God's promises to Abraham and Isaac about the Promised Land (13:15 and note), Jacob arranged for his burial with them in Canaan (49:29–32; cf. 47:29–31). Joseph also instructed his family to bury him in the Promised Land after the Exodus (50:24–26; cf. Josh. 24:32). The burial of Jacob in the ancestral cave and Joseph's determination to be buried in Canaan underscore the covenant family's solidarity and point forward to the Exodus from Egypt. The unity of the family is further emphasized by Joseph's kind words and provisions for his offending brothers (50:15–21).

49:29 in the cave. See ch. 23; 25:9 and notes.

Abraham bought with the field from
Ephron the Hittite to possess as a burying
place. 31 [s]There they buried Abraham and
Sarah his wife. There [t]they buried Isaac and
Rebekah his wife, and there I buried
Leah— 32 the field and the cave that is in it
were bought from the Hittites." 33 When
Jacob finished commanding his sons, he
drew up his feet into the bed and breathed
his last and [u]was gathered to his people.

50

Then Joseph [v]fell on his father's
face and wept over him and kissed
him. 2 And Joseph commanded his servants
the physicians to [w]embalm his father. So
the physicians embalmed Israel. 3 Forty
days were required for it, for that is how
many are required for embalming. And the
Egyptians [x]wept for him seventy days.
4 And when the days of weeping for him
were past, Joseph spoke to the household
of Pharaoh, saying, [y]"If now I have found
favor in your eyes, please speak in the ears
of Pharaoh, saying, 5 My father made me
swear, saying, 'I am about to die: in my
tomb [z]that I hewed out for myself in the
land of Canaan, there shall you bury me.'
Now therefore, let me please go up and
bury my father. Then I will return." 6 And
Pharaoh answered, "Go up, and bury your
father, as he made you swear." 7 So Joseph
went up to bury his father. With him went
up all the servants of Pharaoh, the elders of
his household, and all the elders of the
land of Egypt, 8 as well as all the household
of Joseph, his brothers, and his father's
household. Only their children, their
flocks, and their herds were left [a]in the
land of Goshen. 9 And there went up with
him both chariots and horsemen. It was a
very great company. 10 When they came to
the threshing floor of Atad, which is
beyond the Jordan, [b]they lamented there
with a very great and grievous lamentation,
and he [c]made a mourning for his father
seven days. 11 When the inhabitants of the
land, the Canaanites, saw the mourning on
the threshing floor of Atad, they said, "This
is a grievous mourning by the Egyptians."
Therefore the place was named Abel-
mizraim;[1] it is beyond the Jordan. 12 Thus
his sons did for him as he had commanded them, 13 for [d]his sons carried him to the
land of Canaan and buried him in the cave
of the field at Machpelah, to the east of
Mamre, which Abraham [e]bought with the
field from Ephron the Hittite to possess as
a burying place. 14 After he had buried his
father, Joseph returned to Egypt with his
brothers and all who had gone up with him
to bury his father.

God's Good Purposes

15 When Joseph's brothers saw that their
father was dead, they said, "It may be that
Joseph will hate us and pay us back for all
the evil that we did to him." 16 So they sent
a message to Joseph, saying, "Your father
gave this command before he died, 17 'Say to
Joseph, Please forgive the transgression of
your brothers and their sin, because they
did evil to you.' And now, please forgive the
transgression of the servants of [f]the God of
your father." Joseph wept when they spoke
to him. 18 His brothers also came and [g]fell
down before him and said, "Behold, we are
your servants." 19 But Joseph said to them,
"Do not fear, for [h]am I in the place of God?
20 As for you, you meant evil against me, but
[i]God meant it for good, to bring it about
that many people[2] should be kept alive, as
they are today. 21 So do not fear; [j]I will provide for you and your little ones." Thus he
comforted them and spoke kindly to them.

31 [s]ch. 23:19; 25:9 [t]ch. 35:29
33 [u]ver. 29
Chapter 50
1 [v]ch. 46:4
2 [w]ver. 26; [2 Chr. 16:14; Mark 16:1; Luke 23:56; John 19:39, 40]
3 [x][ver. 10; Num. 20:29; Deut. 34:8; 1 Sam. 31:13; Job 2:13]
4 [y]ch. 47:29; See ch. 33:15
5 [z]2 Chr. 16:14; Isai. 22:16; Matt. 27:60
8 [a]See ch. 45:10
10 [b][2 Sam. 1:17; Acts 8:2] [c][ver. 3]
13 [d]ch. 49:29, 30; [Acts 7:16] [e]ch. 23:16
17 [f]ch. 49:25
18 [g][ch. 37:7, 10]
19 [h]ch. 30:2; [2 Kin. 5:7]
20 [i]ch. 45:5, 7
21 [j]ch. 45:11; 47:12

1 *Abel-mizraim* means *mourning* (or *meadow*) *of Egypt* 2 Or *a numerous people*

50:2 to embalm. An Egyptian practice designed to preserve the body after death and so to maintain personal identity in the afterlife; embalming was not practiced in Israel. Here the embalming preserved the body for transport back to Canaan.

50:4 spoke to the household of Pharaoh. Having just mourned his father's death (Deut. 34:8 note), Joseph's appearance was probably unsuitable for an appearance before Pharaoh (cf. 41:14).

50:5 I hewed out for myself. The Hebrew verb translated "hewed out" can also mean "purchased" (cf. ch. 23). If the text reading is followed, Joseph simply expressed Jacob's instructions in words Pharaoh understood.

50:9 chariots and horsemen. The protection given the burial party by Egyptian arms contrasts with the threat of Egyptian chariots during the Mosaic exodus (Ex. 14:9; 15:4, 5).

50:16 gave this command. It is unclear whether Jacob had actually said this or the fearful brothers simply invented it. In any case, they based their plea for forgiveness on their worship of the same God (v. 17).

50:19 am I in the place of God. Joseph recognized that his captivity had been part of God's gracious plan to save the covenant family (45:5–8); it was not his place to question God's wisdom.

50:20 you meant evil . . . God meant it for good. A classic statement of God's sovereign overruling of human history to accomplish His gracious purposes (24:27; 45:5, 7, 8 and notes). See "Providence"at Prov. 16:33.

that many people should be kept alive. In Egypt, Canaan, and elsewhere (41:57).

The Death of Joseph

22 So Joseph remained in Egypt, he and
his father's house. Joseph lived 110 years.
23 And Joseph saw Ephraim's children [k]of
the third generation. The [l]children also of
Machir the son of Manasseh were [m]counted
as Joseph's own.[1] 24 And Joseph said to his
brothers, "I am about to die, but [n]God will
visit you and bring you up out of this land
to the land [o]that he swore to Abraham, to
Isaac, and to Jacob." 25 Then [p]Joseph made
the sons of Israel swear, saying, "God will
surely visit you, and you shall carry up my
bones from here." 26 So Joseph died, being
110 years old. They [q]embalmed him, and
he was put in a coffin in Egypt.

23 [k][Job 42:16; Ps. 128:6] [l]Num. 32:39; 1 Chr. 7:14, 15 [m][ch. 30:3] 24 [n]ch. 15:14; 46:4; 48:21; Ex. 3:16, 17; [Heb. 11:22] [o]ch. 15:18; 26:3; 28:13; 35:12; 46:4 25 [p]Ex. 13:19; Josh. 24:32 26 [q]See ver. 2

1 Hebrew *were born on Joseph's knees*

50:23 counted as Joseph's own. See notes 30:3 and 48:12. Joseph apparently adopted these great-grandchildren.

50:24 God will visit you. Like his father Jacob on his deathbed (48:21), Joseph expressed firm confidence in God's covenant promises and His gracious visitation. The Hebrew verb translated "visit" denotes a divine encounter that will change one's fortunes for good or ill. For other instances of God's gracious "visitation" see 21:1 (Abraham and Sarah); Ex. 3:16 and 4:31 (the Exodus); Luke 1:68, 78 (the birth of Jesus); and Acts 15:14 (the extension of the gospel to the Gentiles).

Abraham . . . Isaac . . . Jacob. For the first time the three patriarchs are mentioned together; that era passed, but not its hope (Ex. 3:6; Deut. 30:20; 1 Kin. 18:36; 2 Chr. 30:6).

50:25 carry up my bones. Joseph's bones were taken from Egypt by Moses (Ex. 13:19), and later buried at Shechem (Josh. 24:32).

THE SECOND BOOK OF MOSES CALLED

Exodus

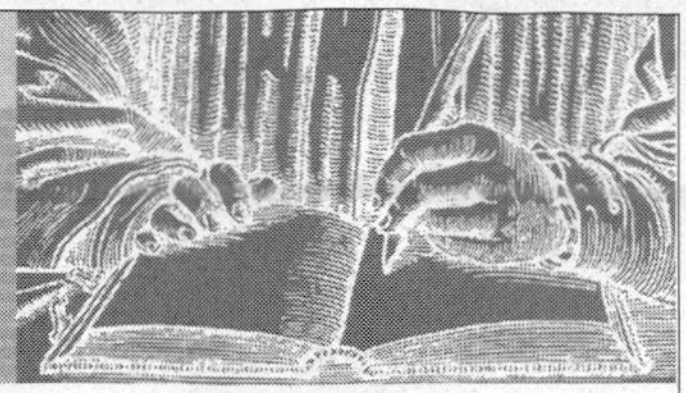

AUTHOR

In the New Testament Jesus calls Exodus "the book of Moses" (Mark 12:26; cf. 7:10), and there are no compelling reasons to deny the Mosaic authorship of the book (Introduction to the Pentateuch: Author and Date).

The title of the book, "Exodus," is derived from the Greek word *exodos* (Luke 9:31), which means "exit" or "departure." The book takes its name from the central event of Israel's departure from Egypt, recorded in the book's first fifteen chapters.

DATE AND OCCASION

Given Moses' authorship of Exodus, we should date the book after the exodus event (c. 1450–1440 B.C.) and before his death about 1406 B.C. According to the dating below, Moses' birth would have just fallen within the reign of Thutmose I. Hatshepsut, the widowed queen of Thutmose II, assumed male titles and even a beard as she reigned from 1504–1483 B.C. Perhaps she was the Pharaoh upon whose death Moses returned to Egypt from Midian.

Exodus carries forward the story of God's fulfillment of His promise to Abraham to bless him and make of him a great nation (Gen. 12:2). It begins by referring to the descent of Israel into Egypt
(1:1–7); this connects through Gen. 46:8–27 with the Genesis narratives. The book concludes with Israel at Sinai where the tabernacle is completed. The events covered in the book may be placed against their historical background as follows.

Joseph's rise to power (1:5) is best set in the favorable conditions for Jacob's family created by the rule over Egypt of the Semitic Hyksos (c. 1700–1550 B.C.). The reference at 1:8 to a new king "who did not know Joseph" likely refers to the expulsion of the Hyksos by the eighteenth dynasty founder Ahmosis I (1570–1546 B.C.). If the Exodus is dated c. 1450–1440 B.C. (Interpretive Difficulties below), the Pharaoh of the oppression was probably Thutmose I (1526–1512 B.C.), while the Pharaoh of the Exodus was Thutmose III (1504–1450 B.C.) or Amenhotep II (1450–1425 B.C.). This dating would allow a possible identification of the incoming Israelites with the Habiru, a group mentioned in the Tell el-Amarna letters (correspondence between Egypt and its Syro-Palestinian vassals during the fourteenth century B.C.). The Habiru were a social or occupational class commonly attested in texts from 2000 B.C. onwards. They were political outcasts in Palestine (Gen. 14:13 note).

The written preservation of the words of God's covenant has central importance for the theology of the Book of Exodus. God not only speaks His words to His assembled people at Sinai, He also gives them His Ten Commandments in writing, "written with the finger of God" on tablets of stone (31:18; cf. 32:15, 16; 34:1, 28). The terms of the covenant were further specified by the so-called "Book of the Covenant" (20:22–23:19), the words of God written down by Moses, the mediator of God's covenant (24:4, 7; 34:27).

The Sinai covenant (19:1–20:21; ch. 24) resembles in both form and content the state treaty form of the second millennium B.C., particularly the Hittite state treaties. These treaties included a preamble (20:2), stipulations (20:3–17), ratification (24:1–11), and blessings and curses. A copy of the treaty was often preserved at the sanctuaries of the parties (e.g., the two tablets of 31:18). Also, the similarity of the content of the case laws of chs. 21–23 to ancient Near Eastern codes (particularly the Code of Hammurabi of Babylon, c. 1750 B.C.) has often been noted.

INTERPRETIVE DIFFICULTIES

The date and route of the Exodus have been subjects of considerable debate. Biblical chronology dates the exodus event at 480 years before the reign of Solomon (1 Kin. 6:1). This would place the event at about 1440 B.C. This early date is consistent with Judg. 11:26, which declares that three hundred years had elapsed since Israel entered Canaan. The c. 1440 B.C. date is also supported by 12:40, 41, where 430 years is the duration of Israel's stay in Egypt. The Pharaoh of the Exodus would then be Thutmose III or Amenhotep II.

Advocates of a much later date appeal to the name "Raamses" (or "Rameses" Gen. 47:11) as one of the store cities built with Israelite labor (1:11). Rameses II (1304–1236 B.C.) is taken to be the Pharaoh of the Exodus, and the approximate date set at 1270 B.C. This is held to be more consistent with the archaeology of cities destroyed in Palestine and with the lack of earlier settlement in Transjordan (the region east of the Jordan River and the Dead Sea). However, more recent discoveries in Transjordan and a new evaluation of the destruction of Jericho have weakened the case for the late date.

The route of the Exodus began at Rameses. Its exact location is the subject of considerable debate, though modern Qantir is the site most favored (Tell el-Daba). From there the Hebrews journeyed south to Succoth (13:20). Here, apparently unable to move on, the Hebrews turned northward (14:2). Three sites are mentioned, Baal-zephon, Migdol, and Pi-hahiroth. Baal-zephon is associated with Tahpanhes, bordering Lake Menzaleh, one of the salt lakes between the Mediterranean and Gulf of Suez. There were three possible routes of Israelite escape. The "way of the land of the Philistines" (13:17) connected Egypt with Canaan by the heavily fortified coastal route. A second route, the way of Shur, began near the Wadi Tumilat in the Delta area, crossed to Kadesh-barnea, and branched off to Canaan. The Egyptian boundary wall of Shur may have been a major obstacle to this route. In leading the people south to southern Sinai, the Lord not only brought them to the mountain He had designated to Moses, but distanced them from further contact with the Egyptians. The deliverance through the sea may have been on a southern extension of Lake Menzaleh.

The Sinai peninsula is a triangle of land measuring approximately 150 miles across at the top and 260 miles along the sides. Two arms of the Red Sea, the Gulf of Suez and the Gulf of Aqaba, flank it. The Hebrews proceeded south along the west coast of the Sinai. The bitter waters of Marah (15:22–25) are usually identified with Ain Hawarah (some forty-five to fifty miles south of the tip of the Gulf of Suez), but Ain Musa may be the correct location. Elim with its many springs and trees has been identified as Wadi Gharandel, the encampment by the Red Sea (Num. 33:10), about seven miles south of Ain Hawarah. The wilderness of Sin would best be identified with Debbet er-Ramleh, a sandy plain along the edge of the Sinai Plateau. If the traditional location of Mount Sinai as Jebel Musa is correct, Israel would have then turned inland by a series of valleys to Jebel Musa, traveling through the desert of Rephidim, where they fought against the Amalekites (17:8–16). Rephidim was the last encampment in the wilderness of Sinai before the sacred mountain. Then they proceeded to Mount Sinai (ch. 19) where they received the law.

CHARACTERISTICS AND THEMES

Several major themes are evident in the Book of Exodus. First, it tells how the Lord liberated Israel from Egypt to fulfill His covenant with the fathers. A second major element of the book is the covenant revelation at Sinai, which specified the terms of relationship between the holy God and His people. The third theme issues from the first two and is their consummation: the reestablishment of God's dwelling with man. Each of these themes involves a triumph of divine grace: God's mighty rescue of His people from slavery in Egypt, His thunderous self-revelation at Sinai, and His gracious condescension to dwell with His erring people in the tabernacle. The unfolding of these themes also reveals the Lord's holiness and grace in His covenant law and in the ceremonial symbolism of Israel's life and worship.

Crucial to the narrative is Moses' role as mediator between God and man. As God's chosen servant, Moses is the mediator of judgment against Egypt, and is the one through whom

God delivers Israel. Through Moses God gives His revelation at Sinai. Moses also shepherds the people through the wilderness to the Promised Land. He pleads for the people, and he is the one through whom the Lord provides food and water. But Moses' role in the history of redemption prepares pointedly for Christ, the Mediator of the new covenant (Deut. 18:15). The revelation that Moses receives of God's name "abounding in steadfast love and faithfulness" (34:6) justifies the building of the tabernacle, but that description of the Lord points forward to the coming of the true tabernacle, the incarnate Christ, the greater Servant of the Lord (John 1:14, 17; Heb. 3:1–6).

God's law reveals His holy nature and requires holiness of the people among whom God will dwell. The ceremonial regulations for Israel's life and worship (chs. 25–31; 35–40) mark out the separation of Israel as the people among whom God lives and rules, demonstrating His kingdom before the nations.

In addition to its description of the historical events by which Israel was delivered to become God's people, Exodus also presents a major illustration of God's saving work throughout history. The savior God redeems His chosen people from the powers of evil, judges those powers, and claims His people as His firstborn son, a holy nation of priests among whom He dwells by His Spirit. The pattern of divine victory over enemies, followed by the establishment of the divine dwelling place, is repeated in Christ's first and second advents (e.g., Eph. 2:14–22; Rev. 20:11–22:5).

The symbolism found in Exodus becomes reality in the new covenant (Jer. 31:31–34; Col. 2:17; Heb. 10:1). The sprinkled blood of animal sacrifice is now replaced by the blood of Christ (24:8; Matt. 26:27, 28; Heb. 12:24; 1 Pet. 1:2). The symbolic substitution of the Passover lamb is fulfilled in Christ, the Lamb of God, our Passover sacrifice (John 1:29; 1 Cor. 5:7). His "exodus" at Jerusalem (Luke 9:31) accomplishes the salvation of the true people of God. God's new covenant people are joined to Jesus Christ, in whom the Gentiles become the people of God, members of the commonwealth of Israel and fellow citizens with the Old Testament saints (19:5, 6; Eph. 2:11–19). The full meaning of the description of Israel in Exodus may now therefore be applied to the churches of the Gentiles (1 Pet. 2:9, 10).

OUTLINE OF EXODUS

I. God Delivers His People: The Exodus (1:1–15:21)
- A. *God in Faithfulness Remembers Israel (chs. 1; 2)*
- B. *God Calls Moses to Deliver Israel (3:1–4:26)*
- C. *Pharaoh Rejects God's Demand (4:27–7:13)*
- D. *God's Judgment Against Egypt (7:14–10:29)*
- E. *God Delivers Israel from Egypt (11:1–13:16)*
- F. *God Saves Israel at the Red Sea (13:17–15:21)*

II. God Leads His People: The Wilderness Testing (15:22–18:27)
- A. *Marah to Elim: God Brings Healing (15:22–27)*
- B. *Wilderness of Sin: God Provides Food (ch. 16)*
- C. *Rephidim: God Provides Water (17:1–7)*
- D. *Rephidim: God Provides Protection (17:8–16)*
- E. *Mountain of God: God Provides Organization (ch. 18)*

III. God and Israel Enter into Covenant (chs. 19–24)
- A. *Preparations for the Covenant (ch. 19)*
- B. *God Proclaims the Covenant (chs. 20–23)*
- C. *Israel Ratifies the Covenant (ch. 24)*

IV. God Reveals the Pattern of the Tabernacle and Its Ministry (chs. 25–31)
- A. *The Tabernacle, Courts, and Furnishings (chs. 25–27)*
- B. *The Priestly Ministry (chs. 28–30)*
- C. *Artisans for the Tabernacle Construction (31:1–11)*
- D. *Sign of the Covenant and the Tablets (31:12–18)*

V. Israel's Rebellion, Judgment, and Restoration (32:1–34:35)
- A. *Israel's Idolatrous Worship (32:1–6)*
- B. *Israel Judged for Idolatry (32:7–29)*
- C. *God Threatens to Withdraw His Presence from Israel (32:30–34:9)*
- D. *God Renews His Covenant (34:10–35)*

VI. Israel's Artisans Prepare the Tabernacle (chs. 35–39)
- A. *Israel Admonished to Remember the Sabbath (35:1–3)*
- B. *Freewill Offerings for the Tabernacle (35:4–29)*
- C. *Craftsmen Called to Begin the Work (35:30–36:17)*
- D. *The Curtains, Boards, and Veils are Made (36:8–38)*
- E. *The Furnishings are Fashioned (37:1–38:8)*
- F. *The Courtyard is Made (38:9–20)*
- G. *Summary: Treasurer's Report (38:21–31)*
- H. *The Priestly Garments Are Sewn (39:1–31)*
- I. *The Work Completed (39:32–43)*

VII. Israel's Artisans Erect the Tabernacle (ch. 40)
- A. *Instructions for the Tabernacle Erection (40:1–16)*
- B. *Moses Supervises the Raising of the Tabernacle (40:17–33)*
- C. *God's Glory Fills the Tabernacle (40:34–38)*

Israel Increases Greatly in Egypt

1 [a]These are the names of the sons of
Israel who came to Egypt with Jacob,
each with his household: 2 Reuben,
Simeon, Levi, and Judah, 3 Issachar,
Zebulun, and Benjamin, 4 Dan and
Naphtali, Gad and Asher. 5 All the descendants of Jacob were [b]seventy persons;
Joseph was already in Egypt. 6 Then [c]Joseph
died, and all his brothers and all that generation. 7 [d]But the people of Israel were
fruitful and increased greatly; they multiplied and grew exceedingly strong, so that
the land was filled with them.

Pharaoh Oppresses Israel

8 Now there arose a new king over Egypt,
[e]who did not know Joseph. 9 And he said to
his people, "Behold, [f]the people of Israel
are too many and too mighty for us.
10 [g]Come, [h]let us deal shrewdly with them,
lest they multiply, and, if war breaks out,
they join our enemies and fight against us
and escape from the land." 11 Therefore
they set taskmasters over them [i]to afflict
them with heavy [j]burdens. They built for
Pharaoh [k]store cities, Pithom and
[l]Raamses. 12 But the more they were
oppressed, the more they multiplied and
the more they spread abroad. And the
Egyptians were in dread of the people of
Israel. 13 So they ruthlessly made the people
of Israel [m]work as slaves 14 and [n]made their
lives bitter with hard service, in mortar and
brick, and in all kinds of work in the field.
In all their work they ruthlessly made them
work as slaves.

15 Then the king of Egypt said to the
Hebrew midwives, one of whom was
named Shiphrah and the other Puah,
16 "When you serve as midwife to the
Hebrew women and see them on the birthstool, if it is a son, you shall kill him, but if
it is a daughter, she shall live." 17 But the
midwives [o]feared God and did not do as
the king of Egypt commanded them, but
let the male children live. 18 So the king of
Egypt called the midwives and said to
them, "Why have you done this, and let
the male children live?" 19 The midwives
said to Pharaoh, "Because the Hebrew
women are not like the Egyptian women,
for they are vigorous and give birth before
the midwife comes to them." 20 [p]So God
dealt well with the midwives. And the people multiplied and grew very strong. 21 And
because the midwives feared God, [q]he gave
them families. 22 Then Pharaoh commanded all his people, [r]"Every son that is born
to the Hebrews[1] you shall cast into [s]the
Nile, but you shall let every daughter live."

The Birth of Moses

2 Now a [t]man from the house of Levi
went and took as his wife a Levite
woman. 2 The woman conceived and bore a
son, and [u]when she saw that he was a fine

1 Samaritan, Septuagint, Targum; Hebrew lacks *to the Hebrews*

Chapter 1
1 [a]For ver. 1-3, see Gen. 35:23-26; 46:8-26
5 [b]Gen. 46:27; Deut. 10:22
6 [c]Gen. 50:26
7 [d]Deut. 26:5; Acts 7:17; [Gen. 46:3]
8 [e]Cited Acts 7:18
9 [f]Ps. 105:24
10 [g]Ps. 83:3, 4 [h]Ps. 105:25; Acts 7:19
11 [i]ch. 3:7; Gen. 15:13; Deut. 26:6 [j]ch. 2:11; 5:4, 5; 6:6, 7; Ps. 81:6 [k][2 Chr. 16:4] [l][ch. 12:37; Gen. 47:11]
13 [m]See ch. 5:7-19
14 [n][ch. 2:23; 6:9; Num. 20:15; Acts 7:19, 34]
17 [o]Prov. 16:6; [Dan. 3:16-18; 6:13; Acts 5:29]
20 [p][Eccles. 8:12]
21 [q][1 Sam. 2:35; 2 Sam. 7:11, 27; 1 Kin. 2:24; 11:38; Ps. 127:1]
22 [r]Acts 7:19 [s]Gen. 41:1
Chapter 2
1 [t]ch. 6:20; Num. 26:59; 1 Chr. 23:14
2 [u]Acts 7:20; Heb. 11:23

1:1–4 Exodus and Genesis are linked by this introduction (Gen. 46:8–27). God's promise to Abraham is fulfilled by Israel's fruitfulness (Gen. 12:2).

1:5 seventy. See notes Gen. 46:15–27. The number going into Egypt is sometimes given as seventy-five (Acts 7:14), with the difference due to who is counted. The Septuagint text (the Greek Old Testament) adds five of Joseph's further male descendants, yielding a total of seventy-five. With women and children the total number was over 150.

1:7 multiplied . . . exceedingly. The terms "fruitful," "multiplied," and "the land was filled" remind us of Gen. 1:26–28. Israel fulfills the mandate given to humankind in Gen. 1. The land was probably the land of Goshen in northeastern Egypt, in the Wadi Tumilat in the Delta, a valley 30 to 40 miles long (cf. Gen. 47:4).

1:8–22 God's multiplication of Israel leads to their oppression by the Egyptians.

1:8 a new king. The beginning of a new era is marked off by the advent of a new Pharaoh. This Pharaoh may have been Ahmosis I (1570–1546 B.C.) of the eighteenth dynasty, who expelled the Hyksos, the Semitic rulers of Egypt from about 1700–1550 B.C. (Introduction: Date and Occasion; Acts 7:18 note).

1:11 Pithom and Raamses. These cities for storing agricultural provisions and military supplies were located in the strategic Nile Delta region. Pithom was probably located at modern Tell er-Ratabah or Tell el Maskhutah, and Raamses is identified as modern Qantir. This item comes too early in the oppression cycle to be identified as the work of Rameses II (1304–1236 B.C.) who is often identified as the Pharaoh of the Exodus (Introduction: Interpretive Difficulties; Gen. 47:11 note). The only other Pharaoh with the necessary forty years' reign was Thutmose III (1504–1450 B.C.). By the nineteenth dynasty the term "Pharaoh" (Egyptian for "great house") became a royal title. Earlier it was a synonym for governmental authority.

1:14 bitter. The bitter oppression of Egypt was later commemorated by the bitter herbs of the Passover meal (12:8).

1:15 Hebrew. See note Gen. 14:13.

midwives. Two midwives to serve such a large population seem far too few; they may have been guild leaders. Their names are Semitic and v. 15 identifies them as Israelite.

1:16 birthstool. These consisted of two stones upon which women in labor squatted.

2:1 a man. The fate of Israel hangs on one family member. Moses has an older sister (v. 4) and brother (7:7). His parents, Amram and Jochebed, were nephew and aunt (6:20).

2:2 fine child. Moses was a healthy child and likely to survive. Jesus Christ, antitype of Moses and founder of the new Israel, was also born under an edict of death and miraculously spared in Egypt (Matt. 2:13–23).

child, she hid him three months. **3** When she could hide him no longer, she took for him a basket made of bulrushes[1] and daubed it with bitumen and pitch. She put the child in it and placed it among the [v]reeds by the river bank. **4** And [w]his sister stood at a distance to know what would be done to him. **5** Now the daughter of Pharaoh came down to bathe at the river, while her young women walked beside the river. She saw the basket among the reeds and sent her servant woman, and she took it. **6** When she opened it, she saw the child, and behold, the baby was crying. She took pity on him and said, "This is one of the Hebrews' children." **7** Then his sister said to Pharaoh's daughter, "Shall I go and call you a nurse from the Hebrew women to nurse the child for you?" **8** And Pharaoh's daughter said to her, "Go." So the girl went and called the child's mother. **9** And Pharaoh's daughter said to her, "Take this child away and nurse him for me, and I will give you your wages." So the woman took the child and nursed him. **10** When the child grew up, she brought him to Pharaoh's daughter, and he became [x]her son. She named him Moses,[2] "Because," she said, "I [y]drew him out of the water."

Moses Flees to Midian

11 One day, [z]when Moses had grown up, he went out to his people and looked on their [a]burdens, and he saw an Egyptian beating a Hebrew, one of his people.[3] **12** He looked this way and that, and seeing no one, he [b]struck down the Egyptian and hid him in the sand. **13** When [c]he went out the next day, behold, two Hebrews were struggling together. And he said to the man in the wrong, "Why do you strike your companion?" **14** He answered, [d]"Who made you a prince and a judge over us? Do you mean to kill me as you killed the Egyptian?" Then Moses was afraid, and thought, "Surely the thing is known." **15** When Pharaoh heard of it, he sought to kill Moses. But [e]Moses fled from Pharaoh and stayed in the land of Midian. And he sat down by [f]a well.

16 Now the [g]priest of Midian had seven daughters, and [h]they came and drew water and filled the troughs to water their father's flock. **17** The shepherds came and drove them away, but Moses stood up and saved them, and [i]watered their flock. **18** When they came home to their father [j]Reuel, he said, "How is it that you have come home so soon today?" **19** They said, "An Egyptian delivered us out of the hand of the shepherds and even drew water for us and [i]watered the flock." **20** He said to his daughters, "Then where is he? Why have you left the man? Call him, that he may [k]eat bread." **21** And Moses was content to dwell with the man, and he gave Moses his daughter [l]Zipporah. **22** She gave birth to a son, and he called his name [m]Gershom, for he said, "I have been a [n]sojourner[4] in a foreign land."

God Hears Israel's Groaning

23 [o]During those many days the king of Egypt died, and the people of Israel [p]groaned because of their slavery and cried out for help. [q]Their cry for rescue from

3 [v]ver. 5; Isai. 19:6
4 [w]ch. 15:20; Num. 26:59
10 [x]Acts 7:21; [Heb. 11:24] [y]2 Sam. 22:17; Ps. 18:16
11 [z]Acts 7:23; Heb. 11:24-26 [a]See ch. 1:11
12 [b]Acts 7:24
13 [c]Acts 7:23-28
14 [d][Luke 12:14]
15 [e]Acts 7:29; Heb. 11:27 [f]Gen. 24:11; 29:2
16 [g]ch. 3:1 [h]Gen. 24:11; 29:10; 1 Sam. 9:11
17 [i][Gen. 29:10]
18 [j]Num. 10:29; [ch. 3:1; 4:18; 18:1, 5, 9, 12]
19 [i][See ver. 17 above]
20 [k]Gen. 31:54; 43:25
21 [l]ch. 4:25; 18:2
22 [m]ch. 18:3 [n]Acts 7:29; [Heb. 11:13, 14]
23 [o][ch 7:7]; Acts 7:23, 30 [p][Deut. 26:7] [q]ch. 3:9; Gen. 18:20, 21; James 5:4

1 Hebrew *papyrus reeds* 2 *Moses* sounds like the Hebrew for *draw out*
3 Hebrew *brothers* 4 *Gershom* sounds like the Hebrew for *sojourner*

2:3 basket made of bulrushes. A box of woven papyrus reeds, daubed with tar to make it watertight (cf. Job 9:26; Is. 18:2). Moses is perhaps depicted as a second Noah—the Hebrew term translated ark is used for Noah's craft in Gen. 7–9. Sargon of Accad (c. 2350 B.C.) was said to have been exposed in a similar chest and left to float in the Euphrates.

2:5 daughter of Pharaoh. Some suppose that this princess became the famous Hatshepsut, the queen of Thutmose II who ruled Egypt after his death (1504–1483 B.C.).

2:10 Moses. This name is Semitic (text note), though perhaps it was compatible with Egyptian *Mose* meaning "is born" (e.g., *Thutmose,* meaning "Thut is born"). There is evidence that Semitic names were not uncommon in the royal court, and it is possible that the child was given a Semitic name by the princess. He was educated in the Egyptian court as a promising young noble (Acts 7:22).

2:11–15 Now forty years old (Acts 7:23), Moses identifies himself with God's people (Heb. 11:24–27). His effort to deliver an Israelite from oppression proves vain when he seeks to be a judge of Israel (v. 14).

2:15 Midian. Probably the name of an early tribal confederacy operating in the Arabian desert. The nomadic Midianites were descendants of Abraham and Keturah (Gen. 25:1–6; Num. 10:29–32; Judg. 6).

2:16 drew water. The women did the difficult task and then were driven off.

2:17 saved them. This was Moses' third intervention in defense of the weak. Nomadic strife over water rights was common.

2:18 Reuel. The name means "Friend of God." Moses' father-in-law was known by two names: Reuel and Jethro (3:1; 4:18). Jethro and Reuel may be variant names, or Reuel a clan name.

2:22 Gershom. See text note. Moses had not forgotten his Egyptian home. Yet he will lead Israel from Egypt to the homeland of the people of God.

2:23 groaned . . . cried out . . . came up. Israel's anguished cry is balanced by a fourfold description of God's response. God "heard . . . remembered . . . saw . . . knew" (vv. 24, 25). This summary prepares for the call of Moses and underscores the book's theme of divine faithfulness to the covenant promises.

slavery came up to God. 24 And [r]God heard
their groaning, and God [s]remembered his
covenant with [t]Abraham, with Isaac, and
with Jacob. 25 God [u]saw the people of
Israel—and God [v]knew.

The Burning Bush

3 Now Moses was keeping the flock of his
father-in-law, Jethro, the priest of
Midian, and he led his flock to the west side
of the wilderness and came to Horeb, the
[w]mountain of God. 2 [x]And [y]the angel of the
LORD appeared to him in a flame of fire out
of the midst of a bush. He looked, and
behold, the bush was burning, yet it was not
consumed. 3 And Moses said, "I will turn
aside to see this great sight, why the bush is
not burned." 4 When the LORD saw that he
turned aside to see, [z]God called to him [a]out
of the bush, "Moses, Moses!" And he said,
"Here I am." 5 Then he said, "Do not come
near; [b]take your sandals off your feet, for the
place on which you are standing is holy
ground." 6 And he said, [c]"I am the God of
your father, the God of Abraham, the God of
Isaac, and the God of Jacob." And Moses hid
his face, for [d]he was afraid to look at God.
7 Then the LORD said, [e]"I have surely seen
the affliction of my people who are in Egypt
and have heard their cry because of their
[f]taskmasters. I know their sufferings, 8 and
[g]I have come down to deliver them out of
the hand of the Egyptians and [h]to bring
them up out of that land to a [i]good and
broad land, a land [j]flowing with milk and

24 [r]ch. 6:5 [s]Ps. 105:8, 42; 106:45 [t]Gen. 15:14; 46:4
25 [u]ch. 3:7; 4:31; [Luke 1:25] [v][ch. 3:16]
Chapter 3
1 [w]ch. 4:27; 18:5; 24:13; Num. 10:33; 1 Kin. 19:8
2 [x]For ver. 2-8, see Acts 7:30-35 [y]Isai. 63:9
4 [z]ch. 19:3 [a]Deut. 33:16
5 [b]Josh. 5:15; [ch. 19:12; Eccles. 5:1]
6 [c]ch. 4:5; Gen. 28:13; 1 Kin. 18:36; Cited Matt. 22:32; Mark 12:26; [Luke 20:37] [d][1 Kin. 19:13; Isai. 6:1, 2, 5]
7 [e]ch. 2:23-25; Neh. 9:9; Ps. 106:44 [f]ch. 5:13, 14 8 [g]Gen. 11:5, 7; 18:21 [h]ch. 6:6; 12:51; [Gen. 50:24] [i]Deut. 1:25; 8:7, 8, 9 [j]ch. 13:5; 33:3; Lev. 20:24; Num. 13:27; Deut. 26:9, 15; Jer. 11:5; 32:22; Ezek. 20:6

3:1 wilderness. An uncultivated area but capable of sustaining grazing. According to 34:3 and Num. 10:11, the wilderness of Sinai sustained Israel's flocks for a year. Horeb and Sinai are terms that possibly distinguish Horeb as an entire range from Mt. Sinai (19:18, 20; cf. Deut. 4:15). **mountain of God.** This term describes the mountain as a sanctuary, a designation that anticipates ch. 19. Moses is now eighty years old (7:7) and has been in Midian forty years.

3:2 angel of the LORD. This was a theophany, a visible manifestation of God (v. 4). See note Gen. 16:7.

fire. A frequent biblical symbol for God's presence (13:21; 19:18; Gen. 3:24; 1 Kin. 18:24, 38); it particularly expresses His all-consuming holiness (Heb. 12:29).

3:3 bush. A real bush was illumined with supernatural fire. God is transcendent, but reveals Himself in the bush to call Moses.

3:5 holy. The spot was made sacred by God's presence. See 19:23; 24:2. The question of how to approach the holy God is central for Exodus. It is resolved in the symbolism of the tabernacle.

3:6 God of your father. God remembers His covenant promises to the patriarchs and identifies Himself as their God. See Gen. 26:24; 28:13; 31:42; 32:9.

3:8 Canaanites. The inhabitants of the Syro-Palestinian coastland.

Hittites. See note Gen. 10:15.

Amorites. See note Gen. 10:16.

Perizzites. Possibly the peasantry located in central Palestine (Josh. 17:15).

Hivites. See note Gen. 10:17.

Jebusites. The original occupants of Jerusalem, later dispossessed by David (Gen. 10:16 note; 2 Sam. 5:6–9).

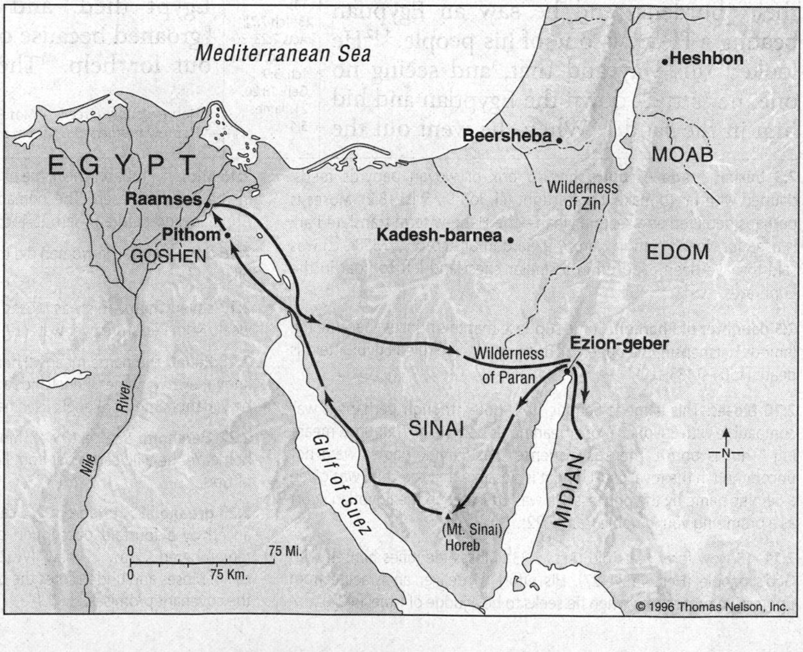

Moses' Flight and Return to Egypt. Being sought by Pharaoh for the slaying of an Egyptian, Moses fled through the Sinai desert and settled in the land of Midian. In the vicinity of Horeb, located by tradition in the Sinaitic Peninsula, Moses was tending the flocks of Jethro, his father-in-law. Here God revealed Himself in the burning bush and called Moses to go back to Egypt. Returning to Jethro in Midian, Moses gathered his family and began the journey to Egypt. He met Aaron at Horeb, and together they returned to Pharaoh's court in Raamses.

honey, to the place of [k]the Canaanites, the
Hittites, the Amorites, the Perizzites, the
Hivites, and the Jebusites. 9 And now,
behold, [l]the cry of the people of Israel has
come to me, and I have also seen the [m]op-
pression with which the Egyptians oppress
them. 10 [n]Come, I will send you to Pharaoh
that you may bring my people, the children
of Israel, out of Egypt." 11 But Moses said to
God, [o]"Who am I that I should go to
Pharaoh and bring the children of Israel out
of Egypt?" 12 He said, [p]"But I will be with
you, and this shall be the sign for you, that
I have sent you: when you have brought the
people out of Egypt, [q]you shall serve God
on this mountain."
13 Then Moses said to God, "If I come to
the people of Israel and say to them, 'The
God of your fathers has sent me to you,' and
they ask me, 'What is his name?' what shall
I say to them?" 14 God said to Moses, "I AM
WHO I AM."[1] And he said, "Say this to the
people of Israel, [r]'I AM has sent me to you.'"
15 God also said to Moses, "Say this to the
people of Israel, 'The LORD,[2] the [s]God of
your fathers, the God of Abraham, the God
of Isaac, and the God of Jacob, has sent me
to you.' This is [t]my name forever, and thus
I am to be remembered throughout all generations. 16 Go and [u]gather the elders of
Israel together and say to them, 'The LORD,
the God of your fathers, the God of Abraham, of Isaac, and of Jacob, has appeared to
me, saying, [v]"I have observed you and what
has been done to you in Egypt, 17 and I
promise that [w]I will bring you up out of
the affliction of Egypt to the land of the
Canaanites, the Hittites, the Amorites, the
Perizzites, the Hivites, and the Jebusites, a
land [w]flowing with milk and honey."' 18 And
[x]they will listen to your voice, and you and
the elders of Israel [y]shall go to the king of
Egypt and say to him, 'The LORD, the God
of the Hebrews, has [z]met with us; and now,
please let us go a three days' journey into
the wilderness, that we may sacrifice to the
LORD our God.' 19 But I know that the king
of Egypt [a]will not let you go unless compelled [b]by a mighty hand.[3] 20 So [c]I will
stretch out my hand and strike Egypt with
[d]all the wonders that I will do in it; [e]after
that he will let you go. 21 And [f]I will give this
people favor in the sight of the Egyptians;
and when you go, you shall not go empty,
22 but each woman shall ask of her neighbor, and any woman who lives in her
house, for [g]silver and gold jewelry, and for
clothing. You shall put them on your sons
and on your daughters. So [h]you shall plunder the Egyptians."

Moses Given Powerful Signs

4 Then Moses answered, "But behold,
they will not believe me or listen to my

8 [k]Gen. 15:18-21
9 [l]ch. 2:23 [m]ch. 1:11-14, 22
10 [n][Ps. 105:26; Mic. 6:4]
11 [o]ch. 6:12; [1 Sam. 18:18; Isai. 6:5, 8; Jer. 1:6]
12 [p]ch. 4:12, 15; Deut. 31:8, 23; Josh. 1:5 [q]See ch. 19
14 [r]ch. 6:3; Ps. 68:4; John 8:58; Heb. 13:8; Rev. 1:4; 4:8
15 [s]ver. 6 [t]Hos. 12:5; [Ps. 135:13]
16 [u]ch. 4:29 [v]ch. 4:31; Gen. 50:24; [Luke 1:68]
17 [w]ver. 8
18 [x]ch. 4:31 [y]ch. 5:1 [z]Num. 23:3, 4, 15, 16
19 [a]ch. 5:2; 7:4 [b]ch. 6:1; 13:3
20 [c]Deut. 6:22; Neh. 9:10; Jer. 32:20; Acts 7:36; See ch. 7–12 [d]ch. 4:21 [e]ch. 12:31
21 [f]ch. 11:2, 3; 12:35, 36; [Gen. 15:14]
22 [g][ch. 33:6] [h][Ezek. 39:10]

[1] Or *I AM WHAT I AM*, or *I WILL BE WHAT I WILL BE* [2] The word *LORD*, when spelled with capital letters, stands for the divine name, *YHWH*, which is here connected with the verb *hayah*, "to be" in verse 14
[3] Septuagint, Vulgate; Hebrew *go, not by a mighty hand*

3:10 Pharaoh. Probably Thutmose III (1504–1450 B.C.). See Introduction: Date and Occasion.

3:11 Who am I. Moses felt inadequate for the task, as did Gideon (Judg. 6:15) and Jeremiah (Jer. 1:6). This is the first of his four objections (v. 14; 4:1, 10).

3:12 sign. God's call will be confirmed by His future action. God will be with Moses to bring him back to worship ("serve God") on this same mountain. Having served the Egyptians, Israel will become God's servants in covenant worship.

3:13 What is his name. Moses anticipates a question from the people that is also his own. Already Moses seeks God's revelation of Himself. If God's deliverance was to be fully appreciated and assured, He who would be worshiped at this mountain must be known (33:12 and note). A personal name was not merely a form of address but a description of character and personality (Ps. 9:10; cf. 1 Sam. 25:25).

3:14 I AM WHO I AM. The Lord is not defined or determined by any other than Himself. As the self-existent One, His promise is sure; He will reveal Himself in His saving deeds.

3:15 The LORD. The Hebrew is *Yahweh,* probably derived from the Hebrew verb for "to be" (thus meaning "he is" or "he will be"). The corresponding first person is *'ehyeh,* "I am." Note the parallels: "I AM has sent me" (v. 14) and "The LORD [Yahweh] . . . has sent me" (v. 15). See theological note "'This Is My Name': God's Self-disclosure" on the next page.

remembered throughout all generations. Yahweh, the divine name particularly associated with God's covenant relationship with Israel, was henceforth to be used in worship. English versions of the Old Testament usually render this Hebrew name as "the LORD," following the practice of the New Testament, and of the Jews in the intertestamental period. The Jews thought the name too holy to pronounce, and when reading the text substituted *'adonay* ("my Lord"). The vowel signs for *'adonay* were later added to the Hebrew consonants of *Yahweh* as a pronunciation reminder, and this hybrid form was rendered "Jehovah" by William Tyndale's English translation (A.D. 1530). In the New Testament, LORD (Yahweh) is applied to Jesus (Rom. 10:13, citing Joel 2:32).

3:16 elders. Lit. "bearded ones." These are family heads who would represent Israel. They will be assembled to hear of God's faithfulness (4:30, 31).

3:17 milk and honey. The usual biblical description of Canaan.

3:18 three days' journey. Possibly an expression for a short period of time.

3:20 wonders. This mention of extraordinary deeds anticipates the plagues (7:14–12:30).

3:21 not go empty. As He promised (Gen. 15:14), God would see that their years of bondage were recompensed.

4:1–9 See "Miracles" at 1 Kin. 17:22.

4:1 But behold. Moses' third objection (3:11 note). Israel must be persuaded. This would be the difficult task, but God had purposed to see

voice, for they will say, 'The LORD did not
appear to you.'" 2 The LORD said to him,
"What is that in your hand?" He said, [i]"A
staff." 3 And he said, "Throw it on the
ground." So he threw it on the ground, and
it became a serpent, and Moses ran from it.
4 But the LORD said to Moses, "Put out your
hand and catch it by the tail"—so he put
out his hand and caught it, and it became
a staff in his hand— 5 "that they may [j]be-
lieve that the LORD, [k]the God of their
fathers, the God of Abraham, the God of
Isaac, and the God of Jacob, has appeared
to you." 6 Again, the LORD said to him, "Put
your hand inside your cloak." [1] And he put
his hand inside his cloak, and when he
took it out, behold, his hand was [l]leprous[2]
like snow. 7 Then God said, "Put your hand
back inside your cloak." So he put his hand
back inside his cloak, and when he took it
out, behold, [m]it was restored like the rest of
his flesh. 8 "If they will not believe you,"
God said, "or listen to the first sign, they
may believe the latter sign. 9 If they will not
believe even these two signs or listen to
your voice, you shall take some water from
the Nile and pour it on the dry ground, and
the water that you shall take from the Nile
[n]will become blood on the dry ground."

Chapter 4
2 [i]ver. 17, 20
5 [j]ch. 19:9
[k]See ch. 3:6
6 [l]Num. 12:10; 2 Kin. 5:27
7 [m][2 Kin. 5:14]
9 [n]ch. 7:19

1 Hebrew *into your bosom*; also verse 7 2 *Leprosy* was a term for several skin diseases; see Leviticus 13

"This is My Name": God's Self-disclosure

In the modern world, a person's name can be merely an identifying label; it does not reveal anything about the person. Biblical names, however, have their background in the widespread tradition that the personal name gives significant information about the one who bears it. The Old Testament constantly celebrates God's making His name known to Israel, and the psalms again and again direct praise to God's name (Ps. 8:1; 113:1–3; 145:1, 2; 148:5, 13). "Name" here means God Himself as He has revealed Himself by word and deed. At the heart of this self-revelation is the name by which He authorized Israel to invoke Him—commonly rendered "the LORD" (for the Hebrew *Yahweh*, as modern scholars pronounce it; or "Jehovah," as it is sometimes written).

God declared this name to Moses when He spoke to him out of the bush that burned steadily without being burned up. God first identified Himself as the God who had committed Himself in covenant to the patriarchs (Gen. 17:1–14); then, when Moses asked Him what he could tell the people who asked what God's name was (the ancients assumed that prayer would only be heard if its addressee was named correctly), God answered first "I AM WHO I AM," then shortened it to "I AM." The name "Yahweh" ("the LORD") sounds like "I am" in Hebrew, and God finally called Himself "the LORD God of your fathers" (Ex. 3:15, 16). The name in all its forms proclaims His eternal, self-sustaining, self-determining, sovereign reality—the supernatural mode of existence that the sign of the burning bush had signified (Ex. 3:2). The bush that was not consumed was God's illustration of His own inexhaustible life. In designating "Yahweh" as "my name forever" (Ex. 3:15), God indicated that His people should always think of Him as the living, reigning, powerful King that the burning bush showed Him to be.

Later Moses asked to see God's "glory." In reply, God proclaimed "the name": "The LORD, the LORD, a God merciful and gracious, slow to anger, and abounding in steadfast love and faithfulness, keeping steadfast love for thousands, forgiving iniquity and transgression and sin, but who will by no means clear the guilty" (Ex. 34:6, 7). At the burning bush, God had addressed the question of the manner of His existence. Here, He answered the question, How can we describe His actions? This foundational announcement of His moral character is often echoed in later passages of Scripture (Neh. 9:17; Ps. 86:15; Joel 2:13; Jon. 4:2). These revelations are all part of His "name," His disclosure of His nature, for which He is to be revered and glorified forever.

In the New Testament, the words and acts of Jesus, the incarnate Son of God, are a full revelation of the mind, character, and purposes of God the Father (John 14:9–11; cf. 1:18). "Hallowed be your name" in the Lord's Prayer (Matt. 6:9) expresses the desire that God will be revered and praised as the splendor of His entire self-disclosure deserves.

that Israel would believe (3:18). Nothing is said about convincing Pharaoh (cf. 6:12).

4:2 hand. The Hebrew word for "hand" often connotes power. Against the oppressing hand of Egypt (3:8; 14:30; 18:10), the mighty hand of God will be stretched out (3:19–20). God will use the hand of Moses to show His power. Moses' staff will become the staff of God (v. 20).

4:6 leprous. Not what is today called Hansen's Disease, but a common skin disease of the time. God shows His power to judge and to heal.

4:9 the Nile. This specific sign was not needed by Moses and was not used, though its force appears in the first plague (7:20). The Nile was revered as a god and was the source of Egypt's life. This sign would have meant the potential death of the Nile and thus of Egypt.

10 But Moses said to the LORD, "Oh, my
Lord, I am not eloquent, either in the past
or since you have spoken to your servant,
but [o]I am slow of speech and of tongue."
11 Then the LORD said to him, "Who has
made man's mouth? Who makes him mute,
or deaf, or seeing, or blind? Is it not I, the
LORD? 12 Now therefore go, and [p]I will be
with your mouth and teach you what you
shall speak." 13 But he said, "Oh, my Lord,
please send someone else." 14 Then the
anger of the LORD was kindled against
Moses and he said, "Is there not Aaron,
your brother, the Levite? I know that he can
speak well. Behold, [q]he is coming out to
meet you, and when he sees you, he will be
glad in his heart. 15 [r]You shall speak to him
and [s]put the words in his mouth, and [p]I will
be with your mouth and with his mouth
and will teach you both what to do. 16 [t]He
shall speak for you to the people, and he
shall be your mouth, and [u]you shall be as
God to him. 17 And take in your hand [v]this
staff, with which you shall do the signs."

Moses Returns to Egypt

18 Moses went back to [w]Jethro his father-
in-law and said to him, "Please let me go
back to my brothers in Egypt to see
whether they are still alive." And Jethro
said to Moses, "Go in peace." 19 And the
LORD said to Moses in Midian, "Go back to
Egypt, for [x]all the men who were seeking
your life are dead." 20 So Moses took [y]his
wife and his sons and had them ride on a
donkey, and went back to the land of
Egypt. And Moses took [z]the staff of God in
his hand.
21 And the LORD said to Moses, "When
you go back to Egypt, see that you do
before Pharaoh all the [a]miracles that I have
put in your power. But [b]I will harden his
heart, so that he will not let the people go.
22 Then you shall say to Pharaoh, 'Thus says
the LORD, [c]Israel is my [d]firstborn son, 23 and
I say to you, "Let my son go that he may
serve me." If you refuse to let him go,
behold, I [e]will kill your firstborn son.'"
24 At a lodging place on the way [f]the LORD
met him and [g]sought to put him to death.
25 Then [h]Zipporah took a [i]flint and cut off
her son's foreskin and touched Moses'[1]
feet with it and said, "Surely you are a
bridegroom of blood to me!" 26 So he let
him alone. It was then that she said, "A
bridegroom of blood," because of the circumcision.
27 The LORD said to Aaron, "Go into the
wilderness [j]to meet Moses." So he went
and met him at the [k]mountain of God and
kissed him. 28 And Moses [l]told Aaron all the
words of the LORD with which he had sent
him to speak, and all [m]the signs that he
had commanded him to do. 29 Then Moses
and Aaron [n]went and gathered together all
the elders of the people of Israel. 30 [o]Aaron
spoke all the words that the LORD had spoken to Moses and did the signs in the sight
of the people. 31 And the people [p]believed;

[1] Hebrew *his*

10 [o][ch. 6:12; Jer. 1:6]
12 [p][ch. 3:12; Isai. 50:4; Jer. 1:9; Ezek. 33:22; Matt. 10:19, 20; Mark 13:11; Luke 12:11, 12; 21:15]
14 [q]ver. 27
15 [r]ch. 7:1, 2 [s]Num. 22:38; 23:5, 12, 16; Deut. 18:18; 2 Sam. 14:3, 19; Isai. 51:16 [p][See ver. 12 above]
16 [t]ver. 30 [u][ch. 7:1; 18:19]
17 [v]ver. 2; ch. 7:15
18 [w][ch. 2:18]
19 [x]ch. 2:15, 23; [Matt. 2:20]
20 [y]ch. 18:2-4 [z]ch. 17:9; Num. 20:8, 9
21 [a]ch. 3:20 [b]ch. 7:13, 22; 8:15, 32; 9:12, 35; 10:1; 14:8; Rom. 9:17, 18; [Deut. 2:30; Josh. 11:20; Isai. 63:17]
22 [c]Hos. 11:1 [d]Jer. 31:9
23 [e]ch. 11:5; 12:29
24 [f][Num. 22:22; 1 Chr. 21:16] [g][Gen. 17:14]
25 [h]ch. 2:21 [i]Josh. 5:2, 3
27 [j]ver. 14 [k]See ch. 3:1
28 [l]ver. 15, 16 [m]See ver. 3-9
29 [n]ch. 3:16
30 [o]ver 16
31 [p]ver. 8, 9; ch. 3:18

4:10 slow of speech. The fourth objection. Moses is not fluent, but God equips whom He calls (Jer. 1:9). God was teaching Moses and his successors to depend on Him for their gifts. If God made the mouth (v. 11), He can enable man to use it.

4:13–16 Left without excuse, Moses still tries to decline his commission. But the Lord has already summoned his brother Aaron. The relation of Moses to Aaron sheds light on the nature of prophecy: Aaron will be a mouthpiece for Moses just as a prophet is for God (v. 16). See also 6:30; 7:1.

4:17 signs. The plagues are again anticipated (3:20 note). These miraculous deeds will be performed with this same staff.

4:19 all the men . . . dead. Including the Egyptian Pharaoh (Introduction: Date and Occasion).

4:20 sons. Gershom (2:22) and Eliezer (18:4).

4:21 I will harden his heart. The Lord's hardening of Pharaoh's heart is a sovereign divine judgment on Pharaoh, who is also said to harden his own heart (8:15; Rom. 9:17, 18). God purposes to display His power over the stubborn hostility of the king so that His people might know that He is the Lord their deliverer (6:6–8).

4:22 Israel is my firstborn son. The Lord puts His claim upon Israel as His firstborn son, His beloved, a title ultimately realized in Jesus Christ (Mark 1:11). God's claim is the reason for God's deliverance and the covenant to be sealed at Sinai ("that he may serve me," v. 23). This claim issues in God's threat against Pharaoh's firstborn (i.e., the firstborn of Egypt).

4:24 put him to death. The Hebrew is unclear. These words echo v. 23 and may refer to Moses' firstborn, Gershom, not to Moses. Alternatively, the attack may have been directed against Moses himself, perhaps because of his failure to circumcise his son.

4:25 flint. Presumably, a ceremonial instrument. Zipporah intervenes to circumcise her son.

Moses' feet. Lit. "his feet"; the word "Moses'" is supplied (cf. 24 note). The connection of Zipporah's action with the "bridegroom of blood" is uncertain. Circumcision, no less than the Passover, requires the shedding of blood for cleansing and protection. The Lord, the God of the fathers, requires the sign He gave to Abraham (Gen. 17:10). Other examples of divine confrontation at the beginning of a mission include Gen. 32:24 and Josh. 5:13.

4:27 to meet Moses. In Hebrew narrative style, this statement takes the reader back in time to explain Aaron's meeting with Moses before Moses left Sinai.

4:30 Aaron. Aaron will now function as Moses' spokesman (vv. 13–16 note).

4:31 believed. Israel now believes as God had said that they would (3:18). They worship, praising God for His care.

and when they heard that the LORD had [q]visited the people of Israel and that he had [r]seen their affliction, [s]they bowed their heads and worshiped.

Making Bricks Without Straw

5 Afterward Moses and Aaron went and said to Pharaoh, "Thus says the LORD, the God of Israel, 'Let my people go, that they may hold [t]a feast to me in the wilderness.'" **2** But Pharaoh said, [u]"Who is the LORD, that I should obey his voice and let Israel go? I do not know the LORD, and moreover, [v]I will not let Israel go." **3** Then they said, "The [w]God of the Hebrews has met with us. Please let us go a three days' journey into the wilderness that we may sacrifice to the LORD our God, lest he fall upon us with pestilence or with the sword." **4** But the king of Egypt said to them, "Moses and Aaron, why do you take the people away from their work? Get back to your [x]burdens." **5** And Pharaoh said, "Behold, [y]the people of the land are now many,[1] and you make them rest from their burdens!" **6** The same day Pharaoh commanded the [z]taskmasters of the people and their [a]foremen, **7** "You shall no longer give the people straw to make bricks, as in the past; let them go and gather straw for themselves. **8** But the number of bricks that they made in the past you shall impose on them, you shall by no means reduce it, for they are idle. Therefore they cry, 'Let us go and offer sacrifice to our God.' **9** Let heavier work be laid on the men that they may labor at it and pay no regard to lying words."

10 So the [b]taskmasters and the foremen of the people went out and said to the people, "Thus says Pharaoh, 'I will not give you straw. **11** Go and get your straw yourselves wherever you can find it, but your work will not be reduced in the least.'" **12** So the people were scattered throughout all the land of Egypt to gather stubble for straw. **13** The [c]taskmasters were urgent, saying, "Complete your work, your daily task each day, as when there was straw." **14** And the foremen of the people of Israel, whom Pharaoh's [c]taskmasters had set over them, were beaten and were asked, "Why have you not done all your task of making bricks today and yesterday, as in the past?"

15 Then the foremen of the people of Israel came and cried to Pharaoh, "Why do you treat your servants like this? **16** No straw is given to your servants, yet they say to us, 'Make bricks!' And behold, your servants are beaten; but the fault is in your own people." **17** But he said, "You are idle, you are idle; that is why you say, 'Let us go and sacrifice to the LORD.' **18** Go now and work. No straw will be given you, but you must still deliver the same number of bricks." **19** The foremen of the people of Israel saw that they were in trouble when they said, "You shall by no means reduce your number of bricks, your daily task each day." **20** They met Moses and Aaron, who were waiting for them, as they came out from Pharaoh; **21** and [d]they said to them, "The LORD look on you and judge, because you have made us stink in the sight of Pharaoh and his servants, and have put a sword in their hand to kill us."

22 Then Moses turned to the LORD and said, "O LORD, why have you done evil to this people? Why did you ever send me? **23** For since I came to Pharaoh to speak in your name, he has done evil to this people, and you have not delivered your people at all."

31 [q]See ch. 3:16 [r]ch. 2:25; 3:7 [s]ch. 12:27; Gen. 24:26; 1 Chr. 29:20
Chapter 5
1 [t]ch. 10:9
2 [u][2 Kin. 18:35; Job 21:15] [v]ch. 3:19
3 [w]ch. 3:18; 7:16; 9:1, 13
4 [x]ch. 1:11
5 [y]ch. 1:7, 9
6 [z]ch. 3:7 [a]ver. 14, 15, 19
10 [b]ch. 3:7
13 [c]ch. 3:7
14 [c][See ver. 13 above]
21 [d]ch. 6:9

1 Samaritan *they are now more numerous than the people of the land*

5:1 Let my people go. The confrontation with Pharaoh begins with God's demand. The people are His, not Pharaoh's.

hold a feast. This was a pilgrimage to a shrine where a festival would be held (3:18).

5:2 Who is the LORD. Pharaoh's question will be answered by the plagues.

5:3 After presenting God's demand, Moses and Aaron seek to reason with Pharaoh. The Lord is the God of the Hebrews; the distance would be only a three-day journey; disobedience to God's command could seriously reduce Pharaoh's work force.

5:5 people of the land. Later this term came to mean the responsible landowners in Israel (2 Kin. 11:18–20; Jer. 34:19), but here it means peasant workers attached to the land.

5:7 straw. The bricks of the time were much larger than modern bricks; they were molded of Nile mud with straw to increase their strength.

5:10 taskmasters. The slave masters and section leaders pass the order down through the ranks. During the events of vv. 6–19 Moses and Aaron do not intervene. This crushing reply of Pharaoh shows his human supremacy.

5:15–21 Israel appeals to Pharaoh for relief and complains to Moses and Aaron about their plight.

5:21 the LORD . . . judge. Not for the last time, leaders of Israel would curse Moses for obeying the command of the Lord.

5:22 Moses . . . said. As a mediator, Moses speaks God's Word to the people, and pleads the plight of the people to God. This pattern is repeated throughout Exodus. God's reply (ch. 6) gives assurance that the hopeless situation will be the occasion for His mighty action.

God Promises Deliverance

6 But the LORD said to Moses, "Now you
shall see what I will do to Pharaoh; for
with a strong hand he will send them out,
and with [e]a strong hand he will [f]drive them
out of his land."
2 God spoke to Moses and said to him, [g]"I
am the LORD. 3 I appeared to Abraham, to
Isaac, and to Jacob, as [h]God Almighty,[1] but
by my name the [i]LORD I did not make myself
known to them. 4 [j]I also established my
covenant with them [k]to give them the land
of Canaan, the land in which they lived as
sojourners. 5 Moreover, [l]I have heard the
groaning of the people of Israel whom the
Egyptians hold as slaves, and I have remembered my covenant. 6 Say therefore to the
people of Israel, [m]'I am the LORD, and [n]I will
bring you out from under the burdens of the
Egyptians, and I will deliver you from slavery to them, and [o]I will redeem you with an
outstretched arm and with great acts of
judgment. 7 I [p]will take you to be my people,
and [q]I will be your God, and you shall know
that [m]I am the LORD your God, who has
brought you out [n]from under the burdens of
the Egyptians. 8 I will bring you into [r]the
land that I [s]swore to give to Abraham, to
Isaac, and to Jacob. I will give it to you for a
possession. [m]I am the LORD.'" 9 Moses spoke
thus to the people of Israel, but they [t]did
not listen to Moses, because of their broken
spirit and harsh slavery.

Chapter 6
1 [e]ch. 3:19; 13:3 [f]ch. 11:1; 12:33, 39
2 [g][Isai. 42:8; Mal. 3:6]
3 [h]Gen. 17:1 [i]Ps. 68:4; 83:18; [John 8:58; Rev. 1:4, 8]
4 [j]Gen. 15:18; 17:4, 7 [k]Gen. 17:8; 28:4
5 [l]ch. 2:24
6 [m][Isai. 42:8; Mal. 3:6] [n]ch. 7:4; Deut. 26:8; Ps. 136:11, 12; [ch. 3:17] [o]ch. 15:13; Deut. 7:8; 2 Kin. 17:36; 1 Chr. 17:21; Neh. 1:10
7 [p]Deut. 4:20; 7:6; 14:2; 26:18; 2 Sam. 7:24; [1 Pet. 2:9] [q]ch. 29:45, 46; Gen. 17:8; Lev. 22:33; Deut. 29:13; [Rev. 21:7] [m][See ver. 6 above] [n][See ver. 6 above]
8 [r]ch. 32:13; Gen. 15:18; 26:3; 28:13; 35:12; Ezek. 20:6, 42 [s][Gen. 14:22; Deut. 32:40; Ezek 20:5, 6; 47:14] [m][See ver. 6 above]
9 [t]ch. 5:21; [Acts 7:25]
12 [t][See ver. 9 above] [u]ver. 30; ch. 4:10; Jer. 1:6; [Jer. 6:10; Ezek. 44:7]
14 [v]Gen. 46:9; 1 Chr. 5:3

10 So the LORD said to Moses, 11 "Go in,
tell Pharaoh king of Egypt to let the people of Israel go out of his land." 12 But
Moses said to the LORD, "Behold, the people of Israel have [t]not listened to me. How
then shall Pharaoh listen to me, for [u]I am
of uncircumcised lips?" 13 But the LORD
spoke to Moses and Aaron and gave them
a charge about the people of Israel and
about Pharaoh king of Egypt: to bring the
people of Israel out of the land of Egypt.

The Genealogy of Moses and Aaron

14 These are the heads of their fathers'
houses: the [v]sons of Reuben, the firstborn
of Israel: Hanoch, Pallu, Hezron, and
Carmi; these are the clans of Reuben. 15 The
[w]sons of Simeon: Jemuel, Jamin, Ohad,
Jachin, Zohar, and Shaul, the son of a
Canaanite woman; these are the clans of
Simeon. 16 These are the names of the [x]sons
of Levi according to their generations:
Gershon, Kohath, and Merari, the years of
the life of Levi being 137 years. 17 The [y]sons
of Gershon: Libni and Shimei, by their
clans. 18 The [z]sons of Kohath: Amram,
Izhar, Hebron, and Uzziel, the years of the
life of Kohath being 133 years. 19 The [a]sons
of Merari: Mahli and Mushi. These are the
clans of the Levites according to their generations. 20 [b]Amram took as his wife

15 [w]Gen. 46:10; 1 Chr. 4:24 16 [x]Gen. 46:11; Num. 3:17; 1 Chr. 6:1, 16 17 [y]Num. 3:18; 1 Chr. 6:17; 23:7 18 [z]Num. 3:19; 26:57; 1 Chr. 6:2, 18 19 [a]Num. 3:20; 1 Chr. 6:19; 23:21 20 [b]See ch. 2:1

[1] Hebrew *El Shaddai*

6:1 drive. The Lord's power will more than prevail. Pharaoh will not only let them go, he will *drive* Israel out.

6:2–8 Note the repeated use of the revelation (authority) formula, "I am the LORD," in these verses (vv. 2, 6–8). The use of God's covenant name underscores the surety of His covenant promises and faithfulness (3:15 and notes).

6:3 God Almighty. God had revealed Himself to the patriarchs as God Almighty (Hebrew *El Shaddai,* Gen. 17:1; 28:3; 35:11). In Genesis, however, the name *Yahweh* is much more commonly used, perhaps only to identify the God of the fathers as Yahweh, the LORD. Nevertheless, while some passages seem to imply the use of *Yahweh* from the earliest time (Gen. 4:26; 9:26; 12:8; 24:12), it is not found as an element in personal names (*Ja-* or *Jo*) before the time of Moses, with the possible exception of Jochebed (6:20). In any case, God identifies Himself as El Shaddai, the God of the patriarchs, but reveals Himself afresh as Yahweh, the covenant God who claims and redeems Israel according to His gracious purpose.

6:4 my covenant. Yahweh is also El Shaddai, the God of Abraham, Isaac, and Jacob. His covenant promise to these earlier patriarchs is His purpose for Israel. The continuity of the covenant is affirmed in vv. 4, 5.

6:5 remembered my covenant. When used of God, "remembered" means that He is prepared to act on His promises, not simply recall them. This narrative affirms the inclusion in the Abrahamic covenant of all Israel.

6:6 bring you out . . . redeem. God's reply to Moses' complaint of 5:22–23. This is the central core of the section, a solemn assurance of redemption and of covenant reaffirmation. **redeem.** This term normally refers to the restoration of rights to a disadvantaged family member by the payment of a price or a ransom; such redemption was normally effected by the next of kin (Lev. 25:25; cf. Ruth 4). Israel, as Yahweh's son (4:22), was redeemed from Egypt to be God's own people. Rescue, redemption, and covenant relation are the keys to the passage. The heart of the covenant is God's claim on His people and the reciprocal claim that He allows them to make on Him.

6:7 my people. This anticipates 19:5–6.

6:9–13 God renews His demand for Israel's release. The discouragement of Israel and Moses shows that the deliverance must be God's work completely. In spite of God's renewed promise, the people will not hear, and even Moses has difficulty believing that his mission will be effective.

6:14–27 In this transitional section, Moses and Aaron are formally identified, and the story of their work is reviewed and resumed in preparation for the description of the ten plagues. The formal identification is accomplished through a genealogy that begins with Reuben, Israel's oldest son, then proceeds to Simeon, the second son, and finally to Levi. Levi's genealogy establishes the link to Moses and Aaron. Among the Levites Amram is singled out, then Aaron and Moses. The subsequent names constitute the priestly line for Israel (Num. 25:10–13; 26:57–62). For Korah, see Num. 16:1–35.

6:20 The record of the marriage of Amram to his paternal aunt would be most unlikely in a fictitious genealogy. Such a marriage was later forbidden in the Mosaic Law (Lev. 18:12). Three women are mentioned in tracing the line: Jochebed, Elisheba, and a daughter of Putiel.

Jochebed his father's sister, and she bore
him Aaron and Moses, the years of the life
of Amram being 137 years. 21 [c]The sons of
Izhar: Korah, Nepheg, and Zichri. 22 The
[d]sons of Uzziel: Mishael, Elzaphan, and
Sithri. 23 Aaron took as his wife Elisheba,
the daughter of [e]Amminadab and the sister
of [f]Nahshon, and she bore him [g]Nadab,
Abihu, Eleazar, and Ithamar. 24 The [h]sons
of Korah: Assir, Elkanah, and Abiasaph;
these are the clans of the Korahites.
25 Eleazar, Aaron's son, took as his wife one
of the daughters of Putiel, and [i]she bore
him Phinehas. These are the heads of the
fathers' houses of the Levites by their clans.
26 These are the Aaron and Moses [j]to
whom the LORD said: "Bring out the people
of Israel from the land of Egypt [k]by their
hosts." 27 It was they who spoke to Pharaoh
king of Egypt about bringing out the people of Israel from Egypt, this Moses and
this Aaron.

28 On the day when the LORD spoke to
Moses in the land of Egypt, 29 the LORD said
to Moses, [l]"I am the LORD; [m]tell Pharaoh
king of Egypt all that I say to you." 30 But
Moses said to the LORD, "Behold, [n]I am of
uncircumcised lips. How will Pharaoh listen to me?"

Moses and Aaron Before Pharaoh

7 And the LORD said to Moses, "See, I
have made you like [o]God to Pharaoh,
and your brother Aaron shall be your
[p]prophet. 2 [q]You shall speak all that I command you, and your brother Aaron shall tell
Pharaoh to let the people of Israel go out of
his land. 3 But [r]I will harden Pharaoh's heart,
and though I [s]multiply my signs and wonders in the land of Egypt, 4 Pharaoh will not
listen to you. Then I will lay my hand on
Egypt and bring my hosts, my people the
children of Israel, out of the land of Egypt by
great acts of judgment. 5 The Egyptians [t]shall
know that I am the LORD, when I stretch out
my hand against Egypt and bring out the
people of Israel from among them." 6 Moses
and Aaron did so; they did just as the LORD
commanded them. 7 Now Moses was [u]eighty
years old, and Aaron eighty-three years old,
when they spoke to Pharaoh.
8 Then the LORD said to Moses and Aaron,
9 "When Pharaoh says to you, [v]'Prove yourselves by working a miracle,' then you shall
say to Aaron, 'Take your staff and cast it
down before Pharaoh, that it may become a
serpent.'" 10 So Moses and Aaron went to
Pharaoh and did just as the LORD commanded. Aaron cast down his staff before Pharaoh
and his servants, and it became a serpent.
11 Then Pharaoh summoned the wise men
and the sorcerers, and they, the [w]magicians
of Egypt, also [x]did the same by their secret
arts. 12 For each man cast down his staff, and
they became serpents. But Aaron's staff swallowed up their staffs. 13 Still [r]Pharaoh's heart
was hardened, and he would not listen to
them, [r]as the LORD had said.

The First Plague: Water Turned to Blood

14 Then the LORD said to Moses,
"Pharaoh's heart is hardened; he refuses to

21 [c]Num. 16:1; 1 Chr. 6:37, 38
22 [d]Lev. 10:4; Num. 3:30
23 [e]Ruth 4:19, 20; 1 Chr. 2:10; Matt. 1:4; Luke 3:33 [f]Num. 1:7; 2:3; 7:12, 17; 10:14; Matt. 1:4; Luke 3:32 [g]Lev. 10:1; Num. 3:2; 26:60; 1 Chr. 6:3; 24:1
24 [h]1 Chr. 6:22, 23, 37
25 [i]Num. 25:7, 11; Josh. 24:33; Ps. 106:30
26 [j]ver. 13 [k]ch. 7:4; 12:17, 51; Num. 33:1
29 [l]See ver. 2 [m]ver. 11; [ch. 7:2]
30 [n][Isai. 6:5]; See ver. 12
Chapter 7
1 [o]ch. 4:16 [p]Gen. 20:7; [1 Sam. 9:9]
2 [q][ch. 4:15; 6:29]
3 [r]See ch. 4:21 [s]ch. 11:9; Ps. 135:9; See Ps. 78:43-51; 105:26-36
5 [t]ver. 17; ch. 8:10, 22; 14:4, 18
7 [u][Deut. 29:5; 31:2; 34:7; Acts 7:23, 30]
9 [v][Isai. 7:11; John 2:18; 4:48; 6:30]
11 [w]Gen. 41:8 [x]ver. 12, 22; ch. 8:7, 18; 9:11; 2 Tim. 3:8
13 [r][See ver. 3 above]

6:23 bore him. No descendant of Moses is named, but those of Aaron continue for the next two generations to establish priestly succession from Aaron through his successor Eleazar. The genealogy spans only four generations for the sojourn in Egypt and is clearly selective (Gen. 5:3–32 note).

6:25 Putiel . . . Phinehas. Like "Merari" in v. 16, these are probably Egyptian names, which occurred frequently among Levites.

6:28–7:7 This section reviews and restates Moses' commission after his hesitation (6:12, 30). The real demand now appears: not a temporary absence, but a definitive exodus from Egypt.

7:1 prophet. The origin of the Hebrew term for "prophet" is disputed, but perhaps it means "one who is called." The function of Aaron in relation to Moses demonstrates the function of a true prophet in relation to God (4:13–16 note).

7:2–5 The theological explanation of the plagues is given in the first five plagues. Pharaoh's obstinacy is self-motivated (7:22; 8:15, 32; 9:7). God is said to have hardened Pharaoh's heart in plagues seven, eight, and nine (10:1, 20, 27). In the sixth plague, the obstinacy stems from Pharaoh himself (9:35), but God also claims to have hardened Pharaoh (10:1). God's purpose is not simply judgment on Pharaoh, but manifesting His power to save His people so that His name might be proclaimed in all the earth (9:16; Rom. 9:17, 18).

7:3 heart. The Hebrew is a broad term describing the center of feeling, thinking, and willing. The Lord causes Pharaoh's heart to become hard (lit. "difficult"), not by implanting evil in it, but by giving it over to its evil direction without restraint (Rom. 1:24, 26, 28). Paul contrasts hardening with showing mercy (Rom. 9:18). God's judgment on Pharaoh issued in mercy to Israel, Egypt, and the nations as they saw His power to save.

though I multiply. Or, "in order that I might multiply."

my signs and wonders. These are the nine plagues and ten miracles of 7:9–11:10, culminating in the death plague.

7:9 serpent. The Hebrew word here (different from the word for "serpent" in 4:3) often refers to a sea reptile or river monster (Gen. 1:21; Ezek. 29:3; 32:2), but can refer to any large reptile. A large snake is probably in view.

7:11 magicians. The Hebrew term indicates an engraver or writer, a learned person. The Egyptian magicians relied on the familiar tricks of magic, Aaron on divine power. See note 9:11.

7:13 as the LORD had said. See 4:21; 7:3, 22; 8:15, 19.

7:14–10:29 A theory of natural causes for the plagues does not do justice to the clear statements of the text (7:17; 9:5 notes). A particular order would be essential for an explanation of the plagues as normal events associated with the overflow of the Nile, but neither the narrative here, nor

let the people go. 15 [y]Go to Pharaoh in the
morning, as he is going out to the water.
Stand on the bank of the Nile to meet him,
and take in your hand [z]the staff that turned
into a [a]serpent. 16 And you shall say to him,
'The [b]LORD, the God of the Hebrews, sent
me to you, saying, "Let my people go, [c]that
they may serve me in the wilderness. But
so far, you have not obeyed." 17 Thus says
the LORD, "By this [d]you shall know that I
am the LORD: behold, with the staff that is
in my hand I will strike the water that is in
the Nile, and [e]it shall turn into blood.
18 The fish in the Nile shall die, and the Nile
will stink, and the Egyptians will [f]grow
weary of drinking water from the Nile."'"
19 And the LORD said to Moses, "Say to
Aaron, 'Take your staff and [g]stretch out
your hand over the waters of Egypt, over
their rivers, their canals, and their ponds,
and all their pools of water, so that they
may become blood, and there shall be
blood throughout all the land of Egypt,
even in vessels of wood and in vessels of
stone.'"
20 Moses and Aaron did as the LORD commanded. In the sight of Pharaoh and in the
sight of his servants he [h]lifted up the staff
and struck the water in the Nile, and all the
[i]water in the Nile turned into blood. 21 And
the fish in the Nile died, and the Nile stank,
so that the Egyptians [j]could not drink water
from the Nile. There was blood throughout
all the land of Egypt. 22 But [k]the magicians
of Egypt did the same by their secret arts.
So [l]Pharaoh's heart remained hardened,
and he would not listen to them, as [m]the
LORD had said. 23 Pharaoh turned and went
into his house, and he did not take even
this to heart. 24 And all the Egyptians dug
along the Nile for water to drink, for they
could not drink the water of the Nile.
25 Seven full days passed after the LORD
had struck the Nile.

15 [y]ch. 8:20; 9:13 [z]ch. 4:2, 17; 17:5 [a]ch. 4:3
16 [b]ch. 3:18; 5:3; 9:1, 13 [c]ch. 3:12, 18; 5:1, 3
17 [d]ver. 5 [e]ch. 4:9; [Rev. 16:4]
18 [f]ver. 21, 24
19 [g]ch. 8:5, 6, 16, 17; 9:22; 10:12, 21; 14:16, 21, 26
20 [h]ch. 17:9 [i]Ps. 78:44; 105:29
21 [j]ver. 18, 24
22 [k]ver. 11 [l]ver. 13; [m]ver. 3, 4

the plague lists in Ps. 78:44–51; 105:28–36, suggest such an order.

The plagues are arranged in three groups of three (7:14–8:19; 8:20–9:12; 9:13–10:29); the tenth is climactic. The first two plagues in each sequence are preceded by a divine warning, but the third comes unheralded. In the first plague of each series Moses contacts Pharaoh in the morning; no time indication is given for the other two. The plagues are the answer to Pharaoh's challenge (5:2; cf. 7:5), and the description of the first plague of each triplet announces the theme of the triplet and gives its purpose. In plagues one through three the theme is the absolute superiority of the Lord (and His agents) over Pharaoh and the Egyptian gods (7:16, 17).

7:14 hardened. Pharaoh's hardening was the necessary prerequisite for the display of divine power (4:21 note).

7:17 The use of the rod with the first three and the last three plagues shows that Yahweh is the real author.

I will strike. Aaron will strike (vv. 19, 20), but the Lord will perform the miracle. The striking is by God's hand, by His rod. The deed of Aaron is owned by God no less than the word that God gave him through Moses.

blood. In Hebrew the word never denotes its red color, but always blood as a substance. The red clay that comes down at the time of flooding from the Ethiopian highlands (coloring the Nile water) is not in view.

7:19 waters. All the natural waters of Egypt were involved, including the natural arms of the Nile, the irrigation canals, and the pools formed by river flooding. The Nile River, the source of Egypt's agricultural life, was revered as a god. Beginning with this plague the Lord's superiority over the Egyptian pantheon of gods is demonstrated.

7:22 magicians. See notes 7:11; 9:11.

The Ten Plagues on Egypt (7:3, 5)

The Plague	The Effect
1. Blood (7:20)	Pharoah hardened (7:22)
2. Frogs (8:6)	Pharaoh begs relief, promises freedom (8:8), but is hardened (8:15)
3. Gnats (8:17)	Pharoah hardened (8:19)
4. Flies (8:24)	Pharoah bargains (8:28), but is hardened (8:32)
5. Livestock died (9:6)	Pharoah hardened (9:7)
6. Boils (9:10)	Pharoah hardened (9:12)
7. Hail (9:23)	Pharoah begs relief (9:27), promises freedom (9:28), but is hardened (9:35)
8. Locusts (10:13)	Pharoah bargains (10:11), begs relief (10:17), but is hardened (10:20)
9. Darkness (10:22)	Pharoah bargains (10:24), but is hardened (10:27)
10. Death of a firstborn (12:29)	Pharoah and Egyptians beg Israel to leave Egypt (12:31–33)

God multiplied His signs and wonders in the land of Egypt that the Egyptians might know that He is the LORD.

The Second Plague: Frogs

8 [1] Then the LORD said to Moses, "Go in
to Pharaoh and say to him, 'Thus says
the LORD, "Let my people go, that [n]they
may serve me. 2 But if you [o]refuse to let
them go, behold, I will plague all your
country with [p]frogs. 3 The Nile shall swarm
with frogs that shall come up into your
house and into [q]your bedroom and on your
bed and into the houses of your servants
and your people,[2] and into your ovens and
your kneading bowls. 4 The frogs shall
come up on you and on your people and
on all your servants."'" 5 [3]And the LORD
said to Moses, "Say to Aaron, [r]'Stretch out
your hand with your staff over the rivers,
over the canals and over the pools, and
make frogs come up on the land of
Egypt!'" 6 So Aaron stretched out his hand
over the waters of Egypt, and [s]the frogs
came up and covered the land of Egypt.
7 But [t]the magicians did the same by their
secret arts and made frogs come up on the
land of Egypt.

8 Then Pharaoh called Moses and Aaron
and said, [u]"Plead with the LORD to take
away the frogs from me and from my people, and [v]I will let the people go to sacrifice to the LORD." 9 Moses said to Pharaoh,
"Be pleased to command me when [u]I am
to plead for you and for your servants and
for your people, that the frogs be cut off
from you and your houses and be left only
in the Nile." 10 And he said, "Tomorrow."
Moses said, "Be it as you say, so [w]that you
may know that [x]there is no one like the
LORD our God. 11 The frogs shall go away
from you and your houses and your servants and your people. They shall be left
only in the Nile." 12 So Moses and Aaron
went out from Pharaoh, and Moses cried
to the LORD about the frogs, as he had
agreed with Pharaoh.[4] 13 And the LORD did
according to the word of Moses. The frogs
died out in the houses, the courtyards,
and the fields. 14 And they gathered them
together in heaps, and the land stank.
15 But when Pharaoh saw that there was a
[y]respite, he [z]hardened his heart and
would not listen to them, as the LORD had
said.

The Third Plague: Gnats

16 Then the LORD said to Moses, "Say to
Aaron, [a]'Stretch out your staff and strike the
dust of the earth, so that it may become
gnats in all the land of Egypt.'" 17 And they
did so. Aaron stretched out his hand with
his staff and struck the dust of the earth,
and [b]there were gnats on man and beast. All
the dust of the earth became gnats in all the
land of Egypt. 18 The [c]magicians tried by
their secret arts to produce gnats, but they
could not. So there were gnats on man and
beast. 19 Then the magicians said to Pharaoh,
"This is [d]the finger of God." But Pharaoh's
heart was hardened, and he would not listen
to them, as the LORD had said.

The Fourth Plague: Flies

20 Then the LORD said to Moses, [e]"Rise up
early in the morning and present yourself
to Pharaoh, as he goes out to the water,
and say to him, 'Thus says the LORD, [f]"Let
my people go, that they may serve me. 21 Or
else, if you will not let my people go,
behold, I will send swarms of flies on you
and your servants and your people, and
into your houses. And the houses of the
Egyptians shall be filled with swarms of
flies, and also the ground on which they
stand. 22 But on that day [g]I will set apart the
land of Goshen, where my people dwell,
so that no swarms of flies shall be there,
[h]that you may know that I am the LORD in
the midst of the earth.[5] 23 Thus I will put a

Chapter 8
1 [n]ver. 20; ch. 3:12, 18
2 [o]ch. 7:14; 9:2 [p][Rev. 16:13]
3 [q]Ps. 105:30
5 [r]See ch. 7:19
6 [s]Ps. 78:45; 105:30
7 [t]See ch. 7:11
8 [u]ver. 28, 30; ch. 9:28; 10:17, 18; [Num. 21:7; 1 Kin. 13:6; Acts 8:24] [v]ver. 25-28; ch. 10:8, 24; 12:31, 32
9 [u][See ver. 8 above]
10 [w]ver. 22; ch. 7:17 [x]ch. 9:14; Deut. 33:26; 2 Sam. 7:22; 1 Chr. 17:20; Ps. 86:8; Isai. 46:9; Jer. 10:6, 7
15 [y][Eccles. 8:11] [z]ver. 32; ch. 7:14; 9:7, 34; 10:1
16 [a]See ch. 7:19
17 [b]Ps. 105:31
18 [c]See ch. 7:11
19 [d]ch. 31:13; Ps. 8:3; Luke 11:20
20 [e]ch. 7:15; 9:13 [f]ver. 1
22 [g]ch. 9:4; 11:7; [Mal. 3:18] [h]ver. 10; ch. 7:17

[1] Ch 7:26 in Hebrew [2] Or *among your people* [3] Ch 8:1 in Hebrew
[4] Or *which he had brought upon Pharaoh* [5] Or *that I the LORD am in the land*

8:3 Nile shall swarm with frogs. Frogs represented the primordial goddess Heket in Egyptian religious life. Here the allegedly divine river and frogs bring misery on the Egyptians—another demonstration of the Lord's supremacy.

8:7 made frogs come up. The magicians can only add to the distress (9:11 note).

8:8 I will let the people go. Pharaoh, personally affected, made his first concession. The plagues were not intended, however, to soften his resistance (7:3), but to magnify Yahweh's power and cause Israel to believe. Pharaoh was tough and shrewd (vv. 15, 25).

8:16–19 God raises His rod against the dust, turning it into a plague of gnats.

8:19 finger of God. The magicians now admit that a divine intervention was directly involved (cf. 31:18; Ps. 8:3), but Pharaoh was not persuaded.

8:20 water. This first plague of the second sequence again finds Pharaoh at the Nile (cf. 7:15).

8:21 swarms. The Hebrew word occurs only here and at Ps. 78:45; 105:31.

8:23 put a division. See text note. In the second set of the three plagues God distinguishes between Goshen and the rest of Egypt. He shows His favor toward His own people. Pharaoh later investigates this (9:7).

division[1] between my people and your people. Tomorrow this sign shall happen.”’”
24 And the LORD did so. [i]There came great
swarms of flies into the house of Pharaoh
and into his servants’ houses. Throughout
all the land of Egypt the land was ruined by
the swarms of flies.
25 Then Pharaoh called Moses and Aaron
and said, “Go, sacrifice to your God within
the land.” 26 But Moses said, “It would not
be right to do so, for the offerings we shall
sacrifice to the LORD our God are an [j]abom-
ination to the Egyptians. If we sacrifice offerings [j]abominable to the Egyptians before
their eyes, will they not stone us? 27 We must
go [k]three days’ journey into the wilderness
and sacrifice to the LORD our God [l]as he tells
us.” 28 So Pharaoh said, “I will let you go to
sacrifice to the LORD your God in the wilderness; only you must not go very far away.
[m]Plead for me.” 29 Then Moses said, “Behold, I am going out from you and I will
plead with the LORD that the swarms of flies
may depart from Pharaoh, from his servants,
and from his people, tomorrow. Only let not
Pharaoh [n]cheat again by not letting the people go to sacrifice to the LORD.” 30 So Moses
went out from Pharaoh and prayed to the
LORD. 31 And the LORD did as Moses asked,
and removed the swarms of flies from
Pharaoh, from his servants, and from his
people; not one remained. 32 But Pharaoh
[o]hardened his heart this time also, and did
not let the people go.

The Fifth Plague: Egyptian Livestock Die

9 Then the LORD said to Moses, [p]“Go in
to Pharaoh and say to him, ‘Thus says
[q]the LORD, the God of the Hebrews, “Let my
people go, that they may serve me. 2 For if
you refuse to let them go and still hold
them, 3 behold, [r]the hand of the LORD will
fall with a very severe plague upon your livestock that are in the field, the horses, the
donkeys, the camels, the herds, and the
flocks. 4 [s]But the LORD will make a distinction between the livestock of Israel and the
livestock of Egypt, so that nothing of all that
belongs to the people of Israel shall die.”’”
5 And the LORD set a time, saying,
“Tomorrow the LORD will do this thing in
the land.” 6 And the next day the LORD did
this thing. [t]All the livestock of the Egyptians
died, but not one of the livestock of the
people of Israel died. 7 And Pharaoh sent,
and behold, not one of the livestock of Israel
was dead. But [u]the heart of Pharaoh was
hardened, and he did not let the people go.

The Sixth Plague: Boils

8 And the LORD said to Moses and Aaron,
“Take handfuls of soot from the kiln, and
let Moses throw them in the air in the sight
of Pharaoh. 9 It shall become fine dust over
all the land of Egypt, and become [v]boils
breaking out in sores on man and beast
throughout all the land of Egypt.” 10 So they
took soot from the kiln and stood before
Pharaoh. And Moses threw it in the air,
and it became boils breaking out in sores
on man and beast. 11 And [w]the magicians
could not stand before Moses because of
the boils, for the boils came upon the magicians and upon all the Egyptians. 12 [x]But
the LORD hardened the heart of Pharaoh,
and he did not listen to them, as [y]the LORD
had spoken to Moses.

1 Septuagint, Vulgate; Hebrew *set redemption*

24 [i]Ps. 78:45; 105:31; [Isai. 7:18]
26 [j][Gen. 43:32; 46:34]
27 [k]ch. 3:18 [l]ch. 3:12
28 [m]See ver. 8
29 [n]ver. 15; [Jer. 42:20, 21]
32 [o]ver. 15
Chapter 9
1 [p]ch. 8:1, 2 [q]See ch. 7:16
3 [r]ch. 7:4
4 [s]ch. 8:22; 11:7
6 [t][ver. 19]
7 [u]ch. 7:14
9 [v]Lev. 13:18; Deut. 28:27; 2 Kin. 20:7; Job 2:7; Isai. 38:21; Rev. 16:2
11 [w]See ch. 7:11; 2 Tim. 3:9
12 [x]See ch. 4:21 [y]ch. 4:21

8:25 During the swarms of flies, Pharaoh offers to negotiate by agreeing to less than the Lord demands. Moses regularly refuses to compromise: he will neither worship in the land nor go less than a three-day journey (v. 28); neither will he leave behind the women and children (10:9–11) nor leave the flocks and herds (10:24). At last, after Pharaoh repeatedly broke faith, God's liberation is total. Israel not only goes out to worship at Sinai but leaves Egypt for Canaan.

8:26 abomination. Egyptians deified the animals customarily sacrificed by the Israelites.

9:3 horses. The horse was brought into Egypt by the Hyksos (c. 1700 B.C.).

camels. Though sporadically used during this period (cf. Gen. 12:16), widespread use of the camel in Egypt only came much later. Perhaps camels of the merchant traders from Arabia and elsewhere are referred to here.

9:5 set a time. The plague has not come by coincidence. The biblical account gives no room for naturalistic explanation (such as an epidemic of anthrax stemming from dead frogs).

Tomorrow. The day's notice suggests that God provided time for God-fearing Egyptians to put their livestock in a place of shelter (cf. vv. 18–19). Not all the Egyptian livestock succumbed to this plague (vv. 9, 19).

9:6 All the livestock. Since the next plague affects livestock also, this phrase must designate either "all kinds of livestock" or all the livestock in the field (v. 5 note; cf. vv. 18–19).

9:7 See 8:23 and note.

9:8 handfuls. This was done before Pharaoh to underscore that the event was supernatural.

9:11 magicians. The defeat of the magicians was clear from the start, when Aaron's staff-become-serpent swallowed up the serpents they produced (7:12). They were able to imitate turning water to blood and producing frogs, but they could only add to, and not reverse, these plagues (7:22; 8:7). When they could not imitate the production of lice, they told Pharaoh the plagues were divine judgments, not magic (8:18, 19). Finally, the magicians are struck with boils and retreat in discomfort and disgrace (9:11).

The Seventh Plague: Hail

13 Then the LORD said to Moses, [z]"Rise up
early in the morning and present yourself
before Pharaoh and say to him, 'Thus says
the LORD, the God of the Hebrews, "Let my
people go, that they may serve me. 14 For
this time I will send all my plagues on you
yourself,[1] and on your servants and your
people, so [a]that you may know that there is
none like me in all the earth. 15 For by now
I could have put out my hand and struck
you and your people with pestilence, and
you would have been cut off from the
earth. 16 [b]But for this purpose I have raised
you up, to show you my power, so [c]that my
name may be proclaimed in all the earth.
17 [d]You are still exalting yourself against my
people and will not let them go. 18 Behold,
about this time tomorrow I will cause very
heavy hail to fall, such as never has been in
Egypt from the day it was founded until
now. 19 Now therefore send, [e]get your livestock and all that you have in the field into
safe shelter, for every man and beast that is
in the field and is not brought home will
die when the hail falls on them."'" 20 Then
whoever feared the word of the LORD
among the servants of Pharaoh hurried his
slaves and his livestock into the houses,
21 but whoever did not pay attention to the
word of the LORD left his slaves and his livestock in the field.

22 Then the LORD said to Moses, "Stretch
out your hand toward heaven, so that there
may be [f]hail in all the land of Egypt, on
man and beast and every plant of the field,
in the land of Egypt." 23 Then Moses
stretched out his staff toward heaven, and
the [g]LORD sent thunder and hail, and fire
ran down to the earth. And the LORD rained
hail upon the land of Egypt. 24 There was
hail and fire flashing continually in the
midst of the hail, very heavy hail, such as
had never been in all the land of Egypt
since it became a nation. 25 The hail struck
down everything that was in the field in all
the land of Egypt, both man and beast.
And the hail [h]struck down every plant of
the field and broke every tree of the field.
26 [i]Only in the land of Goshen, where the
people of Israel were, was there no hail.

27 Then Pharaoh sent and called Moses
and Aaron and said to them, "This time [j]I
have sinned; the [k]LORD is in the right, and
I and my people are in the wrong. 28 [l]Plead
with the LORD, for there has been enough
of God's thunder and hail. I will let you go,
and you shall stay no longer." 29 Moses said
to him, "As soon as I have gone out of the
city, [m]I will stretch out my hands to the
LORD. The thunder will cease, and there
will be no more hail, so that you may know
that [n]the earth is the LORD's. 30 But as for
you and your servants, [o]I know that you do
not yet fear the LORD God." 31 (The flax and
the barley were struck down, for the barley
was in the ear and the flax was in bud.
32 But the wheat and the emmer[2] were not
struck down, for they are late in coming
up.) 33 So Moses went out of the city from
Pharaoh and [m]stretched out his hands to
the LORD, and the thunder and the hail
ceased, and the rain no longer poured
upon the earth. 34 But when Pharaoh saw
that the rain and the hail and the thunder
had ceased, he sinned yet again and [p]hard-
ened his heart, [q]he and his servants. 35 So
[r]the heart of Pharaoh was hardened, and
he did not let the people of Israel go, just
as the LORD had spoken through Moses.

The Eighth Plague: Locusts

10 Then the LORD said to Moses, "Go
in to Pharaoh, for I have hardened
his heart and the heart of his servants, that

13 [z]ch. 7:15; 8:20
14 [a]ch. 8:10
16 [b]Cited Rom. 9:17; [ch. 10:1, 2; 11:9; 14:17; Prov. 16:4] [c][Ps. 83:18]; Isai. 63:12
17 [d][Neh. 9:10]
19 [e][ver. 4]
22 [f]Rev. 16:21
23 [g]Ps. 78:47, 48; 105:32; [Josh. 10:11; 1 Sam. 12:17; Ps. 18:13; 148:8; Isai. 30:30; Ezek. 38:22; Rev. 8:7]
25 [h]Ps. 78:47; 105:33
26 [i]ch. 8:22; 9:4, 6; 10:23; 11:7; 12:13; [Isai. 32:18]
27 [j]ch. 10:16 [k]2 Chr. 12:6; Ps. 129:4; 145:17; Lam. 1:18; Dan. 9:14
28 [l]See ch. 8:8
29 [m]1 Kin. 8:22, 38; Ps. 143:6; Isai. 1:15 [n]Ps. 24:1; 1 Cor. 10:26; [Deut. 10:14]
30 [o]Isai. 26:10
33 [m][See ver. 29 above]
34 [p]See ch. 7:14 [q]1 Sam. 6:6
35 [r]See ch. 4:21

[1] Hebrew *on your heart* [2] A kind of wheat

9:14 These plagues (lit. "blows" or "strokes") show the power of God's hand in smiting Egypt (3:20; 7:25; 12:13). The last three plagues fall when the staff of the Lord is stretched out to heaven, earth, and heaven (9:22; 10:13, 21).

9:15, 16 God's judgments are tempered by mercy. He withholds total destruction so that the Egyptians might know His power and repent (v. 15). Further, God's judgments against Pharaoh will cause God's name to be proclaimed to the nations.

9:20, 21 Some Egyptians learned to fear God's word (10:7).

9:23 thunder. Lit. "voices." This was no earthly hailstorm as the thunderous "voice" of God (signifying His sovereignty over all creation) spoke in judgment (Ps. 29:3–9).

9:25 broke every tree. See Ps. 29:5.

9:27 I have sinned. Pharaoh confesses his guilt for the first time, but the phrase "this time" points to the superficiality of his confession. Though not believing him, Moses nevertheless shows God's power over the earth by stopping the hail.

9:31, 32 in bud . . . late in coming up. This information seems to set the time in January-February, a time when hailstorms are frequent in Egypt. Flax was in the bud in January, and barley was in the ear at that time; it would have been harvested in February.

10:1 hardened his heart. Pharaoh's will is reversed four times in this one narrative: vv. 8, 10–11, 16–17, 20.

I may show these signs of mine among them, 2 and [s]that you may tell in the hearing of your son and of your grandson how I have dealt harshly with the Egyptians and what signs I have done among them, [t]that you may know that I am the LORD."

3 So Moses and Aaron went in to Pharaoh and said to him, "Thus says the LORD, the God of the Hebrews, 'How long will you refuse to [u]humble yourself before me? Let my people go, that they may serve me. 4 For if you refuse to let my people go, behold, tomorrow I will bring [v]locusts into your country, 5 and they shall cover the face of the land, so that no one can see the land. And they shall [w]eat what is left to you after the hail, and they shall eat every tree of yours that grows in the field, 6 and they shall fill [x]your houses and the houses of all your servants and of all the Egyptians, as neither your fathers nor your grandfathers have seen, from the day they came on earth to this day.'" Then he turned and went out from Pharaoh.

7 Then Pharaoh's servants said to him, "How long shall this man be a snare to us? Let the men go, that they may serve the LORD their God. Do you not yet understand that Egypt is ruined?" 8 So Moses and Aaron were brought back to Pharaoh. And he said to them, [y]"Go, serve the LORD your God. But which ones are to go?" 9 Moses said, "We will go with our young and our old. We will go with our sons and daughters and with our flocks and herds, for [z]we must hold a feast to the LORD." 10 But he said to them, "The LORD be with you, if ever I let you and your [a]little ones go! Look, you have some evil purpose in mind.[1] 11 No! Go, the men among you, and serve the LORD, for that is what you are asking." And they were driven out from Pharaoh's presence.

12 Then the LORD said to Moses, [b]"Stretch out your hand over the land of Egypt for the locusts, so that they may come upon the land of Egypt and [c]eat every plant in the land, all that the hail has left." 13 So Moses stretched out his staff over the land of Egypt, and the LORD brought an east wind upon the land all that day and all that night. When it was morning, the east wind had brought the locusts. 14 [d]The locusts came up over all the land of Egypt and settled on the whole country of Egypt, [e]such a dense swarm of locusts as had never been before, nor ever will be again. 15 They covered the face of the whole land, so that the land was darkened, and [f]they ate all the plants in the land and all the fruit of the trees that the hail had left. Not a green thing remained, neither tree nor plant of the field, through all the land of Egypt. 16 Then Pharaoh hastily called Moses and Aaron and said, [g]"I have sinned against the LORD your God, and against you. 17 Now therefore, forgive my sin, please, only this once, and [h]plead with the LORD your God only to remove this death from me." 18 So [i]he went out from Pharaoh and pleaded with the LORD. 19 And the LORD turned the wind into a very strong west wind, which lifted the locusts and drove them [j]into the Red Sea. Not a single locust was left in all the country of Egypt. 20 But the LORD [k]hardened Pharaoh's heart, and he did not let the people of Israel go.

The Ninth Plague: Darkness

21 Then the LORD said to Moses, [l]"Stretch out your hand toward heaven, that there may be [m]darkness over the land of Egypt, a darkness to be felt." 22 So Moses stretched out his hand toward heaven, and there was pitch darkness in all the land of Egypt three days. 23 They did not see one another, nor did anyone rise from his place for three days, but [n]all the people of Israel had light where they lived. 24 Then Pharaoh called

1 Hebrew *before your face*

Chapter 10
2 [s][ch. 13:8, 14; Deut. 4:9; 6:20-22; Ps. 78:5-7; Joel 1:3] [t]ch. 7:17
3 [u]1 Kin. 21:29
4 [v]Lev. 11:22; Prov. 30:27; Joel 1:4; 2:25; Rev. 9:3
5 [w]ch. 9:32
6 [x][ch. 8:3, 21; Joel 2:9]
8 [y]ver. 24
9 [z]ch. 5:1; [ch. 3:18]
10 [a]ver. 24
12 [b]See ch. 7:19
[c]ver. 4, 5
14 [d]Ps. 78:46; 105:34 [e]Joel 2:2
15 [f]Ps. 105:35
16 [g]ch. 9:27
17 [h]See ch. 8:8
18 [i]ch. 8:30; 9:33
19 [j][Joel 2:20]
20 [k]See ch. 4:21
21 [l]ver. 12 [m]Ps. 105:28
23 [n][ch. 8:22; 9:4, 6]

10:2 tell . . . what signs. A clear statement of the divine plan involving Pharaoh. The plagues were to teach Israel and to leave an indelible impression on their posterity (Deut. 6:20–25).

10:9 feast. Moses demands that Israel's permission to worship be unqualified and total. See note 8:25.

10:11 the men among you. Adult males only were necessary at Israel's later festivals (23:17; 34:23). Note the sarcasm of v. 10.

10:12–15 Goshen was presumably exempt.

10:16 hastily. The speed of Pharaoh's action and his confession of sin underscore Egypt's peril. Severe famine threatened ("Not a green thing remained," v. 15).

10:22 pitch darkness. This darkness was clearly more than a blinding sandstorm or an eclipse of the sun. It was an unnatural darkness, like that associated with the day of the Lord (Is. 8:22; 58:10; Joel 2:2; Amos 5:20; Zeph. 1:15; cf. Deut. 28:29). The Egyptians typically celebrated the morning light when the sun god Ra was thought to overcome the dreaded serpent of hostile chaos and darkness. This supernatural darkness was further demonstration of the Lord's superiority over the Egyptian pantheon (7:19; 8:3 notes).

Moses and said, [o]"Go, serve the LORD;
[p]your little ones also may go with you; only
let your flocks and your herds remain
behind." 25 But Moses said, "You must also
let us have sacrifices and burnt offerings,
that we may sacrifice to the LORD our God.
26 Our livestock also must go with us; not a
hoof shall be left behind, for we must take
of them to serve the LORD our God, and we
do not know with what we must serve the
LORD until we arrive there." 27 But the LORD
[q]hardened Pharaoh's heart, and he would
not let them go. 28 Then Pharaoh said to
him, "Get away from me; take care never to
see my face again, for on the day you see
my face you shall die." 29 Moses said, "As
you say! [r]I will not see your face again."

A Final Plague Threatened

11 The LORD said to Moses, "Yet [s]one
plague more I will bring upon
Pharaoh and upon Egypt. Afterward he will
let you go from here. [t]When he lets you go,
he will drive you away completely. 2 Speak
now in the hearing of the people, that [u]they
ask, every man of his neighbor and every
woman of her neighbor, for silver and gold
jewelry." 3 [v]And the LORD gave the people
favor in the sight of the Egyptians.
Moreover, the man Moses was very great in
the land of Egypt, in the sight of Pharaoh's
servants and in the sight of the people.
4 So Moses said, "Thus says the LORD:
[w]About midnight I will go out in the midst
of Egypt, 5 and every firstborn in the land of
Egypt shall die, from the firstborn of
Pharaoh who sits on his throne, even to the
firstborn of the slave girl who is [x]behind
the handmill, and all the firstborn of the
cattle. 6 [y]There shall be a great cry throughout all the land of Egypt, such as there has
never been, nor ever will be again. 7 But not
a dog shall growl [z]against any of the people
of Israel, either man or beast, that you may
know that the LORD [a]makes a distinction
between Egypt and Israel. 8 And [b]all these
your servants shall come down to me and
bow down to me, saying, 'Get out, you and
all the people who follow you.' And after
that I will go out." And he went out from
Pharaoh in hot anger. 9 Then the LORD said
to Moses, [c]"Pharaoh will not listen to you,
that [d]my wonders may be multiplied in the
land of Egypt."
10 Moses and Aaron did all these wonders
before Pharaoh, and the LORD [e]hardened
Pharaoh's heart, and he did not let the people of Israel go out of his land.

The Passover

12 The LORD said to Moses and Aaron
in the land of Egypt, 2 [f]"This month
shall be for you the beginning of months. It
shall be the first month of the year for you.
3 Tell all the congregation of Israel that on
the tenth day of this month every man shall
take a lamb [g]according to their fathers'
houses, a lamb for a household. 4 And if the
household is too small for a lamb, then he
and his nearest neighbor shall take according to the number of persons; according to
what each can eat you shall make your
count for the lamb. 5 Your lamb shall be
[h]without blemish, a male a year old. You
may take it from the sheep or from the
goats, 6 and you shall keep it until the [i]four-
teenth day of this month, when the whole
assembly of the congregation of Israel shall
kill their lambs at twilight.[1]
7 "Then they shall take some of the blood
and put it on the [j]two doorposts and the
lintel of the houses in which they eat it.
8 They shall eat the flesh that night, roasted
on the fire; with [k]unleavened bread and
bitter herbs they shall eat it. 9 Do not eat

[1] Hebrew *between the two evenings*

24 [o]ver. 8 [p]ver. 10
27 [q]ver. 20
29 [r][Heb. 11:27]
Chapter 11
1 [s][ch. 4:23] [t]ch. 12:31, 33, 39
2 [u]ch. 3:22; 12:35
3 [v]ch. 3:21; 12:36
4 [w]ch. 12:29; [Job 34:20; Amos 4:10]
5 [x]Matt. 24:41; Luke 17:35
6 [y]ch. 12:30; [Amos 5:16, 17]
7 [z][ch. 8:22; 9:4]
[a]ch. 9:4
8 [b]ch. 12:33
9 [c]ch. 3:19; 7:4; 10:1 [d]ch. 7:3
10 [e]See ch. 4:21
Chapter 12
2 [f]ch. 13:4; 23:15; 34:18; Deut. 16:1
3 [g]ver. 21
5 [h]Lev. 22:19-21; Deut. 17:1; Mal. 1:8, 14; Heb. 9:14
6 [i]ver. 18; Lev. 23:5; Num. 9:3; 28:16; Josh. 5:10; Ezra 6:19
7 [j]ver. 22
8 [k]ch. 23:18; 34:25; Num. 9:11; Deut. 16:3; 1 Cor. 5:8

11:1 plague. A different Hebrew word for "plague" (cf. 9:14 note) is used to emphasize the climactic act of divine judgment—the death of the firstborn.

11:3 gave . . . favor. All four references to this event (3:21–22; 11:2–3; 12:35–36; Ps. 105:36–38) emphasize that Egypt gave gladly because of the Lord's intervention.

11:5 handmill. The grinding of corn was menial work done by slaves and prisoners of war.

12:2 The first month of the Hebrew year was Abib (March/April). This verse appears to report the institution of this new religious calendar, in commemoration of the Exodus. An autumn calendar is attested at 23:16; 34:22, though these passages may reflect an unofficial agricultural calendar. In the later Babylonian (spring) calendar the month of Abib is called Nisan (Neh. 2:1; Esth. 3:7).

12:5 without blemish. Like the sacrifices of Israel (e.g., Lev. 1:3), the Passover lamb was to be without flaw. The idea of substitution is evident—the lamb died in place of the firstborn. Jesus, whose death was prefigured by the Passover sacrifice, is called the Lamb of God (John 1:29, 36; 1 Pet. 1:19; Rev. 5:6).

12:6 The slaughter occurred at sunset (Deut. 16:6). The act marked the beginning of the Passover.

12:7 blood. Blood symbolizes the life of a victim (Lev. 17:11).

12:8, 9 The Passover meal was to be eaten as if in haste—the lamb roasted whole and accompanied by unleavened bread. The bitter herbs recalled the bitter suffering of slavery in Egypt (1:14).

any of it raw or boiled in water, but [l]roast-
ed, its head with its legs and its inner parts.
10 And [m]you shall let none of it remain until
the morning; anything that remains until
the morning you shall burn. 11 In this manner you shall eat it: with [n]your belt fastened, your sandals on your feet, and your
staff in your hand. And you shall eat it in
haste. [o]It is the LORD's Passover. 12 For [p]I
will pass through the land of Egypt that
night, and I will strike all the firstborn in
the land of Egypt, both man and beast; and
on [q]all the gods of Egypt I will execute
judgments: [r]I am the LORD. 13 [s]The blood
shall be a sign for you, on the houses
where you are. And when I see the blood, I
will pass over you, and no plague will befall
you to destroy you, when I strike the land
of Egypt.
14 "This day shall be [t]for you a memorial
day, and you shall keep it as a feast to the
LORD; throughout your generations, as a
[u]statute forever, you shall keep it as a feast.
15 [v]Seven days you shall eat unleavened
bread. On the first day you shall remove
leaven out of your houses, for if anyone
eats what is leavened, from the first day
until the seventh day, [w]that person shall be
cut off from Israel. 16 On the first day you
shall hold a [x]holy assembly, and on the
seventh day a holy assembly. No work shall
be done on those days. But what everyone
needs to eat, that alone may be prepared by
you. 17 And you shall observe the Feast of
Unleavened Bread, for [y]on this very day I
brought your [z]hosts out of the land of
Egypt. Therefore you shall observe this day,
throughout your generations, as a statute
forever. 18 [a]In the first month, from the
fourteenth day of the month at evening,
you shall eat unleavened bread until the
twenty-first day of the month at evening.
19 [b]For seven days no leaven is to be found
in your houses. If anyone eats what is leavened, [b]that person will be cut off from the
congregation of Israel, [c]whether he is a
sojourner or a native of the land. 20 You
shall eat nothing leavened; in all your
dwelling places you shall eat unleavened
bread."
21 Then Moses called all the elders of
Israel and said to them, "Go and select
lambs for yourselves [d]according to your
clans, and kill the Passover lamb. 22 Take a
bunch of [e]hyssop and [f]dip it in the blood
that is in the basin, and touch [g]the lintel
and the two doorposts with the blood that
is in the basin. [h]None of you shall go out of
the door of his house until the morning.
23 [i]For the LORD will pass through to strike
the Egyptians, and when he sees the blood
on [g]the lintel and on the two doorposts, the
LORD will pass over the door and [j]will not
allow the destroyer to enter your houses to
strike you. 24 You shall observe this rite as a
statute for you and for your sons forever.
25 And when you come to the land that the
LORD will give you, [k]as he has promised,
you shall keep this service. 26 And [l]when
your children say to you, 'What do you
mean by this service?' 27 you shall say, [m]'It is
the sacrifice of the LORD's Passover, for he
passed over the houses of the people of
Israel in Egypt, when he struck the
Egyptians but spared our houses.'" And the
people [n]bowed their heads and worshiped.

9 [l]Deut. 16:7; 2 Chr. 35:13 **10** [m]ch. 23:18; 29:34; 34:25; Deut. 16:4; [Lev. 7:15] **11** [n][Luke 12:35; Eph. 6:14; 1 Pet. 1:13] [o]ver. 27; Lev. 23:5; Deut. 16:5; [1 Cor. 5:7] **12** [p]ver. 23; ch. 11:4, 5 [q]Num. 33:4 [r]ch. 6:2; Isai. 43:11 **13** [s][Heb. 11:28] **14** [t]ch. 13:9 [u]ver. 17, 24, 43; ch. 13:10; 2 Kin. 23:21 **15** [v]ch. 13:6, 7; 23:15; 34:18, 25; Lev. 23:6; Num. 28:17; Deut. 16:3,8; [1 Cor. 5:7,8] [w][Gen. 17:14; Num. 9:13] **16** [x]Lev. 23:7, 8; Num. 28:18, 25 **17** [y]ch. 13:3 [z]ver. 51; ch. 7:4
18 [a]Lev. 23:5; Num. 28:16 **19** [b]ver. 15 [c]ver. 48, 49 **21** [d]ver. 3 **22** [e]Lev. 14:6; Num. 19:18; Ps. 51:7; Heb. 9:19 [f]Heb. 11:28 [g]ver. 7 [h][Isai. 26:20] **23** [i]ver. 12, 13 [g][See ver. 22 above] [j]Heb. 11:28; [Ezek. 9:6; Rev. 7:3; 9:4] **25** [k]ch. 3:8, 17 **26** [l]ch. 13:8, 14; Deut. 6:20; 32:7; Josh. 4:6, 21; Ps. 78:3-6 **27** [m]ver. 11, 21 [n]ch. 4:31

12:11 LORD's Passover. The Hebrew word for "Passover" is of uncertain etymology. The meaning "pass over" is attested here and probably in Is. 31:5. Some suggest a connection with the verb meaning "to limp, hobble," and others propose a derivation from an Accadian word meaning "appease."

The Passover observance is the oldest of the Jewish festivals and was celebrated at twilight on the fourteenth day of the first month (12:6) and for the seven succeeding days (fifteenth through twenty-first). Later participants were garbed for travel to celebrate the exit of Israel from Egypt in haste and anxiety. The practice of ritual questions posed by the children during the Passover celebration is a later development rooted in vv. 26, 27.

Provision was later made for a second or minor Passover one month later for members of the community who missed the initial feast (Num. 9:1–14). The New Testament establishes a direct redemptive connection between the Passover and the death of Jesus, the supreme Passover Lamb, who was sacrificed for us (1 Cor. 5:7).

12:12 firstborn. The firstborn, in whom the hopes of each family were invested, had the right of inheritance. No epidemic or accident could have been so selective.

on all the gods of Egypt . . . judgments. The death of firstborn humans and animals also constituted judgment on the Egyptian pantheon in that many of the sacred animals (which symbolized the gods) were killed. Furthermore, the impotence of Egypt's deities to protect the land's inhabitants was vividly demonstrated to all.

12:15 leaven. Yeast (or leaven) as a product of the previous year's harvest was regarded as a symbol of corruption. No Israelite sacrifice contained leaven.

12:19 cut off from the congregation of Israel. See note Lev. 7:20. Resident aliens and native-born non-Israelites were expected to observe this law.

12:22 hyssop. Hyssop was a species of marjoram used for purification (Lev. 14:4–6; Num. 19:6,18; Ps. 51:7). The richly textured branches and leaves held enough blood to perform the required act.

12:24 See "The Sacraments" at Matt. 28:19.

12:26 your children say to you. See note on v. 11. In Jewish Passover celebrations today, the youngest child asks the ritual question and the father then recites the story of the Exodus (cf. 13:8).

28 Then the people of Israel went and did so; as the LORD had commanded Moses and Aaron, so they did.

The Tenth Plague: Death of the Firstborn

29 [o]At midnight the [p]LORD struck down all the firstborn in the land of Egypt, [q]from the firstborn of Pharaoh who sat on his throne to the firstborn of the captive who was in the dungeon, and all the firstborn of the livestock. 30 And Pharaoh rose up in the night, he and all his servants and all the Egyptians. And there was [r]a great cry in Egypt, for there was not a house where someone was not dead. 31 Then he summoned Moses and Aaron by night and said, "Up, go out from among my people, [s]both you and the people of Israel; and go, serve the LORD, as you have said. 32 [t]Take your flocks and your herds, as you have said, and be gone, and bless me also!"

The Exodus

33 [u]The Egyptians were urgent with the people to send them out of the land in haste. For they said, "We shall all be dead." 34 So the people took their dough before it was leavened, their kneading bowls being bound up in their cloaks on their shoulders. 35 The people of Israel had also done as Moses told them, for they had [v]asked the Egyptians for silver and gold jewelry and for clothing. 36 [w]And the LORD had given the people favor in the sight of the Egyptians, so that [x]they let them have what they asked. Thus they plundered the Egyptians.

37 And the [y]people of Israel journeyed from [z]Rameses to Succoth, [a]about six hundred thousand men on foot, besides women and children. 38 A [b]mixed multitude also went up with them, and very much livestock, both flocks and herds. 39 And they baked unleavened cakes of the dough that they had brought out of Egypt, for it was not leavened, because [u]they were thrust out of Egypt and [c]could not wait, nor had they prepared any provisions for themselves.

40 The time that the people of Israel lived in Egypt was 430 years. 41 At the end of [d]430 years, on that very day, all the hosts of the LORD went out from the land of Egypt. 42 It was a night of watching by the LORD, to bring them out of the land of Egypt; so this same night is a [e]night of watching kept to the LORD by all the people of Israel throughout their generations.

Institution of the Passover

43 And the LORD said to Moses and Aaron, "This is the statute of the Passover: no foreigner shall eat of it, 44 but every slave that is [f]bought for money may eat of it after you have circumcised him. 45 [g]No foreigner or hired servant may eat of it. 46 It shall be eaten in one house; you shall not take any of the flesh outside the house, and [h]you shall not break any of its bones. 47 [i]All the congregation of Israel shall keep it. 48 [j]If a stranger shall sojourn with you and would keep the Passover to the LORD, let all his males be circumcised. Then he may come near and keep it; he [k]shall be as a native of the land. But no uncircumcised person shall eat of it. 49 There shall be [l]one law for the native and for the [j]stranger who sojourns among you."

50 All the people of Israel did just as the LORD commanded Moses and Aaron. 51 And on that very day the [m]LORD brought the people of Israel out of the land of Egypt by their [n]hosts.

29 [o]ch. 11:4 [p]Num. 8:17; 33:4; Ps. 78:51; 105:36; 135:8; 136:10 [q]ch. 4:23; 11:5
30 [r]ch. 11:6; [Amos 5:16, 17]
31 [s][ch. 10:9-11]
32 [t][ch. 10:24-26]
33 [u]ch. 6:1; 11:1, 8; Ps. 105:38
35 [v]ch. 3:22; 11:2
36 [w]ch. 3:21; 11:3 [x]Gen. 15:14; Ps. 105:37
37 [y]Num. 33:3, 5 [z]Gen. 47:11; [ch. 1:11] [a][ch. 38:26; Num. 1:46; 2:32; 11:21; 26:51]
38 [b]Lev. 24:10, 11; Num. 11:4; [Neh. 13:3]
39 [u][See ver. 33 above] [c][Deut. 16:3]
41 [d]Gal. 3:17; [Gen. 15:13; Acts 7:6]
42 [e]See Deut. 16:1-6
44 [f][Gen. 17:12, 13]
45 [g]Lev. 22:10
46 [h]Num. 9:12; Cited John 19:36
47 [i]ver. 6
48 [j]Num. 9:14 [k]ver. 19
49 [l]Num. 9:14; 15:15, 16 [j][See ver. 48 above]
51 [m]ver. 41; Acts 13:17 [n]ver. 17

12:31 Up, go out . . . serve. The threefold command underscores Pharaoh's urgency. He admits defeat.

12:32 bless me also. The blessing sought is presumably to countermand the dreadful curse that had gone through the land.

12:36 given . . . favor. These actions confirm the statement in 11:3.

12:37 Rameses to Succoth. See note 1:11. Succoth cannot be precisely located but must have been in the eastern Delta, possibly at Tell El Maskhutah in the Wadi Tumilat. The coastal routes to Canaan (13:17) were shorter but well-guarded.

six hundred thousand men on foot. Males of military age (v. 41 note; cf. Num. 11:21; 26:51). This number has been thought too large, but four centuries could well produce such numbers (1:7). As is often suggested, the Hebrew word for "thousand" could also be taken as meaning "family" or some subsection of a tribe.

12:38 mixed multitude. Perhaps persecuted minorities or other slaves came with them, as well as other Semites. Egyptians who had intermarried with the Hebrews, and even God-fearing Egyptians, were doubtless also included (cf. 9:19; 12:48; Is. 56:3).

12:40 430 years. See Gen. 15:13; Acts 7:6 note.

12:41 hosts. The Hebrew term denotes military organization (v. 37 note).

12:43–49 This added explanation of the Passover regulations, focusing on the restriction of the ceremony to the covenant community, was occasioned by the mention of non-Israelites leaving Egypt with Israel (v. 38). Only circumcised covenant members were eligible to participate.

12:46 in one house. None of the meat was to be taken outside of the house where non-covenant members could have access to it.

bones. No bones of the animals were to be broken, perhaps as a symbol of covenant unity. As with the Passover lamb, and contrary to Roman custom, no bones of Jesus were broken at His crucifixion (John 19:36; cf. 1 Cor. 5:7).

Consecration of the Firstborn

13 The LORD said to Moses, 2 [o]"Consecrate to me all the firstborn.
Whatever is the first to open the womb
among the people of Israel, both of man and
of beast, is mine."

The Feast of Unleavened Bread

3 Then Moses said to the people,
[p]"Remember this day in which you came out
from Egypt, out of the house of slavery, [q]for
by a strong hand the LORD brought you out
from this place. [r]No leavened bread shall be
eaten. 4 Today, in the month of [s]Abib, you
are going out. 5 And when the LORD brings
you into [t]the land of the Canaanites, the
Hittites, the Amorites, the Hivites, and the
Jebusites, which [u]he swore to your fathers to
give you, a land [v]flowing with milk and
honey, [w]you shall keep this service in this
month. 6 [x]Seven days you shall eat unleavened bread, and on the seventh day there
shall be a feast to the LORD. 7 Unleavened
bread shall be eaten for seven days; no leavened bread shall be seen with you, and no
leaven shall be seen with you in all your territory. 8 [y]You shall tell your son on that day,
'It is because of what the LORD did for me
when I came out of Egypt.' 9 And it shall [z]be
to you as a sign on your hand and as [a]a
memorial [z]between your eyes, that the law of
the LORD may be in your mouth. For with a
strong hand the LORD has brought you out of
Egypt. 10 [b]You shall therefore keep this statute at its appointed time from year to year.
11 "When the LORD brings you into the
land of the Canaanites, [c]as he swore to you
and your fathers, and shall give it to you,
12 [d]you shall set apart to the LORD all that
first opens the womb. All the firstborn of
your animals that are males shall be the
LORD's. 13 [e]Every firstborn of a donkey you
shall redeem with a lamb, or if you will not
redeem it you shall break its neck. Every
[f]firstborn of man among your sons you
shall redeem. 14 [g]And when in time to come
your son asks you, 'What does this mean?'
you shall say to him, [h]'By a strong hand the
LORD brought us out of Egypt, from the
house of [i]slavery. 15 For when Pharaoh stubbornly refused to let us go, the [j]LORD killed
all the firstborn in the land of Egypt, both
the firstborn of man and the firstborn of
animals. Therefore I sacrifice to the LORD all
the males that first open the womb, but [k]all
the firstborn of my sons I redeem.' 16 [l]It
shall be as a mark on your hand or frontlets
between your eyes, for [m]by a strong hand
the LORD brought us out of Egypt."

Pillars of Cloud and Fire

17 When Pharaoh let the people go, God
did [n]not lead them by way of the land of the
Philistines, although that was near. For God
said, "Lest the people [o]change their minds
when they see war and return to Egypt."
18 But God [p]led the people around by the way
of the wilderness toward the Red Sea. And

Chapter 13
2 [o]ver. 12, 13, 15; ch. 22:29, 30; 34:19; Lev. 27:26; Num. 3:13; 8:16, 17; 18:15; Deut. 15:19; Cited Luke 2:23
3 [p]ch. 12:42; Deut. 16:3 [q]ch. 3:19; 6:1 [r]See ch. 2:8
4 [s]ch. 23:15; 34:18; Deut. 16:1
5 [t]ch. 3:8; 23:23; 33:2; 34:11; Josh. 12:8; 24:11 [u]ch. 6:8 [v]See ch. 3:8 [w]ch. 12:25, 26
6 [x]ch. 12:15, 16
8 [y]See ch. 12:26
9 [z]Deut. 6:8; 11:18; [Num. 15:39; Matt. 23:5] [a]ch. 12:14, 24
10 [b][ch.12:14, 17, 24, 43]
11 [c]ver. 5
12 [d]ver. 2
13 [e]ch. 34:20 [f]Num. 3:46, 47; 18:15, 16
14 [g]See ch. 12:26 [h]ver. 3, 16 [i]ver. 3
15 [j]ch. 12:29 [k]ver. 13
16 [l]ver. 9 [m]ver. 14
17 [n][Ps. 107:7] [o]ch. 14:11, 12; [Neh. 9:17]; See Num. 14:1-4
18 [p]ch. 14:2; [Deut. 32:10]; See Num. 33:6-49

13:2 all the firstborn. Firstborn of humans and cattle were sacred to the Lord. Like the firstfruits of the harvest, the firstborn from the womb represented God's claim on all. The principle is enunciated here and the details are given at 13:12–16; 22:29, 30; 34:19, 20. Jesus was so presented as Mary's firstborn (Luke 2:22–23).

13:8 tell your son. See note 12:26.

13:9 sign . . . memorial. Interpreting this figurative expression literally, Jews later put brief passages of the Law (13:1–10, 11–16; Deut. 6:4–9; 11:13–21) in small boxes and attached them to the left arm and forehead. These are the *tephillim,* the phylacteries (protections) of later Judaism, to which Jesus referred in criticizing the Pharisees' ostentatious displays of piety (Matt. 23:5).

13:12 set apart. An animal from the herd or flock could be given to the Lord as a whole burnt offering. The firstborn son was always to be redeemed (v. 13; cf. the pagan use of the firstborn as an offering at 2 Kin. 16:3).

firstborn . . . males. See note on v. 2.

13:13 break its neck. This did not involve the shedding of blood and was not a sacrifice.

13:14 What does this mean. Like the Passover ritual (12:26, 27; 13:8), the redemption of the firstborn was to remind Israel of her redemption from Egypt.

13:15 The Lord's judgment on the firstborn in Egypt is the explanation for His claim on the firstborn in Israel, a claim made both as Creator and as Judge. Israel was not exempted from the death sentence on the firstborn in Egypt. The firstborn were spared only through the blood of the Passover lamb. Subsequent generations must also be redeemed, either through the life consecration of the Levites, chosen by God in place of the firstborn (Num. 3:11–13), or through the redemption price of five shekels (Num. 3:46–51).

13:17 way . . . of the Philistines. The strongly fortified caravan route that ran parallel to the Mediterranean coast (Introduction: Interpretive Difficulties). The Philistines were not in Palestine in considerable numbers until the twelfth century, but undoubtedly there were coastal pockets of Philistine (Minoan) trading colonies there earlier.

13:18 Red Sea. The Hebrew term (*yam suph*) is used to designate the Gulf of Aqaba (23:31), the Gulf of Suez (10:19; Num. 33:10), as well as the body of water crossed in the Exodus. Scholars suggest that the term may mean "sea of reeds" or "sea of the end." The "Red Sea" of the Exodus was probably one of the Bitter Lakes north of the Gulf of Suez. Perhaps it was the southern extension of the present Lake Menzaleh. Archaeological evidence suggests that the Bitter Lakes were at one time joined to the Gulf of Suez, and that shallows existed in them.

the people of Israel went up out of the land
of Egypt equipped for battle. 19 Moses took
the bones of Joseph with him, for Joseph[1]
had made the sons of Israel solemnly swear,
saying, [q]"God will surely visit you, and you
shall carry up my bones with you from here."
20 And [r]they moved on from Succoth and
encamped at Etham, on the edge of the
wilderness. 21 And [s]the LORD went before
them by day in a pillar of cloud to lead them
along the way, and by night in a pillar of fire
to give them light, that they might travel by
day and by night. 22 The pillar of cloud by day
and the pillar of fire by night did not depart
from before the people.

Crossing the Red Sea

14 Then the LORD said to Moses, 2 "Tell
the people of Israel to [t]turn back
and encamp in front of Pi-hahiroth,
between [u]Migdol and the sea, in front of
Baal-zephon; you shall encamp facing it, by
the sea. 3 For Pharaoh will say of the people
of Israel, 'They are wandering in the land;
the wilderness has shut them in.' 4 And [v]I
will harden Pharaoh's heart, and he will
pursue them, and I will [w]get glory over
Pharaoh and all his host, [x]and the
Egyptians shall know that I am the LORD."
And they did so.
5 When the king of Egypt was told that
the people had fled, the [y]mind of Pharaoh
and his servants was changed toward the
people, and they said, "What is this we
have done, that we have let Israel go from
serving us?" 6 So he made ready his chariot
and took his army with him, 7 and took [z]six

19 [q]Gen. 50:25; Josh. 24:32; Heb. 11:22; [Acts 7:16]
20 [r]ch. 12:37; Num. 33:6
21 [s]ch. 14:19, 24; 40:38; Num. 10:34; 14:14; Deut. 1:33; Neh. 9:12, 19; Ps. 78:14; 99:7; 105:39; 1 Cor. 10:1; [Isai. 4:5]; See Num. 9:15-23
Chapter 14
2 [t]ch. 13:18, 20; Num. 33:7, 8 [u]Jer. 44:1
4 [v]See ch. 4:21 [w]Rom. 9:17, 22, 23; See ch. 9:16 [x]ch. 7:5
5 [y]Ps. 105:25
7 [z]ch. 15:4; [Isai. 31:1]

[1] Samaritan, Septuagint; Hebrew *he*

equipped for battle. Israel went out in military formation, disciplined and prepared (12:37 note).

13:19 bones of Joseph. See Gen. 50:25; Josh. 24:32.

13:20 Etham. Israel camped on the edge of the wilderness near what may have been an Egyptian fortress at Etham (since the name seems Egyptian) where they understandably turned back (14:2).

13:21 cloud . . . fire. Customary symbols of the immediate presence of God (3:2 note; 33:9–10; 40:34–38; Num. 9:15–22; 11:25; Ps. 99:7; 105:39). God is not only present; He guides Israel day and night by His presence.

14:2 Pi-hahiroth. By divine command, Israel turned back and camped at Pi-hahiroth, reputedly in the vicinity of Rameses (Qantir). This invited Pharaoh's pursuit (v. 4 note).

Migdol. A general word for "fortification"; its location is presently unknown.

Baal-zephon. This site ("Baal of the North") was reputed to be in the vicinity of Tahpanhes, near Lake Menzaleh, about twenty miles east of Rameses.

14:4 Pharaoh's pursuit of his escaping slaves takes place under God's sovereign direction.

14:6 made ready his chariot. Pharaoh was in earnest since his elite chariot force was deployed. The horse and chariot seem to have been introduced into Egypt by the Hyksos (c. 1700 B.C.). The Egyptian chariot carried three men.

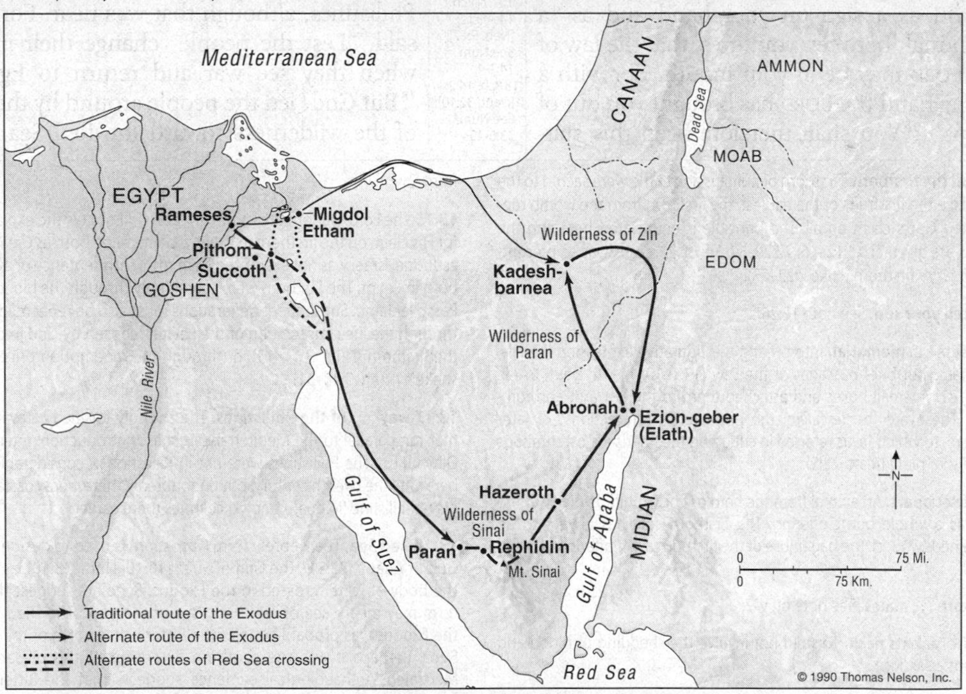

The Exodus from Egypt

hundred chosen chariots and all the other
chariots of Egypt with officers over all of
them. **8** And [v]the LORD hardened the heart
of Pharaoh king of Egypt, and he pursued
the people of Israel while [a]the people of
Israel were going out defiantly. **9** The
[b]Egyptians pursued them, all Pharaoh's
horses and chariots and his horsemen and
his army, and overtook them [c]encamped at
the sea, by Pi-hahiroth, in front of Baal-
zephon.
10 When Pharaoh drew near, the people of
Israel lifted up their eyes, and behold, the
Egyptians were marching after them, and
they feared greatly. And the people of Israel
[d]cried out to the LORD. **11** They [e]said to
Moses, "Is it because there are no graves in
Egypt that you have taken us away to die in
the wilderness? What have you done to us
in bringing us out of Egypt? **12** Is not this
what [f]we said to you in Egypt, 'Leave us
alone that we may serve the Egyptians'? For
it would have been better for us to serve the
Egyptians than to die in the wilderness."
13 And Moses said to the people, [g]"Fear not,
stand firm, and see the salvation of the
LORD, which he will work for you today. For
[h]the Egyptians whom you see today, you
shall never see again. **14** [i]The LORD will fight
for you, and you have only [j]to be silent."
15 The LORD said to Moses, "Why do you
cry to me? Tell the people of Israel to go
forward. **16** [k]Lift up your staff, and [k]stretch
out your hand over the sea and divide it,
that the people of Israel may go through
the sea on dry ground. **17** And [l]I will harden
the hearts of the Egyptians so that they
shall go in after them, and [m]I will get glory
over Pharaoh and all his host, his chariots,
and his horsemen. **18** And the Egyptians
[n]shall know that I am the LORD, [m]when I
have gotten glory over Pharaoh, his chariots, and his horsemen."
19 [o]Then the angel of God who was going
before the host of Israel moved and went
behind them, and the pillar of cloud moved
from before them and stood behind them,
20 coming between the host of Egypt and the
host of Israel. And there was the cloud and
the darkness. And it lit up the night[1] without one coming near the other all night.
21 Then Moses [k]stretched out his hand
over the sea, and the LORD drove the sea
back by [p]a strong east wind all night and
[q]made the sea dry land, and the waters were
[r]divided. **22** And [s]the people of Israel went
into the midst of the sea on dry ground, the
waters being [t]a wall to them on their right
hand and on their left. **23** The Egyptians pursued and went in after them into the midst
of the sea, all Pharaoh's horses, his chariots,
and his horsemen. **24** And in the morning
watch the LORD in the pillar of fire and of
cloud looked down on the Egyptian forces
and threw the Egyptian forces into a panic,
25 clogging[2] their chariot wheels so that they
drove heavily. And the Egyptians said, "Let
us flee from before Israel, for the [u]LORD
fights for them against the Egyptians."
26 Then the LORD said to Moses, [v]"Stretch
out your hand over the sea, that the water
may come back upon the Egyptians, upon
their chariots, and upon their horsemen."
27 [w]So Moses stretched out his hand over the
sea, and the sea [x]returned to its normal

8 [v][See ver. 4 above] [a]ch. 6:1; 13:3, 9, 16; Num. 33:3; Deut. 26:8; Acts 13:17; [ch. 3:19]
9 [b]ch. 15:9; Josh. 24:6 [c]ver. 2
10 [d]Josh. 24:7; Neh. 9:9
11 [e]Ps. 106:7; [ch.13:17]
12 [f]ch. 5:21; 6:9
13 [g]2 Chr. 20:15, 17; Isai. 41:10, 13, 14 [h][ver. 30]
14 [i]ver. 25; Deut. 1:30; 3:22; 20:4; Josh. 10:14, 42; 23:3; 2 Chr. 20:15, 29; Neh. 4:20 [j][Isai. 30:15]
16 [k]See ch. 7:19
17 [l][ver. 4, 8] [m]ver. 4
18 [n]ch. 7:5 [m][See ver. 17 above]
19 [o]ch. 23:20; 32:34; Num. 20:16; Isai. 63:9; [ch. 13:21]
21 [k][See ver. 16 above] [p]ch. 15:10 [q]Ps. 66:6 [r]ch. 15:8; Neh. 9:11; Ps. 74:13; 78:13; 106:9; 114:3; Isai. 51:10; 63:12; [Josh. 3:16; 4:23; Isai. 10:26; 11:15, 16]
22 [s]ver. 29; ch. 15:19; Num. 33:8; Ps. 66:6; Isai. 63:13; 1 Cor. 10:1; Heb. 11:29; [Ps. 77:19] [t]Ps. 78:13; [Hab. 3:10]
25 [u]ver. 14 **26** [v]ver. 16, 21 **27** [w]ver. 21 [x][Josh. 4:18]

1 Septuagint *and the night passed* 2 Or *binding* (compare Samaritan, Septuagint, Syriac); Hebrew *removing*

14:11 They said to Moses. Israel's rebellious complaints against God's leading are a continuing theme in Exodus (5:21; 15:24; 16:3; 17:2; 32:1).

14:13 Fear not. At the crucial point of Israel's deliverance they must see that their salvation is entirely God's work. His judgments on Egypt, His hardening of Pharaoh's heart, His leading Israel to this hopeless impasse, pinned between Pharaoh's chariots and the sea—all prepare for the climactic display of His saving power. The Lord will fight for them; they need only be still. He will gain the glory (14:18).

14:14 The LORD will fight. This phrase indicates the origin of the theme of the Lord as "divine Warrior," celebrated in ch. 15. War in the ancient world was viewed as a sacred undertaking in which the honor of the deity was at stake. In Israel, God was the "God of the armies of Israel" (1 Sam. 17:45), but also the "Lord of Hosts" (i.e., the Lord of the armies of heaven, the architect of Israel's victories and the inflicter of Israel's defeats). An early account of Israel's conquests under the Lord's leadership was called "the Book of the Wars of the LORD" (Num. 21:14). The theology of Holy War, which arose as a result, finds expression throughout both the Old and New Testament.

14:15 cry. A prayer of Moses is to be understood.

14:16 Lift up your staff. The rod of Moses, used in bringing God's judgments on Egypt, will now bring salvation to His people.

14:19 angel . . . cloud. The Angel of the Lord is identified with God's own presence in the cloud (23:20–22). See note Gen. 16:7.

14:21 east wind. God sends the wind to accomplish His purpose, but further supernatural power was needed to maintain the water on either side of the escape route, then return it with sufficient force to destroy Pharaoh's army.

14:24 morning watch. The night was divided into three watches of four hours, the last of which (the morning watch) was from 2:00 to 6:00 A.M., often the time for surprise attack (1 Sam. 11:11). The Lord Himself threw the Egyptian army into confusion.

14:25 The LORD fights. Egypt recognized the victory as God's (cf. v. 14).

14:27 The outstretched hand and staff of Moses are the instruments of destruction for the pursuing army, and bring about Israel's deliverance.

course when the morning appeared. And as
the Egyptians fled into it, the LORD [y]threw[1]
the Egyptians into the midst of the sea.
28 The [z]waters returned and covered the
chariots and the horsemen; of all the host
of Pharaoh that had followed them into the
sea, [a]not one of them remained. 29 But the
[b]people of Israel walked on dry ground
through the sea, the waters being a wall to
them on their right hand and on their left.
30 Thus the LORD [c]saved Israel that day
from the hand of the Egyptians, and Israel
saw the Egyptians dead on the seashore.
31 [d]Israel saw the great power that the LORD
used against the Egyptians, so the people
feared the LORD, and they [e]believed in the
LORD and in his servant Moses.

The Song of Moses

15 Then Moses and the people of Israel
[f]sang this song to the LORD, saying,

[g]"I will sing to the LORD, for he has
triumphed gloriously;
the horse and his rider[2] he has
thrown into the sea.
2 [h]The LORD is my strength and my
[i]song,
and he has become [j]my salvation;
this is my God, and I will praise him,
[k]my father's God, and [l]I will exalt
him.
3 The LORD is [m]a man of war;
[n]the LORD is his name.
4 [o]"Pharaoh's chariots and his host he
cast into the sea,
and his chosen [p]officers were sunk
in the Red Sea.
5 The [q]floods covered them;
they [r]went down into the depths
like a stone.
6 [s]Your right hand, O LORD, glorious in
power,
your right hand, O LORD, [t]shatters
the enemy.
7 In the [u]greatness of your majesty you
overthrow your adversaries;
you send out your fury; it
[v]consumes them like stubble.
8 At the [w]blast of your nostrils the
waters piled up;
the [x]floods stood up in a heap;
the deeps congealed in the heart of
the sea.
9 The enemy said, [y]'I will pursue, I will
overtake,
I [z]will divide the spoil, my desire
shall have its fill of them.
I will draw my sword; my hand
shall destroy them.'
10 You [a]blew with your wind; the [b]sea
covered them;
they sank like lead in the mighty
waters.
11 [c]"Who is like you, O LORD, among the
gods?
Who is like you, majestic in
holiness,
awesome in [d]glorious deeds,
[e]doing wonders?
12 You stretched out [f]your right hand;
the earth swallowed them.

14:27 [y]ch. 15:1, 7; Deut. 11:4; Ps. 78:53; Heb. 11:29
28 [z][Hab. 3:8-13] [a]Ps. 106:11
29 [b]See ver. 22
30 [c]Ps. 106:8, 10 [d]Ps. 92:9-11; [ver. 13]
31 [e]Ps. 106:12; [John 2:11; 11:45]
Chapter 15
1 [f]Ps. 106:12; [Judg. 5:1; 2 Sam. 22:1] [g]ver. 21
2 [h]Ps. 18:1,2; 59:17; 118:14; 140:7; Isai. 12:2 [i]Deut. 10:21; Ps. 109:1 [j]Ps. 18:46; Hab. 3:18 [k]ch. 3:6, 15, 16 [l]2 Sam. 22:47; Ps. 34:3; 99:5, 9; 118:28; 145:1; Isai. 25:1
3 [m]Ps. 24:8; Rev. 19:11 [n]ch. 3:15; 6:3; Ps. 83:18; Isai. 42:8; Mal. 3:6
4 [o]ch. 14:28 [p]ch. 14:7
5 [q]ver. 10; ch. 14:28 [r]Neh. 9:11
6 [s]ver. 12; Ps. 118:15, 16; Isai. 51:9 [t]Ps. 2:9; Rev. 2:27
7 [u]Deut. 33:26 [v][Isai. 5:24; 47:14; Mal. 4:1]
8 [w]ch. 14:21, 22; 2 Sam. 22:16; Job 4:9; Ps. 18:15; [2 Thess. 2:8] [x]Ps. 78:13; [Josh. 3:16; Hab. 3:10]
9 [y]ch. 14:9 [z]Gen. 49:27; Judg. 5:30; Isai. 53:12; Luke 11:22
10 [a]ch. 14:21; [Isai. 11:15; 40:24] [b]ver. 5; ch. 14:28 11 [c]Deut. 3:24; 1 Sam. 2:2; 2 Sam. 7:22; 1 Kin. 8:23; 2 Chr. 6:14; Jer. 10:6 [d][Isai. 6:3; Rev. 4:8] [e]Ps. 77:14 12 [f]ver. 6

[1] Hebrew *shook off* [2] Or *its chariot*; also verse 21

14:30 the LORD saved Israel. Verses 30, 31 summarize God's saving deed and its effect on Israel.

14:31 feared . . . believed in the LORD and in his servant Moses. At this point, Israel is a community that professes faith. Later, in the wilderness, they will apostatize and come under God's wrath (Num. 14; Ps. 95). The church, as a professing community, should avoid this example (Heb. 3; 4).

15:1–21 Moses and Israel sing of deliverance and hope. The poem of vv. 1–18, unique in the Old Testament, is a victory song expressed in the first person singular as a song of Moses. It celebrates the Lord's majestic power in saving Israel at the sea (vv. 1–12) and claims His power in planting Israel in the land (vv. 13–18). The song's many archaic expressions point to its origin in the Mosaic period.

15:1 I will sing. The Lord has shown His glory as He promised, and it is the privilege of His people, led by His servant Moses, to praise the God of their salvation. This Song of Moses becomes Israel's song as well. It is echoed elsewhere in the Old Testament (Ps. 118:14; Is. 12:2), and is sung by the saints in Rev. 15:3.

15:3 The theme of Yahweh as the Divine Warrior is emphasized. See Is. 59:16–18.

15:5 floods. The chaotic waters of the deep, ordered by God at creation (Gen. 1:2), are unleashed by God on the enemy.

15:6 Your right hand. A symbol of power. In Canaanite art the god Baal was sometimes depicted with mace upheld in the right hand. Here, the symbol of divine power was the outstretched hand of Moses holding the rod of the Lord.

15:8 floods stood up. Through the threatening waters of death God brought His people to Himself. The waters were an instrument of judgment for Egypt, and a means of deliverance for Israel. Paul, with some support from Jewish tradition, understood the Red Sea crossing as Israel's "baptism" (1 Cor. 10:2; cf. 1 Pet. 3:21 note).

15:9 I . . . I . . . I . . . I. The staccato repetition of these first person claims reveals an arrogance that is soon silenced.

15:11 Who is like you. The comparison is rhetorical in this threefold presentation of God's nature and power.

15:12 earth swallowed them. An expression for their reception into the underworld, thought to be the abode of the dead (Ps. 63:9; 71:20).

13 “You have [g]led in your steadfast love
the people whom [h]you have
redeemed;
you have [i]guided them by your
strength to your holy abode.
14 [j]The peoples have heard; they tremble;
pangs have seized the inhabitants
of Philistia.
15 Now are the chiefs of Edom
[k]dismayed;
trembling seizes the leaders of [l]Moab;
[m]all the inhabitants of Canaan have
melted away.
16 Terror and [n]dread fall upon them;
because of the greatness of your
arm, they are still [o]as a stone,
till your people, O LORD, pass by,
till the people pass by whom [p]you
have purchased.
17 You will bring them in and [q]plant
them on your own mountain,
the place, O LORD, which you have
made for your abode,
[r]the sanctuary, O Lord, which your
hands have established.
18 [s]The LORD will reign forever and ever.”

19 For when [t]the horses of Pharaoh with
his chariots and his horsemen went into
the sea, [u]the LORD brought back the waters
of the sea upon them, but the people of
Israel walked on dry ground in the midst of
the sea. 20 Then [v]Miriam [w]the prophetess,
the [x]sister of Aaron, took a tambourine in
her hand, and [y]all the women went out
after her with tambourines and dancing.
21 And Miriam sang to them:

[z]“Sing to the LORD, for he has
triumphed gloriously;
the horse and his rider he has
thrown into the sea.”

Bitter Water Made Sweet

22 Then Moses made Israel set out from
the Red Sea, and they went into the wilderness of [a]Shur. They went three days in the
wilderness and found no water. 23 When
they came to [b]Marah, they could not drink
the water of Marah because it was bitter;
therefore it was named Marah.[1] 24 And the
people [c]grumbled against Moses, saying,
“What shall we drink?” 25 And he [d]cried to
the LORD, and the LORD showed him a log,[2]
and he [e]threw it into the water, and the
water became sweet.
There the LORD[3] made for them a statute
and a rule, and there he [f]tested them,

13 [g]Ps. 77:20 [h]Ps. 77:15 [i]Ps. 78:54
14 [j]Num. 14:14; Deut. 2:25; Josh. 2:9,10; 9:24
15 [k][Deut. 2:4] [l]Num. 22:3 [m]Josh. 2:9, 11, 24; 5:1
16 [n]Deut. 2:25; 11:25 [o]1 Sam. 25:37 [p]Ps. 74:2; [1 Pet. 2:9]
17 [q]Ps. 44:2; 80:8; [Jer. 32:41] [r]Ps. 78:54; 132:13, 14
18 [s]Ps. 10:16; 29:10; 45:6; 146:10; Rev. 11:15
19 [t]ch. 14:23 [u]ch. 14:28, 29
20 [v]Mic. 6:4 [w][Judg. 4:4; 2 Kin. 22:14; Neh. 6:14; Luke 2:36] [x]ch. 2:4; Num. 26:59 [y]Judg. 11:34; 1 Sam. 18:6; Ps. 68:25; 149:3; 150:4
21 [z]ver. 1
22 [a]Gen. 16:7; 25:18; 1 Sam. 15:7
23 [b][Ruth 1:20]
24 [c]ch. 16:2; 17:3
25 [d]ch. 14:10; 17:4 [e][2 Kin. 2:21; 4:41] [f]ch. 16:4; Deut. 8:2, 16; Judg. 2:22; 3:1, 4; Ps. 66:10

1 *Marah* means *bitterness* 2 Or *tree* 3 Hebrew *he*

15:13 steadfast love. This translates the Hebrew word *hesed,* the precise sense of which is difficult to render in English. Here it refers to God's loyalty and devotion to His people, a loyalty created by the bond of God's covenant with His people. Though we might expect it to be used for the devotion of God's people to Him, its overwhelming use is as a description of God's devotion to His people. Since God reveals Himself in devotion to His own, there is no stronger term to express the free and faithful grace of His love (34:6, "abounding in steadfast love"; Ps. 136, "his steadfast love endures forever"). God's abiding covenant love and mercy find particular illustration in the Book of Hosea (Hos. 2:19).

15:14 tremble. The extraordinary, divinely induced fear of the inhabitants of Canaan is here depicted (Deut. 2:25 note). The peoples are mentioned in the approximate order they were encountered by Israel during the journey to the Promised Land.

15:17 A brief summary of the aims of the Exodus. The purpose was the settlement of Israel as God's special people in the Promised Land, the sanctuary of God's dwelling.

your own mountain. The point of contact between heaven and earth will be here. Deities in the ancient world were thought to inhabit mountains, and Israel took over this concept poetically. Here the whole of Palestine is viewed as the place of revelation (Deut. 3:25; Ps. 78:54; Is. 11:9).

sanctuary. The land would become such by God's indwelling presence, reminding readers that the goal of the Exodus was the worship of God in the land. Apart from God's gracious presence, there was no point in going to the land (33:15).

15:18 The LORD will reign. There are at least two other references to God's kingship in the Pentateuch (Num. 23:21; Deut. 33:5). The concept of divine covenant with Israel involved a recognition of God's kingship (1 Sam. 8:6–9).

15:22–17:16 As the Lord leads His people into the wilderness, He tests and delivers them in ways that reveal His purposes. He heals bitter water to show Himself as the Healer (15:22–27), gives manna and quail to show Himself as Provider and the One who establishes rest (Sabbath) for His people (16:1–26), and gives the water of life (17:1–7). Finally, in military victory, it is the Lord Himself who is the ensign of His people (17:15).

15:22 wilderness of Shur. Israel travels in the Sinai peninsula (about 260 miles long and 150 miles wide). The word "wilderness" refers here to grazing land as opposed to cultivated land. Shur was located northeast of the Sinai Peninsula, between Egypt and Palestine (Gen. 16:7; 20:1; 25:18).

15:23 Marah. The word means "bitterness." The location is suggested to be modern Ain Hawarah, inland and 50 miles south of the northern end of Suez. Apparently Israel went down the west coast of Sinai until they turned east toward Sinai.

15:24 grumbled. The first instance of Israel's wilderness complaint—behavior that typifies Israel's unbelief in the wilderness. The situation was critical. After nine days the water skins were empty, and death from dehydration was an immediate threat. Further, their hopes were dashed—they had located water, but found it undrinkable (v. 23).

15:25 he cried. The complaint of the people directed to Moses was really against God. Since Moses led at God's command (17:1), he appealed to the Lord.

showed. God instructs Moses by showing him a tree. The general term for God's law (Hebrew *torah*) is a form of the verb "showed." God's revelation in this event is a "statute and a rule," preparing for the statutes and ordinances to be given at Sinai. God's Word instructs Israel as He leads and proves them (cf. Jesus' use of Deut. 8:3 in Matt. 4:4). The tree is a sign of healing and sweetness (Judg. 9:11; Jer. 8:22; Gen. 2:9; Ezek. 47:7, 8).

26 saying, [g]"If you will diligently listen to the voice of the LORD your God, and do that which is right in his eyes, and give ear to his commandments and keep all his statutes, I will put none of the [h]diseases on you that I put on the Egyptians, for I am the LORD, [i]your healer."

27 Then [j]they came to Elim, where there were twelve springs of water and seventy palm trees, and they encamped there by the water.

Bread from Heaven

16 They [k]set out from Elim, and all the congregation of the people of Israel came to the wilderness of Sin, which is between Elim and Sinai, on the fifteenth day of the second month after they had departed from the land of Egypt. **2** And the whole congregation of the people of Israel [l]grumbled against Moses and Aaron in the wilderness, **3** and the people of Israel said to them, [m]"Would that we had died by the hand of the LORD in the land of Egypt, [n]when we sat by the meat pots and ate bread to the full, for you have brought us out into this wilderness to kill this whole assembly with hunger."

4 Then the LORD said to Moses, "Behold, I am about to rain [o]bread from heaven for you, and the people shall go out and gather a day's portion every day, that I may [p]test them, whether they will walk in my law or not. **5** On the sixth day, when they prepare what they bring in, [q]it will be twice as much as they gather daily." **6** So Moses and Aaron said to all the people of Israel, [r]"At evening [s]you shall know that it was the LORD who brought you out of the land of Egypt, **7** and in the morning you shall see the [t]glory of the LORD, because he has heard your grumbling against the LORD. For [u]what are we, that you grumble against us?" **8** And Moses said, "When the LORD gives you in the evening meat to eat and in the morning bread to the full, because the LORD has heard your grumbling that you grumble against him—[v]what are we? Your grumbling is not [w]against us but against the LORD."

9 Then Moses [x]said to Aaron, "Say to the whole congregation of the people of Israel, [y]'Come near before the LORD, for he has heard your grumbling.'" **10** And as soon as Aaron spoke to the whole congregation of the people of Israel, they looked toward the wilderness, and behold, the [t]glory of the LORD appeared in the cloud. **11** And the LORD said to Moses, **12** "I [z]have heard the grumbling of the people of Israel. Say to them, 'At [a]twilight you shall eat meat, and [b]in the morning you shall be filled with bread. Then you shall know that I am the LORD your God.'"

13 In the evening [c]quail came up and covered the camp, and in the morning [d]dew lay around the camp. **14** And when the dew had gone up, there was on the face of the wilderness a fine, flake-like thing, fine as frost on the ground. **15** When the people of Israel saw it, they said to one another, [e]"What is it?"[1] For they [f]did not know what it was. And Moses said to them, [g]"It is the bread that the LORD has given you to eat. **16** This is what the LORD has commanded: 'Gather of it, each one of you, as much

26 [g]See Lev. 26:3-13; Deut. 7:12-15 [h]Deut. 28:27, 60 [i]ch. 23:25; Ps. 103:3; 147:3; Hos. 6:1
27 [j]Num. 33:9
Chapter 16
1 [k]Num. 33:10, 11
2 [l]ch. 15:24; 17:3; 1 Cor. 10:10
3 [m][Num. 20:3-5] [n]Num. 11:4, 5
4 [o]Neh. 9:15; Ps. 78:24, 25; 105:40; John 6:31, 32; 1 Cor. 10:3 [p]See ch. 15:25
5 [q]ver. 22
6 [r]ver. 12, 13 [s]ch. 6:7; [Num. 16:28-30]
7 [t]ch. 40:34; Num. 16:19; 1 Kin. 8:10, 11; [ch. 13:21; 14:24] [u]Num. 16:11
8 [v]ver. 7 [w][Num. 14:27; 1 Sam. 8:7; Luke 10:16; Rom. 13:2]
9 [x][ch. 4:14-16] [y]Num. 16:16
10 [t][See ver. 7 above]
12 [z]ver. 8 [a]ver. 6 [b]ver. 7
13 [c]Num. 11:31; Ps. 78:27, 28; 105:40 [d]Num. 11:9
15 [e]ver. 31 [f]Deut. 8:3 [g]Deut. 8:3; See ver. 4

[1] Or *"It is manna."* Hebrew *man hu*

15:26 diseases . . . I put. See Deut. 28:26, 60–62; 7:15. Diseases mark the effects of divine curse.

I am the LORD, your healer. God has the power (Deut. 32:39) and the mercy to heal (Ps. 103:3). He alone can heal in the peace of His salvation (2 Chr. 16:12; Is. 38:17). To the prayer of anguish (Jer. 17:14), God responds (Jer. 30:17; 33:6). Healing from the damage inflicted by sin and death will come through the Lord's Anointed, by whose wounds we are healed (Is. 53:5; 61:1,2; Matt. 8:17).

15:27 Elim. The site is probably the Wadi Gharandel seven miles south of Ain Hawarah. The Lord, who healed the water of Marah (v. 23), leads His people to a place of rest and refreshment.

16:1–36 Israel arrives in time to observe the Sabbath and a theophany occurs in response to the people's complaints (16:9–13). The chapter draws to a close with a rest on the following Sabbath (16:27–30). Israel's keeping of the Sabbath prior to the revelation at Sinai is highlighted, as is God's continued testing of Israel (v. 4; cf. 15:25; 17:2).

16:1 wilderness of Sin. Situated in the southwest of Sinai, this is perhaps the modern region Debbet er-Ramleh.

16:4 bread. The people cried for bread and meat (v. 3), and God will give both (v. 8). Manna is called the "bread of the angels" (Ps. 78:25). In John 6:26–58, Jesus calls Himself the true manna ("bread of life") of which this provision in the wilderness was a symbol and type.

16:7 glory. The word normally refers to the manifested presence of God. Here, the Lord's gracious provision of the manna is in view.

16:13 quail. These small migratory game birds of the partridge family come from their winter habitat in Africa in the spring. They sometimes rest on the ground exhausted by flight. On a second occasion they are brought by a strong east wind (Num. 11).

16:14 fine, flake-like thing. The manna seems to have been similar to a honey-like secretion of insects that infested the tamarisk plants of the area (called "manna" by the Arabs). It solidifies in the cold desert nights, but must be gathered early. If this is the manna, the miracle would be God's control of the amount. The amount gathered is an omer per man, about two quarts, though a related Arabic word means a cupful, and perhaps this is the meaning here.

as he can eat. You shall each take an
[h]omer,[1] according to the number of the
persons that each of you has in his tent.'"
17 And the people of Israel did so. They
gathered, some more, some less. 18 But
when they measured it with an omer, [i]who-
ever gathered much had nothing left over,
and whoever gathered little had no lack.
Each of them gathered as much as he could
eat. 19 And Moses said to them, "Let no one
leave any of it over till the morning." 20 But
they did not listen to Moses. Some left part
of it till the morning, and [j]it bred worms
and stank. And Moses was angry with
them. 21 Morning by morning they gathered
it, each as much as he could eat; but when
the sun grew hot, it melted.

22 On [k]the sixth day they gathered twice
as much bread, two omers each. And when
all the leaders of the congregation came
and told Moses, 23 he said to them, "This is
what the LORD has commanded: 'Tomorrow is a day of [l]solemn rest, a holy Sabbath
to the LORD; bake what you will bake and
boil what you will boil, and all that is left
over lay aside to be kept till the morning.'"
24 So they laid it aside till the morning, as
Moses commanded them, and [m]it did not
stink, and there were no worms in it.
25 Moses said, "Eat it today, for [l]today is a
Sabbath to the LORD; today you will not
find it in the field. 26 Six days you shall
gather it, but on the seventh day, which is
a Sabbath, there will be none."

27 On the seventh day some of the people
went out to gather, but they found none.
28 And the LORD said to Moses, [n]"How long
will you refuse to keep my commandments
and my laws? 29 See! The LORD has given
you the Sabbath; therefore on the sixth day
he gives you bread for two days. Remain
each of you in his place; let no one go out
of his place on the seventh day." 30 So the
people [o]rested on the seventh day.

31 Now the house of Israel called its name
[p]manna. It was [q]like coriander seed, white,
and the taste of it was like wafers made with
honey. 32 Moses said, "This is what the LORD
has commanded: 'Let an omer of it be kept
throughout your generations, so that they
may see the bread with which I fed you in
the wilderness, when I brought you out of
the land of Egypt.'" 33 And Moses said to
Aaron, "Take a [r]jar, and put an omer of
manna in it, and place it before the LORD to
be kept throughout your generations." 34 As
the LORD commanded Moses, so Aaron
placed it before [s]the testimony to be kept.
35 The people of Israel [t]ate the manna forty
years, till they came to a habitable land.
They ate the manna till [u]they came to the
border of the land of Canaan. 36 (An omer is
[v]the tenth part of an ephah.)[2]

Water from the Rock

17 [w]All the congregation of the people
of Israel moved on from the wilderness of Sin by stages, according to the commandment of the LORD, and camped at
Rephidim, but there was no water for the
people to drink. 2 [x]Therefore the people quarreled with Moses and said, "Give us water
to drink." And Moses said to them, "Why
do you quarrel with me? Why do you [y]test
the LORD?" 3 But the people thirsted there
for water, and [z]the people grumbled against
Moses and said, "Why did you bring us up
out of Egypt, to kill us and our children
and our livestock with thirst?" 4 So Moses
cried to the LORD, "What shall I do with
this people? They are almost ready [a]to stone
me." 5 And the LORD said to Moses, "Pass

16 [h]ver. 36
18 [i]Cited 2 Cor. 8:15
20 [j][ver. 24]
22 [k]ver. 5
23 [l]ch. 35:2, 3; Gen. 2:3; Lev. 23:3; See ch. 20:8-11; 31:14-17
24 [m][ver. 20]
25 [l][See ver. 23 above]
28 [n][Ps. 78:10; Ezek. 20:13]
30 [o]Luke 23:56
31 [p]ver. 15 [q]Num. 11:7, 8
33 [r]Heb. 9:4
34 [s]ch. 25:16, 21; 26:33, 34; 27:21; 30:6, 26, 36; 40:21
35 [t]Deut. 8:2, 3; Neh. 9:20, 21; [u]Josh. 5:12
36 [v]Lev. 5:11; 6:20
Chapter 17
1 [w]ch. 16:1; Num. 33:12, 14
2 [x]Num. 20:3, 4 [y]Deut. 6:16; Ps. 78:18, 41; 95:8, 9; Isai. 7:12; Matt. 4:7; 1 Cor. 10:9; Heb. 3:8, 9
3 [z]ch. 15:24; 16:2
4 [a]Num. 14:10; 1 Sam. 30:6; 2 Chr. 24:21; Matt. 23:37; Luke 13:34; John 8:59; 10:31-33; 11:8; Acts 7:58; 14:5, 19; 2 Cor. 11:25; Heb. 11:37; [Josh. 9:25; 1 Kin. 21:13]

1 An *omer* was about 2 quarts or 2 liters 2 An *ephah* was about 3/5 bushel or 22 liters

16:23 holy Sabbath. An elevated term normally reserved for holy festivals. The implication is that the weekly Sabbath was normally kept by Israel before Sinai. The Sabbath ordinance in the Ten Commandments was a codification of Sabbath observance, not its inauguration.

16:31 coriander. This seed is small, globular, grayish, and aromatic, tasting like honey cakes.

16:33 jar. The manna is set aside in what is called "the golden urn" in Heb. 9:4.

16:35 forty years. The manna continued until they came to Canaan (Josh. 5:10–12). When they reached the Transjordanian country they had fields, vineyards, and wells of water (Num. 21:22), but the manna seems to have continued.

17:1 Rephidim. This region, generally identified with the modern Wadi Refayid, about eight miles south of Jebel Musa, was the last stop before Sinai.

17:2 quarreled. This translates the Hebrew word *rib,* which appears in the name "Meribah" (v. 7). *Rib* is often used in legal contexts with the meaning "to bring suit" (e.g., "plead your case," Mic. 6:1). The move to stone Moses (v. 4) is the execution of judicial sentence for treason. The verdict is threatened if Moses does not provide water.

test the LORD. It is not Moses who is being put on trial, but God. Tempting, or testing, in this setting takes on a judicial meaning. God is being accused of abandoning Israel to die of thirst in the desert.

17:5 Pass on before the people. The people want a trial. God, the just Judge, will give them one. Moses is to pass on before the people, taking in his hand his rod, and accompanied by elders of Israel. The rod of God

on before the people, taking with you some
of the elders of Israel, and take in your
hand the staff with [b]which you struck the
Nile, and go. 6 [c]Behold, I will stand before
you there on the rock at Horeb, and you
shall strike the rock, and water shall come
out of it, and the people will drink." And
Moses did so, in the sight of the elders of
Israel. 7 And he called the name of the place
[d]Massah[1] and [e]Meribah,[2] because of the
quarreling of the people of Israel, and
because they tested the LORD by saying, "Is
the LORD among us or not?"

Israel Defeats Amalek

8 [f]Then Amalek came and fought with
Israel at Rephidim. 9 So Moses said to
[g]Joshua, "Choose for us men, and go out
and fight with Amalek. Tomorrow I will
stand on the top of the hill with [h]the staff
of God in my hand." 10 So [g]Joshua did as
Moses told him, and fought with Amalek,
while Moses, Aaron, and [i]Hur went up to
the top of the hill. 11 Whenever Moses [j]held
up his hand, Israel prevailed, and whenever
he lowered his hand, Amalek prevailed.
12 But Moses' hands grew weary, so they
took a stone and put it under him, and he
sat on it, while Aaron and [i]Hur held up his
hands, one on one side, and the other on
the other side. So his hands were steady
until the going down of the sun. 13 And
[g]Joshua overwhelmed Amalek and his people with the sword.

14 Then the LORD said to Moses, "Write
this as a memorial in a book and recite it in
the ears of [g]Joshua, that [k]I will utterly blot
out the memory of Amalek from under
heaven." 15 And Moses [l]built an altar and
called the name of it, The LORD is my banner, 16 saying, "A hand upon the throne[3] of
the LORD! [k]The LORD will have war with
Amalek from generation to generation."

Jethro's Advice

18 [m]Jethro, [n]the priest of Midian,
Moses' father-in-law, heard of all
that God had done for Moses and for Israel

[1] *Massah* means *testing* [2] *Meribah* means *quarreling* [3] A slight change would yield *upon the banner*

5 [b]ch. 7:20
6 [c]Num. 20:8-11; Deut. 8:15; Neh. 9:15; Ps. 78:15, 16, 20; 105:41; 114:8; Isai. 43:20; 48:21; 1 Cor. 10:4
7 [d]Ps. 95:8 [e]Num. 20:13; Ps. 81:7; 95:8
8 [f]Deut. 25:17; 1 Sam. 15:2
9 [g]ch. 24:13; 32:17; 33:11 [h]ch. 4:20
10 [g][See ver. 9 above] [i]ch. 24:14; 31:2
11 [j][1 Tim. 2:8]
12 [i][See ver. 10 above]
13 [g][See ver. 9 above]
14 [g][See ver. 9 above] [k]Num. 24:20; Deut. 25:19; 1 Sam. 15:3, 7; 30:1, 17; 2 Sam. 8:12
15 [l][Judg. 6:24]
16 [k][See ver. 14 above]
Chapter 18
1 [m][ch. 2:18] [n]ver. 12; ch. 2:16

is identified by the sentence of judgment meted out on Egypt: "with which you struck the Nile," turning it to blood (cf. Is. 30:31, 32). The elders are summoned as representative witnesses (cf. v. 6).

17:6 I will stand before you. An astonishing statement. Man stands before God, not God before man (Deut. 19:17; 25:1–3; 17:8–13). In this trial God takes the place of the accused, standing in the dock.

on the rock. God stands on the rock and is identified with it. God is called the "Rock" in the song of Moses (Deut. 32:4, 15, 18, 31) and in the psalms that speak of this event (Ps. 78:35; 95:1).

strike the rock. Moses lifts the rod of judgment and strikes the rock on which God stands and with which He is symbolically identified. God is not guilty, but He bears the judgment. The fearful solemnity of Moses' blow appears when he later strikes the rock in disobedience, thereby dishonoring the holiness of God (Num. 20:9–12). The rock at Massah, struck for God's people, is a type of Christ, the incarnate and blameless Son of God, who endured the punishment for sin (1 Cor. 10:4).

water. The ultimate reference is to the water of life that flows from the throne of God (Zech. 13:1; 14:8; Ezek. 47:1–12). Jesus offers this water where it was symbolically poured out in the temple at the feast (John 7:37), and John notes the water that flowed from His pierced side on the Cross (John 19:34; cf. 7:38).

17:8 Amalek. The Amalekites, a nomadic group based in southern Palestine, were descendants of Esau (Gen. 36:12–16), indicating the origin of the enmity. The Amalekites attacked from the rear (Deut. 25:18). God had provided manna from heaven and water from the rock; now He provides deliverance from enemies.

17:9 Joshua. Joshua, an Ephraimite previously known as Hoshea ("salvation"), was called Joshua ("Yahweh saves") at Kadesh, possibly as a result of this victory (Num. 13:8, 16).

I will stand . . . with the staff. Joshua will choose men to fight, but they will do so under the uplifted staff, the sign of the Lord's victory.

17:10 Joshua . . . fought. Joshua prevailed in this holy war only when Moses held up to heaven the staff symbolizing the Lord's presence that had brought the plagues on Egypt (4:2; 9:23) and had dried up the sea (14:16).

Hur. Hur, attested in later tradition as the husband of Miriam, Moses' sister, was possibly the grandfather of the famous artisan of the tabernacle, Bezalel (1 Chr. 2:19–20).

17:14 Write this. One of the few references to writing in the Old Testament, though it was widespread at the time. It is linked with oral recitation here. The account was perhaps written in the Book of the Wars of the LORD, mentioned in Num. 21:14.

17:15 The LORD is my banner. The Hebrew word translated "banner" underlies "staff" in v. 9 and is used for the "pole" on which the bronze serpent was later placed (Num. 21:8). Since "banner" suggests cloth to us, this connection is lost. A spear could serve as a standard in battle, with or without bits of cloth tied to it. Later, a staff might have a device on it to mark the rallying point for troops. In the ancient world, these were sometimes images or signs of the gods. Moses' staff is the ensign to which Joshua's army could look and that symbolized God's saving power. Moses declares that God Himself is the Standard, the Ensign of His people.

17:16 A hand . . . the LORD. The Hebrew is difficult to translate and interpret (cf. text note). The central message is nevertheless clear: God gives Israel the victory, and the continuing warfare between Israel and Amalek is the Lord's. On the historic enmity between Israel and Amalek, see Num. 24:20; Deut. 25:17; 1 Sam. 15:2–33; 27:8, 9; 30:1–20; 2 Sam. 8:11, 12; 1 Chr. 4:42, 43; Esth. 3:1 note.

18:1–24:18 The Lord liberated His people from Egypt to bring them to Himself, to make them His special possession among all peoples. In order to enjoy this blessing, however, they were to obey Him and keep His covenant. The revelation at Sinai manifested the holy character of the covenant God and defined the character and behavior appropriate for God's covenant people.

The Sinai covenant also underscores the special role of the mediator. The Lord declared His intention to descend and speak directly to Moses so the people might hear and trust Moses forever (19:9). However, the face-to-face revelation so terrified the people that they pleaded with Moses to go up to God and receive the commands, then return and report to them (20:18–21). Moses was to represent the people before God (19:8), and represent the Lord to the people (19:7).

Another crucial lesson of the theophany and revelation at Sinai is the

his people, how the LORD had brought Israel
out of Egypt. 2 Now Jethro, Moses' father-in-
law, had taken Zipporah, Moses' wife, after
he had sent her home, 3 along with her [o]two
sons. The name of the one was Gershom
([p]for he said, [q]"I have been a sojourner[1] in a
foreign land"), 4 and the name of the other,
Eliezer[2] (for he said, "The God of my father
was my help, and delivered me from the
sword of Pharaoh"). 5 Jethro, Moses' father-
in-law, came with his sons and his wife to
Moses in the wilderness where he was
encamped at the [r]mountain of God. 6 And
when he sent word to Moses, "I,[3] your
father-in-law Jethro, am coming to you with
your wife and her two sons with her,"
7 Moses [s]went out to meet his father-in-law
and bowed down and [t]kissed him. And they
asked each other of their welfare and went
into the tent. 8 Then Moses told his father-
in-law [u]all that the LORD had done to
Pharaoh and to the Egyptians for Israel's
sake, all the hardship that had come upon
them in the way, and how the LORD had
delivered them. 9 And Jethro rejoiced for all
the good that the LORD had done to Israel,
in that he had delivered them out of the
hand of the Egyptians.
10 Jethro said, [v]"Blessed be the LORD, who
has delivered you out of the hand of the
Egyptians and out of the hand of Pharaoh
and has delivered the people from under
the hand of the Egyptians. 11 Now I know
that [w]the LORD is greater than all gods,
because in this affair they [x]dealt arrogantly
with the people."[4] 12 And Jethro, Moses'
father-in-law, brought a burnt offering and
sacrifices to God; and Aaron came with all
the elders of Israel to eat bread with Moses'
father-in-law [y]before God.
13 The next day Moses sat to judge the
people, and the people stood around Moses
from morning till evening. 14 When Moses'
father-in-law saw all that he was doing for
the people, he said, "What is this that you
are doing for the people? Why do you sit
alone, and all the people stand around you
from morning till evening?" 15 And Moses
said to his father-in-law, "Because [z]the people come to me to inquire of God; 16 [a]when
they have a dispute, they come to me and I
decide between one person and another,
and I [b]make them know the statutes of God
and his laws." 17 Moses' father-in-law said to
him, "What you are doing is not good.
18 You and the people with you will certainly wear yourselves out, for the thing is too
heavy for you. [c]You are not able to do it
alone. 19 Now obey my voice; I will give you
advice, and God be with you! You shall
[d]represent the people before God and
[e]bring their cases to God, 20 and you shall
warn them about the statutes and the laws,
and make them know [f]the way in which
they must walk and [g]what they must do.
21 Moreover, look for [h]able men from all the
people, men who fear God, who are trustworthy and hate a bribe, and place such
men over the people as chiefs of thousands,
of hundreds, of fifties, and of tens. 22 And
[i]let them judge the people at all times.
[j]Every great matter they shall bring to you,
but any small matter they shall decide
themselves. So it will be easier for you, and
they will [k]bear the burden with you. 23 If you
do this, God will direct you, you will be
[l]able to endure, and all this people also will
go to their place in peace."
24 So Moses listened to the voice of his
father-in-law and did all that he had said.

3 [o]ch. 4:20; Acts 7:29 [p]ch. 2:22 [q]Ps. 39:12; Heb. 11:13
5 [r]See ch. 3:1
7 [s]Gen. 14:17; 18:2; 19:1; 1 Kin. 2:19 [t][Gen. 29:13; 33:4]; 2 Sam. 19:39
8 [u]See Neh. 9:9-15; Ps. 78:12-28, 42-53; 106:7-12
10 [v]Gen. 14:20; 2 Sam. 18:28; Luke 1:68
11 [w]1 Chr. 16:25; 2 Chr. 2:5; Ps. 95:3; 97:9; 135:5 [x]Neh. 9:10; [Ps. 119:21; Dan. 4:37; Luke 1:51]
12 [y]Deut. 12:7; 14:26; 1 Chr. 29:22; [ch. 24:11; Gen. 31:54]
15 [z][Lev. 24:12; Num. 15:34]
16 [a]ch. 24:14; Deut. 17:8; [2 Sam. 15:2, 3; 1 Cor. 6:1] [b]Deut. 4:5; 5:1
18 [c]Num. 11:14, 17; Deut. 1:9, 12
19 [d]ch. 4:16; [ch. 20:19; Deut. 5:5] [e]Num. 27:5
20 [f]Ps. 143:8 [g]Deut. 1:18
21 [h]Deut. 1:15; 16:18; See 2 Chr. 19:5-10; [Acts 6:3]
22 [i]ver. 26 [j]Lev. 24:11; Num. 15:33; 27:2; 36:1; Deut. 1:17; 17:8 [k]Num. 11:17
23 [l]ver. 18

1 *Gershom* sounds like the Hebrew word for *sojourner* 2 *Eliezer* means *My God is help* 3 Hebrew; Samaritan, Septuagint, Syriac *behold*
4 Hebrew *with them*

importance of separation in preparation for the coming of God. Even Moses objected to the stringent preparations (19:23). The ceremonial law given at Sinai was the Lord's gracious training of the people, a protective measure for a people unaccustomed to the holy presence of God (Gen. 34 note).

18:1–27 Before he narrates the events at Sinai, Moses pauses to report on his visit with Jethro, the priest of Midian and his father-in-law. The focus of Jethro's counsel was Israel's governmental organization.

18:2 sent her home. Moses apparently sent Zipporah and his family back to Jethro some time after the incident of 4:24–26. It may have been after the Exodus from Egypt.

18:11 Now I know. This formula could indicate either the beginning of Jethro's faith (2 Kin. 5:15) or its strengthening (1 Kin. 17:24). In any event, Jethro offered sacrifices and shared the communion meal as a leader, not as a supplicant.

18:12 burnt offering. The whole burnt offering as a dedication sacrifice came first. Fellowship sacrifices, shared by the worshipers, followed. Provisions in Leviticus for sin and guilt offerings would later complete the sacrificial system.

18:16 statutes . . . laws. "Statutes" perhaps suggests standing regulations and "laws" case decisions. They will be codified later.

18:21 look for able men. Delegation is often difficult for an able leader. Men were chosen here on moral rather than intellectual grounds to deal with simple matters. Difficult cases, perhaps those without precedent, were brought to Moses. This is how Israel's legal system would later function. No difference is made between the sacred and the secular. The entire law was God's gift, and obedience to it amounted to obedience to God.

25 [m]Moses chose able men out of all Israel
and made them heads over the people,
chiefs of thousands, of hundreds, of fifties,
and of tens. 26 And [n]they judged the people
at all times. Any hard case they brought to
Moses, but any small matter they decided
themselves. 27 Then Moses let his father-in-
law depart, and [o]he went away to his own
country.

Israel at Mount Sinai

19 On the third new moon after the
people of Israel had gone out of the
land of Egypt, on that day they [p]came into
the wilderness of Sinai. 2 They set out from
[q]Rephidim and came into the wilderness of
Sinai, and they encamped in the wilderness. There Israel encamped before [r]the
mountain, 3 while [s]Moses went up to God.
[t]The LORD called to him out of the mountain, saying, "Thus you shall say to the
house of Jacob, and tell the people of Israel:
4 [u]You yourselves have seen what I did to
the Egyptians, and how [v]I bore you on
eagles' wings and brought you to myself.
5 Now therefore, if you will indeed obey my
voice and keep my covenant, you shall be
[w]my treasured possession among all peoples, for [x]all the earth is mine; 6 and you
shall be to me a [y]kingdom of priests and [z]a
holy nation. These are the words that you
shall speak to the people of Israel."
7 So Moses came and called the elders of
the people and set before them all these
words that the LORD had commanded him.

25 [m]Deut. 1:15
26 [n]ver. 22
27 [o][Num. 10:29, 30]
Chapter 19
1 [p]Num. 33:15
2 [q]ch. 17:1, 8 [r]See ch. 3:1
3 [s]ch. 20:21; [Acts 7:38] [t]ch. 3:4
4 [u]Deut. 29:2 [v]Deut. 32:11, 12; Isai. 63:9 Rev. 12:14
5 [w]Deut. 7:6; 14:2; 26:18; Ps. 135:4; Mal. 3:17; Tit. 2:14 [x]ch. 9:29; Deut. 10:14; Job 41:11; Ps. 24:1; 50:12; 1 Cor. 10:26
6 [y]1 Pet. 2:5, 9; Rev. 1:6; 5:10; 20:6 [z]Lev. 20:26; Deut. 7:6; 14:21; 26:19; 28:9; Isai. 62:12; 1 Pet. 2:9
8 [a]ch. 24:3, 7; Deut. 5:27; 26:17
9 [b]ch. 20:21; 24:16; Deut. 4:11; Ps. 18:11; 97:2; [Matt. 17:5] [c]Deut. 4:12, 36; [John 12:28, 29] [d]ch. 14:31
10 [e]Lev. 11:44, 45; [Josh. 3:5] [f][Gen. 35:2; Lev. 15:5]
11 [g]ch. 34:5; [Deut. 33:2]
12 [h]Cited Heb. 12:20
13 [i]ver. 16, 19

8 [a]All the people answered together and
said, "All that the LORD has spoken we will
do." And Moses reported the words of the
people to the LORD. 9 And the LORD said to
Moses, "Behold, I am coming to you [b]in a
thick cloud, that [c]the people may hear
when I speak with you, and may also [d]be-
lieve you forever."

When Moses told the words of the people to the LORD, 10 the LORD said to Moses,
"Go to the people and [e]consecrate them
today and tomorrow, and let them [f]wash
their garments 11 and be ready for the third
day. For on the third day [g]the LORD will
come down on Mount Sinai in the sight of
all the people. 12 And you shall set limits for
the people all around, saying, 'Take care
not to go up into the mountain or touch
the edge of it. [h]Whoever touches the
mountain shall be put to death. 13 No hand
shall touch him, but he shall be stoned or
shot;[1] whether beast or man, he shall not
live.' When [i]the trumpet sounds a long
blast, they shall come up to the mountain."
14 So Moses [j]went down from the mountain
to the people and [e]consecrated the people;
[f]and they washed their garments. 15 And he
said to the people, "Be ready for the [k]third
day; [l]do not go near a woman."
16 On the morning of the [k]third day there
were [m]thunders and lightnings and [n]a thick
cloud on the mountain and a very loud

14 [j]ver. 3 [e][See ver. 10 above] [f][See ver. 10 above] 15 [k]ver. 11 [l][1 Sam. 21:4, 5; 1 Cor. 7:5] 16 [k][See ver. 15 above] [m]Ps. 77:18; Heb. 12:18; Rev. 4:5; 8:5; 11:19 [n]ver. 9

1 That is, shot with an arrow

19:1 came into . . . Sinai. The wilderness of Sinai lay in the southeast region of the Sinai peninsula. Mount Sinai is traditionally identified as Jebel Musa, a mountain with a broad plain at its base that seems to fit the biblical evidence (v. 2; cf. Deut. 9:21 note). Israel would remain at Sinai for eleven months (Num. 10:11).

19:3–6 God's words begin (v. 3) and end (v. 6) with an instruction of God to Moses. What lies in between is a summary of God's covenant faithfulness and Israel's covenant responsibilities.

19:4 brought you to myself. God's deliverance from slavery was not just liberation, but adoption. He brought them out and carried them through the wilderness to bring them to Himself, to make them His (Gen. 17:7 note).

19:5 obey my voice and keep my covenant. Terms summarizing the proper human response to God's gracious covenant (Gen. 17:2 note). The latter phrase (Gen. 17:9, 10; 1 Kin. 11:11; Ps. 78:10; 103:18; 132:12; Ezek. 17:14) always refers to fidelity to a previously revealed covenant. Since 6:4 has referred to the Exodus as the fulfillment of the patriarchal covenant, the revelation at Sinai must also be seen as an extension of the Abrahamic covenant.

treasured possession. As the following clause shows, God means that Israel will be His personal treasure within what is more generally owned (1 Chr. 29:3). Israel is separated by God's election from the world that belongs to Him.

19:6 kingdom of priests and a holy nation. Israel is to be a priestly royalty, a holy nation set apart from the world as a priest was set apart in ancient society. The emphasis here falls on Israel's relation to God rather than on any priestly ministry to the nations, yet Israel's relation to the Lord also bears witness to the world. Verses 4–6a reflect the Abrahamic covenant of Gen. 12:1–3. What this passage prescribes for Israel, the new covenant makes a reality for believers (1 Pet. 2:9–10; Rev. 1:6; 5:10; 20:6).

19:11 be ready for the third day. Arrangements to ensure ritual purity (washing clothes, v. 10; abstention from sexual intercourse, v. 15; Lev. 15:18; 1 Sam. 21:4) and to safeguard the holiness of the mountain (vv. 12, 13) were commanded in preparation for the theophany, a special visual manifestation of divine presence.

come down on Mount Sinai. The mountain was the LORD's place of meeting with His people, not His residence. The tabernacle was soon to be His earthly dwelling place.

19:16 On the morning of the third day. God comes as promised on the morning of the third day. No natural explanation of vv. 16–19a (e.g., a volcanic eruption) is sufficient. This was a divine manifestation by storm and fire.

a very loud trumpet blast. Later, special occasions of worship were signaled by the blast of the horn (Num. 10:10).

[o] trumpet blast, so that all the people in the
camp [p] trembled. **17** Then [q] Moses brought
the people out of the camp to meet God,
and they took their stand at the foot of
the mountain. **18** Now [r] Mount Sinai was
wrapped in smoke because the LORD had
descended on it in fire. The smoke of it
went up like the smoke of a kiln, and [s] the
whole mountain trembled greatly. **19** And as
the [o] sound of the trumpet grew louder and
louder, Moses spoke, and [t] God answered
him in thunder. **20** The LORD came down on
Mount Sinai, to the top of the mountain.
And the LORD called Moses to the top of
the mountain, and Moses went up.
21 And the LORD said to Moses, "Go down
and warn the people, lest they break
through to the LORD [u] to look and many of
them perish. **22** Also let the priests who
come near to the LORD [v] consecrate themselves, lest the LORD [w] break out against
them." **23** And Moses said to the LORD, "The
people cannot come up to Mount Sinai, for
you yourself warned us, saying, [x] 'Set limits
around the mountain and consecrate it.'"
24 And the LORD said to him, "Go down,
and come up bringing Aaron with you. But
do not let the priests and the people [y] break
through to come up to the LORD, lest he
break out against them." **25** So Moses went
down to the people and told them.

The Ten Commandments

20 [z] And [a] God spoke all these words,
saying,
2 [b] "I am the LORD your God, who brought
you out of the land of Egypt, out of the
house of slavery.
3 [c] "You shall have no other gods before[1]
me.
4 [d] "You shall not make for yourself a carved
image, or any likeness of anything that is in
heaven above, or that is in the earth beneath,
or that is in the water under the earth. **5** [e] You
shall not bow down to them or serve them,
for I the LORD your God am [f] a jealous God,
[g] visiting the iniquity of the fathers on the
children to the third and the fourth generation of those who hate me, **6** but showing
steadfast love to thousands[2] of those who
love me and keep my commandments.
7 [h] "You shall not take the name of the LORD
your God in vain, for the LORD will not hold
him guiltless who takes his name in vain.

16 [o] ver. 13 [p] Heb. 12:21
17 [q] Deut. 4:10
18 [r] ch. 24:17; Judg. 5:5; [Isai. 6:4; Ps. 144:5; Rev. 15:8] [s] Ps. 68:8; Heb. 12:26
19 [o] [See ver. 16 above] [t] Neh. 9:13; Ps. 81:7
21 [u] [ch. 3:6; 1 Sam. 6:19]
22 [v] Lev. 10:3 [w] 2 Sam. 6:8; 1 Chr. 13:11
23 [x] ver. 12; [Josh. 3:4]
24 [y] 2 Sam. 6:8; 1 Chr. 13:11

Chapter 20
1 [z] For ver. 1-17, see Deut. 5:6-21 [a] Deut. 5:22
2 [b] Lev. 26:13; Ps. 81:10; Hos. 13:4
3 [c] 2 Kin. 17:35; Jer. 25:6; 35:15
4 [d] Lev. 26:1; Deut. 27:15; Ps. 97:7; [Acts 17:29]
5 [e] ch. 23:24; Josh. 23:7 [f] ch. 34:14; Deut. 4:24; 6:15; Josh. 24:19; Nah. 1:2 [g] ch. 34:7; Num. 14:18; [Ps. 79:8; 109:14; Isai. 65:6, 7; Jer. 32:18]
7 [h] Lev. 19:12; [Matt. 5:34, 35; James 5:12]

1 Or *besides* 2 Or *to the thousandth generation*

19:24 priests. This may refer to those who discharged the duties of priesthood prior to the establishment of the Levitical priesthood.

20:1–17 The Ten Commandments, or "Ten Words" of the covenant. These are expressions of the eternal law of God that transcend the Old and New Testaments. As God had created order in the heavens and earth with ten words (Gen. 1:3–29), so He creates order in society with ten words. The first four commandments describe how the people are to relate to God, while the remainder describe how God's people are to relate to each other (Deut. 4:13 note). See "The Three Purposes of the Law" at Deut. 13:10.

20:1 See theological note "The Law of God" on the next page.

God spoke all these words. God spoke only these commandments directly to the people (vv. 18–20 and notes; 19:9; Deut. 4:10–14; 5:22–27; 9:10; Neh. 9:13). What are called "words" here are elsewhere called "commandments" (34:28; Deut. 4:13; 10:4). The Hebrew for "word" (*dabar*) was the term for stipulations in the political treaties of the time.

The Decalogue (from the Greek term meaning "ten words") itself reflects the ancient treaty framework (Introduction: Date and Occasion). First comes the treaty preamble ("I am the LORD your God," v. 2), then the historical prologue ("who brought you out of the land of Egypt"). The commandments themselves are the treaty stipulations. God is Israel's Suzerain-King, to whom the people owe complete allegiance. The absence of penalties indicates that the Decalogue is not a legal code but rather a foundational covenant document. These covenant principles are then applied in the "Covenant Code," a set of laws with penalties attached, which follows (20:22–23:19).

20:2 your God. God's claim comes first. Israel is His by right of creation and redemption. The Lord's covenant commands are given to those whom He has already brought to Himself from enslavement to Egypt (19:4), though not from enslavement to sin (chs. 32–34).

20:3 before me. Lit. "before My face" or "in My presence." The Lord is a jealous God who already claims Israel as His (v. 5 note).

20:4 carved image. The term means something hewn from wood or stone. The prohibited image may be that of the Lord, since other deities have been excluded by v. 2, though the qualifying words "any likeness of anything" suggest that pagan idols are in view. Israel was to be distinguished from the nations by her imageless worship. Images are forbidden, not because there could be none, since God made mankind in His own image (Gen. 1:26, 27), but because God must reveal Himself, not be subject to human imagination. In His own time, God did provide His own image—Jesus Christ is the true image of the Godhead in bodily form (Col. 1:15; 2:19). See "Syncretism and Idolatry" at Hos. 2:13.

20:5 jealous. When used of God, this word describes His passion for His holy name, a zeal that demands the exclusive devotion of His people. It is employed when that claim is threatened by other deities (Deut. 6:15; Josh. 24:19).

third and the fourth generation. The longest span of generations represented in a given household at any one time. The severity of God's judgment on subsequent generations warns those who love their children's children of the terrible consequences of their sin.

20:6 showing steadfast love. God's covenant mercy, or steadfast love (Hebrew *ḥesed*) is His devotion to His people (15:13 note).

20:7 takes his name in vain. God's name was a gift of grace to Israel. Not through an idol, but in the name, Israel had access to God in worship. God's name is therefore to be revered. This command forbids the use of God's name in false worship, for incantations or divination, as well as for attesting falsehood or speaking blasphemy (Deut. 28:58). Jesus taught His disciples to pray that God would hallow His name, and Jesus hallowed the Father's name on the Cross (Matt. 6:9; John 12:27, 28).

8 [i] "Remember the Sabbath day, to keep
it holy. 9 [j] Six days you shall labor, and do
all your work, 10 but the [k] seventh day is a
Sabbath to the LORD your God. On it you
shall not do any work, you, or your son,
or your daughter, your male servant, or
your female servant, or your livestock, or
the [l] sojourner who is within your gates.
11 For [m] in six days the LORD made heaven
and earth, the sea, and all that is in them,
and rested the seventh day. Therefore the
LORD blessed the Sabbath day and made it
holy.

8 [i] Lev. 19:3, 30; 26:2; See ch. 31:13-17 **9** [j] ch. 23:12; 34:21; 35:2; Lev. 23:3; Luke 13:14 **10** [k] ch. 16:26; 31:15; Gen. 2:2, 3; Ezek. 20:12; See Num. 15:32-36

[l] See Neh. 13:16-19 **11** [m] See Gen. 1:1–2:3

The Law of God

Human beings were not created autonomous (that is, free to be a law to themselves) but theonomous—subject to the law of God. This was not a hardship, because God had created man in such a way that grateful obedience would bring him the highest happiness. Duty and delight would have coincided, as they did in Jesus (John 4:34; cf. Ps. 112:1; 119:14, 16, 47, 48, 97–113, 127, 128, 163–167). The fallen human heart hates God's law, both because it is a law and because it comes from God. Those who know Christ, however, find not only that they love the law and want to keep it, both to please God and out of gratitude for grace (Rom. 7:18–22; 12:1, 2), but also that the Holy Spirit leads them into a degree of obedience that was never theirs before (Rom. 7:6; 8:4–6; Heb. 10:16).

God's moral law is abundantly set forth in Scripture, in the Decalogue (the Ten Commandments), other statutes of Moses, sermons by the prophets, the teaching of Jesus, and the New Testament letters. The law reflects God's holy character and His purposes for created human beings. God commands the behavior that pleases Him and forbids what offends Him. Jesus summarizes the moral law in the two great commandments, to love God and to love your neighbor (Matt. 22:37–40). He says that on these two depend all the Old Testament moral instructions. The moral teaching of Christ and His apostles is the old law deepened and reapplied to new circumstances—life in the kingdom of God, where the Savior reigns, and in the post-Pentecost era of the Spirit, when God's people are called to live sanctified lives in the midst of a hostile world (John 17:6–19).

Biblical law is of various sorts. Moral laws command the personal and community behavior that is always our duty. The political laws of the Old Testament applied principles of the moral law to Israel's national situation when Israel was a theocracy, God's people on earth. The Old Testament laws about ceremonial purity, diet, and sacrifice were temporary enactments for purposes of instruction. They were canceled by the New Testament because their symbolic meaning had been fulfilled (Matt. 15:20; Mark 7:15–19; Acts 10:9–16; Heb. 10:1–14, 13:9, 10).

The mingling of moral, judicial, and ritual law in the Mosaic books carried the message that life under God is to be seen and lived, not compartmentally, but as a many-sided unity, and also that God's authority as legislator gave equal force to the entire code. However, the laws were of different kinds, with different purposes. The political and ceremonial laws were of limited application, while it seems clear both from the immediate context and from the rest of His teaching that Jesus' affirmation of the unchanging universal force of God's law relates to the moral law as such (Matt. 5:17–19; cf. Luke 16:16, 17).

God requires the total obedience of each person to all the implications of His law. As the *Westminster Larger Catechism*, Q. 99, says, the law binds "the whole man … unto obedience forever"; "it is spiritual, and so reacheth the understanding, will, affections, and all other powers of the soul as well as the words, works, and gestures." In other words, desires as well as actions must be right; Jesus condemns the hypocrisy that tries to hide inner corruption with an outward show (Matt. 15:7, 8, 23:25–28). Furthermore, the corollaries of the law are part of its content: "where a duty is commanded, the contrary sin is forbidden; and, where a sin is forbidden, the contrary duty is commanded."

20:8 Sabbath. The Hebrew word (*shabbat*) apparently derives from the verb meaning "to cease"—the Sabbath being the day that regular labor ceased. Exodus cites God's work of creation as the basis for the command (v. 11), while Deuteronomy bases the Sabbath ordinance on the deliverance from Egypt (Deut. 5:12 and note). The Sabbath ordinance is rooted in both the orders of creation and of redemption—it looks backward to God's good creation (Gen. 2:2, 3) and forward to the final redemptive Sabbath rest for God's people (Heb. 4:1–11). Just as circumcision was the sign of the Abrahamic covenant (Gen. 17), so the Sabbath becomes the sign of the Sinai covenant (31:13), reminding God's people of their place within God's purposes for creation and of their salvation from physical bondage in Egypt. Ultimately, the Sabbath points to Christ, our Creator and Redeemer, who brings rest to the people of God (Matt. 11:28; Col. 2:16, 17).

20:10 shall not do any work. The Sabbath is not designed as a burden, but as a blessed release from hard labor (Mark 2:27). The holiness of the day separates it to the Lord so that it is enjoyed by sharing His rest, celebrating His work of creation and redemption (Deut. 5:15).

12[n] "Honor your father and your mother,
[o]that your days may be long in the land
that the LORD your God is giving you.
13[p] "You shall not murder.[1]
14[q] "You shall not commit adultery.
15[r] "You shall not steal.
16[s] "You shall not bear false witness
against your neighbor.
17[t] "You shall not covet [u]your neighbor's
house; [v]you shall not covet your neighbor's
wife, or his male servant, or his female servant, or his ox, or his donkey, or anything
that is your neighbor's."
18 Now when all the people saw [w]the
thunder and the flashes of lightning and
the sound of the trumpet and the mountain smoking, the people were afraid[2] and
trembled, and they stood far off 19 and said
to Moses, [x]"You speak to us, and we will
listen; but do not let God speak to us, lest
we die." 20[y] Moses said to the people, "Do
not fear, for God has come to [z]test you,
that the fear of him may be before you, that
you may not sin." 21 The people stood far
off, while Moses drew near to the [a]thick
darkness where God was.

Laws About Altars

22 And the LORD said to Moses, "Thus you
shall say to the people of Israel: 'You have
seen for yourselves that I have [b]talked with
you from heaven. 23[c] You shall not make gods
of silver to be with me, nor shall you make
for yourselves gods of gold. 24 An altar of
earth you shall make for me and sacrifice on
it your burnt offerings and your peace offerings, your sheep and your oxen. [d]In every
place where I cause my name to be remembered I will come to you and [e]bless you. 25[f] If
you make me an altar of stone, [g]you shall not
build it of hewn stones, for if you wield your
tool on it you profane it. 26 And you shall not
go up by steps to my altar, that your nakedness be not exposed on it.'

Laws About Slaves

21 "Now these are the [h]rules that you
shall set before them. 2[i] When you
buy a Hebrew slave, he shall serve six
years, and in the seventh he shall go out
free, for nothing. 3 If he comes in single, he
shall go out single; if he comes in married,
then his wife shall go out with him. 4 If his
master gives him a wife and she bears him
sons or daughters, the wife and her children shall be her master's, and he shall go
out alone. 5 But [j]if the slave plainly says, 'I
love my master, my wife, and my children;
I will not go out free,' 6 then his master
shall bring him to [k]God, and he shall bring

12[n]Lev. 19:3; Cited Matt. 15:4; 19:19; Mark 7:10; 10:19; Luke 18:20; Eph. 6:2; [Jer. 35:18, 19] [o]Eph. 6:3 **13**[p]Cited Matt. 5:21; 19:18; Rom. 13:9; [Gen. 9:5, 6; 1 John 3:15] **14**[q]Lev. 18:20; Deut 22:22; Prov. 6:32; 1 Cor. 6:9; Heb. 13:4; Cited Matt. 5:27; Rom. 13:9 **15**[r]Lev. 19:11; Eph. 4:28; Cited Matt. 19:18; Rom. 13:9 **16**[s]ch. 23:1; Prov. 19:5, 9; 21:28; 24:28; 25:18; Cited Matt. 19:18; See Deut. 19:16-20 **17**[t]Luke 12:15; Eph. 5:3, 5; Cited Rom. 7:7; 13:9; [Col. 3:5; Heb. 13:5] [u]Mic. 2:2 [v]Jer. 5:8; Matt. 5:28 **18**[w]Heb. 12:18 **19**[x]Deut. 5:25, 27; 18:16; Gal. 3:19, 20; Heb. 12:19 **20**[y][1 Sam. 12:20] [z][Gen. 22:1]; Deut. 13:3

21[a]Deut. 4:11; 2 Sam. 22:10; 1 Kin. 8:12; Ps. 18:9; 97:2 **22**[b]Deut. 4:36; Neh. 9:13; Heb. 12:25 **23**[c][ch. 32:31; 2 Kin. 17:33; Ezek. 20:39; Zeph. 1:5] **24**[d]Deut. 12:5, 11; 14:23; 16:6, 11; 26:2; 1 Kin. 8:29; 9:3; 2 Chr. 6:6; 7:16; 12:13; Ezra 6:12; Neh. 1:9; Ps. 74:7; Jer. 7:10, 12 [e]Deut. 7:13 **25**[f]Deut. 27:5; Josh. 8:31 [g][1 Kin. 5:17; 1 Chr. 22:2]
Chapter 21 1[h]ch. 24:3; Deut. 4:14; 6:1 **2**[i]Deut. 15:12; Jer. 34:14; See Lev. 25:39-41 **5**[j]Deut. 15:16, 17 **6**[k][Ps. 82:6; John 10:34, 35]

[1] The Hebrew word also covers causing human death through carelessness or negligence [2] Samaritan, Septuagint, Syriac, Vulgate; Masoretic Text *the people saw*

20:12 your father and your mother. With this fifth commandment, the Decalogue turns to human relations, beginning with the family. Honor toward parents anchors society, and binds children to parents in the community of faith. The promise and implied warning of this commandment are unique in this series. Disrespect for parents was a serious matter, for it also dishonored the Lord.

20:13 murder. The law distinguishes between manslaughter and premeditated murder. The verb here is never applied to Israel at war, and capital punishment was already authorized (Gen. 9:6; cf. Lev. 24:17; Num. 35:30–34). Human life is sacred because man bears God's image (Gen. 9:5, 6 and notes).

20:14 adultery. See "Marriage and Divorce" at Mal. 2:16.

20:16 See "Honest Speech, Oaths, and Vows" at Neh. 5:12.

20:18 were afraid and trembled. The awe that recognizes God's power and glory deters sin (v. 20).

20:19 You speak to us. Moses' authority as God's mediator is acknowledged. That God actually did speak distinguishes Him from the false gods who could not (vv. 22, 23).

20:24 burnt offerings . . . peace offerings. See notes Lev. 1:3–17 and 3:1. Only two types of sacrifices are briefly mentioned here; the list of sacrifices will be expanded in Lev. 1–7.

20:25 tool . . . profane. The reasons for this prohibition are no longer clear. Some suggest that this provision was designed to prevent the Israelites from using the altars of Canaanite holy places, which typically were constructed of cut stones. The altar of burnt offering for the tabernacle was of wood, covered with bronze, but was hollow and filled with earth or uncut stones (27:8). See note Deut. 27:5.

20:26 See note 28:42.

21:1–23:33 The Lord sets forth the ordinances of His covenant. Civil and penal laws are presented at 21:1–22:15; laws controlling morality at 22:16–27; 23:1–9; laws of worship at 20:22–26; 22:28–30; 23:10–19. Through 22:17 the statutes are in the form of case law ("If . . . then," with appropriate penalties); afterwards laws of the unconditionally imperative type ("you shall not") predominate. The purpose of these social codes was to regulate Israelite life in the Promised Land.

21:1 rules. The Hebrew word here means "precedents," or guiding principles determined by case decisions. These laws apply the foundational Decalogue (20:1–17) to society.

21:2 buy a Hebrew slave. The case law appropriately commences with laws regulating slavery, for that had been Israel's position in Egypt. A person could sell himself or his wife into slavery because of poverty or debt (2 Kin. 4:1; Neh. 5:1–5; Amos 2:6), and an Israelite could also be sold by his father into slavery (v. 7). Though the Mosaic law allowed the practice of indentured servitude, abuses were carefully limited (Deut. 15:12 note)—such servitude was limited to six years (v. 2) and the rights of slaves were underscored. See note 1 Pet. 2:18.

21:6 to God. The judges probably held court at God's sanctuary. Whether the door or doorpost is at the sanctuary or the home is not specified here, but Deut. 15:17 favors the latter. The piercing of the ear was a public indication of permanent slavery.

him to the door or the doorpost. And his
master shall bore his ear through with an
awl, and he shall be his slave forever.
7 "When a man [l]sells his daughter as a
slave, she shall not go out as the male
slaves do. 8 If she does not please her master, who has designated her[1] for himself,
then he shall let her be redeemed. He shall
have no right to sell her to a foreign people,
since he has broken faith with her. 9 If he
designates her for his son, he shall deal
with her as with a daughter. 10 If he takes
another wife to himself, he shall not diminish her food, her clothing, or [m]her marital
rights. 11 And if he does not do these three
things for her, she shall go out for nothing,
without payment of money.
12 [n]"Whoever strikes a man so that he
dies shall be put to death. 13 [o]But if he did
not lie in wait for him, but God let him fall
into his hand, then [p]I will appoint for you
a place to which he may flee. 14 But if a man
willfully attacks another to kill him by cunning, [q]you shall take him from my altar,
that he may die.
15 "Whoever strikes his father or his
mother shall be put to death.
16 [r]"Whoever steals a man and sells him,
and anyone found [s]in possession of him,
shall be put to death.
17 [t]"Whoever curses[2] his father or his
mother shall be put to death.
18 "When men quarrel and one strikes
the other with a stone or with his fist and
the man does not die but takes to his bed,
19 then if the man rises again and walks
outdoors with his staff, he who struck him
shall be clear; only he shall pay for the loss
of his time, and shall have him thoroughly
healed.
20 "When a man strikes his slave, male or
female, with a rod and the slave dies under
his hand, he shall be avenged. 21 But if the
slave survives a day or two, he is not to be
avenged, for the [u]slave is his money.
22 "When men strive together and hit a
pregnant woman, so that her children
come out, but there is no harm, the one
who hit her shall surely be fined, as the
woman's husband shall impose on him,
and [v]he shall pay as the [w]judges determine.
23 But if there is harm,[3] then you shall pay
[x]life for life, 24 [y]eye for eye, tooth for tooth,
hand for hand, foot for foot, 25 burn for
burn, wound for wound, stripe for stripe.
26 "When a man strikes the eye of his
slave, male or female, and destroys it, he
shall let the slave go free because of his eye.
27 If he knocks out the tooth of his slave,
male or female, he shall let the slave go free
because of his tooth.
28 "When an ox gores a man or a woman to
death, the [z]ox shall be stoned, and its flesh
shall not be eaten, but the owner of the ox
shall not be liable. 29 But if the ox has been
accustomed to gore in the past, and its owner
has been warned but has not kept it in, and
it kills a man or a woman, the ox shall be
stoned, and its owner also shall be put to
death. 30 If [a]a ransom is imposed on him, then
[v]he shall give for the redemption of his life

[1] *Or so that he has not designated her* [2] *Or dishonors*; Septuagint *reviles* [3] *Or so that her children come out and it is clear who was to blame, he shall be fined as the woman's husband shall impose on him, and he alone shall pay. If it is unclear who was to blame . . .*

7 [l]Neh. 5:5
10 [m]1 Cor. 7:5
12 [n]Gen. 9:6; Lev. 24:17; Num. 35:30, 31; [Matt. 26:52]
13 [o]Deut. 19:4, 5; See Num. 35:22-25 [p]Num. 35:11; Deut. 4:41-43; 19:2, 3; See Josh. 20:2-9
14 [q]See 1 Kin. 2:28-34
16 [r]Deut. 24:7; 1 Tim. 1:10 [s]ch. 22:4
17 [t]Lev. 20:9; Deut. 27:16; Cited Matt. 15:4; Mark 7:10; [Prov. 20:20; 30:11]
21 [u][Lev. 25:45, 46]
22 [v][Deut. 22:18, 19] [w][Deut. 32:31; Job 31:11]
23 [x]Deut. 19:21
24 [y]Lev. 24:20; Deut. 19:21; Cited Matt. 5:38
28 [z]Gen. 9:5
30 [a]ch. 30:12; Num. 35:31, 32 [v][See ver. 22 above]

21:7–11 The sale of a woman as a slave-wife seems intended, hence the protection.

21:13 not lie in wait. An instance of unintentional manslaughter is in view. See note Deut. 19:4.

21:15 strikes his father. Such actions transgress the fifth commandment (20:12).

21:16 steals a man. See note 24:7.

21:17 curses. A further transgression of the fifth commandment. The Hebrew word for "curses" may denote other forms of overt dishonor to parents in addition to spoken curses.

21:19 walks outdoors with his staff. Evidence that he is recovering from his injury.

21:20 slave. That the slave did not die immediately was taken as evidence the master did not intend to kill.

21:21 his money. While indentured slavery was accepted in the Old Testament, the clear implications of the Christian gospel led to its removal (1 Pet. 2:18 note). The laws governing Israel's life should be interpreted in light of their cultural and social setting. They restrained exploitation and oppression in recognition of man's "hardness of heart" (cf. Matt. 19:8).

21:22 her children come out. The usual Hebrew word for "child" is used (as in v. 4 and 1:17, 18). The Hebrew verb describes the emergence of a child in Gen. 25:26; 38:28–30. There is no reason to limit the "harm" spoken of to the mother. If there is no lasting harm either to the mother or the child, compensation for the hurt inflicted is to be paid to the husband, fixed by a third party. Otherwise, the penalty is proportionate to the injury to the mother or child, even to "life for life." Although the harm to the woman or child was not intentional, there was culpable negligence in disregarding the welfare of the pregnant woman.

21:24 eye for eye. The fundamental principle is that punishment should fit the crime (Lev. 24:19, 20; Deut. 19:21). Similar statements are found in the laws of Hammurabi (c. 1750 B.C.). It seems that "eye for eye" was idiomatic for the principle of proportional justice, and that such penalties were not literally imposed (Deut. 19:21 note).

21:28 When an ox gores. Harm done by animals is the responsibility of the careless owner, and appropriate compensation must be paid. Since the ox had been involved in blood guilt, its flesh was not to be eaten.

whatever is imposed on him. 31 If it gores a man's son or daughter, he shall be dealt with according to this same rule. 32 If the ox gores a slave, male or female, the owner shall give to their master [b]thirty shekels[1] of silver, and [z]the ox shall be stoned.

Laws About Restitution

33 "When a man opens a pit, or when a man digs a pit and does not cover it, and an ox or a donkey falls into it, 34 the owner of the pit shall make restoration. He shall give money to its owner, and the dead beast shall be his.

35 "When one man's ox butts another's, so that it dies, then they shall sell the live ox and share its price, and the dead beast also they shall share. 36 Or if it is known that the ox has been accustomed to gore in the past, and its owner has not kept it in, he shall repay ox for ox, and the dead beast shall be his.

22 [2] "If a man steals an ox or a sheep, and kills it or sells it, he shall repay five oxen for an ox, and [c]four sheep for a sheep. 2 [3] "If a thief is found [d]breaking in and is struck so that he dies, there shall be no bloodguilt for him, 3 but if the sun has risen on him, there shall be bloodguilt for him. He shall surely pay. If he has nothing, then [e]he shall be sold for his theft. 4 If the stolen beast [f]is found alive in his possession, whether it is an ox or a donkey or a sheep, [g]he shall pay double.

5 "If a man causes a field or vineyard to be grazed over, or lets his beast loose and it feeds in another man's field, he shall make restitution from the best in his own field and in his own vineyard.

6 "If fire breaks out and catches in thorns so that the stacked grain or the standing grain or the field is consumed, he who started the fire shall make full restitution.

7 "If a man gives to his neighbor money or goods to keep safe, and it is stolen from the man's house, then, if the thief is found, [g]he shall pay double. 8 If the thief is not found, the owner of the house shall come near to God to show whether or not he has put his hand to his neighbor's property. 9 For every breach of trust, whether it is for an ox, for a donkey, for a sheep, for a cloak, or for any kind of lost thing, of which one says, 'This is it,' the case of both parties shall come before God. The one whom God condemns shall pay double to his neighbor.

10 "If a man gives to his neighbor a donkey or an ox or a sheep or any beast to keep safe, and it dies or is injured or is driven away, without anyone seeing it, 11 [h]an oath by the LORD shall be between them both to see whether or not he has put his hand to his neighbor's property. The owner shall accept the oath, and he shall not make restitution. 12 But if [i]it is stolen from him, he shall make restitution to its owner. 13 If it is torn by beasts, let him bring it as evidence. He shall not make restitution for what has been torn.

14 "If a man borrows anything of his neighbor, and it is injured or dies, the owner not being with it, he shall make full restitution. 15 If the owner was with it, he shall not make restitution; if it was hired, it came for its hiring fee.[4]

Laws About Social Justice

16 [j]"If a man seduces a virgin[5] who is not engaged to be married and lies with her, he shall give the bride-price[6] for her and make her his wife. 17 If her father utterly refuses to give her to him, [j]he shall pay money equal to the [k]bride-price for virgins.

32 [b][Zech. 11:12, 13; Matt. 26:15] [z][See ver. 28 above]
Chapter 22
1 [c]2 Sam. 12:6; [Prov. 6:31; Luke 19:8]
2 [d]Matt. 24:43
3 [e][ch. 21:2]
4 [f]ch. 21:16 [g][ver. 1]
7 [g][See ver. 4 above]
11 [h]Heb. 6:16
12 [i]Gen. 31:39
16 [j]Deut. 22:28, 29
17 [j][See ver. 10 above] [k]Gen. 34:12; 1 Sam. 18:25

1 A *shekel* was about 2/5 ounce or 11 grams 2 Ch 21:37 in Hebrew 3 Ch 22:1 in Hebrew 4 Or *it is reckoned in* (Hebrew *comes into*) its *hiring fee* 5 Or *a girl of marriageable age*; also verse 17 6 Or *engagement present*; also verse 17

21:32 thirty shekels of silver. The value of a slave's life was less than that of a freeman and was the betrayal value of Jesus (Matt. 26:15; cf. Zech. 11:12).

22:1 repay. Thieves who compounded their guilt by profiting from and disposing the stolen animals were to restore four or fivefold (cf. v. 4). More compensation was required in the case of oxen, which took longer to raise.

22:3 if the sun has risen. The killing of an unknown nighttime burglar did not incur bloodguilt, since confronting the burglar could endanger the homeowner's life. The daytime thief was readily identifiable and killing was not justified.

22:4 double. See note on v. 1.

22:6 in thorns. Thorns were used as hedges to keep animals out of fields (Mic. 7:4); they were also flammable and used for fuel (Ps. 58:9).

22:8 come near to God. If the thief was not found, the entrustee was brought to the sanctuary (21:6 note), where an oath of innocence was presumably sworn.

22:12 is stolen. The entrustee was presumed to have been negligent.

22:14 make full restitution. In the owner's absence, the onus of proof fell on the borrower.

22:15 came for its hiring fee. The cost of renting the animal was to cover the possibility of loss.

22:16 If a man seduces. Laws on premarital intercourse required full responsibility from the male for consequences. The exploited person must be protected. See note Deut. 22:22–29.

18[l] "You shall not permit a sorceress to
live.
19[m] "Whoever lies with an animal shall be
put to death.
20[n] "Whoever sacrifices to any god, other
than the LORD alone, shall be devoted to
destruction.[1]
21[o] "You shall not wrong a sojourner or
oppress him, for you were sojourners in
the land of Egypt. 22[p] You shall not mistreat
any widow or fatherless child. 23 If you do
mistreat them, and they [q]cry out to me, I
will surely [r]hear their cry, 24 and my wrath
will burn, and I will kill you with the
sword, and [s]your wives shall become widows and your children fatherless.
25[t] "If you lend money to any of my people with you who is poor, you shall not be
like a moneylender to him, and you shall
not exact interest from him. 26[u] If ever you
take your neighbor's cloak in pledge, you
shall return it to him before the sun goes
down, 27 for that is his only covering, and it
is his cloak for his body; in what else shall
he sleep? And if he [q]cries to me, I will hear,
for I am [v]compassionate.
28[w] "You shall not revile God, nor [w]curse
a ruler of your people.
29 "You shall not delay to offer from the
fullness of your harvest and from the out-
flow of your presses. [x]The firstborn of your
sons you shall give to me. 30[y] You shall do
the same with your oxen and with your
sheep: [z]seven days it shall be with its mother; on the eighth day you shall give it to me.
31[a] "You shall be consecrated to me.
Therefore [b]you shall not eat any flesh that
is torn by beasts in the field; [c]you shall
throw it to the dogs.

23 [d]"You shall not spread a false
report. You shall not join hands
with a wicked man to be a [e]malicious witness. 2 You shall not fall in with the many
to do evil, nor shall you bear witness in a
lawsuit, siding with the many, so as to pervert justice, 3[f] nor shall you be partial to a
poor man in his lawsuit.
4[g] "If you meet your enemy's ox or his
donkey going astray, you shall bring it back
to him. 5 If you see the donkey of one who
hates you lying down under its burden,
you shall refrain from leaving him with it;
you shall rescue it with him.
6[h] "You shall not pervert the justice due
to your poor in his lawsuit. 7[d] Keep far from
a false charge, and [i]do not kill the innocent
and righteous, for [j]I will not acquit the
wicked. 8[k] And you shall take no bribe, for a
bribe blinds the clear-sighted and subverts
the cause of those who are in the right.
9[l] "You shall not oppress a sojourner. You
know the heart of a sojourner, for you were
sojourners in the land of Egypt.

Laws About the Sabbath and Festivals

10[m] "For six years you shall sow your land
and gather in its yield, 11 but the seventh

18 [l]Lev. 19:26, 31; 20:27; Deut. 18:10, 11; 1 Sam. 28:3, 9
19 [m]Lev. 18:23; 20:15; Deut. 27:21
20 [n][Num. 25:2, 7, 8; Josh. 23:16]; See Deut. 13:1-15; 17:2-5
21 [o]ch. 23:9; Lev. 19:33; Deut. 10:18, 19; Jer. 7:6; Zech. 7:10; Mal. 3:5
22 [p]Deut. 24:17; 27:19; Ps. 94:6; Isai. 1:17, 23; 10:2; Ezek. 22:7; Zech. 7:10; James 1:27
23 [q]Job 34:28; Luke 18:7 [r]Ps. 18:6; 145:19; [James 5:4]
24 [s]Ps. 109:9; Lam. 5:3
25 [t]Lev. 25:35-37; Deut. 23:19, 20; Neh. 5:7; Ps. 15:5; Prov. 28:8; Ezek. 18:8, 13, 17; 22:12
26 [u]Deut. 24:13, 17; Prov. 20:16; Ezek. 18:7, 16; Amos 2:8; [Prov. 22:27]
27 [q][See ver. 23 above] [v]ch. 34:6; 2 Chr. 30:9; Neh. 9:17
28 [w]Cited Acts 23:5; [2 Sam. 19:21; Eccles. 10:20; Jude 8]
29 [x]See ch. 13:2
30 [y]Deut. 15:19 [z]Lev. 22:27 31 [a]ch. 19:6; Lev. 11:44, 45 [b]Lev. 22:8; Ezek. 4:14; 44:31 [c][Matt. 7:6]
Chapter 23 1 [d][Lev. 19:11; Ps. 15:3; 101:5] [e]Deut. 19:16-18; Ps. 35:11; [1 Kin. 21:10, 13; Matt. 26:59-61; Acts 6:11, 13] 3 [f]Lev. 19:15; [Deut. 1:17] 4 [g][Deut. 22:1, 4; Prov. 25:21; Matt. 5:44; Rom. 12:20; 1 Thess. 5:15] 6 [h]Deut. 27:19; Eccles. 5:8; Isai. 10:1, 2; Jer. 5:28, 29; Mal. 3:5 7 [d][See ver. 1 above] [i]Deut. 27:25; [Prov. 17:26] [j]ch. 34:7 8 [k]Deut. 16:19; [1 Sam. 8:3; 2 Chr. 19:7; Ps. 26:10; Prov. 17:23; Isai. 1:23; 5:23; 33:15] 9 [l]See ch. 22:21 10 [m]Lev. 25:3, 4

[1] That is, set apart (devoted) as an offering to the Lord (for destruction)

22:18 sorceress. Sorcery, the attempt to determine and influence the future through occult means, was strongly condemned (Deut. 18:9–13; 2 Kin. 21:6; Jer. 27:9–10; Mic. 5:12; Nah. 3:4). The future lay in God's hands alone (Deut. 18:9 note).

22:20 destruction. Lit. "devoted to sacred use" or "put to the ban" (Deut. 20:17 note). If a sacred use was impossible the item was destroyed, as here. In Israel's holy war—by which God's judgment was executed against the Canaanites—the spoils were under the ban, devoted to God (Num. 21:2, 3; Josh. 7:11).

22:21 sojourner. These individuals were temporary dwellers without family support, much as Israel had been in Egypt. Note that the laws in vv. 21–27 are absolutely stated, in contrast to case law (21:1 note).

22:22 You shall not mistreat. Widows and orphans, who might lack family defenders, are God's special concern. He will hear their cry and avenge them.

22:25 not exact interest. See note Deut. 23:19.

22:26 pledge. See note Deut. 24:6. A pledge was to be returned before hardship was caused by its absence (Deut. 24:10, 11; Amos 2:8).

22:28 revile God. This text is cited by Paul at Acts 23:5. To question duly appointed authority amounted to questioning God's authority (Rom. 13:1, 2). Neither God nor the ruler whose authority comes from Him were to be reviled.

22:29 You shall not delay. Because the firstfruits were symbolic of God's claim on all, Israelites were not to hold back this offering (13:2 note).

22:31 torn by beasts. Since the blood would not have been properly drained (Lev. 3:17; 7:22–27).

23:4 your enemy's ox. The covenant member is not to take advantage of an enemy's misfortune (perhaps a legal opponent here). See Matt. 5:43–48; Rom. 12:20, 21.

23:9 sojourner. The substance of 22:21 is repeated; the legal context here (vv. 6–8) indicates that the stranger was not to be judicially victimized.

23:11 seventh year. Like the weekly Sabbath, on which it was patterned, the sabbatical year was intended for the good of man and of creation (20:8–11 and notes). It reminded Israel that God, the true owner of the land, had entrusted it to them (Lev. 25:2). The land was to lie fallow, and what grew of itself was reserved for the poor, who would not have been able to save sufficient food resources. Leviticus 26:34–35 suggests that the sabbatical year was not always observed, but it is clearly in place at Neh. 10:31.

year you shall let it rest and lie fallow, that
the poor of your people may eat; and what
they leave the beasts of the field may eat.
You shall do likewise with your vineyard,
and with your olive orchard.
12 [n]"Six days you shall do your work, but
on the seventh day you shall rest; that your
ox and your donkey may have rest, and the
son of your servant woman, and the alien,
may be refreshed.
13 [o]"Pay attention to all that I have said to
you, and make no mention of the names of
other gods, nor let it be heard on your lips.
14 [p]"Three times in the year you shall keep
a feast to me. 15 [q]You shall keep the Feast of
Unleavened Bread. As I commanded you,
you shall eat unleavened bread for seven
days at the appointed time in the month of
[r]Abib, for in it you came out of Egypt.
[s]None shall appear before me empty-handed. 16 You shall keep [t]the Feast of Harvest,
of the firstfruits of your labor, of what you
sow in the field. You shall keep the [u]Feast
of Ingathering at the end of the year, when
you gather in from the field the fruit of your
labor. 17 [p]Three times in the year shall all
your males appear before the Lord GOD.
18 [v]"You shall not offer the blood of my
sacrifice with anything leavened, or let the
fat of my feast remain until the morning.
19 "The best of the [w]firstfruits of your
ground you shall bring into the house of
the LORD your God.
[x]"You shall not boil a young goat in its
mother's milk.

12 [n] See ch. 20:9
13 [o] Deut. 4:9; Josh. 22:5; Josh. 23:7; Hos. 2:17; Zech. 13:2
14 [p] ver. 17; ch. 34:23; Deut. 16:16
15 [q] See ch. 12:15 [r] ch. 13:4 [s] ch. 34:20; Deut. 16:16
16 [t] ch. 34:22; See Lev. 23:9-21 [u] Deut. 16:13; See Lev. 23:34-44
17 [p] [See ver. 14 above]
18 [v] ch. 12:8; 34:25; Lev. 2:11
19 [w] ch. 34:26; Lev. 2:12; 23:10, 17; Num. 18:12, 13; Deut. 26:2, 10; Neh. 10:35; Ezek. 44:30 [x] ch. 34:26; Deut. 14:21
20 [y] ch. 14:19; 33:2, 14; Josh. 5:13, 14; 6:2; Isai. 63:9
21 [z] Ps. 78:40, 56 [a] [ch. 32:34; 34:7; Num. 14:35; Josh. 24:19]
22 [b] Gen. 12:3; Deut. 30:7; Jer. 30:20
23 [y] [See ver. 20 above] [c] See ch. 13:5
24 [d] ch. 20:5 [e] Lev. 18:3; Deut. 12:30, 31 [f] ch. 34:13; Num. 33:52; Deut. 7:5, 25; 12:3 [g] See Deut. 16:22

Conquest of Canaan Promised

20 [y]"Behold, I send an angel before you to
guard you on the way and to bring you to
the place that I have prepared. 21 Pay careful attention to him and obey his voice; [z]do
not rebel against him, [a]for he will not pardon your transgression, for my name is in
him.
22 "But if you carefully obey his voice and
do all that I say, then [b]I will be an enemy
to your enemies and an adversary to your
adversaries.
23 [y]"When my angel goes before you and
brings you [c]to the Amorites and the Hittites and the Perizzites and the Canaanites,
the Hivites and the Jebusites, and I blot
them out, 24 you shall [d]not bow down to
their gods nor serve them, [e]nor do as they
do, but [f]you shall utterly overthrow them
and break their [g]pillars in pieces. 25 You
[h]shall serve the LORD your God, and [i]he[1]
will bless your bread and your water, and [j]I
will take sickness away from among you.
26 [k]None shall miscarry or be barren in your
land; I will fulfill the [l]number of your days.
27 I will send [m]my terror before you and will
throw into [n]confusion all the people
against whom you shall come, and I will
make all your enemies turn their backs to
you. 28 And [o]I will send hornets before you,
which shall drive out the Hivites, the

25 [h] Deut. 6:13; 10:12, 20; 11:13; 13:4; Josh. 22:5; Matt. 4:10 [i] Deut. 7:13; 28:5, 8 [j] ch. 15:26; Deut. 7:15 26 [k] Deut. 7:14 [l] [Job 5:26; Ps. 55:23] 27 [m] Deut. 2:25; Josh. 2:9 [n] Deut. 7:23 28 [o] Deut. 7:20; Josh. 24:12

[1] Septuagint, Vulgate *I*

23:14 Three times in the year. Israel's three religious festivals were connected with the nation's agricultural cycle. The Feast of Unleavened Bread occurred in March or April in celebration of the early barley harvest. Seven weeks later came the Feast of Weeks, celebrating the harvest of other cereal crops such as wheat. Finally, the Feast of Tabernacles celebrated the final harvest and end of the agricultural season in the autumn (September).

23:15 Feast of Unleavened Bread. Passover and the Feast of Unleavened Bread were closely associated—the Feast began the day after Passover. Some have argued that the Feast of Unleavened Bread was simply an agricultural festival, but its commemoration of the Exodus is clear here. See note Deut. 16:9–12.

23:16 Feast of Harvest. See v. 14; Deut. 16:9–12 and notes. Also known as the Feast of Weeks or Pentecost, by New Testament times this feast was associated with the giving of the law at Sinai. The new covenant counterpart is the gift of the Spirit at Pentecost (Acts 2:1–39; cf. Rom. 8:23).

Feast of Ingathering. Also called the Feast of Tabernacles or Booths. See v. 14; Deut. 16:13–17 and notes.

end of the year. See note 12:2.

23:18 You shall not offer. Though some argue that the details of this verse applied only to the Passover celebration (cf. 12:10), it is better understood as applying to all offerings. Fat portions kept overnight would not be fresh and were unworthy for offering. Leaven, representing the old harvest, was considered an impurity.

23:19 firstfruits. See notes 13:2; 1 Cor. 15:20.

You shall not boil. See note Deut. 14:21.

23:20 an angel. The Angel of God's presence is mysteriously distinguished from God and yet identified with Him (v. 21; Gen. 16:7 note). The cloud that symbolized God's presence also marked the presence of the Angel (14:19).

23:21 See "'This Is My Name': God's Self-disclosure" at 3:15.

23:22 if you carefully obey. The assurances of this verse resemble the protection clauses in the ancient Near Eastern suzerainty treaties (Introduction: Date and Occasion). See note 20:1.

23:24 pillars. These were stone pillars connected with Canaanite shrines. Though such monuments were earlier used in the worship of the Lord (Gen. 28:18), they were now forbidden.

23:25 he will bless. For a longer list of blessings, see Deut. 28:1–14.

23:27 my terror. See note 15:14.

23:28 hornets. See note Deut. 7:20.

Canaanites, and the Hittites from before
you. 29 [p]I will not drive them out from
before you in one year, lest the land
become desolate and the wild beasts multiply against you. 30 Little by little I will
drive them out from before you, until you
have increased and possess the land.
31 [q]And I will set your border from the Red
Sea to the Sea of the Philistines, and from
the wilderness to the Euphrates, for [r]I will
give the inhabitants of the land into your
hand, and you shall drive them out before
you. 32 [s]You shall make no covenant with
them and their gods. 33 They shall not dwell
in your land, lest they make you sin against
me; for if you serve their gods, [t]it will surely be a snare to you."

The Covenant Confirmed

24 Then he said to Moses, "Come up
to the LORD, you and Aaron, [u]Na-
dab, and Abihu, and [v]seventy of the elders
of Israel, and worship from afar. 2 Moses
[w]alone shall come near to the LORD, but the
others shall not come near, and the people
shall not come up with him."
3 Moses came and told the people all the
words of the LORD and [x]all the rules. And
all the people answered with one voice and
said, [y]"All the words that the LORD has spoken we will do." 4 And [z]Moses wrote down
all the words of the LORD. He rose early in
the morning and built an altar at the foot of
the mountain, and twelve [a]pillars, according to the twelve tribes of Israel. 5 And he
sent young men of the people of Israel,
who offered burnt offerings and sacrificed
peace offerings of oxen to the LORD. 6 And
[b]Moses took half of the blood and put it in
basins, and half of the blood he threw
against the altar. 7 Then he took the Book of
the Covenant and read it in the hearing of
the people. And they said, [x]"All that the
LORD has spoken we will do, and we will be
obedient." 8 [c]And Moses took the blood
and threw it on the people and said,
"Behold the blood of the covenant that the
LORD has made with you in accordance
with all these words."
9 Then Moses and Aaron, Nadab, and
Abihu, and [d]seventy of the elders of Israel
[e]went up, 10 and they [f]saw the God of Israel.
There was under his feet as it were a pavement of [g]sapphire stone, like the very heav-
en for clearness. 11 And he did not lay his
hand on the chief men of the people of
Israel; they beheld God, and [h]ate and
drank.
12 The LORD said to Moses, [i]"Come up to
me on the mountain and wait there, that I
may give you the [j]tablets of stone, with the

29 [p]Deut. 7:22
31 [q]Gen. 15:18; Num. 34:3; Deut. 11:24; Josh. 1:4; [1 Kin. 4:21, 24; Ps. 72:8] [r]Josh. 21:44; Judg. 1:4; 11:21
32 [s]ch. 34:12, 15; Deut. 7:2
33 [t]ch. 34:12; Deut. 7:16; Josh. 23:13; Judg. 2:3; Ps. 106:36
Chapter 24
1 [u]ch. 28:1; See ch. 6:23 [v]Num. 11:16
2 [w]ver. 13, 15, 18
3 [x]ch. 21:1 [y]ch. 19:8; Deut. 5:27
4 [z]Deut. 31:9 [a]Gen. 28:18; 31:45; [ch. 23:24]
6 [b]Heb. 9:18, 19
7 [x][See ver. 3 above]
8 [c]Cited Heb. 9:19, 20; [Heb. 13:20; 1 Pet. 1:2]
9 [d]Num. 11:16 [e][ver. 1]
10 [f]Gen. 32:30; Judg. 13:22; Isai. 6:1, 5; [ch. 33:20, 23; John 1:18; 1 Tim. 6:16; 1 John 4:12, 20] [g]Ezek. 1:26; 10:1
11 [h][ch. 18:12; Gen. 31:54]
12 [i]ver. 2, 15, 18 [j]ch. 31:18; 32:15, 16; Deut. 5:22

23:29 I will not drive them out. The coming conquest would be gradual. The Israelites would not assume responsibility for the whole land until they were able to defend and care for it.

23:31 border. See note Gen. 13:15.

Red Sea. Apparently a reference to the gulf of Aqaba on the southeast (13:18 note).

23:32 make no covenant. Israel was quick to disobey this command (Josh. 9). The collection of covenant laws ends as it had begun—with an emphasis upon the keeping of the first two commandments (20:1–4, 22).

24:1–18 The terms of the covenant having been stipulated, the people ratified the covenant by agreeing to abide by its conditions (v. 3, 7; cf. 19:8).

24:1 Then he said to Moses. The Sinai narrative, which left off at 20:21, is resumed here. The mention of Aaron and his two sons speaks for the authenticity of the narrative, for the sons were later killed for an offence against God (Lev. 10:1–2).

24:3 the words. The Ten Commandments (20:1 note).

rules. Presumably the Covenant Code (20:22–23:19). This may mark Moses' delivery of the Covenant Code, since all Israel had heard the Decalogue (20:1 note).

24:4 Moses wrote. See note Deut. 31:9.

24:5 young men. There was no appointed priesthood as yet. The offerings sealed the covenant, indicating that God's acceptance of Israel was on the basis of blood atonement for sin.

24:7 Book of the Covenant. Usually this phrase is applied to the Covenant Code of 20:22–23:19 (20:1 note). Here it must also include the Ten Commandments (20:2–17) and perhaps other passages such as 19:5, 6.

24:8 threw it on the people. The people are sprinkled with "the blood of the covenant," the blood that puts the covenant into effect (Heb. 9:16–22 and notes). The blood signified cleansing from sin so that the people might enter the covenant relation, and it underscored that the ultimate penalty for breaking the covenant was death. Jesus proclaimed the fulfillment of the symbolism at the Last Supper when He offered the cup: "This is my blood of the covenant, which is poured out for many for the forgiveness of sins" (Matt. 26:28).

24:10 they saw the God of Israel. They saw a visible manifestation of the Lord, but not the fullness of His glory and power. Moses was later privileged to view the "goodness" and the "back" of God (33:19–23 and notes), though the limited character of the manifestation is emphasized.

feet. The description concentrates only on God's feet, an indication of the partial character of the divine manifestation.

pavement. Perhaps the vault of the sky under the throne (cf. Ezek. 1:26).

sapphire. The area beneath God's feet is compared to a pavement of blue lapis lazuli. This semiprecious stone was available in a natural form from Cyprus and Scythia, and in artificial form from Egypt.

24:11 His hand. His power (4:2 note). Not only did they see God, they ate and drank before Him. Similar meals in celebration of the conclusion of a covenant are recorded at Gen. 31:46; Ex. 18:12; Matt. 26:28.

24:12–18 Moses ascends Mount Sinai to receive the covenant tablets and further instructions regarding Israel's worship and the tabernacle.

law and the commandment, which I have
written for their instruction." 13 So Moses
rose with his assistant [k]Joshua, and Moses
went up [l]into the mountain of God. 14 And
he said to the elders, "Wait here for us
until we return to you. And behold, Aaron
and [m]Hur are with you. Whoever has a dispute, let him go to them."
15 Then Moses went up on the mountain,
and [n]the cloud covered the mountain.
16 [o]The glory of the LORD dwelt on Mount
Sinai, and the cloud covered it six days.
And on the seventh day he called to Moses
out of the midst of the cloud. 17 Now the
appearance of the glory of the LORD was
like a [p]devouring fire on the top of the
mountain in the sight of the people of
Israel. 18 Moses entered the cloud and went
up on the mountain. And Moses [q]was on
the mountain forty days and forty nights.

Contributions for the Sanctuary

25 The LORD said to Moses, 2 [r]"Speak to
the people of Israel, that they take for
me a contribution. From [s]every man whose
heart moves him you shall receive the contribution for me. 3 And this is the contribution that you shall receive from them: gold,
silver, and bronze, 4 [t]blue and purple and
scarlet yarns and fine twined linen, goats'
hair, 5 tanned [u]rams' skins, goatskins,[1] acacia wood, 6 [v]oil for the lamps, [w]spices for the
anointing oil and for the fragrant incense,
7 onyx stones, and stones for setting, for the
[x]ephod and for the breastpiece. 8 And let
them make me a [y]sanctuary, that [z]I may
dwell in their midst. 9 [a]Exactly as I show you
concerning the pattern of the [b]tabernacle,
and of all its furniture, so you shall make it.

The Ark of the Covenant

10 [c]"They shall make an ark of acacia
wood. Two cubits[2] and a half shall be its
length, a cubit and a half its breadth, and a
cubit and a half its height. 11 You shall overlay it with [d]pure gold, inside and outside
shall you overlay it, and you shall make on
it a molding of gold around it. 12 You shall
cast four rings of gold for it and put them on
its [e]four feet, two rings on the one side of it,
and two rings on the other side of it. 13 You
shall make poles of acacia wood and overlay
them with gold. 14 And you shall put the

13 [k]ch. 33:11; [ch. 17:9, 10; 24:13] [l]See ch. 3:1 **14** [m]ch. 17:10, 12; 31:2 **15** [n]ch. 19:9, 16; [Matt. 17:5] **16** [o]ch. 16:10; Lev. 9:23; Num. 14:10; 16:42 **17** [p]ch. 3:2; 19:18; Deut. 4:36; Heb. 12:18, 29 **18** [q]ch. 34:28; Deut. 9:9, 18, 25; 10:10
Chapter 25
2 [r]For ver. 1-7, see ch. 35:4-9 [s]ch. 35:5, 21, 29; 36:2; Judg. 5:2; 1 Chr. 29:5; [Ezra 1:6; 2:68; 3:5; 7:16]; Neh. 11:2; [2 Cor. 8:12; 9:7] **4** [t]ch. 26:1, 31, 36 **5** [u]ch. 26:14 **6** [v]ch. 27:20 [w]ch. 30:7, 23, 34; 31:11 **7** [x]ch. 28:4, 15 **8** [y]Heb. 9:1, 2; See ch. 36:1-4 [z]ch. 29:45; 1 Kin. 6:13; 2 Cor. 6:16; Rev. 21:3 **9** [a]ver. 40 [b]ch. 26:1

10 [c]ch. 37:1-3; Deut. 10:3; Heb. 9:4 **11** [d]ver. 24, 25; ch. 30:3, 4; 37:2 **12** [e]ch. 37:3

1 Uncertain; possibly *dolphin skins*, or *dugong skins*; compare 26:14
2 A *cubit* was about 18 inches or 45 centimeters

24:14 Wait here for us. This sets the scene for the golden calf incident in ch. 32.

24:16 glory. The term is used for a manifestation of the divine presence. The remainder of Exodus deals with the terms and conditions of God's dwelling with His people.

25:1–31:8 This section goes into great detail regarding the divine pattern for the place where the Lord Himself would dwell among His people. The tabernacle and its ministry are the two central features—details of the tabernacle construction, and the precise elements, manner, and persons to be employed in God's service are carefully specified. The inauguration of the covenant had established God's kingship over Israel. That kingship was now to be appropriately recognized by the building of a residence for God as a symbol of His royal authority over Israel.

25:1 The materials were to be gathered as freewill offerings from the treasures of the people (12:35, 36). Ironically, while these instructions were being given, the people were contributing gold for an idol at the foot of the mountain (32:1–4).

25:3 gold, silver, and bronze. The nearer the divine presence, the finer the material required. Metals and colored yarns are listed in descending order of value.

25:4 blue. Or, violet. Violet and purple dyes were obtained from shellfish; scarlet from an insect of the cochineal type. These colors were precious because of the cost of the dye. The blue of the tabernacle came to be particularly associated with the Lord (Num. 15:38).

fine twined linen. The fine linen was probably Egyptian.

goats' hair. The goat hair was undyed. It was to be used as a first covering for the tabernacle, and over it other skins would be placed (26:14).

25:5 rams' skins. The ram skin leather was tanned or dyed, perhaps both.

goatskins. The meaning of the Hebrew is uncertain. Dolphin (text note) and sea cow skin are also possible. Such leather may have been cured only, in which case there may be a descending order of value in the skins selected.

acacia wood. A hard, long-lasting wood suitable for carving and overlay.

25:6 spices. See 30:23–25, 34–38.

25:7 onyx stones. The stones set in the two shoulder pieces of the ephod were of an engravable substance such as carnelian, onyx, or lapis lazuli (24:10 note; 28:9–12; 39:6–7).

25:8 sanctuary. This is a broader term than "tabernacle" and refers to any place of God's visible self-revelation, or theophany (15:17; Josh. 24:26; Ezek. 11:16).

25:9 tabernacle. The term means "dwelling place," designating a divine palace or temple. This tabernacle foreshadowed the dwelling of God with man in the Person of Jesus Christ (John 1:14 note).

pattern. The pattern shown to Moses was a model or plan of the tabernacle to be built (cf. the plan of the temple revealed to David in 1 Chr. 28:19). At the same time, it reflected the heavenly reality (Heb. 9:24). See Ezek. 43:10, 11.

25:10 ark. The revelation of the pattern for the earthly sanctuary begins with the plans for the ark of the covenant, the most holy object in the tabernacle. This ornate chest contained the Ten Commandments, the pot of manna, and Aaron's staff (16:33; 25:16; Num. 17:10; Deut. 10:1–5; Heb. 9:4). The cover of the ark was perhaps viewed as a footstool or throne for the Lord (vv. 18, 22 and notes).

cubit. A cubit was roughly the distance from the tip of the middle finger to the elbow—about eighteen inches.

25:13 make poles. So that the ark could be moved without being touched (cf. 2 Sam. 6:6, 7). Its holiness and portability are stressed.

poles into the rings on the sides of the ark to
carry the ark by them. 15 The [f]poles shall
remain in the rings of the ark; they shall not
be taken from it. 16 [g]And you shall put into
the ark the [h]testimony that I shall give you.
17 [i]"You shall make a mercy seat[1] of pure
gold. Two cubits and a half shall be its
length, and a cubit and a half its breadth.
18 And you shall make two cherubim of gold;
of [j]hammered work shall you make them,
on the two ends of the mercy seat. 19 Make
one cherub on the one end, and one cherub
on the other end. [k]Of one piece with the
mercy seat shall you make the cherubim on
its two ends. 20 [l]The cherubim shall spread
out their wings above, overshadowing the
mercy seat with their wings, their faces one
to another; toward the mercy seat shall the
faces of the cherubim be. 21 And you shall
put the mercy seat on the top of the ark, and
in the ark you shall put the testimony that I
shall give you. 22 [m]There I will meet with you,
and from above the mercy seat, from [n]between the two cherubim that are on the ark
of the testimony, I will speak with you about
all that I will give you in commandment for
the people of Israel.

The Table for Bread

23 [o]"You shall make a table of acacia wood.
Two cubits shall be its length, a cubit its
breadth, and a cubit and a half its height.
24 You shall overlay it with [p]pure gold and
make a molding of gold around it. 25 And you
shall make a rim around it a handbreadth[2]
wide, and a molding of gold around the rim.
26 And you shall make for it four rings of gold,
and fasten the rings to the four corners at its
four legs. 27 Close to the frame the rings
shall lie, as [q]holders for the poles to carry
the table. 28 You shall make the poles of acacia wood, and overlay them with gold, and
the table shall be carried with these. 29 And
you shall make its plates and [r]dishes for
incense, and its flagons and bowls with
which to pour drink offerings; you shall
make them of pure gold. 30 And you shall set
the [s]bread of the Presence on the table
before me regularly.

The Golden Lampstand

31 [t]"You shall make a lampstand of pure
gold. The lampstand shall be made of hammered work: its base, its stem, its cups, its
calyxes, and its flowers shall be of one piece
with it. 32 And there shall be six branches
going out of its sides, three branches of the
lampstand out of one side of it and three
branches of the lampstand out of the other
side of it; 33 three cups made like almond
blossoms, each with calyx and flower, on

15 [f]1 Kin. 8:8
16 [g][Deut. 31:26; 1 Kin. 8:9] [h]See ch. 16:34
17 [i]ch. 37:6; Heb. 9:5
18 [j]ver. 31; ch. 37:7, 17, 22; Num. 8:4; 10:2
19 [k]ch. 37:8
20 [l]1 Kin. 8:7; 1 Chr. 28:18; Heb. 9:5
22 [m]ch. 29:42, 43; 30:6, 36; Lev. 16:2; Num. 17:4
22 [n]Num. 7:89
23 [o]For ver. 23-29, see ch. 37:10-16; [1 Kin. 7:48; 2 Chr. 4:8; Heb. 9:2]
24 [p]ver. 11
27 [q]ch. 26:29; 30:4; 36:34; 37:14, 27; 38:5
29 [r]ch. 37:16; Num. 4:7
30 [s]Lev. 24:5, 6
31 [t]For ver. 31-39, see ch. 37:17-24; [1 Kin. 7:49; Zech. 4:2; Heb. 9:2; Rev. 1:12]

[1] Or *cover* [2] A *handbreadth* was about 3 inches or 7.5 centimeters

25:16 testimony. The stone tablets of the Sinai covenant. God's written word is His witness to the terms of His covenant. Scripture is not a fallible human witness to God, but God's infallible witness to man.

25:17 mercy seat. Lit. the "atonement covering," a place at which estranged parties were reconciled. "Atonement" is the normal English translation for the Hebrew root that means "to wipe away" or perhaps "to cover" the guilt of sin from God's eyes so that believers may be reconciled with God. Propitiation (i.e., turning away divine wrath and satisfying the claims of divine justice) is effected by blood sacrifice in the Old Testament (Lev. 17:11). This shedding of blood dramatizes the cost of forgiveness, and points forward to the sacrificial death of Christ on the Cross, where the symbolism of the Day of Atonement was fulfilled. Paul declares that Jesus has been made the propitiation for our sins (Rom. 3:25; cf. 1 John 2:2).

The "mercy seat" was the ark cover, which is sometimes mentioned in distinction from the ark as the place where God was propitiated. In the Septuagint (the Greek Old Testament), the Greek term for "mercy seat" *(hilasterion)* lit. means "place of propitiation" (also in Heb. 9:5).

25:18 cherubim. The cherubs were usually associated with the throne of the Lord as guardians or bearers of the throne (1 Sam. 4:4; Is. 37:16). In the pagan world cherubs were minor deities protective of palaces and temples; here they symbolize angelic guardians (Gen. 3:24). They were perhaps depicted as winged sphinxes (winged lions with human heads).

25:22 I will meet. The Lord is the One "who is enthroned on the cherubim" (1 Sam. 4:4; 2 Sam. 6:2; 2 Kin. 19:15; Ps. 80:1; 99:1; Is. 37:16). The mercy seat becomes the focal point for God's meeting with His people. The purpose of the Exodus was this meeting of God with man (29:45, 46).

25:23–40 The revelation of the earthly sanctuary pattern continues with the plans for objects to be housed in the holy place—the table of the bread of the Presence, its dishes, and the golden lampstand. Instructions for the altar of incense, also housed in the Holy Place, are given in 30:1–10.

25:23 make a table. Called "table of the bread of the Presence" (Num. 4:7) and the "table of pure gold" (Lev. 24:6, 2 Chr. 13:11), on which the bread was arranged (1 Kin. 7:48). It stood on the north side of the holy place (40:22).

25:29 make its . . . dishes. These dishes, all of pure gold, included a plate on which the bread of the Presence was placed, a small pan for the frankincense, a pitcher for the wine libation or drink offering, and a bowl into which this was poured (37:16; Lev. 24:7; Num. 4:7).

25:30 bread of the Presence. This bread could only be eaten by the priests (Lev. 24:8, 9). The careful placement of the twelve loaves (probably symbolizing the twelve tribes of Israel) before the Lord, and the eating of the loaves by the people's religious representatives (the priests) reminded Israel of its constant dependence on God's life-giving presence.

25:31 lampstand. The lampstand, which stood opposite the table in the Holy Place, was constructed of a talent (about seventy-five pounds) of hammered gold and patterned to suggest a growing almond tree. Perhaps symbolic of new life, the almond tree blossomed in late January, before other trees.

25:32 six branches. The pedestal and main upright represented the trunk of the tree, out of which grew three branches on either side. The six branches probably rose to the height of the central shaft, with seven lamps (the number signifying completeness) resting on the topmost ornaments of the shaft and branches (v. 37).

one branch, and three cups made like
almond blossoms, each with calyx and
flower, on the other branch—so for the six
branches going out of the lampstand. 34 And
on the lampstand itself there shall be four
cups made like almond blossoms, with
their calyxes and flowers, 35 and a calyx of
one piece with it under each pair of the six
branches going out from the lampstand.
36 Their calyxes and their branches shall be
of one piece with it, the whole of it a single
piece of hammered work of pure gold.
37 You shall make seven lamps for it. And
the lamps [u]shall be set up so as [v]to give
light on the space in front of it. 38 Its tongs
and their trays shall be of pure gold. 39 It
shall be made, with all these utensils, out of
a talent[1] of pure gold. 40 And [w]see that you
make them after the pattern for them,
which is being shown you on the mountain.

The Tabernacle

26 "Moreover, [x]you shall make the
[y]tabernacle with ten curtains of [z]fine
twined linen and blue and purple and

37 [u]Lev. 24:2-4; 2 Chr. 13:11 [v]Num. 8:2
40 [w]ver. 9; ch. 26:30; 27:8; Num. 8:4; Acts 7:44; Cited Heb. 8:5; [1 Chr. 28:11, 19]
Chapter 26
1 [x]For ver. 1-37, see ch. 36:8-38 [y]ch. 25:9 [z]ver. 31, 36; ch. 28:6, 15; 36:8, 35; 39:3, 8

1 A *talent* was about 75 pounds or 34 kilograms

26:1–37 God reveals the pattern for the tabernacle proper. The tabernacle, God's holy dwelling in the midst of His sinful people, served a double function. On the one hand, it protected the people from the dangers of unauthorized intrusion—the curtains of the Most Holy Place, of the Holy Place, and even of the courtyard stood between the people and the threat of God's consuming holy presence. On the other hand, the tabernacle provided a way of approach to the Lord. Worshipers entered the outer court to pray and offer sacrifices; the priests carried the people's petitions into the holy place; and once a year on the Day of Atonement the high priest entered the Most Holy Place, the very throne-room of the Almighty, with a blood atonement to meet the Lord at the mercy seat.

Nevertheless, the tabernacle was a provisional symbol, rather than the full reality, of God's dwelling with man. It symbolized the heavenly temple of God (Heb. 8:1–6; 9:1–15), and pointed forward to the dwelling of God with man in Jesus Christ, God incarnate in human flesh (John 1:14 note). As the author of Hebrews makes clear, the tabernacle and its ministry were insufficient in themselves (Heb. 10:1–4). Rather, they foreshadowed the final and completely sufficient priestly work of Christ (Heb. 10:11–18).

26:1 tabernacle. The tabernacle itself, which housed the Holy and Most Holy Places, was forty-five feet long, fifteen feet wide, and fifteen feet high. It was covered with ten curtains woven of expensive fabrics

The Plan of the Tabernacle (26:1)

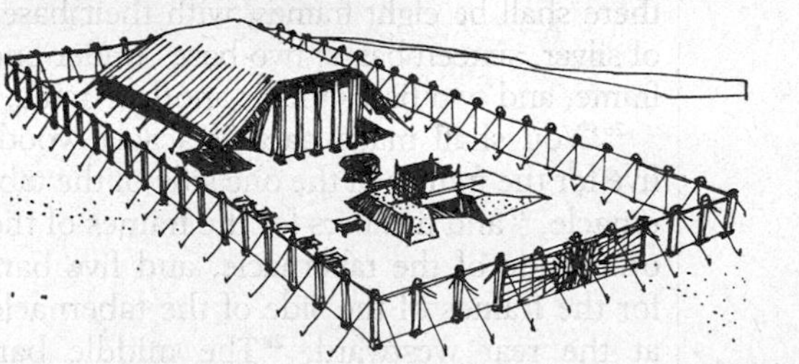

The tabernacle was to provide a place where god might dwell among His people. The term tabernacle sometimes refers to the tent, including the Holy Place and the Most Holy, which was covered with embroidered curtains. But in other places, it refers to the entire complex, including the curtained court in which the tent stood.

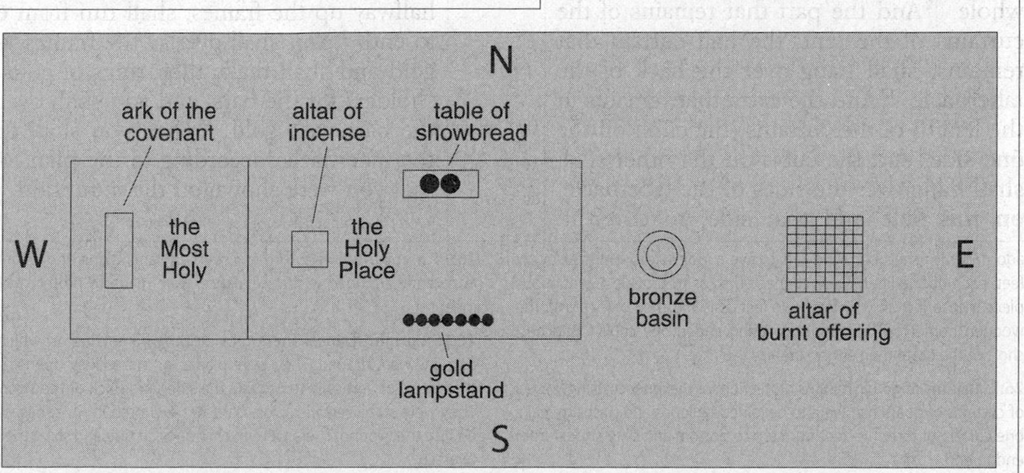

This illustration shows the relative positions of the tabernacle furniture used in Israelite worship. The tabernacle is enlarged for clarity.

scarlet yarns; you shall make them with cherubim [z]skillfully worked into them. [2]The length of each curtain shall be twenty-eight cubits,[1] and the breadth of each curtain four cubits; all the curtains shall be the same size. [3]Five curtains shall be coupled to one another, and the other five curtains shall be coupled to one another. [4]And you shall make loops of blue on the edge of the outermost curtain in the first set. Likewise you shall make loops on the edge of the outermost curtain in the second set. [5]Fifty loops you shall make on the one curtain, and fifty loops you shall make on the edge of the curtain that is in the second set; the loops shall be opposite one another. [6]And you shall make fifty clasps of gold, and couple the curtains one to the other with the clasps, so that the tabernacle may be a single whole.

[7]"You shall also make [a]curtains of goats' hair for a tent over the tabernacle; eleven curtains shall you make. [8]The length of each curtain shall be thirty cubits, and the breadth of each curtain four cubits. The eleven curtains shall be the same size. [9]You shall couple five curtains by themselves, and six curtains by themselves, and the sixth curtain you shall double over at the front of the tent. [10]You shall make fifty loops on the edge of the curtain that is outermost in one set, and fifty loops on the edge of the curtain that is outermost in the second set.

[11]"You shall make fifty clasps of bronze, and put the clasps into the loops, and couple the tent together that it may be a single whole. [12]And the part that remains of the curtains of the tent, the half curtain that remains, shall hang over the back of the tabernacle. [13]And the extra that remains in the length of the curtains, the cubit on the one side, and the cubit on the other side, shall hang over the sides of the tabernacle, on this side and that side, to cover it. [14][b]And you shall make for the tent a covering of tanned [c]rams' skins and a covering of goatskins on top.

[15]"You shall make upright frames for the tabernacle of acacia wood. [16]Ten cubits shall be the length of a frame, and a cubit and a half the breadth of each frame. [17]There shall be two tenons in each frame, for fitting together. So shall you do for all the frames of the tabernacle. [18]You shall make the frames for the tabernacle: twenty frames for the south side; [19]and forty bases of silver you shall make under the twenty frames, two bases under one frame for its two tenons, and two bases under the next frame for its two tenons; [20]and for the second side of the tabernacle, on the north side twenty frames, [21]and their forty bases of silver, two bases under one frame, and two bases under the next frame. [22]And for the rear of the tabernacle westward you shall make six frames. [23]And you shall make two frames for corners of the tabernacle in the rear; [24]they shall be separate beneath, but joined at the top, at the first ring. Thus shall it be with both of them; they shall form the two corners. [25]And there shall be eight frames, with their bases of silver, sixteen bases; two bases under one frame, and two bases under another frame.

[26]"You shall make bars of acacia wood, five for the frames of the one side of the tabernacle, [27]and five bars for the frames of the other side of the tabernacle, and five bars for the frames of the side of the tabernacle at the rear westward. [28]The middle bar, halfway up the frames, shall run from end to end. [29]You shall overlay the frames with gold and shall make their rings of gold for [d]holders for the bars, and you shall overlay the bars with gold. [30]Then you shall erect the tabernacle [e]according to the plan for it that you were shown on the mountain.

1 [z]ver. 31, 36; ch. 28:6, 15; 36:8, 35; 39:3, 8
7 [a]ch. 36:14
14 [b]ch. 36:19
[c]ch. 25:5
29 [d]See ch. 25:27
30 [e]See ch. 25:40

[1] A *cubit* was about 18 inches or 45 centimeters

adorned with cherubim. Two sets of five curtains, forty-two feet by six feet, each of fine linen, were connected so as to provide a continuous piece measuring sixty by forty-two feet. This was then draped over the wooden framework. This inner covering ended one cubit (18 inches) short of the ground on either side (vv. 1–6).

26:7 curtains of goats' hair. As protection for the inner curtain two sets of curtains of goats' hair were to be joined by loops and clasps to make one curtain of forty-five feet from top to bottom and sixty-six feet from end to end.

26:13 the cubit . . . shall hang over. The outer curtains were two cubits (three feet) longer than the inner ones and would barely reach the ground (v. 1 note).

26:14 a covering. Two further covers of rams' skins and goatskins, apparently arranged in that sequence, were made to protect the two inner sets.

26:15 upright frames. These provided the framework on which the curtains were draped. They were planks, or more likely open frames, that were set vertically to provide the sides and back of the structure. They were stabilized with cross bars and anchored in silver bases driven into the ground. There were twenty on each side and six at the back (west).

26:26 make bars. The frames were supported by fifteen cross members overlaid with gold, five for each of the enclosed sides. The entire structure could be dismantled or assembled in a minimum of time.

31 [f]"And you shall make a veil of blue and
purple and scarlet yarns and [g]fine twined
linen. It shall be made with cherubim [g]skill-
fully worked into it. 32 And you shall hang it
on four pillars of acacia overlaid with gold,
with hooks of gold, on four bases of silver.
33 And you shall hang [f]the veil from the
clasps, and bring [h]the ark of the testimony in
there within the veil. And the veil shall separate for you the Holy Place from the Most
Holy. 34 [i]You shall put the mercy seat on the
ark of the testimony in the Most Holy Place.
35 And [j]you shall set the table outside the veil,
and the [k]lampstand on the south side of the
tabernacle opposite the table, and you shall
put the table on the north side.

36 "You shall make a [l]screen for the
entrance of the tent, of [m]blue and purple
and scarlet yarns and [g]fine twined linen,
embroidered with needlework. 37 And you
shall make for the screen five pillars of acacia, and overlay them with gold. Their
hooks shall be of gold, and you shall cast
five bases of bronze for them.

The Bronze Altar

27 "You shall make the [n]altar of acacia
wood, five cubits[1] long and five
cubits broad. The altar shall be square, and
its height shall be three cubits. 2 And you
shall make [o]horns for it on its four corners;
its horns shall be of one piece with it, and
[p]you shall overlay it with bronze. 3 You
shall make pots for it to receive its ashes,
and shovels and basins and [q]forks and fire
pans. You shall make all its utensils of
bronze. 4 You shall also make for it a grating, a network of bronze, and on the net
you shall make four bronze rings at its four
corners. 5 And you shall set it under the
ledge of the altar so that the net extends
halfway down the altar. 6 And you shall
make poles for the altar, poles of acacia
wood, and overlay them with bronze. 7 And
the poles shall be put through the rings, so
that the poles are on the two sides of the
altar when it is carried. 8 You shall make it
hollow, with boards. [r]As it has been shown
you on the mountain, so shall it be made.

The Court of the Tabernacle

9 [s]"You shall make the court of the tabernacle. On the south side the court shall
have hangings of fine twined linen a hundred cubits long for one side. 10 Its twenty
pillars and their twenty bases shall be of
bronze, but the hooks of the pillars and
their fillets shall be of silver. 11 And likewise
for its length on the north side there shall
be hangings a hundred cubits long, its pillars twenty and their bases twenty, of
bronze, but the hooks of the pillars and
their fillets shall be of silver. 12 And for the
breadth of the court on the west side there
shall be hangings for fifty cubits, with ten
pillars and ten bases. 13 The breadth of the
court on the front to the east shall be fifty
cubits. 14 The hangings for the one side of
the gate shall be fifteen cubits, with their
three pillars and three bases. 15 On the
other side the hangings shall be fifteen
cubits, with their three pillars and three
bases. 16 For the gate of the court there shall
be [t]a screen twenty cubits long, of blue and
purple and scarlet yarns and fine twined
linen, embroidered with needlework. It
shall have four pillars and with them four

[1] A *cubit* was about 18 inches or 45 centimeters

31 [f]ch. 36:35; [Lev. 16:2; 2 Chr. 3:14; Matt. 27:51; Heb. 9:3] [g]ver. 1
33 [f][See ver. 31 above] [h]See ch. 16:34
34 [i]ch. 25:21; 40:20
35 [j]ch. 40:22; Heb. 9:2 [k]ch. 40:24
36 [l]ch. 27:16; 36:37 [m]ver. 1, 31; ch. 25:4 [g][See ver. 31 above]
Chapter 27
1 [n]For ver. 1-8, see ch. 38:1-7; [Ezek. 43:13]
2 [o]ch. 29:12; 30:2; [Lev. 4:7, 30; 1 Kin. 1:50; Ps. 118:27] [p][Num. 16:38]
3 [q][1 Sam. 2:13]
8 [r]See ch. 25:40
9 [s]For ver. 9-19, see ch. 38:9-20
16 [t]ch. 26:36

26:31 make a veil. The interior of the tabernacle tent was to be divided by the "veil of the screen" (39:34; 40:21; Num. 4:5), separating the inner Most Holy Place from the outer Holy Place. This veil was a tapestry that hung thirty feet from the entrance to the tent, creating an inner cube fifteen feet square where the ark was kept. This was the Most Holy Place, the throne room where the Lord would meet with Israel's high priest on the Day of Atonement. The Holy Place, a royal antechamber, extended thirty feet from the veil to the tent entrance.

26:36 for the entrance. The gate at the east end was covered by a screen supported by acacia pillars set in bronze sockets. The screen was made of the same material as the inner curtains and the veil, but was of embroidery rather than tapestry since it was further from the Most Holy Place.

27:1 altar. The altar of burnt offering was made of acacia wood overlaid with bronze. The horns at the four corners were important in the ritual and were smeared with blood at the consecration of priests (29:12), in the sin offering (Lev. 4:25, 30), and on the Day of the Atonement (Lev. 16:18). They gave sanctuary to anyone who laid hold of them (1 Kin. 1:50). The altar was hollow and was filled with earth or uncut stones (20:24).

27:3 its utensils. Accessories, being outside of the tabernacle proper, were all of bronze.

27:4 make for it a grating. The grate details and its function are obscure. It was placed halfway down the altar running from below the ledge of the altar to the ground. Perhaps it was for ventilation of the altar fire. The "ledge" of v. 5 was apparently for priests to stand on when offering sacrifice.

27:9 make the court. The court was a rectangle of 150 by 75 feet enclosed by white linen hangings seven and one-half feet high separating it from the surrounding camp of Israel (v. 18).

27:16 For the gate. A thirty-foot opening on the east side was covered by a screen (v. 16). Fifty-six pillars (twenty on the north and south sides, ten on the west, and three on either side of the entrance on the east) in bronze sockets held up the linen hangings. Another four pillars supported the screen. Their arrangement is not specified; neither is the placement of the tabernacle within the courtyard. The pillars may have been held in place by pegs and guy ropes (35:18).

bases. 17 All the pillars around the court
shall be filleted with silver. Their hooks
shall be of silver, and their bases of bronze.
18 The length of the court shall be a hundred cubits, the breadth fifty, and the
height five cubits, with hangings of fine
twined linen and bases of bronze. 19 All the
utensils of the tabernacle for every use, and
all its pegs and all the pegs of the court,
shall be of bronze.

Oil for the Lamp

20 [u]"You shall command the people of Israel
that they bring to you pure beaten olive oil for
the light, that a lamp may regularly be set up
to burn. 21 [v]In the tent of meeting, [w]outside
the veil that is before the testimony, Aaron
and his sons shall tend it from evening to
morning before the LORD. It shall be a statute
forever to be observed throughout their generations by the people of Israel.

The Priests' Garments

28 "Then bring near to you [x]Aaron
your brother, and his sons with
him, from among the people of Israel, to
serve me as priests—Aaron and Aaron's
sons, [y]Nadab and Abihu, Eleazar and
Ithamar. 2 [z]And you shall make holy garments for Aaron your brother, for glory and
for beauty. 3 You shall speak to all the
[a]skillful, whom I have filled with a spirit of
skill, that they make Aaron's garments to
consecrate him for my priesthood. 4 These
are the garments that they shall make: a
[b]breastpiece, an [c]ephod, [d]a robe, [e]a coat of
checker work, [e]a turban, and [e]a sash. They
shall make holy garments for Aaron your
brother and his sons to serve me as priests.
5 They shall receive [f]gold, blue and purple
and scarlet yarns, and fine twined linen.
6 [g]"And they shall make the ephod of
gold, of blue and purple and scarlet yarns,
and of fine twined linen, skillfully worked.
7 It shall have two shoulder pieces attached
to its two edges, so that it may be joined
together. 8 And the [h]skillfully woven band
on it shall be made like it and be of one
piece with it, of gold, blue and purple and
scarlet yarns, and fine twined linen. 9 You
shall take two onyx stones, and engrave on
them the names of the sons of Israel, 10 six
of their names on the one stone, and the
names of the remaining six on the other
stone, in the order of their birth. 11 As a jew-
eler engraves signets, so shall you engrave
the two stones with the names of the sons
of Israel. You shall enclose them in settings
of gold filigree. 12 And you shall set the two
stones on the shoulder pieces of the
ephod, as stones of remembrance for the
sons of Israel. And [i]Aaron shall bear their
names before the LORD on his two shoulders [j]for remembrance. 13 You shall make
settings of gold filigree, 14 and two chains of
pure gold, twisted like cords; and you shall
attach the corded chains to the settings.
15 [k]"You shall make a breastpiece of judgment, in skilled work. In the style of the
ephod you shall make it—of gold, blue and
purple and scarlet yarns, and fine twined
linen shall you make it. 16 It shall be square
and doubled, a span[1] its length and a span
its breadth. 17 [l]You shall set in it four rows of

[1] A *span* was about 9 inches or 22 centimeters

20 [u]Lev. 24:1-4
21 [v]ch. 25:22; 29:42; 30:36 [w]See ch. 26:31
Chapter 28
1 [x]Num. 18:7; Heb. 5:4 [y]See ch. 6:23
2 [z]ver. 40; ch. 29:29; 31:10; 39:1, 2; Lev. 8:7, 30; Num. 20:26, 28; See ch. 29:5-9
3 [a]ch. 31:6; 35:10, 25; 36:1
4 [b]ver. 15 [c]ver. 6 [d]ver. 31 [e]ver. 39; [Lev. 8:7]
5 [f]ch. 25:3
6 [g]For ver. 6-12, see ch. 39:2-7
8 [h]ver. 27, 28; ch. 29:5; 39:5; Lev. 8:7
12 [i]ver. 29, 30 [j][Num. 16:40; Josh. 4:7; Zech. 6:14]
15 [k]For ver. 15-28, see ch. 39:8-21
17 [l][Ezek. 28:13; Rev. 21:19, 20]

27:18 length of the court. The court apparently consisted of two equal seventy-five foot squares containing the tabernacle proper and the open space before it. The ark and the altar of burnt offering were the respective central objects. The eastern, open half of the court provided public space for sacrifices and the gathering of worshipers.

27:20 pure beaten olive oil for the light. Pure olive oil, which provided a virtually smoke-free light. The lamp was the golden lampstand that stood on the south side of the Holy Place (Lev. 24:1–4).

27:21 tent of meeting. The tabernacle was so named because God and Israel's priestly representatives met there as determined by liturgical regulation. It is not identical with the tabernacle of meeting outside the camp where God met Moses (33:7 note; Num. 12:4).

28:1–30:3 Having revealed the pattern of the earthly sanctuary (25:1–27:21), God now reveals the regulations for the priestly ministry of the sanctuary.

28:1 serve me as priests. First and foremost, the priests were to serve as mediators between God and man. As priests and representatives of a holy God, Aaron and his sons participated in the holiness of the tabernacle and were held to strict standards of ritual purity (Lev. 21:1–22:16). In addition to their ceremonial duties, such as offering sacrifices and caring for the place of worship, they acted as judges (Deut. 17:8–13), dispensed blessings (Num. 6:22–27), gave oracles (Num. 27:21), and taught God's law to the people (Deut. 33:10).

Nadab and Abihu. These two sons of Aaron were killed for unlawful activity (Lev. 10:1–2). Aaron was succeeded by Eleazar (Deut. 10:6).

28:2 make holy garments. The vestments of God's holy high priest were of paramount importance. They were designed for beauty and made of the same expensive materials as the tabernacle.

28:6 the ephod. This sleeveless linen garment decorated with colored thread was made from costly materials and reached from the breast down to the hips. It had shoulder straps with two onyx stones engraved with the names of the tribes, and a waistband (39:2–7). The breastpiece that contained the Urim and Thummim was fastened to the ephod (v. 27; 1 Sam. 23:9–10).

28:15 a breastpiece. This was a single piece of fabric, folded double to form a square pouch with gemstones bearing the names of the twelve tribes on its front (v. 21) and the Urim and Thummim inside (v. 30).

stones. A row of sardius,[1] topaz, and carbuncle shall be the first row; 18 and the second
row an emerald, a sapphire, and a diamond;
19 and the third row a jacinth, an agate, and
an amethyst; 20 and the fourth row a beryl, an
onyx, and a jasper. They shall be set in gold
filigree. 21 There shall be twelve stones with
their names according to the names of the
sons of Israel. They shall be like signets, each
engraved with its name, for the twelve tribes.
22 You shall make for the breastpiece twisted
chains like cords, of pure gold. 23 And you
shall make for the breastpiece two rings of
gold, and put the two rings on the two edges
of the breastpiece. 24 And you shall put the
two cords of gold in the two rings at the
edges of the breastpiece. 25 The two ends of
the two cords you shall attach to the two settings of filigree, and so attach it in front to
the shoulder pieces of the ephod. 26 You shall
make two rings of gold, and put them at the
two ends of the breastpiece, on its inside
edge next to the ephod. 27 And you shall
make two rings of gold, and attach them in
front to the lower part of the two shoulder
pieces of the ephod, at its seam above the
[m]skillfully woven band of the ephod. 28 And
they shall bind the breastpiece by its rings to
the rings of the ephod with a lace of blue, so
that it may lie on the skillfully woven band of
the ephod, so that the breastpiece shall not
come loose from the ephod. 29 [n]So Aaron
shall bear the names of the sons of Israel in
the breastpiece of judgment on his heart,
when he goes into the Holy Place, to bring
them to regular [o]remembrance before the
LORD. 30 And in the breastpiece of judgment
[p]you shall put the Urim and the Thummim,
and they shall be on Aaron's heart, when he
goes in before the LORD. Thus Aaron shall
bear the judgment of the people of Israel on
his heart before the LORD regularly.

31 [q]"You shall make the robe of the ephod
all of blue. 32 It shall have an opening for
the head in the middle of it, with a woven
binding around the opening, like the opening in a garment,[2] so that it may not tear.
33 On its hem you shall make pomegranates
of blue and purple and scarlet yarns,
around its hem, with bells of gold between
them, 34 a golden bell and a pomegranate, a
golden bell and a pomegranate, around the
hem of the robe. 35 And it shall be on Aaron
when he ministers, and its sound shall be
heard when he goes into the Holy Place
before the LORD, and when he comes out,
so that he does not die.

36 "You shall make [r]a plate of pure gold
and engrave on it, like the engraving of a
signet, [s]'Holy to the LORD.' 37 And you shall
fasten it on the turban by a cord of blue. It
shall be on the front of the turban. 38 It shall
be on Aaron's forehead, and Aaron shall
[t]bear any guilt from the holy things that the
people of Israel consecrate as their holy
gifts. It shall regularly be on his forehead,
that they may be accepted before the LORD.

39 "You shall weave the coat in checker
work of fine linen, and you shall make a
turban of fine linen, and you shall make a
sash embroidered with needlework.

40 [u]"For Aaron's sons you shall make
coats and sashes and caps. You shall make
them [v]for glory and beauty. 41 And you shall
put them on Aaron your brother, and on
his sons with him, and shall [w]anoint them
and ordain them and [x]consecrate them,
that they may serve me as priests. 42 You
shall make for them [y]linen undergarments
to cover their naked flesh. They shall reach
from the hips to the thighs; 43 and they
shall be on Aaron and on his sons when
they go into the tent of meeting or when

27 [m]ver. 8
29 [n]ver. 12, 30 [o]See ver. 12
30 [p]Lev. 8:8; Num. 27:21; Deut. 33:8; 1 Sam. 28:6; Ezra 2:63; Neh. 7:65; [1 Sam. 23:9; 30:7, 8]

31 [q]For ver. 31-37, see ch. 39:22-31
36 [r]Lev. 8:9 [s]Zech. 14:20
38 [t]Lev. 10:17; Num. 18:1; [Isai. 53:11; Ezek. 4:4-6; John 1:29; Heb. 9:28; 1 Pet. 2:24]
40 [u]ch. 39:27-29, 41; [Ezek. 44:17, 18] [v]ver. 2
41 [w]ch. 29:7; 30:30; 40:13, 15; Lev. 10:7; [x]ch. 29:9; Heb. 7:28; [Lev. 21:10]
42 [y]Lev. 6:10; 16:4; [Ezek. 44:18]

1 The identity of some of these stones is uncertain 2 The meaning of the Hebrew word is uncertain; possibly *coat of mail*

28:22 chains. Ropes of twisted gold thread connected the breastpiece to the shoulder straps of the ephod.

28:29 names of the sons of Israel. Aaron carried this reminder of the nation he represented when he entered the Holy Place.

28:30 the Urim and the Thummim. Lit. "lights and perfections." These two Hebrew words begin with the first and last letters of the alphabet (cf. the "the first and the last" of Rev. 1:17). There is no hint of how they functioned or what they were—perhaps stones of different colors, or two small objects engraved with symbols or letters of the alphabet. Whatever the Urim and Thummim were, they were used to receive oracles from God (Num. 27:21; Deut. 33:8; 1 Sam. 23:6–13; 28:6; Ezra 2:63).

28:31 robe of the ephod. This blue robe with bells was worn under the breastpiece and ephod to identify and protect the priest when he entered an area of special sanctity.

28:36 Holy to the LORD. On the turban of Aaron was fastened a plate or diadem. The same object is called a crown (29:6; 39:30; Lev. 8:9) and worn by kings (2 Sam. 1:10; 2 Kin. 11:12; Ps. 89:39). The engraved plate was of pure gold, and identified Aaron as set apart to the Lord and as Israel's representative.

28:40 make coats . . . sashes . . . caps. The other priestly garments are only briefly described. The coat seems to have been a long shift-like garment worn under the robe. These priestly garments were to be worn in God's presence (v. 43). Ordinary priests wore plain coats, a less ornate sash, and a headdress different from the high priest's.

28:42 linen undergarments. The undergarment was worn so as not to violate the command of 20:26. Ritual nakedness, so common in other ancient religions, was forbidden in Israel.

they come near the altar to minister in the
Holy Place, lest they [z]bear guilt and die.
[a]This shall be a statute forever for him and
for his offspring after him.

Consecration of the Priests

29 "Now this is what you shall do to
them to consecrate them, that they
may serve me as priests. [b]Take one bull of
the herd and two rams without blemish,
2 [c]and unleavened bread, unleavened cakes
mixed with oil, and unleavened wafers
smeared with oil. You shall make them of
fine wheat flour. 3 You shall put them in one
basket and bring them in the basket, and
bring the bull and the two rams. 4 You shall
bring Aaron and his sons to the entrance of
the tent of meeting and [d]wash them with
water. 5 Then [e]you shall take the garments,
and put on Aaron the coat and the robe of
the ephod, and the ephod, and the breastpiece, and gird him with the [f]skillfully
woven band of the ephod. 6 [g]And you shall
set the turban on his head and put the holy
crown on the turban. 7 You shall take [h]the
anointing oil and pour it on his head and
anoint him. 8 Then you [i]shall bring his sons
and put coats on them, 9 and you shall gird
Aaron and his sons with [j]sashes and bind
caps on them. And [k]the priesthood shall be
theirs by a statute forever. Thus you shall
[l]ordain Aaron and his sons.
10 "Then you shall bring the bull before
the tent of meeting. [m]Aaron and his sons
shall lay their hands on the head of the bull.
11 Then you shall kill the bull before the
LORD at the entrance of the tent of meeting,
12 and [n]shall take part of the blood of the
bull and put it on the [o]horns of the altar
with your finger, and the rest of[1] the blood
you shall pour out at the base of the altar.
13 And you shall take all [p]the fat that covers
the entrails, and the long lobe of the liver,
and the two kidneys with the fat that is on
them, and burn them on the altar. 14 But the
flesh of the bull and its skin and its dung
you shall burn with fire [q]outside the camp;
[r]it is a sin offering.
15 "Then [s]you shall take one of the rams,
and [t]Aaron and his sons shall lay their
hands on the head of the ram, 16 and you
shall kill the ram and shall take its blood
and throw it against the sides of the altar.
17 Then you shall [u]cut the ram into pieces,
and wash its entrails and its legs, and put
them with its pieces and its head, 18 and
burn the whole ram on the altar. It is a
burnt offering to the LORD. It is a [v]pleasing
aroma, a food offering[2] to the LORD.
19 [w]"You shall take the other ram, [t]and
Aaron and his sons shall lay their hands on
the head of the ram, 20 and you shall kill the
ram and take part of its blood and put it on
the tip of the right ear of Aaron and on the
tips of the right ears of his sons, and on the
thumbs of their right hands and on the great
toes of their right feet, and throw the rest of
the blood against the sides of the altar.
21 Then you shall take part of the blood that
is on the altar, and of the [x]anointing oil, and
sprinkle it on Aaron and his garments, and
on his sons and his sons' garments with
him. He and his garments shall be holy, and
his sons and his sons' garments with him.
22 "You shall also take the fat from the
ram and the fat tail and the [y]fat that covers
the entrails, and the long lobe of the liver
and the two kidneys with the fat that is on
them, and the right thigh (for it is a ram of
[z]ordination), 23 and [a]one loaf of bread and
one cake of bread made with oil, and one

43 [z]Lev. 5:1, 17; 20:19 [a]ch. 27:21
Chapter 29
1 [b]Lev. 8:2
2 [c]Lev. 2:4; See Lev. 6:20-22
4 [d]ch. 40:12; Lev. 8:6; [Heb. 10:22]
5 [e]ch. 28:2-4 [f]ch. 28:8
6 [g]ch. 28:36, 37; Lev. 8:9; [Num. 6:7]
7 [h]ver. 21; ch. 28:41; 30:25; Lev. 8:12, 30; 10:7; 21:10; Num. 35:25
8 [i]Lev. 8:13
9 [j]ch. 28:4, 39 [k]ch. 27:21; Num. 18:7 [l]ver. 29, 33; Lev. 8:33; 16:32; See ch. 28:41
10 [m]ver. 15, 19; Lev. 1:4; 8:14
12 [n]Lev. 8:15 [o]See ch. 27:2
13 [p]Lev. 3:3, 4
14 [q]Lev. 4:11, 12, 21; Num. 19:3, 5; Heb. 13:11 [r]ver. 36; ch. 30:10
15 [s]ver. 1; Lev. 8:18 [t]ver. 15, 19; Lev. 1:4; 8:14
17 [u]Lev. 8:20
18 [v]ver. 25, 41; See Gen. 8:21
19 [w]ver. 1; Lev. 8:22 [t][See ver. 15 above]
21 [x]ver. 7
22 [y]ver. 13 [z]Lev. 7:37; 8:28, 31, 33
23 [a]ver. 2, 3; Lev. 8:26

[1] Hebrew *all* [2] Or *an offering by fire*; also verses 25, 41

29:1 consecrate. Or, "make them holy," set them apart from their fellow Israelites for God's service.

29:2 bread . . . cakes . . . wafers. Three kinds of grain offering were to be presented (cf. Lev. 2:4–10).

29:4 wash them with water. Aaron and his sons could not enter the tabernacle until they had been ceremonially cleansed by washing, and sacrifice had been made for them (cf. Heb. 7:26–28).

29:5 take the garments. Aaron and his sons were to be clothed with sacred garments symbolic of their office. Only Aaron is anointed (and thereby authorized to act as chief priest).

29:9 ordain. Lit. "fill the hand," a Hebrew idiom for induction into office.

29:10 bring the bull. Priests laid their hands on the bull calf to symbolize personal identification and substitution in this sin offering. Blood was smeared on the horns of the altar of burnt offering as for laymen, since Aaron and his sons were still unconsecrated (Lev. 4:25, 30; cf. Lev. 4:7). The remainder of the blood was poured at the bottom of the altar as for a sin offering. Certain parts were to be burned on the altar (v. 13), but the remainder was to be burned outside the camp as unclean (v. 14).

29:15 one of the rams. This ram was offered as a dedicatory burnt offering (Lev. 1:3–17 note).

29:19 take the other ram. The other ram was offered as a peace offering (Lev. 3:1 note).

29:20 put it on the tip. The ear, hands, and feet of the priests (extremities as parts for the whole) were cleansed from impurities to consecrate for service.

29:22 the right thigh. Normally part of the priest's portion (Lev. 7:32), this was also burned in this sacrifice for the priests.

wafer out of the basket of unleavened
bread that is before the LORD. **24**You shall
put all these on the palms of Aaron and on
the palms of his sons, and [b]wave them for
a wave offering before the LORD. **25**Then
[c]you shall take them from their hands and
burn them on the altar on top of the burnt
offering, as a [d]pleasing aroma before the
LORD. It is a food offering to the LORD.
26"You shall take the [e]breast of the ram of
Aaron's [f]ordination and [g]wave it for a wave
offering before the LORD, and it shall be
your portion. **27**And you shall consecrate
the [h]breast of the wave offering that is
waved and the [i]thigh of the priests' portion
that is contributed from the ram of [f]ordination,
from what was Aaron's and his sons.
28It shall be for Aaron and his sons as a [j]perpetual
due from the people of Israel, for it is
a [g]contribution. It shall be a [g]contribution
from the people of Israel from their peace
offerings, their contribution to the LORD.
29"The holy garments of Aaron [k]shall be
for his sons after him; they shall [l]be anointed
in them and ordained in them. **30**The son
who succeeds him as priest, who comes into
the tent of meeting to minister in the Holy
Place, shall wear them [m]seven days.
31"You shall take the ram of ordination
and [n]boil its flesh in a holy place. **32**And
Aaron and his sons shall eat the flesh of the
ram and the [o]bread that is in the basket in
the entrance of the tent of meeting. **33**[p]They
shall eat those things with which atonement
was made at their ordination and
consecration, but an [q]outsider shall not eat
of them, because they are holy. **34**And if
any of the flesh for the ordination or of the
bread remain until the morning, then you
shall [r]burn the remainder with fire. It shall
not be eaten, because it is holy.
35"Thus you shall do to Aaron and to his
sons, according to all that I have commanded
you. Through [s]seven days shall you
ordain them, **36**and every day you shall offer
a [t]bull as a sin offering for atonement. Also
you shall purify the altar, when you make
atonement for it, and shall [u]anoint it to consecrate
it. **37**Seven days you shall make
atonement for the altar and consecrate it,
and the [v]altar shall be most holy. [w]Whatever
touches the altar shall become holy.
38"Now this is what you shall offer on the
altar: [x]two lambs a year old [y]day by day regularly.
39One lamb you shall offer [z]in the
morning, and the other lamb you shall offer
[a]at twilight. **40**And with the first lamb a tenth
seah[1] of fine flour mingled with a fourth of
a hin[2] of beaten oil, and a fourth of a hin of
wine for a drink offering. **41**The other lamb
you shall offer [a]at twilight, and shall offer
with it a grain offering and its drink offering,
as [b]in the morning, for a [c]pleasing aroma, a
food offering to the LORD. **42**It shall be a [d]regular
burnt offering throughout your generations
at the entrance of the tent of meeting
before the LORD, [e]where I will meet with
you, to speak to you there. **43**There I will
meet with the people of Israel, and it shall
be [f]sanctified by my glory. **44**I will consecrate
the tent of meeting and the altar. [g]Aaron
also and his sons I will consecrate to serve
me as priests. **45**[h]I will dwell among the people
of Israel and will be their God. **46**And
they shall know that [i]I am the LORD their
God, who brought them out of the land of
Egypt that I might dwell among them. I am
the LORD their God.

The Altar of Incense

30 [j]"You shall make [k]an altar on
which to burn incense; you shall
make it of acacia wood. **2**A cubit[3] shall be
its length, and a cubit its breadth. It shall
be square, and two cubits shall be its
height. [l]Its horns shall be of one piece with

24 [b]Lev. 7:30; 8:27, 29; Num. 5:25; 6:20
25 [c]Lev. 6:22; 8:28 [d]ver. 18, 41
26 [e]Lev. 8:29 [f]ver. 22 [g]ver. 24
27 [h]Lev. 7:31, 34; 10:14, 15; Num. 18:11, 18 [i]Lev. 7:32, 34; 10:15; Num. 18:11 [f][See ver. 26 above]
28 [j]Lev. 10:15 [g][See ver. 26 above]
29 [k]Num. 18:8; [Num. 20:26, 28] [l]ver. 9
30 [m]Lev. 8:33, 35
31 [n]Lev. 8:31
32 [o][Matt. 12:4]
33 [p]Lev. 10:14, 15, 17 [q]Lev. 22:10
34 [r]Lev. 8:32
35 [s]Lev. 8:33-35
36 [t]ver. 14; ch. 30:10 [u]ch. 30:26, 28, 29; 40:10
37 [v]ch. 40:10 [w]ch. 30:29; [Matt. 23:19]
38 [x]Num. 28:3; 1 Chr. 16:40; 2 Chr. 2:4; 13:11; 31:3; Ezra 3:3 [y][Dan. 8:11-13; 9:27; 12:11]; Heb. 10:11
39 [z]2 Kin. 16:15; Ezek. 46:13-15 [a]1 Kin. 18:29, 36; Ezra 9:4, 5; Ps. 141:2; Dan. 9:21
41 [a][See ver. 39 above] [b]ch. 30:9; 40:29 [c]ver. 18, 25
42 [d]Num. 28:6 [e]See ch. 25:22
43 [f]ch. 40:34; [1 Kin. 8:11; 2 Chr. 5:14; 7:1-3; Ezek. 43:5; Hag. 2:7, 9; Mal. 3:1]
44 [g]Lev. 21:15; 22:9, 16 **45** [h]ch. 25:8; Lev. 26:12; Zech. 2:10; 2 Cor. 6:16; Rev. 21:3 **46** [i]ch. 20:2
Chapter 30 **1** [j]For ver. 1-5, see ch. 37:25-28 [k]ch. 40:5; Lev. 4:7; Rev. 8:3 **2** [l]See ch. 27:2

1 A *seah* was about 7 quarts or 7.3 liters 2 A *hin* was about 4 quarts or 3.5 liters 3 A *cubit* was about 18 inches or 45 centimeters

29:24 wave them. The ceremonial waving symbolized their dedication as gifts to God.

29:26 your portion. Moses, since he was acting as priest, received the breast and the thigh of the ram as his portion; thereafter the priests were to receive these (Lev. 7:31–32).

29:38 day by day regularly. The requirements for the daily priestly offerings are reviewed (vv. 38–46). The author of Hebrews contrasts these daily sacrifices for sin (whose repetition pointed to their insufficiency) with the once-for-all sacrifice of Christ (Heb. 10:11–14).

29:42–46 This passage states the goal of the Exodus (and of the book). God "brought them out of the land of Egypt" that He might "dwell among them" (v. 46). The covenant relationship between God and His people is fundamentally one of communion between God and man (Gen. 17:7; Ex. 6:7).

30:1 an altar on which to burn incense. The altar was in front of the veil at the entrance to the Most Holy Place (v. 6). It was lit by the high priest morning and evening. The smoke that then covered the mercy seat protected the high priest from the divine presence (Lev. 16:13).

it. 3 You shall [m]overlay it with pure gold, its
top and around its sides and its horns.
And you shall make a molding of gold
around it. 4 And you shall make two gold-
en rings for it. Under its molding on two
opposite sides of it you shall make them,
and they shall be [n]holders for poles with
which to carry it. 5 You shall make the
poles of acacia wood and overlay them
with gold. 6 And you shall put it in front of
the veil that is above the ark of the testimony, in front of the [o]mercy seat that is
above the testimony, where I will meet
with you. 7 And Aaron shall [p]burn fragrant
incense on it. Every morning when he
[q]dresses the lamps he shall burn it, 8 and
when Aaron sets up the lamps at twilight,
he shall burn it, a regular incense offering
before the LORD throughout your generations. 9 You shall not offer [r]unauthorized
incense on it, or a burnt offering, or a grain
offering, and you shall not pour a drink
offering on it. 10 [s]Aaron shall make atonement on its horns once a year. With the
blood of the [t]sin offering of atonement he
shall make atonement for it once in the
year throughout your generations. It is
most holy to the LORD."

The Census Tax

11 The LORD said to Moses, 12 [u]"When
you take the census of the people of
Israel, then each shall give [v]a ransom for
his life to the LORD when you number
them, that there be no plague among
them when you number them. 13 Each one
who is numbered in the census shall give
this: half a shekel[1] according to the
[w]shekel of the sanctuary (the [x]shekel is
twenty gerahs),[2] [y]half a shekel as an offering to the LORD. 14 Everyone who is numbered in the census, from twenty years old
and upward, shall give the LORD's offering. 15 The rich shall not give more, and
the poor shall not give less, than [y]the half
shekel, when you give the LORD's offering
to make atonement for your lives. 16 You
shall take the atonement money from the
people of Israel and shall [z]give it for the
service of the tent of meeting, that it may
bring the people of Israel to [a]remem-
brance before the LORD, so as to make
atonement for your lives."

The Bronze Basin

17 The LORD said to Moses, 18 "You shall
also make a [b]basin of bronze, with its
stand of bronze, for washing. [b]You shall
put it between the tent of meeting and the
altar, and you shall put water in it, 19 with
which Aaron and his sons [c]shall wash their
hands and their feet. 20 When they go into
the tent of meeting, or when they come
near the altar to minister, to burn a food
offering[3] to the LORD, they shall wash with
water, so that they may not die. 21 They
shall wash their hands and their feet, so
that they may not die. It shall [d]be a statute
forever to them, even to him and to his offspring throughout their generations."

The Anointing Oil and Incense

22 The LORD said to Moses, 23 "Take the
[e]finest spices: of liquid myrrh 500
shekels, and of sweet-smelling cinnamon
half as much, that is, 250, and 250 of
[f]aromatic cane, 24 and 500 of cassia,
according to the shekel of the sanctuary,
and a [g]hin[4] of olive oil. 25 And you shall
make of these a sacred anointing oil
blended as by the [h]perfumer; it shall be a
[i]holy anointing oil. 26 [j]With it you shall
anoint the tent of meeting and the ark of
the testimony, 27 and the table and all its
utensils, and the lampstand and its utensils, and the altar of incense, 28 and the
altar of burnt offering with all its utensils
and the [k]basin and its stand. 29 You shall
consecrate them, that they may be most
holy. [l]Whatever touches them will
become holy. 30 [m]You shall anoint Aaron
and his sons, and consecrate them, that

3 [m]ch. 39:38; 40:5, 26; Num. 4:11
4 [n]See ch. 25:27
6 [o]ch. 25:21, 22
7 [p]ver. 34; ch. 31:11; 37:29; 40:27; 1 Sam. 2:28; 1 Chr. 23:13; 2 Chr. 2:4; 29:11; Luke 1:9 [q]See ch. 27:20, 21
9 [r]Lev. 10:1
10 [s]Lev. 16:18; 23:27 [t]ch. 29:36
12 [u]Num. 1:2-4; 26:2; 2 Sam. 24:2 [v]ch. 21:30; Num. 31:50; [Ps. 49:7]
13 [w]ch. 38:24; Lev. 5:15; 27:3, 25 [x]Lev. 27:25; Num. 3:47; 18:16; Ezek. 45:12 [y]ch. 38:26; Matt. 17:24; [Gen. 24:22]
15 [y][See ver. 13 above]
16 [z]See ch. 38:25-31 [a][ch. 28:12; 39:7; Num. 16:40]
18 [b]ch. 40:7, 30; [1 Kin. 7:38]
19 [c]ch. 40:31, 32; Ps. 26:6; [Isai. 52:11; Heb. 10:22]
21 [d]See ch. 27:21
23 [e]S. of S. 4:14; Ezek. 27:22 [f]Ezek. 27:19
24 [g]ch. 29:40
25 [h]ch. 37:29 [i]ch. 37:29; Num. 35:25; Ps. 89:20; 133:2
26 [j]ch. 40:9; Lev. 8:10; Num. 7:1
28 [k]ch. 40:11
29 [l]ch. 29:37
30 [m]See ch. 29:7

[1] A *shekel* was about 2/5 ounce or 11 grams [2] A *gerah* was about 1/50 ounce or 0.6 gram [3] Or *an offering by fire* [4] A *hin* was about 4 quarts or 3.5 liters

30:12 take the census. The half-shekel atonement money that accompanied each census witnessed to Israel's dependence on the Lord's mercy. Their lives were forfeit because of sin, and must be redeemed. The lesson of the Passover and the redemption of the firstborn is applied to all Israel (13:15; 22:29; Num. 3:40–51).

ransom. Lit. "atonement." The payment served as an act of individual atonement and was an assertion of God's rights over Israel.

30:13 half a shekel. In difficult times the amount was apparently reduced (Neh. 10:32).

30:17 21 The priests washed their hands and feet when they approached the altar or entered the tabernacle for ministry. No dimensions are given for the basin, though Solomon's temple basins were massive (1 Kin. 7:38). Neglecting to wash might cause death—the holy God was not to be approached casually (vv. 20, 21).

they may serve me as priests. 31 And you
shall say to the people of Israel, 'This shall
be my holy anointing oil throughout your
generations. 32 It shall not be poured on
the body of an ordinary person, and you
shall make no other like it in composition.
[n]It is holy, and it shall be holy to you.
33 [o]Whoever compounds any like it or
whoever puts any of it on an outsider
shall be cut off from his people.'"
34 The LORD said to Moses, [p]"Take sweet
spices, stacte, and onycha, and galbanum,
sweet spices with pure frankincense (of
each shall there be an equal part), 35 and
make an [q]incense blended as by the [r]per-
fumer, [s]seasoned with salt, pure and holy.
36 You shall beat some of it very small, and
put part of it before the testimony in the
tent of meeting [t]where I shall meet with
you. [u]It shall be most holy for you. 37 And
the incense that you shall make [v]accord-
ing to its composition, you shall not make
for yourselves. It shall be for you holy to
the LORD. 38 [w]Whoever makes any like it to
use as perfume shall be cut off from his
people."

Oholiab and Bezalel

31 The LORD said to Moses, 2 "See, I
have called by name [x]Bezalel the
son of Uri, son of [y]Hur, of the tribe of
Judah, 3 and I have [z]filled him with the
Spirit of God, with ability and intelligence, with knowledge and all craftsmanship, 4 to devise artistic designs, to work
in gold, silver, and bronze, 5 in cutting
stones for setting, and in carving wood,
to work in every craft. 6 And behold, I
have appointed with him [a]Oholiab, the
son of Ahisamach, of the tribe of Dan.
And I have given to all able men [b]ability,
that they may make all that I have commanded you: 7 [c]the tent of meeting, and
[d]the ark of the testimony, and [e]the mercy
seat that is on it, and all the furnishings
of the tent, 8 [f]the table and its utensils,
and [g]the pure lampstand with all its utensils, and [h]the altar of incense, 9 and [i]the
altar of burnt offering with all its utensils,
and [j]the basin and its stand, 10 and [k]the
finely worked garments,[1] the holy garments for Aaron the priest and the garments of his sons, for their service as
priests, 11 and [l]the anointing oil and the
fragrant [m]incense for the Holy Place.
According to all that I have commanded
you, they shall do."

The Sabbath

12 And the LORD said to Moses, 13 "You
are to speak to the people of Israel and
say, 'Above all you shall keep my
Sabbaths, for this is a sign between me
and you throughout your generations,
that you may know that I, the LORD, sanctify you. 14 You shall keep the Sabbath,
because it is holy for you. Everyone who
profanes it shall be put to death.
[n]Whoever does any work on it, that soul
shall be cut off from among his people.
15 [o]Six days shall work be done, but [p]the
seventh day is a Sabbath of solemn rest,
holy to the LORD. [n]Whoever does any
work on the Sabbath day shall be put to
death. 16 Therefore the people of Israel
shall keep the Sabbath, observing the
Sabbath throughout their generations, as
a covenant forever. 17 [q]It is a sign forever
between me and the people of Israel that
[r]in six days the LORD made heaven and
earth, and [s]on the seventh day he rested
and was refreshed.'"
18 And he gave to Moses, when he had
finished speaking with him on Mount
Sinai, the [t]two tablets of the testimony,
tablets of stone, written with [u]the finger of
God.

[1] Or *garments for worship*

32 [n]ver. 25, 37
33 [o]ver. 38
34 [p]ver. 7; ch. 25:6; 37:29
35 [q]ver. 25 [r]See ver. 25 [s][Lev. 2:13]
36 [t]See ch. 25:22 [u][ch. 40:10]
37 [v]ver. 32
38 [w]ver. 33
Chapter 31
2 [x]ch. 35:30; 36:1; 1 Chr. 2:20 [y]ch. 17:10, 12; 24:14
3 [z]ch. 35:31; [1 Kin. 7:14] [a]ch. 35:34 [b]ch. 28:3; 35:10, 35; 36:1
7 [c]See ch. 36:8-38 [d]See ch. 37:1-5 [e]See ch. 37:6-9
8 [f]See ch. 37:10-16 [g]See ch. 37:17-24 [h]See ch. 37:25-28
9 [i]See ch. 38:1-7 [j]ch. 38:8
10 [k]ch. 35:19; 39:1, 41
11 [l]ch. 30:25, 31; 37:29 [m]ch. 30:7, 34
14 [n]ch. 35:2; [Jer. 17:27]; See Num. 15:32-36
15 [o]See ch. 20:9 [p]ch. 16:23; 20:10; Gen. 2:2 [n][See ver. 14 above]
17 [q]ver. 13 [r]Gen. 1:31 [s]Gen. 2:2; Heb. 4:4, 10
18 [t]ch. 24:12; 32:15, 16; Deut. 4:13; 5:22; 9:10, 11; [2 Cor. 3:3] [u]See ch. 8:19

31:1–11 The tabernacle was to be constructed according to the divine design by gifted men who were supernaturally enabled by the Holy Spirit to do all the tasks required (vv. 3–6, 11). All the work was described to Moses by God and little room was left for creative variation (25:9).

31:2 Bezalel. The name is archaic and means "in El's [God's] shadow" (cf. 17:10 note).

31:6 Oholiab. Bezalel's assistant. His name means "the father is my tent."

31:12–17 The Sabbath commandment is reiterated and designated as the covenant sign of the Mosaic covenant (Gen. 9:12 note). To keep God's Sabbath is to keep the covenant since the Sabbath is a sign of the special relationship between God and Israel. To disregard God's Sabbath was to disregard God's purposes for creation through His redemption of Israel.

31:18 two tablets of the testimony. See note Deut. 5:22. Some suggest that these were two identical copies. Consistent with ancient Near Eastern suzerainty treaties, one copy belonged to each treaty partner and the copies were housed in the respective sanctuaries. The ark was both the focal point of Israel's sanctuary and the special dwelling place of God. Hence, both copies were placed in the ark.

finger of God. See 8:19.

The Golden Calf

32 When the people saw that Moses
[v]delayed to come down from the
mountain, the people gathered themselves
together to Aaron and said to him, [w]"Up,
make us gods who shall [x]go before us. As
for this Moses, the man who brought us up
out of the land of Egypt, we do not know
what has become of him." 2 So Aaron said to
them, "Take off the [y]rings of gold that are in
the ears of your wives, your sons, and your
daughters, and bring them to me." 3 So all
the people took off the rings of gold that
were in their ears and brought them to
Aaron. 4 [z]And he received the gold from
their hand and fashioned it with a graving
tool and made a golden[1] calf. And they
said, [a]"These are your gods, O Israel, who
brought you up out of the land of Egypt!"
5 When Aaron saw this, he built an altar
before it. And Aaron [b]made proclamation
and said, "Tomorrow shall be a feast to the
LORD." 6 And they rose up early the next day
and offered burnt offerings and brought
peace offerings. And [c]the people sat down
to eat and drink and rose up [d]to play.
7 And the LORD said to Moses, [e]"Go down,
for your people, whom you brought up out
of the land of Egypt, have [f]corrupted themselves. 8 They have turned aside quickly out
of the way that [g]I commanded them. They
have made for themselves a golden calf and
have worshiped it and sacrificed to it and
said, 'These are your gods, O Israel, who
brought you up out of the land of Egypt!'"
9 And the LORD said to Moses, "I have seen
this people, and behold, [h]it is a stiff-necked
people. 10 Now therefore [i]let me alone, that
[j]my wrath may burn hot against them and [k]I
may consume them, in order that [l]I may
make a great nation of you."
11 But [m]Moses implored the LORD his God
and said, "O LORD, why does your wrath
burn hot against your people, whom you
have brought out of the land of Egypt with
great power and with a mighty hand?
12 [n]Why should the Egyptians say, 'With evil
intent did he bring them out, to kill them in
the mountains and to consume them from
the face of the earth'? Turn from your burning anger and [o]relent from this disaster
against your people. 13 Remember Abraham,
Isaac, and Israel, your servants, to whom
you [p]swore by your own self, and said to
them, [q]'I will multiply your offspring as the
stars of heaven, and all this land that I have
promised I will give to your offspring, and
they shall inherit it forever.'" 14 And the
LORD [r]relented from the disaster that he had
spoken of bringing on his people.

Chapter 32
1 [v]ch. 24:18; Deut. 9:9 [w]ver. 23; Cited Acts 7:40 [x]ch. 13:21
2 [y][ch. 12:35, 36]; See Judg. 8:24-27
4 [z]Deut. 9:16; Neh. 9:18; Ps. 106:19; Acts 7:41; [Judg. 17:3, 4] [a]1 Kin. 12:28
5 [b][2 Kin. 10:20]
6 [c]Cited 1 Cor. 10:7 [d]Gen. 26:8; [Judg. 21:21]
7 [e]Deut. 9:12 [f]Judg. 2:19; [Hos. 9:9]
8 [g]ch. 20:3, 4, 23; Deut. 9:16
9 [h]ch. 33:3, 5; 34:9; Deut. 9:6, 13; 31:27; 2 Chr. 30:8; Acts 7:51; [Isai. 48:4]
10 [i]Deut. 9:14 [j]ch. 22:24 [k]ch. 33:3 [l]Num. 14:12
11 [m]Deut. 9:18, 26-29; Ps. 106:23; [Ps. 74:1, 2]
12 [n][Deut. 32:27]; See Num. 14:13-16 [o]See ver. 14
13 [p]Gen. 22:16; Heb. 6:13 [q]Gen. 12:7; 13:15; 15:7, 18; 26:4; 28:13; 35:11, 12; 48:16
14 [r]Ps. 106:45; [1 Chr. 21:15; Jer. 18:8; 26:13, 15, 19; 26:13, 15; Amos 7:3, 6; Jonah 3:10; 4:2]

1 Hebrew *cast metal*; also verse 8

32:1–34:35 God's continued mercy shown to the people of Israel in these chapters is striking indeed. Even after His mighty Exodus deliverance and miraculous provisions for them in the wilderness, they responded with complaints, recriminations, and the idolatrous worship of the golden calf (16:2, 3; 17:1–3; 32:1–6). We should note, however, that this section displays not only the treachery of Israel and the kindness of their God, but also the central role of Moses the mediator. Because the Lord was pleased with the mediator, He did not cast off the people and start anew to make a great nation out of Moses (32:10–14).

We should not conclude that Israel's continuing in God's favor was due solely to the merit of Moses as God's mediator. Rather, the ground of Moses' plea for mercy was his concern for God's glory and his appeal to the gracious covenant promises God had made to the patriarchs (32:11–14). The crisis of Israel's disloyalty, and the Lord's threat to destroy them, is resolved in the faithfulness of God revealed through the successful appeal of the man Moses, who knew and reached the heart of God.

32:1 gathered themselves together. The phrase is ominous (used of the rebellion of Korah at Num. 16:3; 20:2). The problem is not with Moses' past leadership, but with his absence.

32:4 calf. The bull as a symbol of deity was common in the ancient world. Perhaps a symbol of Apis, the Egyptian fertility bull-god, was meant. Aaron himself may have presented the calf as a symbol of the true God, and he apparently attempted to blunt the apostasy by building an altar and announcing a festival to the Lord (v. 5). Noting that the Hebrew term translated "gods" in vv. 1 and 4 (*'elohim*) can be rendered as singular or plural, some have argued that the people were worshiping the calf as a symbol of the Lord (they would still have been guilty of idolatry, 20:4 note). But the shout of the people is reported here using the plural verb ("brought . . . out") with *'elohim*. The singular form is always used with this noun when it refers to the true God. The people were turning to the bull-god to lead them, in gross violation of 20:2 (cf. Acts 7:39–41).

32:5 feast. The first, second, third, and probably the seventh commandments were violated in this festival (v. 6 note; 20:2–7, 14).

32:6 rose up to play. They rose from their meal to engage in what was probably a fertility cult orgy (the bull-god Apis was the Egyptian god of fertility). That this festival involved sexual immorality is further indicated by the later reference to shameful lack of restraint (v. 25).

32:7 your people. In righteous anger against their idolatry, God does not acknowledge the people as His own. Instead, He designates them to Moses as "your people."

32:10 let me alone. Anticipating the intercession of Moses, God proposes to destroy the stiff-necked apostates and to make a new nation of Moses. If He were to do so, God would be setting aside His promises to Abraham, Isaac, and Jacob (Gen. 12:2; 26:4; 28:14).

32:11 Moses rejects God's offer of v. 10. Instead, arguing on the basis of the honor of God's name (v. 12) and appealing to God's faithfulness to the covenant promises made to the patriarchs (v. 13), Moses pleads that God would continue to acknowledge Israel as His people.

32:13 Israel. The normal sequence would require "Jacob" (cf. 2:24; 3:6; Deut. 1:8), but the substitution is made by Moses to suit the occasion.

32:14 the LORD relented. See note Gen. 6:6. Moses' intercessory prayer itself was also part of God's will and purpose to show His grace. But the effectiveness of Moses' intercession can only be described by characterizing the Lord in human terms: He relents and withholds the total judgment He had threatened. See "The Spiritual Nature of God" at Is. 66:1.

[15]Then [s]Moses turned and went down
from the mountain with the [t]two tablets of
the testimony in his hand, tablets that were
written on both sides; on the front and on
the back they were written. [16][u]The tablets
were the work of God, and the writing was
the writing of God, engraved on the tablets.
[17]When [v]Joshua heard the noise of the people as they shouted, he said to Moses,
"There is a noise of war in the camp." [18]But
he said, "It is not the sound of [w]shouting
for victory, or the sound of the cry of
defeat, but the sound of singing that I
hear." [19]And as soon as he came near the
camp and [x]saw the calf and the dancing,
Moses' anger burned hot, and he threw the
tablets out of his hands and broke them at
the foot of the mountain. [20]He took the calf
that they had made and burned it with fire
and ground it to powder and scattered it
on the water and made the people of Israel
drink it.

15 [s]Deut. 9:15 [t]ch. 34:29
16 [u]ch. 31:18
17 [v]ch. 17:9, 10; 24:13; 33:11
18 [w]Jer. 51:14
19 [x]Deut. 9:16, 17, 21

The Word of God: Scripture as Revelation

Christianity is the true worship and service of the true God, mankind's Creator and Redeemer. It is a religion that rests on revelation: nobody would know the truth about God, nor be able to relate to Him in a personal way, had God not first acted to make Himself known. But God has so acted, and the sixty-six books of the Bible, thirty-nine written before Christ came and twenty-seven after, are together the record, interpretation, and expression of His self-disclosure. God and godliness are the Bible's uniting themes.

From one standpoint, the Scriptures ("scripture" means "writing") are the faithful testimony of the godly to the God whom they loved and served; from another standpoint, because they were composed through a unique exercise of divine superintendence, called "inspiration," they are God's own testimony and teaching in human language. The church calls these writings the Word of God because their authorship and contents are both of divine origin.

Decisive assurance that Scripture is from God and consists entirely of His wisdom and truth comes from Jesus Christ and His apostles, who taught in His name. Jesus, God incarnate, viewed His Bible (our Old Testament) as His heavenly Father's written instruction, which He no less than others must obey (Matt. 4:4, 7, 10; 5:17–20; 19:4–6; 26:31, 52–54; Luke 4:16–21; 16:17; 18:31–33; 22:37; 24:25–27, 45–47; John 10:35), and which He came to fulfill (Matt. 26:24; John 5:46). Paul described the Old Testament as entirely inspired or "God-breathed"—a product of God's Spirit, as is the whole creation also (Ps. 33:6; Gen. 1:2)—and written for our instruction (Rom. 15:4; 1 Cor. 10:11; 2 Tim. 3:15–17). Peter affirms the divine origin of biblical teaching in 2 Pet. 1:21 and 1 Pet. 1:10–12, and so also by his manner of quoting does the writer to the Hebrews (Heb. 1:5–13; 3:7; 4:3; 10:5–7, 15–17; cf. Acts 4:25; 28:25–27).

Since the apostles' teaching about Christ is itself revealed truth in God-taught words (1 Cor. 2:12, 13), the church regards the New Testament, which records the apostolic witness, as completing the Scriptures. During the New Testament period itself Peter refers to Paul's letters as Scripture (2 Pet. 3:15, 16), and Paul apparently calls Luke's Gospel Scripture in 1 Tim. 5:18 (cf. Luke 10:7).

The idea of written directives from God Himself as a basis for godly living goes back to God's inscribing the Ten Commandments on stone tablets and prompting Moses to write His laws and the history of His dealings with His people (Ex. 32:15, 16; 34:1, 27, 28; Num. 33:2; Deut. 31:9). Digesting and living by this material was always central to true devotion for both leaders and others in Israel (Josh. 1:7, 8; 2 Kin. 17:13; 22:8–13; 1 Chr. 22:12, 13; Neh. 8; Ps. 119), and the principle that all must be governed by the Scriptures has passed into Christianity.

What Scripture says, God says; for, in a manner comparable only to the deeper mystery of the Incarnation, the Bible is both fully human and fully divine. So all its manifold contents—histories, prophecies, poems, songs, wisdom writings, sermons, statistics, letters, and whatever else—should be received as from God, and all that biblical writers teach should be revered as God's authoritative instruction. Christians should be grateful to God for the gift of His written Word, and conscientious in basing their faith and life entirely and exclusively upon it.

32:16 work of God . . . writing of God. Attention is emphatically drawn to the divine origin of the tablets to be smashed. See theological note "The Word of God: Scripture as Revelation."

32:18 singing. Moses replies in a short graphic poem with a threefold use of the word for "singing," which lit. reads: "Not the sound of singing victory, not the sound of singing defeat, but the sound of singing I hear."

32:19 broke them. The broken tablets of the covenant law powerfully picture the broken covenant (20:1 note).

32:20 burned it. Perhaps the calf was wooden with a golden overlay. Israel was forced to drink this symbol of their sin to demonstrate that they would bear the responsibility for it (cf. the water of bitterness that later was to be drunk by an adulteress, Num. 5:18–22).

21 And Moses said to Aaron, [y]"What did
this people do to you that you have
brought such a great sin upon them?"
22 And Aaron said, "Let not the anger of my
lord burn hot. [z]You know the people, that
they are set on evil. 23 For [a]they said to me,
'Make us gods who shall go before us. As
for this Moses, the man who brought us up
out of the land of Egypt, we do not know
what has become of him.' 24 So [b]I said to
them, 'Let any who have gold take it off.'
So they gave it to me, and I threw it into
the fire, and out came this calf."

25 And when Moses saw that the people
had broken loose (for Aaron had let them
break loose, [c]to the derision of their enemies), 26 then Moses stood in the gate of
the camp and said, "Who is on the LORD's
side? Come to me." And all the sons of Levi
gathered around him. 27 And he said to
them, "Thus says the LORD God of Israel,
'Put your sword on your side each of you,
and go to and fro from gate to gate
throughout the camp, and each of you [d]kill
his brother and his companion and his
neighbor.'" 28 And the sons of Levi did
according to the word of Moses. And that
day about three thousand men of the people fell. 29 And Moses said, "Today you have
been [e]ordained for the service of the LORD,
each one at the cost of his son and of his
brother, so that he might bestow a blessing
upon you this day."
30 The next day Moses said to the people,
[f]"You have sinned a great sin. And now I
will go up to the LORD; [g]perhaps I can
make atonement for your sin." 31 So Moses
returned to the LORD and said, "Alas, [f]this
people have sinned a great sin. They have
[h]made for themselves gods of gold. 32 But
now, if [i]you will forgive their sin—but if
not, please [j]blot me out of [k]your book that
you have written." 33 But the LORD said to
Moses, [l]"Whoever has sinned against me, I
will blot out of my book. 34 [m]But now go,
lead the people to the place about which I
have spoken to you; [n]behold, my angel
shall go before you. Nevertheless, in the
day when I visit, I will visit their sin upon
them."

35 Then the LORD sent a plague on the
people, because they made the calf, the
one that Aaron made.

The Command to Leave Sinai

33 The LORD said to Moses, "Depart;
go up from here, you [o]and the people whom you have brought up out of the
land of Egypt, to the land of which I swore
to Abraham, Isaac, and Jacob, saying, 'To
[p]your offspring I will give it.' 2 I will send an
[q]angel before you, [r]and I will drive out the
Canaanites, the Amorites, the Hittites, the
Perizzites, the Hivites, and the Jebusites.
3 [s]Go up to a land flowing with milk and
honey; [t]but I will not go up among you,
[u]lest I consume you on the way, for you are
a [v]stiff-necked people."

21 [y][Gen. 20:9]
22 [z][ch. 14:11; 15:24; 16:2, 20; 17:2, 4; 1 Sam. 15:24]
23 [a]ver. 1
24 [b]ver. 2-4
25 [c][ver. 12]
27 [d][Num. 25:5; Deut. 33:9]
29 [e][Zech. 13:3; Matt. 10:37; Luke 14:26]; See Num. 25:11-13; Deut. 13:6-10
30 [f]See ver. 21; [1 Sam. 12:20] [g]2 Sam. 16:12; Amos 5:15
31 [f][See ver. 30 above] [h]ch. 20:23
32 [i][Num. 14:19] [j][Rom. 9:3] [k]Ps. 56:8; 69:28; 139:16; Dan. 12:1; Phil. 4:3
33 [l]Ezek. 18:4, 20
34 [m]ch. 33:12 [n]See ch. 14:19
Chapter 33
1 [o]ch. 32:7 [p]ch. 32:13; See Gen. 12:7
2 [q]See ch. 14:19 [r]See ch. 13:5
3 [s]See ch. 3:8 [t][ver. 15-17] [u]ch. 32:10; Num. 16:21, 45 [v]See ch. 32:9

32:21–24 In Aaron's pathetic defense he blames the people for his own unfaithfulness, and even suggests a miraculous origin for the calf (v. 24). Aaron's conduct throughout this episode suggests that the Levitical priesthood was destined for failure from its inception (Heb. 5:2, 3; 9:7). Divine judgment upon Aaron was averted only by Moses' intercession (Deut. 9:20; 10:6–9 and note on 10:6).

32:26 Who is on the LORD's side. Only the Levites, Moses' own tribe, answered his call to arms to put down the rebellion. They were prepared to use God's sword of judgment against neighbors or even family members (v. 29; cf. Num. 25:1–9).

32:29 ordained. See note 29:9.

32:30 I will go up to the LORD. Although the rebellion had been put down, Israel's guilt before God still loomed. Moses again had to leave Israel and climb the mountain to meet the Lord.

32:32 blot me out of your book. As there was a register of Israel (cf. Num. 1–4), so God Himself has a register of His people (Ps. 56:8; Is. 4:3; Mal. 3:16). If God did not forgive His people, Moses asked to be disinherited with them (cf. vv. 10, 11). Note the similar attitude of Paul in Rom. 9:3.

32:33 Whoever has sinned. Moses' intercession is partially successful: God does not finally reject His people, but the sinful individuals will be judged. The limitations of Moses' mediatorial office and ministry point to the need for a greater Mediator who will present a full and efficacious atonement for sin (Heb. 3:1–6; 10:11–18). See "Christ the Mediator" at 1 Tim. 2:5.

32:34 I will visit their sin. Israel's punishment is presented as certain but undefined. Apparently, a plague was soon added as a temporary punishment (v. 35). Finally, that whole generation, except for a small remnant, died in the wilderness (Num. 14:27–34).

33:1 you have brought up out. "You" suggests that God absolves Himself of responsibility for Israel since the covenant was broken (32:7 note).

33:2 I will send an angel before you. There is no real contrast between the Lord and the Angel here, for the Angel who was to go before Israel had already been identified with the Lord (23:20–23; Gen. 16:7 and notes). The key to understanding God's proposal is found in v. 3 ("I will not go up among you"). At issue was God's gracious dwelling in the midst of the people (29:44–46). If God did not dwell in Israel's midst, then there would be no point in building the tabernacle; indeed, Israel could "depart" immediately without constructing it (v. 1). Instead, another arrangement, already in operation (described in vv. 7–11), would be continued. God would meet with Moses and with inquiring Israelites at a tent "outside the camp, far off from the camp" (v. 7). This new "tent of meeting" was not God's dwelling; Joshua lived there (v. 11). God only came from time to time to the entrance of the tent in the pillar of cloud to speak with Moses (vv. 9, 10).

4 When the people heard this disastrous
word, they [w]mourned, and [x]no one put on
his ornaments. 5 For the LORD had said to
Moses, "Say to the people of Israel, 'You
are a [v]stiff-necked people; if for a single
moment I should go up among you, I
would [y]consume you. So now [x]take off
your ornaments, that I may know what to
do with you.'" 6 Therefore the people of
Israel stripped themselves of their ornaments, from Mount Horeb onward.

The Tent of Meeting

7 Now Moses used to take the tent and
pitch it outside the camp, far off from the
camp, and [z]he called it the tent of meeting.
And everyone who [a]sought the LORD would
go out to the tent of meeting, which was outside the camp. 8 Whenever Moses went out
to the tent, all the people would rise up, and
[b]each would stand at his tent door, and
watch Moses until he had gone into the tent.
9 When Moses entered the tent, the [c]pillar of
cloud would descend and stand at the
entrance of the tent, and the LORD[1] would
speak with Moses. 10 And when all the people
saw the pillar of cloud standing at the
entrance of the tent, all the people would rise
up and worship, each at his tent door.
11 Thus [d]the LORD used to speak to Moses
face to face, as a man speaks to his friend.
When Moses turned again into the camp, his
[e]assistant Joshua the son of Nun, a young
man, would not depart from the tent.

Moses' Intercession

12 Moses said to the LORD, "See, [f]you say
to me, 'Bring up this people,' but you have
not let me know whom you will send with
me. Yet you have said, [g]'I know you by
name, and you have also found favor in my
sight.' 13 Now therefore, if I have found
favor in your sight, please [h]show me now
your ways, that I may know you in order to
find favor in your sight. Consider too that
this nation is [i]your people." 14 And he said,
[j]"My presence will go with you, and [k]I will
give you rest." 15 And he said to him, [l]"If
your presence will not go with me, do not
bring us up from here. 16 For how shall it be
known that I have found favor in your
sight, I and your people? [m]Is it not in your
going with us, [n]so that we are distinct, I
and your people, from every other people
on the face of the earth?"
17 And the LORD said to Moses, "This very thing
that you have spoken I will do, [o]for you have
found favor in my sight, and I know you by
name." 18 Moses said, "Please [p]show me your

4 [w]Num. 14:39 [x][Ezek. 24:17, 23; 26:16]
5 [v][See ver. 3 above] [y]ch. 32:12 [x][See ver. 4 above]
7 [z]ch. 29:42, 43 [a]Deut. 4:29; 2 Sam. 21:1; 1 Chr. 16:10, 11; Ps. 40:16
8 [b][Num. 16:27]
9 [c]See ch. 13:21
11 [d]Num. 12:8; Deut. 34:10; See Gen. 32:30
[e]ch. 17:9, 10; 24:13; 32:17
12 [f]ch. 32:34 [g]ver. 17
13 [h]Ps. 25:4; [Ps. 103:7] [i]Deut. 9:29; [Joel 2:17]
14 [j]Josh. 1:5; Isai. 63:9; See ch. 40:34-38 [k]Deut. 3:20; Josh. 21:44; 22:4; 23:1; [Ps. 95:11]
15 [l][ver. 1-3]
16 [m]Num. 14:14; [n]ch. 19:5, 6; 1 Kin. 8:53
17 [o]ver. 12, 13
18 [p][ver. 20; 1 Tim. 6:16]

1 Hebrew *he*

33:4 they mourned. One might think that Israel would rejoice at the prospect of receiving their inheritance in the land without the threat of God's immediate presence. Instead, they mourned, for no longer would Israel be a nation of priests, enjoying immediate fellowship with God (19:3–6; 29:45, 46). This episode is one of the great crises of the Exodus story.

33:5 take off your ornaments. They stripped off the festive dress associated with idolatry (cf. Gen. 35:4) and assumed the posture of mourners. But this was remorse, not true repentance. They were and would continue to be a stiff-necked people. Still, there was a note of hope in God's words, "that I may know what to do with you."

33:7 take . . . pitch. The Hebrew verbal forms used here indicate this was the customary practice during the period at Sinai. This "tent of meeting" was a temporary structure that served as a meeting place for God and Moses until the tabernacle proper could be built (v. 2 note).

outside . . . far off from. The absence of God's presence from the camp is emphasized.

33:12 Moses said to the LORD. Moses responds to the dismaying threat of vv. 1–3. He could not argue that Israel was not stiff-necked, or that the golden calf was an uncharacteristic aberration. He could only plead God's grace and covenant mercy. He did so by repeatedly asking for precisely what the Lord was threatening to withdraw: the revelation of His own Presence (vv. 13–18). Moses' faithful persistence in intercession was grounded in God's covenant promise of divine-human communion (6:7; 19:5, 6; Gen. 17:7 note), and reminds us of Jacob's persistent struggle with God in quest of divine blessing (Gen. 32:24–30).

whom you will send with me. Moses expresses his objection to the occasional presence of the Angel of the Lord (a mysterious and temporary form of divine manifestation, Gen. 16:7 note; 32:29; Judg. 13:17, 18) acting as a substitute for the immediate presence of God's glory in the midst of the camp (v. 2 note), a relationship epitomized by God's revelation of His covenant Name (3:15 note).

I know you by name. God had declared His electing knowledge of Moses (32:10; 33:11) and would repeat that assurance expressly (v. 17). Because the Lord knew Moses by name personally and intimately, Moses would know the Lord (Num. 12:6–8).

33:13 your ways. Moses would know the Lord Himself and His purposes for Israel.

33:14 presence. Lit. "face." God Himself would go with Moses.

give you rest. Use of the singular pronoun "you" means that the promise of 3:13–15 for all Israel is now repeated for Moses alone.

33:15 me . . . us. Moses prays for the Presence to go with "us," linking Israel with himself. If God chose not to go with His people by dwelling among them, it would be useless to go to the Promised Land. The goal was not just milk and honey in Canaan, but a holy land where God would dwell with His people.

33:16 distinct. Israel's distinctness was grounded in the gracious presence of God Himself.

33:17 found favor in My sight. God includes Israel for Moses' sake; Israel was dependent upon Moses as mediator. Moses' intercession is a type of Christ's work as the new covenant Mediator (cf. Heb. 3; 9:16–22).

33:18 show me your glory. The Lord had sealed His covenant with Israel by revealing Himself (24:9–11), and Moses now seeks a further revelation of God in His glory. His only hope for God's continuing mercy to Israel lay in God Himself. Tasting God's mercy, Moses yearned for a full disclosure. See "The Transfiguration of Jesus" at Mark 9:2.

glory." **19** And he said, [q] "I will make all my
goodness pass before you and will proclaim before you my name 'The LORD.' And
[r] I will be gracious to whom I will be gracious, and will show mercy on whom I will
show mercy. **20** But," he said, "you cannot
see my face, for [s] man shall not see me and
live." **21** And the LORD said, "Behold, there
is a place by me where you shall stand on
the rock, **22** and while my glory passes by I
will put you in a [t] cleft of the rock, and I
will [u] cover you with my hand until I have
passed by. **23** Then I will take away my
hand, and you shall see my back, but my
face shall [v] not be seen."

Moses Makes New Tablets

34 The LORD said to Moses, [w] "Cut for
yourself two tablets of stone like the
first, [x] and I will write on the tablets the
words that were on the first tablets, [y] which
you broke. **2** Be ready by the morning, and
come up in the morning to Mount Sinai,
and present yourself there to me [z] on the
top of the mountain. **3** No [a] one shall come
up with you, and let no one be seen
throughout all the mountain. Let no flocks
or herds graze opposite that mountain."
4 So Moses cut two tablets of stone like the
first. And he rose early in the morning and
went up on Mount Sinai, as the LORD had
commanded him, and took in his hand two
tablets of stone. **5** The LORD [b] descended in
the cloud and stood with him there, and
[c] proclaimed the name of the LORD. **6** The
LORD passed before him and proclaimed,
[d] "The LORD, the LORD, a God merciful and
[e] gracious, slow to anger, and abounding in
steadfast [f] love and faithfulness, **7** [g] keeping
steadfast love for thousands,[1] [h] forgiving
iniquity and transgression and sin, but
[i] who will by no means clear the guilty, [j] visiting the iniquity of the fathers on the children and the children's children, to the
third and the fourth generation." **8** And
Moses quickly [k] bowed his head toward the
earth and worshiped. **9** And he said, "If now
I have found favor in your sight, O Lord,
please [l] let the Lord go in the midst of us,
for [m] it is a stiff-necked people, and pardon
our iniquity and our sin, and take us for
[n] your inheritance."

The Covenant Renewed

10 And he said, "Behold, [o] I am making a
covenant. Before all your people [p] I will do
marvels, such as have not been created in
all the earth or in any nation. And all the
people among whom you are shall see the
work of the LORD, for it is an [q] awesome
thing that I will do with you.
11 "Observe what I command you this
day. Behold, [r] I will drive out before you the
Amorites, the Canaanites, the Hittites, the
Perizzites, the Hivites, and the Jebusites.
12 [s] Take care, lest you make a covenant with

19 [q] Ps. 31:19; Jer. 31:14; [ch. 34:5-7] [r] Cited Rom. 9:15 **20** [s] Gen. 32:30; Deut. 5:24; Judg. 6:22, 23; 13:22; Isai. 6:5; Rev. 1:17; [ch. 24:10, 11] **22** [t] Isai. 2:21 [u] Ps. 91:1, 4 **23** [v] ver. 20; John 1:18; 1 Tim. 6:16; 1 John 4:12
Chapter 34
1 [w] Deut. 10:1 [x] ver. 28; Deut. 10:2, 4 [y] ch. 32:19 **2** [z] ch. 19:20 **3** [a] ch. 19:12, 13, 21 **5** [b] Num. 11:25; [1 Kin. 8:10, 11] [c] ch. 33:19 **6** [d] Num. 14:18; 2 Chr. 30:9; Neh. 9:17; Ps. 86:15; 103:8; 111:4; 112:4; 116:5; 145:8; Joel 2:13 [e] ch. 22:27 [f] Ps. 57:10; 108:4 **7** [g] ch. 20:5, 6; Deut. 5:10; Jer. 32:18; Dan. 9:4 [h] Ps. 103:3; 130:4; Dan. 9:9; 1 John 1:9 [i] ch. 23:21; Josh. 24:19; Job 10:14; Nah. 1:3 [j] Deut. 5:9
8 [k] ch. 4:31; 12:27 **9** [l] ch. 33:15, 16 [m] See ch. 32:9 [n] Deut. 32:9; Ps. 28:9; 33:12; 78:62; 94:14; Jer. 10:16; Zech. 2:12 **10** [o] ver. 27; Deut. 5:2; 29:1 [p] Deut. 4:32-35; Josh. 6:20; 10:12, 13; 2 Sam. 7:23; Ps. 77:14; 78:12 [q] Deut. 10:21; Ps. 145:6; [Isai. 64:3] **11** [r] See ch. 13:5 **12** [s] ch. 23:32; Deut. 7:2; Josh. 23:12, 13; Judg. 2:2

[1] Or *to the thousandth generation*

33:19 my goodness . . . my name. Though the visible magnificence of this theophany is apparent from the text, the emphasis falls on a revelation to Moses of God's sovereign, gracious, and compassionate nature (cf. 34:5–7). In Jesus Christ, the glory of the gracious and compassionate God that was withheld even from Moses is displayed to believers through the Spirit (John 1:14; 2 Cor. 3:18).

to whom . . . on whom. The Lord is sovereign in His purposes of mercy (Rom. 9:14–16). See "The Purpose of God: Predestination and Foreknowledge" at Mal. 1:2.

33:22 See "The Glory of God" at Ezek. 1:28.

33:23 my back. The Lord's goodness withheld what Moses could not bear and revealed all that he could bear.

34:1 two tablets of stone. The replacement of the tablets signals the renewal of the covenant (20:1 note).

34:2, 3 The uniqueness of Moses' mediatorial office is emphasized. The encounter of ch. 19 is to be repeated, but this time with Moses only (cf. 19:24; 24:9).

34:5–7 See "'This Is My Name': God's Self-disclosure" at 3:15.

34:5 The LORD descended. The revelation promised in 33:19–23: Yahweh passed by and proclaimed His name. Moses received an overwhelming answer to his prayer (33:19 note).

34:6, 7 This description of God is foundational for later Israelite piety (Num. 14:18; Neh. 9:17; Ps. 86:15; 103:8; 145:8; Joel 2:13; Jon. 4:2; Nah. 1:3). God's mercy is still proclaimed toward Israel despite her dismal failure (Hos. 11:8).

34:6 abounding in steadfast love. "Steadfast love" here translates the Hebrew term (*hesed*) denoting God's covenant faithfulness and devotion to His people (15:13 note). Because of God's love and faithfulness, He will not abandon His people, but dwell among them in His tabernacle.

34:9 go in the midst of us. This is what the Lord said He would not do, because the people were too sinful, too "stiff-necked" (33:3, 5). Now Moses cites their sin as the very reason for the Presence of God. In effect, he is asking that the compassionate and merciful Lord of grace would dwell in His tabernacle among His people, and forgive their sin. Then comes the amazing request: "take us for your inheritance." Moses does not say "give us our inheritance in the land" (cf. 33:2, 3), but "take us for your special treasure in Your faithful love" (the thought contained in 19:5).

34:11–16 God warns against apostate practices. The selection of cultic laws points to the area where Israel has sinned or is weak. Singular pronouns are used almost totally throughout, for God is making His covenant with Moses and with Israel through him (v. 27).

the inhabitants of the land to which you
go, lest it become a [t]snare in your midst.
13 You shall [u]tear down their altars and
[v]break their pillars and cut down their
[w]Asherim 14 (for [x]you shall worship no
other god, for the LORD, whose name is
Jealous, is a jealous God), 15 [s]lest you make
a covenant with the inhabitants of the
land, and when they [y]whore after their
gods and sacrifice to their gods and [z]you
are invited, you eat of his sacrifice, 16 and
you take of [a]their daughters for your sons,
and their daughters [y]whore after their gods
and make your sons whore after their gods.
17 [b]"You shall not make for yourself any
gods of cast metal.
18 [c]"You shall keep the Feast of
Unleavened Bread. Seven days you shall
eat unleavened bread, as I commanded
you, at the time appointed in [d]the month
Abib, for in the month Abib you came out
from Egypt. 19 [e]All that open the womb are
mine, all your male[1] livestock, the firstborn
of cow and sheep. 20 The [f]firstborn of a donkey you shall redeem with a lamb, or if you
will not redeem it you shall break its neck.
All the firstborn of your sons you shall
redeem. And [g]none shall appear before me
empty-handed.
21 [h]"Six days you shall work, but on the
seventh day you shall rest. In plowing time
and in harvest you shall rest. 22 [i]You shall
observe the Feast of Weeks, the firstfruits
of wheat harvest, and the Feast of
Ingathering at the year's end. 23 [j]Three
times in the year shall all your males
appear before the LORD God, the God of
Israel. 24 For I will [k]cast out nations before
you and [l]enlarge your borders; [m]no one
shall covet your land, when you go up to
appear before the LORD your God three
times in the year.

12 [t]See ch. 23:33
13 [u]Deut. 7:5; 12:3 Judg. 2:2; 6:25; 2 Chr. 34:3, 4 [v]ch. 23:24; 34:13; 2 Kin. 18:4; 23:14; 2 Chr. 31:1 [w]See Deut. 16:21
14 [x]ch. 20:3, 5
15 [s][See ver. 12 above] [y]Lev. 17:7; 20:5; Deut. 31:16; Judg. 2:17; Jer. 3:9; Ezek. 6:9 [z]Num. 25:2; Ps. 106:28; [1 Cor. 8:4, 7, 10; 10:27]
16 [a]Deut. 7:3, 4; 1 Kin. 11:2; Ezra 9:2; Neh. 13:25 [y][See ver. 15 above]
17 [b]Lev. 19:4; Deut. 27:15; [ch. 32:4, 8]
18 [c]See ch. 12:15 [d]ch. 13:4
19 [e]See ch. 13:2
20 [f]ch. 13:13; Num. 18:15 [g]ch. 23:15; Deut. 16:16
21 [h]See ch. 20:9
22 [i]ch. 23:16; Deut. 16:10, 13
23 [j]ch. 23:14, 17; Deut. 16:16
24 [k]ch. 33:2; Deut. 7:1; Ps. 78:55; 80:8; See ch. 23:27-31 [l]Deut. 12:20; 19:8 [m][Prov. 16:7]
25 [n]See ch. 12:8 [o]See ch.12:10
26 [p]See ch. 23:19 [q]Deut. 14:21
27 [r]ver. 10
28 [s]See ch. 24:18 [t][ver. 1; ch. 31:18; 32:16; Deut. 4:13; 10:2, 4]

25 [n]"You shall not offer the blood of my
sacrifice with anything leavened, [o]or let the
sacrifice of the Feast of the Passover remain
until the morning. 26 [p]The best of the firstfruits of your ground you shall bring to the
house of the LORD your God. [q]You shall not
boil a young goat in its mother's milk."
27 And the LORD said to Moses, "Write
these words, for in accordance with these
words [r]I have made a covenant with you
and with Israel." 28 [s]So he was there with
the LORD forty days and forty nights. He
neither ate bread nor drank water. And he
[t]wrote on the tablets the words of the
covenant, the Ten Commandments.[2]

The Shining Face of Moses

29 When Moses came down from Mount
Sinai, with [u]the two tablets of the testimony in his hand as he came down from the
mountain, Moses did not know that the
skin of his face [v]shone because he had
been talking with God.[3] 30 Aaron and all the
people of Israel saw Moses, and behold,
the skin of his face [w]shone, and they were
afraid to come near him. 31 But Moses
called to them, and Aaron and all the leaders of the congregation returned to him,
and Moses talked with them. 32 Afterward
all the people of Israel came near, and he
[x]commanded them all that the LORD had
spoken with him in Mount Sinai. 33 And
when Moses had finished speaking with
them, he put a [y]veil over his face.
34 Whenever Moses [z]went in before the
LORD to speak with him, he would remove
the veil, until he came out. And when he
came out and told the people of Israel what
he was commanded, 35 the people of Israel

29 [u]ch. 32:15 [v]2 Cor. 3:7; [Matt. 17:2] 30 [w]ver. 29 32 [x]ch. 24:3 33 [y]2 Cor. 3:13 34 [z]2 Cor. 3:16

[1] Septuagint, Theodotion, Vulgate, Targum; the meaning of the Hebrew is uncertain [2] Hebrew *the ten words* [3] Hebrew *him*

34:13 Asherim. These were cultic objects that represented the Canaanite goddess of fertility (Asherah), sacred trees or poles that stood beside the Baal altars (cf. Judg. 6:25). Israel must not be compromised by adopting the pagan practices of peoples in the land.

34:14–16 no other god. The theme continues with allusions to the first (vv. 14–16) and second commandments (v. 17). God has begun at the point of Israel's sin and with the Decalogue that was violated.

34:18–26 This section parallels the laws in the Book of the Covenant (23:14–19).

34:27 these words. The commands of vv. 12–26.

34:28 he wrote . . . the words of the covenant. The Lord Himself wrote the Ten Commandments on the tablets (v. 1; 20:1 note).

34:29 shone. Lit. "sent out horns." Although the Hebrew root usually refers to horns, it would seem that rays of light are in view here (cf. Hab. 3:4). Moses' leadership was confirmed by the reflected light of God's glory.

34:30 they were afraid to come near him. The reaction of fear suggests the events of chs. 19; 20. Only when they drew near and conversed without harm were they reassured.

34:33 put a veil over his face. The purpose of the veil was not to calm the anxiety of the people, for Moses put on the veil only after the people had come near and after he had finished declaring the law to the people (vv. 31, 32). Rather, as Paul in 2 Cor. 3:13 makes clear, the veil was to keep the Israelites from seeing that the glory was fading away. According to Paul, this fading glory shows the temporary and inadequate character of the old Mosaic covenant and points to the need for a greater covenant Mediator—Jesus Christ (2 Cor. 3:12–4:6).

would see the face of Moses, that the skin
of Moses' face was [a]shining. And Moses
would put the veil over his face again, until
he went in to speak with him.

Sabbath Regulations

35 Moses assembled all the congregation of the people of Israel and said
to them, [b]"These are the things that the
LORD has commanded you to do. 2 [c]Six days
work shall be done, but on the seventh day
you shall have a Sabbath of solemn rest,
holy to the LORD. Whoever does any work
on it shall be put to death. 3 [d]You shall kindle no fire in all your dwelling places on
the Sabbath day."

Contributions for the Tabernacle

4 Moses said to all the congregation of the
people of Israel, "This is the thing that the
LORD has commanded. 5 [e]Take from among
you a contribution to the LORD. [f]Whoever
is of a generous heart, let him bring the
LORD's contribution: gold, silver, and
bronze; 6 blue and purple and scarlet yarns
and fine twined linen; goats' hair, 7 tanned
rams' skins, and goatskins;[1] acacia wood,
8 oil for the light, spices for the anointing
oil and for the fragrant incense, 9 and onyx
stones and stones for setting, for the ephod
and for the breastpiece.

10 "Let [g]every skillful craftsman among you
come and make all that the LORD has commanded: 11 [h]the tabernacle, its tent and its
covering, its hooks and its frames, its bars,
its pillars, and its bases; 12 [i]the ark with its
poles, the mercy seat, and the [j]veil of the
screen; 13 [k]the table with its poles and all its
utensils, and the [l]bread of the Presence;
14 [m]the lampstand also for the light, with its
utensils and its lamps, and the [n]oil for the
light; 15 [o]and the altar of incense, with its
poles, [p]and the anointing oil and the [q]fra-
grant incense, and [r]the screen for the door,
at the door of the tabernacle; 16 [s]the altar of
burnt offering, with its grating of bronze, its
poles, and all its utensils, the [t]basin and its
stand; 17 [u]the hangings of the court, its pillars and its bases, and the screen for the gate
of the court; 18 [v]the pegs of the tabernacle
and the pegs of the court, and their [w]cords;
19 the [x]finely worked garments for ministering[2] in the Holy Place, the holy garments for
Aaron the priest, and the garments of his
sons, for their service as priests."

20 Then all the congregation of the people of Israel departed from the presence of
Moses. 21 And they came, [y]everyone whose
heart stirred him, and everyone whose
spirit moved him, [z]and brought the
LORD's contribution to be used for the
tent of meeting, and for all its service, and
for the holy garments. 22 So they came,
both men and women. All who were of a
willing heart brought brooches and earrings and signet rings and armlets, all
sorts of gold objects, every man dedicat-
ing an offering of gold to the LORD. 23 And
[a]every one who possessed [b]blue or purple
or scarlet yarns or fine linen or goats' hair
or tanned rams' skins or goatskins
brought them. 24 [c]Everyone who could
make a contribution of silver or bronze
brought it as the LORD's contribution. And
every one who possessed acacia wood of
any use in the work brought it. 25 And
every [d]skillful woman spun with her
hands, and they all brought what they had
spun in blue and purple and scarlet yarns
and fine twined linen. 26 All the women
[y]whose hearts stirred them to use their
skill spun the goats' hair. 27 And the [e]lead-
ers brought onyx stones and stones to be
set, for the ephod and for the breastpiece,
28 and spices and oil for the light, and for
the anointing oil, and for the fragrant
incense. 29 [f]All the men and women, the
people of Israel, whose heart moved them
to bring anything for the work that the
LORD had commanded by Moses to be
done brought it as a freewill offering to
the LORD.

35 [a]ver. 29
Chapter 35
1 [b]ch. 34:32
2 [c]ch. 31:15; See ch. 20:9
3 [d]ch. 16:23
5 [e]For ver. 5-9, see ch. 25:2-7 [f]See ch. 25:2
10 [g]ver. 25; ch. 28:3; 31:6; 36:1, 2
11 [h]See ch. 26:1-30
12 [i]See ch. 25:10-16 [j]ch. 26:31, 33; 39:34; 40:3, 21; Num. 4:5
13 [k]See ch. 25:23-29 [l]ch. 25:30
14 [m]See ch. 25:31-39 [n]ch. 27:20
15 [o]See ch. 30:1-10 [p]See ch. 30:23-33 [q]See ch. 30:34-38 [r]ch. 26:36
16 [s]See ch. 27:1-8 [t]See ch. 30:18-21
17 [u]See ch. 27:9-17
18 [v]ch. 27:19 [w]ch. 39:40
19 [x]ch. 31:10
21 [y]See ch. 25:2 [z]ch. 36:3
23 [a][1 Chr. 29:8] [b]ver. 6, 7; ch. 25:4, 5
24 [c]ch. 36:3, 6
25 [d]ver. 10
26 [y][See ver. 21 above]
27 [e][1 Chr. 29:6-8; Ezra 2:68]
29 [f]ch. 36:3

1 The meaning of the Hebrew word is uncertain; also verse 23; compare 25:5 2 Or *garments for worship*; see 31:10

35:1–3 The work on the tabernacle starts with an admonition to keep the Sabbath, just as the instructions for the work had concluded with such a reminder (31:12–18).

35:4–39:43 This entire section is based on chs. 25–31 but follows a different order. While chs. 25–31 gave the instructions for the tabernacle, this section describes its construction. Beginning with the reiteration of instructions for the gathering of offerings and artisans (35:4–19), the narrative then moves logically to the gathering of materials and the recognition of artisans (35:20–36:7), the construction of the tabernacle parts and contents (36:8–38:31), the preparation of sacred vestments (39:1–31), the erection of the tabernacle (39:32–40:33), and finally to the climactic arrival of the glory of the Lord in the tabernacle (40:34–38).

35:22 women. Women are mentioned for the first time. Their involvement both in the donation and preparation of the materials was significant (vv. 25, 26, 29).

Construction of the Tabernacle

30 [g]Then Moses said to the people of Israel, "See, the LORD has called by name Bezalel the son of Uri, son of Hur, of the tribe of Judah; 31 and he has filled him with the Spirit of God, with [h]skill, with intelligence, with knowledge, and with all craftsmanship, 32 to devise artistic designs, to work in gold and silver and bronze, 33 in cutting stones for setting, and in carving wood, for work in every skilled craft. 34 And he has inspired him to teach, both him and Oholiab the son of Ahisamach of the tribe of Dan. 35 He has [h]filled them with skill to do every sort of work done by an engraver or by a designer or by an embroiderer in blue and purple and scarlet yarns and fine twined linen, or by a weaver—by any sort of workman or skilled designer.

36 "Bezalel and Oholiab and [i]every craftsman in whom the LORD has put skill and intelligence to know how to do any work in the construction of the sanctuary shall work in accordance with all that the LORD has commanded."

2 And Moses called Bezalel and Oholiab and every craftsman in whose mind the LORD had put skill, everyone [j]whose heart stirred him up to come to do the work. 3 And they received from Moses all the [k]contribution that the people of Israel had brought for doing the work on the sanctuary. They still kept bringing him [l]freewill offerings every morning, 4 so that all the craftsmen who were doing every sort of task on the sanctuary came, each from the task that he was doing, 5 and said to Moses, [m]"The people bring much more than enough for doing the work that the LORD has commanded us to do." 6 So Moses gave command, and word was proclaimed throughout the camp, "Let no man or woman do anything more for the [n]contribution for the sanctuary." So the people were restrained from bringing, 7 for the material they had was sufficient to do all the work, and more.

8 [o]And all the craftsmen among the workmen made the tabernacle with ten curtains. They were made of fine twined linen and blue and purple and scarlet yarns, with cherubim skillfully worked. 9 The length of each curtain was twenty-eight cubits,[1] and the breadth of each curtain four cubits. All the curtains were the same size.

10 He coupled five curtains to one another, and the other five curtains he coupled to one another. 11 He made loops of blue on the edge of the outermost curtain of the first set. Likewise he made them on the edge of the outermost curtain of the second set. 12 He made fifty loops on the one curtain, and he made fifty loops on the edge of the curtain that was in the second set. The loops were opposite one another. 13 And he made fifty clasps of gold, and coupled the curtains one to the other with clasps. So the tabernacle was a single whole.

14 He also made curtains of goats' hair for a tent over the tabernacle. He made eleven curtains. 15 The length of each curtain was thirty cubits, and the breadth of each curtain four cubits. The eleven curtains were the same size. 16 He coupled five curtains by themselves, and six curtains by themselves. 17 And he made fifty loops on the edge of the outermost curtain of the one set, and fifty loops on the edge of the other connecting curtain. 18 And he made fifty clasps of bronze to couple the tent together that it might be a single whole. 19 And he made for the tent a covering of tanned rams' skins and goatskins.

20 [p]Then he made the upright frames for the tabernacle of [q]acacia wood. 21 Ten cubits was the length of a frame, and a cubit and a half the breadth of each frame. 22 Each frame had two tenons for fitting together. He did this for all the frames of the tabernacle. 23 The frames for the tabernacle he made thus: twenty frames for the south side. 24 And he made forty bases of silver under the twenty frames, two bases under one frame for its two tenons, and two bases under the next frame for its two tenons. 25 For the second side of the tabernacle, on the north side, he made twenty frames 26 and their forty bases of silver, two bases under one frame and two bases under the next frame. 27 For the rear of the

1 A *cubit* was about 18 inches or 45 centimeters

30 [g]For ver. 30-34, see ch. 31:1-6
31 [h][1 Kin. 7:14; 2 Chr. 2:14]
35 [h][See ver. 31 above]
Chapter 36
1 [i]ch. 28:3; 31:6; 35:10, 25
2 [j]See ch. 25:2
3 [k]ch. 35:24 [l]See ch. 35:29
5 [m][2 Chr. 31:10; 2 Cor. 8:2, 3]
6 [n]ver. 3
8 [o]For ver. 8-19, see ch. 26:1-14
20 [p]For ver. 20-34, see ch. 26:15-29 [q]ch. 25:5, 28; 30:5

36:8–39:43 The work of Bezalel, Oholiab, and their crew of skilled laborers is recounted. The detail of the account underscores the attention paid by the builders to the word of the Lord (39:42–43).

tabernacle westward he made six frames.
28 He made two frames for corners of the
tabernacle in the rear. 29 And they were separate beneath but joined at the top, at the
first ring. He made two of them this way for
the two corners. 30 There were eight frames
with their bases of silver: sixteen bases,
under every frame two bases.
31 He made bars of acacia wood, five for
the frames of the one side of the tabernacle, 32 and five bars for the frames of the
other side of the tabernacle, and five bars
for the frames of the tabernacle at the rear
westward. 33 And he made the middle bar
to run from end to end halfway up the
frames. 34 And he overlaid the frames with
gold, and made their rings of gold for holders for the bars, and overlaid the bars with
gold.
35 [r] He made the veil of blue and purple
and scarlet yarns and fine twined linen;
with cherubim skillfully worked into it he
made it. 36 And for it he made four pillars of
acacia and overlaid them with gold. Their
hooks were of gold, and he cast for them
four bases of silver. 37 He also made a screen
for the entrance of the tent, of blue and purple and scarlet yarns and fine twined linen,

35 [r] For ver. 35-38, see ch. 26:31-37

The Furniture of the Tabernacle (37:1)

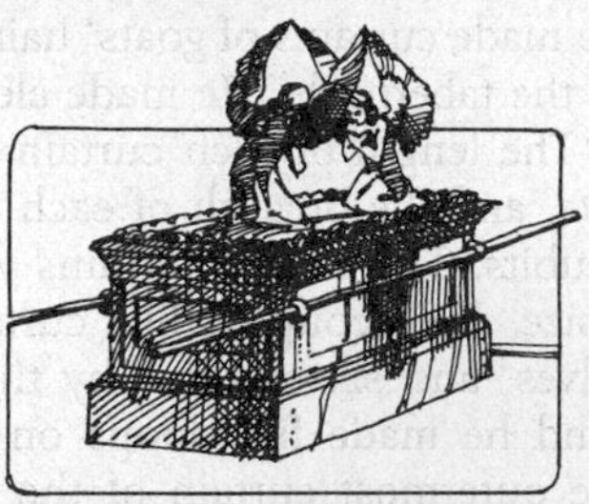

Ark of the Covenant
(Ex. 25:10–22)
The ark was most sacred of all the furniture in the tabernacle. Here the Hebrews kept a copy of the Ten Commandments which summarized the whole covenant.

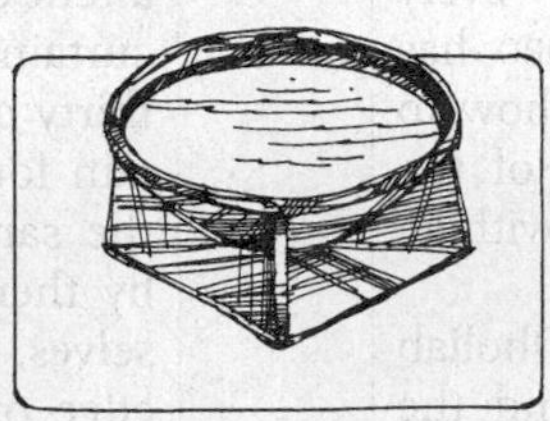

Bronze Basin
(Ex. 30:17–21)
It was to the basin of bronze that the priests would come for cleansing. They must be pure to enter the presence of God

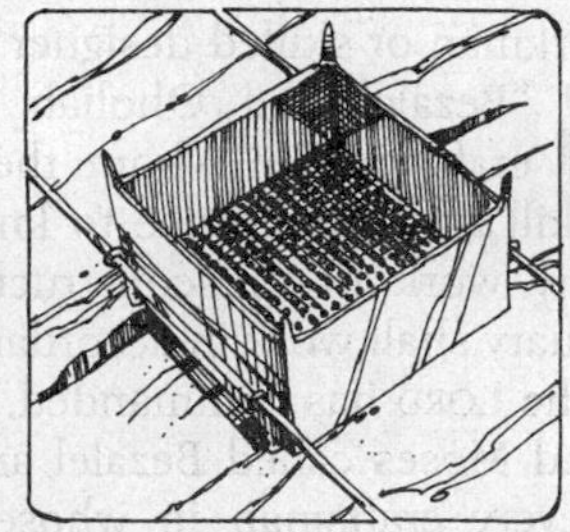

Altar of Burnt Offering
(Ex. 27:1–8)
Animal sacrifices were offered on this altar, located in the court in front of the tabernacle. The blood of the sacrificed was sprinkled on the four horns of the altar.

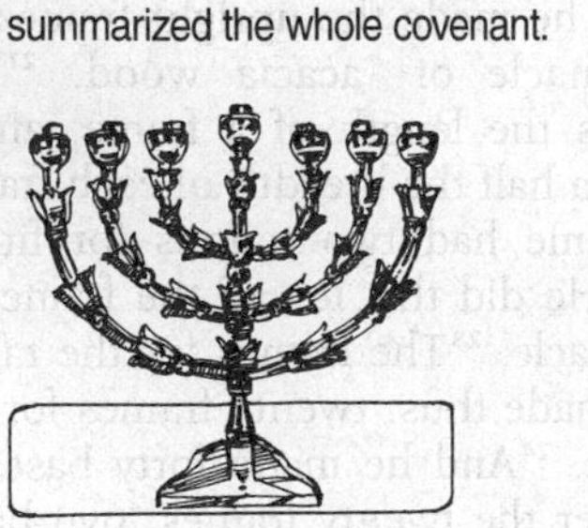

Gold Lampstand
(Ex. 25:31–40)
The gold lampstand stood in the holy place, opposite the table of showbread. It held seven lamps, flat bowls in which a wick lay with one end oin the oil of the bowl and the lightned end hanging out.

Table of Showbread
(Ex. 25:23–30)
The table of showbread was a stand on which the offerings were placed. Always in God's presence on the table were the 12 loaves of bread representing the 12 tribes

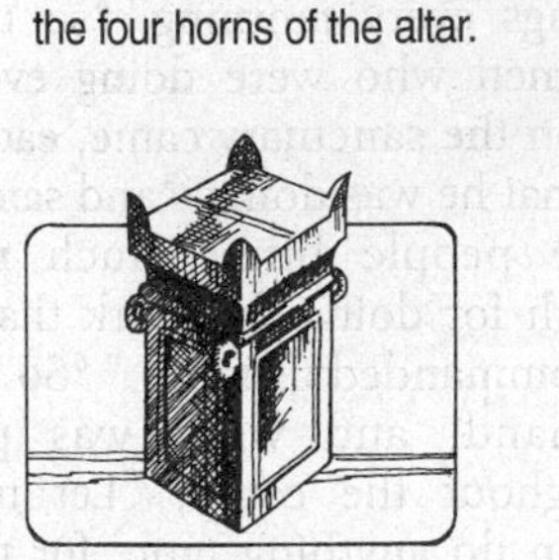

Altar of Incense
(Ex. 30:1–10)
The altar of incense inside the tabernacle was much smaller than the altar of burnt offering outside. The incense burned on the altar was a perfume of a sweet-smelling aroma.

embroidered with needlework, 38 and its five
pillars with their hooks. He overlaid their
capitals, and their fillets were of gold, but
their five bases were of bronze.

Making the Ark

37 [s]Bezalel made the ark of acacia
wood. Two cubits[1] and a half was
its length, a cubit and a half its breadth,
and a cubit and a half its height. 2 And he
overlaid it with pure gold inside and outside, and made a molding of gold around
it. 3 And he cast for it four rings of gold for
its [t]four feet, two rings on its one side and
two rings on its other side. 4 And he made
poles of acacia wood and overlaid them
with gold 5 and put the poles into the rings
on the sides of the ark to carry the ark.
6 And he made a mercy seat of pure gold.
Two cubits and a half was its length, and a
cubit and a half its breadth. 7 And he made
two cherubim of gold. He made them of
hammered work on the two ends of the
mercy seat, 8 one cherub on the one end,
and one cherub on the other end. Of one
piece with the mercy seat he made the
cherubim on its two ends. 9 The cherubim
spread out their wings above, overshadowing the mercy seat with their wings, with
their faces one to another; toward the
mercy seat were the faces of the cherubim.

Making the Table

10 [u]He also made the table of acacia wood.
Two cubits was its length, a cubit its
breadth, and a cubit and a half its height.
11 And he overlaid it with pure gold, and
made a molding of gold around it. 12 And he
made a rim around it a handbreadth[2] wide,
and made a molding of gold around the
rim. 13 He cast for it four rings of gold and
fastened the rings to the four corners at its
four legs. 14 Close to the frame were the
rings, as holders for the poles to carry the
table. 15 He made the poles of acacia wood
to carry the table, and overlaid them with
gold. 16 And he made the vessels of pure
gold that were to be on the table, its plates
and dishes for incense, and its bowls and
flagons with which to pour drink offerings.

Making the Lampstand

17 [v]He also made the lampstand of pure
gold. He made the lampstand of hammered
work. Its base, its stem, its cups, its calyxes, and its flowers were of one piece with it.
18 And there were six branches going out of
its sides, three branches of the lampstand
out of one side of it and three branches of
the lampstand out of the other side of it;
19 three cups made like almond blossoms,
each with calyx and flower, on one branch,
and three cups made like almond blossoms, each with calyx and flower, on the
other branch—so for the six branches
going out of the lampstand. 20 And on the
lampstand itself were four cups made like
almond blossoms, with their calyxes and
flowers, 21 and a calyx of one piece with it
under each pair of the six branches going
out of it. 22 Their calyxes and their branches were of one piece with it. The whole of
it was a single piece of hammered work of
pure gold. 23 And he made its seven lamps
and its tongs and its trays of pure gold.
24 He made it and all its utensils out of a talent[3] of pure gold.

Making the Altar of Incense

25 [w]He made the altar of incense of acacia
wood. Its length was a cubit, and its
breadth was a cubit. It was square, and two
cubits was its height. Its horns were of one
piece with it. 26 He overlaid it with pure
gold, its top and around its sides and its
horns. And he made a molding of gold
around it, 27 and made two rings of gold on
it under its molding, on two opposite sides
of it, as holders for the poles with which to
carry it. 28 And he made the poles of acacia
wood and overlaid them with gold.
29 [x]He made the holy anointing oil also,
and the [y]pure fragrant incense, blended as
by the perfumer.

Making the Altar of Burnt Offering

38 [z]He made the altar of burnt offering
of acacia wood. Five cubits[4] was its
length, and five cubits its breadth. It was
square, and three cubits was its height. 2 He
made horns for it on its four corners. Its
horns were of one piece with it, and he
overlaid it with bronze. 3 And he made all
the utensils of the altar, the pots, the shovels, the basins, the forks, and the fire pans.
He made all its utensils of bronze. 4 And he

Chapter 37
1 [s]For ver. 1-9, see ch. 25:10-20
3 [t]ch. 25:12
10 [u]For ver. 10-16, see ch. 25:23-29
17 [v]For ver. 17-24, see ch. 25:31-39
25 [w]For ver. 25-28, see ch. 30:1-5
29 [x]ch. 30:23, 24, 34, 35 [y]ch. 30:7
Chapter 38
1 [z]For ver. 1-7, see ch. 27:1-8

1 A *cubit* was about 18 inches or 45 centimeters 2 A *handbreadth* was about 3 inches or 7.5 centimeters 3 A *talent* was about 75 pounds or 34 kilograms 4 A *cubit* was about 18 inches or 45 centimeters

made for the altar a grating, a network of bronze, under its ledge, extending halfway down. [5]He cast four rings on the four corners of the bronze grating as holders for the poles. [6]He made the poles of acacia wood and overlaid them with bronze. [7]And he put the poles through the rings on the sides of the altar to carry it with them. He made it hollow, with boards.

Making the Bronze Basin

[8][a]He made the basin of bronze and its stand of bronze, from the mirrors of the [b]ministering women who ministered in the entrance of the tent of meeting.

Making the Court

[9][c]And he made the court. For the south side the hangings of the court were of fine twined linen, a hundred cubits; [10]their twenty pillars and their twenty bases were of bronze, but the hooks of the pillars and their fillets were of silver. [11]And for the north side there were hangings of a hundred cubits, their twenty pillars, their twenty bases were of bronze, but the hooks of the pillars and their fillets were of silver. [12]And for the west side were hangings of fifty cubits, their ten pillars, and their ten bases; the hooks of the pillars and their fillets were of silver. [13]And for the front to the east, fifty cubits. [14]The hangings for one side of the gate were fifteen cubits, with their three pillars and three bases. [15]And so for the other side. On both sides of the gate of the court were hangings of fifteen cubits, with their three pillars and their three bases. [16]All the hangings around the court were of fine twined linen. [17]And the bases for the pillars were of bronze, but the hooks of the pillars and their fillets were of silver. The overlaying of their capitals was also of silver, and all the pillars of the court were filleted with silver. [18]And the screen for the gate of the court was embroidered with needlework in blue and purple and scarlet yarns and fine twined linen. It was twenty cubits long and five cubits high in its breadth, corresponding to the hangings of the court. [19]And their pillars were four in number. Their four bases were of bronze, their hooks of silver, and the overlaying of their capitals and their fillets of silver. [20]And all the pegs for the tabernacle and for the court all around were of bronze.

Materials for the Tabernacle

[21]These are the records of the tabernacle, [d]the tabernacle of the testimony, as they were recorded at the commandment of Moses, the responsibility of the Levites [e]under the direction of Ithamar the son of Aaron the priest. [22][f]Bezalel the son of Uri, son of Hur, of the tribe of Judah, made all that the LORD commanded Moses; [23]and with him was [f]Oholiab the son of Ahisamach, of the tribe of Dan, an engraver and designer and embroiderer in blue and purple and scarlet yarns and fine twined linen.

[24]All the gold that was used for the work, in all the construction of the sanctuary, the gold from the offering, was twenty-nine talents and 730 shekels,[1] by [g]the shekel of the sanctuary. [25]The silver from those of the congregation who were recorded was a hundred talents and 1,775 shekels, by the shekel of the sanctuary: [26]a [g]beka[2] a head (that is, half a shekel, by the shekel of the sanctuary), for everyone who was listed in the records, from twenty years old and upward, for [h]603,550 men. [27]The hundred talents of silver were for casting the [i]bases of the sanctuary and the bases of the veil; a hundred bases for the hundred talents, a talent a base. [28]And of the 1,775 shekels he made hooks for the pillars and overlaid their capitals and made fillets for them. [29]The bronze that was offered was seventy talents and 2,400 shekels; [30]with it he made the [j]bases for the entrance of the tent of meeting, [k]the bronze altar and the bronze grating for it and all the utensils of the altar, [31]the [l]bases around the court, and the [m]bases of the gate of the court, all the [n]pegs of the tabernacle, and all the pegs around the court.

Making the Priestly Garments

39 From the [o]blue and purple and scarlet yarns they made [p]finely woven garments,[3] for ministering in the Holy Place.

8 [a]ch. 30:18 [b]1 Sam. 2:22; [Num. 4:23; 8:24]
9 [c]For ver. 9-20, see ch. 27:9-19
21 [d]Num. 1:50, 53; 9:15; 10:11; 17:7, 8; 18:2; 2 Chr. 24:6; Acts 7:44; [ch. 16:34] [e]ch. 6:23; 28:1; Num. 4:28, 33
22 [f]ch. 31:2, 6
23 [f][See ver. 22 above]
24 [g]See ch. 30:13
26 [g][See ver. 24 above] [h]Num. 1:46
27 [i]ch. 26:19, 21, 25, 32
30 [j]ch. 26:37 [k]ch. 27:2-4
31 [l]ch. 27:10-12 [m]ch. 27:16, 17 [n]ch. 27:19
Chapter 39
1 [o]ch. 35:23, 25 [p]ver. 41; ch. 31:10; 35:19

[1] A *talent* was about 75 pounds or 34 kilograms; a *shekel* was about 2/5 ounce or 11 grams [2] A *beka* was about 1/5 ounce or 5.5 grams
[3] Or *garments for worship*

38:25 talents . . . shekels. At the recognized ratio of three thousand shekels to the talent (a talent was roughly 75 pounds), there were 2193 pounds of gold, 7544 of silver, and 5310 of copper. The amount of silver, a total of 301,175 shekels, is linked to the head count of the Israelites: half a shekel from all males over the age of twenty (603,550 men of military age, Num. 1:46). See note 30:12.

They made the holy garments for Aaron, [q]as the LORD had commanded Moses.

2 [r]He made the ephod of gold, blue and purple and scarlet yarns, and fine twined linen. **3** And they hammered out gold leaf, and he cut it into threads to work into the blue and purple and the scarlet yarns, and into the fine twined linen, in skilled design. **4** They made for the ephod attaching shoulder pieces, joined to it at its two edges. **5** And the skillfully woven band on it was of one piece with it and made like it, of gold, blue and purple and scarlet yarns, and fine twined linen, as the LORD had commanded Moses.

6 They made the onyx stones, enclosed in settings of gold filigree, and engraved like the engravings of a signet, according to the names of the sons of Israel. **7** And he set them on the shoulder pieces of the ephod to be stones of remembrance for the sons of Israel, as the LORD had commanded Moses.

8 [s]He made the breastpiece, in skilled work, in the style of the ephod, of gold, blue and purple and scarlet yarns, and fine twined linen. **9** It was square. They made the breastpiece doubled, a span[1] its length and a span its breadth when doubled. **10** And they set in it four rows of stones. A row of sardius, topaz, and carbuncle was the first row; **11** and the second row, an emerald, a sapphire, and a diamond; **12** and the third row, a jacinth, an agate, and an amethyst; **13** and the fourth row, a beryl, an onyx, and a jasper. They were enclosed in settings of gold filigree. **14** There were twelve stones with their names according to the names of the sons of Israel. They were like signets, each engraved with its name, for the twelve tribes. **15** And they made on the breastpiece twisted chains like cords, of pure gold. **16** And they made two settings of gold filigree and two gold rings, and put the two rings on the two edges of the breastpiece. **17** And they put the two cords of gold in the two rings at the edges of the breastpiece. **18** They attached the two ends of the two cords to the two settings of filigree. Thus they attached it in front to the shoulder pieces of the ephod. **19** Then they made two rings of gold, and put them at the two ends of the breastpiece, on its inside edge next to the ephod. **20** And they made two rings of gold, and attached them in front to the lower part of the two shoulder pieces of the ephod, at its seam above the skillfully woven band of the ephod. **21** And they bound the breastpiece by its rings to the rings of the ephod with a lace of blue, so that it should lie on the skillfully woven band of the ephod, and that the breastpiece should not come loose from the ephod, as the LORD had commanded Moses.

22 [t]He also made the robe of the ephod woven all of blue, **23** and the opening of the robe in it was like the opening in a garment, with a binding around the opening, so that it might not tear. **24** On the hem of the robe they made pomegranates of blue and purple and scarlet yarns and fine twined linen. **25** They also made bells of pure gold, and put the bells between the pomegranates all around the hem of the robe, between the pomegranates— **26** a bell and a pomegranate, a bell and a pomegranate around the hem of the robe for ministering, as the LORD had commanded Moses.

27 [u]They also made the coats, woven of fine [v]linen, for Aaron and his sons, **28** and the [v]turban of fine linen, and the caps of fine linen, and the linen undergarments of fine twined linen, **29** and the sash of fine twined linen and of blue and purple and scarlet yarns, embroidered with needlework, as the LORD had commanded Moses.

30 [w]They made the plate of the holy crown of pure gold, and wrote on it an inscription, like the engraving of a signet, "Holy to the LORD." **31** And they tied to it a cord of blue to fasten it on the turban above, as the LORD had commanded Moses.

32 Thus all the work of the tabernacle of the tent of meeting was finished, and the people of Israel did [x]according to all that the LORD had commanded Moses; so they did. **33** Then they brought the tabernacle to Moses, the tent and all its utensils, its hooks, its frames, its bars, its pillars, and its bases; **34** the covering of tanned rams' skins and goatskins, and the [y]veil of the screen; **35** the ark of the testimony with its poles and the mercy seat; **36** the table with

1 [q]ch. 28:2-4
2 [r]For ver. 2-7, see ch. 28:6-12
8 [s]For ver. 8-21, see ch. 28:15-28
22 [t]For ver. 22-26, see ch. 28:31-34
27 [u]ch. 28:39, 40, 42 [v]Ezek. 44:18
28 [v][See ver. 27 above]
30 [w]ch. 28:36, 37; 29:6
32 [x]ver. 42, 43; ch. 25:40
34 [y]ch. 35:12

[1] A *span* was about 9 inches or 22 centimeters

39:33 they brought . . . to Moses. The finished components were brought to Moses for inspection. Moses had received the instructions from the Lord (chs. 25–31), and only Moses could determine the fitness of what had been made.

all its utensils, and the bread of the Presence; 37 [z]the lampstand of pure gold and its lamps with the lamps set and all its utensils, and the oil for the light; 38 [a]the golden altar, the anointing oil and the fragrant incense, and [b]the screen for the entrance of the tent; 39 the bronze altar, and its grating of bronze, its poles, and all its utensils; the basin and its stand; 40 [c]the hangings of the court, its pillars, and its bases, and the [d]screen for the gate of the court, its [e]cords, and its pegs; and all the utensils for the service of the tabernacle, for the tent of meeting; 41 the finely worked garments for ministering in the Holy Place, the holy garments for Aaron the priest, and the garments of his sons for their service as priests. 42 [f]According to all that the LORD had commanded Moses, so the people of Israel had done all the work. 43 And Moses saw all the work, and behold, they had done it; as the LORD had commanded, so had they done it. Then Moses [g]blessed them.

The Tabernacle Erected

40 The LORD spoke to Moses, saying, 2 "On the [h]first day of the first month you shall [i]erect the tabernacle of the tent of meeting. 3 And you shall put in it the ark of the testimony, and you shall [j]screen the ark with the veil. 4 And [k]you shall bring in the table and arrange it, and [l]you shall bring in the lampstand and set up its lamps. 5 [m]And you shall put the golden altar for incense before the ark of the testimony, and set up the screen for the door of the tabernacle. 6 [n]You shall set the altar of burnt offering before the door of the tabernacle of the tent of meeting, 7 [o]and place the basin between the tent of meeting and the altar, and put water in it. 8 And you shall set up the court all around, and hang up the screen for the gate of the court.

9 "Then you shall take the [p]anointing oil and anoint the tabernacle and all that is in it, and consecrate it and all its furniture, so that it may become holy. 10 You shall also anoint [q]the altar of burnt offering and all its utensils, and consecrate the altar, [r]so that the altar may become most holy. 11 You shall also anoint the basin and its stand, and consecrate it. 12 [s]Then you shall bring Aaron and his sons to the entrance of the tent of meeting and shall wash them with water 13 and put on Aaron the holy garments. And you shall anoint him and consecrate him, that he may serve me as priest. 14 You shall bring his sons also and put coats on them, 15 [t]and anoint them, as you anointed their father, that they may serve me as priests. And their anointing shall admit them to a [u]perpetual priesthood throughout their generations."

16 This Moses did; according to all that the LORD commanded him, so he did. 17 In the first month in the second year, on the first day of the month, [v]the tabernacle was erected. 18 Moses erected the tabernacle. He laid its bases, and set up its frames, and put in its poles, and raised up its pillars. 19 And he spread the tent over the tabernacle and put the covering of the tent over it, as the LORD had commanded Moses. 20 He [w]took the testimony and put it into the ark, and put the poles on the ark and set the mercy seat above on the ark. 21 And he brought the ark into the tabernacle and [x]set up the veil of the screen, and screened [y]the ark of the testimony, as the LORD had commanded Moses. 22 [z]He put the table in the tent of meeting, on the north side of the tabernacle, outside the veil, 23 and arranged the bread on it before the LORD, as the LORD had commanded Moses. 24 [a]He put the lampstand in the tent of meeting, opposite the table on the south side of the tabernacle, 25 [b]and set up the lamps before the LORD, as the LORD had commanded Moses. 26 [c]He put the golden altar in the tent of meeting before the veil, 27 and burned fragrant incense on it, as the LORD had commanded Moses. 28 [d]He put in place the screen for the door of the tabernacle. 29 [e]And he set the altar of burnt offering at the entrance of the tabernacle of the tent of meeting, and offered on it the burnt offering and the [f]grain offering, as the LORD had commanded Moses. 30 [g]He set the basin between the tent of meeting and the altar, and put

37 [z][ch. 25:31]
38 [a]ch. 30:3; 37:26; 40:5, 26 [b]ch. 26:36; 36:37
40 [c]See ch. 27:9-15; 38:9-17; [d]ch. 27:16; 38:18 [e]ch. 35:18
42 [f]ch. 35:10
43 [g]Lev. 9:22, 23; Josh. 22:6; 2 Sam. 6:18; 1 Kin. 8:14; 2 Chr. 6:3; 30:27; See Num. 6:23-27
Chapter 40
2 [h][ch. 12:2; 13:4] [i]ver. 17; ch. 26:30
3 [j]ver. 21; [ch. 35:12]
4 [k]ver. 22; ch. 26:35 [l]ver. 24, 25
5 [m]ver. 26; [ch. 39:38]
6 [n]ver. 29
7 [o]ver. 30; ch. 30:18
9 [p]ch. 30:26
10 [q]ch. 30:28 [r]ch. 29:37
12 [s]See Lev. 8:1-13
15 [t]ch. 28:41; 29:7 [u]Num. 25:13
17 [v]ver. 1; Num. 7:1
20 [w]ch. 25:16; See ch. 16:34
21 [x]ver. 3; See ch. 35:12 [y]ver. 3, 20
22 [z]ver. 4; ch. 26:35
24 [a]ch. 26:35
25 [b]ver. 4; ch. 25:37
26 [c]ver. 5; ch. 30:6, 7
28 [d]ver. 5; ch. 26:36
29 [e]ver. 6 [f]ch. 29:41; 30:9
30 [g]ver. 7

40:1–33 The Lord's detailed instructions to Moses regarding the erection of the tabernacle and the consecration of tabernacle and priests (vv. 1–15) and the subsequent narrative of Moses' obedience (vv. 16–33) emphasize that the tabernacle was completed and its ministry inaugurated in precise obedience to the divine commands.

40:2 erect the tabernacle. The tabernacle is set up about nine months (v. 17; 12:2, 6) after the arrival at Sinai.

water in it for washing, 31 with which Moses
and [h]Aaron and his sons [i]washed their
hands and their feet. 32 When they went into
the tent of meeting, and when they
approached the altar, they washed, as the
LORD commanded Moses. 33 [j]And he erected
the court around the tabernacle and the
altar, and set up the screen of the gate of the
court. So [k]Moses finished the work.

The Glory of the LORD

34 Then [l]the cloud covered the tent of
meeting, and [m]the glory of the LORD filled
the tabernacle. 35 And Moses was not able
to enter the tent of meeting because the
cloud settled on it, and the glory of the
LORD filled the tabernacle. 36 Throughout all
their journeys, [n]whenever the cloud was
taken up from over the tabernacle, the
people of Israel would set out. 37 But [o]if the
cloud was not taken up, then they did not
set out till the day that it was taken up.
38 For the cloud of the LORD was on the tabernacle by day, and fire was in it by night,
in the sight of all the house of Israel
throughout all their journeys.

31 [h]ch. 30:19, 20; [i]ch. 30:21
33 [j]ver. 8; ch. 27:9, 16 [k][Heb. 3:2, 5]
34 [l]See ch. 13:21 [m]ch. 29:43; Lev. 16:2; Num. 9:15; [1 Kin. 8:10, 11; 2 Chr. 5:13, 14; 7:2; Isai. 6:4; Hag. 2:7, 9; Rev. 15:8]
36 [n]Num. 9:17; 10:11; [Neh. 9:19]
37 [o]See Num. 9:19-22

40:31 washed their hands and their feet. Following the placement of the basin, Moses and Aaron complied with the law of priestly washing (30:19–21).

40:34–38 The glory of the Lord filling the tabernacle brings the Book of Exodus to a climax. God, who had brought Israel out of Egypt, has made and renewed His covenant with them and made His dwelling in their midst. A careful recapitulation of the primary theme of the book—the reestablishment of God's dwelling with man—is given in vv. 34–38. This passage also indicates that Israel has begun corporate worship. The history of God's guidance to the Promised Land will follow in the remainder of the Pentateuch.

40:36 Throughout all their journeys. Israel's journeys are linked to the guiding Presence. The covenant God dwells among His people at last and will lead the nation to the land He promised them.

THE THIRD BOOK OF MOSES CALLED

Leviticus

AUTHOR

The conclusion that Moses wrote Leviticus derives from the internal character of Leviticus itself and of the Pentateuch as a whole, as well as from Old and New Testament references to Moses as the author of the Pentateuch. For a more complete discussion of issues relating to Mosaic authorship, see "Introduction to the Pentateuch."

DATE AND OCCASION

Leviticus everywhere reports the words of God to Moses and his brother Aaron, but it never states when and how these words were written down. The precise date Leviticus was committed to writing remains somewhat uncertain, though it doubtless occurred during the wilderness wandering prior to Moses' death (c. 1406 B.C.). The majority of critical scholars place the writing of Leviticus in the postexilic era (c. the sixth century B.C.), many centuries after Moses. This view is improbable, however, because the content of Leviticus does not fit such a late period: the worship of the second temple differed significantly from that enjoined in Leviticus, and Leviticus is presupposed or quoted by earlier books such as Deuteronomy, Amos, and, most obviously, Ezekiel. Other arguments against the origin of Leviticus in Moses' time are also unconvincing. The book reflects the ideals of worship and holiness that were accepted in Israel from the time of Moses to the fall of Jerusalem in 587/86 B.C.

CHARACTERISTICS AND THEMES

No book in the Old Testament presents a greater challenge to the modern reader than Leviticus, and imagination is required to picture the ceremonies and rites that form the bulk of the book. However, it is important to try to understand the rituals in Leviticus for two reasons. First, rituals enshrine, express, and teach those values and ideas that a society holds most dear. By analyzing the ceremonies described in Leviticus, we can learn about what was most important to the Old Testament Israelites. Second, these same ideas are foundational for the New Testament writers. Particularly the concepts of sin, sacrifice, and atonement found in Leviticus are used in the New Testament to interpret the death of Christ.

Precisely because the rituals of Leviticus are so central to Old Testament thinking, they are often obscure to us, because the writers did not need to explain them to their contemporaries. Every Israelite knew why a particular sacrifice was offered on a specific occasion and what a certain gesture meant. For ourselves, every hint in the text must be grasped to understand these things, and a judicious reading between the lines is sometimes required.

Leviticus is part of the covenant law given at Sinai. The ideas that inform the whole Sinaitic covenant, including God's sovereign grace in choosing Israel and His moral demands, are also presupposed here. Certain themes are especially prominent in Leviticus. First, God is present with His people. Second, because God is holy, His people must also be holy (11:45). Since man is sinful, he cannot dwell with the holy God. Contact between the sinner and the divine holiness may result in death. Hence, atonement for sin through the offering of sacrifice is of paramount importance. These themes may be elaborated as follows.

1. The Divine Presence. Every act of worship is performed "to the LORD" (e.g., 1:2), who dwells with His people in the tabernacle of meeting. Because God is present in the Most

Holy Place, entry is barred to all but the high priest once a year on the Day of Atonement (16:17). Though God's presence is usually invisible, He may manifest His glory on special occasions such as the ordination of the priests (9:23, 24). The greatest of God's gifts is that He deigns to dwell with His people (26:12).

2. Holiness. The aims of Leviticus are summarized in 11:45: "You shall therefore be holy; for I am holy." Man is meant to be like God in his character. That involves imitating God in daily life. The holiness of God involves His being the source of perfect life in its physical, spiritual, and moral dimensions. Animals offered to Him in sacrifice must be free of blemish (1:3), and priests who represent God to man and man to God must be free of physical handicaps (21:17–23). Those who suffer discharges, particularly of blood, or who have disfiguring skin diseases are barred from worship until they are cured (chs. 12–15). Physical health is seen to symbolize the perfection of divine life. But holiness is also an inward matter of attitudes issuing in moral behavior. The theme of holiness is especially emphasized in chs. 17–25, which are chiefly concerned with personal ethical conduct, summed up in 19:18 as "you shall love your neighbor as yourself."

3. Atonement Through Sacrifice. Since man failed to live up to God's righteous requirements, a means of atonement was essential so that both his moral lapses and his physical failings could be pardoned. To this end Leviticus gives the most extensive descriptions of the sacrificial system (chs. 1–7), the role of the priests (chs. 8–10; 21–22), and the great national festivals (chs. 16; 23; 25) found in the Old Testament. These great ceremonies were designed to make possible the coexistence of the holy God with His sinful people.

Through the symbols and rites it describes, Leviticus paints a picture of God's character that is presupposed and deepened in the New Testament. Leviticus teaches that God is the source of perfect life, that He loves His people, and that He desires to dwell among them. In this we see a foreshadowing of the Incarnation, when "the Word became flesh and dwelt among us" (John 1:14). Leviticus also shows clearly man's sinfulness: no sooner are Aaron's sons ordained than they profane their office and die in a fearful display of divine judgment (ch. 10). Those suffering from skin disease or bodily discharge, as well as those guilty of grave moral sins, are barred from worship because their imperfections are incompatible with a holy and perfect God (chs. 12–15). The symbols of Leviticus teach the universality of human sin, a doctrine endorsed by Jesus (Mark 7:21–23) and Paul (Rom. 3:23). Caught between divine holiness and human sinfulness, man's paramount need is for atonement. It is here that Leviticus has the most to teach the Christian, for its ideas are taken up and developed by the New Testament in describing the atoning work of Christ. He is the perfect sacrificial Lamb, who takes away the sin of the world (John 1:29). His death is the ransom for many (Mark 10:45). His blood cleanses us from all sin (1 John 1:7). Above all, Jesus is the perfect High Priest who enters not the earthly tabernacle once a year on the Day of Atonement (ch. 16), but has ascended to the heavenly tabernacle forever, because He has not offered merely a goat for the sins of His people, but His own life (Heb. 9; 10). The rending of the temple veil when Jesus was crucified was a visible demonstration that His death opened up the way to God for all believers (Matt. 27:51; Heb. 10:19, 20). Furthermore, Leviticus restricts salvation to the old covenant community of Israel. The food laws (ch. 11) and the prohibitions on mixtures (19:19) reminded Jews of their unique status. But the New Testament opens the kingdom to all nations and abrogates the food laws (Mark 7:14–23; Acts 10), while at the same time insisting on the separation of the church from the world (John 17:16; 2 Cor. 6:14–7:1). And while the Old Testament sufferer had to wait for God to heal him (ch. 14), in the Gospels God in Christ drew near and healed both lepers and those with discharges (Luke 8:43–48; 17:12–19). The God of Leviticus, whose essential character is shown to be holy life, is shown in the Gospels to be present in Christ and His redemptive work.

Leviticus, the Latin form of the Greek title of the book, means "about Levites." The Levites were the tribe of Israel from which the priests were drawn; they were responsible for maintaining Israel's worship facilities and practices. The title is apt, because the book is primarily about worship and fitness for worship. However it is not addressed solely to priests or Levites, but also to lay Israelites, telling them how to offer sacrifices and to enter the presence of God in worship. Leviticus speaks to humanity in every age, reminding us of the depth of our sin, but also pointing us to the sacrifice of Him whose blood is far more effective than the blood of bulls and goats.

OUTLINE OF LEVITICUS

- **I. Laws on Sacrifice (chs. 1–7)**
  - *A. Instructions for the Laity (1:1–6:7)*
    1. The Burnt Offering (ch. 1)
    2. The Grain Offering (ch. 2)
    3. The Peace Offering (ch. 3)
    4. The Sin Offering (4:1–5:13)
    5. The Guilt Offering (5:14–6:7)
  - *B. Instructions for the Priests (6:8–7:38)*
    1. The Burnt Offering (6:8–13)
    2. The Grain Offering (6:14–23)
    3. The Sin Offering (6:24–30)
    4. The Guilt Offering (7:1–10)
    5. The Peace Offering (7:11–36)
    6. Summary (7:37, 38)
- **II. Institution of Priesthood (chs. 8–10)**
  - *A. Consecration of Aaron and His Sons (ch. 8)*
  - *B. Aaron's First Sacrifices (ch. 9)*
  - *C. Judgment on Aaron's Sons (ch. 10)*
- **III. Uncleanness and Its Treatment (chs. 11–16)**
  - *A. Unclean Animals (ch. 11)*
  - *B. Childbirth (ch. 12)*
  - *C. Skin Disease (chs. 13; 14)*
  - *D. Discharges (ch. 15)*
  - *E. The Day of Atonement (ch. 16)*
- **IV. The Practice of Holiness (chs. 17–27)**
  - *A. Sacrifice and Food (ch. 17)*
  - *B. Sexual Behavior (ch. 18)*
  - *C. Principles of Good Neighborliness (ch. 19)*
  - *D. Capital Crimes (ch. 20)*
  - *E. Disqualifications for Priests (ch. 21)*
  - *F. Rules on Sacrifice (ch. 22)*
  - *G. Feasts (ch. 23)*
  - *H. The Tabernacle Lamps and Loaves (24:1–9)*
  - *I. Blasphemy (24:10–23)*
  - *J. Years of Release (ch. 25)*
  - *K. The Blessing and Curse (ch. 26)*
  - *L. Rules on Vows and Tithes (ch. 27)*

Laws for Burnt Offerings

1 [a]The LORD called Moses and spoke to
him [b]from the tent of meeting, saying,
2 "Speak to the people of Israel and say to
them, [c]When any one of you brings an offering to the LORD, you shall bring your offering
of livestock from the herd or from the flock.
3 "If his offering is a burnt offering from
the herd, he shall offer [d]a male without
blemish. He shall bring it to the entrance of
the tent of meeting, that he may be accepted before the LORD. 4 [e]He shall lay his hand
on the head of the burnt offering, and it
shall be [f]accepted for him [g]to make atonement for him. 5 Then he shall kill the bull
before the LORD, and Aaron's sons the
priests shall bring the blood [h]and throw the
blood against the sides of the altar that is at
the entrance of the tent of meeting. 6 Then

Chapter 1
1 [a]Ex. 19:3 [b]Ex. 40:34, 35
2 [c]ch. 22:18, 19
3 [d]See Ex. 12:5
4 [e]Ch. 3:2, 8, 13; 4:4, 15, 24, 29, 33; 8:14, 18, 22; 16:21; Ex. 29:10, 15, 19 [f]ch. 22:21, 27; [Isai. 56:7; Rom. 12:1; Phil. 4:18] [g]ch. 4:20, 26, 31, 35; Num. 15:25; 2 Chr. 29:23, 24; [ch. 9:7; 16:24]
5 [h]ch. 3:8; 2 Chr. 35:11; Heb. 12:24; 1 Pet. 1:2

1:1, 2 Moses begins this manual on worship at the tabernacle by recording the laws of sacrifice. The laws are subdivided into sections addressed to the laity (1:1–6:7) and to the priests (6:8–7:38). Sacrifice in Israel involved the offering of selected domestic animals, grain, oil, and wine. All these products symbolized the worshiping Israelite, who, through the act of sacrifice, was giving himself back to God in some way. In every animal offering the worshiper placed his hand on the victim's head, thereby identifying himself with the animal, saying in effect, "This animal represents me." The animal sacrifices involved the animal's death, and so the sacrifices had atoning symbolism: the animal dying in the sinful worshiper's place represented redemption from the death he deserved. There is then a common core of meaning and significance shared by all the sacrifices. But each sacrifice also had its own distinctive ritual features and religious emphases. This is indicated by the different names of the sacrifices, which sometimes highlight the ritual distinctiveness ("*burnt* offering,") and sometimes the theologically distinctive feature ("*peace* offering, *guilt* offering").

Although the Lord, in response to Moses' intercession (Ex. 32), had rescinded His verdict to judge the people for their idolatrous worship of the golden calf, the removal of their sin remained an unresolved problem. These sacrifices provided an atonement for them and for Aaron, their priest, who led them into that sin (ch. 9). In contrast to Aaron, Jesus Christ, the High Priest of the new Israel, is without sin and never tempts His people to sin (Heb. 9:6–15).

1:1 tent of meeting. The tent shrine or tabernacle described in Ex. 26.

1:2 you shall bring. Israel must obey this manual of instruction on how to be fit to live in the presence of God. God, not humans, prescribes the way His people must live with Him.

of livestock. Only unblemished (v. 3) domesticated animals could be offered. Wild animals, which cost nothing, could not be offered.

1:3–17 The burnt offering begins the list of sacrifices because it was the sacrifice offered most frequently. Its distinctive feature was that the whole animal, except for the skin, was burned on the altar. This symbolized the total consecration of the worshiper to God's service, and served to cover the sins of the worshiper (v. 4 and note). The regulations begin by specifying the most expensive kind of animal that could be offered, the bull (vv. 2–9), and end with the cheapest, the young pigeon (vv. 14–17).

1:3 he shall offer. The layman offering the sacrifice (vv. 4–6, 9) was to kill, skin, cut up, and wash the animal, whereas the priest brings it to God by putting the blood and flesh on the altar.

entrance of the tent. The screened-off courtyard surrounding the tabernacle of meeting. The great altar and a laver for washing the sacrifices stood in the courtyard (v. 9).

1:4 make atonement. Lit. "to cover over." The death of the animal in place of the sinner "covers over" or shields the worshiper from the holy wrath of God.

he shall flay the burnt offering and cut it into pieces, 7 and the sons of Aaron the priest shall put fire on the altar and [i]arrange wood on the fire. 8 And Aaron's sons the priests shall arrange the pieces, the head, and the fat, on the wood that is on the fire on the altar; 9 but its entrails and its legs he shall wash with water. And the priest shall burn all of it on the altar, as [j]a burnt offering, a food offering[1] with a [k]pleasing aroma to the LORD.

10 "If his gift for a burnt offering is from the flock, from the sheep or goats, he shall bring a male without blemish, 11 [l]and he shall kill it on the north side of the altar before the LORD, and Aaron's sons the priests shall throw its blood against the sides of the altar. 12 And he shall cut it into pieces, with its head and its fat, and the priest shall arrange them on the wood that is on the fire on the altar, 13 but the entrails and the legs he shall wash with water. And the priest shall offer all of it and burn it on the altar; it is [j]a burnt offering, a food offering with [k]a pleasing aroma to the LORD.

14 "If his offering to the LORD is a burnt offering of birds, then he shall bring his offering of [m]turtledoves or pigeons. 15 And the priest shall bring it to the altar and wring off its head and burn it on the altar. Its blood shall be drained out on the side of the altar. 16 He shall remove its crop with its contents[2] and cast it [n]beside the altar on the east side, in the place for ashes. 17 He shall tear it open by its wings, but [o]shall not sever it completely. And the priest shall burn it on the altar, on the wood that is on the fire. It is a burnt offering, a food offering with a pleasing aroma to the LORD.

Laws for Grain Offerings

2 "When anyone brings a [p]grain offering as an offering to the LORD, his offering shall be of fine flour. [q]He shall pour oil on it and put frankincense on it 2 and bring it to Aaron's sons the priests. And he shall take from it a handful of the fine flour and oil, with all of its frankincense, and the priest shall burn this as its [r]memorial portion on the altar, a food [s]offering with a pleasing aroma to the LORD. 3 But the [t]rest of the grain offering shall be for Aaron and his sons; [u]it is a most holy part of the LORD's food offerings.

4 "When you bring a grain offering baked in the oven as an offering, it shall be [v]unleavened loaves of fine flour mixed with oil or unleavened wafers smeared with oil. 5 And if your offering is a grain offering [w]baked on a griddle, it shall be of fine flour unleavened, mixed with oil. 6 You shall break it in pieces and pour oil on it; it is a grain offering. 7 And if your offering is a grain offering cooked in a pan, it shall be made of fine flour with oil. 8 And you shall bring the grain offering that is made of these things to the LORD, and when it is presented to the priest, he shall bring it to the altar. 9 And the priest shall take from the grain offering its memorial portion and burn this on the altar, a food [x]offering with a [y]pleasing aroma to the LORD. 10 But the [z]rest of the grain offering shall be for Aaron and his sons; [z]it is a most holy part of the LORD's food offerings.

11 "No grain offering that you bring to the LORD shall be made with [a]leaven, for you shall burn no leaven nor any honey as a food offering to the LORD. 12 [b]As an offering of firstfruits you may bring them to the LORD, but they shall not be offered on the altar for a pleasing aroma. 13 You [c]shall season all your grain offerings with salt. You shall not let the [d]salt of the covenant with your God be missing from your grain offering; [e]with all your offerings you shall offer salt.

14 "If you offer a grain offering of firstfruits to the LORD, you shall offer for the

1 Or *offering by fire*; so throughout Leviticus 2 Or *feathers*

7 [i][Gen. 22:9]
9 [j]ch. 2:3, 9, 10, 11, 16; 3:5, 9, 11, 14, 16; 4:35; Ex. 29:18, 25, 41; [k]See Gen. 8:21
11 [l]ver. 5
13 [j][See ver. 9 above] [k][See ver. 9 above]
14 [m]ch. 5:7; 12:8; [Luke 2:24]
16 [n]ch. 6:10
17 [o][Gen. 15:10]
Chapter 2
1 [p]ch. 6:14; 9:17; Num. 15:4; [q]ver. 15
2 [r]ver. 9, 16; ch. 5:12; 6:15; 24:7; [Acts 10:4] [s]See ch. 1:9
3 [t]ch. 7:9; 10:12, 13 [u][Ex. 40:10]
4 [v]Ex. 29:2
5 [w]ch. 6:21; 7:9; [1 Chr. 23:29; Ezek. 4:3]
9 [x]See ch. 1:9 [y][Phil. 4:18]
10 [z]ver. 3
11 [a]ch. 6:17; [Matt. 16:12; Mark 8:15; Luke 12:1; 1 Cor. 5:8; Gal. 5:9]
12 [b]See Ex. 23:19
13 [c]Col. 4:6 [d]Num. 18:19; [2 Chr. 13:5] [e]Ezek. 43:24

1:9 pleasing aroma to the LORD. The meaning of this phrase is seen most clearly in Gen. 8:21. Sacrifices averted God's anger, causing Him to look benevolently on the worshiper. The New Testament speaks of the death of Christ in similar language (Eph. 5:2).

1:10–13 Sheep and goats were sacrificed in the same way as bulls vv. 3–9.

1:14–17 A simpler procedure was prescribed for doves or pigeons, the offering of the poor. The priest carried out the whole ceremony.

2:1 grain offering. Usually offered in conjunction with an animal sacrifice, it consisted of wheat flour mixed with olive oil, incense, and salt. The mixture was baked, fried, or cooked. Like the other sacrifices, the grain offering symbolized the worshiper's dedication of himself to God.

2:2 memorial. Only a handful of the grain offering was burned; the rest went to the priest (v. 3). Such offerings constituted an important part of a priest's income.

2:11 leaven nor any honey. Possibly omitted because they cause fermentation, which suggests corruption.

2:13 salt. Probably because it is indestructible by fire, salt symbolizes the enduring covenant between God and Israel (Num. 18:19 note).

2:14 firstfruits. See 23:9–14; Deut. 26:1–11. The Israelite was expected to give the first of his harvest to God, and on this occasion the grain offering was prepared differently.

grain offering of your firstfruits fresh [f]ears,
roasted with fire, crushed new grain. 15 And
[g]you shall put oil on it and lay frankincense
on it; it is a grain offering. 16 And the priest
shall burn as its [h]memorial portion some of
the crushed grain and some of the oil with
all of its frankincense; it is a food offering
to the LORD.

Laws for Peace Offerings

3 "If his offering is [i]a sacrifice of peace
offering, if he offers an animal from the
herd, male or female, [j]he shall offer it [k]with-
out blemish before the LORD. 2 And [l]he shall
lay his hand on the head of his offering and
kill it at the entrance of the tent of meeting,
and Aaron's sons the priests shall throw the
blood against the sides of the altar. 3 And
from the sacrifice of the peace offering, as a
food offering to the LORD, he shall offer [m]the
fat covering the entrails and all the fat that
is on the entrails, 4 [n]and the two kidneys
with the fat that is on them at the loins, and
the long lobe of the liver that he shall
remove with the kidneys. 5 Then Aaron's
sons [o]shall burn it on the altar on top of the
burnt offering, which is on the wood on the
fire; it is a food offering with a pleasing
aroma to the LORD.

6 "If his offering for a sacrifice of peace
offering to the LORD is an animal from the
flock, male or female, he shall offer it
[k]without blemish. 7 If he offers a lamb for
his offering, then he shall offer it before
the LORD, 8 lay his hand on the head of his
offering, and kill it in front of the tent of
meeting; and Aaron's sons shall throw its
blood against the sides of the altar. 9 Then
from the sacrifice of the peace offering he
shall offer as a food offering to the LORD its
fat; he shall remove the whole [p]fat tail, cut
off close to the backbone, and the fat that
covers the entrails and all the fat that is on
the entrails 10 and the two kidneys with the
fat that is on them at the loins and the
long lobe of the liver that he shall remove
[q]with the kidneys. 11 And the priest shall
burn it on the altar as [r]a food offering to
the LORD.

12 "If his offering is a goat, then he shall
offer it before the LORD 13 and lay his hand
on its head and kill it in front of the tent of
meeting, and the sons of Aaron shall throw
its blood against the sides of the altar.
14 Then he shall offer from it, as his offering
for a food offering to the LORD, the fat covering the entrails and all the fat that is on
the entrails 15 and the two kidneys with the
fat that is on them at the loins and the long
lobe of the liver that he shall remove [q]with
the kidneys. 16 And the priest shall burn
them on the altar as a [r]food offering with a
pleasing aroma. [s]All fat is the LORD's. 17 It
shall be a statute forever throughout your
generations, in all your dwelling places,
that you eat neither [s]fat nor [t]blood."

Laws for Sin Offerings

4 And the LORD spoke to Moses, saying,
2 "Speak to the people of Israel, saying,
[u]If anyone sins unintentionally[1] in any of
the LORD's commandments [v]about things
not to be done, and does any one of them,

14 [f]ch. 23:14; [Josh. 5:11]
15 [g]ver. 1
16 [h]See ver. 2
Chapter 3
1 [i]ch. 17:5; 22:21; 23:19; Amos 5:22; See ch. 7:11-21, 29-34 [j]ver. 7, 12 [k]See Ex. 12:5
2 [l]See ch. 1:4
3 [m]ch. 4:8, 9; Ex. 29:13, 22
4 [n]ver. 10
5 [o]ch. 6:12
6 [k][See ver. 1 above]
9 [p]ch. 9:19; Ex. 29:22
10 [q]ver. 4
11 [r]ch. 21:6, 8, 17, 21, 22; 22:7, 25; Num. 28:2; Ezek. 44:7; Mal. 1:7
15 [q][See ver. 10 above]
16 [r][See ver. 11 above] [s]ch. 7:23-25; 1 Sam. 2:15; Ezek. 44:7, 15
17 [s][See ver. 16 above] [t]ch. 7:26; 17:10, 14; 19:26; Gen. 9:4; Deut. 12:16, 23; 15:23; 1 Sam. 14:33; Acts 15:20, 29
Chapter 4
2 [u]ch. 5:15, 18; [Ps. 19:12]; See Num. 15:22-29 [v]ver. 13, 22, 27; ch. 5:17

[1] Or *by mistake*; so throughout Leviticus

3:1 peace offering. Also called the "fellowship" or "covenant" offering. The Hebrew term used is related to the word *shalom,* meaning "peace, well-being." This sacrifice was unique in that the worshiper and his family could eat much of the meat, only a part being given to the priests or burned on the altar. It was a sacrifice brought when someone was seeking God's blessing or celebrating blessings received. It was offered to underline a solemn prayer (such as a vow), or when such a prayer was answered, or out of simple gratitude (7:16). Eating meat was a rare luxury in ancient times and was usually something of a celebration. Moses prescribed that every animal killed for food must be offered in sacrifice first (17:3 note), so at least during the wilderness period every meal involving meat was preceded by a peace offering.

3:3, 4 The choicest parts of the carcass were symbolically given to God by being burned. The kidneys symbolized the seat of the emotions (Jer. 17:10 text note).

3:11 as a food offering. The Old Testament insists that God supplies man with food, not vice versa (Gen. 1:29; Ps. 50:12–14). Therefore this comment must be understood figuratively, that God is pleased with the sacrifice offered in faith (cf. Heb. 11:4), just as human beings enjoy food.

3:17 neither fat nor blood. Fat from sacrificial animals belonged to God (v. 3). Eating blood means eating meat from which the blood has not been drained (1 Sam. 14:33). The theological reason for this ban is given in 17:11 (Gen. 9:4 and note).

4:1–5:13 With the words "If anyone sins" (4:2), Moses introduces his instruction to the laity regarding the sin offering. While all sacrifices make atonement for sin to some extent, atonement is the dominant concern of the sin offering. Sin and uncleanness make a person unfit to be in God's presence and also pollute the sanctuary, making it impossible for God to dwell there. The sin offering is designed to cope with this aspect of sin by purifying both the sinner and the sanctuary. The distinctive feature of the sin offering is the use to which the sacrificial blood is put. In other sacrifices the animal's blood is splashed over the side of the altar, but in the case of the sin offering it could be applied to the horned corners of the altar, or sprinkled inside the tabernacle tent (on the incense altar or veil), or even inside the Most Holy Place. Because the tabernacle and its furniture were closely associated with the people who met God there (Heb. 9:22 note), the people's sin defiled the tabernacle as well as themselves. Such pollution required cleansing.

4:2–35 These verses deal with four cases where persons of various ranks do something sinful "unintentionally" (v. 2 text note): the high priest (vv. 3–12), the congregation (vv. 13–21), a ruler (vv. 22–26), a common person (vv. 27–35).

3 if it is the anointed priest who [w]sins, thus
bringing guilt on the people, then he shall
offer for the sin that he has committed [x]a
bull from the herd without blemish to the
LORD for a sin offering. 4 He shall bring the
bull to the [y]entrance of the tent of meeting
before the LORD and lay his hand on the
head of the bull and kill the bull before the
LORD. 5 And the anointed priest [z]shall take
some of the blood of the bull and bring it
into the tent of meeting, 6 and the priest
shall dip his finger in the blood and [z]sprin-
kle part of the blood seven times before the
LORD in front of the veil of the sanctuary.
7 And the priest [a]shall put some of the
blood on the horns of the altar of fragrant
incense before the LORD that is in the tent
of meeting, and [b]all the rest of the blood of
the bull he shall pour out at the base of the
altar of burnt offering that is at the
entrance of the tent of meeting. 8 And all
the fat of the bull of the sin offering he shall
remove from it, [c]the fat that covers the
entrails and all the fat that is on the entrails
9 [d]and the two kidneys with the fat that is
on them at the loins and the long lobe of
the liver that he shall remove with the kidneys 10 (just as these are taken from the ox
of the sacrifice of the peace offerings); and
the priest shall burn them on the altar of
burnt offering. 11 But [e]the skin of the bull
and all its flesh, with its head, its legs, its
entrails, and its dung— 12 all the rest of the
bull—he shall carry [f]outside the camp to a
clean place, to the ash heap, and shall
[g]burn it up on a fire of wood. On the ash
heap it shall be burned up.

13 [h]"If the whole congregation of Israel
sins unintentionally[1] and [i]the thing is hidden from the eyes of the assembly, and
they do any one of the things that by the
LORD's commandments ought not to be
done, and they realize their guilt,[2] 14 [j]when
the sin which they have committed
becomes known, the assembly shall offer a
bull from the herd for a sin offering and
bring it in front of the tent of meeting.
15 And the elders of the congregation [k]shall
lay their hands on the head of the bull
before the LORD, and the bull shall be killed
before the LORD. 16 Then [l]the anointed
priest shall bring some of the blood of the
bull into the tent of meeting, 17 and the
priest shall dip his finger in the blood and
sprinkle it seven times before the LORD in
front of the veil. 18 And he shall put some of
the blood on the horns of the altar that is
in the tent of meeting before the LORD, and
the rest of the blood he shall pour out at
the base of the altar of burnt offering that is
at the entrance of the tent of meeting.
19 And all its fat he shall take from it and
burn on the altar. 20 Thus shall he do with
the bull. As he did [m]with the bull of the sin
offering, so shall he do with this. [n]And the
priest shall make atonement for them, and
they shall be forgiven. 21 And he shall carry
the bull [f]outside the camp and burn it up
as he burned the first bull; it is the sin
offering for the assembly.

22 "When a leader sins, [o]doing unintentionally any one of all the things that by the
commandments of the LORD his God ought
not to be done, and realizes his guilt, 23 or
[p]the sin which he has committed is made
known to him, he shall bring as his offering
a goat, a male without blemish, 24 and
[q]shall lay his hand on the head of the goat
and kill it in the place where they kill the
burnt offering before the LORD; it is a sin
offering. 25 [r]Then the priest shall take some
of the blood of the sin offering with his

3 [w][Heb. 7:27, 28] [x]ch. 9:2
4 [y]ch. 1:3, 4
5 [z]ver. 16, 17; ch. 5:9; 16:14; Num. 19:4; [Isai, 52:15]
7 [a]ch. 8:15; 9:9; 16:18; [Ex. 39:38] [b]ch. 5:9; 8:15; 9:9; Ex. 29:12
8 [c]ch. 3:3
9 [d]ch. 3:4
11 [e]ch. 9:11; Ex. 29:14; Num. 19:5
12 [f]ch. 6:11; 10:4, 5; 14:3; 16:27; 24:14, 23; Ex. 29:14; 33:7; [g]Heb. 13:11
13 [h]Num. 15:24-26 [i]ch. 5:2-4
14 [j]ver. 23
15 [k]See ch. 1:4
16 [l]See ver. 5-12
20 [m]ver. 3 [n]Num. 15:25, 28
21 [f][See ver. 12 above]
22 [o]ver. 2, 13, 27
23 [p]ver. 14
24 [q]See ch. 1:4
25 [r]ver. 7, 18, 30, 34

1 Or *makes a mistake* 2 Or *suffer for their guilt*, or *are guilty*; also verses 22, 27, and chapter 5

4:3 anointed priest. The high priest. His sin has the direct consequence of "bringing guilt on the people" and requires the most expensive atonement, a bull.

he shall offer. The sin and guilt offerings were compulsory after committing certain sins, whereas the other offerings could sometimes be offered voluntarily when the worshiper felt so inclined.

4:6 The serious effects of high priestly sin are shown by the need to purify "the veil of the sanctuary" (the veil separating the Most Holy Place from the Holy Place, Ex. 26:31–35).

4:7 the altar of fragrant incense. This piece of sacred furniture stood in front of the curtain leading into the Most Holy Place. It was cleansed by sprinkling with blood, the holy cleansing agent, making it possible for God to dwell in the tent. At the same time the high priest, who personified the nation, was cleansed.

4:12 outside the camp. See Heb. 13:11–13 and notes.

a clean place. Many places outside the camp contained impurity that would make the priest unfit to officiate in worship. He was to avoid these, and put the ashes left from the burnt offering in a designated clean place, where the remainder of the sacrificial bull was burned.

4:13–21 For sin involving the congregation as a whole, a procedure like that in vv. 3–12 is prescribed, with the community elders representing the people at the altar (v. 15).

4:22–26 A sin by a leader of a tribe or clan was not as serious a threat to the nation's holiness as the first two cases (vv. 3–21). This is reflected in that he was required to offer only a male goat (v. 23), whose blood was applied, not within the tent but outside, to the altar of burnt offering (v. 25).

finger and put it on the horns of the altar of
burnt offering and pour out the rest of its
blood at the base of the altar of burnt offering. 26 And all its fat he shall burn on the
altar, like [s]the fat of the sacrifice of peace
offerings. So [t]the priest shall make atonement for him for his sin, and he shall be
forgiven.

27 "If [u]anyone of the common people sins
unintentionally in doing any one of the
things that by the LORD's commandments
ought not to be done, and realizes his guilt,
28 [v]or the sin which he has committed is
made known to him, he shall bring for his
offering a goat, a female without blemish,
for his sin which he has committed. 29 [w]And
he shall lay his hand on the head of the sin
offering and kill the sin offering in the
place of burnt offering. 30 And the priest
shall take some of its blood with his finger
and put it on the horns of the altar of burnt
offering and pour out all the rest of its
blood at the base of the altar. 31 And [x]all its
fat he shall remove, [y]as the fat is removed
from the peace offerings, and the priest
shall burn it on the altar for a [z]pleasing
aroma to the LORD. [a]And the priest shall
make atonement for him, and he shall be
forgiven.

32 "If he brings a lamb as his offering for
a sin offering, he shall bring [b]a female without blemish 33 [w]and lay his hand on the
head of the sin offering and kill it for a sin
offering in the place where they kill the
burnt offering. 34 Then the priest shall take
some of the blood of the sin offering with
his finger and put it on the horns of the
altar of burnt offering and pour out all the
rest of its blood at the base of the altar.
35 And all its fat he shall remove [c]as the fat
of the lamb is removed from the sacrifice of
peace offerings, and the priest shall burn it
on the altar, on top of the LORD's food
offerings. [d]And the priest shall make atonement for him for the sin which he has
committed, and he shall be forgiven.

5 "If anyone sins in that he hears a public [e]adjuration to testify, and though
he is a witness, whether he has seen or
come to know the matter, yet does not
speak, he shall [f]bear his iniquity; 2 or [g]if
anyone touches an unclean thing, whether
a carcass of an unclean wild animal or a
carcass of unclean livestock or a carcass of
unclean swarming things, and it is hidden
from him and he has become unclean, and
he realizes his guilt; 3 or if he touches [h]hu-
man uncleanness, of whatever sort the
uncleanness may be with which one
becomes unclean, and it is hidden from
him, when he comes to know it, and realizes his guilt; 4 or if anyone utters with his
lips a [i]rash oath to do evil or to do good,
any sort of rash oath that people [j]swear,
and it is hidden from him, when he comes
to know it, and he realizes his guilt in any
of these; 5 when he realizes his guilt in any
of these and [k]confesses the sin he has committed, 6 he shall bring to the LORD as his
compensation[1] for the sin that he has committed, a female from the flock, a lamb or a
goat, for a sin offering. And the priest shall
make atonement for him for his sin.

7 "But [l]if he cannot afford a lamb, then he
shall bring to the LORD as his compensation
for the sin that he has committed two [m]tur-
tledoves or two pigeons,[2] one for a sin offering and the other for a burnt offering. 8 He
shall bring them to the priest, who shall
offer first the one for the sin offering. He
shall [n]wring its head from its neck [n]but
shall not sever it completely, 9 and he shall
sprinkle some of the blood of the sin offering on the side of the altar, while [o]the rest
of the blood shall be drained out [p]at the
base of the altar; it is a sin offering. 10 Then

26 [s]ver. 10:31; ch. 3:3, 5 [t]ver. 20, 31, 35; ch. 5:10, 13, 16, 18; 6:7; 14:18; 15:15
27 [u]ver. 2; Num. 15:27
28 [v]ver. 14, 23
29 [w]ver. 4, 15, 24; See ch. 1:4
31 [x]ch. 3:14 [y]ver. 10, 26; ch. 3:3 [z]ch. 1:9; See Gen. 8:21 [a]ver. 20, 26, 35
32 [b]ver. 28
33 [w][See ver. 29 above]
35 [c]ch. 3:3, 9 [d]ver. 20, 26, 31

Chapter 5
1 [e]1 Kin. 8:31; Prov. 29:24; [1 Sam. 14:24, 26; Matt. 26:63] [f]ver. 17; ch. 7:18; 10:17; 17:16; 19:8; 20:17, 19; Num. 5:31; [Num. 9:13]
2 [g]ch. 11:24, 28, 31, 39; Num. 19:11, 13, 16
3 [h]See ch. 12; ch. 13; ch. 15
4 [i][Judg. 11:30, 31; 1 Sam. 14:24; 25:22; Mark 6:23; Acts 23:12] [j]Eccles. 5:2
5 [k]ch. 16:21; 26:40; Num. 5:7; Ezra 10:1; [Josh. 7:19]
7 [l]ch. 12:8; 14:21 [m]See ch. 1:14
8 [n]ch. 1:15, 17
9 [o]ch. 1:15 [p]ch. 4:7, 18, 30, 34

1 Hebrew *his guilt penalty*; so throughout Leviticus 2 Septuagint *two young pigeons*; also verse 11

4:27–35 Unintentional sins by ordinary Israelites were treated similarly to those of leaders. However they could offer a female goat instead of a male goat, and if they were poor, birds or grain (5:7–13).

5:1–13 It is debated whether this section belongs with what precedes (the sin offering, ch. 4) or with what follows (the guilt offering, 5:14–6:7). Because of the similarity of 4:1 and 5:14, and the occurrence of the Hebrew term for "sin offering" throughout 4:1–5:13, many argue that the description of the guilt offering begins at 5:14. Alternatively, the occurrence of the Hebrew word *'asham* (meaning "guilt," or "guilt offering") in 5:6, 7 has led some to conclude that the discussion of the guilt offering begins in 5:1.

5:1–6 These verses treat sins of omission, inadvertence, or rashness. The cases in view are (a) the sin of withholding evidence (v. 1); (b) the sin of contact with anything unclean (vv. 2, 3); and (c) the sin of careless oath-taking (v. 4).

5:2 unclean. See note on chs. 11–16.

5:5 These sins require confession to God in the presence of a priest and a sin offering for the forgiveness of the sinner (cf. 1 John 1:7, 9).

5:7–10 The poor man's sin offering is like the humblest burnt offering (1:14–17), except for the sprinkling of the blood (5:9; cf. 1:15).

5:10 See "The Atonement" at Rom. 3:25.

he shall offer the second for a burnt offering according to the rule. [q]And the priest shall make atonement for him for the sin that he has committed, and he shall be forgiven.

11 "But if he cannot afford two turtledoves or two pigeons, then he shall bring as his offering for the sin that he has committed a [r]tenth of an ephah[1] of fine flour for a sin offering. He [r]shall put no oil on it and shall put no frankincense on it, for it is a sin offering. 12 And he shall bring it to [s]the priest, and the priest shall take a handful of it as its memorial portion and [t]burn this on the altar, on the LORD's food offerings; it is a sin offering. 13 Thus [q]the priest shall make atonement for him for the sin which he has committed in any one of these things, and he shall be forgiven. And the remainder[2] shall be for the priest, as in the grain offering."

Laws for Guilt Offerings

14 The LORD spoke to Moses, saying, 15 [u]"If anyone commits a breach of faith and sins unintentionally in any of the holy things of the LORD, [v]he shall bring to the LORD as his compensation, a ram without blemish out of the flock, valued[3] in silver shekels,[4] according to the [w]shekel of the sanctuary, for a guilt offering. 16 He shall also make restitution for what he has done amiss in the holy thing and [x]shall add a fifth to it and give it to the priest. [q]And the priest shall make atonement for him with the ram of the guilt offering, and he shall be forgiven.

17 [y]"If anyone sins, doing any of the things that by the LORD's commandments ought not to be done, [z]though he did not know it, then realizes his guilt, he shall bear his iniquity. 18 [a]He shall bring to the priest a ram without blemish out of the flock, or its equivalent for a guilt offering, and [q]the priest shall make atonement for him for the mistake that he made unintentionally, and he shall be forgiven. 19 It is a guilt offering; he has indeed incurred guilt before[5] the LORD."

6

[6] The LORD spoke to Moses, saying, 2 "If anyone sins and [b]commits a breach of faith against the LORD by [c]deceiving his neighbor in [d]a matter of deposit or security, or through robbery, or [e]if he has oppressed his neighbor 3 or [f]has found something lost and lied about it, [g]swearing falsely—in any of all the things that people do and sin thereby— 4 if he has sinned and has realized his guilt and will restore [e]what he took by robbery or what he got by oppression or the deposit that was committed to him or the lost thing that he found 5 or anything about which he has sworn falsely, he shall [h]restore it in full and shall add a fifth to it, and give it to him to whom it belongs on the day he realizes his guilt. 6 And he shall bring to the priest as his compensation to the LORD [i]a ram without blemish out of the flock, or its equivalent for a guilt offering. 7 [j]And the priest shall make atonement for him before the LORD, and he shall be forgiven for any of the things that one may do and thereby become guilty."

The Priests and the Offerings

8 [7]The LORD spoke to Moses, saying, 9 "Command Aaron and his sons, saying, This is the law of the burnt offering. The burnt offering shall be on the hearth on the altar all night until the morning, and the fire of the altar shall be kept burning on it. 10 And [k]the priest shall put on his linen

10 [q]See ch. 4:20, 26, 31, 35
11 [r]Num. 5:15
12 [s]ch. 2:2
[t]ch. 4:35
13 [q][See ver. 10 above]
15 [u]ch. 22:14; [Ezra 10:2]
[v][Ezra 10:19]
[w]See Ex. 30:13
16 [x]ch. 6:5; 22:14; 27:13, 15, 27, 31; Num. 5:7
[q][See ver. 10 above]
17 [y]ch. 4:2
[z]Num. 15:29; [Luke 12:48]
18 [a]ver. 15
[q][See ver. 10 above]
Chapter 6
2 [b]Num. 5:6
[c]ch. 19:11
[d]Ex. 22:7, 10
[e]ch. 19:13; Mic. 2:2
3 [f]Ex. 23:4; Deut. 22:1-3
[g]ch. 19:12; Ex. 22:11
4 [e][See ver. 2 above]
5 [h]Num. 5:7; [ch. 5:16; 2 Sam. 12:6; Luke 19:8]
6 [i]ch. 5:15, 18
7 [j]See ch. 4:26
10 [k]ch. 16:4; Ezek. 44:18; See Ex. 28:39-43

1 An *ephah* was about 3/5 bushel or 22 liters 2 Septuagint; Hebrew *it* 3 Or *flock, or its equivalent* 4 A *shekel* was about 2/5 ounce or 11 grams 5 Or *he has paid full compensation to* 6 Ch 5:20 in Hebrew 7 Ch 6:1 in Hebrew

5:11–13 The items brought here as sin offerings resemble those of the grain offering of ch. 2, but no oil or incense is included.

5:14–6:7 Moses gives instructions to the laity regarding the guilt offering. While the focus of the sin offering was upon the purification of the sinner, the guilt offering was concerned with restitution or reparation. Three types of sins requiring guilt offerings are mentioned: misuse of "the holy things of the LORD" (5:15, 16), supposed sin involving things that "ought not to be done" (5:17–19), and trespass against a neighbor's rights and property (6:2–7).

5:16 holy thing. A reference to tithes and offerings, as well as property dedicated to God (22:7, 10, 14; 27:28).

add a fifth. In cases where a guilt offering was required, misappropriated property also had to be restored plus a fifth (cf. 6:5).

5:17–19 As the phrase "though he did not know it" (v. 17) indicates, these verses concern the person who suspects he has transgressed against divine law or another person but is not sure. Sacrificial remedy is provided for those with an uneasy conscience. In this instance, there is no demand for reparation because the nature of the offense is uncertain.

6:1–7 Trespasses against a neighbor require restoration of the loss plus "a fifth" (v. 5), and the offering of sacrifice to God (cf. Matt. 5:24).

6:8–7:36 Having addressed the laity concerning the laws of sacrifice, Moses now addresses the priests, especially about their entitlement to a share in the sacrifices.

6:9 burnt offering. See note 1:3–17. Christ, the High Priest of the new covenant, offered the final burnt offering in His body: He was wholly consecrated to God, suffering death for sin and bringing about the believer's death to sin (Rom. 6:2–7).

6:10 linen garment. Being white, this apparel probably symbolized purity. These garments were to cover their private parts (Ex. 20:26; 28:42 note; cf. Gen. 3:7, 21).

garment and put his linen undergarment
on his body, and he shall take up the ashes
to which the fire has reduced the burnt
offering on the altar and put them [l]beside
the altar. 11 Then [m]he shall take off his garments and put on other garments and carry
the ashes [n]outside the camp to a clean
place. 12 The fire on the altar shall be kept
burning on it; it shall not go out. The priest
shall burn wood on it every morning, and
he shall arrange the burnt offering on it and
shall burn on it [o]the fat of the peace offerings. 13 Fire shall be kept burning on the
altar continually; it shall not go out.
14 "And this is the law of [p]the grain offering. The sons of Aaron shall offer it before
the LORD in front of the altar. 15 And one
shall take from it a handful of the fine flour
of the grain offering and its oil and all the
frankincense that is on the grain offering
and burn this as its [q]memorial portion on
the altar, a pleasing aroma to the LORD.
16 And [r]the rest of it Aaron and his sons
shall eat. It shall be eaten unleavened [s]in a
holy place. In the court of the tent of meeting they shall eat it. 17 [t]It shall not be baked
with leaven. [u]I have given it as their portion
of my food offerings. [v]It is a thing most
holy, like the sin offering and the guilt
offering. 18 Every male among the children
of Aaron may eat of it, as decreed forever
throughout your generations, from the
LORD's food offerings. Whatever touches
them shall become holy."
19 The LORD spoke to Moses, saying,
20 [w]"This is the offering that Aaron and his
sons shall offer to the LORD on the day
when he is anointed: a [x]tenth of an ephah[1]
of fine flour as a regular grain offering, half
of it in the morning and half in the evening.
21 It shall be made with oil [y]on a griddle.
You shall bring it [z]well mixed, in baked[2]
pieces like a grain offering, and offer it for
a pleasing aroma to the LORD. 22 The priest
from among Aaron's sons, who is anointed
to succeed him, shall offer it to the LORD as
decreed forever. [a]The whole of it shall be
burned. 23 Every grain offering of a priest
shall be wholly burned. It shall not be
eaten."
24 The LORD spoke to Moses, saying,
25 "Speak to Aaron and his sons, saying,
[b]This is the law of the sin offering. [c]In the
place where the burnt offering is killed
shall the sin offering be killed before the
LORD; [d]it is most holy. 26 [e]The priest who
offers it for sin shall eat it. [f]In a holy place
it shall be eaten, in the court of the tent of
meeting. 27 Whatever touches its flesh shall
be holy, and when any of its blood is
splashed on a garment, you shall wash that
on which it was splashed in a holy place.
28 And [g]the earthenware vessel in which it is
boiled [h]shall be broken. But if it is boiled in
a bronze vessel, that shall be scoured and
rinsed in water. 29 Every male among the
priests may eat of it; [d]it is most holy. 30 [i]But
no sin offering shall be eaten from which
any blood is brought into the tent of meeting to make atonement in the Holy Place;
it shall be burned up with fire.

7 [j]"This is the law of the [k]guilt offering.
[l]It is most holy. 2 [m]In the place where
they kill the burnt offering they shall kill
the guilt offering, and its blood shall be
thrown against the sides of the altar. 3 And
[n]all its fat shall be offered, the fat tail, the
fat that covers the entrails, 4 the two kidneys with the fat that is on them at the
loins, and the long lobe of the liver that he
shall remove [o]with the kidneys. 5 The priest
shall burn them on the altar as a food offering to the LORD; it is a guilt offering.
6 [p]Every male among the priests may eat of
it. It shall be eaten in a holy place. [q]It is
most holy. 7 The [r]guilt offering is just like

1 An *ephah* was about 3/5 bushel or 22 liters 2 The meaning of the Hebrew is uncertain

10 [l]ch. 1:16
11 [m]ch. 16:23; Ezek. 42:14; 44:19 [n]See ch. 4:12
12 [o]ch. 3:3, 9, 14
14 [p]ch. 2:1; Num. 15:4
15 [q]ch. 2:2, 9
16 [r]ch. 2:3, 10; Ezek. 44:29; [1 Cor. 9:13] [s]ver. 26; ch. 10:12, 13
17 [t]ch. 2:11 [u]Num. 18:9 [v]ver. 25, 29; ch. 2:3; 7:1
20 [w]Ex. 29:1, 2; [x]ch. 5:11; Ex. 16:36
21 [y]ch. 2:5; 7:9 [z]7:12
22 [a]Ex. 29:25
25 [b]See ch. 4 [c]ch. 1:3, 5, 11; 4:24, 29, 33; [ch. 7:2] [d]ver. 17, 29
26 [e]ch. 10:17, 18; Num. 18:9, 19; Ezek. 44:27-29; [f]ver. 16
28 [g]ch. 11:32, 33; 15:12 [h][ch. 11:33; 15:12]
29 [d][See ver. 25 above]
30 [i]ch. 4:7, 11, 12, 18, 21; 16:27; Heb. 13:11; [ver. 26, 29; ch. 10:18]
Chapter 7
1 [j]See ch. 5:1–6:7 [k]ver. 37 [l]ch. 6:17, 25
2 [m]ch. 6:25
3 [n]ch. 3:3, 4, 9, 10, 14-16; 4:8, 9; Ex. 29:13, 22
4 [o]ch. 3:4
6 [p]ch. 6:18, 29 [q]ver. 1
7 [r]ch.6:25, 26; 14:13

6:12 fire . . . shall be kept burning. This action was perhaps prescribed as a reminder of God's continual presence and the people's need for continual atonement. The first burnt offering at the tabernacle was consumed by fire from God Himself (9:24).

6:14 grain offering. See ch. 2. As the grain offering represented the fruits of obedience, it foreshadowed Christ's life of perfect obedience and thanksgiving to God.

6:18 shall become holy. This is a warning to laity not to touch food consecrated to God in sacrifice. Contact with the sacred food would render a person ritually holy (v. 27 text note; Ex. 29:37). Those who incurred such holiness probably were temporarily placed under restrictions like those governing the activity of priests (21:1–8).

6:19–23 The priest's grain offering, mentioned here for the first time, had to be offered daily (6:20). Unlike these daily sacrifices, Christ our great High Priest offered Himself "once for all" (Heb. 7:27).

6:22 priest . . . who is anointed. The high priest.

6:24–30 sin offering. See 4:1–5:13. Christ, the new covenant High Priest, offered the final sin offering, as He bore the punishment for the believer's sins (1 Pet. 2:24; Is. 53:5).

7:1–10 guilt offering. See 5:14–6:7.

the sin offering; there is one law for them. The priest who makes atonement with it shall have it. 8 And the priest who offers any man's burnt offering shall have for himself the skin of the burnt offering that he has offered. 9 And [s]every grain offering baked [t]in the oven and all that is prepared [u]on a pan or a griddle shall belong to the priest who offers it. 10 And every grain offering, mixed with oil or dry, shall be shared equally among all the sons of Aaron.

11 "And this is the law of the sacrifice of peace offerings that one may offer to the LORD. 12 If he offers it for a thanksgiving, then he shall offer with the thanksgiving sacrifice [v]unleavened loaves mixed with oil, unleavened wafers smeared with oil, and loaves of fine flour [w]well mixed with oil. 13 [x]With the sacrifice of his peace offerings for thanksgiving he shall bring his offering with loaves of leavened bread. 14 And from it he shall offer one loaf from each offering, as a [y]gift to the LORD. [z]It shall belong to the priest who throws the blood of the peace offerings. 15 And the flesh of the sacrifice of his peace offerings [a]for thanksgiving shall be eaten on the day of his offering. He shall not leave any of it until the morning. 16 But [b]if the sacrifice of his offering is a vow offering or a freewill offering, it shall be eaten on the day that he offers his sacrifice, and on the next day what remains of it shall be eaten. 17 But what remains of the flesh of the sacrifice on the third day shall be burned up with fire. 18 If any of the flesh of the sacrifice of his peace offering is eaten on the third day, he who offers it shall not be accepted, neither shall it be credited to him. It is [c]tainted, and he who eats of it shall bear his iniquity.

19 "Flesh that touches any unclean thing shall not be eaten. It shall be burned up with fire. All who are clean may eat flesh, 20 but the person who eats of the flesh of the sacrifice of the LORD's peace offerings [d]while an uncleanness is on him, that person shall be cut off from his people. 21 And if anyone touches an unclean thing, whether [e]human uncleanness or an [f]unclean beast or any [g]unclean detestable creature, and then eats some flesh from the sacrifice of the LORD's peace offerings, that person shall be cut off from his people."

22 The LORD spoke to Moses, saying, 23 "Speak to the people of Israel, saying, [h]You shall eat no fat, of ox or sheep or goat. 24 The fat of an animal [i]that dies of itself and the fat of one that is torn by beasts may be put to any other use, but on no account shall you eat it. 25 For every person who eats of the fat of an animal of which a food offering may be made to the LORD shall be cut off from his people. 26 Moreover, [j]you shall eat no blood whatever, whether of fowl or of animal, in any of your dwelling places. 27 Whoever eats any blood, that person shall be cut off from his people."

28 The LORD spoke to Moses, saying, 29 "Speak to the people of Israel, saying, [k]Whoever offers the sacrifice of his peace offerings to the LORD shall bring his offering to the LORD from the sacrifice of his peace offerings. 30 [l]His own hands shall bring the LORD's food offerings. He shall bring the fat with [m]the breast, that the breast may be waved as a wave offering before the LORD. 31 [n]The priest shall burn the fat on the altar, but [o]the breast shall be for Aaron and his sons. 32 And [o]the right thigh you shall give to the priest as a contribution from the sacrifice of your peace offerings. 33 Whoever among the sons of Aaron offers the blood of the peace offerings and the fat shall have the right thigh for a portion. 34 For the

9 [s]ch. 2:3, 10; Num. 18:9; Ezek. 44:29; [t]ch. 2:7 [u]ch. 2:5; 6:21
12 [v]ch. 2:4; Num. 6:15 [w]ch. 6:21
13 [x]Amos 4:5
14 [y]Ex. 29:27, 28 [z]Num. 18:8, 11, 19
15 [a]ch. 22:29, 30
16 [b]ch. 19:6-8; 22:21
18 [c]ch. 19:7
20 [d]ch. 15:3; 22:3
21 [e]See ch. 12; ch. 13; ch. 15 [f]See ch. 11:24-28; [g]See ch. 11:10-23
23 [h]ch. 3:16, 17
24 [i]ch. 17:15; 22:8; Ex. 22:31; Deut. 14:21; Ezek. 4:14; 44:31
26 [j]See ch. 3:17
29 [k]ch.3:1
30 [l]ch. 3:3, 4, 9, 14 [m]See Ex. 29:24
31 [n]ch. 3:5, 11, 16 [o][ch. 9:21; Num. 6:20]
32 [o][See ver. 31 above]

7:11–36 peace offerings. See note 3:1. Here rules are given about the grain offerings that must accompany peace offerings, and how the meat must be eaten (vv. 15, 16). Christ now spiritually offers believers His flesh to eat (John 6:54–58). In His flesh and blood believers find eternal life and have communion with the Father. Through that communion, believers are transformed more and more into Christ's image (2 Cor. 3:18).

7:12 thanksgiving sacrifice. The Hebrew word here translated "thanksgiving" can also mean "confession" (of sin or of faith in response to God's goodness and mercy). The sacrifice served to underline prayers for forgiveness and healing or as an expression of gratitude for prayers answered.

7:16 vow. People in dire straits might make vows promising something to God if He would answer their prayers (Gen. 28:20–22; 1 Sam. 1:11; 2:21). Such vows were usually accompanied by a peace offering when first made and then again when fulfilled.

freewill offering. This spontaneous offering showed gratitude to God.

7:20 uncleanness. See note on chs. 11–16.

be cut off. This language is a general expression for coming under God's curse, the exact meaning of which is determined by the context of Scripture. It may mean the penalty of execution (e.g., Ex. 31:14–15) or of death without children (18:14, 29; cf. 20:20). In any event, God put the offender to death, with or without human agency.

7:25 fat. See 3:3, 17.

7:26 eat no blood. This phrase refers to eating meat from which the blood has not been drained (1 Sam. 14:33). The reason for this ban is given in 17:11 and Gen. 9:4.

breast that is [o]waved and the thigh that is [o]contributed I have taken from the people of Israel, out of the sacrifices of their peace offerings, and [p]have given them to Aaron the priest and to his sons, as a perpetual due from the people of Israel. 35 This is the portion of Aaron and of his sons from the LORD's food offerings, from the day they were presented to serve as priests of the LORD. 36 The LORD commanded this to be given them by the people of Israel, [q]from the day that he anointed them. It is a perpetual due throughout their generations."

37 This is the law [r]of the burnt offering, of the grain offering, of the sin offering, [s]of the guilt offering, [t]of the ordination offering, and [u]of the peace offering, 38 which the LORD commanded Moses on Mount Sinai, on the day that he commanded the people of Israel [v]to bring their offerings to the LORD, in the wilderness of Sinai.

Consecration of Aaron and His Sons

8 [w]The LORD spoke to Moses, saying, 2 "Take Aaron and his sons with him, and [x]the garments and [y]the anointing oil and the bull of the sin offering and the two rams and the basket of unleavened bread. 3 And assemble all the congregation at the entrance of the tent of meeting." 4 And Moses did as the LORD commanded him, and the congregation was assembled at the entrance of the tent of meeting.

5 And Moses said to the congregation, [z]"This is the thing that the LORD has commanded to be done." 6 And Moses brought Aaron and his sons and washed them with water. 7 And he put [a]the coat on him and tied the sash around his waist and clothed him with the robe and put the ephod on him and tied the skillfully woven band of the ephod around him, binding it to him with the band.[1] 8 And he placed the breastpiece on him, and [b]in the breastpiece he put the Urim and the Thummim. 9 And he set [a]the turban on his head, and [c]on the turban, in front, he set the golden plate, the holy crown, as the LORD commanded Moses.

10 [d]Then Moses took the anointing oil and anointed the tabernacle and all that was in it, and consecrated them. 11 And he sprinkled some of it on the altar seven times, and anointed the altar and all its utensils and the basin and its stand, to consecrate them. 12 And [e]he poured some of the anointing oil on Aaron's head and anointed him to consecrate him. 13 And Moses brought Aaron's sons and clothed them with coats and tied sashes around their waists and bound caps on them, as the LORD commanded Moses.

14 Then he brought [f]the bull of the sin offering, and Aaron and his sons [g]laid their hands on the head of the bull of the sin offering. 15 And he[2] killed it, and [h]Moses took the blood, and with his finger put it on the horns of the altar around it and purified the altar and poured out the blood at the base of the altar and consecrated it to make atonement for it. 16 [i]And he took all the fat that was on the entrails and the long lobe of the liver and the two kidneys with their fat, and Moses burned them on the altar. 17 But [j]the bull and its skin and its flesh and its dung he burned up with fire outside the camp, as the LORD commanded Moses.

18 [k]Then he presented the ram of the burnt offering, and Aaron and his sons laid their hands on the head of the ram. 19 And he killed it, and Moses threw the blood against the sides of the altar. 20 He cut the ram into pieces, and Moses burned [l]the head and the pieces and the fat. 21 He washed the entrails and the legs with water, and Moses burned the whole ram on the altar. It was a burnt offering with a pleasing aroma, a food offering for the LORD, as the LORD commanded Moses.

22 Then [m]he presented the other ram, the ram of ordination, and Aaron and his sons laid their hands on the head of the ram. 23 And he killed it, and Moses took some of its blood and [n]put it on the lobe of Aaron's right ear and on the thumb of his right hand

34 [o][See ver. 31 above] [p]Ex. 29:28; Num. 18:18, 19
36 [q]ch. 8:12, 30; Ex. 40:13-15
37 [r]ch. 6:9, 14, 25 [s]ver. 1 [t]ch. 6:20; Ex. 29:1 [u]ver. 11
38 [v]ch. 1:2
Chapter 8
1 [w]See Ex. 29
2 [x]See Ex. 28:2-4 [y]See Ex. 30:23-25
5 [z]Ex. 29:4
7 [a]Ex. 28:4
8 [b]See Ex. 28:30
9 [a][See ver. 5 above] [c]ch. 21:12; Ex. 28:36, 37
10 [d]See Ex. 30:26-29
12 [e]ch. 21:10, 12; Ex. 30:30; Ps. 133:2
14 [f]Ezek. 43:19 [g]ch. 4:4
15 [h]ch. 4:7; Ezek. 43:20, 26; [Heb. 9:22]
16 [i]ch. 3:4; 4:8
17 [j]ch. 4:11, 12
18 [k]ver. 2
20 [l]ch. 1:8
22 [m]ver. 2
23 [n]See ch. 14:14-17

[1] Hebrew *with it* [2] Probably Aaron or his representative; possibly Moses; also verses 16-23

8:1–10:20 The Lord instructs Moses regarding the institution of the priesthood. The narrative moves from their installation (ch. 8), through their first sacrifices (ch. 9), to God's judgment of two priests (ch. 10).

8:1–36 The instructions for the Levites' consecration (Ex. 29) are carried out. The repetition and elaborateness of the sacrifices (Ex. 29:35–37), and the splendor of Aaron's apparel (vv. 7–9) all point to the importance of the high priesthood. He represented Israel before God.

8:3 at the entrance of the tent of meeting. See note 1:3.

8:7 ephod. See note Ex. 28:6.

8:8 Urim and the Thummim. See note Ex. 28:30.

8:23 Applying the blood to the different parts of Aaron's body symbolized his entire consecration to God (Ex. 29:20 note).

and on the big toe of his right foot. 24 Then he presented Aaron's sons, and Moses put some of the blood on the lobes of their right ears and on the thumbs of their right hands and on the big toes of their right feet. And Moses threw the blood against the sides of the altar. 25 Then he took the fat and the fat tail and all the fat that was on the entrails and the long lobe of the liver and the two kidneys with their fat and the right thigh, 26 and out of the basket of unleavened bread that was before the LORD he took one unleavened loaf and one loaf of bread with oil and one wafer and placed them on the pieces of fat and on the right thigh. 27 And he put all these in the hands of Aaron and in the hands of his sons and waved them as a wave offering before the LORD. 28 Then Moses took them from their hands and burned them on the altar with the burnt offering. This was an ordination offering with a pleasing aroma, a food offering to the LORD. 29 And Moses took the breast and waved it for a wave offering before the LORD. It was Moses' portion of the ram of ordination, as the LORD commanded Moses.

30 Then [o]Moses took some of the anointing oil and of the blood that was on the altar and sprinkled it on Aaron and his garments, and also on his sons and his sons' garments. So he consecrated Aaron and his garments, and his sons and his sons' garments with him.

31 And Moses said to Aaron and his sons, "Boil the flesh at the entrance of the tent of meeting, and there eat it and the bread that is in the basket of ordination offerings, as I commanded, saying, 'Aaron and his sons shall eat it.' 32 And what remains of the flesh and the bread you shall burn up with fire. 33 And you shall not go outside the entrance of the tent of meeting for seven days, until the days of your ordination are completed, for it [p]will take seven days to ordain you. 34 As has been done today, the LORD has commanded to be done to make atonement for you. 35 At the entrance of the tent of meeting you shall remain day and night for seven days, performing what the LORD has [q]charged, so that you do not die, for so I have been commanded." 36 And Aaron and his sons did all the things that the LORD commanded by Moses.

The LORD Accepts Aaron's Offering

9 [r]On the eighth day Moses called Aaron and his sons and the elders of Israel, 2 and he said to Aaron, [s]"Take for yourself a bull calf for a sin offering and [t]a ram for a burnt offering, both without blemish, and offer them before the LORD. 3 And say to the people of Israel, [u]'Take a male goat for a sin offering, and a calf and a lamb, both a year old without blemish, for a burnt offering, 4 and an ox and a ram for peace offerings, to sacrifice before the LORD, and [v]a grain offering mixed with oil, for [w]today the LORD will appear to you.'" 5 And they brought what Moses commanded in front of the tent of meeting, and all the congregation drew near and stood before the LORD. 6 And Moses said, "This is the thing that the LORD commanded you to do, that the glory of the LORD may appear to you." 7 Then Moses said to Aaron, "Draw near to the altar and [x]offer your sin offering and your burnt offering and [y]make atonement for yourself and for the people, and bring the offering of the people and make atonement for them, as the LORD has commanded."

8 So Aaron drew near to the altar and killed the calf of the sin offering, which was for himself. 9 [z]And the sons of Aaron presented the blood to him, and he dipped his finger in the blood and [a]put it on the horns of the altar and poured out the blood at the base of the altar. 10 [b]But the fat and the kidneys and the long lobe of the liver from the sin offering he burned on the altar, [c]as the LORD commanded Moses. 11 [d]The flesh and the skin he burned up with fire outside the camp.

12 Then he killed the burnt offering, and Aaron's sons handed him the blood, and he [e]threw it against the sides of the altar. 13 [f]And they handed the burnt offering to him, piece by piece, and the head, and he burned them on the altar. 14 [g]And he washed the entrails and the legs and burned them with the burnt offering on the altar.

15 [h]Then he presented the people's offering and took the goat of the sin offering that was for the people and killed it and

30 [o]Ex. 30:30; Num. 3:3
33 [p]Ezek. 43:25, 26
35 [q]Num. 3:7; 9:19; Deut. 11:1; 1 Kin. 2:3; Zech. 3:7

Chapter 9
1 [r]Ezek. 43:27
2 [s]ch. 4:3; 8:14; Ex. 29:1
2 [t]ch. 8:18
3 [u]ch. 4:23; [Ezra 6:17]
4 [v]ver. 17; ch. 2:4 [w]ver. 6, 23; Ex. 29:43
7 [x]ch. 4:3; Heb. 5:1-3; 7:27; 9:7 [y]ch. 4:16, 20
9 [z]ch. 4:6; 8:15 [a]See ch. 4:7
10 [b]ch. 8:16 [c]ch. 4:8
11 [d]ch. 4:11; 8:17
12 [e]ch. 1:5; 8:19
13 [f]ch. 8:20
14 [g]ch. 8:21
15 [h]ver. 3, 7; Heb. 2:17; 5:3

9:1–24 The consecration of Aaron and his sons took eight days and culminated in the offering of his first sacrifices and the appearance of God's glory (9:23–24).

9:7 Note that Aaron had to make atonement for himself first and then for the people (cf. Heb. 5:3).

[i]offered it as a sin offering, [j]like the first
one. 16 And he presented the burnt offering
and offered it [k]according to the [l]rule. 17 And
he presented the [m]grain offering, took a
handful of it, and burned it on the altar,
[n]besides the burnt offering of the morning.
18 Then he killed the ox and the ram, [o]the
sacrifice of peace offerings for the people.
And Aaron's sons handed him the blood,
and he threw it against the sides of the
altar. 19 But the fat pieces of the ox and of
the ram, the fat tail and that which covers
[p]the entrails and the kidneys and the long
lobe of the liver— 20 they put the fat pieces
on the breasts, [q]and he burned the fat
pieces on the altar, 21 but the breasts and
the right thigh Aaron waved [r]for a wave
offering before the LORD, as Moses commanded.
22 Then Aaron [s]lifted up his hands toward
the people and [t]blessed them, and he came
down from offering the sin offering and the
burnt offering and the peace offerings.
23 And Moses and Aaron went into the tent
of meeting, and when they came out they
blessed the people, and [u]the glory of the
LORD appeared to all the people. 24 And [v]fire
came out from before the LORD and consumed
the burnt offering and the pieces of
fat on the altar, and when all the people
saw it, [w]they shouted and [x]fell on their
faces.

The Death of Nadab and Abihu

10 Now [y]Nadab and Abihu, the sons of
Aaron, [z]each took his censer and
put fire in it and laid incense on it and
offered [a]unauthorized[1] fire before the
LORD, which he had not commanded them.
2 And fire [b]came out from before the LORD
and consumed them, and they died before
the LORD. 3 Then Moses said to Aaron,
"This is what the LORD has said, 'Among
[c]those who are near me [d]I will be sanctified,
and before all the people I will be glorified.'"
[e]And Aaron held his peace.
4 And Moses called Mishael and Elzaphan,
the sons of [f]Uzziel the uncle of Aaron,
and said to them, "Come near; carry
your brothers away from the front of the
sanctuary and out of the camp." 5 So they
came near and carried them in their coats
out of the camp, as Moses had said. 6 And
Moses said to Aaron and to Eleazar and
Ithamar his sons, [g]"Do not let the hair of
your heads hang loose, and do not tear your
clothes, lest you die, and [h]wrath come upon
all the congregation; but let your brothers,
the whole house of Israel, bewail the burning
that the LORD has kindled. 7 [i]And do not
go outside the entrance of the tent of meeting,
lest you die, [j]for the anointing oil of the
LORD is upon you." And they did according
to the word of Moses.
8 And the LORD spoke to Aaron, saying,
9 [k]"Drink no wine or strong drink, you or
your sons with you, when you go into the
tent of meeting, lest you die. It shall be a
statute forever throughout your generations.
10 You are to [l]distinguish between the holy
and the common, and between the unclean
and the clean, 11 and [m]you are to teach the
people of Israel all the statutes that the LORD
has spoken to them by Moses."
12 Moses spoke to Aaron and to Eleazar

15 [i]See ch. 6:26; [j]ver. 8
16 [k]ch. 1:3, 10 [l]ch. 5:10
17 [m]ver. 4; ch. 2:1, 2 [n]Ex. 29:38, 39
18 [o]ch. 3:1, 12, 16
19 [p]ch. 3:3, 9, 14; 4:8; 7:3
20 [q]ch. 3:5, 16
21 [r]Ex. 29:24, 26; See ch. 7:30-34
22 [s][Luke 24:50] [t]Deut. 21:5; See Num. 6:23-27
23 [u]ver. 4, 6
24 [v][Judg. 6:21; 13:19, 20; 1 Kin. 18:38; 1 Chr. 21:26; 2 Chr. 7:1] [w][Ezra 3:11] [x][1 Kin. 18:39; 2 Chr. 7:3]

Chapter 10
1 [y]ch. 16:1; Ex. 6:23; 28:1; Num. 3:4; 26:61; 1 Chr. 24:2 [z][Num. 16:18] [a]Ex. 30:9
2 [b]ch. 9:24; Num. 16:35; [2 Sam. 6:7]
3 [c]ch. 21:17, 21 [d]Ezek. 28:22 [e][Ps. 39:9]
4 [f]Ex. 6:18, 22; Num. 3:19, 30
6 [g]ch. 13:45; 21:10; Ezek. 24:16, 17; [h]Num. 1:53; 16:22, 46; 18:5; Josh. 7:1; 22:18, 20
7 [i]ch. 21:12 [j]ch. 8:30
9 [k]Ezek. 44:21; [Num. 6:3, 20; Luke 1:15; 1 Tim. 3:3, 8] 10 [l]ch. 11:47; 20:25; Ezek. 22:26; 44:23 11 [m]ch. 14:57; Deut. 24:8; Neh. 8:2, 8, 9; [Jer. 18:18; Mal. 2:7]

[1] Or *strange*

9:22 blessed. The traditional priestly blessing is found in Num. 6:23–26.

9:23 the glory of the LORD. God's appearance signaled His approval of the first sacrifices offered by the newly consecrated priests. The fire that then consumed the offering (v. 24) confirmed God's acceptance of Aaron's ministry (cf. 1 Kin. 18:38; Heb. 12:28–29).

10:1–20 The Lord, who accepted Aaron's sacrifice (9:23, 24), now rejects the ministry of his sons Nadab and Abihu. His sons Eleazar and Ithamar, though sincere, fail in their first ministrations as well (vv. 16–20). These first halting steps of the Levites would characterize their history and lead to Malachi's prophecy of a purified priesthood (Mal. 3:1–5).

10:1 censer. A vessel for burning incense.

unauthorized fire. Lit. "strange fire." Apparently the instructions for offering incense were not properly followed, perhaps by using coals from elsewhere than the altar (Lev. 16:12; cf. Ex. 30:1–9). Some interpreters suggest that the two men were also drunk (cf. v. 9).

10:2 fire came out from before the LORD. The Old Testament frequently warned against approaching God in an unfit state (Ex. 19:12, 21); this principle is also evident in the New Testament (Acts 5:1–10; 1 Cor. 11:29, 30). Eating sacrificial food while unclean (7:21) or entering the Most Holy Place without divine approval might lead to death (16:2). The same divine fire that ignited the inaugural sacrifice, providing atonement for the people (9:24), now engulfed those who encroached upon His altar in an unauthorized fashion. So also the same divine wrath against sin that fell upon Christ in His vicarious sacrifice for His people will blaze against those who reject that sacrifice and yet attempt to approach God in their sin (Heb. 10:26–31).

10:6 let the hair . . . tear. These were signs of mourning (13:45). The high priests were forbidden to mourn even their closest relatives (21:10–12), since total consecration to God meant complete separation from death.

10:10 distinguish between the holy and the common. The priest's job was to teach the people these basic religious distinctions. "Holy" applies to what belongs to God, "clean" to what is fit for Him. Things "unholy" and "unclean" are unfit for God's presence. See note on chs. 11–16.

and Ithamar, his surviving sons: "Take the
[n]grain offering that is left of the LORD's food
offerings, and eat it unleavened beside the
altar, for [o]it is most holy. 13 You shall eat it
in a holy place, because it is your due and
your sons' due, from the LORD's food offerings, for [p]so I am commanded. 14 But the
[q]breast that is waved and the thigh that is
contributed you shall eat in a clean place,
you and your sons and your daughters with
you, for they are given as your due and
your sons' due from the sacrifices of the
peace offerings of the people of Israel.
15 [r]The thigh that is contributed and the
breast that is waved they shall bring with
the food offerings of the fat pieces to wave
for a wave offering before the LORD, and it
shall be yours and your sons' with you as a
due forever, as the LORD has commanded."
16 Now Moses diligently inquired about
[s]the goat of the sin offering, and behold, it
was burned up! And he was angry with
Eleazar and Ithamar, the surviving sons of
Aaron, saying, 17 [t]"Why have you not eaten
the sin offering in the place of the sanctuary, since [o]it is a thing most holy and has
been given to you that you may bear the
iniquity of the congregation, to make
atonement for them before the LORD?
18 Behold, [u]its blood was not brought into
the inner part of the sanctuary. You certainly ought to have eaten it in the sanctuary, [v]as I commanded." 19 And Aaron said
to Moses, "Behold, [w]today they have
offered their sin offering and their burnt
offering before the LORD, and yet such
things as these have happened to me! If I
had eaten the sin offering today, [x]would
the LORD have approved?" 20 And when
Moses heard that, he approved.

Clean and Unclean Animals

11 And the LORD spoke to Moses and
Aaron, saying to them, 2 "Speak to
the people of Israel, saying, [y]These are the
living things that you may eat among all
the animals that are on the earth.
3 Whatever parts the hoof and is cloven-
footed and chews the cud, among the animals, you may eat. 4 Nevertheless, among
those that chew the cud or part the hoof,
you shall not eat these: The camel, because
it chews the cud but does not part the
hoof, is unclean to you. 5 And the [z]rock
badger, because it chews the cud but does
not part the hoof, is unclean to you. 6 And
the hare, because it chews the cud but
does not part the hoof, is unclean to you.
7 And the pig, because it parts the hoof and
is cloven-footed but does not chew the
cud, [a]is unclean to you. 8 You shall not eat
any of their flesh, and you shall not touch
their carcasses; they are unclean to you.
9 "These you may eat, of all that are in the
waters. Everything in the waters that has
fins and scales, whether in the seas or in
the rivers, you may eat. 10 But anything in
the seas or the rivers that has not fins and
scales, of the swarming creatures in the
waters and of the living creatures that are

12 [n]ch. 6:16; Num. 18:9, 10 [o]See ch. 6:17
13 [p]ch. 2:3; 6:16
14 [q]ch. 7:31, 34; Ex. 29:24, 26, 27; Num. 18:11
15 [r]ch. 7:31, 34
16 [s]ch. 9:3, 15
17 [t]ch. 6:26, 29 [o][See ver. 12 above]
18 [u]ch. 6:30 [v]ch. 6:26
19 [w]ch. 9:8, 12
[x]Jer. 6:20; 14:12; Hos. 9:4; Mal. 1:10, 13; 2:13
Chapter 11
2 [y]For ver. 1-47, see Deut. 14:3-20; [Matt. 15:11; Mark 7:15, 18; Acts 10:12-15; 11:6-9; Rom. 14:14; 1 Cor. 8:8; Col. 2:16, 21; Heb. 9:10]
5 [z]Ps. 104:18; Prov. 30:26
7 [a][Isai. 65:4; 66:3, 17]

10:17–20 Aaron and his sons had offered two sin offerings (v. 19; cf. 9:8–17): one for Aaron, the blood of which was sprinkled in the holy place and the remainder burned (4:6, 12), and one for the people, the blood of which was sprinkled on the altar of burnt offering in the courtyard and which was then to be eaten by the priests (6:25, 26). Normally he and his sons should have eaten the meat of the people's sin offering to complete the atonement process, but they had not.

10:19 such things as these have happened to me. Probably a reference to the terrifying events of vv. 1–7. After the display of God's consuming judgment, Aaron was apparently frightened to eat the sacrificial meat, which was holy (6:26–29).

10:20 Moses . . . approved. He realized that the mistake of Aaron and his sons was not motivated by rebellion or by a disregard for the holiness of God.

11:1–16:34 In these chapters, Moses explains the difference between the ceremonially clean and unclean. "Clean" means "fit for God's presence"; "unclean" means "unfit for God's presence." Anyone who was unclean or who had come in contact with uncleanness was to abstain from public worship until he was cleansed. The basic idea is that God is perfect life, while the essence of uncleanness is death. Normal, healthy creatures were clean, but abnormal or unhealthy creatures, and particularly corpses, were unclean. Abnormalities that suggested or that could lead to death were marks of uncleanness. Life and death were not to be mixed, so the unclean was never to enter God's presence. Ultimately, it is Christ, the great Mediator and High Priest, who triumphs over death and corruption on behalf of those who trust in Him (1 Cor. 15:20–28, 50–57).

11:1–47 Moses instructs the Israelites regarding the principles of cleanness, showing them that, though all corpses are unclean (vv. 24, 27, 31–40), some perfectly healthy creatures are also stated to be unclean in a milder sense and therefore must not be eaten. Although some of the forbidden animals posed a possible health threat (e.g., pigs as carriers of trichinosis), this classification is not based simply on health grounds. Rather, the principle teaches basic moral and spiritual truths. Carnivorous animals and birds of prey eat flesh with blood in it, something forbidden to human beings (7:26). Such animals also contact corpses, which are unclean. The clean creatures here symbolize Israelites, while unclean animals symbolize Gentiles. Only domesticated clean animals may be offered in sacrifice, for the sacrificial animal represents the offerer. In restricting his diet to clean animals, the Israelite was reminded that God had chosen Israel alone among the nations. Only when the new covenant admitted Gentiles to the community of God were the food laws abrogated (Mark 7:19; Acts 10:15).

11:2–8 Cud-chewing, cloven-hoofed land animals were clean and so could be eaten. Other animals were unclean.

11:9–12 Only ordinary fish with fins and scales were clean. Other water creatures were unclean and therefore inedible.

in the waters, is [b]detestable to you. 11You
shall regard them as detestable; you shall
not eat any of their flesh, and you shall
detest their carcasses. 12Everything in the
waters that has not fins and scales is
detestable to you.
13"And these you shall detest among the
birds;[1] they shall not be eaten; they are
[b]detestable: [c]the eagle,[2] the bearded vulture, the black vulture, 14the kite, [d]the falcon of any kind, 15every raven of any kind,
16the ostrich, the nighthawk, the sea gull,
the [e]hawk of any kind, 17the [f]little owl, the
cormorant, the [g]short-eared owl, 18the barn
owl, the [h]tawny owl, the carrion vulture,
19the stork, the heron of any kind, the
hoopoe, and [i]the bat.
20"All winged insects that go on all fours
are detestable to you. 21Yet among the
winged insects that go on all fours you may
eat those that have jointed legs above their
feet, with which to hop on the ground.
22Of them you may eat: [j]the locust of any
kind, the bald locust of any kind, the cricket of any kind, and the grasshopper of any
kind. 23But all other winged insects that
have four feet are detestable to you.
24"And by these you shall become
unclean. Whoever touches their carcass
shall be unclean until the evening, 25and
whoever carries any part of their carcass
[k]shall wash his clothes and be unclean
until the evening. 26Every animal that parts
the hoof but is not cloven-footed or does
not chew the cud is unclean to you.
Everyone who touches them shall be
unclean. 27And all that walk on their paws,
among the animals that go on all fours, are
unclean to you. Whoever touches their carcass shall be unclean until the evening,
28and he who carries their carcass [k]shall
wash his clothes and be unclean until the
evening; they are unclean to you.
29"And these are unclean to you among
the swarming things that swarm on the
ground: the mole rat, [l]the mouse, the great
lizard of any kind, 30the gecko, the monitor
lizard, the lizard, the sand lizard, and the
chameleon. 31These are unclean to you

10 [b]ch. 7:21
13 [b][See ver. 10 above] [c]Job 39:26, 30
14 [d]Job 28:7
16 [e]Job 39:26
17 [f]Ps. 102:6 [g]Isai. 34:11
18 [h]Ps. 102:6; Isai. 34:11; Zeph. 2:14
19 [i]Isai. 2:20
22 [j]Ex. 10:4; Joel 1:4; [Matt. 3:4; Mark 1:6]
25 [k]ch. 13:6, 34; 14:8, 9, 47; 15:5; 16:26, 28; 17:15; Num. 19:10; 31:24
28 [k][See ver. 25 above]
29 [l]Isai. 66:17

[1] Or *things that fly*; compare Genesis 1:20 [2] The identity of many of these birds is uncertain

God Is Light: Divine Holiness and Justice

When Scripture calls God, or individual Persons of the Godhead, "holy" (as it often does: Lev. 11:44, 45; Josh. 24:19; 1 Sam. 2:2; Ps. 99:9; Is. 1:4; 6:3; 41:14, 16, 20; 57:15; Ezek. 39:7; Amos 4:2; John 17:11; Acts 5:3, 4, 32; Rev. 15:4), the word signifies everything about God that sets Him apart from us and makes Him an object of awe, adoration, and dread to us. It covers all aspects of His transcendent greatness and moral perfection, and is characteristic of all His attributes, pointing to the "Godness" of God at every point. The core of this truth, however, is God's purity that cannot tolerate any form of sin (Hab. 1:13), and calls sinners to constant self-abasement in His presence (Is. 6:5).

Justice, which means doing in all circumstances things that are right, is one expression of God's holiness. God displays His justice as Lawgiver and Judge, and also as Promise-keeper and Pardoner of sin. His moral law, requiring behavior that matches His own, is "holy and righteous and good" (Rom. 7:12). He judges justly, according to actual desert (Gen. 18:25; Ps. 7:11, 96:13; Acts 17:31). His wrath, His active judicial hostility to sin, is wholly just in its manifestations (Rom. 2:5–16), and His particular judgments (retributive punishments) are glorious and praiseworthy (Rev. 16:5, 7; 19:1–4). Whenever God fulfills His covenant commitment by acting to save His people, it is an act of His righteousness, or justice (Is. 51:5, 6; 56:1; 63:1; 1 John 1:9). When God justifies sinners through faith in Christ, He does so on the basis of justice done—the punishment of our sins in the Person of Christ our substitute. The form taken by His justifying mercy shows Him to be utterly and totally just (Rom. 3:25, 26), and our justification itself is shown to be judicially justified.

When John says that God is "light," with no darkness in Him at all, the imagery affirms God's holy purity, which makes fellowship between Him and the willfully unholy impossible, and requires that the pursuit of holiness and righteousness of life be a central concern for Christian people (1 John 1:5–2:1; 2 Cor. 6:14–7:1; Heb. 12:10–17). The summons to believers, regenerate and forgiven as they are, to practice a holiness that will match God's own, and so please Him, is constant in the New Testament, as indeed it was in the Old (Deut. 30:1–10; Eph. 4:17–5:14; 1 Pet. 1:13–22).

11:13–19 Birds of prey were unclean, but others were clean.

11:20–23 Insects that hop might be eaten (v. 21), but not others.

among all that swarm. Whoever touches
them when they are dead shall be unclean
until the evening. 32 And anything on which
any of them falls when they are dead shall
be unclean, whether it is an article of wood
or a garment or a skin or a sack, any article
that is used for any purpose. [m]It must be
put into water, and it shall be unclean until
the evening; then it shall be clean. 33 And if
any of them falls into any earthenware vessel, all that is in it shall be unclean, and
you [n]shall break it. 34 Any food in it that
could be eaten, on which water comes,
shall be unclean. And all drink that could
be drunk from every such vessel shall be
unclean. 35 And everything on which any
part of their carcass falls shall be unclean.
Whether oven or stove, it shall be broken
in pieces. They are unclean and shall
remain unclean for you. 36 Nevertheless, a
spring or a cistern holding water shall be
clean, but whoever touches a carcass in
them shall be unclean. 37 And if any part of
their carcass falls upon any seed grain that
is to be sown, it is clean, 38 but if water is
put on the seed and any part of their carcass falls on it, it is unclean to you.

39 "And if any animal which you may eat
dies, whoever touches its carcass shall be
unclean until the evening, 40 and [o]whoever
eats of its carcass shall wash his clothes
and be unclean until the evening. And
whoever carries the carcass shall wash his
clothes and be unclean until the evening.

41 [p]"Every swarming thing that swarms
on the ground is detestable; it shall not be
eaten. 42 Whatever goes on its belly, and
whatever goes on all fours, or whatever has
many feet, any swarming thing that swarms
on the ground, you shall not eat, for they
are detestable. 43 [q]You shall not make yourselves detestable with any swarming thing
that swarms, and you shall not defile yourselves with them, and become unclean
through them. 44 For I am the LORD your
God. Consecrate yourselves therefore, and
[r]be holy, for I am holy. [q]You shall not defile
yourselves with any swarming thing that
crawls on the ground. 45 [s]For I am the LORD
who brought you up out of the land of
Egypt to be your God. [r]You shall therefore
be holy, for I am holy."

46 This is the law about beast and bird
and every living creature that moves
through the waters and every creature that
swarms on the ground, 47 [t]to make a distinction between the unclean and the clean
and between the living creature that may
be eaten and the living creature that may
not be eaten.

Purification After Childbirth

12 The LORD spoke to Moses, saying,
2 "Speak to the people of Israel, saying, 'If a woman conceives and bears a
male child, then [u]she shall be unclean
seven days. [v]As at the time of her menstruation, she shall be unclean. 3 And on the
[w]eighth day the flesh of his foreskin shall
be circumcised. 4 Then she shall continue
for thirty-three days in the blood of her
purifying. She shall not touch anything
holy, nor come into the sanctuary, until the
days of her purifying are completed. 5 But if
she bears a female child, then she shall be
unclean two weeks, as in her menstruation.
And she shall continue in the blood of her
purifying for sixty-six days.

6 [u]" 'And when the days of her purifying
are completed, whether for a son or for a
daughter, she shall bring to the priest at
the entrance of the tent of meeting a lamb
a year old for a burnt offering, and a pigeon
or a turtledove for a sin offering, 7 and he

32 [m]ch. 15:12
33 [n]ch. 6:28; 15:12
40 [o]ch. 17:15; 22:8; Deut. 14:21; Ezek. 4:14; 44:31
41 [p][ver. 29]
43 [q]ch. 20:25
44 [r]ch. 19:2; 20:7, 26; 21:8; Ex. 19:6; Cited 1 Pet. 1:16; [1 Thess. 4:7] [q][See ver. 43 above]
45 [s]Ex. 6:7 [r][See ver. 44 above]
47 [t]ch. 10:10; 20:25
Chapter 12
2 [u][Luke 2:22] [v]ch. 15:19
3 [w]Gen. 17:12; Luke 1:59; 2:21; John 7:22, 23
6 [u][See ver. 2 above]

11:44 See theological note "God Is Light: Divine Holiness and Justice."

11:45 be holy. The word "holy" means "separate" or "set apart." Only God is intrinsically holy. He is by nature majestic, awesome, and pure. He demonstrated His transcendent holiness by His creation of the world (Gen. 1:1, 3 and notes), by His great acts in history such as redeeming His people from Egypt, and by His perfect laws. Israel's holiness derived from her unique covenant relationship with the only true and living God. His covenant provided, among other things, moral and judicial laws that reflected God's own righteous standards, and the sacrificial system to cleanse them from sin. The immediate background for this designation of Israel as a "holy nation" is the Lord's appearance on Mount Sinai: they washed their clothes, avoided contact with the mountain, and abstained from sexual intercourse in preparation for that unique event (Ex. 19:10–15, 21–24; Heb. 12:18–21). Jesus Christ, the Mediator of the new covenant (Heb. 8:6; 9:15; 12:24), also demands perfection (Matt. 5:48). But He provides the new Israel with holiness by His perfect sacrifice, which removed the sins of His people forever (Heb. 9; 10), and by His Holy Spirit, who inscribes God's moral law on their hearts (2 Cor. 3:3; cf. Jer. 31:31–34). Without that holiness no one will see God (Heb. 12:14).

12:2 unclean. The flow of blood after childbirth made a mother unclean (vv. 4, 5, 7). Loss of blood could lead to death, thus illustrating the equation of uncleanness with death or the threat thereof (chs. 11–16 note).

12:5 sixty-six days. The text does not explain why the birth of a daughter made a mother unclean for twice as long as the birth of a son. Perhaps a daughter, as a potential mother, was subject to uncleanness in a way a son was not.

shall offer it before the LORD and make atonement for her. Then she shall be clean from the flow of her blood. This is the law for her who bears a child, either male or female. [8]And if she cannot afford a lamb, then she shall take [x]two turtledoves or two pigeons,[1] [y]one for a burnt offering and the other for a sin offering. [z]And the priest shall make atonement for her, and she shall be clean.' "

Laws About Leprosy

13 The LORD spoke to Moses and Aaron, saying, [2]"When a person has on the skin of his body a [a]swelling or an eruption or a spot, and it turns into a case of leprous[2] disease on the skin of his body, [b]then he shall be brought to Aaron the priest or to one of his sons the priests, [3]and the priest shall examine the diseased area on the skin of his body. And if the hair in the diseased area has turned white and the disease appears to be deeper than the skin of his body, it is a case of leprous disease. When the priest has examined him, he shall pronounce him unclean. [4]But if the spot is white in the skin of his body and appears no deeper than the skin, and the hair in it has not turned white, [c]the priest shall shut up the diseased person for seven days. [5]And the priest shall examine him on the seventh day, and if in his eyes the disease is checked and the disease has not spread in the skin, then the [c]priest shall shut him up for another seven days. [6]And the priest shall examine him again on the seventh day, and if the diseased area has faded and the disease has not spread in the skin, then the priest shall pronounce him clean; it is only an eruption. And [d]he shall wash his clothes and be clean. [7]But if the eruption spreads in the skin, after he has shown himself to the priest for his cleansing, he shall appear again before the priest. [8]And the priest shall look, and if the eruption has spread in the skin, then the priest shall pronounce him unclean; it is a leprous disease.

[9]"When a man is afflicted with a leprous disease, he shall be brought to the priest, [10]and the priest shall look. And if there is a [e]white swelling in the skin that has turned the hair white, and there is raw flesh in the swelling, [11]it is a chronic leprous disease in the skin of his body, and the priest shall pronounce him unclean. [f]He shall not shut him up, for he is unclean. [12]And if the leprous disease breaks out in the skin, so that the leprous disease covers all the skin of the diseased person from head to foot, so far as the priest can see, [13]then the priest shall look, and if the leprous disease has covered all his body, he shall pronounce him clean of the disease; it has all turned white, and he is clean. [14]But when raw flesh appears on him, he shall be unclean. [15]And the priest shall examine the raw flesh and pronounce him unclean. Raw flesh is unclean, for it is a leprous disease. [16]But if the raw flesh recovers and turns white again, then he shall come to the priest, [17]and the priest shall examine him, and if the disease has turned white, then the priest shall pronounce the diseased person clean; he is clean.

[18]"If there is in the skin of one's body a [g]boil and it heals, [19]and in the place of the boil there comes a white swelling or a [h]reddish-white spot, then it shall be shown to the priest. [20]And the priest shall look, and if it appears deeper than the skin and its hair has turned white, then the priest shall pronounce him unclean. It is a case of leprous disease that has broken out in the boil. [21]But if the priest examines it and there is no white hair in it and it is not deeper than the skin, but has faded, then the priest shall shut him up seven days. [22]And if it spreads in the skin, then the priest shall pronounce him unclean; it is a disease. [23]But [i]if the spot remains in one place and does not spread, it is the scar of

8 [x]ch. 1:14; 5:7; Cited Luke 2:24 [y]ver. 6 [z]ch. 4:26
Chapter 13
2 [a]ch. 14:56 [b]Deut. 24:8
4 [c][ver. 11]
5 [c][See ver. 4 above]
6 [d]See ch. 11:25
10 [e][Num. 12:10, 12; 2 Kin. 5:27; 15:5; 2 Chr. 26:20, 21]
11 [f][ver. 4, 5]
18 [g]See Ex. 9:9 [h]ver. 24
23 [i]ver. 28

1 Septuagint *two young pigeons* 2 *Leprosy* was a term for several skin diseases

12:8 burnt offering . . . sin offering. These sacrifices for purification were offered after the birth of Jesus (Luke 2:24).

13:1–14:57 These chapters contain God's laws concerning unclean skin diseases referred to as "leprous disease" (13:2, 8). Modern physicians recognize here the symptoms of various modern complaints, but we should remember that the biblical classification is based primarily on spiritual rather than hygienic or medical considerations. The key principle in identifying a skin disease as "unclean" was whether the skin seemed to be rotting away, suggesting the spiritual principle of death. Patchy complaints amounted to uncleanness (vv. 9, 10), but a complaint affecting the whole body did not (vv. 12, 13). Stable conditions were clean, but deteriorating ones were unclean (vv. 5–8, 18–37). Similar principles applied to the diagnosis of uncleanness in clothing: progressive mildews were unclean (vv. 47–52), but stable ones were clean (vv. 53–58). The close association of uncleanness with death is shown in 13:45. The person afflicted with a serious skin disease behaved as a mourner (21:10). He was excluded from the camp, not to protect the health of Israel, but because God was in the camp and uncleanness (death) had to be separated from the presence of God (life). See Num. 5:1–4; 12:14–15.

the boil, and the priest shall pronounce
him clean.
24 "Or, when the body has a burn on its
skin and the raw flesh of the burn becomes
a spot, [j]reddish-white or white, 25 the priest
shall examine it, and if the hair in the spot
has turned white and it appears deeper
than the skin, then it is a leprous disease.
It has broken out in the burn, and the
priest shall pronounce him unclean; it is a
case of leprous disease. 26 But if the priest
examines it and there is no white hair in
the spot and it is no deeper than the skin,
but has faded, the priest shall shut him up
seven days, 27 and the priest shall examine
him the seventh day. If it is spreading in
the skin, then the priest shall pronounce
him unclean; it is a case of leprous disease.
28 But if the spot remains [k]in one place and
does not spread in the skin, but has faded,
it is a swelling from the burn, and the
priest shall pronounce him clean, for it is
the scar of the burn.
29 "When a man or woman has a disease
on the head or the beard, 30 the priest shall
examine the disease. And if it appears
deeper than the skin, and the hair in it is
yellow and thin, then the priest shall pronounce him unclean. It is an itch, a leprous
disease of the head or the beard. 31 And if
the priest examines the itching disease and
it appears no deeper than the skin and
there is no black hair in it, then the priest
shall shut up the person with the itching
disease for seven days, 32 and on the seventh day the priest shall examine the disease. If the itch has not spread, and there is
in it no yellow hair, and the itch appears to
be no deeper than the skin, 33 then he shall
shave himself, but the itch he shall not
shave; and the priest shall shut up the person with the itching disease for another
seven days. 34 And on the seventh day the
priest shall examine the itch, and if the itch
has not spread in the skin and it appears to
be no deeper than the skin, then the priest
shall pronounce him clean. And [l]he shall
wash his clothes and be clean. 35 But if the
itch spreads in the skin after his cleansing,
36 then the priest shall examine him, and if
the itch has spread in the skin, the priest
need not seek for the yellow hair; he is
unclean. 37 But if in his eyes the itch is
unchanged and black hair has grown in it,
the itch is healed and he is clean, and the
priest shall pronounce him clean.
38 "When a man or a woman has spots on
the skin of the body, white spots, 39 the
priest shall look, and if the spots on the
skin of the body are of a dull white, it is
leukoderma that has broken out in the
skin; he is clean.
40 "If a man's hair falls out from his head,
he is bald; he is clean. 41 And if a man's hair
falls out from his forehead, he has baldness
of the forehead; he is clean. 42 But if there is
on the bald head or the bald forehead a
reddish-white diseased area, it is a leprous
disease breaking out on his bald head or
his bald forehead. 43 Then the priest shall
examine him, and if the diseased swelling
is reddish-white on his bald head or on his
bald forehead, like the appearance of leprous disease in the skin of the body, 44 he is
a leprous man, he is unclean. The priest
must pronounce him unclean; his disease
is on his head.
45 "The leprous person who has the disease shall wear torn clothes and [m]let the
hair of his head hang loose, and he shall
[n]cover his upper lip[1] and cry out, [o]'Unclean, unclean.' 46 He shall remain unclean
as long as he has the disease. He is
unclean. He shall live alone. His dwelling
shall be [p]outside the camp.
47 "When there is a case of leprous disease
in a [q]garment, whether a woolen or a linen
garment, 48 in warp or woof of linen or wool,
or in a skin or in anything made of skin, 49 if
the disease is greenish or reddish in the garment, or in the skin or in the warp or the
woof or in any article made of skin, it is a
case of leprous disease, and it shall be
shown to the priest. 50 And the priest shall
examine the disease and shut up that which
has the disease for seven days. 51 Then he
shall examine the disease on the seventh
day. If the disease has spread in the garment, in the warp or the woof, or in the
skin, whatever be the use of the skin, the
disease is a [r]persistent leprous disease; it is
unclean. 52 And he shall burn the garment,
or the warp or the woof, the wool or the
linen, or any article made of skin that is diseased, for it is a persistent leprous disease.
It shall be burned in the fire.

24 [j]ver. 19
28 [k]ver. 23
34 [l]ver. 6
45 [m]ch. 10:6 [n]Ezek. 24:17, 22; Mic. 3:7 [o][Lam. 4:15]
46 [p]Num. 5:2; 12:14, 15; [2 Kin. 7:3; 15:5; 2 Chr. 26:21; Luke 17:12]
47 [q][Jude 23; Rev. 3:4]
51 [r]ch. 14:44

[1] Or *mustache*

53 "And if the priest examines, and if the disease has not spread in the garment, in the warp or the woof or in any article made of skin, 54 then the priest shall command that they wash the thing in which is the disease, and he shall shut it up for another seven days. 55 And the priest shall examine the diseased thing after it has been washed. And if the appearance of the diseased area has not changed, though the disease has not spread, it is unclean. You shall burn it in the fire, whether the rot is on the back or on the front.

56 "But if the priest examines, and if the diseased area has faded after it has been washed, he shall tear it out of the garment or the skin or the warp or the woof. 57 Then if it appears again in the garment, in the warp or the woof, or in any article made of skin, it is spreading. You shall burn with fire whatever has the disease. 58 But the garment, or the warp or the woof, or any article made of skin from which the disease departs when you have washed it, shall then be washed a second time, and be clean."

59 This is the law for a case of leprous disease in a garment of wool or linen, either in the warp or the woof, or in any article made of skin, to determine whether it is clean or unclean.

Laws for Cleansing Lepers

14 The LORD spoke to Moses, saying, 2 "This shall be the law of the leprous person for the day of his cleansing. [s]He shall be brought to the priest, 3 and the priest shall go [t]out of the camp, and the priest shall look. Then, if the case of leprous disease is healed in the leprous person, 4 the priest shall command them to take for him who is to be cleansed two live[1] clean birds and [u]cedarwood and [v]scarlet yarn and [w]hyssop. 5 And the priest shall command them to kill one of the birds in an earthenware vessel over fresh[2] water. 6 He shall take the live bird with the cedarwood and the scarlet yarn and the hyssop, and dip them and the live bird in the blood of the bird that was killed over the fresh water. 7 And he shall [x]sprinkle it [y]seven times on him who is to be cleansed of the leprous disease. Then he shall pronounce him clean and shall [z]let the living bird go [a]into the open field. 8 And he who is to be cleansed [b]shall wash his clothes and shave off all his hair and bathe himself in water, and he shall be clean. And after that he may come into the camp, but [c]live outside his tent seven days. 9 And [d]on the seventh day he shall shave off all his hair from his head, his beard, and his eyebrows. He shall shave off all his hair, and then he [b]shall wash his clothes and bathe his body in water, and he shall be clean.

10 "And on the eighth day he [e]shall take two male lambs without blemish, and one ewe lamb a year old without blemish, and a [f]grain offering of three tenths of an ephah[3] of fine flour mixed with oil, and one log[4] of oil. 11 And the priest who cleanses him shall set the man who is to be cleansed and these things before the LORD, at the entrance of the tent of meeting. 12 And the priest shall take one of the male lambs and [g]offer it for a guilt offering, along with the log of oil, and [h]wave them for a wave offering before the LORD. 13 And he shall kill the lamb [i]in the place where they kill the sin offering and the burnt offering, in the place of the sanctuary. For [j]the guilt offering, like the sin offering, belongs to the priest; [k]it is most holy. 14 The priest shall take some of the blood of the guilt offering, and the priest shall put it [l]on the lobe of the right ear of him who is to be cleansed and on the thumb of his right hand and on the big toe of his right foot. 15 Then the priest shall take some of the log of oil and

Chapter 14
2 [s]Matt. 8:2, 4; Mark 1:40, 44; Luke 5:12, 14; 17:14
3 [t][2 Kin. 7:10; Luke 17:12]
4 [u]Num. 19:6 [v]Heb. 9:19 [w]See Ex. 12:22
7 [x]Heb. 9:13 [y][2 Kin. 5:10, 14] [z][ch. 16:22] [a]ver. 53; [ch. 17:5]
8 [b]ver. 47; See ch. 11:25 [c]Num. 12:15
9 [d][Num. 30:19] [b][See ver. 8 above]
10 [e][Matt. 8:4]; Mark 1:44; Luke 5:14 [f]Num. 15:4; See ch. 2
12 [g]ch. 5:18; 6:6, 7 [h]See Ex. 29:24
13 [i]ch. 1:5, 11; 4:4, 24 [j]ch. 7:7 [k]ch. 2:3; 7:6
14 [l][ch. 8:23; Ex. 29:20]

1 Or *wild* 2 Or *running*; Hebrew *living*; also verses 6, 50, 51, 52 3 An *ephah* was about 3/5 bushel or 22 liters 4 A *log* was about 1/3 quart or 0.3 liter

14:2 cleansing. These ceremonies conducted by the priest did not cure skin disease. A diseased person came to the priest after he had been healed (Luke 5:14). The task of the priest was to make the person who had been excluded from the camp, from his people, and from God, ceremonially clean. Through these ceremonial cleansings, which took place in two stages a week apart, the diseased individual was restored to fellowship with God and with His people.

14:3–8 The first stage of cleansing took place outside the camp. The man washed himself and his clothes, and shaved. Two birds were taken. The blood of one was used to purify the man. The death of that bird portrayed the end of the man's old life outside the camp, and the flight to freedom of the other pictured his liberation from the effects of the disease. Then the man might enter the camp again.

14:9–20 In the second cleansing stage, the Israelite was brought back into full communion with God. The ceremonies here resemble the consecration of the priest (ch. 8). The Israelite was daubed with blood and anointed with oil, being linked to the altar, the symbol of God's presence. A variation on this restoration procedure is prescribed for the poor in vv. 21–31.

pour it into the palm of his own left hand
16 and dip his right finger in the oil that is
in his left hand and sprinkle some oil with
his finger seven times before the LORD.
17 And some of the oil that remains in his
hand the priest shall put on the lobe of the
right ear of him who is to be cleansed and
on the thumb of his right hand and on the
big toe of his right foot, on top of the blood
of the guilt offering. 18 And the rest of the
oil that is in the priest's hand he shall put
on the head of him who is to be cleansed.
[m]Then the priest shall make atonement for
him before the LORD. 19 The priest shall
offer the sin offering, to make atonement
for him who is to be cleansed from his
uncleanness. And afterward he shall kill
the burnt offering. 20 And the priest shall
offer the burnt offering and the [j]grain offering on the altar. [m]Thus the priest shall
make atonement for him, and he shall be
clean.

21 "But [n]if he is poor and cannot afford so
much, then he shall take one male lamb for
a guilt offering [h]to be waved, to make
atonement for him, and a tenth of an
ephah of fine flour mixed with oil for a
grain offering, and a log of oil; 22 [o]also two
turtledoves or two pigeons, whichever he
can afford. The one shall be a sin offering
and the other a burnt offering. 23 [p]And on
the eighth day he shall bring them for his
cleansing to the priest, to the entrance of
the tent of meeting, before the LORD.
24 [q]And the priest shall take the lamb of the
guilt offering and the log of oil, and the
priest shall wave them for a wave offering
before the LORD. 25 And he shall kill the
lamb of the guilt offering. [r]And the priest
shall take some of the blood of the guilt
offering and put it on the lobe of the right
ear of him who is to be cleansed, and on
the thumb of his right hand and on the big
toe of his right foot. 26 And the priest shall
pour some of the oil into the palm of his
own left hand, 27 and shall sprinkle with his
right finger some of the oil that is in his left
hand seven times before the LORD. 28 And
the priest shall put some of the oil that is
in his hand on the lobe of the right ear of
him who is to be cleansed and on the
thumb of his right hand and on the big toe
of his right foot, in the place where the
blood of the guilt offering was put. 29 And
the rest of the oil that is in the priest's
hand he shall put on the head of him who
is to be cleansed, to make atonement for
him before the LORD. 30 And he shall offer,
of the [s]turtledoves or pigeons, whichever
he can afford, 31 one[1] for a sin offering and
the other for a burnt offering, along with a
grain offering. [m]And the priest shall make
atonement before the LORD for him who is
being cleansed. 32 This is the law for him in
whom is a case of leprous disease, who
cannot afford [t]the offerings for his
cleansing."

Laws for Cleansing Houses

33 The LORD spoke to Moses and Aaron,
saying, 34 "When you come into the land of
Canaan, which I give you [u]for a possession, and I put a case of leprous disease in
a house in the land of your possession,
35 then he who owns the house shall come
and tell the priest, 'There seems to me to
be some case of [v]disease in my house.'
36 Then the priest shall command that they
empty the house before the priest goes to
examine the disease, lest all that is in the
house be declared unclean. And afterward
the priest shall go in to see the house.
37 And he shall examine the disease. And if
the disease is in the walls of the house
with greenish or reddish spots, and if it
appears to be deeper than the surface,
38 then the priest shall go out of the house
to the door of the house and shut up the
house seven days. 39 And the priest shall
come again on the seventh day, and look.
If the disease has spread in the walls of the
house, 40 then the priest shall command
that they take out the stones in which is
the disease and throw them into an
unclean place outside the city. 41 And he
shall have the inside of the house scraped
all around, and the plaster that they scrape
off they shall pour out in an unclean place
outside the city. 42 Then they shall take
other stones and put them in the place of
those stones, and he shall take other plaster and plaster the house.
43 "If the disease breaks out again in the

18 [m]See ch. 4:26
20 [j][See ver. 10 above] [m][See ver. 18 above]
21 [n]ch. 5:7, 11; 12:8 [h][See ver. 12 above]
22 [o]See ch. 12:8
23 [p]ver. 10, 11
24 [q]ver. 12
25 [r]For ver. 25-29, see ver. 14-18
30 [s]ver. 22; ch. 15:15
31 [m][See ver. 18 above]
32 [t]ver. 10
34 [u]Gen. 17:8; Num. 32:22; Deut. 32:49
35 [v][Ps. 91:10; Zech. 5:4]

[1] Septuagint, Syriac; Hebrew *afford,* [31]*such as he can afford, one*

14:34–57 This passage adapts principles of diagnosis (13:47–58) and cleansing (14:1–7) to the problem of "disease" (mildew or dry rot) in houses. This problem would have arisen after the settlement in Canaan (v. 34).

house, after he has taken out the stones and scraped the house and plastered it, [44]then the priest shall go and look. And if the disease has spread in the house, it is a [w]persistent leprous disease in the house; it is unclean. [45]And he shall break down the house, its stones and timber and all the plaster of the house, and he shall carry them out of the city to an unclean place. [46]Moreover, whoever enters the house while it is shut up shall be unclean until the evening, [47]and whoever sleeps in the house [x]shall wash his clothes, and whoever eats in the house shall wash his clothes.

[48]"But if the priest comes and looks, and if the disease has not spread in the house after the house was plastered, then the priest shall pronounce the house clean, for the disease is healed. [49]And for the [y]cleansing of the house he shall take [z]two small birds, with cedarwood and scarlet yarn and hyssop, [50]and shall kill one of the birds in an earthenware vessel over fresh water [51]and shall take the cedarwood and the hyssop and the scarlet yarn, along with the live bird, and dip them in the blood of the bird that was killed and in the fresh water and sprinkle the house seven times. [52]Thus he shall cleanse the house with the blood of the bird and with the fresh water and with the live bird and with the cedarwood and hyssop and scarlet yarn. [53]And he shall let the live bird go out of the city [a]into the open country. So he shall [b]make atonement for the house, and it shall be clean."

[54]This is the law for any case of leprous disease: for [c]an itch, [55]for [d]leprous disease in a garment or in [e]a house, [56]and [f]for a swelling or an eruption or a spot, [57]to [g]show when it is unclean and when it is clean. This is the law for leprous disease.

Laws About Bodily Discharges

15 The LORD spoke to Moses and Aaron, saying, [2]"Speak to the people of Israel and say to them, [h]When any man has a discharge from his body,[1] his discharge is unclean. [3]And this is the law of his uncleanness for a discharge: whether his body runs with his discharge, or his body is blocked up by his discharge, it is his uncleanness. [4]Every bed on which the one with the discharge lies shall be unclean, and everything on which he sits shall be unclean. [5]And anyone who touches his bed [i]shall wash his clothes and [j]bathe himself in water and be unclean until the evening. [6]And whoever sits on anything on which the one with the discharge has sat shall wash his clothes and bathe himself in water and be unclean until the evening. [7]And whoever touches the body of the one with the discharge shall wash his clothes and bathe himself in water and be unclean until the evening. [8]And if the one with the discharge spits on someone who is clean, then he shall wash his clothes and bathe himself in water and be unclean until the evening. [9]And any saddle on which the one with the discharge rides shall be unclean. [10]And whoever touches anything that was under him shall be unclean until the evening. And whoever carries such things shall wash his clothes and bathe himself in water and be unclean until the evening. [11]Anyone whom the one with the discharge touches without having rinsed his hands in water shall wash his clothes and bathe himself in water and be unclean until the evening. [12]And an [k]earthenware vessel that the one with the discharge touches shall be broken, and every vessel of wood shall be rinsed in water.

[13]"And when the one with a discharge is cleansed of his discharge, then [l]he shall count for himself seven days for his cleansing, and wash his clothes. And he shall bathe his body in fresh water and shall be clean. [14]And on the eighth day he shall take two [m]turtledoves or two pigeons and come before the LORD to the entrance of the tent of meeting and give them to the priest.

44 [w]ch. 13:51, 52
47 [x]See ch. 11:25
49 [y]ver. 52 [z][ver. 4-6]
53 [a]See ver. 7 [b]ver. 19, 20
54 [c]ch. 13:30
55 [d]ch. 13:47 [e]ver. 34
56 [f]ch. 13:2
57 [g]See ch. 10:10, 11
Chapter 15
2 [h]ch. 22:4; Num. 5:2; 2 Sam. 3:29
5 [i]See ch. 11:25 [j]ch. 16:26; 17:15
12 [k]ch. 6:28; 11:32, 33
13 [l]ver. 28; [ch. 14:8]
14 [m]See ch. 12:8

1 Hebrew *flesh*; also verse 3

15:1–33 This chapter deals with the uncleanness caused by discharges from the sexual organs: (a) long-term male discharge (e.g., gonorrhea; vv. 2–15); (b) short-term male discharges (vv. 16–18); (c) short-term female discharge (menstruation, vv. 19–24); and (d) long-term female discharges (vv. 25–30). That perfectly natural processes like sexual intercourse (v. 18) or menstruation should make someone unclean (i.e., unfit to worship) is surprising. But all these cases involve the loss of bodily fluids (blood or semen), and any loss of a "life fluid" suggested death and was incompatible with the presence of God, who is perfect life.

The New Testament shows God, the giver of perfect life, incarnate in Jesus Christ, healing those who suffered exclusion from His presence under these Old Testament rules (Matt. 9:20–22). The divine program of redemption was historically progressive. The old covenant arrangements that seem so strange to us were early object lessons, a "guardian" pointing forward to the full redemption accomplished in Jesus Christ (Gal. 3:24, 25).

15 And the priest shall use them, [n]one for a sin offering and the other for a burnt offering. [o]And the priest shall make atonement for him before the LORD for his discharge.

16 [p]"If a man has an emission of semen, he shall bathe his whole body in water and be unclean until the evening. 17 And every garment and every skin on which the semen comes shall be washed with water and be unclean until the evening. 18 If a man lies with a woman and has an emission of semen, both of them shall bathe themselves in water and [q]be unclean until the evening.

19 "When a woman has a discharge, and the discharge in her body is blood, she shall be in her menstrual impurity for seven days, and whoever touches her shall be unclean until the evening. 20 [r]And everything on which she lies during her menstrual impurity shall be unclean. Everything also on which she sits shall be unclean. 21 And whoever touches her bed shall wash his clothes and bathe himself in water and be unclean until the evening. 22 And whoever touches anything on which she sits shall wash his clothes and bathe himself in water and be unclean until the evening. 23 Whether it is the bed or anything on which she sits, when he touches it he shall be unclean until the evening. 24 And [s]if any man lies with her and her menstrual impurity comes upon him, he shall be unclean seven days, and every bed on which he lies shall be unclean.

25 "If [t]a woman has a discharge of blood for many days, not at the time of her menstrual impurity, or if she has a discharge beyond the time of her impurity, all the days of the discharge she shall continue in uncleanness. As in the days of her impurity, she shall be unclean. 26 Every bed on which she lies, all the days of her discharge, shall be to her as the bed of her impurity. And everything on which she sits shall be unclean, as in the uncleanness of her menstrual impurity. 27 And whoever touches these things shall be unclean, and shall wash his clothes and bathe himself in water and be unclean until the evening. 28 But [u]if she is cleansed of her discharge, she shall count for herself seven days, and after that she shall be clean. 29 And on the eighth day she shall take two [v]turtledoves or two pigeons and bring them to the priest, to the entrance of the tent of meeting. 30 And the priest shall use one for a sin offering and the other for a burnt offering. And the priest shall make atonement for her before the LORD for her unclean discharge.

31 "Thus you shall keep the people of Israel separate from their uncleanness, lest they die in their uncleanness by [w]defiling my tabernacle that is in their midst."

32 This is the law [x]for him who has a discharge and [y]for him who has an emission of semen, becoming unclean thereby; 33 [z]also for her who is unwell with her menstrual impurity, that is, for anyone, [x]male or [a]female, who has a discharge, and for the [b]man who lies with a woman who is unclean.

The Day of Atonement

16 The LORD spoke to Moses after [c]the death of the two sons of Aaron, when they drew near before the LORD and

15 [n]ch. 14:30, 31; [o]ver. 30; See ch. 4:26 **16** [p]ch. 22:4; Deut. 23:10 **18** [q][1 Sam. 21:4] **20** [r]See ver. 4-10 **24** [s]ch. 18:19; [ch. 20:18] **25** [t]Matt. 9:20; Mark 5:25; Luke 8:43
28 [u]For ver. 28-30, see ver. 13-15 **29** [v]See ch. 12:8 **31** [w]Num. 5:3; 19:13, 20; Ezek. 5:11; 23:38 **32** [x]ver. 2 [y]ver. 16 **33** [z]ver. 19 [x][See ver. 32 above] [a]ver. 25 [b]ver. 24
Chapter 16
1 [c]ch. 10:1, 2

16:1–34 The Day of Atonement, when annual atonement was made for the sins of the nation, was the holiest day in the Old Testament calendar. It fell in the Hebrew seventh month (October) and involved the offering of various sacrifices, the entry of the high priest into the Most Holy Place (in this chapter referred to simply as the "Holy Place" or "holy sanctuary"), and the dispatch of a goat into the wilderness carrying the people's sins. For a summary of the sacrifices see notes on chs. 1; 4; and 5. A summary of the rites is given in vv. 6–10 and fuller details in vv. 11–28. The Day of Atonement proceeded according to the following steps: (a) The high priest washed and dressed (v. 4); (b) he sacrificed a bull as a sin offering for himself (v. 6; cf. v. 11); (c) he entered the Most Holy Place and sprinkled the ark with blood (vv. 12–14); (d) he took two goats and by lot chose one to be the scapegoat (Azazel), the other to be a sin offering (vv. 7–8); (e) he sacrificed one goat as a sin offering (vv. 9, 15); (f) he entered the Most Holy Place and sprinkled the ark with blood (v. 15); (g) he went out to the outer part of the tabernacle of meeting and sprinkled the blood (v. 16); (h) he went out into the courtyard of the tabernacle and sprinkled the main altar with blood (vv. 18–19); (i) he confessed the sins of the Israelites as he laid his hands on the scapegoat's head (v. 21); (j) he sent the scapegoat into the wilderness (vv. 21–22); (k) the scapegoat gone, the high priest changed into his regular garments and washed (vv. 23–24); and (l) finally, he offered burnt offerings for himself and for the people (vv. 24–25).

For the high priest, the most important aspects of the ceremony were his entry into the Most Holy Place with the blood of the sin offerings and the dispatch of the scapegoat into the wilderness. These actions atoned for the sins of repentant Israelites (vv. 16, 19, 21–22). All sin offerings served to cleanse both the earthly sanctuary and the worshipers, but on other occasions the high priest did not enter the (inner) Most Holy Place, but only the anteroom before the separating veil (usually called the "Holy Place"), the chamber containing the altar of incense, the gold lampstand, and the table of showbread. Because the ark of the covenant, the focal point of God's presence in the tabernacle (v. 2 note; Ex. 25:17–22 and notes), was housed in the Most Holy Place, entry to the Most Holy Place was rare and dangerous (v. 2). That the high priest entered the inner chamber only on this one day of the year indicated the depth of atonement being made.

The scapegoat ceremony was also unique to this day. By placing his hands on the goat's head and confessing the nation's sins, the high priest transferred those sins to the goat. The goat then symbolically carried the people's sins away into the wilderness. Christians have long regarded the scapegoat as a type of Christ. The New Testament makes many comparisons between the Day of Atonement and the death of Christ (Heb. 9:6–28; 13:11–13). That Christ was delivered to the Gentiles and killed outside the walls of Jerusalem indicated that He was sent "outside the camp" like the scapegoat of old.

16:1 death of the two sons of Aaron. See 10:1–3.

died, **2**and the LORD said to Moses, "Tell
Aaron your brother not to [d]come at any
time into the Holy Place inside the veil,
before the mercy seat that is on the ark, so
that he may not die. For [e]I will appear in
the cloud over the mercy seat. **3**But in this
way Aaron shall come into the Holy Place:
[f]with a bull from the herd for a sin offering
and [g]a ram for a burnt offering. **4**He shall
put on [h]the holy linen coat and shall have
the linen undergarment on his body, and
he shall tie the linen sash around his waist,
and wear the linen turban; these are the
holy garments. [i]He shall bathe his body in
water and then put them on. **5**And he shall
take from [j]the congregation of the people
of Israel two male goats for a sin offering,
and one ram for a burnt offering.
6"Aaron shall [k]offer the bull as a sin
offering for himself and shall [l]make atonement for himself and for his house. **7**Then
he shall take the two goats and set them
before the LORD at the entrance of the tent
of meeting. **8**And Aaron shall cast lots over
the two goats, one lot for the LORD and the
other lot for [m]Azazel. **9**And Aaron shall
present the goat on which the lot fell for
the LORD and use it as a sin offering, **10**but
the goat on which the lot fell for [m]Azazel
shall be presented alive before the LORD to
make atonement over it, that it may be sent
away into the wilderness to [m]Azazel.
11"Aaron shall present [k]the bull as a sin
offering for himself, and shall make atonement for himself and for his house. He
shall kill the bull as a sin offering for himself. **12**And he shall take [n]a censer full of
coals of fire from the altar before the LORD,
and two handfuls of sweet incense beaten
small, and he shall bring it inside the veil
13[o]and put the incense on the fire before
the LORD, that the cloud of the incense may
cover [p]the mercy seat that is over the testimony, so that he does not die. **14**And [q]he
shall take some of the blood of the bull and
sprinkle it with his finger on the front of
the mercy seat on the east side, and in
front of the mercy seat he shall sprinkle
some of the blood with his finger seven
times.
15[r]"Then he shall kill the goat of the sin
offering that is for the people and bring its
blood [s]inside the veil and do with its blood
as he did with the blood of the bull, sprinkling it over the mercy seat and in front of
the mercy seat. **16**Thus he shall [t]make
atonement for the Holy Place, because of
the uncleannesses of the people of Israel
and because of their transgressions, all
their sins. And so he shall do for the tent of
meeting, which dwells with them in the
midst of their uncleannesses. **17**[u]No one
may be in the tent of meeting from the time
he enters to make atonement in the Holy
Place until he comes out and has made
atonement for himself and for his house
and for all the assembly of Israel. **18**Then he
shall go out to the altar that is [v]before the
LORD and [w]make atonement for it, and
shall take some of the blood of the bull and
some of the blood of the goat, and put it on
the horns of the altar all around. **19**And he
shall sprinkle some of the blood on it with
his finger seven times, and cleanse it and
consecrate it from the uncleannesses of the
people of Israel.

2 [d][Ex. 30:10; Heb. 9:7, 12, 24, 25; 10:19-22] [e]Ex. 25:22; 40:34, 35; [1 Kin. 8:10-12]
3 [f]ch. 4:3 [g]ch. 1:10; 8:18
4 [h]ch. 6:10; 8:7; Ezek. 44:17, 18; See Ex. 28:39-43 [i]ch. 8:6, 7; Ex. 30:20
5 [j]ch. 4:14; Num. 29:11; 2 Chr. 29:21; Ezra 6:17
6 [k]Ezek. 45:22 [l]ver. 17, 24; ch. 9:7; Heb. 7:27, 28; 9:7
8 [m]ver. 26
10 [m][See ver. 8 above]
11 [k][See ver. 6 above]
12 [n]ch. 10:1; Num. 16:46; Rev. 8:3-5
13 [o]Ex. 30:1, 7, 8 [p]Ex. 25:21
14 [q]Heb. 9:13, 25; 10:4; See ch. 4:5, 6
15 [r]Heb. 2:17; 5:1; 9:7 [s]ver. 2; Heb. 6:19; 9:3, 7
16 [t]ver. 18; [Ex. 29:36; Ezek. 45:18; Heb. 9:22, 23]
17 [u][Luke 1:10, 21]
18 [v]ch. 1:5; 4:24 [w]ver. 16; ch. 4:7, 18; Ex. 30:6, 10

16:2 mercy seat. Lit. "atonement covering" or "place of atonement" (Ex. 25:17 note). This slab of pure gold served as a lid for the ark and as a base for the two golden cherubim. The divine presence appeared above the lid of the ark (Ex. 25:22; Ps. 99:1), and Aaron sprinkled the mercy seat with blood on the Day of Atonement. God symbolically revealed the gospel through this cover on the ark. The ark contained the two stone tablets of the law inscribed by the finger of God Himself, representing the eternal moral law of God (Deut. 10:1–5). Since all humans have violated this law, the righteousness of God demands death (Ezek. 18:20; Rom. 6:23). God provided the only means of atonement for His chosen people and for their reconciliation to Him—the atoning blood on the ark's cover. That blood-drenched cover was the meeting point of the holy God with His unholy people. It symbolized the heavenly sanctuary where Christ has entered with His own blood (Heb. 9:12), blood that is efficacious for all the sins of His people, past, present, and future (Rom. 3:21–26; Heb. 9:15).

16:3 Aaron was to offer a bull as a sin offering and a ram as a burnt offering for himself and his family, before offering a goat for the people (v. 5). By contrast, Jesus Christ, the Mediator of the eternal new covenant, was without sin and therefore offered sacrifice for His people only (Heb. 7:26, 27).

16:8 one lot for the LORD. One to be sacrificed.

16:12 take a censer. The smoke from the incense served as a screen between the mercy seat and the high priest, probably to prevent the high priest from seeing the divine presence (v. 13; cf. Ex. 33:20). It also may have served to avert God's wrath (Num. 16:46–50).

16:16 the Holy Place. Here the term denotes the Most Holy Place, or inner sanctuary. The object of the sacrificial ritual was not only the people but the sanctuary itself, which was defiled by their sins. The earthly sanctuary was a representation of the heavenly sanctuary that the blood of Christ also cleansed (Heb. 9:23, 24).

which dwells with them. Lit. "which camps among them." The verb connotes impermanence. God's presence is not finalized in this arrangement. His tent dwelling foreshadowed His dwelling among His people through Christ's Incarnation (John 1:14). Today He has sent His Spirit upon His new covenant people, the church (Acts 2), and His Spirit indwells believers, making them the temples of God (1 Cor. 3:16; 6:19). His final dwelling with His people will occur in the new heavens and the new earth (Rev. 21:1–4).

20 “And when he has made an end of
[x]atoning for the Holy Place and the tent of
meeting and the altar, he shall present the
live goat. 21 And Aaron shall lay both his
hands on the head of the live goat, and confess over it all the iniquities of the people of
Israel, and all their transgressions, all their
sins. And he shall [y]put them on the head of
the goat and send it away into the wilderness
by the hand of a man who is in readiness.
22 The goat shall [z]bear all their iniquities on
itself to a remote area, and [a]he shall let the
goat go free in the wilderness.
23 “Then Aaron shall come into the tent of
meeting and [b]shall take off the linen garments that he put on when he went into the
Holy Place and shall leave them there. 24 And
he shall bathe his body in water in a holy
place and put on his garments and come out
and [c]offer his burnt offering and the burnt
offering of the people and make atonement
for himself and for the people. 25 And [d]the fat
of the sin offering he shall burn on the altar.
26 And he who lets the goat go to [e]Azazel
shall wash his clothes and [f]bathe his body in
water, and afterward he may come into the
camp. 27 [g]And the bull for the sin offering
and the goat for the sin offering, whose
blood was brought in to make atonement in
the Holy Place, shall be carried outside the
camp. Their skin and their flesh and their
dung shall be burned up with fire. 28 And he
who burns them shall wash his clothes and
bathe his body in water, and afterward he
may come into the camp.
29 “And it shall be a statute to you forever that [h]in the seventh month, on the tenth
day of the month, you shall [i]afflict yourselves[1] and shall do no work, either [j]the
native or the stranger who sojourns among
you. 30 For on this day shall atonement be
made for you [k]to cleanse you. You shall be
clean before the LORD from all your sins.
31 [l]It is a Sabbath of solemn rest to you, and
you shall [i]afflict yourselves; it is a statute
forever. 32 [m]And the priest who is anointed
and [n]consecrated as priest in his father's
place [o]shall make atonement, wearing the
holy linen garments. 33 He shall make
atonement for [p]the holy sanctuary, and he
shall make atonement for the tent of meeting and for [q]the altar, and he shall make
atonement for [r]the priests and for [s]all the
people of the assembly. 34 And this shall be
a statute forever for you, that atonement
may be made for the people of Israel [t]once
in the year because of all their sins.” And
Moses did as the LORD commanded him.

The Place of Sacrifice

17 And the LORD spoke to Moses, saying, 2 “Speak to Aaron and his sons
and to all the people of Israel and say to
them, This is the thing that the LORD has
commanded. 3 If any one of the house of
Israel [u]kills an ox or a lamb or a goat in the
camp, or kills it outside the camp, 4 and
[v]does not bring it to the entrance of the tent
of meeting to offer it as a gift to the LORD in
front of the tabernacle of the LORD, bloodguilt shall be imputed to that man. He has
shed blood, and that man [w]shall be cut off
from among his people. 5 This is to the end
that the people of Israel may bring their sacrifices that they sacrifice [x]in the open field,
that they may bring them to the LORD, to
the priest at the entrance of the tent of
meeting, and sacrifice them [y]as sacrifices of
peace offerings to the LORD. 6 And the priest
shall [y]throw the blood on the altar of the
LORD at the entrance of the tent of meeting
and burn the fat [z]for a pleasing aroma to the
LORD. 7 So they shall no more sacrifice their
sacrifices to goat demons, after whom they
[a]whore. This shall be a statute forever for
them throughout their generations.
8 “And you shall say to them, Any one of
the house of Israel, or of the strangers who
sojourn among them, who [b]offers a burnt
offering or sacrifice 9 and [c]does not bring it
to the entrance of the tent of meeting to

[1] Or *shall fast*; also verse 31

20 [x]ver. 16, 18; Ezek. 43:20; 45:20
21 [y][Isai. 53:6; 2 Cor. 5:21]
22 [z][Isai. 53:11, 12; John 1:29; Heb. 9:28; 1 Pet. 2:24] [a][ch. 14:7]
23 [b]See ch. 6:11
24 [c]ver. 3, 5
25 [d]ch. 4:8-10; Ex. 29:13
26 [e]ver. 8, 10 [f][ch. 15:5; 17:15]
27 [g]ch. 4:11, 12, 21; 6:30; Heb. 13:11, 12
29 [h]ch. 23:27; Num. 29:7 [i]ch. 23:32; Ps. 35:13; Isai. 58:3, 5; Dan. 10:12 [j]ch. 17:15; 18:26; 19:34; [Ex. 12:49]
30 [k]Ps. 51:2; Jer. 33:8; Heb. 10:1, 2; 1 John 1:7, 9
31 [l]ch. 23:32 [i][See ver. 29 above]
32 [m][ch. 21:10] [n]Ex. 29:29, 30; [Num. 20:28] [o]ver. 4
33 [p]ver. 16 [q]ver. 18 [r]ver. 6 [s]ver. 24
34 [t]Ex. 30:10; Heb. 9:7, 25
Chapter 17
3 [u][Deut. 12:5, 6, 13-15, 21]
4 [v]ver. 9 [w][Ex. 30:33]
5 [x]ch. 14:7, 53 [y]ch. 1:5
6 [y][See ver. 5 above] [z]See Gen. 8:21
7 [a]See Ex. 34:15
8 [b]ch. 1:2, 3
9 [c]ver. 4

16:29 afflict yourselves. See text note. The ordinary Israelites were to show penitence for their sins by not working, by fasting, and possibly by wearing sackcloth (Ps. 69:10, 11). Failing to observe the Day of Atonement could entail death (23:28–30). This is the only holy day to which this threat is attached.

16:34 once in the year. By contrast, Jesus Christ offered the final and complete sacrifice for sin (Heb. 9:23–28).

17:1–27:34 In these chapters, the Lord's demands for holiness clearly reach into every aspect of Israel's life. In a discussion on topics as diverse as sexual behavior and the Year of Jubilee, capital crimes and the tabernacle loaves, the Lord teaches that Israel must reflect His holiness in their behavior.

17:3–8 In the wilderness period animals could be killed only at the tabernacle, even for ordinary meals. This was to prevent secret sacrifices to idols (v. 7). After entering Canaan this rule was relaxed (Deut. 12:15–16).

17:4 has shed blood. Or, has committed a transgression as grievous as any involving bloodshed.

cut off. See note 7:20.

offer it to the LORD, [w]that man shall be cut
off from his people.

Laws Against Eating Blood

10 “If any one of the house of Israel or of
the strangers who sojourn among them
[d]eats any blood, I will [e]set my face against
that person who eats blood and will cut him
off from among his people. 11 [f]For the life of
the flesh is in the blood, and I have given it
for you on the altar [g]to make atonement for
your souls, [h]for it is the blood that makes
atonement by the life. 12 Therefore I have
said to the people of Israel, No person
among you shall eat blood, neither shall any
stranger who sojourns among you eat blood.
13 “Any one also of the people of Israel, or
of the strangers who sojourn among them,
who takes in hunting any beast or bird that
may be eaten shall [i]pour out its blood and
[j]cover it with earth. 14 For the life of every
creature[1] is its [k]blood: its blood is its life.[2]
Therefore I have said to the people of
Israel, You shall not eat the blood of any
creature, for the life of every creature is its
blood. Whoever eats it shall be cut off.
15 [l]And every person who eats what dies of
itself or what is torn by beasts, [m]whether he
is a native or a sojourner, [n]shall wash his
clothes and [o]bathe himself in water and be
unclean until the evening; then he shall be
clean. 16 But if he does not wash them or
bathe his flesh, [p]he shall bear his iniquity.”

Unlawful Sexual Relations

18 And the LORD spoke to Moses, saying, 2 “Speak to the people of Israel
and say to them, [q]I am the LORD your God.
3 [r]You shall not do as they do in the land of
Egypt, where you lived, and [s]you shall not do
as they do in the land of Canaan, to which I
am bringing you. You shall not walk in their
statutes. 4 [t]You shall follow my rules and
keep my statutes and walk in them. [q]I am the
LORD your God. 5 [t]You shall therefore keep
my statutes and my rules; [u]if a person does
them, he shall live by them: I am the LORD.
6 “None of you shall approach any one of
his close relatives to uncover nakedness. I
am the LORD. 7 [v]You shall not uncover the
nakedness of your father, which is the
nakedness of your mother; she is your mother, you shall not uncover her nakedness.
8 [w]You shall not uncover the nakedness of
your father’s wife; it is your father’s nakedness. 9 [x]You shall not uncover the nakedness
of your sister, your father’s daughter or your
mother’s daughter, whether brought up in
the family or in another home. 10 You shall
not uncover the nakedness of your son’s
daughter or of your daughter’s daughter, for
their nakedness is your own nakedness.
11 You shall not uncover the nakedness of
your father’s wife’s daughter, brought up in
your father’s family, since she is your sister.
12 You shall not uncover the nakedness of
your father’s sister; she is your father’s relative. 13 You shall not uncover the nakedness
of your mother’s sister, for she is your mother’s relative. 14 You shall not uncover the
nakedness of your father’s brother, that is,
you shall not approach his wife; she is your
aunt. 15 [y]You shall not uncover the nakedness
of your daughter-in-law; she is your son’s
wife, you shall not uncover her nakedness.
16 [z]You shall not uncover the nakedness of
your brother’s wife; it is your brother’s

9 [w][See ver. 4 above] 10 [d]See ch. 3:17 [e]ch. 20:3, 6; 26:17; Jer. 44:11; Ezek. 14:8; 15:7; [Ps. 34:16] 11 [f]ver. 14 [g][Matt. 26:28; Mark. 14:24; Rom. 3:25; 5:9; Eph. 1:7; Col. 1:14, 20; Heb. 13:12; 1 John 1:7; Rev. 1:5] [h]Heb. 9:22 13 [i]Deut. 12:16, 24; 15:23; [j]Ezek. 24:7 14 [k]ver. 11; See Gen. 9:4 15 [l]See ch. 22:8 [m]See ch. 16:29 [n]See ch. 11:25 [o]ch. 15:5 16 [p][Num. 19:20]; See ch. 5:1

Chapter 18
2 [q]ch.11:44; 19:4; 20:7; Ex. 6:6, 7 3 [r]Ezek. 20:7, 8; 23:8 [s]Ex. 23:24; Deut. 12:30, 31 4 [t]ver. 26; ch. 19:19, 37; 20:8, 22; 25:18; Deut. 4:1, 6; 5:1; 6:1; 12:1; Ezek. 20:19 [q][See ver. 2 above] 5 [t][See ver. 4 above] [u]Ezek. 20:11, 13, 21; Cited Rom. 10:5; Gal. 3:12; [Luke 10:28] 7 [v]For ver. 7-16, see ch. 20:11-21 8 [w]Deut. 22:30; 27:20; 1 Cor. 5:1; [Gen. 49:4; Amos 2:7]

9 [x][2 Sam. 13:12; Ezek. 22:11] 15 [y][Gen. 38:26; Ezek. 22:11] 16 [z][Gen. 38:8; Deut. 25:5; Matt. 22:24; Mark 12:19; Luke 20:28]

1 Hebrew *all flesh* 2 Hebrew *it is in its life*

17:11 One of the most important theological statements in Leviticus. Life is sacred because it belongs to God. As a mark of respect for life and for its Creator, no Israelite could eat meat with blood in it “for the life of the flesh is in the blood” (cf. Gen. 9:4–6). A second reason is that it is the blood that makes “atonement for your souls.” The blood of animals shed in sacrifice took the place of, and symbolically redeemed, the life of the worshiper. Because animal blood was the sign of salvation, man must not consume it. These ideas are both assumed and transformed in the New Testament. Christ’s shed blood actually atoned for sin (Heb. 9:14, 22; 1 John 1:7), and those who spiritually drink that blood have eternal life (John 6:54).

have given it for you. The sacrificial system of the Old Testament was God’s gracious gift to His people. In anticipation of the final and perfect blood sacrifice offered by Christ, God Himself ordained the procedures whereby His righteous wrath might be averted and His people reconciled to Him.

18:1–30 Moses instructs Israel concerning unlawful practices linked to sex and family, including incest (vv. 6–20), child sacrifice (v. 21), homosexuality (v. 22), and bestiality (v. 23). Israel’s neighbors were much less restrained in their sexual attitudes and behavior (v. 3). They permitted closer intermarriage than allowed here; they allowed homosexuality (cf. v. 22), and even some types of bestiality (cf. v. 23). The laws in this chapter presuppose that an Israelite would normally marry another Israelite. However, unions between blood relatives of the first degree (brother-sister, father-daughter) and the second degree (father-granddaughter, nephew-aunt) were prohibited. Marriage between close relatives by marriage was also banned.

18:8 your father’s wife. Not one’s own mother (cf. v. 7), but the father’s second wife (cf. 1 Cor. 5:1). The phrase “it is your father’s nakedness” recalls the teaching in Gen. 2:24 that the married couple “become one flesh.”

18:9 your sister. A full sister or half sister.

18:11 your sister. A stepsister.

18:16 The law of levirate marriage (Deut. 25:5 note) encouraged a man to marry his widowed sister-in-law if her first marriage was childless. This provision shows the importance of preserving the family inheritance by perpetuating the family line in Old Testament society (Num. 27:1–11 note).

nakedness. 17 You shall not uncover the
nakedness of a woman and of her daughter,
and you shall not take her son's daughter or
her daughter's daughter to uncover her
nakedness; they are relatives; it is depravity.
18 And you shall not take a woman as a [a]rival
wife to her sister, uncovering her nakedness
[b]while her sister is still alive.
19 [c]"You shall not approach a woman to
uncover her nakedness while she is in her
menstrual uncleanness. 20 [d]And you shall not
lie sexually with your neighbor's wife and so
make yourself unclean with her. 21 You shall
not give any of your children to [e]offer them[1]
to [f]Molech, and so [g]profane the name of
your God: I am the LORD. 22 [h]You shall not lie
with a male as with a woman; it is an abomination. 23 [i]And you shall not lie with any
animal and so make yourself unclean with it,
neither shall any woman give herself to an
animal to lie with it: it is [j]perversion.
24 [k]"Do not make yourselves unclean by
any of these things, [l]for by all these the
nations I am driving out before you have
become unclean, 25 and the [m]land became
unclean, so that I punished its iniquity, and
the land [n]vomited out its inhabitants. 26 But
[o]you shall keep my statutes and my rules
and do none of these abominations, either
the [p]native or the stranger who sojourns
among you 27 (for the people of the land,
who were before you, did all of these abominations, so that the land became unclean),
28 lest the land vomit you out when you
make it unclean, as it vomited out the
nation that was before you. 29 For everyone
who does any of these abominations, the
persons who do them shall be cut off from
among their people. 30 [q]So keep my charge
never to practice [r]any of these abominable
customs that were practiced before you,
and never to make yourselves unclean by
them: [s]I am the LORD your God."

18 [a][1 Sam. 1:6] [b][Gen. 31:50]
19 [c][ch. 15:24; 20:18; Ezek. 18:6; 22:10]
20 [d]See Ex. 20:14
21 [e]ch. 20:2-5; Deut. 18:10 [f][1 Kin. 11:7, 33; Acts. 7:43] [g]ch. 19:12; 20:3; 21:6; 22:2, 32; Ezek. 36:20, 22; Mal. 1:12
22 [h]ch. 20:13; [Gen. 19:5; Judg. 19:22; Rom. 1:27; 1 Cor. 6:9, 10; 1 Tim. 1:9, 10]
23 [i]ch. 20:15, 16; Ex. 22:19 [j]ch. 20:12
24 [k]ver. 30; [Matt. 15:19, 20; Mark 7:21-23] [l]ch. 20:23; [Deut. 18:12]
25 [m]Num. 35:34; Jer. 2:7; Ezek. 36:17 [n]ch. 20:22
26 [o]See ver. 4, 5 [p]See ch. 16:29
30 [q]ch. 22:9 [r]ver. 3, 26; ch. 20:23; Deut. 18:9 [s]See ver. 2

Chapter 19
2 [t]See ch. 11:44, 45
3 [u]See Ex. 20:12 [v]See Ex. 20:8
4 [w]ch. 26:1; 1 John 5:21; See Ex. 20:3-5 [x]Ex. 34:17; [Deut. 27:15]
5 [y]See ch. 7:15-18 [z]ch. 1:3; 22:19
7 [a]ch. 7:18
8 [b]See ch. 5:1 [c]ch. 22:15
9 [d]ch. 23:22; Deut. 24:19-21; [Ruth 2:15, 16]

The LORD Is Holy

19 And the LORD spoke to Moses, saying, 2 "Speak to all the congregation
of the people of Israel and say to them, [t]'You
shall be holy, for I the LORD your God am
holy. 3 [u]Every one of you shall revere his
mother and his father, and [v]you shall keep
my Sabbaths: I am the LORD your God. 4 [w]Do
not turn to idols [x]or make for yourselves any
gods of cast metal: I am the LORD your God.
5 [y]"When you offer a sacrifice of peace
offerings to the LORD, you shall offer it so
[z]that you may be accepted. 6 It shall be
eaten the same day you offer it or on the
day after, and anything left over until the
third day shall be burned up with fire. 7 If it
is eaten at all on the third day, it is [a]tainted;
it will not be accepted, 8 and everyone who
eats it shall [b]bear his iniquity, because [c]he
has profaned what is holy to the LORD, and
that person shall be cut off from his people.

Love Your Neighbor As Yourself

9 [d]"When you reap the harvest of your
land, you shall not reap your field right up
to its edge, neither shall you gather the
gleanings after your harvest. 10 And you shall
not strip your vineyard bare, neither shall
you gather the fallen grapes of your vineyard. You shall leave them for the poor and
for the sojourner: I am the LORD your God.
11 [e]"You shall not steal; [f]you shall not
deal falsely; you shall not lie to one another. 12 [g]You shall not swear by my name
falsely, and so [h]profane the name of your
God: I am the LORD.
13 [i]"You shall not oppress your neighbor
or rob him. [j]The wages of a hired servant
shall not remain with you all night until the
morning. 14 [k]You shall not curse the deaf or

11 [e]See Ex. 20:15; [f][ch. 6:2, 3; Eph. 4:15, 25; Col. 3:9] 12 [g]See Ex. 20:7 [h]See ch. 18:21 13 [i]ch. 6:2, 3 [j]Deut. 24:14, 15; Mal. 3:5; [James 5:4] 14 [k]Deut. 27:18

[1] Hebrew *to make them pass through* [the fire]

18:17 her daughter. The daughter of the woman would be the man's step-daughter or step-granddaughter.

18:18 The sad example of Jacob's marriage to Leah and Rachel illustrates the compassionate wisdom of this law (Gen. 29:23–30:24).

18:19 See note on ch. 15.

18:21 offer them to Molech. The custom of sacrificing children was practiced among the ancient Phoenicians and pagan inhabitants of Canaan (Deut. 12:31 note). The cult of Molech, a god of the Ammonites, was a temptation to the Israelites (1 Kin. 11:7; 2 Kin. 23:10).

18:25 the land became unclean. Uncleanness and sin were contagious: all and everything that came in contact with it was infected, including the sanctuary (16:16 note) and the land. **vomited.** This personification of the land underscores the poisonous contagion of uncleanness and sin.

18:29 cut off. See note 7:20.

19:1–37 The theme of holiness is elaborated as God instructs the people on principles of good neighborliness. The chapter illustrates what holiness meant in daily life. See Introduction: Characteristics and Themes (cf. Matt. 5:48; 1 Cor. 11:1; 1 Pet. 1:16).

19:2 See "God Is Light: Divine Holiness and Justice" at 11:44.

19:5 peace offerings. See note 3:1; cf. 7:16–18.

19:9, 10 See Ruth 2:2–23.

19:13 wages of a hired servant. See Deut. 24:14, 15.

put a stumbling block before the blind, but
you shall [l]fear your God: I am the LORD.
15 [m]"You shall do no injustice in court.
You shall not be partial to the poor or defer
to the great, but in righteousness shall you
judge your neighbor. 16 [n]You shall not go
around as a slanderer among your people,
and you shall not [o]stand up against the
life[1] of your neighbor: I am the LORD.
17 [p]"You shall not hate your brother in
your heart, but [q]you shall reason frankly
with your neighbor, lest you [r]incur sin
because of him. 18 [s]You shall not take
vengeance or bear a grudge against the sons
of your own people, but [t]you shall love your
neighbor as yourself: I am the LORD.

You Shall Keep My Statutes

19 [u]"You shall keep my statutes. You shall
not let your cattle breed with a different
kind. [v]You shall not sow your field with two
kinds of seed, nor shall you wear a garment
of cloth made of two kinds of material.
20 "If a man lies sexually with a woman
who is a slave, assigned to another man and
not yet ransomed or given her freedom, a
distinction shall be made. They shall not be
put to death, because she was not free; 21 but
[w]he shall bring his compensation to the
LORD, to the entrance of the tent of meeting,
a ram for a guilt offering. 22 And the priest
shall make atonement for him with the ram
of the guilt offering before the LORD for his
sin that he has committed, and he shall be
forgiven for the sin that he has committed.
23 "When you come into the land and
plant any kind of tree for food, then you
shall regard its fruit as forbidden.[2] Three
years it shall be forbidden to you; it must
not be eaten. 24 And in the fourth year all its
fruit shall be holy, an offering of praise to
the LORD. 25 But in the fifth year you may
eat of its fruit, to increase its yield for you:
I am the LORD your God.
26 [x]"You shall not eat any flesh with the
blood in it. [y]You shall not interpret omens
or [z]tell fortunes. 27 [a]You shall not round off
the hair on your temples or mar the edges
of your beard. 28 You shall not make any
[b]cuts on your body for the dead or tattoo
yourselves: I am the LORD.
29 [c]"Do not profane your daughter by making her a prostitute, lest the land fall into
prostitution and the land become full of
depravity. 30 [d]You shall keep my Sabbaths
and [e]reverence my sanctuary: I am the LORD.
31 [f]"Do not turn to mediums or wizards;[3]
do not seek them out, and so make yourselves unclean by them: I am the LORD your
God.
32 [g]"You shall stand up before the gray
head and honor the face of an old man, and
you shall [h]fear your God: I am the LORD.
33 [i]"When a stranger sojourns with you in
your land, you shall not do him wrong.
34 [j]You shall treat the stranger who sojourns
with you as the native among you, and
[k]you shall love him as yourself, for you
were strangers in the land of Egypt: I am
the LORD your God.
35 [l]"You shall do no wrong in judgment,
in measures of length or weight or quantity. 36 [m]You shall have just balances, just
weights, a just ephah, and a just hin:[4] I am
the LORD your God, who brought you out
of the land of Egypt. 37 And [n]you shall
observe all my statutes and all my rules,
and do them: I am the LORD."

Punishment for Child Sacrifice

20 The LORD spoke to Moses, saying,
2 "Say to the people of Israel, [o]Any
one of the people of Israel or of the
strangers who sojourn in Israel who gives
any of his children to Molech shall surely

14 [l]ver. 32; ch. 25:17; Eccles. 5:7; 12:13; 1 Pet. 2:17 **15** [m]Ex. 23:2, 3; Deut. 1:17; 16:19; 27:19; Ps. 82:2; Prov. 24:23; James 2:9; [2 Chr. 19:6, 7] **16** [n]Prov. 11:13; 20:19 [o]Ex. 23:1, 7; [Matt. 26:60, 61]; See 1 Kin. 21:10-13; Acts 6:11-13 **17** [p]1 John 2:9, 11; 3:15 [q]Prov. 27:5, 6; Matt. 18:15; Luke 17:3; Gal. 6:1; Eph. 5:11 [r][ch. 22:16; Rom. 1:32; 1 Tim. 5:22; 2 John 11] **18** [s]Prov. 20:22; Rom. 12:17, 19; Heb. 10:30 [t]Matt. 5:43; Cited Matt. 19:19; 22:39; Mark 12:31; Luke 10:27; Rom. 13:9; Gal. 5:14; James 2:8 **19** [u]See ch. 18:4, 5 [v]Deut. 22:9-11 **21** [w]ch. 5:15; 6:6, 7 **26** [x]See ch. 3:17 [y]Deut. 18:10; 2 Kin. 17:17 [z]2 Kin. 21:6; 2 Chr. 33:6 **27** [a]ch. 21:5; [Isai. 15:2; Jer. 9:26; 48:37] **28** [b]ch. 21:1, 4, 5; Deut. 14:1; 1 Kin. 18:28; Jer. 16:6; 41:5; 47:5; 48:37 **29** [c][Deut. 23:17] **30** [d]ver. 3; ch. 26:2; See Ex. 20:8 [e]Eccles. 5:1; [Matt. 21:12, 13; Mark 11:15-17; Luke 19:45, 46; John 2:14-16] **31** [f]ch. 20:6, 27; Deut. 18:11; Isai. 8:19; [Ex. 22:18; 1 Sam. 28:3, 7, 9; 1 Chr. 10:13; Acts 16:16] **32** [g]Prov. 20:29; [Lam. 5:12] [h]See ver. 14 **33** [i]Ex. 22:21; 23:9; Mal. 3:5 **34** [j]See ch. 16:29 [k]Deut. 10:19; See ver. 18 **35** [l]See ver. 15 **36** [m]Deut. 25:13, 15; Prov. 11:1; 16:11; 20:10; Ezek. 45:10; [Amos 8:5; Mic. 6:11] **37** [n]See ch. 18:4, 5 **Chapter 20** **2** [o]See ch. 18:21

[1] Hebrew *blood* [2] Hebrew *its uncircumcision* [3] Or *those who consult familiar spirits* [4] An *ephah* was about 3/5 bushel or 22 liters; a *hin* was about 4 quarts or 3.5 liters

19:17 reason frankly . . . because of him. A candid yet tactful reproof of the wrongdoer is better than storing up destructive hatred against that neighbor and so causing oneself to sin as well (Prov. 27:5; Matt. 18:15; Gal. 6:1).

19:18 love your neighbor. A "neighbor" was anyone with whom there was contact, whether Israelite (v. 17) or alien (v. 34; cf. Matt. 22:39, 40; Rom. 13:9).

19:19 Respecting boundaries and distinctions was an aspect of holiness.

19:21 guilt offering. See note 5:14–6:7.

19:24 Firstfruits, like firstborn livestock and children, were to be given to God (Ex. 22:29, 30; 23:19), for Israel was God's firstborn and so was consecrated to Him (Ex. 4:22).

19:28 Mutilation of the body created by God was incompatible with holiness, for the holy God is perfect life (Deut. 14:1 note).

20:1–27 The instruction here repeats many of the same points of chs. 18; 19 (for parallel verses, consult the cross-references), but with the addition of prescribed penalties. The death penalty is indicated for many offenses, pointing to the horror with which God viewed them (cf. Rom. 1:18–32). In

be put to death. The people of the land
shall stone him with stones. 3 [p]I myself will
set my face against that man and will cut
him off from among his people, because he
has given one of his children to Molech, to
make my sanctuary [q]unclean and [r]to profane my holy name. 4 And if the people of
the land do at all close their eyes to that
man when he gives one of his children to
Molech, and do not [s]put him to death,
5 then I will set my face against that man
and against his clan and will cut them off
from among their people, him and all who
follow him in [t]whoring after Molech.
6 "If [u]a person turns to mediums and wizards, whoring after them, [v]I will set my face
against that person and will cut him off from
among his people. 7 [w]Consecrate yourselves,
therefore, and be holy, for I am the LORD
your God. 8 [x]Keep my statutes and do them;
[y]I am the LORD who sanctifies you. 9 For [z]any-
one who curses his father or his mother shall
surely be put to death; he has cursed his
father or his mother; [a]his blood is upon him.

Punishments for Sexual Immorality

10 "If a [b]man commits adultery with the
wife of[1] his neighbor, both the adulterer
and the adulteress shall surely be put to
death. 11 [c]If a man lies with his father's wife,
he has uncovered his father's nakedness;
both of them shall surely be put to death;
their blood is upon them. 12 [d]If a man lies
with his daughter-in-law, both of them shall
surely be put to death; they have committed [e]perversion; their blood is upon them.
13 [f]If a man lies with a male as with a
woman, both of them have committed an
abomination; they shall surely be put to
death; their blood is upon them. 14 [g]If a man
takes a woman and her mother also, it is
depravity; he and they shall be burned with
fire, that there may be no depravity among
you. 15 [h]If a man lies with an animal, he
shall surely be put to death, and you shall
kill the animal. 16 [h]If a woman approaches
any animal and lies with it, you shall kill the
woman and the animal; they shall surely be
put to death; their blood is upon them.
17 [i]"If a man takes his sister, a daughter of
his father or a daughter of his mother, and
sees her nakedness, and she sees his nakedness, it is a disgrace, and they shall be cut
off in the sight of the children of their people. He has uncovered his sister's nakedness, and he shall bear his iniquity. 18 [j]If a
man lies with a woman during her menstrual period and uncovers her nakedness,
he has made naked her fountain, and she
has uncovered the fountain of her blood.
Both of them shall be cut off from among
their people. 19 [k]You shall not uncover the
nakedness of your mother's sister or of your
father's sister, for that is to make naked
[l]one's relative; they shall bear their iniquity.
20 [m]If a man lies with his uncle's wife, he has
uncovered his uncle's nakedness; they shall
bear their sin; they shall die childless. 21 [n]If
a man takes his brother's wife, it is impurity.[2] He has uncovered his brother's nakedness; they shall be childless.

You Shall Be Holy

22 [o]"You shall therefore keep all my
statutes and all my rules and do them, that
the land where I am bringing you to live
may not [p]vomit you out. 23 [q]And you shall
not walk in the customs of the nation that
I am driving out before you, for they did all
these things, and therefore I detested
them. 24 But [r]I have said to you, 'You shall
inherit their land, and I will give it to you
to possess, a land [s]flowing with milk and
honey.' I am the LORD your God, [t]who have
separated you from the peoples. 25 [u]You
shall therefore separate the clean beast
from the unclean, and the unclean bird
from the clean. You shall not make yourselves detestable by beast or by bird or by
anything with which the ground crawls,
which I have set apart for you to hold
unclean. 26 [v]You shall be holy to me, [w]for I
the LORD am holy and have separated you
from the peoples, that you should be mine.
27 [x]"A man or a woman who is a medium
or a wizard shall surely be put to death.
They shall be [y]stoned with stones; [z]their
blood shall be upon them."

[1] Hebrew repeats *if a man commits adultery with the wife of* [2] Literally *menstrual impurity*

3 [p]See ch. 17:10 [q]ch. 19:30; Ezek. 5:11; 23:38, 39 [r]See ch. 18:21
4 [s]Deut. 17:2, 3, 5
5 [t]See Ex. 34:15
6 [u]See ch. 19:31 [v]See ch. 17:10
7 [w]See ch. 11:44
8 [x]See ch. 18:4 [y]ch. 21:8, 15, 23; 22:32; Ex. 31:13; Ezek. 37:28
9 [z]See Ex. 21:17 [a]ver. 11, 12, 13, 16, 27; [2 Sam. 1:16; 1 Kin. 2:32, 33, 37]
10 [b]ch. 18:20; Deut. 22:22; John 8:4, 5
11 [c]See ch. 18:8
12 [d]ch. 18:15 [e]ch. 18:23
13 [f]See ch. 18:22
14 [g]ch. 18:17; Deut. 27:23
15 [h]ch. 18:23; Ex. 22:19; Deut. 27:21
16 [h][See ver. 15 above]
17 [i]ch. 18:9; Deut. 27:22
18 [j]ch. 18:19; [ch. 15:24]
19 [k]ch. 18:12, 13 [l]ch. 18:6
20 [m]ch. 18:14
21 [n]ch. 18:16
22 [o]See ch. 18:4 [p]ch. 18:25, 28
23 [q]ch. 18:3, 24, 30; Deut. 9:5
24 [r]Ex. 3:17; 6:8 [s]See Ex. 3:8 [t]Ex. 33:16; 1 Kin. 8:53; [Ex. 19:5; Deut. 7:6; 14:2; 1 Kin. 8:53]
25 [u]See ch. 11:2-47; Deut. 14:4-20
26 [v]Ex. 19:6 [w]ver. 7; See ch. 11:44
27 [x]See ch. 19:31 [y]ver. 2 [z]ver. 9

other cases divine penalties, such as cutting off (7:20 note), are mentioned; these cover situations where detection might be difficult (v. 18) or family solidarity might make the head of the family reluctant to punish (v. 17).

20:6 See Deut. 18:10, 11; 1 Sam. 28:9.

20:9 Jesus quoted this text in Mark 7:10.

20:25 See notes on ch. 11.

20:27 See note on v. 6.

Holiness and the Priests

21 And the LORD said to Moses, "Speak
to the priests, the sons of Aaron,
and say to them: [a]'No one shall make himself unclean for the dead among his people,
2 except for his closest relatives, his mother,
his father, his son, his daughter, his brother, 3 or his virgin sister (who is near to him
because she has had no husband; for her
he may make himself unclean). 4 He shall
not make himself unclean as a husband
among his people and so profane himself.
5 [b]They shall not make bald patches on
their heads, nor shave off the edges of their
beards, nor make any cuts on their body.
6 They shall be holy to their God and [c]not
profane the name of their God. For they
offer the LORD's food offerings, [d]the bread
of their God; therefore they shall be holy.
7 [e]They shall not marry a prostitute or a
woman who has been defiled, neither shall
they marry a woman [f]divorced from her
husband, for the priest is holy to his God.
8 You shall sanctify him, for he offers the
bread of your God. He shall be holy to you,
for [g]I, the LORD, who sanctify you, [h]am
holy. 9 And the daughter of any priest, if
she profanes herself by whoring, profanes
her father; [i]she shall be burned with fire.
10 [j]"The priest who is chief among his
brothers, on whose head the anointing oil
is poured and who has been consecrated to
wear the garments, [k]shall not let the hair of
his head hang loose nor tear his clothes.
11 He shall not [l]go in to any dead bodies nor
make himself unclean, even for his father
or for his mother. 12 [m]He shall not go out of
the sanctuary, lest he [n]profane the sanctuary of his God, for the [o]consecration of the
anointing oil of his God is on him: I am the
LORD. 13 And he shall take a wife in her virginity.[1] 14 A widow, [p]or a divorced woman,
or a woman who has been defiled, or a
prostitute, these he shall not marry. But he
shall take as his wife a virgin[2] of his own
people, 15 that he may not profane his offspring among his people, for [g]I am the
LORD who sanctifies him."
16 And the LORD spoke to Moses, saying,
17 "Speak to Aaron, saying, None of your
offspring throughout their generations
who has a blemish may [q]approach to offer
the bread of his God. 18 For no one who
has a blemish shall draw near, a man
[r]blind or lame, or one who has a mutilated face [s]or a limb too long, 19 or a man who
has an injured foot or an injured hand,
20 or a hunchback or a dwarf or a man with
a defect in his sight or an [r]itching disease
or scabs or [t]crushed testicles. 21 No man of
the offspring of Aaron the priest who has a
blemish shall come near to [u]offer the
LORD's food offerings; since he has a blemish, he shall not come near to offer the
bread of his God. 22 He may eat the bread
of his God, both of [v]the most holy and of
the [w]holy things, 23 but he shall not go
through the veil or approach the altar,
because he has a blemish, that he may not
[x]profane my sanctuaries, [y]for I am the
LORD who sanctifies them." 24 So Moses
spoke to Aaron and to his sons and to all
the people of Israel.
22 And the LORD spoke to Moses, saying, 2 "Speak to Aaron and his sons
so that they [z]abstain from the holy things
of the people of Israel, which they [a]dedi-
cate to me, so that they do not [b]profane
my holy name: I am the LORD. 3 Say to
them, 'If any one of all your offspring
throughout your generations approaches
the holy things that the people of Israel
dedicate to the LORD, while [c]he has an
uncleanness, that person shall be cut off
from my presence: I am the LORD. 4 None
of the offspring of Aaron who has a leprous disease or a [d]discharge may eat of the
holy things [e]until he is clean. [f]Whoever
touches anything that is unclean through
contact with the dead or [g]a man who has
had an emission of semen, 5 and [h]whoever

1 Or *a young wife* 2 Hebrew *young woman*

Chapter 21
1 [a]Ezek. 44:25
5 [b]Ezek. 44:20; [ch. 19:27, 28; Deut. 14:1]
6 [c]See ch. 18:21 [d]See ch. 3:11
7 [e]ver. 13, 14; Ezek. 44:22 [f]See Deut. 24:1-4
8 [g]ch. 22:9, 16 [h]See ch. 11:44
9 [i][Gen. 38:24]
10 [j]ch. 8:12; 16:32; Ex. 29:29, 30; Num. 35:25 [k]ch. 10:6
11 [l]Num. 19:14; [ver. 1, 2]
12 [m]ch. 10:7 [n]ver. 23 [o][ch. 8:9, 12, 30]
14 [p]ver. 7; Ezek. 44:22
15 [g][see ver. 8 above]
17 [q]ch. 10:3; [Num. 16:5; Ps. 65:4]
18 [r]ch. 22:22 [s][ch. 22:23]
20 [r][See ver. 18 above] [t][Deut. 23:1]
21 [u]ver. 6
22 [v]ch. 2:3, 10; 6:17, 25; 7:1; 10:12, 17; 14:13; 24:9; Num. 18:9 [w]ch. 22:10, 12
23 [x]ver. 12 [y]ch. 22:9, 16
Chapter 22
2 [z][Num. 6:3] [a]ver. 3; Ex. 28:38; Deut. 15:19 [b][Num. 18:32]; See ch. 18:21
3 [c]ch. 7:20
4 [d]ch. 15:2 [e]ch. 14:2; 15:13 [f]Num. 19:11 [g]ch. 15:16
5 [h]ch. 11:24, 43, 44

21:1–24 Ceremonial cleanliness regulations specific to the priests are recorded. These deal with priests in general (vv. 1–9), the high priest (vv. 10–15), and priests suffering from defects (vv. 16–24). All priests represented man as restored to the image of God and therefore had to show God's holiness in their character and in their bodies. Holiness in restored man ultimately involves his perfection and health (fullness of life; freedom from mortality, perishableness, decay), so priests with certain handicaps were forbidden to offer sacrifice (vv. 17–21). But handicapped priests still enjoyed a full share of priestly dues (v. 22).

21:1 Holiness (life) and death are incompatible; therefore priests could not mourn for any save their closest relatives (vv. 2–3).

21:5 Mourning customs involving disfigurement of the body were also banned, for priests as holy men had to have whole bodies (Deut. 14:1 note).

21:10–12 The high priest, representing man restored to fellowship with God, was obliged to avoid all contact with death (cf. 10:6, 7).

22:3 For any unclean person to eat holy food from a sacrifice was to risk death (7:20–21). Uncleanness (death) and holiness (life) were not to mix.

touches a swarming thing by which he
may be made unclean or [i]a person from
whom he may take uncleanness, whatever
his uncleanness may be—6 the person who
touches such a thing shall be unclean until
the evening and shall not eat of the holy
things unless he has [j]bathed his body in
water. 7 When the sun goes down he shall
be clean, and afterward he may eat of the
holy things, because [k]they are his food.
8 [l]He shall not eat what dies of itself or is
torn by beasts, and so make himself
unclean by it: I am the LORD.' 9 They shall
therefore keep my charge, [m]lest they bear
sin for it and die thereby when they profane it: [n]I am the LORD who sanctifies
them.
10 [o]"A lay person shall not eat of a holy
thing; no foreign guest of the priest or
hired servant shall eat of a holy thing,
11 but if a priest buys a slave as his property for money, the slave[1] may eat of it, and
[p]anyone born in his house may eat of his
food. 12 If a priest's daughter marries a layman, she shall not eat of the contribution
of the holy things. 13 But if a priest's
daughter is widowed or divorced and has
no child and [q]returns to her father's
house, [r]as in her youth, she may eat of her
father's food; yet no lay person shall eat of
it. 14 [s]And if anyone eats of a holy thing
unintentionally, he shall add [t]the fifth of
its value to it and give the holy thing to the
priest. 15 They [u]shall not profane the holy
things of the people of Israel, which they
contribute to the LORD, 16 and so cause
them [m]to bear iniquity and guilt, by eating
their holy things: [n]for I am the LORD who
sanctifies them."

Acceptable Offerings

17 And the LORD spoke to Moses, saying,
18 "Speak to Aaron and his sons and all the
people of Israel and say to them, [v]When
any one of the house of Israel or of the
sojourners in Israel presents a burnt offering as his offering, for any of their vows or
freewill offerings that they offer to the
LORD, 19 if it is to be accepted for you it
shall be a [w]male without blemish, of the
bulls or the sheep or the goats. 20 [x]You
shall not offer anything that has a blemish,
for it will not be acceptable for you. 21 And
when anyone [y]offers a sacrifice of peace
offerings to the LORD [z]to fulfill a vow or as
a freewill offering from the herd or from
the flock, to be accepted it must be perfect; there shall be no blemish in it.
22 Animals [a]blind or disabled or mutilated
or having a discharge or [b]an itch or scabs
you shall not offer to the LORD or give
them to the LORD as a food [c]offering on the
altar. 23 You may present a bull or a lamb
that has a part [d]too long or too short for a
freewill offering, but for a vow offering it
cannot be accepted. 24 Any animal that has
its testicles bruised or crushed or torn or
cut you shall not offer to the LORD; you
shall not do it within your land, 25 neither
shall you offer as [e]the bread of your God
any such animals gotten from a foreigner.
Since there is a [f]blemish in them, because
of their mutilation, they will not be accepted for you."
26 And the LORD spoke to Moses, saying,
27 [g]"When an ox or sheep or goat is born, it
shall remain seven days with its mother,
and from the eighth day on it shall be
acceptable as a food offering to the LORD.
28 But you shall not kill an ox or a sheep
[h]and her young in one day. 29 And when
you sacrifice a [i]sacrifice of thanksgiving to
the LORD, you shall sacrifice it so that you
may be accepted. 30 It shall be eaten on the
same day; [j]you shall leave none of it until
morning: I am the LORD.
31 [k]"So you shall keep my commandments and do them: I am the LORD. 32 [l]And
you shall not profane my holy name, that
[m]I may be sanctified among the people of
Israel. [n]I am the LORD who sanctifies you,
33 who brought you out of the land of
Egypt [o]to be your God: I am the LORD."

[1] Hebrew *he*

5 [i]ch. 15:7, 19
6 [j][Heb. 10:22]; See ch. 15:5-11
7 [k]ch. 21:22; [Num. 18:11, 13]; See ch. 3:11
8 [l]See ch. 7:24
9 [m][Ex. 28:43]; See ch. 19:17; [n]ch. 21:8, 15, 23
10 [o]ch. 24:9; [1 Sam. 21:6; Matt. 12:4; Mark 2:26; Luke 6:4]
11 [p]Num. 18:11, 13
13 [q][Gen. 38:11; Ruth 1:8] [r]ch. 10:14; Num. 18:11, 19
14 [s]ch. 4:2; 5:15, 16, 18 [t]ch. 27:13, 15, 19
15 [u]ch. 19:8; Num. 18:32
16 [m][See ver. 9 above] [n][See ver. 9 above]
17 [v]ch. 1:2, 3, 10; Num. 15:14
19 [w]ch. 1:3, 10
20 [x]Deut. 15:21; 17:1; Mal. 1:8, 14; [Heb. 9:14; 1 Pet. 1:19]
21 [y]ch. 3:1, 6 [z]ch. 7:16; Num. 15:3, 8; Deut. 23:21, 23; Ps. 61:8; 65:1; Eccles. 5:4, 5
22 [a]ver. 20; ch. 21:18; Mal. 1:8 [b]ch. 21:20 [c]ch. 1:9, 13; 3:3, 5
23 [d]ch. 21:18
25 [e]See ch. 3:11 [f]Mal. 1:14
27 [g]Ex. 22:30
28 [h][Deut. 22:6]
29 [i]ch. 7:12; Ps. 107:22; 116:17; Amos 4:5
30 [j]ch. 7:15
31 [k]ch. 19:37; Num. 15:40; Deut. 4:40
32 [l]See ch. 18:21; [m]ch. 10:3 [n]See ch. 20:8
33 [o]See Ex. 6:7

22:10–13 These verses define which dependents of the priests were allowed to eat sacrificial food.

22:14 A penalty of restitution was prescribed for non-priests who ate the priestly portions of the sacrifices (cf. 5:14–16).

22:17–25 Only blemish-free animals were to be sacrificed. This was partly because God was not to be given anything but the best (Mal. 1:8), and partly because the holiness of sacrifices was symbolized by a perfect physical body (cf. 21:17–21).

22:23 In the case of the optional freewill offering, a kind of peace offering (ch. 3), minor blemishes could be tolerated.

22:27, 28 Killing an animal soon after birth showed little respect for life and therefore was incompatible with holiness. So, too, did killing an animal and its young on the same day (cf. Deut. 14:21; 22:6, 7).

Feasts of the LORD

23 The LORD spoke to Moses, saying, 2 "Speak to the people of Israel and say to them, [p]These are the appointed feasts of the LORD that you shall [q]proclaim as [r]holy convocations; they are my appointed feasts.

The Sabbath

3 [s]"Six days shall work be done, but on the seventh day is a Sabbath of solemn rest, a holy convocation. You shall do no work. It is a Sabbath to the LORD in all your dwelling places.

The Passover

4 [p]"These are the appointed feasts of the LORD, the [t]holy convocations, which you shall proclaim at the time appointed for them. 5 [u]In the first month, on the fourteenth day of the month at twilight,[1] is the LORD's Passover. 6 And on the fifteenth day of the same month is the Feast of Unleavened Bread to the LORD; for seven days you shall eat unleavened bread. 7 [v]On the first day you shall have a holy convocation; you shall not do any ordinary work. 8 But you shall present a food offering to the LORD for seven days. On the seventh day is a holy convocation; you shall not do any ordinary work."

The Feast of Firstfruits

9 And the LORD spoke to Moses, saying, 10 "Speak to the people of Israel and say to them, [w]When you come into the land that I give you and reap its harvest, you shall bring the sheaf of [x]the firstfruits of your harvest to the priest, 11 and he shall [y]wave the sheaf before the LORD, so that you may be accepted. On the day after the Sabbath the priest shall wave it. 12 And on the day when you [y]wave the sheaf, you shall offer a [z]male lamb a year old without blemish as a burnt offering to the LORD. 13 [a]And the grain offering with it shall be two tenths of an ephah[2] of fine flour mixed with oil, a food offering to the LORD with a pleasing aroma, [b]and the drink offering with it shall be of wine, a fourth of a hin.[3] 14 And you shall eat neither bread nor grain [c]parched or [c]fresh until this same day, until you have brought the offering of your God: it is a statute forever throughout your generations in all your dwellings.

The Feast of Weeks

15 [d]"You shall count seven full weeks from the day after the Sabbath, from the day that you brought the sheaf of the [y]wave offering. 16 You shall count [e]fifty days to the day after the seventh Sabbath. Then you shall present a grain offering of [f]new grain to the LORD. 17 You shall bring from your dwelling places two loaves of bread to be waved, made of two tenths of an ephah. They shall be of fine flour, and they shall be baked with leaven, as [g]firstfruits to the LORD. 18 And you shall present with the bread seven lambs a year old without blemish, and one bull from the herd and two rams. They shall be a burnt offering to the LORD, with their grain offering and their drink offerings, a food offering with a pleasing aroma to the LORD. 19 And you shall offer one [h]male goat for a sin offering, and two male lambs a year old as a sacrifice of [i]peace offerings. 20 And the priest shall [y]wave them with the bread of the firstfruits as a wave offering before the LORD, with the two lambs. [j]They shall be holy to the LORD for the priest. 21 And you shall make proclamation on the same day. You shall hold a holy convocation. You shall not do any ordinary work. It is a statute forever in all your dwelling places throughout your generations.

22 "And [k]when you reap the harvest of your land, you shall not reap your field right up to its edge, nor shall you gather the gleanings after your harvest. You shall leave them for the poor and for the sojourner: I am the LORD your God."

The Feast of Trumpets

23 And the LORD spoke to Moses, saying, 24 "Speak to the people of Israel, saying, In [l]the seventh month, on the first day of the month, you shall observe a day of solemn rest, [m]a memorial proclaimed with blast of trumpets, a holy convocation. 25 You shall not do any ordinary work, and you shall present a food offering to the LORD."

The Day of Atonement

26 And the LORD spoke to Moses, saying, 27 "Now [n]on the tenth day of this seventh

Chapter 23
2 [p]ver. 4, 37; Num. 29:39; See Ex. 23:14-17 [q]Num. 10:10; Ps. 81:3; Joel 2:15 [r]Ex. 12:16
3 [s]ch. 19:3; Ex. 23:12; 31:15; 34:21; Luke 13:14; See Ex. 20:8-11; Deut. 5:12-15
4 [p][See ver. 2 above] [t]Ex. 12:16
5 [u]Ex. 13:3, 10; 23:15; 34:18; Num. 9:2, 3; 28:16, 17; Josh 5:10; 2 Kin. 23:21; Ezra 6:19; [Num. 9:10, 11; 2 Chr. 30:2, 13, 15]; See Ex. 12:2-14; Deut. 16:1-8;
7 [v]Ex. 12:16; Num. 28:18, 25
10 [w]Ex. 23:19; 34:26; Num. 15:18, 19; 28:26; Deut. 26:1, 2 [x]ver. 17
11 [y]ver. 15, 20; Ex. 29:24
12 [y][See ver. 11 above] [z]ch. 1:10
13 [a]ch. 2:14-16 [b]Ex. 29:40
14 [c][ch. 2:14]
15 [d]Ex. 34:22; Deut. 16:9 [y][See ver. 11 above]
16 [e]Acts. 2:1 (Gk.) [f]Num. 28:26
17 [g]See ver. 10
19 [h]ch. 4:23, 28; Num. 28:30; [i]See ch. 3:1
20 [y][See ver. 11 above] [j]Num. 18:12; Deut. 18:4
22 [k]ch. 19:9, 10; Deut. 24:19; [Ruth 2:2, 3]
24 [l]Num. 29:1 [m]ch. 25:9
27 [n]ch. 16:29, 30; Num. 29:7

[1] Hebrew *between the two evenings* [2] An *ephah* was about 3/5 bushel or 22 liters [3] A *hin* was about 4 quarts or 3.5 liters

23:1–44 Attention turns to the calendar of holy days, with specific instructions for the laity (cf. Num. 28, 29, where instructions are given to the priests specifying sacrifices on the different days).

23:4–8 See Ex. 12; 13.

23:26–32 See 16:2–34.

month is the Day of Atonement. It shall
be for you a time of holy convocation,
and you shall afflict yourselves and
present a food offering to the LORD. 28 And
you shall not do any work on that very
day, for it is a Day of Atonement, to make
atonement for you before the LORD your
God. 29 For whoever is not afflicted on
that very day [o]shall be cut off from his
people. 30 And whoever does any work on
that very day, that person I will destroy
from among his people. 31 You shall not
do any work. It is a statute forever
throughout your generations in all your
dwelling places. 32 It shall be to you a
Sabbath of solemn rest, and you shall
afflict yourselves. On the ninth day of the
month beginning at evening, from
evening to evening shall you keep your
Sabbath."

The Feast of Booths

33 And the LORD spoke to Moses, saying,
34 "Speak to the people of Israel, saying,
[p]On the fifteenth day of this seventh
month and for seven days is the Feast of
Booths[1] to the LORD. 35 On the first day
shall be a holy convocation; you shall not
do any ordinary work. 36 For seven days you
shall present food offerings to the LORD.
[q]On the eighth day you shall hold a holy
convocation and present a food offering to
the LORD. It is a [r]solemn assembly; you
shall not do any ordinary work.
37 [s]"These are the appointed feasts of the
LORD, which you shall proclaim as times of
holy convocation, for presenting to the
LORD food offerings, burnt offerings and
grain offerings, sacrifices and drink offerings, each on its proper day, 38 [t]besides the

29 [o]See Ex. 30:33
34 [p]Num. 29:12; Deut. 16:13; Ezra 3:4; Neh. 8:14; Ezek. 45:25; Hos. 12:9; Zech. 14:16; John 7:2
36 [q]Num. 29:35; Neh. 8:18; John 7:37 [r]Num. 29:35; Deut. 16:8; 2 Kin. 10:20; 2 Chr. 7:9; Neh. 8:18; Isai. 1:13; Joel 1:14; 2:15; Amos 5:21
37 [s]ver. 2, 4
38 [t]Num. 29:39

1 Or *tabernacles*

23:33–43 See Deut. 16:13–17.

Israel's Annual Feasts (23:44)

Feast	Month of Sacred Year	Day	Corresponding Month
Passover	1 (Abib)	14	Mar.–Apr.
Ex. 12:1–14; Lev. 23:5; Num. 9:1–14; 28:16; Deut. 16:1–7			
***Unleavened Bread**	1 (Abib)	15–21	Mar.–Apr.
Ex. 12:15–20; 13:3–10; Lev. 23:6–8; Num. 28:17–25; Deut. 16:3, 4, 8			
Firstfruits	1 (Abib) and 3 (Sivan)	16 6	Mar.–Apr. May–June
Lev. 23:9–14; Num. 28:26			
***Weeks** (Harvest or Pentecost)	3 (Sivan)	6 (50 days after barley harvest)	May–June
Ex. 23:16; 34:22; Lev. 23:15–21; Num. 28:26–31; Deut. 16:9–12			
Trumpets *Rosh Hashanah*	7 (Tishri)	1	Sept.–Oct.
Lev. 23:23–25; Num. 19:1–6			
Day of Atonement *Yom Kippur*	7 (Tishri)	10	Sept.–Oct.
Lev. 16; 23:26–32, Num. 29:7–11			
***Booths** (Tabernacles or Ingathering)	7 (Tishri)	15–22	Sept.–Oct.
Ex. 23:16; 34:22; Lev. 23:33–36, 39–43; Num. 29:12–38; Deut. 16:13–15			

*The three major feasts for which all males of Israel were required to travel to the temple in Jerusalem (Ex. 23:14–19).

LORD's Sabbaths and besides your gifts and
besides all your vow offerings and besides
all your freewill offerings, which you give to
the LORD.
39 "On the fifteenth day of the seventh
month, when you have [u]gathered in the
produce of the land, you shall celebrate the
feast of the LORD seven days. On the first
day shall be a solemn rest, and on the
eighth day shall be a solemn rest. 40 And
[v]you shall take on the first day the fruit of
splendid trees, branches of palm trees and
boughs of leafy trees and willows of the
brook, and [w]you shall rejoice before the
LORD your God seven days. 41 [x]You shall
celebrate it as a feast to the LORD for seven
days in the year. It is a statute forever
throughout your generations; you shall celebrate it in the seventh month. 42 [y]You shall
dwell in booths for seven days. All native
Israelites shall dwell in booths, 43 that [z]your
generations may know that I made the people of Israel dwell in booths when I
brought them out of the land of Egypt: I
am the LORD your God."
44 Thus Moses [a]declared to the people of
Israel the appointed feasts of the LORD.

The Lamps

24 [b]The LORD spoke to Moses, saying,
2 "Command the people of Israel to
bring you pure oil from beaten olives for
the lamp, that a light may be kept burning
regularly. 3 Outside the veil of the testimony, in the tent of meeting, Aaron shall
arrange it from evening to morning before
the LORD regularly. It shall be a statute forever throughout your generations. 4 He
shall arrange the lamps on the [c]lampstand
of pure gold[1] before the LORD regularly.

Bread for the Tabernacle

5 "You shall take fine flour and bake
twelve [d]loaves from it; two tenths of an
ephah[2] shall be in each loaf. 6 And you shall
set them in two piles, six in a pile, [e]on the
table of pure gold[3] before the LORD. 7 And
you shall put pure frankincense on each
pile, that it may go with the bread as a
memorial portion as a food offering to the
LORD. 8 [f]Every Sabbath day Aaron shall
arrange it before the LORD regularly; it is
from the people of Israel as a covenant forever. 9 And [g]it shall be for Aaron and his
sons, and [h]they shall eat it in a holy place,
since it is for him a most holy portion out of
the LORD's food offerings, a perpetual due."

Punishment for Blasphemy

10 Now an Israelite woman's son, whose
father was an Egyptian, went out among
the people of Israel. And the Israelite
woman's son and a man of Israel fought in
the camp, 11 and the Israelite woman's son
[i]blasphemed the [j]Name, and cursed. Then
they [k]brought him to Moses. His mother's
name was Shelomith, the daughter of
Dibri, of the tribe of Dan. 12 And [l]they put
him in custody, [m]till the will of the LORD
should be clear to them.
13 Then the LORD spoke to Moses, saying,
14 [n]"Bring out of the camp the one who
cursed, and let all who heard him [o]lay their
hands on his head, and let all the congregation stone him. 15 And speak to the people of Israel, saying, Whoever curses his
God shall [p]bear his sin. 16 Whoever [q]blas-
phemes the name of the LORD shall surely
be put to death. All the congregation shall
stone him. The sojourner as well as the
native, when he blasphemes the Name,
shall be put to death.

An Eye for an Eye

17 [r]"Whoever takes a human life shall
surely be put to death. 18 [s]Whoever takes an
animal's life shall make it good, life for life.
19 If anyone injures his neighbor, [t]as he has
done it shall be done to him, 20 fracture for
fracture, eye for eye, tooth for tooth; what-

39 [u]Ex. 23:16; Deut. 16:13
40 [v]See Neh. 8:14-18 [w]Deut. 16:14, 15
41 [x]See Num. 29:12-38
42 [y]See Neh. 8:14-18
43 [z]See Deut. 31:10-13
44 [a]ver. 2
Chapter 24
1 [b]Ex. 27:20, 21
4 [c]Ex. 31:8; 39:37
5 [d]Ex. 25:30
6 [e]Ex. 25:23, 24; 1 Kin. 7:48; 2 Chr. 4:19; 13:11; Heb. 9:2
8 [f]1 Chr. 9:32; [Num. 4:7; 2 Chr. 2:4]
9 [g]1 Sam. 21:6; Matt. 12:4; Mark 2:26; Luke 6:4 [h][ch. 6:16; 8:31; 21:22; Ex. 29:33]
11 [i]See ver. 16 [j][Ex. 3:14, 15; Phil. 2:9] [k]Ex. 18:22, 26
12 [l][Num. 15:34] [m][Ex. 18:15, 16; Num. 27:5; 36:5, 6]
14 [n][ver. 23] [o][Deut. 13:9; 17:7]
15 [p]ch. 5:1; 20:17, 20; 22:9; Num. 9:13; [Ex. 20:7]
16 [q]ver. 11; 1 Kin. 21:10, 13; Matt. 26:65, 66; Mark 14:63, 64; John 10:33
17 [r]Gen. 9:5, 6; Ex. 21:12; Num. 35:31; Deut. 19:11, 12
18 [s]Ex. 21:33, 34
19 [t]Ex. 21:23-25; Deut. 19:21; Matt. 5:38; 7:2

1 Hebrew *the pure lampstand* 2 An *ephah* was about 3/5 bushel or 22 liters 3 Hebrew *the pure table*

24:2 the lamp. See Ex. 25:31–40 and notes. These formed part of the lampstand that stood in the holy place. Shaped to resemble an almond tree in bloom, the lampstand symbolized the life-giving and light-giving power of God.

24:5 See Ex. 25:23–30 and notes.

24:10 father was an Egyptian. After many years of slavery in Egypt cases of intermarriage were no doubt common. See note Ex. 12:38.

24:11 blasphemed. See Ex. 20:7; 22:28.

24:14 lay their hands on his head. This action was taken to rid themselves of the guilt they had contracted by hearing his blasphemy.

24:20 eye for eye, tooth for tooth. Designed to curb exaggerated revenge (cf. Gen. 4:24), this formula vividly expressed the principle that punishment should be proportionate to the offense. It seems not to have been enforced literally (Ex. 21:26, 27; Deut. 19:21 note). Jesus' opposition to the misuse of this phrase (Matt. 5:38) involved, not an abrogation of this principle of equivalence, but a call to temper its application in light of the love commandment (19:18; cf. Matt. 7:12), in the interests of the kingdom (Matt. 5:10–12), and in the knowledge of God's coming wrath (Rom. 12:17–21; cf. Deut. 32:35).

ever injury he has given a person shall be
given to him. 21 [r]Whoever kills an animal
shall make it good, [s]and whoever kills a
person shall be put to death. 22 You shall
have the [u]same rule for the sojourner and
for the native, for I am the LORD your God."
23 So Moses spoke to the people of Israel,
and [v]they brought out of the camp the one
who had cursed and stoned him with
stones. Thus the people of Israel did as the
LORD commanded Moses.

The Sabbath Year

25 [w]The LORD spoke to Moses on
Mount Sinai, saying, 2 "Speak to the
people of Israel and say to them, When you
come into [x]the land that I give you, the
land shall keep a Sabbath to the LORD. 3 For
six years you shall sow your field, and for
six years you shall prune your vineyard and
gather in its fruits, 4 but in the seventh year
there shall be a Sabbath of solemn rest for
the land, a Sabbath to the LORD. You shall
not sow your field or prune your vineyard.
5 [y]You shall not reap what grows of itself in
your harvest, or gather the grapes of your
undressed vine. It shall be a year of solemn
rest for the land. 6 The Sabbath of the land
shall provide food for you, for yourself and
for your male and female slaves and for
your hired servant and the sojourner who
lives with you, 7 and for your cattle and for
the wild animals that are in your land: [z]all
its yield shall be for food.

The Year of Jubilee

8 "You shall count seven weeks[1] of years,
seven times seven years, so that the time of
the seven weeks of years shall give you
forty-nine years. 9 Then you shall sound
[a]the loud trumpet on the tenth day of the
seventh month. [b]On the Day of Atonement
you shall sound the trumpet throughout all
your land. 10 And you shall consecrate the
fiftieth year, and [c]proclaim liberty throughout the land to all its inhabitants. It shall
be a jubilee for you, when each of you shall
return to his property and each of [d]you
shall return to his clan. 11 That fiftieth year
shall be a jubilee for you; in it [e]you shall
neither sow nor reap [y]what grows of itself
nor gather the grapes from the undressed
vines. 12 For it is a jubilee. It shall be holy to
you. [f]You may eat the produce of the field.[2]

13 [d]"In this year of jubilee each of you
shall return to his property. 14 And if you
make a sale to your neighbor or buy from
your neighbor, [g]you shall not wrong one
another. 15 [h]You shall pay your neighbor
according to the number of years after the
jubilee, and he shall sell to you according
to the number of years for crops. 16 If the
years are many, you shall increase the
price, and if the years are few, you shall
reduce the price, for it is the number of the
crops that he is selling to you. 17 [i]You shall
not wrong one another, but you shall fear
your God, for I am the LORD your God.

18 [j]"Therefore you shall do my statutes
and keep my rules and perform them, and
then [k]you will dwell in the land securely.
19 [l]The land will yield its fruit, and [m]you will
eat your fill [k]and dwell in it securely. 20 And
if you say, [n]'What shall we eat in the seventh year, if [o]we may not sow or gather in
our crop?' 21 I will [p]command my blessing
on you in the sixth year, so that it will produce a crop sufficient for three years.
22 [q]When you sow in the eighth year, you
will be eating some of [r]the old crop; you
shall eat the old until the ninth year, when
its crop arrives.

Redemption of Property

23 "The land shall not be sold in perpetuity, for [s]the land is mine. For you are
strangers and sojourners with me. 24 And in
all the country you possess, you shall allow
a redemption of the land.

1 Or *Sabbaths* 2 Or *countryside*

21 [r][See ver. 17 above] [s][See ver. 18 above]
22 [u]ch. 19:34; Ex. 12:49; Num. 15:16
23 [v][ver. 14]
Chapter 25
1 [w]ch. 26:46
2 [x]Ex. 23:10, 11; [ch. 26:34, 35; 2 Chr. 36:21]
5 [y][2 Kin. 19:29]; Isai. 37:30
7 [z]ver. 12
9 [a][ch. 23:24; Isai. 27:13] [b]ch. 23:24, 27
10 [c]Isai. 61:1; Jer. 34:8, 13, 15, 17; Ezek. 46:17; [Isai. 61:2; 63:4; Luke 4:19] [d]ch. 27:24; Num. 36:4
11 [e]ver. 4, 5 [y][See ver. 5 above]
12 [f]ver. 6, 7
13 [d][See ver. 10 above]
14 [g][ch. 19:33]
15 [h]ch. 27:18, 23
17 [i]ver. 36, 43; ch. 19:14, 32
18 [j]See ch. 18:4, 5 [k]ch. 26:5, 6; Deut. 12:10; [Prov. 1:33; Jer. 23:6; Ezek. 34:25, 28]
19 [l]Ps. 85:12; Ezek. 34:26, 37 [m]ch. 26:5; Deut. 11:15; [Joel 2:19, 26] [k][See ver. 18 above]
20 [n][Matt. 6:25, 31; Luke 12:22, 29] [o]ver. 4, 5
21 [p]Deut. 28:8
22 [q][2 Kin. 19:29] [r]ch. 26:10
23 [s]Deut. 32:43; 2 Chr. 7:20; Ps. 85:1; Hos. 9:3; Joel 2:18; 3:2

25:1–55 The Lord demonstrates His ownership of the Promised Land through laws preventing the exploitation of the land and its tenants (v. 23 note).

25:1–7 Just as man needed a day of rest, land without fertilizers needed to lie fallow for a time. See the similar regulations in Ex. 23:10, 11.

25:10 jubilee. More than a fallow year, it was a year in which all the poor who had fallen into debt were given a fresh start. Loans were written off. Land that had been sold was returned to its original owner, and slaves were released (v. 40).

25:13 return to his property. God protected His gift to each family within the covenant community. In this way He protected the family structure, provided life in perpetuity for them, and prevented commercial exploitation of His gift.

25:23 land is mine. Although God gave Israel the land as one of His good gifts to them to be enjoyed (Deut. 6:10–12; 8:10–13), He still retained final ownership and so might terminate the lease should the people prove undesirable tenants. They did not possess the land as an inalienable right but within the structures of a covenantal relationship with God. The land was not private property to be bought and sold. It symbolized life with God.

25 "If your brother becomes poor and
sells part of his property, [t]then his nearest
redeemer shall come and redeem what his
brother has sold. 26 If a man has no one to
redeem it and then himself becomes prosperous and finds sufficient means to
redeem it, 27 let [u]him calculate the years
since he sold it and pay back the balance to
the man to whom he sold it, and then
return to his property. 28 But if he has not
sufficient means to recover it, then what he
sold shall remain in the hand of the buyer
until the year of jubilee. In the jubilee it
shall [v]be released, and [w]he shall return to
his property.
29 "If a man sells a dwelling house in a
walled city, he may redeem it within a
year of its sale. For a full year he shall
have the right of redemption. 30 If it is not
redeemed within a full year, then the
house in the walled city shall belong in
perpetuity to the buyer, throughout his
generations; [v]it shall not be released in
the jubilee. 31 But the houses of the villages that have no wall around them
shall be classified with the fields of the
land. They may be redeemed, and they
shall be released in the jubilee. 32 As for
[x]the cities of the Levites, the Levites may
redeem at any time the houses in the
cities they possess. 33 And if one of the
Levites exercises his right of redemption,
then the house that was sold in a city
they possess shall be released in the jubilee. For the houses in the cities of the
Levites are their possession among the
people of Israel. 34 But the fields [y]of pastureland belonging to their cities may
not be sold, for that is their possession
forever.

25 [t]Ruth 2:20; 3:9, 12; 4:4, 6; Jer. 32:7, 8
27 [u]See ver. 50-52
28 [v]ch. 27:21 [w]ver. 13, 41
30 [v][See ver. 28 above]
32 [x][Num. 35:2]; See Josh. 21:2-40
34 [y]Num. 35:2; 1 Chr. 13:2; [Acts 4:36, 37]; See Josh. 21:11-42; 1 Chr. 6:55-81

25:25 All the sales described here took place because of hardship. Land was not to be permanently sold from one family to another.

25:26 It was hoped that a relative would buy a poor man's land and return it to him. In any event, he or his family would receive it back in the Year of Jubilee.

25:29, 30 In contrast to agricultural land, houses within cities had to be redeemed within a year or the sale was permanent.

Israel's Other Sacred Times (25:1)

Sabbath Ex. 20:8–11; 31:12–17; Lev. 23:3; Deut. 5:12–15	Every seventh day was a solemn rest from all work.
Sabbath Year Ex. 23:10, 11; Lev. 25:1–7	Every seventh year was designated a "year of release" to allow the land to lie fallow.
Year of Jubilee Lev. 25:8–55; 27:17–24; Ezek. 46:17	The 50th year, which followed seven Sabbath years, was to proclaim liberty to those who were servants because of debt, and to return lands to their former owners.
The New Moon Num. 28:11–15; Ps. 81:3	The first day of the Hebrew 29- or 30-day month was a day of rest, special sacrifices, and the blowing of trumpets.
Dedication (Lights or *Hanukkah*) John 10:22	An eight-day feast in the ninth month (Chislev) commemorating the cleansing of the temple from defilement by Syria, and its rededication.
Purim (Lots) Esth. 9:18–32	A feast on the 14th and 15th of the 12th month (Adar). The name comes form Babylonian *Pur*, meaning "lot".

Kindness for Poor Brothers

35 "If your brother becomes poor and
cannot maintain himself with you, [z]you
shall support him as though he were a
stranger and a sojourner, and he shall live
with you. 36 [a]Take no interest from him or
profit, but [b]fear your God, that your brother may live beside you. 37 [a]You shall not
lend him your money at interest, nor give
him your food for profit. 38 [c]I am the LORD
your God, who brought you out of the land
of Egypt to give you the land of Canaan,
and to be your God.

39 [d]"If your brother becomes poor beside
you and sells himself to you, you shall not
make him serve as a slave: 40 he shall be
with you as a hired servant and as a
sojourner. He shall serve with you until the
year of the jubilee. 41 [v]Then he shall go out
from you, [e]he and his children with him,
and go back to his own clan and return [f]to
the possession of his fathers. 42 For they are
[g]my servants,[1] whom I brought out of the
land of Egypt; they shall not be sold as
slaves. 43 [h]You shall not rule over him [i]ruth-
lessly but [j]shall fear your God. 44 As for
your male and female slaves whom you
may have: you may buy male and female
slaves from among the nations that are
around you. 45 [k]You may also buy from
among the strangers who sojourn with you
and their clans that are with you, who have
been born in your land, and they may be
your property. 46 You may bequeath them
to your sons after you to inherit as a possession forever. You may make slaves of
them, but over your brothers the people of
Israel [l]you shall not rule, one over another
ruthlessly.

Redeeming a Poor Man

47 "If a stranger or sojourner with you
becomes rich, and [m]your brother beside
him becomes poor and sells himself to the
stranger or sojourner with you or to a
member of the stranger's clan, 48 then after
he is sold he may be redeemed. One of his
brothers may redeem him, 49 or his uncle or
his cousin may [n]redeem him, or a close relative from his clan may redeem him. Or if
he [o]grows rich he may redeem himself.
50 He shall calculate with his buyer from the
year when he sold himself to him until the
year of jubilee, and the price of his sale
shall vary with the number of years. The
time he was with his owner shall be [p]rated
as the time of a hired servant. 51 If there are
still many years left, he shall pay proportionately for his redemption some of his
sale price. 52 If there remain but a few years
until the year of jubilee, he shall calculate
and pay for his redemption in proportion
to his years of service. 53 He shall treat him
as a servant hired year by year. [l]He shall
not rule ruthlessly over him in your sight.
54 And if he is not redeemed by these
means, then [q]he and his children with him
shall be released in the year of jubilee.
55 For it is [r]to me that the people of Israel
are servants.[2] They are my servants whom I
brought out of the land of Egypt: I am the
LORD your God.

35 [z]Deut. 15:7, 8; [Ps. 41:1; 112:5, 9; Prov. 14:31; Acts 11:29; 1 John 3:17]
36 [a]See Ex. 22:25 [b]ver. 17, 43; Neh. 5:9; [Mal. 3:5]
37 [a][See ver. 36 above]
38 [c]ver. 42, 55; ch. 22:32, 33; 26:13
39 [d]Ex. 21:2; Deut. 15:12; 1 Kin. 9:22; 2 Kin. 4:1; Neh. 5:5
41 [v][See ver. 28 above] [e][Ex. 21:3] [f]ver. 13, 28
42 [g]ver. 55; [Rom. 6:22; 1 Cor. 7:23]
43 [h][Eph. 6:9; Col. 4:1] [i]Ex. 1:13, 14; Ezek. 34:4 [j]ver. 17, 36
45 [k]Isai. 14:1, 2; 56:3, 6
46 [l]Ex. 1:13, 14; Ezek. 34:4
47 [m]ver. 25, 35, 39
49 [n]See Neh. 5:1-5
[o]ver. 26, 47
50 [p]Job 7:1; Isai. 16:14; 21:16
53 [l][See ver. 46 above]
54 [q]ver. 41; Ex. 21:2, 3
55 [r]ver. 42

Blessings for Obedience

26 "You shall not make [s]idols for yourselves or erect an [t]image or [u]pillar,
and you shall not set up a [v]figured stone in
your land to bow down to it, for I am the
LORD your God. 2 [w]You shall keep my
Sabbaths and reverence my sanctuary: I am
the LORD.

3 [x]"If you walk in my statutes and observe
my commandments and do them, 4 then [y]I
will give you your rains in their season, and
the land shall yield its increase, and the
trees of the field shall yield their fruit.
5 [z]Your threshing shall last to the time of
the grape harvest, and the grape harvest
shall last to the time for sowing. And [a]you
shall eat your bread to the full and [b]dwell
in your land securely. 6 [c]I will give peace in
the land, and [d]you shall lie down, and
none shall make you afraid. And [e]I will
remove harmful beasts from the land, [f]and
the sword shall not go through your land.
7 You shall chase your enemies, and they
shall fall before you by the sword. 8 [g]Five of

Chapter 26
1 [s]See ch. 19:4 [t]See Ex. 20:4, 5 [u]Ex. 23:24 [v]Num. 33:52; [Ezek. 8:10]
2 [w]ch.19:30; See Ex. 20:8
3 [x]Deut. 11:13-15; 28:1-14; See ch. 18:4
4 [y]Ps. 67:6; 85:12; Ezek. 34:26, 27; 36:30; Joel 2:23, 24; Zech. 8:12; [ver. 20; Deut. 11:17]
5 [z][Amos 9:13] [a]See ch. 25:19 [b]See ch. 25:18
6 [c][1 Kin. 4:25; 1 Chr. 22:9] [d]Job 11:19; Jer. 30:10; Zeph. 3:13 [e]Ezek. 34:25; [2 Kin. 17:25; Isai. 35:9; Ezek. 5:17; 14:15] [f][Ezek. 14:17] 8 [g][Deut. 32:30; Josh. 23:10; Isai. 30:17]

1 Hebrew *slaves* 2 Or *slaves*

25:36 See note Deut. 23:19 (Ps. 15:5).

25:39 If a man sold a son or a daughter into slavery because of debt, the servant was released after seven years (Ex. 21:2–11; Deut. 15:12–18). This text deals with an even worse debt where, presumably having sold his land, a man and his whole family were sold as slaves (v. 41). In this case they were released in the Year of Jubilee.

26:1–46 The Lord's instruction to the Israelites culminates in promises of blessings for obedience (vv. 3–13) and of curses for disobedience (vv. 14–39).

you shall chase a hundred, and a hundred
of you shall chase ten thousand, and your
enemies shall fall before you by the sword.
9 [h]I will turn to you and [i]make you fruitful
and multiply you and will confirm my
covenant with you. 10 You shall eat [j]old
store long kept, and you shall clear out the
old to make way for the new. 11 [k]I will make
my dwelling[1] among you, and my soul
shall not abhor you. 12 [l]And I [m]will walk
among you and will be your God, and you
shall be my people. 13 [n]I am the LORD your
God, who brought you out of the land of
Egypt, that you should not be their slaves.
[o]And I have broken the bars of your yoke
and made you walk erect.

Punishment for Disobedience

14 [p]"But if you will not listen to me and
will not do all these commandments, 15 if
you spurn my statutes, and if your soul
abhors my rules, so that you will not do all
my commandments, but [q]break my
covenant, 16 then I will do this to you: I will
visit you with panic, with [r]wasting disease
and fever that consume the eyes and make
the heart ache. And [s]you shall sow your
seed in vain, for your enemies shall eat it.
17 I will [t]set my face against you, and [u]you
shall be struck down before your enemies.
[v]Those who hate you shall rule over you,
and [w]you shall flee when none pursues
you. 18 And if in spite of this you will not
listen to me, then I will discipline you
again [x]sevenfold for your sins, 19 and I will
break [y]the pride of your power, and I [z]will
make your heavens like iron and your earth
like bronze. 20 And [a]your strength shall be
spent in vain, for [b]your land shall not yield
its increase, and the trees of the land shall
not yield their fruit.
21 [c]"Then if you walk contrary to me and
will not listen to me, I will continue striking you, sevenfold for your sins. 22 And [d]I
will let loose the wild beasts against you,
which shall bereave you of your children
and destroy your livestock and make you
few in number, so that [e]your roads shall be
deserted.
23 "And [f]if by this discipline you are not

9 [h]2 Kin. 13:23 [i]Neh. 9:23
10 [j]ch. 25:22
11 [k]Ezek. 37:26-28; [Rev. 21:3]
12 [l]Ex. 29:45; Cited 2 Cor. 6:16 [m]Jer. 7:23; 11:4; 24:7; 30:22; Ezek. 11:20; 14:11; 36:28; 37:27; See Ex. 6:7
13 [n]See ch. 25:38 [o]Ezek. 34:27; [Jer. 27:2; 28:10, 13]
14 [p][Lam. 2:17; Mal. 2:2]; See Deut. 28:15-68
15 [q]ver. 44; Deut. 31:20
16 [r]Deut. 28:21 [s]Deut. 28:33, 51; Job 31:8; Jer. 5:17; Mic. 6:15
17 [t]See ch. 17:10 [u]Deut. 28:25; Judg. 2:14; Jer. 19:7 [v]Ps. 106:41 [w]Prov. 28:1; [ver. 36; Ps. 53:5]
18 [x]ver. 21, 24, 28; 1 Sam. 2:5; Ps. 119:164; Prov. 24:16
19 [y]Ezek. 30:6; [Jer. 13:9] [z]Deut. 28:23
20 [a][Ps. 127:1; Isai. 49:4] [b][Hag. 1:10]; See ver. 4
21 [c]ver. 27
22 [d]Deut. 32:24; See ver. 6 [e]Judg. 5:6; Isai. 33:8; Lam. 1:4; Zech 7:14
23 [f]Jer. 2:30; 5:3; See Amos 4:6-12
[c][See ver. 21 above]
24 [g]2 Sam. 22:27; Ps. 18:26
25 [h]Deut. 32:25; Jer. 14:12; 24:10; 29:17, 18; Ezek. 5:17; 6:3; 14:17; 29:8; 33:2 [i]Num. 14:12; Deut. 28:21

turned to me [c]but walk contrary to me,
24 [g]then I also will walk contrary to you, and
I myself will strike you sevenfold for your
sins. 25 And [h]I will bring a sword upon you,
that shall execute vengeance for the
covenant. And if you gather within your
cities, [i]I will send pestilence among you,
and you shall be delivered into the hand of
the enemy. 26 [j]When I break your supply[2]
of bread, ten women shall bake your bread
in a single oven and shall dole out your
bread again by weight, and [k]you shall eat
and not be satisfied.
27 "But [l]if in spite of this you will not listen to me, but walk contrary to me, 28 then
I will walk contrary to you [m]in fury, and I
myself will discipline you [x]sevenfold for
your sins. 29 [n]You shall eat the flesh of your
sons, and you shall eat the flesh of your
daughters. 30 And [o]I will destroy your high
places and cut down your incense altars
and [p]cast your dead bodies upon the dead
bodies of your idols, and my soul will
abhor you. 31 And I will [q]lay your cities
waste and will [r]make your sanctuaries desolate, and [s]I will not smell your pleasing
aromas. 32 And [t]I myself will devastate the
land, so that your enemies who settle in it
shall be [u]appalled at it. 33 And [v]I will scatter
you among the nations, and I will
unsheathe the sword after you, and your
land shall be a desolation, and your cities
shall be a waste.
34 [w]"Then the land shall enjoy[3] its
Sabbaths as long as it lies desolate, while
you are in your enemies' land; then the
land shall rest, and enjoy its Sabbaths. 35 As
long as it lies desolate it shall have rest, the
rest that it did not have on your Sabbaths
when you were dwelling in it. 36 And as for
those of you who are left, [x]I will send faint-
ness into their hearts in the lands of their

26 [j]Ps. 105:16; Isai. 3:1; Ezek. 4:16; 5:16; 14:13 [k]Isai. 9:20; Mic. 6:14; Hag. 1:6 27 [l]ver. 21, 24 28 [m]Isai. 59:18; 63:3; 66:15; Jer. 21:5; Ezek. 5:13, 15; 8:18 [x][See ver. 18 above] 29 [n]Deut. 28:53; Ezek. 5:10; [2 Kin. 6:29; Lam. 4:10] 30 [o]2 Chr. 14:5; 34:3, 4, 7; See Ezek. 6:3-6 [p][2 Kin. 23:20; 2 Chr. 34:5; Ezek. 6:5] 31 [q]Neh. 2:3; Jer. 4:7; See 2 Kin. 25:4-10 [r]Ps. 74:7; Lam. 1:10; Ezek. 9:6; 21:2 [s]Jer. 6:20; See Isai. 1:11-15; Amos. 5:21-23 32 [t]Jer. 9:11; 25:11, 18 [u]Deut. 28:37; 1 Kin. 9:8; Jer. 18:16; 19:8; Ezek. 5:15 33 [v]Deut. 4:27; 28:64; Neh. 1:8; Ps. 44:11; Jer. 9:16; Ezek. 12:15; 20:23; 22:15; Zech. 7:14; [Luke 21:24] 34 [w]2 Chr. 36:21; See ch. 25:2 36 [x]Ezek. 21:7

1 Hebrew *tabernacle* 2 Hebrew *staff* 3 Or *pay for*; twice in this verse; also verse 43

26:11 Israel's obedience to the covenant requirements would be rewarded with blessing (Ex. 20:12; Deut. 28:1–14; cf. Matt. 6:4), culminating in the greatest of all blessings—the presence of God with His people (Ex. 29:42–46 and note).

26:14–39 Disobedience to God brings suffering (Ex. 20:7; Deut. 28:15–68). Many prophetic passages echo Lev. 26 and Deut. 28, as the prophets argued that the people were suffering, or were about to suffer, God's anger for their sins.

enemies. The [y]sound of a [z]driven leaf shall
put them to flight, and they shall flee as
one flees from the sword, and they shall fall
when none pursues. 37 They shall stumble
over one another, as if to escape a sword,
though none pursues. And [a]you shall have
no power to stand before your enemies.
38 And you shall perish among the nations,
and the land of your enemies shall eat you
up. 39 And those of you who are left shall
[b]rot away in your enemies' lands because
of their iniquity, and also because of the
iniquities of their fathers they shall rot
away like them.
40 "But if [c]they confess their iniquity and
the iniquity of their fathers in their treachery that they [d]committed against me, and
also in walking contrary to me, 41 so that I
walked contrary to them and brought
them into the land of their enemies—if
then their [e]uncircumcised heart is [f]hum-
bled and they make amends for their iniquity, 42 then I will [g]remember my covenant
with Jacob, and I will remember my
covenant with Isaac and my covenant
with Abraham, and I will [h]remember the
land. 43 But [w]the land shall be abandoned
by them and enjoy its Sabbaths while it
lies desolate without them, and they shall
make amends for their iniquity, because
they spurned my rules and their soul
abhorred my statutes. 44 Yet for all that,
when they are in the land of their enemies, [i]I will not spurn them, neither will I
abhor them so as to destroy them utterly
and [j]break my covenant with them, for I
am the LORD their God. 45 But I will for
their sake remember the covenant with
their forefathers, [k]whom I brought out of
the land of Egypt [l]in the sight of the
nations, that I might be their God: I am
the LORD."
46 [m]These are the statutes and rules and
laws that the LORD made between him and
the people of Israel through Moses [n]on
Mount Sinai.

36 [y]ver. 17 [z]Job 13:25 **37** [a]Josh. 7:12, 13; Judg. 2:14 **39** [b]Deut. 28:65; Ezek. 4:17; 24:23; 33:10; [Ezek. 6:9] **40** [c][Neh. 9:2; Prov. 28:13; 1 John 1:9]; See 1 Kin. 8:33-36; Dan. 9:4-19 [d]ch. 6:2; Num. 5:6 **41** [e]See Ex. 6:12 [f][1 Kin. 21:29; 2 Chr. 12:6, 7; 32:26; 33:12, 13] **42** [g]Ex. 2:24; 6:5; Ps. 106:45; Ezek. 16:60 [h][Ps. 85:1] **43** [w][See ver. 34 above] **44** [i][Deut. 4:31; 2 Kin. 13:23; Neh. 9:31; Rom. 11:2] [j]ver. 15 **45** [k]ch. 22:33 [l]Ps. 98:2; Ezek. 20:9, 22 **46** [m]ch. 27:34; Deut. 6:1; 12:1 [n]ch. 25:1

Chapter 27
2 [o][Judg. 11:30, 31, 39; 1 Sam. 1:11, 28; See Num. 30] **3** [p]ver. 25; See Ex. 30:13 **10** [q]ver. 33 **13** [r]ver. 15, 19 [s]ch. 22:14 **15** [t]ver. 13

Laws About Vows

27 The LORD spoke to Moses, saying,
2 "Speak to the people of Israel and
say to them, If anyone [o]makes a special
vow to the LORD involving the valuation of
persons, 3 then the valuation of a male from
twenty years old up to sixty years old shall
be fifty shekels[1] of silver, according to the
[p]shekel of the sanctuary. 4 If the person is a
female, the valuation shall be thirty
shekels. 5 If the person is from five years old
up to twenty years old, the valuation shall
be for a male twenty shekels, and for a
female ten shekels. 6 If the person is from a
month old up to five years old, the valuation shall be for a male five shekels of silver, and for a female the valuation shall be
three shekels of silver. 7 And if the person is
sixty years old or over, then the valuation
for a male shall be fifteen shekels, and for a
female ten shekels. 8 And if someone is too
poor to pay the valuation, then he shall be
made to stand before the priest, and the
priest shall value him; the priest shall value
him according to what the vower can
afford.
9 "If the vow[2] is an animal that may be
offered as an offering to the LORD, all of it
that he gives to the LORD is holy. 10 [q]He
shall not exchange it or make a substitute
for it, good for bad, or bad for good; and if
he does in fact substitute one animal for
another, then both it and the substitute
shall be holy. 11 And if it is any unclean animal that may not be offered as an offering
to the LORD, then he shall stand the animal
before the priest, 12 and the priest shall
value it as either good or bad; as the priest
values it, so it shall be. 13 [r]But if he wishes
to redeem it, he shall add a [s]fifth to the valuation.
14 "When a man dedicates his house as a
holy gift to the LORD, the priest shall value it
as either good or bad; as the priest values it,
so it shall stand. 15 [t]And if the donor wishes

1 A *shekel* was about 2/5 ounce or 11 grams 2 Hebrew *it*

26:40 Even in judgment there was always hope (Deut. 30:1–10). Punishment did not mean an end to the covenant (vv. 44, 45; Gen. 17:2 note; Rom. 11:1–29). God's judgments on His people proved He still cared about them (Heb. 12:5, 6).

26:46 A summary conclusion to the legal material in chs. 1–26.

27:1–34 The final chapter of divine instruction to Israel deals with gifts promised to God, probably by Israelites in dire distress when they made a vow. Later, they might wish to take back the property vowed. The provisions of this chapter showed when and how this could be done.

27:2 persons. It was possible to offer oneself or a member of one's family to the full-time service of God in the temple (1 Sam. 1:11). But only Levites could serve God in this way; other vowed persons had to be redeemed according to the tariff described in vv. 3–8.

27:9–10 Sacrificial animals could not be withdrawn once vowed.

27:11–13 Non-sacrificial animals had to be redeemed.

to redeem his house, he shall add a fifth to the valuation price, and it shall be his.

16 "If a man dedicates to the LORD part of the land that is his possession, then the valuation shall be in proportion to its seed. A homer[1] of barley seed shall be valued at fifty shekels of silver. 17 If he dedicates his field from the year of jubilee, the valuation shall stand, 18 but if he dedicates his field after the jubilee, then the priest shall [u]calculate the price according to the years that remain until the year of jubilee, and a deduction shall be made from the valuation. 19 [v]And if he who dedicates the field wishes to redeem it, then he shall add a fifth to its valuation price, and it shall remain his. 20 But if he does not wish to redeem the field, or if he has sold the field to another man, it shall not be redeemed anymore. 21 But the field, [w]when it is released in the jubilee, shall be a holy gift to the LORD, like a field that has been [x]devoted. The priest shall be in [y]possession of it. 22 If he dedicates to the LORD a field that he has bought, [z]which is not a part of his possession, 23 [a]then the priest shall calculate the amount of the valuation for it up to the year of jubilee, and the man shall give the valuation on that day as a holy gift to the LORD. 24 [b]In the year of jubilee the field shall return to him from whom it was bought, to whom the land belongs as a possession. 25 Every valuation shall be according to [c]the shekel of the sanctuary: [d]twenty gerahs[2] shall make a shekel.

26 "But a [e]firstborn of animals, which as a firstborn belongs to the LORD, no man may dedicate; whether ox or sheep, it is the LORD's. 27 And if it is an unclean animal, then he shall buy it back at the valuation, [f]and add a fifth to it; or, if it is not redeemed, it shall be sold at the valuation.

28 "But [g]no devoted thing that a man devotes to the LORD, of anything that he has, whether man or beast, or of his inherited field, shall be sold or redeemed; every devoted thing is most holy to the LORD. 29 [h]No one devoted, who is to be devoted for destruction[3] from mankind, shall be ransomed; he shall surely be put to death.

30 [i]"Every tithe of the land, whether of the seed of the land or of the fruit of the trees, is the LORD's; it is holy to the LORD. 31 If a man wishes to redeem some of his tithe, he shall add a fifth to it. 32 And every tithe of herds and flocks, every tenth animal of all that [j]pass under the herdsman's staff, shall be holy to the LORD. 33 One shall not differentiate between good or bad, [k]neither shall he make a substitute for it; and if he does substitute for it, then both it and the substitute shall be holy; it shall not be redeemed."

34 [l]These are the commandments that the LORD commanded Moses for the people of Israel [m]on Mount Sinai.

1 A *homer* was about 6 bushels or 220 liters 2 A *gerah* was about 1/50 ounce or 0.6 gram 3 That is, set apart (devoted) as an offering to the Lord (for destruction)

18 [u]ver. 23; ch. 25:15, 16
19 [v]ver. 13
21 [w]ch. 25:28, 30, 31, 33, 41 [x]ver. 28 [y]Num. 18:14; Ezek. 44:29
22 [z]ch. 25:10, 25
23 [a]ver. 18
24 [b]ch. 25:28
25 [c]ver. 3 [d]See Ex. 30:13
26 [e]See Ex. 13:2
27 [f]ver. 11-13
28 [g]ver. 21; Josh. 6:17-19; 1 Sam. 15:21
29 [h][Num. 21:2; Judg. 11:35]
30 [i]Gen. 14:20; 28:22; Num. 18:21, 24; Deut. 14:28; 2 Chr. 31:5, 6, 12; Neh. 13:12; Mal. 3:8, 10
32 [j]Ezek. 20:37; [Jer. 33:13]
33 [k]ver. 10
34 [l]ch. 26:46 [m]ch. 25:1; 26:46

27:28 devoted. Property and persons devoted to God (i.e., placed under the ban) were irrevocably to be placed in the service of God (v. 28), or utterly destroyed (v. 29). This solemn vow was probably pronounced by national leaders, often in time of war (Num. 21:2; 1 Sam. 15) or against those practicing idolatry (Deut. 13:16; 20:17 note).

27:30 tithe. A tenth of all agricultural produce was given to God (i.e., to the priestly tribe of Levi, Num. 18:21–29; Deut. 12:6–18; 14:22–29 and notes).

THE FOURTH BOOK OF MOSES CALLED

Numbers

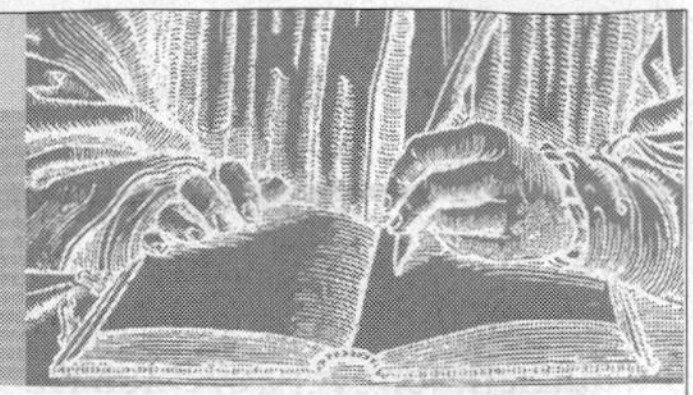

AUTHOR

Together with the rest of the Pentateuch, Numbers has traditionally been ascribed to Moses. This conclusion is based upon the unitary character of the Pentateuch and upon the clear witness of both the Old and New Testaments ascribing these books to Moses (Introduction to the Pentateuch: Author and Date). It is further supported by the obvious antiquity of the materials contained in the Pentateuch. The Book of Numbers itself refers to Moses' activity chronicling the events described in the book (33:2). That much of the book comes from Moses' hand does not rule out the possibility of later editorial activity and the likelihood that some portions were added after Moses' death (e.g., 12:3; and Moses' obituary in Deut. 34).

DATE AND OCCASION

We may reasonably date the composition of the book to the period after the wilderness wandering (which followed the Exodus) and before the death of Moses in about 1406 B.C. The book begins with the preparations for the march across the wilderness, tells of experiences along the way, describes the failure of faith that led the exodus generation of Israelites to refuse to undertake the conquest of the Promised Land, tells of the forty years of waiting until a whole generation would die, and ends with the preparation for entering Canaan. Given its content, Numbers was evidently written as a warning to the generation of Israelites born in the wilderness, that they should persevere in faith and obedience where their parents had not. For future generations of God's people, the book would speak a similar message.

In the Hebrew Bible it was customary to designate each of the five books of Moses by the word with which it began. For Numbers, this practice was modified by using the fifth Hebrew word as a title. This word, translated "in the wilderness," is an apt description of the book's content, since it describes the nation's experience during forty years in the wilderness.

When the Bible was translated into Greek, its books were given Greek names. In the case of Numbers, the Greek translation abandoned the excellent Hebrew name, and used a Greek word meaning "numbers" (*arithmoi*) that actually describes only a few of its chapters. This somewhat inappropriate Greek title was carried over by translation into the English Bible tradition.

CHARACTERISTICS AND THEMES

Two themes—the gracious faithfulness and the sovereign power of Israel's covenant God—are vital to the message of Numbers. The events of Numbers vividly portray the faithfulness of the covenant God despite the failures of an erring humanity. God directs His people as they prepare for their journey through the wilderness, comforts them in difficulties, deals with their fears and failures, and rebukes or punishes them when necessary.

This portrayal of God's covenant faithfulness is in sharp contrast with the book's repeated depiction of human faithlessness, the utter failure of humanity to meet God's standards by its own strength. Human failures are clearly portrayed and contrasted with the wise measures of the ever-faithful covenant God. Even Moses, the greatest leader of all, sinned and was not permitted to enter the Promised Land, although he saw it from a distance (20:9–11 note; 27:12–14). This shows that even the best of persons are still sinners and are saved only through the merits of Christ—salvation comes only through the grace of God.

A second major theme of Numbers is the sovereign power of God in history. Despite imposing obstacles, great dangers, and the failures of His people, God brings them safely through the wilderness. His sovereign power is sufficient for every eventuality.

Throughout the narrative, Numbers pictures the progress of God's people in redemption, pointing forward to Christ who is the true Water that makes life possible and the true Rock that provides safety. The work of Christ is foreshadowed by the typology of the red heifer (19:2–10; Heb. 9:13), the rock that provided water (20:11; 1 Cor. 10:4), and the raised serpent that brought life out of death (21:4–9; John 3:14, 15). The specific prophecy of the conquests of David, the coming one who would defeat Israel's enemies (24:15–19), foreshadows the time when Christ, who is the consummate fulfillment of the Davidic covenant, will universally be recognized as the greatest King of all.

OUTLINE OF NUMBERS

I. Preparation for the Journey Through the Wilderness (1:1–10:10)

- A. *The Men of War Numbered (ch. 1)*
- B. *Positions for the Camp and March Assigned (ch. 2)*
- C. *The Levites Numbered and Their Duties Described (chs. 3; 4)*
- D. *Removal of Defilement from the Camp (ch. 5)*
- E. *A Special Type of Separation—the Nazirite Vow (6:1–21).*
- F. *Arrangements for the Religious Life of the Camp (6:22–9:14)*
- G. *God's Provision for Direction and Guidance (9:15–10:10)*

II. From Sinai to the Plains of Moab (10:11–22:1)

- A. *The First Stage of the Journey (10:11–36)*
- B. *Rebellion and Disaffection (chs. 11; 12)*
- C. *The Crisis at Kadesh-barnea (chs. 13; 14)*
- D. *Laws After the Crisis (ch. 15)*
- E. *The Great Rebellion of Korah, Dathan, and Abiram (ch. 16)*
- F. *The Budding of Aaron's Rod (ch. 17)*
- G. *Duties and Privileges of Priests and Levites (ch. 18)*
- H. *Arrangements for Cleansing (ch. 19)*
- I. *Moses' Sin at Meribah (20:1–13)*
- J. *Events on the Way to the Plains of Moab (20:14–22:1)*

III. The Balaam Incident (22:2–25:18)

- A. *The Summoning of Balaam (22:2–40)*
- B. *Balaam's Prophecies (22:41–24:24)*
- C. *The Aftermath of the Balaam Incident (24:25–25:18)*

IV. Preparations for Entering Canaan (chs. 26–36)

- A. *The New Census (ch. 26)*
- B. *The Problem of Zelophehad's Daughters (27:1–11)*
- C. *Appointment of a Successor for Moses (27:12–23)*
- D. *Rules for Offerings and Special Feasts (chs. 28; 29)*
- E. *Rules About Vows (ch. 30)*
- F. *Vengeance on the Midianites (ch. 31)*
- G. *The Apportionment of Transjordan (ch. 32)*
- H. *A Summary of Journeys from Egypt to the Plains of Moab (33:1–49)*
- I. *Plans for Division of Canaan (33:50–34:29)*
- J. *Levite Towns and Cities of Refuge (ch. 35)*
- K. *The Second Problem of Zelophehad's Daughters (ch. 36)*

A Census of Israel's Warriors

1 The LORD spoke to Moses [a]in the
wilderness of Sinai, [b]in the tent of
meeting, on the first day of the second
month, in the second year after they had
come out of the land of Egypt, saying,
2 [c]"Take a census of all the congregation of
the people of Israel, by clans, [d]by fathers'
houses, according to the number of names,
every male, head by head. 3 [e]From twenty
years old and upward, all in Israel who are
able to go to war, you and Aaron shall list
them, [f]company by company. 4 And there
shall be with you a man from each tribe,
each man being the head of the house of
his fathers. 5 And these are the names of the
men who shall assist you. From Reuben,
[g]Elizur the son of Shedeur; 6 from Simeon,
[h]Shelumiel the son of Zurishaddai; 7 from
Judah, [i]Nahshon the son of Amminadab;
8 from Issachar, [j]Nethanel the son of Zuar;
9 from Zebulun, [k]Eliab the son of Helon;
10 from the sons of Joseph, from Ephraim,
[l]Elishama the son of Ammihud, and from
Manasseh, [m]Gamaliel the son of Pedahzur;
11 from Benjamin, [n]Abidan the son of
Gideoni; 12 from Dan, [o]Ahiezer the son of
Ammishaddai; 13 from Asher, [p]Pagiel the son
of Ochran; 14 from Gad, Eliasaph the son of
[q]Deuel; 15 from Naphtali, [r]Ahira the son of
Enan." 16 These were the ones [s]chosen from
the congregation, [t]the chiefs of their ancestral
tribes, the heads of the clans of
Israel.
17 Moses and Aaron took these men
[u]who had been named, 18 and on the first
day of the second month, they assembled
the whole congregation together, who registered
themselves by clans, by fathers'
houses, according to the number of names
from twenty years old and upward, head
by head, 19 as the LORD commanded
Moses. So he listed them in the wilderness
of Sinai.
20 The people of [v]Reuben, Israel's firstborn,
their generations, by their clans, by
their fathers' houses, according to the
number of names, head by head, every
male from twenty years old and upward, all
who were able to go to war: 21 those listed
of the tribe of Reuben were [w]46,500.
22 Of the people of Simeon, their generations,
by their clans, by their fathers' houses,
those of them who were listed, according
to the number of names, head by head,
every male from twenty years old and
upward, all who were able to go to war:
23 those listed of the tribe of Simeon were
[x]59,300.
24 Of the people of Gad, their generations,
by their clans, by their fathers' houses,
according to the number of the names,
from twenty years old and upward, all who
were able to go to war: 25 those listed of the
tribe of Gad were [y]45,650.
26 Of the people of Judah, their generations,
by their clans, by their fathers' houses,
according to the number of names,
from twenty years old and upward, every
man able to go to war: 27 those listed of the
tribe of Judah were [z]74,600.
28 Of the people of Issachar, their generations,
by their clans, by their fathers' houses,
according to the number of names,
from twenty years old and upward, every
man able to go to war: 29 those listed of the
tribe of Issachar were [a]54,400.
30 Of the people of Zebulun, their generations,
by their clans, by their fathers' houses,
according to the number of names,

Chapter 1
1 [a]ch. 10:11, 12; Ex. 19:1 [b]Ex. 25:22
2 [c]Ex. 30:12; 38:26; 2 Sam. 24:2; 1 Chr. 21:2; See ch. 26:2-51 [d]ver. 18, 20, 22; ch. 3:47; 1 Chr. 23:3, 24
3 [e]ch. 14:29; Ex. 30:14 [f]Ex. 12:51
5 [g]ch. 7:30
6 [h]ch. 7:36
7 [i]See Ex. 6:23
8 [j]ch. 7:18
9 [k]ch. 7:24
10 [l]ch. 7:48; 1 Chr. 7:26 [m]ch. 7:54
11 [n]ch. 7:60
12 [o]ch. 7:66
13 [p]ch. 7:72
14 [q]ch. 7:42
15 [r]ch. 7:78
16 [s]ch. 26:9 [t]ch. 7:2; [Ex. 18:21, 25]; See 1 Chr. 27:16-22
17 [u]1 Chr. 12:31; 16:41; 2 Chr. 28:15; 31:19; Ezra 8:20
20 [v]For ver. 20-46, see ch. 2:3-32
21 [w][ch. 26:7]
23 [x][ch. 26:14]
25 [y][ch. 26:18
27 [z][ch. 26:22; 2 Sam. 24:9]
29 [a][ch. 26:25]

1:1–10:10 With the completion of the tabernacle (Ex. 35:4–40:38) the Lord continues to prepare His people to occupy the Promised Land. A census of fighting men is taken (ch. 1). Then measures to ensure the order and purity of the camp are related—the organization of the camp, the commissioning of the Levites and their ministry, and various provisions for ceremonial purity and religious observance. Finally, provisions are made for direction and guidance of the community (9:15–10:10).

1:1–46 In preparation for the conquest of the land, God commands that a census of the fighting men of Israel be taken. At the end of the book, another census will be taken to establish military strength (26:2). In the ancient Near East, a census could be taken for military, forced labor, or taxation purposes.

1:1 The LORD spoke to Moses. Such statements occur dozens of times in Numbers. Moses was the preeminent prophet. God spoke to the prophets in visions and dreams, but with Moses he spoke face to face (12:8), giving him greater authority. Of all who have lived on earth, only Christ has greater authority than Moses.

the tent of meeting. The tent shrine where God spoke to Moses (Ex. 29:42; 40:34, 35). This term occurs frequently in the Pentateuch and occasionally in later books.

in the second year. Numbers begins thirteen months after the Exodus and relates events that occurred during the next 39 years.

1:5–16 The heads of all the tribes, except the Levites (who had been set apart for the service of the tabernacle), are listed here and also in chs. 2; 7; and 10. The two tribes of Ephraim and Manasseh are listed under Joseph (v. 10), preserving the number of twelve tribes without counting the Levites.

1:20–43 These verses list the number of fighting men in each tribe. Except for the differences in the numbers, these verses follow a strict formula. The tribes are listed in the same order as in vv. 1–15, except that the tribe of Gad is now mentioned third instead of eleventh (vv. 24, 25).

from twenty years old and upward, every
man able to go to war: 31 those listed of the
tribe of Zebulun were [b]57,400.
32 Of the people of Joseph, namely, of the
people of Ephraim, their generations, by
their clans, by their fathers' houses,
according to the number of names, from
twenty years old and upward, every man
able to go to war: 33 those listed of the tribe
of Ephraim were [c]40,500.
34 Of the people of Manasseh, their generations, by their clans, by their fathers'
houses, according to the number of names,
from twenty years old and upward, every
man able to go to war: 35 those listed of the
tribe of Manasseh were [d]32,200.
36 Of the people of Benjamin, their generations, by their clans, by their fathers'
houses, according to the number of names,
from twenty years old and upward, every
man able to go to war: 37 those listed of the
tribe of Benjamin were [e]35,400.
38 Of the people of Dan, their generations, by their clans, by their fathers' houses, according to the number of names,
from twenty years old and upward, every
man able to go to war: 39 those listed of the
tribe of Dan were [f]62,700.
40 Of the people of Asher, their generations, by their clans, by their fathers' houses, according to the number of names,
from twenty years old and upward, every
man able to go to war: 41 those listed of the
tribe of Asher were [g]41,500.
42 Of the people of Naphtali, their generations, by their clans, by their fathers'
houses, according to the number of names,
from twenty years old and upward, every
man able to go to war: 43 those listed of the
tribe of Naphtali were [h]53,400.
44 [i]These are those who were listed,
whom Moses and Aaron listed with the
help of the chiefs of Israel, twelve men,
each representing his fathers' house. 45 So
all those listed of the people of Israel, by
their fathers' houses, from twenty years old
and upward, every man able to go to war in
Israel— 46 all those listed were [j]603,550.

31 [b][ch. 26:27]
33 [c][ch. 26:37]
35 [d][ch. 26:34]
37 [e][ch. 26:41]
39 [f][ch. 26:43]
41 [g][ch. 26:47]
43 [h][ch. 26:50]
44 [i]ch. 26:64
46 [j]Ex. 38:26; [ch. 11:21; 26:51; Ex. 12:37]

Levites Exempted

47 But [k]the Levites were not listed along
with them by their ancestral tribe. 48 For the
LORD spoke to Moses, saying, 49 "Only the
tribe of Levi you shall not list, and you shall
not take a census of them among the people of Israel. 50 [l]But appoint the Levites over
the tabernacle of the testimony, and over all
its furnishings, and over all that belongs to
it. They are to carry the tabernacle and all
its furnishings, and they shall take care of it
[m]and shall camp around the tabernacle.
51 [n]When the tabernacle is to set out, the
Levites shall take it down, and when the
tabernacle is to be pitched, the Levites shall
set it up. [o]And if any outsider comes near,
he shall be put to death. 52 The people of
Israel shall pitch their tents by their companies, each man in his own camp and [p]each
man by his own standard. 53 But the Levites
shall camp around the tabernacle of the testimony, so that there may be no [q]wrath on
the congregation of the people of Israel.
[r]And the Levites shall keep guard over the
tabernacle of the testimony." 54 Thus did the
people of Israel; they did according to all
that the LORD commanded Moses.

Arrangement of the Camp

2 The LORD spoke to Moses and Aaron,
saying, 2 [s]"The people of Israel shall
camp each by his own standard, with the
banners of their fathers' houses. They shall
camp facing the tent of meeting on every
side. 3 Those to camp on the east side toward
the sunrise shall be of the standard of the
camp of Judah by their companies, the chief
of the people of Judah being [t]Nahshon the
son of Amminadab, 4 his company as listed
being 74,600. 5 Those to camp next to him
shall be the tribe of Issachar, the chief of the
people of Issachar being Nethanel the son of
Zuar, 6 his company as listed being 54,400.
7 Then the tribe of Zebulun, the chief of the
people of Zebulun being Eliab the son of
Helon, 8 his company as listed being 57,400.
9 All those listed of the camp of Judah, by
their companies, were 186,400. [u]They shall
set out first on the march.

47 [k]ch. 2:33; [ch. 26:57, 58, 62]; See ch. 3; ch. 4; 1 Chr. 6
50 [l]ch. 3:7, 8; Ex. 38:21; See ch. 4:15-33 [m]See ch. 3:23-38
51 [n]ch. 10:17, 21 [o]ch. 3:10, 38; 18:22; [1 Sam. 6:19; 2 Sam. 6:6, 7; 1 Chr. 13:10]
52 [p]ch. 2:2, 34
53 [q]ch. 8:19; 16:46; 18:5 [r]ch. 3:7, 8, 38; 8:26; 9:19, 23; 18:3-5; 31:30, 47; 1 Chr. 23:32; 2 Chr. 13:11
Chapter 2
2 [s]ch. 1:52
3 [t]See Ex. 6:23
9 [u]ch. 10:14-16

1:45, 46 These two verses give a total for the census.

1:47–54 The Levites were not counted with the others, since they were set apart to care for the tabernacle and were exempt from military service. Their inheritance was also set apart among the Israelites (ch. 3).

2:1–34 Regulations for the placing of the various tribes in the camp and for their order on the march are given. The people were divided into four camps, of three tribes each, located some distance from the tabernacle on the north, south, east, and west. The Levites camped around the tabernacle (1:53). On the march, the tribes are to follow one another in the same order in which they were mentioned. Compare this arrangement with the four-square city of Rev. 21:16, the final dwelling place of God with man.

10 "On the south side shall be the standard of the camp of Reuben by their companies, the chief of the people of Reuben
being Elizur the son of Shedeur, 11 his company as listed being 46,500. 12 And those to
camp next to him shall be the tribe of
Simeon, the chief of the people of Simeon
being Shelumiel the son of Zurishaddai,
13 his company as listed being 59,300.
14 Then the tribe of Gad, the chief of the
people of Gad being Eliasaph the son of
[v]Reuel, 15 his company as listed being
45,650. 16 All those listed of the camp of
Reuben, by their companies, were
151,450. [w]They shall set out second.
17 [x] "Then the tent of meeting shall set
out, with the camp of the Levites in the
midst of the camps; as they camp, so shall
they set out, each in position, standard by
standard.
18 "On the west side shall be the standard
of the camp of Ephraim by their companies, the chief of the people of Ephraim
being Elishama the son of Ammihud, 19 his
company as listed being 40,500. 20 And
next to him shall be the tribe of Manasseh,
the chief of the people of Manasseh being
Gamaliel the son of Pedahzur, 21 his company as listed being 32,200. 22 Then the
tribe of Benjamin, the chief of the people of
Benjamin being Abidan the son of Gideoni,
23 his company as listed being 35,400. 24 All
those listed of the camp of Ephraim, by
their companies, were 108,100. [y]They shall
set out third on the march.
25 "On the north side shall be the standard of the camp of Dan by their companies, the chief of the people of Dan being
Ahiezer the son of Ammishaddai, 26 his
company as listed being 62,700. 27 And
those to camp next to him shall be the tribe
of Asher, the chief of the people of Asher

14 [v][ch. 7:42, 47; 10:20] 16 [w]ch. 10:18-20 17 [x]ch. 10:17, 21
24 [y]ch. 10:22-24; [Ps. 80:2]

2:14 Reuel. Some Hebrew manuscripts have "Deuel." The misspelling "Reuel" is due to the similarity of *R* and *D* in Hebrew writing. It is traditional to note the correction rather than to alter the text.

Placement of Tribes in the Israelite Encampment (2:2)

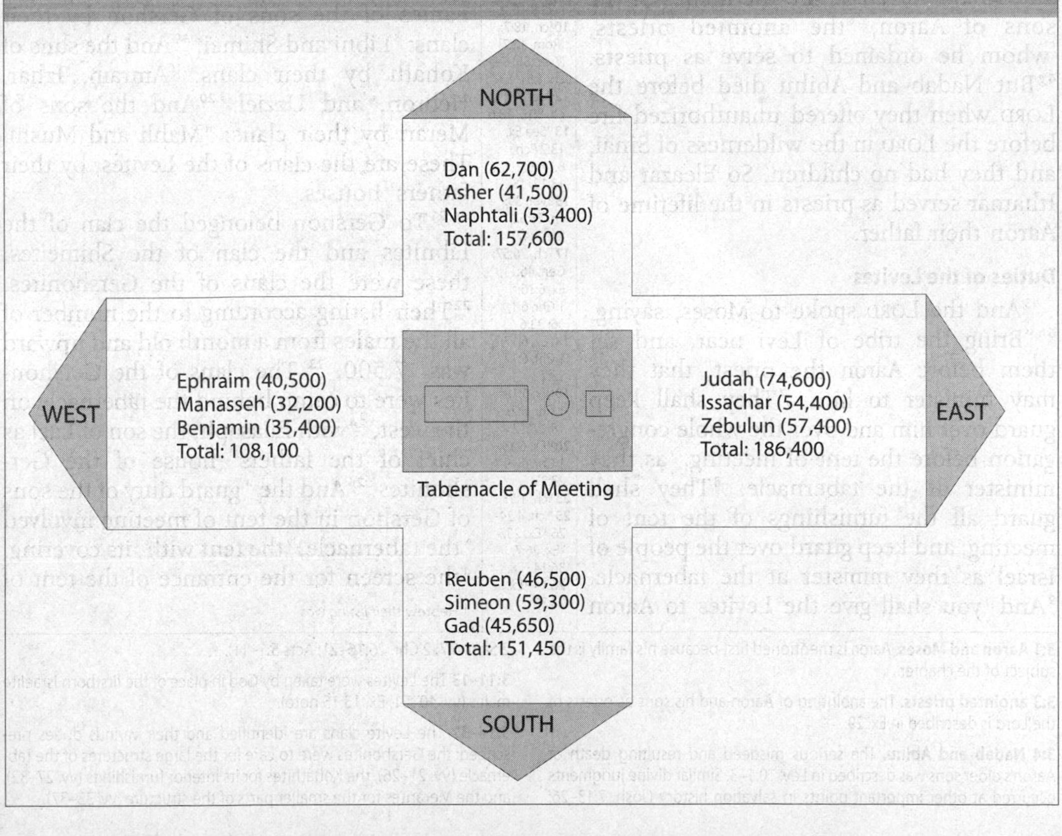

being Pagiel the son of Ochran, 28 his company as listed being 41,500. 29 Then the
tribe of Naphtali, the chief of the people of
Naphtali being Ahira the son of Enan, 30 his
company as listed being 53,400. 31 All
those listed of the camp of Dan were
157,600. [z]They shall set out last, standard
by standard."
32 These are the people of Israel as listed
by their fathers' houses. All those listed in
the camps by their companies were
[a]603,550. 33 But [b]the Levites were not listed among the people of Israel, as the LORD
commanded Moses.
34 Thus did the people of Israel.
According to all that the LORD commanded
Moses, [c]so they camped by their standards,
and so they set out, each one in his clan,
according to his fathers' house.

The Sons of Aaron

3 These are the generations of Aaron
and Moses at the time when the LORD
spoke with Moses on Mount Sinai. 2 These
are the names of the sons of Aaron:
[d]Nadab the firstborn, and Abihu, Eleazar,
and Ithamar. 3 These are the names of the
sons of Aaron, [e]the anointed priests,
[f]whom he ordained to serve as priests.
4 [g]But Nadab and Abihu died before the
LORD when they offered unauthorized fire
before the LORD in the wilderness of Sinai,
and they had no children. So Eleazar and
Ithamar served as priests in the lifetime of
Aaron their father.

Duties of the Levites

5 And the LORD spoke to Moses, saying,
6 [h]"Bring the tribe of Levi near, and set
them before Aaron the priest, that they
may minister to him. 7 They shall keep
guard over him and over the whole congregation before the tent of meeting, [i]as they
minister at the tabernacle. 8 They shall
guard all the furnishings of the tent of
meeting, and keep guard over the people of
Israel as they minister at the tabernacle.
9 And [j]you shall give the Levites to Aaron
and his sons; they are [k]wholly given to him
from among the people of Israel. 10 And you
shall appoint Aaron and his sons, and [l]they
shall guard their priesthood. But if [m]any
outsider comes near, he shall be put to
death."
11 And the LORD spoke to Moses, saying,
12 "Behold, [n]I have taken the Levites from
among the people of Israel instead of every
firstborn who opens the womb among the
people of Israel. The Levites shall be mine,
13 for [o]all the firstborn are mine. [p]On the
day that I struck down all the firstborn in
the land of Egypt, I consecrated for my own
all the firstborn in Israel, both of man and
of beast. They shall be mine: I am the
LORD."
14 And the LORD spoke to Moses in the
wilderness of Sinai, saying, 15 "List the sons
of Levi, by fathers' houses and by clans;
[q]every male from a month old and upward
you shall list." 16 So Moses listed them
according to the word of the LORD, as he
was commanded. 17 [r]And these were the
sons of Levi by their names: Gershon and
Kohath and Merari. 18 And these are the
names of the sons of Gershon by their
clans: [s]Libni and Shimei. 19 And the sons of
Kohath by their clans: [t]Amram, Izhar,
Hebron, and Uzziel. 20 And the sons of
Merari by their clans: [u]Mahli and Mushi.
These are the clans of the Levites, by their
fathers' houses.
21 To Gershon belonged the clan of the
Libnites and the clan of the Shimeites;
these were the clans of the Gershonites.
22 Their listing according to the number of
all the males from a month old and upward
was[1] 7,500. 23 [v]The clans of the Gershonites were to camp behind the tabernacle on
the west, 24 with Eliasaph, the son of Lael as
chief of the fathers' house of the Gershonites. 25 And the [w]guard duty of the sons
of Gershon in the tent of meeting involved
[x]the tabernacle, [y]the tent with [z]its covering,
[a]the screen for the entrance of the tent of

31 [z]ch. 10:25-27
32 [a]See ch. 1:46
33 [b]See ch. 1:47
34 [c][ch. 24:2, 5, 6]
Chapter 3
2 [d]See Ex. 6:23
3 [e]See Lev. ch. 8 [f]See Ex. 28:41
4 [g]ch. 26:61; Lev. 10:1, 2; 1 Chr. 24:2
6 [h]ch. 1:50; 8:6; 18:2
7 [i]ch. 8:11, 15, 24, 26
9 [j]ch. 8:19; 18:6
[k]ch. 8:16
10 [l]ch. 18:7; [Rom. 12:7] [m]ver. 38; See ch. 1:51
12 [n]ver. 41; ch. 8:16; 18:6
13 [o]See Ex. 13:2 [p]ch. 8:17; Ex. 13:12, 15
15 [q]ver. 39; ch. 26:62; [ch. 1:47]
17 [r]ch. 26:57; Gen. 46:11; Ex. 6:16; 1 Chr. 6:1, 16; 23:6
18 [s]Ex. 6:17; 1 Chr. 6:17; 23:7
19 [t]Ex. 6:18; 1 Chr. 6:2, 18; 23:12
20 [u]Ex. 6:19; 1 Chr. 6:19; 23:21
23 [v]ch. 1:53
25 [w]ch. 4:24-26 [x]Ex. 25:9 [y]Ex. 26:7; 36:14 [z]Ex. 26:14 [a]Ex. 26:36

[1] Hebrew *their listing was*

3:1 Aaron and Moses. Aaron is mentioned first because his family is the subject of the chapter.

3:3 anointed priests. The anointing of Aaron and his sons as priests of the Lord is described in Ex. 29.

3:4 Nadab and Abihu. The serious misdeed and resulting death of Aaron's older sons was described in Lev. 10:1–3. Similar divine judgments occurred at other important points in salvation history (Josh. 7:13–26; 2 Sam. 6:7; 2 Chr. 26:16–21; Acts 5:1–11).

3:11–13 The Levites were taken by God in place of the firstborn Israelite males (vv. 40–51; Ex. 13:15 note).

3:14–37 The Levite clans are identified and their various duties prescribed: the Gershonites were to care for the large structures of the tabernacle (vv. 21–26), the Kohathites for its interior furnishings (vv. 27–32), and the Merarites for the smaller parts of the structure (vv. 33–37).

meeting, 26 [b]the hangings of the court, [c]the screen for the door of the court that is around the tabernacle and the altar, and [d]its cords—all the service connected with these.

27 To Kohath belonged the clan of the [e]Amramites and the clan of the Izharites and the clan of the Hebronites and the clan of the Uzzielites; these are the clans of the Kohathites. 28 According to the number of all the males, from a month old and upward, there were 8,600, keeping guard over the sanctuary. 29 The clans of the sons of Kohath were to camp on the south side of the tabernacle, 30 with [f]Elizaphan the son of Uzziel as chief of the fathers' house of the clans of the Kohathites. 31 And their guard duty involved [g]the ark, [h]the table, [i]the lampstand, [j]the altars, the vessels of the sanctuary with which the priests minister, and [k]the screen; all the service connected with these. 32 And Eleazar the son of Aaron the priest was to be chief over the chiefs of the Levites, and to have oversight of those who kept guard over the sanctuary.

33 To Merari belonged the clan of the Mahlites and the clan of the Mushites: these are the clans of Merari. 34 Their listing according to the number of all the males from a month old and upward was 6,200. 35 And the chief of the fathers' house of the clans of Merari was Zuriel the son of Abihail. They were to camp on the north side of the tabernacle. 36 [l]And the appointed guard duty of the sons of Merari involved the [m]frames of the tabernacle, [n]the bars, [o]the pillars, the bases, and all their accessories; all the service connected with these; 37 also [p]the pillars around the court, with their bases and [q]pegs and [r]cords.

38 Those who were to camp before the tabernacle on the east, before the tent of meeting toward the sunrise, were Moses and Aaron and his sons, [s]guarding the sanctuary itself, to protect[1] the people of Israel. And any outsider who came near was to be put to death. 39 All those listed among the Levites, whom Moses and Aaron listed at the commandment of the LORD, by clans, all the males from a month old and upward, were [t]22,000.

Redemption of the Firstborn

40 And the LORD said to Moses, "List all the firstborn males of the people of Israel, from a month old and upward, taking the number of their names. 41 [u]And you shall take the Levites for me—I am the LORD—instead of all the firstborn among the people of Israel, and the cattle of the Levites instead of all the firstborn among the cattle of the people of Israel." 42 So Moses listed all the firstborn among the people of Israel, as the LORD commanded him. 43 And all the firstborn males, according to the number of names, from a month old and upward as listed were 22,273.

44 And the LORD spoke to Moses, saying, 45 [v]"Take the Levites instead of all the firstborn among the people of Israel, and the cattle of the Levites instead of their cattle. The Levites shall be mine: I am the LORD. 46 And [w]as the redemption price for the 273 of the firstborn of the people of Israel, over and above the number of the male Levites, 47 you shall take [x]five shekels[2] per head; you shall take them according to [y]the shekel of the sanctuary (the shekel of twenty gerahs[3]), 48 and give the money to Aaron and his sons as the redemption price for those who are over." 49 So Moses took the redemption money from those who were over and above those redeemed by the Levites. 50 From the firstborn of the people of Israel he took the money, [z]1,365 shekels, by the shekel of the sanctuary. 51 And Moses [a]gave the redemption money to Aaron and his sons, according to the word of the LORD, as the LORD commanded Moses.

Duties of the Kohathites

4 The LORD spoke to Moses and Aaron, saying, 2 "Take a census of the sons of Kohath from among the sons of Levi, by their clans and their fathers' houses,

26 [b]Ex. 27:9 [c]Ex. 27:16 [d]ver. 37; Ex. 35:18; 39:40
27 [e]1 Chr. 26:23
30 [f][Ex. 6:22; Lev. 10:4]
31 [g]Ex. 25:10 [h]Ex. 25:23 [i]Ex. 25:31 [j]Ex. 27:1; 30:1 [k]Ex. 26:36
36 [l]ch. 4:31, 32 [m]Ex. 26:15 [n]Ex. 26:26 [o]Ex. 26:32, 37
37 [p]Ex. 27:10 [q]Ex. 27:19 [r]ver. 26
38 [s]See ch. 1:53
39 [t][ver. 22, 28, 34; See ver. 46-49]
41 [u]ver. 12, 45
45 [v]ver. 12, 41
46 [w]ch. 18:15, 16; Ex. 13:13
47 [x]ch. 18:16; Lev. 27:6 [y]See Ex. 30:13
50 [z]ver. 46, 47
51 [a]ver. 48

[1] Hebrew *guard* [2] A *shekel* was about 2/5 ounce or 11 grams [3] A *gerah* was about 1/50 ounce or 0.6 gram

3:38 Moses and Aaron were to camp in front of the tent of meeting, and to have exclusive approach to the sanctuary.

3:39–49 Firstborn Israelite males were to be redeemed by devoting the Levites to God's service. Money was given for the excess number of firstborn males (vv. 46–49).

4:1–33 The work of the Levitical families—the Kohathites (vv. 1–15), the Gershonites (vv. 21–28), and the Merarites (vv. 29–33)—is further explained. In vv. 16–20, Aaron's son Eleazar is assigned supervision of the entire tabernacle. But all Kohathites, except the descendants of Aaron, were forbidden direct access to the holy things.

3 [b]from thirty years old up to fifty years old, all who can come on duty, to do the work in the tent of meeting. 4 This is the service of the sons of Kohath in the tent of meeting: [c]the most holy things. 5 When the camp is to set out, Aaron and his sons shall go in and take down [d]the veil of the screen and cover [e]the ark of the testimony with it. 6 Then they shall put on it a covering of goatskin[1] and spread on top of that a cloth all of blue, and shall put in its [f]poles. 7 And over the [g]table of the bread of the Presence they shall spread a cloth of blue and put on it the plates, the dishes for incense, the bowls, and the flagons for the drink offering; [h]the regular showbread also shall be on it. 8 Then they shall spread over them a cloth of scarlet and cover the same with a covering of goatskin, and shall [i]put in its poles. 9 And they shall take a cloth of blue and cover [j]the lampstand for the light, with its lamps, its tongs, its trays, and all the vessels for oil with which it is supplied. 10 And they shall put it with all its utensils in a covering of goatskin and put it on the carrying frame. 11 And over [k]the golden altar they shall spread a cloth of blue and cover it with a covering of goatskin, and shall put in its poles. 12 And they shall take all [l]the vessels of the service that are used in the sanctuary and put them in a cloth of blue and cover them with a covering of goatskin and put them on the carrying frame. 13 And they shall take away the ashes from the altar and spread a purple cloth over it. 14 And they shall put on it all the utensils of the altar, which are used for the service there, the fire pans, the forks, the shovels, and the basins, all the utensils of the altar; and they shall spread on it a covering of goatskin, and shall put in its poles. 15 And when Aaron and his sons have finished covering the sanctuary and all the furnishings of the sanctuary, as the camp sets out, after that [m]the sons of Kohath shall come to carry these, [n]but they must not touch the holy things, lest they die. These are the things of the tent of meeting that the sons of Kohath are to carry.

16 "And Eleazar the son of Aaron the priest shall have charge of [o]the oil for the light, the [p]fragrant incense, [q]the regular grain offering, and [r]the anointing oil, with the oversight of the whole tabernacle and all that is in it, of the sanctuary and its vessels."

17 The LORD spoke to Moses and Aaron, saying, 18 "Let not the tribe of the clans of the Kohathites be destroyed from among the Levites, 19 but deal thus with them, that they may live and not die when they come near to [s]the most holy things: Aaron and his sons shall go in and appoint them each to his task and to his burden, 20 [t]but they shall not go in to look on the holy things even for a moment, lest they die."

21 The LORD spoke to Moses, saying, 22 "Take a census of the sons of Gershon also, by their fathers' houses and by their clans. 23 [u]From thirty years old up to fifty years old, you shall list them, all who can [v]come to do duty, to do service in the tent of meeting. 24 This is the service of the clans of the Gershonites, in serving and bearing burdens: 25 [w]they shall carry [x]the curtains of the tabernacle and the tent of meeting with [y]its covering and the covering of goatskin that is on top of it and the screen for the entrance of the tent of meeting 26 and the hangings of the court and the screen for the entrance of the gate of the court that is around the tabernacle and the altar, and their cords and all the equipment for their service. And they shall do all that needs to be done with regard to them. 27 All the service of the sons of the Gershonites shall be at the command of Aaron and his sons, in all that they are to carry and in all that they have to do. And you shall assign to their charge all that they are to carry. 28 This is the service of the clans of the sons of the Gershonites in the tent of meeting, and their guard duty is to be [z]under the direction of Ithamar the son of Aaron the priest.

29 "As for the sons of Merari, you shall list them by their clans and their fathers' houses. 30 [u]From thirty years old up to fifty years old, you shall list them, everyone who can come on duty, to do the service of the tent of meeting. 31 And [a]this is what they are charged to carry, as the whole of their service in the tent of meeting: the frames of the tabernacle, with its bars, pillars, and bases, 32 and the pillars around the court with their bases, pegs, and cords, with all

Chapter 4
3 [b]ver. 23, 30, 35, 39, 43, 47; [ch. 8:24; 1 Chr. 23:3, 24, 27]
4 [c]ver. 19
5 [d]See Ex. 26:31 [e]Ex. 25:10, 16
6 [f]Ex. 25:13
7 [g]Ex. 25:23, 29, 30; 37:16; Lev. 24:6, 8 [h]2 Chr. 2:4
8 [i][Ex. 25:15, 28]
9 [j]See Ex. 25:31-39
11 [k]Ex. 30:1, 3
12 [l][1 Chr. 9:28, 29]
15 [m]ch. 7:9; 10:21; Deut. 31:9 [n]2 Sam. 6:6, 7; 1 Chr. 13:9, 10
16 [o]Ex. 25:6; 27:20; Lev. 24:2 [p]Ex. 25:6; 31:11 [q]Ex. 29:40, 41 [r]Ex. 31:11; See Ex. 30:23-33
19 [s]ver. 4
20 [t][Ex. 19:21; 1 Sam. 6:19]
23 [u]ver. 3 [v]ch. 8:24; [Ex. 38:8; 1 Sam. 2:22]
25 [w][ch. 3:25, 26] [x]See Ex. 26:1-6; 36:8-13 [y]Ex. 36:14, 19
28 [z]ver. 33
30 [u][See ver. 23 above]
31 [a]ch. 3:36, 37

1 The meaning of the Hebrew word is uncertain; compare Exodus 25:5

their equipment and all their accessories. And you shall [b]list by name the objects that they are required to carry. 33 This is the service of the clans of the sons of Merari, the whole of their service in the tent of meeting, [c]under the direction of Ithamar the son of Aaron the priest."

34 And Moses and Aaron and the chiefs of the congregation listed the sons of the Kohathites, by their clans and their fathers' houses, 35 [u]from thirty years old up to fifty years old, everyone who could come on duty, for service in the tent of meeting; 36 and those listed by clans were 2,750. 37 [d]This was the list of the clans of the Kohathites, all who served in the tent of meeting, whom Moses and Aaron listed according to the commandment of the LORD by Moses.

38 Those listed of the sons of Gershon, by their clans and their fathers' houses, 39 [u]from thirty years old up to fifty years old, everyone who could come on duty for service in the tent of meeting— 40 those listed by their clans and their fathers' houses were 2,630. 41 [e]This was the list of the clans of the sons of Gershon, all who served in the tent of meeting, whom Moses and Aaron listed according to the commandment of the LORD.

42 Those listed of the clans of the sons of Merari, by their clans and their fathers' houses, 43 [u]from thirty years old up to fifty years old, everyone who could come on duty, for service in the tent of meeting— 44 those listed by clans were 3,200. 45 [f]This was the list of the clans of the sons of Merari, whom Moses and Aaron listed according to the commandment of the LORD by Moses.

46 All those who were listed of the Levites, whom Moses and Aaron and the chiefs of Israel listed, by their clans and their fathers' houses, 47 [u]from thirty years old up to fifty years old, everyone who could come to do the service of ministry and the service of bearing burdens in the tent of meeting, 48 those listed were 8,580. 49 According to the commandment of the LORD through Moses they were listed, [g]each one with his task of serving or carrying. Thus they were listed by him, [h]as the LORD commanded Moses.

32 [b]Ex. 38:21
33 [c]ver. 28
35 [u][See ver. 23 above]
37 [d]ver. 2
39 [u][See ver. 23 above]
41 [e]ver. 22
43 [u][See ver. 23 above]
45 [f]ver. 29
47 [u][See ver. 23 above]
49 [g]ver. 15, 24, 31 [h]ver. 1, 21, 29

Chapter 5

2 [i]ch. 12:14; Lev. 13:46 [j]Lev. 15:2 [k]ch. 9:6, 10; 19:11, 13; 31:19; Lev. 21:1; [Hag. 2:13]
3 [l]See Lev. 26:11, 12
6 [m]Lev. 6:2, 3
7 [n]Lev. 5:5; 26:40; [Josh. 7:19] [o]Lev. 6:5
8 [p]Lev. 6:6, 7
9 [q]ch. 18:19; Ex. 29:28; Lev. 6:17, 18; 7:6, 7, 9, 10, 14; Deut. 18:3, 4

Unclean People

5 The LORD spoke to Moses, saying, 2 "Command the people of Israel that they [i]put out of the camp everyone who is leprous[1] or has [j]a discharge and everyone who is [k]unclean through contact with the dead. 3 You shall put out both male and female, putting them outside the camp, that they may not defile their camp, [l]in the midst of which I dwell." 4 And the people of Israel did so, and put them outside the camp; as the LORD said to Moses, so the people of Israel did.

Confession and Restitution

5 And the LORD spoke to Moses, saying, 6 "Speak to the people of Israel, [m]When a man or woman commits any of the sins that people commit by breaking faith with the LORD, and that person realizes his guilt, 7 [n]he shall confess his sin that he has committed.[2] [o]And he shall make full restitution for his wrong, adding a fifth to it and giving it to him to whom he did the wrong. 8 But if the man has no next of kin to whom restitution may be made for the wrong, the restitution for wrong shall go to the LORD for the priest, in addition to [p]the ram of atonement with which atonement is made for him. 9 And [q]every contribution, all the holy donations of the people of Israel, which they bring to the priest, shall be his. 10 Each one shall keep his holy donations: whatever anyone gives to the priest shall be his."

A Test for Adultery

11 And the LORD spoke to Moses, saying, 12 "Speak to the people of Israel, If any man's wife goes astray and breaks faith with him, 13 if a man [r]lies with her sexually, and

1 *Leprosy* was a term for several skin diseases; see Leviticus 13
2 Hebrew *they shall confess their sin that they have committed*

5:1–4 Persons physically or ceremonially unclean were sent outside the camp. This action was taken because, as a nation of priests, the Israelites were to represent man restored in the image of God. See note Lev. 13; 14.

5:5–10 When someone wronged another, restitution had to be made, plus an additional fifth (Lev. 5:14–6:7). If the wronged person was not available, and had no relative to whom restitution could be made, it was to be given to the priest, as representing the Lord.

5:11–31 A procedure is described by which the priest could determine whether a woman accused of unfaithfulness by her husband was guilty or innocent. If she was guilty, God would make her sick and unable to bear children (v. 27); if innocent, she would be able to bear children (v. 28).

it is hidden from the eyes of her husband,
and she is undetected though she has
defiled herself, and there is no witness
against her, [s]since she was not taken in the
act, 14 and if the spirit of jealousy comes
over him and he is jealous of his wife who
has defiled herself, or if the spirit of jealousy comes over him and he is jealous of
his wife, though she has not defiled herself,
15 then the man shall bring his wife to the
priest and bring the offering required of
her, a tenth of an ephah[1] of barley flour.
[t]He shall pour no oil on it and put no
frankincense on it, for it is a grain offering
of jealousy, a grain offering of remembrance, [u]bringing iniquity to remembrance.
16 "And the priest shall bring her near
and set her before the LORD. 17 And the
priest shall take holy water in an earthenware vessel and take some of the dust that
is on the floor of the tabernacle and put it
into the water. 18 And the priest shall set
the woman before the LORD and [v]unbind
the hair of the woman's head and place in
her hands the grain offering of remembrance, which is the grain offering of jealousy. And in his hand the priest shall have
the water of bitterness that brings the
curse. 19 Then the priest shall make her take
an oath, saying, 'If no man has lain with
you, and if you have not turned aside to
uncleanness while you were under your
husband's authority, be free from this
water of bitterness that brings the curse.
20 But if you have gone astray, though you
are under your husband's authority, and if
you have defiled yourself, and some man
other than your husband has lain with you,
21 then' (let the priest make the woman take
the oath of the curse, and say to the
woman) [w]'the LORD make you a curse and
an oath among your people, when the
LORD makes your thigh fall away and your
body swell. 22 May this water that brings the
curse [x]pass into your bowels and make
your womb swell and your thigh fall away.'
And the woman shall say, [y]'Amen, Amen.'
23 "Then the priest shall write these curses
in a book and wash them off into the water
of bitterness. 24 And he shall make the
woman drink the water of bitterness that
brings the curse, and the water that brings
the curse shall enter into her and cause bitter pain. 25 And the priest shall take the
grain offering of jealousy out of the
woman's hand [z]and shall wave the grain
offering before the LORD and bring it to the
altar. 26 And the priest [a]shall take a handful
of the grain offering, as its memorial portion, and burn it on the altar, and afterward shall make the woman drink the
water. 27 And when he has made her drink
the water, then, if she has defiled herself
and has broken faith with her husband, the
water that brings the curse shall enter into
her and cause bitter pain, and her womb
shall swell, and her thigh shall fall away,
and the woman [b]shall become a curse
among her people. 28 But if the woman has
not defiled herself and is clean, then she
shall be free and shall conceive children.
29 "This is the law in cases of jealousy,
when a wife, [c]though under her husband's
authority, goes astray and defiles herself,
30 or when the spirit of jealousy comes over
a man and he is jealous of his wife. Then he
shall set the woman before the LORD, and
the priest shall carry out for her all this law.
31 The man shall be free from iniquity, but
the woman [d]shall bear her iniquity."

The Nazirite Vow

6 And the LORD spoke to Moses, saying,
2 "Speak to the people of Israel and say
to them, When either a man or a woman
makes a special vow, the vow of [e]a
Nazirite,[2] [f]to separate himself to the LORD,
3 he [g]shall separate himself from wine and
strong drink. He shall drink no vinegar
made from wine or strong drink and shall
not drink any juice of grapes or eat grapes,
fresh or dried. 4 All the days of his separation[3] he shall eat nothing that is produced
by the grapevine, not even the seeds or the
skins.

13 [r]Lev. 18:20 [s]John 8:4
15 [t][Lev. 2:1, 15; 5:11] [u]1 Kin. 17:18; Ezek. 29:16
18 [v][1 Cor. 11:5-7]
21 [w][Jer. 29:22]
22 [x]Ps. 109:18 [y]See Deut. 27:15-26
25 [z][Lev. 8:27]
26 [a]Lev. 2:2, 9; 5:12
27 [b]Deut. 28:37; Jer. 24:9; 29:18, 22; 42:18; 44:12; Zech. 8:13
29 [c]ver. 19, 20
31 [d]Lev. 20:17, 19, 20
Chapter 6
2 [e]Judg. 13:5; [Acts 21:23] [f][Rom. 1:1]
3 [g]Amos 2:12; Luke 1:15

1 An *ephah* was about 3/5 bushel or 22 liters 2 *Nazirite* means *one separated*, or *one consecrated* 3 Or *Naziriteship*

6:1–21 The Nazirite vow was a special type of voluntary devotion. A person could take a special vow of separation for a limited period of time, during which they were not to eat or drink anything that came from the grapevine, and were not to cut their hair or beard. The grapevine was a source of physical pleasure, and abstention from it represented a life given over to God. Allowing the hair to grow signified abstention from human adornment. During the period for which the vow was taken, the Nazirite was to be careful to avoid becoming ceremonially unclean for any reason (v. 7). If someone should die suddenly in the presence of one who had taken a Nazirite vow, it would be necessary to make certain prescribed offerings (vv. 9–12), shave one's head, and start the period of separation all over again (v. 12). A special ceremony ending the period of Nazirite separation is described (vv. 13–21).

5 “All the days of his vow of separation,
no [h]razor shall touch his head. Until the
time is completed for which he separates
himself to the LORD, he shall be holy. [i]He
shall let the locks of hair of his head grow
long.
6 “All the days that he separates himself
to the LORD [j]he shall not go near a dead
body. **7** [k]Not even for his father or for his
mother, for brother or sister, if they die,
shall he make himself unclean, because his
separation to God is on his head. **8** All the
days of his separation he is holy to the
LORD.
9 “And if any man dies very suddenly
beside him and he defiles his consecrated
head, then [l]he shall shave his head on the
day of his cleansing; on the seventh day he
shall shave it. **10** [m]On the eighth day he shall
bring two turtledoves or two pigeons to the
priest to the entrance of the tent of meeting, **11** and the priest shall offer one for a sin
offering and the other for a burnt offering,
and make atonement for him, because he
sinned by reason of the dead body. And he
shall consecrate his head that same day
12 and separate himself to the LORD for the
days of his separation and bring a male
lamb a year old [n]for a guilt offering. But the
previous period shall be void, because his
separation was defiled.
13 “And this is the law for the Nazirite,
[o]when the time of his separation has been
completed: he shall be brought to the
entrance of the tent of meeting, **14** and he
shall bring his gift to the LORD, one male
lamb a year old without blemish for a burnt
offering, and one ewe lamb a year old without blemish [p]as a sin offering, and one ram
without blemish [q]as a peace offering, **15** and
a basket of unleavened bread, [r]loaves of
fine flour mixed with oil, and unleavened
wafers smeared with oil, and their [s]grain
offering and their [t]drink offerings. **16** And
the priest shall bring them before the LORD
and offer [u]his sin offering and his burnt
offering, **17** and he shall offer the ram as a
sacrifice of peace offering to the LORD, with
the basket of unleavened bread. The priest
shall offer also its grain offering and its
drink offering. **18** And the Nazirite [v]shall
shave his consecrated head at the entrance
of the tent of meeting and shall take the
hair from his consecrated head and put it
on the fire that is under the sacrifice of the
peace offering. **19** And the priest shall take
the [w]shoulder of the ram, when it is boiled,
and one unleavened loaf out of the basket
and one unleavened wafer, and [x]shall put
them on the hands of the Nazirite, after he
has shaved the hair of his consecration,
20 and the priest shall wave them for a wave
offering before the LORD. [y]They are a holy
portion for the priest, together with the
breast that is waved and the thigh that is
contributed. And after that the Nazirite
may drink wine.
21 “This is the law of the Nazirite. But if
he vows an offering to the LORD above his
Nazirite vow, as he can afford, in exact
accordance with the vow that he takes,
then he shall do in addition to the law of
the Nazirite.”

Aaron's Blessing

22 The LORD spoke to Moses, saying,
23 “Speak to Aaron and his sons, saying,
Thus [z]you shall bless the people of Israel:
you shall say to them,

24 The LORD [a]bless you and [b]keep you;
25 the LORD [c]make his face to shine
upon you and be gracious to
you;
26 the LORD [d]lift up his countenance[1]
upon you and give you peace.

27 [e]“So shall they put my name upon the
people of Israel, and I will bless them.”

Offerings at the Tabernacle's Consecration

7 On the day when Moses had finished
[f]setting up the tabernacle and had
anointed and [g]consecrated it with all its

1 Or *face*

5 [h]Judg. 13:5; 16:17; 1 Sam. 1:11 [i]Ezek. 44:20; [1 Cor. 11:14] **6** [j]ch. 19:11, 16; Lev. 21:11 **7** [k]Lev. 21:1, 2, 11 **9** [l]Acts 18:18; 21:24 **10** [m]Lev. 5:7; 14:22; 15:14, 29 **12** [n]Lev. 5:6 **13** [o]Acts 21:26 **14** [p]Lev. 4:32 [q]Lev. 3:6 **15** [r]Ex. 29:2; Lev. 2:4 [s]See Ex. 29:41 [t]ch. 15:5, 7, 10 **16** [u]ver. 14
18 [v]Acts 18:18; 21:24 **19** [w]1 Sam. 2:15 [x]Ex. 29:23, 24 **20** [y][ch. 5:25; Ex. 29:27, 28] **23** [z]Lev. 9:22; Deut. 21:5; 1 Chr. 23:13 **24** [a]Ps. 134:3 [b]See Ps. 121:3-8 **25** [c]Ps. 31:16; 67:1; 80:3, 7, 19; 119:135; [Dan. 9:17] **26** [d]Ps. 4:6 **27** [e]Deut. 28:10; 2 Chr. 7:14; Dan. 9:18, 19
Chapter 7
1 [f]Ex. 40:17, 18 [g]Lev. 8:10, 11

6:24–26 This threefold, divinely inspired blessing was pronounced by the priest with uplifted hands (Lev. 9:22). It moves from a general blessing (v. 24), to an invocation of God's favor and presence (v. 25), and finally to a climactic mention of the peace that comes only with God's gracious presence (v. 26). The pronouncement of this blessing placed God's covenant name LORD (Yahweh) on the people (v. 27).

6:25 make his face to shine upon you. Here is a vivid figure for God looking favorably upon His worshipers. The closer one's access to the face of God, the greater the blessing.

7:1–88 Offerings made at the dedication of the tabernacle are listed. Each of the twelve tribal leaders had a day in which he brought a number of expensive gifts and specified offerings. These gifts and offerings are mentioned in precise detail in each case, even though all the lists are identical—a vivid reminder that God is interested in every part of the spiritual service rendered by His people.

furnishings and had anointed and consecrated the altar with all its utensils, 2 [h]the chiefs of Israel, heads of their fathers' houses, who were the chiefs of the tribes, who were over those who were listed, approached 3 and brought their offerings before the LORD, six wagons and twelve oxen, a wagon for every two of the chiefs, and for each one an ox. They brought them before the tabernacle. 4 Then the LORD said to Moses, 5 "Accept these from them, that they may be used in the service of the tent of meeting, and give them to the Levites, to each man according to his service." 6 So Moses took the wagons and the oxen and gave them to the Levites. 7 Two wagons and four oxen [i]he gave to the sons of Gershon, according to their service. 8 And four wagons and eight oxen [j]he gave to the sons of Merari, according to their service, under the direction of Ithamar the son of Aaron the priest. 9 But to the sons of Kohath he gave none, because they were charged with [k]the service of the holy things that [l]had to be carried on the shoulder. 10 And the chiefs offered offerings for the [m]dedication of the altar on the day it was anointed; and the chiefs offered their offering before the altar. 11 And the LORD said to Moses, "They shall offer their offerings, one chief each day, for the dedication of the altar."

12 He who offered his offering the first day was [n]Nahshon the son of Amminadab, of the tribe of Judah. 13 And his offering was one silver plate whose weight was 130 shekels,[1] one silver basin of 70 shekels, according to [o]the shekel of the sanctuary, both of them full of fine flour mixed with oil for a [p]grain offering; 14 one golden dish of 10 shekels, full of [q]incense; 15 [r]one bull from the herd, one ram, one male lamb a year old, for a burnt offering; 16 one male goat for a [s]sin offering; 17 and for [t]the sacrifice of peace offerings, two oxen, five rams, five male goats, and five male lambs a year old. This was the offering of Nahshon the son of Amminadab.

18 On the second day [u]Nethanel the son of Zuar, the chief of Issachar, made an offering. 19 He offered for his offering one silver plate whose weight was 130 shekels, one silver basin of 70 shekels, according to the shekel of the sanctuary, both of them full of fine flour mixed with oil for a grain offering; 20 one golden dish of 10 shekels, full of incense; 21 one bull from the herd, one ram, one male lamb a year old, for a burnt offering; 22 one male goat for a sin offering; 23 and for the sacrifice of peace offerings, two oxen, five rams, five male goats, and five male lambs a year old. This was the offering of Nethanel the son of Zuar.

24 On the third day [v]Eliab the son of Helon, the chief of the people of Zebulun: 25 his offering was one silver plate whose weight was 130 shekels, one silver basin of 70 shekels, according to the shekel of the sanctuary, both of them full of fine flour mixed with oil for a grain offering; 26 one golden dish of 10 shekels, full of incense; 27 one bull from the herd, one ram, one male lamb a year old, for a burnt offering; 28 one male goat for a sin offering; 29 and for the sacrifice of peace offerings, two oxen, five rams, five male goats, and five male lambs a year old. This was the offering of Eliab the son of Helon.

30 On the fourth day [w]Elizur the son of Shedeur, the chief of the people of Reuben: 31 his offering was one silver plate whose weight was 130 shekels, one silver basin of 70 shekels, according to the shekel of the sanctuary, both of them full of fine flour mixed with oil for a grain offering; 32 one golden dish of 10 shekels, full of incense; 33 one bull from the herd, one ram, one male lamb a year old, for a burnt offering; 34 one male goat for a sin offering; 35 and for the sacrifice of peace offerings, two oxen, five rams, five male goats, and five male lambs a year old. This was the offering of Elizur the son of Shedeur.

36 On the fifth day [x]Shelumiel the son of Zurishaddai, the chief of the people of Simeon: 37 his offering was one silver plate whose weight was 130 shekels, one silver basin of 70 shekels, according to the shekel of the sanctuary, both of them full of fine flour mixed with oil for a grain offering; 38 one golden dish of 10 shekels, full of

2 [h]ch. 1:4
7 [i]ch. 4:25, 28
8 [j]ch. 4:29, 31, 33
9 [k]ch. 3:31; See ch. 4:4-15 [l][2 Sam. 6:13; 1 Chr. 15:5, 15]
10 [m]Deut. 20:5; 1 Kin. 8:63; 2 Chr. 7:5, 9; Ezra 6:16; Neh. 12:27
12 [n]See Ex. 6:23
13 [o]See Ex. 30:13 [p]ch. 8:8; See Ex. 29:41
14 [q]Ex. 30:34, 35
15 [r]Lev. 1:2, 3
16 [s]Lev. 4:23, 24
17 [t]Lev. 3:1
18 [u]ch. 1:8
24 [v]ch. 1:9
30 [w]ch. 1:5
36 [x]ch. 1:6

1 A *shekel* was about 2/5 ounce or 11 grams

7:1–9 The carts and the oxen were presented. The tribal leaders joined together to provide carts, and oxen to pull them, for the use of two of the Levitical clans in carrying the parts of the tabernacle that had been assigned to them (3:21–26, 33–37; 4:21–33). No cart was given to the Kohathites; they were expected to carry the holy things on their shoulders (v. 9).

incense; 39 one bull from the herd, one ram,
one male lamb a year old, for a burnt offering; 40 one male goat for a sin offering;
41 and for the sacrifice of peace offerings,
two oxen, five rams, five male goats, and
five male lambs a year old. This was the
offering of Shelumiel the son of Zurishaddai.

42 On the sixth day [y]Eliasaph the son of
Deuel, the chief of the people of Gad: 43 his
offering was one silver plate whose weight
was 130 shekels, one silver basin of 70
shekels, according to the shekel of the
sanctuary, both of them full of fine flour
mixed with oil for a grain offering; 44 one
golden dish of 10 shekels, full of incense;
45 one bull from the herd, one ram, one
male lamb a year old, for a burnt offering;
46 one male goat for a sin offering; 47 and for
the sacrifice of peace offerings, two oxen,
five rams, five male goats, and five male
lambs a year old. This was the offering of
Eliasaph the son of Deuel.

48 On the seventh day [z]Elishama the son
of Ammihud, the chief of the people of
Ephraim: 49 his offering was one silver plate
whose weight was 130 shekels, one silver
basin of 70 shekels, according to the shekel
of the sanctuary, both of them full of fine
flour mixed with oil for a grain offering;
50 one golden dish of 10 shekels, full of
incense; 51 one bull from the herd, one ram,
one male lamb a year old, for a burnt offering; 52 one male goat for a sin offering;
53 and for the sacrifice of peace offerings,
two oxen, five rams, five male goats, and
five male lambs a year old. This was the
offering of Elishama the son of Ammihud.

54 On the eighth day [a]Gamaliel the son of
Pedahzur, the chief of the people of
Manasseh: 55 his offering was one silver
plate whose weight was 130 shekels, one
silver basin of 70 shekels, according to the
shekel of the sanctuary, both of them full
of fine flour mixed with oil for a grain offering; 56 one golden dish of 10 shekels, full of
incense; 57 one bull from the herd, one ram,
one male lamb a year old, for a burnt offering; 58 one male goat for a sin offering;
59 and for the sacrifice of peace offerings,
two oxen, five rams, five male goats, and
five male lambs a year old. This was the
offering of Gamaliel the son of Pedahzur.

60 On the ninth day [b]Abidan the son of
Gideoni, the chief of the people of
Benjamin: 61 his offering was one silver
plate whose weight was 130 shekels, one
silver basin of 70 shekels, according to the
shekel of the sanctuary, both of them full
of fine flour mixed with oil for a grain offering; 62 one golden dish of 10 shekels, full of
incense; 63 one bull from the herd, one ram,
one male lamb a year old, for a burnt offering; 64 one male goat for a sin offering;
65 and for the sacrifice of peace offerings,
two oxen, five rams, five male goats, and
five male lambs a year old. This was the
offering of Abidan the son of Gideoni.

66 On the tenth day [c]Ahiezer the son of
Ammishaddai, the chief of the people of
Dan: 67 his offering was one silver plate
whose weight was 130 shekels, one silver
basin of 70 shekels, according to the shekel
of the sanctuary, both of them full of fine
flour mixed with oil for a grain offering;
68 one golden dish of 10 shekels, full of incense; 69 one bull from the herd, one ram,
one male lamb a year old, for a burnt offering; 70 one male goat for a sin offering; 71 and
for the sacrifice of peace offerings, two
oxen, five rams, five male goats, and five
male lambs a year old. This was the offering
of Ahiezer the son of Ammishaddai.

72 On the eleventh day [d]Pagiel the son of
Ochran, the chief of the people of Asher:
73 his offering was one silver plate whose
weight was 130 shekels, one silver basin of
70 shekels, according to the shekel of the
sanctuary, both of them full of fine flour
mixed with oil for a grain offering; 74 one
golden dish of 10 shekels, full of incense;
75 one bull from the herd, one ram, one
male lamb a year old, for a burnt offering;
76 one male goat for a sin offering; 77 and for
the sacrifice of peace offerings, two oxen,
five rams, five male goats, and five male
lambs a year old. This was the offering of
Pagiel the son of Ochran.

78 On the twelfth day [e]Ahira the son of
Enan, the chief of the people of Naphtali:
79 his offering was one silver plate whose
weight was 130 shekels, one silver basin of
70 shekels, according to the shekel of the
sanctuary, both of them full of fine flour
mixed with oil for a grain offering; 80 one
golden dish of 10 shekels, full of incense;

42 [y] ch. 1:14; [ch. 2:14]
48 [z] ch. 1:10
54 [a] ch. 1:10
60 [b] ch. 1:11
66 [c] ch. 1:12
72 [d] ch. 1:13
78 [e] ch. 1:15

81 one bull from the herd, one ram, one male lamb a year old, for a burnt offering; 82 one male goat for a sin offering; 83 and for the sacrifice of peace offerings, two oxen, five rams, five male goats, and five male lambs a year old. This was the offering of Ahira the son of Enan.

84 This was the dedication offering for the altar on the day when it was anointed, from the chiefs of Israel: twelve silver plates, twelve silver basins, twelve golden dishes, 85 each silver plate weighing 130 shekels and each basin 70, all the silver of the vessels 2,400 shekels according to the shekel of the sanctuary, 86 the twelve golden dishes, full of incense, weighing 10 shekels apiece according to the shekel of the sanctuary, all the gold of the dishes being 120 shekels; 87 all the cattle for the burnt offering twelve bulls, twelve rams, twelve male lambs a year old, with their grain offering; and twelve male goats for a sin offering; 88 and all the cattle for the sacrifice of peace offerings twenty-four bulls, the rams sixty, the male goats sixty, the male lambs a year old sixty. This was the dedication offering for the altar after it [f]was anointed.

89 And when Moses went into the tent of meeting [g]to speak with the LORD, he heard [h]the voice speaking to him from above the mercy seat that was on the ark of the testimony, from between the two cherubim; and it spoke to him.

The Seven Lamps

8 Now the LORD spoke to Moses, saying, 2 "Speak to Aaron and say to him, When you set up the lamps, the seven lamps shall give light in front of the lampstand." 3 And Aaron did so: he set up its lamps in front of the lampstand, as the LORD commanded Moses. 4 And [i]this was the workmanship of the lampstand, hammered work of gold. From its base to its flowers, it was hammered work; according to the pattern that the LORD had shown Moses, so he made the lampstand.

Cleansing of the Levites

5 And the LORD spoke to Moses, saying, 6 "Take the Levites from among the people of Israel and cleanse them. 7 Thus you shall do to them to cleanse them: sprinkle the [j]water of purification upon them, and [k]let them go with a razor over all their body, and wash their clothes and cleanse themselves. 8 Then let them take a bull from the herd and [l]its grain offering of fine flour mixed with oil, [m]and you shall take another bull from the herd for a sin offering. 9 [n]And you shall bring the Levites before the tent of meeting [o]and assemble the whole congregation of the people of Israel. 10 When you bring the Levites before the LORD, the people of Israel [p]shall lay their hands on the Levites, 11 and Aaron shall offer the Levites before the LORD as a wave offering from the people of Israel, that they may do the service of the LORD. 12 Then the Levites [q]shall lay their hands on the heads of the bulls, and you shall offer [r]the one for a sin offering and the other for a burnt offering to the LORD to make atonement for the Levites. 13 And you shall set the Levites before Aaron and his sons, and shall offer them as [s]a wave offering to the LORD.

14 "Thus you shall separate the Levites from among the people of Israel, and [t]the Levites shall be mine. 15 And after that the Levites shall go in to serve at the tent of meeting, when you have cleansed them and offered them as a [s]wave offering. 16 For they are [u]wholly given to me from among the people of Israel. [v]Instead of all who open the womb, the firstborn of all the people of Israel, I have taken them for myself. 17 [w]For all the firstborn among the people of Israel are mine, both of man and of beast. On the day that I struck down all the firstborn in the land of Egypt I consecrated them for myself, 18 and I have taken the Levites instead of all the firstborn among the people of Israel. 19 [u]And I have given the Levites as a gift to Aaron and his sons from among the people of Israel, to do the service for the people of Israel at the tent of meeting and [x]to make atonement for the people of Israel, [y]that there may be no plague among the people of Israel when the people of Israel come near the sanctuary."

88 [f]ver. 1, 10
89 [g]ch. 12:8; See Ex. 33:9-11 [h]See Ex. 25:22
Chapter 8
4 [i]Ex. 25:31
7 [j]ch. 19:9, 17; [Lev. 8:6] [k][Lev. 14:8, 9]
8 [l]Lev. 2:1; See Ex. 29:41 [m]ver. 12
9 [n][Ex. 29:4; 40:12] [o][Lev. 8:3]
10 [p][Lev. 1:4]
12 [q][Ex. 29:10] [r]ver. 8
13 [s]ver. 11, 21
14 [t]ch. 3:45; [ch. 16:9]
15 [s][See ver. 13 above]
16 [u]ch. 3:9 [v]ch. 3:12, 45
17 [w]See Ex. 13:2
19 [u][See ver. 16 above] [x]ch. 25:11, 13 [y]See ch. 1:53

7:89 the mercy seat. This designation of the ornate cover of the ark represents one Hebrew word (lit. "atonement covering" or "place of atonement"). The mercy seat is mentioned twenty-five times in the Pentateuch, but only once in later books (1 Chr. 28:11). See notes Ex. 25:17 and Lev. 16:2.

8:5–22 This ceremony, which set apart the Levites for service to the Lord, differs significantly from the consecration ceremony of the priests (Ex. 29:1–37; Lev. 8). Key terms in the ordination of Aaron and his sons as priests are "hallow" and "consecrate" (Ex. 29:1, 9 and notes); the Levites were "cleansed" (vv. 6, 15, 21). The priests received new garments; the Levites shaved the hair on their bodies and washed their clothes (Ex. 29:5–9).

8:18 instead of all the firstborn. See note 3:11–13.

20 Thus did Moses and Aaron and all the congregation of the people of Israel to the Levites. According to all that the LORD commanded Moses concerning the Levites, the people of Israel did to them.
21 And [z]the Levites purified themselves from sin and washed their clothes, and [a]Aaron offered them as a wave offering before the LORD, and Aaron made atonement for them to cleanse them.
22 And after that the Levites went in to do their service in the tent of meeting before Aaron and his sons; as the LORD had commanded Moses concerning the Levites, so they did to them.

Retirement of the Levites

23 And the LORD spoke to Moses, saying,
24 "This applies to the Levites: [b]from twenty-five years old and upward they[1] shall come to do duty in the service of the tent of meeting.
25 And from the age of fifty years they shall withdraw from the duty of the service and serve no more.
26 They minister[2] to their brothers in the tent of meeting [c]by keeping guard, but they shall do no service. Thus shall you do to the Levites in assigning their duties."

The Passover Celebrated

9 And the LORD spoke to Moses in the wilderness of Sinai, [d]in the first month of the second year after they had come out of the land of Egypt, saying,
2 "Let the people of Israel keep the Passover at its appointed time.
3 [e]On the fourteenth day of this month, at twilight, you shall keep it at its appointed time; according to all its statutes and all its rules you shall keep it."
4 So Moses told the people of Israel that they should keep the Passover.
5 And they kept the Passover in the first month, on the fourteenth day of the month, at twilight, in the wilderness of Sinai; according to all that the LORD commanded Moses, so the people of Israel did.
6 And there were certain men who were [f]unclean through touching a dead body, so that they could not keep the Passover on that day, and [g]they came before Moses and Aaron on that day.
7 And those men said to him, "We are unclean through touching a dead body. Why are we kept from bringing the LORD's [h]offering at its appointed time among the people of Israel?"
8 And Moses said to them, "Wait, that [i]I may hear what the LORD will command concerning you."
9 The LORD spoke to Moses, saying,
10 "Speak to the people of Israel, saying, If any one of you or of your descendants is unclean through touching a dead body, or is on a long journey, he shall still keep the Passover to the LORD.
11 [j]In the second month on the fourteenth day at twilight they shall keep it. [k]They shall eat it with unleavened bread and bitter herbs.
12 [l]They shall leave none of it until the morning, [m]nor break any of its bones; [n]according to all the statute for the Passover they shall keep it.
13 But if anyone who is clean and is not on a journey fails to keep the Passover, [o]that person shall be cut off from his people because he did not bring the LORD's [p]offering at its appointed time; that man shall bear his sin.
14 And if a stranger sojourns among you and would keep the Passover to the LORD, according to the statute of the Passover and according to its rule, so shall he do. [q]You shall have one statute, both for the sojourner and for the native."

The Cloud Covering the Tabernacle

15 [r]On the day that the tabernacle was set up, the cloud covered the tabernacle, the tent of the testimony. And [s]at evening it was over the tabernacle like the appearance of fire until morning.
16 So it was always: the cloud covered it by day[3] and the

21 [z]ver. 7 [a]ver. 11, 12, 13, 15
24 [b][ch. 4:3; 1 Chr. 23:3, 24, 27]
26 [c]See ch. 1:53
Chapter 9
1 [d][ch. 1:1]
3 [e]See Lev. 23:5
6 [f]ch. 5:2; 19:11, 16; [John 18:28] [g]ch. 27:2; Ex. 18:15, 19, 26
7 [h]ver. 13
8 [i]ch. 27:5
11 [j]See Ex. 12:6; 2 Chr. 30:2-15 [k]Ex. 12:8; [Deut. 16:3]
12 [l]Ex. 12:10 [m]Ex. 12:46; Cited John 19:36 [n]Ex. 12:43, 49
13 [o]Ex. 12:15; [Gen. 17:14] [p]ver. 7
14 [q]Ex. 12:48, 49
15 [r]Ex. 40:17, 34 [s]See Ex. 13:21

[1] Hebrew *he* [2] Hebrew *He ministers* [3] Septuagint, Syriac, Vulgate; Hebrew lacks *by day*

8:24 twenty-five years old. In 4:3, the term of service is listed as from 30 to 50 years old. Rabbinic sources suggest that a five-year apprenticeship was served prior to full service. Alternatively, 4:3 may designate the time when complete responsibility for transporting the tabernacle was undertaken, with lighter duties being assumed at age 25. In 1 Chr. 23:24–26 David lowered the age of Levitical service to 20 because transportation of the tabernacle was no longer necessary.

9:6–13 A special problem is identified and God's answer is given: a person who is unclean or on a journey at the regular time may celebrate Passover exactly one month later. No others may postpone its observance.

9:14 As a covenant rite, the Passover was to be celebrated only by members of the covenant community. Male strangers who wished to participate were to accept the terms of the covenant by being circumcised (Ex. 12:48).

9:15–10:6 Two kinds of guidance were arranged for the march: supernatural guidance by the cloud (9:15–23) and orders from Moses given by trumpet (10:1–6).

appearance of fire by night. 17 And whenever the cloud [t]lifted from over the tent, after
that the people of Israel set out, and in the
place where the cloud settled down, there
the people of Israel camped. 18 At the command of the LORD the people of Israel set
out, and at the command of the LORD they
camped. [u]As long as the cloud rested over
the tabernacle, they remained in camp.
19 Even when the cloud continued over the
tabernacle many days, the people of Israel
[v]kept the charge of the LORD and did not
set out. 20 Sometimes the cloud was a few
days over the tabernacle, and according to
the command of the LORD they remained in
camp; then according to the command of
the LORD they set out. 21 And sometimes the
cloud remained from evening until morning. And when the cloud lifted in the
morning, they set out, or if it continued for
a day and a night, when the cloud lifted
they set out. 22 Whether it was two days, or
a month, or a longer time, that the cloud
continued over the tabernacle, abiding
there, the people of Israel [w]remained in
camp and did not set out, but when it lifted they set out. 23 At the command of the
LORD they camped, and at the command of
the LORD they set out. [v]They kept the
charge of the LORD, at the command of the
LORD by Moses.

The Silver Trumpets

10 The LORD spoke to Moses, saying,
2 "Make two silver trumpets. Of
hammered work you shall make them, and
you shall use them for [x]summoning the
congregation and for breaking camp. 3 And
when [y]both are blown, all the congregation
shall gather themselves to you at the
entrance of the tent of meeting. 4 But if they
blow only one, then [z]the chiefs, the heads
of the tribes of Israel, shall gather themselves to you. 5 When you blow an alarm,
[a]the camps that are on the east side shall
set out. 6 And when you blow an alarm the
second time, [b]the camps that are on the
south side shall set out. An alarm is to be
blown whenever they are to set out. 7 But
when the assembly is to be gathered
together, [c]you shall blow a long blast, but
you shall not [d]sound an alarm. 8 [e]And the
sons of Aaron, the priests, shall blow the
trumpets. The trumpets shall be to you for
a perpetual statute throughout your generations. 9 And [f]when you go to war in your
land against the adversary who [g]oppresses
you, then you shall [d]sound an alarm with
the trumpets, that you may be [h]remem-
bered before the LORD your God, and you
shall be saved from your enemies. 10 [i]On
the day of your gladness also, and at your
appointed feasts and [j]at the beginnings of
your months, you shall blow the trumpets
over your burnt offerings and over the sacrifices of your peace offerings. They shall be
[k]a reminder of you before your God: I am
the LORD your God."

Israel Leaves Sinai

11 In the second year, in the second
month, on the twentieth day of the month,
[l]the cloud lifted from over the tabernacle of
the testimony, 12 and the people of Israel
[m]set out by stages from the [n]wilderness of
Sinai. And the cloud settled down in the
[o]wilderness of Paran. 13 They set out for the
first time [p]at the command of the LORD by
Moses. 14 The standard of the camp of the
people of Judah set out [q]first by their companies, and over their company was
[r]Nahshon the son of Amminadab. 15 And
over the company of the tribe of the people
of Issachar was Nethanel the son of Zuar.
16 And over the company of the tribe of the
people of Zebulun was Eliab the son of
Helon.
17 And when [s]the tabernacle was taken

17 [t]ch. 10:11, 33, 34; Ex. 40:36
18 [u][1 Cor. 10:1]
19 [v]See ch. 1:53
22 [w]Ex. 40:36, 37
23 [v][See ver. 19 above]
Chapter 10
2 [x]Isai. 1:13; Joel 1:14; [Ps. 81:3]
3 [y]Jer. 4:5; Joel 2:15
4 [z]ch. 1:16; 7:2; Ex. 18:21
5 [a]ver. 14; See ch. 2:3-9
6 [b]ver. 18; See ch. 2:10-16
7 [c]ver. 3 [d]Joel 2:1
8 [e]1 Chr. 15:24; 2 Chr. 13:12
9 [f]ch. 31:6; 2 Chr. 13:14; [Josh. 6:5] [g]Judg. 2:18; 4:3; 10:8, 12; 1 Sam. 10:18 [d][See ver. 7 above] [h]See Gen. 8:1
10 [i]ch. 29:1; 1 Chr. 15:24; 2 Chr. 5:12, 13; 7:6; 29:26-28; Ezra 3:10; Neh. 12:35 [j]Ps. 81:3; See ch. 28:11 [k]ver. 9
11 [l]ch. 9:17
12 [m][Ex. 40:36] [n]ch. 1:1; 9:5; Ex. 19:1, 2 [o]ch. 12:16; 13:3, 26; Gen. 21:21; Deut. 1:1
13 [p]ver. 5, 6; ch. 2:34
14 [q]See ch. 2:3-9 [r]For ver. 14-16, see ch. 1:7-9
17 [s]ch. 1:51

10:11–22:1 This section begins with the Lord's guidance of the people immediately to the area of Kadesh in the wilderness of Paran (10:12; 12:16; 13:3, 26), the camp from which they would begin the conquest. Instead of the promised victory, the spies' gloomy report created a rebellion that affected the entire nation, except for Moses, Aaron, Joshua, and Caleb. The Lord pronounced judgment on the whole first generation who were counted in the census, and told them to leave Kadesh and turn back toward Sinai.

In view of this judgment, the laws and results of the meager history following in chs. 15–19 are striking for two reasons: (a) after the judgment the Lord immediately told Israel how to serve Him in the Land of Promise (ch. 15), a clear indication that they would eventually go there as promised; and (b) for the whole period of the wilderness judgment we are given only two events (which were actually one connected incident): Korah's rebellion and the budding of Aaron's rod.

The events in chs. 20; 21 are clearly transitional, beginning with the return to Kadesh, a hint that the conquest was on again. The victory over the king of Arad also signaled the change as the place of victory was named "Hormah," "destruction" (21:3), in contrast to the tragic defeat in ch. 14.

10:11 year . . . month . . . day. Almost fourteen months after the Exodus from Egypt and eleven months after the arrival at Sinai (Ex. 19:1).

10:14–28 The order of march follows the prescription of ch. 2, though more detail about the Levites is given here (vv. 17, 21).

down, the sons of Gershon and the sons of
Merari, [t]who carried the tabernacle, set
out. 18 And [u]the standard of the camp of
Reuben set out by their companies, and
over their company was [v]Elizur the son of
Shedeur. 19 And over the company of the
tribe of the people of Simeon was
[w]Shelumiel the son of Zurishaddai. 20 And
over the company of the tribe of the people
of Gad was [x]Eliasaph the son of [y]Deuel.
21 Then the Kohathites set out, [z]carrying
the holy things, and [a]the tabernacle was set
up before their arrival. 22 And [b]the standard
of the camp of the people of Ephraim set
out by their companies, and over their
company was [c]Elishama the son of
Ammihud. 23 And over the company of the
tribe of the people of Manasseh was
[c]Gamaliel the son of Pedahzur. 24 And over
the company of the tribe of the people of
Benjamin was [d]Abidan the son of Gideoni.
25 Then [e]the standard of the camp of the
people of Dan, acting as the [f]rear guard of
all the camps, set out by their companies,
and over their company was [g]Ahiezer the
son of Ammishaddai. 26 And over the company of the tribe of the people of Asher was
[h]Pagiel the son of Ochran. 27 And over the
company of the tribe of the people of
Naphtali was [i]Ahira the son of Enan.
28 [j]This was the order of march of the people of Israel by their companies, when they
set out.
29 And Moses said to Hobab the son of
[k]Reuel the Midianite, Moses' father-in-law,
"We are setting out for the place of which
the LORD said, [l]'I will give it to you.' Come
with us, and we will do good to you, for
[m]the LORD has promised good to Israel."
30 But he said to him, "I will not go. I will
depart to my own land and to my kindred."
31 And he said, "Please do not leave us, for
you know where we should camp in the
wilderness, and you will serve [n]as eyes for
us. 32 And if you do go with us, [o]whatever
good the LORD will do to us, the same will
we do to you."
33 So they set out from [p]the mount of the
LORD three days' journey. And the ark of
the covenant of the LORD went before them
three days' journey, to seek out [q]a resting
place for them. 34 [r]And the cloud of the
LORD was over them by day, whenever they
set out from the camp.
35 And whenever the ark set out, Moses
said, [s]"Arise, O LORD, and let your enemies
be scattered, and let those who hate you
flee before you." 36 And when it rested, he
said, "Return, O LORD, to the ten thousand
thousands of Israel."

The People Complain

11 And [t]the people complained in the
hearing of the LORD about their misfortunes, and when the LORD heard it, [u]his
anger was kindled, and [v]the fire of the
LORD burned among them and consumed
some outlying parts of the camp. 2 Then
[w]the people cried out to Moses, [x]and
Moses prayed to the LORD, and the fire died
down. 3 So the name of that place was
called [y]Taberah,[1] because the fire of the
LORD burned among them.
4 Now the [z]rabble that was among them
had a strong craving. And the people of
Israel also [a]wept again and said, [b]"Oh that
we had meat to eat! 5 [c]We remember the fish
we ate in Egypt that cost nothing, the
cucumbers, the melons, the leeks, the
onions, and the garlic. 6 But now our
strength is dried up, and there is nothing at
all but this manna to look at."
7 Now [d]the manna was like coriander
seed, and its appearance like that of bdellium. 8 [e]The people went about and gathered it and ground it in handmills or beat
it in mortars and boiled it in pots and
made cakes of it. [f]And the taste of it was
like the taste of cakes baked with oil.
9 [g]When the dew fell upon the camp in the
night, the manna fell with it.
10 Moses heard the people [h]weeping
throughout their clans, everyone at the
door of his tent. And the anger of the LORD
blazed hotly, and Moses was displeased.
11 [i]Moses said to the LORD, "Why have you
dealt ill with your servant? And why have I

17 [t]See ch. 4:24-33; 7:6-8
18 [u]See ch. 2:10-16 [v]ch. 1:5
19 [w]ch. 1:6
20 [x]ch. 1:14 [y][ch. 2:14]
21 [z]ch. 7:9; See ch. 4:4-15 [a][ver. 17]
22 [b]See ch. 2:18-24 [c]ch. 1:10
23 [c][See ver. 22 above]
24 [d]ch. 1:11
25 [e]See ch. 2:25-31 [f][Josh. 6:9] [g]ch. 1:12
26 [h]ch. 1:13
27 [i]ch. 1:15
28 [j]ch. 2:34
29 [k]See Ex. 2:18 [l]Gen. 12:7 [m]Gen. 32:12; Ex. 3:8; 6:7, 8
31 [n][Job 29:15]
32 [o]ver. 29; [Judg. 1:16; 4:11]
33 [p]See Ex. 3:1 [q]Ps. 132:8; Jer. 31:2
34 [r]See Ex. 13:21
35 [s]Ps. 68:1, 2
Chapter 11
1 [t]Deut. 9:22 [u]Ps. 78:21 [v][ch. 16:35; Lev. 10:2; 2 Kin. 1:12; Ps. 106:18; Rev. 13:13]
2 [w][ch. 21:7] [x][James 5:16]; See ch. 16:45-48
3 [y]Deut. 9:22
4 [z]See Ex. 12:38 [a]ch. 14:1 [b]Ps. 78:18; 106:14; 1 Cor. 10:6
5 [c][ch. 21:5; Ex. 16:3; Acts 7:39]
7 [d]Ex. 16:14, 31
8 [e]Ex. 16:16-18 [f][Ex. 16:31]
9 [g]Ex. 16:13, 14
10 [h][Zech. 12:12-14]
11 [i][1 Kin. 19:4; Jonah 4:1-4, 9]

1 *Taberah* means *burning*

10:29 Hobab. Yet another element of guidance is found. Moses asked his Midianite brother-in-law, a man familiar with the wilderness, for assistance (Ex. 2:16–3:1; Judg. 1:16).

10:35–36 Moses was intensely conscious of God's mighty presence with His people. These prayers honor the Lord as the divine Warrior who goes before the host of the people (v. 35), and as the source of divine protection for the camp (v. 36).

11:4 the rabble. These were non-Israelites who came out from Egypt with the Israelites (Ex. 12:38 note).

11:7 manna. See note Ex. 16:14.

not found favor in your sight, that you lay
the burden of all this people on me? **12**Did I
conceive all this people? Did I give them
birth, that you should say to me, [j]'Carry
them in your bosom, as a [k]nurse carries a
nursing child,' to the land [l]that you swore
to give their fathers? **13**[m]Where am I to get
meat to give to all this people? For they
weep before me and say, 'Give us meat, that
we may eat.' **14**[n]I am not able to carry all
this people alone; the burden is too heavy
for me. **15**If you will treat me like this, kill
me at once, if I find favor in your sight, that
I may not see my wretchedness."

Elders Appointed to Aid Moses

16Then the LORD said to Moses, "Gather
for me [o]seventy men of the elders of Israel,
whom you know to be the elders of the
people and [p]officers over them, and bring
them to the tent of meeting, and let them
take their stand there with you. **17**[q]And I
will come down and talk with you there.
And [r]I will take some of the Spirit that is
on you and put it on them, and [s]they shall
bear the burden of the people with you, so
that you may not bear it yourself alone.
18And say to the people, [t]'Consecrate
yourselves for tomorrow, and you shall eat
meat, for you have wept in the hearing of
the LORD, saying, "Who will give us meat
to eat? [u]For it was better for us in Egypt."
Therefore the LORD will give you meat, and
you shall eat. **19**You shall not eat just one
day, or two days, or five days, or ten days,
or twenty days, **20**but a whole month, [v]until it comes out at your nostrils and
becomes loathsome to you, because you
have rejected the LORD who is among you
and have wept before him, saying, [w]"Why
did we come out of Egypt?"'" **21**But Moses
said, [x]"The people among whom I am
number six hundred thousand on foot,
and you have said, 'I will give them meat,
that they may eat a whole month!' **22**[y]Shall
flocks and herds be slaughtered for them,
and be enough for them? Or shall all the
fish of the sea be gathered together for
them, and be enough for them?" **23**And the
LORD said to Moses, [z]"Is the LORD's hand
shortened? Now you shall see whether
[a]my word will come true for you or not."
24So Moses went out and told the people
the words of the LORD. [b]And he gathered
seventy men of the elders of the people and
placed them around the tent. **25**Then [c]the
LORD came down in the cloud and spoke to
him, and took some of the Spirit that was
on him and put it on the seventy elders.
And as soon as the Spirit rested on them,
they prophesied. But they did not continue
doing it.

26Now two men remained in the camp,
one named Eldad, and the other named
Medad, and the Spirit rested on them. They
were among those registered, but they [d]had
not gone out to the tent, and so they prophesied in the camp. **27**And a young man ran
and told Moses, "Eldad and Medad are
prophesying in the camp." **28**And [e]Joshua
the son of Nun, the assistant of Moses from
his youth, said, "My lord Moses, [f]stop
them." **29**But Moses said to him, "Are you
jealous for my sake? [g]Would that all the
LORD's people were prophets, that the LORD
would put his Spirit on them!" **30**And Moses
and the elders of Israel returned to the camp.

Quail and a Plague

31Then a [h]wind from the LORD sprang up,
and it brought quail from the sea and let
them fall beside the camp, about a day's
journey on this side and a day's journey on
the other side, around the camp, and about
two cubits[1] above the ground. **32**And the
people rose all that day and all night and
all the next day, and gathered the quail.
Those who gathered least gathered ten
[i]homers.[2] And they spread them out for
themselves all around the camp. **33**[j]While
the meat was yet between their teeth,
before it was consumed, the anger of the
LORD was kindled against the people, and
[k]the LORD struck down the people with a
very great plague. **34**Therefore the name of
that place was called [l]Kibroth-hattaavah,[3]
because there they buried the people who
had the craving. **35**[m]From Kibroth-hattaavah the people journeyed to [n]Hazeroth,
and they remained at [n]Hazeroth.

12 [j]Isai. 40:11; [Deut. 1:31] [k][Isai. 49:23; 1 Thess. 2:7] [l]Gen. 50:24; Ex. 13:5
13 [m][2 Kin. 7:2; Matt. 15:33; Mark 8:4; John 6:7, 9]
14 [n]Ex. 18:18; Deut. 1:9, 12
16 [o][Ex. 24:1, 9] [p]Deut. 1:15; 16:18
17 [q]ver. 25; ch. 12:5; Gen. 11:5; 18:21; Ex. 19:20 [r][2 Kin. 2:9, 15; Neh. 9:20] [s]Ex. 18:22
18 [t]Ex. 19:10 [u]See ver. 5
20 [v][Ps. 78:29; 106:15] [w]ch. 21:5
21 [x]Ex. 12:37; [ch. 1:46; Ex. 38:26]
22 [y][ver. 13]
23 [z]Isai. 50:2; 59:1
[a]ch. 23:19; Ezek. 12:25; 24:14
24 [b]ver. 16
25 [c]ver. 17
26 [d][1 Sam. 20:26; Jer. 36:5]
28 [e]ch. 26:65; Ex. 24:13; [ch. 13:8]; See ch. 13:16 [f][Mark 9:38; Luke 9:49]
29 [g][1 Cor. 14:5]
31 [h]Ex. 16:13; Ps. 78:26-28; 105:40
32 [i]Ex. 16:36; [Ezek. 45:11]
33 [j]Ps. 78:30, 31 [k][ch. 16:49]
34 [l]Deut. 9:22
35 [m]ch. 33:17 [n]ch. 12:16; 33:17, 18

[1] A *cubit* was about 18 inches or 45 centimeters [2] A *homer* was about 6 bushels or 220 liters [3] *Kibroth-hattaavah* means *graves of craving*

11:25 prophesied. An instance of divinely inspired ecstatic utterance by the elders (cf. 1 Sam. 10:10; 19:24). This apparently temporary phenomenon served to authenticate the leadership of the elders.

11:31 about two cubits above the ground. The quail were not piled to this depth, but flying blindly at a level of about three feet, where they were easily seized or struck down. See note Ex. 16:13.

Miriam and Aaron Oppose Moses

12 Miriam and Aaron spoke against
Moses because of the Cushite
woman whom he had married, for he had
married a Cushite woman. **2**And they said,
"Has the LORD indeed spoken only through
Moses? [o]Has he not spoken through us
also?" And [p]the LORD heard it. **3**Now the
man Moses was very meek, more than all
people who were on the face of the earth.
4And suddenly the LORD said to Moses and
to Aaron and Miriam, "Come out, you three,
to the tent of meeting." And the three of
them came out. **5**And [q]the LORD came down
in a pillar of cloud and stood at the entrance
of the tent and called Aaron and Miriam,
and they both came forward. **6**And he said,
"Hear my words: If there is a prophet among
you, I the LORD make myself known to him
[r]in a vision; I speak with him [s]in a dream.
7Not so with [t]my servant Moses. [u]He is
faithful in all my house. **8**With him I speak
[v]mouth to mouth, clearly, and not in [w]rid-
dles, and he beholds [x]the form of the LORD.
Why then were you not afraid to speak
against my servant Moses?" **9**And the anger
of the LORD was kindled against them, and
he departed.
10When the cloud removed from over the
tent, behold, [y]Miriam was [z]leprous,[1] like
snow. And Aaron turned toward Miriam,
and behold, she was leprous. **11**And Aaron
said to Moses, "Oh, my lord, [a]do not punish
us[2] because we have done foolishly and have
sinned. **12**Let her not be as one dead, whose
flesh is half eaten away when he comes out
of his mother's womb." **13**And Moses cried
to the LORD, "O God, please heal her—
please." **14**But the LORD said to Moses, "If her
father had but [b]spit in her face, should she
not be shamed seven days? Let her be [c]shut
outside the camp seven days, and after that
she may be brought in again." **15**So Miriam
[d]was shut outside the camp seven days, and
the people did not set out on the march till
Miriam was brought in again. **16**After that the
people set out from [e]Hazeroth, and camped
in [f]the wilderness of Paran.

Spies Sent into Canaan

13 The LORD spoke to Moses, saying,
2[g]"Send men to spy out the land of
Canaan, which I am giving to the people
of Israel. From each tribe of their fathers
you shall send a man, every one a chief
among them." **3**So Moses sent them from
[h]the wilderness of Paran, according to the
command of the LORD, all of them men
who were heads of the people of Israel.

Chapter 12
2 [o]Mic. 6:4 [p]ch. 11:1; 2 Kin. 19:4; Isai. 37:4; Ezek. 35:12, 13; [Mal. 3:16]
5 [q]ch. 11:25; 16:19
6 [r]Gen. 46:2; Ezek. 1:1; Dan. 8:2; 10:8, 16; Luke 1:11, 22; Acts 10:11; 22:17, 18 [s]Gen. 20:6; 31:10, 11; 1 Kin. 3:5; Job 33:15; Matt. 1:20; 27:19
7 [t]Ps. 105:26 [u]Heb. 3:2, 5
8 [v]ch. 7:89; [Ex. 33:11; Deut. 34:10; 1 Cor. 13:12] [w]Ps. 49:4; 78:2; Prov. 1:6 [x][Ex. 33:20, 23]
10 [y]Deut. 24:9 [z]See Lev. 13:10
11 [a][2 Sam. 19:19; 24:10; Prov. 30:32]
14 [b]Deut. 25:9; Job 30:10 [c]See Lev. 13:46
15 [d][2 Kin. 15:5; 2 Chr. 26:20, 21; Luke 17:12]
16 [e]ch. 11:35; [ch. 33:18] [f]See ch. 10:12

Chapter 13 2 [g]ch. 32:8; See Deut. 1:22-25 3 [h]ver. 26; ch. 12:16; 32:8; Deut. 1:19; 9:23

[1] *Leprosy* was a term for several skin diseases; see Leviticus 13
[2] Hebrew *lay not sin upon us*

12:1 Cushite. Cush is the region south of Egypt. Zipporah the Midianite (Ex. 2:16–21) might have been referred to as "an Ethiopian," but the directness of the explanation that Moses "had married a Cushite woman" suggests that Zipporah had died and Moses had married again.

12:2 spoken only through Moses. The real reason for the criticism comes to view—jealousy of Moses. Miriam and Aaron had important places in God's plan for Israel (cf. Mic. 6:4), but their jealousy of Moses, if not corrected, could greatly injure the work of God.

12:3 Many suggest that this statement about Moses was added by someone other than Moses, though the Mosaic origin of this verse is not impossible (a unique feature of Scripture is its accurate representation of both the good and bad qualities of its characters, cf. Neh. 13:14, 22; 1 Cor. 4:16, 17). The statement establishes that Moses did not wrongly provoke the complaint of Miriam and Aaron, and explains God's swift defense of His prophet.

12:5 came down. This phrase is often used in Scripture to indicate a special act of God in dealing with earthly events (e.g., Is. 64:1).

12:6–8 The Lord summoned Moses and his two accusers to the tent of meeting. There He rebuked Aaron and Miriam for their arrogant lack of fear in opposing Moses. In light of the clarity and directness of God's self-revelation to Moses, they should have accepted their subordination to his unique status and supported him. See "Prophets" at Deut. 18:18.

12:7 my servant Moses. The New Testament contrasts the great honor of Moses referred to here with the even greater honor of Jesus Christ—Moses was a faithful servant in God's house, but Christ is "faithful over God's house as a son" (Heb. 3:6).

12:8 mouth to mouth. Contrast the way God revealed His will even to Elijah (cf. 1 Kin. 19:9–18). No other Old Testament figure had as intimate a relation to God as Moses, and this description in turn highlights the greater privilege of the Christian—in Jesus Christ, the glory of God's goodness and mercy that was withheld even from Moses is displayed to believers through the Spirit (Ex. 33:19, 20; John 1:14; 2 Cor. 3:18). But the believer also looks forward to a yet greater *visio dei* (vision of God)—seeing Christ "face to face" (1 Cor. 13:12; Rev. 22:4).

clearly, and not in riddles. With respect to the clarity of divine revelation given to him, Moses stands above all other Old Testament prophets (cf. v. 6). The characterization of prophetic revelation as "dark speech" or "riddles" implies that prophetic materials in Scripture are sometimes to be understood figuratively rather than literally.

12:10 leprous. The Hebrew word can refer to various skin diseases. It was clear to anyone who saw Miriam that God had condemned her attitude. Aaron shared the humiliation, for it was evident to all that he too was being chastened for joining her in claiming that they were as great as Moses. God did not make Aaron leprous, however, since his position as high priest (second in importance only to that of Moses) needed to be safeguarded (cf. Num. 16:6–17:11). Later, Uzziah, a beloved king of Judah, was stricken with leprosy when he tried to assume the prerogatives of the high priest (2 Chr. 26:16–21).

12:16 wilderness of Paran. The region southwest of the Promised Land in the east-central portion of the Sinai peninsula (Gen. 21:21).

13:1 The LORD spoke to Moses. God told Moses to send spies apparently in response to an earlier petition of the people, since Deut. 1:22, 23 indicates that they had asked for this. God used the spies to show that the people as a whole were not yet ready to enter the Promised Land.

13:3 heads of the people of Israel. The names of vv. 4–15 are not found

4 And these were their names: From the
tribe of Reuben, Shammua the son of
Zaccur; 5 from the tribe of Simeon,
Shaphat the son of Hori; 6 [i]from the tribe
of Judah, [j]Caleb the son of Jephunneh;
7 from the tribe of Issachar, Igal the son of
Joseph; 8 from the tribe of Ephraim,
[k]Hoshea the son of Nun; 9 from the tribe
of Benjamin, Palti the son of Raphu;
10 from the tribe of Zebulun, Gaddiel the
son of Sodi; 11 from the tribe of Joseph
(that is, from the tribe of Manasseh),
Gaddi the son of Susi; 12 from the tribe of
Dan, Ammiel the son of Gemalli; 13 from
the tribe of Asher, Sethur the son of
Michael; 14 from the tribe of Naphtali,
Nahbi the son of Vophsi; 15 from the tribe
of Gad, Geuel the son of Machi. 16 These
were the names of the men whom Moses
sent to spy out the land. And Moses called
[k]Hoshea the son of Nun Joshua.
17 Moses sent them to spy out the land
of Canaan and said to them, "Go up into
[l]the Negeb and go up into [m]the hill country, 18 and see what the land is, and
whether the people who dwell in it are
strong or weak, whether they are few or
many, 19 and whether the land that they
dwell in is good or bad, and whether the
cities that they dwell in are camps or
strongholds, 20 and whether the land is
[n]rich or poor, and whether there are trees
in it or not. [o]Be of good courage and bring
some of the fruit of the land." Now the
time was the season of the first ripe
grapes.
21 So they went up and spied out the land
[p]from the wilderness of Zin to Rehob, [q]near
Lebo-hamath. 22 They went up into [m]the
Negeb and came to [r]Hebron. [s]Ahiman,
Sheshai, and Talmai, the [t]descendants of
Anak, were there. ([u]Hebron was built seven
years before [u]Zoan in Egypt.) 23 And [v]they
came to the Valley of Eshcol and cut down
from there a branch with a single cluster of
grapes, and they carried it on a pole
between two of them; they also brought
some pomegranates and figs. 24 That place
was called the Valley of Eshcol,[1] because of
the cluster that the people of Israel cut
down from there.

Report of the Spies

25 At the end of forty days they returned
from spying out the land. 26 And they came
to Moses and Aaron and to all the congregation of the people of Israel in the wilderness of Paran, at [w]Kadesh. They brought
back word to them and to all the congregation, and showed them the fruit of the
land. 27 And they told him, "We came to
the land to which you sent us. It [x]flows
with milk and honey, [y]and this is its fruit.
28 [z]However, the people who dwell in the
land are strong, and the cities are fortified and very large. And besides, we saw
the descendants of Anak there. 29 [a]The
Amalekites dwell in the land of the Negeb.
The Hittites, the Jebusites, and the Amorites dwell in the hill country. [b]And the
Canaanites dwell by the sea, and along the
Jordan."
30 But [c]Caleb quieted the people before
Moses and said, "Let us go up at once and
occupy it, for we are well able to overcome
it." 31 [d]Then the men who had gone up with
him said, "We are not able to go up against
the people, for they are stronger than we
are." 32 So [e]they brought to the people of
Israel a bad report of the land that they had
spied out, saying, "The land, through
which we have gone to spy it out, is a land
that devours its inhabitants, and [f]all the
people that we saw in it are of great height.
33 And there we saw the [g]Nephilim (the
sons of Anak, who come from the
[g]Nephilim), and we seemed to ourselves
[h]like grasshoppers, and so we seemed to
them."

6 [i]ch. 34:19; 1 Chr. 4:15 [j]ver. 30; ch. 14:6, 30; 26:65; 32:12; Deut. 1:36; See Josh. 14:6-15; 15:13-18; Judg. 1:12-15
8 [k]ver. 16; ch. 11:28; 14:6, 30, 38; Ex. 24:13; Deut. 32:44; [Neh. 8:17]
16 [k][See ver. 8 above]
17 [l]ver. 22, 29; ch. 21:1; Josh. 15:19; Judg. 1:15 [m]ver. 29; Judg. 1:9, 19
20 [n]Neh. 9:25, 35; Ezek. 34:14 [o]Deut. 31:6, 7, 23
21 [p]ch. 20:1; 33:36; 34:3; Josh. 15:1 [q]ch. 34:8
22 [m][See ver. 17 above] [r]See Josh. 14:15 [s]Josh. 15:14; Judg. 1:10 [t]ver. 33; Deut. 1:28; 2:10; 9:2; Josh. 11:21, 22 [u]Ps. 78:12, 43; Isai. 19:11, 13; 30:4; Ezek. 30:14
23 [v]ch. 32:9; Deut. 1:24, 25
26 [w]ch. 20:1, 16; 32:8; 33:36; Deut. 1:19; Josh. 14:6, 7
27 [x]See Ex. 3:8 [y]Deut. 1:25
28 [z]Deut. 1:28; 9:1, 2
29 [a]ch. 14:43; Ex. 17:8 [b][ch. 14:25]
30 [c][ch. 14:6, 24]
31 [d]ch. 32:9; Deut. 1:28; Josh. 14:8
32 [e]ch. 14:36, 37 [f][Amos 2:9]
33 [g]Gen. 6:4 [h]Isai. 40:22

[1] *Eshcol* means *cluster*

in the earlier lists of leaders and heads of houses (chs. 1; 2; 7; 10). The spies are a separate group of persons specially chosen for the dangerous task of reconnaissance.

13:16 Hoshea . . . Joshua. The first name simply means "salvation"; the new one means "the LORD saves." It was appropriate that the man succeeding Moses as leader should bear a name that pointed to the Lord as the One from whom the nation's salvation must come.

13:22 Hebron. Hebron was well-known as the location of the graves of Abraham, Isaac, and Jacob (Gen. 13:18; 49:29–33; 50:13). Zoan which was built seven years after Hebron is the city of Tanis in Egypt, founded about 1430 B.C. Another name for Hebron is Kiriath-arba, and it was associated with the Anakim or descendents of Anak, a clan of large and intimidating fighters (Josh. 14:15). In later history, David occupied Hebron and was anointed there, first as king of Judah and then as king of Israel and Judah (2 Sam. 2:1–3; 5:1–5).

13:33 Nephilim. See note on Gen. 6:4. The Hebrew term is used in Gen. 6:4 for a group of strong and wicked men who lived in the earth before the Flood. The spies' exaggerated and cowardly report disheartened the people and brought God's judgment on the spies themselves (14:36, 37).

The People Rebel

14 Then all the congregation raised a
loud cry, and the people [i]wept that
night. 2 And all the people of Israel [j]grum-
bled against Moses and Aaron. The whole
congregation said to them, "Would that we
had died in the land of Egypt! Or [k]would
that we had died in this wilderness! 3 Why
is the LORD bringing us into this land, to
fall by the sword? [l]Our wives and our little
ones will become a prey. Would it not be
better for us to go back to Egypt?" 4 And
they said to one another, [m]"Let us choose a
leader and [n]go back to Egypt."
5 Then [o]Moses and Aaron fell on their
faces before all the assembly of the congregation of the people of Israel. 6 [p]And Joshua
the son of Nun and Caleb the son of
Jephunneh, who were among those who
had spied out the land, tore their clothes
7 and said to all the congregation of the people of Israel, [q]"The land, which we passed
through to spy it out, is an exceedingly
good land. 8 If [r]the LORD delights in us, he
will bring us into this land and give it to us,
[s]a land that flows with milk and honey.
9 Only [t]do not rebel against the LORD. And
[u]do not fear the people of the land, for [v]they
are bread for us. Their protection is
removed from them, and the LORD is with
us; do not fear them." 10 [w]Then all the congregation said to stone them with stones.
But [x]the glory of the LORD appeared at the
tent of meeting to all the people of Israel.
11 And the LORD said to Moses, "How
long will this people [y]despise me? And how
long will they not [z]believe in me, in spite of
all the signs that I have done among them?
12 I will strike them with the pestilence and
disinherit them, and I [a]will make of you a
nation greater and mightier than they."

Moses Intercedes for the People

13 But [b]Moses said to the LORD, "Then the
Egyptians will hear of it, for you brought
up this people in your might from among
them, 14 and they will tell the inhabitants of
this land. [c]They have heard that you, O
LORD, are in the midst of this people. For
you, O LORD, are seen face to face, and
[d]your cloud stands over them and you go
before them, in a pillar of cloud by day and
in a pillar of fire by night. 15 Now if you kill
this people as one man, then the nations
who have heard your fame will say, 16 'It is
because the LORD [e]was not able to bring
this people into the land that he swore to
give to them that he has killed them in the
wilderness.' 17 And now, please let the
power of the Lord be great as you have
promised, saying, 18 [f]'The LORD is slow to
anger and abounding in steadfast love, forgiving iniquity and transgression, but he
will by no means clear the guilty, [g]visiting
the iniquity of the fathers on the children,
to the third and the fourth generation.'
19 Please [h]pardon the iniquity of this people, according to the greatness of your
steadfast love, just [i]as you have forgiven
this people, from Egypt until now."

God Promises Judgment

20 Then the LORD said, "I have pardoned,
[j]according to your word. 21 But truly, as I
live, and as all [k]the earth shall be filled with
the glory of the LORD, 22 [l]none of the men
who have seen my glory and my signs that
I did in Egypt and in the wilderness, and yet
have put me to the test these [m]ten times
and have not obeyed my voice, 23 [n]shall see
the land that I swore to give to their fathers.
And none of those who despised me shall
see it. 24 But my servant [o]Caleb, because he
has a different spirit and has [p]followed me
fully, I will bring into the land into which
he went, and his descendants shall possess
it. 25 [q]Now, since the Amalekites and the
Canaanites dwell in the valleys, [r]turn
tomorrow and set out for the wilderness by
the way to the Red Sea."
26 And the LORD spoke to Moses and to
Aaron, saying, 27 "How long shall [s]this
wicked congregation grumble against me?
[t]I have heard the grumblings of the people
of Israel, which they grumble against me.
28 Say to them, [u]'As I live, declares the
LORD, [v]what you have said in my hearing I
will do to you: 29 [w]your dead bodies shall
fall in this wilderness, and [x]of all your
number, listed in the census [y]from twenty
years old and upward, who have grumbled
against me, 30 not one shall come into the

Chapter 14
1 [i]ch. 11:4
2 [j]ver. 27, 29, 33; ch. 16:41; Ex. 15:24; 16:2; 17:3; Ps. 106:25; [Josh. 9:18] [k][ver. 27-29]
3 [l]ver. 31
4 [m]Neh. 9:17 [n][Deut. 17:16; Acts 7:39]
5 [o]ch. 16:4, 22; 20:6
6 [p]ver. 30; ch. 13:6, 8
7 [q]ch. 13:27; Deut. 1:25
8 [r]Deut. 10:15; 2 Sam. 22:20; 1 Kin. 10:9; Ps. 18:19; 22:8; Isai. 62:4 [s]See Ex. 3:8
9 [t]Josh. 22:16, 18, 19, 29 [u]Deut. 7:18; 20:3 [v]ch. 24:8; [Ps. 14:4; 74:14]
10 [w]Ex. 17:4 [x]See Lev. 9:23
11 [y]ver. 23; ch. 16:30 [z]Deut. 1:32; 9:23; Ps. 78:22, 32; 106:24; Heb. 3:18; [John 12:37]
12 [a]Ex. 32:10
13 [b]Ex. 32:12; [Deut. 9:28; 32:27; Ps. 106:23; Ezek. 20:9, 14]
14 [c]Ex. 15:14; Josh. 2:9, 10; 5:1 [d]See Ex. 13:21
16 [e]Deut. 9:28; [Josh. 7:9]
18 [f]See Ex. 34:6, 7 [g]See Ex. 20:5
19 [h]Ex. 34:9 [i]Ps. 78:38; 106:45
20 [j]Ps. 106:23; [James 5:16]; See 1 John 5:14-16
21 [k]Ps. 72:19; Hab. 2:14
22 [l]Deut. 1:35; Ps. 95:11; 106:26; Heb. 3:17, 18 [m][Gen. 31:7; Job 19:3]
23 [n]ch. 32:11; Ezek. 20:15; [ch. 26:64]
24 [o]ver. 6; ch. 13:6 [p]ch. 32:12; Josh. 14:8, 9
25 [q]ver. 43, 45; See ch. 13:29 [r]Deut. 1:40
27 [s]ver. 35 [t]Ex. 16:7, 12 28 [u]ver. 21, 23; ch. 26:65 [v][ver. 2] 29 [w]1 Cor. 10:5; Heb. 3:17 [x]ch. 1:45; 26:64; Deut. 1:35 [y]ch. 1:3; Ex. 30:14

14:1–45 The Exodus generation provided an example of apostasy that the psalmist (Ps. 95:7–11) and New Testament authors (1 Cor. 10:5; Heb. 3:12–4:13) used to warn later generations of God's people.

land where I [z]swore that I would make you
dwell, [a]except Caleb the son of Jephunneh
and Joshua the son of Nun. 31 [b]But your little ones, who you said would become a
prey, I will bring in, and they shall know
the land that [c]you have rejected. 32 But as
for you, [w]your dead bodies shall fall in this
wilderness. 33 And your children [d]shall be
shepherds in the wilderness [e]forty years
and shall [f]suffer for your faithlessness,
until the last of your dead bodies lies in the
wilderness. 34 [g]According to the number of
the days in which you spied out the land,
[h]forty days, a year for each day, you shall
bear your iniquity forty years, and you shall
know my displeasure.' 35 [i]I, the LORD, have
spoken. Surely this will I do to all [j]this
wicked congregation who are gathered
together against me: in this wilderness they
shall come to a full end, and there they
shall die."

36 [k]And the men whom Moses sent to spy
out the land, who returned and made all
the congregation grumble against him by
bringing up a bad report about the land—
37 the men who brought up a bad report of
the land—[l]died by plague before the LORD.
38 Of those men who went to spy out the
land, [m]only Joshua the son of Nun and
Caleb the son of Jephunneh remained
alive.

Israel Defeated in Battle

39 When Moses told these words to all
the people of Israel, the people [n]mourned
greatly. 40 And they rose early in the morning and went up to the heights of the hill
country, saying, [o]"Here we are. We will go
up to the place that the LORD has promised,
for we have sinned." 41 [p]But Moses said,
"Why now are you transgressing the command of the LORD, when that will not succeed? 42 [q]Do not go up, [r]for the Lord is not
among you, lest you be struck down before
your enemies. 43 For there [s]the Amalekites
and the Canaanites are facing you, and you
shall fall by the sword. Because you have
turned back from following the LORD, the
LORD will not be with you." 44 [t]But they presumed to go up to the heights of the hill
country, although neither [u]the ark of the
covenant of the LORD nor Moses departed
out of the camp. 45 Then [v]the Amalekites
and the Canaanites who lived in that hill
country came down and defeated them and
pursued them, even to [w]Hormah.

Laws About Sacrifices

15 The LORD spoke to Moses, saying,
2 "Speak to the people of Israel and
say to them, [x]When you come into the
land you are to inhabit, which I am giving
you, 3 and [y]you offer to the LORD from the
herd or from the flock a food offering[1] or a
burnt offering or a sacrifice, [z]to fulfill a vow
or as a freewill offering or [a]at your appointed feasts, to make a [b]pleasing aroma to the
LORD, 4 then [c]he who brings his offering
shall offer to the LORD [d]a grain offering of a
tenth of an ephah[2] of fine flour, [e]mixed
with a quarter of a hin[3] of oil; 5 and you
shall offer with the burnt offering, or for
the sacrifice, a quarter of a hin of [f]wine for
the drink offering for each lamb. 6 [g]Or for a
ram, you shall offer for a grain offering two
tenths of an ephah of fine flour mixed with
a third of a hin of oil. 7 And for the drink
offering you shall offer a third of a hin of
wine, a [b]pleasing aroma to the LORD. 8 And
when you offer a bull as a burnt offering or
sacrifice, to [z]fulfill a vow or for [h]peace offerings to the LORD, 9 then one shall offer [i]with
the bull a grain offering of three tenths of
an ephah of fine flour, mixed with half a
hin of oil. 10 And you shall offer for the
drink offering half a hin of wine, as a food
offering, a pleasing aroma to the LORD.

11 [j]"Thus it shall be done for each bull or
ram, or for each lamb or young goat. 12 As
many as you offer, so shall you do with
each one, as many as there are. 13 Every
native Israelite shall do these things in this
way, in offering a food offering, with a
pleasing aroma to the LORD. 14 And if a

1 Or *an offering by fire*; so throughout Numbers 2 An *ephah* was about 3/5 bushel or 22 liters 3 A *hin* was about 4 quarts or 3.5 liters

30 [z]See Gen. 14:22 [a]ver. 6, 38; See ch. 13:6
31 [b]ver. 3; Deut. 1:39 [c]Ps. 106:24
32 [w][See ver. 29 above]
33 [d]ch. 32:13; [Ps. 107:40] [e]Ps. 95:10; [Deut. 2:14] [f]Ezek. 23:35
34 [g]ch. 13:25 [h][Ezek. 4:6]
35 [i]ch. 23:19 [j]ver. 27
36 [k]ch. 13:32
37 [l]1 Cor. 10:10; Heb. 3:17; Jude 5
38 [m]ch. 26:65; See ch. 13:16
39 [n]Ex. 33:4
40 [o]Deut. 1:41
41 [p][2 Chr. 24:20]
42 [q]Deut. 1:42 [r][Deut. 31:17]
43 [s]ver. 25, 45; See ch. 13:29
44 [t]Deut. 1:43 [u][1 Sam. 4:3]
45 [v]ver. 43; [Deut. 1:44] [w]ch. 21:3; Judg. 1:17
Chapter 15
2 [x]ver. 18; Lev. 23:10; Deut. 26:1
3 [y]Lev. 1:2, 3 [z]Lev. 22:21; 27:2 [a]ch. 28:19, 27; Lev. 23:8, 12, 36; Deut. 16:10 [b]Ex. 29:18; Lev. 4:31; See Gen. 8:21
4 [c]Lev. 2:1; 6:14 [d]Ex. 29:40; Lev. 23:13 [e]ch. 28:5; Lev. 14:10
5 [f]ch. 28:7, 14
6 [g]ch. 28:12, 14
7 [b][See ver. 3 above]
8 [z][See ver. 3 above] [h]Lev. 7:11
9 [i]ch. 28:12, 14; See Lev. 6:14-17
11 [j]See ch. 28

14:39–45 The Israelites make a futile attempt to conquer Canaan. Despite Moses' opposition, the disappointed people try to enter the Promised Land, and are driven back.

14:45 Hormah. A place of some importance in later history (21:1–3; Josh. 15:30; 19:4; Judg. 1:17; 1 Sam. 30:26–30).

15:1–41 The location of the material in this chapter—between the disastrous defeat at the hands of the Amalekites and Canaanites (14:39–45) and Korah's rebellion (ch. 16)—is significant. In giving this chapter of laws for their behavior in the land (v. 2) God assured Israel that, despite their failures and rebellions, He still planned to give Canaan to them.

15:1 When you come into the land . . . I am giving you. This expectation is a key to the chapter.

stranger is sojourning with you, or anyone
is living permanently among you, and he
wishes to offer a food offering, with a pleasing aroma to the LORD, he shall do as you
do. 15 For the assembly, [k]there shall be one
statute for you and for the stranger who
sojourns with you, a statute forever
throughout your generations. You and the
sojourner shall be alike before the LORD.
16 One law and one rule shall be for you and
for the stranger who sojourns with you."
17 The LORD spoke to Moses, saying,
18 [l]"Speak to the people of Israel and say to
them, When you come into the land to
which I bring you 19 and when you eat of
[m]the bread of the land, you shall present a
contribution to the LORD. 20 [n]Of the first of
your dough you shall present a loaf as a
contribution; like a [o]contribution from the
threshing floor, so shall you present it.
21 [n]Some of the first of your dough you shall
give to the LORD as a contribution throughout your generations.

Laws About Unintentional Sins

22 [p]"But if you sin unintentionally,[1] and
do not observe all these commandments
that the LORD has spoken to Moses, 23 all
that the LORD has commanded you by
Moses, from the day that the LORD gave
commandment, and onward throughout
your generations, 24 then if it was done
unintentionally [q]without the knowledge of
the congregation, all the congregation shall
offer one bull from the herd for a burnt
offering, a pleasing aroma to the LORD,
[r]with its grain offering and its drink offering, according to the rule, and [s]one male
goat for a sin offering. 25 [t]And the priest
shall make atonement for all the congregation of the people of Israel, and they shall
be forgiven, because it was a mistake, and
they have brought their offering, a food
offering to the LORD, and their sin offering
before the LORD for their mistake. 26 And all
the congregation of the people of Israel
shall be forgiven, and the stranger who
sojourns among them, because the whole
population was involved in the mistake.
27 [u]"If one person sins unintentionally, he
shall offer a female goat a year old for a sin
offering. 28 [v]And the priest shall make
atonement before the LORD for the person
who makes a mistake, when he sins unintentionally, to make atonement for him,
and he shall be forgiven. 29 [w]You shall have
one law for him who does anything unintentionally, for him who is native among
the people of Israel and for the stranger
who sojourns among them. 30 [x]But the person who does anything with a high hand,
whether he is native or a sojourner, reviles
the LORD, and that person shall be cut off
from among his people. 31 Because he has
[y]despised the word of the LORD and has
broken his commandment, that person
shall be utterly cut off; his iniquity shall be
on him."

A Sabbathbreaker Executed

32 While the people of Israel were in the
wilderness, they found a man [z]gathering
sticks on the Sabbath day. 33 And those
who found him gathering sticks brought
him to Moses and Aaron and to all the congregation. 34 [a]They put him in custody,
because it had not been made clear what
should be done to him. 35 And the LORD
said to Moses, [b]"The man shall be put to
death; all the congregation shall [c]stone him
with stones outside the camp." 36 And all
the congregation brought him outside the
camp and stoned him to death with stones,
as the LORD commanded Moses.

Tassels on Garments

37 The LORD said to Moses, 38 "Speak to
the people of Israel, and tell them to [d]make
tassels on the corners of their garments
throughout their generations, and to put a
cord of blue on the tassel of each corner.
39 And it shall be a tassel for you to look at
and remember all the commandments of the
LORD, to do them, [e]not to follow[2] after your
own heart and your own eyes, which you are
inclined [f]to whore after. 40 So you shall
remember and do all my commandments,

1 Or *by mistake*; also verses 24, 27, 28, 29 2 Hebrew *to spy out*

15 [k]ver. 29, 30; ch. 9:14; Ex. 12:49
18 [l]ver. 2
19 [m][Josh. 5:11, 12]
20 [n]Deut. 26:2, 10; Neh. 10:37; Ezek. 44:30 [o]Lev. 2:14; See Lev. 23:10-17
21 [n][See ver. 20 above]
22 [p][Lev. 4:2]
24 [q][Lev. 4:13] [r]ver. 8-10 [s]ch. 28:15; Lev. 4:23
25 [t]Lev. 4:20
27 [u]Lev. 4:27, 28
28 [v]Lev. 4:35
29 [w]See ver. 15
30 [x][Deut. 17:12; Ps. 19:13; Heb. 10:26]
31 [y]2 Sam. 12:9; 2 Chr. 36:16; Prov. 13:13
32 [z]Ex. 35:3; See Ex. 20:8, 9
34 [a]Lev. 24:12
35 [b]Ex. 31:14, 15 [c]Lev. 24:14-16; Josh. 7:25; 1 Kin. 21:13; Acts 7:58
38 [d]Deut. 22:12; [Matt. 23:5]
39 [e][Job 31:7; Eccles. 11:9; Ezek. 6:9] [f]Ps. 73:27; 106:39; [Ezek. 6:9]

15:22–29 Sacrifices of atonement for unintentional sins are prescribed. The whole community (vv. 24–26) or an individual alone (v. 27) could be responsible for such transgressions, e.g., of ritual commandments like those given in vv. 1–21.

15:30 does anything with a high hand. The treatment of an individual who sins defiantly is laid down: first the rule (vv. 30, 31) and then the illustration of the Sabbath-breaker (vv. 32–36).

cut off. See note Lev. 7:20.

15:37–41 Tassels with blue threads were to be affixed to garments as reminders to be holy and to keep God's commands (v. 40).

and be [g]holy to your God. 41 [h]I am the LORD your God, who brought you out of the land of Egypt to be your God: I am the LORD your God."

Korah's Rebellion

16 Now [i]Korah the son of Izhar, son of Kohath, son of Levi, and [j]Dathan and Abiram the sons of Eliab, and On the son of Peleth, sons of Reuben, took men. 2 And they rose up before Moses, with a number of the people of Israel, 250 chiefs of the congregation, chosen from the assembly, well-known men. 3 [k]They assembled themselves together against Moses and against Aaron and said to them, [l]"You have gone too far! For [m]all in the congregation are holy, every one of them, and the LORD is among them. Why then do you exalt yourselves above the assembly of the LORD?" 4 When Moses heard it, [n]he fell on his face, 5 and he said to Korah and all his company, "In the morning the LORD will show [o]who is his,[1] and who is [p]holy, and will bring him near to him. The one [q]whom he chooses he will [r]bring near to him. 6 Do this: take [s]censers, Korah and all his company; 7 put fire in them and put incense on them before the LORD tomorrow, and the man whom the LORD chooses shall be the holy one. [t]You have gone too far, sons of Levi!" 8 And Moses said to Korah, "Hear now, you sons of Levi: 9 is it [u]too small a thing for you that the God of Israel has [v]separated you from the congregation of Israel, to bring you near to himself, to do service in the tabernacle of the LORD and to stand before the congregation to minister to them, 10 and that he has brought you near him, and all your brothers the sons of Levi with you? And would you seek the priesthood also? 11 Therefore it is against the LORD that you and all your company have gathered together. What is [w]Aaron that you grumble against him?"

12 And Moses sent to call Dathan and Abiram the sons of Eliab, and they said, "We will not come up. 13 Is it [x]a small thing that you have brought us up out of [y]a land flowing with milk and honey, to kill us in the wilderness, that you must also [z]make yourself a prince over us? 14 Moreover, you have not brought us into a land flowing with milk and honey, nor given us inheritance of fields and vineyards. Will you put out the eyes of these men? We will not come up." 15 And Moses was very angry and said to the LORD, [a]"Do not respect their offering. [b]I have not taken one donkey from them, and I have not harmed one of them."

16 And Moses said to Korah, "Be present, you and all your company, [c]before the LORD, you and they, and Aaron, tomorrow. 17 And [d]let every one of you take his censer and put incense on it, and every one of you bring before the LORD his censer, [e]250 censers; you also, and Aaron, each his censer." 18 So every man took his censer and put fire in them and laid incense on them and stood at the entrance of the tent of meeting with Moses and Aaron. 19 Then Korah assembled all the congregation against them at the entrance of the tent of meeting. [f]And the glory of the LORD appeared to all the congregation.

20 And the LORD spoke to Moses and to Aaron, saying, 21 [g]"Separate yourselves from among this congregation, that I may consume them [h]in a moment." 22 And they [i]fell on their faces and said, "O God, [j]the God of the spirits of all flesh, [k]shall one man sin, and will you be angry with all the congregation?" 23 And the LORD spoke to Moses, saying, 24 "Say to the congregation, Get away from the dwelling of Korah, Dathan, and Abiram."

25 Then Moses rose and went to Dathan and Abiram, and the elders of Israel followed him. 26 And he spoke to the congregation, saying, [l]"Depart, please, from the tents of these wicked men, and touch nothing of theirs, lest you be swept away with

1 Septuagint *The LORD knows those who are his*

40 [g]See Lev. 11:44
41 [h]Lev. 22:33; See Lev. 20:8
Chapter 16
1 [i]ch. 27:3; Ex. 6:16, 18, 21; Jude 11 [j]ch. 26:9
3 [k]Ps. 106:16-18 [l]ver. 7 [m]See Ex. 19:6
4 [n]ch. 14:15; 20:6
5 [o][2 Tim. 2:19] [p]ver. 3 [q]ch. 17:5; 1 Sam. 2:28; Ps. 105:26; [Ex. 28:1] [r]ch. 3:10; Lev. 10:3; Ps. 65:4; Ezek. 40:46; 44:15, 16
6 [s]Lev. 10:1
7 [t]ver. 3
9 [u]ver. 13; 1 Sam. 18:23; Isai. 7:13; [Ezek. 16:20] [v]ch. 8:14; Deut. 10:8
11 [w]Ex. 16:8; [1 Cor. 3:5]
13 [x]ver. 9 [y]See Ex. 3:8 [z]Ex. 2:14; Acts 7:27, 35
15 [a][Gen. 4:4, 5] [b]1 Sam. 12:3; [Acts 20:33; 2 Cor. 7:2]
16 [c]Ex. 16:9; 1 Sam. 12:3, 7
17 [d]ver. 6, 7 [e]ver. 35
19 [f]See Lev. 9:23
21 [g]ver. 45; [Gen. 19:17, 22; Jer. 51:6; Rev. 18:4] [h]Ex. 33:5; Ps. 73:19
22 [i]ver. 45; ch. 14:5; 20:6 [j]ch. 27:16; Job 12:10; Eccles. 12:7; Isai. 57:16; Zech. 12:1 [k][Gen. 18:23-25; 2 Sam. 24:17]
26 [l][Gen. 19:12-14; Isai. 52:11; 2 Cor. 6:17; Rev. 18:4]

16:1–3 This chapter describes a complicated series of events in which two separate movements combined forces to oppose Moses and Aaron. One group, led by Dathan, Abiram, and On from the tribe of Reuben, was jealous of the leadership that God had established, and propagandized against Moses and Aaron. The other disaffected group consisted of Kohathites (Levites), the very group to which Moses and Aaron belonged.

16:4–11 Moses dealt first with the Levite opposition, which had access to the tabernacle. Moses' proposal in vv. 6, 7 set the stage for divine judgment in v. 35.

16:12–14 Moses then dealt with the Reubenites, Dathan and Abiram. After refusing to leave their tents, they were destroyed with their families (vv. 31–33).

16:22 Again Moses acts as an intercessor together with Aaron for the assembly (11:2; 12:13; 14:13–19; and 16:45–48). See notes Ex. 32–34 and 33:17.

all their sins." 27 So they got away from the
dwelling of Korah, Dathan, and Abiram.
And Dathan and Abiram came out and
stood [m]at the door of their tents, together
with their wives, their sons, and their little
ones. 28 And Moses said, "Hereby you shall
know that the LORD has sent me to do all
these works, and that it has not been [n]of
my own accord. 29 If these men die as all
men die, or if they are visited by the fate of
all mankind, [o]then the LORD has not sent
me. 30 But if the LORD creates something
new, and [p]the ground opens its mouth and
swallows them up with all that belongs to
them, and they [q]go down alive into Sheol,
then you shall know that these men have
despised the LORD."
31 [r]And as soon as he had finished speaking all these words, the ground under
them split apart. 32 And the earth opened
its mouth and swallowed them up, with
their households and [s]all the people who
belonged to Korah and all their goods.
33 So they and all that belonged to them
went down alive into Sheol, and the earth
closed over them, and [t]they perished from
the midst of the assembly. 34 And all Israel
who were around them fled at their cry, for
they said, "Lest the earth swallow us up!"
35 And [u]fire came out from the LORD and
consumed [v]the 250 men offering the
incense.
36 [1]Then the LORD spoke to Moses, saying, 37 "Tell Eleazar the son of Aaron the
priest to take up the censers out of the
blaze. Then scatter the fire far and wide,
for they have become holy. 38 As for the
censers of [w]these men who have sinned at
the cost of their lives, let them be made
into hammered plates as a covering for the
altar, for they offered them before the
LORD, and they became holy. [x]Thus they
shall be a sign to the people of Israel." 39 So
Eleazar the priest took the bronze censers,
which those who were burned had offered,
and they were hammered out as a covering
for the altar, 40 to be a reminder to the people of Israel, so [y]that no outsider, who is

27 [m][Ex. 33:8] **28** [n][Jer. 23:16; Ezek. 13:2, 17] **29** [o][1 Kin. 22:28] **30** [p][Gen. 4:11]; [q]ver. 33; Ps. 55:15 **31** [r]ch. 26:10; 27:3; Deut. 11:6; Ps. 106:17 **32** [s][ch. 26:11; 1 Chr. 6:22, 27] **33** [t]Jude 11 **35** [u][ch. 11:1]; Lev. 10:2; Ps. 106:18 [v]ver. 17 **38** [w]Prov. 20:2; Hab. 2:10; [1 Kin. 2:23] [x]ch. 17:10; 26:10 **40** [y]ch. 3:10; 2 Chr. 26:18

not of the descendants of Aaron, should
draw near to burn incense before the
LORD, lest he become like Korah and his
company—as the LORD said to him through
Moses.
41 But on the next day all the congregation of the people of Israel [z]grumbled
against Moses and against Aaron, saying,
"You have killed the people of the LORD."
42 And when the congregation had assembled against Moses and against Aaron, they
turned toward the tent of meeting. And
behold, [a]the cloud covered it, and [b]the
glory of the LORD appeared. 43 And Moses
and Aaron came to the front of the tent of
meeting, 44 and the LORD spoke to Moses,
saying, 45 [c]"Get away from the midst of this
congregation, that I may consume them in
a moment." [d]And they fell on their faces.
46 And Moses said to Aaron, "Take your
censer, and put fire on it from off the altar
and lay incense on it and carry it quickly to
the congregation and make atonement for
them, for [e]wrath has gone out from the
LORD; the plague has begun." 47 So Aaron
took it as Moses said and ran into the
midst of the assembly. And behold, the
plague had already begun among the people. And he put on the incense and made
atonement for the people. 48 And he stood
between the dead and the living, and [f]the
plague was stopped. 49 Now those who died
in the plague were 14,700, [g]besides those
who died in the affair of Korah. 50 And
Aaron returned to Moses at the entrance of
the tent of meeting, when the plague was
stopped.

Aaron's Staff Buds

17 [2] The LORD spoke to Moses, saying,
2 [h]"Speak to the people of Israel,
and get from them staffs, one for each
fathers' house, from all their chiefs according to their fathers' houses, twelve staffs.
Write each man's name on his staff, 3 and
write Aaron's name on the staff of Levi. For
there shall be one staff for the head of each

[1] Ch 17:1 in Hebrew [2] Ch 17:16 in Hebrew

41 [z]See ch. 14:2 **42** [a]Ex. 40:34 [b]ver. 19; See Lev. 9:23 **45** [c]ver. 21, 24 [d]ver. 22 **46** [e]ch. 8:19; 11:33; Lev. 10:6; 1 Chr. 27:24 **48** [f]ver. 50; ch. 25:8; 2 Sam. 24:25; Ps. 106:30 **49** [g]ch. 27:3 **Chapter 17** **2** [h][Ezek. 37:16]

16:28–30 Moses depended on God for his defense (cf. 12:3), relying on divine provision of an irrefutable sign ("something new").

16:32 households and all the people who belonged to Korah. The children of Korah survived (26:11; cf. 1 Chr. 9:19).

16:36–40 The metal censers were removed from the ashes and made into sheets to cover the altar, as a permanent reminder that none but Aaron's descendants were to serve as priests.

16:45b-48 Moses and Aaron again act as intercessors for the sinful people (v. 22 note).

17:1–11 Further evidence of Aaron's unique priesthood is given by God. The blossoms of Aaron's rod taught the leaders of Israel that God had chosen Aaron and his descendants as priests. Aaron's rod was kept permanently in front of the ark as a witness (v. 10).

fathers' house. 4 Then you shall deposit
them in the tent of meeting before the testimony, [i]where I meet with you. 5 And the
staff of the man [j]whom I choose shall
sprout. Thus I will make to cease from me
[k]the grumblings of the people of Israel,
which they grumble against you." 6 Moses
spoke to the people of Israel. And all their
chiefs gave him staffs, one for each chief,
according to their fathers' houses, twelve
staffs. And the staff of Aaron was among
their staffs. 7 And Moses deposited the
staffs before the LORD in [l]the tent of the testimony.
8 On the next day Moses went into the
tent of the testimony, and behold, the staff
of Aaron for the house of Levi had sprouted and put forth buds and produced blossoms, and it bore ripe almonds. 9 Then
Moses brought out all the staffs from
before the LORD to all the people of Israel.
And they looked, and each man took his
staff. 10 And the LORD said to Moses, "Put
back [m]the staff of Aaron before the testimony, to be kept [n]as a sign for the rebels,
[o]that you may make an end of their grumblings against me, lest they die." 11 Thus
did Moses; as the LORD commanded him,
so he did.
12 And the people of Israel said to Moses,
"Behold, we perish, we are undone, we are
all undone. 13 [p]Everyone who comes near,
who comes near to the tabernacle of the
LORD, shall die. Are we all to perish?"

Duties of Priests and Levites

18 So the LORD said to Aaron, "You
and your sons and your father's
house with you shall [q]bear iniquity connected with the sanctuary, [r]and you and
your sons with you shall bear iniquity connected with your priesthood. 2 And with
you bring your brothers also, the tribe of
Levi, the tribe of your father, that they may
[s]join you and [t]minister to you while you
and your sons with you are before the tent
of the testimony. 3 They shall keep guard
over you and [u]over the whole tent, [v]but
shall not come near to the vessels of the
sanctuary or to the altar [w]lest they, and
you, die. 4 They shall join you and keep
guard over the tent of meeting for all the
service of the tent, [x]and no outsider shall
come near you. 5 And you shall [y]keep guard
over the sanctuary and over the altar, [z]that
there may never again be wrath on the people of Israel. 6 [a]And behold, I have taken
your brothers the Levites from among the
people of Israel. [b]They are a gift to you,
given to the LORD, to do the service of the
tent of meeting. 7 And [c]you and your sons
with you shall guard your priesthood for all
that concerns the altar and [d]that is within
the veil; and you shall serve. I give your
priesthood as a gift,[1] and [e]any outsider
who comes near shall be put to death."
8 Then the LORD spoke to Aaron,
"Behold, [f]I have given you charge of the
contributions made to me, all the consecrated things of the people of Israel. I have
given them to you [g]as a portion and to your
sons as a perpetual due. 9 This shall be
yours of the most holy things, reserved
from the fire: every offering of theirs, every
grain offering of theirs and every [h]sin offering of theirs and every [i]guilt offering of
theirs, which they render to me, shall be
most holy to you and to your sons. 10 In a
most holy place shall you eat it. Every male
may eat it; it is holy to you. 11 This also is
yours: the contribution of their gift, all the
[j]wave offerings of the people of Israel. I
have given them to [k]you, and to your sons
and daughters with you, as a perpetual
due. [l]Everyone who is clean in your house
may eat it. 12 [m]All the best of the oil and all
the best of the wine and of the grain, [n]the

1 Hebrew *service of gift*

4 [i]See Ex. 25:22
5 [j]ch. 16:5 [k]ch. 16:11
7 [l]ch. 18:2; Ex. 38:21; 2 Chr. 24:6; Acts 7:44
10 [m]Heb. 9:4 [n]ch. 16:38 [o]ver. 5
13 [p]See ch. 1:51
Chapter 18
1 [q]ver. 23; See Ex. 28:38 [r]ver. 23
2 [s][Gen. 29:34] [t]See ch. 3:6-10
3 [u]ch. 3:25; 31, 36 [v]ch. 16:40 [w]ch. 4:15
4 [x]See ch. 17:13
5 [y]ch. 3:38; Ex. 27:21; 30:7; Lev. 24:3 [z]See Lev. 10:6
6 [a]ch. 3:12, 45 [b]ch. 3:9; 8:19
7 [c]ch. 3:10 [d]Heb. 9:3, 6 [e]See ch. 1:51
8 [f]ch. 5:9; Lev. 7:32 [g]Ex. 29:29; 40:13, 15
9 [h]Lev. 4:22, 27; 6:25, 26 [i]Lev. 7:7; 14:13
11 [j]Ex. 29:27, 28; Lev. 7:30, 34 [k]Lev. 10:14; [Deut. 18:3] [l][Lev. 22:2, 3, 11-13]
12 [m]Deut. 18:4 [n]Ex. 23:19; 34:26; Neh. 10:35, 36

17:4 before the testimony. In front of the ark in the Most Holy Place (cf. vv. 8, 10).

17:13 Everyone who comes near . . . the tabernacle. This terror of approaching God's dwelling highlights the importance of the mediatorial ministry of the priests and Levites described in ch. 18.

18:1–24 The duties and support of the priests and Levites are detailed. Only Aaron and his family could go near the furnishings of the sanctuary or the altar; the other Levites answered to the priests and were to do all the work at the tent of meeting (vv. 1–7). The males of Aaron's family were to receive the parts of the most holy offerings that were kept from the fire (vv. 8–10). All members of this family who were ceremonially clean were to share the wave offerings (v. 11; Ex. 29:24–27; Lev. 7:30–34) and the firstfruits (vv. 12, 13; Ex. 23:16–19; 34:22–26; Lev. 23:20; Deut. 18:4; 26:10). Support for the Levites came from the tithes offered by the people (Deut. 13:22–29 and notes).

18:1 bear iniquity. Aaron and his sons were responsible for offenses against the holiness of the sanctuary and for violations of the rules of the priesthood. The imperfection of their priesthood was indicated by their having to make sacrifices for their own sins, as well as for the sins of others (Ex. 29:38; Heb. 9:7). This imperfection pointed forward to a greater, perfect Priest who did not need to offer sacrifices for His own sin (Heb. 10:11–14).

firstfruits of what they give to the LORD, I give to you. 13 The first ripe fruits of all that is in their land, [o]which they bring to the LORD, shall be yours. [l]Everyone who is clean in your house may eat it. 14 [p]Every devoted thing in Israel shall be yours. 15 [q]Everything that opens the womb of all flesh, whether man or beast, which they offer to the LORD, shall be yours. Nevertheless, [r]the firstborn of man you shall redeem, and the firstborn of unclean animals you shall redeem. 16 And their redemption price [s](at a month old you shall redeem them) you shall fix at five shekels[1] in silver, according to the shekel of the sanctuary, [t]which is twenty gerahs. 17 [u]But the firstborn of a cow, or the firstborn of a sheep, or the firstborn of a goat, you shall not redeem; they are holy. You shall sprinkle their blood on the altar and shall burn their fat as a food offering, with a pleasing aroma to the LORD. 18 But their flesh shall be yours, as [v]the breast that is waved and as the right thigh are yours. 19 [w]All the holy contributions that the people of Israel present to the LORD I give to you, and to your sons and daughters with you, as a perpetual due. [x]It is a covenant of salt forever before the LORD for you and for your offspring with you." 20 And the LORD said to Aaron, "You shall have no inheritance in their land, neither shall you have any portion among them. [y]I am your portion and your inheritance among the people of Israel.

21 [z]"To the Levites I have given every tithe in Israel for an inheritance, in return for their service that they do, their service in the tent of meeting, 22 [a]so that the people of Israel do not come near the tent of meeting, [b]lest they bear sin and die. 23 But [c]the Levites shall do the service of the tent of meeting, [d]and they shall bear their iniquity. It shall be a perpetual statute throughout your generations, and among the people of Israel they shall have no inheritance. 24 For the tithe of the people of Israel, which [e]they present as a contribution to the LORD, I have given to the Levites for an inheritance. Therefore I have said of them that they shall have no inheritance [f]among the people of Israel."

25 And the LORD spoke to Moses, saying, 26 "Moreover, you shall speak and say to the Levites, 'When you take from the people of Israel the tithe that I have given you from them for your inheritance, then you shall present a contribution from it to the LORD, [g]a tithe of the tithe. 27 [h]And your contribution shall be counted to you as though it were the grain of the threshing floor, and as the fullness of the winepress. 28 So you shall also present a contribution to the LORD from all your tithes, which you receive from the people of Israel. And from it you shall give the LORD's contribution to Aaron the priest. 29 Out of all the gifts to you, you shall present every contribution due to the LORD; from each its best part is to be dedicated.' 30 Therefore you shall say to them, 'When you have offered from it the best of it, [i]then the rest shall be counted to the Levites as produce of the threshing floor, and as produce of the winepress. 31 And you may eat it in any place, you and your households, for it is [j]your reward in return for your service in the tent of meeting. 32 And you shall [k]bear no sin by reason of it, when you have contributed the best of it. But you shall not [l]profane the holy things of the people of Israel, lest you die.'"

Laws for Purification

19 Now the LORD spoke to Moses and to Aaron, saying, 2 "This is the statute of the law that the LORD has commanded: Tell the people of Israel to bring you a red heifer without defect, in which there is no blemish, [m]and on which a yoke has never come. 3 And you shall give it to Eleazar the priest, and [n]it shall be taken outside the camp and slaughtered before

13 [o]Ex. 22:29; Lev. 2:14; Deut. 26:2 [l][See ver. 11 above] **14** [p]Lev. 27:28 **15** [q]See Ex. 13:2 [r]Ex. 13:13; 34:20 **16** [s]ch. 3:47; Lev. 27:2, 6 [t]See Ex. 30:13 **17** [u]Deut. 15:19 **18** [v]Ex. 29:26, 28; Lev. 7:31, 32, 34 **19** [w]ver. 11 [x]Lev. 2:13; 2 Chr. 13:5 **20** [y]ver. 23, 24; Deut. 10:9; 12:12; 14:27; 18:1, 2; Josh. 13:33; 14:3; 18:7; Ezek. 44:28 **21** [z]ver. 24, 26; Lev. 27:30, 32; Deut. 14:22; Neh. 10:37; 12:44; Heb. 7:5, 8, 9; [Gen. 14:20; 28:22] **22** [a]See ch. 1:51 [b]Lev. 22:9 **23** [c]ch. 3:7 [d]ver. 1

24 [e]ver. 19, 26, 29 [f]ver. 20, 21, 26 **26** [g]Neh. 10:38 **27** [h]ver. 30 **30** [i]ver. 27 **31** [j][Matt. 10:10; Luke 10:7; 1 Tim. 5:17, 18]; See 1 Cor. 9:4-14 **32** [k]Lev. 19:8; 22:16 [l]Lev. 22:2, 15 **Chapter 19** **2** [m]Deut. 21:3; 1 Sam. 6:7 **3** [n]Lev. 4:12; [Heb. 13:11]

[1] A *shekel* was about 2/5 ounce or 11 grams

18:19 a covenant of salt forever. This phrase indicates the permanent nature of God's promise, based on the apparent indestructibility of salt, which does not burn. The priests had no inheritance in the land. Rather, through the tithes and offerings presented to the Lord by the people, the Lord Himself was to be the Levites' portion (vv. 20, 21).

18:25–32 From the tithes they received from the people, the Levites too were to give a tenth to the priests. It had to be taken from the best and holiest parts (vv. 29–32).

19:1–22 Arrangements for cleansing those ceremonially unclean are presented. Under the direction of Eleazar the priest, a red heifer without blemish (v. 2) is taken outside the camp and killed (v. 3). The priest performs a prescribed ceremony (v. 4) and the heifer is burned (v. 5–6; cf. Heb. 9:11–13). Then the ashes are gathered up and put in a clean place outside the camp, to be kept for use in the water of cleansing (vv. 9–10). Situations of uncleanness requiring ceremonial cleansing are discussed in vv. 11–16, followed by the procedures for use of the water for impurity (vv. 17–22).

him. 4And Eleazar the priest shall take
some of its blood with his finger, and
[o]sprinkle some of its blood toward the
front of the tent of meeting seven times.
5And the heifer shall be burned in his
sight. [p]Its skin, its flesh, and its blood, with
its dung, shall be burned. 6And the priest
shall take [q]cedarwood and hyssop and
scarlet yarn, and throw them into the fire
burning the heifer. 7Then the priest [r]shall
wash his clothes and bathe his body in
water, and afterward he may come into the
camp. But the priest shall be unclean until
evening. 8[s]The one who burns the heifer
[r]shall wash his clothes in water and bathe
his body in water and shall be unclean
until evening. 9And a man who is clean
shall gather up [t]the ashes of the heifer and
deposit them outside the camp in a [u]clean
place. And they shall be kept for the water
for [v]impurity for the congregation of the
people of Israel; it is a sin offering. 10And
the one who gathers the ashes of the heifer
[s]shall wash his clothes and be unclean
until evening. And this shall be a perpetual statute for the people of Israel, and for
the stranger who sojourns among them.
11[w]"Whoever touches the dead body of
any person shall be unclean seven days.
12He [x]shall cleanse himself with the water
on the third day and on the seventh day,
and so be clean. But if he does not cleanse
himself on the third day and on the seventh day, he will not become clean.
13Whoever touches a dead person, the
body of anyone who has died, and does not
cleanse himself, [y]defiles the tabernacle of
the LORD, [z]and that person shall be cut off
from Israel; because the water for impurity
was not thrown on him, he shall be
unclean. His uncleanness is still on him.
14"This is the law when someone dies in
a tent: everyone who comes into the tent
and everyone who is in the tent shall be
unclean seven days. 15And every [a]open vessel that has no cover fastened on it is
unclean. 16[b]Whoever in the open field
touches someone who was killed with a
sword or who died naturally, or touches a
human bone or a [c]grave, shall be unclean
seven days. 17For the unclean they shall
take [d]some ashes of the burnt sin offering,
and fresh[1] water shall be added in a vessel.
18Then a clean person shall take [e]hyssop
and dip it in the water and sprinkle it on
the tent and on all the furnishings and on
the persons who were there and on whoever touched the bone, or the slain or the
dead or the grave. 19And the clean person
shall sprinkle it on the unclean [f]on the third
day and on the seventh day. [g]Thus on the
seventh day he shall cleanse him, and he
shall [h]wash his clothes and bathe himself in
water, and at evening he shall be clean.
20"If the man who is unclean does not
cleanse himself, [i]that person shall be cut off
from the midst of the assembly, since he has
defiled the sanctuary of the LORD. Because
the water for impurity has not been thrown
on him, he is unclean. 21And it shall be a
statute forever for them. The one who sprin-
kles the water for impurity shall wash his
clothes, and the one who touches the water
for impurity shall be unclean until evening.
22And [j]whatever the unclean person touches
shall be unclean, and anyone who touches it
shall be unclean until evening."

The Death of Miriam

20 And the people of Israel, the whole
congregation, came [k]into the wilderness of Zin in the first month, and the
people stayed in Kadesh. And [l]Miriam died
there and was buried there.

The Waters of Meribah

2[m]Now there was no water for the congregation. [n]And they assembled themselves

1 Hebrew *living*

4[o]Lev. 4:6, 17; 16:14, 19]; Heb. 9:13
5[p]Ex. 29:14; Lev. 4:11, 12
6[q]See Lev. 14:4, 6, 49
7[r]See Lev. 11:25
8[s]ver. 5 [r][See ver. 7 above]
9[t]Heb. 9:13 [u]Lev. 4:12; 6:11; 10:14 [v]ver. 13, 20, 21; ch. 31:23
10[r][See ver. 7 above]
11[w]ver. 16; See ch. 5:2; 9:6, 10; 31:19
12[x]ch. 31:19
13[y]ver. 20; Lev. 15:31 [z]See Ex. 30:33
15[a]ch. 31:20; Lev. 11:32
16[b]ver. 11 [c][Matt. 23:27; Luke 11:44]
17[d]Heb. 9:13
18[e]See Ex. 12:22
19[f]ver. 12 [g][Lev. 14:9] [h]See Lev. 11:25
20[i]See Ex. 30:33
22[j][ver. 11; Hag. 2:13]
Chapter 20
1[k]See ch. 13:21 [l]ch. 12:1; 26:59; Ex. 15:20
2[m][Ex. 17:1] [n]ch. 16:19, 42

19:9 outside the camp. Christ, "suffered outside the gate in order to sanctify the people through his own blood" (Heb. 13:12). The ceremonies for cleansing and purification prefigured His death.

19:20 cut off from the midst of the assembly. This exact phrase occurs nowhere else in the Bible. "Cut off from Israel" occurs twice (Ex. 12:15; Num. 19:13). Similar expressions occur in Lev. 17:10; 20:3, 5, 6; 23:29; Num. 9:13; 15:30; Ezek. 14:8. On the meaning of "cut off," see note Lev. 7:20.

20:1–13 In his exasperation with Israel, Moses acted presumptuously and failed to honor the holiness of God (vv. 9–11 note; Ex. 17:6 notes). The seriousness of Moses' sin is evident from the resulting judgment—he was not allowed to enter the Promised Land (v. 12).

20:1 the first month. This would be at the end of the 40 years of wandering decreed in 14:32–34. The period of wandering in the wilderness was nearing its end. Everyone under 40 or even 50 was in effect from a new generation, about to begin the next part of God's plan—entrance into Canaan and conquest of the Promised Land.

Miriam died. Moses' sister was a godly woman. When Moses was a baby she had helped preserve him from destruction (Ex. 2:4–10). After the deliverance at the Red Sea she had led the victory celebration (Ex. 15:20, 21). Yet 12:5–15 shows her serious sin and the resulting punishment.

20:2 no water. Water was the greatest need in wilderness travel (cf. Gen. 21:14–19; Ex. 17:1–7).

together against Moses and against Aaron.
3 And the people [o]quarreled with Moses
and said, "Would that we had perished
[p]when our brothers perished before the
LORD! 4 Why have you brought the assembly of the LORD into this wilderness, that
we should die here, both we and our cattle?
5 And [q]why have you made us come up out
of Egypt to bring us to this evil place? It is
no place for grain or figs or vines or pomegranates, and there is no water to drink."
6 Then Moses and Aaron went from the
presence of the assembly to the entrance of
the tent of meeting and [r]fell on their faces.
[s]And the glory of the LORD appeared to
them, 7 and the LORD spoke to Moses, saying, 8 [t]"Take the staff, and assemble the
congregation, you and Aaron your brother,
and tell the rock before their eyes to yield
its water. So [u]you shall bring water out of
the rock for them and give drink to the
congregation and their cattle." 9 And Moses
took the staff [v]from before the LORD, as he
commanded him.

Moses Strikes the Rock

10 Then Moses and Aaron gathered the
assembly together before the rock, and he
said to them, [w]"Hear now, you rebels: shall
we bring water for you out of this rock?"
11 And Moses lifted up his hand and struck
the rock with his staff twice, [u]and water
came out abundantly, and the congregation drank, and their livestock. 12 And the
LORD said to Moses and Aaron, "Because
[x]you did not believe in me, [y]to uphold me
as holy in the eyes of the people of Israel,
therefore you shall not bring this assembly
into the land that I have given them."
13 [z]These are the waters of Meribah,[1] where
the people of Israel quarreled with the

3 [o]ch. 14:2; [Ex. 17:2] [p]ch. 11:1, 33; 14:37; 16:32, 33, 35, 49
5 [q][Ex. 17:3]
6 [r]ch. 14:5; 16:4, 22, 45 [s]See Lev. 9:23
8 [t][Ex. 17:5] [u]See Ex. 17:6
9 [v]ch. 17:10
10 [w]Ps. 106:32, 33
11 [u][See ver. 8 above]
12 [x]ch. 27:14; Deut. 1:37; 3:26; 32:51 [y]Ezek. 20:41; 36:23; 38:16
13 [z]ch. 27:14; Ex. 17:7; Deut. 32:51; 33:8; Ps. 81:7; 95:8; 106:32
14 [a]Judg. 11:16, 17 [b]See Gen. 36:31-39 [c]Deut. 2:4, 8; 23:7; Obad. 10, 12
15 [d]Gen. 46:6; Acts 7:15 [e]See Ex. 12:40 [f]Ex. 1:11; Deut. 26:6
16 [g]Ex. 2:23; 3:7 [h]Ex. 3:2; 14:19; 23:20; 33:2
17 [i][ch. 21:22; Deut. 2:27]
17 [j][ver. 19]
19 [k][ver. 17] [l]Deut. 2:6, 28
20 [m][Judg. 11:17; Amos 1:11]
21 [n][Deut. 2:29] [o][ch. 21:4; Deut. 2:8; Judg. 11:18]
22 [p]ch. 33:37 [q]ch. 21:4; 33:37

LORD, and through them he showed himself holy.

Edom Refuses Passage

14 [a]Moses sent messengers from Kadesh
to [b]the king of Edom: "Thus says [c]your
brother Israel: You know all the hardship
that we have met: 15 [d]how our fathers went
down to Egypt, [e]and we lived in Egypt a
long time. [f]And the Egyptians dealt harshly with us and our fathers. 16 And [g]when we
cried to the LORD, he heard our voice and
[h]sent an angel and brought us out of Egypt.
And here we are in Kadesh, a city on the
edge of your territory. 17 [i]Please let us pass
through your land. We will not pass
through field or vineyard, [j]or drink water
from a well. We will go along the King's
Highway. We will not turn aside to the
right hand or to the left until we have
passed through your territory." 18 But Edom
said to him, "You shall not pass through,
lest I come out with the sword against
you." 19 And the people of Israel said to
him, "We will go up by the highway, [k]and
if we drink of your water, I and my livestock, [l]then I will pay for it. Let me only
pass through on foot, nothing more." 20 But
he said, [m]"You shall not pass through."
And Edom came out against them with a
large army and with a strong force. 21 Thus
Edom [n]refused to give Israel passage
through his territory, so Israel [o]turned
away from him.

The Death of Aaron

22 And they journeyed from [p]Kadesh, and
the people of Israel, the whole congregation, came to [q]Mount Hor. 23 And the LORD
said to Moses and Aaron at Mount Hor, on

[1] *Meribah* means *quarreling*

20:2–5 The people complain again—an echo of previous complaints (Ex. 15:24; 16:2; 17:3; Num. 11:1; 14:2).

20:9–11 After years of constant service and unparalleled patience Moses fell at his strongest point (12:3): (a) he spoke in anger; (b) he usurped the place of God, saying, "Shall we bring water for you out of this rock?" and (c) he acted violently, striking the rock twice, when God had told him only to speak to it. On the symbolism of the rock, see notes Ex. 17:6.

20:12 God's word of judgment is directed to both Moses and Aaron, for Aaron had accompanied Moses and was implicated in the rashness of his brother's action. Their ministry was coming to an end.

20:13 Meribah. See text note. Together with "Massah" ("testing"), this name was used at the first incident of striking water from a rock (Ex. 17:7; Ps. 95:8 and text notes).

20:14–20 The Edomites, descendants of Jacob's brother Esau (Gen. 25:25–34; 27:1–42; 28:5–9; 32:3–33:16; 35:29; 36:1–43), show an unbrotherly attitude toward Israel. Moses made a courteous request of the Edomites, asking permission to go peacefully through their territory, paying the Edomites for anything the travelers might need on the way. Since Israel was not given this permission, and they did not want to fight their way through, they could not reach the Promised Land without first making a long march through a particularly unpleasant part of the wilderness.

20:14 your brother Israel. Jacob (later called Israel; Gen. 32:28) and his brother Esau had quarreled in their youth, but they were reconciled in later years (Gen. 33:9–16; 35:29).

20:22–29 Eleazar succeeds his father as high priest. Aaron had the joy of seeing his work carried on by a son; Moses, whose ministry as mediator of the Sinai covenant was unique (12:8 note; Ex. 18:1–24:18 note), did not.

the border of the land of Edom, 24 [r]“Let
Aaron be gathered to his people, for he
shall not enter the land that I have given to
the people of Israel, because [s]you rebelled
against my command at the waters of
Meribah. 25 Take Aaron and Eleazar his son
and bring them up to Mount Hor. 26 And
strip Aaron of his garments and put them
on Eleazar his son. And Aaron [r]shall be
gathered to his people and shall die there.”
27 Moses did as the LORD commanded. And
they went up Mount Hor in the sight of all
the congregation. 28 [t]And Moses stripped
Aaron of his garments and put them on
Eleazar his son. And Aaron died there [u]on
the top of the mountain. Then Moses and
Eleazar came down from the mountain.
29 And when all the congregation saw that
Aaron had perished, [v]all the house of Israel
wept for Aaron thirty days.

Arad Destroyed

21 When [w]the Canaanite, the king of
Arad, who lived in [x]the Negeb,
heard that Israel was coming by the way of
Atharim, he fought against Israel, and took
some of them captive. 2 [y]And Israel vowed a
vow to the LORD and said, “If you will
indeed give this people into my hand, then
I will devote their cities to destruction.”[1]
3 And the LORD obeyed the voice of Israel
and gave over the Canaanites, and they
devoted them and their cities to destruction. So the name of the place was called
[z]Hormah.[2]

The Bronze Serpent

4 From Mount Hor [a]they set out by the
way to the Red Sea, [b]to go around the land
of Edom. And the people became impatient on the way. 5 And the people [c]spoke
against God and against Moses, [d]“Why
have you brought us up out of Egypt to die
in the wilderness? For there is no food and
no water, and [e]we loathe this worthless
food.” 6 [f]Then the LORD sent fiery serpents
among the people, and [g]they bit the people, so that many people of Israel died.
7 [h]And the people came to Moses and said,
“We have sinned, for we have spoken
against the LORD and against you. [i]Pray to
the LORD, that he take away the serpents
from us.” So Moses prayed for the people.
8 And the LORD said to Moses, “Make a fiery
serpent and set it on a pole, and everyone
who is bitten, when he sees it, shall live.”
9 So [j]Moses made a bronze[3] serpent and set
it on a pole. And if a serpent bit anyone, he
would look at the bronze serpent and live.

The Song of the Well

10 And the people of Israel set out and
[k]camped in Oboth. 11 [k]And they set out
from Oboth and [k]camped at Iye-abarim, in
the wilderness that is opposite Moab,
toward the sunrise. 12 From there they set
out and camped in [l]the Valley of Zered.
13 From there they set out and camped on
the other side of the Arnon, which is in the
wilderness that extends from the border of
the Amorites, for the [m]Arnon is the border
of Moab, between Moab and the Amorites.
14 Wherefore it is said in the Book of the
Wars of the LORD,

“Waheb in Suphah, and the valleys of
the Arnon,
15 and the slope of the valleys
that extends to the seat of [n]Ar,
and leans to the border of Moab.”

16 And from there they continued [o]to
Beer;[4] that is the well of which the LORD
said to Moses, “Gather the people together, so that [p]I may give them water.” 17 Then
Israel sang this song:

“Spring up, O well!—Sing to it!—
18 the well that the princes dug,

1 That is, set apart (devote) as an offering to the Lord (for destruction); also verse 3 2 *Hormah* means *destruction* 3 Or *copper* 4 *Beer* means *well*

24 [r]ch. 27:13; Deut.32:50; [ch. 31:2; Gen. 25:8] [s]ver. 12
26 [r][See ver. 24 above]
28 [t]Ex. 29:29, 30 [u]ch. 33:38; Deut. 32:50; [Deut. 10:6]
29 [v]Deut. 34:8
Chapter 21
1 [w]ch. 33:40; [Judg. 1:16] [x]See ch. 13:17
2 [y][Gen. 28:20; Judg. 11:30]
3 [z]ch. 14:45; Deut. 1:44; Josh. 19:4; Judg. 1:17
4 [a]ch. 20:22; 33:41 [b]Judg. 11:18
5 [c]Ps. 78:19 [d]Ex. 16:3; 17:3 [e][ch. 11:6]
6 [f]Deut. 8:15; 1 Cor. 10:9; [Isai. 14:29; 30:6] [g]Jer. 8:17
7 [h]Ps. 78:34; [ch. 11:2] [i][Ex. 8:8, 28; 1 Sam. 12:19; 1 Kin. 13:6; Acts 8:24]
9 [j]John 3:14, 15; [2 Kin. 18:4]
10 [k]ch. 33:43, 44
11 [k][See ver. 10 above]
12 [l]Deut. 2:13
13 [m]ch. 22:36; Judg. 11:18
15 [n]ver. 28; Deut. 2:9, 18, 29; Isai. 15:1
16 [o][2 Sam. 20:14] [p][ch. 20:8; Ex. 17:6]

20:29 wept . . . thirty days. See note Deut. 34:8.

21:1–3 The Israelites' first victory against the Canaanites was over Arad at Hormah, where Israel had suffered stinging defeat many years before (14:45). This victory marks a shift in focus from the Exodus generation condemned to die in the wilderness (14:29–35) to the generation born in the wilderness.

21:4–9 This event typifies both the sacrifice of Christ and the faith of His people. Just as the bronze representation of the poisonous serpent was lifted up, so Christ, as one born "in the likeness of sinful flesh" (Rom. 8:3), was lifted up (John 3:14). The afflicted Israelites had no other means of rescue than to look at the bronze snake, just as sinners have no hope for salvation except faith in the crucified Christ (John 3:15, 16). Unfortunately, this bronze serpent later became the object of idolatrous worship (2 Kin. 18:4).

21:14 the Book of the Wars of the LORD. This is the only biblical reference to an uninspired book of victory songs that was apparently current in the land of Israel at the time of David or before. A similar work, the Book of Jashar, is quoted in Josh. 10:12, 13 and 2 Sam. 1:19–27.

Arnon. This perennial stream flowed into the Dead Sea from the east, through a deep ravine. It formed the border between the territory of Moab and the Amorite kingdom of Sihon (21:21–31).

that the nobles of the people delved,
with [q] the scepter and with their
staffs."

And from the wilderness they went on to
Mattanah, 19 and from Mattanah to Nahaliel, and from Nahaliel to Bamoth, 20 and
from Bamoth to the valley lying in the
region of Moab by the top of Pisgah [r] that
looks down on the desert.[1]

King Sihon Defeated

21 Then [s] Israel sent messengers to Sihon
king of the Amorites, saying, 22 [t] "Let me
pass through your land. We will not turn
aside into field or vineyard. We will not
drink the water of a well. We will go by the
King's Highway until we have passed
through your territory." 23 [u] But Sihon would
not allow Israel to pass through his territory. He gathered all his people together and
went out against Israel to the wilderness
and [v] came to Jahaz and fought against
Israel. 24 [w] And Israel defeated him with the
edge of the sword and took possession of
his land from the Arnon to the [x] Jabbok, as
far as to the Ammonites, for the border of
the Ammonites was strong. 25 And Israel
took all these cities, and Israel settled in all
the cities of the Amorites, in Heshbon, and
in all its villages. 26 For Heshbon was the
city of Sihon the king of the Amorites, who
had fought against the former king of Moab
and taken all his land out of his hand, as far
as the Arnon. 27 Therefore the [y] ballad singers say,

"Come to [z] Heshbon, let it be built;
let the city of Sihon be established.
28 For [a] fire came out from Heshbon,
flame from the city of Sihon.
It devoured [n] Ar of Moab,
and swallowed[2] the heights of the
Arnon.
29 [a] Woe to you, O Moab!
You are undone, O people of
[b] Chemosh!
He has made his sons fugitives,
and his daughters captives,
to an Amorite king, Sihon.
30 So we overthrew them;
Heshbon, as far as [c] Dibon,
perished;
and we laid waste as far as Nophah;
fire spread as far as [d] Medeba."[3]

King Og Defeated

31 Thus Israel lived in the land of the
Amorites. 32 And Moses sent to spy out
[e] Jazer, and they captured its villages and dispossessed the Amorites who were there.
33 Then they turned and went up by the way
to Bashan. And Og the king of Bashan came
out against them, he and all his people, to
battle [f] at Edrei. 34 [g] But the LORD said to
Moses, "Do not fear him, for I have given
him into your hand, and all his people, and
his land. And [h] you shall do to him as you
did to Sihon king of the Amorites, who lived
at Heshbon." 35 So they defeated him and his
sons and all his people, until he had no survivor left. And they possessed his land.

Balak Summons Balaam

22 Then [i] the people of Israel set out
and camped in the plains of Moab
beyond the Jordan at Jericho. 2 And [j] Balak
the son of Zippor saw all that Israel had
done to the Amorites. 3 And [k] Moab was in
great dread of the people, because they
were many. Moab was overcome with fear
of the people of Israel. 4 And Moab said to
[l] the elders of Midian, "This horde will now
lick up all that is around us, as the ox licks
up the grass of the field." So Balak the son
of Zippor, who was king of Moab at that
time, 5 [m] sent messengers to Balaam the son

18 [q] See Gen. 49:10
20 [r] [ch. 23:28]
21 [s] Deut. 2:26, 27; Judg. 11:19
22 [t] [ch. 20:17]
23 [u] Deut. 29:7 [v] Deut. 2:32; Judg. 11:20
24 [w] Deut. 2:33; Josh. 12:1, 2; 24:8; Neh. 9:22; Ps. 135:11; 136:19, 20; Amos 2:9 [x] See Gen. 32:22
27 [y] See ch. 23:7 [z] See ch. 32:37
28 [a] Jer. 48:45, 46 [n] [See ver. 15 above]
29 [a] [See ver. 28 above]
[b] Judg. 11:24; 1 Kin. 11:7; 2 Kin. 23:13; Jer. 48:7
30 [c] ch. 32:3; Josh. 13:17; Isai. 15:2; Jer. 48:18; [ch. 33:45, 46] [d] 1 Chr. 19:7; Isai. 15:2
32 [e] ch. 32:1; Josh. 13:25; 2 Sam. 24:5; Jer. 48:32
33 [f] Deut. 1:4; 3:1; Josh. 13:12
34 [g] Deut. 3:2 [h] See ver. 24
Chapter 22
1 [i] ch. 26:3, 63; 31:12; 33:48, 50; 35:1; 36:13
2 [j] Judg. 11:25
3 [k] Ex. 15:15
4 [l] ch. 31:8; Josh. 13:21
5 [m] Deut. 23:4; Josh. 24:9; Neh. 13:2; Mic. 6:5; 2 Pet. 2:15; Jude 11; Rev. 2:14

[1] Or *Jeshimon* [2] Septuagint; Hebrew *the lords of* [3] Compare Samaritan and Septuagint; Hebrew *and we laid waste as far as Nophah, which is as far as Medeba*

21:21–35 Moses narrates Israel's conquest of Heshbon and Bashan. Both of these kingdoms were in eastern Palestine, across the Jordan from Canaan (the Transjordan).

21:33 Bashan. See note Deut. 3:1.

22:1 After the conquest of Heshbon in the southern Transjordan (21:21–26) and Bashan in the north (21:33–35), the Israelites returned south to the area across the Jordan from Jericho and north of the territory of Moab.

22:2–24:25 Though the narrative itself has considerable literary charm (22:28 note), the Balaam incident must also be viewed within the context of God's covenant relationship with His people. In the vivid portrayal of divine opposition to those who curse His people, God's faithfulness to the covenant promises made to Abraham is demonstrated (Gen. 12:3 and note). Ironically, the Lord also used the pagan prophet Balaam, who had been hired by the Moabite king to curse God's people, to bless them instead, and to prophesy the coming of a royal Star out of Jacob—the Messiah Himself—who would triumph over Israel's enemies (24:17–19).

22:4 Moab. The Moabites were descendants of Lot's incestuous relationship with his daughter (Gen. 19:37, 38 note). The Moabites were asking the Midianites to help them resist the Israelite invaders.

22:5 Balaam. The pagan prophet Balaam lived at Pethor, a city in northern Mesopotamia on the banks of the Euphrates river. That Balak sent

of Beor [n]at Pethor, which is near the River
in the land of the people of Amaw,[1] to call
him, saying, "Behold, a people has come
out of Egypt. They cover the face of the
earth, and they are dwelling opposite me.
6 [o]Come now, curse this people for me,
since they are too mighty for me. Perhaps I
shall be able to defeat them and drive them
from the land, for I know that he whom
you bless is blessed, and he whom you
curse is cursed."

7 So the elders of Moab and [l]the elders of
Midian departed with [p]the fees for divination in their hand. And they came to
Balaam and gave him Balak's message.
8 And he said to them, "Lodge here tonight,
and I will bring back word to you, as the
LORD speaks to me." So the princes of
Moab stayed with Balaam. 9 [q]And God
came to Balaam and said, "Who are these
men with you?" 10 And Balaam said to God,
"Balak the son of Zippor, king of Moab, has
sent to me, saying, 11 'Behold, a people has
come out of Egypt, and it covers the face of
the earth. Now come, curse them for me.
Perhaps I shall be able to fight against them
and drive them out.'" 12 God said to
Balaam, "You shall not go with them. You
shall not curse the people, for [r]they are
blessed." 13 So Balaam rose in the morning
and said to the princes of Balak, "Go to
your own land, for the LORD has refused to
let me go with you." 14 So the princes of
Moab rose and went to Balak and said,
"Balaam refuses to come with us."

15 Once again Balak sent princes, more in
number and more honorable than these.
16 And they came to Balaam and said to
him, "Thus says Balak the son of Zippor:
'Let nothing hinder you from coming to
me, 17 [s]for I will surely do you great honor,
and whatever you say to me I will do.
[t]Come, curse this people for me.'" 18 But
Balaam answered and said to the servants
of Balak, [u]"Though Balak were to give me
his house full of silver and gold, [v]I could
not go beyond the command of the LORD
my God to do less or more. 19 So you, too,
[w]please stay here tonight, that I may know
what more the LORD will say to me."
20 [q]And God came to Balaam at night and
said to him, "If the men have come to call
you, rise, go with them; [x]but only do what
I tell you." 21 So Balaam rose in the morning and saddled his donkey and went with
the princes of Moab.

Balaam's Donkey and the Angel

22 But God's anger was kindled because
he went, [y]and the angel of the LORD took
his stand in the way [z]as his adversary. Now
he was riding on the donkey, and his two
servants were with him. 23 And the donkey
saw the angel of the LORD standing in the
road, with a drawn sword in his hand. And
the donkey turned aside out of the road
and went into the field. And Balaam struck
the donkey, to turn her into the road.
24 Then the angel of the LORD stood in a
narrow path between the vineyards, with a
wall on either side. 25 And when the donkey
saw the angel of the LORD, she pushed
against the wall and pressed Balaam's foot
against the wall. So he struck her again.
26 Then the angel of the LORD went ahead
and stood in a narrow place, where there
was no way to turn either to the right or to
the left. 27 When the donkey saw the angel
of the LORD, she lay down under Balaam.
And Balaam's anger was kindled, and he
struck the donkey with his staff. 28 Then the
LORD [a]opened the mouth of the donkey,
and she said to Balaam, "What have I done
to you, that you have struck me these three
times?" 29 And Balaam said to the donkey,
"Because you have made a fool of me. I
wish I had a sword in my hand, for then I

1 Or *his kindred*

5 [n]Deut. 23:4; [ch. 23:7]
6 [o]ch. 23:7
7 [l][See ver. 4 above] [p][1 Sam. 9:7, 8; Mic. 3:11]
9 [q][Gen. 20:3; Job 33:15, 16]
12 [r]See ch. 23:20
17 [s]ver. 37; ch. 24:11 [t]ver. 11
18 [u]ch. 24:13 [v]ver. 38; ch. 23:26; [1 Kin. 22:14; 2 Chr. 18:13]
19 [w]ver. 8
20 [q][See ver. 9 above] [x]ver. 35; ch. 23:12, 26; 24:13
22 [y][Ex. 4:24; 1 Chr. 21:16] [z]ver. 32
28 [a]2 Pet. 2:16

emissaries such a great distance is evidence of Balaam's considerable reputation for supernatural powers.

The nature and extent of Balaam's knowledge of the true God is uncertain. Though a famous sorcerer and prophet (cf. 24:1), Balaam had some regard for the true God (22:8, 18), and the Lord used Balaam to communicate His word (23:7–10, 18–24; 24:3–9, 15–24). Fundamentally, however, Balaam seems to have been a syncretistic opportunist who sought to manipulate the spirit world for his own gain. In the course of this narrative Balaam establishes himself as a prime example of the false prophet and teacher (31:16; 2 Pet. 2:15; Jude 11).

22:22 because he went. In light of God's earlier permission to travel (v. 20), the Lord's response is perhaps surprising. The narrative as a whole indicates, however, that Balaam's trip was perversely motivated and that he certainly hoped to curse Israel (v. 32). God used this confrontation between Balaam and the angel of the Lord to underscore His command to say nothing except what He might direct (v. 35).

the angel of the LORD. See note Gen. 16:7; "Angels" at Zech. 1:9.

22:28 the mouth of the donkey. The story of Balaam abounds in comic irony. The donkey was able to see the path better than the diviner, and then tell him about it (2 Pet. 2:16).

22:29 I wish I had a sword. Balaam was calling for a sword, without knowing that he was about to see one pointed at him.

would kill you." 30 And the donkey said to
Balaam, "Am I not your donkey, on which
you have ridden all your life long to this
day? Is it my habit to treat you this way?"
And he said, "No."
31 Then the LORD [b]opened the eyes of
Balaam, and he saw the angel of the LORD
standing in the way, with his drawn sword
in his hand. And he bowed down and fell
on his face. 32 And the angel of the LORD
said to him, "Why have you struck your
donkey these three times? Behold, I have
come out [c]to oppose you because your way
is perverse[1] before me. 33 The donkey saw
me and turned aside before me these three
times. If she had not turned aside from me,
surely just now I would have killed you and
let her live." 34 Then Balaam said to the
angel of the LORD, [d]"I have sinned, for I did
not know that you stood in the road
against me. Now therefore, if it is evil in
your sight, I will turn back." 35 And the
angel of the LORD said to Balaam, "Go with
the men, [e]but speak only the word that I
tell you." So Balaam went on with the
princes of Balak.
36 When Balak heard that Balaam had
come, he went out to meet him at the city
of Moab, [f]on the border formed by the
Arnon, at the extremity of the border.
37 And Balak said to Balaam, "Did I not
send to you to call you? Why did you not
come to me? Am I not able to [g]honor you?"
38 Balaam said to Balak, "Behold, I have
come to you! Have I now any power of my
own to speak anything? [h]The word that
God puts in my mouth, that must I speak."
39 Then Balaam went with Balak, and they
came to Kiriath-huzoth. 40 And Balak sacrificed oxen and sheep, and sent for Balaam
and for the princes who were with him.
41 And in the morning Balak took Balaam
and brought him up to Bamoth-baal, and
from there he saw a fraction of the people.

Balaam's First Oracle

23 And Balaam said to Balak, [i]"Build
for me here seven altars, and prepare for me here seven bulls and seven
rams." 2 Balak did as Balaam had said. And
Balak and Balaam [j]offered on each altar a
bull and a ram. 3 And Balaam said to Balak,
[k]"Stand beside your burnt offering, and I
will go. Perhaps the LORD will come [l]to
meet me, and whatever he shows me I will
tell you." And he went to a bare height,
4 [m]and God met Balaam. And Balaam said
to him, "I have arranged the seven altars
and I have offered on each altar a bull and
a ram." 5 And the LORD [n]put a word in
Balaam's mouth and said, "Return to
Balak, and thus you shall speak." 6 And he
returned to him, and behold, he and all the
princes of Moab were standing beside his
burnt offering. 7 And Balaam [o]took up his
discourse and said,

"From [p]Aram Balak has brought me,
the king of Moab [q]from the eastern
mountains:
'Come, [r]curse Jacob for me,
and come, denounce Israel!'
8 How can I curse whom God has not
cursed?
How can I denounce whom the
LORD has not denounced?
9 For from the top of the crags [s]I see
him,
from the hills I behold him;
behold, [t]a people dwelling alone,
and [u]not counting itself among the
nations!
10 [v]Who can count the dust of Jacob
or number the fourth part[2] of
Israel?
Let me die [w]the death of the upright,
and let my end be like his!"

11 And Balak said to Balaam, "What have
you done to me? [x]I took you to curse my
enemies, and behold, you have done nothing but bless them." 12 And he answered
and said, [y]"Must I not take care to speak
what the LORD puts in my mouth?"

Balaam's Second Oracle

13 And Balak said to him, "Please come
with me to another place, from which you
may see them. You shall see only a fraction
of them and shall not see them all. Then

31 [b][Gen. 21:19; 2 Kin. 6:17; Luke 24:16, 31]
32 [c]ver. 22
34 [d][1 Sam. 15:24; 26:21; 2 Sam. 12:13; Job 34:31, 32]
35 [e]ver. 20
36 [f]ch. 21:13
37 [g]ver. 17; ch. 24:11
38 [h]ver. 18
Chapter 23
1 [i]ver. 29
2 [j]ver. 14, 30
3 [k]ver. 15 [l][ch. 24:1]
4 [m]ver. 16
5 [n]ver. 12, 16; ch. 22:38; Deut. 18:18; Isai. 51:16; 59:21; Jer. 1:9
7 [o]ver. 18; ch. 24:3, 15, 20, 21, 23; Job 27:1; 29:1; Ps. 49:4; 78:2; Isai. 14:4; Mic. 2:4; [ch. 21:27] [p][ch. 22:5] [q][Gen. 29:1] [r]ch. 22:6
9 [s][ch. 24:17] [t]Deut. 32:28 [u]Ex. 33:16; [Ezra 9:2; Esth. 3:8; Eph. 2:14]
10 [v]See Gen. 13:16 [w]Ps. 37:37; 116:15; Rev. 14:13
11 [x]ch. 22:11; 24:10; Deut. 23:5; Neh. 13:2
12 [y]See ver. 5

1 Or *reckless* 2 Or *dust clouds*

22:40 sent for Balaam . . . princes. Because Balaam and the princes received the meat, this was probably a sacrificial meal, though some suggest a reference to the pagan use of animal entrails for divination (cf. 24:1).

23:1 seven . . . seven . . . seven. The number seven was of profound symbolic significance in the ancient Near East. The sum of the sacred numbers three and four, it often appears in a ritual context (Gen. 21:28; 33:3; Ex. 12:15; 29:35–37).

curse them for me from there." 14 And he
took him to the field of Zophim, to the top
of Pisgah, [z]and built seven altars and offered
a bull and a ram on each altar. 15 Balaam said
to Balak, [a]"Stand here beside your burnt
offering, while I meet the LORD over there."
16 And the LORD met Balaam and [b]put a word
in his mouth and said, "Return to Balak,
and thus shall you speak." 17 And he came to
him, and behold, he was standing beside his
burnt offering, and the princes of Moab with
him. And Balak said to him, "What has the
LORD spoken?" 18 And Balaam took up his
discourse and said,

"Rise, Balak, and hear;
give ear to me, O son of Zippor:
19 [c]God is not man, that he should lie,
or a son of man, that he should
change his mind.
Has he said, and will he not do it?
Or has he spoken, and will he not
fulfill it?
20 Behold, I received a command to
bless:
[d]he has blessed, and [e]I cannot
revoke it.
21 [f]He has not beheld misfortune in
Jacob,
nor has he seen trouble in Israel.
The LORD their God is with them,
and the shout of a king is among
them.
22 [g]God brings them out of Egypt
and is for them like [h]the horns of
the wild ox.
23 For there is no enchantment against
Jacob,
no [i]divination against Israel;
now it shall be said of Jacob and
Israel,
[j]'What has God wrought!'
24 Behold, a people! [k]As a lioness it
rises up
and as a lion it lifts itself;
[l]it does not lie down until it has
devoured the prey
and drunk the blood of the slain."

25 And Balak said to Balaam, "Do not curse
them at all, and do not bless them at all."
26 But Balaam answered Balak, "Did I not tell
you, [m]'All that the LORD says, that I must
do'?" 27 And Balak said to Balaam, [n]"Come
now, I will take you to another place.
Perhaps it will please God that you may
curse them for me from there." 28 So Balak
took Balaam to the top of [o]Peor, which overlooks [p]the desert.[1] 29 And Balaam said to
Balak, [q]"Build for me here seven altars and
prepare for me here seven bulls and seven
rams." 30 [r]And Balak did as Balaam had said,
and offered a bull and a ram on each altar.

Balaam's Third Oracle

24 When Balaam saw that it pleased
the LORD to bless Israel, he did not
go, as at [s]other times, to look for omens,
but set his face toward the wilderness.
2 And Balaam lifted up his eyes and saw
Israel [t]camping tribe by tribe. And [u]the
Spirit of God came upon him, 3 and he
[v]took up his discourse and said,

"The oracle of Balaam the son of Beor,
the oracle of the man whose eye is
opened,[2]
4 the oracle of him who hears the
words of God,
who sees the vision of the Almighty,
[w]falling down with his eyes uncovered:
5 How lovely are your tents, O Jacob,
your encampments, O Israel!
6 Like palm groves[3] that stretch afar,
like gardens beside a river,
[x]like aloes [y]that the LORD has planted,
like cedar trees beside the waters.
7 Water shall flow from his buckets,
and his seed shall be [z]in many
waters;

14 [z]ver. 1, 2
15 [a]ver. 3
16 [b]ver. 5, 12
19 [c]1 Sam. 15:29; Mal. 3:6; Rom. 11:29; Tit. 1:2; Heb. 6:18; James 1:17
20 [d]ch. 22:12; Gen. 12:2; 22:17 [e]ch. 22:18
21 [f][Jer. 50:20]
22 [g]ch. 24:8 [h]Deut. 33:17; Job 39:10, 11; Ps. 22:21; 92:10
23 [i]ch. 22:7 [j]Ps. 44:1
24 [k]Gen. 49:9 [l]Gen. 49:27
26 [m]See ch. 22:18
27 [n]ver. 13
28 [o]ch. 25:18; 31:16; Josh. 22:17; Ps. 106:28, 29; Hos. 9:10; [ch. 25:3, 5] [p]See ch. 21:20
29 [q]ver. 1
30 [r]ver. 2
Chapter 24
1 [s]ch. 23:3, 15
2 [t]See ch. 2:2-31 [u]Judg. 3:10; 1 Sam. 19:20, 23; 2 Chr. 15:1; 20:14
3 [v]See ch. 23:7
4 [w][Ezek. 1:28; 3:23; Rev. 1:10, 17]
6 [x][Ps. 1:3; Jer. 17:8] [y]Ps. 104:16; Isai. 61:3
7 [z][Jer. 51:13; Rev. 17:1]

1 Or *Jeshimon* 2 Or *closed*, or *perfect*; also verse 15 3 Or *valleys*

23:18–24 Balaam's second oracle reaffirms God's determination to bless Israel by giving them victory over the Moabites. Verse 21 is surprising, in view of the sins described in the Book of Numbers. Despite their failings, God regards His people as righteous for the sake of His covenant promises, and He provides the means of their forgiveness (Gen. 17:2 note).

23:27–30 Balak superstitiously decides to see whether another location or additional sacrifices can bring a more favorable result.

24:1–9 Balaam's third oracle pictures the blessings that God plans for Israel, ending with a curse from the Abrahamic promise against those who curse her (v. 9; Gen. 12:3).

24:4 the vision of the Almighty. The word translated "Almighty" (also in v. 16) is the Hebrew word *shaddai,* a divine name associated with the patriarchal narratives (Gen. 17:1; 28:3; 35:11; 43:14; 48:3; 49:25) that also occurs frequently in Job.

24:7 Agag. 1 Samuel 15:32, 33 recounts the death of an Amalekite king who bore this name. Here Balaam may refer to an earlier prominent king of the Amalekites bearing the same personal name. It is also possible that "Agag" was a title, just as the title "Pharaoh" was used by many Egyptian rulers.

his king shall be higher than [a]Agag,
and [b]his kingdom shall be exalted.
8 God brings him out of Egypt
and is for him like the [c]horns of
the wild ox;
he shall [d]eat up the nations, his
adversaries,
and shall [e]break their bones in
pieces
and [f]pierce them through with his
arrows.
9 He crouched, he lay down like a lion
and [g]like a lioness; who will rouse
him up?
[h]Blessed are those who bless you,
and cursed are those who curse
you."

10 And Balak's anger was kindled against
Balaam, and he [i]struck his hands together.
And Balak said to Balaam, [j]"I called you to
curse my enemies, and behold, you have
blessed them these three times. 11 Therefore
now flee to your own place. I said, [k]'I will
certainly honor you,' but the LORD has held
you back from honor." 12 And Balaam said to
Balak, "Did I not tell your messengers whom
you sent to me, 13 [l]'If Balak should give me
his house full of silver and gold, I would not
be able to go beyond the word of the LORD,
to do either good or bad [m]of my own will.
What the LORD speaks, that will I speak'?
14 And now, behold, I am going to my people.
Come, [n]I will let you know what this people
will do to your people [o]in the latter days."

Balaam's Final Oracle

15 [p]And he took up his discourse and
said,

"The oracle of Balaam the son of Beor,
the oracle of the man whose eye is
opened,
16 the oracle of him who hears the
words of God,
and knows the knowledge of [q]the
Most High,
who sees the vision of the Almighty,
[r]falling down with his eyes
uncovered:
17 [s]I see him, but not now;
I behold him, but not near:
[t]a star shall come out of Jacob,
and [u]a scepter shall rise out of
Israel;
it shall [v]crush the forehead[1] of Moab
and break down all the sons of
Sheth.
18 [w]Edom shall be dispossessed;
[x]Seir also, his enemies, shall be
dispossessed.
Israel is doing valiantly.
19 And one from Jacob shall exercise
dominion
and destroy the survivors of cities!"

20 Then he looked on Amalek and [y]took
up his discourse and said,

"Amalek was the first among the
nations,
[z]but its end is utter destruction."

21 And he looked on the Kenite, and took
up his discourse and said,

"Enduring is your dwelling place,
and your nest is set in the rock.
22 Nevertheless, Kain shall be burned
when Asshur takes you away
captive."

23 And he took up his discourse and said,

"Alas, who shall live when God does
this?
24 But ships shall come from [a]Kittim
and shall afflict Asshur and [b]Eber;
and he too [c]shall come to utter
destruction."

[1] Hebrew *corners* [of the head]

7 [a]1 Sam. 15:8 [b]2 Sam. 5:12; 1 Chr. 14:2
8 [c]See ch. 23:22 [d][ch. 14:9; 23:24] [e]Isai. 38:13; Jer. 50:17 [f]Ps. 45:5; Jer. 50:9
9 [g]ch. 23:24; Gen. 49:9 [h]Gen. 12:3; 27:29
10 [i][Job 27:23; Lam. 2:15; Ezek. 21:14, 17; 22:13] [j]See ch. 23:11
11 [k]ch. 22:17, 37
13 [l]ch. 22:18 [m]See ch. 16:28
14 [n][Mic. 6:5; Rev. 2:14] [o]See Gen. 49:1
15 [p][ch. 21:27]; See ch. 23:7
16 [q]Acts 7:48 [r]See ver. 4
17 [s][ch. 23:9] [t]Matt. 2:2; Rev. 22:16 [u]Gen. 49:10 [v]Jer. 48:45; [2 Sam. 8:2]
18 [w][2 Sam. 8:14; Ps. 60:8, 9; Amos 9:12] [x]Gen. 32:3; 36:8
20 [y]See ch. 23:7 [z][Ex. 17:14; 1 Sam. 15:3, 8]
24 [a]Gen. 10:4; Dan. 11:30 [b]Gen. 10:21, 25 [c]ver. 20

24:10, 11 Balak refuses to pay the hired prophet his "wages of unrighteousness"—the "honor" he was expecting (22:7; 2 Pet. 2:15).

24:15–19 In his fourth oracle, Balaam predicts the future advent of a royal conqueror who would triumph over Moab and Edom. An initial fulfillment of these predictions is found in 2 Sam. 8:2–14, which describes David's victory over the Moabites and Edomites. But his accomplishments prefigure the greater conquests of Christ (e.g., Col. 2:15; 1 Cor. 15:25, 26; Rev. 20:10, 14).

24:20–25 In his final oracles, Balaam predicts the downfall of the other nations in the area.

24:20 Amalek. See notes Ex. 17:8, 16.

24:21 Kenite. A nomadic tribe of metalworkers found in Palestine from the Patriarchal period onward (Gen. 15:19). Moses' father-in-law is identified as both a Midianite and a Kenite (Ex. 2:16; Judg. 1:16). The Rechabites of Jer. 35 are thought to be descendants of the Kenites (1 Chr. 2:55; Neh. 3:14).

24:22 Asshur. The Assyrians of northern Mesopotamia were already an important military power, but their greatest conquests would be made centuries later (cf. Is. 36).

24:24 Kittim. The Hebrew name for Cyprus came to represent the Mediterranean region to the west of Palestine. In Dan. 11:30, this word is used to predict the effects of Roman naval power.

25 Then Balaam rose and [d]went back to
his place. And Balak also went his way.

Baal Worship at Peor

25 While Israel lived in [e]Shittim, [f]the
people began to whore with the
daughters of Moab. 2 [g]These invited the people to the sacrifices of their gods, and the
people ate and bowed down to their gods.
3 So Israel yoked himself to Baal of Peor.
And the anger of the LORD was kindled
against Israel. 4 And the LORD said to Moses,
[h]"Take all the chiefs of the people and
[i]hang[1] them in the sun before the LORD,
[j]that the fierce anger of the LORD may turn
away from Israel." 5 And Moses said to [k]the
judges of Israel, [l]"Each of you kill those of
his men who have yoked themselves to Baal
of Peor."
6 And behold, one of the people of Israel
came and brought a Midianite woman to
his family, in the sight of Moses and in the
sight of the whole congregation of the people of Israel, while they were [m]weeping in
the entrance of the tent of meeting.
7 [n]When Phinehas [o]the son of Eleazar, son
of Aaron the priest, saw it, he rose and left
the congregation and took a spear in his
hand 8 and went after the man of Israel into
the chamber and pierced both of them, the
man of Israel and the woman through her
belly. Thus the plague on the people of
Israel was stopped. 9 Nevertheless, [p]those
who died by the plague were twenty-four
thousand.

The Zeal of Phinehas

10 And the LORD said to Moses, 11 "Phinehas the son of Eleazar, son of Aaron the
priest, has turned back my wrath from the
people of Israel, in that he [q]was jealous
with my jealousy among them, so that I did
not consume the people of Israel in [r]my
jealousy. 12 Therefore say, [s]'Behold, I give to
him my covenant of peace, 13 and it shall be
to him and to [t]his descendants after him
the covenant of [u]a perpetual priesthood,
because he was jealous for his God and
made atonement for the people of Israel.'"
14 The name of the slain man of Israel,
who was killed with the Midianite woman,
was Zimri the son of Salu, chief of a father's
house belonging to the Simeonites. 15 And
the name of the Midianite woman who was
killed was Cozbi the daughter of [v]Zur, who
was the tribal head of a father's house in
Midian.
16 And the LORD spoke to Moses, saying,
17 [w]"Harass the Midianites and strike them
down, 18 for they have harassed you with
their [x]wiles, with which they beguiled you
in the matter of [y]Peor, and in the matter of
Cozbi, the daughter of the chief of Midian,
their sister, who was killed on the day of
the plague on account of Peor."

Census of the New Generation

26 [z]After the plague, the LORD said to
Moses and to Eleazar the son of
Aaron, the priest, 2 [a]"Take a census of all
the congregation of the people of Israel,
from twenty years old and upward, by their
fathers' houses, all in Israel who are able to
go to war." 3 And Moses and Eleazar the
priest spoke with them [b]in the plains of
Moab by the Jordan at Jericho, saying,
4 "Take a census of the people,[2] from twenty years old and upward," as the LORD
[c]commanded Moses. The people of Israel
who came out of the land of Egypt were:
5 [d]Reuben, the firstborn of Israel; the sons
of Reuben: of Hanoch, the clan of the Ha-
nochites; of Pallu, the clan of the Palluites;
6 of Hezron, the clan of the Hezronites; of
Carmi, the clan of the Carmites. 7 These are
the clans of the Reubenites, and those listed
were [e]43,730. 8 And the sons of Pallu: Eliab.
9 The sons of Eliab: Nemuel, Dathan, and
Abiram. These are the Dathan and Abiram,
[f]chosen from the congregation, who contended against Moses and Aaron in the

25 [d][ch. 31:8]
Chapter 25
1 [e]ch. 33:49; Josh. 2:1; 3:1; Mic. 6:5 [f][ch. 31:16]
2 [g]Ex. 34:15, 16; Josh. 22:17; Ps. 106:28; Hos. 9:10; [1 Cor. 10:20]
4 [h]See Deut. 4:3 [i][Deut. 21:23; 2 Sam. 21:6; Gal. 3:13] [j]ver. 11; Deut. 13:17
5 [k][ch. 11:16; Ex. 18:21, 25] [l][Ex. 32:27]
6 [m]Joel 2:17
7 [n]Ps. 106:30 [o]Ex. 6:25
9 [p]Deut. 4:3; [1 Cor. 10:8]
11 [q][2 Cor. 11:12] [r]Deut. 32:16, 21; 1 Kin. 14:22; Ps. 78:58; Zeph. 1:18; 3:8; 1 Cor. 10:22; [Ex. 20:5]
12 [s]Mal. 2:4, 5
13 [t]See 1 Chr. 6:4-15 [u]Ex. 40:15
15 [v]ch. 31:8; Josh. 13:21
17 [w]ch. 31:2, 7
18 [x]ch. 31:16; Rev. 2:14 [y]See ch. 23:28
Chapter 26
1 [z]ch. 25:9
2 [a]ch. 1:2, 3; Ex. 30:12; 33:25, 26
3 [b]ver. 63; See ch. 22:1
4 [c]ch. 1:1
5 [d]Gen. 46:8, 9; Ex. 6:14; 1 Chr. 5:1-3
7 [e][ch. 1:21]
9 [f]ch. 1:16; 16:2

1 Or *impale* 2 *Take a census of the people* is implied (compare verse 2)

25:1–3 Fearing to attack the vast throng of Israelites (22:3) and having failed to thwart them through by means of Balaam, the Moabites and Midianites (at Balaam's instigation, 31:16) then sought to subvert and assimilate Israel through idolatry and immorality. When the world cannot eliminate the witness of the elect through direct conflict it often tries to neutralize that witness by absorbing the elect into the world. Old Testament Israel was to survive in physical separation from her neighbors (Lev. 18:24; Deut. 7:3; Josh. 23:12, 13), trusting in God's promises of land and the Messiah.

This incident at the Baal of Peor was later seen as a prime example of the temptations to which the covenant people were exposed by the surrounding peoples (Deut. 4:3; Josh. 22:17; Ps. 106:28; Hos. 9:10).

25:1 Shittim. This Hebrew word identifies the region across the Jordan from Jericho (cf. Josh. 2:1). Here worship of the local fertility god was joined with ritual prostitution (vv. 1–3, 6).

25:3 yoked himself to Baal of Peor. In gross defiance of the covenant between the Lord and Israel, the Israelites yoked themselves to the false god through their idolatrous worship.

25:4 hang them. See note Deut. 21:22.

company of Korah, when they contended
against the LORD 10 and [g] the earth opened its
mouth and swallowed them up together
with Korah, when that company died, when
the fire devoured 250 men, and [h] they
became a warning. 11 But [i] the sons of Korah
did not die.
12 The sons of [j] Simeon according to their
clans: of Nemuel, the clan of the Nem-
uelites; of Jamin, the clan of the Jaminites;
of Jachin, the clan of the Jachinites; 13 of
Zerah, the clan of the Zerahites; of Shaul,
the clan of the Shaulites. 14 These are the
clans of the Simeonites, [k] 22,200.
15 The sons of [l] Gad according to their
clans: of Zephon, the clan of the Zeph-
onites; of Haggi, the clan of the Haggites;
of Shuni, the clan of the Shunites; 16 of
Ozni, the clan of the Oznites; of Eri, the
clan of the Erites; 17 of Arod, the clan of the
Arodites; of Areli, the clan of the Arelites.
18 These are the clans of the sons of Gad as
they were listed, [m] 40,500.
19 The sons of [n] Judah were Er and Onan;
and Er and Onan died in the land of
Canaan. 20 And the sons of Judah according
to their clans were: of Shelah, the clan of
the Shelanites; of Perez, the clan of the
Perezites; of Zerah, the clan of the Zerahites. 21 And the sons of Perez were: of
Hezron, the clan of the Hezronites; of
Hamul, the clan of the Hamulites. 22 These
are the clans of Judah as they were listed,
[o] 76,500.
23 The sons of [p] Issachar according to their
clans: of Tola, the clan of the Tolaites; of
Puvah, the clan of the Punites; 24 of Jashub,
the clan of the Jashubites; of Shimron, the
clan of the Shimronites. 25 These are the
clans of Issachar as they were listed,
[q] 64,300.
26 The sons of [r] Zebulun, according to
their clans: of Sered, the clan of the
Seredites; of Elon, the clan of the Elonites;
of Jahleel, the clan of the Jahleelites.
27 These are the clans of the Zebulunites as
they were listed, [s] 60,500.
28 The sons of [t] Joseph according to their
clans: Manasseh and Ephraim. 29 [u] The sons
of Manasseh: of [v] Machir, the clan of the
Machirites; and Machir was the father of
Gilead; [w] of Gilead, the clan of the Gileadites. 30 These are the sons of Gilead: of
Iezer, the clan of the Iezerites; of Helek,
the clan of the Helekites; 31 and of Asriel, the clan of the Asrielites; and of
Shechem, the clan of the Shechemites;
32 and of Shemida, the clan of the She-
midaites; and of Hepher, the clan of the
Hepherites. 33 Now [x] Zelophehad the son of
Hepher had no sons, but daughters. And
the names of the daughters of Zelophehad
were Mahlah, Noah, Hoglah, Milcah, and
Tirzah. 34 These are the clans of Manasseh,
and those listed were [y] 52,700.
35 These are the sons of Ephraim according to their clans: of Shuthelah, the clan of
the Shuthelahites; of Becher, the clan of
the Becherites; of Tahan, the clan of the
Tahanites. 36 And these are the sons of
Shuthelah: of Eran, the clan of the
Eranites. 37 These are the clans of the sons
of Ephraim as they were listed, [z] 32,500.
These are the sons of Joseph according to
their clans.
38 The sons of [a] Benjamin according to
their clans: of Bela, the clan of the Belaites;
of Ashbel, the clan of the Ashbelites; of
Ahiram, the clan of the Ahiramites; 39 of
Shephupham, the clan of the Shuphamites;
of Hupham, the clan of the Huphamites.
40 And the sons of Bela were Ard and
Naaman: of Ard, the clan of the Ardites; of
Naaman, the clan of the Naamites. 41 These

10 [g] See ch. 16:31-35 [h] ch. 16:38; [1 Cor. 10:6; 2 Pet. 2:6]
11 [i] Ex. 6:24; 1 Chr. 6:22; [ch. 16:32]
12 [j] Gen. 46:10; Ex. 6:15; 1 Chr. 4:24
14 [k] [ch. 1:23]
15 [l] Gen. 46:16
18 [m] [ch. 1:25]
19 [n] Gen. 46:12; 1 Chr. 2:3-5; See Gen. 38:3-10
22 [o] [ch. 1:27]
23 [p] Gen. 46:13; 1 Chr. 7:1
25 [q] [ch. 1:29]
26 [r] Gen. 46:14
27 [s] [ch. 1:31]
28 [t] Gen. 46:20
29 [u] For ver. 29-37; see 1 Chr. 7:14-20 [v] Josh. 17:1 [w] ch. 36:1
33 [x] ch. 27:1; 36:11; Josh. 17:3
34 [y] [ch. 1:35]
37 [z] [ch. 1:33]
38 [a] Gen. 46:21; 1 Chr. 7:6; See 1 Chr. 8:1-5

25:11 Jealous with my jealousy. Note the stress on Phinehas as embodying God's own zeal for the purity of His people. Such zeal earned Phinehas divine commendation and the promise of a perpetual priesthood (v. 13). Later in Jewish history, Phinehas became a symbol of uncompromising loyalty to God's law (Ps. 106:30, 31).

26:1–36:13 The final major section of Numbers concerns preparations for entering the Promised Land, with particular attention paid to matters relevant to life in the land.

26:1–51 Like the census taken 38 years earlier (ch. 1), this second census counted only males, aged twenty or older, and able to serve in the army (v. 2). It records only the total number for each tribe, though in each case the names of the tribe's subdivisions are included. Overall, there was a decline of nearly two thousand in the total number of fighting men.

26:5–11 The tribe of Jacob's eldest son, Reuben, is listed first. Although it had suffered losses because of the rebellion of Dathan and Abiram (vv. 8–10), it had recovered sufficiently to be almost as numerous as at the first census. Korah (of the tribe of Levi) is mentioned here because of his association with Dathan and Abiram, and it is observed that his line did not die out (v. 11).

26:12–14 Simeon's numbers had declined far more than those of any other tribe (from nearly 60,000 to a little over 22,000), probably indicating that the Simeonite leader killed during the Midianite seduction shortly before this census was taken (25:14) was but one of thousands of Simeonites involved in the Midianite seduction (25:1–9). See note Gen. 49:7.

26:19 Er and Onan. See Gen. 38:1–10 and notes.

26:33 Zelophehad. See 27:1–11; 36:1–12.

are the sons of Benjamin according to their
clans, and those listed were [b]45,600.
42 These are the sons of [c]Dan according to
their clans: of Shuham, the clan of the
Shuhamites. These are the clans of Dan
according to their clans. 43 All the clans of
the Shuhamites, as they were listed, were
[d]64,400.
44 The sons of [e]Asher according to their
clans: of Imnah, the clan of the Imnites; of
Ishvi, the clan of the Ishvites; of Beriah, the
clan of the Beriites. 45 Of the sons of Beriah:
of Heber, the clan of the Heberites; of
Malchiel, the clan of the Malchielites.
46 And the name of the daughter of Asher
was Serah. 47 These are the clans of the sons
of Asher as they were listed, [f]53,400.
48 The sons of [g]Naphtali according to
their clans: of Jahzeel, the clan of the
Jahzeelites; of Guni, the clan of the Gu-
nites; 49 of Jezer, the clan of the Jezerites; of
Shillem, the clan of the Shillemites.
50 These are the clans of Naphtali according
to their clans, and those listed were
[h]45,400.
51 This was the list of the people of Israel,
[i]601,730.
52 The LORD spoke to Moses, saying,
53 [j]"Among these the land shall be divided
for inheritance according to the number of
names. 54 [k]To a large tribe you shall give a
large inheritance, and to a small tribe you
shall give a small inheritance; every tribe
shall be given its inheritance in proportion
to its list. 55 But the land shall be [l]divided
by lot. According to the names of the tribes
of their fathers they shall inherit. 56 Their
inheritance shall be divided according to
lot between the larger and the smaller."
57 [m]This was the list of the Levites
according to their clans: of Gershon, the
clan of the Gershonites; of Kohath, the
clan of the Kohathites; of Merari, the clan
of the Merarites. 58 These are the clans of
Levi: the clan of the Libnites, the clan of
the Hebronites, the clan of the Mahlites,
the clan of the Mushites, the clan of the
Korahites. And Kohath was the father of
Amram. 59 The name of Amram's wife was
[n]Jochebed the daughter of Levi, who was
born to Levi in Egypt. And she bore to
Amram Aaron and Moses and Miriam their
sister. 60 [o]And to Aaron were born Nadab,
Abihu, Eleazar, and Ithamar. 61 [p]But Nadab
and Abihu died when they offered unauthorized fire before the LORD. 62 And those
listed were [q]23,000, every male from a
month old and upward. For [r]they were not
listed among the people of Israel, because
[s]there was no inheritance given to them
among the people of Israel.
63 These were those listed by Moses and
Eleazar the priest, who listed the people of
Israel [t]in the plains of Moab by the Jordan
at Jericho. 64 [u]But among these there was
not one of those listed by Moses and Aaron
the priest, who had listed the people of
Israel in the wilderness of Sinai. 65 For the
LORD had said of them, [v]"They shall die in
the wilderness." Not one of them was left,
[w]except Caleb the son of Jephunneh and
Joshua the son of Nun.

The Daughters of Zelophehad

27 Then drew near the daughters of
[x]Zelophehad the son of Hepher,
son of Gilead, son of Machir, son of
Manasseh, from the clans of Manasseh the
son of Joseph. The names of his daughters
were: Mahlah, Noah, Hoglah, Milcah, and
Tirzah. 2 And they stood before Moses and
before Eleazar the priest and before the
chiefs and all the congregation, at the
entrance of the tent of meeting, saying,
3 "Our father [y]died in the wilderness. He
was not among the company of those who
gathered themselves together against the
LORD [z]in the company of Korah, but [a]died
for his own sin. And he had no sons. 4 Why
should the name of our father be taken

41 [b][ch. 1:37]
42 [c]Gen. 46:23
43 [d][ch. 1:39]
44 [e]Gen. 46:17; 1 Chr. 7:30, 31
47 [f][ch. 1:41]
48 [g]Gen. 46:24; 1 Chr. 7:13
50 [h][ch. 1:43]
51 [i][ch. 1:46]
53 [j]Josh. 11:23; 14:1, 2; Ps. 105:44
54 [k]ch. 33:54; 35:8
55 [l]ch. 33:54; 34:13; Josh. 11:23; 14:2
57 [m]Gen. 46:11; See Ex. 6:16-19; 1 Chr. 6:1, 16-30
59 [n]Ex. 2:1, 2, 4; 6:20
60 [o]ch. 3:2; 1 Chr. 24:1
61 [p]ch. 3:4; Lev. 10:1, 2; 1 Chr. 24:2
62 [q][ch. 3:39] [r]ch. 1:49 [s]See ch. 18:20
63 [t]ver. 3; See ch. 22:1
64 [u][ch. 1:44; Deut. 2:14, 15]
65 [v]ch. 14:28, 29; 1 Cor. 10:5 [w]See ch. 13:6
Chapter 27
1 [x]ch. 26:33; 36:11; Josh. 17:3
3 [y]ch. 14:35; 26:64, 65 [z]ch. 16:1, 2 [a][Ezek. 18:4]

26:52–56 The Promised Land was to be divided in proportion to the size of each group, with locations decided by lot.

27:1–11 Rules for inheritance of land, which notably permit women to inherit, are explained after the account of Zelophehad's daughters. Zelophehad had died without leaving a male heir, and his daughters petitioned Moses and the leaders to allow the daughters to inherit their father's portion in the land, and not to let his name be cut off. The names of all five daughters are recorded in v. 1.

In ch. 36 a related question was raised by the tribal leaders: if the daughters of Zelophehad married men of a different tribe, would their father's inheritance be transferred to that tribe? In response to both questions, the Lord answered that the family and tribal legacies should be protected (27:7; 36:6). These protections, as well as the prohibition against permanent transfer of land from one family to another, were rooted in God's ultimate ownership of the Promised Land (Lev. 25:23), and that He had entrusted it to all His people as a good gift and permanent possession to be enjoyed (Lev. 25:34; Deut. 6:10–12; 8:10–13). The land was not simply private property to be transferred on the basis of human convention and agreement. Rather, it symbolized life with God.

away from his clan because he had no son?
[b]Give to us a possession among our
father's brothers."
5 Moses [c]brought their case before the
LORD. 6 And the LORD said to Moses, 7 "The
daughters of Zelophehad [d]are right. [e]You
shall give them possession of an inheritance among their father's brothers and
transfer the inheritance of their father to
them. 8 And you shall speak to the people
of Israel, saying, 'If a man dies and has no
son, then you shall transfer his inheritance
to his daughter. 9 And if he has no daughter, then you shall give his inheritance to
his brothers. 10 And if he has no brothers,
then you shall give his inheritance to his
father's brothers. 11 And if his father has no
brothers, then you shall give his inheritance to the nearest [f]kinsman of his clan,
and he shall possess it. And it shall be for
the people of Israel [g]a statute and rule, as
the LORD commanded Moses.'"

Joshua to Succeed Moses

12 The LORD said to Moses, "Go up into
[h]this mountain of Abarim and see the land
that I have given to the people of Israel.
13 When you have seen it, you also [i]shall be
gathered to your people, as your brother
Aaron was, 14 [j]because you rebelled against
my word in the wilderness of Zin when the
congregation quarreled, failing [k]to uphold
me as holy at the waters before their eyes."
(These are [l]the waters of Meribah of
Kadesh in the wilderness of Zin.) 15 Moses
spoke to the LORD, saying, 16 "Let the LORD,
[m]the God of the spirits of all flesh, appoint
a man over the congregation 17 who [n]shall
go out before them and come in before
them, who shall lead them out and bring
them in, that the congregation of the LORD
may not be [o]as sheep that have no shepherd." 18 So the LORD said to Moses, "Take
[p]Joshua the son of Nun, a man [q]in whom
is the Spirit, and [r]lay your hand on him.
19 Make him stand before Eleazar the priest
and all the congregation, and you shall
[s]commission him in their sight. 20 You shall
invest him with some of your authority,
[t]that all the congregation of the people of
Israel may obey. 21 And he shall stand
before Eleazar the priest, who shall inquire
for him [u]by the judgment of the Urim
before the LORD. At his word they shall go
out, and at his word they shall come in,
both he and all the people of Israel with
him, the whole congregation." 22 And
Moses did as the LORD commanded him.
He took Joshua and made him stand before
Eleazar the priest and the whole congregation, 23 and he laid his hands on him and
[s]commissioned him as the LORD directed
through Moses.

Daily Offerings

28 The LORD spoke to Moses, saying,
2 "Command the people of Israel
and say to them, 'My offering, [v]my food for
my food offerings, my [w]pleasing aroma,
you shall be careful to offer to me at its
appointed time.' 3 [x]And you shall say to
them, This is the food offering that you
shall offer to the LORD: two male lambs a
year old without blemish, day by day, as a
regular offering. 4 The one lamb you shall
offer in the morning, and the other lamb
you shall offer at twilight; 5 also [y]a tenth of
an ephah[1] of fine flour for [z]a grain offering,
mixed [a]with a quarter of a hin[2] of beaten
oil. 6 It is a [b]regular burnt offering, which
was ordained at Mount Sinai for a pleasing
aroma, a food offering to the LORD. 7 Its
drink offering shall be a quarter of a hin for
each lamb. In the Holy Place you shall pour
out a drink offering of strong drink to the
LORD. 8 The other lamb you shall offer at
twilight. Like the grain offering of the
morning, and like its drink offering, you
shall offer it as a food offering, with a pleasing aroma to the LORD.

Sabbath Offerings

9 "On the Sabbath day, two male lambs a
year old without blemish, and two tenths of
an ephah of fine flour for a grain offering,

[1] An *ephah* was about 3/5 bushel or 22 liters [2] A *hin* was about 4 quarts or 3.5 liters

4 [b]Josh. 17:4 **5** [c]Ex. 18:19 **7** [d]ch. 36:5 [e]ch. 36:2 **11** [f]See Ruth 4:3-6; Jer. 32:6-9 [g]ch. 35:29 **12** [h]ch. 21:11; 33:44, 47; Deut. 32:49; [Deut. 3:27; 34:1] **13** [i]See ch. 20:24 **14** [j]ch. 20:12, 24 [k]ch. 20:12, 13 [l]ch. 20:13; Deut. 32: 51; [Ex. 17:7] **16** [m]See ch. 16:22 **17** [n]Deut. 31:2; 1 Sam. 8:20; 18:13; 1 Kin. 3:7; 2 Chr. 1:10; [Josh. 14:11] [o]1 Kin. 22:17; Ezek. 34:5; Zech. 10:2; Matt. 9:36; Mark 6:34 **18** [p]ch. 32:28 [q]Gen. 41:38; See Judg. 3:10 [r]Deut. 34:9 **19** [s]Deut. 3:28; 31:7, 8

20 [t]See Josh. 1:16-18 **21** [u]See Ex. 28:30 **23** [s][See ver. 19 above] **Chapter 28** **2** [v]See Lev. 3:11 [w]See Gen. 8:21 **3** [x]For ver. 3-8, see Ex. 29:38-42 **5** [y]ch. 15:4; Ex. 16:36 [z]Lev. 2:1 [a]Ex. 29:40 **6** [b]Ex. 29:42; [Amos 5:25]

27:12–14 Moses was not permitted to enter the Promised Land, but only to see it from a distance. This was punishment for his failure at Meribah (20:9–13 and notes).

27:18 lay your hand on him. See note Deut. 34:9.

27:20 invest him with some of your authority. Moses' office and ministry were unique (20:22–29 note), but a portion of his honor and authority would be imparted to Joshua.

28:1–29:40 In preparation for entry into the land, the laws of regular sacrifice and celebration already presented earlier (consult cross references) are summarized. Beginning with daily (28:1–8), Sabbath (28:9, 10), and monthly offerings (28:11–15), and then the celebration of annual feasts (28:16–29:40), the summary shows clearly how Israelite life in the land was to revolve around the worship and service of the Lord.

mixed with oil, and its drink offering: 10 this is [c]the burnt offering of every Sabbath, besides the regular burnt offering and its drink offering.

Monthly Offerings

11 [d]"At the beginnings of your months, you shall offer a burnt offering to the LORD: two bulls from the herd, one ram, seven male lambs a year old without blemish; 12 also [e]three tenths of an ephah of fine flour for a grain offering, mixed with oil, for each bull, and two tenths of fine flour for a grain offering, mixed with oil, for the one ram; 13 and a tenth of fine flour mixed with oil as a grain offering for every lamb; for a burnt offering with a pleasing aroma, a food offering to the LORD. 14 Their drink offerings shall be half a hin of wine for a bull, a third of a hin for a ram, and a quarter of a hin for a lamb. This is the burnt offering of each month throughout the months of the year. 15 Also [f]one male goat for a sin offering to the LORD; it shall be offered besides the regular burnt offering and its drink offering.

Passover Offerings

16 [g]"On the fourteenth day of the first month is the LORD's Passover, 17 [h]and on the fifteenth day of this month is a feast. Seven days shall unleavened bread be eaten. 18 [i]On the first day there shall be a holy convocation. You shall not do any ordinary work, 19 but offer a food offering, a burnt offering to the LORD: two bulls from the herd, one ram, and seven male lambs a year old; [j]see that they are without blemish; 20 also their grain offering of fine flour mixed with oil; three tenths of an ephah shall you offer for a bull, and two tenths for a ram; 21 a tenth shall you offer for each of the seven lambs; 22 also [k]one male goat for a sin offering, to make atonement for you. 23 You shall offer these besides the burnt offering of the morning, which is for a regular burnt offering. 24 In the same way you shall offer daily, for seven days, the food of a food offering, with a pleasing aroma to the LORD. It shall be offered besides the regular burnt offering and its drink offering. 25 And [l]on the seventh day you shall have a holy convocation. You shall not do any ordinary work.

Offerings for the Feast of Weeks

26 "On [m]the day of the firstfruits, when you offer a grain offering of new grain to the LORD at your Feast of Weeks, you shall have a holy convocation. You shall not do any ordinary work, 27 but offer a burnt offering, with a pleasing aroma to the LORD: [n]two bulls from the herd, one ram, seven male lambs a year old; 28 also their grain offering of fine flour mixed with oil, three tenths of an ephah for each bull, two tenths for one ram, 29 a tenth for each of the seven lambs; 30 with [o]one male goat, to make atonement for you. 31 Besides the regular burnt offering and its grain offering, you shall offer them and their drink offering. [p]See that they are without blemish.

Offerings for the Feast of Trumpets

29 "On the first day of the seventh month you shall have a holy convocation. You shall not do any ordinary work. [q]It is a day for you to blow the trumpets, 2 and you shall offer a burnt offering, for a pleasing aroma to the LORD: one bull from the herd, one ram, seven male lambs a year old without blemish; 3 also their grain offering of fine flour mixed with oil, three tenths of an ephah[1] for the bull, two tenths for the ram, 4 and one tenth for each of the seven lambs; 5 with [o]one male goat for a sin offering, to make atonement for you; 6 besides [r]the burnt offering of the new moon, and its grain offering, and [s]the regular burnt offering and its grain offering, and their drink offering, according to the rule for them, for a pleasing aroma, a food offering to the LORD.

Offerings for the Day of Atonement

7 [t]"On the tenth day of this seventh month you shall have a holy convocation and [u]afflict yourselves. You shall do no work, 8 but you shall offer a burnt offering to the LORD, a pleasing aroma: one bull from the herd, one ram, seven male lambs a year old: [v]see that they are without blemish. 9 And their grain offering shall be of fine flour mixed with oil, three tenths of an ephah for the bull, two tenths for the one ram, 10 a tenth for each of the seven lambs: 11 also [w]one male goat for a sin offering, besides [x]the sin offering of atonement, and the regular burnt offering and its grain offering, and their drink offerings.

10 [c][Ezek. 46:4, 5]
11 [d]ch. 10:10; 1 Sam. 20:5; 1 Chr. 23:31; 2 Chr. 2:4; Ezra 3:5; Isai. 1:13, 14; Ezek. 45:17; 46:6; Hos. 2:11; Col. 2:16
12 [e]For ver. 12-14, see ch. 15:4-12
15 [f]ver. 22, 30; ch. 15:24; 29:11, 16, 19, 25
16 [g]Deut. 16:1; Ezek. 45:21; See Ex. 12:6
17 [h]Lev. 23:6; [Ex. 12:18]
18 [i]Ex.12:16; Lev. 23:7
19 [j]ver. 31; ch. 29:8, 13; Lev. 22:20; Deut. 15:21; 17:1
22 [k]ver. 15, 30; ch. 29:22, 28, 31, 34, 38
25 [l]Ex. 12:16; 13:6; Lev. 23:8
26 [m]Ex. 23:16; 34:22; Lev. 23:10, 15; Deut. 16:10; [Acts 2:1]
27 [n][Lev. 23:18, 19]
30 [o]ver. 15, 22
31 [p]ver. 19
Chapter 29
1 [q]Lev. 23:24; See ch. 10:1-10
5 [o][See ch. 28:30 above]
6 [r]See ch. 28:11-15 [s]See ch. 28:3-8
7 [t]Lev. 16:29; 23:27 [u]ch. 30:13; Ps. 35:13; Isai. 58:5
8 [v]ver. 13, 17, 20, 23, 26, 29, 32, 36; See ch. 28:19
11 [w]See ch. 28:15 [x]Lev. 16:3, 5

1 An *ephah* was about 3/5 bushel or 22 liters

Offerings for the Feast of Tabernacles

12 [y]"On the fifteenth day of the seventh month you shall have a holy convocation. You shall not do any ordinary work, and you shall keep a feast to the LORD seven days. 13 And [z]you shall offer a burnt offering, a food offering, with a pleasing aroma to the LORD, thirteen bulls from the herd, two rams, fourteen male lambs a year old; they shall be without blemish; 14 and their grain offering of fine flour mixed with oil, three tenths of an ephah for each of the thirteen bulls, two tenths for each of the two rams, 15 and a tenth for each of the fourteen lambs; 16 also one male goat for a sin offering, besides the regular burnt offering, its grain offering and its drink offering.

17 "On the second day twelve bulls from the herd, two rams, fourteen male lambs a year old without blemish, 18 with the grain offering and the drink offerings for the bulls, for the rams, and for the lambs, [a]in the prescribed quantities; 19 also one male goat for a sin offering, besides the regular burnt offering and its grain offering, and their drink offerings.

20 "On the third day eleven bulls, two rams, fourteen male lambs a year old without blemish, 21 with the grain offering and the drink offerings for the bulls, for the rams, and for the lambs, in the prescribed quantities; 22 also one male goat for a sin offering, besides the regular burnt offering and its grain offering and its drink offering.

23 "On the fourth day ten bulls, two rams, fourteen male lambs a year old without blemish, 24 with the grain offering and the drink offerings for the bulls, for the rams, and for the lambs, in the prescribed quantities; 25 also one male goat for a sin offering, besides the regular burnt offering, its grain offering and its drink offering.

26 "On the fifth day nine bulls, two rams, fourteen male lambs a year old without blemish, 27 with the grain offering and the drink offerings for the bulls, for the rams, and for the lambs, in the prescribed quantities; 28 also one male goat for a sin offering; besides the regular burnt offering and its grain offering and its drink offering.

29 "On the sixth day eight bulls, two rams, fourteen male lambs a year old without blemish, 30 with the grain offering and the drink offerings for the bulls, for the rams, and for the lambs, in the prescribed quantities; 31 also one male goat for a sin offering; besides the regular burnt offering, its grain offering, and its drink offerings.

32 "On the seventh day seven bulls, two rams, fourteen male lambs a year old without blemish, 33 with the grain offering and the drink offerings for the bulls, for the rams, and for the lambs, in the prescribed quantities; 34 also one male goat for a sin offering; besides the regular burnt offering, its grain offering, and its drink offering.

35 [b]"On the eighth day you shall have a [c]solemn assembly. You shall not do any ordinary work, 36 but you shall offer a burnt offering, a food offering, with a pleasing aroma to the LORD: one bull, one ram, seven male lambs a year old without blemish, 37 and the grain offering and the drink offerings for the bull, for the ram, and for the lambs, in the prescribed quantities; 38 also one male goat for a sin offering; besides the regular burnt offering and its grain offering and its drink offering.

39 "These you shall offer to the LORD at your [d]appointed feasts, in addition to your [e]vow offerings and your freewill offerings, for your burnt offerings, and for your grain offerings, and for your drink offerings, and for your peace offerings."

40 [1] So Moses told the people of Israel everything just as the LORD had commanded Moses.

Men and Vows

30 Moses spoke to [f]the heads of the tribes of the people of Israel, saying, "This is what the LORD has commanded. 2 [g]If a man vows a vow to the LORD, or [h]swears an oath to bind himself by a pledge, he shall not break his word. [i]He shall do according to all that proceeds out of his mouth.

Women and Vows

3 If a woman vows a vow to the LORD and binds herself by a pledge, while within her father's house in her youth, 4 and her father hears of her vow and of her pledge by

12 [y]See Lev. 23:34
13 [z]Ezra 3:4
18 [a]ver. 21, 24, 27, 30, 33, 37; ch. 15:12; 28:7, 14
35 [b][John 7:37] [c]See Lev. 23:36
39 [d]Lev. 23:2, 4; 1 Chr. 23:31; 2 Chr. 31:3; Ezra 3:5; Neh. 10:33; [Isai. 1:14] [e]Lev. 7:11, 16; 22:21, 23
Chapter 30
1 [f]ch. 1:4, 16; 7:2
2 [g]Deut. 23:21; Eccles. 5:4; See Lev. 27:2 [h]See Lev. 5:4 [i]Job 22:27; Ps. 22:25; 50:14; 66:13, 14; 116:14, 18; Nah. 1:15

1 Ch 30:1 in Hebrew

30:1–16 Ordinarily, people were obliged to fulfill any vow or obligation they had made, including even a rash promise (v. 6). However, the vow of a subordinate member of a household could be cancelled by the head of the house (vv. 5, 8, 12–13, 15). Moses urged the people not to make rash vows, but declared that if made they must be fulfilled (Deut. 23:21–23; cf. Prov. 20:25). For a terrible instance of a rash vow, see Judg. 11:30–40 and notes.

which she has bound herself and says
nothing to her, then all her vows shall
stand, and every pledge by which she has
bound herself shall stand. 5 But if her father
opposes her on the day that he hears of it,
no vow of hers, no pledge by which she has
bound herself shall stand. And the LORD
will forgive her, because her father opposed
her.
6 If she marries a husband, while under
her [j]vows or any thoughtless utterance of
her lips by which she has bound herself,
7 and her husband hears of it and says
nothing to her on the day that he hears,
then her vows shall stand, and her pledges
by which she has bound herself shall
stand. 8 But if, on the day that her husband
comes to hear of it, he opposes her, then
he makes void her [j]vow that was on her,
and the thoughtless utterance of her lips by
which she bound herself. [k]And the LORD
will forgive her. 9 (But any vow of a widow
or of a divorced woman, anything by which
she has bound herself, shall stand against
her.) 10 And if she vowed in her husband's
house or bound herself by a pledge with an
oath, 11 and her husband heard of it and
said nothing to her and did not oppose
her, then all her vows shall stand, and
every pledge by which she bound herself
shall stand. 12 But if her husband makes
them null and void on the day that he
hears them, then whatever proceeds out of
her lips concerning her vows or concerning her pledge of herself shall not stand.
Her husband has made them void, and [l]the
LORD will forgive her. 13 Any vow and any
binding oath to afflict herself, her husband
may establish,[1] or her husband may make
void. 14 But if her husband says nothing to
her from day to day, then he establishes all
her vows or all her pledges that are upon
her. He has established them, because he
said nothing to her on the day that he
heard of them. 15 But if he makes them null
and void after he has heard of them, then
[m]he shall bear her iniquity."
16 These are the statutes that the LORD
commanded Moses about a man and his
wife and about a father and his daughter
while she is in her youth within her father's
house.

6 [i]Ps. 56:12
8 [j][See ver. 6 above] [k]ver. 12
12 [l]ver. 8
15 [m]See Lev. 5:1

Chapter 31
2 [n]ch. 25:17 [o]See ch. 20:24
5 [p]ch. 32:27; Josh. 4:13
6 [q]ch. 10:6, 9; Lev. 23:24
7 [r][Deut. 20:13; Judg. 21:11; 1 Sam. 27:9; 1 Kin. 11:15, 16]
8 [s]Josh. 13:21 [t]ch. 25:15 [u]Josh. 13:22
10 [v]Gen. 25:16
11 [w][Deut. 20:14; Josh. 8:2]
12 [x]See ch. 22:1
14 [y]ver. 48

Vengeance on Midian

31 The LORD spoke to Moses, saying,
2 [n]"Avenge the people of Israel on
the Midianites. Afterward you shall [o]be
gathered to your people." 3 So Moses spoke
to the people, saying, "Arm men from
among you for the war, that they may go
against Midian to execute the LORD's
vengeance on Midian. 4 You shall send a
thousand from each of the tribes of Israel
to the war." 5 So there were provided, out of
the thousands of Israel, a thousand from
each tribe, twelve thousand [p]armed for
war. 6 And Moses sent them to the war, a
thousand from each tribe, together with
Phinehas the son of Eleazar the priest, with
the vessels of the sanctuary and [q]the trumpets for the alarm in his hand. 7 They
warred against Midian, as the LORD commanded Moses, and [r]killed every male.
8 They killed the kings of Midian with the
rest of their slain, [s]Evi, Rekem, [t]Zur, Hur,
and Reba, the five kings of Midian. And
they also killed [u]Balaam the son of Beor
with the sword. 9 And the people of Israel
took captive the women of Midian and
their little ones, and they took as plunder
all their cattle, their flocks, and all their
goods. 10 All their cities in the places where
they lived, and all their [v]encampments,
they burned with fire, 11 [w]and took all the
spoil and all the plunder, both of man and
of beast. 12 Then they brought the captives
and the plunder and the spoil to Moses,
and to Eleazar the priest, and to the congregation of the people of Israel, at the
camp on [x]the plains of Moab by the Jordan
at Jericho.
13 Moses and Eleazar the priest and all
the chiefs of the congregation went to meet
them outside the camp. 14 And Moses was
angry with [y]the officers of the army, the

[1] Or *may allow to stand*

31:1–54 Vengeance against the Midianites for their efforts to seduce the Israelites into idol worship and sexual immorality (ch. 25) is undertaken. This narrative deals particularly with details concerning the plunder taken from the Midianites. Because the plunder of war had to be handled in a fashion that preserved the holiness of God and of the people, the principles stated here helped prepare the Israelites for the coming conquest of the land.

31:6 Phinehas. See note 25:11.

31:8 Balaam. See note 22:5.

31:13–18 Moses' command that all the women who were not virgins must be killed was due to the immorality at Peor. All males were killed, including children, probably to prevent any resurgence of the Midianite clans (cf. v. 7).

commanders of thousands and the commanders of hundreds, who had come from
service in the war. **15** Moses said to them,
"Have you [z]let all the women live?
16 Behold, [a]these, [b]on Balaam's advice,
caused the people of Israel to act treacherously against the LORD in the incident of
[c]Peor, and so [d]the plague came among the
congregation of the LORD. **17** Now therefore,
[e]kill every male among the little ones, and
kill every woman who has known man by
lying with him. **18** But all the young girls
who have not known man by lying with
him [f]keep alive for yourselves. **19** [g]Encamp
outside the camp seven days. Whoever of
you has killed any person and [h]whoever
has touched any slain, purify yourselves
and your captives on the third day and on
the seventh day. **20** You shall purify every
garment, every article of skin, all work of
goats' hair, and every article of wood."
21 Then Eleazar the priest said to the men
in the army who had gone to battle: "This
is the statute of the law that the LORD has
commanded Moses: **22** only the gold, the
silver, the bronze, the iron, the tin, and the
lead, **23** everything that can stand the fire,
you shall pass through the fire, and it shall
be clean. Nevertheless, it shall also be purified [i]with the water for impurity. And
whatever cannot stand the fire, you shall
pass through the water. **24** You must [j]wash
your clothes on the seventh day, and you
shall be clean. And afterward you may
come into the camp."
25 The LORD said to Moses, **26** "Take the
count of the plunder that was taken, both
of man and of beast, you and Eleazar the
priest and the heads of the fathers' houses
of the congregation, **27** and [k]divide the plunder into two parts between the warriors
who went out to battle and all the congregation. **28** And levy for the LORD a tribute
from the men of war who went out to battle, [l]one out of five hundred, of the people
and of the oxen and of the donkeys and of
the flocks. **29** Take it from their half and give
it to Eleazar the priest as a contribution to
the LORD. **30** And from the people of Israel's
half you shall take [m]one drawn out of every
fifty, of the people, of the oxen, of the donkeys, and of the flocks, of all the cattle, and
give them to the Levites [n]who keep guard
over the tabernacle of the LORD." **31** And
Moses and Eleazar the priest did as the
LORD commanded Moses.
32 Now the plunder remaining of the
spoil that the army took was 675,000
sheep, **33** 72,000 cattle, **34** 61,000 donkeys,
35 and 32,000 persons in all, women who
had not known man by lying with him.
36 And the half, the portion of those who
had gone out in the army, numbered
337,500 sheep, **37** and [o]the LORD's tribute
of sheep was 675. **38** The cattle were
36,000, of which the LORD's tribute was
72. **39** The donkeys were 30,500, of which
the LORD's tribute was 61. **40** The persons
were 16,000, of which the LORD's tribute
was 32 persons. **41** And Moses gave the tribute, which was the contribution for the
LORD, to Eleazar the priest, [p]as the LORD
commanded Moses.
42 From the people of Israel's half, which
Moses separated from that of the men who
had served in the army— **43** now the congregation's half was 337,500 sheep,
44 36,000 cattle, **45** and 30,500 donkeys,
46 and 16,000 persons— **47** [q]from the people
of Israel's half Moses took one of every 50,
both of persons and of beasts, and gave
them to the Levites who kept guard over
the tabernacle of the LORD, as the LORD
commanded Moses.
48 Then [r]the officers who were over the
thousands of the army, the commanders of
thousands and the commanders of hundreds, came near to Moses **49** and said to
Moses, "Your servants have counted the
men of war who are under our command,
and there is not a man missing from us.
50 And we have brought the LORD's offering,
what each man found, articles of gold, armlets and bracelets, signet rings, earrings, and
beads, [s]to make atonement for ourselves
before the LORD." **51** And Moses and Eleazar
the priest received from them the gold, all
crafted articles. **52** And all the gold of the contribution that they presented to the LORD,
from the commanders of thousands and the

15 [z][1 Sam. 15:3] **16** [a]ch. 25:2 [b]ch. 24:14; 2 Pet. 2:15; Rev. 2:14 [c]See ch. 23:28 [d]ch. 25:9 **17** [e]Judg. 21:11, 12 **18** [f]See Deut. 21:10-14 **19** [g]ch. 5:2 [h]See ch. 19:12, 22 **23** [i]ch. 19:9 **24** [j]See Lev. 11:25 **27** [k]Josh. 22:8; 1 Sam. 30:24 **28** [l][ch. 18:26]; See ver. 30-41, 47 **30** [m]See ver. 42-47

[n]See ch. 1:53 **37** [o]ver. 28 **41** [p][ch. 18:8, 19] **47** [q]ver. 30 **48** [r]ver. 14 **50** [s]See Ex. 30:12

31:16 on Balaam's advice. See Deut. 23:4, 5; Josh. 13:22; 24:9, 10; Neh. 13:2; Mic. 6:5; 2 Pet. 2:15; Jude 11; Rev. 2:14.

31:25–47 Israel divides the Midianite spoils: half to the soldiers and half to the community (vv. 25–27). As a tribute to the Lord, one out of every five hundred from the soldier's half, and one out of every fifty from the community's half was to be given to the Levites (vv. 28–31, 41). A detailed enumeration of the portions is given (vv. 32–47).

commanders of hundreds, was 16,750
shekels.[1] 53 [t](The men in the army had each
taken plunder for himself.) 54 And Moses
and Eleazar the priest received the gold from
the commanders of thousands and of hundreds, and brought it into the tent of meeting, [u]as a memorial for the people of Israel
before the LORD.

Reuben and Gad Settle in Gilead

32 Now the people of Reuben and the
people of Gad had a very great
number of livestock. And they saw the land
of [v]Jazer and the land of Gilead, and
behold, the place was a place for livestock.
2 So the people of Gad and the people of
Reuben came and said to Moses and to
Eleazar the priest and to the chiefs of the
congregation, 3 [w]"Ataroth, [x]Dibon, Jazer,
Nimrah, Heshbon, Elealeh, Sebam, [y]Nebo,
and Beon, 4 the land [z]that the LORD struck
down before the congregation of Israel, is a
land for livestock, and your servants have
livestock." 5 And they said, "If we have
found favor in your sight, let this land be
given to your servants for a possession. Do
not take us across the Jordan."
6 But Moses said to the people of Gad
and to the people of Reuben, "Shall your
brothers go to the war while you sit here?
7 Why will you discourage the heart of the
people of Israel from going over into the
land that the LORD has given them? 8 Your
fathers did this, [a]when I sent them from
Kadesh-barnea to see the land. 9 For when
they went up to the Valley of Eshcol and
saw the land, they discouraged the heart of
the people of Israel from going into the
land that the LORD had given them. 10 [b]And
the LORD's anger was kindled on that day,
and he swore, saying, 11 'Surely none of the
men who came up out of Egypt, [c]from
twenty years old and upward, shall see the
land that I swore to give [d]to Abraham, to
Isaac, and to Jacob, because they have not
wholly followed me, 12 none except Caleb
the son of Jephunneh the [e]Kenizzite and
Joshua the son of Nun, for [f]they have wholly followed the LORD.' 13 And the LORD's
anger was kindled against Israel, and he
made them [g]wander in the wilderness forty
years, until [h]all the generation that had
done evil in the sight of the LORD was gone.
14 And behold, you have risen in your
fathers' place, a brood of sinful men, to
increase still more the fierce anger of the
LORD against Israel! 15 For if you [i]turn away
from following him, he will again abandon
them in the wilderness, and you will
destroy all this people."
16 Then they came near to him and said,
[j]"We will build sheepfolds here for our
livestock, and cities for our little ones,
17 but [k]we will take up arms, ready to go
before the people of Israel, until we have
brought them to their place. And our little
ones shall live in the fortified cities because
of the inhabitants of the land. 18 [l]We will
not return to our homes until each of the
people of Israel has gained his inheritance.
19 For we will not inherit with them on the
other side of the Jordan and beyond, [m]be-
cause our inheritance has come to us on
this side of the Jordan to the east." 20 So
[n]Moses said to them, "If you will do this, if
you will take up arms to go before the LORD
for the war, 21 and every armed man of you
will pass over the Jordan before the LORD,
until he has [o]driven out his enemies from
before him 22 and the land is subdued
before the LORD; then after that you shall
return and be free of obligation to the LORD
and to Israel, and [p]this land shall be your
possession before the LORD. 23 But if you
will not do so, behold, you have sinned
against the LORD, and [q]be sure your sin will
find you out. 24 [r]Build cities for your little
ones and folds for your sheep, and do what
you have promised." 25 And the people of
Gad and the people of Reuben said to
Moses, "Your servants will do as my lord
commands. 26 [s]Our little ones, our wives,
our livestock, and all our cattle, shall
remain there in the cities of Gilead, 27 [t]but
your servants will pass over, every man
who is [u]armed for war, before the LORD to
battle, as my lord orders."
28 So [v]Moses gave command concerning
them to Eleazar the priest and to [w]Joshua

53 [t]ver. 32; Deut. 20:14
54 [u]Ex. 30:16
Chapter 32
1 [v]ver. 3, 35; See ch. 21:32
3 [w]ver. 34 [x]ver. 34; See ch. 21:30 [y]ver. 38; ch. 33:47; Deut. 32:49; 1 Chr. 5:8; Isai. 15:2; 46:1; Jer. 48:1, 22
4 [z]ch. 21:24, 34; [ver. 33]
8 [a]See ch. 13:3, 21-33; Deut. 1:22-28
10 [b]For ver. 10-12, see Deut. 1:34-36
11 [c]ch. 14:29 [d]See Gen. 50:24
12 [e]Josh. 14:6; 15:17 [f]ch. 14:24; Deut. 1:36; Josh. 14:8, 9
13 [g]See ch. 14:33-35 [h]ch. 26:64, 65
15 [i][Deut. 30:17; Josh. 22:16, 18; 2 Chr. 7:19, 20; 15:2]
16 [j]ver. 24
17 [k]Josh. 4:12, 13
18 [l]Josh. 22:4
19 [m]ver. 33; Josh. 12:1; 13:8
20 [n]Deut. 3:18; Josh. 1:13, 14; 4:12, 13
21 [o]ch. 33:52
22 [p]Deut. 3:12, 15, 16, 18; Josh. 1:15; 13:8, 32; 22:4, 9
23 [q][Gen. 44:16; Isai. 59:12]
24 [r]ver. 16; See ver. 34-38
26 [s]Josh. 1:14
27 [t]Josh. 4:12, 13 [u]ch. 31:5
28 [v]Josh. 1:13 [w]ch. 27:18

[1] A *shekel* was about 2/5 ounce or 11 grams

32:1–42 The tribes of Reuben and Gad, possessors of much livestock, requested permission to settle in the Transjordan territory (the region east of the Jordan River and the Dead Sea) already conquered (vv. 1–5; cf. 21:24–26, 31–35). Because all of Israel was to participate in the conquest and because their departure would dishearten the other tribes, Moses sternly warned them against the sin of the Exodus generation (vv. 6–15). His admonition includes a classic recognition of God's sovereign dominion as judge: "be sure your sin will find you out" (v. 23).

the son of Nun and to the heads of the
fathers' houses of the tribes of the people
of Israel. 29 And Moses said to them, "If the
people of Gad and the people of Reuben,
every man who is armed to battle before
the LORD, will pass with you over the
Jordan and the land shall be subdued
before you, then you shall give them the
land of Gilead for a possession. 30 However,
if they will not pass over with you armed,
they shall have possessions among you in
the land of Canaan." 31 And the people of
Gad and the people of Reuben answered,
"What the LORD has said to your servants,
we will do. 32 We will pass over armed
before the LORD into the land of Canaan,
and the possession of our inheritance shall
remain with us beyond the Jordan."
33 And [x]Moses gave to them, to the people of Gad and to the people of Reuben
and to the half-tribe of Manasseh the son of
Joseph, the kingdom of Sihon king of the
Amorites and the kingdom of Og king of
Bashan, the land and its cities with their
territories, the cities of the land throughout
the country. 34 And the people of Gad built
[y]Dibon, [z]Ataroth, [a]Aroer, 35 Atroth-sho-
phan, [b]Jazer, Jogbehah, 36 [c]Beth-nimrah
and Beth-haran, [d]fortified cities, and folds
for sheep. 37 And the people of Reuben
built [e]Heshbon, [y]Elealeh, Kiriathaim,
38 [f]Nebo, and [g]Baal-meon ([h]their names
were changed), and [c]Sibmah. And they
gave other names to the cities that they
built. 39 And the sons of [i]Machir the son of
Manasseh went to Gilead and captured it,
and dispossessed the Amorites who were
in it. 40 And Moses [j]gave Gilead to Machir
the son of Manasseh, and he settled in it.
41 And [k]Jair the son of Manasseh went and
captured their villages, and called them
Havvoth-jair.[1] 42 And Nobah went and captured Kenath and its villages, and called it
Nobah, after his own name.

Recounting Israel's Journey

33 These are the stages of the people of
Israel, when they went out of the
land of Egypt by their companies under the
leadership of Moses and Aaron. 2 Moses
wrote down their starting places, [l]stage by
stage, by command of the LORD, and these
are their stages according to their starting
places. 3 They [m]set out from Rameses in
[n]the first month, on the fifteenth day of the
first month. On the day after the Passover,
the people of Israel went out [o]triumphant-
ly in the sight of all the Egyptians, 4 while
the Egyptians were burying all their firstborn, [p]whom the LORD had struck down
among them. [q]On their gods also the LORD
executed judgments.
5 So the people of Israel set out from
Rameses and camped at [r]Succoth. 6 And
they set out from Succoth and camped at
[s]Etham, which is on the edge of the wilderness. 7 And they set out from Etham and
turned back to [t]Pi-hahiroth, which is east
of Baal-zephon, and they camped before
Migdol. 8 And they set out from before
Hahiroth[2] and [u]passed through the midst
of the sea into the wilderness, and they
[v]went a three days' journey in the wilderness of Etham and camped at Marah. 9 And
they set out from Marah and came to
[w]Elim; at Elim there were twelve springs of
water and seventy palm trees, and they
camped there. 10 And they set out from
Elim and camped by the Red Sea. 11 And
they set out from the Red Sea and camped
in [x]the wilderness of Sin. 12 And they set
out from the wilderness of Sin and camped
at Dophkah. 13 And they set out from
Dophkah and camped at Alush. 14 And they
set out from Alush and camped at
[y]Rephidim, where there was no water for
the people to drink. 15 And they set out
from Rephidim and camped in the [z]wilder-
ness of Sinai. 16 And they set out from the
wilderness of Sinai and camped at
[a]Kibroth-hattaavah. 17 And they set out
from Kibroth-hattaavah and camped at
[b]Hazeroth. 18 And they [c]set out from
Hazeroth and camped at Rithmah. 19 And

33 [x]Deut. 29:8; Josh. 12:6; 13:8; 22:4; See Deut. 3:12-17
34 [y]ver. 3 [z]ver. 3 [a]See Deut. 2:36
35 [b]ver. 1; See ch. 21:32
36 [c][ver. 3] [d]ver. 17
37 [e]ver. 3; ch. 21:27 [y][See ver. 34 above]
38 [f]See ver. 3 [g][ver. 3; Josh. 13:17; Jer. 48:23] [h][Ex. 23:13; Josh. 23:7] [c][See ver. 36 above]
39 [i]Gen. 50:23; 1 Chr. 7:14, 15
40 [j]Deut. 3:13, 15; Josh. 13:31; 17:1
41 [k]Deut. 3:14; See 1 Chr. 2:21-23

Chapter 33
2 [l]See ch. 9:17-23
3 [m]Ex. 12:37 [n]Ex. 12:2; 13:4 [o]Ex. 14:8
4 [p]Ex. 12:29 [q]Ex. 12:12; [Isai. 19:1]
5 [r]Ex. 12:37
6 [s]Ex. 13:20
7 [t]Ex. 14:2, 9
8 [u]Ex. 14:22 [v]Ex. 15:22, 23
9 [w]Ex. 15:27
11 [x]Ex. 16:1
14 [y]Ex. 17:1
15 [z]Ex. 19:1, 2
16 [a]ch. 11:34
17 [b]ch. 11:35; 12:16
18 [c]ch. 12:16

[1] *Havvoth-jair* means *the villages of Jair* [2] Some manuscripts and versions *Pi-hahiroth*

32:33 the half-tribe of Manasseh. Apparently, many from this tribe had joined Reuben and Gad in wishing to live east of the Jordan. During the time in the wilderness Manasseh had increased from 32,200 to 52,700 (cf. 1:35 and 26:34). Reuben and Gad settled territory already conquered (vv. 33–38), but the half-tribe of Manasseh went further north and made new conquests (vv. 39–42).

33:3, 4 These verses give a vivid summary of the Israelites' departure from Egypt.

33:4 all their firstborn. See Ex. 12:29–33.

On their gods . . . judgments. See note Ex. 12:12.

33:5–48 Many of the names in this list may represent wilderness camps that have since disappeared. For other mention of some locations, see the cross references.

they set out from Rithmah and camped at Rimmon-perez. **20**And they set out from Rimmon-perez and camped at Libnah. **21**And they set out from Libnah and camped at Rissah. **22**And they set out from Rissah and camped at Kehelathah. **23**And they set out from Kehelathah and camped at Mount Shepher. **24**And they set out from Mount Shepher and camped at Haradah. **25**And they set out from Haradah and camped at Makheloth. **26**And they set out from Makheloth and camped at Tahath. **27**And they set out from Tahath and camped at Terah. **28**And they set out from Terah and camped at Mithkah. **29**And they set out from Mithkah and camped at Hashmonah. **30**And they set out from Hashmonah and camped at Moseroth. **31**And they set out from Moseroth and camped at [d]Bene-jaakan. **32**And they set out from Bene-jaakan and camped at [e]Hor-haggidgad. **33**And they set out from Hor-haggidgad and camped at [e]Jotbathah. **34**And they set out from Jotbathah and camped at Abronah. **35**And they set out from Abronah and camped at [f]Ezion-geber. **36**And they set out from Ezion-geber and camped in the [g]wilderness of Zin (that is, Kadesh). **37**And they set out from [h]Kadesh and camped at [i]Mount Hor, on the edge of the land of Edom.

38And Aaron the priest went up [j]Mount Hor at the command of the LORD and died there, in the fortieth year after the people of Israel had come out of the land of Egypt, on the first day of the fifth month. **39**And Aaron was [k]123 years old when he died on Mount Hor.

40And [l]the Canaanite, the king of Arad, who lived in the Negeb in the land of Canaan, heard of the coming of the people of Israel.

41And they set out from Mount Hor and camped at Zalmonah. **42**And they set out from Zalmonah and camped at Punon. **43**And they set out from Punon and camped at [m]Oboth. **44**And they set out from Oboth and camped at [n]Iye-abarim, in the territory of Moab. **45**And they set out from Iyim and camped at [o]Dibon-gad. **46**And they set out from Dibon-gad and camped at Almon-diblathaim. **47**And they set out from Almon-diblathaim [p]and camped in the mountains of Abarim, before Nebo. **48**And they set out from the mountains of Abarim and camped in [q]the plains of Moab by the Jordan at Jericho; **49**they camped by the Jordan from Beth-jeshimoth as far as [r]Abel-shittim in the plains of Moab.

Drive Out the Inhabitants

50And the LORD spoke to Moses in the plains of Moab by the Jordan at Jericho, saying, **51**"Speak to the people of Israel and say to them, [s]When you pass over the Jordan into the land of Canaan, **52**then [t]you shall drive out [u]all the inhabitants of the land from before you and destroy all their [v]figured stones and destroy all their metal images and demolish all their high places. **53**And you shall take possession of the land and settle in it, for I have given the land to you to possess it. **54**[w]You shall inherit the land by lot according to your clans. [x]To a large tribe you shall give a large inheritance, and to a small tribe you shall give a small inheritance. Wherever the lot falls for anyone, that shall be his. According to the tribes of your fathers you shall inherit. **55**But if you do not drive out the inhabitants of the land from before you, then those of them whom you let remain shall be as [y]barbs in your eyes and thorns in your sides, and they shall trouble you in the land where you dwell. **56**And I will do to you [z]as I thought to do to them."

Boundaries of the Land

34 The LORD spoke to Moses, saying, **2**"Command the people of Israel, and say to them, When you enter [a]the land of Canaan [b](this is the land that shall fall to you for an inheritance, the land of Canaan as defined by its borders), **3**[c]your south side shall be from the wilderness of Zin alongside Edom, and your southern border

31 [d][Deut. 10:6] **32** [e]Deut. 10:7 **33** [e][See ver. 32 above] **35** [f]Deut. 2:8; 1 Kin. 9:26; 22:48; 2 Chr. 8:17 **36** [g]ch. 20:1; 27:14 **37** [h]ch. 20:1, 14, 22 [i]ch. 20:23; 21:4; 34:7, 8 **38** [j]ch. 20:25-28; Deut. 32:50; [Deut. 10:6] **39** [k][Ex. 7:7] **40** [l]ch. 21:1 **43** [m]ch. 21:10 **44** [n]ch. 21:11

45 [o]ch. 21:30; [ch. 32:34] **47** [p]Deut. 32:49 **48** [q]ch. 22:1 **49** [r]See ch. 25:1 **51** [s]Deut. 9:1; [Josh. 3:17] **52** [t]ch. 32:21 [u]Ex. 23:24, 33; 34:13; Deut. 7:2, 5; 12:3 [v]Lev. 26:1 **54** [w]ch. 26:53, 55 [x]ch. 26:54; 35:8 **55** [y]Josh. 23:13; Judg. 2:3; Ps. 106:34, 36 **56** [z][Deut. 28:63]

Chapter 34
2 [a]Gen. 17:8; Ex. 3:8; Ps. 105:11 [b]ver. 13 **3** [c]Josh. 15:1; See Gen. 15:18-21; Ezek. 47:13-21

33:31 Bene-jaakan. See Deut. 10:6.

33:36 wilderness of Zin. See 13:21.

33:44 Iye-abarim. See 27:12.

33:52 drive out all the inhabitants. God orders the complete extermination of the Canaanites and the destruction of all marks of idolatry, as had been done to the Midianites (ch. 31).

33:53 settle in it. God sets forth rules for settlement, summarizing the directions in 26:52–56.

34:1–15 These boundaries of Canaan do not include the territory already assigned in Transjordan, east of the Jordan River (vv. 13–15). See ch. 32.

shall run from the end of [d]the Salt Sea on the east. 4 And your border shall turn south of [e]the ascent of Akrabbim, and cross to Zin, and its limit shall be south of Kadesh-barnea. Then it shall go on to [e]Hazar-addar, and pass along to Azmon. 5 And the border shall turn [f]from Azmon to [g]the Brook of Egypt, and its limit shall be at the sea.

6 "For the western border, you shall have the Great Sea and its[1] coast. This shall be your western border.

7 "This shall be your northern border: from the Great Sea you shall draw a line to [h]Mount Hor. 8 From Mount Hor you shall draw a line [i]to Lebo-hamath, and the limit of the border shall be at [j]Zedad. 9 Then the border shall extend to Ziphron, and its limit shall be at [k]Hazar-enan. This shall be your northern border.

10 "You shall draw a line for your eastern border from Hazar-enan to Shepham. 11 And the border shall go down from Shepham to [l]Riblah on the east side of Ain. And the border shall go down and reach to the shoulder of [m]the Sea of Chinnereth on the east. 12 And the border shall go down to the Jordan, and its limit shall be at [n]the Salt Sea. This shall be your land as defined by its borders all around."

13 Moses commanded the people of Israel, saying, [o]"This is the land that you shall inherit by lot, which the LORD has commanded to give to the nine tribes and to the half-tribe. 14 [p]For the tribe of the people of Reuben by fathers' houses and the tribe of the people of Gad by their fathers' houses have received their inheritance, and also the half-tribe of Manasseh. 15 The two tribes and the half-tribe have received their inheritance beyond the Jordan east of Jericho, toward the sunrise."

List of Tribal Chiefs

16 The LORD spoke to Moses, saying, 17 "These are the names of the men who shall divide the land to you for inheritance: [q]Eleazar the priest and Joshua the son of Nun. 18 You shall take one [r]chief from every tribe to divide the land for inheritance. 19 These are the names of the men: Of the tribe of Judah, Caleb the son of Jephunneh. 20 Of the tribe of the people of Simeon, Shemuel the son of Ammihud. 21 Of the tribe of Benjamin, Elidad the son of Chislon. 22 Of the tribe of the people of Dan a chief, Bukki the son of Jogli. 23 Of the people of Joseph: of the tribe of the people of Manasseh a chief, Hanniel the son of Ephod. 24 And of the tribe of the people of Ephraim a chief, Kemuel the son of Shiphtan. 25 Of the tribe of the people of Zebulun a chief, Elizaphan the son of Parnach. 26 Of the tribe of the people of Issachar a chief, Paltiel the son of Azzan. 27 And of the tribe of the people of Asher a chief, Ahihud the son of Shelomi. 28 Of the tribe of the people of Naphtali a chief, Pedahel the son of Ammihud. 29 These are the men whom the LORD commanded to divide the inheritance for the people of Israel in the land of Canaan."

Cities for the Levites

35 The LORD spoke to Moses in [s]the plains of Moab by the Jordan at Jericho, saying, 2 [t]"Command the people of Israel to give to the Levites some of the inheritance of their possession as cities for them to dwell in. And you shall give to the Levites pasturelands around the cities. 3 The cities shall be theirs to dwell in, and their pasturelands shall be for their cattle and for their livestock and for all their beasts. 4 The pasturelands of the cities, which you shall give to the Levites, shall reach from the wall of the city outward a thousand cubits[2] all around. 5 And you shall measure, outside the city, on the east side two thousand cubits, and on the south side two thousand cubits, and on the west side two thousand cubits, and on the north side two thousand cubits, the city being in the middle. This shall belong to them as pastureland for their cities.

6 The cities that you give to the Levites shall be [u]the six cities of refuge, where you

3 [d]ver. 12; Gen. 14:3; Josh. 15:2
4 [e]Josh. 15:3
5 [f]Josh. 15:4 [g]Gen. 15:18; Josh. 15:4, 47; 1 Kin. 8:65; 2 Kin. 24:7; 1 Chr. 13:5; 2 Chr. 7:8; Isai. 27:12
7 [h]ch. 33:37
8 [i]ch. 13:21; 2 Kin. 14:25; Ezek. 48:1 [j]Ezek. 47:15
9 [k]Ezek. 47:17
11 [l]2 Kin. 23:33; Jer. 39:5 [m]Deut. 3:17; Josh. 11:2; 12:3; 19:35; Matt. 4:18; Luke 5:1
12 [n]ver. 3
13 [o]ver. 2; Josh. 14:1, 2
14 [p]ch. 32:33; Josh. 14:3
17 [q]Josh. 14:1; 19:51
18 [r]ch. 1:4, 16

Chapter 35
1 [s]See ch. 22:1
2 [t]Josh. 14:3, 4; 21:2; See Ezek. 45:1-5; 48:8-14
6 [u]ver. 13; Deut. 4:41, 42; Josh. 20:2, 7, 8; 21:3, 13, 21, 27, 32, 36, 38

[1] Syriac; Hebrew lacks *its* [2] A *cubit* was about 18 inches or 45 centimeters

34:16–29 The Lord designates men to assign the portions of the land of Canaan: Eleazar the priest (Num. 20:25–26) and Joshua the commander (Num. 27:18–23) were to be in charge, together with a leader from each of the ten tribes that had not yet been given their inheritance. None of these ten names are included in earlier lists of leaders (Num. 1:5–15; 2:3–29; 7:12–78), nor is any one of them the son of a man included in those lists.

35:1–8 Because the Levites were not given a tribal land inheritance (18:20), they were instead assigned forty-eight towns with surrounding pastureland, including six "cities of refuge."

shall permit the manslayer to flee, and in
addition to them you shall give forty-two
cities. 7 All the cities that you give to the
Levites shall be [v]forty-eight, with their pasturelands. 8 And as for the cities that you
shall give [w]from the possession of the people of Israel, [x]from the larger tribes you
shall take many, and from the smaller
tribes you shall take few; each, in proportion to the inheritance that it inherits, shall
give of its cities to the Levites."

Cities of Refuge

9 And the LORD spoke to Moses, saying,
10 "Speak to the people of Israel and say to
them, [y]When you cross the Jordan into the
land of Canaan, 11 [z]then you shall select
cities to be cities of refuge for you, that the
manslayer who kills any person without
intent may flee there. 12 The cities shall be
for you a refuge from the avenger, that the
manslayer may not die until he stands
before the congregation for judgment.
13 And the cities that you give shall be your
[a]six cities of refuge. 14 [b]You shall give three
cities beyond the Jordan, and three cities in
the land of Canaan, to be cities of refuge.
15 These six cities shall be for refuge for the
people of Israel, and [c]for the stranger and
for the sojourner among them, that anyone
who kills any person without intent may
flee there.
16 [d]"But if he struck him down with an
iron object, so that he died, he is a murderer. The murderer shall be put to death.
17 And if he struck him down with a stone
tool that could cause death, and he died,
he is a murderer. The murderer shall be
put to death. 18 Or if he struck him down
with a wooden tool that could cause death,
and he died, he is a murderer. The murderer shall be put to death. 19 [e]The avenger
of blood shall himself put the murderer to
death; when he meets him, he shall put
him to death. 20 And if he pushed him out
of hatred or hurled something at him, [f]ly-
ing in wait, so that he died, 21 or in enmity
struck him down with his hand, so that he
died, then he who struck the blow shall be
put to death. He is a murderer. [e]The
avenger of blood shall put the murderer to
death when he meets him.
22 "But if he pushed him suddenly without enmity, or hurled anything on him
[g]without lying in wait 23 or used a stone
that could cause death, and without seeing him dropped it on him, so that he
died, though he was not his enemy and
did not seek his harm, 24 then [h]the congregation shall judge between the manslayer
and [e]the avenger of blood, in accordance
with these rules. 25 And the congregation
shall rescue the manslayer from the hand
of the avenger of blood, and the congregation shall restore him to his city of refuge
to which he had fled, and he shall live in it
[i]until the death of the high priest [j]who was
anointed with the holy oil. 26 But if the
manslayer shall at any time go beyond the
boundaries of his city of refuge to which
he fled, 27 and [e]the avenger of blood finds
him outside the boundaries of his city of
refuge, and the avenger of blood kills the
manslayer, he shall not be guilty of blood.
28 For he must remain in his city of refuge
[i]until the death of the high priest, but after
the death of the high priest the manslayer
may return to the land of his possession.
29 And these things shall be for [k]a statute
and rule for you throughout your generations in all your dwelling places.
30 "If anyone kills a person, the murderer
shall be put to death on the [l]evidence of
witnesses. But no person shall be put to
death on the testimony of one witness.
31 Moreover, you shall accept no ransom for
the life of a murderer, who is guilty of
death, but he shall be put to death. 32 And
you shall accept no ransom for him who
has fled to his city of refuge, that he may
return to dwell in the land before the death
of the high priest. 33 You shall not [m]pollute
the land in which you live, for blood [m]pol-
lutes the land, and no atonement can be

7 [v]Josh. 21:41
8 [w]Josh. 21:3 [x]ch. 26:54; 33:54
10 [y]For ver. 10-12, see Deut. 19:2-4; Josh. 20:2-6
11 [z]Ex. 21:13
13 [a]See ver. 6
14 [b]Deut. 4:41; Josh. 20:8
15 [c]ch. 15:16
16 [d]Ex. 21:12, 14; Lev. 24:17; Deut. 19:11, 12
19 [e]Deut. 19:6, 12; Josh. 20:3, 5
20 [f]Ex. 21:14; Deut. 19:11
21 [e][See ver. 19 above]
22 [g]Ex. 21:13
24 [h]ver. 12; Josh. 20:6 [e][See ver. 19 above]
25 [i]Josh. 20:6 [j]Ex. 29:7; Lev. 4:3; 21:10
27 [e][See ver. 19 above]
28 [i][See ver. 25 above]
29 [k]ch. 27:11
30 [l]Deut. 17:6; 19:15; Heb. 10:28; [Matt. 18:16; John 8:17; 2 Cor. 13:1; 1 Tim. 5:19]
33 [m]Ps. 106:38; Jer. 3:1, 2, 9; [Mic. 4:11]

35:9–33 Six cities of refuge were to be established for those who had accidentally killed someone. See note Deut. 4:41–43.

35:12 the avenger. A member of the victim's family was customarily designated to avenge the victim's death by killing the manslayer.

35:25 until the death of the high priest. See also v. 28. The death of the high priest brought a change in the legal status of a manslayer—the guilty one was no longer liable to the penalty for manslaughter.

35:30 No one was to be put to death on the evidence of only one witness.

35:31, 32 Accepting a ransom payment was forbidden in cases of murder and manslaughter. This provision emphasizes the value God places on human life.

35:33, 34 Pollution of the land by bloodshed could be removed only by shedding the blood of the murderer (Gen. 9:5, 6 and notes).

made for the land for the blood that is shed
in it, except [n]by the blood of the one who
shed it. 34 [o]You shall not defile the land in
which you live, in the midst of which I
dwell, [p]for I the LORD dwell in the midst of
the people of Israel."

Marriage of Female Heirs

36 The heads of the fathers' houses of
the clan of the [q]people of Gilead the
son of Machir, son of Manasseh, from the
clans of the people of Joseph, came near
and spoke before Moses and before the
chiefs, the heads of the fathers' houses of
the people of Israel. 2 They said, [r]"The LORD
commanded my lord to give the land for
inheritance by lot to the people of Israel,
and [s]my lord was commanded by the LORD
to give the inheritance of Zelophehad our
brother to his daughters. 3 But if they are
married to any of the sons of the other
tribes of the people of Israel, then their
inheritance will be taken from the inheritance of our fathers and added to the inheritance of the tribe into which they marry.
So it will be taken away from the lot of our
inheritance. 4 And when [t]the jubilee of the
people of Israel comes, then their inheritance will be added to the inheritance of
the tribe into which they marry, and their
inheritance will be taken from the inheritance of the tribe of our fathers."
5 And Moses commanded the people of
Israel according to the word of the LORD,
saying, "The tribe of the people of Joseph
[u]is right. 6 This is what the LORD commands
concerning the daughters of Zelophehad,
'Let them marry whom they think best,
[v]only they shall marry within the clan of
the tribe of their father. 7 The inheritance of
the people of Israel shall not be transferred
from one tribe to another, for every one of
the people of Israel [w]shall hold on to the
inheritance of the tribe of his fathers. 8 And
[x]every daughter who possesses an inheritance in any tribe of the people of Israel
shall be wife to one of the clan of the tribe
of her father, so that every one of the people of Israel may possess the inheritance of
his fathers. 9 So no inheritance shall be
transferred from one tribe to another, for
each of the tribes of the people of Israel
shall hold on to its own inheritance.'"
10 The daughters of Zelophehad did as
the LORD commanded Moses, 11 [y]for Mahlah, Tirzah, Hoglah, Milcah, and Noah, the
daughters of Zelophehad, were married to
sons of their father's brothers. 12 They were
married into the clans of the people of
Manasseh the son of Joseph, and their
inheritance remained in the tribe of their
father's clan.
13 These are the commandments and the
rules that the LORD commanded through
Moses to the people of Israel [z]in the plains
of Moab by the Jordan at Jericho.

33 [n]See Gen. 9:6
34 [o]Lev. 18:25; Deut. 21:23 [p]See Ex. 29:45
Chapter 36
1 [q]ch. 26:20
2 [r]ch. 26:55; 33:54 [s]ch. 27:1, 7; Josh. 17:3, 4
4 [t]Lev. 25:10
5 [u][ch. 27:7]
6 [v]ver. 12
7 [w][1 Kin. 21:3]
8 [x]1 Chr. 23:22
11 [y]ch. 27:1; Josh. 17:3
13 [z]See ch. 22:1

36:1–11 See note 27:1–11.

36:4 the jubilee. In the Jubilee Year, all property would revert to its original owner or heir (Lev. 25:8–17). In the case of the daughters of Zelophehad it had been established that women could inherit land (27:1–11). If a daughter inheriting property were to marry outside her tribe, it appeared that the Law of Jubilee would cause the land to be transfered to the tribe of the new husband. Moses rules that a woman with property may not marry outside her tribe. In agreement with this, the daughters of Zelophehad married relatives in Manasseh.

THE FIFTH BOOK OF MOSES CALLED

Deuteronomy

AUTHOR

By its own testimony (1:1, 5; 31:22), Deuteronomy is the work of Moses. Mosaic authorship is affirmed many times elsewhere in the Old Testament (e.g. 2 Kin. 14:6), in ancient Jewish sources (e.g., Josephus), and in the New Testament. This view was almost universally held until the rise of rationalistic criticism in modern times (Introduction to the Pentateuch: Author and Date).

Critics correctly point out that the last chapter could not have been written by Moses. It is widely agreed that ch. 34 is an addendum, perhaps appended by Joshua. In the same way, the Book of Joshua ends with the death of Joshua, this record clearly having been supplied by the author of the Book of Judges, who appended verses from Judges to the end of Joshua (Judg. 2:7–9; cf. Josh. 24:29–31). Likewise, the first verses of Ezra are copied and appended to the last chapter of Chronicles (Chronicles ends in the middle of a sentence). This way of linking a subsequent book to the preceding one (or variations of this practice) was common in antiquity and was intended to show the proper sequence of scrolls or clay tablets. It is probable that Joshua added the note on Moses' death and Israel's acceptance of Joshua in order to link his own book to Moses' great production. Such obvious additions do not, however, negate the general authorship of Moses.

More controversially, some critics have alleged that the language of 1:1, 5 indicates that the writer of the book must have been located on the west side of the Jordan River, i.e., in Canaan (the Hebrew phrase here translated "beyond the Jordan" is often translated "the other side of the Jordan" or "this side of the Jordan"). Such a description, they argue, belies the credibility of Deuteronomy as a work of Moses, since Moses never crossed the Jordan. This argument assumes that the Hebrew phrase in question must always refer to the region east of the Jordan. It is evident, however, that the precise meaning of the phrase must be determined by the context, and that it can refer either to Transjordan (the region to the east of the Jordan and the Dead Sea, 1:1–5; 3:8; 4:41, 47, 49) or to Canaan itself (3:20, 25; 11:30; Josh. 9:1, 10). Here it clearly means the region east of the Jordan, as the geographical descriptions indicate (1:1, 5).

DATE AND OCCASION

In the nineteenth century, biblical critics contended that Deuteronomy was written about 620 B.C., as part of the religious reform of King Josiah, in which he insisted that worship be centered in Jerusalem. The law of the central sanctuary (ch. 12) was said by these critics to have been the invention of a writer in the time of Josiah. Since the early twentieth century, however, this view has received less favor. Some have dated Deuteronomy as early as Samuel, others as late as the Exile. Many critics still date the book in the seventh century B.C., which is the period of Josiah. But these scholars also question the unity of the book. If some parts seem "early" (from Moses' time), they ascribe those parts to an old tradition that has conveniently been preserved. If other parts seem "late" (during or after the time of Josiah), they are called "later editions" or due to "late editing." Such elastic, subjective, and speculative methods cannot be conclusively disproved without a copy from Moses' own time, which no one possesses. No concrete evidence rules out the composition of Deuteronomy at the time of Moses, making reasonable allowances for additions by someone like Joshua, who appended Moses' obituary to the book, and for some later updating of Hebrew grammar and place names.

The background and setting of the book reflect conditions prior to the conquest of

Canaan under Joshua. There is no mention of a king in Judah or of the city of Jerusalem, which is mentioned over one hundred times by the prophet Jeremiah (who wrote in Josiah's day). It is unlikely that a sixth-century author would make no allusion whatever to that capital city or its temple. The twelve tribes are represented as one nation (instead of, as in Josiah's period, the kingdoms of Judah and Israel). The Transjordan cities of refuge are named, while those in Canaan (which were named later by Joshua) are not. The Babylonian names of months are not used, and there are no Persian loan words in the vocabulary, even though such words would be expected to appear in a work supposedly written during a period when these empires were dominant. Moses, Aaron, and Joshua are named, but no later persons or later historical incidents are mentioned. It is unlikely that a later author, even one well-versed in the lore of the past, could so completely avoid the use of later terms and the mention of persons and events of his own period.

Perhaps most significant is the general conformity of Deuteronomy's structure to the covenant or treaty form of the mid-second millennium B.C. (the approximate time of Moses). We find the following treaty elements in Deuteronomy: (a) a preamble identifying the covenant mediator (1:1–5); (b) a historical prologue reviewing previous covenant history (1:6–4:40); (c) stipulations expounding the covenant way of life (4:44–11:32; 12–26); (d) a declaration of sanctions stating the blessings for obedience and curses for disobedience of the covenant (chs. 27–30); and (e) a provision for the administration of the covenant after the death of the inaugural mediator (chs. 31–34). The main divisions from the covenant documents of Moses' lifetime, then, are discernible in the fifth book of the Pentateuch, Deuteronomy.

We conclude, therefore, that Deuteronomy was written by Moses, Israel's lawgiver, before his death in 1406 B.C.

CHARACTERISTICS AND THEMES

Deuteronomy has been much used both by Christians and ancient Jews. It is quoted in the New Testament over fifty times, a number exceeded only by Psalms and Isaiah. The book contains much exhortation. The detailed legal material (chs. 14–26), much of which parallels Leviticus, is not as familiar or as much used as the rest, although it has importance for special purposes.

The book is a repetition of the law and history of Israel. It consists mainly of three great speeches and a legal compendium given by Moses at the end of his life, while the people were encamped in the plains of Moab, just before Joshua took command and led the people in the conquest of Canaan. The conquest of Transjordan had been successfully concluded, and Moses challenged the people in these farewell addresses.

As Moses' farewell messages to his people, the book combines exhortation and commandments, and serves as an example of how the Law should be taught. The opening address (1:5–4:40) recounts the experiences of Israel under Moses' leadership. Deuteronomy does not speak of how Moses confronted Pharaoh and how the miracles of the ten plagues forced Pharaoh to let the people go, but it alludes to the Exodus repeatedly (five times in the first address: 1:20, 34; 4:20, 34, 37). Moses recounts God's providential and miraculous care for the people during the journey from Egypt to Sinai. Then he details their defeat both spiritually and militarily at Kadesh-barnea. There are references here to events recorded in Numbers, but like the record in Numbers, almost nothing is said about events of the forty years of wilderness wandering. The journey around Edom toward Transjordan is mentioned, and the defeat of the kings Sihon and Og is recorded in fuller detail than in Numbers. Then comes the allocation of land in Transjordan for the tribes of Reuben, Gad, and half of Manasseh (as in Num. 32), and the narrative ends with reference to Moses' plea for himself to enter Canaan, which God disallows (as in Num. 27:12–23). Moses concludes the address with exhortations to be loyal to the Lord.

The second address (4:44–11:32) is composed of exhortations. Some consider this address as continuing to 26:19 with inclusion of the laws and regulations of chs. 12–26. The speech begins with the Ten Commandments, almost exactly like the wording in Ex. 20, aside from the fourth commandment (5:12–15 note). The terror of the theophany (a visible self-revelation of God) is recalled with the call to obedience. Only the Ten Commandments are given directly by the voice of God; the rest of the law is mediated through Moses (5:22 note). The famous *Shema*, "Hear, O Israel: The LORD our God, the LORD is one," is given in 6:4, with the exhortation to teach, remember, and obey. The following chapters are sprinkled with examples of God's care and judgments since leaving Egypt—all allusions to material in Exodus and Numbers. These examples serve to warn Israel to trust the Lord and not themselves. This leads to a promise of success in the coming wars of Canaan.

The laws (chs. 12–26) include regulations for worship, clean foods, slaves and debts, annual feasts, judges, cities of refuge, and various matters of conduct. Most of these have some parallel to material found in the previous books of the Pentateuch, which will be noted at the appropriate places.

The third address (chs. 27–30) is a powerful exhortation to obey the laws of the Lord. It includes the solemn ceremony to be held in the valley between Mount Ebal and Mount Gerizim, near Shechem, after Israel had secured a foothold in Canaan—a ceremony reminiscent of the covenant ceremony of Ex. 20:1–24:8, and duly carried out by Joshua (Josh. 8:30–35). These laws and exhortations were given by Moses with emphasis on Israel's obligation before God to hear and obey the law of the Lord.

The final sections of the book are equally important and powerful (31:1–34:2). They include the installation of Joshua as Moses' successor, the great Song of Moses celebrating the greatness of God and His care for His covenant people (ch. 32), Moses' song of blessing of the twelve tribes after the fashion of Jacob's blessing of his twelve sons in Gen. 49 (ch. 33), and finally, the addendum describing the death of Moses (ch. 34).

Through types and prophecy this book also points us to Christ. He is the Passover Lamb (16:1 note) and the coming Prophet (18:15–19 note). Moses, the founder of Israel's theocracy, mediated the old covenant, but Jesus Christ, the Son of God, mediated the new covenant (Jer. 31:31–34). The substance of the covenants is the same, but their manner of administration differs significantly. Whereas the old covenant was written on tablets of stone, Christ writes the new covenant through the Spirit of the living God on the tablets of human hearts (2 Cor. 3:3). The old covenant was ratified with Israel's promise, "we will hear and do" (5:27; cf. Ex. 19:8; 20:19). But the new covenant depends on God's better promise, "I will write it on their hearts" (Jer. 31:33; Heb. 8:7). The old covenant called for shedding the blood of animals; the everlasting new covenant was instituted once and for all by the blood of Christ (Jer. 32:40; Heb. 9:11–28). The old covenant calls for a heart religion, but it failed through human weakness and became obsolete after its fulfillment at Calvary (Rom. 8:3; Heb. 7:12; 8:13).

The Book of Deuteronomy, the fifth book of Moses, receives its title from the Septuagint, which called it *Deuteronomion*, meaning the "Second Law," or the "Repetition of the Law."

OUTLINE OF DEUTERONOMY

I. Introduction (1:1–5)

II. Moses' First Address (1:6–4:40)

- A. *The Travel from Horeb to the Arnon River (1:6–2:23)*
- B. *The Transjordan Campaign and Settlement (2:24–3:29)*
- C. *Exhortation to Obey God's Law (4:1–14)*
- D. *Warning Against Idolatry (4:15–40)*

III. Interlude: Cities of Refuge in Transjordan (4:41–43)

IV. Moses' Second Address (4:44–11:32)

- A. *Preface and the Ten Commandments (4:44–5:22)*
- B. *Mediation of the Rest of the Law by Moses (5:23–33)*
- C. *Love and Obedience to the One True God (ch. 6)*
- D. *Promise of Victory and Call to Separation (7:1–10:5)*
- E. *Parenthesis: The Levites Set Apart for Service (10:6–9)*
- F. *The Charge to Love and Obey the Great and True God (10:10–11:25)*
- G. *First Mention of Ebal-Gerizim Liturgy (11:26–32)*

V. Reiteration of Laws for Israel's Worship and Conduct (chs. 12–26)

- A. *One Place of Sacrifice, Penalty for Idolatry (chs. 12; 13)*
- B. *Laws of Worship: Cleanness, Judges, King, Priesthood, Prophet (chs. 14–18)*
- C. *Laws of Conduct: Cities of Refuge, War, Purity, Honesty (chs. 19–25)*
- D. *Firstfruits and Tithes, Concluding Exhortations (ch. 26)*

VI. Moses' Third Address: The Covenant and Ebal-Gerizim Liturgy (chs. 27–30)

- A. *The Cursings and Blessings at Ebal and Gerizim (chs. 27; 28)*
- B. *The Moab Covenant (chs. 29; 30)*

VII. The Conclusion of Moses' Ministry (chs. 31–34)

- A. *Transfer of Leadership to Joshua (31:1–29)*
- B. *The Song of Moses (31:30–32:52)*
- C. *Moses' Blessing on the Twelve Tribes (ch. 33)*
- D. *Addendum: The Death of Moses and Eulogy for Him (ch. 34)*

The Command to Leave Horeb

1 These are the words that Moses spoke
to all Israel beyond the Jordan in the
wilderness, in [a]the Arabah opposite [b]Suph,
between [c]Paran and Tophel, Laban,
Hazeroth, and Dizahab. 2 It is eleven days'
journey from Horeb by the way of Mount
Seir to [d]Kadesh-barnea. 3 [e]In the fortieth
year, on the first day of the eleventh
month, Moses spoke to the people of Israel
according to all that the LORD had given
him in commandment to them, 4 after [f]he
had defeated Sihon the king of the
Amorites, who lived in Heshbon, and [g]Og
the king of Bashan, who lived in Ashtaroth
and in [h]Edrei. 5 Beyond the Jordan, [i]in the
land of Moab, Moses undertook to explain
this law, saying, 6 "The LORD our God said
to us in Horeb, [j]'You have stayed long
enough at this mountain. 7 Turn and take
your journey, and go to [k]the hill country of
the Amorites and to all their neighbors in
[a]the Arabah, [l]in the hill country and in the
lowland and in the Negeb and [l]by the seacoast, the land of the Canaanites, and
Lebanon, as far as the great river, the river
Euphrates. 8 See, I have set the land before
you. Go in and take possession of the land
that the LORD swore to your fathers, [m]to
Abraham, to Isaac, and to Jacob, to give to
them and to their offspring after them.'

Leaders Appointed

9 "At that time [n]I said to you, 'I am not
able to bear you by myself. 10 The LORD
your God has multiplied you, and behold,
[o]you are today as numerous as the stars of
heaven. 11 [p]May the LORD, the God of your
fathers, make you a thousand times as
many as you are and bless you, [q]as he has
promised you! 12 [r]How can I bear by myself
the weight and burden of you and your
strife? 13 [s]Choose for your tribes wise,
understanding, and experienced men, and
I will appoint them as your heads.' 14 And
you answered me, 'The thing that you have
spoken is good for us to do.' 15 So I took the
heads of your tribes, wise and experienced
men, [t]and set them as heads over you,
commanders of thousands, commanders of
hundreds, commanders of fifties, commanders of tens, and officers, throughout
your tribes. 16 And I charged your judges at
that time, 'Hear the cases between your
brothers, and [u]judge righteously between a

Chapter 1
1 [a]ch. 3:17 [b][Num. 21:14] [c]1 Sam. 25:1
2 [d]ch. 2:14; 9:23; Num. 13:26; 32:8; 34:4
3 [e][Num. 33:38]
4 [f]See Num. 21:21-32 [g]See Num. 21:33-35 [h]ch. 3:1, 10; Josh. 12:4; 13:12
5 [i]ch. 29:1
6 [j]ch. 2:3; [Ex. 19:1; Num. 10:11]
7 [k][Num. 13:29] [a][See ver. 1 above] [l]Josh. 9:1
8 [m]Gen. 12:7; 13:14, 15; 15:18; 17:7, 8; 26:3, 4; 28:13, 14; 50:24
9 [n]Num. 11:14; [Ex. 18:18]
10 [o][ch. 10:22; 28:62]; See Gen. 15:5
11 [p][2 Sam. 24:3] [q]Gen. 12:2; 22:17; 26:3, 24
12 [r][1 Kin. 3:8, 9]
13 [s][Ex. 18:21; Num. 11:16, 17] 15 [t]Ex. 18:25 16 [u]ch. 16:18; John 7:24

1:1–5 These introductory verses give us the author, Moses, and the circumstances of his addresses to the people just before he died and the people crossed the Jordan.

1:1 beyond the Jordan. See Introduction: Author.

the Arabah opposite Suph. The exact location is uncertain, but taken as a whole, the description points to the region of Moab. This *Arabah* or "plain" extends along the eastern edge of Palestine from the Sea of Galilee south to the Gulf of Aqaba. Suph, meaning "reeds," may refer to a location in Moab near the Arnon River. The names Paran and Hazeroth are mentioned during Israel's travels in the Sinai peninsula (Num. 10:12; 11:35; 12:16; 33:17), but it is unclear whether they are the same places as mentioned here. Tophel, Laban, and Dizahab are mentioned only here.

1:2 eleven days' journey. The distance between Horeb and Kadesh-barnea is about 150 miles. The Israelites went by way of the Mount Seir road, which probably means they traveled part of the time along the valley north of Ezion-geber, a journey of 175 miles or more. They made good time if the whole nation arrived in eleven days. But the "eleven days' journey" could be a conventional expression for the distance involved, rather than the time taken on this particular journey.

1:3 the fortieth year. This date (forty years since the Exodus from Egypt) serves to fix the time for the book as a whole. The years of divine judgment have ended (Num. 14:33, 34), and Israel prepares to enter the Promised Land. This forty-year period included thirty-eight years in the wilderness, followed by two years for the conquest of Transjordan (2:14).

1:4 Sihon . . . Og. The conquest of Transjordan is detailed in 2:24–3:11.

Heshbon. The name has been preserved in the modern Tell Hesban, located in Transjordan some thirty-five miles east of Jerusalem. Extensive excavations have discovered no remains at Hesban from Moses' time (i.e., from the fourteenth century B.C.). It is possible that a nearby mound that does contain fourteenth-century remains is the Heshbon in Moses' day.

Edrei. The name is probably preserved in the town-name of modern Der'a on the border between Syria and Jordan, which does have ruins of this period.

1:5 in the land of Moab. The Israelites are said to have camped in the plains of Moab (e.g., Num. 22:1; 26:3, 63) or in the land of Moab (e.g., Deut. 29:1; 32:49), but Israel was encamped north of the Arnon River, the northern border of Moab. The solution is that Moab earlier had held the northern territory but had been driven south of the Arnon by Sihon the Amorite (Num. 21:26). Jephthah rehearses this history in Judg. 11:14–27.

1:6–4:40 Following the introduction of himself as the covenant mediator (vv. 1–5), Moses turns to a review of the history of Israel prior to this covenant ratification occasion. He provides a travelogue of the nation's movements from the Sinai region to Hormah, on to the Arnon, and into the Transjordan area. This segment of the book concludes with an overview of the covenant now to be renewed with the generation born in the wilderness.

1:6 Horeb. Another name for Sinai, apparently for the area around Mount Sinai. The name Sinai nearly always has the designation "Mount" or "wilderness." Horeb only once has the designation "Mount" (Ex. 33:6).

1:7 the land of the Canaanites. These borders of the Promised Land were given to Abraham in Gen. 15:18, 19. The promise included driving out the Canaanites and the other nations.

1:8 the LORD swore. God's solemn oath to give the land to Abraham's descendants is mentioned at least six times in Genesis, and is found at least twenty-five times in Deuteronomy (it is also mentioned in Exodus, Leviticus, and Numbers).

1:13 Choose . . . wise . . . men. A reference to Ex. 18:24–26 where Moses took the good advice of Jethro, his father-in-law. During the year at Mount Sinai, Moses, under God, organized the nation's judicial system, military power, and worship. Regarding the judges, see 16:18; 17:8; 19:17.

man and his brother or the alien who is
with him. 17 [v]You shall not be partial in
judgment. You shall hear the small and the
great alike. You shall not be intimidated by
anyone, for [w]the judgment is God's. And
the case that is too hard for you, you shall
[x]bring to me, and I will hear it.' 18 And I
commanded you at that time all the things
that you should do.

Israel's Refusal to Enter the Land

19 "Then we set out from Horeb and [y]went
through all that great and terrifying wilderness that you saw, on the way to the hill
country of the Amorites, as the LORD our
God commanded us. And [z]we came to
Kadesh-barnea. 20 And I said to you, 'You
have come to the hill country of the
Amorites, which the LORD our God is giving
us. 21 See, the LORD your God has set the
land before you. Go up, take possession, as
the LORD, the God of your fathers, has told
you. [a]Do not fear or be dismayed.' 22 Then
all of you came near me and said, 'Let us
send men before us, that they may explore
the land for us and bring us word again of
the way by which we must go up and the
cities into which we shall come.' 23 The
thing seemed good to me, and [b]I took
twelve men from you, one man from each
tribe. 24 And [c]they turned and went up into
the hill country, and came to the Valley of
Eshcol and spied it out. 25 And they took in
their hands some of the fruit of the land
and brought it down to us, and brought us
word again and said, 'It is a good land that
the LORD our God is giving us.'

26 "Yet you would not go up, but rebelled
against the command of the LORD your
God. 27 And [d]you murmured in your tents
and said, 'Because the LORD [e]hated us he
has brought us out of the land of Egypt, [f]to
give us into the hand of the Amorites, to
destroy us. 28 Where are we going up? [g]Our
brothers have made our hearts melt,
saying, [h]"The people are greater and taller
than we. The cities are great and fortified
up to heaven. And besides, we have seen
[i]the sons of the Anakim there."' 29 Then I
said to you, 'Do not be in dread or afraid of
them. 30 The LORD your God who goes
before you [j]will himself fight for you, just
as he did for you in Egypt before your eyes,
31 and in the wilderness, where you have
seen how the LORD your God [k]carried you,
as a man carries his son, all the way that
you went until you came to this place.'
32 Yet in spite of this word [l]you did not
believe the LORD your God, 33 [m]who went
before you in the way [n]to seek you out a
place to pitch your tents, in fire by night
and in the cloud by day, to show you by
what way you should go.

The Penalty for Israel's Rebellion

34 "And the LORD heard your words and
was angered, and he swore, 35 [o]'Not one of
these men of this evil generation shall see
the good land that I swore to give to your
fathers, 36 [p]except Caleb the son of Jephunneh. He shall see it, and to him and to his
children I will give the land on which he
has trodden, because he has wholly followed the LORD!' 37 Even with me [q]the LORD
was angry on your account and said, 'You
also shall not go in there. 38 [r]Joshua the son
of Nun, [r]who stands before you, he shall
enter. [s]Encourage him, for he shall cause
Israel to inherit it. 39 And as for [t]your little
ones, who you said would become a prey,
and your children, who today [u]have no
knowledge of good or evil, they shall go in
there. And to them I will give it, and they
shall possess it. 40 But as for you, [v]turn, and
journey into the wilderness in the direction
of the Red Sea.'

41 "Then you answered me, [w]'We have
sinned against the LORD. We ourselves will
go up and fight, just as the LORD our God

17 [v]ch. 16:19; Ex. 23:2, 3; Lev. 19:15; 2 Chr. 19:7; Prov. 24:23; 28:21; Mal. 2:9; James 2:1, 9 [w]2 Chr. 19:6; [Ex. 21:6] [x]Ex. 18:22, 26
19 [y]ch. 8:15; 32:10; Jer. 2:6; [Num. 10:12] [z]See ver. 2
21 [a]ch. 31:8; Josh. 1:9
23 [b]Num. 13:3
24 [c]See Num. 13:22-27
27 [d]Ps. 106:25; See Num. 14:1-4 [e]ch. 9:28 [f][Josh. 7:7]
28 [g]Josh. 14:8 [h]ch. 9:1, 2; See Num. 13:28–33 [i]See Num. 13:22
30 [j]ch. 3:22; Ex. 14:14, 25; Josh. 10:14, 42; 23:3, 10; [Neh. 4:20]
31 [k]ch. 32:11, 12; Ex. 19:4; Isai. 46:3, 4; 63:9; Hos. 11:3
32 [l]Ps. 106:24; Jude 5
33 [m]See Ex. 13:21 [n]Num. 10:33
35 [o]See ch. 2:15; Num. 14:20-30
36 [p]Num. 14:30; Josh. 14:9
37 [q]ch. 4:21; 32:51; 34:4; Num. 20:12; 27:13, 14; [Ps. 106:32]
38 [r]ch. 31:3, 7; Ex. 24:13; [1 Sam. 16:22] [s]ch. 31:7, 23; Num. 27:18-20
39 [t]Num. 14:3, 31 [u]Isai. 7:15, 16
40 [v]ch. 2:1; Num. 14:25
41 [w]Num. 14:40

1:19 Kadesh-barnea. The place was called simply Kadesh in Num. 13:26. Kadesh means "holy place" and the name was doubtless given by the original inhabitants to many supposedly sacred places. This place was called Kadesh-barnea to distinguish it from other such places (e.g., in Naphtali, Judg. 4:6; in Judah, Josh. 15:23).

1:26 but rebelled. This account of the people's failure at Kadesh parallels extensively the account in Num. 13.

1:28 the Anakim. The name Anak appears in Egyptian texts of the early second millennium as the name of a ruler in Palestine. It probably is related to the biblical Anak whose descendants lived in Hebron (Num. 13:22). They were taller than the Israelites and were feared for their military prowess. Joshua conquered them, and their remnants merged with the Philistines (Josh. 12:21, 22).

1:33 in fire by night. The mention of the pillar of fire and the cloud refers to Ex. 13:21, where the pillar guided them out of Egypt, and especially to Num. 9:15–23, which tells of the Lord's guidance through the whole wilderness journey.

1:37 Even with me the LORD was angry. Mention of the doom of the lost generation recalls that God was also displeased with Moses and refused to allow him to enter Canaan (32:51; Num. 20:9–11 note; 27:14). Joshua, a faithful spy, would carry on as leader (Num. 27:12–23).

commanded us.' And every one of you fastened on his weapons of war and thought
it easy to go up into the hill country. 42 And
the LORD said to me, [x]'Say to them, Do not
go up or fight, [y]for I am not in your midst,
lest you be defeated before your enemies.'
43 So I spoke to you, and you would not listen; but you rebelled against the command
of the LORD and [z]presumptuously went up
into the hill country. 44 [a]Then the Amorites
who lived in that hill country came out
against you and chased you [b]as bees do
and beat you down in Seir as far as
[c]Hormah. 45 And you returned and wept
before the LORD, but the LORD did not listen to your voice or give ear to you. 46 So
[d]you remained at Kadesh many days, the
days that you remained there.

The Wilderness Years

2 "Then we turned and journeyed into
the wilderness in the direction of the
Red Sea, [e]as the LORD told me. And for
many days we traveled around Mount Seir.
2 Then the LORD said to me, 3 'You have been
traveling around this mountain country
[f]long enough. Turn northward 4 and command the people, "You are about to pass
through the territory of [g]your brothers, the
people of Esau, [h]who live in Seir; and [i]they
will be afraid of you. So be very careful. 5 Do
not contend with them, for I will not give
you any of their land, no, not so much as
for the sole of the foot to tread on, because
[h]I have given Mount Seir to Esau as a possession. 6 [j]You shall purchase food from

42 [x]Num. 14:42 [y][ch. 31:17]
43 [z]Num. 14:44
44 [a]Num. 14:45 [b][Ps. 118:12; Isai. 7:18] [c]See Num. 21:3
46 [d]Num. 20:1, 22; Judg. 11:17
Chapter 2
1 [e]ch. 1:40; Num. 14:25
3 [f]ch. 1:6
4 [g]ch. 23:7; Amos 1:11; Obad. 10, 12 [h]See Gen. 32:3 [i]See Num. 20:18-21
5 [h][See ver. 4 above]
6 [j]ver. 28
7 [k][Job 23:10] [l]See ch. 8:2-4
8 [m]Judg. 11:18 [n]See ch. 1:1 [o]1 Kin. 9:26; [2 Kin. 14:22; 16:6; 2 Chr. 26:2] [p]See Num. 33:35
9 [q]ver. 19, 29 [r]ver. 18; Num. 21:15; Isai. 15:1 [s]ver. 19; Gen. 19:36, 37
10 [t]Gen. 14:5 [u][ver. 21] [v]See Num. 13:22
11 [w]See Gen. 14:5
12 [x]ver. 22; Gen. 14:6; See Gen. 36:20-30 [y]Num. 21:24, 31, 35
13 [z][Num. 21:12]

them for money, that you may eat, and you
shall also buy water of them for money, that
you may drink. 7 For the LORD your God has
blessed you in all the work of your hands.
[k]He knows your going through this great
wilderness. [l]These forty years the LORD your
God has been with you. You have lacked
nothing."' 8 So [m]we went on, away from our
brothers, the people of Esau, who live in
Seir, away from [n]the Arabah road from
[o]Elath and [p]Ezion-geber.

"And we turned and went in the direction of the wilderness of Moab. 9 And the
LORD said to me, [q]'Do not harass Moab or
contend with them in battle, for I will not
give you any of their land for a possession,
because I have given [r]Ar to [s]the people of
Lot for a possession.' 10 ([t]The Emim formerly lived there, [u]a people great and
many, and tall [v]as the Anakim. 11 Like the
Anakim they are also counted as [w]Reph-
aim, but the Moabites call them Emim.
12 [x]The Horites also lived in Seir formerly,
but the people of Esau dispossessed them
and destroyed them from before them and
settled in their place, [y]as Israel did to the
land of their possession, which the LORD
gave to them.) 13 'Now rise up and go over
[z]the brook Zered.' So we went over [z]the
brook Zered. 14 And the time from our leaving [a]Kadesh-barnea until we crossed [b]the
brook Zered was thirty-eight years, [c]until
the entire generation, that is, the men of
war, had perished from the camp, as the

14 [a]See ch. 1:2, 19 [b][Num. 21:12] [c]Num. 14:33, 35; 26:64; Ps. 78:33; 95:11; 106:26; Ezek. 20:15; [1 Cor. 10:5; Heb. 3:17]; See ch. 1:35

1:46 at Kadesh many days. Little is said in Numbers or Deuteronomy about the forty years of lost time. Numbers gives examples of the people's rebellions against Moses (Num. 16; 17). It is likely that the list of the wanderings in Num. 33:18–49, after they left Hazeroth and the wilderness of Paran, indicates where the tabernacle was set up and the core of the people stayed. As for the rebellious majority, they may have fanned out over the peninsula of Sinai with their flocks in order to find forage.

2:1 direction of the Red Sea. Because the term "Red Sea" could include the Gulf of Aqaba (Ex. 13:18 note), this was likely the desert road to the gulf.

traveled around Mount Seir. Or, "we circled around Mount Seir." The Israelites lived a nomadic life. Moses and those with him continued faithfully in the worship of God.

2:4 your brothers, the people of Esau. As explained in v. 8 and in Num. 20:14–21, the Edomites refused peaceful passage, so Israel went around their territory. Deuteronomy adds to the Numbers account that this was the Lord's command. In Moses' day, the Edomites, according to archaeological study, were apparently not living in fixed locations. They were brothers to Israel in nomadic life as well as in ancestry (Gen. 25:25, 26).

2:8 from Elath and Ezion-geber. Stops at Punon, Oboth, and Iye-abarim are mentioned at Num. 33:43, 44. Punon is probably modern Feinan, in the valley south of the Dead Sea, where there is a good spring. Israel was bypassing Edom and Moab and would attack Canaan from the eastern gateway.

2:10–12 The Emim . . . Horites. We know little about these former inhabitants of Transjordan, but their names occur in Gen. 14, the report of the raid of eastern kings throughout this area in the days of Abraham. The Emim, also called Rephaim (or "giants"), lived where Moab later lived; the Zamzummim, also called Rephaim, lived where the Ammonites later lived; and the Horites preceded the Edomites (vv. 10–12, 20–23). The remark that the Emim and Zamzummim were tall like the Anakim (but had nevertheless been conquered) would help the morale of Israel who had yet to conquer the Anakim (the *im* ending of such names is the Hebrew plural suffix). The identity of the Horites is puzzling. An important early people in Mesopotamia were called Hurrians (an equivalent of the Hebrew term translated "Horite"). Some Horites in Canaan seem to have Hurrian names, but their relationship to the Hurrians is unclear.

2:12 possession, which the LORD gave to them. This phrase might seem to be a later insertion after Israel conquered Canaan, but this could as easily have been spoken by Moses after the significant conquest of Transjordan and settlement of the two-and-a-half tribes there.

2:14 thirty-eight years. See note on 1:3.

LORD had sworn to them. 15 For indeed the
hand of the LORD was against them, to
destroy them from the camp, until they
had perished.

16 "So as soon as all the men of war had
perished and were dead from among the
people, 17 the LORD said to me, 18 'Today you
are to cross the border of Moab at Ar. 19 And
when you approach the territory of the people of Ammon, [d] do not harass them or contend with them, for I will not give you any
of the land of the people of Ammon as a
possession, because I have given it to [e] the
sons of Lot for a possession.' 20 (It is also
counted as a land of [f] Rephaim. Rephaim
formerly lived there—but the Ammonites
call them Zamzummim— 21 [g] a people great
and many, and tall as the Anakim; but the
LORD destroyed them before the Ammonites,[1] and they dispossessed them and
settled in their place, 22 as he did for the
people of Esau, who live in Seir, when he
destroyed [h] the Horites before them and
they dispossessed them and settled in their
place even to this day. 23 As for [i] the Avvim,
who lived in villages as far as [j] Gaza, [k] the
Caphtorim, who came from Caphtor,
destroyed them and settled in their place.)
24 'Rise up, set out on your journey and [l] go
over the Valley of the Arnon. Behold, I have
given into your hand Sihon the Amorite,
king of [m] Heshbon, and his land. Begin to
take possession, and [n] contend with him in
battle. 25 This day I will begin to put [o] the
dread and fear of you on the peoples who
are under the whole heaven, who shall hear
the report of you and shall tremble and be
in anguish because of you.'

The Defeat of King Sihon

26 "So I sent messengers from the wilderness of [p] Kedemoth to Sihon the king of
[m] Heshbon, [q] with words of peace, saying,
27 [r] 'Let me pass through your land. I will go
only by the road; I will turn aside neither
to the right nor to the left. 28 [s] You shall sell
me food for money, that I may eat, and
give me water for money, that I may drink.
Only let me pass through on foot, 29 [t] as the
sons of Esau who live in Seir and the
Moabites who live in Ar did for me, until I
go over the Jordan into the land that the
LORD our God is giving to us.' 30 But [u] Sihon
the king of [m] Heshbon would not let us
pass by him, for the LORD your God [v] hardened his spirit and made his heart obstinate, that he might give him into your
hand, as he is this day. 31 And the LORD
said to me, 'Behold, I have begun to give
Sihon and his land over to you. Begin to
take possession, that you may occupy his
land.' 32 Then [w] Sihon came out against us,
he and all his people, to battle at Jahaz.
33 And [x] the LORD our God gave him over to
us, and [y] we defeated him and his sons and
all his people. 34 And we captured all his
cities at that time and devoted to destruction[2] every [z] city, men, women, and children. We left no survivors. 35 Only the
livestock we took as spoil for ourselves,
with the plunder of the cities that we captured. 36 [a] From Aroer, which is on the edge
of the Valley of the Arnon, and from [b] the
city that is in the valley, as far as Gilead,
there was not a city too high for us. [c] The
LORD our God gave all into our hands.
37 Only to the land of the sons of Ammon
you did not draw near, that is, to all the
banks of the river [d] Jabbok and the cities of
the hill country, whatever the LORD our
God had forbidden us.

19 [d] [ver. 9] [e] Gen. 19:36, 38
20 [f] See Gen. 14:5
21 [g] [ver. 10]
22 [h] ver. 22; Gen. 14:6; See Gen. 36:20-30
23 [i] Josh. 13:3, 4 [j] Gen. 10:19; Jer. 25:20 [k] See Gen. 10:14
24 [l] Num. 21:13, 14; Judg. 11:18, 21 [m] Num. 21:27, 28, 30 [n] [ver. 9]
25 [o] ch. 11:25; 28:10; See Ex. 15:14-16; Josh. 2:9-11
26 [p] Josh. 13:18; 1 Chr. 6:79

[m] [See ver. 24 above] [q] [ch. 20:10]
27 [r] Num. 21:21, 22; Judg. 11:19
28 [s] ver. 6; Num. 20:19
29 [t] ver. 5, 9; [ch. 23:3, 4; Num. 20:18; Judg. 11:17, 18]
30 [u] Num. 21:23 [m] [See ver. 24 above] [v] See Ex. 4:21
32 [w] See Num. 21:23-30
33 [x] [ch. 7:2] [y] ch. 29:7
34 [z] ch. 3:6
36 [a] ch. 3:12; 4:48; Josh. 12:2; 13:9, 16; 2 Kin. 10:33 [b] Josh. 13:9, 16; 2 Sam. 24:5 [c] Ps. 44:3
37 [d] ch. 3:16; Gen. 32:22; Num. 21:24; Josh. 12:2; Judg. 11:22

[1] Hebrew *them* [2] That is, set apart (devoted) as an offering to the Lord (for destruction)

as the LORD had sworn. Another clear reference to Numbers, where God swore that the faithless generation would die in the wilderness (Num. 14:21–23).

2:19 the people of Ammon. The kinship with Ammon, as with Moab and Edom, had long been remembered (Gen. 19:37, 38).

2:23 the Avvim. We know nothing of these people. If the Gaza mentioned is the same as the Gaza in southeastern Canaan, then Moses mentions it here only as part of his survey of earlier dislocations of peoples.

the Caphtorim. If Caphtor means Crete, as is usual, then the reference would be to an early and probably local Philistine community (before the later, great Philistine invasion of c. 1200 B.C.), of which the Abimelech in Gen. 20 was perhaps a member (cf. Jer. 47:4).

2:25 fear of you. Israel now is to begin its conquest, but the people are to remember that it is God who goes before. This was to be the emphasis of God's people ever after (cf. Ps. 44:3).

2:27 Let me pass through. The same offer as was given to Edom and Moab. Here, however, it was God's will for Israel to conquer the territory. Sihon refused Moses' offer, but God was in sovereign control as He had been with Pharaoh (Ex. 4:21). Sihon's resistance became Israel's opportunity.

2:32 at Jahaz. About seven miles south of Heshbon, Sihon was beaten and his territory conquered. The cities were put under the ban (i.e., Israel left no survivors, v. 34; Lev. 27:28 note). The calculated effect of the ban in ancient times was to make the inhabitants of an area flee without putting up resistance. Israel was commanded not to use this procedure except in their conquest of Canaan and Transjordan (20:10–15), where the holy nation would be corrupted by the influence of the remaining pagan culture (Ps. 106:34–39).

The Defeat of King Og

3 "Then we turned and went up the way
to Bashan. And [e]Og the king of Bashan
came out against us, he and all his people,
to battle at [f]Edrei. 2 But the LORD said to
me, 'Do not fear him, for I have given him
and all his people and his land into your
hand. And you shall do to him as you did
to [g]Sihon the king of the Amorites, who
lived at Heshbon.' 3 So the LORD our God
gave into our hand Og also, the king of
Bashan, and all his people, [h]and we struck
him down until he had no survivor left.
4 And we took all his cities at that time—
there was not a city that we did not take
from them—sixty cities, [i]the whole region
of Argob, the kingdom of Og in Bashan.
5 All these were cities fortified with high
walls, gates, and bars, besides very many
unwalled villages. 6 And [j]we devoted them
to destruction,[1] as we did to Sihon the king
of Heshbon, devoting to destruction every
[k]city, men, women, and children. 7 But all
the livestock and the spoil of the cities we
took as our plunder. 8 So we took the land
at that time out of the hand of the two
kings of the Amorites who were beyond the
Jordan, from the Valley of the Arnon to
Mount Hermon 9 (the Sidonians call
[l]Hermon [m]Sirion, while the Amorites call it
[n]Senir), 10 all the cities of the [o]tableland and
all Gilead and all Bashan, as far as [p]Salecah
and Edrei, cities of the kingdom of Og in
Bashan. 11 (For [q]only Og the king of Bashan
was left of the remnant of [r]the Rephaim.
Behold, his bed was a bed of iron. Is it not
in [s]Rabbah of the Ammonites? Nine cubits[2]
was its length, and four cubits its breadth,
according to the [t]common cubit.[3])
12 "When we took possession of this land
at that time, I gave to the Reubenites and
the Gadites the territory beginning [u]at
Aroer, which is on the edge of the Valley
of the Arnon, and half the hill country of
Gilead with [v]its cities. 13 [w]The rest of
Gilead, and all Bashan, the kingdom of Og,
that is, [x]all the region of Argob, I gave to
the half-tribe of Manasseh. (All that portion
of Bashan is called the land of [r]Rephaim.
14 [y]Jair the Manassite took all the region of
Argob, that is, Bashan, as far as the border
of [z]the Geshurites and the Maacathites,
and called the villages [a]after his own name,
Havvoth-jair, as it is to this day.) 15 To
Machir [b]I gave Gilead, 16 and to the Reubenites [c]and the Gadites I gave the territory from Gilead as far as the Valley of the
Arnon, with the middle of the valley as a
border, as far over as the river Jabbok, [d]the
border of the Ammonites; 17 the Arabah
also, with the Jordan as the border, from
[e]Chinnereth as far as [f]the Sea of the
Arabah, [g]the Salt Sea, under [h]the slopes of
Pisgah on the east.
18 "And I commanded you at that time,
saying, 'The LORD your God has given you
this land to possess. [i]All your men of valor
shall cross over armed before your brothers, the people of Israel. 19 Only your wives,
your little ones, and your livestock [j](I know
that you have much livestock) shall remain
in the cities that I have given you, 20 [k]until
the LORD gives rest to your brothers, as to
you, and they also occupy the land that the
LORD your God gives them beyond the
Jordan. Then each of you may return to his

Chapter 3
1 [e]ch. 29:7; Num. 21:33, 35 [f]See ch. 1:4
2 [g]See Num. 21:23-26, 34
3 [h]Num. 21:35
4 [i]1 Kin. 4:13
6 [j]See ch. 7:2; Ps. 135:10-12 [k]ch. 2:34
9 [l]ch. 4:48; Josh. 11:3, 17; 12:5 [m]Ps. 29:6; [ch. 4:48] [n]1 Chr. 5:23; S. of S. 4:8; Ezek. 27:5
10 [o]ch. 4:43; Josh. 13:9, 16, 17, 21; Jer. 48:8, 21 [p]Josh. 12:5; 13:11; 1 Chr. 5:11
11 [q]ch. 2:11, 20 [r]See Gen. 14:5 [s]2 Sam. 11:1; 12:26; Jer. 49:2; Ezek. 21:20; 25:5; Amos 1:14 [t][Rev. 21:17]
12 [u]See ch. 2:36 [v]See Num. 32:32-38; Josh. 13:8-13
13 [w]See Num. 32:39-42; Josh. 13:29-31 [x]1 Kin. 4:13
14 [y]Num. 32:41; [1 Chr. 2:22, 23] [z]Josh 12:5; 13:11, 13; 2 Sam. 3:3; 10:6; 13:37, 38 [a]Num. 32:41
15 [b]Num. 32:39
16 [c][2 Sam. 24:5] [d]Num. 21:24; Josh. 12:2
17 [e]See Num. 34:11 [f]ch. 4:49; Josh. 3:16; 12:3; 2 Kin. 14:25 [g]See Gen. 14:3 [h][Num. 21:15]
18 [i]Num. 32:20, 21; Josh. 1:14; 4:12 19 [j]Num. 32:1, 4 20 [k]Josh. 22:4

[1] That is, set apart (devoted) as an offering to the Lord (for destruction); twice in this verse [2] A *cubit* was about 18 inches or 45 centimeters [3] Hebrew *cubit of a man*

3:1 Og the king of Bashan. Bashan was a fertile region located east of the Jordan and the Sea of Galilee, and extending from the Yarmuk River in the south to Mount Hermon in the north. It is wheat country today and in ancient time was famous for its cattle and flocks (Ps. 22:12; Deut. 32:14). The spoil of this area must have seemed a treasure to the nomadic Israelites.

3:8 beyond the Jordan. The east side of the river. This territory was in extent more than half as large as Canaan proper. From the Arnon River to Mount Hermon is about 150 miles.

3:9 Sirion . . . Senir. Both terms for Mount Hermon are witnessed in ancient Canaanite and Mesopotamian texts.

3:11 a bed of iron. Og's bed, thirteen feet long, suggests he was a giant and that his people, the Rephaim, were also giants (2:10–12 note). The "bed" may actually have been a sarcophagus; the word translated "bed" is rare and could here be a euphemism for a sarcophagus, which would be large enough also to hold tomb objects. The reference to "iron" may only mean that it was joined or trimmed with iron, a new material at this date (before the beginning of the Iron Age c. 1200 B.C.). See note 8:9.

3:12 the Reubenites and the Gadites. These tribes received the southern part of the conquered Transjordan area. Sparsely populated in the modern period, it was more thickly settled in ancient times. Recent excavations have shown a surprising number of Christian churches here before and even after the Muslim conquest.

3:13 half-tribe of Manasseh. The north half of Gilead, beginning near Zarethan, and all of Bashan went to this half-tribe.

3:14 Jair the Manassite. Manasseh had but one son, Machir, and he had one son, Gilead (Num. 26:29–34). Jair's conquest is mentioned in Num. 32:41.

3:18 All your men of valor shall cross. Note the required unity. None could settle until all had conquered. Details are given in Num. 32. See the fulfillment of the pledge in Josh. 22.

possession which I have given you.' 21 And
I commanded [l]Joshua at that time, 'Your
eyes have seen all that the LORD your God
has done to these two kings. So will the
LORD do to all the kingdoms into which
you are crossing. 22 You shall not fear them,
for it is [m]the LORD your God who fights for
you.'

Moses Forbidden to Enter the Land

23 "And I pleaded with the LORD at that
time, saying, 24 'O Lord GOD, you have only
begun to show your servant [n]your greatness and your mighty hand. For [o]what god
is there in heaven or on earth who can do
such works and mighty acts as yours?
25 Please let me go over and see [p]the good
land beyond the Jordan, that good hill
country and [q]Lebanon.' 26 But [r]the LORD
was angry with me because of you and
would not listen to me. And the LORD said
to me, [s]'Enough from you; do not speak to
me of this matter again. 27 [t]Go up to the top
of Pisgah and lift up your eyes westward
and northward and southward and eastward, and look at it with your eyes, for you
shall not go over this Jordan. 28 But [u]charge
Joshua, and encourage and strengthen
him, for he shall go over at the head of this
people, and he shall put them in possession of the land that you shall see.' 29 So we
remained in [v]the valley opposite Beth-peor.

Moses Commands Obedience

4 "And now, O Israel, listen to [w]the
statutes and the rules that I am teaching
you, and do them, [x]that you may live, and go
in and take possession of the land that the
LORD, the God of your fathers, is giving you.
2 [y]You shall not add to the word that I command you, nor take from it, that you may
keep the commandments of the LORD your
God that I command you. 3 Your eyes have
seen what the LORD did [z]at Baal-peor, for the
LORD your God destroyed from among you
all the men who followed the Baal of Peor.
4 But you who held fast to the LORD your God
are all alive today. 5 See, I have taught you
statutes and rules, as the LORD my God commanded me, that you should do them in the
land that you are entering to take possession
of it. 6 [a]Keep them and do them, for [b]that will
be your wisdom and your understanding in
the sight of the peoples, who, when they
hear all these statutes, will say, 'Surely this
great nation is a wise and understanding
people.' 7 For [c]what great nation is there that
has [d]a god so near to it as the LORD our God
is to us, whenever we call upon him? 8 And
what great nation is there, that has statutes
and rules so [e]righteous as all this law that I
set before you today?
9 [f]"Only take care, and [g]keep your soul
diligently, lest you forget the things that
your eyes have seen, and lest they depart
from your heart all the days of your life.
[h]Make them known to your children and
your children's children— 10 how on [i]the day
that you stood before the LORD your God at
Horeb, the LORD said to me, [j]'Gather the
people to me, that I may let them hear my
words, [k]so that they may learn to fear [l]me all
the days that they live on the earth, and that
they may teach their children so.' 11 And
[m]you came near and stood at the foot of the
mountain, while [n]the mountain burned
with fire to the heart of heaven, wrapped in
darkness, cloud, and gloom. 12 Then [o]the
LORD spoke to you out of the midst of the
fire. You heard the sound of words, [p]but saw
no form; [q]there was only a voice. 13 [r]And he
declared to you his covenant, which he

21 [l][Num. 27:18] 22 [m]See Ex. 14:14 24 [n]ch. 5:24; 11:2; 32:3; 1 Chr. 29:11 [o]See Ex. 15:11 25 [p]ch. 4:22; Ex. 3:8 [q][Josh. 1:4] 26 [r]See ch. 1:37 [s][2 Cor. 12:9] 27 [t]Num. 27:12, 13 28 [u]ch. 1:38; 31:3, 7; Num. 27:23 29 [v]ch. 4:46; 34:6
Chapter 4
1 [w]See Lev. 18:4 [x]ch. 6:24; 8:1 2 [y]ch. 12:32; [Josh. 1:7; Prov. 30:6; Rev. 22:18, 19] 3 [z]See Num. 23:28; 25:3-9 6 [a]ch. 29:9 [b]Job 28:28; Ps. 111:10; Prov. 1:7; 9:10 7 [c]2 Sam. 7:23 [d]Ps. 34:18; 46:1; 145:18; 148:14; [James 4:8] 8 [e]Rom. 7:12 9 [f]ver. 23 [g][Prov. 4:23] [h]ch. 6:7; 11:19; 32:46; Gen. 18:19; See Ps. 78:4-6 10 [i]Ex. 19:9, 16; Heb. 12:18, 19 [j]ch. 31:12 [k]ch. 14:23; 17:19 [l]ch. 12:1; 31:13; 1 Kin. 8:40 11 [m]Ex. 19:17 [n]ch. 5:22, 23; Ex. 19:18; 20:18, 21; [Ex. 24:16, 17] 12 [o]ver. 33, 36; ch. 5:4, 22; Ex. 20:1, 19 [p]ver. 15 [q]Ex. 20:22; [1 Kin. 19:12; Job 4:16] 13 [r]ch. 9:9, 11

3:22 the LORD your God . . . fights for you. As Moses passed the command to Joshua, he emphasized the promise: the Lord will give victory.

3:23–28 Moses' prayer in vv. 24, 25 is instructive. He knew of the Lord's anger because of his sin at Meribah (Num. 20:12), but he also knew that God does not "keep his anger forever" (cf. Ps. 103:9). Moses recognized God's great sovereign power and asked for great mercy.

4:2 You shall not add. The word of God to Moses was to be treated as sacred and kept inviolate (12:32). See the similar certification in Rev. 22:18, 19, quite possibly modeled on this prohibition in Deuteronomy.

4:3 Baal-peor. A dreadful warning. The reference is to Num. 25, which details the idolatry at Baal-peor that God judged by killing twenty-four thousand people.

4:6 the peoples. Israel's fidelity would be a testimony to the world that God was near His people and that His laws were righteous.

4:9 Make them known to your children. Deuteronomy stresses the covenant responsibility of parents for their children (6:7; 11:19). This covenant concern for children continues in the New Testament (Matt. 19:14 note; Acts 2:39).

4:10 how on the day that you stood. A reference to the great theophany (visible self-revelation of God) at Mount Sinai recorded in Ex. 19:9–20:19. It was a never-to-be-forgotten experience.

4:13 the Ten Commandments. This title is used also in 10:4 and Ex. 34:28. Protestants usually divide them into four commandments dealing with duty to God and six that give our duty to man. Roman Catholics unite the first and second and divide the tenth resulting in a division of three and seven. The command regarding the Sabbath is pivotal: it has reference to God and also is for the benefit of both men and animals (Mark 2:27); the first three commandments concern God exclusively, the last six deal with humans.

commanded you to perform, that is, [s]the
Ten Commandments,[1] [t]and he wrote them
on two tablets of stone. **14** And [u]the LORD
commanded me at that time to teach you
statutes and rules, that you might do them
in the land that you are going over to
possess.

Idolatry Forbidden

15 [v]"Therefore watch yourselves very carefully. Since [w]you saw no form on the day
that the LORD spoke to you at Horeb out of
the midst of the fire, **16** beware [x]lest you act
corruptly [y]by making a carved image for
yourselves, in the form of any figure, [z]the
likeness of male or female, **17** the likeness of
any animal that is on the earth, the likeness
of any winged bird that flies in the air, **18** the
likeness of anything that creeps on the
ground, the likeness of any fish that is in
the water under the earth. **19** And beware
lest you raise your eyes to heaven, and
when you see [a]the sun and the moon and
the stars, [b]all the host of heaven, you be
drawn away and bow down to them and
serve them, things that the LORD your God
has allotted to all the peoples under the
whole heaven. **20** But the LORD has taken
you and [c]brought you out of the iron furnace, out of Egypt, [d]to be a people of his
own inheritance, as you are this day.
21 Furthermore, [e]the LORD was angry with
me because of you, and he swore that I
should not cross the Jordan, and that I
should not enter the good land that the
LORD your God is giving you for an inheritance. **22** For I must die in this land; [f]I must
not go over the Jordan. But you shall go
over and take possession of [g]that good land.
23 [h]Take care, lest you forget the covenant of
the LORD your God, which he made with
you, and [i]make a carved image, the form of
anything that the LORD your God has forbidden you. **24** For [j]the LORD your God is a
consuming fire, [k]a jealous God.

25 "When you father children and children's children, and have grown old in the
land, [l]if you act corruptly by making a
carved image in the form of anything, and
[m]by doing what is evil in the sight of the
LORD your God, so as to provoke him to
anger, **26** I [n]call heaven and earth to witness
against you today, that you will soon utterly perish from the land that you are going
over the Jordan to possess. You will not live
long in it, but will be utterly destroyed.
27 And the LORD [o]will scatter you among the
peoples, [p]and you will be left few in number among the nations where the LORD will
drive you. **28** And [q]there you will serve gods
of wood and stone, the work of human
hands, [r]that neither see, nor hear, nor eat,
nor smell. **29** [s]But from there you will seek
the LORD your God and you will find him,
if you search after him with all your heart
and with all your soul. **30** When you are in
tribulation, and all these things come upon
you [t]in the latter days, you will return to
the LORD your God and obey his voice.
31 For the LORD your God is [u]a merciful
God. [v]He will not leave you or destroy you
or forget the covenant with your fathers
that he swore to them.

The LORD Alone Is God

32 "For [w]ask now of the days that are past,
which were before you, since the day that
God created man on the earth, and ask
from one end of heaven to the other,
whether such a great thing as this has ever
happened or was ever heard of. **33** [x]Did any

13 [s]Ex. 34:28 [t]See Ex. 24:12
14 [u]See Ex. ch. 21–23
15 [v]Josh. 23:11 [w]ver. 12
16 [x]ver. 25 [y]ver. 23; ch. 5:8; Ex. 20:4; [Acts 17:29] [z]Rom. 1:23
19 [a]ch. 17:3; Job 31:26-28 [b]2 Kin. 17:16; 21:3; [Gen. 2:1]
20 [c]1 Kin. 8:51; Jer. 11:4 [d]ch. 9:29; 32:9
21 [e]See ch. 1:37
22 [f]ch. 3:27 [g]ch. 3:25
23 [h]ver. 9 [i]ver. 23; ch. 5:8; Ex. 20:4; [Acts 17:29]
24 [j]Ex. 24:17; Cited Heb. 12:29; [ch. 9:3; Isai. 10:16-18; 29:6; 30:27, 30; Zeph. 1:18] [k][Isai. 42:8]; See Ex. 20:5
25 [l]ver. 16 [m]ch. 9:18; 2 Kin. 17:17
26 [n]ch. 30:18, 19; 31:28; 32:1; Isai. 1:2; Jer. 2:12; 6:19; Mic. 6:2
27 [o]See Lev. 26:33 [p]ch. 28:62
28 [q]ch. 28:36, 64; Jer. 16:13 [r]Ps. 115:4-7; 135:15-17; Isai. 44:9; 46:7
29 [s]ch. 30:2, 3; Lev. 26:40-42; 2 Chr. 15:4; Neh. 1:9; Isai. 55:6, 7; Jer. 29:13, 14
30 [t]See Gen. 49:1
31 [u]Ex. 34:6; 2 Chr. 30:9; Neh. 9:31; Jonah 4:2 [v]ch. 31:6, 8; Josh. 1:5; 1 Chr. 28:20 **32** [w]Job 8:8 **33** [x]ver. 12; ch. 5:24, 26; Ex. 3:6; 19:21; [Gen. 32:30; Ex. 24:11; 33:20, 23; Judg. 6:22, 23; 13:22]

1 Hebrew *words*

4:15 you saw no form. God is transcendent Spirit (John 4:24), which rules out any idolatrous representation of God in the form of animate objects (vv. 16–18), and any worship of the created order (v. 19).

4:20 the iron furnace. A hot furnace used to smelt iron, a vivid metaphor for a place of great suffering (8:9 note).

4:21 the LORD was angry with me. See 1:37; 3:26; Num. 20:12.

4:24 a jealous God. See note Ex. 20:5.

4:25–29 Here in brief form is found the warning embodied in the curses of 28:15–68. But here also is a promise to the repentant.

4:27 the LORD will scatter you. Such passages have been taken by some as indication that Deuteronomy was not written by Moses, but by someone in the sixth century B.C. during the Jewish exile in Babylon. However, the warning is general, and there is no mention of captivity in Babylon or of conditions in that later period.

4:30 the latter days. This phrase, repeated in 31:29, refers to any general future time of apostasy and renewal (cf. Num. 24:14).

4:31 a merciful God. This description may allude to the name of God given in Ex. 34:6 ("the LORD, a God merciful"). The theme of God's love for His people is highlighted in Deuteronomy (7:7–9, 13; 10:15, 18; 23:5; 33:3), anticipating the more complete revelation of God's love in the New Testament (John 3:16; Rom. 5:8; Eph. 2:4, 5; 1 John 3:1).

the covenant with your fathers. See 1:8.

4:32 the day that God created man. Except for the creation account in the early chapters of Genesis, this is the only mention of the creation of man in the Pentateuch.

people ever hear the voice of a god speaking
out of the midst of the fire, as you have
heard, and still live? 34 Or has any god ever
attempted to go and take a nation for himself from the midst of another nation, by
trials, [y]by signs, by wonders, and [z]by war,
[a]by a mighty hand and [b]an outstretched
arm, and by great deeds of terror, all of
which the LORD your God did for you in
Egypt before your eyes? 35 To you it was
shown, [c]that you might know that the LORD
is God; [d]there is no other besides him.
36 [e]Out of heaven he let you hear his voice,
that he might discipline you. And on earth
he let you see his great fire, and [x]you heard
his words out of the midst of the fire. 37 And
because [f]he loved your fathers and chose
their offspring after them[1] and brought you
out of Egypt [g]with his own presence, by his
great power, 38 [h]driving out before you
nations greater and mightier than yourselves, to bring you in, to give you their
land for an inheritance, as it is this day,
39 know therefore today, and lay it to your
heart, that [i]the LORD is God in heaven
above and on the earth beneath; [j]there is no
other. 40 [k]Therefore you shall keep his
statutes and his commandments, which I
command you today, [l]that it may go well
with you and with your children after you,
and that you may prolong your days in the
land that the LORD your God is giving you
for all time."

Cities of Refuge

41 Then Moses [m]set apart three cities in
the east beyond the Jordan, 42 that [n]the
manslayer might flee there, anyone who
kills his neighbor unintentionally, without
being at enmity with him in time past; he
may flee to one of these cities and save his
life: 43 [o]Bezer in the wilderness on the
[p]tableland for the Reubenites, Ramoth in
Gilead for the Gadites, and Golan in
Bashan for the Manassites.

Introduction to the Law

44 This is the law that Moses set before
the people of Israel. 45 These are the testimonies, the statutes, and the rules, which
Moses spoke to the people of Israel when
they came out of Egypt, 46 beyond the
Jordan [q]in the valley opposite Beth-peor,
in the land of Sihon the king of the
Amorites, who lived at Heshbon, [r]whom
Moses and the people of Israel defeated
when they came out of Egypt. 47 And they
took possession of his land and the land
[s]of Og, the king of Bashan, the two kings
of the Amorites, who lived to the east
beyond the Jordan; 48 [t]from Aroer, which is
on the edge of the Valley of the Arnon, as
far as Mount [u]Sirion[2] (that is, [v]Hermon),
49 together with all the Arabah on the east
side of the Jordan as far as [w]the Sea of the
Arabah, under the slopes of Pisgah.

The Ten Commandments

5 And Moses summoned all Israel and
said to them, "Hear, O Israel, the
statutes and the rules that I speak in your
hearing today, and you shall learn them
and be careful to do them. 2 [x]The LORD our
God made a covenant with us in Horeb.
3 [y]Not with our fathers did the LORD make
this covenant, but with us, who are all of
us here alive today. 4 The LORD spoke with
you [z]face to face at the mountain, out of
the midst of the fire, 5 [a]while I stood

34 [y]ch. 26:8; Ex. 7:3; Jer. 32:21 [z]See Ex. 15:3-10 [a]ch. 7:8; 11:2; 26:8; 34:12 [b]Ex. 6:6; Jer. 32:21 **35** [c][Ex. 10:2] [d]ver. 39; 1 Sam. 2:2; 2 Sam. 22:32; Isai. 45:5, 18, 22; 46:9; Cited Mark 12:32 **36** [e]Ex. 19:9, 19; Neh. 9:13 [x][See ver. 33 above] **37** [f]ch. 10:15 [g]Ex. 33:14; [Isai. 63:9] **38** [h]ch. 7:1; 11:23; Ex. 23:27, 28; 34:24; See ch. 9:1-5 **39** [i]Josh. 2:11; 1 Kin. 8:23; 2 Chr. 20:6; Eccles. 5:2 [j]ver. 39; 1 Sam. 2:2; 2 Sam. 22:32; Isai. 45:5, 18, 22; 46:9; Cited Mark 12:32 **40** [k]Lev. 22:31 [l]ch. 5:16; 6:2, 3; 11:9; 12:25, 28; 22:7; [Prov. 3:1, 2; 10:27] **41** [m]Num. 35:6, 14 **42** [n]ch. 19:4 **43** [o]Josh. 20:8; 21:36; 1 Chr. 6:78 [p]See ch. 3:10 **46** [q]ch. 3:29 [r]ch. 1:4; Num. 21:24 **47** [s]ch. 3:3, 4; Num. 21:33, 35 **48** [t]See ch. 2:36 [u][ch. 3:9] [v]See ch. 3:9 **49** [w]See ch. 3:17

Chapter 5 **2** [x]ch. 4:23; Ex. 19:5 **3** [y][Heb. 8:9] **4** [z][ch. 34:10; Ex. 33:11; Num. 14:14; Judg. 6:22] **5** [a]Ex. 20:21; [Gal. 3:19]

[1] Hebrew *his offspring after him* [2] Syriac; Hebrew *Sion*

4:34 in Egypt. A reference to the deliverance from Egypt, a topic repeatedly mentioned in Deuteronomy.

4:37 his own presence. See Ex. 33:14.

4:41–43 This parenthetical section, in narrative style, marks the close of the first great speech. Moses names the cities of refuge for Transjordan. The principle of having cities of refuge was given in Ex. 21:13; that there should be six was stated in Num. 35:6. This section names the three for Transjordan, while 19:1–13 specifies that three should be designated for Canaan itself. Finally, all six cities are named in Josh. 20:7, 8. This progressive unfolding is consistent with Mosaic authorship and an indication that Deuteronomy was not written after the conquest of Canaan.

4:44–11:32 In this his second address (and in the section to follow, chs. 12–26), Moses expounds the way of life in the covenant. The exposition focuses on love for the Lord, love that issues in obedience and consecration, as exemplified among the Levites set apart for service to the Lord. The sermon closes with a preview of the solemn declaration of covenant obligations elaborated in chs. 27–30.

4:45 testimonies . . . statutes . . . rules. Note the use of covenantal language. This portion of Deuteronomy, with its listing of covenantal requirements, resembles the stipulation sections of ancient treaties, especially those of the second millennium B.C. (Introduction: Date and Occasion).

4:49 the slopes of Pisgah. See the similar area description in 3:17.

5:1 Hear, O Israel. This solemn form of address to Israel is only found in Deuteronomy: first here, then in the great *Shema* of 6:4, and finally in the exhortation of 9:1–3. Here the foundational covenant at Mount Sinai in Horeb is recalled.

5:3 Not with our fathers. Moses is differentiating the Sinai covenant from the promise of the land made to the patriarchs, Abraham, Isaac, and Jacob. It was not the patriarchs who stood before God at Sinai, but the Israelites of Moses' day (11:2 note).

between the LORD and you at that time, to
declare to you the word of the LORD. For
[b]you were afraid because of the fire, and
you did not go up into the mountain. He
said:
6 [c]" 'I am the LORD your God, who
brought you out of the land of Egypt, out
of the house of slavery.
7 " 'You shall have no other gods before[1] me.
8 " 'You shall not make for yourself a
carved image, or any likeness of anything
that is in heaven above, or that is on the
earth beneath, or that is in the water under
the earth. 9 You shall not bow down to
them or serve them; for I the LORD your
God am a jealous God, visiting the iniquity
of the fathers on the children to the third
and fourth generation of those who hate
me, 10 but showing steadfast love to [d]thou-
sands[2] of those who love me and keep my
commandments.
11 " 'You shall not take the name of the
LORD your God in vain, for the LORD will
not hold him guiltless who takes his name
in vain.
12 " 'Observe the Sabbath day, to keep it
holy, as the LORD your God commanded
you. 13 Six days you shall labor and do all
your work, 14 but [e]the seventh day is a
Sabbath to the LORD your God. On it you
shall not do any work, you or your son or
your daughter or your male servant or your
female servant, or your ox or your donkey
or any of your livestock, or the sojourner
who is within your gates, [f]that your male
servant and your female servant may rest as
well as you. 15 [g]You shall remember that
you were a slave[3] in the land of Egypt, and
the LORD your God brought you out from
there [h]with a mighty hand and an outstretched arm. Therefore the LORD your
God commanded you to keep the Sabbath
day.
16 " 'Honor your father and your mother,
as the LORD your God commanded you,
[i]that your days may be long, and that it
may go well with you in the land that the
LORD your God is giving you.
17 [j]" 'You shall not murder.[4]
18 [j]" 'And you shall not commit adultery.
19 " 'And you shall not steal.
20 " 'And you shall not bear false witness
against your neighbor.
21 " 'And you shall not covet your neighbor's wife. And you shall not desire your
neighbor's house, his field, or his male servant, or his female servant, his ox, or his
donkey, or anything that is your neighbor's.'
22 "These words the LORD spoke to all
your assembly [k]at the mountain out of the
midst of the fire, the cloud, and the thick
darkness, with a loud voice; and he added
no more. And [l]he wrote them on two
tablets of stone and gave them to me.
23 And [m]as soon as you heard the voice out
of the midst of the darkness, while the
mountain was burning with fire, you came
near to me, all the heads of your tribes, and
your elders. 24 And you said, 'Behold, the
LORD our God has shown us his glory and
[n]greatness, and [o]we have heard his voice
out of the midst of the fire. This day we
have seen God speak with man and man
[p]still live. 25 Now therefore why should we

1 Or *besides* 2 Or *to the thousandth generation* 3 Or *servant*
4 The Hebrew word also covers causing human death through carelessness or negligence

5 [b]Ex. 19:16; 20:18; 24:2
6 [c]For ver. 6-21, see Ex. 20:2-17
10 [d]Ex. 20:6; Jer. 32:18
14 [e]Ex. 16:29, 30; Heb. 4:4 [f][Ex. 23:12]
15 [g]ch. 15:15; 16:12; 24:18, 22 [h]See ch. 4:34
16 [i]See ch. 4:40
17 [j]Matt. 5:21, 27; Luke 18:20; James 2:11
18 [j][See ver. 17 above]
22 [k]See ch. 4:11 [l]ch. 9:10, 11; Ex. 24:12
23 [m]See ch. 4:12
24 [n]See ch. 3:24 [o]Ex. 19:19 [p]See ch. 4:33

5:6–21 See Ex. 20:2–17 and notes.

5:7 no other gods. The exalted monotheism of this commandment and of the whole Old Testament was unique in ancient times. There are no other gods (4:39), and the worship of anything other than God Himself is forbidden.

5:8 a carved image. See 4:15; note on Ex. 20:4.

5:10 to thousands. Whereas God's anger extends only to the third and fourth generation, His love extends to a thousand generations (7:9).

5:12–15 See "God's Pattern for Worship" at 1 Chr. 16:29.

5:12 Observe the Sabbath day. Most of the commandments in Deuteronomy parallel almost verbatim those in Exodus, with obvious interdependence. Deuteronomy bases this command on the deliverance from the bondage of Egypt, whereas Exodus cites God's work of creation as a basis. The continuing sabbatical principle commands a weekly day of rest. The change from the seventh day to the first day or Lord's Day by the New Testament church (Rev. 1:10), in celebration of Christ's resurrection, points to the inauguration of the new creation (1 Cor. 15:45–49; 2 Cor. 5:17; cf. Ex. 20:11), and to the believer's redemption from bondage to sin through the death and resurrection of Christ.

5:16 that your days may be long. Other passages suggest that this clause may primarily be a promise of settled conditions and long peace for the people in the land, which would also include freedom from early death in war and revolution (5:33; 30:18, 20; cf. 25:15).

5:22 and he added no more. Lit. "and He did not add," perhaps an idiom meaning that He spoke no more. This would fit the statement in Exodus, that the people in their fear asked that God speak no more to them directly, but only through Moses (Ex. 20:19).

two tablets of stone. The tablets are mentioned in Ex. 31:18, where they are called the "two tablets of the testimony . . . written with the finger of God." In addition, the tablets were inscribed on both sides (Ex. 32:15). These tablets were broken (Ex. 32:19), but new ones were made (Ex. 34:1–4, 27). Called "the testimony," the tablets were placed in the ark of the testimony (Ex. 25:16; 40:20), also called the "ark of the covenant" (Num. 10:33). The "testimony" was the written record attesting the terms of the covenant (Ex. 25:16 note).

die? For this great fire will consume us. [q]If
we hear the voice of the LORD our God any
more, we shall die. 26 [p]For who is there of
all flesh, that has heard the voice of the living God speaking out of the midst of fire as
we have, and has still lived? 27 Go near and
hear all that the LORD our God will say and
[r]speak to us all that the LORD our God will
speak to you, and we will hear and do it.'
28 "And the LORD heard your words,
when you spoke to me. And the LORD said
to me, 'I have heard the words of this people, which they have spoken to you. [s]They
are right in all that they have spoken. 29 [t]Oh
that they had such a mind as this always,
to fear me and to keep all my commandments, [u]that it might go well with them
and with their descendants[1] forever! 30 Go
and say to them, "Return to your tents."
31 But you, stand here by me, and [v]I will tell
you the whole commandment and the
statutes and the rules that you shall teach
them, that they may do them in the land
that I am giving them to possess.' 32 You
shall be careful therefore to do as the LORD
your God has commanded you. [w]You shall
not turn aside to the right hand or to the
left. 33 [x]You shall walk in all the way that
the LORD your God has commanded you,
that you may live, and [y]that it may go well
with you, and that you may live long in the
land that you shall possess.

The Greatest Commandment

6 "Now this is [z]the commandment, the
statutes and the rules that the LORD
your God commanded me to teach you,
that you may do them in the land to which
you are going over, to possess it, 2 that [a]you
may fear the LORD your God, you and your
son and your son's son, by keeping all his
statutes and his commandments, which I
command you, all the days of your life, and
[b]that your days may be long. 3 Hear therefore, O Israel, and be careful to do them,
that it may go well with you, and that you
may multiply greatly, [c]as the LORD, the God
of your fathers, has promised you, in a land
flowing with milk and honey.
4 "Hear, O Israel: [d]The LORD our God, the
LORD is one.[2] 5 You [e]shall love the LORD
your God with all your heart and with all
your soul and with all your might. 6 And
[f]these words that I command you today
shall be on your heart. 7 [g]You shall teach
them diligently to your children, and shall
talk of them when you sit in your house,
and when you walk by the way, and when
you lie down, and when you rise. 8 [h]You
shall bind them as a sign on your hand,
and they shall be as frontlets between your
eyes. 9 [i]You shall write them on the doorposts of your house and on your gates.
10 "And when the LORD your God brings
you into the land that he swore to your
fathers, to Abraham, to Isaac, and to Jacob,
to give you—with great and good cities [j]that
you did not build, 11 and houses full of all
good things that you did not fill, and cisterns
that you did not dig, and vineyards and olive
trees that you did not plant—and when you
eat and are full, 12 [k]then take care lest you
forget the LORD, who brought you out of the
land of Egypt, out of the house of slavery. 13 It
is [l]the LORD your God you shall fear. Him
you shall serve and [m]by his name you shall

25 [q]ch. 18:16
26 [p][See ver. 24 above]
27 [r]See Ex. 20:19
28 [s]ch. 18:17
29 [t]ch. 32:29; Ps. 81:13; Isai. 48:18; [Matt. 23:37; Luke 19:42] [u]See ch. 4:40
31 [v]Gal. 3:19
32 [w]ch. 17:20; 28:14; Josh. 1:7; 23:6; 2 Kin. 22:2; Prov. 4:27
33 [x]ch. 10:12; 30:16; Jer. 7:23; [Luke 1:6] [y]See ch. 4:40

Chapter 6
1 [z]ch. 4:1; 5:31; 12:1
2 [a]ch. 5:29; 10:12, 20; 13:4; Ps. 128:1; Eccles. 12:13

[b]See ch. 4:40
3 [c]Gen. 15:5; 22:17; 26:4; 28:14; Ex. 32:13
4 [d]Cited Mark 12:29; [Isai. 42:8; Zech. 14:9; John 17:3; 1 Cor. 8:4, 6]
5 [e]Cited Matt. 22:37; Mark 12:30; Luke 10:27; [2 Kin. 23:25]
6 [f]ch. 11:18; 32:46; Ps. 37:31; Isai. 51:7; Jer. 31:33
7 [g]See ch. 4:9
8 [h]ch. 11:18; Prov. 3:3; 6:21; 7:3; See Ex. 13:9
9 [i]ch. 11:20; [Isai. 57:8]
10 [j]Josh. 24:13; [Josh. 11:13; Neh. 9:25; Ps. 105:44]
12 [k][Prov. 30:8, 9] 13 [l]Cited Matt. 4:10; Luke 4:8 [m]ch. 10:20; Josh. 2:12; Ps. 63:11; Isai. 45:23; 65:16; Jer. 12:16

1 Or *sons* 2 Or *The LORD our God is one LORD*; or *The LORD is our God, the LORD is one*; or *The LORD is our God, the LORD alone*

6:2 days may be long. These words translate the same Hebrew phrase as in 5:33. Here also we may understand the meaning as "long life in the land."

6:4 Hear, O Israel. Often called the *Shema*, from the initial Hebrew word meaning "Hear," this verse became the great confession of Israel's monotheistic faith, and is recited morning and evening by Jews (cf. Mark 12:29). See note 5:1.

The LORD . . . LORD is one. Though the Hebrew may be translated several ways (text note), it is best to understand the verse as affirming both God's uniqueness and unity or singularity—the only God is "one" (Mark 12:29). As the Old Testament implies and the New Testament explicitly teaches, however, there is differentiation of Persons within the unity of the Godhead. See "One and Three: The Trinity" at Is. 44:6.

6:5 all your might. The Hebrew expresses totality. For this reason the New Testament sometimes renders it with "mind and strength" (Mark 12:30). This is the language of devotion. God does not demand mere outward obedience to a law, but the heartfelt love and commitment of the whole person (Prov. 23:26).

6:7 children. See "The Christian Family" at Eph. 5:22.

6:8 frontlets between your eyes. The phrases in this section are multiplied to emphasize the overall importance of God's law. Jews since the time of Christ have taken these verses literally and tie little boxes containing these verses on their arms and foreheads, and fasten them on their doorposts (cf. Matt. 23:5).

6:10 the land that he swore to your fathers. See 5:3 and note. This is one of many references in Deuteronomy to God's solemn promise to the patriarchs.

6:13 by his name you shall swear. The third commandment does not forbid taking an oath on the name of God (cf. Judg. 8:19), but forbids a false oath. Because swearing by the name of a god implied the recognition and worship of that god, the Israelites were not to swear by other gods (cf. Jer. 5:7; Zeph. 1:5).

swear. 14You shall not [n]go after other gods,
[o]the gods of the peoples who are around
you, 15for [p]the LORD your God in your midst
[q]is a jealous God, [r]lest the anger of the LORD
your God be kindled against you, and he
destroy you from off the face of the earth.
16[s]"You shall not put the LORD your God
to the test, [t]as you tested him at Massah.
17You shall [u]diligently keep the commandments of the LORD your God, and his testimonies and his statutes, which he has
commanded you. 18[v]And you shall do what
is right and good in the sight of the LORD,
that it may go well with you, and that you
may go in and take possession of the good
land that the LORD swore to give to your
fathers 19[w]by thrusting out all your enemies
from before you, as the LORD has promised.
20[x]"When your son asks you in time to
come, 'What is the meaning of the testimonies and the statutes and the rules that
the LORD our God has commanded you?'
21then you shall say to your son, [y]'We were
Pharaoh's slaves in Egypt. And the LORD
brought us out of Egypt with a mighty hand.
22And [z]the LORD showed signs and wonders,
great and grievous, against Egypt and against
Pharaoh and all his household, before our
eyes. 23And he brought us out from there,
that he might bring us in and give us the
land that he swore to give to our fathers.
24And the LORD commanded us to do all
these statutes, [a]to fear the LORD our God,
[b]for our good always, that [c]he might preserve
us alive, as we are this day. 25And [d]it will be
righteousness for us, if we are careful to do
all this commandment before the LORD our
God, as he has commanded us.'

14[n]ch. 8:19; 11:16, 28; 13:2, 3; 28:14; Jer. 25:6 [o]ch. 13:7
15[p]ch. 7:21 [q]See Ex. 20:5 [r]ch. 7:4; 11:17
16[s]Cited Matt. 4:7; Luke 4:12 [t]ch. 9:22; 33:8; Ps. 95:8; [1 Cor. 10:9]; See Ex. 17:2-7
17[u]ch. 11:22; Ps. 119:4
18[v]See ch. 12:25
19[w]Ex. 23:28-30; Num. 33:52, 53
20[x]Ex. 12:26; 13:14
21[y][Ex. 20:2]
22[z]Ps. 135:9; See ch. 4:34
24[a]ver. 2, 13 [b]ch. 10:13; Jer. 32:39 [c]ch. 4:1; 8:1; [Lev. 18:5; Ps. 41:2]
25[d]ch. 24:13
Chapter 7
1[e]ch. 31:3; Ps. 44:2, 3 [f]See Ex. 23:23 [g]ch. 4:38; 9:1; 11:23
2[h]ver. 23; ch. 23:14 [i]ch. 20:17; Ex. 22:20; Lev. 27:29; Num. 21:2, 3 [j]Ex. 23:32; 34:12; Judg. 2:2; [ch. 20:10; Josh. 2:14; 9:18; Judg. 1:24]
3[k]Ex. 34:16; Josh. 23:12, 13; 1 Kin. 11:2; [Ezra 9:2]
4[l]ch. 6:15 [m][ch. 4:26; 28:20]

A Chosen People

7 "When the [e]LORD your God brings you
into the land that you are entering to
take possession of it, and clears away many
nations before you, [f]the Hittites, the
Girgashites, the Amorites, the Canaanites,
the Perizzites, the Hivites, and the Jebusites, seven nations [g]more numerous and
mightier than yourselves, 2[h]and when the
LORD your God gives them over to you, and
you defeat them, then you must [i]devote
them to complete destruction.[1] [j]You shall
make no covenant with them and show no
mercy to them. 3[k]You shall not intermarry
with them, giving your daughters to their
sons or taking their daughters for your
sons, 4for they would turn away your sons
from following me, to serve other gods.
[l]Then the anger of the LORD would be kindled against you, and he would destroy
you [m]quickly. 5But thus shall you deal with
them: [n]you shall break down their altars
and dash in pieces their [n]pillars and chop
down their [n]Asherim and [o]burn their
carved images with fire.
6"For [p]you are a people holy to the LORD
your God. The LORD your God has chosen
you to be [p]a people for his treasured possession, out of all the peoples who are on
the face of the earth. 7It was not because
you were more in number than any other
people that the LORD set his love on you
and chose you, for you were the fewest of
all peoples, 8but [q]it is because the LORD
loves you and is keeping [r]the oath that he

5[n]See Ex. 34:13 [o]ver. 25 6[p]ch. 14:2; 26:19; 28:9; Ex. 19:6; 22:31; Jer. 2:3; Amos 3:2; 1 Pet. 2:9; See Ex. 19:5 8[q]ch. 10:15; Isai. 43:4; 63:9; Jer. 31:3; Hos. 11:1; Mal. 1:2 [r]Ex. 32:13; Ps. 105:9-11; Luke 1:72, 73

[1] That is, set apart (devote) as an offering to the Lord (for destruction)

6:15 a jealous God. See note Ex. 20:5.

6:16 Massah. This word means "testing" (Ex. 17:7). Later in Old Testament history, King Ahaz of Judah cited this verse insincerely (Is. 7:12).

6:20–24 See note 4:9.

6:24 to do . . . to fear the LORD. Cf. John 14:23.

7:1 clears away. See note 2:32. Here the Israelites were specifically promised that the Lord would drive out the inhabitants.

seven nations. These seven nations are difficult to identify. In 20:17 only six nations are mentioned (as also in Ex. 3:8, 17; 13:5; 33:2; 34:11), and the Girgashites are omitted. The Jebusites inhabited Jebus, another name for Jerusalem, and there is some indication that they were Hurrians (2:10–12). Amorites are known from ancient Mesopotamia. The ancient lawgiver Hammurabi (1792–1750 B.C.) was an Amorite, as were Og and Sihon, kings of Transjordan. The word "Canaanite" sometimes seems to include them all.

7:2 complete destruction. See note 2:32. Some think that the God of the Old Testament was harsh and vengeful to decree the destruction of the Canaanites, but this is to forget that God is just. The sins of the land's inhabitants were extreme, and the time for judgment had come (cf. Gen. 15:16). God used Israel to punish the Canaanites, but warned that if Israel committed apostasy, leaving the God who had graciously revealed Himself to them, they too would perish (28:15–68).

7:3 You shall not intermarry. Marriage is the closest of human ties and its sacredness was guarded in Old Testament law. The corollary is that marriage must not be contracted with unbelievers, a principle repeated in the New Testament (1 Cor. 7:39). Israel did not maintain her spiritual purity and suffered for it (Ps. 106:37–39).

7:5 break down their altars. Israel was chosen to be a holy people (v. 6), and God would not tolerate pagan religion. Although the means of separation have changed, believers today were chosen for holiness (Eph. 1:4) and are called to separate from false worship (2 Cor. 6:15–18).

7:8 loves you . . . keeping the oath. The election of Israel as a holy nation set apart for God (vv. 6, 7) was grounded, not in any merit or intrinsic goodness in Israel, but in God's love and in His faithfulness to the covenant promises made to the patriarchs (6:10). God's election of the church is based on His oath to Jesus, the son of Abraham, the Son of God (Ps. 110:4; John 17:6). See "God's Covenant of Grace" at Gen. 12:1.

swore to your fathers, that the LORD has
brought you out with a mighty hand and
redeemed you from the house of slavery,
from the hand of Pharaoh king of Egypt.
9 Know therefore that the LORD your God is
God, [s]the faithful God [t]who keeps covenant and steadfast love with those who
love him and keep his commandments, to
a thousand generations, **10** and [u]repays to
their face those who hate him, by destroying them. [v]He will not be slack with one
who hates him. He will repay him to his
face. **11** [w]You shall therefore be careful to do
the commandment and the statutes and
the rules that I command you today.
12 [x]"And because you listen to these rules
and keep and do them, the LORD your God
will keep with you [y]the covenant and the
steadfast love that he swore to your fathers.
13 He will [z]love you, bless you, and multiply
you. [a]He will also bless the fruit of your
womb and the fruit of your ground, your
grain and your wine and your oil, the
increase of your herds and the young of
your flock, in the land that he swore to
your fathers to give you. **14** You shall be
blessed above all peoples. [b]There shall not
be male or female barren among you or
among your livestock. **15** And the LORD will
take away from you all sickness, and none
of the evil [c]diseases of Egypt, which you
knew, will he inflict on you, but he will lay
them on all who hate you. **16** And [d]you shall
consume all the peoples that the LORD your
God will give over to you. [e]Your eye shall
not pity them, neither shall you serve their
gods, for that would be [f]a snare to you.
17 "If you say in your heart, 'These
nations are greater than I. How can I dispossess them?' **18** [g]you shall not be afraid of
them but you shall [h]remember what the
LORD your God did to Pharaoh and to all
Egypt, **19** the great trials that your eyes saw,
[i]the signs, the wonders, the mighty hand,
and the outstretched arm, by which the
LORD your God brought you out. So will
the LORD your God do to all the peoples of
whom you are afraid. **20** Moreover, [j]the
LORD your God will send hornets among
them, until those who are left and hide
themselves from you are destroyed. **21** You
shall not be in dread of them, for the LORD
your God is [k]in your midst, [l]a great and
awesome God. **22** [m]The LORD your God will
clear away these nations before you little by
little. You may not make an end of them at
once,[1] lest the wild beasts grow too numerous for you. **23** [n]But the LORD your God will
give them over to you and throw them into
great confusion, until they are destroyed.
24 And [o]he will give their kings into your
hand, and you shall [p]make their name perish from under heaven. [q]No one shall be
able to stand against you until you have
destroyed them. **25** The carved images of
their gods [r]you shall burn with fire. You
[s]shall not covet the silver or the gold that is
on them or take it for yourselves, lest you
be [t]ensnared by it, for it is an abomination
to the LORD your God. **26** And you shall not
bring an abominable thing into your house
and become devoted to destruction[2] like it.
You shall utterly detest and abhor it, [u]for it
is devoted to destruction.

Remember the LORD Your God

8 "The whole commandment that I
command you today [v]you shall be
careful to do, that you may live and multiply, and go in and possess the land that
the LORD swore to give to your fathers.
2 And you shall remember the whole way
that the LORD your God has led you [w]these

9 [s]Isai. 49:7; 1 Cor. 1:9; 10:13; 2 Cor. 1:18; 1 Thess. 5:24; 2 Thess. 3:3; 2 Tim. 2:13; Heb. 10:23; 1 John 1:9 [t]ch. 5:10; Ex. 20:6; 2 Chr. 6:14; Neh. 1:5; 9:32; Dan. 9:4
10 [u]Job 34:11; Isai. 59:18; Nah. 1:2, 3 [v][2 Pet. 3:9]
11 [w]ch. 10:13
12 [x]For ver. 12-16, see ch. 28:1-14; Lev. 26:3-13 [y]Ps. 105:8; Luke 1:55, 72
13 [z][John 14:21] [a]ch. 30:9
14 [b]Ex. 23:26
15 [c]ch. 28:27, 60; Ex. 9:14; 15:26
16 [d]ver. 2 [e]ch. 13:8; 19:13, 21; 25:12 [f]ver. 25; ch. 12:30; Judg. 8:27; See Ex. 23:33
18 [g]ch. 1:29; 31:6 [h]Ps. 77:11; 105:5
19 [i]ch. 6:22; 11:3
20 [j]Ex. 23:28; Josh. 24:12
21 [k]ch. 6:15; Num. 11:20; 14:14; Josh. 3:10 [l]ch. 10:17; Neh. 1:5; 4:14; 9:32; [ch. 28:58]
22 [m]Ex. 23:29, 30
23 [n]ver. 2
24 [o]Josh. 10:24, 42; 11:12; See Josh. 12:1 [p]See ch. 9:14 [q]ch. 11:25; Josh. 1:5; 10:8; 23:9
25 [r]ver. 5; ch. 12:3; [Ex. 32:20; 1 Chr. 14:12] [s][Josh. 7:1, 21] [t]See ver. 16
26 [u]ch. 13:17; Lev. 27:28; Josh. 6:17, 18; 7:1; [Mic. 4:13]
Chapter 8 **1** [v]ch. 4:1; 5:32, 33; 6:1-3 **2** [w]ch. 1:3; 2:7; 29:5; Amos 2:10

[1] Or *quickly* [2] That is, set apart (devoted) as an offering to the Lord (for destruction); twice in this verse

7:9 a thousand generations. See 5:10 and note.

7:13 He will also bless the fruit of your womb. See 28:4, where a similar verse is included in a liturgy of blessings.

grain . . . wine . . . oil. The three staples of the ancient agricultural economy, here symbolic of prosperity (11:14; 14:23; 18:4); the "oil" is the olive oil used in cooking and lamps.

7:15 the evil diseases of Egypt. The same promise of health is given in Ex. 15:26, and the converse is given as a curse in Deut. 28:60. The dietary laws provided Israel with some protection against common parasites that were rife in Egypt.

7:19 your eyes saw. See note 5:3.

7:20 God will send hornets. The Hebrew word for "hornet" is from the same root as "leprosy" or "leprous disease" (Lev. 14:3). Here it may mean "God will send distress." But the figure of stinging insects chasing the enemy is used elsewhere (1:44; Is. 7:18), and the metaphor of a hornet is quite appropriate (Ex. 23:28 note). God promises to fight for His people with the same power He manifested in the Exodus (v. 18).

7:21 great and awesome. See "The Greatness of God" at 1 Chr. 29:11.

7:25 it is an abomination. Another call for utter hatred of pagan idolatry. But the idols were often made of gold and were valuable. The precious metal was under the ban (Hebrew *ḥerem*); the idols were to be destroyed, and what could pass through the fire was to be given to the Lord (Josh. 6:18, 19).

forty years in the wilderness, that he might
humble you, [x]testing you [y]to know what
was in your heart, [z]whether you would
keep his commandments or not. **3** And he
humbled you and [a]let you hunger and [b]fed
you with manna, which you did not know,
nor did your fathers know, that he might
make you know that [c]man does not live by
bread alone, but man lives by every word[1]
that comes from the mouth of the LORD.
4 [d]Your clothing did not wear out on you
and your foot did not swell these forty
years. **5** Know then in your heart that, [e]as a
man disciplines his son, the LORD your
God disciplines you. **6** So you shall keep
the commandments of the LORD your God
by walking in his ways and by fearing him.
7 For the LORD your God is bringing you
into a good land, [f]a land of brooks of
water, of fountains and springs, flowing
out in the valleys and hills, **8** a land of
wheat and barley, [g]of vines and fig trees
and pomegranates, a land of olive trees
and honey, **9** a land in which you will eat
bread without scarcity, in which you will
lack nothing, a land whose stones are iron,
and out of whose hills you can dig copper.
10 And you shall eat and be full, and you
shall bless the LORD your God for the good
land he has given you.

11 "Take care lest you forget the LORD
your God by not keeping his commandments and his rules and his statutes, which
I command you today, **12** [h]lest, when you
have eaten and are full and have built good
houses and live in them, **13** and when your
herds and flocks multiply and your silver
and gold is multiplied and all that you have
is multiplied, **14** [i]then your heart be lifted
up, and you [j]forget the LORD your God,
who brought you out of the land of Egypt,
out of the house of slavery, **15** who [k]led you
through the great and terrifying wilderness,
[l]with its fiery serpents and scorpions [m]and
thirsty ground where there was no water,
[n]who brought you water out of the flinty
rock, **16** who fed you in the wilderness with
[o]manna that your fathers did not know,
that he might humble you and test you, [p]to
do you good in the end. **17** Beware [q]lest you
say in your heart, 'My power and the might
of my hand have gotten me this wealth.'
18 You shall remember the LORD your God,
for [r]it is he who gives you power to get
wealth, [s]that he may confirm his covenant
that he swore to your fathers, as it is this
day. **19** And if you forget the LORD your God
and go after other gods and serve them and
worship them, [t]I solemnly warn you today
that you shall surely perish. **20** Like the
nations that the LORD makes to perish
before you, [u]so shall you perish, because
you would not obey the voice of the LORD
your God.

Not Because of Righteousness

9 "Hear, O Israel: you are [v]to cross over
the Jordan today, to go in to dispossess
nations [w]greater and mightier than yourselves, cities great and fortified up to heav-
en, **2** a people great and tall, [x]the sons of the
Anakim, [y]whom you know, and of whom
you have heard it said, 'Who can stand

[1] Hebrew *by all*

2 [x]ver. 16; Ex. 15:25 [y][2 Chr. 32:31] [z][Ex. 16:4; Judg. 3:4]
3 [a]Ex. 16:2, 3 [b]Ex. 16:12, 14, 15, 35; [Num. 11:6-9; 21:5] [c]Cited Matt. 4:4; Luke 4:4; [John 6:49-51]
4 [d]ch. 29:5; Neh. 9:21
5 [e]Prov. 3:12; Heb. 12:5, 6; [2 Sam. 7:14; Prov. 29:17; Hos. 10:10; Rev. 3:19]
7 [f]ch. 11:10-12
8 [g][Num. 20:5]
12 [h]ch. 6:11, 12; 28:47; 32:15; Prov. 30:9; Hos. 13:6
14 [i][1 Cor. 4:7] [j]Ps. 78:11; 106:21
15 [k]See ch. 1:19 [l]Num. 21:6; Isai. 30:6 [m]Hos. 13:5 [n]Ex. 17:6; Num. 20:11; Ps. 78:15; 114:8; [ch. 32:13]
16 [o]ver. 3; Ex. 16:15 [p][Jer. 24:5-7; Heb. 12:11]
17 [q][ch. 9:4]
18 [r][Prov. 10:22; Hos. 2:8] [s]ch. 7:8, 12
19 [t][ch. 4:26; 30:18]
20 [u][Dan. 9:11, 12]
Chapter 9
1 [v]ch. 11:31; 12:10; Josh. 1:11 [w]See ch. 4:38
2 [x]See Num. 13:22 [y]ch. 1:28

8:3 manna, which you did not know. The initial giving of manna is mentioned in Ex. 16:15, its cessation in Josh. 5:12. God chose to sustain His people in the wilderness by a means previously unknown to them. Through this miraculous provision God humbled the people (by challenging their self-sufficiency) and tested their obedience (v. 16; cf. Ex. 16:16–30).

man does not live by bread alone. See Matt. 4:4; Luke 4:4.

every word that comes from the mouth of the LORD. Even more basic to life than physical food is the sustaining word of God (Heb. 1:3).

8:4 Your clothing did not wear out. This miraculous preservation is mentioned also in 29:5, but not elsewhere.

8:5 as a man disciplines his son. God let them hunger that He might show them His supply (v. 3). Discipline usually includes initial difficulty followed by blessing (Prov. 3:11, 12; Heb. 12:5, 6).

8:7–9 a good land . . . iron . . . copper. The description is more extensive than the familiar "flowing with milk and honey" found in Exodus, Leviticus, and frequently in Deuteronomy. Palestine certainly had more variety and more rainfall than the flat land of Goshen, but today much of the land is arid. The climate may have been different then, for a small difference in rainfall can significantly affect productivity. The land today has suffered from years of mismanagement—modern hills that were forested within recent memory are now barren. In Assyrian reliefs from about 800 B.C., Israel is depicted with lush vines and grapes, and there is no reason to deny the characterization of the land as pleasant (11:9–12).

8:9 whose stones are iron. The Iron Age (c. 1200–300 B.C.) came to Palestine after Moses died (c. 1406 B.C.), but iron was known before that. Inventories in ancient Ugarit (c. 1400 B.C.) mention two talents of iron. The copper mines of the Sinai Peninsula and the area of south Transjordan were a valuable resource in antiquity, and probably were a source of Solomon's wealth.

8:19 if you forget. Continuing fidelity is the requirement for blessing. Israel without God was no better than the pagans. But God will keep His covenant with the fathers and save a remnant chosen by grace (v. 18; Rom. 11:28, 29).

9:1 Hear, O Israel. See note 5:1. In this long section of exhortation (9:1–11:32), Moses turns toward the future. In the forthcoming conquest of Canaan, God will go before them (v. 3).

9:2 the Anakim. See 1:28; 2:21. The Anakim had frightened the faithless spies forty years earlier (Num. 13:22, 28).

before the sons of Anak?' 3 Know therefore
today that he who [z]goes over before you [a]as
a consuming fire is the LORD your God. He
will destroy them and subdue them before
you. [b]So you shall drive them out and
make them perish quickly, as the LORD has
promised you.
4 [c]"Do not say in your heart, after the
LORD your God has thrust them out before
you, 'It is because of my righteousness that
the LORD has brought me in to possess this
land,' whereas it is [d]because of the wickedness of these nations that the LORD is driving them out before you. 5 [e]Not because of
your righteousness or the uprightness of
your heart are you going in to possess their
land, but because of the wickedness of
these nations the LORD your God is driving
them out from before you, and that he may
confirm [f]the word that the LORD swore to
your fathers, to Abraham, to Isaac, and to
Jacob.
6 "Know, therefore, that the LORD your
God is not giving you this good land to
possess because of your righteousness, for
you are [g]a stubborn people. 7 Remember
and do not forget how you provoked the
LORD your God to wrath in the wilderness.
[h]From the day you came out of the land of
Egypt until you came to this place, you
have been rebellious against the LORD.
8 Even [i]at Horeb you provoked the LORD to
wrath, and the LORD was so angry with you
that he was ready to destroy you. 9 [j]When I
went up the mountain to receive the tablets
of stone, the tablets of the covenant that
the LORD made with you, I remained on the
mountain [k]forty days and forty nights. I
neither ate bread nor drank water. 10 And
[l]the LORD gave me the two tablets of stone
written with the finger of God, and on
them were all the words that the LORD had
spoken with you on the mountain out of
the midst of the fire [m]on the day of the
assembly. 11 And at the end of forty days
and forty nights the LORD gave me the two
tablets of stone, the tablets of the covenant.
12 Then the LORD said to me, [n]'Arise, go
down quickly from here, for your people
whom you have brought from Egypt have
acted corruptly. They have [o]turned aside
quickly out of the way that I commanded
them; they have made themselves a metal
image.'

The Golden Calf

13 [p]"Furthermore, the LORD said to me, 'I
have seen this people, and behold, it is [g]a
stubborn people. 14 [q]Let me alone, that I
may destroy them and [r]blot out their name
from under heaven. And [s]I will make of
you a nation mightier and greater than
they.' 15 [t]So I turned and came down from
the mountain, and [u]the mountain was
burning with fire. And the two tablets of
the covenant were in my two hands. 16 And
[v]I looked, and behold, you had sinned
against the LORD your God. You had made
yourselves a golden[1] calf. [w]You had turned
aside quickly from the way that the LORD
had commanded you. 17 So I took hold of
the two tablets and threw them out of my
two hands and broke them before your
eyes. 18 Then I [x]lay prostrate before the
LORD [y]as before, forty days and forty nights.
I neither ate bread nor drank water,
because of all the sin that you had committed, [z]in doing what was evil in the sight
of the LORD to provoke him to anger. 19 For
I was afraid of the anger and hot displeasure that the LORD bore against you, so that
he was ready to destroy you. [a]But the LORD
listened to me that time also. 20 And the
LORD was so angry with Aaron that he was
ready to destroy him. And I prayed for
Aaron also at the same time. 21 Then [b]I took
the sinful thing, the calf that you had

1 Hebrew *cast-metal*

3 [z]ch. 31:3; [Josh. 3:11] [a]See ch. 4:24 [b]ch. 7:24; Ex. 23:29-31
4 [c][ch. 8:17] [d]ch. 18:12; Lev. 18:24, 25; 20:23; [ch. 20:18]
5 [e][Tit. 3:5] [f]See Gen. 50:24
6 [g]ch. 10:16
7 [h]ver. 24; ch. 31:27; [Ex. 14:11; 15:24; 16:2; 17:2; Num. 11:4; 14:2, 11, 41; 20:2; 21:5; 25:2]
8 [i]Ex. 32:4; Ps. 106:19
9 [j]Ex. 24:12, 15 [k]Ex. 24:18; 34:28; [1 Kin. 19:8; Matt. 4:2; Luke 4:1, 2]
10 [l]Ex. 31:18 [m]ch. 4:10; 10:4; 18:16; Ex. 19:17
12 [n]Ex. 32:7, 8 [o][ch. 31:29; Judg. 2:17]
13 [p]Ex. 32:9 [g][See ver. 6 above]
14 [q]Ex. 32:10 [r]ch. 7:24; 25:19; 29:20; Ex. 17:14 [s]Num. 14:12
15 [t]Ex. 32:15 [u]ch. 4:11; 5:23; Ex. 19:18
16 [v]Ex. 32:19 [w][ch. 31:29; Judg. 2:17]
18 [x]Ex. 34:28; [Ps. 106:23] [y]ver. 9; ch. 10:10 [z]ch. 4:25
19 [a]ch. 10:10; Ex. 32:14; 33:17
21 [b]Ex. 32:20

9:4 because of my righteousness. Note the threefold emphasis in this section (vv. 4–6) that the victory was not because of Israel's goodness, but was entirely the work of God's grace. Repetition was characteristic of Hebrew literature, and aided learning and memorization. Genesis 21:1 is a prime example of this characteristic, misunderstood by critics who insist that ancient Near Eastern literature should resemble the crisp economy that ideally characterizes modern Western journalism. This prejudice has led to the unwarranted conclusion that the Pentateuch must be the product of "cutting and pasting" documents from different authors.

9:9 I went up the mountain. Moses retells the story given in Exodus (Ex. 24:12, 18; 32:7–10, 15–20).

9:21 the brook that ran down from the mountain. Today no stream flows down from Jebel Musa, the peak often identified as Mount Sinai (Ex. 16:1 note). The ground has some moisture, and low bushes grow, but the mention of a stream implies that in Moses' time there was more rainfall than now (8:7–9 note).

9:22 Taberah. See Num. 11:3. On Massah, see 6:16 and Ex. 17:7. On Kibroth-hattaavah, see Num. 11:34.

9:23 you rebelled. The sheer persistence in rebellion by the Israelites (v. 24) points to the importance of Moses' intercession (vv. 25–28; Ex. 32:11–13) and to the gracious power of God, who remains faithful to His covenant despite the failings of the people (v. 29).

made, and burned it with fire and crushed
it, grinding it very small, until it was as fine
as dust. And I threw the dust of it into the
brook that ran down from the mountain.
22 "At [c]Taberah also, and at [d]Massah and
at [e]Kibroth-hattaavah you provoked the
LORD to wrath. 23 And [f]when the LORD sent
you from Kadesh-barnea, saying, 'Go up
and take possession of the land that I have
given you,' then you rebelled against the
commandment of the LORD your God and
[g]did not believe him or obey his voice.
24 [h]You have been rebellious against the
LORD from the day that I knew you.
25 [x]"So I lay prostrate before the LORD for
these forty days and forty nights, because
the LORD had said he would destroy you.
26 [i]And I prayed to the LORD, 'O Lord GOD,
destroy not your people and your heritage,
whom you have redeemed through your
greatness, whom you have brought out of
Egypt with a mighty hand. 27 Remember
your servants, Abraham, Isaac, and Jacob.
Do not regard the stubbornness of this
people, or their wickedness or their sin,
28 lest the land from which you brought us
say, [j]"Because the LORD was not able to
bring them into the land that he promised
them, and because he hated them, he has
brought them out to put them to death in
the wilderness." 29 [k]For they are your people and your heritage, whom you brought
out by your great power and by your outstretched arm.'

New Tablets of Stone

10 "At that time the LORD said to me,
[l]'Cut for yourself two tablets of
stone like the first, and come up to me on
the mountain and [m]make an ark of wood.
2 And I will write on the tablets the words
that were on the first tablets that you
broke, and [n]you shall put them in the ark.'
3 So I made an ark [o]of acacia wood, and
[p]cut two tablets of stone like the first, and
went up the mountain with the two tablets
in my hand. 4 And [q]he wrote on the tablets,
in the same writing as before, the Ten
Commandments[1] [r]that the LORD had spoken to you on the mountain out of the
midst of the fire [s]on the day of the assembly. And the LORD gave them to me. 5 Then
I turned and [t]came down from the mountain and [u]put the tablets in the ark that I
had made. [v]And there they are, as the LORD
commanded me."
6 (The people of Israel [w]journeyed from
Beeroth Bene-jaakan[2] to Moserah. [x]There
Aaron died, and there he was buried. And
his son Eleazar ministered as priest in his
place. 7 [y]From there they journeyed to
Gudgodah, and from Gudgodah to Jotbathah, a land with brooks of water. 8 At
that time [z]the LORD set apart the tribe of
Levi [a]to carry the ark of the covenant of the
LORD [b]to stand before the LORD to minister
to him and [c]to bless in his name, to this
day. 9 [d]Therefore Levi has no portion or
inheritance with his brothers. The LORD is
his inheritance, as the LORD your God said
to him.)
10 [e]"I myself stayed on the mountain, as
at the first time, forty days and forty nights,
[f]and the LORD listened to me that time also.
The LORD was unwilling to destroy you.
11 [g]And the LORD said to me, 'Arise, go on
your journey at the head of the people, so
that they may go in and possess the land,
which I swore to their fathers to give them.'

[1] Hebrew *words* [2] Or *the wells of the Bene-jaakan*

22 [c]Num. 11:1-3 [d]Ex. 17:7 [e]Num. 11:34
23 [f]Num. 13:3; 14:1 [g]Ps. 106:24, 25
24 [h]ver. 7; ch. 31:27
25 [x][See ver. 18 above]
26 [i]See Ex. 32:11-13
28 [j]Num. 14:16
29 [k]ch. 4:20; 1 Kin. 8:51; Neh. 1:19; [Ps. 95:7]
Chapter 10
1 [l]Ex. 34:1, 2 [m]Ex. 25:10
2 [n]Ex. 25:16, 21
3 [o]Ex. 25:10; 37:1 [p]Ex. 34:4
4 [q]Ex. 34:28 [r]Ex. 20:1 [s]See ch. 9:10
5 [t]Ex. 34:29 [u]Ex. 40:20 [v]1 Kin. 8:9
6 [w]Num. 33:30, 31 [x][Num. 20:28; 33:38]
7 [y]Num. 33:32, 33
8 [z]Num. 3:6; 8:14; 16:9; [1 Chr. 23:13] [a]Num. 4:5, 15 [b]ch. 17:12; 18:5, 7 [c]ch. 21:5; Lev. 9:22; See Num. 6:23-26
9 [d]See Num. 18:20
10 [e]ch. 9:18, 25 [f]ch. 9:19
11 [g]Ex. 32:34; 33:1

10:1–5 Summarizing the material in Ex. 34:1–4 and 40:20, Moses here telescopes the receiving of the commandments and the building of the ark. Moses was twice on the Mount. He received the directions for the tabernacle the first time. It and its furniture were built after Moses came down the second time. The tablets were put in the ark when the tabernacle was set up, as mentioned in Ex. 40:20.

10:1 two tablets of stone. It has generally been assumed that the law was written once, the material taking up two tablets or a double tablet. More recently, some have suggested that there were two tablets, each a separate copy of the law. This would reflect the ancient practice of providing each treaty partner with a copy of the agreement. Because the ark was both the place of God's presence with His people, and the focal point of Israel's worship, it was appropriate for both copies of the covenantal terms to be housed in the ark. See note Ex. 31:18.

10:4 the Ten Commandments. See note 4:13.

10:6–9 Some have suggested that this parenthetical section breaks the narrative and is, therefore, a later insertion. It is evident, however, that this section serves to tie together a number of themes from the preceding context: Aaron's role in the golden calf incident, for which he was threatened with death that was averted only by Moses' intercession (9:20); the impending possession of the land (9:1–4), in which the Levites would not participate because the Lord was their inheritance (v. 9; cf. 9:29); and the ark (vv. 1–5), which the Levites were to tend (v. 8).

The journeys in vv. 6, 7 appear to correspond to Num. 33:31–33. These movements are difficult to interpret because we can identify only a few of the places mentioned.

10:6 Moserah . . . Aaron died. This mention of Aaron's death underscores the effectiveness of Moses' intercession (9:20). Aaron was not killed at Sinai, but lived until the fortieth year after the Exodus (Num. 33:38).

10:8 At that time. This does not refer to the time of Aaron's death (v. 6) or to the events of v. 7, but to the time of the revelation at Sinai (Ex. 28; 29).

10:11 to their fathers. To the patriarchs (9:5; Ex. 33:1).

Circumcise Your Heart

12 "And now, Israel, [h]what does the
LORD your God require of you, but [i]to fear
the LORD your God, [j]to walk in all his
ways, [k]to love him, to serve the LORD your
God with all your heart and with all your
soul, 13 and [l]to keep the commandments
and statutes of the LORD, which I am commanding you today [m]for your good?
14 Behold, [n]to the LORD your God belong
heaven and the heaven of heavens, [o]the
earth with all that is in it. 15 Yet [p]the LORD
set his heart in love on your fathers and
chose their offspring after them, you
above all peoples, as you are this day.
16 Circumcise therefore [q]the foreskin of
your heart, and be no longer [r]stubborn.
17 For the LORD your God is [s]God of gods and
[t]Lord of lords, [u]the great, the mighty, and
the awesome God, who is [v]not partial and
takes no bribe. 18 [w]He executes justice for
the fatherless and the widow, and loves
the sojourner, giving him food and clothing. 19 [x]Love the sojourner, therefore, for
you were sojourners in the land of Egypt.
20 [i]You shall fear the LORD your God. You
shall serve him and [y]hold fast to him, and
[z]by his name you shall swear. 21 [a]He is
your praise. He is your God, [b]who has
done for you these great and terrifying
things that your eyes have seen. 22 Your
fathers went down to Egypt [c]seventy persons, and now the LORD your God has
made you [d]as numerous as the stars of
heaven.

12 [h][Mic. 6:8] [i]See ch. 6:2, 13 [j]See ch. 5:33 [k]See ch. 6:5
13 [l]ch. 7:11 [m]ch. 6:24
14 [n]1 Kin. 8:27; 2 Chr. 6:18; Neh. 9:6; Ps. 115:16; Isai. 66:1 [o]Ex. 19:5; Ps. 24:1
15 [p]ch. 4:37; [ch. 7:7]
16 [q]ch. 30:6; Jer. 4:4; [Acts 7:51] [r]See ch. 9:6
17 [s]Josh. 22:22; Ps. 136:2; Dan. 2:47; 11:36 [t]Rev. 17:14; 19:16 [u]Neh. 9:32; See ch. 7:21 [v]2 Chr. 19:7; Job 34:19; Acts 10:34; Rom. 2:11; Gal. 2:6; Eph. 6:9; Col. 3:25; 1 Pet. 1:17
18 [w]Ps. 68:5; 146:9; [ch. 24:17; Ex. 22:22]
19 [x]Ex. 22:21; 23:9; Lev. 19:33, 34
20 [i][See ver. 12 above] [y]ch. 11:22; 13:4; 20:20 [z]See ch. 6:13
21 [a]Ps. 22:3; 109:1; Jer. 17:14 [b]2 Sam. 7:23; Ps. 106:21, 22
22 [c]Gen. 46:27; Ex. 1:5; [Acts 7:14] [d]ch. 28:62; Neh. 9:23; See Gen. 15:5

Love and Serve the LORD

11 [e]"You shall therefore love the LORD
your God and [f]keep his charge, his
statutes, his rules, and his commandments
always. 2 And consider today (since I am not
speaking to [g]your children who have not
known or seen it), consider the discipline[1]
of the LORD your God, [h]his greatness, [i]his
mighty hand and his outstretched arm,
3 [j]his signs and his deeds that he did in
Egypt to Pharaoh the king of Egypt and to
all his land, 4 and what he did to the army
of Egypt, to their horses and to their chariots, [k]how he made the water of the Red Sea
flow over them as they pursued after you,
and how the LORD has destroyed them to
this day, 5 and [l]what he did to you in the
wilderness, until you came to this place,
6 and [m]what he did to Dathan and Abiram
the sons of Eliab, son of Reuben, how the
earth opened its mouth and swallowed
them up, with their households, their tents,
and every living thing that followed them,
in the midst of all Israel. 7 For your eyes
have seen [n]all the great work of the LORD
that he did.

8 "You shall therefore keep the whole
commandment that I command you today,
that you may [o]be strong, and go in and take
possession of the land that you are going
over to possess, 9 and [p]that you may live

Chapter 11 1 [e]See ch. 6:5 [f][Ezek. 44:16]; See Lev. 8:35 2 [g]ch. 31:13 [h]ch. 3:24; 5:24 [i]See ch. 4:34 3 [j]ch. 6:22; 7:19 4 [k]Ex. 14:27, 28; 15:9, 10; Ps. 106:11 5 [l]See Ps. 78:14-40 6 [m]Num. 16:1, 31; 27:3; Ps. 106:17 7 [n]Judg. 2:7 8 [o]ch. 31:6, 7; Josh. 1:6, 7, 9, 18 9 [p]See ch. 4:40

[1] Or *instruction*

10:12 what does the LORD your God require of you. This rhetorical question resembles the much-quoted Mic. 6:8, which calls us to justice, mercy, and humility in our walk with God (cf. Matt. 23:23). To walk with God requires that we love Him with all our being and keep His commandments—love and obedience go together (John 14:23). To love God with our whole being is the greatest commandment (Deut. 6:5; Mark 12:29–34).

10:15 you above all. The contrast is a noble one, between God's sovereignty over and common grace to all creation (v. 14), and His special electing love for the patriarchs and the nation (v. 15).

10:16 Circumcise . . . your heart. This verse (along with Deut. 30:6 and Jer. 4:4) is an effective answer to those who imagine that the Old Testament teaches merely a religion of outward form. Circumcision was a *symbol,* a *sacrament,* an *outward sign* of an *inward grace.* Apart from this, as Paul indicates, circumcision was of no saving significance. True circumcision is "of the heart, by the Spirit, not by the letter" (Rom. 2:29).

10:18 He executes justice. The Lord of surpassing greatness and sovereignty ("God of gods and Lord of lords," v. 17) is also revealed to be the supremely compassionate God, with deep concern for the least in human society: the fatherless, the widow, and the alien. In this He is our example (v. 19).

10:22 seventy. See note Ex. 1:5. Mention of the number who went into Egypt emphasizes God's great love in increasing Israel's population to nearly two million.

11:2 your children. Since the people had seen God's wonderful deliverance (v. 8), they should therefore obey God's commands all the more faithfully. In his mention of "children," it does not seem that Moses distinguishes the adults over age forty in his audience, who had seen the Exodus, from the youths who had not. The younger generation also had seen God's preserving care and discipline in the wilderness (vv. 5, 6). Probably, therefore, Moses is distinguishing the current generation to which he was speaking from their children yet to be born.

11:6 Dathan and Abiram. Moses distinguishes Dathan and Abiram from Korah. Likewise, Ps. 106:17 does not include Korah with those buried alive. This distinction is not because the information about Korah belongs to a later time of writing, as some have held; rather, this distinction by Moses is precise. Closer reading of the record in Num. 16:16–35 shows that Korah was at the tabernacle among the two hundred fifty men with censers. Dathan and Abiram, who were not Levites, were in front of their tents with their families when the earth swallowed them up, and Korah's family with them. But Korah himself perished with the two hundred fifty in the fire from the Lord.

11:9 live long in the land. See note 5:16.

long in the land [q]that the LORD swore to
your fathers to give to them and to their offspring, [r]a land flowing with milk and
honey. 10 For the land that you are entering
to take possession of it is not like the land
of Egypt, from which you have come, where
you sowed your seed and irrigated it,[1] like a
garden of vegetables. 11 [s]But the land that
you are going over to possess is a land of
hills and valleys, which drinks water by the
rain from heaven, 12 a land that the LORD
your God cares for. [t]The eyes of the LORD
your God are always upon it, from the
beginning of the year to the end of the year.
13 [u]"And if you will indeed obey my commandments that I command you today, [u]to
love the LORD your God, and to serve him
with all your heart and with all your soul,
14 [v]he[2] will give the rain for your land in its
season, [w]the early rain and the later rain,
that you may gather in your grain and your
wine and your oil. 15 [x]And he will give grass
in your fields for your livestock, and [y]you
shall eat and be full. 16 Take care [z]lest your
heart be deceived, and you turn aside and
[a]serve other gods and worship them;
17 then [b]the anger of the LORD will be kindled against you, and he [c]will shut up the
heavens, so that there will be no rain, and
the land will yield no fruit, and [d]you will
perish quickly off the good land that the
LORD is giving you.
18 [e]"You shall therefore lay up these words
of mine in your heart and in your soul, and
[f]you shall bind them as a sign on your
hand, and they shall be as frontlets between
your eyes. 19 You shall teach them to your
children, talking of them when you are sitting in your house, and when you are walking by the way, and when you lie down, and
when you rise. 20 [g]You shall write them on
the doorposts of your house and on your
gates, 21 [h]that your days and the days of your
children may be multiplied in the land that
the LORD swore to your fathers to give them,
[i]as long as the heavens are above the earth.
22 For if [j]you will be careful to do all this
commandment that I command you to do,
loving the LORD your God, walking in all his
ways, and [k]holding fast to him, 23 then the
LORD [l]will drive out all these nations before
you, and you will [m]dispossess nations
greater and mightier than yourselves.
24 [n]Every place on which the sole of your
foot treads shall be yours. Your territory
shall be [o]from the wilderness to[3] the
Lebanon and from the River, the river
Euphrates, to the western sea. 25 [p]No one
shall be able to stand against you. The LORD
your God will lay [q]the fear of you and the
dread of you on all the land that you shall
tread, [r]as he promised you.
26 [s]"See, I am setting before you today a
blessing and a curse: 27 [t]the blessing, if you
obey the commandments of the LORD your
God, which I command you today, 28 and
[u]the curse, if you do not obey the commandments of the LORD your God, but
turn aside from the way that I am commanding you today, [v]to go after other gods
that you have not known. 29 And when the
LORD your God brings you into the land
that you are entering to take possession of
it, you shall set [w]the blessing on Mount
Gerizim and the curse on Mount Ebal.
30 Are they not beyond the Jordan, west of
the road, toward the going down of the
sun, in the land of the Canaanites who live

9 [q]See Gen. 50:24 [r]Ex. 3:8
11 [s]ch. 8:7
12 [t][1 Kin. 9:3; Jer. 24:6]
13 [u]See ch. 6:5
14 [v]ch. 28:12; Lev. 26:4 [w][Job 29:23; Jer. 5:24; Hos. 6:3; Joel 2:23; James 5:7]
15 [x]Ps. 104:14 [y]ch. 6:11; [Joel 2:19]
16 [z][Job 31:27] [a]ver. 28; See ch. 6:14
17 [b]ch. 6:15 [c]1 Kin. 8:35; 2 Chr. 6:26; 7:13; [ch. 28:23, 24; Lev. 26:19, 20; Amos 4:7; Zech. 14:17; Rev. 11:6] [d]ch. 4:26; 30:18; Josh. 23:15, 16
18 [e]See ch. 6:6 [f]See ch. 6:8
20 [g]ch. 6:9
21 [h]See ch. 4:40 [i]Ps. 89:29
22 [j]ch. 6:17 [k]See ch. 10:20
23 [l]See ch. 4:38 [m]ch. 9:1
24 [n]Josh. 1:3; [Josh. 14:9] [o]See Ex. 23:31
25 [p]See ch. 7:24 [q]ch. 2:25 [r]Ex. 23:27
26 [s]ch. 30:1, 15, 19
27 [t]See ch. 28:2-14
28 [u]See ch. 28:15-45 [v]See ch. 6:14
29 [w]ch. 27:12, 13; Josh. 8:33

[1] Hebrew *watered it with your feet* [2] Samaritan, Septuagint, Vulgate; Hebrew *I*; also verse 15 [3] Hebrew *and*

11:10 irrigated it. The precise detail of this allusion is unclear. It may refer to the sluice gates of irrigation canals (which were often opened by the gardener's foot), or to the burdensome practice of carrying water by bucket. In contrast to the Promised Land, which had sufficient rainfall for agriculture (vv. 9, 11), arid Egypt depended heavily upon irrigation for farming.

11:13 with all your heart. The command to love the Lord "with all your heart" (6:5) is echoed in Deuteronomy at least six times.

11:14 grain . . . wine . . . oil. See note 7:13.

11:19 teach them to your children. See note 4:9, and the similar exhortations and metaphors in 6:6–9.

11:24 Every place . . . your foot treads. The same expression and the same boundaries of Canaan are repeated in Josh. 1:3–5. Because the boundaries need to include a southern limit, "wilderness" probably means the Sinai Desert. The boundaries include all of modern Israel and Lebanon, together with part of Syria.

11:26 a blessing and a curse. This introduction to the ceremony of blessing and cursing that was to take place at Ebal and Gerizim is reiterated in Deut. 30:19 at the end of Moses' speech. Under divine inspiration, Moses emphasizes the people's obligation to love God and obey His commands.

11:29 Mount Gerizim . . . Mount Ebal. The details of this ceremony are provided in chs. 27; 28; the ceremony itself was performed according to Moses' direction by Joshua (Josh. 8:30–35). The phrases "beyond the Jordan . . . toward the going down of the sun" (v. 30) point to a location in Canaan (i.e., west of the Jordan). According to Gen. 12:6, the "oak of Moreh" is near Shechem. The precise location of Gilgal is uncertain, but it seems to have been near Jericho (Josh. 4:19). The Canaanites inhabited this whole territory, and there is no reason to doubt the usual identification of these mountains as the two mountains near Shechem astride the main north-south road.

in the [x]Arabah, opposite Gilgal, beside [y]the
oak[1] of Moreh? **31** For you are [z]to cross over
the Jordan to go in to take possession of
the land that the LORD your God is giving
you. And when you possess it and live in it,
32 you shall be careful [a]to do all the statutes
and the rules that I am setting before you
today.

The LORD's Chosen Place of Worship

12 [b]"These are the statutes and rules
that you shall be careful to do in the
land that the LORD, the God of your fathers,
has given you to possess, [c]all the days that
you live on the earth. **2** [d]You shall surely
destroy all the places where the nations
whom you shall dispossess served their
gods, [e]on the high mountains and on the
hills and under every green tree. **3** You shall
tear down their altars and dash in pieces
[f]their pillars and burn their [g]Asherim with
fire. You shall chop down the carved
images of their gods and [h]destroy their
name out of that place. **4** [i]You shall not
worship the LORD your God in that way.
5 But you shall seek [j]the place that the LORD
your God will choose out of all your tribes
to put his name and make his habitation[2]
there. There you shall go, **6** and there you
shall bring your burnt offerings and your
sacrifices, [k]your tithes and the contribution
that you present, your vow offerings, your
freewill offerings, and the [l]firstborn of your
herd and of your flock. **7** And [m]there you
shall eat before the LORD your God, and
[n]you shall rejoice, you and your households, in all that you undertake, in which
the LORD your God has blessed you.
8 "You shall not do according to all that
we are doing here today, [o]everyone doing
whatever is right in his own eyes, **9** for you
have not as yet come to [p]the rest and to the
inheritance that the LORD your God is giving you. **10** But when [q]you go over the
Jordan and live in the land that the LORD
your God is giving you to inherit, [r]and
when he gives you rest from all your enemies around, so that you live in safety,
11 then to [j]the place that the LORD your God
will choose, to make his name dwell there,
there you shall bring all that I command
you: your burnt offerings and your sacrifices, [k]your tithes and the contribution that
you present, and all your finest vow offerings that you vow to the LORD. **12** And [n]you
shall rejoice before the LORD your God, you
and your sons and your daughters, your
male servants and your female servants,
and the Levite that is within your towns,
since [s]he has no portion or inheritance
with you. **13** [t]Take care that you do not offer
your burnt offerings at any place that you
see, **14** but at [j]the place that the LORD will
choose in one of your tribes, there you
shall offer your burnt offerings, and there
you shall do all that I am commanding you.
15 "However, you may slaughter and eat
meat within any of your towns, as much as
you desire, [u]according to the blessing of
the LORD your God that he has given you.
[v]The unclean and the clean may eat of it, as
of the gazelle and as of the deer. **16** [w]Only
you shall not eat the blood; you shall pour
it out on the earth like water. **17** You may
not eat within your towns [k]the tithe of your
grain or of your wine or of your oil, or the
firstborn of your herd or of your flock, or
any of your vow offerings that you vow, or
your freewill offerings or the contribution
that you present, **18** but [m]you shall eat them

1 Septuagint, Syriac; see Genesis 12:6. Hebrew *oaks*, or *terebinths*
2 Or *as its habitation*

30 [x]See Deut. 1:1 [y]Judg. 7:1
31 [z]ch. 9:1; 12:10; Josh. 1:11
32 [a]ch. 5:32; 12:32
Chapter 12
1 [b]ch. 6:1 [c]ch. 4:10
2 [d]ch. 7:5; Ex. 34:13 [e]1 Kin. 14:23; 2 Kin. 16:4; 17:10; Jer. 3:6
3 [f]See ch. 16:22 [g]See ch. 16:21 [h][Zeph. 1:4; Zech. 13:2]
4 [i]ver. 31
5 [j]ch. 16:2; 26:2; 1 Kin. 8:29; 2 Chr. 7:12; [Josh. 18:1]
6 [k]ch. 14:22, 23; 15:19, 20 [l]ch. 14:23
7 [m]ch. 14:23, 26; 15:20 [n]ch. 14:26; 16:11, 14, 15; 26:11; 27:7; 28:8; Lev. 23:40
8 [o]Judg. 17:6; 21:25
9 [p]1 Kin. 8:56; Ps. 95:11; [Heb. 4:8]
10 [q]See ch. 11:31 [r]ch. 25:19; Josh. 23:1; [2 Sam. 7:1; 1 Kin. 5:4]
11 [j][See ver. 5 above] [k][See ver. 6 above]
12 [n][See ver. 7 above] [s]See Num. 18:20
13 [t]Lev. 17:3, 4; [1 Kin. 12:28, 33]
14 [j][See ver. 5 above]
15 [u]ch. 16:17 [v]ch. 14:5; 15:22
16 [w]See Lev. 3:17
17 [k][See ver. 6 above]
18 [m][See ver. 7 above]

12:1–26:19 Moses continues to expound the covenant way of life, reiterating laws governing Israel's worship and conduct. The laws pertain to topics from idolatry to tithes, from priests to divorce, from nations to the individual. The section concludes with exhortations to obey the Lord, who is both Redeemer and King.

12:5 the place that the LORD your God will choose. This passage has been used to argue that Deuteronomy was written in the sixth century B.C. so as to support Josiah's centralization of worship at Jerusalem in that period (Introduction: Date and Occasion). But that view, which presupposes an evolutionary theory of the development of Israelite religion, misreads this verse. The reference here to "the place" certainly need not imply that the location of the temple in Jerusalem was known when this text was written. In the course of Israel's history, worship of the Lord was successively centered in several places: Shiloh (Josh. 18:1) and Gibeon (1 Chr. 16:39), as well as later in Jerusalem. The stress here is on the contrast between "the place . . . the LORD your God will choose" and "the places where the nations . . . served their gods" (v. 2). Purity of worship in obedience to divine command, rather than centralization, is primarily in view.

12:7 eat . . . rejoice. Some sacrifices were shared by priests and worshipers. The worship of Israel was holy, reverent, and joyful. The worship of a holy God involved repentance and cleansing, but the redeemed heart was full of joy and praise. The Book of Psalms frequently expresses such joyful devotion.

12:12 no . . . inheritance. The gifts of the worshipers were, in part, to support the priests and Levites, who were allotted no farmland of their own (10:6–9).

12:15 slaughter . . . within any of your towns. The same rule is given in vv. 20, 21. They could slaughter for meat anywhere, but sacrificial meat and foodstuffs devoted to God could only be eaten at the central place of worship. See note Lev. 17:3.

before the LORD your God in [j] the place that
the LORD your God will choose, you and
your son and your daughter, your male servant and your female servant, and the
Levite who is within your towns. And [n] you
shall rejoice before the LORD your God in
all that you undertake. **19** [x] Take care that
you do not neglect the Levite as long as you
live in your land.
20 "When the LORD your God [y] enlarges
your territory, [z] as he has promised you,
and you say, 'I will eat meat,' because you
crave meat, you may eat meat whenever
you desire. **21** If [a] the place that the LORD
your God will choose to put his name there
is too far from you, [b] then you may kill any
of your herd or your flock, which the LORD
has given you, as I have commanded you,
and you may eat within your towns when-
ever you desire. **22** Just [c] as the gazelle or the
deer is eaten, so you may eat of it. [c] The
unclean and the clean alike may eat of it.
23 [d] Only be sure that you do not eat the
blood, [e] for the blood is the life, and you
shall not eat the life with the flesh. **24** You
shall not eat it; you shall pour it out on the
earth like water. **25** You shall not eat it, [f] that
all may go well with you and with your
children after you, [g] when you do what is
right in the sight of the LORD. **26** But the
[h] holy things that are due from you, and
[i] your vow offerings, you shall take, and you
shall go to [a] the place that the LORD will
choose, **27** and [j] offer your burnt offerings,
the flesh and the blood, on the altar of the
LORD your God. The blood of your sacrifices shall be poured out on the altar of the
LORD your God, but the flesh you may eat.
28 Be careful to obey all these words that I
command you, [f] that it may go well with you
and with your children after you forever,

18 [j] [See ver. 5 above] [n] [See ver. 7 above]
19 [x] ch. 14:27; [2 Chr. 31:4]
20 [y] ch. 19:8 [z] ch. 11:24; 19:8, 9; Gen. 28:14; Ex. 34:24
21 [a] See ver. 5 [b] ver. 15
22 [c] ch. 14:5; 15:22
23 [d] See Lev. 3:17 [e] See Gen. 9:4
25 [f] ch. 4:40; [Eccles. 8:12; Isai. 3:10] [g] ch. 6:18; 13:18; Ex. 15:26; 1 Kin. 11:38
26 [h] [Num. 5:9,10; 18:19] [i] [1 Sam. 1:21] [a] [See ver. 21 above]
27 [j] Lev. 1:5, 9, 13; 17:11
28 [f] [See ver. 25 above]

29 [k] ch. 19:1; Josh. 23:4, 5
30 [l] ch. 7:16
31 [m] ver. 4; Lev. 18:3, 26, 30; [2 Kin. 17:15] [n] ch. 7:25; 17:1; 18:12; 23:18; 25:16; 27:15 [o] 2 Kin. 17:31; Jer. 7:31; 19:5
32 [p] See ch. 4:2

Chapter 13
1 [q] Jer. 23:25, 32; 27:9; 29:8; Zech. 10:2
2 [r] [ch. 18:22; Jer. 28:9]
3 [s] ch. 8:2
4 [t] 2 Kin. 23:3; 2 Chr. 34:31 [u] See ch. 10:20
5 [v] ch. 18:20; [Jer. 2:8; 14:14, 15; Zech. 13:3]

when you do what is good and right in the
sight of the LORD your God.

Warning Against Idolatry

29 "When [k] the LORD your God cuts off
before you the nations whom you go in to
dispossess, and you dispossess them and
dwell in their land, **30** take care [l] that you be
not ensnared to follow them, after they have
been destroyed before you, and that you do
not inquire about their gods, saying, 'How
did these nations serve their gods?—that I
also may do the same.' **31** [m] You shall not
worship the LORD your God in that way, for
every [n] abominable thing that the LORD
hates they have done for their gods, for
[o] they even burn their sons and their daughters in the fire to their gods.
32 [1] "Everything that I command you, you
shall be careful to do. [p] You shall not add
to it or take from it.
13 "If a prophet or [q] a dreamer of
dreams arises among you and
gives you a sign or a wonder, **2** and [r] the
sign or wonder that he tells you comes to
pass, and if he says, 'Let us go after other
gods,' which you have not known, 'and
let us serve them,' **3** you shall not listen to
the words of that prophet or that dreamer
of dreams. For the LORD your God [s] is testing you, to know whether you love the
LORD your God with all your heart and
with all your soul. **4** You shall [t] walk after
the LORD your God and fear him and keep
his commandments and obey his voice,
and you shall serve him and [u] hold fast to
him. **5** But [v] that prophet or that dreamer of
dreams shall be put to death, because he
has taught rebellion against the LORD
your God, who brought you out of the

1 Ch 13:1 in Hebrew

12:21 If the place . . . is too far. See 14:24–26.

12:23 the blood is the life. The same principle is given in Gen. 9:4 and Lev. 17:10–14. The treatment of the blood in the sacrificial system shows that it stood for the life of the animal. When the blood is gone, the life is gone. When blood was sprinkled on the altar, innocent life was shed for a guilty sinner. The Old Testament sacrifices show a theology of substitution of the innocent for the guilty. This theology was incomplete, because an animal, no matter how perfect, is by no means as valuable as the human soul (Mic. 6:6, 7). The resolution is found most clearly in Is. 53:10 where the innocent Servant of the Lord dies as a sin offering (cf. John 1:29).

12:31 they even burn their sons and their daughters. Child sacrifice was common in ancient times, especially in the Phoenician colony of Carthage in North Africa. In ancient pagan cultures, children were sometimes sacrificed in times of great need as an expression of devotion to a god (2 Kin. 3:27). Even some Israelites at times engaged in this detestable practice (Judg. 11:30–40; Ps. 106:34–39; Jer. 7:31).

12:32 You shall not add. See 4:2.

13:1–18 Moses issues warnings against apostasy in ch. 13. The first (vv. 1–5) concerns false prophets. The other sections warn against a near relative who tempts to apostasy (vv. 6–11) and the apostasy of a whole town (vv. 12–18). In each case, the penalty is death.

13:1–5 The caution against a false prophet is given to emphasize that even though a prophet seems to carry impressive credentials, the theological test is still crucial. No true prophet could possibly advance a false religion, since Israel's God is the true and only God. All other gods are the creations of men. Those who follow them and worship them must be destroyed from Israel.

land of Egypt and redeemed you out of
the house of slavery, to make you leave
the way in which the LORD your God commanded you to walk. [w]So you shall purge
the evil[1] from your midst.
6 [x]"If your brother, the son of your mother, or your son or your daughter or [y]the
wife you embrace[2] or your friend [z]who is as
your own soul entices you secretly, saying,
'Let us go and serve other gods,' [a]which
neither you nor your fathers have known,
7 some [b]of the gods of the peoples who are
around you, whether near you or far off
from you, from the one end of the earth to
the other, 8 you shall [c]not yield to him or
listen to him, nor [d]shall your eye pity him,
nor shall you spare him, nor shall you conceal him. 9 But you shall kill him. [e]Your
hand shall be first against him to put him
to death, and afterward the hand of all the
people. 10 [f]You shall stone him to death
with stones, because he sought to draw
you away from the LORD your God, who
brought you out of the land of Egypt, out
of the house of slavery. 11 And [g]all Israel
shall hear and fear and never again do any
such wickedness as this among you.

5 [w]ch. 17:7; 19:19; 21:21; 22:21; 24:7; [1 Cor. 5:13]
6 [x]ch. 17:2 [y]ch. 28:54, 56; Mic. 7:5 [z][1 Sam. 18:1, 3; 20:17] [a]ch. 28:64
7 [b]ch. 6:14
8 [c]Prov. 1:10 [d]See ch. 7:16
9 [e]ch. 17:7
10 [f]ch. 17:5; See Josh. 7:25
11 [g]ch. 17:13; 19:20; 21:21
13 [h]Judg. 19:22; 20:13; 1 Sam. 2:12; 25:17; 2 Sam. 16:7; 20:1; 1 Kin. 21:10, 13
14 [i]ch. 17:4; 19:18
16 [j]Josh. 6:24 [k]Josh. 8:28; Jer. 49:2; [Isai. 17:1; 25:2; Jer. 30:18]
17 [l]Josh. 6:18 [m]Josh. 7:26 [n]See Gen. 50:24
18 [o]ch. 12:25, 28

12 "If you hear in one of your cities, which
the LORD your God is giving you to dwell
there, 13 that certain [h]worthless fellows have
gone out among you and have drawn away
the inhabitants of their city, saying, 'Let us
go and serve other gods,' which you have
not known, 14 then you shall inquire and
make search and ask [i]diligently. And
behold, if it be true and certain that such
an abomination has been done among you,
15 you shall surely put the inhabitants of
that city to the sword, devoting it to
destruction,[3] all who are in it and its cattle,
with the edge of the sword. 16 You shall
gather all its spoil into the midst of its open
square and [j]burn the city and all its spoil
with fire, as a whole burnt offering to the
LORD your God. It shall be a [k]heap forever.
It shall not be built again. 17 [l]None of the
devoted things shall stick to your hand,
[m]that the LORD may turn from the fierceness of his anger and show you mercy and
have compassion on you and multiply you,
[n]as he swore to your fathers, 18 if you obey
the voice of the LORD your God, [o]keeping

1 Or *evil person* 2 Hebrew *the wife of your bosom* 3 That is, setting apart (devoting) as an offering to the Lord (for destruction)

The Three Purposes of the Law

Scripture shows that God intends His law to function in three ways, which Calvin crystallized in classic form for the church's benefit as the law's threefold use.

Its first function is to be a mirror reflecting to us both the perfect righteousness of God and our own sinfulness and shortcomings. As Augustine wrote, "the law bids us, as we try to fulfill its requirements, and become wearied in our weakness under it, to know how to ask the help of grace." The law is meant to give knowledge of sin (Rom. 3:20; 4:15; 5:13; 7:7–11), and by showing us our need of pardon and our danger of damnation to lead us in repentance and faith to Christ (Gal. 3:19–24).

A second function, the "civil use," is to restrain evil. Though the law cannot change the heart, it can to some extent inhibit lawlessness by its threats of judgment, especially when backed by a civil code that administers punishment for proven offenses (Deut. 13:6–11; 19:16–21; Rom. 13:3, 4). Thus it secures civil order, and serves to protect the righteous from the unjust.

Its third function is to guide the regenerate into the good works that God has planned for them (Eph. 2:10). The law tells God's children what will please their heavenly Father. It could be called their family code. Christ was speaking of this third use of the law when He said that those who become His disciples must be taught to do all that He had commanded (Matt. 28:20), and that obedience to His commands will prove the reality of one's love for Him (John 14:15). The Christian is free from the law as a system of salvation (Rom. 6:14; 7:4, 6; 1 Cor. 9:20; Gal. 2:15–19; 3:25), but is "under the law of Christ" as a rule of life (1 Cor. 9:21; Gal. 6:2).

13:6–11 Attention turns to the second instance of seduction to apostasy.

13:6 your brother . . . friend. The closest ties on earth do not dissolve the obligation to remain faithful to the true and only God (cf. 21:18–21).

13:10 See theological note "The Three Purposes of the Law."

13:12–18 In the third instance of apostasy the case of a whole town is considered. First, investigation is undertaken (vv. 12–14). If the thing is true, the town must be destroyed (vv. 14–15). Note that the plunder of the town is not to be taken for private gain (vv. 16–18). The thought of gain might cloud the judgment of those who investigated. The Hebrew for "heap" is *tel*, the word now used by archaeologists for the mounds comprising the ruins of successive generations of the buried cities they excavate.

all his commandments that I am commanding you today, and doing what is
right in the sight of the LORD your God.

Clean and Unclean Food

14 "You are [p]the sons of the LORD your
God. [q]You shall not cut yourselves
or make any [r]baldness on your foreheads
for the dead. 2 For [s]you are a people holy to
the LORD your God, and the LORD has chosen you to be a people for his treasured
possession, out of all the peoples who are
on the face of the earth.

3 [t]"You shall not eat any abomination.
4 [u]These are the animals you may eat: the ox,
the sheep, the goat, 5 the deer, the gazelle,
the roebuck, the wild goat, the ibex,[1] the
antelope, and the mountain sheep. 6 Every
animal that parts the hoof and has the hoof
cloven in two and chews the cud, among the
animals, you may eat. 7 Yet of those that
chew the cud or have the hoof cloven you
shall not eat these: the camel, the hare, and
the [v]rock badger, because they chew the cud
but do not part the hoof, are unclean for
you. 8 And the pig, because it parts the hoof
but does not chew the cud, is unclean for
you. Their flesh you shall not eat, and [w]their
carcasses you shall not touch.

9 "Of all that are in the waters you may
eat these: whatever has fins and scales you
may eat. 10 And whatever does not have fins
and scales you shall not eat; it is unclean
for you.

11 "You may eat all clean birds. 12 But
these are the ones that you shall not eat:
the eagle,[2] the bearded vulture, the black
vulture, 13 the kite, the falcon of any kind;
14 every raven of any kind; 15 the ostrich,
the nighthawk, the sea gull, the hawk of
any kind; 16 the little owl and the short-
eared owl, the barn owl 17 and the tawny
owl, the carrion vulture and the cormorant, 18 the stork, the heron of any kind;
the hoopoe and the bat. 19 And all winged
insects are unclean for you; they shall not
be eaten. 20 All clean winged things you
may eat.

21 [x]"You shall not eat anything that has
died naturally. You may give it to the
sojourner who is within your towns, that
he may eat it, or you may sell it to a foreigner. For [y]you are a people holy to the
LORD your God.

[z]"You shall not boil a young goat in its
mother's milk.

Tithes

22 [a]"You shall tithe all the yield of your
seed that comes from the field year by year.
23 And before the LORD your God, in the
place that he will choose, to make his
name dwell there, [b]you shall eat the tithe of
your grain, of your wine, and of your oil,
[c]and the firstborn of your herd and flock,
[d]that you may learn to fear the LORD your
God always. 24 And if the way is too long for
you, so that you are not able to carry the
tithe, when the LORD your God blesses you,

Chapter 14
1 [p][Isai. 1:2; Hos. 1:10; John 1:12; Rom. 9:8, 26; Gal. 3:26] [q]See Lev. 19:28 [r][Isai. 15:2; 22:12; Ezek. 7:18; Amos 8:10]
2 [s]See ch. 7:6
3 [t]Ezek. 4:14; [Acts 10:13, 14]
4 [u]For ver. 4-20, see Lev. 11:2-23
7 [v]Lev. 11:5; [Ps. 104:18; Prov. 30:26]
8 [w][Lev. 11:26]
21 [x]See Lev. 7:24 [y]See ch. 7:6 [z]See Ex. 23:19
22 [a]See Num. 18:21
23 [b]ch. 12:7; 15:20 [c]ch. 12:6 [d]ch. 4:10; 17:19

1 Or *addax* 2 The identity of many of these birds is uncertain

14:1 You shall not cut yourselves . . . for the dead. See Lev. 19:27, 28, where the same rules are given. Details of this custom are unclear, but it doubtless involved practices associated with ancestor worship and pagan ritual mourning. Because Israel was chosen by God as His special possession (v. 2; 26:18), Israel was to be different and was to reject all pagan religion and associated rituals.

14:3–21 This section and Num. 5:1–4 are the main references to the clean-and-unclean legislation outside of Lev. 11–15. The only ground given for the prohibitions is that Israel is to be holy to the Lord. Several reasons, ranging from religious to medical, have been suggested for these laws. In many cases the prohibitions require what would be good public health procedure, but the distinction of clean and unclean was not entirely a matter of health. Rather, it teaches an important moral and spiritual truth: separation from the specified foods and diseases portrayed the holiness of God and of His people. See notes Lev. 11–15.

14:11 all clean birds. No easy formula is given to identify clean birds. In general the scavenger birds are unclean, probably because of their frequent contact with carrion. Such birds might pose a health risk as well. Some of the birds listed in vv. 12–18 can no longer be precisely identified.

14:19 winged insects. But there were exceptions: Lev. 11:22 explicitly mentions the locust, destroying locust, cricket, and grasshopper as clean.

14:21 a young goat in its mother's milk. This prohibition is not fully explained. Appearing also in Ex. 23:19 and 34:26, it is the basis of the practice among orthodox Jews of not eating milk and meat products together. The prohibition may be similar to 22:6, which forbids taking the mother bird with its young. There, the idea is to preserve the mother and nest so as to have more birds for the future. Some have also suggested that cooking a goat in milk may have been a Canaanite practice with pagan religious implications, but the evidence is not clear.

14:22 tithe. A tenth. The law of the tithe was expressed as early as the time of the patriarchs (Gen. 14:20; 28:22). Leviticus 27:32 specifies that the tithe of animals must not be selected, but must be "all that pass under the herdsman's staff."

14:23 before the LORD. The tithe was to be taken to the sanctuary (12:17), where the worshipers were to eat a portion in happy fellowship with the priests, Levites, and the poor. Far from being a burdensome requirement, the giving of the tithe was to be an occasion of joyous celebration and worship (12:7 note; cf. 2 Cor. 9:7).

14:24 if the way is too long. Travel was not easy, and the transportation of agricultural products was harder still. A practical solution was allowed—they could convert the goods to money and carry the money (v. 25).

because [e]the place is too far from you,
which the LORD your God chooses, to set
his name there, 25 then you shall turn it into
money and bind up the money in your
hand and go to the place that the LORD
your God chooses 26 and spend the money
for whatever you desire—oxen or sheep or
wine or strong drink, whatever your
appetite craves. And [b]you shall eat there
before the LORD your God and rejoice, you
and your household. 27 And you shall not
neglect [f]the Levite who is within your
towns, for [g]he has no portion or inheritance with you.

28 [h]"At the end of every three years you
shall bring out all the tithe of your produce
in the same year and lay it up within your
towns. 29 And the Levite, because [g]he has
no portion or inheritance with you, and the
sojourner, the fatherless, and the widow,
who are within your towns, shall come and
eat and be filled, that [i]the LORD your God
may bless you in all the work of your hands
that you do.

The Sabbatical Year

15 "At the end of [j]every seven years
you shall grant a release. 2 And this
is the manner of the release: every creditor
shall release what he has lent to his neighbor. He shall not exact it of his neighbor,
his brother, because the LORD's release has
been proclaimed. 3 [k]Of a foreigner you may
exact it, but whatever of yours is with your
brother your hand shall release. 4 [l]But there
will be no poor among you; [m]for the LORD
will bless you in the land that the LORD
your God is giving you for an inheritance to
possess—5 [n]if only you will strictly obey the
voice of the LORD your God, being careful
to do all this commandment that I command you today. 6 For the LORD your God
will bless you, [o]as he promised you, and
[p]you shall lend to many nations, but you
shall not borrow, and [q]you shall rule over
many nations, but they shall not rule over
you.

7 "If among you, one of your brothers
should become poor, in any of your towns
within your land that the LORD your God is
giving you, [r]you shall not harden your
heart or shut your hand against your poor
brother, 8 but [s]you shall open your hand to
him and lend him sufficient for his need,
whatever it may be. 9 Take care lest there be
an unworthy thought in your heart and you
say, 'The seventh year, the year of release is
near,' and your [t]eye look grudgingly[1] on
your poor brother, and you give him nothing, and he [u]cry to the LORD against you,
and [v]you be guilty of sin. 10 You shall give to
him freely, and [w]your heart shall not be
grudging when you give to him, because
[x]for this the LORD your God will bless you
in all your work and in all that you undertake. 11 For [y]there will never cease to be
poor in the land. Therefore I command
you, 'You shall open wide your hand to
your brother, to the needy and to the poor,
in your land.'

12 [z]"If your brother, a Hebrew man or a
Hebrew woman, is sold[2] to you, he shall
serve you six years, and in the seventh year
you shall let him go free from you. 13 And
when you let him go free from you, you shall
not let him go empty-handed. 14 You shall
furnish him liberally out of your flock, out of

24 [e]ch. 12:21
26 [b][See ver. 23 above]
27 [f]See ch. 12:19 [g]See Num. 18:20
28 [h]ch. 26:12; [Amos 4:4]
29 [f][See ver. 27 above] [i]ch. 15:10; 24:19; Ps. 41:1; Prov. 14:21; 19:17; 22:9; Mal. 3:10

Chapter 15
1 [j]ch. 31:10; Neh. 10:31; [ver. 12; Ex. 23:10, 11; Lev. 25:2-4]
3 [k][ch. 23:20]
4 [l][ver. 11] [m]ch. 28:8
5 [n]ch. 28:1
6 [o]ch. 7:13; Ex. 23:25 [p]ch. 28:12, 44 [q]ch. 28:13; 1 Kin. 4:21, 24; Ezra 4:20; [Prov. 22:7]
7 [r][1 John 3:17]
8 [s]Lev. 25:35; [Matt. 5:42; Luke 6:34, 35]
9 [t]ch. 28:54, 56; Prov. 23:6; 28:22; Matt. 20:15 [u]ch. 24:15 [v][Matt. 25:41, 42]
10 [w][2 Cor. 9:7] [x]Prov. 28:27; See ch. 14:29
11 [y][Matt. 26:11; Mark 14:7; John 12:8]
12 [z]Ex. 21:2; Jer. 34:14; [Lev. 25:39-41]

[1] Or *be evil*; also verse 10 [2] Or *sells himself*

14:28 At the end of every three years. The third-year tithe is mentioned again only in 26:12, and the precise details are unclear. Because it was a special gift for the Levites and the poor, and because the Levitical cities were scattered throughout Israel (Josh. 21), it would have been impractical to take all the tithes at one time to the central place of worship. Thus, these tithe offerings were to be stored in the towns of Israel and used to provide for the needy.

15:1 every seven years . . . grant a release. The sabbatical year was established and described in Ex. 23:10, 11 and Lev. 25:1–7, which require that the land should lie fallow during the seventh year. This passage (15:1–11) adds the provision that debts should be forgiven in that year. Since a loan might be arranged shortly before the sabbatical year, it could amount to a gift. For this reason vv. 7–11 warn against refusing to lend to the poor under these circumstances.

15:4 there will be no poor. The forgiveness of personal loans to the poor is apparently in view here. God desired to bless His people materially in the Land of Promise so that borrowing would be unnecessary (vv. 5, 6). Although full obedience would have resulted in the eradication of poverty from Israel, Moses realistically recognized that some poverty would remain (v. 11; cf. Matt. 26:11). The sabbatical year and the Jubilee provisions (Lev. 25:8–34) were God's gracious provision to minimize the oppression of the poor.

15:12 If your brother . . . is sold. Because this law of servitude is similar to the sabbatical year regulation, it might be thought that the sabbatical year freed all slaves. But that is not stated. Rather, the period of servitude was six years for every Hebrew slave and in the seventh year he went free.

Recalling the nation's experience of servitude in Egypt (v. 15), Israel was to be merciful to slaves. The slave in ancient Israel had rights (Ex. 21:1–11, 20), and the redemption provisions here are generous—the freed slave must be given something with which to start fresh (v. 13, 14; cf. Ex. 12:35, 36). The law of servitude described does not contradict the provision for freedom in the Year of Jubilee (Lev. 25:39–43). That provision probably refers to the special case of an impoverished servant whose ancestral property was gone and who therefore had nowhere to go if freed. When the Year of Jubilee came, his home was restored and he went to it.

your threshing floor, and out of your winepress. [a]As the LORD your God has blessed
you, you shall give to him. 15 [b]You shall
remember that you were a slave in the land
of Egypt, and the LORD your God redeemed
you; therefore I command you this today.
16 But [c]if he says to you, 'I will not go out
from you,' because he loves you and your
household, since he is well-off with you,
17 then you shall take an awl, and put it
through his ear into the door, and he shall be
your slave forever. And to your female slave
you shall do the same. 18 It shall not seem
hard to you when you let him go free from
you, for at half the cost of a hired servant he
has served you six years. So the LORD your
God will bless you in all that you do.
19 [d]"All the firstborn males that are born
of your herd and flock you shall dedicate to
the LORD your God. You shall do no work
with the firstborn of your herd, nor shear
the firstborn of your flock. 20 [e]You shall eat
it, you and your household, before the
LORD your God year by year at the place
that the LORD will choose. 21 [f]But if it has
any blemish, if it is lame or blind or has
any serious blemish whatever, you shall
not sacrifice it to the LORD your God. 22 You
shall eat it within your towns. [g]The
unclean and the clean alike may eat it, as
though it were a gazelle or a deer. 23 [h]Only
you shall not eat its blood; you shall pour
it out on the ground like water.

Passover

16 "Observe the [i]month of Abib and
keep the Passover to the LORD your
God, for [j]in the month of Abib the LORD
your God brought you out of Egypt by
night. 2 And you shall offer the Passover
sacrifice to the LORD your God, from the
flock or [k]the herd, [l]at the place that the
LORD will choose, to make his name dwell
there. 3 You shall eat no leavened bread
with it. [m]Seven days you shall eat it with
unleavened bread, the bread of affliction—for you came out of the land of
Egypt [n]in haste—that all the days of your
life you may remember the day when you
came out of the land of Egypt. 4 [o]No leav-
en shall be seen with you in all your territory for seven days, [p]nor shall any of the
flesh that you sacrifice on the evening of
the first day remain all night until morning. 5 You may not offer the Passover sacrifice within any of your towns that the
LORD your God is giving you, 6 but at the
place that the LORD your God will choose,
to make his name dwell in it, there you
shall offer the Passover sacrifice, in the
evening at sunset, at the time you came
out of Egypt. 7 And you shall cook it and
eat it at the place that the LORD your God
will choose. And in the morning you shall
turn and go to your tents. 8 For [q]six days
you shall eat unleavened bread, and on
the seventh day there shall be [r]a solemn
assembly to the LORD your God. You shall
do no work on it.

The Feast of Weeks

9 [s]"You shall count seven weeks. Begin to
count the seven weeks from the time the
sickle is first put to the standing grain.

14 [a]ch. 8:18; 16:17
15 [b]See ch. 5:15
16 [c]Ex. 21:5, 6
19 [d]See Ex. 13:2
20 [e]ch. 12:7; 14:23, 26
21 [f]See Lev. 22:20
22 [g]ch. 12:15
23 [h]See Lev. 3:17
Chapter 16
1 [i]For ver. 1-8, see Ex. 12:2-39
[j]Ex. 13:4; 34:18
2 [k]Num. 28:19 [l]See ch. 12:5
3 [m]Ex. 13:6 [n]Ex. 12:11; [Isai. 52:12]
4 [o]Ex. 13:7 [p]Ex. 34:25
8 [q][Ex. 13:6] [r]Lev. 23:8, 36
9 [s]Ex. 23:16; 34:22; Lev. 23:15; Num. 28:26; [Acts 2:1]

15:19 All the firstborn . . . dedicate. See 12:17; 15:19 text note.

nor shear. The firstborn ox was not to be worked nor the firstborn sheep shorn, because they were to be given to the Lord while still young.

15:21 any blemish. See 17:1.

16:1–17 Most of ch. 16 deals with the three pilgrimage festivals, so called because they required all grown males to celebrate them at the sanctuary. These feasts are mentioned briefly in Ex. 23:14–17, ending with the same charge given in similar language at Deut. 16:16: Every man must bring his offering. The feasts are listed again in Ex. 34:18–23, where the Passover is simply included with the closely associated Feast of Unleavened Bread (Ex. 23:15 note). All five major feasts are listed more fully in Lev. 23, and they are listed with their offerings in Num. 28 and 29.

16:1 the month of Abib. In Exodus, the Passover (Ex. 12:1–14) and the Feast of Unleavened Bread (Ex. 12:15–20) were instituted in the "first month" (Ex. 12:2, 18), also called the month of Abib, one of the Canaanite month names (Ex. 13:4; 23:15). The Babylonian name of the first month is Nisan, and Babylonian month names appear in Old Testament books of the exilic and postexilic periods (e.g., Esth. 3:7).

keep the Passover. See notes Ex. 12:1–26. The Passover clearly symbolizes substitution, since the lamb is slain in place of the firstborn. Although the blood of animals could not, in itself, redeem human beings, the Passover lamb was a sacramental symbol pointing forward to the effectual sacrifice of Christ (Heb. 10:1–10). So Paul is fully justified in saying, "Christ, our Passover lamb, has been sacrificed" (1 Cor. 5:7).

16:6 at the place . . . God will choose. At the location of the sanctuary. See note 12:5.

16:7 in the morning . . . go to your tents. The lamb or goat was to be slaughtered at the sanctuary at sundown, roasted in that area for several hours, and then eaten at midnight. Following the celebration, the people would return to their tents in the morning. After their settlement in Canaan, when they assembled at the central sanctuary, the majority surely lived in tents again. In modern times the Samaritan Passover on Mount Gerizim is performed precisely in this way.

16:9–12 The Passover was always celebrated on the fourteenth day of the first month (corresponding to the modern March-April). The Israelites used the lunar month, so the Passover was always on a full moon. Associated with Passover was the presentation of the first ripe sheaf of grain (Lev. 23:9). On the day following the seventh Sabbath after that presentation (Lev. 23:15, 16) was the one-day "Feast of Weeks" (v. 10), called "Pentecost" in the New Testament because of this fifty-day calculation.

10 Then you shall keep [t]the Feast of Weeks to
the LORD your God with [u]the tribute of a
freewill offering from your hand, which you
shall give [v]as the LORD your God blesses you.
11 And [w]you shall rejoice before the LORD
your God, you and your son and your
daughter, your male servant and your female
servant, the Levite who is within your towns,
the sojourner, the fatherless, and the widow
who are among you, at the place that the
LORD your God will choose, to make his
name dwell there. 12 [x]You shall remember
that you were a slave in Egypt; and you shall
be careful to observe these statutes.

The Feast of Booths

13 [y]"You shall keep the Feast of Booths
seven days, when you have gathered in the
produce from your threshing floor and
your winepress. 14 [z]You shall rejoice in your
feast, you and your son and your daughter,
your male servant and your female servant,
the Levite, the sojourner, the fatherless,
and the widow who are within your towns.
15 For [a]seven days you shall keep the feast
to the LORD your God at the place that the
LORD will choose, because the LORD your
God will bless you in all your produce and
in all the work of your hands, so that you
will be altogether joyful.
16 [b]"Three times a year all your males
shall appear before the LORD your God at
the place that he will choose: at the Feast
of Unleavened Bread, at the Feast of
Weeks, and at the Feast of Booths. [c]They
shall not appear before the LORD empty-
handed. 17 Every man [d]shall give as he is
able, [v]according to the blessing of the LORD
your God that he has given you.

10 [t]2 Chr. 8:13 [u]See ch. 26:1-11 [v]ch. 12:15; [1 Cor. 16:2]
11 [w]ch. 12:7, 12, 18; 14:26; See Neh. 8:9-12
12 [x]See ch. 5:15
13 [y]Ex. 23:16; See Lev. 23:34
14 [z]ver. 11; See Neh. 8:9-12
15 [a]Lev. 23:39
16 [b]ch. 31:11; Ex. 23:14, 17; 34:23 [c]Ex. 23:15
17 [d][Ezek. 46:5, 11; 2 Cor. 8:12] [v][See ver. 10 above]
18 [e]ch. 1:16; Num. 11:16; Josh. 1:10; 1 Chr. 23:4; 26:29
19 [f]ch. 27:19; Ex. 23:2, 6; Isai. 10:2; Amos 5:12; [Lev. 19:15]; See ch. 24:17 [g]See ch. 1:17 [h]See Ex. 23:8
21 [i]Ex. 34:13; Judg. 6:25; 1 Kin. 14:15; 16:33; 2 Kin. 13:6; 17:16; 2 Chr. 33:3
Chapter 17
1 [j]See Lev. 22:20
2 [k]For ver. 2-7, see ch. 13:6-14 [l]Josh. 7:11, 15; 23:16; Judg. 2:20; 2 Kin. 18:12; Hos. 6:7; 8:1
3 [m]See ch. 4:19 [n][Jer. 7:31; 19:5; 32:35]
4 [o]ch. 13:14; 19:18
5 [p][Lev. 24:14, 16; Josh. 7:25]
6 [q][John 8:17]; See Num. 35:30

Justice

18 "You shall appoint [e]judges and officers
in all your towns that the LORD your God is
giving you, according to your tribes, and
they shall judge the people with righteous
judgment. 19 [f]You shall not pervert justice.
[g]You shall not show partiality, [h]and you
shall not accept a bribe, for a bribe blinds
the eyes of the wise and subverts the cause
of the righteous. 20 Justice, and only justice,
you shall follow, that you may live and
inherit the land that the LORD your God is
giving you.

Forbidden Forms of Worship

21 "You shall not plant any tree as [i]an
Asherah beside the altar of the LORD your
God that you shall make. 22 And you shall
not set up a pillar, which the LORD your
God hates.

17 [j]"You shall not sacrifice to the LORD
your God an ox or a sheep in which
is a blemish, any defect whatever, for that
is an abomination to the LORD your God.
2 [k]"If there is found among you, within
any of your towns that the LORD your God
is giving you, a man or woman who does
what is evil in the sight of the LORD your
God, [l]in transgressing his covenant, 3 and
has gone and served other gods and worshiped them, or [m]the sun or the moon or
any of the host of heaven, [n]which I have
forbidden, 4 and it is told you and you hear
of it, then you shall inquire [o]diligently, and
if it is true and certain that such an abomination has been done in Israel, 5 then you
shall bring out to your gates that man or
woman who has done this evil thing, and
you [p]shall stone that man or woman to
death with stones. 6 [q]On the evidence of

16:13–17 The "Feast of Booths" (v. 13) is so called, because for a week they were to gather at the sanctuary and live in temporary structures. It begins on the fifteenth day of the seventh lunar month (modern September-October), at the end of the agricultural season after the grain was threshed and the grapes harvested. Naturally, the tithe of the harvest was to be brought at this feast, which was also to memorialize Israel's pilgrim experience in leaving Egypt (Lev. 23:43). In addition, this feast was to be a time of reading the law (31:10–13; Neh. 8).

16:18 appoint judges and officers. Moses had appointed leaders at Sinai (1:13), and this section specifies that such an organization should continue. Moreover, the high ideal of justice, and justice alone, was to guide their conduct (19:15–21 note).

16:19 a bribe blinds. This fact is often emphasized (Ex. 23:8; Prov. 17:23).

16:21 Asherah. A reference to the wooden poles, images, or trees that represented the Canaanite goddess Asherah. There was to be no compromise with pagan idolatry (17:2–7). Despite such warnings, these pagan Asherah shrines later became a snare to the Israelites (Judg. 3:7, 8; 2 Kin. 13:6; 17:10).

17:1 blemish . . . defect. It was repeatedly commanded that any flaw or defect would make an animal unsuitable for sacrifice (15:21; Lev. 22:19–25; Num. 19:2). Also, Lev. 21:16–23 specifies that any priest with a physical deformity could not officiate. The symbolism is clear: God is holy (Lev. 21:23), and He demands perfection. As symbols of the coming perfect Savior and His worthy sacrifice, the sacrificial animals were to be without defect.

17:2–7 The sin of idolatry is in view, the seriousness of which is indicated by the consistently prescribed death penalty (v. 5; ch. 13). In such instances, the judicial goal was not rehabilitation or restitution, but to purge Israel of the abomination of idolatry (vv. 4, 7).

17:6 two witnesses or of three witnesses. Condemnation does not take place on the basis of hearsay. Two or three witnesses must agree (v. 6; 19:15–19; Num. 35:30), and must be sufficiently convinced and sincere to take part in the stoning, knowing that the penalty for false witness to a crime was the same as for the crime itself (19:19). There was no torture for confession or torture of witnesses.

two witnesses or of three witnesses the one
who is to die shall be put to death; a person shall not be put to death on the evidence of one witness. 7 [r]The hand of the
witnesses shall be first against him to put
him to death, and afterward the hand of all
the people. So [s]you shall purge[1] the evil[2]
from your midst.

Legal Decisions by Priests and Judges

8 "If any case arises requiring decision
between one kind of homicide and another, one kind of legal right and another, or
one kind of assault and another, any case
within your towns that is too difficult for
you, then you shall arise and go up to [t]the
place that the LORD your God will choose.
9 [u]And you shall come to the Levitical
priests and to the judge who is in office in
those days, and you shall consult them,
and [v]they shall declare to you the decision.
10 Then you shall do according to what they
declare to you from that place that the
LORD will choose. And you shall be careful
to do according to all that they direct you.
11 According to the instructions that they
give you, and according to the decision
which they pronounce to you, you shall
do. You shall not turn aside from the verdict that they declare to you, either to the
right hand or to the left. 12 The man who
[w]acts presumptuously by not obeying the
priest [x]who stands to minister there before
the LORD your God, or the judge, that man
shall die. So [s]you shall purge the evil from
Israel. 13 And all the people [y]shall hear and
fear and not act presumptuously again.

Laws Concerning Israel's Kings

14 "When you come to the land that the
LORD your God is giving you, and you possess it and dwell in it and then say, [z]'I will
set a king over me, like all the nations that
are around me,' 15 you may indeed set a
king over you [a]whom the LORD your God
will choose. One [b]from among your brothers you shall set as king over you. You may
not put a foreigner over you, who is not
your brother. 16 Only he must not acquire
many [c]horses for himself or cause the people [d]to return to Egypt in order to acquire
many horses, since the LORD has said to
you, [e]'You shall never return that way
again.' 17 And he [f]shall not acquire many
wives for himself, lest his heart turn away,
[g]nor shall he acquire for himself excessive
silver and gold.

18 "And when he sits on the throne of his
kingdom, [h]he shall write for himself in a
book a copy of this law, [i]approved by[3] the
Levitical priests. 19 And [j]it shall be with
him, and he shall read in it all the days of
his life, [k]that he may learn to fear the LORD
his God by keeping all the words of this
law and these statutes, and doing them,
20 that his heart may not be lifted up above
his brothers, and that he [l]may not turn
aside from the commandment, either to
the right hand or to the left, [m]so that he
may continue long in his kingdom, he and
his children, in Israel.

Provision for Priests and Levites

18 "The Levitical priests, all the tribe
of Levi, [n]shall have no portion or
inheritance with Israel. They [o]shall eat the
LORD's food offerings[4] as their[5] inheritance.
2 They shall have no inheritance among
their brothers; the LORD is their inheritance, as he promised them. 3 And this
shall be the priests' due from the people,
from those offering a sacrifice, whether an

7 [r]ch. 13:9; [Acts 7:58] [s]ver. 12; See ch. 13:5
8 [t]See ch. 12:5
9 [u]ch. 19:17; 21:5; 2 Chr. 19:8, 10; Ps. 122:5; Jer. 18:18; Hag. 2:11; Mal. 2:7 [v]Ezek. 44:24
12 [w][ch. 18:20, 22; Ezra 10:8] [x]ch. 10:8; 18:5, 7 [s][See ver. 7 above]
13 [y]See ch. 13:11
14 [z][1 Sam. 8:5, 19, 20]
15 [a][1 Sam. 9:15; 10:24; 16:12; 1 Chr. 22:10] [b][Jer. 30:21]
16 [c][1 Kin. 4:26; 10:26, 28; 2 Chr. 1:16; 9:28; Isai. 2:7; 31:1] [d]Isai. 31:1; Ezek. 17:15 [e]ch. 28:68; Hos. 11:5; [Ex. 13:17; 14:13; Num. 14:3, 4]; See Jer. 42:15-19
17 [f][1 Kin. 11:3, 4; Neh. 13:26] [g][Isai. 2:7]
18 [h][2 Kin. 11:12] [i]ch. 31:9, 26; 2 Kin. 22:8; 2 Chr. 34:14
19 [j]Josh. 1:8 [k]ch. 4:10; 14:23
20 [l]ch. 5:32; 1 Kin. 15:5 [m]ch. 4:40
Chapter 18
1 [n]See Num. 18:20 [o]Num. 18:8, 9; Josh. 13:14; 1 Sam. 2:28; [1 Cor. 9:13]

[1] Septuagint *drive out* [2] Or *evil person* [3] Hebrew *from before* [4] Or *the offerings by fire to the LORD* [5] Hebrew *his*

17:8 requiring decision. We do not know the precise details of the Israelite judicial system (19:15–21 note). There were graded courts to take care of difficult cases (Ex. 18:21–26), with priests who judged and also other judges. This passage stresses that the judicial office is divinely ordained, and that verdicts were to be accepted on pain of death (v. 12).

17:14–17 The reference to "a king" (v. 14) is conditional, and need not imply that the text was written when a king ruled Israel, although critics have argued that with its reference to horses, wives, and wealth, the section refers to Solomon and was written long after him by one of his detractors. There was no king in Moses' time, but the future possibility of such a ruler was obvious, since every known ancient nation had a king, and an Israelite king was even predicted in Gen. 49:10. That Israel might have a king was never denied, although it was stated most emphatically that God was their King (33:5). In addition, v. 15 warns against choosing a foreign king, a stipulation that cannot be directed against Solomon and his successors, who were native Israelites.

17:18 write . . . a copy of this law. The phrase "this law" may refer to the Book of Deuteronomy as a whole, or perhaps to the Book of the Covenant (Ex. 24:7) or to the other parts of the Pentateuch. As a covenant nation, Israel was to be governed according to the covenant laws.

18:1 all the tribe of Levi. Not only the priests, but the whole tribe of Levi, numbering twenty-three thousand, was to receive no inheritance (Num. 18:20; 26:62; Deut. 10:9). This tribe would have no farms for livelihood, but would depend on the tithes and offerings of the people (vv. 3–5). Moses specifically allotted them forty-two cities, six of which would be cities of refuge (Num. 35:2–8). In due time these cities were allocated by Joshua (Josh. 21).

18:3 priests' due. In place of a land inheritance, and in recognition of their priestly duties, the priests had a right to specific portions of the animals offered for sacrifice. Later, this practice was sometimes abused by corrupt priests (1 Sam. 2:12–17).

ox or a sheep: [p]they shall give to the priest
the shoulder and the two cheeks and the
stomach. 4 [q]The firstfruits of your grain, of
your wine and of your oil, and the first
fleece of your sheep, you shall give him.
5 For the LORD your God has chosen him
out of all your tribes [r]to stand and minister
in the name of the LORD, him and his sons
for all time.

6 "And if a Levite comes from any of your
towns out of all Israel, [s]where he lives—and
he may come when he desires[1]—[t]to the
place that the LORD will choose, 7 and ministers in the name of the LORD his God, [u]like
all his fellow Levites who stand to minister
there before the LORD, 8 then he may have
equal [v]portions to eat, besides what he
receives from the sale of his patrimony.[2]

Abominable Practices

9 "When you come into the land that the
LORD your God is giving you, [w]you shall not
learn to follow the abominable practices of
those nations. 10 There shall not be found
among you anyone [x]who burns his son or
his daughter as an offering,[3] anyone who
[y]practices divination or [z]tells fortunes or
interprets omens, or [a]a sorcerer 11 or a
charmer or [b]a medium or a wizard or [c]a
necromancer, 12 [d]for whoever does these
things is an abomination to the LORD. And
[e]because of these abominations the LORD
your God is driving them out before you.
13 You shall be blameless before the LORD
your God, 14 for these nations, which you are
about to dispossess, listen to fortune-tellers
and to diviners. But as for you, the LORD
your God has not allowed you to do this.

A New Prophet like Moses

15 [f]"The LORD your God will raise up for
you a prophet like me from among you, from
your brothers—it is to him you shall listen—
16 just as you desired of the LORD your God at
Horeb [g]on the day of the assembly, when
you said, [h]'Let me not hear again the voice of
the LORD my God or see this great fire any
more, lest I die.' 17 And the LORD said to me,

3 [p]See Lev. 7:30-34
4 [q]Num. 18:12; 2 Chr. 31:5
5 [r]ch. 17:12
6 [s]Num. 35:2, 3; Judg. 17:7; 19:1 [t]See ch. 12:5
7 [u][1 Chr. 23:6; 2 Chr. 31:2]
8 [v]2 Chr. 31:4; Neh. 12:44, 47; 13:10
9 [w]ch. 12:29-31; See Lev. 18:26-30
10 [x]See Lev. 18:21 [y]2 Kin. 17:17 [z]See Lev. 19:26 [a][Ex. 22:18]
11 [b]See Lev. 19:31 [c][1 Sam. 28:7]
12 [d]ch. 22:5; 25:16 [e]See ch. 9:4
15 [f]John 1:21, 25, 45; Cited Acts 3:22; 7:37
16 [g]See ch. 9:10 [h]See Ex. 20:19

1 Or *lives—if he comes enthusiastically* 2 The meaning of the Hebrew is uncertain 3 Hebrew *makes his son or his daughter pass through the fire*

Prophets

The canonical prophets, whose books make up over a quarter of the Old Testament, were called by God to be channels of revelation. They were men of God who stood in His council (Jer. 23:22), knew His mind, and were enabled to declare it. God the Holy Spirit spoke in and through them (2 Pet. 1:19–21; Is. 61:1; Mic. 3:8; Acts 28:25–27; 1 Pet. 1:10–12). They knew He was doing so; hence they dared to begin proclamations with "Thus says the LORD," presenting Yahweh Himself as the speaker of what they were saying.

Prophecy involved prediction (foretelling), but usually this was done in a context of declaring God's warnings and exhortations to His covenant people (forthtelling). The prophets looked forward to the coming of the messianic King and His kingdom after purging judgments, but often their chief concern was exhortation to repentance, in hope that impending judgments might be averted. The prophets were primarily reformers, enforcing God's law and recalling God's people to the covenant faithfulness from which they had lapsed.

Along with their preaching to the nation went prayer for the nation—they talked to God about men just as earnestly as they talked to men about God. They fulfilled a unique ministry as intercessors (Ex. 32:30–32; 1 Sam. 7:5–9; 12:19–23; 2 Kin. 19:4; cf. Jer. 7:16; 11:14; 14:11).

False prophets were a bane to Israel. Professionally linked with Israel's organized worship, they said what people wanted to hear and spoke their own dreams and opinions rather than words of God (1 Kin. 22:1–28; Jer. 23:9–40; Ezek. 13).

In the New Testament, one book (Revelation) announces itself as a true and trustworthy prophecy, received directly from God (from God the Father through Jesus Christ, Rev. 1:1–3; 22:12–20). The ministry of the apostles brought instruction directly from God to His people, just as the Old Testament prophetic ministry had done, though the form of presentation was different. The prophets of the New Testament period were linked with the apostles in the foundation of the church (Eph. 2:20; 3:5) as expositors of the fulfillment in Christ of Old Testament prophecy (Rom. 16:25–27).

18:9 the abominable practices of those nations. Anticipating the instructions regarding true and false prophecy in vv. 19–22, Moses forbids all attempts to discern the future through occult, pagan means, as well as resorting to sorcery and witchcraft. The detestable character of these practices is underscored and cited as a reason for divine judgment upon the Canaanites (vv. 9, 12).

[i]‘They are right in what they have spoken.
18 [f]I will raise up for them a prophet like you
from among their brothers. [j]And I will put
my words in his mouth, and [k]he shall speak
to them all that I command him. 19 [l]And
whoever will [m]not listen to my words that he
shall speak in my name, I myself will require
it of him. 20 [n]But the prophet who presumes
to speak a word in my name that I have not
commanded him to speak, or[1] who speaks
in the name of other gods, that same prophet
shall die.’ 21 And if you say in your heart,
‘How may we know the word that the LORD
has not spoken?’— 22 [o]when a prophet
speaks in the name of the LORD, if the word
does not come to pass or come true, that is
a word that the LORD has not spoken; [n]the
prophet has spoken it presumptuously. You
need not be afraid of him.

Laws Concerning Cities of Refuge

19 “When [p]the LORD your God cuts off
the nations whose land the LORD
your God is giving you, and you dispossess
them and dwell in their cities and in their
houses, 2 [q]you shall set apart three cities for
yourselves in the land that the LORD your
God is giving you to possess. 3 You shall
measure the distances[2] and divide into
three parts the area of the land that the
LORD your God gives you as a possession,
so that any manslayer can flee to them.
4 “This is the provision for [r]the manslayer,
who by fleeing there may save his life. If
anyone kills his neighbor unintentionally
without having hated him in the past— 5 as
when someone goes into the forest with his
neighbor to cut wood, and his hand swings
the axe to cut down a tree, and the head
slips from the handle and strikes his neighbor so that he dies—he may flee to one of
these cities and live, 6 lest [s]the avenger of
blood in hot anger pursue the manslayer
and overtake him, because the way is long,
and strike him fatally, though the man did
not deserve to die, since he had not hated
his neighbor in the past. 7 Therefore I command you, You shall set apart three cities.
8 [t]And if the LORD your God enlarges your
territory, [u]as he has sworn to your fathers,
and [v]gives you all the land that he promised to give to your fathers— 9 provided
you are careful to keep all this commandment, which I command you today, by loving the LORD your God and by walking ever
in his ways—[w]then you shall add three
other cities to these three, 10 lest innocent
blood be shed in your land that the LORD
your God is giving you for an inheritance,
and so the guilt of bloodshed be upon you.
11 “But if anyone hates his neighbor and
lies in wait for him and attacks him [x]and
strikes him fatally so that he dies, and he
flees into one of these cities, 12 then the elders of his city shall send and take him
from there, and hand him over to the
avenger of blood, so that he may die.
13 [y]Your eye shall not pity him, [z]but you
shall purge the guilt of innocent blood[3]
from Israel, so that it may be well with you.

Property Boundaries

14 [a]“You shall not move your neighbor’s
landmark, which the men of old have set,
in the inheritance that you will hold in the
land that the LORD your God is giving you
to possess.

17 [i]ch. 5:28
18 [f][See ver. 15 above] [j]Jer. 1:9; 5:14; [John 17:8] [k][John 4:25; 8:28; 12:49, 50]
19 [l][Acts 3:23] [m]Jer. 29:19; 35:13
20 [n]See ch. 13:5
22 [o][ch. 13:1-3; Jer. 28:9] [n][See ver. 20 above]
Chapter 19
1 [p]ch. 12:29
2 [q]Ex. 21:13; Num. 35:10, 14; Josh. 20:2, 8
4 [r]ch. 4:42; Num. 35:15; Josh. 20:3, 5
6 [s]Num. 35:12, 19, 21, 24, 25, 27
8 [t]ch. 12:20 [u]Ex. 34:24 [Ex. 23:31] [v]See Gen. 15:18-21
9 [w]ver. 2; [Josh. 20:7]
11 [x]ch. 27:24; Ex. 21:12, 14; See Num. 35:16-21
13 [y]See ch. 7:16 [z]ch. 21:9; Num. 35:33; [1 Kin. 2:31]
14 [a]ch. 27:17; Job 24:2; Prov. 22:28; 23:10; Hos. 5:10

[1] Or *and* [2] Hebrew *road* [3] Or *the blood of the innocent*

18:18 Moses, the preeminent prophet of the Old Testament period, introduces the topic of Israelite prophecy. God would communicate His word to Israel through a succession of prophets. As mediators of God’s word to the people, the other Old Testament prophets would function in ways similar to Moses (v. 16). But none would be the initial mediators of a covenant, and none would equal Moses’ intimacy with God or receive divine revelations as clear as those given to him (Num. 12:6–8; Deut. 34:10). This passage, then, finds final fulfillment in the Prophet who is equal to, indeed greater than, the prophet Moses—Jesus Christ (Acts 3:22–26; 7:37; cf. John 5:45–47; Heb. 3:2–6). Like Moses, Christ is the Mediator of a covenant between God and His people (Luke 22:20; Heb. 8:7–13). See theological note “Prophets.”

18:20–22 Two means of discerning false prophets from true are given in Deuteronomy. The first is theological integrity—a true prophet will not teach error or lead the people astray (v. 20; 13:1–5). The second is that his prophetic predictions of the future would come true (v. 22). See “The Authentication of Scripture” at 2 Cor. 4:6.

19:2 three cities. These cities of refuge were to be set aside in Canaan. The three cities of refuge for Transjordan had already been named and set aside. See 4:41–43 for the sequence of establishing these cities.

19:4 If anyone kills his neighbor unintentionally. The law of manslaughter is given first in Ex. 21:13, then more fully in Num. 35:6–28. This passage repeats some matters given in Numbers. Other regulations are added, such as the provision for building access roads to the cities of refuge. Also, this passage specifies three extra cities in Canaan if the nation’s territory is greatly enlarged. But it is plain in both Numbers and Deuteronomy that a man guilty of premeditated murder must die. The death penalty is grounded, not in disrespect for life, but in intense respect for the life of the innocent victim, made in the image of God (Gen. 9:6).

19:9 by loving . . . walking ever in his ways. See 6:4.

19:14 your neighbor’s landmark. Though this verse has sometimes been misinterpreted to urge respect for ancient customs and beliefs, the term “landmark” actually refers to stones that served as boundary markers. This law was essential to prevent encroachment and theft of land (27:17; Prov. 22:28; 23:20).

Laws Concerning Witnesses

15 "A single witness shall not suffice
against a person for any crime or for any
wrong in connection with any offense that
he has committed. [b]Only on the evidence
of two witnesses or of three witnesses shall
a charge be established. 16 If [c]a malicious
witness arises to accuse a person of wrongdoing, 17 then both parties to the dispute
shall appear before the LORD, [d]before the
priests and the judges who are in office in
those days. 18 The judges shall [e]inquire diligently, and if the witness is a false witness
and has accused his brother falsely, 19 [f]then
you shall do to him as he had meant to do
to his brother. So you shall purge the evil[1]
from your midst. 20 And the rest [g]shall hear
and fear, and shall never again commit any
such evil among you. 21 [y]Your eye shall not
pity. [h]It shall be life for life, eye for eye,
tooth for tooth, hand for hand, foot for
foot.

Laws Concerning Warfare

20 "When you go out to war against
your enemies, and see [i]horses and
chariots and an army larger than your own,
you shall not be afraid of them, for the LORD
your God is [j]with you, who brought you up
out of the land of Egypt. 2 And when you
draw near to the battle, [k]the priest shall
come forward and speak to the people 3 and
shall say to them, 'Hear, O Israel, today you
are drawing near for battle against your enemies: let not your heart faint. Do not fear or
panic or be in dread of them, 4 for the LORD
your God is he who goes with you [l]to fight
for you against your enemies, to give you
the victory.' 5 Then the officers shall speak
to the people, saying, 'Is there any man
who has built a new house and has not dedicated it? Let him go back to his house, lest
he die in the battle and another man dedicate it. 6 And is there any man who has
planted a vineyard and has not [m]enjoyed its
fruit? Let him go back to his house, lest he
die in the battle and another man enjoy its
fruit. 7 [n]And is there any man who has
betrothed a wife and has not taken her? Let
him go back to his house, lest he die in the
battle and another man take her.' 8 And the
officers shall speak further to the people,
and say, [o]'Is there any man who is fearful
and fainthearted? Let him go back to his
house, lest he make the heart of his fellows
melt like his own.' 9 And when the officers
have finished speaking to the people, then
commanders shall be appointed at the head
of the people.

10 "When you draw near to a city to fight
against it, [p]offer terms of peace to it. 11 And
if it responds to you peaceably and it opens
to you, then all the people who are found
in it shall do forced labor for you and shall
serve you. 12 But if it makes no peace with
you, but makes war against you, then you
shall besiege it. 13 And when the LORD your
God gives it into your hand, [q]you shall put
all its males to the sword, 14 [r]but the
women and the little ones, the livestock,
and everything else in the city, all its spoil,
you [s]shall take as plunder for yourselves.
And [t]you shall enjoy the spoil of your enemies, which the LORD your God has given
you. 15 Thus you shall do to all the cities
that are very far from you, which are not
cities of the nations here. 16 But [u]in the

[1] Or *evil person*

15 [b]Cited Matt. 18:16; 2 Cor. 13:1; See Num. 35:30
16 [c][Ex. 23:1; Ps. 35:11]
17 [d]ch. 17:8, 9; [ch. 21:5]
18 [e]ch. 13:14; 17:4
19 [f]Prov. 19:5, 9; [Dan. 6:24]
20 [g]See ch. 13:11
21 [y][See ver. 13 above] [h]See Ex. 21:23, 24
Chapter 20
1 [i][Josh. 17:18; Ps. 20:7; Isai. 31:1] [j]ch. 31:6, 8; 2 Chr. 13:12; 32:8
2 [k][Num. 10:8, 9; 31:6]
4 [l]ch. 1:30; 3:22; Josh. 23:10
6 [m]ch. 28:30; Lev. 19:23-25; [1 Cor. 9:7]
7 [n][ch. 24:5; 28:30]
8 [o][Judg. 7:3]
10 [p]Judg. 21:13; [ch. 2:26; 2 Sam. 20:18, 20]
13 [q]Num. 31:7
14 [r]Num. 31:9 [s]Josh. 8:2 [t]Josh. 22:8
16 [u]ch. 7:1, 2; Num. 33:52; Josh. 11:14

19:15–21 The general principle was that a conviction was not to be based on the testimony of a single witness (v. 15). When false testimony was detected, the false witness was to receive the same punishment that the falsely accused person would have received (vv. 19–21).

In the jurisprudence of the ancient Near East, much responsibility was given to the judge. He did not simply compare an offense to a particular law and pronounce a verdict. Rather, he compared a case with the principles of the law and with typical cases and gave a decision in accordance with justice and equity (1:13; 16:18; 17:8).

19:15 single witness. See 17:6.

19:20 fear. See "The Three Purposes of the Law" at 13:10.

19:21 eye for eye. Much argument has revolved about this verse. Some contend it is brutal and opposed to New Testament ideas of love and mercy. The phrase "eye for eye" occurs twice more in the Pentateuch (Ex. 21:24; Lev. 24:20). In each case, the verse is in a legal context; it is a principle of public justice—the penalty must fit the crime. There are indications that the term was not taken literally (Ex. 21:18, 26, 27). The only physical penalty mentioned in the law is flogging, and that limited to forty strokes (Deut. 25:3). Christ opposed those who used this verse as an excuse for personal vengeance (Matt. 5:38 note). See notes Ex. 21:24 and Lev. 24:20.

20:1 you shall not be afraid. Morale in the army, particularly the importance of single-minded reliance upon God, is the subject of vv. 1–9. The exemptions cited illustrate the principle that anyone whose heart was not in the fight should not be there (vv. 5–8). The power of God, rather than numerical superiority, would guarantee Israel's victory (v. 4; cf. 32:30 note; Judg. 7:1–8). One result of such an attitude would be high morale, which would itself contribute to victory.

20:10 offer terms of peace. Ancient walled cities could withstand attack for some time, and attackers wanted to avoid the trouble of a lengthy siege. An offer of peace in exchange for vassal tribute (v. 11), coupled with the threat of death for the defending soldiers, could be attractive to both sides. These warfare provisions (comparatively humane for that period) were applied to enemies outside the Promised Land (v. 15).

cities of these peoples that the LORD your
God is giving you for an inheritance, you
shall save alive nothing that breathes, 17 but
[v]you shall devote them to complete
destruction,[1] the Hittites and the Amorites,
the Canaanites and the Perizzites, the
Hivites and the Jebusites, as the LORD your
God has commanded, 18 that [w]they may not
teach you to do according to all their
abominable practices that they have done
for their gods, and so you [x]sin against the
LORD your God.

19 "When you besiege a city for a long
time, making war against it in order to take
it, [y]you shall not destroy its trees by wielding an axe against them. You may eat from
them, but you shall not cut them down.
Are the trees in the field human, that they
should be besieged by you? 20 Only the
trees that you know are not trees for food
you may destroy and cut down, that you
may build siegeworks against the city that
makes war with you, until it falls.

Atonement for Unsolved Murders

21 "If in the land that the LORD your
God is giving you to possess someone is found slain, lying in the open country, and it is not known who killed him,
2 then your elders and your judges shall
come out, and they shall measure the distance to the surrounding cities. 3 And the
elders of the city that is nearest to the slain
man shall take a heifer [z]that has never been
worked and that has not pulled in a yoke.
4 And the elders of that city shall bring the
heifer down to a valley with running water,
which is neither plowed nor sown, and
shall break the heifer's neck there in the valley. 5 Then the priests, the sons of Levi, shall
come forward, for the LORD your God has
chosen [a]them to minister to him and to
bless in the name of the LORD, and [b]by their
word every dispute and every assault shall
be settled. 6 And all the elders of that city
nearest to the slain man [c]shall wash their
hands over the heifer whose neck was broken in the valley, 7 and they shall testify,
'Our hands did not shed this blood, nor did
our eyes see it shed. 8 Accept atonement, O
LORD, for your people Israel, whom you
have redeemed, and [d]do not set the guilt of
innocent blood in the midst of your people
Israel, so that their blood guilt be atoned
for.' 9 So [e]you shall purge the guilt of innocent blood from your midst, when you do
what is right in the sight of the LORD.

Marrying Female Captives

10 "When you go out to war against your
enemies, and the LORD your God gives
them into your hand and you take them
captive, 11 and you see among the captives a
beautiful woman, and you desire to take her
to be your wife, 12 and you bring her home
to your house, she shall shave her head and
pare her nails. 13 And she shall take off the
clothes in which she was captured and shall
remain in your house and [f]lament her
father and her mother a full month. After
that you may go in to her and be her husband, and she shall be your wife. 14 But if
you no longer delight in her, you shall [g]let
her go where she wants. But you shall not
sell her for money, nor shall you [h]treat her
as a slave, since you have humiliated her.

Inheritance Rights of the Firstborn

15 "If a man has two wives, [i]the one loved
and the other unloved, and both the loved
and the unloved have borne him children, and if the firstborn son belongs to the
unloved,[2] 16 then on the day when [j]he assigns
his possessions as an inheritance to his sons,
he may not treat the son of the loved as the
firstborn in preference to the son of the

17 [v]See ch. 7:2
18 [w]ch. 7:4; 12:30, 31; 18:9 [x]Ex. 23:33
19 [y][2 Kin. 3:19, 25]
Chapter 21
3 [z][Num. 19:2]
5 [a]See ch. 10:8 [b]ch. 17:8, 9; 19:17
6 [c][Ps. 26:6; 73:13; Matt. 27:24]
8 [d][Jonah 1:14]
9 [e]ch. 19:13
13 [f][Ps. 45:10]
14 [g][Jer. 34:16] [h]ch. 24:7
15 [i][Gen. 29:30, 33; 1 Sam. 1:4, 5]
16 [j]1 Chr. 5:1, 2; [1 Chr. 26:10; 2 Chr. 11:19, 20, 22]

[1] That is, set apart (devote) as an offering to the Lord (for destruction)
[2] Or *hated*; also verses 16, 17

20:17 complete destruction. The Hebrew word for this practice is *ḥerem,* which means "to put under the ban" (i.e., to devote everything to the Lord), as occurred at Jericho during the conquest (Josh. 6:17–19). See notes Lev. 27:28; Deut. 7:26.

20:19 you shall not destroy its trees. The reference is clearly to fruit trees (v. 20). One of Israel's covenant blessings was to enjoy the fruit of the land God had given them (7:12, 13).

21:1 If . . . someone is found slain. In the case of an unsolved murder, the elders from the nearest town were to take an oath of innocence and ignorance. The symbolism of the heifer, killed while the oath was taken, is clear: it dies as a symbol of the murderer who ought to die. The land was to be purged of serious guilt. The vicarious death of the heifer points to the death of Christ as a satisfaction for the sins, known and unknown, of His people.

21:11 among the captives a beautiful woman. The law preserved the sanctity of marriage. An Israelite man might take a captive woman, but he had to wait a month. She was to be given a chance to adjust and to grieve for her lost family. She was a wife, not chattel, and if the husband divorced her, he could not sell her as a slave.

21:15 two wives. Just as divorce was allowed "because of your hardness of heart" (Matt. 19:8), so polygamy was permitted, but its harsher evils were mitigated. The unloved wife had her rights, and the firstborn son of an unloved wife could not be dispossessed.

unloved, who is the firstborn, 17 but he shall
acknowledge the firstborn, the son of the
unloved, by giving him a double portion of
all that he has, for he is [k]the firstfruits of his
strength. [l]The right of the firstborn is his.

A Rebellious Son

18 "If a man has a stubborn and rebellious
son who will not obey the voice of his father
or the voice of his mother, and, though they
discipline him, will not listen to them, 19 then
his father and his mother shall take hold of
him and bring him out to the elders of his
city at the gate of the place where he lives,
20 and they shall say to the elders of his city,
'This our son is stubborn and rebellious; he
will not obey our voice; he is a glutton and a
drunkard.' 21 [m]Then all the men of the city
shall stone him to death with stones. [n]So you
shall purge the evil from your midst, [o]and all
Israel shall hear, and fear.

A Man Hanged on a Tree Is Cursed

22 "And if a man has committed a crime
punishable by death and he is put to death,
and you hang him on a tree, 23 [p]his body
shall not remain all night on the tree, but
you shall bury him the same day, for [q]a
hanged man is cursed by God. [r]You shall
not defile your land that the LORD your
God is giving you for an inheritance.

Various Laws

22 "You [s]shall not see your brother's
ox or his sheep going astray and
ignore them. You shall take them back to
your brother. 2 And if he does not live near
you and you do not know who he is, you
shall bring it home to your house, and it
shall stay with you until your brother seeks
it. Then you shall restore it to him. 3 And
you shall do the same with his donkey or
with his garment, or with any lost thing of
your brother's, which he loses and you
find; you may not ignore it. 4 [t]You shall not
see your brother's donkey or his ox fallen
down by the way and ignore them. You
shall help him to lift them up again.
5 "A woman shall not wear a man's garment, nor shall a man put on a woman's
cloak, [u]for whoever does these things is an
abomination to the LORD your God.
6 "If you come across a bird's nest in any
tree or on the ground, with young ones or
eggs and the mother sitting on the young
or on the eggs, [v]you shall not take the
mother with the young. 7 You shall let the
mother go, but the young you may take for
yourself, [w]that it may go well with you, and
that you may live long.
8 "When you build a new house, you
shall make a parapet for your roof, that you
may not bring the guilt of blood upon your
house, if anyone should fall from it.
9 [x]"You shall not sow your vineyard with
two kinds of seed, lest the whole yield be
forfeited,[1] the crop that you have sown and
the yield of the vineyard. 10 You shall not

17 [k]Gen. 49:3 [l]Gen. 25:31, 33; 27:36
21 [m]ch. 13:10; See Josh. 7:25 [n]See ch. 13:5 [o]ch. 13:11; 17:13; 19:20
23 [p][Josh. 8:29; 10:26, 27; John 19:31] [q]Cited Gal. 3:13 [r]Num. 35:34
Chapter 22
1 [s]Ex. 23:4
4 [t]Ex. 23:5
5 [u][ch. 18:12; 25:16]
6 [v]Lev. 22:28
7 [w]See ch. 4:40
9 [x]Lev. 19:19

1 Hebrew *become holy*

21:18 a stubborn and rebellious son. In view here is not the petty disobedience of children, but a long-term pattern of rebellion and deep sin. Although "stubborn and rebellious" is not precisely defined, in v. 20 the son is called "a glutton and a drunkard" (cf. Prov. 23:21). In such cases, even the parents were not to shield their offspring (cf. Zech. 13:2, 3).

21:22 hang him on a tree. Hanging as a method of execution is not mentioned in the Old Testament. The practice in view here is the exposure of the corpse of a criminal or an enemy (1 Sam. 31:10–13). Such gruesome exposure, symbolizing divine curse (v. 23), was not to be continued more than a day. This verse motivated the Pharisees' request to have the body of Jesus taken off the cross before nightfall (John 19:31). The point of Gal. 3:13 is that Christ, though innocent, died a criminal's death, taking the curse that we deserved (cf. Acts 5:30).

22:1 take them back. Note the emphasis on the rightful ownership of private property (cf. Ex. 23:4). The law concerning lost property requires that an effort be made to find the owner of strayed or lost property and return the property to him. If the owner cannot be found, the property is to be kept for him until he is found.

22:4 his ox fallen down. Again, accidental loss of private property is to be prevented if possible (cf. Ex. 23:5). Jesus quoted this verse to justify healing a man on the Sabbath. The Pharisees allowed the law of helping a fallen animal to supersede their rules for Sabbath keeping, but had no pity on a man in serious need (Luke 14:5).

22:5 a man's garment . . . a woman's cloak. Women were not to adopt the accoutrements of the male (e.g., carrying weapons), and men were not to dress as women. The symbols of gender difference were to be respected, and while such symbols vary over time and from culture to culture, the principle of gender distinction remains (Gen. 1:27; cf. 1 Tim. 2:13). Violations of the creation order, such as homosexuality and bestiality (Lev. 18:22, 23; 20:13; 1 Cor. 6:9; 1 Tim. 1:10), are an "abomination." It has also been suggested that the interchange of clothing was a part of pagan religious practice.

22:8 parapet for your roof. This is a law against criminal negligence. Roofs in ancient Israel were flat and often reached by an outside stairway. The roof was used for work (Josh. 2:6) or leisure. To prevent accidental injury or death from falling, a parapet or fence was specified.

22:9–11 Similar prohibitions of mixtures are found in Lev. 19:19. Reasons for these regulations are no longer clear. Various suggestions have been made: that these verses teach the importance of creation-order distinctions, that they remind Israel of her call to purity and separation from the surrounding nations (v. 11 note), or that practical considerations were involved (e.g., the mixture of seed as harmful for agriculture).

22:10 an ox and a donkey together. The reason for this may be the impracticality both of making a donkey pull an ox's load and of making an ox go at the faster donkey's pace. Or, the contrast between clean animals (the ox) and unclean (the donkey, 14:1–8) may have served to remind Israel of her call to purity. Paul cites this verse in 2 Cor. 6:14, forbidding the fellowship of believers and unbelievers.

plow with an ox and a donkey together.
11 You shall not wear cloth of wool and
linen mixed together.
12 [y] "You shall make yourself tassels on
the four corners of the garment with which
you cover yourself.

Laws Concerning Sexual Immorality

13 "If any man takes a wife and [z] goes in to
her and then hates her 14 and accuses her of
misconduct and brings a bad name upon
her, saying, 'I took this woman, and when I
came near her, I did not find in her evidence
of virginity,' 15 then the father of the young
woman and her mother shall take and bring
out the evidence of her virginity to the elders
of the city in the gate. 16 And the father of the
young woman shall say to the elders, 'I gave
my daughter to this man to marry, and he
hates her; 17 and behold, he has accused her
of misconduct, saying, "I did not find in
your daughter evidence of virginity." And
yet this is the evidence of my daughter's virginity.' And they shall spread the cloak
before the elders of the city. 18 Then the elders of that city shall take the man and
whip[1] him, 19 and they shall fine him a hundred shekels[2] of silver and give them to the
father of the young woman, because he has
brought a bad name upon a virgin[3] of Israel.
And she shall be his wife. [a] He may not
divorce her all his days. 20 But if the thing is
true, that evidence of virginity was not
found in the young woman, 21 then they
shall bring out the young woman to the
door of her father's house, and [b] the men of
her city shall stone her to death with stones,
because she has [c] done an outrageous thing
in Israel by whoring in her father's house.
[d] So you shall purge the evil from your midst.
22 [e] "If a man is found lying with the wife of
another man, both of them shall die, the man
who lay with the woman, and the woman.
[d] So you shall purge the evil from Israel.
23 "If there is a [f] betrothed virgin, and a
man meets her in the city and lies with her,
24 then you shall bring them both out to the
gate of that city, and you shall stone them
to death with stones, the young woman
because she did not cry for help though
she was in the city, and the man because
he violated his neighbor's wife. [d] So you
shall purge the evil from your midst.
25 "But if in the open country a man meets
a young woman who is betrothed, and the
man seizes her and lies with her, then only
the man who lay with her shall die. 26 But
you shall do nothing to the young woman;
she has committed no offense punishable
by death. For this case is like that of a man
attacking and murdering his neighbor, 27 because he met her in the open country, and
though the betrothed young woman cried
for help there was no one to rescue her.
28 [g] "If a man meets a virgin who is not
betrothed, and seizes her and lies with her,
and they are found, 29 then the man who
lay with her shall give to the father of the
young woman fifty shekels of silver, and
she shall be his wife, because he has violated her. He may not divorce her all his days.
30 [4] [h] "A man shall not take his father's
wife, so that he does not [i] uncover his
father's nakedness.[5]

Those Excluded from the Assembly

23 "No one whose testicles are crushed
or whose male organ is cut off shall
enter the assembly of the LORD.

12 [y] Num. 15:38; [Matt. 23:5]
13 [z] [2 Sam. 13:15]
19 [a] [Matt. 19:8, 9; Mark 10:11; Luke 16:18]
21 [b] [ch. 21:21] [c] See Gen. 34:7 [d] See ch. 13:5
22 [e] Lev. 20:10; [Ezek. 16:38, 40; 23:45, 47; John 8:5]
[d] [See ver. 21 above]
23 [f] [Matt. 1:18, 19]
24 [d] [See ver. 21 above]
28 [g] Ex. 22:16, 17
30 [h] See Lev. 18:8 [i] ch. 27:20; [Ruth 3:9; Ezek. 16:8]

1 Or *discipline* 2 A *shekel* was about 2/5 ounce or 11 grams 3 Or *girl of marriageable age* 4 Ch 23:1 in Hebrew 5 Hebrew *uncover his father's skirt*

22:11 cloth . . . wool and linen. Some suggest that such material would shrink unevenly and therefore not wash well. Others argue that through eating pure food (14:3–21) and not mixing their seeds (Deut. 22:9), their draft animals (22:10), or the materials of their garments, Israel was reminded that they were to be a pure people (7:2–5 and notes).

22:12 make yourself tassels. These tassels were to remind Israel of the Lord's commandments and the nation's responsibility to be holy before God (Num. 15:38–40).

22:14–21 These verses provide for judging a husband's complaint that his wife was not a virgin when they married. Such an accusation, when made by a man who wished to be rid of a wife who displeased him, could be disproved by the wife's parents presenting visible "evidence of . . . virginity," presumably the stained bedclothes of the wedding night (v. 15).

22:22–29 The implications of the seventh commandment are developed (5:18; Ex. 20:14), here with respect to instances of adultery and rape. Particular care is given to guarding the sanctity of the marriage covenant: adultery with a married or betrothed woman is punishable by the death of both consenting parties (vv. 22–24), while lesser penalties are prescribed for a sexual relationship with an unmarried woman (vv. 28, 29). Women depended on their marriage relationship for protection and status in ancient Near Eastern society, and the law provides important protections for women. The penalty for forcible rape of a married woman was the death of the offending man (vv. 25–27). The man who violated the honor of a virgin was compelled to marry her, and could not later divorce her (v. 29).

22:30 A man shall not take his father's wife. Sexual relations with a stepmother are probably in view (Lev. 18:7, 8; 20:11).

23:1 the assembly of the LORD. This phrase refers to the worshiping community gathered before the presence of God, rather than to Israel's population as a whole (Neh. 13:1–3). The Hebrew word for "assembly" (*qahal*) is usually rendered *ekklesia* in the Septuagint (the Greek Old Testament). This is also the term used in the Greek New Testament for "church."

2 [j]"No one born of a forbidden union
may enter the assembly of the LORD. Even
to the tenth generation, none of his
descendants may enter the assembly of the
LORD.
3 [k]"No Ammonite or Moabite may enter
the assembly of the LORD. Even to the tenth
generation, none of them may enter the
assembly of the LORD forever, 4 [l]because
they did not meet you with bread and with
water on the way, when you came out of
Egypt, and because they [m]hired against you
Balaam the son of Beor from Pethor of
[n]Mesopotamia, to curse you. 5 But the LORD
your God would not listen to Balaam;
instead the LORD your God turned [o]the
curse into a blessing for you, because the
LORD your God loved you. 6 You [p]shall not
seek their peace or their prosperity all your
days forever.
7 "You shall not abhor an Edomite, for
[q]he is your brother. You shall not abhor an
Egyptian, because [r]you were a sojourner in
his land. 8 Children born to them in the
third generation may enter the assembly of
the LORD.

Uncleanness in the Camp

9 "When you are encamped against your
enemies, then you shall keep yourself from
every evil thing.
10 "If any man among you becomes [s]un-
clean because of a nocturnal emission,
then he shall go outside the camp. He shall
not come inside the camp, 11 but when
evening comes, he shall [t]bathe himself in
water, and as the sun sets, he may come
inside the camp.
12 "You shall have a place outside the
camp, and you shall go out to it. 13 And you
shall have a trowel with your tools, and
when you sit down outside, you shall dig a
hole with it and turn back and cover up
your excrement. 14 Because [u]the LORD your
God walks in the midst of your camp, to
deliver you and to give up your enemies
before you, therefore your camp must be
holy, so that he may not see anything indecent among you and turn away from you.

Miscellaneous Laws

15 [v]"You shall not give up to his master a
slave who has escaped from his master to
you. 16 He shall dwell with you, in your
midst, in the place that he shall choose
within one of your towns, wherever it suits
him. You shall not wrong him.
17 "None of the [w]daughters of Israel shall
be a cult prostitute, and none [x]of the sons
of Israel shall be a cult prostitute. 18 You
shall not bring the fee of a prostitute or the
wages of a dog[1] into the house of the LORD
your God in payment for any vow, for both
of these are an abomination to the LORD
your God.
19 [y]"You shall not charge interest on loans
to your brother, [z]interest on money, interest on food, interest on anything that is
lent for interest. 20 [a]You may charge a foreigner interest, but you may not charge
your brother interest, [b]that the LORD your
God may bless you in all that you undertake in the land that you are entering to
take possession of it.
21 [c]"If you make a vow to the LORD your
God, you shall not delay fulfilling it, for the
LORD your God will surely require it of you,
and you will be guilty of sin. 22 But if you
refrain from vowing, you will not be guilty
of sin. 23 You shall be careful to do what has
passed your lips, for you have voluntarily

1 Or *male prostitute*

Chapter 23
2 [j][Zech. 9:6]
3 [k]Neh. 13:1, 2
4 [l][ch. 2:29] [m]Num. 22:5, 6; [2 Pet. 2:15] [n]Acts 7:2
5 [o]Num. 23:11; 24:10
6 [p][Ezra 9:12]
7 [q]Gen. 25:24-26; Num. 20:14; Obad. 10, 12 [r]ch. 10:19; Ex. 22:21; 23:9; Lev. 19:34
10 [s]Lev. 15:16
11 [t]See Lev. 15:5
14 [u]Lev. 26:12
15 [v]1 Sam. 30:15
17 [w]Lev. 19:29 [x]1 Kin. 14:24; 15:12; 22:46; 2 Kin. 23:7
19 [y]See Ex. 22:25 [z][Neh. 5:10]
20 [a][ch. 15:3] [b]ch. 15:10
21 [c][Ps. 66:13, 14; 76:11]; See Num. 30:2

23:3 Ammonite or Moabite . . . the tenth generation. As the word "forever" in this verse indicates, "tenth generation" is probably an idiom denoting permanent exclusion from the worshiping community of Israel (cf. Neh. 13:1). This special exclusion of Ammonites and Moabites was due, not to their incestuous origin (Gen. 19:30–38), but to their stubborn opposition to Israel (v. 4; Neh. 13:2). The Old Testament also looks forward to a new covenant in which the exclusions of this passage are transcended (Is. 56:3–8), an event prefigured by Ruth, the Moabite who became the ancestor of David and of the Messiah (Ruth 1:4; 4:17; Matt. 1:5).

23:4 Balaam. Note the clear reference to details in Num. 22–24.

23:9–14 Because the camp of Israelite soldiers was a place of God's presence as divine Warrior (v. 14; 20:4), the camp was to be kept pure of unclean things. In view here are occurrences that were both hygienically and ceremonially unclean: instances of urination or perhaps nocturnal emission (v. 10; cf. Lev. 15:16), and defecation in the camp (v. 13).

23:15 slave who has escaped. Slavery in Israel was carefully regulated and its abuses limited (15:12 note). In view here is an escaped slave from another country who takes refuge in Israel.

23:17 cult prostitute. Ritual prostitution, involving both male and female prostitutes, was characteristic of the Canaanite fertility religions.

23:19 interest. The agricultural economy of ancient Israel was very different from the commercial economy of today, and borrowing was usually due to poverty. God desired to bless an obedient Israel so that borrowing would be unnecessary (15:4 note), and those whom the Lord had blessed materially were to assist fellow Israelites in distress by not charging interest. This regulation did not apply to those outside the covenant (the "foreigner," v. 20).

23:21 a vow to the LORD. Such a vow was given voluntarily (v. 22). It was a serious matter, and if a valid vow, must be kept. The law of vows is given fully in Lev. 27 and Num. 30.

vowed to the LORD your God what you
have promised with your mouth.
24 "If you go into your neighbor's vineyard, you may eat your fill of grapes, as
many as you wish, but you shall not put
any in your bag. 25 If you go into your
neighbor's standing grain, [d]you may pluck
the ears with your hand, but you shall not
put a sickle to your neighbor's standing
grain.

Laws Concerning Divorce

24 "When a man takes a wife and marries her, if then she finds no favor in
his eyes because he has found some indecency in her, and [e]he writes her a certificate
of divorce and puts it in her hand and
sends her out of his house, and she departs
out of his house, 2 and if she goes and
becomes another man's wife, 3 and the latter man hates her and writes her a certificate of divorce and puts it in her hand and
sends her out of his house, or if the latter
man dies, who took her to be his wife,
4 then [f]her former husband, who sent her
away, may not take her again to be his wife,
after she has been defiled, for that is an
abomination before the LORD. And you
shall not bring sin upon the land that the
LORD your God is giving you for an inheritance.

Miscellaneous Laws

5 [g]"When a man is newly married, he
shall not go out with the army or be liable
for any other public duty. He shall be free
at home one year [h]to be happy with his
wife whom he has taken.
6 "No one shall take a mill or an upper
millstone in pledge, for that would be taking a life in pledge.
7 [i]"If a man is found stealing one of his
brothers, of the people of Israel, and if he
[j]treats him as a slave or sells him, then that
thief shall die. [k]So you shall purge the evil
from your midst.
8 "Take care, in [l]a case of leprous[1] disease, to be very careful to do according to
all that the Levitical priests shall direct you.
As I commanded them, so you shall be
careful to do. 9 Remember what the LORD
your God did to [m]Miriam [n]on the way as
you came out of Egypt.
10 "When you make your neighbor a loan
of any sort, you shall not go into his house
to collect his pledge. 11 You shall stand outside, and the man to whom you make the
loan shall bring the pledge out to you.
12 And if he is a poor man, you shall not
sleep in his pledge. 13 [o]You shall restore to
him the pledge as the sun sets, that he may
sleep in his cloak and [p]bless you. And [q]it
shall be righteousness for you before the
LORD your God.
14 "You shall not [r]oppress a hired servant
who is poor and needy, whether he is one
of your brothers or one of the sojourners
who are in your land within your towns.
15 [s]You shall give him his wages on the
same day, before the sun sets (for he is
poor and counts on it), [t]lest he cry against
you to the LORD, and you be guilty of sin.
16 [u]"Fathers shall not be put to death
because of their children, nor shall children
be put to death because of their fathers. Each
one shall be put to death for his own sin.

25 [d][Matt. 12:1; Mark 2:23; Luke 6:1]
Chapter 24
1 [e]Matt. 19:7; Mark 10:4; Cited Matt. 5:31; [Isai. 50:1; Jer. 3:8]
4 [f][Jer. 3:1]
5 [g][ch. 20:7] [h]Prov. 5:18
7 [i]Ex. 21:16; [1 Tim. 1:10] [j]ch. 21:14 [k]See ch. 13:5
8 [l]See Lev. ch. 13; ch. 14
9 [m]See Num. 12:10-15 [n]ch. 25:17
13 [o]See Ex. 22:26 [p]Job 29:13; 31:20 [q]Ps. 112:9; Dan. 4:27; [ch. 6:25]
14 [r]Mal. 3:5; See Lev. 25:39-43
15 [s]Jer. 22:13; See Lev. 19:13 [t]ch. 15:9; James 5:4
16 [u]Cited 2 Kin. 14:6; 2 Chr. 25:4; [Jer. 31:29, 30; Ezek. 18:20]

[1] *Leprosy* was a term for several skin diseases; see Leviticus 13

24:1–4 See "Marriage and Divorce" at Mal. 2:16. The situation described (vv. 1–3) is followed by the legal prescription (v. 4). Divorce was permitted in the Mosaic law, as Jesus later said, "because of your hardness of heart" (Matt. 19:8). The restriction on remarriage of a divorced couple after an intervening marriage (v. 4) served to discourage casual divorces.

24:1 some indecency. The Hebrew of this phrase is the same as "anything indecent" in 23:14, and is rather general. Adultery is apparently not in view, for adultery was punishable by death (22:22). The fact of divorce for a variety of reasons is recognized, but not necessarily condoned (vv. 1–3 are descriptive, not prescriptive).

24:5 newly married. A one-year exemption for the newly married would not only strengthen the marriage relationship and benefit the home, but would also help the morale of the army (20:1 note).

24:6 take . . . in pledge. Because loans were typically given to relieve the economic hardship of the borrower (23:19 note), the material given "in pledge" was likely not collateral property of value equal to the amount of the loan, but a personal possession given as a token of the promise to pay. In keeping with the purpose of the loan, the lender was not to cause further hardship to the borrower by confiscating essential items such as household millstones or outer garments (vv. 10–13, 17). Other references to Old Testament borrowing practices include Ex. 22:26, 27; Job 22:6; 24:3, 9; Amos 2:8.

24:7 stealing . . . his brothers. The chief purpose of kidnapping was the enslavement of others for profit. To sell fellow Israelites into slavery in other countries was forbidden on pain of death, probably because such slaves were cut off from the life of the covenant community (itself a form of "death," Ex. 12:19 and Lev. 7:20 notes). Indentured slavery was allowed within Israel, but was tempered in several important ways (15:12 note). Paul condemns slave traders ("enslavers") together with other violators of the Ten Commandments (1 Tim. 1:10).

24:8 leprous disease. See note Lev. 13; 14.

24:14 a hired servant who is poor. God's concern for the poor and oppressed is emphasized in this passage (Ps. 9:18 note).

24:16 Fathers shall not be put to death because of their children. This interesting and just law is quoted in 2 Kin. 14:6 and 2 Chr. 25:4, where it is cited as from the "Book of the Law of Moses" or the "Law in the Book of Moses."

17 [v]“You shall not pervert the justice due
to the sojourner or to the fatherless, [w]or
take a widow’s garment in pledge, 18 but
[x]you shall remember that you were a slave
in Egypt and the LORD your God redeemed
you from there; therefore I command you
to do this.
19 [y]“When you reap your harvest in your
field and forget a sheaf in the field, you
shall not go back to get it. It shall be for the
sojourner, the fatherless, and the widow,
[z]that the LORD your God may bless you in
all the work of your hands. 20 When you
beat your olive trees, you shall not go over
them again. It shall be for the sojourner,
the fatherless, and the widow. 21 When you
gather the grapes of your vineyard, you
shall not strip it afterward. It shall be for
the sojourner, the fatherless, and the
widow. 22 [x]You shall remember that you
were a slave in the land of Egypt; therefore
I command you to do this.

25 “If there is a [a]dispute between men
and they come into court and the
judges decide between them, [b]acquitting
the innocent and condemning the guilty,
2 then if the guilty man deserves to be beat-
en, the judge shall cause him to lie down
and be beaten in his presence with a number of stripes in proportion to his offense.
3 [c]Forty stripes may be given him, but not
more, lest, if one should go on to beat him
with more stripes than these, your brother
be degraded in your sight.
4 [d]“You shall not muzzle an ox when it is
treading out the grain.

Laws Concerning Levirate Marriage

5 [e]“If brothers dwell together, and one of
them dies and has no son, the wife of the
dead man shall not be married outside the
family to a stranger. Her [f]husband’s brother shall go in to her and take her as his wife
and perform the duty of a husband’s brother
to her. 6 And the first son whom she bears
shall succeed to the name of his dead
brother, that [g]his name may not be blotted
out of Israel. 7 And if the man does not wish
to take his brother’s wife, then his brother’s wife shall [h]go up to the gate to the elders and say, ‘My husband’s brother refuses to perpetuate his brother’s name in Israel;
he will not perform the duty of a husband’s
brother to me.’ 8 Then the elders of his city
shall call him and speak to him, and if he
persists, saying, [i]‘I do not wish to take her,’
9 then his brother’s wife shall go up to him
in the presence of the elders and [j]pull his
sandal off his foot and [k]spit in his face. And
she shall answer and say, ‘So shall it be
done to the man who does not [l]build up
his brother’s house.’ 10 And the name of his
house[1] shall be called in Israel, ‘The house
of him who had his sandal pulled off.’

Miscellaneous Laws

11 “When men fight with one another and
the wife of the one draws near to rescue her
husband from the hand of him who is beating him and puts out her hand and seizes
him by the private parts, 12 then you shall
cut off her hand. [m]Your eye shall have no
pity.
13 “You [n]shall not have in your bag two
kinds of weights, a large and a small. 14 You
shall not have in your house two kinds of
measures, a large and a small. 15 A full and
fair[2] weight you shall have, a full and fair
measure you shall have, [o]that your days
may be long in the land that the LORD your
God is giving you. 16 For [p]all who do such
things, all who act dishonestly, [q]are an
abomination to the LORD your God.
17 [r]“Remember what Amalek did to you
[s]on the way as you came out of Egypt,
18 how he attacked you on the way when
you were faint and weary, and [t]cut off your

1 Hebrew *its name* 2 Or *just*, or *righteous*

17 [v]Ex. 22:21, 22; 23:6; [ch. 10:18; 27:19; Isai. 1:23; Jer. 5:28]; See ch. 16:19 [w][ver. 6, 13; Job 24:3]
18 [x]See ch. 5:15
19 [y]Lev. 19:9; 23:22 [z]See ch. 14:29
22 [x][See ver. 18 above]
Chapter 25
1 [a]ch. 19:17 [b][1 Kin. 8:32; Prov. 17:15]
3 [c][2 Cor. 11:24]
4 [d]Cited 1 Cor. 9:9; 1 Tim. 5:18
5 [e]Matt. 22:24; Mark 12:19; Luke 20:28 [f][Gen. 38:8, 9; Ruth 1:12, 13; 3:9]
6 [g]Ruth 4:10
7 [h][Ruth 4:1, 2]
8 [i][Ruth 4:6]
9 [j][Ruth 4:7] [k][Num. 12:14; Job 30:10; Isai. 50:6] [l]Ruth 4:11
12 [m]See ch. 7:16
13 [n]Lev. 19:35, 36; [Prov. 16:11; Ezek. 45:10; Amos 8:5; Mic. 6:11]
15 [o]See ch. 4:40
16 [p]Prov. 11:1 [q]ch. 18:12; 22:5
17 [r]Ex. 17:8 [s]ch. 24:9
18 [t][Josh. 10:19]

24:19 When you reap your harvest. The compassionate intention of this law is realized in Ruth 2:2–23 (cf. Lev. 19:9, 10; 23:22).

25:3 Forty stripes. This is the background of the Jewish practice of giving “forty lashes less one” (2 Cor. 11:24). The intent was to guard against any possible miscount by erring on the side of mercy.

25:4 You shall not muzzle an ox. According to Paul, this provision for oxen points to the more general principle that those who labor, particularly Christian ministers, deserve fair remuneration for their work (1 Cor. 9:9–12; 1 Tim. 5:18).

25:5 Her husband’s brother. The law of levirate marriage (from the Latin word *levir,* meaning “husband’s brother”) is given only here. The limitation to brothers who “dwell together” may indicate that it applied to an unmarried brother, but it is doubtful that this limitation held in practice. The obvious purpose of the arrangement was to maintain the property rights of the deceased’s family line. The levirate custom dates to patriarchal times and is mentioned in Gen. 38:8–11; Ruth 3:1–4:12; Matt. 22:23–28; Mark 12:18–23; and Luke 20:27–33.

25:13 two kinds of weights. God’s displeasure at dishonest business dealing is stressed (Lev. 19:35, 36; Prov. 11:1; 16:21; 20:10, 23; and Mic. 6:11).

25:17–19 On the historic conflict between Israel and Amalek, see Ex. 17:16 and note.

tail, those who were lagging behind you,
and he did not fear God. **19**Therefore
[u]when the LORD your God has given you
rest from all your enemies around you, in
the land that the LORD your God is giving
you for an inheritance to possess, you shall
[v]blot out the memory of Amalek from
under heaven; you shall not forget.

Offerings of Firstfruits and Tithes

26 "When you come into the land that
the LORD your God is giving you for
an inheritance and have taken possession
of it and live in it, **2** [w]you shall take some of
the first of all the fruit of the ground, which
you harvest from your land that the LORD
your God is giving you, and you shall put it
in a basket, and you shall [x]go to the place
that the LORD your God will choose, to
make his name to dwell there. **3**And you
shall go to the priest who is in office at that
time and say to him, 'I declare today to the
LORD your God that I have come into the
land [y]that the LORD swore to our fathers to
give us.' **4**Then the priest shall take the basket from your hand and set it down before
the altar of the LORD your God.

5"And you shall make response before
the LORD your God, 'A [z]wandering Aramean was my father. And he went down
into Egypt and sojourned there, [a]few in
number, and there he became a nation,
great, mighty, and populous. **6**And [b]the
Egyptians treated us harshly and humiliated us and laid on us hard labor. **7**Then [c]we
cried to the LORD, the God of our fathers,
and the LORD heard our voice and saw our
affliction, our toil, and our oppression.
8And [d]the LORD brought us out of Egypt
[e]with a mighty hand and an outstretched
arm, with great deeds of terror,[1] with signs
and wonders. **9**And he brought us into this
place and gave us this land, [f]a land flowing
with milk and honey. **10**And behold, now I
bring the first of the fruit of the ground,
which you, O LORD, have given me.' And
you shall set it down before the LORD your
God and worship before the LORD your
God. **11**And [g]you shall rejoice in all the
good that the LORD your God has given to
you and to your house, you, and the Levite,
and the sojourner who is among you.

12"When you have finished paying all
[h]the tithe of your produce in the third year,
which is [i]the year of tithing, giving it to the
Levite, the sojourner, the fatherless, and
the widow, so that they may eat within
your towns and be filled, **13**then you shall
say before the LORD your God, 'I have
removed the sacred portion out of my
house, and moreover, I have given it to the
Levite, the sojourner, the fatherless, and
the widow, according to all your commandments that you have commanded me.
I have not transgressed any of your commandment, [j]nor have I forgotten them. **14**[k]I
have not eaten of the tithe while I was
mourning, or removed any of it while I was
unclean, or offered any of it [l]to the dead. I
have obeyed the voice of the LORD my God.
I have done according to all that you have
commanded me. **15**[m]Look down from your
holy habitation, from heaven, and bless
your people Israel and the ground that you
have given us, as you swore to our fathers,
a land flowing with milk and honey.'

16"This day the LORD your God commands you to do these statutes and rules.
You shall therefore be careful to do them
with all your heart and with all your soul.
17[n]You have declared today that the LORD is
your God, and that you will walk in his
ways, and keep his statutes and his commandments and his rules, and will obey his
voice. **18**And the LORD has declared today

[1] Hebrew *with great terror*

19 [u][1 Sam. 15:2, 3] [v]See Ex. 17:8-14
Chapter 26
2 [w]ch. 16:10; Ex. 23:19; 34:26; Num. 15:20; 18:13; Prov. 3:9 [x]See ch. 12:5
3 [y]Ex. 13:5; See ch. 1:8
5 [z]Gen. 43:1, 2 [a][ch. 10:22; Gen. 46:27; Acts 7:14, 15]
6 [b]Ex. 1:11, 14; Num. 20:15
7 [c]Ex. 2:23-25; 3:9; Num. 20:15
8 [d]Ex. 12:37, 51 [e]See ch. 4:34
9 [f]See Ex. 3:8
11 [g]See ch. 12:7
12 [h]See Lev. 27:30 [i]ch. 14:28, 29; [Amos 4:4]
13 [j]Ps. 119:141, 153, 176
14 [k]Lev. 7:20; 21:1, 11; Hos. 9:4 [l][Jer. 16:7]
15 [m]Isai. 63:15; Zech. 2:13
17 [n][Ex. 24:7]

26:2 first of all the fruit. Many scholars suggest that vv. 1–11 refer to a special firstfruits offering that Israel was to bring when they took possession of the land (v. 4), although some relate the ceremony described in these verses to the perpetual firstfruits offering (Lev. 23:9–14). Either way, it is probable that the words of the ceremony reciting God's mighty acts on Israel's behalf (vv. 3–10) continued to be used in Israelite worship.

place . . . God will choose. See note 12:5.

26:5 A wandering Aramean. This verse may refer either to the advanced age of Jacob when he went down to Egypt (Gen. 47:9; cf. 46:30), or to Jacob's changing circumstances and travels to Aram, back to Canaan, throughout Canaan, and finally to Egypt (Gen. 28:2–5; 29:1; 31:20, 21; 33:18; 35:1, 16, 21; 46:1–28).

26:12 the tithe. Regarding the tithe and third year tithe, see notes 14:22 and 14:28.

26:13 sacred portion. As holy things (things set apart for God) the tithes were not to have been put to any unclean or idolatrous use (v. 14). The phrase "offered . . . to the dead" (v. 14) may refer to idolatrous practices (14:1 note).

26:15 Look down from . . . heaven. This phrase was adapted by Solomon in his great prayer at the dedication of the temple (1 Kin. 8:30).

26:16–19 These verses conclude the covenant stipulations section that begins at 12:1. Here the people accepted the terms of God's covenant by their pledge of obedience to the covenant stipulations (v. 17; cf. Ex. 24:7),

that you are [o]a people for his treasured possession, as he has promised you, and that
you are to keep all his commandments,
19 and that he will set you in praise and in
fame and in honor [p]high above all nations
[q]that he has made, and that you shall be [r]a
people holy to the LORD your God, as he
promised."

The Altar on Mount Ebal

27 Now Moses and the elders of Israel
commanded the people, saying,
"Keep the whole commandment that I
command you today. 2 And on the day [s]you
cross over the Jordan to the land that the
LORD your God is giving you, you shall set
up large stones and plaster them with plaster. 3 [t]And you shall write on them all the
words of this law, when you cross over to
enter the land that the LORD your God is
giving you, [u]a land flowing with milk and
honey, as the LORD, the God of your
fathers, has promised you. 4 And when you
have crossed over the Jordan, you shall set
up these stones, concerning which I command you today, [v]on Mount Ebal, and you
shall plaster them with plaster. 5 And there
you shall build an altar to the LORD your
God, an altar of stones. [w]You shall wield no
iron tool on them; 6 you shall build an altar
to the LORD your God of uncut[1] stones.
And you shall offer burnt offerings on it to
the LORD your God, 7 and you shall sacrifice
peace offerings and [x]shall eat there, and
you [x]shall rejoice before the LORD your
God. 8 And [y]you shall write on the stones
all the words of this law very plainly."

Curses from Mount Ebal

9 Then Moses and the Levitical priests
said to all Israel, "Keep silence and hear, O
Israel: [z]this day you have become the people of the LORD your God. 10 You shall
therefore obey the voice of the LORD your
God, keeping his commandments and his
statutes, which I command you today."
11 That day Moses charged the people, saying, 12 "When you have crossed over the
Jordan, [a]these shall stand on Mount Gerizim
to bless the people: Simeon, Levi, Judah,
Issachar, Joseph, and Benjamin. 13 And these
shall stand on Mount Ebal for the curse:
Reuben, Gad, Asher, Zebulun, Dan, and
Naphtali. 14 And [b]the Levites shall declare to
all the men of Israel in a loud voice:
15 [c]"'Cursed be the man who makes a
carved or cast metal image, an abomination
to the LORD, a thing made by the hands of a
craftsman, and sets it up in secret.' [d]And all
the people shall answer and say, 'Amen.'
16 [e]"'Cursed be anyone who dishonors
his father or his mother.' And all the people shall say, 'Amen.'
17 [f]"'Cursed be anyone who moves his
neighbor's landmark.' And all the people
shall say, 'Amen.'
18 [g]"'Cursed be anyone who misleads a
blind man on the road.' And all the people
shall say, 'Amen.'

[1] Hebrew *whole*

18 [o]ch. 7:6; 14:2; See Ex. 19:5
19 [p]ch. 28:1; [ch. 32:8] [q]Ps. 86:9 [r]See ch. 7:6
Chapter 27
2 [s]Josh. 4:1
3 [t]Josh. 8:32 [u]See Ex. 3:8
4 [v]ch. 11:29; Josh. 8:30
5 [w]Ex. 20:25; Josh. 8:31
7 [x]See ch. 12:7
8 [y][Hab. 2:2]
9 [z]ch. 26:18
12 [a]ch. 11:29; Josh. 8:33; [Judg. 9:7]
14 [b][ch. 33:10; Dan. 9:11]
15 [c]See Ex. 20:4; 34:17 [d][Num. 5:22; Neh. 5:13; Ps. 106:48; Jer. 11:5; 28:6; 1 Cor. 14:16]
16 [e]Ex. 20:12; 21:17; Lev. 19:3; See ch. 21:18-21
17 [f]See ch. 19:14
18 [g]Lev. 19:14

and the two parties of the covenant (God and the people) "declared" loyalty to the other (vv. 17, 18).

27:1–30:20 Moses continues his book of farewells with a third address devoted especially to the sanctions by which the covenant requirements will be enforced. After summoning the people to covenant oath in light of their rebelliousness, and prophesying covenant renewal in the future, Moses calls for the people to "choose life" according to the promise given to their fathers, Abraham, Isaac, and Jacob.

27:1 Moses . . . commanded. Moses and the elders specify a ceremony of dedication to be held after the Israelites entered the land. The laws would be published; the ceremony would be impressive; the people would add their "Amen," and a liturgy of promised blessings and curses would follow.

27:2 plaster them with plaster. Moses provides for the publication of the law at the covenant renewal ceremony on Mount Ebal (vv. 3, 8). Large stones were to be whitewashed and the words of the law written on them. This technique of writing upon a whitewashed surface is typically Egyptian (the Canaanite and Mesopotamian practice was to inscribe words into stone surfaces). Because Moses was intimately familiar with Egypt and its practices, these verses provide another indication that the text of Deuteronomy dates to the Mosaic era.

27:5 wield no iron tool. The stones were to be uncut. Because iron was used in the building of Solomon's temple (1 Chr. 22:3, 14), we need not conclude that it was a taboo metal forbidden for religious worship. See note 8:9.

27:12 these . . . on Mount Gerizim to bless. There is no apparent reason for the precise tribal assignments. Here Levi is included among the regular tribes (even among the six that pronounced the blessings), although some of the Levites were to recite the curses the people would answer. The tribe of Joseph united Manasseh and Ephraim, so the enumeration follows the names of the twelve patriarchs rather than the later tribal divisions.

27:15–26 This list of offenses subject to curse is not exhaustive. These offenses may have been chosen as representative of the sorts of sins that might escape detection and so remain secret (cf. vv. 15, 24). Even secret sins would affect Israel's covenant relationship with God (cf. Josh. 7:10–26).

27:15 the man who makes a carved . . . image. The first curse concerns idolatry (5:7–9).

Amen. The Hebrew word means "so be it."

27:16 anyone who dishonors his father or his mother. The second curse concerns the fifth commandment (5:16).

27:17 landmark. See note 19:14.

27:18 misleads a blind man. Leviticus 19:14 commands care for the disabled.

19 [h]"'Cursed be anyone who perverts the
justice due to the sojourner, the fatherless,
and the widow.' And all the people shall
say, 'Amen.'
20 [i]"'Cursed be anyone who lies with his
father's wife, because he has [j]uncovered
his father's nakedness.'[1] And all the people
shall say, 'Amen.'
21 [k]"'Cursed be anyone who lies with any
kind of animal.' And all the people shall
say, 'Amen.'
22 [l]"'Cursed be anyone who lies with his
sister, whether the daughter of his father or
the daughter of his mother.' And all the
people shall say, 'Amen.'
23 [m]"'Cursed be anyone who lies with his
mother-in-law.' And all the people shall
say, 'Amen.'
24 [n]"'Cursed be anyone who strikes down
his neighbor in secret.' And all the people
shall say, 'Amen.'
25 [o]"'Cursed be anyone who takes a bribe
to shed innocent blood.' And all the people
shall say, 'Amen.'
26 [p]"'Cursed be anyone who does not
confirm the words of this law by doing
them.' And all the people shall say,
'Amen.'

Blessings for Obedience

28 "And [q]if you faithfully obey the
voice of the LORD your God, being
careful to do all his commandments that I
command you today, the LORD your God
will set you [r]high above all the nations of
the earth. 2 And all these blessings shall
come upon you and [s]overtake you, if you
obey the voice of the LORD your God.
3 Blessed shall you be in the city, and
[t]blessed shall you be in the field. 4 Blessed
shall be [u]the fruit of your womb and the
fruit of your ground and the fruit of your
cattle, the increase of your herds and the
young of your flock. 5 Blessed shall be your
basket and your [v]kneading bowl. 6 Blessed
shall you be [w]when you come in, and
blessed shall you be when you go out.
7 "The LORD [x]will cause your enemies
who rise against you to be defeated before
you. They shall come out against you one
way and flee before you seven ways. 8 The
LORD [y]will command the blessing on you in
your barns and [z]in all that you undertake.
[a]And he will bless you in the land that the
LORD your God is giving you. 9 [b]The LORD
will establish you as a people holy to himself, as he has sworn to you, if you keep the
commandments of the LORD your God and
walk in his ways. 10 And [c]all the peoples of
the earth shall see that you are [d]called by
the name of the LORD, and they shall be
[e]afraid of you. 11 And [f]the LORD will make
you abound in prosperity, in the fruit of
your womb and in the fruit of your livestock and in the fruit of your ground, within the land that the LORD swore to your
fathers to give you. 12 The LORD will open to
you his good treasury, the heavens, [g]to give
the rain to your land in its season and [h]to

19 [h]See Ex. 22:21, 22
20 [i]See Lev. 18:8 [j]See ch. 22:30
21 [k]See Lev. 18:23
22 [l]Lev. 18:9; 20:17; [Ezek. 22:11]
23 [m]Lev. 18:17; 20:14
24 [n]ch. 19:11; Ex. 21:12, 14
25 [o]ch. 16:19; Ex. 23:7, 8; Ezek. 22:12
26 [p]ch. 28:15; Jer. 11:3; Cited Gal. 3:10
Chapter 28
1 [q][Ex. 15:26; 23:22; Lev. 26:3; Isai. 55:2] [r]ch. 26:19
2 [s]ver. 15; Zech. 1:6
3 [t][Gen. 39:5]
4 [u]ch. 7:13; 30:9; [Gen. 49:25; Ex. 23:26]
5 [v]ver. 17; [Ex. 8:3; 12:34]
6 [w]Ps. 121:8
7 [x]Ex. 23:22, 27; Lev. 26:7, 8; [ver. 25]; See 2 Sam. 22:38-41; Ps. 18:37-40
8 [y]Lev. 25:21; Ps. 133:3 [z]See ch. 12:7 [a]ch. 15:4
9 [b]ch. 7:6; 26:18, 19; 29:13; See Ex. 19:5, 6
10 [c][Isai. 61:9] [d]See Num. 6:27 [e]ch. 2:25; 11:25
11 [f]ch. 30:9
12 [g]ch. 11:14; Lev. 26:4 [h]ch. 14:29

1 Hebrew *uncovered his father's skirt*

27:19 perverts the justice. God upholds the cause of the helpless (10:18).

27:20 lies with his father's wife. See note 22:30.

27:21 lies with any kind of animal. The penalty for this perversion was death (Ex. 22:19; Lev. 18:23; 20:15).

27:22 lies with his sister. This curse concerns both a full sister and a half sister (having the same father but a different mother). See Lev. 18:11; 20:17.

27:23 lies with his mother-in-law. The penalty was death (Lev. 18:17; 20:14).

27:24, 25 Both the secret attacker and the hired assassin fall under divine curse, even though both might expect to avoid detection (vv. 15–26 note).

27:26 does not confirm the words of this law. The final curse covers all the rest of God's commandments. Paul quotes this verse to underscore the stringency of law's demands and the impossibility of meriting salvation by works (Gal. 3:10). Measured by God's standards, all have sinned and fall short of the glory of God (Rom. 3:23). But this does not remove the obligation of the believer to obey the moral laws of God by the enabling of the Holy Spirit.

28:1–68 After recording the liturgy for the covenant ritual at Mount Ebal and Mount Gerizim (ch. 27), Moses calls on the congregation at Moab to obey the commands of God, setting forth God's promised blessings for obedience and His curses for disobedience. The blessings are briefer and come first. The curses are, in some cases, the exact reverse of the blessings, and they continue with awesome emphasis before climaxing on a note of doom (v. 68).

28:4 fruit. Their children, crops, and herds will be blessed. For an agricultural people, these were the crucial elements of physical life.

28:5 your basket and your kneading bowl. Household endeavors would be blessed.

28:6 come in . . . go out. This idiom referring to normal, every-day activities underscores the comprehensiveness of divine blessing (cf. 31:2). God will bless an obedient people in every way.

28:10 See "'This Is My Name': God's Self-disclosure" at Ex. 3:15.

28:11 within the land. The blessings detailed above will be realized in the Land of Promise—itself a major part of the blessing.

28:12 his good treasury, the heavens. This idiom expresses the conviction that the rainfall so crucial to Israel's agricultural prosperity was a gift of God (11:11–17; Ps. 104:13). Here is an implicit warning against the Canaanite fertility religions which ascribed the rainfall to the pagan god Baal.

bless all the work of your hands. And [i]you
shall lend to many nations, but you shall
not borrow. 13 And the LORD will make you
[j]the head and not the tail, and you shall
only go up and not down, if you obey the
commandments of the LORD your God,
which I command you today, being careful
to do them, 14 [k]and if you do not turn aside
from any of the words that I command you
today, to the right hand or to the left, to go
after other gods to serve them.

Curses for Disobedience

15 "But [l]if you will not obey the voice of
the LORD your God or be careful to do all
his commandments and his statutes that I
command you today, then all these curses
shall come upon you and [m]overtake you.
16 Cursed shall you be [n]in the city, and
cursed shall you be in the field. 17 Cursed
shall be your basket and your kneading
bowl. 18 Cursed shall be the fruit of your
womb and the fruit of your ground, the
increase of your herds and the young of
your flock. 19 Cursed shall you be when you
come in, and cursed shall you be when you
go out.
20 "The LORD [o]will send on you curses,
confusion, and [p]frustration in all that you
undertake to do, [q]until you are destroyed
and perish quickly on account of the evil of
your deeds, because you have forsaken me.
21 The LORD will make [r]the pestilence stick
to you until he has consumed you off the
land that you are entering to take possession of it. 22 [s]The LORD will strike you with
wasting disease and with fever, inflamma-
tion and fiery heat, and with drought[1] and
with [t]blight and with mildew. They shall
pursue you until you perish. 23 And [u]the
heavens over your head shall be bronze,
and the earth under you shall be iron.
24 The LORD will make the rain of your land
powder. From heaven dust shall come
down on you until you are destroyed.

25 [v]"The LORD will cause you to be defeated before your enemies. You shall go out
one way against them and flee seven ways
before them. And you [w]shall be a horror to
all the kingdoms of the earth. 26 And [x]your
dead body shall be food for all birds of the
air and for the beasts of the earth, and
[y]there shall be no one to frighten them
away. 27 The LORD will strike you [z]with the
boils of Egypt, and with tumors and [a]scabs
and itch, of which you cannot be healed.
28 The LORD will strike you with [b]madness
and blindness and confusion of mind,
29 and you shall [c]grope at noonday, as the
blind grope in darkness, and you shall not
prosper in your ways.[2] And you shall be
only oppressed and robbed continually,
and there shall be no one to help you.
30 [d]You shall betroth a wife, but another
man shall ravish her. [e]You shall build a
house, but you shall not dwell in it. [f]You
shall plant a vineyard, but you shall not
enjoy its fruit. 31 Your ox shall be slaughtered before your eyes, but you shall not
eat any of it. Your donkey shall be seized
before your face, but shall not be restored
to you. Your sheep shall be given to your
enemies, but there shall be no one to help
you. 32 [g]Your sons and your daughters shall
be given to another people, while your eyes
look on and fail with longing for them all
day long, [h]but you shall be helpless. 33 A
nation that you have not known shall eat
up the fruit of your ground and of all your
labors, and you shall be only oppressed
and crushed continually, 34 so that you are
driven mad [i]by the sights that your eyes
see. 35 The LORD will strike you on the
knees and on the legs [j]with grievous boils
of which you cannot be healed, from the
sole of your foot to the crown of your head.
36 "The LORD will [k]bring you and your
king whom you set over you to a nation

[1] Or *sword* [2] Or *shall not succeed in finding your ways*

12 [i]ch. 15:6; [ver. 44; Ps. 37:26] **13** [j]Isai. 9:14, 15; 19:15 **14** [k]See ch. 5:32 **15** [l]Lev. 26:14; Lam. 2:17; Dan. 9:11, 13; Mal. 2:2 [m]ver. 2 **16** [n][ver. 3-6] **20** [o]Mal. 2:2 [p]Ps. 80:16; Isai. 30:17; 51:20; 66:15 [q]Josh. 23:16 **21** [r]See Lev. 26:25 **22** [s]Lev. 26:16 [t]1 Kin. 8:37; 2 Chr. 6:28; Amos 4:9; Hag. 2:17 **23** [u]Lev. 26:19
25 [v]ch. 32:30; Lev. 26:17, 37; Isai. 30:17; [ver. 7] [w]Ezek. 23:46 **26** [x][1 Sam. 17:44, 46; Ps. 79:2; Jer. 16:4; 19:7; 34:20] [y]Jer. 7:33 **27** [z][ver. 35] [a]Lev. 21:20; 22:22 **28** [b][ver. 34; Zech. 12:4] **29** [c]Job 5:14; Isai. 59:10 **30** [d]ch. 20:5-7; Jer. 8:10 [e]Amos 5:11; Zeph. 1:13 [f]ch. 20:6; Lev. 19:23-25; [Mic. 6:15] **32** [g][2 Chr. 29:9; Joel 3:6] [h]Neh. 5:5 **34** [i]ver. 67 **35** [j][ver. 27] **36** [k]2 Kin. 17:4, 6; 24:12, 14; 25:7, 11; 2 Chr. 33:11; 36:6, 20

28:16–19 The curses here negatively mirror the blessings of vv. 3–6.

28:23 bronze . . . iron. These metaphors of rainless sky and barren land would be frightful to an agricultural people so dependent on rain and soil (cf. Lev. 26:19).

28:25 defeated before your enemies. The expression is the reverse of the blessing in v. 7, with the added horror that their corpses would be exposed with no one to give them decent burial (v. 26).

28:27 The various diseases mentioned here cannot be precisely identified. They may be included in the "diseases of Egypt" (v. 60), from which God had promised to deliver them (7:15; Ex. 15:26) if they would obey His laws. Egyptians suffered from a variety of tropical diseases and parasites (cf. 14:3–21 note).

28:35 sole of your foot . . . head. A description of great torment, also used to describe Job's boils (Job 2:7).

28:36, 37 The covenantal curse of captivity and exile mentioned here becomes an important element of the prophetic covenant lawsuits against disobedient Israel later in the Old Testament (e.g., Is. 5:13; Jer. 13:19; 29:17–19).

28:36 king whom you set over you. See 17:14–17 for another mention of possible future kingship in Israel.

that neither you [l]nor your fathers have
known. And [m]there you shall serve other
gods of wood and stone. 37 And you shall
become [n]a horror, a proverb, and a
byword among all the peoples where the
LORD will lead you away. 38 [o]You shall
carry much seed into the field and shall
gather in little, for [p]the locust shall consume it. 39 [q]You shall plant vineyards and
dress them, but you shall neither drink of
the wine nor gather the grapes, for the
worm shall eat them. 40 You shall have
olive trees throughout all your territory,
but you [r]shall not anoint yourself with the
oil, for your olives shall drop off. 41 You
shall father sons and daughters, but they
shall not be yours, for [s]they shall go into
captivity. 42 [p]The cricket[1] shall possess all
your trees and the fruit of your ground.
43 [t]The sojourner who is among you shall
rise higher and higher above you, and you
shall come down lower and lower. 44 [u]He
shall lend to you, and you shall not lend
to him. [t]He shall be the head, and you
shall be the tail.

45 [v]"All these curses shall come upon you
and pursue you and overtake you till you
are destroyed, because you did not obey
the voice of the LORD your God, to keep
his commandments and his statutes that
he commanded you. 46 They shall be [w]a
sign and a wonder against you and your
offspring forever. 47 [x]Because you did not
serve the LORD your God with joyfulness
and gladness of heart, because of the
abundance of all things, 48 therefore you
shall serve your enemies whom the LORD
will send against you, in hunger and thirst,
in nakedness, and lacking everything. And
he [y]will put a yoke of iron on your neck
until he has destroyed you. 49 [z]The LORD
will bring a nation against you from far
away, from the end of the earth, [a]swoop-
ing down like the eagle, a nation [b]whose
language you do not understand, 50 a hard-
faced nation [c]who shall not respect the old
or show mercy to the young. 51 It shall [d]eat
the offspring of your cattle and the fruit of
your ground, until you are destroyed; it
also shall not leave you grain, wine, or oil,
the increase of your herds or the young of
your flock, until they have caused you to
perish.

52 "They shall [e]besiege you in all your
towns, until your high and fortified walls,
in which you trusted, come down
throughout all your land. And they shall
besiege you in all your towns throughout
all your land, which the LORD your God
has given you. 53 And [f]you shall eat the
fruit of your womb, the flesh of your sons
and daughters, whom the LORD your God
has given you, [g]in the siege and in the
distress with which your enemies shall
distress you. 54 The man who is the most
tender and refined among you will [h]be-
grudge food to his brother, to [i]the wife he
embraces,[2] and to the last of the children
whom he has left, 55 so that he will not
give to any of them any of the flesh of his
children whom he is eating, because he
has nothing else left, [j]in the siege and in
the distress with which your enemy shall
distress you in all your towns. 56 [k]The
most tender and refined woman among
you, who would not venture to set the
sole of her foot on the ground because she
is so delicate and tender, will begrudge to
the husband she embraces,[3] to her son
and to her daughter, 57 her afterbirth that
comes out from between her feet and her
children whom she bears, because lacking
everything she will eat them secretly, [j]in
the siege and in the distress with which
your enemy shall distress you in your
towns.

58 "If you are not careful to do all the
words of this law that are written in this
book, that you may fear this glorious and
awesome name, [l]the LORD your God,
59 then the LORD will bring on you and your
offspring extraordinary afflictions, afflictions severe and lasting, and sicknesses
grievous and lasting. 60 And he will bring

36 [l]Jer. 9:16; 16:13 [m]ver. 64; ch. 4:28
37 [n]1 Kin. 9:7, 8; 2 Chr. 7:20; Jer. 24:9; 25:9; [Ezek. 14:8]
38 [o]Mic. 6:15; Hag. 1:6 [p]Joel 1:4; 2:25
39 [q]Zeph. 1:13
40 [r]Mic. 6:15
41 [s]Lam. 1:5
42 [p][See ver. 38 above]
43 [t][ver. 13]
44 [u][ver. 12] [t][See ver. 43 above]
45 [v]ver. 15
46 [w][Isai. 8:18]
47 [x]Neh. 9:35-37
48 [y]Jer. 28:14
49 [z][Jer. 5:15-17; 6:22, 23]; See Isai. 5:26-30 [a]Jer. 48:40; 49:22; Lam. 4:19; Hos. 8:1; Hab. 1:8; [Ezek. 17:3, 12] [b]Isai. 28:11; 33:19; Jer. 5:15
50 [c][2 Chr. 36:17; Isai. 47:6]
51 [d]ver. 33; Jer. 5:17; [Isai. 62:8, 9]
52 [e][2 Kin. 17:5; 25:1, 2, 4]
53 [f]ver. 57; Lev. 26:29; Jer. 19:9; Ezek. 5:10; [2 Kin. 6:28, 29; Lam. 2:20; 4:10] [g]ver. 55, 57
54 [h]See ch. 15:9 [i]ch. 13:6
55 [j]ver. 53
56 [k]ver. 54; Isai. 47:1
57 [j][See ver. 55 above]
58 [l]Ex. 6:3

[1] Identity uncertain [2] Hebrew *the wife of his bosom* [3] Hebrew *the husband of her bosom*

28:44 He shall lend to you. This curse, like several in this section, is the reverse of an earlier blessing (vv. 12, 13; 23:19 note).

28:49 the end of the earth. This expression for extreme distance is based on how the eye perceives the earth to end where horizon and sky meet; it is equivalent to "far off from you" (cf. 13:7).

28:53 eat the fruit of your womb. Cannibalism was a dreadful accompaniment of ancient sieges, when a city's food supply would be cut off for lengthy periods. This curse found frightful fulfillment during the sieges of Samaria and Jerusalem (2 Kin. 6:28, 29; Jer. 19:9; Lam. 2:20; 4:10).

28:58 this glorious and awesome name. See " 'This Is My Name': God's Self-disclosure" at Ex. 3:15.

upon you again all [m]the diseases of Egypt,
of which you were afraid, and they shall
cling to you. 61 Every sickness also and
every affliction that is not recorded in the
book of this law, the LORD will bring upon
you, until you are destroyed. 62 Whereas
[n]you were as numerous [o]as the stars of
heaven, you shall be left few in number,
because you did not obey the voice of the
LORD your God. 63 And as the LORD [p]took
delight in doing you good and multiplying
you, so the LORD will [q]take delight in bringing ruin upon you and destroying you. And
you shall be plucked off the land that you
are entering to take possession of it.
64 "And the LORD [r]will scatter you among
all peoples, from one end of the earth to
the other, and [s]there you shall serve other
gods [t]of wood and stone, [u]which neither
you nor your fathers have known. 65 And
[v]among these nations you shall find no
respite, and there shall be no resting place
for the sole of your foot, but [w]the LORD will
give you there a trembling heart and failing
eyes and [x]a languishing soul. 66 Your life
shall hang in doubt before you. Night and
day you shall be in dread and have no
assurance of your life. 67 [y]In the morning
you shall say, 'If only it were evening!' and
at evening you shall say, 'If only it were
morning!' because of the dread that your
heart shall feel, and [z]the sights that your
eyes shall see. 68 And the LORD [a]will bring
you back in ships to Egypt, a journey that I
promised that [b]you should never make
again; and there you shall offer yourselves
for sale to your enemies as male and female
slaves, but there will be no buyer."

60 [m]See ch. 7:15
62 [n]ch. 4:27; [2 Kin. 24:14; Neh. 7:4; Jer. 42:2] [o]See ch. 10:22
63 [p]ch. 30:9; Jer. 32:41; Zeph. 3:17 [q][Prov. 1:26; Isai. 1:24; Ezek. 5:13]
64 [r]See Lev. 26:33 [s]ver. 36 [t]ch. 13:6; Jer. 19:4; 44:3 [u]ch. 4:28
65 [v][Amos 9:4] [w][Lev. 26:36] [x]Lev. 26:16
67 [y]Job 7:3, 4 [z]ver. 34
68 [a]Hos. 8:13; 9:3; [Jer. 43:7] [b]See ch. 17:16

Chapter 29
1 [c]ch. 1:5 [d]ch. 5:2, 3
2 [e]Ex. 19:4; [Josh. 23:3]
3 [f]See ch. 4:34
4 [g][Isai. 6:9, 10; 63:17; John 8:43; Acts 28:26, 27; Rom. 11:8, 10]
5 [h]ch. 1:3; 8:2, 4; Amos 2:10; Acts 13:18
6 [i]ch. 8:3; See Ex. 16:4
7 [j]ch. 2:24, 26, 32; 3:1; See Num. 21:21-24, 33-35
8 [k]ch. 3:12, 13; Num. 32:33
9 [l]ch. 4:6
11 [m][Ex. 12:38] [n][Josh. 9:21, 23, 27]

The Covenant Renewed in Moab

29 [1] These are the words of the covenant that the LORD commanded
Moses to make with the people of Israel [c]in
the land of Moab, besides [d]the covenant
that he had made with them at Horeb.
2 [2]And Moses summoned all Israel and
said to them: [e]"You have seen all that the
LORD did before your eyes in the land of
Egypt, to Pharaoh and to all his servants
and to all his land, 3 the great [f]trials that
your eyes saw, the signs, and those great
wonders. 4 But to this day [g]the LORD has
not given you a heart to understand or eyes
to see or ears to hear. 5 [h]I have led you forty
years in the wilderness. Your clothes have
not worn out on you, and your sandals
have not worn off your feet. 6 [i]You have not
eaten bread, and you have not drunk wine
or strong drink, that you may know that I
am the LORD your God. 7 And when you
came to this place, [j]Sihon the king of
Heshbon and Og the king of Bashan came
out against us to battle, but we defeated
them. 8 We took their land and [k]gave it for
an inheritance to the Reubenites, the
Gadites, and the half-tribe of the Manassites. 9 [l]Therefore keep the words of this
covenant and do them, that you may prosper[3] in all that you do.
10 "You are standing today all of you
before the LORD your God: the heads of
your tribes,[4] your elders, and your officers,
all the men of Israel, 11 your little ones, your
wives, and the [m]sojourner who is in your
camp, from [n]the one who chops your wood

1 Ch 28:69 in Hebrew 2 Ch 29:1 in Hebrew 3 Or *deal wisely*
4 Septuagint, Syriac; Hebrew *your heads, your tribes*

28:61 the book of this law. The written record documenting the terms of a covenant had legal status and was a crucial part of the ancient Near Eastern treaty (Introduction: Date and Occasion). Deuteronomy as such is the record of God's covenant with His people (v. 58; 31:24–26).

28:64 will scatter you. Some argue that these threats of exile indicate that portions of Deuteronomy were written during or after the Babylonian exile (sixth century B.C.). This argument is rooted in the view that supernatural predictive prophecy is impossible. But in fact, this covenant curse is couched in more general terms than would apply to the Babylonian exile. It threatens a widespread dispersion "from one end of the earth to the other." It may find fulfillment in the Assyrian and Babylonian exiles, as well as in the dispersion of the Jews after the fall of Jerusalem in A.D. 70.

28:68 there will be no buyer. This theme of abandonment echoes v. 29. The aggregation of curses here is overwhelming. This chapter should be compared with the similar but shorter Lev. 26, which ends with the possibility of confession, repentance, and restoration. Here, the theme of possible restoration is left for ch. 30.

29:1 the covenant . . . in the land of Moab. Scholars debate whether v. 1 concludes what precedes or introduces what follows. The latter, as reflected in the ESV text division, is more likely. This "covenant . . . in the land of Moab" is a renewal of the Sinai covenant ("the covenant . . . at Horeb"). As usual, Moses recites the history of God's mighty acts on Israel's behalf in the Exodus from Egypt and in the wilderness (cf. Moses' speech in 1:6–4:38). There follows a warning against departing from the Lord, a promise of restoration upon repentance, and a solemn charge to obey.

Horeb. See note 1:6.

29:2 in the land of Egypt. The deliverance from Egypt, which occupies a third of the Book of Exodus, is mentioned many times in Deuteronomy (e.g., 1:30; 4:20, 34; 5:6; 11:2–7).

29:4 the LORD has not given . . . eyes to see. Paul combines this verse with Is. 29:10, and applies both verses to the Jews of his day (Rom. 11:8).

29:5 forty years. The special preservation of clothes was mentioned in 8:4. The additional fact given here is that they drank no wine or other fermented drink, since there were no grapes in the desert. They also had no bread, but God supplied them with manna.

to the one who draws your water, 12 so that
you may enter into the [o]sworn covenant of
the LORD your God, which the LORD your
God is making with you today, 13 that he
may [p]establish you today as his people,
and that [q]he may be your God, as he promised you, and [r]as he swore to your fathers,
to Abraham, to Isaac, and to Jacob. 14 It is
not with you alone [s]that I am making this
sworn covenant, 15 but with whoever is
standing here with us today before the
LORD our God, [t]and with whoever is not
here with us today.
16 "You know how we lived in the land of
Egypt, and how we came through the midst
of the nations through which you passed.
17 And you have seen their detestable things,
their idols of wood and stone, of silver and
gold, which were among them. 18 Beware lest
there be among you a man or woman or
clan or tribe whose heart is turning away
today from the LORD our God to go and
serve the gods of those nations. Beware lest
there be among you [u]a root bearing poisonous and bitter fruit, 19 one who, when he
hears the words of this sworn covenant,
blesses himself in his heart, saying, 'I shall
be safe, though I walk in the stubbornness
of my heart.' This will lead to the sweeping
away of moist and dry alike. 20 The LORD will
not be willing to forgive him, but rather [v]the
anger of the LORD and [w]his jealousy will
smoke against that man, and the curses
written in this book will settle upon him,
and the LORD [x]will blot out his name from
under heaven. 21 And the LORD will single
him out from all the tribes of Israel for
calamity, in accordance with all the curses

12 [o]Neh. 10:29
13 [p]ch. 28:9 [q]Ex. 6:7 [r]Gen. 17:7; [Gen. 50:24]
14 [s][Jer. 31:31-33; Heb. 8:8-10]
15 [t][Acts 2:39]
18 [u]Heb. 12:15
20 [v]Ps. 74:1 [w]Ps. 79:5 [x]See ch. 9:14

22 [y]ver. 24
23 [z]Judg. 9:45; Jer. 17:6; Ezek. 47:11; Zeph. 2:9 [a]Gen. 19:24, 25; Jer. 20:16; 49:18; 50:40; 2 Pet. 2:6 [b]Gen. 14:2; Hos. 11:8
24 [c]ver. 22 [d]1 Kin. 9:8, 9; Jer. 22:8, 9
27 [e]See ch. 28:15-68; Lev. 26:14-39; Dan. 9:11-14
28 [f]1 Kin. 14:15; 2 Chr. 7:20; Jer. 12:14 [g]Jer. 22:26
Chapter 30
1 [h]ch. 11:26-28; Lev. 26:40-42 [i]See ch. 28 [j]ch. 4:29-31; See 1 Kin. 8:47-50

of the covenant written in this Book of the
Law. 22 And the next generation, your children who rise up after you, and the foreigner who comes from a far land, [y]will say,
when they see the afflictions of that land
and the sicknesses with which the LORD has
made it sick— 23 the whole land burned out
with brimstone and [z]salt, nothing sown and
nothing growing, where no plant can
sprout, [a]an overthrow like that of Sodom
and Gomorrah, [b]Admah, and Zeboiim,
which the LORD overthrew in his anger and
wrath— 24 all the nations [c]will say, [d]'Why
has the LORD done thus to this land? What
caused the heat of this great anger?' 25 Then
people will say, 'It is because they abandoned the covenant of the LORD, the God of
their fathers, which he made with them
when he brought them out of the land of
Egypt, 26 and went and served other gods
and worshiped them, gods whom they had
not known and whom he had not allotted to
them. 27 Therefore the anger of the LORD was
kindled against this land, [e]bringing upon it
all the curses written in this book, 28 and the
LORD [f]uprooted them from their land in
anger and fury and great wrath, and [g]cast
them into another land, as they are this day.'
29 "The secret things belong to the LORD
our God, but the things that are revealed
belong to us and to our children forever,
that we may do all the words of this law.

Repentance and Forgiveness

30 [h]"And [i]when all these things come
upon you, the blessing and the
curse, which I have set before you, and
[j]you call them to mind among all the

29:12 enter into the sworn covenant. In terming this a renewal of the Sinai covenant, we should remember that the covenant was the same, but the people were not. All those over twenty at Sinai had perished in the wilderness. Many of the people under twenty then, now between forty and sixty, had seen the great events but had not taken part. Now they too were to affirm the covenant.

29:19 the sweeping away of moist and dry alike. The Hebrew of this phrase (apparently an ancient proverb) is difficult to translate. The entire phrase as translated here means that the sinner will not escape judgment by hiding undetected in the company of the righteous (cf. v. 21). Another possibility is to render the phrase "so that the well-watered land is destroyed along with dry land" or "so that the drunkard is destroyed along with the thirsty," indicating that the sin of one brings disaster on many (cf. vv. 22–25). Another possible translation is "to add drunkenness to thirst," meaning that the sinful man compounds his guilt by sinking further into sin.

29:21 this Book of the Law. See note 28:61 (cf. Josh. 1:7, 8).

29:23 Sodom. The four cities of the plain that were destroyed in Abraham's day are named. In Gen. 14 five cities of the plain are mentioned, but not their destruction. In Gen. 19 Sodom and Gomorrah are mentioned and the whole area is said to be destroyed, but Zoar is spared. Deuteronomy puts the two records together and lists the four destroyed cities. The judgment of Sodom was a prophetic model of divine wrath. Like Moses, Isaiah compares the judgment of Israel to that of Sodom (Is. 1:10). Jesus also compares the judgment at His Second Advent to that of Sodom (Luke 17:28–35), as does Peter (2 Pet. 2:6).

29:29 The meaning of the latter part of this verse is apparent: God's revealed law is of vital importance, and the Israelites and their children must follow this revealed law. The reference to "secret things" may suggest that Moses faces the uncertain future of the nation, remembering their waywardness and how they turned to the golden calf at Horeb (Ex. 32). In this uncertainty Moses trusts the hidden future to his trustworthy God.

30:1–10 Anticipating the real possibility of judgment and exile for Israel, Moses looks beyond the time of judgment to Israel's future repentance, restoration, and divine blessing. Significantly, this future blessing will include deliverance from slavery to sin. Moses' reference to the circumcision of the "heart" (v. 6; cf. 10:16) is foundational for the later prophetic

nations where the LORD your God has driv-
en you, 2 and [k]return to the LORD your God,
you and your children, and obey his voice
in all that I command you today, with all
your heart and with all your soul, 3 then the
LORD your God [l]will restore your fortunes
and have compassion on you, and he will
[m]gather you again from all the peoples
where the LORD your God has scattered
you. 4 [n]If your outcasts are in the uttermost
parts of heaven, from there the LORD your
God will gather you, and from there he will
take you. 5 And the LORD your God will
bring you into the land that your fathers
possessed, that you may possess it. [o]And
he will make you more prosperous and
numerous than your fathers. 6 And [p]the
LORD your God will circumcise your heart
and the heart of your offspring, [q]so that
you will love the LORD your God with all
your heart and with all your soul, that you
may live. 7 And the LORD your God will put
all these curses on your foes and enemies
who persecuted you. 8 And you shall again
obey the voice of the LORD and keep all his
commandments that I command you
today. 9 [r]The LORD your God will make you
abundantly prosperous in all the work of
your hand, in the fruit of your womb and
in the fruit of your cattle and in the fruit of
your ground. [s]For the LORD will again take
delight in prospering you, as he took

2 [k]Neh. 1:9; Isai. 55:7; Lam. 3:40; Joel 2:12, 13
3 [l]Ps. 126:1, 4 [m]Jer. 32:37; Ezek. 34:13; 36:24
4 [n]ch. 28:64; Neh. 1:9
5 [o]Zeph. 3:19, 20; See ch. 28:63
6 [p][Jer. 31:33; 32:39, 40; Ezek. 11:19; 36:26, 27]; See ch. 10:16 [q]ver. 16
9 [r]ch. 28:11 [s]Zeph. 3:19, 20; See ch. 28:63
11 [t][Isai. 45:19; 48:16]
12 [u][Rom. 10:6-8]
15 [v][ch. 11:26; 32:47]
16 [w]ver. 6; See ch. 6:5
17 [x]ch. 29:18

delight in your fathers, 10 when you obey
the voice of the LORD your God, to keep his
commandments and his statutes that are
written in this Book of the Law, when you
turn to the LORD your God with all your
heart and with all your soul.

The Choice of Life and Death

11 "For this commandment that I command you today [t]is not too hard for you,
neither is it far off. 12 [u]It is not in heaven,
that you should say, 'Who will ascend to
heaven for us and bring it to us, that we
may hear it and do it?' 13 Neither is it
beyond the sea, that you should say, 'Who
will go over the sea for us and bring it to
us, that we may hear it and do it?' 14 But the
word is very near you. It is in your mouth
and in your heart, so that you can do it.
15 "See, [v]I have set before you today life
and good, death and evil. 16 If you obey the
commandments of the LORD your God[1]
that I command you today, [w]by loving the
LORD your God, by walking in his ways,
and by keeping his commandments and
his statutes and his rules, then you shall
live and multiply, and the LORD your God
will bless you in the land that you are
entering to take possession of it. 17 But if
[x]your heart turns away, and you will not
hear, but are drawn away to worship other

1 Septuagint; Hebrew lacks *If you obey the commandments of the LORD your God*

expectation (Jer. 31:31–34; Ezek. 36:25–27), and finds fulfillment in the New Testament (Rom. 2:29).

30:2 with all your heart and with all your soul. Moses refers again to the great commandment of 6:5, holding out the hope of repentance even where there had been apostasy and judgment.

30:4, 5 The measure of God's compassion in restoration will equal or exceed the measure of His wrath in judgment and exile.

30:6 the LORD . . . will circumcise your heart. See notes on vv. 1–10 and 10:16. The promised restoration and renewal will result from a sovereign work of God in the hearts of His elect. By circumcising (transforming) their hearts, He will replace their total inability and stubbornness (5:29; 10:16; 29:4) with the humility and repentance they need (cf. vv. 1, 2), purifying for Himself a people who will love and obey Him. See "Legalism" at Matt. 23:4.

30:7 on your foes and enemies. The future restoration will bring a fulfillment of the promise made to Abraham and his seed: "Him who dishonors you I will curse" (Gen. 12:3). Moses links the restoration pictured in vv. 3–10 to another judgment by God against the enemies of His people.

30:10 The blessings of the renewed covenant will be inseparable from, but not based on, the obedience of the restored remnant of the people to their Lord's commandments (cf., e.g., Matt. 7:21). The obedience of Christ, which is the victory over sin in which the remnant by faith will share, is the only meritorious basis of such blessings.

30:11–14 Recalling his words in 6:6, Moses maintains that the commandment God revealed through him and the righteousness it required were readily accessible to and attainable by Israel (v. 11). He anticipates, however, that those with uncircumcised hearts and ears will raise questions denying these truths, and will seek to establish a righteousness of their own (vv. 12, 13). Moses rebukes such stubbornness, insisting that the word of righteousness is found "in your mouth and in your heart" (v. 14)—in the mouth and heart that speak not in the unbelief and rebellion of their own righteousness, but in the faith and humility of the Lord's righteousness. This righteousness the Lord demonstrated in the works of salvation and judgment, by which He confirmed His oath to Abraham, Isaac, and Jacob (cf. 8:17, 18; 9:4–6; 30:1–7; especially 1:29–33; 9:23). The commandment that Moses proclaimed here was a word calling for faith, and the righteousness it reveals is a righteousness attained by faith (cf. v. 10 note). Paul alludes to these verses in Rom. 10:6–8, updating Moses' admonition in view of the revelation of God's righteousness in the Person and work of Christ. Paul preaches the word that calls for faith where Moses had to leave off, insisting that Israel (and the Gentiles, Rom. 10:12, 13) must now confess with their mouths that Jesus is Lord (cf. Deut. 6:4), and believe with their hearts that God raised Him from the dead (Rom. 10:9). God's work in Jesus Christ yet again reveals His righteousness (Rom. 3:21–26), and confirms His oath to the fathers (cf. Rom. 4:18–25; Gal. 3). See "The Word of God: Scripture as Revelation" at Ex. 32:16.

30:15 I have set before you. Moses calls for a decision. There are two ways: life or death, God's blessing or sure judgment. Joshua presented the same alternatives (Josh. 24:15), and Jesus, who is greater than Moses or Joshua, calls His disciples to take the narrow path that leads to life (Matt. 7:13, 14).

gods and serve them, 18 [y]I declare to you
today, that you shall surely perish. You
shall not live long in the land that you are
going over the Jordan to enter and possess.
19 I call heaven and earth to witness against
you today, that I have set before you life
and death, [z]blessing and curse. Therefore
choose life, that you and your offspring
may live, 20 loving the LORD your God,
obeying his voice [a]and holding fast to him,
for [b]he is your life and length of days, that
you may dwell in [c]the land that the LORD
swore to your fathers, to Abraham, to
Isaac, and to Jacob, to give them."

Joshua to Succeed Moses

31 So Moses continued to speak these
words to all Israel. 2 And he said to
them, "I am [d]120 years old today. I am no
longer able to [e]go out and come in. The
LORD has said to me, [f]'You shall not go over
this Jordan.' 3 The LORD your God [g]himself
will go over before you. He will destroy
these nations before you, so that you shall
dispossess them, and Joshua will go over at
your head, [h]as the LORD has spoken. 4 And
the LORD will do to them [i]as he did to
Sihon [j]and Og, the kings of the Amorites,
and to their land, when he destroyed them.
5 And the LORD will give them over to you,
and you shall do to them [k]according to the
whole commandment that I have commanded you. 6 [l]Be strong and courageous.
Do not fear or be in dread of them, [m]for it
is the LORD your God who goes with you.
[n]He will not leave you or forsake you."
7 Then [o]Moses summoned Joshua and
said to him in the sight of all Israel, [l]"Be
strong and courageous, for you shall go
with this people into the land that the
LORD has sworn to their fathers to give
them, and you shall put them in possession of it. 8 It is the LORD [p]who goes before
you. He will be with you; [n]he will not leave
you or forsake you. [q]Do not fear or be dismayed."

The Reading of the Law

9 Then Moses [r]wrote this law and gave it
to the priests, the sons of Levi, [s]who carried the ark of the covenant of the LORD,
and to all the elders of Israel. 10 And Moses
commanded them, [t]"At the end of every
seven years, at the set time in the year of
release, at [u]the Feast of Booths, 11 when all
Israel comes [v]to appear before the LORD
your God at the place that he will choose,
[w]you shall read this law before all Israel in
their hearing. 12 [x]Assemble the people,
men, women, and little ones, and the sojourner within your towns, that they may
hear and learn to fear the LORD your God,
and be careful to do all the words of this
law, 13 and that their children, [y]who have
not known it, [z]may hear and learn to fear

18 [y]See ch. 4:26
19 [z]ver. 1
20 [a]See ch. 10:20 [b]Ps. 27:1; 66:9; John 11:25 [c]See ch. 1:8
Chapter 31
2 [d]ch. 34:7; [Ex. 7:7] [e]See Num. 27:17 [f]ch. 3:27; See ch. 1:37
3 [g]ch. 9:3 [h]ch. 1:38; 3:28; Num. 27:18, 21
4 [i]See ch. 2:31-35; Num. 21:21-25 [j]See ch. 3:1-7; Num. 21:33-35
5 [k]See ch. 7:2
6 [l]ver. 23; Josh. 1:6, 7; 10:25; 1 Chr. 22:13; 28:20 [m]See ch. 20:4
[n]Josh. 1:5
7 [o][ch. 3:28] [l][See ver. 6 above]
8 [p]See Ex. 13:21 [n][See ver. 6 above] [q]ch. 1:21; 7:18; Josh. 1:9; 8:1; 10:25
9 [r][ch. 17:18] [s]Num. 4:15; Josh. 3:3; 8:33; 1 Chr. 15:15
10 [t]See ch. 15:1 [u]See Lev. 23:34
11 [v]ch. 16:16; Ex. 23:14, 17; 34:23
[w]Josh. 8:34, 35; 2 Kin. 23:2; See Neh. 8:1-3 12 [x]ch. 4:10 13 [y]ch. 11:2 [z]Ps. 78:5, 6

30:19 heaven and earth to witness. The mention of witnesses recalls the form of ancient Near Eastern treaty documents, which have a list of witnesses at the end, often the names of pagan gods. In the biblical covenant, God's creation is called to witness against His people.

31:1–34:12 In this final section of his work, Moses provides for a smooth transition in covenant administration after his death. Also included are the Song of Moses and Moses' blessing of the twelve tribes. The book concludes with an obituary for Moses.

31:1 Moses continued to speak. This brief exhortation (vv. 1–8) can hardly be called another address, but is part of Moses' arrangement of his final affairs and the transfer of authority to Joshua, his successor (Introduction: Outline).

31:2 120 years old. Acts 7:30 tells us that Moses had spent forty years in Midian tending sheep. This time was not wasted, as he learned the geography and climate of the Sinai peninsula in preparation for leading the Israelites in that area for another forty years. The humiliation of being reduced from a prince in Egypt to being a hired tender of sheep also accomplished the divine disciplinary purpose of preparing Moses for his greater role as shepherd of God's people. This leaves forty years for Moses' youth and training in Egypt. So God ensured that Moses was prepared for his great task.

no longer able to go out and come in. A reference to limitations on Moses' daily activities as leader of the vast company of Israelites (28:6 note). The statement in 34:7 that Moses' "eye was undimmed, and his vigor unabated" need not mean that he felt no effects of his advanced age. Moses' many-faceted role as Israel's leader was coming to an end.

31:3 Joshua will go over. See notes 1:37 and 3:23. Though the aged Moses was still active (34:7), the conquest of Canaan would require some years, and it was time for the younger man to take charge. Most importantly, the Lord Himself would lead as He had done with Moses (Ex. 33:14, 15).

31:6 Be strong and courageous. These and the following words resemble the encouragement God gave Joshua after Moses died (Josh. 1:9).

31:7 Moses summoned Joshua. The transfer of political power is often a delicate matter. Moses wisely, and at God's command, elevated Joshua in the presence of the people.

31:9 Moses wrote this law. The conclusion of Moses' covenant ministry is marked by the completion of the law (vv. 24–26; 28:61 note). Repeatedly in Deuteronomy and Exodus, Moses is said to have written down the law or laws of the Lord. In Leviticus most of the chapters begin with the words, "The LORD spoke to Moses." God used Moses preeminently to speak and write His word for Israel (18:15–19 note).

31:10–13 Moses provides for regular instruction of the people and their children in the covenant law by the priests, at a point in the year when the people had ample time to learn. The Feast of Booths came in the fall and lasted a week (16:13–17 note). During the sabbatical year the land was to lie fallow, and the people would not have been burdened with agricultural duties (15:1 note). This practice of reading the law at regular intervals was characteristic of the suzerainty treaties among nations of Moses' time,

the LORD your God, [a]as long as you live in
the land that you are going over the Jordan
to possess."

Joshua Commissioned to Lead Israel

14 And the LORD said to Moses, [b]"Behold,
the days approach when you must die. Call
Joshua and present yourselves in the tent
of meeting, that [c]I may commission him."
And Moses and Joshua went and presented
themselves in the tent of meeting. 15 And
[d]the LORD appeared in the tent in a pillar of
cloud. And the pillar of cloud stood over
the entrance of the tent.

16 And the LORD said to Moses, [b]"Behold,
you are about to lie down with your
fathers. Then this people will rise and
[e]whore after the foreign gods among them
in the land that they are entering, and they
will [f]forsake me and [g]break my covenant
that I have made with them. 17 Then my
anger will be kindled against them in that
day, and [h]I will forsake them and [i]hide my
face from them, and they will be devoured.
And many evils and troubles will come
upon them, so that they will say in that
day, [j]'Have not these evils come upon us
because [k]our God is not among us?' 18 And
I will surely hide my face in that day
because of all the evil that they have done,
because [l]they have turned to other gods.

19 "Now therefore write [m]this song and
[n]teach it to the people of Israel. Put it in
their mouths, that this song may be [o]a witness for me against the people of Israel.
20 For when I have brought them into the
land [p]flowing with milk and honey, which
I swore to give to their fathers, and they
have eaten and are full and [q]grown fat,
[r]they will turn to other gods and serve
them, and [s]despise me and [g]break my
covenant. 21 And when many evils and troubles have come upon them, this song shall
confront them as [t]a witness (for it will live
unforgotten in the mouths of their offspring). For [u]I know what they are inclined
to do even today, before I have brought

13 [a]See ch. 4:10
14 [b][ch. 34:5; Num. 27:13] [c][ver. 23; Num. 27:19]
15 [d]Ex. 33:9; Num. 12:5
16 [b][See ver. 14 above] [e]Ex. 34:15, 16; Lev. 20:5; Num. 15:39 [f]ch. 32:15; Judg. 2:12; 10:6, 13 [g]Judg. 2:20
17 [h]2 Chr. 12:5; 15:2; 24:20 [i]ch. 32:20; Ps. 30:7; 104:29; Isai. 8:17; 64:7; [Isai. 59:2] [j]Judg. 6:13 [k]Num. 14:42
18 [l]ver. 20
19 [m]See ch. 32:1-43 [n][2 Sam. 1:18] [o]ver. 21, 26
20 [p]See Ex. 3:8 [q]ch. 32:15; Neh. 9:25, 26; Jer. 5:28; Hos. 13:6 [r]ver. 18 [s]Num 14:11, 23; 16:30 [g][See ver. 16 above]
21 [t]ver. 19, 26 [u][Hos. 5:3; 13:5]
23 [v][ver. 14] [w]See ver. 6 [x]ver. 8; Josh. 1:5; 3:7
24 [y]ver. 9
25 [z]See ver. 9
26 [a][2 Kin. 22:8] [b]ver. 19, 21
27 [c]See ch. 9:6 [d]See ch. 9:7
28 [e]See ch. 32:1-43 [f]See ch. 4:26
29 [g]Judg. 2:19; Hos. 9:9 [h][Jer. 44:23] [i]See Gen. 49:1 [j]ch. 4:25; 9:18; 32:16, 21; 1 Kin. 16:7; 2 Kin. 22:17
Chapter 32
1 [k]Ps. 50:4; [Josh. 24:27]; See ch. 4:26 [l]Isai. 34:1; Mic. 1:2; 6:1, 2
2 [m]Isai. 55:10, 11; [Job 29:22, 23] [n]Ps. 72:6; Mic. 5:7
3 [o]See ch. 3:24

them into the land that I swore to give."
22 So Moses wrote this song the same day
and taught it to the people of Israel.

23 [v]And the LORD commissioned Joshua
the son of Nun and said, [w]"Be strong and
courageous, for you shall bring the people
of Israel into the land that I swore to give
them. [x]I will be with you."

24 When Moses had finished [y]writing the
words of this law in a book to the very end,
25 Moses commanded [z]the Levites who carried the ark of the covenant of the LORD,
26 "Take this Book of the Law [a]and put it by
the side of the ark of the covenant of the
LORD your God, that it may be there for [b]a
witness against you. 27 For I know how rebellious and [c]stubborn you are. Behold, even
today while I am yet alive with you, [d]you
have been rebellious against the LORD. How
much more after my death! 28 Assemble to
me all the elders of your tribes and your officers, that I may speak [e]these words in their
ears and [f]call heaven and earth to witness
against them. 29 For I know that after my
death [g]you will surely act corruptly and turn
aside from the way that I have commanded
you. And [h]in the days to come [i]evil will
befall you, because you will do what is evil
in the sight of the LORD, [j]provoking him to
anger through the work of your hands."

The Song of Moses

30 Then Moses spoke the words of this
song until they were finished, in the ears of
all the assembly of Israel:

32 "Give ear, [k]O heavens, and I will
speak,
and let [l]the earth hear the words of
my mouth.
2 May [m]my teaching drop as the rain,
my speech distill as the dew,
like gentle rain upon the tender grass,
and [n]like showers upon the herb.
3 For I will proclaim the name of the
LORD;
ascribe [o]greatness to our God!

which typically provided for the regular publication of the covenantal terms of agreement (Introduction: Date and Occasion).

31:14 the tent of meeting. Joshua's legitimacy and authority as Moses' successor are underscored by his commission at the tent of meeting, accompanied by God's appearance in the pillar of cloud (cf. Num. 12:4–12).

31:19 write this song. Knowing the people's inclination to be unfaithful (v. 21), and realizing the power of song in worship and in memory, the Lord commands Moses to write a song that would serve as a testimony in future days. Other examples of Moses' poetry include Ex. 15:1–18; 32:18; Num. 10:35, 36; and Ps. 90.

32:1 O heavens . . . earth. Moses had called heaven and earth as witnesses at the end of the covenant renewal in 30:19.

32:3 proclaim the name of the LORD. This song was to witness in future days to the Lord, His goodness, and His saving work for Israel (31:19).

4 [p]"The Rock, [q]his work is perfect,
for [r]all his ways are justice.
A God of faithfulness and [s]without iniquity,
just and upright is he.
5 They have dealt corruptly with him;
they are no longer his children
[t]because they are blemished;
they are [u]a crooked and twisted generation.
6 Do you thus repay the LORD,
you foolish and senseless people?
Is not he [v]your father, who [w]created you,
who [x]made you and established you?
7 [y]Remember the days of old;
consider the years of many generations;
[z]ask your father, and he will show you,
your elders, and they will tell you.
8 When the Most High [a]gave to the nations their inheritance,
when he [b]divided mankind,
he fixed the borders[1] of the peoples
according to the number of the sons of God.[2]
9 But the LORD's portion is his people,
Jacob his allotted heritage.
10 "He found him [c]in a desert land,
and in the howling waste of the wilderness;
he [d]encircled him, he cared for him,
he [e]kept him as the apple of his eye.
11 [f]Like an eagle that stirs up its nest,
that flutters over its young,
spreading out its wings, catching them,
bearing them on its pinions,
12 [g]the LORD alone guided him,
[h]no foreign god was with him.
13 [i]He made him ride on the high places of the land,
and he ate the produce of the field,
and he suckled him with [j]honey out of the rock,
and [k]oil out of [l]the flinty rock.
14 Curds from the herd, and milk from the flock,
with fat[3] of lambs,
rams of Bashan and goats,
with the very finest[4] of the wheat—
and you drank foaming wine made from [m]the blood of the grape.
15 "But [n]Jeshurun grew fat, and [o]kicked;
[p]you grew fat, stout, and sleek;
[q]then he forsook God [r]who made him
and scoffed at [s]the Rock of his salvation.
16 [t]They stirred him to jealousy with strange gods;
with abominations they provoked him to anger.
17 [u]They sacrificed to demons that were no gods,
to gods they had never known,
to [v]new gods that had come recently,
whom your fathers had never dreaded.
18 You were unmindful of [w]the Rock
that bore[5] you,
and you [x]forgot the God who gave you birth.
19 [y]"The LORD saw it and spurned them,
because of the provocation of [z]his sons and his daughters.
20 And he said, [a]'I will hide my face from them;

4 [p]ver. 15, 18, 30, 31, 37; Ps. 18:2, 31; Isai. 30:29; Hab. 1:12; See 2 Sam. 22:2 [q][Ps. 18:30] [r]Dan. 4:37; Rev. 15:3 [s]Job 34:10
5 [t][2 Pet. 2:13] [u]Matt. 17:17; Luke 9:41; Phil. 2:15
6 [v]Isai. 63:16; 64:8 [w]Ps. 74:2 [x]ver. 15; Isai. 44:2; 51:13
7 [y][Isai. 63:11] [z]Ps. 44:1
8 [a]Acts 17:26 [b]Gen. 11:8
10 [c]ch. 8:15; Jer. 2:6; Hos. 13:5 [d]Ps. 32:10 [e]Ps. 17:8; Prov. 7:2; Zech. 2:8
11 [f]Ex. 19:4
12 [g]Ps. 78:52, 53 [h]Isai. 43:12
13 [i]ch. 33:29; Isai. 58:14; Ezek. 36:2 [j]Ps. 81:16 [k]Job 29:6 [l]ch. 8:15
14 [m]Gen. 49:11
15 [n]ch. 33:5, 26; Isai. 44:2 [o][1 Sam. 2:29] [p]See ch. 31:20 [q]ch. 31:16 [r]ver. 6 [s]2 Sam. 22:47; Ps. 89:26; 95:1
16 [t]Ps. 78:58; See Num. 25:11
17 [u]Ps. 106:37; [1 Cor. 10:20] [v][Judg. 5:8]
18 [w]2 Sam. 22:47; Ps. 89:26; 95:1 [x]Isai. 17:10; Jer. 2:27, 32; Hos. 8:14
19 [y][Judg. 2:14] [z][Isai. 1:2]
20 [a]See ch. 31:17

1 Or *territories* 2 Compare Dead Sea Scroll, Septuagint; Masoretic Text *Israel* 3 That is, with the best 4 Hebrew *with the kidney fat* 5 Or *fathered*

32:4 Rock. This chapter provides the first instances in Scripture of "Rock" as a name for God (vv. 15, 18, 30; there is a similar image in Gen. 49:24 using a different Hebrew word). Suggesting God's steadfast faithfulness and permanence, the term is common in the Psalms and other poetic passages (Ps. 95:1; Is. 44:8).

32:5 because they are blemished. Note the sharp contrast between the steadfast, righteous God (v. 4) and the corrupt nation (v. 5).

32:8 their inheritance. The meaning here is that God by decree gave the Promised Land to Israel. It was an ancient grant to the patriarchs (v. 7).

according to . . . the sons of God. God is sovereign over all of world history, but world history itself is ordered in the interests of God's plan of redemption for His chosen people Israel (Gen. 12:3).

32:10 as the apple of his eye. A reference to the pupil of the eye. Just as the pupil of the eye is closely guarded against harm, so God protects Israel.

32:11 flutters over its young. The image is of an eagle teaching its young to fly. The poetic figures of the Song of Moses are powerful expressions of God's dealings with His people. See also Gen. 1:2 and note.

32:14 rams of Bashan. See note at 3:1.

32:15 Jeshurun. From the Hebrew term for "upright" *(yashar).* Often used to represent Israel as the upright people of a holy and righteous God (33:5, 26; Is. 44:2), here the term is used ironically.

grew fat, and kicked. Israel is described with the telling figure of a well-fed ox.

32:17 See theological note "Demons" on next page.

I will see what their end will be,
For they are a perverse generation,
children in whom is no faithfulness.
21 [b]They have made me jealous with
what is no god;
they have provoked me to anger
[c]with their idols.
So [d]I will make them jealous with
those who are no people;
I will provoke them to anger with
[e]a foolish nation.
22 For [f]a fire is kindled by my anger,
and it burns to [g]the depths of Sheol,
devours the earth and its increase,
and sets on fire the foundations of
the mountains.
23 "'And I will heap disasters upon them;
[h]I will spend my arrows on them;
24 they shall be wasted with hunger,
and devoured by plague
and poisonous pestilence;
I will send [i]the teeth of beasts
against them,
with the venom of [j]things that
crawl in the dust.
25 [k]Outdoors the sword shall bereave,
and indoors terror,
for young man and woman alike,
the nursing child with the man of
gray hairs.
26 [l]I would have said, "I will cut them to
pieces;
[m]I will wipe them from human
memory,"
27 had I not feared provocation by the
enemy,

21 [b]Ps. 78:58; See Num. 25:11 [c]1 Kin. 16:13, 26; Ps. 31:6; Jonah 2:8; Acts 14:15 [d]Cited Rom. 10:19; [Hos. 1:9, 10] [e][Ps. 74:18]
22 [f]Jer. 15:14; 17:4; Lam. 4:11 [g]Ps. 86:13
23 [h]Job 6:4; Ps. 7:12, 13; 38:2; Lam. 3:12, 13; Ezek. 5:16
24 [i]Lev. 26:22; Ezek. 5:17 [j]Jer. 8:17; Mic. 7:17
25 [k]Lam. 1:20; Ezek. 7:15
26 [l]Ezek. 20:23 [m]Job 18:17; Ps. 34:16; 109:15

Demons

"Demon," or "devil" (as some translations render the words), is from the Greek *daimon* and *daimonion*, the regular terms in the Gospels for the spiritual beings, corrupt and hostile to both God and man, whom Jesus exorcised from their victims during His earthly ministry. The demons are fallen angels, deathless creatures serving Satan (Jesus equated Beelzebub, their reputed ruler, with Satan, Matt. 12:24–29). Having joined Satan's rebellion, they were cast out of heaven to await final judgment (2 Pet. 2:4; Jude 6). Their minds are permanently opposed to God, goodness, truth, the kingdom of Christ, and the welfare of human beings. They have real but limited power and freedom of movement, though in Calvin's picturesque phrase they "drag their chains wherever they go," and can never hope to overcome God.

The level and intensity of demonic manifestations in people during Christ's ministry was unique, having no parallel in Old Testament times or since; it was doubtless part of Satan's desperate battle for his kingdom against Christ's attack on it (Matt. 12:29). Demons have both knowledge and strength (Mark 1:24; 9:17–27). They inflicted or exploited physical and mental maladies (Mark 5:1–15; 9:17, 18; Luke 11:14). They recognized and feared Christ, to whose authority they were subject (Mark 1:25; 3:11, 12; 9:25), though He said that it required effort in prayer to expel them (Mark 9:29).

Christ authorized and equipped the twelve and the seventy to cast out demons in His name (that is, by His power, Luke 9:1; 10:17), and the ministry of exorcism continues to be an occasional pastoral necessity. The sixteenth-century Lutheran church abolished exorcism, believing that Christ's victory over Satan had suppressed demonic invasion forever, but this was premature.

Satan's army of demons uses subtler strategies also—deception and discouragement in many forms. To oppose these is the task of spiritual warfare (Eph. 6:10–18). Though demons can cause trouble of different kinds for regenerate persons in whom the Holy Spirit dwells, they cannot deter God's final purpose of saving His elect, any more than they can escape their own eternal torment. As the devil is God's devil (as Luther put it), so the demons are God's demons, defeated enemies (Col. 2:15) whose limited power is only permitted for the advancement of God's glory as His people contend with them.

32:21 no people. Just as Israel provoked God by worshiping that which was "no God," so God would provoke them by means of "those who are no people" (people outside the sphere of the Mosaic covenant). This prophecy is partly fulfilled in the Old Testament as Israel is defeated by God's instruments of judgment, the Assyrians and Babylonians (Is. 10:5; Jer. 21:4–10). In the New Testament, Paul finds further fulfillment of this verse in the extension of the gospel to the Gentiles (Rom. 10:19; 11:11).

32:22 a fire is kindled . . . to the depths of Sheol. For the figure of God's anger as a consuming fire, see Ps. 21:9; Jer. 15:14; 17:4. The poetic figure here represents God's wrath as an all-devouring fire that burns to the deepest grave, consumes the surface of the earth, and reaches to the roots of the mountains.

32:27 lest their adversaries should misunderstand. Though Israel deserves utter destruction because of her disobedience (v. 26), the Lord preserves a remnant of the people, lest the Gentiles take credit for their victory over Israel and fail to see God's hand in history. Assyria and Babylon were later judged for their arrogant misunderstanding (Is. 10:12–19; 47:6–8).

lest their adversaries should
misunderstand,
lest they should say, [n]"Our hand is
triumphant,
it was not the LORD who did all
this."'

28 "For they are a nation void of counsel,
and there is [o]no understanding
in them.
29 [p]If they were wise, they would
understand this;
they would [q]discern their latter end!
30 How could [r]one have chased a
thousand,
and two have put ten thousand to
flight,
unless their Rock [s]had sold them,
and the LORD had given them up?
31 For [t]their rock is not as our Rock;
[u]our enemies are by themselves.
32 For their vine [v]comes from the vine
of Sodom
and from the fields of Gomorrah;
their grapes are grapes of [w]poison;
their clusters are bitter;
33 their wine is the poison of [x]serpents
and the cruel venom of asps.

34 "'Is not this laid up in store with me,
[y]sealed up in my treasuries?
35 [z]Vengeance is mine, and recompense,[1]
[a]for the time when their foot shall
slip;
for [b]the day of their calamity is at
hand,
and their doom comes swiftly.'
36 For [c]the LORD will vindicate[2] his people
[d]and have compassion on his
servants,
when he sees that their power is
gone
and there is none remaining,
[e]bond or free.

27 [n]Ps. 140:8; Isai. 10:13; [Num. 14:16]
28 [o]Isai. 27:11; Jer. 4:22
29 [p]ch. 5:29; Ps. 81:13; Luke 19:42 [q]Isai. 47:7; Lam. 1:9
30 [r]See Lev. 26:8 [s]See Judg. 2:14
31 [t]1 Sam. 2:2 [u][1 Sam. 4:8]
32 [v][Isai. 1:10; Jer. 23:14; Ezek. 16:46] [w]ch. 29:18
33 [x]Job 20:14, 16; Ps. 58:4 (Heb.)
34 [y][Job 14:17; Hos. 13:12; Rom. 2:5]
35 [z]Ps. 94:1; Isai. 1:24; 59:18; Nah. 1:2; Cited Rom. 12:19; Heb. 10:30 [a][Ps. 94:18] [b][2 Pet. 2:3]
36 [c]Ps. 135:14; Cited Heb. 10:30 [d]Judg. 2:18; Ps. 106:45; [Ps. 90:13] [e]1 Kin. 14:10; 21:21; 2 Kin. 9:8; 14:26

37 [f]Judg. 10:14; 1 Kin. 18:27; Jer. 2:28 [g][ver. 31]
39 [h]Isai. 41:4; 48:12 [i]1 Sam. 2:6; 2 Kin. 5:7 [j]Job 5:18; Hos. 6:1
40 [k]See Gen. 14:22
41 [l]Ps. 7:12; Isai. 27:1; 34:5; 66:16; Ezek. 21:9, 10
42 [m]Jer. 46:10 [n]Judg. 5:2
43 [o]Cited Rom. 15:10 [p]Rev. 6:10; 19:2; [2 Kin. 9:7; Ps. 79:10]

37 Then he will say, [f]'Where are their
gods,
[g]the rock in which they took refuge,
38 who ate the fat of their sacrifices
and drank the wine of their drink
offering?
Let them rise up and help you;
let them be your protection!

39 "'See now that [h]I, even I, am he,
and there is no god beside me;
[i]I kill and I make alive;
[j]I wound and I heal;
and there is none that can deliver
out of my hand.
40 For [k]I lift up my hand to heaven
and swear, As I live forever,
41 if I [l]sharpen my flashing sword[3]
and my hand takes hold on
judgment,
I will take vengeance on my
adversaries
and will repay those who hate me.
42 I will make my arrows drunk with
blood,
and [m]my sword shall devour flesh—
with the blood of the slain and the
captives,
from the [n]long-haired heads of the
enemy.'

43 [o]"Rejoice with him, O heavens;
bow down to him, all gods,[4]
for he [p]avenges the blood of his
children[5]
and takes vengeance on his
adversaries.
He repays those who hate him[6]
and cleanses[7] his people's land."[8]

1 Septuagint *and I will repay* 2 Septuagint *judge* 3 Hebrew *the lightning of my sword* 4 Dead Sea Scroll, Septuagint; Masoretic Text *Rejoice his people, O nations* 5 Dead Sea Scroll, Septuagint; Masoretic Text *servants* 6 Dead Sea Scroll, Septuagint; Masoretic Text lacks *He repays those who hate him* 7 Or *atones for* 8 Septuagint, Vulgate; Hebrew *his land his people*

32:30 one have chased a thousand. Numbers are of no consequence when the Lord intervenes. Israel with God's help would put to flight vast numbers of adversaries (Lev. 26:8), while a numerous but disobedient Israel would be defeated by a few, even fleeing when no one pursued (Lev. 26:17).

32:32 the vine of Sodom. False gods bring evil deeds and poisonous fruit. Sodom was a symbol of awful destruction (29:23 note).

32:35 Vengeance is mine, and recompense. The New Testament quotes this verse twice, using a slightly different wording (Rom. 12:19; Heb. 10:30).

32:36 vindicate . . . have compassion. Israel must see that they have no help apart from the one true God.

32:39 I, even I, am he. The Hebrew emphasizes by repetition. This whole stanza is a towering expression of the uniqueness of God in His being, power, providence, and justice. Because God is both infinitely just and all-powerful, we can be sure that evil will at last be destroyed (Rev. 19:1, 2).

32:43 Rejoice. The Septuagint (Greek Old Testament) and one of the Dead Sea Scrolls contain a longer version of this phrase (text note). This longer version is quoted in Heb. 1:6.

he avenges the blood of his children. This triumphal Song of Moses is echoed at the consummation of human history (Rev. 19:2).

44 Moses came and recited all the words
of this song in the hearing of the people, he
and [q]Joshua[1] the son of Nun. 45 And when
Moses had finished speaking all these
words to all Israel, 46 he said to them,
[r]"Take to heart all the words by which I am
warning you today, [s]that you may command them to your children, that they may
be careful to do all the words of this law.
47 For it is no empty word for you, [t]but your
very life, and by this word you shall live
long in the land that you are going over the
Jordan to possess."

Moses' Death Foretold

48 That very day the LORD spoke to Moses,
49 "Go up [u]this mountain of the Abarim,
Mount Nebo, which is in the land of Moab,
opposite Jericho, and view the land of
Canaan, which I am giving to the people of
Israel for a possession. 50 And die on the
mountain which you go up, and be gathered
to your people, as [v]Aaron your brother died
in Mount Hor and was gathered to his people, 51 [w]because you broke faith with me in
the midst of the people of Israel at the
waters of Meribah-kadesh, in the wilderness
of Zin, and because you did not treat me as
holy in the midst of the people of Israel.
52 For [x]you shall see the land before you, but
you shall not go there, into the land that I
am giving to the people of Israel."

Moses' Final Blessing on Israel

33 This is the blessing with which Moses [y]the man of God blessed the people of Israel before his death. 2 He said,

[z]"The LORD came from Sinai
and dawned from Seir upon us;[2]
he shone forth from Mount Paran;
he came [a]from the ten thousands of
holy ones,
with flaming fire[3] at his right hand.
3 Yes, [b]he loved his people,[4]
[c]all his holy ones were in his[5] hand;
[d]so they followed[6] in your steps,
receiving direction from you,
4 when [e]Moses commanded us a law,
as a possession for the assembly of
Jacob.
5 Thus the LORD [f]became king in
[g]Jeshurun,
when the heads of the people were
gathered,
all the tribes of Israel together.

6 [h]"Let Reuben live, and not die,
but let his men be few."

7 And this he said of Judah:

"Hear, O LORD, the voice of Judah,
and bring him in to his people.
With your hands contend[7] for him,
and be a help against his adversaries."

8 And [i]of Levi he said,

"Give to Levi[8] [j]your Thummim,
and your Urim to your godly one,
[k]whom you tested at Massah,

44 [q]Num. 13:8, 16
46 [r]ch. 11:18; See ch. 6:6 [s]See ch. 4:9
47 [t][Lev. 18:5]; See ch. 30:20
49 [u]See Num. 27:12
50 [v]Num. 20:24, 25, 28; 33:38
51 [w]Num. 20:11-13; 27:14
52 [x]ch. 3:27; 34:4
Chapter 33
1 [y]Josh. 14:6; 1 Chr. 23:14; 2 Chr. 30:16; Ezra 3:2
2 [z][Ex. 19:18, 20; Judg. 5:4, 5; Ps. 68:7, 8; Hab. 3:3] [a][Ps. 68:17; Dan. 7:10; Acts 7:53; Gal. 3:19; Heb. 2:2; Jude 14; Rev. 5:11]
3 [b]ch. 7:7, 8; 10:15; Hos. 11:1 [c][John 10:27-29; Rom. 8:35, 38, 39] [d][Luke 10:39; Acts 22:3]
4 [e]John 1:17; 7:19
5 [f]Num. 23:21; [Judg. 8:23; Isai. 33:22] [g]See ch. 32:15
6 [h][Gen. 49:3, 4]
8 [i][Gen. 49:5] [j]See Ex. 28:30 [k]See Ex. 17:7; Num. 20:13

1 Septuagint, Syriac, Vulgate; Hebrew *Hoshea* 2 Septuagint, Syriac, Vulgate; Hebrew *them* 3 The meaning of the Hebrew word is uncertain 4 Septuagint; Hebrew *peoples* 5 Hebrew *your* 6 The meaning of the Hebrew word is uncertain 7 Probable reading; Hebrew *With his hands he contended* 8 Dead Sea Scroll, Septuagint; Masoretic Text lacks *Give to Levi*

32:47 your very life. Moses emphasizes again that obedience to God's commands, from the heart, is a matter of life—eternal life—and death (30:19, 20).

32:49 Mount Nebo. Usually identified as the modern Jebel Neba, a mountain twelve miles east of the Jordan River's point of entry into the Dead Sea. Rising over four thousand feet above the Dead Sea, Mount Nebo provided Moses a vantage point from which to view the Promised Land.

33:1–29 In Gen. 49, Leah's children are listed first, followed by those of the handmaidens and Rachel. Here the order is different. Reuben, the firstborn, is mentioned first (v. 6), followed by the royal tribe of Judah (v. 7; cf. Gen. 49:10) and the priestly tribe of Levi (vv. 8–11). The tribes descending from Rachel's sons are next (vv. 12–17), followed by two remaining sons of Leah, Zebulun and Issachar (vv. 18, 19). Finally, the servants' children are listed (vv. 20–24). The tribe of Simeon is omitted, perhaps to retain the number twelve, although Jacob's blessing had predicted that Simeon would be scattered throughout Israel (Gen. 49:7).

33:1 the man of God. This expression is used customarily for prophets (1 Sam. 9:6; 1 Kin. 13:1; 17:18; 2 Kin. 4:7), but is applied to Moses only here and in the title of Ps. 90.

33:2 The LORD came from Sinai. The defining event of Moses' ministry, the revelation at Sinai, is recalled in terms describing the theophany on the mountain (Ex. 19:18; cf. Hab. 3:3).

holy ones. This is likely a reference to the angels of the heavenly host surrounding God's throne (cf. 1 Kin. 22:19; Dan. 7:9, 10). The New Testament also mentions the role of angels in giving the Mosaic law (Acts 7:53; Gal. 3:19; Heb. 2:2 and note).

33:5 became king in Jeshurun. A reference to the Lord as king over His people (cf. 1 Sam. 12:12; Ps. 10:16). Moses was never called a king. On "Jeshurun," see note 32:15.

33:6 but let. This reading could reflect the curse on Reuben in Gen. 49:3, 4.

33:7 Judah. This blessing hints at the warrior role of the Davidic kings, descendants of Judah, in leading Israel into battle. But the blessing on Judah is extremely brief in view of the promise of rulership to Judah in Gen. 49:8–12, and in view of Judah's large part in later history. Because a later writer might have wanted to give Judah more prominence, the brevity of this blessing points to a date for Deuteronomy during Moses' lifetime.

33:8 Levi. The blessing on Levi reflects their fidelity at the time of the golden calf, when Levi rallied to Moses' side and acted in judgment against their sinful brethren (Ex. 32:27–29).

Thummim . . . Urim. See note Ex. 28:30.

with whom you quarreled at the
waters of Meribah;
9 who said of his father and mother,
'I regard them not';
[l] he disowned his brothers
and ignored his children.
For [m] they observed your word
and kept your covenant.
10 [n] They shall teach Jacob your rules
and Israel your law;
[o] they shall put incense before you
and [p] whole burnt offerings on your
altar.
11 Bless, O LORD, his substance,
and [q] accept the work of
his hands;
crush the loins of his adversaries,
of those who hate him, that they
rise not again."

12 [r] Of Benjamin he said,
"The beloved of the LORD dwells in
safety.
The High God[1] surrounds him all
day long,
and dwells between his shoulders."

13 And [s] of Joseph he said,
[t] "Blessed by the LORD be his land,
with the choicest gifts of heaven
[u] above,[2]
and of the deep that crouches
beneath,
14 with the choicest fruits of the sun
and the rich yield of the months,
15 with the finest produce of the
ancient mountains
and the abundance of [v] the
everlasting hills,
16 with the best gifts of the earth and
[w] its fullness
and the favor of [x] him who dwells
in the bush.
May these rest on the head of
Joseph,
on the pate of him who is prince
among his brothers.
17 [y] A firstborn bull[3]—he has majesty,
and his horns are the horns of a
[z] wild ox;
with them [a] he shall gore the peoples,
all of them, to the ends of the
earth;
[b] they are the ten thousands of
Ephraim,
and they are the thousands of
Manasseh."

18 And of Zebulun he said,
[c] "Rejoice, Zebulun, in your going out,
and Issachar, in your tents.
19 They shall call peoples [d] to their
mountain;
there they offer [e] right sacrifices;
for they draw from the abundance of
the seas
and the hidden treasures of the
sand."

20 And [f] of Gad he said,
"Blessed be he who enlarges Gad!
Gad crouches [g] like a lion;
he tears off arm and scalp.
21 [h] He chose the best of the land for
himself,
for there a commander's portion
was reserved;
and [i] he came with the heads of the
people,
with Israel he executed the justice
of the LORD,
and his judgments for Israel."

22 And [j] of Dan he said,
[k] "Dan is a lion's cub
[l] that leaps from Bashan."

23 And [m] of Naphtali he said,
"O Naphtali, sated with favor,
and full of the blessing of the LORD,
[n] possess the lake[4] and the south."

9 [l] See Ex. 32:26-29 [m] Mal. 2:4-6
10 [n] ch. 17:9-11; Ezek. 44:23; See Lev. 10:11 [o] Ex. 30:7, 8; 1 Sam. 2:28 [p] Ps. 51:19; Ezek. 43:27
11 [q] Ezek. 20:40, 41; 43:27; [Amos 5:22]
12 [r] [Gen. 49:27]
13 [s] [Gen. 49:22] [t] Gen. 49:25 [u] ver. 28; Gen. 27:28
15 [v] Gen. 49:26; Hab. 3:6; [Ps. 90:2]
16 [w] Ps. 24:1 [x] Ex. 3:2-4; Acts 7:30, 35
17 [y] [1 Chr. 5:1] [z] See Num. 23:22 [a] 1 Kin. 22:11; Ps. 44:5; Dan. 8:4 [b] [Gen. 48:19; Num. 1:33, 35]
18 [c] [Gen. 49:13-15]
19 [d] Ex. 15:17; Isai. 2:3 [e] Ps. 4:5; 51:19
20 [f] [Gen. 49:19] [g] [1 Chr. 12:8]
21 [h] See Num. 32:1-5, 16-19 [i] Num. 32:31, 32; See Josh. 1:12-15; 1 Chr. 5:18-22
22 [j] [Gen. 49:16] [k] [Gen. 49:9] [l] [Josh. 19:47; Judg. 18:27]
23 [m] [Gen. 49:21] [n] See Josh. 19:32-39

1 Septuagint; Hebrew *dwells in safety by him. He* 2 Two Hebrew manuscripts and Targum; Hebrew *with the dew* 3 Dead Sea Scroll, Septuagint, Samaritan; Masoretic Text *His firstborn bull* 4 Or *west*

33:16 who dwells in the bush. Moses alludes to Ex. 3:4.

prince among his brothers. The Hebrew word translated "prince among" is sometimes used for those set apart by the Nazirite vow (cf. Num. 6:1–21 note).

33:17 ten thousands . . . thousands. During this period, Ephraim was smaller than Manasseh (Num. 26:34, 37), but Ephraim was to become more numerous and important (cf. Gen. 48:17–20). Because of the tribe's importance, the name "Ephraim" later was applied to the ten tribes making up the northern kingdom of Israel (2 Chr. 25:7; Hos. 5:3, 11–14).

33:22 Bashan. See note 3:1. This blessing may refer to the northern settlement of Dan, located near Bashan (Judg. 18:27–29). More likely, a comparison of Dan to the strength and ferocity of the lions inhabiting the forests of Bashan may be in view.

24 And [o]of Asher he said,

"Most blessed of sons be Asher;
let him be the favorite of his brothers,
and let him [p]dip his foot in oil.
25 Your bars shall be iron and bronze,
and as your days, so shall your strength be.

26 [q]"There is none like God, O [r]Jeshurun,
[s]who rides through the heavens to your help,
through the skies in his majesty.
27 The eternal God is your [t]dwelling place,[1]
and underneath are the everlasting arms.[2]
And he thrust out the enemy before you
and said, Destroy.
28 So Israel lived in safety,
[u]Jacob lived [v]alone,[3]
in a land of grain and wine,
whose heavens drop down dew.
29 Happy are you, O Israel! [w]Who is like you,
a people [x]saved by the LORD,
[y]the shield of your help,
and the sword of your triumph!
Your enemies shall come fawning to you,
and you shall tread upon [z]their backs."

The Death of Moses

34 Then Moses went up from the
plains of Moab [a]to Mount Nebo, to
the top of Pisgah, which is opposite
Jericho. And the LORD showed him all the
land, Gilead as far as Dan, 2 all Naphtali,
the land of Ephraim and Manasseh, all the
land of Judah [b]as far as the western sea,
3 [c]the Negeb, and [d]the Plain, that is, the
Valley of Jericho [e]the city of palm trees, as
far as [f]Zoar. 4 And the LORD said to him,
[g]"This is the land of which I swore to
Abraham, to Isaac, and to Jacob, 'I will give
it to your offspring.' [h]I have let you see it
with your eyes, but [i]you shall not go over
there." 5 So Moses the servant of the LORD
died there in the land of Moab, according
to the word of the LORD, 6 and he buried
him in the valley in the land of Moab opposite Beth-peor; but [j]no one knows the place
of his burial to this day. 7 [k]Moses was 120
years old when he died. [l]His eye was
undimmed, and his vigor unabated. 8 And
the people of Israel [m]wept for Moses in the
plains of Moab thirty days. Then the days
of weeping and mourning for Moses were
ended.

9 And Joshua the son of Nun was full of
[n]the spirit of wisdom, for [o]Moses had laid
his hands on him. So [p]the people of Israel
obeyed him and did as the LORD had commanded Moses. 10 And there has not
[q]arisen a prophet since in Israel like Moses,
[r]whom the LORD knew face to face, 11 none
like him for all [s]the signs and the wonders
that the LORD sent him to do in the land of
Egypt, to Pharaoh and to all his servants
and to all his land, 12 and for all the mighty
power and all the great deeds of terror that
Moses did in the sight of all Israel.

[1] Or *a dwelling place* [2] Revocalization of verse 27 yields *He subdues the ancient gods, and shatters the forces of old* [3] Hebrew *the abode of Jacob was alone*

24 [o][Gen. 49:20] [p][Job 29:6]
26 [q]See Ex. 15:11 [r]See ch. 32:15 [s]Ps. 68:33, 34; 104:3; Isai. 19:1; Hab. 3:8
27 [t]Ps. 90:1; 91:9
28 [u][Ps. 68:26; Isai. 48:1] [v]Num. 23:9
29 [w][2 Sam. 7:23] [x]Isai. 45:17 [y]Ps. 33:20; 115:9-11 [z]ch. 32:13; Amos 4:13; Mic. 1:3
Chapter 34
1 [a]See Num. 27:12
2 [b]See ch. 11:24
3 [c]ch. 1:7 [d]Gen. 13:12; 19:17, 25, 28, 29; 2 Sam. 18:23 [e]Judg. 1:16; 3:13; 2 Chr. 28:15 [f]Gen. 14:2; 19:22
4 [g]See Gen. 12:7; 50:24 [h]See ch. 1:37 [i]ch. 3:27; 32:52
6 [j][Jude 9]
7 [k]ch. 31:2 [l][Gen. 27:1; 48:10; Josh. 14:10, 11; 1 Sam. 3:2; 4:15
8 [m]Num. 20:29; [Gen. 50:3]
9 [n]Ex. 28:3; Isai. 11:2 [o]Num. 27:18, 23 [p]Josh. 1:17
10 [q][ch. 18:15, 18] [r]ch. 5:4; See Ex. 33:11
11 [s]See ch. 4:34

33:24 dip his foot in oil. Olive oil, valuable for food and also as fuel for lamps, is here symbolic of the tribe's material prosperity (Gen. 49:20; cf. Job 29:6).

33:26–29 This final stanza has blessed the hearts of God's people through the ages. He is the majestic God (v. 26), the eternal God (v. 27), the protecting and providing God (v. 28). The great blessing of Israel was that He was their God. Such a splendid hymn of praise is perhaps only matched by passages in the New Testament such as "the song of Moses, the servant of God, and the song of the Lamb" in Rev. 15:3, 4.

33:26 Jeshurun. See 32:15 and note.

34:1–12 This chapter is a supplement, probably added by the author of the Book of Joshua in order to connect his work with the books of Moses (Introduction: Author).

34:1 Gilead as far as Dan. The descriptions here and in v. 2 name the areas in terms of the tribal areas as designated in the Book of Joshua (Josh. 13–19).

34:7 undimmed . . . unabated. See note 31:2.

34:8 thirty days. The same period of mourning as for Aaron (Num. 20:29; cf. Gen. 50:3, 10; 2 Sam. 1:12). Ritual displays of mourning in the Old Testament included weeping, fasting, tearing of clothing, wearing sackcloth, and throwing dust on the head (Gen. 37:34, 35; Ps. 35:13; Lam. 2:10). Certain mourning practices were forbidden to Israel (14:1 note).

34:9 spirit of wisdom . . . laid his hands on him. Moses had previously put his hand on Joshua to symbolize the transfer of divinely ordained leadership (Num. 27:18). God empowers those whom He chooses and ordains for service.

34:10–12 See note 18:15–19; "Prophets" at 18:18.

34:10 since. Because no length of time is specified, these words need not imply that many generations had passed since Moses' death. Joshua took Moses' place, but he realized that Moses' miracles and access to God had been unique (18:15–19 note; Num. 12:6–8).

34:11 signs and the wonders. Jesus arose as a prophet like Moses, yet superior to him. He did miracles, signs, and wonders before the kings and rulers of the people, and in the sight of all Israel (Matt. 4:23–25; Acts 2:22; 3:22–26).

INTRODUCTION TO THE

Historical Books

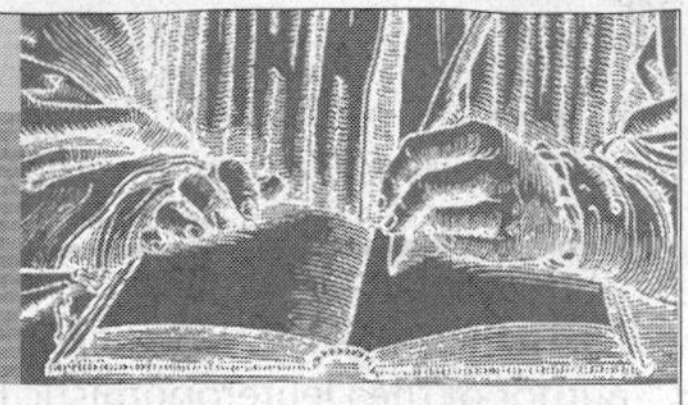

The collection of books in the Protestant Old Testament known as the "historical books" extends from Joshua through Esther. It relates the history of ancient Israel from the conquest of Canaan under Joshua, through the divided kingdoms of Israel and Judah, the fall of the two kingdoms to Assyria and Babylonia, and the restoration of Judah from exile in the sixth century B.C. Each of these twelve books narrates important events in God's dealings with His covenant people.

The books of the Old Testament were first recorded on scrolls and continued to be transmitted in this form through several centuries of use. It was not until the development of the "codex" (the book format first popularized by Christians in the production of the New Testament books) that the order in which the individual books of the Old Testament were to be arranged became an issue. The chronological arrangement of the twelve historical books familiar in Protestant Bibles derives from the order found in the great Septuagint (the Greek translation of the Old Testament) codices produced by Christians in the first four centuries A.D.

The historical books are arranged quite differently in Hebrew Bibles. The books of Joshua, Judges, Samuel, and Kings are grouped together as the "former prophets" and constitute the first half of the second division of the Jewish canon, the "Prophets." The second half of the division, the "latter prophets," consists of Isaiah, Jeremiah, Ezekiel, and the twelve "Minor Prophets." The books of Chronicles, Ezra, and Nehemiah are found in the third division of the Jewish canon, known as the "Writings." Finally, Ruth and Esther are contained in a special subset of five books within the "Writings" known as the "Festival Scrolls," since Jewish tradition required them to be read on certain religious feast days (Ruth at Pentecost, Esther at Purim; the other "scrolls" are Song of Solomon, Ecclesiastes, and Lamentations).

The arrangement of the historical books in the Jewish canon helps us to recognize two important blocks of material within the historical books. Each group of books was completed at a specific time in Israel's history and has particular theological interests and emphases. Scholars now recognize that the books of Joshua, Judges, Samuel, and Kings (the "former prophets") are a carefully constructed history of Israel completed during the Babylonian exile (the component books were actually begun much earlier; see their respective introductions). Similarly, the books of Chronicles, Ezra, and Nehemiah form a second major block of material completed during Judah's restoration from exile. Although there is disagreement among scholars regarding whether they are the work of a single author, these books do share certain theological interests related to their later historical setting.

The books of Joshua, Judges, Samuel, and Kings are referred to by scholars as the "Deuteronomistic History" since the Book of Deuteronomy serves as their historical and theological preamble. Building on Moses' narration of God's saving acts for His people from Abraham through the arrival of the Israelites at the border of the Promised Land, the Deuteronomistic History continues the story from the conquest of that land under Joshua to Jehoiachin, the last surviving Davidic king (2 Kin. 25:27–30). A brief concluding note that Jehoiachin was released from prison to live at the Babylonian court sets the date of the completion of the Deuteronomistic History in the uncertain years of the Babylonian exile. The collection is a serious attempt to write an accurate history of Israel and Judah using the conventions of ancient Near Eastern historiography.

The concerns of these books are not, however, of merely antiquarian interest. This history reiterates from Deuteronomy both such specific issues for the life of the covenant community as the "law of the king" (Deut. 17:14–20; cf. 1 Sam. 8:10–18) and such fundamental theological concepts as blessings for obedience and curses for disobedience (Deut. 28). Indeed, the dominant theological theme of the Deuteronomistic History may be summed up in the statement, "Sin brings punishment; repentance brings restoration" (see especially the repeated cycles of sin, oppression, repentance, and deliverance in the Book of Judges). The repeated sins of idolatry and injustice throughout the histories of Israel and Judah culminated in the ultimate punishment of exile from the Promised Land (Deut. 28:47-68; 2 Kin. 17:7-23; 23:26, 27). The final author of the Deuteronomistic History sees in Jehoiachin's release from prison a glimmer of hope that repentance will again bring restoration; but it remains for him only a hope.

The books of Chronicles, Ezra, and Nehemiah return to telling the story of God's people once that hope has become a reality. Ezra-Nehemiah (originally a single book) extends the history of Judah from the proclamation of Cyrus allowing the first of the Judean exiles to return to Palestine (c. 538 B.C.) through the final resettlement of Jerusalem (c. 400 B.C.). It recounts the rebuilding of the temple under Zerubbabel, the repair of Jerusalem's walls under Nehemiah, and the reconstitution of religious life under Ezra. Chronicles retells the story of the chosen people from Adam (in its genealogies) to Cyrus's proclamation, focusing on the history of Judah under the rule of David and his descendants. Approximately half of Chronicles is taken word for word from the books of Samuel and Kings.

These books are deeply concerned with how God's people should respond to His gracious act of restoring Judah. Since the Babylonian exile had been a punishment for failure to maintain full covenant loyalty to the Lord, the writers of these books were chiefly concerned with the lessons to be drawn from Israel's older and recent history for maintaining the religious purity of the people. Ezra-Nehemiah looks upon God's actions in making a new beginning for His people and emphasizes the need of the newly constituted community to maintain separation from other peoples so as not to fall back into the sin of idolatry. The theological emphases in Chronicles in this regard are twofold. First, Chronicles stresses the importance of the temple, its worship, and its officials in directing the religious life of God's people. Second, it focuses attention on the central role of the Davidic house in the proper administration of the temple and in the religious life of the people.

As the years passed, it became clear that the hopes of the restored community for the resumption of rule by a descendant of David as king over Judah would not be realized. The people continued to read in Chronicles about the glorious history of David's rule and how David and his descendants (most notably Solomon) preserved true worship in Jerusalem. As they reflected on this history, their hopes were directed toward the future Son of David, the Messiah, who would be the perfect leader of the community's religious life. The history of God's saving acts for His people was not to end with Esther's role of rescuing them from destruction by the Persians, or even Ezra and Nehemiah's work of reestablishing them in the Promised Land.

THE BOOK OF

Joshua

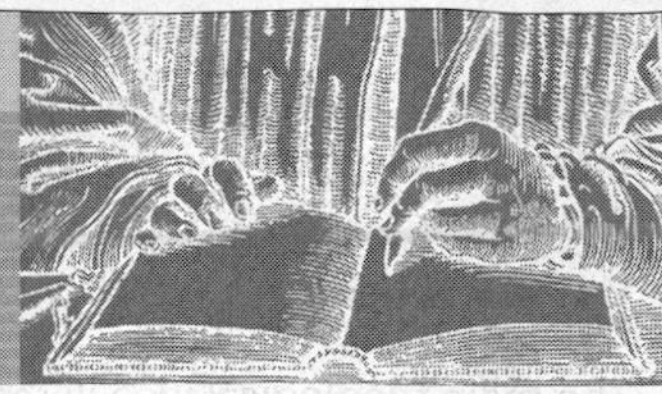

AUTHOR

The author of the Book of Joshua is unknown, and our knowledge of the time it was written depends on the interpretation of certain clues within the book. Theories range from the view that the book was largely composed by Joshua himself (the tradition of the Talmud) to the hypothesis that it was written by someone long after the Jews returned from the exile in Babylon. From the standpoint of the final form of the book, it is probable that a man or group committed to the theological framework of the Book of Deuteronomy gave Joshua its canonical form. See "Date and Occasion" below and "Introduction to the Historical Books."

DATE AND OCCASION

The precise time the Book of Joshua was composed is not clear. Comments within the book itself, such as notices that something is true "to this day," suggest that many of its sources came from a time between the death of Joshua (24:29–31) and the time of Samuel (c. 1050 B.C.). Because Sidon is still reckoned as Phoenicia's leading city (11:8; 19:28), some would date the book no later than 1200 B.C.; after that time Tyre gained the ascendancy. Jerusalem is as yet unconquered (15:63), a feat accomplished by David (2 Sam. 5:6–10), and Gezer is not as yet under Solomon's rule (16:10; 1 Kin. 9:16).

Many scholars today date the final form of the book from its relationship to the Pentateuch and the rest of the Former Prophets ("Characteristics and Themes" below). The introduction of Joshua overlaps with the conclusion of Deuteronomy. Josh. 1:1 matches Deut. 34:1–12, especially v. 5, where Moses is called "the servant of the LORD" for the first time. The conclusion of Joshua (24:29–31) is repeated as part of the introduction to Judges (Judg. 2:6–9).

On balance it appears that the book was written after Joshua's death but before Saul (c. 1050 B.C.) and his successors. The author wrote doubtless to recount the astounding fulfillment of the Lord's promises under Joshua. At the same time, recognizing the need to consolidate the conquest of the land, the author wrote in hope of the rise of another faithful servant who, like Joshua, could lead the Israelites to victory over every enemy still in the land.

INTERPRETIVE DIFFICULTIES

Any attempt to relate the accounts of the Book of Joshua to data gained from archaeological investigations must reckon with the nature of both the biblical record and the archaeological evidence. All historical writing is selective in what it records and interpretive in the manner in which it presents its material. Biblical history has a particular interest in the purposes of God. Archaeological evidence is often ambiguous and illustrative rather than specific in the information it yields.

The task of correlating archaeological data and the biblical record is well illustrated by the debate over the Book of Joshua. Among those who accept the biblical representation of a violent conquest of the land, there are basically two schools of thought. One believes there is persuasive archaeological evidence (such as the destruction of Canaanite cities and occupation patterns) for a violent and successful Israelite invasion of Canaan around 1250 B.C. The other argues that archaeological evidence (such as that at Jericho) together with texts like 1 Kin. 6:1, Judg. 11:26, and Ex. 12:40, indicates that the conquest should be dated earlier, around 1400 B.C. The difficulties arise from uncertainties about the identification of modern sites with biblical locations, disputes over the dating of materials, biblical chronology, and how certain data should be interpreted.

CHARACTERISTICS AND THEMES

The main theological idea in the Book of Joshua is the promise of God to give the land of Canaan to the descendants of Abraham, the people of Israel (Gen. 12:7). This one aspect of the promise to Abraham, Isaac, and Jacob (Gen. 12:1–3) has dominated the contents of Genesis through Deuteronomy. Joshua testifies to God's faithfulness to this promise by recounting the successful entry of the Israelites into the land (2:1–5:12), the dispossession of its inhabitants (5:13–12:24; cf. Gen. 15:13–16 and notes), and the allocation of the territory to the twelve tribes (chs. 13–21). The closing sentence of the main body of the book (21:45) summarizes the theme of the book: "Not one word of all the good promises that the LORD had made to the house of Israel had failed; all came to pass" (21:45; see 23:14). This bold assertion of God's complete faithfulness is accompanied by the recognition that much of what was promised was still unrealized (e.g., 13:1; 23:5; Gen. 13:5 and note), and that the enjoyment of the fulfilled promise was always conditional upon the people's obedience (e.g., 23:12, 13, 15, 16). The full extent of the Promised Land would not be occupied until the reigns of David and Solomon.

Joshua should be understood in relation to the Pentateuch, or Genesis through Deuteronomy in the Hebrew Bible, also called "the Law" (1:7, 8 and notes). The content of these books is summarized in 24:2–10. These verses recount the history of the descendants of Abraham, Isaac, and Jacob from the time the promise was first given to Abraham (Gen. 12:1–3) to the death of Moses (Deut. 34), who had led the Israelites from Egypt to the land promised to them by God. But the Pentateuch ends with the people still outside the Promised Land. Furthermore, the generation of Israelites who came out of Egypt had fallen under God's judgment because of their rebellion in the wilderness (Num. 13; 14; Deut. 1:26–36), and even the death of Moses is understood in these terms (Deut. 1:37; 32:48–52). In this context Joshua speaks of the faithfulness of the Lord to His promises made to the patriarchs, despite the rebellion of the earlier generation of Israelites and the judgment that had fallen on them.

Joshua should also be understood in relation to the history of Israel in the land, recorded in Joshua and the following books, through 2 Kings. The story is a tragic one as far as Israel is concerned. The nation failed to follow the Lord wholeheartedly, and was all but destroyed by God's judgment in the form of the successive assaults by the Assyrians in the eighth century B.C. (2 Kin. 17) and the Babylonians in the sixth century (2 Kin. 25). The Book of Joshua confirms from the outset that the demise of Israel cannot be blamed on the failure of the power or the faithfulness of God.

The New Testament provides a third perspective from which the Book of Joshua should be understood. The promise of God, to which the Book of Joshua points, is the gospel preached to Abraham "beforehand" (Gal. 3:8; Gen. 12:1–3). This promise was kept by God through the time of Joshua and was ultimately fulfilled in Jesus Christ (Acts 13:32, 33; Heb. 4:8–11). The faithfulness of God proclaimed in the Book of Joshua is His faithfulness to the gospel of Christ. Israel's entrance into and occupation of the land prefigures the Christian's life in Christ (Gen. 13:15 and note).

OUTLINE OF JOSHUA

I. Prologue: The Promise and Its Consequences (ch. 1)

II. Entering the Land (2:1–5:12)

- A. *The Promise and a Canaanite Harlot (ch. 2)*
- B. *The Promise and the Crossing of the Jordan (chs. 3; 4)*
- C. *The Promise Remembered in the Land (5:1–12)*

III. Conquering the Land (5:13–12:24)

- A. *The Commander of the Lord's Army (5:13–15)*
- B. *Perishing and Surviving Under the Promise: Jericho and Rahab (ch. 6)*
- C. *Presuming on the Promise: Achan (ch. 7)*
- D. *Promised Victory: Ai (8:1–29)*
- E. *The People of the Promise (8:30–35)*
- F. *Canaanite Fear and Israelite Failure: Gibeon's Treaty and Curse (ch. 9)*
- G. *The Conquest of the South (ch. 10)*

OUTLINE OF JOSHUA (Cont.)

- H. *The Conquest of the North (ch. 11)*
- I. *List of Defeated Kings and Conquered Territory (ch. 12)*

IV. Receiving the Promised Land (13:1–21:45)

- A. *The Command to Allocate the Land (13:1–7)*
- B. *East of the Jordan: The Land Given to Reuben, Gad, and Half-tribe of Manasseh (13:8–33)*
- C. *West of the Jordan (14:1–19:51)*
  1. Introduction (14:1–5)
  2. Caleb: Example of Faithful Obedience (14:6–15)
  3. Judah (ch. 15)
  4. Ephraim and Manasseh (16:1–17:18)
  5. The Other Tribes and Joshua (18:1–19:51)
- D. *Justice in the Promised Land: Cities of Refuge (20:1–9)*
- E. *Cities for the Levites (21:1–42)*
  1. The Levites' Request (21:1–3)
  2. The Allocation of Cities (21:4–8)
  3. Lists of Cities (21:9–40)
     - a. *Cities for the Kohathites (21:9–26)*
     - b. *Cities for the Gershonites (21:27–33)*
     - c. *Cities for the Merarites (21:34–40)*
  4. Total of Cities for the Levities (21:41, 42)
- F. *Concluding summary (21:43–45)*

V. Epilogue: (22:1–24:33)

- A. *Unity of Israel: Its Basis and Its Vulnerability (ch. 22)*
- B. *The Demands of God's Faithfulness (ch. 23)*
- C. *Decision: Israel's Choice at Shechem (24:1–28)*
- D. *The End of an Era: The Deaths of Joshua and Eleazar (24:29–33)*

God Commissions Joshua

1 After the death of Moses the [a]servant of
the LORD, the LORD said to Joshua the
son of Nun, Moses' [b]assistant, 2 "Moses my
servant is dead. Now therefore arise, go over
this Jordan, you and all this people, into the
land that I am giving to them, to the people
of Israel. 3 [c]Every place that the sole of your
foot will tread upon I have given to you, just
as I promised to Moses. 4 [d]From the wilderness and this Lebanon as far as the great
river, the river Euphrates, all the land of the
Hittites to the Great Sea toward the going
down of the sun shall be your territory. 5 [e]No
man shall be able to stand before you all the
days of your life. Just [f]as I was with Moses,
so [g]I will be with you. [h]I will not leave you
or forsake you. 6 [i]Be strong and courageous,
for you shall cause this people to inherit the

Chapter 1
1 [a]ver. 13, 15; Ex. 14:31; Num. 12:7; Deut. 34:5 [b]Deut. 1:38; [Ex. 24:13]
3 [c]Deut. 11:24; [ch. 14:9]
4 [d]Gen. 15:18; Ex. 23:31; See Num. 34:3-12

5 [e]Deut. 7:24 [f]ver. 17; Ex. 3:12 [g]ver. 9, 17; ch. 3:7; 6:27; Deut. 31:8, 23 [h]Gen. 28:15; Deut. 31:6, 8; 1 Chr. 28:20; Cited Heb. 13:5 6 [i]ver. 7, 9, 18; Deut. 31:6, 7

1:1–18 The opening words indicate both the historical starting point of the book and the theological crisis with which it deals. Moses' death concludes the judgment of God on the generation that came out of Egypt (5:4–6; Deut. 1:35; 32:51). What is to be said when Moses had died and the people of Israel had fallen under God's judgment? Ch. 1 introduces the answer to this question, namely, that even "after the death of Moses" the Lord was faithful to His promises. See Introduction: Characteristics and Themes. This reality and its consequences are spelled out by God to Joshua (vv. 1–9), and then by Joshua to the people in general (vv. 10, 11) and the two-and-a-half tribes in particular (vv. 12–15). Finally, the people's response is recorded (vv. 16–18).

1:1 the servant of the LORD. This title of honor suggests the special role of Moses in God's purposes (vv. 1, 2, 7, 13, 15; cf. Is. 42:1). It was also given to Abraham (Gen. 26:24) and will be applied to Joshua on his death (24:29).

Joshua. Joshua's name was changed from "Hoshea" ("salvation") to "Joshua" ("the Lord is salvation") by Moses (Num. 13:16). Joshua appears as Moses' assistant as early as Ex. 17. He was one of the men sent from Kadesh-barnea to explore the land (Num. 13:8), and he joined Caleb in calling on the Israelites to trust the Lord and not to rebel against Him (Num. 14:6–9). Like Caleb (Deut. 1:36), he escaped the judgment that fell on that generation because of its refusal to obey God at Kadesh-barnea. Joshua is presented as the successor to Moses, as was anticipated before Moses' death (Num. 27:12–23; Deut. 3:28; 31:1–8). Joshua's role, however, continues to be subordinate to that of Moses. This is expressed in his submission to the "Book of the Law" (1:8 note) and his obedience to the commands of Moses, something repeatedly emphasized throughout the book (e.g., 1:7; 8:31; 11:12, 15; 14:2, 5; 20:2). In the transition from Moses to Joshua there is continuity because the purpose of God for Israel persists, but there is discontinuity too, because the era of Moses was unique and is the standard of comparison for future generations. There is a similar continuity and discontinuity in the New Testament transition from the Gospels to the Book of Acts.

1:2 go over this Jordan. The people are east of the river (Deut. 1:1), which has a deep valley and forms a formidable boundary between them and the land God has promised to the west. See also 3:15.

into the land. The land is God's gift to the Israelites, in faithfulness to His promise to Abraham (see vv. 3, 6). This is the dominant theme of the book: note the elaboration of this idea in 24:13, echoing Deut. 6:10, 11. The land is an expression of what the New Testament calls "grace" (Eph. 2:8). See note 21:43.

1:3 your foot. "Your" and "you" are plural, indicating the promise is addressed to all Israel.

1:4 The extent of the land promised here exceeds what was actually received in the days of Joshua and corresponds to the dimensions of David's and Solomon's kingdom (1 Kin. 4:21). Despite the emphasis on fulfillment in Joshua (21:45 note), the book sees the promise as still pointing to the future (13:1 note; 23:5, 12–13).

1:5–9 These promises are addressed to Joshua individually, as the successor to Moses. The section begins and ends with God's promise to be with him. Second and second-to-last in order is the exhortation to be strong and courageous. In the middle is the commandment to keep the law together with the promise of success if he does. In ch. 23 Joshua applies these ideas to the whole people of Israel in the light of the faithfulness of God that the whole book proclaims.

1:5 I will be with you. See Gen. 26:3 and notes; Ex. 3:12. The divine presence is not a general concept here, or a mystical experience, but the presence of God to fulfill His promises. Compare the promise of Jesus in Matt. 28:20.

1:6 Be strong and courageous. Confidence based on the promises of God is the essence of biblical faith (vv. 9, 18; 8:1; 10:8, 25; 11:6).

inherit. The idea that the land was an inheritance is important in this book. An inheritance is something handed down from the past, as the

land that I swore to their fathers to give
them. 7 Only be strong and [j]very courageous, being careful to do according to all
the law [k]that Moses my servant commanded you. [l]Do not turn from it to the right
hand or to the left, that you may have good
success[1] wherever you go. 8 This Book of the
Law shall not depart from your mouth, but
[m]you shall meditate on it day and night, so
that you may be careful to do according to
all that is written in it. For then you will
make your way prosperous, and then you
will have good success. 9 Have I not commanded you? [n]Be strong and courageous.
[o]Do not be frightened, and do not be dismayed, for the LORD your God is with you
wherever you go."

Joshua Assumes Command

10 And Joshua commanded the [p]officers
of the people, 11 "Pass through the midst of
the camp and command the people,
'Prepare your provisions, for [q]within three
days [r]you are to pass over this Jordan to go
in to take possession of the land that the
LORD your God is giving you to possess.'"
12 And to the Reubenites, the Gadites,
and the half-tribe of Manasseh Joshua said,
13 "Remember the word that [s]Moses the servant of the LORD commanded you, saying,
'The LORD your God is providing you a
place of rest and will give you this land.'
14 Your wives, your little ones, and your
livestock shall remain in the land that
Moses gave you beyond the Jordan, but all
the men of valor among you shall pass over
armed before your brothers and shall help
them, 15 [t]until the LORD gives rest to your
brothers as he has to you, and they also
take possession of the land that the LORD
your God is giving them. [u]Then you shall
return to the land of your possession and
shall possess it, the land that Moses the
servant of the LORD gave you beyond the
Jordan toward the sunrise."
16 And they answered Joshua, "All that
you have commanded us we will do, and
wherever you send us we will go. 17 Just as
we obeyed Moses in all things, so we will
obey you. Only may the LORD your God [v]be
with you, as he was with Moses! 18 Whoever
rebels against your commandment and dis-
obeys your words, whatever you command
him, shall be put to death. [w]Only be strong
and courageous."

Rahab Hides the Spies

2 And Joshua the son of Nun [x]sent[2] two
men secretly from Shittim as spies,
saying, "Go, view the land, especially
Jericho." And they went and came into the

7 [j]ch. 23:6 [k]ch. 11:15 [l]Deut. 5:32; 28:14
8 [m]Ps. 1:2; 119:15
9 [n]ver. 6, 7, 18 [o]Deut. 1:29; 7:21; 20:3; 31:6, 8
10 [p]Deut. 16:18
11 [q]ch. 3:2 [r]Deut. 9:1; 11:31
13 [s]See Num. 32:20-28
15 [t]Deut. 3:20 [u]ch. 22:4
17 [v]ver. 5
18 [w]ver. 6, 7, 9
Chapter 2
1 [x]Num. 25:1

1 Or *may act wisely* 2 Or *had sent*

land was given in the promise made to Abraham, Isaac, and Jacob. Second, what is inherited brings responsibilities. See 1 Pet. 1:4.

1:7 to do. The essential relationship between faith and obedience is illustrated here. Faith is confidence based on God's promise (v. 6), and such faith issues in obedience (v. 7).

the law. The Hebrew word is broader in meaning than the English word "law." It may include both promises and commands, as well as records of God's activity. See "The Word of God: Scripture as Revelation" at Ex. 32:16.

have good success. Success is understood in terms of what God has promised. Such success cannot be understood simply as a reward earned by obedience, because the promise was issued before any obedience. It would be more accurate to understand the promised success as something that can be forfeited by disobedience.

1:8 Book of the Law. See 8:34–35; 23:6; 24:26; Deut. 31:24–26.

meditate. Cf. Ps. 1:2. From meditation on the Book of the Law flow all the consequences of the promise already seen in vv. 6, 7: obedience and success (v. 8), faith and the presence of God (v. 9). See "Understanding the Word of God" at Ps. 119:34.

1:11 three days. The narrative of Joshua is not arranged in a strictly chronological order (Introduction: Characteristics and Themes). It is possible that the command of v. 11 was spoken after 3:1, but is recorded here to indicate Joshua's role as the people's leader by divine appointment. It is also possible that "three days" is not a precise expression and means "a few days."

to possess. The promise that God has given (v. 2) demands the human act of taking possession, an act of obedient faith (vv. 6; 18:3; and notes).

1:12–15 Num. 32 shows how the Reubenites, Gadites, and half-tribe of Manasseh (13:8 note) had already received their portion of land east of the Jordan. It was understood that they would also join in Israel's conquest of the western portion of the Promised Land (Num. 32:16–32; Deut. 3:18–20). All Israel must participate in taking possession of the land as a whole. There is a dramatic sequel in ch. 22. See notes 12:1; 13:8–33.

1:13 rest. See also v. 15. The goal of God's gift of the land is often referred to as "rest" (11:23; 21:44; 22:4; 23:1), a condition or state that links the land with God's purposes in creation (Gen. 2:2, 3). For the New Testament extension of the idea see Heb. 3:7–4:11.

1:16–18 The people's obedient response to Joshua, and therefore to God, will be echoed and elaborated at the end of the book (24:16–24). The essential connection between faith and obedience is implicit here: the obedience of the people is unambiguous evidence that they believe the promise. The necessary qualities for Joshua's leadership are that God be with him (v. 5 note) and that he be a man of faith (v. 6 note).

2:1–5:12 The first major section of the book recounts the movement of the Israelites from Shittim (2:1), across the Jordan River (chs. 3; 4; cf. 1:2), and into the land of Canaan. This movement marks the end of one era (5:9) and the beginning of the new life in the Land of Promise (5:12). It represents the first main testimony of the book to the faithfulness of God to His promises.

2:1–24 Before the expected sequel to ch. 1 (namely, 3:1) there is the surprising story of the spies who return to Joshua proclaiming the promise of God (v. 24; cf. 1:2–5). Although the Book of Joshua describes in graphic detail the destruction of the Canaanites (chs. 6–12), it gives a prominent place to Rahab, a Canaanite harlot, (Lev. 18:24 in context). It is from

house of [y]a prostitute whose name was
[z]Rahab and lodged there. **2** And it was told
to the king of Jericho, "Behold, men of
Israel have come here tonight to search out
the land." **3** Then the king of Jericho sent to
Rahab, saying, "Bring out the men who
have come to you, who entered your
house, for they have come to search out all
the land." **4** But the woman had taken the
two men and hidden them. And she said,
"True, the men came to me, but I did not
know where they were from. **5** And when
the gate was about to be closed at dark, the
men went out. I do not know where the
men went. Pursue them quickly, for you
will overtake them." **6** But she had brought
them up to the roof and hid them with the
stalks of flax that she had laid in order on
the roof. **7** So the men pursued after them
on the way to the Jordan [a]as far as the
fords. And the gate was shut as soon as the
pursuers had gone out.
8 Before the men[1] lay down, she came
up to them on the roof **9** and said to the
men, "I know that the LORD has given you
the land, [b]and that the fear of you has fall-
en upon us, and that all the inhabitants of
the land [c]melt away before you. **10** For we
have heard how the LORD [d]dried up the
water of the Red Sea before you when you
came out of Egypt, and [e]what you did to
the two kings of the Amorites who were
beyond the Jordan, to [f]Sihon and Og,
whom you devoted to destruction.[2] **11** And
[g]as soon as we heard it, [h]our hearts melted, and there was no spirit left in any man
because of you, for [i]the LORD your God,
he is God in the heavens above and on the
earth beneath. **12** Now then, please swear
to me by the LORD that, as I have dealt
kindly with you, you also will deal kindly
with my father's house, and [j]give me a sure
sign **13** that you will save alive my father and
mother, my brothers and sisters, and all
who belong to them, and deliver our lives
from death." **14** And the men said to her,
"Our life for yours even to death! If you do
not tell this business of ours, then when
the LORD gives us the land [k]we will deal
kindly and faithfully with you."
15 Then she [l]let them down by a rope
through the window, for her house was
built into the city wall, so that she lived in
the wall. **16** And she said[3] to them, "Go into

1 [y]Heb. 11:31; James 2:25 [z]Matt. 1:5
7 [a]Judg. 3:28; 7:24
9 [b]Ex. 15:16; 23:27 [c]ver. 11, 24; Ex. 15:15
10 [d]ch. 4:23; Ex. 14:21 [e]See Num. 21:23-26, 33-35 [f]Ps. 135:11; 136:19, 20
11 [g]Ex. 15:14, 15 [h]ver. 9; ch. 5:1; 7:5; [2 Sam. 17:10; Ps. 22:14; Isai. 13:7; Ezek. 21:7] [i]Deut. 4:39
12 [j]ver. 18
14 [k]Judg. 1:24, 25
15 [l]1 Sam. 19:12; Acts 9:25; 2 Cor. 11:33

1 Hebrew *they* 2 That is, set apart (devoted) as an offering to the Lord (for destruction) 3 Or *had said*

her lips that the spies hear testimony to the promise and the power of God (vv. 9–11), in the light of which she seeks and finds kindness (v. 12). She will be spared from the coming judgment (6:22, 23) and find a place among the people of God (6:25). The chapter testifies to the grace of God in bringing such a woman to seek and find His mercy. The story of Rahab supplies an important perspective on the judgments of God that will occupy much of this book.

2:1 Shittim. The site is a reminder of a time when Israel was guilty of harlotry (both physical and spiritual; Num. 25:1–3), a time not forgotten in this book (22:17).

spies. The role of these spies is as unusual as the conquest that is to follow. Both their role and the conquest are shaped by the promise of God. See their report in v. 24. Cf. Num. 13:17–20.

prostitute . . . Rahab. The narrative does not say why they chose Rahab's house. She is remembered in the New Testament as an ancestor of Christ (Matt. 1:5), and as an example of faith (Heb. 11:31) and good works (James 2:25).

2:2 king of Jericho. Canaan was made up of city-states, each with its own king.

2:3 The skillfully narrated story creates a moment of tension before telling the reader that the men have been hidden (v. 4).

2:4 I did not know. She did know (v. 9). The writer of Joshua does not justify or condemn Rahab for lying, but James approves her action (James 2:25). Deception is a necessary tactic in war. The main point is why Rahab protects the foreign spies (vv. 9–11).

2:6 she had brought them. Note the narrative style in which information is given out of chronological sequence. See Introduction: Characteristics and Themes.

2:7 the gate was shut. The suspense of the narrative increases, since the spies now seem to be trapped.

2:9 I know. Rahab knows what God wants Israel to know (3:10), that the promise of God is true.

fear. This is the inevitable response to finding oneself on the wrong side of what God has promised to do. Contrast 1:6. In holy war panic is incited among God's enemies by the approach of His army (5:1; 9:24; 10:2; Ex. 15:14–16; Deut. 2:25).

2:10 we have heard. The cause of Rahab's knowledge, and the Canaanites' terror, was the news of what God had already done for Israel in faithfulness to His promises. See note 9:3.

Amorites. The term is flexible, sometimes applying to all the peoples of Canaan (e.g., 24:15), sometimes more specifically to people in the hill country (e.g., 5:1), especially as distinct from the Jebusites who also occupied the hill country (e.g., 3:10).

Sihon and Og. See note 12:2–5.

destruction. See notes 6:17, 18.

2:11 the LORD your God, he is God in the heavens above and on the earth beneath. The acknowledgment of God required in Israel (Deut. 4:39) is made by Rahab.

2:12 deal kindly. The Hebrew word often refers to God's mercy to Israel in accordance with His promises.

a sure sign. Probably the oath (v. 14).

2:13 deliver our lives from death. The mercy sought presupposes the certainty of the promise of God. It is no less than deliverance from the coming wrath (cf. 1 Thess. 1:10).

2:14 when the LORD gives us the land. The certainty of the promise is again assumed.

2:15 she let them down . . . the city wall. The suspense created in vv. 2, 3, 7 is resolved.

the hills, or the pursuers will encounter
you, and hide there three days until the
pursuers have returned. Then afterward you
may go your way." 17 The men said to her,
"We will be guiltless with respect to this
oath of yours that you have made us swear.
18 [m]Behold, when we come into the land,
you shall tie this scarlet cord in the window
through which you let us down, [n]and you
shall gather into your house your father and
mother, your brothers, and all your father's
household. 19 Then if anyone goes out of the
doors of your house into the street, [o]his
blood shall be on his own head, and we
shall be guiltless. But if a hand is laid on
anyone who is with you in the house, his
blood shall be on our head. 20 But if you [p]tell
this business of ours, then we shall be guiltless with respect to your oath that you have
made us swear." 21 And she said, "According to your words, so be it." Then she sent
them away, and they departed. And she tied
the scarlet cord in the window.
22 They departed and went into the hills
and remained there three days until the
pursuers returned, and the pursuers
searched all along the way and found nothing. 23 Then the two men returned. They
came down from the hills and [q]passed over
and came to Joshua the son of Nun, and
they told him all that had happened to
them. 24 And they said to Joshua, "Truly
[r]the LORD has given all the land into our
hands. And also, all the inhabitants of the
land [s]melt away because of us."

Israel Crosses the Jordan

3 Then Joshua rose early in the morning
and they set out [t]from Shittim. And
they came to the Jordan, he and all the
people of Israel, and lodged there before
they passed over. 2 [u]At the end of three days
the officers went through the camp 3 and
commanded the people, "As soon as you
see the ark of the covenant of the LORD
your God being carried by [v]the Levitical
priests, then you shall set out from your
place and follow it. 4 [w]Yet there shall be a
distance between you and it, about 2,000
cubits[1] in length. Do not come near it, in
order that you may know the way you shall
go, for you have not passed this way
before." 5 Then Joshua said to the people,
[x]"Consecrate yourselves, for tomorrow the
LORD will do wonders among you." 6 And
Joshua said to the priests, [y]"Take up the
ark of the covenant and pass on before the
people." So they took up the ark of the
covenant and went before the people.
7 The LORD said to Joshua, "Today I will
begin to [z]exalt you in the sight of all Israel,
that they may know that, [a]as I was with
Moses, so I will be with you. 8 And as for
you, command [b]the priests who bear the
ark of the covenant, 'When you come to
the brink of the waters of the Jordan, [c]you
shall stand still in the Jordan.'" 9 And
Joshua said to the people of Israel, "Come
here and listen to the words of the LORD
your God." 10 And Joshua said, "Here is

1 A *cubit* was about 18 inches or 45 centimeters

18 [m]ver. 12 [n]ver. 12; ch. 6:23
19 [o][Matt. 27:25]
20 [p]ver. 14
23 [q]ver. 7
24 [r]ch. 21:44; Ex. 23:31 [s]ver. 9

Chapter 3
1 [t]ch. 2:1
2 [u]ch. 1:10, 11
3 [v]ver. 8; Deut. 31:9, 25
4 [w][Ex. 19:12]
5 [x]ch. 7:13; Ex. 19:10, 14, 15; Lev. 20:7; Num. 11:18; 1 Sam. 16:5; Joel 2:16
6 [y]Num. 4:15
7 [z]ch. 4:14; 1 Chr. 29:25; 2 Chr. 1:1 [a]ch. 1:5
8 [b]ver. 3 [c]ver. 17

2:18 scarlet cord. The cord is not mentioned in ch. 6. It is unlikely that symbolic significance should be seen in the color, although it can be associated with the blood of the Passover lamb and the blood of Christ.

2:24 the LORD has given. These spies return with the news that the promise of God is indeed certain (1:2), news they have learned from Rahab.

3:1–4:24 The crossing of the Jordan River, the river marking the boundary of the Promised Land, was an occasion of wonders comparable to the crossing of the Red Sea (4:23; cf. 3:7; 4:14). The great significance of these wonders is indicated in 4:24. They were to remain a testimony for all peoples and for all time that the hand of the Lord is powerful. The prominence of the ark of the covenant (3:3 note) relates the power of God to the promises of God that are at the heart of the covenant. Ch. 3 gives the events in order; ch. 4 returns to and elaborates on several points, especially the memorial of stones at Gilgal.

3:2 three days. See note 1:11.

3:3 the ark of the covenant of the LORD your God. See Ex. 25:10–22; Deut. 10:5. The ark plays a prominent role in chs. 3; 4; 6; and 8. It signifies not only the presence of the Lord (Num. 10:33–36), but specifically His covenant, which means His commitment to His promises as well as the consequent obligations of Israel. See notes 1:5; 24:25.

the Levitical priests. See Deut. 10:8.

3:4 a distance between you and it. The purpose of the separation may be to ensure that the ark will be visible to the maximum number of people. See 4:11.

3:5 Consecrate yourselves. "Consecrate" means "to make holy" (5:15 note), and probably refers to physical actions like washing that symbolize the holiness of the people. There was a similar requirement when God came down to the people at Mount Sinai (Ex. 19:10, 14, 15).

wonders. The same word is used of the plagues in Egypt (Ex. 3:20; Judg. 6:13; Ps. 78:11; Mic. 7:15) and the conquest of Canaan (Ex. 34:10; 1 Chr. 16:9–24; cf. Jer. 21:2).

3:7 I will begin to exalt you. The Lord validated Joshua's leadership by repeating the wonders He did at the Red Sea through Moses. The God of Joshua is the God of Moses. See note 4:14.

that they may know. God's acts are often said to have the purpose of bringing about knowledge (Ex. 8:10; Deut. 4:35; 2 Kin. 19:19; Is. 45:6). Such knowledge is never merely intellectual. It is, however, attainable through hearing the news of God's acts, as well as by seeing them (2:9, 10; 4:24). Here the object of knowledge is the presence of God with Joshua (1:5 note; cf. Ex. 14:31), which the people will experience through the faithfulness of God to His promises. See notes on v. 10; 4:24.

3:9 listen to the words of the LORD. This is a fundamental duty of the people of God. See 1:8; 24:2.

how you shall know that [d]the living God is
among you and that he will without fail
[e]drive out from before you the Canaanites,
the Hittites, the Hivites, the Perizzites, the
Girgashites, the Amorites, and the Jebusites. **11** Behold, the ark of the covenant of
[f]the Lord of all the earth[1] [g]is passing over
before you into the Jordan. **12** Now therefore [h]take twelve men from the tribes of
Israel, [i]from each tribe a man. **13** And
[j]when the soles of the feet of the priests
bearing the ark of the LORD, [f]the Lord of all
the earth, shall rest in the waters of the
Jordan, the waters of the Jordan shall be
cut off from flowing, and the waters coming down from above shall [k]stand in one
heap."
14 So when the people set out from their
tents to pass over the Jordan with the
priests bearing [l]the ark of the covenant
before the people, **15** and as soon as those
bearing the ark had come as far as the
Jordan, and [m]the feet of the priests bearing
the ark were dipped in the brink of the
water (now [n]the Jordan overflows all its
banks [o]throughout the time of harvest),
16 the waters coming down from above
stood and rose up in a heap very far away,
at Adam, the city that is beside [p]Zarethan,
and those flowing down toward the Sea of
[q]the Arabah, [r]the Salt Sea, were completely
cut off. And the people passed over opposite Jericho. **17** Now the priests bearing the
ark of the covenant of the LORD stood firmly on dry ground in the midst of the Jordan,
[s]and all Israel was passing over on dry
ground until all the nation finished passing
over the Jordan.

10 [d]Deut. 5:26; 1 Sam. 17:26 [e]Ex. 33:2; Deut. 7:1; Ps. 44:2; [Ex. 13:5]
11 [f]Mic. 4:13; Zech. 4:14; 6:5 [g][Deut. 9:3]
12 [h]ch. 4:2, 4 [i][Num. 13:2]
13 [j]ver. 15, 16 [f][See ver. 11 above] [k]Ps. 114:3; [Ex. 15:8; Ps. 78:13]
14 [l]Acts 7:44, 45
15 [m]ver. 13 [n]1 Chr. 12:15; Jer. 12:5; 49:19; 50:44 [o][ch. 4:18; 5:10, 12]
16 [p]1 Kin. 4:12; 7:46 [q]See Deut. 1:1 [r]Gen. 14:3; Num. 34:3
17 [s]ch. 4:22; [Ex. 14:29]

Chapter 4
1 [t]ch. 3:17
2 [u]ch. 3:12
3 [v]Deut. 27:2 [1 Kin. 18:31] [w]ch. 3:13, 15 [x]ver. 8, 19, 20
6 [y]ver. 21; [Ex. 12:26; 13:14; Deut. 6:20]
7 [z]ch. 3:16 [a]Ex. 12:14; Num. 16:40
9 [b]ver. 3

Twelve Memorial Stones from the Jordan

4 When all the nation had finished
passing [t]over the Jordan, the LORD
said to Joshua, **2** [u]"Take twelve men from
the people, from each tribe a man, **3** and
command them, saying, 'Take [v]twelve
stones from here out of the midst of the
Jordan, from the very place [w]where the
priests' feet stood firmly, and bring them
over with you and lay them down in [x]the
place where you lodge tonight.'" **4** Then
Joshua called the twelve men from the
people of Israel, whom he had appointed,
a man from each tribe. **5** And Joshua said
to them, "Pass on before the ark of the
LORD your God into the midst of the
Jordan, and take up each of you a stone
upon his shoulder, according to the number of the tribes of the people of Israel,
6 that this may be a sign among you.
[y]When your children ask in time to come,
'What do those stones mean to you?'
7 then you shall tell them that [z]the waters
of the Jordan were cut off before the ark of
the covenant of the LORD. When it passed
over the Jordan, the waters of the Jordan
were cut off. So these stones shall be to
the people of Israel [a]a memorial forever."
8 And the people of Israel did just as
Joshua commanded and took up twelve
stones out of the midst of the Jordan, according to the number of the tribes of the people
of Israel, just as the LORD told Joshua. And
they carried them over with them to the
place where they lodged and laid them
down[2] there. **9** And Joshua set up twelve
stones in the midst of the Jordan, [b]in the

1 Hebrew *the ark of the covenant, the Lord of all the earth* 2 Or *to rest*

3:10 Here is how. The reference is probably to the whole miracle of the crossing, but attention is focused on the role of the ark (v. 11).

know. That is, "know by experience." Cf. v. 7. What they will know is the presence of God with Israel to bring His promise to certain fulfillment. Remarkably, this knowledge was already attained by Rahab in 2:9.

the living God. Israel's God is opposed to and contrasted with lifeless idols (Deut. 32:21).

Canaanites . . . Jebusites. This is one of several ways of listing the inhabitants of Canaan (Gen. 15:18–21; Deut. 7:1). See note 2:10.

3:11 the ark of the covenant of the Lord of all the earth. Lit. "the ark of the covenant, the Lord of all the earth." Not only the symbol of the covenant, but the Lord Himself will go ahead of His people. The reminder that He is Lord of all the earth suggests that the events that follow will have a purpose which reaches beyond Israel (4:24; cf. 2:11; Gen. 12:3; Ex. 19:5, 6).

3:12 twelve men. This anticipates the main subject of ch. 4; see 4:2.

3:13 stand in one heap. The language has similarities to Ex. 15:8 and Ps. 78:13, which describe the crossing of the Red Sea (4:23). The God of the Exodus is the God of the conquest.

3:14 the people set out. This verse picks up the action from v. 6.

3:15 the Jordan overflows . . . throughout . . . harvest. This vital piece of information takes the reader by surprise. The crossing will be even more remarkable than v. 13 indicated.

3:17 the ark. As instrumental in the miracle, the ark conveys the powerful message of God's faithfulness to His covenant promises.

nation. The Hebrew word used here is not usually applied to Israel; perhaps it is meant to recall Gen. 12:2 and Ex. 19:6, where it is also found.

4:2 twelve. All Israel is to be represented (1:12–15).

4:6 sign. This testimony for future generations of God's faithfulness is the first of several in Joshua (7:26; 8:29). See note on v. 9.

What do those stones mean. Ex. 12:26, 27; Deut. 6:20–25.

4:7 the ark. As the ark is prominent in ch. 3, so is it central to the retelling of the story to future generations. See notes 3:3, 17.

memorial. The purpose of the "sign" (v. 6) and telling about it is for future generations to remember the wonderful faithfulness of God to His promises. On the importance of such remembering for Israel, see Deut. 8:1–20; 1 Cor. 11:25; 2 Tim. 2:8.

place where the feet of the priests bearing the
ark of the covenant had stood; and they are
there to this day. 10 For the priests bearing
the ark stood in the midst of the Jordan until
everything was finished that the LORD commanded Joshua to tell the people, according
to all that Moses had commanded Joshua.
The people passed over in haste. 11 And
when all the people had finished passing
over, the ark of the LORD and the priests
passed over before the people. 12 The sons of
Reuben and the sons of Gad and the half-
tribe of Manasseh [c]passed over armed before
the people of Israel, as Moses had told
them. 13 About 40,000 ready for war passed
over before the LORD for battle, to the plains
of Jericho. 14 On that day the LORD [d]exalted
Joshua in the sight of all Israel, and they
stood in awe of him just as they had stood
in awe of Moses, all the days of his life.
15 And the LORD said to Joshua,
16 "Command the priests bearing [e]the ark of
the testimony to come up out of the Jordan."
17 So Joshua commanded the priests, "Come
up out of the Jordan." 18 And when the
priests bearing the ark of the covenant of the
LORD came up from the midst of the Jordan,
and the soles of the priests' feet were lifted
up on dry ground, the waters of the Jordan
returned to their place and overflowed all its
banks, [f]as before.
19 The people came up out of the Jordan
on the tenth day of the first month, and
they encamped at [g]Gilgal on the east border of Jericho. 20 And [h]those twelve stones,
which they took out of the Jordan, Joshua
set up at Gilgal. 21 And he said to the people of Israel, [i]"When your children ask
their fathers in times to come, 'What do
these stones mean?' 22 then you shall let
your children know, [j]'Israel passed over
this Jordan on dry ground.' 23 For the LORD
your God dried up the waters of the Jordan
for you until you passed over, as the LORD
your God did to the Red Sea, [k]which he
dried up for us until we passed over, 24 [l]so
that all the peoples of the earth may know
that the hand of the LORD is [m]mighty, that
you may [n]fear the LORD your God forever."[1]

The New Generation Circumcised

5 As soon as all the kings of the Amorites
who were beyond the Jordan to the
west, and all the kings of the Canaanites
[o]who were by the sea, [p]heard that the LORD
had dried up the waters of the Jordan for
the people of Israel until they had crossed
over, their hearts [q]melted and [r]there was
no longer any spirit in them because of the
people of Israel.
2 At that time the LORD said to Joshua,
"Make [s]flint knives and circumcise the
sons of Israel a second time." 3 So Joshua
made flint knives and circumcised the sons
of Israel at Gibeath-haaraloth.[2] 4 And this is

1 Or *all the days* 2 *Gibeath-haaraloth* means *the hill of the foreskins*

12 [c]ch. 6:7, 9, 13; Num. 32:20, 21, 27
14 [d]See ch. 3:7
16 [e]Ex. 25:16, 21, 22
18 [f]ch. 3:15
19 [g]ch. 5:9
20 [h]ver. 3, 9
21 [i]ver. 6
22 [j]ch. 3:17
23 [k]ch. 2:10; Ex. 14:21
24 [l]1 Kin. 8:42, 43 [m]Deut. 3:24; Ps. 89:13 [n]Ex. 14:31; Deut. 6:2
Chapter 5
1 [o]Num. 13:29 [p]Ex. 15:14 [q]See ch. 2:11 [r]1 Kin. 10:5
2 [s]Ex. 4:25

4:9 to this day. That is, the day of the narrator. This expression occurs frequently in the Book of Joshua (5:9; 6:25; 7:26; 8:28, 29; 9:27; 10:27; 13:13; 14:14; 15:63; 16:10), pointing to evidence for the truth and relevance of the narrative.

4:12 Reuben . . . Gad . . . Manasseh. See 1:12–15.

4:13 About 40,000. Some scholars suggest the word translated "thousand" means a military unit of unspecified size, a "contingent."

4:14 the LORD exalted Joshua . . . and they stood in awe of him. Joshua's exaltation is in fulfillment of 3:7. See Ex. 14:31. God's powerful faithfulness to His promises has the effect of exalting the one whose leadership is based on those promises.

4:15–18 The conclusion of the miracle is described, with the focus still on the ark.

4:16 the ark of the testimony. Also called the ark of the covenant (Ex. 25:16, 21, 22; 31:18; 32:15; 40:20). The Ten Commandments were deposited in the ark as a testimony to the agreement God made with Israel.

4:19 the tenth day of the first month. This is the day the Passover lamb was to be chosen (Ex. 12:3), underlining the connection between the crossing and the Exodus. See v. 23 and 5:10.

4:23, 24 The pronoun "you" in vv. 23, 24 identifies the later generations with the earlier great acts of God, as Moses did in Deut. 4:9–24; 5:2–5, and as Joshua will do in Josh. 24:5–10 (24:7 note).

4:24 all the peoples of the earth. The wonders of chs. 3 and 4 will have effects far beyond the immediate generation and far beyond the Israelite people (2:10; 5:1; cf. Gen. 12:3). The wonderful works of God in the Bible are expected to affect those who hear about them as powerfully as those who see them (Ex. 10:2; and supremely John 20:30, 31). See notes 2:9, 10.

know. The knowledge of God and His purposes has been the objective of these wonders (3:7, 10 notes). This goal is now shown to apply to all peoples. This knowledge does not necessarily imply salvation (Ex. 14:18).

fear the LORD. A common Old Testament expression for true faith (Ps. 128:1). See 24:14 note.

5:1–12 A significant moment (v. 9), with the wilderness behind them and the new life in the Land of Promise before them (vv. 11, 12), is marked by two symbolic actions: circumcision (vv. 2–8) and the Passover (v. 10). Circumcision was the sign of the covenant with Abraham (Gen. 17:9–14 notes), and was required for participation in the Passover (Ex. 12:48). Circumcision marked the people of the promise; the Passover celebrated their redemption from Egypt. Both the promise to Abraham and the redemption from Egypt looked forward to this day (Gen. 17:8; Ex. 3:8).

5:1 As soon as all the kings . . . heard. See 4:24; note on 2:9.

Amorites. See note 2:10.

5:2 circumcise . . . a second time. See v. 5.

5:4–7 This circumcision was necessary because the generation that came out of Egypt had fallen under God's judgment. In His grace God was raising up a new generation for Himself (v. 7). Physical circumcision

the reason why Joshua circumcised them:
[t]all the males of the people who came out
of Egypt, all the men of war, had died in
the wilderness on the way after they had
come out of Egypt. 5 Though all the people
who came out had been circumcised, yet
all the people who were born on the way in
the wilderness after they had come out of
Egypt had not been circumcised. 6 For the
people of Israel walked [u]forty years in the
wilderness, until all the nation, the men of
war who came out of Egypt, perished,
because they did not obey the voice of the
LORD; the LORD [v]swore to them that he
would not let them see the land that the
LORD had sworn to their fathers to give to
us, [w]a land flowing with milk and honey.
7 So it was [x]their children, whom he raised
up in their place, that Joshua circumcised.
For they were uncircumcised, because they
had not been circumcised on the way.
8 When the circumcising of the whole
nation was finished, they remained in their
places in the camp until they were healed.
9 And the LORD said to Joshua, "Today I
have rolled away the [y]reproach of Egypt
from you." And so the name of that place
is called [z]Gilgal[1] to this day.

First Passover in Canaan

10 While the people of Israel were
encamped at Gilgal, they kept the Passover
[a]on the fourteenth day of the month in the
evening on the plains of Jericho. 11 And the
day after the Passover, on that very day,
they ate of the produce of the land, unleavened cakes and parched grain. 12 And [b]the
manna ceased the day after they ate of the
produce of the land. And there was no
longer manna for the people of Israel, but
they ate of the fruit of the land of Canaan
that year.

The Commander of the LORD's Army

13 When Joshua was by Jericho, he lifted
up his eyes and looked, and behold, [c]a
man was standing before him [d]with his
drawn sword in his hand. And Joshua
went to him and said to him, "Are you for
us, or for our adversaries?" 14 And he said,
"No; but I am the commander of the army
of the LORD. Now I have come." And
Joshua [e]fell on his face to the earth and
worshiped and said to him, "What does
my lord say to his servant?" 15 And the
commander of the LORD's army said to
Joshua, [f]"Take off your sandals from your
feet, for the place where you are standing
is holy." And Joshua did so.

The Fall of Jericho

6 Now Jericho was shut up inside and
outside because of the people of Israel.

[1] *Gilgal* sounds like the Hebrew for *to roll*

4 [t]Num. 14:29; 26:64, 65; Deut. 2:16; Ps. 106:26; 1 Cor. 10:5; Heb. 3:17
6 [u]Num. 14:33; Deut. 1:3; 2:7, 14; 8:4; Ps. 95:10 [v]Num. 14:23; Ps. 95:11; Heb. 3:11 [w]See Ex. 3:8
7 [x]Num. 14:31; Deut. 1:39
9 [y]Gen. 34:14 [z]ch. 4:19
10 [a]Ex. 12:6; Num. 9:5
12 [b]Ex. 16:35
13 [c]Gen. 18:2; 32:24; Acts 1:10; [Ex. 23:20, 23] [d]Num. 22:23, 31
14 [e]Gen. 17:3
15 [f]Ex. 3:5; Acts 7:33

had its spiritual counterpart in circumcised hearts (Deut. 10:16; 30:6 and notes).

5:6 they did not obey . . . the LORD. This is the simplest description of the behavior that brought judgment. The reference is to Num. 14 (Deut. 1:32, 43).

the LORD swore. The promise of God can be a negative one.

5:7 children . . . in their place. These people were, in effect, a "new Israel."

5:9 Today I have rolled away the reproach of Egypt. These words indicate the great significance of this moment. The redemption from Egypt is complete only with the entry into the Promised Land. See the promise of the Exodus and its goal in Ex. 3:8. Had that goal not been reached, the reproach or scorn of Egypt would have remained (Deut. 9:28).

to this day. See note 4:9.

5:12 the manna ceased. This is another indication that a new era has begun and that the first major section of the book is concluded; see Introduction: Outline. On manna and its significance, see Ex. 16; Deut. 8:3.

5:13–12:24 The second major section of the book tells how the Israelites conquered Canaan. The shocking violence and terrible destruction in these chapters trouble many readers. Yet the text seems to ring with praise to God. This is so because the destruction is the true and just judgment of God on sinners (Gen. 15:16; cf. Lev. 18:24–27; Deut. 9:4, 5), through which He fulfilled His gracious promises to Israel (note the connection between salvation and judgment in Ex. 14:13, 14 and Rev. 19:1, 2). These accounts of destruction, no less than anything else in the book, testify to God's faithfulness to His promises (cf. the curse in the promise in Gen. 12:3) and prefigure His final judgment on those who reject His grace (Matt. 25:46; Heb. 9:27; 10:26–31).

5:13–15 The account of the conquest begins with the appearance of "the commander of the army of the LORD." This shows first, that God's sovereignty is free; second, that He and not Joshua controls the ensuing action; and third, that Joshua is the servant of the same God that appeared to Moses in the burning bush (Ex. 3:5).

5:14 No. The commander of the Lord's army encourages Joshua, but He is not under Joshua's command. God is bound neither to destroy all Canaanites nor to deliver all Israelites, as is powerfully illustrated in the subsequent chapters in the experiences of Rahab (6:25) and Achan (ch. 7). See note 6:17, 18.

commander of the army of the LORD. The commander is evidently an appearance of the pre-incarnate Son of God (1:5 and note; Gen. 16:7). The Divine Warrior and His army are prepared for war.

5:15 Take off your sandals. This command is like that of Ex. 3:5, establishing a continuity between what began with Moses and what follows under Joshua. Joshua is the successor to Moses. "Holiness" is fundamentally a quality of God. People (3:5 note) or things are described as holy when they belong to God in some special way.

6:1 Jericho. Its name probably means "Moon City," a center for worship (Gen. 11:27–25:11 note).

6:1–27 The essential elements for a theological understanding of the conquest are indicated in this account of Jericho, the first city to be destroyed. The destruction of the Canaanites, no less than the crossing of the Jordan, is the powerful work of God in faithfulness to the covenant, (note the role of the ark of the covenant in chs. 6 and 3–4, and

None went out, and none came in. 2 And
the LORD said to Joshua, "See, [g]I have given
Jericho into your hand, with its king and
mighty men of valor. 3 You shall march
around the city, all the men of war going
around the city once. Thus shall you do for
six days. 4 Seven priests shall bear seven
[h]trumpets of [i]rams' horns before the ark.
On the seventh day you shall march
around the city seven times, and [j]the
priests shall blow the trumpets. 5 And when
they make a long blast with the ram's horn,
when you hear the sound of the trumpet,
then all the people shall shout with a great
shout, and the wall of the city will fall
down flat,[1] and the people shall go up,
everyone straight before him." 6 So Joshua
the son of Nun called the priests and said
to them, "Take up the ark of the covenant
and let seven priests bear seven trumpets
of rams' horns before the ark of the LORD."
7 And he said to the people, "Go forward.
March around the city and let [k]the armed
men pass on before the ark of the LORD."
8 And just as Joshua had commanded
the people, the seven priests bearing the
seven trumpets of rams' horns before the
LORD went forward, blowing the trumpets,
with the ark of the covenant of the LORD
following them. 9 The armed men were
walking before the priests who were blowing the trumpets, and the [l]rear guard was
walking after the ark, while the trumpets
blew continually. 10 But Joshua commanded
the people, "You shall not shout or make
your voice heard, neither shall any word
go out of your mouth, until the day I tell
you to shout. Then you shall shout." 11 So
he caused the ark of the LORD to circle the
city, going about it once. And they came
into the camp and spent the night in the
camp.
12 Then Joshua rose early in the morning,
and [m]the priests took up the ark of the LORD.
13 And the seven priests bearing the seven
trumpets of rams' horns before the ark of
the LORD walked on, and they blew the
trumpets continually. And the armed men
were walking before them, and the rear
guard was walking after the ark of the
LORD, while the trumpets blew continually.
14 And the second day they marched
around the city once, and returned into the
camp. So they did for six days.
15 On the seventh day they rose early, at
the dawn of day, and marched around the
city in the same manner seven times. It
was only on that day that they marched
around the city seven times. 16 And at the
seventh time, when the priests had blown
the trumpets, Joshua said to the people,
"Shout, for the LORD has given you the
city. 17 And the city and all that is within it
shall be [n]devoted to the LORD for destruction.[2] Only Rahab the prostitute and all
who are with her in her house shall live,

Chapter 6
2 [g]ch. 2:9, 24; Deut. 7:24; Neh. 9:24; [ch. 8:1]
4 [h]Judg. 7:16, 22 [i]ver. 5, 6, 8, 13 [j]Num. 10:8
7 [k]ch. 4:12, 13
9 [l]ver. 13; Num. 10:25; Isai. 52:12; 58:8
12 [m]See ch. 3:6
17 [n]Lev. 27:28; Deut. 20:17

1 Hebrew *under itself*; also verse 20 2 That is, set apart (devoted) as an offering to the Lord (for destruction); also verses 18, 21

see notes 3:3, 11, 14, 17; 4:16). The fearful judgment of God is working to bring about the promised deliverance of His people is an important biblical theme (e.g., Ex. 14:13–14; Rev. 19:1–2). Furthermore, that the grace of God is not restricted to Israel (Gen. 12:3) is evidenced by the experience of Rahab and her household (v. 25). God is not simply anti-Canaanite (see note 5:14).

6:2 the LORD. Although this is sometimes taken to refer to the "commander of the army of the LORD" (5:13–15), the verses are more likely a separate episode introducing the whole of the conquest.

See, I have given. A striking paradox, since all that had been "seen" according to v. 1 was Jericho's shut gates. The promise of God creates possibilities not inherent in the present situation. A similar contrast between present circumstances and what God promises is found often in the Bible, as in the present experience of believers (Gen. 15:2–5; Is. 65:17; Rom. 8:18).

6:4 seven. See note Gen. 4:16.

the seventh day. The number suggests a parallel to the work of creation. Just as the work of creation reached its goal in the seventh day (Gen. 2:1–3), so the work of redemption from Egypt reaches its goal with possession of the Promised Land. Sabbath rest is related to both creation and redemption (Ex. 20:8–11 and Deut. 5:12–15; Josh. 1:13 note). In Heb. 3:7–4:11 "rest" refers to the ultimate goal of God's people.

6:5 straight before him. The collapse of the wall will allow access from every direction.

6:6 the ark of the covenant. See note 3:3. The procession, with the ark at its center, applied the covenant promises of God symbolically to Jericho. For Jericho the covenant promises will mean judgment. The parallel between the role of the ark in crossing the Jordan (chs. 3–4) and the conquest of Canaan is illuminated by Ex. 15:1–18, where the crossing of the Red Sea and the conquest are described in similar terms. All of these events are powerful acts of God in accordance with His covenant, directed to the goal of bringing His people to their promised rest.

6:8 before the LORD. As in 3:11 (note), the presence of the ark is identified with the presence of the Lord Himself. See note 1:5.

6:11 he caused the ark . . . circle. The whole procession can be summed up by referring only to the ark.

in the camp. At Gilgal (5:10).

6:15–19 The description of the seventh day is expanded with a report of Joshua's speech. In accordance with the narrative style noted elsewhere (1:11; 2:6 and notes), the words of vv. 17–19 may have been spoken earlier but are recorded here for dramatic effect.

6:17 devoted . . . for destruction. In the holy war the city was reserved for God. The consequence is seen in v. 21, the awful reality of God's judgment on Jericho, as also on the whole of Canaan (11:11–12, 14, 20; Lev. 27:28–29; Deut. 13:16; 20:10–18).

Only Rahab . . . and all who are with her. Judgment does not exclude grace. The mercy she sought in 2:12 will be extended to her.

because she [o]hid the messengers whom we
sent. 18 But you, keep yourselves from the
things devoted to destruction, lest when
you have devoted them you take any of the
devoted things and make the camp of
Israel [p]a thing for destruction and [q]bring
trouble upon it. 19 But all silver and gold,
and every vessel of bronze and iron, are
holy to the LORD; they shall go into the
treasury of the LORD." 20 So the people
shouted, and the trumpets were blown. As
soon as the people heard the sound of the
trumpet, the people shouted a great shout,
and [r]the wall fell down flat, so that the
people went up into the city, every man
straight before him, and they captured the
city. 21 Then they [s]devoted all in the city to
destruction, both men and women, young
and old, oxen, sheep, and donkeys, with
the edge of the sword.
22 But to the two men who had spied out
the land, Joshua said, "Go into the prostitute's house and bring out from there the
woman and all who belong to her, [t]as you
swore to her." 23 So the young men who
had been spies went in and brought out
Rahab and [u]her father and mother and
brothers and all who belonged to her. And
they brought all her relatives and put them
outside the camp of Israel. 24 And they
burned the city with fire, and everything in
it. [v]Only the silver and gold, and the vessels of bronze and of iron, they put into the
treasury of the house of the LORD. 25 But
Rahab the prostitute and her father's
household and all who belonged to her,
Joshua saved alive. And [w]she has lived in
Israel to this day, because she hid the messengers whom Joshua sent to spy out
Jericho.
26 Joshua laid an oath on them at that
time, saying, [x]"Cursed before the LORD be
the man who rises up and rebuilds this
city, Jericho.

> "At the cost of his firstborn shall he
> lay its foundation,
> and at the cost of his youngest son
> shall he set up its gates."

27 [y]So the LORD was with Joshua, and [z]his
fame was in all the land.

Israel Defeated at Ai

7 But the people of Israel broke faith in
regard to the devoted things, for
[a]Achan the son of Carmi, son of Zabdi, son
of Zerah, of the tribe of Judah, took some
of the devoted things. And the anger of the
LORD burned against the people of Israel.
2 Joshua sent men from Jericho to Ai,
which is near [b]Beth-aven, east of Bethel,
and said to them, "Go up and spy out the
land." And the men went up and spied out
Ai. 3 And they returned to Joshua and said
to him, "Do not have all the people go up,
but let about two or three thousand men
go up and attack Ai. Do not make the
whole people toil up there, for they are
few." 4 So about 3,000 men went up there
from the people. And [c]they fled before the

17 [o]ch. 2:4
18 [p][ch. 7:12] [q]ch. 7:25; 1 Chr. 2:7
20 [r]ver. 5; Heb. 11:30
21 [s][Deut. 7:2]
22 [t]ch. 2:14; Heb. 11:31
23 [u]ch. 2:13
24 [v]ver. 19
25 [w][Matt. 1:5]
26 [x][1 Kin. 16:34]
27 [y]See ch. 1:5 [z]ch. 9:9
Chapter 7
1 [a]ch. 22:20; [1 Chr. 2:6, 7]
2 [b]ch. 18:12; 1 Sam. 13:5; 14:23; Hos. 4:15; 5:8; 10:5
4 [c]Lev. 26:17; Deut. 28:25

6:18 devoted to destruction. The same Hebrew term found in v. 17 occurs three times here, warning Israel not to fall into the same judgment as the Canaanites. Ch. 7 shows the need for this warning.

6:19 holy. See note on 5:15.

6:20, 21 The fall of Jericho is briefly described. Further details may be deduced from v. 24; 8:2; 10:1; 24:11.

6:23 outside the camp. This phrase can describe a temporary state of affairs (v. 25) due to ceremonial uncleanness (e.g., Lev. 13:46).

6:24 the house of the LORD. See note 9:23.

6:25 she has lived in Israel. Rahab is included in the people of God. See Matt. 1:5; Heb. 11:31; James 2:25.

to this day. See note 4:9.

6:26 Cursed . . . who rises up and rebuilds. Jericho was to remain under God's curse, presumably as a sign of the judgment of God that had fallen on the Canaanites and that could fall on Israel. See 1 Kin. 16:34.

6:27 the LORD was with Joshua. See note 4:14.

7:1–26 If Rahab, the Canaanite who found mercy, is a story of God's grace in the midst of judgment (6:25), Achan's story is a reminder of the holiness of God, on which no one may presume (24:19; Num. 17:11–13; Heb. 10:30–31). Ch. 7 recounts the first instance of disobedience in the Promised Land, an ominous event in light of the history that will follow (2 Kin. 17:7–20) and an occasion reminiscent of Gen. 3 (v. 21 note). The incident and its lesson for Israel are recalled in 22:18–20.

7:1 the people of Israel. Although the offense was committed by one man, all Israel is involved and affected (see v. 11; 22:18). The facts stated in v. 1 only gradually became known to the Israelites.

devoted things. See 6:18; note on 6:17.

the anger of the LORD. The anger of God is His personal righteous hostility to evil. Unlike ancient pagan conceptions of divine wrath, in the Bible God's anger is never arbitrary or capricious. It is as much a part of the New Testament message as of the Old (Matt. 3:7; John 3:36; Rom. 1:18; Col. 3:6; 1 Thess. 1:10; Heb. 10:26–31; Rev. 6:16).

7:2–5 In contrast to the stories of the spies (ch. 2), and the conquest of Jericho (ch. 6), Israel is now under God's anger, and the outcome will be different.

7:2 from Jericho to Ai. The movement is westwards and up into the central hill country.

Beth-aven. The name means "house of nothingness" or "house of wickedness." The name may be used disparagingly for Bethel (as in Hos. 4:15; 10:5).

7:3 Do not have all the people go up. Contrast the report of the spies in 2:24.

men of Ai, 5 and the men of Ai killed about
thirty-six of their men and chased them
before the gate as far as Shebarim and
struck them at the descent. And the hearts
of the people [d]melted and became as water.
6 Then Joshua [e]tore his clothes and [f]fell
to the earth on his face before the ark of the
LORD until the evening, he and the elders of
Israel. And they put [g]dust on their heads.
7 And Joshua said, "Alas, O Lord GOD,
[h]why have you brought this people over the
Jordan at all, to give us into the hands of
the Amorites, to destroy us? Would that we
had been content to dwell beyond the
Jordan! 8 O Lord, what can I say, when
Israel has turned their backs before their
enemies! 9 For the Canaanites and all the
inhabitants of the land will hear of it and
will surround us and [i]cut off our name
from the earth. And what will you do for
your great name?"

The Sin of Achan

10 The LORD said to Joshua, "Get up! Why
have you fallen on your face? 11 Israel has
sinned; they have [j]transgressed my
covenant that I commanded them; they
have taken some of the [k]devoted things;
they have stolen and lied and put them
among their own belongings. 12 [l]Therefore
the people of Israel cannot stand before
their enemies. They [m]turn their backs
before their enemies, because they have
become [n]devoted for destruction.[1] I will be
with you no more, unless you destroy [o]the
devoted things from among you. 13 Get up!
Consecrate the people and say, [p]'Consecrate
yourselves for tomorrow; for thus
says the LORD, God of Israel, "There are
devoted things in your midst, O Israel. You
cannot stand before your enemies until you
take away the devoted things from among
you." 14 In the morning therefore you shall
be brought near [q]by your tribes. And the
tribe that the LORD takes by lot shall come
near by clans. And the clan that the LORD
takes shall come near by households. And
the household that the LORD takes shall
come near man by man. 15 [r]And he who is
taken with the devoted things shall be
burned with fire, he and all that he has,
because he has [s]transgressed the covenant
of the LORD, and because he has done [t]an
outrageous thing in Israel."'
16 So Joshua rose early in the morning
and brought Israel near tribe by tribe, and
the tribe of Judah was taken. 17 And he
brought near the clans of Judah, and the
clan of the [u]Zerahites was taken. And he
brought near the clan of the Zerahites man
by man, and Zabdi was taken. 18 And he
brought near his household man by man,
and Achan the son of Carmi, son of Zabdi,
son of Zerah, of the tribe of Judah, was
taken. 19 Then Joshua said to Achan, "My
son, [v]give glory to the LORD God of Israel

5 [d]ch. 2:9, 11
6 [e]Gen. 37:29, 34; Num. 14:6; 2 Sam. 1:11; 13:31 [f]Num. 14:5 [g]1 Sam. 4:12
7 [h]Ex. 5:22; 2 Kin. 3:10
9 [i]Ps. 83:4
11 [j]ver. 15 [k]ch. 6:17, 18
12 [l]Num. 14:45; Judg. 2:14 [m]ver. 8 [n]ch. 6:18
[o]ver. 11
13 [p]ch. 3:5
14 [q]1 Sam. 10:19
15 [r]1 Sam. 14:38, 39 [s]ver. 11 [t]Gen. 34:7; Judg. 20:6
17 [u]Num. 26:20
19 [v]1 Sam. 6:5; Jer. 13:16; Mal. 2:2; John 9:24

[1] That is, set apart (devoted) as an offering to the Lord (for destruction)

7:5 thirty-six. The number of casualties is not great. The fear and dismay of the people were due more to the Lord's anger than to the human scale of the defeat.

the hearts of the people melted. Disobedience in Israel has brought about a great reversal. The Israelites now find themselves in the situation of the Canaanites in 2:11; 5:1.

7:6 tore his clothes . . . put dust on their heads. These are conventional expressions of grief (Job 1:20; 2:12). The cause of grief is the apparent failure of the covenant promises, the symbol of which is the ark. See notes 3:3, 17; 4:16. Joshua's prayer (vv. 7–9) will appeal to those promises. See note 10:6.

7:7–9 Joshua prays for Israel as Moses had done in similar circumstances (cf. Num. 14:13–19).

7:7 why. This question comes to the lips of those who find their experience contradicting their understanding of the promises of God. It can be a rebellious question (as in Num. 14:3), but it can also express a true faith perplexed by circumstances (cf. Ps. 22:1).

Amorites. See note 2:10.

7:9 will hear. See note 9:3.

our name. The promise to Abraham included a great name (Gen. 12:2). Joshua's prayer is based on the promises of God.

your great name. God's reputation is at stake (Ex. 32:12; Num. 14:13–16; Ezek. 36:16–23).

7:11 Israel. The corporate unity of Israel is stressed throughout the chapter. The sin of one man (v. 15) brought guilt on his community (22:18).

transgressed my covenant. This is a further indication of the nature of the sin. The concept of God's covenant includes His commitment to His promises, and the consequent obligations on the people who received the promises. See note 3:3. It is God's covenant because He has set its terms.

devoted things. See 6:18; note on 6:17.

7:12 devoted for destruction. The cause of Israel's defeat at Ai was not a failure of God's promises (7:6 note) but disobedience.

I will be with you no more. This terrible reversal of 1:5 brings the first half of ch. 7 to a climax; the second half will elaborate the words "unless you destroy the devoted things from among you."

7:13 Consecrate. See note 3:5. In contrast to ch. 3, this is preparation to meet God's judgment.

7:14 that the LORD takes. The actual procedure may have been by the Urim and Thummim (Ex. 28:30 note).

7:15 an outrageous thing in Israel. Such an act is contrary to the nature of Israel as the covenant people, and therefore an act of folly. Elsewhere this expression is used of sexual perversions prohibited in Israel (Gen. 34:7; Deut. 22:21; Judg. 20:6, 10; 2 Sam. 13:12; Jer. 29:23).

and [w]give praise[1] to him. And [x]tell me now
what you have done; do not hide it from
me." 20 And Achan answered Joshua, "Truly
[y]I have sinned against the LORD God of
Israel, and this is what I did: 21 when I saw
among the spoil a beautiful cloak from
Shinar, and 200 shekels of silver, and a bar
of gold weighing 50 shekels,[2] then I coveted them and took them. And see, they are
hidden in the earth inside my tent, with
the silver underneath."
22 So Joshua sent messengers, and they
ran to the tent; and behold, it was hidden
in his tent with the silver underneath.
23 And they took them out of the tent and
brought them to Joshua and to all the people of Israel. And they laid them down
before the LORD. 24 And Joshua and all Israel
with him took Achan the son of Zerah, and
the silver and the cloak and the bar of gold,
and his sons and daughters and his oxen
and donkeys and sheep and his tent and all
that he had. And they brought them up to
the [z]Valley of Achor. 25 And Joshua said,
"Why did you [a]bring trouble on us? The
LORD brings trouble on you today." And all
Israel [b]stoned him with stones. [c]They
burned them with fire and stoned them
with stones. 26 And they raised over him [d]a
great heap of stones that remains to this
day. Then [e]the LORD turned from his burning anger. Therefore, to this day the name
of that place is called the Valley of Achor.[3]

The Fall of Ai

8 And the LORD said to Joshua, [f]"Do not
fear and do not be dismayed. Take all
the fighting men with you, and arise, go up
to Ai. See, [g]I have given into your hand the
king of Ai, and his people, his city, and his
land. 2 And you shall do to Ai and its king
as you did [h]to Jericho and its king. Only [i]its
spoil and its livestock you shall take as
plunder for yourselves. Lay an ambush
against the city, behind it."
3 So Joshua and all the fighting men arose
to go up to Ai. And Joshua chose 30,000
mighty men of valor and sent them out
by night. 4 And he commanded them,
"Behold, [j]you shall lie in ambush against
the city, behind it. Do not go very far from
the city, but all of you remain ready. 5 And
I and all the people who are with me will
approach the city. And when they come
out against us [k]just as before, we shall flee
before them. 6 And they will come out after
us, until we have [l]drawn them away from
the city. For they will say, 'They are fleeing
from us, just as before.' So we will flee
before them. 7 Then you shall rise up from
the ambush and seize the city, for the LORD
your God will give it into your hand. 8 And
as soon as you have taken the city, you
shall set the city on fire. You shall do
according to the word of the Lord. [m]See, I
have commanded you." 9 So Joshua sent
them out. And they went to the place of
ambush and lay between Bethel and Ai, to
the west of Ai, but Joshua spent that night
among the people.
10 Joshua arose early in the morning and
mustered the people and went up, he and
the elders of Israel, before the people to Ai.
11 And [n]all the fighting men who were with
him went up and drew near before the city
and encamped on the north side of Ai, with
a ravine between them and Ai. 12 He took
about 5,000 men and set them in ambush

19 [w]Num. 5:6, 7; 2 Chr. 30:22; Ezra 10:11; Dan. 9:4 [x]1 Sam. 14:43
20 [y]2 Sam. 12:13
24 [z]ver. 26; ch.15:7; Isai. 65:10; Hos. 2:15
25 [a]ch. 6:18; 1 Chr. 2:7 [b]Lev. 20:2; 24:14 [c]ch. 22:20
26 [d]ch. 8:29; 2 Sam. 18:17; [Lam. 3:53] [e]Deut. 13:17
Chapter 8
1 [f]ch. 1:9; 10:25; Deut. 1:21; 7:18; 31:8 [g]ch. 2:24; 6:2
2 [h]ch. 6:21 [i]ver. 27; Deut. 20:14
4 [j][Judg. 20:29]
5 [k]ch. 7:5
6 [l]ver. 16
8 [m]2 Sam. 13:28
11 [n]ver. 5

1 Or *and make confession* 2 A *shekel* was about 2/5 ounce or 11 grams
3 *Achor* means *trouble*

7:20 sinned. See note on v. 11.

7:21 saw . . . coveted . . . took. There may be an allusion here to Gen. 3:6, where these three verbs occur in the same order. The pattern of the Garden of Eden has been repeated in the Promised Land: no sooner was the gift of God given than the recipients desired what was forbidden, and took it.

7:23 before the LORD. That is, presumably before the ark. See note 6:8.

7:24 all that he had. God's mercy to Rahab extended to her family (6:23), and the punishment of Achan reached his family.

7:26 from his burning anger. God's wrath, being righteous, ceases when sin has been dealt with. This is fundamental to the New Testament teaching that the death of Christ is an atoning or propitiatory sacrifice (Rom. 3:25, 26).

8:1 Do not fear. Compare 7:5. This call to faith (1:9; 1:6 note) is based on the promises of God despite visible circumstances. It is a common expression of God's favor (Gen. 15:1). It confirms that the Lord's anger has ceased towards Israel.

all the fighting men. Contrast 7:3.

given. The promise of 1:2, 3 (notes) is applied to Ai.

8:2 as you did to Jericho. See 6:21; note on 6:17.

take as plunder. Just as there was an exception to the total destruction of Jericho (6:17), so God makes another exception to that requirement here.

8:3 30,000. See note 4:13.

8:5 just as before. See 7:5.

8:12 5,000. The number differing from the "30,000" in v. 3 may indicate that there were two units assigned to different aspects of the ambush.

between Bethel and Ai, to the west of the
city. 13 So they stationed the forces, the main
encampment that was north of the city and
its rear guard west of the city. But Joshua
spent that night in the valley. 14 And as soon
as the king of Ai saw this, he and all his people, the men of the city, hurried and went
out early to the appointed place[1] toward
[o]the Arabah to meet Israel in battle. [p]But he
did not know that there was an ambush
against him behind the city. 15 And Joshua
and all Israel [q]pretended to be beaten before
them and fled in the direction of the wilderness. 16 So all the people who were in the city
were called together to pursue them, and as
they pursued Joshua they [r]were drawn away
from the city. 17 Not a man was left in Ai or
Bethel who did not go out after Israel. They
left the city open and pursued Israel.

18 Then the LORD said to Joshua, [s]"Stretch
out the javelin that is in your hand toward
Ai, for I will give it into your hand." And
Joshua stretched out the javelin that was in
his hand toward the city. 19 And the men in
the ambush rose quickly out of their place,
and as soon as he had stretched out his
hand, they ran and entered the city and
captured it. And they hurried to set the city
on fire. 20 So when the men of Ai looked
back, behold, the smoke of the city went up
to heaven, and they had no power to flee
this way or that, for the people who fled to
the wilderness turned back against the pursuers. 21 And when Joshua and all Israel saw
that the ambush had captured the city, and
that the smoke of the city went up, then
they turned back and struck down the men
of Ai. 22 And the others came out from the
city against them, so they were in the midst
of Israel, some on this side, and some on
that side. And Israel struck them down,
until there was [t]left none that survived or
escaped. 23 But the king of Ai they took
alive, and brought him near to Joshua.

24 When Israel had finished killing all the
inhabitants of Ai in the open wilderness
where they pursued them, and all of them
to the very last had fallen by the edge of the
sword, all Israel returned to Ai and struck
it down with the edge of the sword. 25 And
all who fell that day, both men and
women, were 12,000, all the people of Ai.
26 But Joshua did not draw back his hand
with which he [u]stretched out the javelin
until he had devoted all the inhabitants of
Ai to destruction.[2] 27 Only the livestock and
the spoil of that city Israel took as their
plunder, according to the word of the LORD
that he [v]commanded Joshua. 28 So Joshua
burned Ai and made it forever a [w]heap of
ruins, as it is to this day. 29 [x]And he hanged
the king of Ai on a tree until evening. [y]And
at sunset Joshua commanded, and they
took his body down from the tree and
threw it at the entrance of the gate of the
city and [z]raised over it a great heap of
stones, which stands there to this day.

Joshua Renews the Covenant

30 At that time Joshua built an altar to the
LORD, the God of Israel, [a]on Mount Ebal,
31 just as Moses the servant of the LORD had
commanded the people of Israel, as it is
written in the Book of the Law of Moses,
"an altar of uncut stones, upon which no
man has wielded an iron tool." And they
offered on it burnt offerings to the LORD
and sacrificed peace offerings. 32 And there,
in the presence of the people of Israel, he

14 [o]See Deut. 1:1 [p]Judg. 20:34
15 [q]Judg. 20:36
16 [r]ver. 6
18 [s]ver. 26
22 [t]Deut. 7:2
26 [u]ver. 18
27 [v]ver. 2
28 [w]Deut. 13:16
29 [x]ch. 10:26 [y]Deut. 21:23 [z]ch. 7:26
30 [a]See Ex. 20:24, 25; Deut. 27:4-6

1 Hebrew *appointed time* 2 That is, set apart (devoted) as an offering to the Lord (for destruction)

8:14 the Arabah. The Jordan Valley.

8:15 the wilderness. Uncultivated land to the east of Ai, not the wilderness on the other side of the Jordan Valley (v. 24).

8:17 or Bethel. The sudden inclusion of Bethel is not explained, but see 12:9, 16.

8:18 the javelin. Compare Moses' action in Ex. 14:16; 17:9.

8:28, 29 to this day. See note 4:9.

8:29 hanged . . . on a tree. This action is a sign of the curse of God (21:22, 23; cf. Gal. 3:13).

8:30–35 The first phase of the account of the conquest (6:1–8:35) concludes with the assembly of the people at Mount Ebal and Mount Gerizim to hear God's promise of blessing and His warning of curse. This assembly was commanded by Moses (Deut. 11:29; 27:1–13); it shows that the life of Israel, including entry into the Promised Land, is established by the covenant and must be lived under the words of God (v. 34).

8:30 Mount Ebal. Just north of Shechem, where Abraham heard God's promise to give the land to his descendants, and where he built an altar to God (Gen. 12:6, 7). Joshua's altar built in the same location many years later accompanied the repetition and renewal of the covenant promises.

8:31 Moses the servant of the LORD. See note 1:1.

the Book of the Law of Moses. See note 1:8. Here the reference is to Deut. 27:5 (cf. Ex. 20:25).

uncut stones. These were used to show it belonged to the Lord (Ex. 20:25 note).

burnt offerings. Offerings were essential for the establishment of the covenant with God. See Gen. 15:9, 10; Ex. 20:24.

8:32 in the presence of the people of Israel . . . the law of Moses. The Word of God is set before the people.

stones. These could be the stones of the altar, but Deut. 27:1–8 indicates that special stones could be set up as writing surfaces.

wrote on [b]the stones a copy of the law of
Moses, which he had written. **33** And all
Israel, [c]sojourner as well as native born,
with their elders and officers and their
judges, stood on opposite sides of the ark
before the Levitical priests [d]who carried the
ark of the covenant of the LORD, half of
them in front of Mount Gerizim and half of
them in front of Mount Ebal, [e]just as
Moses the servant of the LORD had commanded at the first, to bless the people of
Israel. **34** And afterward [f]he read all the words
of the law, [g]the blessing and the curse,
according to all that is written in the Book
of the Law. **35** There was not a word of all
that Moses commanded that Joshua did
not read before all the assembly of Israel,
[h]and the women, and the little ones, and
[i]the sojourners who lived[1] among them.

The Gibeonite Deception

9 As soon as all the kings who were
beyond the Jordan [j]in the hill country
and in the lowland all along the coast [k]of
the Great Sea toward Lebanon, [l]the
Hittites, the Amorites, the Canaanites, the
Perizzites, the Hivites, and the Jebusites,
heard of this, **2** they gathered together as
one to fight against Joshua and Israel.
3 But when the inhabitants of [m]Gibeon
heard what Joshua had done [n]to Jericho
and [o]to Ai, **4** they on their part acted with
cunning and went and made ready provisions and took worn-out sacks for their
donkeys, and wineskins, worn-out and
torn and mended, **5** with worn-out, patched
sandals on their feet, and worn-out clothes.
And all their provisions were dry and crumbly. **6** And they went to Joshua in [p]the camp
at Gilgal and said to him and to the men of
Israel, "We have come from a distant country, so now make a covenant with us." **7** But
the men of Israel said to [q]the Hivites,
"Perhaps you live among us; then [r]how can
we make a covenant with you?" **8** They said
to Joshua, [s]"We are your servants." And
Joshua said to them, "Who are you? And
where do you come from?" **9** They said to
him, [t]"From a very distant country your
servants have come, because of the name
of the LORD your God. [u]For we have heard
a report of him, and all that he did in
Egypt, **10** [v]and all that he did to the two
kings of the Amorites who were beyond the
Jordan, to Sihon the king of Heshbon, and
to Og king of Bashan, who lived in
[w]Ashtaroth. **11** So our elders and all the
inhabitants of our country said to us, 'Take
provisions in your hand for the journey
and go to meet them and say to them, "We
are your servants. Come now, make a
covenant with us."' **12** Here is our bread. It
was still warm when we took it from our
houses as our food for the journey on the
day we set out to come to you, but now,
behold, it is dry and crumbly. **13** These
wineskins were new when we filled them,
and behold, they have burst. And these
garments and sandals of ours are worn out

32 [b]Deut. 27:2-4
33 [c]Deut. 31:12 [d]Deut. 31:9, 25 [e]Deut. 11:29; 27:11-13
34 [f]Deut. 31:11; Neh. 8:2, 3; 13:1 [g]Deut. 30:19; See Deut. 28:2-68
35 [h]Deut. 31:12 [i]ver. 33
Chapter 9
1 [j]Deut. 1:7 [k]Num. 34:6 [l]ch. 3:10; 12:8
3 [m]ch. 10:2, 10, 12; 2 Sam. 21:1, 2; 1 Kin. 3:4, 5; 9:2 [n]ch. 6:21, 24 [o]ch. 8:26, 28
6 [p]ch. 5:10
7 [q]ch. 11:19 [r]Ex. 23:32; Deut. 7:2; Judg. 2:2
8 [s]ver. 11
9 [t]Deut. 20:15 [u]ch. 2:10; 6:27
10 [v]See Num. 21:21-35 [w]ch. 12:4; Deut. 1:4

1 Or *traveled*

8:33 the ark. At the center of the assembly of Israel is the symbol of the covenant that makes them the people of God and according to which they have received the land (3:3; 6:4; 7:6 and notes).

bless the people of Israel. Although blessings and curses will be read (v. 34), blessing has priority in the purpose of God. In Gen. 12:1–3, blessing sums up the good that God promised Abraham (14:13; 22:6).

8:34 the blessing and the curse. Both sides of the covenant of God have already been experienced in the land: blessing in ch. 6 and 8:1–29, cursing in ch. 7. See Deut. 27–28.

8:35 assembly. This gathering of the people of God to hear this word continues in the time of the New Testament church (cf. Deut. 9:10).

9:1, 2 These verses form the background to chs. 9–12. The fear of the Israelites that immobilized the Canaanites in 5:1 here unites them against Joshua and Israel. There is an anticipation of Ps. 2:1–3, the opposition to God and His rule that culminated in the crucifixion of Jesus (Acts 4:25–27). The impotence of the rulers in Ps. 2 is amply illustrated by the list of defeated kings in Josh. 12.

Hittites . . . Jebusites. See note 3:10.

9:3 Gibeon. The action of the people of Gibeon (eight miles north of Jerusalem) is in contrast to the general pattern throughout Canaan (vv. 1, 2).

heard. The effect of the news of God's powerful faithfulness to His promises is an important theme in the account of the conquest (2:10, 11; 5:1; 9:1, 9; 10:1; 11:1; cf. 7:9). For the Canaanites this news was terrifying, for it meant that the God of heaven and earth (2:11) would destroy them (5:13–12:24 note).

9:4 acted with cunning. This deception will bring a curse on the Gibeonites (v. 23) and is a contrast to Rahab's action towards the representatives of Israel in ch. 2.

9:6 We have come from a distant country. The Gibeonites pretend that they live outside Israel's potential zone of interest. The Israelites were prepared to make a treaty with them because of the provisions of Deut. 20:10–18.

covenant. A covenant is a treaty relationship. This covenant would commit Israel to spare the Gibeonites.

9:7 Hivites. This ethnic group, to which the Gibeonites belonged, was one of those God had promised to drive out of Canaan (3:10).

9:9 name. See note 7:9.

heard. See note on v. 3.

9:10 all that he did. The news the Gibeonites had heard is the same as that confessed by Rahab (2:10 note). Their reaction was quite different from hers.

Amorites. See note 2:10.

from the very long journey." 14So the men
took some of their provisions, but [x]did not
ask counsel from the LORD. 15And Joshua
[y]made peace with them and made a
covenant with them, to let them live, and
the leaders of the congregation swore to
them.

16At the end of three days after they had
made a covenant with them, they heard
that they were their neighbors [z]and that
they lived among them. 17And the people
of Israel set out and reached their cities on
the third day. [a]Now their cities were
Gibeon, Chephirah, Beeroth, and Kiriath-
jearim. 18But the people of Israel did not
attack them, because the leaders of the
congregation had sworn to them by the
LORD, the God of Israel. Then all the congregation murmured against the leaders.
19But all the leaders said to all the congregation, "We have sworn to them by the
LORD, the God of Israel, and now we may
not touch them. 20This we will do to them:
let them live, lest [b]wrath be upon us, [c]be-
cause of the oath that we swore to them."
21And the leaders said to them, "Let them
live." So they became [d]cutters of wood and
drawers of water for all the congregation,
just as the leaders [e]had said of them.

22Joshua summoned them, and he said to
them, "Why did you deceive us, saying,
[f]'We are very far from you,' when [g]you dwell
among us? 23Now therefore you are cursed,
and some of you shall never be anything but
servants, [h]cutters of wood and drawers of
water for the house of my God." 24They
answered Joshua, "Because it was told to
your servants for a certainty that the LORD
your God had [i]commanded his servant
Moses to give you all the land and to destroy
all the inhabitants of the land from before
you—so [j]we feared greatly for our lives
because of you and did this thing. 25And
now, behold, we are in your hand. Whatever
seems good and right in your sight to do to
us, do it." 26So he did this to them and delivered them out of the hand of the people of
Israel, and they did not kill them. 27But
Joshua made them that day [k]cutters of wood
and drawers of water for the congregation
and for the altar of the LORD, to this day, [l]in
the place that he should choose.

The Sun Stands Still

10 As soon as Adoni-zedek, king of
Jerusalem, heard how Joshua had
captured Ai and had devoted it to destruction,[1] [m]doing to Ai and its king [n]as he had
done to Jericho and its king, and [o]how the
inhabitants of Gibeon had made peace
with Israel and were among them, 2[p]he[2]
feared greatly, because Gibeon was a great
city, like one of the royal cities, and
because it was greater than Ai, and all its
men were warriors. 3So Adoni-zedek king
of Jerusalem sent to Hoham king of

14 [x]Num. 27:21 15 [y]ch. 11:19 16 [z]ver. 22 17 [a][ch. 18:25-28; Ezra 2:25] 20 [b][Num. 1:53] [c]2 Sam. 21:2 21 [d]ver. 23, 27; Deut. 29:11 [e]ver. 15 22 [f]ver. 6, 9 [g]ver. 16

23 [h]ver. 21, 27 24 [i]Deut. 7:1, 2 [j]Ex. 15:14 27 [k]ver. 21, 23 [1 Chr. 9:2; Ezra 2:43; 8:20; Neh. 7:60; 11:3] [l]Deut. 12:5

Chapter 10
1 [m]See ch. 6:21, 24 [n]ch. 8:22, 26-29 [o]ch. 9:15 2 [p]Deut. 11:25

[1] That is, set apart (devoted) as an offering to the Lord (for destruction); also verses 28, 35, 37, 39, 40 [2] One Hebrew manuscript, Vulgate (compare Syriac); most Hebrew manuscripts *they*

9:14 did not ask counsel from the LORD. How they should have sought counsel is not specified, but as in 5:6, Israel's failure is a failure to obey God.

9:15 made peace. The sense is explained by the following phrase "to let them live."

9:16, 17 three days . . . the third day. If v. 16 anticipates the result of v. 17, then the three days in each verse may be the same. From Gilgal to Gibeon is about nineteen miles.

9:18 murmured. Grumbling (against Moses, Aaron, and ultimately the Lord) was a common activity of Israel in the desert (Ex. 15:24; 16:2, 7–9; 17:3; Num. 14:2, 27, 36).

9:20 wrath. See 7:11 and note. Contrast this oath, kept scrupulously although based on a Gibeonite lie, and the covenant of ch. 7:11, based on the Lord's command, but broken.

9:21 cutters of wood and drawers of water. That is, household slaves.

9:23 house. The tabernacle is called a house in 1 Sam. 1:7. At the time of Solomon the tabernacle was at Gibeon (2 Chr. 1:3, 5).

my God. The danger posed by Canaanites remaining in the land was that they would turn Israel from following the Lord to serve other gods (Deut. 7:4). The implication of this curse is that the Gibeonites would serve in the house of Israel's God without being counted as members of His people. The rituals and sacrifices of the tabernacle required supplies of wood and water.

9:24 feared greatly. See note 2:9.

9:27 the place that he should choose. See Deut. 12; cf. Ex. 20:24.

to this day. See note 4:9.

10:1–43 The hostility anticipated in 9:1, 2 begins to emerge; in ch. 10 the hostile nations to the south are overthrown by remarkable divine intervention. The scheming of the five kings (v. 4) and their destruction (v. 26, 40–42) is like what is described in Ps. 2 (9:1, 2 note), and demonstrates the great power of God to fulfill His promises. This is the kind of battle described in Deut. 20, not ultimately fought by Israel but by God (v. 14 and Deut. 20:4).

10:1 Adoni-zedek. His name means "my Lord is righteous." Compare the name of Melchizedek, who was king in Salem (or Jerusalem); see Gen. 14:18 note.

Jerusalem. This is the first time this form of the city's name occurs in the Bible; in Gen. 14:18 it is referred to as "Salem."

destruction. See notes 6:17, 18.

peace. See 9:15.

10:2 feared. See note 2:9.

a great city, like one of the royal cities. Gibeon did not have a king (9:11) but was as important as the Canaanite city-states with kings.

10:3 Hoham . . . Debir. These were the kings of five southern Canaanite cities.

Hebron, to Piram king of Jarmuth, to
Japhia king of Lachish, and to Debir king of
Eglon, saying, 4 "Come up to me and help
me, and let us strike Gibeon. For [q]it has
made peace with Joshua and with the people of Israel." 5 Then the five kings of the
Amorites, the king of Jerusalem, the king of
Hebron, the king of Jarmuth, the king of
Lachish, and the king of Eglon, [r]gathered
their forces and went up with all their
armies and encamped against Gibeon and
made war against it.
6 And the men of Gibeon sent to Joshua
[s]at the camp in Gilgal, saying, "Do not
relax your hand from your servants. Come
up to us quickly and save us and help us,
for all the kings of the Amorites who dwell
in the hill country are gathered against us."
7 So Joshua went up from Gilgal, he and [t]all
the people of war with him, and all the
mighty men of valor. 8 And the LORD said to
Joshua, [u]"Do not fear them, for I have given
them into your hands. [v]Not a man of them
shall stand before you." 9 So Joshua came
upon them suddenly, having marched up
all night from Gilgal. 10 [w]And the LORD
threw them into a panic before Israel, who [1]
struck them with a great blow at Gibeon
and chased them by the way of [x]the ascent
of Beth-horon and struck them as far as
Azekah and Makkedah. 11 And as they fled
before Israel, while they were [x]going down
the ascent of Beth-horon, [y]the LORD threw
down large stones from heaven on them as
far as Azekah, and they died. There were
more who died because of the hailstones
than the sons of Israel killed with the sword.
12 At that time Joshua spoke to the LORD
in the day when the LORD gave the
Amorites over to the sons of Israel, and he
said in the sight of Israel,

[z]"Sun, stand still at Gibeon,
and moon, in the Valley of Aijalon."
13 And the sun stood still, and the
moon stopped,
until the nation took vengeance on
their enemies.

Is this not written in the Book of Jashar?
The sun stopped in the midst of heaven
and did not hurry to set for about a whole
day. 14 [a]There has been no day like it before
or since, when the LORD obeyed the voice
of a man, for [b]the LORD fought for Israel.
15 So [c]Joshua returned, and all Israel with
him, to the camp at Gilgal.

Five Amorite Kings Executed

16 These five kings fled and hid themselves in the cave at [d]Makkedah. 17 And it
was told to Joshua, "The five kings have
been found, hidden in the cave at Makkedah." 18 And Joshua said, "Roll large stones
against the mouth of the cave and set men
by it to guard them, 19 but do not stay there
yourselves. Pursue your enemies; [e]attack
their rear guard. Do not let them enter their
cities, for the LORD your God has given
them into your hand." 20 When Joshua and
the sons of Israel had finished striking them
with a great blow [f]until they were wiped
out, and when the remnant that remained
of them had entered into the fortified cities,
21 then all the people returned safe to Joshua
in the camp at Makkedah. [g]Not a man

4 [q]ver. 1; ch. 9:15
5 [r]ch. 9:2
6 [s]ch. 5:10; 9:6
7 [t]ch. 8:1, 3
8 [u]ch. 11:6; Judg. 4:14 [v]ch. 1:5
10 [w]Judg. 4:15; 1 Sam. 7:10; Ps. 18:14; Isai. 28:21 [x]ch. 16:3, 5; 18:13, 14; 1 Kin. 9:17; 1 Chr. 7:24; 2 Chr. 8:5
11 [x][See ver. 10 above] [y][Ps. 18:12-14; Isai. 30:30; Rev. 16:21]
12 [z]Hab. 3:11; [Isai. 28:21]
14 [a]Isai. 38:8 [2 Kin. 20:11] [b]ver. 42; ch. 23:3, 10
15 [c]ver. 43
16 [d]ver. 10, 28, 29
19 [e][Deut. 25:18]
20 [f]ch. 8:24
21 [g]Ex. 11:7

[1] Or *and he*

10:5 Amorites. See note 2:10.

10:6 save us and help us. The treaty relationship between Gibeon and Israel (9:15) allowed Gibeon to appeal for help from Israel, the stronger of the treaty partners. This aspect of a human covenant illustrates an aspect of the covenant between God and Israel.

10:8 Do not fear . . . I have given them. The particular actions in this chapter take place under the promises of God introduced in ch. 1. See 1:2, 3, 5–9; 8:1 and notes.

10:9 all night. Gilgal was at the bottom of the Jordan Valley and Gibeon was on top of a mountain twenty miles to the west.

10:10 threw them into a panic. The same expression is often used in descriptions of battles where the Lord is the Divine Warrior (2:9 note; Ex. 14:24; 23:27; Judg. 4:15; 1 Sam. 7:10; 2 Sam. 22:15; cf. Jer. 51:34).

10:11 more who died because of the hailstones. This emphasizes that the victory was a gift to Israel. Experiences like this illuminate the use of storm phenomena in poetic descriptions of God's judgment (Ps. 18:7–16; Is. 30:30).

10:12 in the day. This account may be a flashback; the chronological order of events is hard to discern.

"Sun . . . moon." These rhetorical words addressed to the sun and moon are in reality a prayer to the Lord.

10:13 the sun stood still. The words describe what happened in everyday language that does not explain the nature of the miracle.

the Book of Jashar. A literary work now lost, possibly a celebration of the lives of Israelite heroes (2 Sam. 1:18). The quotation from the Book of Jashar may extend as far as the end of v. 15. The biblical writers often use written sources (Luke 1:1–4).

10:14 the LORD fought for Israel. See Deut. 20, especially v. 4; cf. Ex. 14:14.

10:16–27 The narrative returns to the events of v. 10 to finish the story of the five kings introduced in v. 5.

10:19 the LORD . . . has given. The action of God, in terms of His promise, still dominates the account. See vv. 8, 10, 14.

10:21 Not a man moved his tongue. Not even a word, let alone a weapon, could be raised against God's army.

moved his tongue against any of the people of Israel.

22 Then Joshua said, "Open the mouth of the cave and bring those five kings out to me from the cave." 23 And they did so, and brought those five kings out to him from the cave, the king of Jerusalem, the king of Hebron, the king of Jarmuth, the king of Lachish, and the king of Eglon. 24 And when they brought those kings out to Joshua, Joshua summoned all the men of Israel and said to the chiefs of the men of war who had gone with him, "Come near; put your feet on the necks of these kings." Then they came near and put their feet on their necks. 25 And Joshua said to them, [h]"Do not be afraid or dismayed; be strong and courageous. [i]For thus the LORD will do to all your enemies against whom you fight." 26 And afterward Joshua struck them and put them to death, and he hanged them on five trees. And [j]they hung on the trees until evening. 27 But at the time of the going down of the sun, Joshua commanded, and [k]they took them down from the trees and threw them into the cave where they had hidden themselves, and they set large stones against the mouth of the cave, which remain to this very day.

28 As for [l]Makkedah, Joshua captured it on that day and struck it, and its king, with the edge of the sword. He devoted to destruction every person in it; he left none remaining. And he did to the king of Makkedah [m]just as he had done to the king of Jericho.

Conquest of Southern Canaan

29 Then Joshua and all Israel with him passed on from Makkedah to [n]Libnah and fought against Libnah. 30 And the LORD gave it also and its king into the hand of Israel. And he struck it with the edge of the sword, and every person in it; he left none remaining in it. And he did to its king [m]as he had done to the king of Jericho.

31 Then Joshua and all Israel with him passed on from Libnah to [o]Lachish and laid siege to it and fought against it. 32 And the LORD gave Lachish into the hand of Israel, and he captured it on the second day and struck it with the edge of the sword, and every person in it, as he had done to Libnah.

33 Then Horam king of [p]Gezer came up to help Lachish. And Joshua struck him and his people, until he left none remaining.

34 Then Joshua and all Israel with him passed on from Lachish to [q]Eglon. And they laid siege to it and fought against it. 35 And they captured it on that day, and struck it with the edge of the sword. And he devoted every person in it to destruction that day, as he had done to Lachish.

36 Then Joshua and all Israel with him went up from Eglon to [r]Hebron. And they fought against it 37 and captured it and struck it with the edge of the sword, and its king and its towns, and every person in it. He left none remaining, as he had done to Eglon, and devoted it to destruction and every person in it.

38 Then Joshua and all Israel with him turned back to [s]Debir and fought against it 39 and he captured it with its king and all its towns. And they struck them with the edge of the sword and devoted to destruction every person in it; he left none remaining. Just as he had done to Hebron and to Libnah and its king, so he did to Debir and to its king.

40 So Joshua struck the whole land, the hill country and the Negeb and the lowland [t]and the slopes, and all their kings. He left none remaining, [u]but devoted to destruction all that breathed, just as the LORD God of Israel commanded. 41 And Joshua struck them from [v]Kadesh-barnea as far as Gaza, and all the country of [w]Goshen, as far as Gibeon. 42 And Joshua captured all these kings and their land at one time, [x]because the LORD God of Israel fought for Israel. 43 [y]Then Joshua returned, and all Israel with him, to the camp at Gilgal.

25 [h]ch. 1:6, 9; See Deut. 31:6-8 [i]Deut. 3:21; 7:19
26 [j]ch. 8:29
27 [k]Deut. 21:22, 23
28 [l]ver. 10, 16, 17 [m]ch. 6:21
29 [n]ch. 21:13
30 [m][See ver. 28 above]
31 [o]ver. 3
33 [p]ch. 16:10; Judg. 1:29; See 1 Kin. 9:15-17
34 [q]ver. 3
36 [r]ch. 15:13; Judg. 1:10; See ch. 14:13-15
38 [s]See ch. 15:15-17; Judg. 1:11-13
40 [t]ch. 12:8 [u]Deut. 20:16, 17
41 [v]Deut. 9:23 [w]ch. 11:16
42 [x]ver. 14
43 [y]ver. 15

10:24 your feet on the necks. This is a vivid, symbolic ritual of victory. Defeated enemies are often said to be "under the feet" of the victor (1 Kin. 5:3; Ps. 110:1; 1 Cor. 15:25), and Egyptian royal footstools depict the Pharaoh's feet on his enemies' necks.

10:26 hanged them on five trees. See note 8:29.

10:27 to this very day. See note 4:9.

10:28–39 These verses are a summary account of victories over cities in southern Canaan. The account emphasizes the complete destruction of the towns according to the judgment of God (vv. 28–39; 6:17, 18 and notes). Another emphasis is the unity of Israel (1:12–15) under Joshua's leadership (1:1–9).

Conquests in Northern Canaan

11 When Jabin, king of Hazor, heard of
this, he [z]sent to Jobab king of Madon,
and to the king of Shimron, and to the king
of Achshaph, 2 and to the kings who were in
the northern hill country, and in the [a]Arabah
south of [b]Chinneroth, and in the lowland,
and [c]in Naphoth-dor on the [d]west, 3 to the
Canaanites in the east and the west, the Amorites, the Hittites, the Perizzites, and the
[e]Jebusites in the hill country, and the [f]Hivites
under [g]Hermon in the land of [h]Mizpah.
4 And they came out with all their troops, a
great horde, in number [i]like the sand that is
on the seashore, with very many horses and
chariots. 5 And all these kings joined their
forces and came and encamped together at
the waters of Merom to fight with Israel.
6 And the LORD said to Joshua, [j]"Do not
be afraid of them, for tomorrow at this time
I will give over all of them, slain, to Israel.
You shall [k]hamstring their horses and burn
their [l]chariots with fire." 7 So Joshua and all
his warriors came [m]suddenly against them
by the waters of Merom and fell upon
them. 8 And the LORD gave them into the
hand of Israel, who struck them and
chased them as far as [n]Great Sidon and
[o]Misrephoth-maim, and eastward as far as
the Valley of [p]Mizpeh. And they struck
them until he left none remaining. 9 And
Joshua did to them [q]just as the LORD said
to him: he hamstrung their horses and
burned their chariots with fire.
10 And Joshua turned back at that time
and captured [r]Hazor and struck its king
with the sword, for Hazor formerly was the
head of all those kingdoms. 11 And they
struck with the sword all who were in it,
devoting them to destruction;[1] [s]there was
none left that breathed. And he burned
Hazor with fire. 12 And all the cities of those
kings, and all their kings, Joshua captured,
and struck them with the edge of the
sword, devoting them to destruction, [t]just
as Moses the servant of the LORD had commanded. 13 But none of the cities that stood
on mounds did Israel burn, except Hazor
alone; that Joshua burned. 14 And all the
spoil of these cities and the livestock, the
people of Israel took for their plunder. But
every man they struck with the edge of the
sword until they had destroyed them, and
they did not leave any who breathed. 15 [u]Just
as the LORD had commanded Moses his servant, [v]so Moses commanded Joshua, [w]and
so Joshua did. He left nothing undone of all
that the LORD had commanded Moses.
16 So Joshua took all that land, [x]the hill
country and all the Negeb and [y]all the land
of Goshen [z]and the lowland [z]and the
Arabah [a]and the hill country of Israel and
its lowland 17 [b]from Mount Halak, which
rises toward Seir, as far as [c]Baal-gad in the
Valley of Lebanon below [d]Mount Hermon.
And he captured [e]all their kings and struck
them and put them to death. 18 Joshua
made war [f]a long time with all those kings.
19 There was not a city that made peace
with the people of Israel except [g]the
Hivites, the inhabitants of Gibeon. They
took them all in battle. 20 For it was the

[1] That is, setting apart (devoting) as an offering to the Lord (for destruction); also verses 12, 20, 21

Chapter 11
1 [z]ch. 10:3
2 [a]ch. 3:16; Deut. 1:1
[b]ch. 12:3; 13:27; 19:35; Num. 34:11
[c]ch. 12:23
[d]ch. 17:11; Judg. 1:27
3 [e]ch. 15:63
[f]Judg. 3:3
[g]See Deut. 3:8 [h]ver. 8; Gen. 31:49
4 [i]Gen. 22:17; 32:12; Judg. 7:12; 1 Sam. 13:5
6 [j][ch. 10:8]
[k]ver. 9; 2 Sam. 8:4; 1 Chr. 18:4; [Gen. 49:6]
[l]ch. 17:16-18; Deut. 20:1; Judg. 1:19; 4:3
7 [m]ch. 10:9
8 [n]ch. 19:28
[o]ch. 13:6
[p]ver. 3
9 [q]ver. 6
10 [r][Judg. 4:2]
11 [s]ch. 10:40
12 [t]Deut. 20:16, 17
15 [u]Ex. 34:11, 12 [v]Deut. 7:2
[w]ch. 1:7
16 [x]ch. 12:8
[y]ch. 10:41; 15:51 [z]ver. 2
[a]ver. 21
17 [b]ch. 12:7
[c]ch. 12:7; 13:5 [d]See ch. 11:3 [e]ch. 12:7; Deut. 7:24
18 [f][ch. 14:7, 10]
19 [g]ch. 9:3, 7

11:1–23 The account of the conquest of the northern region of Palestine is similar in its emphases to the report of the southern victories in ch. 10 (10:1–43 note), and brings the book's record of Israel's taking of the land to a conclusion.

11:1–5 Compare the reaction of the Canaanite kings in 10:1–5.

11:1 Jabin, king of Hazor. Hazor was an important city in northern Palestine (v. 10). Jabin was possibly an inherited title (Judg. 4:2).

heard. See note 9:3.

11:2 Chinneroth. Probably near the Sea of Galilee (12:3).

the lowland. The Jordan Valley.

Naphoth-dor. On the Mediterranean coast.

11:4 a great horde. The enormous threat posed by the Canaanites is vividly presented as the background to the promise in v. 6.

11:6 Do not be afraid. The promise of God (1:2, 3, 9), against the background of vv. 4, 5, again creates a possibility not inherent in the situation. See notes 6:2; 8:1; 10:8.

I will give. The Hebrew wording is emphatic and identical to "I am giving" in 1:2.

hamstring their horses and burn their chariots. This is a promise that God will prevail over the most advanced weapons of the time (Ps. 20:7).

11:11 devoting them to destruction. The same term occurs in vv. 12, 20, 21. See note 6:17.

11:12 as Moses the servant of the LORD had commanded. The success of the conquest is emphatically portrayed in terms of obedience to the commands of God given through Moses (1:1–18; 1:1, 3; 5:15 and notes). The writer makes the closest possible connection between the promises of God (v. 6 note) and His commands. Faith and obedience cannot be separated. See note 1:7.

11:16 all that land. In principle the whole land now belonged to the Israelites, although there was "yet very much land to possess" (13:1).

11:18 a long time. This is an indication that the preceding chapters present a greatly condensed account.

11:19 made peace. See 9:6, 15.

11:20 it was the LORD's doing to harden. The relationship between divine sovereignty and human responsibility is seen in the divine hardening of hearts to achieve His purposes. God's sovereign act does not overthrow either His justice or human responsibility (Ex. 10:1, 2; Rom. 9:14–29).

LORD's doing [h]to harden their hearts that they should come against Israel in battle, in order that they should be devoted to destruction and should receive no mercy but be destroyed, [i]just as the LORD commanded Moses.

21 And Joshua came at that time and cut off [j]the Anakim from the hill country, from Hebron, from Debir, from Anab, and from all the hill country of Judah, and from all the hill country of Israel. Joshua devoted them to destruction with their cities. 22 There was none of the Anakim left in the land of the people of Israel. Only in Gaza, [k]in Gath, and in Ashdod did some remain. 23 So Joshua took the whole land, [l]according to all that the LORD had spoken to Moses. [m]And Joshua gave it for an inheritance to Israel [n]according to their tribal allotments. And the land had rest from war.

Kings Defeated by Moses

12 Now these are the kings of the land whom the people of Israel defeated and took possession of their land beyond the Jordan toward the sunrise, from [o]the Valley of the Arnon to Mount Hermon, with all [p]the Arabah eastward: 2 [q]Sihon king of the Amorites who lived at Heshbon and ruled from Aroer, which is on the edge of the Valley of the Arnon, and [r]from the middle of the valley as far as the [s]river Jabbok, the boundary of the Ammonites, that is, half of Gilead, 3 and [p]the Arabah [t]to the Sea of Chinneroth eastward, and in the direction of Beth-jeshimoth, to the Sea of the Arabah, the Salt Sea, southward to the foot of [u]the slopes of Pisgah; 4 and [v]Og[1] king of Bashan, one of the remnant of [w]the Rephaim, [x]who lived at Ashtaroth and at Edrei 5 and ruled over [y]Mount Hermon and [z]Salecah and all Bashan [a]to the boundary of the Geshurites and the Maacathites, and over half of Gilead to the boundary of Sihon king of Heshbon. 6 [b]Moses, the servant of the LORD, and the people of Israel defeated them. And Moses the servant of the LORD [c]gave their land for a possession to the Reubenites and the Gadites and the half-tribe of Manasseh.

Kings Defeated by Joshua

7 And these are the kings of the land whom Joshua and the people of Israel defeated on the west side of the Jordan, from Baal-gad in the Valley of Lebanon to [d]Mount Halak, that rises toward Seir (and Joshua gave their land to the tribes of Israel as a possession [e]according to their allotments, 8 [f]in the hill country, in the lowland, in the Arabah, in the slopes, in the wilderness, and in the Negeb, the land of [g]the Hittites, the Amorites, the Canaanites, the Perizzites, the Hivites, and the Jebusites): 9 [h]the king of Jericho, one; [i]the king of Ai, which is beside Bethel, one; 10 [j]the king of Jerusalem, one; [j]the king of Hebron, one; 11 [j]the king of Jarmuth, one; [j]the king of Lachish, one; 12 [j]the king of Eglon, one; [k]the king of Gezer, one; 13 [l]the king of Debir, one; the king of Geder, one; 14 the king of Hormah, one; the king of Arad, one; 15 [m]the king of Libnah, one; the king of Adullam, one; 16 [n]the king of Makkedah, one; [o]the king of Bethel, one; 17 the king of Tappuah, one; the king of Hepher, one; 18 the king of Aphek, one; the king of Lasharon, one; 19 [p]the king of Madon, one; [q]the king of Hazor, one; 20 [p]the king of Shimron-meron, one; [p]the king of Achshaph, one; 21 [r]the king of Taanach, one; [r]the king of Megiddo, one; 22 the king of

1 Septuagint; Hebrew *the boundary of Og*

20 [h]See Ex. 4:21 [i]Deut. 20:16, 17
21 [j]ch. 15:13, 14; Num. 13:22, 23; Deut. 1:28
22 [k][1 Sam. 17:4]
23 [l]See Num. 34:2-12 [m]See ch. 14–ch. 19; Num. 26:52-56 [n]ch. 12:7; 18:10
Chapter 12
1 [o]Num. 21:13, 24; Deut. 3:8, 9 [p]See Deut. 1:1
2 [q]Deut. 2:32, 33; 3:6, 16; See Num. 21:21-26 [r]Deut. 2:36 [s]Gen. 32:22
3 [p][See ver. 1 above] [t]ch. 11:2 [u]ch. 13:20; Deut. 3:17; 4:49
4 [v]Deut. 3:3, 10; See Num. 21:33-35 [w]ch. 13:12; 15:8; 18:16 [x]ch. 9:10; Deut. 1:4
5 [y]Deut. 3:8, 9 [z]ch. 13:11; Deut. 3:10 [a]Deut. 3:14
6 [b]See Num. 21:23, 24; 33-35 [c]ch. 13:8; Num. 32:29, 33; Deut. 3:11, 12
7 [d]ch. 11:17 [e]ch. 11:23; 18:10
8 [f]ch. 10:40; 11:16 [g]ch. 9:1
9 [h][ch. 6:2] [i]ch. 8:29
10 [j]ch. 10:23
11 [j][See ver. 10 above]
12 [j][See ver. 10 above] [k]ch. 10:33
13 [l]ch. 10:38, 39
15 [m]ch. 10:29
16 [n]ch. 10:28 [o]ch. 8:17; Judg. 1:22
19 [p]ch. 11:1 [q]ch. 11:1, 10
20 [p][See ver. 19 above]
21 [r]ch. 17:11

11:21, 22 Anakim. These people were the fearful inhabitants of Canaan who had frightened the Israelites into disobedience a generation earlier (Num. 13:26–33; Deut. 1:28; 2:10–12 and notes; Josh. 14:12; 15:14). Their destruction concludes the account of the obedient conquest under Joshua.

11:23 an inheritance . . . according to their tribal allotments. This is an anticipatory summary of chs. 13–21. See note 1:6.

the land had rest from war. These words sum up the conquest and the fulfillment of God's promise given in 1:2–5. See notes 1:13; 21:45.

12:1–24 This chapter summarizes the entire conquest under Moses and Joshua with a list of defeated kings and territories. It is an elaboration of 11:17, a striking resolution to 9:1, 2 (note), and a testimony to the truth of the promise in 1:5, providing a fitting conclusion to the whole account of the conquest.

12:1 land. Notice that the territory east of the Jordan is clearly included in the land given by God to Israel (v. 7). See notes 1:12–15; 13:8–33.

Valley of the Arnon. This runs into the Dead Sea from the east and marks the southern boundary here.

Mount Hermon. Northeast of the Sea of Galilee.

12:2–5 See Num. 21:21–35; Deut. 2:24–3:11. The defeat of Sihon and Og marked the beginning of the conquest and is remembered as a testimony to God's power and faithfulness (e.g., Deut. 29:7, 8; 31:4; Josh. 2:10; 9:10; Neh. 9:22; Ps. 135:11; 136:19, 20).

12:6 Moses, the servant of the LORD. See note 1:1.

12:7–24 This summary of the conquest under Joshua approximates the account so far given, but with additions, indicating the incomplete and representative nature of the preceding account.

Kedesh, one; the king of Jokneam in Carmel, one; [23] [r]the king of Dor in [s]Naphath-
dor, one; the king of Goiim in Galilee,[1]
one; [24] the king of Tirzah, one: in all, thirty-
one kings.

Land Still to Be Conquered

13 Now Joshua [t]was old and advanced
in years, and the LORD said to him,
"You are old and advanced in years, and
there remains yet very much land [u]to possess. [2] [v]This is the land that yet remains: all
the [w]regions of the Philistines, and all those
of the Geshurites [3] (from the [x]Shihor,
which is east of Egypt, northward to the
boundary of Ekron, it is counted as

23 [r][See ver. 21 above] [s]ch. 11:2
Chapter 13
1 [t]ch. 14:10; 23:1
[u]Deut. 31:3
2 [v]Judg. 3:1
[w]Joel 3:4
3 [x]1 Chr. 13:5; Jer. 2:18

[1] Septuagint; Hebrew *Gilgal*

13:1–21:45 The third major section of the book details the division of the land among the tribes. The significance of these chapters is made explicit in 21:43–45. The lists of boundaries and towns represent the objective content of the promises of God. Although many of the places are no longer known, and although their allotment here did not in all cases mean that the designated tribe actually occupied them (23:13), they nevertheless are an elaborate testimony to the faithfulness of the Lord.

13:1 Joshua was old. The implication is that further conquest will not take place under him.

very much land. The Book of Joshua speaks of both the complete fulfillment of God's promises (11:23; 21:45) and the incompleteness of the actual possession of the land (e.g., 13:1; 23:4–5). Compare the New Testament perspective of the completeness of what has been given in Christ, and the future expectation that still remains (e.g., Eph. 1:3, 14). While the Book of Joshua testifies to Israel's experience of the Lord's complete faithfulness, the promise remained, pointing to the future. See notes 1:4; 21:45; Gen. 13:15.

13:3 counted as Canaanite. The Philistines were not strictly speaking Canaanites, but their territory was in Canaan and was included in God's promise to Israel.

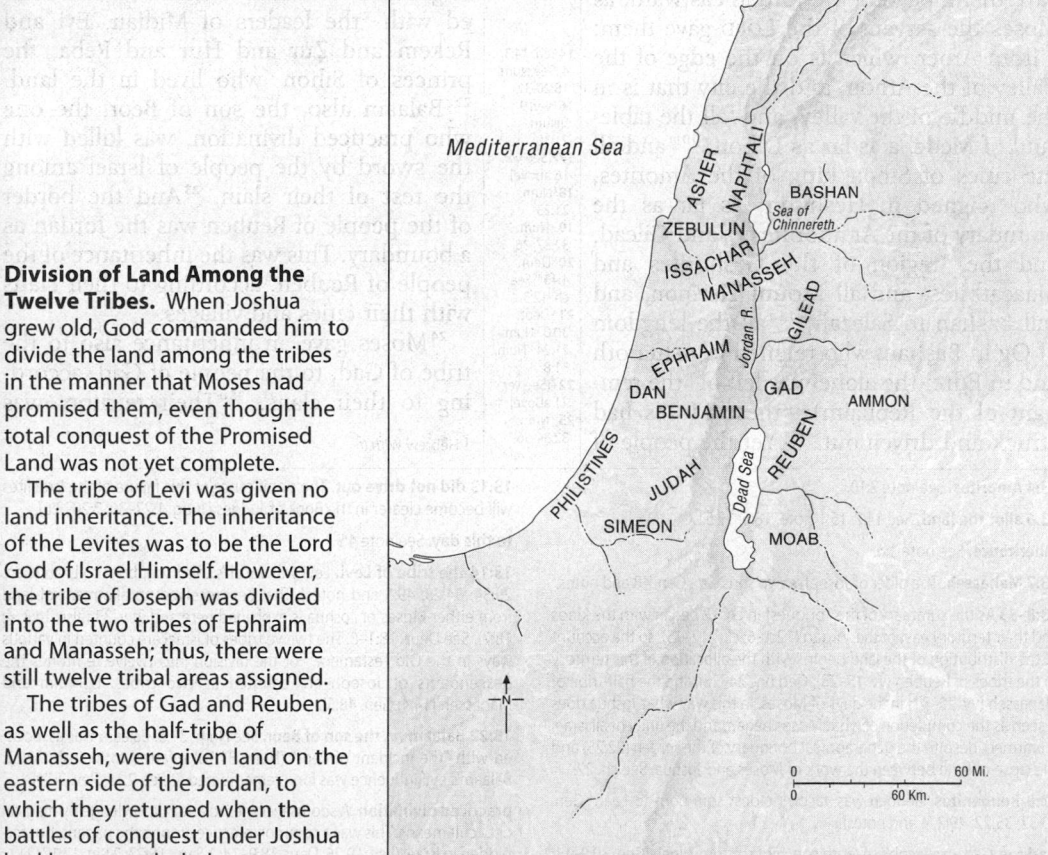

Division of Land Among the Twelve Tribes. When Joshua grew old, God commanded him to divide the land among the tribes in the manner that Moses had promised them, even though the total conquest of the Promised Land was not yet complete.

The tribe of Levi was given no land inheritance. The inheritance of the Levites was to be the Lord God of Israel Himself. However, the tribe of Joseph was divided into the two tribes of Ephraim and Manasseh; thus, there were still twelve tribal areas assigned.

The tribes of Gad and Reuben, as well as the half-tribe of Manasseh, were given land on the eastern side of the Jordan, to which they returned when the battles of conquest under Joshua had been concluded.

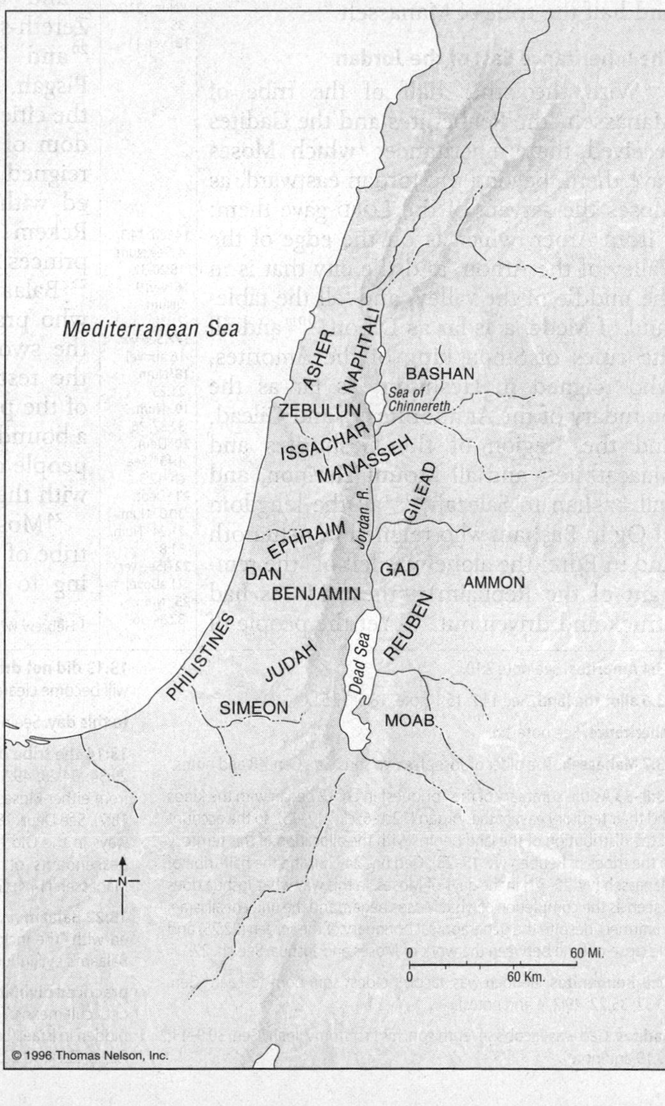

Canaanite; [y]there are five rulers of the
Philistines, those of Gaza, Ashdod, Ashkelon, Gath, and Ekron), and those of [z]the
Avvim, 4 in the south, all the land of the
Canaanites, and Mearah that belongs to
the Sidonians, to Aphek, to the boundary
of [a]the Amorites, 5 and the land of the
[b]Gebalites, and all Lebanon, toward the
sunrise, from [c]Baal-gad below Mount
Hermon to [d]Lebo-hamath, 6 all the inhabitants of the hill country from Lebanon to
[e]Misrephoth-maim, even all the Sidonians.
I myself will drive [f]them out from before
the people of Israel. Only [g]allot the land to
Israel [h]for an inheritance, as I have commanded you. 7 Now therefore [i]divide this
land for an inheritance to the nine tribes
and half the tribe of Manasseh."

The Inheritance East of the Jordan

8 With the other half of the tribe of
Manasseh[1] the Reubenites and the Gadites
received their inheritance, [j]which Moses
gave them, beyond the Jordan eastward, as
Moses the servant of the LORD gave them:
9 [k]from Aroer, which is on the edge of the
Valley of the Arnon, and the city that is in
the middle of the valley, and [l]all the tableland of Medeba as far as Dibon; 10 [m]and all
the cities of Sihon king of the Amorites,
who reigned in Heshbon, as far as the
boundary of the Ammonites; 11 and Gilead,
and the [n]region of the Geshurites and
Maacathites, and all Mount Hermon, and
[n]all Bashan to Salecah; 12 [n]all the kingdom
of Og in Bashan, who reigned in Ashtaroth
and in Edrei (he alone was left of [n]the remnant of the Rephaim); [o]these Moses had
struck and driven out. 13 [p]Yet the people of
Israel did not drive out the Geshurites or
the Maacathites, but Geshur and Maacath
dwell in the midst of Israel to this day.
14 [q]To the tribe of Levi alone Moses gave
no inheritance. The offerings by fire to the
LORD God of Israel are their inheritance, as
he said to him.
15 And Moses gave an inheritance to the
tribe of the people of Reuben according to
their clans. 16 So their territory was from
Aroer, [r]which is on the edge of the Valley
of the Arnon, and the city that is in the
middle of the valley, and all the tableland
by [s]Medeba; 17 with Heshbon, and all its
cities that are in the tableland; [s]Dibon, and
Bamoth-baal, and Beth-baal-meon, 18 [t]and
Jahaz, and Kedemoth, and Mephaath,
19 and [u]Kiriathaim, and [u]Sibmah, and
Zereth-shahar on the hill of the valley,
20 and [v]Beth-peor, and [w]the slopes of
Pisgah, and [w]Beth-jeshimoth, 21 that is, [x]all
the cities of the tableland, and all the kingdom of Sihon king of the Amorites, who
reigned in Heshbon, [y]whom Moses defeated with [z]the leaders of Midian, Evi and
Rekem and Zur and Hur and Reba, the
princes of Sihon, who lived in the land.
22 [z]Balaam also, the son of Beor, the one
who practiced divination, was killed with
the sword by the people of Israel among
the rest of their slain. 23 And the border
of the people of Reuben was the Jordan as
a boundary. This was the inheritance of the
people of Reuben, according to their clans
with their cities and villages.
24 Moses gave an inheritance also to the
tribe of Gad, to the people of Gad, according to their clans. 25 [a]Their territory was

3 [y]Judg. 3:3 [z]Deut. 2:23
4 [a]See Judg. 1:34-36
5 [b]1 Kin. 5:18; Ps. 83:7; Ezek. 27:9 [c]ch. 11:17; 12:7 [d]Num. 34:8
6 [e]ch. 11:8 [f][ch. 23:13; Judg. 2:21-23] [g]ch. 23:4 [h]ch. 23:4; Num. 34:2
7 [i]ch. 14:1, 2
8 [j]ch. 12:6; See Num. 32:33
9 [k]Deut. 2:36 [l]ver. 16; [Num. 21:30]
10 [m]Num. 21:24, 25
11 [n]Deut. 3:14
12 [n][See ver. 11 above] [o]Num. 21:24, 35
13 [p]ver. 11
14 [q]ch. 14:3, 4; See Num. 18:20-32
16 [r]ver. 9 [s][Num. 21:30]
17 [s][See ver. 16 above]
18 [t]Num. 21:23
19 [u]Num. 32:37, 38
20 [v]Deut. 4:46 [w]See ch. 12:3
21 [x]Deut. 3:10 [y]Num. 21:24 [z]Num. 31:8
22 [z][See ver. 21 above]
25 [a]Num. 32:34-36

1 Hebrew *With it*

13:4 Amorites. See note 2:10.

13:6 allot the land. See 14:2; 15:1 note; 18:6; 19:51.

inheritance. See note 1:6.

13:7 Manasseh. The older of Joseph's two sons. See Gen. 48 and notes.

13:8–33 As the summary of the conquest in ch. 12 began with the kings and their territory east of the Jordan (12:1–6; cf. 1:12–15), so the account of the distribution of the land begins with the allocation of this territory to the tribes of Reuben (vv. 15–23), Gad (vv. 24–28), and the half-tribe of Manasseh (vv. 29–31) in the days of Moses. In this way what Joshua does is seen as the completion of what Moses began, and the unity of all Israel is affirmed, despite the geographical boundary of the Jordan (22:25) and the lapse of time between the work of Moses and Joshua. See ch. 22.

13:8 Reubenites. Reuben was Jacob's oldest son, born to Leah (Gen. 29:32; 35:22; 49:3, 4 and notes).

Gadites. Gad was Jacob's seventh son, his first from Zilpah (Gen. 30:9–11; 49:19 and note).

13:13 did not drive out. The significance of this failure of the Israelites will become clearer in the Book of Judges (Judg. 1:27–36; 2:20–3:6).

to this day. See note 4:9.

13:14 the tribe of Levi. Levi was Jacob's third son, born to Leah (Gen. 29:34; 34:25; 49:5 and notes). That Levi received no allotment of land from either Moses or Joshua is explained here and in v. 33 (also 14:3, 4; 18:7). See Deut. 18:1–8. The twelve tribes of Israel are counted in various ways in the Old Testament. For the division into twelve territories the descendants of Joseph are counted as two tribes, Ephraim and Manasseh (14:4; Gen. 48:5).

13:22 Balaam . . . the son of Beor. See Num. 31:8. Balaam was associated with "the incident of Peor" (Num. 31:16) referred to in Josh. 22:17. Balaam's evil influence was long remembered (2 Pet. 2:15; Rev. 2:14).

practiced divination. A soothsayer tries to attain knowledge by magical or occult means. This was a common practice among the pagans, but forbidden in Israel (Lev. 19:26; Deut. 18:9–14; 1 Sam. 15:23; 2 Kin. 17:17; 21:6; Is. 2:6; Ezek. 13:23).

Jazer, and all the cities of Gilead, and half
the land of the Ammonites, to Aroer, which
is east of [b]Rabbah, 26 and from Heshbon to
Ramath-mizpeh and Betonim, and from
[c]Mahanaim to the territory of Debir,[1] 27 and
in the valley Beth-haram, Beth-nimrah,
[d]Succoth, and Zaphon, the rest of the kingdom of Sihon king of Heshbon, having the
Jordan as a boundary, to the lower end of
the Sea of [e]Chinnereth, eastward beyond
the Jordan. 28 This is the inheritance of the
people of Gad according to their clans,
with their cities and villages.
29 And Moses gave an inheritance to the
half-tribe of Manasseh. It was allotted to
the half-tribe of the people of Manasseh
according to their clans. 30 Their region
extended from [f]Mahanaim, through all Bashan, the whole kingdom of Og king of
Bashan, and all [g]the towns of Jair, which
are in Bashan, sixty cities, 31 and half Gilead, and [h]Ashtaroth, and Edrei, the cities
of the kingdom of Og in Bashan. These
were allotted to the people of [i]Machir the
son of Manasseh for the half of the people
of Machir according to their clans.
32 These are the inheritances that Moses
distributed [j]in the plains of Moab, beyond
the Jordan east of Jericho. 33 [k]But to the
tribe of Levi Moses gave no inheritance; the
LORD God of Israel is their inheritance,
[k]just as he said to them.

The Inheritance West of the Jordan

14 These are the inheritances that the
people of Israel received in the land
of Canaan, which [l]Eleazar the priest and
Joshua the son of Nun and the heads of the
fathers' houses of the tribes of the people
of Israel gave them to inherit. 2 Their inheritance was [m]by lot, just as the LORD had
commanded by the hand of Moses for the
nine and one-half tribes. 3 [n]For Moses had
given an inheritance to the two and one-
half tribes beyond the Jordan, [o]but to the
Levites he gave no inheritance among
them. 4 For [p]the people of Joseph were two
tribes, Manasseh and Ephraim. And no
portion was given to the Levites in the
land, but only cities to dwell in, with their
pasturelands for their livestock and their
substance. 5 The people of Israel did [q]as the
LORD commanded Moses; they allotted the
land.

Caleb's Request and Inheritance

6 Then the people of Judah came to
Joshua at Gilgal. And Caleb the son of
Jephunneh the [r]Kenizzite said to him, "You
know [s]what the LORD said to Moses the
man of God in Kadesh-barnea concerning
you and me. 7 I was forty years old when
Moses the servant of the LORD [t]sent me
from Kadesh-barnea to spy out the land,
and I brought him word again as it was in
my heart. 8 But [u]my brothers who went up
with me made the heart of the people melt;
yet I wholly followed the LORD my God.
9 And Moses swore on that day, saying,
[v]'Surely the land [w]on which your foot has
trodden shall be an inheritance for you and
your children forever, because you have
wholly followed the LORD my God.' 10 And
now, behold, the LORD has kept me alive,
[x]just as he said, these [y]forty-five years since
the time that the LORD spoke this word to
Moses, while Israel walked in the wilderness. And now, behold, I am this day
[y]eighty-five years old. 11 [z]I am still as strong
today as I was in the day that Moses sent
me; my strength now is as my strength was

[1] Septuagint, Syriac, Vulgate; Hebrew *Lidebir*

25 [b][Deut. 3:11; 2 Sam. 11:1; 12:26]
26 [c]Gen. 32:2; 2 Sam. 2:8, 12; 17:24
27 [d]Gen. 33:17 [e]See ch. 11:2
30 [f]See ver. 26 [g]Num. 32:41; 1 Chr. 2:23; [Deut. 3:14]
31 [h]ch. 12:4 [i]ch. 17:1; Num. 32:39, 40
32 [j]Num. 22:1
33 [k]ver. 14; ch. 18:7; Num. 18:20
Chapter 14
1 [l]ch. 17:4; 21:1; Num. 34:17, 18
2 [m]Num. 26:56; 33:54; 34:13
3 [n]See ch. 13:8 [o]See ch. 13:33
4 [p]Gen. 48:5; 1 Chr. 5:1, 2
5 [q]ch. 21:2; Num. 35:1, 2
6 [r]ver. 13, 14; Num. 32:12; [ch. 15:17] [s]Num. 14:24, 30; Deut. 1:36, 38
7 [t]Num. 13:6, 16, 30; 14:6-9
8 [u]Deut. 1:28; See Num. 13:31-33
9 [v]Num. 14:24; Deut. 1:36 [w]ch. 1:3
10 [x]Num. 14:30 [y][ver. 7]
11 [z][Deut. 34:7]
11 [a]Deut. 31:2

13:33 the tribe of Levi. See note on v. 14.

14:1–5 This introduces the territories west of the Jordan and relates them to those on the east, explaining again the exception of the Levites. The effect is to keep the reader's attention on the essential unity of all Israel. See note 13:8–33.

14:1 inherit. See note 1:6.

Canaan. Here this means the land west of the Jordan.

Eleazar the priest. Eleazar was the son of Aaron the high priest (Ex. 6:23). He is mentioned before Joshua, possibly because of the priest's role in casting lots (Ex. 28:30; 1 Sam. 2:28).

14:2 by lot. See note 15:1.

14:3, 4 the Levites . . . Manasseh and Ephraim. See note 13:14.

14:6–15 The story of Caleb's inheritance opens the account of the allotment of land under Joshua, while Joshua's inheritance comes at the end (19:49–50). This framework illustrates the principles of human faithfulness to God met by God's faithfulness to His promises. The story of Caleb is concluded in 15:13–19.

14:6 Gilgal. This is probably the same Gilgal as in 10:43, to the east of Jericho.

Caleb. He represented Judah among the twelve spies sent by Moses from Kadesh-barnea into the land (Num. 13:6). Caleb and Joshua represented Ephraim on the same mission (Num. 13:8) and were the only two on that occasion to believe the promise of God (Num. 13:30; 14:6–9, 24, 30, 38; Deut. 1:36).

14:7 as it was in my heart. Caleb's report had expressed his trust in God's promise. See Num. 14:6–9.

14:8 I wholly followed the LORD. Caleb's faith is exemplary.

14:9 Moses swore. This oath is not recorded in Num. 14 or Deut. 1.

then, for war and [a]for going and coming.
12 So now give me this hill country of which
the LORD spoke on that day, for you heard
on that day how the [b]Anakim were there,
with great fortified cities. It may be that the
LORD will be with me, and I shall drive
them out just as the LORD said."
13 Then Joshua [c]blessed him, and he gave
[d]Hebron to Caleb the son of Jephunneh for
an inheritance. 14 Therefore Hebron became
the inheritance of Caleb the son of
Jephunneh the Kenizzite to this day, [e]be-
cause he wholly followed the LORD, the
God of Israel. 15 [f]Now the name of Hebron
formerly was Kiriath-arba.[1] (Arba[2] was the
greatest man among the Anakim.) [g]And the
land had rest from war.

The Allotment for Judah

15 The allotment for the tribe of the
people of Judah according to their
clans reached southward [h]to the boundary
of Edom, to [i]the wilderness of Zin at the farthest south. 2 And their south boundary ran
from the end of the [h]Salt Sea, from the bay
that faces southward. 3 It goes out southward of [j]the ascent of Akrabbim, passes
along to Zin, and goes up south of Kadesh-
barnea, along by Hezron, up to Addar, turns
about to Karka, 4 passes along to Azmon,
goes out by [k]the Brook of Egypt, and comes
to its end at the sea. This shall be your south
boundary. 5 And the east boundary is the
[h]Salt Sea, to the mouth of the Jordan. And
the boundary on the north side runs from
the bay of the sea at the mouth of the
Jordan. 6 And the boundary goes up to [l]Beth-
hoglah and passes along north of [m]Beth-
arabah. And the boundary goes up to [n]the
stone of Bohan the son of Reuben. 7 And the
boundary goes up to Debir from [o]the Valley
of Achor, and so northward, turning toward
Gilgal, which is opposite [p]the ascent of
Adummim, which is on the south side of
the valley. And the boundary passes along
to the waters of [p]En-shemesh and ends at
[q]En-rogel. 8 Then the boundary goes up by
[r]the Valley of the Son of Hinnom at the
southern shoulder of the Jebusite ([s]that is,
Jerusalem). And the boundary goes up to
the top of the mountain that lies over
against the Valley of Hinnom, on the west,
at the northern end of the Valley [t]of
Rephaim. 9 Then the boundary extends
from the top of the mountain [u]to the spring
of the waters of Nephtoah, and from there
to the cities of Mount Ephron. Then the
boundary bends around to Baalah ([v]that is,
Kiriath-jearim). 10 And the boundary circles
west of Baalah to Mount Seir, passes along
to the northern shoulder of Mount Jearim
(that is, Chesalon), and goes down to
[w]Beth-shemesh and passes along by [x]Tim-
nah. 11 The boundary goes out [y]to the shoulder of the hill north of Ekron, then the
boundary bends around to Shikkeron and
passes along to Mount [z]Baalah and goes out
to Jabneel. Then the boundary comes to an
end at the sea. 12 And the west boundary
was [a]the Great Sea with its coastline. This is
the boundary around the people of Judah
according to their clans.
13 According to the commandment of the
LORD to Joshua, he gave to Caleb the son of
Jephunneh a portion among the people of
Judah, [b]Kiriath-arba, that is, [b]Hebron (Arba
was the father of Anak). 14 And Caleb drove
out from there the three sons of Anak,
[c]Sheshai and Ahiman and Talmai, the
descendants of Anak. 15 And he went up
from there against the inhabitants of Debir.
[d]Now the name of Debir formerly was
Kiriath-sepher. 16 And Caleb said, "Whoever strikes Kiriath-sepher and captures it,
to him will I give Achsah my daughter as
wife." 17 [e]And Othniel the son of Kenaz,

12 [b]Num. 13:28, 33
13 [c]ch. 22:6 [d]ch. 10:36, 37; 15:13, 14; 21:11, 12; Judg. 1:20; 1 Chr. 6:55, 56
14 [e]ver. 8, 9
15 [f]ver. 13; Gen. 23:2; 35:27; Judg. 1:10; See ch. 10:36 [g]See ch. 11:23
Chapter 15
1 [h]Num. 34:3 [i]Num. 33:36
2 [h][See ver. 1 above]
3 [j]Num. 34:4; Judg. 1:36
4 [k]ver. 47; Num. 34:5; [ch. 13:3]
5 [h][See ver. 1 above]
6 [l]ch. 18:19, 21 [m]ch. 18:18, 22 [n]ch. 18:17
7 [o]ch. 7:26 [p]ch. 18:17 [q]ch. 18:16 2 Sam. 17:17; 1 Kin. 1:9
8 [r]ch. 18:16; 2 Kin. 23:10 [s]ver. 63; ch. 18:28; [Judg. 19:10; 1 Chr. 11:4] [t]ch. 18:16; See ch. 12:4
9 [u]ch. 18:15 [v]ver. 60; 1 Chr. 13:6
10 [w]1 Sam. 6:9, 12 [x]Gen. 38:12-14; Judg. 14:1
11 [y]ch. 13:3 [z]ver. 9
12 [a]ver. 47; ch. 23:4; Num. 34:6, 7; Ezek. 47:20
13 [b]ver. 54; See ch. 14:13-15
14 [c]Num. 13:22; Judg. 1:10, 20
15 [d]Judg. 1:11; [ver. 49]
17 [e]See Judg. 1:13

[1] *Kiriath-arba* means *the city of Arba* [2] Hebrew *He*

14:12 Anakim. See note 11:21, 22.

I shall drive them out. Faith in God's promise is not expressed in human passivity, but in active obedience. See notes 1:6, 7; 17:15.

14:14 to this day. See note 4:9.

14:15 the land had rest from war. See note 11:23.

15:1–63 The first territory west of the Jordan to be described is Judah's, anticipating the importance of Judah in the later history of Israel as the tribe of David and finally of the Messiah to come (Is. 11:1; see also Gen. 49:8–12). The place names cannot all be identified. Also, the allocation was never followed completely or exactly. The promise was never fully realized in Israel's Old Testament experience. See Introduction: Characteristics and Themes.

15:1 allotment. See 14:2; 18:6. The method of casting lots is not specified. The important point is that the land was not divided by human decision (Prov. 16:33; 18:18).

15:8 Jerusalem. Jerusalem lay outside Judah's territory until the city was finally captured by David (2 Sam. 5:7).

15:14 sons of Anak. See note 11:21–22.

15:17 Othniel. See Judg. 3:7–11 for his later role as judge.

[f]the brother of Caleb, captured it. And he
gave him Achsah his daughter as wife.
18 When she came to him, she urged him to
ask her father for a field. And she got off
her donkey, and Caleb said to her, "What
do you want?" 19 She said to him, "Give me
a blessing. Since you have given me the
land of the Negeb, give me also springs of
water." And he gave her the upper springs
and the lower springs.
20 This is the inheritance of the tribe of the
people of Judah according to their clans.
21 The cities belonging to the tribe of the people of Judah in the extreme south, toward
the boundary of Edom, were Kabzeel, [g]Eder,
Jagur, 22 Kinah, Dimonah, Adadah, 23 Kedesh, Hazor, Ithnan, 24 [h]Ziph, Telem,
Bealoth, 25 Hazor-hadattah, Kerioth-hezron
(that is, Hazor), 26 Amam, Shema, Moladah,
27 Hazar-gaddah, Heshmon, Beth-pelet,
28 Hazar-shual, [i]Beersheba, Biziothiah, 29 Baalah, Iim, Ezem, 30 Eltolad, Chesil, Hormah,
31 [j]Ziklag, Madmannah, Sansannah, 32 Lebaoth, Shilhim, Ain, and Rimmon: in all,
twenty-nine cities with their villages.
33 And in the lowland, [k]Eshtaol, Zorah,
Ashnah, 34 Zanoah, En-gannim, Tappuah,
Enam, 35 [l]Jarmuth, [m]Adullam, [n]Socoh, [n]Aze-
kah, 36 Shaaraim, Adithaim, Gederah, Ged-
erothaim: fourteen cities with their villages.
37 Zenan, Hadashah, Migdal-gad,
38 Dilean, Mizpeh, Joktheel, 39 [o]Lachish,
Bozkath, [p]Eglon, 40 Cabbon, Lahmam, Chit-
lish, 41 Gederoth, Beth-dagon, Naamah, and
[q]Makkedah: sixteen cities with their villages.
42 [r]Libnah, Ether, Ashan, 43 Iphtah, Ashnah, Nezib, 44 [s]Keilah, Achzib, and Mareshah: nine cities with their villages.
45 [t]Ekron, with its towns and its villages;
46 from Ekron to the sea, all that were by
the side of Ashdod, with their villages.
47 [t]Ashdod, its towns and its villages;
[t]Gaza, its towns and its villages; to [u]the
Brook of Egypt, and [v]the Great Sea with its
coastline.
48 And in the hill country, Shamir, Jattir,
Socoh, 49 Dannah, Kiriath-sannah ([w]that is,
Debir), 50 Anab, Eshtemoh, Anim, 51 [x]Goshen,
Holon, and [y]Giloh: eleven cities with their
villages.
52 Arab, Dumah, Eshan, 53 Janim, Beth-
tappuah, Aphekah, 54 Humtah, [z]Kiriath-
arba (that is, [z]Hebron), and Zior: nine
cities with their villages.
55 [a]Maon, [a]Carmel, [b]Ziph, Juttah, 56 Jezreel, Jokdeam, Zanoah, 57 Kain, Gibeah, and
[c]Timnah: ten cities with their villages.
58 Halhul, Beth-zur, Gedor, 59 Maarath,
Beth-anoth, and Eltekon: six cities with
their villages.
60 [d]Kiriath-baal (that is, Kiriath-jearim),
and Rabbah: two cities with their villages.
61 In the wilderness, [e]Beth-arabah, Mid-
din, Secacah, 62 Nibshan, the City of Salt,
and [f]Engedi: six cities with their villages.
63 But the [g]Jebusites, the inhabitants of
Jerusalem, [h]the people of Judah could not
drive out, [h]so the Jebusites dwell with the
people of Judah at Jerusalem to this day.

The Allotment for Ephraim and Manasseh

16 The allotment of the people of
Joseph went from the Jordan by
Jericho, east of the waters of Jericho, [i]into
the wilderness, going up from Jericho into
the hill country to Bethel. 2 Then [j]going
from Bethel to Luz, it passes along to
Ataroth, the territory of the Archites. 3 Then
it goes down westward to the territory of
the Japhletites, as far as the territory of
Lower [k]Beth-horon, then to [l]Gezer, and it
ends at the sea.
4 [m]The people of Joseph, Manasseh and
Ephraim, received their inheritance.
5 The territory of the people of Ephraim
by their clans was as follows: the boundary

17 [f]See ch. 14:6, 13
21 [g]Gen. 35:21
24 [h]1 Sam. 23:14, 15, 19, 24; 26:1, 2
28 [i]Gen. 21:31; 26:23, 33
31 [j]1 Sam. 27:6; 30:1
33 [k][Num. 13:23]
35 [l]ch. 10:3 [m]1 Sam. 22:1 [n]1 Sam. 17:1
39 [o]ch. 10:3, 31, 32 [p]ch. 10:3, 36, 37
41 [q]ch. 10:10, 21
42 [r]ch. 10:29, 30
44 [s]1 Sam. 23:1, 2
45 [t]ch. 13:3
47 [t][See ver. 45 above] [u]See ver. 4 [v]See ver. 12
49 [w][ver. 49]
51 [x]ch. 10:41; 11:16 [y]2 Sam. 15:12
54 [z]For ver. 13, see ch. 14:13-15
55 [a]1 Sam. 23:24, 25; 25:2 [b]ver. 24
57 [c]ver. 10
60 [d]ver. 9
61 [e]ver. 6
62 [f]1 Sam. 23:29; 24:1
63 [g]See ver. 8 [h][Judg. 1:8, 21; 2 Sam. 5:6]
Chapter 16
1 [i]ch. 8:15; 18:12
2 [j][ch. 18:13; Gen. 28:19; Judg. 1:23, 26]
3 [k]See ch. 10:10 [l]See ch. 10:33
4 [m][ch. 17:14]

15:20–62 These verses are a detailed list of towns allotted to Judah. Although many of them can no longer be identified, the extensive enumeration is a clear representation of the promise of God (21:45).

15:20 inheritance. See note 1:6.

15:63 the people of Judah could not drive out. This brief note on Judah's failure is a reminder that the fulfillment of God's promises was not complete. There still remained a "not yet" (21:45 and note). The victory over the Jebusites in Judg. 1:8 apparently was not permanent (cf. Judg. 1:21).

to this day. See note 4:9.

16:1–17:18 These two chapters describe the allotment of land to Joseph's two sons, Ephraim and Manasseh (Gen. 41:50–52; Josh. 13:14 note). Half the tribe of Manasseh had already received their land east of the Jordan (17:1).

16:1 The allotment. See note 15:1.

16:4 Manasseh and Ephraim. Here they are mentioned in the order of birth (Gen. 48:12–20).

inheritance. See note 1:6.

16:5–10 Ephraim was Joseph's younger son (Gen. 41:52), but his territory is described before Manasseh's, probably because of the precedence given him in Gen. 48:12–20.

of their inheritance on the east was
[n]Ataroth-addar as far as Upper Beth-horon,
6 and the boundary goes from there to the
sea. On the north is [o]Michmethath. Then
on the east the boundary turns around
toward Taanath-shiloh and passes along
beyond it on the east to Janoah, 7 then it
goes down from Janoah to Ataroth and [p]to
Naarah, and touches Jericho, ending at the
Jordan. 8 From [q]Tappuah the boundary
goes westward to the brook Kanah and
ends at the sea. Such is the inheritance of
the tribe of the people of Ephraim by their
clans, 9 together with [q]the towns that were
set apart for the people of Ephraim within
the inheritance of the Manassites, all those
towns with their villages. 10 However, [r]they
did not drive out the Canaanites who lived
in Gezer, so the Canaanites have lived in
the midst of Ephraim to this day but have
been made [s]to do forced labor.

17 Then allotment was made to the
people of Manasseh, for he was [t]the
firstborn of Joseph. To [u]Machir the firstborn of Manasseh, the father of Gilead,
[v]were allotted Gilead and Bashan, because
he was a man of war. 2 And allotments were
made [w]to the rest of the people of
Manasseh by their clans, Abiezer, Helek,
Asriel, Shechem, Hepher, and Shemida.
These were the male descendants of
Manasseh the son of Joseph, by their clans.
3 Now [x]Zelophehad the son of Hepher,
son of Gilead, son of Machir, son of
Manasseh, had no sons, but only daughters, and these are the names of his daughters: [x]Mahlah, Noah, Hoglah, Milcah, and
Tirzah. 4 They approached [y]Eleazar the
priest and Joshua the son of Nun and the
leaders and said, [z]"The LORD commanded
Moses to give us an inheritance along with
our brothers." So according to the mouth
of the LORD he gave them an inheritance
among the brothers of their father. 5 Thus
there fell to Manasseh ten portions, besides
[a]the land of Gilead and Bashan, which is
on the other side of the Jordan, 6 because
the daughters of Manasseh received an
inheritance along with his sons. The land
of Gilead was allotted to the rest of the people of Manasseh.
7 The territory of Manasseh reached from
Asher to [b]Michmethath, which is east of
Shechem. Then the boundary goes along
southward to the inhabitants of En-tap-
puah. 8 The land of [c]Tappuah belonged to
Manasseh, but the town of Tappuah on the
boundary of Manasseh belonged to the
people of Ephraim. 9 [c]Then the boundary
went down to the brook Kanah. These
cities, to the south of the brook, among the
cities of Manasseh, belong to Ephraim.
Then the boundary of Manasseh goes on
the north side of the brook and ends at the
sea, 10 the land to the south being Ephraim's and that to the north being Manasseh's, with the sea forming its boundary.
On the north Asher is reached, and on the
east Issachar. 11 Also in Issachar and in
Asher [d]Manasseh had Beth-shean and its
villages, and Ibleam and its villages, and
the inhabitants of [d]Dor and its villages, and
the inhabitants of En-dor and its villages,
and the inhabitants of [d]Taanach and its
villages, and the inhabitants of [d]Megiddo
and its villages; [e]the third is Naphath.[1]
12 [f]Yet the people of Manasseh could not
take possession of those cities, but the
Canaanites persisted in dwelling in that
land. 13 Now when the people of Israel
grew strong, they put the Canaanites [g]to
forced labor, but did not utterly drive them
out.
14 Then [h]the people of Joseph spoke to
Joshua, saying, "Why have you given me
but [i]one lot and one portion as an inheritance, although I am [j]a numerous people,
since all along the LORD has blessed me?"
15 And Joshua said to them, "If you are a

[1] The meaning of the Hebrew is uncertain

5 [n]ch. 18:13
6 [o]ch. 17:7
7 [p]1 Chr. 7:28
8 [q]ch. 17:8, 9
9 [q][See ver. 8 above]
10 [r]Judg. 1:29; 1 Kin. 9:16 [s]ch. 17:13; Gen. 49:15
Chapter 17
1 [t]Gen. 41:51; 46:20; 48:18 [u]Gen. 50:23; Num. 26:29; 32:39, 40; 1 Chr. 7:14 [v]Deut. 3:13, 15
2 [w]See Num. 26:29-32
3 [x]Num. 26:33; 27:1; 36:2, 11
4 [y]ch. 14:1; 21:1; Num. 34:17 [z]Num. 27:6, 7; 36:2
5 [a]ver. 1; ch. 13:30, 31
7 [b]ch. 16:6
8 [c]ch. 16:8, 9
9 [c][See ver. 8 above]
11 [d]1 Chr. 7:29 [1 Kin. 4:11, 12] [e][ch. 11:2; 12:23]
12 [f]Judg. 1:27, 28
13 [g]ch. 16:10; Gen. 49:15
14 [h]ch. 16:4 [i][Gen. 48:22] [j]Gen. 48:19; [Num. 26:34, 37]

16:10 they did not drive out. See note 15:63.

to this day. See note 4:9.

17:1 Manasseh. Manasseh was the older of Joseph's two sons (Gen. 41:50–51; 48:12–20; Josh. 16:5–10 note).

the firstborn of Manasseh. See Gen. 50:23.

17:3–6 It was a provision of the law of Moses that the daughters of a man with no son would inherit from him (Num. 27:1–11, especially v. 8).

17:12, 13 did not utterly drive them out. See notes 15:63; 21:45.

17:14–18 The complaining request of the people of Joseph (v. 14) and their fear of the Canaanites (v. 16) are in contrast to Caleb's faith and courage (14:6–12).

17:14 one lot and one portion. The territory of Manasseh on both sides of the Jordan and of Ephraim is treated as a unit (16:1).

17:15 go up . . . clear ground for yourselves. Faith in the promise of God should be expressed in courageous, obedient action. See notes 1:6, 7; 14:12.

numerous people, go up by yourselves to
the forest, and there clear ground for yourselves in the land of the Perizzites and [k]the
Rephaim, since [l]the hill country of
Ephraim is too narrow for you." 16 The people of Joseph said, "The hill country is not
enough for us. Yet all the Canaanites who
dwell in the plain have [m]chariots of iron,
both those in Beth-shean and its villages
and those in [n]the Valley of Jezreel." 17 Then
Joshua said to the house of Joseph, to
Ephraim and Manasseh, "You are a numerous people and have great power. You shall
not have one allotment only, 18 but the hill
country shall be yours, for though it is a
forest, you shall clear it and possess it to its
farthest borders. For you shall drive out the
Canaanites, [o]though they have chariots of
iron, and though they are strong."

Allotment of the Remaining Land

18 Then the whole congregation of the
people of Israel assembled at
[p]Shiloh and set up [q]the tent of meeting
there. The land lay subdued before them.
2 There remained among the people of
Israel seven tribes whose inheritance had
not yet been apportioned. 3 So Joshua said
to the people of Israel, [r]"How long will
you put off going in to take possession of
the land, which the LORD, the God of your
fathers, has given you? 4 Provide three men
from each tribe, and I will send them out
that they may set out and go up and down
the land. They shall write a description of
it with a view to their inheritances, and
then come to me. 5 They shall divide it into
seven portions. [s]Judah shall continue in
his territory on the south, [t]and the house
of Joseph shall continue in their territory
on the north. 6 And you shall describe the
land in seven divisions and bring the
description here to me. [u]And I will cast
lots for you here before the LORD our God.
7 [v]The Levites have no portion among you,
for the priesthood of the LORD is their heritage. [w]And Gad and Reuben and half the
tribe of Manasseh have received their
inheritance beyond the Jordan eastward,
which Moses the servant of the LORD gave
them."
8 So the men arose and went, and Joshua
charged those who went to write the
description of the land, saying, "Go up and
down in the land and write a description
and return to me. And I will cast lots for
you here before the LORD in Shiloh." 9 So
the men went and passed up and down in
the land and wrote in a book a description
of it by towns in seven divisions. Then they
came to Joshua to the camp at Shiloh,
10 and Joshua [x]cast lots for them in Shiloh
before the LORD. And there Joshua apportioned the land to the people of Israel, [y]to
each his portion.

The Inheritance for Benjamin

11 The lot of the tribe of the people of
Benjamin according to its clans came up,
and the territory allotted to it fell between
the people of Judah and the people of
Joseph. 12 [z]On the north side their boundary began at the Jordan. [a]Then the boundary goes up to the shoulder north of
Jericho, then up through the hill country
westward, and it ends at the wilderness of
[b]Beth-aven. 13 From there the boundary
passes along southward in the direction of

15 [k]See ch. 12:4 [l]ch. 24:33; Judg. 3:27
16 [m]See ch. 11:6 [n]Judg. 6:33
18 [o]Deut. 20:1; See ch. 11:6
Chapter 18
1 [p]ch. 19:51; 21:2; 22:9, 12 [q]ch. 19:51
3 [r][Judg. 18:9]
5 [s][ch. 15:1] [t][ch. 16:1, 4]
6 [u]ver. 10; ch. 14:2
7 [v]See ch. 13:33 [w]See ch. 13:3
10 [x]ver. 6 [y]ch. 11:23; 12:7
12 [z][ch. 16:1] [a]ch. 18:21 [b]See ch. 7:2

17:16 not enough . . . the Canaanites. Their fear and unwillingness to obey are expressions of unbelief.

17:18 you shall drive out. Joshua answers the fears of the people of Joseph with an application of the promise of God (1:2–5).

18:1 the whole congregation . . . assembled. See 8:35 and note.

Shiloh. Located in Ephraim, the city of Shiloh has so far not been prominent in biblical history, but here it becomes what was called in Deut. 12 "the place that the LORD your God will choose" (Deut. 12:5, 11, 18; cf. Jer. 7:12). In the days of David this role will be transferred to Jerusalem. For the role of Shiloh in Israel's history see 22:12; Judg. 18:31; 21:19; 1 Sam. 1:3, 24; 2:14; 3:21; 4:3; 14:3; 1 Kin. 2:27; 11:29; 14:2; Ps. 78:60; Jer. 7:12, 14; 26:6, 9.

tent of meeting. This name is used for the tabernacle in the Book of Joshua only here and at 19:51 ("tabernacle" in 22:19, 29; "house" in 6:24; 9:23). The "meeting" is that of God with His people (1:5 note). The tabernacle contained the ark of the covenant, the wood and gold box containing the Ten Commandments (3:3; 4:16 and notes; Ex. 25:10–22). It was the place where the Old Testament sacrificial system for spiritual cleansing and communication with God was inaugurated, to continue in principle until the time of the New Testament.

18:3 will you put off. Or "be slack" (the same Hebrew verb occurs in Prov. 18:9; 24:10).

take possession. This means to occupy the land completely, something more than the initial conquest (1:11, 15; 13:1; 21:43). It is an act of obedient faith because it is based on the promise of God (1:11 note), hence the note of rebuke in Joshua's question.

the LORD, the God of your fathers. This is an allusion to the promises to the fathers (1:1–9 note).

has given. See notes 1:2, 3, 11.

18:6 before the LORD. God's presence is represented by the tabernacle because He spoke to them "from between the two cherubim" (3:11; 7:23 notes; Ex. 25:22).

18:7 The Levites have no portion . . . Gad and Reuben and . . . Manasseh have received. The means of counting exactly twelve tribes in Israel is explained again. See notes 13:8–33 and 13:14.

Luz, to the shoulder of [c]Luz (that is,
Bethel), then the boundary goes down to
[d]Ataroth-addar, on the mountain that lies
south of Lower [e]Beth-horon. **14** Then the
boundary goes in another direction, turning on the [f]western side southward from
the mountain that lies to the south, opposite Beth-horon, and it ends at Kiriath-
baal ([g]that is, Kiriath-jearim), a city
belonging to the people of Judah. This
forms the western side. **15** And the southern side begins at the outskirts of Kiriath-
jearim. And the boundary goes from there
to Ephron,[1] [g]to the spring of the waters of
Nephtoah. **16** Then the boundary goes
down to the border of the mountain that
overlooks [h]the Valley of the Son of
Hinnom, which is at the north end of the
Valley of [i]Rephaim. And it then goes
down the [h]Valley of Hinnom, south of the
shoulder of the Jebusites, and downward
to [j]En-rogel. **17** Then it bends in a norther-
ly direction going on to En-shemesh, and
from there goes to Geliloth, which is
opposite the ascent of Adummim. Then it
goes down to [k]the stone of Bohan the son
of Reuben, **18** and passing on to the north
of [l]the shoulder of Beth-arabah[2] it goes
down to [l]the Arabah. **19** Then the boundary passes on to the north of the shoulder
of [k]Beth-hoglah. And the boundary ends at
the northern bay of [m]the Salt Sea, at the
south end of the Jordan: this is the southern
border. **20** The Jordan forms its boundary
on the eastern side. This is the inheritance
of the people of Benjamin, according to
their clans, boundary by boundary all
around.
21 Now the cities of the tribe of the people
of Benjamin according to their clans were
[n]Jericho, Beth-hoglah, Emek-keziz, **22** Beth-
arabah, Zemaraim, Bethel, **23** Avvim, Parah,
Ophrah, **24** Chephar-ammoni, Ophni, Geba—
twelve cities with their villages: **25** Gibeon,
Ramah, Beeroth, **26** Mizpeh, Chephirah,
Mozah, **27** Rekem, Irpeel, Taralah, **28** Zela, Ha-
eleph, [o]Jebus[3] (that is, Jerusalem), Gibeah[4]
and Kiriath-jearim[5]—fourteen cities with
their villages. This is the inheritance of the
people of Benjamin according to its clans.

13 [c]See ch. 16:2 [d]ch. 16:5 [e]ch. 16:3; See ch. 10:10
14 [f][ch. 19:11] [g]ch. 15:9
15 [g][See ver. 14 above]
16 [h]See ch. 15:8 [i]See ch. 12:4 [j]See ch. 15:7
17 [k]ch. 15:6
18 [l]ch. 11:2; 15:6
19 [k][See ver. 17 above] [m]ch. 15:2
21 [n]ver. 12
28 [o]See ch. 15:8

Chapter 19
1 [p]ver. 9; [Gen. 49:7]
2 [q]For ver. 2-8, see 1 Chr. 4:28-33
9 [r]ver. 1
11 [s][ch. 18:14; Gen. 49:13] [t]ch. 12:22; 21:34
15 [u]ch. 11:1

The Inheritance for Simeon

19 The second lot came out for
Simeon, for the tribe of the people
of Simeon, according to their clans, [p]and
their inheritance was in the midst of the
inheritance of the people of Judah. **2** [q]And
they had for their inheritance Beersheba,
Sheba, Moladah, **3** Hazar-shual, Balah,
Ezem, **4** Eltolad, Bethul, Hormah, **5** Ziklag,
Beth-marcaboth, Hazar-susah, **6** Beth-
lebaoth, and Sharuhen—thirteen cities
with their villages; **7** Ain, Rimmon, Ether,
and Ashan—four cities with their villages,
8 together with all the villages around these
cities as far as Baalath-beer, Ramah of the
Negeb. This was the inheritance of the
tribe of the people of Simeon according to
their clans. **9** [r]The inheritance of the people
of Simeon formed part of the territory of the
people of Judah. Because the portion of
the people of Judah was too large for them,
the people of Simeon obtained an inheritance in the midst of their inheritance.

The Inheritance for Zebulun

10 The third lot came up for the people of
Zebulun, according to their clans. And the
territory of their inheritance reached as far as
Sarid. **11** Then their boundary goes up [s]west-
ward and on to Mareal and touches
Dabbesheth, then the brook that is east of
[t]Jokneam. **12** From Sarid it goes in the other
direction eastward toward the sunrise to the
boundary of Chisloth-tabor. From there it
goes to Daberath, then up to Japhia. **13** From
there it passes along on the east toward the
sunrise to Gath-hepher, to Eth-kazin, and
going on to Rimmon it bends toward Neah,
14 then on the north the boundary turns
about to Hannathon, and it ends at the
Valley of Iphtahel; **15** and Kattath, Nahalal,
[u]Shimron, Idalah, and Bethlehem—twelve
cities with their villages. **16** This is the inheritance of the people of Zebulun, according to
their clans—these cities with their villages.

The Inheritance for Issachar

17 The fourth lot came out for Issachar,
for the people of Issachar, according to

1 See 15:9; Hebrew *westward* 2 Septuagint; Hebrew *to the shoulder over against the Arabah* 3 Septuagint, Syriac, Vulgate; Hebrew *the Jebusite* 4 Hebrew *Gibeath* 5 Septuagint; Hebrew *Kiriath*

19:1 in the midst . . . Judah. Simeon's allotment was inside the territory of Judah (Gen. 49:7). Judah and Simeon acted together in Judg. 1:3, 17. At some stage the tribe of Simeon seems to have lost its distinct identity.

19:8, 9 inheritance. See note 1:6.

19:15 twelve. It is not clear which twelve cities are meant.

their clans. 18 Their territory included
Jezreel, Chesulloth, [v]Shunem, 19 Hapha-
raim, Shion, Anaharath, 20 Rabbith, Kishion, Ebez, 21 Remeth, En-gannim, En-
haddah, Beth-pazzez. 22 The boundary also
touches Tabor, Shahazumah, and Beth-
shemesh, and its boundary ends at the
Jordan—sixteen cities with their villages.
23 This is the inheritance of the tribe of the
people of Issachar, according to their
clans—the cities with their villages.

The Inheritance for Asher

24 The fifth lot came out for the tribe of
the people of Asher according to their
clans. 25 Their territory included Helkath,
Hali, Beten, Achshaph, 26 Allammelech,
Amad, and Mishal. On the west it touches
[w]Carmel and Shihor-libnath, 27 then it turns
eastward, it goes to Beth-dagon, and touches Zebulun and the Valley of Iphtahel
northward to Beth-emek and Neiel. Then it
continues in the north to [x]Cabul, 28 Ebron,
Rehob, Hammon, Kanah, as far as [y]Sidon
the Great. 29 Then the boundary turns to
Ramah, reaching to the fortified city of
Tyre. Then the boundary turns to Hosah,
and it ends at the sea; Mahalab,[1] Achzib,
30 Ummah, Aphek and Rehob—twenty-two
cities with their villages. 31 This is the inheritance of the tribe of the people of Asher
according to their clans—these cities with
their villages.

The Inheritance for Naphtali

32 The sixth lot came out for the people
of Naphtali, for the people of Naphtali,
according to their clans. 33 And their
boundary ran from Heleph, from [z]the oak
in Zaanannim, and Adami-nekeb, and
Jabneel, as far as Lakkum, and it ended at
the Jordan. 34 Then the boundary turns
[a]westward to Aznoth-tabor and goes from
there to Hukkok, touching Zebulun at the
south and Asher on the west and Judah
on the east at the Jordan. 35 The fortified
cities are Ziddim, Zer, Hammath, Rak-
kath, [b]Chinnereth, 36 Adamah, Ramah,
[c]Hazor, 37 Kedesh, Edrei, En-hazor, 38 Yi-
ron, Migdal-el, Horem, Beth-anath, and
Beth-shemesh—nineteen cities with their
villages. 39 This is the inheritance of the
tribe of the people of Naphtali according
to their clans—the cities with their
villages.

The Inheritance for Dan

40 The seventh lot came out for the tribe
of the people of Dan, according to their
clans. 41 And the territory of its inheritance
included Zorah, Eshtaol, Ir-shemesh,
42 [d]Shaalabbin, [d]Aijalon, Ithlah, 43 Elon,
Timnah, Ekron, 44 Eltekeh, Gibbethon,
Baalath, 45 Jehud, Bene-berak, Gath-rimmon, 46 and Me-jarkon and Rakkon with
the territory over against [e]Joppa. 47 When
[f]the territory of the people of Dan was lost
to them, the people of Dan went up and
fought against Leshem, and after capturing it and striking it with the sword they
took possession of it and settled in it, calling Leshem, Dan, after the name of Dan
their ancestor. 48 This is the inheritance of
the tribe of the people of Dan, according
to their clans—these cities with their villages.

The Inheritance for Joshua

49 When they had finished distributing
the several territories of the land as inheritances, the people of Israel gave an inheritance among them to Joshua the son of
Nun. 50 By command of the LORD they gave
him the city that he asked, [g]Timnath-serah
in the hill country of Ephraim. And he
rebuilt the city and settled in it.
51 [h]These are the inheritances that Eleazar
the priest and Joshua the son of Nun and
the heads of the fathers' houses of the
tribes of the people of Israel distributed by
lot [i]at Shiloh before the LORD, at the
entrance of the tent of meeting. So they finished dividing the land.

18 [v]1 Sam. 28:4
26 [w]1 Kin. 18:19, 20, 42; 2 Kin. 2:25; 4:25; S. of S. 7:5; Isai. 33:9; Jer. 50:19
27 [x][1 Kin. 9:13]
28 [y]ch. 11:8; [Judg. 1:31]
33 [z][Judg. 4:11]
34 [a][Deut. 33:23]
35 [b]See ch. 11:2
36 [c]ch. 11:1
42 [d]Judg. 1:35
46 [e]2 Chr. 2:16; Ezra 3:7
47 [f]Judg. 1:34, 35; 18:1
50 [g]ch. 24:30; Judg. 2:9
51 [h]ch. 14:1; Num. 34:17; [i]See ch. 18:1

1 Compare Septuagint; Hebrew *Mehebel*

19:30 twenty-two. There are more than twenty-two towns mentioned, but some may be noted as points on the boundary.

19:38 nineteen. The list apparently is incomplete.

19:47 Dan. A fuller account of Dan and their conquest of Leshem is given in Judg. 18.

19:49, 50 See notes 14:6–15.

19:50 By command of the LORD. This divine command is not recorded elsewhere (cf. 14:9 note). See Num. 14:30.

Timnath-serah. Joshua would be buried here (24:30).

19:51 Eleazar. See note 14:1.

Shiloh. See note 18:1.

before the LORD. See note 18:6.

tent of meeting. See note 18:1.

The Cities of Refuge

20 Then the LORD said to Joshua, 2 "Say
to the people of Israel, [j]'Appoint the
cities of refuge, of which I spoke to you
through Moses, 3 that the manslayer who
strikes any person without intent or
unknowingly may flee there. They shall be
for you a refuge from the avenger of blood.
4 He shall flee to one of these cities and shall
stand [k]at the entrance of the gate of the city
and explain his case to the elders of that city.
Then they shall take him into the city and
give him a place, and he shall remain with
them. 5 And if the avenger of blood pursues
him, they shall not give up the manslayer
into his hand, because he struck his neighbor unknowingly, and did not hate him in
the past. 6 And he shall remain in that city
[l]until he has stood before the congregation
for judgment, until the death of him who is
high priest at the time. Then the manslayer
may return to his own town and his own
home, to the town from which he fled.'"
7 So they set apart [m]Kedesh in Galilee in
the hill country of Naphtali, and [n]Shechem
in the hill country of Ephraim, and [o]Kiriath-
arba (that is, Hebron) [p]in the hill country of
Judah. 8 And beyond the Jordan east of
Jericho, they appointed [q]Bezer in the
wilderness on the tableland, from the tribe
of Reuben, and [r]Ramoth in Gilead, from the
tribe of Gad, and [s]Golan in Bashan, from
the tribe of Manasseh. 9 These were the
cities designated for all the people of Israel
and [t]for the stranger sojourning among
them, that anyone who killed a person
without intent could flee there, so that he
might not die by the hand of the avenger of
blood, till he stood before the congregation.

Cities and Pasturelands Allotted to Levi

21 Then the heads of the fathers' houses of the Levites came [u]to Eleazar
the priest and to Joshua the son of Nun
and to the heads of the fathers' houses of
the tribes of the people of Israel. 2 And they
said to them [v]at Shiloh in the land of
Canaan, [w]"The LORD commanded through
Moses that we be given cities to dwell in,
along with their pasturelands for our livestock." 3 So by command of the LORD the
people of Israel gave to the Levites the following cities and pasturelands out of their
inheritance.
4 The lot came out for the clans of the
Kohathites. So those Levites who were
descendants of Aaron the priest [x]received
by lot from the tribes of Judah, Simeon,
and Benjamin, thirteen cities.
5 And the rest of the Kohathites received
by lot [y]from the clans of the tribe of
Ephraim, from the tribe of Dan and the
half-tribe of Manasseh, ten cities.
6 The [z]Gershonites received by lot from
the clans of the tribe of Issachar, from the
tribe of Asher, from the tribe of Naphtali,

Chapter 20
2 [j]Ex. 21:13; See Num. 35:6, 11-14; Deut. 4:41-43; 19:2-9
4 [k][Deut. 21:19; Ruth 4:1, 2; Ps. 127:5]
6 [l]Num. 35:12, 24, 25
7 [m]ch. 31:32; 1 Chr. 6:76 [n]ch. 21:21 [o]ch. 21:11, 18; See ch. 14:13-15 [p]ch. 21:11; Luke 1:39
8 [q]ch. 21:36; 1 Chr. 6:78 [r]ch. 21:38; [1 Kin. 22:3] [s]ch. 21:27; 1 Chr. 6:71
9 [t]Num. 35:15
Chapter 21
1 [u]ch. 14:1; 17:4; 19:51; Num. 34:17, 18
2 [v]See ch. 18:1 [w]Num. 35:2
4 [x]See ver. 9-19; Ex. 6:16-19; Num. 3:17-20
5 [y]See ver. 20-26
6 [z]See ver. 27-33

20:1–9 The record of the division of the land is followed by a provision for basic justice in it, illustrating God's concern for justice and the preservation of life. The provision implies the idea of just retribution, while restraining the injustice that could flow from vengeance (Deut. 4:41–43).

20:2 cities of refuge. These were places where certain offenders could escape unjust vengeance and seek a fair trial. Similar cities will also be given to the Levites (21:1–42; Num. 35:6), and by implication will be places where the law of God can be found.

through Moses. See Ex. 21:12–14; Num. 35:6–34; Deut. 19:1–13.

20:3 without intent or unknowingly. Unintentional sin receives specific treatment in the law (Lev. 4:2, 13, 22, 27; 5:15, 18; Num. 15:22–29; 35:22; Deut. 4:42; 19:4; Ezek. 45:20; cf. Heb. 9:7).

avenger of blood. This would be the victim's nearest male relative or possibly an official of the city where the killing occurred (Num. 35:19–21).

20:4 the gate of the city. This was the usual place for legal transactions (Ruth 4:1–12).

elders. Apparently the elders held a preliminary hearing of the accused man's case.

20:5 they shall not give up. There is a presumption in favor of the accused.

20:6 death of . . . high priest. His death marked the end of an era and provided a convenient limitation to the provisions made here.

20:7 set apart. The Hebrew verb can also be translated "sanctified."

20:8 beyond. See Deut. 4:41–43.

20:9 the stranger. Concern for the foreigner in Israel was a regular feature of the law (e.g., Ex. 12:48–49; 20:10; 22:21; 23:9, 12).

21:1–42 The last part of the division of the land is the assignment of towns to the Levites, whose lack of an inheritance in the land has been mentioned in 13:14 (note), 33; 14:3–4; 18:7. These towns continued to belong to the tribes to which they had been assigned, but were provided, along with adjoining pasturelands (v. 8), for the Levites to live in.

21:2 The LORD commanded through Moses. Refers to Num. 35:1–8. The request of the Levites, like that of Caleb in 14:6–12, was an expression of faith in the promise of God.

21:3 inheritance. See note 1:6.

21:4 lot. See note 15:1.

Kohathites. Kohath was Levi's second son (Ex. 6:16; Num. 3:17), but his descendants have precedence because the priestly line through Aaron descended from him (Ex. 6:18, 20). Aaron and his sons were chosen by God to be priests (Ex. 28:1; Lev. 8:1–36).

Judah, Simeon, and Benjamin. The towns allotted for these tribes were near Jerusalem, where the temple would later be built, although Jerusalem itself is not mentioned in this chapter.

21:6 Gershonites. Descendants of Levi's first son (Ex. 6:16; Num. 3:17).

and from the half-tribe of Manasseh in
Bashan, thirteen cities.
7 The [a]Merarites according to their clans
received from the tribe of Reuben, the tribe
of Gad, and the tribe of Zebulun, twelve
cities.
8 These cities and their pasturelands the
people of Israel [b]gave by lot to the Levites,
[c]as the LORD had commanded through
Moses.
9 Out of the tribe of the people of Judah
and the tribe of the people of Simeon they
gave the following cities mentioned by
name, 10 which went to [d]the descendants of
Aaron, one of the clans of the Kohathites
who belonged to the people of Levi; since
the lot fell to them first. 11 [e]They gave them
[f]Kiriath-arba (Arba being the father of
Anak), that is Hebron, [g]in the hill country
of Judah, along with the pasturelands
around it. 12 But the fields of the city and its
villages had been given to Caleb the son of
Jephunneh as his possession.
13 And to the descendants of Aaron the
priest they gave Hebron, [h]the city of refuge
for the manslayer, with its pasturelands,
[i]Libnah with its pasturelands, 14 Jattir with
its pasturelands, Eshtemoa with its pasturelands, 15 Holon with its pasturelands,
Debir with its pasturelands, 16 Ain with its
pasturelands, Juttah with its pasturelands,
Beth-shemesh with its pasturelands—nine
cities out of these two tribes; 17 then out of
the tribe of Benjamin, [j]Gibeon with its pasturelands, Geba with its pasturelands,
18 Anathoth with its pasturelands, and
Almon with its pasturelands—four cities.
19 The cities of the descendants of Aaron,
the priests, were in all thirteen cities with
their pasturelands.
20 [k]As to the rest of the Kohathites belonging to the Kohathite clans of the
Levites, the cities allotted to them were out
of the tribe of Ephraim. 21 To them were
given Shechem, [l]the city of refuge for the
manslayer, with its pasturelands in the hill
country of Ephraim, Gezer with its pasturelands, 22 Kibzaim with its pasturelands,
Beth-horon with its pasturelands—four
cities; 23 and out of the tribe of Dan, Elteke
with its pasturelands, Gibbethon with its
pasturelands, 24 Aijalon with its pasturelands,
Gath-rimmon with its pasturelands—four
cities; 25 and out of the half-tribe of
Manasseh, Taanach with its pasturelands,
and Gath-rimmon with its pasturelands—
two cities. 26 The cities of the clans of the
rest of the Kohathites were ten in all with
their pasturelands.
27 [m]And to the Gershonites, one of the
clans of the Levites, were given out of the
half-tribe of Manasseh, Golan in Bashan
with its pasturelands, [l]the city of refuge for
the manslayer, and Beeshterah with its
pasturelands—two cities; 28 and out of the
tribe of Issachar, Kishion with its pasturelands, Daberath with its pasturelands,
29 Jarmuth with its pasturelands, En-gannim with its pasturelands—four cities;
30 and out of the tribe of Asher, Mishal with
its pasturelands, Abdon with its pasturelands, 31 Helkath with its pasturelands, and
Rehob with its pasturelands—four cities;
32 and out of the tribe of Naphtali, Kedesh
in Galilee with its pasturelands, [l]the city of
refuge for the manslayer, Hammoth-dor
with its pasturelands, and Kartan with its
pasturelands—three cities. 33 The cities of
the several clans of the Gershonites were
in all thirteen cities with their pasturelands.
34 [n]And to the rest of the Levites, the
Merarite clans, were given out of the tribe
of Zebulun, Jokneam with its pasturelands,
Kartah with its pasturelands, 35 Dimnah
with its pasturelands, Nahalal with its pasturelands—four cities; 36 and out of the
tribe of Reuben, [o]Bezer with its pasturelands, Jahaz with its pasturelands, 37 Kedemoth with its pasturelands, and Mephaath
with its pasturelands—four cities; 38 and
out of the tribe of Gad, [o]Ramoth in Gilead
with its pasturelands, the city of refuge for
the manslayer, [p]Mahanaim with its pasturelands, 39 [p]Heshbon with its pasturelands, Jazer with its pasturelands—four
cities in all. 40 As for the cities of the several Merarite clans, that is, the remainder of
the clans of the Levites, those allotted to
them were in all twelve cities.

7 [a]See ver. 34-40
8 [b]ver. 3
[c]Num. 35:2; See ch. 14:3-5
10 [d]ver. 4
11 [e]For ver. 11-19, see 1 Chr. 6:54-60 [f]See ch. 14:13-15
[g]ch. 20:7; Luke 1:39
13 [h]ch. 20:7
[i]ch. 10:29
17 [j]ch. 9:3
20 [k]For ver. 20-26, see 1 Chr. 6:66-70
21 [l]ch. 20:7, 8
27 [m]For ver. 27-33, see 1 Chr. 6:71-76 [l][See ver. 21 above]
32 [l][See ver. 21 above]
34 [n]For ver. 34-40, see 1 Chr. 6:77-81
36 [o]ch. 20:8
38 [o][See ver. 36 above]
[p]See ch. 13:26
39 [p][See ver. 38 above]

21:7 Merarites. Descendants of Levi's third son (Ex. 6:16; Num. 3:17).

21:10 first. The precedence of the priestly line is emphasized (v. 4).

21:12 Caleb. See note 14:6.

21:13 city of refuge. See note 20:2.

21:17 Gibeon. See note 9:3. The Gibeonites had to serve in the house of God (9:23 and note).

41 [q]The cities of the Levites in the midst of
the possession of the people of Israel were
in all forty-eight cities with their pasturelands. 42 These cities each had its pasturelands around it. So it was with all these
cities.
43 [r]Thus the LORD gave to Israel all the
land that he swore to give to their fathers.
And they took possession of it, and they
settled there. 44 [s]And the LORD gave them
rest on every side just as he had sworn to
their fathers. [t]Not one of all their enemies
had withstood them, for [u]the LORD had
given all their enemies into their hands.
45 [v]Not one word of all the good promises
that the LORD had made to the house of
Israel had failed; all came to pass.

The Eastern Tribes Return Home

22 At that time Joshua summoned the
Reubenites and the Gadites and the
half-tribe of Manasseh, 2 and said to them,
"You have kept [w]all that Moses the servant
of the LORD commanded you [x]and have
obeyed my voice in all that I have commanded you. 3 You have not forsaken your
brothers these many days, down to this
day, but have been careful to keep the
charge of the LORD your God. 4 [y]And now
the LORD your God has given rest to your
brothers, as he promised them. Therefore
turn and go to your tents in the land where
your possession lies, [z]which Moses the servant of the LORD gave you on the other side
of the Jordan. 5 [a]Only be very careful to
observe the commandment and the law
that Moses the servant of the LORD commanded you, [b]to love the LORD your God,
and to walk in all his ways and to keep his
commandments and to cling to him and to
serve him with all your heart and with all
your soul." 6 So Joshua [c]blessed them and
sent them away, and they went to their
tents.
7 Now to the one half of the tribe of
Manasseh Moses had given a possession in
Bashan, [d]but to the other half Joshua had
given a possession beside their brothers in
the land west of the Jordan. And when
Joshua sent them away to their homes and
blessed them, 8 he said to them, "Go back
to your tents with much wealth and with
very much livestock, with silver, gold,
bronze, and iron, and with much clothing.
[e]Divide the spoil of your enemies with your
brothers." 9 So the people of Reuben and
the people of Gad and the half-tribe of
Manasseh returned home, parting from the
people of Israel at Shiloh, which is in the
land of Canaan, to go [f]to the land of
Gilead, their own land of which they had
possessed themselves by command of the
LORD through Moses.

The Eastern Tribes' Altar of Witness

10 And when they came to the region of
the Jordan that is in the land of Canaan,
the people of Reuben and the people of
Gad and the half-tribe of Manasseh built
there an altar by the Jordan, an altar of
imposing size. 11 And the people of Israel
[g]heard it said, "Behold, the people of
Reuben and the people of Gad and the
half-tribe of Manasseh have built the altar
at the frontier of the land of Canaan, in the
region about the Jordan, on the side that

41 [q]Num. 35:7
43 [r]Gen. 13:15; 15:18; 26:3; 28:4, 13
44 [s]See ch. 11:23 [t]ch. 10:8; 23:9 [u]ch. 2:24; Deut. 7:24
45 [v]ch. 23:14, 15
Chapter 22
2 [w]See Num. 32:20-22; Deut. 3:18-20 [x]ch. 1:16, 17
4 [y]See ch. 11:23 [z]See ch. 13:8
5 [a]Deut. 6:6, 17; 11:22 [b]ch. 23:11; Deut. 6:5; 10:12; 11:1, 13, 22
6 [c]ch. 14:13
7 [d]ch. 17:5
8 [e]Num. 31:27; 1 Sam. 30:24
9 [f]Num. 32:1, 26, 29
11 [g]See Deut. 13:12-15

21:43–45 This summary reviews the whole book, not just chs. 13–21. The idea that dominates the entire book is the faithfulness of God to His promises (v. 45).

21:43 he swore to give to their fathers. The faithfulness of God attested in this book is His faithfulness to the promises made to Abraham, Isaac, and Jacob. In the New Testament, these promises are identified as the gospel (Gal. 3:8; Introduction: Characteristics and Themes).

21:44 Not one . . . withstood. This sums up chs. 1–12, fulfilling the promise of 1:5.

enemies. See note 23:1.

21:45 Not one word . . . failed. The writer speaks of the conquest as completed (vv. 43–45 note; 10:40–42; 11:23; 23:1, 14), while continuing to describe the occupation as incomplete (13:1–7; 15:63; 17:12–13; 18:3; 23:5). A country may officially be defeated and occupied before every part of it ceases resistance.

the house of Israel. Israel is considered as a unity (1:12–15; 13:8–33 notes).

22:1–24:33 The book closes with three chapters about Israel's faithfulness, following God's faithfulness that has been the main subject so far (21:43–45 and note). The human response demanded by God's remarkable grace is the recurring theme of the final chapters. Each chapter begins with Joshua summoning the people (22:1; 23:1–2; 24:1), and focuses on the faithfulness God now requires of them.

22:1 Reubenites . . . Manasseh. See note 13:8–33.

22:4 rest. See 21:44; 1:13 and note.

22:5 to observe . . . to love . . . to walk. The various expressions used to describe the proper human response to the grace of God are found in Deuteronomy (4:9, 29; 6:5; 10:12–13; 11:13 and notes). They portray a wholehearted and confident love and obedience (23:11 and note; John 14:23).

22:6, 7 blessed. See 8:33 note.

22:8 Go back. Joshua's words of blessing are in the form of commands (like Gen. 1:28). To obey them is to receive the benefit.

22:9 Shiloh. See note 18:1.

Gilead. Referring generally to the land east of the Jordan.

22:10 an altar of imposing size. It would serve as a monument (v. 27).

belongs to the people of Israel." **12** And when the people of Israel heard of it, [h]the whole assembly of the people of Israel gathered at Shiloh to make war against them.

13 Then the people of Israel [h]sent to the people of Reuben and the people of Gad and the half-tribe of Manasseh, in the land of Gilead, [i]Phinehas the son of Eleazar the priest, **14** and with him ten chiefs, one from each of the tribal families of Israel, [j]every one of them the head of a family among the clans of Israel. **15** And they came to the people of Reuben, the people of Gad, and the half-tribe of Manasseh, in the land of Gilead, and they said to them, **16** "Thus says the whole congregation of the LORD, 'What is this breach of faith that you have committed against the God of Israel in turning away this day from following the LORD by building yourselves an altar this day [k]in rebellion against the LORD? **17** Have we not had enough of [l]the sin at Peor from which even yet we have not cleansed ourselves, and for which there came a plague upon the congregation of the LORD, **18** that you too must turn away this day from following the LORD? And if [k]you too rebel against the LORD today then tomorrow [m]he will be angry with the whole congregation of Israel. **19** But now, if the land of your possession is unclean, pass over into the LORD's land [n]where the LORD's tabernacle stands, and take for yourselves a possession among us. [o]Only do not rebel against the LORD or make us as rebels by building for yourselves an altar other than the altar of the LORD our God. **20** [p]Did not Achan the son of Zerah break faith in the matter of the devoted things, and [m]wrath fell upon all the congregation of Israel? And he did not perish alone for his iniquity.'"

21 Then the people of Reuben, the people of Gad, and the half-tribe of Manasseh said in answer to the heads of the families of Israel, **22** "The Mighty One, [q]God, the LORD! The Mighty One, God, the LORD! [r]He knows; and let Israel itself know! If it was in rebellion or in breach of faith against the LORD, do not spare us today **23** for building an altar to turn away from following the LORD. Or if we did so to offer burnt offerings or grain offerings or peace offerings on it, may the LORD himself [s]take vengeance. **24** No, but we did it from fear that [t]in time to come your children might say to our children, 'What have you to do with the LORD, the God of Israel? **25** For the LORD has made the Jordan a boundary between us and you, you people of Reuben and people of Gad. You have no portion in the LORD.' So your children might make our children cease to worship the LORD. **26** Therefore we said, 'Let us now build an altar, not for burnt offering, nor for sacrifice, **27** but to be [u]a witness between us and you, and between our generations after us, that we [v]do perform the service of the LORD in his presence with our burnt offerings and sacrifices and peace offerings, so your children will not say to our children in time to come, "You have no portion in the LORD."'

12 [h]Judg. 20:1
13 [h][See ver. 12 above] [i]Ex. 6:25; Num. 25:7; Judg. 20:28
14 [j]Num. 1:4
16 [k]ver. 18, 19; Num. 14:9; [Lev. 17:8, 9; Deut. 12:13, 14]
17 [l]Num. 25:3; Deut. 4:3; Ps. 106:28
18 [k][See ver. 16 above] [m]Num. 16:22
19 [n]ch. 18:1 [o]ver. 16, 18
20 [p]ch. 7:1, 5 [m][See ver. 18 above]
22 [q]Deut. 10:17 [r]1 Kin. 8:39
23 [s]Deut. 18:19; 1 Sam. 20:16
24 [t]See ch. 4:6, 21
27 [u]ver. 34; ch. 24:27; Gen. 31:48 [v]Deut. 12:5, 6, 17, 18

22:12 the whole assembly. See 8:35 and note.

to make war. The reaction of the Israelites can be understood in light of the command to have no rival altars to the one at the central sanctuary (Lev. 17:8–9). The law demanded disciplinary action against apostasy (Deut. 13:12–18).

22:13 Phinehas. His action at Peor (v. 17; Num. 25:7–8) adds solemnity to his being chosen for this mission.

22:16 the whole congregation. The unity of Israel is emphasized throughout Joshua. Geographical boundaries and differences of experience are transcended by the one God, under whose promises all Israel is one people (13:8–33 note). The corollary is that apostasy and rebellion against God will destroy this unity.

turning away. Apostasy is turning away from the Lord; repentance is turning away from sin and toward the Lord (1 Kin. 8:33; Jer. 3:7; Hos. 6:1).

an altar . . . in rebellion. The altar is understood by the rest of Israel in the light of such teaching as Lev. 17:8–9; Deut. 12. But the accusation is rash. The law requires careful investigation before taking action (Deut. 13:12–14).

22:17 the sin at Peor. This was an occasion of great apostasy before entering Canaan (Num. 25; Josh. 2:1 note).

not cleansed. For cleansing see Lev. 11–16. An inner cleansing also is implied here. The Israelites are not yet rid of the tendency they displayed at Peor.

22:18 angry. See note 7:1.

22:19 if the land . . . is unclean. That is, if the land is not made holy by God's presence. The land east of the Jordan was as much God's gift as the land on the west, despite the geographical separation (13:8–33 and note).

tabernacle. See note 18:1.

make us as rebels. Apostasy offends not only God but His people also.

22:23 building an altar. Both groups accept the teaching of passages such as Lev. 17:8, 9 and Deut. 12 (v. 16 note).

offerings. See Lev. 1–3.

22:25 a boundary between us and you. The Book of Joshua has repeatedly rejected disunity (v. 16 note).

no portion in the LORD. To deny that their land was God's land (v. 19) was to deny that they shared in God's promise.

22:27 witness. The altar was to function as a testimony (cf. the stones at Gilgal, 4:20–24), not a place of sacrifice.

28 And we thought, If this should be said to
us or to our descendants in time to come,
we should say, 'Behold, the copy of the
altar of the LORD, which our fathers made,
not for burnt offerings, nor for sacrifice,
but to be [u]a witness between us and you.'
29 Far be it from us that we should [w]rebel
against the LORD and turn away this day
from following the LORD [w]by building an
altar for burnt offering, grain offering, or
sacrifice, other than the altar of the LORD
our God that stands before his tabernacle!"
30 When [x]Phinehas the priest and the
chiefs of the congregation, the heads of the
families of Israel who were with him, heard
the words that the people of Reuben and
the people of Gad and the people of
Manasseh spoke, [y]it was good in their eyes.
31 And Phinehas the son of Eleazar the
priest said to the people of Reuben and the
people of Gad and the people of Manasseh,
"Today we know that [z]the LORD is in our
midst, because you have not committed
this breach of faith against the LORD. Now
you have delivered the people of Israel
from the hand of the LORD."
32 Then Phinehas the son of Eleazar the
priest, and the chiefs, returned from the
people of Reuben and the people of Gad [a]in
the land of Gilead to the land of Canaan, to
the people of Israel, and brought back word
to them. 33 And the report [b]was good in the
eyes of the people of Israel. And the people
of Israel [c]blessed God and spoke no more of
making war against them to destroy the
land where the people of Reuben and the
people of Gad were settled. 34 The people of
Reuben and the people of Gad called the
altar Witness, "For," they said, [d]"it is a witness between us that the LORD is God."

Joshua's Charge to Israel's Leaders

23 A long time afterward, when the
LORD had given [e]rest to Israel from
all their surrounding enemies, and Joshua
[f]was old and well advanced in years,
2 Joshua [g]summoned all Israel, its elders
and heads, its judges and officers, and said
to them, "I am now old and well advanced
in years. 3 And you have seen all that the
LORD your God has done to all these
nations for your sake, [h]for it is the LORD
your God who has fought for you. 4 Behold,
[i]I have allotted to you as an inheritance for
your tribes those nations that remain,
along with all the nations that I have
already cut off, from the Jordan to the
Great Sea in the west. 5 The LORD your God
[j]will push them back before you and drive
them out of your sight. And you shall possess their land, [k]just as the LORD your God
promised you. 6 Therefore, [l]be very strong
to keep and to do all that is written in the
Book of the Law of Moses, [m]turning aside
from it neither to the right hand nor to the
left, 7 [n]that you may not mix with these
nations remaining among you [o]or make
mention of the names of their gods [p]or
swear by them or serve them or bow down
to them, 8 [q]but you shall cling to the LORD

28 [u][See ver. 27 above]
29 [w]See ver. 16
30 [x]ver. 13, 14 [y]ver. 33
31 [z]Lev. 26:11, 12
32 [a]ver. 10, 11, 15
33 [b]ver. 30 [c]1 Chr. 29:20; Neh. 8:6; Dan. 2:19; Luke 2:28
34 [d]ver. 27
Chapter 23
1 [e]See ch. 11:23 [f]ch. 13:1
2 [g]ch. 24:1; [Deut. 31:28; 1 Chr. 28:1]
3 [h]ch. 10:14, 42; Ex. 14:14
4 [i]See ch. 13:2-7
5 [j]ch. 13:6; Ex. 23:30; 33:2; 34:11; Deut. 4:28; 11:23 [k]Num. 33:53
6 [l]ch. 1:7 [m]ch. 1:7; Deut. 5:32; 28:14
7 [n]Ex. 23:33; Deut. 7:2, 3 [o]Ex. 23:13; [Ps. 16:4] [p]Jer. 5:7; [Zeph. 1:5]
8 [q]ch. 22:5; Deut. 10:20; 11:22; 13:4

22:30 good in their eyes. Contrast Phinehas's reaction to actual apostasy in Num. 25:7–8.

22:31 the LORD is in our midst. The fears of v. 18 would not be realized because the suspected unfaithfulness had not occurred.

you have delivered. This is an unusual way of making an important point: by not turning from God they had saved Israel from God's wrath.

22:34 Witness. The altar witnessed (v. 27) to the one reality that united all Israel and, by implication, to the offense that could destroy Israel (v. 16).

23:1–16 Joshua in his old age addresses all Israel, probably at Shiloh (18:1; 19:51; 21:2). Chs. 23 and 24 take up the exhortations of ch. 1 and apply them to Israel following the substantial fulfillment of God's promises. The beginning and end of the book (chs. 1 and 23–24) convey the purpose of the whole, namely, an exhortation to faithful obedience based on the complete faithfulness of God to His promises. Joshua's speech in ch. 23 expresses this three times over (vv. 3–8, 9–13, 14–16), with variations in emphasis.

23:1 rest. See note 1:13. The experience of "rest . . . from all their surrounding enemies," here incompletely realized, will become part of Israel's hope (Deut. 12:10; 2 Sam. 7:11; 1 Chr. 22:9; cf. Mic. 5:9; Luke 1:71).

enemies. Israel represents God's kingship to the world (Ex. 19:5–6) and will ultimately bring blessing to the nations (Gen. 12:3). The nations' hostility to Israel is an expression of their hostility to God (cf. Gen. 3:15; Ex. 23:22 notes).

old. Joshua died at the age of 110 (24:29 note).

23:2 all Israel. He called representatives of every tribe.

23:3–8 In these verses the call to obedience is introduced by a reminder of God's faithfulness (vv. 5, 9, 14).

23:3 God . . . fought for you. See note 10:14.

23:4 nations that remain. Affirmation of the complete faithfulness of God to His promises and the incompleteness of the actual conquest stand side by side in this chapter (21:45 note).

inheritance. See note 1:6.

23:6 be very strong. The consequences of God's promises applied to Joshua in 1:6 (note) are now applied to all Israel.

and to do. See note 1:7.

Book of the Law. See note 1:8.

23:7 that you may not mix with these nations. The Hebrew makes a close connection between vv. 6 and 7. Faithful obedience to the Book of the Law will avoid religious association with the pagan nations.

23:8 cling to. See note 22:5.

your God just as you have done to this day.
9 [r]For the LORD has driven out before you
great and strong nations. And as for you,
[s]no man has been able to stand before you
to this day. **10** [t]One man of you puts to
flight a thousand, since it is the LORD your
God [u]who fights for you, just as he promised you. **11** [v]Be very careful, therefore, to
love the LORD your God. **12** For if you turn
back and cling to the remnant of these
nations remaining among you [w]and make
marriages with them, so that you associate
with them and they with you, **13** know for
certain that [x]the LORD your God will no
longer drive out these nations before you,
[y]but they shall be a snare and a trap for
you, a whip on your sides and thorns in
your eyes, until you perish from off this
good ground that the LORD your God has
given you.
14 "And now [z]I am about to go the way of
all the earth, and you know in your hearts
and souls, all of you, that [a]not one word
has failed of all the good things[1] that the
LORD your God promised concerning you.
All have come to pass for you; not one of
them has failed. **15** But just as all the good
things that the LORD your God promised
concerning you have been fulfilled for you,
so the LORD will bring upon you [b]all the
evil things, until he has destroyed you from
off this good land that the LORD your God
has given you, **16** if you transgress the
covenant of the LORD your God, which he
commanded you, and go and serve other
gods and bow down to them. Then the
anger of the LORD will be kindled against
you, and you shall perish quickly from off
the good land that he has given to you."

The Covenant Renewal at Shechem

24 Joshua gathered all the tribes of
Israel [c]to Shechem and [d]summoned
the elders, the heads, the judges, and the
officers of Israel. And [e]they presented themselves before God. **2** And Joshua said to all
the people, "Thus says the LORD, the God of
Israel, 'Long ago, [f]your fathers lived beyond
the Euphrates, Terah, the father of Abraham
and of Nahor; and [g]they served other gods.
3 [h]Then I took your father Abraham from

9 [r]ch. 13:6; Ex. 23:30; 33:2; 34:11; Deut. 4:28; 11:23 [s]ch. 1:5; 10:8; 21:44
10 [t][Lev. 26:8; Deut. 32:30] [u]ver. 3; Ex. 14:14; Deut. 3:22
11 [v]ch. 22:5
12 [w]Ex. 34:16; Deut. 7:3
13 [x]Judg. 2:3,
21 [y]Ex. 23:33; Num. 33:55; Deut. 7:16; Judg. 2:3
14 [z]1 Kin. 2:2 [a]ch. 21:45
15 [b]See Lev. 26:14-39; Deut. 28:15-68
Chapter 24
1 [c]ver. 25, 32 [d]See ch. 23:2 [e]1 Sam. 10:19
2 [f]See Gen. 11:27-32 [g][Gen. 31:30; 35:2]
3 [h]See Gen. 12:1-5; Acts 7:2-4

1 Or *words;* also twice in verse 15

as you have done. The previous generation who rebelled in the wilderness and the generations to follow did not do as well (cf. 24:31).

23:9 no man has been able to stand before you. The promise to Joshua in 1:5 has been fulfilled for the Israelites (Deut. 7:24; 11:25).

23:11 love the LORD your God. In the Bible love can be commanded. This does not mean that such love lacks emotional depth. It is actually more than emotion. It is expressed in glad and willing obedience (22:5 note).

23:12 turn back. See 22:16 and note.

make marriages with them. See notes Gen. 26:34, 35; 34:1–31; 38:1–30.

23:13 God will no longer drive out. The validity of God's promise (v. 5) is not dependent on human cooperation. The history of Israel shows this, as does the rest of the Bible, culminating in the work of Christ. But the promise will not benefit those who reject the grace of God. This provision was part of the promise from the beginning (Gen. 12:3).

23:14–16 See note on vv. 3–8. In this final section of Joshua's speech the exhortation is again based on a reminder of God's faithfulness, but consists entirely of warnings of the consequences of turning away from the Lord.

23:14 know in your hearts and souls. Knowledge of God's faithfulness can never be merely intellectual, but pervades and shapes every aspect of a person's life.

not one word has failed. See note 21:45.

23:15 good things . . . evil things. There are two sides to God's faithfulness, because there are two sides to His covenant: promises and warnings. God can be trusted to enforce the warnings as fully as He can be trusted to keep His promises.

23:16 transgress the covenant. See note 7:11.

anger. See note 7:1.

24:1–28 At the end of his life, Joshua led Israel in a reaffirmation of the covenant, much as Moses did before he died (Deut. 32:46). As with Deuteronomy, there may be an analogy between this covenant renewal and the kind of treaties that were typically used to formalize relations between powerful sovereign nations and weaker client states (see Deuteronomy: Introduction). These treaties, called "suzerainty treaties," commonly included elements like those found in Josh. 24, such as a historical prologue reviewing the care given by the powerful party to the client (vv. 2–13); a prohibition of any outside alliance (vv. 14, 23); and provision for a written document (vv. 25, 26). There are also significant differences between such ancient treaties and Josh. 24.

24:1 Joshua gathered all the tribes. See 8:33–35; 23:2 and note.

Shechem. The very place where God had first promised the land to the descendants of Abraham (Gen. 12:6–7) is the place where the descendants assemble, having received the land. See note 8:30.

before God. This does not necessarily imply the movement of the tabernacle from Shiloh (19:51) to Shechem for the occasion. The presence of God was not restricted to the tabernacle (cf. 1 Kin. 8:27), just as His presence was not guaranteed by physical possession of the ark (1 Sam. 4:3–11).

24:2 Thus says the LORD. Joshua speaks with the authority of Moses (Deut. 5:27) and of a prophet (Deut. 18:15–19).

beyond the Euphrates. The reference is presumably to Ur (Gen. 11:28) or Haran (Gen. 11:31).

other gods. The pagan beginning underlines the grace of God to which this history testifies, and provides the background for the exhortation in v. 14.

24:3–13 The word of God to the people on this occasion is not a new word. The books of Genesis (vv. 2–4), Exodus (vv. 5–7), Numbers (vv. 8–10), and Joshua (vv. 11–13) are reviewed by way of rehearsing God's dealings with the people since the time of Abraham, focusing on the gift of the land promised to Abraham and now received by his descendants. The review begins with a digest of Genesis from the promise to Abraham through the descent to Egypt (Gen. 11–50).

24:3 Then I. God is the dominant subject of the verbs in vv. 3–13.

beyond the River and [i]led him through all
the land of Canaan, and made his offspring
many. [j]I gave him Isaac. 4 And to Isaac I gave
[k]Jacob and Esau. [l]And I gave Esau the hill
country of Seir to possess, [m]but Jacob and
his children went down to Egypt. 5 [n]And I
sent Moses and Aaron, [o]and I plagued Egypt
with what I did in the midst of it, and [p]after-
ward I brought you out.
6 "'Then [p]I brought your fathers out of
Egypt, and [q]you came to the sea. [r]And the
Egyptians pursued your fathers with chariots
and horsemen to the Red Sea. 7 [s]And when
they cried to the LORD, [t]he put darkness
between you and the Egyptians [u]and made
the sea come upon them and cover them;
[v]and your eyes saw what I did in Egypt. [w]And
you lived in the wilderness a long time.
8 Then I brought you to the land of the
Amorites, who lived on the other side of the
Jordan. [x]They fought with you, and I gave
them into your hand, and you took possession of their land, and I destroyed them
before you. 9 [y]Then Balak the son of Zippor,
king of Moab, arose and fought against
Israel. [z]And he sent and invited Balaam the
son of Beor to curse you, 10 [a]but I would not
listen to Balaam. [a]Indeed, he blessed you. So
I delivered you out of his hand. 11 [b]And you
went over the Jordan and came to Jericho,
[c]and the leaders of Jericho fought against
you, and also [c]the Amorites, the Perizzites,
the Canaanites, the Hittites, the Girgashites,
the Hivites, and the Jebusites. And I gave
them into your hand. 12 And I sent [d]the hornet before you, which drove them out before
you, the two kings of the Amorites; it was
[e]not by your sword or by your bow. 13 I gave
you a land on which you had not labored
[f]and cities that you had not built, and you
dwell in them. You eat the fruit of vineyards
and olive orchards that you did not plant.'

Choose Whom You Will Serve

14 [g]"Now therefore fear the LORD and
serve him in sincerity and in faithfulness.
[h]Put away the gods that your fathers served
beyond the River and in Egypt, and serve
the LORD. 15 [i]And if it is evil in your eyes to
serve the LORD, [j]choose this day whom you
will serve, whether [h]the gods your fathers
served in the region beyond the River, or
[k]the gods of the Amorites in whose land
you dwell. [l]But as for me and my house, we
will serve the LORD."
16 Then the people answered, "Far be it
from us that we should forsake the LORD to
serve other gods, 17 for it is the LORD our God
who brought us and our fathers up from the

3 [i]Gen. 12:6 [j]Gen. 21:2, 3
4 [k]Gen. 25:24-26 [l]Gen. 36:8; Deut. 2:5 [m]Gen. 46:1, 6; Acts 7:15
5 [n]Ex. 3:10; 4:14 [o]See Ex. ch. 7–ch. 12 [p]Ex. 12:37, 51
6 [p][See ver. 5 above] [q]Ex. 14:2 [r]Ex. 14:9
7 [s]Ex. 14:10 [t]Ex. 14:20 [u]Ex. 14:27, 28 [v]Deut. 4:34; 29:2 [w]See ch. 5:6
8 [x]See Num. 21:21-35
9 [y][Judg. 11:25] [z]Num. 22:5; Deut. 23:4
10 [a]Num. 23:11, 20; 24:1, 10
11 [b]ch. 3:14, 17; 4:10-13
[c]ch. 6:1; See ch. 10:1-3; 11:1-3
12 [d]Ex. 23:28; Deut. 7:20 [e]Ps. 44:3
13 [f]Deut. 6:10, 11; [ch. 11:13]
14 [g]Deut. 10:12; 1 Sam. 12:24 [h]ver. 2, 23
15 [i]1 Kin. 18:21; Ezek. 20:39 [j]ver. 22 [h][See ver. 14 above] [k]Ex. 23:24, 32, 33; 34:15; Deut. 13:7; 29:18; Judg. 6:10 [l]Gen. 18:19

made his offspring many. The promise of many descendants to Abraham is a preeminent concern in Genesis (Gen. 12:2; 15:5; 17:2 and notes), and is related to God's blessing on humanity in Gen. 1:26–18 (cf. Ex. 1:7 note).

24:4 Jacob and Esau. The principle of divine election was clear in the choice of Jacob over Esau (Gen. 25:23; Rom. 9:11 and note). So also is the reality that God's promises are often in apparent conflict with the immediate course of history. Jacob had to go to Egypt.

24:5–7 Joshua's summary of Exodus is remarkable for its failure to mention the giving of the Law at Mount Sinai. The account concentrates on the actions leading directly to occupation of the Promised Land.

24:6 Red Sea. See note Ex. 13:18.

24:7 your eyes saw. The people of Joshua's day are spoken of as having participated in the redemptive events of the past. This emphasizes that they must see the goodness of God towards them not only in their personal experience, but also in the larger history of their people. See note 4:23, 24.

in the wilderness a long time. A few words summarize everything from the crossing of the sea to the arrival at the land. See note on vv. 5–7.

24:8–10 Joshua's summary of Numbers does not mention the rebellions that took place in the wilderness (Num. 14; 25), probably because the emphasis of his review is on the deeds of God.

24:8 Amorites. See note 2:10.

24:9 Balaam. See Num. 22–24; note on Josh. 13:22.

24:10 Indeed, he blessed you. Balaam illustrates God's complete power over those who would bring harm to His people.

24:11 Amorites . . . Jebusites. See 3:10 and note.

24:12 hornet. This is possibly a metaphor for sudden panic (2:9; 5:1; Ex. 23:28; Deut. 7:20).

not by your sword. The Israelites received the land as a gift that must not be understood as based on their own achievement (1:2 note; cf. Eph. 2:8).

24:14 fear the LORD. See 4:24. This response is demanded by the history of God's faithfulness to His promises in vv. 2–13. The fear of God is associated with knowledge of His grace and is fully compatible with love for Him (Deut. 10:12, 13; Ps. 130:4). Contrast 2:9, where the Canaanites fear God because of His coming judgment; and 7:5, where the Israelites experience His anger.

Put away the gods. This may refer literally to idols, or metaphorically to abandoning the gods they represent, or to both. The goodness of God to Israel (vv. 2–13) demands exclusive allegiance, summed up by the first commandment (Ex. 20:3).

the River. See note on v. 2.

and in Egypt. Israel's idolatry in Egypt will be remembered by Ezekiel (20:7–10; 23:3–8, 19–21, 27).

24:15 choose this day whom you will serve. There is some irony in offering a kind of choice after the Lord is rejected. The choice is between the gods Abraham left behind (vv. 2, 3) and the gods of the dispossessed Amorites (vv. 12; 2:10 note).

me and my house. See 6:25; 7:24; Acts 16:15.

24:16–18 In response to the call of v. 14, the people repudiate other gods (v. 16), acknowledge the Lord's goodness from the Exodus to the conquest, and conclude by promising obedience to the Lord.

land of Egypt, out of the house of slavery,
and who did those great signs in our sight
and preserved us in all the way that we
went, and among all the peoples through
whom we passed. **18** And the LORD drove out
before us all the peoples, the Amorites who
lived in the land. Therefore we also will
serve the LORD, for he is our God."
19 But Joshua said to the people, "You are
not able to serve the LORD, for he is [m]a holy
God. He is [n]a jealous God; [o]he will not forgive your transgressions or your sins. **20** [p]If
you forsake the LORD and serve foreign gods,
then [q]he will turn and do you harm and consume you, after having done you good."
21 And the people said to Joshua, "No, but we
will serve the LORD." **22** Then Joshua said to
the people, "You are witnesses against yourselves that [r]you have chosen the LORD, to
serve him." And they said, "We are witnesses." **23** He said, "Then [s]put away the foreign
gods that are among you, and incline your
heart to the LORD, the God of Israel." **24** And
the people said to Joshua, "The LORD our
God we will serve, and his voice we will
obey." **25** So Joshua [t]made a covenant with
the people that day, and put in place [u]stat-
utes and rules for them at Shechem. **26** And
Joshua [v]wrote these words in the Book of the
Law of God. And [w]he took a large stone and
set it up there [x]under the terebinth that was
by the sanctuary of the LORD. **27** And Joshua
said to all the people, "Behold, [y]this stone
shall be a witness against us, for [z]it has heard
all the words of the LORD that he spoke to us.
Therefore it shall be a witness against you,
lest you deal falsely with your God." **28** So
Joshua [a]sent the people away, every man to
his inheritance.

Joshua's Death and Burial

29 [b]After these things Joshua the son of
Nun, the servant of the LORD, died, being
110 years old. **30** And they buried him in
his own inheritance at [c]Timnath-serah,
which is in the hill country of Ephraim,
north of the mountain of Gaash.
31 [d]Israel served the LORD all the days of
Joshua, and all the days of the elders who
outlived Joshua [e]and had known all the
work that the LORD did for Israel.
32 [f]As for the bones of Joseph, which the
people of Israel brought up from Egypt,
they buried them at Shechem, in the piece
of land [g]that Jacob bought from the sons of
Hamor the father of Shechem for a hundred pieces of money.[1] It became an inheritance of the descendants of Joseph.
33 And Eleazar the son of Aaron died, and
they buried him at Gibeah, the town of
[h]Phinehas his son, which had been given
him in [i]the hill country of Ephraim.

1 Hebrew *for a hundred qesitah*; a unit of money of unknown value

19 [m]Lev. 19:2 1 Sam. 6:20; Ps. 99:5, 9; Isai. 5:16 [n]Ex. 20:5; Nah. 1:2 [o]Ex. 23:21
20 [p][1 Chr. 28:9; 2 Chr. 15:2; Ezra 8:22; Isai. 1:28; 65:11, 12; Jer. 17:13] [q]ch. 23:15; Isai. 63:10; [Acts 7:42]
22 [r]ver. 15
23 [s]ver. 14; Judg. 10:16; 1 Sam. 7:3
25 [t]2 Kin. 11:17 2 Chr. 23:16; Neh. 9:38 [u]Ex. 15:25
26 [v]Deut. 31:24 [w][ch. 4:3; Gen. 28:18] [x]Gen. 35:4; Judg. 9:6
27 [y]ch. 22:27, 28, 34; Gen. 31:48, 52; Deut. 31:19, 21, 26 [z][Deut. 32:1]
28 [a]Judg. 2:6
29 [b]For ver. 29-31, see Judg. 2:7-9
30 [c][ch. 19:50]
31 [d]Judg. 2:7 [e]Deut. 11:2; 31:13
32 [f]Gen. 50:25; Ex. 13:19 [g]Gen. 33:19
33 [h]ch. 22:13 [i]ver. 30; ch. 17:15

24:19 You are not able to serve the LORD. This paradoxical statement will all too soon be proved true (v. 31 note; 7:1–26 note; 23:12, 13 note; Judg. 2:7, 10–13; 2 Kin. 17:7–23; Deut. 31:16). It is based on the holiness of God, who cannot be approached casually (Ps. 15:1, 2; Eccl. 5:1, 2). Also, Joshua warns the people because he knows their rebelliousness himself (22:17 and note).

holy. Only a people separated from pagan ways (Lev. 18:3; 20:26) can serve the God who is holy, entirely separate from other gods (Lev. 19:2).

jealous. See Ex. 20:5 and note.

will not forgive. The transgressions in view here amount to the apostasy described in the following verse.

24:20 he will turn. God's dealing will change from grace to judgment (Gen. 6:7). In another sense God never changes (1 Sam. 15:29), since His promise has always included the threat of judgment (23:15; Gen. 6:6 and notes).

24:21 we will serve the LORD. The people reject the possibility envisaged or predicted in v. 20.

24:22 witnesses against yourselves. When they are accused of forsaking the Lord the case against them will be supported by their decision on this occasion.

24:23 put away. See note on v. 14.

24:25 made a covenant. Joshua formalized the relationship (cf. Gen. 15:18; Deut. 4:23; 29:1; see also notes on 3:3; 9:6).

statutes and rules. These would specify the content of Israel's obedience to the Lord.

24:26 Book of the Law of God. This is probably to be identified with the Book of the Law in 1:8; 8:31; 23:6.

terebinth. Compare Gen. 12:6; 35:4; Judg. 9:6.

24:27 witness. Compare how the stones at Gilgal were to provide a testimony to what God had done (4:20–24 and note).

24:28 every man to his inheritance. These words are an appropriate concluding note to the book that tells of God's giving the promised inheritance to Israel. Similar words occur, after a considerably different period, at the end of the Book of Judges (Judg. 21:24). See note 1:6.

24:29–33 The deaths of Joshua and Eleazar mark the end of the period that has been the subject of this book. Their burials, along with the burial of the bones of Joseph, in the land that is now Israel's possession symbolizes God's faithful fulfillment of His promises to the patriarchs.

24:29 servant of the LORD. See note 1:1.

110. This age is the same as Joseph's at his death (Gen. 50:22 and note). Such long lives signified God's blessing (cf. Deut. 34:7).

24:30 his own inheritance. See 19:49–50. Unlike Abraham, who had to purchase land for a burial plot (Gen. 23:4; cf. Gen. 33:19), Joshua is buried in his own land.

24:31 Israel served the LORD all the days of Joshua. The faithfulness of the generation of Joshua and the elders is testimony to the Lord's power in everything He had done for Israel. That such faithfulness would be so short-lived supports Joshua's assertion in vv. 19–20 (notes; Judg. 2:7, 10–13).

24:32 the bones of Joseph. The promise believed by Joseph (Gen. 50:24, 25 and notes) now comes to fulfillment.

Jacob bought. See Gen. 33:19. The new situation of owning the land is again contrasted with the time of the patriarchs, who had only the promise of it.

24:33 Eleazar. See note 14:1.

Phinehas. See note 22:13.

THE BOOK OF

Judges

AUTHOR

The original author of Judges is unknown, though we may infer certain things about him from his work. He evidently supported David's kingship over that of Saul's son Ish-bosheth, who was from the tribe of Benjamin. The author's loyalty to David and the tribe of Judah would indicate that he lived and wrote during the early period of David's reign at Hebron. The writer of Judges addresses the Israelites of his day from the same theological point of view as the Book of Deuteronomy. The final form of the Book of Judges is doubtless the work of a person or group that shared this perspective. See also "Characteristics and Themes," below, and "Introduction to the Historical Books" on page 295.

DATE AND OCCASION

The subject matter of Judges suggests that the book was composed during a period when there was strong controversy about whether the king should be from the house of David and the tribe of Judah, or from the house of Saul and the tribe of Benjamin. There were rival kings from these tribes when David ruled in Hebron, and Ish-bosheth, Saul's son, ruled in the north. Judges ends with events that severely compromise the reputation of the tribe of Benjamin.

The events narrated in Judges span about 350 years, from the conquest of Canaan (c. 1400 B.C.) until just before Samuel, who anointed the first king of Israel (c. 1050 B.C.). The first of the judges in the book, Othniel, appears during the generation following Joshua. Samson, the last judge in the book, was a contemporary of Samuel. During this period Israel was oppressed from within by the Canaanites and from without by the Arameans, Moabites, Midianites, Ammonites, Amalekites, Amorites, and Philistines.

Like the other historical books of the Old Testament, Judges might be treated as a sermon addressed to the covenant community at a time of crisis. The readers had not themselves experienced the events described in the book. Rather, the readers were of a later generation facing their own crisis in keeping the covenant. The stories of successes and failures either encouraged or sobered the later generation. Judges records a period of gross ignorance and sin. The people are depicted as unstable and easily led into idolatry. Extreme crimes are described in the book.

Gideon asks the question that is central to Judges: "if the LORD is with us, why then has all this happened to us?" (6:13). There was warning in Deuteronomy that the result of turning away from God and serving idols would be the sort of suffering that took place during the period of the judges. God would seem to be absent and the land would be filled with sorrows (Deut. 31:16,17). Israel needed a king who could teach them how to keep their covenant with the Lord.

CHARACTERISTICS AND THEMES

Judges can be divided into three distinct sections (Introduction: Outline). Each section has its own internal style and consistency, containing lively narration of God's people and leaders in action. Occasionally humorous, sometimes tragic, but never dull, the individual stories within the sections are complete in themselves.

Each episode and section employs verbal repetition, historical comparison, and quotations from the Book of Joshua to emphasize the connections between people, places, and events. The reader is invited to search for the pattern and moral framework of the history.

The central section of Judges (3:7–16:31), the bulk of the book, makes an extensive use of repetition. The author describes a repeating sequence of events. The Israelites do evil in the eyes of the Lord, turning to serve other gods. God becomes angry and delivers them up to oppressors. They cry out for help, and God raises up a judge to deliver them. The judge brings peace, but the nation returns to sin as soon as the judge dies. The repeated phrasing describing this pattern reinforces the point that the Israelites were unrepentant. While each judge and the details of the deliverance he brought varies, the end was inevitable: the people again did evil in the eyes of the Lord.

Six major judges are described, interspersed with the mention of six lesser judges. The opening and closing sections of the book are like bookends, enclosing the cyclical narratives about the judges. The introduction (1:1–2:5) points out Israel's general failure to conquer the land according to the provisions of the covenant God had made with them. The cycles of the twelve judges show that the judges could not lead the people into faithfulness to the covenant. There was a downward spiral of increasing disobedience. The conclusion (chs. 17–21) recounts two especially grievous examples of covenant disobedience. The writer repeats the brief, tragic observation, "There was no king in Israel. Everyone did what was right in his own eyes."

The writer of Judges, like the authors of the other historical books, calls the community of faith to obey the covenant, applying to their lives the teaching of Deuteronomy. He points to the successes and failures of previous generations, and challenges the people of David's time to be faithful to the covenant. He warns them prophetically about the dangers of the wrong kind of leadership.

According to Judges, Israel was falling away from the covenant and worshiping false gods as they forgot the Lord's acts of salvation in the past (2:10; 6:13). As in Deuteronomy, the sin of seeking other gods is the continuing pattern of covenant disobedience (Judg. 2:11, 12; 3:7, 12; 8:33; 10:6, 10; Deut. 4:23). The repeated cycles with the constant refrains, "the people of Israel did what was evil in the sight of the LORD" (2:11; 3:7, 12; 4:1; 6:1; 10:6; 13:1) and "everyone did what was right in his own eyes" (17:6; 21:25; cf. Deut. 12:8; 31:16, 17), were a sharp warning to Israel in David's early kingship that they absolutely needed a king who could enable the nation to keep the terms of their covenant with God.

Beyond these immediate applications for the original audience of Judges, we should observe that later readers doubtless saw in the book the hope for a new David who would teach them to keep their covenant with the Lord. This would be especially true of those who read the book in the days of the divided monarchy or during and after the exile to Babylon. In New Testament days, the gospel of Jesus, the son of David (Matt. 1:1), answers the longing of the readers of Judges for the presence of a godly king, and heightens the church's expectation of His return in glory.

TITLE

The title "Judges" refers to the twelve men God raised up prior to the time of Samuel to deliver Israel from their oppressors (2:11–19). The normal translation of the Hebrew noun and verb as "judge" and "to judge" can be misleading to modern readers, since the judges of Israel were military and political leaders rather than officials presiding over courts of law. Deborah is the only judge who is mentioned as having a judicial function in the usual sense (4:4, 5). The last judge, Samuel, was a priest and prophet. At one point God is called "the Judge" (11:27).

OUTLINE OF JUDGES

I. Introduction: Questions of Leadership and Conquest Completion (1:1–2:5)
- A. *The Promise to Judah (1:1, 2)*
- B. *Various Tribes in the Conquest (1:3–36)*
  1. Judah's Successes (1:3–20)
  2. Benjamin's Failure to Take Jerusalem (1:21)
  3. Joseph's Success at Bethel (1:22–26)
  4. Failures in Conquest by the Rest of the Tribes (1:27–36)
- C. *God's Judgment for Disobedience (2:1–5)*

II. Cycles of the Judges (2:6–16:31)
- A. *Pattern for All That Follows (2:6–3:6)*
  1. Joshua and the Generation After Him (2:6–10)
  2. The Pattern of Israel's Covenant Obedience (2:11–19)
  3. God's Judgment for Covenant Disobedience (2:20–3:6)
     - a. *The Purpose in God's Judgment (2:20–23)*
     - b. *The Instruments of God's Judgment (3:1–6)*

OUTLINE OF JUDGES (Cont.)

- B. *The Failure of Twelve Judges to Maintain Faithfulness to the Covenant (3:7–16:31)*
  1. Othniel (3:7–11)
  2. Ehud (3:12–30)
  3. Shamgar (3:31)
  4. Deborah and Barak (chs. 4; 5)
  5. Gideon and His Son Abimelech (chs. 6–9)
     - a. *Gideon (6:1–8:32)*
     - b. *Abimelech (8:33–9:57)*
  6. Tola (10:1, 2)
  7. Jair (10:3–5)
  8. Jephthah (10:6–12:7)
  9. Ibzan (12:8–10)
  10. Elon (12:11, 12)
  11. Abdon (12:13–15)
  12. Samson (chs. 13–16)

III. Two Grievous Sins (chs. 17–21)

- A. *The Danites and Idolatry (chs. 17; 18)*
- B. *Civil War: Israel Against Benjamin (chs. 19–21)*

The Continuing Conquest of Canaan

1 After the death of Joshua, the people of
Israel [a]inquired of the LORD, [b]"Who
shall go up first for us against the
Canaanites, to fight against them?" 2 The
LORD said, "Judah shall go up; behold, I
have given the land into his hand." 3 And
Judah said to Simeon his brother, "Come
up with me into the territory allotted to
me, that we may fight against the
Canaanites. [c]And I likewise will go with
you into the territory allotted to you." So
Simeon went with him. 4 Then Judah went
up and the LORD gave the Canaanites and
the Perizzites into their hand, and they
defeated 10,000 of them at Bezek. 5 They
found Adoni-bezek at Bezek and fought
against him and defeated the Canaanites
and the Perizzites. 6 Adoni-bezek fled, but
they pursued him and caught him and cut
off his thumbs and his big toes. 7 And
Adoni-bezek said, "Seventy kings with their
thumbs and their big toes cut off [d]used to
pick up scraps under my table. [e]As I have
done, so God has repaid me." And they
brought him to Jerusalem, and he died
there.
8 [f]And the men of Judah fought against
Jerusalem and captured it and struck it
with the edge of the sword and set the city
on fire. 9 And afterward the men of Judah
went down to fight against the Canaanites
who lived in [g]the hill country, in the
Negeb, and in [g]the lowland. 10 [h]And Judah
went against the Canaanites who lived in
Hebron [i](now the name of Hebron was formerly Kiriath-arba), and they defeated
[j]Sheshai and Ahiman and Talmai.
11 From there they went against the
inhabitants of Debir. The name of Debir
was formerly Kiriath-sepher. 12 And Caleb
said, "He who attacks Kiriath-sepher and
captures it, I will give him Achsah my
daughter for a wife." 13 And Othniel the son
of Kenaz, [k]Caleb's younger brother, captured it. And he gave him Achsah his
daughter for a wife. 14 When she came to
him, she urged him to ask her father for a
field. And she dismounted from her donkey, and Caleb said to her, "What do you
want?" 15 She said to him, "Give me a blessing. Since you have set me in the land of
the Negeb, give me also springs of water."
And Caleb gave her the upper springs and
the lower springs.
16 And the descendants of the [l]Kenite,
Moses' father-in-law, went up with the
people of Judah [m]from the city of palms

Chapter 1
1 [a]Num. 27:21; 1 Sam. 22:10; 2 Sam. 2:1 [b]ch. 20:18
3 [c]ver. 17
7 [d][Luke 16:21] [e][Lev. 24:19; 1 Sam. 15:33]
8 [f][Josh. 15:63]
9 [g]Josh. 9:1; 11:2, 16; 12:8
10 [h]For ver. 10-15, see Josh. 15:13-19 [i]Josh. 14:15; 15:13 [j]Num. 13:22; Josh. 15:14
13 [k]ch. 3:9
16 [l]ch. 4:11, 17; 1 Sam. 15:6 [m]Deut. 34:3

1:1–2:5 This introduction to Judges, in which covenant keeping finds expression in dispossessing and destroying the Canaanites, raises the question of leadership for fighting them (v. 1). The covenant-keeping successes and failures of the various tribes, and God's judgment on Israel for the covenant failure of letting the Canaanites live in the land, are recounted (cf. Deut. 7:1–2; 20:16–20). The space and detail given to Judah's successes (vv. 3–20) contrast strongly with the brief accounts of the failures of the other tribes (vv. 21–36), although the house of Joseph is treated positively (vv. 22–26).

1:1 After. The Book of Joshua opens similarly: "After the death of Moses" (Josh. 1:1).

Who. The Israelites ask an almost identical question at the end of the book—"Who shall go up first for us to fight against the people of Benjamin?" (20:18). The choice of God is Judah. David and his heirs would come from this tribe.

Canaanites. The Canaanites were one of several groups inhabiting the land of Canaan. The Israelites were commanded to annihilate them (Deut. 7:1–2; 20:16–20), and whether they could obey these terms of the covenant will be the issue for this entire introductory section.

1:8 sword. Judah obeyed the covenant by destroying the inhabitants without mercy (Deut. 7:1–2; 20:16–20). Judah did not occupy Jerusalem at this point (v. 21).

1:10–15 These verses describing the victories of Caleb and Othniel are quoted from Josh. 15:13–19.

1:12 Caleb. Caleb, though of Kenizzite ancestry (Gen. 15:19; Num. 32:12), was counted as belonging to the tribe of Judah. He represented Judah when the spies were sent into Canaan (Num. 13:6).

1:13 Othniel . . . Caleb's younger brother. See Josh. 15:17–19. Judg. 1:12–15 provides the only real picture of this first judge.

into the wilderness of Judah, which lies in
the Negeb near [n]Arad, [o]and they went and
settled with the people. 17 [p]And Judah went
with Simeon his brother, and they defeated
the Canaanites who inhabited Zephath and
devoted it to destruction. So the name of
the city was called [q]Hormah.[1] 18 Judah also
[r]captured Gaza with its territory, and
Ashkelon with its territory, and Ekron with
its territory. 19 [p]And the LORD was with
Judah, and he took possession of the [s]hill
country, but he could not drive out the
inhabitants of the plain because they had
[t]chariots of iron. 20 [u]And Hebron was given
to Caleb, as Moses had said. And he drove
out from it [v]the three sons of Anak. 21 But
the people of Benjamin did not drive out
the Jebusites who lived in Jerusalem, [w]so the
Jebusites have lived with the people of
Benjamin in Jerusalem to this day.
22 The house of Joseph also went up
against Bethel, [x]and the LORD was with
them. 23 And the house of Joseph scouted
out Bethel. ([y]Now the name of the city was
formerly Luz.) 24 And the spies saw a man
coming out of the city, and they said to
him, "Please show us the way into the city,
[z]and we will deal kindly with you." 25 And
he showed them the way into the city. And
they struck the city with the edge of the
sword, but they let the man and all his family go. 26 And the man went to [a]the land of
the Hittites and built a city and called its
name Luz. That is its name to this day.

Failure to Complete the Conquest

27 [b]Manasseh did not drive out the inhabitants of Beth-shean and its villages, or
Taanach and its villages, or the inhabitants
of Dor and its villages, or the inhabitants of
Ibleam and its villages, or the inhabitants
of Megiddo and its villages, for the
Canaanites persisted in dwelling in that
land. 28 When Israel grew strong, they put
the Canaanites to forced labor, but did not
drive them out completely.
29 [c]And Ephraim did not drive out the
Canaanites who lived in Gezer, so the
Canaanites lived in Gezer among them.
30 Zebulun did not drive out the inhabitants of Kitron, or the inhabitants of
[d]Nahalol, so the Canaanites lived among
them, but became subject to forced labor.
31 [e]Asher did not drive out the inhabitants of Acco, or the inhabitants of Sidon
or of Ahlab or of Achzib or of Helbah or of
Aphik or of Rehob, 32 so the Asherites lived
among the Canaanites, the inhabitants of
the land, for they did not drive them out.
33 Naphtali did not drive out the inhabitants of [f]Beth-shemesh, or the inhabitants
of Beth-anath, so they lived among the
Canaanites, the inhabitants of the land.
Nevertheless, the inhabitants of Beth-
shemesh and of Beth-anath became subject
to forced labor for them.
34 [g]The Amorites pressed the people of
Dan back into the hill country, for they did
not allow them to come down to the plain.
35 The Amorites persisted in dwelling in
Mount Heres, [h]in Aijalon, and in Shaalbim,
but the hand of the house of Joseph rested
heavily on them, and they became subject
to forced labor. 36 And the border of the
Amorites ran from [i]the ascent of Akrabbim,
from Sela and upward.

Israel's Disobedience

2 Now the angel of the LORD went up
from Gilgal to [j]Bochim. And he said, "I
brought you up from Egypt and brought

16 [n]Num. 21:1 [o]See Num. 10:29-32
17 [p]ver. 3 [q]ver. 2, 22; Num. 21:3
18 [r][ch. 3:3; Josh. 11:22]
19 [p][See ver. 17 above] [s]See ver. 9 [t]Josh. 17:16, 18
20 [u]Num. 14:24; Deut. 1:36; Josh. 14:9, 13; 15:13, 14 [v]ver. 10
21 [w][Josh. 15:63]
22 [x]ver. 19
23 [y]Gen. 28:19; 35:6; 48:3; Josh. 18:13
24 [z]Josh. 2:12, 14
26 [a]Josh. 1:4
27 [b]For ver. 27, 28, see Josh. 17:11-13
29 [c]Josh. 16:10; 1 Kin. 9:16
30 [d][Josh. 19:15; 21:35]
31 [e]For ver. 31, 32, see Josh. 19:24-30
33 [f]For ver. 33, see Josh. 19:32-39
34 [g][Josh. 19:47, 48]
35 [h]Josh. 19:42
36 [i]Num. 34:4; Josh. 15:3
Chapter 2
1 [j]ver. 5

1 *Hormah* means *utter destruction*

1:19 the LORD was with Judah. God kept His covenant promise (v. 2). With the exception of the house of Joseph, the writer deals briefly with the rest of the tribes, describing as failures their efforts at settlement (1:27–36 note).

chariots of iron. Such chariots, with their wooden wheels overlaid with iron, were powerful weapons, especially on the level plains. In effect, Judah is excused for failing to dislodge the Canaanites.

1:20 Caleb. Caleb, from the tribe of Judah, is an example of faithfulness to the covenant. In Deut. 1:36–37, Caleb is rewarded for his covenant obedience, an obedience flowing from faith in God's promise.

1:21 people of Benjamin. The writer specifies that Benjamin, Saul's tribe, did not make a final conquest of Jerusalem. According to Joshua 15:63, the tribe of Judah also failed to drive the Jebusites out of Jerusalem. The city was on the border between the two tribes. The complete conquest of Jerusalem was left for David to accomplish (2 Sam. 5:7).

1:22 the LORD was with them. Besides Judah (v. 19), only with regard to the house of Joseph is it said that "the LORD was with them."

1:27–36 Judah, Benjamin, and Joseph have already been mentioned. The shortcomings of the remaining tribes are briefly presented in outline fashion.

1:34 people of Dan. See chs. 17–18.

2:1–5 This passage reviews the preceding chapter, and like 2:20–3:6, provides the background for the narrative that follows. The covenant was made between God and "your fathers"; these are the parties to the covenant. The covenant terms forbid treaties or mixed worship with the Canaanites. Failure to observe these requirements brought the judgment of the covenant on Israel (Deut. chs. 28–31).

2:1 the angel of the LORD. A theophany, that is, a visible revelation of God. See 6:11–24; 13:2–23. The words of God's preeminent messenger (6:11–24; Ex. 3:1–17) are the words of the Lord Himself. The Angel of the Lord led Israel out of captivity in Egypt and fought for them (Ex. 14:19; 23:20–23; 33:2; Num. 20:16; Is. 63:9).

Gilgal. The ark of the covenant was at Gilgal (Josh. 5:1–12).

you into the land that I swore to give to
your fathers. I said, [k]'I will never break my
covenant with you, 2 [l]and you shall make
no covenant with the inhabitants of this
land; [m]you shall break down their altars.'
But you have not obeyed my voice. What is
this you have done? 3 So now I say, [n]"I will
not drive them out before you, but they
shall become [o]thorns in your sides,[1] and
their gods shall be a snare to you." 4 As
soon as the angel of the LORD spoke these
words to all the people of Israel, the people
lifted up their voices and wept. 5 And they
called the name of that place Bochim.[2] And
they sacrificed there to the LORD.

The Death of Joshua

6 When Joshua dismissed the people, the
people of Israel went each to his inheritance to take possession of the land. 7 [p]And
the people served the LORD all the days of
Joshua, and all the days of the elders who
outlived Joshua, who had seen all the great
work that the LORD had done for Israel.
8 And Joshua the son of Nun, the servant of
the LORD, died at the age of 110 years.
9 And they buried him within the boundaries of [q]his inheritance in Timnath-heres,
[r]in the hill country of Ephraim, north of
the mountain of Gaash. 10 And all that generation also were gathered to their fathers.
And there arose another generation after
them who did not know the LORD or the
work that he had done for Israel.

Israel's Unfaithfulness

11 [s]And the people of Israel did what was
evil in the sight of the LORD and served the
Baals. 12 [t]And they abandoned the LORD, the
God of their fathers, who had brought them
out of the land of Egypt. [u]They went after
other gods, from among the gods of the peoples who were around them, and [v]bowed
down to them. [w]And they provoked the
LORD to anger. 13 They abandoned the LORD
[x]and served the Baals and the Ashtaroth.
14 [y]So the anger of the LORD was kindled
against Israel, and he [z]gave them over to
plunderers, who plundered them. [a]And he
sold them into the hand of their surrounding enemies, [b]so that they could no longer
withstand their enemies. 15 Whenever they
marched out, the hand of the LORD was
against them for harm, as the LORD had

1 [k]Gen. 17:7; Ex. 6:4; Deut. 31:16
2 [l]Deut. 7:2 [m]Deut. 12:3
3 [n]ver. 21 [o]Num. 33:55; Josh. 23:13
7 [p]For ver. 7-9, see Josh. 24:29-31
9 [q]Josh. 19:50 [r]Josh. 24:33
11 [s]ch. 3:7; 4:1; 6:1; 10:6; 13:1
12 [t]Deut. 31:16 [u][Deut. 6:14] [v]ver. 17, 19; [Ex. 20:5] [w]Deut. 31:29
13 [x]ch. 3:7; 10:6; Ps. 106:36; [1 Sam. 7:4]
14 [y]ver. 20 [z]2 Kin. 17:20 [a]ch. 3:8; 4:2; [Deut. 32:30; 1 Sam. 12:9] [b]Lev. 26:37; Josh. 7:12, 13

[1] Vulgate, Old Latin (compare Septuagint); Hebrew *sides* [2] *Bochim* means *weepers*

I brought you up from Egypt. The Ten Commandments begin with the same statement (Ex. 20:2; Deut. 5:6), a reminder that the history of what God has done is linked to His commands. The Sovereign God who publishes the covenant identifies Himself as the Benefactor of His people.

and brought you into the land that I swore. God kept His oath (Josh. 23:3–16). The chief difference here between God and His people is that God keeps His vow while the people break theirs.

I will never break my covenant. See Deut. 7:9.

2:2 you shall break down their altars. Idolatry is taken as the leading, typical act of covenant breaking (v. 11; Ex. 34:13; Num. 33:52; Deut. 7:5; 12:3; Josh. 23:16).

you have not obeyed. Israel contracted marriages with the people of the land (3:5–6) and did not tear down their altars (6:25–32). The Canaanites could not be driven out because of Israel's sin.

2:3 thorns . . . a snare. Intermarriage and all other relationships with the Canaanites had been forbidden because such contact would lead to idolatry (Ex. 34:12; Num. 33:55; Deut. 7:16; Josh. 23:12–13). For disobeying the terms of the covenant, Israel would suffer what Canaan suffered, removal from the land (Num. 33:56; Josh. 23:13; 2 Kin. 17:5–8; 25:1–11).

2:6–10 This section, except for v. 10, is closely similar to Josh. 24:28–31 and introduces the pattern for the cycles of the judges that follows.

2:6 When Joshua. See 1:1; Introduction: Date and Occasion.

2:7 the people served the LORD. See Josh. 24:16–18, 21–22, 31. Covenant obedience led to blessing in the land for that generation.

had seen all the great work. See v. 10; Deut. 4:9; 6:22; 7:19; 11:2–7; Josh. 23:3.

2:10 who did not know the LORD or the work that he had done for Israel. One generation was to declare God's wonders to the next (Deut. 4:9; 6:1–6). Later psalmists extol them (Ps. 44:1–3; 78:2–8). If God's people knew what He had done they would obey the commands of His covenant. But the leaders—heads of families, priests, and judges—failed to keep the covenant or to tell the next generation about God's mighty deeds.

2:11–19 These verses give the pattern for chs. 3–16. They show the sovereignty of God in history as He executes the judgment of the covenant. It was He who sold the people and fought against them, and it was He also who raised up the judges to deliver them. Idolatry was the sin on account of which God punished Israel. Vv. 11–19 are elaborated in 1 Sam. 12:9–11 and Ps. 106:34–46.

2:11 did what was evil. This refrain occurs at 2:11; 3:7, 12; 4:1; 6:1; 10:6; 13:1.

served the Baals. Israel's evil is summed up in their worship of false gods (v. 2 note). They chose Baal, the Canaanite storm god, and rejected the Lord, who had brought them through the Red Sea and was the true Lord of the storm. "Baals" is plural because Baal was worshiped differently in each Canaanite locality.

2:13 Ashtaroth. These were the goddesses of fertility in the Canaanite pantheon.

2:14 he gave them over. See Deut. 28:48; 1 Sam. 12:9. Israel's enemies and oppressors had no power over God's people unless God allowed it. Israel's conquest is now reversed, as people from outside Canaan (Arameans, Moabites, Midianites, Amalekites, and Philistines) oppress Israel, the new inhabitants of the land (3:8–12; 4:2; 6:1; 10:7; 13:1).

2:15 the hand of the LORD was against them. The hand of the Lord was associated with the saving power of God (Ex. 3:20; 6:1; 13:3; Deut. 4:34). Now the same hand was turned against them in punishment. The Lord was faithful both to bless and to judge. When God rescues His people, He rescues them from their enemies as an act of grace. It is His own judgment that allows their enemies to prevail, and in rescuing them He must turn this judgment aside.

warned, [c]and as the LORD had sworn to
them. And they were in terrible distress.

The LORD Raises Up Judges

16 [d]Then the LORD raised up judges, [e]who
saved them out of the hand of those who
plundered them. 17 Yet they did not listen to
their judges, for [f]they whored after other
gods and bowed down to them. [g]They soon
turned aside from the way in which their
fathers had walked, who had obeyed the
commandments of the LORD, and they did
not do so. 18 Whenever the LORD raised up
judges for them, [h]the LORD was with the
judge, and he saved them from the hand of
their enemies all the days of the judge. [i]For
the LORD was moved to pity by [j]their groaning because of those who afflicted and
oppressed them. 19 But [k]whenever the judge
died, they turned back and were more corrupt than their fathers, going after other
gods, serving them and bowing down to
them. They did not drop any of their practices or their stubborn ways. 20 [l]So the anger
of the LORD was kindled against Israel, and
he said, "Because this people [m]have transgressed my covenant that I commanded
their fathers and have not obeyed my voice,
21 [n]I will no longer drive out before them any
of the nations that Joshua left when he
died, 22 in order [o]to test Israel by them,
whether they will take care to walk in the
way of the LORD as their fathers did, or not."
23 So the LORD left those nations, not driving
them out quickly, and he did not give them
into the hand of Joshua.

3 [p]Now these are the nations that the
LORD left, to test Israel by them, that is,
all in Israel who had not experienced all the
wars in Canaan. 2 It was only in order that
the generations of the people of Israel might
know war, to teach war to those who had not
known it before. 3 These are the nations: [q]the
five lords of the Philistines and all the
Canaanites and the Sidonians and the Hivites who lived on Mount Lebanon, from
Mount Baal-hermon as far as Lebo-hamath.
4 They were for [r]the testing of Israel, to know
whether Israel would obey the commandments of the LORD, which he commanded
their fathers by the hand of Moses. 5 So the
people of Israel lived [s]among the Canaanites,
the Hittites, the Amorites, the Perizzites, the
Hivites, and the Jebusites. 6 [t]And their
daughters they took to themselves for wives,
and their own daughters they gave to their
sons, and they served their gods.

Othniel

7 [u]And the people of Israel did what was
evil in the sight of the LORD. They forgot the
LORD their God and served the Baals and
[v]the Asheroth. 8 Therefore the anger of the
LORD was kindled against Israel, [w]and he
sold them into the hand of [x]Cushan-
rishathaim king of Mesopotamia. And the
people of Israel served Cushan-rishathaim
eight years. 9 But when the people of Israel
[y]cried out to the LORD, the LORD raised up a
[z]deliverer for the people of Israel, who
saved them, [a]Othniel the son of Kenaz,
Caleb's younger brother. 10 [b]The Spirit of the
LORD was upon him, and he judged Israel.
He went out to war, and the LORD gave
Cushan-rishathaim king of Mesopotamia
into his hand. And his hand prevailed over

15 [c]See Lev. 26:14-46; Deut. 28:15-68
16 [d]ch. 3:9, 15; 1 Sam. 12:11; Acts 13:20 [e]ch. 3:31; 10:1, 12, 13; 12:2, 3; 13:5; [ch. 3:9; Neh. 9:27]
17 [f]ch. 8:33; Ex. 34:15 [g]Deut. 9:12
18 [h][Josh. 1:5] [i]Gen. 6:6; Deut. 32:36; Ps. 106:45; Jer. 18:8; 26:3; [Num. 23:19] [j]Ex. 2:24; 6:5
19 [k][ch. 3:12; 4:1; 6:1; 8:33]
20 [l]ver. 14 [m]Deut. 17:2; Josh. 23:16
21 [n]ver. 3; Josh. 23:13
22 [o]ch. 3:1, 4; Ex. 15:25; [Deut. 8:2, 16; 13:3]
Chapter 3
1 [p]ver. 4; ch. 2:21, 22
3 [q]See Josh. 13:2-6
4 [r]ver. 1
5 [s]Ex. 3:8; Ps. 106:35
6 [t][Ex. 34:16; Deut. 7:3; Ezra 9:12]
7 [u]ch. 2:11-13 [v]ch. 6:25; Ex. 34:13
8 [w]ch. 2:14 [x]Hab. 3:7
9 [y]ver. 15; ch. 4:3; 6:7; 10:10 [z]ver. 15; ch. 2:16; Neh. 9:27 [a]ch. 1:13
10 [b]ch. 6:34; 11:29; 13:25; 14:6, 19; 15:14

2:16 judges. The role of the judges was primarily to rescue the nation from its enemies (3:9, 15; 1 Sam. 12:11).

2:17 they whored after. Since the covenant agreement can be compared to marriage, harlotry is a standard metaphor for faithlessness and disobedience (8:33; Deut. 31:16; the Book of Hosea).

2:18 was moved to pity. The people's groaning moved their God (Ex. 2:24; 6:5).

2:19 They did not drop. Neither their judges (v. 17) nor the memory of how they had been delivered was enough to make the people keep the covenant (v. 10).

2:23 left those nations. See Deut. 7:22–23; Josh. 13:1–7. This explains why there were still Canaanites during a period when Israel had been faithful (vv. 6–9). Vv. 20–22 and 3:1–4 provide a new reason for God's leaving the Canaanites, to test the hearts of the people.

3:1 not experienced. See 2:10. Even God's judgment was not without grace. The testing was an opportunity for a generation who had not seen the Lord work on their behalf to exercise faith and see His might with their own eyes (v. 2).

3:3 Philistines . . . Canaanites . . . Sidonians . . . Hivites. The Canaanites and the Hivites were to be utterly destroyed (1:1). David defeated or destroyed them.

3:5 among the Canaanites . . . Jebusites. All these were nations devoted to destruction (1:1). Israel violated the covenant by living among them and not destroying them.

3:6 their daughters they took. This had the effect of leading the Israelites into idolatry. The result of making covenants with the Canaanites rather than destroying that population is repeatedly explained in the following narrative cycles (2:2). It becomes clear that the people cared more about covenants with their pagan neighbors than their covenant with God.

3:7 the Baals and the Asheroth. See 2:11, 13 and notes.

3:9 Othniel. See 1:13 note. The prominence of Judah in Israel is highlighted, since the first judge was from Judah and was the only judge without an explicit failure in his own covenant keeping. The success of Judah promotes David, who was from that tribe.

3:10 Spirit of the LORD. The Spirit is also mentioned in connection with Gideon, Jephthah, and Samson. By the gift of the Spirit the judge was empowered to deliver the people (6:34; 11:29; 13:25; 14:6, 19; 15:14).

he judged Israel. This means he fought for Israel and delivered them. See Introduction: Title.

Cushan-rishathaim. 11 [c]So the land had rest
forty years. Then Othniel the son of Kenaz
died.

Ehud

12 [d]And the people of Israel again did
what was evil in the sight of the LORD, and
the LORD strengthened Eglon [e]the king of
Moab against Israel, because they had done
what was evil in the sight of the LORD. 13 He
gathered to himself the Ammonites and the
[f]Amalekites, and went and defeated Israel.
And they took possession of [g]the city of
palms. 14 And the people of Israel served
Eglon the king of Moab eighteen years.
15 Then the people of Israel [h]cried out to
the LORD, and the LORD raised up for them
[h]a deliverer, Ehud, the son of Gera, the
Benjaminite, [i]a left-handed man. The people of Israel sent tribute by him to Eglon
the king of Moab. 16 And Ehud made for
himself a sword with two edges, a cubit[1] in
length, and he bound it on his right thigh
under his clothes. 17 And he presented the
tribute to Eglon king of Moab. Now Eglon
was a very fat man. 18 And when Ehud had
finished presenting the tribute, he sent
away the people who carried the tribute.
19 But he himself turned back [j]at the idols
near Gilgal and said, "I have a secret message for you, O king." And he commanded,
"Silence." And all his attendants went out
from his presence. 20 And Ehud came to
him as he was sitting alone in his [k]cool roof
chamber. [l]And Ehud said, "I have a message from God for you." And he arose from
his seat. 21 And Ehud reached with his left
hand, took the sword from his right thigh,
and thrust it into his belly. 22 And the hilt
also went in after the blade, and the fat
closed over the blade, for he did not pull
the sword out of his belly; and the dung
came out. 23 Then Ehud went out into the
porch[2] and closed the doors of the roof
chamber behind him [m]and locked them.
24 When he had gone, the servants came,
and when they saw that the doors of the
roof chamber were locked, they thought,
[n]"Surely he is relieving himself in the closet
of the cool chamber." 25 And they waited till
they were embarrassed. But when he still
did not open the doors of the roof chamber,
they took the key and opened them, and
there lay their lord dead on the floor.
26 Ehud escaped while they delayed, and
he passed beyond [o]the idols and escaped
to Seirah. 27 When he arrived, [p]he sounded
the trumpet in [q]the hill country of
Ephraim. Then the people of Israel went
down with him from the hill country, and
he was their leader. 28 And he said to them,
"Follow after me, [r]for the LORD has given
your enemies the Moabites into your
hand." So they went down after him and
seized [s]the fords of the Jordan against the
Moabites and did not allow anyone to pass
over. 29 And they killed at that time about
10,000 of the Moabites, all strong, able-
bodied men; not a man escaped. 30 So
Moab was subdued that day under the
hand of Israel. [t]And the land had rest for
eighty years.

Shamgar

31 After him was [u]Shamgar the son of
Anath, who killed 600 of the Philistines
[v]with an oxgoad, and he also [w]saved Israel.

Deborah and Barak

4 [x]And the people of Israel again did
what was evil in the sight of the LORD

11 [c][ver. 30; ch. 5:31; 8:28; Josh. 11:23]
12 [d]ch. 2:19 [e]1 Sam. 12:9
13 [f]ch. 5:14; 6:33; Ps. 83:7 [g]ch. 1:16; Deut. 34:3
15 [h]See ver. 9 [i]ch. 20:16; [1 Chr. 12:2]
19 [j]ver. 26; [Josh. 4:20]
20 [k]Amos 3:15 [l][2 Sam. 20:9, 10]
23 [m][2 Sam. 13:17, 18]
24 [n]1 Sam. 24:3
26 [o]ver. 19
27 [p]ch. 6:34; 1 Sam. 13:3 [q]See Josh. 24:33
28 [r]ch. 4:7, 14; 7:9, 15; 1 Sam. 17:47; 2 Chr. 16:8; [1 Kin. 22:12, 15] [s]ch. 12:5; Josh. 2:7; [ch. 7:24]
30 [t]ver. 11
31 [u]ch. 5:6 [v][ch. 5:8; 1 Sam. 13:19, 22] [w]See ch. 2:16
Chapter 4
1 [x]See ch. 2:19

[1] A *cubit* was about 18 inches or 45 centimeters [2] The meaning of the Hebrew word is uncertain

3:11 the land had rest forty years. Though the pattern in 2:11–19 does not mention the time length of peace, the stories themselves end with a comment about peace or the lack of it (v. 30; 5:31; 8:28; 12:7; 15:20; 16:31).

3:12–30 The story of Ehud humiliates the oppressor of God's people.

3:12 See 2:11 note.

Eglon the king of Moab. The Lord strengthened the pagan king to be used as His instrument of judgment.

3:15 left-handed. Lit. "with his right hand restricted." This is not the usual Hebrew word for "left-handed." It is used elsewhere only in 20:16, also for the men of Benjamin. "Benjamin" can be translated "son of the right hand," and the writer may be making a pun about a left-handed son of the right hand.

3:20 I have a message from God for you. The secret message of v. 19 here becomes a divine message. It was not a false word, but the true word of God working against the same rod raised up by God to punish His people (v. 12 note). Eglon was useful as a tool of God's wrath against Israel, but now that wrath comes back upon him.

3:28 the LORD has given. Each major judge except for Othniel verbally acknowledges God's control in Israel's victory (4:14; 7:15; 11:21–30; 15:18; 16:28).

3:30 rest for eighty years. See v. 11 note.

3:31 Shamgar the son of Anath. Shamgar is mentioned only here and in the song of Deborah (5:6). Since Anath was a Canaanite goddess of war, perhaps "son of Anath" was a war hero's nickname.

600 . . . with an oxgoad. Samson slew one thousand Philistines with the jawbone of a donkey (15:15–17).

after Ehud died. 2 And the LORD [y]sold them
into the hand of [z]Jabin king of Canaan,
who reigned in [z]Hazor. The commander
of his army was [a]Sisera, who lived in
[b]Harosheth-hagoyim. 3 Then the people of
Israel [c]cried out to the LORD for help, for he
had [d]900 chariots of iron and he oppressed
the people of Israel cruelly for twenty years.
4 Now Deborah, a prophetess, the wife of
Lappidoth, was judging Israel at that time.
5 She used to sit under the palm of Deborah
between Ramah and Bethel in [e]the hill
country of Ephraim, and the people of
Israel came up to her for judgment. 6 She
sent and summoned [f]Barak the son of
Abinoam from [g]Kedesh-naphtali and said
to him, "Has not the LORD, the God of
Israel, commanded you, 'Go, gather your
men at Mount [h]Tabor, taking 10,000 from
the people of Naphtali and the people of
Zebulun. 7 And I will draw out Sisera, the
general of Jabin's army, to meet you by [i]the
river Kishon with his chariots and his
troops, [j]and I will give him into your
hand'?" 8 Barak said to her, "If you will go
with me, I will go, but if you will not go
with me, I will not go." 9 And she said, "I
will surely go with you. Nevertheless, the
road on which you are going will not lead
to your glory, for the LORD will [k]sell Sisera
into the hand of a woman." Then Deborah
arose and went with Barak to Kedesh.
10 And Barak called out [l]Zebulun and
Naphtali to Kedesh. And 10,000 men went
up at his heels, and Deborah went up with
him.
11 Now Heber [m]the Kenite had separated
from the Kenites, the descendants of
[n]Hobab the father-in-law of Moses, and
had pitched his tent as far away as the oak
in [o]Zaanannim, which is near Kedesh.
12 When Sisera was told that Barak the
son of Abinoam had gone up to Mount
Tabor, 13 Sisera called out all his chariots,
[p]900 chariots of iron, and all the men who
were with him, from Harosheth-hagoyim to
the river Kishon. 14 And Deborah said to
Barak, "Up! For this is the day in which
[q]the LORD has given Sisera into your hand.
[r]Does not the LORD go out before you?" So
Barak went down from Mount Tabor with
10,000 men following him. 15 [s]And the
LORD routed Sisera and all his chariots and
all his army before Barak by the edge of the
sword. And Sisera got down from his chariot and fled away on foot. 16 And Barak pursued the chariots and the army to
Harosheth-hagoyim, and all the army of
Sisera fell by the edge of the sword; not a
man was left.
17 But Sisera fled away on foot to the tent
of Jael, the wife of Heber the Kenite, for
there was peace between Jabin the king of
Hazor and the house of Heber the Kenite.
18 And Jael came out to meet Sisera and said
to him, "Turn aside, my lord; turn aside to
me; do not be afraid." So he turned aside
to her into the tent, and she covered him
with a rug. 19 And he said to her, "Please
give me a little water to drink, for I am
thirsty." So she opened [t]a skin of milk and
gave him a drink and covered him. 20 And
he said to her, "Stand at the opening of the
tent, and if any man comes and asks you,
'Is anyone here?' say, 'No.'" 21 But Jael the
wife of Heber took a tent peg, and took a
hammer in her hand. Then she went softly
to him and drove the peg into his temple

2 [y]ch. 2:14 [z][Josh. 11:1, 10] [a]1 Sam. 12:9; Ps. 83:9 [b]ver. 13, 16
3 [c]See ch. 3:9 [d]ver. 13; [ch. 1:19]
5 [e]See Josh. 24:33
6 [f]Heb. 11:32 [g]Josh. 19:37 [h]ch. 8:18
7 [i]ver. 13; ch. 5:21; 1 Kin. 18:40; Ps. 83:9 [j]See ch. 3:28
9 [k]See ch. 2:14
10 [l]ch. 5:18
11 [m]ch. 1:16 [n]Num. 10:29 [o]Josh. 19:33
13 [p]ver. 3
14 [q]ver. 7 [r]Deut. 9:3; 2 Sam. 5:24; Ps. 68:7; Isai. 52:12
15 [s]ver. 23; Ps. 83:9; [Josh. 10:10]
19 [t]ch. 5:25

4:2 Jabin. This Jabin is a descendant of the Jabin mentioned in Josh. 11:1–9.

4:4 Deborah, a prophetess, the wife of Lappidoth. Lit. "a woman, a prophetess, the wife of Lappidoth." The emphasis is that a woman is the leader in Israel. Deborah, a prophetess, is introduced at the point where the narrator usually mentions the deliverer (6:8 note).

4:5 sit . . . for judgment. That is, she was a magistrate, handing down legal decisions.

4:6 Mount Tabor. This was a rounded hillock standing isolated on the north side of the plain in the Jezreel Valley.

4:7 river Kishon. The river Kishon was near the base of Mount Tabor and was virtually dry for much of the year (v. 15 note).

4:8 If you will go. Barak was asking Deborah to risk her life to verify the truth of her words, and he was also asking a woman to do what he had been assigned to do. From his point of view the mission was suicidal, since the exposed Mount Tabor could easily be surrounded by the chariots of Sisera, cutting off any escape. Barak's faith was not equal to this danger.

4:9 will not lead to your glory. Barak was punished for doubting (v. 8).

for the LORD will sell Sisera into the hand of a woman. The enemy will not be delivered to Barak, but to a woman. As God would have it, Jael (v.17) will succeed where faithless Barak will fail (vv. 18–22).

4:10 Zebulun and Naphtali. See 5:13–18.

4:13 river Kishon. See vv. 7, 15.

4:14 the LORD has given Sisera. Deborah confirms her word from the Lord (v. 7).

4:15 the LORD routed. From Deborah's song we learn that the Lord sent rain that would cause flash floods, trapping the chariots.

4:18–21 See 5:24–27 for the poetic account.

4:21 drove the peg. No motive is given for Jael's action. A woman killed

until it went down into the ground while
he was lying fast asleep from weariness. So
he died. 22 And behold, as Barak was pursuing Sisera, Jael went out to meet him and
said to him, "Come, and I will show you
the man whom you are seeking." So he
went in to her tent, and there lay Sisera
dead, with the tent peg in his temple.
23 [u]So on that day God subdued Jabin the
king of Canaan before the people of Israel.
24 And the hand of the people of Israel
pressed harder and harder against Jabin
the king of Canaan, until they destroyed
Jabin king of Canaan.

The Song of Deborah and Barak

5 [v]Then sang Deborah and Barak the son of Abinoam on that day:

2 "That the leaders took the lead in
Israel,
that [w]the people offered
themselves willingly,
bless the LORD!

3 "Hear, O kings; give ear, O princes;
to the LORD I will sing;
I will make melody to the LORD,
the God of Israel.

4 "LORD, [x]when you went out from
Seir,
when you marched from the region
of Edom,
[y]the earth trembled
and the heavens dropped,
yes, the clouds dropped water.
5 The mountains [z]quaked before the
LORD,
[a]even Sinai before the LORD, the
God of Israel.

6 "In the days of [b]Shamgar, son of
Anath,
in the days of [c]Jael, [d]the highways
were abandoned,
and travelers kept to the byways.
7 The villagers ceased in Israel;
they ceased to be until I arose;
I, Deborah, arose as a mother in
Israel.
8 [e]When new gods were chosen,
then war was in the gates.
[f]Was shield or spear to be seen
among forty thousand in Israel?
9 My heart goes out to the
commanders of Israel
who [g]offered themselves willingly
among the people.
Bless the LORD.

10 "Tell of it, [h]you who ride on white
donkeys,
you who sit on rich carpets[1]
and you who walk by the way.
11 To the sound of musicians[2] at the
watering places,
there they repeat the righteous
triumphs of the LORD,
the righteous triumphs of his
villagers in Israel.

"Then down to the gates marched the
people of the LORD.

12 [i]"Awake, awake, Deborah!
Awake, awake, break out in a song!
Arise, Barak, [j]lead away your
captives,
O son of Abinoam.

23 [u]ver. 15
Chapter 5
1 [v][Ex. 15:1]
2 [w]ver. 9; [2 Chr. 17:16]
4 [x]Deut. 33:2; [Ps. 68:7]
[y]2 Sam. 22:8; Ps. 18:7; 68:8; 77:18; Nah. 1:5; Hab. 3:10
5 [z]Isai. 64:1, 3
[a][Ex. 19:18; Deut. 4:11]
6 [b]ch. 3:31
[c]ch. 4:17
[d]Lev. 26:22; Isai. 33:8; Lam. 1:4
8 [e]ch. 2:12, 17; Deut. 32:16
[f][1 Sam. 13:19, 22]
9 [g]ver. 2
10 [h][ch. 10:4; 12:14; Zech. 9:9]
12 [i]Ps. 57:8
[j]Ps. 68:18; Eph. 4:8

1 The meaning of the Hebrew word is uncertain; it may connote *saddle blankets* 2 Or *archers*; the meaning of the Hebrew word is uncertain

Sisera, and the Lord's word to Barak was fulfilled (v. 9). Women were not normally warriors, and it was considered shameful to die at the hands of a woman (9:53–54).

5:1–32 "The Song of Deborah" is famous for its age and for its outstanding literary quality.

5:2 That the leaders took the lead. Leadership is a major theme in Judges.

5:4 from Seir . . . from the region of Edom. Mount Seir was the main mountain ridge running through Edom, Israel's point of departure for the battles of conquest (Deut. 33:2). God is pictured as the mighty Warrior going before His people.

5:4, 5 the earth trembled . . . before the LORD. God is pictured as a warrior who fights by means of the created elements. The portrayal of God as ruling the storm is doubly appropriate: by defeating Sisera with a cloudburst (v. 20) God refutes Baal's claim to be lord of the storm.

5:6, 7 the highways were abandoned. Israel's failed leadership had resulted in chaos and foreign domination. It was not like the days in which God had been the warrior at the front of Israel (vv. 4–5). The roads were abandoned because they were not safe for travel on account of the foreign oppressors and robbers. No one provided protection.

5:7 a mother in Israel. The princes would not lead (implied by v. 2), but a woman was raised up to lead Israel. Contrast this "mother in Israel" with the despairing mother of Sisera (v. 28).

5:8 When new gods were chosen, then war was in the gates. This is a poetic representation of the cycle of sin and punishment (2:11–19). Idolatry brings suffering to the city.

5:9 offered themselves. Later in the song there is a pointed comparison of those who volunteered to fight and those who for some reason refused (v. 13–23).

5:10 ride on white donkeys. Donkeys were ridden by nobility; the song is addressed to the princes mentioned in vv. 2, 9.

5:11 the righteous triumphs of the LORD. The Lord's righteous acts are His intervention and defeat of His people's enemies. These are His judgments in the earth (cf. Rev. 15:4).

13 Then down marched the remnant of
the noble;
the people of the LORD marched
down for me against the mighty.
14 From Ephraim [k]their root [l]they
marched down into the valley,[1]
following you, Benjamin, with your
kinsmen;
from [m]Machir marched down the
commanders,
and from Zebulun those who bear
the lieutenant's[2] staff;
15 the princes of Issachar came with
Deborah,
and Issachar faithful to [n]Barak;
into the valley they rushed at his
heels.
Among the clans of Reuben
there were great searchings of heart.
16 Why did you sit still [o]among the
sheepfolds,
to hear the whistling for the flocks?
Among the clans of Reuben
there were great searchings of heart.
17 [p]Gilead stayed beyond the Jordan;
[q]and Dan, why did he stay with the
ships?
[r]Asher sat still [s]at the coast of the sea,
staying by his landings.
18 [t]Zebulun is a people who risked their
lives to the death;
[t]Naphtali, too, on the heights of the
field.

19 "The kings came, they fought;
then fought the kings of Canaan,
at [u]Taanach, by the waters of
[v]Megiddo;
[w]they got no spoils of silver.
20 [x]From heaven the stars fought,
from their courses they fought
against Sisera.
21 [y]The torrent Kishon swept them away,
the ancient torrent, the torrent
Kishon.
March on, my soul, with might!

22 "Then loud beat the horses' hoofs
with the galloping, galloping of his
steeds.

14 [k]ch. 3:27; 12:15 [l][ch. 12:15] [m]Num. 32:39, 40
15 [n]ch. 4:14
16 [o]Gen. 49:14; Ps. 68:13; [Num. 32:1]
17 [p]See Josh. 13:24-28 [q][Josh. 19:46] [r][Josh. 19:29, 31] [s]Gen. 49:13
18 [t]ch. 4:10
19 [u]ch. 1:27; Josh. 17:11; 1 Kin. 4:12 [v]2 Kin. 9:27; 23:29, 30; 2 Chr. 35:22 [w][ver. 30]
20 [x]Josh. 10:11
21 [y]ch. 4:7
23 [z][ch. 21:9, 10]
24 [a]ch. 4:17
25 [b]ch. 4:19
26 [c]ch. 4:21
28 [d][2 Sam. 6:16] [e][Prov. 7:6]
30 [f]Ex. 15:9
31 [g][Ps. 83:9, 10] [h][2 Sam. 23:4; Dan. 12:3; Matt. 13:43] [i]Ps. 19:5; 37:6 [j]See ch. 3:11

23 "Curse Meroz, says the angel of the
LORD,
curse its inhabitants thoroughly,
[z]because they did not come to the
help of the LORD,
to the help of the LORD against the
mighty.

24 "Most blessed of women be [a]Jael,
the wife of Heber the Kenite,
of tent-dwelling women most
blessed.
25 [b]He asked water and she gave him milk;
she brought him curds in a noble's
bowl.
26 [c]She sent her hand to the tent peg
and her right hand to the
workmen's mallet;
she struck Sisera,
she crushed his head;
she shattered and pierced his temple.
27 Between her feet
he sank, he fell, he lay still;
between her feet
he sank, he fell;
where he sank,
there he fell—dead.

28 [d]"Out of the window she peered,
the mother of Sisera wailed
through [e]the lattice:
'Why is his chariot so long in coming?
Why tarry the hoofbeats of his
chariots?'
29 Her wisest princesses answer,
indeed, she answers herself,
30 'Have they not found and [f]divided
the spoil?—
A womb or two for every man;
spoil of dyed materials for Sisera,
spoil of dyed materials embroidered,
two pieces of dyed work
embroidered for the neck as spoil?'

31 [g]"So may all your enemies perish,
O LORD!
But your friends be [h]like the sun
[i]as he rises in his might."

[j]And the land had rest for forty years.

[1] Septuagint; Hebrew *in Amalek* [2] Hebrew *commander's*

5:15 great searchings. The failure of Reuben, Gilead, Dan, and Asher (v. 17) to participate shows that Israel was not united.

5:20 the stars fought. The participation of the heavens means that God was intervening, fighting as the divine Warrior from heaven. This text has been appealed to in history as biblical grounds for astrology, but this distorts the sense of the passage.

5:23 Meroz. A city of uncertain location.

5:24–27 This section of the song closely parallels the narrative of 4:18–22.

5:31 rest for forty years. This standard conclusion ties Deborah's and Barak's song to ch. 4 (cf. 2:19; 3:11).

Midian Oppresses Israel

6 [k]The people of Israel did what was evil in
the sight of the LORD, and the LORD gave
them into the hand of [l]Midian seven years.
2 And the hand of Midian overpowered Israel,
and because of Midian the people of Israel
made for themselves the dens that are in the
mountains and [m]the caves and the strongholds. 3 For whenever the Israelites planted
crops, the Midianites and [n]the Amalekites
and [o]the people of the East would come up
against them. 4 They would encamp against
them [p]and devour the produce of the land,
as far as Gaza, and leave no sustenance in
Israel and no sheep or ox or donkey. 5 For
they would come up with their livestock and
their tents; they would come [q]like locusts in
number—both they and their camels could
not be counted—so that they laid waste the
land as they came in. 6 And Israel was brought
very low because of Midian. And the people
of Israel [r]cried out for help to the LORD.

7 When the people of Israel cried out to
the LORD on account of the Midianites,
8 the LORD sent a prophet to the people of
Israel. And he said to them, "Thus says the
LORD, the God of Israel: [s]I led you up from
Egypt and brought you out of the house of
bondage. 9 And I delivered you from the
hand of the Egyptians and from the hand
of all who oppressed you, and [t]drove them
out before you and gave you their land.
10 And I said to you, 'I am the LORD your
God; [u]you shall not fear the gods of the
Amorites in whose land you dwell.' But
you have not obeyed my voice."

The Call of Gideon

11 Now the angel of the LORD came and
sat under the terebinth at Ophrah, which
belonged to Joash [v]the Abiezrite, while his
son [w]Gideon was beating out wheat in the
winepress to hide it from the Midianites.
12 And [x]the angel of the LORD appeared to
him and said to him, [y]"The LORD is with
you, O mighty man of valor." 13 And
Gideon said to him, "Please, sir,[1] if the
LORD is with us, why then has all this happened to us? And where are [z]all his wonderful deeds [a]that our fathers recounted to
us, saying, 'Did not the LORD bring us up
from Egypt?' But now the LORD has forsak-
en us and given us into the hand of
Midian." 14 And the LORD[2] turned to him
and said, "Go in this might of yours and
save Israel from the hand of Midian; [b]do
not I send you?" 15 And he said to him,
[c]"Please, Lord, how can I save Israel?
Behold, [d]my clan is the weakest in
Manasseh, and I am the least in my father's
house." 16 And the LORD said to him, [e]"But
I will be with you, and you shall strike the
Midianites as one man." 17 And he said to
him, [f]"If now I have found favor in your
eyes, then [g]show me a sign that it is you
who speaks with me. 18 Please [h]do not
depart from here until I come to you and
bring out my present and set it before
you." And he said, "I will stay till you
return."

19 So Gideon went into his house [i]and prepared a young goat and unleavened cakes

Chapter 6
1 [k]See ch. 2:19 [l]Gen. 25:2; Num. 25:17, 18; Hab. 3:7
2 [m]1 Sam. 13:6; Heb. 11:38
3 [n]ch. 3:13 [o]ver. 33; ch. 7:12; 8:10; Gen. 29:1; 1 Kin. 4:30; Job 1:3
4 [p][Lev. 26:16]; See Deut. 28:30-33, 51; Mic. 6:15
5 [q]ch. 7:12
6 [r]See ch. 3:9
8 [s]1 Sam. 10:18
9 [t]Ps. 44:2, 3
10 [u]Josh. 24:15; See 2 Kin. 17:35-38
11 [v]ch. 8:2; Josh. 17:2 [w]Heb. 11:32
12 [x]ch. 13:3; Luke 1:11; [Acts 10:3] [y]Josh. 1:5
13 [z]Ps. 89:49; Isai. 63:15 [a]Ps. 44:1
14 [b]1 Sam. 12:11; [Josh. 1:9]
15 [c][Ex. 3:11] [d]1 Sam. 9:21; 18:18
16 [e]Ex. 3:12; Josh. 1:5
17 [f]Ex. 33:13 [g]2 Kin. 20:8, 9; Isai. 7:11; [ver. 36, 37]; See Ex. 4:1-8
18 [h]ch. 13:15; Gen. 18:3-5
19 [i]Gen. 18:6-8

1 Or *Please, my Lord* 2 Septuagint *the angel of the LORD*; also verse 16

6:1–8:32 Gideon was the greatest of the judges. The following facts bear out this judgment. (a) His story is the longest in the book. (b) The Lord is more visibly active in his story than in any of the others. (c) The Angel of the Lord appeared to him, but to no other judge (vv. 11–24). (d) Centuries later Isaiah remembers Gideon's defeat of Midian as a significant victory (Is. 9:4; 10:26). (e) He is listed first in Samuel's list of deliverers ("Jerubbaal," 1 Sam. 12:11). (f) He is paralleled with Moses (6:11–24 note). (g) The people sought to make him king (8:22–23). (h) He lived like a king (8:26–27, 30, 32). Yet for all this, Gideon failed badly at one point. Gideon made a gold ephod that drew him and others into sin (8:27). In his greatness and in his deficiency, Gideon pointed to the need for a better deliverer, a king who would truly keep the covenant. In this way he points to Christ.

6:2 Midian overpowered. None of the other stories in Judges devotes such attention to the details of the oppression as this one. Homes, crops, and livestock were subject to the covenant curse (Deut. 28:30–33, 38–42). The Midianite oppression was so great that Isaiah mentioned it centuries later (Is. 9:4; 10:26).

6:6 was brought very low. Lit. "made small." The covenant curse was a reversal of God's promise to Abraham (Gen. 15:5; 22:17; Deut. 28:62; Ps. 107:38–39).

cried out. See 2:19; 3:9.

6:8 a prophet. The prophets constantly reminded the people of their covenant obligations. The words of this unnamed prophet (vv. 8–10) are virtually identical to the words of the Angel of the Lord in 2:1–3.

6:8, 9 brought . . . delivered . . . drove them . . . gave you. Remembering these saving actions of God is the first part of covenant keeping. In Israel religious apostasy was linked to forgetting God's saving acts, and His law.

6:11–24 This is the heart of the Gideon narrative. His call is similar to Moses' call (Ex. 3); he asks the question that is central to the book's message (v. 13); and his search for faith begins with signs (6:1–8:32 note). The search for and need for a covenant-keeping deliverer like the prophet Moses is the focus of Judges.

6:11 angel of the LORD came. See 2:1; 13:3.

6:13 why. This question is central to the Book of Judges. The Angel did not answer the question, since the prophet had already answered it (vv. 8–10; Deut. 28:47–52; 29:24–27; 31:17–18). Some of the psalms ask a similar question (Ps. 44:20; 74:9–11).

6:14 Go in this might of yours. See v. 34; 7:2, 7. God would be his strength, though Gideon did not yet know it.

6:15 weakest. When asked about kingship, Saul used similar words (1 Sam. 9:21).

from an ephah[1] of flour. The meat he put in
a basket, and the broth he put in a pot, and
brought them to him under the terebinth
and presented them. 20 And the angel of God
said to him, "Take the meat and the unleavened cakes, and put them [j] on this rock, and
[k] pour the broth over them." And he did so.
21 Then the angel of the LORD reached out
the tip of the staff that was in his hand and
touched the meat and the unleavened cakes.
[l] And fire sprang up from the rock and consumed the flesh and the unleavened cakes.
And the angel of the LORD vanished from his
sight. 22 Then Gideon perceived that he was
the angel of the LORD. And Gideon said,
[m] "Alas, O Lord GOD! For now I have seen
the angel of the LORD face to face." 23 But the
LORD said to him, [n] "Peace be to you. Do not
fear; you shall not die." 24 Then Gideon built
an altar there to the LORD and called it, [o] The
LORD is Peace. To this day it still stands at
[p] Ophrah, which belongs to the Abiezrites.
25 That night the LORD said to him, "Take
your father's bull, and the second bull seven
years old, and pull down the altar of Baal
that your father has, and cut down [q] the
Asherah that is beside it 26 and build an altar
to the LORD your God on the top of the
[r] stronghold here, with stones laid in due
order. Then take the second bull and offer it
as a burnt offering with the wood of the
Asherah that you shall cut down." 27 So
Gideon took ten men of his servants and did
as the LORD had told him. But because he
was too afraid of his family and the men of
the town to do it by day, he did it by night.

Gideon Destroys the Altar of Baal

28 When the men of the town rose early
in the morning, behold, the altar of Baal
was broken down, and the Asherah beside
it was cut down, and the second bull was
offered on the altar that had been built.
29 And they said to one another, "Who has
done this thing?" And after they had
searched and inquired, they said, "Gideon
the son of Joash has done this thing."

20 [j] ch. 13:19 [k] [1 Kin. 18:33, 34]
21 [l] Lev. 9:24; 1 Kin. 18:38; 2 Chr. 7:1
22 [m] ch. 13:21, 22; [Gen. 32:30; Ex. 33:20; Deut. 5:26]
23 [n] Dan. 10:19
24 [o] [Gen. 22:14; Ex. 17:15; Ezek. 48:35] [p] ver. 11; ch. 8:27, 32
25 [q] ch. 3:7
26 [r] Dan. 11:7, 10, 31 (Heb.)

32 [s] ch. 7:1; 1 Sam. 12:11; [2 Sam. 11:21]
33 [t] ver. 3 [u] Josh. 17:16
34 [v] See ch. 3:10 [w] ch. 3:27
35 [x] ch. 7:24
36 [y] For ver. 36-40, see Ex. 4:1-7
39 [z] Gen. 18:32

30 Then the men of the town said to Joash,
"Bring out your son, that he may die, for he
has broken down the altar of Baal and cut
down the Asherah beside it." 31 But Joash
said to all who stood against him, "Will
you contend for Baal? Or will you save
him? Whoever contends for him shall be
put to death by morning. If he is a god, let
him contend for himself, because his altar
has been broken down." 32 Therefore on
that day Gideon[2] was called [s] Jerubbaal,
that is to say, "Let Baal contend against
him," because he broke down his altar.
33 Now [t] all the Midianites and the
Amalekites and the people of the East came
together, and they crossed the Jordan and
encamped in [u] the Valley of Jezreel. 34 But
[v] the Spirit of the LORD clothed Gideon, [w] and
he sounded the trumpet, and the Abiezrites
were called out to follow him. 35 [x] And he
sent messengers throughout all Manasseh,
and they too were called out to follow him.
[x] And he sent messengers to Asher, Zebulun,
and Naphtali, and they went up to meet
them.

The Sign of the Fleece

36 [y] Then Gideon said to God, "If you will
save Israel by my hand, as you have said,
37 behold, I am laying a fleece of wool on
the threshing floor. If there is dew on the
fleece alone, and it is dry on all the
ground, then I shall know that you will
save Israel by my hand, as you have said."
38 And it was so. When he rose early next
morning and squeezed the fleece, he
wrung enough dew from the fleece to fill a
bowl with water. 39 Then Gideon said to
God, [z] "Let not your anger burn against
me; let me speak just once more. Please let
me test just once more with the fleece.
Please let it be dry on the fleece only, and
on all the ground let there be dew." 40 And
God did so that night; and it was dry on
the fleece only, and on all the ground there
was dew.

[1] An *ephah* was about 3/5 bushel or 22 liters [2] Hebrew *he*

6:22 I have seen . . . face. See 13:22; Deut. 5:24; Is. 6:5; 1 Tim. 6:16.

6:25–32 This episode in Gideon's life reveals how he came to be known as Jerubbaal. His immediate father's idolatry is tragic in light of what Gideon says about "our fathers" in v. 13.

6:25, 26 pull down the altar. See Deut. 12:3.

6:26 due order. That is, according to the prescriptions of the Law of Moses.

6:31 If he is a god. See 10:14.

6:33–40 Gideon sought confidence through signs (v. 17), which the Lord did not refuse to give him (cf. Luke 1:18–20).

6:34 Spirit of the LORD. See 3:10 and note; 11:29; 13:25; 14:6, 19; 15:14.

6:36 If you will save. Even though the Spirit had come upon him, Gideon still struggled with faith (6:27 note).

Gideon's Three Hundred Men

7 Then [a]Jerubbaal (that is, Gideon) and
all the people who were with him rose
early and encamped beside [b]the spring of
Harod. And the camp of Midian was north
of them, [c]by the hill of Moreh, in the valley.
2 The LORD said to Gideon, "The people
with you are too many for me to give the
Midianites into their hand, [d]lest Israel
boast over me, saying, 'My own hand has
saved me.' 3 Now therefore proclaim in the
ears of the people, saying, [e]'Whoever is
fearful and trembling, let him return home
and hurry away from Mount Gilead.'"
Then 22,000 of the people returned, and
10,000 remained.
4 And the LORD said to Gideon, "The people are still too many. Take them down to
the water, and I will test them for you
there, and anyone of whom I say to you,
'This one shall go with you,' shall go with
you, and anyone of whom I say to you,
'This one shall not go with you,' shall not
go." 5 So he brought the people down to the
water. And the LORD said to Gideon, "Every
one who laps the water with his tongue, as
a dog laps, you shall set by himself.
Likewise, every one who kneels down to
drink." 6 And the number of those who
lapped, putting their hands to their
mouths, was 300 men, but all the rest of
the people knelt down to drink water.
7 And the LORD said to Gideon, [f]"With the
300 men who lapped I will save you and
give the Midianites into your hand, and let
all the others go every man to his home."
8 So the people took provisions in their
hands, and their trumpets. And he sent all
the rest of Israel every man to his tent, but
retained the 300 men. And the camp of
Midian was below him [g]in the valley.
9 That same [h]night the LORD said to him,
"Arise, go down against the camp, [i]for I
have given it into your hand. 10 But if you
are afraid to go down, go down to the camp
with Purah your servant. 11 [j]And you shall
hear what they say, and afterward your
hands shall be strengthened to go down
against the camp." [k]Then he went down
with Purah his servant to the outposts of
the armed men who were in the camp.
12 And the Midianites and the Amalekites
and [l]all the people of the East lay along the
valley like locusts in abundance, and their
camels were without number, [m]as the sand
that is on the seashore in abundance.
13 When Gideon came, behold, a man was
telling a dream to his comrade. And he
said, "Behold, I dreamed a dream, and
behold, a cake of barley bread tumbled into
the camp of Midian and came to the tent
and struck it so that it fell and turned it
upside down, so that the tent lay flat."
14 And his comrade answered, "This is no
other than the sword of Gideon the son of
Joash, a man of Israel; God has given into
his hand Midian and all the camp."
15 As soon as Gideon heard the telling of
the dream and its interpretation, he worshiped. And he returned to the camp of
Israel and said, "Arise, for the LORD has
given the host of Midian into your hand."
16 And he divided the 300 men into three
companies and put trumpets into the
hands of all of them and empty jars, with
[n]torches inside the jars. 17 And he said to
them, "Look at me, and do likewise. When
I come to the outskirts of the camp, do as
I do. 18 When I blow the trumpet, I and all
who are with me, then blow the trumpets
also on every side of all the camp and
shout, [o]'For the LORD and for Gideon.'"

Gideon Defeats Midian

19 So Gideon and the hundred men who
were with him came to the outskirts of the
camp at the beginning of the middle watch,
when they had just set the watch. And they
blew the trumpets and smashed the jars
that were in their hands. 20 Then the three
companies blew the trumpets and broke
the jars. They held in their left hands the
torches, and in their right hands the trumpets to blow. [o]And they cried out, "A
sword for the LORD and for Gideon!"
21 Every man stood in his place around the
camp, [p]and all the army ran. They cried out
and fled. 22 [q]When they blew the 300 trumpets, [r]the LORD set [s]every man's sword

Chapter 7
1 [a]ch. 6:32 [b][1 Sam. 29:1] [c]Gen. 12:6; Deut. 11:30
2 [d]Deut. 8:17; [Isai. 10:13]
3 [e]Deut. 20:8
7 [f][1 Sam. 14:6; 2 Chr. 14:11]
8 [g]ver. 1
9 [h]Gen. 46:2, 3; 1 Kin. 3:5 [i]See ch. 3:28
11 [j]See ver. 13-15 [k][1 Sam. 14:9, 10]
12 [l]See ch. 6:3 [m]Josh. 11:4
16 [n]ch. 15:4; Gen. 15:17
18 [o][Ex. 14:13, 14; 2 Chr. 20:17]
20 [o][See ver. 18 above]
21 [p][2 Kin. 7:7]
22 [q][Josh. 6:4, 16, 20] [r][Ps. 83:9; Isai. 9:4] [s]1 Sam. 14:20; [2 Chr. 20:23]

7:1–8 The drastic reduction of troops demonstrated God's power to save Israel and brought Him glory. It also challenged Gideon and encouraged Israel to trust him.

7:17 Look at me. These words are similar to those of Gideon's son Abimelech (9:48–49).

7:23–8:21 Israel's lack of unity is apparent in the difficulties between Gideon, Ephraim, Succoth, and Penuel.

against his comrade and against all the
army. And the army fled as far as Beth-
shittah toward Zererah,[1] as far as the border of Abel-meholah, by Tabbath. 23 And
the men of Israel were called out from
Naphtali and from Asher and from all
Manasseh, and they pursued after Midian.
24 [t]Gideon sent messengers throughout
[u]all the hill country of Ephraim, saying,
"Come down against the Midianites and
capture the waters against them, as far as
[v]Beth-barah, and also the Jordan." So all
the men of Ephraim were called out, and
they captured the waters as far as Beth-
barah, and also the Jordan. 25 And they captured [w]the two princes of Midian, Oreb and
Zeeb. They killed Oreb [x]at the rock of
Oreb, and Zeeb they killed at the winepress
of Zeeb. Then they pursued Midian, and
they brought the heads of Oreb and Zeeb
to Gideon [y]across the Jordan.

Gideon Defeats Zebah and Zalmunna

8 [z]Then the men of Ephraim said to him,
"What is this that you have done to us,
not to call us when you went to fight with
Midian?" And they accused him fiercely.
2 And he said to them, "What have I done
now in comparison with you? Is not [a]the
gleaning of the grapes of Ephraim better
than the grape harvest of Abiezer? 3 [b]God
has given into your hands the princes of
Midian, Oreb and Zeeb. What have I been
able to do in comparison with you?" [c]Then
their anger[2] against him subsided when he
said this.
4 And Gideon came to the Jordan and
crossed over, he and [d]the 300 men who
were with him, exhausted yet pursuing.
5 So he said to the men of [e]Succoth, "Please
give loaves of bread to the people who follow me, for they are exhausted, and I am
pursuing after Zebah and Zalmunna, the
kings of Midian." 6 And the officials of
Succoth said, [f]"Are the hands of Zebah and
Zalmunna already in your hand, [g]that we
should give bread to your army?" 7 So
Gideon said, "Well then, when the LORD
has given Zebah and Zalmunna into my
hand, [h]I will flail your flesh with the thorns
of the wilderness and with briers." 8 And
from there he went up to [i]Penuel, and
spoke to them in the same way, and the
men of Penuel answered him as the men of
Succoth had answered. 9 And he said to the
men of Penuel, [j]"When I come again in
peace, [k]I will break down this tower."
10 Now Zebah and Zalmunna were in
Karkor with their army, about 15,000 men,
all who were left of all the army of [l]the people of the East, for there had fallen 120,000
men [m]who drew the sword. 11 And Gideon
went up by the way of the tent dwellers
east of [n]Nobah and Jogbehah and attacked
the army, for the army felt [o]secure. 12 And
Zebah and Zalmunna fled, and he pursued
them [p]and captured the two kings of
Midian, Zebah and Zalmunna, and he
threw all the army into a panic.
13 Then Gideon the son of Joash returned
from the battle by the ascent of Heres.
14 And he captured a young man of Succoth
and questioned him. And he wrote down
for him the officials and elders of Succoth,
seventy-seven men. 15 And he came to the
men of Succoth and said, "Behold Zebah
and Zalmunna, about whom you taunted
me, saying, [q]'Are the hands of Zebah and
Zalmunna already in your hand, that we
should give bread to your men who are
exhausted?'" 16 And he took the elders of
the city, and he took thorns of the wilderness and briers and with them taught the
men of Succoth a lesson. 17 [r]And he broke
down the tower of Penuel and killed the
men of the city.
18 Then he said to Zebah and Zalmunna,
"Where are the men whom you killed at
[s]Tabor?" They answered, "As you are, so
were they. Every one of them resembled
the son of a king." 19 And he said, "They
were my brothers, the sons of my mother.
[t]As the LORD lives, if you had saved them
alive, I would not kill you." 20 So he said to
Jether his firstborn, "Rise and kill them!"
But the young man did not draw his sword,
for he was afraid, because he was still a
young man. 21 Then Zebah and Zalmunna
said, "Rise yourself and fall upon us, for as
the man is, so is his strength." And Gideon

24 [t]ch. 6:35 [u]See Josh. 24:33 [v][ch. 3:28]
25 [w]ch. 8:3; Ps. 83:11 [x]Isai. 10:26 [y]ch. 8:4
Chapter 8
1 [z][ch. 12:1; 2 Sam. 19:41]
2 [a]Isai. 24:13; Jer. 49:9; Obad. 5; Mic. 7:1
3 [b]ch. 7:24, 25 [c][Prov. 15:1]
4 [d]ch. 7:6
5 [e]Gen. 33:17; Ps. 60:6
6 [f][1 Kin. 20:11] [g][1 Sam. 25:11]
7 [h]ver. 16
8 [i]Gen. 32:30, 31; 1 Kin. 12:25
9 [j][1 Kin. 22:27, 28] [k]ver. 17
10 [l]See ch. 6:3 [m]ch. 20:2, 15, 17, 25, 35, 46; 2 Sam. 24:9; 2 Kin. 3:26; 1 Chr. 21:5
11 [n]Num. 32:35, 42 [o]ch. 18:27
12 [p]Ps. 83:11
15 [q]ver. 6
17 [r][1 Kin. 12:25]
18 [s][ch. 4:6]
19 [t]See Ruth 3:13

[1] Some Hebrew manuscripts *Zeredah* [2] Hebrew *their spirit*

7:25 at the rock of Oreb. See Is. 10:26.

8:1–3 The conflict here between Ephraim and Gideon is similar to the conflict between Ephraim and Jephthah; see 12:1–6.

8:4–21 Gideon has problems with the men of Succoth and Penuel and ultimately punished both for failing to help him in his pursuit of the Midianite leaders.

arose and [u]killed Zebah and Zalmunna,
and he took [v]the crescent ornaments that
were on the necks of their camels.

Gideon's Ephod

22 Then the men of Israel said to Gideon,
"Rule over us, you and your son and your
grandson also, for you have saved us from
the hand of Midian." 23 Gideon said to them,
"I will not rule over you, and my son will not
rule over you; [w]the LORD will rule over you."
24 And Gideon said to them, "Let me make
a request of you: every one of you give me
the earrings from his spoil." (For they had
golden earrings, [x]because they were Ishmaelites.)
25 And they answered, "We will
willingly give them." And they spread a
cloak, and every man threw in it the earrings
of his spoil. 26 And the weight of the golden
earrings that he requested was 1,700
shekels[1] of gold, besides [y]the crescent ornaments and [z]the pendants and the purple
garments worn by the kings of Midian, and
besides the collars that were around the
necks of their camels. 27 And Gideon [a]made
an ephod of it and put it in his city, [b]in
Ophrah. And all Israel [c]whored after it there,
and it became a [d]snare to Gideon and to his
family. 28 So Midian was subdued before the
people of Israel, and they raised their heads
no more. [e]And the land had rest forty years
in the days of Gideon.

The Death of Gideon

29 [f]Jerubbaal the son of Joash went and
lived in his own house. 30 Now Gideon had
[g]seventy sons, his own offspring,[2] for he
had many wives. 31 And his concubine
[h]who was in Shechem also bore him a son,
and he called his name Abimelech. 32 And
Gideon the son of Joash died [i]in a good old
age and was buried in the tomb of Joash
his father, [j]at Ophrah of the Abiezrites.
33 [k]As soon as Gideon died, the people of
Israel turned again and [l]whored after the
Baals and made [m]Baal-berith their god.
34 And the people of Israel [n]did not remember the LORD their God, who had delivered
them from the hand of all their enemies on
every side, 35 [o]and they did not show steadfast love to the family of Jerubbaal (that is,
Gideon) in return for all the good that he
had done to Israel.

Abimelech's Conspiracy

9 Now Abimelech the son of Jerubbaal
went to Shechem to [p]his mother's relatives and said to them and to the whole
clan of his mother's family, 2 "Say in the
ears of all the leaders of Shechem, 'Which
is better for you, that all [q]seventy of the
sons of Jerubbaal rule over you, or that one
rule over you?' Remember also that [p]I am
[r]your bone and your flesh."
3 And his mother's relatives spoke all
these words on his behalf in the ears of all
the leaders of Shechem, and their hearts
inclined to follow Abimelech, for they said,
[s]"He is our brother." 4 And they gave him
seventy pieces of silver out of the house of
[t]Baal-berith with which Abimelech hired
[u]worthless and reckless fellows, who followed him. 5 And he went to his father's
house at [v]Ophrah [w]and killed his brothers
the sons of Jerubbaal, seventy men, on one

21 [u]Ps. 83:11 [v]ver. 26; Isai. 3:18
23 [w][1 Sam. 8:7; 10:19; 12:12, 17, 19]
24 [x][Gen. 37:25, 28, 36; 39:1]
26 [y]ver. 21 [z]Isai. 3:19
27 [a]ch. 17:5; 18:14, 17; See Ex. 28:6-35 [b]ch. 6:24 [c]ver. 33; ch. 2:17; Ex. 34:15; Ps. 106:39 [d]Ex. 23:33; Deut. 7:16
28 [e][ch. 3:11; 5:31]
29 [f]ch. 6:32; 7:1
30 [g]ch. 9:2, 5
31 [h]ch. 9:1, 2
32 [i]Gen. 15:15; 25:8; Job 5:26 [j]ch. 6:24
33 [k][ch. 2:19] [l]See ver. 27 [m]ch. 9:4, 46
34 [n]Ps. 78:11, 42; 106:13, 21
35 [o]See ch. 9:16-18
Chapter 9
1 [p]ch. 8:31
2 [q]ch. 8:30 [p][See ver. 1 above] [r]Gen. 29:14
3 [s]ver. 18
4 [t]ch. 8:33; [ver. 46] [u]ch. 11:3; 2 Chr. 13:7; [Prov. 12:11; Acts 17:5]
5 [v]ch. 6:24 [w][2 Kin. 11:1, 2]

1 A *shekel* was about 2/5 ounce or 11 grams 2 Hebrew *who came from his own loins*

8:22 Rule over us. Gideon was such an outstanding judge that the people wished to make him king.

8:23 the LORD will rule. This verse, like 1 Sam. 8:7–9, says that kingship in Israel was a mistake. Yet Judges demonstrates that it had become necessary. With no king, society disintegrated (21:25).

8:24 give me the earrings. Though Gideon rejected kingship, he acted like a king (v. 30).

8:27 ephod. The genuine ephod of the high priest was employed for seeking the Lord's will (1 Sam. 23:9–11; 30:7, 8).

whored after it. Gideon, the greatest of the judges until Samuel, gave the people occasion to sin (2:17 and notes).

a snare to Gideon and to his family. Gideon's father had been an idolater (6:25), and now Gideon fell into the same sin.

8:31 Abimelech. Gideon names the son of his concubine "Abimelech" ("my father is king") notwithstanding all Gideon's claims to the contrary. See vv. 23, 24.

8:33–9:57 The Abimelech story demonstrates the disaster the wrong kind of king could be. Abimelech was an anti-deliverer, an oppressor of the people, and a breaker of the covenant. His story raises the question of who should be king (9:2, 8–20, 28, 29). In light of this question, it is significant that Abimelech and Saul resemble each other in important ways (9:23 note; 9:54 note). This would imply that Saul was the same sort of king that Abimelech was. The message to the readers of Judges was that they should no more want Ish-bosheth the son of Saul to be their king, than Israel had wanted Abimelech, the son of Gideon.

8:33 Baal-berith. Lit. "Baal (lord) of the covenant." This god was a counterfeit of the God who truly was the Lord of the covenant. See 9:4 note.

8:34 did not remember. Remembering God and His works of salvation is a first step in covenant obedience (2:10 note).

8:35 they did not show steadfast love. See 9:5, 16–19.

9:1 Abimelech. See 8:31 note.

9:4 Baal-berith. See notes on v. 46; 8:33. The temple of Baal-berith paid the wages of those who oppressed Israel under Abimelech.

9:5 on one stone. The men were in effect sacrificed to Baal-berith (v. 53 note).

stone. But Jotham the youngest son of
Jerubbaal was left, for he hid himself. 6 And
all the leaders of Shechem came together,
and all [x]Beth-millo, and they went and
made Abimelech king, by the oak of the
pillar at Shechem.
7 When it was told to Jotham, he went
and stood on top of [y]Mount Gerizim and
cried aloud and said to them, "Listen to
me, you leaders of Shechem, that God may
listen to you. 8 [z]The trees once went out to
anoint a king over them, and they said to
the olive tree, [a]'Reign over us.' 9 But the
olive tree said to them, 'Shall I leave my
abundance, by which gods and men are
honored, and go hold sway over the trees?'
10 And the trees said to the fig tree, 'You
come and reign over us.' 11 But the fig tree
said to them, 'Shall I leave my sweetness
and my good fruit and go hold sway over
the trees?' 12 And the trees said to the vine,
'You come and reign over us.' 13 But the
vine said to them, 'Shall I leave my wine
that [b]cheers God and men and go hold
sway over the trees?' 14 Then all the trees
said to the bramble, 'You come and reign
over us.' 15 And the bramble said to the
trees, 'If in good faith you are anointing me
king over you, then come and [c]take refuge
in my shade, but if not, [d]let fire come out
of the bramble and devour [e]the cedars of
Lebanon.'
16 "Now therefore, if you acted in good
faith and integrity when you made
Abimelech king, and if you have dealt well
with [f]Jerubbaal and his house and have
done to him [g]as his deeds deserved—17 for
my father fought for you and risked his life
and delivered you from the hand of
Midian, 18 and you have risen up against my
father's house this day [h]and have killed his
sons, seventy men on one stone, and have
made [i]Abimelech, the son of his female servant, king over the leaders of Shechem, [j]be-
cause he is your relative—19 if you then
have acted in good faith and integrity with
Jerubbaal and with his house this day, then
[k]rejoice in Abimelech, and let him also
rejoice in you. 20 But if not, [l]let fire come
out from Abimelech and devour the leaders
of Shechem and Beth-millo; and let fire
come out from the leaders of Shechem and
from Beth-millo and devour Abimelech."
21 And Jotham ran away and fled and went
to [m]Beer and lived there, because of
Abimelech his brother.

The Downfall of Abimelech

22 Abimelech ruled over Israel three years.
23 [n]And God sent an evil spirit between
Abimelech and the leaders of Shechem,
and the leaders of Shechem [o]dealt treacherously with Abimelech, 24 [p]that the violence done to the seventy sons of Jerubbaal
might come, and their blood be laid on
Abimelech their brother, who killed them,
and on the men of Shechem, who strengthened his hands to kill his brothers. 25 And
the leaders of Shechem put men in ambush
against him on the mountaintops, and they
robbed all who passed by them along that
way. And it was told to Abimelech.
26 And Gaal the son of Ebed moved into
Shechem with his relatives, and the leaders
of Shechem put confidence in him. 27 And
they went out into the field and gathered
the grapes from their vineyards and trod
them and held a festival; and they went
into [q]the house of their god and ate and
drank and reviled Abimelech. 28 And Gaal
the son of Ebed said, [r]"Who is Abimelech,
and who are we of Shechem, that we
should serve him? Is he not the son of
Jerubbaal, and is not Zebul his officer?
Serve the men of [s]Hamor the father of
Shechem; but why should we serve him?
29 Would that this people were under my
hand! Then I would remove Abimelech. I
would say[1] to Abimelech, 'Increase your
army, and come out.'"
30 When Zebul the ruler of the city heard
the words of Gaal the son of Ebed, his anger
was kindled. 31 And he sent messengers to

1 Septuagint; Hebrew *and he said*

6 [x]ver. 20; [2 Sam. 5:9] **7** [y]Deut. 11:29; 27:12; Josh. 8:33; [John 4:20] **8** [z][2 Kin. 14:9] [a]ch. 8:22, 23 **13** [b]Ps. 104:15 **15** [c]Dan. 4:12; Hos. 14:7; [Isai. 30:2] [d]ver. 20; [Num. 21:28; Ezek. 19:14] [e]1 Kin. 4:33; 2 Kin. 14:9; 19:23; Ps. 104:16; Isai. 2:13; 37:24. **16** [f]See ch. 6:32 [g]Prov. 12:14; Isai. 3:11; [ch. 8:35] **18** [h]ver. 5, 6 [i]ch. 8:31 [j]ver. 3
19 [k][Isai. 8:6] **20** [l]ver. 15; [ver. 56, 57] **21** [m]Num. 21:16 **23** [n][1 Sam. 16:14; 18:10; 19:9] [o]Isai. 33:1 **24** [p]ver. 56; [1 Kin. 2:32; Esth. 9:25; Ps. 7:16; Matt. 23:35, 36] **27** [q]ver. 4, 46 **28** [r][1 Sam. 25:10] [s]Gen. 34:2, 6

9:7 Mount Gerizim. The mount of blessing (Deut. 27:12) was used for a curse. This reversal highlights the reversal theme that permeates the Abimelech story (8:33–9:57 note).

9:14 bramble. The product of idolatry (v. 4), Abimelech's kingship would be a thorn to Israel (2:3 note).

9:20 let fire. Jotham's curse is fulfilled in vv. 45–52.

9:23 an evil spirit. The historical parallel with Saul is significant. Both Abimelech and Saul had an evil spirit come against them as they began to lose their kingdoms (1 Sam. 16:14). This is the first mention of God's direct action in the story of Abimelech.

9:26 Gaal. Gaal is another "Abimelech," a lost brother claiming the right to rule by right of his ancestry.

9:28 Who is Abimelech. Note the similar speech at v. 2, also delivered in Shechem.

Abimelech secretly,[1] saying, "Behold, Gaal
the son of Ebed and his relatives have come
to Shechem, and they are stirring up[2] the
city against you. **32** Now therefore, go by
night, you and the people who are with
you, and set an ambush in the field. **33** Then
in the morning, as soon as the sun is up,
rise early and rush upon the city. And
when he and the people who are with him
come out against you, you may do to them
[t]as your hand finds to do."
34 So Abimelech and all the men who
were with him rose up by night and set an
ambush against Shechem in four companies. **35** And Gaal the son of Ebed went out
and stood in the entrance of the gate of the
city, and Abimelech and the people who
were with him rose from the ambush.
36 And when Gaal saw the people, he said
to Zebul, "Look, people are coming down
from [u]the mountaintops!" And Zebul said
to him, "You mistake[3] the shadow of the
mountains for men." **37** Gaal spoke again
and said, "Look, people are coming down
from the center of the land, and one company is coming from the direction of the
Diviners' Oak." **38** Then Zebul said to him,
"Where is your mouth now, you who said,
[v]'Who is Abimelech, that we should serve
him?' Are not these the people whom you
despised? Go out now and fight with
them." **39** And Gaal went out at the head of
the leaders of Shechem and fought with
Abimelech. **40** And Abimelech chased him,
and he fled before him. And many fell
wounded, up to the entrance of the gate.
41 And Abimelech lived at Arumah, and
Zebul drove out Gaal and his relatives, so
that they could not dwell at Shechem.
42 On the following day, the people went
out into the field, and Abimelech was told.
43 He took his people and divided them into
three companies and set an ambush in the
fields. And he looked and saw the people
coming out of the city. So he rose against
them and killed them. **44** Abimelech and the
company that was with him [w]rushed forward and stood at the entrance of the gate
of the city, while the two companies
rushed upon all who were in the field and
killed them. **45** And Abimelech fought
against the city all that day. He captured
the city and killed the people who were in
it, and [x]he razed the city and [y]sowed it with
salt.
46 When all the leaders of the Tower of
Shechem heard of it, they entered [z]the
stronghold of the house of [a]El-berith.
47 Abimelech was told that all the leaders of
the Tower of Shechem were gathered
together. **48** And Abimelech went up to
Mount [b]Zalmon, he and all the people who
were with him. And Abimelech took an axe
in his hand and cut down a bundle of
brushwood and took it up and laid it on
his shoulder. And he said to the men who
were with him, "What you have seen me
do, hurry and do as I have done." **49** So
every one of the people cut down his bundle and following Abimelech put it against
[c]the stronghold, and they set the stronghold on fire over them, so that all the people of the Tower of Shechem also died,
about 1,000 men and women.
50 Then Abimelech went to Thebez and
encamped against Thebez and captured it.
51 But there was a strong tower within the
city, and all the men and women and all
the leaders of the city fled to it and shut
themselves in, and they went up to the roof
of the tower. **52** And Abimelech came to the
tower and fought against it and drew near
to the door of the tower to burn it with fire.
53 [d]And a certain woman threw an upper
millstone on Abimelech's head and
crushed his skull. **54** [e]Then he called quickly to the young man his armor-bearer and
said to him, "Draw your sword and kill me,
lest they say of me, 'A woman killed him.'"
And his young man thrust him through,
and he died. **55** And when the men of Israel
saw that Abimelech was dead, everyone

33 [t]Eccles. 9:10 **36** [u]ver. 7, 25 **38** [v]ver. 28, 29 **44** [w]ch. 20:37
45 [x]2 Kin. 3:25 [y]Deut. 29:23 **46** [z]ver. 49 [a]ver. 4; ch. 8:33 **48** [b]Ps. 68:14 **49** [c]ver. 46 **53** [d]2 Sam. 11:21 **54** [e][1 Sam. 31:4]

[1] Or *at Tormah* [2] Hebrew *besieging*, or *closing up* [3] Hebrew *You see*

9:45 sowed it with salt. This would ruin it for farming.

9:46 El-berith. Lit. "god of the covenant." El was the father of the gods in the Canaanite pantheon. This was probably the same temple as the one mentioned at 9:4, which supplied Abimelech money. Now he returned to destroy it.

9:48 do as I have done. Abimelech's words, as he leads his men, resemble his father's (7:17).

9:49 set the stronghold on fire. This fulfilled Jotham's curse (v. 20).

9:53 an upper millstone. A stone figured prominently in Abimelech's death, as it had in the murder of all his brothers (9:5 note).

9:54 Draw your sword and kill me. Like Saul (1 Sam. 31:4), Abimelech sought to die proudly. This incident, like the presence of an evil spirit from God (9:23 and note), is a strong point of resemblance between Saul and Abimelech.

A woman killed him. He had to share this indignity with Sisera (4:9).

departed to his home. 56 [f]Thus God returned the evil of Abimelech, which he
committed against his father in killing his
seventy brothers. 57 And God also made all
the evil of the men of Shechem return on
their heads, and upon them came [g]the
curse of Jotham the son of Jerubbaal.

Tola and Jair

10 After Abimelech there arose to [h]save
Israel Tola the son of Puah, son of
Dodo, a man of Issachar, and he lived at
Shamir in [i]the hill country of Ephraim.
2 And he judged Israel twenty-three years.
Then he died and was buried at Shamir.
3 After him arose Jair the Gileadite, who
judged Israel twenty-two years. 4 And he
had thirty sons who [j]rode on thirty donkeys, and they had thirty cities, called
Havvoth-jair to this day, [k]which are in the
land of Gilead. 5 And Jair died and was
buried in Kamon.

Further Disobedience and Oppression

6 [l]The people of Israel again did what was
evil in the sight of the LORD [m]and served the
Baals and the Ashtaroth, the gods of Syria,
[n]the gods of Sidon, the gods of Moab, the
gods of the Ammonites, and the gods of the
Philistines. And they [o]forsook the LORD and
did not serve him. 7 So the anger of the LORD
was kindled against Israel, and [p]he sold
them into the hand of the Philistines and
into the hand of the Ammonites, 8 and they
crushed and oppressed the people of Israel
that year. For eighteen years they oppressed
all the people of Israel who were beyond the
Jordan in the land of the Amorites, which is
in Gilead. 9 And the Ammonites crossed the
Jordan to fight also against Judah and
against Benjamin and against the house of
Ephraim, so that Israel was severely distressed.
10 And the people of Israel [q]cried out to the
LORD, saying, "We have sinned against you,
because [r]we have forsaken our God and
have served the Baals." 11 And the LORD said
to the people of Israel, "Did I not save you
[s]from the Egyptians and [t]from the Amorites,
[u]from the Ammonites and [v]from the
Philistines? 12 The Sidonians also, and [w]the
Amalekites and the Maonites oppressed
you, and you cried out to me, and I [x]saved
you out of their hand. 13 Yet you have [y]for-
saken me and served other gods; therefore I
will save you no more. 14 Go and cry out [z]to
the gods whom you have chosen; let them
save you in the time of your distress." 15 And
the people of Israel said to the LORD, "We
have sinned; do to us whatever seems good
to you. Only please deliver us this day." 16 So
they put away the foreign gods from among
them and served the LORD, and [a]he became
impatient over the misery of Israel.
17 Then the Ammonites were called to
arms, and they encamped in Gilead. And
the people of Israel came together, and
they encamped at [b]Mizpah. 18 And the people, the leaders of Gilead, said one to

56 [f][Job 31:8; Ps. 94:23; Prov. 5:22]; See ver. 24
57 [g]ver. 20
Chapter 10
1 [h]ver. 12, 13; See ch. 2:16 [i]See Josh. 24:33
4 [j]ch. 5:10; 12:14 [k]Deut. 3:14
6 [l]See ch. 2:11 [m]See ch. 2:13 [n]1 Kin. 11:5, 7, 33; 2 Kin. 23:13 [o]ver. 10, 13; Deut. 31:16
7 [p]See ch. 2:14
10 [q]See ch. 3:9 [r]ver. 6, 13
11 [s]Ex. 14:30 [t]See Num. 21:21-32 [u][ch. 3:13] [v]ch. 3:31
12 [w][ch. 3:13; 5:14; 6:3] [x]See ch. 2:16
13 [y]ver. 6, 10; [Deut. 32:15; Jer. 2:13]
14 [z]Deut. 32:37, 38
16 [a]ch. 2:18; Isai. 63:9
17 [b]ch. 11:11, 29

9:56 Thus God returned. God is not highly visible in this narrative (9:23 note). But He brought Abimelech to judgment.

10:1–5 Two judges, Tola and Jair, are introduced with few details. Four other minor judges are described in similar fashion (3:31; 12:8–15).

10:1 Tola. Tola is mentioned only here in Scripture.

10:3 Jair. Like Tola, Jair is not mentioned anywhere else in the Bible.

10:4 who rode on thirty donkeys. Thirty sons, thirty donkeys, and the control of thirty towns indicate great wealth and power (5:10).

10:6–12:7 Cf. 1 Sam. 12:11. The list of idols Israel followed (10:6) and the internal chaos of Israel became more pronounced (12:1–7). Jephthah brought only six years of peace (12:7) instead of peace for a generation (3:11, 30; 5:31; 8:28). Finally, Jephthah rashly and sinfully sacrificed his daughter (11:30–40 note).

Many things about Jephthah are reminiscent of Gideon, Abimelech, or Saul. Jephthah like Gideon was a "mighty man of valor" (6:12; 11:1). Both men made the Ephraimites angry by not calling them out to participate in battle (8:1–3; 12:1–6). Jephthah and Abimelech were both outcast sons, one born to a concubine and the other to a harlot. They gathered to themselves bands of adventurers (9:4; 11:3). Both Jephthah and Saul were made leaders in Mizpah (11:11; 1 Sam. 10:17). Both men faced Ammonites as their first adversaries (11:12–29; 1 Sam. 11:1–11). Jepthah and Saul each made an unwise vow that returned to threaten their firstborn, and each offered an unlawful sacrifice (11:30–40; 1 Sam. 13:8–14; 14:24–25).

10:6 gods. In previous accounts only the Baals and the Ashtaroths were mentioned (2:11, 13; 3:7). This longer list of gods indicates a downward spiral in Israel's violations of the covenant. See also vv. 11–12 and note. The peoples mentioned surrounded Israel on its borders.

10:10–16 This is the only account in the Book of Judges where Israel not only cries out to God, but also puts away their idols. Elsewhere, they simply cried out to the Lord and He delivered them (10:10; 2:19; 3:9). God saw through their superficial repentance but chose to deliver them anyway (cf. Deut. 32:15–38).

10:10 forsaken our God and have served the Baals. The same language is used in their indictment in v. 6.

10:12 oppressed you. The list of gods in v. 6 coincides almost identically with the list of oppressing nations. Israel rejected the God who had saved them, and instead followed the compassionless gods of their oppressors.

10:13 no more. See Deut. 8:19–20; 31:16–17; Num. 33:55–56; Josh. 23:13; Judg. 2:3.

10:14 cry out to the gods whom you have chosen. See Deut. 32:37–38. The same taunt is made in Jer. 2:28; 11:12–13.

10:15 deliver us. The desire to be delivered, rather than to serve the Lord, was Israel's true motive in repenting.

10:17 Mizpah. See 11:11; 20:1.

another, "Who is the man who will begin
to fight against the Ammonites? [c]He shall
be head over all the inhabitants of Gilead."

Jephthah Delivers Israel

11 Now [d]Jephthah the Gileadite was [e]a
mighty warrior, but he was the son
of a prostitute. Gilead was the father of
Jephthah. **2** And Gilead's wife also bore him
sons. And when his wife's sons grew up,
they drove Jephthah out and said to him,
"You shall not have an inheritance in our
father's house, for you are the son of
another woman." **3** Then Jephthah fled
from his brothers and lived in the land of
[f]Tob, and [g]worthless fellows collected
around Jephthah and went out with him.
4 After a time the Ammonites made war
against Israel. **5** And when the Ammonites
made war against Israel, the elders of
Gilead went to bring Jephthah from the
land of [f]Tob. **6** And they said to Jephthah,
"Come and be our leader, that we may
fight with the Ammonites." **7** But Jephthah
said to the elders of Gilead, "Did you not
hate me and drive me out of my father's
house? Why have you come to me now
when you are in distress?" **8** And the elders
of Gilead said to Jephthah, "That is why we
have turned to you now, that you may go
with us and fight with the Ammonites and
[h]be our head over all the inhabitants of
Gilead." **9** Jephthah said to the elders of
Gilead, "If you bring me home again to
fight with the Ammonites, and the LORD
gives them over to me, I will be your head."
10 And the elders of Gilead said to Jephthah, [i]"The LORD will be witness between
us, if we do not do as you say." **11** So
Jephthah went with the elders of Gilead,
and the people [j]made him head and leader
over them. And Jephthah spoke all his
words [k]before the LORD at [l]Mizpah.
12 Then Jephthah sent messengers to the
king of the Ammonites and said, "What do
you have against me, that you have come to
me to fight against my land?" **13** And the
king of the Ammonites answered the messengers of Jephthah, [m]"Because Israel on
coming up from Egypt took away my land,
from the [n]Arnon to the [o]Jabbok and to the
Jordan; now therefore restore it peaceably."
14 Jephthah again sent messengers to the
king of the Ammonites **15** and said to him,
"Thus says Jephthah: [p]Israel did not take
away the land of Moab or the land of the
Ammonites, **16** but when they came up from
Egypt, Israel went through the wilderness
[q]to the Red Sea and [r]came to Kadesh.
17 [s]Israel then sent messengers to the king
of Edom, saying, 'Please let us pass
through your land,' [t]but the king of Edom
would not listen. And they sent also to the
king of Moab, but he would not consent.
So Israel [u]remained at Kadesh.
18 "Then they journeyed through the
wilderness and [v]went around the land of
Edom and the land of Moab and [w]arrived
on the east side of the land of Moab and
[x]camped on the other side of the Arnon.
But they did not enter the territory of
Moab, for the Arnon was the boundary of
Moab. **19** [y]Israel then sent messengers to
Sihon king of the Amorites, king of
Heshbon, and Israel said to him, 'Please let
us pass through your land to our country,'
20 but Sihon did not trust Israel to pass
through his territory, so Sihon gathered all
his people together and encamped at Jahaz
and fought with Israel. **21** And the LORD, the
God of Israel, gave Sihon and all his people
into the hand of Israel, and they defeated
them. So Israel took possession of all the
land of the Amorites, who inhabited that
country. **22** And they took possession of all
the territory of the Amorites from the
Arnon to the Jabbok and from the wilderness to the Jordan. **23** So then the LORD, the

18 [c][ch. 11:5, 6, 8, 11]
Chapter 11
1 [d]Heb. 11:32 [e]ch. 6:12; 2 Kin. 5:1
3 [f]2 Sam. 10:6, 8 [g]See ch. 9:4; [1 Sam. 22:2]
5 [f][See ver. 3 above]
8 [h]ch. 10:18
10 [i]Jer. 42:5
11 [j]ver. 6, 8; ch. 10:18 [k]1 Sam. 10:19, 25; 11:15; 12:7; [ch. 20:1; 1 Sam. 10:17] [l]ch. 10:17
13 [m]See Num. 21:24-26 [n]Num. 21:13 [o]Gen. 32:22
15 [p]Deut. 2:9, 19
16 [q]Num. 14:25; Deut. 1:40 [r]Num. 13:26
17 [s]Num. 20:14 [t]See Num. 20:18-21 [u]Num. 20:1; Deut. 1:46
18 [v]Num. 21:4; See Deut. 2:1-8 [w]Num. 21:11 [x]Num. 21:13; 22:36
19 [y]For ver. 19-22, see Num. 21:21-26; Deut. 2:26-37

11:1 a mighty warrior. This is what Gideon was called (6:12).

son of a prostitute. Jephthah's heritage made him an outcast (v. 2).

11:3 worthless fellows. Another similarity between Jephthah and Abimelech was their followers (9:4).

11:9 the LORD gives them. Jephthah showed his faith that it was God who gave him victory.

11:10 The LORD will be witness. The elders were swearing an oath in order to confirm a covenant.

11:11 Jephthah spoke all his words before the LORD at Mizpah. The covenant is confirmed before the Lord in Mizpah. Years later the people made Saul king, also before the Lord, at Mizpah (1 Sam. 10:17).

11:12–29 For the historical background to this conflict, see Num. 20:14–21; 21:10–35; Deut. 2:16–3:11. At the time of Jephthah, the Ammonites hoped to extend their territory into what once had been their land, but had now been Israel's for three hundred years. Jephthah countered Ammonite demands by rehearsing this history and showing that they took no more than what the God of Israel had given them and, having been instructed by Him (Deut. 2:18–19), did not take anything from Ammon.

11:12 king of the Ammonites. Like Saul, Jephthah's first adversary was the Ammonites (1 Sam. 11:1–11). Gilead was the region threatened in Saul's story as well.

God of Israel, dispossessed the Amorites
from before his people Israel; and are you
to take possession of them? **24** Will you not
possess what [z]Chemosh your god gives you
to possess? [a]And all that the LORD our God
has dispossessed before us, we will possess. **25** Now are you any better than [b]Balak
the son of Zippor, king of Moab? Did he
ever contend against Israel, or did he ever
go to war with them? **26** While Israel lived
[c]in Heshbon and its villages, and [d]in Aroer
and its villages, and in all the cities that are
on the banks of the Arnon, 300 years, why
did you not deliver them within that time?
27 I therefore have not sinned against you,
and you do me wrong by making war on
me. [e]The LORD, the Judge, decide this day
between the people of Israel and the people of Ammon." **28** But the king of the
Ammonites did not listen to the words of
Jephthah that he sent to him.

Jephthah's Tragic Vow

29 [f]Then the Spirit of the LORD was upon
Jephthah, and he passed through Gilead
and Manasseh and passed on to Mizpah of
Gilead, and from Mizpah of Gilead he
passed on to the Ammonites. **30** And
Jephthah [g]made a vow to the LORD and
said, "If you will give the Ammonites into
my hand, **31** then whatever[1] comes out from
the doors of my house to meet me when I
return in peace from the Ammonites [h]shall
be the LORD's, and [i]I will offer it[2] up for a
burnt offering." **32** So Jephthah crossed over
to the Ammonites to fight against them,
and the LORD gave them into his hand.
33 And he struck them from Aroer to the
neighborhood of [j]Minnith, twenty cities,
and as far as Abel-keramim, with a great
blow. So the Ammonites were subdued
before the people of Israel.
34 Then Jephthah came to his home at
[k]Mizpah. And behold, his daughter came
out to meet him [l]with tambourines and
with dances. She was his only child; beside
her he had neither son nor daughter. **35** And
as soon as he saw her, he tore his clothes
and said, "Alas, my daughter! You have
brought me very low, and you have become
the cause of great trouble to me. For I have
opened my mouth to the LORD, [m]and I cannot take back my vow." **36** And she said to
him, "My father, you have opened your
mouth to the LORD; do to me according to
what has gone out of your mouth, now that
the LORD has avenged you on your enemies, on the Ammonites." **37** So she said to
her father, "Let this thing be done for me:
leave me alone two months, that I may go
up and down on the mountains and weep
for my virginity, I and my companions."
38 So he said, "Go." Then he sent her away
for two months, and she departed, she and
her companions, and wept for her virginity
on the mountains. **39** And at the end of two
months, she returned to her father, [n]who
did with her according to his vow that he
had made. She had never known a man,
and it became a custom in Israel **40** that the
daughters of Israel went year by year to
lament the daughter of Jephthah the
Gileadite four days in the year.

Jephthah's Conflict with Ephraim

12 [o]The men of Ephraim were called to
arms, and they crossed to Zaphon and

24 [z]Num. 21:29; 1 Kin. 11:7 [a]Deut. 9:5; 18:12; Josh. 3:10
25 [b]Num. 22:2; Josh. 24:9; Mic. 6:5
26 [c]Num. 21:25 [d]Deut. 2:36
27 [e]Gen. 16:5; 18:25; 31:53; 1 Sam. 24:12, 15
29 [f]See ch. 3:10
30 [g]Gen. 28:20; 1 Sam. 1:11
31 [h][Lev. 27:2; 1 Sam. 1:28] [i]Ps. 66:13
33 [j]Ezek. 27:17
34 [k]ver. 11; ch. 10:17 [l]Ex. 15:20; 1 Sam. 18:6; Ps. 68:25; Jer. 31:4
35 [m]Num. 30:2; [Eccles. 5:4, 5]
39 [n]ver. 31
Chapter 12
1 [o]ch. 8:1

1 Or *whoever* 2 Or *him*

11:23 the LORD, the God of Israel. Warfare was viewed as a battle between the gods of the opposing forces. If Israel won, it was because the God of Israel had done it, and no one could dispute the result (v. 24). See v. 21.

11:27 The LORD, the Judge, decide this day. See vv. 21, 23. Jephthah declared that God was the Judge over all peoples and gods. Here the word is used in a legal sense, as in handing down a decision, although God would ultimately be a deliverer as well (vv. 32–33). The Book of Judges affirms that God is the true King (8:23) and true Judge, who alone could solve Israel's woes.

11:29 Spirit of the LORD. See 3:10 and note.

11:30–40 Jephthah defeated the Ammonites, but in the process made a rash vow to the Lord and sacrificed his daughter as a burnt offering. God was not to be worshiped in the way the pagans worshiped their gods, namely, by human sacrifice (Deut. 12:31; 18:10; Ps. 106:37–38). As a deliverer, Jephthah did not show the people how to keep the covenant, despite giving evidence of his faith (vv. 10–11, 21, 23, 27). Like Jephthah, Saul also made a rash vow that turned out to be a threat to his own child (1 Sam. 14:24–45).

11:35 tore his clothes. This was the sign of mourning over death.

opened my mouth. Although vows were sacred (Deut. 23:21–23), Jephthah's action was wrong. Human sacrifice was absolutely forbidden in Israel (v. 39 note). It is evil to keep an evil vow. Unlawful oaths and vows must not be made or, if made, not kept (cf. Matt. 14:1–12).

11:36 do to me according to what has gone out of your mouth. That is, "offer me as a sacrifice" (vv. 30–31).

11:37 weep for my virginity. This probably means to lament that she would never marry or have children (vv. 38, 39).

11:39 according to his vow. Though stated delicately, the text is clear: Jephthah sacrificed his daughter as a burnt offering. It is observed that she was a virgin, but this was not the content of the vow. Human sacrifice was sin, an imitation of pagan practice (11:30–40 note; Deut. 12:31; Ps. 106:38).

12:1 men of Ephraim. Like Gideon, Jephthah had trouble with Ephraim (8:1–5); unlike Gideon, they brought it to civil war. Unity was sorely lacking in Israel.

12:1–7 Following immediately after the sacrifice of his daughter (11:30–40), this story implies that Jephthah's struggle with Ephraim and

said to Jephthah, "Why did you cross over to
fight against the Ammonites and did not call
us to go with you? We will burn your house
over you with fire." 2 And Jephthah said to
them, "I and my people had a great dispute
with the Ammonites, and when I called you,
you did not save me from their hand. 3 And
when I saw that you would not save me, [p]I
took my life in my hand and crossed over
against the Ammonites, and the LORD gave
them into my hand. Why then have you
come up to me this day to fight against me?"
4 Then Jephthah gathered all the men of
Gilead and fought with Ephraim. And the
men of Gilead struck Ephraim, because they
said, [q]"You are fugitives of Ephraim, you
Gileadites, in the midst of Ephraim and
Manasseh." 5 And the Gileadites captured
[r]the fords of the Jordan against the
Ephraimites. And when any of the fugitives
of Ephraim said, "Let me go over," the men
of Gilead said to him, "Are you an Ephraimite?" When he said, "No," 6 they said to
him, "Then say Shibboleth," and he said,
"Sibboleth," for he could not pronounce it
right. Then they seized him and slaughtered
him at [r]the fords of the Jordan. At that time
42,000 of the Ephraimites fell.
7 Jephthah judged Israel six years. Then
Jephthah the Gileadite died and was buried
in his city in Gilead.[1]

Ibzan, Elon, and Abdon

8 After him Ibzan of Bethlehem judged
Israel. 9 He had thirty sons, and thirty
daughters he gave in marriage outside his
clan, and thirty daughters he brought in
from outside for his sons. And he judged
Israel seven years. 10 Then Ibzan died and
was buried at Bethlehem.
11 After him Elon the Zebulunite judged
Israel, and he judged Israel ten years.
12 Then Elon the Zebulunite died and was
buried at Aijalon in the land of Zebulun.
13 After him Abdon the son of Hillel the
Pirathonite judged Israel. 14 He had forty
[s]sons and thirty grandsons, who [t]rode on
seventy donkeys, and he judged Israel eight
years. 15 Then Abdon the son of Hillel the
Pirathonite died and was buried at Pirathon
in the land of Ephraim, in the hill country
of the Amalekites.

The Birth of Samson

13 And the people of Israel again [u]did
what was evil in the sight of the
LORD, so the LORD gave them [v]into the
hand of the Philistines for forty years.
2 There was a certain man of [w]Zorah, of
the tribe of the Danites, whose name was
Manoah. [x]And his wife was barren and had

3 [p] 1 Sam. 19:5; 28:21; Job 13:14; [Ps. 119:109]
4 [q] [1 Sam. 25:10]
5 [r] See ch. 3:28
6 [r] [See ver. 5 above]
14 [s] Job 18:19; Isai. 14:22; [1 Tim. 5:4] [t] ch. 5:10
Chapter 13
1 [u] See ch. 2:11 [v] [ch. 3:31; 10:7; 1 Sam. 12:9]
2 [w] Josh. 19:41; [Josh. 15:33] [x] [1 Sam. 1:2; Luke 1:7]

1 Septuagint; Hebrew *in the cities of Gilead*

his abbreviated judgeship (v. 7) were God's judgment on him for sacrificing his daughter. Ps. 78 (esp. vv. 9–11, 67) reflects on Ephraim's failure to fight and explains God's rejection of Ephraim as Israel's leader. Judah, the tribe of David, and not Ephraim would lead Israel (Ps. 78:68–72).

Why. See 8:1 for an almost identical question put to Gideon.

12:4 the midst of Ephraim and Manasseh. The Gileadites were descended from Joseph, as were Ephraim and Manasseh.

12:5 fords of the Jordan. Gilead was on the east side of the Jordan, Ephraim on the west.

12:6 Shibboleth . . . Sibboleth. The Ephraimites could be recognized by the way certain words were pronounced in their dialect.

12:7 Jephthah judged Israel six years. Previous judges led for forty or eighty years, and peace lasted a generation or two. Jephthah's abbreviated rule, the increased number of gods being worshiped, and the civil war with Ephraim contribute to a picture of Israel's downward spiral.

12:8–15 Ibzan, Elon, and Abdon are briefly mentioned (10:1–5 note). Nothing more is known about these men. They bring the total of judges mentioned in the Book of Judges to twelve.

12:14 seventy donkeys. Abdon wielded virtually royal power and wealth (10:4).

13:1–16:31 Samson's story is the last in the cycles of the judges. He had great promise. He was a Nazirite from the womb, and his birth was a supernatural gift to barren parents; like the great judge Gideon, the Angel of the Lord appeared at his calling; unlike any other judge, he was called from the womb; and more than any other judge, he experienced the Spirit coming upon him (13:25; 14:6, 19; 15:14). Yet, of all the judges, Samson was most clearly a rogue. Having taken the vow to be a Nazirite (13:4–5, 7, 14; 16:17; Num. 6:1–21), he kept only the part about not cutting his hair. He repeatedly broke God's covenant and his vow by seeking foreign wives, sleeping with prostitutes, touching dead things, and drinking wine. He showed no interest in delivering Israel. The fanfare of his calling and the circumstances surrounding his birth and life only heighten the tragedy of his life and emphasize the depths to which Israel had descended. But God had raised him up to deliver Israel from the Philistines (v. 5), and He used even the sins of Samson as an occasion against them (14:4).

Samson was not like Gideon or Samuel. Though the Spirit came upon him repeatedly, this had no impact on his character. Like Saul, Samson lost the Spirit's empowerment as a result of God's judgment. Yet the account of the end of his life (16:25–31) reflects a renewal of his faith while a prisoner of his (and God's) enemies. Heb. 11:32 lists Samson on the honor roll of faith.

13:1 the people of Israel again did what was evil. The usual introductory formula is especially abbreviated (cf. 2:11–19).

gave them . . . Philistines. See 2:14; 1 Sam. 12:9.

13:2–25 Like Gideon (6:11–24), Samson's parents did not recognize the Angel of the Lord. They saw a miraculous fire, and then feared the consequences of having seen the Angel of the Lord. These strong parallels pose the question whether Samson might not become as great a judge as Gideon (13:1–16:31 note). Three times the Nazirite requirements are spelled out even before Samson is born (vv. 4–5, 7, 14). This repetition heightens their importance.

13:2 barren. Samson's mother was barren, like Sarah, Rebekah, Rachel (Gen. 16:1; 25:21; 29:31), and the mother of Samuel (1 Sam. 1:2, 5; Judg. 13:1–16:31 note).

no children. 3 [y]And the angel of the LORD
appeared to the woman and said to her,
"Behold, you are barren and have not
borne children, but you shall conceive and
bear a son. 4 Therefore be careful [z]and
drink no wine or strong drink, and eat
nothing unclean, 5 for behold, you shall
conceive and bear a son. [a]No razor shall
come upon his head, for the child shall be
[z]a Nazirite to God from the womb, and he
shall [b]begin to save Israel from the hand of
the Philistines." 6 Then the woman came
and told her husband, [c]"A man of God
came to me, and his appearance was like
the appearance of the angel of God, very
awesome. [d]I did not ask him where he was
from, and he did not tell me his name, 7 but
he said to me, [e]'Behold, you shall conceive
and bear a son. So then drink no wine or
strong drink, and eat nothing unclean, for
the child shall be a Nazirite to God from
the womb to the day of his death.'"
8 Then Manoah prayed to the LORD and
said, "O Lord, please let the man of God
whom you sent come again to us and teach
us what we are to do with the child who
will be born." 9 And God listened to the
voice of Manoah, and the angel of God
came again to the woman as she sat in the
field. But Manoah her husband was not
with her. 10 So the woman ran quickly and
told her husband, "Behold, the man who
came to me the other day has appeared to
me." 11 And Manoah arose and went after
his wife and came to the man and said to
him, "Are you the man who spoke to this
woman?" And he said, "I am." 12 And
Manoah said, "Now when your words
come true, [f]what is to be the child's manner of life, and what is his mission?" 13 And
the angel of the LORD said to Manoah, "Of
all that I said to the woman let her be careful. 14 She may not eat of anything that
comes from the vine, [g]neither let her drink
wine or strong drink, or eat any unclean

3 [y]ch. 6:12; Luke 1:11, 13
4 [z]ver. 7, 14; [Num. 6:2, 3; Luke 1:15]
5 [a]ch. 16:17; 1 Sam. 1:11; [Num. 6:5] [z][See ver. 4 above] [b][1 Sam. 7:13; 2 Sam. 8:1; 1 Chr. 18:1]
6 [c]See Deut. 33:1 [d][ver. 17, 18]
7 [e]ver. 3-5
12 [f][Luke 1:66]
14 [g]ver. 4, 7
15 [h]ch. 6:19; [Gen. 18:5-8]
17 [i][ver. 6]
18 [j]Gen. 32:29 [k][Isai. 9:6]
19 [l]ch. 6:19-21
20 [m]Lev. 9:24; 1 Chr. 21:16; Ezek. 1:28
21 [n]ch. 6:22
24 [o]1 Sam. 2:21; 3:19; Luke 1:80; [Luke 2:52]
25 [p]See ch. 3:10 [q]ch. 18:11; Josh. 15:33
Chapter 14
1 [r]Heb. 11:32 [s]Gen. 38:12, 13; Josh. 15:10; 19:43

thing. All that I commanded her let her
observe."
15 Manoah said to the angel of the LORD,
"Please let us detain you and [h]prepare a
young goat for you." 16 And the angel of the
LORD said to Manoah, "If you detain me, I
will not eat of your food. But if you prepare
a burnt offering, then offer it to the LORD."
(For Manoah did not know that he was the
angel of the LORD.) 17 And Manoah said to
the angel of the LORD, [i]"What is your
name, so that, when your words come true,
we may honor you?" 18 And the angel of the
LORD said to him, [j]"Why do you ask my
name, seeing [k]it is wonderful?" 19 So
[l]Manoah took the young goat with the
grain offering, and offered it on the rock to
the LORD, to the one who works[1] wonders,
and Manoah and his wife were watching.
20 And when the flame went up toward
heaven from the altar, the angel of the
LORD went up in the flame of the altar.
Now Manoah and his wife were watching,
[m]and they fell on their faces to the ground.
21 The angel of the LORD appeared no
more to Manoah and to his wife. [n]Then
Manoah knew that he was the angel of the
LORD. 22 And Manoah said to his wife, [n]"We
shall surely die, for we have seen God."
23 But his wife said to him, "If the LORD had
meant to kill us, he would not have accepted a burnt offering and a grain offering at
our hands, or shown us all these things, or
now announced to us such things as
these." 24 And the woman bore a son and
called his name Samson. [o]And the young
man grew, and the LORD blessed him.
25 [p]And the Spirit of the LORD began to stir
him in Mahaneh-dan, between [q]Zorah and
Eshtaol.

Samson's Marriage

14 [r]Samson went down to [s]Timnah,
and at Timnah he saw one of the

1 Septuagint, Vulgate; Hebrew *and working*

13:3 the angel of the LORD. See 2:1; 6:11–24; 13:1–16:31 note; "Angels" at Zech. 1:9.

13:5 Nazirite . . . from the womb. For background see Num. 6:1–21. Normally the Nazirite vow was taken for a set amount of time, and not from birth (13:1–16:31 note).

13:6 the appearance of the angel of God. She failed to recognize that it really was the Angel of the Lord (6:22; 13:16).

13:15 prepare a young goat. They repeated Gideon's hospitality (6:19).

13:17 What is your name. Jacob asked the same question (Gen. 32:29).

13:19–22 The incidents here parallel those in Gideon's life (6:20–22).

13:24 the young man grew, and the LORD blessed him. In spite of God's blessing, Samson was weak in faith (13:1–16:31 note), in contrast to Samuel (1 Sam. 2:26; 3:19) or Jesus (Luke 2:52).

13:25 the Spirit of the LORD. See 3:10 note.

14:1–15:20 Immediately after learning that the Lord was with Samson and that the Spirit began to stir in him (13:25), the reader is told that

daughters of the Philistines. 2 Then he
came up and told his father and mother, "I
saw one of the daughters of the Philistines
at Timnah. [t]Now get her for me as my
wife." 3 But his father and mother said to
him, "Is there not a woman among the
daughters [u]of your relatives, or among all
our people, that you must go to take a wife
from the [v]uncircumcised Philistines?" But
Samson said to his father, "Get her for me,
for she is right in my eyes."
4 His father and mother did not know that
it was [w]from the LORD, for he was seeking
an opportunity against the Philistines. [x]At
that time the Philistines ruled over Israel.
5 Then Samson went down with his father
and mother to Timnah, and they came to
the vineyards of Timnah. And behold, a
young lion came toward him roaring.
6 [y]Then the Spirit of the LORD rushed upon
him, and although he had nothing in his
hand, he tore the lion in pieces as one tears
a young goat. But he did not tell his father
or his mother what he had done. 7 Then he
went down and talked with the woman,
and she was right in Samson's eyes.
8 After some days he returned to take her.
And he turned aside to see the carcass of
the lion, and behold, there was a swarm of
bees in the body of the lion, and honey.
9 He scraped it out into his hands and went
on, eating as he went. And he came to his
father and mother and gave some to them,
and they ate. But he did not tell them that
he had scraped the honey from the carcass
of the lion.
10 His father went down to the woman, and
Samson prepared a feast there, for so the
young men used to do. 11 As soon as the people saw him, they brought thirty companions
to be with him. 12 And Samson said to them,
[z]"Let me now put a riddle to you. If you can
tell me what it is, within [a]the seven days of
the feast, and find it out, then I will give you
thirty linen garments and thirty [b]changes of
clothes, 13 but if you cannot tell me what it is,
then you shall give me thirty linen garments
and thirty changes of clothes." And they said
to him, "Put your riddle, that we may hear
it." 14 And he said to them,

"Out of the eater came something to
eat.
Out of the strong came something
sweet."

And in three days they could not solve the
riddle.
15 On the fourth[1] day they said to
Samson's wife, [c]"Entice your husband to
tell us what the riddle is, [d]lest we burn you
and your father's house with fire. Have you
invited us here to impoverish us?" 16 And
Samson's wife wept over him and said,
[e]"You only hate me; you do not love me.
You have put a riddle to my people, and
you have not told me what it is." And he
said to her, "Behold, I have not told my
father nor my mother, and shall I tell you?"
17 She wept before him the seven days that
their feast lasted, and on the seventh day
he told her, because [f]she pressed him hard.
Then she told the riddle to her people.
18 And the men of the city said to him on
the seventh day before the sun went down,

"What is sweeter than honey?
What is stronger than a lion?"

And he said to them,

"If you had not plowed with my
heifer,
you would not have found out my
riddle."

19 [g]And the Spirit of the LORD rushed upon
him, and he went down to [h]Ashkelon and

2 [t][Gen. 34:4] 3 [u][Gen. 24:3, 4; 28:1, 2] [v]ch. 15:18; 1 Sam. 14:6; 17:26, 36; 31:4; 2 Sam. 1:20 4 [w]Josh. 11:20 [x]ch. 13:1; 15:11 6 [y]ver. 19; ch. 15:14; 1 Sam. 11:6; [ch. 3:10] 12 [z]Ezek. 17:2; [1 Kin. 10:1; Ps. 78:2; Prov. 1:6] [a]Gen. 29:27

[b]Gen. 45:22; 2 Kin. 5:5, 22, 23 15 [c]ch. 16:5 [d]ch. 15:6 16 [e][ch. 16:15] 17 [f][ch. 16:16] 19 [g]See ver. 6 [h]ch. 1:18

1 Septuagint, Syriac; Hebrew *seventh*

Samson sought a wife from among the Philistines (14:1–2). In this section, Samson's prodigious strength, poetic abilities, and intense pride and temper are revealed. The narrative revolves around the pursuit and loss of the Philistine wife and the consequences for both Philistia and Samson. In the course of these events, Samson broke the Nazirite vow by touching a dead thing (14:8–9) and by drinking wine (v. 10). All that remained was for him to cut his hair. Three times the Spirit of the Lord came on him and he killed his enemies. He led Israel for twenty years (15:20). Normally this would be the end of the narrative. But Samson continued to be distracted by foreign women, and the story concludes with the narrative of his consequent demise (ch. 16).

14:2 daughters of the Philistines. Israelites must not marry foreign wives (3:1–6; 14:3; Deut. 7:3–4; 1 Kin. 11:1–6; Ezra 9–10).

14:4 that it was from the LORD. While Samson's desire was sinful, God used it for His own purposes to bring judgment on the Philistines.

14:6 Spirit of the LORD. See 3:10 note.

14:8, 9 the carcass of the lion. Part of the Nazirite vow was to avoid even approaching a dead body (Num. 6:6). Samson touched the carcass, which should have annulled his vow. He did not tell his parents. On the surface one is led to believe that he was silent for the sake of making his riddle, but he was also hiding the transgression of his vow.

14:10 prepared a feast. At such a feast wine was usual. Yet as a Nazirite, Samson was forbidden to drink wine (13:1–16:31 note; 13:2–25 note).

14:19 the Spirit of the LORD. See 3:10 note.

struck down thirty men of the town and
took their spoil and gave the garments to
those who had told the riddle. In hot anger
he went back to his father's house. 20 And
Samson's wife was given to [i]his companion, [j]who had been his best man.

Samson Defeats the Philistines

15 After some days, at the time of
wheat harvest, Samson went to visit
his wife with [k]a young goat. And he said, "I
will go in to my wife in the chamber." But
her father would not allow him to go in.
2 And her father said, "I really thought that
you utterly hated her, [l]so I gave her to your
companion. Is not her younger sister more
beautiful than she? Please take her
instead." 3 And Samson said to them, "This
time I shall be innocent in regard to the
Philistines, when I do them harm." 4 So
Samson went and caught 300 foxes and
took torches. And he turned them tail to
tail and put a torch between each pair of
tails. 5 And when he had set fire to the
torches, he let the foxes go into the standing grain of the Philistines and set fire to
the stacked grain and the standing grain, as
well as the olive orchards. 6 Then the
Philistines said, "Who has done this?" And
they said, "Samson, the son-in-law of the
Timnite, because he has taken his wife
[m]and given her to his companion." And the
Philistines came up and [n]burned her and
her father with fire. 7 And Samson said to
them, "If this is what you do, I swear I will
be avenged on you, and after that I will
quit." 8 And he struck them hip and thigh
with a great blow, and he went down and
stayed in the [o]cleft of the rock of Etam.
9 Then the Philistines came up and
encamped in Judah and [p]made a raid on
[q]Lehi. 10 And the men of Judah said, "Why
have you come up against us?" They said,
"We have come up to bind Samson, to do
to him as he did to us." 11 Then 3,000 men
of Judah went down to the cleft of the rock
of Etam, and said to Samson, "Do you not
know that [r]the Philistines are rulers over
us? What then is this that you have done to
us?" And he said to them, "As they did to
me, so have I done to them." 12 And they
said to him, "We have come down to bind
you, that we may give you into the hands
of the Philistines." And Samson said to
them, "Swear to me that you will not attack
me yourselves." 13 They said to him, "No;
we will only bind you and give you into
their hands. We will surely not kill you."
So they bound him with two [s]new ropes
and brought him up from the rock.
14 When he came to Lehi, the Philistines
came shouting to meet him. [t]Then the
Spirit of the LORD rushed upon him, and
the ropes that were on his arms became as
flax that has caught fire, and his bonds
melted off his hands. 15 And he found a
fresh jawbone of a donkey, and put out his
hand and took it, [u]and with it he struck
1,000 men. 16 And Samson said,

"With the jawbone of a donkey,
heaps upon heaps,
with the jawbone of a donkey
have I struck down a thousand
men."

17 As soon as he had finished speaking, he
threw away the jawbone out of his hand.
And that place [v]was called Ramath-lehi.[1]
18 And he was very thirsty, and he called
upon the LORD and said, [w]"You have granted this great salvation by the hand of your
servant, and shall I now die of thirst and
fall into the hands of the uncircumcised?"
19 And God split open the hollow place that
is [v]at Lehi, and water came out from it. And
when he drank, [x]his spirit returned, and he
revived. Therefore the name of it was called

[1] *Ramath-lehi* means *the hill of the jawbone*

20 [i]ch. 15:2, 6 [j]John 3:29
Chapter 15
1 [k][Gen. 38:17]
2 [l]ver. 6; ch. 14:20
6 [m]ver. 2 [n]ch. 14:15
8 [o]ver. 11; Isai. 2:21; 57:5
9 [p]2 Sam. 5:18, 22 [q]ver. 14, 17, 19
11 [r]ch. 13:1; 14:4
13 [s]ch. 16:11, 12
14 [t]ch. 14:6, 19; 1 Sam. 11:6; [ch. 3:10]
15 [u]Josh. 23:10; [ch. 3:31; Lev. 26:8]
17 [v]ver. 9, 14
18 [w][Ps. 3:7]
19 [v][See ver. 17 above] [x]Gen. 45:27

14:20 was given to his companion. This was not a custom but an attempt by an embarrassed father to save face (15:1–2). Even the Philistines continued to refer to Samson as "the son-in-law of the Timnite" (15:6).

15:1 at the time of wheat harvest. This was a dry time when fields burned easily (vv. 4–5).

his wife. Legally she was Samson's wife.

15:2 I gave her to your companion. See 14:20 and note.

15:6 the son-in-law of the Timnite. See 14:20 and note.

15:13 bound him with two new ropes. See 16:11–12.

15:14 the Spirit of the LORD. See 3:10 note; 14:6, 19.

15:15 a fresh jawbone . . . 1,000 men. See the parallel with Shamgar, son of Anath (3:31).

15:18 he called upon. This is one of only two times that Samson is mentioned as having spoken to the Lord (16:28).

shall I now die of thirst. Like the Israelites who experienced miracle upon miracle in the wilderness, Samson complained to God. The parallel is marked by the cry for water and the miraculous manner in which God supplied it (v. 19; Ex. 17:1–7; Num. 20:1–13). Both Israel and Samson were complaining to God, but God in His mercy and compassion met their need (Judg. 10:10–16).

En-hakkore;[1] it is at Lehi to this day. 20 And
he judged Israel [y]in the days of the
Philistines twenty years.

Samson and Delilah

16 Samson went to [z]Gaza, and there he
saw a prostitute, and he went in to
her. 2 The Gazites were told, "Samson has
come here." And they [a]surrounded the
place and set an ambush for him all night
at the gate of the city. They kept quiet all
night, saying, "Let us wait till the light of
the morning; then we will kill him." 3 But
Samson lay till midnight, and at midnight
he arose and took hold of the doors of the
gate of the city and the two posts, and
pulled them up, bar and all, and put them
on his shoulders and carried them to the
top of the hill that is in front of Hebron.
4 After this he loved a woman in the
Valley of Sorek, whose name was Delilah.
5 And [b]the lords of the Philistines came up
to her and said to her, [c]"Seduce him, and
see where his great strength lies, and by
what means we may overpower him, that
we may bind him to [d]humble him. And we
will each give you 1,100 pieces of silver."
6 So Delilah said to Samson, "Please tell me
where your great strength lies, and how
you might be bound, that one could [d]sub-
due you."
7 Samson said to her, "If they bind me
with seven fresh bowstrings that have not
been dried, [e]then I shall become weak and
be like any other man." 8 Then the lords of
the Philistines brought up to her seven
fresh bowstrings that had not been dried,
and she bound him with them. 9 Now she
had men lying in ambush in an inner
chamber. And she said to him, "The
Philistines are upon you, Samson!" But he
snapped the bowstrings, as a thread of flax
snaps when it touches the fire. So the
secret of his strength was not known.
10 Then Delilah said to Samson, "Behold,
you have mocked me and told me lies.
Please tell me how you might be bound."
11 And he said to her, "If they bind me with
[f]new ropes that have not been used, then I
shall become weak and be like any other
man." 12 So Delilah took new ropes and
bound him with them and said to him,
"The Philistines are upon you, Samson!"
And the men lying in ambush were in an
inner chamber. But he snapped the ropes
off his arms like a thread.
13 Then Delilah said to Samson, "Until
now you have mocked me and told me lies.
Tell me how you might be bound." And he
said to her, "If you weave the seven locks of
my head with the web and fasten it tight
with the pin, then I shall become weak and
be like any other man." 14 So while he slept,
Delilah took the seven locks of his head
and wove them into the web.[2] And she
made them tight with the pin and said to
him, "The Philistines are upon you,
Samson!" But he awoke from his sleep and
pulled away the pin, the loom, and the
web.
15 And she said to him, [g]"How can you
say, 'I love you,' when your heart is not
with me? You have mocked me these three
times, and you have not told me where
your great strength lies." 16 And [h]when she
pressed him hard with her words day after
day, and urged him, his soul was vexed to
death. 17 And he told her all his heart, and
said to her, [i]"A razor has never come upon
my head, for I have been a Nazirite to God
from my mother's womb. If my head is
shaved, then my strength will leave me,
and I shall become weak and be like any
other man."
18 When Delilah saw that he had told her
all his heart, she sent and called the lords
of the Philistines, saying, "Come up again,
for he has told me all his heart." Then the

20 [y]ch. 13:1
Chapter 16
1 [z]Josh. 15:47
2 [a][1 Sam. 23:26; Ps. 118:10-12; Acts 9:24]
5 [b]Josh. 13:3 [c]ch. 14:15 [d]ver. 19
6 [d][See ver. 5 above]
7 [e]ver. 11, 17
11 [f]ch. 15:13, 14
15 [g]ch. 14:16
16 [h][ch. 14:17]
17 [i][ch. 13:5]

[1] *En-hakkore* means *the spring of him who called* [2] Compare Septuagint; Hebrew lacks *and fasten it tight . . . into the web*

15:20 twenty years. Normally this would signal the end of the story, but not so here (14:1–15:20 note). Like Jephthah (12:7), Samson did not lead Israel for a full generation (forty years), as had the earlier judges.

16:1–22 This account contains two parallel stories showing Samson's desire for women, his prodigious strength, and the efforts the Philistines made to capture him. Samson's continual covenant breaking was judged by God; he was captured by the Philistines and blinded (vv. 21–22). Delilah's attempts to snare Samson reveal Samson to be a fool for remaining with her. It is even more strange that the Spirit of God leaves him only when his hair is cut, not at an earlier point of his covenant breaking. God was patient with Samson until the last sign of his vow was gone, and then God judged him.

16:1 a prostitute. Samson once again broke the covenant (14:2).

16:11 new ropes. See 15:13.

16:15 How can you say. See 14:16–17.

16:17 from my mother's womb. See 13:5.

If my head is shaved. Samson had always ignored the other aspects of his vow (13:1–16:31 note). His true strength was the Spirit of the Lord (v. 20).

lords of the Philistines came up to her and
brought [j]the money in their hands. 19 She
made him sleep on her knees. And she
called a man and had him shave off the
seven locks of his head. Then she began [k]to
torment him, and his strength left him.
20 And she said, "The Philistines are upon
you, Samson!" And he awoke from his
sleep and said, "I will go out as at other
times and shake myself free." But he did
not know that [l]the LORD had left him.
21 And the Philistines seized him and
gouged out his eyes and brought him down
to Gaza and bound him with bronze shackles. [m]And he ground at the mill in the
prison. 22 But the hair of his head began to
grow again after it had been shaved.

The Death of Samson

23 Now the lords of the Philistines gathered to offer a great sacrifice to [n]Dagon
their god and to rejoice, and they said,
"Our god has given Samson our enemy
into our hand." 24 And when the people
saw him, [o]they praised their god. For they
said, "Our god has given our enemy into
our hand, the ravager of our country, who
has killed many of us."[1] 25 And [p]when their
hearts were merry, they said, "Call Samson,
that he may entertain us." So they called
Samson out of the prison, and he entertained them. They made him stand
between the pillars. 26 And Samson said to
the young man who held him by the hand,
"Let me feel the pillars on which the house
rests, that I may lean against them." 27 Now
the house was full of men and women. All
the lords of the Philistines were there, and
[q]on the roof there were about 3,000 men
and women, who looked on while Samson
entertained.
28 Then Samson called to the LORD and
said, "O Lord GOD, [r]please remember me
and please strengthen me only this once, O
God, that I may be avenged on the
Philistines for my two eyes." 29 And Samson
grasped the two middle pillars on which
the house rested, and he leaned his weight
against them, his right hand on the one
and his left hand on the other. 30 And
Samson said, "Let me die with the
Philistines." Then he bowed with all his
strength, and the house fell upon the lords
and upon all the people who were in it. So
the dead whom he killed at his death were
more than those whom he had killed during his life. 31 Then his brothers and all his
family came down and took him and
brought him up and buried him [s]between
Zorah and Eshtaol in the tomb of Manoah
his father. He had judged Israel twenty
years.

Micah and the Levite

17 There was a man of [t]the hill country
of Ephraim, whose name was
Micah. 2 And he said to his mother, "The
1,100 pieces of silver that were taken from
you, about which you uttered a curse, and
also spoke it in my ears, behold, the silver
is with me; I took it." And his mother said,
[u]"Blessed be my son by the LORD." 3 And he
restored the 1,100 pieces of silver to his
mother. And his mother said, "I dedicate
the silver to the LORD from my hand for my
son, to make [v]a carved image and [w]a metal
image. Now therefore I will restore it to
you." 4 So when he restored the money to
his mother, his mother [x]took 200 pieces of
silver and gave it to the silversmith, who
made it into a carved image and a metal
image. And it was in the house of Micah.
5 And the man Micah had a shrine, and he
made [y]an ephod and [z]household gods, and

18 [j]ver. 5
19 [k]ver. 5, 6
20 [l]1 Sam. 28:15, 16
21 [m][Ex. 11:5; Matt. 24:41]
23 [n]1 Chr. 10:10; See 1 Sam. 5:2-7
24 [o][Dan. 5:4]
25 [p]ch. 19:6; [2 Sam. 13:28]
27 [q][Deut. 22:8; 2 Sam. 11:2; Neh. 8:16; Matt. 24:17; Mark 13:15; Luke 17:31]
28 [r]Jer. 15:15
31 [s]ch. 13:25
Chapter 17
1 [t]ver. 8; ch. 18:2; See Josh. 24:33
2 [u]Ruth 3:10; 1 Sam. 15:13
3 [v][Ex. 20:4] [w][Lev. 19:4]
4 [x][Isa. 46:6]
5 [y]ch. 8:27; 18:14, 17; See Ex. 28:6-35 [z][Gen. 31:19; Hos. 3:4]

[1] *Or who has multiplied our slain*

16:20 the LORD had left him. The Spirit of the Lord was not giving him strength (13:25; 14:6, 19; 15:14). Like Saul (cf. Is. 16:14 with 1 Sam. 15:23), Samson lost the power of the Spirit because he disobeyed. God was his power, not magic associated with long hair.

16:23 Our god has given. God is the Judge who allowed oppressors to mistreat His people on account of their sin (v. 20); it was not the power of the gods of the nations that enabled them to overcome Israel (2:14–15).

16:28 O Lord GOD. Samson's final plea is to take revenge for the loss of his sight. The writer does not comment on this motive. God in His grace answered the prayer and allowed Samson to kill the enemies of Israel (10:10–16; 15:18–19).

16:30 more than . . . he had killed during his life. See 13:1–16:31 note.

16:31 He had judged . . . twenty years. See 15:20 note.

17:1–18:31 This section, recounting the Danite idolatry, is part of the conclusion to the Book of Judges. The phrases, "In those days there was no king in Israel" (17:6; 18:1), and "everyone did what was right in his own eyes" (17:6) are repeated in the last section of the narrative cycles (19:1; 21:25). Without a king the people were miserable.

17:2 The story starts abruptly with the return of stolen goods. The mother seems not to be surprised.

17:3 dedicate . . . to the LORD . . . to make a carved image and a metal image. This statement is highly ironic. However well-intentioned, consecrating this silver in this way violated the second commandment (Deut. 5:8), an indication of the spiritual ignorance of the period.

17:5 an ephod. See 8:27 and note.

[a]ordained[1] one of his sons, who became
his priest. 6 [b]In those days there was no
king in Israel. [c]Everyone did what was right
in his own eyes.
7 Now there was a young man of
[d]Bethlehem in Judah, of the family of Judah, who was a Levite, and he sojourned
there. 8 And the man departed from the
town of Bethlehem in Judah to sojourn
where he could find a place. And as he
journeyed, he came to [e]the hill country of
Ephraim to the house of Micah. 9 And
Micah said to him, "Where do you come
from?" And he said to him, "I am a Levite
of Bethlehem in Judah, and I am going to
sojourn where I may find a place." 10 And
Micah said to him, "Stay with me, and be
to me [f]a father and a priest, and I will give
you ten pieces of silver a year and a suit of
clothes and your living." And the Levite
went in. 11 And the Levite [g]was content to
dwell with the man, and the young man
became to him like one of his sons. 12 And
Micah [h]ordained the Levite, and the young
man [i]became his priest, and was in the
house of Micah. 13 Then Micah said, "Now
I know that the LORD will prosper me,
because I have a Levite as priest."

Danites Take the Levite and the Idol

18 [j]In those days there was no king in
Israel. And in those days [k]the tribe
of the people of Dan was seeking for itself
an inheritance to dwell in, for until then no
inheritance among the tribes of Israel had
fallen to them. 2 So the people of Dan sent
five able men from the whole number of
their tribe, [l]from Zorah and from Eshtaol,
[m]to spy out the land and to explore it. And
they said to them, "Go and explore the
land." And they came [n]to the hill country
of Ephraim, to the house of Micah, and
lodged there. 3 When they were by the
house of Micah, they recognized the voice
of the young Levite. And they turned aside
and said to him, "Who brought you here?
What are you doing in this place? What is
your business here?" 4 And he said to them,
"This is how Micah dealt with me: [o]he has
hired me, and I have become his priest."
5 And they said to him, [p]"Inquire of God,
please, that we may know whether the
journey on which we are setting out will
succeed." 6 And the priest said to them,
[q]"Go in peace. The journey on which you
go is under the eye of the LORD."
7 Then the five men departed and came to
[r]Laish and saw the people who were there,
how they lived in security, after the manner
of the Sidonians, [s]quiet and unsuspecting,
lacking[2] nothing that is in the earth and
possessing wealth, and how [t]they were far
from the Sidonians and had no dealings
with anyone. 8 And when they came to their
brothers at [u]Zorah and Eshtaol, their brothers said to them, "What do you report?"
9 They said, [v]"Arise, and let us go up against
them, for we have seen the land, and
behold, it is very good. [w]And will you do
nothing? [x]Do not be slow to go, to enter in
and possess the land. 10 As soon as you go,
you will come to an [y]unsuspecting people.
The land is spacious, for God has given it
into your hands, [z]a place where there is no
lack of anything that is in the earth."

5 [a]ver. 12; [1 Kin. 13:33] 6 [b]ch. 18:1; 19:1; 21:25 [c][Deut. 12:8] 7 [d]ch. 19:1; Ruth 1:1, 2; Mic. 5:2; Matt. 2:1, 5, 6 8 [e]See Josh. 24:33 10 [f]ch. 18:19 11 [g][Ex. 2:21] 12 [h]ver. 5 [i][ch. 18:30]
Chapter 18
1 [j]ch. 17:6; 21:25 [k][ch. 1:34; Josh. 19:47, 48] 2 [l]ver. 8, 11; ch. 13:25 [m][Num. 13:17; Josh. 2:1]
[n]ch. 17:1, 8; See Josh. 24:33 4 [o]ch. 17:10 5 [p]Num. 27:21 6 [q]1 Sam. 1:17; [1 Kin. 22:6] 7 [r][Josh. 19:47] [s]ver. 10, 27 [t]ver. 28 8 [u]ver. 2, 11 9 [v][Num. 13:20; Josh. 2:23, 24] [w]1 Kin. 22:3 [x][Josh. 18:3] 10 [y]ver. 7, 27 [z][ch. 19:19; Deut. 8:9]

1 Hebrew *filled the hand of*; also verse 12 2 Compare 18:10; the meaning of the Hebrew word is uncertain

17:6 In those days. See 18:1; 19:1; 21:25. The refrain comments on the ignorance of Micah and his mother that was typical of the time. They made idols in the name of the Lord, and appointed their own priest.

17:7 Levite. The Levites' inheritance was to serve the Lord at His dwelling place, the tabernacle (Deut. 18:1–8; Josh. 13:14, 33; 14:3–4).

17:10 be to me a father. That is, in a religious sense.

17:11 like one of his sons. That the Levite was "content" with the arrangement shows complete insensitivity to apostasy. An appointed officer of the tabernacle was serving an idol.

17:13 prosper me. This is a foolish statement (v. 3 note; 17:1–18:31 note), further illustrating the darkened understanding of the time, descending to the level of superstition.

18:1 In those days . . . in those days. The repetition (see also 17:6) subtly indicates from the very outset of the narrative that the Danites were doing what was right in their own eyes.

no king in Israel. See 17:6 note.

no inheritance . . . had fallen to them. The Danites had failed to conquer the portion assigned to them (1:34–36). They were in violation of the covenant.

18:2 to spy out the land. They were imitating their forefathers (Num. 13:2, 12).

18:3 they recognized the voice. That is, the distinctive accent of the young man from the south of Israel (cf. 12:6).

18:5 Inquire of God. Priests apparently used an ephod to seek the will of the Lord (8:27 and note).

18:6 The journey on which you go is under the eye of the LORD. The tragic irony of this story—the Levite ministering to idols; Micah's absurd confidence (17:13)—cancels the validity of such a benediction uttered by unholy lips.

18:7 quiet and unsuspecting. Their peaceful, defenseless nature is emphasized by repetition (vv. 10, 27–28).

18:9 the land . . . is very good. Unlike the original spies that entered Canaan, these spies brought back a good report. Conquest would be easy because the people were unsuspecting and peaceful (vv. 7, 10).

11 So 600 men of the tribe of Dan, [a]armed
with weapons of war, set out from Zorah and
Eshtaol, 12 and went up and encamped at
Kiriath-jearim in Judah. On this account that
place is called [b]Mahaneh-dan[1] to this day;
behold, it is west of [c]Kiriath-jearim. 13 And
they passed on from there to [d]the hill country
of Ephraim, and came to the house of Micah.
14 Then the five men who had gone to
scout out the country of Laish said to their
brothers, "Do you know that [e]in these houses there are an ephod, household gods, a
carved image, and a metal image? Now therefore consider what you will do." 15 And they
turned aside there and came to the house of
the young Levite, at the home of Micah, and
[f]asked him about his welfare. 16 Now the 600
men of the Danites, [g]armed with their
weapons of war, stood by the entrance of the
gate. 17 And [h]the five men who had gone to
scout out the land went up and entered and
took [i]the carved image, the ephod, the
household gods, and the metal image, while
the priest stood by the entrance of the gate
with the 600 men armed with weapons of
war. 18 And when these went into Micah's
house and took [i]the carved image, the
ephod, the household gods, and the metal
image, the priest said to them, "What are
you doing?" 19 And they said to him, "Keep
quiet; [j]put your hand on your mouth and
come with us and be to us [k]a father and a
priest. Is it better for you to be priest to the
house of one man, or to be priest to a tribe
and clan in Israel?" 20 And the priest's heart
was glad. He took the ephod and the household gods and the carved image and went
along with the people.

11 [a]ver. 16
12 [b]Josh. 15:60 [c]ch. 13:25
13 [d]ver. 2
14 [e]ch. 17:4, 5
15 [f]Gen. 43:27
16 [g]ver. 11
17 [h]ver. 2, 14 [i]ver. 14; ch. 17:4, 5
18 [i][See ver. 17 above]
19 [j]Job 21:5; 29:9; 40:4; Prov. 30:32; Mic. 7:16 [k]ch. 17:10
21 [l][1 Sam. 17:22; Isai. 10:28; Acts 21:15
24 [m][Gen. 31:30]
27 [n]ver. 7, 10 [o]Josh. 19:47
28 [p]ver. 7 [q]2 Sam. 10:6; [Num. 13:21; Josh. 19:28]
29 [r]ch. 20:1; Gen. 14:14; 1 Kin. 12:29, 30; 15:20 [s]ver. 7
30 [t]Ex. 2:22; 18:3 [u][ch. 17:12]

21 So they turned and departed, putting
the little ones and the livestock and [l]the
goods in front of them. 22 When they had
gone a distance from the home of Micah, the
men who were in the houses near Micah's
house were called out, and they overtook
the people of Dan. 23 And they shouted to
the people of Dan, who turned around and
said to Micah, "What is the matter with you,
that you come with such a company?"
24 And he said, [m]"You take my gods that I
made and the priest, and go away, and what
have I left? How then do you ask me, 'What
is the matter with you?'" 25 And the people
of Dan said to him, "Do not let your voice
be heard among us, lest angry fellows fall
upon you, and you lose your life with the
lives of your household." 26 Then the people
of Dan went their way. And when Micah
saw that they were too strong for him, he
turned and went back to his home.
27 But the people of Dan took what Micah
had made, and the priest who belonged to
him, and they came to Laish, to a people
[n]quiet and unsuspecting, and [o]struck them
with the edge of the sword and burned the
city with fire. 28 And there was no deliverer
because it was [p]far from Sidon, and they
had no dealings with anyone. It was in the
valley that belongs to [q]Beth-rehob. Then
they rebuilt the city and lived in it. 29 And
they named the city [r]Dan, after the name of
Dan their ancestor, who was born to Israel;
but [s]the name of the city was Laish at the
first. 30 And the people of Dan set up the
carved image for themselves, and Jonathan
the son of Gershom, [t]son of Moses,[2] [u]and

[1] *Mahaneh-dan* means *camp of Dan* [2] Or *Manasseh*

18:14 an ephod, household gods, a carved image, and a metal image. This whole list (17:5) is repeated three times in the next six verses (vv. 17, 18, 20) and is twice referred to more generally (vv. 27, 30–31).

18:16 600 men . . . armed . . . by the entrance. The Danites' action is a kind of parody of the conquest of the land begun earlier under Joshua. They go in the strength of overwhelming numbers against a single household, rather than in the strength of the Lord against a fierce enemy. The armed men are mentioned twice as standing outside the door.

18:19 be to us a father and a priest. See 17:10 note.

18:20 And the priest's heart was glad. He was happy for advancement.

He took the ephod . . . carved image. The priest was going to lead Dan in false worship as he had Micah's household.

18:21 in front of them. That is, to protect them from an attack from behind.

18:24 How then do you ask me. Micah is a pathetic figure, believing that God would bless "obedience" in any way that he chose to offer it (17:13).

18:27 took what Micah had made. See v. 14.

a people quiet and unsuspecting. The Israelites were to destroy only the seven proscribed Canaanite nations (Deut. 7:1). To other peoples they were first to offer peace (Deut. 20:10–18). Dan did not ask who these people were (Josh. 9:1–27) and may have destroyed an innocent population. Moreover, this was not the land God had allotted them (Josh. 19:47).

18:30 set up the carved image for themselves. This is an example of what it meant for everyone to do what was right in his own eyes in the absence of a king (v. 14; 17:6).

Jonathan the son of Gershom, son of Moses. (See text note). This was the Levite Micah had hired (17:10, 13).

until the day. Since v. 31 specifies that Micah's idol was set up as long as "the house of God was at Shiloh," the captivity mentioned here would be the time of oppression that began with the Philistine victory near Shiloh, when the ark was removed from there (1 Sam. 4:4, 11). The captivity in Babylon occurred much later.

his sons were priests to the tribe of the
Danites until the day [v]of the captivity of the
land. 31So they set up Micah's carved image
that he made, [w]as long as the house of God
was at Shiloh.

A Levite and His Concubine

19 In those days, [x]when there was no
king in Israel, a certain Levite was
sojourning in the remote parts of [y]the hill
country of Ephraim, who took to himself a
concubine from [z]Bethlehem in Judah.
2And his concubine was unfaithful to[1]
him, and she went away from him to her
father's house at Bethlehem in Judah, and
was there some four months. 3Then her
husband arose and went after her, to speak
kindly to her and bring her back. He had
with him his servant and a couple of donkeys. And she brought him into her father's
house. And when the girl's father saw him,
he came with joy to meet him. 4And his
father-in-law, the girl's father, made him
stay, and he remained with him three days.
So they ate and drank and spent the night
there. 5And on the fourth day they arose
early in the morning, and he prepared to
go, but the girl's father said to his son-in-
law, [a]"Strengthen your heart with a morsel
of bread, and after that you may go." 6So
the two of them sat and ate and drank
together. And the girl's father said to the
man, "Be pleased to spend the night, and
[b]let your heart be merry." 7And when the
man rose up to go, his father-in-law
pressed him, till he spent the night there
again. 8And on the fifth day he arose early
in the morning to depart. And the girl's
father said, [c]"Strengthen your heart and
wait until the day declines." So they ate,
both of them. 9And when the man and his
concubine and his servant rose up to
depart, his father-in-law, the girl's father,
said to him, "Behold, now the day has
waned toward evening. Please, spend the
night. Behold, the day draws to its close.
Lodge here and let your heart be merry,
and tomorrow you shall arise early in the
morning for your journey, and go home."
10But the man would not spend the
night. He rose up and departed and arrived
opposite [d]Jebus (that is, Jerusalem). He had
with him a couple of saddled donkeys, and
his concubine was with him. 11When they
were near Jebus, the day was nearly over,
and the servant said to his master, "Come
now, let us turn aside to this city of the
Jebusites and spend the night in it." 12And
his master said to him, "We will not turn
aside into the city of foreigners, who do not
belong to the people of Israel, but we will
pass on to [e]Gibeah." 13And he said to his
young man, "Come and let us draw near to
one of these places and spend the night at
Gibeah or at [f]Ramah." 14So they passed on
and went their way. And the sun went
down on them near Gibeah, which belongs
to Benjamin, 15and they turned aside there,
to go in and spend the night at Gibeah. And
he went in and sat down in the open square
of the city, [g]for no one took them into his
house to spend the night.

30 [v]ch. 13:1; 1 Sam. 4:2, 3, 10, 11; See Ps. 78:60-64
31 [w]Josh. 18:1; 1 Sam. 1:3
Chapter 19
1 [x]ch. 17:6; 18:1; 21:25 [y]See Josh. 24:33 [z]See ch. 17:7
5 [a]ver. 8; Gen. 18:5
6 [b]ver. 9, 22; ch. 16:25; Ruth 3:7; 2 Sam. 13:28
8 [c]ver. 5
10 [d]See Josh. 15:8, 63
12 [e]Josh. 18:28
13 [f]Josh. 18:25
15 [g]ver. 18

1 Septuagint, Old Latin *became angry with*

18:31 house of God. That is, the tabernacle, which was at Shiloh up to the time of Samuel (Josh. 18:1; 1 Sam. 3:21; 4:3). This was before David's reign. The ark was taken by Eli's sons from Shiloh into battle and lost to the Philistines (1 Sam. 4:4–11). After that the ark was never in Shiloh again.

19:1–21:25 The situation in Israel had deteriorated so much that some of God's people behaved like the people of Sodom and Gomorrah (Gen. 19:1–11). Civil war between the tribes was the result. This final story in the conclusion of Judges blames the misery of Israel on the lack of a king (19:1; 21:25; cf. 17:6; 18:1). Benjamin was the tribe that sinned. Even more, it was the men of Gibeah, Saul's hometown, that behaved like the people of Sodom. Saul's action in 1 Sam. 11:6–8 is clearly parallel to the Levite's desecration of his concubine (19:29 note). Finally, Judah, the tribe of David, was the Lord's choice to be the leader against Benjamin (note the similarity of wording between 1:1–2 and 20:18). The Benjaminites had practically become Canaanites. No one was without fault, however. Each tribe was doing as it saw fit (21:25). The conclusion to be drawn is that a king was needed, a king from Judah and not Benjamin. David and not Saul would initially qualify. Yet, being a man, even David would prove unequal to the task, as later developments would show (2 Sam. 12:10, 11). The Lord whom the people had rejected (1 Sam. 8:7, 8) alone could be their true King (8:22, 23).

19:1 Levite. This man was from the tribe that served the Lord as His priests.

concubine. A concubine was usually a slave and had a lower legal status than a wife (8:31; 9:18).

19:2 unfaithful. The law demanded the stoning of adulterers (Deut. 22:22), but the people were not following the law (17:6; 21:25).

19:10 Jebus . . . Jerusalem. See 1:21 and note.

19:12 We will not turn aside. Ironically, they refuse to lodge with foreigners, only to find that their fellow Israelites are no better than Sodom and Gomorrah (19:1–21:25 note).

Gibeah. When the Book of Judges was written, Gibeah would have been well known as the home town of Saul (19:1–21:25 note).

19:14–20:48 The story of what happened to the Levite in Gibeah is similar to the story of Sodom and Gomorrah (Gen. 19:1–13). Gibeah's sin was like that of Sodom and Gomorrah, and the Benjaminites were destroyed by the LORD's permission and assistance (20:18, 28, 35). Saul was from Benjamin, and it would not have helped him or his descendants for these events to be remembered.

19:15 sat down in the open square. In this manner the travelers advertised their need for hospitality (vv. 16–20).

16 And behold, an old man was coming
from his work in the field at evening. The
man was from [h] the hill country of Ephraim,
and he was sojourning in Gibeah. [i]The
men of the place were Benjaminites. 17 And
he lifted up his eyes and saw the traveler in
the open square of the city. And the old
man said, "Where are you going? and
where do you come from?" 18 And he said
to him, "We are passing from Bethlehem in
Judah to the remote parts of the hill country of Ephraim, from which I come. I went
to Bethlehem in Judah, and I am going [j] to
the house of the Lord,[1] [g]but no one has
taken me into his house. 19 We have straw
and feed for our donkeys, with bread and
wine for me and your female servant and
the young man with your servants. [k]There
is no lack of anything." 20 And the old man
said, [l]"Peace be to you; I will care for all
your wants. [m]Only, do not spend the night
in the square." 21 So he brought him into
his house and gave the donkeys feed. [n]And
they washed their feet, and ate and drank.

Gibeah's Crime

22 As they were [o]making their hearts
merry, behold, the men of the city, worthless fellows, [p]surrounded the house, beating on the door. And they said to the old
man, the master of the house, "Bring out
the man who came into your house, that we
may know him." 23 And the man, the master
of the house, went out to them and said to
them, "No, my brothers, [q]do not act so
wickedly; since this man has come into my
house, [r]do not do this vile thing. 24 [s]Behold,
here are my virgin daughter and his concubine. Let me bring them out now. [t]Violate
them and do with them what seems good to
you, but against this man [q]do not do this
outrageous thing." 25 But the men would
not listen to him. So the man seized his
concubine and made her go out to them.
And they knew her and abused her all night
until the morning. And as the dawn began
to break, they let her go. 26 And as morning
appeared, the woman came and fell down
at the door of the man's house where her
master was, until it was light.

27 And her master rose up in the morning, and when he opened the doors of the
house and went out to go on his way,
behold, there was his concubine lying at
the door of the house, with her hands on
the threshold. 28 He said to her, "Get up, let
us be going." [u]But there was no answer.
Then he put her on the donkey, and the
man rose up and went away to his home.
29 And when he entered his house, he took
a knife, and taking hold of his concubine
he [v]divided her, limb by limb, into twelve
pieces, and sent her throughout all the territory of Israel. 30 [w]And all who saw it said,
"Such a thing has never happened or been
seen from the day that the people of Israel
came up out of the land of Egypt until this
day; [x]consider it, take counsel, and speak."

Israel's War with the Tribe of Benjamin

20 Then [y]all the people of Israel came
out, [z]from Dan to Beersheba,
including the land of Gilead, and the congregation assembled as one man to the
LORD at [a]Mizpah. 2 And the [b]chiefs of all the
people, of all the tribes of Israel, presented
themselves in the assembly of the people of

1 Septuagint *my home*; compare verse 29

16 [h]ver. 1; See Josh. 24:33 [i]ver. 14; ch. 20:4
18 [j]ch. 18:31 [g][See ver. 15 above]
19 [k][ch. 18:10]
20 [l]Gen. 43:23 [m]Gen. 19:2
21 [n]Gen. 18:4; 24:32; 43:24; [John 13:5]
22 [o]See ver. 6 [p]ch. 20:5; [Gen. 19:4]
23 [q]Gen. 19:7 [r]ch. 20:6; Gen. 34:7; Deut. 22:21; 2 Sam. 13:12; [Josh. 7:15]
24 [s][Gen. 19:8] [t]Gen. 34:2; Deut. 21:14
[q][See ver. 23 above]
28 [u][ch. 20:5]
29 [v]ch. 20:6; [1 Sam. 11:7]
30 [w][Hos. 9:9; 10:9] [x]ch. 20:7

Chapter 20
1 [y]ch. 21:5; [Josh. 22:12; 1 Sam. 11:7] [z]1 Sam. 3:20; 2 Sam. 3:10; 24:2 [a][1 Sam. 7:5; 10:17]
2 [b]1 Sam. 14:38

19:16 an old man . . . of Ephraim. It took another "foreigner" from another generation to show hospitality.

19:18 to the house of the Lord. That is, to the tabernacle in Shiloh (18:31).

19:22 Bring out the man. See Gen. 19:5.

19:23 do not do this vile thing. Whatever else may be said, according to the customs of hospitality the host cannot contemplate surrendering his guest to violence. In the law, the sexual act contemplated is described as "an abomination" (Lev. 18:22; 20:13).

19:24 my virgin daughter. As Lot offered his daughters to protect his guests (Gen. 19:8), the host offers his daughter to protect the Levite. The author does not comment on the morality of this offer, but the whole story is presented as a final illustration of the evil consequences of forsaking God's rule and doing what is right in one's own eyes.

19:28 But there was no answer. She was dead.

19:29 twelve pieces. The original audience of Judges would have been well aware of how Saul later cut up oxen into twelve parts in order to summon Israel to fight against the Ammonites (1 Sam. 11:6–8).

19:30 Such a thing. This would be the grotesque use of the woman's body.

20:1–48 The attack upon the Levite and his concubine resulted in civil war between all Israel and Benjamin (ch. 19). Repeated reference to Israel's oneness (vv. 1–2, 8, 11) makes an important point: Israel was united for the first time in the Book of Judges. Although their action was not unjust, it is sad that they were united only in order to punish one of their own number (v. 23). Judah was to lead against Benjamin as it had led against the Canaanites (v. 18; 1:1, 2 and notes).

20:1 from Dan to Beersheba. The extreme north and south of Israel.

assembled as one man. For the first time Israel was united, but the purpose was to wage war against their brothers.

to the LORD at Mizpah. See 11:11 note. Saul was later made king at Mizpah.

20:2 in the assembly of the people of God. After the repeated cycles of sin, judgment, and deliverance, it is an evidence of God's mercy that Israel was still called His people.

God, 400,000 men on foot [c]that drew the
sword. 3 (Now the people of Benjamin
heard that the people of Israel had gone up
to Mizpah.) And the people of Israel said,
"Tell us, how did this evil happen?" 4 And
the Levite, the husband of the woman who
was murdered, answered and said, [d]"I
came to Gibeah that belongs to Benjamin,
I and my concubine, to spend the night.
5 [e]And the leaders of Gibeah rose against
me and surrounded the house against me
by night. They meant to kill me, and they
violated my concubine, and she is dead.
6 [f]So I took hold of my concubine and cut
her in pieces and sent her throughout all
the country of the inheritance of Israel, for
they have committed abomination and
[g]outrage in Israel. 7 Behold, you people of
Israel, all of you, [h]give your advice and
counsel here."
8 And all the people arose as one man,
saying, "None of us will go to his tent, and
none of us will return to his house. 9 But
now this is what we will do to Gibeah: we
will go up against it by lot, 10 and we will
take ten men of a hundred throughout all
the tribes of Israel, and a hundred of a
thousand, and a thousand of ten thousand,
to bring provisions for the people, that
when they come they may repay Gibeah of
Benjamin, for all the outrage that they have
committed in Israel." 11 So all the men of
Israel gathered against the city, united as
one man.
12 [i]And the tribes of Israel sent men
through all the tribe of Benjamin, saying,
"What evil is this that has taken place
among you? 13 Now therefore give up the
men, [j]the worthless fellows in Gibeah, that
we may put them to death [k]and purge evil
from Israel." But the Benjaminites would
not listen to the voice of their brothers, the
people of Israel. 14 Then the people of
Benjamin came together out of the cities to
Gibeah to go out to battle against the people of Israel. 15 And the people of Benjamin
mustered out of their cities on that day
[l]26,000 men [m]who drew the sword,
besides the inhabitants of Gibeah, who
mustered 700 chosen men. 16 Among all
these were 700 chosen men who were [n]left-
handed; every one could sling a stone at a
hair and not miss. 17 And the men of Israel,
apart from Benjamin, mustered [m]400,000
men who drew the sword; all these were
men of war.
18 The people of Israel arose and went up
to [o]Bethel and inquired of God, [p]"Who
shall go up first for us to fight against the
people of Benjamin?" And the LORD said,
[p]"Judah shall go up first."
19 Then the people of Israel rose in the
morning and encamped against Gibeah.
20 And the men of Israel went out to fight
against Benjamin, and the men of Israel
drew up the battle line against them at
Gibeah. 21 [q]The people of Benjamin came
out of Gibeah and destroyed on that day
22,000 men of the Israelites. 22 But the people, the men of Israel, took courage, and
again formed the battle line in the same
place where they had formed it on the first
day. 23 [r]And the people of Israel went up
and wept before the LORD until the
evening. And they inquired of the LORD,
"Shall we again draw near to fight against
our brothers, the people of Benjamin?"
And the LORD said, "Go up against them."
24 So the people of Israel came near
against the people of Benjamin the second
day. 25 And Benjamin [s]went against them
out of Gibeah the second day, and
destroyed 18,000 men of the people of
Israel. All these were men who [t]drew the
sword. 26 Then all the people of Israel, the
whole army, went up and came to [u]Bethel
and wept. They sat there before the LORD
and fasted that day until evening, and
offered burnt offerings and peace offerings
before the LORD. 27 And the people of Israel
inquired of the LORD [v](for the ark of the
covenant of God was there in those days,

2 [c]ver. 15, 17, 25, 35, 46; See ch. 8:10
4 [d]ch. 19:15
5 [e]ch. 19:22, 25, 26
6 [f]ch. 19:29 [g]See ch. 19:23
7 [h]ch. 19:30
12 [i][Deut. 13:14; Josh. 22:13, 16]
13 [j]ch. 19:22; See Deut. 13:13 [k]Deut. 13:5; 17:2
15 [l][Num. 1:37; 26:41] [m]ver. 2
16 [n]ch. 3:15; [1 Chr. 12:2]
17 [m][See ver. 15 above]
18 [o]ver. 26, 31 [p][ch. 1:1]
21 [q]ver. 25
23 [r]ver. 26-28
25 [s]ver. 21 [t]ver. 2
26 [u]ver. 18, 31
27 [v][Josh. 18:1; 1 Sam. 4:3, 4]

20:5 they violated my concubine. The Levite omits the details of how the concubine had been offered (19:23–24).

20:8 as one man. See vv. 1, 11, and 20:1–48 note. The Israelites took an oath to see this through to the end.

20:13 purge evil. The Israelites did not see the evil that pervaded their community.

20:16 were left-handed. See 3:15 note.

20:18 to Bethel. The ark of the Lord and the priest with the ephod were at Bethel at this time (v. 27).

Who shall go up first. This is the same language that is used at the beginning of Judges, where the question to be decided was who should lead against the Canaanites (1:1).

Judah. The Lord gave the same answer as in 1:2, but in a different situation.

20:23 inquired of the LORD. See vv. 18, 27–28; cf. 1 Sam. 28:6.

our brothers, the people of Benjamin. Note how the Israelites now add the word "brothers" to their inquiry (v. 18).

28 and [w]Phinehas the son of Eleazar, son of Aaron, [x]ministered before it in those days), saying, "Shall we go out once more to battle against our brothers, the people of Benjamin, or shall we cease?" And the LORD said, "Go up, for tomorrow I will give them into your hand."

29 [y]So Israel set men in ambush around Gibeah. 30 And the people of Israel went up against the people of Benjamin on the third day and set themselves in array against Gibeah, as at other times. 31 And the people of Benjamin went out against the people and were drawn away from the city. And as at other times they began to strike and kill some of the people in the highways, [z]one of which goes up to [a]Bethel and the other to Gibeah, and in the open country, about thirty men of Israel. 32 And the people of Benjamin said, [b]"They are routed before us, as at the first." But the people of Israel said, "Let us flee and draw them away from the city to the highways." 33 And all the men of Israel rose up out of their place and set themselves in array at Baal-tamar, and the men of Israel who were in ambush rushed out of their place from Maareh-geba.[1] 34 And there came against Gibeah 10,000 chosen men out of all Israel, and the battle was hard, [c]but the Benjaminites did not know that disaster was close upon them. 35 And the LORD defeated Benjamin before Israel, and the people of Israel destroyed 25,100 men of Benjamin that day. All these were men who [d]drew the sword. 36 So the people of Benjamin saw that they were defeated.

The men of Israel gave ground to Benjamin, because they trusted the men in ambush whom they had set against Gibeah. 37 [e]Then the men in ambush hurried and rushed against Gibeah; the men in ambush moved out and struck all the city with the edge of the sword. 38 Now the appointed signal between the men of Israel and the men in the main ambush was that when they made a great cloud of smoke rise up out of the city 39 the men of Israel should turn in battle. Now Benjamin had begun to strike and kill about thirty men of Israel. They said, [f]"Surely they are defeated before us, as in the first battle." 40 But when the signal began to rise out of the city in a column of smoke, the Benjaminites looked behind them, and behold, [g]the whole of the city went up in smoke to heaven. 41 Then the men of Israel turned, and the men of Benjamin were dismayed, [h]for they saw that disaster was close upon them. 42 Therefore they turned their backs before the men of Israel in [i]the direction of the wilderness, but the battle overtook them. And those who came out of the cities were destroying them in their midst. 43 Surrounding the Benjaminites, they pursued them and trod them down from Nohah[2] as far as opposite Gibeah on the east. 44 Eighteen thousand men of Benjamin fell, all of them men of valor. 45 And they turned [i]and fled toward the wilderness to the rock of [j]Rimmon. Five thousand men of them were cut down in the highways. And they were pursued hard to Gidom, and 2,000 men of them were struck down. 46 So all who fell that day of Benjamin were 25,000 men who drew the sword, all of them men of valor. 47 But 600 men turned and [i]fled toward the wilderness to the rock of [j]Rimmon and remained at the rock of Rimmon four months. 48 And the men of Israel turned back against the people of Benjamin and struck them with the edge of the sword, the city, men and beasts and all that they found. And all the towns that they found they set on fire.

Wives Provided for the Tribe of Benjamin

21 Now the men of Israel had sworn [k]at Mizpah, "No one of us shall give his daughter in marriage to Benjamin." 2 And the people came to [l]Bethel and sat there till evening before God, and they lifted up their voices and wept bitterly. 3 And they said, "O LORD, the God of Israel, why has this happened in Israel, that today there should be one tribe lacking in Israel?" 4 And the next day the people rose early

1 Some Septuagint manuscripts *place west of Geba* 2 Septuagint; Hebrew [at their] *resting place*

28 [w]Num. 25:7; 31:6; Josh. 24:33 [x]Deut. 10:8; 18:5, 7
29 [y][Josh. 8:4]
31 [z]ch. 21:19 [a]ver. 18, 26
32 [b][Josh. 8:5, 6]
34 [c]ver. 41
35 [d]ver. 2
37 [e][Josh. 8:19]
39 [f]ver. 31, 32
40 [g][Josh. 8:20]
41 [h]ver. 34
42 [i][Josh. 8:15, 24]
45 [i][See ver. 42 above] [j]ch. 21:13; Josh. 15:32
47 [i][See ver. 42 above] [j][See ver. 45 above]
Chapter 21
1 [k]ver. 18; ch. 20:1
2 [l]ch. 20:18, 26, 31

20:48 struck them with the edge of the sword. The Israelites treated the Benjaminites like the Canaanites (1:8, 17). Moreover, the Benjaminites' end was like that of the inhabitants of Sodom (19:14–20:48 note).

21:1–25 The actions of Israel in this final episode of the book should be interpreted in light of the concluding comment: "In those days there was no king in Israel. Everyone did what was right in his own eyes" (v. 25). The Israelites wondered why this evil had come upon them (vv. 3, 15; 6:13 note). As with Gideon (6:13), no answer was given. Yet the book's larger context gives the clear answer that Israel had sinned and continued to sin in horrible ways.

and [m]built there an altar and offered burnt
offerings and peace offerings. 5 And the
people of Israel said, "Which of all the
tribes of Israel did not come up in the assembly to the LORD?" [n]For they had taken
a great oath concerning him who did not
come up to the LORD to Mizpah, saying,
"He shall surely be put to death." 6 And the
people of Israel [o]had compassion for
Benjamin their brother and said, "One
tribe is cut off from Israel this day. 7 [p]What
shall we do for wives for those who are left,
since we have sworn by the LORD that we
will not give them any of our daughters for
wives?"

8 And they said, "What one is there of the
tribes of Israel that did not come up to the
LORD to Mizpah?" And behold, no one had
come to the camp from [q]Jabesh-gilead, to
the assembly. 9 For when the people were
mustered, behold, not one of the inhabitants of [q]Jabesh-gilead was there. 10 So the
congregation sent 12,000 of their bravest
men there and commanded them, [r]"Go
and strike the inhabitants of Jabesh-gilead
with the edge of the sword; also the
women and the little ones. 11 This is what
you shall do: [s]every male and every woman
that has lain with a male you shall devote
to destruction." 12 And they found among
the inhabitants of Jabesh-gilead 400 young
virgins who had not known a man by lying
with him, and they brought them to the
camp at [t]Shiloh, which is in the land of
Canaan.

13 Then the whole congregation sent
word to the people of Benjamin who were
at the [u]rock of Rimmon and [v]proclaimed
peace to them. 14 And Benjamin returned at
that time. And they gave them the women
whom they had saved alive of the women
of Jabesh-gilead, but they were not enough
for them. 15 And the people [w]had compassion on Benjamin because the LORD had
made a breach in the tribes of Israel.

16 Then the elders of the congregation
said, [x]"What shall we do for wives for those
who are left, since the women are destroyed
out of Benjamin?" 17 And they said, "There
must be an inheritance for the survivors of
Benjamin, that a tribe not be blotted out
from Israel. 18 Yet we cannot give them
wives from our daughters." [y]For the people
of Israel had sworn, "Cursed be he who
gives a wife to Benjamin." 19 So they said,
"Behold, there is the yearly feast of the
LORD at Shiloh, which is north of Bethel, on
the east of [z]the highway that goes up from
Bethel to Shechem, and south of Lebonah."
20 And they commanded the people of
Benjamin, saying, "Go and lie in ambush in
the vineyards 21 and watch. If the daughters
of Shiloh come out to [a]dance in the dances,
then come out of the vineyards and snatch
each man his wife from the daughters of
Shiloh, and go to the land of Benjamin.
22 And when their fathers or their brothers
come to complain to us, we will say to
them, 'Grant them graciously to us,
because we did not take for each man of
them his wife in battle, neither did you give
them to them, else you would now be
guilty.'" 23 And the people of Benjamin did
so and took their wives, according to their
number, from the dancers whom they carried off. Then they went and returned to
their inheritance [b]and rebuilt the towns and
lived in them. 24 And the people of Israel
departed from there at that time, every man
to his tribe and family, and they went out
from there every man to his inheritance.

25 [c]In those days there was no king
in Israel. Everyone did what was right in
his own eyes.

4 [m][2 Sam. 24:25]
5 [n][ch. 5:23]
6 [o]ver. 15
7 [p]ver. 16
8 [q]1 Sam. 11:1; 31:11-13
9 [q][See ver. 8 above]
10 [r][ver. 5]
11 [s]Num. 31:17
12 [t]Josh. 18:1
13 [u]ch. 20:47 [v]Deut. 20:10
15 [w]ver. 6
16 [x]ver. 7
18 [y]ver. 1
19 [z][ch. 20:31]
21 [a]ch. 11:34; Ex. 15:20
23 [b][ch. 20:48]
25 [c]ch. 17:6; 18:1; 19:1

21:8 Jabesh-gilead. Saul's first act as king was to defend Jabesh-gilead. Since he was a Benjaminite from Gibeah, Saul may have descended from one of the women taken from Jabesh-gilead (v. 12).

21:15 the LORD had made a breach in the tribes of Israel. God did this to punish the Benjaminites for their sin.

21:19–23 Israel's degeneracy was now so complete that they even proposed and allowed the kidnapping of their own women to avoid breaking a rash vow. The nation was indeed acting, unchecked, in accord with their own sinful inclinations (v. 25; cf. 17:6).

21:25 In those days. While Israel's only hope was in allegiance to her divine King, the nation rather settled for a human monarchy (1 Sam. 8:7, 22), which inevitably would fail them.

THE BOOK OF

Ruth

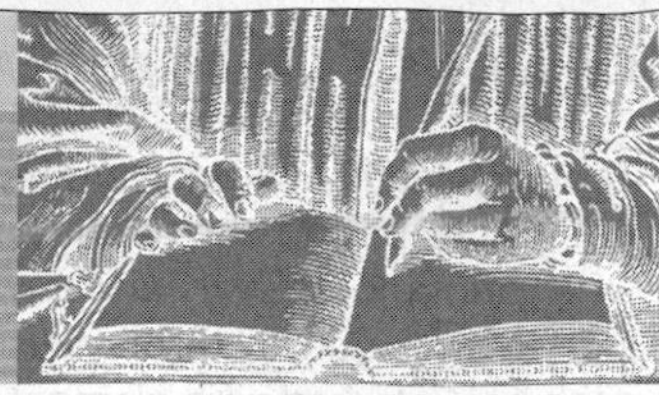

AUTHOR

The Book of Ruth, named after its principal character, is an anonymous short story. Rabbinic tradition held that the book, with Judges and Samuel, was written by the prophet Samuel. This is possible only if the book is dated early. Some would date Ruth as late as after the Jewish exile in Babylon, which took place during the sixth century B.C.

DATE AND OCCASION

The Book of Ruth can be dated in the time of Samuel (c. 1050 B.C., at the beginning of Israel's monarchy), the time of David (c. 1000 B.C.), or the century following the exile in Babylon (c. 450 B.C.). The reference to David in 4:17, the genealogy of 4:18–22, and the explanation of an apparently antiquated custom in 4:7 indicate a time after David had begun to reign. The book's portrayal of good relations between Moabites and Israelites suits best the early period of David's rule. All told, a time early in the monarchy may be affirmed as readily as any other.

This universally appealing narrative has evoked diverse conclusions concerning its purpose. Such a story does not need a moral to justify its popularity, but that it had a moral, or at least a theological purpose, is beyond doubt. Biblical interpreters have had no trouble finding a purpose; the challenge is to find a single, dominant theme.

Ruth has been understood to celebrate the following: (a) that a proselyte, even from Moab, can be faithful to the Lord and gain full membership in Israel; (b) that qualities of loyalty and covenant faithfulness in a foreigner can be a model for Israel's response to the Lord; (c) that the Lord as Redeemer will restore the exiled family of Israel to its land. In light of the epilogue (4:18–22), however, and assuming a date close to the time of David, the major purpose seems to include showing that David's kingship is legitimate. The primacy of the tribe of Judah (the father of Perez; 4:12, 18) had already been established in Israel, despite Tamar's strange act of desperation (Gen. 38). Now the primacy of David must be established, even though there is a Moabite in the line. Boaz is the model for the relative who redeems, while Ruth beautifully reflects God's faithful covenant love, claiming refuge under the Lord's wings, and clinging to Naomi. If God has drawn together all these disparate strands so carefully to bless the line of David, is that not one more reason to affirm David's initially fragile claim to the throne?

INTERPRETIVE DIFFICULTIES

The issues that have fascinated scholars arise directly from puzzling elements in the narrative. These may be divided into the following groups: (a) questions about purpose, related to difficulties in dating and origin; (b) questions about legal customs, especially the family obligations of a close relative of a deceased person; and (c) internal difficulties, such as the relationship between 4:12, 17 and the genealogy in 4:18–22. An abundant literature addresses each of these areas, with sometimes little agreement. It is one of the remarkable phenomena of biblical research that such debates leave unaffected the powerful impact this simple account has on every generation of readers.

CHARACTERISTICS AND THEMES

Though clearly an important historical document of its period, the narrative of Ruth is told with dramatic intensity and movement. The story moves quickly through its various stages, each part marked with elements of irony and suspense, all contributing to a symphony of divine providential fulfillment. The Lord inspires Naomi's return, Ruth's covenant faithfulness, and Boaz's righteous adherence to the law. The book closes with a genealogy of King David, the descendant of Boaz the Israelite and Ruth the Moabite, a young woman who took refuge under the Lord's wings (2:12) and was rewarded by God, who "gave her conception" (4:13).

Ruth and Boaz are part of a longer line that often shows God's grace combined with human frailty. One of David's ancestors was Perez (4:12, 18), son of an irregular union between Judah and his own daughter-in-law, Tamar, who was "more righteous" than the patriarch himself (Gen. 38:26). The closing few verses of Ruth (4:18–22) are commonly said to be a later addition to the book, but genealogies are not unusual in ancient narratives. Also, this genealogy underlines a particular value of Ruth, its revelation of the mixed ancestry of King David and through him, of Jesus Christ.

Looking beyond this witness to the legitimacy of David's kingship, we should note the significance of the book in the light of the gospel. Ruth follows the faith of Abraham, as she leaves home and family to go to a foreign land under the Lord's care. The universal scope of the gospel comes to light as Ruth the Moabite finds the blessing promised to all the nations in Abraham's descendants. Finally, Ruth becomes an ancestor of Christ, who in Himself will reconcile to God such different nations as Moab and Israel.

OUTLINE OF RUTH

I. The Death of Elimelech and His Sons (1:1–5)

II. Naomi and Ruth Return to Bethlehem in Judah (1:6–22)

- A. *Naomi and Her Daughters-in-law Leave Moab (1:6, 7)*
- B. *Naomi Urges Orpah to Go Back Home (1:8–14)*
- C. *Ruth's Solemn Promise (1:15–18)*
- D. *Naomi's Bitter Homecoming (1:19–22)*

III. Ruth Gleans in the Fields of Boaz (ch. 2)

- A. *Ruth Goes Out to Glean (2:1–3)*
- B. *Boaz Meets Ruth (2:4–16)*
- C. *Naomi's Assessment of Boaz (2:17–23)*

IV. Ruth Visits Boaz at the Threshing Floor (ch. 3)

- A. *Naomi's Plan (3:1–5)*
- B. *Boaz Discovers Ruth (3:6–13)*
- C. *Ruth Returns to Naomi (3:14–18)*

V. Boaz Redeems Ruth (ch. 4)

- A. *The Close Relative Excuses Himself (4:1–6)*
- B. *Ruth and Boaz Are Married Before Witnesses (4:7–12)*
- C. *The First Child Is Welcomed and Blessed (4:13–17)*
- D. *Genealogy from Perez to David (4:18–22)*

Naomi Widowed

1 In the days [a]when the judges ruled
there was [b]a famine in the land, and a
man of [c]Bethlehem in Judah went to
sojourn in the country of Moab, he and his
wife and his two sons. 2 The name of the
man was Elimelech and the name of his
wife Naomi, and the names of his two sons
were Mahlon and Chilion. They were
[d]Ephrathites from Bethlehem in Judah.
They went into the country of Moab and
remained there. 3 But Elimelech, the husband of Naomi, died, and she was left with
her two sons. 4 These took Moabite wives;
the name of the one was Orpah and the
name of the other Ruth. They lived there
about ten years, 5 and both Mahlon and
Chilion died, so that the woman was left
without her two sons and her husband.

Ruth's Loyalty to Naomi

6 Then she arose with her daughters-in-
law to return from the country of Moab, for
she had heard in the fields of Moab that
[e]the LORD had visited his people and [f]given
them food. 7 So she set out from the place
where she was with her two daughters-in-
law, and they went on the way to return to
the land of Judah. 8 But Naomi said to her
two daughters-in-law, "Go, return each of
you to her mother's house. May the LORD
[g]deal kindly with you, as you have dealt
with [h]the dead and with me. 9 The LORD
grant that you may find [i]rest, each of you in
the house of her husband!" Then she
kissed them, and they lifted up their voices
and wept. 10 And they said to her, "No, we
will return with you to your people." 11 But
Naomi said, "Turn back, my daughters;
why will you go with me? Have I yet sons
in my womb [j]that they may become your
husbands? 12 Turn back, my daughters; go
your way, for I am too old to have a husband. If I should say I have hope, even if I
should have a husband this night and
should bear sons, 13 would you therefore
wait till they were grown? Would you
therefore refrain from marrying? No, my
daughters, for it is exceedingly bitter to me
for your sake that [k]the hand of the LORD
has gone out against me." 14 Then they lifted up their voices and wept again. And
Orpah kissed her mother-in-law, but Ruth
clung to her.
15 And she said, "See, your sister-in-law
has gone back to her people and to [l]her
gods; return after your sister-in-law." 16 But
Ruth said, "Do not urge me to leave you or
to return from following you. For where

Chapter 1
1 [a]Judg. 2:16 [b]Gen. 12:10; 26:1; 43:1; 2 Kin. 8:1 [c]See Judg. 17:7
2 [d]Gen. 35:19
6 [e]Ex. 3:16; 4:31; Luke 1:68 [f]Ps. 132:15
8 [g]Josh. 2:12, 14; Judg. 1:24 [h]ver. 5; ch. 2:20
9 [i]ch. 3:1
11 [j]Gen. 38:11; Deut. 25:5
13 [k]Judg. 2:15; [Job 19:21; Ps. 32:4; 38:2; 39:10]
15 [l]Judg. 11:24; 1 Kin. 11:7; Jer. 48:7, 13, 46

1:1–5 The preface moves quickly through the necessary background (time, place, and source of conflict), setting the stage for the scenes that follow.

1:1 In the days. In Hebrew this is a standard formula for opening a historical book. The period of the judges in Israel was infamous as a time of instability and apostasy.

a famine. Events in the Book of Ruth turn on the curse of famine, and its corresponding reversal in blessing. Famines were sometimes a sign of divine displeasure (1 Kin. 17:1). Naomi (1:21) bitterly acknowledges God's sovereign hand in her circumstances, and in any case, events are never outside His decree.

country of Moab. Lit. "fields of Moab." Moabites, who were related to Israel through Lot (Gen. 19:37), occupied parts of central Transjordan at various times. Although God protected them at first from the Israelite invaders (Deut. 2:9), the Moabites were subjugated by Saul (1 Sam. 14:47) and then by David (2 Sam. 8:2). See also Deut. 23:3. There were some periods of friendly relations, with considerable cultural and economic interchange, as shown by David's placement of his parents with the king of Moab while he was a fugitive (1 Sam. 22:3). Elimelech's sojourn in Moab takes place during one such period.

1:2 Elimelech. Although the story might have climaxed with God's provision of an immediate heir for the deceased Elimelech, the drama emphasizes the role of the women in the family (4:14, 16) and the passing significance of Elimelech as a remote ancestor of David (4:17–22).

Naomi. Lit. "pleasant" (vv. 20–21). Naomi's story is told first.

1:4 Moabite wives. This action was not forbidden, though Deut. 23:3–6 would prohibit the male descendants access to the temple. The irony is that an heir, and an ancestor of the great king David, would come through one of these foreigners.

1:5 the woman was left without. Naomi was an old, barren woman, in a foreign country, with two alien and childless daughters-in-law. She seems an unlikely prospect for any role in the Lord's covenantal history of redemption.

1:6, 7 These verses set the stage for vv. 8–18. The women must decide what factors will determine their paths: finding a husband and having children, living in one's own country, being close to one's family, or finally, for Ruth, trusting in the Lord as sovereign God. Naomi's love for her daughters-in-law, and her reaction to bitter experiences at God's hand, dominate this scene. Ruth's decision, and her irrevocable vow of fidelity to Naomi's people and her God, says much about the impact of Naomi's character and faith on her daughter-in-law.

1:6 the LORD had visited his people. A note of hope is sounded. Ruth's story never loses sight of God, whose faithful love determines history.

1:9, 10 we will return with you. This initial declaration of both daughters heightens the dramatic tension.

1:11 Have I yet sons. Naomi's talk of raising up sons to replace the missing husbands only exaggerates her loss. The idea itself may refer to the law of levirate marriage. According to this law, if a man died leaving a widow, his brother was obliged to marry the widow, taking his place and preserving the family lines (Deut. 25:5, 6). There was also a custom that when someone died a close relative (or "redeemer") was supposed to buy (or "redeem") the deceased's estate. Just how these customs functioned in the history of Ruth and Boaz is a matter of continuing debate (2:20 note).

1:15 her gods. A new element is introduced. Up to now it might have been assumed that the daughters had become worshipers of the Lord. Now it becomes clear that the choice of homeland is a choice for or against the true God. Against the background of Orpah's choice, the courage and beauty of Ruth's declaration (vv. 16–17) is all the more obvious.

you go I will go, and where you lodge I will
lodge. [m]Your people shall be my people,
and your God my God. 17 [n]Where you die I
will die, and there will I be buried. [n]May
the LORD do so to me and more also if anything but death parts me from you."
18 [o]And when Naomi saw that she was
determined to go with her, she said no
more.

Naomi and Ruth Return

19 So the two of them went on until they
came to Bethlehem. And when they came
to Bethlehem, [p]the whole town was stirred
because of them. And the women said, "Is
this Naomi?" 20 She said to them, "Do not
call me Naomi;[1] call me [q]Mara,[2] for the
Almighty has dealt very bitterly with me.
21 [r]I went away full, and the LORD has
brought me back empty. Why call me
Naomi, when the LORD has testified against
me and the Almighty has brought calamity
upon me?"
22 So Naomi returned, and Ruth the
Moabite her daughter-in-law with her, who
returned from the country of Moab. And
they came to Bethlehem [s]at the beginning
of barley harvest.

16 [m][ch. 2:11, 12]
17 [n]1 Sam. 3:17; 25:22; 2 Sam. 19:13; 1 Kin. 2:23
18 [o][Acts 21:14]
19 [p][Matt. 21:10]
20 [q]Ex. 15:23
21 [r]Job 1:21
22 [s]2 Sam. 21:9; [ch. 2:23]

Chapter 2
1 [t]ch. 3:2, 12 [u]ch. 4:21; Matt. 1:5
2 [v][Deut. 24:19] [w]ver.

Ruth Meets Boaz

2 Now Naomi had [t]a relative of her husband's, a worthy man of the clan of
Elimelech, whose name was [u]Boaz. 2 And
Ruth the Moabite said to Naomi, "Let me go
to the field and [v]glean among the ears of
grain after him [w]in whose sight I shall find
favor." And she said to her, "Go, my daughter." 3 So she set out and went and gleaned
in the field after the reapers, and she happened to come to the part of the field
belonging to Boaz, who was of the clan of
Elimelech. 4 And behold, Boaz came from
Bethlehem. And he said to the reapers,
[x]"The LORD be with you!" And they
answered, "The LORD bless you." 5 Then
Boaz said to his young man who was in
charge of the reapers, "Whose young
woman is this?" 6 And the servant who was
in charge of the reapers answered, "She is
the young Moabite woman, [y]who came back
with Naomi from the country of Moab. 7 She
said, 'Please let me glean and gather among
the sheaves after the reapers.' So she came,
and she has continued from early morning
until now, except for a short rest."[3]

1 *Naomi* means *pleasant* 2 *Mara* means *bitter* 3 Compare Septuagint, Vulgate; the meaning of the Hebrew phrase is uncertain

1:19–21 Naomi . . . empty. The women's question (v. 19) expresses their amazement that this woman, whose circumstances had once reflected her name ("pleasant"), should now have fallen upon such hard times. Naomi does not hesitate to say it was the Lord's doing. She does not give a reason, and the narrator does not suggest anything, about why she was suffering.

1:22 Ruth the Moabite. She is not just any Ruth. For the story it is crucial that she be remembered as the foreigner (1:4; 2:2, 6, 21; 4:5, 10; especially 2:10). Also, the reader may be prompted to think of Ruth's ancestor, Lot's daughter, and the incestuous beginnings of the Moabite nation (Gen. 19:30–38). In both cases the problem is childlessness or lack of a male heir.

barley harvest. Early calendars, like the Gezer Calendar from the tenth century B.C., associated months with the agricultural cycle. Barley was the first of the cereals to be harvested, in April; wheat was the last. In later tradition the barley and wheat harvests came to be identified with the festivals of Passover and Pentecost. The season of harvest was a time of celebration, rejoicing together before God, and remembering the poor. The narrative development is tied to this scheme. The women return home at the barley harvest, a time of God's favor and the beginning of fruitful restoration for Naomi.

2:1–23 Chapter two introduces the last main character, Boaz, and the major theme, that of the close relative, or redeemer, who has certain responsibilities for the family and property of a relative who dies (2:20 note). The narrator, who already knows what is ahead, gives only a hint with the description of Boaz as "a relative" in v. 1. Only after the natural kindness of Boaz, and the natural winsomeness of Ruth, have taken their course, does Naomi reveal the key to the entire story: Boaz is "a close relative" (2:20). Even then, no claims are made; there is no appeal to custom. Events must wait their time, while Naomi schemes, Ruth serves quietly, and Boaz finishes the harvest. However, God had already provided an answer through the law (Lev. 25).

2:1 relative. Or "friend." The Hebrew text leaves the technical status of Boaz unclear, but the story unfolds as if he were the "nearest redeemer" described in Lev. 25:25, whose responsibility relates primarily but not exclusively to the property of an impoverished relative (1:11; 2:20 and notes). Later on (e.g., 2:20; 3:9) Boaz will be identified as such a "close relative," but at this point he is introduced to prepare the reader for the occurrence that places Ruth in his field.

worthy. The Hebrew usually means an outstanding fighter, but here it means someone powerful and important in society.

2:2 Let me go to the field. Ruth's initiative, on the surface, is simply to keep herself and Naomi alive, according to a custom codified in Leviticus (19:9–10; 23:22) and Deuteronomy (24:19). As poor people, Ruth and Naomi would receive some help, but much more is about to come their way. A hint of this provision is given in Ruth's plaintive request that she might glean "after him in whose sight I shall find favor."

2:3 she happened to come. It seems as if she came to the field of her relative by coincidence, yet God is causing the event.

2:4 behold. Boaz's arrival satisfies the expectations raised in vv. 1–3.

2:6, 7 The servant's answer establishes Ruth's character. She is faithful, having come while still in her youth to a foreign country for the sake of her relative. She is modest, asking permission for what might have been considered a right. She is hardworking, having been busy since morning.

2:7 among the sheaves. Ruth's request seems not to go beyond what was her right as a widow (Deut. 24:19–21). But the response of Boaz will prove to go far beyond the legal requirement (v. 15).

has continued. This is usually taken to mean that she was working all morning, but it could mean that she had been waiting for her request to be granted by the owner of the field. It is more likely that it refers to work, since she interrupted the morning with a rest.

8 Then Boaz said to Ruth, "Now, listen,
my daughter, do not go to glean in another
field or leave this one, but keep close to my
young women. 9 Let your eyes be on the
field that they are reaping, and go after
them. Have I not charged the young men
not to touch you? And when you are
thirsty, go to the vessels and drink what the
young men have drawn." 10 Then [z]she fell
on her face, bowing to the ground, and
said to him, "Why have I found favor in
your eyes, that you should [a]take notice of
me, since I am a foreigner?" 11 But Boaz
answered her, [b]"All that you have done for
your mother-in-law since the death of your
husband has been fully told to me, and
how you left your father and mother and
your native land and came to a people that
you did not know before. 12 [c]The LORD
repay you for what you have done, and a
full reward be given you by the LORD, the
God of Israel, under whose wings you have
come to take refuge!" 13 Then she said, [d]"I
have found favor in your eyes, my lord, for
you have comforted me and spoken kindly
to your servant, though I am not one of
your servants."

14 And at mealtime Boaz said to her,
"Come here and eat some bread and dip
your morsel in the wine." So she sat beside
the reapers, and he passed to her roasted
grain. And she ate until [e]she was satisfied,
and she had some left over. 15 When she
rose to glean, Boaz instructed his young
men, saying, "Let her glean even among
the sheaves, and do not reproach her.
16 And also pull out some from the bundles
for her and leave it for her to glean, and do
not rebuke her."

17 So she gleaned in the field until
evening. Then she beat out what she had
gleaned, and it was about an ephah[1] of barley. 18 And she took it up and went into the
city. Her mother-in-law saw what she had
gleaned. She also brought out and gave her
what food she had left over [f]after being satisfied. 19 And her mother-in-law said to her,
"Where did you glean today? And where
have you worked? Blessed be the man
[g]who took notice of you." So she told her
mother-in-law with whom she had worked
and said, "The man's name with whom I
worked today is Boaz." 20 And Naomi said
to her daughter-in-law, [h]"May he be
blessed by the LORD, whose kindness has
not forsaken [i]the living or the dead!"
Naomi also said to her, "The man is a close
relative of ours, one of [j]our redeemers."
21 And Ruth the Moabite said, "Besides, he
said to me, 'You shall keep close by my
young men until they have finished all my
harvest.'" 22 And Naomi said to Ruth, her
daughter-in-law, "It is good, my daughter,
that you go out with his young women, lest
in another field you be assaulted." 23 So she
kept close to the young women of Boaz,
gleaning until the end of the barley and
wheat harvests. And she lived with her
mother-in-law.

10, 13
4 [x]Ps. 129:7, 8
6 [y]ch. 1:22
10 [z][1 Sam. 25:23, 41]
[a]ver. 19
11 [b]ch. 1:14, 16, 17
12 [c][1 Sam. 24:19]
13 [d]ver. 2, 10; Gen. 33:15; 1 Sam. 1:18
14 [e]ver. 18

18 [f]ver. 14
19 [g]ver. 10
20 [h]ch. 3:10; Judg. 17:2; 1 Sam. 15:13; 23:21;

Ruth and Boaz at the Threshing Floor

3 Then Naomi her mother-in-law said to
her, "My daughter, should I not seek

1 An *ephah* was about 3/5 bushel or 22 liters

2:8–12 Events unfold quickly as Boaz accedes to the request and offers his protection and provision (vv. 8–9). Ruth acknowledges his favor to her, an undeserving "foreigner" (v. 10). Only then (vv. 11–12) does the narrative give some inkling of God's providential working. Boaz has known already that Ruth is no ordinary foreigner. She has taken "refuge" under the "wings" of the Lord, and she will receive "a full reward" from Him (v. 12). Though a foreigner, Ruth's loyalty to God will become a key element in God's great plan of redemption. The plan will be worked out through David, the covenant king, and through Christ, David's greater Son. The reward of Ruth's faith far transcends local time and circumstances.

2:14–16 Boaz's permission is clearly extraordinary.

2:14 wine. This was a sour but refreshing drink or dip (cf. Num. 6:3).

2:17 beat out . . . about an ephah. Beating out the grain, or threshing it, separated the kernels from the husks, chaff, and stalks. An ephah was about half a bushel, a large amount to have gleaned.

2:18 what food she had left over. This would be what she had set aside from her noon meal (v. 14).

2:20 whose kindness has not forsaken. God's love is faithful, and He will not forget the ones He loves. The blessings He promised will pass from Boaz to Ruth to Naomi, and eventually to all the elect.

close relative of ours. See Introduction: Interpretive Difficulties. The law of redemption now comes into view. According to this law, the nearest male blood relative had the duty of preserving the family name and property. This duty could entail (a) avenging the death of a family member (Num. 35:19–21); (b) buying back family property that had been sold to pay debts (Lev. 25:25); (c) buying back a relative who had sold himself into slavery to pay debts (Lev. 25:47–49); and (d) marrying the widow of a deceased relative (Deut. 25:5–10). Apparently these duties could be renounced or declined under certain circumstances (cf. Ruth 3:12; 4:1–8). Boaz was such a "close relative" (or "redeemer") to Ruth, and this fact now determines the course of action (see 1:11; 2:1 and notes). Ruth's destiny will proceed according to law, unlike her ancestor, Lot's daughter, who committed incest (Gen. 19:30–38).

2:23 until the end of . . . harvests. The two-month delay prepares for the threshing floor incident (ch. 3).

3:1–18 Now the narrative moves toward resolution. In a midnight visit, Ruth carries out and expands Naomi's plan, putting her own reputation and all her expectations at risk. She claims the protection of Boaz as a "redeemer" (v. 9). Her trust in his character is vindicated, and she is unharmed. God's activity behind the scenes continues without a break. But even at this moment, the engagement must be delayed; there is a

[k]rest for you, that it may be well with you?
2 Is not Boaz [l]our relative, [m]with whose
young women you were? See, he is winnowing barley tonight at the threshing
floor. 3 [n]Wash therefore and anoint yourself, and put on your cloak and go down to
the threshing floor, but do not make yourself known to the man until he has finished
eating and drinking. 4 But when he lies
down, observe the place where he lies.
Then go and uncover his feet and lie down,
and he will tell you what to do." 5 And she
replied, "All that you say I will do."
6 So she went down to the threshing floor
and did just as her mother-in-law had commanded her. 7 And when Boaz had eaten
and drunk, and [o]his heart was merry, he
went to lie down at the end of the heap of
grain. Then she came softly and uncovered
his feet and lay down. 8 At midnight the
man was startled and turned over, and
behold, a woman lay at his feet! 9 He said,
"Who are you?" And she answered, "I am
Ruth, your servant. [p]Spread your wings[1]
over your servant, for you are [q]a redeemer."
10 And he said, [r]"May you be blessed by the
LORD, my daughter. You have made this
last kindness greater than [s]the first in that
you have not gone after young men,
whether poor or rich. 11 And now, my
daughter, do not fear. I will do for you all
that you ask, for all my fellow townsmen
know that you are [t]a worthy woman. 12 And
now it is true that I am [u]a redeemer. Yet
there is a redeemer nearer than I. 13 Remain
tonight, and in the morning, if he will [v]re-
deem you, good; let him do it. But if he is
not willing to redeem you, then, [w]as the
LORD lives, I will redeem you. Lie down
until the morning."
14 So she lay at his feet until the morning,
but arose before one could recognize
another. And he said, "Let it not be known
that the woman came to the threshing
floor." 15 And he said, "Bring the garment
you are wearing and hold it out." So she
held it, and he measured out six measures
of barley and put it on her. Then she went
into the city. 16 And when she came to her
mother-in-law, she said, "How did you
fare, my daughter?" Then she told her all
that the man had done for her, 17 saying,
"These six measures of barley he gave to
me, for he said to me, 'You must not go
back empty-handed to your mother-in-
law.'" 18 She replied, "Wait, my daughter,
until you learn how the matter turns out,
for the man will not rest but will settle the
matter today."

2 Sam. 2:5 [i]ch. 1:8 [j]ch. 3:9; 4:14
Chapter 3
1 [k]ch. 1:9
2 [l]ch. 2:1 [m]ch. 2:8
3 [n]2 Sam. 12:20; 14:2
7 [o]See Judg. 19:6
9 [p]Ezek. 16:8; [Deut. 22:30] [q]ch. 2:20
10 [r]See ch. 2:20 [s]ch. 1:8
11 [t]Prov. 12:4; 31:10
12 [u]ch. 4:1
13 [v]ch. 4:5; [Deut. 25:5] [w]Judg. 8:19; 1 Sam. 14:39;

1 Compare 2:12; the word for *wings* can also mean *corners of a garment*

closer relative (3:12), and Boaz, a man of outstanding honor, will not rest until this obstacle is removed.

3:1 Like Lot's two daughters (Gen. 19:31–32), Naomi and Ruth had lost their husbands and children. Again, Naomi acted to preserve her family line, but in quite a different way from Lot's daughters.

rest for you. This means that Ruth should be married, a need that Naomi had taken to heart (1:9).

3:3, 4 The instructions, presented to Ruth so precisely, have strong overtones of intrigue.

the threshing floor. This was a cleared area where grain was crushed or torn to separate the chaff, straw, and grains. The harvest was then winnowed, or thrown into the air for the wind to blow away the chaff and let the grains fall directly to the ground. All this took place in the spring at the time of the harvest festivals. The prophet Hosea refers to the threshing floor as a common site of sexual immorality (Hos. 9:1).

3:4 uncover his feet. A comparison of this scene with the history of Lot's daughters (Gen. 19:30–38) is instructive. At Naomi's suggestion, Ruth was approaching Boaz with some boldness. But her purpose was to become engaged. Her answer (v. 9) shows that she was not thinking of becoming pregnant outside wedlock.

lie down. Ruth lies patiently at Boaz's feet until he wakes (vv. 8–9); nothing unseemly happens between them during the night (v. 11).

3:7 merry. Boaz had been drinking, but was hardly drunk. After all the work and festivity of the day, Boaz went to "the end of the heap of grain," a place where Ruth was able to meet him privately. God's providence was clearing a path for her.

3:9 Spread your wings over your servant. See text note. Ezek. 16:8 explains the idiom. Ruth asks directly for the favor of marriage, although Naomi's instructions were not quite so bold (v. 4).

redeemer. The law does not specify marriage as the responsibility of such a person, though an extension of Lev. 25 can readily be envisioned. Mahlon's name and property will be preserved (4:10), suggesting the levirate marriage, but it is difficult to see how Deut. 25:5–6 could be strictly applied. See Introduction: Interpretive Difficulties and note on 2:20. Again, Ruth goes far beyond Naomi's specified plan.

3:10 kindness. Lit. "covenant love." Throughout the book, God's own covenant love (1:8; 2:20) is mirrored by that of Ruth (1:8, 16–17). Now her faithfulness is proved as (a) she invokes the duties of a close relative, and (b) she has declined to follow any of the young men. The "kindness" Boaz refers to is evidently Ruth's proposal to follow the custom that would provide an heir for Naomi.

the first. That is, when she chose to accompany Naomi.

3:11 a worthy woman. This is the feminine equivalent of the Hebrew phrase in 2:1. Ruth has risen from being a Moabite and servant to becoming attractive to Boaz as a possible marriage partner.

3:12 a redeemer nearer than I. Boaz suddenly mentions a complicating factor. If Naomi was thinking of a relative, why was this closer relative not introduced earlier? The custom of redemption seems to be leading to a solution, but now it creates a problem along the way. The engagement must be postponed.

3:15 six measures of barley. This gift of barley shows Boaz's magnanimity toward Ruth (v. 17), and is a symbol of Naomi's changed estate (1:21). Ruth receives grain from Boaz as an emblem of her future fruitfulness.

3:16 How did you fare. The same Hebrew words are translated "Who are you?" in v. 9.

3:18 Wait. This is an ironic touch, for the time to wait will be very short. Naomi does not expect a conclusion to be long in coming.

Boaz Redeems Ruth

4 Now Boaz had gone up to [x]the gate
and sat down there. And behold, [y]the
redeemer, of whom Boaz had spoken,
came by. So Boaz said, "Turn aside,
friend; sit down here." And he turned
aside and sat down. **2** And he took ten
men [z]of the elders of the city and said,
"Sit down here." So they sat down. **3** Then
he said to the redeemer, "Naomi, who has
come back from the country of Moab, is
selling the parcel of land that belonged to
our relative Elimelech. **4** So I thought I
would tell you of it and say, [a]'Buy it in the
presence of those sitting here and in the
presence of the elders of my people.' If
you will redeem it, redeem it. But if you[1]
will not, tell me, that I may know, for
there is no one besides you to redeem it,
and I come after you." And he said, "I will
redeem it." **5** Then Boaz said, "The day
you buy the field from the hand of Naomi,
you also acquire Ruth[2] the Moabite, the
widow of the dead, in order [b]to perpetuate
the name of the dead in his inheritance."
6 [c]Then the redeemer said, "I cannot
redeem it for myself, lest I impair my own
inheritance. Take my right of redemption
yourself, for I cannot redeem it."
7 [d]Now this was the custom in former
times in Israel concerning redeeming and
exchanging: to confirm a transaction, the
one drew off his sandal and gave it to the
other, and this was the manner of attesting in Israel. **8** So when the redeemer said
to Boaz, "Buy it for yourself," he drew off
his sandal. **9** Then Boaz said to the elders
and all the people, "You are witnesses
this day that I have bought from the
hand of Naomi all that belonged to
Elimelech and all that belonged to
[e]Chilion and to Mahlon. **10** Also Ruth the
Moabite, the widow of Mahlon, I have
bought to be my wife, [f]to perpetuate the
name of the dead in his inheritance, that
the name of the dead may not be cut off
from among his brothers and from the
gate of his native place. You are witnesses this day." **11** Then all the people who
were [g]at the gate and the elders said, "We
are witnesses. May the LORD make the
woman, who is coming into your house,
like Rachel and Leah, [h]who together
[i]built up the house of Israel. May you act
worthily in [j]Ephrathah and [k]be renowned
in Bethlehem, **12** and may your house be
like the house of Perez, [l]whom Tamar
bore to Judah, because [m]of the offspring
that the LORD will give you by this young
woman."

Ruth and Boaz Marry

13 So Boaz took Ruth, and she became
his wife. And he went in to her, [n]and the
LORD gave her conception, and she bore a
son. **14** [o]Then the women said to Naomi,
"Blessed be the LORD, who has not left you
this day without [p]a redeemer, and may his

1 Hebrew *he* 2 Masoretic Text *you also buy it from Ruth*

2 Sam. 4:9; 12:5; 2 Kin. 2:2, 6
Chapter 4
1 [x]2 Sam. 15:2; 18:4, 24, 33; 19:8; Ps. 127:5 [y]ch. 2:20
2 [z]1 Kin. 21:8; Prov. 31:23
4 [a]Lev. 25:25; [Jer. 32:7, 8]
5 [b]ver. 10; ch. 3:13; Deut. 25:5, 6
6 [c]ch. 3:12, 13
7 [d]See Deut. 25:7-10
9 [e]ch. 1:2, 4, 5
10 [f]ver. 5
11 [g]See ver. 1 [h]See Gen. 29:31–30:24; 35:16-18 [i]Deut. 25:9 [j]Gen. 35:16, 19 [k]ver. 14
12 [l]Gen. 38:29; 1 Chr. 2:4; Matt. 1:3 [m]1 Sam. 2:20
13 [n]Gen. 29:31; 33:5
14 [o][Luke 1:58] [p]ch. 2:20

4:1–17 The fourth chapter brings out the divine purpose behind Ruth's original decision to follow Naomi and Naomi's God. The necessary arrangements seem to turn on a combination of levirate marriage (Deut. 25:5–10) and the laws for a redeeming relative (Lev. 25). Ruth is taken as a wife, and ancient blessings for fruitfulness are invoked. Naomi's bitterness turns to joy, and her grandson is to become the grandfather of King David. In these events the Lord's hidden providence is revealed.

4:1 the gate. The entranceway to a city was a usual site of legal and commercial transactions.

friend. Boaz must have known the man's name. The narrator quotes Boaz with an indefinite phrase, something like the English expression "so and so." Perhaps he did not want to memorialize a selfish person in his story.

4:2 took ten men. There is no recorded legal requirement for a particular number of men. The later Jewish tradition by which ten men make up a quorum for worship may derive from this incident. In a rural culture, where the use of writing is limited, it is important for a contract to be made with a number of official witnesses.

4:3 selling the parcel of land. This sale is a surprising new element, no hint of which has been given up to now. Details about the sale are not necessary for the story and are omitted.

4:5 you also acquire Ruth. This association of Ruth and Naomi under the laws about the property and family of a deceased relative is an unusual application of the laws. But an understanding of these details is not essential to the purpose of the narrative.

4:7 drew off his sandal. Little is known about the symbolism of this custom. Its point clearly was to confirm the transaction legally. See Deut. 25:9–10 (a different setting) and Amos 8:6.

4:10 to perpetuate the name of the dead. The disappearance of one's name was considered to be an extreme misfortune (1 Sam. 24:21; 2 Sam. 14:7).

4:11 like Rachel and Leah. These are the two wives of Jacob (Israel), who were the mothers, either naturally or through their maids Zilpah and Bilhah, of all the sons of Israel, the heads of the twelve tribes.

Ephrathah . . . Bethlehem. As in 1:1–2, these place names, associated with David, are given special prominence.

4:12 be like . . . Perez. In a much earlier time, Judah had become the father of Perez because Onan refused to carry out his obligation as a close relative (Gen. 38:29). Perez became a symbol of the fruitful offspring. Now in the same way Boaz becomes the father of Obed (v. 21) because another person refused to carry out the levirate obligation. Despite human failures, the messianic line was preserved (Matt. 1:3, 5, 16).

4:14–17 The women's praises celebrate the fulfillment of God's covenant love to Naomi. Her daughter-in-law Ruth is more to her than seven sons would be (v. 15). Moreover, Naomi in effect has a son in her grandson Obed (v. 17). He will become the grandfather of David.

name [q]be renowned in Israel! 15 He shall be
to you a restorer of life and a nourisher of
your old age, for your daughter-in-law who
loves you, [r]who is more to you than seven
sons, has given birth to him." 16 Then
Naomi took the child and laid him on her
lap and became his nurse. 17 [s]And the
women of the neighborhood gave him
a name, saying, "A son has been born
to Naomi." They named him Obed. He
was the father of Jesse, the father of David.

The Genealogy of David

18 Now these are the generations of Perez:
[t]Perez fathered Hezron, 19 Hezron fathered
Ram, Ram fathered Amminadab, 20 [u]Am-
minadab fathered Nahshon, Nahshon
fathered Salmon, 21 Salmon fathered Boaz,
Boaz fathered Obed, 22 Obed fathered Jesse,
and Jesse fathered David.

14 [q]ver. 11
15 [r]1 Sam. 1:8
17 [s]Luke 1:59
18 [t]For ver. 18-22, see 1 Chr. 2:4-15; Matt. 1:3-6
20 [u]Num. 1:7; [Ex. 6:23]

4:16 Naomi took the child. Possibly this means that there was a formal adoption procedure. Whatever the case, this closing scene is the happy ending of what is truly "Naomi's Story." The sorrowful widow who thought she had returned empty (1:21) has been filled beyond expectation (Ps. 126:5, 6).

4:18–22 The closing genealogy (Introduction: Characteristics and Themes) shifts the focus from Naomi back to Boaz, and fulfills a larger purpose of the narrative. The genealogy begins with Perez, someone who could "breach" (Gen. 38:29, text note), and whom the women in their blessing remembered as the vigorous son of Tamar (v. 12). Like Ruth, Tamar became an ancestor of David in an unexpected way. For New Testament readers, David is not the end of God's provisions for the people of His choice, His covenant bride. But for her own time, Ruth's journey had reached its divinely appointed goal.

THE FIRST BOOK OF

Samuel

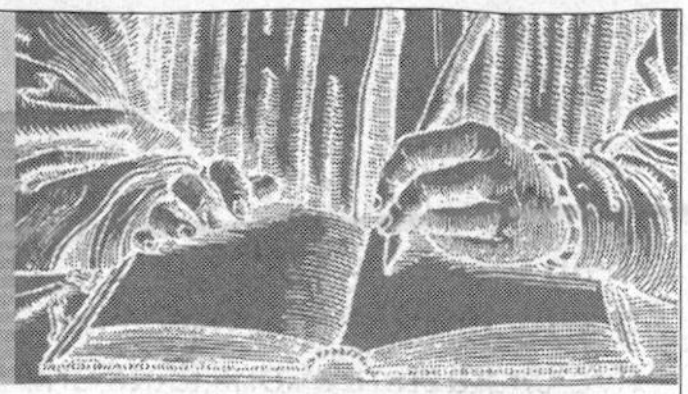

AUTHOR

The books of Samuel do not directly name their author, and it seems likely that the association of Samuel's name with these books reflects the role he played in anointing Israel's first kings. Samuel is described as an old man in 8:1 and as having already died in 25:1, long before many of the events of 1 and 2 Samuel had even taken place. However, 1 Chr. 29:29 attaches the names of Samuel and his prophetic successors Nathan and Gad to certain written sources, portions of which may have been incorporated into the written history of Israel as it took shape. The books of Samuel were probably given their final form by someone deeply influenced by the theology of the Book of Deuteronomy ("Introduction to the Historical Books" on page 295).

DATE AND OCCASION

As with authorship, the books of Samuel give no clear indication of the date they were written. Joshua, Judges, Samuel, and Kings all clearly contain information from sources contemporary with the events narrated in them, but their final form was not set until the time of Judah's exile in Babylon (see "Introduction to the Historical Books").

In the latter half of the eleventh century B.C., a time when the international powers of the ancient Near East were preoccupied with internal conflicts, Israel was transformed from a loosely knit tribal confederation into a united monarchy. The institution of the monarchy was a new stage in the political and religious history of Israel, although the idea of kingship itself would have been known to Israel from the practice of its neighbors (Judg. 3:12; 4:2; 8:5). What is remarkable is not that Israel eventually installed a king, but that it resisted doing so for so long. One cause of Israel's reluctance is revealed in the words of Gideon, "I will not rule over you, and my son will not rule over you; the LORD will rule over you" (Judg. 8:23). A fundamental tenet of Israel's faith was that the Lord Himself (Yahweh) was Israel's Sovereign, their Great King (8:7; 12:12; Num. 23:21; Ps. 5:2; Mal. 1:14). Nevertheless, the opening books of the Bible contain indications that Israel, in accordance with the divine will, would one day have a human monarch (Gen. 49:10; Num. 24:7, 17–19; cf. Gen. 17:6, 16; 35:11). Moses anticipated a time when Israel would be settled in the Promised Land and would desire a king, and he gave instructions to regulate kingship when it came (Deut. 17:14–20; cf. 28:36). As 1 Samuel opens, that time has almost arrived.

It is difficult to attach firm dates to most of the events recounted in Samuel. Although definite figures are given for the duration of David's reign over Judah and Israel (2 Sam. 5:4, 5), there is no clear indication of how long Saul reigned (13:1 note). The specific years of David's and Saul's reigns have to be established by working back from the dates of events recorded in Kings, which have their own chronological difficulties (see Introduction to 1 Kings). There is broad consensus that David had consolidated his rule over both Judah and Israel shortly before 1000 B.C. (Judah, c. 1010 B.C.; Israel, c. 1003 B.C.). David's lifetime can be dated about 1040 to 970 B.C. Samuel could have been born about 1100 B.C.

CHARACTERISTICS AND THEMES

The books of 1 and 2 Samuel are masterpieces of literature. Their basic purpose is to give a historical account of the emergence and early development of the Israelite monarchy under Saul and David. The history is selective, and the nature of the selections reveals the theological concerns of the books. Kingship in Israel came into being through the mediation of a prophet, and the written history of this change has a prophetic point of view.

The narratives of 1 and 2 Samuel are written in an economical style, using a variety of narrative techniques: keywords (2:29 note); comparative characterizations (Saul and Jonathan, David and Uriah; see 13:22 note, 14:6 note, and 2 Sam. 11); repetition and variation (Saul's two confessions in 15:24, 25, 30); and analogy (Nabal compared with Saul, ch. 25). Sensitivity to such literary features can open the door to theological and historical understanding, and to a sense of the unity of the text.

The basic plot of 1 Samuel is Saul's rise to power and subsequent rejection. As noted above, the books of Samuel focus on an important innovation in Israel's religious and political life—having an earthly king. The subject of 1 Samuel is largely the intersecting careers of three figures: Samuel, Saul, and David. The key issue is how a human king can be accommodated in the framework of the covenant relationship existing between God and Israel. How can Israel have a king without compromising God's kingship?

In the Hebrew Bible, 1 Samuel follows the Book of Judges, which ends with the doleful refrain, "In those days there was no king in Israel. Everyone did what was right in his own eyes" (21:25; cf. 17:6; 18:1; 19:1). This refrain can also describe the first chapters of 1 Samuel. As the book opens, Israel is without a human king, and the Israelites are unconcerned with honoring their divine King. Even the priests, the sons of Eli, simply do what is right in their own eyes (2:12–17).

The first unit relates the birth of Samuel and his call to be a prophet (chs. 1–3). In a famous song, Hannah praises God for the birth of Samuel (2:1–10). Her song introduces basic theological themes of the books—the sovereignty and holiness of God, divine reversal of human fortune, divine deliverance, and the futility of trusting human strength. Kingship is anticipated in a reference to the Lord's "anointed," "his king" (2:10). The story of the downfall of the priestly house of Eli introduces the theme of divine rejection and its causes.

The section 4:1–7:1 is often called "the ark narrative." In these chapters the Lord demonstrates His power, first against Israel's attempt to exploit the ark as if it were a magical talisman, and second in a devastating march through the Philistine cities. In 7:2–17 God's power to deliver Israel and defeat Israel's enemies is displayed through God's man, Samuel. Against this backdrop, the sinfulness of the people's demand for a human ruler (ch. 8) is clearly seen. It is not that Israel is never to have a human monarch, for a king has long been anticipated. What is objectionable is for the people to want a king "like all the nations" (8:5), because this desire is a rejection of the greatest King, God Himself (8:7). In spite of the folly of the people's request, God will grant it, provided the people are warned about the potential abuses of monarchy, and provided the king himself is willing to submit to God's rule.

Israel's first king proves to be a disappointment. Saul is introduced in 9:2 as an impressive person of striking proportion, presumably what the people wanted. The prophet Samuel told Saul that he would rule Israel, and then anointed him in the Lord's name (9:26–10:1). Soon afterward the Spirit of God overcame Saul and he prophesied with a company of prophets. He gathered a force from all Israel and led them to victory over the Ammonites. He was approved by the people, and Samuel publicly anointed him king (10:24; 11:14, 15). Clearly the kingship in Israel is conceived of as requiring the special direction of God.

On two important occasions Saul fell short of what God required. When he was instructed to wait for Samuel, Saul's patience expired and he offered a sacrifice that Samuel should have performed (13:8–14). Secondly, when God issued a commandment to destroy the Amalekites, Saul followed only half-way (ch. 15). He preserved the life of the king and many of the animals. Samuel denounced him sternly and took sword in hand himself to cut down the king. At this time Samuel prophesied that Saul had been rejected and that God had given the kingdom to someone else (15:28). God's favor was removed from Saul (28:17).

The fall of Saul's dynasty is coincident with the rise of David. David, like Saul, was chosen by God to be king. But in his case God's choice was somehow deeper. David was not without faults, but ultimately God promised him that He would not reject him on that account (2 Sam. 7:8–16). He would punish him, but He would preserve him. David married Saul's daughter Michal and became the intimate friend of his son Jonathan, yet even as he did so Saul's jealousy and suspicion fell on him. Saul became deranged and tried to kill both David and Jonathan (18:11; 19:1; 20:33). David was forced to flee from the court and become a fugitive in his own country.

At the last Saul's original calling to deliver his people from the Philistines was reawakened in him, and he fought a disastrous battle at Gilboa.

Unwilling to be captured, King Saul committed suicide, opening David's path to the throne.

In many ways David's career typifies that of his greater Son, Jesus Christ. Both were sanctioned by a prophet, David by Samuel (3:20; 16:13) and Jesus by John the Baptist (Matt. 14:5; John 1:29–31; 5:31–35). The Spirit of the Lord came upon both (16:13; Mark 1:9–11). Both were rejected by jealous kings (18:9; Matt. 2:16) and were warned to flee for their lives (ch. 20; Matt. 2:13–15). Rejected also by their own people without cause (23:12; John 19:15), both learned in exile to depend on God.

TITLE

The books of Samuel have had various titles. The Septuagint (the Greek translation of the Old Testament) and the Vulgate (a Latin translation of the whole Bible) group them with 1 and 2 Kings as First, Second, Third, and Fourth "Kingdoms" or "Kings." Jewish tradition distinguished Samuel and Kings, but did not divide Samuel into two books until the fifteenth century A.D.

OUTLINE OF 1 SAMUEL

I. Before the Monarchy: God Rules and Rescues His People (chs. 1–7)

A. God's Man: Samuel and Eli at Shiloh (chs. 1–3)

1. Samuel's Birth and Hannah's Song of Thanksgiving (1:1–2:10)
2. The Rejection of the House of Eli (2:11–36)
3. The Initiation of Samuel as Prophet (ch. 3)

B. God's Power: The Ark of God and Philistia (4:1–7:1)

1. The Ark Is Captured by the Philistines (ch. 4)
2. The Ark in Philistia (ch. 5)
3. The Ark Is Returned to Israel (6:1–7:1)

C. God's Victory: Samuel Versus the Philistines at Mizpah (7:2–17)

II. The Beginning of Monarchy: The People Demand a King (chs. 8–12)

A. Samuel Hears and God Grants the People's Request (ch. 8)

B. Saul's Rise: Designation by Samuel and Demonstration in Battle (chs. 9–12)

1. Saul Anointed by Samuel (9:1–10:16)
2. Saul Publicly Selected by Lot at Mizpah (10:17–27)
3. Saul Rescues Jabesh-gilead from the Ammonites (ch. 11)

C. Samuel Issues Warnings About Monarchy (ch. 12)

III. The People's Choice: The Reign and Rejection of King Saul (chs. 13–15)

A. Saul Versus the Philistines: Saul's First Rejection (chs. 13; 14)

1. Jonathan Attacks the Philistines; Saul Fails the Test (ch. 13)
2. Jonathan Leads the People to Victory; Saul Becomes Isolated (ch. 14)

B. Saul Versus the Amalekites: Saul Rejected (ch. 15)

IV. God's Choice: The Rise of David and Fall of Saul (chs. 16–31)

A. David's Rise Delights All but Saul (chs. 16–18)

1. David Anointed by Samuel and Introduced to Saul (ch. 16)
2. David and Goliath (ch. 17)
3. David and the House of Saul (ch. 18)

B. Saul Seeks David's Life (chs. 19–23)

1. Saul's Attempts to Kill David Are Thwarted (ch. 19)
2. Jonathan Aids and Encourages David (ch. 20)
3. David Deceives Ahimelech at Nob and Escapes to Gath (ch. 21)
4. Saul Destroys the Priests of Nob; David Delivers the People of Keilah (22:1–23:6)
5. Saul Pursues David but Is Thwarted by the Philistines (23:7–29)

C. David Protects Saul's Life (chs. 24–26)

1. David Spares Saul's Life in the Cave (ch. 24)
2. Abigail Keeps David from Murder in His Dispute with Nabal (ch. 25)
3. David Spares Saul's Life in the Camp (ch. 26)

D. David Hides with the Philistines; Saul Takes His Own Life (chs. 27–31)

1. David Flees to the Philistines (ch. 27)
2. Saul and the Medium at En-dor (ch. 28)
3. David Rejected by the Philistines (ch. 29)
4. David Recovers What Had Been Taken by the Amalekites (ch. 30)
5. Saul, Wounded on Mount Gilboa, Takes His Own Life (ch. 31)

The Birth of Samuel

1 There was a certain man of
[a]Ramathaim-zophim of [b]the hill country of Ephraim whose name was Elkanah
the son of Jeroham, son of Elihu, son of
Tohu, son of Zuph, [c]an Ephrathite. 2 He
had two wives. The name of the one was
Hannah, and the name of the other,
Peninnah. And Peninnah had children, but
Hannah had no children.
3 Now this man used to go up [d]year by
year from his city [e]to worship and to sacrifice to the LORD of hosts [f]at Shiloh, where
the two sons of Eli, Hophni and Phinehas,
were priests of the LORD. 4 On the day when
Elkanah sacrificed, [g]he would give portions
to Peninnah his wife and to all her sons
and daughters. 5 But to Hannah he gave a
double portion, because he loved her,
though the LORD had closed her womb.[1]
6 And her rival used to provoke her grievously to irritate her, because the LORD had
closed her womb. 7 So it went on year by
year. As often as she went up to the house
of the LORD, she used to provoke her.
Therefore Hannah wept and would not eat.
8 And Elkanah, her husband, said to her,
"Hannah, why do you weep? And why do
you not eat? And why is your heart sad?
[h]Am I not more to you than ten sons?"
9 After they had eaten and drunk in
Shiloh, Hannah rose. Now Eli the priest
was sitting on the seat beside the doorpost
of [i]the temple of the LORD. 10 She was
[j]deeply distressed and prayed to the LORD
and wept bitterly. 11 And she [k]vowed a vow
and said, "O LORD of hosts, if you will
indeed [l]look on the affliction of your servant and [m]remember me and not forget
your servant, but will give to your servant a
son, then I will give him to the LORD all the
days of his life, [n]and no razor shall touch
his head."
12 As she continued praying before the
LORD, Eli observed her mouth. 13 Hannah
was speaking in her heart; only her lips

Chapter 1
1 [a][ver. 19] [b]See Josh. 24:33 [c][1 Kin. 11:26]
3 [d]ver. 21; Ex. 23:14; Deut. 16:16; [Luke 2:41] [e]See Deut. 12:5-7 [f][Josh. 18:1]
4 [g]Deut. 12:17, 18; 16:11; [Neh. 8:10, 12]
8 [h]Ruth 4:15
9 [i]ch. 3:3
10 [j]Job 7:11; 10:1
11 [k]Gen. 28:20; Judg. 11:30 [l]Gen. 29:32 [m]ver. 19; [Gen. 30:22] [n]Judg. 13:5; [Num. 6:5]

1 Syriac; the meaning of the Hebrew is uncertain. Septuagint *And, although he loved Hannah, he would give Hannah only one portion, because the LORD had closed her womb*

1:1–7:17 God rules and delivers His people before the time of the monarchy. He does so by raising up Samuel (chs. 1–3), intervening directly against the Philistines (4:1–7:1), and giving Samuel victory over the Philistines (7:2–17).

1:1 a certain man. This expression and the accompanying genealogy suggest that Elkanah was a man of standing. The reference to a barren wife (v. 2) resembles the introduction to the birth of Samson (Judg. 13:2).

Ramathaim-zophim. Possibly meaning "twin heights," the name occurs only here in the Old Testament. It may be the same as the New Testament Arimathea (northwest of Bethel). Samuel's hometown is usually called Ramah, about five miles north of Jerusalem (1:19; 2:11; 7:17; 8:4; 15:34; 19:18; 25:1).

of Zuph. "Zuph" is both a personal name (1 Chr. 6:35) and a territory (9:5).

Ephrathite. Ephraim was the place he was from, not necessarily the tribe of his ancestry (1 Chr. 6:16–30, 33–37).

1:2 two wives. Polygamy is first mentioned in Gen. 4:19. It is recognized and regulated, though not endorsed, in Deut. 21:15–17.

no children. Hannah was childless and was provoked by her prolific rival (vv. 6, 7). A barren though favored wife who receives a special offspring from Yahweh is not uncommon in the Old Testament. See Gen. 18:1–15 (Sarah-Isaac); 25:21–26 (Rebekah-Esau and Jacob); 30:22–24 (Rachel-Joseph); Judg. 13:2–5 (Manoah's wife-Samson). In the New Testament see Luke 1:5–25 (Elizabeth-John).

1:3 This man used to go up. Perhaps he was observing "the yearly feast of the LORD at Shiloh" (Judg. 21:19), or perhaps he went for a family ceremony (20:6). In the Pentateuch (the five books of Moses, or Torah) reference is made to three annual pilgrim-feasts (Ex. 23:14–17; 34:18–23; Deut. 16:1–17).

LORD of hosts. This title occurs here for the first time in the Old Testament. "LORD" represents "Yahweh" in Hebrew, the personal name of the God of Israel, as distinct from the general designation "God." "Hosts" or "armies" is the traditional translation of the other word. Depending on the context, it could include the hosts of Israel (17:45), the cosmic hosts or celestial bodies (Deut. 4:19), and the angelic hosts (Josh. 5:14). As a whole the title expresses the Lord's sovereignty over all earthly and heavenly powers.

Shiloh. Halfway between Shechem and Bethel, Shiloh (modern Seilun) was an important Israelite religious center in the period before the monarchy (Josh. 18:1; Judg. 21:19). At least the sanctuary there (Jer. 7:12) may have been destroyed by the Philistines after the battle of Aphek (4:1–11).

Eli. As with some other well-known people in the Old Testament (Joshua, Ex. 17:9; and Jonathan, 1 Sam. 13:2), Eli is first introduced by name only.

1:5 double portion. The Hebrew is difficult but has usually been interpreted as an especially honorable portion. Elkanah's attempts to lessen Hannah's sorrow by expressing his love for her (v. 8) were ineffective.

the LORD had closed her womb. Hannah's barrenness came not by chance nor as a form of punishment (2 Sam. 6:23), but was under the Lord's sovereign control.

1:6 her rival. See note 1:2.

1:7 would not eat. Hannah refused to eat until the Lord answered her prayer; compare David's actions in 2 Sam. 12:16–20, and contrast Saul's in 1 Sam. 28:23–25. In the New Testament, fasting often accompanies serious dealings with the Lord (Acts 13:2–3; 14:23).

1:9 temple. The mention of a "doorpost" here and "doors" in 3:15, as well as sleeping quarters in 3:2, 3, may suggest a more permanent structure than the tent of Moses' time. Other designations for the structure in Samuel are "the house of the LORD" (v. 7; 3:15) and "the tent of meeting" (2:22). From 2 Sam. 7:6 it is clear that before the time of David the tabernacle or temple was a tent and not a permanent structure.

1:11 vow. On the making of vows by married women, and the husbands' responsibility to confirm or nullify, see Num. 30:6–15.

remember me. Hannah asks not simply for the Lord to keep her in mind but for Him to do something special to help her.

no razor. Hannah's vow reflects elements of the Nazirite vow (Num. 6:1–21). Specifically, these are: abstaining from grapes or anything made from grapes, not cutting the hair, and avoiding all contact with anything dead. While such vows were generally made for a limited period of time, Hannah's was for "all the days" of her son's life (see Judg. 13:5 note).

1:13 drunken. Eli's conclusion that Hannah was drunk is an unsettling element in the narrative because it suggests that he was unfamiliar with fervency in prayer.

moved, and her voice was not heard.
Therefore Eli took her to be a drunken
woman. **14** And Eli said to her, "How long
will you go on being drunk? Put away your
wine from you." **15** But Hannah answered,
"No, my lord, I am a woman troubled in
spirit. I have drunk neither wine nor strong
drink, but [o]I have been pouring out my
soul before the LORD. **16** Do not regard your
servant as [p]a worthless woman, for all
along I have been speaking out of my
great anxiety and vexation." **17** Then Eli
answered, [q]"Go in peace, and the God of Israel [r]grant your petition that you have
made to him." **18** And she said, [s]"Let your
servant find favor in your eyes." Then the
woman [t]went her way and ate, and her face
was no longer sad.
19 They rose early in the morning and
worshiped before the LORD; then they went
back to their house at [u]Ramah. And
Elkanah knew Hannah his wife, and the
LORD [v]remembered her. **20** And in due time
Hannah conceived and bore a son, and she
called his name Samuel, for she said, "I
have asked for him from the LORD."[1]

Samuel Given to the LORD

21 The man Elkanah and all his house
[w]went up to offer to the LORD the yearly
sacrifice and to pay his vow. **22** But Hannah
did not go up, for she said to her husband,
"As soon as the child is weaned, I will
bring him, so that he may appear in the
presence of the LORD [x]and dwell there forever." **23** [y]Elkanah her husband said to her,
"Do what seems best to you; wait until you
have weaned him; [z]only, may the LORD
establish his word." So the woman
remained and nursed her son until she
weaned him. **24** And when she had weaned
him, [a]she took him up with her, along with
a three-year-old bull,[2] an ephah[3] of flour,
and a skin of wine, and she brought him to
[b]the house of the LORD at Shiloh. And the
child was young. **25** Then they slaughtered
the bull, and they brought the child to Eli.
26 And she said, "Oh, my lord! [c]As you live,
my lord, I am the woman who was standing here in your presence, praying to the
LORD. **27** For this child I prayed, [d]and the
LORD has granted me my petition that I
made to him. **28** Therefore I have lent him to
the LORD. As long as he lives, he is lent to
the LORD."

[e]And he worshiped the LORD there.

Hannah's Prayer

2 And Hannah prayed and said,

[f]"My heart exults in the LORD;
[g]my strength is exalted in the LORD.
My mouth derides my enemies,
because [h]I rejoice in your salvation.

2 [i]"There is none holy like the LORD;
there is none besides you;
there is [j]no rock like our God.
3 Talk no more so very proudly,
let not arrogance come from your
mouth;
for the LORD is a God of knowledge,
and by him actions are weighed.

15 [o]Job 30:16; Ps. 42:4; Lam. 2:19; [Ps. 62:8] **16** [p]ch. 2:12; Judg. 19:22 **17** [q]ch. 20:42; Judg. 18:6; 2 Kin. 5:19; Mark 5:34 [r]Ps. 20:4, 5 **18** [s]Gen. 33:15; Ruth 2:13 [t][Eccles. 9:7] **19** [u]ch. 2:11; [ver. 1] [v]ver. 11 **21** [w]ver. 3 **22** [x]ver. 11, 28; [ch. 2:11, 18; 3:1] **23** [y][Num. 30:7] [z]2 Sam. 7:25 **24** [a]Deut. 12:5, 6, 11 [b]ver. 3, 9; [Josh. 18:1] **26** [c]ch. 17:55; 20:3; 2 Sam. 11:11; 2 Kin. 2:2, 4, 6; 4:30 **27** [d]ver. 17; [Ps. 6:9] **28** [e]Gen. 24:26, 52
Chapter 2
1 [f]For ver. 1-10, see Luke 1:46-53 [g]ver. 10; Ps. 75:10; 89:17, 24; 92:10; 112:9; 148:14 [h]Ps. 9:14; 13:5; 20:5; 35:9 **2** [i]Ex. 15:11; Ps. 86:8; 89:6, 8 [j]Deut. 32:30, 31

[1] *Samuel* sounds like the Hebrew for *heard of God* [2] Septuagint, Syriac; Hebrew *three bulls* [3] An *ephah* was about 3/5 bushel or 22 liters

1:16 worthless. See 2:12.

1:18 her face was no longer sad. Hannah's actions in response to the benediction of v. 17 give evidence of her belief.

1:20 Samuel. Various meanings of the name "Samuel" have been suggested, including "heard by God," "he who is from God," "name of God," and even "son of God" (as one "given" or "promised" by God). "Saul" is also from the Hebrew verb "to ask," (8:10 note).

1:21 vow. See Lev. 7:16 and note.

1:22 weaned. In the ancient Near East a child was weaned later than is often customary today (2 Macc. 7:27; "I carried you nine months in my womb, and nursed you for three years"). Weaning may also have been celebrated with a feast (Gen. 21:8).

1:23 his word. "Your word" is probably to be preferred here. Elkanah, as Hannah's husband (1:11 note), invokes the Lord's assistance in Hannah's fulfillment of her vow.

1:24 three-year-old bull . . . skin of wine. According to Num. 15:8–10, the fulfillment of a vow was to be accompanied by an offering of a young bull, fine flour, and wine. Hannah brings all three, but in larger measure than required.

2:1–10 Her prayer for a son having been answered, Hannah offers a jubilant song of thanksgiving. Focusing on the Lord's sovereignty and grace to the humble, Hannah anticipates the major themes of the books of Samuel. The same themes of sovereignty, grace, and deliverance are reiterated in David's song of thanksgiving near the end of 2 Samuel (ch. 22). The two songs provide a poetic frame for 1 and 2 Samuel. Mary's briefer song of praise (the Magnificat, Luke 1:46–55) seems to have been modeled on Hannah's. Both songs open with rejoicing in the Lord's deliverance (v. 1; Luke 1:46–48), extol the Lord's uniqueness and holiness (v. 2; Luke 1:49, 50), condemn proud boasting (v. 3; Luke 1:51), point to reversals of human fortune as the result of interventions by the sovereign Lord (vv. 4–8; Luke 1:52, 53), and express the Lord's faithful care for His own (v. 9; Luke 1:54, 55). Hannah's song concludes with the assertion that the Lord Himself will give strength to His king, His anointed (vv. 9–10).

2:1 strength. It is God who exalts the strength of the righteous but cuts off the strength of the wicked (Ps. 75:10).

2:2 rock. As a metaphor for God, this term is concentrated in poetic passages such as the song of Moses in Deut. 32; the song of David in 2 Sam. 22; Psalms; and Isaiah. The metaphor suggests God's strength and sovereignty, and the security of those who trust in Him. Here the focus is on the uniqueness of the one true God as opposed to false sources of security (compare the contrast with false gods, also called "rock," in Deut. 32:31, 37; Is. 44:8).

4 [k]The bows of the mighty are broken,
but the feeble bind on strength.
5 Those who were full have hired
themselves out for bread,
but those who were hungry have
ceased to hunger.
[l]The barren has borne seven,
[m]but she who has many children is
forlorn.
6 [n]The LORD kills and brings to life;
he brings down to Sheol and
raises up.
7 [o]The LORD makes poor and makes rich;
[p]he brings low and he exalts.
8 [q]He raises up the poor from the dust;
he lifts the needy from the ash heap
[r]to make them sit with princes
and inherit a seat of honor.
[s]For the pillars of the earth are the
LORD's,
and on them he has set the world.

9 [t]"He will guard the feet of his faithful
ones,
but the wicked shall be cut off in
darkness,
for not by might shall a man prevail.
10 [u]The adversaries of the LORD shall be
broken to pieces;
[v]against them he will thunder in
heaven.
[w]The LORD will judge the ends of the
earth;
he will give strength to his king
[x]and exalt the power of his anointed."

4 [k]Ps. 37:15; 46:9; 76:3
5 [l]Ps. 113:9; Isai. 54:1 [m]Jer. 15:9
6 [n]Deut. 32:39
7 [o][Job 1:21] [p]Job 5:11; Ps. 75:7
8 [q]Ps. 113:7, 8; [Dan. 4:17; Luke 1:52] [r]Job 36:7 [s][Job 38:4-6; Ps. 24:2; 102:25; 104:5]
9 [t]Ps. 121:3; Prov. 3:26; [Ps. 91:11]
10 [u]Ps. 2:9 [v]ch. 7:10; Ps. 18:13; [2 Sam. 22:14] [w]Ps. 96:10, 13; 98:9 [x]ver. 1; [Ps. 89:24]
11 [y]ch. 1:19 [z]ver. 18; ch. 3:1
12 [a]See ch. 1:16 [b]Judg. 2:10
15 [c]Lev. 3:5, 16; 7:23, 25, 31
17 [d][Gen. 6:11] [e][Mal. 2:8]
18 [f]ver. 11; ch. 3:1 [g]Ex. 28:4; 2 Sam. 6:14; 1 Chr. 15:27

11 Then Elkanah went home [y]to Ramah.
[z]And the boy ministered to the LORD in the
presence of Eli the priest.

Eli's Worthless Sons

12 Now the sons of Eli were [a]worthless
men. [b]They did not know the LORD. 13 The
custom of the priests with the people was
that when any man offered sacrifice, the
priest's servant[1] would come, while the
meat was boiling, with a three-pronged
fork in his hand, 14 and he would thrust it
into the pan or kettle or cauldron or pot.
All that the fork brought up the priest
would take for himself. This is what they
did at Shiloh to all the Israelites who came
there. 15 Moreover, [c]before the fat was
burned, the priest's servant would come
and say to the man who was sacrificing,
"Give meat for the priest to roast, for he
will not accept boiled meat from you but
only raw." 16 And if the man said to him,
"Let them burn the fat first, and then take
as much as you wish," he would say, "No,
you must give it now, and if not, I will take
it by force." 17 Thus the sin of the young
men was very great [d]in the sight of the
LORD, [e]for the men treated the offering of
the LORD with contempt.
18 [f]Samuel was ministering before the
LORD, a boy [g]clothed with a linen ephod.
19 And his mother used to make for him a
little robe and take it to him each year

1 Hebrew *young man*; also verse 15

2:5 has borne seven. The number seven represented ideal completeness (Ruth 4:15).

2:9 for not by might shall a man prevail. The subsequent narratives confirm that it is not physical prowess but God's presence that brings success. In the ark narrative of chs. 4–6, the Lord makes His hand felt by the Philistines without the assistance of human agents (5:6). Other such examples are the Lord's victory through Samuel in ch. 7; the contrasting successes of Saul and Jonathan in chs. 13 and 14; the choice of David, the youngest of Jesse's sons, in ch. 16; and David's victory over Goliath in ch. 17.

2:10 his king. The reference to the Lord's king here points forward to the central event of the books of Samuel, namely, the institution of a monarchy, and implies that the idea of kingship, properly conceived, is not wrong. That Israel would have a king is anticipated in various places in the Pentateuch (Gen. 49:10; Num. 24:7, 17–19; Deut. 17:14–20).

his anointed. Numerous objects and persons were subject to religious anointing in ancient Israel (Ex. 30:22–33), but it was the king ultimately who had the title of the "LORD's anointed" or simply "the anointed." Persons chosen for divine service were anointed to signify that this was their calling, that they were authorized to perform it, and that God would give them the help they needed. References to the king as the Lord's anointed are prevalent in the books of Samuel (v. 35; 12:3, 5; 16:6; 24:6) and Psalms (Ps. 2:2; 18:50). The present passage is the first reference to a king of Israel as God's "anointed," though the idea of anointing a king is found already in Jotham's fable (Judg. 9:8, 15). The English word "messiah" represents the Hebrew word meaning "anointed." In the New Testament, "Christ" represents the Greek word *Christos*, also meaning "anointed."

2:12 worthless. This Hebrew phrase (lit. "sons of Belial") connotes vile persons. It is used of those who incite to idolatry (Deut. 13:13) or insurrection (10:27; 2 Sam. 16:7; 20:1); who are sexually immoral (Judg. 19:22); or who are liars (1 Kin. 21:10, 13). Unfortunately the phrase could be applied to Eli's sons.

did not know. Use of the verb "know" here and in 3:7 sets up an ironic contrast between Eli's sons and Samuel (3:7 note).

2:13 custom of the priests. The practice described in vv. 13, 14 is different from the prescriptions of Lev. 7:28–36 and Deut. 18:3. The greed of the sons of Eli caused the people to treat "the offering of the LORD with contempt" (v. 17).

2:15 before the fat was burned. Since the time of Abel's offering of the fat of the firstborn of his flock (Gen. 4:4), the fat portion was considered to be the best, and as such, to belong to the Lord. The priests had the duty of burning the fat on the altar as an offering to the Lord (Lev. 3:16; 7:31). Like blood, the fat was strictly forbidden for human consumption, and anyone who ate it would be expelled from the people (Lev. 3:17; 7:23–25).

2:18 Samuel. The behavior of Samuel, who ministers faithfully before the Lord, and also of Eli, who regularly blesses Elkanah and his wife (v. 20), is in sharp contrast with the abuses of Eli's sons.

linen ephod. A short inner garment of some sort, and associated with priestly service (22:18), the linen ephod was worn also by King David when he brought the ark to Jerusalem (2 Sam. 6:14). See also 2:28, note.

2:19 robe. An outer garment to be worn over the linen ephod.

[h]when she went up with her husband to
offer the yearly sacrifice. 20 Then Eli would
bless Elkanah and his wife, and say, "May
the LORD give you children by this woman
[i]for the petition she asked of the LORD." So
then they would return to their home.
21 [j]Indeed the LORD visited Hannah, and
she conceived and bore three sons and two
daughters. [k]And the young man Samuel
grew in the presence of the LORD.

Eli Rebukes His Sons

22 Now Eli was very old, and he kept
hearing all that his sons were doing to all
Israel, and how they lay with the women
who [l]were serving at the entrance to the
tent of meeting. 23 And he said to them,
"Why do you do such things? For I hear of
your evil dealings from all the people.
24 No, my sons; it is no good report that I
hear the people of the LORD spreading
abroad. 25 If someone sins against a man,
God will mediate for him, but if someone
sins against the LORD, who can intercede
for him?" But they would not listen to the
voice of their father, [m]for it was the will of
the LORD to put them to death.

19 [h]ch. 1:3
20 [i]ch. 1:28
21 [j]Gen. 21:1 [k]ver. 26; ch. 3:19; [Judg. 13:24; Luke 1:80; 2:40]
22 [l]Ex. 38:8
25 [m][Josh. 11:20]
26 [n]Luke 2:52
27 [o]1 Kin. 13:1 [p]Ex. 4:14, 27
28 [q]Ex. 28:1; Num. 18:1, 7 [r][ch. 14:3; 22:18] [s]Lev. 2:3, 10; 6:16; 7:7, 8, 34; 10:14, 15; Num. 5:9, 10; See Num. 18:8-19
29 [t]Deut. 32:15 [u]ver. 32; Deut. 12:5, 6; 26:15; Ps. 26:8; 68:5
30 [v]Ex. 27:21; 29:9 [w][Jer. 18:9, 10]

26 Now the young man Samuel [n]contin-
ued to grow both in stature and in favor
with the LORD and also with man.

The LORD Rejects Eli's Household

27 And there came [o]a man of God to Eli
and said to him, "Thus the LORD has said,
[p]'Did I indeed reveal myself to the house
of your father when they were in Egypt
subject to the house of Pharaoh? 28 [q]Did I
choose him out of all the tribes of Israel to
be my priest, to go up to my altar, to burn
incense, [r]to wear an ephod before me? [s]I
gave to the house of your father all my
offerings by fire from the people of Israel.
29 Why then do you [t]scorn[1] my sacrifices
and my offerings that I [u]commanded, and
honor your sons above me by fattening
yourselves on the choicest parts of every
offering of my people Israel?' 30 Therefore
the LORD the God of Israel declares: [v]'I
promised that your house and the house
of your father should go in and out before
me forever,' [w]but now the LORD declares:
'Far be it from me, for those who honor
me I will honor, and those who despise me

[1] Septuagint; Hebrew *kick at*

2:20 petition she asked. Eli's words recall those of Hannah in 1:27, 28. Both "petition" and "asked" in Hebrew derive from the same word as the name "Saul" (1:20 note).

2:21 in the presence of the LORD. Or "with the LORD"; the same Hebrew expression is used in v. 26.

2:22 Now Eli. Again as at v. 12, the focus shifts from the boy Samuel to the house of Eli.

kept hearing. Eli had to be told about what he should have already observed and controlled on his own. But his offenses run much deeper than mere inattentiveness (v. 29).

lay with the women. On the "tent of meeting," see note 1:9; on "the women who were serving," see Ex. 38:8. Though explicitly condemned by the Law (Deut. 23:17, 18), religious prostitution was practiced by the Canaanites and posed a constant danger to the Israelites (1 Kin. 15:12; 2 Kin. 23:7; Hos. 4:14).

2:25 God will mediate. Eli's point is that while there may be some mediation of disputes between people, when someone offends God there is no one who can intervene. Eli's sons sinned first and foremost against the Lord (v. 17), and they sealed their doom by refusing to hear Eli's warning.

it was the will of the LORD to put them to death. This clear statement of God's sovereignty over the destiny of the wicked does not diminish people's responsibility for their own actions. An example of the relation between divine sovereignty and human responsibility is found in the hardening of Pharaoh's heart in the early chapters of Exodus. About half the time Pharaoh is said to have hardened his own heart (Ex. 8:15); the rest of the time God is said to harden it (Ex. 4:21; Rom. 9:17, 18). God can punish persistent, willful sin by taking away the power to repent (Josh. 11:20; Rom. 1:24, 26, 28).

2:26 in favor with the LORD. The gravity of Eli's sons' refusal to listen to man or God is emphasized by the striking contrast with Samuel, who grows in favor with God and men. The emphasis on Samuel's growth as more than merely physical foreshadows a theme that is later developed in contrasting portraits of Saul and David. The expression of v. 6 is used by Luke to describe the childhood of Jesus (Luke 2:52; see Prov. 3:4).

2:27–36 The words of the man of God to Eli exhibit features typical of prophetic judgment speeches. There is an accusation (expressed here through accusing questions that emphasize the contrast between the Lord's grace and Eli's disobedience) and an announcement of judgment confirmed by a sign. Other examples of prophetic speeches of this type are found in chs. 13; 15; and 2 Sam. 12:7–12.

2:27 man of God. In the Old Testament this designation is often used interchangeably with "prophet" (9:8–11; 1 Kin. 13:15–18; 2 Kin. 5:8; 6:10–12).

house of your father . . . in Egypt. Although Eli's genealogy is nowhere recorded in the Old Testament, v. 28 implies that he was a descendant of Aaron. The assertion that the Lord revealed Himself and selected Eli's house as far back as the period of Israelite servitude in Egypt underscores the gross ingratitude of the house of Eli.

2:28 wear an ephod. Or perhaps "carry" an ephod. The ephod mentioned here is not the garment mentioned in v. 18, but the high-priestly ephod bearing the "breastpiece of judgment" and the "Urim and Thummim," through which the Lord's will could be determined (Ex. 28:4–30).

gave . . . my offerings. Both in the Old Testament (Num. 18:8; Deut. 18:1) and in the New (1 Cor. 9:13, 14; 1 Tim. 5:17, 18) God provides for the support of those who are in His service.

2:29 honor. Though the offenses of his sons are more blatant, Eli himself does not escape blame. As father and high priest, he should have confronted his sons with more than words (vv. 23–25). His failure to take action amounts to honoring his sons above the Lord (v. 30). The Hebrew word for "honor" is a key word in the subsequent accounts of the fall of the family of Eli and the capture and return of the ark (chs. 4–7); see the notes on 4:21; 6:5, 6.

2:30 forever. That is, continually or indefinitely.

shall be lightly esteemed. 31 Behold, [x]the
days are coming when I will cut off your
strength and the strength of your father's
house, so that there will not be an old man
in your house. 32 Then [y]in distress you will
look with envious eye on all the prosperity
that shall be bestowed on Israel, [z]and
there shall not be an old man in your
house forever. 33 The only one of you
whom I shall not cut off from my altar
shall be spared to weep his[1] eyes out to
grieve his heart, and all the descendants[2]
of your house shall die by the sword of
men.[3] 34 [a]And this that shall come upon
your two sons, Hophni and Phinehas,
shall be the sign to you: both of them shall
die [b]on the same day. 35 [c]And I will raise up
for myself a faithful priest, who shall do
according to what is in my heart and in my
mind. [d]And I will build him a sure house,
and he shall go in and out before [e]my
anointed forever. 36 And everyone who is
left in your house shall come to implore
him for a piece of silver or a loaf of bread
and shall say, "Please put me in one of the
priests' places, that I may eat a morsel of
bread."'"

The Lord Calls Samuel

3 [f]Now the young man Samuel was ministering to the Lord under Eli. [g]And
the word of the Lord was rare in those
days; there was no frequent vision.
2 At that time Eli, [h]whose eyesight had
begun to grow dim so that he could not
see, was lying down in his own place. 3 [i]The
lamp of God had not yet gone out, and
Samuel was lying down [j]in the temple of
the Lord, where the ark of God was.
4 Then the Lord called Samuel, and he
said, "Here I am!" 5 and ran to Eli and said,
"Here I am, for you called me." But he said,
"I did not call; lie down again." So he went
and lay down.
6 And the Lord called again, "Samuel!"
and Samuel arose and went to Eli and said,
"Here I am, for you called me." But he said,
"I did not call, my son; lie down again."
7 Now Samuel did not yet know the Lord,
and the word of the Lord had not yet been
revealed to him.
8 And the Lord called Samuel again the
third time. And he arose and went to Eli
and said, "Here I am, for you called me."
Then Eli perceived that the Lord was calling the young man. 9 Therefore Eli said to
Samuel, "Go, lie down, and if he calls you,
you shall say, 'Speak, Lord, for your servant hears.'" So Samuel went and lay down
in his place.
10 And the Lord came and stood, calling as
at other times, "Samuel! Samuel!" And
Samuel said, "Speak, for your servant
hears." 11 Then the Lord said to Samuel,
"Behold, I am about to do a thing in Israel
[k]at which the two ears of everyone who

31 [x]1 Kin. 2:27; [ch. 4:11, 18, 20; 22:18, 19] **32** [y]ch. 4:11; [Judg. 18:30]; See Ps. 78:59-64 [z][Zech. 8:4] **34** [a]1 Kin. 13:3 [b]ch. 4:11 **35** [c]1 Kin. 2:35; 1 Chr. 29:22 [d]ch. 25:28; 1 Kin. 11:38; [2 Sam. 7:11, 27] [e]2 Sam. 22:51; Ps. 18:50; [Ps. 89:20]
Chapter 3
1 [f]ch. 2:11, 18 [g][ver. 21; Ps. 74:9; Amos 8:11] **2** [h]ch. 4:15; Gen. 27:1; 48:10; [Deut. 34:7] **3** [i]Ex. 27:20, 21; Lev. 24:2, 3; 2 Chr. 13:11 [j]ch. 1:9 **11** [k]2 Kin. 21:12; Jer. 19:3

1 Septuagint; Hebrew *your*; twice in this verse 2 Hebrew *increase*
3 Septuagint; Hebrew *die as men*

2:31 will not be an old man in your house. The decimation of Eli's house begins with the death of his sons (4:11) and himself (4:18). It is continued with Saul's massacre of the priests of Nob (22:17–19) and culminates in Solomon's removal of Abiathar from the priesthood (1 Kin. 2:26, 27).

2:32 in distress you will look with envious eye. The Hebrew is difficult and parts of vv. 31, 32 are lacking in the Septuagint and the Dead Sea Scrolls.

2:34 sign. Prophetic utterances were often confirmed by signs (2:27–36 note; cf. 10:7, 9; 1 Kin. 13:3, 5; 2 Kin. 19:29; 20:8, 9).

2:35 faithful priest. While the statement in 3:20 that Samuel was "established" as a prophet of the Lord suggests Samuel may have been the fulfillment of this prediction, the clearer fulfillment comes in the person of Zadok, who served as high priest alongside Abiathar under David (2 Sam. 8:17 note) and came to preeminence under Solomon (1 Kin. 2:35). The descendants of Zadok held the high priesthood from the time of Solomon to the time of Antiochus Epiphanes and the Maccabees (for details see "Introduction to the Intertestamental Period").

my anointed. This is the second allusion to the coming king in this chapter (v. 10 note).

2:36 eat a morsel of bread. Prophetic judgments were characterized by a correspondence of crime and punishment. The hunger threatened in this verse corresponds to the greedy satisfaction described in vv. 12–27 and 29.

3:1 the word of the Lord was rare. The Lord's withholding His word is a sign of His displeasure (14:37; Ps. 74:9; Lam. 2:9; Amos 8:11, 12). Conversely, His communication to Samuel is a sign of favor.

vision. The Hebrew word often denotes an auditory encounter rather than a visual one. Such revelations were necessary for the well-being of God's people (Prov. 29:18).

3:3 The lamp of God had not yet gone out. This notice may be simply a time reference (Ex. 27:20–21; Lev. 24:1–4). The use of "lamp" as a metaphor of hope and promise is very common (2 Sam. 21:17; 22:29; 1 Kin. 11:36; 15:4; Job 18:5; Ps. 132:17; Prov. 13:9), and is possible here. With Samuel on the scene, there is still a flicker of hope.

temple. See note 1:9.

ark of God. Elsewhere called "the ark of the testimony" and "the ark of the covenant," this chest of acacia wood overlaid with gold is described in Ex. 25:10–22. The ark is important in chs. 4–6 and again in 2 Sam. 6.

3:7 Samuel did not yet know the Lord. The repetition of terminology from 2:12 about "knowing" God only emphasizes the contrast in meaning. Eli's sons "did not know the Lord" because they wickedly disregarded Him. Samuel was a child and no revelation had yet come to him.

3:8 Then Eli perceived. Eli's slowness to recognize that God was calling Samuel recalls earlier instances of misperception (1:12–16) and unawareness (2:22 note), contributing to the reader's impression of Eli as an aged priest whose eyes have grown dim (v. 2) in more ways than one.

hears it will tingle. 12 On that day I will fulfill
against Eli [l]all that I have spoken concerning
his house, from beginning to end. 13 [l]And I
declare to him that I am about to punish his
house forever, for the iniquity that he knew,
[m]because his sons were blaspheming God,[1]
[n]and he did not restrain them. 14 Therefore I
swear to the house of Eli [o]that the iniquity of
Eli's house shall not be atoned for by sacrifice or offering forever."
15 Samuel lay until morning; then he
opened the doors of the house of the LORD.
And Samuel was afraid to tell the vision to
Eli. 16 But Eli called Samuel and said,
"Samuel, my son." And he said, "Here I
am." 17 And Eli said, "What was it that he
told you? Do not hide it from me. [p]May
God do so to you and more also if you hide
anything from me of all that he told you."
18 So Samuel told him everything and hid
nothing from him. And he said, [q]"It is the
LORD. Let him do what seems good to him."
19 [r]And Samuel grew, and the LORD was
with him [s]and let none of his words fall to
the ground. 20 And all Israel [t]from Dan to
Beersheba knew that Samuel was established as a prophet of the LORD. 21 And the
LORD appeared again at Shiloh, for the

12 [l]See ch. 2:30-36
13 [l][See ver. 12 above] [m]ch. 2:12, 17, 22 [n]ch. 2:23-25
14 [o][Isai. 22:14]
17 [p][Ruth 1:17]
18 [q][2 Sam. 10:12; Job 1:21; 2:10; Ps. 39:9; Isai. 39:8]
19 [r]See ch. 2:21 [s][ch. 9:6]
20 [t]See 2 Sam. 3:10
21 [u][Josh. 18:1] [v]ver. 1, 4
Chapter 4
1 [w][ch. 5:1; 7:12] [x]ch. 29:1; Josh. 12:18
3 [y]Josh. 18:1
4 [z]Ex. 25:22; 2 Sam. 6:2; Ps. 80:1; 99:1; [Num. 7:89]

LORD revealed himself to Samuel [u]at Shiloh
[v]by the word of the LORD.

The Philistines Capture the Ark

4 And the word of Samuel came to all
Israel.
Now Israel went out to battle against the
Philistines. They encamped at [w]Ebenezer,
and the Philistines encamped at [x]Aphek.
2 The Philistines drew up in line against
Israel, and when the battle spread, Israel
was defeated by the Philistines, who killed
about four thousand men on the field of battle. 3 And when the troops came to the
camp, the elders of Israel said, "Why has the
LORD defeated us today before the Philistines? Let us bring the ark of the covenant
of the LORD here [y]from Shiloh, that it may
come among us and save us from the power
of our enemies." 4 So the people sent to
Shiloh and brought from there the ark of the
covenant of the LORD of hosts, [z]who is
enthroned on the cherubim. And the two
sons of Eli, Hophni and Phinehas, were
there with the ark of the covenant of God.
5 As soon as the ark of the covenant of
the LORD came into the camp, all Israel

[1] *Or blaspheming for themselves*

3:12 all that I have spoken. See 2:27–36. The repetition to Samuel of the oracle against Eli confirms the oracle itself and establishes Samuel as a prophet of the Lord (v. 20).

3:13 were blaspheming God. If Eli's sons were cursing God they were committing an offense worthy of death (Lev. 24:15, 16).

did not restrain them. Eli, in view of his position as high priest, should have taken action to restrain his sons once verbal rebuke proved ineffective (2:29 note; 2 Sam. 13:21 note).

3:14 not be atoned for by sacrifice or offering forever. While there was provision to atone for unintentional priestly sins (Lev. 4:1–12), the sins of Eli's house were clearly acts of open defiance (Num. 15:30–31). They had scorned the normal means of atonement, that is, sacrifice and offering (2:17, 29).

3:18 It is the LORD. Let him do what seems good to him. Eli humbly accepts his rejection and confesses God's right to rule in the affairs of men. His words establish a benchmark by which later characters in the narrative should be judged: Saul (20:30, 31) and David (2 Sam. 15:25, 26).

3:19 the LORD was with him. From the perspective of the books of Samuel, it is God's presence with someone that makes the difference between success and failure (16:18; 18:12, 14, 28).

let none of his words fall to the ground. See 9:6. Samuel thus passed the test of a true prophet (Deut. 18:21, 22).

3:20 Dan to Beersheba . . . prophet of the LORD. While Samuel's responsibilities as judge would take him on a circuit of the central hill country (7:15–17), his reputation as a prophet spread throughout "all Israel" (2 Sam. 3:10; 17:11; 24:25; 1 Kin. 4:25).

3:21 Shiloh. See note 1:3.

4:1 the word of Samuel came to all Israel. The episode that began with a notice of the rarity of the word of the Lord (3:1) concludes with a notice of the change brought by the selection of Samuel to be "a prophet of the LORD" (3:20 and note).

Philistines. The Philistines are one of the "Sea Peoples" named in Egyptian texts from the time of Rameses III. By the time of the judges (Judg. 3:31; 13–16), the Philistines had settled along the coastlands of southern Canaan in a league of five cities: Ashdod, Ashkelon, Ekron, Gath, and Gaza (6:17; Judg. 3:3). The Philistines often tried to expand their territory, and in the time of Samuel and the early monarchy they were in direct conflict with the Israelites to the north and east.

Ebenezer. This may be an archaeological site about two miles east of Aphek (cf. v. 6). Ebenezer (meaning "stone of help") is mentioned again in 5:1. The Ebenezer of 7:12 recalls these earlier references (7:12 note), but it is a different place, near Mizpah.

Aphek. Aphek was at the southern end of the plain of Sharon, about five miles inland from the Mediterranean, near the source of the Yarkon River (29:1). It was among the cities conquered by Joshua (Josh. 12:18).

4:3 Why has the LORD defeated us. The elders' question is appropriate insofar as it reflects the belief that "the battle is the LORD's" (17:47). They do not wait for an answer, however, but immediately take matters into their own hands.

Let us bring the ark. The elders' apparent conviction that the ark was a magical guarantee of the Lord's presence is similar to that of the Philistines (vv. 7–9). Salvation depends on God's free initiative and sovereign grace, not on human techniques or schemes (2 Sam. 15:25 and note).

4:4 LORD of hosts. See note 1:3.

Hophni and Phinehas. With his two wicked sons (2:12–17, 27–36) in charge of the ark, it is not surprising that Eli's "heart trembled for the ark of God" (v. 13).

[a]gave a mighty shout, so that the earth
resounded. 6 And when the Philistines
heard the noise of the shouting, they said,
"What does this great shouting in the
camp of the Hebrews mean?" And when
they learned that the ark of the LORD had
come to the camp, 7 the Philistines were
afraid, for they said, "A god has come into
the camp." And they said, "Woe to us! For
nothing like this has happened before.
8 Woe to us! Who can deliver us from the
power of these mighty gods? These are the
gods who struck the Egyptians with every
sort of plague in the wilderness. 9 [b]Take
courage, and be men, O Philistines, lest
you become slaves to the Hebrews [c]as they
have been to you; be men and fight."
10 So the Philistines fought, [d]and Israel
was defeated, [e]and they fled, every man to
his home. And there was a very great
slaughter, for there fell of Israel thirty thousand foot soldiers. 11 [f]And the ark of God
was captured, [g]and the two sons of Eli,
Hophni and Phinehas, died.

The Death of Eli

12 A man of Benjamin ran from the battle
line and came to Shiloh the same day, [h]with
his clothes torn and with dirt on his head.
13 When he arrived, [i]Eli was sitting on his
seat by the road watching, for his heart
trembled for the ark of God. And when the
man came into the city and told the news,
all the city cried out. 14 When Eli heard the
sound of the outcry, he said, "What is this
uproar?" Then the man hurried and came
and told Eli. 15 Now Eli was ninety-eight
years old [j]and his eyes were set so that he
could not see. 16 And the man said to Eli, "I
am he who has come from the battle; I fled
from the battle today." And he said, [k]"How
did it go, my son?" 17 He who brought the
news answered and said, "Israel has fled
before the Philistines, and there has also
been a great defeat among the people. Your
two sons also, Hophni and Phinehas, are
dead, and the ark of God has been captured." 18 As soon as he mentioned the ark
of God, Eli fell over backward [l]from his seat
by the side of the gate, and his neck was
broken and he died, for the man was old
and heavy. He had judged Israel forty years.
19 Now his daughter-in-law, the wife of
Phinehas, was pregnant, about to give birth.
And when she heard the news that the ark of
God was captured, and that her father-in-law
and her husband were dead, she bowed and
gave birth, for her pains came upon her.
20 And about the time of her death the women
attending her said to her, [m]"Do not be afraid,
for you have borne a son." But she did not
answer or pay attention. 21 And she named
the child [n]Ichabod, saying, [o]"The glory has
departed[1] from Israel!" because [p]the ark of
God had been captured and because of her
father-in-law and her husband. 22 And she
said, "The glory has departed from Israel, [p]for
the ark of God has been captured."

The Philistines and the Ark

5 When the Philistines captured the ark
of God, they brought it from [q]Ebenezer

5 [a]Josh. 6:5, 20
9 [b]Cited 1 Cor. 16:13; [2 Sam. 10:12] [c]Judg. 13:1
10 [d]ver. 2; Ps. 78:62; [Lev. 26:17; Deut. 28:25] [e]2 Sam. 18:17; 19:8; 2 Kin. 14:12; 2 Chr. 25:22
11 [f][ch. 2:32; Ps. 78:60, 61] [g]ch. 2:34; Ps. 78:64
12 [h]See Josh. 7:6
13 [i]ver. 18; ch. 1:9
15 [j]1 Kin. 14:4; [ch. 3:2]
16 [k]2 Sam. 1:4
18 [l]ver. 13
20 [m]Gen. 35:17
21 [n]ch. 14:3 [o]Ps. 78:61; [Ps. 26:8] [p]ver. 11
22 [p][See ver. 21 above]
Chapter 5
1 [q]ch. 4:1; 7:12

[1] Or *gone into exile*; also verse 22

4:6 Hebrews. This word first occurs in Gen. 14:13 as a description of Abram. Extrabiblical documents of the second millennium B.C. mention a diverse and widespread people called "Habiru." This has caused considerable debate about whether the biblical Hebrews are the same as these people. The Habiru seem to have been a landless class of aliens or refugees, who survived either by hiring themselves out as soldiers or farmers, or by plundering.

4:8 mighty gods . . . who struck the Egyptians. The Philistines' cry of woe betrays their polytheistic perspective but nevertheless leaves little doubt of the impact that event had on surrounding nations (6:6; Josh. 2:9–11).

4:10 thirty thousand. Far from bringing relief, the Israelites' attempt to manipulate the Lord for their own ends resulted in even greater defeat (v. 2).

4:11 the ark of God was captured. An event as astonishing as it was disastrous, the loss of the ark must surely have made "two ears . . . tingle" (3:11).

Hophni and Phinehas, died. In fulfillment of 2:34 and 3:12.

4:13 his heart trembled for the ark of God. Earlier rebuked for honoring his sons more than the Lord (2:29), Eli now shows a concern for the ark of God that surpasses his concern for his own sons (vv. 17–18).

4:18 mentioned the ark. Not the news of heavy losses suffered by the Israelites, nor the news of the death of his own sons (v. 17), but the announcement that the ark of God had been captured prompted the reaction that resulted in Eli's own death.

He had judged Israel. There is no necessary contradiction in Eli's being described as both priest and judge (Deut. 17:8–12; 19:17; 1 Chr. 23:2–4; 2 Chr. 19:8; Ezek. 44:24). "Judged" associates him with the leaders God raised up between the death of Joshua and the institution of kingship.

forty years. Eli's forty-year tenure of leadership would have overlapped the exploits of Samson (Judg. 13–16) and possibly also the activity of the judges mentioned in Judg. 12:8–15.

4:21 Ichabod . . . The glory has departed. Phinehas's wife, as she dies, names their newborn son Ichabod, meaning either "No glory" or "Where is the glory?" (2:29 note). As v. 22 makes clear, the "glory" to which she refers is not primarily the house of Eli but the ark of God now lost. See also note on 14:3.

5:1 Ebenezer. See 4:1 note.

Ashdod. One of the five main Philistine cities (4:1), Ashdod is about thirty miles south of Ebenezer and three miles inland from the Mediterranean. Philistine occupation of Ashod is attested archaeologically for the twelfth and eleventh centuries B.C. In the New Testament period, the site was called Azotus (Acts 8:40).

to [r]Ashdod. **2**Then the Philistines took the
ark of God and brought it into the house of
Dagon and set it up beside [s]Dagon. **3**And
when the people of Ashdod rose early the
next day, behold, [t]Dagon had fallen face
downward on the ground before the ark of
the LORD. So they took Dagon and put him
back in his place. **4**But when they rose early
on the next morning, behold, Dagon had
fallen face downward on the ground before
the ark of the LORD, [u]and the head of
Dagon and both his hands were lying cut
off on the threshold. Only the trunk of
Dagon was left to him. **5**This is why the
priests of Dagon and all who enter the
house of Dagon [v]do not tread on the threshold of Dagon in Ashdod to this day.
6[w]The hand of the LORD was heavy
against the people of Ashdod, and he terrified and afflicted them with [x]tumors, both
Ashdod and its territory. **7**And when the
men of Ashdod saw how things were, they
said, "The ark of the God of Israel must not
remain with us, for his hand is hard against
us and against Dagon our god." **8**So they
sent and gathered together all [y]the lords of
the Philistines and said, "What shall we do
with the ark of the God of Israel?" They
answered, "Let the ark of the God of Israel
be brought around to Gath." So they
brought the ark of the God of Israel there.
9But after they had brought it around, [z]the
hand of the LORD was against the city, causing a very great panic, and he afflicted the
men of the city, both young and old, so
that [x]tumors broke out on them. **10**So they
sent the ark of God to Ekron. But as soon
as the ark of God came to Ekron, the people of Ekron cried out, "They have brought
around to us the ark of the God of Israel to
kill us and our people." **11**[y]They sent therefore and gathered together all the lords of
the Philistines and said, "Send away the
ark of the God of Israel, and let it return to
its own place, that it may not kill us and
our people." For there was a deathly panic
throughout the whole city. [w]The hand of
God was very heavy there. **12**The men who
did not die were struck with [x]tumors, and
the cry of the city went up to heaven.

The Ark Returned to Israel

6 The ark of the LORD was in the country
of the Philistines seven months. **2**And
the Philistines called for the priests and
[a]the diviners and said, "What shall we do
with the ark of the LORD? Tell us with what

1 [r]Josh. 13:3
2 [s]Judg. 16:23
3 [t][Isai. 46:1, 2]
4 [u][Jer. 50:2; Ezek. 6:4, 6; Mic. 1:7]
5 [v][Zeph. 1:9]
6 [w][Ex. 9:3; Ps. 32:4; Acts 13:11] [x]ch. 6:5
8 [y]Josh. 13:3
9 [z]ch. 7:13; 12:15; Deut. 2:15 [x][See ver. 6 above]
11 [y][See ver. 8 above] [w][See ver. 6 above]
12 [x][See ver. 6 above]
Chapter 6
2 [a]Deut. 18:10; [Gen. 41:8; Ex. 7:11; Dan. 2:2; 5:7]

5:2 Dagon. A prominent deity among the Philistines as well as in Mesopotamia, Syria, and Phoenicia from the middle of the third millennium B.C., Dagon was once thought to be a fish deity because of the similarity between the name Dagon and the Hebrew word for fish (*dag*). It now appears more likely that the name should be associated with the Hebrew word for grain (*dagan*), making Dagon an agricultural or fertility god. Dagon seems to have headed the Philistine pantheon (Judg. 16:23; 1 Chr. 10:10), which included the goddess Ashtoreth (31:8–10) and the god Baal-zebul ("Baal the prince"). Baal-zebul was worshiped at Ekron, and his name was intentionally distorted by the Israelites to Baal-zebub ("lord of the flies"; 2 Kin. 1:1–6, 16). The worship of Dagon is attested as late as the Maccabean period (second century B.C.; 1 Macc. 10:83, 84).

set it up beside Dagon. In the ancient Near East the victorious army would carry off the gods of the vanquished and deposit them in the temple of their own gods as a sign of the inferiority and subordination of the captured gods. Though not an idol, the ark of God was treated that way by the Philistines.

5:3 Dagon had fallen face downward. The supposedly victorious deity lies on his face doing homage to the ostensibly vanquished one (v. 2 note).

5:4 head . . . hands were lying cut off. The specific damage to the idol is to be understood in light of the common practice in antiquity of removing the head and hands of the enemy dead (Judg. 7:25; 8:6; 1 Sam. 17:54; 31:9; 2 Sam. 4:12).

5:5 tread on the threshold. Thresholds are often invested with special significance, and the practice of not stepping on the threshold of a sacred place was known, if not approved, in Israel (Zeph. 1:9). Linking the custom of the priests of Dagon with this humiliating incident may be intended more to ridicule them than to convey information about their ritual practice.

to this day. This phrase suggests a significant interval of time between the event and the account of it (cf. 6:18).

5:6 The hand of the LORD was heavy. See v. 11 and notes on vv. 1, 4; 2:9. The Lord is not tamed by friend or foe. Refusing to be manipulated by Israel, God departed to the territory of Israel's enemies (4:21). There He demonstrated His sovereignty, causing the Philistines to feel the weight of His hand in judgment.

tumors. The most plausible explanation of the tumors is that they were symptoms of bubonic plague, transmitted by rodents.

5:8 lords of the Philistines. The reference is apparently to the rulers of the Philistine league (4:1 note), who could cooperate in times of emergency.

Gath. The location of Gath is debated, but the best candidate is Tel es-Safi, about twelve miles east of Ashdod. Possibly the Philistine plan was to move the ark to another town in the hope that the plague would not break out there, showing that it had been a coincidence that a plague had broken out in Ashdod. This hope was dramatically dashed (v. 9).

5:10 the people of Ekron. After the failed experiment in Gath, the people of Ekron at least are no longer skeptical about the danger of keeping the ark (v. 8 note). Ekron was five miles due north of Gath and was the closest of the Philistines' major cities to Israelite territory.

5:11 Send away the ark. Unable to bear up under the heavy "hand of the LORD" (v. 6 note), the Ekronites now plead that the ark be returned "to its own place."

6:1 seven months. The events recorded in the previous chapter took place not in a matter of days but months. The number seven often signifies completeness.

6:2 diviners. Together with witchcraft and sorcery (Num. 23:23), divination was explicitly condemned in Israel (Deut. 18:10, 14; Jer. 27:9; Ezek. 13:23). It was practiced by some of Israel's neighbors (Num. 22:7; Ezek. 21:21).

What shall we do. They had the same problem faced by the people of

we shall send it to its place." **3**They said, "If
you send away the ark of the God of Israel,
do not send it empty, but by all means
return him [b]a guilt offering. Then you will
be healed, and it will be known to you why
[c]his hand does not turn away from you."
4And they said, "What is the guilt offering
that we shall return to him?" They
answered, "Five golden [d]tumors and five
golden mice, [e]according to the number of
the lords of the Philistines, for the same
plague was on all of you and on your lords.
5So you must make images of your [d]tumors
and images of your mice that ravage the
land, [f]and give glory to the God of Israel.
Perhaps [g]he will lighten his hand from off
you [h]and your gods and your land. **6**Why
should you harden your hearts as [i]the
Egyptians and [j]Pharaoh hardened their
hearts? After he had dealt severely with
them, [k]did they not send the people away,
and they departed? **7**Now then, take and
prepare [l]a new cart and two milk cows [m]on
which there has never come a yoke, and
yoke the cows to the cart, but take their
calves home, away from them. **8**And take
the ark of the LORD and place it on the cart
and put in a box at its side [n]the figures of
gold, which you are returning to him as [b]a
guilt offering. Then send it off and let it go
its way **9**and watch. If it goes up on the way
to its own land, to [o]Beth-shemesh, then it
is he who has done us this great harm, but
if not, then we shall know that it is not [p]his
hand that struck us; it happened to us by
coincidence."
10The men did so, and took two milk
cows and yoked them to the cart and shut
up their calves at home. **11**And they put the
ark of the LORD on the cart and the box
with the golden mice and the images of
their tumors. **12**And the cows went straight
in the direction of [q]Beth-shemesh along
[r]one highway, lowing as they went. They
turned neither to the right nor to the left,
and the lords of the Philistines went after
them as far as the border of [q]Beth-
shemesh. **13**Now the people of Beth-
shemesh were reaping their wheat harvest
in the valley. And when they lifted up their
eyes and saw the ark, they rejoiced to see
it. **14**The cart came into the field of Joshua
of Beth-shemesh and stopped there. [s]A
great stone was there. And they split up the
wood of the cart and offered the cows as a
burnt offering to the LORD. **15**And the
Levites took down the ark of the LORD and
the box that was beside it, in which were
the golden figures, and set them upon [s]the
great stone. And the men of [q]Beth-shemesh
offered burnt offerings and sacrificed sacrifices on that day to the LORD. **16**And when
[t]the five lords of the Philistines saw it, they
returned that day to Ekron.

3 [b][Lev. 5:15, 16] [c]ver. 9
4 [d]ch. 5:6, 9,12 [e]ver. 17, 18; Josh. 13:3; Judg. 3:3
5 [d][See ver. 4 above] [f][Josh. 7:19] [g][ch. 5:6, 9, 11] [h]ch. 5:3, 4, 7
6 [i][Ex. 14:17] [j]Ex. 8:15, 32; [Ex. 7:13; 9:7, 35; 10:1] [k]Ex. 12:31
7 [l][2 Sam. 6:3] [m][Num. 19:2]
8 [n]ver. 4, 5 [b][See ver. 3 above]
9 [o]Josh. 15:10 [p]ver. 3
12 [q]Josh. 21:16 [r]Num. 20:19
14 [s]ver. 18
15 [s][See ver. 14 above] [q][See ver. 12 above]
16 [t]See ver. 4

Ashdod (5:8). Moving the ark from place to place inside Philistine territory had failed, making it clear that the only solution was to return the ark to Israel.

6:3 guilt offering. The offering is intended to acknowledge guilt and to compensate for the offense of taking the ark (v. 4).

6:5 make images of your tumors. The procedure adopted by the Philistines had several purposes. The gold used for the models was a kind of compensation for having taken the ark (v. 4), while the images of tumors and rats were probably a form of sympathetic magic. The Philistines' stated purpose, however, was to "give glory" to Israel's God. With this announcement, the ark narrative comes almost full circle. It was for Israel's failure to honor the Lord and handle the ark properly that God had removed it from them.

your gods. The Lord's oppressive treatment of the gods of the Philistines is like His treatment of "the gods of Egypt" (Ex. 12:12). As the next verse indicates, this comparison was not lost on the Philistines themselves.

6:6 Why should you harden your hearts. Forms of the Hebrew word translated "harden" in this sentence are encountered often in the story of the rejection of the priesthood of Eli's house and the loss of the ark. Elsewhere the word is translated "glory" (v. 5; 4:21), and "honor" (see 2:29 and note).

dealt severely with them. Or "toyed with them," "abused them." The same expression is used in 31:4; Ex. 10:2; Jer. 38:19.

6:7–9 An ancient Hittite ritual text shows some parallels to the procedure described in these verses. In the Hittite ritual, relief from a plague thought to be caused by an enemy god is sought by ceremonially crowning a ram to pacify the enemy god, and then driving the ram down a road leading to enemy territory. In the Philistine version, the point of choosing cows that have never been yoked and of locking away their calves is apparently to make it certain that if the cows do head for Israel it will not be from natural causes nor by coincidence, but by the influence of Israel's God.

6:9 Beth-shemesh. Lit. "House of the Sun." One of several places in Israel with this name, this Beth-shemesh has been identified with Tel er-Rumeileh, seven miles east of Ekron (5:10 note). Beth-shemesh was a border city (v. 12; Josh. 15:10) frequently in dispute between the Philistines and Israelites (2 Chr. 28:18).

6:12 lowing as they went. Obviously not happy to be leaving their calves behind, the cows nevertheless do not deviate from their divinely directed path.

6:13 their wheat harvest. See 12:17 note.

6:14 Joshua of Beth-shemesh. Although this Joshua is not mentioned elsewhere in the Bible, his field and the prominent rock located in it were apparently well known at the time the present account was written (v. 18).

burnt offering. See note 10:8.

6:15 Levites. Beth-shemesh was assigned to the Levites, specifically, the descendants of Aaron (Josh. 21:16).

set them upon the great stone. The large rock was used as a pedestal for the ark and the gold objects, not as an impromptu altar.

17 These are the golden tumors that the
Philistines returned as a [u]guilt offering to
the LORD: one for Ashdod, one for Gaza,
one for Ashkelon, one for Gath, one for
Ekron, 18 and the golden mice, according to
the number of all the cities of the
Philistines belonging to the five lords,
[v]both fortified cities and unwalled villages.
[w]The great stone beside which they set
down the ark of the LORD is a witness to
this day in the field of Joshua of Beth-
shemesh.

19 [x]And he struck some of the men of
Beth-shemesh, because they looked upon
the ark of the LORD. He struck seventy
men of them,[1] and the people mourned
because the LORD had struck the people
with a great blow. 20 Then the men of
Beth-shemesh said, [y]"Who is able to
stand before the LORD, this holy God?
And to whom shall he go up away from
us?" 21 So they sent messengers to the
inhabitants of [z]Kiriath-jearim, saying,
"The Philistines have returned the ark of
the LORD. Come down and take it up to
you."

7 And the men of Kiriath-jearim came
and took up the ark of the LORD and
brought it to the house of [a]Abinadab on the
hill. And they consecrated his son Eleazar
to have charge of the ark of the LORD. 2 From
the day that the ark was lodged at Kiriath-
jearim, a long time passed, some twenty
years, and all the house of Israel lamented
after the LORD.

Samuel Judges Israel

3 And Samuel said to all the house of
Israel, [b]"If you are returning to the LORD
with all your heart, then [c]put away the foreign gods and the [d]Ashtaroth from among
you and [e]direct your heart to the LORD [f]and
serve him only, and he will deliver you out
of the hand of the Philistines." 4 So the people of Israel put away the Baals and the
Ashtaroth, and they served the LORD only.

5 Then Samuel said, "Gather all Israel at
[g]Mizpah, and I will pray to the LORD for
you." 6 So they gathered at [g]Mizpah [h]and
drew water and poured it out before the
LORD [i]and fasted on that day and said
there, [j]"We have sinned against the LORD."
And Samuel judged the people of Israel at
Mizpah. 7 Now when the Philistines heard
that the people of Israel had gathered at
Mizpah, the lords of the Philistines went
up against Israel. And when the people of
Israel heard of it, they were afraid of the
Philistines. 8 And the people of Israel said
to Samuel, "Do not cease to cry out to the
LORD our God for us, that he may save us
from the hand of the Philistines." 9 So
Samuel took a nursing lamb and offered it
as a whole burnt offering to the LORD. And
[k]Samuel cried out to the LORD for Israel,
and the LORD answered him. 10 As Samuel
was offering up the burnt offering, the
Philistines drew near to attack Israel. [l]But
the LORD thundered with a mighty sound
that day against the Philistines and threw

17 [u]ver. 3, 8
18 [v][Deut. 3:5] [w]ver. 14, 15
19 [x][Ex. 19:21; Num. 4:15, 20; 2 Sam. 6:7]
20 [y][2 Sam. 6:9]
21 [z]1 Chr. 13:5, 6; [Josh. 9:17; 18:14]
Chapter 7
1 [a]2 Sam. 6:3
3 [b]1 Kin. 8:48; Isai. 55:7; Hos. 6:1; Joel 2:12; See Deut. 30:2-10 [c]Gen. 35:2; Josh. 24:14, 23; [Judg. 10:16] [d]Judg. 2:13 [e][2 Chr. 19:3; 30:19; Ezra 7:10] [f]Deut. 6:13; 10:20; 13:4; Cited Matt. 4:10; Luke 4:8
5 [g][Judg. 20:1]
6 [g][See ver. 5 above] [h][2 Sam. 14:14] [i]ch. 31:13; Neh. 9:1 [j]Judg. 10:10
9 [k]Ps. 99:6; Jer. 15:1
10 [l]ch. 2:10; [2 Sam. 22:14, 15; Ps. 18:13]

[1] Hebrew *of the people seventy men, fifty thousand men*

6:18 to this day. See note on v. 14.

6:19 looked upon the ark. See Num. 4:5, 20. Presumptuous handling of the ark led to its capture, and a similar offense must now be purged on the occasion of its return. The problem of handling the ark improperly will arise again in 2 Sam. 6.

6:20 Who is able to stand. Cf. Ex. 9:11.

6:21 Kiriath-jearim. Located nine miles northeast of Beth-shemesh, Kiriath-jearim is also called Kiriath-baal (Josh. 15:60; 18:14), Baalah (Josh. 15:9), and Baale-judah (2 Sam. 6:2).

7:2 twenty years . . . lamented after the LORD. In light of Samuel's reference to "foreign gods" among the Israelites (v. 3), it seems that it was only at the close of these twenty years that Israel began to seek the Lord.

7:3 direct your heart to the LORD . . . and he will deliver you. The cycle of apostasy, oppression, repentance, and deliverance so typical of the Book of Judges (Judg. 3:7–9) is repeated in the events of this chapter.

7:4 the Baals and the Ashtaroth. See notes 5:2; 31:10.

7:5 Mizpah. A town in Benjamin seven miles north of Jerusalem and eight miles northeast of Kiriath-jearim, Mizpah played a prominent role in Israel before the monarchy (10:17; Judg. 20:1; 21:1, 5, 8). It was one of the regular stops in Samuel's circuit (v. 16). The name, meaning something like "place of watching," implies a high vantage point and was given to a number of sites (e.g., 22:3).

7:6 drew water and poured it out before the LORD. Although this action is not paralleled elsewhere in Scripture, it seems to signify sorrow and, along with fasting, a desire to seek God earnestly (cf. 1:15; Ps. 62:8; Lam. 2:19). David's action in 2 Sam. 23:16 occurs in a different context and has a different meaning.

We have sinned against the LORD. The words and actions (v. 4) of the Israelites give evidence of true repentance. The time is ripe for the Lord to deliver His people from their Philistine oppressors. The response of the Philistines to the convocation at Mizpah (v. 7) provides an opportunity for this deliverance.

7:8 cry out to the LORD. In the Book of Judges, "crying out" to the Lord was answered through a deliverer whom the Lord would raise up (Judg. 3:9, 15). Here Samuel functions as intercessor and intermediary, while the victory is clearly the Lord's doing (v. 10).

7:9 burnt offering. See note 10:8.

7:10 the LORD thundered . . . against the Philistines. This statement dramatically recalls the earlier words of Hannah that "the adversaries . . . shall be broken to pieces; against them he will thunder in heaven" (2:10; cf. 2 Sam. 22:14). Hannah's words are immediately preceded by the statement that "not by might shall a man prevail" (2:9). Human strength is of little consequence when the Lord decides to act.

them into confusion, and they were routed before Israel. 11 And the men of Israel went out from Mizpah and pursued the Philistines and struck them, as far as below Beth-car.

12 Then Samuel [m]took a stone and set it up between Mizpah and Shen[1] and called its name Ebenezer;[2] for he said, "Till now the LORD has helped us." 13 [n]So the Philistines were subdued and did not again enter the territory of Israel. And the hand of the LORD was against the Philistines all the days of Samuel. 14 The cities that the Philistines had taken from Israel were restored to Israel, from Ekron to Gath, and Israel delivered their territory from the hand of the Philistines. There was peace also between Israel and the Amorites.

15 [o]Samuel judged Israel all the days of his life. 16 And he went on a circuit year by year to Bethel, Gilgal, and Mizpah. And he judged Israel in all these places. 17 Then he would return to [p]Ramah, for his home was there, and there also he judged Israel. [q]And he built there an altar to the LORD.

Israel Demands a King

8 When Samuel became old, [r]he made his sons judges over Israel. 2 The name of his firstborn son was Joel, and the name of his second, Abijah; they were judges in Beersheba. 3 Yet his sons did not walk in his ways [s]but turned aside after gain. [t]They took bribes and perverted justice.

4 Then all the elders of Israel gathered together and came to Samuel at [p]Ramah 5 and said to him, "Behold, you are old and your sons do not walk in your ways. [u]Now appoint for us a king to judge us like all the nations." 6 But the thing displeased Samuel when they said, "Give us a king to judge us." And Samuel prayed to the LORD. 7 And the LORD said to Samuel, "Obey the voice of the people in all that they say to you, [v]for they have not rejected you, [w]but they have rejected me from being king over them. 8 According to all the deeds that they have done, from the day I brought them up out of Egypt even to this day, forsaking me and serving other gods, so they are also doing to you. 9 Now then, obey their voice; only you shall solemnly warn them [x]and show them the ways of the king who shall reign over them."

Samuel's Warning Against Kings

10 So Samuel told all the words of the LORD to the people who were asking for a king from him. 11 He said, [y]"These will be the ways of the king who will reign over you: [z]he will take your sons and appoint them to his chariots and to be his horsemen and to run before his chariots. 12 And

12 [m]Gen. 28:18; 31:45; 35:14; Josh. 4:9; 24:26
13 [n][Judg. 13:1]
15 [o]ver. 6; ch. 12:11; [Judg. 2:16]
17 [p]ch. 1:19 [q][ch. 14:35; Judg. 21:4]
Chapter 8
1 [r]Deut. 16:18
3 [s][Ex. 18:21] [t][Ex. 23:8; Deut. 16:19; Ps. 15:5]
4 [p][See ver. 17 above]
5 [u]ver. 19, 20; [Deut. 17:14; Hos. 13:10; Acts 13:21]
7 [v][Ex. 16:8] [w]ch. 10:19
9 [x]See ver. 11-18
11 [y]ch. 10:25; See Deut. 17:16-20 [z]ch. 14:52

1 Hebrew; Septuagint, Syriac *Jeshanah* 2 *Ebenezer* means *stone of help*

7:11 Beth-car. Location not known.

7:12 Ebenezer. A different site than that mentioned in 4:1 (note) and 5:1, this Ebenezer nevertheless recalls the earlier episode, when the Israelites tried to manipulate their God by carrying the ark into battle only to suffer a resounding defeat. Now God has given them a great victory over the same enemies. Samuel sets up a memorial stone with the name Ebenezer, "Stone of Help," not only to commemorate the victory but also as reminder of the different results brought about by presumption on the one hand and by repentance on the other.

Till now the LORD has helped us. The saying means that the Lord had been with them all the way "to this place," or "to this hour."

7:13 did not again enter the territory of Israel. The reference is to the tactical situation and not to the continuing history of Israel. The Philistines were convincingly defeated and attempted no counterattack (compare 2 Sam. 2:28 with 3:1; also 2 Kin. 6:23 with 6:24), but this does not rule out subsequent Philistine aggression (9:16; 10:5; 13:3; 14:52).

the hand of the LORD was against the Philistines. What God had done during the tenure of the ark in Philistine territory (5:4, 6; 6:5 and notes), He now continues through the leadership of Samuel. Throughout Samuel's lifetime God continued to give Israel victory, though the fighting at times was fierce (14:52). The defeat recounted in ch. 31 came only after Samuel's death (25:1).

7:16 Bethel. Ten miles north of Jerusalem.

Gilgal. Gilgal was probably in the Jordan Valley near Jericho (Josh. 5:10).

Mizpah. See note 7:5.

7:17 Ramah. See note 1:1.

8:5 appoint for us a king. The reasons given by the elders for wanting a king, though acceptable in themselves (as confirmed by the narrator in vv. 1–3), are really a pretext; what they really wanted was to become like "all the nations" (cf. v. 20).

8:7 they have not rejected you. Since the elders couch their request in terms of a "king to judge us" (v. 5 note), Samuel initially interprets their overture as an attack on his own leadership (v. 6). But the Lord points out to him that the affront is far graver than that.

they have rejected me. The offense of the elders' request lies not in the concept of human kingship in itself, for kingship in Israel had long been anticipated (2:10 note), but in breaking their covenant relationship with God. Their sin was to reject God as their king and to take instead a human monarch (10:19; 12:12–20; and contrast Gideon's refusal in Judg. 8:23).

8:10 who were asking for a king. For the second time in 1 Samuel an individual is "asked for." The individual given in response to the first request was Samuel (1:20 note), and it is Saul (whose name is based on the Hebrew root meaning "ask for") who will be given in response to the second request.

8:11 These will be the ways of the king. Israel's Canaanite neighbors and many of the Israelite kings were guilty of harsh practices like those described in vv. 11–17.

run before. Compare the actions of Absalom in 2 Sam. 15:1 with Adonijah in 1 Kin. 1:5.

chariots. See 2 Sam. 8:4; 15:1; 1 Kin. 4:26; 10:26–29.

he will appoint for himself commanders of
thousands and commanders of fifties, and
some [a]to plow his ground and to reap his
harvest, and to make his implements of
war and the equipment of his chariots.
13 He will take your daughters to be perfumers and cooks and bakers. 14 [b]He will
take the best of your fields and vineyards
and olive orchards and give them to his
servants. 15 He will take the tenth of your
grain and of your vineyards and give it to
his officers and to his servants. 16 He will
take your male servants and female servants and the best of your young men[1] and
your donkeys, and put them to his work.
17 He will take the tenth of your flocks, and
you shall be his slaves. 18 And in that day
you will cry out because of your king,
whom you have chosen for yourselves, [c]but
the LORD will not answer you in that day."

The LORD Grants Israel's Request

19 But the people refused to obey the
voice of Samuel. And they said, "No! But
there shall be a king over us, 20 [d]that we
also may be like all the nations, and that
our king may judge us and go out before us
and fight our battles." 21 And when Samuel
had heard all the words of the people, he
repeated them in the ears of the LORD.
22 And the LORD said to Samuel, [e]"Obey
their voice and make them a king." Samuel
then said to the men of Israel, "Go every
man to his city."

Saul Chosen to Be King

9 There was a man of Benjamin whose
name was [f]Kish, the son of Abiel, son
of Zeror, son of Becorath, son of Aphiah, a
Benjaminite, a man of wealth. 2 And he had
a son whose name was Saul, [g]a handsome
young man. There was not a man among
the people of Israel more handsome than
he. [h]From his shoulders upward he was
taller than any of the people.
3 Now the donkeys of Kish, Saul's father,
were lost. So Kish said to Saul his son, "Take
one of the young men with you, and arise,
go and look for the donkeys." 4 And he
passed through [i]the hill country of Ephraim
and passed through the land of [j]Shalishah,
but they did not find them. And they passed
through the land of Shaalim, but they were
not there. Then they passed through the
land of Benjamin, but did not find them.
5 When they came to the land of Zuph,
Saul said to his servant[2] who was with him,
"Come, let us go back, [k]lest my father
cease to care about the donkeys and
become anxious about us." 6 But he said to
him, "Behold, there is [l]a man of God in
this city, and he is a man who is held in
honor; [m]all that he says comes true. So
now let us go there. Perhaps he can tell us
the way we should go." 7 Then Saul said to
his servant, "But if we go, [n]what can we
bring the man? For the bread in our sacks
is gone, and there is no present to bring to

12 [a]See Gen. 45:6
14 [b]1 Kin. 21:7; [Ezek. 46:18]
18 [c]Prov. 1:28; Isai. 1:15; Mic. 3:4
20 [d]ver. 5
22 [e]ver. 7; [Hos. 13:11]

Chapter 9
1 [f]ch. 14:51; 1 Chr. 8:33; 9:39
2 [g][ch. 8:16] [h]ch. 10:23
4 [i]See Josh. 24:33 [j]2 Kin. 4:42
5 [k]ch. 10:2
6 [l]Deut. 33:1; Judg. 13:6; 1 Kin. 13:1 [m]ch. 3:19
7 [n][1 Kin. 14:3; 2 Kin. 4:42; 8:8]

1 Septuagint *cattle* 2 Hebrew *young man*; also verses 7, 8, 10, 27

8:14 fields . . . vineyards. See note 22:7.

8:15–17 tenth. The demands of the king will either take from what belongs to the Lord (Lev. 27:30–32; Deut. 14:22, 28) or create a tax burden for his subjects.

8:18 your king. See 12:13 and contrast 16:1.

the LORD will not answer you. Judging by the consequences, Israel's rejection of the Lord in favor of a human king is the moral and religious equivalent of forsaking the Lord to serve other gods (Judg. 10:10–14).

8:20 like all the nations. See note on v. 5.

fight our battles. To be contrasted with "the LORD's battles" (18:17; 25:28).

8:22 Obey their voice and make them a king. The Lord's concession to the people's sinful request is, at this point in the account, perplexing. If their desire for a king is sinful, amounting to a rejection of God as king (vv. 7, 18 and notes), how can God grant it? One answer lies in the standards of acceptable kingship that the Lord will establish. God is graciously willing to give the people a king and even to bless him, although not the sort of king they envisage (10:1, 7, 8 and notes). At the same time, because they adopted kingship in unbelief, they came to suffer under kings like those of the nations.

Go every man to his city. Samuel's dismissal of the men of Israel implies that appointing a king will require some preparation. The course of that preparation will be related in the chapters that follow.

9:1 a man of wealth. The opening verse of the account of Saul's adventures is formally similar to the beginning of the birth narrative of Samuel (1:1). In both instances the father of the principal character is introduced with sufficient genealogical references to suggest a man of standing. In Samuel's introduction we are also told of the father's faithful religious observance (1:3–5), whereas in this account we are introduced immediately to Saul (v. 2), and the focus remains exclusively on external qualities.

9:2 a handsome young man. The emphasis of this description is Saul's physical stature and impressive appearance. Compare the description of Absalom in 2 Sam. 14:25, 26.

9:6 there is a man of God in this city. That Saul is unaware of the presence and reputation of the man of God or has not thought of consulting him reflects negatively on his judgment.

all that he says comes true. The man of God is Samuel, of whom it is said in 3:19 that the Lord "let none of his words fall to the ground."

9:7 there is no present to bring to the man of God. Josephus (*Antiquities* 6.4.1) interprets Saul's words as a sign that he was ignorant that a true prophet would accept no reward. Israel's writing prophets express disdain for those who prophesy for money (Mic. 3:5, 11), although there are various references to goods being offered in return for prophetic favors (e.g., 1 Kin. 14:3; 2 Kin. 4:42; 8:8). In two instances payment is explicitly refused (1 Kin. 13:7–9; 2 Kin. 5:15, 16), and in one instance where goods are accepted, the payment does not benefit the prophet personally but is distributed among the people (2 Kin. 4:42).

the man of God. What do we have?" 8 The
servant answered Saul again, "Here, I have
with me a quarter of a shekel[1] of silver, and
I will give it to the man of God to tell us
our way." 9 (Formerly in Israel, when a man
[o]went to inquire of God, he said, "Come,
let us go to the seer," for today's "prophet"
was formerly called a seer.) 10 And Saul said
to his servant, "Well said; come, let us go."
So they went to the city where the man of
God was.

11 As they went up the hill to the city,
[p]they met young women coming out to
draw water and said to them, "Is the seer
here?" 12 They answered, "He is; behold, he
is just ahead of you. Hurry. He has come
just now to the city, because the people
[q]have a sacrifice today on [r]the high place.
13 As soon as you enter the city you will find
him, before he goes up to the high place to
eat. For the people will not eat till he
comes, since he must bless the sacrifice;
afterward those who are invited will eat.
Now go up, for you will meet him immediately." 14 So they went up to the city. As
they were entering the city, they saw
Samuel coming out toward them on his
way up to the high place.

15 Now the day before Saul came, [s]the
LORD had [t]revealed to Samuel: 16 "Tomorrow about this time I will send to you
a man from the land of Benjamin, [u]and
you shall anoint him to be prince over my
people Israel. He shall save my people from
the hand of the Philistines. [v]For I have
seen[2] my people, because their cry has
come to me." 17 When Samuel saw Saul, the
LORD told him, [w]"Here is the man of whom
I spoke to you! He it is who shall restrain
my people." 18 Then Saul approached
Samuel in the gate and said, "Tell me
where is the house of the seer?" 19 Samuel
answered Saul, "I am the seer. Go up
before me to the high place, for today you
shall eat with me, and in the morning I will
let you go and will tell you all that is on
your mind. 20 [x]As for your donkeys that
were lost three days ago, do not set your
mind on them, for they have been found.
And for whom is all that is desirable in
Israel? Is it not for you and for all your
father's house?" 21 Saul answered, "Am I
not a Benjaminite, [y]from the least of the
tribes of Israel? [z]And is not my clan the
humblest of all the clans of the tribe of
Benjamin? Why then have you spoken to
me in this way?"

22 Then Samuel took Saul and his young
man and brought them into the hall and
gave them a place at the head of those who
had been invited, who were about thirty persons. 23 And Samuel said to the cook, "Bring
the portion I gave you, of which I said to
you, 'Put it aside.'" 24 So the cook took up
[a]the leg and what was on it and set them
before Saul. And Samuel said, "See, what
was kept is set before you. Eat, because it
was kept for you until the hour appointed,
that you might eat with the guests."[3]

So Saul ate with Samuel that day. 25 And
when they came down from the high place
into the city, a bed was spread for Saul[4] [b]on
the roof, and he lay down to sleep. 26 Then
at the break of dawn[5] Samuel called to Saul
on the roof, "Up, that I may send you on
your way." So Saul arose, and both he and
Samuel went out into the street.

9 [o]Gen. 25:22
11 [p]Gen. 24:11
12 [q]ch. 16:2; 20:29; Gen. 31:54 [r]ch. 10:5; 1 Kin. 3:2-4
15 [s]ch. 15:1; [Acts 13:21] [t]Ruth. 4:4
16 [u]ch. 10:1 [v]Ex. 2:25; 3:7, 9
17 [w][ch. 16:12]
20 [x]ver. 3
21 [y][Judg. 20:46; 21:6; Ps. 68:27] [z]ch. 15:17; [Judg. 6:15]
24 [a]Ex. 29:22, 27; Lev. 7:32, 33; [Ezek. 24:4]
25 [b][Deut. 22:8; 2 Sam. 11:2; 16:22; Neh. 8:16; Matt. 24:17; Acts 10:9]

1 A *shekel* was about 2/5 ounce or 11 grams 2 Septuagint adds *the affliction of* 3 Hebrew *appointed, saying, 'I have invited the people'* 4 Septuagint; Hebrew *and he spoke with Saul* 5 Septuagint; Hebrew *and they arose early and at the break of dawn*

9:9 today's "prophet" was formerly called a seer. The terms are synonymous.

9:12 They answered. In the Hebrew, vv. 12, 13 convey excitement and animation as the girls urge Saul to hurry up to the city, where he will be just in time to meet Samuel.

high place. Although it was recognized that such high places (often sites of Canaanite worship) posed a clear danger to the purity of Israelite worship (e.g., Lev. 26:30; Num. 33:52; Deut. 12:2, 3; Jer. 2:20), it is apparent from passages such as this that worship of Yahweh was sometimes conducted there, especially during the early monarchy (10:5; 1 Kin. 3:2–4). Such worship may have been made necessary by the loss of the sanctuary at Shiloh (1:3 note). After the division of the kingdom, worship at "high places" was a serious problem both in the north (1 Kin. 12:31, 32; 13:32–34) and in the south (1 Kin. 14:22–24). Removal of the "high places" was a major goal of reform movements under southern kings like Hezekiah (2 Kin. 18:4) and Josiah (2 Kin. 23:5).

9:16 anoint him. See note 2:10.

prince. The word appears to be a title for "one designated to rule" (cf. its use with reference to Solomon as crown prince in 1 Kin. 1:35). Saul's assignment in the immediate context is to deliver Israel from the Philistines, and against the background of ch. 8 the logical assumption is that he will go on to become king.

Philistines. See note 4:1.

9:18 Saul approached Samuel. Saul's failure to recognize Samuel is a troubling hint of spiritual insensitivity and inattentiveness that will increasingly characterize Saul as the narrative progresses.

9:20 all that is desirable in Israel. This expression may suggest that Saul is just the kind of king the people want in ch. 8.

9:24 took up the leg . . . set them before Saul. The special treatment given Saul illustrates not only his newly elevated status but also Samuel's divinely enabled anticipation of his arrival (vv. 15, 16).

27 As they were going down to the outskirts of the city, Samuel said to Saul, "Tell
the servant to pass on before us, and when
he has passed on, stop here yourself for a
while, that I may make known to you the
word of God."

Saul Anointed King

10 [c]Then Samuel took a flask of oil and
poured it on his head [d]and kissed
him and said, "Has not the LORD anointed
you to be prince over [e]his people Israel?
And you shall reign over the people of the
LORD and you will save them from the hand
of their surrounding enemies. And this
shall be the sign to you that the LORD has
anointed you to be prince[1] over his heritage. 2 When you depart from me today,
you will meet two men by [f]Rachel's tomb in
the territory of Benjamin at Zelzah, and they
will say to you, [g]'The donkeys that you
went to seek are found, and now [h]your
father has ceased to care about the donkeys
and is anxious about you, saying, "What
shall I do about my son?"' 3 Then you shall
go on from there further and come to the
[i]oak of Tabor. Three men [j]going up [k]to God
at Bethel will meet you there, one carrying
three young goats, another carrying three
loaves of bread, and another carrying a skin
of wine. 4 And they will greet you and give
you two loaves of bread, which you shall
accept from their hand. 5 After that you shall
come to [l]Gibeath-elohim,[2] [m]where there is
a garrison of the Philistines. And there, as
soon as you come to the city, you will meet
a group of prophets coming down [n]from
the high place with harp, tambourine, flute,
and lyre before them, prophesying. 6 [o]Then
the Spirit of the LORD will rush upon you,
[p]and you will prophesy with them and be
turned into another man. 7 Now when
[q]these signs meet you, do what your hand
finds to do, [r]for God is with you. 8 Then go
down before me [s]to Gilgal. And behold, I
am coming to you to offer burnt offerings
and [t]to sacrifice peace offerings. [u]Seven
days you shall wait, until I come to you and
show you what you shall do."
9 When he turned his back to leave
Samuel, God gave him another heart. And
all these signs came to pass that day.
10 When they came to [v]Gibeah,[3] behold, a
group of prophets met him, [o]and the Spirit
of God rushed upon him, and he prophesied among them. 11 And when all who
knew him previously saw how he prophesied with the prophets, the people said to
one another, "What has come over the son
of Kish? [w]Is Saul also among the prophets?"

Chapter 10
1 [c]ch. 9:16; 16:13; 2 Sam. 2:4; 1 Kin. 1:34, 39; 2 Kin. 9:1, 3, 6 [d][Ps. 2:12] [e]Deut. 32:9; Ps. 78:71
2 [f]Gen. 35:19, 20 [g]ch. 9:3, 4 [h]ch. 9:5
3 [i]Gen. 13:18 [j][Judg. 20:31] [k]Gen. 28:22; 35:1, 3, 7
5 [l]ver. 10 [m]ch. 13:3, 4 [n][ch. 9:12]
6 [o]ver. 10; ch. 11:6; 16:13; [Num. 11:25; Judg. 3:10; 14:6, 19] [p]ver. 10; ch. 19:23, 24
7 [q]Ex. 4:8; Judg. 6:17; Luke 2:12 [r]Josh. 1:5; Judg. 6:12
8 [s]ch. 11:14, 15; 13:4 [t]ch. 11:15 [u]ch. 13:8
10 [v]ver. 5 [o][See ver. 6 above]
11 [w]ch. 19:24; [Matt. 13:54, 55; John 7:15]

1 Septuagint; Hebrew lacks *over his people Israel? And you shall. . . . to be prince* 2 *Gibeath-elohim* means *the hill of God* 3 *Gibeah* means *the hill*

10:1 anointed you to be prince. See note 9:16.

his heritage. See 9:16 ("my people Israel"); 2 Sam. 20:19 and note; Deut. 32:9. The Lord's willingness to grant the people a human king does not mean that He forfeited His rule over His own people, Israel. The appointed king was always subordinate to God.

10:2–6 Samuel's words will be confirmed to Saul as the sequence of events comes to pass in the order foretold. Finally, Saul will come under the power of the Spirit (vv. 5, 6).

10:5 a garrison of the Philistines. The mention of a Philistine garrison foreshadows the task ahead for the one designated to deliver the people of God from the Philistines (9:16). On the stationing of garrisons in subject territories, see David's practice in 2 Sam. 8:6.

group of prophets. Samuel is associated with a group of prophets in 19:20, where he is described as their leader. Note the similar association of Elisha with the "sons of the prophets" in 2 Kin. 2; 6:1; 9:1; etc. These prophetic guilds appear to have been made up of defenders of true religion in times of widespread apostasy and spiritual indifference.

prophesying. Prophecy in the Old Testament is often, though not exclusively, associated with the giving of a message (see Aaron's role as Moses' "prophet" or spokesman in Ex. 7:1; and compare Ezek. 21:9; Amos 3:8). God's prophets were His messengers (2 Sam. 7:1–5; 12:1; 24:11–12). In some places, prophecy is associated with music (Ex. 15:20, 21; 1 Chr. 25:1). The prophesying in view here seems to be praising God and exhorting the people with musical accompaniment.

10:6 Spirit of the LORD will rush upon you. See v. 10; 11:6 note. The activity of the Spirit with Samson is expressed in identical terms (Judg. 14:6, 19; 15:14). Whereas the Spirit was ultimately withdrawn from Saul (cf. 16:14; 18:10), David's endowment with the Spirit was permanent (16:13). Frequently in the Old Testament the bestowal of the Spirit is an empowerment by God of an individual for a particular task. Conversely, God can send a lying spirit (1 Kin. 22:23) or an evil ("distressing") spirit (16:14–16, 23; 18:10; 19:9; Judg. 9:23).

10:7 do what your hand finds to do. In the light of Saul's general commission to deliver Israel from the Philistines (9:16) and of Samuel's specific mention of a visible symbol of Philistine domination at the site of the third and final sign (v. 5), Samuel's words could be taken to imply that Saul should respond to his anointing by attacking the Philistine outpost. In the event, this possibility is not realized. Samuel's words can also be interpreted as an encouragement for Saul to submit to the prophetic influence mentioned in v. 6.

10:8 go down before me to Gilgal. When Saul has done what his "hand finds to do," he is to meet Samuel in Gilgal, so the latter can offer sacrifices and give Saul further instructions.

burnt offerings. A full description of the ritual of the burnt offering can be found in Lev. 1:3–17. Burnt offerings are also mentioned in 6:14, 15; 7:9, 10; 13:9, 12; 15:22; 2 Sam. 6:17, 18; 24:22–25.

peace offerings. The peace offering is described in Lev. 3 and is first mentioned in Ex. 20:24. Other references in Samuel to peace offerings are 11:15; 13:9; 2 Sam. 6:17, 18; 24:25.

10:9 God gave him another heart. The language is similar to Ezek. 11:19; 36:26, if not John 3:3 (see also Jer. 31:31). But it is difficult to say what Saul's experience was precisely.

10:11 Is Saul also among the prophets. Or, "Is even Saul among the prophets?" The proverb (v. 12) expresses surprise at something very improbable. The onlookers who knew Saul are surprised to find him associating with religious enthusiasts.

12 And a man of the place answered, [x]"And
who is their father?" Therefore it became a
proverb, [w]"Is Saul also among the
prophets?" 13 When he had finished prophesying, he came to the high place.
14 [y]Saul's uncle said to him and to his servant, "Where did you go?" And he said,
[z]"To seek the donkeys. And when we saw
they were not to be found, we went to
Samuel." 15 And Saul's uncle said, "Please
tell me what Samuel said to you." 16 And
Saul said to his uncle, [a]"He told us plainly
that the donkeys had been found." But
about the matter of the kingdom, of which
Samuel had spoken, he did not tell him
anything.

Saul Proclaimed King

17 Now Samuel called the people together
[b]to the LORD [c]at Mizpah. 18 And he said to
the people of Israel, [d]"Thus says the LORD,
the God of Israel, 'I brought up Israel out
of Egypt, and I delivered you from the hand
of the Egyptians and from the hand of all
the kingdoms that were oppressing you.'
19 [e]But today you have rejected your God,
who saves you from all your calamities and
your distresses, and you have said to him,
'Set a king over us.' Now therefore [f]present
yourselves before the LORD by your tribes
and by your thousands."
20 Then Samuel [g]brought all the tribes of
Israel near, and the tribe of Benjamin was
taken by lot. 21 He brought the tribe of
Benjamin near by its clans, and the clan of
the Matrites was taken by lot;[1] and Saul the
son of Kish was taken by lot. But when they
sought him, he could not be found. 22 [h]So
they inquired again of the LORD, "Is there a
man still to come?" and the LORD said,
"Behold, he has hidden himself among the
baggage." 23 Then they ran and took him
from there. And when he stood among the
people, [i]he was taller than any of the people
from his shoulders upward. 24 And Samuel
said to all the people, "Do you see him
[j]whom the LORD has chosen? There is none
like him among all the people." And all the
people shouted, [k]"Long live the king!"
25 Then Samuel told the people [l]the rights
and duties of the kingship, and he wrote
them in a book and laid it up before the
LORD. Then Samuel sent all the people
away, each one to his home. 26 Saul also
went to his home [m]at Gibeah, and with
him went men of valor whose hearts God
had touched. 27 But some [n]worthless fellows said, "How can this man save us?"
And they despised him and brought him
no present. But he held his peace.

Saul Defeats the Ammonites

11 [o]Then Nahash the Ammonite went
up and besieged [p]Jabesh-gilead,
and all the men of Jabesh said to Nahash,
[q]"Make a treaty with us, and we will serve
you." 2 But Nahash the Ammonite said to
them, "On this condition I will make a
treaty with you, [r]that I gouge out all your
right eyes, and thus [s]bring disgrace on all

12 [x][Isai. 54:13; John 6:45] [w][See ver. 11 above]
14 [y]ch. 14:50 [z]See ch. 9:4-6
16 [a]ch. 9:20
17 [b][ch. 11:15] [c]ch. 7:5, 6
18 [d]Judg. 6:8, 9; [ch. 12:8]
19 [e]ch. 8:7, 19; 12:12 [f]Josh. 24:1
20 [g]Josh. 7:14, 16, 17
22 [h]See ch. 22:10
23 [i]ch. 9:2
24 [j]2 Sam. 21:6 [k]2 Sam. 16:16; 1 Kin. 1:25, 39; 2 Kin. 11:12; 2 Chr. 23:11
25 [l]See ch. 8:11-18; Deut. 17:14-20
26 [m]ch. 11:4
27 [n]ch. 2:12; Deut. 13:13
Chapter 11
1 [o]ch. 12:12 [p]Judg. 21:8 [q]Gen. 26:28; 1 Kin. 20:34; Ezek. 17:13; [Ex. 23:32; 34:12, 15; Deut. 7:2]
2 [r][Num. 16:14] [s]ch. 17:26; Gen. 34:14

1 Septuagint adds *finally he brought the family of the Matrites near, man by man*

10:12 who is their father. Since leaders of prophetic guilds were sometimes called "father" (2 Kin. 2:12; 6:21), this question might be asking for the leader of this particular guild. If, on the other hand, the onlookers are contemptuous of prophecy, their surprise might be that a man like Saul, of good family and social standing, would associate with such "mad fellows" (cf. 2 Kin. 9:11), whose fathers were inferior to his. Still another possibility is that the question means that the "Father" or origin of the prophetic band does not follow normal rules, and Saul, unlikely as it may seem, has found a place with them. See "Prophets" at Deut. 18:18.

10:14–16 The significance of this conversation has long puzzled commentators. Some have understood Saul's reluctance to mention the kingship (v. 16) as a sign of humility.

10:17 Samuel called the people. The Lord's choice of Saul is now made public at Mizpah, apparently through casting a lot or using the Urim and Thummim (v. 20 and note).

10:20 Benjamin was taken. Casting lots was probably the method of selection (cf. Lev. 16:8–10; Num. 26:55), and it may have involved the Urim and Thummim (2:28; Ex. 28:30 note; Num. 27:21; Deut. 33:8).

10:22 hidden himself among the baggage. The Lord singles out Saul even though he is not immediately present. Something similar occurs with David (16:11).

10:25 rights and duties of the kingship. A similar expression in 8:9–11 refers to the negative consequences of having a king. Here it means the regulations that a king must follow (Deut. 17:14–20; 2 Kin. 11:12 note).

laid it up before the LORD. See Deut. 31:26; Josh. 24:26.

10:27 How can this man save us. Those who pose this question are "rebels" because they call into question the Lord's process of selection.

11:1 Nahash the Ammonite. Descended from Lot, the Ammonites were a Semitic people (Gen. 19:38; Deut. 2:19) whose kingdom was on the east side of the Jordan, south of the Jabbok River. While Ammon was sometimes on friendly terms with Israel (2 Sam. 10:2), the Ammonites often exerted pressure on Israel's eastern border (Judg. 3:13; 11:4–32), as the Philistines did on the west. According to the Dead Sea Scrolls and Josephus (*Antiquities* 6.5.1), the siege of Jabesh-gilead was part of a larger campaign by Nahash.

Jabesh-gilead. A principal city in what was probably the territory of Gad, Jabesh-gilead was east of the Jordan River, twenty-two miles south of the Sea of Chinnereth (Galilee).

11:2 gouge out all your right eyes. While the stated reason for such treatment is to "bring disgrace on all Israel," Josephus (*Antiquities* 6.5.1) remarks that the loss of the right eye would have made military service impossible, since the sight of the left eye would be hindered by the shield.

Israel." 3 The elders of Jabesh said to him,
"Give us seven days' respite that we may
send messengers through all the territory of
Israel. Then, if there is no one to save us,
we will give ourselves up to you." 4 When
the messengers came to [t]Gibeah of Saul,
they reported the matter in the ears of the
people, [u]and all the people wept aloud.
5 Now, behold, Saul was coming from the
field behind the oxen. And Saul said,
"What is wrong with the people, that they
are weeping?" So they told him the news of
the men of Jabesh. 6 [v]And the Spirit of God
rushed upon Saul when he heard these
words, and his anger was greatly kindled.
7 He took a yoke of oxen [w]and cut them in
pieces and sent them throughout all the
territory of Israel by the hand of messengers, saying, [x]"Whoever does not come out
after Saul and Samuel, so shall it be done
to his oxen!" Then the dread of the LORD
fell upon the people, and they came out [y]as
one man. 8 When he mustered them at
[z]Bezek, [a]the people of Israel were three
hundred thousand, and the men of Judah
thirty thousand. 9 And they said to the messengers who had come, "Thus shall you say
to the men of Jabesh-gilead: 'Tomorrow, by
the time the sun is hot, you shall have [b]de-
liverance.'" When the messengers came
and told the men of Jabesh, they were glad.
10 Therefore the men of Jabesh said,
[c]"Tomorrow we will give ourselves up to
you, and you may do to us whatever seems
good to you." 11 [d]And the next day Saul put
the people [e]in three companies. And they
came into the midst of the camp in the
morning watch and struck down the
Ammonites until the heat of the day. And
those who survived were scattered, so that
no two of them were left together.

The Kingdom Is Renewed

12 Then the people said to Samuel, [f]"Who
is it that said, 'Shall Saul reign over us?'
[g]Bring the men, that we may put them to
death." 13 But Saul said, [h]"Not a man shall
be put to death this day, for today [i]the
LORD has worked [j]salvation in Israel."
14 Then Samuel said to the people, "Come,
let us go to Gilgal and there renew the
kingdom." 15 So all the people went to
[k]Gilgal, and there they made Saul king [l]be-
fore the LORD in Gilgal. There [m]they sacrificed peace offerings before the LORD, and
there Saul and all the men of Israel rejoiced
greatly.

Samuel's Farewell Address

12 And Samuel said to all Israel,
"Behold, I have obeyed [n]your voice
in all that you have said to me [o]and have
made a king over you. 2 And now, behold,
the king [p]walks before you, [q]and I am old
and gray; and behold, my sons are with

4 [t]ch. 10:26 [u]Judg. 2:4; 21:2
6 [v]See ch. 10:6, 10
7 [w][Judg. 19:29] [x]Judg. 21:5, 8, 10 [y]Judg. 20:1
8 [z]Judg. 1:5 [a][Judg. 20:15-17; 2 Sam. 24:9]
9 [b]ver. 13
10 [c]ver. 3
11 [d][ch. 31:11] [e]Judg. 7:16
12 [f]ch. 10:27 [g][Luke 19:27]
13 [h]2 Sam. 19:22 [i][ch. 19:5; Ex. 14:13] [j]ver. 9
15 [k]ch. 10:8; [l]ch. 15:33; [ch. 10:17; Judg. 11:11] [m]ch. 10:8
Chapter 12
1 [n]ch. 8:5, 19, 20 [o]ch. 10:24; 11:14, 15
2 [p][ch. 8:20; Num. 27:17] [q]ch. 8:1, 5

11:3 we will give ourselves up to you. While the elders of Jabesh clearly intend Nahash to understand their words as a surrender, the Hebrew verb employed is often used in the sense of soldiers "going out" to battle (8:20; 18:30; 2 Sam. 18:2–4, 6). When in v. 10 the men of Jabesh again promise to give up to the Ammonites, it is with some irony, because the Ammonites are still thinking of "surrender," but the townspeople are planning to fight.

11:6 Spirit of God rushed upon Saul. The phrase recalls the activity of the Spirit with Samson (10:6 note), except that here (as in 10:10) "God" is used in place of the personal name "LORD."

11:7 cut them in pieces. Saul's action roughly parallels that of the Levite in Judg. 19. The Levite's sin was notorious and the comparison would not be at all complimentary.

and Samuel. See notes 10:1, 7, 8.

11:8 Bezek. Located nine miles west of the Jordan River, opposite Jabesh-gilead.

people of Israel . . . men of Judah. Even before the division of the kingdom (1 Kin. 12), a distinction was often made between the northern and southern tribes (17:52; 18:16; 2 Sam. 2:10; 3:10; 5:5; 11:11; 12:8; 19:11, 40–43; 20:2; 21:2; 24:1, 9).

11:10 we will give ourselves up to you. See note on v. 3.

11:11 three companies. See 13:17; Judg. 7:16; 9:43; 2 Sam. 18:2.

in the morning watch. Between 2:00 and 6:00 A.M., taking advantage of the cover of darkness.

11:12 Bring the men. The reference includes, but may not be limited to, the "worthless fellows" of 10:27.

11:13 the LORD has worked salvation in Israel. Saul interrupts a question directed to Samuel with a confession that marks a high point in his own life. His amnesty or pardon of those "worthless fellows" (10:27) who rejected him can possibly be compared to his reluctance to kill Agag and the flocks of Amalek (15:9), if it is thought of as a failure to carry out the harsher aspects of a divine commission.

11:14 let us go to Gilgal and there renew the kingdom. On one level it is the process of Saul's accession to the throne that can now be resumed (v. 15 note), but on a deeper level it is the continued reign of the Lord that must be renewed (ch. 12).

Gilgal. See note 13:4.

11:15 made Saul king. A person's rise to leadership in ancient Israel can be analyzed as following a three-step process: (a) designation as the Lord's choice; (b) demonstration of valor and of having the Lord's power through performing a heroic feat; and (c) confirmation by the people. Saul was designated by Samuel, and he had a prophetic experience (ch. 10). Although he might immediately have attacked the Philistine garrison at Gibeah (10:5, 8), he soon after gains an important victory by delivering Jabesh-gilead (v. 13). He is then crowned at Gilgal.

peace offerings. See note 10:8.

12:1 have made a king over you. The process of accession to the throne has been completed, and Samuel's speech in ch. 12 marks the end of the period of the judges.

you. I have walked before you from my
youth until this day. 3 Here I am; testify
against me before the LORD and before [r]his
anointed. [s]Whose ox have I taken? Or
whose donkey have I taken? Or whom have
I defrauded? Whom have I oppressed? Or
from whose hand have I taken a bribe to
blind my eyes with it? Testify against me[1]
and I will restore it to you." 4 They said,
"You have not defrauded us or oppressed
us or taken anything from any man's
hand." 5 And he said to them, "The LORD is
witness against you, and [r]his anointed is
witness this day, that you have not found
anything [t]in my hand." And they said, "He
is witness."
6 And Samuel said to the people, [u]"The
LORD is witness,[2] who appointed Moses
and Aaron and brought your fathers up out
of the land of Egypt. 7 Now therefore stand
still that I may plead with you before the
LORD concerning all the righteous deeds of
the LORD that he performed for you and for
your fathers. 8 [v]When Jacob went into
Egypt, and the Egyptians oppressed them,[3]
[w]then your fathers cried out to the LORD
and [x]the LORD sent Moses and Aaron, [y]who
brought your fathers out of [z]Egypt and
made them dwell in this place. 9 But they
forgot the LORD their God. [a]And he sold
them into the hand of Sisera, commander
of the army of Hazor,[4] [b]and into the hand
of the Philistines, [c]and into the hand of the
king of Moab. And they fought against
them. 10 [d]And they cried out to the LORD
and said, 'We have sinned, because we
have forsaken the LORD [e]and have served
the Baals and the Ashtaroth. But now [f]de-
liver us out of the hand of our enemies,
that we may serve you.' 11 And the LORD
sent [g]Jerubbaal [h]and Barak[5] [i]and Jephthah
and [j]Samuel and delivered you out of the
hand of your enemies on every side, and
you lived in safety. 12 And when you saw
that [k]Nahash the king of the Ammonites
came against you, [l]you said to me, 'No, but
a king shall reign over us,' [m]when the LORD
your God was your king. 13 And now [n]be-
hold the king whom you have chosen, for
whom you have asked; behold, [o]the LORD
has set a king over you. 14 If you will [p]fear
the LORD and serve him and obey his voice
and not rebel against the commandment of
the LORD, and if both you and the king who
reigns over you will follow the LORD your
God, it will be well. 15 But [q]if you will not
obey the voice of the LORD, but rebel
against the commandment of the LORD,
then [r]the hand of the LORD will be against
you and [s]your king.[6] 16 Now therefore
[t]stand still and see this great thing that the
LORD will do before your eyes. 17 [u]Is it not
wheat harvest today? [v]I will call upon the
LORD, that he may send thunder and rain.
And you shall know and see that [w]your
wickedness is great, which you have done
in the sight of the LORD, in asking for your-

1 Septuagint; Hebrew lacks *Testify against me* 2 Septuagint; Hebrew lacks *is witness* 3 Septuagint; Hebrew lacks *and the Egyptians oppressed them* 4 Septuagint *the army of Jabin king of Hazor* 5 Septuagint, Syriac; Hebrew *Bedan* 6 Septuagint; Hebrew *fathers*

3 [r]ch. 24:6; 26:9, 11, 16; 2 Sam. 1:14, 16; [ch. 10:1] [s][Ex. 20:17; Num. 16:15]
5 [r][See ver. 3 above] [t]Ex. 21:16; 22:4
6 [u][Mic. 6:4]
8 [v]Gen. 46:5, 6 [w]Ex. 2:23 [x]Ex. 3:10; 4:14-16 [y][ch. 10:18] [z]Judg. 3:7
9 [a]Judg. 4:2 [b]Judg. 10:7; 13:1; [Judg. 3:31] [c]Judg. 3:12
10 [d]Judg. 10:10; [Judg. 3:9] [e]Judg. 2:13 [f]Judg. 10:15
11 [g]Judg. 6:14, 32 [h]1 Chr. 7:17 [i]Judg. 11:1 [j]See ch. 7:10-13
12 [k]ch. 11:1 [l]ch. 8:5, 19 [m][ch. 8:7; 10:19; Judg. 8:23]
13 [n]ch. 10:24 [o]ch. 9:16, 17; [Hos. 13:11]
14 [p]ver. 24; Deut. 6:2; Josh. 24:14
15 [q]Lev. 26:14, 15; Deut. 28:15; Josh. 24:20 [r]ch. 5:9 [s][ver. 9]
16 [t]Ex. 14:13
17 [u][Prov. 26:1] [v]ch. 7:9, 10; [James 5:16-18] [w]ch. 8:7

12:3–15 Samuel advances a three-pronged argument to compel the people to recognize their guilt for requesting a king. First, he invites agreement from the people that his leadership has been blameless (vv. 4, 5). Second, he points out that in the past it was always the Lord who appointed leaders (v. 6), and these proved fully adequate (vv. 7, 8). Third, he emphasizes that even when Israel "forgot the LORD their God," the Lord was gracious to them. Although He subjected them to enemy oppression (v. 9), He heard their confessions of sin and cries for deliverance (v. 10) and raised up judges, among them Samuel himself (v. 11). Against this background of the sufficiency of the Lord's provision, the people's demand to have a human king, even though the Lord was their king (v. 12), can be seen for what it is (8:7). Nevertheless, kingship can succeed, if both king and people "fear the LORD and serve him and obey his voice" (v. 14).

12:3 his anointed. See note 2:10. Saul's anointing is ordered in 9:16 and performed in 10:1.

Whose ox . . . whose donkey have I taken. Valuable possessions in biblical times, ox and donkey are mentioned in the tenth commandment as typical objects of covetousness (Ex. 20:17; Deut. 5:21).

12:7 may plead with you. Samuel has taken the stand himself as a defendant and been acquitted (vv. 3–5); now he takes the role of prosecutor and the people become the defendants. Their crime is having desired a king in total disregard of all the "righteous deeds of the LORD" throughout the time of the Exodus and the judges (vv. 7–11).

12:12 when you saw that Nahash the king of the Ammonites came against you. Though it is not explicitly mentioned in ch. 8, it is possible that the Ammonite threat was already a concern at that time (11:1 note). Alternatively, Samuel may simply be citing the Ammonite episode as the most recent example of the people's faithless tendency to seek help from men rather than God. Saul himself gave the Lord credit for the victory (11:13).

12:13 the king whom you have chosen. See 8:18 and contrast 16:1.

for whom you have asked. See 8:10 note.

12:14 fear the LORD. A fundamental prerequisite for covenant blessing in Moses' day (Deut. 6:2, 24; 10:12; 31:12, 13), in Joshua's (Josh. 4:24; 24:14), and now in the new era of the monarchy, "fear of the LORD" means standing in awe of Him and giving Him the honor and obedience that is His due as God and gracious Father.

12:16–19 Having made his case against the people in vv. 3–15, Samuel now invokes a dramatic sign to drive home the point of the people's guilt. The sign achieves the desired result, and the people repent for having "added to all our sins this evil, to ask for ourselves a king" (v. 19). On signs accompanying prophetic utterances, see 2:34 note.

12:17 wheat harvest. The wheat harvest probably took place in May and June, early in Israel's dry season.

selves a king." 18 So Samuel called upon the
LORD, and the LORD sent thunder and rain
that day, [x]and all the people greatly feared
the LORD and Samuel.
19 And all the people said to Samuel,
[y]"Pray for your servants to the LORD your
God, that we may not die, for we have
added to all our sins this evil, to ask for
ourselves a king." 20 And Samuel said to the
people, "Do not be afraid; you have done
all this evil. Yet [z]do not turn aside from following the LORD, but serve the LORD with
all your heart. 21 And [z]do not turn aside
after [a]empty things that cannot profit or
deliver, for they are empty. 22 [b]For the LORD
will not forsake his people, [c]for his great
name's sake, because [d]it has pleased the
LORD to make you a people for himself.
23 Moreover, as for me, far be it from me
that I should sin against the LORD by ceasing [e]to pray for you, [f]and I will instruct you
in the good and the right way. 24 [g]Only fear
the LORD and serve him faithfully with all
your heart. For consider [h]what great things
he has done for you. 25 But if you still do
wickedly, [i]you shall be swept away, [j]both
you and your king."

Saul Fights the Philistines

13 Saul was . . .[1] years old when he began to reign, and he reigned . . . and
two[2] years over Israel.
2 Saul chose three thousand men of
Israel. Two thousand were with Saul in
[k]Michmash and the hill country of Bethel,
and a thousand were with Jonathan in
[l]Gibeah of Benjamin. The rest of the people
he sent home, every man to his tent.
3 Jonathan defeated [m]the garrison of the
Philistines that was [n]at Geba, and the Philistines heard of it. And Saul [o]blew the
trumpet throughout all the land, saying,
"Let the Hebrews hear." 4 And all Israel
heard it said that Saul had defeated the garrison of the Philistines, and also that Israel
had become a stench to the Philistines.
And the people were called out to join Saul
at Gilgal.
5 And the Philistines mustered to fight
with Israel, thirty thousand chariots and
six thousand horsemen and troops [p]like
the sand on the seashore in multitude.
They came up and encamped in Michmash, to the east of [q]Beth-aven. 6 When the
men of Israel saw that they were in trouble
(for the people were hard pressed), the
people hid themselves [r]in caves and in
holes and in rocks and in tombs and in cisterns, 7 and some Hebrews crossed the
fords of the Jordan to the land of Gad and
Gilead. Saul was still at Gilgal, and all the
people followed him trembling.

Saul's Unlawful Sacrifice

8 [s]He waited seven days, the time
appointed by Samuel. But Samuel did not
come to Gilgal, and the people were scattering from him. 9 So Saul said, "Bring the
burnt offering here to me, and the peace
offerings." And he offered the burnt offering. 10 As soon as he had finished offering

18 [x]Ex. 14:31; [Ezra 10:9]
19 [y]ver. 23; [Ex. 9:28; 10:17; Jer. 15:1]
20 [z]Deut. 11:16
21 [z][See ver. 20 above] [a]Jer. 16:19; Hab. 2:18; [1 Cor. 8:4]
22 [b]1 Kin. 6:13; Ps. 94:14; [1 Kin. 8:57] [c]Josh. 7:9; Ps. 106:8; Jer. 14:21; Ezek. 20:9, 14, 22 [d]Deut. 7:7, 8; 14:2; [1 Pet. 2:9]
23 [e]See ver. 19 [f]1 Kin. 8:36; 2 Chr. 6:27; Ps. 27:11; [Prov. 4:11; Jer. 6:16]
24 [g]ver. 14; [Eccles. 12:13] [h]Deut. 10:21; Ps. 126:2, 3
25 [i]Josh. 24:20; [Num. 16:26] [j][Deut. 28:36]
Chapter 13
2 [k]ver. 5, 11, 16, 23; ch. 14:31 [l]ver. 15; ch. 10:26
3 [m]ch. 10:5 [n]ver. 16; ch. 14:5 [o][Judg. 3:27]
5 [p]Josh. 11:4 [q]ch. 14:23
6 [r]Judg. 6:2; Heb. 11:38
8 [s]ch. 10:8

1 The number is lacking in Hebrew and Septuagint 2 *Two* may not be the entire number; something may have dropped out

12:20–25 In response to the people's repentance, Samuel comforts them, "Do not be afraid," and challenges them to renewed commitment (v. 20).

12:23 pray for you . . . instruct you. Samuel's responsibilities in the kingdom will include intercession and instruction (12:1 note; for other duties of Samuel see 10:8).

12:24 fear the LORD. See note on v. 14.

with all your heart. See v. 20; 16:7.

13:1–14:52 Saul's reign officially begins. Compare the chronological notice of 13:1 with similar formulas in 2 Sam. 2:10; 5:4; 1 Kin. 14:21; 22:42). The narrative turns to Saul's first encounters with the Philistines, who were a continuing threat to Israel.

13:1 The preservation of this verse in the manuscript tradition has some defect, since as it stands the Hebrew says that Saul was one year old when he began to rule. But Saul was already a soldier. Saul probably reigned about twenty years, and the number "forty" in Acts 13:21 would be a round figure meaning "a long time." See the chronology in Introduction: Date and Occasion.

13:2 Michmash. Some four miles southeast of Bethel on the north side of the Wadi Suwenet, a seasonal river valley used for travel between the Jordan Valley and the central hill country.

Gibeah of Benjamin. This may be the Gibeah three miles north of Jerusalem, or possibly it was a village facing Michmash from the south side of the Wadi Suwenet.

13:3 Jonathan defeated the garrison . . . at Geba. This could be the same garrison near where Saul prophesied.

blew the trumpet. Trumpets were used in war as a signaling device (2 Sam. 2:28; 18:16; 20:1).

Hebrews. See note 4:6.

13:4 Gilgal. Saul responds to the crisis precipitated by Jonathan (v. 3), gathering the people at Gilgal in accordance with Samuel's instructions (10:8). Gilgal's situation in the Jordan Valley near Jericho placed it outside immediate Philistine control, making it a strategic site for a general muster. Gilgal had figured prominently in Israel's earlier history (Josh. 4:19, 20; 5:10; 9:6; 10:6–15, 43; 1 Sam. 7:16; 11:14).

13:7 all the people. These are the people summoned in v. 4, and not the troops already deployed in v. 2.

13:8 the time appointed by Samuel. Samuel had previously specified seven days (10:8).

13:9 burnt offering . . . peace offerings. See 10:8 note.

the burnt offering, behold, Samuel came.
And Saul went out to meet him and greet
him. **11** Samuel said, "What have you
done?" And Saul said, "When I saw that
the people were scattering from me, and
that you did not come within the days
appointed, and that the Philistines had
mustered at Michmash, **12** I said, 'Now the
Philistines will come down against me at
Gilgal, and I have not sought the favor of
the LORD.' So I forced myself, and offered
the burnt offering." **13** And Samuel said to
Saul, [t]"You have done foolishly. [u]You have
not kept the command of the LORD your
God, with which he commanded you. For
then the LORD would have established your
kingdom over Israel forever. **14** But now
[v]your kingdom shall not continue. The
LORD has sought out a man [w]after his own
heart, and the LORD has commanded him
to be prince over his people, because you
have not kept what the LORD commanded
you." **15** And Samuel arose and went up
from Gilgal. The rest of the people went
up after Saul to meet the army; they went
up from Gilgal[1] to [x]Gibeah of Benjamin.
And Saul numbered the people who
were present with him, [y]about six hundred
men. **16** And Saul and Jonathan his son and
the people who were present with them
stayed in [z]Geba of Benjamin, but the
Philistines encamped in Michmash. **17** And
[a]raiders came out of the camp of the
Philistines in three companies. One company turned toward Ophrah, to the land of
Shual; **18** another company turned toward
[b]Beth-horon; and another company turned
toward the border that looks down on the
valley of [c]Zeboim toward the wilderness.
19 [d]Now there was no blacksmith to be
found throughout all the land of Israel, for
the Philistines said, "Lest the Hebrews
make themselves swords or spears." **20** But
every one of the Israelites went down to the
Philistines to sharpen his plowshare, his
mattock, his axe, or his sickle,[2] **21** and the
charge was two-thirds of a shekel[3] for the
plowshares and for the mattocks, and a
third of a shekel[4] for sharpening the axes
and for setting the goads.[5] **22** So on the day
of the battle [e]there was neither sword nor
spear found in the hand of any of the people with Saul and Jonathan, but Saul and
Jonathan his son had them. **23** And [f]the garrison of the Philistines went out to the
[g]pass of [h]Michmash.

Jonathan Defeats the Philistines

14 One day Jonathan the son of Saul
said to the young man who carried
his armor, "Come, let us go over to the
Philistine garrison on the other side." But
he did not tell his father. **2** Saul was staying
in the outskirts of Gibeah in the pomegranate cave[6] at [h]Migron. The people who
were with him were about [i]six hundred
men, **3** including [j]Ahijah the son of Ahitub,

1 Septuagint; Hebrew lacks *The rest of the people . . . from Gilgal*
2 Septuagint; Hebrew *plowshare* 3 Hebrew *was a pim* 4 A *shekel* was about 2/5 ounce or 11 grams 5 The meaning of the Hebrew verse is uncertain 6 Or *under the pomegranate* [tree]

13 [t]2 Sam. 24:10; 1 Chr. 21:8; 2 Chr. 16:9 [u]ch. 15:11
14 [v]ch. 15:28 [w]Cited Acts 13:22
15 [x]ver. 2 [y]ch. 14:2
16 [z]ver. 3; ch. 14:5
17 [a]ch. 14:15
18 [b]See Josh. 10:10 [c]Neh. 11:34
19 [d][2 Kin. 24:14]
22 [e][Judg. 5:8]
23 [f]ch. 14:1, 4, 6, 11; 2 Sam. 23:14 [g]ch. 14:4, 5; Isai. 10:28, 29 [h]Isai. 10:28
Chapter 14
2 [h][See 13:23 above] [i]ch. 13:15
3 [j]ch. 22:9, 11, 20

13:11 What have you done. See note 2:27–36.

When I saw. From a purely human perspective Saul's excuses would seem to carry some weight. But they do not take into account the freedom of God to act on behalf of His people, as Jonathan's testimony in 14:6 confirms.

13:13 You have done foolishly. This Hebrew expression implies both intellectual and moral failure. For a similar confrontation between a prophet and a king, see 2 Chr. 16:7–9.

You have not kept the command. In this context, Saul had transgressed by offering sacrifices on his own authority.

13:14 your kingdom shall not continue. Saul's hopes of establishing a dynasty are dashed, though Saul himself will not yet be deposed (15:23).

a man after his own heart. The phrase might also be rendered "a man of His own choosing," placing the accent on the Lord's sovereign election. Nevertheless, in the light of passages such as 2:35 and 16:7, the text is also saying that the Lord's chosen one, David, was "after God's heart" in the sense of being committed to His will and purposes.

13:15 And Samuel arose. Because of Saul's foolish action, Samuel apparently departed without giving Saul any further instructions (10:8). The longer reading of the Septuagint (the early Greek translation of the Old Testament; see text note) is probably correct, suggesting that after Samuel's departure Saul rejoined Jonathan at Geba (v. 2 note; v. 16 note).

13:17 raiders came out . . . in three companies. Raiding parties would plunder and terrorize, as well as keep up military pressure by reconnoitering and controlling important routes.

13:19–21 The Israelites were short of weapons and depended on the Philistines even for making their tools. Archaeological evidence suggests that the Philistines learned how to work iron earlier than their neighbors.

13:22 with Saul and Jonathan. This notice pins the hopes of Israel on two people in particular, and the following chapter compares them to the disadvantage of Saul.

14:1 But he did not tell his father. Jonathan's decision not to tell his father of his daring plan may imply a lack of confidence in him (cf. Abigail's similar action in response to her husband Nabal in 25:19).

14:3 son of Ahitub, Ichabod's brother. The presence of a member of the rejected priestly house of Eli (2:30) in Saul's camp is a reminder of the recent rejection of Saul's own royal house (13:14).

wearing an ephod. The presence in Saul's camp of the ephod useful for seeking God's will (2:28 note) encourages the expectation that he will use it to ask the Lord's guidance, as David does later (23:9–12; 30:7–8). In this instance however, Saul leaves it to Jonathan to discover the Lord's will (v. 10 note). In v. 19 (note) Saul shows a lack of respect for the ephod; later he savagely turns against those whose task it is to oversee its care and use (22:18; cf. 21:9). In the end, Saul's efforts to discover the Lord's will are met with silence (28:6 note).

[k]Ichabod's brother, son of Phinehas, son of
Eli, the priest of the LORD [l]in Shiloh, [m]wear-
ing an ephod. And the people did not
know that Jonathan had gone. **4** Within
[n]the passes, by which Jonathan sought to
go over to the Philistine garrison, there was
a rocky crag on the one side and a rocky
crag on the other side. The name of the one
was Bozez, and the name of the other
Seneh. **5** The one crag rose on the north in
front of Michmash, and the other on the
south in front of [o]Geba.
6 Jonathan said to the young man who
carried his armor, "Come, let us go over to
the garrison of these [p]uncircumcised. It
may be that the LORD will work for us, [q]for
nothing can hinder the LORD from saving
by many or by few." **7** And his armor-bearer
said to him, "Do all that is in your heart.
Do as you wish.[1] Behold, I am with you
heart and soul." **8** Then Jonathan said,
"Behold, we will cross over to the men, and
we will show ourselves to them. **9** If they say
to us, 'Wait until we come to you,' then we
will stand still in our place, and we will not
go up to them. **10** But if they say, 'Come up
to us,' then we will go up, for the LORD has
given them into our hand. And this shall be
the sign to us." **11** So both of them showed
themselves to the garrison of the Philistines. And the Philistines said, "Look,
Hebrews are coming [r]out of the holes
where they have hidden themselves."
12 And the men of the garrison hailed
Jonathan and his armor-bearer and said,
"Come up to us, and we will show you a
thing." And Jonathan said to his armor-
bearer, "Come up after me, for the LORD
has given them into the hand of Israel."
13 Then Jonathan climbed up on his hands
and feet, and his armor-bearer after him.
And they fell before Jonathan, and his
armor-bearer killed them after him. **14** And
that first strike, which Jonathan and his
armor-bearer made, killed about twenty
men within as it were half a furrow's length
in an acre[2] of land. **15** And there was a panic
in the camp, in the field, and among all the
people. The garrison and even [s]the raiders
trembled, the earth quaked, and it became
a very great panic.
16 And the watchmen of Saul in Gibeah
of Benjamin looked, and behold, the multitude [t]was dispersing here and there.[3]
17 Then Saul said to the people who were
with him, "Count and see who has gone
from us." And when they had counted,
behold, Jonathan and his armor-bearer
were not there. **18** So Saul said to Ahijah,
"Bring the ark of God here." For the ark of
God went at that time with the people of
Israel.[4] **19** Now [u]while Saul was talking to
the priest, the tumult in the camp of the
Philistines increased more and more. So
Saul said to the priest, "Withdraw your
hand." **20** Then Saul and all the people who
were with him rallied and went into the
battle. And behold, [v]every Philistine's
sword was against his fellow, and there
was very great confusion. **21** Now the
Hebrews who had been with the
Philistines before that time and who had
gone up with them into the camp, [w]even
they also turned to be with the Israelites
who were with Saul and Jonathan.
22 Likewise, when all the men of Israel
[x]who had hidden themselves [y]in the hill
country of Ephraim heard that the
Philistines were fleeing, they too followed
hard after them in the battle. **23** [z]So the
LORD saved Israel that day. And the battle
passed beyond [a]Beth-aven.

1 Septuagint *Do all that your mind inclines to* 2 Hebrew *yoke*
3 Septuagint; Hebrew *they went here and there* 4 Hebrew; Septuagint *Bring the ephod. For at that time he wore the ephod before the people*

3 [k]ch. 4:21 [l]See Josh. 18:1 [m]ch. 2:28
4 [n]ch. 13:23
5 [o]ch. 13:3, 16
6 [p]ch. 17:26; Judg. 14:3 [q][Judg. 7:4, 7; 2 Chr. 14:11]
11 [r]ch. 13:6
15 [s]ch. 13:17
16 [t]Josh. 2:9
19 [u]Num. 27:21
20 [v][Judg. 7:22; 2 Chr. 20:23]
21 [w][ch. 29:4]
22 [x]ver. 11; ch. 13:6 [y]See Josh. 24:33
23 [z]Ex. 14:39 [a]ch. 13:5

14:4 Bozez . . . Seneh. These names possibly mean "slippery" and "thorny" and so dramatize the challenge facing Jonathan.

14:6 uncircumcised. The uncircumcised were people like the Philistines, who stood outside God's covenant (Gen. 17:14; Ex. 12:48; Judg. 14:3; 15:18).

nothing can hinder the LORD from saving. Compare David's confidence in 17:47. Although the narrator does not offer a criticism of Saul's excuse in 13:11 (that "the people were scattering," and so forth), Jonathan's bold confession makes an indirect commentary on the inadequacy of that excuse.

14:10 the sign to us. Jonathan is not willing to move ahead without the Lord's approval. In this regard he is more faithful than his father, who seems to show a declining commitment to obtaining divine guidance (13:8–15; 14:18, 19, 36 and notes).

14:11 Hebrews. See note 4:6.

14:18 ark of God. The Septuagint (early Greek translation of the Old Testament) reads "ephod" and is probably correct since the ephod was clearly present in Gibeah (v. 3 note) and was used to inquire of the Lord (2:28 note). The Hebrew reading, "ark," is doubtful because the ark was in Kiriath-jearim at this time (7:1, 2); the ark is never said to have been used as a means of divine omen; and to touch the ark (cf. v. 19) resulted in death (6:19; 2 Sam. 6:6, 7).

14:19 Withdraw your hand. In ordering the priest to let go of the instrument by which the will of the Lord could have been determined, Saul takes matters back into his own hands (cf. 13:9).

14:21 Hebrews. See note 4:6.

Saul's Rash Vow

24 And the men of Israel had been hard
pressed that day, [b]so Saul had laid an oath
on the people, saying, "Cursed be the man
who eats food until it is evening and I am
avenged on my enemies." So none of the
people had tasted food. 25 Now when all the
people[1] came to the forest, behold, there
was honey on the ground. 26 And when the
people entered the forest, behold, the
honey was dropping, but no one put his
hand to his mouth, for the people feared
the oath. 27 But Jonathan had not heard his
father charge the people with the oath, [c]so
he put out the tip of the staff that was in
his hand and dipped it in the honeycomb
and put his hand to his mouth, and his
eyes became bright. 28 Then one of the people said, "Your father strictly charged the
people with an oath, saying, 'Cursed be
the man who eats food this day.'" And the
people were [d]faint. 29 Then Jonathan said,
"My father has troubled the land. See how
my eyes have become bright because I tasted a little of this honey. 30 How much better if the people had eaten freely today of
the spoil of their enemies that they found.
For now the defeat among the Philistines
has not been great."

31 They struck down the Philistines that
day from [e]Michmash to [f]Aijalon. And the
people were very [d]faint. 32 The people
[g]pounced on the spoil and took sheep and
oxen and calves and slaughtered them
on the ground. And the people ate them
[h]with the blood. 33 Then they told Saul,
"Behold, the people are sinning against the
LORD by eating [h]with the blood." And he said,
"You have dealt treacherously; roll a great
stone to me here."[2] 34 And Saul said, "Disperse yourselves among the people and say
to them, 'Let every man bring his ox or his
sheep and slaughter them here and eat,
and do not sin against the LORD by eating
with the blood.'" So every one of the people brought his ox with him that night and
they slaughtered them there. 35 And Saul
[i]built an altar to the LORD; it was the first
altar that he built to the LORD.

36 Then Saul said, "Let us go down after
the Philistines by night and plunder them
until the morning light; let us not leave a
man of them." And they said, "Do whatever seems good to you." But [j]the priest said,
"Let us draw near to God here." 37 And Saul
inquired of God, "Shall I go down after the
Philistines? Will you give them into the
hand of Israel?" [k]But he did not answer
him that day. 38 And Saul said, "Come here,
all you leaders of the people, and know and
see how this sin has arisen today. 39 For [l]as
the LORD lives who saves Israel, [m]though it
be in Jonathan my son, he shall surely die."
But there was not a man among all the people who answered him. 40 Then he said to
all Israel, "You shall be on one side, and I
and Jonathan my son will be on the other
side." And the people said to Saul, "Do
what seems good to you." 41 Therefore Saul
said, "O LORD God of Israel, why[3] have you
not answered your servant this day? If this
guilt is in me or in Jonathan my son, O
LORD, God of Israel, give Urim. But if this
guilt is in your people Israel, give
Thummim." [n]And Jonathan and Saul were
taken, but the people escaped. 42 Then Saul
said, [n]"Cast the lot between me and my
son Jonathan." And Jonathan was taken.

43 Then Saul said to Jonathan, [o]"Tell me
what you have done." And Jonathan told
him, [p]"I tasted a little honey with the tip of
the staff that was in my hand. Here I am; I
will die." 44 And Saul said, [q]"God do so to
me and more also; [r]you shall surely die,

24 [b][Josh. 6:26]
27 [c]ver. 43
28 [d]Judg. 8:4, 5
31 [e]ch. 13:2 [f]Josh. 10:12 [d][See ver. 28 above]
32 [g]ch. 15:19 [h][Lev. 3:17]
33 [h][See ver. 32 above]
35 [i][ch. 7:12, 17]
36 [j]ver. 3, 18, 19
37 [k]ch. 28:6
39 [l]See Ruth 3:13 [m]ver. 44
41 [n][ch. 10:20, 21; Josh. 7:16-18; Acts 1:24-26]
42 [n][See ver. 41 above]
43 [o][Josh. 7:19] [p]ver. 27
44 [q]See Ruth 1:17 [r]ver. 39

1 Hebrew *land* 2 Septuagint; Hebrew *this day* 3 Vulgate (compare Septuagint); Hebrew *Saul said to the LORD, the God of Israel, "Why . . .*

14:24 had been hard pressed. This is an account of something that took place earlier the same day, that is, after Jonathan left to make an attack on the Philistines (vv. 13, 14) but before Saul joined the battle (v. 20).

14:27 But Jonathan had not heard. Probably Jonathan did not hear because he had left the camp before the oath was imposed (v. 24 note).

14:29 My father has troubled the land. The lack of confidence implicit in Jonathan's exclusion of his father from his plans (v. 1) now rises to an outright condemnation of his father's foolish action in binding the people under an oath. As in the case of Achan (Josh. 7:16–18, 25), a lot will be cast to uncover the guilty party, the "troubler" of the land. The lot reveals Jonathan as the one who violated the oath (v. 42), but the real troubler of Israel was Saul.

14:31 Aijalon. About fifteen miles west of Michmash in the Valley of Aijalon, the route the Philistines seem to have followed back to their homeland.

14:33 eating with the blood. Prohibitions against eating blood are recorded often in the Old Testament (Gen. 9:4; Lev. 3:17; 7:26, 27; 17:10, 12; 19:26; Deut. 15:23; Ezek. 33:25).

14:35 the first altar. This is also the only altar to be mentioned.

14:36 But the priest said. It is unusual that the priest, probably Ahijah (v. 3), should take the initiative. But this agrees with the pattern of Saul's declining commitment to obtaining the Lord's guidance (v. 10 note).

14:39 not a man . . . answered him. The people protected Jonathan.

Jonathan." 45 Then the people said to Saul,
"Shall Jonathan die, who has worked this
great salvation in Israel? Far from it! [l]As the
LORD lives, [s]there shall not one hair of his
head fall to the ground, for he has worked
with God this day." So the people ransomed
Jonathan, so that he did not die. 46 Then Saul
went up from pursuing the Philistines, and
the Philistines went to their own place.

Saul Fights Israel's Enemies

47 When Saul had taken the kingship over
Israel, he fought against all his enemies on
every side, against Moab, [t]against the Ammonites, against Edom, against the kings
of [u]Zobah, and against the Philistines.
Wherever he turned he routed them. 48 And
he did valiantly [v]and struck the Amalekites
and delivered Israel out of the hands of
those who plundered them.
49 [w]Now the sons of Saul were Jonathan,
Ishvi, and Malchi-shua. And the names of his
two daughters were these: the name of the
firstborn was [x]Merab, and the name of the
younger Michal. 50 And the name of Saul's
wife was Ahinoam the daughter of Ahimaaz.
[y]And the name of the commander of his
army was Abner the son of Ner, [z]Saul's
uncle. 51 [a]Kish was the father of Saul, and Ner
the father of Abner was the son of [a]Abiel.
52 There was hard fighting against the
Philistines all the days of Saul. And when
Saul saw any strong man, or any valiant
man, [b]he attached him to himself.

45 [l][See ver. 39 above] [s]2 Sam. 14:11; 1 Kin. 1:52; Luke 21:18; Acts 27:34; [Matt. 10:30; Luke 12:7]
47 [t]ch. 11:11 [u]2 Sam. 8:3; 10:6
48 [v]ch. 15:3, 7
49 [w][ch. 31:2; 2 Sam. 2:8-10; 1 Chr. 8:33; 9:39] [x]ch. 18:17, 19
50 [y]2 Sam. 2:8 [z][ch. 10:14]
51 [a]ch. 9:1
52 [b]ch. 8:11

Chapter 15
1 [c]ch. 9:16
2 [d]See Ex. 17:8-16; Deut. 25:17-19
3 [e]Lev. 27:28, 29; Josh. 6:17, 21 [f][ch. 22:19]
6 [g]ch. 27:10; Judg. 1:16 [h][Ex. 18:10, 19; Num. 10:29, 32]
7 [i]ch. 14:48 [j]Gen. 2:11; 25:18 [k]ch. 27:8; [Gen. 16:7; Ex. 15:22]
8 [l][ch. 27:8, 9; 30:1]
9 [m]ver. 15, 21; [ch. 28:18]

The LORD Rejects Saul

15 And Samuel said to Saul, [c]"The
LORD sent me to anoint you king
over his people Israel; now therefore listen
to the words of the LORD. 2 Thus says the
LORD of hosts, 'I have noted what Amalek
did to Israel [d]in opposing them on the way
when they came up out of Egypt. 3 Now go
and strike Amalek and [e]devote to destruction[1] all that they have. Do not spare them,
[f]but kill both man and woman, child and
infant, ox and sheep, camel and donkey.'"
4 So Saul summoned the people and numbered them in Telaim, two hundred thousand men on foot, and ten thousand men of
Judah. 5 And Saul came to the city of Amalek
and lay in wait in the valley. 6 Then Saul said
to [g]the Kenites, "Go, depart; go down from
among the Amalekites, lest I destroy you
with them. [h]For you showed kindness to all
the people of Israel when they came up out
of Egypt." So the Kenites departed from
among the Amalekites. 7 [i]And Saul defeated
the Amalekites from [j]Havilah as far as [k]Shur,
which is east of Egypt. 8 And he took Agag
the king of the Amalekites alive [l]and devoted to destruction all the people with the
edge of the sword. 9 [m]But Saul and the people spared Agag and the best of the sheep
and of the oxen and of the fattened calves[2]
and the lambs, and all that was good, and

1 That is, set apart (devote) as an offering to the Lord (for destruction); also verses 8, 9, 15, 18, 20, 21 2 The meaning of the Hebrew term is uncertain

14:45 Far from it. When forced by Saul's hardness (vv. 39, 44) to choose between Saul and Jonathan, the people choose Jonathan, whom they clearly recognize as the one the Lord used in the battle that day. Saul's foolish behavior has alienated him from everyone around him, even his own people. His isolation is not permanent, however, for Jonathan becomes his confidant again later (20:2), and the people show signs of renewed loyalty (23:19; 24:1). Even Samuel has further dealings with him (ch. 15).

14:47–51 This gives a summary of Saul's military accomplishments (vv. 47, 48) and details about his family and Abner's (vv. 49–51). A comparison of this section with the longer summary of David's victories and officers in 2 Sam. 8 reveals a number of similarities, but also a telling difference: nowhere in the summation of Saul is there anything akin to the statement repeated about David, that "the LORD gave victory to David wherever he went" (2 Sam. 8:6, 14).

14:52 hard fighting. See notes 7:13.

15:1 The LORD sent me to anoint you. Samuel mentions his role in anointing Saul to set the context for his continuing service as mediator of God's orders to Saul (10:1 note).

listen to the words of the LORD. The Hebrew word translated "listen" is repeated several times in this chapter, underscoring the central theme of obedience ("listen," "hear," "obey," and "voice," "bleating," "lowing" in vv. 1, 14, 19, 20, 22, 24).

15:2 Amalek. Descendants of Esau (according to Gen. 36:12, 16), the Amalekites were a nomadic desert people who lived in southern Judah and beyond, toward Egypt. They fought frequently with the Israelites.

15:3 devote to destruction. Lit. "place them under the ban." This meant to devote persons or things completely to the Lord. In war it usually required the total destruction of properties and execution of people. The inclusion of animals in this verse is especially striking. The ban was an element of "holy war" and could not be decreed by anyone but God.

man and woman, child and infant. See 22:19 and note.

15:4 Telaim. This is probably the Telem listed in Josh. 15:24 as one of the cities of Judah. The Septuagint (early Greek translation of the Old Testament) has Gilgal instead, which some have suggested was the site of Samuel's instructions to Saul (vv. 1–3).

15:6 For you showed kindness. Perhaps an allusion to the kindness of Moses' Kenite father-in-law (Judg. 1:16) recorded in Ex. 18.

15:7 from Havilah . . . Shur. See Gen. 25:18. Shur is mentioned in 27:8 as lying at the frontiers of the territory of the Amalekites, near the eastern border of Egypt. The location of Havilah remains uncertain, but the general sense of the reference is that Saul's victory was extensive.

15:8 Agag. This is either a personal name or a title, like "Pharaoh"; see Num. 24:7; "Agagite" in Esth. 3:1.

all the people. This is not "all" without exception, but all who fell into Saul's hands (there are later references to Amalekites in 27:8; 30:1, 18). For this limited sense of "all," cf. 13:7; 31:6.

15:9 Saul and the people spared. They went against the Lord's

would not utterly destroy them. All that was
despised and worthless they devoted to
destruction.
10 The word of the LORD came to
Samuel: 11 [n]"I regret that I have made Saul
king, for he has turned back from following me and [o]has not performed my commandments." And Samuel was angry, and
he cried to the LORD all night. 12 And
Samuel rose early to meet Saul in the
morning. And it was told Samuel, "Saul
came to [p]Carmel, and behold, he set up a
monument for himself and turned and
passed on and went down to Gilgal."
13 And Samuel came to Saul, and Saul said
to him, [q]"Blessed be you to the LORD. I
have performed the commandment of the
LORD." 14 And Samuel said, "What then is
this bleating of the sheep in my ears and
the lowing of the oxen that I hear?" 15 Saul
said, "They have brought them from the
Amalekites, [r]for the people spared the
best of the sheep and of the oxen to sacrifice to the LORD your God, and the rest we
have devoted to destruction." 16 Then
Samuel said to Saul, "Stop! I will tell you
what the LORD said to me this night." And
he said to him, "Speak."
17 And Samuel said, [s]"Though you are little in your own eyes, are you not the head
of the tribes of Israel? The LORD anointed
you king over Israel. 18 And the LORD sent
you on a mission and said, 'Go, devote to
destruction the sinners, the Amalekites,
and fight against them until they are consumed.' 19 Why then did you not obey the
voice of the LORD? [t]Why did you pounce on
the spoil and do what was evil in the sight
of the LORD?" 20 And Saul said to Samuel,
[u]"I have obeyed the voice of the LORD. I
have gone on the mission on which the
LORD sent me. I have brought Agag the king
of Amalek, and I have devoted the Amalekites to destruction. 21 [v]But the people
took of the spoil, sheep and oxen, the best
of the things devoted to destruction, to
sacrifice to the LORD your God in Gilgal."
22 And Samuel said,

> [w]"Has the LORD as great delight in
> burnt offerings and sacrifices,
> as in obeying the voice of the LORD?
> Behold, [x]to obey is better than
> sacrifice,
> and to listen than the fat of rams.
> 23 For rebellion is as the sin of
> divination,
> and presumption is as iniquity and
> [y]idolatry.
> Because [z]you have rejected the word
> of the LORD,
> [a]he has also rejected you from
> being king."

11 [n]ver. 35; [ver. 29]; See Gen. 6:6 [o]ver. 3, 9; [ch. 13:13] 12 [p]Josh. 15:55 13 [q]See Ruth 2:20 15 [r]ver. 9, 21 17 [s][ch. 9:21]
19 [t]ch. 14:32 20 [u]ver. 13 21 [v]ver. 15 22 [w]Ps. 40:6-8; 50:8, 9; Prov. 21:3; Isai. 1:11-13, 16, 17; Jer 7:22, 23. Mic. 6:6-8; Heb. 10:6-9 [x]Eccles. 5:1; Hos. 6:6; Matt. 9:13; 12:7; Mark 12:33 23 [y]See Gen. 31:19, 34 [z]ver. 26 [a]ch. 13:14

command (v. 3). A desire to profit from the victory may underlie the unwillingness to destroy anything that was good. Achan kept back goods that were devoted to destruction, apparently because he was greedy (Josh. 7:1). The reader is not told Saul's motive for sparing Agag, whether political, like Ahab's mercy to Ben-hadad (1 Kin. 20:30–34), or pride, a desire to parade his captive as a trophy of war. Saul did set up a victory monument "for himself" (v. 12).

15:11 I regret. See note on v. 29.

turned back. This is a serious indictment in view of 12:14, where obedience and following the Lord are named as the essential requirements for a successful reign.

Samuel was angry. The same Hebrew expression is used in 18:8 and 2 Sam. 6:8.

he cried to the LORD all night. Clearly Samuel takes no pleasure in Saul's rejection (v. 35; 16:1).

15:12 Carmel. About seven miles south of Hebron (25:2; Josh. 15:55). This is not the Mount Carmel in the north.

monument for himself. The closest parallel is in 2 Sam. 18:18, where Absalom erects a pillar "for himself" to commemorate his name.

15:14–23 These verses display the standard features of a prophetic judgment speech to an individual (2:27–36 note), but in this instance the accused, Saul, vigorously contests the charges.

15:15 They have brought them . . . to sacrifice. In response to Samuel's accusation Saul offers two excuses: First, the people are responsible and not he; second, the animals will be killed as sacrifices. Samuel will answer these excuses.

15:17 little in your own eyes. Whatever ideas Saul had about his role as king, Samuel rejects his attempt to avoid personal responsibility for what had happened.

15:19 pounce on the spoil. Samuel rejects Saul's claim that the animals were spared because they were needed for sacrifice. On the verb translated "pounce," see 25:14 note.

15:20, 21 Ignoring Samuel's refusal to accept his excuses, Saul repeats them adamantly.

15:22, 23 The poetic form of these two verses highlights their climactic importance in the episode.

15:22 burnt offerings. See note 10:8.

to obey is better than sacrifice. Although Samuel clearly disbelieves Saul's excuse (v. 19 note), he accepts it for the sake of argument, and makes the point that ritual performance is worthless when not accompanied by a sincere and submissive spirit. For similar denunciations of empty ritual by Israel's later prophets, see Is. 1:10–17; Jer. 6:19, 20; 7:21–26; Hos. 6:6; Amos 5:21–24; Mic. 6:6–8; also Ps. 51:16, 17; Prov. 15:8; 21:3, 27.

15:23 rebellion . . . divination . . . idolatry. Witchcraft and idolatry were especially serious sins.

Because you have rejected . . . he has also rejected. As Samuel comes to the announcement of judgment upon Saul, he expresses it in a manner that makes plain the justice of God's verdict. Offense and punishment correspond (2:27–36 note). While Saul's failure in ch. 13 meant the end of any hopes for his dynasty (13:14), his disobedience in the present context means the end of his personal right to be king. The next chapter recounts the anointing of David and the departure of the Spirit of the Lord from Saul (16:13, 14).

24 Saul said to Samuel, [b]"I have sinned,
for I have transgressed the commandment
of the LORD and your words, because I
feared the people and obeyed their voice.
25 Now therefore, please pardon my sin and
[c]return with me that I may worship the
LORD." **26** And Samuel said to Saul, "I will
not return with you. [d]For you have rejected
the word of the LORD, [e]and the LORD has
rejected you from being king over Israel."
27 [f]As Samuel turned to go away, Saul seized
the skirt of his robe, and it tore. **28** And
Samuel said to him, [g]"The LORD has torn
the kingdom of Israel from you this day
and has given it to a neighbor of yours,
who is better than you. **29** And also the
Glory of Israel [h]will not lie or have regret,
for he is not a man, that he should have
regret." **30** Then he said, "I have sinned; yet
[i]honor me now before the elders of my
people and before Israel, [j]and return with
me, that I may bow before the LORD your
God." **31** So Samuel turned back after Saul,
and Saul bowed before the LORD.
32 Then Samuel said, "Bring here to me
Agag the king of the Amalekites." And Agag
came to him cheerfully.[1] Agag said, "Surely
the bitterness of death is past." **33** And
Samuel said, [k]"As your sword has made
women childless, so shall your mother be
childless among women." And Samuel
hacked Agag to pieces before the LORD [l]in
Gilgal.
34 Then Samuel went [m]to Ramah, and
Saul went up to his house in [n]Gibeah of
Saul. **35** [o]And Samuel did not see Saul again
until the day of his death, [p]but Samuel
grieved over Saul. [q]And the LORD regretted
that he had made Saul king over Israel.

David Anointed King

16 The LORD said to Samuel, [r]"How
long will you grieve over Saul, since
[s]I have rejected him from being king over
Israel? [t]Fill your horn with oil, and go. I
will send you to Jesse the Bethlehemite,
[u]for I have provided for myself a king
among his sons." **2** And Samuel said, "How
can I go? If Saul hears it, he will kill me."
And the LORD said, "Take a heifer with you
and say, [v]'I have come to sacrifice to the
LORD.' **3** And invite Jesse to the sacrifice, and
I will show you what you shall do. [w]And
you shall anoint for me him whom I declare
to you." **4** Samuel did what the LORD commanded and came to Bethlehem. The elders of the city [x]came to meet him trembling and said, [y]"Do you come peaceably?"
5 And he said, "Peaceably; I have come to sacrifice to the LORD. [z]Consecrate yourselves,
and come with me to the sacrifice." And he

1 Or *haltingly* (compare Septuagint); the Hebrew is uncertain

24 [b][2 Sam. 12:13]
25 [c]ver. 30
26 [d]ver. 23 [e]ch. 16:1
27 [f][1 Kin. 11:30, 31]
28 [g]ch. 28:17, 18
29 [h]Num. 23:19; [Ezek. 24:14]
30 [i][John 5:44; 12:43] [j]ver. 25
33 [k][Judg. 1:7] [l]ver. 12, 21
34 [m][ch. 1:19] [n]ch. 11:4
35 [o][ch. 19:24] [p]ch. 16:1 [q]ver. 11
Chapter 16
1 [r]ch. 15:35 [s]ch. 15:23, 26 [t]See ch. 10:1 [u]Ps. 78:70; 89:19, 20; Acts 13:22
2 [v][ch. 9:12; 26:29]
3 [w]ch. 9:16
4 [x]ch. 21:1 [y]1 Kin. 2:13; [2 Kin. 9:22]
5 [z]Josh. 3:5

15:24, 25 At last Saul begins to accept responsibility ("I have sinned"), though he still blames the people for initiating the unfortunate events ("I feared the people and obeyed their voice"). On the surface, Saul's confession sounds adequate, but against the background of Samuel's warnings in 12:14, 15, his admissions lead not so much to a possibility that there will be reconciliation as to the certainty that he will be "swept away" (12:25). Saul will offer a second, more candid confession in v. 30.

15:26 I will not return with you. Samuel's refusal to return with Saul suggests Samuel is not satisfied with the sincerity of the confession as a whole (v. 30 note).

15:28 torn the kingdom. Samuel seizes upon the tearing of the robe as a fitting symbol of the Lord's having "torn the kingdom" from Saul (cf. 24:4, 5; 1 Kin. 11:29–33).

15:29 will not lie or have regret. Saul's rejection is final, and no attempt to mitigate its consequences will avail. There is no contradiction between this statement and the notices in vv. 11 and 35 that the Lord "regretted" having made Saul king. As in Num. 23:19, the point is that when the Lord makes a pronouncement intended to be final, He cannot be talked out of it.

15:30 honor me. Saul's real concern becomes clear in this his second confession (cf. vv. 24, 25 and note). As Samuel seems already to suspect (v. 26 note), Saul is less concerned with being reconciled to the Lord than with finding honor before the elders of "my people." In return for this honor, Saul offers to do obeisance before the Lord "your" God.

15:31 Samuel turned back. Several reasons for Samuel's reversal of his earlier decision (v. 26) may be suggested: (a) Saul has at last issued a candid confession; (b) there is no danger after vv. 28, 29 that Saul might interpret Samuel's actions as a retraction of his judgment; (c) Samuel must still deal with Agag.

15:35 Samuel grieved over Saul. See note on v. 11.

16:1–31:13 These chapters narrate David's rise to power and Saul's fall from power and his death. David's rise is marked by his anointing by Samuel and his time in Saul's service (chs. 16–18), his flight from Saul (chs. 19–23), his avoidance of bloodguilt (chs. 24–26), and his escape to the Philistines (chs. 27–31).

16:1 Bethlehemite. First mentioned in Gen. 35:19, Bethlehem is David's hometown (17:12, 15). On the significance of this site for the Messiah ("the anointed one"), see Mic. 5:2; Matt. 2:5, 6; John 7:42.

I have provided for myself. The selection of a king for "myself" (the Lord), contrasts with the choice of a king for "them" (the people) in 8:22 (8:18; 12:13).

16:2 I have come to sacrifice. While true insofar as it goes, this statement does not disclose the real reason for Samuel's journey to Bethlehem (v. 1). There may well be an ironic tone in the Lord's instruction to Samuel, coming as it does on the heels of Saul's claim to have spared animals only "to sacrifice" them (15:15, 21). Cases of deception like this one must be weighed in their particular circumstances (20:6; 21:2; 27:10; 2 Sam. 16:17–19; Josh. 2:4 and notes).

16:3 anoint. See note 2:10.

16:4 the elders of the city . . . trembling. See the similar response of Ahimelech upon David's arrival alone in Nob (21:1). No reason is given for the elders' trembling. It probably has to do with Samuel's prophetic function as an instrument of God's judgment.

consecrated Jesse and his sons and invited
them to the sacrifice.
6 When they came, he looked on [a]Eliab
and thought, "Surely the LORD's anointed is
before him." 7 But the LORD said to Samuel,
[b]"Do not look on his appearance or on the
height of his stature, because I have rejected him. For the LORD sees not as man sees:
man looks on the outward appearance, [c]but
the LORD looks on the heart." 8 Then Jesse
called [d]Abinadab and made him pass before
Samuel. And he said, "Neither has the LORD
chosen this one." 9 Then Jesse made
[d]Shammah pass by. And he said, "Neither
has the LORD chosen this one." 10 And Jesse
made seven of his sons pass before Samuel.
And Samuel said to Jesse, "The LORD has
not chosen these." 11 Then Samuel said to
Jesse, "Are all your sons here?" And he said,
[e]"There remains yet the youngest,[1] but
behold, he is keeping the sheep." And
Samuel said to Jesse, [f]"Send and get him,
for we will not sit down till he comes here."
12 And he sent and brought him in. Now he
was [g]ruddy and had beautiful eyes and was
handsome. And the LORD said, [h]"Arise,
anoint him, for this is he." 13 Then Samuel
took [i]the horn of oil [j]and anointed him in
the midst of his brothers. [k]And the Spirit of
the LORD rushed upon David from that day
forward. And Samuel rose up and went to
Ramah.

David in Saul's Service

14 [l]Now the Spirit of the LORD departed
from Saul, [m]and an evil[2] spirit from the
LORD tormented him. 15 And Saul's servants
said to him, "Behold now, an evil spirit
from God is tormenting you. 16 Let our lord
now command your servants [n]who are
before you to seek out a man who is skillful
in playing the lyre, and when the evil spirit
from God is upon you, he will [o]play it, and
you will be well." 17 So Saul said to his servants, "Provide for me a man who can play
well and bring him to me." 18 One of the
young men answered, "Behold, I have seen
a son of Jesse the Bethlehemite, who is skillful in playing, [p]a man of valor, a man of
war, prudent in speech, and a man of good
presence, [q]and the LORD is with him."
19 Therefore Saul sent messengers to Jesse
and said, "Send me David your son, [r]who is
with the sheep." 20 [s]And Jesse took a donkey
laden with bread and a skin of wine and a
young goat and sent them by David his son
to Saul. 21 And David came to Saul [t]and
entered his service. And Saul loved him
greatly, and he became his armor-bearer.
22 And Saul sent to Jesse, saying, "Let David
remain in my service, for he has found favor
in my sight." 23 And [u]whenever the evil spirit from God was upon Saul, David took the
lyre [o]and played it with his hand. So Saul
was refreshed and was well, and the evil
spirit departed from him.

David and Goliath

17 Now the Philistines [v]gathered their
armies for battle. And they were
gathered at [w]Socoh, which belongs to
Judah, and encamped between Socoh and

6 [a]ch. 17:13
7 [b]Ps. 147:10, 11 [c]1 Kin. 8:39; 1 Chr. 28:9; Ps. 7:9; Jer. 11:20; 17:10; 20:12; [Acts 1:24]
8 [d]ch. 17:13
9 [d][See ver. 8 above]
11 [e]ch. 17:13; [2 Sam. 13:3; 1 Chr. 2:13] [f][2 Sam. 7:8; Ps. 78:70, 71]
12 [g]ch. 17:42 [h][ch. 9:17]
13 [i]ver. 1 [j][ch. 10:1; Ps. 89:20] [k]ch. 10:6, 10; 11:6; See Judg. 3:10
14 [l]ch. 18:12; 28:15, 16; [Judg. 16:20] [m]ch. 18:10; 19:9; [Judg. 9:23]
16 [n]ver. 21, 22; 1 Kin. 10:8 [o]ch. 18:10; 19:9; [2 Kin. 3:15]
18 [p]See ch. 17:32, 34-36 [q]ch. 3:19; 18:12, 14
19 [r]ver. 11; ch. 17:15, 34
20 [s][ch. 10:27; 17:18]
21 [t]See ver. 16
23 [u]ver. 14, 16 [o][See ver. 16 above]
Chapter 17
1 [v]ch. 13:5 [w]Josh. 15:35

[1] Or *smallest* [2] Or *a harmful*; also verses 15, 16, 23

16:7 stature, because I have rejected him. The reference to "stature" as a false measure of an individual's qualification to be king, along with the notice that this son of Jesse is "rejected," is reminiscent of Saul, who was notable for his height (9:2; 10:23) but was rejected (15:23, 26).

the LORD looks on the heart. It is an axiom that God's standards are inward, not outward (13:14 note; Rom. 2:28, 29). See "God Sees and Knows: Divine Omniscience" at Prov. 15:3.

16:13 in the midst of his brothers. It is likely that the elders also witnessed David's being anointed (vv. 4, 5). The emphasis on the brothers being present at the event may shed light on Eliab's behavior in 17:28.

Spirit of the LORD rushed upon David. See notes 10:6; 11:6. David's endowment with the Spirit "from that day forward" sets him apart from Saul (and also Samson) upon whom the Spirit descended only sporadically.

16:14 Spirit of the LORD departed from Saul. The empowering and validating presence of God's Spirit must have been removed from Saul at his definitive rejection as king in ch. 15 (cf. also v. 1).

evil spirit. Cf. 1 Kin. 22:21–23. The Hebrew word may describe something that is troubling, annoying, or harmful.

16:18 man of war. This speech may seem to conflict with Saul's statement in 17:33 that David, who is but a youth, will be no match for Goliath. In response one can say that the servant's recommendation of David is doubtless exaggerated, like a modern letter of reference. Saul for his part was comparing David to Goliath and was reluctant to take the risk of sending anyone against the Philistine giant.

the LORD is with him. This fact more than any human quality will account for David's persistent, if circuitous, rise to power, while Saul's increasing recognition that David is preferred to him will play no small part in his own psychological disintegration (3:19; 17:37; 18:12, 28, 29; 20:13; 2 Sam. 7:9 and notes).

16:19 Send me David your son, who is with the sheep. Saul unwittingly invites his eventual replacement to enter his court. David's rise to power is providentially directed, and is not the result of human effort or grasping for power.

16:21 Saul loved him greatly. Note Jonathan's response to David (18:1, 3; 20:17), as well as that of Michal (18:20, 28), the people (18:16), and possibly even Saul's other servants (18:22).

17:1 between Socoh and Azekah, in Ephes-dammim. Socoh was fifteen miles west of Bethlehem, near the Philistine border, and Azekah was two miles northwest of Socoh.

[x]Azekah, in [y]Ephes-dammim. **2** And Saul
and the men of Israel were gathered, and
encamped in [z]the Valley of Elah, and drew
up in line of battle against the Philistines.
3 And the Philistines stood on the mountain on the one side, and Israel stood on
the mountain on the other side, with a valley between them. **4** And there came out
from the camp of the Philistines a champion named [a]Goliath of [b]Gath, whose height
was six[1] cubits and a span. **5** He had a helmet of bronze on his head, and he was
armed with a coat of mail, and the weight
of the coat was five thousand shekels[2] of
bronze. **6** And he had bronze armor on his
legs, and a [c]javelin of bronze slung between
his shoulders. **7** The shaft of his spear was
like a weaver's beam, and his spear's head
weighed six hundred shekels of iron. [d]And
his shield-bearer went before him. **8** He
stood and shouted to the ranks of Israel,
"Why have you come out to draw up for
battle? Am I not a Philistine, and [e]are you
not servants of Saul? Choose a man for
yourselves, and let him come down to me.
9 If he is able to fight with me and kill me,
then we will be your servants. But if I prevail against him and kill him, then you
shall be our servants [f]and serve us." **10** And
the Philistine said, [g]"I defy the ranks of
Israel this day. Give me a man, that we may
fight together." **11** When Saul and all Israel
heard these words of the Philistine, they
were dismayed and greatly afraid.

12 Now David was [h]the son of an
[i]Ephrathite of Bethlehem in Judah, [j]named
Jesse, [k]who had eight sons. In the days of
Saul the man was already old and advanced
in years.[3] **13** The three oldest sons of Jesse
had followed Saul to the battle. And [l]the
names of his three sons who went to the
battle were Eliab the firstborn, and next to
him Abinadab, and the third Shammah.
14 [m]David was the youngest. The three eldest followed Saul, **15** but David went back
and forth from Saul [n]to feed his father's
sheep at Bethlehem. **16** For forty days the
Philistine came forward and took his stand,
morning and evening.

17 And Jesse said to David his son, "Take
for your brothers an ephah[4] of this parched
grain, and these ten loaves, and carry them
quickly to the camp to your brothers.
18 [o]Also take these ten cheeses to the commander of their thousand. [p]See if your
brothers are well, and bring some token
from them."

19 Now Saul and they and all the men of
Israel were in the valley of Elah, fighting
with the Philistines. **20** And David rose early
in the morning and left the sheep with a
keeper and took the provisions and went,
as Jesse had commanded him. And he
came to [q]the encampment as the host was
going out to the battle line, shouting the
war cry. **21** And Israel and the Philistines
drew up for battle, army against army.
22 And David left the [r]things in charge of
the keeper of the [r]baggage and ran to the
ranks and went and greeted his brothers.
23 As he talked with them, behold, [s]the
champion, the Philistine of Gath, Goliath
by name, came up out of the ranks of the
Philistines and spoke [t]the same words as
before. And David heard him.

24 All the men of Israel, when they saw
the man, fled from him and were much
afraid. **25** And the men of Israel said, "Have
you seen this man who has come up?
Surely he has come up to [u]defy Israel. And
the king will enrich the man who kills him
with great riches [v]and will give him his
daughter and make his father's house free
in Israel." **26** And David said to the men

1 [x]Josh. 10:10; Neh. 11:30 [y][1 Chr. 11:13]
2 [z]ver. 19; ch. 21:9
4 [a][2 Sam. 21:19; 1 Chr. 20:4] [b]ch. 21:10; Josh. 11:22; 13:3
6 [c]ver. 45
7 [d]ver. 41
8 [e]ch. 8:17
9 [f][ch. 11:1]
10 [g]ver. 25, 26, 36, 45; [2 Sam. 21:21]
12 [h]ver. 58; ch. 16:1, 18; Ruth 4:22 [i]Gen. 35:19 [j]ver. 58; ch. 16:1, 18 [k]ch. 16:10, 11; [1 Chr. 2:13-15]
13 [l]ch. 16:6, 8, 9; [1 Chr. 2:13]
14 [m]ch. 16:11
15 [n]ch. 16:19
18 [o][ch. 16:20] [p][Gen. 37:14]
20 [q]ch. 26:5, 7
22 [r]Isai. 10:28; Acts 21:15
23 [s]ver. 4 [t]ver. 8
25 [u]ver. 10, 36, 45 [v][Josh. 15:16]

1 Hebrew; Septuagint, Dead Sea Scroll and Josephus *four* 2 A *shekel* was about 2/5 ounce or 11 grams 3 Septuagint, Syriac; Hebrew *among men* 4 An *ephah* was about 3/5 bushel or 22 liters

17:2 Valley of Elah. The valley descends from east to west, passing just north of Socoh and Azekah.

17:4 champion. Trial by single combat, where the outcome of a fight to the death between two champions is taken as the will of the gods, is rare in the Old Testament (compare 2 Sam. 2:14–16). It is well attested, however, among some of Israel's neighbors.

six cubits and a span. That is, nine feet, nine inches. The Septuagint (Greek Old Testament translation), Dead Sea Scrolls, and Josephus (*Antiquities* 6.9.1) all have four cubits instead of six, making Goliath six and a half feet tall, still a remarkable height by ancient standards.

17:5–7 The detailed description of Goliath's armor and weapons is striking. David does not have to trust in equipment (vv. 39, 50).

17:11 Saul. The Philistine challenge to the "servants of Saul" had been to "choose a man" (v. 8). The logical choice would have been Saul (9:2; 10:23, 24), but he was terrified like everyone else.

17:12 Ephrathite. See Gen. 35:19; 48:7; Ruth 1:2; 4:11; 1 Chr. 4:4; Mic. 5:2.

17:15 David went back and forth from Saul. David's time was split between duties to his king (16:21–23) and to his father. David's whole family is introduced with him (vv. 12–14).

17:25 give him his daughter. See notes 18:17–19, 20–27.

who stood by him, "What shall be done for
the man who kills this Philistine and takes
away [w]the reproach from Israel? For who is
this [x]uncircumcised Philistine, that he
should [u]defy the armies of [y]the living
God?" 27 And the people answered him in
the same way, [z]"So shall it be done to the
man who kills him."

28 Now Eliab his eldest brother heard
when he spoke to the men. And Eliab's
anger was kindled against David, and he
said, "Why have you come down? And
with whom have you left those few sheep
in the wilderness? I know your presumption and the evil of your heart, for you have
come down to see the battle." 29 And David
said, "What have I done now? [a]Was it not
but a word?" 30 And he turned away from
him toward another, and spoke [b]in the
same way, and the people answered him
again as before.

31 When the words that David spoke were
heard, they repeated them before Saul, and
he sent for him. 32 And David said to Saul,
[c]"Let no man's heart fail because of him.
[d]Your servant will go and fight with this
Philistine." 33 And Saul said to David, "You
are not able to go against this Philistine to
fight with him, for you are but a youth, and
he has been a man of war from his youth."
34 But David said to Saul, "Your servant
used to keep sheep for his father. And
when there came a lion, or a bear, and took
a lamb from the flock, 35 I went after him
and struck him and delivered it out of his
mouth. And if he arose against me, I
caught him by his beard and struck him
and killed him. 36 Your servant has struck
down both lions and bears, and this
uncircumcised Philistine shall be like one
of them, [e]for he has defied the armies of
the living God." 37 And David said, [f]"The
LORD who delivered me from the paw of
the lion and from the paw of the bear will
deliver me from the hand of this
Philistine." And Saul said to David, "Go,
[g]and the LORD be with you!"

38 Then Saul clothed David with his
armor. He put a helmet of bronze on his
head and clothed him with a coat of mail,
39 and David strapped his sword over his
armor. And he tried in vain to go, for he
had not tested them. Then David said to
Saul, "I cannot go with these, for I have not
tested them." So David put them off.
40 Then he took his staff in his hand and
chose five smooth stones from the brook
and put them in his shepherd's pouch. His
sling was in his hand, and he approached
the Philistine.

41 And the Philistine moved forward and
came near to David, [h]with his shield-bearer
in front of him. 42 And when the Philistine
looked and saw David, he disdained him,
for he was but a youth, [i]ruddy and handsome in appearance. 43 And the Philistine
said to David, "Am I [j]a dog, that you come
to me with sticks?" And the Philistine
cursed David by his gods. 44 The Philistine
said to David, "Come to me, and I will give
your flesh [k]to the birds of the air and to the
beasts of the field." 45 Then David said to
the Philistine, "You come to me with a
sword and with a spear and with [l]a javelin,
but I come to you in the name of the LORD
of hosts, the God of the armies of Israel,
[e]whom you have defied. 46 This day the
LORD will deliver you into my hand, and I

26 [w]ch. 11:2 [x]See Judg. 14:3 [u][See ver. 25 above] [y]Deut. 5:26; Josh. 3:10
27 [z]ver. 25
29 [a]ver. 17
30 [b]ver. 26, 27
32 [c][Deut. 20:3] [d][ch. 16:18]

36 [e]ver. 10, 26
37 [f][2 Tim. 4:17] [g][ch. 20:13; 1 Chr. 22:11, 16]
41 [h]ver. 7
42 [i]ch. 16:12
43 [j]ch. 24:14; 2 Sam. 3:8; 9:8; 16:9; 2 Kin. 8:13
44 [k]ver. 46
45 [l]ver. 6 [e][See ver. 36 above]

17:26 uncircumcised Philistine. See note 14:6.

17:28 Eliab's anger was kindled. Eliab's sudden anger is the reaction of a man who was unable to meet a challenge and who resented being outdone by his little brother. David's having been anointed would only increase Eliab's jealousy. In Genesis 37, Joseph's older brothers react in the same way to the knowledge that he would one day be superior to them (Gen. 37:2–19).

with whom have you left those few sheep. Whatever his excitement about the battle, David had acted responsibly in regard to his more mundane duties (vv. 20, 22).

your presumption. Or, "your insolence."

the evil of your heart. Contrast Eliab's judgment of David with God's, as indicated by statements like "a man after his own heart" (13:14), and "the LORD looks on the heart" (16:7).

17:33–37 The conversation between Saul and David vividly illustrates the radical difference in perspective between them. Saul continues to think in terms of what is humanly possible ("You are not able," v. 33), while David is confident that "The LORD . . . will deliver me" (v. 37).

17:36 uncircumcised Philistine. See 14:6 note.

17:37 the LORD be with you. David's rise to power continues to be furthered, if unwittingly, by Saul. Having brought him into his court (16:19 note), Saul now sends him out to fight his battle. Most ironic of all, Saul invokes over David the benediction that most clearly distinguishes them and will account for David's ultimate success—"the LORD be with you" (16:18 and note).

17:38, 39 David's rejection of Saul's armor and weapons supports the point of the narrative that "the LORD saves not with sword and spear. For the battle is the LORD's" (v. 47).

17:45 in the name of the LORD of hosts. See note 1:3. David comes "in the name" of God, that is, by the authority and power of God. On the significance of God's name as expressing His character, see, for example, Ex. 34:5–7.

17:46 dead bodies . . . of the Philistines. David outdoes Goliath's threat (v. 44) by extending his counterthreat to encompass the entire Philistine army.

will strike you down and cut off your head.
[m]And I will give the dead bodies of the host
of the Philistines this day [n]to the birds of
the air and to the wild beasts of the earth,
[o]that all the earth may know that there is a
God in Israel, 47 and that all this assembly
may know that [p]the LORD saves not with
sword and spear. [q]For the battle is the
LORD's, and he will give you into our
hand."
48 When the Philistine arose and came
and drew near to meet David, David ran
quickly toward the battle line to meet the
Philistine. 49 And David put his hand in his
bag and took out a stone and slung it and
struck the Philistine on his forehead. The
stone sank into his forehead, and he fell on
his face to the ground.
50 So David prevailed over the Philistine
with a sling and with a stone, and struck
the Philistine and killed him. There was no
sword in the hand of David. 51 Then David
ran and stood over the Philistine [r]and took
his sword and drew it out of its sheath and
killed him and cut off his head with it.
When the Philistines saw that their champion was dead, [s]they fled. 52 And the men
of Israel and Judah rose with a shout and
pursued the Philistines as far as Gath[1] and
the gates of [t]Ekron, so that the wounded
Philistines fell on the way from [u]Shaaraim
as far as [v]Gath and Ekron. 53 And the people of Israel came back from chasing the
Philistines, and they plundered their camp.
54 And David took [w]the head of the
Philistine [x]and brought it to Jerusalem, but
he put his armor in his tent.
55 As soon as Saul saw David go out
against the Philistine, he said to Abner,
[y]the commander of the army, "Abner,
[z]whose son is this youth?" And Abner said,
[a]"As your soul lives, O king, I do not
know." 56 And the king said, "Inquire
whose son the boy is." 57 And as soon as
David returned from the striking down of
the Philistine, Abner took him, and
brought him before Saul [b]with the head of
the Philistine in his hand. 58 And Saul said
to him, "Whose son are you, young man?"
And David answered, [c]"I am the son of
your servant Jesse the Bethlehemite."

David and Jonathan's Friendship

18 As soon as he had finished speaking
to Saul, the soul of Jonathan was
knit to the soul of David, and Jonathan
[d]loved him as his own soul. 2 And Saul took
him that day [e]and would not let him return
to his father's house. 3 Then Jonathan made
a covenant with David, because [d]he loved
him as his own soul. 4 And Jonathan
stripped himself of the robe that was on
him and gave it to David, and his armor,
and even his sword and his bow and his
belt. 5 And David went out [f]and was successful wherever Saul sent him, so that
Saul set him over the men of war. And this
was good in the sight of all the people and
also in the sight of Saul's servants.

Saul's Jealousy of David

6 As they were coming home, when David
returned from striking down the Philistine,
[g]the women came out of all the cities of
Israel, singing and dancing, to meet King
Saul, with tambourines, with songs of joy,

[1] Septuagint; Hebrew *Gai*

46 [m]Deut. 28:26 [n]ver. 44 [o]1 Kin. 18:36; [Josh. 4:24]
47 [p]Hos. 1:7; [Ps. 44:6, 7; Zech. 4:6] [q]2 Chr. 20:15
51 [r]ch. 21:9; [2 Sam. 23:21] [s][Heb. 11:34]
52 [t]Josh. 15:11 [u]Josh. 15:36 [v]See ver. 4
54 [w]ver. 57 [x][2 Sam. 5:6, 7]
55 [y]2 Sam. 2:8 [z][ch. 16:21, 22] [a]See ch. 1:26
57 [b]ver. 54
58 [c]ver. 12
Chapter 18
1 [d]ch. 20:17; Deut. 13:6; [ch. 19:2; 2 Sam. 1:26]
2 [e][ch. 17:15]
3 [d][See ver. 1 above]
5 [f]ver. 14, 15, 30
6 [g]Ex. 15:20; Judg. 11:34

17:47 battle is the LORD's. See notes on vv. 38, 39; 14:6.

17:50 killed. That is, dealt him the mortal wound (v. 51) note.

There was no sword. This verse marks the climax of the contest between Goliath, who physically speaking had all the advantages, and David, who had God on his side, and was able to triumph even without a sword (cf. vv. 45–47).

17:51 killed. A different form of the Hebrew verb is used than in v. 50; the sense is "dispatched," as in 14:13.

17:52 Gath and Ekron. See notes 4:1; 5:8, 10.

17:54 brought it to Jerusalem. Since Jerusalem was at this time in Jebusite hands (2 Sam. 5:6–9 and notes), this remark should be understood as referring to a later time.

17:55 whose son is this youth. Saul's question and Abner's response appear to conflict with the events described in 16:18–22. At the same time a chronological relationship between chs. 16 and 17 seems to be warranted (v.15 and 18:2). Saul's question may have been prompted by concerns about the social status of someone who might receive the position promised in 17:25, including marriage to his daughter. The intensity of Saul's interest may also reflect his knowledge that the kingdom will ultimately be given to "a neighbor of yours, who is better than you" (15:28). See 18:8 and note.

18:2 would not let him return. See note 17:15.

18:3 covenant. The nature of the covenant is not explicitly stated, but see the note on v. 4. Further references to the covenant between Jonathan and David include 20:8, 13–17, 42; 22:8; 23:18.

18:4 Jonathan stripped himself of the robe. As crown prince (20:31), Jonathan would have expected to succeed his father as king. In 13:22 Jonathan and Saul had been distinguished from the rest of the people by their possession of swords and spears. Here Jonathan's gifts of his robe and weapons to David not only signifies his loyalty but implies his recognition of David as God's choice for the next king. See Jonathan's explicit confession in 23:17; also 2 Sam. 1:10 note.

18:5 Saul set him over the men of war. Military success continues to be David's hallmark, and Saul gives David a rank in the army commensurate with his accomplishments.

and with musical instruments.[1] **7**And the
women [h]sang to one another as they celebrated,

[i]"Saul has struck down his thousands,
and David his ten thousands."

8And Saul was very angry, and this saying
displeased him. He said, "They have
ascribed to David ten thousands, and to
me they have ascribed thousands, and
what more can he have but [j]the kingdom?"
9And Saul eyed David from that day on.
10The next day [k]a harmful spirit from
God rushed upon Saul, and [l]he raved within his house while David was [m]playing the
lyre, as he did day by day. [n]Saul had his
spear in his hand. **11**And Saul [o]hurled the
spear, for he thought, "I will pin David to
the wall." But David evaded him twice.
12[p]Saul was afraid of David because [q]the
LORD was with him [r]but had departed from
Saul. **13**So Saul removed him from his presence and made him a commander of a
thousand. [s]And he went out and came in
before the people. **14**And David [t]had success in all his undertakings, [q]for the LORD
was with him. **15**And when Saul saw that
[t]he had great success, he stood in fearful
awe of him. **16**[u]But all Israel and Judah
loved David, for he went out and came in
before them.

David Marries Michal

17Then Saul said to David, "Here is [v]my
elder daughter Merab. [w]I will give her to
you for a wife. Only be valiant for me [x]and
fight the LORD's battles." For Saul thought,
"Let not my hand be against him, [y]but let
the hand of the Philistines be against him."
18And David said to Saul, [z]"Who am I, and
who are my relatives, my father's clan in
Israel, that I should be son-in-law to the
king?" **19**But at the time when Merab,
Saul's daughter, should have been given
to David, she was given to [a]Adriel the
[b]Meholathite for a wife.
20Now [v]Saul's daughter Michal [c]loved
David. And they told Saul, and the thing
pleased him. **21**Saul thought, "Let me give
her to him, that she may [d]be a snare for
him [e]and that the hand of the Philistines
may be against him." Therefore Saul said to
David a second time,[2] [f]"You shall now be
my son-in-law." **22**And Saul commanded
his servants, "Speak to David in private and
say, 'Behold, the king has delight in you,
and all his servants love you. Now then
become the king's son-in-law.'" **23**And
Saul's servants spoke those words in the
ears of David. And David said, [g]"Does it
seem to you a little thing to become the
king's son-in-law, since I am a poor man
and have no reputation?" **24**And the servants of Saul told him, "Thus and so did
David speak." **25**Then Saul said, "Thus
shall you say to David, 'The king desires no
[h]bride-price except a hundred foreskins of
the Philistines, [i]that he may be avenged of
the king's enemies.'" [j]Now Saul thought to
make David fall by the hand of the
Philistines. **26**And when his servants told
David these words, it pleased David well to
be the king's son-in-law. [k]Before the time
had expired, **27**David arose and went, [l]along
with his men, and killed two hundred of
the Philistines. [m]And David brought their
foreskins, which were given in full number
to the king, that he might become the
king's son-in-law. And Saul gave him his

1 Or *triangles, or three-stringed instruments* 2 Hebrew *by two*

7 [h][Ex. 15:21] [i]ch. 21:11; 29:5
8 [j]ch. 15:28
10 [k]ch. 16:14; [Judg. 9:23] [l]ch. 19:23, 24; [1 Kin. 18:29; Acts 16:16] [m]See ch. 16:16 [n]ch. 19:9
11 [o]ch. 19:10; 20:33
12 [p]ver. 15, 29 [q]ver. 28; ch. 16:18 [r]ch. 16:14; 28:15
13 [s]ver. 16; [Num. 27:17; 2 Sam. 5:2]
14 [t]ver. 5 [q][See ver. 12 above]
15 [t][See ver. 14 above]
16 [u][ver. 5]
17 [v]ch. 14:49 [w]ch. 17:25 [x]ch. 25:28 [y]ver. 21, 25
18 [z]ver. 23; 2 Sam. 7:18
19 [a][2 Sam. 21:8] [b]Judg. 7:22
20 [v][See ver. 17 above] [c]ver. 28
21 [d]Ex. 10:7 [e]ver. 17 [f][ver. 26]
23 [g][Num. 16:9]
25 [h]Gen. 34:12; Ex. 22:17 [i]ch. 14:24 [j]ver. 17, 21
26 [k][ver. 21]
27 [l]ver. 13 [m]2 Sam. 3:14

18:7 David his ten thousands. See 21:11; 29:5. It is a common feature of Hebrew poetry for one or more terms in the first half of a verse to be increased or intensified in the second half. For the thousand-ten thousand parallelism, see Deut. 32:30; Ps. 91:7; 144:13; Mic. 6:7. Whether the women's song praises Saul and David as equals or implies that David is better than Saul, Saul certainly takes offense to it (v. 8).

18:8 what more can he have but the kingdom. Saul rightly senses that David may be the "neighbor" who will replace him (15:28; 17:55 note).

18:10 a harmful spirit. See note 16:14.

raved. Ecstatic experiences could be caused by God's Spirit (10:6, 15), but also by evil spirits or false prophets (1 Kin. 18:29).

18:12 the LORD was with him. See 16:18 and note.

had departed from Saul. See 16:14 and note.

18:13–16 Saul's removal of David from the court, with an accompanying demotion in military rank, may be intended to decrease David's visibility and popularity, as well as to increase the risk of his dying in battle. The effect of Saul's scheming, however, is actually the reverse. David is brought into closer contact with the people, so that "all Israel and Judah loved David" (v. 16).

18:17–19 In view of David's great popularity, Saul cannot continue to delay fulfilling his promise (17:25). Nevertheless, he adds a further condition, that David "fight the LORD's battles," in the hope that the Philistines would kill David for him (vv. 17, 21, 25). David says that he lacks the social standing to marry the king's daughter, a conventional protest in such circumstances (cf. 9:21). At the last minute, Saul reneges on his promise and gives Merab to someone else.

18:20–27 When Saul's second daughter Michal falls in love with David, Saul offers David another chance to become his son-in-law (vv. 20, 21). He adds again to the conditions David must fulfill (v. 25). David wastes no time (v. 26) in meeting Saul's requirement twice over, and becomes the king's son-in-law (v. 27).

daughter Michal for a wife. 28 But when
Saul saw and knew that [n] the LORD was with
David, [o] and that Michal, Saul's daughter,
loved him, 29 Saul was even more afraid of
David. So Saul was David's enemy continually.
30 [p] Then the princes of the Philistines
came out to battle, and as often as they
came out [q] David had more success than all
the servants of Saul, so that his name was
highly esteemed.

Saul Tries to Kill David

19 And Saul spoke to Jonathan his son
and to all his servants, that they
should kill David. [r] But Jonathan, Saul's
son, delighted much in David. 2 And
Jonathan told David, "Saul my father seeks
to kill you. Therefore be on your guard in
the morning. Stay in a secret place and
hide yourself. 3 And I will go out and stand
beside my father in the field where you
are, and I will speak to my father about
you. And if I learn anything I will tell you."
4 And Jonathan spoke well of David to Saul
his father and said to him, "Let not the
king [s] sin against his servant David, because he has not sinned against you, and
because his deeds have brought good to
you. 5 For [t] he took his life in his hand [u] and
he struck down the Philistine, [v] and the
LORD worked a great salvation for all Israel.
You saw it, and rejoiced. Why then will
you sin against [w] innocent blood by killing
David without cause?" 6 And Saul listened
to the voice of Jonathan. Saul swore, [x] "As
the LORD lives, he shall not be put to
death." 7 And Jonathan called David, and
Jonathan reported to him all these things.
And Jonathan brought David to Saul,
and he was in his presence [y] as before.
8 And there was war again. And David
went out and fought with the Philistines
and struck them with a great blow, so that
they fled before him. 9 [z] Then a harmful
spirit from the LORD came upon Saul, as he
sat in his house with his spear in his hand.
[a] And David was playing the lyre. 10 [b] And
Saul sought to pin David to the wall with
the spear, but he eluded Saul, so that he
struck the spear into the wall. And David
fled and escaped that night.
11 [c] Saul sent messengers to David's
house to watch him, that he might kill him
in the morning. But Michal, David's wife,
told him, "If you do not escape with your
life tonight, tomorrow you will be killed."
12 [d] So Michal let David down through the
window, and he fled away and escaped.
13 Michal took [e] an image and laid it on the
bed and put a pillow of goats' hair at its
head and covered it with the clothes.
14 And when Saul sent messengers to take
David, she said, "He is sick." 15 Then Saul
sent the messengers to see David, saying,
"Bring him up to me in the bed, that I may
kill him." 16 And when the messengers
came in, behold, [e] the image was in the
bed, with the pillow of goats' hair at its
head. 17 Saul said to Michal, "Why have
you deceived me thus and let my enemy
go, so that he has escaped?" And Michal
answered Saul, "He said to me, 'Let me go.
[f] Why should I kill you?'"
18 Now David fled and escaped, and he
came to Samuel at [g] Ramah and told him all
that Saul had done to him. And he and
Samuel went and lived at Naioth. 19 And it
was told Saul, "Behold, David is at Naioth

28 [n] ver. 12 [o] ver. 20
30 [p] ch. 19:8; [2 Sam. 11:1] [q] ver. 5
Chapter 19
1 [r] ch. 18:1
4 [s] [Gen. 42:22]
5 [t] ch. 28:21; Judg. 12:3; [Judg. 9:17] [u] ch. 17:49, 50 [v] [ch. 11:13; 1 Chr. 11:14] [w] Matt. 27:4
6 [x] See Ruth 3:13
7 [y] ch. 16:21; 18:2, 13
9 [z] See ch. 16:14 [a] See ch. 16:16
10 [b] ch. 18:11; 20:33
11 [c] See Ps. 59
12 [d] [Josh. 2:15; Acts 9:24, 25]; 2 Cor. 11:33
13 [e] See Gen. 31:19
16 [e] [See ver. 13 above]
17 [f] [2 Sam. 2:22]
18 [g] 1 Sam. 1:19

18:28, 29 the LORD was with David. Saul's increasing fear of David is well-founded, since the Lord is with David (vv. 12, 14). David's success would not have distressed Saul so much if, like Jonathan, Saul had been able to accept his rejection with equanimity.

19:1 they should kill David. Saul's covert attempts on David's life having come to nothing (ch. 18), he decides to take a direct approach.

19:4 Jonathan spoke well of David. Jonathan's magnanimity towards David stands in stark contrast to Saul's malevolence, continuing the unfavorable comparison of father and son noted earlier (13:22; 14:1, 6, 10, 29 and notes). It seems likely that Jonathan's loyalty to David stems not from ignorance of David's destiny, but from a willing acceptance of it (18:4 note; 23:17 note).

19:9 a harmful spirit. See note 16:14.

19:10 Saul sought to pin David to the wall. Perhaps again galled by David's military success (v. 8; 18:8), Saul resorts to one of his old tricks (18:10, 11).

19:11 Michal, David's wife, told him. As Saul's designs on David's life become increasingly intense and overt, David is warned first by Saul's son (v. 2) and then by his daughter.

19:12 he fled away and escaped. Henceforth, David will be on the run from Saul.

19:13 an image. The Hebrew same term is translated "household gods" in Gen. 31:19, 34, 35; Judg. 18:14. The Genesis references imply small objects, while the present reference suggests something larger.

19:17 He said to me. Michal's deception here has an element of self-preservation. In light of Saul's later behavior (20:32, 33), Michal had reason to be afraid of him (cf. 16:2).

19:18 Ramah. See note 1:1.

Naioth. This word, which occurs only in this chapter, is associated with the place name Ramah. It is quite possibly not a proper noun at all, but a word meaning the "camps" in which the prophets at Ramah were active (compare the prophets' lodge in 2 Kin. 6:1, 2).

in Ramah." 20 Then Saul sent messengers to
take David, and when they saw the company of the prophets prophesying, and
Samuel standing as head over them, [h]the
Spirit of God came upon the messengers of
Saul, [i]and they also prophesied. 21 When it
was told Saul, he sent other messengers,
[i]and they also prophesied. And Saul sent
messengers again the third time, [i]and they
also prophesied. 22 Then he himself went to
Ramah and came to the great well that is in
Secu. And he asked, "Where are Samuel
and David?" And one said, "Behold, they
are at Naioth in [g]Ramah." 23 And he went
there to Naioth in Ramah. [j]And the Spirit
of God came upon him also, and as he
went he prophesied until he came to
Naioth in Ramah. 24 [k]And he too stripped
off his clothes, and he too prophesied
before Samuel and lay naked all that day
and all that night. Thus it is said, [l]"Is Saul
also among the prophets?"

Jonathan Warns David

20 Then David fled from Naioth [m]in
Ramah and came and said before
Jonathan, "What have I done? What is my
guilt? And what is my sin before your
father, that he seeks my life?" 2 And he said
to him, "Far from it! You shall not die.
Behold, my father does nothing either great
or small without disclosing it to me. And
why should my father hide this from me? It
is not so." 3 But David vowed again, saying,
"Your father knows well that [n]I have found
favor in your eyes, and he thinks, 'Do not
let Jonathan know this, lest he be grieved.'
But truly, [o]as the LORD lives and [p]as your
soul lives, there is but a step between me
and death." 4 Then Jonathan said to David,
"Whatever you say, I will do for you."
5 David said to Jonathan, "Behold, tomorrow is [q]the new moon, and I should not fail
to sit at table with the king. But let me go,
[r]that I may hide myself in the field till the
third day at evening. 6 [s]If your father misses
me at all, then say, 'David earnestly asked
leave of me to run [t]to Bethlehem his city,
for there is a yearly [u]sacrifice there for all
the clan.' 7 If he says, 'Good!' it will be well
with your servant, but if he is angry, then
know that [v]harm is determined by him.
8 Therefore deal kindly with your servant,
[w]for you have brought your servant into a
covenant of the LORD with you. [x]But if
there is guilt in me, kill me yourself, for
why should you bring me to your father?"
9 And Jonathan said, "Far be it from you! If
I knew that [v]it was determined by my
father that harm should come to you,
would I not tell you?" 10 Then David said to
Jonathan, "Who will tell me if your father
answers you roughly?" 11 And Jonathan said
to David, "Come, let us go out into the
field." So they both went out into the field.
12 And Jonathan said to David, "The
LORD, the God of Israel, be witness![1] When
I have sounded out my father, about this
time tomorrow, or the third day, behold, if
he is well disposed toward David, shall I
not then send and disclose it to you? 13 But

20 [h][ch. 10:5, 6, 10] [i][Num. 11:25; Joel 2:28]
21 [i][See ver. 20 above]
22 [g][See ver. 18 above]
23 [j][ch. 18:10]
24 [k]Isai. 20:2; Mic. 1:8; [2 Sam. 6:20] [l]ch. 10:11, 12
Chapter 20
1 [m]ch. 1:19
3 [n]See Gen. 33:15 [o]ch. 25:26; 2 Kin. 2:2, 4, 6; 4:30; See Ruth 3:13 [p]ch. 1:26
5 [q]ver. 18; Num. 10:10; 28:11 [r]ch. 19:2, 3
6 [s]ver. 18 [t]ch. 16:4 [u][ch. 9:12]
7 [v]ch. 25:17; Esth. 7:7; [ver. 33]
8 [w]ver. 16, 42; ch. 18:3; 23:18; [2 Sam. 21:7] [x]2 Sam. 14:32

1 Hebrew lacks *be witness*

19:20 the company of the prophets prophesying. See note 10:5.

19:22 great well . . . in Secu. Secu is unknown, but it may be a site about two miles north of Ramah. Some have suggested reconstructing the difficult Hebrew on the basis of Septuagint (the Old Testament Greek translation) to read "well of the threshing floor on the bare height." This could have been a familiar landmark, such as are mentioned more than once in Samuel (20:19; 2 Sam. 20:8).

19:23 the Spirit of God came upon him. Having set out to destroy David, Saul has been frustrated by Jonathan, Michal, Samuel, and now finally by God Himself.

19:24 he too stripped off his clothes. Robes in the books of Samuel often seem to have a symbolic significance, frequently pertaining to the kingship (15:28; 18:4; 24:4–6 and notes). While Jonathan's gift of his robe to David in 18:4 was voluntary, Saul's action here is under the compulsion of God's Spirit.

20:1 Naioth. See note 19:18.

20:2 Far from it. Apparently Jonathan is unaware of the most recent attempts on David's life (19:9–24) and assumes that the oath of 19:6 still stands.

20:5 the new moon. This festival was a time of rejoicing at the beginning of each month. It was marked by the sounding of trumpets (Num. 10:10; Ps. 81:3) and special sacrifices (Num. 28:11–15). The festival is often mentioned in conjunction with the Sabbath (2 Kin. 4:23; 1 Chr. 23:31; Neh. 10:33; Is. 66:23; Ezek. 46:3) and may have been subject to similar regulations (Amos 8:5). The new moon celebration is mentioned once in the New Testament (Col. 2:16).

20:6 then say. Jonathan goes along with David's pretext in vv. 28, 29. In evaluating the ethics of such actions, one might compare the Lord's instructions to Samuel in 16:2 (note), although in that context the excuse was a half-truth and not an outright untruth, as it seems to be here.

Bethlehem. See note 16:1.

yearly sacrifice. See note 1:3; cf. 1:21.

20:7 your servant. This address expresses humility and deference (1:11, 16; 3:10; 17:32; 22:15; 23:10; 25:24).

20:8 covenant. See 18:3, 4 and notes. Pledges of friendship and loyalty are reiterated in vv. 13–17, 42.

20:13 the LORD be with you, as he has been with my father. This single reference to the Lord as being "with Saul" should be understood as referring to the kingship. Recognizing that David is now God's chosen king (18:4 note; 23:17 and note), Jonathan gives him allegiance over and above his allegiance to his own father (v. 16).

should it please my father to do you harm,
[y]the LORD do so to Jonathan and more also
if I do not disclose it to you and send you
away, that you may go in safety. [z]May the
LORD be with you, as he has been with my
father. 14 If I am still alive, show me the
steadfast love of the LORD, that I may not
die; 15 [a]and do not cut off[1] your steadfast
love from my house forever, when the LORD
cuts off every one of the enemies of David
from the face of the earth." 16 And Jonathan
made a covenant with the house of David,
saying,[2] [b]"May the LORD take vengeance on
David's enemies." 17 And Jonathan made
David swear again by his love for him, [c]for
he loved him as he loved his own soul.
18 Then Jonathan said to him, [d]"Tomorrow is the new moon, and [e]you will be
missed, because [f]your seat will be empty.
19 On the third day go down quickly to the
place where you hid yourself when the
matter was in hand, and remain beside
the stone heap.[3] 20 And I will shoot three
arrows to the side of it, as though I shot at
a mark. 21 And behold, I will send the
young man, saying, 'Go, find the arrows.' If
I say to the young man, 'Look, the arrows
are on this side of you, take them,' then
you are to come, for, [g]as the LORD lives, it
is safe for you and there is no danger. 22 But
if I say to the youth, [h]'Look, the arrows are
beyond you,' then go, for the LORD has sent
you away. 23 [i]And as for the matter of which
you and I have spoken, behold, [j]the LORD
is between you and me forever."
24 So David hid himself in the field. And
when the new moon came, the king sat
down to eat food. 25 The king sat on his seat,
as at other times, on the seat by the wall.
Jonathan sat opposite,[4] and Abner sat by
Saul's side, [k]but David's place was empty.
26 Yet Saul did not say anything that day,
for he thought, "Something has happened
to him. [l]He is not clean; surely he is not
clean." 27 But on [m]the second day, the day
after the new moon, [k]David's place was
empty. And Saul said to Jonathan his son,
"Why has not the son of Jesse come to the
meal, either yesterday or today?" 28 Jonathan answered Saul, [n]"David earnestly
asked leave of me to go to Bethlehem. 29 He
said, 'Let me go, for our clan holds a sacrifice in the city, and my brother has commanded me to be there. So now, if I have
found favor in your eyes, let me get away
and see my brothers.' For this reason he
has not come to the king's table."
30 Then Saul's anger was kindled against
Jonathan, and he said to him, "You son of a
perverse, rebellious woman, do I not know
that you have chosen the son of Jesse to
your own shame, and to the shame of your
mother's nakedness? 31 For as long as the
son of Jesse lives on the earth, neither you
nor your kingdom shall be established.
Therefore send and bring him to me, for he
shall surely die." 32 Then Jonathan answered
Saul his father, [o]"Why should he be put to
death? What has he done?" 33 [p]But Saul
hurled his spear at him to strike him. So
Jonathan knew [q]that his father was determined to put David to death. 34 And
Jonathan rose from the table in fierce anger
and ate no food the second day of the
month, for he was grieved for David,
because his father had disgraced him.

13 [y][Ruth 1:17] [z]Josh. 1:5, 17; 1 Kin. 1:37; 1 Chr. 22:11, 16; [ch. 17:37]
15 [a]2 Sam. 9:1, 3, 7; 21:7
16 [b][ch. 25:22; Josh. 22:23]
17 [c]ch. 18:1, 3
18 [d]ver. 5 [e]ver. 6 [f]ver. 25, 27
21 [g]ver. 3; See Ruth 3:13
22 [h]ver. 37
23 [i]ver. 14, 15 [j]ver. 42
25 [k]ver. 18
26 [l]Lev. 7:21; See Lev. 11:24-28; 15:1-4
27 [m][ver. 34] [k][See ver. 25 above]
28 [n]ver. 6
32 [o]ch. 19:5
33 [p]ch. 18:11; 19:10 [q]ver. 7

[1] Or *but if I die, do not cut off* [2] Septuagint *earth, let not the name of Jonathan be cut off from the House of David* [3] Septuagint; Hebrew *the stone Ezel* [4] Compare Septuagint; Hebrew *stood up*

20:15 do not cut off your steadfast love. For the fulfillment of this request, see 2 Sam. 9:1–8; 21:7.

20:16 David's enemies. See note on v. 13. Since it is David himself who will be accountable to keep covenant with Jonathan, "enemies" is probably a euphemistic reference to Saul, Jonathan's father (cf. 25:22; 2 Sam. 12:14).

20:17 swear. See note on v. 8.

20:18 new moon. See note on v. 5.

20:19 the stone heap. The site is otherwise unknown. The Hebrew may mean something like "Departure Stone." The stone was possibly a familiar landmark on the way out of town; for other such landmarks mentioned in Samuel, see 19:22; 2 Sam. 20:8 and notes.

20:23 LORD is between you and me. See Gen. 31:50, 53.

20:24 new moon. See note on v. 5.

20:25 Abner. He was Saul's relative and military commander (14:50).

20:26 not clean. See especially Lev. 7:19–21. Laws of cleanliness are covered most fully in Lev. 11–15, though references to "clean" and "unclean" are frequent throughout the Pentateuch (Gen. 7:2; Lev. 5:2; Num. 5:2; Deut. 14:3–21; etc.). The point is not physical but ritual or religious uncleanness.

20:28, 29 See note on v. 6.

20:30 son of a perverse, rebellious woman. As in similar modern expressions, the insult is meant for Jonathan and not necessarily his mother.

20:31 neither you nor your kingdom shall be established. Despite Samuel's words in 13:14, Saul still clings to hope for his dynasty (cf. 18:8 note). Contrast Jonathan's ready acceptance of the Lord's will (v. 13; 18:4; 23:17 and notes). It may be inferred from Saul's words that Jonathan was his firstborn and thus in line for the throne.

20:33 Saul hurled his spear at him. Saul's and Jonathan's opposite reactions to David have driven a wedge between them. Saul's attempt on Jonathan's life matches his earlier attempts on David's (18:11; 19:10).

35 In the morning Jonathan went out into
the field to the appointment with David,
and with him a little boy. 36 And he said to
his boy, "Run and find the arrows that I
shoot." As the boy ran, he shot an arrow
beyond him. 37 And when the boy came to
the place of the arrow that Jonathan had
shot, Jonathan called after the boy and
said, [r]"Is not the arrow beyond you?"
38 And Jonathan called after the boy,
"Hurry! Be quick! Do not stay!" So
Jonathan's boy gathered up the arrows and
came to his master. 39 But the boy knew
nothing. Only Jonathan and David knew
the matter. 40 And Jonathan gave his
weapons to his boy and said to him, "Go
and carry them to the city." 41 And as soon
as the boy had gone, David rose from
beside the stone heap[1] and fell on his face
to the ground and bowed three times. And
they kissed one another and wept with one
another, David weeping the most. 42 Then
Jonathan said to David, [s]"Go in peace,
because we have sworn both of us in the
name of the LORD, saying, [t]'The LORD shall
be between me and you, [u]and between my
offspring and your offspring, forever.'" And
he rose and departed, and Jonathan went
into the city.[2]

David and the Holy Bread

21 [3] Then David came to [v]Nob to
[w]Ahimelech the priest. And Ahimelech [x]came to meet David trembling and
said to him, "Why are you alone, and
no one with you?" 2 And David said to
Ahimelech the priest, "The king has
charged me with a matter and said to me,
'Let no one know anything of the matter
about which I send you, and with which I
have charged you.' I have made an
appointment with the young men for such
and such a place. 3 Now then, what do you
have on hand? Give me five loaves of
bread, or whatever is here." 4 And the
priest answered David, "I have no common bread on hand, but there is [y]holy
bread—[z]if the young men have kept themselves from women." 5 And David
answered the priest, "Truly women have
been kept from us as always when I go on
an expedition. The vessels of the young
men are holy even when it is an ordinary
journey. How much more today will their
vessels be holy?" 6 So the priest gave him
[y]the holy bread, for there was no bread
there but the bread of the Presence,
[a]which is removed from before the LORD,
to be replaced by hot bread on the day it is
taken away.
7 Now a certain man of the servants of
Saul was there that day, detained before
the LORD. His name was [b]Doeg the
Edomite, the chief of Saul's herdsmen.
8 Then David said to Ahimelech, "Then
have you not here a spear or a sword at
hand? For I have brought neither my sword
nor my weapons with me, because the
king's business required haste." 9 And
the priest said, [c]"The sword of Goliath the
Philistine, whom you struck down in [d]the
valley of Elah, behold, it is here wrapped in
a cloth behind the ephod. If you will take
that, take it, for there is none but that
here." And David said, "There is none like
that; give it to me."

David Flees to Gath

10 And David rose and fled that day from
Saul and went to [e]Achish the king of Gath.

37 [r]ver. 22
42 [s]ver. 13; ch. 1:17 [t]ver. 23 [u]ver. 15
Chapter 21
1 [v]ch. 22:9, 11, 19; Neh. 11:32; Isai. 10:32 [w][ch. 14:3; Mark 2:26] [x][ch. 16:4]
4 [y]Ex. 25:30; Lev. 24:5; Matt. 12:3, 4; Mark 2:25, 26; Luke 6:3, 4 [z]Ex. 19:15
6 [y][See ver. 4 above] [a]Lev. 24:8, 9
7 [b]ch. 22:9; See Ps. 52
9 [c]ch. 17:51 [d]ch. 17:2
10 [e]See Ps. 34

[1] Septuagint; Hebrew *from beside the south* [2] This sentence is 21:1 in Hebrew [3] Ch 21:2 in Hebrew

20:42 sworn. See note on v. 8.

21:1 Nob. Probably located less than two miles northeast of Jerusalem (Is. 10:32), Nob became "the city of the priests" (22:19) sometime after the disaster that came upon Shiloh (1:3 note; 2:32 note) at the hands of the Philistines (4:1–11).

Ahimelech. Either Ahijah's brother or simply another name for Ahijah (14:3), Ahimelech occupies the position of high priest once held by his great-grandfather Eli (1:9). See also Mark 2:26 and note.

21:2 king has charged me. Having employed a pretext to good advantage not long before (20:6 note), David does so again, with disastrous results for Ahimelech and the priests at Nob (22:6–19).

21:4 holy bread. That is, "the showbread" (v. 6; Ex. 25:30; 35:13; Lev. 24:5–9; 1 Chr. 9:32). See Jesus' reference to this episode in Matt. 12:3, 4; Mark 2:25, 26; Luke 6:3, 4.

kept themselves from women. Ritual cleanliness was a part of consecration prior to battle or other important occasions (Ex. 19:15; Lev. 15:18; Deut. 23:9–14; Josh. 3:5; 2 Sam. 11:11–12).

21:6 bread of the Presence. See v. 4 and note.

21:7 Doeg the Edomite. The presence of Doeg at these transactions arouses apprehensions in the reader as it did in David (22:22). These apprehensions prove well founded as the narrative progresses (22:9, 10, 18, 19). Doeg is also mentioned in the title of Ps. 52.

21:9 sword of Goliath. See 17:51, 54.

ephod. See 2:28 note.

21:10 Achish. See 27:2–12; 29:1–11; title to Ps. 34, where "Abimelech" may be a name for Philistine kings.

Gath. See notes 4:1; 5:8.

11 And the servants of Achish said to him,
"Is not this David the king of the land? [f]Did
they not sing to one another of him in
dances,

> 'Saul has struck down his thousands,
> and David his ten thousands'?"

12 And David [g]took these words to heart
and was much afraid of Achish the king of
Gath. 13 So he changed his behavior before
them and pretended to be insane in their
hands and made marks on the doors of the
gate and let his spittle run down his beard.
14 Then Achish said to his servants,
"Behold, you see the man is mad. Why
then have you brought him to me? 15 Do I
lack madmen, that you have brought this
fellow to behave as a madman in my presence? Shall this fellow come into my
house?"

David at the Cave of Adullam

22 David departed from there and
escaped to [h]the cave of [i]Adullam.
And when his brothers and all his father's
house heard it, they went down there to
him. 2 [j]And everyone who was in distress,
and everyone who was in debt, and everyone who was bitter in soul,[1] gathered to
him. And he became captain over them.
And there were with him [k]about four hundred men.

3 And David went from there to Mizpeh
of Moab. And he said to the king of Moab,
"Please let my father and my mother stay[2]
with you, till I know what God will do for
me." 4 And he left them with the king of
Moab, and they stayed with him all the
time that David was in the stronghold.
5 Then the prophet [l]Gad said to David, "Do
not remain in the stronghold; depart, and
go into the land of Judah." So David
departed and went into the forest of
Hereth.

Saul Kills the Priests at Nob

6 Now Saul heard that David was discovered, and the men who were with him. Saul
was sitting at Gibeah under [m]the tamarisk
tree on the height with his spear in his
hand, and all his servants were standing
about him. 7 And Saul said to his servants
who stood about him, "Hear now, people of
Benjamin; will the son of Jesse [n]give every
one of you fields and vineyards, will he
make you all commanders of thousands
and commanders of hundreds, 8 that all of
you have conspired against me? No one discloses to me [o]when my son makes a
covenant with the son of Jesse. None of you
[p]is sorry for me or discloses to me that my
son has stirred up my servant against me,
[q]to lie in wait, as at this day." 9 Then
answered [r]Doeg the Edomite, who stood by
the servants of Saul, "I saw the son of Jesse
[s]coming to Nob, to [t]Ahimelech the son of
Ahitub, 10 [u]and he inquired of the LORD for
him and [v]gave him provisions and gave him
the sword of Goliath the Philistine."

11 Then the king sent to summon
Ahimelech the priest, the son of Ahitub,

1 Or *discontented* 2 Syriac, Vulgate; Hebrew *go out*

11 [f]ch. 18:7; 29:5
12 [g][Luke 2:19]
Chapter 22
1 [h]See Ps. 57; 142 [i]2 Sam. 23:13; 1 Chr. 11:15
2 [j][Judg. 9:4; 11:3] [k][ch. 23:13; 25:13]
5 [l]2 Sam. 24:11, 18, 19; 1 Chr. 21:9, 11, 13, 18, 19; 29:29; 2 Chr. 29:25
6 [m][ch. 31:13; Gen. 21:33]
7 [n][ch. 8:14]
8 [o]ch. 18:3 [p][ch. 23:21] [q]ver. 13
9 [r]ch. 21:7; See Ps. 52 [s]ch. 21:1 [t][ch. 14:3]
10 [u]ch. 23:2, 4; 30:8; 2 Sam. 5:19, 23; [Num. 27:21] [v]ch. 21:6, 9

21:11 David the king. Outside as well as inside Israel, David's royal destiny seems to be recognized, even if the Philistines' statement is best understood as popular exaggeration.

David his ten thousands. See note 18:7.

22:1 cave of Adullam. Adullam, which may mean "refuge," has been identified with a site seventeen miles southwest of Jerusalem, midway between Gath and Hebron. See also 2 Sam. 23:13; Josh. 12:15; titles to Ps. 57 and 142.

his father's house . . . went down there to him. The vehemence that drove Saul to attack even his own family (20:33) left David's family with little reason to feel secure.

22:3 Mizpeh of Moab. The specific location of this city is unknown. On the name Mizpeh ("watchtower"), see 7:5 note.

king of Moab. Moab had a king already in Judg. 3:12.

stay with you. David's decision to seek sanctuary in Moab may be based not only on the assumption that a nation at odds with Saul (14:47) might well wish to side with a rival, but also on David's family ties to the Moabites (Ruth 4:13–17).

what God will do for me. While taking whatever practical measures he can, David nevertheless sees God in sovereign control of his situation (2 Sam. 15:25, 26).

22:4 the stronghold. See note 23:14.

22:5 prophet Gad. Later to serve as King David's seer (2 Sam. 24:11; 2 Chr. 29:25; cf. 1 Chr. 29:29), Gad's presence at this point is a reminder that David's destiny is divinely appointed and that he is under the Lord's protection. David will later be joined by a priest (vv. 20–23).

22:6 spear in his hand. The mention of Saul's spear here may be a reminder of Saul's violent temper (18:10, 11; 19:10; 20:33), which comes to full expression in this episode.

22:7 people of Benjamin. Having apparently surrounded himself with members of his own tribe (9:1, 2; 10:21), Saul seeks to reinforce their loyalty with an appeal to self-interest: is David, of the tribe of Judah, likely to be fair to Benjaminites?

fields and vineyards. The questions addressed by Saul to his officials suggest that he engaged in at least some of the abusive royal practices about which Samuel had warned (8:10–18).

22:8 when my son makes a covenant. See notes 18:3, 4.

22:9 Doeg the Edomite. See 21:7 and note.

Ahimelech the son of Ahitub. See 21:1 and notes.

and all his father's house, the priests who
were at Nob, and all of them came to the
king. 12 And Saul said, "Hear now, son of
Ahitub." And he answered, "Here I am, my
lord." 13 And Saul said to him, "Why have
you conspired against me, you and the son
of Jesse, in that you have given him bread
and a sword and [u]have inquired of God for
him, so that he has risen against me, [w]to lie
in wait, as at this day?" 14 Then Ahimelech
answered the king, "And who among all
your servants is so faithful as David, who is
the king's son-in-law, and captain over[1]
your bodyguard, and honored in your
house? 15 Is today the first time [u]that I have
inquired of God for him? No! Let not the
king impute anything to his servant or to
all the house of my father, for your servant
has known nothing of all this, [x]much or little." 16 And the king said, "You shall surely
die, Ahimelech, you and all your father's
house." 17 And the king said to [y]the guard
who stood about him, "Turn and kill the
priests of the LORD, because their hand also
is with David, and they knew that he fled
and did not disclose it to me." But the servants of the king would not put out their
hand to strike the priests of the LORD.
18 Then the king said to Doeg, "You turn
and strike the priests." And Doeg the
Edomite turned and struck down the
priests, [z]and he killed on that day eighty-
five persons who wore the linen ephod.
19 And Nob, the city of the priests, he put to
the sword; [a]both man and woman, child
and infant, ox, donkey and sheep, he put
to the sword.

20 But one of the sons of Ahimelech the
son of Ahitub, named [b]Abiathar, escaped
and fled after David. 21 And Abiathar told
David that Saul had killed the priests of the
LORD. 22 And David said to Abiathar, "I
knew on that day, [c]when Doeg the Edomite
was there, that he would surely tell Saul. I
have occasioned the death of all the persons of your father's house. 23 [d]Stay with
me; do not be afraid, for he who seeks my
life seeks your life. With me you shall be in
safekeeping."

David Saves the City of Keilah

23 Now they told David, "Behold, the
Philistines are fighting against
[e]Keilah and are robbing the threshing
floors." 2 Therefore David [f]inquired of the
LORD, "Shall I go and attack these
Philistines?" And the LORD said to David,
"Go and attack the Philistines and save
Keilah." 3 But David's men said to him,
"Behold, we are afraid here in Judah; how
much more then if we go to Keilah against
the armies of the Philistines?" 4 Then David
[f]inquired of the LORD again. And the LORD
answered him, "Arise, go down to Keilah,
[g]for I will give the Philistines into your
hand." 5 And David and his men went to
Keilah and fought with the Philistines and
brought away their livestock and struck
them with a great blow. So David saved the
inhabitants of Keilah.
6 [h]When Abiathar the son of Ahimelech
had fled to David to Keilah, he had come
down with an ephod in his hand. 7 Now it

[1] Septuagint, Targum; Hebrew *and has turned aside to*

13 [u][See ver. 10 above] [w]ver. 8
15 [u][See ver. 10 above] [x]ch. 25:36
17 [y][2 Kin. 10:25; 11:4, 6; 2 Chr. 12:10]
18 [z][ch. 2:31]
19 [a][ch. 15:3]
20 [b]ch. 23:6, 9
22 [c]ch. 21:7
23 [d][1 Kin. 2:26]
Chapter 23
1 [e]Josh. 15:44
2 [f]See ch. 22:10
4 [f][See ver. 2 above] [g]ver. 14; Josh. 24:11; Judg. 7:7; 20:28
6 [h]ch. 22:20

22:13 conspired against me. Saul's assumption that Ahimelech has plotted with David against the king is baseless; Ahimelech was simply misled by David (21:2 note).

risen against me, to lie in wait. Saul's assumption of hostile motives on David's part is as ill-founded as his assumption about Ahimelech.

22:14 captain over your bodyguard. Ahimelech may still think that David was doing covert work for Saul (21:2) when he came for help.

22:17 would not . . . strike the priests. Saul's command that the priests of the Lord be slaughtered is so evil and irrational that his own men refuse to carry it out. At least once before, Saul's men found it necessary to go against him (14:45 and note).

22:18 killed . . . eighty-five persons. See note 2:31.

linen ephod. See note 2:18.

22:19 both man and woman, child and infant. It is an irony extremely damaging to Saul's image that the description of the total slaughter of the inhabitants of Nob, "the city of the priests," matches almost verbatim the order that had been given for the slaughter of the Amalekites (15:3) that Saul failed to carry out.

22:20 Abiathar . . . fled after David. Support for David continues to build, chiefly as a result of Saul's own misguided attempts at self-preservation. David now has the support of both prophet (v. 5) and priest. Abiathar brings to David the ephod (23:6), which was a means of discerning the Lord's will (2:28 note; 14:3 note).

22:22 I have occasioned. It would be easy for David to excuse himself for the massacre at Nob by simply condemning Saul. Instead, he readily admits his own share of responsibility for the disaster (21:2 note). In this admission the reader glimpses a major difference between David and his predecessor, the quality of their repentance (15:24–26, 30 and notes; 2 Sam. 12:13 note).

23:1 Keilah. Located about three miles south of Adullam (22:1) near Philistine territory, Keilah is also mentioned in Josh. 15:44.

robbing the threshing floors. Cf. Judg. 6:3–6.

23:6 ephod. Not the "linen ephod" traditionally worn by all priests (cf. 22:18), but the ephod associated with divine inquiry (2:28 note).

23:7 God has given him into my hand. Saul's interpretation of events is without foundation, as the narrator's diametrically opposed assertion makes clear: "God did not give him into his hand" (v. 14).

was told Saul that David had come to
Keilah. And Saul said, "God has given him
into my hand, for he has shut himself in by
entering a town that has gates and bars."
8 And Saul summoned all the people to
war, to go down to Keilah, to besiege David
and his men. 9 David knew that Saul was
plotting harm against him. And he said to
Abiathar the priest, [i]"Bring the ephod
here." 10 Then said David, "O LORD, the
God of Israel, your servant has surely heard
that Saul seeks to come to Keilah, to
destroy the city on my account. 11 Will the
men of Keilah surrender me into his hand?
Will Saul come down, as your servant has
heard? O LORD, the God of Israel, please
tell your servant." And the LORD said, "He
will come down." 12 Then David said, "Will
the men of Keilah surrender me and my
men into the hand of Saul?" And the LORD
said, [j]"They will surrender you." 13 Then
David and his men, [k]who were about six
hundred, arose and departed from Keilah,
and they went [l]wherever they could go.
When Saul was told that David had
escaped from Keilah, he gave up the expedition. 14 And David remained in the
strongholds in the wilderness, in the hill
country [m]of the Wilderness of [n]Ziph. And
Saul sought him every day, but God did
not give him into his hand.

Saul Pursues David

15 David saw that Saul had come out to
seek his life. David was in the Wilderness
of Ziph at Horesh. 16 And Jonathan, Saul's
son, rose and went to David at Horesh, and
strengthened his hand in God. 17 And he
said to him, "Do not fear, for the hand of
Saul my father shall not find you. You shall
be king over Israel, and I shall be next to
you. [o]Saul my father also knows this."
18 [p]And the two of them made a covenant
before the LORD. David remained at
Horesh, and Jonathan went home.

19 [q]Then the Ziphites went up to Saul at
Gibeah, saying, "Is not David hiding
among us in the strongholds at Horesh, on
the hill of Hachilah, which is south of
[r]Jeshimon? 20 Now come down, O king,
according to all your heart's desire to come
down, [s]and our part shall be to surrender
him into the king's hand." 21 And Saul said,
[t]"May you be blessed by the LORD, [u]for you
have had compassion on me. 22 Go, make
yet more sure. Know and see the place
where his foot is, and who has seen him
there, for it is told me that he is very cunning. 23 See therefore and take note of all
the lurking places where he hides, and
come back to me with sure information.
Then I will go with you. And if he is in the
land, I will search him out among all the
thousands of Judah." 24 And they arose and
went to Ziph ahead of Saul.

Now David and his men were [v]in the
wilderness of Maon, [w]in the Arabah to the
south of [r]Jeshimon. 25 And Saul and his
men went to seek him. And David was
told, so he went down to the rock and
lived in the wilderness of Maon. And when
Saul heard that, he pursued after David in
the wilderness of Maon. 26 Saul went on
one side of the mountain, and David and
his men on the other side of the mountain.
And David was hurrying to get away from
Saul. As Saul and his men were closing in
on David and his men to capture them,

9 [i]ch. 30:7; [Num. 27:21]
12 [j]ver. 20
13 [k]ch. 25:13; 27:2; [ch. 22:2; 30:9, 10] [l][2 Sam. 15:20]
14 [m]See Ps. 63 [n]Josh. 15:24
17 [o]ch. 24:20; [ch. 20:31]
18 [p]ch. 18:3; 20:8, 16, 42; [2 Sam. 21:7]
19 [q]ch. 26:1; See Ps. 54 [r]Num. 21:20
20 [s]ver. 12
21 [t]See Ruth 2:20 [u][ch. 22:8]
24 [v]ch. 25:2; Josh. 15:55 [w]See Deut. 1:1 [r][See ver. 19 above]

23:12 Will the men of Keilah surrender me. In view of Saul's ruthless treatment of the city of Nob, the behavior of the Keilahites probably reflects fear rather than ingratitude to David.

23:13 men, who were about six hundred. The growth of David's company from four hundred (22:2) to six hundred is an indication of his increasing strength (22:20 note).

23:14 strongholds in the wilderness. The term "strongholds" suggests a geographical area and not a single location (22:4; 2 Sam. 5:17; 23:14).

Wilderness of Ziph. The village of Ziph is thirteen miles southeast of Keilah and five miles southeast of Hebron. The wilderness would be the desert area south of Hebron. Ziph is mentioned in Josh. 15:55, along with Maon (v. 24) and Carmel (15:12; 25:2).

God did not give him into his hand. God is in sovereign control of David's destiny (v. 7; 22:20 and notes).

23:16 Jonathan, Saul's son . . . strengthened his hand in God. No longer ignorant of his father's malevolence toward David (contrast 20:2), Jonathan acts as a true friend by aiding David in finding strength where true strength can alone be found. See 30:6, where David once more "strengthened himself in the LORD his God."

23:17 I shall be next to you. Though Jonathan will not survive to serve David (31:2), his readiness to let go of personal ambition for the sake of God's chosen king (18:4; 20:13) is a foil to Saul's desperate efforts to hang on to a kingdom that is no longer his (15:23).

Saul . . . knows this. See 20:30, 31. Saul's refusal to accept his rejection (compare Eli's response in 3:18) cannot be excused on the grounds that he does not know to whom the kingdom should go.

23:18 covenant. See notes 18:3, 4.

23:19 Ziphites. See note on v. 14; 26:1.

Gibeah. This was Saul's hometown (10:26).

23:24 wilderness of Maon. About eight miles south of Hebron, Maon is mentioned in 25:2 as the hometown of Nabal.

27 a messenger came to Saul, saying,
"Hurry and come, for the Philistines have
made a raid against the land." 28 So Saul
returned from pursuing after David and
went against the Philistines. Therefore that
place was called the Rock of Escape.[1]
29 [2] And David went up from there and lived
in the strongholds of [x]Engedi.

David Spares Saul's Life

24 [3] [y]When Saul returned from following the Philistines, he was told,
"Behold, David is in the wilderness of
Engedi." 2 Then Saul took [z]three thousand
chosen men out of all Israel and went to
seek David and his men in front of the
Wildgoats' Rocks. 3 And he came to the
sheepfolds by the way, where there was a
cave, and Saul went in [a]to relieve himself.[4]
Now David and his men were sitting in the
innermost parts [b]of the cave. 4 And the men
of David said to him, [c]"Here is the day of
which the LORD said to you, 'Behold, I will
give your enemy into your hand, and you
shall do to him as it shall seem good to
you.'" Then David arose and stealthily cut
off a corner of Saul's robe. 5 And afterward
[d]David's heart struck him, because he had
cut off a corner of Saul's robe. 6 He said to
his men, [e]"The LORD forbid that I should
do this thing to my lord, the LORD's anointed, to put out my hand against him, seeing
he is [f]the LORD's anointed." 7 So David persuaded his men with these words [g]and did
not permit them to attack Saul. And Saul
rose up and left the cave and went on his
way.
8 Afterward David also arose and went
out of the cave, and called after Saul, "My
lord the king!" And when Saul looked
behind him, David bowed with his face to
the earth and paid homage. 9 And David
said to Saul, "Why do you listen to the
words of men who say, 'Behold, David
seeks your harm'? 10 Behold, this day your
eyes have seen how the LORD gave you
today into my hand in the cave. [h]And some
told me to kill you, but I spared you.[5] I
said, 'I will not put out my hand against
my lord, [f]for he is the LORD's anointed.'
11 See, my father, see the corner of your
robe in my hand. For by the fact that I cut
off the corner of your robe and did not kill
you, you may know and see that [i]there is
no wrong or treason in my hands. I have
not sinned against you, though [j]you hunt
my life to take it. 12 [k]May the LORD judge
between me and you, may the LORD avenge
me against you, but my hand shall not be
against you. 13 As the proverb of the
ancients says, 'Out of the wicked comes
wickedness.' But my hand shall not be
against you. 14 After whom has the king of
Israel come out? After whom do you pur-
sue? [l]After a dead dog! [m]After a flea! 15 [k]May
the LORD therefore be judge and give sentence between me and you, and see to it
and [n]plead my cause and deliver me from
your hand."
16 As soon as David had finished speaking
these words to Saul, Saul said, [o]"Is this your
voice, my son David?" And Saul lifted up
his voice and wept. 17 He said to David,
"You are more righteous than I, [p]for you

29 [x]Josh. 15:62; 2 Chr. 20:2; S. of S. 1:14; Ezek. 47:10
Chapter 24
1 [y]ch. 23:28
2 [z]ch. 23:2
3 [a]Judg. 3:24 [b]See Ps. 57; 142
4 [c]ver. 7; [ch. 26:8]
5 [d]2 Sam. 24:10
6 [e]ch. 26:11 [f]See ch. 12:3
7 [g][Ps. 7:4]
10 [h]ver. 4 [f][See ver. 6 above]
11 [i]Ps. 7:3 [j]ch. 26:29
12 [k]Gen. 16:5; Judg. 11:27
14 [l]See ch. 17:43 [m]ch. 26:20
15 [k][See ver. 12 above] [n]ch. 25:39; Ps. 35:1; 43:1; 119:154
16 [o]ch. 26:17
17 [p][ch. 26:21]

1 Or *Rock of Divisions* 2 Ch 24:1 in Hebrew 3 Ch 24:2 in Hebrew
4 Hebrew *cover his feet* 5 Septuagint, Syriac, Targum; Hebrew *it* (my eye) *spared you*

23:27 Philistines have made a raid against the land. The providential timing of this Philistine incursion is obvious.

23:28 Saul returned from pursuing after David. Saul distinguishes himself by sacrificing personal concerns for the sake of national security.

23:29 strongholds of Engedi. Engedi was a large spring on the steep western shore of the Dead Sea. Its vicinity afforded David provisions and protection in his flight from Saul.

24:1 wilderness of Engedi. See note 23:29.

24:4 Here is the day of which the LORD said to you. While it is providential that Saul should enter the very cave where David and his men are hidden, there has been no hint that God wanted David to lift a hand against Saul (cf. v. 6). The suggestion by David's men that he do so would be a mistaken conclusion of their own.

cut off a corner of Saul's robe. David restricts himself to a symbolic act (v. 5 note).

24:5 David's heart struck him. Although David later displays the corner of Saul's robe as evidence of his goodwill towards Saul (v. 11), his pangs of conscience (cf. 2 Sam. 24:10) suggest that a desire to secure such proof may not have been his only reason for going so close to Saul. In view of the royal significance of robes (15:28; 18:4; 19:24 and notes), David may have felt guilty of an inappropriate grasping after the kingship and of an act of aggression against the Lord's anointed (v. 6). See theological note "Conscience and the Law."

24:6 LORD's anointed. David recognizes and safeguards the sanctity of the Lord's anointed (26:9; cf. 2:10 note), leaving judgment and vengeance to the Lord (v. 12).

24:13 proverb. David's point seems to be like Jesus' teaching, "You will recognize them by their fruits" (Matt. 7:16, 20). David is known by his restraint, but Saul is known from his efforts to harm David.

24:14 A dead dog. David abases himself before Saul, as Mephibosheth will later do before David (2 Sam. 9:8). The expression "dead dog" occurs only one other time in the Old Testament, 2 Sam. 16:9. "Dog" is usually an insult (17:43; 2 Sam. 3:8; 2 Kin. 8:13).

24:17 You are more righteous than I. Having just escaped with his life, Saul experiences a rare moment of remorse. His testimony to David's righteousness recognizes David's right to rule; even Saul acknowledges that David did not rise to power by illicit means.

have repaid me good, whereas I have repaid
you evil. 18 And you have declared this day
how you have dealt well with me, in that
you did not kill me when the LORD put me
into your hands. 19 For if a man finds his
enemy, will he let him go away safe? So may
the LORD reward you with good for what
you have done to me this day. 20 And now,
behold, [q]I know that you shall surely be
king, and that the kingdom of Israel shall be
established in your hand. 21 [r]Swear to me
therefore by the LORD that you will not cut
off my offspring after me, and [s]that you will
not destroy my name out of my father's
house." 22 And David swore this to Saul.
Then Saul went home, but David and his
men went up [t]to the stronghold.

The Death of Samuel

25 [u]Now Samuel died. And all Israel
assembled [v]and mourned for him,
and they buried him [w]in his house at
[x]Ramah.

David and Abigail

Then David rose and went down to [y]the
wilderness of Paran. 2 And there was a man
in [z]Maon whose business was in [a]Carmel.
The man was very rich; he had three thousand sheep and a thousand goats. [b]He was
shearing his sheep in Carmel. 3 Now the
name of the man was Nabal, and the name
of his wife Abigail. The woman was discerning and beautiful, but the man was
harsh and badly behaved; [c]he was a
Calebite. 4 David heard in the wilderness
that Nabal [b]was shearing his sheep. 5 So
David sent ten young men. And David said
to the young men, "Go up to Carmel, and
go to Nabal and greet him in my name.
6 And thus you shall greet him: [d]'Peace be
to you, and peace be to your house, and
peace be to all that you have. 7 I hear that
you have shearers. Now your shepherds
have been with us, and we did them no
harm, [e]and they missed nothing all the
time they were in Carmel. 8 Ask your young

20 [q]ch. 23:17
21 [r][Gen. 21:23] [s][2 Sam. 21:7]
22 [t]ch. 23:29
Chapter 25
1 [u]ch. 28:3 [v]Gen. 50:10; [Num. 20:29; Deut. 34:8] [w][1 Kin. 2:34] [x]ch. 1:19
[y]Num. 10:12
2 [z]ch. 23:24 [a]Josh. 15:55 [b][Gen. 38:13; 2 Sam. 13:23]
3 [c][ch. 30:14]
4 [b][See ver. 2 above]
6 [d][1 Chr. 12:18; Matt. 10:13; Luke 10:5]
7 [e]ver. 15, 21

Conscience and the Law

Conscience is the built-in power of our minds to pass moral judgments on ourselves, approving or disapproving our actions, thoughts, and plans, and telling us, if what we have done is assessed as wrong, that we deserve to suffer for it. Conscience has in it two elements: an awareness of certain things as being right or wrong, and an ability to apply laws and rules to specific situations. Conscience insists on judging us, and insists on judging us by the highest standard we know. Hence we call it God's voice in the soul, and in a sense it is.

Paul says that God has written a certain knowledge of His law on every human heart (Rom. 2:14, 15), and experience confirms this. But conscience can be misinformed, or conditioned to regard evil as good, or become seared and dull through repeated sin (1 Tim. 4:2). The judgments of conscience are only to be received as God's voice when they match God's own truth and law in Scripture. The conscience must be educated to judge scripturally.

Superstition or scruple may lead a person to count as sinful an action that according to God's word is not sinful. But for such a "weak" conscience (Rom. 14:1, 2; 1 Cor. 8:7, 12) to go against itself and do what it mistakenly judges to be wrong would be sin (Rom. 14:23). Those whose conscience is "weak" should never be pressed or cajoled to do what destroys their good conscience.

The New Testament ideal is a conscience free from guilt and able to guide us in a holy direction. The conscience can only be freed from guilt by the power of Christ's blood. Once freed and protected in its freedom by the gift of justification, the conscience is able to grow through the teaching of Scripture and the means of grace in Christian life.

24:20 you shall surely be king. Contrast Samuel's rebuke of Saul in 13:14, "But now your kingdom shall not continue." Yet in contrast to Jonathan's action in 18:4 (note), Saul gives no sign of being ready to give the throne to David (see 26:25 note).

25:1 all Israel . . . mourned for him. The extent of mourning is a sign of Samuel's prominence as a leader. Compare the mourning that accompanied the deaths of Jacob (Gen. 50:10), Aaron (Num. 20:29), and Moses (Deut. 34:8).

Ramah. Samuel's hometown (1:1 note).

25:2 Carmel. The same Carmel where Saul erected a monument in his own honor (15:12 notes). The setting of this incident near Carmel is the first of many reminders of Saul in this chapter.

25:3 Nabal. In v. 25 Abigail explains the name as meaning "folly." If it seems unlikely that parents would name a child "fool," it may simply be that this is a disparaging play on a name which sounded like "fool."

Calebite. On Caleb's tribal holdings, see Josh. 14:13; 15:13. The similarity of the name "Caleb" to the Hebrew word for "dog" (cf. 24:14 note) may account for the inclusion of this particular detail in the introduction of Nabal.

men, and they will tell you. Therefore let
my young men find favor in your eyes, for
we come [f] on a feast day. Please give whatever you have at hand to your servants and
to your son David.' "
9 When David's young men came, they
said all this to Nabal in the name of David,
and then they waited. 10 And Nabal
answered David's servants, [g] "Who is
David? Who is the son of Jesse? [h] There are
many servants these days who are breaking
away from their masters. 11 Shall I take [i] my
bread and my water and my meat that I
have killed for my shearers and give it to
[j] men who come from I do not know
where?" 12 So David's young men turned
away and came back and told him all this.
13 And David said to his men, "Every man
strap on his sword!" And every man of
them strapped on his sword. David also
strapped on his sword. And [k] about four
hundred men went up after David, [k] while
two hundred [l] remained with the baggage.
14 But one of the young men told Abigail,
Nabal's wife, "Behold, David sent messengers out of the wilderness to greet our master, and he [m] railed at them. 15 Yet the men
were very good to us, and we suffered no
harm, [n] and we did not miss anything when
we were in the fields, as long as we went
with them. 16 They were [o] a wall to us both
by night and by day, all the while we were
with them keeping the sheep. 17 Now therefore know this and consider what you
should do, [p] for harm is determined against
our master and against all his house, and
he is such [q] a worthless man that one cannot speak to him."
18 Then Abigail made haste and took two
hundred loaves and two skins of wine and
five sheep already prepared and five seahs[1]
of parched grain and a hundred clusters of
raisins and two hundred cakes of figs, and
laid them on donkeys. 19 And she said to
her young men, "Go on before me; behold,
I come after you." But she did not tell her
husband Nabal. 20 And as she rode on the
donkey and came down under cover of the
mountain, behold, David and his men
came down toward her, and she met them.
21 Now David had said, "Surely in vain have
I guarded all that this fellow has in the
wilderness, [r] so that nothing was missed of
all that belonged to him, and he has [s] returned me evil for good. 22 [t] God do so to
the enemies of David[2] and more also, if by
morning I leave so much as one male of all
who belong to him."
23 When Abigail saw David, she hurried
[u] and got down from the donkey [v] and fell
before David on her face and bowed to the
ground. 24 She fell at his feet and said, [w] "On
me alone, my lord, be the guilt. Please let
your servant speak in your ears, and hear
the words of your servant. 25 Let not my
lord regard [q] this worthless fellow, Nabal,
for as his name is, so is he. Nabal[3] is his
name, and folly is with him. But I your servant did not see the young men of my lord,
whom you sent. 26 Now then, my lord, [x] as
the LORD lives, and as your soul lives,
because [y] the LORD has restrained you from
bloodguilt and from [z] saving with your own
hand, now then [a] let your enemies and
those who seek to do evil to my lord be as
Nabal. 27 And now let this [b] present that
your servant has brought to my lord be
given to the young men who follow my
lord. 28 Please forgive the trespass of your
servant. For the LORD will certainly make

8 [f] Esth. 8:17; 9:19, 22
10 [g] [Judg. 9:28] [h] [Judg. 12:4]
11 [i] [Judg. 8:6] [j] [ch. 22:2]
13 [k] ch. 23:13; 27:2; [ch. 22:2] [l] ch. 30:24
14 [m] ch. 14:32; 15:19
15 [n] ver. 7, 21
16 [o] [Job 1:10]
17 [p] [ch. 20:7] [q] Deut. 13:13
21 [r] ver. 7, 15 [s] Ps. 109:5; [Prov. 17:13]
22 [t] See Ruth 1:17
23 [u] Josh. 15:18; Judg. 1:14; [Gen. 24:64] [v] ver. 41; Ruth 2:10
24 [w] [2 Sam. 14:9]
25 [q] [See ver. 17 above]
26 [x] See ch. 20:3 [y] [Gen. 20:6] [z] [Rom. 12:19; Heb. 10:30] [a] [2 Sam. 18:32]
27 [b] ch. 30:26; Gen. 33:11; [2 Kin. 5:15; 18:31]

1 A *seah* was about 7 quarts or 7.3 liters 2 Septuagint *to David*
3 *Nabal* means *fool*

25:8 your son David. Compare the attitude of respect and deference adopted by David in addressing Saul as "my father" in 24:11.

25:14 he railed at them. Nabal's attack on David's messengers is vicious. The Hebrew verb translated "railed" means "to shriek" or "to fly at" something and is closely related to the Hebrew noun for "birds of prey." The same verb is used of Saul in 15:19 to describe his unrestrained "pouncing" upon the Amalekite spoils (cf. 14:32).

25:16 They were a wall to us. Not only did David's men refrain from inflicting harm (v. 7), their presence also gave protection to the shepherds of Nabal (v. 21).

25:17 he is such a worthless man that one cannot speak to him. Nabal's plight springs from his own wickedness. His lack of knowledge is a refusal to know.

25:19 But she did not tell her husband Nabal. In refusing to confide in her husband, Abigail shows her lack of confidence in him. In view of Abigail's insight into the Lord's choice of David (v. 28 and note), her decision to go against her husband's wishes seems to fall under the category of obeying God rather than men (Acts 5:29).

25:22 if by morning I leave . . . one male. Unrestrained by any special status of the man Nabal (contrast 24:9–12), David is intent upon exacting personal revenge.

25:25 as his name is, so is he. See note on v. 3.

25:28 a sure house. Abigail's perception of David is as right as her husband's is wrong (vv. 10, 11; 2 Sam. 7:11–16).

fighting the battles of the LORD. Abigail's words hint at the difference between David's proper military role and the personal vendetta he is now pursuing. Righteous engagement in conflict means standing boldly for God and leaving personal injuries to be dealt with by the Lord (24:12).

evil shall not be found in you. To have taken his own revenge on an enemy

my lord [c]a sure house, because my lord [d]is
fighting the battles of the LORD, and evil
shall not be found in you so long as you
live. 29 If men rise up to pursue you and to
seek your life, the life of my lord shall be
bound in the bundle of the living in the
care of the LORD your God. And the lives of
your enemies [e]he shall sling out as from
the hollow of a sling. 30 And when the LORD
has done to my lord according to all the
good that he has spoken concerning you
and has appointed you prince over Israel,
31 my lord shall have no cause of grief or
pangs of conscience for having shed blood
without cause or for my lord taking
vengeance himself. And when the LORD has
dealt well with my lord, then remember
your servant."
32 And David said to Abigail, [f]"Blessed be
the LORD, the God of Israel, who sent you
this day to meet me! 33 Blessed be your discretion, and blessed be you, [y]who have
kept me this day from bloodguilt [z]and from
avenging myself with my own hand! 34 For
as surely [g]as the LORD the God of Israel
lives, [y]who has restrained me from hurting
you, unless you had hurried and come to
meet me, truly by morning there had not
been left to Nabal so much as one male."
35 Then David received from her hand what
she had brought him. And he said to her,
[h]"Go up in peace to your house. See, I have
obeyed your voice, and I have granted your
petition."
36 And Abigail came to Nabal, and
behold, [i]he was holding a feast in his
house, like the feast of a king. And Nabal's
heart [j]was merry within him, for he was
very drunk. So she told him nothing [k]at all
until the morning light. 37 In the morning,
when the wine had gone out of Nabal, his
wife told him these things, and his heart
died within him, and he became as a stone.
38 And about ten days later [l]the LORD struck
Nabal, and he died.
39 When David heard that Nabal was
dead, he said, [f]"Blessed be the LORD who

28 [c]1 Kin. 11:38; [ch. 2:35; 2 Sam. 7:11, 27; 1 Kin. 9:5; 1 Chr. 17:10, 25] [d]ch. 18:17
29 [e]Jer. 10:18
32 [f]Gen. 24:27; Ps. 41:13; 72:18; Luke 1:68
33 [y][See ver. 26 above] [z][See ver. 26 above]
34 [g]See Ruth 3:13 [y][See ver. 26 above]
35 [h]See ch. 1:17
36 [i][2 Sam. 13:23] [j][2 Sam. 13:28; 1 Kin. 21:7] [k]ch. 22:15
38 [l]ch. 26:10
39 [f][See ver. 32 above]
[m]See ch. 24:15 [n]ver. 26, 33, 34 [o]1 Kin. 2:44; [Ps. 7:16; Ezek. 17:19] [p][S. of S. 8:8]
41 [q][Ruth 2:10]
43 [r]Josh. 15:56 [s]ch. 27:3; 30:5; 2 Sam. 2:2; 3:2, 3; 1 Chr. 3:1
Chapter 26
1 [t]ch. 23:19; See Ps. 54
2 [u]ch. 23:14 [v]ch. 24:2
5 [w]ch. 14:50; 17:55; 2 Sam. 2:8 [x]ch. 17:20
6 [y]2 Sam. 2:18; 3:39; 16:10; 19:22; 1 Chr. 2:16 [z][Judg. 7:9-11]

has [m]avenged the insult I received at the
hand of Nabal, [n]and has kept back his servant from wrongdoing. [o]The LORD has
returned the evil of Nabal on his own
head." Then David sent and [p]spoke to
Abigail, to take her as his wife. 40 When the
servants of David came to Abigail at
Carmel, they said to her, "David has sent
us to you to take you to him as his wife."
41 And she rose [q]and bowed with her face to
the ground and said, "Behold, your hand-
maid is a servant to wash the feet of the servants of my lord." 42 And Abigail hurried
and rose and mounted a donkey, and her
five young women attended her. She followed the messengers of David and
became his wife.
43 David also took Ahinoam of [r]Jezreel,
[s]and both of them became his wives. 44 Saul
had given Michal his daughter, David's
wife, to Palti the son of Laish, who was of
Gallim.

David Spares Saul Again

26 [t]Then the Ziphites came to Saul at
Gibeah, saying, "Is not David hiding himself on the hill of Hachilah, which
is on the east of Jeshimon?" 2 So Saul arose
and went down to [u]the wilderness of Ziph
with [v]three thousand chosen men of Israel
to seek David in the wilderness of Ziph.
3 And Saul encamped on the hill of
Hachilah, which is beside the road on the
east of Jeshimon. But David remained in
the wilderness. When he saw that Saul
came after him into the wilderness, 4 David
sent out spies and learned that Saul had
come. 5 Then David rose and came to the
place where Saul had encamped. And
David saw the place where Saul lay, with
[w]Abner the son of Ner, the commander of
his army. Saul was lying within [x]the
encampment, while the army was encamped around him.
6 Then David said to Ahimelech the
Hittite, and to Joab's brother [y]Abishai the
son of Zeruiah, [z]"Who will go down with

would have made David little better than Saul, and David later praises the Lord for sending Abigail to deter him from such a transgression (v. 32).

25:29 bound . . . bundle . . . sling . . . sling. Note the poetic repetition in Abigail's speech.

25:36 like the feast of a king. This phrase invites the thought that Nabal is somehow like another king, Saul.

25:39 Blessed be the LORD. It would have been wrong for David to take matters into his own hands, but not because Nabal was innocent. Having heard of Nabal's death, David thanks the Lord for keeping him from personal wrongdoing while at the same time upholding his cause.

25:40–44 Abigail . . . Ahinoam . . . Michal. David now has three wives: Michal, Saul's daughter, who has been given to someone else; Ahinoam; and Abigail. See also 2 Sam. 2:2; 3:2, 3.

26:1 Ziphites came to Saul. See note 23:19.

26:6 Abishai the son of Zeruiah. See note 2 Sam. 2:18.

me into the camp to Saul?" And Abishai
said, "I will go down with you." 7 So David
and Abishai went to the army by night.
And there lay Saul sleeping within [x]the encampment, with his spear stuck in the
ground [a]at his head, and Abner and the
army lay around him. 8 Then said Abishai
to David, [b]"God has given your enemy into
your hand this day. Now please let me pin
him to the earth with one stroke of the
spear, and I will not strike him twice." 9 But
David said to Abishai, "Do not destroy
him, for who can put out his hand [c]against
the LORD's anointed and be guiltless?"
10 And David said, [d]"As the LORD lives, [e]the
LORD will strike him, or [f]his day will come
to die, [g]or he will go down into battle and
perish. 11 [h]The LORD forbid that I should
put out my hand against the LORD's anointed. But take now the spear that is [i]at his
head and the jar of water, and let us go."
12 So David took the spear and the jar of
water from Saul's head, and they went
away. No man saw it or knew it, nor did
any awake, for they were all asleep,
because [j]a deep sleep from the LORD had
fallen upon them.
13 Then David went over to the other side
and stood far off on the top of the hill, with
a great space between them. 14 And David
called to the army, and to Abner the son of
Ner, saying, "Will you not answer, Abner?"
Then Abner answered, "Who are you who
calls to the king?" 15 And David said to
Abner, "Are you not a man? Who is like
you in Israel? Why then have you not kept
watch over your lord the king? For one of
the people came in to destroy the king your
lord. 16 This thing that you have done is not
good. [k]As the LORD lives, you deserve to
die, because you have not kept watch over
your lord, the LORD's anointed. And now
see where the king's spear is and the jar of
water that was [l]at his head."

17 Saul recognized David's voice and said,
[m]"Is this your voice, my son David?" And
David said, "It is my voice, my lord, O
king." 18 And he said, [n]"Why does my lord
pursue after his servant? For what have I
done? What evil is on my hands? 19 Now
therefore let my lord the king hear the
words of his servant. If it is the LORD who
has stirred you up against me, may he
accept an offering, but if it is men, may
they be cursed before the LORD, [o]for they
have driven me out this day that I should
have no share in [p]the heritage of the LORD,
saying, 'Go, serve other gods.' 20 Now
therefore, let not my blood fall to the earth
away from the presence of the LORD, for the
king of Israel has come out to seek [q]a single flea like one who hunts a partridge in
the mountains."
21 Then Saul said, [r]"I have sinned.
Return, my son David, for I will no more
do you harm, because my life was precious
in your eyes this day. Behold, I have acted
foolishly, and have made a great mistake."
22 And David answered and said, "Here is
the spear, O king! Let one of the young
men come over and take it. 23 [s]The LORD
rewards every man for his righteousness
and his faithfulness, for the LORD gave you
into my hand today, and I would not put
out my hand against the LORD's anointed.
24 Behold, as your life was precious this day
in my sight, so may my life be precious in
the sight of the LORD, and may he deliver
me out of all tribulation." 25 Then Saul said
to David, "Blessed be you, my son David!
You will do many things and will [t]succeed
in them." So David went his way, and Saul
returned to his place.

David Flees to the Philistines

27 Then David said in his heart, "Now
I shall perish one day by the hand
of Saul. There is nothing better for me than

7 [x][See ver. 5 above] [a]ver. 11, 16
8 [b][ch. 24:4, 18]
9 [c]ver. 11, 16, 23; ch. 24:6, 10; [2 Sam. 1:16]
10 [d][Ruth 3:13] [e][ch. 25:38] [f][Gen. 47:29; Deut. 31:14] [g]ch. 31:6
11 [h]ch. 24:6 [i]ver. 7, 16
12 [j]Gen. 2:21; 15:12
16 [k][Ruth 3:13] [l]ver. 7, 11
17 [m]ch. 24:16
18 [n]ch. 24:9, 11
19 [o][Ps. 120:5] [p]2 Sam. 14:16; 20:19; 21:3
20 [q]ch. 24:14
21 [r]ch. 15:24; [ch. 24:17, 18]
23 [s][Ps. 7:8; 18:20]
25 [t][Gen. 32:28]

26:8 God has given your enemy. See note 24:4.

26:9 against the LORD's anointed. See 24:6 and note.

26:10 the LORD will strike him. David's words express an assurance gained or at least reinforced by the Lord's recent dealings with Nabal (25:38, 39).

26:12 a deep sleep from the LORD. David's survival and ultimate success are divinely overseen and directed (see also 30:2, 19 and notes).

26:19 the heritage of the LORD. See note 2 Sam. 20:19.

Go, serve other gods. David means that he was expelled to live among aliens, away from the people of God.

26:20 a partridge. The partridge, whose name in Hebrew means "caller," is a cleverly chosen name for David, who stands on the crest of a mountain and "calls" (vv. 13, 14).

26:21 I have sinned. Return. David's response to Saul's confession and invitation (v. 22) indicates he doubts Saul's sincerity; compare Samuel's response to a similar invitation by Saul in 15:24–26.

26:25 Blessed be you, my son David. Saul's behavior is erratic, and David trusts neither his confessions nor his blessings (27:1; see note 24:20).

27:1 one day by the hand of Saul. Despite recently learned lessons of faith (26:10), David tires of being a fugitive in constant danger and gives

that I should escape to the land of the
Philistines. Then Saul will despair of seeking me any longer within the borders of
Israel, and I shall escape out of his hand."
2 So David arose and went over, he and [u] the
six hundred men who were with him, [v] to
Achish the son of Maoch, king of Gath.
3 And David lived with Achish at Gath, he
and his men, every man with his household, and David with [w] his two wives,
Ahinoam of Jezreel, and Abigail of Carmel,
Nabal's widow. 4 And when it was told Saul
that David had fled to Gath, he no longer
sought him.
5 Then David said to Achish, "If [x] I have
found favor in your eyes, let a place be
given me in one of the country towns, that
I may dwell there. For why should your servant dwell in the royal city with you?" 6 So
that day Achish gave him [y] Ziklag. Therefore
Ziklag has belonged to the kings of Judah
to this day. 7 [z] And the number of the days
that David lived in the country of the
Philistines was a year and four months.
8 Now David [a] and his men went up and
made raids against [b] the Geshurites, [c] the
Girzites, and [d] the Amalekites, for these
were the inhabitants of the land from of
old, [e] as far as Shur, to the land of Egypt.
9 And David would strike the land and
would leave neither man nor woman alive,
but would take away the sheep, the oxen,
the donkeys, the camels, and the garments,
and come back to Achish. 10 When Achish
asked, "Where have you [f] made a raid
today?" David would say, "Against the
Negeb of Judah," or, "Against the Negeb of
[g] the Jerahmeelites," or, "Against the Negeb
of [h] the Kenites." 11 And David would leave
neither man nor woman alive to bring news
to Gath, thinking, "Lest they should tell
about us and say, 'So David has done.'"
Such was his custom all the while he lived
in the country of the Philistines. 12 And
Achish trusted David, thinking, "He has
made himself an utter stench to his people
Israel; therefore he shall always be my
servant."

Chapter 27
2 [u] ch. 23:13; [2 Sam. 15:18] [v] ch. 21:10; [1 Kin. 2:39]
3 [w] See ch. 25:43
5 [x] See Gen. 33:15
6 [y] Josh. 15:31
7 [z] [ch. 29:3]
8 [a] See 1 Chr. ch. 12 [b] Josh. 13:2 [c] [Josh. 16:10; Judg. 1:29] [d] [ch. 15:7, 8] [e] See ch. 15:7
10 [f] [ch. 23:27] [g] ch. 30:29 [h] See Judg. 1:16

Saul and the Medium of En-dor

28 In those days [i] the Philistines gathered their forces for war, to fight
against Israel. And Achish said to David,
"Understand that you and your men are to
go out with me in the army." 2 David said to
Achish, "Very well, you shall know what
your servant can do." And Achish said to
David, "Very well, I will make you my
bodyguard for life."
3 Now [j] Samuel had died, and all Israel
had mourned for him and buried him [k] in
Ramah, his own city. And Saul had put

Chapter 28
1 [i] [ch. 29:1]
3 [j] ch. 25:1 [k] ch. 1:19

in to the human fear that Saul will eventually succeed in destroying him. David's anxiety may be heightened since he and his men have their families with them (v. 3). For the second time (21:10), David seeks refuge among Israel's archenemies, the Philistines.

27:2 Achish. Now that the rift between David and Saul is conspicuous and indisputable, Achish readily accepts David's presence, doubtless hoping to benefit from David's allegiance in his own struggles against Saul (29:6).

27:3 his two wives. See note 25:40–44.

27:5 in the royal city with you. While David's request to be assigned to "one of the country towns" is ostensibly based on a desire not to burden the royal city, it promises him a greater freedom of action by removing him from the eyes of Achish (vv. 8–11).

27:6 Ziklag. Listed among the cities of Judah (Josh. 15:31; 19:5), ancient Ziklag may have been at Tel esh-Shariah, fifteen miles northwest of Beersheba. Once an Israelite possession, Ziklag was under Philistine control at this time.

kings of Judah. This expression is from the viewpoint of a time after the division of Israel into the northern and southern kingdoms (1 Kin. 12).

27:8 Geshurites. Neighbors of the Philistines (Josh. 13:2), these people are not the same as the Geshurites from east of the Jordan (Josh. 13:11; 2 Sam. 15:8; 1 Chr. 2:23). David's wife, Absalom's mother (2 Sam. 3:3), was from the Geshurites east of the Jordan.

Girzites. Not identifiable; Gezer is quite distant.

Amalekites. See note 15:2.

Shur. See note 15:7.

27:9 leave neither man nor woman alive. David's practice would conceal his double-dealings from Achish (v. 11). Whether it was right is doubtful at best in the absence of any indication that the Lord had ordered his actions.

27:10 David would say. This is not the first time David thinks it necessary to deceive (20:6; 21:2 and notes; cf. 16:2 note).

the Negeb of Judah. See 2 Sam. 24:7; 2 Chr. 28:18. The large southern region of Israel, the Negeb, extended from Beersheba south to the Gulf of Aqaba.

Jerahmeelites. 1 Chr. 2:9–15 mentions Jerahmeel as a descendant of Judah through Hezron and as a brother of Ram, an ancestor of David.

Kenites. Kenites and Jerahmeelites are mentioned together in 30:29.

27:12 Achish trusted David. Achish was deceived by David's pretense of raiding villages in Judah and its environs.

28:1 Understand. Achish points out that his benevolence to David has certain strings attached. The same Hebrew phrase is used in Solomon's warning to Shimei in 1 Kin. 2:37, 42.

28:2 what your servant can do. The irony of David's ambiguous answer (will David fight for or against him?) has a counterpoint in the perhaps unconscious irony of Achish's reply.

my bodyguard for life. Presumably Achish's offer is contingent on David's performance in battle. The Hebrew term used by Achish for "bodyguard" means literally "keeper of my head," an unfortunate choice of words in view of David's treatment of Goliath (17:49–54).

28:3 Samuel had died. The death of Samuel signals the passing of an era.

[l]the mediums and the necromancers out
of the land. [4]The Philistines assembled
and came and encamped [m]at Shunem.
And Saul gathered all Israel, and they
encamped [n]at Gilboa. [5]When Saul saw the
army of the Philistines, he was afraid, and
his heart trembled greatly. [6]And when
Saul inquired of the LORD, [o]the LORD did
not answer him, either [p]by dreams, or [q]by
Urim, or by prophets. [7]Then Saul said to
his servants, [r]"Seek out for me a woman
who is a medium, that I may go to her and
inquire of her." And his servants said to
him, "Behold, there is a medium at
[s]En-dor."

[8]So Saul [t]disguised himself and put on
other garments and went, he and two men
with him. And they came to the woman by
night. And he said, [u]"Divine for me by a
spirit and bring up for me whomever I
shall name to you." [9]The woman said to
him, "Surely you know what Saul has
done, [l]how he has cut off the mediums
and the necromancers from the land. Why
then are you laying a trap for my life to
bring about my death?" [10]But Saul swore
to her by the LORD, [v]"As the LORD lives, no
punishment shall come upon you for this
thing." [11]Then the woman said, "Whom
shall I bring up for you?" He said, "Bring
up Samuel for me." [12]When the woman
saw Samuel, she cried out with a loud
voice. And the woman said to Saul, "Why
have you deceived me? You are Saul."
[13]The king said to her, "Do not be afraid.
What do you see?" And the woman said to
Saul, "I see a god coming up out of the
earth." [14]He said to her, "What is his
appearance?" And she said, "An old man
is coming up, and he is wrapped [w]in a
robe." And Saul knew that it was Samuel,
and he bowed with his face to the ground
and paid homage.

[15]Then Samuel said to Saul, "Why have
you disturbed me by bringing me up?" Saul
answered, "I am in great distress, for the
Philistines are warring against me, and
[x]God has turned away from me and [y]an-
swers me no more, either by prophets or by
dreams. Therefore I have summoned you
to tell me what I shall do." [16]And Samuel
said, "Why then do you ask me, since the
LORD has turned from you and become
your enemy? [17]The LORD has done to you
as he spoke by me, for [z]the LORD has torn
the kingdom out of your hand and given it
to your neighbor, David. [18][a]Because you
did not obey the voice of the LORD and did
not carry out his fierce wrath against
Amalek, therefore the LORD has done this
thing to you this day. [19]Moreover, the LORD
will give Israel also with you into the hand
of the Philistines, and tomorrow you [b]and
your sons shall be with me. The LORD will
give the army of Israel also into the hand of
the Philistines."

[20]Then Saul fell at once full length on the
ground, filled with fear because of the
words of Samuel. And there was no
strength in him, for he had eaten nothing

3 [l][Ex. 22:18; Lev. 19:31; 20:27; Deut. 18:10, 11]
4 [m]Josh. 19:18 [n]ch. 31:1
6 [o]ver. 15; ch. 14:37 [p]Num. 12:6 [q][Ex. 28:30; Num. 27:21; Deut. 33:8]
7 [r][1 Chr. 10:13] [s]Josh. 17:11; Ps. 83:10
8 [t]1 Kin. 20:38; 22:30; 2 Chr. 18:29; 35:22 [u][Deut. 18:10]
9 [l][See ver. 3 above]
10 [v]See Ruth 3:13
14 [w]ch. 15:27
15 [x]ch. 16:14; 18:12 [y]ver. 6
17 [z]ch. 15:28
18 [a]ch. 15:9
19 [b]ch. 31:2

the mediums and the necromancers. Although Saul's expulsion of mediums and necromancers is fully in keeping with Mosaic law (Lev. 19:31; 20:6, 27; Deut. 18:11), it is only a partial proof of zeal for the religion of Israel. Saul's consultation of a medium is a clear indication of unfaithfulness and disobedience (1 Chr. 10:13), while Lev. 20:6 says that such a person is to be "cut . . . off from among his people."

28:4 Shunem. Located just southwest of the hill of Moreh and sixteen miles southwest of the Sea of Chinnereth (Galilee). Shunem was the site of the Philistine camp on the eve of the battle in which Saul died (ch. 31).

Gilboa. This is probably the mountain range that begins five miles south of Shunem and extends south along the eastern edge of the plain of Jezreel. It could also be a village located in the heart of the Gilboa range eleven miles south of Shunem. See 29:1 and note.

28:5 his heart trembled greatly. See 17:11 and note.

28:6 the LORD did not answer him. Saul's inquiry is prompted by anxiety (v. 5), not piety, and the Lord's refusal to answer is reminiscent of the threat of 8:18.

by dreams, or by Urim, or by prophets. Saul rejected the Lord and as a consequence was rejected by the Lord (15:23 and note). This cut him off from the usual means of divine inquiry. Whereas David had the prophet Gad in his retinue (22:5), it is unlikely that a true prophet accompanied Saul. Moreover, the authentic ephod containing the Urim and Thummim (2:28 note) had come into David's possession through Abiathar (23:6).

28:7 Seek out for me a woman who is a medium. His purge of the land notwithstanding (v. 3 note), Saul seems to have no doubt that a medium can be found, and his attendants can name one immediately.

En-dor. Josh. 17:11, 12 attests to a persistent Canaanite influence at En-dor, which was about five miles north of Shunem (v. 4 note). Saul's recourse to En-dor took him behind Philistine lines.

28:12 the woman saw Samuel. Probably this was Samuel, and not merely an apparition. The consternation of the medium shows that the figure was something outside her usual experience of magic arts. The narrator calls it simply "Samuel," and what the figure says is consistent with Samuel's pronouncements when alive (especially ch. 15). For some reason the Lord allowed Samuel to visit Saul. It is clear from the medium's reaction that she could not compel him to appear.

28:14 Saul knew that it was Samuel. Apparently Saul recognized Samuel when the woman described his mantle. Robes have symbolized the fate of Saul's kingship in a variety of ways, and mention of Samuel's mantle recollects the devastating pronouncement of 15:28 (see also 18:4; 24:4–6).

28:19 you and your sons shall be with me. That is, among the dead (31:2–4).

all day and all night. 21 And the woman
came to Saul, and when she saw that he
was terrified, she said to him, "Behold,
your servant has obeyed you. [c]I have taken
my life in my hand and have listened to
what you have said to me. 22 Now therefore,
you also obey your servant. Let me set a
morsel of bread before you; and eat, that
you may have strength when you go on
your way." 23 He refused and said, "I will
not eat." But his servants, together with the
woman, urged him, and he listened to their
words. So he arose from the earth and sat
on the bed. 24 Now the woman had a fattened calf in the house, and she quickly
killed it, and she took flour and kneaded it
and baked unleavened bread of it, 25 and
she put it before Saul and his servants, and
they ate. Then they rose and went away
that night.

The Philistines Reject David

29 [d]Now the Philistines had gathered
all their forces at [e]Aphek. And the
Israelites were encamped by [f]the spring
that is in [g]Jezreel. 2 As [h]the lords of the
Philistines were passing on by hundreds
and by thousands, and David and his men
were passing on in the rear [i]with Achish,
3 the commanders of the Philistines said,
"What are these Hebrews doing here?" And
Achish said to the commanders of the
Philistines, "Is this not David, the servant
of Saul, king of Israel, who has been with
me [j]now for days and years, and since he
deserted to me [k]I have found no fault in
him to this day." 4 But [h]the commanders of
the Philistines were angry with him. And
the commanders of the Philistines said to
him, "Send the man back, that he may
return [l]to the place to which you have
assigned him. He shall not go down with
us to battle, [m]lest in the battle he become
an adversary to us. For how could this fellow reconcile himself to his lord? Would it
not be with the heads of the men here? 5 Is
not this David, of whom they sing to one
another in dances,

[n]'Saul has struck down his thousands,
and David his ten thousands'?"

6 Then Achish called David and said to
him, [o]"As the LORD lives, you have been
honest, and to me it seems right that [p]you
should march out and in with me in the
campaign. For I have found nothing wrong
in you from the day of your coming to me
to this day. Nevertheless, the lords do not
approve of you. 7 So go back now; and go
peaceably, that you may not displease the
lords of the Philistines." 8 And David said
to Achish, "But what have I done? What
have you found in your servant from the
day I entered your service until now, that I
may not go and fight against the enemies of
my lord the king?" 9 And Achish answered
David and said, "I know that you are as
blameless in my sight [q]as an angel of God.
Nevertheless, [r]the commanders of the
Philistines have said, 'He shall not go up
with us to the battle.' 10 Now then rise early
in the morning [s]with the servants of your
lord who came with you, and start early in
the morning, and depart as soon as you
have light." 11 So David set out with his
men early in the morning to return to the
land of the Philistines. But the Philistines
went up to [t]Jezreel.

21 [c]See Judg. 12:3
Chapter 29
1 [d]ch. 28:1 [e]ch. 4:1; Josh. 12:18 [f]Judg. 7:1 [g]Josh. 17:16
2 [h]Josh. 13:3 [i]ch. 28:1, 2
3 [j][ch. 27:7] [k][Dan. 6:5]
4 [h][See ver. 2 above]
[l]ch. 27:6; 30:1 [m][ch. 14:21]
5 [n]ch. 18:7; 21:11
6 [o]See ch. 20:3 [p]2 Sam. 3:25; 2 Kin. 19:27; Ps. 121:8; Isai. 37:28
9 [q]2 Sam. 14:17, 20; 19:27 [r]Josh. 13:3
10 [s][1 Chr. 12:19, 22]
11 [t]Josh. 17:16

28:23 I will not eat. See note 1:7.

28:24 fattened calf. Much has changed since Saul's first encounter with Samuel, when he was designated as the one to deliver Israel from the Philistines (9:16) and was treated to a festal meal by the prophet (9:22–24). Now in his last encounter with Samuel, on the eve of his own death and the crushing Philistine defeat of Israel, Saul is treated to a fatted calf by a medium.

29:1 The Philistines had gathered. This notice resumes the account initiated in 28:1, 2 but suspended in order to relate Saul's visit with the medium (28:3–25).

Aphek. Probably the same Aphek mentioned in 4:1 (note), twenty-eight miles north of Gath. The Philistines assembled their forces at Aphek before continuing their northward march (v. 2).

Jezreel. North of Mount Gilboa, a few miles south of Shunem, and forty miles northeast of Aphek.

29:3 Hebrews. See note 4:6.

I have found no fault in him. This judgment is a measure of Achish's gullibility, not David's sincerity (27:8–12).

29:4 lest in the battle he become an adversary. The other Philistine commanders are less gullible than Achish and perhaps still carry painful memories of mid-battle defection in an earlier war with Israel (14:21).

29:5 Is not this David, of whom they sing. See note 18:7; 21:11.

29:8 But what have I done. A protest of genuine innocence when spoken to Saul (26:18), the question is now no more than a ruse. David has indeed done much (27:8–12), if Achish only could see it.

that I may not go and fight against the enemies of my lord the king. As in 28:2, David again deals in ambiguities apparent to the reader, if not to Achish. The ambiguity here is the identity of "my lord the king." It could be Achish, Saul, or possibly God Himself.

29:9 you are as blameless in my sight as an angel of God. Achish's grossly misplaced confidence makes him appear practically a fool. On the expression "angel of God," see 2 Sam. 14:17, 20; 19:27.

David's Wives Are Captured

30 Now when David and his men
came to [u]Ziklag on the third day,
[v]the Amalekites had [w]made a raid against
the Negeb and against Ziklag. They had
overcome Ziklag and burned it with fire
2 and taken captive the women and all[1]
who were in it, both small and great. They
killed no one, but carried them off and
went their way. 3 And when David and his
men came to the city, they found it burned
with fire, and their wives and sons and
daughters taken captive. 4 Then David and
the people who were with him raised their
voices and wept until they had no more
strength to weep. 5 David's [x]two wives also
had been taken captive, Ahinoam of Jezreel
and Abigail the widow of Nabal of Carmel.
6 And David was greatly distressed, for the
people spoke [y]of stoning him, because all
the people were bitter in soul,[2] each for his
sons and daughters. But David strengthened himself in the LORD his God.
7 [z]And David said to Abiathar the priest,
the son of Ahimelech, "Bring me the
ephod." So Abiathar brought the ephod to
David. 8 [a]And David inquired of the LORD,
"Shall I pursue after this [b]band? Shall I
overtake them?" He answered him,
"Pursue, for you shall surely overtake [c]and
shall surely rescue." 9 So David set out, and
[d]the six hundred men who were with him,
and they came to the brook Besor, where
those who were left behind stayed. 10 But
David pursued, he and four hundred men.
[e]Two hundred stayed behind, who were
too exhausted to cross the brook Besor.
11 They found an Egyptian in the open
country and brought him to David. And
they gave him bread and he ate. They gave
him water to drink, 12 and they gave him a
piece of a cake of figs and two clusters of
raisins. And when he had eaten, [f]his spirit
revived, for he had not eaten bread or
drunk water for three days and three
nights. 13 And David said to him, "To whom
do you belong? And where are you from?"
He said, "I am a young man of Egypt, servant to an Amalekite, and my master left
me behind because I fell sick three days
ago. 14 [g]We had made a raid against the
Negeb of [h]the Cherethites and against that
which belongs to Judah and against the
Negeb of Caleb, and we burned Ziklag with
fire." 15 And David said to him, "Will you
take me down to this band?" And he said,
"Swear to me by God that you will not kill
me or deliver me into the hands of my master, and I will take you down to this
[i]band."

David Defeats the Amalekites

16 And when he had taken him down,
behold, they were spread abroad over all
the land, eating and drinking and dancing,
because of all the great spoil they had
taken from the land of the Philistines and
from the land of Judah. 17 And David struck
them down from twilight until the evening
of the next day, and not a man of them
escaped, except four hundred young men,
who mounted camels and fled. 18 [j]David
recovered all that the Amalekites had
taken, and David rescued his two wives.
19 Nothing was missing, whether small or
great, sons or daughters, spoil or anything

1 Septuagint; Hebrew lacks *and all* 2 Compare 22:2

Chapter 30
1 [u]ch. 29:4, 11 [v]ch. 27:8; [ch. 15:3, 7] [w]ver. 14
5 [x]See ch. 25:42, 43
6 [y][Ex. 17:4; Num. 14:10]
7 [z]ch. 23:6, 9
8 [a]See ch. 22:10 [b][1 Chr. 12:21] [c]ver. 18
9 [d]See ch. 23:13
10 [e]ver. 21
12 [f]Judg. 15:19; [ch. 14:27]
14 [g]ver. 1 [h]2 Sam. 8:18; 15:18; 20:7, 23; 1 Kin. 1:38, 44; 1 Chr. 18:17; [Ezek. 25:16; Zeph. 2:5]
15 [i][ch. 25:3]
18 [j]ver. 8

30:1 Ziklag. See note 27:6.

Amalekites had made a raid. See notes 15:2, 8. Having been the victims of David's forays (27:8), the Amalekites have taken the opportunity of David's absence from Ziklag to retaliate.

the Negeb. See note 27:10.

30:2 They killed no one. A remarkable evidence of the Lord's providential protection of David (v. 19; 26:12), whose own practice had been quite different (27:9).

30:3 their wives and sons and daughters taken captive. This turn of events is especially troubling, inasmuch as concern for the safety of their families may have motivated the retreat of David and his men to Philistine territory in the first place (27:1 note).

30:6 David strengthened himself in the LORD his God. See note 23:16.

30:7 Abiathar brought the ephod. See note 22:20.

30:9 brook Besor. Seasonal rivers (or "wadis") from the vicinity of Beersheba and south converge to form the brook Besor, which runs northwest to empty into the Mediterranean. David and his men would have come to the ravine some thirteen miles south of Ziklag.

30:10 too exhausted. Their exhaustion is not surprising after a march of over sixty miles from Aphek (29:1–11) to the brook Besor.

30:14 the Negeb of the Cherethites. The Cherethites were probably from Crete. They are often mentioned alongside the Philistines (Ezek. 25:16; Zeph. 2:5). The "Cherethites and Pelethites" served under the command of Benaiah, son of Jehoiada, as professional troops loyal to David (2 Sam. 8:18; 15:18; 20:7, 23) and, for a short time at least, to Solomon (1 Kin. 1:44). They seem to have been the king's bodyguard (2 Sam. 23:20, 23).

the Negeb of Caleb. Caleb, son of Jephunneh, is first mentioned in Num. 13:6 as one of the spies chosen to scout out the land of Canaan. He is commended in Num. 14:24 as one who followed the Lord "fully" and who therefore would receive an inheritance in the Promised Land. His inheritance included Hebron (Josh. 14:13, 14; Judg. 1:20).

30:19 Nothing was missing. This is further, striking evidence of the Lord's watchful care over David's affairs (v. 2 note).

that had been taken. [j]David brought back
all. 20 David also captured all the flocks and
herds, and the people drove the livestock
before him,[l] and said, "This is David's
spoil."
21 Then David came to [k]the two hundred
men who had been too exhausted to follow
David, and who had been left [k]at the brook
Besor. And they went out to meet David
and to meet the people who were with him.
And when David came near to the people
he greeted them. 22 Then all the wicked and
worthless fellows among the men who had
gone with David said, "Because they did
not go with us, we will not give them any
of the spoil that we have recovered, except
that each man may lead away his wife and
children, and depart." 23 But David said,
"You shall not do so, my brothers, with
what the LORD has given us. He has preserved us and given into our hand the band
that came against us. 24 Who would listen
to you in this matter? [l]For as his share is
who goes down into the battle, so shall his
share be who stays by the baggage. They
shall share alike." 25 And he made it a
statute and a rule for Israel from that day
forward to this day.
26 When David came to Ziklag, he sent
part of the spoil to his friends, the elders of
Judah, saying, "Here is a present for you
from the spoil of the enemies of the LORD."
27 It was for those in [m]Bethel, in Ramoth of
the Negeb, in [n]Jattir, 28 in [o]Aroer, in
Siphmoth, in [p]Eshtemoa, 29 in Racal, in the
cities of [q]the Jerahmeelites, in the cities of
[r]the Kenites, 30 in [s]Hormah, in Bor-ashan,
in Athach, 31 in [t]Hebron, for all the places
where David and his men had roamed.

The Death of Saul

31 [u]Now the Philistines fought against
Israel, and the men of Israel fled
before the Philistines and fell slain [v]on
Mount Gilboa. 2 And the Philistines overtook Saul and his sons, and the Philistines
struck down [w]Jonathan and [x]Abinadab
and Malchi-shua, the sons of Saul. 3 [y]The
battle pressed hard against Saul, and the
archers found him, and he was badly
wounded by the archers. 4 [z]Then Saul said
to his armor-bearer, "Draw your sword,
and thrust me through with it, lest these
[a]uncircumcised come and thrust me
through, and mistreat me." But his armor-
bearer would not, [b]for he feared greatly.
Therefore Saul took his own sword [c]and
fell upon it. 5 And when his armor-bearer
saw that Saul was dead, he also fell upon
his sword and died with him. 6 Thus Saul
died, and his three sons, and his armor-
bearer, and all his men, on the same day
together. 7 And when the men of Israel
who were on the other side of the valley
and those beyond the Jordan saw that the
men of Israel had fled and that Saul and
his sons were dead, they abandoned their
cities and fled. And the Philistines came
and lived in them.
8 The next day, when the Philistines came
to strip the slain, they found Saul and his
three sons fallen on Mount Gilboa. 9 So
they cut off his head and stripped off his
armor and sent messengers throughout
the land of the Philistines, [d]to carry the
good news [e]to the house of their idols and
to the people. 10 [f]They put his armor in the
temple of [g]Ashtaroth, and they fastened

1 The meaning of the Hebrew clause is uncertain

19 [j][See ver. 18 above]
21 [k]ver. 10
24 [l][Num. 31:27; Josh. 22:8]
27 [m]Gen. 28:19; See Judg. 1:22-26 [n]Josh. 15:48
28 [o]Deut. 2:36; Josh. 13:16 [p]Josh. 15:50
29 [q]ch. 27:10 [r]See Judg. 1:16
30 [s]Judg. 1:17
31 [t]Josh. 14:13-15; Judg. 1:10; 2 Sam. 2:1-4

Chapter 31
1 [u]For ver. 1-13, see 1 Chr. 10:1-12 [v]ch. 28:4; [2 Sam. 1:6, 21; 21:12]
2 [w]1 Chr. 8:33 [x][ch. 14:49]
3 [y][2 Sam. 1:6]
4 [z][Judg. 9:54] [a]See Judg. 14:3 [b][2 Sam. 1:14] [c][2 Sam. 1:10]
9 [d][2 Sam. 1:20] [e][Judg. 16:23, 24]
10 [f][ch. 21:9] [g]See Judg. 2:13

30:21 brook Besor. See note on v. 9.

30:22 worthless fellows. See note 2:12, where the same Hebrew expression is used.

30:23 what the LORD has given us. David recognizes that the successful rescue is not his doing, but the Lord's (vv. 2, 19 and notes). This leads him to reject the idea that the front line troops have a right to more spoil than those who stayed behind.

30:26 spoil to . . . the elders of Judah. Probably he was thanking them for the help he received in escaping from Saul (v. 31), though it was also in this area that David's kingship was first officially recognized (2 Sam. 2:1–4).

30:27–31 As v. 31 says, these cities were within the range of David's roamings as a fugitive. All of them are in the south of Judah. This Bethel (v. 27), for example, should not be confused with the more northern city of the same name (7:16 note).

31:1 Mount Gilboa. See note 28:4.

31:2 Jonathan and Abinadab and Malchi-shua, the sons of Saul. See 14:49. For a listing of all four sons of Saul, see 1 Chr. 8:33. Chronicles gives the name Eshbaal, which was probably altered later to Ish-bosheth ("man of shame") to avoid any association with the Canaanite god Baal. Ish-bosheth was the only son of Saul left alive after the defeat on Mount Gilboa.

31:4 uncircumcised. See note 14:6.

Saul took his own sword and fell upon it. While some praise Saul's action as worthy of a tragic hero, the tenor of the books of Samuel points in another direction. To be commended are those who like David in times of distress find strength in God (23:16; 30:6), and who like Jonathan yield fully to His will (18:4, 28, 29; 19:4; 20:31; 23:17 and notes).

31:6 all his men. On the qualified sense of "all," see the note on 15:8.

31:10 Ashtaroth. These were the fertility goddesses of the Canaanites.

his body to the wall of [h]Beth-shan. 11 [i]But
when the inhabitants of Jabesh-gilead
heard what the Philistines had done to
Saul, 12 [j]all the valiant men arose and went
all night and took the body of Saul and the
bodies of his sons from the wall of Beth-
shan, and they came to Jabesh [k]and
burned them there. 13 And they took their
bones [l]and buried them under [m]the
tamarisk tree in Jabesh and [n]fasted seven
days.

10 [h]Josh. 17:11
11 [i]2 Sam. 21:10; See ch. 11:1-11
12 [j]2 Sam. 2:4-7

[k][2 Chr. 16:14; 21:19; Jer. 34:5] 13 [l]2 Sam. 21:12, 14 [m][ch. 22:6] [n][Gen. 50:10]

Beth-shan. Located in the Jordan Valley some sixteen miles south of the Sea of Chinnereth (Galilee), this border city of the territory of Manasseh is listed in Josh. 17:11, 16; Judg. 1:27 among those cities that resisted Israelite occupation and remained Canaanite and Philistine strongholds.

31:11 Jabesh-gilead. See note 11:1.

31:12 took the body of Saul . . . from the wall. This courageous act of the "valiant men" of Jabesh-gilead is an expression of gratitude for their own rescue by Saul recounted in ch. 11. It was also regarded as extremely shameful for the dead to be unburied.

THE SECOND BOOK OF Samuel

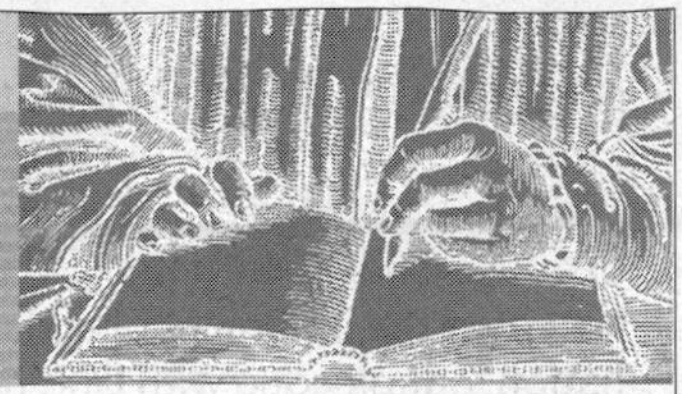

AUTHOR

The author of 2 Samuel is unknown. Although some of the material recounted in 1 Samuel may have been derived from writings by the prophet Samuel (cf. 1 Chr. 29:29), all the events reported in 2 Samuel occurred after his lifetime.

DATE AND OCCASION

In their original form, 1 and 2 Samuel were a single book. This book was completed as part of the "Deuteronomic History" during the exile of Judah in Babylon (see "Introduction to the Historical Books" on page 295). The narratives are based on sources and traditions contemporary with the events themselves.

CHARACTERISTICS AND THEMES

With Saul now dead (1 Sam. 31), the way is open for David to take the throne without lifting his hand against "the LORD's anointed" (cf. 1 Sam. 24:5, 6). David became a king by stages, first over Judah and then over all Israel (1:1–5:5). Though his ascendancy over Judah proceeds smoothly, blood is spilled before he becomes king over the whole nation. The narratives emphasize that David is innocent of the deaths of Abner (Saul's former general) and Ish-bosheth (Saul's only surviving son), as he was innocent of the deaths of Saul and Jonathan.

The attention of the narrative then shifts to the transactions, both political and theological, by which David's throne is established. David's acquisition of a capital city, his resounding defeat of the Philistines, and his transfer of the ark of God to his newly established capital, Jerusalem, are recounted in chs. 5 and 6. Then the Lord, after refusing David's offer to build a house for Him, makes a covenant with David that He will build a house or dynasty for David that will endure forever. This promise is the continuation and specification of the divine covenant with the patriarchs and is a major development of the messianic hope that will be fulfilled in Christ (7:4–17 note). David's principal achievements included his military victories (expanding Israel's borders to the limits promised to Abraham in Gen. 15:18) and his covenant faithfulness to Jonathan, which David expresses by showing kindness to Mephibosheth (chs. 6–8).

The Davidic covenant of ch. 7 establishes that the purposes of God for the house of David are sure. The promise does not make it impossible for David or his descendants to forfeit some of the temporal benefits of their privileged position if they should fall into sin. Domestic and political chaos followed David's sin against Uriah and Bathsheba (ch. 11). When confronted by Nathan (ch. 12), David's repentance is genuine, and God's forgiveness is immediate. Yet sin still has its consequences. With his ability to exercise proper authority impaired (perhaps by a sense of guilt), David witnesses his own sins replicated in the lives of his sons (13:21 note). Not until he has survived two rebellions, first by his own son Absalom and then by Sheba, son of Bichri (ch. 20), does David's reign regain a measure of equilibrium.

Thematic closure is provided for the books of Samuel by a kind of epilogue in chs. 21–24. The chapters are symmetrical in outline, and at the center are two poems celebrating the two fundamental reasons for David's blessedness. First, the Lord is his deliverer (22:2–51), and second, the Lord has made an "everlasting covenant" with him (23:1–7). Framing this poetic core are lists of David's champions (21:15–22; 23:8–39), the human agents of his success. Finally, the first and last sections are accounts of how David made atonement for Saul's sin against the

Gibeonites (21:3), and then for his own sin of taking a census of the people (ch. 24). In the first case David averted a famine by handing over for death seven of Saul's family. In the second, he accepted the judgment of a plague upon the nation, but pleaded with God that it be cut short before Jerusalem was struck. David's prayer was heard. David was disqualified from building a temple because of the blood he had shed during his life (1 Chr. 22:8; 28:3), but these books reveal the fervency of his heart and how he valued his relationship with God above all else.

OUTLINE OF 2 SAMUEL

I. God Enthrones David over Judah and Israel (1:1–5:5)

A. David Becomes King over Judah (1:1–2:7)

1. David Avenges and Laments the Deaths of Saul and Jonathan (ch. 1)
2. David Anointed King over Judah (2:1–7)

B. David Becomes King over Israel (2:8–5:5)

1. Abner Makes Ish-bosheth King over Israel, and There Is War Between the Houses of Saul and David (2:8–32)
2. Abner Goes over to David and Is Murdered by Joab (ch. 3)
3. Ish-bosheth Is Assassinated, and David Becomes King over All Israel (4:1–5:5)

II. David Gains a City and a Promise of an Everlasting Dynasty (5:6–10:19)

A. David Establishes His Capital in Jerusalem (5:6–6:23)

1. David Captures Jerusalem and Defeats the Philistines (5:6–25)
2. David Brings the Ark of God to Jerusalem (ch. 6)

B. God Promises David an Everlasting Dynasty (ch. 7)

C. David's Achievements as King (chs. 8–10)

1. David's Victories and Officers (ch. 8)
2. David's Kindness to Mephibosheth (ch. 9)
3. David's Kindness to Hanun Is Rebuffed, and War with Ammon Ensues (ch. 10)

III. David Sins and Suffers the Consequences (chs. 11–20)

A. David Sins and Finds Reconciliation (chs. 11; 12)

1. Bathsheba and Uriah (ch. 11)
2. David Repents, but His Sin Carries Consequences (ch. 12)

B. David's Sons Sin, but Reconciliation Is Incomplete (chs. 13; 14)

1. Amnon Commits Sexual Sin, and Absalom Commits Murder (ch. 13)
2. Absalom Returns to Jerusalem but Is Not Fully Reconciled to David (ch. 14)

C. Absalom Rebels and Dies (chs. 15–18)

1. Absalom Revolts Against David and David Flees Jerusalem (ch. 15)
2. Shimei Curses David (ch. 16)
3. Hushai Confuses the War Council of Absalom (ch. 17)
4. Absalom Is Killed by Joab and Mourned by David (ch. 18)

D. God Restores David's Reign (chs. 19; 20)

1. David Returns to Jerusalem (ch. 19)
2. Sheba's Attempts to Secede (ch. 20)

IV. Epilogue: Last Words About David's Reign (chs. 21–24)

A. A Famine Resulting from Saul's Sin Is Stopped (21:1–14)

B. Human Agents of David's Success (21:15–22)

C. David Sings the Praises of God (ch. 22)

D. David's "Last Words" (23:1–7)

E. More Human Agents of David's Success (23:8–39)

F. A Plague Resulting from David's Sin Is Stopped (ch. 24)

David Hears of Saul's Death

1 After the death of Saul, when David
had returned [a]from striking down the
Amalekites, David remained two days in
Ziklag. 2 And on the third day, behold, [b]a
man came from Saul's camp, [c]with his
clothes torn and dirt on his head. And
when he came to David, [d]he fell to the
ground and paid homage. 3 David said to
him, "Where do you come from?" And he
said to him, "I have escaped from the camp
of Israel." 4 And David said to him, [e]"How
did it go? Tell me." And he answered, "The
people fled from the battle, and also many
of the people have fallen and are dead, and
Saul and his son Jonathan are also dead."
5 Then David said to the young man who
told him, "How do you know that Saul and
his son Jonathan are dead?" 6 And the
young man who told him said, [f]"By chance
I happened to be on Mount Gilboa, and
there was Saul leaning on his spear, and
behold, the chariots and the horsemen
were close upon him. 7 And when he
looked behind him, he saw me, and called
to me. And I answered, 'Here I am.' 8 And
he said to me, 'Who are you?' I answered
him, 'I am an Amalekite.' 9 And he said to
me [g]'Stand beside me and kill me, for
anguish has seized me, and yet my life still
lingers.' 10 So I stood beside him and killed
him, because I was sure that he could not
live after he had fallen. [h]And I took the
crown that was on his head and the armlet
that was on his arm, and I have brought
them here to my lord."
11 Then David took hold of his clothes and
[i]tore them, and so did all the men who were
with him. 12 And they mourned and wept
[j]and fasted until evening for Saul and for
Jonathan his son and for the people of the
LORD and for the house of Israel, because
they had fallen by the sword. 13 And David
said to the young man who told him,
"Where do you come from?" And he
answered, "I am the son of a sojourner, an
Amalekite." 14 David said to him, "How is it
you were not [k]afraid to put out your hand to
destroy [l]the LORD's anointed?" 15 Then
[m]David called one of the young men and
said, "Go, execute him." And he struck him
down so that he died. 16 And David said to
him, [n]"Your blood be on your head, for your
own mouth has testified against you, saying,
'I have killed [o]the LORD's anointed.'"

David's Lament for Saul and Jonathan

17 And David [p]lamented with this lamentation over Saul and Jonathan his son,
18 and he said it[1] should be taught to the
people of Judah; behold, it is written in
[q]the Book of Jashar.[2] He said:

19 "Your glory, O Israel, is slain on your
high places!
[r]How the mighty have fallen!
20 [s]Tell it not in Gath,
[t]publish it not in the streets of
Ashkelon,
[u]lest the daughters of the Philistines
rejoice,

Chapter 1
1 [a]See 1 Sam. 30:17-20
2 [b]ch. 4:10 [c]See Josh. 7:6 [d]ch. 14:4
4 [e][1 Sam. 4:16]
6 [f]For ver. 6-10, see 1 Sam. 31:1-4; 1 Chr. 10:1-6
9 [g][Judg. 9:54]
10 [h][2 Kin. 11:12]
11 [i]ch. 13:31; [ch. 3:31]; See Josh. 7:6
12 [j][ch. 3:35]
14 [k][1 Sam. 24:6, 10; 26:9; 31:4] [l]See 1 Sam. 12:3
15 [m]ch. 4:10
16 [n][ch. 3:29; Josh. 2:19; 1 Kin. 2:32, 37; Matt. 27:25] [o]See 1 Sam. 12:3
17 [p][ch. 3:33; 2 Chr. 35:25]
18 [q]Josh. 10:13
19 [r]ver. 25, 27
20 [s]Mic. 1:10 [t][1 Sam. 31:9; Amos 3:9] [u][Ex. 15:20; Judg. 11:34]

1 Septuagint; Hebrew *the Bow*, which may be the name of the lament's tune 2 Or *of the upright*

1:1 Ziklag. See 1 Sam. 30:1; note on 1 Sam. 27:6.

1:2 clothes torn and dirt on his head. In the wake of Israel's devastating defeat (1 Sam. 31:1), the messenger apparently thinks it appropriate to take on the appearance of mourning (cf. Josh. 7:6; 1 Sam. 4:12). His claim to have had a hand in Saul's death (v. 10), however, shows that he expects at least this item of news to please David.

1:6 chariots and the horsemen were close upon him. Chariots often carried archers (cf. Saul's injury, 1 Sam. 31:3).

1:10 I stood beside him and killed him. The Amalekite must have happened upon Saul's body before the Philistines (1 Sam. 31:8). In the hopes of receiving a reward from David he fabricated a part for himself in Saul's death.

crown . . . armlet. The crown in view is presumably a lighter version of the heavy state crown. The way in which Saul's regalia came into David's possession is a stark contrast to Jonathan's voluntary surrender of his robe and weapons to David (1 Sam. 18:4 and note). This contrast epitomizes the radically different responses of Saul and Jonathan to the divine will with respect to David and the house of Saul (e.g., 1 Sam. 18:28, 29; 19:4; 20:30, 31; 23:17, 18).

1:14 the LORD's anointed. By not sharing David's conviction about the sacrosanct status of "the LORD's anointed" (1 Sam. 24:6; 26:9), the Amalekite signs his own death warrant (vv. 15, 16).

1:15 Go, execute him. David's severe reaction to the Amalekite's story provides evidence that he was not involved in Saul's death (cf. 4:10).

1:17 David lamented. The lament opens with an introduction presenting the refrain, "How the mighty have fallen!" The first section exhorts the people to mourn for Saul, and is marked by the references to "the daughters of the Philistines" (v. 20) and the "daughters of Israel" (v. 24). The second section (vv. 25, 26) expresses David's personal mourning for Jonathan. The lament closes with a final repetition of the mournful refrain.

1:18 it should be taught. "Weapons of war" (v. 27) probably stands for Saul and Jonathan. Compare the designation of Elijah and Elisha as "the chariots of Israel and its horsemen" (2 Kin. 2:12; 13:14).

Book of Jashar. See note Josh. 10:13.

1:19 How the mighty have fallen. This phrase, which refers to Saul and Jonathan (v. 17), is repeated as a refrain in vv. 25 and 27. "Mighty" occurs also in v. 21 in parallel to "Saul."

1:20 Tell it not in Gath. David implores his listeners not to let the news be heard among the Philistine cities, lest the daughters of the Philistines rejoice over Israel's defeat, as the daughters of Israel had earlier rejoiced over the defeat of the Philistines (1 Sam. 18:7).

lest the daughters of [v]the
uncircumcised exult.

21 [w]"You mountains of Gilboa,
let there be no dew or rain upon you,
nor fields of offerings![1]
For there the shield of the mighty
was defiled,
the shield of Saul, not [x]anointed
with oil.

22 "From the blood of the slain,
from the fat of the mighty,
[y]the bow of Jonathan turned not back,
and the sword of Saul returned not
empty.

23 "Saul and Jonathan, beloved and lovely!
In life and in death they were not
divided;
they were [z]swifter than eagles;
they were [a]stronger than lions.

24 "You daughters of Israel, weep over
Saul,
who clothed you luxuriously in
scarlet,
[b]who put ornaments of gold on
your apparel.

25 [c]"How the mighty have fallen
in the midst of the battle!

"Jonathan lies slain on your high places.
26 I am distressed for you, my brother
Jonathan;
very pleasant have you been to me;
[d]your love to me was extraordinary,
surpassing the love of women.

27 [c]"How the mighty have fallen,
and the weapons of war perished!"

20[v]See Judg. 14:3
21[w]1 Sam. 31:1 [x][1 Sam. 10:1]
22[y][1 Sam. 18:4]
23[z][Jer. 4:13; Hab. 1:8] [a][Judg. 14:18]
24[b][Ezek. 16:11]
25[c]ver. 19
26[d]See 1 Sam. 18:1, 3
27[c][See ver. 25 above]
Chapter 2
1[e]See 1 Sam. 22:10 [f]See Josh. 14:13
2[g]See 1 Sam. 25:42, 43
3[h]1 Sam. 27:2, 3; 30:1; See 1 Chr. 12:1-22
4[i]ch. 5:5 [j]1 Sam. 31:11-13
5[k]See Ruth 2:20
7[i][See ver. 4 above]
8[l]1 Sam. 14:50 [m]See Josh. 13:26

David Anointed King of Judah

2 After this David [e]inquired of the LORD,
"Shall I go up into any of the cities of
Judah?" And the LORD said to him, "Go
up." David said, "To which shall I go up?"
And he said, "To [f]Hebron." 2 So David went
up there, and [g]his two wives also, Ahinoam
of Jezreel and Abigail the widow of Nabal
of Carmel. 3 And David brought up [h]his
men who were with him, everyone with his
household, and they lived in the towns of
Hebron. 4 And the men of Judah came, and
there they anointed David [i]king over the
house of Judah.

When they told David, [j]"It was the men
of Jabesh-gilead who buried Saul," 5 David
sent messengers to the men of Jabesh-
gilead and said to them, [k]"May you be
blessed by the LORD, because you showed
this loyalty to Saul your lord and buried
him. 6 Now may the LORD show steadfast
love and faithfulness to you. And I will do
good to you because you have done this
thing. 7 Now therefore let your hands be
strong, and be valiant, for Saul your lord [i]is
dead, and the house of Judah has anointed
me king over them."

Ish-bosheth Made King of Israel

8 But [l]Abner the son of Ner, commander
of Saul's army, took Ish-bosheth the son of
Saul and brought him over to [m]Mahanaim,

1 Septuagint *firstfruits*

1:21 not anointed with oil. It was customary to condition and preserve leather shields by rubbing them with oil (Is. 21:5). It may be more than coincidental that the particular wording is associated with royalty. Not only were kings "anointed" (1 Sam. 2:10 note) for their office, but the word "shield" is sometimes used in the Old Testament as a figure for "sovereign" or "chieftain." Beneath the literal meaning of the words is perhaps the implication, "sovereign Saul, no longer anointed with oil."

1:22 the sword of Saul returned not empty. The intent of this line is to praise Saul's military prowess.

1:26 surpassing the love of women. David's praise of Jonathan's love (cf. 1 Sam. 18:3) does not mean that love between friends is inherently superior to marital love. Rather, the point seems to be the astonishingly selfless quality of Jonathan's love for David. David was himself not selfless in his relations with women (3:2 note).

2:1 David inquired of the LORD. Though aware of his divine appointment to become Israel's next king, David seeks the Lord's guidance, as he has done so often before (e.g., 1 Sam. 23:2, 4, 9–12; 30:7, 8).

Hebron. Located nineteen miles southwest of Jerusalem, Hebron has the highest elevation of any town in Israel and was strategically well suited for the inauguration of David's rule over Judah. Hebron was a Canaanite royal city when the Israelites came from Egypt (Josh. 10:3), but its links with the people of God extend back to the patriarchs (e.g., Gen. 13:18; 23:2, 19; 35:27).

2:2 Ahinoam . . . Abigail. See 1 Sam. 25:40–44 note.

Jezreel. Listed in Josh. 15:56 as one of the hill country villages south of Hebron, this Jezreel is not the better-known Jezreel in the north (v. 9).

Carmel. See notes 1 Sam. 15:12; 25:2.

2:4 anointed David king. On anointing, see 1 Sam. 2:10 note. David had already been anointed by Samuel (1 Sam. 16:3, 12, 13) and is now anointed again, this time as king over Judah. He will be anointed a third time, as king over Israel (5:3).

2:5 May you be blessed by the LORD. David's commendation of the Jabeshites for their kindness to Saul accomplishes two things. It shows he has no malice towards the now deceased king, and it sets the stage for his own bid for leadership over the Gileadites east of the Jordan River.

2:8–32 Abner's installation of Saul's son Ish-bosheth as king over Israel results in war between the houses of Saul and David.

2:8 Ish-bosheth. See note 1 Sam. 31:2. As will become apparent, this last surviving son of Saul is little more than a pawn in the hand of Abner.

brought him over to Mahanaim. Abner brought Ish-bosheth across the

9 and he made him king over Gilead and
the Ashurites and Jezreel and Ephraim and
Benjamin and all Israel. 10 Ish-bosheth,
Saul's son, was forty years old when he
began to reign over Israel, and he reigned
two years. But the house of Judah followed
David. 11 [n]And the time that David was king
in Hebron over [i]the house of Judah was
seven years and six months.

The Battle of Gibeon

12 Abner the son of Ner, and the servants
of Ish-bosheth the son of Saul, went out
from Mahanaim to Gibeon. 13 And Joab the
son of Zeruiah and the servants of David
went out and met them at [o]the pool of
Gibeon. And they sat down, the one on the
one side of the pool, and the other on the
other side of the pool. 14 And Abner said to
Joab, "Let the young men arise and compete before us." And Joab said, "Let them
arise." 15 Then they arose and passed over
by number, twelve for Benjamin and Ish-
bosheth the son of Saul, and twelve of the
servants of David. 16 And each caught his
opponent by the head and thrust his sword
in his opponent's side, so they fell down
together. Therefore that place was called
Helkath-hazzurim,[1] which is at Gibeon.
17 And the battle was very fierce that day.
And Abner and the men of Israel were beat-
en before the servants of David.

18 And the [p]three sons of Zeruiah were
there, Joab, Abishai, and Asahel. Now
Asahel was [q]as swift of foot as a wild
gazelle. 19 And Asahel pursued Abner, and
as he went, he turned neither to the right
hand nor to the left from following Abner.
20 Then Abner looked behind him and said,
"Is it you, Asahel?" And he answered, "It is
I." 21 Abner said to him, "Turn aside to your
right hand or to your left, and seize one of
the young men and take his spoil." But
Asahel would not turn aside from following
him. 22 And Abner said again to Asahel,
"Turn aside from following me. Why
should I strike you to the ground? How
then could I lift up my face to your brother Joab?" 23 But he refused to turn aside.
Therefore Abner struck him [r]in the stomach with the butt of his spear, so that the
spear came out at his back. And he fell
there and died where he was. And all who
came to the place where Asahel had fallen
and died, stood still.

24 But Joab and Abishai pursued Abner.
And as the sun was going down they came
to the hill of Ammah, which lies before
Giah on the way to the wilderness of Gibeon. 25 And the people of Benjamin gathered themselves together behind Abner
and became one group and took their
stand on the top of a hill. 26 Then Abner
called to Joab, "Shall the sword devour forever? Do you not know that the end will be
bitter? How long will it be before you tell
your people to turn from the pursuit of
their brothers?" 27 And Joab said, "As God
lives, if [s]you had not spoken, surely the
men would not have given up the pursuit
of their brothers until the morning." 28 So
Joab blew the trumpet, and all the men
stopped and pursued Israel no more, nor
did they fight anymore.

11 [n]ch. 5:5; 1 Kin. 2:11 [i][See ver. 4 above]
13 [o][Jer. 41:12]
18 [p]1 Chr. 2:16; [1 Sam. 26:6] [q][ch. 22:34; 1 Chr. 12:8; Ps. 18:33; S. of S. 2:17; 8:14; Hab. 3:19]
23 [r]ch. 3:27; 4:6; 20:10
27 [s]ver. 14; [Prov. 17:14]

[1] *Helkath-hazzurim* means *the field of sword-edges*

Jordan River, probably in an effort to escape Philistine pressure. Two sites near the Jabbok River have been suggested for Mahanaim, one seven miles and the other seventeen miles from the river.

2:9 king over Gilead, . . . all Israel. The way specific parts are listed suggests that Ish-bosheth's control of these areas was more complete than his control of Israel as a whole.

2:11 seven years and six months. See note 5:4, 5.

2:12 Gibeon. Gibeon was a Benjaminite town, now called el-Jib, about five miles north of Jerusalem.

2:13 Joab the son of Zeruiah. See note on v. 18.

2:14 Let the young men arise and compete. Abner suggests a form of representative combat similar to the contest between David and Goliath (1 Sam. 17:4 note). Large-scale bloodshed was not averted either time (vv. 17, 31).

2:18 three sons of Zeruiah. According to 1 Chr. 2:16, Zeruiah was one of David's two sisters, which would make her sons his nephews.

Joab. Joab played an important role throughout David's reign, serving as commander of David's forces (8:16). Though an ardent supporter of David, Joab at times proved to be uncontrollable (3:39), acting in his own interests (3:26, 27) and even defying David's orders (18:5, 9–14). Joab was executed by King Solomon (1 Kin. 2:28–35).

Abishai. Abishai served alongside Joab in David's army (10:10; 18:2; 23:18).

Asahel. Also listed among David's mighty men (23:24), Asahel's relentless pursuit of Abner in this present episode will lead to a violent death (v. 23).

2:22 How then could I . . . your brother Joab. Abner's attempts to avoid striking down Asahel may be motivated not simply by fear of reprisal from Joab, but also by a desire not to erect unnecessary barriers to eventual compromise with David. See note on v. 26.

2:26 tell your people to turn from the pursuit of their brothers. Abner's reference to "their brothers" may suggest a shift in a more conciliatory direction; perhaps Abner senses that David cannot be stopped. Abner would prefer truce to defeat, especially if he could remain autonomous.

2:28 trumpet. See note 1 Sam. 13:3.

29 And Abner and his men went all that
night through [t]the Arabah. They crossed
the Jordan, and marching the whole morning, they came to [u]Mahanaim. 30 Joab
returned from the pursuit of Abner. And
when he had gathered all the people
together, there were missing from David's
servants nineteen men besides Asahel.
31 But the servants of David had struck
down of Benjamin 360 of Abner's men.
32 And they took up Asahel and buried him
in the tomb of his father, which was at
Bethlehem. And Joab and his men
marched all night, and the day broke upon
them at Hebron.

Abner Joins David

3 There was a long war between the
house of Saul and the house of David.
And David grew stronger and stronger,
while the house of Saul became weaker and
weaker.
2 [v]And sons were born to David at Hebron: his firstborn was Amnon, of [w]Ahin-
oam of Jezreel; 3 and his second, Chileab, of
[w]Abigail the widow of Nabal of Carmel;
and the third, Absalom the son of Maacah
[x]the daughter of Talmai king of [y]Geshur;
4 and the fourth, [z]Adonijah the son of Haggith; and the fifth, Shephatiah the son of
Abital; 5 and the sixth, Ithream, of Eglah,
David's wife. These were born to David in
Hebron.
6 While there was war between the house
of Saul and the house of David, Abner was
making himself strong in the house of Saul.
7 Now Saul had a concubine whose name
was [a]Rizpah, the daughter of Aiah. And
Ish-bosheth said to Abner, [b]"Why have you
gone in to my father's concubine?" 8 Then
Abner was very angry over the words of Ish-
bosheth and said, "Am I [c]a dog's head of
Judah? To this day I keep showing steadfast love to the house of Saul your father, to
his brothers, and to his friends, and have
not given you into the hand of David. And
yet you charge me today with a fault concerning a woman. 9 [d]God do so to Abner
and more also, if I do not accomplish for
David [e]what the LORD has sworn to him,
10 to transfer the kingdom from the house
of Saul and set up the throne of David over
Israel and over Judah, [f]from Dan to
Beersheba." 11 And Ish-bosheth could not
answer Abner another word, because he
feared him.
12 And Abner sent messengers to David
on his behalf,[1] saying, "To whom does the
land belong? Make your covenant with me,
and behold, my hand shall be with you to
bring over all Israel to you." 13 And he said,
"Good; I will make a covenant with you.
But one thing I require of you; that is, [g]you
shall not see my face unless you first bring
[h]Michal, Saul's daughter, when you come
to see my face." 14 Then David sent messengers to Ish-bosheth, Saul's son, saying,

[1] Or *where he was*; Septuagint *at Hebron*

29 [t]See Deut. 1:1 [u]ver. 8; See Josh. 13:26
Chapter 3
2 [v]For ver. 2-5, see 1 Chr. 3:1-4 [w]1 Sam. 25:42, 43
3 [w][See ver. 2 above] [x]ch. 13:37, 38 [y]ch. 14:32; 15:8; [1 Sam. 27:8]
4 [z]1 Kin. 1:5
7 [a]ch. 21:8-10 [b][ch. 16:21]
8 [c]See 1 Sam. 17:43
9 [d]ver. 35; See Ruth 1:17 [e]1 Sam. 15:28; 16:1, 12; 28:17; 1 Chr. 12:23
10 [f]ch. 17:11; 24:2, 15; Judg. 20:1; 1 Sam. 3:20; 1 Kin. 4:25
13 [g][Gen. 43:3] [h]1 Sam. 14:49

2:30, 31 The disparity between the number of casualties suffered by David's troops and by the Benjaminites is a token of things to come.

3:1 war between the house of Saul and the house of David. At least in the northern tribes, the transfer of power to David after the death of Saul was not unopposed. A key figure supporting Saul was Abner, Saul's military commander who had installed Saul's surviving son, Ish-bosheth, as king in Mahanaim (2:8, 9). But the tide was running in David's favor (2:30, 31 note).

3:2–11 The list of six sons born to David (vv. 2–5) amplifies the statement in v. 1 that "David grew stronger and stronger," while the wrangling between Abner and Ish-bosheth over a concubine (vv. 6–11) dramatizes the final statement in v. 1 that "the house of Saul became weaker and weaker."

3:2 sons were born to David at Hebron. As the list that follows reveals, David took additional wives in Hebron. In 5:13–16, after David's arrival in Jerusalem, yet more wives and concubines are added, and at least eleven more children will be born to David (see the cumulative list in 1 Chr. 3:1–9). While the narrator offers no explicit evaluation of David's behavior (ancient Near Eastern kings commonly multiplied wives and children), it violates the standards of Deut. 17:17.

3:3 Maacah the daughter of Talmai king of Geshur. David's marrying a foreign wife from the small Aramean kingdom of Geshur may have been politically motivated, giving him an ally north of Ish-bosheth's shaky realm.

3:7 Why have you gone in to my father's concubine. Abner's appropriation of Saul's concubine would amount to a claim on the throne (12:8 note; 16:21 note; 1 Kin. 2:22). The reader is not told whether Ish-bosheth's suspicion is well-founded or simple paranoia. Whatever the case, Abner uses the accusation as an occasion to shift his allegiance to David (vv. 8–10).

3:9 what the LORD has sworn to him. See 5:2 note; 1 Sam. 13:14 note; 15:28; 24:20 note.

3:10 Dan to Beersheba. A proverbial expression for "the whole country" (Judg. 20:1).

3:11 he feared him. Ish-bosheth's reaction indicates that Abner was in a position not only to make a threat but to carry it out.

3:12 To whom does the land belong. Abner means that the land is his own, as one who controls it and can give it to David, or else that the land is David's by right, and that David should enlist Abner's help to secure it.

3:13 bring Michal, Saul's daughter. Returning David's wife Michal to him (1 Sam. 18:27) would not only make right Saul's wrong of having given her to another in David's absence (1 Sam. 25:44), but would also strengthen David's claim to the throne over Saul's former realm. The restrictions of Deut. 24:1–4 do not apply in this situation, since David's separation from Michal was involuntary.

3:14 David sent messengers to Ish-bosheth. The insecurity of Ish-bosheth's position is evident not only in his fear of Abner (v. 11) but also in his inability to resist David's orders.

"Give me my wife Michal, [i]for whom I paid
the bridal price of a hundred foreskins of
the Philistines." 15 And Ish-bosheth sent
and took her from her husband Paltiel the
son of Laish. 16 But her husband went with
her, weeping after her all the way to
[j]Bahurim. Then Abner said to him, "Go,
return." And he returned.
17 And Abner conferred with the elders of
Israel, saying, "For some time past you
have been seeking David as king over you.
18 Now then bring it about, [k]for the LORD
has promised David, saying, 'By the hand
of my servant David I will save my people
Israel from the hand of the Philistines, and
from the hand of all their enemies.'"
19 Abner also spoke to [l]Benjamin. And then
Abner went to tell David at Hebron all that
Israel and the whole house of Benjamin
thought good to do.
20 When Abner came with twenty men to
David at Hebron, David made a feast for
Abner and the men who were with him.
21 And Abner said to David, "I will arise and
go and [m]will gather all Israel to my lord the
king, that they may make a covenant with
you, and that you may [n]reign over all that
your heart desires." So David sent Abner
away, and he went in peace.
22 Just then the servants of David arrived
with Joab from a raid, bringing much spoil
with them. But Abner was not with David
at Hebron, for he had sent him away, and
he had gone in peace. 23 When Joab and all
the army that was with him came, it was
told Joab, "Abner the son of Ner came to
the king, and he has let him go, and he has
gone in peace." 24 Then Joab went to the
king and said, "What have you done?
Behold, Abner came to you. Why is it that
you have sent him away, so that he is gone?
25 You know that Abner the son of Ner
came to deceive you and to know [o]your
going out and your coming in, and to know
all that you are doing."

Joab Murders Abner

26 When Joab came out from David's
presence, he sent messengers after Abner,
and they brought him back from the cistern of Sirah. But David did not know
about it. 27 And when Abner returned to
Hebron, Joab took him aside into the midst
of the gate to speak with him privately,
[p]and there he struck him [q]in the stomach,
so that he died, for the blood of Asahel his
brother. 28 Afterward, when David heard of
it, he said, "I and my kingdom are forever
guiltless before the LORD for the blood of
Abner the son of Ner. 29 [r]May it fall upon
the head of Joab and upon all his father's
house, and may the house of Joab never be
without [s]one who has a discharge or who is
[t]leprous or who holds a spindle or who
falls by the sword or who lacks bread!" 30 So
Joab and Abishai his brother killed Abner,
because [u]he had put their brother Asahel
to death in the battle at Gibeon.

David Mourns Abner

31 Then David said to Joab and to all the
people who were with him, [v]"Tear your
clothes and [w]put on sackcloth and mourn
before Abner." And King David followed
the bier. 32 They buried Abner at Hebron.
And the king lifted up his voice and wept

14 [i]1 Sam. 18:25, 27 **16** [j]ch. 16:5; 17:18; 19:16; 1 Kin. 2:8 **18** [k]See ver. 9 **19** [l][1 Chr. 12:29] **21** [m]ver. 12 [n]1 Kin. 11:37

25 [o]See 1 Sam. 29:6 **27** [p]1 Kin. 2:5, 32; [ch. 20:9, 10] [q]See ch. 2:23 **29** [r]See ch. 1:16 [s]Lev. 15:2 [t]Lev. 14:2 **30** [u]ch. 2:23 **31** [v]See Josh. 7:6 [w]Gen. 37:34; 1 Kin. 20:31

a hundred foreskins of the Philistines. David refers to the bride-price that Saul had set for Michal (1 Sam. 18:25); his payment had actually been twice the amount (1 Sam. 18:27).

weeping. A vivid glimpse of suffering caused by deeds outside the man's control.

3:16 Bahurim. Tentatively identified with a site about 1.5 miles east of Jerusalem in the territory of Benjamin. Bahurim was the hometown of Shimei, son of Gera (16:5; 1 Kin. 2:8).

3:17 you have been seeking David as king over you. See v. 1 note. Apparently Ish-bosheth and Abner are all that have stood in the way of harmonious relations between David and Israel. Abner here steps aside, and Ish-bosheth will not stand long without him (ch. 4).

3:18 my servant David. David is now recognized as the recipient of a commission like the one first given to Saul (1 Sam. 9:16).

3:21 that they may make a covenant with you. See 5:3.

in peace. The repetition of this phrase twice more in vv. 22, 23 underscores that David was not involved in Abner's death; see also vv. 26, 28, 29, 37.

3:24 Joab's agitation at the thought of Abner's peaceful departure is apparent in his words to David.

3:26 cistern of Sirah. A few miles north of Hebron.

But David did not know about it. This note is another confirmation of David's innocence in the death of Abner (vv. 21–23, 28, 29, 37).

3:27 for the blood of Asahel his brother. See also v. 30. In 2:18–23 Abner's slaying of Asahel is depicted as essentially a matter of self-defense, and the battle context of Abner's action makes it doubtful that Joab had the right to act as an "avenger of blood" (14:11; Num. 35:16–25; Deut. 19:11–13; Josh. 20:3). Joab may also have wanted to eliminate a potential rival in David's court (see his murder of Amasa in 20:10).

3:28 I and my kingdom are forever guiltless. See vv. 21–23, 26, 37.

3:29 May it fall upon the head of Joab. David's decision only to utter a curse upon Joab's house rather than take direct disciplinary action may have been a result of the ambiguous circumstances of Joab's crime. More likely, however, such factors as Joab's considerable power and reputation and his familial relationship with David influenced his decision. Ultimately Joab's crime did not go unpunished (1 Kin. 2:5, 6, 28–35).

at the grave of Abner, and all the people
wept. 33 And the king [x]lamented for Abner,
saying,

[y]"Should Abner die [z]as a fool dies?
34 Your hands were not bound;
your feet were not fettered;
as one falls before the wicked
you have fallen."

And all the people wept again over him.
35 Then all the people came [a]to persuade
David to eat bread while it was yet day. But
David swore, saying, [b]"God do so to me and
more also, if I taste bread or anything else
[c]till the sun goes down!" 36 And all the people took notice of it, and it pleased them, as
everything that the king did pleased all the
people. 37 So all the people and all Israel
understood that day that it had not been the
king's will to put to death Abner the son of
Ner. 38 And the king said to his servants, "Do
you not know that a prince and a great man
has fallen this day in Israel? 39 And I was gentle today, though anointed king. [d]These
men, the sons of Zeruiah, are more severe
than I. [e]The LORD repay the evildoer according to his wickedness!"

Ish-bosheth Murdered

4 When Ish-bosheth, Saul's son, heard
that Abner had died at Hebron, [f]his
courage failed, and all Israel was dismayed.
2 Now Saul's son had two men who were
captains of raiding bands; the name of the
one was Baanah, and the name of the other
Rechab, sons of Rimmon a man of
Benjamin from Beeroth ([g]for Beeroth also
is counted part of Benjamin; 3 [h]the
Beerothites fled [i]to Gittaim and have been
sojourners there to this day).
4 [j]Jonathan, the son of Saul, had a son
who was crippled in his feet. He was five
years old when the news about Saul and
Jonathan [k]came from Jezreel, and his nurse
took him up and fled, and as she fled in her
haste, he fell and became lame. And his
name was Mephibosheth.
5 Now the sons of Rimmon the
Beerothite, Rechab and Baanah, set out,
and about the heat of the day they came to
the house of Ish-bosheth as he was taking
his noonday rest. 6 And they came into the
midst of the house as if to get wheat, and
they stabbed him [l]in the stomach. Then
Rechab and Baanah his brother escaped.[1]
7 When they came into the house, as he lay
on his bed in his bedroom, they struck him
and put him to death and beheaded him.
They took his head and went by the way of
[m]the Arabah all night, 8 and brought the
head of Ish-bosheth to David at Hebron.
And they said to the king, "Here is the
head of Ish-bosheth, the son of Saul, your
enemy, [n]who sought your life. The LORD
has avenged my lord the king this day on
Saul and on his offspring." 9 But David
answered Rechab and Baanah his brother,
the sons of Rimmon the Beerothite, [o]"As
the LORD lives, [p]who has redeemed my life
out of every adversity, 10 [q]when one told
me, 'Behold, Saul is dead,' and thought he
was bringing good news, [r]I seized him and
killed him at Ziklag, which was the reward
I gave him for his news. 11 How much more,
when wicked men have killed a righteous
man in his own house on his bed, shall I
not now [s]require his blood at your hand
and destroy you from the earth?" 12 And
David commanded his young men, and
they killed them and cut off their hands

33 [x][ch. 1:17; 2 Chr. 35:25] [y][Eccles. 2:16] [z]ch. 13:12, 13
35 [a]ch. 12:17 [b]See Ruth 1:17 [c][ch. 1:12]
39 [d][ch. 16:10; 19:22] [e][Ps. 28:4; 2 Tim. 4:14]
Chapter 4
1 [f]Ezra 4:4; Isai. 13:7; Jer. 6:24
2 [g]Josh. 18:25
3 [h][1 Sam. 31:7] [i]Neh. 11:33
4 [j]ch. 9:3, 6
[k]1 Sam. 29:1, 11
6 [l]See ch. 2:23
7 [m]ch. 2:29; See Deut. 1:1
8 [n]1 Sam. 19:10, 11; 23:15
9 [o]See Ruth 3:13 [p]1 Kin. 1:29
10 [q]See ch. 1:4-10 [r]ch. 1:15
11 [s][Gen. 9:5, 6]

1 Septuagint *And behold, the doorkeeper of the house had been cleaning wheat, but she grew drowsy and slept. So Rechab and Baanah his brother slipped in*

3:39 more severe. That is, "too hard" or "ruthless." See v. 29 note; cf. 16:10; 19:22.

4:1 Abner had died. The death of Abner affected Ish-bosheth and "all Israel" the same way, but for different reasons. Ish-bosheth's "courage failed" because he knew that Abner's death meant the loss of the backbone of his government. Israel, on the other hand, "was dismayed" by what may have appeared as a rejection of their friendly overture to David (3:17–21).

4:2 part of Benjamin. The Benjaminite origin of Ish-bosheth's assassins is stressed (two verses are dedicated to establishing it), perhaps to show that disenchantment with the house of Saul extended even into his own tribe.

4:3 the Beerothites fled to Gittaim. Although Beeroth was one of the four major cities of the Gibeonites (an Amorite people who duped Joshua into making a peace treaty with them; Josh. 9:17), Josh. 18:25 indicates that the town was allotted to Benjamin. King Saul had attempted to annihilate the Gibeonites (21:1, 2), and this aggression may explain the flight of the Beerothites to Gittaim.

4:4 news about Saul and Jonathan. That is, of their deaths (1 Sam. 31).

Mephibosheth. Mephibosheth will appear again in 9:6–13; 16:1–4; 19:24–30; 21:7 (21:8 mentions a different Mephibosheth).

4:9 who has redeemed my life out of every adversity. Whereas Rechab and Baanah have tried to portray themselves as agents of the Lord's judgment against Saul (v. 8), David's response makes clear that with the Lord as his deliverer David has no need of human assistance.

4:12 And David commanded. David shows none of the hesitation to act in this instance that he had shown in the case of Joab (3:29 note).

cut off their hands and feet. Mutilation of this sort was not uncommon in the ancient Near East.

and feet and hanged them beside the pool
at Hebron. But they took the head of Ish-
bosheth and buried it [t]in the tomb of
Abner at Hebron.

David Anointed King of Israel

5 Then all the tribes of Israel [u]came to
David at Hebron and said, "Behold,
[v]we are your bone and flesh. 2 In times past,
when Saul was king over us, [w]it was you
who led out and brought in Israel. And the
LORD said to you, [x]'You shall be shepherd
of my people Israel, and you shall be prince
over Israel.'" 3 So all the elders of Israel
came to the king at Hebron, [y]and King
David made a covenant with them at
Hebron [z]before the LORD, and they anointed David king over Israel. 4 David was thirty years old when he began to reign, and
[a]he reigned forty years. 5 [a]At Hebron he
reigned over Judah [b]seven years and six
months, and at Jerusalem he reigned over
all Israel and Judah thirty-three years.[1]
6 [c]And the king and his men went to
Jerusalem [d]against the Jebusites, the inhabitants of the land, who said to David, "You
will not come in here, but the blind and the
lame will ward you off"—thinking, "David
cannot come in here." 7 Nevertheless, David
took the stronghold of Zion, [e]that is, the city
of David. 8 And David said on that day,
"Whoever would strike the Jebusites, let him
get up the water shaft to attack 'the lame and
the blind,' who are hated by David's soul."
Therefore it is said, "The blind and the lame
shall not come into the house." 9 And David
lived in the stronghold and called it [e]the city
of David. And David built the city all around
from the [f]Millo inward. 10 And David became
greater and greater, for the LORD, the God of
hosts, was with him.
11 [g]And [h]Hiram king of Tyre sent messengers to David, and cedar trees, also carpenters and masons who built David a house.
12 And David knew that the LORD had established him king over Israel, and that he had
exalted his kingdom for the sake of his people Israel.
13 And David took more [i]concubines and
wives from Jerusalem, after he came from
Hebron, and more sons and daughters
were born to David. 14 [j]And these are the

12 [t]ch. 3:32
Chapter 5
1 [u]For ver. 1-3, see 1 Chr. 11:1-3 [v]See Gen. 29:14
2 [w][1 Sam. 18:13] [x]ch. 7:7; 1 Chr. 17:6; Ps. 78:71, 72; [Matt. 2:6]
3 [y]ch. 3:12, 13, 21; [2 Kin. 11:17] [z]Judg. 11:11; 1 Sam. 23:18
4 [a]1 Kin. 2:11; 1 Chr. 3:4; 29:27
5 [a][See ver. 4 above] [b]ch. 2:11
6 [c]For ver. 6-10, see 1 Chr. 11:4-9 [d]Judg. 19:11; [Josh. 15:63; Judg. 1:21]
7 [e]ch. 6:12, 16
9 [f]1 Kin. 9:15, 24; 11:27; 2 Kin. 12:20; 2 Chr. 32:5
11 [g]For ver. 11-25, see 1 Chr. 14:1-16 [h]1 Kin. 5:6
13 [i][1 Chr. 3:9]
14 [j][1 Chr. 3:5-8]

[1] Dead Sea Scroll lacks verses 4-5

5:1 all the tribes of Israel. That is, their leaders; cf. "all the elders" in v. 3. It has been suggested that the Hebrew word here translated "tribes" may also mean "rulers."

your bone and flesh. This is an expression of kinship (19:12–13; Gen. 29:14; Judg. 9:2) and the first of three reasons given by the Israelites in vv. 1, 2 for wanting to make David king.

5:2 led out and brought in Israel. An idiom for leading military campaigns (1 Sam. 18:13, 16). The second reason for wanting to make David king was his military success (1 Sam. 17:32, 45–47; 18:7; 25:28).

the LORD said to you. The third reason is David's divine appointment (1 Sam. 16:1 note).

shepherd. This designation is often used metaphorically in the Bible, either for God (Gen. 49:24; Ps. 23:1; 80:1; etc.), for His Son Jesus (John 10:11; Heb. 13:20; 1 Pet. 5:4; Rev. 7:17; etc.), or for divinely appointed human leaders (7:7; Num. 27:15–17; etc.). The image is one of intimate, caring leadership (v. 12 note).

5:3 King David made a covenant. See 3:21. The covenant establishing David's rule over the northern tribes likely consisted of regulations for the kingship (cf. 1 Sam. 10:25), including their rights and responsibilities to one another and to the Lord (2 Kin. 11:17). That this covenant did not end the sense of separate identity felt by Israel and Judah is evident in the revolt of Sheba (20:1) and particularly in the dissolution of the united kingdom under Rehoboam (1 Kin. 12:16).

they anointed David. See note 2:4.

5:4, 5 In the Old Testament, a stereotyped formula often introduces the account of a king's official tenure in office (e.g., 1 Sam. 13:1; 2 Sam. 2:10; 1 Kin. 14:21; 22:42; etc.). In this case it appropriately marks David's assumption of power over all Israel.

5:6 Jerusalem. A city of great antiquity (occupied as early as the third millennium B.C.), Jerusalem was in Benjamin, near the northern border of Judah. The city had earlier been conquered by Judah (Judg. 1:8), but neither Judah nor Benjamin had been successful in permanently dislodging its Jebusite inhabitants (Josh. 15:63; Judg. 1:21). David may well have thought that Jerusalem's strategic location and relatively independent status made the city well suited to the establishment of a national capital that would not imply favoritism to any particular region.

Jebusites . . . said to David. The Jebusites' taunt, whether suggestive of overconfidence or simply of a determination to fight to the last man (even be he blind or lame), reflects the hostility between the Jebusites and David (see v. 8; 1 Sam. 17:54 note).

5:7 stronghold of Zion. This marks the first occurrence of "Zion" in the Bible and the only one in Samuel. The name originally designated a fortified mound located at the southern end of the Ophel ridge. Eventually the name came to be used in an extended sense for all of Jerusalem (2 Kin. 19:21; Is. 2:3) and even for the entire nation of Israel (Ps. 149:2; Is. 46:13). The name occurs frequently in Israel's poetic and prophetic literature, where it is often presented as the place of God's mighty acts of salvation and judgment (e.g., Ps. 14:7; Is. 4:4; Lam. 4:11).

5:10 became greater. Just as chs. 3 and 4 detail how "the house of Saul became weaker and weaker" (3:1; 3:2–11 note), so chs. 5–10 show David growing "stronger and stronger" (3:1). The fundamental reason for David's success is that the Lord was with him (see note 1 Sam. 16:18).

5:11 Hiram king of Tyre. Tyre was a Phoenician port city about thirty-five miles north of Mount Carmel and twenty-five miles south of Sidon. Hiram's generosity to David may have been motivated by the impressiveness of David's recent accomplishments, but it also involved an element of self-interest. Tyre needed the inland trade routes now controlled by David and the agricultural produce of central Palestine (cf. Ezra 3:7). Hiram's friendship with Israel continued well into Solomon's reign (1 Kin. 5:1–12; 9:11; etc.).

5:12 the LORD had established him king. See note on v. 10.

for the sake of his people Israel. David understands not only that his kingship is dependent entirely upon God, but also that it is intended for the benefit of God's people (v. 2; 8:15).

5:13–16 See 3:2 note, and the slightly longer list in 1 Chr. 14:3–7.

names of those who were born to him in
Jerusalem: Shammua, Shobab, Nathan,
Solomon, **15** Ibhar, Elishua, Nepheg, Japhia,
16 Elishama, Eliada, and Eliphelet.

David Defeats the Philistines

17 When the Philistines heard that David
had been anointed king over Israel, all the
Philistines went up to search for David. But
David heard of it and went down [k]to the
stronghold. **18** Now the Philistines had
come and spread out in [l]the Valley of
Rephaim. **19** And David [m]inquired of the
LORD, "Shall I go up against the Philistines?
Will you give them into my hand?" And the
LORD said to David, "Go up, for I will certainly give the Philistines into your hand."
20 And David came to Baal-perazim, and
David defeated them there. And he said,
"The LORD has burst through my enemies
before me like a bursting flood." [n]Therefore
the name of that place is called Baal-perazim.[1] **21** And the Philistines left their idols
there, and David and his men carried them
away.

22 And the Philistines came up yet again
[o]and spread out in the Valley of Rephaim.
23 [p]And when David inquired of the LORD,
he said, "You shall not go up; go around to
their rear, and come against them opposite
the balsam trees. **24** And [q]when you hear the
sound of marching in the tops of the balsam trees, then rouse yourself, [r]for then
the LORD has gone out before you to strike
down the army of the Philistines." **25** And
David did as the LORD commanded him,
and struck down the Philistines from Geba
[s]to Gezer.

The Ark Brought to Jerusalem

6 [t]David again gathered all the chosen
men of Israel, thirty thousand. **2** And
David arose and went with all the people
who were with him from [u]Baale-judah [v]to
bring up from there the ark of God, which
is called by the name of the LORD of hosts
[w]who sits enthroned on the cherubim.
3 And they carried the ark of God [x]on a new
cart and brought it [y]out of the house of
Abinadab, which was on the hill. And
Uzzah and Ahio,[2] the sons of Abinadab,
were driving the new [y]cart,[3] **4** with the ark
of God, and Ahio went before the ark.

Uzzah and the Ark

5 And David and all the house of Israel
were making merry before the LORD, with
[z]songs[4] and lyres and harps and tambourines and castanets and cymbals. **6** And
when they came to the threshing floor of
[a]Nacon, Uzzah [b]put out his hand to the ark
of God and took hold of it, for the oxen
stumbled. **7** And the anger of the LORD was
kindled against Uzzah, and [c]God struck
him down there because of his error, and he
died there beside the ark of God. **8** And
David was angry because the LORD had
burst forth against Uzzah. And that place is

17 [k]ch. 23:14; 1 Sam. 22:4, 5
18 [l]ver. 22; ch. 23:13; Josh. 15:8; 18:16; [Josh. 17:15]
19 [m]See ch. 2:1
20 [n]Isai. 28:21
22 [o]ver. 18
23 [p]See 1 Sam. 22:10
24 [q][2 Kin. 7:6] [r][Judg. 4:14]
25 [s]Josh. 10:33
Chapter 6
1 [t]For ver. 1-11, see 1 Chr. 13:6-14
2 [u]Josh. 15:9, 60 [v]2 Chr. 1:4 [w]Ex. 25:22; 1 Sam. 4:4; Ps. 80:1
3 [x][1 Sam. 6:7]
4 [y][1 Sam. 7:1]
5 [z][1 Chr. 13:8]; See Ps. 150:3-5
6 [a][1 Chr. 13:9] [b][Num. 4:15; 1 Chr. 15:2]
7 [c][1 Sam. 6:19]

1 *Baal-perazim* means *lord of bursting through* 2 Or *and his brother;* also verse 4 3 Compare Septuagint; Hebrew *the new cart, and brought it out of the house of Abinadab, which was on the hill* 4 Septuagint, 1 Chronicles 13:8; Hebrew *fir trees*

5:17 When the Philistines heard. While David's reign over Judah had not been contested by the Philistines, the extension of his domain to the northern tribes posed a threat to Philistine interests that they could not ignore.

stronghold. See 1 Sam. 23:14 note.

5:18 Valley of Rephaim. This valley begins a few miles southwest of Jerusalem and descends in a westward direction toward Philistine territory (21:16 note; 23:13; Josh. 15:8; 18:16).

5:19 David inquired of the LORD. See note 2:1.

5:20 Baal-perazim. Baal-perazim has been identified with a site three miles southwest of Jerusalem.

5:21 left their idols. David inflicts on the Philistines a loss similar to what Israel suffered with the capture of the ark in 1 Sam. 4.

carried them away. See note 1 Sam. 5:2; 1 Chr. 14:12 says that David burned them.

5:24 the LORD has gone out before you. The Lord is a warrior (Ex. 15:3) who goes before His people to fight for them (Ex. 14:14; Deut. 1:30).

5:25 from Geba to Gezer. David's rout of the Philistines was far more decisive than Jonathan's (1 Sam. 14:31). Defeating the Philistines in particular (8:1) was of special significance (3:18; 19:9; 1 Chr. 14:17; cf. 1 Sam 9:16).

6:2 Baale-judah. See note on 1 Sam. 6:21.

ark of God. See note 1 Sam. 3:3.

the name. See 1 Sam. 17:45 and note; cf. Deut. 12:5, 11, 21.

LORD of hosts. See note 1 Sam. 1:3.

6:3 new cart. This mode of transporting the ark recalls the Philistine precedent set in 1 Sam. 6:7 but neglects the divine directive that the ark, equipped with rings and poles (Ex. 25:12–14; 37:5), is to be carried on the shoulders of priests (Num. 4:15, 19; 7:9; Deut. 10:8; Josh. 3:8; etc.).

house of Abinadab. See 1 Sam. 7:1.

Uzzah and Ahio. While attempts have been made to identify Uzzah with Eleazar in 1 Sam. 7:1, it is more likely that the two sons mentioned here were brothers of Eleazar, or possibly even grandsons of Abinadab. The Hebrew word "son" can also mean "descendant."

6:7 because of his error. The Hebrew here is difficult, but compare the explanation given in 1 Chr. 13:10, "because he put out his hand to the ark." It may be that the punishment relates not only to Uzzah's touching the ark, but, more importantly, to the irregular way the ark was being carried (v. 3 note; 1 Chr. 15:13–15).

6:8 David was angry. The reader is not told whether the main cause of David's anger was Uzzah's death, Uzzah's recklessness, or his own cavalier handling of the ark.

called Perez-uzzah,[1] to this day. 9 And David
was afraid of the LORD that day, and he said,
"How can the ark of the LORD come to me?"
10 So David was not willing to take the ark of
the LORD into the city of David. But David
took it aside [d]to the house of Obed-edom
the Gittite. 11 And the ark of the LORD
remained in the house of Obed-edom the
Gittite three months, [e]and the LORD blessed
Obed-edom and all his household.
12 And it was told King David, "The LORD
has blessed the household of Obed-edom
and all that belongs to him, because of the
ark of God." [f]So David went and brought
up the ark of God from the house of Obed-
edom [g]to the city of David with rejoicing.
13 And when [h]those who bore the ark of the
LORD had gone six steps, [i]he sacrificed an
ox and a fattened animal. 14 And David
[j]danced before the LORD with all his might.
And David was [k]wearing a linen ephod.
15 So David and all the house of Israel
brought up the ark of the LORD with shouting and with the sound of the horn.

David and Michal

16 As the ark of the LORD came into the
city of David, Michal the daughter of Saul
looked out of the window and saw King
David leaping and dancing before the
LORD, and she despised him in her heart.
17 And they brought in the ark of the LORD
and set it [l]in its place, inside the tent that
David had pitched for it. [m]And David
offered burnt offerings and peace offerings
before the LORD. 18 And when David had
finished offering the burnt offerings and
the peace offerings, [n]he blessed the people
in the name of the LORD of hosts 19 and distributed among all the people, the whole
multitude of Israel, both men and women,
a cake of bread, a portion of meat,[2] and a
cake of raisins to each one. [o]Then all the
people departed, each to his house.
20 And David returned to bless his household. But Michal the daughter of Saul came
out to meet David and said, "How the king
of Israel honored himself today, [p]uncover-
ing himself today before the eyes of his servants' female servants, as one of the [q]vulgar
fellows shamelessly uncovers himself!"
21 And David said to Michal, "It was before
the LORD, [r]who chose me above your father
and above all his house, to appoint me as
prince over Israel, the people of the LORD—
and I will make merry before the LORD. 22 I
will make myself yet more contemptible
than this, and I will be abased in your[3]
eyes. But by the female servants of whom
you have spoken, by them I shall be held in
honor." 23 And Michal the daughter of Saul
had no child to the day of her death.

God's Covenant with David

7 [s]Now when the king lived in his house
and the LORD [t]had given him rest from
all his surrounding enemies, 2 the king said
to [u]Nathan the prophet, "See now, I dwell
[v]in a house of cedar, but the ark of God
dwells [w]in a tent." 3 And Nathan said to the

10 [d][1 Chr. 15:25] 11 [e]1 Chr. 26:5 12 [f]For ver. 12-19, see 1 Chr. 15:25–16:3 [g][1 Kin. 8:1] 13 [h][Num. 4:15; 7:9; Josh. 3:3; 1 Chr. 15:2, 15] [i][1 Kin. 8:5] 14 [j][Ex. 15:20; Ps. 30:11; 150:4] [k]1 Sam. 2:18 17 [l][1 Chr. 15:1; 2 Chr. 1:4; Ps. 132:8] [m][1 Kin. 8:5, 62, 63]
18 [n][1 Kin. 8:14, 55] 19 [o]1 Chr. 16:43 20 [p]ver. 14, 16; [1 Sam. 19:24] [q]Judg. 9:4 21 [r]1 Sam. 13:14; 15:28
Chapter 7
1 [s]For ver. 1-29, see 1 Chr. 17:1-27 [t]See Josh. 11:23 2 [u]ver. 17; ch. 12:1 [v]ch. 5:11 [w]Ex. 26:1

1 *Perez-uzzah* means *the bursting forth upon Uzzah* 2 Vulgate; the meaning of the Hebrew term is uncertain 3 Septuagint; Hebrew *my*

6:10 Obed-edom the Gittite. That is, a man of Gath. Whether the reference is to the Philistine city of Gath (1 Sam. 4:1 note; 5:8 note) or to Gath Rimmon (a Levitical city in Dan or Manasseh; Josh. 21:23–25) is uncertain. Obed-edom is frequently referred to as a Levite in Chronicles (e.g., 1 Chr. 15:17–25; 16:5, 38; 26:4, 5, 8, 15; 2 Chr. 25:24).

6:13 bore the ark. This time the ark is transported according to the Mosaic legislation (vv. 3, 7 and notes).

he sacrificed. David's sacrifice is perhaps a symbol of thanksgiving and intercession—thanksgiving that the procession has begun with God's blessing, and intercession that it may so continue.

6:14 linen ephod. See note 1 Sam. 2:18.

6:16 she despised him. Suggestions about the cause of Michal's displeasure are given only later, in vv. 20–22.

6:17 burnt offerings and peace offerings. See note 1 Sam. 10:8.

6:20 How the king of Israel honored himself today. Michal's comment is heavy with sarcasm. She mentions his being king, his immodesty, and his other women. Her jealousy may have been aroused because her father had been displaced by David.

uncovering. David had taken off his robes and had worn only a linen ephod (v. 14).

6:21 It was before the LORD. David will not accept Michal's indictment. It was not before the "female servants" (that is, for their eyes) but "before the LORD" that he celebrated. David pointedly mentions that the Lord displaced Saul and chose him instead.

6:22 I will make myself yet more contemptible than this. Or, "I will humble myself even more than this." Unlike Eli and his sons (1 Sam. 2:29, 30 and notes), and Michal's own father Saul (1 Sam. 15:12, 30 and notes), David is willing to be abased that the Lord may receive the honor due Him.

by them I shall be held in honor. David replies that he has no reason to feel embarrassed before the maids. Michal's displeasure in him is wrong.

6:23 Michal the daughter of Saul had no child. This was either because of the direct decision of the Lord, or because David excluded Michal from marital relations. It was a reproach to be childless (1 Sam. 1:5, 6).

7:1 rest from all his surrounding enemies. See notes on vv. 6, 9. See also v. 11; Deut. 12:10; 25:19; Josh. 23:1.

7:2 Nathan. Mentioned here for the first time, Nathan the prophet will also play a significant role in ch. 12 and 1 Kin. 1. See also 1 Chr. 29:29; 2 Chr. 9:29; 29:25.

in a tent. David apparently views his palace as symbolic of his now-

king, [x]"Go, do all that is in your heart, for
the LORD is with you."
4But that same night the word of the
LORD came to Nathan, **5**"Go and tell my
servant David, 'Thus says the LORD:
[y]Would you build me a house to dwell in?
6I have not lived in a house [z]since the day
I brought up the people of Israel from
Egypt to this day, but I have been moving
about [a]in a tent for my dwelling. **7**In all
places where [b]I have moved with all the
people of Israel, did I speak a word with
[c]any of the judges[1] of Israel, whom I commanded [d]to shepherd my people Israel,
saying, "Why have you not built me a
house of cedar?"' **8**Now, therefore, thus
you shall say to my servant David, 'Thus
says the LORD of hosts, [e]I took you from the
pasture, from following the sheep, that you
should be prince over my people Israel.
9[f]And I have been with you wherever you
went and have cut off all your enemies
from before you. And I will make for you a
great name, like the name of the great ones
of the earth. **10**And I will appoint a place for
my people Israel [g]and will plant them, so
that they may dwell in their own place [h]and
be disturbed no more. [i]And violent men
shall afflict them no more, as formerly,
11[j]from the time that I appointed judges
over my people Israel. And [k]I will give you
rest from all your enemies. Moreover, the
LORD declares to you that [l]the LORD will
make you a house. **12**[m]When your days are
fulfilled and [n]you lie down with your
fathers, [o]I will raise up your offspring after
you, who shall come from your body, and
I will establish his kingdom. **13**[p]He shall
build a house for my name, and [q]I will
establish the throne of his kingdom forever. **14**[r]I will be to him a father, and he shall
be to me a son. When he commits iniqui-
ty, [s]I will discipline him with the rod of
men, with the stripes of the sons of men,
15[s]but my steadfast love will not depart
from him, [t]as I took it from Saul, whom I
put away from before you. **16**[u]And your
house and your kingdom shall be made
sure forever before me.[2] [u]Your throne shall
be established forever.'" **17**In accordance
with all these words, and in accordance
with all this vision, Nathan spoke to David.

David's Prayer of Gratitude

18Then King David went in and sat before
the LORD and said, [v]"Who am I, O Lord
GOD, and what is my house, that you have

3[x]1 Kin. 8:17, 18; 1 Chr. 22:7; 28:2; [Acts 7:46] **5**[y]1 Kin. 5:3; 8:19; 1 Chr. 22:8; 28:3 **6**[z]1 Kin. 8:16 [a]Ex. 40:18, 19, 34 **7**[b]Lev. 26:11, 12; Deut. 23:14 [c][1 Chr. 17:6] [d]See ch. 5:2 **8**[e]1 Sam. 16:11; Ps. 78:70 **9**[f]ch. 5:10; 8:6, 14; 1 Sam. 18:14 **10**[g]Ps. 44:2; 80:8; Jer. 24:6; Amos 9:15 [h]2 Kin. 21:8 [i][Ps. 89:22] **11**[j]See Judg. 2:14-16; 1 Sam. 12:9-11 [k]ver. 1; See Josh. 11:23 [l]ver. 27; 1 Kin. 11:38; [Ex. 1:21; 1 Sam. 2:35] **12**[m][1 Kin. 2:1] [n]1 Kin. 1:21; 2:10; Acts 13:36; [Deut. 31:16] [o]1 Kin. 8:20; Ps. 132:11 **13**[p]1 Kin. 5:5; 6:12; 8:19; 1 Chr. 22:10; 28:6 [q]ver. 16; Ps. 89:4, 29, 36, 37 **14**[r]Ps. 89:26, 27; Cited Heb. 1:5 **15**[s]Ps. 89:32, 33 [t]1 Sam. 15:23, 28; [1 Kin. 11:13, 34] **16**[u]ver. 13; Ps. 89:36, 37; [Luke 1:33] **18**[v][Gen. 32:10]

[1] Compare 1 Chronicles 17:6; Hebrew *tribes* [2] Septuagint; Hebrew *you*

established rule (5:11, 12), and he proposes that God's rule should be similarly symbolized with a permanent dwelling.

7:3 Go. David's plan seems reasonable to Nathan, but he is quick to reverse himself when ordered by the Lord (v. 4). Nathan is no flatterer (12:7–14).

7:4–17 The theological and historical significance of the divine promise to David recorded in these verses (paralleled in 1 Chr. 17:3–15) can hardly be overestimated. Indeed, the promise of an enduring Davidic kingdom has been called the summit of the entire Old Testament. Looking back, it takes up the promises of blessing made to Abraham and his elect seed (Gen. 17:16) and brings them to rest on David (vv. 9, 10, 12). Looking forward, it prepares for the messianic hope that inspires Israel's faith before and after the exile in Babylon (Is. 11:1; Jer. 23:5, 6; Zech. 3:8; 6:12). The hope for a Messiah culminates in the coming of Jesus Christ (Is. 9:1–7; Luke 1:32, 33, 69, 70; Acts 2:30, 31; 13:22, 23; Rom. 1:1–4; 2 Tim. 2:8; Rev. 22:16).

7:5 my servant David. Cf. 3:18; Ps. 89:3. The Lord's reference to David as "my servant" places him in a select company, which includes Abraham (Gen. 26:24), Moses (Num. 12:7, 8; Deut. 34:5), Caleb (Num. 14:24), and Joshua (Josh. 24:29).

7:6 I have not lived in a house. God has accompanied His elect people throughout their wanderings (vv. 6, 7). Not until He has planted them in their place (v. 10) and they enjoy "rest" (v. 11) that exceeds what they already have under David (v. 1) will He allow a permanent house to be built for His name (v. 13).

7:9 I have been with you. See note 1 Sam. 16:18.

a great name. The declaration of a great name recalls the divine promise made to the patriarch Abraham in Gen. 12:2. Cf. 8:13, where David "made a name for himself."

7:11 the LORD will make you a house. Having declined David's offer to build Him a house (temple; v. 5), the Lord counters with the gracious announcement that He will instead establish a dynasty for David.

7:12 your offspring. Solomon.

who shall come from your body. The same words were spoken to Abraham in Gen. 15:4.

7:13 for my name. It was "for his great name's sake" that the Lord refused to reject His people after their sinful request for a king (1 Sam. 12:22). Now He announces to David that his own son, who will succeed him as king, will build a temple "for my name." For an explication of the significance of God's name, see Ex. 34:5–7, and note on 1 Sam. 17:45.

7:14–16 father . . . a son. The full significance of this promise, expressive of the special relationship that the Lord establishes with the Davidic kings (Ps. 2:7; 89:18–37), is ultimately realized in Christ (Mark 1:11; Acts 13:33; Heb. 1:5).

7:14 I will discipline him. As a father, the Lord will discipline the royal son when he does wrong, but His covenantal love will never be taken away from him. Though the punishment is severe, extending even to the loss of land and temple (1 Kin. 9:6–9), God's promise to establish forever the throne of David cannot fail. This promise will increasingly come to be understood in messianic terms (Is. 9:7; 11:1–5; Jer. 33:14–26; Mic. 5:2–5).

7:18 David went in and sat before the LORD. Presumably David sat in front of the ark, the symbol of the Lord's presence (Ex. 25:22; 30:6; Deut. 10:8; Josh. 6:8). It was not usual to sit while praying (Deut. 10:7).

Who am I. Having offered God a house, David is overwhelmed by the Lord's declaration that He will build David a house. The humility evident in David's "Who am I" agrees with his recognition that it is the sovereign Lord who has been with him (1 Sam. 16:18 note) to bring him this far.

brought me thus far? **19** And yet this was a
small thing in your eyes, O Lord GOD. [w]You
have spoken also of your servant's house for
a great while to come, and this is instruction
for mankind, O Lord GOD! **20** And what more
can David say to you? [x]For you know your
servant, O Lord GOD! **21** Because of your
promise, and according to your own heart,
you have brought about all this greatness, to
make your servant know it. **22** [y]Therefore you
are great, O LORD God. [z]For there is none
like you, and there is no God besides you,
according to all that we have heard with our
ears. **23** [a]And who is like your people Israel,
the one nation on earth whom God went to
redeem to be his people, making himself a
name [b]and doing for them[1] great and awesome things by driving out[2] before your people, whom [c]you redeemed for yourself from
Egypt, a nation and its gods? **24** [d]And you
established for yourself your people Israel to
be your people forever. And you, O LORD,
became their God. **25** And now, O LORD God,
confirm forever the word that you have spoken concerning your servant and concerning
his house, and do as you have spoken. **26** And
your name will be magnified forever, saying,
'The LORD of hosts is God over Israel,' and
the house of your servant David will be
established before you. **27** For you, O LORD of
hosts, the God of Israel, have made this revelation to your servant, saying, 'I will build
you a house.' Therefore your servant has
found courage to pray this prayer to you.
28 And now, O Lord GOD, you are God, and
[e]your words are true, and you have promised
this good thing to your servant. **29** Now therefore may it please you to bless the house of
your servant, so that it may continue forever
before you. For you, O Lord GOD, have spoken, [f]and with your blessing shall the house
of your servant be blessed forever."

David's Victories

8 [g]After this David defeated the Philistines and subdued them, and David
took [h]Metheg-ammah out of the hand of
the Philistines.
2 [i]And he defeated Moab and he measured them with a line, making them lie
down on the ground. Two lines he measured to be put to death, and one full line
to be spared. And the Moabites [j]became
servants to David and [k]brought tribute.
3 David also defeated [l]Hadadezer the son
of Rehob, king of [m]Zobah, as he went to
restore his power at the river Euphrates.
4 [n]And David took from him 1,700 horsemen, and 20,000 foot soldiers. And David
[o]hamstrung all the chariot horses but left
enough for a hundred chariots. **5** [p]And when
the [q]Syrians of Damascus came to help
[l]Hadadezer king of [m]Zobah, David struck
down 22,000 men of the Syrians. **6** Then
David put garrisons in Aram of Damascus,
and the Syrians [r]became servants to David
and brought tribute. [s]And the LORD gave victory to David wherever he went. **7** And David
took [t]the shields of gold that were carried by
the servants of Hadadezer and brought them
to Jerusalem. **8** And from Betah and from
Berothai, cities of Hadadezer, King David
took very much bronze.

19 [w]ver. 12, 13; 1 Chr. 17:17
20 [x]See Ps. 139:1-4
22 [y]1 Chr. 16:25; 2 Chr. 2:5 [z]Ex. 15:11; Deut. 3:24; Ps. 86:8; 89:6, 8; Isai. 45:5; Jer. 10:6
23 [a]Deut. 4:7, 34; 33:29; Ps. 147:20 [b]Deut. 10:21 [c]Deut. 9:26; Neh. 1:10
24 [d]ver. 13, 16, 26; Deut. 26:18
28 [e]John 17:17
29 [f]ch. 22:51; Ps. 89:28, 29
Chapter 8
1 [g]For ver. 1-18, see 1 Chr. 18:1-17; Ps. 60 [h][1 Chr. 18:1]
2 [i]Num. 24:17 [j]ver. 6, 14; [Ps. 60:8] [k][1 Sam. 10:27; 2 Kin. 17:3; Ps. 72:10]
3 [l][ch. 10:16, 19; 1 Chr. 18:3] [m]ch. 10:6; 1 Sam. 14:47; 1 Kin. 11:23
4 [n][1 Chr. 18:4] [o]See Josh. 11:6
5 [p][1 Kin. 11:23-25] [q]See Josh. 11:6 [l][See ver. 3 above] [m][See ver. 3 above]
6 [r]ver. 2, 14 [s]ver. 14
7 [t][2 Kin. 11:10; 2 Chr. 23:9; S. of S. 4:4]

[1] With a few Targums, Vulgate, Syriac; Hebrew *you* [2] Septuagint (compare 1 Chronicles 17:21); Hebrew *for your land*

7:19 this is instruction for mankind. The Hebrew of this phrase is difficult. The parallel verse at 1 Chr. 17:17 reads quite differently: you "have shown me future generations."

7:22–24 David is moved by consideration of his own unique status and that of his house (vv. 18–21) to contemplate the uniqueness of his God. He is the only true God, and in His unmerited favor He chose David, and the nation of Israel itself, to be the people through whom His great name would become known (Ex. 15:11–13; Deut. 7:6–8).

8:1 David defeated the Philistines and subdued them. In this summary of David's victories, pride of place is given to his defeat of the Philistines, Israel's archenemy (3:18; 1 Sam. 9:16) and against whom David's successes far surpass those of his predecessor, Saul (1 Sam. 14:52). See also 5:25 note.

Metheg-ammah. The name is otherwise unattested. The parallel in 1 Chr. 18:1 reads "Gath and its villages," and "Metheg-ammah" may refer in some way to the Philistine capitals.

8:2 he measured them. David executed two-thirds of his Moabite opponents and reduced the survivors to tributary status. The cause of David's ruthless treatment of a people whom he had earlier trusted (1 Sam. 22:3) is not stated.

Moabites. See notes 1 Sam. 22:3.

8:3 Hadadezer. This name appears to be a compound of "Hadad," the Syrian storm-god or Baal, and "ezer," meaning "help." Though defeated by David, Hadadezer later assists the Ammonites in their opposition to David (10:15–19).

Zobah. Already during Saul's reign there had been conflict between Israel and the "kings of Zobah" (1 Sam. 14:47), a Syrian region north of Israel.

8:4 hamstrung all the chariot horses. According to Deut. 17:16, the kings of Israel were not to "acquire many horses." Nevertheless, two of David's sons, Absalom and Adonijah, later dramatize their bids for the throne by preparing chariots and having fifty men run before them (15:1; 1 Kin. 1:5; cf. 1 Sam. 8:11). A third son, Solomon, will become well-known for his chariot (1 Kin. 4:26–28; 9:22; 10:26–29).

8:6 the LORD gave victory to David wherever he went. This statement, repeated in v. 14, sets the summary of David's victories apart from that of Saul's (1 Sam. 14:47–51 note; 16:18 note).

8:8 bronze. 1 Chr. 18:8 notes that Solomon used this bronze in the construction of the temple.

9 When Toi king of [u]Hamath heard that
David had defeated the whole army of Hadadezer, 10 Toi sent his son Joram to King
David, to ask about his health and to bless
him because he had fought against Hadadezer and defeated him, for Hadadezer
had often been at war with Toi. And Joram
brought with him articles of silver, of
gold, and of bronze. 11 [v]These also King
David dedicated to the LORD, together
with the silver and gold that he dedicated
from all the nations he subdued, 12 from
Edom, [w]Moab, [x]the Ammonites, [y]the Philistines, [z]Amalek, and from the spoil of
Hadadezer the son of Rehob, king of [m]Zo-
bah.
13 And David made a name for himself
when he returned from striking down
18,000 Edomites in [a]the Valley of Salt.
14 Then he put garrisons in Edom; throughout all Edom he put garrisons, [b]and all the
Edomites became David's servants. And
the LORD gave victory to David wherever he
went.

David's Officials

15 So David reigned over all Israel. And
David administered justice and equity to
all his people. 16 [c]Joab the son of Zeruiah
was over the army, and [d]Jehoshaphat the
son of Ahilud was recorder, 17 and [e]Zadok
the son of Ahitub and Ahimelech the son
of Abiathar were priests, and [f]Seraiah was
secretary, 18 and [g]Benaiah the son of
Jehoiada was over[1] the [h]Cherethites and
the Pelethites, and David's sons were
priests.

David's Kindness to Mephibosheth

9 And David said, "Is there still anyone
left of the house of Saul, that I may
[i]show him kindness for Jonathan's sake?"
2 Now there was a servant of the house of
Saul whose name was [j]Ziba, and they
called him to David. And the king said to
him, "Are you Ziba?" And he said, "I am
your servant." 3 And the king said, "Is there
not still someone of the house of Saul, that
I may show [k]the kindness of God to him?"
Ziba said to the king, "There is still a son of
[l]Jonathan; he is crippled in his feet." 4 The
king said to him, "Where is he?" And Ziba
said to the king, "He is in the house of
[m]Machir the son of Ammiel, at Lo-debar."

[1] Compare 20:23, 1 Chronicles 18:17, Syriac, Targum, Vulgate; Hebrew lacks *was over*

9 [u]1 Kin. 8:65; 2 Kin. 18:34 **11** [v]1 Kin. 7:51; 1 Chr. 26:26 **12** [w]ver. 2 [x]ch. 10:14; 12:30 [y]See ch. 5:17-25 [z]1 Sam. 30:20 [m][See ver. 3 above] **13** [a]2 Kin. 14:7; [Josh 15:62] **14** [b]Gen. 25:23; 27:29, 37, 40; Num. 24:18 **16** [c]For ver. 16-18, see ch. 20:23-26 [d]1 Kin. 4:3 **17** [e]1 Chr. 24:3, 6 [f][1 Chr. 18:16] **18** [g]1 Kin. 4:4; [ch. 23:20-23] [h]ch. 15:18; 20:7; 1 Sam. 30:14; 1 Kin. 1:38
Chapter 9
1 [i]1 Sam. 18:3; 20:14, 15, 42 **2** [j]ch. 16:1-4; 19:17, 29 **3** [k]1 Sam. 20:14 [l]ch. 4:4 **4** [m]ch. 17:27

8:11 These also King David dedicated to the LORD. David's action is perhaps in preparation for the temple to be built by Solomon (1 Chr. 22:1–5, 14; 29:1–5, 16–19).

8:13 Edomites. The slaughter of eighteen thousand Edomites in the Valley of Salt, south or southwest of the Dead Sea, is credited to Abishai in 1 Chr. 18:12. It may be that Abishai received credit as one of David's generals. See also Ps. 60, title.

8:15 David administered justice and equity. As the prototypical theocratic king, David not only subjugated Israel's enemies (vv. 1–14), but also knew that his calling was to be just (23:3). His descendants did not always follow his example, despite prophetic exhortation (Jer. 22:3). Ultimately they saw the ruin of Jerusalem (foretold in, e.g., Jer. 22:5; cf. 52:12–14). But even before the fall of Jerusalem, there arose a hope for a "righteous Branch" from the line of David, "a king [who] shall deal wisely, and shall execute justice and righteousness in the land" (Jer. 23:5; 33:15). On this messianic expectation, see note 7:4–17.

to all his people. See note 5:12.

8:16 Joab. See note 2:18.

recorder. The specific nature of this office is hard to determine. Conjectures include keeper of state records, secretary of state, and plausibly royal herald. Jehoshaphat continued to hold this office under the Solomonic administration (1 Kin. 4:3).

8:17 Zadok the son of Ahitub. Zadok was a Levite priest descended from Aaron through Eleazar (1 Chr. 6:3–8, 50–53). Although he was one of two chief priests under David, he became the sole high priest in Solomon's administration (1 Kin. 2:35). From that time on, the Zadokite priests were one of the most important and influential priestly families (Ezra 7:1, 2; Ezek. 40:46; 44:15).

Ahimelech the son of Abiathar. According to 20:25 and 1 Kin. 4:4, Zadok and Abiathar were David's priests (see 15:24, 35; 19:11). It was earlier reported that Abiathar, "one of the sons of Abimelech," had joined David during his exile from Saul's court (1 Sam. 22:20). It seems likely, therefore, that the names of father and son have somehow been reversed here (as also in 1 Chr. 18:16). Abiathar was a descendant of Eli through a different Ahitub than Zadok's father (1 Sam. 14:3; 22:20). His removal by Solomon for having supported Adonijah's bid for the throne (1 Kin. 1:7, 8) brought to fulfillment the judgment on the house of Eli (1 Sam. 2:31 note; 1 Kin. 2:26, 27).

Seraiah was secretary. Variations in the recording of this name (20:25; 1 Chr. 18:16; possibly 1 Kin. 4:3) may suggest a non-Israelite origin—perhaps Egypt, where the scribal tradition was well established. The scribe would have been among the highest ranking civil servants (2 Kin. 12:10; 18:18).

8:18 Benaiah. A man of outstanding military credentials (23:20–22), Benaiah demonstrated his intense loyalty to David and Solomon (1 Kin. 1:8, 36, 37), and, after carrying out Solomon's order to execute Joab, became commander-in-chief of Solomon's army (1 Kin. 2:34, 35; 4:4).

Cherethites and the Pelethites. See note 1 Sam. 30:14.

priests. This was an officer for which they were not clearly eligible. The parallel at 1 Chr. 18:17 reads "chief officials in the service of the king." David and Solomon at least supervised sacrifices (6:17, 18; 1 Chr. 21:28; 2 Chr. 5:6).

9:1 house of Saul. On the progressive decline of the "house of Saul," see note 5:10.

kindness for Jonathan's sake. On the covenant between David and Jonathan, see 1 Sam. 18:3, 4; 20:15 and notes.

9:4 Machir the son of Ammiel. Mentioned also in 17:27–29, Machir appears to have been a wealthy man in a good position to host a descendant of Israel's first king.

Lo-debar. This city has been tentatively located in Gilead about four miles northwest of Mahanaim, Ish-bosheth's short-lived capital east of the Jordan River (2:8 note).

5 Then King David sent and brought him
from the house of Machir the son of
Ammiel, at Lo-debar. 6 And [n]Mephibosheth
the son of Jonathan, son of Saul, came to
David and fell on his face and paid homage. And David said, "Mephibosheth!" And
he answered, "Behold, I am your servant."
7 And David said to him, "Do not fear, [i]for
I will show you kindness for the sake of
your father Jonathan, and I will restore to
you all the land of Saul your father, and
[o]you shall eat at my table always." 8 And he
paid homage and said, "What is your servant, that you should show regard for [p]a
dead dog such as I?"
9 Then the king called Ziba, Saul's servant, and said to him, "All that belonged to
Saul and to all his house I have given to
your master's grandson. 10 And you and
your sons and your servants shall till the
land for him and shall bring in the produce, that your master's grandson may
have bread to eat. But Mephibosheth your
master's grandson [o]shall always eat at my
table." Now Ziba had [q]fifteen sons and
twenty servants. 11 Then Ziba said to the
king, "According to all that my lord the
king commands his servant, so will your
servant do." So Mephibosheth [o]ate at
David's[1] table, like one of the king's sons.
12 And Mephibosheth had a young son,
[r]whose name was Mica. And all who lived
in Ziba's house became Mephibosheth's
servants. 13 So Mephibosheth lived in
Jerusalem, for [o]he ate always at the king's
table. Now [k]he was lame in both his feet.

David Defeats Ammon and Syria

10 [s]After this the king of the Ammonites
died, and Hanun his son reigned in
his place. 2 And David said, "I will deal loyally[2] with Hanun the son of [t]Nahash, as his
father dealt loyally with me." So David sent
by his servants to console him concerning
his father. And David's servants came into
the land of the Ammonites. 3 But the princes
of the Ammonites said to Hanun their lord,
"Do you think, because David has sent comforters to you, that he is honoring your
father? Has not David sent his servants to
you to search the city and to spy it out and
to overthrow it?" 4 So Hanun took David's
servants and shaved off half the beard of
each and cut off their garments in the middle, [u]at their hips, and sent them away.
5 When it was told David, he sent to meet
them, for the men were greatly ashamed.
And the king said, "Remain at Jericho until
your beards have grown and then return."
6 When the Ammonites saw that they had
become a stench to David, the Ammonites
sent and hired the Syrians of [v]Beth-rehob,
and [w]the Syrians of Zobah, 20,000 foot soldiers, and the king of [x]Maacah with 1,000
men, and the men of [y]Tob, 12,000 men.
7 And when David heard of it, he sent Joab
and all the host of [z]the mighty men. 8 And
the Ammonites came out and drew up in
battle array at the entrance of the gate, and
[w]the Syrians of Zobah and of Rehob and
[y]the men of Tob and Maacah were by
themselves in the open country.

1 Septuagint; Hebrew *my* 2 Or *kindly*; twice in this verse

6 [n]ch. 16:4; 19:24, 25, 30; 21:7; [1 Chr. 8:34; 9:40]
7 [i][See ver. 1 above] [o]ch. 19:28; 1 Kin. 2:7; [2 Kin. 25:29]
8 [p]ch. 16:9; 1 Sam. 24:14
10 [o][See ver. 7 above] [q]ch. 19:17
11 [o][See ver. 7 above]
12 [r]1 Chr. 8:34
13 [o][See ver. 3 above] [k][See ver. 3 above]

Chapter 10
1 [s]For ver. 1-19, see 1 Chr. 19:1-19
2 [t]1 Sam. 11:1
4 [u][Isai. 20:4]
6 [v]Judg. 18:28 [w]ch. 8:3, 5 [x][Josh. 13:11, 13] [y]Judg. 11:3, 5
7 [z]ch. 23:8
8 [w][See ver. 6 above] [y][See ver. 6 above]

9:6 Mephibosheth. See note 4:4.

9:7 land of Saul your father. The property that David restored to Mephibosheth may well have been substantial (v. 10 note).

you shall eat at my table. David also offers Mephibosheth a place of honor at his own table (on the practice, see 2 Kin. 25:29). It has been suggested David was somewhat self-serving, since the arrangement would enable him to keep Mephibosheth under surveillance. But this suggestion seems unlikely for several reasons. The text offers no hint of such a motive; Mephibosheth's crippled condition made him less of a threat; and David would surely have known from his own experience that it was dangerous for a rival to be at court (see 16:3).

9:8 dead dog. See note 1 Sam. 24:14.

9:10 fifteen sons and twenty servants. The number of men put to work farming the land shows that the properties were extensive. The number also indicates Ziba's own power and his potential threat to Mephibosheth (16:3; 19:26).

9:12 a young son, whose name was Mica. See also the genealogies of 1 Chr. 8:34, 35; 9:40, 41. David's beneficence "for Jonathan's sake" (v. 1) was not limited to Mephibosheth.

10:1 Ammonites. See note 1 Sam. 11:1.

10:2 I will deal loyally with Hanun the son of Nahash. The Hebrew phrase translated "deal loyally" suggests that there was a covenant between David and Nahash, even though Nahash's aggression towards Israel had helped Saul rise to power (1 Sam. 11:1–11; 12:12). The friendly relationship between David and Nahash may have been established during the period when David was a fugitive from Saul.

10:3 the city. Presumably this is a reference to the capital city, Rabbah (11:1 note).

10:4 shaved off half the beard. Hanun humiliated the emissaries.

10:5 Jericho. The first site west of the Jordan that would be reached by the delegation returning from Rabbah.

10:6 the Syrians of Beth-rehob . . . of Zobah. See note 8:3. Beth-rehob lay southwest of Zobah (cf. Num. 13:21; Judg. 18:28).

Maacah. Maacah was the region just north of Lake Huleh (Deut. 3:14; Josh. 13:11–13).

Tob. A city east of the Jordan River and forty-eight miles north of Rabbah (11:1 note; Judg. 11:3, 5).

10:7 Joab. See note 2:18.

9 When Joab saw that the battle was set
against him both in front and in the rear,
he chose some of the best men of Israel
and arrayed them against the Syrians.
10 The rest of his men he put in the charge
of Abishai his brother, and he arrayed them
against the Ammonites. 11 And he said, "If
the Syrians are too strong for me, then you
shall help me, but if the Ammonites are too
strong for you, then I will come and help
you. 12 [a]Be of good courage, and [b]let us be
courageous for our people, and for the
cities of our God, and [c]may the LORD do
what seems good to him." 13 So Joab and
the people who were with him drew near to
battle against the Syrians, and they fled
before him. 14 And when the Ammonites
saw that the Syrians fled, they likewise fled
before Abishai and entered the city. Then
Joab returned from fighting against the
Ammonites and came to Jerusalem.
15 But when the Syrians saw that they had
been defeated by Israel, they gathered
themselves together. 16 And Hadadezer sent
and brought out the Syrians who were
beyond [d]the Euphrates.[1] They came to
Helam, with [e]Shobach the commander of
the army of Hadadezer at their head. 17 And
when it was told David, he gathered all
Israel together and crossed the Jordan and
came to Helam. The Syrians arrayed themselves against David and fought with him.
18 And the Syrians fled before Israel, and
David killed of the Syrians the men of 700
chariots, and 40,000 horsemen, and
wounded [f]Shobach the commander of
their army, so that he died there. 19 And
when all the kings who were servants of
Hadadezer saw that they had been defeated by Israel, they made peace with Israel
[g]and became subject to them. So the
Syrians were afraid to save the Ammonites
anymore.

David and Bathsheba

11 [h, i]In the spring of the year, the time
when kings go out to battle, David
sent Joab, and his servants with him, and
all Israel. And they ravaged the Ammonites
and besieged [j]Rabbah. But David remained
at Jerusalem.
2 It happened, late one afternoon, when
David arose from his couch and was walking on [k]the roof of the king's house, that he
saw from the roof a woman bathing; and
the woman was very beautiful. 3 And David
sent and inquired about the woman. And
one said, "Is not this [l]Bathsheba, the
daughter of Eliam, the wife of [m]Uriah the
Hittite?" 4 So David sent messengers and
took her, and she came to him, and he lay
with her. ([n]Now she had been purifying
herself from her uncleanness.) Then she
returned to her house. 5 And the woman
conceived, and she sent and told David, "I
am pregnant."
6 So David sent word to Joab, "Send me
Uriah the Hittite." And Joab sent Uriah to
David. 7 When Uriah came to him, David
asked how Joab was doing and how the

12 [a]See Deut. 31:6 [b]1 Sam. 4:9; [1 Cor. 16:13] [c]1 Sam. 3:18
16 [d][ch. 8:3] [e][1 Chr. 19:16]
18 [f][1 Chr. 19:18]
19 [g]ch. 8:6
Chapter 11
1 [h]1 Chr. 20:1 [i]1 Kin. 20:22, 26; 2 Chr. 36:10 [j]ch. 12:26; Deut. 3:11
2 [k]See 1 Sam. 9:25
3 [l][1 Chr. 3:5] [m]ch. 23:39
4 [n]Lev. 15:19, 28; 18:19

[1] Hebrew *the River*

10:10 Abishai. See note 2:18.

10:12 Be of good courage . . . may the LORD do what seems good to him. Finding himself in the difficult military position of having to fight on two fronts, Joab urges courage but recognizes that the outcome of the conflict will depend ultimately on the Lord (cf. David's words in 15:26).

10:14 Joab returned. Apparently he did not capture the city of Rabbah on this occasion (11:1; 12:26–29).

10:16 Hadadezer. See note 8:3.

Helam. About twelve miles north of Tob (v. 6 note).

10:19 the Syrians were afraid to save. The door was opened to a second campaign against the Ammonites.

11:1 when kings go out to battle. See 1 Kin. 20:22, 26. In the Near East, springtime was a logical time for military campaigns, since the winter rains would have ceased and the labor-intensive harvest would not have begun.

David sent Joab. This is not the first time that David has sent Joab on a military expedition (10:7), but since it was the time when "kings go out to battle" and yet "David remained at Jerusalem," there may be some criticism of David for remaining behind.

besieged Rabbah. Called "Rabbah of the Ammonites" in Deut. 3:11 and elsewhere (12:26; 17:27; Jer. 49:2; Ezek. 21:20), this city was the capital of Ammon (Amos 1:13–15). It is twenty-four miles east of the Jordan River opposite Jericho. In New Testament times it was called Philadelphia, and today it is Amman, Jordan. See also 10:14 and note.

11:2 late one afternoon . . . David arose from his couch. David's luxury is in marked contrast to the activities of Joab and his men (vv. 1, 11).

11:3 Bathsheba. Not until 12:24 will the name "Bathsheba" be mentioned again; in the intervening verses the reference will be to "the woman" (v. 5) or to "the wife of Uriah" (v. 26; 12:10, 15). The focus is not on Bathsheba herself so much as on her status as the wife of another man.

Eliam. If Bathsheba's father is the same as "Eliam the son of Ahithophel" (23:34), this might help to explain Ahithophel's later betrayal of David in favor of Absalom's conspiracy (15:12; 16:15), which ostensibly was motivated by a sense of David's injustice (15:4, 6). Notice especially the nature of Ahithophel's advice in 16:20, 21.

Uriah. Uriah is a Hebrew name, meaning "the LORD is my light."

11:4 her uncleanness. If the reference is to menstruation (Lev. 15:19–30), the point would be to remove all doubt that David is responsible for Bathsheba's pregnancy (v. 5).

11:5 I am pregnant. Bathsheba leaves it to David to decide what to do.

people were doing and how the war was
going. 8 Then David said to Uriah, "Go
down to your house and [o]wash your feet."
And Uriah went out of the king's house,
and there followed him a present from the
king. 9 But Uriah slept at the door of the
king's house with all the servants of his
lord, and did not go down to his house.
10 When they told David, "Uriah did not go
down to his house," David said to Uriah,
"Have you not come from a journey? Why
did you not go down to your house?"
11 Uriah said to David, [p]"The ark and Israel
and Judah dwell in booths, and my lord
Joab and [q]the servants of my lord are camping in the open field. Shall I then go to my
house, to eat and to drink and to lie with
my wife? As you live, and [r]as your soul lives,
I will not do this thing." 12 Then David said
to Uriah, "Remain here today also, and
tomorrow I will send you back." So Uriah
remained in Jerusalem that day and the
next. 13 And David invited him, and he ate
in his presence and drank, [s]so that he made
him drunk. And in the evening he went out
to lie on his couch with the servants of his
lord, but he did not go down to his house.
14 In the morning David [t]wrote a letter to
Joab and sent it by the hand of Uriah. 15 In
the letter he wrote, "Set Uriah in the forefront of the hardest fighting, and then
draw back from him, [u]that he may be
struck down, and die." 16 And as Joab was
besieging the city, he assigned Uriah to the
place where he knew there were valiant
men. 17 And the men of the city came out
and fought with Joab, and some of the servants of David among the people fell.
Uriah the Hittite also died. 18 Then Joab
sent and told David all the news about the
fighting. 19 And he instructed the messenger, "When you have finished telling all
the news about the fighting to the king,
20 then, if the king's anger rises, and if he
says to you, 'Why did you go so near the
city to fight? Did you not know that they
would shoot from the wall? 21 [v]Who killed
Abimelech the son of Jerubbesheth? Did
not a woman cast an upper millstone on
him from the wall, so that he died at
Thebez? Why did you go so near the wall?'
then you shall say, 'Your servant Uriah the
Hittite is dead also.'"
22 So the messenger went and came and
told David all that Joab had sent him to
tell. 23 The messenger said to David, "The
men gained an advantage over us and came
out against us in the field, but we drove
them back to the entrance of the gate.
24 Then the archers shot at your servants
from the wall. Some of the king's servants
are dead, and your servant Uriah the
Hittite is dead also." 25 David said to the
messenger, "Thus shall you say to Joab,
'Do not let this matter trouble you, for the
sword devours now one and now another.
Strengthen your attack against the city and
overthrow it.' And encourage him."
26 When the wife of Uriah heard that
Uriah her husband was dead, she lamented
over her husband. 27 And when the mourning was over, David sent and brought her to
his house, and [w]she became his wife and
bore him a son. But the thing that David
had done displeased the LORD.

8 [o]See Gen. 18:4
11 [p]ch. 7:2, 6 [q]ch. 20:6; 1 Kin. 1:33 [r]See 1 Sam. 1:26
13 [s][Gen. 19:33, 35]
14 [t]1 Kin. 21:8, 9
15 [u]ch. 12:9
21 [v]Judg. 9:53
27 [w]ch. 12:9

11:8 wash your feet. Uriah understands David to be suggesting that he sleep with his wife. This might make possible the deception that Uriah was the child's father.

a present. David perhaps wanted to encourage the couple.

11:9 But Uriah . . . did not go down to his house. Despite David's efforts, Uriah does not do what he considers wrong. It is not impossible that Uriah knew about David's relationship with Bathseba (perhaps from the messengers of v. 4), but this is unlikely in view of his willingness to carry a letter from David to Joab (v. 14). Uriah explains his abstinence in v. 11.

11:11 The ark and Israel and Judah. Uriah's insistence that he will not fare better than his fellow combatants again underscores by contrast the reprehensible nature of David's sin. Even though the Lord Himself (as symbolized by the presence of the ark) was on the field of battle, the king has been in Jerusalem (vv. 1, 2 and notes).

11:13 made him drunk. See note on v. 8. Uriah still remained faithful to his duty and did not go home.

11:15 Set Uriah in the forefront. Having failed to bend Uriah, David now feels compelled to take another course, and Joab, not surprisingly (2:18; 3:27; 20:10 and notes), is willing to help.

11:21 Jerubbesheth. "Besheth," meaning "shame," was sometimes substituted for "Baal."

11:22 all that Joab had sent him. The Septuagint (the Greek translation of the Old Testament) has a longer reading in which this statement is followed by an angry response from David along the lines anticipated by Joab in vv. 20, 21.

11:25 Do not let this matter trouble you. David's answer is cynical. He pretends to console his accomplice in murder. Note the similar phrasing of v. 27.

11:27 when the mourning was over. The customary period of mourning for her was probably seven days (Gen. 50:10; 1 Sam. 31:13). National leaders were sometimes mourned for longer periods. Aaron was mourned thirty days (Num. 20:29), likewise Moses (Deut. 34:8). The Egyptians mourned seventy days for Jacob (Gen. 50:3).

bore him a son. See 12:14.

displeased the LORD. Lit. "was evil in the eyes of the LORD"; see v. 25. David has broken at least four of the Ten Commandments (Ex. 20:2–17; Deut. 5:6–21), namely, murder, adultery, lying, and coveting his neighbor's wife.

Nathan Rebukes David

12 And the LORD sent [x]Nathan to
David. He came to him and said to
him, [y]"There were two men in a certain city,
the one rich and the other poor. 2 The rich
man had very many flocks and herds, 3 but
the poor man had nothing but one little ewe
lamb, which he had bought. And he
brought it up, and it grew up with him and
with his children. It used to eat of his morsel
and drink from his cup and lie in his arms,[1]
and it was like a daughter to him. 4 Now
there came a traveler to the rich man, and he
was unwilling to take one of his own flock or
herd to prepare for the guest who had come
to him, but he took the poor man's lamb
and prepared it for the man who had come
to him." 5 Then David's anger was greatly
kindled against the man, and he said to
Nathan, [z]"As the LORD lives, the man who
has done this deserves to die, 6 and he shall
restore the lamb [a]fourfold, because he did
this thing, and because he had no pity."
7 Nathan said to David, "You are the
man! Thus says the LORD, the God of Israel,
[b]'I anointed you king over Israel, and I
delivered you out of the hand of Saul. 8 And
I gave you your master's house and your
master's wives into your arms and gave you
the house of Israel and of Judah. And if this
were too little, I would add to you as much
more. 9 [c]Why have you despised the word
of the LORD, [d]to do what is evil in his sight?
[e]You have struck down Uriah the Hittite
with the sword and [f]have taken his wife to
be your wife and have killed him with the
sword of the Ammonites. 10 Now therefore
the sword shall never depart from your
house, because you have despised me and
have taken the wife of Uriah the Hittite to
be your wife.' 11 Thus says the LORD,
'Behold, I will raise up evil against you out
of your own house. And I will take your
wives before your eyes and give them to
your neighbor, and he shall lie with your
wives in the sight of this sun. 12 For you did
it secretly, [g]but I will do this thing before
all Israel and before the sun.'" 13 [h]David
said to Nathan, [i]"I have sinned against the
LORD." And Nathan said to David, [j]"The
LORD also has put away your sin; you shall
not die. 14 Nevertheless, because by this
deed you have utterly [k]scorned the LORD,[2]
the child who is born to you shall die."
15 Then Nathan went to his house.

David's Child Dies

And the LORD afflicted the child that
Uriah's wife bore to David, and he became
sick. 16 David therefore sought God on
behalf of the child. And David [l]fasted and
went in [m]and lay all night on the ground.
17 And the elders of his house stood beside
him, to raise him from the ground, but he
would not, nor did he eat food with them.

1 Hebrew *bosom*; also verse 8 2 Masoretic Text *the enemies of the LORD*; Dead Sea Scroll *the word of the LORD*

Chapter 12
1 [x]ver. 7, 13, 15, 25; ch. 7:2, 4, 17; 1 Kin. 1:10, 22, 34; 4:5; 1 Chr. 29:29; 2 Chr. 9:29 [y][ch. 14:5-7; Judg. 9:8-15]; 1 Kin. 20:35-41
5 [z]See Ruth 3:13
6 [a][Ex. 22:1; Luke 19:8]
7 [b]1 Sam. 16:13
9 [c]Num. 15:31 [d]1 Sam. 15:19 [e]ch. 11:15, 17 [f]ch. 11:27
12 [g]ch. 16:22
13 [h][1 Sam. 15:24] [i]ch. 24:10; Ps. 32:5; 51:4 [j]Ps. 32:1; Mic. 7:18; Zech. 3:4
14 [k]Isai. 52:5; [Ezek. 36:20, 23; Rom. 2:24]
16 [l][1 Kin. 21:27] [m]ch. 13:31

12:1 the LORD sent Nathan. The prophets were servants of the word of God, which has authority even over kings. The prophets needed courage and were sometimes in sharp conflict with the kings (1 Kin. 22:8; 2 Kin. 1:3, 4; Mark 6:17; cf. Acts 7:52).

one rich and the other poor. The rich man is David and the poor man is Uriah. The parable was also fulfilled by Ahab and Jezebel against Naboth (1 Kin. 21:1–14).

12:3 like a daughter to him. The verse ends with the Hebrew word for "daughter," not coincidentally also the first syllable of the name "Bathsheba."

12:5 the man who has done this deserves to die. Nathan's parable has succeeded; in pronouncing judgment on the rich man, David has condemned himself. His response is an exclamation, not a legal decision. He mentions first death, then restitution.

12:6 fourfold. Ex. 22:1 orders fourfold restitution for stolen sheep. Some commentators have detected here a hint of David's subsequent loss of four sons: the first son of Bathsheba (vv. 14, 18), Amnon (13:28, 29), Absalom (18:14, 15), and Adonijah (1 Kin. 2:24, 25).

12:7–12 In a manner typical of prophetic judgment speeches (1 Sam. 2:27–36 note), Nathan begins with an accusation including a description of the Lord's providence (vv. 7, 8) and an accusing question and indictment (v. 9). He concludes by announcing the judgment and the penalties corresponding to the crime.

12:7 I anointed you. Compare Samuel's indictment of Saul (1 Sam. 15:17).

12:8 your master's wives. It is uncertain whether this statement is to be taken literally (only one wife and one concubine of Saul are mentioned, 3:7; 1 Sam. 14:50) or simply refers to the full extent of David's inheritance of Saul's kingdom. On the matter of kings acquiring their predecessors' harems, see 3:7 and note.

12:9 evil in his sight. This same idiom appears in 11:25, 27.

You have struck down Uriah. Because David causes Uriah to die in battle, he is as guilty as if he had murdered him with his own hand.

12:10 the sword shall never depart from your house. As Uriah was killed by violence, the house of David will be plagued by violence. Absalom killed Amnon (13:28, 29); Joab killed Absalom (18:14, 15); and Solomon ordered the deaths of Adonijah (1 Kin. 2:24, 25) and Joab (1 Kin. 2:29–34).

12:11 I will raise up evil. The prophecy is fulfilled by the rebellion of Absalom (chs. 15–18).

lie with your wives in the sight of this sun. This prediction is fulfilled in 16:21, 22.

12:13 I have sinned against the LORD. When charged by God's prophet, David responds with an immediate and unqualified confession; contrast Saul's confessions in 1 Sam. 15:24, 25, 30 (notes). Ps. 51, according to its superscription, is a fuller picture of David's repentance.

you shall not die. See notes 11:5; 12:5.

12:17 nor did he eat food with them. See note 1 Sam. 1:7.

18 On the seventh day the child died. And
the servants of David were afraid to tell him
that the child was dead, for they said,
"Behold, while the child was yet alive, we
spoke to him, and he did not listen to us.
How then can we say to him the child is
dead? He may do himself some harm."
19 But when David saw that his servants
were whispering together, David understood that the child was dead. And David
said to his servants, "Is the child dead?"
They said, "He is dead." 20 Then David arose
from the earth [n]and washed and anointed
himself and changed his clothes. And he
went into the house of the LORD [o]and worshiped. He then went to his own house.
And when he asked, they set food before
him, and he ate. 21 Then his servants said to
him, "What is this thing that you have
done? You fasted and wept for the child
while he was alive; but when the child died,
you arose and ate food." 22 He said, "While
the child was still alive, I fasted and wept,
for I said, [p]'Who knows whether the LORD
will be gracious to me, that the child may
live?' 23 But now he is dead. Why should I
fast? Can I bring him back again? I shall go
to him, [q]but he will not return to me."

Solomon's Birth

24 Then David comforted his wife,
Bathsheba, and went in to her and lay with
her, and [r]she bore a son, and he called his
name [s]Solomon. And the LORD loved him
25 and sent a message by Nathan the
prophet. So he called his name Jedidiah,[1]
because of the LORD.

Rabbah Is Captured

26 [t]Now Joab [u]fought against [v]Rabbah of
the Ammonites and took the royal city.
27 And Joab sent messengers to David and
said, "I have fought against Rabbah; moreover, I have taken the city of waters. 28 Now
then gather the rest of the people together
and encamp against the city and take it,
lest I take the city and it be called by my
name." 29 So David gathered all the people
together and went to Rabbah and fought
against it and took it. 30 And he took the
crown of their king from his head. The
weight of it was a talent[2] of gold, and in it
was a precious stone, and it was placed on
David's head. And he brought out the spoil
of the city, a very great amount. 31 And he
brought out the people who were in it and
set them to labor with saws and iron picks
and iron axes and made them toil at[3] the
brick kilns. And thus he did to all the cities
of the Ammonites. Then David and all the
people returned to Jerusalem.

Amnon and Tamar

13 Now [w]Absalom, David's son, had a
beautiful sister, whose name was
[x]Tamar. And after a time Amnon, David's
son, loved her. 2 And Amnon was so tormented that he made himself ill because of
his sister Tamar, for she was a virgin, and it
seemed impossible to Amnon to do anything to her. 3 But Amnon had a friend,
whose name was Jonadab, the son of
[y]Shimeah, David's brother. And Jonadab
was a very crafty man. 4 And he said to him,
"O son of the king, why are you so haggard
morning after morning? Will you not tell
me?" Amnon said to him, "I love Tamar, my
brother Absalom's sister." 5 Jonadab said to
him, "Lie down on your bed and pretend to
be ill. And when your father comes to see

20 [n]Ruth 3:3 [o]Job 1:20
22 [p][Jonah 3:9]
23 [q]Job 7:8-10
24 [r]Matt. 1:6 [s]1 Chr. 22:9
26 [t]For ver. 26-31, see 1 Chr. 20:1-3 [u]ch. 11:1 [v]Deut. 3:11

Chapter 13
1 [w]ch. 3:2, 3; 1 Chr. 3:2 [x]1 Chr. 3:9
3 [y]1 Chr. 2:13; [1 Sam. 16:9; 17:13]

[1] *Jedidiah* means *beloved of the LORD* [2] A *talent* was about 75 pounds or 34 kilograms [3] Hebrew *pass through*

12:20 worshiped. Like Eli, but unlike Saul, David humbly accepts the Lord's discipline (15:26; 16:11; 1 Sam. 3:18 and notes).

12:23 I shall go to him. That is, in the place of the dead (1 Sam. 28:19 note; Gen. 37:35).

12:24 his wife. Here for the first time Bathsheba is called David's wife (11:3 note).

Solomon. This name is usually considered to be derived from the Hebrew word for "peace" (cf. 1 Chr. 22:9). Another possibility is that it means "replacement"; the birth of Solomon compensates for the loss of the first child.

12:25 Jedidiah. See text note. This name confirms that "the LORD loved him" (v. 24) and bodes well for the future of the Davidic house. Despite the sin of David and his descendants, the Lord's favor will not be withdrawn (7:14 note).

12:26–31 The narrative once again returns to the Ammonite campaign (11:1 and note). This time it is not David who sends Joab, but Joab who sends for David (v. 27).

12:28 called by my name. Joab's concern may have been prompted by an interest in David's reputation and the propriety of having the king receive the captive crown.

12:30 the crown of their king. A crown weighing as much as seventy-five pounds ("a talent") would have been too heavy to wear except for brief ceremonies. The crown could have been from a statue of Milcom or Molech. The same Hebrew letters translated as "their king" could also be read as "Milcom" (i.e., Molech, the chief god of the Ammonites; see 1 Kin. 11:5, 33).

12:31 set them to labor. Subjugation of defeated enemies was common practice for David (8:2) and in the culture of the ancient Near East generally (Ex. 1:11; Josh. 9:22–27; 1 Kin. 9:20, 21).

13:1–39 David's sons follow their father's example of adultery (Amnon, vv. 1–22) and murder (Absalom, vv. 23–39).

you, say to him, 'Let my sister Tamar come
and give me bread to eat, and prepare the
food in my sight, that I may see it and eat it
from her hand.' " 6 So Amnon lay down and
pretended to be ill. And when the king
came to see him, Amnon said to the king,
"Please let my sister Tamar come and
[z]make a couple of cakes in my sight, that I
may eat from her hand."
7 Then David sent home to Tamar, saying, "Go to your brother Amnon's house
and prepare food for him." 8 So Tamar went
to her brother Amnon's house, where he
was lying down. And she took dough and
kneaded it and made cakes in his sight and
baked the cakes. 9 And she took the pan
and emptied it out before him, but he
refused to eat. And Amnon said, [a]"Send
out everyone from me." So everyone went
out from him. 10 Then Amnon said to
Tamar, "Bring the food into the chamber,
that I may eat from your hand." And Tamar
took the cakes she had made and brought
them into the chamber to Amnon her
brother. 11 But when she brought them near
him to eat, he took hold of her and said to
her, "Come, lie with me, my sister." 12 She
answered him, "No, my brother, do not
violate[1] me, for [b]such a thing is not done in
Israel; do not do this [c]outrageous thing.
13 As for me, where could I carry my shame?
And as for you, you would be as one of [d]the
outrageous fools in Israel. Now therefore,
please speak to the king, for he will not
withhold me from you." 14 But he would
not listen to her, and being stronger than
she, he violated her and lay with her.
15 Then Amnon hated her with very great
hatred, so that the hatred with which he
hated her was greater than the love with
which he had loved her. And Amnon said
to her, "Get up! Go!" 16 But she said to him,
"No, my brother, for this wrong in sending
me away is greater than the other that you
did to me."[2] But he would not listen to her.
17 He called the young man who served him
and said, "Put this woman out of my presence and bolt the door after her." 18 Now
she was wearing [e]a long robe[3] with sleeves,
for thus were the virgin daughters of the
king dressed. So his servant put her out
and bolted the door after her. 19 And Tamar
[f]put ashes on her head and [g]tore the long
robe that she wore. And [h]she laid her hand
on her head and went away, crying aloud
as she went.
20 And her brother Absalom said to her,
"Has Amnon your brother been with you?
Now hold your peace, my sister. He is your
brother; do not take this to heart." So Tamar
lived, a desolate woman, in her brother
Absalom's house. 21 When King David heard
of all these things, he was very angry.[4] 22 But
Absalom spoke to Amnon [i]neither good nor
bad, for Absalom hated Amnon, because he
had violated his sister Tamar.

6 [z]Gen. 18:6
9 [a][Gen. 45:1]
12 [b]Lev. 18:9, 11; 20:17 [c]Gen. 34:7; Judg. 19:23; 20:6
13 [d][ch. 3:33]
18 [e]Gen. 37:3; Judg. 5:30; Ps. 45:14
19 [f]See Josh. 7:6 [g]See ch. 1:11 [h]Jer. 2:37
22 [i]Gen. 24:50; 31:24

1 Or *humiliate*; also verses 14, 22, 32 2 Compare Septuagint, Vulgate; the meaning of the Hebrew is uncertain 3 Or *a robe of many colors* (compare Genesis 37:3); also verse 19 4 Dead Sea Scroll, Septuagint add *But he would not punish his son Amnon, because he loved him, since he was his firstborn*

13:6 make a couple of cakes. Both the words used for the "cakes" and their preparation ("make") are cognates of the Hebrew word for "heart" and may have an amorous connotation. A more common word for food is used by Jonadab in v. 5 and by David in v. 7. Unfortunately, David seems to have missed the innuendo in Amnon's overture.

in my sight. This emphasis (also in vv. 5, 8) is suggestive of a lustful aspect in Amnon's request.

13:12–14 Tamar's desperate appeal to Amnon points first to the distinctive moral standards of Israel ("such a thing is not done in Israel," v. 12), then to the claims of human decency ("my shame"), then to Amnon's self-interest ("you would be as one of the outrageous fools"), and finally to marriage as a better means of fulfilling Amnon's desire (v. 13). But he does not listen (v. 14).

13:12 do not violate me. The verb is used elsewhere to describe acts of rape (Gen. 34:2; Deut. 22:24, 29) and sexual violence (Judg. 19:24; 20:5).

13:13 he will not withold me from you. It is uncertain whether David would have allowed such a marriage (see Lev. 18:9, 11; 20:17; Deut. 27:22), or whether Tamar is simply trying every possible argument.

13:15 the hatred . . . was greater than the love. With keen psychological insight, the narrator notes that Amnon no sooner violates Tamar than he is suddenly repulsed by the victim of his crime.

13:16 this wrong in sending me away is greater. See Ex. 22:16; Deut. 22:28, 29.

13:17 this woman. This is a rude and abrupt way of referring to Tamar. Compare Amnon's terse dismissal of her (v. 15).

13:18 a long robe. A garment of similar description was given to Joseph by his father Jacob (Gen. 37:3).

13:20 Has Amnon your brother been with you. Absalom's ability to discern the wrong suffered by Tamar suggests that Amnon's infatuation with her was not a deep secret.

hold your peace . . . do not take this to heart. Though seeking to calm his sister, Absalom would soon seek revenge against Amnon (vv. 22, 32).

13:21 David . . . was very angry. That David was furious at Amnon's violation of Tamar is understandable; that he took no disciplinary action is not (1 Sam. 3:13 and note). The Septuagint translation and the Dead Sea Scrolls add, "he would not hurt Amnon because he was his eldest son and he loved him." Whether original or not, the sentence accurately highlights a weakness in David's handling of his sons (14:24, 33; 1 Kin. 1:6 and notes). It was David's duty as father and as king to "administer justice and equity to all his people" (8:15 and note). His failure to do this contributed to the greatest political crisis of his life, Absalom's rebellion. One of Absalom's complaints was that David withheld justice (15:4–6).

Absalom Murders Amnon

23 After two full years Absalom had
[j]sheepshearers at Baal-hazor, which is near
Ephraim, and Absalom invited all the king's
sons. 24 And Absalom came to the king and
said, "Behold, your servant has sheepshearers. Please let the king and his servants go
with your servant." 25 But the king said to
Absalom, "No, my son, let us not all go, lest
we be burdensome to you." He pressed
him, but he would not go but gave him his
blessing. 26 Then Absalom said, "If not,
please let my brother Amnon go with us."
And the king said to him, "Why should he
go with you?" 27 But Absalom pressed him
until he let Amnon and all the king's sons
go with him. 28 Then Absalom commanded
his servants, "Mark when Amnon's [k]heart is
merry with wine, and when I say to you,
'Strike Amnon,' then kill him. Do not fear;
have I not commanded you? Be courageous
and be valiant." 29 So the servants of
Absalom did to Amnon as Absalom had
commanded. Then all the king's sons arose,
and each mounted his mule and fled.
30 While they were on the way, news
came to David, "Absalom has struck down
all the king's sons, and not one of them is
left." 31 Then the king arose and [l]tore his
garments and [m]lay on the earth. And all his
servants who were standing by tore their
garments. 32 But [n]Jonadab the son of
Shimeah, David's brother, said, "Let not
my lord suppose that they have killed all
the young men the king's sons, for Amnon
alone is dead. For by the command of
Absalom this has been determined from
the day he violated his sister Tamar. 33 Now
therefore let not my lord the king so [o]take
it to heart as to suppose that all the king's
sons are dead, for Amnon alone is dead."

23 [j]Gen. 31:19; 38:12, 13; 1 Sam. 25:4, 36
28 [k]See Judg. 19:6
31 [l]See ch. 1:11 [m]ch. 12:16
32 [n]ver. 3
33 [o]ch. 19:19
34 [p]ver. 37, 38
37 [q]ver. 34 [r]ch. 3:3; 1 Chr. 3:2 [s]ch. 14:23, 32; 15:8
38 [q][See ver. 37 above]
39 [t]Gen. 24:67; 38:12; [Gen. 37:35]
Chapter 14
1 [u]ch. 13:39
2 [v]2 Chr. 11:6; 20:20; Amos 1:1 [w][ch. 12:20; Ruth 3:3]
3 [x]ver. 19; [Ex. 4:15]
4 [y]ch. 1:2 [z]2 Kin. 6:26
5 [a]See ch. 12:1

Absalom Flees to Geshur

34 [p]But Absalom fled. And the young man
who kept the watch lifted up his eyes and
looked, and behold, many people were
coming from the road behind him[1] by the
side of the mountain. 35 And Jonadab said
to the king, "Behold, the king's sons have
come; as your servant said, so it has come
about." 36 And as soon as he had finished
speaking, behold, the king's sons came and
lifted up their voice and wept. And the king
also and all his servants wept very bitterly.
37 [q]But Absalom fled and went to [r]Talmai
the son of Ammihud, king of [s]Geshur. And
David mourned for his son day after day.
38 [q]So Absalom fled and went to Geshur,
and was there three years. 39 And the spirit
of the king[2] longed to go out[3] to Absalom,
because [t]he was comforted about Amnon,
since he was dead.

Absalom Returns to Jerusalem

14 Now Joab the son of Zeruiah knew
[u]that the king's heart went out to
Absalom. 2 And Joab sent to [v]Tekoa and
brought from there a wise woman and said
to her, "Pretend to be a mourner and put
on mourning garments. [w]Do not anoint
yourself with oil, but behave like a woman
who has been mourning many days for the
dead. 3 Go to the king and speak thus to
him." So Joab [x]put the words in her
mouth.
4 When the woman of Tekoa came to the
king, [y]she fell on her face to the ground
and paid homage and said, [z]"Save me, O
king." 5 And the king said to her, "What is
your trouble?" She answered, [a]"Alas, I am
a widow; my husband is dead. 6 And your
servant had two sons, and they quarreled

[1] Septuagint *the Horonaim Road* [2] Dead Sea Scroll, Septuagint; Hebrew *David* [3] Compare Vulgate *ceased to go out*

13:23 Baal-hazor. Not the better known Hazor in Galilee, this site was some five miles from Bethel. It may have been chosen by Absalom to facilitate his imminent escape to relatives in Geshur, across the Jordan River (v. 37).

Absalom invited all the king's sons. The invitation was to participate in the feasting that accompanied the shearing of sheep (cf. 1 Sam. 25:4–8).

13:26 let my brother Amnon go with us. Amnon was the oldest son and crown prince, but even so his being singled out by Absalom aroused suspicion. David questions the request—"Why should he go with you?"

13:27 But Absalom pressed him. David sends not only Amnon but the rest of his sons, perhaps to deter Absalom from taking revenge against Amnon.

13:28 kill him. In one stroke Absalom will avenge his sister Tamar and move himself closer to the throne (3:3; 15:1–6). He will also become a murderer, repeating his father's sin as Amnon repeated David's sin of sexual immorality.

13:29 his mule. See note 18:9.

13:32 Amnon alone is dead. Jonadab seems to have known something about Absalom's plans.

13:37 Talmai. Absalom's maternal grandfather (3:3).

Geshur. See note on v. 23.

13:39–14:1 the king longed . . . the king's heart went out. It is hard to determine what emotions or reactions precisely are specified in these sentences.

14:2 Tekoa. Later known as the birthplace of Amos, Tekoa was a town ten miles south of Jerusalem.

with one another in the field. There was no
one to separate them, and one struck the
other and killed him. 7 And now the whole
clan has risen against your servant, and
they say, 'Give up the man who struck his
brother, that we may put him to death for
the life of his brother whom he killed.' And
so they would [b]destroy the heir also. Thus
they would quench my coal that is left and
leave to my husband neither name nor
[c]remnant on the face of the earth."
8 Then the king said to the woman, "Go
to your house, and I will give orders concerning you." 9 And the woman of Tekoa
said to the king, [d]"On me be the guilt, my
lord the king, and on my father's house; let
the king and his throne be guiltless." 10 The
king said, "If anyone says anything to you,
bring him to me, and he shall never touch
you again." 11 Then she said, "Please let the
king invoke the LORD your God, that [e]the
avenger of blood kill no more, and my son
be not destroyed." He said, [f]"As the LORD
lives, [g]not one hair of your son shall fall to
the ground."
12 Then the woman said, "Please let your
servant speak a word to my lord the king."
He said, "Speak." 13 And the woman said,
"Why then have you planned such a thing
against [h]the people of God? For in giving
this decision the king convicts himself,
inasmuch as the king does not bring [i]his
banished one home again. 14 We must all
die; we are [j]like water spilled on the
ground, which cannot be gathered up
again. But God will not take away life, and
he devises means [k]so that the banished one
will not remain an outcast. 15 Now I have
come to say this to my lord the king
because the people have made me afraid,
and your servant thought, 'I will speak to
the king; it may be that the king will perform the request of his servant. 16 For the
king will hear and deliver his servant from
the hand of the man who would destroy
me and my son together from [l]the heritage
of God.' 17 And your servant thought, 'The
word of my lord the king will set me at
rest,' for my lord the king is [m]like the angel
of God to discern good and evil. The LORD
your God be with you!"
18 Then the king answered the woman,
"Do not hide from me anything I ask you."
And the woman said, "Let my lord the king
speak." 19 The king said, "Is the hand of
Joab with you in all this?" The woman
answered and said, [n]"As surely as you live,
my lord the king, one cannot turn to the
right hand or to the left from anything that
my lord the king has said. It was your servant Joab who commanded me; [o]it was he
who put all these words in the mouth of
your servant. 20 In order to change the
course of things your servant Joab did this.
But my lord has wisdom like the wisdom of
[m]the angel of God to know all things that
are on the earth."
21 Then the king said to Joab, "Behold
now, I grant this; go, bring back the young
man Absalom." 22 And Joab fell on his face
to the ground and paid homage [p]and
blessed the king. And Joab said, "Today
your servant knows that I have found favor
in your sight, my lord the king, in that the
king has granted the request of his servant." 23 So Joab arose and went to [q]Geshur
and brought Absalom to Jerusalem. 24 And
the king said, "Let him dwell apart in his
own house; he is not to come into my presence." So Absalom lived apart in his own
house and did not come into the king's
presence.

7 [b][Matt. 21:38; Mark 12:7; Luke 20:14] [c][Gen. 45:7]
9 [d]1 Sam. 25:24
11 [e]Num. 35:19, 21; Deut. 19:12 [f]See Ruth 3:13 [g]1 Sam. 14:45; Acts 27:34
13 [h]Judg. 20:2 [i][ch. 13:37, 38]
14 [j][1 Sam. 7:6] [k]Num. 35:15, 25, 28
16 [l]See 1 Sam. 26:19
17 [m]ch. 19:27; 1 Sam. 29:9
19 [n]1 Sam. 1:26 [o]ver. 3
22 [p]1 Kin. 8:66
23 [q]ch. 13:38

14:7 the whole clan has risen against your servant. The tale which the wise women concocts raises not only the issue of blood revenge (v. 11; 3:27; Num. 35:16–25; Deut. 19:11–13; Josh. 20:3) but also the continuance of her family line on its ancestral property, for her enemies propose to execute the surviving son. As she points out, this would leave her with no name or descendant, something that Israelite law sought to avoid (Deut. 25:5–10). The woman skillfully introduces in her fictional story the same dilemma that David had. His duty to avenge the blood of Amnon conflicted with his anxiety that Absalom, now presumably his heir, not be cut off. Compare Nathan's parable in 12:1–4.

14:9 On me be the guilt. The woman is either expressing her willingness to shoulder whatever blame might arise, or is requesting, in polite court language, permission to speak further (1 Sam. 25:24).

14:11 invoke the LORD your God. The woman requests and secures an oath from David, in the name of the Lord, that "the avenger of blood kill no more." As was the case in Nathan's parable (12:1–6), a judgment is elicited from David's own mouth that will then be used to judge him (v. 13).

14:14 God will not take away life, and he devises means. The woman seems to mean that God does not desire to take away lives, but is ready to see the banishment ended. Some translations read that "God will not take away the life of someone who arranges for a banishment to end."

14:15, 16 While the woman has accomplished her objective of pleading for Absalom, she now returns to the matter of her own son, perhaps hoping that David will continue to believe her story and not discover that she and Joab have conspired together (vv. 1–3).

14:17 angel of God. The woman flatters David by praising his judgment. See also v. 20; 19:27; 1 Sam. 29:9.

14:23 Geshur. See 13:37 note.

14:24 he is not to come into my presence. David allows Absalom to return to Jerusalem, but the estrangement continues.

25 Now in all Israel there was no one so
much to be praised for his handsome
appearance as Absalom. [r]From the sole of
his foot to the crown of his head there was
no blemish in him. 26 And when he cut the
hair of his head (for at the end of every year
he used to cut it; when it was heavy on
him, he [s]cut it), he weighed the hair of his
head, two hundred shekels[1] by the king's
weight. 27 There were born [t]to Absalom
three sons, and one daughter whose name
was Tamar. She was a beautiful woman.
28 So Absalom lived two full years in
Jerusalem, without coming into the king's
presence. 29 Then Absalom sent for Joab, to
send him to the king, but Joab would not
come to him. And he sent a second time, but
Joab would not come. 30 Then he said to his
servants, "See, Joab's field is next to mine,
and he has barley there; go and set it on fire."
So Absalom's servants set the field on fire.[2]
31 Then Joab arose and went to Absalom at
his house and said to him, "Why have your
servants set my field on fire?" 32 Absalom
answered Joab, "Behold, I sent word to you,
'Come here, that I may send you to the king,
to ask, "Why have I come from [q]Geshur? It
would be better for me to be there still."
Now therefore let me go into the presence of
the king, [u]and if there is guilt in me, let him
put me to death.'" 33 Then Joab went to the
king and told him, and he summoned
Absalom. So he came to the king and bowed
himself on his face to the ground before the
king, and the king kissed Absalom.

Absalom's Conspiracy

15 After this Absalom [v]got himself a
chariot and horses, and fifty men to
run before him. 2 And Absalom used to rise
early and stand beside [w]the way of the gate.
And when any man had a dispute to come
before the king for judgment, Absalom
would call to him and say, "From what city
are you?" And when he said, "Your servant
is of such and such a tribe in Israel,"
3 Absalom would say to him, "See, your
claims are good and right, but there is no
man designated by the king to hear you."
4 Then Absalom would say, [x]"Oh that I
were judge in the land! Then every man
with a dispute or cause might come to me,
and I would give him justice." 5 And whenever a man came near to pay homage to
him, he would put out his hand and take
hold of him and kiss him. 6 Thus Absalom
did to all of Israel who came to the king for
judgment. So Absalom stole the hearts of
the men of Israel.
7 And [y]at the end of four[3] years Absalom
said to the king, "Please let me go and pay
my vow, which I have vowed to the LORD,
in Hebron. 8 For your servant [z]vowed a vow
[a]while I lived at Geshur in Aram, saying, 'If
the LORD will indeed bring me back to
Jerusalem, then I will offer worship to[4] the
LORD.'" 9 The king said to him, [b]"Go in
peace." So he arose and went to Hebron.
10 But Absalom sent secret messengers
throughout all the tribes of Israel, saying,
"As soon as you hear the sound of the
trumpet, then say, 'Absalom is king at
Hebron!'" 11 With Absalom went two hundred men from Jerusalem [c]who were invited guests, and they went in their innocence

25 [r]Deut. 28:35; Job 2:7; Isai. 1:6
26 [s]Ezek. 44:20
27 [t][ch. 18:18]
32 [q][See ver. 23 above] [u]1 Sam. 20:8
Chapter 15
1 [v]1 Kin. 1:5
2 [w]See Ruth 4:1
4 [x]Judg. 9:29
7 [y][1 Sam. 16:1]
8 [z]Gen. 28:20, 21; 1 Sam. 1:11 [a]ch. 13:38
9 [b]1 Sam. 1:17
11 [c][1 Sam. 9:13; 16:3, 5]

[1] A *shekel* was about 2/5 ounce or 11 grams [2] Septuagint, Dead Sea Scroll add *So Joab's servants came to him with their clothes torn, and they said to him, "The servants of Absalom have set your field on fire."* [3] Septuagint, Syriac; Hebrew *forty* [4] Or *will serve*

14:25, 26 As was with Saul before him, Absalom is described in exclusively physical terms (1 Sam. 9:1, 2 and notes). The description of how his hair was cut and weighed not only hints at Absalom's vanity, but also foreshadows the way he was to die (18:9–15).

14:27 three sons. See note 18:18.

daughter whose name was Tamar. That only the daughter's name is recorded is sometimes taken to imply that Absalom's sons all died young, but the significance of this notice may lie elsewhere. The daughter's name was the same as the sister whose violation had brought Absalom into conflict with David.

14:32 put me to death. Absalom hopes to win David over, and whatever happens he does not expect to be executed. David had not taken any dire action so far in the affair, and Absalom had some justification for killing Amnon. In effect his request is that he should be completely punished or completely forgiven, and not be left in between.

14:33 the king kissed Absalom. The narrative ends abruptly. Though David's action is sometimes referred to as the "kiss of reconciliation," it is doubtful that a real reconciliation was effected. Ironically, by giving kisses to those who approached him with petitions, Absalom was soon to steal away the hearts of the people and launch a rebellion against his father (15:5, 6).

15:1 a chariot and horses, and fifty men. See notes 8:4; 1 Sam. 8:11.

15:4 I would give him justice. See note 13:21.

15:7 four years. Four years from the meeting of v. 33 would be six years from Absalom's return to Jerusalem (14:28).

Hebron. See note 2:1. Hebron was Absalom's birthplace (3:2, 3), but also the place where David was first anointed king over Judah (2:4) and subsequently also over Israel (5:3).

15:8 Geshur. See note 13:23.

15:9 Go in peace. Though employing a standard expression (e.g., 1 Sam. 1:17; 20:42; 29:7), David's farewell to Absalom adds a touch of irony to the story, since Absalom planned to make war.

15:10 Absalom is king at Hebron. See note on v. 7.

and knew nothing. 12 And while Absalom
was offering the sacrifices, he sent for[1]
[d]Ahithophel the Gilonite, [e]David's counselor, from his city [f]Giloh. And the conspiracy grew strong, and the people with
Absalom [g]kept increasing.

David Flees Jerusalem

13 And a messenger came to David, saying, [h]"The hearts of the men of Israel have
gone after Absalom." 14 Then David said to
all his servants who were with him at
Jerusalem, "Arise, and let us [i]flee, or else
there will be no escape for us from
Absalom. Go quickly, lest he overtake us
quickly and bring down ruin on us and
strike the city with the edge of the sword."
15 And the king's servants said to the king,
"Behold, your servants are ready to do
whatever my lord the king decides." 16 So
the king went out, and all his household
after him. And the king left [j]ten concubines
to keep the house. 17 And the king went
out, and all the people after him. And they
halted at the last house.
18 And [k]all his servants passed by him,
and all the Cherethites, and all the
Pelethites, and all the six hundred Gittites
who had followed him from [l]Gath, passed
on before the king. 19 Then the king said to
[m]Ittai the Gittite, "Why do you also go with
us? Go back and stay with the king, for you
are a foreigner and also an exile from your
home. 20 You came only yesterday, and
shall I today make you wander about with
us, since I go [n]I know not where? Go back
and take your brothers with you, and may
the LORD show[2] steadfast love and faithfulness to you." 21 But Ittai answered the king,
[o]"As the LORD lives, and as my lord the
king lives, [p]wherever my lord the king shall
be, whether for death or for life, there also
will your servant be." 22 And David said to
Ittai, "Go then, pass on." So Ittai the Gittite
passed on with all his men and all the little
ones who were with him. 23 And all the land
wept aloud as all the people passed by, and
the king crossed [q]the brook [r]Kidron, and
all the people passed on toward [s]the wilderness.
24 And [t]Abiathar came up, and behold,
[u]Zadok came also with all the Levites,
[v]bearing the ark of the covenant of God.
And they set down the ark of God until the
people had all passed out of the city.
25 Then the king said to Zadok, "Carry the
ark of God back into the city. If I find favor
in the eyes of the LORD, he will [w]bring me
back and let me see both it and his [x]dwell-
ing place. 26 But if he says, 'I have no [y]plea-
sure in you,' behold, here I am, [z]let him do
to me what seems good to him." 27 The king
also said to Zadok the priest, "Are you not
a [a]seer?[3] Go back to the city in peace, with
[b]your two sons, Ahimaaz your son, and
Jonathan the son of Abiathar. 28 See, I will
wait at [c]the fords of [v]the wilderness until
word comes from you to inform me." 29 So
Zadok and Abiathar carried the ark of God
back to Jerusalem, and they remained
there.
30 But David went up the ascent of the
Mount of Olives, weeping as he went,
[d]barefoot and [e]with his head covered. And

12 [d]ver. 31; ch. 16:20; 17:1, 14, 23 [e]1 Chr. 27:33; [Ps. 41:9; 55:12-14] [f]Josh. 15:51 [g]Ps. 3:1
13 [h]Judg. 9:3
14 [i]ch. 19:9
16 [j]ch. 16:21, 22; 20:3
18 [k]See ch. 8:18 [l]1 Sam. 27:2
19 [m]ch. 18:2
20 [n][1 Sam. 23:13]
21 [o]See Ruth 3:13 [p][Ruth 1:16, 17]
23 [q]1 Kin. 2:37; 15:13; 2 Kin. 23:4, 6, 12 [r][John 18:1] [s]ch. 16:2; 17:16, 29
24 [t]ch. 8:17; 20:25 [u]Num. 4:15 [v]1 Sam. 22:20
25 [w]Ps. 43:3 [x]Ex. 15:13; Jer. 25:30
26 [y]ch. 22:20; Num. 14:8; 1 Kin. 10:9; 2 Chr. 9:8; Ps. 18:19; 22:8; Isai. 62:4 [z]1 Sam. 3:18
27 [a]See 1 Sam. 9:9 [b]ch. 17:17
28 [c]ch. 17:16 [v][See ver. 24 above]
30 [d]ch. 19:4; Esth. 6:12; Jer. 14:3, 4 [e]Isai. 20:2-4

1 Or *sent* 2 Septuagint; Hebrew lacks *may the LORD show*
3 Septuagint *Look*

15:12 Ahithophel. See note 11:3 ("Eliam").

Giloh. A town in the hill country of Judah (Josh. 15:48, 51), probably not far from Hebron.

15:17 the last house. The Hebrew reads lit. "the Far House," perhaps denoting a well-known landmark on the outskirts of the city.

15:18 Cherethites . . . Pelethites. See note 1 Sam. 30:14.

six hundred. This number, which occurs frequently in military contexts (e.g., Judg. 3:31; 18:11; 20:47; 1 Sam. 13:15), may designate a standard military unit.

Gittites. That is, from Gath. Perhaps David won the loyalty of these troops during his time in the Philistine region ruled by Achish of Gath (1 Sam. 27).

15:19 Ittai the Gittite. This foreigner became one of David's trusted military commanders, alongside Joab and Abishai (vv. 21, 22; 18:2, 5, 12).

15:20 yesterday. Presumably this is to be understood figuratively and not literally.

15:21 there also will your servant be. Ittai and his men were evidently mercenaries, but Ittai's loyalty was still outspoken.

15:23 brook Kidron. A valley running from north to south along the eastern side of Jerusalem and separating Jerusalem from the Mount of Olives.

15:24 Abiathar . . . Zadok. See note 8:17.

ark of the covenant of God. See notes 1 Sam. 3:3; 4:3.

15:25 Carry the ark of God back. David clearly resists any magical understanding of the ark's power (contrast the elders of Israel, 1 Sam. 4:3). Rather, he casts himself on the Lord's mercy.

15:26 let him do to me what seems good to him. David humbly accepts the Lord's will (10:12 note; 1 Sam. 3:18), yet this does not prevent him from taking steps to secure his survival (vv. 28, 32–36).

15:27 Go back to the city. Zadok, Abiathar, and their sons will prove useful to David's cause in 17:15–21.

15:28 fords of the wilderness. Probably the region along the western shore of the Dead Sea; see 17:16.

15:30 Mount of Olives. See note on v. 23.

barefoot . . . head covered. These are signs of grief and sorrow (Esth. 6:12; Is. 20:2–4; Jer. 14:3, 4; Mic. 1:8).

all the people who were with him covered
their heads, and they went up, [f]weeping as
they went. 31 And it was told David,
"Ahithophel is among the conspirators
with Absalom." And David said, "O LORD,
please [g]turn the counsel of Ahithophel into
foolishness."
32 While David was coming to the summit, where God was worshiped, behold,
Hushai [h]the Archite came to meet him [i]with
his coat torn and [i]dirt on his head. 33 David
said to him, "If you go on with me, you will
be [j]a burden to me. 34 But if you return to
the city and say to Absalom, [k]'I will be your
servant, O king; as I have been your father's
servant in time past, so now I will be your
servant,' then you will defeat for me the
counsel of Ahithophel. 35 Are not Zadok and
Abiathar the priests with you there? So
whatever you hear from the king's house,
[l]tell it to Zadok and Abiathar the priests.
36 Behold, [m]their two sons are with them
there, Ahimaaz, Zadok's son, and Jonathan,
Abiathar's son, [m]and by them you shall
send to me everything you hear." 37 So
Hushai, [n]David's friend, came into the city,
[o]just as Absalom was entering Jerusalem.

Ziba Lies to David

16 When David had passed a little
beyond [p]the summit, [q]Ziba the servant of Mephibosheth met him, with a couple of donkeys saddled, bearing two hundred loaves of bread, [r]a hundred bunches of
raisins, a hundred of summer fruits, and a
skin of wine. 2 And the king said to Ziba,
"Why have you brought these?" Ziba
answered, [s]"The donkeys are for the king's
household to ride on, the bread and summer fruit for the young men to eat, and the
wine for those who [t]faint in the wilderness
to drink." 3 And the king said, "And where
is your master's son?" [u]Ziba said to the
king, "Behold, he remains in Jerusalem, for
he said, 'Today the house of Israel will give
me back the kingdom of my father.'" 4 Then
the king said to Ziba, "Behold, all that
belonged to Mephibosheth is now yours."
And Ziba said, "I pay homage; let me ever
find favor in your sight, my lord the king."

Shimei Curses David

5 When King David came to [v]Bahurim,
there came out a man of the family of the
house of Saul, whose name was [w]Shimei,
the son of Gera, and as he came [x]he cursed
continually. 6 And he threw stones at David
and at all the servants of King David, and
all the people and all the mighty men were
on his right hand and on his left. 7 And
Shimei said as he [x]cursed, "Get out, get
out, you man of blood, you worthless man!
8 The LORD [y]has avenged on you all [z]the
blood of the house of Saul, in whose place
you have reigned, and the LORD has given
the kingdom into the hand of your son
Absalom. See, your evil is on you, for you
are a man of blood."
9 Then Abishai the son of Zeruiah said to
the king, "Why should this [a]dead dog
[b]curse my lord the king? Let me go over
and take off his head." 10 But the king said,
[c]"What have I to do with you, [d]you sons of
Zeruiah? If he is cursing because the LORD
has said to him, 'Curse David,' who then
shall say, 'Why have you done so?'" 11 And
David said to Abishai and to all his servants, "Behold, [e]my own son seeks my life;
how much more now may this Benjaminite! Leave him alone, and let him curse,

30 [f]Ps. 126:6
31 [g]ch. 16:23; 17:14, 23
32 [h]Josh. 16:2 [i]See Josh. 7:6
33 [j]ch. 19:35
34 [k]ch. 16:19
35 [l]ch. 17:15, 16
36 [m]ch. 17:17
37 [n]ch. 16:16; 1 Chr. 27:33 [o]ch. 16:15
Chapter 16
1 [p]ch. 15:30, 32 [q]See ch. 9:2-13 [r][1 Sam. 25:18]
2 [s][Judg. 5:10; 10:4] [t]ver. 14; ch. 17:29
3 [u]ch. 19:26, 27
5 [v]See ch. 3:16 [w]ch. 19:16; See 1 Kin. 2:8, 36-46 [x]ch. 19:21
7 [x][See ver. 5 above]
8 [y]Judg. 9:24, 56, 57; 1 Kin. 2:32, 33 [z]See ch. 1:16
9 [a]ch. 9:8; 1 Sam. 24:14; [ch. 3:8] [b][Ex. 22:28]
10 [c]ch. 19:22 [d]See 1 Sam. 26:6
11 [e]ch. 12:11

15:32 Hushai. No sooner does David pray that Ahithophel's counsel be confounded than he is presented, in the person of Hushai, with the means of accomplishing his objective.

the Archite. The Archites were of Canaanite descent (Gen. 10:15-17) and their territory was west of Bethel (Josh. 16:2).

15:37 Hushai, David's friend. Probably an official counselor. See 1 Chr. 27:33.

16:1 Mephibosheth. See note 4:4.

16:4 all that belonged to Mephibosheth is now yours. While David appears to believe Ziba's tale of Mephibosheth's treachery, he will change his ruling after hearing Mephibosheth's side of the story (19:24–30).

16:5 Bahurim. See note 3:16.

Shimei. As a kinsman of Saul, Shimei may have held David responsible for the deaths of Abner and Ish-bosheth (vv. 7, 8; on David's innocence, see 3:21, 26, 28; 4:9, 12 and notes). He may also have resented David's permitting seven of Saul's descendants to be executed by the Gibeonites (21:1 note). As a resident of Bahurim, moreover, Shimei may have been upset by David's treatment of Michal, Saul's daughter, for it was there that her second husband was ordered to cease following her as she was being taken back to David (3:16).

16:8 The LORD has avenged on you. Shimei is correct that divine retribution plays a part in David's distress, but it is not because of any injustice to the house of Saul. It was the result of David's sin against Uriah and Bathsheba (12:11).

16:9 Abishai the son of Zeruiah. See note 2:18.

dead dog. See note 1 Sam. 24:14.

16:11 let him curse. David refuses to silence Shimei for several reasons. The Lord has prompted him to curse (v. 10); if his own son wants to kill him, how much more a kinsman of Saul; if the cursing is unjust, the Lord may repay David with good (v. 12). David's ready submission to God's judgment is consistent with his character (12:20–23; 15:26) and reminiscent of Eli (1 Sam. 3:18 note).

for the LORD has told him to. **12** It may be
that the LORD will look on the wrong done
to me,[1] and that the LORD will repay me
with good for his cursing today." **13** So
David and his men went on the road, while
Shimei went along on the hillside opposite
him and [f]cursed as he went and threw
stones at him and flung dust. **14** And the
king, and all the people who were with
him, [g]arrived weary at the Jordan.[2] And
there he refreshed himself.

Absalom Enters Jerusalem

15 [h]Now Absalom and all the people, the
men of Israel, came to Jerusalem, and
Ahithophel with him. **16** And when Hushai
the Archite, [h]David's friend, came to
Absalom, Hushai said to Absalom, [i]"Long
live the king! Long live the king!" **17** And
Absalom said to Hushai, "Is this your loyalty to your friend? [j]Why did you not go
with your friend?" **18** And Hushai said to
Absalom, "No, for whom the LORD and this
people and all the men of Israel have chosen, his I will be, and with him I will
remain. **19** And again, [k]whom should I
serve? Should it not be his son? As I have
served your father, so I will serve you."
20 Then Absalom said to Ahithophel,
"Give your counsel. What shall we do?"
21 Ahithophel said to Absalom, "Go in to
[l]your father's concubines, whom he has
left to keep the house, and all Israel will
hear that you have made yourself a stench
to your father, and [m]the hands of all who
are with you will be strengthened." **22** So
they pitched a tent for Absalom [n]on the
roof. And Absalom went in to his father's
concubines [o]in the sight of all Israel.
23 Now in those days the counsel that
Ahithophel gave was as if one consulted
the word of God; so was all the counsel of
Ahithophel esteemed, [p]both by David and
by Absalom.

Hushai Saves David

17 Moreover, Ahithophel said to
Absalom, "Let me choose twelve
thousand men, and I will arise and pursue
David tonight. **2** I will come upon him while
he is [q]weary and discouraged and throw
him into a panic, and all the people who
are with him will flee. [r]I will strike down
only the king, **3** and I will bring all the people back to you as a bride comes home to
her husband. You seek the life of only one
man,[3] and all the people will be at peace."
4 And the advice seemed right in the eyes of
Absalom and all the elders of Israel.
5 Then Absalom said, "Call [s]Hushai the
Archite also, and let us hear what he has to
say." **6** And when Hushai came to Absalom,
Absalom said to him, "Thus has Ahithophel spoken; shall we do as he says? If
not, you speak." **7** Then Hushai said to
Absalom, "This time the counsel that
Ahithophel has given is not good." **8** Hushai
said, "You know that your father and his
men are mighty men, and that they are
enraged,[4] [t]like a bear robbed of her cubs in
the field. Besides, your father is expert in
war; he will not spend the night with the
people. **9** Behold, even now he has hidden
himself in one of the pits or in some other
place. And as soon as some of the people
fall[5] at the first attack, whoever hears it will
say, 'There has been a slaughter among the
people who follow Absalom.' **10** Then even
the valiant man, whose heart is like the
heart of a lion, will utterly [u]melt with fear,
for all Israel knows that your father is a
mighty man, and that those who are with
him are valiant men. **11** But my counsel is
that all Israel be gathered to you, [v]from
Dan to Beersheba, [w]as the sand by the sea

[1] Septuagint, Vulgate *will look upon my affliction* [2] Septuagint; Hebrew lacks *at the Jordan* [3] Septuagint; Hebrew *like the return of the whole* [is] *the man whom you seek* [4] Hebrew *bitter of soul* [5] Or *as he falls on them*

13 [f]ch. 19:21
14 [g]ver. 2
15 [h]ch. 15:37
16 [h][See ver. 5 above] [i]1 Sam. 10:24; 1 Kin. 1:25, 39; 2 Kin. 11:12
17 [j][ch. 19:25]
19 [k]ch. 15:34
21 [l]ch. 15:16; 20:3 [m]ch. 2:7; Zech. 8:9, 13
22 [n]See 1 Sam. 9:25 [o]ch. 12:11, 12
23 [p]ch. 15:12

Chapter 17
2 [q]ch. 16:14; [Deut. 25:18] [r][1 Kin. 22:31]
5 [s]ch. 16:16-18
8 [t]Prov. 17:12; Hos. 13:8
10 [u]See Josh. 2:11
11 [v]See ch. 3:10 [w]See Gen. 22:17

16:15 Ahithophel. See note 11:3 ("Eliam").

16:16 Hushai the Archite. See note 15:32.

16:17–19 Absalom's suspicion of David's "friend" (v. 16; 15:37) elicits from him a clever reply that he will be loyal to the one whom the Lord and all Israel have chosen. Moreover, it is a natural thing for one who served a father to serve his son also.

16:21 Go in to your father's concubines. To remove any thought among Absalom's followers of a reconciliation with David, Ahithophel counsels Absalom to lie with David's concubines who had been left behind (15:16). This would make clear Absalom's desire for the throne (3:7 note; 12:8 note; 1 Kin. 2:22). Whatever the motivation, such behavior was detestable to God (Lev. 18).

16:22 Absalom went in. This action fulfills the judgment announced by Nathan in 12:11, 12.

17:5 Hushai the Archite. See note 15:32.

17:6 Thus has Ahithophel spoken. Absalom explained Ahithophel's advice to Hushai.

17:7–13 After declaring Ahithophel's advice "not good" (v. 7), Hushai offers an alternative plan, emphasizing not quick action but overpowering numbers (vv. 11–13). The plan he suggested gained time for David to escape across the Jordan River (vv. 16, 22).

17:11 from Dan to Beersheba. See Judg. 20:1; 1 Sam. 3:20.

for multitude, and that you go to battle in
person. 12 So we shall come upon him in
some place where he is to be found, and
we shall light upon him as the dew falls on
the ground, and of him and all the men
with him not one will be left. 13 If he withdraws into a city, then all Israel will bring
ropes to that city, and we shall drag it into
the valley, until not even a pebble is to be
found there." 14 And Absalom and all the
men of Israel said, "The counsel of Hushai
the Archite is better than the counsel of
Ahithophel." [x]For the LORD had ordained[1]
to defeat the good counsel of Ahithophel,
so that the LORD might bring harm upon
Absalom.
15 [y]Then Hushai said to Zadok and
Abiathar the priests, "Thus and so did
Ahithophel counsel Absalom and the elders
of Israel, and thus and so have I counseled.
16 Now therefore send quickly and tell
David, 'Do not stay tonight at [z]the fords of
the wilderness, but by all means pass over,
lest the king and all the people who are with
him be [a]swallowed up.'" 17 Now [b]Jonathan
and Ahimaaz were waiting at [c]En-rogel. A
female servant was to go and tell them, and
they were to go and tell King David, for they
were not to be seen entering the city. 18 But
a young man saw them and told Absalom.
So both of them went away quickly and
came to the house of a man at [d]Bahurim,
who had a well in his courtyard. And they
went down into it. 19 [e]And the woman took
and spread a covering over the well's mouth
and scattered grain on it, and nothing was
known of it. 20 When Absalom's servants
came to the woman at the house, they said,
"Where are Ahimaaz and Jonathan?" And
the woman said to them, "They have gone
over the brook[2] of water." And when they
had sought and could not find them, they
returned to Jerusalem.
21 After they had gone, the men came up
out of the well, and went and told King
David. They said to David, [f]"Arise, and go
quickly over the water, for thus and so has
Ahithophel counseled against you." 22 Then
David arose, and all the people who were
with him, and they crossed the Jordan. By
daybreak not one was left who had not
crossed the Jordan.
23 When Ahithophel saw that his counsel
was not followed, he saddled his donkey
and went off home to [g]his own city. He [h]set
his house in order and [i]hanged himself,
and he died and was buried in the tomb of
his father.
24 Then David came to [j]Mahanaim. And
Absalom crossed the Jordan with all the
men of Israel. 25 Now Absalom had set
[k]Amasa over the army instead of Joab.
Amasa was the son of a man named Ithra
the Ishmaelite,[3] who had married Abigal
the daughter of [l]Nahash, sister of Zeruiah,
Joab's mother. 26 And Israel and Absalom
encamped in the land of Gilead.
27 When David came to Mahanaim,
[m]Shobi the son of Nahash from [n]Rabbah of

14 [x]ch. 15:31, 34
15 [y]ch. 15:35, 36
16 [z]ch. 15:28 [a]ch. 20:19
17 [b]ch. 15:27, 36 [c]Josh. 15:7; 18:16
18 [d]See ch. 3:16
19 [e][Josh. 2:6]
21 [f]ver. 15, 16
23 [g]ch. 15:12 [h][2 Kin. 20:1] [i][Matt. 27:5]
24 [j]See Josh. 13:26
25 [k]ch. 19:13; 20:9, 12; 1 Kin. 2:5, 32 [l][1 Chr. 2:13, 16]
27 [m][ch. 10:1, 2] [n]ch. 12:26, 29

1 Hebrew *commanded* 2 The meaning of the Hebrew word is uncertain 3 Compare 1 Chronicles 2:17; Hebrew *Israelite*

17:12 we shall light upon him as the dew falls on the ground. Hushai's simile evokes a sense of the all-encompassing power of a "blanketing" mass attack, and also tends, by its use of serene imagery, to lessen the sense of urgency and to suggest that the victory will be effortless.

17:14 the LORD had ordained. Though the Lord does not openly intervene, He is far from inactive.

to defeat the good counsel. This is an answer to David's prayer in 15:31.

17:15 Zadok and Abiathar. In 15:27–29 David sent them, along with their sons Ahimaaz and Jonathan, back to Jerusalem in order to gather and convey information to him (15:35, 36). For general information on Zadok and Abiathar, see note 8:17.

17:16 fords of the wilderness. See note 15:28.

17:17 Jonathan and Ahimaaz. See note on v. 15.

En-rogel. A spring outside the walls of Jerusalem, probably on the south.

a female servant. Drawing water was a normal task for a young woman, and these visits to the spring would not be noticed.

17:18 came to the house of a man at Bahurim. From David's recent trip through Bahurim, the site of Shimei's cursing (16:5–14), he would know who his supporters were. On Bahurim, see note 3:16.

17:23 his own city. See 15:12 and note.

hanged himself. Ahithophel's suicide was presumably prompted not only because his most recent advice was ignored, but also because he knew Absalom's chances of success had become slim. Neither could there be any reconciliation with David (16:21 and note).

17:24 Mahanaim. See note 2:8.

17:25 Amasa. According to 1 Chr. 2:13–17, Amasa was David's nephew. This would make Amasa a cousin of both Absalom and Joab (2:18 note). Absalom appoints Amasa to replace Joab as commander of the army, and David will later do the same (19:13). Amasa's tenure will be short, however, for Joab was never slow in dealing with a competitor (20:9, 10).

Abigail. Amasa's mother was either David's sister (1 Chr. 2:15–17) or perhaps his half-sister since she is here described as "the daughter of Nahash, sister of Zeruiah."

Nahash. This is presumably a different Nahash than the Ammonite "Nahash from Rabbah" in v. 27.

17:27 Shobi the son of Nahash. Like Hanun, Shobi was a member of the Ammonite royal family (10:1, 2), but unlike Hanun he was friendly towards David and may even have been David's appointee to govern the city of Rabbah after its capture (12:26–31).

Rabbah of the Ammonites. See note 11:1.

the Ammonites, and [o]Machir the son of
Ammiel from Lo-debar, and [p]Barzillai the
Gileadite from Rogelim, **28**brought beds,
basins, and earthen vessels, wheat, barley,
flour, parched grain, beans and lentils,[1]
29honey and curds and sheep and cheese
from the herd, for David and the people
with him to eat, for they said, "The people
are hungry and [q]weary and thirsty [r]in the
wilderness."

Absalom Killed

18 Then David mustered the men who
were with him and set over them
commanders of thousands and commanders of hundreds. **2**And David sent out the
army, one third under the command of
Joab, one third under the command of
Abishai the son of Zeruiah, Joab's brother,
and one third under the command of [s]Ittai
the Gittite. And the king said to the men, "I
myself will also go out with you." **3**[t]But the
men said, "You shall not go out. For if we
flee, they will not care about us. If half of us
die, they will not care about us. But you are
worth ten thousand of us. Therefore it is
better that you send us help from the city."
4The king said to them, "Whatever seems
best to you I will do." So the king stood at
the side of the gate, while all the army
marched out by hundreds and by thousands. **5**And the king ordered Joab and
Abishai and Ittai, "Deal gently for my sake
with the young man Absalom." [u]And all the
people heard when the king gave orders to
all the commanders about Absalom.

6So the army went out into the field
against Israel, and the battle was fought in
the [v]forest of Ephraim. **7**And the men of
Israel were defeated there by the servants
of David, and the loss there was great on
that day, twenty thousand men. **8**The battle spread over the face of all the country,
and the forest devoured more people that
day than the sword.

9And Absalom happened to meet the servants of David. Absalom was riding on his
mule, and the mule went under the thick
branches of a great terebinth, [w]and his head
caught fast in the oak, and he was suspended between heaven and earth, while
the mule that was under him went on.
10And a certain man saw it and told Joab,
"Behold, I saw Absalom hanging in an
oak." **11**Joab said to the man who told him,
"What, you saw him! Why then did you not
strike him there to the ground? I would
have been glad to give you ten pieces of silver and a belt." **12**But the man said to Joab,
"Even if I felt in my hand the weight of a
thousand pieces of silver, I would not reach
out my hand against the king's son, for [x]in
our hearing the king commanded you and
Abishai and Ittai, 'For my sake protect the
young man Absalom.' **13**On the other hand,
if I had dealt treacherously against his life[2]
(and there is nothing hidden from the
king), then you yourself would have stood
aloof." **14**Joab said, "I will not waste time
like this with you." And he took three
javelins in his hand and thrust them into
the heart of Absalom while he was still alive
in the oak. **15**And ten young men, Joab's
armor-bearers, surrounded Absalom and
struck him and killed him.

27 [o]ch. 9:4 [p]ch. 19:31, 32; 1 Kin. 2:7; [Ezra 2:61]
29 [q]ch. 16:2 [r]ch. 15:23
Chapter 18
2 [s]ch. 15:19
3 [t]ch. 21:17
5 [u]ver. 12
6 [v]ver. 17; [Josh. 17:15, 18]
9 [w][ch. 14:26]
12 [x]ver. 5

[1] Hebrew adds *and parched grain* [2] Or *at the risk of my life*

Machir. See note 9:4.

Barzillai. For more on this benefactor of David and David's attempt to reward him, see 19:31–39; 1 Kin. 2:7.

18:1 thousands . . . hundreds. These are standard military units, (Ex. 18:21; Num. 31:14; Deut. 1:15; 1 Sam. 8:12; 22:7; 29:2).

18:2 one third. It was a conventional practice to divide troops into three parts (1 Sam. 11:11).

Abishai. See note 2:18.

18:3 You shall not go out. In response to David's emphatic pronouncement in v. 2, the troops are adamant that he must not accompany them. Perhaps they fear that David's feelings for Absalom (v. 5; 18:33–19:7) or simply his advancing age (21:15–17) might prove a liability in the campaign. They recognize, moreover, that the death of David would mean sure defeat, as Ahithophel had earlier pointed out to Absalom (17:2, 3).

18:4 at the side of the gate. That is, in Mahanaim (17:24, 27). See note 19:8.

18:6 the forest of Ephraim. Though the territory of Ephraim was west of the Jordan, the present context implies that "the forest of Ephraim" was east of the Jordan. Ephraim may have taken some territory in the east.

18:8 the forest devoured more. The enemy would be lost in the unfamiliar, rough terrain. Some might take the opportunity to desert and others become easy prey for more experienced soldiers.

18:9 riding on his mule. Mules were the royal mount of choice (13:29; 1 Kin. 1:33).

his head caught fast in the oak. The text does not say that Absalom's famous hair was caught in the branches, but it seems likely (14:25, 26 and note).

18:11 I would have been glad to give you. Joab has no qualms about violating David's express command (v. 5).

18:12, 13 The man obviously does not share Joab's cavalier attitude towards David's orders. Moreover, he astutely concludes that, if he killed Absalom, Joab would deny having any part in it and leave him to take the blame.

16 Then Joab blew the trumpet, and the
troops came back from pursuing Israel, for
Joab restrained them. 17 And they took
Absalom and threw him into a great pit in
the forest and raised over him [y]a very great
heap of stones. And all Israel [z]fled every
one to his own home. 18 Now Absalom in
his lifetime had taken and set up for himself [a]the pillar that is in [b]the King's Valley,
for he said, [c]"I have no son to keep my
name in remembrance." He called the pillar after his own name, and it is called
Absalom's monument[1] to this day.

David Hears of Absalom's Death

19 Then Ahimaaz the son of Zadok said,
[d]"Let me run and carry news to the king
that [e]the LORD has delivered him from the
hand of his enemies." 20 And Joab said to
him, "You are not to carry news today. You
may carry news another day, but today you
shall carry no news, because the king's son
is dead." 21 Then Joab said to the Cushite,
"Go, tell the king what you have seen." The
Cushite bowed before Joab, and ran.
22 Then Ahimaaz the son of Zadok said again
to Joab, "Come what may, let me also run
after the Cushite." And Joab said, "Why
will you run, my son, seeing that you will
have no reward for the news?" 23 "Come
what may," he said, "I will run." So he said
to him, "Run." Then Ahimaaz ran by the
way of [f]the plain, and outran the Cushite.
24 Now David [g]was sitting between the
two gates, and [h]the watchman went up to
the roof of the gate by the wall, and when
he lifted up his eyes and looked, he saw a
man running alone. 25 The watchman called
out and told the king. And the king said,
"If he is alone, there is news in his mouth."
And he drew nearer and nearer. 26 The
watchman saw another man running. And
the watchman called to the gate and said,
"See, another man running alone!" The
king said, "He also brings news." 27 The
watchman said, "I think the running of
the first is [i]like the running of Ahimaaz the
son of Zadok." And the king said, [j]"He is a
good man and comes with good news."
28 Then Ahimaaz cried out to the king, "All
is well." And he bowed before the king with
his face to the earth and said, [k]"Blessed be
the LORD your God, who has delivered up
the men who raised their hand against my
lord the king." 29 And the king said, [l]"Is it
well with the young man Absalom?"
Ahimaaz answered, "When Joab sent the
king's servant, your servant, I saw a great
commotion, but I do not know what it was."
30 And the king said, "Turn aside and stand
here." So he turned aside and stood still.

David's Grief

31 And behold, the Cushite came, and the
Cushite said, "Good news for my lord the
king! For [m]the LORD has delivered you this
day from the hand of all who rose up against
you." 32 The king said to the Cushite, [l]"Is it
well with the young man Absalom?" And the
Cushite answered, [n]"May the enemies of my
lord the king and all who rise up against you
for evil be like that young man." 33[2] And the
king was deeply moved and went up to the
chamber over the gate and wept. And as he
went, he said, [o]"O my son Absalom, my son,
my son Absalom! Would I had died instead
of you, O Absalom, my son, my son!"

17 [y]Josh. 7:26; 8:29 [z]ch. 19:8; 20:1, 22; 1 Sam. 4:10; 2 Kin. 8:21
18 [a]Gen. 28:18 [b][Gen. 14:17] [c]ch. 14:27
19 [d]ch. 15:33 [e]ver. 31
23 [f][Deut. 34:3]
24 [g]ch. 19:8 [h][ch. 13:34; 2 Kin. 9:17]
27 [i][2 Kin. 9:20] [j][1 Kin. 1:42]
28 [k]See Gen. 14:20
29 [l]ch. 20:9
31 [m]ver. 19
32 [l][See ver. 29 above] [n]1 Sam. 25:26
33 [o]ch. 19:4

1 Or *Absalom's hand* 2 Ch 19:1 in Hebrew

18:16 blew the trumpet. See note 1 Sam. 13:3.

18:17 raised over him a very great heap of stones. Such burial was often reserved for criminals or enemies (Josh. 7:26; 8:29).

18:18 pillar. Compare Saul's action in 1 Sam. 15:12. In life Absalom had envisaged for himself a king's career and had erected a pillar of remembrance in his own honor; in death he was branded a traitor and buried under a pile of stones.

King's Valley. Probably near Jerusalem (Gen. 14:17).

no son. Absalom's three sons, mentioned but not named in 14:27, presumably were not yet born or were already deceased when Absalom erected his monument.

18:19 Ahimaaz. Ahimaaz has previously served as a messenger for David (15:36; 17:15–21) and wishes to do so again.

18:20 You are not to carry news today. It can be inferred from v. 27 that there was a correlation between the messenger chosen and the content of the message. Joab's decision not to send Ahimaaz may have been prompted by a desire not to appear as personally taking too much pleasure in Absalom's death.

18:21 Cushite. Cush is the area south of Egypt.

18:25 alone, there is news in his mouth. Were he fleeing the battlefield he would not likely be alone, nor would he be approaching so energetically and openly (compare 19:3, which speaks of people "who are ashamed when they flee in battle" and so steal into the city).

18:27 good man . . . good news. See note on v. 20.

18:29 I saw a great commotion, but I do not know what it was. Ahimaaz conceals his knowledge of Absalom's death (v. 20).

18:32 like that young man. The Cushite offers a conventionally phrased response (1 Sam. 25:26), which David readily understands (v. 33).

18:33 O my son Absalom. The awful repetition in David's outburst conveys his anguish at the loss of his son (19:4). In spite of all the harm that Absalom caused, David's grief blinds him to everything else (19:5 note).

Joab Rebukes David

19 It was told Joab, "Behold, the king is weeping and mourning for Absalom." 2 So the victory that day was turned into mourning for all the people, for the people heard that day, "The king is grieving for his son." 3 And the people stole into the city that day as people steal in who are ashamed when they flee in battle. 4 The king [p]covered his face, and the king cried with a loud voice, [q]"O my son Absalom, O Absalom, my son, my son!" 5 Then Joab came into the house to the king and said, "You have today covered with shame the faces of all your servants, who have this day saved your life and the lives of your sons and your daughters and the lives of your wives and your concubines, 6 because you love those who hate you and hate those who love you. For you have made it clear today that commanders and servants are nothing to you, for today I know that if Absalom were alive and all of us were dead today, then you would be pleased. 7 Now therefore arise, go out and speak [r]kindly to your servants, for I swear by the LORD, if you do not go, not a man will stay with you this night, and this will be worse for you than all the evil that has come upon you from your youth until now." 8 Then the king arose and took his [s]seat in the gate. And the people were all told, "Behold, the king is sitting in the gate." And all the people came before the king.

David Returns to Jerusalem

Now Israel had [t]fled every man to his own home. 9 And all the people were arguing throughout all the tribes of Israel, saying, [u]"The king delivered us from the hand of our enemies and [v]saved us from the hand of the Philistines, and now [w]he has fled out of the land from Absalom. 10 But Absalom, whom we anointed over us, is dead in battle. Now therefore why do you say nothing about bringing the king back?"

11 And King David sent this message to [x]Zadok and Abiathar the priests, "Say to the elders of Judah, 'Why should you be the last to bring the king back to his house, when the word of all Israel has come to the king?[1] 12 You are my brothers; [y]you are my bone and my flesh. Why then should you be the last to bring back the king?' 13 And say to Amasa, [z]'Are you not my bone and my flesh? [a]God do so to me and more also, if you are not [b]commander of my army from now on in place of Joab.'" 14 And he swayed the heart of all the men of Judah [c]as one man, so that they sent word to the king, "Return, both you and all your servants." 15 So the king came back to the Jordan, and Judah came to Gilgal to meet the king and to bring the king over the Jordan.

David Pardons His Enemies

16 And [d]Shimei the son of Gera, the Benjaminite, from Bahurim, hurried to come down with the men of Judah to meet King David. 17 And with him were a thousand men from Benjamin. And [e]Ziba the servant of the house of Saul, with his fifteen sons and his twenty servants, rushed down to the Jordan before the king, 18 and they crossed the ford to bring over the king's household and to do his pleasure. And Shimei the son of Gera fell down before the king, as he was about to cross the Jordan, 19 and said to the king, [f]"Let not my lord hold me guilty or remember how your servant [g]did wrong on the day my lord the king left Jerusalem. Do not let the king take it to heart. 20 For your servant knows that I have sinned. Therefore, behold, I

Chapter 19
4 [p]ch. 15:30 [q]ch. 18:33
7 [r]Gen. 34:3 (Heb.)
8 [s]ch. 18:4, 24, 33; See Ruth 4:1 [t]See ch. 18:17
9 [u]See ch. 8:1-14 [v]ch. 5:20; 8:1 [w]ch. 15:14
11 [x]ch. 15:29
12 [y]ch. 5:1; [Gen. 29:14]
13 [z]ch. 17:25 [a]See Ruth 1:17 [b]ch. 8:16
14 [c][Judg. 20:1]
16 [d]ch. 16:5; 1 Kin. 2:8
17 [e]ch. 9:2, 10; See ch. 16:1-4
19 [f][1 Sam. 22:15] [g]See ch. 16:5-13

1 Septuagint; Hebrew *to the king, to his house*

19:5 You have today covered with shame. What might, under different circumstances, be an understandable display of grief is totally unacceptable here. Joab forcefully declares to David the demoralizing effect his behavior is having on those who have just saved his life. If the actions of later usurpers is any guide, Absalom's success could have cost the lives of David and his whole household (1 Kin. 15:29; 16:11, 12; 2 Kin. 10:6, 7, 17).

19:7 not a man will stay with you. Joab practically threatens to lead a rebellion himself if David does not correct his behavior and show his troops proper honor.

19:8 the king is sitting in the gate. Heeding Joab's words, David takes his place in the gate of Mahanaim (18:4 note), the same spot where he had earlier given orders concerning the treatment of Absalom (18:5). The two gateway scenes provide a frame for the account of the death of Absalom.

19:13 Amasa. See note 17:25.

commander of my army . . . in place of Joab. David's promotion of Amasa over Joab appears to be politically astute and magnanimous, since Amasa had sided with Absalom and was deserving of a traitor's death. But it turned out to be a mistake (20:8–10).

19:15 Gilgal. See 1 Sam. 13:4 note.

19:16 Shimei the son of Gera. See 16:5–14 and notes.

Bahurim. See note 3:16.

19:20 house of Joseph. Strictly speaking, the "house of Joseph" would include only the descendants of Joseph's two sons, Ephraim and Manasseh (Gen. 48:5, 20; Josh. 17:17). The expression is frequently used, however, to describe all the northern tribes (Josh. 18:5; 1 Kin. 11:28; Amos 5:6; Zech. 10:6). In the present context, even Benjamin, Shimei's tribe, is included.

have come this day, the first [h]of all the
house of Joseph to come down to meet my
lord the king." 21 Abishai the son of Zeruiah
answered, "Shall not Shimei be put to
death for this, because [i]he cursed the
LORD's anointed?" 22 But David said,
[j]"What have I to do with you, you sons of
Zeruiah, that you should this day be as an
adversary to me? [k]Shall anyone be put to
death in Israel this day? For do I not know
that I am this day king over Israel?" 23 [l]And
the king said to Shimei, "You shall not
die." And the king gave him his oath.
24 And [m]Mephibosheth the son of Saul
came down to meet the king. He had neither taken care of his feet nor trimmed his
beard nor washed his clothes, from the day
the king departed until the day he came
back in safety. 25 And when he came to
Jerusalem to meet the king, the king said to
him, [n]"Why did you not go with me,
Mephibosheth?" 26 He answered, "My lord,
O king, my servant deceived me, for your
servant said to him, 'I will saddle a donkey
for myself,[1] that I may ride on it and go
with the king.' For [o]your servant is lame.
27 [p]He has slandered your servant to my
lord the king. But my lord the king is [q]like
the angel of God; do therefore what seems
good to you. 28 For all my father's house
were but men doomed to death before my
lord the king, but [r]you set your servant
among those who eat at your table. What
further right have I, then, to cry to the
king?" 29 And the king said to him, "Why
speak any more of your affairs? I have
decided: you and Ziba shall divide the
land." 30 And Mephibosheth said to the
king, "Oh, let him take it all, since my lord
the king has come safely home."
31 Now [s]Barzillai the Gileadite had come
down from Rogelim, and he went on with
the king to the Jordan, to escort him over
the Jordan. 32 Barzillai was a very aged man,
eighty years old. [t]He had provided the king
with food while he stayed at Mahanaim, for
he was a very wealthy man. 33 And the king
said to Barzillai, "Come over with me, and
I will provide for you with me in Jerusalem." 34 But Barzillai said to the king,
[u]"How many years have I still to live, that I
should go up with the king to Jerusalem?
35 I am this day [v]eighty years old. Can I discern what is pleasant and what is not? Can
your servant taste what he eats or what he
drinks? Can I still listen to the voice of
singing men and singing women? Why
then should your servant be [w]an added
burden to my lord the king? 36 Your servant
will go a little way over the Jordan with the
king. Why should the king repay me with
such a reward? 37 Please let your servant
return, that I may die in my own city near
the grave of my father and my mother. But
here is your servant [x]Chimham. Let him go
over with my lord the king, and do for him
whatever seems good to you." 38 And the
king answered, "Chimham shall go over
with me, and I will do for him whatever
seems good to you, and all that you desire
of me I will do for you." 39 Then all the people went over the Jordan, and the king
went over. And [y]the king kissed Barzillai
and blessed him, and he returned to his
own home. 40 The king went on to Gilgal,
and Chimham went on with him. All the
people of Judah, and also half the people of
Israel, brought the king on his way.
41 Then all the men of Israel came to the
king and said to the king, "Why have our
brothers the men of Judah stolen you away
and [z]brought the king and his household
over the Jordan, and all David's men with
him?" 42 All the men of Judah answered the
men of Israel, "Because the king is [a]our
close relative. Why then are you angry over
this matter? Have we eaten at all at the

1 Septuagint, Syriac, Vulgate *Saddle a donkey for me*

20 [h][ch. 16:5]
21 [i][Ex. 22:28]
22 [j]ch. 16:10 [k][1 Sam. 11:13]
23 [l][1 Kin. 2:8, 9, 37, 46]
24 [m]ch. 9:6
25 [n][ch. 16:17]
26 [o]ch. 9:3
27 [p]ch. 16:3 [q]ch. 14:17, 20; 1 Sam. 29:9
28 [r]ch. 9:7, 10, 13
31 [s]1 Kin. 2:7
32 [t]ch. 17:27-29
34 [u]Gen. 47:8
35 [v][Ps. 90:10] [w]ch. 15:33
37 [x]1 Kin. 2:7; Jer. 41:17
39 [y]See ch. 14:33
41 [z]ver. 15
42 [a]ver. 12

19:21 cursed the LORD's anointed. This was a grave offense. See note 1 Sam. 2:10.

19:22 Shall anyone be put to death in Israel this day. For a similar sentiment under similar circumstances, see 1 Sam. 11:13.

19:23 You shall not die. Although David will remember his oath, he will not forget Shimei's offense, and on his deathbed will remind Solomon of it (1 Kin. 2:8, 9).

19:24 Mephibosheth. See note 4:4.

neither taken care of his feet. Mephibosheth's neglect of personal hygiene signified his distress over David's predicament and may also have been intended to serve as evidence of his loyalty, when and if David should return.

19:27 angel of God. See note 14:17.

19:29 divide the land. David either is unwilling to call Ziba to account for his betrayal or is uncertain of the truth of Mephibosheth's story, so he settles for a compromise arrangement.

19:37 Chimham. In the light of the circumstances and of David's words in 1 Kin. 2:7, it is reasonable to assume that Chimham was a son of Barzillai. The later place-name "Geruth Chimham, near Bethlehem" (Jer. 41:17) may suggest that a land grant was part of Chimham's reward.

king's expense? Or has he given us any
gift?" 43 And the men of Israel answered the
men of Judah, "We have [b]ten shares in the
king, and in David also we have more than
you. Why then did you despise us? Were
we not the first to speak of bringing back
our king?" [c]But the words of the men of
Judah were fiercer than the words of the
men of Israel.

The Rebellion of Sheba

20 Now there happened to be there [d]a
worthless man, whose name was
Sheba, the son of Bichri, a Benjaminite.
And he blew the trumpet and said,

[e]"We have no portion in David,
and we have no inheritance in the
son of Jesse;
[f]every man to his tents, O Israel!"

2 So all the men of Israel withdrew from
David and followed Sheba the son of Bichri.
But the men of Judah followed their king
steadfastly from the Jordan to Jerusalem.
3 And David came to his house at
Jerusalem. And the king took [g]the ten concubines whom he had left to care for the
house and put them in a house under guard
and provided for them, but did not go in to
them. So they were shut up until the day of
their death, living as if in widowhood.
4 Then the king said to [h]Amasa, "Call the
men of Judah together to me within three
days, and be here yourself." 5 So Amasa
went to summon Judah, but he delayed
beyond the set time that had been appointed him. 6 And David said to Abishai, "Now
Sheba the son of Bichri will do us more
harm than Absalom. Take [i]your lord's servants and pursue him, lest he get himself to
fortified cities and escape from us."[1] 7 And
there went out after him Joab's men and the
[j]Cherethites and the Pelethites, and all the
mighty men. They went out from Jerusalem
to pursue Sheba the son of Bichri. 8 When
they were at the great stone that is in
Gibeon, Amasa came to meet them. Now
Joab was wearing a soldier's garment, and
over it was a belt with a sword in its sheath
fastened on his thigh, and as he went forward it fell out. 9 And Joab said to Amasa,
"Is it well with you, my brother?" And Joab
took Amasa by the beard with his right
hand [k]to kiss him. 10 But Amasa did not
observe the sword that was in Joab's hand.
[l]So Joab struck him with it [m]in the stomach
and spilled his entrails to the ground without striking a second blow, and he died.

Then Joab and Abishai his brother pursued Sheba the son of Bichri. 11 And one of
Joab's young men took his stand by Amasa

[1] Hebrew *snatches away our eyes*

43 [b][1 Kin. 11:30, 31] [c]Isai. 9:21; 11:13
Chapter 20
1 [d]See Deut. 13:13 [e][ch. 19:43] [f]ver. 22; 1 Kin. 12:16; 2 Chr. 10:16
3 [g]ch. 15:16; 16:21, 22
4 [h]ch. 17:25; 19:13
6 [i]ch. 11:11; 1 Kin. 1:33
7 [j]ver. 23; See ch. 8:18
9 [k][Matt. 26:49; Mark 14:45; Luke 22:47]
10 [l]1 Kin. 2:5 [m]See ch. 2:23

19:43 ten shares in the king. Whereas there are ten northern tribes, there are only two southern tribes, Judah and Simeon. The northerners felt slighted.

you despise us. The north-south hostility so much in evidence will fuel Sheba's revolt (ch. 20) and eventually bring about the division of the kingdom (1 Kin. 12). See note 1 Sam. 11:8.

20:1 worthless man. See note on 1 Sam. 2:12.

Sheba, the son of Bichri, a Benjaminite. From the same tribe as Saul, Sheba may even have been his relative.

no portion in David. See note 19:43. Although the aggressive behavior of the men of Judah was certainly a factor, residual allegiance to Saul must have also played a part in the mass withdrawal of support from David among the northern tribes.

every man to his tents. This archaic turn of phrase should not be taken to imply that the Israelites at this stage in their history were still tent-dwellers. See Judg. 19:9 where the ESV renders the Hebrew word for "tent" simply as "home."

20:3 the ten concubines. See 15:16; notes on 16:21, 22.

20:4 Amasa. See notes 17:25; 19:13.

three days. This was a limited, though not impossible, amount of time for the task set by David.

20:5 he delayed. The reason for Amasa's delay is not stated. Perhaps he did not entirely support David's cause or, alternatively, was unable to gain an immediate following among the Judahites, whose loyalties may still have been with Joab (v. 11 and note).

20:6 said to Abishai. Though Amasa is proving unsatisfactory, David is still unwilling to reinstate Joab (19:13), so he addresses Joab's brother Abishai instead. By the end of the episode, however, Joab will have retaken his former position, regardless of David's wishes (vv. 13, 23).

your lord's servants. They are called "Joab's men" in v. 7.

20:7 the Cherethites and the Pelethites. See note 1 Sam. 30:14.

mighty men. They are presumably the same as those listed in 23:8–39.

20:8 the great stone. This was possibly a well-known landmark, on the order of those mentioned elsewhere in Samuel (15:17; 1 Sam. 19:22; 20:19). The large stone may have been an altar (cf. 1 Sam. 14:33, 34), and some have suggested a link with the "great high place" in Gibeon (1 Kin. 3:4).

Gibeon. See note 2:12.

it fell out. Whether the sword fell to the ground, or into the folds of Joab's tunic (possibly girded up for marching), is not stated. See note on v. 10.

20:9 took Amasa by the beard. This was a normal gesture in administering the kiss of greeting and was not likely to arouse suspicion.

20:10 the sword that was in Joab's hand. It is unclear whether this is the sword that had fallen and so was retrieved, either from the ground or the folds of Joab's tunic (v. 8 note), or a second weapon that had been concealed on Joab's person (in which case the dropped sword was a decoy). At any rate, Joab is able to catch Amasa completely off guard and kill him, as he had killed Abner (3:27).

20:11 Whoever favors Joab . . . David. Two things might be inferred from this summons. Joab continued to enjoy the personal loyalty of at least some of the troops, despite his having been ousted by David (19:13), and Amasa's loyalty to David was not beyond question. See note on v. 5.

and said, "Whoever favors Joab, and whoever is for David, let him follow Joab."
12 And Amasa lay wallowing in his blood in
the highway. And anyone who came by,
seeing him, stopped. And when the man
saw that all the people stopped, he carried
Amasa out of the highway into the field
and threw a garment over him. 13 When he
was taken out of the highway, all the people went on after Joab to pursue Sheba the
son of Bichri.
14 And Sheba passed through all the
tribes of Israel to [n]Abel of [n]Beth-maacah,[1]
and all [o]the Bichrites[2] assembled and followed him in. 15 And all the men who were
with Joab came and besieged him in Abel
of Beth-maacah. [p]They cast up a mound
against the city, and it stood against the
rampart, and they were battering the wall
to throw it down. 16 Then a wise woman
called from the city, "Listen! Listen! Tell
Joab, 'Come here, that I may speak to
you.'" 17 And he came near her, and the
woman said, "Are you Joab?" He answered,
"I am." Then she said to him, "Listen to
the words of your servant." And he
answered, "I am listening." 18 Then she
said, "They used to say in former times,
'Let them but ask counsel at [n]Abel,' and so
they settled a matter. 19 I am one of those
who are peaceable and faithful in Israel.
You seek to destroy a city that is a mother
in Israel. Why will you [q]swallow up [r]the
heritage of the LORD?" 20 Joab answered,
"Far be it from me, far be it, that I should
[q]swallow up or destroy! 21 That is not true.
But a man of [s]the hill country of Ephraim,
called Sheba the son of Bichri, has lifted up
his hand against King David. Give up him
alone, and I will withdraw from the city."
And the woman said to Joab, "Behold, his
head shall be thrown to you over the wall."
22 Then the woman went to all the people
[t]in her wisdom. And they cut off the head
of Sheba the son of Bichri and threw it out
to Joab. So he blew the trumpet, and they
dispersed from the city, [u]every man to his
home. And Joab returned to Jerusalem to
the king.
23 [v]Now Joab was in command of all the
army of Israel; and Benaiah the son of
Jehoiada was in command of the Cherethites and the Pelethites; 24 and [w]Adoram
was in charge of the forced labor; and
Jehoshaphat the son of Ahilud was the
recorder; 25 and Sheva was secretary; and
[x]Zadok and Abiathar were priests; 26 and
[y]Ira the Jairite was also David's priest.

David Avenges the Gibeonites

21 Now there was a famine in the days
of David for three years, year after
year. And David [z]sought the face of the

14 [n][2 Kin. 15:29] [o]Num. 21:16
15 [p]2 Kin. 19:32; Isai. 37:33; Jer. 6:6; Ezek. 4:2; 26:8
18 [n][See ver. 14 above]
19 [q]ch. 17:16 [r]See 1 Sam. 26:19
20 [q][See ver. 19 above]
21 [s]See Josh. 24:33
22 [t]ver. 16; [Eccles. 9:14, 15] [u]See 1 Sam. 4:10
23 [v]For ver. 23-26, see ch. 8:16-18; 1 Kin. 4:3-6
24 [w][1 Kin. 12:18]
25 [x]ch. 15:24; 19:11
26 [y][ch. 23:38]
Chapter 21
1 [z][Num. 27:21]

1 Compare 20:15; Hebrew *and Beth-maacah* 2 Hebrew *Berites*

20:14 Abel of Beth-maacah. This city is mentioned also in 1 Kin. 15:20; 2 Kin. 15:29. On the kingdom of Maacah, see 10:6 and note. Abel is usually identified with a site about twelve miles north of Lake Huleh and four miles west of Dan.

20:19 a city that is a mother in Israel. The phrase "a mother in Israel" is one of veneration and honor (Judg. 5:7). This "peaceable and faithful" city deserves to be treated with respect rather than destroyed as a rebellious traitor.

the heritage of the LORD. That is, Israel—its land and its people, as a whole and in its parts (14:16; 21:3; 1 Sam. 10:1 and note; 26:19).

20:21 hill country of Ephraim. This name may apply to a geographical area which extended into Benjaminite territory, or else Sheba, although of Benjaminite ancestry (v. 1), was living in Ephraim.

20:23–26 This summary of David's officers parallels the list in 8:15–18, with several differences. The opening formula regarding "David's reign" (8:15) is lacking, as is any mention of David's sons (cf. 8:18). Seraiah (8:17) is here called Sheva (v. 25), and two new names are added to the list: Adoram and Ira (vv. 24, 26). 1 Kin. 4:1–6 indicates that many of David's officers continued in their duties during at least the early part of Solomon's reign.

20:23 Joab was in command of all the army of Israel. See note on v. 6. Having regained his former position, apparently without protest from David, Joab retained it until he was executed by Solomon for treason (1 Kin. 1:7; 2:22, 28–35).

Benaiah . . . the Cherethites and the Pelethites. See 1 Sam. 30:14 note.

20:24 Adoram. After serving not only under David but also under Solomon (1 Kin. 4:6 note), Adoram will be stoned by "all Israel" during the early days of King Rehoboam (1 Kin. 12:18).

forced labor. The Hebrew word translated "forced labor" here and in 1 Kin. 12:18 is used to describe the hard labor imposed on subjugated peoples like the Israelites in Egypt (Ex. 1:11), or the surviving Canaanites after the Israelite conquest (Josh. 16:10; Judg. 1:28). It also describes the labor done by conscripts from Israel itself on the building projects of Solomon (1 Kin. 9:15). Neither Adoram nor forced laborers are included in the first summary of David's government (8:15–18), which may suggest that forced labor was not introduced until later on in David's reign (see perhaps 12:31).

Jehoshaphat . . . recorder. That is, perhaps a "royal herald" (see 8:16 note).

20:25 Sheva was secretary. He was a high ranking official, perhaps akin to "secretary of state" (see note 8:17).

20:26 Ira. Ira is not mentioned elsewhere in the Old Testament, unless he is "Ira the son of Ikkesh" (23:26) or "Ira the Ithrite" (23:38), both listed among David's mighty men (23:24–39).

Jairite. Some have attempted to associate "Ira the Jairite" with the Levitical city of "Jattir" (Josh. 21:14). Others refer to "Jair the son of Manasseh" (Num. 32:41; Deut. 3:14) or to "Jair the Gileadite" (Judg. 10:3).

21:1 there was a famine. Not uncommon in the land of Canaan (Gen. 12:10; 26:1; Ruth 1:1), famine is often recognized in the Bible as a manifestation of God's judgment (e.g., 24:13; Deut. 32:24; 2 Kin. 8:1; Ps. 105:16; Is. 14:30; Jer. 11:22; Ezek. 14:21; Rev. 6:8).

in the days of David. The time frame is stated quite generally. Perhaps

LORD. And the LORD said, "There is bloodguilt on Saul and on his house, because he
put the Gibeonites to death." **2**So the king
called the Gibeonites and spoke to them.
Now the Gibeonites were not of the people
of Israel but [a]of the remnant of the
Amorites. Although the people of Israel
had sworn to spare them, Saul had sought
to strike them down in his zeal for the people of Israel and Judah. **3**And David said to
the Gibeonites, "What shall I do for you?
And how shall I make atonement, that you
may bless [b]the heritage of the LORD?" **4**The
Gibeonites said to him, "It is not a matter
of silver or gold between us and Saul or his
house; neither is it for us to put any man to
death in Israel." And he said, "What do
you say that I shall do for you?" **5**They said
to the king, "The man who consumed us
and planned to destroy us, so that we
should have no place in all the territory of
Israel, **6**let seven of his sons be given to us,
so that we may hang them before the LORD
at [c]Gibeah of Saul, [d]the chosen of the
LORD." And the king said, "I will give
them."

7But the king spared Mephibosheth, the
son of Saul's son Jonathan, because of [e]the
oath of the LORD that was between them,
between David and Jonathan the son of
Saul. **8**The king took the two sons of
[f]Rizpah the daughter of Aiah, whom she
bore to Saul, Armoni and Mephibosheth;
and the five sons of Merab[1] the daughter of
Saul, whom [g]she bore to [h]Adriel the son of
Barzillai the Meholathite; **9**and he gave
them into the hands of the Gibeonites, and
they hanged them on the mountain before
the LORD, and the seven of them perished
together. They were put to death in the first
days of harvest, [i]at the beginning of barley
harvest.

10[j]Then Rizpah the daughter of Aiah
took sackcloth and spread it for herself on
the rock, from the beginning of harvest
until rain fell upon them from the heavens. And she did not allow the birds of the
air to come upon them by day, or the
beasts of the field by night. **11**When David
was told what Rizpah the daughter of
Aiah, the concubine of Saul, had done,
12David went and took the bones of Saul
and the bones of his son Jonathan from
the men of Jabesh-gilead, [k]who had stolen
them from the public square of [l]Beth-
shan, where the Philistines had hanged
them, on the day the Philistines killed Saul
on Gilboa. **13**And he brought up from
there the bones of Saul and the bones of
his son Jonathan; and they gathered the
bones of those who were hanged. **14**And
they buried the bones of Saul and his son
Jonathan in the land of Benjamin in [m]Zela,
in the tomb of Kish his father. And they
did all that the king commanded. And
after that [n]God responded to the plea for
the land.

War with the Philistines

15There was war again between the
Philistines and Israel, and David went

1 Two Hebrew manuscripts, Septuagint; most Hebrew manuscripts *Michal*

2 [a]See Josh. 9:3-17
3 [b]See 1 Sam. 26:19
6 [c]1 Sam. 10:26; 11:4 [d]1 Sam. 10:24
7 [e]1 Sam. 20:8, 42; 23:18
8 [f]ch. 3:7 [g][Gen. 50:23] [h][1 Sam. 18:19]
9 [i]Ruth 1:22
10 [j][Deut. 21:23]
12 [k]1 Sam. 31:10-13; [ch. 2:4] [l]Josh. 17:11
14 [m]Josh. 18:28 [n]ch. 24:25

the famine should be placed about the time that Mephibosheth came to David's court (v. 7; ch. 9) and before Absalom's rebellion (16:5 note), but this is uncertain.

on Saul and on his house. Saul had tried to annihilate the Gibeonites (v. 2; 4:3 note), though obviously with only partial success.

21:2 the people of Israel had sworn. Israel's treaty with the Gibeonites is recorded in Josh. 9. Although Israel had been remiss in entering into such a treaty without inquiring of the Lord (Josh. 9:14), they still felt obliged to honor their word (Josh. 9:19).

in his zeal for the people of Israel and Judah. Saul's attempt to annihilate the Gibeonites was motivated by nationalistic, not religious, zeal. He may have wanted to rid his home tribe, Benjamin, of unwanted Amorite survivors. For Saul's ancestral association with Gibeon, see 1 Chr. 9:35–39.

21:3 the heritage of the LORD. See note 20:19.

21:6 seven. This number symbolizes completeness, not the number of Gibeonites slain by Saul.

Gibeah of Saul, the chosen of the LORD. Some scholars think the text should read "Gibeon—on the mountain of the LORD"; cf. "on the mountain before the LORD" in v. 9 and "the great high place" in 1 Kin. 3:4.

21:7 spared Mephibosheth. See note 9:1; ch. 9.

the oath of the LORD . . . between David and Jonathan. See notes 1 Sam. 18:3; 20:13.

21:8 Rizpah. See vv. 10, 11; 3:7.

Mephibosheth. A son of Saul, not to be confused with Mephibosheth, the son of Jonathan (4:4).

21:9 the beginning of barley harvest. That is, in April.

21:10 she did not allow the birds of the air to come upon them. It was considered a disgrace when the bodies of the slain were allowed to become carrion for birds and beasts (Deut. 28:26; 1 Sam. 17:44, 46; Ps. 79:2; Is. 18:6; Jer. 7:33; 16:4). Rizpah guarded the bodies until they could be buried (vv. 11–14).

21:11–14 David is prompted by Rizpah's vigil to gather the bones of the recently slain (so the Septuagint Greek translation of v. 13) and of Saul and Jonathan as well, and to give them a proper burial in the tomb of Kish, Saul's father.

21:14 God responded to the plea for the land. An almost identical statement occurs in 24:25 after the lifting of the plague brought on by David's census.

21:15–22 These verses describe briefly the defeat of four Philistine champions at the hands of David and his men. While it is difficult to

down together with his servants, and they
fought against the Philistines. And David
grew weary. 16 And Ishbi-benob, one of the
descendants [o]of the giants, whose spear
weighed three hundred shekels[1] of bronze,
and who was armed with a new sword,
thought to kill David. 17 But Abishai the son
of Zeruiah came to his aid and attacked the
Philistine and killed him. Then David's
men swore to him, [p]"You shall no longer
go out with us to battle, lest you quench
[q]the lamp of Israel."

18 [r]After this there was again war with the
Philistines at Gob. Then [s]Sibbecai [t]the
Hushathite struck down Saph, who was
one of the descendants [u]of the giants.
19 And there was again war with the
Philistines at Gob, and [v]Elhanan the son of
Jaare-oregim, the Bethlehemite, struck
down Goliath the Gittite, [w]the shaft of
whose spear was like a weaver's beam.[2]
20 And there was again war at Gath, where
there was a man of great stature, who had
six fingers on each hand, and six toes on
each foot, twenty-four in number, and he
also was descended [x]from the giants.
21 And when [y]he taunted Israel, Jonathan
the son of Shimei, David's brother, struck
him down. 22 These four were descended
[x]from the giants in Gath, and they fell by
the hand of David and by the hand of his
servants.

16 [o]ver. 18, 20, 22
17 [p][ch. 18:3] [q]ch. 22:29; 1 Kin. 11:36; 15:4; 2 Kin. 8:19; 2 Chr. 21:7; Ps. 132:17
18 [r]For ver. 18-22, see 1 Chr. 20:4-8 [s]1 Chr. 11:29; 27:11 [t]ch. 23:27 [u]ver. 16, 20, 22
19 [v][ch. 23:24] [w]1 Sam. 17:7; 1 Chr. 20:5
20 [x]ver. 16, 18
21 [y]1 Sam. 17:10, 25, 26, 36, 45
22 [x][See ver. 20 above]

Chapter 22
1 [z][Ex. 15:1; Judg. 5:1; 1 Chr. 16:7]
2 [a]For ver. 1-51, see Ps. 18:2-50 [b]Deut. 32:4; Ps. 31:3; 71:3; 91:2; 144:2
3 [c]ver. 32, 47 [d]Cited Heb. 2:13 [e]ver. 31; Gen. 15:1 [f]Luke 1:69 [g]Ps. 9:9; 59:9, 16, 17; 62:2, 6; [Prov. 18:10] [h]Ps. 14:6; 46:7, 11; 71:7; Jer. 16:19
4 [i]1 Chr. 16:25; Ps. 48:1; 96:4

David's Song of Deliverance

22 And David spoke [z]to the LORD the
words of this song on the day when
the LORD delivered him from the hand of
all his enemies, and from the hand of Saul.
2 [a]He said,

[b]"The LORD is my rock and my fortress
and my deliverer,
3 [c]my[3] God, my rock, [d]in whom I
take refuge,
[e]my shield, and [f]the horn of my
salvation,
[g]my stronghold and [h]my refuge,
my savior; you save me from
violence.
4 I call upon the LORD, who is [i]worthy
to be praised,
and I am saved from my enemies.

5 [j]"For the waves of death
encompassed me,
the torrents of destruction
assailed me;[4]
6 [k]the cords of Sheol entangled me;
the snares of death confronted me.

7 [l]"In my distress I called upon the LORD;
to my God I called.

5 [j][Ps. 42:7; 93:4; Jonah 2:3] 6 [k]Ps. 116:3 7 [l]Ps. 116:4; 120:1; Jonah 2:2

1 A *shekel* was about 2/5 ounce or 11 grams 2 Contrast 1 Chronicles 20:5, which may preserve the original reading 3 Septuagint (compare Psalm 18:2); Hebrew lacks *my* 4 Or *terrified me*

locate these events chronologically with any precision, their literary placement provides a fitting preface to David's song of praise (ch. 22).

21:16 descendants of the giants. The term "Rephaim" is sometimes applied to such peoples as the Emim, Zamzummim, and Anakim (Deut. 2:10, 11, 20, 21), all distinguished for their size and strength. According to Josh. 11:21, 22, the Anakim were driven from the hill country of Israel and Judah by Joshua, but remained in the Philistine cities of Gaza, Gath, and Ashdod.

three hundred shekels. That is, just over seven pounds. Goliath's spearhead had weighed twice as much (1 Sam. 17:7).

21:17 Abishai. See note 2:18.

lamp of Israel. This metaphor expresses the belief that Israel's hope and promise of blessing resided in David and his house (1 Sam. 3:3 note).

21:18 giants. See note on v. 16.

21:19 Elhanan . . . Goliath. The corresponding verse in 1 Chr. 20:5 contains the words "brother of." It has been suggested that "Elhanan" is another name for David (as "Jedidiah" for Solomon, 2 Sam. 12:24, 25). This would make 2 Sam. say that Elhanan (David) killed Goliath, but it makes 1 Chr. 20:5 difficult, unless Elhanan (David) killed both Goliath and Lahmi. Neither Samuel nor Chronicles supposes that anyone except David killed Goliath, and it remains unclear why they introduce the name Elhanan in two verses.

21:20 giants. See note on v. 16.

21:22 by the hand of David and . . . his servants. David was directly involved in the encounter with Ishbi-benob (vv. 16, 17).

22:1 this song. David's song of praise (which appears also in Ps. 18, with minor variations), together with the prayer of Hannah, forms a fitting frame for the books of 1 and 2 Samuel (1 Sam. 2:1–10 note). This song focuses on the Lord's deliverance of David. It may be outlined as follows: introductory praise of God as "savior" (vv. 2–4); the psalmist's distress (vv. 5, 6); the psalmist's petition (v. 7); the Lord's response in cosmic demonstration (vv. 8–16) and personal rescue (vv. 17–20); the psalmist's innocence (vv. 21–25) and the Lord's faithfulness (vv. 26–30); the Lord's deliverance (vv. 31–37) and the psalmist's resultant victories (vv. 38–46); concluding praise of God as Savior (vv. 47–51). Ps. 144, also ascribed to David, shows many similarities in theme and language.

all his enemies. See 8:1–14; cf. 5:8; 7:1, 9, 11; 18:32.

from the hand of Saul. See 12:7; 1 Sam. 18–31 (especially 18:9–11; 19:2, 10–11, 15–16).

22:2 rock. See also vv. 32, 47; note on 1 Sam. 2:2.

22:3 horn. See notes 1 Sam. 2:1, 10.

22:5 waves . . . torrents. See v. 17. The image of overflowing water recurs frequently in Old Testament poetry as a symbol of distress and destruction (Ps. 32:6; 69:1, 2, 14; 144:7; Is. 43:2; Jon. 2:5).

22:7 In my distress. Being in a narrow or tightly confined space is a common figure for distress. In v. 20 (note) relief is described as being brought into a "broad place."

From his temple he heard my voice,
and my cry [m] came to his ears.

8 "Then [n] the earth reeled and rocked;
[o] the foundations of the heavens trembled
and quaked, because he was angry.
9 Smoke went up from his nostrils,[1]
and devouring fire from his mouth;
[p] glowing coals flamed forth from him.
10 [q] He bowed the heavens and [r] came down;
[s] thick darkness was under his feet.
11 He rode on a cherub and flew;
he was seen on [t] the wings of the wind.
12 He made [s] darkness around him [u] his canopy,
thick clouds, a gathering of water.
13 Out of the brightness before him
[v] coals of fire flamed forth.
14 [w] The LORD thundered from heaven,
and the Most High uttered his voice.
15 And he sent out [x] arrows and scattered them;
lightning, and routed them.
16 Then the channels of the sea were seen;
the foundations of the world were laid bare,
at the rebuke of the LORD,
at the [y] blast of the breath of his nostrils.

17 [z] "He sent from on high, he took me;
he drew me out of many waters.
18 He rescued me from my strong enemy,
from those who hated me,
for they were too mighty for me.
19 They confronted me in the day of my calamity,
but the LORD was my support.
20 [a] He brought me out into a broad place;
he rescued me, because [b] he delighted in me.

21 "The LORD [c] dealt with me according to my righteousness;
according to the [d] cleanness of my hands he rewarded me.
22 [e] For I have kept the ways of the LORD
and have not wickedly departed from my God.
23 [f] For all his rules were before me,
and from his statutes I did not turn aside.
24 I was [g] blameless before him,
and I kept myself from guilt.
25 [d] And the LORD has rewarded me according to my righteousness,
according to my cleanness in his sight.

26 [h] "With the merciful you show yourself merciful;
with the [g] blameless man you show yourself blameless;
27 with the purified you deal purely,
and with the crooked you make yourself seem tortuous.
28 [i] You save a humble people,
[j] but your eyes are on the haughty to bring them down.
29 [k] For you are my lamp, O LORD,
and my God lightens my darkness.
30 For by you I can run against a troop,
and by my God I can leap over a wall.
31 This God—[l] his way is perfect;
the [m] word of the LORD proves true;
he is [n] a shield for all those who take refuge in him.

32 "For who is God, but the LORD?
[o] And who is a rock, except our God?

7 [m] Ps. 18:6
8 [n] Judg. 5:4; Ps. 77:18; 97:4 [o] [Job 26:11]
9 [p] ver. 13
10 [q] Ps. 144:5 [r] Isai. 64:1 [s] [Ex. 20:21; 1 Kin. 8:12; Ps. 97:2]
11 [t] Ps. 104:3
12 [s] [See ver. 10 above] [u] Job 36:29
13 [v] ver. 9
14 [w] Job 37:4; Ps. 29:3
15 [x] Deut. 32:23; Ps. 7:13; 77:17; 144:6; Hab. 3:11
16 [y] Ex. 15:8
17 [z] Ps. 144:7
20 [a] Ps. 31:8; 118:5 [b] See ch. 15:26
21 [c] 1 Sam. 26:23; 1 Kin. 8:32; Ps. 7:8 [d] [Ps. 24:4]
22 [e] Gen. 18:19; Prov. 8:32
23 [f] Ps. 119:30, 102
24 [g] [Gen. 6:9; 17:1; Job 1:1]
25 [d] [See ver. 21 above]
26 [h] [Matt. 5:7] [g] [See ver. 24 above]
28 [i] [Ps. 72:12, 13] [j] [Isai. 2:11, 12, 17; Luke 1:51]
29 [k] Job 29:3; Ps. 27:1; [ch. 21:17]
31 [l] Deut. 32:4; Matt. 5:48 [m] Prov. 30:5 [n] ver. 3; Ps. 5:12; 33:20; 59:11; 84:9
32 [o] See ver. 2

[1] Or *in his wrath*

From his temple. This probably means God's heavenly sanctuary (1 Kin. 8:27, 38–39; Ps. 11:4; Is. 6:1; Jon. 2:7; Rev. 11:19; 14:17; 15:5).

22:9 Smoke went up from his nostrils. Compare the imagery used to describe the awesome power of Leviathan in Job 41:18–21.

22:11 rode on a cherub and flew. See Ex. 25:17–22; Num. 7:89; Ezek. 10:19; 11:22.

22:14 The LORD thundered. See 1 Sam. 2:10; 7:10. The Lord's voice is often likened to thunder (Job 37:4, 5; 40:9; Ps. 29:3; Is. 33:3).

Most High. See Gen. 14:19 and notes.

22:15 he sent out arrows. For similar imagery, see Deut. 32:23, 42; Job 6:4; Ps. 64:7. Lightning is sometimes described as the Lord's arrows (Ps. 77:17; cf. Hab. 3:11; Zech. 9:14).

22:17 many waters. See v. 5 note.

22:20 broad place. See v. 7 note.

22:21–25 David is not laying claim to righteousness or sinlessness in any absolute sense. Rather he asserts his blamelessness with respect to his enemies and his confidence that the Lord rewards those who seek to be faithful to Him (v. 26; 1 Sam. 26:23). If this were not the case, David would surely be classed among "the haughty" (v. 28).

22:27 tortuous. Lit. "And with the twisted you will deal tortuously." In the economy of God's justice, those who take "twisted" paths will find the way tortuous.

22:28 humble . . . haughty. See the theme of divine reversal of fortunes in Hannah's prayer (1 Sam. 2:1–10 and note; especially v. 7).

22:29 my lamp. Cf. notes on 21:17; 1 Sam. 3:3.

33 This God is my [p] strong refuge
and has made my[1] way blameless.[2]
34 [q] He made my feet like the feet of a deer
and set me secure [r] on the heights.
35 [s] He trains my hands for war,
so that my arms can bend a bow of
bronze.
36 You have given me the shield of your
salvation,
and your gentleness made me great.
37 [t] You gave a wide place for my steps
under me,
and my feet[3] did not slip;
38 I pursued my enemies and destroyed
them,
and did not turn back until they
were consumed.
39 I consumed them; I thrust them
through, so that they did not rise;
they fell [u] under my feet.
40 For you equipped me with strength
for the battle;
you made [v] those who rise against
me sink under me.
41 You [w] made my enemies turn their
backs to me,[4]
those who hated me, and I
destroyed them.
42 They looked, but there was none to
save;
they cried to the LORD, but [x] he did
not answer them.
43 I beat them fine [y] as the dust of the
earth;
I crushed them and stamped them
down [z] like the mire of the streets.
44 "You delivered me from strife with my
people;[5]
you kept me as the head of [a] the
nations;
[b] people whom I had not known
served me.
45 Foreigners came cringing to me;
as soon as they heard of me, they
obeyed me.
46 Foreigners lost heart
and came trembling[6] [c] out of their
fortresses.
47 "The LORD lives, and blessed be my
rock,
and exalted be [d] my God, [e] the rock
of my salvation,
48 the God who gave me vengeance
and [f] brought down peoples
under me,
49 who brought me out from my enemies;
you exalted me above [v] those who
rose against me;
you delivered me from [g] men of
violence.
50 [h] "For this I will praise you, O LORD,
among the nations,
and sing praises to your name.
51 [i] Great salvation he brings[7] to his king,
and shows steadfast love to [j] his
anointed,
to David and his offspring [k] forever."

33 [p] ver. 2; Ps. 28:8; 31:3, 4
34 [q] See ch. 2:18 [r] Deut. 32:13; 33:29; Isai. 58:14
35 [s] Ps. 144:1
37 [t] Prov. 4:12
39 [u] [Mal. 4:3]
40 [v] Ps. 44:5; 59:1
41 [w] Ex. 23:27
42 [x] 1 Sam. 28:6; Prov. 1:28; [Isai. 1:15; Mic. 3:4]
43 [y] 2 Kin. 13:7 [z] Isai. 10:6; Mic. 7:10; Zech. 10:5; [Deut. 28:13]
44 [a] See ch. 8:1-14 [b] Isai. 55:5
46 [c] Mic. 7:17
47 [d] ver. 3, 32 [e] Deut. 32:15; Ps. 89:26; 95:1
48 [f] Ps. 144:2
49 [v] [See ver. 40 above] [g] Ps. 140:1
50 [h] Cited Rom. 15:9
51 [i] [Ps. 144:10] [j] [1 Sam. 16:12, 13; Ps. 89:20] [k] ch. 7:12, 13; Ps. 89:29

The Last Words of David

23 Now these are the last words of David:
The oracle of David, the son of Jesse,
the oracle of [l] the man who was
raised on high,
[j] the anointed of the God of Jacob,
the sweet psalmist of Israel:[8]
2 [m] "The Spirit of the LORD speaks by me;
his word is on my tongue.

Chapter 23
1 [l] [ch. 7:8, 9; Ps. 78:70, 71] [j] [See ch. 22:51 above]
2 [m] [2 Pet. 1:21]

[1] Or *his*; also verse 34 [2] Compare Psalm 18:32; Hebrew *he has blamelessly set my way free*, or *he has made my way spring up blamelessly* [3] Hebrew *ankles* [4] Or *you gave me my enemies' necks* [5] Septuagint *with the peoples* [6] Compare Psalm 18:45; Hebrew *equipped themselves* [7] Or *He is a tower of salvation* [8] Or *the favorite of the songs of Israel*

22:32 rock. See v. 2 and note.

22:44 my people. This is possibly a reference to the many perils that David experienced at the hands of Saul, Absalom, and others. The corresponding verse in Ps. 18:43 reads simply "the people," as does the Septuagint (Greek Old Testament translation) of this verse.

22:51 his king . . . anointed. The mention of the Lord's "king" and His "anointed" is reminiscent of the closing verse of Hannah's prayer in 1 Sam. 2:10. After the dynastic promise of 2 Sam. 7:5–16, David can speak confidently of God's unfailing mercy to his descendants forever. The dynastic theme is the transition to ch. 23, where David celebrates the "everlasting covenant" he has with the Lord (23:5).

23:1 last words. That is, his last poem. See 1 Kin. 2:1–10 for David's final instructions to Solomon.

oracle. Or "utterance." The Hebrew word is often, though not exclusively, associated with prophecy (e.g., 1 Sam. 2:30; 2 Kin. 9:26), an association not inappropriate for David (v. 2 and note; Acts 2:30).

the sweet psalmist of Israel. Another translation of the Hebrew is "the beloved of Israel's Protector."

23:2–4 The Lord revealed to David the essential character and glorious benefits of the ideal theocratic king. Only in the Christ, the greater Son of David, will such qualities of character be fully displayed and such benefits fully realized (7:4–17 note).

23:2 The Spirit of the LORD speaks by me. Other references to David acting or speaking under divine inspiration include 1 Chr. 28:11, 12; Matt. 22:43; Acts 1:16; 4:25. David's empowerment by the Spirit is recounted in 1 Sam. 16:13.

3 The God of Israel has spoken;
[n] the Rock of Israel has said to me:
When one rules justly over men,
ruling [o] in the fear of God,
4 he [p] dawns on them like the morning light,
like the sun shining forth on a cloudless morning,
like rain[1] that makes grass to sprout from the earth.
5 For does not my house stand so with God?
[q] For he has made with me an everlasting covenant,
ordered in all things and secure.
For will he not cause to prosper
all my help and my desire?
6 But worthless men[2] are all like thorns that are thrown away,
for they cannot be taken with the hand;
7 but the man who touches them
arms himself with iron and the shaft of a spear,
and they are utterly consumed with fire."[3]

David's Mighty Men

8 [r] These are the names of the mighty men
whom David had: [s] Josheb-basshebeth a
Tahchemonite; he was chief of the three.[4]
He wielded his spear[5] against eight hundred whom he killed at one time.
9 And next to him among the three mighty
men was Eleazar the son of [t] Dodo, son of
[u] Ahohi. He was with David when they
defied the Philistines who were gathered
there for battle, and the men of Israel withdrew. 10 He rose and struck down the
Philistines until his hand was weary, and his
hand clung to the sword. And the LORD
brought about a great victory that day, and
the men returned after him only to strip the
slain.
11 And next to him was Shammah, the
son of Agee the [v] Hararite. The Philistines
gathered together at Lehi, where there was
a plot of ground full of lentils, and the men
fled from the Philistines. 12 But he took his
stand in the midst of the plot and defended it and struck down the Philistines, and
the LORD worked a great victory.
13 And three of the thirty chief men went
down and came about harvest time to David
at the [w] cave of Adullam, when a band of
Philistines was encamped [x] in the Valley of
Rephaim. 14 David was then [y] in the stronghold, and [z] the garrison of the Philistines was
then at Bethlehem. 15 And David said longingly, "Oh, that someone would give me
water to drink from the well of Bethlehem
that is by the gate!" 16 Then the three mighty
men broke through the camp of the
Philistines and drew water out of the well of
Bethlehem that was by the gate and carried
and brought it to David. But he would not
drink of it. He poured it out to the LORD
17 and said, "Far be it from me, O LORD, that
I should do this. Shall I drink [a] the blood of
the men who went at the risk of their lives?"
Therefore he would not drink it. These
things the three mighty men did.

3 [n] See ch. 22:2, 3, 32, 47 [o] Ex. 18:21; 2 Chr. 19:7, 9
4 [p] [Judg. 5:31; Prov. 4:18; Hos. 6:5]
5 [q] ch. 7:15, 16; Ps. 89:29; Isai. 55:3
8 [r] For ver. 8-39, see 1 Chr. 11:11-47 [s] [1 Chr. 27:2, 3]
9 [t] 1 Chr. 27:4 [u] ver. 28
11 [v] ver. 33
13 [w] See 1 Sam. 22:1 [x] See ch. 5:18
14 [y] 1 Sam. 22:4, 5 [z] [1 Sam. 13:23]
17 [a] [Lev. 17:10]

1 Hebrew *from rain* 2 Hebrew *worthlessness* 3 Hebrew *fire in the sitting* 4 Or *of the captains* 5 1 Chronicles 11:11; the meaning of the Hebrew expression is uncertain

23:3 Rock. See v. 32; notes on 22:2; 1 Sam. 2:2.

justly. Righteous rule is possible only for one who lives in a right relationship with God. On what it means to "fear" God, see 1 Sam. 12:14 note.

23:4 the morning light . . . sun shining forth. The benefits of righteous rule are enlightenment, fruitfulness, and refreshment. For a fuller development of similar themes, see Ps. 72.

23:5 does not my house stand so with God. David's confidence rests not in his own righteousness but in the everlasting covenant made with him by a gracious God (7:11–16; 2 Chr. 13:5; 21:7; Ps. 89:3, 4, 28, 29; Is. 55:3; Ezek. 37:25, 26).

23:6 worthless men. The Hebrew term is "Belial"; see note 1 Sam. 2:12. The focus here may be on those who had opposed the rule of David.

23:8–39 The presentation of David's "mighty men" in these verses forms a counterpart to the much shorter description of Davidic champions in 21:15–22. According to v. 39, the warriors listed should total thirty-seven. They are presented in two sets of three (vv. 8–12 and 13–17), plus Abishai (vv. 18, 19), Benaiah (vv. 20–23), and the thirty-one listed in vv. 24–39. However, the "three" of vv. 13–17 are apparently to be counted among "the thirty" (v. 13; v. 24 note) and not separately. Thus, this list would contain thirty-six mighty men, and Joab would make thirty-seven. A similar list is given in 1 Chr. 11:10–47 with more than fifteen additional names and no summary total.

23:8 eight hundred. 1 Chr. 11:11 has "300," probably a copyist's error.

23:10 The LORD brought about a great victory that day. This statement, repeated in v. 12, serves as a reminder that, whatever the heroic qualities of the human agent, it is God who ultimately brings victory (8:6, 14; 1 Sam. 14:15, 23; 19:5).

23:11 ground full of lentils. Destroying crops was a common tactic of war (Judg. 6:3–6, 11).

23:13 Valley of Rephaim. See note 5:18.

23:14 stronghold. See note 1 Sam. 23:14.

23:16 poured it out to the LORD. The brave exploit of the three men is a testimony to their devotion to David, while David's refusal to drink (v. 17) what had been procured at such great risk to his loyal followers is testimony to his love for them.

18 Now Abishai, the brother of Joab, the
son of Zeruiah, was chief of the thirty.[1] And
he wielded his spear against three hundred
men[2] and killed them and won a name beside the three. 19 He was the most renowned
of the thirty[3] and became their commander,
but he did not attain to [b]the three.
20 And [c]Benaiah the son of Jehoiada was a
valiant man[4] of [d]Kabzeel, a doer of great
deeds. He struck down two ariels[5] of Moab.
He also went down and struck down a lion
in a pit on a day when snow had fallen.
21 And he struck down an Egyptian, a handsome man. The Egyptian had a spear in his
hand, but Benaiah went down to him with a
staff and snatched the spear out of the
Egyptian's hand and killed him with his own
spear. 22 These things did Benaiah the son of
Jehoiada, and won a name beside the three
mighty men. 23 He was renowned among the
thirty, but he did not attain to the three. And
David set him over his bodyguard.
24 [e]Asahel the brother of Joab was one of
the thirty; Elhanan the son of Dodo of
Bethlehem, 25 [f]Shammah of Harod, Elika
of Harod, 26 Helez the Paltite, Ira the son of
Ikkesh [g]of Tekoa, 27 Abiezer [h]of Anathoth,
Mebunnai [i]the Hushathite, 28 Zalmon [j]the
Ahohite, Maharai [k]of Netophah, 29 Heleb
the son of Baanah [k]of Netophah, Ittai the
son of Ribai of [l]Gibeah of the people of
Benjamin, 30 Benaiah [m]of Pirathon, Hiddai
of the brooks of [n]Gaash, 31 Abi-albon the
Arbathite, Azmaveth of [o]Bahurim, 32 Eliahba
the Shaalbonite, the sons of Jashen,
Jonathan, 33 [p]Shammah the Hararite, Ahiam
the son of Sharar the Hararite, 34 Eliphelet
the son of Ahasbai [q]of Maacah, [r]Eliam the
son of [s]Ahithophel of Gilo, 35 Hezro[6] [t]of
Carmel, Paarai the Arbite, 36 Igal the son of
Nathan [u]of Zobah, Bani the Gadite, 37 Zelek
the Ammonite, Naharai [v]of Beeroth, the
armor-bearer of Joab the son of Zeruiah,
38 [w]Ira the [x]Ithrite, Gareb the Ithrite,
39 [y]Uriah the Hittite: thirty-seven in all.

David's Census

24 [z, a]Again the anger of the LORD was
kindled against Israel, and he incited David against them, saying, [b]"Go, number Israel and Judah." 2 So the king said to
Joab, the commander of the army,[7] who
was with him, "Go through all the tribes of
Israel, [c]from Dan to Beersheba, and number
the people, that I may know the number of
the people." 3 But Joab said to the king,
[d]"May the LORD your God add to the people a hundred times as many as they are,
while the eyes of my lord the king still see
it, but why does my lord the king delight in
this thing?" 4 But the king's word prevailed
against Joab and the commanders of the
army. So Joab and the commanders of the

19 [b]1 Chr. 11:21
20 [c]ch. 8:18; 20:23 [d]Josh. 15:21
24 [e]ch. 2:18; 1 Chr. 27:7
25 [f][1 Chr. 11:27; 27:8]
26 [g]See ch. 14:2
27 [h]Josh. 21:18 [i]ch. 21:18
28 [j]ver. 9 [k]2 Kin. 25:23
29 [k][See ver. 28 above] [l]Josh. 18:28; Judg. 19:14
30 [m]Judg. 12:13, 15; 1 Chr. 27:14 [n]Josh. 24:30; Judg. 2:9
31 [o][ch. 3:16]
33 [p]ver. 11
34 [q]ch. 10:6, 8 [r]ch. 11:3 [s]ch. 15:12
35 [t]Josh. 15:55
36 [u]ch. 8:3
37 [v]ch. 4:2
38 [w][ch. 20:26] [x]1 Chr. 2:53
39 [y]ch. 11:3, 6
Chapter 24
1 [z]For ver. 1-25, see 1 Chr. 21:1-28 [a][1 Chr. 21:1] [b][1 Chr. 27:23, 24]
2 [c]ver. 15; See ch. 3:10
3 [d]Deut. 1:11

1 Two Hebrew manuscripts, Syriac; most Hebrew manuscripts *three* 2 Or *slain ones* 3 1 Chronicles 11:25; Hebrew *Was he the most renowned of the three?* 4 Or *the son of Ishhai* 5 The meaning of the word *ariel* is unknown 6 Or *Hezrai* 7 Septuagint *to Joab and the commanders of the army*

23:18 Abishai. See note 2:18.

23:20 Benaiah. See note 8:18.

23:23 bodyguard. David's bodyguard presumably comprised Cherethites and Pelethites (1 Sam. 30:14 note).

23:24 Asahel. See note 2:18.

the thirty. "Thirty" may be a round number. Not surprisingly, more of David's men are from the tribe of Judah than from any other.

Elhanan. He is not necessarily the same Elhanan as in 21:19 (note).

23:29 Gibeah of the people of Benjamin. David received support even from Saul's hometown (1 Sam. 10:26; 11:4).

23:30 Benaiah. Not the same as Benaiah in vv. 20–23.

23:34 Eliam the son of Ahithophel. See note 11:3.

23:36 Zobah. See note 8:3.

23:37 Beeroth. See note 4:3.

23:39 Uriah the Hittite. By concluding the list of David's mighty men with Uriah, the victim of David's great sin in ch. 11, the chapter ends with a poignant reminder that David was, like all men, a sinner and in need of God's forgiveness (ch. 12). This theme is continued in the next chapter.

thirty-seven in all. See note on vv. 8–39.

24:1–25 This chapter is a fitting conclusion to the books of Samuel. David is shown for what he is, a sinner, but a sinner who is ready to repent and to cast himself upon God's mercy (12:13 and note). Another appropriate note is the association of the threshing floor of Araunah (vv. 18–25) with Mount Moriah, the future site of the temple (1 Chr. 22:1; 2 Chr. 3:1; Gen. 22:2).

24:1 Again. If a specific occasion is in view, a probable one is the famine of 21:1.

he incited David. The antecedent of "he" is the Lord (cf. 1 Sam. 26:19). According to 1 Chr. 21:1, however, it was Satan who moved David. At issue here is the mystery of the presence and practice of evil. The Scripture is clear that God is not the author of evil (James 1:13–15), but it also teaches that the wicked acts of men and of Satan do not fall outside God's sovereign determination (Ex. 4:21; 1 Sam. 2:25 and note; 1 Kin. 22:20–23; Job 1:12; Ezek. 14:9; Acts 4:27, 28). Satan is a creature, absolutely subordinate to the sovereignty of God. Satan's activities and desires cannot create a space that is free from God's control or that escapes God's purposes.

number Israel and Judah. Taking a census does not appear to have been wrong in itself (Num. 1:1, 2; 4:1, 2; 26:1–4), but see Ex. 30:11, 12. This act of census may have pointed to a lack of trust in David's heart, or even to a desire to gain control of God's providence by making an inventory of His apparent resources. That the report (v. 9) emphasizes military strength may suggest that David wanted to take more territory than what the Lord had granted him.

24:2 from Dan to Beersheba. A proverbial expression for all the land.

24:3 but why. The reason for Joab's reluctance is not stated. It could as easily have been political as religious, since the people might have taken a census as a sign that David planned to raise taxes or to draft more soldiers.

army went out from the presence of the
king to number the people of Israel. 5 They
crossed the Jordan and began from [e]Aroer,[1]
and from the city that is in the middle of
the [f]valley, toward Gad and on to [g]Jazer.
6 Then they came to Gilead, and to Kadesh
in the land of the Hittites;[2] and they came
to Dan, and from Dan[3] they went around to
[h]Sidon, 7 and came to the fortress of Tyre
and to all the cities of the [i]Hivites and
[i]Canaanites; and they went out to the
Negeb of Judah at Beersheba. 8 So when
they had gone through all the land, they
came to Jerusalem at the end of nine
months and twenty days. 9 And Joab gave
the sum of the numbering of the people to
the king: in Israel there were 800,000
valiant men [j]who drew the sword, and the
men of Judah were 500,000.

5 [e]Deut. 2:36; Josh. 13:9, 16 [f][Num. 13:23] [g]Num. 21:32; 32:1, 3
6 [h]Josh. 19:28; Judg. 18:28
7 [i]Josh. 11:3; Judg. 3:3
9 [j]Judg. 8:10
10 [k]1 Sam. 24:5 [l]ch. 12:13

The LORD's Judgment of David's Sin

10 But [k]David's heart struck him after he
had numbered the people. And David said
to the LORD, [l]"I have sinned greatly in what
I have done. But now, O LORD, please take

[1] Septuagint; Hebrew *encamped in Aroer* [2] Septuagint; Hebrew *to the land of Tahtim-hodshi* [3] Septuagint; Hebrew *they came to Dan-jaan and*

24:5–7 These verses indicate that the census was begun in the south, east of the Jordan River, and continued in a counterclockwise direction through the the land, finally arriving in Beersheba.

24:8 nine months and twenty days. Most of this time was needed for taking the census; the travel itself could have been accomplished in a matter of weeks.

24:9 in Israel there were 800,000 . . . Judah were 500,000. 1 Chr. 21:5 has "1,100,000" and "470,000," respectively. On this difference, see notes 1 Chr. 21:5.

24:10 take away the iniquity. David's plea for forgiveness may have been granted by God before the arrival of Gad (vv. 11–13). Nevertheless, as in the case of David's sin against Uriah and Bathsheba, for-

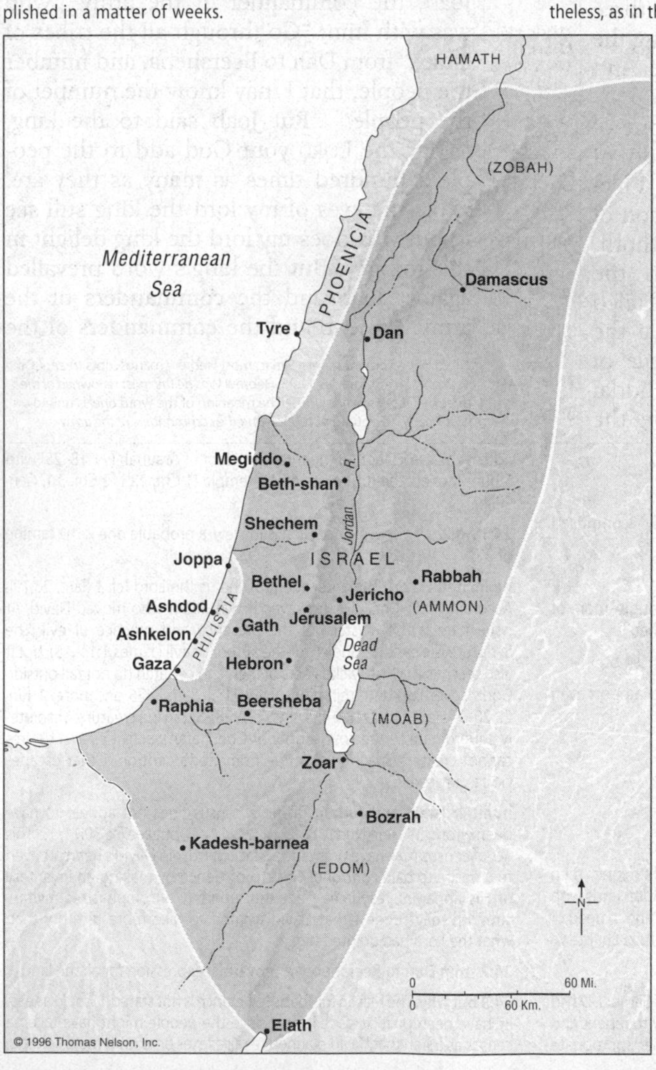

The Davidic Kingdom. The military successes of David led to the unprecedented expansion of the borders of his kingdom. His victories against the Moabites and Edomites to the east and south of Jerusalem greatly expanded and solidified his control of those areas. Repelling frequent attacks from the west, he succeeded in isolating Philistine control to a few coastal cities. Victory against Zobag and the Arameans in the northeast greatly extended his borders in that direction, and the subsequent victory against the Ammonites cemented his control over the central regions. Joab's census, taken prior to David's death, confirms the vast extent of David's kingdom.

away the iniquity of your servant, for I have
done [m]very foolishly." 11 And when David
arose in the morning, the word of the LORD
came to [n]the prophet Gad, David's [o]seer,
saying, 12 "Go and say to David, 'Thus says
the LORD, Three things I offer[1] you. Choose
one of them, that I may do it to you.'" 13 So
Gad came to David and told him, and said
to him, "Shall [p]three[2] years of famine come
to you in your land? Or will you flee three
months before your foes while they pursue
you? Or shall there be three days' pestilence in your land? Now consider, and
decide what answer I shall return to him
who sent me." 14 Then David said to Gad,
"I am in great distress. Let us fall into the
hand of the LORD, [q]for his mercy is great;
but let me not fall into the hand of man."
15 [r]So the LORD sent a pestilence on Israel
from the morning until the appointed time.
And there died of the people from [s]Dan to
Beersheba 70,000 men. 16 And when [t]the
angel stretched out his hand toward
Jerusalem [u]to destroy it, [v]the LORD relented
from the calamity and said to the angel
[u]who was working destruction among the
people, "It is enough; now stay your hand."
And [t]the angel of the LORD was by the
threshing floor of [w]Araunah the Jebusite.
17 Then David spoke to the LORD when he
saw the angel who was striking the people,
and said, "Behold, I have sinned, and I have
done wickedly. But these sheep, what have
they done? Please let your hand be against
me and against my father's house."

10 [m]See 1 Sam. 13:13
11 [n]See 1 Sam. 22:5 [o]See 1 Sam. 9:9
13 [p][1 Chr. 21:12]
14 [q]Ps. 119:156
15 [r]1 Chr. 27:24 [s]ver. 2
16 [t]2 Kin. 19:35; 2 Chr. 32:21; Isai. 37:36; Acts 12:23 [u]Ex. 12:13, 23 [v]Gen. 6:6; 1 Sam. 15:11; Joel 2:13, 14; Jonah 3:10 [w][2 Chr. 3:1]
18 [x][2 Chr. 3:1]
21 [y]Num. 16:48, 50
22 [z]1 Kin. 19:21
23 [a]Deut. 33:11; [Ps. 20:3]
25 [b]ch. 21:14

David Builds an Altar

18 And Gad came that day to David and
said to him, "Go up, raise an altar to the
LORD on the threshing floor of [x]Araunah
the Jebusite." 19 So David went up at Gad's
word, as the LORD commanded. 20 And
when Araunah looked down, he saw the
king and his servants coming on toward
him. And Araunah went out and paid homage to the king with his face to the ground.
21 And Araunah said, "Why has my lord the
king come to his servant?" David said, "To
buy the threshing floor from you, in order
to build an altar to the LORD, that the
plague [y]may be averted from the people."
22 Then Araunah said to David, "Let my
lord the king take and offer up what seems
good to him. Here are the oxen for the
burnt offering and the [z]threshing sledges
and the yokes of the oxen for the wood.
23 All this, O king, Araunah gives to the
king." And Araunah said to the king, "The
LORD your God [a]accept you." 24 But the
king said to Araunah, "No, but I will buy it
from you for a price. I will not offer burnt
offerings to the LORD my God that cost me
nothing." So David bought the threshing
floor and the oxen for fifty shekels[3] of silver. 25 And David built there an altar to the
LORD and offered burnt offerings and peace
offerings. [b]So the LORD responded to the
plea for the land, and the plague was averted from Israel.

1 Or *hold over* 2 Compare 1 Chronicles 21:12, Septuagint; Hebrew *seven* 3 A *shekel* was about 2/5 ounce or 11 grams

giveness does not mean that sin will have no further consequences (v. 13; 12:13, 14).

24:12 Go and say to David. The Lord sends Gad to confront David, as He had earlier sent the prophet Nathan (12:1 and note).

24:13 famine . . . foes . . . pestilence. Implicit in the threat of pursuit by "foes" is loss of life by the sword, as 1 Chr. 21:12 makes explicit. Famine, sword, and plague are the Old Testament's triad of woes regularly threatened for obdurate covenant-breaking (Lev. 26:23–26; Deut. 28:21–26; 32:24, 25; 1 Kin. 8:37; 2 Chr. 20:9; Is. 51:19; Jer. 14:12; Ezek. 6:11, 12).

24:14 Let us fall into the hand of the LORD. Technically, this would allow either the first or third option, that is, famine or plague. The inference is sometimes made that David's choice is selfish, but all three options, including flight before enemies, would have cost lives (v. 13 note). David's motivation is entirely different, for he had learned that the Lord's mercy is great (v. 16; cf. Ex. 34:6, 7; Neh. 9:17; Ps. 30:5; 86:14–16; 103:8–10; Is. 54:7, 8; 60:10; Hos. 11:8, 9; Joel 2:13).

24:15 Dan to Beersheba. See v. 2.

24:16 angel of the LORD. See note Gen. 16:7. On the Lord's angels as agents of judgment, see Ex. 33:2; Ps. 35:5, 6; 78:49; Matt. 13:41; Acts 12:23.

threshing floor of Araunah. See note 24:1–25.

24:17 let your hand be against me. The heart of David, like the heart of God (v. 16), is grieved by the suffering he sees among his people, his "sheep." As their shepherd-king, he is moved to compassion and, not knowing that God in His mercy has already stayed His hand (vv. 16, 21), asks that the hand of judgment fall upon him alone. David deserved punishment for his sin, and the people were innocent. David's offer as a guilty person to suffer in the place of innocent "sheep" is not a very close analogy of Christ's death for the sake of His sheep (John 10:11), although the language is similar. Christ was innocent and died for the guilty.

24:22 burnt offering. See note 1 Sam. 10:8.

24:24 I will not offer burnt offerings to the LORD my God that cost me nothing. While God's grace and forgiveness are free, David understands that proper worship of God is never to be cheap or careless (cf. Mal. 1:6–14; 2 Cor. 8:1–5). The consistent testimony of Scripture is that God deserves our best, the "firstfruits" (Num. 18:12; Deut. 18:3–5; 26:10; Neh. 12:44; Prov. 3:9).

fifty shekels of silver. 1 Chr. 21:25 records a much larger sum of six hundred shekels of gold, possibly referring to a larger transaction of which the fifty shekels was a part.

24:25 burnt offerings and peace offerings. See note 1 Sam. 10:8.

the LORD responded to the plea for the land. An almost identical statement is made in 21:14.

THE FIRST BOOK OF THE

Kings

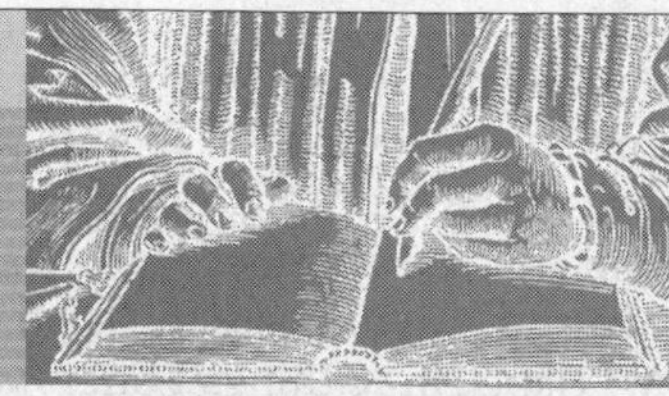

AUTHOR

Jewish tradition held that Jeremiah wrote 1 and 2 Kings and Lamentations as well as the prophecy under his name. The points of view of Joshua, Judges, 1 and 2 Samuel, and 1 and 2 Kings, are very similar, and because they develop the theological ideas expressed in Deuteronomy, they are often called "the Deuteronomic History" by modern authors. But the author of 1 and 2 Kings is not identified in the books themselves, and his identity cannot be known with certainty.

DATE AND OCCASION

Indications are that the books were compiled from historical sources during the time the Jews were exiles in Babylon. Second Kings ends while the last king of Judah, Jehoiachin, is detained in Babylon (2 Kin. 25:27–30). Since there is no mention of the return of the people from exile in 538 B.C., it is probable that the final edition of the work was completed at the midpoint of the Babylonian exile (560–550 B.C.).

Earlier materials are no doubt also present. First, the author clearly had access to a variety of sources, both administrative and prophetic. The names of his sources: "the Book of the Acts of Solomon" (1 Kin. 11:41), "the Chronicles of the Kings of Israel" (1 Kin. 14:19), and "the Chronicles of the Kings of Judah" (1 Kin. 14:29). Probably the author also had access to material recounting the lives and ministries of the prophets. Second, there are a number of statements in 1 and 2 Kings that describe conditions that prevailed before the time of the captivity, and yet say of them that they continue "to this day" (1 Kin. 8:8; 9:21; 12:19; 2 Kin. 8:22). Such statements point to the existence of pre-exilic material that was subsequently included in Kings. Third, the final chapter of 2 Kings is distinguished by a detailed chronology by day, month, and year of events surrounding the final siege of Jerusalem and the destruction of the temple.

Second Kings has a somewhat unusual ending. The book seems to reach its climax with the reign of Josiah (2 Kin. 23:25), but this optimism is clouded by a prophecy of impending judgment (2 Kin. 23:26, 27). Moreover, the narrative stops abruptly with Judah in Babylon, with no theological summary or conclusion. For these reasons, some scholars believe that the main work of writing Kings was done before the time of the Exile. In this theory, the original book of Kings was composed during the reign of King Josiah, and someone living during the Exile updated this history with a brief record of Judah's final years. But whether one holds to this two-edition hypothesis or to a one-edition (exilic) hypothesis, the book has a unified perspective.

CHARACTERISTICS AND THEMES

Kings as History. Characteristic of the author is a fondness for recording in detail many features of his nation's past. This genuine interest in the dates, figures, and institutions of the kingdom of Israel appears in his record of preparations for the temple (1 Kin. 5), its dimensions and decoration (1 Kin. 6), and its furniture and vessels (1 Kin. 7:13–51). The writer gives the length of reigns for monarchs in both kingdoms, and he synchronizes their reigns with each other.

The author organizes and presents Israel's experience with kingship in periods in order to provide a clear and meaningful account of his nation's past. Beginning with an evaluation of the united monarchy under Solomon (1 Kin. 1–11), the author carefully depicts its dissolution (1 Kin. 12:1–24) and the formation of two separate entities, Israel in the north and Judah in the south. He goes on to present the separate history of each realm, until the fall of the northern kingdom in 722 B.C. (2 Kin. 17). The alternation between the northern kingdom (usually called Israel) and the southern kingdom (usually called Judah) can be confusing, but it is central to the author's purpose of presenting a unified history of all the Israelite tribes.

In portraying the divided kingdom, the writer points out important differences between the two realms. Kingship in Judah was relatively stable, under the descendants of David, but kingship in Israel was unstable, and there was a succession of dynasties. Twenty kings from nine different families ruled over Israel in the northern kingdom during its existence of about two hundred years. In contrast, twenty kings from one family ruled over the southern kingdom for about three hundred fifty years. The writer concludes his coverage of the northern kingdom with a lengthy commentary on its major shortcomings (2 Kin. 17:7–34).

To consider Kings as no more than history of the monarchy would strip the book of its theological value, since the author is not a dispassionate observer, merely chronicling his nation's past. Nevertheless, the historical value of his work should not be underestimated. In composing a coherent and meaningful account of his nation's past, the biblical writer has provided an invaluable service to anyone who wants to understand this momentous era in Israelite history.

Kings as Theology. Kings is not only a history, but also a work of theology, a reflection on God's ways with His people Israel, whom He had delivered from the "iron furnace" of Egypt to be His own "heritage" (1 Kin. 8:51–53). In composing a work of theological history, the writer takes lessons from the past to serve his people in the present and future. There are a number of central themes that inform his overall point of view and his evaluation of the monarchy.

1. The People as God's Elect. Israel was not in itself better than any of the other nations. Israel did not first choose God; rather, God "separated them from among all the peoples of the earth" according to His unfathomable grace (1 Kin. 8:53). Holiness results not from any intrinsic merit, but from God's election (Deut. 7:6; 26:18, 19).

Kings emphasizes the solidarity of Israel. The writer is concerned for all the tribes of Israel. Although he severely criticizes the northern kingdom and its monarchs because of their cultic apostasy, the writer still considers these tribes to be part of Israel, and he shows sustained interest in them. Even after the northern tribes are exiled by the Assyrians, the author does not forget them. He both documents and commends Josiah's reforms in Samaria (2 Kin. 23:15–20).

2. "My Servants the Prophets." Prophets play a major role during the Israelite monarchy. In writing about the prophets, the author is interested in their ministry as bearers of God's Word. The prophets passionately insist on undivided allegiance to the Lord, opposing any alliance or political posture that might jeopardize the distinctiveness of Israelite religion. Not surprisingly, this strict adherence to the covenant often pits the prophets against kings and queens who were willing to compromise in politics and religion with Israel's neighbors. Although the writer gives most of his attention to Elijah and Elisha, he mentions many other prophets: Nathan (1 Kin. 1:22), Ahijah (1 Kin. 11:29–39; 14:1–18), Shemaiah (1 Kin. 12:21–24), Micaiah (1 Kin. 22:8–28), Jonah (2 Kin. 14:25), Isaiah (2 Kin. 19:1–7, 20:14), and Huldah (2 Kin. 22:14–20).

3. One God, One Sanctuary. Yahweh is Lord of the cosmos and ruler over the kingdoms of the earth (2 Kin. 19:15). God leads His people into battle, answers their prayers, honors their sacrifices, and displays a special concern for the poor and oppressed. Undivided devotion to God is a hallmark of the covenant (1 Kin. 18:21, 39).

Related to the existence of the one supreme God is the author's contention that there can be only one central sanctuary (Deut. 12). The construction of the temple by Solomon is a major event in Israelite history. Accordingly, great attention is given in 1 Kings to the preparations for and construction of this edifice, including detailed descriptions of its dimensions and furnishings.

Consistent with this emphasis on one God and one temple is the prohibition of worshiping other gods or worshiping at other cult sites. As the books of Kings depict the deterioration in devotion toward God during the course of the divided kingdom, the problem is not so much a wholesale abandonment of Yahweh for other gods, but combining worship of Yahweh with worship of foreign gods. The influence of Canaanite worship was especially strong in northern Israel which, with the sponsorship of its monarchs, used Canaanite rituals, beliefs, and cult objects. This type of religious syncretism also affected Judah. The writer cites the worship of other gods as a major reason for the defeat and exile of both Israel and Judah (2 Kin. 17:7, 16, 19; 21:3–5).

4. Covenant and Kingship. Both the Mosaic and the Davidic covenants figure prominently in Kings. The writer evaluates the conduct of king and people alike on the basis of the covenant established at Mount Sinai.

Viewing the relationship between God and Israel as a covenant means that every human institution is subject to the authority of God. Thus, although the monarchy is God-ordained, its power is by no means absolute. King and people alike are responsible for remaining faithful to their covenant with God. Each king is evaluated according to whether he kept the Torah (or Law).

The author gives particular attention to loyalty toward God as manifested by justice and unwavering support of the temple in Jerusalem. Of the eight southern kings who receive positive estimations, only Hezekiah and Josiah are singled out for their devotion to Yahweh (2 Kin. 18:5; 23:25). Hezekiah is esteemed for removing the high places in Judah and for his unwavering trust in God during Sennacherib's invasion (2 Kin. 18:3–7). The author bestows high honor on Josiah for refurbishing the temple and carrying out sweeping reforms in both Judah and Samaria (2 Kin. 22:2; 23:25). Because Jehu purged Israel of Baal worship, he is the only one of the northern kings to receive a commendation (2 Kin. 10:30).

Chronology. The Book of Kings is filled with chronological data. The author dates the building of the temple 480 years after the Exodus (1 Kin. 6:1). He provides figures for the length of David's and Solomon's reigns, and he gives explicit information on the reigns of all of Judah's and Israel's kings. During the period of the divided kingdom, the author synchronizes the start of each king's reign with the regnal year of the king in the other kingdom. The author also lists the king's age upon accession and the name of his mother for the Judean kings.

Coordinating this data with Assyrian, Babylonian, and other extrabiblical records is a challenging task, since knowing how long a given king reigned does not establish precisely when he reigned. The dates of the fall of Israel and the fall of Judah are known with some certainty, and other major dates can be calculated from them. One scheme is as follows:

970 B.C.	End of David's Reign
970–930 B.C.	Solomon's Reign
930 B.C.	Division of the Kingdom
722 B.C.	Fall of Israel
586 B.C.	Fall of Judah

TITLE

The books of Kings concern the history and demise of the monarchy in Israel from the last days of David (970 B.C.) to the exile in Babylon almost four centuries later (586 B.C.). The two books comprise one unit within a larger group of books—Joshua, Judges, 1 and 2 Samuel, and 1 and 2 Kings—traditionally called the "former prophets" and more recently known as the Deuteronomistic (or Deuteronomic) History. These books are a continuous narrative, and it is helpful to recognize their essential unity.

The two books of Kings were originally one book. In the Septuagint (the Greek translation of the Old Testament), the Vulgate (the Latin translation), and most other versions, the work is divided in two. This division was for convenience of copying or publication and was not based on content. The reigns of Ahaziah (1 Kin. 22:51–53; 2 Kin. 1) and Jehoshaphat (1 Kin. 22:41–50; 2 Kin. 3) overlap both books. In the same way the prophetic ministry of Elijah appears in both volumes (1 Kin. 17–19 and 2 Kin. 1; 2).

OUTLINE OF 1 KINGS

I. The Reign of Solomon (chs. 1–11)

A. Solomon Established as David's Rightful Successor (chs. 1–4)

1. Solomon's Succession to the Throne (1:1–2:11)
2. Solomon's Consolidation of Power (2:12–46)
3. The Gift of Wisdom (3:1–15)
4. Solomon's Wisdom Exemplified (3:16–4:34)

B. Major Accomplishments of Solomon's Reign (chs. 5–10)

1. Preparations for Building the Temple (ch. 5)
2. Construction of the Temple (ch. 6)
3. Construction of a Royal Palace (7:1–12)
4. Furnishing the Temple (7:13–51)
5. Solomon's Temple Prayer and Dedication (ch. 8)
6. God's Twofold Response (9:1–9)
7. Solomon in All of His Glory (9:10–10:29)

C. Solomon's Spiritual and Political Decline (ch. 11)

1. Solomon's Sins (11:1–13)

OUTLINE OF 1 KINGS (Cont.)

2. Punishments Against Solomon (11:14–25)
3. Jeroboam's Rise: Punishment and New Hope (11:26–43)

II. The Early Divided Kingdom (chs. 12–16)

A. The Secession of the Northern Tribes (12:1–24)

B. Jeroboam I of Israel (12:25–14:20)

1. Jeroboam's Gold Calves (12:25–33)
2. Two Prophets (ch. 13)
3. Judgment Against Jeroboam Decreed (14:1–20)

C. Rehoboam of Judah (14:21–31)

D. Abijam of Judah (15:1–8)

E. Asa of Judah (15:9–24)

F. Nadab of Israel (15:25–32)

G. Baasha of Israel (15:33–16:7)

H. Elah of Israel (16:8–14)

I. Zimri of Israel (16:15–20)

J. Omri of Israel (16:21–28)

K. Ahab of Israel (16:29–34)

III. Prophets and Kings (1 Kin. 17:1–2 Kin. 8:15)

A. The Prophets and Ahab (17:1–22:40)

1. Elijah the Tishbite (ch. 17)
2. Elijah Against the Canaanite Prophets (ch. 18)
3. The Revelation to Elijah on Mount Horeb (ch. 19)
4. Ahab's Misconduct in Holy War (ch. 20)
5. Ahab and Jezebel Seize Naboth's Vineyard (ch. 21)
6. Micaiah's Judgment Against Ahab (22:1–40)

B. Jehoshaphat of Judah (22:41–50)

C. Ahaziah of Israel Defies Elijah (22:51–2 Kin. 1:18)

David in His Old Age

1 Now King David was old and advanced
in years. And although they covered
him with clothes, he could not get warm.
2 Therefore his servants said to him, "Let a
young woman be sought for my lord the
king, and let her wait on the king and be in
his service. Let her lie in your arms,[1] that my
lord the king may be warm." 3 So they
sought for a beautiful young woman
throughout all the territory of Israel, and
found Abishag the [a]Shunammite, and
brought her to the king. 4 The young
woman was very beautiful, and she was of
service to the king and attended to him,
but the king knew her not.

Adonijah Sets Himself Up As King

5 Now [b]Adonijah the son of Haggith
exalted himself, saying, "I will be king."
[c]And he prepared for himself chariots and
horsemen, and fifty men to run before him.
6 His father had never at any time displeased him by asking, "Why have you
done thus and so?" He was also a very
handsome man, [d]and he was born next
after Absalom. 7 He conferred with [e]Joab
the son of Zeruiah and with [f]Abiathar the
priest. And they followed Adonijah and
helped him. 8 But [f]Zadok the priest and
[g]Benaiah the son of Jehoiada and [h]Nathan
the prophet and [i]Shimei and Rei and

Chapter 1
3 [a]Josh. 19:18
5 [b]2 Sam. 3:4 [c]2 Sam. 15:1
6 [d]2 Sam. 3:3, 4; 1 Chr. 3:2
7 [e]2 Sam. 2:13, 18 [f]2 Sam. 20:25
8 [f][See ver. 7 above] [g]2 Sam. 8:18 [h]2 Sam. 12:1 [i]ch. 4:18

[1] Or *in your bosom*

1:1–2:11 Solomon succeeds David as king in spite of political turmoil and intrigue by Adonijah, Abiathar, Joab, and Shimei.

1:1 old and advanced in years. As 1 Kings begins, David is about seventy years old (2 Sam. 5:4; 1 Kin. 2:11).

1:3 Abishag the Shunammite. Shunem was sixteen miles southwest of the Sea of Chinneroth (Galilee), near Mount Gilboa (Josh. 19:18; 1 Sam. 28:4; 2 Kin. 4:8).

1:4 the king knew her not. Since David did not have sexual relations with Abishag, Adonijah's later request to marry her (2:17) was not against the law of Deut. 22:30.

1:5 Adonijah. Probably the oldest living son of David (2 Sam. 3:2–5; 13:28; 18:14). As such, he may have thought he would succeed his father. At this time, however, there was no custom or law dictating who would be David's successor, other than his own decision (vv. 13, 17, 20, 30).

chariots and horsemen. Like Absalom before him (2 Sam. 15:1), Adonijah signals his ambitions and positions himself to take the throne.

1:6 had never at any time displeased him. As in dealing with his other rebellious sons, David made no attempt either to question or discipline Adonijah. But his patience and forgiveness only seemed to invite further rebellion (2 Sam. 13:32, 39; 14:33; 18:5).

very handsome. Handsome features were an asset for someone aspiring to the throne (1 Sam. 9:2; 16:12; 2 Sam. 14:25, 26).

1:7 Joab the son of Zeruiah. Joab was the commander of the army of Israel and one of David's longstanding supporters (2 Sam. 2:13; 8:16; 18:2; 20:10, 23). His relationship with David was strained by his harsh actions in putting down rebellions (2 Sam. 18:5; 19:5–8, 13; 1 Kin. 2:5, 6).

Abiathar the priest. He and Zadok were the two high priests appointed by David (1 Sam. 22:20–22; 2 Sam. 8:17 note).

1:8 Benaiah the son of Jehoiada. Benaiah was the commander of the Cherethites and Pelethites, mercenary forces who functioned in large measure as David's royal guard (2 Sam. 8:18; 20:7; 23:20; 1 Chr. 18:17).

Nathan the prophet. The most prominent prophet during David's reign (2 Sam. 7:1–17; 12:1–15).

Shimei. A different man than the one referred to in 2 Sam. 16:5–8; 1 Kin. 2:8, 36–46. Perhaps this person is the "Shimei the son of Ela" who was one of Solomon's governors (4:18).

[j]David's mighty men were not with Adonijah.

9 Adonijah sacrificed sheep, oxen, and fattened cattle by the Serpent's Stone, which is beside [k]En-rogel, and he invited all his brothers, the king's sons, and all the royal officials of Judah, 10 but he did not invite Nathan the prophet or Benaiah or the mighty men or [l]Solomon his brother.

Nathan and Bathsheba Before David

11 Then Nathan said to Bathsheba the mother of Solomon, "Have you not heard that [b]Adonijah the son of Haggith has become king and David our lord does not know it? 12 Now therefore come, let me give you advice, that you may save your own life and the life of your son Solomon. 13 Go in at once to King David, and say to him, 'Did you not, my lord the king, swear to your servant, saying, [m]"Solomon your son shall reign after me, and he shall sit on my throne"? Why then is Adonijah king?' 14 Then while you are still speaking with the king, I also will come in after you and confirm your words."

15 So Bathsheba went to the king in his chamber (now the king was very old, and Abishag the Shunammite was attending to the king). 16 Bathsheba bowed and paid homage to the king, and the king said, "What do you desire?" 17 She said to him, "My lord, you swore to your servant by the LORD your God, saying, [m]'Solomon your son shall reign after me, and he shall sit on my throne.' 18 And now, behold, Adonijah is king, although you, my lord the king, do not know it. 19 [n]He has sacrificed oxen, fattened cattle, and sheep in abundance, and has invited all the sons of the king, [f]Abiathar the priest, and Joab the commander of the army, but [l]Solomon your servant he has not invited. 20 And now, my lord the king, the eyes of all Israel are on you, to tell them who shall sit on the throne of my lord the king after him. 21 Otherwise it will come to pass, when my lord the king [o]sleeps with his fathers, that I and my son Solomon will be counted offenders."

22 While she was still speaking with the king, Nathan the prophet came in. 23 And they told the king, "Here is Nathan the prophet." And when he came in before the king, he bowed before the king, with his face to the ground. 24 And Nathan said, "My lord the king, have you said, 'Adonijah shall reign after me, and he shall sit on my throne'? 25 For he has gone down this day and [n]has sacrificed oxen, fattened cattle, and sheep in abundance, and has invited all the king's sons, the commanders[1] of the army, and Abiathar the priest. And behold, they are eating and drinking before him, and saying, [p]'Long live King Adonijah!' 26 [q]But me, your servant, and Zadok the priest, and Benaiah the son of Jehoiada, and your servant Solomon he has not invited. 27 Has this thing been brought about by my lord the king and you have not told your servants who should sit on the throne of my lord the king after him?"

Solomon Anointed King

28 Then King David answered, "Call Bathsheba to me." So she came into the king's presence and stood before the king. 29 And the king swore, saying, [r]"As the LORD lives, who has redeemed my soul out of every adversity, 30 [s]as I swore to you by the LORD, the God of Israel, saying, 'Solomon

8 [j]See 2 Sam. 23:8-39
9 [k]Josh. 15:7; 2 Sam. 17:17
10 [l]2 Sam. 12:24
11 [b][See ver. 5 above]
13 [m]ver. 30; [1 Chr. 22:9]
17 [m][See ver. 13 above]
19 [n]ver. 9
[f][See ver. 7 above]
[l][See ver. 10 above]
21 [o]ch. 2:10; 2 Sam. 7:12; [Deut. 31:16]
25 [n][See ver. 19 above]
[p]See 1 Sam. 10:24
26 [q]ver. 8, 10, 32
29 [r]See Ruth 3:13
30 [s]ver. 13, 17

1 Hebrew; Septuagint *Joab the commander*

mighty men. See 2 Sam. 23:8–39.

1:9 sacrificed. Again, Adonijah follows the example of Absalom (2 Sam. 15:7–12; 1:5 note).

En-rogel. This spring was located south of the city. Because of their importance to the city, springs were considered to be an appropriate place for such activity (v. 33; cf. 2 Sam. 17:17).

1:11 Bathsheba the mother of Solomon. Queen mothers could play an influential role in the affairs of state (2:19; 15:13; 2 Kin. 10:13). As Solomon's mother, Bathsheba had a major interest in seeing that Adonijah was thwarted in his plans to become king.

1:12 save your own life and the life of your son. Since contenders for the throne in the ancient Near East sometimes sought to consolidate their own positions by eliminating all potential rivals, Nathan's advice conveys a sense of urgency (cf. 15:29; 2 Kin. 10:11; 11:1).

1:13 Why then is Adonijah king. Nathan's advice plays on the ambiguity and instability inherent during a coup attempt. Actually David is still king, but Nathan's words underscore the fact that Adonijah has also publicly claimed this status (vv. 5, 9). By having both Bathsheba and himself speak with David, Nathan underscores the gravity of the situation to the "very old" king (v. 15).

1:17 you swore. In ancient Israel an oath taken in the Lord's name constituted a sacred obligation and, as such, was considered inviolable (Ex. 20:7; Lev. 19:12; Josh. 9:15, 18, 20; Judg. 11:30, 35; Eccl. 5:4–7).

1:20 tell them who shall sit on the throne. Only a public declaration that Solomon will succeed David as king will suffice to turn back Adonijah's revolt.

1:24–27 have you said. Nathan incisively attacks the issue. Either David has privately affirmed Adonijah as heir apparent (and hence Nathan, Zadok, and Benaiah have been shunned), or David has not done so (and hence Adonijah has rebelled against his own father).

1:30 Solomon your son shall reign after me. Solomon will be the "offspring" through whom God will fulfill His promise of establishing "the throne of his kingdom forever" (2 Sam. 7:12, 13).

your son shall reign after me, and he shall
sit on my throne in my place,' even so will
I do this day." 31 Then Bathsheba bowed
with her face to the ground and paid homage to the king and said, [t]"May my lord
King David live forever!"
32 King David said, "Call to me Zadok the
priest, Nathan the prophet, and Benaiah
the son of Jehoiada." So they came before
the king. 33 And the king said to them,
"Take with you [u]the servants of your lord
and have Solomon my son ride on my own
mule, and bring him down to [v]Gihon.
34 And let Zadok the priest and Nathan the
prophet there [w]anoint him king over Israel.
[x]Then blow the trumpet and say, [y]'Long
live King Solomon!' 35 You shall then come
up after him, and he shall come and sit on
my throne, for he shall be king in my place.
And I have appointed him to be ruler over
Israel and over Judah." 36 And Benaiah the
son of Jehoiada answered the king, "Amen!
May the LORD, the God of my lord the king,
say so. 37 [z]As the LORD has been with my
lord the king, even so may he be with
Solomon, [a]and make his throne greater
than the throne of my lord King David."
38 So Zadok the priest, Nathan the
prophet, and Benaiah the son of Jehoiada,
[b]and the Cherethites and the Pelethites
went down and had Solomon ride on King
David's mule and brought him to Gihon.
39 There Zadok the priest took the horn of
[c]oil from the tent and [d]anointed Solomon.
[x]Then they blew the trumpet, and all the
people said, [y]"Long live King Solomon!"
40 And all the people went up after him,
playing on pipes, and rejoicing with great
joy, so that the earth was split by their
noise.
41 Adonijah and all the guests who were
with him heard it as they finished feasting.
And when Joab heard the sound of the
trumpet, he said, "What does this uproar in
the city mean?" 42 While he was still speaking, behold, [e]Jonathan the son of Abiathar
the priest came. And Adonijah said, "Come
in, [f]for you are a worthy man and bring
good news." 43 Jonathan answered Adonijah, "No, for our lord King David has made
Solomon king, 44 and the king has sent with
him Zadok the priest, Nathan the prophet,
and Benaiah the son of Jehoiada, and the
[b]Cherethites and the Pelethites. And they
had him ride on the king's mule. 45 And
Zadok the priest and Nathan the prophet
have anointed him king at [v]Gihon, and they
have gone up from there rejoicing, so that
the city is in an uproar. This is the noise
that you have heard. 46 [g]Solomon sits on the
royal throne. 47 Moreover, the king's servants came to congratulate our lord King
David, saying, [h]'May your God make the
name of Solomon more famous than yours,
and make his throne greater than your
throne.' And the king [i]bowed himself on
the bed. 48 And the king also said, 'Blessed
be the LORD, the God of Israel, [j]who has
granted someone[1] to sit on my throne this
day, my own eyes seeing it.'"
49 Then all the guests of Adonijah trembled and rose, and each went his own way.
50 And Adonijah feared Solomon. So he
arose and went [k]and took hold of [l]the
horns of the altar. 51 Then it was told

31 [t]Neh. 2:3; Dan. 2:4; 3:9; 5:10; 6:6, 21
33 [u]2 Sam. 11:11; 20:6 [v]2 Chr. 32:30; 33:14
34 [w]See 1 Sam. 10:1 [x]2 Sam. 15:10; 2 Kin. 9:13; 11:14 [y][ver. 25]; See 1 Sam. 10:24
37 [z]See 1 Sam. 20:13 [a]ver. 47
38 [b]See 2 Sam. 8:18
39 [c][Ps. 89:20]; See Ex. 30:23-32 [d]1 Chr. 29:22 [x][See ver. 34 above] [y][See ver. 34 above]
42 [e]2 Sam. 15:27, 36; 17:17 [f]2 Sam. 18:27
44 [b][See ver. 38 above]
45 [v][See ver. 33 above]
46 [g]1 Chr. 29:23
47 [h]ver. 37 [i][Gen. 47:31]
48 [j]ch. 3:6; [Ps. 132:11, 12]
50 [k]ch. 2:28 [l]Ex. 27:2

1 Septuagint *one of my offspring*

1:33 Solomon . . . on my own mule. Mules and donkeys were used as mounts of royalty (Judg. 10:4; 2 Sam. 13:29; 18:9; Zech. 9:9). David is therefore making a public declaration that Solomon is the heir.

Gihon. The Gihon spring, located about one-half mile north of En-rogel (v. 9), was a major supply of water for Jerusalem (2 Chr. 32:30; 33:14). Due to topography, En-rogel is not visible from Gihon; however, the two are within earshot (v. 41).

1:34 anoint him king over Israel. Priests (Ex. 28:41; 29:4–9; Lev. 4:3, 5, 16), kings (1 Sam. 2:10; 9:16; 10:1), and occasionally prophets (1 Kin. 19:16), were anointed in ancient Israel. The Hebrew for "anointed" became a technical term for the Lord's anointed, usually with royal connotations. The title is usually transliterated "messiah." The Greek word for "anointed" is *Christos* (English "Christ," Matt. 1:17). Although Solomon received God's promises to David, those promises were fully realized only with the coming of Jesus Christ.

blow the trumpet and say, 'Long live King Solomon!' A public celebration of Solomon's new status as crown prince (cf. 1 Sam. 10:24; 2 Sam. 15:10; 16:16; 2 Kin. 9:13; 11:12).

1:35 Israel and . . . Judah. Although made up of twelve tribes, the nation was composed of two major units, Israel in the north and Judah in the south. When David became king, he had to command assent from both Judah (2 Sam. 2:4) and Israel (2 Sam. 5:3). As heir to the Davidic dynasty, Solomon became king of both areas at once.

1:38 Cherethites and the Pelethites. See note on v. 8.

1:39 Zadok the priest. In ancient Israel both priests and prophets could officiate at the anointing of a king (1 Sam. 9:16; 16:12; 2 Kin. 9:1–3; 11:12).

tent. A reference to the tent David pitched (2 Sam. 6:17) to house the ark of the covenant (Ex. 37:1–9), not the same as the tabernacle of Moses (Ex. 35:4–29; 36:8–38; 1 Kin. 3:4; 1 Chr. 16:39; 21:29).

1:41 Adonijah . . . heard it. See note on v. 33.

1:47 the king bowed himself. David praises God (v. 48), because his prayer for succession has been granted (cf. Gen. 47:31).

1:50 horns of the altar. These were projections resembling horns at the four corners on the top of the altar (Ex. 27:2; 29:12; Lev. 4:7; Ps. 118:27). The place of sacrifice was sacred, and Adonijah was seeking sanctuary there before God in the hope that he would not be killed (Ex. 21:12–14; 1 Kin. 2:28–34).

Solomon, "Behold, Adonijah fears King
Solomon, for behold, he has laid hold of
the horns of the altar, saying, 'Let King
Solomon swear to me first that he will not
put his servant to death with the sword.' "
52 And Solomon said, "If he will show himself a worthy man, [m]not one of his hairs
shall fall to the earth, but if wickedness is
found in him, he shall die." 53 So King
Solomon sent, and they brought him down
from the altar. And he came and paid homage to King Solomon, and Solomon said to
him, "Go to your house."

David's Instructions to Solomon

2 [n]When David's time to die drew near,
he commanded Solomon his son, say-
ing, 2 [o]"I am about to go the way of all the
earth. [p]Be strong, and show yourself a
man, 3 and keep the charge of the LORD
your God, walking in his ways and keeping
his statutes, his commandments, his rules,
and his testimonies, as it is written in the
Law of Moses, [q]that you may prosper in all
that you do and wherever you turn, 4 that
the LORD may [r]establish his word that he
spoke concerning me, saying, [s]'If your
sons pay close attention to their way, [t]to
walk before me in faithfulness with all
their heart and with all their soul, [u]you
shall not lack[1] a man on the throne of
Israel.'
5 "Moreover, you also know what Joab
the son of Zeruiah [v]did to me, how he
dealt with the two commanders of the
armies of Israel, [w]Abner the son of Ner,
[x]and Amasa the son of Jether, whom he
killed, avenging[2] in time of peace for
blood that had been shed in war, and putting the blood of war[3] on the belt around
his[4] waist and on the sandals on his feet.
6 Act therefore [y]according to your wisdom,
but do not let his gray head go down to
Sheol in peace. 7 But deal loyally with the
sons of [z]Barzillai the Gileadite, and let
them be [a]among those who eat at your
table, [b]for with such loyalty[5] they met me
when I fled from Absalom your brother.
8 And there is also with you [c]Shimei the
son of Gera, the Benjaminite from
Bahurim, who cursed me with a grievous
curse on the day [d]when I went to
Mahanaim. [e]But when he came down to
meet me at the Jordan, I swore to him by
the LORD, saying, 'I will not put you to
death with the sword.' 9 Now therefore do
not hold him guiltless, [f]for you are a wise
man. You will know what you ought to do
to him, and you shall [g]bring his gray head
down with blood to Sheol."

The Death of David

10 [h]Then David slept with his fathers and
was buried in [i]the city of David. 11 And the
time that David reigned over Israel was
[j]forty years. He reigned seven years in
Hebron and thirty-three years in Jerusalem.
12 [k]So Solomon sat on the throne of David
his father, and his kingdom was firmly
established.

52 [m]See 1 Sam. 14:45
Chapter 2
1 [n][Gen. 47:29]
2 [o]Josh. 23:14 [p]See Josh. 1:6, 7
3 [q]Deut. 29:9; 1 Chr. 22:12, 13
4 [r]2 Sam. 7:25 [s]Ps. 132:12 [t][ch. 3:6; 9:4; 2 Kin. 20:3] [u]ch. 8:25; 9:5; 2 Sam. 7:12, 13
5 [v]2 Sam. 18:5, 12, 14; [2 Sam. 3:39] [w]ver. 32; 2 Sam. 3:27 [x]2 Sam. 20:10
6 [y][ver. 9]
7 [z]See 2 Sam. 19:31-38 [a]2 Sam. 9:7, 10 [b]2 Sam. 17:27-29
8 [c]2 Sam. 16:5 [d]2 Sam. 17:24 [e]2 Sam. 19:18
9 [f][ver. 6] [g][Gen. 42:38; 44:31]
10 [h]ch. 1:21; Acts 2:29; 13:36 [i]ch. 3:1; 9:24
11 [j]2 Sam. 5:4, 5; 1 Chr. 29:26, 27
12 [k]1 Chr. 29:23; 2 Chr. 1:1

1 Hebrew *there shall not be cut off for you* 2 Septuagint; Hebrew *placing* 3 Septuagint *innocent blood* 4 Septuagint *my*; twice in this verse 5 Or *steadfast love*

1:52 If he will show himself a worthy man. Solomon spares Adonijah on condition that he conduct himself as a loyal citizen of Solomon's kingdom.

2:1 he commanded Solomon. David, like Jacob (Gen. 49), Moses (Deut. 31:1–8), Joshua (Josh. 23), and Samuel (1 Sam. 12) before him, gives a final speech before his death. These speeches mark the transition from one era to another and the transfer of authority.

2:2 the way of all the earth. That is, the grave (Josh. 23:14).

Be strong, and show yourself a man. These instructions were suitable either before a warrior went into battle or before a person undertook a difficult task (Deut. 31:7, 23; Josh. 1:6, 7, 9, 18; 1 Sam. 4:9).

2:3 walking in his ways and keeping his statutes. David admonishes Solomon to be faithful to God and so experience blessing (cf. Deut. 4:40; 6:2; 8:6, 11; 10:12–11:1).

2:4 If your sons pay close attention to their way. David's instructions to Solomon echo God's promises to David through the prophet Nathan in 2 Sam. 7:8–16 and reaffirmed in David's prayer in 2 Sam. 7:18–29. Here David underscores the need for covenant faithfulness (cf. 8:25, 26; 9:4, 5).

with all their heart and . . . soul. These words are an allusion to Deut. 4:29 and 6:5. When Jesus is asked what is the greatest commandment, He too quotes from Deut. 6:5 (Matt. 22:35–40).

2:5 Joab the son of Zeruiah. Joab was the most successful, but also the most unscrupulous, of David's generals (1:7 note). David calls on Solomon to see to it that the crimes Joab committed against his rivals "Abner the son of Ner" (2 Sam. 3:22–30) and "Amasa" (cf. 2 Sam. 20:4–10) do not go unpunished. The way Joab tricked Abner and Amasa and murdered them was unlawful (Deut. 19:1–13; 21:1–9).

2:7 eat at your table. That is, enjoy a position of honor at the court and share in the bounty of the state (2 Sam. 9:7; 19:28; 2 Kin. 25:29; Neh. 5:17).

2:8 Shimei the son of Gera. He had cursed and stoned David when the latter was running from his son Absalom (2 Sam. 16:5–8). Shimei later begged for pardon and David promised that Shimei would not die (2 Sam. 19:16–23).

2:9 do not hold him guiltless. Cursing a ruler violated God's law (Ex. 22:28; cf. 1 Kin. 21:10).

2:10 the city of David. One of David's major accomplishments was to capture Jerusalem, which became the nation's capital. The city afterward bore the name of David in his honor (2 Sam. 5:7).

2:11 David reigned . . . forty years. David ruled approximately 1010–970 B.C. During his last years he may have shared the throne with Solomon (1:38–40).

The Kings of Israel and Judah

The United Kingdom

Saul 1050–1010 B.C.
David 1010–970 B.C.
Solomon 970–930 B.C.

The Divided Kingdom

Judah		B.C.	Israel	
		950		
Rehoboam	930-913		Jeroboam I	930-909
		925		
Abijah	913-910		Nadab	909-908
			Baasha	908-886
Asa	910-869	900	Elah	886-885
			Zimri	885
			Tibni	885-880
Jehoshaphat	872-848	875	Omri	885-874
			Ahab	874-853
			Ahaziah	853-852
Jehoram	848-841	850	Joram	852-841
Ahaziah	841		Jehu	841-814
Athaliah	841-835	825		
Joash	835-796			
			Jehoahaz	814-798
		800		
Amaziah	796-767		Jehoash	798-782
Azariah	792-740		Jeroboam II	793-753
		775		
Jotham	750-735	750	Zechariah	753
			Shallum	752
Ahaz	735-715		Menahem	752-742
		725	Pekahiah	742-740
Hezekiah	715-686		Pekah	752-732
			Hoshea	732-722
		700		
Manasseh	697-642			
		675		
		650		
Amon	642-640			
Josiah	640-609			
		625		
Jehoahaz	609			
Jehoiakim	609-598	600		
Jehoiachin	598-597			
Zedekiah	597-586			
		586		

Solomon's Reign Established

13 Then Adonijah the son of Haggith
came to Bathsheba the mother of Solomon.
And she said, [l]"Do you come peacefully?"
He said, "Peacefully." 14 Then he said, "I
have something to say to you." She said,
"Speak." 15 He said, "You know that [m]the
kingdom was mine, and that all Israel fully
expected me to reign. However, the kingdom has turned about and become my
brother's, [n]for it was his from the LORD.
16 And now I have one request to make of
you; do not refuse me." She said to him,
"Speak." 17 And he said, "Please ask King
Solomon—he will not refuse you—to give
me [o]Abishag the Shunammite as my wife."
18 Bathsheba said, "Very well; I will speak
for you to the king."

19 So Bathsheba went to King Solomon to
speak to him on behalf of Adonijah. And
the king rose to meet her and bowed down
to her. Then he sat on his throne and had
a seat brought for the king's mother, [p]and
she sat on his right. 20 Then she said, "I
have one small request to make of you; do
not refuse me." And the king said to her,
"Make your request, my mother, for I will
not refuse you." 21 She said, "Let [o]Abishag
the Shunammite be given to Adonijah your
brother as his wife." 22 King Solomon
answered his mother, "And why do you
ask [o]Abishag the Shunammite for
Adonijah? Ask for him the kingdom also,
[q]for he is my older brother, and on his side
[r]are Abiathar[1] the priest and Joab the son
of Zeruiah." 23 Then King Solomon swore
by the LORD, saying, [s]"God do so to me and
more also if this word does not cost
Adonijah his life! 24 Now therefore [t]as the
LORD lives, who has established me and
placed me on the throne of David my
father, and who has made me a house, [u]as
he promised, Adonijah shall be put to
death this day." 25 So King Solomon sent
[v]Benaiah the son of Jehoiada, and he struck
him down, and he died.

26 And to Abiathar the priest the king
said, "Go to [w]Anathoth, to your estate, for
you deserve death. But I will not at this
time put you to death, [x]because you carried the ark of the Lord GOD before David
my father, [y]and because you shared in all
my father's affliction." 27 [z]So Solomon
expelled Abiathar from being priest to the
LORD, thus fulfilling [a]the word of the LORD
that he had spoken concerning the house
of Eli in Shiloh.

28 When the news came to Joab—for Joab
[b]had supported Adonijah although [c]he had
not supported Absalom—Joab fled to the
tent of the LORD and caught hold of the
[d]horns of the altar. 29 And when it was told
King Solomon, "Joab has fled to the tent of
the LORD, and behold, he is beside the
altar," Solomon sent Benaiah the son of
Jehoiada, saying, "Go, strike him down."
30 So Benaiah came to the tent of the LORD
and said to him, "The king commands,
'Come out.'" But he said, "No, I will die
here." Then Benaiah brought the king word
again, saying, "Thus said Joab, and thus he
answered me." 31 The king replied to him,
[e]"Do as he has said, strike him down and
bury him, [f]and thus take away from me and
from my father's house the guilt for the

13 [l]1 Sam. 16:4
15 [m][ch. 1:5, 25] [n]1 Chr. 22:9, 10; 28:5-7
17 [o]ch. 1:3, 4
19 [p][Ps. 45:9]
21 [o][See ver. 17 above]
22 [o][See ver. 17 above] [q]ch. 1:6; 1 Chr. 3:2, 5 [r]ch. 1:7
23 [s]See Ruth 1:17
24 [t]See Ruth 3:13 [u]2 Sam. 7:11, 13; 1 Chr. 22:10
25 [v]2 Sam. 8:18
26 [w]Josh. 21:18 [x]1 Sam. 23:6; 2 Sam. 15:24, 29 [y]See 1 Sam. 22:20-23
27 [z][ver. 35] [a]See 1 Sam. 2:27-36
28 [b]ch. 1:7 [c]2 Sam. 17:25; 18:2 [d]ch. 1:50
31 [e][Ex. 21:14] [f]Num. 35:33; Deut. 19:13; 21:8, 9

1 Septuagint, Syriac, Vulgate; Hebrew *and for him and for Abiathar*

2:15 all Israel fully expected me to reign. This was wishful thinking on Adonijah's part (1:7–10).

it was his from the LORD. Adonijah claims to recognize the sanctity of Solomon's reign, but his request for Abishag suggests otherwise.

2:17 give me Abishag the Shunammite. In the ancient Near East, a large court and family was a sign of royal status. Abishag remained a virgin while she stayed with David (1:1–4) and so Adonijah would not be technically breaking the law by marrying her (Deut. 22:30). Nonetheless, should Adonijah prove successful in marrying Abishag from David's harem, this would constitute a claim to the throne and an open affront to Solomon's power (cf. 2 Sam. 3:6, 7; 12:7, 8; 16:20–24).

2:18–21 Bathsheba accedes to Adonijah's request. It is unclear whether she was taken in by Adonijah's ruse, or whether she is merely playing along, confident of what Solomon's response will be.

2:19 his right. The "right" was a position of high honor (Ps. 110:1; Matt. 20:21).

2:24 established. See v. 12.

a house, as he promised. According to 1 Kin. 11:42 and 14:21, Solomon's son Rehoboam was born about a year before Solomon came to power (cf. 1 Chr. 22:9, 10).

2:26 Because Abiathar, as a holy priest, carried the ark (2 Sam. 15:24, 29) and shared David's hardships (1 Sam. 22:20–23; 23:6–9; 30:7; 2 Sam. 17:15; 19:11), Solomon tempers the penalty he metes out to Abiathar, banishing him to Anathoth (his ancestral home). Anathoth was four miles from Jerusalem.

2:27 fulfilling the word. The writer of Kings is fond of pointing out God's fulfillment of earlier promises (8:20; 12:15; 15:29; 16:12). In this case, the prophecy of a man of God concerning the demise and removal of Eli's descendants from priestly office (1 Sam. 2:30–36) is realized during the reign of Solomon.

2:28 Having heard of Adonijah's execution and Abiathar's banishment, Joab flees to "the tent of the LORD" (1:39 note), and grasps "the horns of the altar" (1:50 note) in the vain hope of escaping retribution.

2:29 Go, strike him down. Joab could have found asylum at the altar only if he had accidentally caused the death of another (Ex. 21:14). Instead, Joab's role in Adonijah's sedition gave Solomon the opportunity to honor one of his father's last requests (vv. 5, 6; 1:7 note).

blood that Joab shed without cause. 32 The
LORD will [g]bring back his bloody deeds on
his own head, because, without the knowledge of my father David, he attacked and
killed with the sword two men [h]more righteous and better than himself, [i]Abner the
son of Ner, commander of the army of
Israel, and [j]Amasa the son of Jether, commander of the army of Judah. 33 [g]So shall
their blood come back on the head of Joab
and on the head of his descendants forever.
But for David and for his descendants and
for his house and for his throne there shall
be peace from the LORD forevermore."
34 Then Benaiah the son of Jehoiada went
up and struck him down and put him to
death. And he was buried in his own house
in the wilderness. 35 [k]The king put Benaiah
the son of Jehoiada over the army in place
of Joab, and the king put [l]Zadok the priest
[m]in the place of Abiathar.
36 Then the king sent and summoned
[n]Shimei and said to him, "Build yourself
a house in Jerusalem and dwell there, and
do not go out from there to any place
whatever. 37 For on the day you go out
and cross [o]the brook Kidron, know for
certain that you shall die. [p]Your blood
shall be on your own head." 38 And Shimei
said to the king, "What you say is good; as
my lord the king has said, so will your servant do." So Shimei lived in Jerusalem
many days.
39 But it happened at the end of three years
that two of Shimei's servants ran away to
[q]Achish, son of Maacah, king of Gath. And
when it was told Shimei, "Behold, your servants are in Gath," 40 Shimei arose and saddled a donkey and went to Gath to Achish
to seek his servants. Shimei went and
brought his servants from Gath. 41 And
when Solomon was told that Shimei had
gone from Jerusalem to Gath and returned, 42 the king sent and summoned
Shimei and said to him, "Did I not make
you swear by the LORD and solemnly warn
you, saying, 'Know for certain that on the
day you go out and go to any place whatever, you shall die'? And you said to me,
'What you say is good; I will obey.' 43 Why
then have you not kept your oath to the
LORD and the commandment with which I
commanded you?" 44 The king also said to
Shimei, "You know in your own heart [r]all
the harm that you did to David my father.
So the LORD will [s]bring back your harm on
your own head. 45 But King Solomon shall
be blessed, [t]and the throne of David shall
be established before the LORD forever."
46 Then the king commanded Benaiah the
son of Jehoiada, and he went out and
struck him down, and he died.
[u]So the kingdom was established in the
hand of Solomon.

Solomon's Prayer for Wisdom

3 [v]Solomon made a marriage alliance
with Pharaoh king of Egypt. He took
Pharaoh's daughter and brought her into
[w]the city of David until he had finished
[x]building his own house [y]and the house of
the LORD [z]and the wall around Jerusalem.
2 [a]The people were sacrificing at the high
places, however, because no house had yet
been built for the name of the LORD.
3 Solomon [b]loved the LORD, [c]walking in
the statutes of David his father, only he
sacrificed and made offerings at the high
places. 4 And the king went to Gibeon to
sacrifice there, [d]for that was the great high
place. Solomon used to offer a thousand
burnt offerings on that altar. 5 [e]At Gibeon

32 [g]See Judg. 9:24 [h]2 Chr. 21:13 [i]ver. 5; 2 Sam. 3:27 [j]2 Sam. 20:9, 10
33 [g][See ver. 32 above]
35 [k]ch. 4:4 [l]1 Chr. 29:22 [m]ver. 27
36 [n]ver. 8
37 [o]2 Sam. 15:23 [p]See 2 Sam. 1:16
39 [q][1 Sam. 27:2]
44 [r]See 2 Sam. 16:5-14 [s]See 1 Sam. 25:39
45 [t][Prov. 25:5]
46 [u]ver. 12; [2 Chr. 1:1]
Chapter 3
1 [v]ch. 7:8; 9:16, 24; 2 Chr. 8:11 [w]See ch. 2:10 [x]ch. 7:1 [y]See ch. 6 [z]ch. 9:15
2 [a]ch. 22:43; [Deut. 12:2, 3]
3 [b]Deut. 6:5; 30:16, 20; [Ps. 31:23] [c]ver. 6, 14
4 [d]2 Chr. 1:3, 6, 13; [1 Chr. 16:39; 21:29]
5 [e]For ver. 5-14, see 2 Chr. 1:7-12

2:32 Despite their earlier loyalties to Saul and Absalom, Abner became commander of the army of Israel (2 Sam. 2:8, 9) and Amasa commander of the army of Judah (2 Sam. 19:13; 20:4–10); hence, they were perceived by Joab as threats to his control of the military.

2:35 Both Zadok and Abiathar previously had played leading roles in Israel as priests appointed by David (2 Sam. 8:17 note). Zadok and his descendants now become the sole high priestly family in Israel (1 Sam. 2:35).

2:39 Gath. One of the five major Philistine cities (Josh. 13:3; 1 Sam. 21:11; 27:2).

3:1 a marriage alliance with Pharaoh. The name of the pharaoh mentioned here is not known, but could be one of the last monarchs of the twenty-first Egyptian dynasty. This marriage alliance attests the international prominence of Israel during the period of the united monarchy.

3:2 sacrificing at the high places. When the Israelites entered the land of Canaan, they were supposed to destroy all the hilltop shrines of the Canaanites (Num. 33:52; Deut. 7:5; 12:3) and build instead their own centers of worship at divinely approved sites (Ex. 20:24; Judg. 6:24; 13:19; 1 Sam. 7:17; 9:12, 13). Worship at these sites was acceptable until the central sanctuary discussed at length in Deut. 12 was built.

3:3 the statutes. That is, the stipulations of the Mosaic covenant (2:3 note).

only. The author will return to this exception later in Solomon's reign (11:1–13). Even after the temple was built, Solomon continued to worship indiscriminately at the high places.

3:4 the great high place. Chronicles says that the tabernacle of Moses and the ancient bronze altar were located at Gibeon (1 Chr. 21:29; 2 Chr. 1:2–6).

burnt offerings. Used for thanksgiving and atonement, burnt offerings were the most common type of offering. The animal was burned completely except for the hide, which was taken by the priest (Lev. 7:8).

[f]the LORD appeared to Solomon [g]in a
dream by night, and God said, "Ask what I
shall give you." 6 And Solomon said, "You
have shown great and steadfast love to your
servant David my father, because [h]he
walked before you in faithfulness, in righteousness, and in uprightness of heart
toward you. And you have kept for him this
great and steadfast love and [i]have given
him a son to sit on his throne this day.
7 And now, O LORD my God, [j]you have
made your servant king in place of David
my father, [k]although I am but a little child.
I do not know [l]how to go out or come in.
8 [m]And your servant is in the midst of your
people whom you have chosen, a great
people, [n]too many to be numbered or
counted for multitude. 9 [o]Give your servant
therefore an understanding mind [p]to govern your people, that I may [q]discern
between good and evil, for who is able to
govern this your great people?"
10 It pleased the Lord that Solomon had
asked this. 11 And God said to him,
"Because you have asked this, and have
not asked for yourself long life or riches or
the life of your enemies, but have asked
for yourself understanding to discern
what is right, 12 behold, [r]I now do according to your word. Behold, [s]I give you a
wise and discerning mind, so that none
like you has been before you and none
like you shall arise after you. 13 [t]I give you
also what you have not asked, [u]both riches and honor, so that no other king shall
compare with you, all your days. 14 And if
you will walk in my ways, keeping my
statutes and my commandments, [v]as your
father David walked, then [w]I will lengthen
your days."
15 And Solomon [x]awoke, and behold, it
was a dream. Then he came to Jerusalem
and stood before the ark of the covenant of
the LORD, and offered up burnt offerings
and peace offerings, and made a feast for
all his servants.

Solomon's Wisdom

16 Then two prostitutes came to the king
[y]and stood before him. 17 The one woman
said, "Oh, my lord, this woman and I live
in the same house, and I gave birth to a
child while she was in the house. 18 Then
on the third day after I gave birth, this
woman also gave birth. And we were alone.
There was no one else with us in the
house; only we two were in the house.
19 And this woman's son died in the night,
because she lay on him. 20 And she arose at
midnight and took my son from beside me,
while your servant slept, and laid him at
her breast, and laid her dead son at my
breast. 21 When I rose in the morning to
nurse my child, behold, he was dead. But
when I looked at him closely in the morning, behold, he was not the child that I had
borne." 22 But the other woman said, "No,
the living child is mine, and the dead child
is yours." The first said, "No, the dead
child is yours, and the living child is mine."
Thus they spoke before the king.
23 Then the king said, "The one says,
'This is my son that is alive, and your son
is dead'; and the other says, 'No; but your
son is dead, and my son is the living one.'"
24 And the king said, "Bring me a sword."
So a sword was brought before the king.
25 And the king said, "Divide the living
child in two, and give half to the one and
half to the other." 26 Then the woman
whose son was alive said to the king,
because [z]her heart yearned for her son,

5 [f]ch. 9:2; 11:9 [g][Num. 12:6; Matt. 1:20; 2:13, 19]
6 [h]ch. 2:4; 9:4; [Ps. 15:2] [i]ch. 1:48
7 [j][1 Chr. 28:5] [k][1 Chr. 29:1] [l]Num. 27:17
8 [m]Deut. 7:6 [n]Gen. 13:16; 15:5
9 [o][Prov. 2:6, 9; James 1:5] [p]Ps. 72:1, 2 [q][2 Sam. 14:17; Isai. 7:15; Heb. 5:14]
12 [r][1 John 5:14, 15] [s]ch. 4:29-31; 5:12; 10:23, 24; Eccles. 1:16
13 [t][Matt. 6:33] [u]ch. 4:21-24; 10:23, 27; [Prov. 3:16]
14 [v]ver. 6; ch. 15:5 [w][Ps. 91:16; Prov. 3:2]
15 [x]Gen. 41:7
16 [y]Num. 27:2
26 [z]Gen. 43:30; Jer. 31:20; [Isai. 49:15]

3:5 dream. This dream sets the stage for the first major period in Solomon's tenure as king. For dreams as vehicles of revelation in the Bible, see Gen. 26:24; 28:12; 31:11; 46:2; Num. 12:6; Judg. 7:13; Dan. 2:4; 7:1; Matt. 1:20; 2:12, 19, 22.

3:7 little child. Solomon was possibly about twenty years old at his accession. He was young and inexperienced, but was humble enough to admit it (cf. Jer. 1:6).

3:8 a great people. Since the Exodus from Egypt, the Israelites had grown in population to the point that the promises to Abraham (Gen. 12:2; 13:16; 22:17, 18) and Jacob (Gen. 32:12) were now being realized. This large population faced its leader with considerable challenges.

3:10 pleased the Lord. Solomon did not ask for the usual wishes of an oriental king: long life, wealth, or the death of his enemies (v. 11).

3:12 none like you. Solomon's wisdom is incomparable in the history of Israel (4:29–34; 10:6–9).

3:14 if you will walk in my ways . . . I will lengthen your days. Unlike the other divine gifts, a long life is contingent upon Solomon's continuing faithfulness to God—a condition he will fail to fulfill (11:1–13).

3:15 In gratitude to God, Solomon returns to Jerusalem, stands before the ark, the central symbol of God's presence (Ex. 37:1–9), and offers burnt offerings (v. 4 note) and peace offerings (Lev. 3).

3:16 came to the king. In the ancient Near East it was expected of a king that he would hear special cases and appeals (2 Sam. 14:4–21; 15:1). In this way the monarch was directly responsible to the people.

3:25 give half to the one and half to the other. A legal tradition in the ancient Near East stipulated that if a judge could not determine who owned a disputed piece of property, he should divide it evenly between the two contestants (cf. Ex. 21:35). Solomon's application of this tradition in this case is brilliant.

"Oh, my lord, give her the living child, and
by no means put him to death." But the
other said, "He shall be neither mine nor
yours; divide him." 27 Then the king
answered and said, "Give the living child to
the first woman, and by no means put him
to death; she is his mother." 28 And all
Israel heard of the judgment that the king
had rendered, and they stood in awe of the
king, because they perceived that [a]the wisdom of God was in him to do justice.

Solomon's Officials

4 King Solomon was king over all Israel,
2 and these were his high officials:
Azariah the son of Zadok was [b]the priest;
3 Elihoreph and Ahijah the sons of Shisha
were secretaries; [c]Jehoshaphat the son of
Ahilud was recorder; 4 [d]Benaiah the son of
Jehoiada was in command of the army;
[e]Zadok and Abiathar were priests; 5 Azariah
the son of Nathan was over [f]the officers;
Zabud the son of Nathan was priest and
[g]king's friend; 6 Ahishar was in charge of
the palace; and [h]Adoniram the son of Abda
was in charge of [i]the forced labor.
7 Solomon had twelve officers over all
Israel, who provided food for the king and
his household. Each man had to make provision for one month in the year. 8 These
were their names: Ben-hur, in [j]the hill
country of Ephraim; 9 Ben-deker, in Makaz,
Shaalbim, Beth-shemesh, and Elonbeth-
hanan; 10 Ben-hesed, in Arubboth (to him
belonged Socoh and all the land of
Hepher); 11 Ben-abinadab, in all [k]Naphath-
dor (he had Taphath the daughter of
Solomon as his wife); 12 Baana the son of
Ahilud, in [l]Taanach, Megiddo, and all
[l]Beth-shean that is beside Zarethan below
Jezreel, and from Beth-shean to Abel-
meholah, as far as the other side of
Jokmeam; 13 Ben-geber, [m]in Ramoth-gilead
(he had [n]the villages of Jair the son of
Manasseh, which are in Gilead, and he had
[o]the region of Argob, which is in Bashan,
sixty great cities with walls and bronze
bars); 14 Ahinadab the son of Iddo, in
Mahanaim; 15 Ahimaaz, in Naphtali (he had
taken Basemath the daughter of Solomon
as his wife); 16 Baana the son of Hushai, in
Asher and Bealoth; 17 Jehoshaphat the son
of Paruah, in Issachar; 18 [p]Shimei the son of
Ela, in Benjamin; 19 Geber the son of Uri, in
the land of Gilead, [q]the country of Sihon
king of the Amorites and of Og king of
Bashan. And there was one governor who
was over the land.

Solomon's Wealth and Wisdom

20 Judah and Israel were as many [r]as the
sand by the sea. They ate and drank and
were happy. 21 [1] [s]Solomon ruled over all the
kingdoms from the [t]Euphrates to the land
of the Philistines and to the border of
Egypt. [u]They brought tribute and served
Solomon all the days of his life.
22 Solomon's provision for one day was
thirty cors[2] of fine flour and sixty cors of
meal, 23 ten fat oxen, and twenty pasture-
fed cattle, a hundred sheep, besides deer,

28 [a]ver. 9, 11, 12; [Ezra 7:25]
Chapter 4
2 [b]1 Chr. 6:10
3 [c]2 Sam. 8:16; 20:24
4 [d]ch. 2:35 [e]2 Sam. 20:25; [ch. 2:27, 35]
5 [f]ver. 7 [g][2 Sam. 15:37; 16:16; 1 Chr. 27:33]
6 [h]ch. 5:14; [ch. 12:18; 2 Sam. 20:24; 2 Chr. 10:18] [i][ch. 9:15]
8 [j]See Josh. 24:33
11 [k]Josh. 11:2
12 [l][Josh. 17:11]
13 [m][ch. 22:3] [n]Num. 32:41 [o]Deut. 3:4
18 [p]ch. 1:8
19 [q]Deut. 3:8-10
20 [r]Gen. 22:17; [ch. 3:8; 2 Chr. 1:9]
21 [s]2 Chr. 9:26 [t]Gen. 15:18; Ex. 23:31; Josh. 1:4; Ps. 72:8 [u]Ps. 68:29; 72:10, 11

1 Ch 5:1 in Hebrew 2 A *cor* was about 6 bushels or 220 liters

3:28 they stood in awe of the king. Solomon's ruling demonstrated that God had indeed given him "wisdom . . . to do justice" (cf. v. 11; Prov. 16:10).

4:1 all Israel. Solomon, like David before him, ruled over a united kingdom (1:35 note).

4:2 son. In Hebrew, the word "son" can mean "descendant" (Gen. 31:28, 43). In this case, Azariah is probably the son of Ahimaaz (1 Chr. 6:8, 9), and thus the grandson of Zadok the priest.

4:4 Zadok and Abiathar. These were the two leading priests during the reign of David and the beginning of Solomon's reign. Solomon deposed Abiathar for joining Adonijah in his sedition (1:7; 2:27), while Azariah succeeded Zadok as priest during the reign of Solomon (v. 2).

4:5 Nathan. His identity is unclear. Possibilities include the prophet Nathan (2 Sam. 7:2–17; 12:1–15; 1 Kin. 1:11) and the son of David (2 Sam. 5:14).

4:6 in charge of the palace. This important post involved administering the palace and overseeing the king's properties (1 Kin. 16:9; 18:3; 2 Kin. 18:18, 37; 19:2).

Adoniram. Also known as "Adoram," he was in charge of forced labor during the reigns of David (2 Sam. 20:24), Solomon, and Rehoboam (12:18).

forced labor. This conscripted labor was performed primarily, but not exclusively, by captives of war from defeated nations (5:13–16; 9:15, 23; Num. 31:25–47; Josh. 9:23).

4:7 twelve officers. The new administrative districts overseen by these governors are not exactly the same as the old Israelite tribal areas, possibly because the tribes varied greatly in population and land holdings, and Solomon desired a steady monthly income for his government.

4:19 Geber . . . Gilead. For Sihon see Num. 32:33; Deut. 2:24–37. Subsequent to the Israelite capture of Sihon's territory, the Israelites defeated King Og of Bashan and captured all his lands (east of the Sea of Chinneroth; see Num. 32:33; Deut. 3:1–11). Geber was therefore governor over a large district east of the Jordan.

4:20 as many as the sand by the sea. This is a fulfillment of the promises to the patriarchs (3:8 note; Gen. 22:17; 32:12).

4:21 to the border of Egypt. The borders of Solomon's kingdom are in essence the borders promised to Abraham (Gen. 15:18; 17:8; Deut. 1:7; 11:24; Josh. 1:4). Hence, in the presentation of Kings, Solomon ruled over an empire representing the long-awaited fulfillment of the patriarchal promises (cf. vv. 24, 25).

4:22 provision for one day. These were for Solomon's court, palace, and extended family.

gazelles, roebucks, and fattened fowl. 24 For
he had dominion over all the region west of
the Euphrates from Tiphsah to [v]Gaza, over
all the kings west of the Euphrates. [w]And
he had peace on all sides around him.
25 And Judah and Israel [x]lived in safety,
[y]from Dan even to Beersheba, [z]every man
under his vine and under his fig tree, all the
days of Solomon. 26 [a]Solomon also had
40,000 stalls of horses for his chariots, and
12,000 horsemen. 27 And those officers
supplied provisions for King Solomon, and
for all who came to King Solomon's table,
each one in his month. They let nothing be
lacking. 28 Barley also and straw for the
horses and [b]swift steeds they brought to
the place where it was required, each
according to his duty.
29 [c]And God gave Solomon wisdom and
understanding beyond measure, and
breadth of mind [d]like the sand on the
seashore, 30 so that Solomon's wisdom surpassed the wisdom of all [e]the people of the
east [f]and all the wisdom of Egypt. 31 For he
was [c]wiser than all other men, wiser than
Ethan the Ezrahite, and Heman, Calcol,
and Darda, the sons of Mahol, and his
fame was in all the surrounding nations.
32 [g]He also spoke 3,000 proverbs, [h]and his
songs were 1,005. 33 He spoke of trees,
from the cedar that is in Lebanon to the
hyssop that grows out of the wall. He
spoke also of beasts, and of birds, and of
reptiles, and of fish. 34 And people of all
nations came to hear the wisdom of
Solomon, and from [i]all the kings of the
earth, who had heard of his wisdom.

Preparations for Building the Temple

5 [1] Now [j]Hiram king of Tyre sent his servants to Solomon when he heard that
they had anointed him king in place of his
father, [k]for Hiram always loved David.
2 And Solomon sent word to Hiram, 3 [l]"You
know that David my father could not build
a house for the name of the LORD his God
[m]because of the warfare with which his
enemies surrounded him, until the LORD
put them under the soles of his feet. 4 [n]But
now the LORD my God has given me rest on
every side. There is neither adversary nor
misfortune. 5 And so I intend to build a
house for the name of the LORD my God,
[o]as the LORD said to David my father, 'Your
son, whom I will set on your throne in your
place, shall build the house for my name.'
6 Now therefore command that cedars of
Lebanon be cut for me. And my servants
will join your servants, and I will pay you
for your servants such wages as you set, for
you know that there is no one among us
who knows how to cut timber like the
Sidonians."

24 [v]Gen. 10:19 [w]1 Chr. 22:9
25 [x]Jer. 23:6; 32:37; Ezek. 28:26 [y]See 2 Sam. 3:10 [z]Mic. 4:4; Zech. 3:10; [2 Kin. 18:31; Isai. 36:16]
26 [a][ch. 10:26; 2 Chr. 1:14; 9:25]
28 [b]Esth. 8:10, 14; Mic. 1:13
29 [c]ch. 3:12 [d][ver. 20]
30 [e]Judg. 6:3 [f]Acts 7:22; [Isai. 19:11]
31 [c][See ver. 29 above]
32 [g]Prov. 1:1; Eccles. 12:9 [h]S. of S. 1:1
34 [i]2 Chr. 9:23; [ch. 10:1]
Chapter 5
1 [j][2 Chr. 2:3] [k]2 Sam. 5:11; 1 Chr. 14:1
3 [l]For ver. 3-11, see 2 Chr. 2:3-16 [m]1 Chr. 22:8; 28:3
4 [n][ch. 4:24; 1 Chr. 22:9]
5 [o]2 Sam. 7:13; 1 Chr. 17:12; 22:10; 28:6

[1] Ch 5:15 in Hebrew

4:24 Tiphsah to Gaza. Tiphsah was located on the west bank of the Euphrates, and Gaza is located on the southeastern Mediterranean coast.

peace on all sides. David had to fight many wars to secure the kingdom, and Solomon enjoyed the result. Conditions of peace were a prerequisite for building major projects such as the temple and palace (2 Sam. 7:10, 11; 1 Kin. 5:3–5).

4:26 40,000 stalls. There are variations in the versions as to how many stalls for chariot horses Solomon had. If the "12,000 horsemen" means "12,000 horses" then each stall had three horses, the normal complement for a chariot being two primary horses and one reserve. According to 10:26, Solomon had fourteen hundred chariots. Solomon's chariot force and bureaucracy required ample, regular provisions (vv. 27, 28).

4:30 the east. That is, Mesopotamia to the northeast (Gen. 29:1) and Arabia to the east (Jer. 49:28; Ezek. 25:4, 10).

Egypt. Examples of wisdom literature from both Mesopotamia and Egypt have been discovered and translated.

4:32 proverbs . . . songs. Solomon was a lover and supporter of wisdom literature, and was himself an accomplished author.

4:33 trees . . . beasts . . . birds. Solomon took a special interest in nature. By writing proverbs Solomon gave order to social relations; by listing fauna and flora, he gave order to the elements of his kingdom.

4:34 people of all nations. Solomon acquired an international reputation for wisdom. The monarchs of various nations sent emissaries to learn from Solomon's erudition. The Ebla texts from 2350 B.C. mention learned men from many nations "lecturing" in Ebla, showing how early such travel was possible.

5:1 Hiram king of Tyre. Tyre is a city on the Mediterranean coast, now in modern Lebanon. Since Hiram ruled about 980–947 B.C., his reign overlapped both David's and Solomon's.

Hiram always loved David. Hiram supplied materials and workers when David built himself a palace (2 Sam. 5:11).

5:3 the warfare with which his enemies surrounded him. Even though David wanted to build the temple himself, he spent much of his reign expanding and consolidating the kingdom (2 Sam. 7:10, 11). In a play on the Hebrew word for "house," the prophet Nathan told David that God would build a "house," or dynasty, for him, while David's offspring would build a "house," or temple, for God (2 Sam. 7:12–16). Through God's grace, Solomon is implementing the promise made to his father David.

5:4 rest on every side. The rest that many of Israel's leaders had hoped for (Ex. 33:14; Deut. 25:19; Josh. 1:13, 15; 2 Sam. 7:11) is now a reality.

5:5 the name of the LORD. In Semitic culture, a name was thought to reveal something of a person's character and identity (Gen. 17:5; 32:28; Ex. 3:13, 14; 34:6, 7; Deut. 12:5).

Your son. Solomon refers explicitly to God's promise in 2 Sam. 7:12, 13.

5:6 cedars of Lebanon. These trees were famous in the ancient Near East and often used in building royal palaces and temples.

no one . . . who knows how. The Israelites did not have the craftsmen and artisans needed to construct the temple by themselves.

Sidonians. Taken in a narrow sense, they were the residents of the port city of Sidon north of Tyre. Here the term probably refers to the inhabitants of Tyre, Gebal (Byblos), and Sidon, the people who were later called the Phoenicians.

7 As soon as Hiram heard the words of
Solomon, he rejoiced greatly and said,
"Blessed be the LORD this day, who has
given to David a wise son to be over this
great people." 8 And Hiram sent to
Solomon, saying, "I have heard the message that you have sent to me. I am ready
to do all you desire in the matter of cedar
and cypress timber. 9 My servants shall
bring it down to the sea from Lebanon, and
I will make it into rafts to go by sea to the
place you direct. And I will have them broken up there, and you shall receive it. And
you shall meet my wishes [p]by providing
food for my household." 10 So Hiram supplied Solomon with all the timber of cedar
and cypress that he desired, 11 while
Solomon gave Hiram 20,000 cors[1] of wheat
as food for his household, and 20,000[2] cors
of beaten oil. Solomon gave this to Hiram
year by year. 12 And the LORD gave Solomon
wisdom, [q]as he promised him. And there
was peace between Hiram and Solomon,
and the two of them made a treaty.
13 King Solomon drafted [r]forced labor out
of all Israel, and the draft numbered
30,000 men. 14 And he sent them to
Lebanon, 10,000 a month in shifts. They
would be a month in Lebanon and two
months at home. [s]Adoniram was in charge
of the draft. 15 Solomon also [t]had 70,000
burden-bearers and 80,000 stonecutters in
the hill country, 16 besides Solomon's 3,300
[u]chief officers who were over the work,
[v]who had charge of the people who carried
on the work. 17 At the king's command
[w]they quarried out great, costly stones in
order to lay the foundation of the house
with dressed stones. 18 So Solomon's
builders and Hiram's builders and [x]the
men of Gebal did the cutting and prepared
the timber and the stone to build the
house.

Solomon Builds the Temple

6 [y]In the four hundred and eightieth year
after the people of Israel came out of
the land of Egypt, in the fourth year of
Solomon's reign over Israel, in the month of
Ziv, which is the second month, [z]he began
to build the house of the LORD. 2 [a]The
house that King Solomon built for the LORD
was sixty cubits[3] long, twenty cubits wide,
and thirty cubits high. 3 The vestibule in
front of the nave of the house was twenty
cubits long, equal to the width of the
house, and ten cubits deep in front of the
house. 4 And [b]he made for the house windows with recessed frames.[4] 5 [c]He also built
a structure[5] against the wall of the house,
running around the walls of the house,
both the nave and [d]the inner sanctuary.
And he made [e]side chambers all around.
6 The lowest story[6] was five cubits broad,
the middle one was six cubits broad, and
the third was seven cubits broad. For
around the outside of the house he made
offsets on the wall in order that the

9 [p][Ezra 3:7; Ezek. 27:17; Acts 12:20]
12 [q]ch. 3:12
13 [r]ch. 4:6; 9:15
14 [s]See ch. 4:6
15 [t]2 Chr. 2:18; [ch. 9:20-22]
16 [u]ch. 4:5 [v]ch. 9:23
17 [w][ch. 6:7; 1 Chr. 22:2]
18 [x]Josh. 13:5; Ezek. 27:9
Chapter 6
1 [y]2 Chr. 3:1, 2 [z]Acts 7:47
2 [a]2 Chr. 3:3, 4; See Ezek. ch. 40-42
4 [b]Ezek. 40:16; 41:16, 26
5 [c]Ezek. 41:6 [d]ver. 16, 19, 20, 23, 31; ch. 7:49; 8:6, 8; 2 Chr. 3:16; 4:20; 5:7, 9; Ps. 28:2 [e]Ezek. 41:5, 6

1 A *cor* was about 6 bushels or 220 liters 2 Septuagint; Hebrew *twenty* 3 A *cubit* was about 18 inches or 45 centimeters 4 Or *blocked lattice windows* 5 Or *platform*; also verse 10 6 Septuagint; Hebrew *structure*, or *platform*

5:7 Blessed be the LORD this day. Even a foreign king acknowledges the accomplishments of Israel's God manifested through King Solomon (cf. 10:6–9).

5:9 food for my household. In exchange for Hiram's help Solomon is expected to supply food for Hiram's court (v. 11) and wages for his workers (v. 6).

5:12 the LORD gave Solomon wisdom. Solomon's administrative and political talents are again associated with God's gift of wisdom. (cf. Deut. 1:15; Is. 11:2–4).

5:13 drafted forced labor out of all Israel. Solomon pressed some of his own people into service as forced laborers on his building projects. This policy was deeply resented and contributed in no small way to the division of the kingdom following Solomon's death (9:22; 12:4, 16 and notes).

5:14 Adoniram. See note 4:6.

5:18 men of Gebal. Gebal (or Byblos) was known internationally for its trade in papyrus, the ancient form of paper made from pressed and dried cuttings of papyrus reed.

6:1 four hundred and eightieth year. The author's chronology reflects how momentous the construction of the temple was for Israel's life under God. The building of the temple under Solomon was the culmination of a long series of events that began with the deliverance out of Egypt. **fourth year of Solomon's reign.** Approximately 966 B.C., placing the Exodus in the year 1446 B.C. Some scholars date the Exodus in the thirteenth century B.C. They understand four hundred eighty years in one of two ways. Some take it as a figurative number representing twelve generations of forty years each. Others, on the basis of ancient Near Eastern custom, argue that the figure is the total of a sequence of periods, some of them overlapping.

6:2 the house . . . for the LORD. There are a number of similarities between the tabernacle and the temple, although the temple was twice the size of the tabernacle (Ex. 26:15–30; 36:20–34). Both were divided into three main sections: a vestibule, a sanctuary (the Holy Place), and an inner sanctuary (the Most Holy Place). This three-part structure was common in other ancient Near Eastern temples. Israel's sanctuary differed radically from a pagan sanctuary because it had no idols. At its center was the ark of the covenant containing the Ten Commandments, the moral will of God that ordered Israel's life (Deut. 10:4, 5; 1 Kin. 8:6–9).

6:4 windows with recessed frames. Wide on the inner side of the wall, these windows would gradually slope to form a slit on the outer wall.

6:5 chambers. These rooms surrounded the Most Holy Place and the Holy Place but not the vestibule. They were used for storage.

6:6 The lowest story. The total height of the three stories of side rooms was not as high as the main temple itself.

supporting beams should not be inserted
into the walls of the house.
7 When the house was built, [f]it was with
stone prepared at the quarry, so that neither hammer nor axe nor any tool of iron
was heard in the house while it was being
built.
8 The entrance for the lowest[1] story was
on the south side of the house, and one
went up by stairs to the middle story, and
from the middle story to the third. 9 [g]So he
built the house and finished it, and he
made the ceiling of the house of beams and
planks of cedar. 10 He built the structure
against the whole house, five cubits high,
and it was joined to the house with timbers
of cedar.
11 Now the word of the LORD came to
Solomon, 12 "Concerning this house that
you are building, [h]if you will walk in my
statutes and obey my rules and keep all my
commandments and walk in them, then I
will establish my word with you, [i]which I
spoke to David your father. 13 And [j]I will
dwell among the children of Israel [k]and
will not forsake my people Israel."
14 [l]So Solomon built the house and finished it. 15 He lined the walls of the house
on the inside with boards of cedar. From
the floor of the house to the walls of the
ceiling, he covered them on the inside with
wood, [m]and he covered the floor of the
house with boards of cypress. 16 [n]He built
twenty cubits of the rear of the house with
boards of cedar from the floor to the walls,
and he built this within as an inner sanctuary, as [o]the Most Holy Place. 17 The
house, that is, the nave in front of the inner
sanctuary, was forty cubits long. 18 The
cedar within the house was carved in the
form of [p]gourds and open flowers. All was
cedar; no stone was seen. 19 The inner sanctuary he prepared in the innermost part of
the house, to set there the ark of the
covenant of the LORD. 20 The inner sanctuary[2] was twenty cubits long, twenty cubits
wide, and twenty cubits high, and he overlaid it with pure gold. He also overlaid[3] an
altar of cedar. 21 And Solomon overlaid the
inside of the house with pure gold, and he
drew chains of gold across, in front of the
inner sanctuary, and overlaid it with gold.
22 And he overlaid the whole house with
gold, until all the house was finished. [q]Also
the whole altar that belonged to the inner
sanctuary he overlaid with gold.
23 [r]In the inner sanctuary [s]he made two
cherubim of olivewood, each ten cubits high.
24 Five cubits was the length of one wing of
the cherub, and five cubits the length of the
other wing of the cherub; it was ten cubits
from the tip of one wing to the tip of the
other. 25 The other cherub also measured ten
cubits; both cherubim had the same measure and the same form. 26 The height of one
cherub was ten cubits, and so was that of the
other cherub. 27 He put the cherubim in the
innermost part of the house. [t]And the wings
of the cherubim were spread out so that a
wing of one touched the one wall, and a
wing of the other cherub touched the other
wall; their other wings touched each other in
the middle of the house. 28 And he overlaid
the cherubim with gold.

1 Septuagint, Targum; Hebrew *middle* 2 Vulgate; Hebrew *and before the inner sanctuary* 3 Septuagint *made*

7 [f]ch. 5:18; Deut. 27:5, 6 **9** [g]ver. 14, 38 **12** [h]ch. 9:4; [ch. 2:4] [i]2 Sam. 7:13; 1 Chr. 22:10 **13** [j]Ex. 25:8 [k]Deut. 31:6, 8; Josh. 1:5 **14** [l]ver. 9, 38 **15** [m][ch. 7:7] **16** [n]2 Chr. 3:8 [o]ch. 7:50; 8:6; Ex. 26:33, 34; 2 Chr. 3:8; Ezek. 45:3; Heb. 9:3
18 [p]ch. 7:24 **22** [q]Ex. 30:1, 3, 6 **23** [r]For ver. 23-27, see 2 Chr. 3:10-12 [s]Ex. 37:7-9 **27** [t]ch. 8:7; Ex. 25:20; 37:9; 2 Chr. 5:8

6:8 entrance for the lowest story. That is, of the side rooms (see text note).

6:11 the word of the LORD came to Solomon. God characteristically speaks to Solomon, not through other prophets, but as a prophet himself (3:5, 11–14; 9:2–9; 11:11–13).

6:12 if you will walk in my statutes. With special reference to the building of the temple, God reminds Solomon that the promises to David require covenant fidelity on Solomon's part (2:3, 4 and notes).

6:13 will not forsake my people. The existence of the temple did not in and of itself guarantee the presence of God with Israel. Loyalty to the Torah is the main issue in the people's relationship with God (2:3 note and 9:6–9).

6:16 an inner sanctuary, as the Most Holy Place. The Most Holy Place, a perfect cube about 30 feet on a side (v. 20), was the most sacred area of the temple. It contained the ark of the covenant (v. 19) and the cherubim. Only the High Priest was allowed to enter this room and then only on one day a year, the Day of Atonement (Hebrew *Yom Kippur;* Lev. 16; 23:26–32; Num. 29:7–11). The tabernacle had such "a Most Holy Place" (Ex. 26:33; cf. Heb. 9:12, 14).

6:19 the ark of the covenant of the LORD. The central symbol of the Israelite's communion with God, the ark contained the two tablets of the covenant (Ex. 25:21; Deut. 9:9).

6:20 overlaid it with pure gold. The temple was beautiful and costly. In its glory and beauty, this earthly temple was a symbol of God's heavenly temple (8:36, 39; Heb. 9:11).

6:22 altar that belonged to the inner sanctuary. This was probably an incense altar (7:48; Ex. 30:1, 6; 37:25–28; Heb. 9:4).

6:23 two cherubim. These were winged creatures with human faces (cf. Gen. 3:24; Ezek. 41:18, 19). The two cherubim stood as guardians on either side of the ark (8:6, 7; 2 Chr. 3:10–13). The tips of their unfolded wings reached ten cubits high, or half the height of the Most Holy Place itself (v. 16). In the ancient Near East, kings were sometimes depicted as sitting upon a throne supported by cherubim. The cherubim in the temple may have represented God's symbolic enthronement in the Most Holy Place. God was present with His people and associated Himself in a special way with this place of worship (1 Sam. 4:4; 6:2; 1 Kin. 8:10–13; 2 Kin. 19:15; Ps. 80:1; 99:1).

29 Around all the walls of the house he
carved engraved figures of cherubim and
palm trees and open flowers, in the inner
and outer rooms. 30 The floor of the house
he overlaid with gold in the inner and outer
rooms.
31 For the entrance to the inner sanctuary
he made doors of olivewood; the lintel and
the doorposts were five-sided.[1] 32 He covered
the two doors of olivewood with carvings of
cherubim, palm trees, and open flowers. He
overlaid them with gold and spread gold on
the cherubim and on the palm trees.
33 So also he made for the entrance to the
nave doorposts of olivewood, in the form of
a square, 34 and two doors of cypress wood.
[u]The two leaves of the one door were folding, and the two leaves of the other door
were folding. 35 On them he carved cherubim and palm trees and open flowers, and
he overlaid them with gold evenly applied
on the carved work. 36 [v]He built the inner
court with three courses of cut stone and
one course of cedar beams.
37 [w]In the fourth year the foundation of
the house of the LORD was laid, in the
month of Ziv. 38 And in the eleventh year, in
the month of Bul, which is the eighth
month, the house was finished in all its
parts, and according to all its specifications. He was seven years in building it.

Solomon Builds His Palace

7 Solomon was [x]building his own house
thirteen years, and he finished his
entire house.
2 He built [y]the House of the Forest of
Lebanon. Its length was a hundred cubits[2]
and its breadth fifty cubits and its height
thirty cubits, and it was built on four[3] rows
of cedar pillars, with cedar beams on the
pillars. 3 And it was covered with cedar
above the chambers that were on the forty-
five pillars, fifteen in each row. 4 There were
window frames in three rows, and window
opposite window in three tiers. 5 All the
doorways and windows[4] had square
frames, and window was opposite window
in three tiers.
6 And he made [z]the Hall of Pillars; its
length was fifty cubits, and its breadth thirty cubits. There was a porch in front with
pillars, and [a]a canopy in front of them.
7 And he made the Hall of the Throne
where he was to pronounce judgment,
even the Hall of Judgment. [b]It was finished
with cedar from floor to rafters.[5]
8 His own house where he was to dwell,
in the other court back of the hall, was of
like workmanship. Solomon also made a
house like this hall for Pharaoh's daughter
[c]whom he had taken in marriage.
9 All these were made of costly stones, cut
according to measure, sawed with saws,
back and front, even from the foundation to
the coping, and from the outside to the
great court. 10 The foundation was of costly
stones, huge stones, stones of eight and ten
cubits. 11 And above were costly stones, cut
according to measurement, and cedar.
12 [d]The great court had three courses of cut
stone all around, and a course of cedar
beams; so had the inner court of the house
of the LORD and [e]the vestibule of the house.

The Temple Furnishings

13 And King Solomon sent and brought
[f]Hiram from Tyre. 14 He was the son of a
widow of the tribe of Naphtali, and his

34 [u][Ezek. 41:24]
36 [v]ch. 7:12
37 [w]ver. 1
Chapter 7
1 [x]ch. 3:1; 9:10; 2 Chr. 8:1
2 [y]ch. 10:17, 21
6 [z][ver. 12] [a]Ezek. 41:25, 26
7 [b]ch. 6:15, 16
8 [c]ch. 3:1; 2 Chr. 8:11
12 [d]ch. 6:36 [e][ver. 6]
13 [f][2 Chr. 2:14]

1 The meaning of the Hebrew phrase is uncertain 2 A *cubit* was about 18 inches or 45 centimeters 3 Septuagint *three* 4 Septuagint; Hebrew *posts* 5 Syriac, Vulgate; Hebrew *floor*

6:29 palm trees and open flowers. An image reminiscent of the Garden of Eden in Gen. 2. Though our first ancestors were expelled from paradise because of their rebellion against God (Gen. 3:24), and we share their expulsion, communion with God is still possible through His grace.

6:36 the inner court. Part of the exterior courtyard surrounding the temple, where the great altar and the molten Sea were situated (cf. 7:23–26). Access to this area nearest the temple itself may have been restricted to the priests (2 Chr. 4:9).

three courses. Each layer of stone was separated by a layer of cedar beams (cf. Ezra 6:4). Similar constructions have been unearthed at Megiddo.

6:38 seven years. It took Solomon seven years to build the temple, whereas it took him thirteen years to build his palace (7:1).

7:2 the House of the Forest of Lebanon. Probably so named because of the extensive use of Lebanon cedar inside. This complex was probably located immediately south of the temple.

length . . . a hundred cubits and its breadth fifty . . . and its height thirty. Although the same height as the temple, Solomon's palace was considerably longer and more than twice as wide (6:2).

7:6 the Hall of Pillars. Half the length of the palace and about two-thirds of the width (7:2), this colonnade was probably an impressive entrance hall.

7:7 the Hall of Judgment. The place where Solomon formally carried out his duties as administrator of God's holy kingdom (3:16 note).

7:13–51 This part of the account is not placed chronologically; Solomon actually began making arrangements for equipping the temple prior to its actual completion (2 Chr. 2:7, 13, 14).

7:13 Hiram. He should not be confused with Hiram, the king of Tyre, with whom Solomon ratified a treaty for the supply of materials and craftsmen (5:1–12).

father was a man of Tyre, a worker in
bronze. And [g]he was full of wisdom,
understanding, and skill for making any
work in bronze. He came to King Solomon
and did all his work.
15 [h]He cast [i]two pillars of bronze.
[j]Eighteen cubits was the height of one pillar, and a line of twelve cubits measured its
circumference. It was hollow, and its thickness was four fingers. The second pillar
was the same.[1] 16 He also made two capitals
of cast bronze to set on the tops of the pillars. The height of the one capital was five
cubits, and [j]the height of the other capital
was five cubits. 17 There were lattices of
checker work with wreaths of chain work
for the capitals on the tops of the pillars, a
lattice[2] for the one capital and a lattice for
the other capital. 18 Likewise he made
pomegranates[3] in two rows around the one
latticework to cover the capital that was on
the top of the pillar, and he did the same
with the other capital. 19 Now the capitals
that were on the tops of the pillars in the
vestibule were of lily-work, four cubits.
20 The capitals were on the two pillars and
also above the rounded projection which
was beside the latticework. There were
[k]two hundred pomegranates in two rows
all around, and so with the other capital.
21 [l]He set up the pillars at the vestibule of
the temple. He set up the pillar on the
south and called its name Jachin, and he
set up the pillar on the north and called its
name Boaz. 22 And on the tops of the pillars
was lily-work. Thus the work of the pillars
was finished.
23 [m]Then he made [n]the sea of cast metal.
It was round, ten cubits from brim to brim,
and five cubits high, and a line of thirty
cubits measured its circumference. 24 Under
its brim were [o]gourds, for ten cubits, compassing the sea all around. The gourds were
in two rows, cast with it when it was cast.
25 It stood on [p]twelve oxen, three facing
north, three facing west, three facing south,
and three facing east. The sea was set on
them, and all their rear parts were inward.
26 Its thickness was a handbreadth,[4] and its
brim was made like the brim of a cup, like
the flower of a lily. It held two thousand
baths.[5]
27 He also made the [q]ten stands of bronze.
Each stand was four cubits long, four cubits
wide, and three cubits high. 28 This was the
construction of the stands: they had panels,
and the panels were set in the frames, 29 and
on the panels that were set in the frames
were lions, oxen, and cherubim. On the
frames, both above and below the lions and
oxen, there were wreaths of beveled work.
30 Moreover, each stand had four bronze
wheels and axles of bronze, and at the four
corners were supports for a basin. The supports were cast with wreaths at the side of
each. 31 Its opening was within a crown that
projected upward one cubit. Its opening
was round, as a pedestal is made, a cubit
and a half deep. At its opening there were
carvings, and its panels were square, not
round. 32 And the four wheels were underneath the panels. The axles of the wheels
were of one piece with the stands, and the
height of a wheel was a cubit and a half.
33 The wheels were made like a chariot
wheel; their axles, their rims, their spokes,
and their hubs were all cast. 34 There were
four supports at the four corners of each
stand. The supports were of one piece with
the stands. 35 And on the top of the stand
there was a round band half a cubit high;
and on the top of the stand its stays and its
panels were of one piece with it. 36 And on
the surfaces of its stays and on its panels, he
carved cherubim, lions, and palm trees,
according to the space of each, with

14 [g][Ex. 31:3-5; 35:31] **15** [h]For ver. 15-21, see 2 Chr. 3:15-17 [i]2 Kin. 25:17; 1 Chr. 18:8; 2 Chr. 4:12; Jer. 52:21-23 [j]ver. 41 **16** [j][See ver. 15 above] **20** [k][ver. 42; 2 Chr. 3:16; 4:13; Jer. 52:23] **21** [l]2 Chr. 3:17 **23** [m]For ver. 23-26, see 2 Chr. 4:2-5 [n]2 Kin. 16:17; 25:13; 1 Chr. 18:8; Jer. 52:17; [Ex. 30:18] **24** [o][ch. 6:18] **25** [p]Jer. 52:20 **27** [q]2 Kin. 25:13; 2 Chr. 4:14; Jer. 52:17

1 Targum, Syriac (compare Septuagint and Jeremiah 52:21); Hebrew *and a line of twelve cubits measured the circumference of the second pillar* 2 Septuagint; Hebrew *seven*; twice in this verse 3 Two manuscripts (compare Septuagint); Hebrew *pillars* 4 A *handbreadth* was about 3 inches or 7.5 centimeters 5 A *bath* was about 6 gallons or 22 liters

7:15 two pillars of bronze. One pillar was on each side of the temple's entrance (v. 21). It is unclear whether they were freestanding or whether they supported a roof which may have also covered the porch of the temple.

7:16 two capitals. It was common in the ancient Near East to lavish capitals with ornate decoration.

7:23 the sea of cast metal. A huge circular basin holding up to eight thousand gallons of water (2 Chr. 4:5 note). According to Chronicles, the priests used the Sea for cleansing (2 Chr. 4:6). Its symbolic significance is disputed. Some scholars highlight the positive attributes of water as life-giving, while others argue that the bronze Sea commemorates God's power over the forces of chaos, typified by the sea (cf. Rev. 21:1).

7:25 twelve oxen. The Sea rested on four triads of oxen pointed in the four cardinal directions. In the ancient Near East, oxen symbolized physical and reproductive potency. Their arrangement is indicative of God's universal lordship.

7:27 ten stands of bronze. These portable and highly decorated wagons held water basins (v. 38). The priests used the water to wash sections of animals that had been slaughtered for burnt offerings (Lev. 1:9, 13; 2 Chr. 4:6).

wreaths all around. 37 After this manner he
made [q] the ten stands. All of them were cast
alike, of the same measure and the same
form.
38 And he made [r] ten basins of bronze.
Each basin held forty baths, each basin
measured four cubits, and there was a
basin for each of the ten stands. 39 And he
set the stands, five on the south side of the
house, and five on the north side of the
house. And he set the sea at the southeast
corner of the house.
40 [s] Hiram also made [t] the pots, the shovels, and the basins. So Hiram finished all
the work that he did for King Solomon on
the house of the LORD: 41 the two pillars, the
two bowls of the capitals that were on the
tops of the pillars, and the two [u] latticeworks to cover the two bowls of the capitals
that were on the tops of the pillars; 42 and
the [v] four hundred pomegranates for the
two latticeworks, two rows of pomegranates
for each latticework, to cover the two bowls
of the capitals that were on the pillars; 43 the
ten stands, and the ten basins on the
stands; 44 and [w] the one sea, and the twelve
oxen underneath the sea.
45 Now [x] the pots, the shovels, and the
basins, all these vessels in the house of
the LORD, which Hiram made for King
Solomon, were of burnished bronze. 46 In
the plain of the Jordan the king cast them,
in the clay ground between [y] Succoth and
[z] Zarethan. 47 And Solomon left all the vessels unweighed, because there were so
many of them; [a] the weight of the bronze
was not ascertained.
48 So Solomon made all the vessels that
were in the house of the LORD: [b] the golden
altar, [c] the golden table for [d] the bread of the
Presence, 49 [e] the lampstands of pure gold,
five on the south side and five on the north,
before the inner sanctuary; [f] the flowers, the
lamps, and the tongs, of gold; 50 the cups,
snuffers, basins, dishes for incense, and
[g] fire pans, of pure gold; and the sockets of
gold, for the doors of the innermost part of
the house, [h] the Most Holy Place, and for
the doors of the nave of the temple.
51 Thus all the work that King Solomon
did on the house of the LORD was finished.
And Solomon brought in [i] the things that
David his father had dedicated, the silver,
the gold, and the vessels, and stored them
in the treasuries of the house of the LORD.

The Ark Brought into the Temple

8 [j] Then Solomon assembled the elders
of Israel and all the heads of the tribes,
[k] the leaders of the fathers' houses of the
people of Israel, before King Solomon in
Jerusalem, [l] to bring up the ark of the
covenant of the LORD out of [m] the city of
David, which is Zion. 2 And all the men of
Israel assembled to King Solomon at [n] the
feast in the month Ethanim, which is the
seventh month. 3 And all the elders of Israel
came, and [o] the priests took up the ark.
4 And they brought up the ark of the LORD,
[p] the tent of meeting, and all the holy vessels that were in the tent; the priests and
the Levites brought them up. 5 And King
Solomon and all the congregation of Israel,
who had assembled before him, were with
him before the ark, [q] sacrificing so many
sheep and oxen that they could not be
counted or numbered. 6 [r] Then the priests
brought the ark of the covenant of the LORD
[s] to its place in [t] the inner sanctuary of the
house, in the Most Holy Place, [t] underneath

37 [q] [See ver. 27 above]
38 [r] 2 Chr. 4:6; [Ex. 30:18]
40 [s] For ver. 40-51, see 2 Chr. 4:11-5:1 [t] Ex. 27:3; 38:3
41 [u] ver. 17, 18
42 [v] [ver. 20]
44 [w] ver. 23, 25
45 [x] Ex. 27:3; 38:3
46 [y] Josh. 13:27 [z] Josh. 3:16
47 [a] [1 Chr. 22:3, 14]
48 [b] See Ex. 37:25-29 [c] [2 Chr. 4:8]; See Ex. 37:10-16 [d] Ex. 25:30; See Lev. 24:5-8
49 [e] 2 Chr. 4:7 [f] See Ex. 25:31-38
50 [g] Ex. 27:3 [h] See ch. 6:16
51 [i] 2 Sam. 8:11
Chapter 8
1 [j] For ver. 1-9, see 2 Chr. 5:2-10 [k] Num. 1:16 [l] [2 Sam. 6:17] [m] See 2 Sam. 5:7
2 [n] ver. 65; Lev. 23:34; See 2 Chr. 7:8-10
3 [o] [Num. 4:15; Deut. 31:9; Josh. 3:3, 6; 1 Chr. 15:14, 15]
4 [p] [ch. 3:4; 2 Chr. 1:3]
5 [q] 2 Sam. 6:17
6 [r] Ex. 26:33, 34 [s] See ch. 6:5 [t] ch. 6:27

7:40 shovels, and the basins. Priests used the shovels to remove ashes from the altar, and the bowls for rituals involving blood or water (Ex. 27:3; Jer. 52:18).

7:46 Succoth. This center of metallurgy was located east of the Jordan, north of the Wadi Jabbok (Gen. 33:17; Josh. 13:27; Judg. 8:4, 5). Zarethan was nearby.

7:48 the golden altar . . . table. The same altar described in 6:22. The "bread of the Presence" or holy bread (1 Sam. 21:4, 6) arranged on the golden table was understood as an offering before God (Ex. 25:23–30; Lev. 24:5–9; Num. 4:7; 2 Chr. 13:11; Matt. 12:4).

7:49 lampstands. There were ten lampstands in the temple, as compared to only one in the tabernacle (Ex. 25:31–40; 26:35).

7:51 David his father. During his reign David accumulated booty from military campaigns and received tribute from a variety of states (2 Sam. 8:9–12; 1 Chr. 18:7–11; 2 Chr. 5:1).

treasuries of the house of the LORD. Depositories for the government's wealth, sometimes used as tribute by the kings to ward off foreign invaders (15:18; 2 Kin. 12:18; 18:13–16). The treasure was also the object of raids by opposing kings (14:25, 26; 2 Kin. 14:13, 14).

8:1 the elders of Israel. Senior leaders who were in charge of local government and justice throughout Old Testament history (Ex. 18:13–26; Num. 11:16–30; Judg. 21:16–24; 1 Sam. 8:1–9).

the city of David, which is Zion. This oldest section of Jerusalem was south of the temple. David had earlier brought the ark from the house of Obed-edom to Zion (2 Sam. 6:1–19).

8:2 the feast. Solomon apparently waited eleven months to dedicate the temple (6:38) so that the ceremony could be part of the Feast of Booths in the New Year, which was commemorated during the seventh month (Lev. 23:34; Deut. 16:13–15).

8:4 the tent of meeting. The tabernacle along with all its furnishings is brought, presumably from Gibeon (3:4 note), by the priests and the Levites.

8:6 underneath the wings of the cherubim. See note 6:23.

the wings of the cherubim. **7** For the cherubim spread out their wings over the place
of the ark, so that the cherubim overshadowed the ark and its poles. **8** [u]And the poles
were so long that the ends of the poles
were seen from the Holy Place before [t]the
inner sanctuary; but they could not be seen
from outside. And they are there to this
day. **9** There was nothing in the ark except
[v]the two tablets of stone that Moses put
there at Horeb, where [w]the LORD made a
covenant with the people of Israel, when
they came out of the land of Egypt. **10** And
when the priests came out of the Holy
Place, [x]a cloud filled the house of the LORD,
11 so that the priests could not stand to
minister because of the cloud, for the glory
of the LORD filled the house of the LORD.

Solomon Blesses the LORD

12 [y]Then Solomon said, "The LORD[1] has
said that he would dwell [z]in thick darkness. **13** [a]I have indeed built you an exalted
house, [b]a place for you to dwell in forever."
14 Then the king turned around and
[c]blessed all the assembly of Israel, while all
the assembly of Israel stood. **15** And he said,
[d]"Blessed be the LORD, the God of Israel,
who with his hand has fulfilled [e]what he
promised with his mouth to David my
father, saying, **16** [f]'Since the day that I
brought my people Israel out of Egypt, I
chose no city out of all the tribes of Israel
in which to build a house, [g]that my name
might be there. [h]But I chose David to be
over my people Israel.' **17** [i]Now it was in the
heart of David my father to build a house
for the name of the LORD, the God of Israel.
18 But the LORD said to David my father,
'Whereas it was in your heart to build a
house for my name, you did well that it
was in your heart. **19** [j]Nevertheless, you
shall not build the house, but your son
who shall be born to you shall build the
house for my name.' **20** Now the LORD has
fulfilled his promise that he made. For I
have risen in the place of David my father,
and sit on the throne of Israel, [k]as the LORD
promised, and I have built the house for
the name of the LORD, the God of Israel.
21 And there I have provided a place for the
ark, [l]in which is the covenant of the LORD
that he made with our fathers, when he
brought them out of the land of Egypt."

Solomon's Prayer of Dedication

22 Then Solomon [m]stood before the altar
of the LORD in the presence of all the assembly of Israel and [n]spread out his hands
toward heaven, **23** and said, "O LORD, God
of Israel, [o]there is no God like you, in heav-
en above or on earth beneath, [p]keeping
covenant and showing steadfast love to
your servants who walk before you with all
their heart, **24** who have kept with your servant David my father what you declared to
him. [e]You spoke with your mouth, and with
your hand have fulfilled it this day. **25** Now
therefore, O LORD, God of Israel, keep for
your servant David my father what you have
promised him, saying, [q]'You shall not lack a
man to sit before me on the throne of Israel,
if only your sons pay close attention to their
way, to walk before me as you have walked
before me.' **26** [r]Now therefore, O God of
Israel, let your word be confirmed, which
you have spoken to your servant David my
father.
27 "But will God indeed dwell on the

1 Septuagint *The LORD has set the sun in the heavens, but*

8 [u]Ex. 25:13-15 [t][See ver. 6 above]
9 [v]Ex. 25:21; 40:20; Deut. 10:2, 5; Heb. 9:4 [w]Ex. 34:27, 28; Deut. 4:13
10 [x]Ex. 40:34, 35; 2 Chr. 5:13, 14; 7:1, 2; [Ezek. 10:3, 4]
12 [y]For ver. 12-50, see 2 Chr. 6:1-39 [z]Ps. 18:11; 97:2; [Lev. 16:2]
13 [a]2 Sam. 7:13 [b]Ex. 15:17; [Ps. 132:14]
14 [c]ver. 55; 2 Sam. 6:18
15 [d]Luke 1:68 [e]ch. 6:12
16 [f]See 2 Sam. 7:4-16, 25 [g]ver. 29; Deut. 12:11 [h]1 Sam. 16:1; 2 Sam. 7:8; 1 Chr. 28:4
17 [i]2 Sam. 7:2, 3; 1 Chr. 17:1, 2
19 [j]ch. 5:3, 5; 2 Sam. 7:5, 12, 13
20 [k]1 Chr. 28:5, 6
21 [l]ver. 9; Deut. 31:26
22 [m]ver. 54; 2 Chr. 6:12, 13 [n][Ex. 9:33; Ezra 9:5; Isai. 1:15]
23 [o]Ex. 15:11; 2 Sam. 7:22 [p]See Deut. 7:9
24 [e][See ver. 15 above]
25 [q]See ch. 2:4
26 [r]2 Sam. 7:25

8:8 to this day. Statements to this effect (9:13, 21; 10:12; 12:19) were written from the perspective of a writer who lived before the destruction of the temple (586 B.C.). See Introduction: Author.

8:9 the two tablets of stone. The copy of the covenant (cf. v. 21; Ex. 25:16, 21; 40:20).

Horeb. Following the pattern established in Deuteronomy, the writers of the Deuteronomic History call the site where the covenant was made "Mount Horeb" and not "Mount Sinai." "Horeb" is used eleven times in Deuteronomy (cf. Deut. 5:2) and twice in the history (here and 19:8); "Sinai" occurs only once in each (Deut. 33:2; Judg. 5:5).

8:10 a cloud filled the house of the LORD. After the Exodus from Egypt, God led His people through the wilderness with a pillar of cloud by day and a pillar of fire by night (Ex. 13:21; 40:36–38). At Mount Sinai God revealed Himself in a cloud (Ex. 19:9; 24:15–18). When the tabernacle was constructed God covered it with the cloud of His glory (Ex. 40:34, 35; cf. Lev. 16:2). Now He shows His approval of the newly constructed sanctuary.

8:12 dwell in thick darkness. No one can see God and live, but God can reveal Himself and manifest His love toward His people in indirect ways (v. 10 note).

8:13 a place for you to dwell in forever. The temple, as a divinely sanctioned place for prayer and sacrifice, was a special sign of God's presence among His people (Ps. 76:2; 132:13, 14; Is. 8:18; Amos 1:2).

8:22 spread out his hands. This gesture signified prayer (Ex. 9:29; Is. 1:15; 1 Tim. 2:8).

8:23 there is no God like you. The incomparability of God is a prominent theme throughout the Scriptures (Ex. 15:11; Deut. 4:39; Ps. 86:8; Mark 12:29; Eph. 4:6; Rev. 19:6). God's fidelity is not temporary (3:6; 8:16; Deut. 7:9, 12; Ps. 52:8; Heb. 13:8), nor is His power limited to a specific country (vv. 41–43; Jonah).

8:25 if only your sons pay close attention. Solomon repeats the condition that his dynasty would continue to rule Israel if David's sons remained faithful to God (2:3, 4; 6:11–13; 9:4–9; 11:11–13).

earth? Behold, [s]heaven and the highest
heaven cannot contain you; how much less
this house that I have built! **28** Yet have
regard to the prayer of your servant and to
his plea, O LORD my God, listening to the
cry and to the prayer that your servant
prays before you this day, **29** [t]that your eyes
may be open night and day toward this
house, the place of which you have said,
[u]'My name shall be there,' that you may listen to the prayer that your servant offers
toward this place. **30** And listen to the plea
of your servant and of your people Israel,
when they pray toward this place. And listen in heaven your dwelling place, and
when you hear, forgive.

31 "If a man sins against his neighbor and
is made to take [v]an oath and comes and
swears his oath before your altar in this
house, **32** then hear in heaven and act and
judge your servants, [w]condemning the guilty
by bringing his conduct on his own head,
and vindicating the righteous by rewarding
him according to his righteousness.

33 [x]"When your people Israel are defeated
before the enemy because they have sinned
against you, and [y]if they turn again to you
and acknowledge your name and pray and
plead with you in this house, **34** then hear in
heaven and forgive the sin of your people
Israel and bring them again to the land that
you gave to their fathers.

35 [z]"When heaven is shut up and there is
no rain because they have sinned against
you, if they pray toward this place and
acknowledge your name and turn from
their sin, when you afflict them, **36** then
hear in heaven and forgive the sin of your
servants, your people Israel, when [a]you
teach them [b]the good way in which they
should walk, and grant rain upon your
land, which you have given to your people
as an inheritance.

37 [c]"If there is famine in the land, if there
is pestilence or blight or mildew or locust
or caterpillar, if their enemy besieges them
in the land at their gates,[1] whatever plague,
whatever sickness there is, **38** whatever
prayer, whatever plea is made by any man
or by all your people Israel, each knowing
the affliction of his own heart and stretching out his hands toward this house, **39** then
hear in heaven your dwelling place and forgive and act and render to each whose
heart you know, according to all his ways
([d]for you, you only, know the hearts of all
the children of mankind), **40** that they may
fear you [e]all the days that they live in the
land that you gave to our fathers.

41 "Likewise, when a foreigner, who is not
of your people Israel, comes from a far
country for your name's sake **42** (for they
shall hear of your great name [f]and your
mighty hand, and of your outstretched
arm), when he comes and prays toward
this house, **43** hear in heaven your dwelling
place and do according to all for which the
foreigner calls to you, in order [g]that all the
peoples of the earth may know your name
and [h]fear you, as do your people Israel, and
that they may know that this house that I
have built is called by your name.

44 "If your people go out to battle against
their enemy, by whatever way you shall send
them, and they pray to the LORD [i]toward the
city that you have chosen and the house that
I have built for your name, **45** then hear in
heaven their prayer and their plea, and
maintain their cause.

1 Septuagint, Syriac *in any of their cities*

27 [s]2 Chr. 2:6; [Isai. 66:1; Jer. 23:24; Acts 7:49; 17:24]
29 [t]ver. 52; [2 Chr. 7:15; Neh. 1:6] [u]ver. 16; ch. 9:3; Deut. 12:11
31 [v][Ex. 22:11]
32 [w]Deut. 25:1
33 [x]Lev. 26:17; Deut. 28:45 [y]Lev. 26:40; [Neh. 1:9]
35 [z]Deut. 11:17; Luke 4:25; [Lev. 26:17; Deut. 28:25]
36 [a][Ps. 25:4; 27:11; 86:11] [b]1 Sam. 12:23
37 [c][Lev. 26:16, 25, 26; Deut. 28:21, 22, 37, 38, 42, 52; 2 Chr. 20:9]
39 [d]1 Chr. 28:9; Acts 1:24; [1 Sam. 16:7; Jer. 17:10]
40 [e]Deut. 12:1
42 [f]Deut. 3:24; 2 Chr. 6:32
43 [g]ver. 60; [Josh. 4:24] [h]Ps. 102:15
44 [i][ver. 48]

8:29 My name shall be there. God had promised that He would be present in a special way in the Jerusalem temple, and Solomon implores God to hear the prayers that are directed toward the temple (Dan. 6:10; 9:17; Jon. 2:4).

8:31 an oath. In certain trials the suspect might be required to take an oath of innocence at the sanctuary to corroborate his defense (Ex. 22:7–12; Num. 5:11–31). Solomon prays that God, through His involvement in the suspects' lives, would condemn the guilty and declare the innocent not guilty (v. 32).

8:33 because they have sinned against you. Defeat by an enemy was not a defeat by that enemy's god, but a defeat of Israel by God Himself due to Israel's own infidelity (Deut. 28:25; Josh. 7; 2 Chr. 36:15–19; Lam. 2:1–8).

8:34 bring them again to the land. It was not unusual for the army and people defeated in war to be deported to another land. Solomon asks God to be merciful and restore those who ask His forgiveness.

8:35 When heaven is shut up. Just as God directs the fate of His people in war, so also God controls the world of nature. Drought was one of the curses of the covenant (17:1; Deut. 28:22–24; Amos 4:7, 8).

8:37 famine . . . sickness. Solomon mentions a wide variety of afflictions: famine, pestilence, locusts, war, and sickness, all mentioned in Deut. 28.

8:39 render to each . . . according to all his ways. Solomon prays that God would use His infinite knowledge to establish justice among His people.

8:43 that all the peoples of the earth may know your name. Solomon prays that one day all peoples will commit their lives to God, just as Israel does (cf. Is. 56:6–8; Zech. 8:23; Matt. 28:19).

8:44 If your people go out to battle. Solomon is referring to military endeavors taken at divine behest (20:13–30; Lev. 26:7; Deut. 20; 21:10; 1 Sam. 23:2, 4; 2 Sam. 5:19, 24).

46 "If they sin against you—[j]for there is no
one who does not sin—and you are angry
with them and give them to an enemy, so
that they are carried away captive [k]to the
land of the enemy, far off or near, 47 yet [l]if
they turn their heart in the land to which
they have been carried captive, and repent
and plead with you in the land of their captors, saying, [m]'We have sinned and have
acted perversely and wickedly,' 48 [n]if they
repent with all their mind and with all their
heart in the land of their enemies, who carried them captive, and pray to you [o]toward
their land, which you gave to their fathers,
the city that you have chosen, and the house
that I have built for your name, 49 then hear
in heaven your dwelling place their prayer
and their plea, and maintain their cause
50 and forgive your people who have sinned
against you, and all their transgressions that
they have committed against you, and [p]grant
them compassion in the sight of those who
carried them captive, that they may have
compassion on them 51 ([q]for they are your
people, and your heritage, which you
brought out of Egypt, [r]from the midst of the
iron furnace). 52 [s]Let your eyes be open to the
plea of your servant and to the plea of your
people Israel, giving ear to them whenever
they call to you. 53 For you separated them
from among all the peoples of the earth to be
your heritage, [t]as you declared through
Moses your servant, when you brought our
fathers out of Egypt, O Lord GOD."

Solomon's Benediction

54 [u]Now as Solomon finished offering all
this prayer and plea to the LORD, he arose
from before the altar of the LORD, where he
had [v]knelt with hands outstretched toward
heaven. 55 And he stood and [w]blessed all the
assembly of Israel with a loud voice, saying,
56 "Blessed be the LORD who has given rest to
his people Israel, according to all that he
promised. [x]Not one word has failed of all his
good promise, which he spoke by Moses his
servant. 57 The LORD our God be with us, as
he was with our fathers. [y]May he not leave us
or forsake us, 58 that he may [z]incline our
hearts to him, to walk in all his ways and to
keep his commandments, his statutes, and
his rules, which he commanded our fathers.
59 Let these words of mine, with which I have
pleaded before the LORD, be near to the LORD
our God day and night, and may he maintain the cause of his servant and the cause of
his people Israel, as each day requires, 60 that
[a]all the peoples of the earth may know that
[b]the LORD is God; there is no other. 61 [c]Let
your heart therefore be wholly true to the
LORD our God, walking in his statutes and
keeping his commandments, as at this day."

Solomon's Sacrifices

62 [d]Then [e]the king, and all Israel with him,
offered sacrifice before the LORD. 63 Solomon
offered as peace offerings to the LORD
22,000 oxen and 120,000 sheep. So the
king and all the people of Israel dedicated
the house of the LORD. 64 The same day the
king consecrated the middle of the court
that was before the house of the LORD, for
there he offered the burnt offering and the
grain offering and the fat pieces of the
peace offerings, because [f]the bronze altar
that was before the LORD was too small to
receive the burnt offering and the grain
offering and the fat pieces of the peace
offerings.

46 [j]Prov. 20:9; Eccles. 7:20; Rom. 3:23; James 3:2; 1 John 1:8, 10 [k]Lev. 26:34, 44; Deut. 28:36, 64
47 [l]Lev. 26:40 [m]Neh. 1:6; Ps. 106:6; Dan. 9:5
48 [n]1 Sam. 7:3; Jer. 29:12-14 [o]Dan. 6:10; [ver. 44; Ps. 5:7; Jonah 2:4]
50 [p]Ps. 106:46
51 [q]Deut. 9:29; [Neh. 1:10] [r]Deut. 4:20; Jer. 11:4
52 [s][ver. 29]
53 [t]Ex. 19:5, 6; Deut. 9:26, 29; 14:2
54 [u]2 Chr. 7:1
[v][2 Chr. 6:13]
55 [w]ver. 14
56 [x]Josh. 21:45; 23:14
57 [y][Deut. 31:6; Josh. 1:5; 1 Sam. 12:22]
58 [z]Ps. 119:36
60 [a]ver. 43 [b]Deut. 4:35, 39; [ch. 18:39]
61 [c]2 Kin. 20:3; [ch. 11:4; 15:3, 14]
62 [d]For ver. 62-66 see 2 Chr. 7:4-10 [e][Ezra 6:16, 17]
64 [f]See 2 Chr. 4:1

8:46 no one who does not sin. See "Original Sin and Total Depravity" at Ps. 51:5.

they are carried away captive. Exile from the land is one of the most severe curses in the Sinaitic covenant (v. 33 note; Lev. 26:33–45; Deut. 28:64–68; 30:1–5). Exile is also a curse in a number of ancient Near Eastern treaties.

8:50 forgive your people. Being outside the land of Israel does not mean that God's promises are no longer operative (Neh. 1:11). Solomon beseeches God to cause the exiles' captors to show mercy toward their captives (Ps. 106:46).

8:53 For you separated them. Since God specifically chose Israel and liberated them from Egypt to become His own special inheritance (Ex. 19:3–6; Deut. 4:20; 9:26), Solomon prays that God will not forget this history of redemption when Israel finds itself in exile.

8:56 the LORD who has given rest to his people. After considerable upheaval in the period of wilderness wandering and conquest, Israel had experienced the fulfillment of the good promise, which He promised through His servant Moses (5:4 note; Ex. 33:14; Deut. 12:10). In the New Testament, Christians are exhorted to make every effort to enter God's rest (Heb. 4:11; cf. Rev. 14:13).

8:60 there is no other. The other gods whom people worship are fictional; the only real God is the God of Israel (cf. Deut. 4:35).

8:63 22,000 oxen. Over the course of fourteen days of dedicatory festivities, Solomon and the great many people present in Jerusalem offer a multitude of sacrifices, far more than at the comparatively modest dedication of the second temple (Ezra 6:16–18).

8:64 offering. For burnt offerings, see note 3:4. Grain offerings often accompanied animal sacrifices (Lev. 2; 7:11–14; 8:26; 9:4; 14:20; Num. 15:1–10) and were indications of the worshiper's gratitude and praise. For peace offerings, see Lev. 3.

the bronze altar. This altar on which sacrifices were burned was located in front of the temple (vv. 22, 54) and is different from the incense altar inside the temple (6:22 note).

65 So Solomon held [g]the feast at that
time, and all Israel with him, a great assembly, from [h]Lebo-hamath to [i]the Brook of
Egypt, before the LORD our God, seven
days.[1] **66** On the eighth day he sent the people away, and they blessed the king and
went to their homes joyful and glad of
heart for all the goodness that the LORD
had shown to David his servant and to
Israel his people.

The LORD Appears to Solomon

9 [j]As soon as Solomon had finished
building the house of the LORD [k]and
the king's house and [l]all that Solomon
desired to build, **2** [m]the LORD appeared to
Solomon a second time, as he had
appeared to him at Gibeon. **3** And the LORD
said to him, "I have heard your prayer and
your plea, which you have made before me.
I have consecrated this house that you have
built, [n]by putting my name there forever.
[o]My eyes and my heart will be there for all
time. **4** And as for you, if you will [p]walk
before me, [q]as David your father walked,
with integrity of heart and uprightness,
doing according to all that I have commanded you, and keeping my statutes and
my rules, **5** [r]then I will establish your royal
throne over Israel forever, as I promised
David your father, saying, 'You shall not
lack a man on the throne of Israel.' **6** [s]But if
you turn aside from following me, you or
your children, and do not keep my commandments and my statutes that I have set
before you, but go and serve other gods
and worship them, **7** [t]then I will cut off
Israel from the land that I have given them,
[u]and the house that I have consecrated for
my name I will cast out of my sight, [v]and
Israel will become a proverb and a byword
among all peoples. **8** And this house will
become a heap of ruins.[2] Everyone passing
by it will be astonished and will hiss, and
they will say, [w]'Why has the LORD done
thus to this land and to this house?' **9** Then
they will say, 'Because [x]they abandoned
the LORD their God who brought their
fathers out of the land of Egypt and laid
hold on other gods and worshiped them
and served them. Therefore the LORD has
brought all this disaster on them.'"

Solomon's Other Acts

10 [y]At the end of [z]twenty years, in which
Solomon had built the two houses, the
house of the LORD and the king's house,
11 and Hiram king of Tyre had supplied
Solomon with cedar and cypress timber and
gold, as much as he desired, King Solomon
gave to Hiram twenty cities in the land of
Galilee. **12** But when Hiram came from Tyre
to see the cities that Solomon had given him,
they did not please him. **13** Therefore he said,
"What kind of cities are these that you have
given me, my brother?" So they are called the
land of [a]Cabul to this day. **14** Hiram had sent
to the king 120 talents[3] of gold.
15 And this is the account of [b]the forced
labor that King Solomon drafted to build
the house of the LORD and his own house
and [c]the Millo and the wall of Jerusalem

65 [g]ver. 2; Lev. 23:34 [h]Num. 13:21; 34:8 [i]Num. 34:5; 2 Kin. 24:7
Chapter 9
1 [j]For ver. 1-9, see 2 Chr. 7:11-22 [k]ch. 7:1; 2 Chr. 8:1 [l]ver. 19; 2 Chr. 8:6
2 [m]ch. 3:5; 11:9
3 [n]ch. 8:16, 29 [o]Deut. 11:12
4 [p][Gen. 17:1] [q]ch. 11:4, 6, 38; 14:8; 15:5
5 [r]ch. 6:12; 1 Chr. 22:10; See ch. 2:4
6 [s][2 Sam. 7:14; Ps. 89:30, 32]
7 [t]Deut. 4:26; 2 Kin. 17:23; 25:21 [u]Jer. 7:14 [v]Deut. 28:37; [Ps. 44:14]
8 [w]Deut. 29:24-26; Jer. 22:8, 9
9 [x]ch. 18:18
10 [y]For ver. 10-28, see 2 Chr. 8:1-18 [z][ch. 6:37, 38; 7:1]
13 [a][Josh. 19:27]
15 [b]ch. 5:13 [c]ver. 24; See 2 Sam. 5:9

1 Septuagint; Hebrew *seven days and seven days, fourteen days*
2 Syriac, Old Latin; Hebrew *will become high* 3 A *talent* was about 75 pounds or 34 kilograms

8:65 Lebo-hamath. This area near the northern limit of the territory controlled by Israel was located about 20 miles south of Kadesh on the Orontes River (Josh. 13:5; 2 Kin. 14:25).

Brook of Egypt. Probably to be equated with Wadi El-Arish, in northeastern Sinai. People from the entire extent of Solomon's kingdom were present for these festivities (4:21).

8:66 all the goodness that the LORD had shown to David his servant and to Israel his people. God graciously fulfilled His commitment to David that one of his offspring would build the temple he had wanted to build (2 Sam. 7:1–16). God also gave Israel a central sanctuary (Deut. 12) and rest from their enemies (1 Kin. 5:4).

9:3 have consecrated. God made the temple holy by being present in a special way (8:10–13, 29).

9:4 if you will walk. The attention shifts to the conduct of Solomon and future kings. As stated previously (2:3, 4 and notes; 8:25), the future dominion of David's descendants over Israel is contingent on their fidelity to the Torah.

9:7 cut off. The presence of the temple is not an unchangeable guarantee against the consequences of prolonged covenant infidelity (6:13 note). The covenant curses will come into effect if the king and people are unfaithful (Deut. 28:37; Jer. 19:8).

9:9 abandoned. Other peoples will understand the cause of the unusual spectacle of God destroying His own temple and exiling His people (Deut. 29:24–28).

9:10–10:29 This section highlights Solomon's glory by summarizing his building projects (9:10–28), his fame (10:1–13), and his great riches (10:14–29).

9:10 At the end of twenty years. Given the earlier chronological notices (6:1, 37, 38; 7:1), this would be around 946 B.C.

9:11 Solomon gave to Hiram twenty cities. Although Solomon and Hiram had made an earlier agreement (5:1–12), it appears that Solomon was now in financial difficulty. In exchange for Hiram sending Solomon 120 talents (4 1/2 tons) of gold (v. 14), Solomon granted Hiram the use of twenty cities in Galilee (cf. 2 Chr. 8:2 and note).

9:14 120 talents of gold. At first glance, this seems like a huge amount of gold. Nevertheless, the gold Solomon received from Hiram is not as much as the 150 talents of gold Tiglath-pileser III of Assyria claimed to have received from Tyre in about 730 B.C.

9:15 the Millo. As the city of Jerusalem expanded northward along the Ophel ridge, it was necessary to build supporting earthworks for the

and [d]Hazor and [e]Megiddo and Gezer
16 (Pharaoh king of Egypt had gone up and
captured Gezer and burned it with fire,
and had killed [f]the Canaanites who lived
in the city, and had given it as dowry to
[g]his daughter, Solomon's wife; 17 so
Solomon rebuilt Gezer) and [h]Lower Beth-
horon 18 and Baalath and Tamar in the
wilderness, in the land of Judah,[1] 19 and all
the store cities that Solomon had, and [i]the
cities for his chariots, and the cities for [j]his
horsemen, and whatever Solomon [k]desired
to build in Jerusalem, in Lebanon, and in
all the land of his dominion. 20 All the people who were left of the Amorites, the
Hittites, the Perizzites, the Hivites, and the
Jebusites, who were not of the people of
Israel— 21 [l]their descendants who were left
after them in the land, [m]whom the people
of Israel were unable to devote to destruction[2]—[n]these Solomon drafted to be
[o]slaves, and so they are to this day. 22 But
[p]of the people of Israel Solomon made no
slaves. They were the soldiers, they were
his officials, his commanders, his captains, his chariot commanders and his
horsemen.

23 These were the chief officers who were
over Solomon's work: [q]550 [r]who had charge
of the people who carried on the work.

24 But [g]Pharaoh's daughter went up from
the city of David to [s]her own house that
Solomon had built for her. [t]Then he built
[u]the Millo.

25 Three times a year Solomon used to
offer up burnt offerings and peace offerings
on the altar that he built to the LORD, making offerings with it[3] before the LORD. So he
finished the house.

26 King Solomon built a fleet of ships at
[v]Ezion-geber, which is near Eloth on the
shore of the Red Sea, in the land of Edom.
27 And Hiram sent [w]with the fleet his servants, seamen who were familiar with the
sea, together with the servants of Solomon.
28 And they went to [x]Ophir and brought
from there gold, 420 talents, and they
brought it to King Solomon.

The Queen of Sheba

10 [y]Now when [z]the queen of [a]Sheba
heard of the fame of Solomon concerning the name of the LORD, she came [b]to
test him with hard questions. 2 She came to
Jerusalem with a very great retinue, with
camels [c]bearing spices and very much gold
and precious stones. And when she came
to Solomon, she told him all that was on
her mind. 3 And Solomon answered all her
questions; there was nothing hidden from
the king that he could not explain to her.
4 And when the queen of Sheba had seen all
the wisdom of Solomon, the house that he

15 [d]Josh. 11:1 [e]Josh. 17:11
16 [f]Josh. 16:10 [g]ch. 3:1; 7:8
17 [h]See Josh. 10:10
19 [i]ch. 10:26; 2 Chr. 1:14; 9:25 [j]ch. 4:26 [k]ver. 1
21 [l][Judg. 1:21, 27, 29; 3:1] [m][Josh. 15:63; 17:12] [n]Judg. 1:28 [o]Ezra 2:55-58; Neh. 7:57-60; 11:3
22 [p]Lev. 25:39
23 [q][2 Chr. 8:10] [r]ch. 5:16
24 [g][See ver. 16 above] [s]ch. 7:8
[t]ch. 11:27; [2 Sam. 5:9; 2 Chr. 32:5] [u]See ver. 15
26 [v]ch. 22:48; Num. 33:35; Deut. 2:8
27 [w]ch. 10:11
28 [x]ch. 10:11; 22:48; 1 Chr. 29:4; Job 22:24; 28:16; Ps. 45:9; Isai. 13:12
Chapter 10
1 [y]For ver. 1-13, see 2 Chr. 9:1-12 [z][Matt. 12:42; Luke 11:31] [a]Ps. 72:10, 15; Isai. 60:6; Jer. 6:20; Ezek. 27:22, 23; 38:13; Joel 3:8 [b]See Judg. 14:12
2 [c]ver. 10

1 Hebrew lacks *of Judah* 2 That is, set apart (devote) as an offering to the Lord (for destruction) 3 Septuagint lacks *with it*

city's fortifications. The "Millo" (lit. "filling") was apparently such a restraining structure constructed east of the palace to fill in a depression along the ridgetop (cf. v. 24; 11:27; 2 Sam. 5:9; 2 Kin. 12:20; 2 Chr. 32:5).

Hazor and Megiddo and Gezer. These towns are strategically located along major trade routes. Hazor is ten miles north of the Sea of Chinneroth (Galilee); Megiddo is at the opening onto the Jezreel Valley of a strategic pass through the Carmel ridge. Gezer was twenty miles west of Jerusalem. Archaeological excavation has revealed identical Solomonic gates at each of these sites. By fortifying these three sites, Solomon consolidated his control of trade and commerce.

9:16 Pharaoh . . . had gone up and captured Gezer. Gezer had remained in Canaanite hands, despite the Israelite conquest (Josh. 16:10; Judg. 1:29). The pharaoh captured Gezer, perhaps from the Philistines. Since Egypt and Israel had a treaty (3:1), it was in the interest of both countries not to have Gezer in hostile hands.

9:17 Lower Beth-horon. Eleven miles northwest of Jerusalem (cf. Josh. 16:3) at the foot of a strategic pass controlling access to the Judean highlands.

9:18 Baalath. Eight miles northeast of Ashdod, near the Mediterranean coast (cf. Josh. 19:44).

Tamar. Sixteen miles southwest of the Dead Sea (Judg. 1:16. Tamar means "palm"; Ezek. 47:19; 48:28).

9:20 the Amorites, the Hittites, the Perizzites, the Hivites, and the Jebusites. When Israel entered the land of Canaan, they were to destroy completely the nations who were living there (Deut. 7:1; 20:17; Josh. 3:10; 9:1). The Israelites did not do this in any systematic fashion (Josh. 16:10; Judg. 1–2; 3:5), and Solomon's policy was to conscript the descendants of these peoples permanently (v. 21).

9:22 Solomon made no slaves. Solomon conscripted permanently foreign peoples living in the land, but the Israelite workers he conscripted served for fixed periods of time (5:13 note; 12:4 note).

9:26 Ezion-geber. So as not to be dependent on the merchant navies and ports of other nations, Solomon built ships at Ezion-geber, his own port. This was a new venture for Israel, and Solomon enlisted the help of his ally, Hiram of Tyre, who supplied sailors to accompany Solomon's own (v. 27).

Red Sea. That is, the Gulf of Aqaba (Jer. 49:20, 21).

9:28 Ophir. The location of Ophir is disputed (Job 28:16; Ps. 45:9; Is. 13:12). Suggestions include western Arabia, the Horn of Africa, and India.

10:1 Sheba. Two main suggestions for this location are southwest Arabia (modern Yemen) and northern Arabia, the land of the Sabeans (Job 1:15; 6:19; Ps. 72:10).

concerning the name of the LORD. The Queen of Sheba comes to Jerusalem not simply because of Solomon's fame, but because she recognizes the relationship between Solomon's fame and the Lord.

hard questions. Wishing to discover whether Solomon's reputation is deserved, the Queen of Sheba tests him with hard questions (cf. Judg. 14:12).

had built, 5 the food of his table, the seating
of his officials, and the attendance of his
servants, their clothing, his cupbearers,
[d]and his burnt offerings that he offered at
the house of the LORD, there was no more
breath in her.
6 And she said to the king, "The report was
true that I heard in my own land of your
words and of your wisdom, 7 but I did not
believe the reports until I came and my own
eyes had seen it. And behold, the half was
not told me. Your wisdom and prosperity
surpass the report that I heard. 8 [e]Happy are
your men! Happy are your servants, who
continually stand before you and hear your
wisdom! 9 [f]Blessed be the LORD your God,
who has delighted in you and set you on the
throne of Israel! [g]Because the LORD loved
Israel forever, he has made you king, [h]that
you may execute justice and righteousness."
10 [i]Then she gave the king 120 talents[1] of
gold, and a very great quantity of spices and
precious stones. Never again came such an
abundance of spices as these that the queen
of Sheba gave to King Solomon.
11 Moreover, [j]the fleet of Hiram, which
brought [k]gold from Ophir, brought from
Ophir a very great amount of almug wood
and precious stones. 12 And the king made of
the almug wood supports for the house of
the LORD and for the king's house, also lyres
and harps for the singers. No such almug
wood has come or been seen to this day.
13 And King Solomon gave to the queen of
Sheba all that she desired, whatever she
asked besides what was given her by the
bounty of King Solomon. So she turned and
went back to her own land with her servants.

Solomon's Great Wealth

14 [l]Now the weight of gold that came to
Solomon in one year was 666 talents of
gold, 15 besides that which came from the
explorers and from the business of the merchants, and from all the kings of the west
and from the governors of the land. 16 King
Solomon made 200 large shields of beaten
gold; 600 shekels[2] of gold went into each
shield. 17 And he made 300[m] shields of beat-
en gold; three minas[3] of gold went into each
shield. And the king put them in [n]the House
of the Forest of Lebanon. 18 The king also
made a great ivory throne and overlaid it
with the finest gold. 19 The throne had six
steps, and at the back of the throne was a
calf's head, and on each side of the seat were
armrests and two lions standing beside the
armrests, 20 while twelve lions stood there,
one on each end of a step on the six steps.
The like of it was never made in any kingdom. 21 All King Solomon's drinking vessels
were of gold, and all the vessels of [n]the
House of the Forest of Lebanon were of pure
gold. None were of silver; silver was not considered as anything in the days of Solomon.
22 For the king had [o]a fleet of ships of
Tarshish at sea with the fleet of Hiram. Once
every three years the fleet of ships of
Tarshish used to come bringing gold, silver,
ivory, apes, and peacocks.[4]

5 [d][1 Chr. 26:16]
8 [e][Prov. 8:34]
9 [f]ch. 5:7 [g]2 Chr. 2:11 [h]2 Sam. 8:15; [Ps. 72:2]
10 [i]ver. 2
11 [j]ch. 9:27 [k]See ch. 9:28
14 [l]For ver. 14-28, see 2 Chr. 9:13-28
17 [m]ch. 14:26 [n]ch. 7:2
21 [n][See ver. 17 above]
22 [o]ch. 22:48; Gen. 10:4; 1 Chr.1:7; 2 Chr. 20:36, 37; Ps. 48:7; 72:10

1 A *talent* was about 75 pounds or 34 kilograms 2 A *shekel* was about 2/5 ounce or 11 grams 3 A *mina* was about 1 1/4 pounds or 0.6 kilogram 4 Or *baboons*

10:5 the food of his table. See notes 2:7 and 4:22.

his cupbearers. The cupbearer was an important post in ancient Near Eastern governments (Gen. 40; 41:9; Neh. 1:11).

10:9 Blessed be the LORD your God. The Queen of Sheba specifically mentions the personal name of the God of Israel in her statement to Solomon (vv. 6–9). Jesus cites the Queen of Sheba in His indictment against the people of His own day (Matt. 12:42; Luke 11:31).

10:11 fleet of Hiram. In addition to helping Solomon build his own fleet, Hiram of Tyre used some of his own ships to transport goods for Solomon (9:26–28; 10:22).

almug wood. Suggestions about the nature of this wood include red sandalwood and juniper.

10:12 lyres and harps for the singers. Israelite royalty probably sponsored musicians to compose appropriate hymns and psalms for worship.

10:13 Solomon gave. They exchanged gifts (v. 10).

10:14 came to Solomon in one year. Annual, steady tribute was necessary to support all of Solomon's major projects and outlays.

10:15 from the explorers . . . merchants. Solomon controlled a large territory on the trade routes north to Mesopotamia and south to Egypt. Tariffs on the goods transported through Israel would have been substantial.

governors of the land. See 4:7–19.

10:16, 17 large shields. These extremely heavy and valuable shields were made chiefly for ceremonial and aesthetic reasons. The use of such shields as a visible sign of a king's wealth and status is not unique to Solomon. After a campaign of about 714 B.C., King Sargon II claims to have taken "six shields of gold" from a temple.

10:18 a great ivory throne. Solomon used the great influx of tribute to support an extravagant lifestyle (vv. 18–21, 23–25). His throne was probably made of wood inlaid with ivory and gold. Ivory carvings plated with gold have been found in the Assyrian royal palaces at Nimrud. Solomon's desire for the finest in furnishings and buildings burdened his subjects (12:4).

10:21 drinking vessels were of gold. Beautiful golden vessels from ancient times have been found in Egypt (thirteenth century B.C.), Ugarit (on the Mediterranean coast in modern Syria, thirteenth century B.C.), and Persia (sixth to fourth centuries B.C.).

10:22 a fleet of ships. These so-called "ships of Tarshish" were built to make long ocean voyages.

with the fleet of Hiram. See note 9:26.

23 [p]Thus King Solomon excelled all the
kings of the earth in riches and in wisdom.
24 And the whole earth sought the presence
of Solomon to hear his wisdom, which God
had put into his mind. 25 Every one of them
brought his present, articles of silver and
gold, garments, myrrh, spices, horses, and
mules, so much year by year.

26 [q]And Solomon gathered together [r]char-
iots and horsemen. He had 1,400 chariots
and 12,000 horsemen, whom he stationed
in the [s]chariot cities and with the king in
Jerusalem. 27 And the king made silver as
common in Jerusalem as stone, and he
made cedar as plentiful as [t]the sycamore of
the Shephelah. 28 And Solomon's [u]import
of horses was from Egypt and Kue, and the
king's traders received them from Kue at a
price. 29 A chariot could be imported from
Egypt for 600 shekels of silver and a horse
for 150, and so through the king's traders
they were exported to all the kings of [v]the
Hittites and the kings of Syria.

Solomon Turns from the LORD

11 Now [w]King Solomon loved many foreign women, along with the daughter of Pharaoh: Moabite, Ammonite,
Edomite, Sidonian, and Hittite women,
2 from the nations concerning which the
LORD had said to the people of Israel, [x]"You
shall not enter into marriage with them,
neither shall they with you, for surely they
will turn away your heart after their gods."
Solomon clung to these in love. 3 He had
700 wives, princesses, and 300 concubines. And his wives turned away his heart.
4 For when Solomon was old his wives
turned away his heart after other gods, and
[y]his heart was not wholly true to the LORD
his God, [z]as was the heart of David his
father. 5 For Solomon went after [a]Ashtoreth
the goddess of the Sidonians, and after
[b]Milcom the abomination of the Ammonites. 6 So Solomon did what was evil in
the sight of the LORD and did not wholly
follow the LORD, as David his father had
done. 7 Then Solomon built a high place
for [c]Chemosh the abomination of Moab,
and for [d]Molech the abomination of the
Ammonites, on the mountain east of Jerusalem. 8 And so he did for all his foreign
wives, who made offerings and sacrificed
to their gods.

The LORD Raises Adversaries

9 And the LORD was angry with Solomon,
because [e]his heart had turned away from
the LORD, the God of Israel, [f]who had
appeared to him twice 10 and [g]had commanded him concerning this thing, that he
should not go after other gods. But he did
not keep what the LORD commanded.
11 Therefore the LORD said to Solomon,
"Since this has been your practice and you
have not kept my covenant and my statutes
that I have commanded you, [h]I will surely
tear the kingdom from you and will give it
to your servant. 12 Yet for the sake of David
your father I will not do it in your days, but

23 [p][ch. 3:12, 13; 4:30]
26 [q]For ver. 26-29, see 2 Chr. 1:14-17 [r][ch. 4:26; 2 Chr. 9:25] [s]ch. 9:19
27 [t]1 Chr. 27:28
28 [u]2 Chr. 9:28; [Deut. 17:16]
29 [v]Judg. 1:26
Chapter 11
1 [w]Neh. 13:26; [Deut. 17:17]
2 [x]See Ex. 34:16
4 [y][ch. 8:61] [z]ch. 9:4
5 [a]ver. 33; Judg. 2:13; 2 Kin. 23:13 [b][ver. 7]
7 [c]Num. 21:29; 2 Kin. 23:13 [d]Lev. 18:21; 20:2-4; 2 Kin. 23:10; Acts 7:43; [ver. 5]
9 [e]ver. 2, 4 [f]ch. 3:5; 9:2
10 [g]ch. 6:12; 9:6
11 [h]ver. 31; [ch. 12:15, 16]

10:26 chariots and horsemen. The "law of the king" in Deut. 17:16 forbids the monarch to accumulate great numbers of chariots and horses.

10:28 Egypt and Kue. Kue was in what is now Turkey. It may be that "Egypt" (Hebrew *misrayim*) has been confused with "Musri," also in Turkey (see also 2 Kin. 7:6). Solomon may have financed the buildup of his own military forces by his trading in the famous Cilician horses and the superior chariots of Egypt (v. 29).

10:29 imported . . . they were exported. Not only did Solomon amass chariots and horses, he also initiated substantial trade in these commodities through "the king's traders" (v. 28). In doing this Solomon was exploiting Israel's strategic geographic location.

the kings of the Hittites. The Hittites lived in Anatolia (Asia Minor). During Solomon's reign they were no longer the unified empire they had been between 1375–1240 B.C. They were now ruled by a number of minor kings, each with his own domain.

11:1 loved many foreign women. Whereas in the first part of his reign, "Solomon loved the LORD, walking in the statutes of David his father" (3:3), he later "loved many foreign women." Diplomatic marriages between the dynasties of various kingdoms were common in the ancient Near East as a means of ratifying treaties, but the multiplication of royal wives is forbidden in Deut. 17:17. Moreover, there were prohibitions against marrying foreign wives in the land Israel was to possess (Ex. 34:16; Deut. 7:1–4; Josh. 23:12, 13).

11:2 turn away your heart. The phrase alludes to the warning of Deut. 7:4.

11:4 as was the heart of David his father. David is consistently presented as a model king (3:14; 9:4; 14:8; 15:3; 2 Kin. 8:19; 22:2). He was not without sins (2 Sam. 11; 12; 24:1–15; 1 Kin. 15:5), but when he sinned, his repentance was exemplary (2 Sam. 12:16, 17; 24:10–17). David's devotion to God was unparalleled.

11:5 Ashtoreth. The Phoenician goddess of love and fertility, called Astarte by the Greeks (cf. Judg. 2:13; 2 Kin. 23:13).

Milcom. Or Molech. He was the national god of the Ammonites.

11:6 Solomon did what was evil. Solomon's many sins violated fundamental principles of Israelite religion: multiplying wives (v. 1 note), worshiping other gods (Ex. 20:3, 5), and building sanctuaries for the foreign gods (vv. 7, 8; Ex. 20:4).

11:7 Chemosh. He was the national god of the Moabites (2 Kin. 3:26, 27). See "Syncretism and Idolatry" at Hos. 2:13.

11:10 after other gods. See 3:14; 9:6–9.

11:11 tear the kingdom from you. See vv. 29–39.

11:12 I will not do it in your days. God's great love for David causes Him to temper His judgment on Solomon in two respects: first, God postpones the division until the reign of Solomon's son; and second, God does not remove the entire kingdom from the Davidic dynasty (v. 13).

I will tear it out of the hand of your son.
13 However, [i]I will not tear away all the
kingdom, but [j]I will give one tribe to your
son, for the sake of David my servant and
for the sake of Jerusalem [k]that I have chosen."
14 And the LORD raised up an adversary
against Solomon, Hadad the Edomite. He
was of the royal house in Edom. 15 For
[l]when David was in Edom, and Joab the
commander of the army went up to bury
the slain, he struck down every male in
Edom 16 (for Joab and all Israel remained
there six months, until he had cut off
every male in Edom). 17 But Hadad fled to
Egypt, together with certain Edomites of
his father's servants, Hadad still being a
little child. 18 They set out from Midian
and came to [m]Paran and took men with
them from Paran and came to Egypt, to
Pharaoh king of Egypt, who gave him a
house and assigned him an allowance of
food and gave him land. 19 And Hadad
found great favor in the sight of Pharaoh,
so that he gave him in marriage the sister
of his own wife, the sister of Tahpenes
the queen. 20 And the sister of Tahpenes
bore him Genubath his son, whom
Tahpenes weaned in Pharaoh's house.
And Genubath was in Pharaoh's house
among the sons of Pharaoh. 21 But when
Hadad heard in Egypt [n]that David slept
with his fathers and that Joab the commander of the army was dead, Hadad said
to Pharaoh, "Let me depart, that I may go
to my own country." 22 But Pharaoh said
to him, "What have you lacked with me
that you are now seeking to go to your
own country?" And he said to him, "Only
let me depart."
23 God also raised up as an adversary to
him, Rezon the son of Eliada, who had fled
from his master [o]Hadadezer king of Zobah.
24 And he gathered men about him and
became leader of a marauding band, [p]after
the killing by David. And they went to
Damascus and lived there and made him
king in Damascus. 25 He was an adversary
of Israel all the days of Solomon, doing
harm as Hadad did. And he loathed Israel
and reigned over Syria.
26 [q]Jeroboam the son of Nebat, [r]an
Ephraimite of Zeredah, a servant of Solomon, whose mother's name was Zeruah, a
widow, also [s]lifted up his hand against the
king. 27 And this was the reason why he lifted up his hand against the king. [t]Solomon
built the Millo, and closed up the breach of
the city of David his father. 28 The man
Jeroboam was very able, and when Solomon
saw that the young man was industrious he
gave him charge over all the forced labor of
the house of Joseph. 29 And at that time,
when Jeroboam went out of Jerusalem, the
prophet [u]Ahijah the Shilonite found him on
the road. Now Ahijah had dressed himself
in a new garment, and the two of them were
alone in the open country. 30 Then Ahijah
laid hold of the new garment that was on
him, [v]and tore it into twelve pieces. 31 And

13 [i][2 Sam. 7:15; Ps. 89:33] [j]ver. 32, 36; [ch. 12:20] [k]Deut. 12:5, 11
15 [l]2 Sam. 8:14; 1 Chr. 18:12, 13
18 [m]Num. 10:12; Deut. 33:2
21 [n]ch. 2:10
23 [o][2 Sam. 10:16]
24 [p]2 Sam. 8:3; 10:8, 18
26 [q]ch. 12:2; 2 Chr. 13:6 [r]1 Sam. 1:1 [s]2 Sam. 20:21
27 [t]ch. 9:24; [2 Sam. 5:9]
29 [u]ch. 12:15; 14:2; 15:29; 2 Chr. 9:29
30 [v][1 Sam. 15:27]

11:13 one tribe. This probably refers to Judah (12:20; 2 Kin. 17:18). If Judah is already understood without being mentioned, another tribe is meant, such as Benjamin (12:21) or Simeon.

for the sake of Jerusalem. Jerusalem was God's chosen city, the site of Israel's central sanctuary anticipated in Deut. 12 and constructed by Solomon. Jerusalem is a central symbol of God's love for His people and the communion between God and His people throughout the Bible (Ps. 68:29; 122:2–6; 135:21; 137:5–7; Is. 62:1; Dan. 9:25; Rev. 3:12; 21:2, 10).

11:15 when David was in Edom. See 2 Sam. 8:14. An earlier victory by Joab is reversed, as Hadad returns from exile in Egypt and successfully rebels against Solomon (v. 25).

11:18 from Midian. The Midianites lived east of Moab and Edom.

Paran. This area was in the Sinai peninsula southeast of Kadesh.

gave him a house. Taking notice of the emerging power of David, Pharaoh was ready to shelter David's foes in the hope that one day they would curtail Israel's power (v. 21). Ancient treaties forbid providing asylum to political rebels.

11:22 Only let me depart. Following David's death, Hadad wanted to return to his own land, despite the Pharaoh's objections, probably because he wanted to liberate it from Israelite domination (v. 25).

11:23 adversary. Formerly Solomon could boast that in his reign there was "neither adversary nor misfortune" (5:4), but now God afflicted him with a succession of enemies.

Hadadezer king of Zobah. On David's conquest of Hadadezer and Syria, see 2 Sam. 8:3–6; 10:15–19.

11:24 king in Damascus. From his base in Damascus, Rezon persistently caused trouble for Solomon.

11:26–43 Jeroboam rebels against Solomon and escapes to Egypt until Solomon's death.

11:26 Jeroboam the son of Nebat . . . against the king. Whereas Hadad and Rezon are external enemies raised up by God, Jeroboam, an Ephraimite, is an internal foe.

Zeredah. Twenty-one miles east of Joppa in the territory of Ephraim.

11:27 the Millo. See note 9:15.

11:28 over all the forced labor of the house of Joseph. Jeroboam was in charge of the laborers Solomon drafted from the tribes of Ephraim and Manasseh (5:13–16), and was well aware of the resentment these tribes felt toward Solomon (12:4).

11:29 Shilonite. Shiloh was in Ephraim, about twelve miles east of Zeredah.

11:30 tore it into twelve pieces. Ahijah performs a symbolic action, that is, he acts out a parable. Such colorful actions dramatize the reality

he said to Jeroboam, "Take for yourself ten
pieces, for thus says the LORD, the God of
Israel, 'Behold, [w]I am about to tear the kingdom from the hand of Solomon and will
give you ten tribes 32 (but [x]he shall have one
tribe, for the sake of my servant David and
for the sake of Jerusalem, [y]the city that I
have chosen out of all the tribes of Israel),
33 because they have[1] forsaken me [z]and worshiped Ashtoreth the goddess of the Sidonians, Chemosh the god of Moab, and
Milcom the god of the Ammonites, and they
have not walked in my ways, doing what is
right in my sight and keeping my statutes
and my rules, as David his father did.
34 Nevertheless, I will not take the whole
kingdom out of his hand, but I will make
him ruler all the days of his life, for the sake
of David my servant whom I chose, who
kept my commandments and my statutes.
35 [a]But I will take the kingdom out of his
son's hand and will give it to you, ten tribes.
36 Yet to his son [x]I will give one tribe, that
David my servant may always have [b]a lamp
before me in Jerusalem, [y]the city where I
have chosen to put my name. 37 And I will
take you, and you shall reign over all that
your soul desires, and you shall be king over
Israel. 38 And if you will listen to all that I
command you, and will walk in my ways,
and do what is right in my eyes by keeping
my statutes and my commandments, as
David my servant did, [c]I will be with you
and [d]will build you a sure house, as I built
for David, and I will give Israel to you. 39 And
I will afflict the offspring of David because of
this, but not forever.'" 40 Solomon sought
therefore to kill Jeroboam. But Jeroboam
arose and fled into Egypt, to [e]Shishak king
of Egypt, and was in Egypt until the death of
Solomon.

41 [f]Now the rest of the acts of Solomon,
and all that he did, and his wisdom, are
they not written in the Book of the Acts of
Solomon? 42 And the time that Solomon
reigned in Jerusalem over all Israel was
forty years. 43 And Solomon [g]slept with his
fathers and was buried in the city of David
his father. And [h]Rehoboam his son reigned
in his place.

Rehoboam's Folly

12 [i]Rehoboam went to [j]Shechem, for
all Israel had come to Shechem to
make him king. 2 And as soon as [k]Jeroboam
the son of Nebat heard of it (for [l]he was
still in Egypt, where he had fled from King
Solomon), then Jeroboam returned from[2]
Egypt. 3 And they sent and called him, and
Jeroboam and all the assembly of Israel
came and said to Rehoboam, 4 [m]"Your

31 [w]ver. 11-13
32 [x]ver. 13; ch. 12:21 [y]ch. 14:21; See Deut. 12:5
33 [z]ver. 5, 7
35 [a]ver. 12; ch. 12:16, 17
36 [x][See ver. 32 above] [b]ch. 15:4; 2 Sam. 21:17; 2 Kin. 8:19; 2 Chr. 21:7 [y][See ver. 32 above]
38 [c]Josh. 1:5 [d]1 Sam. 2:35; 2 Sam. 7:11, 27
40 [e]ch. 14:25; 2 Chr. 12:2, 5, 7, 9
41 [f]For ver. 41-43, see 2 Chr. 9:29-31
43 [g]ch. 2:10; 14:20 [h]Matt. 1:7

Chapter 12
1 [i]For ver. 1-19, see 2 Chr. 10:1-19 [j][Judg. 9:6]
2 [k]ch. 11:26 [l]ch. 11:40
4 [m]ch. 4:7, 22; 9:15; See 1 Sam. 8:11-18

[1] Septuagint, Syriac, Vulgate *he has*; twice in this verse [2] Septuagint, Vulgate (compare 2 Chronicles 10:2); Hebrew *lived in*

of the spoken word and God's intervention in history (cf. 22:11; Is. 20; Jer. 13:1–11). In this case, the torn pieces of Ahijah's robe illustrate the impending division of the kingdom.

11:31 Take for yourself ten pieces. On behalf of the Lord, Ahijah summons Jeroboam to take ten of the twelve pieces, symbolizing the ten northern tribes over which Jeroboam will shortly become king. As with the earlier rebellions of Hadad and Rezon, Jeroboam's insurrection is a divine judgment against Solomon.

11:32 one tribe. See note on v. 13.

11:34 I will make him ruler. See note on v. 12.

11:35 out of his son's hand. That is, from Solomon's successor, Rehoboam (12:1–24).

11:36 that David my servant may always have a lamp. The metaphor of a lamp signifies the permanence of the Davidic dynasty in the city of Jerusalem (15:4; 2 Sam. 21:17; 2 Kin. 8:19; 2 Chr. 21:7; Ps. 132:17).

11:37 over all that your soul desires. A similar promise is given to David (2 Sam. 3:21).

king over Israel. That is, over the ten northern tribes. During the period of the divided kingdom, the term "Israel" most often designates these ten tribes. "Judah" denotes the domain still ruled by David's descendants.

11:38 listen to all that I command you. Jeroboam will be subject to the same covenantal stipulations that were operative for Saul, David, and Solomon (2:3, 4 and notes).

I will be with you. These words are an assurance of God's presence and sustenance (Deut. 31:8; Judg. 2:18; 6:12, 16; 1 Sam. 3:19; 2 Sam. 5:10; 7:9). Ahijah hopes that Jeroboam will be more loyal to the covenant than Solomon.

11:39 but not forever. This phrase looks forward to a restoration of Davidic power. Such a restoration was attempted by Josiah of Judah, but he could not complete it (2 Kin. 22; 23). The prophets also look for a renewal of Davidic rule (Jer. 30:9; Ezek. 34:23; 37:15–28; Hos. 3:5; Amos 9:11). These hopes are fulfilled in Jesus Christ, the Messiah (Matt. 1:1; Mark 1:1).

11:40 Shishak. Shishak was the first king over the twenty-second dynasty and ruled from 945–924 B.C. (14:25, 26). Solomon was married to a daughter of a pharaoh from the twenty-first dynasty (3:1 note).

11:41 the Book of the Acts of Solomon. One of the sources (no longer in existence) used by the writer of 1 and 2 Kings. Other official sources are mentioned in 14:19 and 29.

11:42 forty years. Approximately 970–930 B.C.

12:1–24 King Rehoboam's refusal to listen to the people's request to lighten their burden sparks secession by the northern tribes. From this point on the northern kingdom is usually referred to as Israel, and the southern kingdom as Judah.

12:1 Shechem. This major Israelite center associated with the renewal of the covenant with the Lord (Josh. 24:1–33) was in northern Ephraim, thirty miles north of Jerusalem.

to make him king. Rehoboam traveled to Shechem to be made king by acclamation (see 1 Sam. 11:15 and the covenant the northern tribes made with David in 2 Sam. 5:1–3). As it turned out, the northern tribes did not accept Rehoboam.

12:2 as soon as Jeroboam . . . heard of it. That is, about the death of Solomon (11:43).

father made our yoke heavy. Now therefore
lighten the hard service of your father and
his heavy yoke on us, and we will serve
you." 5 He said to them, [n]"Go away for
three days, then come again to me." So the
people went away.
6 Then King Rehoboam took counsel
with the old men, who had stood before
Solomon his father while he was yet alive,
saying, "How do you advise me to answer
this people?" 7 And they said to him, "If
you will be a servant to this people today
and serve them, and speak good words to
them when you answer them, then they
will be your servants forever." 8 But he
abandoned the counsel that the old men
gave him and took counsel with the young
men who had grown up with him and
stood before him. 9 And he said to them,
"What do you advise that we answer this
people who have said to me, 'Lighten the
yoke that your father put on us'?" 10 And
the young men who had grown up with
him said to him, "Thus shall you speak to
this people who said to you, 'Your father
made our yoke heavy, but you lighten it for
us,' thus shall you say to them, 'My little
finger is thicker than my father's thighs.
11 And now, whereas [m]my father laid on you
a heavy yoke, I will add to your yoke. My
father disciplined you with whips, but I
will discipline you with scorpions.'"
12 So Jeroboam and all the people came
to Rehoboam the third day, as the king
said, [o]"Come to me again the third day."
13 And the king answered the people harshly, and forsaking the counsel that the old
men had given him, 14 he spoke to them
according to the counsel of the young men,
saying, [m]"My father made your yoke heavy,
but I will add to your yoke. My father disciplined you with whips, but I will discipline you with scorpions." 15 So the king
did not listen to the people, for [p]it was a
turn of affairs brought about by the LORD
that he might fulfill his word, which [q]the
LORD spoke by Ahijah the Shilonite to
Jeroboam the son of Nebat.

The Kingdom Divided

16 And when all Israel saw that the king
did not listen to them, the people
answered the king, "What portion do we
have in David? We have no inheritance in
the son of Jesse. [r]To your tents, O Israel!
Look now to your own house, David." So
Israel went to their tents. 17 But Rehoboam
reigned over [s]the people of Israel who lived
in the cities of Judah. 18 Then King
Rehoboam sent [t]Adoram, who was
taskmaster over the forced labor, and all
Israel stoned him to death with stones.
And King Rehoboam hurried to mount his
chariot to flee to Jerusalem. 19 [u]So Israel has
been in rebellion against the house of
David to this day. 20 And when all Israel
heard that Jeroboam had returned, they
sent and called him to the assembly and
made him king over all Israel. There was
none that followed the house of David but
[v]the tribe of Judah only.
21 [w]When Rehoboam came to Jerusalem,
he assembled all the house of Judah and
the tribe of Benjamin, 180,000 chosen
warriors, to fight against the house of
Israel, to restore the kingdom to Rehoboam
the son of Solomon. 22 But the word of God
came to [x]Shemaiah the man of God: 23 "Say

5 [n]ver. 12
11 [m][See ver. 4 above]
12 [o]ver. 5
14 [m][See ver. 4 above]
15 [p]ver. 24 [q]ch. 11:11, 31
16 [r]See 2 Sam. 20:1
17 [s]ch. 11:13, 36
18 [t]ch. 4:6; 5:14
19 [u]2 Kin. 17:21
20 [v]ch. 11:13, 32, 36
21 [w]For ver. 21-24, see 2 Chr. 11:1-4
22 [x]2 Chr. 12:5, 7, 15

12:4 Your father made our yoke heavy. The expression "yoke" is characteristically used for the oppression of the Israelites by foreign rulers (Lev. 26:13; Deut. 28:48; Is. 9:4; 10:27; 14:25; Jer. 27:8, 11; Ezek. 34:27). Its use here is an indictment of Solomon for imposing harsh labor on his own people (5:13; 9:22; 11:28 and notes).

12:6 the old men. These older and experienced advisers were well acquainted with the traditions of Israel and understood how the monarchy affected the lives of ordinary Israelites.

12:7 If you will be a servant. Though entrusted with power, the Israelite king was to establish justice and so serve both God and His people (Deut. 17:14–20; Ps. 72).

12:8 the young men. These young advisers, like Rehoboam himself, had grown up in the royal court. Apparently they thought that Rehoboam's privileges were inalienable like those of an oriental monarch.

12:10 My little finger is thicker than my father's thighs. These words are an arrogant and unwise boast about how much more oppressive Rehoboam's yoke will be than his father's (v. 11).

12:15 by the LORD. The writer does not mention God's agency in order to excuse Rehoboam's foolishness. God is using Rehoboam's misguided actions as an instrument for fulfilling Ahijah's prophecy (11:31–39).

12:16 Look now to your own house, David. The northern tribes secede from Judah and from the authority of David's descendants. For an identical taunt against David himself, see 2 Sam. 20:1.

12:17 people of Israel. That is, members of the northern tribes who had settled in the south.

12:18 Adoram. Rehoboam unwisely sent out the chief of forced labor to quell the uprising (4:6; 5:14, where the name is spelled "Adoniram").

all Israel. That is, representatives of the northern tribes (12:1).

12:19 to this day. See 8:8 note.

12:20 to the assembly. Jeroboam does not seem to have played an active role in the assembly at Shechem. Once he is made king, however, he takes charge over Israelite affairs (vv. 25–33).

12:22 the man of God. This common expression designates a prophet (1 Sam. 2:27; 1 Kin. 13:1; 2 Kin. 4:7).

to Rehoboam the son of Solomon, king of
Judah, and to all the house of Judah and
Benjamin, and to the [y]rest of the people,
24 'Thus says the LORD, You shall not go up
or fight against your relatives the people of
Israel. Every man return to his home, [z]for
this thing is from me.'" So they listened to
the word of the LORD and went home
again, according to the word of the LORD.

Jeroboam's Golden Calves

25 Then Jeroboam [a]built Shechem in the
hill country of Ephraim and lived there.
And he went out from there and [b]built
Penuel. 26 And Jeroboam said in his heart,
"Now the kingdom will turn back to the
house of David. 27 If this people [c]go up to
offer sacrifices in the temple of the LORD at
Jerusalem, then the heart of this people
will turn again to their lord, to Rehoboam
king of Judah, and they will kill me and
return to Rehoboam king of Judah." 28 So
the king took counsel and [d]made two
calves of gold. And he said to the people,
"You have gone up to Jerusalem long
enough. [e]Behold your gods, O Israel, who
brought you up out of the land of Egypt."
29 And he set one in Bethel, and the other
he put in Dan. 30 Then [f]this thing became a
sin, for the people went as far as Dan to be
before one.[1] 31 He also made [g]temples on
high places and [h]appointed priests from
among all the people, who were not of the
Levites. 32 And Jeroboam appointed a feast
on the fifteenth day of the eighth month
like [i]the feast that was in Judah, and he
offered sacrifices on the altar. So he did in
Bethel, sacrificing to the calves that he
made. And he placed in Bethel [j]the priests
of the high places that he had made. 33 He
went up to the altar that he had made in
Bethel on the fifteenth day in the eighth
month, in the month that he had devised
from his own heart. And he instituted a
feast for the people of Israel and went up to
the altar [k]to make offerings.

A Man of God Confronts Jeroboam

13 And behold, [l]a man of God came
out of Judah by the word of the
LORD to Bethel. Jeroboam was standing by
the altar [m]to make offerings. 2 [n]And the
man cried against the altar by the word of
the LORD and said, "O altar, altar, thus
says the LORD: 'Behold, a son shall be born
to the house of David, [o]Josiah by name,
and he shall sacrifice on you the priests of
the high places who make offerings on
you, and human bones shall be burned on

23 [y][ver. 17]
24 [z]ver. 15
25 [a][Judg. 9:45] [b][Judg. 8:17]
27 [c]Deut. 12:5, 6
28 [d]2 Kin. 10:29; 17:16; 2 Chr. 11:15; 13:8; Hos. 8:5, 6; 10:5; 13:2; [ch. 14:9] [e][Ex. 32:4, 8]
30 [f]ch. 13:34; 2 Kin. 17:21
31 [g]ch. 13:32 [h]ch. 13:33; 2 Kin. 17:32; 2 Chr. 11:14, 15; 13:9
32 [i]Lev. 23:33, 34; Num. 29:12 [j]ch. 13:2; [Amos 7:13]
33 [k]ch. 13:1
Chapter 13
1 [l]2 Kin. 23:17 [m]ch. 12:33
2 [n]ver. 32 [o]2 Kin. 23:15, 16

1 Septuagint *went to the one at Bethel and to the other as far as Dan*

12:23 the rest of the people. Probably a reference to members of the northern tribes who had settled in Judah (v. 17).

12:24 return to his home, for this thing is from me. The prophet Shemaiah reaffirms what the prophet Ahijah had earlier declared (11:29–39): the division of the kingdom conforms to the will of God. The existence of two realms is ordained by God, and each now has the opportunity to prove their loyalty to His covenant.

12:25–33 In an effort to retain the people's loyalty, Jeroboam makes golden calves at Bethel and Dan and institutes a counter-system of worship for Israel.

12:25 Penuel. Jeroboam consolidates his rule by fortifying Shechem and Penuel, two critical cities along the River Jabbok.

12:27 If this people go up to offer sacrifices. Jeroboam fears that religious unity between north and south will lead to a return to political unity as well.

12:28 two calves of gold. Canaanites characteristically depicted their gods standing on bulls, calves, or other animals. Jeroboam probably prepared his golden calves as a kind of throne platform for God, and not as images of the Lord. Nevertheless, his innovation was an invitation for Canaanite religious practices to enter the northern kingdom (cf. Ex. 32:4).

12:29 Bethel, and . . . Dan. These sites are the centers farthest south and north in Jeroboam's kingdom. Bethel (lit. "house of God") was a historic Israelite worship center (Gen. 12:8; 28:11–19; 35:6, 7; Judg. 20:26–28; 1 Sam. 7:16).

12:30 this thing became a sin. The establishment of national religious centers in competition with the one in Jerusalem is repeatedly referred to in the books of Kings as the sin of Jeroboam (13:34; 14:16; 15:26, 30; 16:2; 2 Kin. 3:3; 10:29; 13:2; 17:22). Unfortunately, every northern king followed the path first blazed by Jeroboam. None of them tried to institute a thorough reform. Without determined opposition, the sin of Jeroboam brought about the deterioration and demise of Israel (2 Kin. 17:22, 23).

12:31 temples on high places. See note 3:2. By promoting worship at the high places, Jeroboam introduced further innovations into his cult.

priests from among all the people. Jeroboam created his own priesthood, without regard to their priestly qualifications or Levitical genealogy (Deut. 18:1–8; Judg. 17:10–13).

12:32 appointed a feast. Perhaps he imitated the Feast of Booths (Lev. 23:34; 1 Kin. 8:2).

12:33 the month that he had devised. That is, one not sanctioned by God. By instituting his own religious centers, festival, and priesthood, Jeroboam deliberately wished to disassociate himself and his people from the Jerusalem temple and the worship practiced there. This clearly goes against the intent of Jeroboam's commission from God as described in 11:36–39 and 12:15, which mandated a political but not a religious separation between Israel and Judah. Loyalty to the covenant (11:38) requires loyalty to the temple established for God's honor and to its priests, festivals, and sacrifices.

13:1 man of God. See note 12:22.

Judah. God sent a southern prophet to denounce Jeroboam's northern cult.

13:2 Josiah. He ruled Judah 640–609 B.C., three hundred years after Jeroboam.

sacrifice . . . the priests of the high places. This prophecy is realized during Josiah's reign (2 Kin. 23:15–20). By burning human bones on the altar, Josiah desecrated it and made it unfit for continued use as a sacred precinct.

you.'" 3 And he gave [p]a sign the same day,
saying, "This is the sign that the LORD has
spoken: 'Behold, the altar shall be torn
down, and the ashes that are on it shall be
poured out.'" 4 And when the king heard
the saying of the man of God, which he
cried against the altar at Bethel, Jeroboam
stretched out his hand from the altar, saying, "Seize him." And his hand, which he
stretched out against him, dried up, so
that he could not draw it back to himself.
5 The altar also was torn down, and the
ashes poured out from the altar, according
to the sign that the man of God had given
by the word of the LORD. 6 And the king
said to the man of God, [q]"Entreat now the
favor of the LORD your God, and pray for
me, that my hand may be restored to me."
And the man of God entreated the LORD,
and the king's hand was restored to him and
became as it was before. 7 And the king said
to the man of God, "Come home with me,
and refresh yourself, and [r]I will give you a
reward." 8 And the man of God said to the
king, [s]"If you give me half your house, [t]I
will not go in with you. And I will not eat
bread or drink water in this place, 9 for so
was it commanded me by the word of the
LORD, saying, 'You shall neither eat bread
nor drink water nor return by the way that
you came.'" 10 So he went another way and
did not return by the way that he came to
Bethel.

The Prophet's Disobedience

11 Now [u]an old prophet lived in Bethel.
And his sons[1] came and told him all that
the man of God had done that day in
Bethel. They also told to their father the
words that he had spoken to the king.
12 And their father said to them, "Which
way did he go?" And his sons showed him
the way that the man of God who came
from Judah had gone. 13 And he said to his
sons, "Saddle the donkey for me." So they
saddled the donkey for him and he mounted it. 14 And he went after the man of God
and found him sitting under an oak. And
he said to him, "Are you the man of God
who came from Judah?" And he said, "I
am." 15 Then he said to him, "Come home
with me and eat bread." 16 And he said, [v]"I
may not return with you, or go in with you,
neither will I eat bread nor drink water
with you in this place, 17 for it was said to
me [w]by the word of the LORD, 'You shall
neither eat bread nor drink water there, nor
return by the way that you came.'" 18 And
he said to him, "I also am a prophet as you
are, and an angel spoke to me by the word
of the LORD, saying, 'Bring him back with
you into your house that he may eat bread
and drink water.'" But he lied to him. 19 So
he went back with him and ate bread in his
house and drank water.

20 And as they sat at the table, the word
of the LORD came to the prophet who had
brought him back. 21 And he cried to the
man of God who came from Judah, "Thus
says the LORD, 'Because you have disobeyed the word of the LORD and have not
kept the command that the LORD your God
commanded you, 22 but have come back
and have eaten bread and drunk water in
the place of which he said to you, "Eat no
bread and drink no water," your body shall
not come to the tomb of your fathers.'"
23 And after he had eaten bread and drunk,
he saddled the donkey for the prophet
whom he had brought back. 24 And as he
went away [x]a lion met him on the road and
killed him. And his body was thrown in the
road, and the donkey stood beside it; the

3 [p] See Judg. 6:17
6 [q] Ex. 8:8; 9:28; 10:17; Num. 21:7; Acts 8:24
7 [r] [1 Sam. 9:7; 2 Kin. 5:15]
8 [s] Num. 22:18; 24:13 [t] ver. 16, 17
11 [u] ver. 25; [2 Kin. 23:18]
16 [v] ver. 8, 9
17 [w] ch. 20:35; 1 Thess. 4:15
24 [x] ch. 20:36

1 Septuagint, Syriac, Vulgate; Hebrew *son*

13:3 sign. The prophets sometimes gave a sign, an immediate proof, to corroborate a prophecy (2 Kin. 19:29; 20:8–11; Jer. 44:29, 30).

the ashes that are on it shall be poured out. The altar was thereby profaned (Lev. 6:10–13).

13:5 The altar also was torn down. This sign (v. 3) confirms the prophecy about Josiah and shows God's condemnation of Jeroboam's religious system.

13:6 that my hand may be restored. God, in generously healing Jeroboam's hand, reaffirms the authority of His prophet.

13:8 eat bread or drink water. For the prophet to accept this hospitality would imply his approval of Jeroboam's policies.

13:9 You shall neither eat . . . nor drink . . . nor return. The prophet has explicit instructions from God about his personal conduct (v. 17).

13:11 lived in Bethel. The old prophet is from the north, unlike the man of God from Judah.

13:18 he lied to him. The man of God from Judah could not have known this, except that the new revelation violated his own orders from God.

13:20 the word of the LORD. Ironically, God uses the old "lying" prophet of Bethel to deliver a true prophecy (v. 18).

13:22 your body shall not come to the tomb of your fathers. It was considered important to be buried along with one's ancestors in the family burial plot (1:21; Gen. 47:30; Josh. 24:32; 2 Sam. 2:32; 17:23).

13:24 the donkey . . . lion. The strange behavior of the animals is understood to be miraculous, and when news of it reaches the old prophet he immediately understands its significance.

lion also stood beside the body. 25 And
behold, men passed by and saw the body
thrown in the road and the lion standing
by the body. And they came and told it in
the city where [y]the old prophet lived.
26 And when the prophet who had
brought him back from the way heard of it,
he said, "It is the man of God who disobeyed the word of the LORD; therefore the
LORD has given him to the lion, which has
torn him and killed him, according to the
word that the LORD spoke to him." 27 And he
said to his sons, "Saddle the donkey for
me." And they saddled it. 28 And he went
and found his body thrown in the road, and
the donkey and the lion standing beside the
body. The lion had not eaten the body or
torn the donkey. 29 And the prophet took up
the body of the man of God and laid it on
the donkey and brought it back to the city[1]
to mourn and to bury him. 30 And he laid the
body in his own grave. And they mourned
over him, saying, [z]"Alas, my brother!" 31 And
after he had buried him, he said to his sons,
"When I die, bury me in the grave in which
the man of God is buried; [a]lay my bones
beside his bones. 32 [b]For the saying that he
called out by the word of the LORD against
the altar in Bethel and against [c]all the houses of the high places that are in the cities of
[d]Samaria shall surely come to pass."
33 After this thing Jeroboam did not turn
from his evil way, but made priests for the
high places again from among all the people. Any who would, he ordained to be
priests of the high places. 34 [e]And this thing
became sin to the house of Jeroboam, [f]so
as to cut it off and to destroy it from the
face of the earth.

Prophecy Against Jeroboam

14 At that time Abijah the son of
Jeroboam fell sick. 2 And Jeroboam
said to his wife, "Arise, and disguise yourself, that it not be known that you are the
wife of Jeroboam, and go to [g]Shiloh.
Behold, Ahijah the prophet is there, [h]who
said of me that I should be king over this
people. 3 [i]Take with you ten loaves, some
cakes, and a jar of honey, and go to him.
He will tell you what shall happen to the
child."
4 Jeroboam's wife did so. She arose and
went to [g]Shiloh and came to the house of
[j]Ahijah. Now [j]Ahijah could not see, for his
eyes were dim because of his age. 5 And the
LORD said to [j]Ahijah, "Behold, the wife of
Jeroboam is coming to inquire of you concerning her son, for he is sick. Thus and
thus shall you say to her."
When she came, she pretended to be
another woman. 6 But when [j]Ahijah heard
the sound of her feet, as she came in at the
door, he said, "Come in, wife of Jeroboam.
Why do you pretend to be another? For I
am charged with unbearable news for you.
7 Go, tell Jeroboam, 'Thus says the LORD,
the God of Israel: [k]"Because I exalted you
from among the people and made you
leader over my people Israel 8 and [l]tore the
kingdom away from the house of David
and gave it to you, and yet you have not
been [m]like my servant David, who kept my
commandments and followed me with all
his heart, doing only that which was right
in my eyes, 9 but you have done evil above
all who were before you and have gone and
[n]made for yourself other gods and [o]metal
images, provoking me to anger, and [p]have
cast me behind your back, 10 therefore
behold, I will bring harm upon the house
of Jeroboam and [q]will cut off from
Jeroboam every male, [r]both bond and free
in Israel, and [s]will burn up the house of
Jeroboam, as a man burns up dung until
it is all gone. 11 [t]Anyone belonging to
Jeroboam who dies in the city the dogs
shall eat, and anyone who dies in the open
country the birds of the heavens shall eat,

25 [y]ver. 11
30 [z][Jer. 22:18]
31 [a][2 Kin. 23:17, 18]
32 [b]ver. 2; See 2 Kin. 23:16-19 [c]ch. 12:31 [d][ch. 16:24]
34 [e]ch. 12:30; 2 Kin. 17:21 [f]ch. 14:10; [ch. 15:29, 30]

Chapter 14
2 [g]See Josh. 18:1 [h]See ch. 11:29-31
3 [i][1 Sam. 9:7, 8]
4 [g][See ver. 2 above] [j]ch. 11:29
5 [j][See ver. 4 above]
6 [j][See ver. 4 above]
7 [k]ch. 16:2; [2 Sam. 12:7, 8]
8 [l]ch. 11:31 [m]ch. 11:33, 38; 15:5; [ch. 9:4]
9 [n]ch. 12:28; 2 Chr. 11:15 [o][Ex. 34:17] [p]Ezek. 23:35; [Neh. 9:26; Ps. 50:17]
10 [q]ch. 21:21; 2 Kin. 9:8 [r]Deut. 32:36; 2 Kin.14:26 [s]ch. 16:3
11 [t]ch. 16:4; 21:24

1 Septuagint; Hebrew *he came to the city of the old prophet*

13:30 Alas, my brother. This lament is appropriate for an equal and not for a superior (cf. Jer. 22:18).

13:31 lay my bones beside his bones. The old prophet identifies himself with the prophecy of the man from Judah by having himself buried in the same tomb. When Josiah later desecrates the Bethel altar, he does not disturb the bones out of respect for the prophet from Judah (2 Kin. 23:17, 18).

13:34 sin to the house of Jeroboam. See note 12:30.

14:1 Abijah the son of Jeroboam fell sick. People in Old Testament times sometimes looked to prophets to heal diseases (2 Kin. 4:18–22; 5:1–14) or to predict the fate of someone who was ill (2 Kin. 1:2–4; 8:8).

14:2 disguise yourself. Jeroboam evidently feared the prophet and thought his son would be treated better if he was not associated with him.

14:3 take . . . ten loaves. Jeroboam's wife is to carry these gifts fit for a commoner but not for royalty (1 Sam. 9:6–8; 2 Kin. 5:15; 8:8), to ingratiate herself with Ahijah.

14:11 dogs shall eat . . . the birds of the heavens. See Deut. 28:26. Such curses are typical of the ancient world, including Homer (Iliad 1.4).

for the LORD has spoken it.”’ 12 Arise therefore, go to your house. [u]When your feet
enter the city, the child shall die. 13 And all
Israel shall mourn for him and bury him,
for he only of Jeroboam shall come to the
grave, because in him [v]there is found
something pleasing to the LORD, the God
of Israel, in the house of Jeroboam.
14 [w]Moreover, the LORD will raise up for
himself a king over Israel who shall cut off
the house of Jeroboam today. And henceforth, 15 the LORD will strike Israel as a reed
is shaken in the water, and [x]root up Israel
out of [y]this good land that he gave to their
fathers and scatter them [z]beyond the
Euphrates, because they have made their
[a]Asherim, provoking the LORD to anger.
16 And he will give Israel up because of the
sins of Jeroboam, which he sinned and
made Israel to sin.”

17 Then Jeroboam’s wife arose and
departed and came to [b]Tirzah. And [c]as she
came to the threshold of the house, the
child died. 18 And all Israel buried him and
mourned for him, [d]according to the word
of the LORD, which he spoke by his servant
Ahijah the prophet.

The Death of Jeroboam

19 Now the rest of the acts of Jeroboam,
[e]how he warred and how he reigned,
behold, they are written in the Book of the
Chronicles of the Kings of Israel. 20 And the
time that Jeroboam reigned was twenty-
two years. And he slept with his fathers,
and Nadab his son reigned in his place.

Rehoboam Reigns in Judah

21 [f]Now Rehoboam the son of Solomon
reigned in Judah. Rehoboam was forty-one
years old when he began to reign, and he
reigned seventeen years in Jerusalem, [g]the
city that the LORD had chosen out of all the
tribes of Israel, to put his name there. [h]His
mother’s name was Naamah the Am-
monite. 22 [i]And Judah did what was evil in
the sight of the LORD, and they [j]provoked
him to jealousy with their sins that they
committed, more than all that their fathers
had done. 23 For they also built for themselves [k]high places [l]and pillars and
[m]Asherim on every high hill and [n]under
every green tree, 24 and there were also
[o]male cult prostitutes in the land. They did
according to all the abominations of the
nations that the LORD drove out before the
people of Israel.
25 [p]In the fifth year of King Rehoboam,
Shishak king of Egypt came up against
Jerusalem. 26 He took away the treasures of
the house of the LORD and the treasures of
the king’s house. [q]He took away everything. He also took away all the shields of
gold [r]that Solomon had made, 27 and King
Rehoboam made in their place shields of
bronze, and committed them to the hands

12 [u]ver. 17
13 [v]2 Chr. 12:12; 19:3
14 [w]See ch. 15:27-29
15 [x]Deut. 29:28; Ps. 52:5; Prov. 2:22 [y]Josh. 23:15, 16 [z][2 Kin. 15:29] [a]Ex. 34:13; Deut. 12:3
17 [b]ch. 15:21, 33; 16:6, 8, 15, 23 [c]ver. 12
18 [d]ver. 13
19 [e]See 2 Chr. 13:2-20
21 [f]2 Chr. 12:13 [g]ch. 11:32, 36 [h]2 Chr. 12:13
22 [i][2 Chr. 12:1, 14] [j]See Num. 25:11
23 [k]See Deut. 12:2 [l]See Ex. 23:24 [m]ver. 15 [n]Deut. 12:2; 2 Kin. 16:4; Isai. 57:5; Jer. 2:20
24 [o]See Deut. 23:17
25 [p]2 Chr. 12:2, 9-11
26 [q][ch. 15:18] [r]ch. 10:17

14:15 the LORD will . . . root up Israel out of this good land. The possibility of exile for apostasy is raised in the Mosaic covenant (Deut. 28:63, 64; 29:28), in Joshua’s farewell speech (Josh. 23:15, 16), and in Solomon’s temple prayer (8:33, 34, 46–53).

Asherim. Probably carved figures of the Canaanite goddess Asherah, a consort of Baal (Ex. 34:13; Deut. 12:3; Judg. 3:7).

14:17 Tirzah. Tirzah was fourteen miles west of the Jordan River, about halfway between Jerusalem and the Sea of Chinneroth (Galilee). It was Jeroboam’s place of residence and later the capital of Israel (15:33) until Omri built the city of Samaria (16:24).

as she came to the threshold. The death of Abijah was an indication that Ahijah’s other prophecies would come true (v. 18).

14:19 the rest of the acts. The biblical writer does not claim to write an exhaustive account of Jeroboam’s reign. Rather, he has written what he considers important for his readers to know (Introduction: Characteristics and Themes).

Chronicles of the Kings of Israel. See note 11:41 and Introduction: Author.

14:20 twenty-two years. That is, 930–909 B.C.

14:21–31 These verses summarize the reign of Rehoboam, Solomon’s son and immediate successor. His reign is marked by growing idolatry and immorality, loss of treasures to the king of Egypt, and continual warfare with Jeroboam.

14:21 Rehoboam. The author switches his attention to the southern kingdom, recording events that chronologically overlap with events in the north.

seventeen years. That is, 930–913 B.C.

14:22 Judah. The Septuagint (Old Testament Greek translation) reads “Rehoboam” (cf. 2 Chr. 12:14 which reads “he did evil”).

14:23 high places. See note 3:2.

pillars. Basically stones set up on the ground. Many of these sacred stones were used by the Canaanites in their worship. Such pillars were forbidden in Israel’s law (Ex. 23:24; Lev. 26:1; Deut. 12:3; 16:22).

Asherim. See note on v. 15.

under every green tree. Religious activities carried out near certain trees in Old Testament times were considered of special significance (Deut. 12:2; 2 Kin. 17:10; Is. 57:5; Jer. 2:20; Ezek. 6:13; Hos. 4:13).

14:24 male cult prostitutes. The Canaanites believed that ritual prostitution helped to ensure the fertility of land, flocks, and people. It was forbidden in Israel (Deut. 23:17, 18; 1 Kin. 15:12; 22:46; 2 Kin. 23:7; Hos. 4:14).

14:25 Shishak. He founded the twenty-second dynasty over Egypt and began to rule around 945 B.C. According to Egyptian sources, including a fragment of a stele from Shishak’s campaign, Shishak also invaded Israel and inflicted widespread destruction.

14:26 He took away the treasures. That is, treasures stored in the temple by King Solomon (7:51).

14:27 shields of bronze. The independent kingdom of Judah was too small and too poor to be able to replace Solomon’s shields exactly.

of the officers of the guard, who kept the
door of the king's house. 28 And as often as
the king went into the house of the LORD,
the guard carried them and brought them
back to the guardroom.
29 [s]Now the rest of the acts of Rehoboam
and all that he did, are they not written in
the Book of the Chronicles of the Kings of
Judah? 30 [t]And there was war between
Rehoboam and Jeroboam continually.
31 And Rehoboam slept with his fathers and
was buried with his fathers in the city of
David. [u]His mother's name was Naamah
the Ammonite. And [v]Abijam his son
reigned in his place.

Abijam Reigns in Judah

15 [w]Now in the eighteenth year of King
Jeroboam the son of Nebat, Abijam
began to reign over Judah. 2 He reigned for
three years in Jerusalem. His mother's
name was Maacah the daughter of Abishalom. 3 And he walked in all the sins that
his father did before him, and [x]his heart
was not wholly true to the LORD his God, as
the heart of David his father. 4 Nevertheless, for David's sake the LORD his God
gave him [y]a lamp in Jerusalem, setting up
his son after him, and establishing Jerusalem, 5 because [z]David did what was right
in the eyes of the LORD and did not turn
aside from anything that he commanded
him all the days of his life, [a]except in the
matter of Uriah the Hittite. 6 [b]Now there
was war between Rehoboam and Jeroboam
all the days of his life. 7 [c]The rest of the acts
of Abijam and all that he did, are they not
written in the Book of the Chronicles of the
Kings of Judah? [d]And there was war
between Abijam and Jeroboam. 8 [e]And
Abijam slept with his fathers, and they
buried him in the city of David. And Asa
his son reigned in his place.

Asa Reigns In Judah

9 In the twentieth year of Jeroboam king
of Israel, Asa began to reign over Judah,
10 and he reigned forty-one years in
Jerusalem. His mother's name was Maacah
the daughter of Abishalom. 11 [f]And Asa did
what was right in the eyes of the LORD, as
David his father had done. 12 He put away
the [g]male cult prostitutes out of the land
and removed [h]all the idols that his fathers
had made. 13 [i]He also removed Maacah his
mother from being queen mother because
she had made an abominable image for
Asherah. And Asa cut down her image and
[j]burned it at the brook Kidron. 14 [k]But the
high places were not taken away. Nevertheless, [l]the heart of Asa was wholly true to
the LORD all his days. 15 And [m]he brought
into the house of the LORD the sacred gifts
of his father and his own sacred gifts, silver, and gold, and vessels.
16 [n]And there was war between Asa and
Baasha king of Israel all their days.
17 [o]Baasha king of Israel went up against
Judah and [p]built Ramah, [q]that he might
permit no one to go out or come in to Asa

29 [s]For ver. 29-31, see 2 Chr. 12:15, 16
30 [t]ch. 15:6; [ch. 12:21-24]
31 [u]2 Chr. 12:13 [v][Matt. 1:7]
Chapter 15
1 [w]2 Chr. 13:1, 2
3 [x]ch. 11:4; [ver. 14; ch. 8:61]
4 [y]See ch. 11:36
5 [z]ch. 9:4; 14:8 [a]2 Sam. 11:4, 15; 12:9
6 [b]ch. 14:30
7 [c][2 Chr. 13:22] [d]See 2 Chr. 13:2-20
8 [e]2 Chr. 14:1
11 [f]2 Chr. 14:2
12 [g]See ch. 14:24 [h][2 Chr. 15:8]
13 [i]For ver. 13-15, see 2 Chr. 15:16-18 [j][Ex. 32:20]
14 [k]ch. 22:43; [2 Kin. 12:3; 14:4] [l][ver. 3]
15 [m][ch. 7:51]
16 [n]ver. 32
17 [o]For ver. 17-22, see 2 Chr. 16:1-6 [p]ver. 21, 22 [q][ch. 12:27]

14:29 Book of the Chronicles of the Kings of Judah. See note 11:41.

14:30 war . . . continually. Minor border skirmishes and full-fledged wars between Israel and Judah characterized the early history of the divided monarchy (12:24; 14:19; 15:6; 2 Chr. 13:1–20).

14:31 Naamah the Ammonite. Rehoboam was born of one of Solomon's marriages to foreign women (11:1).

15:2 He reigned for three years in Jerusalem. That is, 913–910 B.C.

His mother's name was Maacah. Probably because of his sources, the author lists the name of the king's mother for the monarchs of Judah only (see Introduction: Chronology).

Abishalom. A variant spelling of "Absalom" (cf. 2 Sam. 3:3; 14:27; 2 Chr. 13:2).

15:3 sins that his father did. See 14:22–24.

the heart of David his father. David was a model king (11:4 note).

15:5 Uriah the Hittite. The husband of Bathsheba and a general in David's army, whom David murdered (2 Sam. 11).

15:7 the Book of the Chronicles of the Kings of Judah. See note 11:41 and Introduction: Author.

war between Abijam and Jeroboam. See note 14:30; 2 Chr. 13:1–20.

15:10 he reigned forty-one years. That is, 910–869 B.C.

Maacah the daughter of Abishalom. See note on v. 2.

15:11 Asa did what was right. Asa earned this praise by expunging Canaanite religious symbols (vv. 12–14).

15:12 male cult prostitutes. See note 14:24.

the idols that his fathers had made. See note 14:23.

15:13 queen mother. The queen mother could at times exercise considerable influence in the royal court (1:11–14, 28–31; 2 Kin. 11:1–20).

brook Kidron. This wadi (seasonal stream bed) runs through the valley that marks the eastern boundary of Jerusalem.

15:14 high places. Such rural centers of worship could be devoted to the Lord, to one of the Canaanite deities, or to some combination of both (3:2 note).

15:15 brought into the house of the LORD. Asa tries to replace some of the treasures lost during Shishak's invasion (14:25, 26).

15:16 war . . . all their days. The reference is most likely not to a full-fledged war, but to a continuing series of skirmishes and battles (14:30 note).

15:17 Ramah. This town was in Benjamin, only six miles north of Jerusalem. Since Ramah was strategically located at the junction of several routes leading into the Judean highlands, the Israelite king could limit access to Jerusalem. Moreover, Israel was much larger than Judah. Baasha's campaign and blockade was a serious threat.

king of Judah. 18 Then Asa took all the silver
and the gold [r]that were left in the treasures
of the house of the LORD and the treasures
of the king's house and gave them into the
hands of his servants. [s]And King Asa sent
them to Ben-hadad the son of Tabrimmon,
the son of Hezion, king of Syria, [t]who lived
in Damascus, saying, 19 "Let there be [u]a
covenant[1] between me and you, as there
was between my father and your father.
Behold, I am sending to you a present of silver and gold. Go, break your covenant with
Baasha king of Israel, that he may withdraw
from me." 20 And Ben-hadad listened to
King Asa and sent the commanders of his
armies against the cities of Israel and conquered [v]Ijon, [w]Dan, [x]Abel-beth-maacah,
and all [y]Chinneroth, with all the land of
Naphtali. 21 And when Baasha heard of it,
[z]he stopped building Ramah, and he lived
in [a]Tirzah. 22 Then King Asa made a proclamation to all Judah, none was exempt, and
they carried away the stones of Ramah and
its timber, with which Baasha had been
building, and with them King Asa built
[b]Geba of Benjamin and [c]Mizpah. 23 [d]Now
the rest of all the acts of Asa, all his might,
and all that he did, and the cities that he
built, are they not written in the Book of the
Chronicles of the Kings of Judah? But in his
old age he was diseased in his feet. 24 And
Asa slept with his fathers and was buried
with his fathers in the city of David his
father, and [e]Jehoshaphat his son reigned in
his place.

Nadab Reigns in Israel

25 [f]Nadab the son of Jeroboam began to
reign over Israel in the second year of Asa
king of Judah, and he reigned over Israel
two years. 26 He did what was evil in the
sight of the LORD [g]and walked in the way of
his father, and in his sin [h]which he made
Israel to sin.
27 [i]Baasha the son of Ahijah, of the
house of Issachar, conspired against him.
And Baasha struck him down at [j]Gib-
bethon, which belonged to the Philistines,
for Nadab and all Israel were laying siege
to Gibbethon. 28 So Baasha killed him in
the third year of Asa king of Judah and
reigned in his place. 29 And as soon as he
was king, he killed all the house of
Jeroboam. He left to the house of Jeroboam not one that breathed, until he had
destroyed it, [k]according to the word of the
LORD that he spoke by his servant Ahijah
the Shilonite. 30 It was for the sins of
Jeroboam that he sinned and [h]that he made
Israel to sin, and because of the anger to
which he provoked the LORD, the God of
Israel.
31 Now the rest of the acts of Nadab and
all that he did, are they not written in the
Book of the Chronicles of the Kings of
Israel? 32 [l]And there was war between Asa
and Baasha king of Israel all their days.

Baasha Reigns in Israel

33 In the third year of Asa king of Judah,
Baasha the son of Ahijah began to reign
over all Israel at Tirzah, and he reigned
twenty-four years. 34 He did what was evil
in the sight of the LORD [m]and walked in the
way of Jeroboam and in his sin which he
made Israel to sin.

18 [r]ch. 14:26 [s][2 Kin. 12:18] [t]ch. 11:24
19 [u][2 Chr. 16:7]
20 [v]2 Kin. 15:29 [w]Judg. 18:29 [x]2 Sam. 20:14; 2 Kin. 15:29 [y]See Josh. 11:2
21 [z]ver. 17 [a]ch. 14:17; 16:6, 9
22 [b]Josh. 21:17 [c]Josh. 18:26
23 [d]For ver. 23, 24, see 2 Chr. 16:11-14
24 [e]2 Chr. 17:1; [Matt. 1:8]
25 [f]ch. 14:20
26 [g][ver. 34] [h]ver. 30; ch. 12:30; 14:16
27 [i]ch. 14:14 [j]ch. 16:15; Josh. 19:44; 21:23
29 [k]ch. 14:10, 14
30 [h][See ver. 26 above]
32 [l]ver. 16
34 [m][ver. 26]

[1] Or *treaty*; twice in this verse

15:18 sent them to Ben-hadad. Asa used the temple money to bribe the Syrians to help him against the Israelites under Baasha. The Syrians would have to breach a treaty to do this, as Asa himself acknowledges.

15:20 Ben-hadad listened. The Syrian king gained money from Judah and territory from Israel by betraying Baasha.

Ijon, Dan . . . Naphtali. This area is north of the Sea of Chinneroth (Galilee). Subduing it gave Syria control of trade routes as well as access to the Phoenician cities of Tyre and Acco.

15:21 Tirzah. See note 14:17.

15:22 none was exempt. Asa conscripted forced labor to destroy Ramah and build the fortifications at Geba and Mizpah (5:13 note; 9:22 note).

Geba of Benjamin. Ramah, Geba, and Mizpah are all five to ten miles north of Jerusalem. By fortifying them, Asa discouraged another Israelite campaign against Judah (cf. 2 Chr. 14:6, 7).

15:23 Book of the Chronicles of the Kings of Judah. See note 11:41.

15:24 Jehoshaphat. For his reign, see 22:41–50.

15:25–32 These verses summarize the reign of Nadab, king of Israel, but give more attention to the subsequent actions of his assassin and successor, Baasha. As soon as he becomes king, Baasha kills Jeroboam's whole family in fulfillment of Ahijah's prophecy (14:10, 11).

15:25 two years. That is, 909–908 B.C.

15:26 his sin which he made Israel to sin. See note 12:30.

15:27 Gibbethon. This city was assigned to the tribe of Dan but usually controlled by the Philistines (Josh. 19:44). It was west of Jerusalem and five miles north of Ekron.

15:29 he killed all the house of Jeroboam. In order to consolidate his position as king, Baasha disposes of all potential claimants to the throne in Jeroboam's family. This fulfills the prophecy of Ahijah to Jeroboam (14:10–11). The author does not commend Baasha's actions; on the contrary, he later condemns him (16:7).

15:31 Book of the Chronicles of the Kings of Israel. See note 11:41.

15:32 war between Asa and Baasha. See note 14:30.

15:33 Tirzah. See note 14:17.

15:34 the way of Jeroboam. See note 12:30.

16 And the word of the LORD came to [n]Jehu the son of [o]Hanani against Baasha, saying, 2 "Since I [p]exalted you out of the dust and made you leader over my people Israel, and [q]you have walked in the way of Jeroboam and have made my people Israel to sin, provoking me to anger with their sins, 3 behold, I will utterly [r]sweep away [s]Baasha and his house, and I will make your house [t]like the house of Jeroboam the son of Nebat. 4 [u]Anyone belonging to Baasha who dies in the city the dogs shall eat, and anyone of his who dies in the field the birds of the heavens shall eat."

5 Now the rest of the acts of Baasha and what he did, and his might, are they not written in the Book of the Chronicles of the Kings of Israel? 6 And Baasha slept with his fathers and was buried at [v]Tirzah, and Elah his son reigned in his place. 7 Moreover, the word of the LORD came by the prophet [n]Jehu the son of Hanani against Baasha and his house, both because of all the evil that he did in the sight of the LORD, provoking him to anger with the work of his hands, in being like the house of Jeroboam, and also because [w]he destroyed it.

Elah Reigns in Israel

8 In the twenty-sixth year of Asa king of Judah, Elah the son of Baasha began to reign over Israel in Tirzah, and he reigned two years. 9 But his servant [x]Zimri, commander of half his chariots, conspired against him. When he was at Tirzah, drinking himself drunk in the house of Arza, [y]who was over the household in Tirzah, 10 Zimri came in and struck him down and killed him, in the twenty-seventh year of Asa king of Judah, and reigned in his place.

11 When he began to reign, as soon as he had seated himself on his throne, he struck down [z]all the house of Baasha. He [a]did not leave him a single male of his relatives or his friends. 12 Thus Zimri destroyed all the house of Baasha, [b]according to the word of the LORD, which he spoke against Baasha by [n]Jehu the prophet, 13 for all the sins of Baasha and the sins of Elah his son, which they sinned and which they made Israel to sin, [c]provoking the LORD God of Israel to anger with their idols. 14 Now the rest of the acts of Elah and all that he did, are they not written in the Book of the Chronicles of the Kings of Israel?

Zimri Reigns in Israel

15 In the twenty-seventh year of Asa king of Judah, Zimri reigned seven days in Tirzah. Now the troops were encamped against [d]Gibbethon, which belonged to the Philistines, 16 and the troops who were encamped heard it said, "Zimri has conspired, and he has killed the king." Therefore all Israel made Omri, the commander of the army, king over Israel that day in the camp. 17 So Omri went up from Gibbethon, and all Israel with him, and they besieged Tirzah. 18 And when Zimri saw that the city was taken, he went into the citadel of the king's house and burned the king's house over him with fire and died, 19 because of his sins that he committed, doing evil in the sight of the LORD, [e]walking in the way of Jeroboam, and for his sin which he committed, making Israel to sin. 20 Now the rest of the acts of Zimri, and the conspiracy that he made, are they not written in the Book of the Chronicles of the Kings of Israel?

Chapter 16
1 [n]2 Chr. 19:2; 20:34 [o]2 Chr. 16:7
2 [p][ch. 14:7] [q]ch. 15:34
3 [r][ch. 14:10; 21:21] [s]ver. 11 [t][ch. 15:29]
4 [u][ch. 14:11; 21:24]
6 [v]ch. 14:17; 15:21
7 [n][See ver. 1 above] [w]ch. 15:27, 29; [Hos. 1:4]
9 [x]2 Kin. 9:31 [y][ch. 18:3]
11 [z][ver. 3] [a][1 Sam. 25:22]
12 [b]ver. 3 [n][See ver. 1 above]
13 [c]ver. 26; Deut. 32:21
15 [d]ch. 15:27
19 [e][ch. 15:26, 34]

16:2 I exalted you out of the dust. As with Ahijah's condemnation of Jeroboam (14:7, 8), Jehu begins his prophetic speech by rehearsing God's kindness to Baasha.

the way of Jeroboam. See note 12:30.

16:3 Baasha and his house. Because Baasha followed the policies set by Jeroboam, Baasha and his house will suffer the same fate (15:29).

16:4 dogs. See 14:11 and note.

16:5 Book of the Chronicles of the Kings of Israel. See note 11:41.

16:8 reigned two years. That is, 886–885 B.C.

16:11, 12 He did not leave him a single male. This action fulfilled the prophecy of 16:3, 4 (15:29 note).

16:14 the Book of the Chronicles of the Kings of Israel. See note 11:41.

16:15 the twenty-seventh year. That is, 885 B.C.

reigned seven days in Tirzah. The history of Israel, the northern kingdom, was plagued by frequent coups and coup attempts. Judah, the southern kingdom, was somewhat more stable, perhaps because their kings continued to be descendants of David. But the instability of Israel in the north can also be blamed on their kings' disregard for the covenant. Political upheaval was God's way of disciplining and renewing Israel's leadership (11:29–39; 14:7–11; 16:1–4; 21:19–22; 22:17; 2 Kin. 1:2–4).

Gibbethon. About twenty-five miles west of Jerusalem, and five miles north of Ekron, an important Philistine city.

16:16 Zimri has conspired. The Israelite soldiers refuse to accept Zimri's kingship.

Omri, the commander. Omri held a higher rank than Zimri (v. 9). The troops may have felt more obligation to follow Omri than Zimri.

16:19 the way of Jeroboam. See note 12:30.

16:20 the Book. See note 11:41.

Omri Reigns in Israel

21 Then the people of Israel were divided
into two parts. Half of the people followed
Tibni the son of Ginath, to make him king,
and half followed Omri. 22 But the people
who followed Omri overcame the people
who followed Tibni the son of Ginath. So
Tibni died, and Omri became king. 23 In
the thirty-first year of Asa king of Judah,
Omri began to reign over Israel, and he
reigned for twelve years; six years he
reigned in Tirzah. 24 He bought the hill of
[f]Samaria from Shemer for two talents[1] of
silver, and he fortified the hill and called
the name of the city that he built [g]Samaria,
after the name of Shemer, the owner of the
hill.
25 [h]Omri did what was evil in the sight of
the LORD, and did more evil [i]than all who
were before him. 26 For [e]he walked in all the
way of Jeroboam the son of Nebat, and in
the sins that he made Israel to sin, [j]pro-
voking the LORD, the God of Israel, to anger
by their idols. 27 Now the rest of the acts of
Omri that he did, and the might that he
showed, are they not written in the Book of
the Chronicles of the Kings of Israel? 28 And
Omri slept with his fathers and was buried
in Samaria, and Ahab his son reigned in his
place.

Ahab Reigns in Israel

29 In the thirty-eighth year of Asa king of
Judah, Ahab the son of Omri began to
reign over Israel, and Ahab the son of Omri
reigned over Israel in Samaria twenty-two
years. 30 And Ahab the son of Omri did evil
in the sight of the LORD, [k]more than all
who were before him. 31 And as if it had
been a light thing for him to walk in the
sins of Jeroboam the son of Nebat, [l]he
took for his wife Jezebel the daughter of
Ethbaal king of the [m]Sidonians, [n]and went
and served Baal and worshiped him. 32 He
erected an altar for Baal in [o]the house of
Baal, which he built in Samaria. 33 And
Ahab made an [p]Asherah. Ahab did more
to provoke the LORD, the God of Israel, to
anger [k]than all the kings of Israel who
were before him. 34 [q]In his days Hiel of
Bethel built [r]Jericho. He laid its foundation at the cost of Abiram his firstborn,
and set up its gates at the cost of his
youngest son Segub, according to the
word of the LORD, which he spoke by
Joshua the son of Nun.

Elijah Predicts a Drought

17 Now Elijah the Tishbite, of [s]Tishbe[2]
in Gilead, said to Ahab, [t]"As the
LORD the God of Israel lives, [u]before whom
I stand, [v]there shall be neither dew nor rain
these years, except by my word." 2 And the
word of the LORD came to him, 3 "Depart
from here and turn eastward and hide
yourself by the brook Cherith, which is

24 [f][ch. 13:32] [g]ver. 28, 29, 32
25 [h]Mic. 6:16 [i]ver. 30
26 [e][See ver. 19 above] [j]ver. 13
30 [k]ch. 21:25; [ver. 25]
31 [l][Ex. 34:16; Deut. 7:3] [m]Judg. 18:7 [n]ch. 21:25, 26; [2 Kin. 3:2; 10:18; 17:16]
32 [o]2 Kin. 10:21, 26, 27
33 [p]ch. 18:19; 2 Kin. 13:6; 17:10; 21:3; 2 Chr. 14:3; [Ex. 34:13; Jer. 17:2] [k][See ver. 30 above]
34 [q][Josh. 6:26] [r]See 2 Kin. 2:4, 18-22
Chapter 17
1 [s][Judg. 12:4] [t]ch. 18:10, 15; 22:14; 2 Kin. 3:14; 5:16; See Ruth 3:13 [u]ch. 18:15; [Deut. 10:8] [v]Luke 4:25; James 5:17; [ch. 18:1]

[1] A *talent* was about 75 pounds or 34 kilograms [2] Septuagint; Hebrew *of the settlers*

16:21 were divided. Tibni contested Omri's right to the throne.

16:22 Tibni died, and Omri became king. This terse statement leaves the impression that Tibni was killed in the struggle with Omri and his followers, but natural causes cannot be ruled out.

16:23 In the thirty-first year of Asa. That is, 880 B.C. The struggle between Omri and Tibni lasted four years (v. 15).

he reigned for twelve years. That is, 885–874 B.C.

16:24 Samaria. Like David (2 Sam. 5:6–12), Omri founded his own capital, Samaria. It was halfway between the Jordan River and the Mediterranean Sea, about thirty-seven miles north of Jerusalem. Samaria was easily defended and became the permanent capital of Israel (20:1; 2 Kin. 6:24; 10:17; 13:6; 18:9, 10). "Samaria" sometimes refers to the northern kingdom as a whole (2 Kin. 17:24; Amos 3:9, 12).

16:26 the way of Jeroboam. See note 12:30.

16:27 the might that he showed. Politically and militarily Omri was quite successful. The Moabite stone, an inscription from one of Israel's neighbors, states that Omri subjugated Moab and captured Medeba. Much later, the annals of the Assyrian king Tiglath-pileser III (c. 732 B.C.) still speak of Israel as the "house of Omri."

16:29 twenty-two years. That is, 874–853 B.C.

16:30 Ahab . . . did evil. Note that the same phrase is applied to Jeroboam (14:9). The phrase means "extremely bad."

16:31 he took for his wife Jezebel. This marriage of Omri's son to Ethbaal's daughter may have been arranged by Omri for diplomatic reasons. Jezebel's presence gave official support in Israel to the worship of Baal.

served Baal. "Baal" means "lord," "husband." Baal was a storm god, a dominant deity in Canaanite religion. He was considered instrumental in bringing life-giving rains and fertility to the land.

16:33 Asherah. See note 14:15.

16:34 Hiel of Bethel built Jericho. After its earlier destruction (Josh. 5:13–6:27), Jericho had been inhabited as a settlement (Josh. 18:21; 2 Sam. 10:5). Hiel's wish to turn the site of Jericho into a full-fledged city brought on the curse of Josh. 6:26, which prohibited rebuilding the city and outlined the consequences of doing so.

17:1 Elijah. The name means "Yah is God." "Yah" or "Jah" is a short form of the divine name "Yahweh," translated as "LORD" (cf. Ex. 3:14, 15). Elijah's name corresponds to the theme of his ministry: the Lord is God and there is no other. Elijah was the major prophet of Yahweh when Ahab and Jezebel were promoting Baal worship in Israel.

Tishbite. Probably Elijah was from a town called Tishbe.

Gilead. Gilead is an area of undefined extent east of the Jordan River.

neither dew nor rain. Baal (16:31 note) was the Canaanite storm god, and this drought questioned Baal's ability to control the weather.

except by my word. The drought will demonstrate to a wayward Israel who truly is God.

east of the Jordan. 4You shall drink from
the brook, and I have commanded the
ravens to feed you there." 5So he went and
did according to the word of the LORD. He
went and lived by the brook Cherith that is
east of the Jordan. 6And the ravens brought
him bread and meat in the morning, and
bread and meat in the evening, and he
drank from the brook. 7And after a while
the brook dried up, because there was no
rain in the land.

The Widow of Zarephath

8Then the word of the LORD came to
him, 9"Arise, go to [w]Zarephath, which
belongs to Sidon, and dwell there. Behold,
I have commanded a widow there to feed
you." 10So he arose and went to [w]Zare-
phath. And when he came to the gate of
the city, behold, a widow was there [x]gath-
ering sticks. And he called to her and said,
"Bring me a little water in a vessel, that I
may drink." 11And as she was going to
bring it, he called to her and said, "Bring
me a morsel of bread in your hand." 12And
she said, [t]"As the LORD your God lives, I
have nothing baked, only a handful of flour
in a jar and a little oil in a jug. And now I
am gathering a couple of sticks that I may
go in and prepare it for myself and my son,
that we may eat it and die." 13And Elijah
said to her, "Do not fear; go and do as you
have said. But first make me a little cake of
it and bring it to me, and afterward make
something for yourself and your son. 14For
thus says the LORD the God of Israel, 'The
jar of flour shall not be spent, and the jug
of oil shall not be empty, until the day that
the LORD sends rain upon the earth.'"
15And she went and did as Elijah said. And
she and he and her household ate for many
days. 16The jar of flour was not spent, neither did the jug of oil become empty,
according to the word of the LORD that he
spoke by Elijah.

Elijah Raises the Widow's Son

17After this the son of the woman, the
mistress of the house, became ill. And his
illness was so severe that there was no
breath left in him. 18And she said to Elijah,
[y]"What have you against me, O [z]man of
God? You have come to me to bring my sin
to remembrance and to cause the death of
my son!" 19And he said to her, "Give me
your son." And he took him from her arms
and carried him up into the upper chamber
where he lodged, and laid him on his own
bed. 20And he cried to the LORD, "O LORD
my God, have you brought calamity even
upon the widow with whom I sojourn, by
killing her son?" 21[a]Then he stretched himself upon the child three times and cried to
the LORD, "O LORD my God, let this child's
life come into him again." 22And the LORD
listened to the voice of Elijah. And the life
of the child came into him again, and [b]he
revived. 23And Elijah took the child and
brought him down from the upper chamber into the house and delivered him to his
mother. And Elijah said, "See, your son
lives." 24And the woman said to Elijah,
[c]"Now I know that you are a man of God,
and that the word of the LORD in your
mouth is truth."

Elijah Confronts Ahab

18 [d]After many days the word of the
LORD came to Elijah, in the third
year, saying, "Go, show yourself to Ahab,
and I will send rain upon the earth." 2So
Elijah went to show himself to Ahab. Now

9[w]Obad. 20; Luke 4:26
10[w][See ver. 9 above] [x]Num. 15:32, 33
12[t][See ver. 1 above]
18[y][Luke 4:34; 5:8] [z]See Deut. 33:1
21[a]2 Kin. 4:34, 35; Acts 20:10
22[b][Heb. 11:35]
24[c][John 3:2]
Chapter 18
1[d]See ch. 17:1

17:4 ravens to feed you. Although Elijah was in the wilderness, the Lord could provide for him, much as He had for the nation of Israel centuries earlier during the Exodus (Ex. 16:4–36). Ironically, Israel is in the Promised Land, but has forgotten who sustains her.

17:5 brook Cherith. This brook probably flowed into the Jordan from the east. It may have been in northern Gilead, toward the Sea of Chinneroth (Galilee).

17:9 Zarephath. This town was on the Mediterranean coast between Tyre and Sidon. God commands Elijah to travel away from Israel into the area where Canaanite religion is supreme.

widow. The word is practically synonymous with "poor," because in the ancient Near East widows were largely unprotected by the law and were easily exploited (Deut. 14:29; 16:11; 24:20; 26:12; Ps. 94:6; Is. 47:8, 9). This particular widow was not an Israelite.

17:12 As the LORD your God lives. This is an oath formula (1:17 note) taken in the name of Elijah's God. The widow may have been deferring to Elijah, or she may have had a genuine interest in the God of Israel.

17:13 first make me a little cake. Elijah presents her with a test of faith, demanding complete commitment. Despite the scarcity of food, she is to feed God's prophet before she takes care of herself and her son.

17:18 What have you against me, O man of God. The widow was upset with God because her son was dead, and she complained to Elijah by suggesting that it was his mission to punish her for her sin.

17:21 he stretched himself upon the child three times. Elijah performs a symbolic action together with his prophetic prayer (11:30 note). His repeated physical contact with the boy's body emphasizes the request for warmth and life to be returned to the boy (cf. 2 Kin. 4:34; Acts 20:10).

17:22 See theological note "Miracles."

the famine was severe in Samaria. [3]And
Ahab called Obadiah, who was [e]over the
household. (Now Obadiah feared the LORD
greatly, [4]and [f]when Jezebel cut off the
prophets of the LORD, Obadiah took a hundred prophets and hid them by fifties in a
cave and fed them with bread and water.)
[5]And Ahab said to Obadiah, "Go through
the land to all the springs of water and to
all the valleys. Perhaps we may find grass
and save the horses and mules alive, and
not lose some of the animals." [6]So they
divided the land between them to pass
through it. Ahab went in one direction by
himself, and Obadiah went in another
direction by himself.
[7]And as Obadiah was on the way,
behold, Elijah met him. And Obadiah recognized him and fell on his face and said,
"Is it you, my lord Elijah?" [8]And he
answered him, "It is I. Go, tell your lord,
'Behold, Elijah is here.'" [9]And he said,
"How have I sinned, that you would give
your servant into the hand of Ahab, to kill
me? [10][g]As the LORD your God lives, there is
no nation or kingdom where my lord has
not sent to seek you. And when they would
say, 'He is not here,' he would take an oath
of the kingdom or nation, that they had not
found you. [11]And now you say, 'Go, tell
your lord, "Behold, Elijah is here."' [12]And
as soon as I have gone from you, [h]the Spirit
of the LORD will carry you I know not
where. And so, when I come and tell Ahab
and he cannot find you, he will kill me,
although I your servant have feared the
LORD from my youth. [13]Has it not been told
my lord what I did [i]when Jezebel killed the
prophets of the LORD, how I hid a hundred
men of the LORD's prophets by fifties in a
cave and fed them with bread and water?
[14]And now you say, 'Go, tell your lord,
"Behold, Elijah is here"'; and he will kill
me." [15]And Elijah said, [g]"As the LORD of

3 [e]ch. 16:9
4 [f]ver. 13
10 [g]See ch. 17:1
12 [h]2 Kin. 2:16; Ezek. 3:12, 14; 8:3; Acts 8:39
13 [i]ver. 4
15 [g][See ver. 10 above]

Miracles

Scripture has no single word for miracle. The concept includes thoughts expressed by several terms: "wonder," "mighty work," and "sign."

"Wonder" calls attention to the impression made by miracles. "Miracle," from the Latin *miraculum*, means something that evokes wonder. A miracle is an event beyond the normal, triggering awareness of God's presence and power. Striking providences and coincidences, as well as the phenomena of nature, can communicate a similar awareness, as they give evidence of God's "eternal power and divine nature" (Rom. 1:20).

"Mighty work" points to the presence in biblical history of supernatural acts of God involving the power that created the world from nothing. Raising the dead to life, which Jesus did more than once (Luke 7:11–17; 8:49–56; John 11:38–44), and Elijah, Elisha, Peter, and Paul did also (1 Kin. 17:17–24; 2 Kin. 4:18–37; Acts 9:36–41; 20:9–12), is a work of such creative power; it is not chance or coincidence, and cannot be explained from the course of nature.

"Sign" is a term regularly used for miracles in the Gospel of John, where seven key miracles are recorded, indicating that miracles point to something; they carry a message. The miracles in Scripture are nearly all clustered in the time of the Exodus, of Elijah and Elisha, and of Christ and His apostles. They authenticate the miracle-workers themselves as God's representatives and messengers (cf. Ex. 4:1–9; 1 Kin. 17:24; John 10:38; 14:11; 2 Cor. 12:12; Heb. 2:3, 4), and beyond this, they show God's power bringing about salvation and executing judgment, despite all opposition. The miracles of the Bible are not absurd, irrational, or mere displays of power undertaken for their own sake. They directly fulfill God's purposes and are consistent with His majesty and holiness.

Belief in the miraculous is integral to Christianity. Jesus' incarnation and resurrection are the two supreme miracles of Scripture, defining the Christian faith. No one can refuse Jesus' life or His resurrection without refusing the faith itself. There is nothing irrational about believing that God who made the world can intervene creatively in it at any time; in truth, it would be irrational to believe in any other God. Not faith in the Biblical miracles, but doubt about them, is unreasonable in the end.

18:3 over the household. This was an important position in the royal administration (4:6 note).

18:4 Jezebel cut off the prophets of the LORD. Not content to promote her native religion, Jezebel persecuted followers of the Lord and murdered His prophets.

18:5 horses and mules. The drought threatened Ahab's government because the army depended on these animals, for example, in the chariot forces. Ahab's reaction to the drought was practical, to find water, and did not reach the heart of the issue: who is sovereign over nature and life.

18:12 the Spirit of the LORD will carry you. Earlier Elijah had disappeared across the Jordan only to emerge in Zarephath.

hosts lives, before whom I stand, I will
surely show myself to him today." 16 So
Obadiah went to meet Ahab, and told him.
And Ahab went to meet Elijah.
17 When Ahab saw Elijah, Ahab said to
him, [j]"Is it you, you [k]troubler of Israel?"
18 And he answered, "I have not troubled
Israel, but you have, and your father's house,
because you have [l]abandoned the commandments of the LORD and [m]followed the
Baals. 19 Now therefore send and gather all
Israel to me at Mount [n]Carmel, and the [o]450
prophets of Baal and [p]the 400 prophets of
Asherah, [q]who eat at Jezebel's table."

The Priests of Baal Defeated

20 So Ahab sent to all the people of Israel
and gathered the prophets together at
Mount Carmel. 21 And Elijah came near to
all the people and said, "How long [r]will
you go limping between two different opinions? [s]If the LORD is God, follow him; but if
Baal, then follow him." And the people did
not answer him a word. 22 Then Elijah said
to the people, [t]"I, even I only, am left a
prophet of the LORD, but Baal's prophets
are [u]450 men. 23 Let two bulls be given to
us, and let them choose one bull for themselves and cut it in pieces and lay it on the
wood, but put no fire to it. And I will prepare the other bull and lay it on the wood
and put no fire to it. 24 And you call upon
the name of your god, and I will call upon
the name of the LORD, and the God who
[v]answers by fire, he is God." And all the
people answered, "It is well spoken."
25 Then Elijah said to the prophets of Baal,
"Choose for yourselves one bull and prepare it first, for you are many, and call
upon the name of your god, but put no fire
to it." 26 And they took the bull that was
given them, and they prepared it and called
upon the name of Baal from morning until
noon, saying, "O Baal, answer us!" But
there was no voice, and no one answered.
And they limped around the altar that they
had made. 27 And at noon Elijah mocked
them, saying, "Cry aloud, for he is a god.
Either he is musing, or he is relieving himself, or he is on a journey, or perhaps he is
asleep and must be awakened." 28 And they
cried aloud and [w]cut themselves after their
custom with swords and lances, until the
blood gushed out upon them. 29 And as
midday passed, they raved on until the
time of [x]the offering of the oblation, but
there was no voice. No one answered; no
one paid attention.
30 Then Elijah said to all the people,
"Come near to me." And all the people
came near to him. And he repaired the altar
of the LORD that had been [y]thrown down.
31 Elijah took twelve stones, according to
the number of the tribes of the sons of
Jacob, to whom the word of the LORD
came, saying, [z]"Israel shall be your name,"
32 and with the stones he built an altar in
the name of the LORD. And he made a
trench about the altar, as great as would
contain two seahs[1] of seed. 33 [a]And he put
the wood in order and cut the bull in
pieces and laid it on the wood. And he
said, "Fill four jars with water and [b]pour it
on the burnt offering and on the wood."
34 And he said, "Do it a second time." And
they did it a second time. And he said, "Do
it a third time." And they did it a third
time. 35 And the water ran around the altar
and filled the trench also with water.

17 [j][ch. 21:20] [k][Josh. 7:25]
18 [l]ch. 9:9; 2 Chr. 15:2; 24:20 [m]ch. 16:31
19 [n]See Josh. 19:26 [o]ver. 22 [p]See ch. 16:33 [q][2 Kin. 3:13]
21 [r][2 Kin. 17:41] [s]Josh. 24:15; [Matt. 6:24]
22 [t]ch. 19:10, 14 [u]ver. 19
24 [v]See ver. 38
28 [w][Lev. 19:28; Deut. 14:1]
29 [x][Ex. 29:39, 41]
30 [y]ch. 19:10, 14
31 [z]Gen. 32:28; 35:10; 2 Kin. 17:34
33 [a]Gen. 22:9; Lev. 1:7 [b][Judg. 6:20]

[1] A *seah* was about 7 quarts or 7.3 liters

18:17 you troubler of Israel. Ahab views Elijah as a troublemaker, a threat to the normal functioning of society. His understanding is shallow.

18:18 the Baals. These were local manifestations of the god Baal.

18:19 Mount Carmel. This mountain juts out along the Mediterranean coast due west of the Sea of Chinneroth (Galilee). Because it was near the Phoenician cities, the influence of Baal religion was probably strong.

Asherah. See note 14:15.

who eat at Jezebel's table. These prophets are supported by the state (2:7 note).

18:24 the God who answers by fire. Since Baal's followers believed that Baal controlled thunder, lightning, and storms, Elijah's challenge struck at the core of his alleged power (16:31 note).

18:26 they limped around the altar. The Baal prophets engaged in a ritual dance to arouse the unresponsive Baal.

18:27 Cry aloud. Myths of Baal portray him traveling, fighting war, visiting the underworld, and even dying and coming back to life. Elijah knows these beliefs and plays on them when he taunts Baal's followers.

18:28 after their custom. They cut themselves to provoke Baal. Self-laceration was prohibited in Old Testament law (Lev. 19:28; Deut. 14:1), but nevertheless was practiced by some (Jer. 41:5; 47:5).

18:29 they raved on. This description probably indicates a trance or ecstatic state.

the time of the offering of the oblation. That is, around 3:00 P.M. (Ex. 29:38–41; Num. 28:3–8; 2 Kin. 16:15; Acts 3:1).

18:31 twelve stones. Elijah emphasizes the oneness of the people, despite the division of the kingdom. In this way he also underscores that the contest at Mount Carmel is not significant for the northern tribes only, but for the southern tribes as well (Ex. 20:25; 24:4; Josh. 4).

Israel shall be your name. The words are a quotation of Gen. 35:10, where God affirmed the special name He had earlier given Jacob.

36 And at the time of [c]the offering of the
oblation, Elijah the prophet came near and
said, "O LORD, [d]God of Abraham, Isaac,
and Israel, let it be known this day that
[e]you are God in Israel, and that I am your
servant, and that [f]I have done all these
things at your word. 37 Answer me, O
LORD, answer me, that this people may
know that you, O LORD, are God, and that
you have turned their hearts back."
38 [g]Then the fire of the LORD fell and consumed the burnt offering and the wood
and the stones and the dust, and licked up
the water that was in the trench. 39 And
when all the people saw it, they fell on
their faces and said, [h]"The LORD, he is
God; the LORD, he is God." 40 And Elijah
said to them, "Seize the prophets of Baal;
let not one of them escape." And they
seized them. And Elijah brought them
down to [i]the brook Kishon and [j]slaugh-
tered them there.

The LORD Sends Rain

41 And Elijah said to Ahab, "Go up, eat
and drink, for there is a sound of the rushing of rain." 42 So Ahab went up to eat and
to drink. And Elijah went up to the top of
Mount Carmel. [k]And he bowed himself
down on the earth and put his face
between his knees. 43 And he said to his servant, "Go up now, look toward the sea."
And he went up and looked and said,
"There is nothing." And he said, "Go
again," seven times. 44 And at the seventh
time he said, "Behold, [l]a little cloud like a
man's hand is rising from the sea." And he
said, "Go up, say to Ahab, 'Prepare your
chariot and go down, lest the rain stop
you.'" 45 And in a little while the heavens
grew black with clouds and wind, and
there was a great rain. And Ahab rode and
went to [m]Jezreel. 46 [n]And the hand of the
LORD was on Elijah, [o]and he gathered up
his garment and ran before Ahab to the
entrance of [p]Jezreel.

36 [c]ver. 29 [d]See Ex. 3:6 [e]Josh. 4:24; 1 Sam. 17:46 [f][Num. 16:28]
38 [g]ver. 24; See Lev. 9:24
39 [h]ver. 24
40 [i]Judg. 4:7 [j][2 Kin. 10:25]
42 [k][James 5:17, 18]
44 [l][Luke 12:54]
45 [m]Josh. 17:16
46 [n]2 Kin. 3:15; Ezek. 1:3; 3:14 [o]Ex. 12:11; 2 Kin. 4:29; 9:1; Jer. 1:17 [p]Josh. 17:16
Chapter 19
1 [q]ch. 18:40
2 [r][ch. 20:10]; See Ruth 1:17
3 [s]See Gen. 21:31
4 [t][Num. 11:15; Jonah 4:3, 8]
8 [u]Ex. 24:18; 34:28; Deut. 9:9, 18; Matt. 4:2; Mark 1:13; Luke 4:2 [v]Ex. 3:1

Elijah Flees Jezebel

19 Ahab told Jezebel all that Elijah had
done, and how [q]he had killed all
the prophets with the sword. 2 Then Jezebel
sent a messenger to Elijah, saying, [r]"So
may the gods do to me and more also, if I
do not make your life as the life of one of
them by this time tomorrow." 3 Then he
was afraid, and he arose and ran for his life
and came to [s]Beersheba, which belongs to
Judah, and left his servant there.

4 But he himself went a day's journey into
the wilderness and came and sat down
under a broom tree. [t]And he asked that he
might die, saying, "It is enough; now, O
LORD, take away my life, for I am no better
than my fathers." 5 And he lay down and
slept under a broom tree. And behold, an
angel touched him and said to him, "Arise
and eat." 6 And he looked, and behold,
there was at his head a cake baked on hot
stones and a jar of water. And he ate and
drank and lay down again. 7 And the angel
of the LORD came again a second time and
touched him and said, "Arise and eat, for
the journey is too great for you." 8 And he
arose and ate and drank, and went in the
strength of that food [u]forty days and forty
nights to [v]Horeb, the mount of God.

18:36 Elijah . . . came near and said. In contrast to the elaborate and frantic activities of the Baal prophets, Elijah's prayer is simple and direct.

18:37 you have turned their hearts back. The human act of repentance is not possible without divine grace.

18:40 brook Kishon. This brook runs toward the north in the plain below Mount Carmel.

slaughtered them there. Israel was a theocracy, a society founded by and constituted under God. Deut. 13:1–5 mandates the death of false prophets; Deut. 13:13–18 and 17:2–7 prescribe death to anyone embracing idolatry or inciting others to it.

18:41 eat and drink. Ahab's austerity can end, because the famine will soon be over (cf. James 5:17, 18).

18:45 Ahab rode and went to Jezreel. Ahab used the town of Jezreel (located near Mount Gilboa) as a second residence (in addition to Samaria; 20:43; 21:1).

19:1 Ahab told Jezebel. Jezebel plays a major role in governing Israel (18:4 note). Together with Ahab, she wants to punish Elijah for killing the prophets of Baal (v. 2).

19:2 So may the gods do to me. Jezebel's oath calls down a penalty on herself if she should fail to kill Elijah within a day's time (1:17 note).

19:3 Beersheba. In the southern territory of Judah, 130 miles south of Jezreel. As he did before, Elijah flees outside the borders of the northern kingdom (17:3–6, 9).

19:4 broom tree. This desert bush grows as high as nine feet and provides some shade.

It is enough. After waging and winning a titanic struggle with God's help against the prophets of Baal, Elijah is discouraged and depressed. Although the Lord had defeated Baal, Elijah has become a fugitive from Ahab and Jezebel. Because of the incongruity between the visible (the promoters of Baal who still govern Israel) and the invisible (the lordship of Yahweh), Elijah wants to die.

19:7 the journey is too great for you. Elijah is to travel all the way to Mount Horeb (that is, Mount Sinai), the original site of God's revelation to Moses. Horeb was in the arid Sinai Peninsula between Israel and Egypt, but the exact location is unknown (Ex. 3:1; 17:6; 33:6; Deut. 1:2, 6, 19; 4:10, 15).

The LORD Speaks to Elijah

9 There he came to a cave and lodged in
it. And behold, [w]the word of the LORD
came to him, and he said to him, "What
are you doing here, Elijah?" 10 He said, "I
have been very [x]jealous for the LORD, the
God of hosts. For the people of Israel have
forsaken your covenant, [y]thrown down
your altars, and [z]killed your prophets with
the sword, [a]and I, even I only, am left, and
they seek my life, to take it away." 11 And
he said, "Go out and [b]stand on the mount
before the LORD." And behold, the LORD
passed by, and [c]a great and strong wind
tore the mountains and broke in pieces
the rocks before the LORD, but the LORD
was not in the wind. And after the wind
[d]an earthquake, but the LORD was not in
the earthquake. 12 And after the earthquake
a fire, but the LORD was not in the fire.
And after the fire the sound of a low whisper.[1] 13 And when Elijah heard it, [e]he
wrapped his face in his cloak and went out
and stood at the entrance of the cave. And
behold, [f]there came a voice to him and
said, "What are you doing here, Elijah?"
14 He said, [x]"I have been very jealous for
the LORD, the God of hosts. For the people
of Israel have forsaken your covenant,
[y]thrown down your altars, and killed your
prophets with the sword, and I, even I
only, am left, and they seek my life, to take
it away." 15 And the LORD said to him, "Go,
return on your way to the wilderness of
Damascus. And when you arrive, you shall
anoint Hazael to be king over Syria. 16 [g]And
Jehu the son of Nimshi you shall anoint to
be king over Israel, and [h]Elisha the son of
Shaphat of Abel-meholah you shall anoint
to be prophet in your place. 17 And the one
who escapes from [i]the sword of Hazael
[j]shall Jehu put to death, and the one who
escapes from the sword of Jehu [k]shall
Elisha put to death. 18 [l]Yet I will leave
seven thousand in Israel, all the knees that
have not bowed to Baal, and every mouth
that has not [m]kissed him."

The Call of Elisha

19 So he departed from there and found
Elisha the son of Shaphat, who was plowing with twelve yoke of oxen in front of
him, and he was with the twelfth. Elijah
passed by him and cast [n]his cloak upon
him. 20 And he left the oxen and ran after
Elijah and said, [o]"Let me kiss my father
and my mother, and then I will follow
you." And he said to him, "Go back again,
for what have I done to you?" 21 And he
returned from following him and took the
yoke of oxen and sacrificed them and
boiled their flesh [p]with the yokes of the
oxen and gave it to the people, and they
ate. Then he arose and went after Elijah
and assisted him.

Ahab's Wars with Syria

20 [q]Ben-hadad the king of Syria gathered all his army together. [r]Thirty-
two kings were with him, and horses and

[1] *Or a sound, a thin silence*

9 [w]ver. 13 **10** [x]Num. 25:11, 13 [y]ch. 18:30; Cited Rom. 11:3 [z]ch. 18:4 [a]ch. 18:22 **11** [b]Ex. 24:12; 34:2 [c]Ezek. 1:4 [d]Ezek. 37:7 **13** [e][Ex. 3:6] [f]ver. 9 **14** [x][See ver. 10 above] [y][See ver. 10 above]

16 [g]See 2 Kin. 9:1-6 [h][ver. 19-21; 2 Kin. 2:9, 15] **17** [i]2 Kin. 8:12; 13:3, 22 [j]See 2 Kin. ch. 9–10 [k][Hos. 6:5] **18** [l]Cited Rom. 11:4 [m][Hos. 13:2] **19** [n]2 Kin. 2:8 **20** [o][Matt. 8:21, 22; Luke 9:61, 62] **21** [p][2 Sam. 24:22] **Chapter 20** **1** [q]2 Kin. 6:24; 8:7; [ch. 15:18] [r]ch. 22:31

19:11, 12 the LORD passed by. God summons Elijah to prepare for a divine revelation, in much the same way He prepared Moses at Mount Sinai (Ex. 33:30–33; 34:2).

wind . . . earthquake . . . fire. These phenomena were indications of God's presence on Mount Sinai (Ex. 19:18, 19; 20:18; 24:17; Deut. 4:11, 12; 5:22–25), but God does not reveal Himself to Elijah through them.

a low whisper. The Lord answers Elijah in an unexpected way. God is present in near silence. Contrary to the notions of Elijah, divine silence does not mean divine inactivity.

19:13 wrapped his face. Moses was covered by God's "hand" before He passed by (Ex. 33:20–23), and Elijah covers his face upon hearing the "low whisper" (v.12). No one can see God and live (1 Tim. 6:16).

19:15 anoint Hazael to be king over Syria. Although it was common for prophets to anoint kings, it was most unusual for them to anoint foreign kings. God's purpose was to use this king from Damascus to bring His judgment against the house of Ahab (2 Kin. 8:7–15, 28, 29; 10:32; 12:17, 18; 13:3, 22).

19:16 Jehu . . . anoint. Jehu was a military commander under both Ahab and his son, Joram (2 Kin. 9:5, 6). At the behest of Elisha, Jehu would launch a complete purge of the house of Ahab (2 Kin. 9:1–10:17).

Elisha the son of Shaphat. The name "Elisha" means "God is salvation" or "God saves" and is an apt characterization of Elisha's mission. There are many parallels between the work of Elijah and that of Elisha. Both uphold the standards of the covenant of Sinai despite the opposition of kings (18:17–46; 21:19–22; 2 Kin. 3:13; 9:1–10).

19:18 seven thousand. Elijah had thought he was the only one left.

every mouth that has not kissed him. That is, has kissed the image of Baal (cf. Hos. 13:2).

19:20 what have I done to you. With this elliptic and enigmatic statement, Elijah apparently permits Elisha to make a visit to his home, because what has happened to him was great, and will not lose its effectiveness through such a delay.

19:21 sacrificed them. Elisha makes a total commitment to his new prophetic calling by ending his old way of life. The call of Jesus to His disciples is a comprehensive claim (Mark 1:16–20; 2:14). The same can be said for Jesus' demands upon any who would follow Him (Mark 8:34–38).

assisted him. Elisha does not begin as an equal with Elijah, but as his apprentice or aide. Moses also had Joshua as his servant, and trained him to be his successor (Ex. 24:13; 33:11).

20:1 Ben-hadad the king of Syria. This is probably Ben-hadad II, grandson of the Ben-hadad mentioned in 15:18–20.

Thirty-two kings. Ben-hadad II assembled a coalition of thirty-two kings of client city-states and tribal chieftains to campaign against Ahab.

chariots. And he went up and closed in on
[s]Samaria and fought against it. 2 And he
sent messengers into the city to Ahab king
of Israel and said to him, “Thus says Ben-
hadad: 3 ‘Your silver and your gold are
mine; your best wives and children also
are mine.’ ” 4 And the king of Israel
answered, “As you say, my lord, O king, I
am yours, and all that I have.” 5 The messengers came again and said, “Thus says
Ben-hadad: ‘I sent to you, saying, “Deliver
to me your silver and your gold, your wives
and your children.” 6 Nevertheless I will
send my servants to you tomorrow about
this time, and they shall search your house
and the houses of your servants and lay
hands on whatever pleases you and take it
away.’ ”

7 Then the king of Israel called all the
[t]elders of the land and said, [u]“Mark, now,
and see how this man is seeking trouble,
for he sent to me for my wives and my children, and for my silver and my gold, and I
did not refuse him.” 8 And all the elders
and all the people said to him, “Do not listen or consent.” 9 So he said to the messengers of Ben-hadad, “Tell my lord the king,
‘All that you first demanded of your servant
I will do, but this thing I cannot do.’ ” And
the messengers departed and brought him
word again. 10 Ben-hadad sent to him and
said, [v]“The gods do so to me and more
also, if the dust of Samaria shall suffice for
handfuls for all the people [w]who follow
me.” 11 And the king of Israel answered,
“Tell him, ‘Let not him who straps on his
armor boast himself like he who takes it
off.’ ” 12 When Ben-hadad heard this message as [x]he was drinking with the kings in
the booths, he said to his men, “Take your
positions.” And they took their positions
against the city.

Ahab Defeats Ben-hadad

13 And behold, a prophet came near to
Ahab king of Israel and said, “Thus says the
LORD, Have you seen all this great multitude? Behold, [y]I will give it into your hand
this day, [z]and you shall know that I am the
LORD.” 14 And Ahab said, “By whom?” He
said, “Thus says the LORD, By the servants of
the governors of the districts.” Then he said,
“Who shall begin the battle?” He answered,
“You.” 15 Then he mustered the servants of
the governors of the districts, and they were
232. And after them he mustered all the
people of Israel, seven thousand.

16 And they went out at noon, while Ben-
hadad [x]was drinking himself drunk in the
booths, he and the thirty-two kings who
helped him. 17 The servants of the governors
of the districts went out first. And Ben-
hadad sent out scouts, and they reported to
him, “Men are coming out from Samaria.”
18 He said, “If they have come out for peace,
take them alive. Or if they have come out
for war, take them alive.”

19 So these went out of the city, the servants of the governors of the districts and
the army that followed them. 20 And each
struck down his man. The Syrians fled, and
Israel pursued them, but Ben-hadad king
of Syria escaped on a horse with horsemen.
21 And the king of Israel went out and
struck the horses and chariots, and struck
the Syrians with a great blow.

22 Then [a]the prophet came near to the
king of Israel and said to him, “Come,
strengthen yourself, and consider well
what you have to do, for [b]in the spring the
king of Syria will come up against you.”

23 And the servants of the king of Syria
said to him, “Their gods are gods of the
hills, and so they were stronger than we.
But let us fight against them in the plain,

1 [s]ch. 16:24
7 [t]ch. 21:8, 11 [u][2 Kin. 5:7]
10 [v]ch. 19:2 [w][Ex. 11:8]
12 [x][ch. 16:9]
13 [y]ver. 28 [z][ch. 18:36]
16 [x][See ver. 12 above]
22 [a]ver. 13 [b]2 Sam. 11:1

20:4 my lord, O king. Ahab addresses Ben-hadad as an inferior to a superior. Ahab hoped that by surrendering he could preserve his own life and prevent his city from being destroyed.

20:9 this thing I cannot do. In his surrender (v. 4) Ahab did not contemplate actually handing over women and children, at least not those in his own palace and retinue.

20:10 The gods do so to me. Enraged at Ahab's refusal, Ben-hadad promises to reduce Samaria to a heap of dust.

20:11 him who straps on his armor. Ahab responds with a proverb that it is foolish to boast about winning before the fight has begun.

20:13 I will give it into your hand this day. This is the form of assurance given before battles when the Lord is about to fight on Israel's side (Josh. 6:2, 16; 8:1, 18; Judg. 7:2; 18:10; 2 Chr. 13:16; 16:8). God defends the cause of His people against oppressors and enemies (Ex. 15:1–21; Judg. 5; Hab. 3:3–19; Rev. 18).

20:16 drinking himself drunk. The thirty-two kings were over-confident and callous about their responsibilities.

20:23 Their gods are gods of the hills. Both Samaria and Jerusalem in the central hill country. In the polytheistic conceptions of the time, each god had specific zones of influence and strengths.

fight against them in the plain. It was understood that wars were fought not only by armies but also by their gods, and the Syrians wanted to fight in the plains where they thought Yahweh would be outside his sphere of influence and hence in a weak position.

and surely we shall be stronger than they.
24 And do this: remove the kings, each from
his post, and put commanders in their
places, 25 and muster an army like the army
that you have lost, horse for horse, and
chariot for chariot. Then we will fight
against them in the plain, and surely we
shall be stronger than they." And he listened to their voice and did so.

Ben-hadad Captured

26 [b]In the spring, Ben-hadad mustered
the Syrians and went up to [c]Aphek to fight
against Israel. 27 And the people of Israel
were mustered and were provisioned and
went against them. The people of Israel
encamped before them like two little
flocks of goats, but the Syrians filled the
country. 28 And a [d]man of God came near
and said to the king of Israel, "Thus says
the LORD, 'Because the Syrians have said,
[e]"The LORD is a god of the hills but he is
not a god of the valleys," therefore [f]I will
give all this great multitude into your
hand, and you shall know that I am the
LORD.'" 29 And they encamped opposite
one another seven days. Then on the seventh day the battle was joined. And the
people of Israel struck down of the
Syrians 100,000 foot soldiers in one day.
30 And the rest fled into the city of [c]Aphek,
and the wall fell upon 27,000 men who
were left.

Ben-hadad Released

Ben-hadad also fled and entered [g]an
inner chamber in the city. 31 And his servants said to him, "Behold now, we have
heard that the kings of the house of Israel
are merciful kings. Let us [h]put sackcloth
around our waists and ropes on our heads
and go out to the king of Israel. Perhaps he
will spare your life." 32 So they [h]tied sackcloth around their waists and put ropes on
their heads and went to the king of Israel
and said, "Your servant Ben-hadad says,
'Please, let me live.'" And he said, "Does
he still live? He is my brother." 33 Now the
men were watching for a sign, and they
quickly took it up from him and said,
"Yes, your brother Ben-hadad." Then he
said, "Go and bring him." Then Ben-
hadad came out to him, and he caused
him to come up into the chariot. 34 And
Ben-hadad said to him, [i]"The cities that
my father took from your father I will
restore, and you may establish bazaars for
yourself in [j]Damascus, as my father did in
Samaria." And Ahab said, "I will let you go
on these terms." So he made a covenant
with him and let him go.
35 And a certain man of [k]the sons of the
prophets said to his fellow [l]at the command
of the LORD, "Strike me, please." But the
man refused to strike him. 36 Then he said
to him, "Because you have not obeyed the
voice of the LORD, behold, as soon as you
have gone from me, a lion shall strike you
down." And as soon as he had departed
from him, [m]a lion met him and struck him
down. 37 Then he found another man and
said, "Strike me, please." And the man
struck him—struck him and wounded him.
38 So the prophet departed and waited for
the king by the way, [n]disguising himself
with a bandage over his eyes. 39 And as the
king passed, he cried to the king and said,
"Your servant went out into the midst of
the battle, and behold, a soldier turned and
brought a man to me and said, 'Guard this
man; if by any means he is missing, [o]your

26 [b][See ver. 22 above] [c]2 Kin. 13:17
28 [d]ch. 17:13 [e]ver. 23 [f]ver. 13
30 [c][See ver. 26 above] [g]ch. 22:25; 2 Kin. 9:2; 2 Chr. 18:24
31 [h]See 2 Sam. 3:31
32 [h][See ver. 31 above]
34 [i]ch. 15:20 [j][ch. 11:24]
35 [k]2 Kin. 2:3, 5, 7, 15 [l]ch. 13:17, 18
36 [m][ch. 13:24]
38 [n]1 Sam. 28:8
39 [o][2 Kin. 10:24]

20:24 remove the kings. The kings had been getting drunk (vv. 12, 16) and it would be wise to replace them with fighting men.

20:26 Aphek. About four miles east of the Sea of Chinneroth (Galilee).

20:31 the kings of . . . Israel are merciful. Certain powers in the Near East, such as Assyria, were brutal toward the vanquished.

sackcloth . . . ropes. The Syrians were dramatizing their humility and submission to the Israelites.

20:32 Your servant. Earlier, Ahab had addressed Ben-hadad as a superior (vv. 4, 9); now the tables are turned.

He is my brother. Ahab's surprising response depicts Ben-hadad as an equal in a treaty relationship (9:13), a concession Ben-hadad's men were quick to exploit (v. 33).

20:34 you may establish bazaars. International trade could bring substantial income (10:23–29), and the guarantee of a market in another country would afford a distinct economic advantage for the merchants of Israel.

these terms. The two kings formalize their negotiations by ratifying a covenant or treaty.

20:35 sons of the prophets. This designation does not mean physical children, but members of a prophetic guild or association. Elijah and Elisha were probably leaders of such groups (2 Kin. 2:3, 15; 4:1, 38; 6:1; 9:1).

20:36 Because you have not obeyed the . . . LORD. This highly unusual incident needs to be understood in the context of the previous story in which Ahab did not obey the dictates of holy war. Aware of Ahab's treaty with Ben-hadad II, the prophet is dramatizing the consequences of refusing to heed the word of God.

a lion shall strike you. The old prophet from Bethel uttered a similar decree of judgment against the man of God from Judah (13:20–25).

20:39 a talent of silver. This was a huge quantity (about 75 pounds), more than a common soldier could afford.

life shall be for his life, or else you shall pay
a talent[1] of silver.’ 40 And as your servant
was busy here and there, he was gone.” The
king of Israel said to him, “So shall your
judgment be; you yourself have decided it.”
41 Then he hurried to take the bandage away
from his eyes, and the king of Israel recognized him as one of the prophets. 42 And he
said to him, “Thus says the LORD, ‘Because
you have let go out of your hand the man
whom I had devoted to destruction,[2] therefore [o]your life shall be for his life, and your
people for his people.’” 43 And the king of
Israel [p]went to his house vexed and sullen
and came to Samaria.

Naboth's Vineyard

21 Now Naboth the Jezreelite had a
vineyard in [q]Jezreel, beside the
palace of Ahab king of Samaria. 2 And after
this Ahab said to Naboth, [r]“Give me your
vineyard, that I may have it for a vegetable
garden, because it is near my house, and I
will give you a better vineyard for it; or, if it
seems good to you, I will give you its value
in money.” 3 But Naboth said to Ahab,
“The LORD forbid [s]that I should give you
the inheritance of my fathers.” 4 And Ahab
[t]went into his house vexed and sullen
because of what Naboth the Jezreelite had
said to him, for he had said, “I will not give
you the inheritance of my fathers.” And he
lay down on his bed and turned away his
face and would eat no food.
5 But Jezebel his wife came to him and
said to him, “Why is your spirit so vexed
that you eat no food?” 6 And he said to her,
“Because I spoke to Naboth the Jezreelite
and said to him, ‘Give me your vineyard for
money, or else, if it please you, I will give
you another vineyard for it.’ And he
answered, ‘I will not give you my vineyard.’” 7 And Jezebel his wife said to him,
“Do you now govern Israel? Arise and eat
bread and let your heart be cheerful; I will
give you the vineyard of Naboth the
Jezreelite.”
8 [u]So she wrote letters in Ahab’s name
and sealed them with his seal, and she sent
the letters to [v]the elders and the leaders
who lived with Naboth in his city. 9 And
she wrote in the letters, “Proclaim a fast,
and set Naboth at the head of the people.
10 And set two [w]worthless men opposite
him, and let them bring a charge against
him, saying, [x]‘You have cursed[3] God and
the king.’ Then take him out and stone
him to death.” 11 And the men of his city,
[v]the elders and the leaders who lived in his
city, did as Jezebel had sent word to them.
As it was written in the letters that she had
sent to them, 12 [y]they proclaimed a fast and
set Naboth at the head of the people.
13 And the two worthless men came in and
sat opposite him. And the worthless men
brought a charge against Naboth in the
presence of the people, saying, “Naboth
cursed God and the king.” So they took
him outside the city and stoned him to

42 [o][See ver. 39 above]
43 [p]ch. 21:4
Chapter 21
1 [q]ch. 18:45, 46
2 [r][1 Sam. 8:14]
3 [s]Lev. 25:23; Num. 36:7; Ezek. 46:18
4 [t]ch. 20:43
8 [u][Esth. 3:12] [v]ch. 20:7; Ruth 4:2
10 [w]See Deut. 13:13 [x]Ex. 22:28; Lev. 24:16; [Acts 6:11; 23:5]
11 [v][See ver. 8 above]
12 [y][Isai. 58:4]

1 A *talent* was about 75 pounds or 34 kilograms 2 That is, set apart (devoted) as an offering to the Lord (for destruction) 3 Hebrew *blessed*; also verse 13

20:40 So shall your judgment be. Ahab shows no mercy, and so passes judgment on himself (v. 42; 2 Sam. 12:7).

20:42 whom I had devoted to destruction. See Lev. 27:28; Josh. 6:17; 7:1, 20–26. The wars were campaigns fought and won by God Himself, using the Israelites as His agents. In fighting these wars Israel was to conduct itself in a prescribed manner, observing stipulations of holy conduct. Ahab was willing to accept divine victory, but he violated the rules for the holy war by making a treaty with Ben-hadad and yoking Israel to a foreign power (Deut. 7:1–6; 20:16–18).

your life shall be for his life, and your people for his people. Even though each person is responsible for his own conduct before God, the actions of each person inevitably affect the lives of others for good or ill.

21:1 Jezreel. About twenty-four miles north of Samaria. Ahab maintained a palace here in addition to one in the capital (18:45).

21:2 Give me your vineyard. In Canaanite nations a king could seize property and personal belongings at pleasure, because in theory all the property was owned by the royal family and only entrusted to their subjects. In Israel, God owned the land (Ex. 19:3–8; Lev. 25:23) and the people held it as His stewards (Num. 14:8; 35:34; Deut. 1:8). The powers of an Israelite monarch were limited in contrast to the powers of a Canaanite king (Deut. 17:14–20; 1 Sam. 8:9–19; 10:25). When Ahab wanted his neighbor’s vineyard, his thought was to negotiate a purchase (cf. 16:24).

21:3 The LORD forbid. Naboth’s reaction was quick, because his land was a sacred inheritance from the Lord. When the land was distributed following the conquest (Josh. 13–21), each family received its own inheritance as a divine gift and a trust. Since Naboth’s vineyard was his portion of his family’s inheritance, to sell it would mean cutting off his own descendants (Lev. 25:23; Num. 27:1–11; 36:1–12).

21:8 she wrote letters . . . to the elders and the leaders. Jezebel used the royal power to have Naboth falsely accused and executed.

21:9 Proclaim a fast. Jezebel, with Ahab’s complicity, fosters apprehensiveness among the town’s inhabitants, because fasting was a characteristic response to a crisis or major transgression (Judg. 20:26; 1 Sam. 7:5, 6; 2 Chr. 20:3; Jon. 3:5, 7–9).

21:10 two worthless men. The law of Israel stipulated that at least two witnesses were required to convict a person of a capital offense (Num. 35:30; Deut. 17:5, 6; 19:15).

cursed God and the king. The penalty for cursing God was death (Ex. 22:28; Lev. 24:10–16).

21:13 outside the city. In accordance with the Law, the murderers avoided ritual impurity (Lev. 24:14; Num. 15:35, 36). Second Kings 9:26 adds that Naboth’s sons were also killed, eliminating any possible heirs.

death with stones. 14 Then they sent to
Jezebel, saying, "Naboth has been stoned;
he is dead."
15 As soon as Jezebel heard that Naboth
had been stoned and was dead, Jezebel
said to Ahab, "Arise, take possession of the
vineyard of Naboth the Jezreelite, which he
refused to give you for money, for Naboth
is not alive, but dead." 16 And as soon as
Ahab heard that Naboth was dead, Ahab
arose to go down to the vineyard of Naboth
the Jezreelite, to take possession of it.

The LORD Condemns Ahab

17 [z]Then the word of the LORD came to
Elijah the Tishbite, saying, 18 "Arise, go
down to meet Ahab king of Israel, who is in
[a]Samaria; behold, he is in the vineyard of
Naboth, where he has gone to take possession. 19 And you shall say to him, 'Thus
says the LORD, "Have you killed and also
taken possession?"' And you shall say to
him, 'Thus says the LORD: [b]"In the place
where dogs licked up the blood of Naboth
shall dogs lick your own blood."'"
20 Ahab said to Elijah, [c]"Have you found
me, O my enemy?" He answered, "I have
found you, because [d]you have sold yourself
to do what is evil in the sight of the LORD.
21 Behold, I will bring disaster upon you. I
will utterly burn you up, and [e]will cut off
from Ahab every male, bond or free, in
Israel. 22 And I will make your house like
[f]the house of Jeroboam the son of Nebat,
and like [g]the house of Baasha the son of
Ahijah, for the anger to which you have
provoked me, and because you [h]have made
Israel to sin. 23 And of Jezebel the LORD also
said, [i]'The dogs shall eat Jezebel within [j]the
walls of Jezreel.' 24 [k]Anyone belonging to
Ahab who dies in the city the dogs shall
eat, and anyone of his who dies in the open
country the birds of the heavens shall eat."

Ahab's Repentance

25 ([l]There was none who sold himself to
do what was evil in the sight of the LORD
like Ahab, whom Jezebel his wife incited.
26 He acted very abominably in going after
[m]idols, as [n]the Amorites had done, whom
the LORD cast out before the people of
Israel.)
27 And when Ahab heard those words, he
[o]tore his clothes and [p]put sackcloth on his
flesh and [q]fasted and lay in sackcloth and
went about dejectedly. 28 And the word of
the LORD came to Elijah the Tishbite, saying, 29 "Have you seen how Ahab has humbled himself before me? Because he has
humbled himself before me, I will not
bring the disaster in his days; [r]but in his
son's days I will bring the disaster upon his
house."

Ahab and the False Prophets

22 For three years Syria and Israel continued without war. 2 [s]But in the
third year [t]Jehoshaphat the king of Judah
came down to the king of Israel. 3 And the
king of Israel said to his servants, "Do you
know that [u]Ramoth-gilead belongs to us,
and we keep quiet and do not take it out of
the hand of the king of Syria?" 4 And he said
to Jehoshaphat, "Will you go with me to
battle at Ramoth-gilead?" And Jehoshaphat
said to the king of Israel, [v]"I am as you are,
my people as your people, my horses as
your horses."

17 [z][Ps. 9:12]
18 [a]ch. 16:24
19 [b]ch. 22:38; 2 Kin. 9:26
20 [c][ch. 18:17] [d]ver. 25; 2 Kin. 17:17; Rom. 7:14
21 [e]2 Kin. 9:8; [ch. 14:10]
22 [f]ch. 15:29 [g]ch. 16:3, 11 [h]ch. 14:16
23 [i]2 Kin. 9:36 [j]2 Sam. 20:15
24 [k][ch. 14:11; 16:4]
25 [l]See ch. 16:30-33
26 [m][ch. 15:12; 2 Kin. 17:12; 21:11] [n]Gen. 15:16
27 [o]2 Kin. 6:30 [p]See 2 Sam. 3:31 [q]2 Sam. 12:16
29 [r]2 Kin. 9:25
Chapter 22
2 [s]For ver. 1-35, see 2 Chr. 18:2-34 [t]ch. 15:24
3 [u]Deut. 4:43; Josh. 21:38; 2 Kin. 8:28; 9:1, 14; 2 Chr. 22:5
4 [v]2 Kin. 3:7

21:24 dogs . . . birds of the heavens shall eat. See 14:11 and note.

21:25 There was none . . . like Ahab. See 16:30–33 and notes.

21:26 Amorites. The word here refers to the pre-Israelite inhabitants of Canaan (Gen. 15:16; Deut. 1:7; 2 Sam. 21:2).

21:27 tore his clothes and put sackcloth on. God's judgment, uttered through Elijah, changes Ahab's attitude. Tearing clothes and wearing sackcloth were marks of mourning and repentance (Gen. 37:34; 2 Sam. 3:31; 2 Kin. 6:30; Lam. 2:10; Joel 1:13).

21:29 I will not bring the disaster in his days. God revises the punishment He gave in vv. 21–24. The penalty was not rescinded but delayed a generation due to God's mercy.

his son's days. That is, Joram (2 Kin. 9:25, 26). Though Ahab would not live to see the end of his dynasty, he and Jezebel died shameful deaths (22:37, 38; 2 Kin. 9:10, 34–37).

22:1 three years. Israel had peace for three years following the two-year war between Syria and Israel described in 20:1–34. During this peace, Hadadezer (Ben-hadad II) of Syria, Ahab of Israel, and ten other kings formed a coalition to ward off an Assyrian invasion led by Shalmaneser III. Assyrian records report that in the major battle of this campaign fought at Qarqar, Syria, on the Orontes River (853 B.C.), Ahab contributed two hundred chariots and ten thousand soldiers. Assyria's claim to have won a great victory seems to be an exaggeration, because the Assyrians withdrew and did not try to invade again for about four years.

22:2 Jehoshaphat the king of Judah. On his reign, see vv. 41–50 and 2 Kin. 3:7–27.

22:3 Ramoth-gilead. Located about twenty-eight miles east of the Jordan River, near a tributary to the Yarmuk River, Ramoth-gilead became Israel's possession during the conquest (Deut. 4:43; Josh. 20:8; cf. 1 Kin. 4:13), and Ahab thought it was time to retrieve it from the Syrians (v. 4).

22:4 I am as you are. This diplomatic language signifies Jehoshaphat's agreement to join the campaign against the Syrians. Jehoshaphat seems to be a junior partner in this coalition rather than an equal of Ahab, because Ahab tells him what to do (v. 30). Since formerly Judah was

5And Jehoshaphat said to the king of
Israel, "Inquire first for the word of the
LORD." **6**Then the king of Israel [w]gathered
the prophets together, about four hundred
men, and said to them, "Shall I go to battle
against Ramoth-gilead, or shall I refrain?"
And they said, "Go up, for the Lord will give
it into the hand of the king." **7**But
[x]Jehoshaphat said, "Is there not here another prophet of the LORD of whom we may
inquire?" **8**And the king of Israel said to
Jehoshaphat, "There is yet one man by
whom we may inquire of the LORD, Micaiah
the son of Imlah, but I hate him, for he
never prophesies good concerning me, but
evil." And Jehoshaphat said, "Let not the
king say so." **9**Then the king of Israel summoned an officer and said, "Bring quickly
Micaiah the son of Imlah." **10**Now the king
of Israel and Jehoshaphat the king of Judah
were sitting on their thrones, arrayed in
their robes, at the threshing floor [y]at the
entrance of the gate of Samaria, and all the
prophets were prophesying before them.
11And Zedekiah the son of Chenaanah made
for himself [z]horns of iron and said, "Thus
says the LORD, 'With these [a]you shall push
the Syrians until they are destroyed.'" **12**And
all the prophets prophesied so and said,
"Go up to Ramoth-gilead and triumph; the
LORD will give it into the hand of the king."

Micaiah Prophesies Against Ahab

13And the messenger who went to summon Micaiah said to him, "Behold, the
words of the prophets with one accord are
favorable to the king. Let your word be like
the word of one of them, and speak favorably." **14**But Micaiah said, [b]"As the LORD
lives, [c]what the LORD says to me, that I will
speak." **15**And when he had come to the
king, the king said to him, "Micaiah, shall
we go to Ramoth-gilead to battle, or shall
we refrain?" And he answered him, "Go up
and triumph; the LORD will give it into the
hand of the king." **16**But the king said to
him, "How many times shall I make you
swear that you speak to me nothing but the
truth in the name of the LORD?" **17**And he
said, "I saw all Israel scattered on the
mountains, [d]as sheep that have no shepherd. And the LORD said, 'These have no
master; let each return to his home in
peace.'" **18**And the king of Israel said to
Jehoshaphat, [e]"Did I not tell you that he
would not prophesy good concerning me,
but evil?" **19**And Micaiah said, "Therefore
hear the word of the LORD: [f]I saw the LORD
sitting on his throne, [g]and all the host of
heaven standing beside him on his right
hand and on his left; **20**and the LORD said,
'Who will entice Ahab, that he may go up
and fall at Ramoth-gilead?' And one said
one thing, and another said another.
21Then a spirit came forward and stood
before the LORD, saying, 'I will entice him.'
22And the LORD said to him, 'By what
means?' And he said, 'I will go out, and will
be [h]a lying spirit in the mouth of all his

6[w]ch. 18:19 **7**[x]2 Kin. 3:11 **10**[y]See Ruth 4:1 **11**[z][Zech. 1:18, 19] [a][Deut. 33:17]

14[b]See ch. 17:1 [c]Num. 22:18; 24:13 **17**[d]Num. 27:17; Matt. 9:36 **18**[e]ver. 8 **19**[f]Isai. 6:1; Dan. 7:9; Rev. 4:2 [g][Deut. 33:2; Job 1:6; 2:1; Ps. 103:21; Dan. 7:10; Heb. 12:22] **22**[h][Judg. 9:23; Ezek. 14:9; 2 Thess. 2:11]

allied with the Syrians against Israel (15:16–21), this new arrangement marks a change in the foreign policies of both Israel and Judah. At some point in Ahab's reign, he formalized his relationship with Judah by giving his daughter Athaliah in marriage to Jehoram the son of the king of Judah (2 Kin. 8:18, 26). Athaliah was a devoted Baal worshiper, and the diplomatic marriage introduced state-sponsored Baal worship to Judah, corrupting the worship of Yahweh (2 Kin. 11).

22:5 Inquire first for the word of the LORD. It was usual to consult with God or His prophets before embarking on a major campaign (1 Sam. 23:1–4; 2 Sam. 2:1; 2 Kin. 3:11; 2 Chr. 20:3–17).

22:6 prophets . . . about four hundred men. The prophets whose words are recorded in the Scriptures are only a fraction of the total number of people who called themselves prophets in those times (18:19; 2 Kin. 3:13; Jer. 28). Prophets were also common in other societies of the ancient Near East.

they said, "Go up." Most of the Israelite prophets were eager to please their patrons, usually the kings, by pronouncing flatteries and agreeable messages (Jer. 28:1–4; Amos 7:10–13).

22:7 Is there not here another prophet of the LORD. Jehoshaphat is skeptical of his prophets.

22:8 Micaiah the son of Imlah. The name "Micaiah" means "Who is like Yahweh?" He appears only in this chapter.

he never prophesies good concerning me. According to Jeremiah, one should be wary of prophets who prophesy too optimistically about the nation's future (Jer. 29:8, 9).

22:10 sitting on their thrones. Ahab and Jehoshaphat sit in the city at the place where judicial and municipal decisions were made (Deut. 21:19; 25:7; Ruth 4:1–12; Amos 5:10–15).

22:11 Zedekiah. This man is one of the prophets sought out by Ahab.

horns of iron. The horns symbolize power (Deut. 33:17; Zech. 1:18–21). On symbolic actions of prophets, see 11:30 note.

22:14 As the LORD lives. A conventional oath (1:17 note).

what the LORD says to me. Even if he wanted to say something else, Micaiah can only speak the word of the Lord.

22:15 Go up and truimph. Micaiah is being sarcastic, and Ahab knows it.

22:17 I saw all Israel scattered. Micaiah depicts the defeated and leaderless armies of Israel in a state of anarchy.

that have no shepherd. The term "shepherd" can refer to a king (Zech. 13:7). Micaiah does not identify which shepherd is meant.

22:22 I will go out, and will be a lying spirit. One of the celestial beings carries out God's wishes by using the four hundred prophets as a means of reinforcing a false sense of security in Ahab (1 Sam. 16:14–16; Job 1:6–8, 12; Jer. 14:14–16; 23:16, 26; Ezek. 14:9; Gal. 1:6–9).

prophets.' And he said, 'You are to entice
him, and you shall succeed; go out and do
so.' **23** Now therefore behold, the LORD has
put a lying spirit in the mouth of all these
your prophets; the LORD has declared disaster for you."
24 Then Zedekiah the son of Chenaanah
came near [i]and struck Micaiah on the
cheek and said, "How did the Spirit of the
LORD go from me to speak to you?" **25** And
Micaiah said, "Behold, you shall see on
that day when you go [j]into an inner chamber to hide yourself." **26** And the king of
Israel said, "Seize Micaiah, and take him
back to Amon the governor of the city and
to Joash the king's son, **27** and say, 'Thus
says the king, [k]"Put this fellow in prison
and feed him meager rations of bread and
water, [l]until I come in peace."'" **28** And
Micaiah said, "If you return in peace, [m]the
LORD has not spoken by me." And he said,
[n]"Hear, all you peoples!"

Ahab Killed in Battle

29 So the king of Israel and Jehoshaphat
the king of Judah went up to Ramoth-
gilead. **30** And the king of Israel said to
Jehoshaphat, [o]"I will disguise myself and
go into battle, but you wear your robes."
And the king of Israel disguised himself
and went into battle. **31** Now the king of
Syria had commanded [p]the thirty-two captains of his chariots, "Fight with neither
small nor great, but only with the king of
Israel." **32** And when the captains of the
chariots saw Jehoshaphat, they said, "It is
surely the king of Israel." So they turned to
fight against him. And Jehoshaphat cried
out. **33** And when the captains of the chariots saw that it was not the king of Israel,
they turned back from pursuing him. **34** But
a certain man drew his bow at random[1]
and struck the king of Israel between the
scale armor and the breastplate. Therefore
he said to the driver of his chariot, "Turn
around and carry me out of the battle, [q]for
I am wounded." **35** And the battle continued that day, and the king was propped up
in his chariot facing the Syrians, until at
evening he died. And the blood of the
wound flowed into the bottom of the chariot. **36** And about sunset a cry went through
the army, "Every man to his city, and every
man to his country!"
37 So the king died, and was brought to
Samaria. And they buried the king in
Samaria. **38** And they washed the chariot by
the pool of Samaria, and the dogs licked up
his blood, and the prostitutes washed
themselves in it, [r]according to the word of
the LORD that he had spoken. **39** Now the
rest of the acts of Ahab and all that he did,
and [s]the ivory house that he built and all
the cities that he built, are they not written
in the Book of the Chronicles of the Kings
of Israel? **40** So Ahab slept with his fathers,
and Ahaziah his son reigned in his place.

Jehoshaphat Reigns in Judah

41 [t]Jehoshaphat the son of [u]Asa began to
reign over Judah in the fourth year of Ahab
king of Israel. **42** Jehoshaphat was thirty-five
years old when he began to reign, and he
reigned twenty-five years in Jerusalem. His
mother's name was Azubah the daughter of
Shilhi. **43** [v]He walked in all the way of Asa
his father. He did not turn aside from it,
doing what was right in the sight of the
LORD. Yet [w]the high places were not taken

1 Hebrew *in his innocence*

24 [i][Lam. 3:30; Mic. 5:1; Matt. 5:39; Acts 23:2] **25** [j]ch. 20:30 **27** [k][2 Chr. 16:10] [l][Judg. 8:9] **28** [m][Num. 16:29; Deut. 18:22] [n]Mic. 1:2 **30** [o]2 Chr. 35:22 **31** [p][ch. 20:1, 16, 24] **34** [q][2 Chr. 35:23] **38** [r]ch. 21:19 **39** [s][Amos 3:15] **41** [t]For ver. 41-43, see 2 Chr. 20:31-33 [u]ver. 51 **43** [v][2 Chr. 17:3] [w][ch. 15:14; 2 Kin. 12:3]

22:25 an inner chamber to hide. When the battle is over, Zedekiah will be disgraced and forced to seek refuge.

22:28 If you return in peace. Regardless of Ahab's will, the prophecy stands.

22:30 I will disguise myself. Ahab's disguise indicates that he fears Micaiah's words.

your robes. Ahab cynically has Jehoshaphat dress in royal robes, hoping that if a king has to be killed in battle (v. 17), it will be Jehoshaphat.

22:31 Fight with neither. Neutralizing the leader of an opposing army was critical, because the opposing army might then collapse.

22:38 the dogs licked up his blood. This action is a partial realization of Elijah's prophecy in 21:19 (cf. 2 Kin. 9:25, 26).

the prostitutes washed. The reference is possibly to sacred prostitutes from the temple of Baal.

22:39 the ivory house that he built. Archaeological excavations at Samaria have discovered decorative ivory inlays dating to this period. Such extravagance is criticized by Amos (Amos 3:15).

cities that he built. Archaeological excavations reveal that Samaria and Megiddo were refortified during this period.

Book of the Chronicles of the Kings of Israel. See note 11:41.

22:40 Ahaziah. On the reign of Ahaziah, see vv. 51–53; 2 Kin. 1.

22:41 in the fourth year. If Jehoshaphat was co-regent with his father Asa for three years, as some scholars believe, the fourth year would be 869 B.C. and would refer to the beginning of his independent reign.

22:42 he reigned twenty-five years. That is, 872–848 B.C.

22:43 doing what was right in the sight of the LORD. Jehoshaphat is one of the southern kings depicted in a positive light by the author of Kings.

the high places were not taken away. See note 3:2.

away, and the people still sacrificed and
made offerings on the high places.
44 [x]Jehoshaphat also made peace with the
king of Israel.
45 Now the rest of the acts of Jehoshaphat, and his might that he showed, and
how he warred, are they not written [y]in the
Book of the Chronicles of the Kings of
Judah? 46 And from the land he exterminat-
ed the remnant [z]of the male cult prostitutes who remained in the days of his
father Asa.
47 [a]There was no king in Edom; a deputy
was king. 48 Jehoshaphat made [b]ships of
Tarshish to go to [c]Ophir for gold, but they
did not go, for the ships were wrecked at
[d]Ezion-geber. 49 Then Ahaziah the son of
Ahab said to Jehoshaphat, "Let my servants
go with your servants in the ships," but
Jehoshaphat was not willing. 50 [e]And Jehoshaphat slept with his fathers and was
buried with his fathers in the city of David
his father, and Jehoram his son reigned in
his place.

Ahaziah Reigns in Israel

51 Ahaziah the son of Ahab [f]began to
reign over Israel in Samaria in the seventeenth year of Jehoshaphat king of Judah,
and he reigned two years over Israel. 52 He
did what was evil in the sight of the LORD
[g]and walked in the way of his father and in
the way of his mother and in the way of
Jeroboam the son of Nebat, who made
Israel to sin. 53 [h]He served Baal and worshiped him and provoked the LORD, the
God of Israel, to anger [i]in every way that
his father had done.

44[x][2 Chr. 18:1; 20:35, 36]
45[y][2 Chr. 20:34]
46[z]ch. 14:24; 15:12
47[a][2 Sam. 8:14; 2 Kin. 3:9; 8:20]
48[b]See ch. 10:22 [c]See ch. 9:28 [d]See ch. 9:26
50[e]2 Chr. 21:1
51[f]ver. 40
52[g][ch. 15:26]
53[h]ch. 16:30 [i][ch. 16:31, 32]

22:44 Jehoshaphat also made peace with the king of Israel. Whereas the early years of the divided kingdom were characterized by intermittent warfare, the treaty between Jehoshaphat and Ahab was the start of a period of peaceful relations between Judah and Israel (cf. 2 Kin. 8:18, 26).

22:45 how he warred. See 2 Kin. 3:7–27; 2 Chr. 17:11; 20.

Book of the Chronicles of the Kings of Judah. See note 11:41.

22:46 male cult prostitutes. See note 14:24.

22:47 a deputy was king. There was "no king in Edom," because in all likelihood Edom was a vassal of Judah. The king of Judah then decided who would rule in Edom (2 Kin. 8:20–22).

22:48 made ships. Jehoshaphat, like Solomon before him, wants to establish a navy of his own based at Ezion Geber (9:26–28; 10:22; 2 Chr. 20:35–37).

Ophir. See note 9:28.

22:49 Ahaziah the son of Ahab. See 1 Kin. 22:51–2 Kin. 1:18.

Let my servants go with your servants. See 2 Chr. 20:35–37.

22:51 and he reigned two years. That is, 853–852 B.C.

22:52 his father and . . . mother. Ahab and Jezebel (16:29–34).

in the way of Jeroboam. See note 12:30.

22:53 He served Baal and worshiped him. The worship of Baal, introduced and supported by Ahab and Jezebel, is perpetuated by their son (16:31 note).

THE SECOND BOOK OF THE

Kings

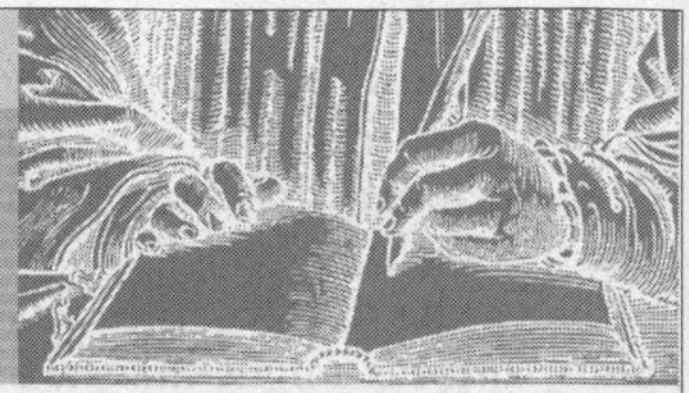

AUTHOR

The two books of Kings were originally one book that has been divided for the convenience of scribes or printers. Although Jeremiah was traditionally considered the author of Kings, most scholars now believe that it was the work of an unknown writer or group of writers who finished compiling it during the Judean Exile (see "Introduction to 1 Kings: Author").

DATE AND OCCASION

Second Kings begins during the reign of Ahaziah in Israel and Jehoshaphat in Judah. It carries the history through the exile of King Jehoiachin in Babylon. One of the high points of the book is the reign of Hezekiah, the first great reformer of worship at the temple (18:4). After the fall of Samaria, the northern kingdom of Israel, Hezekiah began the process of reunifying the people of the divided kingdom. The climax of the book is the reign of Josiah, the second reformer of the temple (22:3–23:24). Both Hezekiah and Josiah are singled out for their incomparable devotion to the Lord (18:5; 23:25). See "Introduction to 1 Kings: Characteristics and Themes."

CHARACTERISTICS AND THEMES

In the concluding chapters of the book, Jerusalem is captured by the Babylonians. The account of the fall emphasizes the rapid sequence of events culminating in the theft of the temple furniture and treasures. The ending of the book is abrupt and has led scholars to propose that the last two chapters were written during the exile in Babylon. See "Introduction to 1 Kings: Date and Occasion."

OUTLINE OF 2 KINGS

(Continued from Outline of 1 Kings)

III. Prophets and Kings (1 Kin. 17:1–2 Kin. 8:15)

- A. *The Prophets and Ahab (1 Kin. 17:1–22:40)*
- B. *Jehoshaphat of Judah (1 Kin. 22:41–50)*
- C. *Ahaziah of Israel Defies Elijah (1 Kin. 22:51–2 Kin. 1:18)*
- D. *Elijah Succeeded by Elisha (2:1–18)*
- E. *The Ministry of Elisha (2:19–8:15)*
  1. Elisha and the Prophets (2:19–25)
  2. Elisha and the War Against Moab (ch. 3)
  3. Elisha's Ministry to the Needy (ch. 4)
  4. Elisha and Naaman of Syria (ch. 5)
  5. Elisha and the Prophets (6:1–7)
  6. Elisha and the Syrian Siege of Samaria (6:8–7:20)
  7. Elisha and the Shunammite Woman (8:1–6)
  8. Elisha and Hazael of Syria (8:7–15)

IV. The Late Divided Kingdom (8:16–17:41)

- A. *Jehoram of Judah (8:16–24)*
- B. *Ahaziah of Judah (8:25–29)*
- C. *Jehu of Israel (chs. 9; 10)*
  1. Jehu Anointed King (9:1–13)
  2. Jehu's Bloody Coup (9:14–37)
  3. Jehu Massacres Ahab's Family (10:1–17)
  4. Jehu's Campaign Against Baal Worship (10:18–36)
- D. *The Coup Against Athaliah of Judah (ch. 11)*
- E. *Jehoash of Judah (ch. 12)*
- F. *Jehoahaz of Israel (13:1–9)*
- G. *Jehoash of Israel (13:10–25)*
- H. *Amaziah of Judah (14:1–22)*
- I. *Jeroboam II of Israel (14:23–29)*
- J. *Azariah of Judah (15:1–7)*

OUTLINE OF 2 KINGS (Cont.)

- K. *Zechariah of Israel (15:8–12)*
- L. *Shallum of Israel (15:13–16)*
- M. *Menahem of Israel (15:17–22)*
- N. *Pekahiah of Israel (15:23–26)*
- O. *Pekah of Israel (15:27–31)*
- P. *Jotham of Judah (15:32–38)*
- Q. *Ahaz of Judah (ch. 16)*
- R. *Hoshea of Israel (17:1–6)*
- S. *Reflection on the Exile of Israel (17:7–23)*
- T. *Resettlement by Assyrian Deportees (17:24–41)*

V. Judah Alone (18:1–25:30)

- A. *Hezekiah (chs. 18–20)*
  1. Summary (18:1–8)
  2. Assyrian Invasion (18:9–37)
  3. Divine Deliverance (ch. 19)
  4. Hezekiah's Illness (20:1–11)
  5. The Babylonian Envoy (20:12–21)
- B. *Manasseh (21:1–18)*
- C. *Amon (21:19–26)*
- D. *Josiah (22:1–23:30)*
  1. Repairing the Temple and the Discovery of the Book of the Law (ch. 22)
  2. Reforms in Jerusalem, Judah, and Samaria (23:1–20)
  3. Covenant Renewal and Passover (23:21–28)
  4. Death in Battle with Neco of Egypt (23:29, 30)
- E. *Jehoahaz (23:31–34)*
- F. *Jehoiakim (23:35–24:7)*
- G. *Jehoiachin (24:8–16)*
- H. *Zedekiah (24:17–20)*
- I. *The Babylonian Exile of Judah (25:1–21)*
- J. *The Assassination of Gedaliah (25:22–26)*
- K. *Jehoiachin in Exile (25:27–30)*

Elijah Denounces Ahaziah

1 [a]After the death of Ahab, Moab [b]re-
belled against Israel.
2 Now Ahaziah fell through the lattice in
his upper chamber in Samaria, and lay
sick; so he sent messengers, telling them,
"Go, inquire of [c]Baal-zebub, the god of
Ekron, [d]whether I shall recover from this
sickness." 3 But the angel of the LORD said
to Elijah [e]the Tishbite, "Arise, go up to
meet the messengers of the king of
Samaria, and say to them, 'Is it because
there is no God in Israel that you are going
to inquire of [c]Baal-zebub, the god of
Ekron? 4 Now therefore thus says the LORD,
[f]You shall not come down from the bed to
which you have gone up, but you shall
surely die.'" So Elijah went.
5 The messengers returned to the king,
and he said to them, "Why have you
returned?" 6 And they said to him, "There
came a man to meet us, and said to us, 'Go
back to the king who sent you, and say to
him, Thus says the LORD, Is it because
there is no God in Israel that you are sending to inquire of [c]Baal-zebub, the god of
Ekron? Therefore you shall not come down
from the bed to which you have gone up,
but you shall surely die.'" 7 He said to
them, "What kind of man was he who
came to meet you and told you these
things?" 8 They answered him, [g]"He wore a
garment of hair, with a belt of leather about
his waist." And he said, "It is Elijah the
Tishbite."
9 Then the king sent to him a captain of
fifty men with his fifty. He went up to
Elijah, who was sitting on the top of a hill,
and said to him, [h]"O man of God, the king
says, 'Come down.'" 10 But Elijah answered
the captain of fifty, "If I am a man of God,
[i]let fire come down from heaven and consume you and your fifty." Then fire came
down from heaven and consumed him and
his fifty.
11 Again the king sent to him another
captain of fifty men with his fifty. And he
answered and said to him, "O man of God,
this is the king's order, 'Come down quickly!'" 12 But Elijah answered them, "If I am a
man of God, [j]let fire come down from
heaven and consume you and your fifty."

Chapter 1
1 [a]ch. 3:5 [b][2 Sam. 8:2]
2 [c][Matt. 10:25; 12:24, 27; Mark 3:22; Luke 11:15, 18, 19] [d][ch. 8:8]
3 [e]1 Kin. 17:1; 21:17 [c][See ver. 2 above]
4 [f]ver. 6, 16
6 [c][See ver. 2 above]
8 [g][Zech. 13:4; Matt. 3:4; Mark 1:6]
9 [h]Deut. 33:1; Judg. 13:6; 1 Sam. 2:27; 9:6
10 [i]Luke 9:54
12 [j]Job 1:16

1:3 Elijah the Tishbite. See note 1 Kin. 17:1.

king of Samaria. See note 1 Kin. 16:24.

1:8 a garment of hair . . . a belt of leather. In his appearance, his ascetic life, and his prophetic boldness, John the Baptist resembles Elijah (Matt. 3:4). Both prophets carried out a ministry of judgment and repentance (Matt. 3:1–12; Luke 3:2–17).

1:9 man of God, the king says, 'Come down.' For Ahaziah, Elijah's prophecy constituted interference in the affairs of state, and he should therefore be held accountable to the king for his actions. Ahaziah's response reveals a characteristically Canaanite understanding of the unbridled powers of kingship (1 Sam. 8:11–17; 1 Kin. 21:2 note; cf. Deut. 17:14–20).

Then the fire of God came down from heaven and consumed him and his fifty.

13 Again the king sent the captain of a third fifty with his fifty. And the third captain of fifty went up and came and fell on his knees before Elijah and entreated him, "O man of God, please let my life, and the life of these fifty servants of yours, [k]be precious in your sight. 14 Behold, fire came down from heaven and consumed the two former captains of fifty men with their fifties, but now let my life be precious in your sight." 15 Then the angel of the LORD said to Elijah, "Go down with him; do not be afraid of him." So he arose and went down with him to the king 16 and said to him, "Thus says the LORD, 'Because you have sent messengers to inquire of [c]Baal-zebub, the god of Ekron—is it because there is no God in Israel to inquire of his word?—therefore you shall not come down from the bed to which you have gone up, but you shall surely die.'"

17 So he died according to the word of the LORD that Elijah had spoken. Jehoram became king in his place [l]in the second year of Jehoram the son of Jehoshaphat, king of Judah, because Ahaziah had no son. 18 Now the rest of the acts of Ahaziah that he did, are they not written in the Book of the Chronicles of the Kings of Israel?

Elijah Taken to Heaven

2 Now when the LORD was about to [m]take Elijah up to heaven by a whirlwind, Elijah and [n]Elisha were on their way from [o]Gilgal. 2 And Elijah said to Elisha, [p]"Please stay here, for the LORD has sent me as far as Bethel." But Elisha said, [q]"As the LORD lives, and as you yourself live, I will not leave you." So they went down to Bethel. 3 And [r]the sons of the prophets who were in Bethel came out to Elisha and said to him, "Do you know that today the LORD will take away your master [s]from over you?" And he said, "Yes, I know it; keep quiet."

4 Elijah said to him, "Elisha, [p]please stay here, for the LORD has sent me to [t]Jericho." But he said, [q]"As the LORD lives, and as you yourself live, I will not leave you." So they came to Jericho. 5 [r]The sons of the prophets who were at Jericho drew near to Elisha and said to him, "Do you know that today the LORD will take away your master [s]from over you?" And he answered, "Yes, I know it; keep quiet."

6 Then Elijah said to him, [p]"Please stay here, for the LORD has sent me to the Jordan." But he said, "As the LORD lives, and as you yourself live, I will not leave you." So the two of them went on. 7 Fifty men of [r]the sons of the prophets also went and stood at some distance from them, as they both were standing by the Jordan. 8 Then Elijah [u]took his cloak and rolled it up and struck the water, [v]and the water was parted to the one side and to the other, till the two of them could go over on dry ground.

9 When they had crossed, Elijah said to Elisha, "Ask what I shall do for you, before I am taken from you." And Elisha said, "Please let there be a double portion of your spirit on me." 10 And he said, "You have asked a hard thing; yet, if you see me as I am being taken from you, it shall be so for you, but if you do not see me, it shall not be so." 11 And as they still went on and talked, behold, [w]chariots of fire and horses of fire separated the two of them. And Elijah went up by a whirlwind into heaven.

13 [k][1 Sam. 26:21; Ps. 72:14]
16 [c][See ver. 2 above]
17 [l][ch. 3:1; 8:16]
Chapter 2
1 [m][Gen. 5:24] [n]See 1 Kin. 19:19-21 [o]ch. 4:38; [Josh. 5:9]
2 [p][Ruth 1:15, 16] [q]See Ruth 3:13
3 [r]ch. 4:1, 38; 5:22; 6:1; 9:1; 1 Kin. 20:35 [s]See ch. 4:38
4 [p][See ver. 2 above] [t][Josh. 6:26; 1 Kin. 16:34] [q][See ver. 2 above]
5 [r][See ver. 3 above] [s][See ver. 3 above]
6 [p][See ver. 2 above]
7 [r][See ver. 3 above]
8 [u][1 Kin. 19:19] [v][Ex. 14:21; Josh. 3:16]
11 [w]See ch. 6:17

1:17 Jehoram. Jehoram, like Ahaziah, was a son of Ahab (3:1; 1 Kin. 22:51). This Jehoram of the northern kingdom of Israel should not be confused with Jehoram (or Joram), the son and successor to Jehoshaphat (see 8:16, 23), who ruled in the southern kingdom (Judah) at about the same time.

1:18 Book of the Chronicles of the Kings of Israel. See note 1 Kin. 11:41.

2:1 up to heaven by a whirlwind. In the Bible only Elijah and Enoch (Gen. 5:24) are privileged not to die but to be directly taken up to heaven.

Gilgal. Located west of the Jordan near Jericho.

2:2 Bethel. Bethel is a major Israelite city in the central highlands (1 Kin. 12:29 note).

2:8 struck the water. Elijah, like Moses and Joshua before him, witnesses a division of waters that allows God's chosen to pass through safely on dry ground (Ex. 14:21, 22; Josh. 3:14–17).

2:9 a double portion. In Israel the oldest son received a double share of the family inheritance and with it the right of succession (Deut. 21:17). Elisha's desire for "a double portion of your spirit" was therefore a bold request to carry on Elijah's ministry.

2:10 You have asked a hard thing. It was not up to Elijah but to God to determine whether Elisha's daring request would be met.

2:11 chariots of fire and horses of fire. God's heavenly attendants escort Elijah to heaven "by a whirlwind." Fire appears several times in Elijah's ministry as a sign of God's all-consuming power (1:10, 12, 14; 1 Kin. 18:38; cf. 1 Kin. 19:12).

12 And Elisha saw it and he cried, "My
father, my father! [x]The chariots of Israel
and its horsemen!" And he saw him no
more.

Then he took hold of his own clothes
[y]and tore them in two pieces. 13 And he
took up the cloak of Elijah that had fallen
from him and went back and stood on the
bank of the Jordan. 14 Then he took the
cloak of Elijah that had fallen from him and
struck the water, saying, "Where is the
LORD, the God of Elijah?" And when he
had struck the water, [v]the water was parted to the one side and to the other, and
Elisha went over.

Elisha Succeeds Elijah

15 Now when [r]the sons of the prophets
who were at Jericho saw him opposite
them, they said, "The spirit of Elijah rests
on Elisha." And they came to meet him
and bowed to the ground before him.
16 And they said to him, "Behold now, there
are with your servants fifty strong men.
Please let them go and seek your master. It
may be that [z]the Spirit of the LORD has
caught him up and cast him upon some
mountain or into some valley." And he
said, "You shall not send." 17 But when
they urged him [a]till he was ashamed, he
said, "Send." They sent therefore fifty
men. And for three days they sought him
but did not find him. 18 And they came
back to him while he was staying at
Jericho, and he said to them, "Did I not say
to you, 'Do not go'?"

19 Now the men of the city said to Elisha,
"Behold, the situation of this city is pleasant, as my lord sees, but the water is bad,
and the land is unfruitful." 20 He said,
"Bring me a new bowl, and put salt in it."
So they brought it to him. 21 Then he went
to the spring of water and [b]threw salt in it
and said, "Thus says the LORD, I have
healed this water; from now on neither
death nor miscarriage shall come from it."
22 So the water has been healed to this day,
according to the word that Elisha spoke.

23 He went up from there to Bethel, and
while he was going up on the way, some
small boys came out of the city and jeered
at him, saying, "Go up, you baldhead! Go
up, you baldhead!" 24 And he turned
around, and when he saw them, [c]he cursed
them in the name of the LORD. And two
she-bears came out of the woods and tore
forty-two of the boys. 25 From there he went
on to [d]Mount Carmel, and from there he
returned [e]to Samaria.

Moab Rebels Against Israel

3 [f]In the eighteenth year of Jehoshaphat
king of Judah, Jehoram the son of
Ahab became king over Israel in Samaria,
and he reigned twelve years. 2 He did what
was evil in the sight of the LORD, though
not like his father and mother, for he put
away the [g]pillar of Baal [h]that his father
had made. 3 Nevertheless, he clung to [i]the
sin of Jeroboam the son of Nebat, [j]which
he made Israel to sin; he did not depart
from it.

12 [x]ch. 13:14 [y][1 Kin. 11:30]
14 [v][See ver. 8 above]
15 [r][See ver. 3 above]
16 [z]See 1 Kin. 18:12
17 [a]ch. 8:11
21 [b][ch. 4:41; Ex. 15:25]
24 [c][Neh. 13:25]
25 [d]Josh. 19:26; 1 Kin. 18:19, 20 [e][ch. 3:11]
Chapter 3
1 [f][ch. 1:17]
2 [g][ch. 10:26, 27; Ex. 23:24] [h]1 Kin. 16:31, 32
3 [i]1 Kin. 12:28, 31, 32 [j]See 1 Kin. 14:16

2:12 My father, my father. This title of respect for a person of authority (Gen. 45:8; Judg. 17:10; Matt. 23:9) will later be used for Elisha (6:21; 13:14). The prophet Malachi declared that Elijah would return before the coming of the "day of the LORD" (Mal. 4:5 and note). Elijah would prepare the people for the Lord's ministry (1:8 note).

2:13 took up the cloak. Earlier Elijah had cast his cloak upon Elisha as a sign that Elisha would be his successor (1 Kin. 19:19). Now what was promised takes place.

2:14 the water was parted . . . and Elisha went over. God designated Joshua as the approved successor to Moses (Num. 27:12–23; Deut. 31:1–8; 34:9; Josh. 1:1–9) by having Joshua lead the people across the Jordan River into the Promised Land, much as Moses led the people through the Red Sea (Ex. 14; 15; Josh. 3). Now God designates Elisha as the successor to Elijah by dividing the Jordan for him as He did for Elijah (v. 8).

2:15 the sons of the prophets . . . bowed to the ground before him. See note 1 Kin. 20:35.

2:19 the men of the city. These men are probably the leaders of Jericho (v. 18).

2:20 new bowl. A new vessel would be free from any ceremonial pollution.

put salt in it. Salt is a preservative, and is an appropriate symbol for how God is faithful to His promises and maintains His people (Lev. 2:13; Num. 18:19; 2 Chr. 13:5; Ezek. 43:24; Matt. 5:13; Mark 9:49, 50).

2:23 baldhead. It may be that the youths were sarcastically comparing Elisha with his teacher Elijah, who "wore a garment of hair" (1:8), and taunting him to "go up" to heaven as Elijah had done (v. 11).

2:24 cursed. Elisha in his ministry is characteristically compassionate toward the repentant and hard on the unresponsive and obstinate. The mauling of the Bethel youths becomes another public manifestation of the power of God present in His spokesman, Elisha (vv. 14, 21).

3:1 In the eighteenth year of Jehoshaphat. Probably Jehoram of Judah and his father Jehoshaphat ruled together as co-regents for approximately five years (853–848 B.C.). "The second year of Jehoram" (1:17) would be the same as "the eighteenth year of Jehoshaphat" (3:1).

twelve years. That is, 852–841 B.C.

3:2 pillar of Baal. See note 1 Kin. 14:23. Jehoram initiates a minor reform, attempting to undo some of the damage of his parents.

3:3 sin of Jeroboam. See note 1 Kin. 12:30. Jehoram's reform was not thoroughgoing; he did not address the fundamental flaw in the worship of the northern kingdom.

4 Now Mesha king of Moab was a sheep
breeder, [k]and he had to deliver to the king
of Israel 100,000 lambs and the wool of
100,000 rams. 5 But [l]when Ahab died, the
king of Moab rebelled against the king of
Israel. 6 So King Jehoram marched out of
Samaria at that time and mustered all
Israel. 7 And he went and sent word to
Jehoshaphat king of Judah, "The king of
Moab has rebelled against me. Will you go
with me to battle against Moab?" And he
said, "I will go. [m]I am as you are, my people as your people, my horses as your horses." 8 Then he said, "By which way shall we
march?" Jehoram answered, "By the way of
the wilderness of Edom."
9 So the king of Israel went with the king
of Judah and [n]the king of Edom. And when
they had made a circuitous march of seven
days, there was no water for the army or for
the animals that followed them. 10 Then the
king of Israel said, "Alas! [o]The LORD has
called these three kings to give them into
the hand of Moab." 11 [p]And Jehoshaphat
said, "Is there no prophet of the LORD here,
through whom we may inquire of the
LORD?" Then one of the king of Israel's servants answered, [q]"Elisha the son of
Shaphat is here, [r]who poured water on the
hands of Elijah." 12 And Jehoshaphat said,
"The word of the LORD is with him." So the
king of Israel and Jehoshaphat and the king
of Edom went down to him.
13 And Elisha said to the king of Israel,
[s]"What have I to do with you? Go to [t]the
prophets of your father and to [u]the
prophets of your mother." But the king of
Israel said to him, "No; it is [o]the LORD who
has called these three kings to give them
into the hand of Moab." 14 And Elisha said,
[v]"As the LORD of hosts lives, before whom
I stand, were it not that I have regard for
Jehoshaphat the king of Judah, I would
neither look at you nor see you. 15 But now
[w]bring me a musician." And when the
musician played, [x]the hand of the LORD
came upon him. 16 And he said, "Thus says
the LORD, 'I will make this dry streambed
full of pools.' 17 For thus says the LORD,
'You shall not see wind or rain, but that
streambed shall be filled with water, so
that you shall drink, you, your livestock,
and your animals.' 18 This is a light thing in
the sight of the LORD. He will also give the
Moabites into your hand, 19 and you shall
attack every fortified city and every choice
city, and shall fell every good tree and stop
up all springs of water [y]and ruin every good
piece of land with stones." 20 The next
morning, about the time of [z]offering the
sacrifice, behold, water came from the
direction of Edom, till the country was
filled with water.
21 When all the Moabites heard that the
kings had come up to fight against them, all
who were able to put on armor, from the
youngest to the oldest, were called out and
were drawn up at the border. 22 And when
they rose early in the morning and the sun
shone on the water, the Moabites saw the
water opposite them as red as blood. 23 And
they said, "This is blood; the kings have
surely fought together and struck one
another down. Now then, Moab, to the
spoil!" 24 But when they came to the camp
of Israel, the Israelites rose and struck the
Moabites, till they fled before them. And
they went forward, striking the Moabites as
they went. [1] 25 And they overthrew the cities,

4 [k][Isai. 16:1, 2] 5 [l]ch. 1:1 7 [m]1 Kin. 22:4 9 [n][1 Kin. 22:47] 10 [o][Josh. 7:7] 11 [p]1 Kin. 22:7 [q][ch. 2:25] [r][1 Kin. 19:21; John 13:4, 5] 13 [s][Ezek. 14:3] [t]1 Kin. 22:6 [u]1 Kin. 18:19 [o][See ver. 10 above]

14 [v]ch. 5:16; 1 Kin. 17:1 15 [w][1 Sam. 10:5; 1 Chr. 25:1] [x]1 Kin. 18:46; Ezek. 1:3; 3:14, 22; 8:1; 37:1; 40:1 19 [y][ver. 25; Isai. 25:2] 20 [z][Ex. 29:39, 40]

1 Septuagint; the meaning of the Hebrew is uncertain

3:4 Mesha king of Moab. According to the Moabite Stone, Mesha acknowledged that, like his predecessors, he also was a vassal to Israel. He claimed to have freed his land from subjection to Israel and boasted that "Israel has perished forever."

he had to deliver to the king. Part of Mesha's obligations as a vassal would be to pay tribute regularly to his superior.

3:9 king of Edom. The ruler of Edom was likely a vassal to the king of Judah and therefore obliged to assist him (cf. 8:20; 1 Kin. 22:47).

3:11 Is there no prophet of the LORD here. Jehoshaphat posed a similar question to Ahab (1 Kin. 22:7).

3:14 regard for Jehoshaphat. Elisha consents to prophesy for the coalition, but only for the sake of Jehoshaphat, whose reign was viewed positively (1 Kin. 22:43).

3:15 bring me a musician. The musician was employed to provide an atmosphere suitable for the reception of divine revelation (cf. 1 Sam. 10:5, 6; 19:20–24).

the hand of the LORD. The phrase is a symbol of prophetic inspiration (Ezek. 1:3; 8:1; 13:9).

3:16 this dry streambed. This is usually identified as the Valley of Zered, a wadi (seasonal stream) that flows into the southern end of the Dead Sea and formed the border between Edom and Moab (Deut. 2:13).

3:20 water came from the direction of Edom. Flash floods in the mountains of Edom flowed rapidly through the stream bed in the direction of the Dead Sea.

3:22 the water . . . as red as blood. The water was colored by Edom's red sandstone (cf. Gen. 25:30).

3:25 Kir-haraseth. Probably this was the capital of Moab (Is. 16:7, 11; Jer. 48:31, 36), about eleven miles east of the Dead Sea and fourteen miles north of the Valley of Zered.

and [a]on every good piece of land every man
threw a stone until it was covered. They
stopped every spring of water and felled all
the good trees, till only its stones were left
in [b]Kir-hareseth, and the slingers surrounded and attacked it. 26 When the king of
Moab saw that the battle was going against
him, he took with him 700 [c]swordsmen to
break through, opposite the king of Edom,
but they could not. 27 Then he took his oldest son who was to reign in his place [d]and
offered him for a burnt offering on the wall.
And there came great wrath against Israel.
And they withdrew from him and returned
to their own land.

Elisha and the Widow's Oil

4 Now the wife of one of the [e]sons of the
prophets cried to Elisha, "Your servant
my husband is dead, and you know that
your servant feared the LORD, [f]but the creditor has come to take my two children to be
his slaves." 2 And Elisha said to her, "What
shall I do for you? Tell me; what have you in
the house?" And she said, "Your servant has
nothing in the house except a jar of oil."
3 Then he said, "Go outside, borrow vessels
from all your neighbors, empty vessels and
not too few. 4 Then go in and shut the door
behind yourself and your sons and pour
into all these vessels. And when one is full,
set it aside." 5 So she went from him and
shut the door behind herself and her sons.
And as she poured they brought the vessels
to her. 6 When the vessels were full, she said
to her son, "Bring me another vessel." And
he said to her, "There is not another." Then
the oil stopped flowing. 7 She came and told
the [g]man of God, and he said, "Go, sell the
oil and pay your debts, and you and your
sons can live on the rest."

Elisha and the Shunammite Woman

8 One day Elisha went on to [h]Shunem,
where a [i]wealthy woman lived, who urged
him to eat some food. So whenever he
passed that way, he would turn in there to
eat food. 9 And she said to her husband,
"Behold now, I know that this is a holy
[g]man of God who is continually passing
our way. 10 Let us make a small room on the
roof with walls and put there for him a bed,
a table, a chair, and a lamp, so that whenever he comes to us, he can go in there."
11 One day he came there, and he turned
into the chamber and rested there. 12 And
he said to [j]Gehazi his servant, "Call this
Shunammite." When he had called her,
she stood before him. 13 And he said to
him, "Say now to her, 'See, you have taken
all this trouble for us; what is to be done
for you? Would you have a word spoken
on your behalf to the king or to [k]the commander of the army?'" She answered, "I
dwell among my own people." 14 And he
said, "What then is to be done for her?"
Gehazi answered, "Well, she has no son,
and her husband is old." 15 He said, "Call
her." And when he had called her, she
stood in the doorway. 16 And he said, "At
this season, [l]about this time next year, you
shall embrace a son." And she said, "No,
my lord, [g]O man of God; [m]do not lie to
your servant." 17 But the woman conceived, and she bore a son about that time
[l]the following spring, as Elisha had said to
her.

Elisha Raises the Shunammite's Son

18 When the child had grown, he went
out one day to his father among the
reapers. 19 And he said to his father, "Oh,
[n]my head, my head!" The father said to his
servant, "Carry him to his mother." 20 And
when he had lifted him and brought him to
his mother, the child sat on her lap till
noon, and then he died. 21 And she went up
[o]and laid him on the bed of the [g]man of
God and shut the door behind him and

25 [a][ver. 19] [b]Isai. 16:7; [Isai. 15:1; 16:11; Jer. 48:31, 36] **26** [c][Judg. 20:2] **27** [d]Amos 2:1; [Mic. 6:7]
Chapter 4
1 [e]See ch. 2:3 [f][Lev. 25:39-41; 1 Sam. 22:2; Neh. 5:5; Matt. 18:25] **7** [g]See Deut. 33:1 **8** [h]Josh. 19:18 [i][1 Sam. 25:2; 2 Sam. 19:32]
9 [g][See ver. 7 above] **12** [j]ch. 5:20, 21, 25; 8:4, 5 **13** [k]2 Sam. 19:13; [ch. 5:1] **16** [l]Gen. 18:14; [Gen. 17:21] [g][See ver. 7 above] [m]ver. 28 **17** [l][See ver. 16 above] **19** [n][Ps. 121:6] **21** [o]ver. 32 [g][See ver. 7 above]

3:27 his oldest son. This grisly act was meant to induce the god Chemosh to deliver the Moabites from certain defeat. Child sacrifice was expressly forbidden in Israel (Ex. 34:20; Deut. 18:10); nevertheless, two later kings of Judah (Ahaz and Manasseh) apparently practiced it (16:3; 21:6).

4:1 sons of the prophets. See note 1 Kin. 20:35.

my two children to be his slaves. The Mosaic law allows taking children as bond servants (or slaves) for a limited period of time (Ex. 21:2, 7; Lev. 25:39–46; Deut. 15:12–18). Unfortunately, this provision was often abused (Neh. 5:5–8; Jer. 34:8–22; Amos 2:6; 8:6).

4:8 Shunem. In northern Canaan, outside Israel (1 Kin. 1:3 note).

4:12 Gehazi. Elisha's personal attendant (5:20–27; 6:15).

4:14 she has no son, and her husband is old. An heir was of great importance because the family name and possessions would be passed on to the children. Without a son, a family's home and goods would be given to others. Moreover, living as a widow, a real prospect for this woman, would be very difficult (1 Kin. 17:9 note).

4:17 bore a son. Throughout the Bible, God's grace to childless women, such as Sarah (Gen. 17:16–19), Rebekah (Gen. 25:21–26), Rachel (Gen. 29:31; 30:22–24), and Elizabeth (Luke 1:5–25), shows His love and compassion for the poor and downtrodden.

4:21 laid him on the bed of the man of God. She refuses to accept the death of her son and conceals his body in Elisha's room so that the ritual

went out. 22 Then she called to her husband
and said, "Send me one of the servants and
one of the donkeys, that I may quickly go
to [g]the man of God and come back again."
23 And he said, "Why will you go to him
today? It is neither [p]new moon nor
Sabbath." She said, "All is well." 24 Then
she saddled the donkey, and she said to
her servant, "Urge the animal on; do not
slacken the pace for me unless I tell you."
25 So she set out and came to the man of
God [q]at Mount Carmel.

When the man of God saw her coming,
he said to Gehazi his servant, "Look, there
is the Shunammite. 26 Run at once to meet
her and say to her, 'Is all well with you? Is
all well with your husband? Is all well with
the child?'" And she answered, "All is
well." 27 And when she came [r]to the mountain to the man of God, she caught hold of
his feet. And Gehazi came to push her
away. But the man of God said, "Leave her
alone, for she is in bitter distress, and the
LORD has hidden it from me and has not
told me." 28 Then she said, "Did I ask my
lord for a son? [s]Did I not say, 'Do not
deceive me?'" 29 He said to Gehazi, [t]"Tie up
your garment and [u]take my staff in your
hand and go. If you meet anyone, [v]do not
greet him, and if anyone greets you, do not
reply. And [u]lay my staff on the face of the
child." 30 Then the mother of the child said,
[w]"As the LORD lives and as you yourself
live, I will not leave you." So he arose and
followed her. 31 Gehazi went on ahead and
laid the staff on the face of the child, but
there was no sound or sign of life.
Therefore he returned to meet him and
told him, "The child [x]has not awakened."
32 When Elisha came into the house, he
saw the child lying dead on his bed. 33 So
he went in and [y]shut the door behind the
two of them [z]and prayed to the LORD.
34 Then he went up and lay on the child,
putting his mouth on his mouth, his eyes
on his eyes, and his hands on his hands.
And as [a]he stretched himself upon him,
the flesh of the child became warm. 35 Then
he got up again and walked once back and
forth in the house, and went up [a]and
stretched himself upon him. The child
sneezed seven times, and the child opened
his eyes. 36 Then he summoned Gehazi and
said, "Call this Shunammite." So he called
her. And when she came to him, he said,
"Pick up your son." 37 She came and fell at
his feet, bowing to the ground. [b]Then she
picked up her son and went out.

Elisha Purifies the Deadly Stew

38 And Elisha came again to [c]Gilgal when
[d]there was a famine in the land. And as
[e]the sons of the prophets [f]were sitting
before him, he said to his servant, [g]"Set on
the large pot, and boil stew for the sons of
the prophets." 39 One of them went out
into the field to gather herbs, and found a
wild vine and gathered from it his lap full
of wild gourds, and came and cut them up
into the pot of stew, not knowing what
they were. 40 And they poured out some for
the men to eat. But while they were eating
of the stew, they cried out, "O man of God,
there is death in the pot!" And they could
not eat it. 41 He said, "Then bring flour."
[h]And he threw it into the pot and said,
"Pour some out for the men, that they may
eat." And there was no harm in the pot.
42 A man came from [i]Baal-shalishah,
[j]bringing the man of God bread of the firstfruits, twenty loaves of barley and fresh
ears of grain in his sack. And Elisha said,
[k]"Give to the men, that they may eat."
43 But his servant said, "How can I set this
before a hundred men?" So he repeated,
"Give them to the men, that they may eat,
for thus says the LORD, 'They shall eat and
have some left.'" 44 So he set it before them.
And they ate and had some left, according
to the word of the LORD.

22 [g][See ver. 7 above] 23 [p][Num. 28:11] 25 [q]ch. 2:25 27 [r]ver. 25 28 [s]ver. 16 29 [t]See 1 Kin. 18:46 [u][Ex. 7:19; 14:16; Acts 19:12] [v]Luke 10:4 30 [w]See Ruth 3:13 31 [x][John 11:11] 33 [y]ver. 4; Matt. 6:6; [Matt. 9:25; Mark 5:37, 40; Luke 8:51] [z]1 Kin. 17:20

34 [a]1 Kin. 17:21; [Acts 20:10] 35 [a][See ver. 34 above] 37 [b]1 Kin. 17:23; Heb. 11:35; [ch. 8:1, 5] 38 [c]ch. 2:1 [d]ch. 8:1 [e]See ch. 2:3 [f]Deut. 33:3; Luke 10:39; Acts 22:3; [ch. 2:3, 5] [g]Ezek. 24:3 41 [h][ch. 2:21; Ex. 15:25] 42 [i][1 Sam. 9:4] [j][1 Sam. 9:7] [k]See Matt. 14:16-21; 15:32-38; Mark 6:37-44; 8:4-9; Luke 9:13-17; John 6:5-13

of mourning will not begin (Gen. 50:10; 2 Chr. 35:25; Job 2:12, 13; Dan. 10:2; Mark 5:38; John 11:33).

4:23 It is neither new moon nor Sabbath. Ancient Israel had a lunar calendar, and a festival was celebrated at each New Moon (Num. 10:10; 28:11–15; Ezra 3:5; Neh. 10:33; Is. 1:13, 14; Amos 8:5). The law did not permit work on the Sabbath, and possibly not on the New Moon either (Ex. 16:23; 20:8–10; 1 Sam. 20:5; 1 Chr. 23:31).

4:27 caught hold of his feet. Doing this was a sign of respect (John 11:32).

4:38 Set on the large pot. During a famine, Elisha's request was not trivial (cf. 1 Kin. 17:11–13).

4:39 wild gourds. There exist in this area several more or less poisonous gourds that resemble edible plants.

4:42 Baal-shalishah. In the hill country of Ephraim, on the Brook of Kanah.

bread of the firstfruits. By bringing the firstfruits of the harvest, the man showed his dedication to Elijah and his gratitude for his prophetic work (Lev. 2:14; 23:9–21; Deut. 18:3–5).

Naaman Healed of Leprosy

5 [l]Naaman, [m]commander of the army of
the king of Syria, was a great man with
his master and in high favor, because by
him the LORD had given victory to Syria. He
was a mighty man of valor, but he was a
leper.[1] **2**Now the Syrians on [n]one of their
raids had carried off a little girl from the
land of Israel, and she worked in the service of Naaman's wife. **3**She said to her
mistress, "Would that my lord were with
the prophet who is in Samaria! He would
cure him of his leprosy." **4**So Naaman went
in and told his lord, "Thus and so spoke
the girl from the land of Israel." **5**And the
king of Syria said, "Go now, and I will send
a letter to the king of Israel."
So he went, [o]taking with him ten talents
of silver, six thousand shekels[2] of gold, and
ten [p]changes of clothes. **6**And he brought
the letter to the king of Israel, which read,
"When this letter reaches you, know that I
have sent to you Naaman my servant, that
you may cure him of his leprosy." **7**And
when the king of Israel read the letter, [q]he
tore his clothes and said, [r]"Am I God, to
kill and to make alive, that this man sends
word to me to cure a man of his leprosy?
Only [s]consider, and see how he is seeking
a quarrel with me."
8But when Elisha the [t]man of God heard
that the king of Israel had torn his clothes,
he sent to the king, saying, "Why have you
torn your clothes? Let him come now to
me, that he may know that there is a
prophet in Israel." **9**So Naaman came with
his horses and chariots and stood at the
door of Elisha's house. **10**And Elisha sent a
messenger to him, saying, [u]"Go and wash
in the Jordan seven times, and your flesh
shall be restored, and you shall be clean."
11But Naaman was angry and went away,
saying, "Behold, I thought that he would
surely come out to me and stand and call
upon the name of the LORD his God, and
wave his hand over the place and cure
the leper. **12**Are not Abana[3] and Pharpar,
the rivers of [v]Damascus, better than all the
waters of Israel? Could I not wash in them
and be clean?" So he turned and went away
in a rage. **13**But his servants came near and
said to him, [w]"My father, it is a great word
the prophet has spoken to you; will you
not do it? Has he actually said to you,
'Wash, and be clean'?" **14**So he went down
and dipped himself seven times in the
Jordan, according to the word of the man
of God, [x]and his flesh was restored like the
flesh of a little child, [y]and he was clean.

Gehazi's Greed and Punishment

15Then he returned to the man of God,
he and all his company, and he came and
stood before him. And he said, "Behold, I
know that [z]there is no God in all the earth
but in Israel; so [a]accept now a present from
your servant." **16**But he said, [b]"As the LORD
lives, before whom I stand, [c]I will receive
none." And he urged him to take it, but he
refused. **17**Then Naaman said, "If not,
please let there be given to your servant
two mules' load of earth, for from now on

Chapter 5
1 [l]Luke 4:27 [m][ch. 4:13]
2 [n]ch. 6:23
5 [o][ch. 4:42; 8:8, 9; 1 Sam. 9:7] [p]Ver. 22, 23; [Judg. 14:12]
7 [q]See Gen. 44:13 [r][Gen. 30:2; Deut. 32:39; 1 Sam. 2:6] [s][1 Kin. 20:7]
8 [t]See Deut. 33:1
10 [u][John 9:7]
12 [v][1 Kin. 11:24]
13 [w][ch. 6:21; 8:9; Judg. 17:10]
14 [x]ver. 10; [Job 33:25] [y]Luke 4:27
15 [z][Dan. 2:47; 3:29; 6:26, 27] [a][Gen. 33:11]
16 [b]ch. 3:14; 1 Kin. 17:1 [c][Gen. 14:23]

1 *Leprosy* was a term for several skin diseases; see Leviticus 13 2 A *talent* was about 75 pounds or 34 kilograms; a *shekel* was about 2/5 ounce or 11 grams 3 Or *Amana*

5:1 the king of Syria. This king and the king of Israel (v. 5) are probably Ben-hadad II (8:7; 13:3; 1 Kin. 20:1) and Jehoram (1:17; 3:1; 9:24).

5:2 raids. During the long history of tension between Israel and Syria there were often skirmishes and raids along the border.

5:5 a letter to the king of Israel. The Syrian king sends an official letter to the king of Israel introducing Naaman and asking for a favor on his behalf. The Syrian king has mistakenly supposed that Elisha's work is at the command of the Israelite king.

ten talents of silver, six thousand shekels of gold. That is, about 750 pounds of silver and 150 pounds of gold.

5:7 he tore his clothes. This was a sign of great distress (1 Kin. 21:27 note).

5:8 Why have you torn your clothes. Elisha scolds the king for reacting to the Syrian request with such alarm and not believing that God could help him.

he may know that there is a prophet in Israel. See 3:11; 8:7, 8; 1 Kin. 17:24; 18:36. Elisha responds affirmatively to the Syrian gesture (v. 3).

5:10 Elisha sent a messenger. Both Elijah and Elisha would often test the faith of the people to whom they ministered (1 Kin. 17:13; 2 Kin. 4:3, 4). In this case, Elisha does not even meet with Naaman but sends instructions through a messenger instead.

5:11 wave his hand over the place. Not realizing the importance of divine freedom and the critical role of faith, Naaman thought there was something contemptible about having to bathe seven times in the river.

5:12 Abana and Pharpar, the rivers of Damascus. If the prophetic healing was a meaningless ritual, Naaman might as well have stayed at home.

5:15 there is no God in all the earth but in Israel. Naaman was not merely saying that the Lord was more powerful than the Syrian gods; he was confessing that there is only one God, the Lord. In saying this, Naaman adopts the faith of Israel as his own (1 Kin. 18:39).

5:16 As the LORD lives. The words are an oath (1 Kin. 1:17 note).

5:17 two mules' load of earth. People in the ancient Near East believed that the gods were tied to the lands they ruled. Naaman asks for dirt from the Lord's land to sanctify the altar he plans to build for Him in another country.

your servant will not offer burnt offering or
sacrifice to any god but the LORD. 18 In this
matter may the LORD pardon your servant:
when my master goes into the house of
[d]Rimmon to worship there, [e]leaning on my
arm, and I bow myself in the house of
Rimmon, when I bow myself in the house
of Rimmon, the LORD pardon your servant
in this matter." 19 He said to him, [f]"Go in
peace."
But when Naaman had gone from him a
short distance, 20 [g]Gehazi, the servant of
Elisha the man of God, said, "See, my master has spared this Naaman the Syrian, in
not accepting from his hand what he
brought. [h]As the LORD lives, I will run after
him and get something from him." 21 So
Gehazi followed Naaman. And when
Naaman saw someone running after him,
he got down from the chariot to meet him
and said, [i]"Is all well?" 22 And he said, "All
is well. My master has sent me to say,
'There have just now come to me from [j]the
hill country of Ephraim two young men of
the sons of the prophets. Please give them
a talent of silver and [k]two festal garments.'" 23 And Naaman said, [l]"Be pleased
to accept two talents." And he urged him
and tied up two talents of silver in two
bags, with two festal garments, and laid
them on two of his servants. And they carried them before Gehazi. 24 And when he
came to the hill, he took them from their
hand and put them in the house, and he
sent the men away, and they departed.
25 He went in and stood before his master,
and Elisha said to him, "Where have you
been, Gehazi?" And he said, "Your servant
went nowhere." 26 But he said to him, "Did
not my heart go when the man turned from
his chariot to meet you? Was it a time to
accept money and garments, olive orchards
and vineyards, sheep and oxen, male servants and female servants? 27 Therefore the
leprosy of Naaman shall cling to you and to
your descendants forever." So he went out
from his presence [m]a leper, like snow.

18 [d][1 Kin. 15:18; Zech. 12:11] [e]ch. 7:2, 17
19 [f]1 Sam. 1:17
20 [g]ch. 4:12 [h]See Ruth 3:13
21 [i]ch. 9:11
22 [j]See Josh. 24:33 [k]ver. 5
23 [l]ch. 6:3
27 [m]Ex. 4:6; Num. 12:10; [ch. 15:5]
Chapter 6
1 [n]See ch. 2:3
6 [o][ch. 2:21]

The Axe Head Recovered

6 Now [n]the sons of the prophets said to
Elisha, "See, the place where we dwell
under your charge is too small for us. 2 Let
us go to the Jordan and each of us get there
a log, and let us make a place for us to
dwell there." And he answered, "Go."
3 Then one of them said, "Be pleased to go
with your servants." And he answered, "I
will go." 4 So he went with them. And when
they came to the Jordan, they cut down
trees. 5 But as one was felling a log, his axe
head fell into the water, and he cried out,
"Alas, my master! It was borrowed." 6 Then
the man of God said, "Where did it fall?"
When he showed him the place, [o]he cut off
a stick and threw it in there and made the
iron float. 7 And he said, "Take it up." So he
reached out his hand and took it.

Horses and Chariots of Fire

8 Once when the king of Syria was warring against Israel, he took counsel with his
servants, saying, "At such and such a place
shall be my camp." 9 But the man of God
sent word to the king of Israel, "Beware
that you do not pass this place, for the
Syrians are going down there." 10 And the
king of Israel sent to the place about which
the man of God told him. Thus he used to
warn him, so that he saved himself there
more than once or twice.
11 And the mind of the king of Syria was
greatly troubled because of this thing, and
he called his servants and said to them,
"Will you not show me who of us is for the
king of Israel?" 12 And one of his servants
said, "None, my lord, O king; but Elisha,
the prophet who is in Israel, tells the king
of Israel the words that you speak in your
bedroom." 13 And he said, "Go and see
where he is, that I may send and seize
him." It was told him, "Behold, he is in

5:18 Rimmon. The word "Rimmon" (lit. "pomegranate") is a parody of the name Ramanu, the Syrian storm god corresponding to Baal. This chief deity of Syria was also known by the name Hadad (Zech. 12:11).

5:22 sons of the prophets. See note 1 Kin. 20:35.

5:26 money. The word refers not to coins (which were probably not yet in use), but to quantities of gold or silver.

5:27 to you and to your descendants. Sin is not only individual, but corporate (Ex. 20:5).

6:1 the sons of the prophets. See note 1 Kin. 20:35.

6:5 axe head. This tool was expensive and relatively rare in Israel at this time. Because the prophet borrowed the axe head from a friend, its loss was a problem.

6:8 king of Syria. As in ch. 5, the kings of Syria and Israel (v. 9) are unnamed. They are most likely Ben-hadad II (8:7; 13:3; 1 Kin. 20:1) and Jehoram (1:17; 3:1; 9:24).

warring against Israel. Despite the ratification of a treaty between Israel and Syria (1 Kin. 20:34; 22:1), the two nations continued to fight.

[p]Dothan." 14 So he sent there horses and
chariots and a great army, and they came
by night and surrounded the city.
15 When the servant of the man of God
rose early in the morning and went out,
behold, an army with horses and chariots
was all around the city. And the servant
said, "Alas, my master! What shall we do?"
16 He said, "Do not be afraid, [q]for those
who are with us are more than those who
are with them." 17 Then Elisha prayed and
said, "O LORD, please [r]open his eyes that
he may see." So the LORD opened the eyes
of the young man, and he saw, and behold,
the mountain was full of [s]horses and chariots of fire all around Elisha. 18 And when
the Syrians came down against him, Elisha
prayed to the LORD and said, "Please strike
this people with blindness." [t]So he struck
them with blindness in accordance with
the prayer of Elisha. 19 And Elisha said to
them, "This is not the way, and this is not
the city. Follow me, and I will bring you to
the man whom you seek." And he led them
to Samaria.
20 As soon as they entered Samaria, Elisha
said, "O LORD, [r]open the eyes of these
men, that they may see." So the LORD
opened their eyes and they saw, and
behold, they were in the midst of Samaria.
21 As soon as the king of Israel saw them, he
said to Elisha, [u]"My father, shall I strike
them down? Shall I strike them down?"
22 He answered, "You shall not strike them
down. Would you strike down those whom
you have taken captive [v]with your sword
and with your bow? [w]Set bread and water
before them, that they may eat and drink
and go to their master." 23 So he prepared
for them a great feast, and when they had
eaten and drunk, he sent them away, and
they went to their master. And the Syrians
did not come again [x]on raids into the land
of Israel.

Ben-hadad's Siege of Samaria

24 Afterward [y]Ben-hadad king of Syria
mustered his entire army and went up and
besieged Samaria. 25 And there was a great
famine in Samaria, as they besieged it, until
a donkey's head was sold for eighty shekels
of silver, and the fourth part of a kab[1] of
dove's dung for five shekels of silver.
26 Now as the king of Israel was passing by
on the wall, a woman cried out to him, saying, "Help, my lord, O king!" 27 And he
said, "If the LORD will not help you, how
shall I help you? From the threshing floor,
or from the winepress?" 28 And the king
asked her, "What is your trouble?" She
answered, "This woman said to me, 'Give
your son, that we may eat him today, and
we will eat my son tomorrow.' 29 [z]So we
boiled my son and ate him. And on the
next day I said to her, 'Give your son, that
we may eat him.' But she has hidden her
son." 30 When the king heard the words of
the woman, [a]he tore his clothes—now he
was passing by on the wall—and the people looked, and behold, [a]he had sackcloth
beneath on his body— 31 and he said,
[b]"May God do so to me and more also, if
the head of Elisha the son of Shaphat
remains on his shoulders today."
32 Elisha was sitting in his house, [c]and the
elders were sitting with him. Now the king
had dispatched a man from his presence,
but before the messenger arrived Elisha said
to the elders, "Do you see how this [d]mur-
derer has sent to take off my head? Look,
when the messenger comes, shut the door
and hold the door fast against him. Is not
the sound of his master's feet behind him?"

1 A *shekel* was about 2/5 ounce or 11 grams; a *kab* was about 1 quart or 1 liter

13 [p]Gen. 37:17
16 [q]2 Chr. 32:7; [Ps. 55:18; Rom. 8:31]
17 [r]ver. 20 [s]ch. 2:11; [Ps. 34:7; 68:17]; See Zech. 1:8-10; 6:1-7
18 [t][Gen. 19:11]
20 [r][See ver. 17 above]
21 [u]ch. 5:13; 8:9; Judg. 17:10
22 [v]Gen. 48:22 [w]Rom. 12:20
23 [x]ver. 8, 9; ch. 5:2; 24:2
24 [y]1 Kin. 20:1
29 [z][Lev. 26:29; Deut. 28:53, 57; Ezek. 5:10]
30 [a]1 Kin. 21:27
31 [b][1 Kin. 19:2]; See Ruth 1:17
32 [c]Ezek. 8:1; 14:1; 20:1 [d][1 Kin. 18:4; 21:13]

6:16 those who are with us. Elisha is referring to God's heavenly host or army (cf. Josh. 5:13–15; 2 Chr. 32:7, 8; Dan. 10:20; 12:1). In fighting wars for God, the Israelites believed that they were not fighting alone, but with the power of God (Ex. 15:1–12; Deut. 20:1–4; 2 Sam. 22:7–16, 31–51). See also Matt. 26:53.

6:17 open his eyes. Elisha prays that the servant would see something that does not appear to the naked eye: God's heavenly armies waiting to do battle with the Syrians.

6:21 My father. The kings called Elisha "father" by way of respect (2:12 note; 13:14).

6:22 Would you strike down. Elisha's point is twofold. First, the captives do not belong to the king because the victory was God's. Second, captives who are at the mercy of their captors were not normally killed (Deut. 20:11; 2 Sam. 8:2).

6:24 Ben-hadad. Most likely Ben-hadad II (8:7; 1 Kin. 20:1 note).

6:25 a donkey's head was sold for eighty shekels of silver. An undesirable part of an unclean animal (Lev. 11:2–7; Deut. 14:4–8) was selling for two pounds of silver.

6:28 Give your son, that we may eat him. The curses of the Sinai covenant envision exactly this sort of cannibalism (Lev. 26:29; Deut. 28:52–57; cf. Lam. 2:20; 4:10; Ezek. 5:10).

6:30 tore his clothes. Doing this was a sign of distress (1 Kin. 21:27 note).

he had sackcloth beneath on his body. It became known that even the king was in a state of mourning (Gen. 37:34; 1 Kin. 21:27; Jon. 3:5, 6).

6:32 the elders were sitting with him. The leaders of the city were conferring with Elisha, not with the king (1 Kin. 8:1 note).

33 And while he was still speaking with
them, the messenger came down to him
and said, "This trouble is from the LORD!
[e]Why should I wait for the LORD any
longer?"

Elisha Promises Food

7 But Elisha said, "Hear the word of the
LORD: thus says the LORD, [f]Tomorrow
about this time a seah[1] of fine flour shall be
sold for a shekel,[2] and two seahs of barley
for a shekel, at the gate of Samaria." 2 Then
[g]the captain on whose hand the king
leaned said to the man of God, [h]"If the
LORD himself should make windows in
heaven, could this thing be?" But he said,
"You shall see it with your own eyes, but
you shall not eat of it."

The Syrians Flee

3 Now there were four men who were lepers[3] [i]at the entrance to the gate. And they
said to one another, "Why are we sitting
here until we die? 4 If we say, 'Let us enter
the city,' the famine is in the city, and we
shall die there. And if we sit here, we die
also. So now come, let us go over to the
camp of the Syrians. If they spare our lives
we shall live, and if they kill us we shall but
die." 5 So they arose at twilight to go to the
camp of the Syrians. But when they came
to the edge of the camp of the Syrians,
behold, there was no one there. 6 For the
Lord had made the army of the Syrians
[j]hear the sound of chariots and of horses,
the sound of a great army, so that they said
to one another, "Behold, the king of Israel
has hired against us [k]the kings of the
Hittites and the kings of Egypt to come
against us." 7 [l]So they fled away in the twilight and abandoned their tents, their horses, and their donkeys, leaving the camp as
it was, and fled for their lives. 8 And when
these lepers came to the edge of the camp,
they went into a tent and ate and drank,
and they carried off silver and gold and
clothing and went and hid them. Then they
came back and entered another tent and
carried off things from it and went and hid
them.

9 Then they said to one another, "We are
not doing right. This day is a day of good
news. If we are silent and wait until the
morning light, punishment will overtake
us. Now therefore come; let us go and tell
the king's household." 10 So they came and
called to the gatekeepers of the city and
told them, "We came to the camp of the
Syrians, and behold, there was no one to
be seen or heard there, nothing but the
horses tied and the donkeys tied and the
tents as they were." 11 Then the gatekeepers
called out, and it was told within the king's
household. 12 And the king rose in the night
and said to his servants, "I will tell you
what the Syrians have done to us. They
know that we are hungry. Therefore they
have gone out of the camp to hide themselves in the open country, thinking,
'When they come out of the city, we shall
take them alive and get into the city.'"
13 And one of his servants said, "Let some
men take five of the remaining horses, seeing that those who are left here will fare
like the whole multitude of Israel who have
already perished. Let us send and see."
14 So they took two horsemen, and the king
sent them after the army of the Syrians,
saying, "Go and see." 15 So they went after
them as far as the Jordan, and behold, all
the way was littered with garments and
equipment that the Syrians had thrown
away in their haste. And the messengers
returned and told the king.

16 Then the people went out and plundered the camp of the Syrians. So a seah of
fine flour was sold for a shekel, and two
seahs of barley for a shekel, [m]according to
the word of the LORD. 17 Now the king had
appointed [n]the captain on whose hand he
leaned to have charge of the gate. And the
people trampled him in the gate, so that he
died, as the man of God had said [o]when
the king came down to him. 18 For when
the man of God had said to the king, "Two
seahs of barley shall be sold for a shekel,
and a seah of fine flour for a shekel, about

33 [e][Job 2:9]
Chapter 7
1 [f]ver. 18
2 [g]ver. 17, 19; [ch. 5:18] [h]Mal. 3:10; [Gen. 7:11]
3 [i][Lev. 13:46]
6 [j][ch. 6:17; 2 Sam. 5:24; Job 15:21] [k][1 Kin. 10:29]
7 [l][Ps. 48:4-6; Prov. 28:1]
16 [m]ver. 1
17 [n]ver. 2 [o]ch. 6:32

[1] A *seah* was about 7 quarts or 7.3 liters [2] A *shekel* was about 2/5 ounce or 11 grams [3] *Leprosy* was a term for several skin diseases; see Leviticus 13

7:1 a seah of fine flour shall be sold for a shekel. Elisha prophesies a sudden reversal of the famine; seven quarts of flour will sell for less than one-half ounce of silver (cf. 6:25).

7:3 at the entrance to the gate. The Mosiac law prohibited people with skin diseases from living in the community (Lev. 13:46; Num. 5:1–4; 12:14, 15).

7:6 the Hittites and . . . Egypt. The Hittites lived in Asia Minor (Num. 13:29). Egypt (Hebrew *misrayim*) may have been confused with a minor state next to the Hittites whose name is similar to the Hebrew name for Egypt (cf. 1 Kin. 10:28, 29 notes).

this time tomorrow in the gate of Samaria,"
19 [n]the captain had answered the man of
God, "If the LORD himself should make
windows in heaven, could such a thing
be?" And he had said, [p]"You shall see it
with your own eyes, but you shall not eat
of it." **20** And so it happened to him, for the
people trampled him in the gate and he
died.

The Shunammite's Land Restored

8 Now Elisha had said to the woman
[q]whose son he had restored to life,
"Arise, and depart with your household, and
sojourn wherever you can, for the LORD [r]has
called for a famine, and it will come upon the
land for [s]seven years." **2** So the woman arose
and did according to the word of the man of
God. She went with her household and
sojourned in the land of the Philistines seven
years. **3** And at the end of the seven years,
when the woman returned from the land of
the Philistines, she went to appeal to the
king for her house and her land. **4** Now the
king was talking with [t]Gehazi the servant of
the man of God, saying, "Tell me all the
great things that Elisha has done." **5** And
while he was telling the king how [q]Elisha
had restored the dead to life, behold, the
woman whose son he had restored to life
appealed to the king for her house and her
land. And Gehazi said, "My lord, O king,
here is the woman, and here is her son
whom Elisha restored to life." **6** And when
the king asked the woman, she told him. So
the king appointed an official for her, saying,
"Restore all that was hers, together with all
the produce of the fields from the day that
she left the land until now."

Hazael Murders Ben-hadad

7 Now Elisha came to [u]Damascus. [v]Ben-
hadad the king of Syria was sick. And when
it was told him, "The man of God has come
here," **8** the king said to [w]Hazael, [x]"Take a
present with you and go to meet the man of
God, [y]and inquire of the LORD through him,
saying, 'Shall I recover from this sickness?' "
9 So Hazael went to meet him, and took a
present with him, all kinds of goods of
Damascus, forty camel loads. When he
came and stood before him, he said, [z]"Your
son Ben-hadad king of Syria has sent me to
you, saying, 'Shall I recover from this sickness?' " **10** And Elisha said to him, [a]"Go, say
to him, 'You shall certainly recover,' but the
LORD has shown me that [b]he shall certainly
die." **11** And he fixed his gaze and stared at
him, [c]until he was embarrassed. And the
man of God wept. **12** And Hazael said, "Why
does my lord weep?" He answered, "Because I know [d]the evil that you will do to
the people of Israel. You will set on fire their
fortresses, and you will kill their young men
with the sword [e]and dash in pieces their
little ones and rip open their pregnant
women." **13** And Hazael said, "What is your
servant, [f]who is but a dog, that he should
do this great thing?" Elisha answered, [g]"The
LORD has shown me that you are to be king
over Syria." **14** Then he departed from Elisha
and came to his master, who said to him,
"What did Elisha say to you?" And he
answered, "He told me [h]that you would certainly recover." **15** But the next day he took
the bed cloth[1] and dipped it in water and
spread it over his face, till he died. And
Hazael became king in his place.

1 The meaning of the Hebrew is uncertain

19 [n][See ver. 17 above] [p]ver. 2
Chapter 8
1 [q]ch. 4:35 [r]Ps. 105:16; Hag. 1:11 [s][Gen. 41:27]
4 [t]See ch. 4:12
5 [q][See ver. 1 above]
7 [u][1 Kin. 11:24] [v]ch. 6:24; 1 Kin. 20:1
8 [w]1 Kin. 19:15, 17 [x]See 1 Sam. 9:7 [y][ch. 1:2]
9 [z][ch. 5:13]
10 [a]ver. 14 [b]ver. 15
11 [c]ch. 2:17
12 [d]ch. 10:32; 12:17; 13:3, 7, 22; Amos 1:3, 4 [e]Isai. 13:16; Hos. 13:16; Nah. 3:10; [Ps. 137:9; Hos. 10:14]
13 [f]See 1 Sam. 17:43 [g][1 Kin. 19:15]
14 [h]ver. 10

8:1 a famine. The writer does not state how much time had elapsed between the events of ch. 4 and this incident.

8:2 in the land of the Philistines. That is, on the southwestern plain, where rainfall was quite adequate for agriculture.

8:3 to appeal. In his capacity as overseer of the nation's judicial system, the king hears special cases (1 Kin. 3:16 note).

8:4 the king. He is unnamed, but if this king is Jehoram (1:17; 3:13), it is surprising that he knows nothing of Elisha's activities. Either this incident took place soon after the events of 4:8–37 or the king referred to here is Jehu (ch. 9).

Gehazi. He was Elisha's personal attendant (4:12 note; 5:27 note).

8:7 Elisha came to Damascus. It was unusual for prophets to visit foreign capitals, but Elisha was on an unusual mission: to implement the first of the three commands God had given to Elijah on Mount Horeb (1 Kin. 19:15, 16).

Ben-hadad. Probably Ben-hadad II (6:24; 1 Kin. 20:1 note).

8:8 Hazael. The Lord had told Elijah that he should anoint Hazael as king over Syria, to be part of God's judgment against the house of Ahab (1 Kin. 19:15).

8:9 all kinds of goods of Damascus. The city of Damascus had an international reputation as a trade center of the ancient Near East.

Your son Ben-hadad. This is a diplomatic indication of the high regard Ben-hadad held for Elisha (6:21; 13:14).

8:12 set on fire . . . rip open. Such atrocities were common in ancient wars (Gen. 34:29; Ps. 137:9; Is. 13:16; Hos. 10:14; 13:16; Amos 1:13; Nah. 3:10). Elisha does not approve of such actions; he mourns them.

8:13 your servant . . . a dog. This expression of self-deprecation before a superior occurs in a number of extrabiblical documents (the Lachish and Amarna letters) from early sixth century Judah (see also a similar formula in 1 Sam. 17:43; 24:14; 2 Sam. 3:8). Assyrian inscriptions refer to Hazael as "the son of a nobody," that is, a commoner.

8:15 he took the bed cloth. Hazael takes Elisha's prophecy as a license to commit murder, an indication of Hazael's ruthlessness.

Jehoram Reigns in Judah

16In the fifth year of [i]Joram the son of
Ahab, king of Israel, when Jehoshaphat was
king of Judah,[1] Jehoram the son of
Jehoshaphat, king of Judah, began to reign.
17He was [j]thirty-two years old when he
became king, and he reigned eight years in
Jerusalem. **18**And he walked in the way of
the kings of Israel, as the house of Ahab had
done, for [k]the daughter of Ahab was his
wife. And he did what was evil in the sight
of the LORD. **19**Yet the LORD was not willing
to destroy Judah, for the sake of David his
servant, [l]since he promised to give [m]a lamp
to him and to his sons forever.
20In his days Edom revolted from the
rule of Judah and set up [n]a king of their
own. **21**Then Joram[2] passed over to Zair
with all his chariots and rose by night, and
he and his chariot commanders struck the
Edomites who had surrounded him, but
his army [o]fled home. **22**[p]So Edom revolted
from the rule of Judah to this day. Then
[q]Libnah revolted at the same time. **23**Now
the rest of the acts of Joram, and all that he
did, are they not written in the Book of the
Chronicles of the Kings of Judah? **24**So
Joram slept with his fathers and was buried
[r]with his fathers in the city of David, and
[s]Ahaziah his son reigned in his place.

Ahaziah Reigns in Judah

25[t]In the [u]twelfth year of Joram the son of
Ahab, king of Israel, Ahaziah the son of
Jehoram, king of Judah, began to reign.
26Ahaziah was [v]twenty-two years old when
he began to reign, and he reigned one year
in Jerusalem. His mother's name was
Athaliah; she was [w]a granddaughter of
Omri king of Israel. **27**He also walked in the
way of the house of Ahab and did what was
evil in the sight of the LORD, as the house
of Ahab had done, for he was son-in-law to
the house of Ahab.
28He went with Joram the son of Ahab to
make war against [x]Hazael king of Syria at
[y]Ramoth-gilead, and the Syrians wounded
Joram. **29**[z]And King Joram returned to be
healed in Jezreel of the wounds that the
Syrians had given him at [a]Ramah, when he
fought against Hazael king of Syria. And
[b]Ahaziah the son of Jehoram king of Judah
went down to see Joram the son of Ahab in
Jezreel, because he was sick.

Jehu Anointed King of Israel

9 Then Elisha the prophet called one of
[c]the sons of the prophets and said to
him, [d]"Tie up your garments, and take this
[e]flask of oil in your hand, and go to
[f]Ramoth-gilead. **2**And when you arrive, look
there for Jehu [g]the son of Jehoshaphat, son
of Nimshi. And go in and have him rise from
among [h]his fellows, and lead him to an
inner chamber. **3**Then take the flask of oil
and pour it on his head and say, 'Thus says
the LORD, [i]I anoint you king over Israel.'
Then open the door and flee; do not linger."

1 Septuagint, Syriac lack *when Jehoshaphat was king of Judah* 2 *Joram* is another spelling of *Jehoram* (the son of Jehoshaphat) as in verse 16; also verses 23, 24

16[i][ch. 1:17; 3:1] 17[j]For ver. 17-24, see 2 Chr. 21:5-10 18[k][ver. 26] 19[l]2 Sam. 7:12, 13; Ps. 132:11 [m]1 Kin. 11:36; 15:4; [2 Sam. 21:17] 20[n]ch. 3:9; [1 Kin. 22:47] 21[o]See 2 Sam. 18:17 22[p][Gen. 27:40] [q]Josh. 10:29, 30 24[r][2 Chr. 21:20] [s][2 Chr. 21:17; 22:6; 25:23] 25[t]For ver. 25-29, see 2 Chr. 22:1-6 [u][ch. 9:29] 26[v][2 Chr. 22:2] [w][1 Kin. 15:10] 28[x]ver. 15 [y][1 Kin. 22:3] 29[z]ch. 9:15 [a]2 Chr. 22:6; [ver. 28; 2 Chr. 22:5] [b]ch. 9:16

Chapter 9

1[c]See ch. 2:3 [d]See 1 Kin. 18:46 [e]1 Sam. 10:1 [f]ch. 8:28; [1 Kin. 22:3] 2[g]ver. 14; [ver. 20; 1 Kin. 19:16] [h][ver. 5, 11] 3[i][1 Kin. 19:16; 2 Chr. 22:7]

8:16 Jehoram. Jehoram probably reigned together with his father Jehoshaphat for five years before becoming the sole monarch of Judah (1:17; 1 Kin. 22:42). This verse marks the death of Jehoshaphat and the beginning of (Jehoram's) Joram's independent rule (848–841 B.C.).

8:18 walked in the way of the kings of Israel. Usually Judah's kings are evaluated with reference to their own predecessors. Jehoram is purposely contrasted with the "house of Ahab" because he imitated their policies. Ahab introduced and sanctioned Baal worship in the northern kingdom of Israel, and now Jehoram does the same in Judah.

the daughter of Ahab. The ruling dynasties of north and south were now linked by ideology and by blood (v. 26; 2 Chr. 21:6). Athaliah promoted Baal worship in the south much as her mother Jezebel promoted Baal religion in the north (1 Kin. 16:31; 18:4; 19:2).

8:19 for the sake of David his servant. Because of God's love for David, He was longsuffering with Judah (2 Sam. 7:12–16 notes; 1 Kin. 11:4 note).

give a lamp . . . forever. See note 1 Kin. 11:36.

8:22 to this day. See note 1 Kin. 8:8.

Libnah revolted. Libnah was near the border with Philistia, about fifteen miles southeast of Ashdod.

8:23 Book of the Chronicles of the Kings of Judah. See note 1 Kin. 11:41.

8:24 Ahaziah. He should not be confused with his maternal uncle, King Ahaziah of Israel (1 Kin. 22:40, 51–2 Kin. 1:18).

8:25 twelfth year of Joram the son of Ahab. That is, 841 B.C.

8:26 Athaliah. See note on v. 18.

8:27 He also walked in the way of the house of Ahab and did what was evil. Like his father Jehoram, Ahaziah imitated the religious policies of Ahab, sanctioning the worship in Judah of the Canaanite god Baal (1 Kin. 16:31 note).

8:28 He went with Joram the son of Ahab to make war. Earlier Jehoshaphat of Judah aligned himself with Ahab of Israel in a campaign against the Syrians at Ramoth-gilead (1 Kin. 22). This campaign, like the earlier one, ends in disaster (1 Kin. 22:32–37).

8:29 King Joram returned to be healed in Jezreel. A royal residence for the northern kings was maintained at Jezreel (1 Kin. 18:45 note). It was also the site of Ahab's and Jezebel's horrendous crime against Naboth (1 Kin. 21).

Ramah. That is, Ramoth-gilead.

9:1 sons of the prophets. See note 1 Kin. 20:35.

9:3 take . . . oil and pour it on his head. Elisha directs one of the prophets to perform a ritual of anointing used to designate a (future) king (11:12; 23:30; 1 Sam. 9:16; 10:1; 16:13; 2 Sam. 2:7).

4 So the young man, the servant of the prophet, went to Ramoth-gilead. 5 And when he came, behold, the commanders of the army were in council. And he said, "I have a word for you, O commander." And Jehu said, "To which of us all?" And he said, "To you, O commander." 6 So he arose and went into the house. And the young man poured the oil on his head, saying to him, "Thus says the LORD the God of Israel, [i]I anoint you king over the people of the LORD, over Israel. 7 And you shall strike down the house of Ahab your master, so that I may avenge [j]on Jezebel the blood of my servants the prophets, and the blood of all the servants of the LORD. 8 For the whole house of Ahab shall perish, [k]and I will cut off from Ahab [l]every male, [m]bond or free, in Israel. 9 And I will make the house of Ahab like [n]the house of Jeroboam the son of Nebat, and like [o]the house of Baasha the son of Ahijah. 10 [p]And the dogs shall eat Jezebel in the territory of Jezreel, and none shall bury her." Then he opened the door and fled.

11 When Jehu came out to the servants of his master, they said to him, [q]"Is all well? Why did [r]this mad fellow come to you?" And he said to them, "You know the fellow and his talk." 12 And they said, "That is not true; tell us now." And he said, "Thus and so he spoke to me, saying, 'Thus says the LORD, I anoint you king over Israel.'" 13 Then in haste [s]every man of them took his garment and put it under him on the bare[1] steps, and they blew the trumpet and proclaimed, [t]"Jehu is king."

Jehu Assassinates Joram and Ahaziah

14 Thus Jehu the son of Jehoshaphat the son of Nimshi conspired against Joram. ([u]Now Joram with all Israel had been on guard at Ramoth-gilead against [v]Hazael king of Syria, 15 [w]but King Joram had returned to be healed in Jezreel of the wounds that the Syrians had given him, when he fought with Hazael king of Syria.) So Jehu said, "If this is your decision, then let no one slip out of the city to go and tell the news in Jezreel." 16 Then Jehu mounted his chariot and went to Jezreel, for Joram lay there. And Ahaziah king of Judah had come down to visit Joram.

17 Now the watchman was standing on the tower in Jezreel, and he saw the company of Jehu as he came and said, "I see a company." And Joram said, "Take a horseman and send to meet them, and let him say, 'Is it peace?'" 18 So a man on horseback went to meet him and said, "Thus says the king, 'Is it peace?'" And Jehu said, "What do you have to do with peace? Turn around and ride behind me." And the watchman reported, saying, "The messenger reached them, but he is not coming back." 19 Then he sent out a second horseman, who came to them and said, "Thus the king has said, 'Is it peace?'" And Jehu answered, "What do you have to do with peace? Turn around and ride behind me." 20 Again the watchman reported, "He reached them, but he is not coming back. And the driving [x]is like the driving of Jehu [y]the son of Nimshi, for he drives furiously."

21 Joram said, [z]"Make ready." And they made ready his chariot. [a]Then Joram king of Israel and Ahaziah king of Judah set out, each in his chariot, and went to meet Jehu, and met him [b]at the property of Naboth the Jezreelite. 22 And when Joram saw Jehu, he said, "Is it peace, Jehu?" He answered, "What peace can there be, so long as [c]the whorings and the sorceries of your mother Jezebel are so many?" 23 Then Joram reined about and fled, saying to Ahaziah, "Treachery, O Ahaziah!" 24 And Jehu drew his bow with his full strength, and shot Joram between the shoulders, so that the arrow pierced his heart, and he sank in his chariot. 25 Jehu said to Bidkar [d]his aide, "Take him up and throw him [b]on the plot of ground belonging to Naboth the Jezreelite. For remember, when you and I rode side by side behind Ahab his father,

6 [i][See ver. 3 above]
7 [j][1 Kin. 18:4]; See 1 Kin. 21:5-15
8 [k]ch. 10:17; 1 Kin. 21:21; [1 Kin. 14:10] [l]See 1 Sam. 25:22 [m]Deut. 32:36
9 [n]1 Kin. 14:10; 15:29; 21:22 [o]1 Kin. 16:3, 11; 21:22
10 [p]ver. 35, 36; 1 Kin. 21:23
11 [q]ch. 5:21 [r]Jer. 29:26; Hos. 9:7; [John 10:20; Acts 26:24]
13 [s][Matt. 21:8; Mark 11:8] [t][1 Kin. 1:34]
14 [u][ch. 8:28] [v][1 Kin. 19:17]
15 [w]ch. 8:29
20 [x][2 Sam. 18:27] [y]1 Kin. 19:17; [ver. 2, 14]
21 [z]1 Kin. 18:44 [a]2 Chr. 22:7 [b]1 Kin. 21:1; [ver. 26]
22 [c][2 Chr. 21:13]
25 [d][ch. 7:2] [b][See ver. 21 above]

[1] The meaning of the Hebrew word is uncertain

9:9 like the house of Jeroboam . . . like the house of Baasha. God had destroyed these two earlier Israelite dynasties due to their unfaithfulness (1 Kin. 15:27–30; 16:8–13).

9:10 none shall bury her. The lack of a burial was a sign of disgrace (Jer. 8:2; 16:4–6; 22:19; 25:33).

9:11 this mad fellow. Because of their unusual lifestyle, eccentric habits, and ecstatic prophetic messages, the prophets struck some people as deranged (cf. Jer. 29:26; Hos. 9:7).

9:13 they blew the trumpet. The trumpets announced the anointing of a king (cf. 2 Sam. 15:10; 1 Kin. 1:34).

9:21 Naboth the Jezreelite. Jehu's coup reaches its climax at the very place Ahab and Jezebel had Naboth killed (1 Kin. 21:1–16).

9:22 What peace. Jehu's question addresses the heart of the issue. There can be no true peace where there is idolatry and witchcraft (cf. 17:17; 21:6; Judg. 2:17; 8:33; Hos. 2; 3; Nah. 3:4).

how [e]the LORD made this [f]pronouncement
against him: 26 'As surely as I saw yesterday
the blood of Naboth and the blood of his
sons—declares the LORD—I will repay you
on this plot of ground.' Now therefore take
him up and throw him on the plot of
ground, in accordance with the word of the
LORD."
27 [g]When Ahaziah the king of Judah saw
this, he fled in the direction of Beth-
haggan. And Jehu pursued him and said,
"Shoot him also." And they shot him[1] in
the chariot at the ascent of Gur, which is
by [h]Ibleam. And he fled to [h]Megiddo and
died there. 28 [i]His servants carried him in a
chariot to Jerusalem, and buried him in his
tomb with his fathers in the city of David.
29 In the [j]eleventh year of Joram the son
of Ahab, Ahaziah began to reign over
Judah.

Jehu Executes Jezebel

30 When Jehu came to Jezreel, Jezebel
heard of it. And [k]she painted her eyes and
adorned her head and looked out of the
window. 31 And as Jehu entered the gate,
she said, [l]"Is it peace, you Zimri, murderer
of your master?" 32 And he lifted up his face
to the window and said, "Who is on my
side? Who?" Two or three eunuchs looked
out at him. 33 He said, "Throw her down."
So they threw her down. And some of her
blood spattered on the wall and on the
horses, and they trampled on her. 34 Then
he went in and ate and drank. And he said,
"See now to this cursed woman and bury
her, [m]for she is a king's daughter." 35 But
when they went to bury her, they found no
more of her than the skull and the feet and
the palms of her hands. 36 When they came
back and told him, he said, "This is the
word of the LORD, which he spoke by his
servant Elijah the Tishbite, [n]'In the territory of Jezreel the dogs shall eat the flesh of
Jezebel, 37 and the corpse of Jezebel shall be
[o]as dung on the face of the field in the territory of Jezreel, so that no one can say,
This is Jezebel.'"

Jehu Slaughters Ahab's Descendants

10 Now Ahab had seventy sons in
[p]Samaria. So Jehu wrote letters and
sent them to Samaria, to the rulers of the
city,[2] to the elders, and to [q]the guardians of
the sons[3] of Ahab, saying, 2 "Now then, as
soon as this letter comes to you, seeing
your master's sons are with you, and there
are with you chariots and horses, fortified
cities also, and weapons, 3 select the best
and fittest of your master's sons and set
him on his father's throne and fight for
your master's house." 4 But they were
exceedingly afraid and said, "Behold, the
two kings could not stand before him. How
then can we stand?" 5 So he who was over
the palace, and he who was over the city,
together with the elders and the guardians,
sent to Jehu, saying, [r]"We are your servants, and we will do all that you tell us.
We will not make anyone king. Do whatever is good in your eyes." 6 Then he wrote to

25 [e]1 Kin. 21:19, 29 [f]See Isai. 13:1
27 [g][2 Chr. 22:9] [h]Josh. 17:11
28 [i][2 Kin. 23:30; 2 Chr. 35:24]
29 [j][ch. 8:25; 2 Chr. 21:17-19]
30 [k][Jer. 4:30; Ezek. 23:40]
31 [l]See 1 Kin. 16:9-20
34 [m]1 Kin. 16:31
36 [n]1 Kin. 21:23
37 [o][Ps. 83:10; Jer. 8:2; 9:22; 16:4; 25:33]
Chapter 10
1 [p]1 Kin. 16:24 [q][Esth. 2:7]
5 [r]Josh. 9:8, 11

1 Syriac, Vulgate (compare Septuagint); Hebrew lacks *and they shot him* 2 Septuagint, Vulgate; Hebrew *rulers of Jezreel* 3 Hebrew lacks *of the sons*

9:25 the LORD made this pronouncement against him. See 1 Kin. 21:21–24.

9:27 Ahaziah the king of Judah . . . died. Jehu was not authorized to kill the descendants of David who were related to the house of Ahab through his daughter Athaliah (cf. vv. 8–10). Jehu was too zealous in carrying out his commission. Hosea criticizes him for "the blood of Jezreel" (Hos. 1:4).

9:29 In the eleventh year. This figure may count only the whole years of his reign, leaving out the year he took the throne. This would agree with the figures given in 8:25.

9:30 Jezreel. Again the scene of action ominously returns to the site of Naboth's murder.

9:31 Zimri. In referring to Jehu in this way, Jezebel is sarcastically alluding to Zimri's bloody purge almost half a century earlier (1 Kin. 16:9–15).

9:32 eunuchs. This word could refer to men who were employed as guards and attendants of royal harems in the ancient Near East (as here) or to officials who served in the royal court (20:18; Is. 39:7; Jer. 29:2; 34:19; 38:7; Dan. 1:3, 7–10).

9:34 a king's daughter. Jehu does not dignify Jezebel with the title Queen of Israel, but refers to her as the daughter of Ethbaal, the Sidonian king (1 Kin. 16:31).

9:36 dogs shall eat the flesh of Jezebel. The judgment oracle Jezebel so contemptuously scorned in her life is now fulfilled in her death (1 Kin. 21:23). Dogs were also present at Ahab's death (1 Kin. 22:38).

10:1 seventy sons. This figure probably included grandsons. How many wives (1 Kin. 20:5) Ahab had is not known.

elders. See note 1 Kin. 8:1.

guardians of the sons. These guardians were responsible for bringing up and educating children in the royal household. The king was dead and Jehu addressed various lesser figures.

10:5 over the palace. See note 1 Kin. 4:6.

over the city. This position is similar to the "governor of the city" in 1 Kin. 22:26.

10:6 take the heads of your master's sons. Jehu's demand takes the form of a pun. In Hebrew "head" can mean part of the body or it can mean "leader" or "chief." It is uncertain whether Jehu is asking for the death of all Ahab's male descendants, or for the leaders among the royal princes.

them a second letter, saying, "If you are on
my side, and if you are ready to obey me,
take the heads of your master's sons and
come to me at Jezreel tomorrow at this
time." Now the king's sons, seventy persons, were with the great men of the city,
[q]who were bringing them up. 7 And as soon
as the letter came to them, they took the
king's sons [s]and slaughtered them, seventy
persons, and put their heads in baskets
and sent them to him at Jezreel. 8 When the
messenger came and told him, "They have
brought the heads of the king's sons," he
said, "Lay them in two heaps at the
entrance of the gate until the morning."
9 Then in the morning, when he went out,
he stood and said to all the people, "You
are innocent. [t]It was I who conspired
against my master and killed him, but who
struck down all these? 10 Know then that
there shall [u]fall to the earth nothing of the
word of the LORD, which the LORD spoke
concerning the house of Ahab, for the LORD
has done [v]what he said by his servant
Elijah." 11 So Jehu struck down all who
remained of the house of Ahab in Jezreel,
all his great men and his close friends and
his priests, until he left him none remaining.

12 Then he set out and went to Samaria.
On the way, when he was at Beth-eked of
the Shepherds, 13 Jehu met [w]the relatives of
Ahaziah king of Judah, and he said, "Who
are you?" And they answered, "We are the
relatives of Ahaziah, and we came down to
visit the royal princes and the sons of the
queen mother." 14 He said, "Take them
alive." And they took them alive and
slaughtered them at the pit of Beth-eked,
forty-two persons, and he spared none of
them.

15 And when he departed from there, he
met [x]Jehonadab the son of [y]Rechab coming
to meet him. And he greeted him and said
to him, "Is your heart true to my heart as
mine is to yours?" And Jehonadab
answered, "It is." Jehu said,[1] "If it is, [z]give
me your hand." So he gave him his hand.
And Jehu took him up with him into the
chariot. 16 And he said, "Come with me,
and see [a]my zeal for the LORD." So he[2] had
him ride in his chariot. 17 And when he
came to Samaria, [b]he struck down all who
remained to Ahab in Samaria, till he had
wiped them out, according to the word of
the LORD [v]that he spoke to Elijah.

Jehu Strikes Down the Prophets of Baal

18 Then Jehu assembled all the people and
said to them, [c]"Ahab served Baal a little, but
Jehu will serve him much. 19 Now therefore
call to me all the [d]prophets of Baal, all his
worshipers and all his priests. Let none be
missing, for I have a great sacrifice to offer to
Baal. Whoever is missing shall not live." But
Jehu did it with cunning in order to destroy
the worshipers of Baal. 20 And Jehu ordered,
[e]"Sanctify [f]a solemn assembly for Baal." So
[g]they proclaimed it. 21 And Jehu sent
throughout all Israel, and all the worshipers
of Baal came, so that there was not a man left
who did not come. And they entered [h]the
house of Baal, and the house of Baal was
filled from one end to the other. 22 He said to
him who was in charge of the wardrobe,
"Bring out the vestments for all the worshipers of Baal." So he brought out the vestments for them. 23 Then Jehu went into the
house of Baal with Jehonadab the son of
Rechab, and he said to the worshipers of
Baal, "Search, and see that there is no servant of the LORD here among you, but only
the worshipers of Baal." 24 Then they[3] went
in to offer sacrifices and burnt offerings.

6 [q][See ver. 1 above]
7 [s][1 Kin. 21:21]
9 [t]ch. 9:14, 24
10 [u][1 Sam. 3:19] [v]1 Kin. 21:19, 21, 29
13 [w][ch. 8:29; 9:16; 2 Chr. 21:17; 22:8]
15 [x]See Jer. 35:6-10, 14, 16, 18
[y]1 Chr. 2:55
[z]Ezra 10:19; Ezek. 17:18
16 [a][1 Kin. 19:10]
17 [b]ch. 9:8; 2 Chr. 22:8
[v][See ver. 10 above]
18 [c]1 Kin. 16:31, 32
19 [d]1 Kin. 18:19; 22:6
20 [e][Joel 1:14]
[f][Lev. 23:36]
[g][Ex. 32:5]
21 [h]ch. 11:18; 1 Kin. 16:32

1 Septuagint; Hebrew lacks *Jehu said* 2 Septuagint, Syriac, Targum; Hebrew *they* 3 Septuagint *he* (compare verse 25)

10:7 slaughtered . . . seventy persons. The leaders of Samaria take no chances; they carry out Jehu's command literally. In this way another component of Elijah's prophecy comes to pass (1 Kin. 21:21–24).

10:8 Lay them in two heaps. Assyrian kings, like Ashurbanipal and Shalmaneser III, intimidated populations by leaving heaps of heads by the city gates.

10:11 Jehu struck down all. Jehu's actions went far beyond the mandate of Elijah's oracle (1 Kin. 21:21–24) and the oracle delivered personally to Jehu (9:7–10).

10:12 Beth-eked of the Shepherds. Probably located a few miles northeast of Jenin.

10:13 relatives of Ahaziah. These relatives do not realize that a coup has taken place.

10:15 Jehonadab the son of Rechab. He was from a family or clan in Israel that led a life of austerity and abstinence. Following their convictions about worshiping God, the Rechabites did not plant fields or drink wine (Jer. 35).

10:18 Ahab served Baal a little, but Jehu will serve him much. Jehu's ruse was designed to entice Baal supporters to reveal their allegiance publicly. Having utterly destroyed the house of Ahab (v. 17), Jehu now begins his purge of Baal worship in Israel.

10:21 the house of Baal. Ahab built this structure in Samaria (1 Kin. 16:32).

Now Jehu had stationed eighty men outside and said, "The man who allows any of
those whom I give into your hands to
escape [i]shall forfeit his life." 25 So as soon as
he had made an end of offering the burnt
offering, Jehu said to the guard and to the
officers, [j]"Go in and strike them down; let
not a man escape." So when they put them
to the sword, the guard and the officers
cast them out and went into the inner
room of the house of Baal, 26 and they
brought out the [k]pillar that was in [h]the
house of Baal and burned it. 27 And they
demolished the [k]pillar of Baal, and demolished the house of Baal, and made it [l]a
latrine to this day.

Jehu Reigns in Israel

28 Thus Jehu wiped out Baal from Israel.
29 But Jehu did not turn aside from [m]the
sins of Jeroboam the son of Nebat, [n]which
he made Israel to sin—that is, the golden
calves that were in Bethel and in Dan.
30 And the LORD said to Jehu, "Because you
have done well in carrying out what is right
in my eyes, and have done to the house of
Ahab according to all that was in my heart,
[o]your sons of the fourth generation shall sit
on the throne of Israel." 31 But Jehu was not
careful to walk in the law of the LORD the
God of Israel with all his heart. [p]He did not
turn from the sins of Jeroboam, which he
made Israel to sin.
32 In those days the LORD [q]began to cut
off parts of Israel. [r]Hazael defeated them
throughout the territory of Israel: 33 from
the Jordan eastward, all the land of Gilead,
the Gadites, and the Reubenites, and the
Manassites, from [s]Aroer, which is by the
Valley of the Arnon, that is, [t]Gilead and
Bashan. 34 Now the rest of the acts of Jehu
and all that he did, and all his might, are
they not written in the Book of the
Chronicles of the Kings of Israel? 35 So Jehu
slept with his fathers, and they buried him
in Samaria. And Jehoahaz his son reigned
in his place. 36 The time that Jehu reigned
over Israel in Samaria was twenty-eight
years.

Athaliah Reigns in Judah

11 [u]Now when [v]Athaliah the mother of
Ahaziah saw that her son was dead,
she arose and destroyed all the royal family. 2 But Jehosheba, the daughter of King
Joram, sister of Ahaziah, took [w]Joash the
son of Ahaziah and stole him away from
among the king's sons who were being put
to death, and she put[1] him and his nurse
in a bedroom. Thus they[2] hid him from
Athaliah, so that he was not put to death.
3 And he remained with her six years, hidden in the house of the LORD, while
Athaliah reigned over the land.

Joash Anointed King in Judah

4 [x]But in the seventh year [y]Jehoiada sent
and brought the captains of [z]the Carites

24 [i][1 Kin. 20:39, 42]
25 [j][1 Kin. 18:40]
26 [k]ch. 3:2; 1 Kin. 14:23 [h][See ver. 21 above]
27 [k][See ver. 26 above] [l][Ezra 6:11; Dan. 2:5; 3:29]
29 [m]See 1 Kin. 12:28-31 [n]See 1 Kin. 14:16
30 [o]ch. 15:12; [ver. 35; ch. 13:1, 10; 14:23; 15:8]
31 [p]ver. 29
32 [q][ch. 13:25; 14:25] [r][ch. 8:12; 1 Kin. 19:17]
33 [s]Deut. 2:36 [t][Amos 1:3, 4]
Chapter 11
1 [u]For ver. 1-3, see 2 Chr. 22:10-12 [v]ch. 8:26
2 [w][ver. 21; ch. 12:1]
4 [x]For ver. 4-20, see 2 Chr. 23:1-21 [y]ver. 9 [z]ver. 19

1 Compare 2 Chronicles 22:11; Hebrew lacks *and she put* 2 Septuagint, Syriac, Vulgate (compare 2 Chronicles 22:11) *she*

10:26 the pillar. See note 1 Kin. 14:23.

burned it. Stone monuments can be shattered by heating them with fire and then pouring cold water on them.

10:27 made it a latrine. This desecrated the site and discouraged any future Baal worshipers from trying to rebuild their temple.

10:31 law of the LORD. On the importance of keeping the law, see note 1 Kin. 2:3.

10:33 from the Jordan eastward. Hazael succeeds in capturing the Israelite tribal territories located in the Transjordan, thus realizing Elisha's prophecy (8:12).

Aroer. The city was located just a few miles north of the River Arnon east of the Dead Sea (Deut. 2:36; Josh. 12:2; 13:9, 16).

10:34 the rest of the acts of Jehu. In an inscription on the "Black Obelisk," the Assyrian ruler Shalmaneser III records that "Jehu, son of Omri" paid him tribute of silver, gold, and other articles. Nothing is said of this in Kings.

Book of the Chronicles of the Kings of Israel. See note 1 Kin. 11:41.

10:35 Jehoahaz. For his reign, see 13:1–9.

10:36 twenty-eight years. That is, 841–814 B.C.

11:1–21 Jehoiada the priest leads a coup against the usurper Athaliah, mother of Ahaziah, and installs young Joash (Jehoash), son of Ahaziah, as rightful king of Judah.

11:1 Athaliah. A daughter of Ahab, she was dedicated to seeing Baal worship flourish in Judah (8:18; 11:18). Athaliah's attempted purge of the royal house of Judah brought the dynasty of David to the brink of extinction.

11:2 Jehosheba. Probably not a daughter of Athaliah, Jehosheba would be a half-sister of Ahaziah. In 2 Chr. 22:11, she is identified as the wife of Jehoiada the priest (cf. vv. 4, 9).

Joash. He was the son of Ahaziah and consequently a grandson of Athaliah.

in a bedroom. Joash, less than a year old (vv. 3, 21) and not yet weaned, is providentially saved from Athaliah's persecution.

11:3 six years. The writer acknowledges that Athaliah had control over Judah for at least six years, but because he regards her reign as illegitimate, he does not dignify it with the usual introduction and conclusion (cf. vv. 1, 20 with 11:21–12:3, 19–21). Her years as Judah's head of state are counted as part of Joash's reign.

in the house of the LORD. In the temple Joash would have been instructed in God's Law.

11:4 the guards. That is, the royal guard (cf. the Cherethites in 2 Sam. 8:18; 20:23). They are of uncertain origin, although some scholars depict them as mercenaries from Caria in southeast Asia Minor.

and of the guards, and had them come to
him in the house of the LORD. And he made
a covenant with them and put them under
oath in the house of the LORD, and he
showed them the king's son. 5 And he commanded them, "This is the thing that you
shall do: one third of you, [a] those who come
off duty on the Sabbath and guard the
king's house 6 ([b] another third being at the
gate Sur and a third at the gate behind
the guards) shall guard the palace.[1] 7 And
the two divisions of you, which come on
duty in force on the Sabbath and guard the
house of the LORD on behalf of the king,
8 shall surround the king, each with his
weapons in his hand. And whoever
approaches the ranks is to be put to death.
Be with the king [c] when he goes out and
when he comes in."
9 The captains did according to all that
Jehoiada the priest commanded, and they
each brought his men who were to go off
duty on the Sabbath, with those who were
to come on duty on the Sabbath, and came
to Jehoiada the priest. 10 And the priest
gave to the captains the spears and
[d] shields that had been King David's,
which were in the house of the LORD.
11 And the guards stood, every man with
his weapons in his hand, from the south
side of the house to the north side of the
house, around the altar and the house on
behalf of the king. 12 Then he brought out
the king's son and put [e] the crown on him
and gave him [f] the testimony. And they
proclaimed him king and anointed him,
and they clapped their hands and said,
[g] "Long live the king!"
13 When Athaliah heard the noise of the
guard and of the people, she went into the
house of the LORD to the people. 14 And
when she looked, there was the king standing [h] by the pillar, according to the custom,
and the captains and the trumpeters beside
the king, and all the people of the land
rejoicing and [i] blowing trumpets. And
Athaliah [j] tore her clothes and cried,
"Treason! Treason!" 15 Then Jehoiada the
priest commanded the captains who were
set over the army, "Bring her out between
the ranks, and put to death with the sword
anyone who follows her." For the priest
said, "Let her not be put to death in the
house of the LORD." 16 So they laid hands
on her; and she went through the horses'
entrance to the king's house, and there she
was put to death.
17 And Jehoiada [k] made a covenant between the LORD and the king and people,
that they should be the LORD's people, and
also [l] between the king and the people.
18 Then all the people of the land went to
[m] the house of Baal and tore it down; [n] his
altars and his images they broke in pieces,
and they killed Mattan the priest of Baal
before the altars. And the priest posted
watchmen over the house of the LORD.
19 And he took the captains, [o] the Carites,
the guards, and all the people of the land,
and they brought the king down from the
house of the LORD, marching through [p] the
gate of the guards to the king's house. And

5 [a] [1 Chr. 9:25]
6 [b] [2 Chr. 23:5]
8 [c] [Num. 27:17]
10 [d] 2 Sam. 8:7; 1 Chr. 18:7
12 [e] [2 Sam. 1:10] [f] Ex. 25:16; 31:18; See Deut. 17:18-20
[g] 1 Sam. 10:24; 2 Sam. 16:16; 1 Kin. 1:39
14 [h] ch. 23:3; [2 Chr. 34:31] [i] 1 Kin. 1:34 [j] See Gen. 44:13
17 [k] [Josh. 24:25] [l] 2 Sam. 5:3
18 [m] ch. 10:21, 23, 26 [n] [Deut. 12:3]
19 [o] ver. 4 [p] ver. 6; [2 Chr. 23:20]

[1] The meaning of the Hebrew word is uncertain

11:6 the gate behind the guards. This gate was probably in the southern wall separating the temple from the palace.

11:10 spears and shields. These articles may have been part of the booty David captured from King Hadadezer of Zobah (2 Sam. 8:3–11). Dedicated by David to the Lord (2 Sam. 8:7, 11), these spears and shields were stored in the temple. Another explanation is that they are David's personal spears and shields.

11:12 the testimony. This refers either to the Sinaitic covenant as a whole (Ex. 25:16; cf. 23:3) or to a more limited document that specifies the duties and limitations of kingship (Deut. 17:14–20).

11:14 standing by the pillar. Pillars called "Jachin" and "Boaz" framed the vestibule of the temple (1 Kin. 7:15–22). When people gathered at the temple on important occasions, such as a royal speech, they would stand in this area in front of the temple proper.

people of the land. The precise meaning of this term is disputed by scholars, and it is likely that its meaning changed during the course of Israelite history (Ezra 9:1, 2). Here it seems to designate leaders of the people who had remained faithful to the Lord and to the Davidic dynasty.

tore her clothes. See note 1 Kin. 21:27.

11:15 put to death with the sword. This command follows the stipulations of Deut. 13:12–18.

put to death in the house of the LORD. Bloodshed within the temple precincts was sacrilege.

11:17 a covenant. Jehoiada leads the people and Joash in renewing their allegiance to the Mosaic covenant. Other covenant renewals had taken place in Israel's past (Deut. 29:1; Josh. 8:30–35; 24:1–28). Chronicles mentions a number of covenant renewals during the course of the monarchy (2 Chr. 15:12; 23:16; 29:10; 34:31). Considering the influx of Baal worship in Judah's recent past, it was appropriate for all parties to make a new beginning by rededicating themselves to the Lord.

between the king and the people. See 2 Chr. 23:3. Such an agreement would delineate the responsibilities of both parties within the larger context of the Mosaic covenant (Deut. 17:14–20; 2 Sam. 5:3).

11:18 people of the land. See note on v. 14.

the house of Baal. Jehoiada leads the people in a thorough reformation, which parallels the earlier reformation led by Jehu in the north (10:18–29).

11:19 the guards. See note on v. 4.

he took his seat on the throne of the kings.
20 So all the people of the land rejoiced, and
the city was quiet after Athaliah had been
put to death with the sword at the king's
house.

Jehoash Reigns in Judah

21[1] [q]Jehoash[2] was seven years old when
he began to reign.

12 In the seventh year of Jehu,
Jehoash[3] began to reign, and he
reigned forty years in Jerusalem. His mother's name was Zibiah of Beersheba. 2 And
Jehoash did what was right in the eyes of
the LORD all his days, because Jehoiada the
priest instructed him. 3 Nevertheless, [r]the
high places were not taken away; the people continued to sacrifice and make offerings on the high places.

Jehoash Repairs the Temple

4 Jehoash said to the priests, "All the
money of the holy things [s]that is brought
into the house of the LORD, the money for
which each man is assessed—the money
from the assessment of persons—and [t]the
money that a man's heart prompts him to
bring into the house of the LORD, 5 let the
priests take, each from his donor, and let
them repair the house wherever any need
of repairs is discovered." 6 But by the
twenty-third year of King Jehoash, the
priests had made no repairs on the house.
7 Therefore King Jehoash summoned
Jehoiada the priest and the other priests
and said to them, "Why are you not repairing the house? Now therefore take no more
money from your donors, but hand it over
for the repair of the house." 8 So the priests
agreed that they should take no more
money from the people, and that they
should not repair the house.

9 Then Jehoiada the priest took [u]a chest
and bored a hole in the lid of it and set it
beside the altar on the right side as one
entered the house of the LORD. And the
priests who guarded the threshold put in it
all the money that was brought into the
house of the LORD. 10 And whenever they
saw that there was much money in the
chest, the king's secretary and the high
priest came up and they bagged and counted [v]the money that was found in the house
of the LORD. 11 Then they would give the
money that was weighed out into the
hands of the workmen who had the oversight of the house of the LORD. And they
paid it out to the carpenters and the
builders who worked on the house of the
LORD, 12 and [w]to the masons and the stonecutters, as well as to buy timber and quarried stone for making repairs on the house
of the LORD, and for any outlay for the
repairs of the house. 13 [x]But there were not
made for the house of the LORD [y]basins of
silver, snuffers, bowls, trumpets, or any
vessels of gold, or of silver, from the money
that was brought into the house of the
LORD, 14 for that was given to the workmen
who were repairing the house of the LORD
with it. 15 And [z]they did not ask an account-
ing from the men into whose hand they
delivered the money to pay out to the workmen, for they dealt honestly. 16 The money
from [a]the guilt offerings and the money
from the [b]sin offerings was not brought into
the house of the LORD; [c]it belonged to the
priests.

17 At that time [d]Hazael king of Syria went
up and fought against Gath and took it.
But when Hazael set his face [e]to go up
against Jerusalem, 18 Jehoash king of Judah

21 [q]For ch. 11:21–12:15, see 2 Chr. 24:1-14
Chapter 12
3 [r]ch. 14:4; 15:35; 1 Kin. 15:14; 22:43
4 [s]ch. 22:4 [t][Ex. 35:5; 1 Chr. 29:9]
9 [u][Mark 12:41; Luke 21:1]
10 [v][ch. 22:4]
12 [w][ch. 22:5, 6]
13 [x][2 Chr. 24:14] [y]1 Kin. 7:50
15 [z]ch. 22:7
16 [a]Lev. 5:15, 18 [b]Lev. 4:24, 29 [c]Lev. 7:7; Num. 18:19
17 [d]ch. 8:12; [1 Kin. 19:17] [e][2 Chr. 24:23, 24]

[1] Ch 12:1 in Hebrew [2] *Jehoash* is another spelling of *Joash* (son of Ahaziah) as in verse 2 [3] *Jehoash* is another spelling of *Joash* (son of Ahaziah) as in 11:2; also verses 2, 4, 6, 7, 18

11:21 Jehoash was seven years old. Jehoiada was a significantly positive influence on Jehoash during the first part of his reign (12:2; 2 Chr. 24:22).

12:1 seventh year of Jehu . . . reigned forty years. That is, 835–796 B.C.

12:2 did what was right. Jehoash is one of several Judean kings who receive positive evaluations (Introduction to 1 Kings: Characteristics and Themes).

12:3 the high places. Jehoash's reign was not without its religious shortcomings. The people continued to worship at "the high places" (1 Kin. 3:2 note).

12:4 the holy things. Jehoash proposes to use the revenue of the temple to refurbish the temple (cf. Neh. 10:32). The temple had suffered neglect during the years of Athaliah (v. 5; 2 Chr. 24:7).

assessment. Israelite young men at the age of twenty were obliged to enlist for a year of military service and donate half a shekel to the sanctuary (Ex. 30:11–16).

12:9 the priests. See 22:4; 23:4; 25:18; Jer. 35:4; 52:24.

12:13 any vessels. See 1 Kin. 7:50. Priority was given to repairing the temple building. During Athaliah's regime, temple furnishings were used for the worship of Baal (2 Chr. 24:7).

12:16 guilt offerings. See Lev. 5:16; 6:6, 7; Num. 5:7–10.

sin offerings. See Lev. 4. Jehoash's restoration did not deprive priests of the main sources of their income (Lev. 7:7).

12:17 Gath. One of the five major Philistine cities, it had previously belonged to Judah (1 Chr. 18:1; 2 Chr. 11:8).

12:18 all the sacred gifts. Jehoash plunders his own palace and temple for a bribe or tax to pay Hazael to withdraw.

[f]took all the sacred gifts that Jehoshaphat
and Jehoram and Ahaziah his fathers, the
kings of Judah, had dedicated, [g]and his
own sacred gifts, and all the gold that was
found in the treasuries of the house of the
LORD and of the king's house, and sent
these to Hazael king of Syria. Then Hazael
went away from Jerusalem.

The Death of Joash

19 Now the rest of the acts of Joash and all
that he did, are they not written in the Book
of the Chronicles of the Kings of Judah?
20 [h]His servants arose and made a conspiracy [i]and struck down Joash in the house of
[j]Millo, on the way that goes down to Silla.
21 It was [k]Jozacar the son of Shimeath and
Jehozabad the son of [k]Shomer, his servants,
who struck him down, so that he died. And
they buried him with his fathers in the city
of David, [l]and Amaziah his son reigned in
his place.

Jehoahaz Reigns in Israel

13 In the twenty-third year of Joash the
son of Ahaziah, king of Judah,
Jehoahaz the son of Jehu began to reign
over Israel in Samaria, and he reigned seventeen years. 2 He did what was evil in the
sight of the LORD and followed the sins of
Jeroboam the son of Nebat, [m]which he
made Israel to sin; he did not depart from
them. 3 [n]And the anger of the LORD was kindled against Israel, and he gave them continually into the hand of [o]Hazael king of
Syria and into the hand of [p]Ben-hadad the
son of Hazael. 4 Then Jehoahaz [q]sought the
favor of the LORD, and the LORD listened to
him, [r]for he saw the oppression of Israel,

18 [f]ch. 16:8; 18:15, 16; 1 Kin. 15:18; [ch. 14:14; 1 Kin. 14:26] [g]ver. 4
20 [h]For ver. 20, 21, see 2 Chr. 24:25-27 [i]ch. 14:5 [j][2 Sam. 5:9]
21 [k][2 Chr. 24:26] [l]ch. 14:1
Chapter 13
2 [m]See 1 Kin. 14:16
3 [n][Judg. 2:14] [o]ch. 8:12; [1 Kin. 19:17] [p]ver. 24, 25
4 [q]Ex. 32:11; [Ps. 78:34] [r]ch. 14:26; Ex. 3:7, 9
5 [s][Judg. 3:9; Neh. 9:27] [t]See 2 Sam. 18:17
6 [m][See ver. 2 above] [u]1 Kin. 16:33
7 [v][Amos 1:3]
11 [m][See ver. 2 above]
12 [w]ch. 14:15 [x]See ver. 14-19, 25 [y]See ch. 14:8-14

how the king of Syria oppressed them.
5 (Therefore the LORD gave Israel [s]a savior,
so that they escaped from the hand of the
Syrians, and the people of Israel lived in
[t]their homes as formerly. 6 Nevertheless,
they did not depart from the sins of the
house of Jeroboam, [m]which he made Israel
to sin, but walked[1] in them; and [u]the
Asherah also remained in Samaria.) 7 For
there was not left to Jehoahaz an army of
more than fifty horsemen and ten chariots
and ten thousand footmen, for the king of
Syria had destroyed them and made them
like the dust [v]at threshing. 8 Now the rest of
the acts of Jehoahaz and all that he did,
and his might, are they not written in the
Book of the Chronicles of the Kings of
Israel? 9 So Jehoahaz slept with his fathers,
and they buried him in Samaria, and Joash
his son reigned in his place.

Jehoash Reigns in Israel

10 In the thirty-seventh year of Joash king
of Judah, Jehoash[2] the son of Jehoahaz
began to reign over Israel in Samaria, and
he reigned sixteen years. 11 He also did
what was evil in the sight of the LORD. He
did not depart from all the sins of
Jeroboam the son of Nebat, [m]which he
made Israel to sin, but he walked in them.
12 [w]Now the rest of the acts of Joash [x]and all
that he did, [y]and the might with which he
fought against Amaziah king of Judah, are
they not written in the Book of the
Chronicles of the Kings of Israel? 13 So
Joash slept with his fathers, and Jeroboam

1 Septuagint, Syriac, Targum, Vulgate; Hebrew *he walked* 2 *Jehoash* is another spelling for *Joash* (son of Jehoahaz) as in verses 9, 12-14; also verse 25

12:19 the rest of the acts. See 2 Chr. 22:10–24:27.

Book of the Chronicles of the Kings of Judah. See note 1 Kin. 11:41.

12:20 servants. Joash's servants were sons of foreign women in the government's employ (14:5; 2 Chr. 24:26).

house of Millo. The term may refer either to a building constructed upon the "Millo" in Jerusalem (the earthworks built by Solomon; 1 Kin. 9:15 note) or to a site within Jerusalem northwest of the City of David (cf. Judg. 9:6, 20).

12:21 Amaziah. For the reign of Amaziah, see 14:1–22.

13:1 twenty-third year of Joash . . . reigned seventeen years. That is, 814–798 B.C.

13:2 the sins of Jeroboam. See note 1 Kin. 12:30.

13:3 Ben-hadad the son of Hazael. That is, Ben-hadad III. For Ben-hadad I, see 1 Kin. 15:18–21; for Ben-hadad II, see 1 Kin. 20:1 note; 2 Kin. 6:24; 8:7.

13:5 gave Israel a savior. Much as in the time of the judges (Judg. 2:16–23), God provides temporary help from the Syrian onslaught. The deliverer is not named.

13:6 the sins of the house of Jeroboam. See note 1 Kin. 12:30.

Asherah. This object was set up by Ahab (1 Kin. 16:33) and apparently was left untouched by Jehu's reforms (2 Kin. 10:18–28).

13:7 fifty horsemen and ten chariots and ten thousand footmen. The king is left with a large number of infantry, but only a very few chariots. This crippled his ability to react quickly to a military crisis.

13:8 Book of the Chronicles of the Kings of Israel. See note 1 Kin. 11:41.

13:10 the thirty-seventh year of Joash. That is, 798 B.C. Jehoash reigned 798–782 B.C.

13:11 the sins of Jeroboam. See note 1 Kin. 12:30.

13:12 Book of the Chronicles of the Kings of Israel. See note 1 Kin. 11:41.

13:13 Jeroboam. Jeroboam II ruled from 793–753 B.C., including eleven years as co-regent with his father Jehoash. Jeroboam began his independent reign when Jehoash died in 782 B.C. See 14:23–29.

sat on his throne. And Joash was buried in
Samaria with the kings of Israel.

The Death of Elisha

14 Now when Elisha had fallen sick with
the illness of which he was to die, Joash
king of Israel went down to him and wept
before him, crying, [z]"My father, my father!
The chariots of Israel and its horsemen!"
15 And Elisha said to him, "Take a bow and
arrows." So he took a bow and arrows.
16 Then he said to the king of Israel, "Draw
the bow," and he drew it. And Elisha laid
his hands on the king's hands. **17** And he
said, "Open the window eastward," and he
opened it. Then Elisha said, "Shoot," and
he shot. And he said, "The LORD's arrow of
victory, the arrow of victory over Syria! For
you shall fight the Syrians in [a]Aphek until
you have made an end of them." **18** And he
said, "Take the arrows," and he took them.
And he said to the king of Israel, "Strike
the ground with them." And he struck
three times and stopped. **19** Then [b]the man
of God was angry with him and said, "You
should have struck five or six times; then
you would have struck down Syria until
you had made an end of it, but now you
will strike down Syria only [c]three times."
20 So Elisha died, and they buried him.
Now bands of [d]Moabites used to invade
the land in the spring of the year. **21** And as
a man was being buried, behold, a marauding band was seen and the man was
thrown into the grave of Elisha, and as
soon as the man touched the bones of
Elisha, he revived and stood on his feet.
22 [e]Now Hazael king of Syria oppressed
Israel all the days of Jehoahaz. **23** [f]But the
LORD was gracious to them and had compassion on them, [g]and he turned toward

14 [z]ch. 2:12
17 [a]1 Kin. 20:26
19 [b]See Deut. 33:1 [c]ver. 25
20 [d]ch. 1:1; 3:7; 24:2
22 [e]ch. 8:12
23 [f]ch. 14:27 [g][Ex. 2:24, 25]
[h]Ex. 32:13
25 [i][ch. 10:32; 14:25] [j]ver. 18, 19; [Amos 1:4]
Chapter 14
1 [k]For ver. 1-6, see 2 Chr. 25:1-4 [l][ch. 13:10] [m]ch. 12:21
4 [n]See ch. 12:3 [o][ch. 16:4]
5 [p][ch. 15:19] [q]ch. 12:20
6 [r]Deut. 24:16; [Jer. 31:30; Ezek. 18:4, 20]
7 [s]2 Chr. 25:11 [t]2 Sam. 8:13; 1 Chr. 18:12; See Ps. 60 [u]Isai. 16:1 [v][Josh. 15:38]

them, [h]because of his covenant with
Abraham, Isaac, and Jacob, and would not
destroy them, nor has he cast them from
his presence until now.
24 When Hazael king of Syria died, Ben-
hadad his son became king in his place.
25 Then Jehoash the son of Jehoahaz took
again from Ben-hadad the son of Hazael
the cities [i]that he had taken from Jehoahaz
his father in war. [j]Three times Joash defeated him and recovered the cities of Israel.

Amaziah Reigns in Judah

14 [k]In the [l]second year of Joash the son
of Joahaz, king of Israel, [m]Amaziah
the son of Joash, king of Judah, began to
reign. **2** He was twenty-five years old when
he began to reign, and he reigned twenty-
nine years in Jerusalem. His mother's name
was Jehoaddin of Jerusalem. **3** And he did
what was right in the eyes of the LORD, yet
not like David his father. He did in all
things as Joash his father had done. **4** [n]But
the high places were not removed; [o]the people still sacrificed and made offerings on the
high places. **5** And as soon as the royal
power was [p]firmly in his hand, he struck
down his servants [q]who had struck down
the king his father. **6** But he did not put to
death the children of the murderers,
according to what is written in the Book of
the Law of Moses, where the LORD commanded, [r]"Fathers shall not be put to death
because of their children, nor shall children
be put to death because of their fathers. But
each one shall die for his own sin."
7 [s]He struck down ten thousand
Edomites in [t]the Valley of Salt and took
[u]Sela by storm, and called it [v]Joktheel,
which is its name to this day.

13:14 My father. See note 2:12.

The chariots of Israel and its horsemen. Earlier, Elisha used this expression of Elijah; now Jehoash applies the compliment to Elisha.

13:17 eastward. This window opened toward the region controlled by Syria (10:32, 33).

the arrow of victory over Syria. The symbolic action is a prophecy that Jehoash himself will fulfill.

Aphek. See note 1 Kin. 20:26.

13:18 and stopped. Somehow Jehoash failed to perceive the inner meaning of what the prophet was urging him to do. Elisha considered that Jehoash was clearly guilty for his lack of enthusiasm.

13:20 Elisha died. Presumably Elisha died of old age.

13:23 because of His covenant with Abraham, Isaac, and Jacob. Divine commitment is steadfast and eternal (cf. 1 Kin. 18:36).

13:24 Ben-hadad. That is, Ben-hadad III (v. 3 note).

13:25 Three times Joash defeated him. Fulfilling the last prophecy of Elisha (v. 19), the victories of Joash stopped the Syrian expansion. Later, Jeroboam II would also defeat the Syrians (14:25).

14:1 In the second year of Joash. That is, 796 B.C.

14:3 he did what was right in the eyes of the LORD. He followed the laws of the covenant (1 Kin. 2:3 note).

yet not like David his father. See note 1 Kin. 11:4.

14:4 the high places were not removed. Amaziah is one of several kings of Judah praised by the author, but his praise is qualified because Amaziah tolerated worship at the hilltop shrines (1 Kin. 3:2 note).

14:5 struck down his servants. See 12:20, 21.

14:7 struck down ten thousand Edomites. This major victory temporarily reversed earlier losses (cf. 8:20–22; 2 Chr. 25:11, 12).

8 [w]Then Amaziah sent messengers to
Jehoash[1] the son of Jehoahaz, son of Jehu,
king of Israel, saying, “Come, [x]let us look
one another in the face.” 9 And Jehoash
king of Israel sent word to Amaziah king of
Judah, [y]“A thistle on Lebanon sent to a
cedar on Lebanon, saying, ‘Give your
daughter to my son for a wife,’ and a wild
beast of Lebanon passed by and trampled
down the thistle. 10 You have indeed
[z]struck down Edom, [a]and your heart has
lifted you up. Be content with your glory,
and stay at home, for why should you provoke trouble so that you fall, you and
Judah with you?”
11 But Amaziah would not listen. So
Jehoash king of Israel went up, and he and
Amaziah king of Judah [x]faced one another
in battle at [b]Beth-shemesh, which belongs
to Judah. 12 And Judah was defeated by
Israel, [c]and every man fled to his home.
13 And Jehoash king of Israel captured
Amaziah king of Judah, the son of Jehoash,
son of Ahaziah, at Beth-shemesh, and came
to Jerusalem and broke down the wall of
Jerusalem for four hundred cubits,[2] from
[d]the Ephraim Gate to [e]the Corner Gate.
14 And he seized [f]all the gold and silver, and
all the vessels that were found in the house
of the LORD and in the treasuries of the
king's house, also hostages, and he returned to Samaria.
15 [g]Now the rest of the acts of Jehoash
that he did, and his might, and how he

8 [w]For ver. 8-14, see 2 Chr. 25:17-24 [x][ch. 23:29]
9 [y][Judg. 9:8-15]
10 [z]ver. 7 [a]Deut. 8:14; 2 Chr. 26:16; 32:25; Ezek. 28:2, 5, 17
11 [x][See ver. 8 above] [b]Josh. 15:10
12 [c]See 1 Sam. 4:10
13 [d]Neh. 8:16; 12:39 [e]2 Chr. 25:23; 26:9; Jer. 31:38; Zech. 14:10
14 [f]ch. 12:18; 1 Kin. 7:51
15 [g]ch. 13:12, 13
17 [h]For ver. 17-22, see 2 Chr. 25:25-26:2
19 [i]See Josh. 10:3
22 [j]ch. 16:6; Deut. 2:8; [2 Chr. 8:17; 26:2]
24 [k]See 1 Kin. 14:16

fought with Amaziah king of Judah, are
they not written in the Book of the
Chronicles of the Kings of Israel? 16 And
Jehoash slept with his fathers and was
buried in Samaria with the kings of Israel,
and Jeroboam his son reigned in his place.
17 [h]Amaziah the son of Joash, king of
Judah, lived fifteen years after the death of
Jehoash son of Jehoahaz, king of Israel.
18 Now the rest of the deeds of Amaziah, are
they not written in the Book of the
Chronicles of the Kings of Judah? 19 And
they made a conspiracy against him in
Jerusalem, and he fled to [i]Lachish. But they
sent after him to Lachish and put him to
death there. 20 And they brought him on
horses; and he was buried in Jerusalem
with his fathers in the city of David. 21 And
all the people of Judah took Azariah, who
was sixteen years old, and made him king
instead of his father Amaziah. 22 He built
[j]Elath and restored it to Judah, after the
king slept with his fathers.

Jeroboam II Reigns in Israel

23 In the fifteenth year of Amaziah the son
of Joash, king of Judah, Jeroboam the son
of Joash, king of Israel, began to reign in
Samaria, and he reigned forty-one years.
24 And he did what was evil in the sight of
the LORD. He did not depart from all the
sins of Jeroboam the son of Nebat, [k]which

[1] *Jehoash* is another spelling for *Joash* (son of Jehoahaz) as in 13:9, 12-14; also verses 9, 11-16 [2] A *cubit* was about 18 inches or 45 centimeters

Valley of Salt. Probably this is the salt flats south of the Dead Sea (cf. 2 Sam. 8:13; Ps. 60:title).

Sela. The Septuagint (Old Testament Greek translation) identifies Sela (meaning “rock” in Hebrew) as Petra (meaning “rock” in Greek), located along the Rift Valley about fifty miles south of the Dead Sea. Some modern scholars place it in northern Edomite territory near Bozrah (Judg. 1:36).

to this day. This phrase reflects a time before the Jews were taken captive to Babylon (1 Kin. 8:8 note).

14:8 Jehoash. See 13:10–25.

14:9 A thistle. The northern kingdom was larger and more powerful than the southern kingdom (1 Kin. 14:30; 15:16, 17 and notes). In this fable (cf. Judg. 9:8–15) the little thistle (Amaziah) thinks it is equal to a cedar of Lebanon (Jehoash) only to be trampled underfoot.

14:11 Beth-shemesh. A city fifteen miles west of Jerusalem (1 Kin. 4:9).

14:13 Jehoash . . . captured Amaziah. Jehoash probably brought Amaziah back to Samaria (v. 14). Amaziah was forced to stay there until the death of Jehoash (v. 17).

Ephraim Gate. This main gate was in the north wall (Neh. 8:16; 12:39).

Corner Gate. At the northwest angle of the wall (2 Chr. 26:9; Jer. 31:38; Zech. 14:10).

14:15 Book of the Chronicles of the Kings of Israel. See note 1 Kin. 11:41.

14:16 Jeroboam. Jeroboam II, who ruled from 793–753 B.C. (vv. 23–29).

14:18 Book of the Chronicles of the Kings of Judah. See note 1 Kin. 11:41.

14:19 Lachish. An important city of Judah fifteen miles west of Hebron.

14:21 sixteen years old. Probably Azariah was made king during his father's absence, and the reigns of father and son overlapped for many years (vv. 13, 17).

14:22 Elath. A seaport on the Gulf of Aqaba, Elath was first used by Solomon to foster sea trade with other nations (1 Kin. 9:26–28). Because Amaziah defeated Edom (v. 7), his son Azariah was able to rebuild Elath and again use it as a Judean port (cf. 1 Kin. 22:47–49; 2 Kin. 8:20–22; 16:6).

14:23 In the fifteenth year of Amaziah. That is, 782 B.C., the beginning of Jeroboam's independent reign.

Jeroboam. That is, Jeroboam II. For the reign of Jeroboam I, see 1 Kin. 11:26–14:19.

forty-one years. That is, 793–753 B.C. It is likely that Jeroboam II was coregent with his father Jehoash for eleven years at the start of his reign (Introduction to 1 Kings: Characteristics and Themes).

14:24 the sins of Jeroboam. See note 1 Kin. 12:30. Politically and economically, Jeroboam II was one of the most successful monarchs in the entire history of the northern kingdom (v. 25). He forced the Syrians to retreat from Damascus into central Syria. He also expanded Israelite territory toward the Dead Sea.

he made Israel to sin. 25 [l]He restored the
border of Israel [m]from Lebo-hamath as far
as the Sea of [n]the Arabah, according to the
word of the LORD, the God of Israel, which
he spoke by his servant [o]Jonah the son of
Amittai, the prophet, who was from [p]Gath-
hepher. 26 For the LORD [q]saw that the affliction of Israel was very bitter, [r]for there was
none left, bond or free, and there was none
to help Israel. 27 [s]But the LORD had not said
that he would blot out the name of Israel
from under heaven, so he saved them by
the hand of Jeroboam the son of Joash.

28 Now the rest of the acts of Jeroboam
and all that he did, and his might, how he
fought, and how he restored [t]Damascus
and [u]Hamath to Judah in Israel, are they
not written in the Book of the Chronicles
of the Kings of Israel? 29 And Jeroboam slept
with his fathers, the kings of Israel, and
Zechariah his son reigned in his place.

Azariah Reigns in Judah

15 [v]In the twenty-seventh year of
Jeroboam king of Israel, [w]Azariah
the son of Amaziah, king of Judah, began
to reign. 2 He was [x]sixteen years old when
he began to reign, and he reigned fifty-two
years in Jerusalem. His mother's name was
Jecoliah of Jerusalem. 3 And he did what
was right in the eyes of the LORD, according
to all that his father Amaziah had done.
4 [y]Nevertheless, the high places were not
taken away. The people still sacrificed and
made offerings on the high places. 5 [z]And
the LORD touched the king, so that he was
a leper[1] to the day of his death, [a]and he
lived in a separate house.[2] And Jotham the
king's son was over the household, governing the people of the land. 6 Now the rest of
the acts of Azariah, and all that he did, are
they not written in the Book of the
Chronicles of the Kings of Judah? 7 And
Azariah slept with his fathers, and they
buried him with his fathers [b]in the city of
David, and Jotham his son reigned in his
place.

Zechariah Reigns in Israel

8 In the thirty-eighth year of Azariah king
of Judah, Zechariah the son of Jeroboam
reigned over Israel in Samaria six months.
9 And he did what was evil in the sight of
the LORD, as his fathers had done. He did
not depart from the sins of Jeroboam the
son of Nebat, [c]which he made Israel to sin.
10 Shallum the son of Jabesh conspired
against him and [d]struck him down at
Ibleam and put him to death and reigned
in his place. 11 Now the rest of the deeds of

1 *Leprosy* was a term for several skin diseases; see Leviticus 13 2 The meaning of the Hebrew word is uncertain

25 [l][ch. 10:32; 13:25] [m]See 1 Kin. 8:65 [n]See Deut. 3:17
25 [o]Jonah 1:1; [Matt. 12:39, 40] [p]Josh. 19:13
26 [q]Ex. 3:7; [ch. 13:4] [r]See Deut. 32:36
27 [s][ch. 13:5, 23]
28 [t][2 Sam. 8:6; 1 Kin. 11:24; 1 Chr. 18:5, 6] [u]2 Chr. 8:3
Chapter 15
1 [v][ch. 14:17] [w][ver. 13, 30, 32, 34; 2 Chr. 26:1]
2 [x]2 Chr. 26:3, 4
4 [y]See ch. 12:3
5 [z]For ver. 5-7, see 2 Chr. 26:21-23 [a]See Lev. 13:46
7 [b][2 Chr. 26:23]
9 [c]See 1 Kin. 14:16
10 [d][Amos 7:9]

14:25 Lebo-hamath. This area was the northernmost part of Israel (Num. 13:21; 34:7–9; 1 Kin. 8:65 note).

Sea of the Arabah. That is, the Dead Sea (Josh. 3:16; 12:3). Jeroboam expanded Israel's territory to the south on the eastern side of the Jordan, the lands of Ammon and Moab. Jeroboam II controlled more land than any previous northern king (cf. Amos 6:14).

Jonah the son of Amittai. See Introduction to Jonah.

Gath-hepher. About fourteen miles west of the southern part of the Sea of Chinneroth (Galilee). See Josh. 19:13.

14:27 blot out the name. In the ancient Near East names were erased from inscriptions as a sign of rejection or loss of power (Ex. 32:32, 33; Deut. 9:14; 29:20).

14:28 Damascus. The capital of Syria.

Hamath. That is, "Lebo-hamath." See note on v. 25.

Judah. David and Solomon had controlled both Damascus and Hamath (2 Sam. 8:6; 1 Kin. 8:65; 2 Chr. 8:3).

Book of the Chronicles of the Kings of Israel. See note 1 Kin. 11:41.

14:29 Zechariah. On the reign of Zechariah, see 15:8–12.

15:1 In the twenty-seventh year of Jeroboam. That is, 767 B.C., when Amaziah died and Azariah began his independent rule.

15:2 He was sixteen years old. Azariah, also called Uzziah (15:30, 32, 34; Is. 6:1), was likely co-regent for many years with his father Amaziah, who was captured by Jehoash of Israel (14:13 note).

fifty-two years. That is, 792–740 B.C. Azariah, like Jeroboam II in the north, enjoyed a long reign, though in the end he suffered from a skin disease (v. 5).

15:3 he did what was right in the eyes of the LORD. He followed the dictates of the covenant (1 Kin. 2:3 note).

15:4 the high places were not taken away. Azariah, like his father Amaziah (14:3, 4), is praised, but the praise is qualified because Azariah did not stop worship at the hilltop shrines (1 Kin. 3:2 note).

15:5 leper. Azariah suffered from some form of skin disease distinct from Hansen's disease (2 Chr. 26:16–21).

Jotham . . . was over the household. He held the highest post in the government of Judah (18:18; Is. 22:15–23). Jotham acted as the king when Azariah became incapacitated and became king when Azariah died (vv. 32–38).

15:6 Book of the Chronicles of the Kings of Judah. See note 1 Kin. 11:41.

15:7 Jotham. See vv. 32–38.

15:8 In the thirty-eighth year of Azariah. That is, 753 B.C. Zechariah was the last king in the dynasty of Jehu (10:30).

15:9 the sins of Jeroboam. See note 1 Kin. 12:30.

15:10 Shallum . . . struck him down. Zechariah's death precipitated a long struggle for power that involved a series of revolutions and counter-revolutions. Including Zechariah, Israel had four different kings (Shallum, Menahem, Pekahiah) in only thirteen years. These kings did not have the prophetic sanction (cf. Hos. 8:4).

15:11 Book of the Chronicles of the Kings of Israel. See note 1 Kin. 11:41.

Zechariah, behold, they are written in the
Book of the Chronicles of the Kings of
Israel. 12 (This was [e] the promise of the LORD
that he gave to Jehu, "Your sons shall sit on
the throne of Israel to the fourth generation." And so it came to pass.)

Shallum Reigns in Israel

13 Shallum the son of Jabesh began to
reign in the thirty-ninth year of [f] Uzziah
king of Judah, and he reigned one month
in [g] Samaria. 14 Then Menahem the son of
Gadi came up from [h] Tirzah and came to
Samaria, and he struck down Shallum the
son of Jabesh in Samaria and put him to
death and reigned in his place. 15 Now the
rest of the deeds of Shallum, and the conspiracy that he made, behold, they are written in the Book of the Chronicles of the
Kings of Israel. 16 At that time Menahem
sacked Tiphsah and all who were in it and
its territory from Tirzah on, because they
did not open it to him. Therefore he sacked
it, [i] and he ripped open all the women in it
who were pregnant.

Menahem Reigns in Israel

17 In the thirty-ninth year of Azariah king
of Judah, Menahem the son of Gadi began
to reign over Israel, and he reigned ten years
in Samaria. 18 And he did what was evil in
the sight of the LORD. He did not depart all
his days from all the sins of Jeroboam the
son of Nebat, which he made Israel to sin.
19 [j] Pul[1] the king of Assyria came against the
land, and Menahem gave [j] Pul a thousand
talents[2] of silver, that he might help him [k] to
confirm his hold on the royal power.
20 Menahem exacted the money from Israel,
that is, from all the wealthy men, fifty
shekels[3] of silver from every man, to give to
the king of Assyria. So the king of Assyria
turned back and did not stay there in the
land. 21 Now the rest of the deeds of
Menahem and all that he did, are they not
written in the Book of the Chronicles of the
Kings of Israel? 22 And Menahem slept with
his fathers, and Pekahiah his son reigned in
his place.

Pekahiah Reigns in Israel

23 In the fiftieth year of Azariah king of
Judah, Pekahiah the son of Menahem
began to reign over Israel in Samaria, and
he reigned two years. 24 And he did what
was evil in the sight of the LORD. He did not
turn away from the sins of Jeroboam the
son of Nebat, which he made Israel to sin.
25 And Pekah the son of Remaliah, his captain, conspired against him with fifty men
of the people of Gilead, and struck him
down in Samaria, in the citadel of the king's
house with Argob and Arieh; he put him to
death and reigned in his place. 26 Now the
rest of the deeds of Pekahiah and all that he
did, behold, they are written in the Book of
the Chronicles of the Kings of Israel.

12 [e] ch. 10:30
13 [f] [ver. 1]
[g] 1 Kin. 16:24
14 [h] 1 Kin. 14:17
16 [i] See ch. 8:12
19 [j] 1 Chr. 5:26
[j] 1 Chr. 5:26
[k] [ch. 14:5]

1 Another name for *Tiglath-pileser III* (compare verse 29) 2 A *talent* was about 75 pounds or 34 kilograms 3 A *shekel* was about 2/5 ounce or 11 grams

15:13–16 Having usurped the throne of Israel by assassinating Zechariah, Shallum reigns only one month before he himself is killed.

15:13 in the thirty-ninth year of Uzziah. That is, 752 B.C. Uzziah is also called Azariah (v. 2 note).

15:14 Tirzah. The former capital of Israel (1 Kin. 14:17; 15:21, 33).

15:15 Book of the Chronicles of the Kings of Israel. See note 1 Kin. 11:41.

15:16 Tiphsah. There is a place called Tiphsah on the Euphrates River in the far north (1 Kin. 4:24), but the text probably means "Tappuah" on the border between Manasseh and Ephraim (Josh. 16:8; 17:7, 8).

ripped open. See note 8:12.

15:17 reigned ten years. That is, 752–742 B.C.

15:18 the sins of Jeroboam. See note 1 Kin. 12:30.

15:19 Pul. The Babylonian throne name of the Assyrian king Tiglath-pileser III (745–727 B.C.; cf. 1 Chr. 5:26). The Assyrian Empire was growing stronger. The annals of Tiglath-pileser III claim that he received tribute from a number of western kings, including Menahem of Samaria.

thousand talents of silver. This sum is consistent with the tribute demanded by other kings during this period.

confirm his hold on the royal power. Ironically, Menahem uses his vassal relationship with the dreaded Assyrians to consolidate his own rule over Israel. This willing subservience to the Assyrians is decried by the prophet Hosea (Hos. 5:13, 14).

15:20 from all the wealthy men, fifty shekels. A conversion of the figures indicates that sixty thousand men paying twenty ounces of silver each would have raised the one thousand talents required.

15:21 Book of the Chronicles of the Kings of Israel. See note 1 Kin. 11:41.

15:23 fiftieth year . . . reigned two years. That is, 742–740 B.C.

15:24 the sins of Jeroboam. See note 1 Kin. 12:31.

15:25 Pekah the son of Remaliah. A high-ranking official in the northern kingdom, he was evidently part of an anti-Assyrian faction within the northern kingdom (v. 29). He pursued improved relations with the Syrians during his reign as a way to offset Assyrian designs in the west (16:1–9; Is. 7:1).

fifty men of the people of Gilead. Pekah, like the rebels before him (vv. 10, 14), may have been from Gilead. Pekah may have reigned over Gilead before attempting to overthrow Pekahiah in Samaria.

15:26 Book of the Chronicles of the Kings of Israel. See note 1 Kin. 11:41.

Pekah Reigns in Israel

27 In the fifty-second year of Azariah king
of Judah, Pekah the son of Remaliah began
to reign over Israel in Samaria, and he
reigned twenty years. 28 And he did what
was evil in the sight of the LORD. He did
not depart from the sins of Jeroboam the
son of Nebat, [l]which he made Israel to sin.
29 In the days of Pekah king of Israel,
[m]Tiglath-pileser king of Assyria came and
captured [n]Ijon, [o]Abel-beth-maacah, Janoah, [p]Kedesh, [q]Hazor, Gilead, and [r]Gali-
lee, all the land of Naphtali, and he carried
the people captive to Assyria. 30 Then
Hoshea the son of Elah made a conspiracy
against Pekah the son of Remaliah and
struck him down and put him to death and
reigned in his place, [s]in the twentieth year
of Jotham the son of Uzziah. 31 Now the
rest of the acts of Pekah and all that he did,
behold, they are written in the Book of the
Chronicles of the Kings of Israel.

Jotham Reigns in Judah

32 In the second year of Pekah the son of
Remaliah, king of Israel, Jotham the son of
Uzziah, king of Judah, began to reign. 33 He
was [t]twenty-five years old when he began
to reign, and he reigned sixteen years in
Jerusalem. His mother's name was Jerusha
the daughter of Zadok. 34 And he did what
was right in the eyes of the LORD, [u]accord-
ing to all that his father Uzziah had done.
35 [v]Nevertheless, the high places were not
removed. The people still sacrificed and
made offerings on the high places. He built
[w]the upper gate of the house of the LORD.
36 Now the rest of the acts of Jotham and all
that he did, are they not written in the
Book of the Chronicles of the Kings of
Judah? 37 In those days the LORD began to
send [x]Rezin the king of Syria and [x]Pekah
the son of Remaliah against Judah.
38 Jotham slept with his fathers and was
buried with his fathers in the city of David
his father, and Ahaz his son reigned in his
place.

Ahaz Reigns in Judah

16 In the seventeenth year of Pekah
the son of Remaliah, Ahaz the son
of Jotham, king of Judah, began to reign.
2 Ahaz was [y]twenty years old when he
began to reign, and he reigned sixteen
years in Jerusalem. And he did not do what
was right in the eyes of the LORD his God,
as his father David had done, 3 but he
walked in the way of the kings of Israel.

28 [l]See 1 Kin. 14:16
29 [m]ch. 16:7; [1 Chr. 5:6, 26; 2 Chr. 28:20] [n]1 Kin. 15:20 [o]2 Sam. 20:14, 15 [p]Josh. 19:37 [q]Josh. 11:1; Judg. 4:2; 1 Kin. 9:15 [r]Isai. 9:1
30 [s][ch. 17:1]
33 [t]For ver. 33, 34, see 2 Chr. 27:1, 2
34 [u]ver. 3; [2 Chr. 27:6]
35 [v]See ch. 12:3 [w]2 Chr. 23:20; 27:3
37 [x]ch. 16:5; Isai. 7:1
Chapter 16
2 [y]For ver. 2-4, see 2 Chr. 28:1-4

15:27–31 Having assassinated Pekahiah, Pekah succeeds him as king of Israel. The king of Assyria captures part of Israel's territory during Pekah's reign.

15:27 In the fifty-second year of Azariah. That is, 740 B.C.

twenty years. That is, 752–732 B.C. The chronology of Pekah's rule is difficult to establish. It is possible that he led a rebellion during the politically unstable reign of Menahem (vv. 17–22) and that his reign is calculated from this point (v. 25 note).

15:28 the sins of Jeroboam. See note 1 Kin. 12:30.

15:29 Tiglath-pileser. That is, Tiglath-pileser III. All the cities and areas listed are in the northern part of the Israelite kingdom. During his campaign of 733–732 B.C., Tiglath-pileser also ravaged Syria and captured its capital, Damascus (16:9).

carried the people captive to Assyria. As is remarked in 10:32, God was reducing Israel in land and population.

15:30 in the twentieth year of Jotham. That is, 732 B.C. For the reign of Hoshea, see 17:1–6.

15:31 Book of the Chronicles of the Kings of Israel. See note 1 Kin. 11:41.

15:32 In the second year of Pekah. That is, 750 B.C.

15:33 He was twenty-five years old. Jotham was likely co-regent with his father Azariah (Uzziah) for the first ten years of his reign (v. 2 note).

sixteen years. That is, 750–735 B.C.

15:34 he did what was right in the eyes of the LORD. He was loyal to the covenant (1 Kin. 2:3 note).

15:35 the high places were not removed. See note 1 Kin. 3:2.

upper gate of the house of the LORD. Also called the "upper Benjamin gate" (Jer. 20:2), this gate was in the northern part of the temple complex, facing the territory of Benjamin.

15:36 Book of the Chronicles of the Kings of Judah. See note 1 Kin. 11:41.

15:37 Rezin. He was the last king of Syria. Syria and Israel had forged an alliance to combat the Assyrians and were prepared to force the king of Judah to join them by invading Judah (v. 29 note; 16:5–12 and notes).

16:1 In the seventeenth year of Pekah. That is, 735 B.C. Scholars disagree over the precise chronology of Ahaz's reign (cf. 15:33, 37; 17:1; 18:1; and also Introduction to 1 Kings: Characteristics and Themes).

16:2 sixteen years. That is, 732–715 B.C. This figure would represent the length of his reign from his official recognition as king of Judah by the Assyrians.

16:3 he walked in the way of the kings of Israel. The sin of Jeroboam I (1 Kin. 12:26–33), continued by all subsequent Israelite kings, was the construction of ritual religious centers in Bethel and Dan. These northern cult sites were conduits for bringing foreign religions into the northern kingdom. In the southern kingdom, Ahaz built a foreign altar in Jerusalem. Like Jeroboam I, Ahaz officiated at inaugural sacrifices for the new altar (vv. 10–13; 1 Kin. 12:32, 33).

burned his son as an offering. The atrocity of child sacrifice was practiced by some of Judah's neighbors, although it was outlawed by the law of Moses (Lev. 18:21; Deut. 18:10; cf. 2 Kin. 3:27). Ahaz was not the only Judean king who disobeyed this law (21:6; 23:10; Jer. 7:31; 32:35).

the despicable practices of the nations. In its behavior, Judah was becoming indistinguishable from the nations that God drove out of Canaan so that the Israelites could inhabit the land. The people were betraying their sacred calling to be "a kingdom of priests and a holy nation" (Ex. 19:6).

[z]He even burned his son as an offering,[1]
[a]according to the despicable practices of
the nations whom the LORD drove out
before the people of Israel. 4 [b]And he sacrificed and made offerings [c]on the high
places and on the hills and under every
green tree.
5 [d]Then Rezin king of Syria and [d]Pekah
the son of Remaliah, king of Israel, came
up to wage war on Jerusalem, and they
besieged Ahaz [e]but could not conquer him.
6 At that time Rezin the king of Syria recovered [f]Elath for Syria and drove the men of
Judah from [f]Elath, and the Edomites came
to Elath, where they dwell to this day. 7 [g]So
Ahaz sent messengers to [h]Tiglath-pileser
king of Assyria, saying, "I am your servant
and your son. Come up and rescue me
from the hand of the king of Syria and from
the hand of the king of Israel, who are
attacking me." 8 Ahaz also [i]took the silver
and gold that was found in the house of the
LORD and in the treasures of the king's
house and sent a present to the king of
Assyria. 9 [j]And the king of Assyria listened
to him. The king of Assyria marched up
against Damascus [k]and took it, carrying its
people captive to [l]Kir, and he killed Rezin.
10 When King Ahaz went to Damascus to
meet [m]Tiglath-pileser king of Assyria, he
saw the altar that was at Damascus. And
King Ahaz sent to [n]Uriah the priest a model
of the altar, and its pattern, exact in all its
details. 11 And Uriah the priest built the
altar; in accordance with all that King Ahaz
had sent from Damascus, so Uriah the
priest made it, before King Ahaz arrived
from Damascus. 12 And when the king
came from Damascus, the king viewed the
altar. [o]Then the king drew near to the altar
and went up on it 13 and burned his burnt
offering and his grain offering and poured
his drink offering and threw the blood of
his peace offerings on the altar. 14 And [p]the
bronze altar that was before the LORD he
removed [q]from the front of the house, from
the place between [r]his altar and the house
of the LORD, and put it on the north side of
[r]his altar. 15 And King Ahaz commanded
Uriah the priest, saying, "On the great altar
burn [s]the morning burnt offering and the
evening grain offering and the king's burnt
offering and his grain offering, with the
burnt offering of all the people of the land,
and their grain offering and their drink
offering. And throw on it all the blood of
the burnt offering and all the blood of the
sacrifice, but [t]the bronze altar shall be for
me to inquire by." 16 Uriah the priest did all
this, as King Ahaz commanded.
17 And King Ahaz cut off the frames of the
stands and removed the basin from them,
and he took down [u]the sea[2] from off the
bronze oxen that were under it and put it
on a stone pedestal. 18 And the covered way
for the Sabbath that had been built inside
the house and the outer entrance for the
king he caused to go around the house of
the LORD, because of the king of Assyria.
19 Now the rest of the acts of Ahaz that he
did, are they not written [v]in the Book of the
Chronicles of the Kings of Judah? 20 And
Ahaz slept with his fathers and [w]was buried

3 [z][Ps. 106:37, 38]; See Lev. 18:21 [a]ch. 21:2; [Deut. 12:31; 18:9]
4 [b][ch. 14:4] [c]Deut. 12:2; 1 Kin. 14:23
5 [d]ch. 15:37 [e][2 Chr. 28:5, 6]
6 [f]See ch. 14:22
7 [g]See 2 Chr. 28:16 [h]See ch. 15:29
8 [i]See ch. 12:18
9 [j][2 Chr. 28:21] [k][Amos 1:5] [l]Isai. 22:6; Amos 1:5; 9:7
10 [m]See ch. 15:29 [n]Isai. 8:2
12 [o]See 2 Chr. 26:16-19
14 [p]2 Chr. 4:1 [q][Ex. 40:6, 29] [r]ver. 11
15 [s]Ex. 29:39-41 [t]ver. 14
17 [u]1 Kin. 7:23, 25
19 [v][2 Chr. 28:26]
20 [w][2 Chr. 28:27]

1 Or *made his son pass through the fire* 2 Compare 1 Kings 7:23

16:5 Rezin . . . and Pekah. The Israelite and Syrian kings wanted to bring Judah forcibly under their control so that they could make a united front against Assyria (15:19, 25, 37). Into this crisis stepped the prophet Isaiah, who counseled the irresolute Ahaz (Is. 7:1–17).

16:6 Rezin . . . recovered Elath. This undid Azariah's earlier victory (14:22).

Edomites came to Elath. Edom exploited Judah's defeat for its own gain.

to this day. See note 1 Kin. 8:8.

16:7 Tiglath-pileser. See notes 15:19, 29.

16:8 Ahaz also took the silver and gold. Ahaz, like a number of kings before him, attempted to buy security with a large tribute payment given as a bribe to a foreign power (12:18; Ex. 23:8; Deut. 16:19; 1 Kin. 15:18; Is. 5:23; Ezek. 22:12). A list from Assyria of rulers who brought tribute to Tiglath-pileser in 734 B.C. includes the name of "Jehoahaz of Judah" (Ahaz).

16:9 carrying its people captive to Kir. The destruction of Syria fulfilled prophecies of both Isaiah (Is. 7:16) and Amos (Amos 1:5). The exact location of Kir is not known (Is. 22:6; Amos 9:7).

16:13 peace offerings. See Lev. 7:11–21. Most of these sacrifices were also offered at the dedication of the temple under Solomon (1 Kin. 8:64). Ahaz considered the construction of this foreign altar to be of great importance for his kingdom.

16:15 morning burnt offering. See Ex. 29:38, 39.

evening grain offering. See note 1 Kin. 18:29.

king's burnt offering and his grain offering. See Ezek. 46:12.

the bronze altar shall be for me to inquire by. Ahaz perverted the old altar from its normal use and instead employed it for divination, a foreign practice in which priests tried to tell the future by examining the entrails of sacrificial animals. Divination was rigorously outlawed in Israel (Lev. 19:26; Deut. 18:10).

16:17 frames . . . basin. See 1 Kin. 7:27–37.

sea. See 1 Kin. 7:22–26.

bronze oxen. Ahaz probably used the bronze to pay tribute to Assyria.

16:19 Book of the Chronicles of the Kings of Judah. See note 1 Kin. 11:41.

with his fathers in the city of David, and
Hezekiah his son reigned in his place.

17 In the twelfth year of Ahaz king of
Judah, [x]Hoshea the son of Elah
began to reign in Samaria over Israel, and
he reigned nine years. 2 And he did what
was evil in the sight of the LORD, yet not as
the kings of Israel who were before him.
3 [y]Against him came up [z]Shalmaneser king
of Assyria. And Hoshea became his vassal
and paid him tribute. 4 But the king of
Assyria found treachery in Hoshea, for he
had sent messengers to So, king of Egypt,
and offered no tribute to the king of
Assyria, as he had done year by year.
Therefore the king of Assyria shut him up
and bound him in prison. 5 Then the king
of Assyria invaded all the land and came to
Samaria, and for three years he besieged it.

The Fall of Israel

6 In the ninth year of Hoshea, the king of
Assyria [a]captured Samaria, [b]and he carried
the Israelites away to Assyria [c]and placed
them in Halah, and on the Habor, the river
of [d]Gozan, and in the cities of [e]the Medes.

Exile Because of Idolatry

7 And this occurred because the people of
Israel had sinned against the LORD their
God, [f]who had brought them up out of the
land of Egypt from under the hand of
Pharaoh king of Egypt, and had feared
other gods 8 [g]and walked in the customs of
the nations whom the LORD drove out
before the people of Israel, [h]and in the customs that the kings of Israel had practiced.
9 And the people of Israel did secretly
against the LORD their God things that were
not right. They built for themselves high
places in all their towns, [i]from watchtower
to fortified city. 10 They set up for themselves [j]pillars and Asherim on every high
hill and under every green tree, 11 and there
they made offerings on all the high places,
as the nations did whom the LORD carried
away before them. And they did wicked
things, provoking the LORD to anger, 12 and
they served idols, [k]of which the LORD had
said to them, "You shall not do this." 13 Yet
the LORD [l]warned Israel and Judah [m]by
every prophet [n]and every seer, saying,
[o]"Turn from your evil ways and keep my
commandments and my statutes, in accordance with all the Law that I commanded
your fathers, and that I sent to you by my
servants the prophets."

14 But they would not listen, [p]but were
stubborn, as their fathers had been, who
did not believe in the LORD their God.
15 They despised his statutes [q]and his
covenant that he made with their fathers
and the warnings that he gave them. They

Chapter 17
1 [x][ch. 15:30]
3 [y]For ver. 3-7, see ch. 18:9-12 [z][Hos. 10:14]
6 [a][Hos. 13:16] [b][Lev. 26:32, 33; Deut. 28:36, 64; 29:27, 28] [c]ch. 18:11; [1 Chr. 5:26] [d]Isai. 37:12 [e]Ezra 6:2; Isai. 13:17; 21:2; Jer. 51:11, 28
7 [f]ver. 36; Lev. 25:38; See Ex. 20:2
8 [g]Lev. 18:3; Deut. 18:9 [h]ver. 19; ch. 16:3
9 [i]ch. 18:8
10 [j]See Ex. 23:24
12 [k]See Ex. 20:4
13 [l]Neh. 9:30 [m]ver. 23 [n]See 1 Sam. 9:9 [o]Jer. 18:11; 25:5; 35:15
14 [p]Deut. 9:6; 2 Chr. 30:8; [Deut. 31:27; Acts 7:51]
15 [q]Deut. 29:25

16:20 Hezekiah. For his reign, see chs. 18–20.

17:1–6 This section narrates the reign of Hoshea, the last king of Israel. In 722 B.C. the king of Assyria conquered Samaria and deported the people of Israel to Assyria.

17:1 Ahaz. The synchronism with Ahaz's reign is difficult to unravel. See 16:1 and note.

Hoshea . . . reigned nine years. That is, 732–723 B.C., ending with his imprisonment for three years preceding the fall of Samaria (vv. 4, 5).

17:3 Shalmaneser. Shalmaneser V, who succeeded Tiglath-pileser III as king of Assyria, ruled from 727–722 B.C. Hoshea, unlike his predecessor Pekah (15:27–31 and notes), was a vassal of Assyria.

17:4 So, king of Egypt. "So" may be the name of a place in the eastern delta of Egypt, where the king of Egypt was. Switching his allegiance, Hoshea hoped that Egypt would protect him from any Assyrian reprisals. The prophet Hosea condemns this diplomacy as "without sense" (Hos. 7:11).

offered no tribute to the king of Assyria. Withholding tribute from a suzerain (overlord) was tantamount to rebellion.

17:5 for three years he besieged it. The Assyrian campaign followed the arrest of Hoshea in 724/23 B.C. During this long siege, Shalmaneser V died and was succeeded by Sargon II (Is. 20:1), who exiled the inhabitants of Samaria (v. 6).

17:6 In the ninth year of Hoshea. That is, 722/21 B.C. The figure given ("ninth year") counts his reign from 730, perhaps because his having the Assyrians as sponsors delayed his official recognition. Another possibility is that it leaves out the three years he was in prison.

the king of Assyria. Sargon II, who ruled Assyria 722–705 B.C.

carried the Israelites away. Sargon II claims in his annals to have deported 27,290 inhabitants to distant locations. The capture of Samaria marked the end of the northern kingdom (1 Chr. 5:25, 26). It never rose again (vv. 7–23 and notes). Archaeological evidence suggests that many people fled Israel during the succession of Assyrian attacks on the north and settled in Judah. This influx of northern refugees significantly increased the population of Jerusalem during the late eighth and early seventh century B.C.

Gozan. This Assyrian provincial capital was near the Habor River, a northern tributary of the Euphrates.

cities of the Medes. Though not identified by name, they were probably in the area northeast of the Tigris River and south of the Caspian Sea.

17:8 customs. Not only did Israel imitate the practices of its pagan neighbors (Ex. 34:15; Deut. 18:9; Judg. 2:13), but it also followed the cultic innovations of its wayward kings (1 Kin. 12:26–33; 16:30–34).

17:9 high places. See note 1 Kin. 3:2.

17:10 pillars. See note 1 Kin. 14:23.

Asherim. See note 1 Kin. 14:15.

on every high hill and under every green tree. See Deut. 12:2; Jer. 2:20; 3:6, 13; 17:2.

17:12 idols. Any representation of a pagan deity or of the Lord was expressly forbidden (Ex. 20:4; Deut. 4:15–19, 23–28).

17:13 all the Law. That is, the Mosaic law with all the provisions of the covenant (1 Kin. 2:3 note).

went after [r]false idols [s]and became false,
and they followed the nations that were
around them, concerning whom the [t]LORD
had commanded them that they should
not do like them. 16 And they abandoned all
the commandments of the LORD their God,
and made for themselves metal images of
[u]two calves; and they [v]made an Asherah
and [w]worshiped all the host of heaven and
served [x]Baal. 17 [y]And they burned their sons
and their daughters as offerings[1] and used
[z]divination and [a]omens and [b]sold themselves to do evil in the sight of the LORD,
provoking him to anger. 18 Therefore the
LORD was very angry with Israel and
removed them out of his sight. None was
left but [c]the tribe of Judah only.
19 [d]Judah also did not keep the commandments of the LORD their God, but
walked in the customs that Israel had
introduced. 20 And the LORD rejected all the
descendants of Israel and afflicted them
[e]and gave them into the hand of plunderers, until he had cast them out of his sight.
21 [f]When he had torn Israel from the
house of David, [g]they made Jeroboam the
son of Nebat king. And Jeroboam drove
Israel from following the LORD [h]and made
them commit great sin. 22 The people of
Israel walked in all the sins that Jeroboam
did. They did not depart from them, 23 until the LORD removed Israel out of his sight,
[i]as he had spoken by all his servants the
prophets. [j]So Israel was exiled from their
own land to Assyria until this day.

Assyria Resettles Samaria

24 [k]And the king of Assyria brought people from [l]Babylon, Cuthah, [m]Avva, [n]Ha-
math, and [o]Sepharvaim, and placed them
in the cities of Samaria instead of the people of Israel. And they took possession of
Samaria and lived in its cities. 25 And at the
beginning of their dwelling there, they did
not fear the LORD. Therefore the LORD sent
lions among them, which killed some of
them. 26 So the king of Assyria was told,
"The nations that you have carried away
and placed in the cities of Samaria do not
know the law of the god of the land.
Therefore he has sent lions among them,
and behold, they are killing them, because
they do not know the law of the god of the
land." 27 Then the king of Assyria commanded, "Send there one of the priests
whom you carried away from there, and let
him[2] go and dwell there and teach them
the law of the god of the land." 28 So one of
the priests whom they had carried away
from Samaria came and lived in [p]Bethel
and taught them how they should fear the
LORD.
29 But every nation still made gods of its
own and put them [q]in the shrines of the
high places that the Samaritans had made,

15 [r]Deut. 32:21; [1 Kin. 16:13] [s]Jer. 2:5; Rom. 1:21 [t]Deut. 12:30, 31
16 [u]See 1 Kin. 12:28 [v]1 Kin. 14:15, 23; 15:13; 16:33 [w]ch. 21:3; 23:5; [Deut. 4:19] [x]ch. 11:18; 1 Kin. 16:31; 22:53
17 [y]ch. 16:3; [Lev. 18:21; Ezek. 23:37] [z][Deut. 18:10] [a][Lev. 19:26] [b]See 1 Kin. 21:20
18 [c][1 Kin. 11:13, 32; 12:20]
19 [d][Jer. 3:8]
20 [e]Judg. 2:14; [ch. 13:3; 15:29]
21 [f]1 Kin. 11:11, 31 [g]1 Kin. 12:20 [h]See 1 Kin. 14:16
23 [i]ver. 13 [j]ver. 6
24 [k]Ezra 4:2, 10 [l]ver. 30 [m][ch. 18:34] [n]See 1 Kin. 8:65 [o]ver. 31; ch. 18:34; 19:13
28 [p]1 Kin. 12:29
29 [q]1 Kin. 12:31; 13:32

[1] Or *made their sons and their daughters pass through the fire* [2] Syriac, Vulgate; Hebrew *them*

17:16 metal images of two calves. The religious idols of Jeroboam I at Bethel and Dan (1 Kin. 12:28, 29) were in part modeled on the construction of the golden calf by Aaron (Ex. 32:4, 8; Deut. 9:12, 16; Hos. 13:2).

the host of heaven. Although condemned in the Mosaic law (Deut. 4:19; 17:3), some Israelites participated in such astral cults (21:5; 23:4, 5; Amos 5:26).

served Baal. See 1 Kin. 16:31, 32.

17:17 burned their sons and their daughters as offerings. See notes 3:27; 16:3.

divination and omens. See note 16:15.

17:19 the customs that Israel had introduced. See 8:18; 11:18–21.

17:20 the LORD rejected all the descendants of Israel. God's rejection was demonstrated by their exile from the land He had given them (v. 6).

17:21 When he had torn Israel from the house of David. The creation of the northern kingdom was a punishment against Solomon (1 Kin. 11:11–13), but it also was a promising beginning for the northern tribes (1 Kin. 11:29–39).

made them commit great sin. The reference is to Jeroboam's fashioning of two calves at Bethel and Dan (1 Kin. 12:25–33; 14:7–16 and notes).

17:24 king of Assyria. This king was most likely Sargon II. As the Assyrians deported people from Israel, they imported people from other countries. This policy was intended to ensure that the defeated nation would not reassert itself. Assyrian records attest that later Assyrian kings brought more foreign immigrants to Samaria.

Babylon, Cuthah. At this point Babylon was under Assyrian control. Cuthah was about eight miles northeast of Babylon.

Avva, Hamath, and Sepharvaim. Avva or "Ivvah" and Sepharvaim were probably in Syria (18:34; 19:13). Hamath was on the Orontes River (cf. 14:25 note).

Samaria. After its fall to the Assyrians, the region of the former northern kingdom of Israel is usually called "Samaria" (1 Kin. 16:24 note).

17:25 lions among them. Lions were often used by God as an instrument of judgment (1 Kin. 13:24; 20:36; Amos 3:12).

17:26 the law of the god of the land. The Assyrians, like many other peoples in the ancient Near East, believed that the gods of a particular land would trouble the people who lived there if they failed to perform the appropriate rituals for those gods.

17:29 gods of its own. Bringing back an Israelite priest to serve at Bethel did not oblige the immigrants settling in Samaria to follow the local religion. On the contrary, they continued to follow their own religious practices, taking over local sanctuaries and worshiping there.

the Samaritans. See 23:19; 1 Kin. 12:31; 13:32. Although the expression "Samaritans" appears only here in the Old Testament, it occurs in extrabiblical documents as early as the eighth century B.C. referring to the residents of the northern kingdom.

every nation in the cities in which they
lived. 30 The men of [r]Babylon made
Succoth-benoth, the men of Cuth made
Nergal, the men of Hamath made Ashima,
31 and the Avvites made Nibhaz and
Tartak; and the Sepharvites [s]burned their
children in the fire to [t]Adrammelech and
Anammelech, the gods of [u]Sepharvaim.
32 [v]They also feared the LORD [w]and appointed from among themselves all sorts of
people as priests of the high places, who
sacrificed for them in the shrines of [x]the
high places. 33 So they feared the LORD but
also served their own gods, after the manner of the nations from among whom they
had been carried away.
34 To this day they do according to the
former manner. They do not fear the LORD,
and they do not follow the statutes or the
rules or the law or the commandment that
the LORD commanded the children of
Jacob, [y]whom he named Israel. 35 The LORD
made a covenant with them and commanded them, [z]"You shall not fear other
gods [a]or bow yourselves to them or serve
them or sacrifice to them, 36 but [b]you shall
fear the LORD, [c]who brought you out of the
land of Egypt with great power and [d]with
an outstretched arm. You shall bow yourselves to him, and to him you shall sacrifice. 37 And the statutes and the rules and
the law and the commandment that he
wrote for you, [e]you shall always be careful
to do. [z]You shall not fear other gods, 38 and
[f]you shall not forget the covenant that I
have made with you. [z]You shall not fear

30 [r]ver. 24
31 [s]See ver. 17 [t][ch. 19:37] [u]ver. 24
32 [v][Zeph. 1:5] [w]See 1 Kin. 12:31 [x]ver. 29
34 [y]Gen. 32:28; 35:10; 1 Kin. 18:31
35 [z]Judg. 6:10 [a]See Ex. 20:5
36 [b]Deut. 6:13 [c]ver. 7 [d]Ex. 6:6; Deut. 6:13
37 [e]Deut. 5:32 [z][See ver. 35 above]
38 [f]Deut. 4:23 [z][See ver. 35 above]
39 [b][See ver. 36 above]
41 [g][Zeph. 1:5]
Chapter 18
1 [h][ch. 16:2; 17:1] [i]2 Chr. 28:27; Matt. 1:9
2 [j]For ver. 2, 3, see 2 Chr. 29:1, 2 [k][2 Chr. 29:1]
3 [l]ch. 20:3; 2 Chr. 31:20
4 [m]ver. 22; 2 Chr. 31:1 [n]ch. 17:10; See Ex. 23:24 [o]ch. 17:16; See Deut. 16:21 [p]Num. 21:8, 9
5 [q]ch. 19:10 [r]ch. 23:25
6 [s][Deut. 10:20; Josh. 23:8]
7 [t]2 Chr. 15:2

other gods, 39 but [b]you shall fear the LORD
your God, and he will deliver you out of
the hand of all your enemies." 40 However,
they would not listen, but they did according to their former manner.
41 [g]So these nations feared the LORD and
also served their carved images. Their children did likewise, and their children's children—as their fathers did, so they do to
this day.

Hezekiah Reigns in Judah

18 [h]In the third year of Hoshea son of
Elah, king of Israel, [i]Hezekiah the
son of Ahaz, king of Judah, began to reign.
2 He was [j]twenty-five years old when he
began to reign, and he reigned twenty-nine
years in Jerusalem. His mother's name was
[k]Abi the daughter of Zechariah. 3 [l]And he
did what was right in the eyes of the LORD,
according to all that David his father had
done. 4 [m]He removed the high places and
broke the [n]pillars and cut down [o]the
Asherah. And he broke in pieces [p]the
bronze serpent that Moses had made, for
until those days the people of Israel had
made offerings to it (it was called Nehushtan).[1] 5 [q]He trusted in the LORD the
God of Israel, [r]so that there was none like
him among all the kings of Judah after him,
nor among those who were before him.
6 [s]For he held fast to the LORD. He did not
depart from following him, but kept the
commandments that the LORD commanded Moses. 7 [t]And the LORD was with him;

1 *Nehushtan* sounds like the Hebrew for both *bronze* and *serpent*

17:33 served their own gods. The religion was syncretistic—it combined elements of the worship of the Lord with the worship of many other deities.

17:34 To this day. See note 1 Kin. 8:8.

the children of Jacob, whom he named Israel. The relationship between God and the people He elected was the covenant ratified on Mount Sinai (v. 35; Ex. 19–24) and renewed on the plains of Moab (Deuteronomy). Being an Israelite was in the end not an ethnic classification, but a religious one, to belong to the God of the covenant (Ex. 12:38; Deut. 26:5; Rom. 9:8).

17:39 he will deliver you out of the hand of all your enemies. Just as God had delivered His people in the past, He could do so again in the future (Ex. 20:2; 23:22; Deut. 20:1–4; 23:14).

17:41 to this day. See note 1 Kin. 8:8. Despite the Assyrian conquest and its aftermath, some of the Samaritans and their descendants continued to embrace monotheism and to follow the Sinaitic covenant throughout the biblical period and even into modern times.

18:1 In the third year of Hoshea. That is, 729 B.C., referring to the beginning of Hezekiah's reign as co-regent with his father Ahaz (cf. 16:1; 17:1; and Introduction to 1 Kings: Characteristics and Themes).

18:2 twenty-nine years. His reign as sole king of Judah lasted from 715–686 B.C.

18:3 he did what was right in the eyes of the LORD. Hezekiah is one of the most highly praised kings in the entire history of Judah (vv. 4, 7 notes).

David his father. On David's reign as the standard by which all other reigns are judged, see note 1 Kin. 11:4.

18:4 He removed the high places. Hezekiah, unlike earlier Judean kings of Judah, reformed the people's worship by destroying the local shrines (1 Kin. 3:2 note).

pillars . . . Asherah. See notes 1 Kin. 14:15, 23.

the bronze serpent. Originally preserved to commemorate God's mercy to the Israelites when they were in the wilderness (Num. 21:6–9), this bronze serpent had become in itself an object of worship, hence an idol (cf. John 3:14, 15).

18:7 He rebelled against the king of Assyria and would not serve him. Hezekiah's father Ahaz had been a vassal of Assyria and modified temple arrangements to reflect this fact (16:7–18). Hezekiah's rebellion against the Assyrians probably involved withholding tribute from them.

wherever he went out, [u]he prospered. He
rebelled against the king of Assyria and
would not serve him. 8 [v]He struck down the
Philistines as far as Gaza and its territory,
[w]from watchtower to fortified city.
9 In the fourth year of King Hezekiah,
which was the seventh year of Hoshea son of
Elah, king of Israel, [x]Shalmaneser king of
Assyria came up against Samaria and
besieged it, 10 and at the end of three years he
took it. In the sixth year of Hezekiah, which
was the ninth year of Hoshea king of Israel,
Samaria was taken. 11 The king of Assyria carried the Israelites away to Assyria and put
them in [y]Halah, and on the [y]Habor, [y]the river
of Gozan, and in the cities of the Medes,
12 because they did not obey the voice of
the LORD their God but transgressed his
covenant, even all that Moses the servant of
the LORD commanded. They neither listened
nor obeyed.

Sennacherib Attacks Judah

13 [z]In the fourteenth year of King
Hezekiah, Sennacherib king of Assyria
came up against all the fortified cities of
Judah and took them. 14 And Hezekiah king
of Judah sent to the king of Assyria at
Lachish, saying, "I have done wrong; withdraw from me. Whatever you impose on
me I will bear." [a]And the king of Assyria
required of Hezekiah king of Judah three
hundred talents[1] of silver and thirty talents
of gold. 15 And Hezekiah [b]gave him all the
silver that was found in the house of the
LORD and in the treasuries of the king's
house. 16 At that time Hezekiah stripped
the gold from the doors of the temple of
the LORD and from the doorposts that
Hezekiah king of Judah had overlaid and
gave it to the king of Assyria. 17 And the
king of Assyria sent the [c]Tartan, the Rab-
saris, and the Rabshakeh with a great army
from Lachish to King Hezekiah at Jerusalem. And they went up and came to
Jerusalem. When they arrived, they came
and stood by [d]the conduit of the upper
pool, which is on the highway to the
Washer's Field. 18 And when they called for
the king, there came out to them [e]Eliakim
the son of Hilkiah, who was over the
household, and [f]Shebnah the •secretary,
and Joah the son of Asaph, the recorder.
19 And the Rabshakeh said to them, "Say
to Hezekiah, 'Thus says the great king, the
king of Assyria: On what do you rest this
trust of yours? 20 Do you think that mere
words are strategy and power for war? In
whom do you now trust, that you have
rebelled against me? 21 Behold, you are
trusting now in Egypt, that broken reed of
[g]a staff, which will pierce the hand of any
man who leans on it. Such is Pharaoh king
of Egypt to all who trust in him. 22 But if
you say to me, "We trust in the LORD our
God," is it not he [h]whose high places and
altars Hezekiah has removed, saying to
Judah and to Jerusalem, "You shall worship before this altar in Jerusalem"?
23 Come now, make a wager with my master the king of Assyria: I will give you two
thousand horses, if you are able on your

7 [u][ch. 16:7]
8 [v][Isai. 14:29] [w]ch. 17:9
9 [x]For ver. 9-12, see ch. 17:3-7
11 [y]ch. 17:6; 1 Chr. 5:26
13 [z]For ver. 13-37, see 2 Chr. 32:1-20; Isai. 36:1-22
14 [a][ch. 23:33]
15 [b][ch. 12:18; 16:8]
17 [c]Isai. 20:1 [d]Isai. 7:3; [ch. 20:20]
18 [e]Isai. 22:20 [f]Isai. 22:15
21 [g][Ezek. 29:6, 7]; See Isai. 30:2, 3, 7
22 [h][ver. 4; 2 Chr. 31:1]

1 A *talent* was about 75 pounds or 34 kilograms

18:8 He struck down the Philistines. During Ahaz's reign the Philistines were able to capture Judean territory (2 Chr. 28:18).

Gaza and its territory. Gaza was near the Mediterranean coast; Hezekiah had penetrated far into Philistine territory.

18:9–37 The Assyrians invade Judah and, advancing to Jerusalem, demand Judah's surrender.

18:9–12 The writer provides a summary of the fall of Samaria narrated and commented upon more fully in ch. 17. In so doing, he underscores the threat Assyria poses to Judah.

18:13–20:19 The story of Sennacherib's campaign and its aftermath is found also in Is. 36–39, with a few additions and omissions.

18:13 In the fourteenth year. 701 B.C., dated from the beginning of his independent reign (vv. 1, 2 and notes).

Sennacherib king of Assyria. Sennacherib succeeded Sargon II in 705 B.C.

came up against all the fortified cities of Judah. The annals of Sennacherib record his campaign against Phoenicia, Judah, the Philistine cities, and Egypt. He claims to have taken forty-six cities and "countless small villages." He also boasts of having shut up Hezekiah in Jerusalem "like a bird in a cage." His annals, however, do not claim that Sennacherib captured Jerusalem (Mic. 1:9 and note).

18:14–16 Hezekiah attempts to convince Sennacherib to withdraw by offering a huge tribute payment (v. 7 note). In using temple and palace treasuries to influence the actions of a foreign king, Hezekiah follows the example of Asa (1 Kin. 15:18) and his own father Ahaz (16:8, 9). The annals of Sennacherib confirm that Hezekiah sent tribute at this time.

18:17 the king of Assyria sent. Some scholars believe that this refers to a second campaign of Sennacherib against Hezekiah about twelve to thirteen years after the first. While this view is possible, there is no solid evidence to support it and, in any event, it is unnecessary. Sennacherib's annals consistently report that Sennacherib not only demanded tribute from kings who "did not bow in submission to my yoke," but also insisted on deposing such rebellious kings and replacing them with monarchs of his own choosing. Hezekiah only sends tribute; he does not abdicate (vv. 14–16).

Lachish. This Judean fortress was located twenty-eight miles southwest of Jerusalem (cf. Mic. 1:13).

18:18 The three Assyrian officials confer with three Judean officials: the palace administrator (cf. 1 Kin. 4:6), the secretary (cf. 2 Sam. 8:17), and the recorder (cf. 2 Sam. 8:16).

part to set riders on them. 24 How then can
you repulse a single captain among the
least of my master's servants, when you
trust in Egypt for chariots and for horsemen? 25 Moreover, is it without the LORD
that I have come up against this place to
destroy it? The LORD said to me, Go up
against this land, and destroy it.'"

26 Then [e]Eliakim the son of Hilkiah, and
[f]Shebnah, and Joah, said to the Rabshakeh,
"Please speak to your servants in [i]Aramaic,
for we understand it. Do not speak to us in
the language of Judah within the hearing of
the people who are on the wall." 27 But the
Rabshakeh said to them, "Has my master
sent me to speak these words to your master
and to you, and not to the men sitting on the
wall, who are doomed with you to eat their
own dung and to drink their own urine?"

28 Then the Rabshakeh stood and called
out in a loud voice in the language of
Judah: "Hear the word of the great king,
the king of Assyria! 29 Thus says the king:
'Do not let Hezekiah deceive you, for he
will not be able to deliver you out of my[1]
hand. 30 Do not let Hezekiah make you
trust in the LORD by saying, The LORD will
surely deliver us, and this city will not be
given into the hand of the king of Assyria.'
31 Do not listen to Hezekiah, for thus says
the king of Assyria: 'Make your peace with
me and come out to me. Then [j]each one of
you will eat of his own vine, and each one
of his own fig tree, and each one of you will
drink the water of his own cistern, 32 until I
come and take you away to a land like your
own land, [k]a land of grain and wine, a land
of bread and vineyards, a land of olive trees
and [l]honey, that you may live, and not die.
And do not listen to Hezekiah when he
misleads you by saying, The LORD will
deliver us. 33 [m]Has any of the gods of the
nations ever delivered his land out of the
hand of the king of Assyria? 34 [n]Where are
the gods of [o]Hamath and [p]Arpad? Where
are the gods of Sepharvaim, Hena, and
[q]Ivvah? Have they delivered Samaria out of
my hand? 35 Who among all the gods of the
lands have delivered their lands out of my
hand, [r]that the LORD should deliver
Jerusalem out of my hand?'"

36 But the people were silent and
answered him not a word, for the king's
command was, "Do not answer him."
37 Then [s]Eliakim the son of Hilkiah, who
was over the household, and Shebna the
secretary, and Joah the son of Asaph, the
recorder, came to Hezekiah [t]with their
clothes torn and told him the words of the
Rabshakeh.

Isaiah Reassures Hezekiah

19 [u]As soon as King Hezekiah heard it,
[t]he tore his clothes and [v]covered
himself with sackcloth and went into the
house of the LORD. 2 And he sent Eliakim,
who was over the household, and Shebna
the secretary, and the senior priests, [v]cov-
ered with sackcloth, to the prophet Isaiah
the son of Amoz. 3 They said to him, "Thus
says Hezekiah, This day is a day of distress,
of rebuke, and of disgrace; children have
come to the point of birth, and there is no
strength to bring them forth. 4 [w]It may be
that the LORD your God heard all the words
of the Rabshakeh, whom his master the

26 [e][See ver. 18 above] [f][See ver. 18 above] [i][Ezra 4:7; Dan. 2:4]
31 [j][1 Kin. 4:25]
32 [k]Deut. 8:7, 8
[l]See Ex. 3:8
33 [m]ch. 19:12; [Isai. 10:10, 11]
34 [n][ch. 19:13] [o]See 1 Kin. 8:65 [p]Isai. 10:9 [q][ch. 17:24]
35 [r][Dan. 3:15]
37 [s]ver. 18, 26; ch. 19:2 [t]See Josh. 7:6
Chapter 19
1 [u]For ver. 1-37, see 2 Chr. 32:20-22; Isai. 37:1-38 [t][See ver. 37 above] [v]See 2 Sam. 3:31
2 [v][See ver. 1 above]
4 [w][2 Sam. 16:12]

1 Hebrew *his*

18:26 Please speak to your servants in Aramaic. Aramaic (the language of ancient Syria) had become by this time the international language of diplomacy. By asking the Assyrian officials to use Aramaic, the official hoped to prevent the inhabitants of Jerusalem from understanding the field commander's speech.

18:31 vine . . . fig tree, and . . . cistern. The description is indicative of normal, peaceful everyday life (1 Kin. 4:25; Mic. 4:4; Zech. 3:10).

18:32 take you away to a land. These words are a parody of God's gift of the promised land to the Israelites. The Assyrian king thereby offers to replace the Lord's promises with his own. Hezekiah will later refer to these claims as blasphemous (19:1–6).

18:33 In the Bible the Lord is utterly distinct from other gods. The Assyrian field commander, however, makes no distinction. In the field commander's opinion, if the gods of the nations could not defeat Assyria, neither will the Lord.

18:34 Hamath . . . Sepharvaim . . . and Ivvah. See note 17:24.

Arpad. Located near Hamath in Syria, Arpad was captured in 740 B.C.

18:36 the people were silent. The Assyrian effort to rouse the populace against their king (vv. 29, 31, 32) was a total failure.

18:37 with their clothes torn. The torn clothes indicate emotional duress (1 Kin. 21:27 note).

19:1 tore his clothes. See 1 Kin. 21:27.

covered himself with sackcloth. See note 6:30.

19:2 who was over the household. See 1 Kin. 4:6 note.

the secretary. See 2 Sam. 8:17.

the senior priests. These elders were probably the heads of the various priestly families in Jerusalem.

the prophet Isaiah. Isaiah plays a pivotal role by providing Hezekiah with good counsel during this crisis (Is. 37).

19:4 the remnant that is left. This remnant includes all the people left in Judah, whether from Judah or Israel, after the Assyrian attacks and deportations (17:6 note).

king of Assyria has sent [x]to mock the living
God, and will rebuke the words that the
LORD your God has heard; therefore lift up
your prayer for [y]the remnant that is left."
5When the servants of King Hezekiah came
to Isaiah, **6**Isaiah said to them, "Say to your
master, 'Thus says the LORD: Do not be
afraid because of the words that you have
heard, with which [z]the servants of the king
of Assyria have [a]reviled me. **7**Behold, I will
put a spirit in him, so that [b]he shall hear a
rumor and return to his own land, and I
will make him [c]fall by the sword in his own
land.'"

Sennacherib Defies the LORD

8The Rabshakeh returned, and found the
king of Assyria fighting against [d]Libnah, for
he heard that the king had left [e]Lachish.
9[f]Now the king heard concerning Tirhakah
king of Cush, "Behold, he has set out to
fight against you." So he sent messengers
again to Hezekiah, saying, **10**"Thus shall you
speak to Hezekiah king of Judah: 'Do not let
your God [g]in whom you trust deceive you
by promising that [h]Jerusalem will not be
given into the hand of the king of Assyria.
11Behold, you have heard what the kings of
Assyria have done to all lands, devoting
them to destruction.[1] And shall you be
delivered? **12**[i]Have the gods of the nations
delivered them, the nations that my fathers
destroyed, [j]Gozan, [k]Haran, Rezeph, and the
people of [l]Eden who were in Telassar?
13[m]Where is the king of Hamath, the king of
Arpad, the king of the city of Sepharvaim,
the king of Hena, or the king of Ivvah?'"

Hezekiah's Prayer

14Hezekiah received [n]the letter from the
hand of the messengers and read it; and
Hezekiah went up to the house of the LORD
and spread it before the LORD. **15**And
Hezekiah prayed before the LORD and said:
"O LORD the God of Israel, [o]who is
enthroned above the cherubim, [p]you are
the God, you alone, of all the kingdoms of
the earth; you have made heaven and
earth. **16**[q]Incline your ear, O LORD, and
hear; [r]open your eyes, O LORD, and see;
and hear the words of Sennacherib, which
he has sent [s]to mock the living God.
17Truly, O LORD, the kings of Assyria have
laid waste the nations and their lands **18**and
have cast their gods into the fire, for they
were not gods, [t]but the work of men's
hands, wood and stone. Therefore they
were destroyed. **19**So now, O LORD our
God, save us, please, from his hand, [u]that
all the kingdoms of the earth may know
that [p]you, O LORD, are God alone."

Isaiah Prophesies Sennacherib's Fall

20Then Isaiah the son of Amoz sent to
Hezekiah, saying, "Thus says the LORD, the
God of Israel: Your prayer to me about
Sennacherib king of Assyria [v]I have heard.
21This is the word that the LORD has spo-
ken concerning him:

"She despises you, she
scorns you—
[w]the virgin daughter of Zion;
she [x]wags her head behind you—
the daughter of Jerusalem.

22 "Whom have you [y]mocked and
[z]reviled?
Against whom have you raised
your voice
and lifted your eyes to the heights?
Against [a]the Holy One of Israel!

1 That is, setting apart (devoting) as an offering to the Lord (for destruction)

4 [x]ver. 16 [y][Isai. 1:9]
6 [z]ch. 18:17 [a]See ch. 18:22-25, 30-35
7 [b]ver. 9 [c]ver. 37
8 [d]Josh. 10:29 [e]ch. 18:14; Josh. 10:31
9 [f][1 Sam. 23:27] [g]ch. 18:5
10 [h]ch. 18:30
12 [i]ch. 18:33 [j]ch. 17:6 [k]Gen. 11:31; Ezek. 27:23 [l]Ezek. 27:23; Amos 1:5
13 [m]ch. 18:34
14 [n][2 Chr. 32:17]
15 [o]See Ex. 25:22 [p]1 Kin. 18:39; Neh. 9:6; Ps. 86:10; Isai. 37:16, 20; 44:6; Jer. 10:10, 12
16 [q]Ps. 31:2; 71:2; Dan. 9:18 [r]2 Chr. 6:40; Dan. 9:18 [s]ver. 4
18 [t]2 Chr. 32:19; Ps. 115:4
19 [u]Josh. 4:24; Ps. 83:18 [p][See ver. 15 above]
20 [v][ch. 20:5]
21 [w]Lam. 2:13 [x]Job 16:4; Ps. 22:7; 109:25; Lam. 2:15
22 [y]ver. 4 [z]ver. 6 [a]Ps. 71:22; Isai. 5:24; 60:9; Jer. 51:5

19:8 Libnah. This town was on the Judean border with Philistia, twelve miles southeast of Ashdod. In his annals, Sennacherib boasts of how he compelled Hezekiah to surrender into his custody the king of Ekron, whom Hezekiah was holding in Jerusalem. Sennacherib was evidently successful in reversing most of Hezekiah's earlier gains against the Philistines (18:8).

Lachish. See 18:17 and note.

19:9 Tirhakah king of Cush. The Biblical "Cush" or Ethiopia refers to southern Egypt and the land to the south. Tirhakah was the brother of the pharaoh Shebteko, who launched a campaign into Palestine to counter the Assyrians under Sennacherib. Although Tirhakah did not become king until 690 or 688 B.C., by the time of the composition of this passage it was natural to refer to him with his characteristic title.

19:12 Gozan. See 17:6.

Haran. See Gen. 11:31.

Rezeph. A town in Syria northeast of Hamath.

the people of Eden who were in Telassar. Eden was a district in Syria south of Haran.

19:13 Hamath . . . Ivvah. Sennacherib provided this litany of names, including cities where the Assyrians had deported people from Israel (17:24 and note), to impress on Hezekiah that Judah would suffer as Israel had.

19:18 they were not gods. See Deut. 4:28, 35; 32:17–21; Ps. 115:3–8; Is. 40:18–20; 44:9–20.

19:21 the virgin daughter of Zion. The phrase refers affectionately to Jerusalem (Is. 1:8).

wags her head behind you. The words describe a gesture of mocking as Assyria runs away (Jer. 18:16).

23 [b]By your messengers you have
mocked the Lord,
and you have said, [c]'With my
many chariots
I have gone up the heights of the
mountains,
to the far recesses of [d]Lebanon;
I felled its tallest cedars,
its choicest cypresses;
I entered its farthest lodging place,
its most [e]fruitful forest.
24 I dug wells
and drank foreign waters,
and I dried up with the sole of my foot
all the streams [f]of Egypt.'
25 "Have you not heard
that [g]I determined it long ago?
I planned from days of old
what [h]now I bring to pass,
that you should turn fortified cities
into heaps of ruins,
26 while their inhabitants, shorn of
strength,
are dismayed and confounded,
and have become [i]like plants of the
field
and like tender grass,
like grass on the housetops,
blighted before it is grown.
27 "But I know your sitting down
[j]and your going out and coming in,
and your raging against me.
28 Because you have raged against me
and your complacency has come
into my ears,
I will [k]put my hook in your nose
and my bit in your mouth,
and [l]I will turn you back on the way
by which you came.

23 [b]ch. 18:17 [c]Ps. 20:7 [d]See Judg. 9:15 [e]2 Chr. 26:10; [Isai. 10:18]
24 [f]Isai. 19:6
25 [g][Isai. 45:7] [h][Isai. 10:5]
26 [i]Ps. 129:6
27 [j][1 Sam. 29:6]
28 [k]Ezek. 29:4; 38:4; [Job 41:2; Isai. 30:28; Amos 4:2] [l]ver. 33, 36
29 [m]ch. 20:8, 9; 1 Sam. 2:34; Isai. 7:11, 14
30 [n][2 Chr. 32: 22, 23]
31 [o][Isai. 10:20] [p]Isai. 9:7
32 [q]2 Sam. 20:15
33 [r]ver. 28
34 [s]ch. 20:6; [Isai. 31:5] [t]1 Kin. 11:13
35 [u][Ex. 12:23; 2 Sam. 24:16]
36 [v]Gen. 10:11; Jonah 1:2
37 [w][ch. 17:31]
Chapter 20
1 [x]For ver. 1-11, see Isai. 38:1-22 [y]2 Chr. 32:24 [z][2 Sam. 17:23]

29 "And this shall be [m]the sign for you:
this year eat what grows of itself, and in the
second year what springs of the same.
Then in the third year sow and reap and
plant vineyards, and eat their fruit.
30 [n]And
the surviving remnant of the house of
Judah shall again take root downward and
bear fruit upward.
31 For out of Jerusalem
shall go a remnant, and out of Mount Zion
[o]a band of survivors. [p]The zeal of the LORD
will do this.
32 "Therefore thus says the LORD concerning the king of Assyria: He shall not come
into this city or shoot an arrow there, or
come before it with a shield or [q]cast up a
siege mound against it.
33 [r]By the way that
he came, by the same he shall return, and
he shall not come into this city, declares
the LORD.
34 [s]For I will defend this city to
save it, for my own sake [t]and for the sake
of my servant David."
35 And that night [u]the angel of the LORD
went out and struck down 185,000 in the
camp of the Assyrians. And when people
arose early in the morning, behold, these
were all dead bodies.
36 Then Sennacherib
king of Assyria departed and went home
and lived at [v]Nineveh.
37 And as he was
worshiping in the house of Nisroch his
god, [w]Adrammelech and Sharezer, his
sons, struck him down with the sword and
escaped into the land of Ararat. And
Esarhaddon his son reigned in his place.

Hezekiah's Illness and Recovery

20 [x]In those days [y]Hezekiah became
sick and was at the point of death.
And Isaiah the prophet the son of Amoz
came to him and said to him, "Thus says
the LORD, [z]'Set your house in order, for you

19:25 Have you not heard. The Assyrians mistakenly believe that their great victories stem from their own might. They do not recognize that God is ultimately responsible for their success (cf. Is. 10:5–12; 14:24–27).

19:28 I will put my hook in your nose and my bit in your mouth. This reference is to the Assyrian custom of treating captured enemies like animals in a caravan (2 Chr. 33:11; cf. Ezek. 19:4, 9). God will turn the tables on Assyria.

19:29 sign. That is, a verification of a future event (1 Kin. 13:3 note).

19:30 remnant. See notes on v. 4 and Is. 1:9. The remnant will not only survive, but flourish.

19:34 for the sake of my servant David. See note 1 Kin. 11:36.

19:35 angel of the LORD. For the angel as an instrument of destruction, see Gen. 19:15; 2 Sam. 24:16. The massive destruction of the Assyrian army carries out the prophecies of vv. 21, 32–34.

19:36 Nineveh. The capital of the Assyrian Empire.

19:37 Nisroch. This god is not found in Assyrian records.

struck him down. Assyrian documents record that in a struggle for the throne in 681 B.C. one of Sennacherib's sons killed him. The author of Kings has telescoped the events surrounding Sennacherib's shameful defeat (701 B.C.) and his assassination (681 B.C.).

Ararat. The word is another name for Urartu, present day Armenia (Gen. 8:4).

Esarhaddon. He ruled Assyria from 681–669 B.C.

20:1 In those days. There is good reason to believe that this incident and the reception of the Babylonian envoys (vv. 12–19) occurred before the Assyrian invasion of Judah in 701 B.C., because according to Babylonian documents, Merodach-baladan (v. 12) died in 703 B.C. Since God added fifteen years to Hezekiah's life (v. 6), he would have been ill in 702 B.C. or before.

shall die; you shall not recover.'" 2 Then
Hezekiah turned his face to the wall and
prayed to the LORD, saying, 3 "Now, O
LORD, [a]please remember how I have walked
before you in faithfulness and [b]with a
whole heart, [c]and have done what is good
in your sight." [d]And Hezekiah wept bitterly.
4 And before Isaiah had gone out of the
middle court, the word of the LORD came
to him: 5 "Turn back, and say to Hezekiah
[e]the leader of my people, Thus says the
LORD, the God of David your father: [f]I have
heard your prayer; [g]I have seen your tears.
Behold, I will heal you. On the third day
you shall go up to the house of the LORD,
6 and I will add fifteen years to your life. I
will deliver you and this city out of the
hand of the king of Assyria, [h]and I will
defend this city for my own sake and for
my servant David's sake." 7 And Isaiah said,
"Bring a cake of figs. And let them take and
lay it on the boil, that he may recover."
8 And Hezekiah said to Isaiah, "What
shall be the sign that the LORD will heal me,
and that I shall go up to the house of the
LORD on the third day?" 9 And Isaiah said,
"This shall be [i]the sign to you from the
LORD, that the LORD will do the thing that
he has promised: shall the shadow go forward
ten steps, or go back ten steps?"
10 And Hezekiah answered, "It is an easy
thing for the shadow [j]to lengthen ten steps.
Rather let the shadow go back ten steps."
11 And Isaiah the prophet called to the
LORD, [k]and he brought the shadow back
ten steps, by which it had gone down on
the steps of Ahaz.

3 [a][Neh. 5:19; 13:14, 22, 31] [b]See 1 Kin. 8:61 [c]ch. 18:3 [d][Ps. 39:12, 13]
5 [e]1 Sam. 9:16; 10:1 [f]ch. 19:20; [Ps. 65:2] [g]Ps. 39:12; 56:8
6 [h]ch. 19:34
9 [i]See ch. 19:29
10 [j]Ps. 102:11
11 [k][Josh. 10:12, 13]
12 [l]For ver. 12-19, see Isai. 39:1-8 [m][Isai. 39:1] [n][2 Chr. 32:31]
13 [o][2 Chr. 32:27]
17 [p]ch. 24:13; Jer. 20:5; [ch. 25:13]; See Jer. 27:19-22
18 [q]ch. 24:12; 2 Chr. 33:11 [r][Dan. 1:3]
19 [s]1 Sam. 3:18; [2 Chr. 32:25, 26]
20 [t][2 Chr. 32:32] [u]ch. 18:17; Neh. 2:14; 3:16

Hezekiah and the Babylonian Envoys

12 [l]At that time [m]Merodach-baladan the
son of Baladan, king of Babylon, [n]sent
envoys with letters and a present to
Hezekiah, for he heard that Hezekiah had
been sick. 13 And Hezekiah welcomed
them, and he showed them [o]all his treasure
house, the silver, the gold, the spices, the
precious oil, his armory, all that was found
in his storehouses. There was nothing in
his house or in all his realm that Hezekiah
did not show them. 14 Then Isaiah the
prophet came to King Hezekiah, and said
to him, "What did these men say? And
from where did they come to you?" And
Hezekiah said, "They have come from a far
country, from Babylon." 15 He said, "What
have they seen in your house?" And
Hezekiah answered, "They have seen all
that is in my house; there is nothing in my
storehouses that I did not show them."
16 Then Isaiah said to Hezekiah, "Hear
the word of the LORD: 17 Behold, the days
are coming, when [p]all that is in your house,
and that which your fathers have stored up
till this day, shall be carried to Babylon.
Nothing shall be left, says the LORD. 18 [q]And
some of your own sons, who shall be born
to you, shall be taken away, [r]and they shall
be eunuchs in the palace of the king of
Babylon." 19 Then said Hezekiah to Isaiah,
[s]"The word of the LORD that you have spoken
is good." For he thought, "Why not, if
there will be peace and security in my
days?"
20 [t]The rest of the deeds of Hezekiah and
all his might and how he made [u]the pool

20:5 I have heard your prayer; I have seen your tears. God compassionately adds fifteen years (v. 6) to Hezekiah's life. Hezekiah's reforms (18:4, 5), together with his abiding trust in God during the Assyrian invasion (18:7, 22, 32; 19:4), reveal a consistency of character. In this respect Hezekiah's conduct is exemplary. Not only does this passage underscore the importance of prayer, but also divine freedom, compassion, and omnipotence (cf. 1 Kin. 21:27–29).

20:6 I will deliver you and this city out of the hand of the king of Assyria. See notes on v. 1 and 1 Kin. 11:13.

20:7 cake of figs. Divine agency in healing does not rule out the use of medicine (v. 5).

20:10 ten steps. The reference is to index marks on the steps (dial) of Ahaz (v. 11; Is. 38:8; cf. Josh. 10:12–14).

20:12 Merodach-baladan. Merodach-baladan was king over Babylon from 721 B.C. until forced by the Assyrian King Sargon II into a vassal relationship (710 B.C.). Shortly after Sargon's death (705 B.C.), Merodach-baladan led his country to a short-lived independence in 704 B.C. before Sennacherib forced him out in 703 B.C. (v. 1 note).

sent . . . letters and a present to Hezekiah. Assyria was the dominant world empire at this time, and it is likely that Merodach-baladan, together with the king of Egypt, was seeking to encourage Hezekiah's independence from the Assyrians.

20:13 his armory, all that was found in his storehouses. This display probably occurred before Hezekiah sent his treasures as tribute to the Assyrians (v. 1 note; 18:14–16 note). Hezekiah was attempting to impress his Babylonian visitors with his nation's wealth and power. Hezekiah was receptive to the idea of an alignment with Egypt and Babylon. Isaiah opposed Ahaz's treaty with Assyria (Is. 7:1–17), and he opposed this attempt to make a treaty with Babylon and Egypt (vv. 16–18; Is. 30; 31).

20:17 shall be carried to Babylon. Isaiah rebukes a naive Hezekiah. The same treasures which might induce a treaty, might also attract an invasion. This prophecy was fulfilled by a Babylonian invasion in 598 B.C. and by the Babylonian exile of 586 B.C. Having sought refuge with the Babylonians, Hezekiah discovers that the Babylonians will ultimately be Judah's ruin.

20:18 your own sons, who shall be born to you. Hezekiah's son Manasseh was exiled by the Assyrians and held captive in Babylon (2 Chr. 33:11). Other descendants followed later (24:15; 25:7).

20:20 the pool and the conduit and brought water into the city. Hezekiah made improvements in Jerusalem's water supply in advance of

and the conduit [v]and brought water into
the city, are they not written in the Book of
the Chronicles of the Kings of Judah?
21 [w]And Hezekiah slept with his fathers, and
Manasseh his son reigned in his place.

Manasseh Reigns in Judah

21 [x]Manasseh was twelve years old
when he began to reign, and he
reigned fifty-five years in Jerusalem. His
mother's name was Hephzibah. **2** And he
did what was evil in the sight of the LORD,
[y]according to the despicable practices of
the nations whom the LORD drove out
before the people of Israel. **3** For he rebuilt
the high places [z]that Hezekiah his father
had destroyed, and he erected altars for
Baal and made [a]an Asherah, [b]as Ahab king
of Israel had done, [c]and worshiped all the
host of heaven and served them. **4** [d]And he
built altars in the house of the LORD, of
which the LORD had said, [e]"In Jerusalem
will I put my name." **5** And he built altars
[c]for all the host of heaven in [f]the two courts
of the house of the LORD. **6** [g]And he burned
his son as an offering[1] and [h]used fortune-
telling and [i]omens and dealt [j]with mediums and with wizards. He did much evil in
the sight of the LORD, provoking him to
anger. **7** And the carved image of [a]Asherah
that he had made he set in the house of
which the LORD said to David and to
Solomon his son, "In this house, [e]and in
Jerusalem, which I have chosen out of all
the tribes of Israel, I will put my name forever. **8** [k]And I will not cause the feet of
Israel to wander anymore out of the land
that I gave to their fathers, if only they will
be careful to do according to all that I have
commanded them, and according to all the
Law that my servant Moses commanded
them." **9** But they did not listen, and
Manasseh led them astray to do more evil
than the nations had done whom the LORD
destroyed before the people of Israel.

Manasseh's Idolatry Denounced

10 And the LORD said by his servants the
prophets, **11** [l]"Because Manasseh king of
Judah has committed these abominations
and has done things [m]more evil than all
that the Amorites did, who were before
him, [n]and has made Judah also to sin [o]with
his idols, **12** therefore thus says the LORD,
the God of Israel: Behold, I am bringing
upon Jerusalem and Judah such disaster[2]
that the ears of everyone who hears of it
[p]will tingle. **13** [q]And I will stretch over
Jerusalem the measuring line of Samaria,
and the plumb line of the house of Ahab,

20 [v]2 Chr. 32:30; [Isai. 22:9, 11]
21 [w]2 Chr. 32:33
Chapter 21
1 [x]For ver. 1-9, see 2 Chr. 33:1-9
2 [y][ch. 16:3]
3 [z]ch. 18:4 [a]See Deut. 16:21 [b]1 Kin. 16:32, 33 [c]ch. 17:16; 23:5; [Deut. 4:19]
4 [d]Jer. 7:30; 32:34 [e]ver. 7; ch. 23:27; 2 Sam. 7:13; 1 Kin. 8:29; 9:3; [Deut. 12:11]
5 [c][See ver. 3 above] [f]ch. 23:12; 1 Kin. 6:36; 7:12
6 [g]See Lev. 18:21 [h]See Lev. 19:26 [i]ch. 17:17 [j]ch. 23:24; See Lev. 19:31
7 [a][See ver. 3 above]
[e][See ver. 4 above]
8 [k][2 Sam. 7:19]
11 [l]ver. 2; ch. 23:26; 24:3, 4; Jer. 15:4 [m]1 Kin. 21:26 [n]ver. 16 [o]ver. 21
12 [p]1 Sam. 3:11; Jer. 19:3
13 [q]Isai. 34:11; [Isai. 28:17; Lam. 2:8; Amos 7:7, 8]

1 Hebrew *made his son pass through the fire* 2 Or *evil*

the Assyrian invasion. An inscription in the Siloam Tunnel celebrates the completion of an impressive engineering feat. The conduit runs from the Gihon spring outside the city wall (cf. 1 Kin. 1:33 note) through seventeen hundred feet of solid rock to the Pool of Siloam inside the city.

Book of the Chronicles of the Kings of Judah. See note 1 Kin. 11:41.

21:1–18 These verses summarize the evil reign of Manasseh, king of Judah. Manasseh leads Judah into sin by reintroducing idolatry into Judah; he is also guilty of shedding "much innocent blood" (v. 16). So great is Manasseh's sin that God pronounces disaster on Judah and Jerusalem.

21:1 twelve years old. Manasseh most likely began his reign as coregent with his father, Hezekiah.

fifty-five years. That is, 697–642 B.C., including a ten-year co-regency with Hezekiah. Manasseh's reign was the longest of any Judean king. Assyrian records say that Manasseh was a vassal of both Esarhaddon (681–669 B.C.) and Ashurbanipal (669–627 B.C.).

21:2 he did what was evil. Manasseh presided over the worst period of infidelity in Judah's history. The reforms instituted by Hezekiah were reversed by his son. Manasseh also introduced pagan elements into Judean worship that were unprecedented during the entire period of the monarchy (vv. 3–11 notes).

21:3 the high places that Hezekiah his father had destroyed. See 18:4 and note on 1 Kin. 3:2.

altars for Baal. State-sanctioned Baal worship had previously been eradicated in the reforms led by the priest Jehoiada (11:18).

Asherah. See note 1 Kin. 14:15.

as Ahab king of Israel had done. Manasseh imitated the policies of the worst king of the northern kingdom (1 Kin. 16:30–33).

worshiped all the host of heaven. In Babylon and other nations, the sun, moon, and stars were personified as gods (17:16: 23:5). Star worship was forbidden in Israel (Deut. 4:19; 17:3).

21:4 altars in the house of the LORD. These altars were dedicated to "the host of heaven" (v. 5).

Jerusalem. See note 1 Kin. 11:13.

21:6 burned his son as an offering. On the gruesome practice of child sacrifice, see note 16:3 and Deut. 12:29–31.

mediums . . . wizards. See note 16:15.

21:7 to David and to Solomon his son. David wished to build the temple himself (2 Sam. 7:1–3), but the Lord instead promised David that He would build David a dynasty and that his son (Solomon) would build the temple (2 Sam. 7:8–16). That promise was fulfilled during Solomon's reign, and God blessed the temple as the divinely ordained place for sacrifice and prayer (1 Kin. 9:1–3; cf. Deut. 12:5).

21:8 if only they will be careful to do. The land was a gift, and its possession was predicated upon Israelite fidelity (Deut. 1:8; 3:18; 4:1, 25–28; 1 Kin. 9:4–9).

my servant Moses. See note 1 Kin. 2:3.

21:11 Amorites. Here a general designation of the original inhabitants of Canaan (1 Kin. 21:26 note).

21:13 measuring line . . . the plumb line. Both Samaria (17:5, 6) and the house of Ahab (10:10, 11) were destroyed. Yahweh uses for destruction the tools normally employed for construction (Is. 34:11; Lam. 2:8; Amos 7:7–9).

and I will wipe Jerusalem as one wipes a
dish, wiping it and turning it upside down.
14 And I will forsake the remnant of my heritage and give them into the hand of their
enemies, and they shall become a prey and
a spoil to all their enemies, 15 because they
have done what is evil in my sight and have
provoked me to anger, since the day their
fathers came out of Egypt, even to this
day."

16 [r]Moreover, Manasseh shed very much
innocent blood, till he had filled Jerusalem
from one end to another, besides the sin
[s]that he made Judah to sin so that they did
what was evil in the sight of the LORD.

17 [t]Now the rest of the acts of Manasseh
and all that he did, and the sin that he
committed, are they not written in the
Book of the Chronicles of the Kings of
Judah? 18 [u]And Manasseh slept with his
fathers and was buried in the garden of his
house, [v]in the garden of Uzza, and Amon
his son reigned in his place.

Amon Reigns in Judah

19 Amon was twenty-two years old when
he began to reign, and he reigned two years
in Jerusalem. His mother's name was
Meshullemeth the daughter of Haruz of
Jotbah. 20 And he did what was evil in the
sight of the LORD, [w]as Manasseh his father
had done. 21 He walked in all the way in
which his father walked and served [x]the
idols that his father served and worshiped
them. 22 [y]He abandoned the LORD, the God
of his fathers, and did not walk in the way
of the LORD. 23 And the servants of Amon
conspired against him and put the king to
death in his house. 24 But the people of the
land struck down all those who had conspired against King Amon, and the people
of the land made Josiah his son king in his
place. 25 Now the rest of the acts of Amon
that he did, are they not written in the
Book of the Chronicles of the Kings of
Judah? 26 And he was buried in his tomb [z]in
the garden of Uzza, and Josiah his son
reigned in his place.

Josiah Reigns in Judah

22 [a]Josiah was eight years old when he
began to reign, and he reigned thirty-one years in Jerusalem. His mother's
name was Jedidah the daughter of Adaiah
of [b]Bozkath. 2 And he did what was right in
the eyes of the LORD and walked in all the
way of David his father, [c]and he did not
turn aside to the right or to the left.

Josiah Repairs the Temple

3 In the eighteenth year of King Josiah, the
king sent Shaphan the son of Azaliah, son
of Meshullam, the secretary, to the house of
the LORD, saying, 4 "Go up to [d]Hilkiah the
high priest, that he may count the money
[e]that has been brought into the house of
the LORD, which [f]the keepers of the threshold have collected from the people. 5 [g]And

16 [r]ch. 24:4 [s]ver. 11 **17** [t]See 2 Chr. 33:11-19 **18** [u]For ver. 18-24, see 2 Chr. 33:20-25 [v]ver. 26 **20** [w]See ver. 2-6, 11 **21** [x]ver. 11

22 [y]ch. 22:17; [1 Kin. 11:33] **26** [z]ver. 18 **Chapter 22** **1** [a]See 2 Chr. 34:1, 2 [b]Josh. 15:39 **2** [c]See Deut. 5:32 **4** [d][ch. 12:10] [e]ch. 12:4 [f]ch. 12:9 **5** [g]ch. 12:11, 12, 14

21:14 I will forsake. The time for patience and forbearance is over. Jerusalem and Judah will not be defeated by a superior people or a superior god. On the contrary, God is abandoning what is left of the original twelve tribes (the "remnant") to their enemies as punishment (Is. 1:5). The exile to Babylon of 586 B.C. is in view (25:1–17).

21:15 since the day. After liberating His people from slavery in Egypt, God made a covenant with Israel at Mount Sinai (Ex. 19:1–Num. 10:10). Although both God and Israel made promises in this covenant, only God remained faithful. Israel's history was characterized by constant rebellion.

21:16 shed very much innocent blood. This expression refers to oppression and persecution of the weak (Jer. 7:6; 22:3, 17; Ezek. 22:6–31).

21:17 Book of the Chronicles of the Kings of Judah. See note 1 Kin. 11:41.

21:19 Amon . . . reigned two years. That is, 642–640 B.C. It is probable that Amon, like Manasseh before him, was an Assyrian vassal.

21:24 the people of the land. See note 11:14. Desiring thorough reforms and not merely the removal of Amon, the people step forward and install a descendant of David who will be loyal to the Davidic legacy.

21:25 Book of the Chronicles of the Kings of Judah. See note 1 Kin. 11:41.

22:1 thirty-one years. That is, 640–609 B.C.

Bozkath. A town in Judah, mentioned in Josh. 15:39 but of unknown location.

22:2 David his father. The writer commends several kings of Judah—Asa (1 Kin. 15:11), Jehoshaphat (1 Kin. 22:43), Joash (2 Kin. 12:2), Amaziah (14:3), Azariah (15:3), Jotham (15:34), and Hezekiah (18:3), but he gives Josiah the highest praise (23:25). Josiah instituted the most thoroughgoing reforms of any king (23:1–24). The prophet Jeremiah also spoke well of Josiah's reign (Jer. 22:15, 16).

did not turn aside. His actions were wholly in accord with the mandate of the covenant (Deut. 5:32; 17:11, 20; 28:14; Josh. 1:7; Prov. 4:27).

22:3 eighteenth year. That is, when Josiah was twenty-six years old.

secretary. Or "scribe," see 2 Sam. 8:17; Ezra 7:6 and notes. By the time of Josiah's reign, the Assyrian Empire was in a state of decline. Josiah, unlike Manasseh, asserted Judah's independence from Assyria. Josiah was able to gain control over at least part of the former northern kingdom (23:4, 15–20).

22:4 Hilkiah. Probably not the same man who is mentioned as the father of Jeremiah (Jer. 1:1), this Hilkiah was the grandfather of the high priest Seraiah who was exiled to Babylon (25:18–20).

which the keepers of the threshold have collected from the people. King Joash earlier had used the same technique for collecting funds to refurbish the temple (12:4, 5). Josiah was restoring the temple after its neglect in the days of Manasseh and Amon.

let it be given into the hand of the workmen
who have the oversight of the house of the
LORD, and let them give it to the workmen
who are at the house of the LORD, repairing
the house ([6]that is, to the carpenters, and
to the builders, and to the masons), and let
them use it for buying timber and quarried
stone to repair the house. 7 But [h]no account-
ing shall be asked from them for the money
that is delivered into their hand, for they
deal honestly."

Hilkiah Finds the Book of the Law

8 And Hilkiah the high priest said to
Shaphan the secretary, "I have found [i]the
Book of the Law in the house of the LORD."
And Hilkiah gave the book to Shaphan,
and he read it. 9 And Shaphan the secretary
came to the king, and reported to the king,
"Your servants have emptied out the
money that was found in the house and
have delivered it into the hand of the workmen who have the oversight of the house of
the LORD." 10 Then Shaphan the secretary
told the king, "Hilkiah the priest has given
me a book." And Shaphan read it before
the king.

11 When the king heard the words of the
Book of the Law, [j]he tore his clothes. 12 And
the king commanded Hilkiah the priest,
and [k]Ahikam the son of Shaphan, and
[l]Achbor the son of [l]Micaiah, and Shaphan
the secretary, and Asaiah the king's servant, saying, 13 "Go, inquire of the LORD for
me, and for the people, and for all Judah,
concerning the words of this book that has
been found. For great is [m]the wrath of the
LORD that is kindled against us, because
our fathers have not obeyed the words of
this book, to do according to all that is
written concerning us."

14 So Hilkiah the priest, and Ahikam, and
Achbor, and Shaphan, and Asaiah went to
Huldah the prophetess, the wife of
Shallum the son of [n]Tikvah, son of
[n]Harhas, keeper of the wardrobe (now she
lived in Jerusalem in [o]the Second Quarter),
and they talked with her. 15 And she said to
them, "Thus says the LORD, the God of
Israel: 'Tell the man who sent you to me,
16 Thus says the LORD, behold, I will bring
disaster upon this place and upon its
inhabitants, all the words of the book that
the king of Judah has read. 17 [p]Because they
have forsaken me and have made offerings
to other gods, that they might provoke me
to anger with all the work of their hands,
therefore [m]my wrath will be kindled against
this place, and it will not be quenched.
18 But to the king of Judah, who sent you to
inquire of the LORD, thus shall you say to
him, Thus says the LORD, the God of Israel:
Regarding the words that you have heard,
19 [q]because your heart was penitent, and
you [r]humbled yourself before the LORD,
when you heard how I spoke against this
place and against its inhabitants, that they
should become [s]a desolation and [t]a curse,
and you [u]have torn your clothes and wept
before me, I also have heard you, declares
the LORD. 20 Therefore, behold, I will gather
you to your fathers, and [v]you shall be gathered to your grave in peace, and your eyes
shall not see all the disaster that I will bring
upon this place.'" And they brought back
word to the king.

Josiah's Reforms

23 [w]Then the king sent, and all the elders of Judah and Jerusalem were
gathered to him. 2 And the king went up to
the house of the LORD, and with him all the
men of Judah and all the inhabitants of
Jerusalem and the priests and the prophets,
all the people, both small and great. And
[x]he read in their hearing all the words of the

7 [h]ch. 12:15
8 [i]Deut. 31:24-26; 2 Chr. 34:14
11 [j]See Josh. 7:6
12 [k]ch. 25:22; Jer. 26:24; 39:14; 40:5 [l][2 Chr. 34:20]
13 [m]Deut. 29:27
14 [n][2 Chr. 34:22] [o]Zeph. 1:10; [ch. 20:4]
17 [p]ch. 21:22; Deut. 29:25, 26 [m][See ver. 13 above]
19 [q][Ps. 51:17; Isai. 57:15] [r]1 Kin. 21:29 [s]Lev. 26:31, 32; 2 Chr. 30:7; Jer. 25:18; 44:22; Mic. 6:16 [t]Jer. 24:9; 26:6; 44:22 [u]ver. 11
20 [v]Ps. 37:37; Isai. 57:1,2
Chapter 23
1 [w]For ver. 1-3, see 2 Chr. 34:29-32
2 [x]See Deut. 31:11

22:8 the Book of the Law. Actually a scroll, this document was probably a version of the Book of Deuteronomy (Deut. 28:61; 31:24, 26). The reforms which Josiah initiates (23:1–24) follow Deuteronomy.

22:11 he tore his clothes. See note 1 Kin. 21:27. Josiah was disturbed because the Law was not being kept, and he realized that this displeased God (v. 13; Deut. 6:10–19; 28:15–68).

22:12 Ahikam the son of Shaphan. Ahikam was the father of Gedaliah, who was later appointed by Nebuchadnezzar to be governor of Judah (25:22; Jer. 26:24).

22:13 Go, inquire of the LORD. Josiah, like a number of kings before him, consults a prophet or prophetess in a dire situation (19:2; 20:1–5; 1 Kin. 14:1–18; 20:13, 14).

22:14 Huldah the prophetess. She was probably a court prophet, consulted on matters of state (Deut. 18:14–22).

the Second Quarter. Probably a recently developed quarter on the western hill of Jerusalem (cf. 2 Chr. 33:14; Zeph. 1:10).

23:1 elders. See 1 Kin. 8:1 note.

23:2 Book of the Covenant. Scholars debate the precise contents of this book or scroll. Although Ex. 20–23 is called the "Book of the Covenant" (Ex. 24:7), it is unlikely that only these chapters in Exodus are meant. Judging from the kinds of reform Josiah pursues in vv. 4–24, the book was a version of Deuteronomy (22:8 note) or a larger group of laws including Deuteronomy.

Book of the Covenant [y] that had been found
in the house of the LORD. **3** And the king
stood [z] by the pillar and [a] made a covenant
before the LORD, [b] to walk after the LORD and
to keep his commandments and his testimonies and his statutes with all his heart
and all his soul, to perform the words of
this covenant that were written in this
book. And all the people joined in the
covenant.

4 And the king commanded Hilkiah the
high priest and the priests [c] of the second
order and the keepers of the threshold to
bring out of the temple of the LORD all the
vessels made for [d] Baal, for [e] Asherah, and
for all the host of heaven. [f] He burned them
outside Jerusalem in the fields of the
Kidron and carried their ashes to Bethel.
5 And he deposed the priests whom the
kings of Judah had ordained to make offerings in the high places at the cities of Judah
and around Jerusalem; those also who
burned incense to Baal, to the sun and the
moon and the constellations [g] and all the
host of the heavens. **6** And he brought out
[h] the Asherah from the house of the LORD,
outside Jerusalem, to the brook Kidron,
[i] and burned it at the brook Kidron [j] and
beat it to dust and cast the dust of it upon
the graves [k] of the common people. **7** And he
broke down the houses of [l] the male cult
prostitutes who were in the house of the
LORD, [m] where the women wove hangings
for [h] the Asherah. **8** And he brought all the
priests out of the cities of Judah, and
defiled the high places where the priests
had made offerings, from [n] Geba to
Beersheba. And he broke down the high
places of the gates that were at the entrance
of the gate of Joshua the governor of the
city, which were on one's left at the gate of
the city. **9** [o] However, the priests of the high
places did not come up to the altar of the
LORD in Jerusalem, but they ate unleavened
bread among their brothers. **10** And he
defiled [p] Topheth, which is [q] in the Valley of
the Son of Hinnom, [r] that no one might
burn his son or his daughter as an offering
to [s] Molech. [1] **11** And he removed the horses
that the kings of Judah had dedicated to
the sun, at the entrance to the house of the
LORD, by the chamber of Nathan-melech
the chamberlain, which was in the
precincts. [2] And he burned the chariots of
the sun with fire. **12** And the altars [t] on the
roof of the upper chamber of Ahaz, which
the kings of Judah had made, and the altars
[u] that Manasseh had made in the two courts
of the house of the LORD, he pulled down
and broke in pieces [3] and cast the dust of
them [v] into the brook Kidron. **13** And the
king defiled the high places that were east

2 [y] ch. 22:8
3 [z] ch. 11:14 [a] [ch. 11:17] [b] Deut. 13:4
4 [c] [ch. 25:18; Jer. 52:24] [d] ch. 21:3 [e] See Deut. 16:21 [f] ver. 15
5 [g] ch. 21:3
6 [h] See Deut. 16:21 [i] ver. 15 [j] ver. 15; [2 Chr. 15:16] [k] [2 Chr. 34:4]
7 [l] 1 Kin. 14:24; 15:12; See Deut. 23:17 [m] [Ezek. 16:16] [h] [See ver. 6 above]
8 [n] 1 Kin. 15:22
9 [o] See Ezek. 44:10-14
10 [p] Isai. 30:33; Jer. 7:31, 32; 19:6, 11-14 [q] See Josh. 15:8 [r] See Lev. 18:21 [s] See 1 Kin. 11:7
12 [t] [Jer. 19:13; 32:29; Zeph. 1:5] [u] ch. 21:5 [v] ver. 4, 6

1 Hebrew *might cause his son or daughter to pass through the fire for Molech* 2 The meaning of the Hebrew word is uncertain 3 Hebrew *pieces from there*

23:3 by the pillar. See 11:14 note; 1 Kin. 7:15 note.

made a covenant. Josiah, like Moses (Ex. 24:1–8; Deut. 29:1), Joshua (Josh. 24:1–28), and Jehoiada (2 Kin. 11:17) before him, leads the people in renewing their commitment to God. During the liturgy, the people pledged themselves to "keep his commandments and his testimonies and his statutes."

with all his heart and all his soul. See Deut. 6:5, and Jesus' summary of the law in Matt. 22:36–40.

23:4 Baal. See note 1 Kin. 16:32.

Asherah. See note 1 Kin. 14:15.

the host of heaven. See notes 17:16 and 21:4.

ashes to Bethel. Bethel was one of the two original places where Jeroboam I used golden calves in a rival cult (1 Kin. 12:26–33). By depositing ashes at Bethel, Josiah desecrates Jeroboam's religious center (cf. vv. 15–20).

23:5 priests. See Hos. 10:5; Zeph. 1:4.

high places. See note 1 Kin. 3:2.

23:6 burned it . . . and beat it to dust. This is like what Moses did after the Israelites worshiped a golden calf (Ex. 32:20; Deut. 9:21).

the graves of the common people. Josiah does this to desecrate the wooden image, not to contaminate the graves of the poor (Num. 19:16; Jer. 26:23).

23:7 male cult prostitutes. See note 1 Kin. 14:24.

23:8 from Geba to Beersheba. Geba was at the far north of Judah and Beersheba at the far south. Josiah is centralizing the worship of the southern kingdom in accord with the prescriptions of Deut. 12.

23:9 did not come up to the altar of the LORD. Deut. 18:6–8 allows local priests the option of joining the staff of the central sanctuary. However, the uncertain ancestry of these priests may have rendered them unfit for this task (1 Kin. 12:31; 13:33). They could aspire to a secondary role in the temple service.

ate unleavened bread. The priests from the high places were allowed a portion of the priestly provisions (Lev. 2:10; 6:16–20).

23:10 Topheth. Child sacrifice occurred at this location in the Valley of the Son of Hinnom outside Jerusalem (16:3; 21:6; Is. 30:33; Jer. 7:31, 32; 19:5, 6).

Molech. See note 1 Kin. 11:5.

23:11 horses . . . dedicated to the sun. The sun was regarded as divine by some of Israel's neighbors (17:16), and the Assyrian sun-god was known by the title "chariot-rider." Miniature clay horses with solar disks on their foreheads have been found in excavations near the temple area. See also Ezek. 8:16.

23:12 pulled down. By tearing down the altars used for astral worship, Josiah reversed the policies of Ahaz (16:3, 4, 10–16), Manasseh (21:3), and Amon (21:21).

23:13 the high places . . . which Solomon the king of Israel had built. Of all the Judean kings, only Josiah was bold enough to tear down the high places Solomon built for the gods of his foreign wives (1 Kin. 11:1–8, 33).

of Jerusalem, to the south of [w]the mount of
corruption, which Solomon the king of
Israel had built for [x]Ashtoreth the abomination of the Sidonians, and for [y]Chemosh the
abomination of Moab, and for [z]Milcom the
abomination of the Ammonites. 14 And he
broke in pieces the [a]pillars and cut down
the Asherim and filled their places with the
bones of men.
15 Moreover, the altar at Bethel, the high
place erected [b]by Jeroboam the son of
Nebat, [c]who made Israel to sin, [d]that altar
with the high place he pulled down and
burned,[1] reducing it to dust. He also burned
the Asherah. 16 And as Josiah turned, he saw
the tombs there on the mount. And he sent
and took the bones out of the tombs and
burned them on the altar and defiled it, [e]ac-
cording to the word of the LORD that the
man of God proclaimed, who had predicted
these things. 17 Then he said, "What is that
monument that I see?" And the men of the
city told him, [f]"It is the tomb of the man of
God who came from Judah and predicted[2]
these things that you have done against the
altar at Bethel." 18 And he said, "Let him be;
let no man move his bones." So they let his
bones alone, with the bones [g]of the prophet
who came out of Samaria. 19 And Josiah
removed all the shrines also of the high
places that were [h]in the cities of Samaria,
which kings of Israel had made, provoking
the LORD to anger. He did to them according
to all that he had done at Bethel. 20 And [i]he
sacrificed all the priests of the high places
who were there, on the altars, [j]and burned
human bones on them. Then he returned to
Jerusalem.

13 [w][1 Kin. 11:7] [x]See 1 Kin. 11:5 [y][Num. 21:29] [z][1 Kin. 11:5]
14 [a]See Ex. 23:24
15 [b]1 Kin. 12:28, 29, 33 [c]See 1 Kin. 14:16 [d]ver. 6
16 [e]1 Kin. 13:2
17 [f]1 Kin. 13:1, 30
18 [g]1 Kin. 13:11, 31
19 [h][2 Chr. 34:6, 7]
20 [i][ch. 11:18; Ex. 22:20; 1 Kin. 18:40] [j]2 Chr. 34:5
21 [k]See 2 Chr. 35:1-17 [l]See Ex. 12:3-11; Lev. 23:5, 8; Num. 9:2-4; Deut. 16:2-8
22 [m]2 Chr. 35:18, 19
24 [n]ch. 21:6; See Lev. 19:31 [o]See Gen. 31:19 [p]ch. 21:11, 21 [q]Lev. 19:31; 20:27; Deut. 18:11 [r]ch. 22:8
25 [s][ch. 18:5]
26 [t]ch. 21:11; 24:3, 4; Jer. 15:4
27 [u]ch. 17:18, 20; 18:11; 21:13 [v]See ch. 21:4

Josiah Restores the Passover

21 And the king commanded all the people, [k]"Keep the Passover to the LORD your
God, [l]as it is written in this Book of the
Covenant." 22 [m]For no such Passover had
been kept since the days of the judges who
judged Israel, or during all the days of the
kings of Israel or of the kings of Judah. 23 But
in the eighteenth year of King Josiah this
Passover was kept to the LORD in Jerusalem.
24 Moreover, Josiah put away [n]the mediums and the necromancers and [o]the
household gods and [p]the idols and all the
abominations that were seen in the land of
Judah and in Jerusalem, that he might
establish [q]the words of the law that were
written in the book [r]that Hilkiah the priest
found in the house of the LORD. 25 [s]Before
him there was no king like him, who
turned to the LORD with all his heart and
with all his soul and with all his might,
according to all the Law of Moses, nor did
any like him arise after him.
26 Still the LORD did not turn from the
burning of his great wrath, by which his
anger was kindled against Judah, [t]because
of all the provocations with which
Manasseh had provoked him. 27 And the
LORD said, "I will remove Judah also out of
my sight, [u]as I have removed Israel, and I
will cast off this city that I have chosen,
Jerusalem, [v]and the house of which I said,
My name shall be there."

Josiah's Death in Battle

28 Now the rest of the acts of Josiah and
all that he did, are they not written in the

[1] Septuagint *broke in pieces its stones* [2] Hebrew *called*

23:14 broke . . . cut down. Josiah defiles sacred precincts dating to the time of Rehoboam, where there were "pillars" and "Asherim" (1 Kin. 14:23).

23:15 the altar at Bethel. See 1 Kin. 12:32, 33. It is unclear whether Josiah defiled the cult center Jeroboam I established at Dan (1 Kin. 12:29, 30) or whether this cult center was still functioning.

23:16 tombs. These tombs belonged to the Bethel priests appointed by Jeroboam I (1 Kin. 12:31, 32; 13:2).

according to the word of the LORD. See the prophecy of 1 Kin. 13:2, 32 and the story of which it is a part (1 Kin. 13).

23:18 Samaria. The name here probably designates the former northern kingdom (v. 19 and 17:24; 1 Kin. 13:32) and not the city. The northern prophet was from Bethel (1 Kin. 13:11), and Omri built the city of Samaria sometime after this prophecy (1 Kin. 16:24 and note).

23:19 in the cities of Samaria. Josiah began his northern reforms at Bethel and extended them into the former northern kingdom.

23:20 sacrificed all the priests. See the statutes dealing with those advocating the worship of other gods, Deut. 13:6–18; 17:2–7.

23:21–28 Josiah reinstitutes the Passover.

23:21 this Book of the Covenant. This refers to Deuteronomy, especially 16:1–8, that authorizes eating the Passover only at the central sanctuary. The Passover was originally observed in a family setting (Ex. 12:1–28, 43–49).

23:23 in the eighteenth year. That is, when Josiah was twenty-six years old.

23:24 mediums and the necromancers. These were introduced by Manasseh (21:6).

household gods. On these small idols, see Gen. 31:19; Judg. 17:5; 1 Sam. 19:13.

words of the law. See notes on v. 2; 22:8.

23:26 the LORD did not turn from the burning of his great wrath. The reforms of Josiah delayed but did not change God's decision to exile His people because of the sins of Manasseh (21:12–15 and notes).

23:28 Book of the Chronicles of the Kings of Judah. See note 1 Kin. 11:41.

Book of the Chronicles of the Kings of
Judah? 29 [w]In his days [x]Pharaoh Neco king
of Egypt went up to the king of Assyria to
the river Euphrates. King Josiah went to
meet him, and Pharaoh Neco killed him at
[y]Megiddo, as soon as he saw him. 30 [z]And
his servants carried him dead in a chariot
from [y]Megiddo and brought him to
Jerusalem and buried him in his own
tomb. [a]And the people of the land took
Jehoahaz the son of Josiah, and anointed
him, and made him king in his father's
place.

Jehoahaz's Reign and Captivity

31 [b]Jehoahaz was twenty-three years old
when he began to reign, and he reigned
three months in Jerusalem. His mother's
name was [c]Hamutal the daughter of
Jeremiah of Libnah. 32 And he did what was
evil in the sight of the LORD, [d]according to
all that his fathers had done. 33 And
[x]Pharaoh Neco put him in bonds at [e]Riblah
in the land of [f]Hamath, that he might not
reign in Jerusalem, and laid on the land a
tribute of a hundred talents[1] of silver and a
talent of gold. 34 And [x]Pharaoh Neco made
Eliakim the son of Josiah king in the place
of Josiah his father, and [g]changed his name
to Jehoiakim. But he took Jehoahaz away,
[h]and he came to Egypt and died there.
35 And Jehoiakim [i]gave the silver and the
gold to Pharaoh, but he taxed the land to
give the money according to the command
of Pharaoh. He exacted the silver and the
gold of the people of the land, from everyone according to his assessment, to give it
to Pharaoh Neco.

Jehoiakim Reigns in Judah

36 [j]Jehoiakim was twenty-five years old
when he began to reign, and he reigned
eleven years in Jerusalem. His mother's
name was Zebidah the daughter of Pedaiah
of Rumah. 37 And he did what was evil in
the sight of the LORD, [d]according to all that
his fathers had done.

24

[k]In his days, Nebuchadnezzar king
of Babylon came up, and Jehoiakim
became his servant three years. Then he
turned and rebelled against him. 2 And the
LORD sent against him bands of the
[l]Chaldeans and [m]bands of the Syrians and
bands of the Moabites and bands of the
Ammonites, and sent them against Judah
to destroy it, [n]according to the word of the
LORD that he spoke by his servants the
prophets. 3 Surely this came upon Judah at
the command of the LORD, to remove them
out of his sight, [o]for the sins of Manasseh,
according to all that he had done, 4 and also
[p]for the innocent blood that he had shed.
For he filled Jerusalem with innocent

[1] A *talent* was about 75 pounds or 34 kilograms

29 [w]For ver. 29, 30, see 2 Chr. 35:20-24 [x]Jer. 46:2 [y][Judg. 5:19; Zech. 12:11]
30 [z][ch. 9:28] [y][See ver. 29 above] [a]For ver. 30-34, see 2 Chr. 36:1-4
31 [b][1 Chr. 3:15; Jer. 22:11] [c]ch. 24:18
32 [d][ch. 24:9, 19]
33 [x][See ver. 29 above] [e]ch. 25:6, 20, 21; Jer. 39:5, 6; 52:9, 10, 26, 27 [f]See 1 Kin. 8:65
34 [x][See ver. 29 above] [g][ch. 24:17; Dan. 1:7] [h]Jer. 22:11, 12; [Ezek. 19:3, 4]
35 [i]ver. 33
36 [j]2 Chr. 36:5
37 [d][See ver. 32 above]
Chapter 24
1 [k]2 Chr. 36:6; Jer. 25:1, 9; Dan. 1:1
2 [l]ch. 25:4; Jer. 32:28, 29; 35:11; [Ezek. 19:8] [m]Jer. 35:11 [n]ch. 20:17; 21:12-14; 23:27
3 [o]ch. 21:11; 23:26
4 [p]ch. 21:16

23:29 Neco. This pharaoh ruled from 610–595 B.C.

to the king of Assyria. Babylon was now the most powerful nation in the Near East, and the Assyrian Empire was in decline. Neco was probably marching to aid the Assyrians against the resurgent Babylonians.

23:30 people of the land. See note 11:14.

Jehoahaz. Jehoahaz (or Shallum) was chosen to replace the fallen Josiah even though he was Josiah's youngest son (1 Chr. 3:15; Jer. 22:11). He may have been selected over his older brothers because he pursued an anti-Egyptian posture, like that of his father (cf. Ezek. 19:3, 4).

anointed him. See note 1 Kin. 1:34.

23:31–35 These verses summarize the brief reign of Jehoahaz, King of Judah, who did "evil in the sight of the LORD" (v. 32). Jehoahaz was captured and deported to Egypt, and his son Eliakim (Jehoiakim) replaced him.

23:31 three months. During 609 B.C.

Jeremiah. Not the prophet Jeremiah, who was from Anathoth (Jer. 1:1).
Libnah. See note 8:22.

23:33 Riblah in the land of Hamath. Located on the Orontes River in the north Lebanon Valley, Riblah was used first by Neco and later by Nebuchadnezzar as a military headquarters (25:6).

23:34 Eliakim . . . Jehoiakim. When obliging their vassals to take a loyalty oath, Assyrian kings sometimes changed their vassals' names. Neco's ability to make Eliakim change his name may be such an attempt to make a show of power.

23:35 exacted the silver and the gold of the people of the land. Jehoiakim taxes the very people who had brought Jehoahaz to the throne (v. 30).

23:36–24:7 The writer makes it clear that the disasters befalling Judah at the hands of foreign invaders are in fulfillment of God's word of judgment against Judah for Manasseh's sin (21:10–15; 24:2–4).

23:36 eleven years. That is, 609–598 B.C.

Rumah. The town was located about fourteen miles west of the Sea of Chinneroth (Galilee).

24:1 Nebuchadnezzar. Nebuchadnezzar II was king of Babylon from 605–562 B.C. Babylon defeated Neco of Egypt in a major battle at Carchemish (Jer. 46:2), and Judah was now ruled by Babylon instead of Egypt.

came up. According to Babylonian records, Nebuchadnezzar II subdued the "Hatti land," including the "city of Judah" (that is, Jerusalem).
three years. That is, 604–602 B.C.

he turned and rebelled. Going against Jeremiah's counsel (Jer. 27:9–11), Jehoiakim's decision to rebel may have been influenced by Egypt's successful defense against Nebuchadnezzar in 601 B.C.

24:2 the LORD sent . . . bands. God's reaction against Judah's rebellion was swift. The Syrians, Moabites, and Ammonites were vassals of Babylon, and were probably compelled to participate in the invasion of Judah.

24:4 innocent blood that he had shed. See note 21:16. The violation of the covenant was so reprehensible that the Lord "would not pardon" it.

blood, and the LORD would not pardon.
5 [q]Now the rest of the deeds of Jehoiakim
and all that he did, are they not written in
the Book of the Chronicles of the Kings of
Judah? 6 So Jehoiakim [r]slept with his
fathers, and Jehoiachin his son reigned in
his place. 7 [s]And the king of Egypt did not
come again out of his land, [t]for the king of
Babylon had taken all that belonged to the
king of Egypt [u]from the Brook of Egypt to
the river Euphrates.

Jehoiachin Reigns in Judah

8 [v]Jehoiachin was [w]eighteen years old
when he became king, and he reigned
three months in Jerusalem. His mother's
name was Nehushta the daughter of
Elnathan of Jerusalem. 9 And he did what
was evil in the sight of the LORD, [x]accord-
ing to all that his father had done.

Jerusalem Captured

10 At that time the servants of [y]Neb-
uchadnezzar king of Babylon came up to
Jerusalem, and the city was besieged. 11 And
[y]Nebuchadnezzar king of Babylon came to
the city while his servants were besieging it,
12 [z]and Jehoiachin the king of Judah gave
himself up to the king of Babylon, himself
and his mother and his servants and his officials and his palace officials. [a]The king of
Babylon took him prisoner [b]in the eighth
year of his reign 13 and carried off all the
treasures of the house of the LORD [c]and the
treasures of the king's house, [d]and cut in
pieces all the vessels of gold in the temple of
the LORD, [e]which Solomon king of Israel had
made, [f]as the LORD had foretold. 14 [g]He carried away all Jerusalem and all the officials
and all the mighty men of valor, [h]10,000
captives, [i]and all the craftsmen and the
smiths. None remained, [j]except the poorest
people of the land. 15 [k]And he carried away
Jehoiachin to Babylon. The king's mother,
the king's wives, his officials, and the chief
men of the land he took into captivity from
Jerusalem to Babylon. 16 And the king of
Babylon brought captive to Babylon all the
men of valor, [l]7,000, and the craftsmen and
the metal workers, 1,000, all of them strong
and fit for war. 17 [m]And the king of Babylon
[n]made Mattaniah, [o]Jehoiachin's uncle, king
in his place, [p]and changed his name to
Zedekiah.

Zedekiah Reigns in Judah

18 [q]Zedekiah was twenty-one years old
when he became king, and he reigned
eleven years in Jerusalem. His mother's
name was [r]Hamutal the daughter of
Jeremiah of Libnah. 19 And he did what was
evil in the sight of the LORD, [s]according to
all that Jehoiakim had done. 20 For because
of the anger of the LORD it came to the
point in Jerusalem and Judah that he cast
them out from his presence.

[t]And Zedekiah rebelled against the king
of Babylon.

Fall and Captivity of Judah

25 [u]And in the ninth year of his reign,
in the tenth month, on the tenth

5 [q]2 Chr. 36:8 6 [r][2 Chr. 36:6; Jer. 22:18, 19; 36:30] 7 [s]Jer. 37:5-7 [t][Jer. 46:2, 20, 24, 26] [u]See Num. 34:5 8 [v][1 Chr. 3:16; Jer. 22:24, 28; 24:1; 37:1; Esth. 2:6] [w][2 Chr. 36:9] 9 [x]ch. 23:37 10 [y]Dan. 1:1 11 [y][See ver. 10 above] 12 [z][Jer. 24:1; 29:1, 2; Ezek. 17:12] [a][2 Chr. 36:10] [b][ch. 25:27] 13 [c]ch. 20:17; Isai. 39:6 [d]2 Chr. 36:7; Ezra 1:7; Dan. 1:2; 5:2, 3 [e]See 1 Kin. 7:48-50 [f]Jer. 20:5 14 [g]Jer. 24:1 [h][ver. 16; Jer. 52:28] [i]Jer. 24:1; 29:2; [1 Sam. 13:19, 22] [j]ch. 25:12 15 [k]2 Chr. 36:10; Esth. 2:6; [Jer. 22:24-26] 16 [l][ver. 14] 17 [m]For ver. 17-20, see 2 Chr. 36:10-13 [n][Jer. 37:1] [o][1 Chr. 3:15] [p][ch. 23:34; 2 Chr. 36:4] 18 [q]For ch. 24:18–25:21, see Jer. 52:1-27 [r]ch. 23:31 19 [s]ch. 23:37 20 [t]Ezek. 17:18
Chapter 25 1 [u]For ver. 1-7, see 2 Chr. 36:17-20; Jer. 39:1-7; 52:4-11

24:5 Book of the Chronicles of the Kings of Judah. See note 1 Kin. 11:41.

24:6 Jehoiachin. He is also called "Jeconiah" (1 Chr. 3:16) and "Coniah" (Jer. 22:24).

reigned in his place. Jehoiakim died (598 B.C.) before Jerusalem surrendered to the Babylonians (vv. 8–12).

24:7 Brook of Egypt. See 1 Kin. 8:65 note.

24:8 three months. According to Babylonian records Jerusalem fell March 16, 597 B.C. The reign of Jehoiachin must have begun in December, 598.

24:13 all the vessels of gold. See 1 Kin. 7:51.

24:14 10,000 captives. Jer. 52:28 gives a figure of "3,023" deportees, but that may not include women and children.

except the poorest. The Babylonians deported the upper classes and leaders from captured lands. In this way they crippled the economies of those societies.

24:16 all the men of valor . . . and the craftsmen and the metal workers. These may be part of the round figure of "10,000 captives" in v. 14.

24:17 Mattaniah. A brother of Jehoiakim (Jehoiachin's father) and son of Josiah (1 Chr. 3:15; Jer. 1:3).

Zedekiah. Mattaniah's name was probably changed to show that he was a vassal under Nebuchadnezzar (23:34 note).

24:18–25:21 This section of Kings is paralleled by Jer. 52:1–27.

24:18 eleven years. That is, 597–586 B.C.

Jeremiah. Not the prophet Jeremiah. See 23:31 and note.

Libnah. See note 8:22.

24:19 according to all that Jehoiakim had done. The biblical writer does not tell all of the evil Zedekiah committed during his reign. God's judgment had already been decreed, and Judah was sliding into oblivion (20:17, 18; 21:12–15; 22:16, 17). Further information on Zedekiah's reign can be found in Jer. 21; 24; 27; 29; 32; 37–39; Ezek. 17:11–21.

24:20 Zedekiah rebelled against the king of Babylon. Despite being a vassal appointed by Nebuchadnezzar, Zedekiah plotted with Egypt and other nations against the Babylonians (Jer. 27:3–8; Ezek. 17:11–21). Zedekiah's ill-fated decision to rebel against Babylon may have been encouraged by Pharaoh Hophra (Apries), who came to power in 589 B.C.

25:1 in the ninth year. That is, January, 588 B.C.

day of the month, [v]Nebuchadnezzar king
of Babylon came with all his army against
Jerusalem and laid siege to it. [w]And they
built siegeworks all around it. **2** So the city
was besieged till the eleventh year of King
Zedekiah. **3** On the ninth day of the fourth
month [x]the famine was so severe in the city
that there was no food for the people of the
land. **4** Then a breach was made in the city,
and all the men of war fled by night by the
way of the gate between the two walls, by
[y]the king's garden, though [z]the Chaldeans
were around the city. And they went in the
direction of the [a]Arabah. **5** But the army of
the Chaldeans pursued the king and overtook him in the plains of Jericho, and all
his army was scattered from him. **6** Then
they captured the king [b]and brought him
up to the king of Babylon at [c]Riblah, and
they passed sentence on him. **7** They
slaughtered the sons of Zedekiah before his
eyes, [d]and put out the eyes of Zedekiah and
bound him in chains and took him to
Babylon.
8 [e]In the fifth month, on [f]the seventh day
of the month—that was the nineteenth
year of King Nebuchadnezzar, king of
Babylon—Nebuzaradan, the captain of the
bodyguard, a servant of the king of
Babylon, came to Jerusalem. **9** [g]And he
burned the house of the LORD [h]and the
king's house and all the houses of
Jerusalem; every great house he burned
down. **10** And all the army of the Chaldeans,
who were with the captain of the guard,
[i]broke down the walls around Jerusalem.
11 [j]And the rest of the people who were left
in the city and the deserters who had
deserted to the king of Babylon, together
with the rest of the multitude, Nebuzaradan
the captain of the guard carried into exile.
12 But the captain of the guard left [k]some of
the poorest of the land to be vinedressers
and plowmen.
13 [l]And the pillars [m]of bronze that were
in the house of the LORD, and [n]the stands
and [o]the bronze sea that were in the
house of the LORD, the Chaldeans broke
in pieces and carried the bronze to
Babylon. **14** [p]And they took away the pots
and the shovels and the snuffers and the
dishes for incense and all the vessels of
bronze used in the temple service, **15** the
fire pans also and the bowls. What was of
gold the captain of the guard took away as
gold, and what was of silver, as silver. **16** As
for the two pillars, the one sea, and the
stands that Solomon had made for the
house of the LORD, [q]the bronze of all these
vessels was beyond weight. **17** [r]The height
of the one pillar was eighteen cubits,[1] and
on it was a capital of bronze. The height of
the capital was three cubits. A latticework
and pomegranates, all of bronze, were all
around the capital. And the second pillar
had the same, with the latticework.
18 [s]And the captain of the guard took
[t]Seraiah the chief priest and [u]Zephaniah
the second priest and the three keepers of
the threshold, **19** and from the city he took
an officer who had been in command of
the men of war, and [v]five men of the king's
council who were found in the city, and
the secretary of the commander of the army
who mustered the people of the land, and
sixty men of the people of the land who
were found in the city. **20** And Nebuzaradan
the captain of the guard took them and
brought them to the king of Babylon at

1 [v]Jer. 34:1, 2; 39:1, 2; Ezek. 24:2 [w][Ezek. 21:22; 26:8]
3 [x][Lam. 4:9, 10]
4 [y]Neh. 3:15 [z]See ch. 24:2 [a]See Deut. 1:1
6 [b]Jer. 32:4 [c][ch. 23:33]
7 [d][Ezek. 12:13]
8 [e]For ver. 8-12, see Jer. 39:8-12; 52:12-16 [f][Jer. 52:12]
9 [g]2 Chr. 36:19; Ps. 79:1 [h][Hos. 8:14; Amos 2:5]
10 [i]Neh. 1:3
11 [j]2 Chr. 36:20
12 [k]ch. 24:14; Jer. 40:7
13 [l][Jer. 27:19, 22]; For ver. 13-17, see 2 Chr. 36:18-20; Jer. 52:17-23 [m]1 Kin. 7:15 [n]1 Kin. 7:27 [o]1 Kin. 7:23
14 [p]Ex. 27:3; 1 Kin. 7:45, 50
16 [q]1 Kin. 7:47
17 [r][1 Kin. 7:15-18; 2 Chr. 3:15]
18 [s]For ver. 18-21, see Jer. 52:24-27 [t]1 Chr. 6:14; Ezra 7:1 [u]Jer. 21:1; 29:25; 37:3
19 [v]Esth. 1:14; [Jer. 52:25]

[1] A *cubit* was about 18 inches or 45 centimeters

25:2 till the eleventh year. That is, July, 586 B.C. (Jer. 39:2; 52:5–7).

25:3 famine. During the siege, Jerusalem experienced terrible privation (Jer. 38:2–3; Lam. 4:10).

25:4 gate between the two walls. This gate was in the southeastern wall of the City of David and may have been the "Fountain Gate" (Neh. 3:15).

25:6 the king of Babylon at Riblah. See note 23:33.

25:7 put out the eyes of Zedekiah. Blinding was a common punishment for rebellious captives in the ancient Near East (Ezek. 12:13).

took him to Babylon. Zedekiah ignored the counsel of Jeremiah (Jer. 38:14–28). Jeremiah had urged the king to surrender to Babylon because the Lord's judgment was inevitable. Through a peaceful surrender, Jerusalem could be spared destruction. Zedekiah's stubborn resistance brought only horrible results for both his family and the people. Zedekiah himself died in Babylon (Jer. 52:11).

25:8 In the fifth month. That is, August, 586 B.C.

25:9 every great house. The terrible carnage and destruction was deliberate. Nebuchadnezzar did not rebuild Judah with Jerusalem as a Babylonian provincial capital. And unlike the Assyrians in their dealings with Israel (17:24–31; Ezra 4:2), he did not import new settlers from other areas to replace the dead and exiled.

25:11 who had deserted. Apparently some of the people had given their allegiance to the Babylonians, even before the final siege. The Babylonians took them to Babylon.

carried into exile. The Babylonians implemented a second deportation (24:12–16), leaving only the poor to till the land (v. 12).

25:15 fire pans also and the bowls. See 24:13; 1 Kin. 7:50; Jer. 15:13; 20:5; 27:16–22.

25:18 Seraiah the chief priest. The grandson of Hilkiah (22:4, 8; 1 Chr. 6:13, 14) and ancestor of Ezra (Ezra 7:1).

[w]Riblah. 21 And the king of Babylon struck
them down and put them to death at
[w]Riblah in the land of Hamath. [x]So Judah
was taken into exile out of its land.

Gedaliah Made Governor of Judah

22 And over the people who remained in
the land of Judah, whom Nebuchadnezzar
king of Babylon had left, he appointed
[y]Gedaliah the son of [z]Ahikam, son of
Shaphan, governor. 23 [a]Now when all the
captains and their men heard that the king
of Babylon had appointed Gedaliah governor, they came with their men to Gedaliah
at [b]Mizpah, namely, Ishmael the son of
Nethaniah, and Johanan the son of Kareah,
and Seraiah the son of Tanhumeth the
Netophathite, and Jaazaniah the son of the
Maacathite. 24 And Gedaliah swore to them
and their men, saying, "Do not be afraid
because of the Chaldean officials. Live in
the land and serve the king of Babylon, and
it shall be well with you." 25 [c]But in the seventh month, [d]Ishmael the son of
Nethaniah, son of Elishama, of the royal
family, came with ten men and struck
down Gedaliah and put him to death along
with the Jews and the Chaldeans who were
with him at Mizpah. 26 [e]Then all the people,
both small and great, and the captains of
the forces arose and went to Egypt, for they
were afraid of the Chaldeans.

Jehoiachin Released from Prison

27 [f]And in the thirty-seventh year of [g]the
exile of Jehoiachin king of Judah, in the
twelfth month, on the twenty-seventh day
of the month, Evil-merodach king of
Babylon, in the year that he began to reign,
graciously [h]freed[1] Jehoiachin king of Judah
from prison. 28 And he spoke kindly to him
and gave him a seat above the seats of the
kings who were with him in Babylon. 29 So
Jehoiachin put off his prison garments.
And every day of his life [i]he dined regularly at the king's table, 30 and for his
allowance, a regular allowance was given
him by the king, according to his daily
needs, as long as he lived.

20 [w]ch. 23:33
21 [w][See ver. 20 above] [x][ch. 23:27; Lev. 26:33; Deut. 28:64]
22 [y]Jer. 39:14; 40:5 [z]ch. 22:12
23 [a]For ver. 23, 24, see Jer. 40:7-9 [b]Josh. 18:26
25 [c]Jer. 41:1, 2 [d]Jer. 40:14, 15
26 [e]See Jer. 43:4-7
27 [f]For ver. 27-30, see Jer. 52:31-34 [g]ch. 24:12, 15 [h]Gen. 40:13, 20
29 [i]2 Sam. 9:7, 13

1 Hebrew *lifted up the head of*

25:21 put them to death. The Babylonian forces eliminated all the remaining leaders, not all of whom were soldiers.

25:22 Gedaliah. Having abolished the monarchy, Nebuchadnezzar appointed Gedaliah as governor. Gedaliah's father Ahikam supported Jeremiah (Jer. 26:24). Nebuchadnezzar chose a well-known citizen of Judah as governor to bring stability to the land (Jer. 40:9–12).

Ahikam. Gedaliah's father had been a close adviser of Josiah (22:12).

25:23 Mizpah. Gedaliah lived in Mizpah, 8 miles north of Jerusalem (Jer. 40:6).

25:24 swore. See note 1 Kin. 1:17.

25:25 seventh month. That is, October, 586 B.C.

Ishmael . . . of the royal family. Ishmael's grandfather, Elishama, was royal secretary under Jehoiakim (Jer. 36:12; 41:1). Ishmael was part of a faction in Judah which viewed Gedaliah as a collaborator and wanted to resist the Babylonians (see the detailed account in Jer. 40:13–41:18). Ishmael probably had set his sights on reestablishing the throne of Judah with himself as king.

struck down Gedaliah. This action created even worse conditions in Judah (Jer. 44:1–14). The exiles considered Gedaliah's death a great loss. They instituted fast days to mourn his death as well as the destruction of Judah and Jerusalem (Zech. 7:5; 8:19).

25:26 went to Egypt. Fearing reprisals from the Babylonians, these coup leaders sought refuge in Egypt where an anti-Babylonian pharaoh ruled (24:20 note). The law of the king in Deut. 17:14–20 forbids any king in Israel to lead the people back to Egypt (Deut. 17:16). Ironically, these coup leaders in their quest for power enact one of the curses of the covenant—returning to Egypt, the land of bondage and slavery (Deut. 28:68).

25:27–30 The writer of Kings ends his work on a hopeful note by calling attention to the mercy shown to Jehoiachin, king of Judah, while in exile in Babylon.

25:27 in the thirty-seventh year. That is, March, 561 B.C.

Evil-merodach . . . began to reign. Evil-merodach was the son and successor of Nebuchadnezzar (24:1 note).

freed Jehoiachin . . . from prison. Administrative texts from Babylonia mention payment of rations in oil and barley to Jehoiachin, king of Judah, and five of his sons. Evil-merodach may have initiated this act of mercy on the occasion of his enthronement.

25:28 a seat above the seats. Deut. 4:25–31; 30:1–10 and King Solomon's temple prayer (1 Kin. 8:46–53) all address conditions of exile. These texts urge repentance (Deut. 4:30; 30:2; 1 Kin. 8:47). Solomon's prayer that the exiles might find compassion at the hands of their captors is realized in the kind treatment of Jehoiachin. Deut. 30:3–5 promises restoration to the people of God, and in 538 B.C. the Jews were allowed to return home (Ezra 1:1–4; Is. 44:24–28; 45:1–6). Christians understand the promise of Deut. 30:6, that God will circumcise the hearts of His people so that they will obey Him, to be fulfilled by the coming of the Holy Spirit (Acts 2:14–21; 2 Cor. 3:1–6).

25:29 he dined regularly at the king's table. See note 1 Kin. 2:7. The preferential treatment of Jehoiachin is a glimmer of hope for the continuance of the promises to David (2 Sam. 7:8–16). The somber final chapters of Kings emphasize the divine judgment on Judah (21:10–15; 23:26, 27; 24:3, 4, 20; 25:21), but they also reveal in the last few verses that the destruction of Judah and Jerusalem did not cut off the line of David. There is reason to look to the future with trust in God.

THE FIRST BOOK OF THE Chronicles

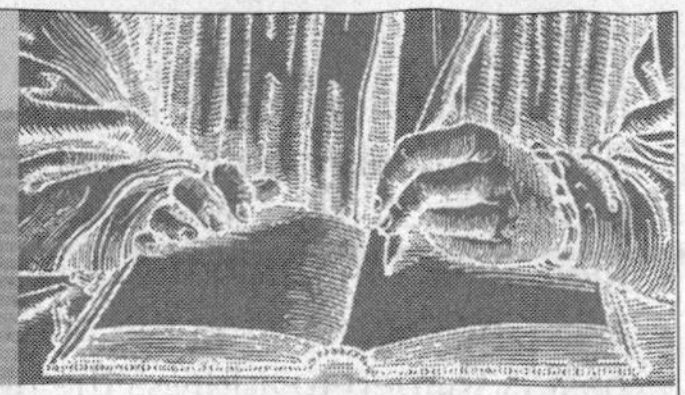

AUTHOR

Jewish tradition regarded Ezra as the primary author of Chronicles, Ezra, and Nehemiah. At least two reasons make this identification plausible: the book was written following the Babylonian exile of the Jews, near the time of Ezra's ministry (Date and Occasion below), and many passages in Chronicles sympathize with the priestly concerns of Ezra (Characteristics and Themes below).

Other considerations cast doubt on the traditional view of authorship. The date of composition for Chronicles cannot be limited to Ezra's lifetime (Date and Occasion); the focus on kingship characteristic of Chronicles is not present in Ezra's teaching; and Ezra's distress over the apostasy associated with intermarriage is not a prominent theme in Chronicles. In other words, historical and scriptural evidence does not point decisively to Ezra. By convention, the anonymous author is known as "the Chronicler."

The Chronicler had more than one written source. He depended on a number of biblical texts, especially Samuel and Kings, but also the Pentateuch, Judges, Ruth, Psalms, Isaiah, Jeremiah, and Zechariah. There are specific citations of several royal sources not otherwise known, such as "the chronicles of King David" (27:24), "the Book of the Kings" (2 Chr. 24:27), "the Book of the Kings of Israel" (9:1; 2 Chr. 20:34), "the Book of the Kings of Judah and Israel" (2 Chr. 16:11; 25:26; 28:26; 32:32), and "the Book of the Kings of Israel and Judah" (2 Chr. 27:7; 35:27; 36:8). The Chronicler used prophetic sources, including the writings of Samuel (29:29), Nathan (29:29; 2 Chr. 9:29), Gad (29:29), and others (9:29; 12:15; 13:22; 26:22; 32:32). Variations of style and content in the work suggest that there may have been still other unspecified sources.

DATE AND OCCASION

The final verses of 2 Chronicles indicate that it was written after the release of the exiles from Babylon in 538 B.C. The absence of Hellenistic influences suggests that the history was composed before the Alexandrian period (that is, before 331 B.C.). Nevertheless, opinions vary over the precise date of composition.

Some interpreters have proposed that the Chronicler wrote as early as the reconstruction of the temple under Zerubbabel (c. 520–515 B.C.). At least three pieces of evidence support this view. First, the Chronicler consistently presents the temple and its personnel in close partnership with the royal line of David. This emphasis suggests a date near the time of Zerubbabel, when expectations of royal and priestly partnership were high (Zech. 4). Second, there is close attention to the details of priestly and Levitical duties (1 Chr. 6:1–53 note). This suggests a connection with the time when the new temple order was being established. Third, the writer's omission of Solomon's downfall due to intermarriage with pagan women (1 Kin. 11:1–40; Neh. 13:26) suggests that Chronicles may have been written before intermarriage had become a major issue in the community following the exile in Babylon.

The majority of interpreters have dated Chronicles during or shortly after the ministries of Ezra and Nehemiah, in the latter half of the fifth century or the early decades of the fourth century B.C. It is reasonable to locate the book during the period from about the time of Zerubbabel to soon after the ministries of Ezra and Nehemiah. The major themes of the book fit well within these boundaries (between 515 and 400 B.C.).

The Chronicler wrote for historical and theological reasons. His extensive use of historical documents and devotion to numerical and chronological details (e.g., 1 Chr. 5:18; 2 Chr. 14:1, 9; 16:1, 12, 13) indicate that he intended to give his readers an accurate historical record. But he did not merely offer information about the past; he also wrote to convey a relevant theological message. Comparing the Chronicles with Samuel and Kings reveals that this account of Israel's past is shaped to address the needs of the community recently returned from Babylonian exile. It was written to encourage and guide the readers as they sought the full restoration of the kingdom.

The people who had returned from the exile faced many difficulties. The restoration had not brought about the dramatic changes for which many had hoped. Instead, they had to endure discouraging economic hardship, foreign opposition, and internal conflict. These difficulties raised many questions. Who are the legitimate heirs to the promises God gave His people? What political and religious institutions should be embraced? Was there hope for a new Davidic king? The historian who wrote Chronicles addressed these and similar questions.

CHARACTERISTICS AND THEMES

The theological message of Chronicles may be summarized in many ways, but three concerns are prominent. These are the people of God, the king and temple, and divine blessing and judgment.

First, the people of God. Throughout his history the writer identifies the people who should be counted as heirs of God's covenant promises. The prominence of this theme appears in his frequent use of the expression "all Israel" (1 Chr. 11:1; 2 Chr. 10:1; 29:24). On the one hand, the author considered those who had been released from Babylonian exile to be the people of God. Representatives of Judah, Benjamin, Ephraim, and Manasseh, who had returned to the land were the chosen people (1 Chr. 9:3 note). On the other hand, the author considered the restoration of Israel to be incomplete as long as any of the tribes remained outside the land, separated from the Davidic king and the Jerusalem temple. As a result, the Chronicler is careful to include both the northern and southern tribes in his genealogies (2:3–9:1), to present the picture of the united monarchy under David and Solomon extending to all the people (11:1 note), and to depict the reunification of the northern and southern kingdoms in the days of Hezekiah. The returned exiles were the remnant of God's people, but they looked forward to the restoration of all the people of God. As Hezekiah put it, "For if you return to the LORD, your brothers and your children will find compassion with their captors and return to this land. For the LORD your God is gracious and merciful" (2 Chr. 30:9).

Second, the king and temple. Chronicles presents the people of God as organized around two central institutions, the Davidic throne and the Jerusalem temple. The genealogies give special attention to David's lineage (1 Chr. 2:10–17; ch. 3) and to the organization of priests and Levites (1 Chr. 6). David's line had been chosen by God as the permanent dynasty over the nation (1 Chr. 17; 2 Chr. 13:5; 21:7; 23:3), and the establishment of David's throne was a demonstration of divine love and blessing for Israel (1 Chr. 14:2; 2 Chr. 2:11). The historian also focuses on the temple as the place where God's name resides (2 Chr. 7:12, 16; 33:7). The joy and splendor of music in temple worship is revealed (6:31–47; 9:15–16, 33; 13:8; 15:16–24, 28; 23:5; ch. 25; 2 Chr. 5:1–13; 7:6; 23:13; 29:25–30; 34:12; and notes).

The full restoration of the kingdom could not take place apart from the Davidic king and the Jerusalem temple. As the Lord said to David, "I will raise up your offspring after you, one of your own sons, and I will establish his kingdom. He shall build a house for me, and I will establish his throne forever" (1 Chr. 17:11, 12).

The third concern is divine blessing and judgment. The author shows his readers how to receive God's blessings in their day. He stresses the close connection between fidelity and blessing, infidelity and judgment (1 Chr. 28:9; 2 Chr. 6:14; 7:2–22; 15:2; 16:7–9; 21:12–15; 24:20; 28:9; 34:24–28). The king and the temple could not in themselves secure God's blessing for Israel; there had to be obedience to the Mosaic law and to prophetic and priestly instruction. The Lord blessed those who upheld the purity of temple worship and relied on Him alone (1 Chr. 5:20; 2 Chr. 13:18; 14:7; 32:20, 21). When the people or the kings turned to sin, an immediate retribution of illness and military defeat often followed (1 Chr. 10; 2 Chr. 13:1–16; 16:12; 28:1–5; 33:1–11). Even so, the people could be restored to blessing by seeking God in repentance and prayer (1 Chr. 21:1–22:1; 2 Chr. 7:13–15; 12:1–12; 33:10–13). The Chronicler shows that the full restoration of God's people would come only as they lived in fidelity to the Lord. Azariah says it well: "If you seek him, he will be found by you, but if you forsake him, he will forsake you" (2 Chr. 15:2).

The book's treatment of the people of God, the kingship and temple, and divine blessing and judgment, has immediate reference to the Jewish community in reconstruction following the Babylonian exile. The New Testament reveals that the kingdom will ultimately be restored in Christ, the promised Son of David.

The book's concept of the people of God becomes a reality in Christ. Like the community of the restoration, those who follow Christ are the heirs of Israel's promises (Gal. 3:14, 29; 4:28; Eph. 2:11–22; 3:6). The church extends beyond Israel to include the Gentiles (Luke 2:32; Acts 9:15; 11:1, 18), and in the end all of God's elect "the Israel of God" (Gal. 6:16), will be united under the lordship of Christ.

The hope for David's throne to be restored was fulfilled in Christ. He was born the Son of David, the heir to the Davidic covenant (Luke 1:32; Rom. 1:3; Rev. 22:16). Christ met all the conditions of obedience placed on David's line (Rom. 5:19; Phil. 2:8; Heb. 5:7–10). In the Resurrection, Christ took His throne in heaven (Acts 2:33–35; Eph. 1:20–23; Phil. 2:9; Rev. 3:21), from which He leads His people into blessing and victory (Rom. 8:37; Eph. 4:7–13). He will reign until all His enemies are defeated (1 Cor. 15:24–26).

The purposes of the temple are fulfilled in Christ. Christ was Himself the perfect sacrifice for sin (Heb. 9:11–28; 1 Pet. 3:18; 1 John 2:2). He mediates our prayers and intercedes on our behalf in heaven (Heb. 3:1; 4:14–16; 6:20; 7:26; 8:1). As our High Priest and Captain, He will bring all His people into the presence of God (John 14:1–4; 1 Thess. 4:16–17).

Finally, the book's revelation of divine blessing and judgment is realized in Christ. Jesus bore the judgment of God on sin and set His people free to follow the path of obedience (Rom. 3:21–26). He gives His people new life and makes them citizens of God's kingdom (John 3:16; Phil. 3:20).

As the following outline indicates, the book may be divided into four sections. Each part contributes specific elements to the overall theological purpose. The first concerns genealogies and is discussed below. The united monarchy, its division, and its reunion, are discussed in the Introduction to 2 Chronicles.

Genealogies in the Ancient Near East had a variety of forms and functions. Some of the passages in Chronicles trace a single family line through many generations (2:34–41). Others sketch several family lines together (6:1–3). The genealogies sometimes skip generations without notice, emphasizing significant persons and events (6:4–15). Ancient genealogies often included brief narratives highlighting important events, and the writer of Chronicles pauses on occasion to tell a story (1 Chr. 4:9–10; 5:18–22).

Ancient genealogies set out not only family relations, but political, geographical, and social connections. The Chronicles contain an assortment of lists, including families (e.g., 1 Chr. 3:17–24), political relations (e.g., 1 Chr. 2:24, 42, 45, 49–52), and trade guilds (e.g., 1 Chr. 4:14, 21–23).

An essential purpose of the extensive genealogies is to establish that the returned exiles are the legitimate continuation of God's elect people. The writer works this out by reporting the election of Israel from all peoples (1 Chr. 1:2–2:2), the arrangement of the tribes of Israel (1 Chr. 2:3–9:1), and the representation of the tribes that returned from Babylon (1 Chr. 9:16–34).

The genealogies focus on the order of the tribes of Israel, especially the role of the families of David and Levi. If the people were to receive the blessings of God, they must observe carefully the divinely ordained arrangements. Their responsibility for obeying is established by their designation as God's elect people.

The Book of Chronicles, now in two parts as 1 and 2 Chronicles, was originally without title. The words of its traditional Hebrew name appear often in the books of Kings as part of longer phrases (e.g., 1 Kin. 14:29), and in other places by themselves (Neh. 12:23; Esth. 2:23; 6:1). Jerome in the fourth century, and Luther in the sixteenth, called the book "The Chronicle of the Entire Sacred History." The modern English title is from this tradition.

OUTLINE OF 1 CHRONICLES

I. The Genealogies of God's People (1 Chr. 1:1–9:34)

- A. *Adam to Israel (1:1–2:2)*
- B. *The Tribes of Israel (2:3–9:1)*
  1. Judah (2:3–4:23)
  2. Simeon, Reuben, Gad, and the Half-tribe of Manasseh (4:24–5:26)
  3. Levi (ch. 6)
  4. Issachar, Benjamin, Naphtali, Manasseh, Ephraim, and Asher (ch. 7)
  5. Benjamin (ch. 8)
  6. Summary (9:1a)
- C. *Returnees from Exile (9:1b-34)*

II. The United Monarchy (1 Chr. 9:35–2 Chr. 9:31)

- A. *Saul (9:35–10:14)*
  1. Genealogy (9:35–44)
  2. Death (ch. 10)
- B. *David (chs. 11–29)*
  1. Widespread Support (chs. 11; 12)
  2. Preparations for the Temple (chs. 13–29)
     - a. *Centralization of Worship (chs. 13–16)*
     - b. *Commission to Prepare (ch. 17)*
     - c. *Military Preparations (chs. 18–20)*
     - d. *Discovery of Temple Site (21:1–22:1)*
     - e. *Commission of Builders (22:2–19)*
     - f. *Arrangement of Personnel (chs. 23–27)*
     - g. *National Celebration and Solomon's Commission (chs. 28; 29)*

From Adam to Abraham

1 [1] [a]Adam, Seth, Enosh; **2** [b]Kenan, Mahalalel, Jared; **3** Enoch, Methuselah,
Lamech; **4** Noah, [c]Shem, Ham, and Japheth.
5 [d]The sons of Japheth: Gomer, Magog,
Madai, Javan, Tubal, Meshech, and Tiras.
6 The sons of Gomer: Ashkenaz, Riphath,[2]
and Togarmah. **7** The sons of Javan: Elishah, Tarshish, Kittim, and Rodanim.
8 [e]The sons of Ham: Cush, Egypt, Put, and
Canaan. **9** The sons of Cush: Seba, Havilah,
Sabta, Raama, and Sabteca. The sons of
Raamah: Sheba and Dedan. **10** Cush fathered
Nimrod. He was the first on earth to be a
mighty man.[3]
11 [f]Egypt fathered Ludim, Anamim,
Lehabim, Naphtuhim, **12** Pathrusim, Casluhim (from whom the Philistines came),
and Caphtorim.
13 Canaan fathered Sidon his firstborn and
Heth, **14** and the Jebusites, the Amorites, the
Girgashites, **15** the Hivites, the Arkites, the
Sinites, **16** the Arvadites, the Zemarites, and
the Hamathites.
17 [g]The sons of Shem: Elam, Asshur,
Arpachshad, Lud, and Aram. And the sons
of Aram:[4] Uz, Hul, Gether, and Meshech.
18 Arpachshad fathered Shelah, and Shelah
fathered Eber. **19** To Eber were born two
sons: the name of the one was Peleg[5] (for
in his days the earth was divided), and his
brother's name was Joktan. **20** Joktan
fathered Almodad, Sheleph, Hazarmaveth,
Jerah, **21** Hadoram, Uzal, Diklah, **22** Obal,[6]
Abimael, Sheba, **23** Ophir, Havilah, and Jobab; all these were the sons of Joktan.
24 [h]Shem, Arpachshad, Shelah; **25** Eber,
Peleg, Reu; **26** Serug, Nahor, Terah; **27** Abram,
that is, Abraham.

From Abraham to Jacob

28 The sons of Abraham: [i]Isaac and
[j]Ishmael. **29** [k]These are their genealogies: the
firstborn of Ishmael, Nebaioth, and Kedar,
Adbeel, Mibsam, **30** Mishma, Dumah, Massa, Hadad, Tema, **31** Jetur, Naphish, and

Chapter 1
1 [a]Gen. 4:25, 26; 5:3, 6
2 [b]For ver. 2-4, see Gen. 5:9-32
4 [c]Gen. 6:10; 9:18
5 [d]For ver. 5-7, see Gen. 10:2-4
8 [e]For ver. 8-10, see Gen. 10:6-8
11 [f]For ver. 11-16, see Gen. 10:10-18
17 [g]For ver. 17-23, see Gen. 10:22-29
24 [h]For ver. 24, 27, see Gen. 11:10-26; Luke 3:34-36
28 [i]Gen. 21:2, 3 [j]Gen. 16:11, 15
29 [k]For ver. 29-31, see Gen. 25:13-16

[1] Many names in these genealogies are spelled differently in other biblical books [2] Septuagint; Hebrew *Diphath* [3] Or *He began to be a mighty man on the earth* [4] Septuagint; Hebrew lacks *And the sons of Aram* [5] *Peleg* means *division* [6] Septuagint, Syriac (compare Genesis 10:28); Hebrew *Ebal*

1:1–9:34 The writer establishes the election and arrangement of the people of God from the beginning of history until the return of Judah from the Babylonian exile of the sixth century B.C. This election is the basis of the privileges and responsibilities of the readers as the continuing people of God.

1:4–27 Beginning with Noah, the account shows how God chose some nations over others. The sons of Noah are treated separately: Japheth (1:5–7), Ham (1:8–16), and Shem (1:17–27). Relying selectively on Gen. 10:1–32 (Gen. 10 note), the Chronicler places the chosen line last. From the descendants of Noah, the Shemites (Semitic peoples) alone were in special covenant relationship with God.

1:5 sons. In ancient Near Eastern genealogies, the terms "sons" and "fathers" are often used literally. But they may be used more loosely, referring to relatively distant family relations or other social or geographical connections. Here "sons" points to cultural and geographical relationships. Compare the geographical focus of 2:42–55; 4:1–23; 28:43; 6:54–81; 7:20–29; 9:2; 11:10–47.

1:8 sons of Ham. More attention is given to the Hamites than the Japhethites because Israel had more dealings with them. The list begins with all four sons of Ham, but records only the descendants of Cush, Egypt, and Canaan. "Cush" is the Hebrew for "Ethiopia," meaning the remote areas south of Egypt.

1:17 sons of Shem. Divine election narrows within the Shemites to Abraham's family. The writer follows Gen. 10:21–31 closely and adds a brief summary of Gen. 11:10–27 to extend the genealogy to Abraham.

1:28 Abraham. The plan of sovereign election is shown in the descendants of Abraham. As before, the writer deals first with those not chosen (1:29–33) and then with the chosen line in Isaac (1:34–2:2).

1:31 sons of Ishmael. Following Genesis, the account distinguishes Ishmael's descendants from the covenant line.

Ishmael. He was promised great blessings from God (Gen. 16:11, 12), but he was not the heir of the covenant of grace God made with Abraham (Gen. 17:18–21).

Kedemah. These are the sons of Ishmael.
32 [l]The sons of Keturah, Abraham's concu-
bine: she bore Zimran, Jokshan, Medan,
Midian, Ishbak, and Shuah. The sons of
Jokshan: Sheba and Dedan. **33** The sons of
Midian: Ephah, Epher, Hanoch, Abida, and
Eldaah. All these were the descendants of
Keturah.
34 Abraham fathered [i]Isaac. The sons of
Isaac: [m]Esau and [n]Israel. **35** [o]The sons of
Esau: Eliphaz, Reuel, Jeush, Jalam, and
Korah. **36** The sons of Eliphaz: Teman, Omar,
Zepho, Gatam, Kenaz, and of Timna,[1]
Amalek. **37** The sons of Reuel: Nahath, Zerah,
Shammah, and Mizzah.
38 [p]The sons of Seir: Lotan, Shobal,
Zibeon, Anah, Dishon, Ezer, and Dishan.
39 The sons of Lotan: Hori and Hemam;[2]
and Lotan's sister was Timna. **40** The sons of
Shobal: Alvan,[3] Manahath, Ebal, Shepho,[4]
and Onam. The sons of Zibeon: Aiah and
Anah. **41** The son[5] of Anah: Dishon. The
sons of Dishon: Hemdan,[6] Eshban, Ithran,
and Cheran. **42** The sons of Ezer: Bilhan,
Zaavan, and Akan.[7] The sons of Dishan: Uz
and Aran.
43 [q]These are the kings who reigned in the
land of Edom before any king reigned over
the people of Israel: Bela the son of Beor, the
name of his city being Dinhabah. **44** Bela
died, and Jobab the son of Zerah of [r]Bozrah
reigned in his place. **45** Jobab died, and
Husham of the land of the [s]Temanites
reigned in his place. **46** Husham died, and
Hadad the son of Bedad, who defeated
Midian in the country of Moab, reigned in
his place, the name of his city being Avith.
47 Hadad died, and Samlah of Masrekah
reigned in his place. **48** Samlah died, and
Shaul of Rehoboth on the Euphrates reigned
in his place. **49** Shaul died, and Baal-hanan,
the son of Achbor, reigned in his place.
50 Baal-hanan died, and Hadad reigned in his
place, the name of his city being Pai; and his
wife's name was Mehetabel, the daughter of
Matred, the daughter of Mezahab. **51** And
Hadad died.
The chiefs of Edom were: chiefs Timna,
Alvah, Jetheth, **52** Oholibamah, Elah, Pinon,
53 Kenaz, Teman, Mibzar, **54** Magdiel, and
Iram; these are the chiefs of Edom.

A Genealogy of David

2 These are the sons of [t]Israel: [u]Reuben,
Simeon, Levi, Judah, [v]Issachar, Zebulun,
2 [w]Dan, [x]Joseph, [y]Benjamin, [z]Naphtali, [a]Gad,
and Asher. **3** [b]The sons of Judah: [c]Er, Onan
and Shelah; these three Bath-shua the
Canaanite bore to him. Now Er, Judah's firstborn, was evil in the sight of the LORD, and
he put him to death. **4** His daughter-in-law
[d]Tamar also bore him Perez and Zerah.
Judah had five sons in all.
5 The [e]sons of Perez: Hezron and Hamul.
6 The sons of Zerah: Zimri, Ethan, Heman,
Calcol, and Dara, five in all. **7** The son[8] of
Carmi: Achan, the troubler of Israel, who
[f]broke faith in the matter of the devoted
thing; **8** and Ethan's son was Azariah.
9 The sons of Hezron that were born to him:
Jerahmeel, [g]Ram, and [h]Chelubai. **10** [g]Ram
fathered Amminadab, and [i]Amminadab
fathered [j]Nahshon, prince of the sons of
Judah. **11** Nahshon fathered [k]Salmon,[9] Salmon
fathered [l]Boaz, **12** Boaz fathered Obed, Obed
fathered Jesse. **13** [m]Jesse fathered Eliab his firstborn, Abinadab the second, [n]Shimea the
third, **14** Nethanel the fourth, Raddai the fifth,

[1] Septuagint (compare Genesis 36:12); Hebrew lacks *and of* [2] Septuagint (compare Genesis 36:22); Hebrew *Homam* [3] Septuagint (compare Genesis 36:23); Hebrew *Alian* [4] Septuagint (compare Genesis 36:23); Hebrew *Shephi* [5] Hebrew *sons* [6] Septuagint (compare Genesis 36:26); Hebrew *Hamran* [7] Septuagint (compare Genesis 36:27); Hebrew *Jaakan* [8] Hebrew *sons* [9] Septuagint (compare Ruth 4:21); Hebrew *Salma*

32 [l]For ver. 32, 33, see Gen. 25:1-4
34 [i][See ver. 28 above] [m]Gen. 25:25, 26 [n]Gen. 32:28
35 [o]For ver. 35-37, see Gen. 36:4, 5, 9-13
38 [p]For ver. 38-42, see Gen. 36:20-28
43 [q]For ver. 43-54, see Gen. 36:31-43
44 [r]Isai. 34:6; 63:1
45 [s]Gen. 36:11; Job 2:11; Jer. 49:7, 20; Ezek. 25:13

Chapter 2
1 [t]ch. 1:34 [u]Gen. 29:32-35 [v]Gen. 30:18-20
2 [w]Gen. 30:6 [x]Gen. 30:22-24 [y]Gen. 35:18 [z]Gen. 30:8 [a]Gen. 30:10-13
3 [b]Gen. 38:2-5; 46:12 [c]Gen. 38:7
4 [d]Gen. 38:11, 14, 29, 30; Ruth 4:12; Matt. 1:3
5 [e]Gen. 46:12; Ruth 4:18
7 [f]Josh. 6:18; 7:1
9 [g]Ruth 4:19; Matt. 1:3, 4 [h][ver. 13, 42]
10 [g][See ver. 9 above] [i]Ruth 4:19; Matt. 1:4 [j]Num. 1:7; 2:3
11 [k][Ruth 4:20; 21; Matt. 1:4] [l]Ruth 4:21, 22; Matt. 1:5, 6
13 [m]1 Sam. 16:6, 8; 17:13 [n][1 Sam. 16:9; 17:13]

1:32 sons of Keturah. See note Gen. 25:1–4. Abraham's descendants through Keturah were not from the line of promise in Isaac.

1:34 sons of Isaac. That is, Esau and Jacob. See Gen. 25:27–34; 27:1–40.

1:35 sons of Esau. See Gen. 36:10–43.

2:1 sons of Israel. This list follows Gen. 35:23–26 except for the position of Dan.

2:3–9:1 The writer has presented the twelve tribes of Israel as the goal of divine election. Now he describes the extent and order of the covenant nation, covering prominent figures in all the tribes except Dan and Zebulun. The lists involve not only people but also tribal territories. This is suggestive of a hope that the community of those returned from exile would eventually grow to include all the tribes and their territories (1:5 note).

2:3–4:23 Judah is placed first, a departure from the order of names announced in 2:1, 2. The priority of Judah reflects the importance of the throne of David for the hope of the returned exiles.

2:3–9 sons of Judah. These were Er, Onan, Shelah (by a Canaanite woman, Gen. 38:2), Perez, and Zerah (by Tamar, Judah's daughter-in-law, Gen. 38:11–30). Perez and Hezron were ancestors of David.

2:6 Ethan, Heman, Calcol, and Dara. These are traditional wise men compared with Solomon in 1 Kin. 4:31. Ethan and Heman probably should be distinguished from David's musicians having the same names (15:19 and Ps. 88; 89).

2:7 Carmi. A son of Zimri, who is mentioned in 2:6 (Josh. 7:1).

2:10 Ram. Departing from the order of Hezron's sons presented in 2:9, Ram is placed first, as part of the line of David (2:3–4:23 note). This genealogical information is probably from the Book of Ruth (Ruth 4:18–22).

15 Ozem the sixth, [o]David the seventh. 16 And their sisters were Zeruiah and Abigail. [p]The sons of Zeruiah: Abishai, Joab, and Asahel, three. 17 [q]Abigail bore Amasa, and the father of Amasa was [q]Jether the Ishmaelite.

18 [r]Caleb the son of Hezron fathered children by his wife Azubah, and by Jerioth; and these were her sons: Jesher, Shobab, and Ardon. 19 When Azubah died, [r]Caleb married [s]Ephrath, who bore him [t]Hur. 20 Hur fathered Uri, and Uri fathered [u]Bezalel.

21 Afterward Hezron went in to the daughter of [v]Machir the father of Gilead, whom he married when he was sixty years old, and she bore him Segub. 22 And Segub fathered Jair, who had twenty-three cities in the land of Gilead. 23 [w]But Geshur and Aram took from them Havvoth-jair, Kenath, and its villages, sixty towns. All these were descendants of Machir, the father of Gilead. 24 After the death of Hezron, [x]Caleb went in to Ephrathah,[1] the wife of Hezron his father, and she bore him [y]Ashhur, the father of Tekoa.

25 The sons of [z]Jerahmeel, the firstborn of Hezron: Ram, his firstborn, Bunah, Oren, Ozem, and Ahijah. 26 Jerahmeel also had another wife, whose name was Atarah; she was the mother of Onam. 27 The sons of Ram, the firstborn of Jerahmeel: Maaz, Jamin, and Eker. 28 The sons of Onam: Shammai and Jada. The sons of Shammai: Nadab and Abishur. 29 The name of Abishur's wife was Abihail, and she bore him Ahban and Molid. 30 The sons of Nadab: Seled and Appaim; and Seled died childless. 31 The son[2] of Appaim: Ishi. [a]The son of Ishi: Sheshan. The son of Sheshan: Ahlai. 32 The sons of Jada, Shammai's brother: Jether and Jonathan; and Jether died childless. 33 The sons of Jonathan: Peleth and Zaza. These were the descendants of Jerahmeel. 34 Now Sheshan had no sons, only daughters, but Sheshan had an Egyptian slave whose name was Jarha. 35 So Sheshan gave his daughter in marriage to Jarha his slave, and she bore him Attai. 36 Attai fathered Nathan, and Nathan fathered [b]Zabad. 37 [b]Zabad fathered Ephlal, and Ephlal fathered [c]Obed. 38 Obed fathered Jehu, and Jehu fathered Azariah. 39 Azariah fathered Helez, and Helez fathered Eleasah. 40 Eleasah fathered Sismai, and Sismai fathered Shallum. 41 Shallum fathered Jekamiah, and Jekamiah fathered [d]Elishama.

42 The sons of [e]Caleb the brother of Jerahmeel: Mareshah[3] his firstborn, who fathered Ziph. The son[4] of Mareshah: [f]Hebron.[5] 43 The sons of Hebron: Korah, Tappuah, Rekem and Shema. 44 Shema fathered Raham, the father of Jorkeam; and Rekem fathered Shammai. 45 The son of Shammai: Maon; and Maon fathered Beth-zur. 46 Ephah also, Caleb's concubine, bore Haran, Moza, and Gazez; and Haran fathered Gazez. 47 The sons of Jahdai: Regem, Jotham, Geshan, Pelet, Ephah, and Shaaph. 48 Maacah, Caleb's concubine, bore Sheber and Tirhanah. 49 She also bore Shaaph the father of Madmannah, Sheva the father of Machbenah and the father of Gibea; and the [g]daughter of Caleb was Achsah. 50 These were the descendants of Caleb.

The sons[6] of Hur the firstborn of [h]Ephrathah: Shobal the father of Kiriath-jearim, 51 [i]Salma, the father of Bethlehem, and Hareph the father of Beth-gader. 52 Shobal the father of Kiriath-jearim had other sons: [j]Haroeh, half of the Menuhoth. 53 And the clans of Kiriath-jearim: the Ithrites, the Puthites, the Shumathites, and the Mishraites; from these came the [k]Zorathites and the Eshtaolites. 54 The sons of Salma: Bethlehem, the Netophathites,

15 [o][1 Sam. 16:10; 17:12, 14]
16 [p]2 Sam. 2:18
17 [q][2 Sam. 17:25]
18 [r][ver. 9]
19 [r][See ver. 18 above] [s][ver. 50] [t]Ex. 17:10, 12; 24:14
20 [u]Ex. 31:2
21 [v]Num. 27:1
23 [w][Num. 32:41, 42; Deut. 3:14; Josh. 13:30]
24 [x]ver. 19, 50 [y]ch. 4:5
25 [z]ver. 9
31 [a][ver. 34, 35]
36 [b]ch. 11:41
37 [b][See ver. 36 above] [c][2 Chr. 23:1]
41 [d]2 Kin. 25:25
42 [e]ver. 9 [f]See Josh. 14:13
49 [g][Josh. 15:17; Judg. 1:13]
50 [h]ch. 4:4; [ver. 19]
51 [i][ch. 4:4]
52 [j][ch. 4:2]
53 [k]ch. 4:2

1 Septuagint, Vulgate; Hebrew *in Caleb Ephrathah* 2 Hebrew *sons*; three times in this verse 3 Septuagint; Hebrew *Mesha* 4 Hebrew *sons* 5 Hebrew *the father of Hebron* 6 Septuagint, Vulgate; Hebrew *son*

2:15 David the seventh. According to 1 Sam. 17:12–14, David was Jesse's eighth son. Elihu is omitted here, although he is mentioned in 27:18. Perhaps Elihu is omitted because he had no children.

2:18–24 This Caleb is not "Caleb the son of Jephunneh" (Num. 13:6; 1 Chr. 4:15), but "Chelubai" (v. 9).

2:20 Bezalel. The line of Ram (v. 10) leads to Jesse, David's father, and the line of Caleb leads to Bezalel, supervisor of the tabernacle construction in the days of Moses (Ex. 31:1–5; 35:30–36:7). The proximity of the royal family (2:10–17) to the family of Bezalel reflects the association of the throne of David with temple worship following the exile (6:1 note).

2:25 Jerahmeel. This is the only place where the Bible gives genealogical information about the family of Jerahmeel, who lived in southern Judah (1 Sam. 27:10; 30:27–29).

2:34 Sheshan. This additional information about the family of Jerahmeel concentrates on the line from Sheshan (2:31) to Elishama (2:41). It is possible that Elishama was a contemporary of David (the twenty-third generation of Judah), but he may have been the scribe of King Jehoiakim (Jer. 36:12, 20).

2:42 fathered Ziph . . . Hebron. When the word "father" is associated with the name of a town or village, it probably means "founder" or "head" (1:5 note). The inclusion of settlements lying outside the control of the community would encourage readers of the time to consider regaining all the territories once occupied by the people of God (2:3–9:1 note).

Atroth-beth-joab and half of the Manahathites,
the Zorites. 55 The clans also of the scribes who
lived at Jabez: the Tirathites, the Shimeathites
and the Sucathites. These are the [l]Kenites who
came from Hammath, the father of [m]the house
of Rechab.

Descendants of David

3 [n]These are the sons of David who were
born to him in Hebron: the firstborn,
Amnon, by Ahinoam the Jezreelite; the second, [o]Daniel, by Abigail the Carmelite, 2 the
third, Absalom, whose mother was Maacah,
the daughter of Talmai, king of Geshur; the
fourth, Adonijah, whose mother was
Haggith; 3 the fifth, Shephatiah, by Abital; the
sixth, Ithream, by his wife Eglah; 4 six were
born to him in Hebron, [p]where he reigned
for seven years and six months. [q]And he
reigned thirty-three years in Jerusalem.
5 [r]These were born to him in Jerusalem:
[s]Shimea, Shobab, Nathan and [t]Solomon,
four by [u]Bath-shua, the daughter of
[u]Ammiel; 6 then Ibhar, [v]Elishama, Eliphelet,
7 Nogah, Nepheg, Japhia, 8 Elishama, [w]Eliada,
and Eliphelet, nine. 9 All these were David's
sons, besides the sons of the concubines,
[x]and Tamar was their sister.
10 The son of Solomon was [y]Rehoboam,
[z]Abijah his son, [a]Asa his son, [b]Jehoshaphat
his son, 11 [c]Joram his son, [d]Ahaziah his son,
[e]Joash his son, 12 [f]Amaziah his son, [g]Aza-
riah his son, [h]Jotham his son, 13 [i]Ahaz his
son, [j]Hezekiah his son, [k]Manasseh his son,
14 [l]Amon his son, [m]Josiah his son. 15 The
sons of Josiah: [n]Johanan the firstborn, the
second [o]Jehoiakim, the third [p]Zedekiah,
the fourth Shallum. 16 The descendants of
[q]Jehoiakim: [r]Jeconiah his son, [s]Zedekiah
his son; 17 and the sons of Jeconiah, the
[t]captive: [u]Shealtiel his son, 18 Malchiram,
Pedaiah, Shenazzar, Jekamiah, Hoshama
and Nedabiah; 19 and the sons of Pedaiah:
[v]Zerubbabel and Shimei; and the sons of
[v]Zerubbabel: Meshullam and Hananiah,
and Shelomith was their sister; 20 and
Hashubah, Ohel, Berechiah, Hasadiah, and
Jushab-hesed, five. 21 The sons of Hananiah: Pelatiah and Jeshaiah, his son[1]
Rephaiah, his son Arnan, his son Obadiah,
his son Shecaniah. 22 The son[2] of Shecaniah: [w]Shemaiah. And the sons of Shemaiah: [x]Hattush, Igal, Bariah, Neariah, and
Shaphat, six. 23 The sons of Neariah: Elioenai, Hizkiah, and Azrikam, three. 24 The
sons of Elioenai: Hodaviah, Eliashib,
Pelaiah, Akkub, Johanan, Delaiah, and
Anani, seven.

Descendants of Judah

4 [y]The sons of Judah: [z]Perez, Hezron,
[a]Carmi, Hur, and Shobal. 2 [b]Reaiah the

55 [l]Judg. 1:16 [m]2 Kin. 10:15; Jer. 35:2
Chapter 3
1 [n]For ver. 1-4, see 2 Sam. 3:2-5 [o][2 Sam. 3:3]
4 [p]2 Sam. 2:11 [q]2 Sam. 5:5
5 [r]For ver. 5-8, see ch. 14:4-7; 2 Sam. 5:14-16 [s][ch. 14:4; 2 Sam. 5:14] [t]2 Sam. 12:24 [u][2 Sam. 11:3]
6 [v][ch. 14:5; 2 Sam. 5:15]
8 [w][ch.14:7]
9 [x]2 Sam. 13:1
10 [y]1 Kin. 11:43 [z][1 Kin. 14:31; 15:1] [a]1 Kin. 15:8 [b]1 Kin. 15:24
11 [c]2 Kin. 8:16 [d]2 Kin. 8:24; [2 Chr. 21:17; 22:6] [e]2 Kin. 11:2
12 [f]2 Kin. 12:21 [g][2 Kin. 15:30] [h]2 Kin. 15:7
13 [i]2 Kin. 15:38 [j]2 Kin. 16:20 [k]2 Kin. 20:21
14 [l]2 Kin. 21:18 [m]2 Kin. 21:26

15 [n][2 Kin. 23:30] [o][2 Kin. 23:34] [p][2 Kin. 24:17] 16 [q][Matt. 1:11] [r][2 Kin. 24:6; Jer. 22:24] [s][2 Kin. 24:17] 17 [t]2 Kin.24:15 [u]Ezra 3:2; 5:2; Hag. 1:1, 12, 14; 2:2, 23; Matt. 1:12; Luke 3:27 19 [v]Ezra 2:2; Hag. 1:1, 12, 14; Zech. 4:6 22 [w]Neh. 3:29 [x]Ezra 8:2
Chapter 4 1 [y][Gen. 46:12] [z]Gen. 38:29 [a]ch. 2:7 2 [b][ch. 2:52]

[1] Septuagint (compare Syriac, Vulgate); Hebrew *sons of*; four times in this verse [2] Hebrew *sons*

2:55 Kenites. These were foreigners related by marriage to Moses and adopted by Judah (Judg. 1:16; 4:11). They are included as legitimate members of the people of God.

3:1 sons of David. This material on the line of Ram, David's ancestor (2:3–4:23 note), shows that Zerubbabel (3:19) is the legitimate heir of the Davidic line. The record of David's family covers his children born in Hebron and Jerusalem (3:1–9); Solomon's descendants (3:10–16); and the descendants of Jehoiachin (3:17–24). The list of these sons is from 2 Sam. 3:2–5; 5:13–16; 13:1.

3:10 son of Solomon. David's other sons are passed over to focus on Solomon, the chosen descendant. The royal line moves unchallenged from David to Solomon (23:1 note). Azariah (3:12) is the same person later called Uzziah (2 Chr. 26:1 note).

3:15 sons of Josiah. Josiah's firstborn, Johanan (otherwise unknown), did not succeed him. Shallum (Jehoahaz) followed Josiah (2 Chr. 36:1, 2; 2 Kin. 23:30, 31). Pharaoh Neco removed Shallum from power and replaced him with his brother, Eliakim (Jehoiakim, 2 Chr. 36:3, 4; 2 Kin. 23:32–34). Jehoiakim was succeeded by his son Jehoiachin (2 Chr. 36:9, 10; 2 Kin. 24:8–16), but Nebuchadnezzar replaced Jehoiachin with Josiah's third son Zedekiah (2 Chr. 36:10–14; 2 Kin. 24:18–20).

3:17 Jeconiah. Also called Jehoiachin or Coniah. The prophet Jeremiah, whose life and words were known to the writer (2 Chr. 35:25; 36:12, 21, 22), announced that God would remove Jeconiah's family from the throne (Jer. 22:30 note). In His mercy, however, God withdrew this curse and established Jeconiah's line once again. Jeconiah was released from prison in Babylon (2 Kin. 25:27–30). Sheshbazzar (spelled Shenazzar in 3:18) brought temple treasures back to Judah (Ezra 1:11; 5:14–16). Zerubbabel (3:19) was governor over the restored community following the exile in Babylon and rebuilt the temple (Ezra 3:1–13). God declared Zerubbabel His "signet ring" (Hag. 2:23), reversing the curse on Jeconiah (Jer. 22:24). Zerubbabel never became king, but his line represented the royal hopes of the community. Both Matthew (Matt. 1:12, 13) and Luke (Luke 3:27) identify Jesus, the supreme King, with this lineage.

3:19 Pedaiah . . . Zerubbabel. Zerubbabel is called the son of Shealtiel (3:17) elsewhere (Ezra 3:2, 8; Neh. 12:1; Hag. 1:12, 14; 2:2, 23; Matt. 1:12; Luke 3:27). This may mean that Zerubbabel succeeded Pedaiah. Alternatively, Pedaiah may have become the head of the family at Shealtiel's death, adopting Zerubbabel as his own.

3:21 his son Rephaiah . . . Shecaniah. Probably not descendants of Zerubbabel, but other Davidic families contemporary with Zerubbabel. If this is correct, the genealogy goes only two generations beyond Zerubbabel (Introduction: Date and Occasion).

3:22 six. The verse mentions only five. One name may have been lost as the text was copied later. It is also possible that "six" includes Shemaiah with the five sons as the descendants of Shechaniah.

4:1–23 Judah. In this section, personal and clan names are mixed with place-names, some of them outside the boundaries of the territory of the returned exiles (2:42 note).

4:1 Carmi. Probably this refers to Caleb (2:9). If so, the verse gives a linear genealogy from Judah to Shobal (2:4, 5, 9, 50).

son of Shobal fathered Jahath, and Jahath
fathered Ahumai and Lahad. These were
the clans of the [c]Zorathites. 3 These were the
sons[1] of Etam: Jezreel, Ishma, and Idbash;
and the name of their sister was
Hazzelelponi, 4 and [d]Penuel fathered [e]Gedor,
and Ezer fathered Hushah. These were the
sons of Hur, the firstborn of [f]Ephrathah, the
father of Bethlehem. 5 [g]Ashhur, the father of
Tekoa, had two wives, Helah and Naarah;
6 Naarah bore him Ahuzzam, Hepher,
Temeni, and Haahashtari. These were the
sons of Naarah. 7 The sons of Helah: Zereth,
Izhar, and Ethnan. 8 Koz fathered Anub,
Zobebah, and the clans of Aharhel, the son
of Harum. 9 Jabez was [h]more honorable
than his brothers; and his mother called his
name Jabez,[2] saying, "Because I bore him in
pain." 10 Jabez called upon the God of Israel,
saying, "Oh that you would bless me and
enlarge my border, and that your hand
might be with me, and that you would keep
me from harm[3] so that it might not bring
me pain!" And God granted what he asked.
11 Chelub, the brother of Shuhah, fathered
Mehir, who fathered Eshton. 12 Eshton
fathered Beth-rapha, Paseah, and Tehinnah,
the father of Ir-nahash. These are the men
of Recah. 13 The sons of [i]Kenaz: [j]Othniel
and Seraiah; and the sons of Othniel:
Hathath and Meonothai.[4] 14 Meonothai
fathered Ophrah; and Seraiah fathered
Joab, the father of Ge-harashim,[5] so-called
because they were craftsmen. 15 The sons of
[k]Caleb the son of Jephunneh: Iru, Elah, and
Naam; and the son[6] of Elah: Kenaz. 16 The
sons of Jehallelel: Ziph, Ziphah, Tiria, and
Asarel. 17 The sons of Ezrah: Jether, Mered,
Epher, and Jalon. These are the sons of
Bithiah, the daughter of Pharaoh, whom
Mered married;[7] and she conceived and
bore[8] Miriam, Shammai, and Ishbah, the
father of Eshtemoa. 18 And his Judahite wife
bore [l]Jered the father of Gedor, Heber the
father of Soco, and Jekuthiel the father of
Zanoah. 19 The sons of the wife of Hodiah,
the sister of Naham, were the fathers of
Keilah the Garmite and Eshtemoa the
Maacathite. 20 The sons of Shimon: Amnon,
Rinnah, Ben-hanan, and Tilon. The sons of
Ishi: Zoheth and Ben-zoheth. 21 The sons of
[m]Shelah the son of Judah: Er the father
of Lecah, Laadah the father of Mareshah,
and the clans of the house of linen workers
at Beth-ashbea; 22 and Jokim, and the men
of Cozeba, and Joash, and Saraph, who
ruled in Moab and returned to Lehem[9]
(now the records[10] are ancient). 23 These
were the potters who were inhabitants of
Netaim and Gederah. They lived there in
the king's service.

Descendants of Simeon

24 [n]The sons of Simeon: Nemuel, Jamin,
Jarib, Zerah, Shaul; 25 Shallum was his son,
Mibsam his son, Mishma his son. 26 The
sons of Mishma: Hammuel his son, Zaccur
his son, Shimei his son. 27 Shimei had sixteen sons and six daughters; but his brothers did not have many children, [o]nor did all
their clan multiply [p]like the men of Judah.
28 [q]They lived in Beersheba, Moladah,
Hazar-shual, 29 [r]Bilhah, Ezem, [s]Tolad, 30 [s]Be-
thuel, Hormah, Ziklag, 31 Beth-marcaboth,
[t]Hazar-susim, [t]Beth-biri, and [t]Shaaraim.
These were their cities until David reigned.
32 And their villages were Etam, Ain,
Rimmon, Tochen, and Ashan, five cities,
33 along with all their villages that were
around these cities as far as [u]Baal. These
were their settlements, and they kept a
genealogical record.

2 [c]ch. 2:53 **4** [d][ver. 18] [e]ver. 18, 39 [f][Gen. 35:19; ch. 2:50, 51] **5** [g]ch. 2:24 **9** [h][Gen. 34:19] **13** [i]Josh. 15:17 [j]Judg. 1:13; 3:9, 11 **15** [k]Num. 13:6 **18** [l][ver. 4] **21** [m]ch. 2:3; Gen. 38:1, 5; 46:12; Num. 26:20 **24** [n]Num. 26:12 **27** [o][ver. 38] [p][Num. 2:4, 13; 26:14, 22] **28** [q]For ver. 28-33, see Josh. 19:2-8 **29** [r][Josh. 19:3] [s][Josh. 19:4] **30** [s][See ver. 29 above] **31** [t][Josh. 19:6] **33** [u][Josh. 19:8]

1 Septuagint (compare Vulgate); Hebrew *father* 2 *Jabez* sounds like the Hebrew for *pain* 3 Or *evil* 4 Septuagint, Vulgate; Hebrew lacks *Meonothai* 5 *Ge-harashim* means *valley of craftsmen* 6 Hebrew *sons* 7 The clause *These are . . . married* is transposed from verse 18 8 Hebrew lacks *and bore* 9 Vulgate (compare Septuagint); Hebrew *and Jashubi-lahem* 10 Or *matters*

4:9 Jabez was more honorable. This is a brief example of extraordinary piety in the line of Judah. Blessing through prayer and trust in God is a major theme in Chronicles (1 Chr. 5:18–22; 17:16–27; 21:1–22:1; 2 Chr. 6:12–42; 7:12–16; 13:14–16; 14:11–13; 18:31; 20:5–30; 30:18–20; 32:20–24; 33:11–13). In line with the geographical references in this chapter, the focus is on territorial expansion (1:5 note), victory, and safety through prayer (2 Chr. 6:34 note).

4:13 Othniel. Israel's first judge (Josh. 15:17; Judg. 1:13; 3:9–11).

4:17 Bithiah, the daughter of Pharaoh. Mered's marriage to Pharaoh's daughter is otherwise not recorded. It suggests a time when Israelites were prominent in Egypt, possibly during the days of Joseph.

4:21–23 Shelah. Judah's oldest surviving son (2:3). The record of Shelah includes personal names, place-names, and trade guilds (linen workers, potters, and royal servants; see note 1:5).

4:24 Simeon. The tribe of Simeon was closely associated with the tribe of Judah (Josh. 19:1–9; Judg. 1:3). This material is of several types: genealogies (4:24–27, 34–38), geography (4:28–33), and historical notes on territorial expansion (4:39–43). For other genealogical records of the tribe of Simeon, see Gen. 46:10; Ex. 6:15; Num. 26:12–14.

4:28 Beersheba. This list of settlements in Simeon is drawn from Josh. 19:2–8 (cf. Josh. 15:26–32, where several of these villages are given to Judah). Knowledge of territories held before the Babylonian exile would instill hopes for geographical expansion after the people returned (2:3–9:1 note).

34 Meshobab, Jamlech, Joshah the son of Amaziah, 35 Joel, Jehu the son of Joshibiah, son of Seraiah, son of Asiel, 36 Elioenai, Jaakobah, Jeshohaiah, Asaiah, Adiel, Jesimiel, Benaiah, 37 Ziza the son of Shiphi, son of Allon, son of Jedaiah, son of Shimri, son of Shemaiah—38 these mentioned by name were princes in their clans, [v]and their fathers' houses increased greatly. 39 They journeyed to the entrance of [w]Gedor, to the east side of the valley, to seek pasture for their flocks, 40 where they found rich, good pasture, and the land was very broad, [x]quiet, and peaceful, for the former inhabitants there belonged to Ham. 41 [y]These, registered by name, came in the days of Hezekiah, king of Judah, and destroyed their tents and the Meunites who were found there, and marked them for destruction to this day, [z]and settled in their place, because there was pasture there for their flocks. 42 And some of them, five hundred men of the Simeonites, went to [a]Mount Seir, having as their leaders Pelatiah, Neariah, Rephaiah, and Uzziel, the sons of Ishi. 43 And they defeated [b]the remnant of the Amalekites who had escaped, and they have lived there to this day.

Descendants of Reuben

5 The sons of Reuben the firstborn of Israel ([c]for he was the firstborn, but because [d]he defiled his father's couch, [e]his birthright was given to the sons of Joseph the son of Israel, so that he could not be enrolled as the oldest son; 2 [f]though Judah became strong among his brothers and a [g]chief came from him, yet the birthright belonged to Joseph), 3 the [h]sons of Reuben, the firstborn of Israel: Hanoch, Pallu, Hezron, and Carmi. 4 The sons of Joel: Shemaiah his son, Gog his son, Shimei his son, 5 Micah his son, Reaiah his son, Baal his son, 6 Beerah his son, whom [i]Tiglath-pileser[1] king of Assyria carried away into exile; he was a chief of the Reubenites. 7 And his kinsmen by their clans, [j]when the genealogy of their generations was recorded: the chief, Jeiel, and Zechariah, 8 and Bela the son of Azaz, son of [k]Shema, son of Joel, who lived in [l]Aroer, as far as [m]Nebo and [n]Baal-meon. 9 He also lived to the east as far as the entrance of the desert this side of the Euphrates, because their livestock had multiplied [o]in the land of Gilead. 10 And in the days of Saul they waged war against the [p]Hagrites, who fell into their hand. And they lived in their tents throughout all the region east of Gilead.

Descendants of Gad

11 The sons of Gad lived over against them in the land of Bashan as far as [q]Salecah: 12 Joel the chief, Shapham the second, Janai, and Shaphat in Bashan. 13 And their kinsmen according to their fathers' houses: Michael, Meshullam, Sheba, Jorai, Jacan, Zia and Eber, seven. 14 These were the sons of Abihail the son of Huri, son of Jaroah, son of Gilead, son of Michael, son of Jeshishai, son of Jahdo, son of Buz. 15 Ahi the son of Abdiel, son of Guni, was chief in their fathers' houses, 16 and they lived in Gilead, in Bashan and in its towns, and in all the pasturelands of [r]Sharon to their limits. 17 All of these were recorded in genealogies in the days of [s]Jotham king of Judah, and in the days of [t]Jeroboam king of Israel.

18 The Reubenites, the Gadites, and the

38 [v][ver. 27]
39 [w]ver. 4, 18
40 [x][Judg. 18:7, 27]
41 [y]See ver. 34-38 [z][ch. 5:22]
42 [a]Gen. 36:8
43 [b][1Sam. 15:8; 30:17]
Chapter 5
1 [c]Gen. 29:32; 49:3 [d]Gen. 35:22; 49:4 [e]See Gen. 48: 15-22
2 [f]See Gen. 49:8-10 [g]Mic. 5:2; Matt. 2:6
3 [h]Gen. 46:9; Ex. 6:14; Num. 26:5, 6
6 [i]2 Chr. 28:20
7 [j]ver. 17
8 [k][ver. 4] [l]Deut. 2:36; Josh. 13:16 [m]Num. 32:3 [n]Num. 32:38
9 [o]Josh. 22:9
10 [p]ver. 19, 20; ch. 11:38; 27:31
11 [q]Josh. 12:5; 13:11
16 [r]ch. 27:29
17 [s]2 Kin. 15:5, 32 [t]2 Kin. 14:16, 28

[1] Hebrew *Tilgath-pilneser*; also verse 26

4:34 Meshobab. The writer lists some prominent leaders from Simeon (4:34–38) and then describes how they expanded their territories in several directions (4:39–43). Neh. 11:26–29 indicates that some of these cities (Moladah, Hazar-shual, Beersheba, Ziklag, and En-rimmon) were resettled after the Babylonian exile. The point is to tell the readers how far the Promised Land extends.

4:41 to this day. Also v. 43. The expression "today" or "this day" in Chronicles may refer to the writer's own time (5:26; 2 Chr. 20:26; 35:25), or it may refer to the earlier days of the sources being quoted. At times, it may even indicate the times of the sources used by the sources (13:11; 2 Chr. 5:9; 8:8; 10:19; 21:10). Sometimes the expression is an idiom for "from then on" or "in perpetuity."

5:1–26 The tribes east of the Jordan River are discussed. This material is in four sections: Reuben (vv. 1–10); Gad (vv. 11–17); a brief narrative (vv. 18–22); and the half-tribe of Manasseh (vv. 23–26). The hope is that these tribes will be included in the nation after the return from exile in Babylon (2:42 note).

5:1 he was the firstborn. The writer explains why Reuben the firstborn is given so little prominence among the tribes. He defiled his father's bed (Gen. 35:22; 49:4) and lost his right as firstborn to the double portion of the inheritance (Deut. 21:15–17). Instead, Joseph received Reuben's double portion through his sons Ephraim and Manasseh, who were treated as separate tribes (Gen. 48:1–22).

5:2 a chief came from him. The ruler mentioned here is David, and by implication Zerubbabel, his descendant (2 Sam. 5:2; 6:21; 1 Chr. 11:2; 17:7).

5:6 Tiglath-pileser. A king of Assyria (745–727 B.C.), also called Pul (v. 26). He invaded Israel (2 Kin. 15:29) and required Ahaz to pay tribute (2 Chr. 28:21 note). See the introductions to Amos, Isaiah, Hosea, and Micah.

5:8 Aroer . . . Baal-meon. This geographical information comes from Num. 32:37, 38 and Josh. 13:15–23.

5:18–22 The Reubenites, the Gadites, and the half-tribe of Manasseh. This brief narrative concerns all three tribes from east of the Jordan River (cf. 4:9, 10). The story illustrates the importance of prayer and reliance on God in battle, a theme appearing frequently in this history (2 Chr. 6:34 note).

half-tribe of Manasseh had valiant men
who carried shield and sword, and drew
the bow, [u]expert in war, 44,760, able to go
to war. 19 They waged war against the
[v]Hagrites, [w]Jetur, Naphish, and Nodab.
20 And when they prevailed over them, the
Hagrites and all who were with them were
given into their hands, [x]for they cried out
to God in the battle, and he granted their
urgent plea [y]because they trusted in him.
21 They carried off their livestock: 50,000 of
their camels, 250,000 sheep, 2,000 donkeys, and 100,000 men alive. 22 For many
fell, because the war was of God. And they
lived [z]in their place until [a]the exile.

The Half-Tribe of Manasseh

23 The members of the half-tribe of
Manasseh lived in the land. They were very
numerous from Bashan to Baal-hermon,
[b]Senir, and Mount Hermon. 24 These were
the heads of their fathers' houses: Epher,[1]
Ishi, Eliel, Azriel, Jeremiah, Hodaviah, and
Jahdiel, mighty warriors, famous men, heads
of their fathers' houses. 25 But they broke
faith with the God of their fathers, and
[c]whored [d]after the gods of the peoples of the
land, whom God had destroyed before them.
26 So the God of Israel stirred up the spirit of
[e]Pul king of Assyria, the spirit of [f]Tiglath-
pileser king of Assyria, and he took them
into exile, namely, the Reubenites, the
Gadites, and the half-tribe of Manasseh, and
brought them [g]to Halah, [g]Habor, Hara, and
[g]the river Gozan, to this day.

Descendants of Levi

6 [2] [h]The sons of Levi: Gershon, Kohath,
and Merari. 2 [i]The sons of Kohath:
Amram, Izhar, Hebron, and Uzziel. 3 [j]The
children of Amram: Aaron, Moses, and
Miriam. [k]The sons of Aaron: Nadab, Abihu,
Eleazar, and Ithamar. 4 [l]Eleazar fathered
[m]Phinehas, Phinehas fathered Abishua,
5 Abishua fathered Bukki, Bukki fathered
Uzzi, 6 [n]Uzzi fathered Zerahiah, Zerahiah
fathered [o]Meraioth, 7 Meraioth fathered Amariah, Amariah fathered Ahitub, 8 [p]Ahitub
fathered [q]Zadok, Zadok fathered Ahimaaz,
9 Ahimaaz fathered Azariah, Azariah fathered
Johanan, 10 and Johanan fathered Azariah ([r]it
was he who served as priest [s]in the house
that Solomon built in Jerusalem). 11 Azariah
fathered [t]Amariah, Amariah fathered Ahitub, 12 Ahitub fathered Zadok, Zadok
fathered [u]Shallum, 13 Shallum fathered
[v]Hilkiah, Hilkiah fathered Azariah, 14 Azariah
fathered [w]Seraiah, Seraiah fathered Jehozadak; 15 and [x]Jehozadak went into exile
when the LORD sent Judah and Jerusalem
into exile [y]by the hand of Nebuchadnezzar.
16 [3] The [z]sons of Levi: Gershom, Kohath,
and Merari. 17 And these are the names of
the sons of Gershom: [a]Libni and Shimei.
18 [b]The sons of Kohath: Amram, Izhar,
Hebron and Uzziel. 19 [c]The sons of Merari:
Mahli and Mushi. These are the clans of
the Levites according to their fathers. 20 [d]Of
Gershom: Libni his son, [e]Jahath his son,
Zimmah his son, 21 Joah his son, Iddo his
son, Zerah his son, Jeatherai his son. 22 [f]The
sons of Kohath: Amminadab his son,
Korah his son, Assir his son, 23 Elkanah his

18 [u]Num. 1:3
19 [v]See ver. 10 [w]ch. 1:31; [Gen. 25:15]
20 [x][2 Chr. 14:11; 18:31] [y]Ps. 22:4, 5
22 [z]ch. 4:41 [a]ver. 6; 2 Kin. 15:29; 17:6
23 [b]Deut. 3:9; Ezek. 27:5
25 [c]See Ex. 34:15 [d]2 Kin. 17:7
26 [e]2 Kin. 15:19 [f]See ver. 6 [g]2 Kin. 17:6; 18:11
Chapter 6
1 [h]ch. 23:6; Gen. 46:11; Ex. 6:16; Num. 26:57; [ch. 5:27 in Heb.]
2 [i]Ex. 6:18; [ver. 22]
3 [j]Ex. 6:20; 15:20 [k]Lev. 10:1, 12
4 [l]For ver. 4-6; 11-14, see Ezra 7:1-5 [m]See Ex. 6:25
6 [n]For ver. 6-8, see ver. 50-53 [o][ch. 9:11; Neh. 11:11]
8 [p]2 Sam. 8:17 [q]2 Sam. 15:27
9 [r]2 Chr. 26:17, 18 [s]See 1 Kin. 6; 2 Chr. 3
11 [t]2 Chr. 19:11; Ezra 7:3
12 [u][Neh. 11:11]
13 [v]2 Kin. 22:4; Ezra 7:1
14 [w]2 Kin. 25:18
15 [x][Ezra 3:2] [y]See 2 Kin. 25:8-21; [ch. 6:1 in Heb.]
16 [z]For ver. 16-19, see Ex. 6:16-19 17 [a][ch. 23:7] 18 [b]ch. 23:12 19 [c]ch. 23:21; [ver. 44, 47] 20 [d]For ver. 20:21, see ver. 41-43 [e]ver. 43 22 [f]For ver. 22-28, see ver. 33-38

1 Septuagint, Vulgate; Hebrew *and Epher* 2 Ch 5:27 in Hebrew
3 Ch 6:1 in Hebrew

5:21 100,000. The Israelites overcame an army much larger than their own (v. 18; 19:7 and note).

5:22 until the exile. This remark refers to the deportation of the tribes east of the Jordan River by the Assyrians in 734 B.C. (vv. 6, 26).

5:23–26 The tribes east of the Jordan River suffered exile because the infidelity of the half-tribe of Manasseh invited divine retribution. These events stand in contrast to the preceding narrative of prayer and blessing (vv. 18–22; cf. 4:9, 10).

5:25 whored after the gods. See note 2 Chr. 21:11.

5:26 to this day. See note 4:41.

6:1 Levi. A lengthy account of the tribe of Levi provides the background for the arrangement of the temple personnel in the restored community following the exile in Babylon. The writer connects the Davidic monarchy with temple worship in his conception of a restored people. The discussion covers people and territories (1:5; 2:3–9:1 note). The attention given to Levi reveals the importance of the temple and priesthood. If the returning exiles are to see God's blessing, then the royal family (Judah) and the temple personnel also (Levi) must carry out their proper functions (29:22 note). The material covers the priests descended from Aaron, a survey of three clans of Levi, the temple musicians appointed by David (6:31–47), and the duties of the sons of Aaron and other families. These materials provide a rationale for ordering the tribe of Levi in the period after the exile in Babylon.

6:8 Zadok. See note 15:11.

6:10 Azariah. An interest in Solomon's temple arrangement as a model for the community returning from the exile explains the relevance of a comment on Azariah (1 Kin. 4:2 and Introduction: Characteristics and Themes).

6:14, 15 Jehozadak. The high-priestly line is traced to Jehozadak, father of Jeshua (usually spelled Joshua), who was high priest in the early period following the exile to Babylon (Ezra 3:2; 5:2; 10:18; Hag. 1:1; 2:2; Zech. 3:1; 6:11).

6:16–19 Drawn from Ex. 6:16–19 and Num. 3:17–20; 26:57–61.

6:22 Amminadab. Probably another name for Izhar (vv. 2, 37, 38; Ex. 6:18, 21).

6:22, 23 Assir . . . Elkanah . . . Ebiasaph. These men were all sons of Korah (Ex. 6:24; cf. v. 37).

son, Ebiasaph his son, Assir his son,
24 Tahath his son, Uriel his son, Uzziah his
son, and Shaul his son. 25 The sons of
Elkanah: Amasai and Ahimoth, 26 Elkanah
his son, Zophai his son, Nahath his son,
27 Eliab his son, Jeroham his son, Elkanah
his son. 28 The sons of Samuel: Joel[1] his
firstborn, the second Abijah.[2] 29 [g]The sons
of Merari: Mahli, Libni his son, Shimei his
son, Uzzah his son, 30 Shimea his son,
Haggiah his son, and Asaiah his son.
31 These are the men [h]whom David put in
charge of the service of song in the house
of the LORD [i]after the ark rested there.
32 They ministered with song before the tabernacle of the tent of meeting until
Solomon built the house of the LORD in
Jerusalem, and they performed their service
according to their order. 33 These are the
men who served and their sons. Of the
sons of the Kohathites: Heman the singer
the son of Joel, son of [j]Samuel, 34 son of
Elkanah, son of Jeroham, son of Eliel, son
of Toah, 35 son of Zuph, son of Elkanah,
son of Mahath, son of Amasai, 36 son of
Elkanah, son of Joel, son of Azariah, son of
Zephaniah, 37 son of Tahath, son of Assir,
son of Ebiasaph, son of Korah, 38 son of
Izhar, son of Kohath, son of Levi, son of
Israel; 39 and his brother [k]Asaph, who stood
on his right hand, namely, Asaph the son
of Berechiah, son of Shimea, 40 son of
Michael, son of Baaseiah, son of Malchijah,
41 son of Ethni, son of Zerah, son of Adaiah,
42 son of Ethan, son of Zimmah, son of
Shimei, 43 son of Jahath, son of Gershom,
son of Levi. 44 On the left hand were their
brothers, the sons of Merari: Ethan the son
of Kishi, son of Abdi, son of Malluch, 45 son
of Hashabiah, son of Amaziah, son of
Hilkiah, 46 son of Amzi, son of Bani, son of
Shemer, 47 son of Mahli, son of Mushi, son
of Merari, son of Levi. 48 And their brothers
the Levites were appointed for all the
service of the tabernacle of the house of God.
49 But Aaron and his sons made offerings
[l]on the altar of burnt offering and on [m]the
altar of incense for all the work of the Most
Holy Place, and [n]to make atonement for
Israel, according to all that Moses the servant of God had commanded. 50 [o]These are
the sons of Aaron: Eleazar his son, Phinehas
his son, Abishua his son, 51 Bukki his son,
Uzzi his son, Zerahiah his son, 52 Meraioth
his son, Amariah his son, Ahitub his son,
53 Zadok his son, Ahimaaz his son.
54 These are their dwelling places according to their [p]settlements within their borders: to the sons of Aaron of the [q]clans of
Kohathites, for theirs was the first lot, 55 to
them they gave Hebron in the land of
Judah and its surrounding pasturelands,
56 [r]but the fields of the city and its villages
they gave to Caleb the son of Jephunneh.
57 [s]To the sons of Aaron they gave the cities
of refuge: Hebron, Libnah with its pasturelands, Jattir, Eshtemoa with its pasturelands, 58 Hilen with its pasturelands, Debir
with its pasturelands, 59 Ashan with its pasturelands, and Beth-shemesh with its pasturelands; 60 and from the tribe of
Benjamin, Gibeon,[3] Geba with its pasturelands, Alemeth with its pasturelands, and
Anathoth with its pasturelands. All their
cities throughout their clans were thirteen.
61 [t]To the rest of the Kohathites were
given by lot out of the clan of the tribe, out
of the half-tribe, the half of Manasseh, ten
cities. 62 To the Gershomites according to
their clans were allotted thirteen cities out
of the tribes of Issachar, Asher, Naphtali
and Manasseh in Bashan. 63 [u]To the
Merarites according to their clans were
allotted twelve cities out of the tribes of
Reuben, Gad and Zebulun. 64 [v]So the people of Israel gave the Levites the cities with

29 [g][ver. 19, 44-47] 31 [h]See ch. 16:4-6 [i]See ch. 15:25-16:1; 2 Sam. 6:12-17 33 [j][ver. 28] 39 [k]ch. 15:17, 19; 2 Chr. 5:12; Ezra 2:41; Neh. 7:44

49 [l]Lev. 1:7, 9 [m]Ex. 30:7 [n]Ex. 30:10; Lev. 4:20 50 [o]For ver. 50-53, see ver. 4-8 54 [p]Gen. 25:16; Num. 31:10 [q]Josh. 21:4, 10 56 [r][Josh. 14:13; 15:13] 57 [s]For ver. 57-60, see Josh. 21:13-19 61 [t][ver. 66-70; Josh. 21:5] 63 [u]Josh. 21:7 64 [v]Josh. 21:3

[1] Septuagint, Syriac (compare verse 33 and 1 Samuel 8:2); Hebrew lacks *Joel* [2] Hebrew *and Abijah* [3] Septuagint, Syriac (compare Joshua 21:17); Hebrew lacks *Gibeon*

6:26, 27 Zophai . . . Nahath . . . Eliab. Probably alternative names for Zuph, Toah, and Eliel (vv. 34, 35).

6:27, 28 Elkanah . . . Samuel. 1 Sam. 1:1 traces Elkanah and his ancestors back to Zophia (Zuph) as Ephraimites. This designation may have indicated the location of his home, not his tribe (1 Sam. 1:1 note).

6:31 David put in charge. David appointed groups from each of the three clans of Levi as musicians (15:16–26; 2 Chr. 35:3): the family of Heman from Kohath (vv. 33–38), the family of Asaph from Gershon (vv. 39–43), and the family of Ethan from Merari (vv. 44–47). The importance of music in worship is stressed (15:16 note), and what is said also gives a basis for the functions of these clans in the period following the exile in Babylon.

6:49 all that Moses . . . had commanded. See note 16:40.

6:53 Zadok. Discussion of the Levitical families concludes with the exclusive right of the Zadokites to offer sacrifices because of their direct descent from Aaron. There may have been some controversy about this among the Levitical families at the time of writing (15:11 note).

6:60 pasturelands. Areas of countryside used for grazing.

6:64 In this account (vv. 54–81), drawing from Josh. 21:4–48, the writer points to the wide area that had belonged to Levi. Most of the places named were outside the boundaries of the province occupied following the return from exile, suggesting a hope that the restored community would expand (2:42 note).

their pasturelands. 65 They gave by lot out of the tribes of Judah, Simeon, and Benjamin [w]these cities that are mentioned by name.

66 [x]And some of the clans of the sons of Kohath had cities of their territory out of the tribe of Ephraim. 67 They were given the cities of refuge: Shechem with its pasturelands in the hill country of Ephraim, Gezer with its pasturelands, 68 [y]Jokmeam with its pasturelands, Beth-horon with its pasturelands, 69 Aijalon with its pasturelands, Gath-rimmon with its pasturelands, 70 and out of the half-tribe of Manasseh, Aner with its pasturelands, and Bileam with its pasturelands, for the rest of the clans of the Kohathites.

71 [z]To the Gershomites were given out of the clan of the half-tribe of Manasseh: Golan in Bashan with its pasturelands and [a]Ashtaroth with its pasturelands; 72 and out of the tribe of Issachar: Kedesh with its pasturelands, Daberath with its pasturelands, 73 Ramoth with its pasturelands, and Anem with its pasturelands; 74 out of the tribe of Asher: Mashal with its pasturelands, Abdon with its pasturelands, 75 Hukok with its pasturelands, and Rehob with its pasturelands; 76 and out of the tribe of Naphtali: Kedesh in Galilee with its pasturelands, Hammon with its pasturelands, and Kiriathaim with its pasturelands. 77 [b]To the rest of the Merarites were allotted out of the tribe of Zebulun: [c]Rimmono with its pasturelands, [c]Tabor with its pasturelands, 78 and [d]beyond the Jordan at Jericho, on the east side of the Jordan, out of the tribe of Reuben: Bezer in the wilderness with its pasturelands, Jahzah with its pasturelands, 79 Kedemoth with its pasturelands, and Mephaath with its pasturelands; 80 and out of the tribe of Gad: [e]Ramoth in Gilead with its pasturelands, [f]Mahanaim with its pasturelands, 81 [g]Heshbon with its pasturelands, and [h]Jazer with its pasturelands.

Descendants of Issachar

7 The sons[1] of Issachar: Tola, [i]Puah, [j]Jashub, and Shimron, four. 2 The sons of Tola: Uzzi, Rephaiah, Jeriel, Jahmai, Ibsam, and Shemuel, heads of their fathers' houses, namely of Tola, mighty warriors of their generations, their number [k]in the days of David being 22,600. 3 The son[2] of Uzzi: Izrahiah. And the sons of Izrahiah: Michael, Obadiah, Joel, and Isshiah, all five of them were chief men. 4 And along with them, by their generations, according to their fathers' houses, were units of the army for war, 36,000, for they had many wives and sons. 5 Their kinsmen belonging to all the clans of Issachar were in all 87,000 mighty warriors, enrolled by genealogy.

Descendants of Benjamin

6 [l]The sons of Benjamin: Bela, Becher, and Jediael, three. 7 The sons of Bela: Ezbon, Uzzi, Uzziel, Jerimoth, and Iri, five, heads of fathers' houses, mighty warriors. And their enrollment by genealogies was 22,034. 8 The sons of Becher: Zemirah, Joash, Eliezer, Elioenai, Omri, Jeremoth, Abijah, [m]Anathoth, and Alemeth. All these were the sons of Becher. 9 And their enrollment by genealogies, according to their generations, as heads of their fathers' houses, mighty warriors, was 22,200. 10 The son of Jediael: Bilhan. And the sons of Bilhan: Jeush, Benjamin, Ehud, Chenaanah, Zethan, Tarshish, and Ahishahar. 11 All these were the sons of Jediael according to the heads of their fathers' houses, mighty warriors, 17,200, able to go to war. 12 And Shuppim and Huppim were the sons of Ir, Hushim the son of [n]Aher.

Descendants of Naphtali

13 [o]The sons of Naphtali: [p]Jahziel, Guni, Jezer and [q]Shallum, the descendants of Bilhah.

Descendants of Manasseh

14 [r]The sons of Manasseh: Asriel, whom his Aramean concubine bore; she bore [s]Machir the father of Gilead. 15 And Machir took a wife for Huppim and for Shuppim.

1 Syriac (compare Vulgate); Hebrew *And to the sons* 2 Hebrew *sons;* also verses 10, 12, 17

65 [w]See ver. 57-60
66 [x]For ver. 66-70, see Josh. 21:20-26
68 [y]Josh. 12:22; 1 Kin. 4:12
71 [z]For ver. 71-76, see Josh. 21:27-33 [a]Josh. 9:10
77 [b]For ver. 77-81, see Josh. 21:34-39 [c][Josh. 19:12, 13]
78 [d]Josh. 13:32
80 [e]1 Kin. 22:3, 4; 2 Kin. 9:1, 14 [f]See Gen. 32:2
81 [g]Josh. 13:17; 21:39 [h]Num. 21:32; Josh. 21:39
Chapter 7
1 [i][Num. 26:23] [j][Gen. 46:13]
2 [k]2 Sam. 24:1, 2, 9
6 [l]Gen. 46:21; Num. 26:38; See ch. 8:1-40
8 [m][ch. 6:60]
12 [n][ch. 8:1]
13 [o]Num. 26:48-50 [p][Num. 26:48] [q][Num. 26:49]
14 [r]For ver. 14-19, see Num. 26:29-33 [s]See Josh. 17:1

7:1 Issachar. The record of Issachar is drawn from Gen. 46:13; Num. 1:28; 26:23–25. Some portions of the material stem from military lists (vv. 2, 4, 5). For the numbers of fighting men, see note 12:23.

7:6–12 Benjamin. The writer will return to the tribe of Benjamin again in ch. 8 to trace the lineage of Saul. Here he draws upon military lists (vv. 7, 9, 11). For the numbers of fighting men see note 12:23.

7:13 sons of Naphtali. This list repeats information found in Gen. 46:24 and Num. 26:48–50.

7:14 Manasseh. See 5:23–26 note. Much of the data here is taken from Num. 26:29–34 and Josh. 17:1–13. The focus on women in this line may stem from the importance of Zelophehad's daughters in Num. 26:33.

The name of his sister was Maacah. And
the name of the second was Zelophehad,
and [t]Zelophehad had daughters. 16 And
Maacah the wife of Machir bore a son, and
she called his name Peresh; and the name
of his brother was Sheresh; and his sons
were Ulam and Rakem. 17 The son of Ulam:
[u]Bedan. These were the sons of Gilead the
son of Machir, son of Manasseh. 18 And his
sister Hammolecheth bore Ishhod, Abiezer
and Mahlah. 19 The sons of Shemida were
Ahian, Shechem, Likhi, and Aniam.

Descendants of Ephraim

20 The [v]sons of Ephraim: Shuthelah, and
Bered his son, Tahath his son, Eleadah his
son, Tahath his son, 21 Zabad his son,
Shuthelah his son, and Ezer and Elead,
whom the men of Gath who were born in
the land killed, because they came down to
raid their livestock. 22 And Ephraim their
father mourned many days, and his brothers came to comfort him. 23 And Ephraim
went in to his wife, and she conceived and
bore a son. And he called his name
Beriah,[1] because disaster had befallen his
house. 24 His daughter was Sheerah, who
built both Lower and Upper [w]Beth-horon,
and Uzzen-sheerah. 25 Rephah was his son,
Resheph his son, Telah his son, Tahan his
son, 26 Ladan his son, Ammihud his son,
[x]Elishama his son, 27 Nun[2] his son, [y]Joshua
his son. 28 [z]Their possessions and settlements were Bethel and its towns, and to
the east Naaran, and to the west [a]Gezer
and its towns, Shechem and its towns, and
Ayyah and its towns; 29 [b]also in possession
of the Manassites, [c]Beth-shean and its
towns, Taanach and its towns, Megiddo
and its towns, Dor and its towns. In these
lived the sons of Joseph the son of Israel.

Descendants of Asher

30 [d]The sons of Asher: Imnah, Ishvah,
Ishvi, Beriah, and their sister Serah. 31 The
sons of Beriah: Heber, and Malchiel, who
fathered Birzaith. 32 Heber fathered Japhlet,
Shomer, Hotham, and their sister Shua.
33 The sons of Japhlet: Pasach, Bimhal, and
Ashvath. These are the sons of Japhlet.
34 The sons of Shemer his brother: Rohgah,
Jehubbah, and Aram. 35 The sons of Helem
his brother: Zophah, Imna, Shelesh, and
Amal. 36 The sons of Zophah: Suah,
Harnepher, Shual, Beri, Imrah. 37 Bezer,
Hod, Shamma, Shilshah, Ithran, and Beera.
38 The sons of Jether: Jephunneh, Pispa,
and Ara. 39 The sons of Ulla: Arah, Hanniel,
and Rizia. 40 All of these were men of Asher,
heads of fathers' houses, approved, mighty
warriors, chiefs of the princes. Their number enrolled by genealogies, for service in
war, was 26,000 men.

A Genealogy of Saul

8 [e]Benjamin fathered Bela his firstborn,
Ashbel the second, [f]Aharah the third,
2 Nohah the fourth, and Rapha the fifth.
3 And Bela had sons: Addar, Gera, Abihud,
4 Abishua, [g]Naaman, Ahoah, 5 Gera, [h]She-
phuphan, and Huram. 6 These are the sons
of Ehud (they were heads of fathers' houses
of the inhabitants of Geba, and they were
carried into exile to [i]Manahath): 7 Naaman,[3]
Ahijah, and Gera, that is, Heglam,[4] who
fathered Uzza and Ahihud. 8 And Shaharaim
fathered sons in the country of Moab after
he had sent away Hushim and Baara his
wives. 9 He fathered sons by Hodesh his
wife: Jobab, Zibia, Mesha, Malcam, 10 Jeuz,
Sachia, and Mirmah. These were his sons,
heads of fathers' houses. 11 He also fathered
sons by Hushim: Abitub and Elpaal. 12 The
sons of Elpaal: Eber, Misham, and Shemed,
who built [j]Ono and [k]Lod with its towns,
13 and Beriah and [l]Shema (they were heads
of fathers' houses of the inhabitants of
[m]Aijalon, who caused the inhabitants of
Gath to flee); 14 and Ahio, Shashak, and
Jeremoth. 15 Zebadiah, Arad, Eder, 16 Michael, Ishpah, and Joha were sons of Beriah.
17 Zebadiah, Meshullam, Hizki, Heber,

15 [t]Num. 27:1; 36:11; Josh. 17:3
17 [u]1 Sam. 12:11
20 [v]Num. 26:35
24 [w]See Josh. 10:10, 11
26 [x]Num. 1:10; 7:48
27 [y]Num. 13:8, 16
28 [z]Josh. 16:2, 3
[a]Josh. 16:3
29 [b]Josh. 17:7
[c]Josh. 17:11
30 [d]Gen. 46:17; Num. 26:44

Chapter 8
1 [e][ch. 7:6; Gen. 46:21; Num. 26:38]
[f][ch. 7:12]
4 [g]Num. 26:40
5 [h][ch. 7:12]
6 [i][ch. 2:52, 54]
12 [j]Ezra 2:33; Neh. 6:2; 7:37; 11:35
[k][Acts 9:32, 35, 38]
13 [l][ver. 21]
[m]Josh. 10:12

[1] *Beriah* sounds like the Hebrew for *disaster* [2] Hebrew *Non* [3] Hebrew *and Naaman* [4] Or *he carried them into exile*

7:20 Ephraim. Matters of lineage and geography appear again (2:3–9:1 note).

7:30 Asher. The genealogy of Asher is drawn from Gen. 46:17 and Num. 26:44–46. For the numbers of fighting men, see note 12:23.

8:1 Benjamin. The survey of the tribes of Israel concludes with a second, more extensive treatment of Benjamin (cf. 7:6–12). The genealogy of Benjamin is comparable in length to the treatment of Judah (2:3–4:23) and Levi (6:1–81). The tribe of Benjamin is of special importance because of its close association with Judah in the days before and after the Babylonian exile (1 Kin. 12:20, 21; 1 Chr. 9:4–9). Saul, the first king of Israel, was from the tribe of Benjamin (1 Sam. 9:1–10:27; 1 Chr. 9:35–44). This chapter is arranged according to geography: Geba (vv. 1–7), Moab (vv. 8–13), Jerusalem (vv. 14–28), and Gibeon (8:29–40).

8:1–7 Compare the various lists in 7:6–12; Gen. 46:21; Num. 26:38–41.

8:8–13 Moab. For Israelites living in Moab (v. 8), see 1 Sam. 22:3–5 and Ruth 1:1, 2.

18 Ishmerai, Izliah, and Jobab were the sons
of Elpaal. 19 Jakim, Zichri, Zabdi, 20 Elienai,
Zillethai, Eliel, 21 Adaiah, Beraiah, and
Shimrath were the sons of Shimei. 22 Ishpan,
Eber, Eliel, 23 Abdon, Zichri, Hanan, 24 Han-
aniah, Elam, Anthothijah, 25 Iphdeiah, and
Penuel were the sons of Shashak. 26 Sham-
sherai, Shehariah, Athaliah, 27 Jaareshiah,
Elijah, and Zichri were the sons of Jeroham.
28 These were the heads of fathers' houses,
according to their generations, chief men.
These lived in Jerusalem.

29 [n] [o]Jeiel[1] the father of Gibeon lived in
Gibeon, and the name of his wife was
Maacah. 30 His firstborn son: Abdon, then
Zur, Kish, Baal, Nadab, 31 Gedor, Ahio,
Zecher, 32 and Mikloth (he fathered Shimeah). Now these also lived opposite their
kinsmen in Jerusalem, with their kinsmen.
33 [p]Ner was the father of Kish, Kish of Saul,
Saul of [q]Jonathan, Malchi-shua, Abinadab
and Eshbaal; 34 and the son of Jonathan
was Merib-baal; and Merib-baal was the
father of [r]Micah. 35 The sons of Micah:
Pithon, Melech, Tarea, and Ahaz. 36 Ahaz
fathered Jehoaddah, and Jehoaddah fathered Alemeth, Azmaveth, and Zimri.
Zimri fathered Moza. 37 Moza fathered
Binea; Raphah was his son, Eleasah his
son, Azel his son. 38 Azel had six sons, and
these are their names: Azrikam, Bocheru,
Ishmael, Sheariah, Obadiah, and Hanan.
All these were the sons of Azel. 39 The sons
of Eshek his brother: Ulam his firstborn,
Jeush the second, and Eliphelet the third.
40 The sons of Ulam were men who were
mighty warriors, bowmen, having many
sons and grandsons, 150. All these were
Benjaminites.

29 [n][ch. 9:35] [o]For ver. 29-38, see ch. 9:35-38
33 [p]For ver. 33-38, see ch. 9:39-44; [1 Sam. 9:1; 14:51] [q]ch. 10:2; 1 Sam. 31:2
34 [r]2 Sam. 9:12

Chapter 9
1 [s]ch. 5:25, 26
2 [t]For ver. 2-22, see Neh. 11:3-22 [u]Ezra 2:70; Neh. 7:73 [v]Ezra 2:43, 58; 7:7; 8:17, 20; Neh. 3:26; 7:60, 73; 10:23; 11:3, 21; [Josh. 9:27]
4 [w][ch. 2:5, 6]
9 [x][Neh. 11:8] [y][2 Chr. 35:4, 5]
10 [z]For ver. 10-13, see Neh. 11:10-14
11 [a][Jer. 20:1; Acts 4:1]

A Genealogy of the Returned Exiles

9 So all Israel was recorded in genealogies, and these are written in the Book
of the Kings of Israel. And [s]Judah was
taken into exile in Babylon because of their
breach of faith. 2 [t]Now the first to [u]dwell
again in their possessions in their cities
were Israel, the priests, the Levites, and the
[v]temple servants. 3 And some of the people
of Judah, Benjamin, Ephraim, and
Manasseh lived in Jerusalem: 4 Uthai the
son of Ammihud, son of Omri, son of
Imri, son of Bani, from the sons of [w]Perez
the son of Judah. 5 And of the Shilonites:
Asaiah the firstborn, and his sons. 6 Of the
sons of Zerah: Jeuel and their kinsmen,
690. 7 Of the Benjaminites: Sallu the son of
Meshullam, son of Hodaviah, son of
Hassenuah, 8 Ibneiah the son of Jeroham,
Elah the son of Uzzi, son of Michri, and
Meshullam the son of Shephatiah, son of
Reuel, son of Ibnijah; 9 and their kinsmen
according to their generations, [x]956. All
these were heads of fathers' houses according [y]to their fathers' houses.

10 [z]Of the priests: Jedaiah, Jehoiarib,
Jachin, 11 and Azariah the son of Hilkiah,
son of Meshullam, son of Zadok, son of
Meraioth, son of Ahitub, the [a]chief officer
of the house of God; 12 and Adaiah the son
of Jeroham, son of Pashhur, son of
Malchijah, and Maasai the son of Adiel, son
of Jahzerah, son of Meshullam, son of
Meshillemith, son of Immer; 13 besides their
kinsmen, heads of their fathers' houses,
1,760, mighty men for the work of the service of the house of God.

[1] Compare 9:35; Hebrew lacks *Jeiel*

8:29–40 Much of this list is repeated in 9:35–44. It traces the Benjaminites in Gibeon to Saul (8:33) and many generations after him.

8:33 Eshbaal. This is probably his original name, meaning "man of Baal." He is also called Ishvi, or "man of the LORD" (1 Sam. 14:49), and Ish-bosheth, "man of shame" (2 Sam. 2:8).

8:34 Merib-baal. This name for Mephibosheth was probably first spelled Meri-baal ("hero of Baal" or "loved of Baal") and later changed to Merib-baal (perhaps "opponent of Baal"). "Mephibosheth" itself means "from the mouth of shame" (2 Sam. 4:4; 9:6).

9:1–34 This chapter contains a selective summary of Israelites who made up the early community of those returning from exile in Babylon. Much of this material also appears in Neh. 11.

9:1 all Israel. The lists of the tribes of Israel represent the entire nation. The historical people of God and their territories are presented as a model for the community of those returning from exile in Babylon (11:1; 2 Chr. 10:1; 29:24 and notes).

9:2 their possessions. The account emphasizes that the returnees took possession of land that was rightfully theirs.

Israel, the priests, the Levites, and the temple servants. The lists that follow (9:4–34) cover each of these categories except the temple servants, who may have been descendants of the Gibeonites (Josh. 9:23) pressed into the mundane work required for maintaining the tabernacle (Ezra 8:20).

9:3 Judah, Benjamin, Ephraim, and Manasseh. The northern and southern kingdoms are considered to have been reunited under Hezekiah (2 Chr. 29:1 note). Representatives of the entire nation went into the Babylonian exile and returned to the land. For this reason, the writer does not overlook Ephraim and Manasseh among those returning. Yet Judah and Benjamin are given special attention because they represent the southern kingdom, the home of the line of David and the location of the temple.

9:4–6 Those belonging to the tribe of Judah are traced to Judah's sons: Perez (9:4), Shelah (9:5—"Shilonites" probably stands for "Shelanites"; cf. 2:3; 4:21–23; and Num. 26:20), and Zerah (9:6).

14 [b]Of the Levites: Shemaiah the son of
Hasshub, son of Azrikam, son of Hashabiah, of the sons of Merari; 15 and Bak-
bakkar, Heresh, Galal and Mattaniah the
son of Mica, son of Zichri, son of Asaph;
16 and Obadiah the son of Shemaiah, son of
Galal, son of Jeduthun, and Berechiah the
son of Asa, son of Elkanah, who lived in the
villages of the Netophathites.
17 The gatekeepers were Shallum, Akkub,
Talmon, Ahiman, and their kinsmen
(Shallum was the chief); 18 until then they
were [c]in the king's gate on the east side as
the gatekeepers of the camps of the Levites.
19 Shallum the son of Kore, son of [d]Ebi-
asaph, son of Korah, and his kinsmen of his
fathers' house, the [e]Korahites, were in
charge of the work of the service, keepers of
the thresholds of the tent, as their fathers
had been in charge of the camp of the LORD,
keepers of the entrance. 20 And [f]Phinehas
the son of Eleazar was the chief officer over
them in time past; the LORD was with him.
21 [g]Zechariah the son of Meshelemiah was
gatekeeper at the entrance of the tent of
meeting. 22 All these, who were chosen as
gatekeepers at the thresholds, were 212.
They were enrolled by genealogies in their
villages. [h]David and Samuel [i]the seer established them in their office of trust. 23 So they
and their sons were in charge of the gates of
the house of the LORD, that is, the house of
the tent, as guards. 24 The gatekeepers were
on the four sides, east, west, north, and
south. 25 And their kinsmen who were [j]in
their villages were obligated to come [k]in
every seven days, in turn, to be with these,
26 for the four chief gatekeepers, who were
Levites, were entrusted to be over [l]the
chambers and the treasures of the house of
God. 27 And they lodged around the house
of God, for on them lay the duty of watching, and [m]they had charge of opening it
every morning.

14 [b]For ver. 14-17, see Neh. 11:15-19
18 [c]Ezek. 46:1, 2
19 [d][ch. 26:1] [e]ch. 12:6; Num. 26:58; 2 Chr. 20:19
20 [f][Num. 25:11-13]
21 [g]ch. 26:2
22 [h][ch. 26:1, 2] [i]See 1 Sam. 9:9
25 [j]ver. 16 [k][2 Kin. 11:5]
26 [l]1 Kin. 6:5, 8]
27 [m]See Num. 1:53
29 [n]ch. 23:23; Lev. 6:20, 21
30 [o]See Ex. 30:23-25
31 [p]ver. 19 [e][See ver. 19 above] [i][See ver. 22 above] [q]ch. 23:29
32 [r]See Lev. 24:5-8
33 [s]ch. 6:31; 25:1
35 [t]For ver. 35-38, see ch. 8:29-32
39 [u]For ver. 39-44, see ch. 8:33-38
40 [v][2 Sam. 4:4; 9:6, 10]
41 [w]ch.8:35
42 [x][ch.8:36]
43 [y][ch. 8:37]

28 Some of them had charge of the utensils
of service, for they were required to count
them when they were brought in and taken
out. 29 Others of them were appointed over
the furniture and over all the holy utensils,
also over the [n]fine flour, the wine, the oil,
the incense, and the spices. 30 Others, of the
sons of the priests, [o]prepared the mixing of
the spices, 31 and Mattithiah, one of the
Levites, the firstborn of [p]Shallum the
[e]Korahite, was [i]entrusted with [q]making
the flat cakes. 32 Also some of their kinsmen
of the Kohathites had [r]charge of the showbread, to prepare it every Sabbath.
33 Now these, the [s]singers, the heads of
fathers' houses of the Levites, were in the
chambers of the temple free from other
service, for they were on duty day and
night. 34 These were heads of fathers' houses of the Levites, according to their generations, leaders. These lived in Jerusalem.

Saul's Genealogy Repeated

35 [t]In Gibeon lived the father of Gibeon,
Jeiel, and the name of his wife was Maacah,
36 and his firstborn son Abdon, then Zur,
Kish, Baal, Ner, Nadab, 37 Gedor, Ahio,
Zechariah, and Mikloth; 38 and Mikloth was
the father of Shimeam; and these also lived
opposite their kinsmen in Jerusalem, with
their kinsmen. 39 [u]Ner fathered Kish, Kish
fathered Saul, Saul fathered Jonathan,
Malchi-shua, Abinadab, and Eshbaal. 40 And
the son of Jonathan was [v]Merib-baal, and
Merib-baal fathered Micah. 41 The sons of
Micah: Pithon, Melech, Tahrea, and [w]Ahaz.[1]
42 And Ahaz fathered [x]Jarah, and Jarah
fathered Alemeth, Azmaveth, and Zimri.
And Zimri fathered Moza. 43 Moza fathered
Binea, and [y]Rephaiah was his son, Eleasah
his son, Azel his son. 44 Azel had six sons
and these are their names: Azrikam,
Bocheru, Ishmael, Sheariah, Obadiah, and
Hanan; these were the sons of Azel.

1 Compare 8:35; Hebrew lacks *and Ahaz*

9:15, 16, 33 Asaph . . . Jeduthun. Levites in charge of music (6:39; 9:33; 16:41, 42). Their prominence in this list reflects the importance of music in worship (15:16 note).

9:16 Netophathites. Netophah was a town about three miles south of Bethlehem (Neh. 7:26; 12:28).

9:17 gatekeepers. There is a list of gatekeepers in 26:1–19. This list reaches to the time of David (vv. 23, 24). The cycles of duty of the gatekeepers is described, evidently as a model for the new generation. David's tabernacle required twenty-four guards. Assignments and rotations were made by lot (26:12–18).

9:28–34 The Levites performed a variety of functions in the temple. Special exemption was made for the musicians (15:16 note).

9:39 Saul. The writer has now established the identity, order, and territory of the people of God by lists and genealogies. His next task, occupying many chapters, is to give a portrait of the united monarchy. The united monarchy is presented as an ideal for the community of returned exiles engaged in restoring the kingdom in their own day. Unlike the lengthy record of Saul's rise and fall in the books of Samuel, Chronicles simply reports Saul's genealogy (9:35–44) and the transfer of power from Saul to David (10:1–14) before turning to the history of David (chs. 11–29) and Solomon (2 Chr. 1–9).

The Death of Saul and His Sons

10 [z]Now the Philistines fought against
Israel, and the men of Israel fled
before the Philistines and fell slain on
Mount Gilboa. 2 And the Philistines overtook Saul and his sons, and the Philistines
struck down Jonathan and Abinadab and
Malchi-shua, the sons of Saul. 3 The battle
pressed hard against Saul, and the archers
found him, and he was wounded by the
archers. 4 Then Saul said to his armor-bearer, "Draw your sword and thrust me
through with it, lest these uncircumcised
come and mistreat me." But his armor-
bearer would not, for he feared greatly.
Therefore Saul took his own sword and fell
upon it. 5 And when his armor-bearer saw
that Saul was dead, he also fell upon his
sword and died. 6 Thus Saul died; he and
his three sons and all his house died
together. 7 And when all the men of Israel
who were in the valley saw that the army[1]
had fled and that Saul and his sons were
dead, they abandoned their cities and fled,
and the Philistines came and lived in them.
8 The next day, when the Philistines came
to strip the slain, they found Saul and his
sons fallen on Mount Gilboa. 9 And they
stripped him and took his head and his
armor, and sent messengers throughout
the land of the Philistines to carry the good
news to their idols and to the people.
10 And they put his armor in the temple of
their gods and fastened his head in the
temple of Dagon. 11 But when all Jabesh-
gilead heard all that the Philistines had
done to Saul, 12 all the valiant men arose
and took away the body of Saul and the
bodies of his sons, and brought them to
Jabesh. And they buried their bones under
the oak in Jabesh and fasted seven days.
13 So Saul died [a]for his breach of faith. He
broke faith with the LORD in that he did not
keep the command of the LORD, and also
[b]consulted a medium, seeking guidance.
14 He [c]did not seek guidance from the LORD.
Therefore the LORD put him to death and
[d]turned the kingdom over to David the son
of Jesse.

David Anointed King

11 [e]Then all Israel gathered together to
David at Hebron and said, "Behold,
we are your bone and flesh. 2 In times past,
even when Saul was king, it was you who
led out and brought in Israel. And the LORD
your God said to you, [f]'You shall be shepherd of my people Israel, and you shall be
prince over my people Israel.'" 3 So all the
elders of Israel came to the king at Hebron,
and David made a covenant with them at
Hebron before the LORD. And they anointed David king over Israel, [g]according to the
word of the LORD by Samuel.

David Takes Jerusalem

4 And David and all Israel went to
Jerusalem, [h]that is Jebus, where the Jeb-
usites were, [i]the inhabitants of the land.
5 The inhabitants of Jebus said to David,
"You will not come in here." Nevertheless,
David took the stronghold of Zion, that is,

1 Hebrew *they*

Chapter 10
1 [z]For ver. 1-12, see 1 Sam. 31:1-13
13 [a]1 Sam. 13:13, 14; 15:23 [b]1 Sam. 28:7
14 [c][1 Sam. 28:6] [d]ch. 12:23; 1 Sam. 15:28; 2 Sam. 3:9, 10
Chapter 11
1 [e]For ver. 1-9, see 2 Sam. 5:1-3; 6-10
2 [f]Ezek. 34:23
3 [g]ver. 10; ch. 12:23; 1 Sam. 16:1, 3, 12, 13
4 [h]See Josh. 15:8 [i]Judg. 1:21

10:1 fell slain. The soldiers (10:1), Saul (10:4, 6–8, 12–14), his sons (10:2, 6–8, 12), and his armor-bearer (10:5) all died, indicating that Saul was under severe divine judgment (10:13). The writer follows 1 Sam. 31 in his report of Saul's suicide, defilement, and burial. He adds vv. 13, 14 to give the reason for these tragic events.

10:6 all his house. Saul's three sons (10:2) and his chief officers died, but Ish-bosheth (also called Eshbaal) survived (8:33; 9:39; 2 Sam. 2:8). Saul's ruling house had come to an abrupt end, unlike David's house (dynasty) which God established permanently over Israel (17:1–15 note).

10:9 took his head. See the parallel with David and Goliath (1 Sam. 17:54). The treatment of Saul's body by his enemies highlights the dishonor of his defeat and death.

10:13 breach of faith. In 10:1–12, Saul's demise is seen to be the result of divine judgment. Saul died because he had been unfaithful to the Lord by failing to "keep the command" and to "seek guidance" from God. Saul's consultation with the medium at En-dor (strictly forbidden in Deut. 18:9–14) was the climax of his failures (1 Sam. 28).

10:14 seek guidance from the LORD. See note 2 Chr. 7:14.

David. The reign of David is central to the history of this period. David is a model monarch for the generation returning from exile in Babylon. The books of Chronicles acknowledge that David had faults (13:7–11; 21:1–7), but did not record the major failures and troubles recorded in Samuel (2 Sam. 11:1–21:14). The account of David's reign focuses on two major concerns: David's great popularity (chs. 11–12) and his preparations for the temple (chs. 13–29). The section is arranged primarily by topic rather than chronology. The enthusiastic support for David from all over Israel should be an encouragement and model for the returned exiles.

11:1 all Israel. This and similar expressions are used in the narrative about the united monarchy to refer to the nation as a whole under the rule of David and Solomon (11:10; 12:38; 14:8; 15:3, 28; 18:14; 19:17; 21:5; 28:4, 8; 2 Chr. 1:2; 7:8; 9:30). Although there still was hope for an inclusive, unified kingdom under a new Davidic king, this hope could not be realized until the coming of Christ, the Son of David and messianic King (2 Chr. 10:1 note; 29:24 note; also Introduction: Characteristics and Themes).

11:2 the LORD your God said to you. On several occasions in this section it is explained that the popular support David received was the result of God's sovereign decree (11:3, 9, 10; 12:18, 23). A legitimate king of Israel had to be chosen by God, not merely by popular sentiment (Deut. 17:14, 15). David met this qualification (2 Chr. 6:6).

11:5 Nevertheless, David took the stronghold. David's success is demonstrated by reporting the conquest and fortification of his capital city. Successful building projects often displayed the blessing of God on a king. See notes 2 Chr. 2:1–8:16; 11:5–12; 14:6, 7; 17:12; 26:9; 27:3, 4; 32:27–29.

the city of David. 6 David said, "Whoever
strikes the Jebusites first [j] shall be chief and
commander." And Joab the son of Zeruiah
went up first, so he became chief. 7 And
David lived in the stronghold; therefore it
was called the city of David. 8 And he built
the city all around from the Millo in complete circuit, and Joab repaired the rest of
the city. 9 And David [k] became greater and
greater, for the LORD of hosts was with him.

David's Mighty Men

10 [l] Now these are the chiefs of David's
mighty men, who gave him strong support
in his kingdom, together with all Israel, to
make him king, [m] according to the word of
the LORD concerning Israel. 11 This is an
account of David's mighty men: [n] Jashobeam, a [n] Hachmonite, was [o] chief of the
three.[1] He wielded his spear against 300
whom he killed at one time.
12 And next to him among the three
mighty men was Eleazar the son of [p] Dodo,
the Ahohite. 13 He was with David at Pas-
dammim [q] when the Philistines were gathered there for battle. There was a plot of
ground full of barley, and the men fled
from the Philistines. 14 But he took his[2]
stand in the midst of the plot and defended it and killed the Philistines. And the
LORD saved them by a great victory.
15 Three of the thirty chief men went
down to the rock to David at the cave of
Adullam, when the army of Philistines was
encamped in the [r] Valley of Rephaim.
16 David was then in the stronghold, and
[s] the garrison of the Philistines was then at
Bethlehem. 17 And David said longingly,
"Oh that someone would give me water to
drink from the well of Bethlehem that is by
the gate!" 18 Then the three mighty men
broke through the camp of the Philistines
and drew water out of the well of
Bethlehem that was by the gate and took it
and brought it to David. But David would
not drink it. He poured it out to the LORD
19 and said, "Far be it from me before my
God that I should do this. Shall I drink the
lifeblood of these men? For at the risk of
their lives they brought it." Therefore he
would not drink it. These things did the
three mighty men.
20 Now Abishai, the brother of Joab, was
chief of the thirty.[3] And he wielded his
spear against 300 men and killed them and
won a name beside the three. 21 He was the
most renowned[4] of the thirty[5] and became
their commander, but he did not attain to
the three.
22 And Benaiah the son of Jehoiada was a
valiant man[6] of Kabzeel, a doer of great
deeds. He struck down two heroes of Moab.
He also went down and struck down a lion
in a pit on a day when snow had fallen.
23 And he struck down an Egyptian, a man of
great stature, five cubits[7] tall. The Egyptian
had in his hand a spear [t] like a weaver's
beam, but Benaiah went down to him with a
staff and snatched the spear out of the
Egyptian's hand and killed him with his own
spear. 24 These things did Benaiah the son of
Jehoiada and won a name beside the three
mighty men. 25 He was renowned among the
thirty, but he did not attain to the three. And
David set him over his bodyguard.
26 The mighty men were [u] Asahel the brother of Joab, Elhanan the son of Dodo of
Bethlehem, 27 Shammoth of Harod,[8] Helez
the Pelonite, 28 Ira the son of Ikkesh of
Tekoa, Abiezer of Anathoth, 29 Sibbecai the
Hushathite, Ilai the Ahohite, 30 Maharai
of Netophah, Heled the son of Baanah of
Netophah, 31 Ithai the son of Ribai of Gibeah
of the people of Benjamin, Benaiah of
Pirathon, 32 Hurai of the brooks of Gaash,
Abiel the Arbathite, 33 Azmaveth of Ba-
harum, Eliahba the Shaalbonite, 34 Hashem[9]
the Gizonite, Jonathan the son of Shagee
the Hararite, 35 Ahiam the son of Sachar the
Hararite, Eliphal the son of Ur, 36 Hepher the
Mecherathite, Ahijah the Pelonite, 37 Hezro
of Carmel, Naarai the son of Ezbai, 38 Joel
the brother of Nathan, Mibhar the son of

6 [j] 2 Sam. 8:16
9 [k] Esth. 9:4
10 [l] For ver. 10-41, see 2 Sam. 23:8-39 [m] ver. 3
11 [n] [2 Sam. 23:8] [o] [ch. 12:18]
12 [p] [ch. 27:4]
13 [q] [2 Sam. 23:11, 12]
15 [r] ch. 14:8
16 [s] [1 Sam. 10:5]
23 [t] 1 Sam. 17:7
26 [u] ch. 27:7

[1] Compare 2 Samuel 23:8; Hebrew *thirty*, or *captains* [2] Compare 2 Samuel 23:12; Hebrew *they . . . their* [3] Syriac; Hebrew *three* [4] Compare 2 Samuel 23:19; Hebrew *more renowned among the two* [5] Syriac; Hebrew *three* [6] Syriac; Hebrew *the son of a valiant man* [7] A *cubit* was about 18 inches or 45 centimeters [8] Compare 2 Samuel 23:25; Hebrew *the Harorite* [9] Compare Septuagint and 2 Samuel 23:32; Hebrew *the sons of Hashem*

11:10–47 On the whole, this list of chiefs and mighty men is derived from 2 Sam. 23:8–39. The purpose is stated in the opening verse: these leaders supported David's kingship with "all Israel . . . according to the word of the LORD." The mighty acts of David's men highlight their outstanding qualities, placing David himself in a duly favorable light.

11:10 all Israel. See note 11:1.

11:15–19 David's mighty men displayed skill and courage by fetching water for him from behind enemy lines. In response, David showed humility by offering the water as a drink offering to the Lord (Gen. 35:14; 2 Kin. 16:13; Jer. 7:18).

[v]Hagri, 39 Zelek the Ammonite, Naharai of
Beeroth, the armor-bearer of Joab the son of
Zeruiah, 40 Ira the Ithrite, Gareb the Ithrite,
41 Uriah the Hittite, [w]Zabad the son of Ahlai,
42 Adina the son of Shiza the Reubenite, a
leader of the Reubenites, and thirty with
him, 43 Hanan the son of Maacah, and
Joshaphat the Mithnite, 44 Uzzia the
Ashterathite, Shama and Jeiel the sons of
Hotham the Aroerite, 45 Jediael the son of
Shimri, and Joha his brother, the Tizite,
46 Eliel the Mahavite, and Jeribai, and
Joshaviah, the sons of Elnaam, and Ithmah
the Moabite, 47 Eliel, and Obed, and Jaasiel
the Mezobaite.

The Mighty Men Join David

12 [x]Now these are the men who came
to David at Ziklag, while he could
not move about freely because of Saul the
son of Kish. And they were among the
mighty men who helped him in war. 2 They
[y]were bowmen and could shoot arrows and
sling stones with either the right or the [z]left
hand; they were Benjaminites, [a]Saul's kinsmen. 3 The chief was Ahiezer, then Joash,
both sons of Shemaah of [b]Gibeah; also
Jeziel and Pelet, the sons of Azmaveth;
Beracah, Jehu of [c]Anathoth, 4 Ishmaiah of
[d]Gibeon, a mighty man among the thirty
and a leader over the thirty; Jeremiah,[1]
Jahaziel, Johanan, Jozabad of Gederah,
5 Eluzai,[2] Jerimoth, Bealiah, Shemariah,
Shephatiah the Haruphite; 6 Elkanah,
Isshiah, Azarel, Joezer, and Jashobeam, the
[e]Korahites; 7 And Joelah and Zebadiah, the
sons of Jeroham of Gedor.

8 From the Gadites there went over to
David at the stronghold in the wilderness
mighty and experienced warriors, expert
with shield and spear, whose faces were
like the faces of lions and who were [f]swift
as gazelles upon the mountains: 9 Ezer the
chief, Obadiah second, Eliab third, 10 Mish-
mannah fourth, Jeremiah fifth, 11 Attai
sixth, Eliel seventh, 12 Johanan eighth,
Elzabad ninth, 13 Jeremiah tenth, Mach-
bannai eleventh. 14 These Gadites were officers of the army; the least was a [g]match for
a hundred men and the greatest for a thousand. 15 These are the men who crossed the
Jordan in the first month, when it was
[h]overflowing all its banks, and put to flight
all those in the valleys, to the east and to
the west.

16 And some of the men of Benjamin and
Judah came to the stronghold to David.
17 David went out to meet them and said to
them, "If you have come to me in friendship to help me, my heart will be joined to
you; but if to betray me to my adversaries,
although there is no wrong in my hands,
then may the God of our fathers see and
rebuke you." 18 Then [i]the Spirit clothed
Amasai, chief of the thirty, and he said,

"We are yours, O David,
and with you, O son of Jesse!
[j]Peace, peace to you,
and peace to your helpers!
For your God helps you."

Then David received them and made them
officers of his troops.

19 Some of the men of Manasseh deserted
to David [k]when he came with the
Philistines for the battle against Saul. (Yet
he did not help them, for the rulers of the
Philistines took counsel and sent him
away, saying, [l]"At peril to our heads he will
desert to his master Saul.") 20 As he went to
Ziklag, these men of Manasseh deserted to
him: Adnah, Jozabad, Jediael, Michael,
Jozabad, Elihu, and Zillethai, chiefs of
thousands in Manasseh. 21 They helped
David against [m]the band of raiders, for they
were all mighty men of valor and were
commanders in the army. 22 For from day to

38 [v][ch. 5:10]
41 [w][ch. 2:36]
Chapter 12
1 [x]See 1 Sam. 27:2-6
2 [y]2 Chr. 17:17; Ps. 78:9 [z][Judg. 3:15; 20:16] [a]ver. 29
3 [b]Josh. 18:28 [c]ch. 11:28; 27:12
4 [d]Josh. 9:3
6 [e]ch. 9:19
8 [f]2 Sam. 2:18
14 [g][Lev. 26:8]
15 [h]See Josh. 3:15
18 [i]See Judg. 3:10 [j][2 Sam. 17:25]
19 [k][1 Sam. 25:6] [l]See 1 Sam. 29:2-9
21 [m][1 Sam. 29:4]

[1] Hebrew verse 5 [2] Hebrew verse 6

11:41–47 The Chronicler adds to the list of David's supporters recorded in 2 Sam. 23:39. Repeated references to tribes and locations illustrates the diverse and widespread support David enjoyed.

12:8–19 At David's wilderness stronghold (cf. 1 Sam. 22:14, 29; 24:1), Israelites from various locations joined him. There were supporters from Gad, Benjamin, Judah, and Manasseh. See note 11:10–47.

12:8 faces of lions . . . swift as gazelles. Animal metaphors are common for warriors and leaders, and the men from Gad were swift and fierce.

12:15 overflowing. In March and April, northern melting snows frequently swell the rivers of Palestine, making the Jordan River particularly treacherous to cross. This detail emphasizes the superior courage of David's supporters from Gad.

12:18 the Spirit. By mentioning the Holy Spirit, the writer explains that the defection of men from Benjamin, the tribe of Saul, to David was not misguided. The Spirit of God directed David's supporters.

12:19 he did not help them. While significantly abbreviating the account of 1 Sam. 29, the writer is clear that David did not fight against his fellow Israelites.

12:20 Ziklag. David received further support at Ziklag (12:8–19 note).

12:22 like an army of God. The writer gives high praise to David's army by comparing it to the innumerable heavenly army.

day men came to David to help him, until
there was a great army, like an [n]army of
God.
23 These are the numbers of the divisions
of the armed troops [o]who came to David in
Hebron [p]to turn the kingdom of Saul over
to him, [q]according to the word of the LORD.
24 The men of Judah bearing shield and
spear were 6,800 armed troops. 25 Of the
Simeonites, mighty men of valor for war,
7,100. 26 Of the Levites 4,600. 27 The prince
Jehoiada, of the house of Aaron, and with
him 3,700. 28 [r]Zadok, a young man mighty
in valor, and twenty-two commanders from
his own fathers' house. 29 Of the
Benjaminites, [s]the kinsmen of Saul, 3,000,
of whom the [t]majority had to that point
kept their allegiance to the house of Saul.
30 Of the Ephraimites 20,800, mighty men
of valor, famous men in their fathers' houses. 31 Of the half-tribe of Manasseh 18,000,
who were [u]expressly named to come and
make David king. 32 Of Issachar, men who
[v]had understanding of the times, to know
what Israel ought to do, 200 chiefs, and
all their kinsmen under their command.
33 Of Zebulun 50,000 seasoned troops,
[w]equipped for battle with all the weapons
of war, to help David[1] with [x]singleness of
purpose. 34 Of Naphtali 1,000 commanders
with whom were 37,000 men armed with
shield and spear. 35 Of the Danites 28,600
men equipped for battle. 36 Of [y]Asher
40,000 [z]seasoned troops [z]ready for battle.
37 Of the Reubenites and Gadites and the half-
tribe of Manasseh from beyond the Jordan,
120,000 men armed with all the weapons of
war.

38 All these, men of war, arrayed in battle
order, came to Hebron with [a]full intent to
make David king over all Israel. Likewise,
all the rest of Israel were of a [b]single mind
to make David king. 39 And they were there
with David for three days, eating and
drinking, for their brothers had made
preparation for them. 40 And also their relatives, from as far as Issachar and Zebulun
and Naphtali, came bringing food on donkeys and on camels and on mules and on
oxen, abundant provisions of flour, [c]cakes
of figs, clusters of raisins, and wine and oil,
oxen and sheep, for there was joy in Israel.

The Ark Brought from Kiriath-Jearim

13 David consulted with the commanders of thousands and of hundreds,
with every leader. 2 And David said to all the
assembly of Israel, "If it seems good to you
and from the LORD our God, let us send
abroad to our brothers [d]who remain in all
the lands of Israel, as well as to the priests
and Levites in the cities that have pasturelands, that they may be gathered to us. 3 Then
let us bring again the ark of our God to us,
[e]for we did not seek it[2] in the days of Saul."
4 All the assembly agreed to do so, for the
thing was right in the eyes of all the people.

Uzzah and the Ark

5 [f]So David assembled all Israel [g]from the
[h]Nile[3] of Egypt to Lebo-hamath, to bring
the ark of God [i]from Kiriath-jearim. 6 [j]And
David and all Israel went up to [k]Baalah,
that is, to Kiriath-jearim that belongs to
Judah, to bring up from there the ark of
God, which is called by the name of the

22 [n]1 Sam. 30:1 **23** [o]ch. 11:1; 2 Sam. 2:3, 4; 5:1 [p]ch. 10:14 [q]ch. 11:3, 10; 1 Sam. 16:1, 3 **28** [r]ch. 6:8; 2 Sam. 8:17 **29** [s]ver. 2 [t][2 Sam. 2:8, 9] **31** [u]See Num. 1:17 **32** [v][Esth. 1:13] **33** [w]ver. 36, 38 [x][Ps. 12:2] **36** [y][2 Sam. 2:9] [z]ver. 33
38 [a][1 Kin. 8:61] [b][ver.33] **40** [c][1 Sam. 25:18; 30:12]
Chapter 13
2 [d][1 Sam. 31:1] **3** [e][1 Sam. 7:1, 2] **5** [f]ch. 15:3; 2 Sam. 6:1 [g][1 Kin. 8:65] [h]See Num. 34:5 [i][1 Sam. 6:21; 7:1] **6** [j]For ver. 6-14, see 2 Sam. 6:2-11 [k]Josh. 15:9, 60

[1] Septuagint; Hebrew lacks *David* [2] Or *him* [3] Hebrew *Shihor*

12:23 Hebron. David found other supporters at Hebron, with representatives coming from each tribe. The numbers appear very high. Several explanations of these large numbers are possible. The Hebrew word translated "thousand" may be a technical term referring to a military unit of considerably smaller size. In that case, v. 24 would read "men of Judah, carrying shield and spear, six units with eight hundred armed for war." Second, the Hebrew consonants translated "thousand" could also be read with other vowel points, to mean "chiefs." On this account, v. 24 would read "six chiefs with eight hundred armed for war." Finally, it is possible that there is a figurative or rhetorical exaggeration (12:22 note).

12:38–40 The report of David's widespread support closes with the observation that the people at Hebron, and the rest of the nation, were of "a single mind" in their support of David. They celebrated their new king with joy and feasting. This happy event would have been a model for the community returning from exile in Babylon.

12:38 all Israel. See note 11:1.

13:1–29:30 The second essential component of David's model kingdom, his enthusiastic preparations for the temple, is recounted here. The account has two parts: centralization of worship in Jerusalem (chs. 13–16) and temple preparations (chs. 17–29). Comparison with 2 Sam. 5 and 6 indicates that the materials in Samuel and Chronicles are arranged topically and not in strict chronological order. The Chronicles account is in three parts: the failed attempt to transfer the ark to Jerusalem (ch. 13); David's blessings (ch. 14); and the successful recovery of the ark (chs. 15; 16).

13:1–4 This introduction does not appear in 2 Sam. 5 and 6. It focuses on the support of "all the assembly" for worship centralized at Jerusalem (13:4–8; also 11:1 note).

13:2 good to you . . . from the LORD. The harmony between David and the people as they seek to obey God is a model for the returned exiles (2 Chr. 30:4, 5).

13:3 we did not seek it. The Chronicler contrasts David and Saul (11:2). David was concerned for the ark, while Saul neglected it.

13:6 called by the name. The "name" of God indicates the nearness of God, the divine power dwelling in the temple and accessible through prayer and sacrifice (16:10; 22:7, 8, 10, 19; 28:3; 29:16; 2 Chr. 2:1, 4; 6:5–10, 20, 32–38; 7:16, 20; 12:13; 20:8, 9; 33:4, 7). The New Testament teaches Christians to pray "in the name" of Jesus, meaning "by authority of" Jesus (John 12:28; 14:13, 14; 16:24).

LORD who [l]sits enthroned above the cherubim. 7 And they carried the ark of God on a
new cart, from the house of [m]Abinadab,
and Uzzah and Ahio[1] were driving the cart.
8 And David and all Israel were rejoicing
before God with all their might, with song
and [n]lyres and harps and tambourines and
cymbals and trumpets.
9 And when they came to the threshing
floor of [o]Chidon, Uzzah put out his hand
to take hold of the ark, for the oxen stumbled. 10 And the anger of the LORD was kindled against Uzzah, and he struck him
down [p]because he put out his hand to the
ark, and [q]he died there before God. 11 And
David was angry because the LORD had broken out against Uzzah. And that place is
called Perez-uzza[2] to this day. 12 And David
was afraid of God that day, and he said,
"How can I bring the ark of God home to
me?" 13 So David did not take the ark home
into the city of David, but took it aside to
the house [r]of Obed-edom the Gittite.
14 And the ark of God remained with the
household of Obed-edom in his house
three months. [s]And the LORD blessed the
household of Obed-edom and all that he
had.

David's Wives and Children

14 [t]And Hiram king of Tyre sent messengers to David, and cedar trees,
also masons and carpenters to build a
house for him. 2 And David knew that the
LORD had established him as king over
Israel, and that his kingdom was highly
exalted for the sake of his people Israel.
3 And David took more wives in Jerusalem, and David fathered more sons
and daughters. 4 [u]These are the names of
the children born to him in Jerusalem:
[v]Shammua, Shobab, Nathan, Solomon,
5 Ibhar, Elishua, Elpelet, 6 Nogah, Nepheg,
Japhia, 7 Elishama, [w]Beeliada and [x]Eliph-
elet.

Philistines Defeated

8 When the Philistines heard that David
had been anointed king over all Israel, all
the Philistines went up to search for David.
But David heard of it and went out against
them. 9 Now the Philistines had come and
[y]made a raid in the [z]Valley of Rephaim.
10 And David inquired of God, "Shall I go
up against the Philistines? Will you give
them into my hand?" And the LORD said to
him, "Go up, and I will give them into your
hand." 11 And he went up to Baal-perazim,
and David struck them down there. And
David said, "God has broken through[3] my
enemies by my hand, like a bursting
flood." Therefore the name of that place is
called Baal-perazim. 12 And they left their
gods there, and David gave command, and
they were burned.
13 And the Philistines yet again [a]made a
raid in the valley. 14 And when David again
inquired of God, [b]God said to him, "You
shall not go up after them; go around and
come against them opposite the balsam
trees. 15 And when you hear the sound of
marching in the tops of the balsam trees,
then go out to battle, for God has gone out
before you to strike down the army of the
Philistines." 16 And David did as God commanded him, and they struck down the

6 [l]See 1 Sam. 4:4
7 [m][1 Sam. 7:1]
8 [n][ch. 15:16]
9 [o][2 Sam. 6:6]
10 [p][ch. 15:13, 15; Num. 4:15] [q]Lev. 10:2
13 [r][2 Chr. 25:24]
14 [s][ch. 26:4, 5]
Chapter 14
1 [t]For ver. 1-16, see 2 Sam. 5:11-25
4 [u]For ver. 4-7, see ch. 3:5-8 [v][ch. 3:5]
7 [w][ch. 3:8 [x]2 Sam. 5:16]
9 [y]ver. 13 [z]ch. 11:15
13 [a]ver. 9
14 [b]ver. 16

1 Or *and his brother* 2 *Perez-uzza* means *the breaking out against Uzzah* 3 *Baal-perazim* means *Lord of breaking through*

who sits enthroned above the cherubim. The ark of the covenant represented the presence of God among His people.

13:7 on a new cart. The Israelites did not observe the law of God about transporting the ark with poles on the priests' shoulders (Ex. 25:12–15). Instead, they handled it with disregard for the holiness of God and the divine regulation of worship (15:2, 11–15).

13:8 rejoicing before God. See note 15:16.

13:10 he struck him. Uzzah demonstrated a disregard for the sanctity of worship by touching the ark (Num. 4:15). Although seemingly a minor offense, Uzzah's violation involved carelessness for the holiness of God, which called for judgment that would be a warning to all (v. 7 note).

13:11 to this day. See note 4:41.

13:13 Obed-edom. A Levite (15:18, 21, 24) who was blessed with many sons (26:4, 5) presumably because he cared properly for the ark. Chronicles often mentions numerous children as a sign of divine approval and blessing (14:3; 2 Chr. 11:18–23; 13:21).

14:1 This account illustrates that despite David's failure (ch. 13), God established and blessed him. Three items appear: palace preparations (14:1, 2), David's children in Jerusalem (14:3–7), and David's victory over the Philistines (14:8–17).

14:2 the LORD had established . . . exalted for the sake of his people. David recognized that the establishment of his kingdom was a blessing for the people. Following their exile in Babylon, readers would be encouraged by these remarks in their hope for a new Davidic king (2 Chr. 2:11 note).

14:8–12 David's victory over the Philistines contrasts with Saul's defeat (10:1–7). David inquired of the Lord (14:10, 14); Saul had consulted a medium (10:13). This event also contrasts with David's failed attempt to retrieve the ark (13:1–14). While David had been angered because the Lord had "broken out" against Uzzah (13:11), he now declares that "God has broken through" against the Philistines (14:11).

14:8 all Israel. See note 11:1.

14:12 they were burned. David followed Mosaic regulations in these actions (Deut. 7:5, 25).

Philistine army from Gibeon to Gezer. 17 And the fame of David went out into all lands, and the LORD brought the [c]fear of him upon all nations.

The Ark Brought to Jerusalem

15 David[1] built houses for himself in the city of David. And he prepared a place for the ark of God and [d]pitched a tent for it. 2 Then David said that no one but the Levites may carry [e]the ark of God, for the LORD had chosen them to carry the ark of the LORD and to minister to him forever. 3 [f]And David assembled all Israel at Jerusalem to bring up the ark of the LORD [g]to its place, which he had prepared for it. 4 And David gathered together the sons of Aaron and [h]the Levites: 5 of the sons of Kohath, Uriel the chief, with 120 of his brothers; 6 of the sons of Merari, Asaiah the chief, with 220 of his brothers; 7 of the sons of Gershom, Joel the chief, with 130 of his brothers; 8 of the sons of Elizaphan, Shemaiah the chief, with 200 of his brothers; 9 of the sons of Hebron, Eliel the chief, with 80 of his brothers; 10 of the sons of Uzziel, Amminadab the chief, with 112 of his brothers. 11 Then David summoned the priests [i]Zadok and [j]Abiathar, and the Levites Uriel, Asaiah, Joel, Shemaiah, Eliel, and Amminadab, 12 and said to them, "You are the heads of the fathers' houses of the Levites. [k]Consecrate yourselves, you and your brothers, so that you may bring up the ark of the LORD, the God of Israel, [l]to the place that I have prepared for it. 13 [m]Because you did not carry it the first time, the LORD our God broke out against us, because we did not seek him according to the rule." 14 So the priests and the Levites consecrated themselves to bring up the ark of the LORD, the God of Israel. 15 And the Levites carried the ark of God on their shoulders [n]with the poles, [o]as Moses had commanded according to the word of the LORD.

16 David also commanded the chiefs of the Levites to appoint their brothers as the singers who should play loudly on [p]musical instruments, on harps and lyres and cymbals, to raise sounds of joy. 17 So the Levites appointed [q]Heman the son of Joel; and of his brothers [r]Asaph the son of Berechiah; and of the sons of Merari, their brothers, [s]Ethan the son of Kushaiah; 18 and with them their brothers of the second order, Zechariah, Jaaziel, Shemiramoth, Jehiel, Unni, Eliab, Benaiah, Maaseiah, Mattithiah, Eliphelehu, and Mikneiah, and the gatekeepers Obed-edom and Jeiel. 19 The singers, Heman, Asaph, and Ethan, were to sound bronze cymbals; 20 Zechariah, [t]Aziel, Shemiramoth, Jehiel, Unni, Eliab, Maaseiah, and Benaiah were to play harps according to [u]Alamoth; 21 but Mattithiah, Eliphelehu, Mikneiah, [v]Obed-edom, Jeiel, and Azaziah were to lead with lyres according to [w]the Sheminith. 22 Chenaniah, leader of the Levites in music, should direct the music, for he understood it. 23 Berechiah and Elkanah were to be gatekeepers for the ark. 24 Shebaniah, Joshaphat, Nethanel, Amasai, Zechariah, Benaiah, and Eliezer, the priests, should [x]blow the trumpets before the ark of God. [v]Obed-edom and Jehiah were to be gatekeepers for the ark.

25 [y]So David and the elders of Israel and the commanders of thousands went to bring up the ark of the covenant of the LORD from the house of [v]Obed-edom with rejoicing. 26 And because God helped the

17 c[Deut. 2:25]
Chapter 15
1 d ch. 16:1
2 e ver. 15, 26; Num. 4:2, 15
3 f ch. 13:5; [1 Kin. 8:1] g ver. 1, 12; 2 Sam. 6:17
4 h See ch. 6:16-30
11 i ch.6:8; 16:39 j 1 Sam. 22:20; 1 Kin. 2:26
12 k 2 Chr. 35:6 l ver. 1, 3
13 m ch. 13:7; 2 Sam. 6:3
15 n Ex. 25:14 o Num. 4:15; 7:9
16 p [ch. 13:8; 16:5, 42]
17 q ch. 6:33 r ch. 6:39 s ch. 6:44
20 t [ver.18] u See Ps. 40 title
21 v ch. 26:4 w See Ps. 6 title
24 x ver. 28; ch. 16:6; Num. 10:8 v [See ver. 21 above]
25 y For ver. 25-28, see 2 Sam. 6:12-15 v [See ver. 21 above]

1 Hebrew *He*

14:17 fear of him upon all nations. This verse is in addition to the account of 2 Sam. 5, highlighting David's international fame (v. 1 note). David stood strong against his enemies. Other nations saw the power of God in the king's victory and feared (Josh. 2:11; 2 Chr. 17:10; 20:29). Readers of the book are encouraged to hope for a new David who would overthrow secular worldly powers (Hag. 2:6, 7, 20–23; Zech. 9:1–13).

15:1–16:43 This account of the successful recovery of the ark explains David's order for the Levites and worship. Eight verses (15:25–16:3) are like 2 Sam. 6:12–19.

15:1 pitched a tent. The tabernacle was still in Gibeon (16:39). David constructed a new tabernacle for the ark.

15:2 This verse and vv. 13–15 show that David transferred the ark in compliance with Mosaic law (Ex. 25:12–15; Deut. 10:8; 18:5).

15:4–10 All three divisions of the tribe of Levi (Kohathites, Merarites, and Gershonites) were included in David's worship organization, providing a model for Levitical orders following the nation's exile in Babylon (6:1–53 and notes).

15:11 Zadok and Abiathar. The two high priests during David's reign. Zadok served at the tabernacle in Gibeon (16:39) and Abiathar served in Jerusalem (18:16; 27:34 and notes). Solomon later excluded Abiathar because of his support of Adonijah's bid for the throne (1 Kin. 1:7; 2:26, 27). This left Zadok and his descendants as the high priestly family in Jerusalem (6:1, 53 and notes).

15:15 as Moses had commanded. See note 16:40.

15:16 An interest in the music of worship is apparent in 1 and 2 Chronicles; see 1 Chr. 6:31–47; 9:15–16, 33; 13:8; 15:28; 16:4–6; 23:5; 25:1–7; 2 Chr. 5:12, 13; 7:6; 23:13; 29:25–30; 34:12. This emphasis is doubtless related to a concern for the restoration of proper worship in the period following the return from exile in Babylon (6:1 note).

Levites who were carrying the ark of the
covenant of the LORD, they sacrificed [z]sev-
en bulls and seven rams. 27 David was
clothed with a robe of fine linen, as also
were all the Levites who were carrying the
ark, and the singers and Chenaniah the
leader of the music of the singers. And
David wore a linen ephod. 28 So all Israel
brought up the ark of the covenant of the
LORD with shouting, to the sound of the
horn, [a]trumpets, and cymbals, and made
loud music on [b]harps and lyres.
29 And as the ark of the covenant of the
LORD came to the city of David, Michal the
daughter of Saul looked out of the window
and saw King David dancing and rejoicing,
and she despised him in her heart.

The Ark Placed in a Tent

16 And they brought in the ark of God
and set it inside [c]the tent that David
had pitched for it, and they offered burnt
offerings and peace offerings before God.
2 And when David had finished offering the
burnt offerings and the peace offerings, he
blessed the people in the name of the LORD
3 and distributed to all Israel, both men and
women, to each a loaf of bread, a portion of
meat,[1] and a cake of raisins.
4 Then he appointed some of the Levites
as ministers before the ark of the LORD, to
invoke, to thank, and to praise the LORD,
the God of Israel. 5 [d]Asaph was the chief,
and second to him were Zechariah, Jeiel,
Shemiramoth, Jehiel, Mattithiah, Eliab,
Benaiah, Obed-edom, and Jeiel, who were
to play harps and lyres; Asaph was to
sound the cymbals, 6 and Benaiah and
Jahaziel the priests were to blow trumpets
regularly before the ark of the covenant of
God. 7 Then on that day [e]David first
appointed that thanksgiving be sung to the
LORD by Asaph and his brothers.

26 [z]Num. 23:1; Job 42:8
28 [a][ver. 24] [b]ver. 16
Chapter 16
1 [c]ch. 15:1
5 [d]ch. 6:39
7 [e][2 Sam. 22:1; 23:1]
8 [f]For ver. 8-22, see Ps. 105:1-15 [g]Isai. 12:4 [h][Ps. 145:11, 12]
11 [i]Ps. 24:6; 27:8
12 [j][Ps. 77:11; 143:5] [k]Ps. 78:43
14 [l]Isai. 26:9
16 [m]Gen. 17:2; 22:16; 26:3; 28:13; [Luke 1:73]
17 [n]Gen. 35:11, 12
18 [o]Gen. 13:15; 15:18-21
19 [p]Deut. 7:7; 26:5 [q]Heb. 11:9

David's Song of Thanks

8 [f]Oh give thanks to the LORD; [g]call
upon his name;
[h]make known his deeds among
the peoples!
9 Sing to him; sing praises to him;
tell of all his wondrous works!
10 Glory in his holy name;
let the hearts of those who seek
the LORD rejoice!
11 [i]Seek the LORD and his strength;
seek his presence continually!
12 [j]Remember the wondrous works that
he has done,
[k]his miracles and the judgments
he uttered,
13 O offspring of Israel his servant,
sons of Jacob, his chosen ones!
14 He is the LORD our God;
[l]his judgments are in all the earth.
15 Remember his covenant forever,
the word that he commanded, for
a thousand generations,
16 the covenant [m]that he made with
Abraham,
his sworn promise to Isaac,
17 which [n]he confirmed as a statute to
Jacob,
as an everlasting covenant
to Israel,
18 saying, [o]"To you I will give the land
of Canaan,
as your portion for an
inheritance."
19 When you were [p]few in number,
and of little account, and
[q]sojourners in it,
20 wandering from nation to nation,
from one kingdom to another
people,

1 Compare Septuagint, Syriac, Vulgate; the meaning of the Hebrew is uncertain

15:27 a robe of fine linen. The robe of fine linen and the linen ephod were the usual clothing of priests (1 Sam. 2:18; 22:18).

15:28 all Israel. See note 11:1.

15:29 Michal the daughter of Saul. Attention is drawn to the hardened heart of Saul's daughter. In contrast to the people, the Levites, and David, Michal was disgusted by the enthusiastic worship. Michal's sarcastic rebuke (2 Sam. 6:20) is not repeated here, perhaps to avoid casting doubt on the purity of David's worship.

16:4 Levites. The Davidic arrangement of the Levites is noted (6:1 note). **to invoke, to thank, and to praise.** These correspond to the three principal kinds of psalms.

16:5 harps and lyres. See note 15:16.

16:7–36 thanksgiving . . . sung to the LORD. There is a psalm of celebration not found in Samuel. The passage is similar to portions of several psalms (compare vv. 8–22 with Ps. 105:1–15; vv. 23–33 with Ps. 96; vv. 34–36 with Ps. 106:1, 47, 48). David celebrated the entry of the ark into Jerusalem as a mighty act of God, and his words had continuing value for those returning to Jerusalem from the exile in Babylon. David calls for the praise of God (vv. 8–13). He remembers the promise of the land and the protection of God in the wanderings of the past (vv. 15–22). Later readers experienced similar blessings in their return to the land. David invites the people to cry out for further protection and deliverance (v. 35). Those returned from Babylon needed the same help from God. Finally, the people responded with praise and joy at the blessings of God (v. 36), just as the later readers should praise God in their day.

16:11 Seek. See note 2 Chr. 7:14.

21 he allowed no one to oppress them;
he [r]rebuked kings on their
account,
22 saying, "Touch not my
anointed ones,
do my [s]prophets no harm!"
23 [t]Sing to the LORD, all the earth!
Tell of his salvation from day
to day.
24 Declare his glory among the nations,
his marvelous works among all
the peoples!
25 For [u]great is the LORD, and greatly to
be praised,
and he is to be held in awe [v]above
all gods.
26 For all the gods of the peoples
are idols,
[w]but the LORD made the heavens.
27 Splendor and majesty are before him;
strength and joy are in his place.
28 Ascribe to the LORD, O clans
of the peoples,
[x]ascribe to the LORD glory
and strength!
29 Ascribe to the LORD the glory due
his name;
bring an offering and come
before him!
[y]Worship the LORD in the splendor of
holiness;[1]
30 tremble before him, all the earth;
yes, the world is established; it
shall never be moved.
31 [z]Let the heavens be glad, and let the
earth rejoice,
and let them say among the
nations, [a]"The LORD reigns!"
32 [b]Let the sea roar, and all that fills it;
let the field exult, and everything
in it!
33 Then shall the trees of the forest sing
for joy
before the LORD, for he comes to
judge the earth.
34 Oh give thanks to the LORD,
for he is good;
for his steadfast love endures
forever!

35 [c]Say also:
"Save us, O God of our salvation,
and gather and deliver us from
among the nations,
that we may give thanks to your
holy name,
and glory in your praise.
36 [d]Blessed be the LORD, the God
of Israel,
from everlasting to everlasting!"

[e]Then all the people said, "Amen!" and
praised the LORD.

Worship Before the Ark

37 So David left Asaph and his brothers
there [f]before the ark of the covenant of the
LORD to minister regularly before the ark
[g]as each day required, 38 and also [h]Obed-
edom and his[2] sixty-eight brothers, while
[h]Obed-edom, the son of Jeduthun, and
[i]Hosah were to be gatekeepers. 39 And he
left [j]Zadok the priest and his brothers the
priests before the tabernacle of the LORD
[k]in the high place that was at Gibeon 40 to
offer burnt offerings to the LORD [l]on the
altar of burnt offering [m]regularly morning
and evening, to do all that is written in the
Law of the LORD that he commanded Israel.
41 With them were [n]Heman and Jeduthun
[o]and the rest of those chosen and [p]express-
ly named to give thanks to the LORD, [q]for
his steadfast love endures forever. 42 Heman
and Jeduthun had trumpets and cymbals
for the music and instruments [r]for sacred
song. The sons of Jeduthun were appointed to the gate.
43 [s]Then all the people departed each to
his house, and David went home to bless
his household.

The LORD's Covenant with David

17 [t]Now when David lived in his
house, David said to Nathan the
prophet, "Behold, I dwell in a house of

21 [r][Gen. 12:17; 20:3]
22 [s][Gen. 20:7]
23 [t]For ver. 23-33, see Ps. 96:1-13
25 [u]Ps. 145:3 [v][Ps. 95:3]
26 [w][Ps. 115:15; Isai. 42:5; 44:24; Jer. 10:11, 12]
28 [x][Ps. 29:1]
29 [y][Ps. 110:3]
31 [z][Isai. 49:13] [a]Ps. 93:1; 97:1; 99:1; [Isai. 52:7; Rev. 11:15, 17; 19:6]
32 [b]Ps. 98:7
35 [c]For ver. 35, 36, see Ps. 106:47, 48
36 [d]Ps. 41:13; [1 Kin. 8:15] [e][Deut. 27:15; Ps. 106:48]
37 [f]ver. 4, 5 [g]2 Chr. 31:16
38 [h]ch. 26:4 [i]ch. 26:10, 16
39 [j]ch. 15:11 [k]See 1 Kin. 3:4
40 [l]Ex. 27:1 [m]See Ex. 29:38-41; Num. 28:3-8
41 [n]See ch. 6:33 [o][ch. 25:1, 3, 6] [p]Num. 1:17 [q]2 Chr. 5:13; 7:3, 6; 20:21; Ezra 3:11; Jer. 33:11; See ver. 34
42 [r][1 Chr. 25:7; 29:27]
43 [s]2 Sam. 6:19, 20
Chapter 17
1 [t]For ver. 1-27, see 2 Sam. 7:1-29

1 Or *in holy attire* 2 Hebrew *their*

16:29 Worship. See theological note "God's Pattern for Worship."

16:40 all that is written in the Law of the LORD. David's commitment to observing Mosaic law is presented as a model for the reorganization of the community following the return from exile in Babylon (6:49; 15:15; 22:12, 13; 2 Chr. 6:16; 12:1, 2; 14:4; 17:3–9; 24:6, 9; 25:4; 30:15, 16; 31:3–21; 33:8; 34:19–33; 35:6–26). See Introduction: Characteristics and Themes.

17:1–29:30 David made a most important contribution to Israel's history by preparing for the temple. This account has six major sections: being commissioned by God (ch. 17); making military preparation (chs. 18–20); discovering the temple site (21:1–22:1); commissioning the builders (22:2–19); arranging personnel (chs. 23–27); and leading national celebration and exhortation (chs. 28; 29).

God's Pattern for Worship

Biblical worship is the due response of rational creatures to the self-revelation of their Creator. It honors and glorifies God by gratefully offering back to Him all the good gifts, and all the knowledge of His greatness and graciousness, that He has given. His servants praise Him for what He is, thank Him for what He has done, desire Him to increase in glory through continuing acts of mercy, judgment, and power, and trust Him with their prayers for their own and others' well-being. Learning from God is worship too: attention to His word of instruction honors Him, while inattention is an offense. Acceptable worship requires "clean hands and a pure heart" (Ps. 24:4), and a willingness to express devotion in works of service as well as words of adoration.

The basis of worship is the covenant relationship whereby God has bound Himself to those whom He has saved and claimed (see "God's Covenant of Grace" at Gen. 12:1). This grounding in covenant was true of Old Testament worship, as it is now of Christian worship. The spirit of covenant worship, as the Old Testament reveals it, is a blend of awe and joy at the privilege of drawing near to the mighty Creator, with radical self-humbling and honest confession of sin and need. Since God is holy and man is fallen, it must always be so in this world. Worship will be central in the life of heaven (Rev. 4:8–11; 5:9–14; 7:9–17; 11:15–18; 15:2–4; 19:1–10), and so it must be central in the life of the church on earth. It should already be the main activity, both private and corporate, in each believer's life (Col. 3:17).

In the Mosaic law God gave His covenant people a pattern for their worship. All the elements of true worship were included in it, though some of them were typical, pointing forward to Christ and ceasing to be valid after He came. The Book of Psalms provided hymns and prayers for use in Israel's worship; Christians use the psalms in worship today, distinguishing between the demands of the Old and New Testament administrations of the one covenant of grace.

The main features in the pattern for public worship that God gave to Israel were:

(a) The Sabbath, the seventh day following each six days of work: a holy day of rest, to be observed as a memorial of creation (Gen. 2:3; Ex. 20:8–11) and redemption (Deut. 5:12–15). God required Sabbath-keeping (Ex. 16:21–30; 20:8–9; 31:12–17; 34:21; 35:1–3; Lev. 19:3, 30; 23:3; cf. Is. 58:13–14) and made Sabbath-breaking a capital offense (Ex. 31:14; Num. 15:32–36).

(b) Three annual feasts were held (Ex. 23:14–17; 34:23; Deut. 16:16) at which the people gathered at God's sanctuary and offered sacrifices celebrating His bounty. They sought and acknowledged reconciliation and fellowship with Him, and ate and drank together as an expression of joy. The Passover was held on the fourteenth day of the first month and commemorated the Exodus (Ex. 12; Lev. 23:5–8; Num. 28:16–25; Deut. 16:1–8). The Feast of Weeks, also called the Feast of Harvest, Firstfruits, or Pentecost, was held fifty days after Passover and marked the end of the grain harvest (Ex. 23:16; 34:22; Lev. 23:15–22; Num. 28:26–31; Deut. 16:9–12). The Feast of Booths (or "Tabernacles") was held in the seventh month and celebrated the end of the agricultural year; it also reminded the people how God had led them through the wilderness (Lev. 23:39–43; Num. 29:12–38; Deut. 16:13–15).

(c) The Day of Atonement was held on the tenth day of the seventh month. Once each year the high priest took blood into the innermost room of the sanctuary to atone for Israel's sins, and a scapegoat was sent into the wilderness as a sign that those sins were taken away (Lev. 16).

(d) The regular sacrificial system required daily and monthly burnt offerings (Num. 28:1–15), as well as certain personal sacrifices. The common features of these sacrifices were that the offering must be flawless, and the blood of the sacrifice must be poured out on the altar to make atonement (Lev. 17:11).

Rituals of personal purification (Lev. 12–15; Num. 19) and devotion (e.g., consecration of the firstborn, Ex. 13:1–16) were also part of the God-given pattern.

Under the new covenant, in which Old Testament types have given way to their antitypes, Christ's priesthood, sacrifice, and intercession supersede the entire Mosaic system for putting away sin (Heb. 7–10). Baptism (Matt. 28:19) and the Lord's Supper (Matt. 26:26–29; 1 Cor. 11:23–26) replace circumcision (Gal. 2:3–5; 6:12–16) and Passover (1 Cor. 5:7, 8); the Jewish festal calendar no longer applies (Gal. 4:10; Col. 2:16); ceremonial defilement and rites of purification have passed away (Mark 7:19; 1 Tim. 4:3, 4); and the Sabbath is renewed, with the day changed from the last to the first day of the week. The apostles and the early Christians worshiped on the first day of the week (Acts 20:7; 1 Cor. 16:2), celebrating the day Jesus rose from the dead, "the Lord's day" (Rev. 1:10), and regarding it as the Christian Sabbath. These changes from old to new were momentous, but the pattern of true worship, with its essential elements, continues unchanged to this day.

cedar, but the ark of the covenant of the
LORD is under a tent." [2]And Nathan said to
David, "Do all that is in your heart, for God
is with you."
[3]But that same night the word of the
LORD came to Nathan, [4]"Go and tell my
servant David, 'Thus says the LORD: [u]It is
not you who will build me a house to dwell
in. [5]For I have not lived in a house since
the day I brought up Israel to this day, [v]but
I have gone from tent to tent and from
dwelling to dwelling. [6]In all places where I
have moved with all Israel, did I speak a
word with any of the judges of Israel,
whom I commanded to shepherd my people, saying, "Why have you not built me a
house of cedar?"' [7]Now, therefore, thus
shall you say to my servant David, 'Thus
says the LORD of hosts, I took you from the
pasture, from following the sheep, to be
prince over my people Israel, [8]and I have
been with you wherever you have gone and
have cut off all your enemies from before
you. And I will make for you a name, like
the name of the great ones of the earth.
[9]And I will appoint a place for my people
Israel and will plant them, that they may
dwell in their own place and be disturbed
no more. And violent men shall waste
them no more, as formerly, [10]from the time
that I appointed judges over my people
Israel. And I [w]will subdue all your enemies.
Moreover, I declare to you that the LORD
will build you a house. [11]When your days
are fulfilled to walk with your fathers, I will
raise up your offspring after you, one of
your own sons, and I will establish his

4 [u]ch. 28:3
5 [v][2 Sam. 7:6]
10 [w][2 Sam. 7:11]

13 [x]Cited Heb. 1:5
[y][1 Sam. 15:23, 28]
19 [z][2 Sam. 7:21]

kingdom. [12]He shall build a house for me,
and I will establish his throne forever. [13][x]I
will be to him a father, and he shall be to
me a son. I will not take my steadfast love
from him, [y]as I took it from him who was
before you, [14]but I will confirm him in my
house and in my kingdom forever, and his
throne shall be established forever.'" [15]In
accordance with all these words, and in
accordance with all this vision, Nathan
spoke to David.

David's Prayer

[16]Then King David went in and sat
before the LORD and said, "Who am I, O
LORD God, and what is my house, that you
have brought me thus far? [17]And this was a
small thing in your eyes, O God. You have
also spoken of your servant's house for a
great while to come, and have shown me
future generations,[1] O LORD God! [18]And
what more can David say to you for honoring your servant? For you know your servant. [19][z]For your servant's sake, O LORD,
and according to your own heart, you have
done all this greatness, in making known
all these great things. [20]There is none like
you, O LORD, and there is no God besides
you, according to all that we have heard
with our ears. [21]And who is like your people Israel, the one[2] nation on earth whom
God went to redeem to be his people, making for yourself a name for great and awesome things, in driving out nations before
your people whom you redeemed from
Egypt? [22]And you made your people Israel

[1] The meaning of the Hebrew is uncertain [2] Septuagint, Vulgate *other*

17:1–27 David's commission from God to prepare for the temple is in two parts: Nathan's dynastic oracle (17:1–15) and David's prayer of acceptance (17:16–27). The writer follows 2 Sam. 7 closely.

17:1–15 The word "house" lies at the heart of this passage. David saw his own house ("palace") and desired to build a "house" (a temple) for God. But God declared that He would build a "house" (a dynasty, v. 10) for David. David's son would build a "house" (a temple, v. 12) for the Lord.

17:1, 10 The Chronicler does not repeat the references to David's rest from enemies found in 2 Sam. 7:1, 11. The emphasis is that David was a man of war (but see 17:8; 22:18), and therefore unqualified to build the temple (22:6–10 note).

17:7–14 Nathan announces the dynastic promises associated with the Davidic covenant. The covenant with David is also celebrated in Ps. 89 and 132. God promised that David's descendants would become a dynasty ruling always over Israel. Individual kings were subject to severe chastisement (2 Sam. 7:14; Ps. 89:30–32), but the line of David would never be permanently rejected from the throne (2 Sam. 7:15, 16; 2 Chr. 6:16; Ps. 89:33–37; 132:11, 12). This covenant was a basis for hope that Israel could be fully restored (Introduction: Characteristics and Themes). The New Testament reveals that the promises to David were fulfilled in Christ. Christ kept the conditions of the covenant perfectly (Heb. 4:15); He serves as the Mediator of the covenant of grace (Acts 2:25–36; Heb. 9:15); and He promised to return as conquering King (Matt. 24:29–31; Mark 13:24–27; Luke 21:25–28).

17:13 to him a father . . . to me a son. This language indicates a special adoption of the chosen king, not a belief in the divinity of the king as in other ancient Near Eastern cultures (Ps. 2:7; 45:6; 89:27 and note). New Testament writers understand these words about Solomon as a foreshadowing of Christ, the final Davidic King (Mark 1:11; Luke 1:32, 33; Heb. 1:5). Christ was the Son of David, but He was also the Son of God. He was conceived by the Holy Spirit (Luke 1:35) and is the Second Person of the Godhead (John 1:1–18; 17:1).

17:14 his throne shall be established forever. God designated David's line as the permanent dynasty over His people. When David's descendants failed they were chastised (2 Sam. 7:14), but God always raised up another son of David to continue the line. This promise gave hope to the community following the exile of the sixth century B.C., and came to fulfillment in Jesus, who reigns on the throne of David forever (vv. 7–14 note; 2 Chr. 21:7).

17:16 Who am I. David's sincere expression of humility sets an attractive and valuable example (29:14–16; 2 Chr. 2:6).

to be your people forever, and you, O
LORD, became their God. 23 And now, O
LORD, let the word that you have spoken
concerning your servant and concerning
his house be established forever, and do as
you have spoken, 24 and your name will be
established and magnified forever, saying,
'The LORD of hosts, the God of Israel, is
Israel's God,' and the house of your servant
David will be established before you. 25 For
you, my God, have revealed to your servant
that you will build a house for him.
Therefore your servant has found courage
to pray before you. 26 And now, O LORD,
you are God, and you have promised this
good thing to your servant. 27 Now you
have been pleased to bless the house of
your servant, that it may continue forever
before you, for it is you, O LORD, who have
blessed, and it is blessed forever."

David Defeats His Enemies

18 [a]After this David defeated the
Philistines and subdued them, and
he took Gath and its villages out of the
hand of the Philistines.
2 And he defeated Moab, and the
Moabites became servants to David and
brought tribute.
3 David also defeated [b]Hadadezer king of
[c]Zobah-Hamath, as he went to set up his
monument[1] at the river Euphrates. 4 And
David took from him 1,000 chariots,
[d]7,000 horsemen and 20,000 foot soldiers.
And David hamstrung all the chariot horses,
but left enough for 100 chariots. 5 And
when the Syrians of Damascus came to
help Hadadezer king [e]of Zobah, David
struck down 22,000 men of the Syrians.
6 Then David put garrisons[2] in Syria of
Damascus, and the Syrians became servants
to David and brought tribute. And
the LORD gave victory to David[3] wherever
he went. 7 And David took the shields of
gold that were carried by the servants of
Hadadezer and brought them to Jerusalem.
8 And from [f]Tibhath and from Cun, cities of
Hadadezer, David took a large amount of
bronze. [g]With it Solomon made the bronze
sea and the pillars and the vessels of
bronze.
9 When [h]Tou king of Hamath heard that
David had defeated the whole army of
Hadadezer, king of Zobah, 10 he sent his
son [i]Hadoram to King David, to ask about
his health and to bless him because he had
fought against [b]Hadadezer and defeated
him; for [b]Hadadezer had often been at war
with Tou. And he sent all sorts of articles of
gold, of silver, and of bronze. 11 These also
King David dedicated to the LORD, together
with the silver and gold that he had carried
off from all the nations, from [j]Edom,
Moab, the Ammonites, the Philistines and
Amalek.
12 And [k]Abishai, the son of Zeruiah, killed
18,000 Edomites in the Valley of Salt.
13 Then he put garrisons in Edom, and all
the Edomites became David's servants.
And the LORD gave victory to David wherever
he went.

David's Administration

14 So David reigned over all Israel, and he
administered justice and equity to all his
people. 15 And [l]Joab the son of Zeruiah was
over the army; and Jehoshaphat the son of
Ahilud was recorder; 16 [m]and Zadok the son

Chapter 18
1 [a]For ver. 1-17, see 2 Sam. 8:1-18
3 [b][2 Sam. 8:3] [c]See 1 Kin. 8:65
4 [d][2 Sam. 8:4]
5 [e]ch. 19:6
8 [f][2 Sam. 8:8] [g]1 Kin. 7:15, 23; 2 Chr. 4:12, 15, 16
9 [h][2 Sam. 8:9]
10 [i][2 Sam. 8:10] [b][See ver. 3 above]
11 [j][2 Sam. 8:12]
12 [k]1 Sam. 26:6; [2 Sam. 8:13]
15 [l][ch. 11:6]
16 [m][2 Sam. 8:17; 20:25]

[1] Hebrew *hand* [2] Septuagint, Vulgate, 2 Samuel 8:6 (compare Syriac); Hebrew lacks *garrisons* [3] Hebrew *the LORD saved David*

17:24 name. See note 13:6.

18:1–20:8 This section concerns David's military and political accomplishments. Relying on 2 Sam. 8; 10; 11; and 21, it is organized in four sections: a survey of victories (18:1–13); a list of officials (18:14–17); victory over the Ammonites (19:1–20:3); and victory over the Philistines (20:4–8). This material demonstrates how David established the political security necessary for temple construction in Solomon's day (18:13 note; 22:17–19). Second, it offers the background for David's enormous contributions to the temple construction (18:8, 11 note). Third, it anticipates David's disqualification from temple building because of his warfare (22:6–10 note; 28:3). Fourth, David's victories inspired the readers to hope for victory over the enemies of their day (19:1–20:3 note). David's involvement with Mephibosheth (2 Sam. 9; 21:1–14) is omitted, as is his adultery with Bathsheba and its aftermath (2 Sam. 11–20; see 10:14 note).

18:1–13 See 2 Sam. 8:1–14 and notes. The only noteworthy omission in the account is David's severe treatment of the Moabites (2 Sam. 8:2).

18:4 7,000. According to the parallel text in 2 Sam. 8:4, David captured "1,700." However, an ancient translation of 2 Sam. agrees with 1 Chr. in reading "7,000" and it may be that the Hebrew text of 2 Sam. was miscopied at some point (see 19:18 note).

18:8, 11 Solomon made . . . David dedicated. David devoted the spoils of warfare to temple construction, preparing the way for Solomon to build.

18:11 Edom . . . Amalek. This list of enemies covers most of the armies mentioned in chs. 18–20.

18:13 the LORD gave victory to David. David's victories provided a secure political environment that allowed Solomon to concentrate on building (19:1–20:3 note).

18:14 David reigned over all Israel. David's domestic arrangements also contributed to the political stability necessary for building projects (18:1–20:8 note).

all Israel. The Chronicler carries this expression over from 2 Sam. 8:15.

of Ahitub and [n]Ahimelech the son of
Abiathar were priests; and [o]Shavsha was
secretary; 17 and Benaiah the son of
Jehoiada was over the Cherethites and the
Pelethites; and David's sons were the
[p]chief officials in the service of the king.

The Ammonites Disgrace David's Men

19 [q]Now after this Nahash the king of the
Ammonites died, and his son reigned
in his place. 2 And David said, "I will deal kindly with Hanun the son of Nahash, for his father
dealt kindly with me." So David sent messengers to console him concerning his father. And
David's servants came to the land of the
Ammonites to Hanun to console him. 3 But
the princes of the Ammonites said to Hanun,
"Do you think, because David has sent comforters to you, that he is honoring your father?
Have not his servants come to you to search
and to overthrow and to spy out the land?"
4 So Hanun took David's servants and shaved
them and cut off their garments in the middle,
at their hips, and sent them away; 5 and they
departed. When David was told concerning
the men, he sent messengers to meet them,
for the men were greatly ashamed. And the
king said, "Remain at Jericho until your
beards have grown and then return."
6 When the Ammonites saw that they had
become a stench to David, Hanun and the
Ammonites sent 1,000 talents[1] of silver to
hire chariots and horsemen [r]from Mesopotamia, from Aram-maacah and from
[s]Zobah. 7 They hired 32,000 chariots and the
king of Maacah with his army, who came
and encamped before [t]Medeba. And the
Ammonites were mustered from their cities
and came to battle. 8 When David heard of it,
he sent Joab and all the army of the mighty
men. 9 And the Ammonites came out and
drew up in battle array at the entrance of the
city, and the kings who had come were by
themselves in the open country.

16 [n][ch. 24:3, 6] [o][2 Sam. 8:17; 1 Kin. 4:3]
17 [p][2 Sam. 8:18]
Chapter 19
1 [q]For ver. 1-19, see 2 Sam. 10:1-19
6 [r][2 Sam. 10:6] [s]ch. 18:5, 9
7 [t]Num. 21:30; Josh. 13:9, 16
11 [u]ch. 18:12
16 [v][2 Sam. 10:16, 18] [w]2 Sam. 10:16
18 [x][2 Sam. 10:18] [v][See ver. 16 above]
19 [w][See ver. 16 above]

Ammonites and Syrians Defeated

10 When Joab saw that the battle was set
against him both in front and in the rear, he
chose some of the best men of Israel and
arrayed them against the Syrians. 11 The rest
of his men he put in the charge of [u]Abishai
his brother, and they were arrayed against
the Ammonites. 12 And he said, "If the
Syrians are too strong for me, then you shall
help me, but if the Ammonites are too
strong for you, then I will help you. 13 Be
strong, and let us use our strength for our
people and for the cities of our God, and
may the LORD do what seems good to him."
14 So Joab and the people who were with him
drew near before the Syrians for battle, and
they fled before him. 15 And when the
Ammonites saw that the Syrians fled, they
likewise fled before Abishai, Joab's brother,
and entered the city. Then Joab came to
Jerusalem.
16 But when the Syrians saw that they
had been defeated by Israel, they sent messengers and brought out the Syrians who
were beyond the Euphrates, with [v]Sho-
phach the commander of the army of
[w]Hadadezer at their head. 17 And when it
was told to David, he gathered all Israel
together and crossed the Jordan and came
to them and drew up his forces against
them. And when David set the battle in
array against the Syrians, they fought with
him. 18 And the Syrians fled before Israel,
and David killed of the Syrians the men of
[x]7,000 chariots and 40,000 [x]foot soldiers,
and put to death also [v]Shophach the commander of their army. 19 And when the servants of [w]Hadadezer saw that they had
been defeated by Israel, they made peace
with David and became subject to him. So
the Syrians were not willing to save the
Ammonites any more.

1 A *talent* was about 75 pounds or 34 kilograms

18:16 Zadok . . . Ahimelech the son of Abiathar. See note 15:11.

18:17 Cherethites . . . Pelethites. Foreign mercenaries among the king's guards (1 Sam. 30:14 note).

chief officials. Chronicles uses a word more definitely referring to high political office. David and his sons were not technically priests, and the writer is being more precise about the proper ordering of royalty and priesthood (6:1 note).

19:1–20:3 Compare 2 Sam. 10:1–19; 11:1; 12:29–31 and notes. For the omission of David's sin with Bathsheba and the ensuing troubles in the Davidic house (2 Sam. 11:1–21:14) see note 18:1–20:8.

19:1 Ammonites. The Ammonites were longstanding enemies of Israel (Judg. 10:7–9; 10:17–11:40; 1 Sam. 11:1–11; 14:47). They also troubled the community following the return from exile in Babylon (Neh. 2:19; 4:3, 7, 8).

19:6 Mesopotamia. Chronicles replaces the less familiar Beth-rehob with Mesopotamia and omits the reference to Tob (2 Sam. 10:6).

19:7 32,000. Israel's victory is frequently highlighted by reporting the numbers of the opposing army (15:18–22; 2 Chr. 12:2–4; 13:3; 14:9).

19:17 all Israel. See note 11:1.

19:18 7,000. 2 Sam. 10:18 reads "700." It is possible that the higher number in Chronicles is due to a copyist's error in transmission of the text.

The Capture of Rabbah

20 [y]In the spring of the year, the time when kings go out to battle, Joab led out the army and ravaged the country of the Ammonites and came and besieged Rabbah. But David remained at Jerusalem. And [z]Joab struck down Rabbah and overthrew it. 2 [a]And David took the crown of their king from his head. He found that it weighed a talent[1] of gold, and in it was a precious stone. And it was placed on David's head. And he brought out the spoil of the city, a very great amount. 3 And he brought out the people who were in it and set them to labor[2] [b]with saws and iron picks and axes.[3] And thus David did to all the cities of the Ammonites. Then David and all the people returned to Jerusalem.

Philistine Giants Killed

4 [c]And after this there arose war with the Philistines at Gezer. Then Sibbecai the Hushathite struck down Sippai, who was one of the descendants of the giants, and the Philistines were subdued. 5 And there was again war with the Philistines, and Elhanan the son of [d]Jair struck down Lahmi [d]the brother of Goliath the Gittite, the shaft of whose spear was like a weaver's beam. 6 And there was again war at Gath, where there was a man of great stature, who had six fingers on each hand and six toes on each foot, twenty-four in number, and he also was descended from the giants. 7 And when he taunted Israel, Jonathan the son of [e]Shimea, David's brother, struck him down. 8 These were descended from the giants in Gath, and they fell by the hand of David and by the hand of his servants.

David's Census Brings Pestilence

21 [f]Then [g]Satan stood against Israel and incited David to number Israel. 2 So David said to Joab and the commanders of the army, "Go, number Israel, from Beersheba to Dan, and bring me a report, that I may know their number." 3 But Joab said, "May the LORD add to his people a hundred times as many as they are! Are they not, my lord the king, all of them my lord's servants? Why then should my lord require this? Why should it be a cause of guilt for Israel?" 4 But the king's word prevailed against Joab. So Joab departed and went throughout all Israel and came back to Jerusalem. 5 And Joab gave the sum of the numbering of the people to David. In all Israel there were [h]1,100,000 men who drew the sword, and in Judah [h]470,000 who drew the sword. 6 [i]But he did not include Levi and Benjamin in the numbering, for the king's command was abhorrent to Joab.

7 But God was displeased with this thing, and he struck Israel. 8 And David said to God, "I have sinned greatly in that I have done this thing. But now, please [j]take away the iniquity of your servant, for I have acted very foolishly." 9 And the LORD spoke to

Chapter 20
1 [y]2 Sam. 11:1 [z]2 Sam. 12:26
2 [a]For ver. 2, 3, see 2 Sam. 12:30, 31
3 [b][2 Sam. 12:31]
4 [c]For ver. 4-8, see 2 Sam.21:18-22
5 [d][2 Sam. 21:19]
7 [e]ch. 2:13; 2 Sam. 13:3; [1 Sam. 16:9; 17:13]

Chapter 21
1 [f]For ver. 1-28, see 2 Sam. 24:1-25 [g]Zech. 3:1, 2 [2 Sam. 24:1] See Job 1:6-12; 2:1-7
5 [h][2 Sam. 24:9]
6 [i]ch. 27:24
8 [j][2 Sam. 12:13]

1 A *talent* was about 75 pounds or 34 kilograms 2 Compare 2 Samuel 12:31; Hebrew *he sawed* 3 Compare 2 Samuel 12:31; Hebrew *saws*

20:1 In the spring. Armies typically advanced after the first spring harvest when food was more abundant (2 Sam. 11:1; 1 Kin. 20:22, 26).

20:2 spoil . . . a very great amount. See note 18:8, 11.

20:4 were subdued. Not found in 2 Sam. 21:18. The sentence indicates that the promise of 17:10 was fulfilled (2 Chr. 13:18; and contrast 28:19).

21:1–22:1 The history continues with David's discovery of the temple site (17:1–29:30 note). The theme of military victory (19:1–20:8) leads to an account of David's census. With two major exceptions, the account follows 2 Sam. 24 closely (21:1; 21:28–22:1 and notes). Second Samuel reports how David brought trouble on the nation but successfully interceded on its behalf. In Chronicles the point of the story is to tell how God led David to discover the holy site for the temple.

21:1 Satan. When the Hebrew word *satan* is used with a definite article, it means lit. "the adversary" (Job 1:6; Zech. 3:1). Here *satan* is used for the first time without a definite article, probably as a proper name. See "Satan" at Job 1:6.

Satan stood. According to 1 Sam. 24:1, it was God who moved David. God Himself tempts no one (James 1:13), but He employs created means under His sovereign control. Chronicles identifies Satan as the instrument by which David was led astray. The two passages together remind us that God is sovereign over all events, not excepting temptation and sin (11:4; 25:20 note; Ex. 4:21 note; Josh. 11:20; 1 Kin. 22:22–23; 2 Chr. 10:15 note; Job 1:12; 2:10; Ezek. 3:20; 14:9; Matt. 6:13; Acts 4:27, 28).

21:3 a cause of guilt for Israel. Taking a census was not prohibited by Old Testament law, though there were specific regulations (Ex. 30:12; Num. 1:2; 26:2). David's desire for a count of his military personnel may have been an indication of reliance on human might rather than on divine power (2 Chr. 13:18 and note). In the light of Joab's response (21:6; 27:24), David may have insisted that the tribe of Levi be counted for military service as well (v. 6 note).

21:5 All Israel. 2 Sam. 24:9 reads simply "Israel." See note 11:1.

1,100,000. The differences of these numbers from those in 2 Sam. 24:9 are problematic. It may be that the number of men from Judah is included in the total for "all Israel" (that is, *including* Judah with 470,000 not "and in Judah"). The Book of Chronicles may exclude some elements, such as Levi and Benjamin, from its count (21:6 note). Or the numbers may be approximations. Beyond this, one or both texts may suffer from errors of copying.

21:6 he did not include. Joab did not carry through completely the census David had ordered (v. 3 note).

Levi and Benjamin. These tribes were not included in the census. The tribe of Levi was to be excluded from any military census, according to Mosaic Law (Num. 1:49; 2:33). Benjamin may have been excluded because the tabernacle was in Gibeon at the time (v. 29).

Gad, David's [k]seer, saying, 10 "Go and say
to David, 'Thus says the LORD, Three things
I offer you; choose one of them, that I may
do it to you.'" 11 So Gad came to David and
said to him, "Thus says the LORD, 'Choose
what you will: 12 either [l]three years of
famine, or three months of devastation by
your foes while the sword of your enemies
overtakes you, or else three days of the
sword of the LORD, pestilence on the land,
with the angel of the LORD destroying
throughout all the territory of Israel.' Now
decide what answer I shall return to him
who sent me." 13 Then David said to Gad,
"I am in great distress. Let me fall into the
hand of the LORD, for his mercy is very
great, but do not let me fall into the hand
of man."

14 So the LORD sent a pestilence on Israel,
and 70,000 men of Israel fell. 15 And God
sent the angel to Jerusalem to destroy it,
but as he was about to destroy it, the LORD
saw, and he [m]relented from the calamity.
And he said to the angel who was working
destruction, "It is enough; now stay your
hand." And the angel of the LORD was
standing by the threshing floor of Ornan
the Jebusite. 16 And David lifted his eyes
and saw the angel of the LORD standing
between earth and heaven, and in his
hand a drawn sword stretched out over
Jerusalem. Then David and the elders,
[n]clothed in sackcloth, fell upon their faces.
17 And David said to God, "Was it not I
who gave command to number the people? It is I who have sinned and done great
evil. But these sheep, what have they
done? Please let your hand, O LORD my
God, be against me and against my father's
house. But do not let the plague be on
your people."

9 [k]ch. 29:29; See 1 Sam. 9:9
12 [l][2 Sam. 24:13]
15 [m]See Gen. 6:6
16 [n]1 Kin. 20:31; See 2 Sam. 3:31
18 [o][2 Chr. 3:1]
25 [p][2 Sam. 24:24]
26 [q]See Lev. 9:24

David Builds an Altar

18 Now [o]the angel of the LORD had commanded Gad to say to David that David
should go up and raise an altar to the LORD
on the threshing floor of Ornan the
Jebusite. 19 So David went up at Gad's
word, which he had spoken in the name of
the LORD. 20 Now Ornan was threshing
wheat. He turned and saw the angel, and
his four sons who were with him hid themselves. 21 As David came to Ornan, Ornan
looked and saw David and went out from
the threshing floor and paid homage to
David with his face to the ground. 22 And
David said to Ornan, "Give me the site of
the threshing floor that I may build on it an
altar to the LORD—give it to me at its full
price—that the plague may be averted from
the people." 23 Then Ornan said to David,
"Take it, and let my lord the king do what
seems good to him. See, I give the oxen for
burnt offerings and the threshing sledges
for the wood and the wheat for a grain
offering; I give it all." 24 But King David said
to Ornan, "No, but I will buy them for the
full price. I will not take for the LORD what
is yours, nor offer burnt offerings that cost
me nothing." 25 So David paid Ornan [p]600
shekels[1] of gold by weight for the site.
26 And David built there an altar to the
LORD and presented burnt offerings and
peace offerings and called on the LORD, and
the LORD[2] [q]answered him with fire from
heaven upon the altar of burnt offering.
27 Then the LORD commanded the angel,
and he put his sword back into its sheath.

28 At that time, when David saw that the
LORD had answered him at the threshing
floor of Ornan the Jebusite, he sacrificed

1 A *shekel* was about 2/5 ounce or 11 grams 2 Hebrew *he*

21:13 his mercy is very great. Despite the severity of divine chastisement, David trusts in the abundant mercy of God. Undoubtedly, the promises to David in 17:1–14 supply a background to David's confident trust in God's mercy.

21:16 This verse is not found in the traditional Hebrew text of 2 Sam. 24. However, recently discovered texts of Samuel (Dead Sea Scrolls) and other witnesses suggest that the verse was probably originally in Samuel.

21:20, 21 Although these verses about Ornan (spelled "Araunah" in 2 Sam. 24) do not appear in the traditional Hebrew text of 2 Sam. 24:20, recently discovered texts of Samuel (Dead Sea Scrolls) and other witnesses suggest that the information was originally in Samuel.

21:22 at its full price. This portion of the account is reminiscent of Abraham's purchase of the burial site for Sarah (Gen. 23). David purchased the site at full price. As a result, the future temple site (21:28–22:1 note) was a royal possession devoted to the temple.

21:25 600 shekels . . . for the site. 2 Sam. 24:24 reads "the threshing floor and the oxen for fifty shekels of silver." It has been suggested that Samuel focuses on the threshing floor with its oxen, while Chronicles gives the value of the whole site.

21:26 the LORD answered him with fire. A rare occurrence, indicating God's special approval of David's actions (Lev. 9:24; 1 Kin. 18:37, 38). This event anticipates Solomon's temple dedication later at this same site (2 Chr. 7:1).

21:28–22:1 These verses are not found in 2 Sam. 24. They show an interest in sacrifice (21:28), and possibly help explain David's neglect of the tabernacle (21:29, 30). The main point is that David recognized the threshing floor of Ornan as the site for the future temple (22:1). This remarkable ending with its clear account of moral failure in David's life indicates vividly the place to which the community must turn for sacrifice, forgiveness, and answered prayer (2 Chr. 3:1; 6:12–42 and notes).

there. 29 For the tabernacle of the LORD,
which Moses had made in the wilderness,
and the altar of burnt offering [r]were at that
time in the high place at Gibeon, 30 but
David could not go before it to inquire of
God, for he was afraid of the sword of the
angel of the LORD.

22 Then David said, [s]"Here shall be the
house of the LORD God and here the
altar of burnt offering for Israel."

David Prepares for Temple Building

2 David commanded to gather together
the [t]resident aliens who were in the land
of Israel, and he [u]set stonecutters to prepare dressed stones for building the house
of God. 3 David also provided great quantities of iron for nails for the doors of the
gates and for clamps, [v]as well as bronze in
quantities beyond weighing, 4 and cedar
timbers without number, [w]for the Sidonians and Tyrians brought great quantities of cedar to David. 5 For David said,
[x]"Solomon my son is young and inexperienced, and the house that is to be built for
the LORD must be exceedingly magnificent,
of fame and glory throughout all lands. I
will therefore make preparation for it." So
David provided materials in great quantity
before his death.

Solomon Charged to Build the Temple

6 Then he called for Solomon his son and
charged him to build a house for the LORD,
the God of Israel. 7 David said to Solomon,
"My son, [y]I had it in my heart to build a
house to the name of the LORD my God.
8 But the word of the LORD came to me,
saying, [z]'You have shed much blood and
have waged great wars. You shall not build
a house to my name, because you have
shed so much blood before me on the
earth. 9 Behold, a son shall be born to you
who shall be a man of rest. [a]I will give him
rest from all his surrounding enemies. [b]For
his name shall be Solomon, and I will give
peace and quiet to Israel in his days. 10 [c]He
shall build a house for my name. [d]He shall
be my son, and I will be his father, and I
will establish his royal throne in Israel forever.'

11 "Now, my son, [e]the LORD be with you,
so that you may succeed in building the
house of the LORD your God, as he has spoken concerning you. 12 [f]Only, may the LORD
grant you discretion and understanding,
that when he gives you charge over Israel
you may keep the law of the LORD your
God. 13 [g]Then you will prosper if you are
careful to observe the statutes and the rules
that the LORD commanded Moses for
Israel. [h]Be strong and courageous. Fear
not; do not be dismayed. 14 With great
pains I have provided for the house of the
LORD [i]100,000 talents[1] of gold, a million
talents of silver, and [j]bronze and iron
beyond weighing, for there is so much of it;
timber and stone, too, I have provided. To
these you must add. 15 You have an abundance of workmen: stonecutters, masons,
carpenters, and all kinds of craftsmen without number, skilled in working 16 gold, silver, bronze, and iron. Arise and work! [k]The
LORD be with you!"

1 A *talent* was about 75 pounds or 34 kilograms

29 [r]ch. 16:39; 2 Chr. 1:3; [1 Kin. 3:4]
Chapter 22
1 [s]ch. 21:18, 19, 26, 28; 2 Chr. 3:1; [Deut. 12:5]
2 [t][1 Kin. 9:20, 21; 2 Chr. 2:17] [u][1 Kin. 5:17]
3 [v]ver.14; 1 Kin. 7:47
4 [w][1 Kin. 5:6]
5 [x]ch. 29:1; [1 Kin. 3:7; Prov. 4:3]
7 [y]ch. 17:1, 2; 28:2; 2 Sam. 7:2, 3; 1 Kin. 8:17; See Ps. 132:1-5
8 [z]ch. 28:3; [1 Kin. 5:3]
9 [a]1 Kin. 5:4; [ver. 18; 1 Kin. 4:25] [b]2 Sam. 12:24
10 [c]See 2 Sam. 7:13 [d]ch. 28:6; 2 Sam. 7:14; Heb. 1:5
11 [e]ver 16; [1 Sam. 20:13]
12 [f][1 Kin. 3:9, 12; Ps. 72:1]
13 [g]ch. 28:7 [h]ch. 28:20; [Deut. 31:6, 7; Josh. 1:6, 7, 9]
14 [i][ch. 29:4] [j]ver. 3
16 [k]ver. 11

22:2–29:20 This is the longest section about David's life in the Bible and is found only in Chronicles. The history of how David completed temple preparations begins and ends with descriptions of royal assemblies (22:2–19 and 28:1–29:20) that are similar at several points (compare 22:8 with 28:3; 22:13 with 28:20; and 22:17 with 28:21).

22:2–19 This is the first assembly in which David gave commissions to foreign laborers (22:2–4), Solomon (22:5–16), and the Israelite leaders (22:17–19) to construct the temple of God.

22:2 aliens. David and Solomon used conscripted labor made up primarily of foreigners (1 Kin. 5:13–18; 9:15–23; 11:28; 2 Chr. 2:2, 17–18; 8:7–10). The mention of "aliens" participating in the construction of the first temple corresponds to the participation of foreigners in the reconstruction of the temple following the Babylonian exile of the Jews (Is. 60:10–12).

22:3 iron. Presumably taken from the Philistines whom David had conquered (1 Sam. 13:19–22).

bronze. Taken from the spoils of war (18:8, 11 note).

22:5 young and inexperienced. Solomon was not experienced enough to handle the responsibility of preparing for the temple (cf. 29:1; 2 Chr. 13:7).

preparation. The central theme of this section is how David provided virtually everything for the temple built by Solomon, including plans, materials, workers, work assignments, political stability, and popular support. In effect, the temple was a joint project of David and Solomon (22:2–29:20; 2 Chr. 2:3 and notes). See Introduction: Characteristics and Themes.

22:6–10 The writer explains why David himself could not build the temple. 1 Kin. 5:3–5 states that David was preoccupied with warfare, and this passage states specifically that David was ritually defiled by bloodshed so that he could not be directly involved in the building (2 Chr. 6:9).

22:7, 8, 10, 19 name. See note 13:6.

22:9 rest . . . peace and quiet. On several occasions peace and rest from warfare are seen as God's reward to His faithful people (v. 18; 2 Chr. 14:6, 7; 15:15; 20:30; 23:21). This blessing was held out to those returned from Babylonian exile as a basis for hope in their troubled days.

22:12, 13 keep the law of the LORD. See note 16:40.

22:13 Be strong and courageous. David's commission to Solomon (22:12, 13) is reminiscent of Joshua's commission from God (cf. 28:20 and Josh. 1:6–9).

17 David also commanded [l]all the leaders
of Israel to help Solomon his son, saying,
18 “Is not the LORD your God with you? And
[m]has he not given you peace on every side?
For he has delivered the inhabitants of the
land into my hand, and the land is subdued before the LORD and his people.
19 Now [n]set your mind and heart to seek the
LORD your God. Arise and build the sanctuary of the LORD God, [o]so that the ark of
the covenant of the LORD and the holy vessels of God may be brought into a house
built [p]for the name of the LORD.”

David Organizes the Levites

23 [q]When David was old and full of
days, [r]he made Solomon his son
king over Israel.
2 David[1] assembled all the leaders of
Israel and the priests and the Levites. 3 The
Levites, [s]thirty years old and upward, were
numbered, and [t]the total was [u]38,000
men. 4 “Twenty-four thousand of these,”
David said,[2] [v]“shall have charge of the
work in the house of the LORD, 6,000 shall
be [w]officers and judges, 5 4,000 gatekeepers, and 4,000 shall offer praises to the
LORD with the instruments [x]that I have
made for praise.” 6 [y]And David organized
them in divisions [z]corresponding to the
sons of Levi: Gershon, Kohath, and Merari.
7 [a]The sons of Gershon[3] were Ladan and
Shimei. 8 The sons of Ladan: [b]Jehiel the chief,
and Zetham, and Joel, three. 9 The sons of
Shimei: Shelomoth, Haziel, and Haran, three.
These were the heads of the fathers’ houses
of Ladan. 10 And the sons of Shimei: Jahath,
Zina, and Jeush and Beriah. These four were
the sons of Shimei. 11 Jahath was the chief,
and Zizah the second; but Jeush and Beriah
did not have many sons, therefore they
became counted as a single father’s house.

12 [c]The sons of Kohath: Amram, Izhar,
Hebron, and Uzziel, four. 13 [d]The sons of
Amram: Aaron and Moses. [e]Aaron was set
apart to dedicate the most holy things, that
he and his sons forever should [f]make offerings before the LORD and [g]minister to him
and [h]pronounce blessings in his name forever. 14 But the sons of Moses the [i]man of
God were named among the [j]tribe of Levi.
15 The sons of Moses: Gershom and Eliezer.
16 The [k]sons of Gershom: [l]Shebuel the chief.
17 The sons of Eliezer: Rehabiah the chief. Eliezer had no other sons, but the sons of
Rehabiah were very many. 18 The sons of Izhar:
Shelomith the chief. 19 The [m]sons of Hebron:
Jeriah the chief, Amariah the second, Jahaziel
the third, and Jekameam the fourth. 20 [n]The
sons of Uzziel: Micah the chief and Isshiah
the second.
21 [o]The sons of Merari: Mahli and Mushi.
The sons of Mahli: Eleazar and [p]Kish.
22 Eleazar died [q]having no sons, but only
daughters; their [r]kinsmen, the sons of
Kish, married them. 23 [s]The sons of Mushi:
Mahli, Eder, and Jeremoth, three.
24 [t]These were the sons of Levi by their
fathers’ houses, the heads of fathers’ houses [u]as they were listed according to the
number of the names of the individuals
from [v]twenty years old and upward who
were to do the work for the service of the
house of the LORD. 25 For David said, “The
LORD, the God of Israel, [w]has given rest to
his people, and he dwells in Jerusalem forever. 26 And so the Levites no longer need
[x]to carry the tabernacle or any of the things
for its service.” 27 For by the last words of
David the sons of Levi were numbered

17 [l]See ch. 28:1-6 **18** [m]ch. 23:25; [Deut. 12:10; Josh. 21:44; 23:1; 2 Sam. 7:1]; See ver. 9 **19** [n][2 Chr. 20:3] [o]1 Kin. 8:6, 21; 2 Chr. 5:7; 6:11 [p]ver. 7; 1 Kin. 5:3
Chapter 23
1 [q]ch. 29:28 [r][ch. 28:5; 29:22, 28]; See 1 Kin. 1:33-39 **3** [s]Num. 4:3, 47 [t]ver. 24; Num. 1:2 [u][Num. 4:47, 48] **4** [v][2 Chr. 2:2, 18; 34:12; Ezra 3:8, 9] [w]ch. 26:29; [Deut. 16:18; 2 Chr. 19:8] **5** [x]2 Chr. 29:25, 26; Neh. 12:36; Amos 6:5 **6** [y][2 Chr. 8:14; 23:18; 35:4; Ezra 6:18] [z]ch. 6:1, 16; Ex. 6:16; Num. 26:57 **7** [a]ch. 26:21 **8** [b]ch. 15:18; 29:8; [ch. 26:21] **12** [c]ch. 6:18; 26:23; Ex. 6:18; Num. 3:19 **13** [d]Ex. 6:20 [e]Ex. 28:1; [Heb. 5:4] [f]Ex. 30:7; Num. 16:40; 1 Sam 2:28 [g]Deut. 21:5 [h]Num. 6:23 **14** [i]Deut 33:1 [j][ch. 26:23-25] **16** [k]Ex. 2:22; 18:3, 4 [l]ch. 26:24 **19** [m]ch. 24:23; [ch. 26:31] **20** [n]ch. 24:24, 25

21 [o]ch. 6:19, 29; 24:26; Ex. 6:19; [Num. 26:58] [p]ch. 24:29 **22** [q]ch. 24:28 [r][Num. 36:6, 8] **23** [s]ch. 24:30 **24** [t][Num. 10:17, 21] [u]ver. 3 [v]2 Chr. 31:17; Ezra 3:8; [ver. 3; Num. 4:3; 8:24] **25** [w]See ch. 22:18 **26** [x]2 Chr. 34:3; See Num. 4:5-15

1 Hebrew *He* 2 Hebrew lacks *David said* 3 Vulgate (compare Septuagint, Syriac); Hebrew *to the Gershonite*

22:17–19 David’s success in war provided the political stability necessary for constructing the temple (18:1–20:8 note).

22:18 peace. See note on v. 9.

22:19 seek the LORD. See note 2 Chr. 7:14.

23:1 This opening verse is a topical heading for 23:1–29:20.

he made Solomon his son king over Israel. Apparently assuming his readers’ knowledge of the Book of Kings, the writer of Chronicles says little about the checkered history of David’s rise to power (11:1–9 note). He also does not discuss Solomon’s struggle for kingship (1 Kin. 1; 2), presenting a smooth transition of power from David to Solomon. See 3:10–16 note, and Introduction: Characteristics and Themes.

23:2–27:34 David’s organization of religious (23:2–26:32) and civil (ch. 27) personnel established arrangements for Solomon’s administration, and it also provided a model for the reorganization of the people in the community after the return from exile in Babylon.

23:2–32 the priests and the Levites. Between introductory (23:2–6) and concluding remarks (23:24–32) comes the list of divisions of Levites into Gershonites (23:7–11), Kohathites (23:12–20), and Merarites (23:21–23). See note 6:1.

23:3 thirty years old. Apparently the age at which Levites began service was adjusted according to need: thirty years (Num. 4:1–3), twenty-five years (Num. 8:23–25), and twenty years (1 Chr. 23:24, 27). A period of apprenticeship may be in view in some passages.

23:5 instruments. See note 15:16.

23:6–23 Compare similar lists in 6:16–30; 24:20–30.

23:24, 27 twenty years. See note on v. 3.

from [v]twenty years old and upward. **28** For
their duty was to assist the sons of Aaron
for the service of the house of the LORD,
having the care of the courts and the
chambers, the cleansing of all that is holy,
and any work for the service of the house
of God. **29** Their duty was also to assist with
the [y]showbread, the [z]flour for the grain
offering, the wafers of unleavened bread,
the [a]baked offering, the [b]offering mixed
with oil, and all [c]measures of quantity or
size. **30** And they were to stand every morning, thanking and praising the LORD, and
likewise at evening, **31** and whenever burnt
offerings were offered to the LORD [d]on
Sabbaths, [e]new moons and feast days, [f]ac-
cording to the number required of them,
regularly before the LORD. **32** Thus [g]they
were to keep charge of the tent of meeting
and the sanctuary, and to attend the sons
of Aaron, their brothers, for the [h]service of
the house of the LORD.

David Organizes the Priests

24 The divisions of the sons of Aaron
were these. The sons of [i]Aaron:
Nadab, Abihu, Eleazar, and Ithamar. **2** [j]But
Nadab and Abihu died before their father
and had no children, so Eleazar and
Ithamar became the priests. **3** With the help
of [k]Zadok of the sons of Eleazar, and
Ahimelech of the sons of Ithamar, David
organized them according to the appointed
duties in their service. **4** Since more chief
men were found among the sons of Eleazar
than among the sons of Ithamar, they
organized them under sixteen heads of
fathers' houses of the sons of Eleazar, and
eight of the sons of Ithamar. **5** They divided
them [l]by lot, all alike, for there were sacred
officers and officers of God among both the
sons of Eleazar and the sons of Ithamar.
6 And the scribe Shemaiah, the son of
Nethanel, a Levite, recorded them in the
presence of the king and the princes and
Zadok the priest and [m]Ahimelech the son
of Abiathar and the heads of the fathers'
houses of the priests and of the Levites,
one father's house being chosen for Eleazar
and one chosen for Ithamar.
7 The first lot fell to Jehoiarib, the second
to Jedaiah, **8** the third to Harim, the fourth
to Seorim, **9** the fifth to Malchijah, the sixth
to Mijamin, **10** the seventh to Hakkoz, the
eighth to [n]Abijah, **11** the ninth to Jeshua,
the tenth to Shecaniah, **12** the eleventh to
Eliashib, the twelfth to Jakim, **13** the thirteenth to Huppah, the fourteenth to
Jeshebeab, **14** the fifteenth to Bilgah, the sixteenth to Immer, **15** the seventeenth to
Hezir, the eighteenth to Happizzez, **16** the
nineteenth to Pethahiah, the twentieth to
Jehezkel, **17** the twenty-first to Jachin, the
twenty-second to Gamul, **18** the twenty-
third to Delaiah, the twenty-fourth to
Maaziah. **19** These had as their appointed
duty in their service [o]to come into the
house of the LORD according to the procedure established for them by Aaron their
father, as the LORD God of Israel had commanded him.
20 And of the rest of the sons of Levi: [p]of
the sons of Amram, Shubael; of the sons of
Shubael, Jehdeiah. **21** [q]Of Rehabiah: of the
sons of Rehabiah, Isshiah the chief. **22** Of
the Izharites, Shelomoth; of the sons of
Shelomoth, Jahath. **23** [r]The sons of Hebron:[1]
Jeriah the chief,[2] Amariah the second,
Jahaziel the third, Jekameam the fourth.
24 [s]The sons of Uzziel, Micah; of the sons of
Micah, Shamir. **25** The brother of Micah,
Isshiah; of the sons of Isshiah, Zechariah.
26 [t]The sons of Merari: Mahli and Mushi.
The sons of Jaaziah: Beno.[3] **27** The sons of
Merari: of Jaaziah, Beno, Shoham, Zaccur
and Ibri. **28** Of Mahli: Eleazar, [u]who had no
sons. **29** Of Kish, the sons of Kish: Jerah-
meel. **30** [v]The sons of Mushi: Mahli, Eder,

27 [v][See ver. 24 above]
29 [y]See Lev. 24:5-8 [z]ch. 9:29; Lev. 6:20, 21 [a]ch. 9:31 [b]Lev. 6:21; 7:12 [c][Lev. 19:35]
31 [d]Isai. 1:13 [e]See Num. 28:11 [f]See Lev. 23:2, 4
32 [g]Num. 1:53 [h]See Num. 3:6-9
Chapter 24
1 [i]Lev. 10:1, 6; Num. 26:60
2 [j]Lev. 10:2; Num. 26:61
3 [k]ver. 31; 2 Sam. 8:17
5 [l] ver. 31
6 [m]2 Sam. 8:17; [ch. 18:16; 1 Sam. 22:20; 23:6]
10 [n]Luke 1:5
19 [o]ch. 9:25
20 [p]ch. 23:13
21 [q]ch. 23:17
23 [r]ch. 23:19
24 [s]ch. 23:20
26 [t]ch. 23:21
28 [u]ch. 23:22
30 [v] ch. 23:23

1 Compare 23:19; Hebrew lacks *Hebron* 2 Compare 23:19; Hebrew lacks *the chief* 3 Or *his son*; also verse 27

23:28 to assist the sons of Aaron. The Levites were under the authority of the Aaronic priests. See notes 6:53 and 15:11.

24:1, 2 The account follows the traditional division of the sons of Aaron (cf. 6:3; Ex. 6:23; Num. 3:2–4). The descendants of Eleazar and Ithamar alone served as priests (6:1 note; Lev. 10:1–3).

24:3 Zadok. See notes 6:53 and 15:11.

24:5 divided them by lot. Casting lots in careful accord with revealed standards was designed to ensure that decisions were made according to divine direction rather than human prejudice (Prov. 16:33; Luke 1:8, 9; Acts 1:26).

24:6 Ahimelech the son of Abiathar. See note 18:16.

24:7–18 Twenty-four divisions were established to provide for regular rotation of duty among the priestly families. See the similar practice in New Testament times (Luke 1:8, 9).

24:7 Jehoiarib. The father of the Maccabees (Mattathias) was in the division of Jehoiarib (cf. 1 Macc. 2:1).

24:10 Abijah. The father of John the Baptist (Zechariah) was in the division of Abijah (Luke 1:5).

and Jerimoth. These were the sons of the
Levites according to their fathers' houses.
31 These also, the head of each father's
house and his younger brother alike,
[w]cast lots, just as their brothers the sons of
Aaron, in the presence of King David,
[x]Zadok, Ahimelech, and the heads of
fathers' houses of the priests and of the
Levites.

David Organizes the Musicians

25 David and the chiefs of the service
also set apart for the service the sons
of [y]Asaph, and of [z]Heman, and of
[a]Jeduthun, who [b]prophesied with lyres,
with [c]harps, and with cymbals. The list of
those who did the work and of their duties
was: 2 Of the sons of Asaph: Zaccur, Joseph,
Nethaniah, and Asharelah, sons of Asaph,
under the direction of Asaph, who [b]proph-
esied under the direction of the king. 3 Of
Jeduthun, the sons of Jeduthun: Gedaliah,
Zeri, Jeshaiah, Shimei,[1] Hashabiah, and
Mattithiah, six, under the direction of their
father Jeduthun, [b]who prophesied with the
lyre in thanksgiving and praise to the LORD.
4 Of Heman, the sons of Heman: Bukkiah,
Mattaniah, Uzziel, Shebuel and Jerimoth,
Hananiah, Hanani, Eliathah, Giddalti, and
Romamti-ezer, Joshbekashah, Mallothi,
Hothir, Mahazioth. 5 All these were the sons
of Heman [d]the king's seer, according to the
promise of God to exalt him, for God had
given Heman fourteen sons and three
daughters. 6 They were all under the direction of their father in the music in the
house of the LORD with cymbals, [c]harps,
and lyres for the service of the house of
God. Asaph, Jeduthun, and Heman were
under the order of the king. 7 The number of
them along with their brothers, who were
trained in singing to the LORD, all who were
skillful, was [e]288. 8 And they cast lots for
their duties, [f]small and great, teacher and
pupil alike.

31 [w]ver. 5; ch. 25:8; 26:13, 14; Neh. 11:1 [x]ver. 6
Chapter 25
1 [y]See ch. 6:39 [z]See ch. 6:33 [a]ch. 16:41 [b][Ex. 15:20; 2 Kin. 3:15] [c]ch. 15:16; Neh. 12:27
2 [b][See ver. 1 above]
3 [b][See ver. 1 above]
5 [d][2 Sam. 24:11]
6 [c][See ver. 1 above]
7 [e][ch. 23:5]
8 [f]ch. 26:13
Chapter 26
2 [g]ch. 9:21

9 The first lot fell for Asaph to Joseph;
the second to Gedaliah, to him and his
brothers and his sons, twelve; 10 the third
to Zaccur, his sons and his brothers,
twelve; 11 the fourth to Izri, his sons and
his brothers, twelve; 12 the fifth to
Nethaniah, his sons and his brothers,
twelve; 13 the sixth to Bukkiah, his sons
and his brothers, twelve; 14 the seventh to
Jesharelah, his sons and his brothers,
twelve; 15 the eighth to Jeshaiah, his sons
and his brothers, twelve; 16 the ninth to
Mattaniah, his sons and his brothers,
twelve; 17 the tenth to Shimei, his sons and
his brothers, twelve; 18 the eleventh to
Azarel, his sons and his brothers, twelve;
19 the twelfth to Hashabiah, his sons and
his brothers, twelve; 20 to the thirteenth,
Shubael, his sons and his brothers, twelve;
21 to the fourteenth, Mattithiah, his sons
and his brothers, twelve; 22 to the fifteenth,
to Jeremoth, his sons and his brothers,
twelve; 23 to the sixteenth, to Hananiah, his
sons and his brothers, twelve; 24 to the seventeenth, to Joshbekashah, his sons and
his brothers, twelve; 25 to the eighteenth, to
Hanani, his sons and his brothers, twelve;
26 to the nineteenth, to Mallothi, his sons
and his brothers, twelve; 27 to the twentieth, to Eliathah, his sons and his brothers,
twelve; 28 to the twenty-first, to Hothir, his
sons and his brothers, twelve; 29 to the
twenty-second, to Giddalti, his sons and his
brothers, twelve; 30 to the twenty-third, to
Mahazioth, his sons and his brothers,
twelve; 31 to the twenty-fourth, to Romamti-
ezer, his sons and his brothers, twelve.

Divisions of the Gatekeepers

26 As for the divisions of the gatekeepers: of the Korahites, Meshelemiah
the son of Kore, of the sons of Asaph.
2 And Meshelemiah had sons: [g]Zechariah

1 One Hebrew manuscript, Septuagint; most Hebrew manuscripts lack *Shimei*

24:31 just as their brothers. The equal treatment of all the families was a model to be followed by the readers in the period following the Babylonian exile (24:5 note). Possibly there was a controversy that required emphasis on this fairness.

Zadok. See notes 6:53 and 15:11.

25:1–31 The music of worship is mentioned many times in this chapter (15:16 note).

25:1 chiefs of the service. The name of David together with his captains recommends their assignments (11:10; 12:32) as a model for the organization of the community.

prophesied. Temple personnel are seen in prophetic roles on several occasions (2 Chr. 20:14–17; 24:19–22; 29:30; 35:15; cf. 2 Kin. 23:2 with 2 Chr. 34:30). This theme suggests the role of priests as guides for the restoration of the community after the return from exile in Babylon (Zech. 6:9–15).

25:8 cast lots for their duties. See note 24:5.

25:9–31 first . . . twenty-fourth. See note 24:7–18.

26:1–19 gatekeepers. The specific duties of gatekeepers are described in 9:22–29.

the firstborn, Jediael the second, Zebadiah the third, Jathniel the fourth, 3 Elam the fifth, Jehohanan the sixth, Eliehoenai the seventh. 4 And [h]Obed-edom had sons: Shemaiah the firstborn, Jehozabad the second, Joah the third, Sachar the fourth, Nethanel the fifth, 5 Ammiel the sixth, Issachar the seventh, Peullethai the eighth, [i]for God blessed him. 6 Also to his son Shemaiah were sons born who were rulers in their fathers' houses, for they were men of great ability. 7 The sons of Shemaiah: Othni, Rephael, Obed and Elzabad, whose brothers were able men, Elihu and Semachiah. 8 All these were of the sons of Obed-edom with their sons and brothers, able men qualified for the service; sixty-two of Obed-edom. 9 And Meshelemiah had sons and brothers, able men, eighteen. 10 And [j]Hosah, of the sons of Merari, had sons: Shimri the chief (for though he was not the firstborn, his father made him chief), 11 Hilkiah the second, Tebaliah the third, Zechariah the fourth: all the sons and brothers of Hosah were thirteen.

12 These divisions of the gatekeepers, corresponding to their chief men, had duties, just as their brothers did, ministering in the house of the LORD. 13 And they cast lots by fathers' houses, [k]small and great alike, for their gates. 14 The lot for the east fell to Shelemiah. They cast lots also for his son Zechariah, a shrewd counselor, and his lot came out for the north. 15 Obed-edom's came out for the south, and to his sons was allotted [l]the gatehouse. 16 For Shuppim and [j]Hosah it came out for the west, at the gate of Shallecheth on [m]the road that goes up. Watch corresponded to watch. 17 On the east there were six each day,[1] on the north four each day, on the south four each day, as well as two and two at the gatehouse. 18 And for the [n]colonnade[2] on the west there were four at [m]the road and two at the colonnade. 19 These were the divisions of the gatekeepers among the Korahites and the sons of Merari.

Treasurers and Other Officials

20 And of the Levites, Ahijah had charge of [o]the treasuries of the house of God and the treasuries of the dedicated gifts. 21 The sons of Ladan, the sons of the Gershonites belonging to Ladan, the heads of the fathers' houses belonging to Ladan the Gershonite: [p]Jehieli.[3]

22 [q]The sons of Jehieli, Zetham, and Joel his brother, were in charge of the treasuries of the house of the LORD. 23 [r]Of the Amramites, the Izharites, the Hebronites, and the Uzzielites— 24 and [s]Shebuel the son of Gershom, son of Moses, was chief officer in charge of the treasuries. 25 His brothers: from [t]Eliezer were his son Rehabiah, and his son [u]Jeshaiah, and his son Joram, and his son Zichri, and his son [v]Shelomoth. 26 This Shelomoth and his brothers were in charge of all the treasuries of the dedicated gifts that David the king and the heads of the fathers' houses and the officers of the thousands and the hundreds and the commanders of the army [w]had dedicated. 27 From spoil won in battles they dedicated gifts for the maintenance of the house of the LORD. 28 Also all that [x]Samuel the seer and Saul the son of Kish and Abner the son of Ner and Joab the son of Zeruiah had dedicated—all dedicated gifts were in the care of [v]Shelomoth[4] and his brothers.

29 Of the Izharites, Chenaniah and his sons were appointed to [y]external duties for Israel, [z]as officers and judges. 30 Of the Hebronites, [a]Hashabiah and his brothers, 1,700 men of ability, had the oversight of Israel westward of the Jordan for all the

4 [h]ch. 15:18, 24; 16:38
5 [i]ch. 13:14; 2 Sam. 6:11
10 [j]ch. 16:38
13 [k]ch. 25:8
15 [l]Neh. 12:25; [2 Chr. 25:24]
16 [j][See ver. 10 above] [m]1 Kin. 10:5; 2 Chr. 9:4; [Neh. 3:31]
18 [n]2 Kin. 23:11 [m][See ver. 16 above]
20 [o]ver. 22, 24, 26; ch. 28:12; Ezra 2:69; Neh. 10:38
21 [p][ch. 29:8]
22 [q][ch. 23:8]
23 [r]ch. 23:12
24 [s]ch. 23:16; [ch. 24:20]
25 [t][ch. 23:17] [u][ch. 24:21] [v][ch. 23:18]
26 [w]2 Sam. 8:11
28 [x]ch. 29:29; See 1 Sam 9:9 [v][See ver. 25 above]
29 [y]Neh. 11:16 [z]ch. 23:4; See Deut. 16:18
30 [a]ch. 27:17

1 Septuagint; Hebrew *six Levites* 2 Or *court*; Hebrew *parbar* (meaning unknown); twice in this verse 3 The Hebrew of verse 21 is uncertain 4 Hebrew *Shelomith*

26:4 Obed-edom. See note 13:13.

26:5 for God blessed him. Numerous children are a sign of divine blessing (13:13 note).

26:13–16 cast lots. For the casting of lots see note 24:5.

26:14 east. The main entrance to the temple, with six gatekeepers (26:17).

26:15 Obed-edom's came out for the south. The South Gate was the main entrance for the king. Obed-edom was highly honored by this assignment.

26:20 Levites. The Levites were given responsibilities in the temple (26:20–28) and away from Jerusalem (26:29–32).

treasuries. The temple was a storehouse of great wealth (29:6–9; 2 Chr. 4; 34:9–11; 36:7–19). The Levites were in charge of collecting and managing its extensive resources.

26:26–28 David . . . Samuel . . . Saul . . . Abner . . . Joab. Apparently, special attention was given to temple donations made by important figures.

26:29–32 Legal and administrative functions for Levites were established in Mosaic legislation (Deut. 17:8–13). See notes 2 Chr. 17:7, 8 and 19:5–11.

work of the LORD and for the service of the
king. 31 Of the Hebronites, [b]Jerijah was
chief of the Hebronites of whatever genealogy or fathers' houses. (In the fortieth year
of David's reign search was made and men
of great ability among them were found at
[c]Jazer in Gilead.) 32 King David appointed
him and his brothers, 2,700 men of ability,
heads of fathers' houses, to have the oversight of the Reubenites, the Gadites and
the half-tribe of the Manassites for everything pertaining to God and for [d]the affairs
of the king.

Military Divisions

27 This is the number of the people of
Israel, the heads of fathers' houses,
the commanders of thousands and hundreds, and their officers who served the
king in all matters concerning the divisions
that came and went, month after month
throughout the year, each division numbering 24,000:
2 [e]Jashobeam the son of Zabdiel was in
charge of the first division in the first
month; in his division were 24,000. 3 He
was a [f]descendant of Perez and was chief of
all the commanders. He served for the first
month. 4 [g]Dodai the Ahohite[1] was in charge
of the division of the second month; in his
division were 24,000. 5 The third commander, for the third month, was [h]Benaiah,
the son of Jehoiada the chief priest; in his
division were 24,000. 6 This is the Benaiah
[i]who was a mighty man of the thirty and in
command of the thirty; Ammizabad his son
was in charge of his division.[2] 7 [j]Asahel the
brother of Joab was fourth, for the fourth
month, and his son Zebadiah after him; in
his division were 24,000. 8 The fifth commander, for the fifth month, was
[k]Shamhuth the Izrahite; in his division were
24,000. 9 Sixth, for the sixth month, was
[l]Ira, the son of Ikkesh the Tekoite; in his
division were 24,000. 10 Seventh, for the
seventh month, was [m]Helez the Pelonite, of
the sons of Ephraim; in his division were
24,000. 11 Eighth, for the eighth month, was
[n]Sibbecai the Hushathite, of the Zerahites;
in his division were 24,000. 12 Ninth, for the
ninth month, was [o]Abiezer of Anathoth, a
Benjaminite; in his division were 24,000.
13 Tenth, for the tenth month, was [p]Maharai
of Netophah, of the Zerahites; in his division were 24,000. 14 Eleventh, for the
eleventh month, was [q]Benaiah of Pirathon,
of the sons of Ephraim; in his division were
24,000. 15 Twelfth, for the twelfth month,
was [r]Heldai the Netophathite, of [s]Othniel;
in his division were 24,000.

Leaders of Tribes

16 Over the tribes of Israel, for the
Reubenites, Eliezer the son of Zichri was
chief officer; for the Simeonites, Shephatiah the son of Maacah; 17 for Levi, [t]Hash-
abiah the son of Kemuel; for Aaron,
[u]Zadok; 18 for Judah, Elihu, one of David's
brothers; for Issachar, Omri the son of
Michael; 19 for Zebulun, Ishmaiah the son
of Obadiah; for Naphtali, Jeremoth the son
of Azriel; 20 for the Ephraimites, Hoshea the
son of Azaziah; for the half-tribe of
Manasseh, Joel the son of Pedaiah; 21 for
the half-tribe of Manasseh in Gilead,
Iddo the son of Zechariah; for Benjamin,
Jaasiel the son of Abner; 22 for Dan, Azarel
the son of Jeroham. These were the [v]lead-
ers of the tribes of Israel. 23 David did not
count those below twenty years of age, for
the [w]LORD had promised to make Israel as
many as the stars of heaven. 24 Joab the son
of Zeruiah began to count, but [x]did not finish. Yet [y]wrath came upon Israel for this,
and the number was not entered in the
chronicles of King David.
25 Over the king's treasuries was [z]Az-
maveth the son of Adiel; and over
the treasuries in the country, in the cities,
in the villages and in the towers, was

1 Septuagint; Hebrew *Ahohite and his division and Mikloth the chief officer* 2 Septuagint, Vulgate; Hebrew *was his division*

31 [b]ch. 24:23; [ch. 23:19] [c]ch. 6:81; Num. 21:32; Josh. 21:39
32 [d]2 Chr. 19:11
Chapter 27
2 [e]ch. 11:11; [2 Sam. 23:8]
3 [f]Num. 26:20
4 [g]2 Sam. 23:9; [ch.11:12]
5 [h]2 Sam. 8:18
6 [i]ch. 11:24, 25; 2 Sam. 23:20-28
7 [j]ch. 11:26; 2 Sam. 23:24
8 [k][ch. 11:27; 2 Sam. 23:25]
9 [l]ch. 11:28
10 [m]ch. 11:27
11 [n]ch. 11:29; 20:4; 2 Sam. 21:18
12 [o]ch.11:28
13 [p]ch. 11:30
14 [q]ch. 11:31
15 [r][2 Sam. 23:29] [s]ch. 4:13; Judg. 1:13; 3:9
17 [t]ch. 26:30 [u]ch. 24:3
22 [v]ch. 28:1
23 [w]See Gen. 15:5
24 [x][ch. 21:5, 6] [y]ch. 21:7; 2 Sam. 24:12-15
25 [z]ch 11:33; 2 Sam. 23:31

27:1–34 The writer turns to questions of military order (27:1–15), tribal heads (27:16–24), royal overseers (27:25–31), and royal counselors (27:32–34). David's extensive organization of his kingdom laid the groundwork for Solomon's temple project (22:5 note).

27:1 month after month. Military duties rotated much as did priestly responsibilities (24:7–18 note).

27:2 24,000. See note 12:23. Many officers listed here appear in a similar list in 11:11–47 (cf. 2 Sam. 23:8–39).

27:16–22 tribes of Israel. Gad and Asher are omitted, perhaps because Ephraim and the two halves of Manasseh are counted. The total remains twelve.

27:23, 24 These verses refer to David's census in 21:1–22:1 (2 Sam. 24). Because of God's reaction to the census, the count never became part of the official court record.

27:25–31 This is probably a partial list indicating how much property and wealth David had acquired in preparation for Solomon's construction of the temple (22:5 note).

Jonathan the son of Uzziah; 26 and over
those who did the work of the field for till-
ing the soil was Ezri the son of Chelub;
27 and over the vineyards was Shimei the
Ramathite; and over the produce of the
vineyards for the wine cellars was Zabdi
the Shiphmite. 28 Over the olive and [a]syc-
amore trees in the Shephelah was Baal-
hanan the Gederite; and over the stores of
oil was Joash. 29 Over the herds that pastured in [b]Sharon was Shitrai the Sharonite;
over the herds in the valleys was Shaphat
the son of Adlai. 30 Over the camels was
Obil the Ishmaelite; and over the donkeys
was Jehdeiah the Meronothite. Over the
flocks was Jaziz the [c]Hagrite. 31 All these
were stewards of King David's property.
32 Jonathan, David's uncle, was a counselor, being a man of understanding and a
scribe. He and Jehiel the son of Hachmoni
attended the king's sons. 33 [d]Ahithophel
was the [e]king's counselor, and Hushai the
Archite was the king's friend. 34 Ahithophel
was succeeded by Jehoiada the son of
[f]Benaiah, and [g]Abiathar. Joab was [h]com-
mander of the king's army.

David's Charge to Israel

28 [i]David assembled at Jerusalem all the
officials of Israel, the [j]officials of the
tribes, the officers of the divisions that served
the king, the [k]commanders of thousands, the
commanders of hundreds, the [l]stewards of
all the property and livestock of the king and
his sons, together with the palace officials,
the [m]mighty men and all the seasoned warriors. 2 Then King David rose to his feet and
said: "Hear me, my brothers and my people.
[n]I had it in my heart to build a house of rest
for the ark of the covenant of the LORD and
for the [o]footstool of our God, and I made
preparations for building. 3 But God said to
me, [p]'You may not build a house for my
name, for you are a man of war and have
shed blood.' 4 Yet the LORD God of Israel
[q]chose me from all my father's house to be
king over Israel [r]forever. [s]For he chose Judah
as leader, and in the house of Judah my
father's [t]house, and among my father's sons
he took pleasure in me to make me king over
all Israel. 5 And of [u]all my sons (for the LORD
has given me many sons) he [v]has chosen
Solomon my son to sit on the throne of the
kingdom of the LORD over Israel. 6 He said to
me, 'It is [w]Solomon your son who shall build
my house and my courts, for I have chosen
him to be my son, and I will be his father. 7 I
will establish his kingdom [r]forever [x]if he continues strong in keeping my commandments
and my rules, as he is today.' 8 Now therefore
in the sight of all Israel, the assembly of the
LORD, and in the hearing of our God, observe
and seek out all the commandments of the
LORD your God, that you may possess this
good land and leave it for an inheritance to
your children after you forever.

David's Charge to Solomon

9 "And you, Solomon my son, know the
God of your father and serve him with a
[y]whole heart and with a willing mind, [z]for
the LORD searches all hearts and understands
every plan and thought. [a]If you seek him, he
will be found by you, but if you forsake him,
he will cast you off forever. 10 Be careful now,
for the LORD has chosen you to build a house
for the sanctuary; [b]be strong and do it."
11 Then David gave Solomon his son the
[c]plan of the [d]vestibule of the temple,[1] and of
its houses, its treasuries, its upper rooms,
and its inner chambers, and of the room for
the [e]mercy seat; 12 and the plan of all that he
had in mind for the courts of the house of

[1] Hebrew lacks *of the temple*

28 [a]1 Kin. 10:27; 2 Chr. 1:15; 9:27
29 [b]ch. 5:16
30 [c]See ch. 5:10
33 [d]See 2 Sam. 15:12 [e]See 2 Sam. 15:37
34 [f][ver.5] [g]1 Kin. 1:7; [ch. 24:6] [h][ch. 11:6]
Chapter 28
1 [i]ch. 23:2 [j]See ch. 27:16-22 [k]See ch. 27:1-15 [l]See ch. 27:25-31 [m]See ch. 11:10-47
2 [n]See ch. 22:7 [o]Ps. 99:5; 132:7; Isai. 66:1; Lam. 2:1; [Ps. 110:1]
3 [p]See 2 Sam. 7:5, 13
4 [q]1 Sam. 16:12, 13 [r]ch. 17:23, 27 [s]ch. 5:2; Gen. 49:8; Ps. 78:68 [t]1 Sam. 16:1
5 [u]See ch.3:1-9; 14:3-7 [v]ch. 22:9; 23:1
6 [w]See 2 Sam. 7:13, 14
7 [r][See ver. 4 above] [x][ch. 22:13]
9 [y][1 Kin. 8:61] [z]See 1 Sam. 16:7 [a]See 2 Chr. 16:2
10 [b]ver. 20; Ezra 10:4; Hag. 2:4
11 [c]ver.19; See Ex. 25:40 [d]1 Kin. 6:3; 2 Chr. 3:4 [e]Ex. 25:17

27:32–34 A list of David's closest advisers (18:14–17) highlights the organizational preparations David made for Solomon's construction of the temple.

28:1–29:20 The writer describes David's final assembly in which he charged the officials of Israel and Solomon (ch. 28), collected contributions for the temple (29:1–9), and offered praise and petitions (29:10–20). See note 22:2–29:20.

28:1 all the officials of Israel. These are the officials listed in ch. 27, representing the entire nation (11:1 note).

28:3 my name. See note 13:6.

28:4, 8 all Israel. See note 11:1.

28:5 he has chosen. Solomon was designated as David's successor by divine election, not because of human maneuvering. Being chosen by God was the essential requirement for a legitimate Israelite king (Deut. 17:15).

28:6 my son. See note 17:13.

28:7 keeping my commandments and my rules. See note 16:40.

28:9 If you seek him . . . if you forsake him. Basic covenantal conditions apply to the promises given to David and his line. Though the Davidic dynasty itself would not be rejected, individual kings and the nation could suffer severely under God's judgment for apostasy. For similar expressions of this principle see 2 Chr. 6:14, 16; 7:17–22; 15:2; 16:7–9; 19:2, 3; 21:12–15; 24:20; 34:23–28. See also Introduction: Characteristics and Themes.

28:12 the plan. Although David actively planned for the temple, his efforts were directed by the Holy Spirit. This underlines the need for the community after the Babylonian exile to follow the patterns established for the temple by David and Solomon.

the LORD, all the surrounding chambers, [f]the
treasuries of the house of God, and the treasuries for dedicated gifts; 13 for the [g]divisions
of the priests and of the [h]Levites, and all the
work of the service in the house of the LORD;
for all the vessels for the service in the house
of the LORD, 14 the weight of gold for all gold-
en vessels for each service, the weight of silver vessels for each service, 15 the weight of
the golden [i]lampstands and their lamps, the
weight of gold for each lampstand and its
lamps, the weight of silver for a lampstand
and its lamps, according to the use of each
lampstand in the service, 16 the weight of gold
for each table for the showbread, the silver
for the silver tables, 17 and pure gold for the
forks, the basins and the cups; for the gold-
en bowls and the weight of each; for the silver bowls and the weight of each; 18 for the
[j]altar of incense made of refined gold, and its
weight; also his plan for the golden chariot of
the [k]cherubim that spread their wings and
covered the ark of the covenant of the LORD.
19 All this he made clear to me in writing from
the hand of the LORD, [l]all the work to be
done according to the plan.
20 Then David said to Solomon his son,
[m]"Be strong and courageous and do it. Do
not be afraid and do not be dismayed, for
the LORD God, even my God, is with you.
He will not leave you or forsake you, until
all the work for the service of the house of
the LORD is finished. 21 And behold the [n]di-
visions of the priests and the Levites for all
the service of the house of God; and with
you in all the work will be [o]every willing
man who has skill for any kind of service;
also the officers and all the people will be
wholly at your command."

Offerings for the Temple

29 And David the king said to all the
assembly, "Solomon my son, whom
alone God has chosen, is [p]young and inexperienced, and the work is great, for [q]the
palace will not be for man but for the LORD
God. 2 So I have provided for the house of my
God, so far as I was able, the gold for the
things of gold, the silver for the things of silver, and the bronze for the things of bronze,
the iron for the things of iron, and wood for
the things of wood, besides great quantities
of [r]onyx and stones for setting, antimony,
colored stones, all sorts of precious stones
and marble. 3 Moreover, in addition to all
that I have provided for the holy house, I
have a treasure of my own of gold and silver,
and because of my devotion to the house of
my God I give it to the house of my God:
4 [s]3,000 talents[1] of gold, of the gold of
[t]Ophir, and 7,000 talents of refined silver,
for overlaying the walls of the house,[2] 5 and
for all the work to be done by craftsmen,
gold for the things of gold and silver for the
things of silver. Who then will offer willingly,
consecrating himself[3] today to the LORD?"
6 Then [u]the leaders of fathers' houses
made their freewill offerings, as did also the
leaders of the tribes, the commanders of
thousands and of hundreds, and [v]the officers over the king's work. 7 They gave for the
service of the house of God 5,000 talents
and 10,000 [w]darics[4] of gold, 10,000 talents
of silver, 18,000 talents of bronze and
100,000 talents of iron. 8 And whoever had
precious stones gave them to the treasury of
the house of the LORD, in the care of [x]Jehiel
the Gershonite. 9 Then the people rejoiced
because they had given willingly, for with a
[y]whole heart they had offered freely to the
LORD. David the king also rejoiced greatly.

David Prays in the Assembly

10 Therefore David blessed the LORD in
the presence of all the assembly. And

12 [f]See ch. 26:20
13 [g]ch. 24:1 [h]ch. 23:6
15 [i]See Ex. 25:31-37
18 [j]See Ex. 30:1 [k]See Ex. 25:18-22; 1 Kin. 6:23-28
19 [l]ver. 11, 12; Ex. 25:40
20 [m]See ch. 22:13; Josh. 1:5
21 [n]ver. 13; See ch. 24-26 [o][Ex. 35:25, 26; 36:1, 2]
Chapter 29
1 [p]ch. 22:5; [1 Kin. 3:7] [q]ver. 19
2 [r][Isai. 54:11, 12; Rev. 21:19-21]
4 [s][ch.22:14] [t]See 1 Kin. 9:28
6 [u]ch. 27:1; 28:1 [v]See ch. 27:25-31
7 [w]Ezra 2:69; 8:27; Neh. 7:70-72
8 [x]ch. 23:8; [ch. 26:21]
9 [y][2 Kin. 12:4; 2 Cor. 9:7]

1 A *talent* was about 75 pounds or 34 kilograms 2 Septuagint; Hebrew *houses* 3 Or *ordaining himself*; Hebrew *filling his hand*
4 A *daric* was a coin weighing about 1/4 ounce or 8.5 grams

28:20 Be strong and courageous. The language resembles Joshua's commission (22:13 note).

28:21 will be wholly at your command. David's organization of the priests, Levites, and artisans was for the sake of building Solomon's temple (22:5 note).

29:1–9 David followed Moses' example in asking for contributions to the temple project (Ex. 25:1–8; 35:4–9, 20–29). These directions would remind the exiles returned from Babylon of the importance of continuing contributions to the new temple (Hag. 1:2–11; Mal. 3:8–10). See notes 2 Chr. 24:10–12.

29:1 young and inexperienced. See note 22:5.

29:2–5 David declared the purpose behind his previous accomplishments. All was done to prepare for Solomon's temple (22:5; 27:1–34 and notes).

29:3 I have a treasure . . . I give it. David gave from his own wealth in addition to the spoils of war (18:8, 11; 2 Chr. 30:24 and notes). David served as an example of generous contribution to the temple (29:18 note).

29:7 darics. The daric was a Persian coin used in the Chronicler's day. He uses this terminology for the sake of his readers (Introduction: Author).

29:10–19 David praises God for what has been accomplished (29:10–13) and asks for continued empowerment of the people and of Solomon (29:14–19).

David said: [z]"Blessed are you, O LORD, the
God of Israel our father, forever and ever.
11 [a]Yours, O LORD, is the greatness and the
power and the glory and the victory and
the majesty, for all that is in the heavens
and in the earth is yours. Yours is the kingdom, O LORD, and you are exalted as head
above all. 12 [b]Both riches and honor come
from you, and you rule over all. [c]In your
hand are power and might, and in your
hand it is to make great and to give
strength to all. 13 And now we thank you,
our God, and praise your glorious name.
14 "But who am I, and what is my people, that we should be able thus to offer
willingly? For all things come from you,
and of your own have we given you. 15 [d]For
we are strangers before you and sojourners, as all our fathers were. Our days on
the earth are [e]like a shadow, and there is
no abiding.[1] 16 O LORD our God, all this
abundance that we have provided for
building you a house for your holy name
comes from your hand and is all your
own. 17 I know, my God, [f]that you test the
heart and [g]have pleasure in uprightness.
In the uprightness of my heart I have
freely offered all these things, and now I
have seen your people, who are present
here, offering freely and joyously to you.
18 O LORD, the God of Abraham, Isaac, and
Israel, our fathers, keep forever such purposes and thoughts in the hearts of your

10 [z]Luke 1:68
11 [a][1 Tim. 1:17; Rev. 5:13]
12 [b][1 Kin. 3:13; 2 Chr. 1:12; Rom. 11:36]
[c]2 Chr. 20:6
15 [d]See Lev. 25:23
[e]Job 14:2; Ps. 102:11; 144:4
17 [f]ch. 28:9; Prov. 17:3; [1 Sam. 16:7]
[g][Prov. 11:20]

[1] Septuagint, Vulgate; Hebrew *hope*, or *prospect*

The Greatness of God

God is great (Deut. 7:21; Neh. 4:14; Ps. 48:1; 86:10; 95:3; 145:3; Dan. 9:4), greater than we can grasp. Theology states this truth by describing Him as "incomprehensible"—not that He is irrational or illogical, so as to prevent us from following His thoughts at all, but that our minds cannot contain Him, because He is infinite and we are finite. Scripture portrays God not only as dwelling in thick and impenetrable darkness, but also as dwelling in unapproachable light (Ps. 97:2; 1 Tim. 6:16). These two images express the same thought: our Creator is above us, and it is beyond our power to take His measure.

God tells us in the Bible that creation, providence, the Trinity, the incarnation, the regenerating work of the Spirit, union with Christ in His death and resurrection, and the inspiration of Scripture—to go no further—are facts, and we accept them on the strength of His word, without knowing how they can be. As creatures, we are unable fully to comprehend either the being or the actions of the Creator.

As it would be wrong, however, to suppose ourselves to know everything about God (and so in effect to imprison Him in the box of our own limited notion of Him), so it would be wrong to doubt that our concept of God constitutes real knowledge of Him. One of the consequences of being made in God's image is that we are able both to know about Him and to know Him relationally, in a true if limited way. Calvin speaks of God as condescending to our weakness and accommodating Himself to our incapacity, both in the inspiration of the Scriptures and the incarnation of the Son, in order to give us genuine understanding of Himself. By analogy, the form and substance of a parent's baby-talk bears no comparison with the full contents of the parent's mind, which might be expressed in conversation with another adult; but still the child receives true information about the parent from the baby-talk, and responds with growing love and trust.

This is why the Creator presents Himself to us anthropomorphically, as having a face (Ex. 33:11), ears (Neh. 1:6), and eyes (Job 28:10); or as having feet (Nah. 1:3), sitting on a throne (1 Kin. 22:19), flying on the wind (Ps. 18:10), or fighting in battle (2 Chr. 32:8; Is. 63:1–6). These are not descriptions of what God is in Himself, but of what He is to us: the transcendent Lord who relates to His people as Father and Friend. God comes to us in this way to draw us out in love and trust, even though in a way we are always like little children who understand only in part (1 Cor. 13:12).

We should never forget that the purpose of theology is doxology; we study in order to praise. The truest expression of trust in God will always be worship, and it will always be proper worship to praise God for being greater than we know.

29:11 Yours, O LORD. This is probably the source of the longer ending of the Lord's prayer (Matt. 6:13; cf. Luke 11:4). See theological note "The Greatness of God."

29:14–16 Although David worked hard to prepare for Solomon's temple, he acknowledged that all of his accomplishments came from the sovereign hand of God. David saw himself as powerless and hopeless apart from God's blessing (2 Chr. 1:9; 20:6, 12).

29:14 who am I. See note 17:16; 2 Chr. 2:6.

29:16 name. See note 13:6.

29:18 keep forever. David's words speak directly to the readers of a later time, who must continue to give freely to temple worship.

people, and direct their hearts toward
you. 19 [h]Grant to Solomon my son a whole
heart that he may keep your commandments, your testimonies, and your
statutes, performing all, and that he may
[i]build the palace [j]for which I have made
provision."
20 Then David said to all the assembly,
[k]"Bless the LORD your God." And all the
assembly blessed the LORD, the God of
their fathers, [l]and bowed their heads and
paid homage to the LORD and to the king.
21 And they offered sacrifices to the LORD,
and on the next day offered burnt offerings
to the LORD, 1,000 bulls, 1,000 rams, and
1,000 lambs, with their [m]drink offerings,
and sacrifices in abundance for all Israel.
22 And they ate and drank before the LORD
on that day with great gladness.

Solomon Anointed King

And they made Solomon the son of
David king [n]the second time, and they
[o]anointed him as prince for the LORD, and
[p]Zadok as priest.
23 [q]Then Solomon sat on the [r]throne of
the LORD as king in place of David his
father. And he prospered, and all Israel
obeyed him. 24 All the leaders and the
mighty men, and also all the sons of King
David, pledged their allegiance to King
Solomon. 25 And the LORD made Solomon
very [s]great in the sight of all Israel and
[t]bestowed on him such royal majesty as
had not been on any king before him in
Israel.

The Death of David

26 Thus David the son of Jesse reigned
over all Israel. 27 The [u]time that he reigned
over Israel was forty years. He reigned seven
years in Hebron and thirty-three years in
Jerusalem. 28 Then he died [v]at a good age,
[w]full of days, riches, and honor. And
Solomon his son reigned in his place.
29 Now the acts of King David, from first to
last, are written in the Chronicles [x]of
Samuel the seer, and in the Chronicles of
[y]Nathan the prophet, and in the Chronicles of [z]Gad the seer, 30 with accounts of all
his rule and his might and of the circum-
stances [a]that came upon him and upon
Israel and upon all the kingdoms of the
countries.

19 [h][Ps. 72:1] [i]ver. 1, 2 [j]ch. 22:14
20 [k]See Josh. 22:33 [l]See Ex. 4:31
21 [m]Gen. 35:14
22 [n][ch. 23:1] [o]See 1 Kin. 1:38-39 [p]1 Kin. 2:35
23 [q]1 Kin. 2:12 [r]ch. 28:5; [2 Chr. 9:8]
25 [s]2 Chr. 1:1; [Josh. 3:7] [t]1Kin. 3:13; 2 Chr. 1:12; [Eccles. 2:9]
27 [u]2 Sam. 5:4, 5; 1 Kin. 2:11
28 [v][Gen. 15:15; 25:8] [w]ch. 23:1
29 [x]ch. 26:28; [1 Sam. 9:9] [y]See 2 Sam. 12:1 [z]See 1 Sam. 22:5
30 [a][Dan. 4:23, 25]

29:19 keep Your commandments. See note 16:40.

29:21–25 The transfer of power to Solomon culminates in a grand celebration of sacrifice (v. 21), feasting (v. 22), and national harmony (vv. 22–25). See note 23:1.

29:22 the second time. This phrase is omitted from some ancient translations, possibly because its exact reference is hard to determine. It may be that 1 Kin. 1:32–36 is the first anointing, accomplished in private and followed by the more public one. Both Saul (1 Sam. 10:1; 11:14–15) and David (1 Sam. 16:13; 2 Sam. 2:4; 5:3) received more than one anointing.

Zadok as priest. The writer associates closely the Davidic monarchy and the Zadokite priestly line (6:1 note).

29:24 pledged their allegiance. The writer omits discussion of the attempted rebellion of Adonijah (1 Kin. 1), apparently counting it as a failed attempt that does not color the unanimity of support for Solomon.

29:25 had not been on any king before him. Especially in the building of the temple, Solomon's reign was more glorious than his father David's.

29:29, 30 the Chronicles of. The writer of Chronicles refers to several sources for David's reign, in addition to the books of Samuel and Kings (see Introduction).

THE SECOND BOOK OF THE

Chronicles

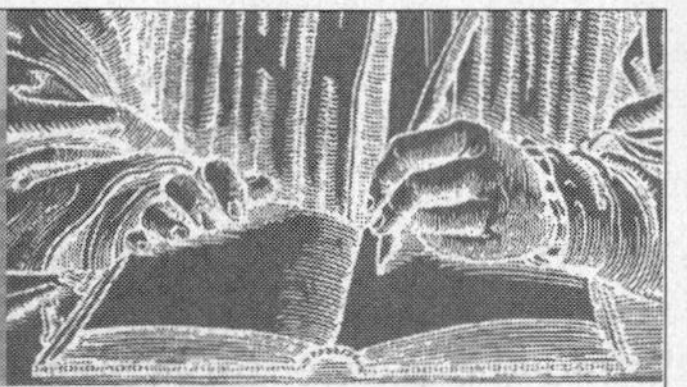

AUTHOR

Early Jewish tradition regarded Ezra as the author of the Chronicles, but it is doubtful that the work can be decisively dated within his lifetime (see "Date and Occasion"). The book is widely considered to be by an anonymous author, usually called "the Chronicler," who composed his history of Israel and Judah by drawing on a number of biblical (e.g., Samuel and Kings) and extra-biblical sources (e.g., the no longer extant writings of Nathan, Ahijah, and Iddo, 9:29). See "Introduction to 1 Chronicles: Author."

DATE AND OCCASION

Chronicles was written to encourage and guide the community that had returned from exile in Babylonia as they sought to reestablish their lives as the people of God in the land He had promised to the patriarchs. Exactly when in this period of restoration the book was completed, however, is difficult to ascertain. Although some evidence points to the social and political situation among the first groups of returnees, the genealogies in the early part of the book (see especially 1 Chr. 3:17–24 and notes) suggest a date shortly after the ministries of Ezra and Nehemiah, c. 400 B.C. (see "Introduction to 1 Chronicles").

CHARACTERISTICS AND THEMES

The Chronicler retells the history of Israel and Judah in order to provide theological answers to three fundamental questions which arose after the Jews returned from exile in Babylonia. How can it be known who are the heirs to God's covenant promises after the dislocation of exile and return? What was to become of their central political and religious institutions, the Davidic throne and the Jerusalem temple, and how would they be related to one another in the restored community? Thirdly, how were the people to understand the experience of exile and restoration in the light of God's law and grace, His judgment and forgiveness? The discussion of these themes begun in the Introduction to 1 Chronicles is continued here with respect to 2 Chronicles.

The United Monarchy under Solomon (1:1–9:31). The opening section of 2 Chronicles depicts Solomon as the divinely blessed successor of David. The Chronicler passes over Solomon's struggle for power (1 Chr. 23:1 note) and his later downfall due to intermarriage (1 Kin. 11:1–40). He shows Solomon as the king of "all Israel" (1 Chr. 11:1 note), and as the prime instrument for constructing the temple in Jerusalem (2:1–8:16). There is a brief notice of his death (9:29–31).

Solomon's reign is narrated in a topical and symmetrical form, opening and closing with passages describing the king's wisdom and wealth (ch. 1; 9:13–28). Just inside these passages are sections about his international relations (ch. 2; 8:17–9:12). Inserted between these passages are sections about the building of the temple and Solomon's other projects throughout Israel (3:1–5:1; 8:1–16), and in the center is the description of the temple dedication (5:2–7:10) and the divine response to it (7:12–22). A concentric outline of this kind emphasizes the topics in the middle, in this case the dedication of the temple.

The Divided Kingdom (10:1–28:26). The record of Israel's history from Rehoboam to Ahaz focuses on events in the southern kingdom of Judah. Although the Book of Kings is the source of much of the information, Chronicles omits large blocks of material dealing with the northern kingdom of Israel. The focus of

Chronicles is Judah and its capital Jerusalem, the place of the Davidic king and the temple of God.

The kings of the period are measured by the ideal of the united monarchy. The king must be faithful to the Law of Moses; he must support the temple order established by David and Solomon; and he must listen to prophetic and priestly instruction. Some kings are evaluated negatively (Jehoram, 21:4–20; Ahaziah, 22:1–9; Ahaz, 28:1–27), others positively (Abijah, 13:1–14:1; Jotham, 27:1–9). For the most part the records are mixed (Rehoboam, 10:1–12:16; Asa, 14:2–16:14; Jehoshaphat, 17:1–21:3; Joash, 22:10–24:27; Amaziah, 25:1–28; Uzziah, 26:1–23).

God blessed His people when they were faithful, and chastised them when they turned away from Him. Victory, security, and prosperity came to those who sought the Lord. Defeat, trouble, and illness came upon those who forgot Him.

The Reunited Kingdom (29:1–36:23). Beginning with Hezekiah, Israel entered a new phase of her history. Like David and Solomon, Hezekiah was able to unite the faithful of Israel and Judah around the Davidic throne through worship and celebration at the temple (29:1 note and 29:24 note). This reunited people experienced periods of failure: Manasseh's apostasy (33:1–10), the reign of Amon (33:21–25), and the kings of Judah just before the Babylonian exile (36:2–14). But each failure was followed by God's gracious renewal of the people: Manasseh's restoration (33:11–17), Josiah's reforms (34:3–35:19), and the return from exile in Babylonia (36:22–23).

Despite the failures of the reunited kingdom, God continued to grant blessings to His repentant people. He extended His mercy to them, offering them His blessing. At the same time, the events of the period demonstrate the requirements placed on those who longed for the full restoration of the kingdom. The nation must turn to the Lord in humility and live faithfully before Him.

OUTLINE OF 2 CHRONICLES

(Continued from Outline of 1 Chronicles)

II. The United Monarchy (1 Chr. 9:35–2 Chr. 9:31)

- A. *Saul (1 Chr. 9:35–10:14)*
- B. *David (1 Chr. 11–29)*
- C. *Solomon (2 Chr. 1–9)*
  1. Wisdom and Wealth (ch. 1)
  2. International Assistance (ch. 2)
  3. Temple Building and Furnishings (3:1–5:1)
  4. Temple Dedication (5:2–7:11)
  5. Divine Response to Dedication (7:12–22)
  6. Conclusion to Temple Building (8:1–16)
  7. International Recognition (8:17–9:12)
  8. Wisdom and Wealth (9:13–28)
  9. End of Reign and Death (9:29–31)

III. The Divided Kingdom (2 Chr. 10–28)

- A. *Rehoboam (chs. 10–12)*
- B. *Abijah (13:1–14:1)*
- C. *Asa (14:2–16:14)*
- D. *Jehoshaphat (17:1–21:1)*
- E. *Jehoram (21:2–20)*
- F. *Ahaziah (22:1–9)*
- G. *Athaliah (22:10–23:15)*
- H. *Joash (23:16–24:27)*
- I. *Amaziah (ch. 25)*
- J. *Uzziah (ch. 26)*
- K. *Jotham (ch. 27)*
- L. *Ahaz (ch. 28)*

IV. The Reunited Kingdom (2 Chr. 29–36)

- A. *Hezekiah (chs. 29–32)*
- B. *Manasseh (33:1–20)*
- C. *Amon (33:21–25)*
- D. *Josiah (chs. 34; 35)*
- E. *Josiah's Successors (36:1–14)*
- F. *Exile and Release (36:15–23)*

Solomon Worships at Gibeon

1 [a]Solomon the son of David established
himself in his kingdom, [b]and the LORD
his God was with him and made him
exceedingly great.
2 Solomon spoke to all Israel, to the [c]com-
manders of thousands and of hundreds, to
the judges, and to all the leaders in all Israel,
the heads of fathers' houses. 3 And Solomon,
and all the assembly with him, went to [d]the
high place that was at Gibeon, [e]for [f]the tent
of meeting of God, which Moses the servant
of the LORD had made in the wilderness, was
there. 4 [g](But David had brought up the ark
of God from Kiriath-jearim to the place that
David had prepared for it, for he had pitched
a tent for it in Jerusalem.) 5 Moreover, [h]the
bronze altar that [i]Bezalel the son of Uri, son
of Hur, had made, was there before the tabernacle of the LORD. And Solomon and the
assembly [j]resorted to it. 6 And Solomon went
up there to the bronze altar before the LORD,
which was at the tent of meeting, [k]and
offered a thousand burnt offerings on it.

Solomon Prays for Wisdom

7 [l]In that night God appeared to Solomon,
and said to him, "Ask what I shall give you."
8 And Solomon said to God, "You have
shown great and steadfast love to David my
father, [m]and have made me king in his
place. 9 O LORD God, [n]let your word to David
my father be now fulfilled, for you have
made me king over a people as numerous
[o]as the dust of the earth. 10 Give me now wisdom and knowledge to [p]go out and come in
before this people, for who can govern this
people of yours, which is so great?" 11 God
answered Solomon, "Because this was in
your heart, and you have not asked [q]posses-
sions, wealth, honor, or the life of those who
hate you, and have not even asked long life,
but have asked wisdom and knowledge for
yourself that you may govern my people
over whom I have made you king, 12 wisdom
and knowledge are granted to you. I will
also give you [q]riches, possessions, and
honor, [r]such as none of the kings had who
were before you, and none after you shall
have the like." 13 So Solomon came from[1]
the [s]high place at Gibeon, from before [t]the
tent of meeting, to Jerusalem. And he
reigned over Israel.

Solomon Given Wealth

14 [u]Solomon gathered together chariots
and horsemen. [v]He had 1,400 chariots and
12,000 horsemen, whom he stationed [w]in
the chariot cities and with the king in
Jerusalem. 15 And the king made silver and
gold as common in Jerusalem as stone, and
he made cedar as plentiful as the sycamore
of the Shephelah. 16 And Solomon's import
of horses was from Egypt and Kue, and the
king's traders would buy them from Kue
for a price. 17 They imported a chariot from
Egypt for 600 shekels[2] of silver, and a
horse for 150. Likewise through them
these were exported to all the kings of the
Hittites and the kings of Syria.

[1] Septuagint, Vulgate; Hebrew *to* [2] A *shekel* was about 2/5 ounce or 11 grams

Chapter 1
1 [a]1 Kin.2:46 [b]1 Chr. 29:25
2 [c]1 Chr. 27:1
3 [d]See 1 Kin. 3:4 [e]1 Chr. 16:39; 21:29 [f]Ex. 29:10; Lev. 10:7; Num. 14:10
4 [g]See 2 Sam. 6:2-17; 1 Chr. 15:25– 16:1
5 [h]Ex. 27:1, 2; 38:1, 2 [i]Ex. 31:2 [j][1 Chr. 13:3]
6 [k]1 Kin. 3:4
7 [l]For ver. 7-12, see 1 Kin. 3:5-14
8 [m]1 Chr. 28:5
9 [n]ch. 6:17; 1 Kin. 8:26 [o]Gen. 13:16
10 [p][Num. 27:17; Deut. 31:2]
11 [q] Eccles. 5:19; 6:2
12 [q] [See ver. 11 above] [r]ch. 9:22; [1 Chr. 29:25]
13 [s]See 1 Kin. 3:4 [t]ver. 3
14 [u]For ver. 14-17, see ch. 9:25-28; 1 Kin. 10:26-29 [v][1 Kin. 4:26] [w][1 Kin. 9:19]

1:1–17 This section is balanced by a parallel section on Solomon's wisdom and wealth (9:13–28).

1:1 established himself. The historian frequently uses expressions like this to indicate success after difficulty (12:13; 13:21; 17:1; 25:11; 27:6). Indirectly he acknowledges that Solomon's rise to power was tumultuous, although he omits the details given in 1 Kin. 2 (1 Chr. 23:1 note).

God was with him. Solomon's success was the result of God's sovereign blessing in fulfillment of David's hopes (1 Chr. 22:11, 16; 28:20).

1:2–13 This passage roughly follows 1 Kin. 3:4–15, but the account is expanded somewhat, emphasizing the theme of Solomon's reign over "all Israel" (v. 2) and explaining why Solomon went to Gibeon to sacrifice (vv. 3–6).

1:2 all Israel. See note 1 Chr. 11:1.

1:5 Bezalel. In the course of building the temple, Solomon emerges as a kind of counterpart of Bezalel who had helped construct the tabernacle. See notes 1 Chr. 2:20 and Ex. 31:1–11.

1:7 appeared . . . said. As does the Book of 1 Kings, Chronicles reports that God spoke directly to Solomon in dreams (7:12). Solomon, like David, was an instrument of revelation for Israel (1 Chr. 22:8; 28:6, 19).

1:9 let your word to David my father be now fulfilled. This request ties the reign of Solomon to David (1 Chr. 17:1–15 note; 22:5 note). Solomon depended fully on God for the ability to carry out his role as king (cf. 1 Chr. 29:14–16 note).

as numerous as the dust of the earth. Solomon recognized the multiplication of Israel as fulfillment of God's promise to Abraham (Gen. 13:16; 22:17). The promise would encourage readers in the time following the Babylonian exile to hope for successful repopulation of the Promised Land in their own day (Neh. 1:8, 9; Zech. 8:7, 8).

1:10 wisdom. The splendor and power of Solomon's reign was the result of divinely bestowed wisdom. In his wisdom Solomon foreshadowed Christ, who is the Wisdom of God incarnate (Is. 11:1, 2; Col. 2:3).

1:13 The account in Kings ends with Solomon's sacrifice in Jerusalem (1 Kin. 3:15). Passing over this as well as Solomon's judgment between the two mothers (1 Kin. 3:16–28), Chronicles focuses on Solomon's temple construction as a demonstration of his wisdom.

1:14–17 God kept His promise to make Solomon wealthy (v. 12). This passage is connected with its parallel (9:13–28) in the overall narrative by the repetition of the topic of horse trade (compare 1:14, 16, 17 with 9:25–28) and abundance of "silver and gold" like "stone" and "cedar" as common as sycamore trees (1:15; 9:27).

Preparing to Build the Temple

2 [1] [x]Now Solomon purposed to build a
temple for the name of the LORD, and a
royal palace for himself. **2** [2] [y]And Solomon
assigned 70,000 men to bear burdens and
80,000 to quarry in the hill country, and
[z]3,600 to oversee them. **3** [a]And Solomon
sent word to Hiram the king of Tyre: [b]"As
you dealt with David my father and sent him
cedar to build himself a house to dwell in,
so deal with me. **4** Behold, I am about to
build a house for the name of the LORD my
God and dedicate it to him for the burning
of [c]incense of sweet spices before him, and
for [d]the regular arrangement of the showbread, and for [e]burnt offerings morning and
evening, [f]on the Sabbaths and the new
moons and the appointed feasts of the LORD
our God, as ordained forever for Israel. **5** The
house that I am to build will be great, [g]for
our God is greater than all gods. **6** [h]But who
is able to build him a house, since [h]heaven,
even highest heaven, cannot contain him?
Who am I to build a house for him, except
as a place to make offerings before him? **7** So
now [i]send me a man skilled to work in gold,
silver, bronze, and iron, and in purple, crimson, and blue fabrics, trained also in engraving, to be with the skilled workers who are
with me in Judah and Jerusalem, [j]whom
David my father provided. **8** Send me also
cedar, cypress, and algum timber from
Lebanon, for I know that [k]your servants
know how to cut timber in Lebanon. And
my servants will be with your servants, **9** to
prepare timber for me in abundance, for the
house I am to build will be great and wonderful. **10** [l]I will give for your servants, the
woodsmen who cut timber, 20,000 cors[3] of
crushed wheat, 20,000 cors of barley, 20,000
baths[4] of wine, and 20,000 baths of oil."
11 Then Hiram the king of Tyre answered in
a letter that he sent to Solomon, [m]"Because
the LORD loves his people, he has made you
king over them." **12** Hiram also said, "Blessed
be the LORD God of Israel, [n]who made heav-
en and earth, who has given King David a
wise son, who has discretion and understanding, [o]who will build a temple for the
LORD and a royal palace for himself.
13 "Now I have sent a skilled man, who
has understanding, Huram-abi, **14** [p]the son of
a woman of the daughters of Dan, and his
father was a man of Tyre. He is [q]trained to
work in gold, silver, bronze, iron, stone, and
wood, and in purple, blue, and crimson fabrics and fine linen, and to do all sorts of
engraving and execute any design that may
be assigned him, with your craftsmen, the
craftsmen of my lord, David your father.
15 Now therefore the wheat and barley, oil
and wine, [r]of which my lord has spoken, let
him send to his servants. **16** [s]And we will cut
whatever timber you need from Lebanon
and bring it to you in rafts by sea to [t]Joppa,
so that you may take it up to Jerusalem."
17 Then Solomon counted all the resident
aliens who were in the land of Israel, [u]after
the census of them that David his father
had taken, and there were found 153,600.
18 [v]Seventy thousand of them he assigned to
bear burdens, 80,000 to quarry in the hill
country, and 3,600 as overseers to make
the people work.

Solomon Builds the Temple

3 [w]Then Solomon began to build the
house of the LORD in Jerusalem [x]on

[1] Ch 1:18 in Hebrew [2] Ch 2:1 in Hebrew [3] A *cor* was about 6 bushels or 220 liters [4] A *bath* was about 6 gallons or 22 liters

Chapter 2
1 [x]1 Kin. 5:5
2 [y]ver. 18; 1 Kin. 5:15; 16; [ch. 8:7, 8; 1 Kin. 9:20; 21] [z][1 Kin. 5:16]
3 [a]For ver. 3-16, see 1 Kin. 5:2-11 [b]1 Chr. 14:1
4 [c]See Ex. 30:7 [d]See Lev. 24:5-8 [e]See Num. 28:3-8 [f]ch. 8:13; Num. 28:9, 11, 19, 26
5 [g]Ps. 135:5; [Ex. 15:11; 1 Chr. 16:25; Ps. 86:8]
6 [h]ch. 6:18; 1 Kin. 8:27; Isai. 66:1; Acts 7:49
7 [i]ver. 13, 14 [j]1 Chr. 22:15
8 [k]ch. 9:10; 11
10 [l][1 Kin. 5:11]
11 [m]ch. 9:8; 1 Kin. 10:9
12 [n]See Gen. 1:1 [o][ver. 1]
14 [p]1 Kin. 7:14 [q][ver. 7]
15 [r]ver. 10
16 [s][1 Kin. 5:9] [t]See Josh. 19:46
17 [u][1 Chr. 22:2]
18 [v]See ver. 2
Chapter 3
1 [w]For ver. 1, 2, see 1 Kin. 6:1 [x]Gen. 22:2, 14

2:1–18 Solomon's most prominent work in the Chronicles is the building of the temple. The mention of the temple and palace (v. 1) and Hiram (v. 3) connects this passage with the parallel account in 8:1–16.

2:1 name. See note 1 Chr. 13:6.

royal palace for himself. Solomon's palace is mentioned on several occasions (2:12; 7:11; 8:1; 9:3, 11), but there is no description of its elaborate construction as in 1 Kin. 7:1–12. Attention is focused on the temple.

2:2 assigned 70,000 men. See note 1 Chr. 22:2.

2:3 David my father. This account of Solomon's message to Hiram makes it clear that David laid the foundation on which Solomon is building (v. 7; and cf. 1 Kin. 5:3–5). See note 1 Chr. 22:5.

2:4 name. See note 1 Chr. 13:6.

as ordained forever for Israel. This is a reminder that Solomon's temple services were to be observed in their day.

2:6 cannot contain him. Solomon recognized that his temple was incapable of containing the omnipresent Creator (6:18). Nevertheless, the splendor of the temple must reflect the greatness of God.

Who am I. Solomon recognized he was unworthy of God's blessing, as his father had been before him (1 Chr. 17:16 note).

2:11 Because the LORD loves his people. The establishment of the Davidic line was an act of divine love toward Israel (1 Chr. 14:2 note).

2:12 wise son. This verse makes it explicit that Solomon's wisdom was visible in his construction of the temple (1:13 note).

2:14 Dan. 1 Kin. 7:14 reports that the mother of Huram-abi (Hebrew *Hiram)* was from Naphtali. She may have been from Dan but living in Naphtali.

2:17, 18 aliens . . . to bear burdens . . . to quarry . . . overseers to make the people work. See note 1 Chr. 22:2.

Mount Moriah, where the LORD[1] had
appeared to David his father, at the place
that David had appointed, [y]on the threshing floor of Ornan the Jebusite. 2 He began
to build in the second month of the fourth
year of his reign. 3 These are Solomon's
[z]measurements[2] for building the house of
God: [a]the length, in cubits[3] of the old standard, was sixty cubits, and the breadth
twenty cubits. 4 The vestibule in front of the
nave of the house was twenty cubits long,
equal to the width of the house,[4] and its
height was 120 cubits. He overlaid it on
the inside with pure gold. 5 [b]The nave he
lined with cypress and covered it with fine
gold [c]and made palms and chains on it.
6 He adorned the house with settings of
precious stones. The gold was gold of
Parvaim. 7 So he lined the house with
gold—its beams, its thresholds, its walls,
and its doors—[c]and he carved cherubim
on the walls.
8 [d]And he made the Most Holy Place. Its
length, corresponding to the breadth of the
house, was twenty cubits, and its breadth
was twenty cubits. He overlaid it with 600
talents[5] of fine gold. 9 The weight of gold
for the nails was fifty shekels.[6] And he
overlaid [e]the upper chambers with gold.
10 [f]In the Most Holy Place he made two
cherubim of wood[7] and overlaid[8] them
with gold. 11 The wings of the cherubim
together extended twenty cubits: one wing
of the one, of five cubits, touched the wall
of the house, and its other wing, of five
cubits, touched the wing of the other
cherub; 12 and of this cherub, one wing, of
five cubits, touched the wall of the house,
and the other wing, also of five cubits, was
joined to the wing of the first cherub. 13 The
wings of these cherubim extended twenty

1 [y][1 Chr. 21:15, 18, 28]
3 [z][Ezra 3:11] [a]For ver. 3, 4, see 1 Kin. 6:2, 3
5 [b]1 Kin. 6:17 [c]1 Kin. 6:29, 32
7 [c][See ver. 5 above]
8 [d][1 Kin. 6:16]
9 [e]1 Chr. 28:11
10 [f]For ver. 10-13, see 1 Kin. 6:23-28

1 Septuagint; Hebrew lacks *the LORD* 2 Syriac; Hebrew *foundations* 3 A *cubit* was about 18 inches or 45 centimeters 4 Compare 1 Kings 6:3; the meaning of the Hebrew is uncertain 5 A *talent* was about 75 pounds or 34 kilograms 6 A *shekel* was about 2/5 ounce or 11 grams 7 Septuagint; the meaning of the Hebrew is uncertain 8 Hebrew *they overlaid*

3:1 Mount Moriah . . . the threshing floor of Ornan. The place of Solomon's temple is holy, corresponding to the site where Abraham was tried (Gen. 22:2–14). David purchased this site after his census (1 Chr. 21:1–22:1), securing the place for Solomon to work (1 Chr. 22:5 note).

3:3–17 Compared to the account of temple construction in 1 Kin. 6:4–20, this account gives more details of ornamentation (3:4–9), including the decorations of the main hall ("the vestibule," 3:4–7), the Most Holy Place (3:8–14), and the pillars (3:15–17).

3:4 vestibule. The vestibule of the temple brought the length of the entire structure to eighty cubits (120 feet).

3:5 The nave. That is, the Holy Place.

3:10 cherubim. These decorations were free-standing statues (vv. 11–18), much larger than the cherubim on the mercy seat of the ark of the covenant itself (Ex. 25:18–20).

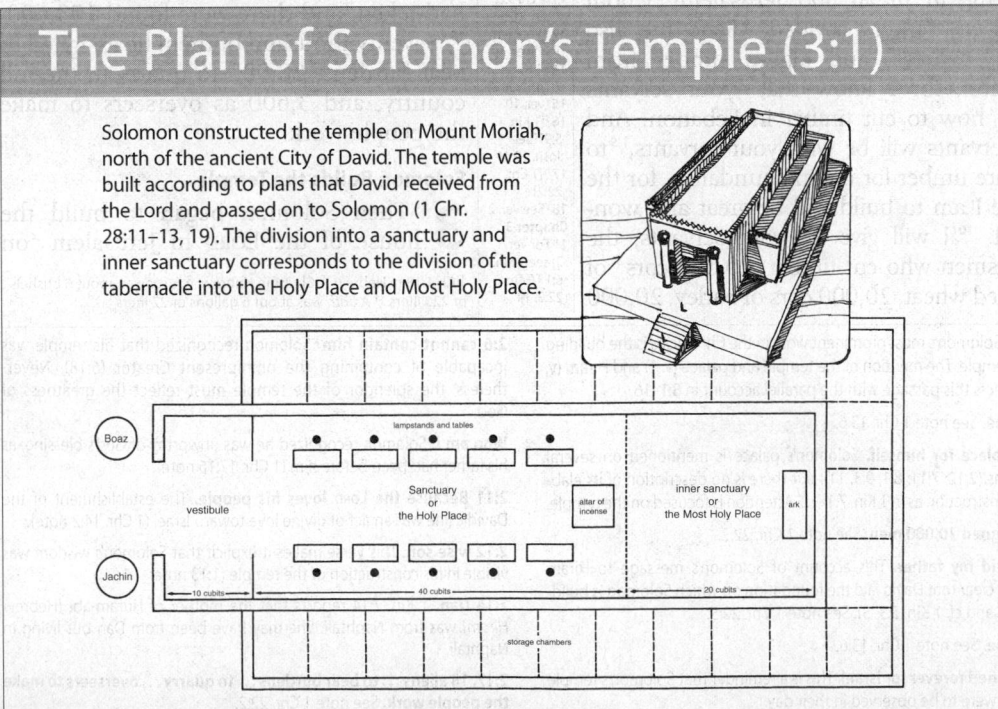

The Plan of Solomon's Temple (3:1)

Solomon constructed the temple on Mount Moriah, north of the ancient City of David. The temple was built according to plans that David received from the Lord and passed on to Solomon (1 Chr. 28:11–13, 19). The division into a sanctuary and inner sanctuary corresponds to the division of the tabernacle into the Holy Place and Most Holy Place.

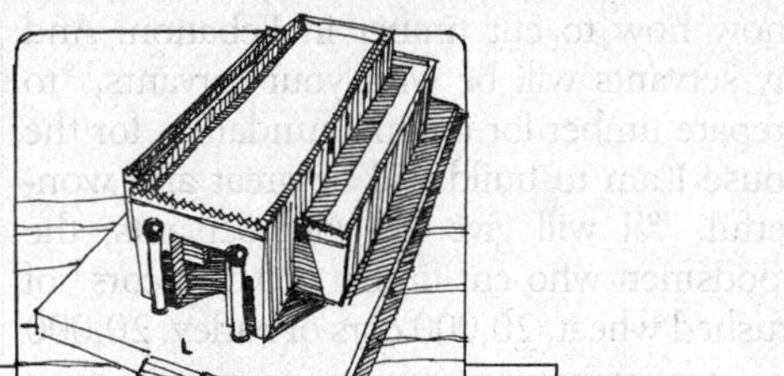

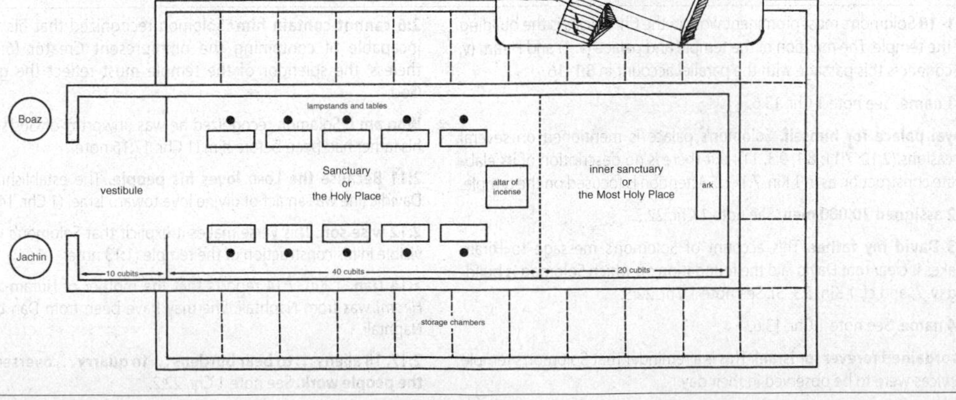

cubits. The cherubim[1] stood on their feet,
[g]facing the nave. **14** [h]And he made the veil of
blue and purple and crimson fabrics and
fine linen, and he worked cherubim on it.
15 [i]In front of the house he made two pillars thirty-five cubits high, with a capital of
five cubits on the top of each. **16** He made
chains like a necklace[2] and put them on
the tops of the pillars, and he made a hundred pomegranates and put them on the
chains. **17** [j]He set up the pillars in front of
the temple, one on the south, the other on
the north; that on the south he called
Jachin, and that on the north Boaz.

The Temple's Furnishings

4 He made [k]an altar of bronze, twenty
cubits[3] long and twenty cubits wide
and ten cubits high. **2** [l]Then he made the
sea of cast metal. It was round, ten cubits
from brim to brim, and five cubits high,
and a line of thirty cubits measured its circumference. **3** Under it were figures of
gourds,[4] for ten cubits, compassing the sea
all around. The gourds were in two rows,
cast with it when it was cast. **4** It stood on
twelve oxen, three facing north, three facing west, three facing south, and three facing east. The sea was set on them, and all
their rear parts were inward. **5** Its thickness
was a handbreadth.[5] And its brim was
made like the brim of a cup, like the flower
of a lily. [m]It held 3,000 baths.[6] **6** [n]He also
made ten basins in which to wash, and set
five on the south side, and five on the
north side. In these they were to rinse off
what was used for the burnt offering, and
the sea was for the priests to wash in.
7 And he made ten golden lampstands [o]as
prescribed, and set them in the temple, five
on the south side and five on the north.
8 [p]He also made ten tables and placed them
in the temple, five on the south side and
five on the north. And he made a hundred
basins of gold. **9** He made [q]the court of the
priests [r]and the great court and doors for
the court and overlaid their doors with
bronze. **10** [s]And he set the sea at the southeast corner of the house.
11 [t]Hiram also made the pots, the shovels,
and the basins. [u]So Hiram finished the
work that he did for King Solomon on the
house of God: **12** the two pillars, [v]the bowls,
and the two capitals on the top of the pillars; and the two latticeworks to cover the
two bowls of the capitals that were on the
top of the pillars; **13** [w]and the 400 pomegranates for the two latticeworks, two rows
of pomegranates for each latticework, to
cover the two bowls of the capitals that
were on the pillars. **14** [n]He made the stands
also, and the basins on the stands, **15** and
the one sea, and the twelve oxen underneath it. **16** The pots, the shovels, [x]the forks,
and all the equipment for these [t, y]Huram-
abi made of burnished bronze for King
Solomon for the house of the LORD. **17** In
the plain of the Jordan the king cast them,
in the clay ground between Succoth and
Zeredah.[7] **18** [z]Solomon made all these
things in great quantities, for the weight of
the bronze was not sought.
19 So Solomon made all the vessels that
were in the house of God: the golden altar,
[a]the tables for the bread of the Presence,
20 the lampstands and their lamps of pure
gold [b]to burn before the inner sanctuary, as
prescribed; **21** the flowers, the lamps, and

13 [g]Ezek. 40:9
14 [h]See Ex. 26:31
15 [i]For ver. 15, 16, see 1 Kin. 7:15-20; [1 Kin. 7:15; 2 Kin. 25:17; Jer. 52:21]
17 [j]1 Kin. 7:21
Chapter 4
1 [k]ch. 7:7; 8:12; [ch. 15:8; 1 Kin. 8:64; 2 Kin. 16:14] See Ezek. 43:13-17
2 [l]For ver. 2-5, see 1 Kin. 7:23-26
5 [m][1 Kin. 7:26]
6 [n]1 Kin. 7:38, 39
7 [o]ver. 20; 1 Kin. 7:49; See Ex. 25:31-39; 27:20, 21
8 [p]ver. 19; [1 Kin. 7:48]
9 [q]1 Kin. 6:36 [r][ch. 6:13; 2 Kin. 21:5]
10 [s]1 Kin. 7:39
11 [t]For ver. 11–ch. 5:1, see 1 Kin. 7:40-51 [u][1 Kin. 7:13, 14]
12 [v]1 Kin. 7:41
13 [w][1 Kin. 7:20]
14 [n][See ver. 6 above]
16 [x]1 Chr. 28:17 [t][See ver. 11 above] [y]ch. 2:13; [1 Kin. 7:14]
18 [z]1 Kin. 7:47
19 [a]ver. 8
20 [b]ver. 7

1 Hebrew *they* 2 Hebrew *chains in the inner sanctuary* 3 A *cubit* was about 18 inches or 45 centimeters 4 Compare 1 Kings 7:24; Hebrew *oxen*; twice in this verse 5 A *handbreadth* was about 3 inches or 7.5 centimeters 6 A *bath* was about 6 gallons or 22 liters 7 Spelled *Zarethan* in 1 Kings 7:46

3:14 veil. Solomon's temple was according to the pattern of Moses' tabernacle but twice the size (Ex. 26:31–35). In Solomon's temple also a veil separated the Most Holy Place from the Holy Place ("the nave"). The veil prohibited access to the Most Holy Place. It symbolized restriction of access to God's presence, a restriction done away with in the mediating work of Christ's death (Matt. 27:51 note; Heb. 9:1–14 note; 10:11–22 note).

3:15 thirty-five cubits high. 1 Kin. 7:15 reads "eighteen cubits" (cf. 2 Kin. 25:17; Jer. 52:21). It has been suggested that "thirty-five" represents the sum of the lengths of the two pillars (eighteen plus eighteen) or the sum of the dimensions given (eighteen in height, twelve around, and five for the capital). It is also possible that a later copyist has introduced an error.

4:1 altar of bronze. Mentioned also in 1 Kin. 8:64; 2 Kin. 16:14. The bronze altar was the main altar. The large measurements are the dimensions of the base, from which steps went to the altar (Ezek. 43:13–17).

4:2 sea of cast metal. Solomon's version of the "basin of bronze" in Moses' tabernacle (Ex. 30:18). The water of this basin was used for rituals of cleansing (4:6; 1 Kin. 7:23 note).

4:3 gourds. Though the Hebrew reads "oxen," the ornamental border was probably gourds of some kind (cf. 1 Kin. 7:24).

4:4 twelve oxen. See note 1 Kin. 7:25. The twelve bulls pointed to the four directions of the compass (cf. Num. 2 on the encampment of the tribes; Rev. 21:12–14).

4:5 3,000 baths. 1 Kin. 7:26 reads "two thousand baths." These are round numbers and not exact statements of volume.

4:9 court of the priests and the great court. Both courtyards are mentioned in Kings (1 Kin. 6:36; 7:12). The great court was for the laity.

4:11–22 The text follows 1 Kin. 7:40–50 in the description of Hiram's work.

the tongs, of purest gold; 22 the snuffers,
basins, dishes for incense, and fire pans, of
pure gold, and the sockets[1] of the temple,
for the inner doors to the Most Holy Place
and for the doors of the nave of the temple
were of gold.

5 [c]Thus all the work that Solomon did
for the house of the LORD was finished.
And Solomon brought in the things that
David his father had dedicated, and stored
the silver, the gold, and all the vessels in
the treasuries of the house of God.

The Ark Brought to the Temple

2 Then Solomon assembled the elders of
Israel and all the heads of the tribes, the
leaders of the fathers' houses of the people
of Israel, in Jerusalem, to bring up the
ark of the covenant of the LORD out of
[d]the city of David, which is Zion. 3 And all
the men of Israel assembled before the king
at the feast that is in the seventh month.
4 And all the elders of Israel came, [e]and the
Levites took up the ark. 5 And they brought
up the ark, the tent of meeting, and all the
holy vessels that were in the tent; [f]the
Levitical priests brought them up. 6 And
King Solomon and all the congregation of
Israel, who had assembled before him,
were before the ark, sacrificing so many
sheep and oxen that they could not be
counted or numbered. 7 Then the priests
brought the ark of the covenant of the LORD
to its place, in the inner sanctuary of the
house, in the Most Holy Place, underneath
the wings of the cherubim. 8 The cherubim
spread out their wings over the place of the
ark, so that the cherubim made a covering
above the ark and its poles. 9 And the poles
were so long that the ends of the poles
were seen [g]from the Holy Place before the
inner sanctuary, but they could not be seen
from outside. And they are[2] there to this
day. 10 There was nothing in the ark except
the two tablets [h]that Moses put there at
Horeb, where the LORD made a covenant
with the people of Israel, when they came
out of Egypt. 11 And when the priests came
out of the Holy Place (for all the priests who
were present had consecrated themselves,
without regard to [i]their divisions, 12 and all
the Levitical [j]singers, [k]Asaph, [l]Heman, and
Jeduthun, their sons and kinsmen, arrayed
in fine linen, with [m]cymbals, harps, and
lyres, stood east of the altar with 120
[n]priests who were trumpeters; 13 and it was
the duty of the trumpeters and singers to
make themselves heard in unison in praise
and thanksgiving to the LORD), and when
the song was raised, [o]with trumpets and
cymbals and other musical instruments, in
praise to the LORD,

[p]"For he is good,
for his steadfast love endures
forever,"

the house, the house of the LORD, was filled
with a cloud, 14 so that the priests could not
stand to minister because of the cloud, [q]for
the glory of the LORD filled the house of
God.

Solomon Blesses the People

6 [r]Then Solomon said, "The LORD has
said that he would dwell in thick darkness. 2 But I have built you [s]an exalted
house, a place for you to dwell in forever."
3 Then the king turned around and blessed
all the assembly of Israel, while all the

Chapter 5
1 [c]For ver. 1-10, see 1 Kin. 8:1-9
2 [d]2 Sam. 6:12
4 [e][ver. 7; 1 Kin. 8:3]
5 [f]ch. 23:18; 30:27
9 [g][1 Kin. 8:8]
10 [h]Deut. 10:2, 5; [ch. 6:11]
11 [i]1 Chr. 24:1, 5; [Luke 1:5]
12 [j]See 1 Chr. 25:1-4 [k]See 1 Chr. 6:39 [l]See 1 Chr. 6:33 [m]1 Chr. 15:16; Ps. 150:3-5 [n]ch. 7:6; 1 Chr. 15:24
13 [o]1 Chr. 16:42 [p]See 1 Chr. 16:34
14 [q]ch. 7:2; 1 Kin. 8:11; [Ex. 40:35; Ezek. 10:3, 4]
Chapter 6
1 [r]For ver. 1-39, see 1 Kin. 8:12-50; [Ex. 20:21; Heb. 12:18]
2 [s][Ps. 135:21]

[1] Compare 1 Kings 7:50; Hebrew *the entrance of the house* [2] Hebrew *it is*

5:1 David his father. The historian ties Solomon's temple directly to David's preparations (2:3 note).

5:2–7:10 The text closely follows the account of temple dedication in 1 Kin. 8. The report is in four balanced sections: an opening celebration of the transfer of the ark (5:2–6:2); Solomon's blessing (6:3–11); Solomon's prayer (6:12–42); and concluding celebrations (7:1–10).

5:3 all the men of Israel. Like David, Solomon received widespread support from Israel (1 Chr. 11:1 note).

seventh month. This was Tishri, when the Feast of Booths was celebrated. Since the temple was completed in the eighth month of Solomon's eleventh year (1 Kin. 6:38), the ark would have been brought in eleven months later.

5:5 Levitical priests. Repeated references to priests and Levites in this account indicates that Solomon observed carefully the tabernacle and temple regulations (1 Chr. 6 notes).

5:9 there to this day. See note 1 Chr. 4:41.

5:10 Nothing . . . except the two tablets. In the tabernacle of Moses' time the ark also contained Aaron's staff (Num. 17:10, 11) and the jar of manna (Ex. 16:32–34).

5:11–13 See 1 Kin. 8:10, 11. The books of Chronicles emphasize the use of music in worship (1 Chr. 15:16 note).

5:13 he is good . . . forever. A familiar line of descriptive praise honoring God for His enduring goodness and mercy (7:3, 6; Ps. 106:1; 107:1; 136).

5:13, 14 cloud . . . glory. God blessed Solomon's temple with His presence as He had blessed the tabernacle (Ex. 40:34–38). The prophets hoped for God's glory to return to the temple after the exile in Babylonia (Ezek. 43:1–5; Hag. 2:7–9; Zech. 2:10; 8:3).

6:1, 2 Solomon expresses his hope for the permanence of the presence of God in the temple. This was a keen concern for the community seeking to reestablish itself after returning from exile in Babylonia in the sixth century B.C. (5:13, 14 note).

assembly of Israel stood. 4 And he said,
"Blessed be the LORD, the God of Israel,
who with his hand has fulfilled what he
promised with his mouth to David my
father, saying, 5 'Since the day that I
brought my people out of the land of
Egypt, I chose no city out of all the tribes
of Israel in which to build a house, that my
name might be there, and I chose no man
as prince over my people Israel; 6 [t]but I
have chosen Jerusalem that my name may
be there, [u]and I have chosen David to be
over my people Israel.' 7 [v]Now it was in the
heart of David my father to build a house
for the name of the LORD, the God of Israel.
8 But the LORD said to David my father,
'Whereas [v]it was in your heart to build a
house for my name, you did well that it
was in your heart. 9 Nevertheless, it is not
you who shall build the house, but your
son who shall be born to you shall build
the house for my name.' 10 Now the LORD
has fulfilled his promise that he made. For
I have risen in the place of David my father
and sit on the throne of Israel, as the LORD
promised, and I have built the house for
the name of the LORD, the God of Israel.
11 And there I have set the ark, [w]in which is
the covenant of the LORD that he made
with the people of Israel."

Solomon's Prayer of Dedication

12 Then Solomon stood before the altar of
the LORD in the presence of all the assembly
of Israel and spread out his hands.
13 [x]Solomon had made a bronze platform
five cubits[1] long, five cubits wide, and three
cubits high, and had set it in the court, and
he stood on it. [y]Then he knelt on his knees
in the presence of all the assembly of Israel,
and spread out his hands toward heaven,
14 and said, "O LORD, God of Israel, [z]there is
no God like you, in heaven or on earth,
[a]keeping covenant and showing steadfast
love to your servants who walk before you
with all their heart, 15 [b]who have kept with
your servant David my father what you
declared to him. You spoke with your
mouth, and with your hand have fulfilled it
this day. 16 Now therefore, O LORD, God of
Israel, keep for your servant David my
father what you have promised him, saying,
[c]'You shall not lack a man to sit before me
on the throne of Israel, [d]if only your sons
pay close attention to their way, to walk in
my law as you have walked before me.'
17 Now therefore, O LORD, God of Israel, let
your word be confirmed, which you have
spoken to your servant David.

18 "But will God indeed dwell with man
on the earth? Behold, [e]heaven and the
highest heaven cannot contain you, how
much less this house that I have built!
19 Yet have regard to the prayer of your servant and to his plea, O LORD my God, listening to the cry and to the prayer that
your servant prays before you, 20 [f]that your
eyes may be open day and night toward
this house, the place where you have promised to set your name, that you may listen
to the prayer that your servant offers toward
this place. 21 And listen to the pleas of your
servant and of your people Israel, when
they pray toward this place. And listen from

6 [t]ch. 12:13; Ps. 78:68 [u]1 Chr. 28:4; See 1 Sam. 16:11-13
7 [v]2 Sam. 7:2; 1 Chr. 17:1; 28:2
8 [v][See ver. 7 above]
11 [w][ch. 5:10]
13 [x][2 Kin. 11:14; 23:3]
[y][1 Kin. 8:54]
14 [z]See Ex. 15:11 [a]See Deut. 7:9
15 [b]1 Chr. 22:9, 10
16 [c]ch. 7:18; See 1 Kin. 2:4 [d]Ps. 132:12
18 [e]See ch. 2:6
20 [f][ver. 40]

[1] A *cubit* was about 18 inches or 45 centimeters

6:5–10, 20, 32–34, 38 name. See note 1 Chr. 13:6; " 'This Is My Name': God's Self-disclosure" at Ex. 3:15.

6:9 it is not you who shall build. For the explanation of David's disqualification, see 1 Chr. 22:6–10 and note.

6:10 fulfilled his promise. See notes 1 Chr. 17:1–15.

6:13 This verse does not appear in the traditional Hebrew (Masoretic) text of 1 Kin. 8. The repetition of "spread out his hands" at the end of vv. 12 and 13 may have caused a scribe to skip the intervening material at some point in the copying of manuscripts.

court. That is, the "great court" outside the temple proper (4:9 note).

6:14 keeping covenant and showing steadfast love. Solomon's words of praise touch on both sides of the covenant relationship between God and His people. God keeps His covenant, and the people must walk in it "with all their heart." Violation of the covenant invites divine retribution (Deut. 7:9–12; 30:15–20). This idea of the covenant is central in the books of the Chronicles (1 Chr. 28:9 note).

6:16, 17 Solomon refers to the promise given through Nathan of a permanent dynasty (1 Chr. 17:7–14 notes).

6:16 if only your sons pay close attention. The responsibility to persevere is emphasized.

walk in my law. See note 1 Chr. 16:40.

6:18–39 Solomon turns to the heart of his concern. He prays that the temple will be the national center for effective prayer. He begins with a general request to God to hear the people's prayers (vv. 18–21) listing seven specific situations in which prayers may be offered in or toward the temple (vv. 22–39). This aspect of Solomon's prayer would encourage readers in the time of restoration following the exile in Babylonia to make the restored temple the center of prayer in that time.

6:18 heaven and the highest heaven cannot contain you. See note 2:6.

6:19–21 prayer . . . prays. See note 7:14.

6:21 listen from heaven your dwelling place. Solomon uses this expression four times in his prayer (vv. 21, 30, 33, 39). The temple was the earthly place that provided access to the heavenly court through the sacrifices offered there and the promise of God's gracious presence (1 Chr. 13:6 note).

heaven your dwelling place, [g]and when you
hear, forgive.
[22]“If a man sins against his neighbor and
is made to take an oath and comes and
swears his oath before your altar in this
house, [23]then hear from heaven and act
and judge your servants, repaying the
guilty by bringing his conduct on his own
head, and vindicating the righteous by
rewarding him according to his righteousness.
[24]“If your people Israel are defeated
before the enemy because they have sinned
against you, and they turn again and
acknowledge your name and pray and
plead with you in this house, [25][g]then hear
from heaven and forgive the sin of your
people Israel and bring them again to the
land that you gave to them and to their
fathers.
[26][h]“When heaven is shut up and there is
no rain because they have sinned against
you, if they pray toward this place and
acknowledge your name and turn from
their sin, when you afflict[1] them, [27][g]then
hear in heaven and forgive the sin of your
servants, your people Israel, when you
teach them the good way[2] in which they
should walk, and grant rain upon your
land, which you have given to your people
as an inheritance.
[28][i]“If there is famine in the land, if there
is pestilence or blight or mildew or locust
or caterpillar, if their enemies besiege them
in the land at their gates, whatever plague,
whatever sickness there is, [29]whatever
prayer, whatever plea is made by any man
or by all your people Israel, each knowing
his own affliction and his own sorrow and
stretching out his hands toward this house,

21 [g][Dan. 9:19]
25 [g][See ver. 21 above]
26 [h]ch. 7:13; [1 Kin. 17:1]
27 [g][See ver. 21 above]
28 [i][ch. 20:9]
30 [g][See ver. 21 above] [j]See 1 Sam. 16:7
33 [k]ch. 7:14; [James 2:7]
36 [l]Eccles. 7:20; James 3:2; 1 John 1:8

[30][g]then hear from heaven your dwelling
place and forgive and render to each whose
heart you know, according to all his ways,
[j]for you, you only, know the hearts of the
children of mankind, [31]that they may fear
you and walk in your ways all the days that
they live in the land that you gave to our
fathers.
[32]“Likewise, when a foreigner, who is
not of your people Israel, comes from a far
country for the sake of your great name
and your mighty hand and your outstretched arm, when he comes and prays
toward this house, [33]hear from heaven
your dwelling place and do according to
all for which the foreigner calls to you, in
order that all the peoples of the earth may
know your name and fear you, as do your
people Israel, and that they may know that
this house [k]that I have built is called by
your name.
[34]“If your people go out to battle against
their enemies, by whatever way you shall
send them, and they pray to you toward
this city that you have chosen and the
house that I have built for your name,
[35]then hear from heaven their prayer and
their plea, and maintain their cause.
[36]“If they sin against you—[l]for there is no
one who does not sin—and you are angry
with them and give them to an enemy, so
that they are carried away captive to a land
far or near, [37]yet if they turn their heart in the
land to which they have been carried captive,
and repent and plead with you in the land of
their captivity, saying, ‘We have sinned and
have acted perversely and wickedly,’ [38]if
they repent with all their mind and with all

[1] Septuagint, Vulgate; Hebrew *answer* [2] Septuagint, Syriac, Vulgate (compare 1 Kings 8:36); Hebrew *toward the good way*

6:22 made to take an oath. For the kinds of legal procedures in mind here, see Ex. 22:10, 11; Lev. 6:1–7.

6:24 defeated . . . because they have sinned. Military defeat is often listed as a consequence of violating the covenant (Lev. 26:14–17; Deut. 28:25, 26, 47–52).

6:24, 26 turn again . . . turn. See note 7:14.

6:24, 32 pray . . . prays. See note 7:14.

6:26 no rain. Rain and drought are presented as covenant blessings and curses (Lev. 26:3, 4; Deut. 11:13, 14; Jer. 3:3; Joel 2:23–27; Hag. 1:9–11).

6:28 famine . . . locust. Famines and plagues of various sorts are often listed as covenant curses (Lev. 26:16, 20, 25, 26; Deut. 28:20–22, 27, 28, 35, 42).

6:32, 33 foreigner. Solomon asked that foreigners would also receive answers to prayer at the temple. The prophets looked forward to the inclusion of Gentiles among the people of God (Is. 56:6–8; Zech. 8:20–23; 14:16–21). The form of the petition emphasizes the centrality of the temple even as the kingdom expands to other nations. The inclusion of many Gentiles in the kingdom was ultimately fulfilled in Christ (Rom. 3:29; Gal. 3:14; Eph. 2:14–22).

6:34 go out to battle. The writer frequently reports how God answered prayer offered in battle (1 Chr. 5:18–22 note; 2 Chr. 13:14 note; 14:11 note; 18:31 note; 32:20 note).

6:36–39 carried away captive . . . maintain their cause. Exile and captivity are often listed as curses for violating the covenant (Deut. 28:36, 37, 64). Solomon's request was realized twice within the history of Chronicles itself. First Manasseh (33:10–13) and later the entire remnant of Israel (36:20–23) suffered exile in Babylonia and were restored to the Promised Land.

6:37 repent. See note 7:14.

6:38 toward their land . . . city . . . house. See the practice of Daniel (Dan. 6:10) and Jonah (Jon. 2:4).

their heart in the land of their captivity to
which they were carried captive, and pray
toward their land, which you gave to their
fathers, the city that you have chosen and
the house that I have built for your name,
39 then hear from heaven your dwelling place
their prayer and their pleas, and maintain
their cause and forgive your people who
have sinned against you. 40 Now, O my God,
[m]let your eyes be open [n]and your ears attentive to the prayer of this place.

41 "And now arise, O LORD God, and go
to your [o]resting place,
you and the ark of your might.
Let your priests, O LORD God, be
[p]clothed with salvation,
and let your saints [q]rejoice in your
goodness.
42 O LORD God, [r]do not turn away the
face of your anointed one!
[s]Remember your steadfast love for
David your servant."

Fire from Heaven

7 [t]As soon as Solomon finished his
prayer, [u]fire came down from heaven
and consumed the burnt offering and the
sacrifices, [v]and the glory of the LORD filled
the temple. 2 And the priests could not
enter the house of the LORD, because the
glory of the LORD filled the LORD's house.
3 When all the people of Israel saw the fire
come down and the glory of the LORD on
the temple, they bowed down with their
faces to the ground on the pavement and
worshiped and gave thanks to the LORD,
saying, "For he is good, [w]for his steadfast
love endures forever."

The Dedication of the Temple

4 [x]Then the king and all the people
offered sacrifice before the LORD. 5 King
Solomon offered as a sacrifice 22,000 oxen
and 120,000 sheep. So the king and all the
people dedicated the house of God. 6 The
priests stood at their posts; [y]the Levites
also, with the instruments for music to the
LORD that King David had made for giving
thanks to the LORD—[w]for his steadfast love
endures forever—whenever David offered
praises by their ministry;[1] [z]opposite them
the priests sounded trumpets, and all Israel
stood.
7 [a]And Solomon consecrated the middle
of the court that was before the house of
the LORD, for there he offered the burnt
offering and the fat of the peace offerings,
because the bronze altar Solomon had
made could not hold the burnt offering
and the grain offering and the fat.
8 At that time Solomon held the feast for
seven days, and all Israel with him, a very
great assembly, from [b]Lebo-hamath to the
[c]Brook of Egypt. 9 And on the eighth day
they held a solemn assembly, for they had
kept the dedication of the altar seven days
and the feast seven days. 10 On the twenty-
third day of the seventh month he sent the
people away to their homes, joyful and
glad of heart for the prosperity that the
LORD had granted to David and to Solomon
and to Israel his people.

If My People Pray

11 [d]Thus Solomon finished the house of
the LORD and the king's house. All that
Solomon had planned to do in the house
of the LORD and in his own house he successfully accomplished. 12 Then the LORD
appeared to Solomon in the night and said
to him: "I have heard your prayer [e]and
have chosen this place for myself as a
house of sacrifice. 13 [f]When I shut up the

[1] Hebrew *by their hand*

40 [m]Neh. 1:6, 11; [ver. 20; ch. 7:15] [n]Ps. 130:2
41 [o]Ps. 132:8, 9; [1 Chr. 28:2] [p][Isai. 61:10] [q][ch. 7:10; Neh. 9:25]
42 [r]Ps. 132:10 [s][Ps. 132:1]
Chapter 7
1 [t]1 Kin. 8:54 [u]Lev. 9:24; 1 Kin. 18:38; 1 Chr. 21:26 [v]See ch. 5:13
3 [w]See ch. 5:13
4 [x]1 Kin. 8:62; 63
6 [y][1 Chr. 15:16] [w][See ver. 3 above] [z]ch. 5:12
7 [a]For ver. 7-10, see 1 Kin. 8:64-66
8 [b]See Num. 34:8 [c]See Num. 34:5
11 [d]For ver. 11-22, see 1 Kin. 9:1-9
12 [e]See Deut. 12:5
13 [f][ch. 6:26, 28]

6:40 Now, O my God. Solomon's prayer ends with an adaptation of Ps. 132:8–10 about the joy of worship in the place chosen by God. The concluding words of the prayer given in 1 Kin. 8:50, 51 specify that the people were chosen by God and brought out of Egypt. Solomon asks God to remember the people and the place that He chose, and there to receive graciously all who turn to Him. Solomon's appeal is based on God's initiative in election.

7:1 fire came down. See note 1 Chr. 21:26.

glory. See "The Glory of God" at Ezek. 1:28.

7:2, 3 The repetition of elements from 5:13, 14 balances the initial celebration with the closing celebration. Note especially the praise for God's enduring mercy (7:3, 6; 5:13 and note).

7:6 The music of worship adds to the splendor of the celebration (1 Chr. 15:16 note).

all Israel. The whole nation was involved (1 Chr. 11:1 note).

7:8 feast. The Feast of Booths (5:3 note).

7:10 to David and to Solomon. 1 Kin. 8:66 simply reads "David." The writer of Chronicles regards the temple construction as a joint effort of David and Solomon (1 Chr. 22:5 note).

7:13–15 These verses do not appear in Kings. They report God's response to several requests mentioned in Solomon's prayer (6:14–42). Readers of the time following the return of exiles from Babylonia were looking to God to help them restore or "heal" the land (Introduction to 1 Chronicles: Date and Occasion).

heavens so that there is no rain, or command the locust to devour the land, or send pestilence among my people, 14 if my people who are called by my name [g]humble themselves, and pray and seek my face and turn from their wicked ways, then I will hear from heaven and will forgive their sin and heal their land. 15 [h]Now my eyes will be open and my ears attentive to the prayer that is made in this place. 16 [e]For now I have chosen and consecrated this house that my name may be there forever. My eyes and my heart will be there for all time. 17 And as for you, if you will walk before me as David your father walked, doing according to all that I have commanded you and keeping my statutes and my rules, 18 then I will establish your royal throne, as I covenanted with David your father, saying, [i]'You shall not lack a man to rule Israel.'

19 [j]"But if you[1] turn aside and forsake my statutes and my commandments that I have set before you, and go and serve other gods and worship them, 20 [k]then I will pluck you[2] up from my land that I have given you, and this house that I have consecrated for my name, I will cast out of my sight, and I will make it [l]a proverb and a byword among all peoples. 21 And at this house, which was exalted, everyone passing by will be astonished and say, [m]'Why has the LORD done thus to this land and to this house?' 22 Then they will say, 'Because they abandoned the LORD, the God of their fathers who brought them out of the land of Egypt and laid hold on other gods and worshiped them and served them. Therefore he has brought all this disaster on them.'"

14 [g][ch. 12:7]
15 [h]See ch. 6:40
16 [e][See ver. 12 above]
18 [i]1 Kin. 8:25; See ch. 6:16
19 [j][Lev. 26:14; Deut. 28:15]
20 [k][Deut. 29:28] [l]See Deut. 28:37
21 [m] Deut. 29:24; Jer. 22:8, 9

Chapter 8
1 [n]For ver. 1-18, see 1 Kin. 9:10-28
5 [o]See Josh. 16:3, 5 [p]ch. 14:7; Deut. 3:5
7 [q]See Gen. 15:18-21
8 [r]ch. 10:18; 1 Kin. 4:6; 9:21; 12:18; [Josh. 16:10]
11 [s]1 Kin. 3:1; 7:8; 9:24
12 [t]ch. 4:1; 15:8
13 [u][Ex. 29:38]

Solomon's Accomplishments

8 [n]At the end of twenty years, in which Solomon had built the house of the LORD and his own house, 2 Solomon rebuilt the cities that Hiram had given to him, and settled the people of Israel in them.

3 And Solomon went to Hamath-zobah and took it. 4 He built Tadmor in the wilderness and all the store cities that he built in Hamath. 5 He also built [o]Upper Beth-horon and Lower Beth-horon, [p]fortified cities [p]with walls, gates, and bars, 6 and Baalath, and all the store cities that Solomon had and all the cities for his chariots and the cities for his horsemen, and whatever Solomon desired to build in Jerusalem, in Lebanon, and in all the land of his dominion. 7 [q]All the people who were left of the Hittites, the Amorites, the Perizzites, the Hivites, and the Jebusites, who were not of Israel, 8 from their descendants who were left after them in the land, whom the people of Israel had not destroyed—these Solomon drafted [r]as forced labor, and so they are to this day. 9 But of the people of Israel Solomon made no slaves for his work; they were soldiers, and his officers, the commanders of his chariots, and his horsemen. 10 And these were the chief officers of King Solomon, 250, who exercised authority over the people.

11 [s]Solomon brought Pharaoh's daughter up from the city of David to the house that he had built for her, for he said, "My wife shall not live in the house of David king of Israel, for the places to which the ark of the LORD has come are holy."

12 Then Solomon offered up burnt offerings to the LORD on the altar of the LORD [t]that he had built before the vestibule, 13 [u]as

1 The Hebrew for *you* is plural here 2 Hebrew *them*; twice in this verse

7:13 rain . . . locust . . . pestilence. Refers directly to 6:26–31.

7:14 if my people. God promised that the nation would receive relief from the hardships caused by their sin if the people would turn to Him in humility and prayer. This promise was especially relevant to the restored community following the Babylonian exile. A number of events in the divided and reunited kingdoms illustrate the principles of this passage (12:6; 13:14; 14:8–15; 18:31; 20:5–19; 32:20; 33:12, 13 and notes). Many times in Chronicles the concepts in this passage appear as the decisive factor for divine blessing and curses.

humble. An attitude of contrition and dependence on God (12:6, 7, 12; 30:11; 33:12, 19, 23; 34:27).

7:16, 20 name. See note 1 Chr. 13:6.

7:17–22 The promise that the dynasty founded by David would remain forever, gave hope to those seeking to restore the nation following their return from exile in Babylonia. While the promise to David's line was irrevocable, the nation always faced the threat of punishment if they should be unfaithful (1 Chr. 17:7–14 note; and 28:9 note).

7:17 keeping my statutes and my rules. See note 1 Chr. 16:40.

8:1–16 This account of Solomon's building projects and temple arrangements balances with 3:1–5:1. Its content follows 1 Kin. 9:10–28.

8:2 Hiram had given to him. Solomon gave these cities to Hiram, who later returned them (1 Kin. 9:10–14).

8:8 Solomon drafted as forced labor. See note 1 Chr. 22:2.

to this day. See note 1 Chr. 4:41.

8:11 the places . . . are holy. Solomon moved his Egyptian wife out of regard for the holiness of the ark and the places associated with it. Unlike the books of Kings (1 Kin. 11:1–13) and Nehemiah (Neh. 13:26, 27), Chronicles reserves negative comment on Solomon's international marriages. These sad facts were well known.

8:12–16 Again the account of details concerning worship, Levites, and priests, is more full than that in Kings (cf. 1 Kin. 9:25; 1 Chr. 6:1 note).

the duty of each day required, offering [v]according to the commandment of Moses for the Sabbaths, the new moons, and the [w]three annual feasts—the Feast of Unleavened Bread, the Feast of Weeks, and the Feast of Booths. **14** According to the ruling of David his father, he appointed [x]the divisions of the priests for their service, [y]and the Levites for their offices of praise and [z]ministry before the priests [u]as the duty of each day required, and [a]the gatekeepers in their divisions at each gate, for so David [b]the man of God had commanded. **15** And they did not turn aside from what the king had commanded the priests and Levites concerning any matter and concerning the treasuries.

16 Thus was accomplished all the work of Solomon from[1] the day the foundation of the house of the LORD was laid until it was finished. So the house of the LORD was completed.

17 Then Solomon went to [c]Ezion-geber and [d]Eloth on the shore of the sea, in the land of Edom. **18** And Hiram sent to him by the hand of his servants ships and servants familiar with the sea, and they went to Ophir together with the servants of Solomon and brought from there [e]450 talents[2] of gold and brought it to King Solomon.

The Queen of Sheba

9 [f]Now when [g]the queen of Sheba heard of the fame of Solomon, she came to Jerusalem to test him with hard questions, having a very great retinue and camels bearing spices and very much gold and precious stones. And when she came to Solomon, she told him all that was on her mind. **2** And Solomon answered all her questions. There was nothing hidden from Solomon that he could not explain to her. **3** And when [g]the queen of Sheba had seen the wisdom of Solomon, the house that he had built, **4** the food of his table, the seating of his officials, and the attendance of his servants, and their clothing, his cupbearers, and their clothing, and his burnt offerings that he offered at the house of the LORD, there was no more breath in her.

5 And she said to the king, "The report was true that I heard in my own land of your words and of your wisdom, **6** but I did not believe the[3] reports until I came and my own eyes had seen it. And behold, half the greatness of your wisdom was not told me; you surpass the report that I heard. **7** Happy are your wives![4] Happy are these your servants, who continually stand before you and hear your wisdom! **8** Blessed be the LORD your God, who has delighted in you [h]and set you on his throne as king for the LORD your God! [i]Because your God loved Israel and would establish them forever, he has made you king over them, that you may execute justice and righteousness." **9** Then she gave the king 120 talents[5] of gold, and a very great quantity of spices, and precious stones. There were no spices such as those that the queen of Sheba gave to King Solomon.

10 Moreover, the servants of Hiram and the servants of Solomon, [j]who brought gold from Ophir, brought algum wood and precious stones. **11** And the king made from the algum wood [k]supports for the house of the LORD and for the king's house, lyres also and harps for the singers. There never was seen the like of them before in the land of Judah.

12 And King Solomon gave to the queen of Sheba all that she desired, whatever she asked [l]besides what she had brought to the king. So she turned and went back to her own land with her servants.

Solomon's Wealth

13 [m]Now the weight of gold that came to Solomon in one year was 666 talents of gold, **14** besides that which the explorers and merchants brought. [n]And all the kings of Arabia and the governors of the land brought gold and silver to Solomon. **15** King Solomon made 200 large shields of beaten gold; 600 shekels[6] of beaten gold went into each shield. **16** And he made 300 shields of beaten gold; [o]300 shekels of gold went into each shield; and the king put them in the

13 [v]Num. 28:3, 9, 11, 26; 29:2 [w]Ex. 23:14; Deut. 16:16
14 [x]See 1 Chr. ch. 24 [y]See 1 Chr. ch. 25 [z]ch. 7:6 [u][See ver. 13 above] [a]See 1 Chr. 9:17-23; 1 Chr. ch. 26 [b]Neh. 12:24, 36
17 [c]1 Kin. 9:26 [d][Deut. 2:8; 2 Kin. 14:22]
18 [e]ch. 9:10; [1 Kin. 9:28]
Chapter 9
1 [f]For ver. 1-12, see 1 Kin. 10:1-13 [g][Matt. 12:42; Luke 11:31]
3 [g][See ver. 1 above]
8 [h]1 Chr. 29:23 [i]ch. 2:11
10 [j]ch. 8:18
11 [k][1 Kin. 10:12]
12 [l][1 Kin. 10:13]
13 [m]For ver. 13-28, see 1 Kin. 10:14-28
14 [n]Ps. 68:29; 72:10
16 [o][1 Kin. 10:17]

1 Septuagint, Syriac, Vulgate; Hebrew *to* 2 A *talent* was about 75 pounds or 34 kilograms 3 Hebrew *their* 4 Septuagint (compare 1 Kings 10:8); Hebrew *men* 5 A *talent* was about 75 pounds or 34 kilograms 6 A *shekel* was about 2/5 ounce or 11 grams

9:8 establish them forever. The queen of Sheba recognized Solomon's wise rule as God's provision for the well-being of Israel. Solomon's wealth and wisdom (2:13–28), like the international favor he enjoyed (v. 23), was a high point for the covenant community. The generation that returned from the distress of exile in Babylonia looked to it for inspiration and courage in their work of rebuilding.

House of the Forest of Lebanon. [17]The king
also made a great ivory throne and overlaid
it with pure gold. [18]The throne had six
steps and a footstool of gold, which were
attached to the throne, and on each side of
the seat were arm rests and two lions
standing beside the arm rests, [19]while
twelve lions stood there, one on each end
of a step on the six steps. Nothing like it
was ever made for any kingdom. [20]All King
Solomon's drinking vessels were of gold,
and all the vessels of the House of the
Forest of Lebanon were of pure gold. Silver
was not considered as anything in the days
of Solomon. [21]For the king's ships went to
[p]Tarshish with the servants of Hiram. Once
every three years the ships of Tarshish used
to come bringing gold, silver, ivory, apes,
and peacocks.[1]
[22]Thus King Solomon [q]excelled all the
kings of the earth in riches and in wisdom.
[23]And all the kings of the earth sought the
presence of Solomon to hear his wisdom,
which God had put into his mind. [24]Every
one of them brought his present, articles
of silver and of gold, garments, myrrh,
spices, horses, and mules, so much year
by year. [25]And Solomon had [r]4,000 stalls
for horses and chariots, and 12,000 horsemen, whom he stationed in the chariot
cities and with the king in Jerusalem.
[26][s]And he ruled over all the kings [t]from the
Euphrates to the land of the Philistines
and to the border of Egypt. [27][u]And the
king made silver as common in Jerusalem
as stone, and he made cedar as plentiful as
the sycamore of the Shephelah. [28][v]And
horses were imported for Solomon from
Egypt and from all lands.

Solomon's Death

[29][w]Now the rest of the acts of Solomon,
from [x]first to last, are they not written in the
history of [y]Nathan the prophet, and in the
prophecy of [z]Ahijah the Shilonite, and in
the visions of [a]Iddo [b]the seer concerning
Jeroboam the son of Nebat? [30]Solomon
reigned in Jerusalem over all Israel forty years.
[31]And Solomon slept with his fathers and
was buried in [c]the city of David his father,
and Rehoboam his son reigned in his place.

The Revolt Against Rehoboam

10 [d]Rehoboam went to Shechem, for
all Israel had come to Shechem to
make him king. [2]And as soon as Jeroboam
the son of Nebat heard of it (for he was in
Egypt, [e]where he had fled from King
Solomon), then Jeroboam returned from
Egypt. [3]And they sent and called him. And
Jeroboam and all Israel came and said to
Rehoboam, [4][f]"Your father made our yoke
heavy. Now therefore lighten the hard service of your father and his heavy yoke on
us, and we will serve you." [5]He said to
them, "Come to me again in three days."
So the people went away.
[6]Then King Rehoboam took counsel
with the old men,[2] who had stood before
Solomon his father while he was yet alive,
saying, "How do you advise me to answer
this people?" [7]And they said to him, [g]"If
you will be good to this people and please
them and speak good words to them, then
they will be your servants forever." [8]But he
abandoned the counsel that the old men
gave him, and took counsel with the young

21 [p]ch. 20:36, 37
22 [q]1 Kin. 3:13
25 [r][ch. 1:14; 1 Kin. 4:26; 10:26]
26 [s]1 Kin. 4:21 [t]Gen. 15:18; Ex. 23:31; Ps. 72:8
27 [u]ch. 1:15
28 [v]ch. 1:16
29 [w]For ver. 29-31, see 1 Kin. 11:41-43 [x]1 Chr. 29:29 [y]2 Sam. 12:1 [z]1 Kin. 11:29 [a]ch. 12:15; 13:22 [b]2 Sam. 24:11; See 1 Sam. 9:9
31 [c][1 Kin. 2:10]
Chapter 10
1 [d]For ver. 1-19, see 1 Kin. 12:1-20
2 [e]1 Kin. 11:40
4 [f][1 Kin. 5:15]
7 [g][1 Kin. 12:7]

1 Or *baboons* 2 Or *the elders*; also verses 8, 13

9:23 all the kings of the earth. See 9:8 note.

9:27, 28 silver . . . cedar . . . horses. See note 1:14–17.

9:29–31 Writing for a generation in need of encouragement (v. 8 note), the author does not discuss the well-known trouble caused by Solomon's foreign wives (1 Kin. 11:1–40). He moves directly from the king's glory to the end of his reign. In the same way he does not bring up David's sin with Bathsheba and the troubles this caused.

9:29 written in the history of. See Introduction to 1 Chronicles: Author.

10:1–28:27 The Divided Kingdom. In this section the writer makes use of 1 Kin. 12–2 Kin. 17. His record of the period of the divided monarchy does not rehearse the harsh condemnation of the northern tribes found in Kings, focusing instead on events in Judah where the temple was and the Davidic king lived. Throughout this section, the writer reports how the conditions in the kingdom depended on the nation's faithfulness to God. As readers considered these events, they could see clearly the choices for blessing and curse in their own day.

In telling about Rehoboam's kingship, the writer makes broad use of Kings (cf. 10:1–11:4 with 1 Kin. 12:1–24; 12:9–16 with 1 Kin. 14:21, 25–31), while presenting the material in accord with his own theological understanding and emphasis. The account is presented in two parts (chs. 10; 11 and 12:1–14), each part narrating a problematic situation, prophetic encounter, and divine blessing. The conclusion is a notice of his wars with Jeroboam and his death (12:15, 16). The chapters impress on the readers God's curse against pride and infidelity and the benefits of living in humility and obedience to the prophetic word (20:20 note).

10:1–11:23 The first section recounting Rehoboam's reign focuses on his first three years as king (11:17), in which there is conflict (ch. 10), obedience to the prophetic word (11:1–4), and divine blessing (11:5–23). 10:1–11:4 is derived from 1 Kin. 12:1–24 (notes); the Chronicler adds 11:5–23.

10:1 Rehoboam. Reigned 931–913 B.C.

all Israel. In the discussion of the period of the divided monarchy, this expression and others like it can refer to: the southern kingdom alone (11:3; 12:1; 24:5; 28:23); the northern kingdom alone (10:16; 11:13; 13:4, 15); or both kingdoms together (18:16; cf. 1 Chr. 11:1 note; 2 Chr. 29:24 note).

men who had grown up with him and
stood before him. 9 And he said to them,
"What do you advise that we answer this
people who have said to me, 'Lighten the
yoke that your father put on us'?" 10 And
the young men who had grown up with
him said to him, "Thus shall you speak to
the people who said to you, 'Your father
made our yoke heavy, but you lighten it
for us'; thus shall you say to them, 'My
little finger is thicker than my father's
thighs. 11 And now, whereas my father laid
on you a heavy yoke, I will add to your
yoke. My father disciplined you with whips,
but I will discipline you with scorpions.'"
12 So Jeroboam and all the people came
to Rehoboam the third day, as the king
said, "Come to me again the third day."
13 And the king answered them harshly;
and forsaking the counsel of the old men,
14 King Rehoboam spoke to them according to the counsel of the young men, saying, "My father made your yoke heavy, but
I will add to it. My father disciplined you
with whips, but I will discipline you with
scorpions." 15 So the king did not listen to
the people, for it was a turn of affairs
brought about by God that the LORD might

10:15 by God that the LORD might fulfill his word. The author points out that Rehoboam's reaction must be seen in the light of God's sovereign purposes. Ahijah's prophecy concerning Jeroboam (1 Kin. 11:29–39) was fulfilled by this turn of events. Divine sovereignty extends over the sinful actions of human beings (1 Chr. 21:1 note).

A Kingdom Divided. The glory of the united kingdom faded at the death of Solomon. Bitter feelings had been aroused by some of the harsh policies of Solomon's rule. The system of forced labor for building projects (1 Kin. 5:13) and the administrative districts that cut across old tribal boundaries (1 Kin. 4:7-19) were not popular with the people.

When Solomon's son Rehoboam ascended the throne, he inherited an internal tension between north and south that had to be addressed if the kingdom were to remain united. At Shechem the people, with Jeroboam as their leader, asked for change. Rehoboam's harsh rejection of their demands led to the people's rebellious response: "Each of you to your tents, O Israel! Look now to your own house, David!" The Kingdom split. Rehoboam reigned over Judah to the south, but Jeroboam became king of Israel to the north.

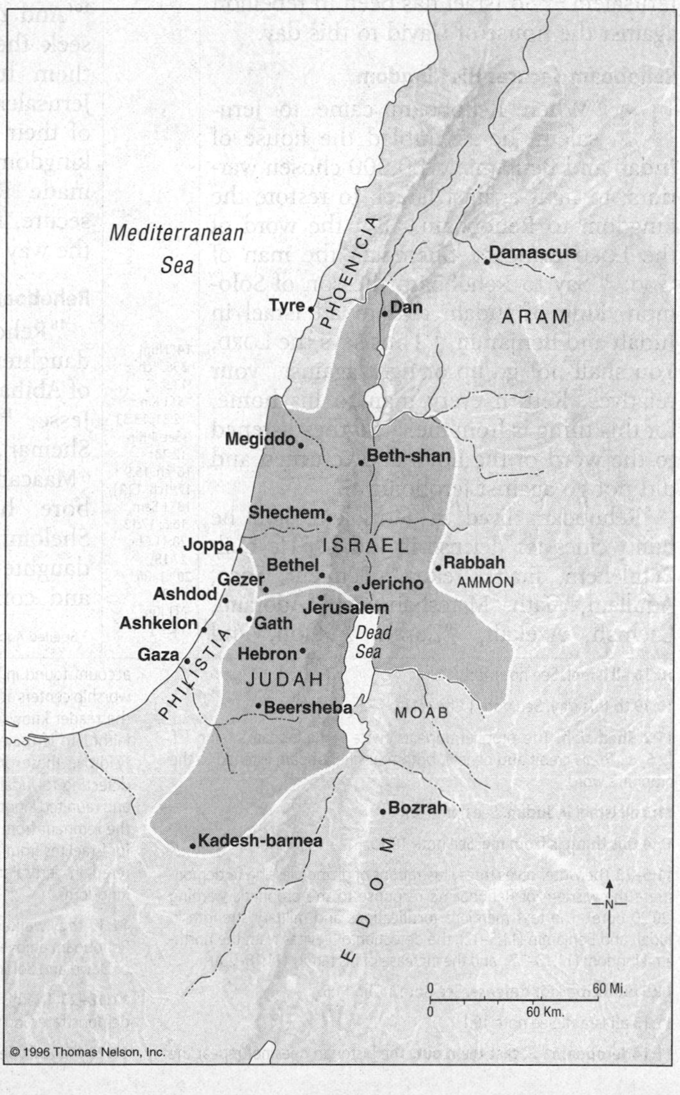

fulfill his word, [h]which he spoke by Ahijah
the Shilonite to Jeroboam the son of
Nebat.
16 And when all Israel saw that the king
did not listen to them, the people
answered the king, "What portion have we
in David? We have no inheritance in the
son of Jesse. [i]Each of you to your tents, O
Israel! Look now to your own house,
David." So all Israel went to their tents.
17 But Rehoboam reigned over the people of
Israel who lived in the cities of Judah.
18 Then King Rehoboam sent [j]Hadoram,[1]
who was taskmaster over the forced labor,
and the people of Israel stoned him to
death with stones. And King Rehoboam
quickly mounted his chariot to flee to
Jerusalem. 19 So Israel has been in rebellion
against the house of David to this day.

Rehoboam Secures His Kingdom

11 [k]When Rehoboam came to Jerusalem, he assembled the house of
Judah and Benjamin, 180,000 chosen warriors, to fight against Israel, to restore the
kingdom to Rehoboam. 2 But the word of
the LORD came to [l]Shemaiah the man of
God: 3 "Say to Rehoboam the son of Solomon, king of Judah, and to all Israel in
Judah and Benjamin, 4 'Thus says the LORD,
You shall not go up or fight against [m]your
relatives. Return every man to his home,
for this thing is from me.'" So they listened
to the word of the LORD and returned and
did not go against Jeroboam.
5 Rehoboam lived in Jerusalem, and he
built [n]cities for defense in Judah. 6 He built
Bethlehem, Etam, Tekoa, 7 Beth-zur, Soco,
Adullam, 8 Gath, [o]Mareshah, Ziph, 9 Adoraim,
Lachish, Azekah, 10 Zorah, Aijalon, and
Hebron, fortified cities that are in Judah and
in Benjamin. 11 He made the fortresses strong,
and put commanders in them, and stores of
food, oil, and wine. 12 And he put shields and
spears in all the cities and made them very
strong. So he held Judah and Benjamin.

Priests and Levites Come to Jerusalem

13 And the priests and the Levites who
were in all Israel presented themselves to
him from all places where they lived. 14 For
the Levites left [p]their common lands and
their holdings and came to Judah and
Jerusalem, [q]because Jeroboam and his sons
cast them out from serving as priests of the
LORD, 15 and he appointed his own [r]priests
for the high places and for the goat idols
and for [s]the calves that he had made.
16 [t]And those who had set their hearts to
seek the LORD God of Israel came after
them from all the tribes of Israel to
Jerusalem to sacrifice to the LORD, the God
of their fathers. 17 [u]They strengthened the
kingdom of Judah, and for three years they
made Rehoboam the son of Solomon
secure, for they walked for three years in
the way of David and Solomon.

Rehoboam's Family

18 Rehoboam took as wife Mahalath the
daughter of Jerimoth the son of David, and
of Abihail the daughter of [v]Eliab the son of
Jesse, 19 and she bore him sons, Jeush,
Shemariah, and Zaham. 20 After her he took
[w]Maacah the daughter of Absalom, who
bore him [x]Abijah, Attai, Ziza, and
Shelomith. 21 Rehoboam loved Maacah the
daughter of Absalom above all his wives
and concubines (he took eighteen wives

15 [h]See 1 Kin. 11:29-39
16 [i]See 2 Sam. 20:1
18 [j][1 Kin. 4:6; 5:14]
Chapter 11
1 [k]For ver. 1-4, see 1 Kin. 12:21-24
2 [l]ch. 12:5, 15
4 [m]ch. 28:8, 11
5 [n]ver. 23; ch. 8:5; 12:4; 14:6; 17:2, 19; 21:3
8 [o]ch. 14:9

14 [p]Num. 35:2 [q]ch. 13:9
15 [r]1 Kin. 12:31; 13:33 [s]See 1 Kin. 12:28
16 [t]ch. 15:9
17 [u][ch. 12:1]
18 [v]1 Sam. 16:6; 17:13, 28; [1 Chr. 27:18]
20 [w]1 Kin. 15:2 [x][1 Kin. 14:31]

[1] Spelled *Adoram* in 1 Kings 12:18

10:16 all Israel. See note 10:1.

10:19 to this day. See note 1 Chr. 4:41.

11:2 Shemaiah. The prophet appears twice in Rehoboam's reign (cf. 12:5–8). To his credit and benefit, both times Rehoboam listened to the prophet's word.

11:3 all Israel in Judah. See note 10:1.

11:4 this thing is from me. See note 10:15.

11:5–23 The writer gives three illustrations of divine blessing to demonstrate the wisdom of Rehoboam's response to the prophetic warning (20:20 note). The text mentions fortifications and military strength in Judah and Benjamin (11:5–12), the defection of Levites from the northern kingdom (11:13–17), and the increase of his family (11:18–23).

11:5 built cities for defense. See note 1 Chr. 11:5.

11:13 all Israel. See note 10:1.

11:14 Jeroboam . . . cast them out. The historian does not repeat the account found in 1 Kings about how Jeroboam established idolatrous worship centers at Dan and Bethel (1 Kin. 12:25–33), but he assumes that the reader knows it. Jeroboam rejected priests and Levites who were faithful to Jerusalem as the proper site for worship. Jeroboam's animosity drove these priests to Rehoboam. The theme of faithful Israelites defecting to Judah appears several times in the periods of the divided and reunited kingdoms (13:8–11; 15:9; 30:10–12). Following the return of the remnant from exile in Babylonia, these accounts were a precedent for Israelites from the northern kingdom, since the restoration was centered in Jerusalem (1 Chr. 9:3 note; see Introduction: The Divided Kingdom).

11:17 they walked for three years in the way of David and Solomon. Rehoboam enjoyed God's blessing because he imitated the faithfulness of David and Solomon for the early years of his reign.

11:18–23 The historian frequently mentions the increase of family to demonstrate God's blessing (1 Chr. 13:13 note).

11:20 Maacah. See 13:2 note.

and sixty concubines, and fathered twenty-
eight sons and sixty daughters). 22 [y]And
Rehoboam appointed [x]Abijah the son of
Maacah as chief prince among his brothers,
for he intended to make him king. 23 And
he dealt wisely and distributed some of his
sons through all the districts of Judah and
Benjamin, in all the fortified cities, and he
gave them abundant provisions and procured wives for them.[1]

Egypt Plunders Jerusalem

12 [z]When the rule of Rehoboam was
established [a]and he was strong, [b]he
abandoned the law of the LORD, and all Israel
with him. 2 [c]In the fifth year of King
Rehoboam, because they had been unfaithful to the LORD, [d]Shishak king of Egypt came
up against Jerusalem 3 with 1,200 chariots
and 60,000 horsemen. And the people were
without number who came with him from
Egypt—[e]Libyans, Sukkiim, and Ethiopians.
4 And he took [f]the fortified cities of Judah
and came as far as Jerusalem. 5 Then
[g]Shemaiah the prophet came to Rehoboam
and to the princes of Judah, who had gathered at Jerusalem because of Shishak, and
said to them, "Thus says the LORD, [h]'You
abandoned me, so I have abandoned you to
the hand of Shishak.'" 6 Then the princes of
[i]Israel and the king humbled themselves and
said, [j]"The LORD is righteous." 7 When the
LORD saw that they humbled themselves, the
word of the LORD came to Shemaiah: [k]"They
have humbled themselves. I will not destroy
them, but I will grant them some deliverance, [l]and my wrath shall not be poured out
on Jerusalem by the hand of Shishak.
8 Nevertheless, they shall be servants to him,
[m]that they may know my service and the
service of the kingdoms of the countries."

9 [n]So Shishak king of Egypt came up
against Jerusalem. He took away the treasures of the house of the LORD and the
treasures of the king's house. He took away
everything. He also took away [o]the shields
of gold that Solomon had made, 10 and King
Rehoboam made in their place shields of
bronze and committed them to the hands
of the officers of the guard, who kept the
door of the king's house. 11 And as often as
the king went into the house of the LORD,
the guard came and carried them and
brought them back to the guardroom.
12 And when [p]he humbled himself the wrath
of the LORD turned from him, so as not to
make a complete destruction. Moreover,
[q]conditions were good[2] in Judah.
13 [r]So King Rehoboam grew strong in
Jerusalem and reigned. Rehoboam was
forty-one years old when he began to reign,
and he reigned seventeen years in
Jerusalem, the city that the LORD had chosen
out of all the tribes of Israel to put his name
there. His mother's name was Naamah the
Ammonite. 14 And he did evil, [s]for he did not
set his heart to seek the LORD.
15 [t]Now the acts of Rehoboam, [u]from first
to last, are they not written in the chronicles of [v]Shemaiah the prophet and of [w]Iddo
[x]the seer?[3] There were continual wars
between Rehoboam and Jeroboam. 16 And
Rehoboam slept with his fathers and was
buried in the city of David, and [y]Abijah[4]
his son reigned in his place.

Abijah Reigns in Judah

13 [z]In the eighteenth year of King
Jeroboam, [y]Abijah began to reign

22 [y][Deut. 21:15-17] [x][See ver. 20 above]
Chapter 12
1 [z]ch. 11:17 [a]ch. 26:16 [b]See 1 Kin. 14:22-24
2 [c]1 Kin. 14:25 [d]1 Kin. 11:40
3 [e]ch. 16:8; Nah. 3:9; [Dan. 11:43]
4 [f]See ch. 11:5-12
5 [g]ch. 11:2; 1 Kin. 12:22 [h][ch. 15:2]
6 [i][ch. 21:2] [j]Ex. 9:27
7 [k][ch. 7:14; 1 Kin. 21:29; James 4:10] [l][ch. 34:25]
8 [m][Deut. 28:47, 48; Isai. 26:13]
9 [n]For ver. 9-11, see 1 Kin. 14:26-28 [o]ch. 9:15, 16; 1 Kin. 10:16, 17
12 [p][ch. 7:14; 1 Kin. 21:29; James 4:10] [q][ch. 19:3]
13 [r]1 Kin. 14:21
14 [s][ch. 19:3]
15 [t][1 Kin. 14:29] [u]ch. 9:29; 1 Chr. 29:29 [v]ver. 5; 1 Kin. 12:22 [w]ch. 9:29; 13:22 [x]See 1 Sam. 9:9
16 [y][1 Kin. 14:31]
Chapter 13
1 [z]1 Kin. 15:1, 2 [y][See ch. 12:16 above]

1 Hebrew *and sought a multitude of wives* 2 Hebrew *good things were found* 3 After *seer*, Hebrew adds *according to genealogy* 4 Spelled *Abijam* in 1 Kings 14:31

12:1–12 For the second major portion of the account of Rehoboam's reign (chs. 10–12 note) the historian expands the account of 1 Kin. 14:25–28. He reports Rehoboam's disobedience in his fourth year and the divine retribution by Shishak's invasion in the fifth year (12:2).

12:1, 2 abandoned the law . . . unfaithful to the LORD. See 1 Kin. 14:22–24 for more details on this apostasy. See also note on 1 Chr. 16:40.

12:1 all Israel. See note 10:1.

12:2 Shishak. The founder of the twenty-second dynasty of Egypt (c. 945–924 B.C.), whose military campaign extended to the plains of Jezreel and Megiddo.

12:3–9 The author adds these verses to complete the parallel with Rehoboam's previous encounter with Shemaiah (cf 11:2–4; 10:1–11:23 note).

12:3 1,200 . . . 60,000 . . . without number. See note 1 Chr. 19:7.

12:6 humbled themselves. See also vv. 7, 12. This event illustrates God's response to Solomon's prayer (7:14 note).

12:7, 8 Although Shemaiah modified his first warning, God's sovereign plan was not overturned. Prophetic warnings were designed to stir repentance. If they succeeded in this, the threat of judgment was often removed, postponed, or softened (Jer. 18:1–12; Joel 2:12–14; Jon. 3).

12:12 good in Judah. While Rehoboam continued to suffer for his sins, God graciously established his kingdom and blessed the nation.

12:14 he did evil. Probably a reference to the sins of Rehoboam's fourth year (vv. 1, 2 note). 1 Kin. 14:29–31 does not include this observation.

12:15 written in the chronicles. See Introduction to 1 Chronicles: Author.

13:1–14:1 The account of Abijah's reign in Chronicles (13:2–21) differs considerably from that in Kings (1 Kin. 15:3–5). Chronicles emphasizes the positive side of Abijah's reign while the writer of Kings focuses on the negative side (1 Kin. 15:3). Chronicles reports Abijah's speech against the northern kingdom (13:4–12) and his prayerful reliance on God in battle (13:14).

over Judah. **2** He reigned for three years in
Jerusalem. His mother's name was [a]Mi-
caiah[1] the daughter of Uriel of Gibeah.
[b]Now there was war between Abijah and
Jeroboam. **3** Abijah went out to battle, having an army of valiant men of war, 400,000
chosen men. And Jeroboam [c]drew up his
line of battle against him with 800,000
chosen mighty warriors. **4** Then Abijah
stood up on Mount [d]Zemaraim that is in
[e]the hill country of Ephraim and said,
"Hear me, O Jeroboam and all Israel!
5 Ought you not to know that the LORD God
of Israel [f]gave the kingship over Israel forever to David and his sons by [g]a covenant
of salt? **6** Yet Jeroboam the son of Nebat, a
servant of Solomon the son of David, rose
up [h]and rebelled against his lord, **7** and certain [i]worthless scoundrels gathered about
him and defied Rehoboam the son of
Solomon, when Rehoboam was [j]young and
irresolute[2] and could not withstand them.
8 "And now you think to withstand the
kingdom of the LORD in the hand of the
sons of David, because you are a great multitude and have with you [k]the golden calves
that Jeroboam made you for gods. **9** [l]Have
you not driven out the priests of the LORD,
the sons of Aaron, and the Levites, and
made priests for yourselves like the peoples
of other lands? Whoever comes [m]for ordination[3] with a young bull or seven rams
becomes a priest of what are [n]no gods.
10 But as for us, the LORD is our God, and
we have not forsaken him. We have priests
ministering to the LORD who are sons of
Aaron, and Levites for their service. **11** They
offer to the LORD [o]every morning and every
evening burnt offerings and incense of
sweet spices, set out [p]the showbread on
the table of pure gold, [q]and care for the
golden lampstand that its lamps may [r]burn
every evening. For we [s]keep the charge of
the LORD our God, but you have forsaken
him. **12** Behold, God is with us at our head,
and his priests [t]with their battle trumpets
to sound the call to battle against you. O
sons of Israel, [u]do not fight against the
LORD, the God of your fathers, for you cannot succeed."
13 Jeroboam had sent [v]an ambush around
to come upon them from behind. Thus his
troops[4] were in front of Judah, and the
ambush was behind them. **14** And when
Judah looked, behold, the battle was in
front of and behind them. [w]And they cried
to the LORD, and the priests [t]blew the
trumpets. **15** Then the men of Judah raised
the battle shout. And when the men of
Judah shouted, [x]God defeated Jeroboam
and all Israel before Abijah and Judah.
16 The men of Israel fled before Judah, [y]and
God gave them into their hand. **17** Abijah
and his people struck them with great
force, so there fell slain of Israel 500,000
chosen men. **18** Thus the men of Israel were
subdued at that time, and the men of
Judah prevailed, [z]because they relied on

2 [a][ch. 11:20] [b]1 Kin. 15:7 **3** [c]ch. 14:10; Judg. 20:22; 1 Sam. 17:2 **4** [d]Josh. 18:22 [e]See Josh. 24:33 **5** [f]2 Sam. 7:12, 13, 16 [g]Num. 18:19 **6** [h]1 Kin. 11:26; 12:19, 20 **7** [i]See Judg. 9:4 [j][ch. 12:13; 1 Kin. 14:21] **8** [k]See 1 Kin. 12:28 **9** [l]ch. 11:14, 15 [m]ch. 29:31 [n]Jer. 5:7 **11** [o]ch. 2:4 [p]See Lev. 24:5-9 [q]See Ex. 25:31-39 [r]Ex. 27:20, 21; Lev. 24:2-4 [s]Num. 1:53 **12** [t]Num. 10:9 [u][Acts 5:39] **13** [v][Josh. 8:9] **14** [w]ch. 14:11 [t][See ver. 12 above] **15** [x]ch. 14:12 **16** [y]ch. 16:8 **18** [z][ch. 14:11; 16:7, 8]

1 Spelled *Maacah* in 1 Kings 15:2 2 Hebrew *soft of heart* 3 Hebrew *to fill his hand* 4 Hebrew *they*

13:1 Abijah. He reigned 913–910 B.C. while Jeroboam I ruled the northern kingdom (930–909 B.C.).

13:2 Micaiah. A variant spelling of "Maacah" (see 11:20; 1 Kin. 15:2). Maacah was apparently the granddaughter of Absalom through his daughter Tamar and her husband Uriel of Gibeah.

war between Abijah and Jeroboam. 1 Kin. 15:6, 7 mentions this war, but Chronicles has more details including the drawing of battle lines, Abijah's speech, the battle itself, and its outcome.

13:3 400,000 . . . 800,000. Judah was greatly outnumbered, highlighting the power of God at work on behalf of faithful Judah (1 Chr. 12:23 note; 19:7 note).

13:4–12 Abijah's speech against the northern kingdom makes clear that David's dynasty was approved by God, and that the temple worship in Jerusalem was established by God.

13:4 Mount Zemaraim. This was in the border regions between Judah and Israel, probably in the territory of Benjamin (cf. Josh. 18:22).

13:6 Jeroboam . . . rebelled. Abijah appeals to the northern army by blaming Jeroboam for the rebellion against Rehoboam.

13:7 young and irresolute and could not withstand them. Abijah explains that Rehoboam's offense against the northern tribes (10:1–17) was the result of his youth and inexperience (cf. 1 Chr. 22:5; 29:1; 2 Chr. 12:13).

13:8 kingdom of the LORD. Despite Rehoboam's offense, to oppose David's dynasty was to resist God Himself.

13:9 driven out the priests . . . and the Levites. The writer of Chronicles has already mentioned the defection of these Levites as an indication of God's blessing on Rehoboam (11:13–17 and notes).

13:10 we have not forsaken. In contrast with the northern kingdom, Judah had remained fundamentally loyal to the temple, priests, and Levites (but see 12:1, 2). This assessment of Judah's condition is reversed later in Hezekiah's day (29:4–11 note; 30:6–9 note).

13:11, 12 Abijah's speech refers to his care for proper worship. The original readers of Chronicles were reestablishing worship in Jerusalem following the return of the Jews from exile in Babylonia.

13:12 God is with us. See Is. 7:14 notes; Num. 14:9; Ps. 46:7; Matt. 1:23. The presence of God with the army of Judah secured victory. Abijah asserted that God was with Judah, even in a fight against the northern kingdom.

13:14 cried to the LORD. In his dedicatory prayer Solomon had spoken of praying to God in battle (6:34 note). Prayer appears as the decisive factor in the battle (1 Chr. 4:9 note).

13:15 all Israel. In this context, the northern kingdom.

13:18 were subdued. See note 1 Chr. 20:4.

the LORD, the God of their fathers. 19 And
Abijah pursued Jeroboam [a]and took cities
from him, Bethel with its villages and
Jeshanah with its villages and [b]Ephron[1]
with its villages. 20 Jeroboam did not recover his power in the days of Abijah. [c]And the
LORD struck him down, [d]and he died. 21 But
Abijah grew mighty. And he took fourteen
wives and had twenty-two sons and sixteen
daughters. 22 The rest of the acts of Abijah,
his ways and his sayings, are written in the
[e]story of the prophet [f]Iddo.

Asa Reigns in Judah

14 [2] [g]Abijah slept with his fathers, and
they buried him in the city of
David. And Asa his son reigned in his
place. In his days the land had rest for ten
years. [3] 2 And Asa did what was good and
right in the eyes of the LORD his God. 3 He
took away the foreign altars [h]and the high
places and broke down [i]the pillars and cut
down the [j]Asherim 4 and commanded
Judah to seek the LORD, the God of their
fathers, and to keep the law and the commandment. 5 He also took out of all the
cities of Judah [h]the high places and the [k]in-
cense altars. And the kingdom had rest
under him. 6 He built [l]fortified cities in
Judah, for the land had rest. He had no war
in those years, [m]for the LORD gave him
peace. 7 And he said to Judah, "Let us build
these cities and surround them with [n]walls
and towers, gates and bars. The land is still
ours, because we have sought the LORD our
God. We have sought him, [m]and he has
given us peace on every side." So they built
and prospered. 8 And Asa had an army of
[o]300,000 from Judah, armed with large
shields and spears, and 280,000 men from
Benjamin that carried shields and drew
bows. All these were mighty men of valor.
9 Zerah [p]the Ethiopian came out against
them with an army of a million men and
300 chariots, and came as far as
[q]Mareshah. 10 And Asa went out to meet
him, and [r]they drew up their lines of battle
in the Valley of Zephathah at [q]Mareshah.
11 And Asa [s]cried to the LORD his God, "O
LORD, there is none like you to help,
between the mighty and the weak. Help us,
O LORD our God, [t]for we rely on you, [u]and
in your name we have come against this
multitude. O LORD, you are our God; let
not man prevail against you." 12 [v]So the
LORD defeated the Ethiopians before Asa
and before Judah, and the Ethiopians fled.
13 Asa and the people who were with him
pursued them as far as [w]Gerar, and the
Ethiopians fell until none remained alive,
for they were broken before the LORD and

19 [a][ch. 15:8; 17:2] [b][Josh. 15:9]
20 [c]1 Sam. 25:38 [d]1 Kin. 14:20
22 [e]ch. 24:27 [f]ch. 9:29; 12:15
Chapter 14
1 [g][1 Kin. 15:8]
3 [h][ch. 15:17; 1 Kin. 15:14] [i]See Ex. 23:24 [j]Ex. 34:13
5 [h][See ver. 3 above] [k]ch. 34:4, 7; Lev. 26:30; Isai. 17:8; 27:9; Ezek. 6:4, 6
6 [l]See ch. 11:5 [m]ch. 15:15; 20:30
7 [n]ch. 8:5 [m][See ver. 6 above]
8 [o][ch. 13:3]
9 [p]ch. 12:3; 16:8; [q]ch. 11:8; Josh 15:44
10 [r]ch. 13:3 [q][See ver. 9 above]
11 [s]ch. 13:14; Ex. 14:10 [t]ch. 13:18 [u][1 Sam. 17:45]
12 [v]ch. 13:15
13 [w]Gen. 10:19; 20:1; 26:1, 6

[1] Or *Ephrain* [2] Ch 13:23 in Hebrew [3] Ch 14:1 in Hebrew

because they relied on the LORD. Reliance on the power of the Lord instead of human strength is a dominant theme in 1 and 2 Chronicles (16:2 note).

13:20, 21 The outcomes for Jeroboam and Abijah indicate whether God approved or disapproved of them. Jeroboam never recovered from his defeat. Abijah, however, grew stronger and had many children (1 Chr. 13:13 note).

13:22 the story of the prophet Iddo. See Introduction to 1 Chronicles: Author.

14:1 the land had rest. See note 1 Chr. 22:9.

14:2–16:14 This account of Asa's reign is considerably longer than that of 1 Kin. 15:9–24. Asa's reign is presented in two parts: years of fidelity and blessing (14:2–15:19) and later years of infidelity and curse (ch. 16). These two parts form a pattern of contrasting parallels. Asa's growing prosperity (14:2–7) is balanced by the concluding section on his illness and death (16:11–14). The main section concerns warfare, prophetic encouragement, and the royal response (14:8–15:19 and 16:1–10). The historian contrasts the results of relying on God (15:8–19) with the results of relying on human power (16:2 note; 20:20 note).

14:2 Asa. Reigned from 911 to 870 B.C.

14:3 took away . . . the high places. Asa removed pagan high places from both Jerusalem and "all the cities of Judah" (14:5), but 15:17 (1 Kin. 15:14) indicates that these initial efforts were not continued throughout his life. A similar explanation holds for the descriptions of Jehoshaphat's removal of high places (cf. 17:6; 20:33).

14:4 seek the LORD. See note 7:14.

keep the law and the commandment. See note 1 Chr. 16:40.

14:6 He had no war. Apparently, this means that there were no major wars in this period. The writer says later that Asa had captured some towns in Ephraim during this time (15:8).

the LORD gave him peace. Chronicles presents peace in Asa's reign as a blessing for devotion and obedience to God (14:2–16:14 note; 1 Chr. 22:9 note).

14:6, 7 He built . . . Let us build. God also assisted Asa's building projects (1 Chr. 11:5 note).

14:7 because we have sought the LORD. Asa plainly said that his success came from having sought God (v. 4).

14:8–15 When Zerah attacked, Asa sought the Lord and gained victory, fulfilling Solomon's request in his prayer (6:34 note). This battle directly contrasts with Asa's later battle against Baasha (16:1–6; see note 14:2–16:14).

14:8 Asa's army totaled 580,000. The attacking army was nearly twice as large ("a million men," v. 9). On these large numbers, see note 1 Chr. 12:23.

14:9 Zerah the Ethiopian. Possibly a general of Pharaoh Osorkon I, second ruler of the twenty-second dynasty of Egypt. "Ethiopia" in the Bible is the remote region south of Egypt, including parts of modern Eritrea, Ethiopia, and Sudan.

a million men. See 1 Chr. 19:7 note.

14:11 weak. Asa expressed his utter inadequacy for battle against Zerah (20:12 note).

we rely on you. Reliance on the Lord's power was the key to Asa's victory (16:2 note).

his army. The men of Judah[1] carried away
very much spoil. 14 And they attacked all
the cities around [w]Gerar, [x]for the fear of the
LORD was upon them. They plundered all
the cities, for there was much plunder in
them. 15 And they struck down the tents of
those who had livestock and carried away
sheep in abundance and camels. Then they
returned to Jerusalem.

Asa's Religious Reforms

15 [y]The Spirit of God came upon
Azariah the son of Oded, 2 and he
went out to meet Asa and said to him,
"Hear me, Asa, and all Judah and
Benjamin: [z]The LORD is with you while you
are with him. [a]If you seek him, he will be
found by you, [b]but if you forsake him, he
will forsake you. 3 [c]For a long time Israel
was without the true God, and without a
teaching priest and without law, 4 [d]but
when in their distress they turned to the
LORD, the God of Israel, and sought him,
he was found by them. 5 In those times
there was no peace [e]to him who went out
or to him who came in, for great disturbances afflicted all the inhabitants of the
lands. 6 They were broken in pieces. Nation
was crushed by nation and city by city, for
God troubled them with every sort of distress. 7 [f]But you, take courage! Do not let
your hands be weak, [g]for your work shall
be rewarded."

8 As soon as Asa heard these words, [h]the
prophecy of Azariah the son of Oded, he
took courage and put away the detestable
idols from all the land of Judah and
Benjamin and from [i]the cities that he had
taken in [j]the hill country of Ephraim, and
he repaired the altar of the LORD [k]that was
in front of the vestibule of the house of the
LORD.[2] 9 And he gathered all Judah and
Benjamin, [l]and those from Ephraim,
Manasseh, and Simeon who were residing
with them, for great numbers had deserted
to him from Israel when they saw that the
LORD his God was with him. 10 They were
gathered at Jerusalem in the third month of
the fifteenth year of the reign of Asa. 11 They
sacrificed to the LORD on that day [m]from
the spoil that they had brought 700 oxen
and 7,000 sheep. 12 [n]And they entered into
a covenant to seek the LORD, the God of
their fathers, with all their heart and with
all their soul, 13 but that whoever would not
seek the LORD, the God of Israel, [o]should
be put to death, whether young or old,
man or woman. 14 They swore an oath to
the LORD with a loud voice and with shouting and with trumpets and with horns.
15 And all Judah rejoiced over the oath, for
they had sworn with all their heart and had
sought him with their whole desire, and he
was found by them, [p]and the LORD gave
them rest all around.

16 [q]Even Maacah, [r]his mother, King Asa
removed from being queen mother because
she had made a detestable image [s]for
Asherah. Asa cut down her image, [t]crushed
it, and burned it at the brook Kidron. 17 [u]But
the high places were not taken out of Israel.
Nevertheless, the heart of Asa was wholly
true all his days. 18 And he brought into the
house of God the sacred gifts of his father
and his own sacred gifts, silver, and gold,
and vessels. 19 And there was no more war
until the thirty-fifth year of the reign of Asa.

Asa's Last Years

16 [v]In the [w]thirty-sixth year of the
reign of Asa, Baasha king of Israel

14 [w][See ver. 13 above] [x]ch. 17:10; 20:29; [Gen. 35:5]
Chapter 15
1 [y]ch. 20:14; 24:20; Num. 24:2; Judg. 3:10; [ver. 8]
2 [z]ch. 20:17 [a]1 Chr. 28:9; Isai. 55:6; Jer. 29:13; [b]ch. 12:5; 24:20
3 [c][Hos. 3:4]
4 [d]Deut. 4:30, 31
5 [e]Judg. 5:6
7 [f]Josh. 1:6, 7, 9 [g]Gen. 15:1; [Ps. 62:12]
8 [h][ver. 1] [i]ch. 17:2; [ch. 13:19] [j]See Josh. 24:33 [k]Ch. 8:12
9 [l]ch. 11:16
11 [m]See ch. 14:13-15
12 [n]ch. 29:10; 34:31; 2 Kin. 23:3; Neh. 10:29
13 [o]See Deut. 13:6-9
15 [p]ch. 14:7; 20:30
16 [q]For ver. 16-18, see 1 Kin. 15:13-15 [r][1 Kin. 15:2, 10] [s]Ex. 34:13 [t][ch. 30:14; 2 Kin. 23:6, 15]
17 [u][ch. 14:3, 5]
Chapter 16
1 [v]For ver. 1-6, see 1 Kin. 15:17-22 [w][1 Kin. 16:8]

1 Hebrew *they* 2 Hebrew *the vestibule of the LORD*

15:1–7 Azariah proclaims the principle of retribution so often illustrated in this account of the divided monarchy. Faithfulness to God will bring blessing; disloyalty will result in chastisement.

15:2 If you seek him. See notes 7:14 and 1 Chr. 28:9.

15:4 turned to the LORD. See note 7:14.

15:8–19 Asa responded to the prophets with further reforms (v. 8) and an assembly of covenant renewal (vv. 9–15); he went so far as to depose Maacah, his relative, because of her religious apostasy (vv. 16–19).

15:9 deserted to him. Israelites from the northern tribes (11:14 note) defected and joined Asa as he suppressed idolatry and reestablished worship in Jerusalem.

15:12 entered into a covenant. Covenant renewal here continues God's relationship with His people through the generations. Asa (15:12), Jehoiada (23:16), Hezekiah (29:10), and Josiah (34:30–32) lead the nation in such renewals.

15:13 put to death. The Law of Moses prescribed capital punishment for those who sought other gods (Ex. 22:20; Deut. 13:6–16).

15:15 rest all around. See note 1 Chr. 22:9.

15:17 all his days. See note 14:3.

15:19 no more war. See note 14:6.

15:19–16:1 thirty-fifth year . . . thirty-sixth year. Kings reports that Elah succeeded Baasha in Asa's 26th year (1 Kin. 15:33; 16:8), Zimri in Asa's 27th year (1 Kin. 16:10, 15) and Omri in Asa's 31st year (1 Kin. 16:23). Consequently, this battle could not have taken place in the 36th year of Asa (16:1) since Baasha would have been dead for ten years. No simple solution to this difficulty has been found.

16:1–6 Asa's battle with Baasha of Israel began his downfall. He sought the assistance of Ben-hadad of Syria, in sharp contrast with his battle against Zerah when he relied on the Lord (14:2–16:14 note).

went up against Judah and built Ramah,
[x]that he might permit no one to go out or
come in to Asa king of Judah. 2 Then Asa
took silver and gold from the treasures of
the house of the LORD and the king's house
and sent them to Ben-hadad king of Syria,
who lived in Damascus, saying, 3 "There is
a covenant[1] between me and you, as there
was between my father and your father.
Behold, I am sending to you silver and
gold. Go, break your covenant with Baasha
king of Israel, that he may withdraw from
me." 4 And Ben-hadad listened to King Asa
and sent the commanders of his armies
against the cities of Israel, and they conquered Ijon, Dan, Abel-maim, and all the
[y]store cities of Naphtali. 5 And when
Baasha heard of it, he stopped building
Ramah and let his work cease. 6 Then King
Asa took all Judah, and they carried away
the stones of Ramah and its timber, with
which Baasha had been building, and with
them he built Geba and Mizpah.
7 At that time [z]Hanani [a]the seer came to
Asa king of Judah and said to him,
[b]"Because you relied on the king of Syria,
and did not rely on the LORD your God, the
army of the king of Syria has escaped you.
8 Were not [c]the Ethiopians and [d]the
Libyans a huge army with very many chariots and horsemen? Yet [e]because you relied
on the LORD, he gave them into your hand.
9 [f]For the eyes of the LORD run to and fro
throughout the whole earth, to give strong
support to those [g]whose heart is blameless
toward him. [h]You have done foolishly in
this, for from now on [i]you will have wars."
10 Then Asa was angry with the seer and put
him [j]in the stocks in prison, for he was in
a rage with him because of this. And Asa
inflicted cruelties upon some of the people
at the same time.
11 [k]The acts of Asa, from first to last, are
written in the Book of the Kings of Judah
and Israel. 12 In the thirty-ninth year of his
reign Asa was diseased in his feet, and his
disease became severe. Yet even in his disease he did not seek the LORD, but sought
help from physicians. 13 And Asa slept with
his fathers, dying in the forty-first year of
his reign. 14 They buried him in the tomb
that he had cut for himself in the city of
David. They laid him on a bier [l]that had
been filled with various kinds of spices prepared by the perfumer's art, [m]and they
made a very great fire in his honor.

Jehoshaphat Reigns in Judah

17 Jehoshaphat his son reigned in his
place and strengthened himself
against Israel. 2 He placed forces in all the
[n]fortified cities of Judah and set garrisons
in the land of Judah, and in the cities of
Ephraim [o]that Asa his father had captured. 3 The LORD was with Jehoshaphat,
because he walked in the earlier ways of
his father David. He did not seek the
Baals, 4 but sought the God of his father
and walked in his commandments, [p]and
not according to the practices of Israel.
5 Therefore the LORD established the kingdom in his hand. And all Judah [q]brought
tribute to Jehoshaphat, [r]and he had great

1 [x][ch. 15:9] 4 [y][Ex. 1:11] 7 [z]ch. 19:2; 1 Kin. 16:1 [a]See 1 Sam. 9:9 [b][Isai. 31:1; Jer. 17:5] 8 [c]ch. 14:9 [d]ch. 12:3 [e][ch. 13:16, 18] 9 [f]Zech. 4:10; [Prov. 15:3] [g][1 Kin. 8:61] [h]1 Sam. 13:13 [i]1 Kin. 15:16, 32

10 [j][ch. 18:26] 11 [k]For ver. 11-14, see 1 Kin. 15:23, 24 14 [l][Gen. 50:2; Mark 16:1; John 19:39, 40] [m][ch. 21:19; Jer. 34:5]

Chapter 17
2 [n]See ch. 11:5 [o]ch. 15:8 4 [p][1 Kin. 12:28] 5 [q][ch. 32:23] [r]ch. 18:1

[1] Or *treaty*; twice in this verse

16:2 treasures of the house of the LORD . . . to Ben-hadad. Asa's actions were wrong on two counts. He took from the temple treasuries, showing disregard for the temple and its worship (cf. 28:21). Second, he allied himself with a foreign power instead of relying on the Lord. The historian demonstrates the benefits of relying on God many times (1 Chr. 5:20; 2 Chr. 13:18; 14:11–15; 16:7, 8; 32:20–22). He also deplores foreign alliances and points to their dire consequences (18:1; 19:2; 20:35–37; 22:3–9; 25:7; 28:16–21; 35:21 note), a suitable warning to those engaged in rebuilding the nation following the return from exile in Babylonia.

16:7–10 In contrast to the earlier episode of Azariah's encouragement and Asa's reforms (ch. 15), Hanani now rebuked King Asa, who reacted negatively (14:2–16:14 note).

16:7 escaped you. Baasha deserted his position before the arrival of Asa and Ben-hadad, cutting short Asa's victory (16:5).

16:8 Were not the Ethiopians. Hanani referred directly to the contrast with Asa's victory over Zerah (14:8–15). "Ethiopians" means people from south of Egypt. The Libyans were from north Africa.

16:9 from now on you will have wars. Hanani threatens divine judgment because of Asa's infidelity (1 Chr. 28:9 note; 2 Chr. 14:6 note).

16:10 some of the people. Presumably those who agreed with Hanani the prophet.

16:11–14 Asa's rejection of the prophetic word led to his disease and death (14:2–16:14 note).

16:12 physicians. Asa continued to turn away from the Lord and rely on human strength. The Old Testament does not hesitate to prescribe medical treatment for physical maladies (2 Kin. 20:5–7 and the use of balm in Jer. 8:22; 51:8), but it never divorces natural remedies from seeking divine assistance (Deut. 32:39).

16:14 made a very great fire in his honor. These fires were not cremations, but memorials honoring deceased kings. Contrast the honor bestowed on Asa with the response to Jehoram's death (21:19).

17:1–21:3 The account of Jehoshaphat's reign incorporates most of the record in Kings (cf. 1 Kin. 22:1–35 with 2 Chr. 18:2–34; 1 Kin. 22:41–46, 49 with 2 Chr. 20:31–36), adding some material and a summary of his reign.

17:1 Jehoshaphat. He reigned 872–848 B.C. Jehoshaphat was probably co-regent with Asa for three years (872–869 B.C.) because of Asa's illness (16:11–14; cf. 20:31 note).

17:2 cities of Ephraim. See note 14:6.

riches and honor. 6 His heart was courageous in the ways of the LORD. And furthermore, [s]he took the high places and the Asherim out of Judah.

7 In the third year of his reign he sent his officials, Ben-hail, Obadiah, Zechariah, Nethanel, and Micaiah, [t]to teach in the cities of Judah; 8 [u]and with them the Levites, Shemaiah, Nethaniah, Zebadiah, Asahel, Shemiramoth, Jehonathan, Adonijah, Tobijah, and Tobadonijah; and with these Levites, the priests Elishama and Jehoram. 9 And [t]they taught in Judah, having the Book of the Law of the LORD with them. They went about through all the cities of Judah and taught among the people.

10 [v]And the fear of the LORD fell upon all the kingdoms of the lands that were around Judah, and they made no war against Jehoshaphat. 11 Some of the Philistines [w]brought Jehoshaphat presents and silver for tribute, and the Arabians also brought him 7,700 rams and 7,700 goats. 12 And Jehoshaphat grew steadily greater. He built in Judah fortresses and store cities, 13 and he had large supplies in the cities of Judah. He had soldiers, mighty men of valor, in Jerusalem. 14 This was the muster of them by fathers' houses: Of Judah, the commanders of thousands: Adnah the commander, with 300,000 mighty men of valor; 15 and next to him Jehohanan the commander, with 280,000; 16 and next to him Amasiah the son of Zichri, [x]a volunteer for the service of the LORD, with 200,000 mighty men of valor. 17 Of Benjamin: Eliada, a mighty man of valor, with 200,000 men [y]armed with bow and shield; 18 and next to him Jehozabad with 180,000 armed for war. 19 These were in the service of the king, besides [z]those whom the king had placed in the fortified cities throughout all Judah.

Jehoshaphat Allies with Ahab

18 Now Jehoshaphat [a]had great riches and honor, [b]and he made a marriage alliance with Ahab. 2 [c]After some years he went down to Ahab in Samaria. And Ahab killed an abundance of sheep and oxen for him and for the people who were with him, and induced him to go up against Ramoth-gilead. 3 Ahab king of Israel said to Jehoshaphat king of Judah, "Will you go with me to Ramoth-gilead?" He answered him, "I am as you are, my people as your people. We will be with you in the war."

4 And Jehoshaphat said to the king of Israel, "Inquire first for the word of the LORD." 5 Then the king of Israel gathered the prophets together, four hundred men, and said to them, "Shall we go to battle against Ramoth-gilead, or shall I refrain?" And they said, "Go up, for God will give it into the hand of the king." 6 But Jehoshaphat said, "Is there not here another prophet of the LORD of whom we may inquire?" 7 And the king of Israel said to Jehoshaphat, "There is yet one man by whom we may inquire of the LORD, Micaiah the son of Imlah; but I hate him, for he never prophesies good concerning me, but always evil." And Jehoshaphat said, "Let not the king say so." 8 Then the king of Israel summoned an officer and said, "Bring quickly Micaiah the son of Imlah." 9 Now the king of Israel and Jehoshaphat the king of Judah were sitting on their thrones, arrayed in their robes. And they were sitting at the threshing floor [d]at the entrance of the gate of Samaria, and all the

6 [s][ch. 15:17; 20:33; 1 Kin. 22:43]
7 [t]See ch. 35:3
8 [u]ch. 19:8
9 [t][See ver. 7 above]
10 [v]ch. 14:14; 20:29
11 [w][ch. 26:8; 2 Sam. 8:2]
16 [x]Judg. 5:2, 9; Neh. 11:2
17 [y][1 Chr. 12:2]
19 [z]ver. 2

Chapter 18
1 [a]ch. 17:5 [b]ch. 21:6; 2 Kin. 8:18
2 [c]For ver. 2-34, see 1 Kin. 22:2-35
9 [d]See Ruth 4:1

17:6 high places. See note 14:3.

17:7 In the third year. This teaching mission probably took place just after Asa's death (17:1 note).

17:7, 8 officials . . . Levites. The royal officials were accompanied by Levites whom Moses had ordained to be teachers of the people (1 Chr. 26:29–32 note; 2 Chr. 19:5–11 note).

17:9 the Book of the Law of the LORD. The identity of this book is uncertain. It may have included the entire Pentateuch, but in light of the nature of Jehoshaphat's reforms (19:4–11), it may have been limited to the Book of Deuteronomy.

17:10 fear of the LORD. Fear of the divine power displayed in Jehoshaphat's military strength gave him peace with other nations (1 Chr. 14:17 note).

17:12 fortresses and store cities. See note 1 Chr. 11:5.

17:14–18 For these large numbers see note 1 Chr. 12:23.

18:1–19:3 In contrast with his early years, Jehoshaphat came under God's curse because he ignored the prophetic warning and made an alliance with the northern kingdom (16:2 note; 20:20 note).

18:1 he made a marriage alliance. The author refers to the marriage of Jehoshaphat's son, Jehoram, to Athaliah, daughter of Ahab (21:6; 22:2). In Kings, Ahab represents the depths of apostasy in the northern kingdom (1 Kin. 16:30). Cf. 19:1–3 and see note 16:2.

18:2 induced. The Hebrew expression can have the connotation of enticing to apostasy (Deut. 13:6; 1 Chr. 21:1).

Ramoth-gilead. A city thirty miles east of the Jordan River, closer to the Sea of Galilee than the Dead Sea. It had belonged to Israel since the time of Moses (Deut. 4:43; Josh. 20:8). Ben-hadad failed to return the city to Israel as he had agreed (1 Kin. 20:34).

prophets were prophesying before them.
10 And Zedekiah the son of Chenaanah
made for himself horns of iron and said,
"Thus says the LORD, 'With these you shall
push the Syrians until they are destroyed.'"
11 And all the prophets prophesied so and
said, "Go up to Ramoth-gilead and triumph. The LORD will give it into the hand
of the king."
12 And the messenger who went to summon Micaiah said to him, "Behold, the
words of the prophets with one accord are
favorable to the king. Let your word be like
the word of one of them, and speak favorably." 13 But Micaiah said, [e]"As the LORD
lives, [f]what my God says, that I will speak."
14 And when he had come to the king, the
king said to him, "Micaiah, shall we go to
Ramoth-gilead to battle, or shall I refrain?"
And he answered, "Go up and triumph;
they will be given into your hand." 15 But
the king said to him, "How many times
shall I make you swear that you speak to
me nothing but the truth in the name of
the LORD?" 16 And he said, "I saw all Israel
scattered on the mountains, [g]as sheep that
have no shepherd. And the LORD said,
'These have no master; let each return to
his home in peace.'" 17 And the king of
Israel said to Jehoshaphat, "Did I not tell
you that he would not prophesy good concerning me, but evil?" 18 And Micaiah said,
"Therefore hear the word of the LORD: [h]I
saw the LORD sitting on his throne, and all
the host of heaven standing on his right
hand and on his left. 19 And the LORD said,
'Who will entice Ahab the king of Israel, that
he may go up and fall at Ramoth-gilead?'
And one said one thing, and another said
another. 20 Then a spirit came forward and
stood before the LORD, saying, 'I will entice
him.' And the LORD said to him, 'By what
means?' 21 And he said, 'I will go out, and
will be [i]a lying spirit in the mouth of all his
prophets.' And he said, 'You are to entice
him, and you shall succeed; go out and do
so.' 22 Now therefore behold, the LORD has
put a lying spirit in the mouth of these

13 [e]1 Kin. 17:1 [f]Num. 22:18; 24:13
16 [g]Num. 27:17; Matt. 9:36
18 [h]See 1 Kin. 22:19
21 [i]See 1 Kin. 22:22

your prophets. The LORD has declared disaster concerning you."
23 Then Zedekiah the son of Chenaanah
came near [j]and struck Micaiah on the
cheek and said, "Which way did the Spirit
of the LORD go from me to speak to you?"
24 And Micaiah said, "Behold, you shall see
on that day when you go into an inner
chamber to hide yourself." 25 And the king
of Israel said, "Seize Micaiah and take him
back to Amon [k]the governor of the city and
to Joash the king's son, 26 and say, 'Thus
says the king, [l]Put this fellow in prison and
feed him with meager rations of bread and
water until I return in peace.'" 27 And
Micaiah said, "If you return in peace, the
LORD has not spoken by me." And he said,
[m]"Hear, all you peoples!"

The Defeat and Death of Ahab

28 So the king of Israel and Jehoshaphat
the king of Judah went up to Ramoth-gilead.
29 And the king of Israel said to Jehoshaphat, "I will disguise myself and go
into battle, but you wear your robes." And
the king of Israel disguised himself, and
they went into battle. 30 Now the king of
Syria had commanded the captains of his
chariots, "Fight with neither small nor
great, but only with the king of Israel." 31 As
soon as the captains of the chariots saw
Jehoshaphat, they said, "It is the king of
Israel." So they turned to fight against him.
And Jehoshaphat cried out, and the LORD
helped him; God drew them away from
him. 32 For as soon as the captains of the
chariots saw that it was not the king of Israel,
they turned back from pursuing him. 33 But a
certain man drew his bow at random[1] and
struck the king of Israel between the scale
armor and the breastplate. Therefore he said
to the driver of his chariot, "Turn around
and carry me out of the battle, for I am
wounded." 34 And the battle continued that
day, and the king of Israel was propped up in
his chariot facing the Syrians until evening.
Then at sunset he died.

23 [j]See 1 Kin. 22:24
25 [k]ch. 34:8
26 [l]See ch. 16:10
27 [m]Mic. 1:2

1 Hebrew *in his innocence*

18:18 I saw the LORD. Micaiah's vision of heavenly deliberations (cf. Job 1:6–12; Is. 6:1–8; Zech. 3) demonstrates that the sovereignty of God extends over evil events (1 Chr. 21:1 note).

18:28 In contrast with Rehoboam (11:4) and Asa after his first battle (15:1–8), Jehoshaphat paid no attention to the prophet's warning. As a result, Jehoshaphat barely escaped with his life (18:31). See note 20:20.

18:31 Jehoshaphat cried out. The writer adds to the words of 1 Kings 22:32 the explicit statement that "the LORD helped him," recalling the request of Solomon's dedicatory prayer (6:34 note; 7:14 note).

18:34 he died. The writer does not repeat the details of Ahab's death found in 1 Kin. 22:36–40.

Jehoshaphat's Reforms

19 Jehoshaphat the king of Judah
returned in safety to his house in
Jerusalem. 2 But [n]Jehu the son of [o]Hanani
[p]the seer went out to meet him and said to
King Jehoshaphat, "Should you [q]help the
wicked and love those who hate the LORD?
Because of this, [r]wrath has gone out
against you from the LORD. 3 Nevertheless,
[s]some good is found in you, for [t]you
destroyed the Asherahs out of the land,
and have [u]set your heart to seek God."
4 Jehoshaphat lived at Jerusalem. And he
went out again among the people, from
Beersheba to [v]the hill country of Ephraim,
and brought them back to the LORD, the
God of their fathers. 5 He appointed
[w]judges in the land in all [x]the fortified
cities of Judah, city by city, 6 and said to the
judges, "Consider what you do, [y]for you
judge not for man but for the LORD. He is
with you in giving judgment. 7 Now then,
let the fear of the LORD be upon you. Be
careful what you do, for [z]there is no injustice with the LORD our God, [a]or partiality or
taking bribes."
8 Moreover, in Jerusalem Jehoshaphat
[b]appointed certain Levites and priests and
heads of families of Israel, [y]to give judgment for the LORD and to decide disputed
cases. They had their seat at Jerusalem.
9 And he charged them: [c]"Thus you shall
do in the fear of the LORD, in faithfulness,
[d]and with your whole heart: 10 [e]whenever a
case comes to you from your brothers who
live in their cities, concerning bloodshed,
law or commandment, statutes or rules,
then you shall warn them, that they may
not incur guilt before the LORD and [f]wrath
may not come upon you and your brothers. Thus you shall do, and you will not
incur guilt. 11 And behold, Amariah the
chief priest is over you [g]in all matters of
the LORD; and Zebadiah the son of Ishmael, the governor of the house of Judah,
in all the king's matters, and the Levites
will serve you as officers. [h]Deal coura-
geously, and may the LORD be with the
upright!"[1]

Jehoshaphat's Prayer

20 After this [i]the Moabites and Ammonites, and with them some of
the Meunites,[2] came against Jehoshaphat
for battle. 2 Some men came and told
Jehoshaphat, "A great multitude is coming
against you from Edom,[3] from beyond the
sea; and, behold, they are in [j]Hazazon-
tamar" (that is, [k]Engedi). 3 Then Jehoshaphat was afraid and set his face [l]to seek
the LORD, and [m]proclaimed a fast throughout all Judah. 4 And Judah assembled to
seek help from the LORD; from all the cities
of Judah they came to seek the LORD.
5 And Jehoshaphat stood in the assembly
of Judah and Jerusalem, in the house of the
LORD, before the new court, 6 and said, "O
LORD, God of our fathers, are you not [n]God
in heaven? You [o]rule over all the kingdoms
of the nations. [p]In your hand are power and
might, so that none is able to withstand
you. 7 Did you not, our God, [q]drive out the
inhabitants of this land before your people
Israel, and give it forever to the descendants
of [r]Abraham your friend? 8 And they have
lived in it and have built for you in it a sanctuary for your name, saying, 9 [s]'If disaster
comes upon us, the sword, judgment,[4] or
pestilence, or famine, [t]we will stand before
this house and before you—[u]for your name
is in this house—and cry out to you in our
affliction, and you will hear and save.'

[1] Hebrew *the good* [2] Compare 26:7; Hebrew *Ammonites* [3] One Hebrew manuscript; most Hebrew manuscripts *Aram* (Syria) [4] Or *the sword of judgment*

Chapter 19
2 [n]ch. 20:34; 1 Kin. 16:1 [o]ch. 16:7 [p]See 1 Sam. 9:9 [q][ch. 18:1; 20:37; Ps. 139:21] [r]ver. 10; ch. 24:18; 32:25
3 [s]ch. 12:12; 1 Kin. 14:13 [t]ch. 17:6 [u]ch. 30:19; Ezra 7:10
4 [v]See Josh. 24:33
5 [w][Deut. 16:18] [x]See ch. 11:5
6 [y]Deut. 1:17
7 [z]Deut. 32:4; Job 8:3; 34:10; [Gen. 18:25; Rom. 9:14] [a]See Deut. 10:17
8 [b]ch. 17:8, 9 [y][See ver. 6 above]
9 [c]2 Sam. 23:3 [d]1 Kin. 8:61
10 [e]See Deut. 17:8 [f]ver. 2
11 [g]1 Chr. 26:30, 32 [h]1 Chr. 28:10; [Ezra 10:4]
Chapter 20
1 [i]2 Kin. 1:1; 3:4, 7
2 [j]Gen. 14:7 [k]See 1 Sam. 23:29
3 [l]ch. 19:3; [1 Chr. 22:19] [m]Ezra 8:21; Jer. 36:9; Jonah 3:5; [Joel 1:14; 2:15]
6 [n]See Deut. 4:39 [o][Dan. 4:17, 25, 32] [p]1 Chr. 29:12
7 [q]Ps. 44:2 [r]Isai. 41:8; James 2:23
9 [s]ch. 6:28-30; 1 Kin. 8:33, 37; [Ezek. 14:21] [t][Ezra 10:1] [u]ch. 6:20

19:1–3 Jehoshaphat escaped death after crying out to the Lord (18:31). Even so, Jehu rebukes him for his sin. God had chastised Jehoshaphat for depending on a foreign alliance (16:7–10 note; 1 Chr. 28:9 note).

19:5–11 Jehoshaphat established a system of courts throughout Judah to enforce Mosaic law (1 Chr. 26:20–32). He had earlier sent out leaders, Levites, and priests to teach (17:7–9).

19:6 He is with you. This does not mean that their decisions were inspired, but that God approved of the work of the courts in general, and wanted their decisions to be made according to His law first of all.

20:1–30 This battle is not found in Kings. Jehoshaphat responded to a serious military threat with exemplary reliance on the Lord (contrast his approach to the battle in 18:1–19:3).

20:1 Moabites . . . Ammonites. The descendants of these enemies were still a threat to Israel after the return from exile in Babylonia (Neh. 2:19; 4:1–3; 13).

20:2 A great multitude . . . against you. See note 1 Chr. 19:7.

20:3, 4 proclaimed a fast. Jehoshaphat responded immediately by calling Judah to fast and seek the Lord; these actions recall Solomon's dedicatory prayer (see notes 6:34).

20:5–19 Jehoshaphat's assembly followed the liturgical pattern often associated with prayers of lament: corporate prayer is offered (20:5–13); there is an oracle of deliverance from God (20:14–17); and the people respond with praise (20:18, 19).

20:9 Jehoshaphat applied Solomon's dedicatory prayer explicitly to his situation (6:12–42 and notes).

10 And now behold, the men of [v]Ammon
and Moab and [w]Mount Seir, whom [x]you
would not let Israel invade when they came
from the land of Egypt, [y]and whom they
avoided and did not destroy— 11 behold,
they reward us [z]by coming to drive us out
of your possession, which you have given
us to inherit. 12 O our God, will you not [a]ex-
ecute judgment on them? For we are powerless against this great horde that is coming against us. We do not know what to do,
but [b]our eyes are on you."
13 Meanwhile all Judah stood before the
LORD, with their little ones, their wives, and
their children. 14 And [c]the Spirit of the LORD
came upon Jahaziel the son of Zechariah,
son of Benaiah, son of Jeiel, son of
Mattaniah, a Levite of the sons of Asaph, in
the midst of the assembly. 15 And he said,
"Listen, all Judah and inhabitants of
Jerusalem and King Jehoshaphat: Thus says
the LORD to you, [d]'Do not be afraid and do
not be dismayed at this great horde, [e]for the
battle is not yours but God's. 16 Tomorrow
go down against them. Behold, they will
come up by the ascent of Ziz. You will find
them at the end of [f]the valley, east of the
wilderness of Jeruel. 17 [g]You will not need to
fight in this battle. Stand firm, hold your
position, and see the salvation of the LORD
on your behalf, O Judah and Jerusalem.' Do
not be afraid and do not be dismayed.
Tomorrow go out against them, [h]and the
LORD will be with you."
18 Then Jehoshaphat [i]bowed his head
with his face to the ground, and all Judah
and the inhabitants of Jerusalem fell down
before the LORD, worshiping the LORD.
19 And the Levites, of the [j]Kohathites and
the [k]Korahites, stood up to praise the LORD,
the God of Israel, with a very loud voice.
20 And they rose early in the morning and
went out into [l]the wilderness of Tekoa.
And when they went out, Jehoshaphat
stood and said, "Hear me, Judah and
inhabitants of Jerusalem! [m]Believe in the
LORD your God, and you will be established; believe his prophets, and you will
succeed." 21 And when he had taken counsel with the people, he appointed those
who were to sing to the LORD and praise
him [n]in holy attire, as they went before the
army, and say,

[o]"Give thanks to the LORD,
for his steadfast love endures
forever."

22 And when they began to sing and praise,
the LORD set [p]an ambush against the men
of [q]Ammon, Moab, and Mount Seir, who
had come against Judah, so that they were
routed. 23 For the men of Ammon and
Moab rose against the inhabitants of
Mount Seir, devoting them to destruction,[1]
and when they had made an end of the
inhabitants of Seir, [r]they all helped to
destroy one another.

The LORD Delivers Judah

24 When Judah came to the watchtower of
the wilderness, they looked toward the
horde, and behold, there[2] were dead bodies
lying on the ground; none had escaped.
25 When Jehoshaphat and his people came
to take their spoil, they found among them,
in great numbers, goods, clothing, and precious things, which they took for themselves until they could carry no more. They
were three days in taking the spoil, it was so
much. 26 On the fourth day they assembled
in the Valley of Beracah,[3] for there they
blessed the LORD. Therefore the name of
that place has been called the Valley of
Beracah to this day. 27 Then they returned,
every man of Judah and Jerusalem, and
Jehoshaphat at their head, returning to
Jerusalem with joy, [s]for the LORD had made
them rejoice over their enemies. 28 They
came to Jerusalem with harps and lyres and
trumpets, to the house of the LORD. 29 [t]And
the fear of God came on all the kingdoms of

10 [v]ver. 1, 22, 23 [w]ch. 25:11, 14; Gen 32:3; 36:8 [x]Deut. 2:4, 5, 9, 19 [y]Num. 20:21
11 [z]Ps. 83:6, 7, 12
12 [a][1 Sam. 3:13] [b]Ps. 25:15; 123:1, 2; 141:8
14 [c]See ch. 15:1
15 [d]ch. 32:7; [Deut. 1:29, 30; 31:6, 8] [e]1 Sam. 17:47
16 [f]Num 13:23
17 [g][Ex. 14:13, 14] [h]ch. 15:2; 32:8; [Num. 14:9]
18 [i]ch. 29:29, 30; Ex. 4:31; Neh. 8:6
19 [j]Ex. 6:16, 18 [k]See 1 Chr. 9:19
20 [l][2 Sam. 14:2] [m]Isai. 7:9
21 [n]See 1 Chr. 16:29 [o]See 1 Chr. 16:34
22 [p][ch. 13:13] [q]ver. 10
23 [r][Judg. 7:22; 1 Sam. 14:20]
27 [s]Neh. 12:43
29 [t]ch. 14:14; 17:10

1 That is, setting apart (devoting) as an offering to the Lord (for destruction) 2 Hebrew *they* 3 *Beracah* means *blessing*

20:12 we are powerless. Confession of human impotence, humility, and reliance on divine power also appear in Asa's prayer (14:11 note).

20:15 not yours but God's. Human effort in Israel's warfare was overshadowed by divine power. The prophet reminded Jehoshaphat that human responsibility depends on the sovereignty of God (v. 17).

20:20–30 The strategy and outcome of this battle form a striking contrast to Jehoshaphat's previous battle (18:28–34 and notes).

20:20 believe his prophets, and you will succeed. 2 Chronicles frequently emphasizes the importance of trusting and obeying the prophetic word (chs. 10–12 note; 14:2–16:14 note; 18:1–19:3 note; 24:19 note; 25:1–13 note; 25:15, 16 note; 28:5–15 note; 36:15 note; see also Introduction to 1 Chronicles: Characteristics and Themes). Jehoshaphat's instruction contrasts with his earlier rejection of Micaiah (18:1–32).

20:21 his steadfast love endures forever. See note 5:13.

20:26 to this day. See note 1 Chr. 4:41.

20:29 fear of God. See note 17:10.

the countries when they heard that the
LORD had fought against the enemies of
Israel. 30 So the realm of Jehoshaphat was
quiet, [u]for his God gave him rest all around.
31 [v]Thus Jehoshaphat reigned over Judah.
He was thirty-five years old when he began
to reign, and he reigned twenty-five years in
Jerusalem. His mother's name was Azubah
the daughter of Shilhi. 32 He walked in the
way of Asa his father and did not turn aside
from it, doing what was right in the sight of
the LORD. 33 [w]The high places, however, were
not taken away; [x]the people had not yet set
their hearts upon the God of their fathers.
34 Now the rest of the acts of Jehoshaphat,
from first to last, are written in the chronicles of [y]Jehu the son of Hanani, [z]which are
recorded in the Book of the Kings of Israel.

The End of Jehoshaphat's Reign

35 [a]After this Jehoshaphat king of Judah
joined with Ahaziah king of Israel, who acted
wickedly. 36 He joined him in building ships
to go to [b]Tarshish, and they built the ships
in Ezion-geber. 37 Then Eliezer the son of
Dodavahu of Mareshah prophesied against
Jehoshaphat, saying, [c]"Because you have
joined with Ahaziah, the LORD will destroy
what you have made." And the ships were
wrecked and were not able to go to Tarshish.

Jehoram Reigns in Judah

21 [d]Jehoshaphat slept with his fathers
and was buried with his fathers in the
city of David, and Jehoram his son reigned in
his place. 2 He had brothers, the sons of
Jehoshaphat: Azariah, Jehiel, Zechariah,
Azariah, Michael, and Shephatiah; all these
were the sons of Jehoshaphat king of [e]Judah.
3 Their father gave them great gifts of silver,
gold, and valuable possessions, together
with [f]fortified cities in Judah, but he gave
the kingdom to Jehoram, because he was the
firstborn. 4 When Jehoram had ascended the
throne of his father and was established,
he killed all his brothers with the sword, and
also some of the princes of [e]Israel. 5 [g]Jehoram
was [h]thirty-two years old when he became
king, and he reigned eight years in
Jerusalem. 6 [i]And he walked in the way of the
kings of Israel, as the house of Ahab had
done, for [j]the daughter of Ahab was his wife.
And he did what was evil in the sight of the
LORD. 7 Yet the LORD was not willing to
destroy the house of David, because of the
covenant that he had made with David, and
since he had promised to give [k]a lamp to him
and to his sons forever.
8 In his days Edom revolted from the [l]rule
of Judah and set up a king of their own.
9 Then Jehoram passed over with his commanders and all his chariots, and he rose
by night and struck the Edomites who had
surrounded him and his chariot commanders. 10 So Edom revolted from [m]the rule of
Judah to this day. At that time Libnah also
revolted from his rule, because he had forsaken the LORD, the God of his fathers.
11 Moreover, he made high places in the
hill country of Judah and led the inhabitants of Jerusalem [n]into whoredom and

30 [u][ch. 14:6, 7; 15:15]
31 [v] For ver. 31-33, see 1 Kin. 22:41-43
33 [w][ch. 17:6] [x]ch. 12:14
34 [y]ch. 19:2 [z]1 Kin. 16:1, 7
35 [a]1 Kin. 22:48, 49
36 [b]ch. 9:21
37 [c][ch. 19:2]
Chapter 21
1 [d]1 Kin. 22:50
2 [e][ch. 12:6; 23:2; 24:5, 16]
3 [f]See ch. 11:5
4 [e][See ver. 2 above]
5 [g]For ver. 5-10, see 2 Kin. 8:17-22 [h][ver. 20]
6 [i]See 1 Kin. 12:28-30; 16:31-33 [j]ch. 18:1; 2 Kin. 8:18
7 [k]See 1 Kin. 11:36; [2 Sam. 21:17]
8 [l]ver. 10
10 [m]ver. 8
11 [n]Ex. 34:16; Lev. 17:7; 20:5

20:30 quiet . . . rest. See note 1 Chr. 22:9.

20:31 twenty-five years. 2 Kin. 3:1 (eighteen years) and 8:16 (four years) bring Jehoshaphat's reign to twenty-two years. Chronicles and 1 Kin. 22:42 include the three years in which Jehoshaphat was co-regent with Asa (17:1 note).

20:33 high places. See note 14:3.

20:34 recorded in the Book. See Introduction to 1 Chronicles: Author.

20:35–37 The text includes a brief notice of another time Jehoshaphat received a prophetic rebuke for making an alliance with the northern kingdom (16:2 note).

20:37 Eliezer . . . prophesied. See note 20:20.

21:2–20 The historian supplements the record of Jehoram's reign in Kings (2 Kin. 8:16–24); in Kings the assessment is negative. Jehoram reigned as co-regent with Jehoshaphat 853–848 B.C. (2 Kin. 1:17; 3:1), and by himself 848–841 B.C. He murdered his brothers (21:2–7); Edom and Libnah rebelled against him (21:8–10); he fell into idolatry (21:11); and Elijah prophesied an impending judgment (21:12–20).

21:2 brothers. The murder of Jehoram's brothers recorded here is additional to the account in Kings (2 Kin. 8:16–22). On the other side, Kings describes how Solomon disposed of Adonijah, an event omitted from Chronicles (1 Kin. 2:24).

21:4 Israel. See note 10:1.

21:5 eight years. As sole monarch (21:2–20 note).

21:7 not willing to destroy the house of David. The house of David was on the brink of annihilation. Jehoram deserved to die, but God preserved his life to fulfill His promise of a permanent dynasty to David. Despite the sins of individual descendants of David, the Davidic line would never be entirely rejected (1 Chr. 17:7–14 note).

21:8–10 God's displeasure toward Jehoram became evident when these two nations subject to Judah successfully rebelled against him.

21:8 Edom. Jehoshaphat had subjugated Edom through righteous dependence on God (20:1–30). Jehoram, however, failed in his attempt.

21:10 to this day. See note 1 Chr. 4:41.

Libnah. An area between Judah and Philistia.

21:11–20 This episode illustrating the depths of Jehoram's sin is additional to the account in Kings.

21:11 made high places. While Asa and Jehoshaphat failed to rid the land of all high places (14:3 note), Jehoram actively built them (cf. 28:25).

whoredom. Perhaps literally through involvement with prostitution in pagan worship rituals, or metaphorically through spiritual infidelity (1 Chr. 5:25).

made Judah go astray. 12 And a letter came
to him from Elijah the prophet, saying,
"Thus says the LORD, the God of David
your father, [o]'Because you have not
walked in the ways of Jehoshaphat your
father, or [p]in the ways of Asa king of
Judah, 13 [i]but have walked in the way of
the kings of Israel and have enticed Judah
and the inhabitants of Jerusalem [n]into
whoredom, [q]as the house of Ahab led
Israel into whoredom, and also you [r]have
killed your brothers, of your father's
house, who were better than yourself,
14 behold, the LORD will bring a great
plague on your people, your children, your
wives, and all your possessions, 15 and you
yourself will have a severe sickness [s]with a
disease of your bowels, until your bowels
come out because of the disease, day by
day.'"

16 [t]And the LORD stirred up against
Jehoram the anger[1] of the Philistines and of
[u]the Arabians who are near the Ethiopians.
17 And they came up against Judah and
invaded it and carried away all the possessions they found that belonged to the
king's house, and also his sons and his
wives, so that no son was left to him except
[v]Jehoahaz, his youngest son.

18 And after all this the LORD struck him
[w]in his bowels with an incurable disease.
19 In course of time, at the end of two
years, his bowels came out because of the
disease, and he died in great agony. His
people made no fire in his honor, [x]like the
fires made for his fathers. 20 [y]He was thirty-two years old when he began to reign,
and he reigned eight years in Jerusalem.
And he departed [z]with no one's regret.
[a]They buried him in the city of David, but
not in the tombs of the kings.

12 [o]ch. 17:3 [p]ch. 14:2-5
13 [i][See ver. 6 above] [n][See ver. 11 above] [q]See 1 Kin. 16:31-33 [r]ver. 4
15 [s]ver. 18, 19
16 [t][1 Kin. 11:14, 23] [u]ch. 17:11; 22:1; 26:7
17 [v]ch. 25:23; [ch. 22:6]
18 [w]ver. 15
19 [x]ch. 16:14
20 [y][ver. 5] [z][Jer. 22:18] [a][ch. 24:25; 28:27]

Chapter 22
1 [b]For ver. 1-6, see 2 Kin. 8:24-29 [c]See ch. 21:16
2 [d][ch. 21:6]
7 [e]2 Kin. 9:21 [f]2 Kin. 9:6, 7
8 [g]See 2 Kin. 10:11-14 [h][ch. 24:24]
9 [i][2 Kin. 9:27] [j]2 Kin. 9:28

Ahaziah Reigns in Judah

22 [b]And the inhabitants of Jerusalem
made Ahaziah his youngest son king
in his place, for the band of men that came
with [c]the Arabians to the camp had killed
all the older sons. So Ahaziah the son of
Jehoram king of Judah reigned. 2 Ahaziah
was twenty-two years old when he began to
reign, and he reigned one year in Jerusalem.
His mother's name was Athaliah, [d]the
granddaughter of Omri. 3 He also walked in
the ways of the house of Ahab, for his
mother was his counselor in doing wickedly. 4 He did what was evil in the sight of the
LORD, as the house of Ahab had done. For
after the death of his father they were his
counselors, to his undoing. 5 He even followed their counsel and went with Jehoram
the son of Ahab king of Israel to make war
against Hazael king of Syria at Ramoth-
gilead. And the Syrians wounded Joram,
6 and he returned to be healed in Jezreel of
the wounds that he had received at Ramah,
when he fought against Hazael king of
Syria. And Ahaziah the son of Jehoram king
of Judah went down to see Joram the son of
Ahab in Jezreel, because he was wounded.

7 But it was ordained by God that the
downfall of Ahaziah should come about
through his going to visit Joram. For when
he came there, [e]he went out with Jehoram
to meet Jehu the son of Nimshi, [f]whom the
LORD had anointed to destroy the house of
Ahab. 8 [g]And when Jehu was [h]executing
judgment on the house of Ahab, he met the
princes of Judah and the sons of Ahaziah's
brothers, who attended Ahaziah, and he
killed them. 9 [i]He searched for Ahaziah,
and he was captured while hiding in
Samaria, and he was brought to Jehu and
put to death. [j]They buried him, for they

1 Hebrew *spirit*

21:12 Elijah. The only mention of the prophet in Chronicles; compare the lengthy account of his prophetic activities in 1 Kin. 17–2 Kin. 2.

21:14–19 The judgment against Jehoram was twofold. God promises "a great plague" on the people and on Jehoram's family, a threat fulfilled by the attacks of Philistines and Arabs. Second, Jehoram becomes terminally ill, as promised. The emphasis is on immediate retribution (1 Chr. 28:9 note).

21:19 made no fire. Contrast with the response to Asa's death (16:14). Jehoram (21:20), Joash (24:25), Ahaz (28:27), and Manasseh (33:20) died in ignominy. Amon was disgracefully assassinated (cf. 33:24).

21:20 Chronicles supplements the record given in 2 Kin. 8:24 of Jehoram's death and burial with details that reveal his utter disgrace.

eight years. See note on v. 5.

22:1–9 The record of Chronicles ties Ahaziah (841 B.C.) closely to his father Jehoram (21:4–20). Both kings were deeply influenced by Athaliah and so are evaluated negatively (21:6; 22:3, 4). In both reigns, the Davidic dynasty barely escaped annihilation (21:16, 17; 22:7–9).

22:3–9 Chronicles presents Ahaziah's rapid downfall as divine chastisement for his alliance with the northern kingdom (16:2 note).

22:5 Hazael. See 1 Kin. 19:15 and 2 Kin. 8:7–15.

22:8 Jehu was executing judgment. Kings reports that Elisha anointed Jehu to destroy the house of Omri (2 Kin. 9:1–10:31). The death of Ahaziah was part of this judgment.

22:9 They buried him. Ahaziah received an honorable burial, not because of his own character, but because of his grandfather Jehoshaphat.

said, "He is the grandson of Jehoshaphat,
[k]who sought the LORD with all his heart."
And the house of Ahaziah had no one able
to rule the kingdom.

Athaliah Reigns in Judah

10 [l]Now when Athaliah the mother of
Ahaziah saw that her son was dead, she
arose and destroyed all the royal family of
the house of Judah. 11 But Jehoshabeath,[1]
the daughter of the king, took Joash the
son of Ahaziah and stole him away from
among the king's sons who were about to
be put to death, and she put him and his
nurse in a bedroom. Thus Jehoshabeath,
the daughter of King Jehoram and wife of
Jehoiada the priest, because she was a sister of Ahaziah, hid him from Athaliah, so
that she did not put him to death. 12 And he
remained with them six years, hidden in
the house of God, while Athaliah reigned
over the land.

Joash Made King

23 [m]But in the seventh year Jehoiada
took courage and entered into a
covenant with the commanders of hundreds, Azariah the son of Jeroham, Ishmael
the son of Jehohanan, Azariah the son of
Obed, Maaseiah the son of Adaiah, and
Elishaphat the son of Zichri. 2 And they
went about through Judah and gathered
the Levites from all the cities of Judah, and
the heads of fathers' houses of [n]Israel, and
they came to Jerusalem. 3 And all the
assembly made a covenant with the king in
the house of God. And Jehoiada[2] said to
them, "Behold, the king's son! Let him
reign, [o]as the LORD spoke concerning the
sons of David. 4 This is the thing that you
shall do: [p]of you priests and Levites who
come off duty on the Sabbath, one third
shall be gatekeepers, 5 and one third shall
be at the king's house and one third at the
Gate of the Foundation. And all the people
shall be in the courts of the house of the
LORD. 6 Let no one enter the house of the
LORD except the priests [q]and ministering
Levites. They may enter, for they are holy,
but all the people shall keep the charge of
the LORD. 7 The Levites shall surround the
king, each with his weapons in his hand.
And whoever enters the house shall be put
to death. Be with the king when he comes
in and when he goes out."

8 The Levites and all Judah did according
to all that Jehoiada the priest commanded,
and they each brought his men, who were
to go off duty on the Sabbath, with those
who were to come on duty on the Sabbath,
for Jehoiada the priest did not dismiss [r]the
divisions. 9 And Jehoiada the priest gave to
the captains the spears and the large and
small shields that had been King David's,
which were in the house of God. 10 And he
set all the people as a guard for the king,
every man with his weapon in his hand,
from the south side of the house to the
north side of the house, around the altar
and the house. 11 Then they brought out
the king's son and put the crown on him
and gave him [s]the testimony. And they proclaimed him king, and Jehoiada and his
sons anointed him, and they said, [t]"Long
live the king."

Athaliah Executed

12 When Athaliah heard the noise of the
people running and praising the king, she
went into the house of the LORD to the people. 13 And when she looked, there was the
king standing by his pillar at the entrance,
and the captains and the trumpeters beside
the king, and all the people of the land
rejoicing and blowing trumpets, and the
singers with their musical instruments leading in the celebration. And Athaliah tore her

9 [k]ch. 17:4
10 [l]For ver. 10-12, see 2 Kin. 11:1-3
Chapter 23
1 [m]For ver. 1-21, see 2 Kin. 11:4-20
2 [n]See ch. 21:2
3 [o]See ch. 6:16
4 [p][1 Chr. 24:4]; [1 Chr. 9:25]
6 [q]See 1 Chr. 23: 27-29
8 [r]See 1 Chr. ch. 24
11 [s]Deut. 17:18, 19 [t]See 1 Sam. 10:24

1 Spelled *Jehosheba* in 2 Kings 11:2 2 Hebrew *he*

22:10–24:27 Compare 2 Kin. chs. 11 and 12 on the record of Joash. This portion of Chronicles illustrates the close association between king and priest. The Davidic line was preserved by Jehoshabeath and her husband, the priest Jehoiada (22:10–23:21); the Davidic king served faithfully under the influence of Jehoiada (24:1–16); the king failed when he rejected the instruction of Jehoiada's son, and put him to death (24:17–27). Cooperation of king and priest was essential. See also Zech. 3; 4; 6:9–15.

22:10–12 Jehoshaphat's marriage alliance (18:1 note) finally yielded its worst result. Athaliah nearly destroyed the Davidic line in her quest to establish herself as queen.

22:11 Joash. Reigned 835–796 B.C.

22:12 Athaliah. Athaliah was the only queen to rule in Judah (841–835 B.C.).

23:1–11 The Zadokite priest Jehoiada resisted Queen Athaliah and gained the military support necessary for temple and political reform.

23:2 through Judah . . . all the cities. This verse expands the account in Kings depicting Joash's widespread support in Judah (1 Chr. 11:1 note).

23:3 as the LORD spoke. See note 1 Chr. 17:14.

23:11 the testimony. Probably the covenant made in 23:3; compare also Deut. 17:18–20.

23:13 trumpeters . . . singers . . . musical instruments. See 1 Chr. 15:16 note.

clothes and cried, "Treason! Treason!"
14 Then Jehoiada the priest brought out the
captains who were set over the army, saying
to them, "Bring her out between the ranks,
and anyone who follows her is to be put to
death with the sword." For the priest said,
"Do not put her to death in the house of the
LORD." 15 So they laid hands on her,[1] and
she went into the entrance of [u]the horse
gate of the king's house, and they put her to
death there.

Jehoiada's Reforms

16 And Jehoiada made a covenant between
himself and all the people and the king that
they should be the LORD's people. 17 Then all
the people went to the house of Baal and
tore it down; his altars and his images they
broke in pieces, [v]and they killed Mattan the
priest of Baal before the altars. 18 And
Jehoiada posted watchmen for the house of
the LORD under the direction of [w]the Levitical
priests and the Levites [x]whom David had
organized to be in charge of the house of the
LORD, to offer burnt offerings to the LORD, [y]as
it is written in the Law of Moses, with rejoicing and with singing, [z]according to the order
of David. 19 He stationed [a]the gatekeepers at
the gates of the house of the LORD so that no
one should enter who was in any way
unclean. 20 And he took the captains, the
nobles, the governors of the people, and all
the people of the land, and they brought the
king down from the house of the LORD,
marching [b]through the upper gate to the
king's house. And they set the king on the
royal throne. 21 So all the people of the land
rejoiced, and the city was quiet after Athaliah
had been put to death with the sword.

Joash Repairs the Temple

24 [c]Joash[2] was seven years old when
he began to reign, and he reigned
forty years in Jerusalem. His mother's
name was Zibiah of Beersheba. 2 [d]And
Joash did what was right in the eyes of the
LORD all the days of Jehoiada the priest.
3 Jehoiada got for him two wives, and he
had sons and daughters.
4 After this Joash [e]decided to [f]restore the
house of the LORD. 5 And he gathered the
priests and the Levites and said to them,
"Go out to the cities of Judah and gather
from all [g]Israel money to repair the house
of your God from year to year, and see that
you act quickly." But the Levites did not
act quickly. 6 So the king summoned
Jehoiada the chief and said to him, "Why
have you not required the Levites to bring
in from Judah and Jerusalem [h]the tax levied
by Moses, the servant of the LORD, and the
congregation of Israel for [i]the tent of testimony?" 7 For [j]the sons of Athaliah, that
wicked woman, had broken into the house
of God, and had also used all [k]the dedicated things of the house of the LORD for the
Baals.
8 So the king commanded, and they
made a chest and set it outside the gate of
the house of the LORD. 9 And [l]proclamation
was made throughout Judah and Jerusalem
to bring in for the LORD [h]the tax that Moses
the servant of God laid on Israel in the
wilderness. 10 And all the princes and all
the people rejoiced and brought their tax
and dropped it into the chest until they
had finished.[3] 11 And whenever the chest
was brought to the king's officers by the
Levites, when they saw that there was
much money in it, the king's secretary and
the officer of the chief priest would come
and empty the chest and take it and return
it to its place. Thus they did day after day,
and collected money in abundance. 12 And

15 [u]Neh. 3:28; Jer. 31:40; [2 Kin. 11:16]
17 [v]Deut. 13:9
18 [w]ch. 5:5; 30:27; [x]1 Chr. 23:6, 30, 31; 24:1 [y]Num. 28:2 [z][1 Chr. 25:2]
19 [a]See 1 Chr. 26:1-19
20 [b][2 Kin. 11:19; 15:35]
Chapter 24
1 [c]For ver. 1-14, see 2 Kin. 11:21–12:15
2 [d][ch. 26:5]
4 [e][1 Chr. 22:7] [f]ver. 12
5 [g]See ch. 21:2
6 [h]See Ex. 30:12-16 [i]See Num. 17:7, 8
7 [j][ch. 21:17] [k][1 Kin. 15:15]
9 [l][Ezra 1:1] [h][See ver. 6 above]

1 Or *they made a passage for her* 2 Spelled *Jehoash* in 2 Kings 12:1
3 Or *until it was full*

23:16 made a covenant. See note 15:12.

23:17 house of Baal. Probably a shrine to Baal erected for Athaliah (cf. 1 Kin. 11:1–8).

23:18, 19 This account emphasizes more than 2 Kin. 11:18 that the new temple order under Jehoiada and Joash was according to Mosaic and Davidic design. The books of Chronicles were written in the time of reconstruction following the return of the Jews from exile in Babylonia, and such encouragement was appropriate.

23:21 quiet. See note 1 Chr. 22:9.

24:1–22 This account should be compared with 2 Kin. 12. Note that vv. 15–22 are a lengthy supplement.

24:2 all the days of Jehoiada. Joash's positive accomplishments were the result of the influence of Jehoiada (24:14). After Jehoiada's death, Joash turned away from the Lord (24:17–19; cf. 26:5). The historian illustrates the importance of mutual support between king and priest (22:10–24:27 note).

24:5 priests and the Levites. Chronicles more than 2 Kin. 12:1–3 emphasizes the need for proper Levitical order (23:18, 19 note).

money . . . from year to year. This requirement was the half-shekel tax of Ex. 30:11–16; 38:24–26 (see 24:9).

24:6, 9 Moses . . . laid on Israel. See note 1 Chr. 16:40.

24:10–12 The generous and joyful giving of the officials and people was a good example for those engaged in restoring temple worship following the return from exile in Babylonia (1 Chr. 29:1–9 note).

the king and Jehoiada gave it to those who had charge of the work of the house of the LORD, and they hired masons and carpenters to restore the house of the LORD, and also workers in iron and bronze to repair the house of the LORD. 13 So those who were engaged in the work labored, and the repairing went forward in their hands, and they restored the house of God to its proper condition and strengthened it. 14 And when they had finished, they brought the rest of the money before the king and Jehoiada, and with it [m]were made utensils for the house of the LORD, both for the service and for the burnt offerings, and dishes for incense and vessels of gold and silver. And they offered burnt offerings in the house of the LORD regularly all the days of Jehoiada.

15 But Jehoiada grew old and full of days, and died. He was 130 years old at his death. 16 And they buried him in the city of David among the kings, because he had done good in [n]Israel, and toward God and his house.

17 Now after the death of Jehoiada the princes of Judah came and paid homage to the king. Then the king listened to them. 18 And they abandoned the house of the LORD, the God of their fathers, and served [o]the Asherim and the idols. And [p]wrath came upon Judah and Jerusalem for this guilt of theirs. 19 [q]Yet he sent prophets among them to bring them back to the LORD. [r]These testified against them, but they would not pay attention.

Joash's Treachery

20 [s]Then the Spirit of God clothed Zechariah [t]the son of Jehoiada the priest, and he stood above the people, and said to them, "Thus says God, [u]'Why do you break the commandments of the LORD, so that you cannot prosper? [v]Because you have forsaken the LORD, he has forsaken you.'" 21 But [w]they conspired against him, [x]and by command of the king they stoned him with stones in the court of the house of the LORD. 22 Thus Joash the king did not remember the kindness that Jehoiada, Zechariah's father, had shown him, but killed his son. And when he was dying, he said, "May the LORD see [y]and avenge!"[1]

Joash Assassinated

23 At the end of the year [z]the army of the Syrians came up against Joash. They came to Judah and Jerusalem and destroyed all the princes of the people from among the people and sent all their spoil to the king of Damascus. 24 Though the army of the Syrians had come with few men, [a]the LORD delivered into their hand a very great army, [v]because Judah[2] had forsaken the LORD, the God of their fathers. Thus they [b]executed judgment on Joash.

25 When they had departed from him, leaving him [c]severely wounded, [d]his servants conspired against him because of the blood of [e]the son[3] of Jehoiada the priest, and killed him on his bed. So he died, and they buried him in the city of David, [f]but they did not bury him in the tombs of the kings. 26 Those who conspired against him were Zabad the son of Shimeath the Ammonite, and Jehozabad the son of Shimrith the Moabite. 27 Accounts of his sons and of the many oracles against him and of [g]the rebuilding[4] of the house of God are written in the [h]Story of the Book of the Kings. And Amaziah his son reigned in his place.

Amaziah Reigns in Judah

25 [i]Amaziah was twenty-five years old when he began to reign, and he reigned twenty-nine years in Jerusalem. His mother's name was Jehoaddan of Jerusalem.

14 [m][2 Kin. 12:13]
16 [n]See ch. 21:2
18 [o]See Deut. 16:21 [p]ch. 19:2, 10; 28:11, 13; 29:8; 32:25
19 [q]Jer. 25:4; [Matt. 23:34; Luke 11:49]; See ch. 36:15 [r]Neh. 13:15, 21
20 [s]ch. 15:1; 20:14; [t][Matt. 23:35] [u][Num. 14:41] [v]ch. 15:2
21 [w][Neh. 9:26] [x]Matt. 23:35; Luke 11:51
22 [y][Gen. 9:5]
23 [z][2 Kin. 12:17, 18]
24 [a]Isai. 30:17; [Lev. 26:8, 36, 37] [v][See ver. 20 above] [b][ch. 22:8]
25 [c][Deut. 28:35] [d]For ver. 25-27, see 2 Kin. 12:20, 21 [e][ver. 21, 22] [f][ch. 21:20; 28:27]
27 [g]ver. 12 [h]ch. 13:22
Chapter 25
1 [i]For ver. 1-4, see 2 Kin. 14:1-6

1 Hebrew *and seek* 2 Hebrew *they* 3 Septuagint, Vulgate; Hebrew *sons* 4 Hebrew *founding*

24:19 prophets . . . they would not pay attention. Apostasy is tied to the rejection of God's prophets (20:20 note).

24:20 you have forsaken . . . he has forsaken. See note 1 Chr. 28:9.

24:23, 24 Chronicles frequently mentions military defeat as the judgment of God against sin (1 Chr. 10; 2 Chr. 13:1–16; 18:33, 34; 21:16, 17; 25:14–24; 28:1–5; 33:1–11).

24:24 Judah had forsaken. The tables are turned against Judah as had been threatened in the covenant (Deut. 28:25; 32:30; 1 Chr. 28:9 note).

24:26 Ammonite . . . Moabite. Jehoshaphat had earlier defeated Ammon and Moab (20:1 note).

24:27 Story of the Book of the Kings. See Introduction to 1 Chronicles: Author.

25:1–28 The account of Amaziah's reign (796–767 B.C.) should be compared with 2 Kin. 14. Note that the war against Edom is recorded only in Chronicles (vv. 5–16). The writer of Chronicles shows how foreign alliances, response to prophetic instruction, and idolatry affect Israel's military security. The account describes fidelity and infidelity, much as in the accounts of Joash and Uzziah (22:10–24:27 note).

25:1–13 Ahaziah was not devoted wholeheartedly to the Lord, but he responded properly to prophetic warning (20:20 note).

2 And he did what was right in the eyes of the LORD, [j]yet not with a whole heart. 3 And as soon as the royal power was firmly his, he killed his servants who had struck down the king his father. 4 But he did not put their children to death, according to what is written in the Law, in the Book of Moses, where the LORD commanded, [k]"Fathers shall not die because of their children, nor children die because of their fathers, but each one shall die for his own sin."

Amaziah's Victories

5 Then Amaziah assembled the men of Judah and set them by fathers' houses under commanders of thousands and of hundreds for all Judah and Benjamin. He mustered those [l]twenty years old and upward, and found that they were [m]300,000 choice men, fit for war, [n]able to handle spear and shield. 6 He hired also 100,000 mighty men of valor from Israel for 100 talents[1] of silver. 7 But [o]a man of God came to him and said, "O king, do not let the army of Israel go with you, for the LORD is not with Israel, with all these Ephraimites. 8 But go, act, be strong for the battle. Why should you suppose that God will cast you down before the enemy? [p]For God has power to help or to cast down." 9 And Amaziah said to the man of God, "But what shall we do about the hundred talents that I have given to the army of Israel?" The man of God answered, "The LORD is able to give you much more than this." 10 Then Amaziah discharged the army that had come to him from Ephraim to go home again. And they became very angry with Judah and returned home in fierce anger. 11 But Amaziah took courage and led out his people and went to the [q]Valley of Salt and struck down [r]10,000 men of Seir. 12 The men of Judah captured another 10,000 alive and took them to the top of a rock and threw them down from the top of the rock, and they were all dashed to pieces. 13 But the men of the army whom Amaziah sent back, not letting them go with him to battle, raided the cities of Judah, [s]from Samaria to Beth-horon, and struck down 3,000 people in them and took much spoil.

Amaziah's Idolatry

14 After Amaziah came from striking down the Edomites, [t]he brought the gods [r]of the men of Seir and set them up as his gods and worshiped them, making offerings to them. 15 Therefore the LORD was angry with Amaziah and sent to him a prophet, who said to him, "Why have you sought the gods of a people [u]who did not deliver their own people from your hand?" 16 But as he was speaking, the king said to him, "Have we made you a royal counselor? Stop! Why should you be struck down?" So the prophet stopped, but said, "I know that [v]God has determined to destroy you, because you have done this and have not listened to my counsel."

Israel Defeats Amaziah

17 [w]Then Amaziah king of Judah took counsel and sent to Joash the son of Jehoahaz, son of Jehu, king of Israel, saying, "Come, let us look one another in the face." 18 And Joash the king of Israel sent word to Amaziah king of Judah, [x]"A thistle on Lebanon sent to a cedar on Lebanon, saying, 'Give your daughter to my son for a wife,' and a wild beast of Lebanon passed by and trampled down the thistle. 19 You say, 'See, I[2] have struck down Edom,' and [y]your heart has lifted you up in boastful-

2 [j][ver. 14] **4** [k]Deut. 24:16; [Jer. 31:30; Ezek. 18:20] **5** [l]Num. 1:3 [m][ch. 11:1; 13:3; 17:14-18; 26:13] [n]1 Chr. 12:8 **7** [o]Deut. 33:1 **8** [p][ch. 20:6] **11** [q]2 Kin. 14:7 [r]ch. 20:10 **13** [s][ch. 15:8; 19:4] **14** [t][ch. 28:23] [r][See ver. 11 above] **15** [u][ver. 11] **16** [v][Josh. 11:20] **17** [w]For ver. 17-24, see 2 Kin. 14:8-14 **18** [x][Judg. 9:8] **19** [y]See ch. 26:16

1 A *talent* was about 75 pounds or 34 kilograms 2 Hebrew *you*

25:4 Book of Moses. See 1 Chr. 16:40.

25:5, 6 300,000 . . . 100,000. For these large numbers, see note 1 Chr. 12:23.

25:7 do not let the army of Israel go. The prophet again condemns an alliance with the northern kingdom (16:2 note).

the LORD is not with Israel. Abijah had voiced a similar opinion concerning the northern kingdom (13:9, 10).

25:8 God has power. In typical fashion, the man of God proclaims the need to rely solely upon divine power in battle (16:2 note).

25:10 angry with Judah. Although Amaziah obeyed the prophetic word, the northern mercenaries were angry. If not their pay, they had lost their chance for booty (cf. v. 13).

25:12 all dashed to pieces. Amaziah followed Mosaic instructions for holy war (Deut. 20:13–18).

25:13 Samaria. An unidentified town in Judah, not the better-known capital of the northern kingdom.

25:14 brought the gods. In contrast with Amaziah's earlier obedience (v. 12), he now disobeyed Mosaic instructions (Ex. 20:3; Deut. 7:25) and David's example (1 Chr. 14:12), bringing the Edomite gods to Jerusalem. He eventually worshiped these gods.

25:15, 16 In contrast with his earlier repentance at the prophetic word (25:7–10), Amaziah rebuffed the prophet and received a stern warning (20:20 note).

25:16 God has determined to destroy you. See note 1 Chr. 28:9.

ness. But now stay at home. Why should
you provoke trouble so that you fall, you
and Judah with you?"
20 But Amaziah would not listen, for it
was of God, in order that he might give
them into the hand of their enemies, [z]be-
cause they had sought the gods of Edom.
21 So Joash king of Israel went up, and he
and Amaziah king of Judah faced one
another in battle at Beth-shemesh, which
belongs to Judah. 22 And Judah was defeated by Israel, and every man fled to his
home. 23 And Joash king of Israel captured
Amaziah king of Judah, the son of Joash,
son of [a]Ahaziah, at Beth-shemesh, and
brought him to Jerusalem and broke down
the wall of Jerusalem for 400 cubits,[1] from
[b]the Ephraim Gate to the Corner Gate.
24 And he seized all the gold and silver, and
all the vessels that were found in the house
of God, in the care of [c]Obed-edom. He
seized also the treasuries of the king's
house, also hostages, and he returned to
Samaria.
25 [d]Amaziah the son of Joash, king of
Judah, lived fifteen years after the death of
Joash the son of Jehoahaz, king of Israel.
26 Now the rest of the deeds of Amaziah,
from first to last, are they not written in the
Book of the Kings of Judah and Israel?
27 From the time when he turned away from
the LORD they made a conspiracy against
him in Jerusalem, and he fled to Lachish.
But they sent after him to Lachish and put
him to death there. 28 And they brought
him upon horses, and he was buried with
his fathers in the city of David.[2]

Uzziah Reigns in Judah

26 And all the people of Judah took
Uzziah,[3] who was sixteen years old,
and made him king instead of his father
Amaziah. 2 He built Eloth and restored it to
Judah, after the king slept with his fathers.
3 Uzziah was [e]sixteen years old when he
began to reign, and he reigned fifty-two
years in Jerusalem. His mother's name was
Jecoliah of Jerusalem. 4 And he did what
was right in the eyes of the LORD, according
to all that his father Amaziah had done.
5 He set himself to seek God [f]in the days of
Zechariah, [g]who instructed him in the fear
of God, and as long as he sought the LORD,
God made him prosper.
6 He went out and [h]made war against the
Philistines and broke through the wall of
Gath and the wall of Jabneh and the wall of
Ashdod, and he built cities in the territory
of Ashdod and elsewhere among the
Philistines. 7 God helped him [i]against the
Philistines and against the Arabians who
lived in Gurbaal and against the [j]Meunites.
8 The Ammonites [k]paid tribute to Uzziah,
and his fame spread even to the border of
Egypt, for he became very strong.
9 Moreover, Uzziah built towers in Jerusalem at [l]the Corner Gate and at [m]the
Valley Gate and at [n]the Angle, and fortified
them. 10 And he built towers in the wilderness and [o]cut out many cisterns, for he had
large herds, both in the Shephelah and in
the plain, and he had farmers and vinedressers in the hills and in the fertile lands,
for he loved the soil. 11 Moreover, Uzziah
had an army of soldiers, fit for war, in divisions according to the numbers in the
muster made by Jeiel the secretary and
Maaseiah the officer, under the direction of
Hananiah, one of the king's commanders.
12 The whole number of the heads of

20 [z]ver. 14, 15
23 [a]ch. 21:17 [b]Neh. 8:16
24 [c]1 Chr. 26:15
25 [d]For ver. 25–ch. 26:2, see 2 Kin. 14:17-22

Chapter 26
3 [e]For ver. 3, 4, see 2 Kin. 15:2, 3
5 [f][ch. 24:2] [g][Dan. 1:17; 10:1]
6 [h][Isai. 14:29]
7 [i]ch. 21:16 [j][ch. 20:1]
8 [k][ch. 17:11; 2 Sam. 8:2]
9 [l]See 2 Kin. 14:13 [m]Neh. 2:13, 15; 3:13 [n]Neh. 3:19
10 [o]Deut. 6:11; Neh. 9:25

1 A *cubit* was about 18 inches or 45 centimeters 2 Hebrew *of Judah*
3 Spelled *Azariah* in 2 Kings 14:21

25:20 it was of God. The sovereignty of God includes hardening the hearts of sinners so that they no longer respond to warnings (1 Chr. 21:1 note; cf. Ex. 3:19; 4:12; 7:3, 4).

25:22–24 The defeat of Amaziah contrasts with his earlier victory (vv. 11–13).

25:26 Book of the Kings. See Introduction to 1 Chronicles: Author.

26:1–23 The historian who composed Chronicles adds a long section (vv. 5–20) to the brief notices about Uzziah in 2 Kings 14 and 15. His account is in four stages: rise to power (vv. 1–2), obedience and blessing (vv. 3–15), disobedience and curse (vv. 16–20), and summary and death (vv. 22, 23).

26:1 Uzziah. Uzziah reigned 792/91–740/39 B.C. In 2 Kings he is frequently, but not always, called Azariah.

26:4 according to . . . his father Amaziah. The historian compares Uzziah with his father, whose reign was also divided between blessing and curse.

26:5 seek God . . . sought the LORD. See note 7:14.

in the days of Zechariah. An unknown royal adviser. It is unlikely that this is the person named in Is. 8:2, since "in the days of" suggests that Zechariah died during Uzziah's reign and could not have been an adviser to his grandson. Joash was obedient as long as Jehodiah was alive, and Uzziah did well under Zechariah's tutelage (24:2 note).

26:6–15 Uzziah was blessed in international conflict (vv. 6–8), domestic affairs (vv. 9, 10), and military strength (vv. 11–15).

26:7 Meunites. Uzziah's blessing recalls Jehoshaphat's victory (20:1–30).

26:8 Ammonites. See note 1 Chr. 19:1.

26:9 Uzziah built. A reversal of the destruction in Amaziah's defeat (25:23). See note 1 Chr. 11:5.

fathers' houses of mighty men of valor was 2,600. [13]Under their command was an army of [p]307,500, who could make war with mighty power, to help the king against the enemy. [14]And Uzziah prepared for all the army shields, spears, helmets, [q]coats of mail, bows, and stones for slinging. [15]In Jerusalem he made engines, invented by skillful men, to be on the towers and the corners, to shoot arrows and great stones. And his fame spread far, for he was marvelously helped, till he was strong.

Uzziah's Pride and Punishment

[16]But when [r]he was strong, [s]he grew proud, to his destruction. For he was unfaithful to the LORD his God and entered the temple of the LORD to burn incense on the altar of incense. [17]But [t]Azariah the priest went in after him, with eighty priests of the LORD who were men of valor, [18]and they withstood King Uzziah and said to him, [u]"It is not for you, Uzziah, to burn incense to the LORD, [v]but for the priests the sons of Aaron, who are consecrated to burn incense. Go out of the sanctuary, for you have done wrong, and it will bring you no honor from the LORD God." [19]Then Uzziah was angry. Now he had a censer in his hand to burn incense, and when he became angry with the priests, [w]leprosy[1] broke out on his forehead in the presence of the priests in the house of the LORD, by the altar of incense. [20]And Azariah the chief priest and all the priests looked at him, and behold, he was leprous in his forehead! And they rushed him out quickly, and he himself hurried to go out, because the LORD had struck him. [21][x]And King Uzziah was a leper to the day of his death, and being a leper lived [y]in a separate house, for he was excluded from the house of the LORD. And Jotham his son was over the king's household, governing the people of the land.

[22]Now the rest of the acts of Uzziah, from first to last, [z]Isaiah the prophet the son of Amoz wrote. [23]And Uzziah slept with his fathers, and they buried him with his fathers in the burial field that belonged to the kings, for they said, "He is a leper." And Jotham his son reigned in his place.

Jotham Reigns in Judah

27 [a]Jotham was twenty-five years old when he began to reign, and he reigned sixteen years in Jerusalem. His mother's name was Jerushah the daughter of Zadok. [2]And he did what was right in the eyes of the LORD according to all that his father Uzziah had done, [b]except he did not enter the temple of the LORD. But the people still followed corrupt practices. [3]He built the upper gate of the house of the LORD and did much building on the wall of [c]Ophel. [4]Moreover, he built cities in the hill country of Judah, and forts and towers on the wooded hills. [5]He fought with the king of the Ammonites and prevailed against them. And the Ammonites gave him that year 100 talents[2] of silver, and 10,000 cors[3] of wheat and 10,000 of barley. The

13 [p][ch. 25:5]
14 [q]Neh. 4:16
16 [r][ch.12:1; Deut. 32:15] [s]ch. 32:25; Ezek. 28:2, 5, 17; [ch. 25:19; Deut. 8:14; 2 Kin. 14:10]
17 [t]1 Chr. 6:10
18 [u]Num. 16:40; 18:7 [v]Ex. 30:7, 8
19 [w][Ex. 4:6; Num. 12:10; 2 Kin. 5:27]
21 [x]For ver. 21-23, see 2 Kin. 15:5-7 [y][Lev. 13:46; Num. 5:2]
22 [z]Isai. 1:1; 6:1
Chapter 27
1 [a]For ver. 1-3, see 2 Kin. 15:33-35
2 [b][ch. 26:16]
3 [c]ch. 33:14; Neh. 3:26, 27; 11:21

1 *Leprosy* was a term for several skin diseases; see Leviticus 13 2 A *talent* was about 75 pounds or 34 kilograms 3 A *cor* was about 6 bushels or 220 liters

26:13 307,500. For the large number, see note 1 Chr. 12:23.

26:16–20 This episode shows God's judgment against Uzziah's pride. As with Rehoboam (12:1), initial success led to disregard for God and His law. Uzziah's leprosy is mentioned only briefly in 2 Kin. 15:5.

26:16 when he was strong. Moses warned Israel to be careful not to let success make them proud and rely on themselves rather than on God (Deut. 8:10–18).

26:17 Azariah. An otherwise unknown priest. He and eighty courageous priests delivered God's judgment to Uzziah. The writer of Chronicles highlights the role of priests as instructors of royalty for a third time (24:2 and note).

26:18 for the priests. Burning incense was restricted to the priests in Mosaic legislation (Ex. 30:7–9; Num. 16:39, 40). See "Christians and Civil Government" at Rom. 13:1.

26:21 excluded from the house of the LORD. Uzziah was quarantined and kept out of the temple, in agreement with the Law of Moses (Lev. 13:46; Num. 5:1–4).

26:22 Isaiah the prophet . . . wrote. See Introduction to 1 Chronicles: Author.

26:23 in the burial field. Uzziah was buried away from the royal family in relative dishonor because of the curse of leprosy.

27:1–9 In contrast to the records from Joash to Uzziah, where each reign has a balance of obedience and disobedience (22:10–24:27 note), the writer's evaluation of Jotham is fully positive. This is followed with a negative treatment of Ahaz (ch. 28). Chronicles points out that faithfulness to God is the way to success in construction projects and military conflict.

27:1 Jotham . . . sixteen years. Reigned 750–732 B.C. Jotham reigned during the period of his father Uzziah's leprosy (750–740 B.C.), and had co-regency with his son Ahaz (735–732 B.C.). For six years he was the sole monarch. The figure "sixteen years" here and in v. 8 probably refers to his co-regency with his father and his independent reign. Adding his four years with Ahaz brings the total to twenty years (2 Kin. 15:30).

27:2 did not enter the temple. Jotham did not violate priestly regulations as Uzziah had done (26:18 note).

the people still followed corrupt practices. The historian explains that the people and not Jotham were guilty of continuing corruption. (cf. 2 Kin. 15:35).

27:5, 6 This record of victory over the Ammonites highlights God's approval of Jotham.

Ammonites paid him the same amount in
the second and the third years. 6 So Jotham
became mighty, because he ordered his
ways before the LORD his God. 7 [d]Now the
rest of the acts of Jotham, and all his wars
and his ways, behold, they are written in
the Book of the Kings of Israel and Judah.
8 He was [e]twenty-five years old when he
began to reign, and he reigned sixteen years
in Jerusalem. 9 And Jotham slept with his
fathers, and they buried him in the city of
David, and Ahaz his son reigned in his
place.

Ahaz Reigns in Judah

28 [f]Ahaz was twenty years old when he
began to reign, and he reigned sixteen years in Jerusalem. And he did not do
what was right in the eyes of the LORD, as
his father David had done, 2 but he walked
in the ways of the kings of Israel. He even
made [g]metal images for [h]the Baals, 3 and
[i]he made offerings in the [j]Valley of the Son
of Hinnom and [k]burned his sons as an
offering,[1] according to [l]the abominations
of the nations whom the LORD drove out
before the people of Israel. 4 And he sacrificed and [i]made offerings on the high
places and on the hills and under every
green tree.

Judah Defeated

5 [m]Therefore the LORD his God gave him
into the hand of the king of Syria, who
defeated him and took captive a great number of his people and brought them to
Damascus. He was also given into the hand
of the king of Israel, who struck him with
great force. 6 For [n]Pekah the son of
Remaliah killed 120,000 from Judah in one
day, all of them men of valor, because they
had forsaken the LORD, the God of their
fathers. 7 And Zichri, a mighty man of
Ephraim, killed Maaseiah the king's son
and Azrikam the commander of the palace
and Elkanah the next in authority to the
king.
8 The men of Israel took captive 200,000
[o]of their relatives, women, sons, and
daughters. They also took much spoil from
them and brought the spoil to Samaria.
9 But a prophet of the LORD was there,
whose name was Oded, and he went out to
meet the army that came to Samaria and
said to them, "Behold, because the LORD,
the God of your fathers, [p]was angry with
Judah, he gave them into your hand, but
you have killed them in a rage [q]that has
reached up to heaven. 10 And now you
intend to subjugate the people of Judah
and Jerusalem, male and female, as your
slaves. Have you not sins of your own
against the LORD your God? 11 Now hear
me, and send back the captives [o]from your
relatives whom you have taken, for the
fierce wrath of the LORD is upon you."
12 Certain chiefs also of the men of
Ephraim, Azariah the son of Johanan,
Berechiah the son of Meshillemoth,
Jehizkiah the son of Shallum, and Amasa
the son of Hadlai, stood up against those
who were coming from the war 13 and said
to them, "You shall not bring the captives
in here, for you propose to bring upon us
guilt against the LORD in addition to our
present sins and guilt. For our guilt is
already great, and there is fierce wrath
against Israel." 14 So the armed men left the
captives and the spoil before the princes
and all the assembly. 15 And [r]the men who
have been mentioned by name rose and
took the captives, and with the spoil they
clothed all who were naked among them.
They clothed them, gave them sandals,
[s]provided them with food and drink, and
anointed them, and carrying all the feeble

1 Hebrew *made his sons pass through the fire*

7 [d][2 Kin. 15:36]
8 [e]ver. 1
Chapter 28
1 [f]For ver. 1-4, see 2 Kin. 16:2-4
2 [g][Ex. 34:17] [h]Judg. 2:11
3 [i]ver. 25 [j]See Josh. 15:8 [k]ch. 33:6; [Lev. 18:21] [l]ch. 33:2; Deut. 18:9
4 [i][See ver. 3 above]
5 [m]Isai. 7:1; [2 Kin. 16:5, 6]
6 [n]2 Kin. 15:27; 16:5
8 [o]ch. 11:4
9 [p]Isai. 47:6; Ezek. 25:12, 15; 26:2 [q]Ezra 9:6; Rev. 18:5
11 [o][See ver. 8 above]
15 [r]ver. 12 [ch. 31:19; Num. 1:17] [s]2 Kin. 6:22; Prov. 25:21, 22; Rom. 12:20

27:7 in the Book of the Kings. See Introduction to 1 Chronicles: Author.

28:1–27 The account of Ahaz in 2 Kin. 16 is supplemented in 2 Chronicles. Ahaz's reign contrasts sharply with his father's kingdom (ch. 27 note), and the account focuses on how infidelity leads to military defeat.

28:1 Ahaz. Ahaz reigned together with Jotham 735–732 B.C., and then as sole monarch for sixteen years, 732–716 B.C. If he was twenty when he took office, he was thirty-six when he died, and he would have been only eleven when his son Hezekiah was born (29:1). Some ancient sources give the figure "twenty-five" instead of "twenty" for his age at succession.

28:3 burned his sons. Ahaz's apostasy was so complete that he practiced human sacrifice. See Lev. 18:21; Deut. 12:31; 18:10; 2 Kin. 16:3; 17:17; 21:6; 23:10; 2 Chr. 33:6; Ps. 106:37, 38; Is. 57:5; Jer. 7:30, 31; 19:5; 32:35; Ezek. 16:20, 21; Mic. 6:7.

28:5–15 Ahaz is defeated in battle as a divine judgment on his flagrant apostasy (v. 5).

28:5 king of Syria . . . king of Israel. Rezin (king of Syria) and Pekah (king of Israel) joined forces against Ahaz (2 Kin. 16:5, 6; Is. 7:1–17).

28:9 Samaria. Turning from his usual focus on the southern kingdom (Judah), the historian reports that citizens of Samaria, capital of the northern kingdom, obeyed when a prophet spoke to them. This obedience was an instructive contrast to the apostasy of Judah, the southern kingdom.

among them on donkeys, they brought
them to their kinsfolk at Jericho, [t]the city
of palm trees. Then they returned to
Samaria.
16 [u]At that time King Ahaz sent to the
king[1] of Assyria for help. 17 For the
Edomites had again invaded and defeated
Judah and carried away captives. 18 [v]And
the Philistines had made raids on [w]the
cities in the Shephelah and the Negeb of
Judah, and had taken Beth-shemesh,
Aijalon, Gederoth, Soco [x]with its villages,
Timnah with its villages, and Gimzo with
its villages. And they settled there. 19 For
the LORD humbled Judah because of Ahaz
king of [y]Israel, for he had made Judah act
sinfully[2] and had been very unfaithful to
the LORD. 20 So [z]Tiglath-pileser[3] king of
Assyria came against him and afflicted him
instead of strengthening him. 21 [a]For Ahaz
took a portion from the house of the LORD
and the house of the king and of the
princes, and gave tribute to the king of
Assyria, but it did not help him.

Ahaz's Idolatry

22 In the time of his distress he became
yet more faithless to the LORD—this same
King Ahaz. 23 For [b]he sacrificed to the gods
of Damascus that had defeated him and
said, [c]"Because the gods of the kings of
Syria helped them, I will sacrifice to them
that they may help me." But they were the
ruin of him and of all Israel. 24 And Ahaz
gathered together the vessels of the house
of God and [d]cut in pieces the vessels of the
house of God, and he shut up the doors of
the house of the LORD, and he made himself [e]altars in every corner of Jerusalem.
25 In every city of Judah he made high
places to [f]make offerings to other gods,

15 [t]Deut. 34:3; Judg. 1:16
16 [u][2 Kin. 16:7, 8]
18 [v][Ezek. 16:27, 57] [w]See Josh. 15:33-36 [x][Num. 21:25]
19 [y]See ch. 21:2
20 [z][2 Kin. 15:29; 16:7]
21 [a]2 Kin. 16:8, 9
23 [b][ch. 25:14] [c][Jer. 44:17, 18]
24 [d][2 Kin. 16:17] [e][ch. 30:14]
25 [f]ver. 3
26 [g]For ver. 26, 27, see 2 Kin. 16:19, 20
27 [h][ch. 21:20; 24:25] [i]See ch. 21:2
Chapter 29
1 [j]For ver. 1, 2, see 2 Kin. 18:1-3 [k][ch. 26:5]
3 [l][ver. 7; ch. 28:24]
5 [m]ver. 15, 34; ch. 35:6; 1 Chr. 15:12; Ezra 6:20
6 [n]Jer. 2:27; Ezek. 8:16
7 [o]ch. 28:24
8 [p]See ch. 24:18

provoking to anger the LORD, the God of
his fathers. 26 [g]Now the rest of his acts and
all his ways, from first to last, behold, they
are written in the Book of the Kings of
Judah and Israel. 27 And Ahaz slept with his
fathers, and they buried him in the city, in
Jerusalem, for [h]they did not bring him into
the tombs of the kings of [i]Israel. And
Hezekiah his son reigned in his place.

Hezekiah Reigns in Judah

29 [j]Hezekiah began to reign when he
was twenty-five years old, and he
reigned twenty-nine years in Jerusalem. His
mother's name was Abijah[4] the daughter of
[k]Zechariah. 2 And he did what was right in
the eyes of the LORD, according to all that
David his father had done.

Hezekiah Cleanses the Temple

3 In the first year of his reign, in the first
month, he [l]opened the doors of the house
of the LORD and repaired them. 4 He
brought in the priests and the Levites and
assembled them in the square on the east
5 and said to them, "Hear me, Levites! Now
[m]consecrate yourselves, and consecrate the
house of the LORD, the God of your fathers,
and carry out the filth from the Holy Place.
6 For our fathers have been unfaithful and
have done what was evil in the sight of the
LORD our God. They have forsaken him and
[n]have turned away their faces from the
habitation of the LORD and turned their
backs. 7 They also [o]shut the doors of the
vestibule and put out the lamps and have
not burned incense or offered burnt offerings in the Holy Place to the God of Israel.
8 Therefore [p]the wrath of the LORD came on
Judah and Jerusalem, and he has made

1 Septuagint, Syriac, Vulgate (compare 2 Kings 16:7); Hebrew *kings*
2 Or *wildly* 3 Hebrew *Tilgath-pilneser* 4 Spelled *Abi* in 2 Kings 18:2

28:21 took . . . from the house of the LORD. See note 16:2.

did not help him. Tiglath-pileser of Assyria (745–727 B.C.) gave some temporary relief to Judah from the threats of Syria and Israel (2 Kin. 16:7–9), but Judah became subservient to Assyria.

28:25 made high places. See note 21:11.

28:26 the Book of the Kings. See Introduction to 1 Chronicles: Author.

28:27 not . . . tombs. See note 21:19.

29:1 Hezekiah. The reign of Hezekiah (716–687 B.C.) begins a new era in the history of Israel and Judah. The northern kingdom had been destroyed by the Assyrians and only Judah remained. Hezekiah brought together representatives from both kingdoms to form a single, reunited kingdom with one king and one temple in Jerusalem. The writer of Chronicles devotes more attention to Hezekiah than any other king except David and Solomon. He uses material from 2 Kin. 18–20, but he supplements it broadly, including an extensive account of Hezekiah's temple reforms and Passover celebration (29:3–31:1). Hezekiah's reign appears as a return to the glory of Solomon's kingdom.

29:3 opened the doors . . . and repaired them. Hezekiah overturns the actions of his father Ahaz (28:25 note) and restores the gold ornamentation stripped from the temple doors (2 Kin. 16:8, 9).

29:4 Chronicles normally gives attention to matters concerning the priests and Levites (1 Chr. 6:1 note).

29:4–11 Hezekiah's speech stands in contrast with Abijah's earlier assessments (13:6–12 notes). Judah is no longer different from Israel; both have forsaken God. Judah must repent as well.

29:7 shut the doors. As Ahaz did (28:24).

29:8 on Judah and Jerusalem. Hezekiah asserts that Judah and Jerusalem were under the curse of God for their neglect of the temple.

them [q]an object of horror, of astonishment,
[r]and of hissing, as you see with your own
eyes. 9 For behold, [s]our fathers have fallen
by the sword, and our sons and our daughters and our wives are in captivity for this.
10 Now [t]it is in my heart [u]to make a
covenant with the LORD, the God of Israel,
in order that his fierce anger may turn away
from us. 11 My sons, do not now be negligent, [v]for the LORD has chosen you to stand
in his presence, to minister to him and to
be his ministers and make offerings to
him."
12 Then the Levites arose, [w]Mahath the
son of Amasai, and Joel the son of Azariah,
of the sons of [x]the Kohathites; and of the
sons of [x]Merari, Kish the son of Abdi, and
Azariah the son of Jehallelel; and of the
[x]Gershonites, Joah the son of Zimmah, and
Eden the son of Joah; 13 and of the sons of
[y]Elizaphan, Shimri and Jeuel; and of the
sons of [z]Asaph, Zechariah and Mattaniah;
14 and of the sons of [a]Heman, Jehuel and
Shimei; and of the sons of [b]Jeduthun,
Shemaiah and Uzziel. 15 They gathered their
brothers and [c]consecrated themselves and
went in as the king had commanded, [d]by
the words of the LORD, [e]to cleanse the
house of the LORD. 16 The priests went into
the inner part of the house of the LORD to
cleanse it, and they brought out all the
uncleanness that they found in the temple
of the LORD into the court of the house of
the LORD. And the Levites took it and carried it out to [f]the brook Kidron. 17 They
began to consecrate [g]on the first day of
the first month, and on the eighth day of
the month they came to the vestibule of the
LORD. Then for eight days they consecrated
the house of the LORD, and on the sixteenth day of the first month they finished.
18 Then they went in to Hezekiah the king
and said, "We have cleansed all the house
of the LORD, the altar of burnt offering and
all its utensils, and the table for the showbread and all its utensils. 19 All the utensils
[h]that King Ahaz discarded in his reign
when he was faithless, we have made ready
and consecrated, and behold, they are
before the altar of the LORD."

Hezekiah Restores Temple Worship

20 Then Hezekiah the king rose early and
gathered the officials of the city and went
up to the house of the LORD. 21 And they
brought seven bulls, seven rams, seven
lambs, and seven male goats [i]for a sin offering for the kingdom and for the sanctuary
and for Judah. And he commanded the
priests the sons of Aaron to offer them on
the altar of the LORD. 22 So they slaughtered
the bulls, and the priests received the
blood [j]and threw it against the altar. And
they slaughtered the rams and their blood
was thrown against the altar. And they
slaughtered the lambs and their blood was
thrown against the altar. 23 Then the goats
for the sin offering were brought to the
king and the assembly, [k]and they laid their
hands on them, 24 and the priests slaughtered them and made a sin offering with
their blood on the altar, [l]to make atonement for all Israel. For the king commanded that the burnt offering and the sin offering should be made for all Israel.
25 [m]And he stationed the Levites in the
house of the LORD with cymbals, harps,
and lyres, [n]according to the commandment of David and of Gad [o]the king's seer
and of [p]Nathan the prophet, for the commandment was from the LORD through his
prophets. 26 The Levites stood with [q]the

8 [q]Deut. 28:25; [r]Jer. 19:8; 25:9, 18; 29:18; Mic. 6:16
9 [s]ch. 28:5, 6, 8, 17
10 [t]See 1 Chr. 22:7 [u]See ch. 15:12
11 [v]Num. 3:6; 8:14; 18:2, 6
12 [w]ch. 31:13 [x]Num. 3:17
13 [y]1 Chr. 15:8 [z]1 Chr. 6:39
14 [a]1 Chr. 6:33 [b]1 Chr. 9:16
15 [c]See ver. 5 [d]ch. 30:12 [e][Neh. 13:9]
16 [f]See 2 Sam. 15:23
17 [g]ver. 3
19 [h][ch. 28:24]
21 [i][Lev. 4:14]
22 [j]Lev. 8:15, 19, 24; Heb. 9:21; [ch. 35:11]
23 [k]Lev. 4:15
24 [l]Lev. 4:26
25 [m]1 Chr. 16:4; 25:6; [1 Chr. 15:16] [n]ch. 8:14; 1 Chr. 23:5; 25:1; [o]See 1 Sam. 9:9 [p]2 Sam. 12:1
26 [q]1 Chr. 23:5; [Amos 6:5]

29:9 in captivity. During the reign of Ahaz, many people from Judah were taken into exile by the Syrians (28:5–8) and Edomites (28:17). These events foreshadowed the Babylonian captivity to come (36:15–23), making the reign of Hezekiah a persuasive example for restoration after exile.

29:10 in my heart. The anger of God turned Hezekiah toward Him in repentance, not away from Him in fear.

make a covenant. See note 15:12.

29:12–14 The historian mentions representatives of the three divisions of the tribe of Levi (v. 12) and the three families of singers (vv. 13, 14). Hezekiah's reforms were widely supported by the Levites and in accordance with the order established under David and Solomon (1 Chr. 6:1 note).

29:13 Elizaphan. A prominent leader of the Kohathites (Num. 3:30).

29:16 priests went into the inner part. The historian offers these details to demonstrate that Hezekiah's renovation strictly accorded with Mosaic legislation.

29:20–36 Hezekiah's dedication of the temple is reported in three parts: sacrifices brought by the leaders (vv. 20–24), arrangement of music (vv. 25–30), and sacrifices brought by the people (vv. 31–36).

29:21 for the kingdom . . . sanctuary . . . Judah. Sacrifices were made on behalf of the royal family, the priests and Levites, and the people. All three groups were involved in the apostasy under Ahaz (2 Kin. 16).

29:24 all Israel. In connection with the reunited kingdom (chs. 29–36), the expression "all Israel" (30:1; 31:1; 35:3) refers to both Judah together with the refugees from the northern tribes (1 Chr. 11:1 note; 2 Chr. 10:1 note). Hezekiah ordered sacrifices to be offered, not for Judah only (v. 21), but for all the descendants of Israel. This desire to unite is clearly expressed in his arrangements for the Passover (30:1–6).

29:25 cymbals, harps, and lyres. See note 1 Chr. 15:16.

instruments of David, [r]and the priests
with the trumpets. [27]Then Hezekiah commanded that the burnt offering be offered
on the altar. And when the burnt offering
began, [s]the song to the LORD began also,
and the trumpets, accompanied by the
instruments of David king of Israel. [28]The
whole assembly worshiped, and the singers sang and the trumpeters sounded. All
this continued until the burnt offering was
finished. [29]When the offering was finished,
[t]the king and all who were present with
him bowed themselves and worshiped.
[30]And Hezekiah the king and the officials
commanded the Levites to sing praises to
the LORD with the words of David and of
Asaph the seer. And they sang praises with
gladness, and they bowed down and worshiped.
[31]Then Hezekiah said, [u]"You have now
consecrated yourselves to[1] the LORD. Come
near; bring sacrifices and thank offerings to
the house of the LORD." And the assembly
brought sacrifices and thank offerings, and
all who were [v]of a willing heart brought
burnt offerings. [32]The number of the burnt
offerings that the assembly brought was 70
bulls, 100 rams, and 200 lambs; all these
were for a burnt offering to the LORD. [33]And
the consecrated offerings were 600 bulls
and 3,000 sheep. [34]But the priests were too
few and could not flay all the burnt offerings, so until other priests had consecrated
themselves, [w]their brothers the Levites
helped them, until the work was finished—[x]for the Levites were more upright
in heart than the priests in consecrating
themselves. [35]Besides the great number of
burnt offerings, there was [y]the fat of the
peace offerings, and there were [z]the drink
offerings for the burnt offerings. Thus the
service of the house of the LORD was

26 [r]See 1 Chr. 15:24
27 [s][ch. 23:18]
29 [t][ch. 20:18]
31 [u]ch. 13:9; [Ex. 28:41] [v]Ex. 35:5, 22
34 [w][ch. 35:11] [x][ch. 30:3]
35 [y]Lev. 3:1, 16 [z]Num. 15:5, 7, 10

restored. [36]And Hezekiah and all the people rejoiced because God had prepared for
the people, for the thing came about suddenly.

Passover Celebrated

30 Hezekiah sent to all Israel and
Judah, and wrote letters also to
Ephraim and Manasseh, that they should
come to the house of the LORD at Jerusalem
to keep the Passover to the LORD, the God
of Israel. [2]For the king and his princes and
all the assembly in Jerusalem had taken
counsel to keep the Passover [a]in the second month— [3]for they could not keep it
[b]at that time [c]because the priests had not
consecrated themselves in sufficient number, nor had the people assembled in
Jerusalem— [4]and the plan seemed right to
the king and all the assembly. [5]So they
decreed to make a proclamation throughout all Israel, [d]from Beersheba to Dan, that
the people should come and keep the
Passover to the LORD, the God of Israel, at
Jerusalem, for they had not kept it as often
as prescribed. [6][e]So couriers went throughout all Israel and Judah with letters from
the king and his princes, as the king had
commanded, saying, "O people of Israel,
[f]return to the LORD, the God of Abraham,
Isaac, and Israel, that he may turn again to
the remnant of you who have escaped from
the hand of [g]the kings of Assyria. [7][h]Do not
be like your fathers and your brothers, who
were faithless to the LORD God of their
fathers, so that he made them a desolation,
as you see. [8][i]Do not now be stiff-necked as
your fathers were, but yield yourselves to
the LORD and come to his sanctuary, which
he has consecrated forever, and serve the
LORD your God, [j]that his fierce anger may

Chapter 30
2 [a]ver. 13, 15; Num. 9:10, 11
3 [b][ch. 29:17; Ex. 12:6, 18] [c]ch. 29:34; [ver. 24]
5 [d]See 2 Sam. 3:10
6 [e][Esth. 3:13, 15; 8:10, 14; Jer. 51:31] [f]Jer. 4:1; Joel 2:12, 13 [g]2 Kin. 15:19, 29
7 [h][Ezek. 20:18]
8 [i]Ex. 32:9; Deut. 9:6; 10:16; 2 Kin. 17:14; Neh. 9:16, 29; Jer. 7:26; 17:23; [Acts 7:51] [j]ch. 29:10

1 Hebrew *filled your hand for*

29:32–35 These sacrifices were fewer in number, but still a reminder of what Solomon had offered when the temple was dedicated (7:4–6).

29:36 came about suddenly. The restoration of the temple took less than three weeks (vv. 3, 17), an evidence that God was working in the people.

30:1 the Passover. The writer of Kings emphasizes the Passover under Josiah (2 Kin. 23:21–23) without discussing the celebration arranged by Hezekiah. The writer of Chronicles exalts this celebration that reunited the northern and southern tribes in temple worship. Such reunion was of striking relevance for those who were working for the restoration of Israel in the time following the return of the exiles from Babylon (Introduction to 1 Chronicles: Characteristics and Themes).

30:2 king . . . princes . . . all the assembly. Hezekiah followed the good example of David (1 Chr. 13:1).

the second month. Normally, the Unleavened Bread and Passover feasts were to be observed in the first month (Ex. 12:2, 6; Deut. 16:1–8; cf. 2 Chr. 35:1). However, exceptions were made for those who were traveling or were unclean (Num. 9:9–13). Hezekiah applied the exception generously to the entire nation (v. 3).

30:6–9 Hezekiah sent the same letter to both Israel and Judah (v. 6). His letter contrasts with Abijah's speech to the northerners (13:4–12). By Hezekiah's day, Judah and Israel were both in need of repentance and renewal.

30:6 return to the LORD. See note 7:14.

the remnant of you who have escaped. The historian uses this terminology in a technical sense, meaning those who had been spared by God to represent the continuation of the nation.

turn away from you. **9**For [f]if you return to
the LORD, your brothers and your children
[k]will find compassion with their captors
and return to this land. For [l]the LORD your
God is gracious and merciful and will not
turn away his face from you, [m]if you return
to him."
10[e]So the couriers went from city to city
through the country of [n]Ephraim and
Manasseh, and as far as Zebulun, but [o]they
laughed them to scorn and mocked them.
11However, [p]some men of Asher, of
Manasseh, and of Zebulun humbled themselves and came to Jerusalem. **12**The hand
of God was also on Judah to give them one
heart to do what the king and the princes
commanded [q]by the word of the LORD.
13And many people came together in
Jerusalem to keep the Feast of Unleavened
Bread [r]in the second month, a very great
assembly. **14**They set to work and removed
[s]the altars that were in Jerusalem, and all
the altars for burning incense they took
away [t]and threw into the Kidron valley.
15[u]And they slaughtered the Passover lamb
on the fourteenth day of the second
month. [v]And the priests and the Levites
were ashamed, [w]so that they consecrated
themselves and brought burnt offerings
into the house of the LORD. **16**[x]They took
their accustomed posts according to the
Law of Moses [y]the man of God. The priests
threw the blood that they received from the
hand of the Levites. **17**For there were many
in the assembly who had not consecrated
themselves. Therefore the Levites had to
slaughter the Passover lamb for everyone
who was not clean, to consecrate it to the
LORD. **18**For a majority of the people, [z]many
of them from Ephraim, Manasseh,
Issachar, and Zebulun, had not cleansed
themselves, yet they ate the Passover otherwise [a]than as prescribed. For Hezekiah
had prayed for them, saying, "May the
good LORD pardon everyone **19**[b]who sets his
heart to seek God, the LORD, the God of his
fathers, even though not according to the
sanctuary's rules of cleanness."[1] **20**And the
LORD heard Hezekiah and healed the people. **21**And the people of Israel who were
present at Jerusalem kept [c]the Feast of
Unleavened Bread seven days with great
gladness, and the Levites and the priests
praised the LORD day by day, singing with
all their might[2] to the LORD. **22**And
Hezekiah spoke [d]encouragingly to all the
Levites who showed good skill in the service of the LORD. So they ate the food of the
festival for seven days, sacrificing peace
offerings and [e]giving thanks to the LORD,
the God of their fathers.
23Then the whole assembly agreed
together to keep the feast [f]for another
seven days. So they kept it for another
seven days with gladness. **24**For Hezekiah
king of Judah [g]gave the assembly 1,000
bulls and 7,000 sheep for offerings, and
the princes gave the assembly 1,000 bulls
and 10,000 sheep. And the priests [h]conse-
crated themselves in great numbers. **25**The
whole assembly of Judah, and the priests
and the Levites, [i]and the whole assembly
that came out of Israel, and the sojourners
who came out of the land of Israel, and the
sojourners who lived in Judah, rejoiced.
26So there was great joy in Jerusalem, for
[j]since the time of Solomon the son of David
king of Israel there had been nothing like
this in Jerusalem. **27**Then [k]the priests and
the Levites arose and [l]blessed the people,
and their voice was heard, and their prayer
came to [m]his holy habitation in heaven.

Hezekiah Organizes the Priests

31 Now when all this was finished, all
Israel who were present went out to
the cities of Judah and [n]broke in pieces the
[o]pillars and cut down [p]the Asherim and
broke down the high places and the altars

9[f][See ver. 6 above] [k][Ps. 106:46] [l]Ex. 34:6; Dan. 9:9 [m]See 1 Sam. 7:3
10[e][See ver. 6 above] [n]ver. 1 [o][ch. 36:16]
11[p]ver. 18, 21, 25
12[q][ch. 29:15]
13[r]ver. 2
14[s]ch. 28:24 [t][ch. 15:16; 2 Kin. 23:6]
15[u]ch. 35:11 [v][ch. 29:34] [w][Ezra 6:20]
16[x]ch. 35:10 [y]Deut.33:1
18[z]ver. 11, 25 [a]See Ex. 12:43-49
19[b]ch. 19:3
21[c]Ex. 12:15; 13:6; Ezra 6:22
22[d]ch. 32:6; Isai. 40:2 [e][Lev. 5:5; Ezra 10:11]
23[f][1 Kin. 8:65]
24[g][ch. 35:7-9] [h]ver. 3; ch. 29:34
25[i] ver. 11, 18
26[j]See ch. 7:8-10
27[k]ch. 5:5; 23:18 [l]See Num. 6:23-27 [m]Deut. 26:15; Ps. 68:5

Chapter 31
1[n]2 Kin. 18:4 [o]See Deut. 16:22 [p]See Deut. 16:21

1 Hebrew *not according to the cleanness of holiness* 2 Compare 1 Chronicles 13:8; Hebrew *with instruments of might*

30:9 compassion . . . return to this land. Hezekiah recalls Solomon's dedicatory prayer (6:36–39). His concern for the return of those who had been taken into exile was instructive for anyone hoping to see the nation restored in the time following the Babylonian exile (Zech. 8:7, 8).

30:11 However, some men. The presence of some was important, even if all would not come.

30:16 Law of Moses. See note 1 Chr. 16:40.

30:17–20 The failure of some to be ritually cleansed threatened the reunification of the tribes. Hezekiah interceded for the offenders, and God made the reunification of the nation possible (cf. Ex. 32:30–32).

30:23–27 Just as Solomon's temple celebration was extended (7:8, 9), Hezekiah's feast continued for another week.

30:24 Hezekiah . . . gave. Hezekiah followed the example of David in supporting the temple at his own expense (1 Chr. 29:3 note; 2 Chr. 35:7, 8 note).

30:27 his holy habitation in heaven. Note the similar language in Solomon's prayer (6:21, 30, 33, 39).

throughout all Judah and Benjamin, and in
Ephraim and Manasseh, until they had
destroyed them all. Then all the people of
Israel returned to their cities, every man to
his possession.
2 And Hezekiah appointed [q]the divisions of
the priests and of the Levites, division by
division, each according to his service, the
priests and the Levites, [r]for burnt offerings
and peace offerings, to minister in the gates
of the camp of the LORD and to give thanks
and praise. 3 [s]The contribution of the king
from his own possessions was for the burnt
offerings: the burnt offerings of morning and
evening, and the burnt offerings for the
Sabbaths, the new moons, and the appointed feasts, [t]as it is written in the Law of the
LORD. 4 And he commanded the people who
lived in Jerusalem to give [u]the portion due to
the priests and the Levites, that they might
give themselves to the Law of the LORD. 5 As
soon as the command was spread abroad,
the people of Israel gave in abundance the
firstfruits of grain, wine, oil, honey, and of all
the produce of the field. And they brought in
abundantly [v]the tithe of everything. 6 And the
people of Israel and Judah who lived in the
cities of Judah also brought in the tithe of
cattle and sheep, and [w]the tithe of the dedicated things that had been dedicated to the
LORD their God, and laid them in heaps. 7 In
the third month they began to pile up the
heaps, and finished them in the seventh
month. 8 When Hezekiah and the princes
came and saw the heaps, they blessed the
LORD and his people Israel. 9 And Hezekiah
questioned the priests and the Levites about
the heaps. 10 Azariah the chief priest, who
was [x]of the house of Zadok, answered him,
"Since they began to bring the contributions
into the house of the LORD, we have eaten
and had enough and have plenty left, [y]for the
LORD has blessed his people, so that we have
this large amount left."
11 Then Hezekiah commanded them to
prepare [z]chambers in the house of the LORD,
and they prepared them. 12 And they faithfully brought in the contributions, the tithes,
and the dedicated things. The chief officer
[a]in charge of them was Conaniah the Levite,
with [b]Shimei his brother as second, 13 [b]while
Jehiel, Azaziah, Nahath, Asahel, Jerimoth,
Jozabad, Eliel, Ismachiah, [b]Mahath, and
Benaiah were overseers assisting Conaniah
and Shimei his brother, by the appointment
of Hezekiah the king and [x]Azariah the chief
officer of the house of God. 14 And Kore the
son of Imnah the Levite, keeper of the east
gate, was over the freewill offerings to God,
to apportion the contribution reserved for
the LORD and the most holy offerings.
15 [b]Eden, Miniamin, Jeshua, Shemaiah,
Amariah, and Shecaniah were [c]faithfully
assisting him in [d]the cities of the priests, to
distribute the portions to their brothers, old
and young alike, by divisions, 16 except those
enrolled by genealogy, males from three
years old and upward—all who entered the
house of the LORD [e]as the duty of each day
required—for their service according to their
offices, by their divisions. 17 The enrollment
of the priests was according to their fathers'
houses; that of the Levites [f]from twenty years
old and upward was according to their
offices, by their divisions. 18 They were
enrolled with all their little children, their
wives, their sons, and their daughters, the
whole assembly, for they were faithful in
keeping themselves holy. 19 And for the sons
of Aaron, the priests, who were in the fields
of common land belonging to their cities,
there were men in the several cities who were
[g]designated by name to distribute portions
to every male among the priests and to everyone among the Levites who was enrolled.
20 Thus Hezekiah did throughout all Judah,
[h]and he did what was good and right and
faithful before the LORD his God. 21 And every
work that he undertook in the service of the
house of God and in accordance with the law
and the commandments, seeking his God,
he did with all his heart, and prospered.

2 [q]1 Chr. 23:6; 24:1 [r]1 Chr. 23:30, 31
3 [s][ch. 35:7] [t]See Num. 28:3–29:40
4 [u][Neh. 13:10]; See Num. 18:8-24
5 [v]Neh. 13:12
6 [w]Lev. 27:30; Deut. 14:28
10 [x]1 Chr. 6:8 [y][Mal. 3:10]
11 [z]1 Chr. 9:26, 33 [2 Kin. 23:11; Neh. 10:39]
12 [a][ch. 35:9; Neh. 13:13] [b][2 Chr. 29:12, 14]
13 [b][See ver. 12 above] [x][See ver. 10 above]
15 [b][See ver. 12 above] [c]1 Chr. 9:22 [d]See Josh. 21:9-19
16 [e]1 Kin. 8:59; Ezra 3:4; Neh. 11:23; 12:47
17 [f]1 Chr. 23:24, 27
19 [g][ch. 28:15; Num. 1:17]; See ver. 12-15
20 [h]2 Kin. 18:3; 20:3

31:2–21 Apart from 31:20, 21 (cf. 2 Kin. 18:5–7), this material is not in Kings. The author of Chronicles writes in a time when temple worship was being reestablished, and the provisions of Hezekiah would have been of obvious relevance for that task.

31:2 appointed the divisions of the priests and of the Levites. Hezekiah returned to the order of Solomon (8:14), who followed David's design (1 Chr. 6:1 note).

31:3, 4 the Law of the LORD. See note 1 Chr. 16:40.

he commanded the people. As David had done, Hezekiah gave from his own treasury before appealing to the people (1 Chr. 29:3 note).

31:16 three years old. Perhaps this refers to the inclusion of children in the distribution of food (see also v. 18). However, "three" could be a copyist's error for "thirty," the age of active service in the temple (1 Chr. 23:3 note).

31:21 prospered. The Lord rewarded Hezekiah for his faithfulness and obedience. He delivered him from invasion (32:1), healed his illness (32:24), forgave his pride (32:26), and gave him wealth (32:27–31).

Sennacherib Invades Judah

32 [i]After these things and these acts of
faithfulness, Sennacherib king of
Assyria came and invaded Judah and
encamped against the fortified cities, thinking to win them for himself. 2 And when
Hezekiah saw that Sennacherib had come
and intended to fight against Jerusalem,
3 he planned with his officers and his
mighty men to stop the water of the
springs that were outside the city; and they
helped him. 4 A great many people were
gathered, and they stopped all the springs
and [j]the brook that flowed through the
land, saying, "Why should the kings of
Assyria come and find much water?" 5 He
set to work resolutely and built up [k]all the
wall that was broken down and raised towers upon it,[1] and outside it he built another wall, and he strengthened the [l]Millo in
the city of David. He also made weapons
and shields in abundance. 6 And he set
combat commanders over the people and
gathered them together to him in the
square at the gate of the city and spoke
[m]encouragingly to them, saying, 7 [n]"Be
strong and courageous. [o]Do not be afraid
or dismayed before the king of Assyria and
all the horde that is with him, [p]for there are
more with us than with him. 8 With him is
[q]an arm of flesh, [r]but with us is the LORD
our God, to help us and to fight our battles." And the people took confidence from
the words of Hezekiah king of Judah.

Sennacherib Blasphemes

9 After this, Sennacherib, king of Assyria,
who was besieging Lachish with all his
forces, sent his servants to Jerusalem to
Hezekiah king of Judah and to all the people of Judah who were in Jerusalem, saying,
10 "Thus says Sennacherib king of Assyria,
'On what are you trusting, that you endure
the siege in Jerusalem? 11 Is not Hezekiah
misleading you, that he may give you over
to die by famine and by thirst, when he
tells you, "The LORD our God will deliver
us from the hand of the king of Assyria"?
12 [s]Has not this same Hezekiah taken away
his high places and his altars and commanded Judah and Jerusalem, "Before one
altar you shall worship, and on it you shall
burn your sacrifices"? 13 Do you not know
what I and my fathers have done to all the
peoples of other lands? Were the gods of
the nations of those lands at all able to
deliver their lands out of my hand? 14 Who
among all the gods of those nations that
my fathers devoted to destruction[2] was
able to deliver his people from my hand,
that your God should be able to deliver you
from my hand? 15 Now, therefore, do not let
Hezekiah deceive you or mislead you in
this fashion, and do not believe him, for no
god of any nation or kingdom has been
able to deliver his people from my hand or
from the hand of my fathers. How much
less will your God deliver you out of my
hand!'"

16 And his servants said still more against
the Lord GOD and against his servant
Hezekiah. 17 And he wrote letters to cast
contempt on the LORD, the God of Israel
and to speak against him, saying, "Like the
gods of the nations of the lands who have
not delivered their people from my hands,
so the God of Hezekiah will not deliver his
people from my hand." 18 And they shouted it with a loud voice in the language of
Judah to the people of Jerusalem who were
on the wall, to frighten and terrify them, in
order that they might take the city. 19 And
they spoke of the God of Jerusalem as they
spoke of the gods of the peoples of the
earth, which are the work of men's hands.

The LORD Delivers Jerusalem

20 Then Hezekiah the king and Isaiah the
prophet, the son of Amoz, prayed because
of this and cried to heaven. 21 And the LORD
sent an angel, who cut off all the mighty
warriors and commanders and officers in
the camp of the king of Assyria. So he
returned with [t]shame of face to his own

Chapter 32
1 [i]For ver. 1-22, see 2 Kin. 18:13–19:37; Isai. 36:1–37:38
4 [j]ver. 30
5 [k]ch. 25:23; [Isai. 22:9, 10] [l]See 2 Sam. 5:9
6 [m]ch. 30:22; Isai. 40:2
7 [n]See Deut. 31:6 [o]ch. 20:15 [p]2 Kin. 6:16
8 [q]Jer. 17:5 [r]ch. 15:2; 20:17
12 [s][ch. 31:1]
21 [t][Ps. 44:15; Jer. 7:19]

1 Vulgate; Hebrew *and raised upon the towers* 2 That is, set apart (devoted) as an offering to the Lord (for destruction)

32:1–23 In Kings the account of Sennacherib's invasion is the most prominent episode of Hezekiah's reign (2 Kin. 18:17–19:37). Chronicles gives a shorter account, using it to illustrate the divine blessing granted because of fidelity, trust, and prayer.

32:7, 8 Hezekiah's speech demonstrated his full reliance on divine power to overcome his great enemy.

32:9 The writer of Chronicles does not repeat what 2 Kings says about Hezekiah's payment of tribute to Sennacherib from the treasures of the temple, or the Assyrian's charge that Hezekiah had an alliance with Egypt (2 Kin. 18:14–27). He emphasizes Hezekiah's virtues.

32:20 Hezekiah . . . Isaiah . . . prayed. There is a more detailed account of these events in 2 Kin. 19:1–34. On the value of prayer in battle, see 6:34 note.

land. And when he came into the house of
his god, some of his own sons struck him
down there with the sword. 22 So the LORD
saved Hezekiah and the inhabitants of
Jerusalem from the hand of Sennacherib
king of Assyria and from the hand of all his
enemies, and he provided for them on
every side. 23 And many [u]brought gifts to
the LORD to Jerusalem and precious things
to Hezekiah king of Judah, so that he was
exalted in the sight of all nations from that
time onward.

Hezekiah's Pride and Achievements

24 [v]In those days Hezekiah became sick
and was at the point of death, and he
prayed to the LORD, and he answered him
and gave him a sign. 25 But Hezekiah [w]did
not make return according to the benefit
done to him, for [x]his heart was proud.
Therefore [y]wrath came upon him and
Judah and Jerusalem. 26 But Hezekiah
[z]humbled himself for the pride of his heart,
both he and the inhabitants of Jerusalem,
so that the wrath of the LORD did not come
upon them in the days of Hezekiah.
27 And Hezekiah had very great riches
and honor, and he made for himself treasuries for silver, for gold, for precious
stones, for spices, for shields, and for all
kinds of [a]costly vessels; 28 storehouses also
for the yield of grain, wine, and oil; and
stalls for all kinds of cattle, and sheepfolds.
29 He likewise provided cities for himself,
and flocks and herds in abundance, for
God had given him very great possessions.
30 This same Hezekiah [b]closed the upper
outlet of the waters of [c]Gihon and directed
them down to the west side of the city of
David. And Hezekiah prospered in all his
works. 31 And so in the matter of the envoys
of the princes of Babylon, [d]who had been
sent to him to inquire about [e]the sign that
had been done in the land, God left him to
himself, [f]in order to test him and to know
all that was in his heart.
32 Now the rest of the acts of Hezekiah
and his good deeds, behold, they are written [g]in the vision of Isaiah the prophet the
son of Amoz, [h]in the Book of the Kings of
Judah and Israel. 33 And Hezekiah slept
with his fathers, and they buried him in the
[i]upper part of the tombs of the sons of
David, and all Judah and the inhabitants of
Jerusalem did him honor at his death. And
Manasseh his son reigned in his place.

Manasseh Reigns in Judah

33 [j]Manasseh was twelve years old
when he began to reign, and he
reigned fifty-five years in Jerusalem. 2 And
he did what was evil in the sight of the
LORD, according to [k]the abominations of
the nations whom the LORD drove out
before the people of Israel. 3 For he rebuilt
the high places [l]that his father Hezekiah
had broken down, and he erected altars to
the Baals, and made [m]Asherahs, and worshiped all the host of heaven and served
them. 4 And he built altars in the house of
the LORD, of which the LORD had said, [n]"In
Jerusalem shall my name be forever." 5 And
he built altars for all the host of heaven in
[o]the two courts of the house of the LORD.
6 [p]And he burned his sons as an offering [q]in
the Valley of the Son of Hinnom, and [r]used
fortune-telling and omens and sorcery, and
dealt with [s]mediums and with wizards. He
did much evil in the sight of the LORD, provoking him to anger. 7 And [t]the carved

23 [u][ch. 17:5]
24 [v]See 2 Kin. 20:1-11; Isai. 38:1-8
25 [w][Ps. 116:12] [x]See ch. 26:16 [y]ch. 19:2; 24:18
26 [z]Jer. 26:18, 19; [ch. 33:12]
27 [a]ch. 36:10
30 [b]2 Kin. 20:20; [Isai. 22:9, 11] [c]1 Kin. 1:33
31 [d]2 Kin. 20:12; Isai. 39:1 [e]ver. 24 [f]Deut. 8:2
32 [g]See Isai. ch. 36–39 [h]See 2 Kin. 18-20
33 [i][2 Sam. 15:30]
Chapter 33
1 [j]For ver. 1-9, see 2 Kin. 21:1-9
2 [k]ch. 28:3
3 [l]ch. 30:14; 31:1; 2 Kin. 18:4 [m]See Deut. 16:21; [Deut. 17:3]
4 [n]ch. 6:6
5 [o]ch. 4:9
6 [p]ch. 28:3 [q]See Josh. 15:8 [r]Deut. 18:10 [s]See 1 Sam. 28:3
7 [t]ver. 15

32:24–26 There is a fuller account of this illness and prayer in 2 Kin. 20:1–11.

32:25 heart was proud. See note 26:16.

32:27–29 very great riches. Hezekiah's wealth recalls the wealth of Solomon's kingdom (ch. 1; 9:13–28).

32:31 The historian abbreviates the record of 2 Kin. 20:12–19 (cf. Is. 39) in which Isaiah told Hezekiah that his treasures would be taken to Babylon. The author, apparently assuming that his readers are familiar with the account in Kings, leaves out Isaiah's harsh rebuke.

envoys . . . of Babylon. The Babylonian ambassadors came to investigate reports of Hezekiah's "sign" (v. 24; cf. 2 Kin. 20:8–11). Apparently, they desired a military alliance with Hezekiah against Assyria.

to test him. Hezekiah was tested to see whether he would form an alliance with Babylon against Assyria. As the Book of Kings reports, Hezekiah failed the test (2 Kin. 20:12–19).

32:32 written in the vision of Isaiah the prophet. The historian may be referring to the canonical Book of Isaiah (called a "vision," Is. 1:1).

33:1–20 This portrait of Manasseh forms a striking contrast with 2 Kin. 21:1–18. The harsh condemnation of Manasseh (2 Kin. 21:10–16) is omitted, and there is instead an account of his exile, repentance, return, and reforms (vv. 11–17). The writer of Kings blames Manasseh for the downfall of Jerusalem (2 Kin. 21:11–15). Knowing this, the historian of Chronicles encourages his readers by demonstrating that even the worst of sinners can be forgiven and restored through repentance, humility, and prayer.

33:1 Manasseh . . . fifty-five years. Manasseh reigned 696–642 B.C., the longest reign of any king in Judah.

33:2 abominations of the nations. Note the repetition of this theme in v. 9. See the similar evaluation of Ahaz (28:3). Manasseh's sins were so great that he deserved destruction as much as the Canaanites whom God destroyed during the conquest (Gen. 15:16).

33:4 my name. See v. 7 and note on 1 Chr. 13:6.

33:6 he burned his sons as an offering. This is another terrible similarity between Manasseh and Ahaz (28:3 note; 33:2 note).

image of the idol that he had made he set
in the house of God, of which God said to
David and to Solomon his son, "In this
house, and in Jerusalem, which I have chosen out of all the tribes of Israel, [n]I will put
my name forever, 8 and I will no more
remove the foot of Israel from the land
[u]that I appointed for your fathers, if only
they will be careful to do all that I have
commanded them, all the law, the statutes,
and the rules given through Moses."
9 Manasseh led Judah and the inhabitants
of Jerusalem astray, to do more evil than
the nations whom the LORD destroyed
before the people of Israel.

Manasseh's Repentance

10 The LORD spoke to Manasseh and to his
people, but they paid no attention.
11 [v]Therefore the LORD brought upon them
the commanders of the army of the king of
Assyria, who captured Manasseh with hooks
and [w]bound him with chains of bronze and
brought him to Babylon. 12 And when he
was in distress, he entreated the favor of the
LORD his God [x]and humbled himself greatly
before the God of his fathers. 13 He prayed to
him, and [y]God was moved by his entreaty
and heard his plea and brought him again to
Jerusalem into his kingdom. [z]Then
Manasseh knew that the LORD was God.
14 Afterward he built an outer wall for the
city of David west of [a]Gihon, in the valley,
and for the entrance into [b]the Fish Gate,
and carried it around [c]Ophel, and raised it
to a very great height. He also put commanders of the army in all the fortified
cities in Judah. 15 And [d]he took away the
foreign gods and the idol from the house of
the LORD, and all the altars that he had
built on the mountain of the house of the
LORD and in Jerusalem, and he threw them

7 [n][See ver. 4 above]
8 [u]2 Sam. 7:10
11 [v][Deut. 28:36] [w][ch. 36:6; Judg. 6:21]
12 [x][ch. 32:26]
13 [y]1 Chr. 5:20; Ezra 8:23 [z][Dan. 4:25]
14 [a]1 Kin. 1:33 [b]Neh. 3:3; 12:39; Zeph. 1:10 [c]ch. 27:3
15 [d]ver. 3, 5, 7
17 [e] [ch. 32:12]
18 [f]ver. 13, 19 [g]See 1 Sam. 9:9 [h]See ch. 21:2
19 [y][See ver. 13 above] [i]ver. 3 [x][See ver. 12 above]
21 [j]For ver. 21-25, see 2 Kin. 21:19-24
22 [k]ver. 7; [ch. 34:3, 4]
23 [l]ver. 12

outside of the city. 16 He also restored the
altar of the LORD and offered on it sacrifices
of peace offerings and of thanksgiving, and
he commanded Judah to serve the LORD,
the God of Israel. 17 [e]Nevertheless, the people still sacrificed at the high places, but
only to the LORD their God.
18 Now the rest of the acts of Manasseh,
and [f]his prayer to his God, and the words
of [g]the seers who spoke to him in the name
of the LORD, the God of Israel, behold, they
are in the Chronicles of the Kings [h]of Israel.
19 And his prayer, and how [y]God was
moved by his entreaty, and all his sin and
his faithlessness, and the sites [i]on which
he built high places and set up the
[i]Asherim and the images, before [x]he humbled himself, behold, they are written in
the Chronicles of the Seers.[1] 20 So Manasseh slept with his fathers, and they buried
him in his house, and Amon his son
reigned in his place.

Amon's Reign and Death

21 [j]Amon was twenty-two years old when
he began to reign, and he reigned two years
in Jerusalem. 22 And he did what was evil in
the sight of the LORD, as Manasseh his
father had done. Amon sacrificed to all the
images [k]that Manasseh his father had
made, and served them. 23 And he did not
humble himself before the LORD, [l]as
Manasseh his father had humbled himself,
but this Amon incurred guilt more and
more. 24 And his servants conspired against
him and put him to death in his house.
25 But the people of the land struck down
all those who had conspired against King
Amon. And the people of the land made
Josiah his son king in his place.

1 One Hebrew manuscript, Septuagint; most Hebrew manuscripts *of Hozai*

33:8 Moses. See note 1 Chr. 16:40.

33:10 The LORD spoke. The historian abbreviates the fuller description in 2 Kin. 21:10–15.

33:11–13 The author adds a report of Manasseh's exile, repentance, and return.

33:11 the king of Assyria. Either Esarhaddon (681–669 B.C.) or Ashurbanipal (669–627 B.C.).

to Babylon. It is possible that Manasseh was involved in the rebellion (652–648 B.C.) of Shamash-Shum-Ukin of Babylon against the Assyrian king, Ashurbanipal. Manasseh's captivity in Babylon and his return to the Promised Land might remind the readers of their own deportation to Babylon and their recent restoration.

33:12, 13 Manasseh's prayer and restoration were in line with Solomon's temple dedication (6:36–39) and God's response to it (7:14 note).

33:14–16 For similar reforms see 17:1–6.

33:14 The historian notes Manasseh's building projects as a sign of God's blessing.

33:15 all the altars. The writer of Kings notes that Josiah had to destroy altars Manasseh had erected (2 Kin. 23:12). Apparently, Manasseh's reforms were incomplete.

33:18, 19 the Chronicles of the Kings of Israel . . . Chronicles of the Seers. See Introduction to 1 Chronicles: Author.

33:20 buried him in his house. See note 21:19.

33:21–25 See 2 Kin. 21:19–26.

33:21 Amon . . . two years. He reigned 642–640 B.C.

Josiah Reigns in Judah

34 [m]Josiah was eight years old when he
began to reign, and he reigned thirty-one years in Jerusalem. 2 And he did
what was right in the eyes of the LORD, and
walked in the ways of David his father; and
he did not turn aside to the right hand or
to the left. 3 For in the eighth year of his
reign, while he was yet a boy, he began to
seek the God of David his father, and in the
twelfth year he began to purge Judah and
Jerusalem of the high places, the [n]Asherim,
and the carved and the metal images. 4 And
they chopped down the altars of the Baals
in his presence, and he cut down the [o]in-
cense altars that stood above them. And he
broke in pieces the [n]Asherim and the
carved and the metal images, and he made
dust of them and [o]scattered it over the
graves of those who had sacrificed to them.
5 [p]He also burned the bones of the priests
on their altars and cleansed Judah and
Jerusalem. 6 And in the [q]cities of Manasseh,
Ephraim, and Simeon, and as far as
Naphtali, in their ruins[1] all around, 7 he
broke down the altars and beat the
[n]Asherim and the images [r]into powder and
cut down all the incense altars throughout
all the land of Israel. Then he returned to
Jerusalem.

The Book of the Law Found

8 [s]Now in the eighteenth year of his reign,
when he had cleansed the land and the
house, he sent Shaphan the son of Azaliah,
and Maaseiah the [t]governor of the city, and
Joah the son of Joahaz, [u]the recorder, to
repair the house of the LORD his God.
9 They came to [v]Hilkiah the high priest and
gave him the money that had been brought
into the house of God, which the Levites,
the keepers of the threshold, had collected
from [q]Manasseh and Ephraim and from all
the remnant of Israel and from all Judah
and Benjamin and from the inhabitants of
Jerusalem. 10 And they gave it to the workmen who were working in the house of the
LORD. And the workmen who were working
in the house of the LORD gave it for repairing and restoring the house. 11 They gave it
to the carpenters and the builders to buy
quarried stone, and timber for binders and
[w]beams for the buildings that the kings of
Judah had let go to ruin. 12 And the men
did the work faithfully. Over them were set
Jahath and Obadiah the Levites, of the
sons of Merari, and Zechariah and Meshullam, of the sons of the Kohathites, to
have oversight. [x]The Levites, all who were
skillful with instruments of music, 13 were
over [y]the burden-bearers and directed all
who did work in every kind of service, and
some of the Levites were scribes and officials and gatekeepers.
14 While they were bringing out the
money that had been brought into the
house of the LORD, [v]Hilkiah the priest
found the Book of the Law of the LORD
given through Moses. 15 Then Hilkiah
answered and said to Shaphan the secretary, "I have found the Book of the Law
in the house of the LORD." And Hilkiah
gave the book to Shaphan. 16 Shaphan
brought the book to the king, and further
reported to the king, "All that was committed to your servants they are doing. 17 They
have emptied out the money that was
found in the house of the LORD and have
given it into the hand of the overseers and
the workmen." 18 Then Shaphan the secretary told the king, "Hilkiah the priest has
given me a book." And Shaphan read from
it before the king.
19 And when the king heard the words of
the Law, [z]he tore his clothes. 20 And the
king commanded Hilkiah, Ahikam the son
of Shaphan, Abdon the son of Micah,

Chapter 34
1 [m]For ver. 1, 2, see 2 Kin. 22:1, 2
3 [n]See ch. 14:3
4 [o][2 Kin. 23:6] [n][See ver. 3 above]
5 [p]2 Kin. 23:20; [1 Kin. 13:2]
6 [q]2 Kin. 23:15, 19
7 [n][See ver. 3 above] [r][Deut. 9:21]
8 [s]For ver. 8-28, see 2 Kin. 22:3-20 [t]ch. 18:25 [u]2 Sam. 8:16
9 [v]ch. 35:8 [q][See ver. 6 above]
11 [w]Neh. 2:8
12 [x]1 Chr. 23:5
13 [y]ch. 2:2, 18; Neh. 4:10
14 [v][See ver. 9 above]
19 [z]See Josh. 7:6

[1] The meaning of the Hebrew is uncertain

34:1–36:1 Josiah's reign is also recorded in 2 Kin. 22:1–23:30.

34:1 Josiah . . . thirty-one years. Josiah reigned 640–609 B.C.

34:3–35:19 The historian bases his account of Josiah's reforms on 2 Kin. 22:3–23:23, but the order of events differs. Broadly speaking, in 2 Kings Josiah's reforms are summarized geographically: discovery of the book in the temple (2 Kin. 22:3–23:3), reformation of city and nation (2 Kin. 23:4–20), and Passover celebration at the temple (2 Kin. 23:21–23). The historian of Chronicles orders the events chronologically: reforming the city and nation (34:3–7), discovering the book in the temple (34:8–33), and celebrating the Passover (35:1–19). References to the eighth and twelfth years (34:3) and the eighteenth year (34:8; 35:19) indicate that the reforms began before the discovery of the book.

34:3 while he was yet a boy. Josiah began to reverse the policies of Amon at an early age.

he began to purge. Josiah's removal of idolatry is reported more completely in 2 Kin. 23:4–20.

34:12 the Levites. The involvement of the Levites would ensure that Josiah's reforms were according to the patterns established by David (1 Chr. 6), Solomon (2 Chr. 7:6; 8:14) and Hezekiah (29:2–19).

instruments of music. See note 1 Chr. 15:16.

34:15 the Book of the Law . . . of the LORD. Probably Deuteronomy (2 Kin. 22:8 note). The priests delivered the book to Josiah, who accepted it as the guide for his reforms (cf. Ezra 7:6–10; Neh. 8; 9).

Shaphan the secretary, and Asaiah the king's servant, saying, 21 "Go, inquire of the LORD for me and for those who are left in Israel and in Judah, concerning the words of the book that has been found. For great is [a]the wrath of the LORD that is poured out on us, because our fathers have not kept the word of the LORD, to do according to all that is written in this book."

Huldah Prophesies Disaster

22 So Hilkiah and those whom the king had sent[1] went to Huldah the prophetess, the wife of Shallum the son of Tokhath, son of Hasrah, keeper of the wardrobe (now she lived in Jerusalem in the Second Quarter) and spoke to her to that effect. 23 And she said to them, "Thus says the LORD, the God of Israel: 'Tell the man who sent you to me, 24 Thus says the LORD, behold, I will bring disaster upon this place and upon its inhabitants, all the curses that are written in the book that was read before the king of Judah. 25 Because they have forsaken me and [b]have made offerings to other gods, that they might provoke me to anger with all the works of their hands, therefore [a]my wrath will be poured out on this place and will not be quenched. 26 But to the king of Judah, who sent you to inquire of the LORD, thus shall you say to him, Thus says the LORD, the God of Israel: Regarding the words that you have heard, 27 because your heart was tender and you humbled yourself before God when you heard his words against this place and its inhabitants, and you have humbled yourself before me and have torn your clothes and wept before me, I also have heard you, declares the LORD. 28 Behold, I will gather you to your fathers, and you shall be gathered to your grave in peace, and your eyes shall not see all the disaster that I will bring upon this place and its inhabitants.'" And they brought back word to the king.

29 [c]Then the king sent and gathered together all the elders of Judah and Jerusalem. 30 And the king went up to the house of the LORD, with all the men of Judah and the inhabitants of Jerusalem and the priests and the Levites, all the people both great and small. And he read in their hearing all the words of the Book of the Covenant that had been found in the house of the LORD. 31 And the king [d]stood in his place [e]and made a covenant before the LORD, to walk after the LORD and to keep his commandments and his testimonies and his statutes, with all his heart and all his soul, to perform the words of the covenant that were written in this book. 32 Then he made all who were present in Jerusalem and in Benjamin stand to it. And the inhabitants of Jerusalem did according to the covenant of God, the God of their fathers. 33 And Josiah took away [f]all the abominations from all the territory that belonged to the people of Israel and made all who were present in Israel serve the LORD their God. All his days they did not turn away from following the LORD, the God of their fathers.

Josiah Keeps the Passover

35 [g]Josiah kept a Passover to the LORD in Jerusalem. And they slaughtered the Passover lamb [h]on the fourteenth day of the first month. 2 He appointed the priests to their offices [i]and encouraged them in the service of the house of the LORD. 3 And he said to the Levites [j]who taught all Israel and who were holy to the LORD, "Put the holy ark in the house that Solomon the son of David, king of Israel, built. You need not carry it on your shoulders. Now serve the LORD your God and his people Israel. 4 Prepare yourselves [k]according to your fathers' houses by your divisions, [l]as prescribed in the writing of David king of Israel [m]and the document of Solomon his son. 5 And [n]stand in the Holy Place [o]according to the groupings of the

21 [a]ch. 12:7
25 [b]ch. 28:3, 4, 25 [a][See ver. 21 above]
29 [c]For ver. 29-32, see 2 Kin. 23:1-3
31 [d]ch. 6:13; 2 Kin. 11:14; [ch. 30:16] [e]See ch. 15:12
33 [f]ch. 28:3; 33:2
Chapter 35
1 [g]2 Kin. 23:21-23 [h]Ex. 12:6; Ezra 6:19
2 [i]ch. 29:11
3 [j]ch. 17:9; Neh. 8:7, 9; [ch. 15:3; 30:22; Lev. 10:11; Deut. 33:10; Ezra 7:10; Mal. 2:7]
4 [k]1 Chr. 9:9 [l]See 1 Chr. ch. 23–26 [m]ch. 8:14
5 [n]Ps. 134:1 [o][Ezra 6:18]

1 Syriac, Vulgate; Hebrew lacks *had sent*

34:23–28 Huldah the prophetess announced divine judgment because of the violation of God's law, but Josiah's humility had the effect of postponing disaster (1 Chr. 28:9 note).

34:30 the Covenant. Josiah promulgated the law of God to the people and swore himself to obey it. He required the people to join him in this public renewal of God's relationship with them (v. 32).

35:1 Passover. The Passover celebrated in Josiah's eighteenth year is mentioned briefly in 2 Kin. 23:21–23, but described here in detail. Like Hezekiah before him (30:1 note), Josiah enthusiastically observed this national celebration in the temple at Jerusalem (see also Ezra 6:19–22).

first month. See note 30:2.

35:3 all Israel. This includes people from the northern and southern kingdoms. Like Hezekiah, Josiah presided over a reunion of the people (30:1 note).

35:4 the writing of David . . . and . . . Solomon. Josiah's celebration could stand as an example to future generations because it was conducted according to the recognized standards of David and Solomon.

fathers' houses of your brothers the lay
people, and according to the division of the
Levites by fathers' household. 6 And slaughter the Passover lamb, and [p]consecrate
yourselves, and prepare for your brothers,
to do according to the word of the LORD by
Moses."

7 Then Josiah contributed to the lay people, as Passover offerings for all who were
present, lambs and young goats from the
flock to the number of 30,000, and 3,000
bulls; [q]these were from the king's possessions. 8 And his officials contributed willingly to the people, to the priests, and to the
Levites. [r]Hilkiah, Zechariah, and Jehiel, the
chief officers of the house of God, gave to
the priests for the Passover offerings 2,600
Passover lambs and 300 bulls. 9 Conaniah
also, and Shemaiah and Nethanel his brothers, and Hashabiah and Jeiel and Jozabad,
the chiefs of the Levites, gave to the Levites
for the Passover offerings 5,000 lambs and
young goats and 500 bulls.

10 When the service had been prepared
for, the priests [s]stood in their place, [t]and
the Levites in their divisions according to
the king's command. 11 [u]And they slaughtered the Passover lamb, and the priests
[v]threw the blood that they received from
them [w]while the Levites flayed the sacrifices. 12 And they set aside the burnt offerings that they might distribute them
according to the groupings of the fathers'
houses of the lay people, to offer to the
LORD, as it is written in the Book of Moses.
And so they did with the bulls. 13 [x]And they
roasted the Passover lamb with fire according to the rule; and they [y]boiled the holy
offerings in pots, in cauldrons, and in pans,
and carried them quickly to all the lay people. 14 And afterward they prepared for
themselves and for the priests, because the
priests the sons of Aaron were offering the
burnt offerings and the fat parts until night;
so the Levites prepared for themselves and

6 [p]See ch. 29:5
7 [q][ch. 31:3]
8 [r]ch. 34:9, 14
10 [s]ch. 30:16 [t]Ezra 6:18
11 [u]ch. 30:15; Ezra 6:20 [v]See ch.29:22 [w][ch. 29:34]
13 [x]Ex. 12:8, 9; Deut. 16:7 [y][1 Sam. 2:13-15]
15 [z]See 1 Chr. ch. 25 [a]See 1 Sam. 9:9 [b]See 1 Chr. 9:17-29; 26:1-19
17 [c]See ch.30:21
18 [d]2 Kin. 23:22, 23
20 [e]2 Kin. 23:29, 30 [f][Jer. 46:2]
22 [g][1 Kin. 22:30] [h]Judg. 5:19
23 [i][1 Kin. 22:34]

for the priests the sons of Aaron. 15 The
singers, the sons of Asaph, were in their
place [z]according to the command of David,
and Asaph, and Heman, and Jeduthun the
king's [a]seer; [b]and the gatekeepers were at
each gate. They did not need to depart from
their service, for their brothers the Levites
prepared for them.

16 So all the service of the LORD was prepared that day, to keep the Passover and to
offer burnt offerings on the altar of the
LORD, according to the command of King
Josiah. 17 And the people of Israel who were
present kept the Passover at that time, [c]and
the Feast of Unleavened Bread seven days.
18 [d]No Passover like it had been kept in
Israel since the days of Samuel the prophet.
None of the kings of Israel had kept such a
Passover as was kept by Josiah, and the
priests and the Levites, and all Judah and
Israel who were present, and the inhabitants of Jerusalem. 19 In the eighteenth year
of the reign of Josiah this Passover was kept.

Josiah Killed in Battle

20 [e]After all this, when Josiah had prepared the temple, Neco king of Egypt went
up to fight at [f]Carchemish on the
Euphrates and Josiah went out to meet
him. 21 But he sent envoys to him, saying,
"What have we to do with each other, king
of Judah? I am not coming against you this
day, but against the house with which I am
at war. And God has commanded me to
hurry. Cease opposing God, who is with
me, lest he destroy you." 22 Nevertheless,
Josiah did not turn away from him, but
[g]disguised himself in order to fight with
him. He did not listen to the words of Neco
from the mouth of God, but came to fight
in the plain of [h]Megiddo. 23 And the archers
shot King Josiah. And the king said to his
servants, [i]"Take me away, for I am badly
wounded." 24 So his servants took him out
of the chariot and carried him in his second chariot and brought him to Jerusalem.

35:6 the word of the LORD by Moses. See note 1 Chr. 16:40.

35:7, 8 Josiah followed a pattern similar to David (1 Chr. 29:3 note) and Hezekiah (30:24 note). His own contributions were followed by enthusiastic contributions from others.

35:18 No Passover like it . . . since the days of Samuel. The writer makes a similar observation about Hezekiah's Passover (30:26).

35:20 Even a king who "had prepared the temple" would suffer divine retribution if he ignored the word of God. Josiah fell in battle because he refused to obey the divinely directed words of Pharaoh Neco (v. 22).

35:21 house with which I am at war. It is not clear why Josiah wanted to impede the progress of Pharaoh Neco. He may have been entangled in an alliance with Neco's enemies (cf. 2 Kin. 23:29).

35:22 from the mouth of God. In some way God had conveyed His purposes to the foreign king, as He had to Ahimelech through a dream (Gen. 20:3), but Josiah would not listen.

And he died and was buried in the tombs of his fathers. [j]All Judah and Jerusalem mourned for Josiah. 25 [k]Jeremiah also uttered a lament for Josiah; and all [l]the singing men and singing women have spoken of Josiah in their laments to this day. They made these a rule in Israel; behold, they are written in the Laments. 26 Now the rest of the acts of Josiah, and his good deeds according to what is written in the Law of the LORD, 27 and his acts, first and last, behold, they are written in the Book of the Kings of Israel and Judah.

Judah's Decline

36 [m]The people of the land took Jehoahaz the son of Josiah and made him king in his father's place in Jerusalem. 2 Jehoahaz was twenty-three years old when he began to reign, and he reigned three months in Jerusalem. 3 Then the king of Egypt deposed him in Jerusalem and [n]laid on the land a tribute of a hundred talents of silver and a talent[1] of gold. 4 And the king of Egypt made Eliakim his brother king over Judah and Jerusalem, and changed his name to Jehoiakim. But Neco took Jehoahaz his brother and carried him to Egypt.

5 [o]Jehoiakim was twenty-five years old when he began to reign, and he reigned eleven years in Jerusalem. He did what was evil in the sight of the LORD his God. 6 [p]Against him came up Nebuchadnezzar king of Babylon [q]and bound him in chains [r]to take him to Babylon. 7 [s]Nebuchadnezzar also carried part of the vessels of the house of the LORD to Babylon and put them in his palace in Babylon. 8 [t]Now the rest of the acts of Jehoiakim, and the abominations that he did, and what was found against him, behold, they are written in the Book of the Kings of Israel and Judah. And Jehoiachin his son reigned in his place.

9 [u]Jehoiachin was eight years old when he became king, and he reigned three months and ten days in Jerusalem. He did what was evil in the sight of the LORD. 10 In [v]the spring of the year King Nebuchadnezzar sent and brought him to Babylon, [w]with the precious vessels of the house of the LORD, and made his brother [x]Zedekiah king over Judah and Jerusalem.

11 [y]Zedekiah was twenty-one years old when he began to reign, and he reigned eleven years in Jerusalem. 12 He did what was evil in the sight of the LORD his God. He did not humble himself before [z]Jeremiah the prophet, who spoke from the mouth of the LORD. 13 [a]He also rebelled against King Nebuchadnezzar, who had made him swear by God. [b]He stiffened his neck and hardened his heart against turning to the LORD, the God of Israel. 14 All the officers of the priests and the people likewise were exceedingly unfaithful, following all the abominations of the nations. And they polluted the house of the LORD that he had made holy in Jerusalem.

15 The LORD, the God of their fathers, [c]sent persistently to them by his messengers, because he had compassion on his people and on his dwelling place. 16 [d]But they kept mocking the messengers of God, [e]despising his words and scoffing at his prophets, [f]until the wrath of the LORD

24 [j][Zech. 12:11]
25 [k]Lam. 4:20; [2 Sam. 1:17] [l]2 Sam. 19:35; Ezra 2:65; Neh. 7:67; [Matt. 9:23]
Chapter 36
1 [m]For ver. 1-4, see 2 Kin. 23:30-34
3 [n]Deut. 22:19
5 [o]2 Kin. 23:36, 37
6 [p]2 Kin. 24:1 [q][ch. 33:11] [r][2 Kin. 24:6; Jer. 22:18, 19; 36:30]
7 [s]2 Kin. 24:13; Ezra 1:7; Dan. 1:1, 2; 5:2; [ver. 10, 18]
8 [t]2 Kin. 24:5, 6
9 [u]For ver. 9, 10, see 2 Kin. 24:8-17
10 [v]2 Sam. 11:1 [w][ver. 7, 18] [x]Jer. 37:1; [2 Kin. 24:17]
11 [y]For ver. 11-13, see 2 Kin. 24:18-20; Jer. 52:1, 2
12 [z]See Jer. 21:3-7; 27:12-22; 32:1-5; 37:6-10; 38:17-26
13 [a]Jer. 52:3; Ezek. 17:15, 18 [b]See ch. 30:8
15 [c]Jer. 7:13, 25; 25:3, 4; 26:5; 29:19; 35:15; 44:4; [Jer. 11:7; 32:33]
16 [d][Jer. 5:12, 13] [e][Prov. 1:25, 30] [f][Ezra 5:12]

1 A *talent* was about 75 pounds or 34 kilograms

35:24 Jerusalem mourned. Despite his final weakness, Josiah was an honorable king of Judah (21:19 note).

35:25 Jeremiah also uttered a lament. This passage has been taken to show that Jeremiah wrote the Book of Lamentations, but the identification is uncertain.

to this day. See note 1 Chr. 4:41.

35:27 the Book of the Kings. See the introduction to 1 Chronicles.

36:2–14 The historian quickly traces the reigns of Josiah's three sons (Jehoahaz, Jehoiakim, and Zedekiah) and his grandson (Jehoiachin). His account is shorter than Kings (2 Kin. 23:31–24:20); he reports the failures and disobedience leading to exile in Babylonia (1 Chr. 3:15 note; 3:17 note).

36:2 Jehoahaz. Reigned for three months in 609 B.C.

36:3 king of Egypt. After Josiah's defeat by Neco (609 B.C.), Egypt dominated Judah.

36:4 changed his name. To change another king's name demonstrated political dominance.

36:5–8 An abbreviation of 2 Kin. 23:36–24:7.

36:5 Jehoiakim. Reigned 609–598 B.C.

36:6 Nebuchadnezzar king of Babylon. After Egypt was defeated by the Babylonians at Carchemish (605 B.C.), Judah was subjected to Babylonian power.

36:9 Jehoiachin. Reigned for just over three months in 597 B.C. This capture and release is reported in 2 Kin. 24:8–12; 25:27–30. Chronicles passes over his release from Babylon, electing instead to end with the edict of Cyrus permitting the exiles to return to Jerusalem.

36:11 Zedekiah. Reigned 597–586 B.C. Zedekiah sought help from Egypt, but to no avail. The Babylonians laid siege to Jerusalem for two years and finally took the city in 586 B.C.

36:14 All the officers. Not only the kings, but the priests and the people also committed sins that subjected them to the retribution of exile in Babylonia.

36:15 his messengers. The warnings of prophets appear often in Chronicles (20:20 note). Jeremiah was active during the reign of Zedekiah (Jer. 1; 21; 34; 37; 38; 52).

36:16 no remedy. Compare Heb. 6:4–6.

rose against his people, until there was no
remedy.

Jerusalem Captured and Burned

17 [g]Therefore he brought up against them
the king of the Chaldeans, who killed their
young men with the sword in the house of
their sanctuary and had no compassion on
young man or virgin, old man or aged. He
gave them all into his hand. 18 [h]And all the
vessels of the house of God, great and
small, and the treasures of the house of the
LORD, and the treasures of the king and of
his princes, all these he brought to
Babylon. 19 [i]And they burned the house of
God and broke down the wall of Jerusalem
and burned all its palaces with fire and
destroyed all its precious vessels. 20 He
[j]took into exile in Babylon those who had
escaped from the sword, [k]and they became
servants to him and to his sons until the
establishment of the kingdom of Persia,
21 to fulfill the word of the LORD by the
mouth of Jeremiah, until the land had [l]en-
joyed its Sabbaths. All the days that it lay
desolate [m]it kept Sabbath, to fulfill seventy
years.

The Proclamation of Cyrus

22 [n]Now in the first year of Cyrus king of
Persia, [o]that the word of the LORD by the
mouth of Jeremiah might be fulfilled, [p]the
LORD stirred up the spirit of Cyrus king of
Persia, so that he made a proclamation
throughout all his kingdom and also put it
in writing: 23 "Thus says Cyrus king of
Persia, 'The LORD, the God of heaven, has
given me all the kingdoms of the earth, and
he has charged me to build him a house at
Jerusalem, which is in Judah. Whoever is
among you of all his people, may the LORD
his God be with him. Let him go up.' "

17 [g]For ver. 17-20, see 2 Kin. 25:1-7; [Deut. 28:49; Ezra 9:7]
18 [h]2 Kin. 25:13-15; [ver. 7, 10]
19 [i]2 Kin. 25:9
20 [j]2 Kin. 25:11 [k]Jer. 27:7
21 [l]Lev. 26:34, 35, 43; [Dan. 9:2] [m][Lev. 25:4, 5]
22 [n]For ver. 22, 23, see Ezra 1:1-3 [o]Jer. 25:12, 13; 29:10; 33:10, 11, 14 [p]Isai. 44:28

36:21 land had enjoyed its Sabbaths. This observation shows that God had His own purposes in allowing the Babylonian exile of the Jews. During it the land could enjoy the Sabbath rests it had been denied (Lev. 26:40–45).

seventy years. See Jer. 25:1–14 and Dan. 9. Chronicles takes the end of the seventy years to be the first year of Cyrus (538 B.C.). Perhaps the calculation is from the first deportation (605 or 604 B.C.) under Jehoiakim. Zech. 1:12–17 may indicate that the seventy years was measured from the destruction of the temple in 586 B.C. to its rededication in 516 B.C.

36:22, 23 This passage is repeated with some variation in Ezra 1:1–4. Cyrus exercised a liberal policy toward many people deported by the Babylonians. Israel's release recalls Solomon's prayer of dedication (6:36–39 note).

36:23 charged me to build him a house at Jerusalem. God caused Cyrus to return the people to Israel with the specific purpose of rebuilding the temple. In the course of his work the writer of Chronicles has given due emphasis to the temple and its services, showing how its renewal could be accomplished under God's guidance.

THE BOOK OF

Ezra

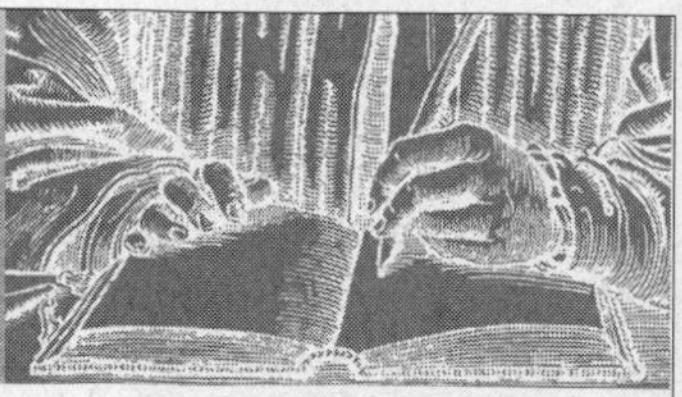

AUTHOR

It is not known who wove together into their present form all the documents included in Ezra and Nehemiah (Characteristics and Themes below). Despite an earlier view that a single author wrote the books of Chronicles, Ezra, and Nehemiah, the consensus among scholars is that the historian who wrote Chronicles ("the Chronicler") was probably not the author of Ezra and Nehemiah ("Introduction to 1 Chronicles: Author"). Ezra kept a journal or "memoirs" (7:28 note), as Nehemiah did also. Given his literary skills (7:6 and note), Ezra may well have been the compiler of the books of Ezra and Nehemiah, as is held by Jewish tradition.

DATE AND OCCASION

Ezra and Nehemiah can be dated in the period 430–400 B.C. The narratives were written to encourage the Jews who had returned from exile by revealing to them that though Israel was still under Persian rule, their sovereign God was continuing His redemptive work and reestablishing true worship among them.

CHARACTERISTICS AND THEMES

Although modern Bibles treat Ezra and Nehemiah as two separate books, they were originally a single work. They are treated as one composition in the Hebrew Bible, the Talmud, Josephus (C. A.D. 37–100), and the oldest manuscripts of the Septuagint (the Old Testament Greek translation). Origen (A.D. 185–253) was the first to separate Ezra and Nehemiah into two books.

Ezra-Nehemiah is a historical narrative composed of numerous originally separate documents, woven together to form a beautiful and powerful whole. Lists play a significant role in Ezra and Nehemiah. There are lists regarding (a) the temple articles (1:9–11), (b) those who initially returned from exile (2:3–70, repeated in Neh. 7:8–73), (c) the leaders who returned with Ezra (8:2–14), (d) those involved in mixed marriages (10:18–43), (e) those who rebuilt the wall (Neh. 3), (f) those who sealed the covenant (Neh. 10:1–27), (g) new residents in Jerusalem and those in the villages (Neh. 11), and (h) the priests and Levites who returned with Zerubbabel (Neh. 12:1–26).

Much official correspondence has also been included. These letters were written in Aramaic, the language of international diplomacy at that time. There is (a) the letter of Rehum to Artaxerxes (4:11–16), (b) the reply of Artaxerxes (4:17–22), (c) the letter of Tattenai to Darius (5:7–17), (d) the memorandum regarding the decree of Cyrus (6:2–5), (e) the reply of Darius to Tattenai (6:6–12), and (f) the letter of Artaxerxes on behalf of Ezra (7:12–26).

In addition, the decree of Cyrus (1:2–4) and materials from Ezra and Nehemiah themselves have been included (7:27–9:15; Neh. 1:1–7:5; 12:27–43; 13:14–31).

Three themes of Ezra and Nehemiah can be found in the decree of Cyrus (1:2–4). First, rebuilding the temple in Jerusalem is God's objective in the history of redemption at this point; second, the people of God as a whole, and not merely the great leaders, are vital for accomplishing this purpose. Third, the written word is a powerful tool used by God to accomplish His objective.

Cyrus commissioned the return from exile for the express purpose of rebuilding "the house of the LORD, the God of Israel" (1:3). Cyrus's commission was directed toward the people of God as a whole, not toward this or that leader. The long lists of otherwise unknown people testify that the people of God as a whole are responsible for rebuilding.

Cyrus's written decree was the human instrument generating the action in Ezra and Nehemiah. Written documents play a major role in the subordinate actions as well. Letters stop and start the work on the temple (4:23; 6:6–7). A letter gives Ezra authority to carry out reforms (7:25–26). The written word of God is a moving force in the narrative (3:2; 10:3; Neh. 8:1; 9:13). This theme is significant, since the era involved is that of the last Old Testament prophets (Haggai, Zechariah, and Malachi). There was to be a period of silence after them, during which the people of God would be governed exclusively by the written word. The silence was broken by John the Baptist, the forerunner of Christ.

The overall purpose of Ezra and Nehemiah is to affirm that God works sovereignly through responsible human agents to accomplish His redemptive objective. Cyrus issued his decree because the Lord had moved his spirit (1:1). Those who returned came back because the Lord had moved their spirits (1:5). Ezra succeeded because the good hand of God was upon him (7:9). Artaxerxes supported the work of rebuilding because the Lord had put it in his spirit (7:27). Human beings acted freely and responsibly under the providence of God to bring His plans to fruition (see "God Reigns: Divine Sovereignty" at Dan. 4:34).

OUTLINE OF EZRA

I. Return of the Exiles and Rebuilding of the Temple (chs. 1–6)

- A. *Return of the Exiles (chs. 1; 2)*
  1. The Decree of Cyrus (1:1–4)
  2. Preparations for Returning (1:5–11)
  3. The List of Returnees (ch. 2)
- B. *Rebuilding of the Temple (chs. 3–6)*
  1. Rebuilding of the Altar (3:1–6)
  2. Rebuilding of the Temple Proper (3:7–6:22)
     - a. *Rebuilding Begun (3:7–13)*
     - b. *Opposition to Rebuilding (ch. 4)*
     - c. *Rebuilding Resumed (5:1, 2)*
     - d. *Opposition to Rebuilding (5:3–6:12)*
     - e. *Rebuilding Completed (6:13–22)*

II. Return of Ezra and Rebuilding of the Community (chs. 7–10)

- A. *Return of Ezra (chs. 7; 8)*
  1. Ezra's Return (7:1–10)
  2. Ezra's Commission (7:11–26)
  3. Ezra's Doxology (7:27, 28)
  4. Ezra's Companions (8:1–14)
  5. Ezra's Return (8:15–36)
- B. *Rebuilding of the Community (chs. 9; 10)*
  1. Ezra's Reaction to Intermarriage (ch. 9)
     - a. *Ezra Hears (9:1, 2)*
     - b. *Ezra Grieves (9:3, 4)*
     - c. *Ezra Confesses (9:5–15)*
  2. The People's Reaction to Ezra (ch. 10)
     - a. *The People Grieve (10:1)*
     - b. *The People Confess (10:2)*
     - c. *The People Repent (10:3–17)*
     - d. *The People Who Were Guilty (10:18–44)*

The Proclamation of Cyrus

1 [a]In the first year of Cyrus king of Persia,
[b]that the word of the LORD by the mouth
of Jeremiah might be fulfilled, the LORD
stirred up the spirit of Cyrus king of Persia,
so [c]that he made a proclamation throughout
all his kingdom and also put it in writing:
2 "Thus says Cyrus king of Persia: The
LORD, the God of heaven, has given me all
the kingdoms of the earth, and [d]he has
charged me to build him a house at
Jerusalem, which is in Judah. 3 Whoever is
among you of all his people, may his God
be with him, and let him go up to
Jerusalem, which is in Judah, and rebuild
the house of the LORD, the God of Israel—
[e]he is the God who is in Jerusalem. 4 And
let each survivor, in whatever place he
sojourns, be assisted by the men of his
place with silver and gold, with goods and
with beasts, besides freewill offerings for
the house of God that is in Jerusalem."
5 Then rose up the heads of the fathers'
houses of Judah and Benjamin, and the
priests and the Levites, [f]everyone whose
spirit [g]God had stirred to go up to rebuild
the house of the LORD that is in Jerusalem.
6 And all who were about them [h]aided them
with vessels of silver, with gold, with goods,
with beasts, and with costly wares, besides
all that was freely offered. 7 [i]Cyrus the king
also brought out the vessels of the house of
the LORD that [j]Nebuchadnezzar had carried
away from Jerusalem and placed in the
house of his gods. 8 Cyrus king of Persia
brought these out in charge of [k]Mithredath
the treasurer, who counted them out to
[l]Sheshbazzar the prince of Judah. 9 And this
was the number of them: [m]30 basins of
gold, 1,000 basins of silver, 29 censers,
10 30 bowls of gold, 410 bowls of silver, and
1,000 other vessels; 11 all the vessels of gold
and of silver were 5,400. All these did
Sheshbazzar bring up, when the exiles were
brought up from Babylonia to Jerusalem.

The Exiles Return

2 [n]Now these were the people of the province who came up out of the captivity of

Chapter 1
1 [a]For ver. 1-3, see 2 Chr. 36:22, 23 [b]Jer. 25:12, 13; 29:10 [c]ch. 5:13
2 [d]Isai. 44:28; [Isai. 45:1, 13]
3 [e]Dan. 6:26
5 [f][Phil. 2:13] [g]ver. 1
6 [h][ch. 4:4]; Jer. 38:4
7 [i]ch. 5:14; 6:5 [j]2 Kin. 24:13; 2 Chr. 36:7
8 [k]ch. 4:7 [l]ch. 5:14
9 [m][ch. 8:27; 1 Chr. 28:17]
Chapter 2
1 [n]For ver. 1-70, see Neh. 7:6-73

1:1–3 The same words, with minor differences, close 2 Chronicles. Ezra picks up the history of redemption where Chronicles leaves off.

1:1 first year. 538 B.C., the first year of Cyrus's reign. He conquered Babylon in October 539 and reigned over Persia from 550 to 530.

that the word of the LORD . . . might be fulfilled. Jeremiah had prophesied seventy years of captivity in Babylon (Jer. 25:11–12; 29:10; see Dan. 9:2). From 605 when the first captives were deported, to 538 when the decree to return was issued, is sixty-seven years. Other prophecies may also be in view (Jer. 16:14–15; 27:22). The Lord was sovereignly bringing to pass the word He had spoken over half a century before.

the LORD stirred up the spirit. This phrase expresses the main theme of the book: God works sovereignly through responsible human agents to accomplish His redemptive plan (6:22; 7:27). In the words of Prov. 21:1, the Lord directed Cyrus's spirit like "a stream of water . . . he turns it wherever he will."

1:2–4 The decree may have been written with the help of Jewish advisers.

1:2 The LORD, the God of heaven. A title identifying the Lord as the supreme authority and power (5:12; 6:9, 10; 7:12, 21, 23; Neh. 1:4, 5; 2:4, 20; Dan. 2:18, 19, 37, 44; Jon. 1:9).

has given me . . . has charged me. Cyrus's testimony to the sovereignty of God was probably a formality for him, since the Cylinder of Cyrus says similar things about other gods (1:3 note).

a house at Jerusalem. This "house" refers in the first place to the temple, but in the end will include the city of God and the people of God. The rebuilding of the "house" of God is a dominant theme in Ezra and Nehemiah (Introduction: Characteristics and Themes).

1:3 Cyrus treated Israel in the same way as his other subject peoples. His purpose was to enlist the gods of these peoples in his own service (note the motivation of Darius in 6:10 and of Artaxerxes in 7:23). The Lord's controlling purpose, however, is to continue the progress of redemption.

of all His people. Cyrus's commission is directed to all the people, not the leaders, expressing a major theme of the book (Introduction: Characteristics and Themes): the people of God as a whole are vital to the accomplishing of God's redemptive plan.

1:4 in whatever place he sojourns. This phrase refers to Jews who stayed in Babylon, and perhaps to Gentiles.

be assisted. In the Exodus from Egypt, the Egyptians sent Israel out with gifts (Ex. 12:35–36).

1:5 The response is described in language parallel to the decree, emphasizing the immediate response of the people to Cyrus's decree and God's prompting.

heads of the fathers' houses. These were the patriarchs of extended families.

Judah and Benjamin. The two tribes exiled by the Babylonians.

the priests and the Levites. Restoration of the temple service required their return (8:15–17).

God had stirred. The same Hebrew phrase as in v. 1. God's sovereign power generated the decree and the response.

1:8 Mithredath. A Persian official.

Sheshbazzar. Identified by some as Zerubbabel. However, Sheshbazzar seems to be a somewhat unknown figure in 5:14–16, whereas Zerubbabel is well known (5:2–3). Probably Sheshbazzar was the official leader, perhaps a Persian, designated by Cyrus, while Zerubbabel was the popular leader.

1:9–11 The total of the numbers in vv. 9–10 is 2,499, not 5,400 as reported in v. 11. The reason for this discrepancy is not known. The difficulty is compounded by not knowing exactly what the "basins" and "bowls" were. The production of these treasures must have encouraged the spirits of God's people, since Jeremiah had prophesied that they would be preserved and carried back to Jerusalem (Jer. 27:22).

1:11 The exiles returned to Jerusalem with the articles for the temple according to the decree of Cyrus. The Lord kept His promise that after chastening His people for breaking the covenant He would bring them back to the Promised Land (Deut. 30:1–5).

2:1–70 This list of exiles who returned may not appear theologically important, but the repetition of the same list, with some variations, in

those exiles [o]whom Nebuchadnezzar the
king of Babylon had carried captive to
Babylonia. They returned to Jerusalem and
Judah, each to his own town. **2** They came
with Zerubbabel, Jeshua, Nehemiah, Seraiah, Reelaiah, [p]Mordecai, Bilshan, Mispar,
Bigvai, Rehum, and Baanah.
The number of the men of the people of
Israel: **3** [q]the sons of Parosh, 2,172. **4** The
sons of Shephatiah, 372. **5** The sons of Arah,
775. **6** The sons of Pahath-moab, namely the
sons of Jeshua and Joab, 2,812. **7** The sons of
Elam, 1,254. **8** The sons of Zattu, 945. **9** The
sons of Zaccai, 760. **10** The sons of Bani, 642.
11 The sons of Bebai, 623. **12** The sons of
Azgad, 1,222. **13** The sons of Adonikam,
666. **14** The sons of Bigvai, 2,056. **15** The sons
of Adin, 454. **16** The sons of Ater, namely of
Hezekiah, 98. **17** The sons of Bezai, 323.
18 The sons of Jorah, 112. **19** The sons of
Hashum, 223. **20** The sons of Gibbar, 95.
21 The sons of Bethlehem, 123. **22** The men of
Netophah, 56. **23** The men of Anathoth, 128.
24 The sons of Azmaveth, 42. **25** The sons of
Kiriath-arim, Chephirah, and Beeroth, 743.
26 The sons of Ramah and Geba, 621. **27** The
men of Michmas, 122. **28** The men of Bethel
and Ai, 223. **29** The sons of Nebo, 52. **30** The
sons of Magbish, 156. **31** The sons of [r]the
other Elam, 1,254. **32** The sons of Harim,
320. **33** The sons of Lod, Hadid, and Ono,
725. **34** The sons of Jericho, 345. **35** The sons
of Senaah, 3,630.
36 The priests: the [s]sons of Jedaiah, of the
house of Jeshua, 973. **37** The sons of Immer,
1,052. **38** The [t]sons of Pashhur, 1,247.
39 The sons of Harim, 1,017.
40 The Levites: the sons of [u]Jeshua and
Kadmiel, of the sons of Hodaviah, 74. **41** The
singers: the sons of [v]Asaph, 128. **42** The sons
of the [w]gatekeepers: the sons of Shallum,
the sons of Ater, the sons of Talmon, the
sons of Akkub, the sons of Hatita, and the
sons of Shobai, in all 139.
43 [x]The temple servants: the sons of Ziha,
the sons of Hasupha, the sons of Tabbaoth,
44 the sons of Keros, the sons of Siaha,
the sons of Padon, **45** the sons of Lebanah, the
sons of Hagabah, the sons of Akkub, **46** the
sons of Hagab, the sons of Shamlai, the sons
of Hanan, **47** the sons of Giddel, the
sons of Gahar, the sons of Reaiah, **48** the sons
of Rezin, the sons of Nekoda, the sons of
Gazzam, **49** the sons of Uzza, the sons
of Paseah, the sons of Besai, **50** the sons of
Asnah, the sons of Meunim, the sons of
Nephisim, **51** the sons of Bakbuk, the sons
of Hakupha, the sons of Harhur, **52** the sons of
Bazluth, the sons of Mehida, the sons of
Harsha, **53** the sons of Barkos, the sons of Sisera, the sons of Temah, **54** the sons of Neziah,
and the sons of Hatipha.
55 [y]The sons of Solomon's servants: the
sons of Sotai, the sons of Hassophereth,
the sons of Peruda, **56** the sons of Jaalah,
the sons of Darkon, the sons of Giddel,
57 the sons of Shephatiah, the sons of
Hattil, the sons of Pochereth-hazzebaim,
and the sons of Ami.
58 All the temple servants and the sons of
Solomon's servants were 392.
59 The following were those who came up
from Tel-melah, Tel-harsha, Cherub, Ad-
dan, and Immer, [z]though they could not
prove their fathers' houses or their descent,
whether they belonged to Israel: **60** the sons
of Delaiah, the sons of Tobiah, and the
sons of Nekoda, 652. **61** Also, of the sons of
the priests: the sons of Habaiah, the sons
of Hakkoz, and the sons of [a]Barzillai (who

1 [o]2 Kin. 24:14-16; 25:11; 2 Chr. 36:29
2 [p]Esth. 2:5, 6
3 [q]ch. 8:3; 10:25
31 [r][ver. 7]
36 [s]For ver. 36-39, see 1 Chr. 24:7-18
38 [t]1 Chr. 9:12
40 [u][Neh. 10:9]
41 [v]See 1 Chr. 6:39
42 [w]1 Chr. 9:17, 18
43 [x]1 Chr. 9:2; Neh. 11:3
55 [y]Neh. 11:3; [1 Kin. 9:21]
59 [z][1 Chr. 9:1]
61 [a]2 Sam. 17:27

Neh. 7 would suggest otherwise. First, the Lord knows His people personally. The covenant relation between the Lord and His people is a bond of intimate friendship. Second, common people are vital to the accomplishing of God's redemptive plan (Introduction: Characteristics and Themes). Not only are the religious and political leaders important in rebuilding the house of God, but so are the common people. In fact, "the rest of the people" contributed more to the rebuilding than did "the heads of the fathers' houses" and the governor (Neh. 7:70–72). Third, the enumeration resembles those found in Numbers and Joshua (Num. 1; 26; Josh. 18; 19). As the Lord formed the covenant community following the Exodus from Egypt, so He re-creates it following the return from Babylon.

2:2 Zerubbabel. A descendant of David and a grandson of King Jehoiachin, he was the leader responsible for laying the temple's foundation (3:8–10).

Jeshua. He was high priest at the time of the restoration (Hag. 1:1; Zech. 3:1).

Nehemiah. Not the same Nehemiah who later oversaw the reconstruction of Jerusalem's walls.

Mordecai. Not the same Mordecai who was Esther's cousin.

2:2–35 The first group listed is the laity. The list is in two parts: part one (vv. 3–20) gives the family names of the returnees, and part two (vv. 21–35) lists their towns. The laity are mentioned ahead of the clergy, in keeping with the emphasis in Ezra and Nehemiah on the significance of the common people in rebuilding the kingdom (2:1–70 note).

2:36–58 The next groups were officially associated with the temple service: priests (vv. 36–39), Levites (v. 40), singers (v. 41), gatekeepers (v. 42), temple servants (vv. 43–54), and Solomon's servants (vv. 55–57). Solomon's servants probably served in the temple, since they are counted together with the temple servants in v. 58.

2:59–63 The final group of returnees is made up of those who could not prove that they were Israelites. Again, the laity is listed first (v. 60), then the priests (v. 61).

had taken a wife from the daughters of
Barzillai the Gileadite, and was called by
their name). 62 These sought their registration among those enrolled in the genealogies, but they were not found there, and
[b]so they were excluded from the priesthood as unclean. 63 The [c]governor told
them that they were not [d]to partake of the
most holy food, until there should be a
priest to consult [e]Urim and Thummim.
64 [f]The whole assembly together was
42,360, 65 besides their male and female
servants, of whom there were 7,337, and
they had 200 male and female [g]singers.
66 Their horses were 736, their mules were
245, 67 their camels were 435, and their
donkeys were 6,720.
68 [h]Some of the heads of families, when
they came to the house of the LORD that is
in Jerusalem, made freewill offerings for the
house of God, to erect it on its site.
69 According to their ability they gave to [i]the
treasury of the work 61,000 darics[1] of gold,
5,000 minas[2] of silver, and 100 priests'
garments.
70 [j]Now the priests, the Levites, some of
the people, the singers, the gatekeepers, and
the temple servants lived in their towns, and
all the rest of Israel[3] in their towns.

Rebuilding the Altar

3 [k]When the seventh month came, and
the children of Israel were in the towns,
the people gathered as one man to
Jerusalem. 2 Then arose Jeshua the son of
Jozadak, with his fellow priests, and
[l]Zerubbabel the son of [m]Shealtiel with his
kinsmen, and they built the altar of the God
of Israel, to offer burnt offerings on it, [n]as it
is written in the Law of Moses the [o]man of
God. 3 They set the altar in its place, [p]for fear
was on them because of the peoples of the
lands, and [q]they offered burnt offerings on it
to the LORD, burnt offerings morning and
evening. 4 [r]And they kept the Feast of Booths,
[s]as it is written, [t]and offered the daily burnt
offerings by number according to the rule, as
each day required, 5 and after that the regular burnt [u]offerings, the offerings at the new
moon [v]and at all the appointed feasts of the
LORD, and the offerings of everyone who
made a freewill offering to the LORD. 6 From
the first day of the seventh month they
began to offer burnt offerings to the LORD.
But the foundation of the temple of the
LORD was not yet laid. 7 So they gave money
to the masons and the carpenters, [w]and
food, drink, and oil to the Sidonians and the
Tyrians [x]to bring cedar trees from Lebanon
to the sea, to Joppa, [y]according to the grant
that they had from Cyrus king of Persia.

Rebuilding the Temple

8 Now in the second year after their coming
to the house of God at Jerusalem, in the sec-

62 [b][Num. 3:10]
63 [c]Neh. 8:9 [d]Lev. 22:2, 10, 15, 16 [e]See Ex. 28:30
64 [f]Neh. 7:66, 67
65 [g]See 2 Chr. 35:25
68 [h]Neh. 7:70-72
69 [i][1 Chr. 26:20]
70 [j]Neh. 7:73
Chapter 3
1 [k]Neh. 7:73; 8:1
2 [l]Matt. 1:12; Luke 3:27 [m]1 Chr. 3:17; Matt. 1:12; Luke 3:27 [n]Deut. 12:5, 6 [o]See Deut. 33:1
3 [p][ch. 4:4] [q]Ex. 29:38; Num. 28:3, 4
4 [r]Zech. 14:16; See Neh. 8:14-17 [s]Ex. 23:16; Lev. 23:34 [t]See Num. 29:12-38
5 [u]See Num. 28:11-15 [v]Num. 29:39
7 [w]1 Kin. 5:6, 9; 2 Chr. 2:10 [x]2 Chr. 2:16 [y]ch. 1:3, 4; 6:3

1 A *daric* was a coin weighing about 1/4 ounce or 8.5 grams 2 A *mina* was about 1 1/4 pounds or 0.6 kilogram 3 Hebrew *all Israel*

2:62 excluded . . . as unclean. A man had to be descended from Aaron in order to be a priest (Ex. 29:44; Num. 3:3).

2:63 the most holy food. Only a priest or a member of his household could eat the portion of the sacrifice allotted to the priests (Lev. 22:10).

Urim and Thummim. A device for making decisions (Ex. 28:30), needed in this case to determine the ancestry of these priests.

2:64 42,360. This is the same total as in Neh. 7:66. The sum of the figures in the list in Ezra is, however, only 29,818, while the sum of the list in Neh. 7 is 31,089. Certain groups may have been counted without being listed, or an error might have occurred in copying manuscripts.

2:68 freewill offerings. The first temple was also built with freewill offerings (1 Chr. 29:1–9), not with the tithe. The principle of giving beyond the tithe willingly and according to one's ability is still at work in building the kingdom under the new covenant (2 Cor. 8:11).

2:70 This final verse closes off the section by echoing v. 1. In v. 1 they "came" and "returned"; in v. 70 they have "lived in their towns." The Lord had returned the people of promise to the Land of Promise.

3:1–6:22 The people rebuild the altar, resume the sacrifices (3:1–6), and then rebuild the temple itself (3:7–6:22). Spurred on by the prophets Haggai and Zechariah (5:1–2) and blessed by God (5:5), they succeed in spite of opposition from the peoples around them (ch. 4) and the governor of "the province Beyond the River," (5:3–6:12).

3:1 the seventh month. This was Tishri (September-October), the month of the Feast of Booths (Lev. 23:33–44). The desire to celebrate this feast (3:4) no doubt provided the stimulus needed to rebuild the altar.

3:2 burnt offerings. Burnt offerings were the primary offerings (Lev. 1), but others are also in view (v. 5). The burnt offering was the continuing basis on which a sinful people could live in the presence of a holy God (Ex. 29:42), looking forward as it did to the sacrifice of Christ, as the final sacrifice that brings sinners into the presence of God (Heb. 10:19–20).

as it is written. The written word was a powerful tool used by God to accomplish His redemptive plan.

3:3 fear was on them. They had the courage to build the altar and lay the foundation of the temple. But their courage would soon be tested (4:4–5), and the work would be stopped (4:24).

3:4–6 Not only was the Feast of Booths celebrated, but the entire sacrificial system was set in motion, because the sacrifices were a part of maintaining the covenant relationship (Heb. 9:22). So important were the sacrifices that they were started before the temple itself was finished.

3:7 Provisions were made immediately to begin rebuilding the temple. The language of v. 7 recalls the materials assembled for Solomon's temple (1 Chr. 22:2–4; 2 Chr. 2:8–16).

3:8 the second year. 536 B.C.

the second month. This is Ziv (or Iyar, April-May), the same time of year that Solomon began building the original temple (2 Chr. 3:2).

to supervise the work of the house of the LORD. This phrasing is virtually identical to the language used about Solomon's temple (1 Chr. 23:4).

ond month, [z]Zerubbabel the son of Shealtiel
and [z]Jeshua the son of Jozadak made a
beginning, together with the rest of their
kinsmen, the priests and the Levites and all
who had come to Jerusalem from the captivity. They [a]appointed the Levites, from twenty years old and upward, to [b]supervise the
work of the house of the LORD. 9 And [z]Jeshua
with his sons and his brothers, and Kadmiel
and his sons, the sons of Judah, together [b]su-
pervised the workmen in the house of God,
along with the [c]sons of Henadad and the
Levites, their sons and brothers.
10 And when the builders laid the foundation of the temple of the LORD, the
priests in their vestments came forward
with trumpets, and the Levites, the sons of
Asaph, with cymbals, to praise the LORD,
[d]according to the directions of David king
of Israel. 11 And they sang responsively,
praising and giving thanks to the LORD,

[e]"For he is good,
for his steadfast love endures
forever toward Israel."

And all the people shouted with a great
shout when they praised the LORD, because
the foundation of the house of the LORD was
laid. 12 But many of the priests and Levites
and heads of fathers' houses, [f]old men who
had seen the first house, wept with a loud
voice when they saw the foundation of this
house being laid, though many shouted
aloud for joy, 13 so that the people could not
distinguish the sound of the joyful shout
from the sound of the people's weeping, for
the people shouted with a great shout, and
the sound was heard far away.

Adversaries Oppose the Rebuilding

4 Now when [g]the adversaries of Judah
and Benjamin heard that the returned
exiles were building a temple to the LORD,
the God of Israel, 2 they approached
Zerubbabel and the heads of fathers' houses and said to them, "Let us build with
you, for we worship your God as you do,
and we have been sacrificing to him ever
[h]since the days of [i]Esarhaddon king of
Assyria [j]who brought us here." 3 But
Zerubbabel, Jeshua, and the rest of the
heads of fathers' houses in Israel said to
them, [k]"You have nothing to do with us in
building a house to our God; but we alone
will build to the LORD, the God of Israel, [l]as
King Cyrus the king of Persia has commanded us."
4 [m]Then the people of the land discouraged the people of Judah and made them
afraid to build 5 and bribed counselors
against them to frustrate their purpose, all
the days of Cyrus king of Persia, even until
the reign of Darius king of Persia.
6 And in the reign of [n]Ahasuerus, in the
beginning of his reign, they wrote an
accusation against the inhabitants of Judah
and Jerusalem.

8 [z]ch. 2:2; 4:3 [a]1 Chr. 23:24 [b]1 Chr. 23:4
9 [z][See ver. 8 above] [b][See ver. 8 above] [c]Neh. 10:10
10 [d]1 Chr. 6:31; 16:4-6; 25:1, 2
11 [e]See 1 Chr. 16:34, 41
12 [f]Hag. 2:3

Chapter 4
1 [g]See ver. 7-10
2 [h]2 Kin. 17:24, 32, 33 [i]2 Kin. 19:37 [j][ver. 10]
3 [k]Neh. 2:20 [l]ch. 1:1-3
4 [m]Neh. 3:3
6 [n]Esth. 1:1; Dan. 9:1

3:10 when the builders laid the foundation. The focus of the narrative is the response of the people rather than the mechanics of construction. If the return of the temple articles encouraged the spirits of the people (1:9–11 note), much more did the laying of the foundation confirm their faith in God, who had promised restoration after exile (Deut. 30:1–5). Their expression of praise echoes exactly the dedication of Solomon's temple (2 Chr. 5:13).

3:12 But many . . . wept. The tears of the older members of the community were not tears of joy, but tears of disappointment because of the contrast between this small beginning (cf. Zech. 4:10) and the splendor of Solomon's temple. Similar disappointment would later call for rebuke (Hag. 2:1–5), but for the moment the joy of the Lord was the strength of many.

4:1 the adversaries. Though these people came with apparently good intentions, they are referred to as "adversaries," since they later tried to undermine the work of restoration. There was some political motivation in this conflict, because only returnees had authorization from Cyrus to undertake construction (1:2–4). But ultimately the trouble was religious. The "adversaries" were people from various places who had been transplanted into Samaria, the area north of Judah, after the destruction of the northern kingdom of Israel in 722 B.C. (4:9–10 note). They worshiped many gods and incorporated worship of the Lord into their polytheism (2 Kin. 17:24–41). The animosity between the Jews and the Samaritans who descended from these "adversaries" forms part of the background of the New Testament (cf. John 4:1–42).

4:3 we alone will build. The discrimination was not racial or political, but religious. From the early days of living in the Promised Land (Judg. 3:6) and throughout their history (2 Kin. 17:7–17), alliances with foreigners led the Israelites into idolatry and ultimately to exile from the land (2 Kin. 17:18–23). The failure of the returnees to separate themselves from the indigenous population became a problem before long (Ezra 9; 10). The same principle of religious separation is still operative under the new covenant (2 Cor. 6:14–7:1).

4:4 the people of the land. The "adversaries" of v. 1.

4:5 bribed counselors. Perhaps these were Persian officials. The obstructive efforts of the adversaries caused a delay in the work from the time of Cyrus (550–530 B.C.) until the second year of Darius (522–486 B.C.).

4:6–23 This material is a separate section, describing opposition to rebuilding the wall after Darius and during the reigns of Xerxes (486–465 B.C.) and Artaxerxes I (465–424 B.C.). The narrative justifies calling the neighboring peoples in v. 1 "adversaries." Second, it shows that opposition was not a brief and passing problem, but a foretaste of prolonged opposition to the people of God in rebuilding God's "house"—the temple, but also the city and the nation.

4:6 Ahasuerus. Ahasuerus (Xerxes) succeeded Darius and was king of Persia from 486 to 465 B.C.

they wrote an accusation. The subject of the verb is not specified, but the context shows that the troublemakers were a later generation of the "adversaries" of v. 1. Nothing is said about the nature of the accusation.

The Letter to King Artaxerxes

7 In the days of Artaxerxes, Bishlam and
[o]Mithredath and Tabeel and the rest of their
associates wrote to Artaxerxes king of
Persia. The letter was written [p]in Aramaic
and translated.[1] 8 Rehum the commander
and Shimshai the scribe wrote a letter
against Jerusalem to Artaxerxes the king as
follows: 9 Rehum the commander, Shimshai
the scribe, and the rest of their associates,
the [q]judges, the [r]governors, the officials, the
Persians, the men of Erech, the Babylonians, the men of Susa, that is, the [s]Elam-
ites, 10 and the rest of the nations whom the
great and noble [t]Osnappar deported and
settled in the cities of Samaria and in the
rest of the province [u]Beyond the River.
11 (This is a copy of the letter that they sent.)
"To Artaxerxes the king: Your servants, the
men of the province [u]Beyond the River,
send greeting. And now 12 be it known to
the king that the Jews who came up from
you to us have gone to Jerusalem. They are
rebuilding that rebellious and wicked city.
They are [v]finishing the walls and repairing
the foundations. 13 Now be it known to the
king that if this city is rebuilt and the walls
finished, they will not pay [w]tribute, custom,
or toll, and the royal revenue will be
impaired. 14 Now because we eat the salt of
the palace and it is not fitting for us to witness the king's dishonor, therefore we send
and inform the king, 15 in order that search
may be made in the book of the records
of your fathers. You will find in the book
of the records and learn that this city is
a rebellious city, hurtful to kings and
provinces, and that sedition was stirred up
in it from of old. That was why this city was
laid waste. 16 We make known to the king
that if this city is rebuilt and its walls finished, you will then have no possession in
the province Beyond the River."

The King Orders the Work to Cease

17 The king sent an answer: "To Rehum
the commander and Shimshai the scribe
and the rest of their associates who live in
Samaria and in the rest of the province
Beyond the River, greeting. And now 18 the
letter that you sent to us has been [x]plainly
read before me. 19 And I made a decree, and
search has been made, and it has been
found that this city from of old has risen
against kings, and that rebellion and sedition have been made in it. 20 And mighty
kings have been over Jerusalem, [y]who ruled
over the whole province Beyond the River,
to whom [z]tribute, custom, and toll were
paid. 21 Therefore make a decree that these
men be made to cease, and that this city be
not rebuilt, until a decree is made by me.
22 And take care not to be slack in this matter. Why should damage grow to the hurt
of the king?"
23 Then, when the copy of King Artaxerxes' letter was read before Rehum and
Shimshai the scribe and their associates,
they went in haste to the Jews at Jerusalem
and by force and power made them cease.
24 Then the work on the house of God that
is in Jerusalem stopped, and it ceased until

7 [o]ch. 1:8 [p][2 Kin. 18:26]
9 [q][2 Kin. 17:24, 30, 31] [r][ch. 5:6; 6:6] [s]Isai. 11:11
10 [t][ver. 2] [u]ch. 7:12
11 [u][See ver. 10 above]
12 [v]ch. 5:3, 9
13 [w]ver. 20; ch. 7:24
18 [x][Neh. 8:8]
20 [y]1 Kin. 4:21; Ps. 72:8; [Gen. 15:18; Josh. 1:4] [z]ver. 13; [ch. 7:24]

[1] Hebrew *written in Aramaic and translated in Aramaic,* indicating that 4:8–6:18 is in Aramaic; another interpretation is *The letter was written in the Aramaic script and set forth in the Aramaic language*

4:7 Artaxerxes. Artaxerxes I, successor to Ahasuerus (Xerxes) and king of Persia from 465 to 424 B.C.

wrote to Artaxerxes. There is no information about the content of this letter, but considering the context it was doubtless an effort to prevent rebuilding the wall.

Aramaic. This was the language of international diplomacy in the ancient Near East.

4:8–6:18 This section is written not in Hebrew, but Aramaic, the language of the original documents. The correspondence expresses the concern of various Gentile officials about the progress of the Jews' work.

4:8 scribe. Scribes were high officials who wrote official correspondence and kept archival records for the provincial government (7:6 note).

4:9 the rest of their associates. The opposition did not come from a few, but was broadly based.

4:10 Osnappar. Probably Ashurbanipal, the last successful king of Assyria (668–627 B.C.), who transplanted various peoples into Samaria. This practice was begun after the fall of Samaria in 722 B.C., probably by Sargon II (2 Kin. 17:24).

Beyond the River. The area west of the Euphrates, including Aram, Phoenicia, and Palestine.

4:12 finishing the walls. See note 4:6–23.

4:14 we eat the salt of the palace. Lit. "we have salted with the salt of the palace." Probably this is a way of referring to the covenantal obligation of a vassal to his overlord (cf. Lev. 2:13; Num. 18:19; 2 Chr. 13:5).

4:15 book of the records. The various Aramaic documents used in writing this section of Ezra would have been kept in a similar archive.

a rebellious city . . . was laid waste. See 2 Kin. 18:7; 24:1.

4:16 have no possession. Obviously an exaggeration, these words were intended to sway Artaxerxes.

4:18 has been plainly read. The king was not given a summary of the letter; it was read to him word for word.

4:20 Israel once received tribute from other nations, under David and Solomon. Now, even though they have returned to the Land of Promise, God's people must submit to the rule of the ungodly (9:9 and note).

4:24 After the section dealing with opposition to the rebuilding of the wall (vv. 6–23), the author returns to the topic of vv. 1–5, rebuilding the temple.

the second year of the reign of Darius king
of Persia.

Rebuilding Begins Anew

5 Now the prophets, [a]Haggai and
[b]Zechariah the son of Iddo, prophesied
to the Jews who were in Judah and
Jerusalem, in the name of the God of Israel
who was over them. 2 [c]Then Zerubbabel the
son of Shealtiel and [d]Jeshua the son of
Jozadak arose and began to rebuild the
house of God that is in Jerusalem, and the
prophets of God were [e]with them, supporting them.
3 At the same time [f]Tattenai the governor
of the province Beyond the River and
Shethar-bozenai and their associates came to
them and spoke to them thus, [g]"Who gave
you a decree to build this house and to finish this structure?" 4 They[1] also asked them
this: "What are the names of the men who
are building this building?" 5 But [h]the eye of
their God was on the elders of the Jews, and
they did not stop them until the report
should reach Darius and then an answer be
returned by letter concerning it.

Tattenai's Letter to King Darius

6 This is a copy of the letter that [f]Tattenai
the governor of the province Beyond the
River and Shethar-bozenai and his associates the [i]governors who were in the province
Beyond the River sent to Darius the king.
7 They sent him a report, in which was written as follows: "To Darius the king, all
peace. 8 Be it known to the king that we
went to the province of Judah, to the house
of the great God. It is being built with huge
stones, and timber is laid in the walls. This
work goes on diligently and prospers in their
hands. 9 Then we asked those elders and
spoke to them thus, '[g]Who gave you a
decree to build this house and to finish this
structure?' 10 We also asked them their
names, for your information, that we might
write down the names of their leaders.[2]
11 And this was their reply to us: 'We are the
servants of the God of heaven and earth,
and we are rebuilding the house that was
built many years ago, [j]which a great king of
Israel built and [k]finished. 12 [l]But because our
fathers had angered the God of heaven, he
[m]gave them into the hand of Nebuchadnezzar king of Babylon, the Chaldean, who
destroyed this house and carried away the
people to Babylonia. 13 [n]However, in the first
year of Cyrus king of Babylon, Cyrus the
king made a decree that this house of God
should be rebuilt. 14 [o]And the gold and silver
vessels of the house of God, which Nebuchadnezzar had taken out of the temple
that was in Jerusalem and brought into the
temple of Babylon, these Cyrus the king
took out of the temple of Babylon, and they
were delivered to one whose name was
[p]Sheshbazzar, whom he had made governor;
15 and he said to him, "Take these vessels, go
and put them in the temple that is in
Jerusalem, and let the house of God be
rebuilt on its site." 16 Then this [p]Sheshbazzar

Chapter 5
1 [a]Hag. 1:1 [b]Zech. 1:1
2 [c]ch. 3:2 [d]See ch. 3:2 [e][ch. 6:14]
3 [f]ch. 6:6, 13 [g]ch. 4:12
5 [h]Ps. 33:18; [ch. 7:6, 28]
6 [f][See ver. 3 above] [i][ch. 4:9]
9 [g][See ver. 3 above]
11 [j]1 Kin. 6:1 [k]ch. 4:12
12 [l]2 Chr. 36:16, 17 [m]2 Kin. 24:2; See 2 Kin. 25:8-11
13 [n]ch. 1:1
14 [o]ch. 1:7, 8; 6:5 [p]ch. 1:8
16 [p][See ver. 14 above]

1 Septuagint, Syriac; Aramaic *We* 2 Aramaic *of the men at their heads*

5:1, 2 The year Haggai and Zechariah began to prophesy was the same year referred to in 4:24, the second year of Darius (Hag. 1:1; Zech. 1:1). Work on the temple did not resume because of a decree from Darius, but because of the preaching of God's prophets and the obedient response of God's people (Hag. 1:14, 15).

5:1 over them. Both the people (Deut. 28:10) and the prophets (Jer. 15:16) belonged to God.

5:2 supporting them. The help took the form of courageous preaching and constant encouragement (as in the books of Haggai and Zechariah).

5:3, 4 As soon as the work on the temple was renewed, the Persian officials of the area renewed their opposition to it.

5:5 This time God chose to intervene, and the officials permitted the work to continue until they should hear from Darius. Here, as throughout Ezra and Nehemiah, God intervened through the actions of people (cf. note on 1:1).

5:8 province of Judah. Judea was a province in the Persian Empire, not an independent political state.

prospers in their hands. It prospered due to the care of God (v. 5), the preaching of the prophets (vv. 1, 2), and the leadership of Zerubbabel and Jeshua (v. 2).

5:9 Who gave you a decree. The question underscores Judah's lack of independence.

5:11–16 The reply of the Jewish leaders to the questions of the Persian officials (vv. 3–4) is included in the letter to Darius.

5:11 God of heaven and earth. This was a fuller form of the more frequent title "God of heaven" (1:2 note).

a great king of Israel. Solomon built the original temple in the years 966–959 B.C. (1 Kin. 6:1, 38).

5:12 gave them into the hand. God gave Israel into the hand of Nebuchadnezzar to punish them for breaking the covenant. Those who trust in Christ are safe from God's righteous anger (1 John 4:17–18), because God the Father gave Christ into the hands of wicked men, and Christ endured God's wrath on behalf of the elect (Mark 9:31; Luke 9:44; 24:7; Rom. 8:32).

Chaldean. The Chaldeans lived in southern Mesopotamia and established the Neo-Babylonian Empire by overthrowing the Assyrians in 612 B.C. The new empire continued until overthrown by the Persians in 539.

5:13 made a decree. Here is the answer, on the human level, to the question posed in 5:3.

5:14 Sheshbazzar. See note 1:8.

5:16 from that time . . . building. The work was not done continuously, but with a break of about seventeen years (4:24 note).

came and [q]laid the foundations of the house
of God that is in Jerusalem, and from that
time until now it has been in building, and
it is [r]not yet finished.' [17]Therefore, if it
seems good to the king, [s]let search be made
in the royal archives there in Babylon, to see
whether a decree was issued by Cyrus the
king for the rebuilding of this house of God
in Jerusalem. And let the king send us his
pleasure in this matter."

The Decree of Darius

6 Then Darius the king made a decree,
and [t]search was made in Babylonia, in
the house of the archives where the documents were stored. [2]And in Ecbatana, the
capital that is [u]in the province of Media, a
scroll was found on which this was written:
"A record. [3]In the first year of Cyrus the
king, Cyrus the king issued a decree:
Concerning the house of God at Jerusalem,
let the house be rebuilt, the place where
sacrifices were offered, and let its foundations be retained. Its height shall be sixty
cubits[1] and its breadth sixty cubits, [4][v]with
three layers of great stones and one layer of
timber. Let the cost be paid from the royal
treasury. [5]And also [w]let the gold and silver
vessels of the house of God, which
Nebuchadnezzar took out of the temple
that is in Jerusalem and brought to
Babylon, be restored and brought back to
the temple that is in Jerusalem, each to its
place. You shall put them in the house of
God.

[6]"Now therefore, [x]Tattenai, governor of
the province Beyond the River, Shethar-
bozenai, [y]and your associates the governors
who are in the province Beyond the River,
keep away. [7]Let the work on this house of
God alone. Let the governor of the Jews and
the elders of the Jews rebuild this house of
God on its site. [8]Moreover, [z]I make a decree
regarding what you shall do for these elders
of the Jews for the rebuilding of this house
of God. The cost is to be paid to these men
in full and without delay from the royal revenue, the tribute of the province from
Beyond the River. [9]And whatever is needed—bulls, rams, or sheep for burnt offerings to the God of heaven, wheat, salt,
wine, or oil, as the priests at Jerusalem
require—let that be given to them day by
day without fail, [10]that they may offer pleasing sacrifices to the God of heaven [a]and
pray for the life of the king and his sons.
[11]Also I make a decree that if anyone alters
this edict, a beam shall be pulled out of his
house, and he shall be impaled on it, and
[b]his house shall be made a dunghill. [12]May
the God [c]who has caused his name to dwell
there overthrow any king or people who
shall put out a hand to alter this, or to
destroy this house of God that is in
Jerusalem. I Darius make a decree; let it be
done with all diligence."

The Temple Finished and Dedicated

[13]Then, according to the word sent by
Darius the king, [x]Tattenai, the governor of
the province Beyond the River, Shethar-
bozenai, and their associates did with all
diligence what Darius the king had
ordered. [14][d]And the elders of the Jews built
and prospered through the prophesying of
Haggai the prophet and Zechariah the son
of Iddo. They finished their building by
decree of the God of Israel and [e]by decree
of Cyrus and [f]Darius and [g]Artaxerxes king

16[q]ch. 3:8, 10 [r][ch. 6:15]
17[s]ch. 6:1, 2
Chapter 6
1[t]ch. 5:17
2[u][2 Kin. 17:6]
4[v]1 Kin. 6:36
5[w]ch. 1:7, 8; 5:14
6[x]ch. 5:3, 6 [y]ch. 5:6
8[z]ch. 7:13, 21
10[a]Jer. 29:7; [1 Tim. 2:2]
11[b]Dan. 2:5; 3:29
12[c]1 Kin. 9:3
13[x][See ver. 6 above]
14[d]ch. 5:1, 2 [e]ver. 3; ch. 1:1; 5:13 [f]ver. 12; [ch. 4:24] [g]ch. 7:1

[1] A *cubit* was about 18 inches or 45 centimeters

5:17 let search be made. This is the second reference to an archival search, underscoring the theme of the power of written documents (Introduction: Characteristics and Themes). The first search (4:15) had stopped the building of the wall. The second search would result in the completion of the temple.

6:1, 2 Darius responded to Tattenai's request. The search began in the treasury at Babylon, but the decree was found in Achmetha (Ecbatana), a city almost three hundred miles northeast of Babylon, and probably the city from which Cyrus issued the decree.

6:3–5 This copy of the decree differs somewhat from that in 1:2–4; for example, God's name is not used ("LORD"). The copy in 1:2–4 is what the heralds proclaimed to the Jews, while this copy is the minutes kept as an official record.

6:3 Its height shall be sixty cubits and its breadth sixty cubits. These dimensions are larger than those of Solomon's temple (1 Kin. 6:2). They may give the maximum size allowed rather than the size planned.

6:6–12 Having found Cyrus's decree, Darius issued a second decree reinforcing it. In God's providence the opposition of Tattenai and his associates turned out for the good of the project (cf. Gen. 50:20).

6:9 whatever is needed. As a result of the opposition, provision was made for continuing the temple services.

6:10 pray for the life of the king. See note 1:3.

6:11 if anyone alters this edict. It was customary to pronounce curses on anyone who changed an official document (cf. Rev. 22:18–19). As a result of the opposition, God's people were granted irrevocable support to rebuild the temple.

6:13 did with all diligence what Darius the king had ordered. Darius had ordered that his decree be "with all diligence" (6:12), and it was.

6:14 the prophesying of Haggai . . . and Zechariah. The preaching of the prophets moved the people to start the work again (5:1–2) and to complete it.

of Persia; 15 and this house was finished on
the third day of the [h]month of Adar, in the
sixth year of the reign of Darius the king.
16 And the people of Israel, the priests
and the Levites, and the rest of the
returned exiles, celebrated the [i]dedication
of this house of God with joy. 17 They
offered at the dedication of this house of
God 100 bulls, 200 rams, 400 lambs, and
as a sin offering for all Israel [j]12 male goats,
according to the number of the tribes of
Israel. 18 And they set the priests [k]in their
divisions and the Levites [l]in their divisions,
for the service of God at Jerusalem, [m]as it is
written in the Book of Moses.

Passover Celebrated

19 [n]On the fourteenth day of the first
month, the returned exiles kept the
Passover. 20 [o]For the priests and the Levites
had purified themselves together; all of
them were clean. [p]So they slaughtered the
Passover lamb for all the returned exiles,
for their fellow priests, and for themselves.
21 It was eaten by the people of Israel who
had returned from exile, and [q]also by
everyone who had joined them and separated himself [r]from the uncleanness of the
peoples of the land to worship the LORD,
the God of Israel. 22 And they kept the Feast
of Unleavened Bread [s]seven days with joy,
for the LORD had made them joyful [t]and
had turned the heart of [u]the king of Assyria
to them, so that he aided them in the work
of the house of God, the God of Israel.

Ezra Sent to Teach the People

7 Now after this, [v]in the reign of
[v]Artaxerxes king of Persia, [w]Ezra the
son of Seraiah, son of Azariah, son of
Hilkiah, 2 son of Shallum, son of Zadok,
son of Ahitub, 3 son of Amariah, son of
Azariah, son of Meraioth, 4 son of Zerahiah,
son of Uzzi, son of Bukki, 5 son of Abishua,
son of Phinehas, son of Eleazar, son of
Aaron the chief priest— 6 this Ezra went up
from Babylonia. He was a scribe [x]skilled in
the Law of Moses that the LORD the God of
Israel had given, and the king granted him
all that he asked, [y]for the hand of the LORD
his God was on him.
7 And there went up also to Jerusalem, in
the seventh year of Artaxerxes the king,
some of the people of Israel, and [z]some of
the priests and [a]Levites, the singers and
gatekeepers, and the temple [b]servants.
8 And he came to Jerusalem in the fifth
month, which was in the seventh year of
the king. 9 For on the first day of the first
month he began to go up from Babylonia,
and on the first day of the fifth month he
came to Jerusalem, [c]for the good hand of

15 [h]Esth. 3:7
16 [i]1 Kin. 8:63; 2 Chr. 7:5
17 [j][ch. 8:35]
18 [k]1 Chr. 24:1; 2 Chr. 35:5 [l]1 Chr. 23:6 [m]Num. 3:6; 8:9
19 [n]Ex. 12:6
20 [o]2 Chr. 30:15 [p]2 Chr. 35:11
21 [q]Neh. 9:2; 10:28; [ch. 9:1] [r]ch. 9:11
22 [s]Ex. 12:15; 13:6; 2 Chr. 30:21; 35:17
[t]ch. 7:27; [Prov. 21:1] [u][Neh. 13:6]
Chapter 7
1 [v]Neh. 2:1 [w]For ver. 1-5, see 1 Chr. 6:4-14
6 [x]ver. 11, 12, 21; Neh. 8:1, 4, 13; 12:26, 36 [y]ver. 9, 28; ch. 8:18, 22, 31; Neh. 2:8, 18 [ch. 5:5]
7 [z]See ch. 8:1-14 [a]ch. 8:15-19 [b]ch. 8:17, 20; [ch. 2:43]
9 [c]See ver. 6

God . . . Cyrus. The same word is used for the command of God and the decrees of the Persian kings. God's sovereign decree does not negate human responsibility, but rather establishes it. The reference to Artaxerxes may seem to be out of place, since the temple proper was completed before he became king. However, the temple is not explicitly mentioned in the Aramaic text of v. 14, so the reference could be a preview to the finishing of the rebuilding of the entire "house of God," including the community and the wall that were rebuilt under the authority of Artaxerxes (7:11–26; Neh. 2:1, 8).

6:15 this house was finished. The date was March 12, 515 B.C., four years after the work was renewed (Hag. 1:15), twenty years after the work was begun (3:8), and almost exactly seventy years after the Solomonic temple was destroyed in 586.

6:16 the dedication of this house of God. With the dedication of the temple a major milestone has been reached. The parenthetical section of 4:6–23 has already given a preview of trouble to come. The dedication of the wall (Neh. 12:27) and the final reforms (Neh. 13) will complete the restoration of the Jewish community.

6:17 They offered. The number of offerings is small in comparison to those of Solomon (1 Kin. 8:62, 63). Reference to a sin offering shows an awareness of sin and faith in God who keeps His covenant of love (Deut. 7:9).

6:18 written in the Book of Moses. The written text prescribed the temple duties and ensured that they would be carried out. The first Aramaic section of Ezra ends with this verse.

7:1 Now after this. About sixty years passed between the events at the end of ch. 6 and those at the beginning of ch. 7. The only information we have on this period from Ezra and Nehemiah concerns opposition in the days of Ahasuerus (4:6 note)—the events in the Book of Esther occurred during this period (Esth. 1:1).

Artaxerxes. Artaxerxes I, king of Persia from 465–424 B.C.

Ezra. The lengthy introduction of Ezra (vv. 1–10) signals his importance for what follows. The first information given about Ezra is his ancestry. The genealogy is full but not complete; the phrase "son of" is often used to mean "descendant." Ezra's line goes back to Aaron, establishing his priestly authority for his subsequent actions.

7:6 went up from Babylonia. Not all the pious exiles had returned with Sheshbazzar in 538 B.C. Ezra's family had not. Ezra had probably not been born at the time of the first return. He grew up in Babylon, where most of the exiles lived.

a scribe skilled. In the Old Testament, scribes were often government officials who composed official documents (4:8 note; 2 Sam. 8:17; 1 Kin. 4:3), administered temple treasuries (2 Kin. 12:10, 11; 22:3, 4, 9; Neh. 13:13), served as court emissaries (2 Kin. 18:18–37), and provided literary functions like taking dictation (Jer. 36:32). Ezra had governmental authority (v. 25), but his most important qualification was as a teacher of God's law (vv. 10, 11, 14; Neh. 8:1–9).

that the LORD . . . had given. The "Law of Moses" is divine in origin (cf. 2 Tim. 3:16). The reference here may be to the first five books of the Bible.

the king granted him all that he asked. The actions of responsible human beings are traced back to the sovereign action of God: Ezra asked and Artaxerxes complied because God favored Ezra.

7:7 there went up . . . some. Ezra was not alone, but leading a second group of returning exiles.

the seventh year. 458 B.C.

7:9 he came to Jerusalem. The trip took place in the spring, when there would have been ample water along the way. It took about four months.

his God was on him. 10 For Ezra had set his
heart to study the Law of the LORD, and to
do it [d]and to [e]teach his statutes and rules
in Israel.
11 This is a copy of the letter that King
Artaxerxes gave to Ezra the priest, the
scribe, a man learned in matters of the commandments of the LORD and his statutes for
Israel: 12 "Artaxerxes, [f]king of kings, to Ezra
the priest, the [g]scribe of the Law of the God
of heaven. Peace.[1] [h]And now 13 [i]I make a
decree that anyone of the people of Israel or
their priests or Levites in my kingdom, who
freely offers to go to Jerusalem, may go with
you. 14 For you are sent by the king [j]and his
seven counselors to make inquiries about
Judah and Jerusalem according to the Law
of your God, which is in your hand, 15 and
also to carry the silver and gold that the
king [j]and his counselors have freely offered
to the God of Israel, [k]whose dwelling is in
Jerusalem, 16 [l]with all the silver and gold
that you shall find in the whole province of
Babylonia, and [m]with the freewill offerings
of the people and the priests, vowed willingly for the house of their God that is in
Jerusalem. 17 With this money, then, you
shall with all diligence buy bulls, rams, and
lambs, with their grain offerings and their
drink offerings, and [n]you shall offer them
on the altar of the house of your God that is
in Jerusalem. 18 Whatever seems good to
you and your brothers to do with the rest of
the silver and gold, you may do, according
to the will of your God. 19 The vessels that
have been given you for the service of the
house of your God, you shall deliver before
the God of Jerusalem. 20 And whatever else
is required for the house of your God,
which it falls to you to provide, you may
provide it out of the king's treasury.
21 "And I, Artaxerxes the king, make a
decree to all the treasurers in the province
Beyond the River: Whatever Ezra the priest,
the scribe of the Law of the God of heaven,
requires of you, let it be done with all diligence, 22 up to 100 talents[2] of silver, 100
cors[3] of wheat, 100 baths[4] of wine, 100
baths of oil, and salt without prescribing
how much. 23 Whatever is decreed by the
God of heaven, let it be done in full for the
house of the God of heaven, lest his wrath be
against the realm of the king and his sons.
24 We also notify you that it shall not be lawful to impose [o]tribute, custom, or toll on
anyone of the priests, the Levites, the
singers, the doorkeepers, the temple servants, or other servants of this house of God.
25 "And you, Ezra, according to the wisdom of your God that is in your hand, [p]ap-
point magistrates and judges who may
judge all the people in the province Beyond
the River, all such as know the laws of your
God. [q]And those who do not know them,
you shall teach. 26 Whoever will not obey
the law of your God and the law of the
king, let judgment be strictly executed on

10 [d]ver. 25; [Deut. 33:10 [e]2 Chr. 17:7; Mal. 2:7; Matt. 23:2, 3]; See Neh. 8:1-8
12 [f]Ezek. 26:7; Dan. 2:37 [g]See ver. 6 [h]ch. 4:10, 11, 17
13 [i]ch. 6:8
14 [j]ver. 15, 28; ch. 8:25; [Esth. 1:14]
15 [j][See ver. 14 above] [k]2 Chr. 6:2; [Ps. 135:21]
16 [l]ch. 8:25 [m]1 Chr. 29:6, 9
17 [n]Deut. 12:5, 11
24 [o]ch. 4:13, 20
25 [p]Ex. 18:21, 22; Deut. 16:18 [q]See ver. 10

1 Aramaic *Perfect* (probably a greeting) 2 A *talent* was about 75 pounds or 34 kilograms 3 A *cor* was about 6 bushels or 220 liters 4 A *bath* was about 6 gallons or 22 liters

the good hand of his God. Success is attributed to God's providence.

7:10 For. Ezra's goal in going to Jerusalem is now given. As a diligent hearer and doer of the Word (James 1:22), Ezra's goal was to teach others to do the same.

7:11–26 A copy of a letter from King Artaxerxes records his commission of Ezra to return to Jerusalem to inquire about the spiritual state of the people (v. 14), to provide supplies for the temple (vv. 15–24), and to arrange for the administration of justice (vv. 25, 26).

7:11 letter. The letter (vv. 12–26), written in Aramaic (4:7 note), gives Ezra the authority to carry out the reforms recorded in the following chapters. The letter may have been written by Ezra and then signed by Artaxerxes, or Artaxerxes may have had Jewish advisers help compose the letter, as some of the details seem to indicate.

7:12 king of kings. A title used by Persian monarchs to indicate their supremacy over all subject kings. That God is the true King of kings is implicit in the Book of Ezra (1:1 note) and explicit elsewhere in Scripture (Rev. 17:14; 19:16).

scribe. See note on v. 6.

7:13 This permission to return extends to all who are willing, as did the original decree of Cyrus in 1:3.

7:14 to make inquiries. Whereas Cyrus commissioned the first returnees "to build" a temple, Artaxerxes commissioned Ezra to inquire about the spiritual condition of the people. His efforts would help rebuild the community of God's people, God's "house" (Num. 12:7).

7:15–17 Artaxerxes' knowledge of the details of Israelite worship indicates that Ezra or Jewish advisers wrote the letter themselves or assisted in writing it (1:2–4 note).

7:18 the will of your God. Conformity to God's will is a major theme in the rest of the book.

7:20 whatever else is required. The generosity of Artaxerxes was like that of Darius (6:9).

7:23 lest his wrath. See note 1:3.

7:25 Ezra's role was twofold: exercising governmental authority and teaching the law of God (7:6 note).

all the people . . . Beyond the River. This means the Jews who had returned to Judah and Jerusalem.

7:26 the law of your God and the law of the king. The two are not identical. The distinction between religious and civil law was more important for the Jews in exile under a foreign civil power, than during the monarchy, when the state was of the same religion as the people. The second Aramaic section of Ezra ends with this verse.

let judgment be strictly executed. Ezra himself is not given the authority to punish in this verse; the "officials and the elders" exercise it in 10:8.

him, whether for death or for banishment
or for confiscation of his goods or for
imprisonment."
27 [r]Blessed be the LORD, the God of our
fathers, [s]who put such a thing as this into
the heart of the king, to beautify the house
of the LORD that is in Jerusalem, 28 [t]and
who extended to me his steadfast love
before the king and his counselors, and
before all the king's mighty officers. I took
courage, for the hand of the LORD my God
was on me, and I gathered leading men
from Israel to go up with me.

Genealogy of Those Who Returned with Ezra

8 These are the heads of their fathers'
houses, and this is the genealogy of
those who went up with me from
Babylonia, in the reign of Artaxerxes the
king: 2 Of the sons of Phinehas, Gershom.
Of the sons of [u]Ithamar, Daniel. Of the
sons of David, [v]Hattush. 3 Of the sons of
Shecaniah, who was of the sons of [w]Parosh,
Zechariah, with whom were registered 150
men. 4 [x]Of the sons of Pahath-moab,
Eliehoenai the son of Zerahiah, and with
him 200 men. 5 Of the sons of Zattu,[1]
Shecaniah the son of Jahaziel, and with
him 300 men. 6 Of the sons of Adin, Ebed
the son of Jonathan, and with him 50 men.
7 Of the sons of Elam, Jeshaiah the son of
Athaliah, and with him 70 men. 8 Of the
sons of Shephatiah, Zebadiah the son of
Michael, and with him 80 men. 9 Of the
sons of Joab, Obadiah the son of Jehiel,
and with him 218 men. 10 Of the sons of
Bani,[2] Shelomith the son of Josiphiah, and
with him 160 men. 11 [y]Of the sons of Bebai,
Zechariah, the son of Bebai, and with him

27 [r]1 Chr. 29:10 [s]ch. 6:22
28 [t]ch. 9:9
Chapter 8
2 [u]1 Chr. 24:3, 4 [v][1 Chr. 3:22]
3 [w]For ver. 3, see ch. 2:3-15
4 [x]ch. 10:30
11 [y]ch. 10:28
15 [z]ver. 21, 31 [a][ch. 7:7]
16 [b]ch. 10:15
18 [c]See ch. 7:6 [d]1 Chr. 6:19
19 [e]Neh. 12:24 [f]1 Chr. 6:1, 16
20 [g]ch. 2:43; 7:7 [h]Num. 1:17
21 [i]See 2 Chr. 20:3 [j]ver. 15, 31 [k][Ps. 5:8]

28 men. 12 Of the sons of Azgad, Johanan
the son of Hakkatan, and with him 110
men. 13 Of the sons of Adonikam, those
who came later, their names being
Eliphelet, Jeuel, and Shemaiah, and with
them 60 men. 14 Of the sons of Bigvai,
Uthai and Zaccur, and with them 70 men.

Ezra Sends for Levites

15 I gathered them to the river that runs to
[z]Ahava, and there we camped three days.
As I reviewed the people and the priests, I
found there [a]none of the sons of Levi.
16 Then I sent for Eliezer, Ariel, Shemaiah,
Elnathan, Jarib, Elnathan, Nathan,
Zechariah, and [b]Meshullam, leading men,
and for Joiarib and Elnathan, who were
men of insight, 17 and sent them to Iddo,
the leading man at the place Casiphia,
telling them what to say to Iddo and his
brothers and[3] the temple servants at the
place Casiphia, namely, to send us ministers for the house of our God. 18 And [c]by the
good hand of our God on us, they brought
us a man of discretion, of the sons of [d]Mah-
li the son of Levi, son of Israel, namely
Sherebiah with his sons and kinsmen, 18;
19 also [e]Hashabiah, and with him Jeshaiah of
[f]the sons of Merari, with his kinsmen and
their sons, 20; 20 [g]besides 220 of the temple
servants, whom David and his officials had
set apart to attend the Levites. These were
all [h]mentioned by name.

Fasting and Prayer for Protection

21 [i]Then I proclaimed a fast there, at the
river [j]Ahava, that we might humble ourselves before our God, [k]to seek from him a

1 Septuagint; Hebrew lacks *Zattu* 2 Septuagint; Hebrew lacks *Bani* 3 Hebrew lacks *and*

7:27 put such a thing . . . into the heart of the king. The actions of Artaxerxes are traced to the sovereign action of God.

7:28 extended to me his steadfast love. "Steadfast love" represents the Hebrew word *ḥesed* which refers to God's covenant loyalty. The same word occurs in 9:9. Artaxerxes' favor toward Ezra is owing to God's covenant loyalty to His people.

to me. The first reference to Ezra in the first person and the beginning of the Ezra's "memoirs" (Introduction: Author).

the hand of the LORD. Ezra's awareness of God's providential control was a source of encouragement for the tasks that lay ahead.

8:1–14 Not all the exiles returned in response to the decree of Cyrus in 538 B.C. A second but significantly smaller group returned with Ezra about eighty years after the first return.

8:15 none of the sons of Levi. Ezra wanted more Levites for service in the temple (v. 17), and perhaps to help with the sacrifices mentioned in v. 35. He may also have wanted Levites to be part of the caravan to the Promised Land, as they had been at the time of the Exodus from Egypt and the first return from Babylon (1:2 note).

8:16 Then I sent for. Ezra selected a group of influential men to persuade some Levites to return with him.

8:17 the leading man at the place Casiphia. The location is not certain, but it could be Ctesiphon on the Tigris River north of Babylon. Since in earlier (Deut. 12:5; Jer. 7:2–3) and later times, "the place" refers to a holy place, it seems that Casiphia was the site of a sanctuary. There was a Jewish sanctuary at Elephantine, Egypt, at this same time. Levites would have been concentrated at such a sanctuary, explaining why Ezra sent the delegation to Casiphia. Iddo would have been the leader at the sanctuary.

8:18–20 the good hand of our God. Ezra did not weary of ascribing his success to God's providential control (7:6 note). Thirty-eight Levites were persuaded to return along with three key levitical leaders and 220 temple servants ("Nethinim"). Just as the Lord had stirred the spirits of Cyrus (1:1), the first returnees (1:5), and Artaxerxes (7:27), so His good hand moved these Levites to accept Ezra's call.

8:21 a fast. Fasting is an aspect of "humbling ourselves" for the purpose of requesting something from God (2 Chr. 20:3).

safe journey for ourselves, our children,
and all our goods. 22 For I was ashamed to
ask the king for a band of soldiers and
horsemen to protect us against the enemy
on our way, since we had told the king,
[l]"The hand of our God is for good on [m]all
who seek him, and the power of his wrath
is against all who forsake him." 23 So we
fasted and implored our God for this, and
he listened to our entreaty.

Priests to Guard Offerings

24 Then I set apart twelve of the leading
priests: [e]Sherebiah, [e]Hashabiah, and ten of
their kinsmen with them. 25 And I weighed
out to them the [n]silver and the gold and the
vessels, the offering for the house of our
God that the king and his [o]counselors and
his lords and all Israel there present had
offered. 26 [p]I weighed out into their hand
650 talents[1] of silver, and silver vessels
worth 200 talents,[2] and 100 talents of gold,
27 20 bowls of gold worth 1,000 darics,[3] and
two vessels of fine bright bronze as precious
as gold. 28 And I said to them, [q]"You are
holy to the LORD, and [r]the vessels are holy,
and the silver and the gold are a freewill
offering to the LORD, the God of your
fathers. 29 Guard them and keep them until
you weigh them before the chief priests and
the Levites and the heads of fathers' houses
in Israel at Jerusalem, [s]within the chambers
of the house of the LORD." 30 So the priests
and the Levites [p]took over the weight of the
silver and the gold and the vessels, to bring
them to Jerusalem, to the house of our God.
31 Then we departed from the river Ahava
[t]on the twelfth day of the first month, to go
to Jerusalem. [u]The hand of our God was on
us, and he delivered us from the hand of
the enemy and from ambushes by the way.
32 [v]We came to Jerusalem, and there we
remained three days. 33 On the fourth day,
within the house of our God, the silver and
the gold and the vessels were [w]weighed
into the hands of [x]Meremoth the priest,
son of Uriah, and with him was Eleazar the
son of Phinehas, and with them were the
Levites, [y]Jozabad the son of Jeshua and
Noadiah the son of [z]Binnui. 34 The whole
was counted and weighed, and the weight
of everything was recorded.
35 At that time [a]those who had come from
captivity, the returned exiles, offered burnt
offerings to the God of Israel, [b]twelve bulls
for all Israel, ninety-six rams, seventy-seven
lambs, and as a sin offering twelve male
goats. All this was a burnt offering to the
LORD. 36 [c]They also delivered the king's
commissions to the king's [d]satraps[4] and to
the governors of the province Beyond the
River, and they aided the people and the
house of God.

Ezra Prays About Intermarriage

9 After these things had been done,
the officials approached me and said,
"The people of Israel and the priests and

22 [l]See ch. 7:6 [m][2 Chr. 15:2]
24 [e][See ver. 19 above]
25 [n]ch. 7:15, 16 [o]See ch. 7:14
26 [p][ch. 1:9-11]
28 [q]Lev. 21:6 [r]Lev. 22:2, 3
29 [s][ch. 10:6]
30 [p][See ver. 26 above]
31 [t][ch. 7:9] [u]See ch. 7:6
32 [v]Neh. 2:11
33 [w][ch. 1:9-11] [x]Neh. 3:4, 21 [y]Neh. 11:16 [z]Neh. 3:24
35 [a]ch. 2:1 [b][ch. 6:17]
36 [c]ch. 7:21 [d]Esth. 3:12; 8:9; 9:3; Dan. 3:2, 3, 27; 6:2, 3

[1] A *talent* was about 75 pounds or 34 kilograms [2] Revocalization; the number is missing in the Masoretic Text [3] A *daric* was a coin weighing about 1/4 ounce or 8.5 grams [4] A *satrap* was a Persian official

a safe journey. Safety from bandits, among other dangers, is in view (v. 31).

8:22 I was ashamed. Ezra had testified to God's providential control, not only before the saints but also before Artaxerxes. It would have seemed inconsistent with this testimony to ask for a military escort in addition. See note Neh. 2:7–9 for a contrast between Ezra and Nehemiah on this point.

8:23 he listened to our entreaty. Not then and there with words, but throughout the journey with actions (vv. 31, 32).

8:24 twelve. Twelve priests and twelve Levites, perhaps as representatives of all Israel (cf. v. 35).

8:25 the king . . . had offered. The total contribution listed in v. 26 is enormous, such that critics have doubted the authenticity of the list. However, the Persian kings were known for their great wealth and generosity toward the religions of subject peoples. There were also wealthy Jewish families in Babylon by this time.

8:28 holy to the LORD. Holiness is an attribute of God (Lev. 19:2) and, by extension, of anyone or anything belonging to Him, especially priests (Lev. 21:6), Levites (Num. 3:11–13, where "consecrated" means dedicated to God), and temple articles (Ex. 30:22–29). Ezra's strict command arises from the spiritual threat that contact with the profane represented for the holy.

8:31 twelfth day. According to 7:9, departure was on the first day. The difference is due to the delay experienced in order to find the needed Levites.

he delivered us. Again Ezra attributes his success to God's providential control. The fasting and prayer for a safe journey was answered with the arrival of people and possessions in Jerusalem (vv. 21, 32).

8:32 there we remained three days. Compare the similar rest of Nehemiah in Neh. 2:11 (cf. Josh. 3:2).

8:35 offered burnt offerings. Just as the provisions had been made (7:17), so the sacrifices were offered. This is a picture of complete success.

9:1 After these things had been done. That is, four and a half months after arrival (7:9; 10:9).

the officials approached me and said. Ezra had come to teach the law (7:10 note) and now some of the leaders came to him to report certain sins. Possibly they were responding to his teaching.

have not separated themselves. The point was the difference of religion, not race, as the following verses indicate (vv. 10–12; 4:3 note).

the peoples of the lands. Of those listed, only the Ammonites, Moabites, and Egyptians were present in the days of Ezra. The others were in the land during the Conquest under Joshua, and the mention of them could have brought to mind the original prohibitions against intermarriage (Ex. 34:10–16; Deut. 7:1–4).

the [e]Levites have not separated themselves
from the peoples of the lands [f]with their
abominations, from the [g]Canaanites, the
Hittites, the Perizzites, the Jebusites, the
Ammonites, the Moabites, the Egyptians,
and the Amorites. **2** [h]For they have taken
some of their daughters to be wives for
themselves and for their sons, so that the
[i]holy race[1] has [j]mixed itself with the peoples of the lands. And in this faithlessness
the hand of the officials and chief men has
been foremost." **3** As soon as I heard this, I
[k]tore my garment and my cloak and pulled
hair from my head and beard and [l]sat
appalled. **4** Then all who [m]trembled at the
words of the God of Israel, because of the
faithlessness of the returned exiles, gathered around me while I sat [n]appalled until
the evening sacrifice. **5** And at the [n]evening
sacrifice I rose from my fasting, with my
garment [k]and my cloak torn, and fell upon
my knees [o]and spread out my hands to the
LORD my God, **6** saying:
"O my God, I am ashamed and blush to
lift my face to you, my God, for our iniquities
[p]have risen higher than our heads, and our
[q]guilt has [r]mounted up to the heavens.
7 [s]From the days of our fathers to this day we
have been in great [q]guilt. And for our iniquities we, our kings, and our priests have been
given into the hand of the kings of the lands,
to the sword, to captivity, to plundering,
[t]and to utter shame, as it is today. **8** But now
for a brief moment favor has been shown by
the LORD our God, to leave us a [u]remnant
and to give us a [v]secure hold[2] within his holy
place, that our God may [w]brighten our eyes
and grant us a little reviving in our slavery.
9 [x]For we are slaves. Yet our God has not forsaken us in our slavery, [y]but has extended to
us his steadfast love before the kings of
Persia, to grant us some reviving to set up the
house of our God, to repair its ruins, and to
give us protection[3] in Judea and Jerusalem.
10 "And now, O our God, what shall we
say after this? For we have forsaken your
commandments, **11** which you commanded
by your servants the prophets, saying, 'The

Chapter 9
1 [e][ch. 6:21; Neh. 9:2] [f]Deut. 12:30, 31 [g]See Ex. 13:5
2 [h]ch. 10:2; Neh. 13:23, 27; [Ex. 34:16; Deut. 7:3; Neh. 10:30] [i]See Deut. 7:6 [j]Ps. 106:35; [2 Cor. 6:14]
3 [k]See Josh. 7:6 [l][Neh. 1:4]
4 [m]ch. 10:3; Isai. 66:2, 5 [n]Ex. 29:39, 41
5 [n][See ver. 4 above] [k][See ver. 3 above] [o]1 Kin. 8:22
6 [p][Ps. 38:4] [q]ver. 7, 13, 15; ch. 10:10, 19; 2 Chr. 24:18 [r][2 Chr. 28:9; Rev. 18:5]
7 [s]Ps. 106:6; Dan. 9:5, 6 [q][See ver. 6 above] [t]Dan. 9:7, 8
8 [u]ver. 13, 14, 15 [v]Isai. 22:23 [w]Ps. 13:3 9 [x][Neh. 9:36] [y]ch. 7:28

1 Hebrew *offspring* 2 Hebrew *nail*, or *tent-pin* 3 Hebrew *a wall*

9:2 the holy race has mixed. The problem was not intermarriage of different ethnic groups, but the confusion of those set apart as holy by covenant with the Lord with those who were outside the covenant and therefore unclean (8:28, 29 note; 9:11–12 note).

the officials. The word for "officials" here is the same as in v. 1. Not all the leaders led people to sin; some led the way to reform.

9:3 I tore my garment and my cloak. This action was a typical way of expressing grief (2 Sam. 13:19).

pulled hair from my head and beard. This action is unusual. Some years later, Nehemiah would encounter the same sin, but rather than pulling out his own hair, he would pull out the hair of the offenders (Neh. 13:25).

9:4 all who trembled. There was a group who had not intermarried, but who had feared the Lord and kept His law (cf. Is. 66:2).

the evening sacrifice. Mid-afternoon, a time of prayer as well as sacrifice (Ps. 141:2).

9:5 fell upon my knees and spread out my hands. See 1 Kin. 8:54. Kneeling expresses humility before the majestic Lord (Ps. 95:6), and spreading the hands often accompanies petitions (Ps. 28:2).

9:6 ashamed and blush. Previously, Ezra had been ashamed to ask Artaxerxes for protection on the return trip (8:22). Now his shame is of a different kind, a shame joined with the guilt that results from sin.

our iniquities . . . our guilt. Ezra is acutely aware of the people's sin and guilt before God. Note also the sudden shift from "my" to "our." Though Ezra was not guilty of marrying into paganism, he identified himself with the people in their sin, as did the Suffering Servant of Isaiah (Is. 53:12; 2 Cor. 5:21).

9:7 From the days of our fathers. There was a sense of corporate solidarity and mutual responsibility that spanned the generations.

9:8 a brief moment. The status of the returnees as the recipients of God's favor was in jeopardy.

favor has been shown by the LORD . . . a remnant. Justice demanded the absolute end of the people of God, but grace preserved a remnant. Through this remnant the Messiah would come and redemption would be accomplished.

secure hold. The word translated "secure hold" means a stake that holds a tent in position (Judg. 4:21) or a nail that holds up objects that are hung on it (Is. 22:23–25). The Lord had given Israel a place in His temple, like the peg of a tent, and had made Ezra someone who could be trusted with burdens.

brighten our eyes. An idiom for increased vigor (Ps. 13:3).

9:9 we are slaves. Though restored to their land, the people of God were not politically independent, as they had been during the monarchy (4:19–23 note).

God has not forsaken us. God's promise not to forsake the nation was, in its outer, typological aspect, conditional (10:5 note). If Israel forsook God and the covenant by disregarding the law, she would forfeit the blessings and experience the curses (Deut. 28:20; 29:24–25; 31:16–17). But even so God would never finally desert Israel, through whom Christ would come. See Lev. 26:44, 45; Ps. 89:30–37; Is. 54:7; Rom. 11.

the kings of Persia. Specifically, Cyrus (550–530 B.C.), who issued the decree to return, Darius (522–486 B.C.), who confirmed the decree, and Artaxerxes (465–424 B.C.), who commissioned Ezra to teach the people.

protection in Judea and Jerusalem. This phrase does not refer to the wall built later by Nehemiah, but is a figure for the protection afforded the returnees (note the other figurative language in v. 8, and that the wall of Nehemiah was not built around all of Judah).

9:10 forsaken your commandments. Forsaking the commandments meant that covenant curses could fall upon the people at any time (v. 9 note on "forsaken us").

9:11 you commanded . . . saying. Moses was the prophet who gave the command initially (Deut. 7:1–3). The words are not a quotation of a single text, but a summary of the theology of separation taken from numerous texts, such as Lev. 18:25; Deut. 4:5; 7:3; 18:9; 27:3; 2 Kin. 21:16. The separation was not ethnic or racial but religious. Intermarriage with people outside the covenant introduced a relentless temptation to corrupt or abandon worship of the true and living God (cf. Deut. 7:3, 4; Judg. 14:1–4; 1 Kin. 11:1–4; 2 Cor. 6:14).

land that you are entering, to take possession of it, is a land impure with the impurity of the peoples of the lands, with their
abominations that have filled it from end to
end with [z]their uncleanness. 12 [a]Therefore
do not give your daughters to their sons,
neither take their daughters for your sons,
and never seek their peace or prosperity,
that you may be strong and eat the good of
the land [b]and leave it for an inheritance to
your children forever.' 13 And after all that
has come upon us for our evil deeds and
for [c]our great guilt, seeing that you, our
[d]God, have punished us less than our iniquities deserved and have given us such a
[e]remnant as this, 14 shall we break your
commandments again and [f]intermarry with
the peoples who practice these abominations? Would you not be angry with us
[g]until you consumed us, so that there
should be no [e]remnant, nor any to escape?
15 O LORD the God of Israel, you are just, for
we are left a [e]remnant that has escaped, as
it is today. Behold, we are before you in our
[h]guilt, [i]for none can stand before you
because of this."

The People Confess Their Sin

10 [j]While Ezra prayed and [k]made confession, weeping and [l]casting himself down [m]before the house of God, a very
great assembly of men, women, and children, gathered to him out of Israel, for the
people wept bitterly. 2 And Shecaniah the
son of Jehiel, of the sons of Elam,
addressed Ezra: [n]"We have broken faith
with our God and have married foreign
women from the peoples of the land, but
even now there is hope for Israel in spite of
this. 3 Therefore [o]let us make a covenant
with our God to put away all these wives
and [p]their children, according to the counsel of my lord and of [q]those who tremble at
the commandment of our God, and let it
be done [r]according to the Law. 4 Arise, for
it is your task, and we are with you; [s]be
strong and do it." 5 Then Ezra arose and
made the leading priests and Levites and
all Israel [t]take oath that they would do as
had been said. So they took the oath.
6 Then Ezra withdrew [u]from before the
house of God and went to the [v]chamber of
[w]Jehohanan the son of [x]Eliashib, where he
spent the night,[1] neither [y]eating bread nor
drinking water, for he was mourning over
the faithlessness of the exiles. 7 And a
proclamation was made throughout Judah
and Jerusalem to all the returned exiles
that they should assemble at Jerusalem,
8 and that if anyone did not come within
three days, by order of the officials and the
elders all his property should be forfeited,
and he himself banned from the congregation of the exiles.
9 Then all the men of Judah and
Benjamin assembled at Jerusalem within
the three days. It was the ninth month, on

11 [z]ch. 6:21
12 [a]See ver. 2 [b][Prov. 13:22]
13 [c]ver. 6, 7 [d]Job 11:6; Ps. 103:10 [e]ver. 8
14 [f]See ver. 2 [g][Deut. 9:8] [e][See ver. 13 above]
15 [e][See ver. 13 above] [h]Neh. 9:33; Ps. 119:137; Jer. 12:1; Dan. 9:14 [i]Ps. 130:3

Chapter 10
1 [j]Neh. 1:4, 5 [k]Neh. 1:6; Dan. 9:20 [l]Deut. 9:18 [m][2 Chr. 20:9]
2 [n]See 9:2
3 [o]2 Chr. 34:31 [p][ch. 10:44] [q]ch. 9:4 [r]Deut. 7:2, 3
4 [s]1 Chr. 28:10; [2 Chr. 19:11]
5 [t]Neh. 5:12; 13:25
6 [u]ver. 1 [v]ch. 8:29 [w]Neh. 12:22, 23 [x]Neh. 3:1 [y]Deut. 9:18

1 Probable reading; Hebrew *where he went*

9:13 less than our iniquities deserved. The restoration was on the basis of grace and the promise of the Abrahamic covenant (Deut. 4:25–31). So also was the initial entrance into the land (Deut. 9:5).

9:14 no remnant. Ezra fears that the current covenant breach might result in ultimate judgment. Though judgment would later come upon the nation (Luke 20:9–19), even then there would be a remnant according to grace (Rom. 11:1–5).

9:15 Ezra's conclusion is that even now the people live only because of God's grace.

10:1 Ezra . . . weeping. Other leaders had set the pace for sin (9:2). Now Ezra set the pace for repentance, not by exhorting the people to mourn, but by mourning himself.

10:2 Ezra's confession in 9:13, 14 became the confession of the people through one of their leaders, Shecaniah.

there is hope. Shecaniah encouraged Ezra that all was not lost.

10:3 make a covenant. This was not an entirely new covenant, but the renewal of the Mosaic covenant in terms of an oath (v. 5) to keep the stipulation regarding intermarriage (Deut. 7:3; cf. Jer. 34:8–22 for a similar covenant renewal).

to put away. This is not the usual Hebrew phrase for divorce, and is used only here for putting away a wife. The Hebrew expression in v. 2 ("have married . . . women") is not the usual phrase for marriage, and is used in the same way only in Neh. 13, in an analogous situation. The author's choice of language seems to indicate that he did not regard the unions as legitimate marriages, nor the sending away as actual divorce.

according to the Law. The law does not provide explicitly for this exact situation. The phrase may refer to sending a woman away with her children, some provisions (Gen. 21:14), and certain legal rights (Deut. 21:10–14).

10:5 Ezra arose. Ezra responded to the encouragement of Shecaniah and put his advice into practice.

made . . . all Israel take oath. The covenant was conditional, as the swearing of the oath by the Israelites and not by the Lord indicates (9:9 note; Jer. 34:8–22).

10:6 the chamber. Located in the temple.

neither eating bread nor drinking water. A total fast was rare (Deut. 9:18). The fast indicates that Ezra did not think the exiles were immune to the covenant punishments on the basis of an oath alone.

10:8 within three days. Three days was sufficient time for any who wished to travel to Jerusalem, owing to the reduced territory of Judah.

forfeited . . . banned. Failure to comply would have resulted in the loss of property and excommunication (7:26).

10:9 Judah and Benjamin. See note 1:5.

the ninth month, on the twentieth day of the month. It was December, in the cold and rainy season. Jerusalem is colder than most of

the twentieth day of the month. And all the
people sat in the open square before the
house of God, trembling because of this
matter and because of the [z]heavy rain.
10 And Ezra the priest stood up and said to
them, "You have broken faith and married
foreign women, and so increased the guilt
of Israel. 11 Now then [a]make confession to
the LORD, the God of your fathers and do
his will. [b]Separate yourselves from the peoples of the land and from the foreign
wives." 12 Then all the assembly answered
with a loud voice, "It is so; we must do as
you have said. 13 But the people are many,
and it is a time of heavy rain; we cannot
stand in the open. Nor is this a task for one
day or for two, for we have greatly transgressed in this matter. 14 Let our officials
stand for the whole assembly. Let all in our
cities who have taken foreign wives come
[c]at appointed times, and with them the
elders and judges of every city, [d]until the
fierce wrath of our God over this matter is
turned away from us." 15 Only Jonathan the
son of Asahel and Jahzeiah the son of
Tikvah opposed this, and [e]Meshullam and
[f]Shabbethai the Levite supported them.

16 Then the returned exiles did so. Ezra the
priest selected men,[1] heads of fathers' houses, according to their fathers' houses, each of
them designated by name. On the first day of
the tenth month they sat down to examine
the matter; 17 and by the first day of the first
month they had come to the end of all the
men who had married foreign women.

Those Guilty of Intermarriage

18 Now there were found some of the sons
of the priests who had married foreign
women: Maaseiah, Eliezer, Jarib, and
Gedaliah, some of the sons of [g]Jeshua the
son of Jozadak and his brothers. 19 They
[h]pledged themselves to put away their wives,
and their guilt offering was [i]a ram of the flock
for their guilt.[2] 20 [j]Of the sons of Immer:
Hanani and Zebadiah. 21 [k]Of the sons of
Harim: Maaseiah, Elijah, Shemaiah, Jehiel,
and Uzziah. 22 Of the sons of Pashhur:
Elioenai, Maaseiah, Ishmael, Nethanel, Jozabad, and Elasah.

23 Of the Levites: Jozabad, Shimei,
Kelaiah (that is, Kelita), Pethahiah, Judah,
and Eliezer. 24 Of the singers: Eliashib. Of
the gatekeepers: Shallum, Telem, and Uri.

25 And of Israel: of the sons of Parosh:
Ramiah, Izziah, Malchijah, Mijamin, Eleazar,
Hashabiah,[3] and Benaiah. 26 Of the sons of
Elam: Mattaniah, Zechariah, Jehiel, Abdi,
Jeremoth, and Elijah. 27 Of the sons of Zattu:
Elioenai, Eliashib, Mattaniah, Jeremoth,
Zabad, and Aziza. 28 Of the sons of Bebai
were Jehohanan, Hananiah, Zabbai, and
Athlai. 29 Of the sons of Bani were Meshul-
lam, Malluch, Adaiah, Jashub, Sheal, and
Jeremoth. 30 Of the sons of Pahath-moab:
Adna, Chelal, Benaiah, Maaseiah, Mattaniah,
Bezalel, Binnui, and Manasseh. 31 Of the
[l]sons of Harim: Eliezer, Isshijah, Malchijah,
Shemaiah, Shimeon, 32 Benjamin, Malluch,
and Shemariah. 33 Of the sons of Hashum:
Mattenai, Mattattah, Zabad, Eliphelet, Jere-
mai, Manasseh, and Shimei. 34 Of the sons of
[m]Bani: Maadai, Amram, Uel, 35 Benaiah,
Bedeiah, Cheluhi, 36 Vaniah, Meremoth,
Eliashib, 37 Mattaniah, Mattenai, Jaasu. 38 Of
the sons of Binnui:[4] Shimei, 39 Shelemiah,
Nathan, Adaiah, 40 Machnadebai, Shashai,
Sharai, 41 Azarel, Shelemiah, Shemariah,
42 Shallum, Amariah, and Joseph. 43 Of the
sons of Nebo: Jeiel, Mattithiah, Zabad,
Zebina, Jaddai, Joel, and Benaiah. 44 All these
had married foreign women, and some of the
women [n]had even borne children.[5]

9 [z][1 Sam. 12:18]
11 [a][Josh. 7:19] [b]ver. 3
14 [c]Neh. 13:31 [d]2 Chr. 29:10; 30:8; [Num. 25:4
15 [e]ch. 8:16 [f]Neh. 11:16
18 [g]ch. 3:2
19 [h]See 2 Kin. 10:15
[i]Lev. 6:6
20 [j]For ver. 20, 43, see ch. 2:3, 41
21 [k][ver. 31]
31 [l]ver. 21
34 [m][ver. 29]
44 [n][ver. 3]

1 Syriac; Hebrew *And there were selected Ezra . . .* 2 Or *as their reparation* 3 Septuagint; Hebrew *Malchijah* 4 Septuagint; Hebrew *Bani, Binnui* 5 Or *and they put them away with their children*

the countryside around it, and rainfall in the region is more concentrated than in temperate climates.

all the people. The people as a whole responded to the proclamation.

trembling because of this matter. Ezra's distress had spread throughout the populace (v. 1 note).

10:11 make confession. Lit. "give thanks and praise to." When a person confesses sin and trusts in God for mercy, praise is given to God. In Psalm 103 the psalmist "blesses" God by confessing who God is and what He has done.

do his will. Confession must lead to repentance (v. 6 note).

Separate yourselves. See note 9:11–12.

10:12 all the assembly answered. Not only had all the men assembled and expressed their distress (v. 9), but they also agreed with Ezra as to their sin and guilt.

10:13 But. This was not an attempt to escape the responsibility to repent, but an expression of genuine concern that the repentance be carried out well.

10:15 opposed this. They probably opposed the delay, though they may have opposed the sending away of the foreign women.

10:18–44 From this list of those guilty of intermarriage it is evident that the individual who sins cannot find sanctuary within the larger community (Deut. 29:19–21). But for those who will avail themselves of the sacrifice provided by God there is always forgiveness (v. 19).

THE BOOK OF

Nehemiah

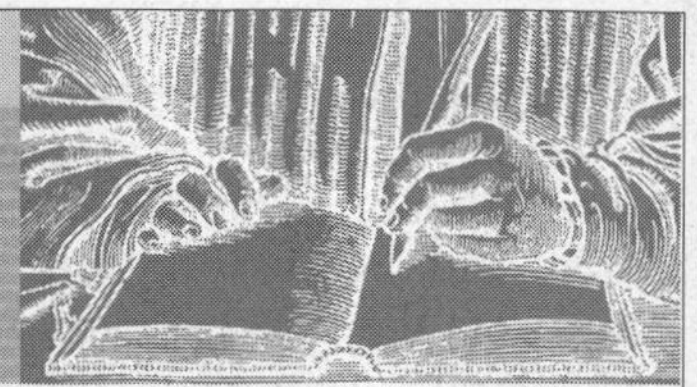

AUTHOR

Ezra and Nehemiah were originally a single book composed from a variety of historical sources, including the personal memoirs of Ezra and Nehemiah. According to Jewish tradition, Ezra was responsible for compiling these sources into their current form (see "Introduction to Ezra: Author").

DATE AND OCCASION

Assuming the traditional view of authorship, these narratives were written during the period 430–400 B.C. to encourage the Judeans who had returned from exile in Babylon and were reestablishing their community in and around Jerusalem (see "Introduction to Ezra: Date and Occasion").

CHARACTERISTICS AND THEMES

The major theme of Ezra and Nehemiah is that God works sovereignly through responsible human agents to accomplish His redemptive purpose. The author develops this theme in Nehemiah with particular attention to the rebuilding and dedication of the defensive walls of Jerusalem (1:1–7:3; 12:27–43) and the reconstitution of the whole people called "Israel" in their covenant relationship with God (7:4–13:31). See "Introduction to Ezra: Characteristics and Themes" for further discussion of the themes of Ezra and Nehemiah as a whole.

OUTLINE OF NEHEMIAH

I. Return of Nehemiah and Rebuilding of the Wall (1:1–7:3)

- *A. Return of Nehemiah (1:1–2:10)*
  1. Preparations for the Return (1:1–2:8)
     - *a. Report from Judah (1:1–3)*
     - *b. Response of Nehemiah (1:4–11)*
     - *c. Request Before the King (2:1–8)*
  2. The Trip and the Beginning of the Conflict (2:9, 10)
- *B. Rebuilding the Wall (2:11–7:3)*
  1. Inspection and Proposal (2:11–18)
  2. First Escalation of the Conflict (2:19, 20)
  3. Rebuilding Begun (ch. 3)
  4. Second Escalation of the Conflict (4:1–6)
  5. Rebuilding Continued (4:7–23)
  6. Internal Problems Threaten the Rebuilding (ch. 5)
  7. Climax of the Conflict (6:1–14)
  8. End of the Conflict (6:15–7:3)

II. Return of the Exiles and Rebuilding the Community (7:4–13:31)

- *A. Return of the Exiles (7:4–73)*
  1. The Need to Repopulate Jerusalem (7:4, 5)
  2. Record of Returnees (7:6–73)
- *B. Rebuilding the Community (7:73–13:31)*
  1. Renewing the Covenant (7:73–10:39)
     - *a. Reading of the Law (7:73–8:18)*
     - *b. Confession of Sin (9:1–37)*
     - *c. Ratification of the Oath (9:38–10:39)*
  2. Dedication of the Wall (chs. 11; 12)
     - *a. Listing of Residents (ch. 11)*
     - *b. Listing of Priests and Levites (12:1–26)*
     - *c. The Dedication Proper (12:27–43)*
     - *d. Provisions for Clergy (12:44–47)*
  3. Reformation of the People (ch. 13)
     - *a. Exclusion of Foreigners (13:1–3)*
     - *b. Attention to the Temple (13:4–14)*
     - *c. Observance of the Sabbath (13:15–22)*
     - *d. The End of Intermarriage (13:23–31)*

Report from Jerusalem

1 The words of [a]Nehemiah the son of
Hacaliah.
Now it happened in the month of
[b]Chislev, [c]in the twentieth year, as I was in
[d]Susa the capital,[1] **2** that [e]Hanani, one of
my brothers, came with certain men from
Judah. And I asked them concerning the
Jews who escaped, who had survived the
exile, and concerning Jerusalem. **3** And they
said to me, "The remnant there in the
province who had survived the exile is in
great trouble and [f]shame. [g]The wall of
Jerusalem is broken down, [h]and its gates
are destroyed by fire."

Nehemiah's Prayer

4 As soon as I heard these words I [i]sat
down and wept and mourned for days, and
I continued fasting and praying before the
[j]God of heaven. **5** And I said, "O LORD God
of heaven, [k]the great and awesome God
who keeps covenant and steadfast love
with those who love him and keep his
commandments, **6** [l]let your ear be attentive
and your eyes open, to hear the prayer of
your servant that I now pray before you day
and night for the people of Israel your servants, [m]confessing the sins of the people of
Israel, which we have sinned against you.
Even [n]I and my father's house have sinned.
7 [o]We have acted very corruptly against you
and have not kept the commandments, the
statutes, and the rules [p]that you commanded your servant Moses. **8** Remember
the word that you commanded your servant Moses, saying, 'If you are unfaithful, [q]I
will scatter you among the peoples, **9** [r]but if
you return to me and keep my commandments and do them, [s]though your dispersed be under the farthest skies, I will
gather them from there and bring them [t]to
the place that I have chosen, to make my
name dwell there.' **10** [u]They are your servants and your people, whom you have
redeemed by your great power and by your
strong hand. **11** O Lord, [l]let your ear be
attentive to the prayer of your servant, and
to the prayer of your servants who delight
to fear your name, and give success to your
servant today, and grant him mercy in the
sight of this man."
Now I was [v]cupbearer to the king.

Nehemiah Sent to Judah

2 In the month of Nisan, [w]in the twentieth year of King [x]Artaxerxes, when
wine was before him, [y]I took up the wine
and gave it to the king. Now I had not been
sad in his presence. **2** And the king said to
me, "Why is your face sad, seeing you are

Chapter 1
1 [a]ch. 10:1 [b]Zech. 7:1 [c]ch. 2:1 [d]Esth. 1:2, 5; 2:3, 5
2 [e]ch. 7:2
3 [f]ch. 2:17 [g]ch. 2:13; 2 Kin. 25:10 [h]ch. 2:3, 13, 17
4 [i][Ezra 9:3] [j]ch. 2:4
5 [k]ch. 9:32; Dan. 9:4; [Deut. 7:21]
6 [l]Dan. 9:18; [1 Kin. 8:29; 2 Chr. 6:40] [m]Ezra 10:1; Dan. 9:20 [n][Ps. 106:6]
7 [o]Dan. 9:5 [p]Deut. 28:15
8 [q]Lev. 26:33; Deut. 28:64; See Deut. 4:25-27
9 [r]Lev. 26:39-42; Deut. 4:29-31; 30:2, 3 [s]Deut. 30:4 [t]Deut. 12:5
10 [u]Deut. 9:29
11 [l][See ver. 6 above] [v][ch. 2:1]
Chapter 2
1 [w]ch. 1:1; 5:14 [x]Ezra 7:1 [y][ch. 1:11]

[1] Or *the fortified city*

1:1 The words of. The introductory phrase does not mean that the Book of Nehemiah was originally separate. It may indicate the beginning of personal records or memoirs by Nehemiah (Introduction: Author).

Nehemiah. The name means "the LORD has comforted."

Chislev . . . twentieth year. November-December 446 B.C., the twentieth year of Artaxerxes I (2:1; Ezra 7:1).

Susa. This city was a winter residence of the Persian kings (Esth. 1:2 note).

1:2 Hanani. A short form of Hananiah, it means "the LORD is gracious." A certain Hananiah who was head of Jewish affairs is mentioned in the Elephantine papyri, and is believed by some to have been the brother of Nehemiah (7:2).

1:3 its gates are destroyed by fire. Perhaps this destruction was the result of the events recorded in Ezra 4:7–23, but the reference to "gates" makes the destruction by Nebuchadnezzar in 586 B.C. more likely.

1:4 fasting and praying. Fasting is here connected with mourning (1 Sam. 31:13) as well as with making a request of God (Ezra 8:21 note). Nehemiah was a man of prayer (2:4; 4:4, 9; 5:19; 6:9, 14; 13:14, 22, 29, 31).

the God of heaven. See notes Ezra 1:2; Dan. 4:37.

1:5 In this address Nehemiah captures both the transcendence of God and His immanence. The true God is not only far above His people as the God of heaven (v. 4 note); He is near His people as the God of the covenant (Deut. 4:7).

steadfast love. See note Ezra 7:28.

1:6 day and night. The reference is to the prayer of one particular day (v. 11), after four months of prayer and fasting (1:4; 2:1 note). "Day and night" means "continually" (Josh. 1:8; Ps. 1:2).

1:7 The Mosaic covenant was conditional: the Lord would keep His promises if Israel obeyed His commands (v. 5). Israel failed to obey His commands and the result was exile (Ezra 9:9 note).

1:8 Remember. A common petition (Deut. 9:27; Ps. 132:1; Jer. 14:21), particularly in Nehemiah (5:19; 6:14; 13:14, 22, 29, 31).

1:9 I will gather them. The Mosaic covenant promised restoration of a remnant after exile (Deut. 30:1–5) on the basis of the covenant made with Abraham (Deut. 4:25–31).

make my name dwell there. The name of God symbolizes God Himself, as He reveals Himself to His people. A place for His name to dwell is a place for Him to be with the people and to receive their worship (Deut. 12:5 note).

1:10 redeemed. The reference is to the Exodus (Ex. 32:11; Mic. 6:4).

1:11 who delight to fear your name. The fear of the Lord is the proper response to God's self-revelation. To fear God is to know Him (Prov. 9:10), to trust Him (Ps. 34:11, 22), to obey Him (Prov. 8:13), and to show Him reverence.

this man. Artaxerxes I.

cupbearer. A member of the royal court, whose responsibility was to choose wine (2:1) and safeguard it from poison. The steward's access to the king secured prestige and influence at court.

2:1 Nisan . . . twentieth year. The date was March-April 445 B.C., four months after Nehemiah received the report about Jerusalem. The Persian New Year or another holiday may be indicated by the use of wine (cf. 1:11 note).

King Artaxerxes. See note Ezra 4:7.

not sick? This is nothing but [z]sadness of
the heart." Then I was very much afraid. 3 I
said to the king, [a]"Let the king live forever!
Why should not my face be sad, [b]when the
city, the place of my fathers' graves, lies in
ruins, and its gates have been destroyed by
fire?" 4 Then the king said to me, "What are
you requesting?" So I prayed [c]to the God of
heaven. 5 And I said to the king, "If it pleases the king, and if your servant has found
favor in your sight, that you send me to
Judah, to the city of my fathers' graves, that
I may rebuild it." 6 And the king said to me
([d]the queen sitting beside him), "How long
will you be gone, and when will you
return?" So it pleased the king to send me
[e]when I had given him a time. 7 And I said
to the king, "If it pleases the king, let letters
be given me [f]to the governors of the
province Beyond the River, that they may
let me pass through until I come to Judah,
8 and a letter to Asaph, the keeper of the
king's forest, that he may give me timber to
make beams for the gates of [g]the fortress of
the temple, and for the wall of the city, and
for the house that I shall occupy." And the
king granted me what I asked, [h]for the
good hand of my God was upon me.

Nehemiah Inspects Jerusalem's Walls

9 Then I came to [i]the governors of the
province Beyond the River and gave them
the king's letters. Now the king had sent
with me officers of the army and horsemen.

2 [z]Prov. 15:13
3 [a]1 Kin. 1:31; Dan. 2:4; 5:10; 6:21 [b]ver. 13, 17; ch. 1:3
4 [c]ver. 20; ch. 1:4, 5; Ezra 5:12; Dan. 2:18
6 [d][Ps. 45:9] [e][ch. 5:14; 13:6]
7 [f]Ezra 8:36
8 [g]ch. 7:2 [h]ver. 18; See Ezra 7:6
9 [i]Ezra 8:36
10 [j]ver. 19; ch. 4:1, 7; 6:1, 2, 5, 12, 14; 13:28 [k]ch. 13:4
11 [l]Ezra 8:32
13 [m]ch. 3:13; 2 Chr. 26:9 [n]ch. 3:13, 14; 12:31 [o]ch. 1:3 [p]ver. 3, 17
14 [q]ch. 3:15; 12:37 [r]2 Kin. 20:20; [ch. 3:16; 2 Chr. 32:3, 30]
15 [s]2 Sam. 15:23
17 [t]ver. 3:13; ch. 1:3 [u]ch. 1:3; Ps.44:13; 79:4; Jer. 24:9; Ezek. 5:14, 15; 22:4
18 [v]ver. 8

10 But when [j]Sanballat the Horonite and
[k]Tobiah, the Ammonite servant, heard this,
it displeased them greatly that someone
had come to seek the welfare of the people
of Israel.
11 [l]So I went to Jerusalem and was there
three days. 12 Then I arose in the night, I
and a few men with me. And I told no one
what my God had put into my heart to do
for Jerusalem. There was no animal with me
but the one on which I rode. 13 I went out by
night by [m]the Valley Gate to the Dragon
Spring and to [n]the Dung Gate, and I
inspected the walls of Jerusalem [o]that were
broken down [p]and its gates that had been
destroyed by fire. 14 Then I went on to [q]the
Fountain Gate and to [r]the King's Pool, but
there was no room for the animal that was
under me to pass. 15 Then I went up in the
night [s]by the valley and inspected the wall,
and I turned back and entered by the Valley
Gate, and so returned. 16 And the officials
did not know where I had gone or what I
was doing, and I had not yet told the Jews,
the priests, the nobles, the officials, and the
rest who were to do the work.
17 Then I said to them, "You see the trouble we are in, [t]how Jerusalem lies in ruins
with its gates burned. Come, let us build
the wall of Jerusalem, that we may no
longer [u]suffer derision." 18 And I told them
[v]of the hand of my God that had been
upon me for good, and also of the words

2:2 very much afraid. Nehemiah feared the king's wrath (Prov. 16:14) because he was sad on a festive occasion, or because he was about to ask the king to reverse a previous decision (Ezra 4:21). Nehemiah may also have feared that he would be refused the permission he sought.

2:5 that I may rebuild it. Rebuilding the city is one aspect of rebuilding the "house of God" (cf. Num. 12:7), a major theme in Ezra and Nehemiah (Introduction to Ezra: Characteristics and Themes). It is the focus of Neh. 1:1–7:3.

2:6 How long . . . given him a time. It may seem doubtful that Nehemiah requested the twelve-year absence presumed in 5:14, but his request to rebuild his personal residence (v. 8) seems to indicate that more than a brief leave was in view from the beginning.

2:7 And I said. Nehemiah now makes his specific requests.

letters. The two references to letters in vv. 7, 8 are part of a major theme in Ezra and Nehemiah: the written word is an effective instrument used by God to accomplish His redemptive purpose (Introduction to Ezra: Characteristics and Themes).

2:8 timber . . . for the gates. The scope of the building project becomes clear: fortress, walls, governor's residence.

the good hand of my God. Nehemiah acts as a responsible human agent in making the request, but the success is from God's sovereign good pleasure (Ezra 7:6). This theme expresses the overarching message of Ezra and Nehemiah (Introduction to Ezra: Characteristics and Themes).

2:10 Sanballat. A Babylonian name, meaning "Sin (the moon god) gives life." Sanballat and his descendants served for more than a century as the governors of Samaria, the area north of Judah. He may have worshiped the God of Israel in some fashion (2 Kin. 17:24–41), since the names of his sons, Delaiah and Shelemiah, end with a short form of "Yahweh."

Tobiah. Probably the governor of Ammon, east of Judah. The name means "the LORD is good," indicating that he, too, may have worshiped the God of Israel (6:17, 18; 13:4).

heard. References to the enemies having "heard" will punctuate the rest of 1:1–7:3 like a refrain (v. 19; 4:1, 7, 15; 6:1, 16). The conflict escalates until it is resolved in 6:16.

displeased them greatly. The opposition had a political aspect, but was religious at its root (v. 20; Ezra 4:13 notes).

2:11–18 Soon after returning to Jerusalem, Nehemiah conducts a night-time inspection of the walls and, aware of God's blessing upon him, advises the officials of the city to rebuild them.

2:11–16 Nehemiah's three-day wait after arriving in Jerusalem invites a comparison with Ezra (Ezra 8:32). Ezra acted publicly, Nehemiah secretly (that Nehemiah had "told no one" is emphasized in v. 12; cf. v. 16).

2:17 in ruins. The city had lain in ruins for almost 150 years (1:3 note). An earlier attempt to rebuild the wall had been stopped (Ezra 4:7–23). Nehemiah's presence would change all that.

build the wall. See note on v. 5.

2:18 also of the words that the king had spoken. Nehemiah's acknowledgment of God's sovereignty as the ultimate source of his plan does not exclude the providentially ordered actions of the king (v. 8 note).

that the king had spoken to me. And they
said, "Let us rise up and build." [w]So they
strengthened their hands for the good
work. **19** But when Sanballat the Horonite
and Tobiah the Ammonite servant and
[x]Geshem the Arab heard of it, [y]they jeered
at us and despised us and said, "What is
this thing that you are doing? [z]Are you
rebelling against the king?" **20** Then I replied
to them, [a]"The God of heaven will make us
prosper, and we his servants will arise and
build, but you have no portion or right or
claim[1] in Jerusalem."

Rebuilding the Wall

3 Then [b]Eliashib the high priest rose up
with his brothers the priests, and they
built [c]the Sheep Gate. They consecrated it
and [d]set its doors. They consecrated it as
far as the Tower of the Hundred, as far as
the [e]Tower of Hananel. **2** And next to him
[f]the men of Jericho built. And next to
them[2] Zaccur the son of Imri built.
3 The sons of Hassenaah built [g]the Fish
Gate. [h]They laid its beams and [d]set its doors,
its bolts, and its bars. **4** And next to them
[i]Meremoth the son of Uriah, son of Hakkoz
repaired. And next to them [j]Meshullam the
son of Berechiah, son of Meshezabel
repaired. And next to them Zadok the son of
Baana repaired. **5** And next to them [k]the
Tekoites repaired, but their nobles would
not stoop to serve their Lord.[3]
6 [l]Joiada the son of Paseah and Meshullam the son of Besodeiah [l]repaired the
Gate of Yeshanah.[4] [h]They laid its beams
and [d]set its doors, its bolts, and its bars.
7 And next to them repaired Melatiah the
Gibeonite and Jadon the Meronothite, the
men of Gibeon and of Mizpah, the seat of
[m]the governor of the province Beyond the
River. **8** Next to them Uzziel the son of
Harhaiah, goldsmiths, repaired. Next to
him Hananiah, one of the perfumers,
repaired, and they restored Jerusalem as far
as [n]the Broad Wall. **9** Next to them
Rephaiah the son of Hur, [o]ruler of half the
district of[5] Jerusalem, repaired. **10** Next to
them Jedaiah the son of Harumaph
repaired opposite his house. And next to
him Hattush the son of Hashabneiah
repaired. **11** Malchijah the son of Harim and
Hasshub the son of Pahath-moab repaired
another section and [p]the Tower of the
Ovens. **12** Next to him Shallum the son of
Hallohesh, [q]ruler of half the district of
Jerusalem, repaired, he and his daughters.
13 Hanun and the inhabitants of Zanoah
repaired [r]the Valley Gate. They rebuilt it
and [s]set its doors, its bolts, and its bars,
and repaired a thousand cubits[6] of the
wall, as far as [t]the Dung Gate.
14 Malchijah the son of Rechab, ruler of
the district of [u]Beth-haccherem, repaired

18 [w][2 Sam. 2:7]
19 [x][ch. 6:6] [y]ch. 4:1; Ps. 44:13 [z]ch. 6:6
20 [a]ver. 4
Chapter 3
1 [b]ver. 20, 21; ch. 13:4, 7, 28 [c]ver. 32; ch. 12:39; John 5:2 [d]ch. 6:1; 7:1 [e]Jer. 31:38; Zech. 14:10
2 [f]Ezra 2:34
3 [g]ch. 12:39; 2 Chr. 33:14; Zeph. 1:10 [h][ch. 2:8] [d][See 2:6 above]
4 [i]ver. 21; Ezra 8:33 [j]ver. 30; Ezra 8:16
5 [k]ver. 27; [2 Sam. 14:2]
6 [l]ch. 12:39 [h][See ver. 3 above] [d][See ver. 1 above]
7 [m]ch. 2:7, 9
8 [n]ch. 12:38
9 [o]ver. 12
11 [p]ch. 12:38
12 [q]ver. 9
13 [r]ch. 2:13, 15; 2 Chr. 26:9 [s]See ver. 1 [t]ch. 2:13; 12:31
14 [u]Jer. 6:1

[1] Or *memorial* [2] Hebrew *him* [3] Or *lords* [4] Or *of the old city*
[5] Or *foreman of half the portion assigned to*; also verses 12, 14, 15, 16, 17, 18 [6] A *cubit* was about 18 inches or 45 centimeters

Let us rise up. Nehemiah's initiative met with wholehearted support on the part of the leaders of Judah; by now the reader knows that this response, too, is governed by God's purpose (Ezra 1:5 note).

2:19 Sanballat . . . Tobiah. See v. 10 and note.

Geshem the Arab. This third opponent of Nehemiah was probably an Arab chief controlling the area south of Judah. Nehemiah is pictured as virtually surrounded by enemies—Sanballat to the north, Tobiah to the east, and Geshem to the south (4:7, 8 note).

2:20 God of heaven. See note 1:4.

prosper. Nehemiah had requested success from God in 1:11. Now he expresses confidence that the sovereign God will prosper the people.

you have no portion. On this religious exclusivity, see the note on Ezra 4:3.

3:1–32 This chapter underscores an important theme of Ezra and Nehemiah: the people of God as a whole and not just the great leaders are vital for accomplishing God's redemptive purpose. All of God's people worked together to rebuild the wall: clergy and laity, craftsmen and tradesmen, by town and by family, each contributing to the completion of the whole (cf. Eph. 4:16).

3:1 Eliashib. He was the grandson of Jeshua, the High Priest during the days of Zerubbabel.

Sheep Gate. This gate was at the northeast corner of the city (cf. John 5:2). The description in the following verses moves counterclockwise until the Sheep Gate is mentioned again in v. 32.

Tower of the Hundred. This would have been somewhere on the north side, the side with the poorest natural defenses.

Tower of Hananel. A tower on the north side.

3:3 Fish Gate. A main gate on the north side (2 Chr. 33:14; Zeph. 1:10), this was probably the gate used by merchants (cf. 13:16).

3:5 their nobles would not. Though the text presents an amazing picture of unanimity, it notes realistically that not all of God's people were in harmony with what the Lord was doing through Nehemiah.

3:6 Gate of Yeshanah. A gate on the northwest corner of the city.

3:8 Broad Wall. A wall on the west side of the northern half of the city.

3:10 opposite his house. Probably others too, like Jedaiah, worked on the sections near their homes.

3:11 Tower of the Ovens. A tower on the west side of the city, perhaps midway.

3:12 he and his daughters. This phrase is an extraordinary testimony to the dedication of the whole community to the task of rebuilding (5:1 note; 12:43 note).

3:13 Valley Gate. On the west side of the city facing the Tyropean Valley.

Dung Gate. On the southwest corner of the city facing the Hinnom Valley.

[t]the Dung Gate. He rebuilt it and [s]set its
doors, its bolts, and its bars.
15 And Shallum the son of Col-hozeh,
ruler of the district of Mizpah, repaired [v]the
Fountain Gate. He rebuilt it and covered it
and [s]set its doors, its bolts, and its bars.
And he built the wall of [w]the Pool of Shelah
of [x]the king's garden, as far as [y]the stairs
that go down from the City of David.
16 After him Nehemiah the son of Azbuk,
ruler of half the district of Beth-zur,
repaired to a point opposite [z]the tombs of
David, as far as [a]the artificial pool, and as
far as the house of the mighty men. 17 After
him the Levites repaired: Rehum the son of
Bani. Next to him Hashabiah, ruler of half
the district of Keilah, repaired for his district. 18 After him their brothers repaired:
Bavvai the son of Henadad, ruler of half the
district of Keilah. 19 Next to him Ezer the
son of Jeshua, ruler of Mizpah, repaired
another section opposite the ascent to the
armory at [b]the buttress.[1] 20 After him
Baruch the son of Zabbai repaired another
section from the buttress to the door of the
house of [c]Eliashib the high priest. 21 After
him [d]Meremoth the son of Uriah, son of
Hakkoz repaired another section from the
door of the house of Eliashib to the end of
the house of Eliashib. 22 After him the
priests, the men of [e]the surrounding area,
repaired. 23 After them Benjamin and
Hasshub repaired opposite their house.
After them Azariah the son of Maaseiah,
son of Ananiah repaired beside his own
house. 24 After him Binnui the son of
Henadad repaired another section, from
the house of Azariah to the buttress 25 and
to [f]the corner. Palal the son of Uzai
repaired opposite the buttress and the
tower projecting from the upper house of
the king at [g]the court of the guard. After
him Pedaiah the son of Parosh 26 [h]and the
temple servants living on [i]Ophel repaired
to a point opposite [j]the Water Gate on the
east and the projecting tower. 27 After him
[k]the Tekoites repaired another section
opposite the great projecting tower as far as
the wall of Ophel.
28 Above [l]the Horse Gate the priests
repaired, each one opposite his own house.
29 After them Zadok the son of Immer
repaired opposite his own house. After him
Shemaiah the son of Shecaniah, the keeper
of the East Gate, repaired. 30 After him
Hananiah the son of Shelemiah and Hanun
the sixth son of Zalaph repaired another
section. After him [m]Meshullam the son of
Berechiah repaired opposite [n]his chamber.
31 After him Malchijah, one of the goldsmiths, repaired as far as the house of the
temple servants and of the merchants,
opposite the Muster Gate,[2] and to the
upper chamber of the corner. 32 And between the upper chamber of the corner and
[o]the Sheep Gate the goldsmiths and the
merchants [p]repaired.

Opposition to the Work

4 [3] Now when [q]Sanballat heard that we
were building the wall, he was angry and
greatly enraged, and he jeered at the Jews.
2 And he said in the presence of his brothers
and of the army of [r]Samaria, "What are these
feeble Jews doing? Will they restore it for
themselves?[4] Will they sacrifice? Will they
finish up in a day? Will they revive the stones
out of the heaps of rubbish, and burned ones
at that?" 3 [q]Tobiah the Ammonite was beside
him, and he said, "Yes, what they are building—[s]if a fox goes up on it he will break
down their stone wall!" 4 [t]Hear, O our God,
for we are despised. [u]Turn back their taunt
on their own heads and give them up to
be plundered in a land where they are
captives. 5 [v]Do not cover their guilt, and let

14 [t][See ver. 13 above] [s][See ver. 13 above]
15 [v]ch. 2:14 [s][See ver. 13 above] [w][Luke 13:4; John 9:7, 11] [x]2 Kin. 25:4 [y]ch. 12:37
16 [z]1 Kin. 2:10; Acts 2:29 [a]2 Kin. 20:20; Isai. 22:11
19 [b]2 Chr. 26:9
20 [c]ver. 1
21 [d]ver. 4
22 [e]ch. 12:28
25 [f][2 Kin. 14:13] [g]Jer. 32:2; 33:1; 37:21; 38:6, 13, 28; 39:14; [ch. 12:39]
26 [h]ch. 11:21 [i]2 Chr. 27:3
[j]ch. 8:1, 3, 16; 12:37
27 [k]ver. 5
28 [l]See 2 Chr. 23:15
30 [m]ver. 4 [n][ch. 12:44; 13:7]
32 [o]See ver. 1 [p]ch. 3:33
Chapter 4
1 [q]ver. 7; ch. 2:10, 19
2 [r]1 Kin. 16:24
3 [q][See ver. 1 above] [s][Lam. 5:18]
4 [t]Ps. 123:3, 4 [u]Ps. 79:12
5 [v]Ps. 69:27, 28; 109:14, 15; Jer. 18:23

[1] Or *corner*; also verses 20, 24, 25 [2] Or *Hammiphkad Gate*
[3] Ch 3:33 in Hebrew [4] Or *Will they commit themselves to God?*

3:15 Fountain Gate. On the southeast corner of the city facing the Kidron Valley.

City of David. Though in disrepair, it was still the city David established to be the political and religious capital of the theocracy. There is continuity between the past and present generations (Ezra 2:1–70 note).

3:26 Ophel. Ophel has usually been located south of the temple mount, but more probably it included also the southern part of the city below the Water Gate.

Water Gate. About halfway up the east side of the city, this gate faced the Kidron Valley and the main water source, the Gihon Spring.

3:28 Horse Gate. On the northeast side of the city.

3:29 East Gate. Just north of the Horse Gate.

3:31 Muster Gate. Between the East Gate and the Sheep Gate.

3:32 Sheep Gate. The counterclockwise description has come full circle (v. 1 note).

4:1–3 when Sanballat heard. The conflict between Israel and their Gentile rulers is escalating (2:10 note). The intent of the mockery is to stop the work.

4:4, 5 This is the first of three such imprecatory prayers (6:14; 13:29). An imprecatory prayer is one that calls for the enemy to be cursed (e.g., Ps. 79:12; 94:1–3; 137:7–9). See Introduction to Psalms: The Curses of the Psalms.

not their sin be blotted out from your sight,
for they have provoked you to anger in the
presence of the builders.
6 So we built the wall. And all the wall
was joined together to half its height, for
the people had a mind to work.
7 [1] But when [q]Sanballat and Tobiah and
the Arabs and the Ammonites and the
Ashdodites heard that the repairing of the
walls of Jerusalem was going forward and
that the breaches were beginning to be
closed, they were very angry. 8 [w]And they all
plotted together to come and fight against
Jerusalem and to cause confusion in it.
9 And we prayed to our God and set a guard
as a protection against them day and night.
10 In Judah it was said,[2] "The strength of
those who bear the burdens is failing. There
is too much rubble. By ourselves we will
not be able to rebuild the wall." 11 And our
enemies said, "They will not know or see
till we come among them and kill them and
stop the work." 12 At that time the Jews who
lived near them came from all directions
and said to us ten times, "You must return
to us."[3] 13 So in the lowest parts of the space
behind the wall, in open places, I stationed
the people by their clans, with their swords,
their spears, and their bows. 14 And I looked
and arose and said to the nobles and to the
officials and to the rest of the people, [x]"Do
not be afraid of them. Remember the Lord,
[y]who is great and awesome, [z]and fight for
your brothers, your sons, your daughters,
your wives, and your homes."

The Work Resumes

15 When our enemies heard that it was
known to us [a]and that God had frustrated
their plan, we all returned to the wall, each
to his work. 16 From that day on, half of my
servants worked on construction, and half
held the spears, shields, bows, and [b]coats
of mail. And the leaders stood behind the
whole house of Judah, 17 who were building
on the wall. Those who carried burdens
were loaded in such a way that each
labored on the work with one hand and
held his weapon with the other. 18 And
each of the builders had his sword
strapped at his side while he built. The
man who sounded the trumpet was beside
me. 19 And I said to [c]the nobles and to the
officials and to the rest of the people, "The
work is great and widely spread, and we are
separated on the wall, far from one another. 20 In the place where you hear the sound
of the trumpet, rally to us there. [d]Our God
will fight for us."
21 So we labored at the work, and half of
them held the spears from the break of
dawn until the stars came out. 22 I also said
to the people at that time, "Let every man
and his servant pass the night within
Jerusalem, that they may be a guard for us
by night and may labor by day." 23 So neither I nor my brothers nor my servants nor
the men of the guard who followed me,
none of us took off our clothes; [e]each kept
his weapon at his right hand.[4]

Nehemiah Stops Oppression of the Poor

5 Now there arose [f]a great outcry of the
people and of their wives [g]against their

7 [q][See ver. 1 above]
8 [w]See Ps. 83:3-5
14 [x][Num. 14:9]; Deut. 1:29 [y]Deut. 7:21; 10:17 [z]2 Sam. 10:12
15 [a][Job 5:12]
16 [b]2 Chr. 26:14
19 [c]ver. 14
20 [d]Ex. 14:14, 25; Deut. 1:30; 3:22; 20:4; Josh. 23:10
23 [e][Judg. 5:11]
Chapter 5
1 [f][Ex. 3:9; Isai. 5:7] [g]Lev. 25:35, 37; Deut. 15:7

[1] Ch 4:1 in Hebrew [2] Hebrew *Judah said* [3] The meaning of the Hebrew is uncertain [4] Probable reading; Hebrew *each his weapon the water*

4:7 when Sanballat . . . heard. One more group, the Ashdodites, is added to the list of enemies. Nehemiah is now completely encircled by the enemy, as Ashdod lies on the Philistine plain to his west (2:19 note).

4:10 In Judah it was said. A collective term is used, emphasizing that discouragement was widespread.

The strength . . . the wall. Perhaps this poetic couplet was chanted by the people. Part of the reason that they were discouraged was simply that the work was hard.

4:12 said to us ten times. Ten is a symbolic number for completeness. The fear of violence was growing in the minds of the people.

4:13 I stationed the people. Nehemiah's first action was to station additional guards at the most vulnerable points. The tension continues to rise as the people of Judah take up arms for the first time.

4:14 great and awesome. See "The Greatness of God" at 1 Chr. 29:11.

4:15 God had frustrated their plan. In Ezra 4:5, 24 the enemy frustrated the plan to build the temple; now God responds in kind by frustrating the plan to stop building.

we all returned to the wall. Nehemiah responded successfully to the tide of discouragement by adding guards and exhorting the people.

4:16 spears . . . coats of mail. The arms first mentioned in v. 13 are supplemented here with shield and armor (a breastplate of metal).

4:17 Those who carried . . . held his weapon. The porters had a hand free to hold a weapon, which may have been no more than a stone for throwing.

4:18 each of the builders had his sword. The builders needed two hands to work, so they wore swords at their sides.

the trumpet. The trumpet, or *shofar,* had numerous functions in the Old Testament. Here, as in Judg. 3:27, it would rally the troops.

4:21 until the stars came out. This shows how strong their dedication was, since work usually ended at sundown.

5:1–13 This section leaves the main topic of opposition by outsiders to consider the difficulties that arose from within. Probable causes of the economic stress mentioned are that Judah was cut off from trading with neighbors; farmers were away from their fields, because they stayed in Jerusalem, (4:22); there was a famine (v. 3); and previous administrators

Jewish brothers. 2 For there were those who
said, "With our sons and our daughters,
we are many. So let us get grain, that we
may eat and keep alive." 3 There were also
those who said, "We are mortgaging our
fields, our vineyards, and our houses to get
grain because of the famine." 4 And there
were those who said, "We have borrowed
money for [h] the king's tax on our fields and
our vineyards. 5 Now [i] our flesh is as the
flesh of our brothers, our children are as
their children. Yet [j] we are forcing our sons
and our daughters to be slaves, and some
of our daughters have already been
enslaved, but it is not in our power to help
it, for other men have our fields and our
vineyards."
6 I was very angry when I heard [f] their outcry and these words. 7 I took counsel with
myself, and I brought charges against the
nobles and the officials. I said to them,
[k] "You are exacting interest, each from his
brother." And I held a great assembly
against them 8 and said to them, "We, as far
as we are able, [l] have bought back our
Jewish brothers who have been sold to the
nations, but you even sell your brothers
that they may be sold to us!" They were
silent and could not find a word to say. 9 So
I said, "The thing that you are doing is not
good. Ought you not to walk [m] in the fear of
our God [n] to prevent the taunts of the
nations our enemies? 10 Moreover, I and my
brothers and my servants are lending them
money and grain. Let us abandon this
exacting of interest. 11 Return to them this
very day their fields, their vineyards, their
olive orchards, and their houses, and the
percentage of money, grain, wine, and oil
that you have been exacting from them."
12 Then they said, "We will restore these
and [o] require nothing from them. We will
do as you say." And I called the priests and
[p] made them swear [q] to do as they had
promised. 13 [r] I also shook out the fold[1] of
my garment and said, "So may God shake
out every man from his house and from his
labor who does not keep this promise. So
may he be shaken out and emptied." [s] And
all the assembly said "Amen" and praised
the LORD. And the people did as they had
promised.

Nehemiah's Generosity

14 Moreover, from the time that I was
appointed to be their governor in the land
of Judah, from [t] the twentieth year to [u] the
thirty-second year of Artaxerxes the king,
twelve years, [v] neither I nor my brothers ate
the food allowance of the governor. 15 The
former governors who were before me laid
heavy burdens on the people and took
from them for their daily ration[2] forty
shekels[3] of silver. Even their servants lord-
ed it over the people. But I did not do so,
[w] because of the fear of God. 16 I also perse-
vered in the work on this wall, and we

4 [h] Ezra 4:13, 20; 7:24
5 [i] Isai. 58:7; [Gen. 29:14] [j] [Ex. 21:7; Lev. 25:39; 2 Kin. 4:1]
6 [f] [See ver. 1 above]
7 [k] [Ex. 22:25; Lev. 25:36; Ps. 15:5; Ezek. 22:12]
8 [l] Lev. 25:48, 49
9 [m] Lev. 25:36 [n] ch. 4:4; [2 Sam. 12:14]
12 [o] [ch. 10:31] [p] Ezra 10:5 [q] Jer. 34:8, 9
13 [r] [Acts 18:6] [s] ch. 8:6; [Deut. 27:15]; 1 Chr. 16:36; Ps. 106:48
14 [t] ch. 2:1 [u] ch. 13:6 [v] [2 Thess. 3:8]
15 [w] ver. 9

1 Hebrew *bosom* 2 Compare Vulgate; Hebrew *with food and wine afterward* 3 A *shekel* was about 2/5 ounce or 11 grams

had burdened the people (v. 15). Times were so bad that children were sold into slavery, houses and vineyards were mortgaged, and money was borrowed at interest. The crushing realization for Nehemiah was that not foreigners but the people themselves were forcing these intolerable measures on each other.

5:1 their wives. Since women play a minor role in Ezra and Nehemiah, mentioning them here emphasizes how severe the crisis was (3:12 note; 12:43 note).

5:3 famine. Famines were often signs of God's judgment (Deut. 11:16, 17; 1 Chr. 21:12; Hag. 1:7–11). Perhaps this famine was God's judgment upon the leaders' failure to do what was right.

5:5 enslaved. According to Lev. 25:39–43, a man who became poor could sell himself, along with his family, to a fellow Israelite in order to get back on his feet financially; he was to be treated as a hired worker, not as a slave. The error in Nehemiah's day seems to be twofold: (a) only the children were being sold, resulting in the breakup of family units; (b) the children were being treated as slaves, not as hired workers.

5:7 brought charges against. A bold step on Nehemiah's part.

exacting interest. The law prohibited not only usury, but interest of any kind (Ex. 22:25–27; Lev. 25:35–37; Deut. 23:20).

5:10 I and my brothers. Nehemiah too seems to have made interest-bearing loans. He includes himself in the call to repent.

5:11 grain, wine, and oil. This familiar triad is in the order of the agricultural harvests: first grain, then grapes, and finally olives ripened.

5:12 made them swear. This act was a renewal of their commitment to keep the law of Moses concerning lending and debt-slavery. See theological note "Honest Speech, Oaths, and Vows."

5:13 shook out the fold. In this covenant renewal Nehemiah dramatized the curses for failing to keep the oath (cf. Jer. 34:8–22).

5:14 twentieth year . . . thirty-second year. 445 B.C. to 433 B.C. This twelve-year period was Nehemiah's first term as governor; after it he was recalled to the Persian court (13:6, 7), and then he returned to Jerusalem for a second term of unknown length.

the food allowance of the governor. A governor had the right to collect taxes for his personal support. Nehemiah waived this right for the benefit of the people (v. 18; cf. 1 Cor. 9:4, 12; 2 Thess. 3:8, 9).

5:15 former governors . . . laid heavy burdens. Sheshbazzar (Ezra 5:14) and Zerubbabel (Hag. 1:1) were former governors, but their terms were almost one hundred years earlier. The oppressive governors were Nehemiah's more immediate predecessors, whose policies had been harmful (5:1–13 note).

fear of God. See note 1:11.

5:16 Nehemiah's reason for being governor was service, not personal advancement, corresponding to his reason for going to Judah in the first place (2:5).

acquired no land, and all my servants were
gathered there for the work. 17 Moreover,
there were [x] at my table 150 men, Jews and
officials, besides those who came to us
from the nations that were around us.
18 [y] Now what was prepared at my expense [1]
for each day was one ox and six choice
sheep and birds, and every ten days all
kinds of wine in abundance. Yet for all this
[v] I did not demand the food allowance of
the governor, because the service was too
heavy on this people. 19 [z] Remember for my
good, O my God, all that I have done for
this people.

17 [x] [2 Sam. 9:7, 10]; 1 Kin. 18:19
18 [y] [1 Kin. 4:22, 23] [v] [See ver. 14 above]
19 [z] ch. 13:14, 22, 31

Chapter 6
1 [a] ch. 2:10, 19; 4:1, 7 [b] [ver. 6] [c] [ch. 3:1, 3]
2 [d] 1 Chr. 8:12

Conspiracy Against Nehemiah

6 Now when [a] Sanballat and Tobiah and
[b] Geshem the Arab and the rest of our
enemies heard that I had built the wall and
that there was no breach left in it ([c] although up to that time I had not set up the
doors in the gates), 2 Sanballat and Geshem
sent to me, saying, "Come and let us meet
together at Hakkephirim in the plain of
[d] Ono." But they intended to do me harm.
3 And I sent messengers to them, saying, "I
am doing a great work and I cannot come

1 Or *prepared for me*

Honest Speech, Oaths, and Vows

Truth in relationships, especially between Christians, is divinely commanded (Eph. 4:25; Col. 3:9), and truth-telling is integral to authentic godliness (Ps. 15:1–3). God forbids lying, deception, and malicious misrepresentation (Ex. 20:16; Lev. 19:11). Jesus traces lying back to Satan (John 8:44). Those who, like Satan, lie in order to deceive and harm others are sternly condemned in Scripture (Ps. 5:9; 12:1–4; 52:2–5; Jer. 9:3–6; Rev. 22:15). One way of acknowledging the dignity of our neighbors, who bear God's image, is to recognize that they have a right to the truth. Telling the truth shows proper respect for our neighbor and for God, and is fundamental to true religion and the love of one's neighbor.

In the ninth commandment God prohibits false witness (Ex. 20:16). Using the principle that the commandments require what is good as they forbid what is evil, the *Westminster Larger Catechism* (Q. 144) observes that the ninth commandment requires:

> the preserving and promoting of truth between man and man, and the good name of our neighbor, as well as our own; appearing and standing for the truth; and from the heart, sincerely, freely, clearly, and fully, speaking the truth, and only the truth, in matters of judgment and justice, and in all other things whatsoever.

Oaths are solemn declarations invoking God as a witness to statements and promises, inviting Him to punish anything false. Scripture approves oaths as appropriate on solemn occasions (Gen. 24:1–9; Ezra 10:5; Neh. 5:12; cf. 2 Cor. 1:23; Heb. 6:13–17). During the Reformation, the Anabaptists refused to take oaths as part of their rejection of involvement in the life of the secular world. They understood Jesus' condemnation of oaths as if it were a rejection of oath-taking as such, rather than a condemnation of false or improper oaths, used to create a false impression, to manipulate, or to deceive (Matt. 5:33–37; cf. James 5:12).

Vows to God are the devotional equivalent of oaths, and must be treated with equal seriousness (Deut. 21:23; Eccl. 5:4–6). What one swears or vows to do must at all costs be done (Ps. 15:4; cf. Josh. 9:15–18). God requires us to take His words seriously, and our own as well. However, "no man may vow to do anything forbidden in the Word of God, or what would hinder any duty therein commanded" (*Westminster Confession*, XXII. 7).

5:17 at my table. According to Persian custom, Nehemiah as governor had to entertain the officials under his authority as well as visiting dignitaries from other countries.

5:18 for each day. The food listed could have fed hundreds of people. Nehemiah was as generous as he was rich.

5:19 Remember. The second use of "remember" in a prayer (1:8 note) and the first of four prayers asking God to "remember me" (13:14, 22, 31).

6:1 when Sanballat . . . heard. The phrase continues the series of similar phrases (2:10 note) and brings the reader back to the main topic of Neh. 1:1–7:3, from which ch. 5 was a digression (5:1–13 note). The conflict that has been steadily escalating here reaches its climax, as the wall is virtually complete. This final attempt to stop the work is threefold: to harm (vv. 2–4), to frighten (vv. 5–9), and to discredit (vv. 10–13) Nehemiah.

6:2 Ono. Ono was in the northwestern corner of Judah, as far from the safety of Jerusalem as is possible without leaving the country.

to do me harm. A vague phrase, perhaps referring to murder (v. 10) or to a later allegation that Nehemiah's trip to Ono was to enlist others in revolt against Persia (v. 6).

down. Why should the work stop while I
leave it and come down to you?" 4 And they
sent to me four times in this way, and I
answered them in the same manner. 5 In
the same way Sanballat for the fifth time
sent his servant to me with an open letter
in his hand. 6 In it was written, "It is
reported among the nations, and Geshem[1]
also says it, that you and [e]the Jews intend
to rebel; that is why you are building the
wall. And according to these reports you
wish to become their king. 7 And you have
also set up prophets to proclaim concerning you in Jerusalem, 'There is a king in
Judah.' And now the king will hear of these
reports. So now come and let us take counsel together." 8 Then I sent to him, saying,
"No such things as you say have been
done, for you are inventing them out of
your own mind." 9 For they all wanted to
frighten us, thinking, "Their hands will
drop from the work, and it will not be
done." But now, O God,[2] strengthen my
hands.

10 Now when I went into the house of
Shemaiah the son of Delaiah, son of
Mehetabel, who was [f]confined to his
home, he said, "Let us meet together in the
house of God, within the temple. Let us
close the doors of the temple, for they are
coming to kill you. They are coming to kill
you by night." 11 But I said, "Should such a
man as I run away? And what man such as
I could go into the temple and live?[3] I will
not go in." 12 And I understood and saw
that God had not sent him, [g]but he had
pronounced the prophecy against me
because Tobiah and Sanballat had hired
him. 13 For this purpose he was hired, that
I should be afraid and act in this way and
sin, and so they could give me a bad name
in order to taunt me. 14 [h]Remember Tobiah
and Sanballat, O my God, according to
these things that they did, and also [i]the
prophetess Noadiah and the rest of the
prophets who wanted to make me afraid.

The Wall Is Finished

15 So the wall was finished on the twenty-
fifth day of the month Elul, in fifty-two
days. 16 And [j]when all our enemies heard of
it, all the nations around us were afraid and
fell greatly in their own esteem, [k]for they
perceived that this work had been accomplished with the help of our God.
17 Moreover, in those days the nobles of
Judah sent many letters to Tobiah, and
Tobiah's letters came to them. 18 For many
in Judah were bound by oath to him,
because he was the son-in-law of Shecaniah
the son of [l]Arah: and his son Jehohanan
had taken the daughter of [m]Meshullam the
son of Berechiah as his wife. 19 Also they
spoke of his good deeds in my presence and
reported my words to him. And Tobiah sent
letters to make me afraid.

7 Now when the wall had been built
[n]and I had set up the doors, and the
gatekeepers, the singers, and the Levites
had been appointed, 2 I gave [o]my brother
Hanani and Hananiah the governor of [p]the

6 [e]ch. 2:19
10 [f]Jer. 36:5
12 [g][Ezek. 13:17, 22]
14 [h]ch. 13:29 [i][Ezek. 13:17]
16 [j]ch. 2:10; 4:1, 7 [k][Ps. 126:2]
18 [l]Ezra 2:5 [m]Ezra 8:16
Chapter 7
1 [n][ch. 6:1]
2 [o]ch. 1:2 [p]ch. 2:8

1 Hebrew *Gashmu* 2 Hebrew lacks *O God* 3 Or *would go into the temple to save his life*

6:3 Why should the work stop. Nehemiah saw that the basic purpose of the plot was to stop the work on the wall.

6:4 four times. Both sides are persistent as the conflict reaches its climax.

6:5 open letter. Letters were normally sealed, but Sanballat wanted this letter to be public, so as to stop the work.

6:6, 7 The accusation was plausible: the wall was being rebuilt, Judah had a history of rebellion against her overlords, and Nehemiah was a skillful leader with a passion for his homeland.

6:9 now . . . strengthen my hands. Another of the brief prayers so characteristic of Nehemiah (1:4 note).

6:10 Shemaiah. He may have been not only a prophet (v. 12) but a priest, giving him access to the temple.

in the house of God. The final ploy now unfolds. Nehemiah might have sought asylum in the courtyard of the temple (Ex. 21:12–14), but he was not allowed to enter the temple itself since he was not a priest (Num. 18:7).

6:11 Nehemiah's courage shines through again (5:7 note).

6:13 I should be afraid . . . taunt me. The idea was to make Nehemiah behave like a coward and a lawbreaker, so that his reputation would be ruined and he could not finish the wall.

6:14 Remember. The third use of "remember" in a prayer (1:8 note) and the second imprecatory prayer (4:4, 5 note), as the "remembering" here is unto judgment.

6:15 So the wall was finished. This verse actually forms the conclusion to the section that began in v. 1, with v. 16 opening the final episode of Neh. 1:1–7:3. The last of six attempts to stop the work had failed.

Elul. August-September 445 B.C.

6:16–7:3 Although opposition to rebuilding the walls ceases with their completion (v. 16), attempts to intimidate Nehemiah continue (6:17–19). Nehemiah takes measures to secure the gates of the city against possible continued aggression by Israel's enemies (7:1–3).

6:17–19 Tobiah's relation by marriage to those at work on the wall would have provided a natural channel for the transfer of information about the circumstances in Jerusalem to Nehemiah's opponents.

7:1 set up the doors. This showed that the wall was now complete (6:1).

7:2 gave . . . charge. Leaders were appointed to oversee the security of the city.

Hananiah. See note 1:2.

God-fearing. See note 1:11.

castle charge over Jerusalem, for he was [q]a more faithful and God-fearing man than many. 3 And I said to them, "Let not the gates of Jerusalem be opened until the sun is hot. And while they are still standing guard, let them shut and bar the doors. Appoint guards from among the inhabitants of Jerusalem, some at their guard posts and some in front of their own homes." 4 The city was wide and large, but the people within it were few, and no houses had been rebuilt.

Lists of Returned Exiles

5 Then my God put it into my heart to assemble the nobles and the officials and the people to be enrolled by genealogy. And I found the book of the genealogy of [r]those who came up at the first, and I found written in it:

6 [s]These were the people of the province who came up out of the captivity of those exiles whom Nebuchadnezzar the king of Babylon had carried into exile. They returned to Jerusalem and Judah, each to his town. 7 They came with Zerubbabel, Jeshua, Nehemiah, [t]Azariah, Raamiah, Nahamani, Mordecai, Bilshan, Mispereth, Bigvai, Nehum, Baanah.

The number of the men of the people of Israel: 8 the sons of Parosh, 2,172. 9 The sons of Shephatiah, 372. 10 The sons of Arah, [u]652. 11 The sons of Pahath-moab, namely the sons of Jeshua and Joab, 2,818. 12 The sons of [v]Elam, 1,254. 13 The sons of Zattu, 845. 14 The sons of Zaccai, 760. 15 The sons of [w]Binnui, 648. 16 The sons of Bebai, 628. 17 The sons of Azgad, 2,322. 18 The sons of Adonikam, 667. 19 The sons of Bigvai, 2,067. 20 The sons of Adin, 655. 21 The sons of Ater, namely of Hezekiah, 98. 22 The sons of Hashum, 328. 23 The sons of Bezai, 324. 24 The sons of [x]Hariph, 112. 25 The sons of [y]Gibeon, 95. 26 The men of Bethlehem and Netophah, 188. 27 The men of Anathoth, 128. 28 The men [z]of Beth-azmaveth, 42. 29 The men of [a]Kiriath-jearim, Chephirah, and Beeroth, 743.

2 [q][ch. 13:13]
5 [r]Ezra 1:11
6 [s]For ver. 6-73, see Ezra 2:1-70
7 [t][Ezra 2:2]
10 [u][Ezra 2:5]
12 [v][ver. 34]
15 [w][Ezra 2:10]
24 [x][Ezra 2:17]
25 [y][Ezra 2:20]
28 [z][Ezra 2:24]
29 [a][Ezra 2:25]

34 [b][ver. 12]
39 [c]1 Chr. 9:10; 24:7
40 [d]1 Chr. 9:12; 24:14
41 [e]1 Chr. 9:12
42 [f]1 Chr. 24:8
43 [g][Ezra 2:40; 3:9]
47 [h][Ezra 2:44]
48 [i][Ezra 2:46]
52 [j][Ezra 2:50]
54 [k][Ezra 2:52]
57 [l][Ezra 2:55]
59 [m][Ezra 2:57]
61 [n]Ezra 2:59
[o][Ezra 2:59]

30 The men of Ramah and Geba, 621. 31 The men of Michmas, 122. 32 The men of Bethel and Ai, 123. 33 The men of the other Nebo, 52. 34 The sons of [b]the other Elam, 1,254. 35 The sons of Harim, 320. 36 The sons of Jericho, 345. 37 The sons of Lod, Hadid, and Ono, 721. 38 The sons of Senaah, 3,930.

39 The priests: the sons of [c]Jedaiah, namely the house of Jeshua, 973. 40 The sons of [d]Immer, 1,052. 41 The sons of [e]Pashhur, 1,247. 42 The sons of [f]Harim, 1,017.

43 The Levites: the sons of Jeshua, namely of Kadmiel of the sons of [g]Hodevah, 74. 44 The singers: the sons of Asaph, 148. 45 The gatekeepers: the sons of Shallum, the sons of Ater, the sons of Talmon, the sons of Akkub, the sons of Hatita, the sons of Shobai, 138.

46 The temple servants: the sons of Ziha, the sons of Hasupha, the sons of Tabbaoth, 47 the sons of Keros, the sons of [h]Sia, the sons of Padon, 48 the sons of Lebana, the sons of [i]Hagaba, the sons of [i]Shalmai, 49 the sons of Hanan, the sons of Giddel, the sons of Gahar, 50 the sons of Reaiah, the sons of Rezin, the sons of Nekoda, 51 the sons of Gazzam, the sons of Uzza, the sons of Paseah, 52 the sons of Besai, the sons of Meunim, the sons of [j]Nephushesim, 53 the sons of Bakbuk, the sons of Hakupha, the sons of Harhur, 54 the sons of [k]Bazlith, the sons of Mehida, the sons of Harsha, 55 the sons of Barkos, the sons of Sisera, the sons of Temah, 56 the sons of Neziah, the sons of Hatipha.

57 The sons of Solomon's servants: the sons of Sotai, the sons of Sophereth, the sons of [l]Perida, 58 the sons of Jaala, the sons of Darkon, the sons of Giddel, 59 the sons of Shephatiah, the sons of Hattil, the sons of Pochereth-hazzebaim, the sons of [m]Amon. 60 All the temple servants and the sons of Solomon's servants were 392.

61 [n]The following were those who came up from Tel-melah, Tel-harsha, Cherub, [o]Addon, and Immer, but they could not

7:3 until the sun is hot. Guards were appointed to secure the gates at night. The gates were usually opened at dawn; waiting until later was a security measure for the city.

7:4–73 Nehemiah prepares to meet the need to repopulate Jerusalem (vv. 4, 5) by consulting a genealogical record of exiles who had returned earlier (vv. 5–73).

7:5 my God put it into my heart. See note on "hand of my God" at 2:8.

enrolled by genealogy. The purpose of this registration is to help repopulate Jerusalem, as will become clear when this topic is resumed in 11:1, 2.

book of the genealogy . . . at the first. On the theological significance of this list, see the note at Ezra 2:1–70. The repetition of the list underscores the continuity of Nehemiah's generation with the first ones to return.

prove their fathers' houses nor their
descent, whether they belonged to Israel:
62 the sons of Delaiah, the sons of Tobiah,
the sons of Nekoda, 642. 63 Also, of the
priests: the sons of Hobaiah, the sons of
Hakkoz, the sons of Barzillai (who had
taken a wife of the daughters of Barzillai the
Gileadite and was called by their name).
64 These sought their registration among
those enrolled in the genealogies, but it was
not found there, so they were excluded
from the priesthood as unclean. 65 [p]The
[q]governor told them that they were not to
partake of the most holy food until a priest
with Urim and Thummim should arise.

Totals of People and Gifts

66 The whole assembly together was
42,360, 67 besides their male and female servants, of whom there were 7,337. And they
had 245 singers, male and female. 68 Their
horses were 736, their mules 245,[1] 69 their
camels 435, and their donkeys 6,720.
70 Now some of the heads of fathers'
houses gave to the work. The [q]governor gave
to the treasury 1,000 darics[2] of gold, 50
basins, 30 priests' garments and 500 minas[3]
of silver.[4] 71 And some of the heads of
fathers' houses gave into the treasury of the
work 20,000 darics of gold and 2,200 minas
of silver. 72 [r]And what the rest of the people
gave was 20,000 darics of gold, 2,000 minas
of silver, and 67 priests' garments.
73 So the priests, the Levites, the gatekeepers, the singers, some of the people,
the temple servants, and all Israel, lived in
their towns.
[s]And when the seventh month had come,
the people of Israel were in their towns.

Ezra Reads the Law

8 And all the people gathered as one man
into the square before [t]the Water Gate.
And they told [u]Ezra the scribe to bring the
Book of the Law of Moses that the LORD had
commanded Israel. 2 So Ezra the priest
[v]brought the Law before the assembly, both
men and women and all who could understand what they heard, [w]on the first day of
the seventh month. 3 [x]And he read from it
facing the square before the Water Gate from
early morning until midday, in the presence
of the men and the women and those who
could understand. And the ears of all the
people were attentive to the Book of the Law.
4 And Ezra the scribe stood on a wooden platform that they had made for the purpose.
And beside him stood Mattithiah, Shema,
Anaiah, Uriah, Hilkiah, and Maaseiah on his
right hand, and Pedaiah, Mishael, Malchijah,
Hashum, Hashbaddanah, Zechariah, and
Meshullam on his left hand. 5 And Ezra
opened the book in the sight of all the people, for he was above all the people, and as
he opened it all the people stood. 6 And Ezra
blessed the LORD, the great God, and all the
people answered, [y]"Amen, Amen," [z]lifting
up their hands. [a]And they bowed their heads
and worshiped the LORD with their faces to
the ground. 7 [b]Also Jeshua, Bani, Sherebiah,
Jamin, Akkub, Shabbethai, Hodiah, Maaseiah, Kelita, Azariah, Jozabad, Hanan,
Pelaiah, the Levites,[5] [c]helped the people to
understand the Law, [d]while the people
remained in their places. 8 They read from
the book, from the Law of God, clearly,[6] and
they gave the sense, so that the people
understood the reading.

This Day Is Holy

9 And Nehemiah, who was [e]the governor,
and Ezra [f]the priest and scribe, and the

65 [p]Ezra 2:63 [q]ch. 8:9; 10:1
70 [q][See ver. 65 above]
72 [r][Ezra 2:69]
73 [s]Ezra 3:1
Chapter 8
1 [t]ch. 3:26
[u]See Ezra 7:6
2 [v]See Deut. 31:11 [w]Lev. 23:24
3 [x]See ch. 13:1
6 [y]See ch. 5:13 [z]Ps. 134:2; Lam. 3:41; [1 Tim. 2:8] [a]See 2 Chr. 20:18
7 [b][ch. 9:4] [c]See 2 Chr. 35:3 [d]ch. 9:3
9 [e]ch. 7:65, 70; 10:1; Ezra 2:63 [f]ch. 12:26

[1] Ezra 2:66 and the margins of some Hebrew manuscripts; Hebrew lacks *Their horses . . . 245* [2] A *daric* was a coin weighing about 1/4 ounce or 8.5 grams [3] A *mina* was about 1 1/4 pounds or 0.6 kilogram [4] Probable reading; Hebrew lacks *minas of silver* [5] Vulgate; Hebrew *and the Levites* [6] Or *with interpretation*, or *paragraph by paragraph*

7:73–13:31 The covenant community itself is rebuilt as Israel renews the covenant with God (7:73–10:39), dedicates the walls of the city (chs. 11; 12), and obeys other aspects of the law (ch. 13).

8:2 before the assembly. The participants (repeated in v. 3) are in keeping with those required to be present at the reading of the Law prescribed for the Feast of Booths in Deut. 31:10–13.

first day of the seventh month. This was the time for celebrating the Feast of Trumpets (Num. 29:1–6).

8:3 he read from it facing the square. For the public reading of the Law in the context of covenant ratification or renewal, see Ex. 24:7; Josh. 8:30–35; 2 Kin. 23:1–3.

8:5 book. A scroll.

all the people stood. By standing they expressed their reverence for the Law (cf. v. 6).

8:6 Amen, Amen. The people concurred in the praise offered by Ezra; the repetition expresses the emphatic degree of assent.

lifting up their hands. Lifting the hands often accompanies prayer and praise to God (Ps. 28:2; 63:4; 134:2; 1 Tim. 2:8).

8:8 gave the sense. The Law was not only read but explained, to ensure that the people grasped the meaning. There may also have been translation from Hebrew to Aramaic. The doctrine of the perspicuity ("clarity") of Scripture is that the things necessary for salvation can be understood from the Bible without special techniques or higher education. This truth does not eliminate the need for faithful exposition of the Scriptures by persons trained for this (Ezra 7:6–10).

8:9 Nehemiah . . . Ezra . . . Levites. There was unity among all the leaders on this occasion.

Levites who taught the people said to all
the people, [g]"This day is holy to the LORD
your God; [h]do not mourn or weep." For all
the people wept as they heard the words of
the Law. 10 Then he said to them, "Go your
way. Eat the fat and drink sweet wine and
[i]send portions to anyone who has nothing
ready, for this day is holy to our Lord. And
do not be grieved, for the joy of the LORD is
your strength." 11 So the Levites calmed all
the people, saying, "Be quiet, for this day is
holy; do not be grieved." 12 And all the
people went their way to eat and drink and
to send portions and to make great rejoicing, because [j]they had understood the
words that were declared to them.

Feast of Booths Celebrated

13 On the second day the heads of
fathers' houses of all the people, with the
priests and the Levites, came together to
Ezra the scribe in order to study the words
of the Law. 14 And they found it written in
the Law that the LORD had commanded by
Moses [k]that the people of Israel should
dwell in booths[1] during the feast of the
seventh month, 15 and that they should
proclaim it and [l]publish it in all their towns
and [m]in Jerusalem, "Go out to the hills and
bring [n]branches of olive, wild olive, myrtle,
palm, and other leafy trees to make booths,
as it is written." 16 So the people went out
and brought them and made booths for
themselves, each [o]on his roof, and in their
courts and in the courts of the house of
God, and in the square at [p]the Water Gate
and in the square at [q]the Gate of Ephraim.
17 And all the assembly of those who had
returned from the captivity made booths
and lived in the booths, for from the days
of Jeshua the son of Nun to that day [r]the
people of Israel had not done so. And there
was [s]very great rejoicing. 18 And day by day,
from the first day to the last day, [t]he read
from the Book of the Law of God. They
kept the feast seven days, and [u]on the
eighth day there was a solemn assembly,
according to the rule.

The People of Israel Confess Their Sin

9 Now on the twenty-fourth day of [v]this
month the people of Israel were assembled [w]with fasting [x]and in sackcloth, [y]and
with earth on their heads. 2 [z]And the
Israelites separated themselves from all foreigners and stood and confessed their sins
and the iniquities of their fathers. 3 [a]And
they stood up in their place and read from
the Book of the Law of the LORD their God
for a quarter of the day; for another quarter
of it they made confession and worshiped
the LORD their God. 4 On the stairs of the
Levites stood [b]Jeshua, Bani, Kadmiel,
Shebaniah, Bunni, Sherebiah, Bani, and
Chenani; and they cried with a loud voice
to the LORD their God. 5 Then the Levites,
Jeshua, Kadmiel, Bani, Hashabneiah,
Sherebiah, Hodiah, Shebaniah, and Pethahiah, said, "Stand up and bless the LORD
your God from everlasting to everlasting.
[c]Blessed be your glorious name, which is
exalted above all blessing and praise.
6 [2] [d]"You are the LORD, you alone. [e]You
have made heaven, [f]the heaven of heavens,
[g]with all their host, [e]the earth and all that
is on it, the seas and all that is in them;
[h]and you preserve all of them; and the host
of heaven worships you. 7 You are the LORD,
the God [i]who chose Abram and brought
him out of [j]Ur of the Chaldeans [k]and gave
him the name Abraham. 8 [l]You found his
heart faithful before you, [m]and made with
him the covenant to give to his offspring
[n]the land of the Canaanite, the Hittite, the
Amorite, the Perizzite, the Jebusite, and the

9 [g]ver. 2; Lev. 23:24; Num. 29:1 [h][Eccles. 3:4]
10 [i]Esth. 9:19, 22
12 [j]ver. 7, 8
14 [k]Lev. 23:34, 40, 42
15 [l]Lev. 23:4 [m]Deut. 16:16 [n][Lev. 23:40]
16 [o]See 1 Sam. 9:25 [p]ver. 1,3; ch. 3:26 [q]ch. 12:39; 2 Kin. 14:13; 2 Chr. 25:23
17 [r][1 Kin. 8:2; 2 Chr. 7:9; 8:13; Ezra 3:4] [s][2 Chr. 30:21]
18 [t]Deut 31:10, 11 [u]Lev. 23:36; Num. 29:35
Chapter 9
1 [v][ch. 8:2] [w][1 Sam. 7:6] [x]See 2 Sam. 3:31 [y]See Josh. 7:6
2 [z]ch. 10:28; ch. 13:3, 30; [Ezra 6:21; 10:11]
3 [a]ch. 8:7, 8
4 [b][ch. 8:7]
5 [c][1 Chr. 29:13]
6 [d]See 2 Kin. 19:15 [e]See Gen. 1:1 [f]See Deut. 10:14 [g]See Gen. 2:1 [h][Ps. 36:6]
7 [i]See Gen. 11:31 [j]Gen. 11:31 [k]Gen. 17:5
8 [l]Gen. 15:6 [m]Gen. 12:7; 15:18; 17:7-9 [n]See Ex. 13:5

1 Or *temporary shelters* 2 Septuagint adds *And Ezra said*

This day is holy . . . do not mourn. Holiness and mourning are not mutually exclusive (Lev. 23:26–32; Is. 6:3–5), but it was clear that on this occasion sorrow would be inappropriate.

8:10 anyone who has nothing. Those who had plenty to eat were to share with those who did not (cf. Ps. 22:26). This incident provides an illustration for understanding the sin in 1 Cor. 11:17–34.

8:14 dwell in booths. This temporary living arrangement was a reminder of life in the wilderness after the redemption from Egypt and before entering the Promised Land (Lev. 23:42, 43).

the feast of the seventh month. The Feast of Booths (Lev. 23:34–40).

9:1 were assembled. In 8:1 the people had gathered to hear the Law; here they gather to confess their sins in response to it (v. 3).

9:2 their sins . . . their fathers. See note Ezra 9:7.

9:3 Law of the LORD. The Law calls for at least two responses: confession and worship.

9:5–37 In this prayer of praise, the Levites (vv. 4, 5) address God on behalf of the people, extolling Him as Creator (v. 6) and Redeemer (vv. 7–12), Lawgiver and Disciplinarian, Savior and Judge (vv. 13–31). On the basis of His character and covenant, they petition God to take notice of their distress (vv. 32–37) in preparation for their covenant renewal (9:38–10:39 and note).

9:7, 8 The people praise God for choosing Abraham and giving him the covenant of promise (Gen. 12–22).

9:8 made with him the covenant. This covenant with Abraham (Gen.

Girgashite. [o]And you have kept your promise, for you are righteous.
9 [p]“And you saw the affliction of our
fathers in Egypt and heard [q]their cry at the
Red Sea, 10 [r]and performed signs and wonders against Pharaoh and all his servants and
all the people of his land, for you knew that
[s]they acted arrogantly against our fathers.
And [t]you made a name for yourself, as it is to
this day. 11 [u]And you divided the sea before
them, so that they went through the midst of
the sea on dry land, and you cast their pursuers into the depths, [v]as a stone into mighty
waters. 12 By [w]a pillar of cloud you led them
in the day, and by a pillar of fire in the night
to light for them the way in which they
should go. 13 [x]You came down on Mount
Sinai [y]and spoke with them from heaven and
gave them [z]right rules and true laws, good
statutes and commandments, 14 [a]and you
made known to them your holy Sabbath and
commanded them commandments and
statutes and a law by Moses your servant.
15 [b]You gave them bread from heaven for
their hunger and [c]brought water for them
out of the rock for their thirst, and you [d]told
them to go in to possess the land that you
had sworn to give them.
16 “But they and our fathers [e]acted presumptuously and stiffened their neck and
did not obey your commandments. 17 They
refused to obey [f]and were not mindful of the
wonders that you performed among them,
but they stiffened their neck and appointed
a leader to return to their slavery in Egypt.
But you are a God ready to forgive, [g]gracious
and merciful, slow to anger and abounding
in steadfast love, and did not forsake them.
18 Even [h]when they had made for themselves
a golden[1] calf and said, ‘This is your God

8 [o][Josh. 23:14]
9 [p]Ex. 3:7 [q]Ex. 14:10
10 [r]See Ex. ch. 7–14 [s]Ex. 18:11 [t]Isai. 63:12, 14; Jer. 32:20; Dan. 9:15; [Ex. 9:16]
11 [u]Ex. 14:21, 22, 27, 28; Ps. 78:13 [v]Ex. 15:5, 10
12 [w]ver. 19; Ex. 13:21, 22; Num. 14:14; 1 Cor. 10:1
13 [x]Ex. 19:20 [y]See Ex. 20:1-17 [z]Ps. 19:8:9; [Rom. 7:12]; See Ps. 119
14 [a]Ex. 16:23; 20:8-11; [Gen. 2:2, 3; Ezek. 20:12, 20]
15 [b][Ex. 16:14, 15; Ps. 78:25; 105:40; 1 Cor. 10:3]; Cited John 6:31 [c]Ex. 17:6; Num. 20:10; Ps. 78:15-17; 105:41; 1 Cor. 10:4 [d]Deut. 1:8
16 [e]Ex. 18:11
17 [f]Ps. 78:11, 42, 43; [g]ver. 31; Ex. 34:6; Num. 14:18; Ps. 86:5, 15; Joel 2:13
18 [h]Ex. 32:4; Ps. 106:19, 20; Acts 7:41
[i]ver. 26; Ps. 78:41, 58; [Heb. 3:15]
19 [j]ver. 27, 31; Ps. 106:45 [k]See ver. 12
20 [l]Isai. 63:11; [Num. 11:17] [m][Ex. 16:35]; See ver. 15
21 [n]Deut. 2:7

who brought you up out of Egypt,’ [i]and had
committed great blasphemies, 19 you [j]in your
great mercies did not forsake them in the
wilderness. [k]The pillar of cloud to lead them
in the way did not depart from them by day,
[k]nor the pillar of fire by night to light for
them the way by which they should go.
20 [l]You gave your good Spirit to instruct them
[m]and did not withhold your manna from
their mouth and gave them water for their
thirst. 21 [n]Forty years you sustained them in
the wilderness, and they lacked nothing.
Their clothes did not wear out and their feet
did not swell.
22 “And you gave them kingdoms and
peoples and allotted to them every corner.
[o]So they took possession of the land of
Sihon king of Heshbon [p]and the land of Og
king of Bashan. 23 You multiplied their children [q]as the stars of heaven, and you
brought them into the land that you had
told their fathers to enter and possess. 24 [r]So
the descendants went in and possessed the
land, [s]and you subdued before them the
inhabitants of the land, the Canaanites, and
gave them into their hand, with their kings
and the peoples of the land, that they might
do with them as they would. 25 And they
captured [t]fortified cities and [u]a rich land,
and took possession of [v]houses full of all
good things, cisterns already hewn, vineyards, olive orchards and fruit trees in
abundance. So they ate and were filled [w]and
became fat and delighted themselves in
[x]your great goodness.
26 [y]“Nevertheless, they were disobedient

22 [o]See Num. 21:21-31 [p]See Num. 21:33-35 23 [q]Gen. 15:5; 22:17 24 [r]See Josh. ch. 1–12 [s]Ps. 44:2, 3 25 [t]Deut. 3:5; 9:1; Josh. 10:20; 14:12 [u]ver. 35; [Num. 13:20, 27; Deut. 8:7, 8; Ezek. 20:6] [v]Deut. 6:11 [w]Deut. 32:15 [x]ver. 35; Hos. 3:5 26 [y]Judg. 2:11, 12; Ezek. 20:21

1 Hebrew *metal*

15) is the basis upon which God's grace is extended time and again to His unfaithful people, as is brought out in the remainder of this prayer of praise.

you have kept your promise. God's promise to Abraham was conditioned only upon God's righteous oath (Gen. 15:9–21; Deut. 9:4–6).

9:9–12 God is praised for redeeming Israel from Egypt (Ex. 1–19).

9:13–21 The praise of God continues with an account of the giving of the Law at Mount Sinai and God's gracious provisions in the wilderness.

9:13 Mount Sinai. See Ex. 20.

right rules . . . good statutes. The Law was not perceived to be a burden, but a delight (Ps. 119:5–16; Rom. 7:12).

9:14 Sabbath. The Sabbath was a key symbol in the Law (Is. 56:2, 4, 6; Ezek. 20:13, 16, 21, 24; 22:8; 23:38).

9:15 sworn. The reference is to God's oath to Abraham (Ex. 6:8).

9:16, 17 The first confession of sin.

9:17 appointed a leader. See Num. 14:1–4. In contrast to the unfaithfulness of Israel is the faithfulness of God to His oath to Abraham (vv. 8, 15; Ezra 9:13 note).

9:18 Even when. God's grace shines all the more brightly when juxtaposed against Israel's sin (Rom. 9:22–24).

9:19–21 God's continual care in the wilderness was not due to Israel's obedience, but to His own compassion, stemming from His promise to Abraham (vv. 7, 8).

9:22–25 God enabled the Israelites to conquer the land of Canaan in keeping with His promise to Abraham (vv. 7–8).

9:26–28 Israel responded to God's faithfulness with disobedient rebellion during the days of the judges. For the pattern of rebellion, oppression, petition, and salvation, see Judg. 2:10–19.

and rebelled against you [z]and cast your law
behind their back [a]and killed your
prophets, who [b]had warned them in order
to turn them back to you, [c]and they committed great blasphemies. 27 [d]Therefore you
gave them into the hand of their enemies,
who made them suffer. [e]And in the time of
their suffering they cried out to you and
you heard them from heaven, and according to your great mercies you gave them
[f]saviors who saved them from the hand of
their enemies. 28 [g]But after they had rest
they did evil again before you, and you
abandoned them to the hand of their enemies, so that they had dominion over
them. Yet when they turned and cried to
you, you heard from heaven, [h]and many
times you delivered them according to your
mercies. 29 [b]And you warned them in order
to turn them back to your law. Yet [i]they
acted presumptuously and did not obey
your commandments, but sinned against
your rules, [j]which if a person does them,
he shall live by them, [k]and turned a stubborn shoulder [l]and stiffened their neck and
would not obey. 30 Many years [m]you bore
with them [n]and warned them [o]by your
Spirit through your prophets. [p]Yet they
would not give ear. [q]Therefore you gave
them into the hand of the peoples of the
lands. 31 Nevertheless, [r]in your great mercies [s]you did not make an end of them or
forsake them, [t]for you are a gracious and
merciful God.
32 "Now, therefore, our God, [u]the great,
the mighty, and the awesome God, who
keeps covenant and steadfast love, let not
all the hardship seem little to you that has
come upon us, upon our kings, our
princes, our priests, our prophets, our
fathers, and all your people, [v]since the time
of the kings of Assyria until this day. 33 [w]Yet
you have been righteous in all that has
come upon us, for you have dealt faithfully
[x]and we have acted wickedly. 34 Our kings,
our princes, our priests, and our fathers
have not kept your law or paid attention to
your commandments and your warnings
that you gave them. 35 Even in their own
kingdom, [y]enjoying your great goodness
that you gave them, and in the large and
[y]rich land that you set before them, [z]they
did not serve you or turn from their wicked
works. 36 Behold, [a]we are slaves this day; in
the land that you gave to our fathers to
enjoy its fruit and its good gifts, behold, we
are slaves. 37 [b]And its rich yield goes to the
kings whom you have set over us because
of our sins. They rule over our bodies and
over our livestock as they please, and we
are in great distress.
38 [1] "Because of all this [c]we make a firm
covenant in writing; on [d]the sealed document are the names of[2] our princes, our
Levites, and our priests."

The People Who Sealed the Covenant

10 [3] [e]On the seals are the names of[4]
Nehemiah [f]the governor, [g]the son
of Hacaliah, Zedekiah, 2 [h]Seraiah, Azariah,
Jeremiah, 3 Pashhur, Amariah, Malchijah,

26 [z]Ps. 50:17; [1 Kin. 14:9] [a]1 Kin. 18:4; 19:10; 2 Chr. 24:20, 21; Matt. 23:37; Acts 7:52 [b]See ver. 30 [c]See ver. 18 **27** [d]Judg. 2:14; Ps. 106:41, 42 [e]Ps. 106:44, 45 [f]Judg. 2:16; 3:9 **28** [g]Judg. 3:11, 12, 30; 4:1; 5:31; 6:1 [h]Ps. 106:43 **29** [b][See ver. 26 above] [i]ver. 10, 16 [j]See Lev. 18:5 [k]Zech. 7:11 [l]See ver. 16 **30** [m][Acts 13:18] [n]ver. 26, 29, 34; 2 Kin. 17:13 [o]1 Pet. 1:10, 11; 2 Pet. 1:21 [p]Acts 7:51 [q]Ezra 9:7; [Isai. 42:24] **31** [r]ver. 19, 27 [s]Jer. 4:27; 5:10, 18 [t]ver. 17 **32** [u]ch. 1:5; Deut. 7:21 [v]2 Kin. 17:3 **33** [w]See Ezra 9:15 [x]Ps. 106:6; Dan. 9:5 **35** [y]ver. 25 [z]Deut. 28:47 **36** [a]Ezra 9:9 **37** [b]Deut. 28:33, 51 **38** [c]2 Kin. 23:3; 2 Chr. 29:10; 34:31; Ezra 10:3; [ch. 10:29]; ch. 10:1 [d][ch. 10:1]

Chapter 10 1 [e]ch. 9:38 [f]See ch. 8:9 [g]ch. 1:1 **2** [h]For ver. 2-27, see ch. 12:2-21

[1] Ch 10:1 in Hebrew [2] Hebrew lacks *the names of* [3] Ch 10:2 in Hebrew [4] Hebrew lacks *the names of*

9:28 many times . . . your mercies. Where sin abounded grace abounded all the more (Rom. 5:20).

9:29–31 The praise of God continues with mention of His patience during the monarchy.

9:29 he shall live by them. The Mosaic covenant offered life for obedience (Lev. 18:5; Rom. 10:5). Israel's failure to merit life in the land testifies to the universal need for a Substitute through whom the righteous requirements of the law might be fully met on behalf of those who could not meet these terms on their own (Rom. 8:3, 4).

9:32 hardship seem little. The petition is that God would do again what He had done in the past, to see the distress of His people and come to their aid.

kings of Assyria. These are the Neo-Assyrian kings of the late tenth century B.C. After them came the Neo-Babylonian kings in the late seventh century, and then the Persian kings in the mid-sixth century.

9:33 you have been righteous. The execution of the covenant curses throughout Israel's history was in perfect harmony with the principle of divine justice, which lay at the foundation of the Mosaic covenant (Ezra 9:9 note).

9:34, 35 The leaders are singled out as particularly responsible.

9:36 slaves. See note on "we are slaves" at Ezra 9:9.

9:37 we are in great distress. Implicit in this statement is a request for aid (v. 32 note).

9:38–10:39 The people not only prayed for aid, but also renewed their obligations under the Mosaic covenant. From the beginning, the Mosaic covenant had to be renewed after periods of covenant violation (Ex. 34; 1 Sam. 12; 2 Kin. 23).

9:38 in writing. When the law was written down and sealed it could become an effective instrument in the redemptive purposes of God (Introduction to Ezra: Characteristics and Themes).

10:1–27 The leaders who renewed the covenant are listed. Surprisingly Ezra is absent. He played a significant role in ch. 8, but has now quietly disappeared from the scene. His job was successfully completed when the people themselves were reading from the Law and understanding it on their own.

10:1 On the seals are the names. This list of people, who for the most part are not known elsewhere, reinforces one of the major themes of Ezra and Nehemiah: the people of God as a whole, not just the great leaders, are vital for the accomplishing of God's redemptive plan (Introduction to Ezra: Characteristics and Themes).

4 [i]Hattush, Shebaniah, Malluch, 5 Harim,
Meremoth, Obadiah, 6 Daniel, Ginnethon,
Baruch, 7 Meshullam, Abijah, Mijamin,
8 Maaziah, Bilgai, Shemaiah; these are the
priests. 9 And the Levites: [j]Jeshua the son of
Azaniah, Binnui of the sons of [k]Henadad,
Kadmiel; 10 and their brothers, Shebaniah,
Hodiah, Kelita, Pelaiah, Hanan, 11 Mica,
Rehob, Hashabiah, 12 Zaccur, Sherebiah,
Shebaniah, 13 Hodiah, Bani, Beninu. 14 The
chiefs of the people: [l]Parosh, Pahath-moab,
Elam, Zattu, Bani, 15 Bunni, Azgad, Bebai,
16 Adonijah, Bigvai, Adin, 17 Ater, Hezekiah,
Azzur, 18 Hodiah, Hashum, Bezai, 19 Hariph,
Anathoth, Nebai, 20 Magpiash, Meshullam,
Hezir, 21 Meshezabel, Zadok, Jaddua,
22 Pelatiah, Hanan, Anaiah, 23 Hoshea,
Hananiah, Hasshub, 24 Hallohesh, Pilha,
Shobek, 25 Rehum, Hashabnah, Maaseiah,
26 Ahiah, Hanan, Anan, 27 Malluch, Harim,
Baanah.

The Obligations of the Covenant

28 [m]The rest of the people, the priests, the
Levites, the gatekeepers, the singers, the
temple servants, [n]and all who have separated themselves from the peoples of the
lands to the Law of God, their wives, their
sons, their daughters, all who have knowledge and understanding, 29 join with their
brothers, their nobles, [o]and enter into a
curse and an oath [p]to walk in God's Law
that was given by Moses the servant of
God, and to observe and do all the commandments of the LORD our Lord and his
rules and his statutes. 30 [q]"We will not give
our daughters to the peoples of the land or
take their daughters for our sons. 31 [r]And if
the peoples of the land bring in goods or
any grain on the Sabbath day to sell, we
will not buy from them on the Sabbath or
on a holy day. And we will forego the crops
of the [s]seventh year and the [t]exaction of
every debt.

32 "We also take on ourselves the obligation to give yearly [u]a third part of a shekel[1]
for the service of the house of our God:
33 [v]for the showbread, [w]the regular grain offering, [w]the regular burnt offering, the
Sabbaths, the new moons, the appointed
feasts, the holy things, and the sin offerings
to make atonement for Israel, and for all
the work of the house of our God. 34 [x]We,
the priests, the Levites, and the people,
have likewise cast lots [y]for the wood offering, to bring it into the house of our God,
according to our fathers' houses, at times
appointed, year by year, to burn on the
altar of the LORD our God, [z]as it is written
in the Law. 35 We obligate ourselves [a]to
bring the firstfruits of our ground and the
firstfruits of all fruit of every tree, year by
year, to the house of the LORD; 36 also to
bring to the house of our God, to the
priests who minister in the house of our
God, the firstborn of our sons and of our
cattle, [b]as it is written in the Law, and the
firstborn of our herds and of our flocks;
37 [c]and to bring the first of our dough, and
our contributions, the fruit of every tree,
the wine and the oil, to the priests, [d]to the
chambers of the house of our God; and to
bring to the Levites the tithes from our
ground, for it is the Levites who collect the
tithes in all our towns where we labor.
38 And the priest, the son of Aaron, shall be
with the Levites when the Levites receive
the tithes. And the Levites shall bring up
the tithe of the tithes to the house of our
God, to the chambers of [e]the storehouse.
39 For the people of Israel and the sons of
Levi [f]shall bring the contribution of grain,
wine, and oil to the chambers, where the
vessels of the sanctuary are, as well as the
priests who minister, and the gatekeepers
and the singers. [g]We will not neglect the
house of our God."

4 [i]Ezra 8:2
9 [j]Ezra 2:40 [k]Ezra 3:9
14 [l]See ch. 7:8-42; Ezra 2:3-35
28 [m]See Ezra 2:36-54 [n]See ch. 9:2
29 [o]ch. 5:12, 13; Deut. 29:12, 14; [Ps. 119:106] [p][2 Kin. 23:3; 2 Chr. 34:31]
30 [q]Ex. 34:16; Deut. 7:3; Ezra 9:12, 14
31 [r]Ex. 20:10; Lev. 23:3; Deut. 5:12; See ch. 13:15-22 [s]Ex. 23:10, 11; Lev. 25:4 [t]Deut. 15:1, 2; [ch. 5:12]
32 [u][Matt. 17:24]
33 [v]2 Chr. 2:4; [1 Chr. 9:32]; See Lev. 24:5-9 [w]See Num. 28; 29
34 [x][ch. 11:1] [y]ch. 13:31; [Isai. 40:16] [z]Lev. 6:12
35 [a]Ex. 23:19; 34:26; Lev. 19:23, 24; Num. 18:12; Deut. 26:2
36 [b]Ex. 13:2, 12, 13; Lev. 27:26, 27; Num. 18:15, 16
37 [c]Lev. 23:17; Num. 15:20, 21; 18:12; Deut. 18:4 [d]1 Chr. 9:26; 2 Chr. 31:11
38 [e]1 Chr. 26:20
39 [f][ch. 13:12; Deut. 12:6, 11; 2 Chr. 31:12] [g][ch. 13:11]

1 A *shekel* was about 2/5 ounce or 11 grams

10:29 enter into . . . an oath. The swearing of the oath by the people (9:15; Ezra 10:5 note) emphasizes the distinctively legal nature of the Mosaic covenantal arrangement, as compared to the Abrahamic covenant of grace (Gen. 12:1–3), in which the oath is taken by God alone. As the apostle Paul would later reveal, the Mosaic covenant was a kind of "guardian" whose introduction would not annul the covenant of promise already made with Abraham (Gal. 3:17, 24). Throughout the history of redemption, all of God's covenantal arrangements call for an obedience springing from faith in God and willing to observe the terms of the covenant.

10:30–39 Particular pledges of obedience are elaborated.

10:30 give our daughters. Intermarriage with people outside the covenant was a recurring problem in the history of Israel (cf. Ezra 4:3 note).

10:31 Sabbath. See Ex. 20:8–11; Deut. 5:12–15. See note 9:14.

10:32 a third part. Ex. 30:13, 14 prescribes half a shekel. The difference could be from the use of a new monetary system under the Persians, or it could be a concession to the hard economic times.

10:33 offerings. See Lev. 1–7.

10:39 not neglect the house of our God. Rebuilding the house of God is a major theme in Ezra and Nehemiah (Introduction to Ezra: Characteristics and Themes).

The Leaders in Jerusalem

11 Now the leaders of the people
[h]lived in Jerusalem. And the rest of
the people [i]cast lots to bring one out of ten
to live in Jerusalem [j]the holy city, while
nine out of ten[1] remained in the other
towns. **2** And the people blessed all the men
[k]who willingly offered to live in Jerusalem.
3 [l]These are the chiefs of the province who
lived in Jerusalem; but in the towns of Judah
[m]everyone lived on his property in their
towns: Israel, the priests, the Levites, [n]the
temple servants, [o]and the descendants of
Solomon's servants. **4** And in Jerusalem lived
certain of the sons of Judah and of the sons
of Benjamin. Of the sons of Judah: Athaiah
the son of Uzziah, son of Zechariah, son of
Amariah, son of Shephatiah, son of Mahalalel, of the sons of [p]Perez; **5** and Maaseiah
the son of Baruch, son of Col-hozeh, son of
Hazaiah, son of Adaiah, son of Joiarib, son
of Zechariah, son of the Shilonite. **6** All the
sons of Perez who lived in Jerusalem were
468 valiant men.
7 And these are the sons of Benjamin:
Sallu the son of Meshullam, son of Joed, son
of Pedaiah, son of Kolaiah, son of Maaseiah,
son of Ithiel, son of Jeshaiah, **8** and his brothers, men of valor, 928.[2] **9** Joel the son of
Zichri was their overseer; and Judah the son
of Hassenuah was second over the city.
10 Of the priests: Jedaiah the son of Joiarib,
Jachin, **11** Seraiah the son of Hilkiah, son of
Meshullam, son of Zadok, son of Meraioth,
son of Ahitub, ruler of the house of God,
12 and their brothers who did the work of the
house, 822; and Adaiah the son of Jeroham,
son of Pelaliah, son of Amzi, son of
Zechariah, son of Pashhur, son of Malchijah,
13 and his brothers, heads of fathers' houses,
242; and Amashsai, the son of Azarel, son of
Ahzai, son of Meshillemoth, son of Immer,
14 and their brothers, mighty men of valor,
128; their overseer was Zabdiel the son of
Haggedolim.

Chapter 11
1 [h][1 Chr. 9:3] [i]ch. 10:34 [j]ver. 18; Isai. 48:2; 52:1 Matt. 4:5; 27:53
2 [k][Judg. 5:9; 2 Chr. 17:16]
3 [l]For ver. 3-19, see 1 Chr. 9:2-34 [m]ver. 20 [n]Ezra 2:43 [o]Ezra 2:55
4 [p][Gen. 38:29]
16 [q]Ezra 8:33 [r]1 Chr. 26:29
17 [s]ch. 12:8, 24
18 [t]See ver. 1
20 [u]ver. 3
21 [v]ch. 3:26
23 [w]Ezra 6:8, 9; 7:20 [x]ch. 12:47; 2 Chr. 31:16
25 [y]Josh. 14:15; 21:11

15 And of the Levites: Shemaiah the son
of Hasshub, son of Azrikam, son of
Hashabiah, son of Bunni; **16** and Shabbethai
and [q]Jozabad, of the chiefs of the Levites,
who were over [r]the outside work of the
house of God; **17** and [s]Mattaniah the son of
Mica, son of Zabdi, son of Asaph, who was
the leader of the praise,[3] who gave thanks,
and Bakbukiah, the second among his
brothers; and Abda the son of Shammua,
son of Galal, son of Jeduthun. **18** All the
Levites in [t]the holy city were 284.
19 The gatekeepers, Akkub, Talmon and
their brothers, who kept watch at the gates,
were 172. **20** And the rest of Israel, and of
the priests and the Levites, were in all the
towns of Judah, [u]every one in his inheritance. **21** [v]But the temple servants lived on
Ophel; and Ziha and Gishpa were over the
temple servants.
22 The overseer of the Levites in Jerusalem
was Uzzi the son of Bani, son of Hashabiah,
son of Mattaniah, son of Mica, of the sons
of Asaph, the singers, over the work of the
house of God. **23** [w]For there was a command
from the king concerning them, and a fixed
provision for the singers, [x]as every day
required. **24** And Pethahiah the son of
Meshezabel, of the sons of Zerah the son of
Judah, was at the king's side[4] in all matters
concerning the people.

Villages Outside Jerusalem

25 And as for the villages, with their fields,
some of the people of Judah lived in
[y]Kiriath-arba and its villages, and in Dibon
and its villages, and in Jekabzeel and its villages, **26** and in Jeshua and in Moladah and
Beth-pelet, **27** in Hazar-shual, in Beersheba
and its villages, **28** in Ziklag, in Meconah and
its villages, **29** in En-rimmon, in Zorah, in
Jarmuth, **30** Zanoah, Adullam, and their villages, Lachish and its fields, and Azekah and

1 Hebrew *nine hands* 2 Compare Septuagint; Hebrew *And after him Gabbai, Sallai, 928* 3 Compare Septuagint, Vulgate; Hebrew *beginning* 4 Hebrew *hand*

11:1 cast lots. This phrase ties this list to the pledges in 10:30–39 (cf. 10:34) and shows the quick implementation of those pledges.

one out of ten. Populating the city by means of a tithe (a tenth) of the people is the first step in not neglecting the house of God, as pledged in 10:39.

the holy city. A rare phrase, used elsewhere only in v. 18; Is. 48:2; 52:1. Holiness has been expanding—from holy vessels (Ezra 1:7; cf. 8:28) to priests (Ezra 8:28), people (Ezra 9:2), the holy place (Ezra 9:8), the gates (3:1), the Sabbaths (9:14)—the entire city is now holy. The city with all that is in it has become holy, "God's house," which the Lord purposed to build (Heb. 3:1–6).

11:2 who willingly offered. This probably does not refer to a second group in addition to the tenth chosen by lot, but to a willing spirit in those who were chosen.

11:4 Judah . . . Benjamin. See note Ezra 1:5.

11:23 a command from the king. The reference may be to David (12:24; 1 Chr. 25) or to King Artaxerxes (Ezra 7:21–24).

11:25–36 This list is of those who resettled the surrounding area. It links with Ezra 2:21–35, binding Ezra and Nehemiah into a whole.

its villages. So they encamped from
Beersheba to [z]the valley of Hinnom. 31 The
people of Benjamin also lived from Geba
onward, at Michmash, Aija, Bethel and its
villages, 32 Anathoth, Nob, Ananiah, 33 Hazor,
Ramah, Gittaim, 34 Hadid, Zeboim, Neballat,
35 Lod, and [a]Ono, the valley of craftsmen.
36 And certain divisions of the Levites in
Judah were assigned to Benjamin.

Priests and Levites

12 These are [b]the priests and the Levites
who came up with [c]Zerubbabel the
son of Shealtiel, and [d]Jeshua: [e]Seraiah,
Jeremiah, Ezra, 2 Amariah, Malluch, Hattush,
3 Shecaniah, Rehum, Meremoth, 4 Iddo,
Ginnethoi, Abijah, 5 Mijamin, Maadiah,
Bilgah, 6 Shemaiah, Joiarib, Jedaiah, 7 Sallu,
Amok, Hilkiah, Jedaiah. These were the
chiefs of the priests and of their brothers in
the days of Jeshua.
8 And the Levites: Jeshua, Binnui,
Kadmiel, Sherebiah, Judah, and Mattaniah,
who with his brothers was [f]in charge of the
songs of thanksgiving. 9 And Bakbukiah
and Unni and their brothers stood opposite them [g]in the service. 10 And Jeshua was
the father of Joiakim, Joiakim the father of
Eliashib, Eliashib the father of Joiada,
11 Joiada the father of Jonathan, and
Jonathan the father of Jaddua.
12 [h]And in the days of Joiakim were
priests, heads of fathers' houses: of Seraiah,
Meraiah; of Jeremiah, Hananiah; 13 of Ezra,
Meshullam; of Amariah, Jehohanan; 14 of
Malluchi, Jonathan; of Shebaniah, Joseph;
15 of Harim, Adna; of Meraioth, Helkai; 16 of
Iddo, Zechariah; of Ginnethon, Meshullam;
17 of Abijah, Zichri; of Miniamin, of Moadiah,
Piltai; 18 of Bilgah, Shammua; of Shemaiah,
Jehonathan; 19 of Joiarib, Mattenai; of
Jedaiah, Uzzi; 20 of Sallai, Kallai; of Amok,
Eber; 21 of Hilkiah, Hashabiah; of Jedaiah,
Nethanel.
22 In the days of Eliashib, Joiada, Johanan,
and Jaddua, the Levites were recorded as
heads of fathers' houses; so too were the
priests in the reign of Darius the Persian.
23 As for the sons of Levi, their heads of
fathers' houses [i]were written in the Book of
the Chronicles until the days of Johanan the
son of Eliashib. 24 And the chiefs of the
Levites: Hashabiah, Sherebiah, and [j]Jeshua
the son of Kadmiel, with their brothers who
stood opposite them, [k]to praise and to give
thanks, [l]according to the commandment of
David [m]the man of God, [n]watch by watch.
25 Mattaniah, Bakbukiah, Obadiah, Meshullam, Talmon, and Akkub were gatekeepers
standing guard at [o]the storehouses of the
gates. 26 These were in the days of Joiakim the
son of Jeshua son of Jozadak, and in the days
of [p]Nehemiah the governor and of [p]Ezra, the
priest and scribe.

Dedication of the Wall

27 And at [q]the dedication of the wall of
Jerusalem they sought the Levites in all
their places, to bring them to Jerusalem to
celebrate the dedication with gladness,
with thanksgivings and with singing, [r]with
cymbals, harps, and lyres. 28 And the sons
of the singers gathered together from the
district surrounding Jerusalem and from
the villages of the Netophathites; 29 also
from Beth-gilgal and from the region of
Geba and Azmaveth, for the singers had
built for themselves villages around
Jerusalem. 30 And the priests and the
Levites [s]purified themselves, and they purified the people and the gates and the wall.
31 Then I brought the leaders of Judah up

30 [z]See Josh. 15:8
35 [a]ch. 6:2; 1 Chr. 8:12
Chapter 12
1 [b]Ezra 2:1, 2 [c]ver. 47; See 1 Chr. 3:19 [d]See Ezra 3:2 [e]For ver. 1-7, see ver. 12-21; ch. 10:2-8
8 [f]ver. 24; ch. 11:17; [2 Chr. 5:13]
9 [g][ver. 24]
12 [h]ver. 26
23 [i]See 1 Chr. 9:14-16
24 [j]ch. 10:9; Ezra 2:40 [k]ver. 24; ch. 11:17; [2 Chr. 5:13] [l]See 1 Chr. ch. 25 [m]ver. 36 [n][ver. 9; Ezra 3:11]
25 [o][1 Chr. 26:15]
26 [p]ch. 8:9
27 [q]See Num. 7:10 [r]See 1 Chr. 15:16
30 [s]ch. 13:22, 30

12:1–10 This list of priests and Levites who returned under Zerubbabel connects the end of Nehemiah to the beginning of Ezra, uniting the whole work.

12:1 Zerubbabel . . . Jeshua. See note Ezra 2:2.

Ezra. This is not the same Ezra as the leading figure of Ezra and Nehemiah. That Ezra returned eighty years after Zerubbabel (Ezra 7:6 note).

12:9 opposite them. For antiphonal singing, see v. 24.

12:10 Eliashib. See 3:1 and note.

12:12–21 This list is repeated with certain variations from vv. 1–7.

12:22–26 This is a list of heads of Levitical families.

12:22 Darius the Persian. This is Darius II (423–404 B.C.) or more probably Darius III (336–331).

12:27–43 The dedication ceremony is for the wall surrounding God's "house," the temple as such and the community, which is now complete. In this section Nehemiah writes in the first person (v. 31).

12:27 sought the Levites. The dedication could not take place without the help of the Levites, who are included in the preceding lists (vv. 1–26).

12:28, 29 the singers gathered. Hence the list in 11:22, 23.

12:30 purified. Ritual purification was a representation or symbol of moral purity (Lev. 16:30).

12:31–39 A grand procession took place, apparently beginning at the Valley Gate (3:13). Part of the procession, led by Ezra (v. 36), moved counterclockwise (v. 31), passing the Dung Gate, the Fountain Gate, and the Water Gate before proceeding to the temple. The other part of the procession, accompanied by Nehemiah (v. 38), moved clockwise (v. 38), passing the gates on the north side of the city before going to the temple. For the locations, see ch. 3 and notes.

onto the wall and appointed two great
choirs that gave thanks. [t]One went to the
south on the wall to [u]the Dung Gate. 32 And
after them went Hoshaiah and half of the
leaders of Judah, 33 and Azariah, Ezra,
Meshullam, 34 Judah, Benjamin, Shemaiah,
and Jeremiah, 35 and certain of the priests'
sons [v]with trumpets: Zechariah the son of
Jonathan, son of Shemaiah, son of
Mattaniah, son of Micaiah, son of Zaccur,
son of Asaph; 36 and his relatives, Shemaiah,
Azarel, Milalai, Gilalai, Maai, Nethanel,
Judah, and Hanani, [w]with the musical
instruments of David [x]the man of God. And
Ezra the scribe went before them. 37 At [y]the
Fountain Gate they went up straight before
them by [z]the stairs of the city of David, at
the ascent of the wall, above the house of
David, to [a]the Water Gate on the east.
38 [b]The other choir of those who gave
thanks went to the north, and I followed
them with half of the people, on the wall,
above [c]the Tower of the Ovens, to [d]the Broad
Wall, 39 and above [e]the Gate of Ephraim, and
by [f]the Gate of Yeshanah,[1] and by [g]the Fish
Gate and [h]the Tower of Hananel and [h]the
Tower of the Hundred, to [i]the Sheep Gate;
and they came to a halt at [j]the Gate of the
Guard. 40 So both choirs of those who gave
thanks stood in the house of God, and I and
half of the officials with me; 41 and the priests
Eliakim, Maaseiah, Miniamin, Micaiah,
Elioenai, Zechariah, and Hananiah, [k]with
trumpets; 42 and Maaseiah, Shemaiah,
Eleazar, Uzzi, Jehohanan, Malchijah, Elam,
and Ezer. And the singers sang with
Jezrahiah as their leader. 43 And they offered
great sacrifices that day and rejoiced, for God
had made them rejoice with great joy; the
women and children also rejoiced. And the
joy of Jerusalem was heard far away.

Service at the Temple

44 [l]On that day men were appointed over
the storerooms, the contributions, the firstfruits, and the tithes, to gather into them
the portions required by the Law for the
priests and for the Levites according to the
fields of the towns, for Judah rejoiced over
the priests and the Levites who ministered.
45 And they performed the service of their
God and the service of purification, as did
the singers and the gatekeepers, [m]accord-
ing to the command of David and his son
Solomon. 46 For long ago in the days of
David and [n]Asaph there were directors of
the singers, and there were songs[2] of praise
and thanksgiving to God. 47 And all Israel in
the days of Zerubbabel and in the days of
Nehemiah gave the [o]daily portions for the
singers and the gatekeepers; [p]and they set
apart that which was for the Levites; [q]and
the Levites set apart that which was for the
sons of Aaron.

Nehemiah's Final Reforms

13 On that day [r]they read from the
Book of Moses in the hearing of the
people. And in it was found written [s]that
no Ammonite or Moabite should ever enter
the assembly of God, 2 for they did not
meet the people of Israel with bread and
water, but hired Balaam against them to
curse them—yet our God turned the curse
into a blessing. 3 As soon as the people
heard the law, [t]they separated from Israel
all [u]those of foreign descent.
4 Now before this, [v]Eliashib the priest,
who [w]was appointed over the chambers of
the house of our God, and who was related
to [x]Tobiah, 5 prepared for Tobiah a large
chamber where they had previously put the
grain offering, the frankincense, the vessels,

1 Or *of the old city* 2 Or *leaders*

31 [t][ver. 38] [u]ch. 2:13; 3:13
35 [v]See 1 Chr. 15:24
36 [w]1 Chr. 23:5 [x]ver. 24
37 [y]ch. 2:14; 3:15 [z]ch. 3:15 [a]ch. 3:26; 8:1, 3, 16
38 [b][ver. 31] [c]ch. 3:11 [d]ch. 3:8
39 [e]See ch. 8:16 [f]ch. 3:6 [g]See ch. 3:3 [h]ch. 3:1 [i]See ch. 3:1 [j]See ch. 3:25
41 [k]See 1 Chr. 15:24
44 [l]ch. 13:5, 12, 13; [2 Chr. 31:11, 12]
45 [m]See 1 Chr. 25:26
46 [n]1 Chr. 25:1; 2 Chr. 29:30
47 [o]ch. 11:23; 2 Chr. 31:16 [p]Num. 18:21, 24 [q]See Num. 18:26-28
Chapter 13
1 [r]ch. 8:3, 8, 9, 18; 9:3; [Deut. 31:11, 12; 2 Kin. 23:2] [s]See Deut. 23:3-5
3 [t]See ch. 9:2 [u][Ex. 12:38; Num. 11:4]
4 [v]ver. 28; ch. 3:1 [w][ch. 12:44] [x]ch. 2:10

12:43 God had made them rejoice. The people rejoiced, because God had given them cause to do so by His sovereign work through human agents (Introduction to Ezra: Characteristics and Themes).

the women and children. Including women and children underlines the great size of the celebration (3:12 note; 5:1 note).

12:44–47 These verses show that the people had honored their pledge (10:39) and not neglected the house of God.

12:45 command of David and his son Solomon. See 1 Chr. 25; 2 Chr. 8:14.

12:47 all Israel. The people of God as a whole, not just the great leaders, are vital for accomplishing God's redemptive plan.

13:1–3 The pledge of general obedience to the Law of Moses (10:28, 29) included separation from neighboring peoples (10:28). The people did not conform to this aspect of the law (Deut. 23:3–6). The exclusion of "those of foreign descent" was in keeping with the pledge in 10:28, 29. It was religious separation, not racial or political (Ezra 4:3 note).

13:1 On that day. This was during Nehemiah's second term as governor, as indicated by the chronological references in vv. 4, 6.

13:3 heard the law. Though Ezra is not on the scene, his labor is still bearing fruit (10:1–27 note).

13:4–14 The final pledge, not to neglect the house of God (10:39), had been violated during Nehemiah's absence (v. 11), as had the pledges regarding the storehouse and the tithes (10:37–39). Reform was needed.

13:4 Eliashib. This Eliashib was possibly the high priest (3:1 note), but more likely another priest with the same name; the high priest would probably not have been put in charge of the storehouse.

Tobiah. See note 2:10.

and the tithes of grain, wine, and oil,
[y]which were given by commandment to the
Levites, singers, and gatekeepers, and the
contributions for the priests. 6 While this
was taking place, I was not in Jerusalem, for
[z]in the thirty-second year of Artaxerxes
[a]king of Babylon I went to the king. And
after some time I asked leave of the king
7 and came to Jerusalem, and I then discovered the evil that Eliashib had done for
Tobiah, [b]preparing for him a chamber in
the courts of the house of God. 8 And I was
very angry, and I threw all the household
furniture of Tobiah out of the chamber.
9 Then I gave orders, and they [c]cleansed the
chambers, and I brought back there the vessels of the house of God, with the grain
offering and the frankincense.

10 I also found out that [d]the portions of
the Levites had not been given to them, so
that the Levites and the singers, who did
the work, had fled each [e]to his field. 11 [f]So
I confronted the officials and said, [g]"Why
is the house of God forsaken?" And I
gathered them together and set them in
their stations. 12 Then all Judah brought
[h]the tithe of the grain, wine, and oil into
the storehouses. 13 And [i]I appointed as
treasurers over the storehouses Shelemiah
the priest, Zadok the scribe, and Pedaiah
of the Levites, and as their assistant
Hanan the son of Zaccur, son of Mattaniah, [j]for they were considered reliable,
and their duty was to distribute to their
brothers. 14 [k]Remember me, O my God,
concerning this, and do not wipe out my
good deeds that I have done for the house
of my God and for his service.

15 In those days I saw in Judah people
treading winepresses [l]on the Sabbath, and
bringing in heaps of grain and loading them
on donkeys, and also wine, grapes, figs, and
all kinds of loads, [m]which they brought into
Jerusalem on the Sabbath day. And [n]I
warned them on the day when they sold
food. 16 Tyrians also, who lived in the city,
brought in fish and all kinds of goods and
sold them on the Sabbath to the people of
Judah, in Jerusalem itself! 17 [o]Then I confronted the nobles of Judah and said to
them, "What is this evil thing that you are
doing, [p]profaning the Sabbath day? 18 [q]Did
not your fathers act in this way, and did not
our God bring all this disaster[1] on us and
on this city? Now you are bringing more
wrath on Israel by profaning the Sabbath."

19 As soon as it [r]began to grow dark at the
gates of Jerusalem before the Sabbath, I
commanded that the doors should be shut
and gave orders that they should not be
opened until after the Sabbath. And I stationed some of my servants at the gates,
that no load might be brought in on the
Sabbath day. 20 Then the merchants and
sellers of all kinds of wares lodged outside
Jerusalem once or twice. 21 [s]But I warned
them and said to them, "Why do you lodge
outside the wall? If you do so again, I will
lay hands on you." From that time on they
did not come on the Sabbath. 22 Then I
commanded the Levites [t]that they should
purify themselves and come and guard the
gates, to keep the Sabbath day holy.
[u]Remember this also in my favor, O my
God, and spare me according to the greatness of your steadfast love.

23 In those days also I saw the Jews [v]who
had married women [w]of Ashdod, [x]Ammon,

5 [y]Num. 18:21, 24
6 [z]ch. 5:14 [a]Ezra 6:22
7 [b]ver. 5
9 [c]2 Chr. 29:15, 16, 18
10 [d]2 Chr. 31:4; [Mal. 3:8] [e]ch. 12:28, 29
11 [f]ver. 17, 25 [g][ch. 10:39]
12 [h][ch. 10:38, 39; 12:44]
13 [i][2 Chr. 31:12, 13] [j]ch. 7:2; [1 Cor. 4:2]
14 [k]ver. 22, 31; ch. 5:19
15 [l][Ex. 20:10] [m]See ch. 10:31 [n]ver. 21
17 [o]ver. 11 [p][Matt. 12:5]
18 [q]See Jer. 17:19-23
19 [r]Lev. 23:32
21 [s]ver. 15
22 [t]ch. 12:30 [u][ver. 14, 31]
23 [v]Ezra 9:2; 10:10 [w][ch. 4:7] [x][ver. 1; Ezra 9:1]

1 The Hebrew word can mean *evil, harm,* or *disaster*, depending on context

13:6 I was not in Jerusalem. See note 5:14.

king of Babylon. The Persian kings bore this title after the conquest of the Babylonian Empire (Ezra 5:13).

13:8 threw. Compare Matt. 21:12, 13.

13:10 portions of the Levites. These words link this section to the pledge in 10:37. The Levites possessed no land (Num. 18:20–24; Deut. 14:29; 18:1), though some may have had private income (Deut. 18:8). The dependence of the Levites on the support of the people may explain the reluctance of many Levites to leave Babylonia (Ezra 8:15–20).

13:11 So I confronted. See note 5:7.

forsaken. The pledge not to neglect the house of God (10:39) had been violated.

13:12 brought the tithe. They did so in keeping with the pledge in 10:37.

13:13 reliable. Cf. Acts 6:1–5; 2 Cor. 8:16–21.

13:14 Remember me. The fourth use of "remember" in a prayer (1:8 note), and the second of four prayers by Nehemiah with the theme "remember me" (5:19 note).

13:15 Sabbath . . . bringing . . . sold. Three links with the pledge in 10:31 that had been violated.

13:16 Tyrians. These men were one of the "peoples of the land" in view in 10:31.

13:19 began to grow dark. The Israelites usually counted days from sunset to sunset (Lev. 23:32; Esth. 4:16; Dan. 8:14 text note).

13:22 Remember. See note on v. 14.

13:23 married. Ezra had dealt with this perennial problem twenty-five years before (Ezra 9:1 note).

Ashdod. See note 4:7, 8.

and [x]Moab. 24 And half of their children
spoke the language of Ashdod, and they
could not speak the language of Judah, but
the language of each people. 25 [o]And I confronted them and cursed them and beat
some of them and pulled out their hair.
[y]And I made them take oath in the name of
God, saying, "You shall not give your
daughters to their sons, or take their
daughters for your sons or for yourselves.
26 [z]Did not Solomon king of Israel sin on
account of such women? [a]Among the many
nations there was no king like him, and he
was [b]beloved by his God, and God made
him king over all Israel. Nevertheless, foreign women made even him to sin. 27 Shall
we then listen to you and do all this great
evil and [c]act treacherously against our God
by marrying foreign women?"
28 And one of the sons of [d]Jehoiada, the
son of [e]Eliashib the high priest, was the son-
in-law of [f]Sanballat the Horonite. Therefore
I chased him from me. 29 [g]Remember them,
O my God, because they have desecrated
the priesthood [h]and the covenant of the
priesthood and the Levites.
30 [i]Thus I cleansed them from everything
foreign, and I established the duties of the
priests and Levites, each in his work; 31 and
I provided [j]for the wood offering [k]at
appointed times, and for the firstfruits.
[l]Remember me, O my God, for good.

23 [x][ver. 1; Ezra 9:1]
25 [o][See ver. 17 above] [y]Ezra 10:5; [ch. 10:29, 30]
26 [z]See 1 Kin. 11:1-8 [a]1 Kin. 3:13; 2 Chr. 1:12 [b][2 Sam. 12:24]
27 [c]Ezra 10:2
28 [d]ch. 12:10, 11, 22 [e]ver. 4, 7; ch. 3:1; 13:4, 7 [f]ch. 2:10, 19
29 [g][ch. 6:14] [h]Mal. 2:4
30 [i]ch. 10:30
31 [j]ch. 10:34 [k]Ezra 10:14 [l]ver. 14, 22

13:25 pulled out their hair. Nehemiah's action can be contrasted with that of Ezra in Ezra 9:3.

shall not give. Ezra actually dissolved the illegitimate unions (Ezra 10:3 note), whereas Nehemiah only attempted to prevent such unions in the future.

13:26 even him. The argument is from the greater to the less: "If Solomon was not spared, how much less will we be spared."

13:28 son-in-law. His marriage was doubly grievous, first, because a high priest in particular was not to marry a foreigner (Lev. 21:14), and second, because Sanballat was an enemy (2:19; 4:1; 6:1).

13:29 Remember them. The sixth use of "remember" in a prayer (1:8 note), and the third imprecatory prayer (4:4, 5 note).

13:31 wood. Contributions of wood are made in keeping with the pledge in 10:34.

Remember me. See note on v. 14. The book does not end on the high note of 12:27–47, but on the note of failure to carry out the pledges of 10:30–39 and the continuing need for reform. The people of God had not arrived at a resting place. Ezra and Nehemiah show the devotion of the faithful to the temple of God and the community surrounding it, a devotion that comes to maturity in Christ and the church (1 Cor. 3:5–17; Eph. 2:21, 22; 4:16; Heb. 3:1–6).

THE BOOK OF

Esther

AUTHOR

Although the author of the Book of Esther is unknown, his interest in the origin and observance of the festival of Purim, his intense nationalism, and his intimate knowledge of the Persian court, customs, and geography suggest that he was a Persian Jew living in Susa.

DATE AND OCCASION

The earliest possible date for the book is sometime after the events described in it, that is, the fifth century B.C. The latest possible date is during the first century B.C. A late fifth- or fourth-century dating is now generally preferred by scholars, who point to linguistic evidence as well as the author's favorable attitude toward the Persian king and Gentiles in general as evidence for an early date.

The writer of Esther clearly intended his book to explain the origin of the celebration of Purim, to establish Purim as a festival celebrated by each new generation of Jews, and to regulate its observance (9:20–32).

INTERPRETIVE DIFFICULTIES

The question of whether the Book of Esther belongs in the canon of Scripture has been raised from an early period by both Jews and Christians, though the book's commendation of the popular festival of Purim argued strongly in favor of its inclusion in the Jewish canon. Objections voiced by some Christians to Esther's canonicity included its absence from some of the earliest lists of canonical books, its lack of citation in the New Testament, its lack of overt references to God and to religious practices, its excessive Jewish nationalism, and its spirit of vengeance. Some of these objections were alleviated when the early church adopted an expanded version of the Book of Esther found in the Septuagint (the Greek translation of the Old Testament). This Septuagint text contains over one hundred verses, not found in the Hebrew text, that made the book more religiously acceptable to some. These additions include a dream of Mordecai about the coming destruction of the Jews and prayers of Mordecai and Esther for deliverance. However, when the Protestant churches judged the shorter Hebrew version of Esther to be the authoritative version, objections to the book's canonicity resurfaced.

The violence in the Book of Esther is a kind of civil war, which Cicero called the worst of all calamities. The author of Esther shows the relief of the people when justice triumphs, and does not criticize the means employed, such as the hanging of Haman's sons. But it would be a mistake to consider these events as models for behavior. The extreme situation and threat under which they happened limits what can be concluded from them. The author does not engage in moral reflection about the massive killing and the motives of avengers. The reader struggling with some of the questions that arise needs to go to other places, such as the prophets, Job, or Revelation, where the discussion includes them and answers may be found. Positively, the Book of Esther testifies clearly to the invisible hand of Providence, which will not allow the covenant people to be utterly destroyed.

CHARACTERISTICS AND THEMES

The Book of Esther is renowned for the high quality of its literary artistry, which functions as the principal vehicle for its religious meaning. The author skillfully uses narrative tensions created by reversals or sharp contrasts of fortunes and expectations, and by roles that are often highly ironic in nature. Notice the two descriptions of banquets of Ahasuerus and his wife, the first described in full detail and the second presented tersely (1:1–8, 9); the striking contrast between the initial portrait of the king as powerful and pompous (1:1–8) and the subsequent revelation of his incompetence and weakness; the effective contrast between the king's response when Vashti failed to appear before him and when Esther appeared unannounced (1:11–21; 5:1–3); the ironic reversal of Haman's career (6:4–12); the pathetic scene in which Haman pleads for Esther's mercy, only to be accused of attempted rape (7:7–9); and the poetic justice of hanging Haman on his own gallows. The last is an example of the ironic reversals in the fortunes and position of Haman and Mordecai (7:9–10; 8:1–2; 9:25). Such reversals, when compared with those of the Exodus, the Babylonian exile, and even the Crucifixion and Resurrection, subtly reveal God's hand in the salvation history of His people.

The writer also uses repetition or duplication to weave the various parts of the story together. For example, notice the three references to official records ("chronicles") located at significant turning points in the narrative (2:23; 6:1; 10:2). There are three sets of paired banquets marking the beginning, middle, and end of the book: the banquets of Ahasuerus (1:3–4, 5–8), Esther (5:4–8; 7:1–10), and the two celebrations of Purim (9:18–32). See also the banquet theme in 1:9; 2:18; 3:15; 8:17; 9:17; the threefold mention of the size of Ahasuerus's empire (1:1; 8:9; 9:30); the repeated promise to Esther of "even to the half of my kingdom" (5:3, 6; 7:2; cf. 9:12); the repeated insistence that the Hebrews did not plunder their enemies (9:10, 15–16); the two accounts of Esther's hidden identity (2:10, 20); the double assembling of virgins (2:8, 19); Haman's two interchanges with his wife and friends (5:10–14; 6:13–14); the two veilings of Haman's head (6:12; 7:8); the two references to the subsiding of Ahasuerus's anger (2:1; 7:10); and the two reminders that the laws of the Medes and Persians cannot be altered (1:19; 8:8). The use of the number "seven" is noteworthy (1:5, 10, 14), as is Esther's repeated request and reception of favor (2:9, 15, 17; 5:2, 8; 7:3; 8:9).

The literary technique of foreshadowing is also employed in the Book of Esther. Most striking is the prediction of Haman's wife that he would "surely fall" because Mordecai was a Jew (6:13). The author is a master of suspense and paces the speed of the narrative well. The constant references to time not only present the events as history (1:1, 2) and underscore the theme of God's providential working in history, but also keep the story moving (e.g., 2:1, 15, 19, 21; 3:1).

The writer of Esther creatively builds upon the symbolic or typical aspects of the names of two of the main characters to show how the personal antagonism between Haman, the archenemy of the Jews, and Mordecai, the faithful Jew, was part of the historic conflict between Israel and the Amalekites. This conflict provides the foundation for the plot against all the Jews (2:5 note; 3:1 note). Similarities in phrasing, setting, story line, and emphasis also suggest that the Joseph story was an important model for the writer of Esther (note the similarities between 2:2–4 and Gen. 41:34–37; 3:10 and Gen. 41:42; 8:6 and Gen. 44:34).

A number of important themes are intertwined in the book. The theme of feasting or banquets establishes the setting of the main action of the narrative, culminating with the celebration of Purim, and contrasting with the theme of fasting (4:3, 16; 9:31). A contrast of obedience and disobedience also runs through the book. The initial disobedience of Vashti in ch. 1 sets the stage for the challenges facing Esther about obeying Mordecai (2:10, 20; 4:8–16) and standing up against the king's law (4:11, 16; 5:1, 2). The stage is also set for Mordecai's refusal to obey Haman's command, and his contrary willingness to carry out Esther's instructions (4:17) and to serve both the Persian king and the best interests of the Jews (10:3). The theme of providential protection of the Jews, as indicated in 4:14, is basic to the narrative and is a reason for the book's continuing significance among the community of faith. Related to this theme is that of rest and relief from enemies, which the feast of Purim commemorates (9:16, 22, cf. Deut. 25:19). Though God is not explicitly mentioned in this book, the reader nevertheless learns through the narrative that God is always, if invisibly, present with His people. He continues to guide and protect them today, even as He defended them in ancient Persia.

OUTLINE OF ESTHER

I. Selection of Esther as Queen (chs. 1; 2)
- A. *The Downfall of Queen Vashti (ch. 1)*
- B. *The Rise of Queen Esther (2:1–18)*
- C. *A Conspiracy Discovered (2:19–23)*

II. Plot to Destroy the Jews (chs. 3; 4)
- A. *Haman's Promotion and Plot (ch. 3)*
- B. *Mordecai's Counterplan (ch. 4)*

III. Esther Saves the Jews (5:1–9:15)
- A. *Esther's Uninvited Audience with the King (5:1–8)*
- B. *Haman's Plan to Hang Mordecai (5:9–14)*
- C. *Haman's Humiliation and Mordecai's Reward (6:1–13)*
- D. *Haman's Execution (6:14–7:10)*
- E. *Plan for Deliverance of the Jews (ch. 8)*
- F. *Victory for the Jews (9:1–15)*

IV. Establishment of the Feast of Purim (9:16–32)

V. Epilogue (ch. 10)

The King's Banquets

1 Now in the days of Ahasuerus, the
Ahasuerus who reigned [a]from India to
Ethiopia over [b]127 provinces, 2 in those
days when King Ahasuerus [c]sat on his royal
throne in [d]Susa, the capital,[1] 3 in the third
year of his reign [e]he gave a feast for all his
officials and servants. The army of Persia
and Media and the nobles and governors of
the provinces were before him, 4 while he
showed the riches of his royal glory and the
splendor and pomp of his greatness for
many days, 180 days. 5 And when these
days were completed, the king gave for all
the people present in Susa, the citadel,
both great and small, a feast lasting for
seven days in the court of [f]the garden of the
king's palace. 6 There were white cotton
curtains and violet hangings fastened with
cords of fine linen and purple to silver
rods[2] and marble pillars, and also [g]couch-
es of gold and silver on a mosaic pavement
of porphyry, marble, mother-of-pearl and
precious stones. 7 Drinks were served in
golden vessels, vessels of different kinds,
and the royal wine was lavished according
to the bounty of the king. 8 And drinking
was according to this edict: "There is no
compulsion." For the king had given
orders to all the staff of his palace to do as
each man desired. 9 Queen Vashti also gave
a feast for the women in the palace that
belonged to King Ahasuerus.

Queen Vashti's Refusal

10 On the seventh day, [h]when the heart of
the king was merry with wine, he commanded Mehuman, Biztha, [i]Harbona,
[j]Bigtha and Abagtha, Zethar and Carkas,
the seven eunuchs who served in the presence of King Ahasuerus, 11 to bring Queen
Vashti before the king with [k]her royal
crown,[3] in order to show the peoples and
the princes her beauty, for she was lovely
to look at. 12 But Queen Vashti refused to
come at the king's command delivered by
the eunuchs. At this the king became
enraged, and his anger burned within him.
13 Then the king said to [l]the wise men
[m]who knew the times (for this was the
king's procedure toward all who were
versed in law and judgment, 14 the men
next to him being Carshena, Shethar,

Chapter 1
1 [a]ch. 8:9 [b]ch. 8:9; 9:30; [Dan. 6:1]
2 [c]1 Kin. 1:46 [d]See Neh. 1:1
3 [e]ch. 2:18; [Gen. 40:20; 1 Kin. 3:15; Mark 6:21]
5 [f]ch. 7:7, 8
6 [g][Ezek. 23:41; Amos 6:4]
10 [h][2 Sam. 13:28] [i]ch. 7:9 [j][ch. 2:21; 6:2]
11 [k]ch. 2:17; 6:8
13 [l]Jer. 10:7; Dan. 2:12, 13; Matt. 2:1 [m]1 Chr. 12:32

[1] *Or the fortified city* [2] *Or rings* [3] *Or headdress*

1:1 Ahasuerus. Also known as Xerxes (486–465 B.C.), Ahasuerus was the Persian king mentioned in Ezra 4:6. He was renowned for consolidating his father Darius's empire, for his successful building projects, and for his wars against the Greeks from 480–470 B.C.

Ethiopia. In Hebrew, "Cush," the region south of Egypt, now part of northern Sudan.

127 provinces. The reference here to the large number of divisions within the twenty larger administrative districts, or satrapies, in the Persian Empire is intended to impress.

1:2 Susa, the capital. This acropolis, a fortified palace 120 feet above the surrounding city of Susa, was one of the three Persian capitals and the royal winter residence. It has been excavated several times since 1851.

1:3 in the third year. 483 B.C.

1:4–7 For 180 days the king ostentatiously displayed the royal wealth. The extravagant seven-day outdoor feast was the climax of the celebrations. The elaborate details about the drinking vessels and the abundance of the wine stress the king's lavish generosity.

1:9 Vashti. This name, not found elsewhere, may be related to the Persian word meaning "the beloved" or "the best." Extrabiblical sources name Ahasuerus's queen as Amestris. He may have had other queens.

1:12 Reasons for Vashti's disobedience are not given in the Hebrew text, though early Jewish interpreters explained that she was commanded to appear naked, wearing only her crown, or that she had some disfigurement. The queen's refusal to obey introduces the theme of obedience and disobedience.

1:13, 14 the times. This expression usually refers to astrology, though in this context it probably means "the proper course to follow" (cf. 1 Chr. 12:32). The satirical flavor of the narrative is evident as the king, who has just displayed all the power and glory of his magnificent kingdom, has to consult experts on matters of law and justice, and to go to the nobles (cf. Ezra 7:14) for advice on how to deal with his wife's behavior.

Admatha, Tarshish, Meres, Marsena, and
[n]Memucan, [o]the seven princes of Persia
and Media, [p]who saw the king's face, and
sat first in the kingdom): 15 "According to
the law, what is to be done to Queen
Vashti, because she has not performed the
command of King Ahasuerus delivered by
the eunuchs?" 16 Then Memucan said in the
presence of the king and the officials, "Not
only against the king has Queen Vashti
done wrong, but also against all the officials and all the peoples who are in all the
provinces of King Ahasuerus. 17 For the
queen's behavior will be made known to all
women, causing them to look at their husbands with contempt, since they will say,
'King Ahasuerus commanded Queen
Vashti to be brought before him, and she
did not come.' 18 This very day the noble
women of Persia and Media who have
heard of the queen's behavior will say the
same to all the king's officials, and there
will be contempt and wrath in plenty. 19 If
it please the king, let a royal order go out
from him, and let it be written among the
laws of the Persians and the Medes so [q]that
it may not be repealed, that Vashti is never
again to come before King Ahasuerus. And
let the king give her royal position to
another who is better than she. 20 So when
the decree made by the king is proclaimed
throughout all his kingdom, for it is vast,
[r]all women will give honor to their husbands, high and low alike." 21 This advice
pleased the king and the princes, and the
king did as Memucan proposed. 22 He sent
letters to all the royal provinces, [s]to every
province in its own script and to every people in its own language, that every man be
master in his own household and speak
according to the language of his people.

14 [n]ver. 16, 21 [o]Ezra 7:14 [p]2 Kin. 25:19
19 [q]ch. 8:8; Dan. 6:8, 12, 15
20 [r][Eph. 5:22, 24, 33; Col. 3:18; 1 Tim. 2:12; 1 Pet. 3:1]
22 [s]ch. 3:12; 8:9
Chapter 2
1 [t][ch. 7:10] [u]ch. 1:19, 20

Esther Chosen Queen

2 After these things, [t]when the anger of
King Ahasuerus had abated, he remembered Vashti [u]and what she had done and
what had been decreed against her. 2 Then
the king's young men who attended him
said, "Let beautiful young virgins be sought
out for the king. 3 And let the king appoint
officers in all the provinces of his kingdom to
gather all the beautiful young virgins to the

1:19 laws of the Persians . . . may not be repealed. The permanency of royal law is an important feature in the development of the story (4:11; 8:8). The plan to banish Vashti and to give her position to someone better, more beautiful or more obedient, had to be carried out.

1:21, 22 letters to all the royal provinces. The Persian postal system, renowned for its efficiency, was used to publish the irrevocable royal edicts (3:12–14; 8:9, 10; cf. 9:20, 30).

2:1 abated. The use of the same rare verb in 7:10 suggests a parallel between the dismissal of Vashti and the hanging of Haman.

he remembered Vashti. The king may have regretted his actions, but it was too late; the legislation had made his actions permanent.

Persian Empire (500 B.C.). The rise of Persia was rapid. In 550 B.C. Cyrus the Persian inherited the kingdom of the Medes. In 546 B.C. he captured the Lydian capital of Sardis. In 539 B.C. he took Babylon without a fight. In 538 B.C. he permitted the Jews to begin returning to Palestine and supported their cause in rebuilding their homeland. By 500 B.C. the Persian Empire stretched from India in the east through Asia Minor to Greece in the west, and included Egypt and some of coastal Africa to the south.

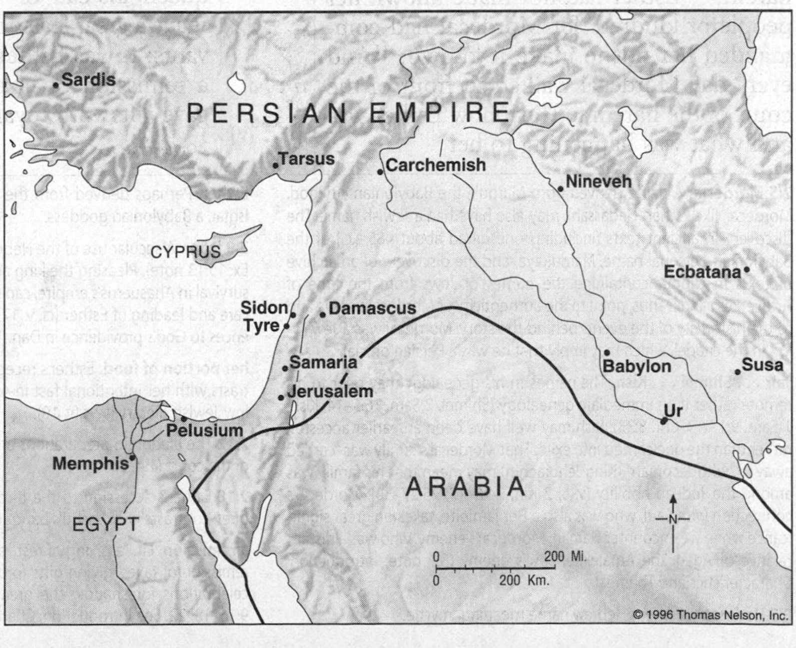

harem in Susa the capital, under custody of
[v]Hegai, the king's eunuch, who is in charge
of the women. [w]Let their cosmetics be given
them. 4 And let the young woman who pleases the king be queen instead of Vashti." This
pleased the king, and he did so.
5 Now there was a Jew in Susa the citadel
whose name was [x]Mordecai, the son of Jair,
son of Shimei, son of Kish, a Benjaminite,
6 [y]who had been carried away from
Jerusalem among the captives carried away
with Jeconiah king of Judah, whom
Nebuchadnezzar king of Babylon had carried away. 7 He was bringing up Hadassah,
that is Esther, [z]the daughter of his uncle,
for she had neither father nor mother. The
young woman had a beautiful figure and
was lovely to look at, and when her father
and her mother died, Mordecai took her as
his own daughter. 8 So when the king's
order and his edict were proclaimed, and
[a]when many young women were gathered
in Susa the citadel in custody of [b]Hegai,
Esther also was taken into the king's palace
and put in custody of Hegai, who had
charge of the women. 9 And the young
woman pleased him and won his favor.
And he quickly provided her [c]with her cosmetics and her portion of food, and with
seven chosen young women from the
king's palace, and advanced her and her
young women to the best place in the
harem. 10 [d]Esther had not made known her
people or kindred, for Mordecai had commanded her not to make it known. 11 And
every day Mordecai walked in front of the
court of the harem to learn how Esther was
and what was happening to her.

12 Now when the turn came for each
young woman to go in to King Ahasuerus,
after being twelve months under the regulations for the women, since this was the regular period of their beautifying, six months
with oil of myrrh and six months with spices
and ointments for women— 13 when the
young woman went in to the king in this
way, she was given whatever she desired to
take with her from the harem to the king's
palace. 14 In the evening she would go in,
and in the morning she would return to
the second harem in custody of Shaashgaz,
the king's eunuch, who was in charge of the
concubines. She would not go in to the king
again, unless the king delighted in her and
she was summoned by name.
15 When the turn came for Esther [e]the
daughter of Abihail the uncle of Mordecai,
who had taken her as his own daughter, to
go in to the king, she asked for nothing
except what [f]Hegai the king's eunuch, who
had charge of the women, advised. Now
Esther was winning favor in the eyes of all
who saw her. 16 And when Esther was taken
to King Ahasuerus into his royal palace in
the tenth month, which is the month of
Tebeth, in the seventh year of his reign,
17 the king loved Esther more than all the
women, and she won grace and favor in his
sight more than all the virgins, so that he set
[g]the royal crown[1] on her head and made her
queen instead of Vashti. 18 Then the king
[h]gave a great feast for all his officials and servants; it was Esther's feast. He also granted
a remission of taxes to the provinces and
gave gifts with royal generosity.

[1] Or *headdress*

3 [v]ver. 8, 15 [w]ver. 9, 12
5 [x]Ezra 2:2
6 [y]2 Kin. 24:14, 15; 2 Chr. 36:10, 20; Jer. 24:1; 29:1, 2
7 [z]ver. 15
8 [a]ver. 3 [b]ver. 3
9 [c]ver. 3, 12
10 [d]ver. 20
15 [e]ver. 7; ch. 9:29
15 [f]ver. 3, 8
17 [g]ch. 1:11; 6:8
18 [h]See ch. 1:3

2:5 Mordecai. A name derived from Marduk, the Babylonian city-god. Mordecai, like Esther (Hadassah), may also have had a Jewish name. The discovery in ancient texts (including one dated about 485 B.C.) of the Babylonian personal name, Mardukaya, and the discovery of an archive of texts in Nippur containing the names of Jews from the time of Artaxerxes I and Darius, point to the authenticity of Mordecai's name and to the historicity of the events behind the story. Mordecai was a Jew living in the citadel, which may imply that he was a Persian official.

Jair . . . Shimei . . . Kish. The names in his genealogy may refer to his remote rather than immediate genealogy (Shimei, 2 Sam. 16:5–14; Kish, 1 Sam. 9:1–2; 1 Chr. 8:33). Kish may well have been an earlier ancestor, rather than the one carried into exile. That Mordecai's family was "carried away . . . with Jeconiah" (King Jehoiachin) may mean that his family was among the Judean nobility (v. 6; 2 Kin. 24:6–17; 25:27–30). Mordecai's connection with Saul, who was also a Benjaminite, takes on great significance when we encounter Haman, Mordecai's enemy, who was a distant relative of Agag, the Amalekite, Saul's enemy (3:1 note; Introduction: Characteristics and Themes).

2:7 Hadassah. Esther's Hebrew name meaning "myrtle."

Esther. Perhaps derived from the Persian word for "star," or a form of Ishtar, a Babylonian goddess.

2:9 favor. A secular use of the Hebrew word for covenant loyalty (*hesed*, Ex. 15:13 note). Pleasing the king and gaining his favor, so necessary for survival in Ahasuerus's empire, can be seen as signs of God's providential care and leading of Esther (cf. v. 17; 5:2; contrast the more explicit references to God's providence in Dan. 1:9).

her portion of food. Esther's reception of special portions of food contrasts with her intentional fast in 4:16. Unlike Daniel, Esther did not follow Jewish dietary laws (v. 10).

2:12 The elaborate preparations are in keeping with the other excesses of the court (1:4–8).

2:18 Esther's accession to the throne, which is celebrated with a banquet, contrasts with Vashti's banquet in 1:9.

a remission. Lit. "a giving of rest," a celebration that may have included remission of taxes, giving gifts (probably food), and other favors. These celebrations foreshadow the great banquet and rest for the Jews in 9:16–18, 22. See Introduction: Characteristics and Themes.

Mordecai Discovers a Plot

19 Now when the virgins were gathered
together [i]the second time, Mordecai was
sitting [j]at the king's gate. 20 [k]Esther had not
made known her kindred or her people, as
Mordecai had commanded her, for Esther
obeyed Mordecai just [l]as when she was
brought up by him. 21 In those days, as
Mordecai was sitting at the king's gate,
[m]Bigthan and [n]Teresh, two of the king's
eunuchs, who guarded the threshold,
became angry and sought to lay hands on
King Ahasuerus. 22 And this came to the
knowledge of Mordecai, [o]and he told it to
Queen Esther, and Esther told the king in
the name of Mordecai. 23 When the affair
was investigated and found to be so, the
men were both hanged on the gallows.[1]
And it was recorded in [p]the book of the
chronicles in the presence of the king.

Haman Plots Against the Jews

3 After these things King Ahasuerus
[q]promoted Haman [r]the Agagite, the
son of Hammedatha, [s]and advanced him
and set his throne above all the officials
who were with him. 2 And all the king's servants who were at the king's gate bowed
down and paid homage to Haman, for the
king had so commanded concerning him.
[t]But Mordecai did not bow down or pay
homage. 3 Then the king's servants who
were [u]at the king's gate said to Mordecai,
"Why do you transgress [v]the king's command?" 4 And when they spoke to him day
after day and he would not listen to them,
they told Haman, in order to see whether
Mordecai's words would stand, for he had
told them that he was a Jew. 5 And when
Haman saw that [t]Mordecai did not bow
down or pay homage to him, Haman was
[w]filled with fury. 6 But he disdained to lay
hands on Mordecai alone. So, as they had
made known to him the people of
Mordecai, Haman sought to destroy all the
Jews, the people of Mordecai, throughout
the whole kingdom of Ahasuerus.
7 In the first month, which is the month
of Nisan, in the twelfth year of King
Ahasuerus, [x]they cast Pur (that is, they cast
lots) before Haman day after day; and they
cast it month after month till the twelfth
month, which is [y]the month of Adar.
8 Then Haman said to King Ahasuerus,
"There is a certain people scattered abroad
and dispersed among the peoples in all the
provinces of your kingdom. [z]Their laws are
different from those of every other people,
and they do not keep the king's laws, so
that it is not to the king's profit to tolerate
them. 9 If it please the king, let it be
decreed that they be destroyed, and I will
pay 10,000 talents[2] of silver into the hands
of those who have charge of the king's
business, that they may put it into the
king's treasuries." 10 [a]So the king took his
signet ring from his hand and gave it to
Haman [b]the Agagite, the son of Hammedatha, [c]the enemy of the Jews. 11 And
the king said to Haman, "The money is
given to you, the people also, to do with
them as it seems good to you."

19 [i]ver. 3, 4 [j]ver. 21; ch. 3:2, 3; 5:9, 13; 6:10, 12
20 [k]ver. 10 [l]ver. 7
21 [m][ch. 1:10; 6:2] [n]ch. 6:2
22 [o]ch. 6:2; [ch. 7:9]
23 [p]ch. 6:1; 10:2
Chapter 3
1 [q]ch. 5:11 [r]ver. 10; ch. 8:3, 5; 9:24 [s]ch. 5:11
2 [t]ch. 5:9
3 [u]See ch. 2:19 [v]ver. 2
5 [t][See ver. 2 above] [w]Dan. 3:19
7 [x]ch. 9:24, 26 [y]Ezra 6:15
8 [z][Ezra 4:12, 13; Acts 16:20, 21]
10 [a]ch. 8:2; Gen. 41:42 [b]ver. 1 [c]ch. 7:6; 8:1; 9:10, 24

[1] Or *suspended on a stake* [2] A *talent* was about 75 pounds or 34 kilograms

2:19 at the king's gate. This expression (cf. v. 21; 3:2; 5:9, 13; 6:10, 12) may imply that Mordecai had been made a palace official, a position that not only enabled him to discover the conspiracy to assassinate the king (v. 21), but also may have incited Haman's jealousy (5:13).

2:23 on the gallows. Lit. "on a tree." This refers to impalement on wooden stakes, a Persian and Assyrian form of execution. To the Jews, this would be a sign that the two officials were under God's curse (Deut. 21:22, 23 and note), confirming the appropriateness of Mordecai's loyalty to the pagan king.

recorded in the book of the chronicles. Mordecai was not rewarded at this time (6:1–11); instead, the account of Haman's promotion is given (3:1).

3:1 Haman the Agagite. Although the names "Haman" and "Hammedatha" may be Persian, the identification of Haman as "the Agagite" suggests an important association with Agag, the king of the Amalekites, the archenemies of Israel, who were opposed by Saul (Ex. 17:8–16; Deut. 25:17–19; 1 Sam. 14:47–15:35).

3:2 Mordecai did not bow down or pay homage. Mordecai's refusal to honor Haman cannot be explained on the basis of Old Testament law, since Jews did not regard bowing before kings and other honored persons as a violation of the first and second commandments (Ex. 20:3–6; 1 Sam. 25:23; 2 Sam. 18:28; 2 Kin. 4:37). Haman and Mordecai are best understood as representatives of two hostile nations—Israel and its enemy Amalek, a nation under divine curse (v. 1 note). Mordecai's refusal to bow down to his hereditary enemy because he (Mordecai) "was a Jew" is understandable (v. 4). Similarly, Haman's seemingly excessive passion to destroy the entire Jewish nation for Mordecai's insolence is explained (v. 6).

3:7 Pur (that is, they cast lots). Haman used the ancient practice of casting lots (1 Sam. 14:41–42; Prov. 16:33) to determine the most propitious time to set in motion his plan to destroy the Jews. The plural form of *Pur, Purim,* is the name of the celebration that commemorates the death of Haman, the enemy of all the Jews (9:23–32).

3:9 10,000 talents of silver. This enormous bribe is calculated to have been about two-thirds the annual revenue of the Persian Empire under King Darius.

3:10 signet ring. Yet another of the king's impulsive responses authorized Haman to issue royal edicts (cf. Gen. 41:42). The repetition of Haman's full name together with the added phrase, "the enemy of the Jews," underlines the terrible predicament of the Jews at this point.

12 [d]Then the king's scribes were summoned on the thirteenth day of the first
month, and an edict, according to all that
Haman commanded, was written to the
king's [e]satraps and to the governors over all
the provinces and to the officials of all the
peoples, [f]to every province in its own script
and every people in its own language. It
was written [g]in the name of King
Ahasuerus [h]and sealed with the king's
signet ring. 13 Letters were sent [i]by couriers
to all the king's provinces with instruction
[j]to destroy, to kill, and to annihilate all
Jews, young and old, women and children,
[k]in one day, the thirteenth day of the
twelfth month, which is the month of
Adar, [l]and to plunder their goods. 14 [m]A
copy of the document was to be issued as
a decree in every province by proclamation
to all the peoples to be ready for that day.
15 [i]The couriers went out hurriedly by order
of the king, and the decree was issued in
Susa the citadel. And the king and Haman
sat down to drink, [n]but the city of Susa was
thrown into confusion.

Esther Agrees to Help the Jews

4 When Mordecai learned all that had
been done, Mordecai tore his clothes
[o]and put on sackcloth and ashes, and went
out into the midst of the city, and he cried
out with a loud and bitter cry. 2 He went up
to the entrance of the king's gate, for no
one was allowed to enter the king's gate
clothed in sackcloth. 3 And in every
province, wherever the king's command
and his decree reached, there was great
mourning among the Jews, [p]with fasting
and weeping and lamenting, and many of
them [q]lay in sackcloth and ashes.
4 When Esther's young women and her
eunuchs came and told her, the queen was
deeply distressed. She sent garments to
clothe Mordecai, so that he might take off
his sackcloth, but he would not accept
them. 5 Then Esther called for Hathach, one
of the king's eunuchs, who had been
appointed to attend her, and ordered him
to go to Mordecai to learn what this was
and why it was. 6 Hathach went out to
Mordecai in the open square of the city in
front of the king's gate, 7 and Mordecai told
him all that had happened to him, [r]and the
exact sum of money that Haman had
promised to pay into the king's treasuries
for the destruction of the Jews. 8 Mordecai
also gave him [s]a copy of the written decree
issued in Susa for their destruction, that he
might show it to Esther and explain it to
her and command her to go to the king to
beg his favor and plead with him on behalf
of her people. 9 And Hathach went and told
Esther what Mordecai had said. 10 Then
Esther spoke to Hathach and commanded
him to go to Mordecai and say, 11 "All the
king's servants and the people of the king's
provinces know that if any man or woman
goes to the king inside [t]the inner court
without being called, [u]there is but one
law—to be put to death, except the one [v]to
whom the king holds out the golden
scepter so that he may live. But as for me,
I have not been called to come in to the
king these thirty days."
12 And they told Mordecai what Esther
had said. 13 Then Mordecai told them to
reply to Esther, "Do not think to yourself
that in the king's palace you will escape
any more than all the other Jews. 14 For if
you keep silent at this time, relief and
deliverance will rise for the Jews from
another place, but you and your father's
house will perish. And who knows whether
you have not come to the kingdom for such

12 [d]ch. 8:9 [e]See Ezra 8:36 [f]ch. 1:22; 8:9 [g]ch. 8:8, 10; [1 Kin. 21:8] [h]ch. 8:8, 10
13 [i]ch. 8:10; [2 Chr. 30:6] [j]ch. 7:4; 8:11 [k]ch. 8:12; [ch. 9:1] [l]ch. 8:11
14 [m]ch. 8:13, 14
15 [i][See ver. 13 above] [n][ch. 8:15]
Chapter 4
1 [o]See 2 Sam. 3:31
3 [p]ver. 16; ch. 9:31 [q]Dan 9:3; [Isai. 58:5]
7 [r]ch. 3:9
8 [s]ch. 3:14; 8:13
11 [t]ch. 5:1; [ch. 6:4] [u]Dan. 2:9 [v]ch. 5:2; 8:4

3:12–14 Haman's plans were set in motion. The elaborate descriptive language (e.g., the multiple verbs in the edict "to destroy, to kill, and to annihilate") highlights the painfulness of the senseless edict and emphasizes the extreme danger to God's covenant people. See Introduction: Characteristics and Themes.

3:13 to plunder their goods. To be compared with the Jews' refusal to plunder (9:10, 15–16).

4:1–3 tore his clothes . . . bitter cry . . . fasting . . . ashes. These responses by Mordecai (vv. 1, 2) and by Jews in every province (v. 3), are conventional signs of intense grief and horror at the reception of bad news (cf. Gen. 37:29, 34; Dan. 9:3; Jon. 3:6). The Persians responded similarly after their defeat by the Greeks at the battle of Salamis.

4:4 sent garments. Esther may have wanted Mordecai to be attired properly so that she could speak with him in person (v. 2).

4:5 Hathach. His name may mean "the good one," or perhaps "courier."

4:8 decree. Mordecai made sure that Esther not only was given a copy of the edict but had it explained to her (perhaps translated) before he charged her to entreat the king for mercy for her people. Mordecai's previous command that Esther conceal her identity as a Jew is reversed (2:10).

4:12–14 Mordecai subtly alludes to his belief that God, in His sovereignty, has providentially ordered the events of Esther's life to put her in a position where she can act to deliver all the Jews. Mordecai believed that the sovereign God would bring relief and deliverance to the Jews, that Esther could be the means through which that deliverance would come, and that God was not restricted to this plan if Esther decided to remain quiet.

a time as this?" 15 Then Esther told them to
reply to Mordecai, 16 "Go, gather all the
Jews to be found in Susa, and hold a fast
on my behalf, and do not eat or drink for
[w]three days, night or day. I and my young
women will also fast as you do. Then I will
go to the king, though it is against the law,
[x]and if I perish, I perish." 17 Mordecai then
went away and did everything as Esther
had ordered him.

Esther Prepares a Banquet

5 [y]On the third day Esther put on her
royal robes and stood in [z]the inner
court of the king's palace, in front of the
king's quarters, while the king was sitting on
his royal throne inside the throne room
opposite the entrance to the palace. 2 And
when the king saw Queen Esther standing
in the court, [a]she won favor in his sight,
[b]and he held out to Esther the golden
scepter that was in his hand. Then Esther
approached and touched the tip of the
scepter. 3 And the king said to her, "What is
it, Queen Esther? What is your request? It
shall be given you, even [c]to the half of my
kingdom." 4 And Esther said, "If it please the
king, let the king and Haman come today to
a feast that I have prepared for the king."
5 Then the king said, "Bring Haman quickly,
so that we may do as Esther has asked." So
the king and Haman came to the feast that
Esther had prepared. 6 [d]And as they were
drinking wine after the feast, the king said to
Esther, [e]"What is your wish? It shall be
granted you. And what is your request?
[c]Even to the half of my kingdom, it shall be
fulfilled." 7 Then Esther answered, "My wish
and my request is: 8 [f]If I have found favor in
the sight of the king, and if it please the king
to grant my wish and fulfill my request, let
the king and Haman come to [g]the feast that
I will prepare for them, and tomorrow I will
do as the king has said."

16 [w][ch. 5:1] [x][Gen. 43:14]
Chapter 5
1 [y][ch. 4:16] [z]ch. 4:11; [ch. 6:4]
2 [a][ch. 2:9] [b]ch. 4:11; 8:4
3 [c]ch. 7:2; [Mark 6:23]
6 [d]ch. 7:2 [e]ver. 3; ch. 7:2; 9:12 [c][See ver. 3 above]
8 [f]ch. 7:3; 8:5 [g]ch. 6:14

Haman Plans to Hang Mordecai

9 And Haman went out that day [h]joyful
and glad of heart. But when Haman saw
Mordecai [i]in the king's gate, [j]that he neither rose nor trembled before him, he was
filled with wrath against Mordecai.
10 Nevertheless, Haman restrained himself
and went home, and he sent and brought
his friends and [k]his wife Zeresh. 11 And
Haman recounted to them the splendor of
his riches, [l]the number of his sons, all the
promotions with which [m]the king had honored him, and how he had advanced him
above the officials and the servants of the
king. 12 Then Haman said, "Even Queen
Esther let no one but me come with the
king to the feast she prepared. And tomorrow also I am invited by her together with
the king. 13 Yet all this is worth nothing to
me, so long as I see Mordecai the Jew sitting [i]at the king's gate." 14 Then [k]his wife
Zeresh and all his friends said to him, [n]"Let
a gallows[1] fifty cubits[2] high be made, and
in the morning tell the king to have
Mordecai hanged upon it. Then go joyfully
with the king to the feast." This idea
pleased Haman, and he had the gallows
made.

The King Honors Mordecai

6 On that night the king could not sleep.
And he gave orders to bring [o]the book
of memorable deeds, the chronicles, and
they were read before the king. 2 And it was
found written how [p]Mordecai had told
about [q]Bigthana and [r]Teresh, two of the
king's eunuchs, who guarded the threshold,
and who had sought to lay hands on King
Ahasuerus. 3 And the king said, "What
honor or distinction has been bestowed on
Mordecai for this?" The king's young men
who attended him said, "Nothing has been

9 [h]1 Kin. 8:66 [i]See ch. 2:19 [j]ch. 3:5
10 [k]ch. 6:13
11 [l]See ch. 9:7-10; [m]ch. 3:1
13 [i][See ver. 9 above]
14 [k][See ver. 10 above] [n]ch. 6:4; 7:9, 10; [ch. 8:7; 9:13, 25]
Chapter 6
1 [o]ch. 2:23; 10:2
2 [p]ch. 2:22 [q][ch. 1:10; 2:21] [r]ch. 2:21

[1] Or *stake*; twice in this verse [2] A *cubit* was about 18 inches or 45 centimeters

4:16 Go, gather . . . fast on my behalf. With conviction, faith, and fear, Esther directs that a fast (prayer always accompanied religious fasting, Deut. 9:9; Judg. 20:26, 27; Ezra 8:21–23; 2 Sam. 12:16; Dan. 9:3) be undertaken on her behalf. God honored the faith of the Jews at this time by saving them from destruction.

three days, night or day. Fasts generally were prescribed for only one day. This unusually long fast points to the seriousness of the situation and effectively contrasts with the feasts that stand at the beginning and end of the book (1:3, 5, 9; 2:18; 9:17–18).

against the law. Esther's dilemma reintroduces the theme of obedience, since obedience to Mordecai meant disobeying the law.

if I perish, I perish. Courage, rather than passive resignation, is seen here (cf. Gen. 43:14).

5:1, 2 Wearing royal robes that undoubtedly enhanced her beauty (contrast the mourning attire in 4:15–16), Esther approached the king, who granted her request for an audience.

5:3 half of my kingdom. This generous offer reflects a courtly convention and should not be taken literally (v. 6; cf. Mark 6:23). Esther's first request is that the king and Haman attend a banquet (v. 4). Her second response (v. 8) effectively obliges the king to grant her petition. But it is not until 7:2–6 that Esther finally answers the king's question. Esther's delaying tactics not only demonstrate her wisdom and sense of control, but also raise the suspense in the story.

done for him.” 4 And the king said, “Who is
in the court?” Now Haman had just entered
[s]the outer court of the king’s palace to speak
to the king about having Mordecai hanged
on [t]the gallows[1] that he had prepared for
him. 5 And the king’s young men told him,
“Haman is there, standing in the court.”
And the king said, “Let him come in.” 6 So
Haman came in, and the king said to him,
“What should be done to the man [u]whom
the king delights to honor?” And Haman
said to himself, “Whom would the king
delight to honor more than me?” 7 And
Haman said to the king, “For the man
whom the king delights to honor, 8 let royal
robes be brought, which the king has worn,
[v]and the horse that the king has ridden, and
on whose head [w]a royal crown[2] is set. 9 And
let the robes and the horse be handed over
to one of the king’s most noble officials. Let
them dress the man whom the king delights
to honor, and let them lead him on the
horse through the square of the city, [x]pro-
claiming before him: ‘Thus shall it be done
to the man whom the king delights to
honor.’” 10 Then the king said to Haman,
“Hurry; take the robes and the horse, as you
have said, and do so to Mordecai the Jew
who sits [y]at the king’s gate. Leave out nothing that you have mentioned.” 11 So Haman
took the robes and the horse, and he
dressed Mordecai and led him through the
square of the city, proclaiming before him,
“Thus shall it be done to the man whom the
king delights to honor.”

12 Then Mordecai returned to the king’s
gate. But Haman hurried to his house,
mourning [z]and with his head covered.
13 And Haman told [a]his wife Zeresh and all
his friends everything that had happened
to him. Then his wise men and his wife
Zeresh said to him, “If Mordecai, before
whom you have begun to fall, is of the
Jewish people, you will not overcome him
but will surely fall before him.”

Esther Reveals Haman’s Plot

14 While they were yet talking with him,
the king’s eunuchs arrived and hurried to
bring Haman [b]to the feast that Esther had
prepared.

7 So the king and Haman went in to feast
with Queen Esther. 2 And on the second
day, as they were drinking wine after the
feast, the king again said to Esther, [c]“What is
your wish, Queen Esther? It shall be granted
you. And what is your request? [d]Even to the
half of my kingdom, it shall be fulfilled.”
3 Then Queen Esther answered, [e]“If I have
found favor in your sight, O king, and if it
please the king, let my life be granted me for
my wish, and my people for my request.
4 [f]For we have been sold, I and my people,
[g]to be destroyed, to be killed, and to be annihilated. If we had been sold merely as slaves,
men and women, I would have been silent,
for our affliction is not to be compared with
the loss to the king.” 5 Then King Ahasuerus
said to Queen Esther, “Who is he, and where
is he, who has dared[3] to do this?” 6 And
Esther said, [h]“A foe and enemy! This wicked
Haman!” Then Haman was terrified before
the king and the queen.

Haman Is Hanged

7 And the king arose in his wrath from
the wine-drinking and went into [i]the
palace garden, but Haman stayed to beg for
his life from Queen Esther, for he saw that
harm was determined against him by the
king. 8 And the king returned from [i]the

4 [s][ch. 4:11; 5:1] [t]ch. 5:14 **6** [u]ver. 7, 9, 11 **8** [v][1 Kin. 1:33] [w]ch. 1:11; 2:17 **9** [x][Gen. 41:43] **10** [y]See ch. 2:19 **12** [z]See 2 Sam. 15:30 **13** [a]ch. 5:10, 14

14 [b]ch. 5:8 **Chapter 7** **2** [c]ch. 5:6; 9:12 [d]ch. 5:3 **3** [e]ch. 5:8 **4** [f]ch. 3:9; 4:7 [g]ch. 3:13; 8:11 **6** [h]See ch. 3:10 **7** [i]ch. 1:5 **8** [i][See ver. 7 above]

1 Or *suspended on a stake* 2 Or *headdress* 3 Hebrew *whose heart has filled him*

6:6–9 The identity of the one to be honored is concealed (cf. Haman’s intentional veiling of the identity of the people to be destroyed, 3:8). Assuming that he himself was the man to be honored, Haman unveiled his personal dream list, which focused not on material gain or position, but rather on public acclaim and adulation (cf. Gen. 41:42, 43).

6:13 you will not overcome him. Haman’s wife and advisers give voice to the belief that the Jewish people were indomitable and, perhaps, even to the view that their God was the living God. See the predictions about the fall of Amalek before Israel (Ex. 17:16; Num. 24:20; Deut. 25:17–19; 1 Sam. 15; 2 Sam. 1:8–16; cf. Dan. 6:26, 27; Josh. 2:11; 9:29; Ezek. 38:23). See also Introduction: Characteristics and Themes.

6:14 hurried to bring Haman. The affairs of the court were always carried out in haste. It was oriental custom for servants to escort guests to special functions.

7:3 The drama of the scene is heightened by Esther’s slow unveiling of her petition for her own life and her request that her people be spared.

7:4 sold. A reference to Haman’s initial bribe (3:9; 4:7).

destroyed . . . killed . . . annihilated. The Hebrew verbs are precisely those used in the initial decree (3:13).

not to be compared. The Hebrew is somewhat difficult to translate. Esther seems to argue that Haman’s financial offer (3:9) would not compensate for the king’s damages (i.e., lost revenue from the Jews).

7:8 falling on the couch. Haman’s violations of etiquette seal his fate.

covered Haman’s face. The court attendants understood the implications of the king’s word (v. 8). As always, the king welcomed the advice of others—here, the eunuch, Harbona (1:10; cf. the speech in 5:14). The order to hang Haman on the gallows intended for Mordecai is the great ironic reversal of the story. See Introduction: Characteristics and Themes.

palace garden to the place where they were
drinking wine, as Haman was falling on
[j]the couch where Esther was. And the king
said, "Will he even assault the queen in my
presence, in my own house?" As the word
left the mouth of the king, they covered
Haman's face. **9** Then [k]Harbona, one of the
eunuchs in attendance on the king, said,
"Moreover, [l]the gallows[1] that Haman has
prepared for Mordecai, [m]whose word saved
the king, is standing at Haman's house,
fifty cubits[2] high." **10** And the king said,
"Hang him on that." [n]So they hanged
Haman on the gallows that he had prepared for Mordecai. [o]Then the wrath of the
king abated.

Esther Saves the Jews

8 On that day King Ahasuerus gave to
Queen Esther the house of Haman,
[h]the enemy of the Jews. And Mordecai
came before the king, for Esther had told
[p]what he was to her. **2** [q]And the king took
off his signet ring, which he had taken from
Haman, and gave it to Mordecai. And
Esther set Mordecai over the house of
Haman.

3 Then Esther spoke again to the king.
She fell at his feet and wept and pleaded
with him to avert the evil plan of Haman
[r]the Agagite and the plot that he had
devised against the Jews. **4** [s]When the king
held out the golden scepter to Esther,
5 Esther rose and stood before the king.
And she said, "If it please the king, [t]and if
I have found favor in his sight, and if the
thing seems right before the king, and I am
pleasing in his eyes, let an order be written
to revoke [u]the letters devised by Haman
[r]the Agagite, the son of Hammedatha,
which he wrote to destroy the Jews who are
in all the provinces of the king. **6** For how
can I bear [v]to see the calamity that is coming to my people? Or how can I bear to see
the destruction of my kindred?" **7** Then
King Ahasuerus said to Queen Esther and
to Mordecai the Jew, "Behold, [w]I have
given Esther the house of Haman, and they
have hanged him on the gallows,[3] because
he intended to lay hands on the Jews. **8** But
you may write as you please with regard to
the Jews, in the name of the king, [x]and seal
it with the king's ring, for an edict written
in the name of the king and sealed with the
king's ring [y]cannot be revoked."

9 [z]The king's scribes were summoned at
that time, in the third month, which is the
month of Sivan, on the twenty-third day.
And an edict was written, according to all
that Mordecai commanded concerning the
Jews, to [a]the satraps and the governors and
the officials of the provinces [b]from India to
Ethiopia, [b]127 provinces, [c]to each province
in its own script and to each people in its
own language, and also to the Jews in their
script and their language. **10** [d]And he wrote
in the name of King Ahasuerus [e]and sealed
it with the king's signet ring. Then he sent
the letters by mounted couriers riding on
[f]swift horses that were used in the king's
service, bred from the royal stud, **11** saying
that the king allowed the Jews who were in
every city [g]to gather and defend their lives,
[h]to destroy, to kill, and to annihilate any
armed force of any people or province that
might attack them, children and women
included, [i]and to plunder their goods,
12 [j]on one day throughout all the provinces
of King Ahasuerus, on the thirteenth day of
the twelfth month, which is the month of
Adar. **13** [k]A copy of what was written was to
be issued as a decree in every province,
being publicly displayed to all peoples, and
the Jews were to be ready on that day to
take vengeance on their enemies. **14** So the
couriers, mounted on their [f]swift horses
that were used in the king's service, rode
out hurriedly, urged by the king's command. And the decree was issued in Susa
the citadel.

15 Then Mordecai went out from the presence of the king [l]in royal robes of blue and
white, with a great golden crown[4] and [m]a
robe of fine linen and purple, [n]and the city
of Susa shouted and rejoiced. **16** The Jews
had [o]light and gladness and joy and honor.

8 [j][ch. 1:6]
9 [k]ch. 1:10 [l]See ch. 5:14 [m][ch. 2:22]
10 [n][Ps. 7:16; Prov. 11:5, 6; Dan. 6:24] [o][ch. 2:1]
Chapter 8
1 [h][See ch. 7:6 above] [p][ch. 2:7, 15]
2 [q]ch 3:10
3 [r]ch. 3:1; 9:24
4 [s]ch. 4:11; 5:2
5 [t]ch. 5:8; 8:5 [u][ch. 3:13] [r][See ver. 3 above]
6 [v][ch. 7:4]
7 [w]ver. 1
8 [x]ver. 10; ch. 3:12 [y][ch. 1:19; Dan. 6:8, 12, 15]
9 [z]ch. 3:12 [a]See Ezra 8:36 [b]ch. 1:1 [c]ch. 1:22; 3:12
10 [d]ch. 3:12, 13 [e]ver. 10; ch. 3:12 [f]1 Kin. 4:28
11 [g]ch. 9:2, 15, 16, 18 [h]ch. 3:13; 7:4 [i][ch. 9:10, 15, 16]
12 [j]ch. 3:13; 9:1
13 [k]ch. 3:14; 4:8
14 [f][See ver. 10 above]
15 [l][Gen. 41:42; Dan. 5:29] [m][1 Chr. 15:27] [n][ch. 3:15]
16 [o][Ps. 97:11]

[1] Or *stake*; also verse 10 [2] A *cubit* was about 18 inches or 45 centimeters [3] Or *stake* [4] Or *headdress*

8:1 gave to Queen Esther the house of Haman. According to Persian custom, the property of a traitor was confiscated by the crown. **Mordecai came before the king.** Mordecai was given official status (1:14) and effectively took over Haman's official and personal position.

8:7, 8 Although the king is not able to revoke the decree formally (1:19), he authorizes Esther and Mordecai to issue another decree that will effectively nullify the first edict.

8:9–14 The new decree, issued two months and ten days after the first (3:12), is almost identical to Haman's first decree (3:12–15).

17 [p]ch. 9:19, 22; 1 Sam. 25:8 [q]ch. 9:27 [r]ch. 9:2
Chapter 9
1 [s]ch. 8:12 [t]ver. 17 [u]ch. 3:13 [j][See ch. 8:12 above]
2 [v]ver. 15, 16, 18; ch. 8:11 [w]ch. 8:17
3 [x]See Ezra 8:36
4 [y][2 Sam. 3:1]; 1 Chr. 11:9
10 [z]ch. 9:13, 14; [ch. 5:11] [a]See ch. 3:10 [b][ch. 8:11]
12 [c]ch. 5:6; 7:2
13 [d]ver. 15; ch. 8:11
16 [e]ver. 2 [f]ver. 2; [ch. 8:11]
17 [g]ver. 1
18 [g][See ver. 17 above] [h]ver. 21
19 [i]Deut. 3:5; Ezek. 38:11; Zech. 2:4; [j]ch. 8:17 [k]Neh. 8:10, 12

17 And in every province and in every city,
wherever the king's command and his
edict reached, there was gladness and joy
among the Jews, a feast and [p]a holiday.
[q]And many from the peoples of the country
declared themselves Jews, [r]for fear of the
Jews had fallen on them.

The Jews Destroy Their Enemies

9 [s]Now in the twelfth month, which is the
month of Adar, [t]on the thirteenth day of
the same, [u]when the king's command and
edict were about to be carried out, [j]on the
very day when the enemies of the Jews
hoped to gain the mastery over them, the
reverse occurred: the Jews gained mastery
over those who hated them. **2** [v]The Jews
gathered in their cities throughout all the
provinces of King Ahasuerus to lay hands on
those who sought their harm. And no one
could stand against them, [w]for the fear of
them had fallen on all peoples. **3** All the officials of the provinces and [x]the satraps and
the governors and the royal agents also
helped the Jews, for the fear of Mordecai
had fallen on them. **4** For Mordecai was great
in the king's house, and his fame spread
throughout all the provinces, for the man
Mordecai grew [y]more and more powerful.
5 The Jews struck all their enemies with the
sword, killing and destroying them, and did
as they pleased to those who hated them.
6 In Susa the citadel itself the Jews killed and
destroyed 500 men, **7** and also killed
Parshandatha and Dalphon and Aspatha
8 and Poratha and Adalia and Aridatha **9** and
Parmashta and Arisai and Aridai and
Vaizatha, **10** [z]the ten sons of Haman the son
of Hammedatha, [a]the enemy of the Jews,
[b]but they laid no hand on the plunder.

11 That very day the number of those
killed in Susa the citadel was reported to
the king. **12** And the king said to Queen
Esther, "In Susa the citadel the Jews have
killed and destroyed 500 men and also the
ten sons of Haman. What then have they
done in the rest of the king's provinces!
[c]Now what is your wish? It shall be granted
you. And what further is your request? It
shall be fulfilled." **13** And Esther said, "If it
please the king, let the Jews who are in Susa
be allowed [d]tomorrow also to do according
to this day's edict. And let the ten sons of
Haman be hanged on the gallows."[1] **14** So
the king commanded this to be done. A
decree was issued in Susa, and the ten sons
of Haman were hanged. **15** The Jews who
were in Susa gathered also on the fourteenth day of the month of Adar and they
killed 300 men in Susa, but they laid no
hands on the plunder.
16 [e]Now the rest of the Jews who were in
the king's provinces also [f]gathered to
defend their lives, and got relief from their
enemies and killed 75,000 of those who
hated them, but they laid no hands on the
plunder. **17** This was [g]on the thirteenth day
of the month of Adar, and on the fourteenth day they rested and made that a day
of feasting and gladness. **18** But the Jews who
were in Susa gathered [g]on the thirteenth
day and on the fourteenth, and rested [h]on
the fifteenth day, making that a day of feasting and gladness. **19** Therefore the Jews of
the villages, who live in [i]the rural towns,
hold the fourteenth day of the month of
Adar as a day for gladness and feasting, as
[j]a holiday, and [k]as a day on which they
send gifts of food to one another.

[1] Or *stake*

8:17 many from the peoples . . . declared themselves Jews. The conversion of those from other nations who feared the Jews marks a climax in the story (cf. Josh. 2:9; Ex. 15:14–16; Ps. 105:38).

9:1 the reverse occurred. The theme of ironic reversal is again stressed. See Introduction: Characteristics and Themes.

9:2 fear of them. Fear of the God of the Jews was behind the Persians' pervasive fear of the Jews (cf. Ex. 15:14–16). The reversal (v. 1 note) was so complete that all the officials who were to have enforced the extermination of the Jews aided them.

9:5 did as they pleased. The extent of the killing is emphasized (vv. 6–11), but so is the Jews' not plundering their enemies (v. 10). Their refusal to plunder recalls the plundering of the Amalekites that led to Saul's demise (1 Sam. 15:17–19). This contrast (cf. 8:11) suggests the propriety of their conduct in this final encounter with the Amalekites, despite the extent of the killing.

9:12–15 Esther's requests for further vengeance (v. 13), which may have been due to the great degree of anti-Semitism in that city, led to a second day of bloodshed in Susa (v. 15). Notably, the emphasis in the narrative is on killing enemies and not just on winning a victory. The two days of bloodshed have led to differences among Jews over which day to observe Purim (vv. 17–19).

9:14 the ten sons of Haman were hanged. The bodies of the dead sons (v. 12) were displayed as a warning and a sign of ultimate dishonor (2:23 note).

9:16, 17 The slaughter of a further seventy-five thousand enemies emphasizes the extent of the antagonism towards the Jews throughout the empire, which in turn explains the celebrations that followed.

9:16 relief from their enemies. The rest granted to the Jews at this time became the basis for the annual celebration of Purim (also v. 22).

9:19 send gifts of food to one another. The exchange of gifts, usually food (v. 22), enabled even the poorest Jew to join in the celebrations (Neh. 8:10, 12; Deut. 16:11, 14) and is a further instance of providential care for the oppressed, here within the Jewish community itself.

The Feast of Purim Inaugurated

20 And Mordecai recorded these things
and sent letters to all the Jews who were in
all the provinces of King Ahasuerus, both
near and far, 21 obliging them to keep the
fourteenth day of the month Adar and also
the fifteenth day of the same, year by year,
22 as the days on which the Jews got relief
from their enemies, and as the month that
had been turned for them from sorrow into
gladness and from mourning into [j]a holiday; that they should make them days of
feasting and gladness, days for sending gifts
of food to one another and gifts to the poor.
23 So the Jews accepted what they had
started to do, and what Mordecai had written to them. 24 For Haman the Agagite, the
son of Hammedatha, [l]the enemy of all the
Jews, [m]had plotted against the Jews to
destroy them, and [n]had cast Pur (that is,
cast lots), to crush and to destroy them.
25 But when it came before the king, he
gave orders in writing [o]that his evil plan
that he had devised against the Jews
[p]should return on his own head, and that
he and his sons should be hanged on the
gallows.[1] 26 Therefore they called these
days Purim, after the term [n]Pur. Therefore,
because of all that was written in [q]this letter, and of what they had faced in this matter, and of what had happened to them,
27 the Jews firmly obligated themselves and
their offspring and [r]all who joined them,
that without fail they would keep [s]these
two days according to what was written
and at the time appointed every year,
28 that these days should be remembered
and kept throughout every generation, in
every clan, province, and city, and that
these days of Purim should never fall into
disuse among the Jews, nor should the
commemoration of these days cease
among their descendants.
29 Then Queen Esther, [t]the daughter of
Abihail, and Mordecai the Jew gave full
written authority, confirming [u]this second
letter about Purim. 30 Letters were sent to
all the Jews, [v]to the 127 provinces of the
kingdom of Ahasuerus, in words of peace
and truth, 31 that these days of Purim
should be observed at their appointed seasons, as Mordecai the Jew and Queen
Esther obligated them, and as they had
obligated themselves and their offspring,
with regard to [w]their fasts and their lamenting. 32 The command of Queen Esther confirmed these practices of [x]Purim, and it was
recorded in writing.

The Greatness of Mordecai

10 King Ahasuerus imposed tax on the
land and on [y]the coastlands of the
sea. 2 And all the acts of his power and
might, and the full account of the high
honor of Mordecai, [z]to which the king
advanced him, are they not written in [a]the
Book of the Chronicles of the kings of
Media and Persia? 3 For Mordecai the Jew
was [b]second in rank to King Ahasuerus,
and he was great among the Jews and popular with the multitude of his brothers, for
he [c]sought the welfare of his people and
spoke peace to all his people.

[1] Or *suspended on a stake*

22 [j][See ver. 19 above] 24 [l]See ch. 3:10 [m]ch. 3:6, 7 [n]ch. 3:7 25 [o]ch. 7:9, 10; 8:3, 7 [p][Ps. 7:16] 26 [n][See ver. 24 above] [q]ver. 20 27 [r][Isai. 56:3, 6; Zech. 2:11] [s]ver. 21

29 [t]ch. 2:15 [u]ver. 20; ch. 8:10 30 [v]ch. 1:1; 8:9 31 [w]ch. 4:3 32 [x]ver. 26 Chapter 10 1 [y]Isai. 11:11; 24:15 2 [z]ch. 8:15; 9:4 [a]ch. 2:23; 6:1 3 [b]2 Chr. 28:7; [Gen. 41:40] [c][Neh. 2:10; Ps. 122:8, 9]

9:20–32 These verses clarify that the purpose of the book is to establish Purim as a festival to be celebrated by each new generation of Jews, and to give instructions for its observance.

9:20 Mordecai recorded these things. He sent the letters of instruction regarding the festival.

9:24, 25 This brief summary of the events of the preceding chapters focuses, not on Esther and Mordecai, but on the king and Haman, and presents Haman as the archetypal adversary of all Jews, past and present (3:10; 8:1; 9:10).

9:29–32 Esther and Mordecai sent a final official letter regarding Purim that carefully places the feast within the setting of the more established Israelite practices of fasting and lamentation (v. 31). In this way Purim was made an official religious celebration of the Jews, a task the writer of Esther seemed to view as important because of the non-Mosaic origin of the feast.

10:1–3 This postscript to the book focuses attention on King Ahasuerus and Mordecai and directs the reader to the book of the official records ("chronicles") of the kings of Media and Persia for further information (cf. 1 Kin. 14:19, 29). For some reason Esther's name is not included in the postscript.

10:3 Mordecai is esteemed as an ideal Jewish statesman. His importance as a model for the Jews and in the establishment of the Feast of Purim was acknowledged in the apocryphal Book of Maccabees, where Purim is called "the day before Mordecai's day" (2 Macc. 15:36).

THE BOOK OF

Job

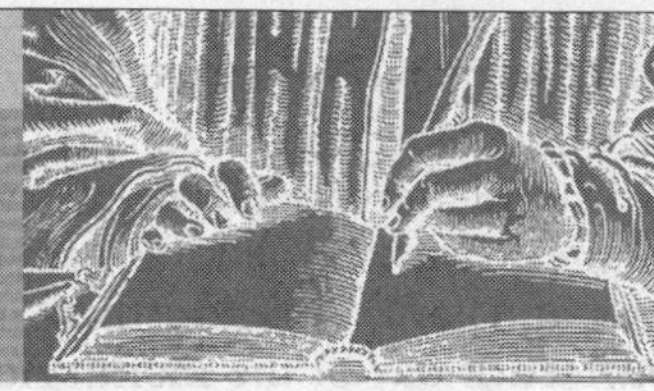

AUTHOR

The relationship between the opening narrative of the book (the prologue, chs. 1; 2) and the content of Job's discussions with his friends (the dialogue, chs. 3–27) make it clear that Job was not the author of this book. Had he known what took place in the divine council, there would have been no point to the debate over whether Job had brought on his sufferings by sinful conduct. Rather, God used a skillful poet from the covenant community to write this remarkable book. The language presents many challenges to the translator because of its poetic grammar and its rich vocabulary. We know that the author was an Israelite since he refers to God by the covenant name "Yahweh," while Job and his companions (see 1:1) use such terms as "God" and "the Almighty" (12:9 is the only exception). The probability is that the poet used sources from patriarchal times, including some from Job himself, in composing the book.

DATE AND OCCASION

We do not know exactly when the author of Job lived and wrote, but the classical Hebrew of the prologue places him after 1500 B.C. The final form of the book may not have appeared until the era of Solomon or somewhat later when Hebrew wisdom literature reached its zenith. The discovery of fragments from Job among the Dead Sea scrolls has ruled out attempts to date Job as late as the second century B.C.

Among the wisdom writings of the Old Testament the Book of Job stands with Ecclesiastes as a kind of anti-wisdom. It counters the traditional wisdom as it wrestles with the difficult question of suffering along with the affirmation that God is just and good. The book deals with this subject with a frankness that is often baffling. The book does not suggest that there is an evil deity, or that God's power is limited. Instead it praises the Creator's sovereignty, wisdom, and glory. That the God of Job is neither evil nor limited is seen in two portrayals of Job's relationship with God.

The first is taken from the book's prologue and epilogue. The prologue depicts Job's submission to the divine will in the midst of suffering. There Job appears as a good man trusting the goodness of his God. Finally, in the epilogue (42:7–17), God honors his trust by restoring him.

The second portrait shows Job's indignation over his plight. He thinks that God has become his enemy and is unjustly afflicting him. Job comes to this conclusion because he knows that God is sovereign. Had he believed in a limited deity, he would have had no problem with God's justice or goodness, since then he could not hold God responsible for every event, including his misfortune.

The church has often emphasized only the message of the prologue and epilogue because it is easier to understand. The reference of James 5:11 to the "patience" or "perseverance" of Job is not based on a shallow interpretation that ignores the central section of dialogues. James is not stressing Job's passivity, but his "perseverance" and, with it, God's compassion and mercy in accomplishing His purposes. God's purpose in Job's suffering is the key to understanding the seeming discrepancy between the tranquil Job of the prologue (chs. 1; 2) and the raging Job of the central section. God's purpose is complex, involving more than one question of faith.

CHARACTERISTICS AND THEMES

Compositions similar to the Book of Job appear in Mesopotamian and Egyptian sources from Old Testament times. One ("A Dialogue About Human Misery") is about a counselor who criticizes a sufferer for his impiety while the sufferer struggles over the character of the gods. The literary format of Job is not unique among documents from the ancient Near East, consisting of a prose prologue, a poetic dialogue, and finally a prose epilogue. But there is no other work dealing with the problem of human suffering in light of the transcendence and goodness of God that approaches the theological depth, literary sophistication, and practical application of the Book of Job.

The book's exploration of the themes associated with God's purpose in human suffering unfolds in the following manner. In the prologue we view the God-Job relationship from the divine perspective. God chose Job to be one of His suffering servants, an instrument through whom to accomplish a spiritual triumph: "Have you considered my servant Job?" (1:8, 2:3). Satan falsely accuses Job of serving God for the sake of material blessings (1:9–11). Job is given the high calling of remaining true to God even when everything is taken away, and grim suffering becomes his daily lot. Will Job do as the Adversary predicts, and curse God to His face? This is the question that drives the moving drama of the book as Job loses his initial confidence and sinks into despair. If Job remains faithful, God through Job will show that the Adversary is a liar.

While the prologue gives us the divine perspective, the central section of speeches presents the human perspective. As a human being he is ignorant of what took place in the divine council. He struggles with a traditional view, a perversion of Proverbs, that all suffering is an immediate punishment of human sins. Job's counselors, like many others, considered the depth of Job's suffering to be adequate evidence that his sin was great (cf. John 9:2).

As Job confronts the heartless counselors used by Satan to accuse him falsely, he says things for which he must later repent (42:5, 6). He knows the counselors are wrong, but he cannot understand how a pious person like himself should suffer so much when the godless enjoy prosperity and health (12:6).

Like the psalmists, Job often complains to God in the language of legal disputes. Some of what Job says shocks his friends. While they say all the right things *about* God, they never say anything *to* Him. Job wrestles with God and tells Him every doubt and fear. His relationship with God is vital while theirs consists of dead aphorisms. It is not so much what they say, as how they apply it to Job, that shows the arrogance of their insisting that they know why Job is suffering. They are insensitive (13:4, 5; 16:2; 19:21), as well as shallow and presumptuous regarding divine things. Job has been falsely accused; he is not suffering for his sins, though he cannot avoid wondering about this. But even though he imagines God is angry with him, in his better moments he still believes God is just and will provide a Redeemer (16:19–21; 19:23–27).

This hope becomes a reality when Job finally has the face-to-face audience with God that he requested (13:15–18; 31:35–37). When God appears in the storm (chs. 38–41), Job is not rebuked as one suffering for his sins, but is humbled before the Lord as one whose ill-advised speech had obscured God's purpose (38:2; 42:2, 3). God reveals Himself as Job's friend, bringing him before the astonishing works of creation to show him that the One he has reproached is sovereign in goodness and power. Job recognizes that God is and remains his friend.

When his eyes have seen the Lord and he has repented in dust and ashes, Job has come to understand that God on His throne is sovereign, and rewards those who belong to Him despite times of pressure and pain. The reader learns that Job suffered, not because he was one of the worst of men, but because he was one of the best, and that his ordeal glorified his God.

OUTLINE OF JOB

I. Prologue (1:1–2:13)

- A. *Job Blessed and Blameless (1:1–5)*
- B. *Job Tested (1:6–2:13)*
  1. Satan Accuses Job (1:6–12)
  2. Job's Commitment Despite Tragedy (1:13–22)
  3. Satan Accuses Job Again (2:1–6)
  4. Job's Faith Despite Personal Suffering (2:7–10)
  5. The Arrival of the Counselors (2:11–13)

II. Dialogue (chs. 3–27)

- A. *Job Laments His Birth (ch. 3)*
- B. *The First Cycle of Speeches (chs. 4–14)*
  1. Eliphaz (chs. 4; 5)
  2. Job's Reply (chs. 6; 7)
  3. Bildad (ch. 8)
  4. Job's Reply (chs. 9; 10)
  5. Zophar (ch. 11)
  6. Job's Reply (chs. 12–14)
- C. *The Second Cycle of Speeches (chs. 15–21)*
  1. Eliphaz (ch. 15)
  2. Job's Reply (chs. 16; 17)
  3. Bildad (ch. 18)

OUTLINE OF JOB (Cont.)

4. Job's Reply (ch. 19)
5. Zophar (ch. 20)
6. Job's Reply (ch. 21)

D. *The Third Cycle of Speeches (chs. 22–26)*

1. Eliphaz (ch. 22)
2. Job's Reply (chs. 23; 24)
3. Bildad (ch. 25)
4. Job's Reply (ch. 26)

E. *Job's Closing Discourse (ch. 27)*

III. Interlude on Wisdom (ch. 28)

IV. Monologues (chs. 29–41)

A. *Job's Final Oration (chs. 29–31)*

1. Past Blessing, Honor, and Personal Benevolence (ch. 29)
2. Present Dishonor and Suffering and No Benevolence (ch. 30)
3. A Protestation of Innocence Under Sanctions and Oath (ch. 31)

B. *Elihu's Speeches (chs. 32–37)*

1. Apology for Speaking (32:1–5)
2. The First Speech (32:6–33:33)
3. The Second Speech (ch. 34)
4. The Third Speech (ch. 35)
5. The Fourth Speech (chs. 36; 37)

C. *God's Responses (38:1–42:6)*

1. God's First Discourse (38:1–40:2)
2. Job Humbled (40:3–5)
3. God's Second Discourse (40:6–41:34)
4. Job Repentant (42:1–6)

V. Epilogue (42:7–17)

A. *The Counselors Rebuked (42:7–9)*

B. *Job Restored (42:10–17)*

Job's Character and Wealth

1 There was a man in the land of [a]Uz
whose name was [b]Job, and that man
was [c]blameless and upright, one who
[d]feared God and [e]turned away from evil.
2 There were born to him [f]seven sons and
three daughters. **3** He possessed 7,000
sheep, 3,000 camels, 500 yoke of oxen, and
500 female donkeys, and very many servants, so that this man was the greatest of
all [g]the people of the east. **4** His sons used to
go and hold a feast in the house of each one
on his day, and they would send and invite
their three sisters to eat and drink with
them. **5** And when the days of the feast had
run their course, Job would send and [h]consecrate them, and he would rise early in the
morning and [i]offer burnt offerings according to the number of them all. For Job said,
"It may be that my children have sinned,
and [j]cursed[1] God in their hearts." Thus Job
did continually.

Chapter 1
1 [a]Jer. 25:20; Lam. 4:21 [b]Ezek. 14:14, 20; James 5:11 [c]ver. 8; ch. 2:3; [ch. 9:20; Gen. 6:9; 17:1] [d]ch. 4:6; Prov. 16:6 [e][ch. 28:28; Ps. 34:14]
2 [f]ch. 42:13
3 [g]See Judg. 6:3
5 [h]1 Sam. 16:5 [i]ch. 42:8; Gen. 8:20 [j]ch. 2:5; [Ps. 10:3]
6 [k]ch. 2:1; 38:7; Gen. 6:2, 4 [l][1 Chr. 21:1; Zech. 3:1; Rev. 12:9, 10]
7 [m]ch. 2:2; [1 Pet. 5:8]

Satan Allowed to Test Job

6 Now there was a day when [k]the sons of
God came to present themselves before the
LORD, and [l]Satan[2] also came among them.
7 The LORD said to Satan, "From where have
you come?" Satan answered the LORD and
said, "From [m]going to and fro on the earth,
and from walking up and down on it." **8** And
the LORD said to Satan, "Have you [n]considered my [o]servant Job, that there is none like
him on the earth, [p]a blameless and upright
man, who fears God and turns away from
evil?" **9** Then Satan answered the LORD and
said, "Does Job fear God for no reason?
10 Have you not put [q]a hedge around him and
his house and all that he has, on every side?
You have [r]blessed the work of his hands, and
his possessions have increased in the land.

8 [n]ch. 2:3 [o]Num. 12:7; 2 Sam. 7:5; Isai. 20:3 [p]ver. 1 **10** [q][Ps. 3:3; 34:7] [r][Ps. 128:1, 2]

[1] The Hebrew word *bless* is used euphemistically for *curse* in 1:5, 11; 2:5, 9 [2] Hebrew *the Adversary*

1:1–5 The prologue (1; 2) begins with a depiction of Job blessed by and devoted to his God.

1:1 Uz. Uz was an extended region east of Judah, perhaps on the edge of the desert, but conducive to raising crops (v. 14) and livestock (v. 3). Job was not a nomad but an elder in a major town (29:7).

blameless and upright. This is ordinary language and does not mean that Job was sinless.

1:3 sheep . . . camels . . . oxen . . . donkeys. Patriarchal wealth was measured by amount of livestock (cf. Gen. 30:43).

1:5 consecrate them. Job was rightly concerned for the spiritual welfare of his children.

offer burnt offerings. By this means of grace the patriarch Job, like Abraham (Gen. 15:9, 10), filled the role of priest for the family, consecrating his children to the Lord.

cursed God in their hearts. The Hebrew reads lit. "blessed God," but that is a euphemism. Cursing God was a sin about which Job himself would be tested (v. 11).

1:6–2:13 The writer reveals the developments in heaven and their consequences on earth that led to Job's suffering.

1:6–12 This is the first of two scenes in heaven depicting the divine council and focusing on the encounter between God (Yahweh) and Satan. Satan is more than prosecutor. He opposes the will of God, in keeping with the role of the serpent in Gen. 3. In v. 9 he questions Job's religious motive. The use of "Yahweh," the covenant name of God, throughout chs. 1 and 2 (also in 38:1; 40:1; and ch. 42) indicates that God was in a covenant relation with Job in love and mercy from first to last.

1:6 Satan. See theological note "Satan."

1:8 Job is honored by God, who approves of him as a true and faithful servant, i.e., one keeping the solemn oaths of the covenant relationship. It is God, not Satan, who singles out Job for testing.

11 But [s]stretch out your hand and [t]touch all
that he has, and he will [u]curse you [v]to your
face." 12 And the LORD said to Satan, "Behold,
all that he has is in your hand. Only against
him do not stretch out your hand." So Satan
went out from the presence of the LORD.

Satan Takes Job's Property and Children

13 Now there was a day when his sons and
daughters were eating and drinking wine in
their oldest brother's house, 14 and there
came a messenger to Job and said, "The
oxen were plowing and the donkeys feeding
beside them, 15 and [w]the Sabeans fell upon
them and took them and struck down the
servants[1] with the edge of the sword, and I
alone have escaped to tell you." 16 While he
was yet speaking, there came another and
said, [x]"The fire of God fell from heaven and
burned up the sheep and the servants and
consumed them, and I alone have escaped
to tell you." 17 While he was yet speaking,
there came another and said, [y]"The
Chaldeans formed [z]three groups and made
a raid on the camels and took them and
struck down the servants with the edge of
the sword, and I alone have escaped to tell
you." 18 While he was yet speaking, there
came another and said, [a]"Your sons and
daughters were eating and drinking wine in
their oldest brother's house, 19 and behold, a
great wind came across [b]the wilderness and
struck the four corners of the house, and it
fell upon the young people, and they are
dead, and I alone have escaped to tell you."
20 Then Job arose and [c]tore his [d]robe and
[e]shaved his head [f]and fell on the ground

11 [s]ch. 2:5 [t]ch. 19:21; Isai. 53:4; (Heb.) [u]ver. 5 [v]Isai. 65:3
15 [w]ch. 6:19; See 1 Kin. 10:1
16 [x]2 Kin. 1:12
17 [y]Gen. 11:28; 2 Kin. 24:2 [z][Judg. 7:16; 1 Sam. 11:11]
18 [a]ver. 4, 13
19 [b]Isai. 21:1; Jer. 4:11; Hos. 13:15
20 [c]See Gen. 37:29 [d]Erza 9:3 [e]Jer. 7:29 [f][1 Pet. 5:6]

[1] Hebrew *the young men*; also verses 16, 17

Satan

Satan is the leader of the fallen angels, and like them he comes into full view only in the New Testament. His name means "adversary" (opponent of God and His people), and the Old Testament introduces him as such (1 Chr. 21:1; Job 1; 2; Zech. 3:1, 2). The New Testament gives him revealing titles: Devil (*diabolos*), meaning "accuser" (that is, of God's people; Rev. 12:9, 10); Apollyon, meaning "destroyer" (Rev. 9:11); tempter (Matt. 4:3; 1 Thess. 3:5); and wicked one (1 John 5:18, 19). "Ruler of this world" (John 12:31; 14:30; 16:11) and "god of this world" (2 Cor. 4:4) point to Satan as presiding over mankind's anti-God lifestyles (cf. Eph. 2:2; 1 John 5:19; Rev. 12:9). Jesus said that Satan was always a murderer, and is the father of lies. As such, he is both the original liar and the sponsor of all subsequent falsehood and deceits (John 8:44). Finally, he is identified as the serpent who fooled Eve in Eden (Rev. 12:9; 20:2). The picture is one of malice, fury, and cruelty, directed against God, against God's truth, and against those whom God loves.

Satan's deceptive cunning is highlighted by Paul's statement that he becomes an angel of light, disguising evil as good (2 Cor. 11:14). His destructive ferocity comes out in the description of him as a roaring, devouring lion (1 Pet. 5:8) and as a dragon (Rev. 12:9). As he was Christ's sworn foe (Matt. 4:1–11; 16:23; Luke 4:13; cf. Luke 22:3), so now he opposes the Christian, always probing for weaknesses, misdirecting strengths, and undermining faith, hope, and love (Luke 22:32; 2 Cor. 2:11; 11:3–15; Eph. 6:16). Satan's malice and cunning should be taken seriously, but the Christian should not lapse into abject terror of him, for he is a defeated enemy. Satan is stronger than human beings, but Christ has triumphed over him (Matt. 12:29), and Christians will triumph over him as well, resisting him with the resources Christ supplies (Eph. 6:10–18; James 4:7; 1 Pet. 5:9, 10). "He who is in you is greater than he who is in the world" (1 John 4:4).

Acknowledging Satan's reality, taking his opposition seriously, noting his strategy, and reckoning on continual war with him, is not a lapse into a dualistic concept of two gods, one good, one evil, fighting it out. Satan is a creature, superhuman but not divine; he has much knowledge and power, but he is neither omniscient nor omnipotent; he is not omnipresent; and he is an already defeated rebel, having no more power than God allows him and being destined for the lake of fire (Rev. 20:10).

1:11 Will Job, who was so sensitive to the possibility of his children cursing God, now sin that way himself?

1:12 The Adversary is allowed to test Job, but at this point, only with regard to his possessions and family. His power is restricted to what is permitted by the Lord.

1:13–22 Despite Satan's divinely-permitted (and divinely-limited) assaults on his possessions, servants, and children, Job remains steadfast in his belief that God is good.

1:20–22 Job utters a wisdom poem that portrays the wisdom of quiet submission to the secret will of God. Everything belongs to the Creator who gave it. God's people must praise Him for whatever He does with what is His. The word "blessed," (or "praised," v. 21) is the same used in v. 11 for "cursed." By using it here, the author is stressing how Job has frustrated Satan's predictions in v. 11. But v. 22 implies the testing is not yet over.

and worshiped. 21 And he said, [g]"Naked I
came from my mother's womb, and naked
shall I [h]return. The LORD [i]gave, and the
LORD has taken away; [j]blessed be the name
of the LORD."
22 [k]In all this Job did not sin or charge
God with [l]wrong.

Satan Attacks Job's Health

2 Again [m]there was a day when the sons
of God came to present themselves
before the LORD, and Satan also came
among them to present himself before the
LORD. 2 And the LORD said to Satan, "From
where have you come?" Satan answered
the LORD and said, "From going to and fro
on the earth, and from walking up and
down on it." 3 And the LORD said to Satan,
"Have you considered my servant Job, that
there is none like him on the earth, a
blameless and upright man, who fears God
and turns away from evil? He still [n]holds
fast his integrity, although you incited me
against him to destroy him [o]without reason." 4 Then Satan answered the LORD and
said, "Skin for skin! All that a man has he
will give for his life. 5 But [p]stretch out your
hand and touch his bone and his flesh,
and he will [q]curse you to your face." 6 And
the LORD said to Satan, "Behold, he is in
your hand; only spare his life."
7 So Satan went out from the presence of
the LORD and struck Job with loathsome
[r]sores from [s]the sole of his foot to the
crown of his head. 8 And he took [t]a piece of
broken pottery with which to scrape himself while he sat in [u]the ashes.
9 Then his wife said to him, "Do you still
[v]hold fast your integrity? [q]Curse God and
die." 10 But he said to her, "You speak as
one of the [w]foolish women would speak.
[x]Shall we receive good from God, and shall
we not receive evil?"[1] [y]In all this Job did
not [z]sin with his lips.

Job's Three Friends

11 Now when Job's three [a]friends heard of
all this evil that had come upon him, they
came each from his own place, Eliphaz [b]the
Temanite, Bildad [c]the Shuhite, and Zophar
the Naamathite. They made an appointment together to come to [d]show him sympathy and comfort him. 12 And when they
saw him from a distance, they did not recognize him. And they raised their voices
and wept, and they [e]tore their robes and
sprinkled [f]dust on their heads toward
heaven. 13 And they sat with him on the
ground [g]seven days and seven nights, and
no one spoke a word to him, for they saw
that his suffering was very great.

Job Laments His Birth

3 After this Job [h]opened his mouth and
cursed the day of his birth. 2 And Job
said:

21 [g]Eccles. 5:15; [Ps. 49:17; 1 Tim. 6:7] [h][Gen. 3:19; Ps. 90:3; Eccles. 12:7] [i][Eccles. 5:19; James 1:17] [j]Ps. 113:2; Dan. 2:20; [Eph. 5:20; 1 Thess. 5:18]
22 [k]ch. 2:10 [l]ch. 24:12
Chapter 2
1 [m]ch. 1:6
3 [n]ver. 9; [ch. 27:5, 6] [o]ch. 9:17
5 [p]ch. 1:11 [q]ch. 1:5
7 [r]Ex. 9:9; Lev. 13:18; [Deut. 28:27] [s]Deut. 28:35; Isai. 1:6
8 [t]ch. 41:30 [u]ch. 42:6; Ezek. 27:30; Jonah 3:6; Matt. 11:21
9 [v]ver. 3 [q][See ver. 5 above]
10 [w][Ps. 74:18, 22] [x][Ps. 39:1; James 5:10, 11] [y]ch. 1:22 [z][Ps. 39:1]
11 [a][Prov. 17:17] [b]See 1 Chr. 1:45 [c]Gen. 25:2; 1 Chr. 1:32 [d]ch. 42:11; [Rom. 12:15]
12 [e]See Gen. 37:29 [f]See Josh. 7:6; Neh. 9:1; Lam. 2:10; Ezek. 27:30
13 [g]Ezek. 3:15; [Gen. 50:10]
Chapter 3 1 [h]ch. 33:2; Ps. 78:2

1 Or *disaster*; also verse 11

2:1–6 Further developments in heaven—another round of accusations from Satan—precede more suffering for Job on earth.

2:3 holds fast his integrity . . . without reason. The sudden change from the words of 1:6–8 at the end of 2:1–3 shows how the Adversary, who has lost the first round, is humiliated by God through a bit of irony. The same word Satan had used to accuse Job is used here, translated "without reason." It is the Adversary who has done wrong, not Job.

2:4 Skin for skin. Satan is suggesting that even Job's statement of faith in 1:21 is nothing but a ploy. He is willing to sacrifice anything for his own skin. If God will only stretch out His hand and strike Job's body, then he would curse God to His face.

2:6 spare his life. God permits the Adversary to be used as His instrument to strike Job. This brings up the problem of evil. Satan, as a creature, is reined in. He is allowed to go only as far as God permits. The word translated "spare" can be translated "safeguard"; it would appear that Satan is being held responsible for Job's life.

2:7–10 Despite Satan's divinely-permitted (and divinely-limited) attacks on his body, Job holds firmly committed to his conviction that God is praiseworthy.

2:7 loathsome sores. We have no way of knowing the exact nature of Job's disease.

2:8 sat in the ashes. Perhaps by trial and error the ancients learned that the ashes were a place where disease would not spread. Or it may simply have been a way of lamenting.

2:9 Job's wife was unaware of God's guarantee that Job's life would not be taken.

2:10 foolish. The Hebrew word for "foolish" or "fool" has to do with faithlessness and religious apostasy, as in Ps. 14:1 (cf. 53:1). It is more an ethical judgment than an intellectual one.

Job did not sin with his lips. This stress on the purity of Job's speech is an anticipation of the contrast that will come in the dialogue, where Job's words are less pure.

2:11–13 Job's friends arrive to comfort him in the midst of his terrible suffering.

2:13 they sat with him on the ground seven days and seven nights, and no one spoke a word to him. This behavior, tied to the number of completeness (seven), expresses the most intense form of grief they could display. Near Eastern protocol demanded that Job should be the first to speak. For the practice of mourning seven days over the dead, see Gen. 50:10.

3:1–27:23 In three cycles of speeches, the writer explores human perspectives on Job's suffering.

3:1–26 Job breaks the silence with a fiercely emotional lamentation. He expresses the same kind of depression that overtook the psalmist (Ps. 88) and also Jeremiah (Jer. 20:14, 15), whose bitter lament is, in language, similar to Job's.

3 [i]"Let the day perish on which I
was born,
and the night that said,
'A man is conceived.'
4 Let that day be darkness!
May God above not seek it,
nor light shine upon it.
5 Let gloom and [j]deep darkness claim it.
Let clouds dwell upon it;
let the blackness of the day
terrify it.
6 That night—let thick darkness seize it!
Let it not rejoice among the days
of the year;
let it not come into the number of
the months.
7 Behold, let that night be barren;
let no joyful cry enter it.
8 Let those curse it who curse the day,
who are ready to rouse up
[k]Leviathan.
9 Let the stars of its dawn be dark;
let it hope for light, but have none,
nor see [l]the eyelids of
the morning,
10 because it did not shut the doors of
my mother's womb,
nor hide trouble from my eyes.

11 "Why [m]did I not die at birth,
come out from the womb and
expire?
12 Why did [n]the knees receive me?
Or why the breasts, that I should
nurse?
13 For then I would have lain down and
been quiet;
I would have slept; then I would
have been at rest,
14 with kings and counselors of the
earth
who [o]rebuilt ruins for themselves,
15 or with princes who had gold,
who filled their houses with silver.
16 Or why was I not as a hidden
[p]stillborn child,
as infants who never see the light?
17 There the wicked cease from troubling,
and there the weary are at [q]rest.
18 There the prisoners are at ease
together;
they hear not the voice of [r]the
taskmaster.
19 The small and the great are there,
and the slave is free from his
master.

20 "Why is light given to him who is in
misery,
and life to [s]the bitter in soul,
21 who [t]long for death, but it comes not,
and dig for it more than for
[u]hidden treasures,
22 who rejoice exceedingly
and are glad when they find the
grave?
23 Why is light given to a man whose
[v]way is hidden,
whom God has [w]hedged in?
24 For my sighing comes [x]instead of[1]
my bread,
and my [y]groanings are poured out
like water.
25 [z]For the thing that I fear comes
upon me,
and what I dread befalls me.
26 I am not at ease, nor am I quiet;
I have no rest, but trouble comes."

Eliphaz Speaks: The Innocent Prosper

4 Then Eliphaz the Temanite answered and said:
2 "If one ventures a word with you, will
you be impatient?
Yet who can keep from speaking?
3 Behold, you have instructed many,
and you have [a]strengthened the
weak hands.
4 Your words have upheld him who
was stumbling,
and you have [a]made firm the
feeble knees.

3 [i][ch. 10:18, 19]; See Jer. 20:14-18
5 [j]ch. 10:21, 22; 12:22; 24:17; 28:3; 34:22; 38:17; Ps. 23:4; Isai. 9:2; Matt. 4:16
8 [k]ch. 41:1
9 [l]ch. 41:18
11 [m]ch. 10:18, 19
12 [n]Gen. 30:3; 50:23; Isai. 66:12
14 [o][Isai. 58:12]
16 [p]Ps. 58:8; Eccles. 6:3; [1 Cor. 15:8]
17 [q]ch. 17:16
18 [r]Ex. 3:7
20 [s]Prov. 31:6
21 [t]Rev. 9:6 [u]Prov. 2:4
23 [v]Isai. 40:27 [w][ch. 1:10]; See ch. 19:8
24 [x][Ps. 42:3; 80:5; 102:9] [y]Ps. 22:1; 38:8
25 [z][Prov. 10:24]
Chapter 4
3 [a]Isai. 35:3; [Heb. 12:12]
4 [a][See ver. 3 above]

[1] Or *like*; Hebrew *before*

3:3–10 Job does not curse God, but he goes so far as to question God's wisdom in giving him life.

3:11–26 Vv. 3–10 were set in the form of curses, while these are rhetorical questions. Job gives vent to his frustration, asking why he was not stillborn (vv. 11, 12, 16). Since that did not happen, his frustration moves on to ask rhetorically why he should not have experienced premature death (vv. 20, 23).

4:1–5:27 Eliphaz begins the first cycle of speeches (chs. 4–14) in which Job and his friends debate the reasons for his predicament.

4:2–6 Eliphaz is the least caustic of Job's three friends, at least in his first speech. These opening words, which assume Job is innocent (v. 7), should be compared with 22:1–11, where he is fully convinced Job is getting what he deserves. Job is complimented for being a wisdom teacher (vv. 3, 4), but in v. 5 he is warned lest he fail to apply to himself what he has taught others.

5 But now it has come to you, and you
are impatient;
it touches you, and you are
dismayed.
6 [b] Is not your fear of God[1]
your [c] confidence,
and the integrity of your ways your
hope?

7 "Remember: [d] who that was innocent
ever perished?
Or where were the upright
cut off?
8 As I have seen, those who [e] plow
iniquity
and sow trouble reap the same.
9 By [f] the breath of God they perish,
and by [g] the blast of his anger they
are consumed.
10 The roar of the lion, the voice of the
fierce lion,
[h] the teeth of the young lions are
broken.
11 The strong lion perishes for lack of
prey,
and the cubs of the lioness are
scattered.

12 "Now a word was brought to me
stealthily;
my ear received [i] the whisper of it.
13 Amid [j] thoughts from [k] visions of the
night,
when [k] deep sleep falls on men,
14 dread came upon me, and trembling,
which made all my bones shake.
15 A spirit glided past my face;
the hair of my flesh stood up.
16 It stood still,
but I could not discern its
appearance.
[l] A form was before my eyes;
there was silence, then I heard [m] a
voice:
17 [n] 'Can mortal man be in the right
before[2] God?
Can a man be pure before his
Maker?
18 Even in his servants [o] he puts no trust,
and his angels he charges with error;
19 how much more those who dwell in
houses of [p] clay,
whose foundation is in [q] the dust,
who are crushed like [r] the moth.
20 Between [s] morning and evening they
are beaten to pieces;
they perish forever [t] without
anyone regarding it.
21 Is not their tent-cord plucked up
within them,
[u] do they not die, and that without
wisdom?'

5 "Call now; is there anyone who will
answer you?
To which of [v] the holy ones will
you turn?
2 Surely vexation kills the fool,
and jealousy slays the simple.
3 [w] I have seen the fool taking root,
but suddenly I cursed his dwelling.
4 His children are [x] far from safety;
they are crushed in [y] the gate,
and there is no one to deliver them.
5 The hungry eat his harvest,
and he takes it even out of
thorns,[3]
and the thirsty[4] pant after his[5]
wealth.
6 For affliction does not come from the
dust,
nor does trouble sprout from the
ground,
7 but man is [z] born to trouble
as the sparks fly upward.

6 [b] ch. 1:1 [c] ch. 31:24; Prov. 3:26
7 [d] [Ps. 37:25]
8 [e] Hos. 10:13; [Ps. 7:14; Prov. 22:8; Gal. 6:7, 8]
9 [f] Isai. 30:33 [g] ch. 15:30; Ex. 15:8; Ps. 18:15; [Isai. 11:4; 2 Thess. 2:8]
10 [h] Ps. 58:6; [ch. 29:17; Ps. 3:7]
12 [i] ch. 26:14
13 [j] ch. 20:2 [k] ch. 33:15; Gen. 2:21; 15:12; 1 Sam. 26:12; Isai. 29:10
16 [l] Num. 12:8 [m] [1 Kin. 19:12]
17 [n] ch. 9:2; 10:4; 25:4; 32:2
18 [o] ch. 15:15
19 [p] ch. 10:9; 13:12; 33:6; Isai. 64:8; 2 Cor. 4:7; 5:1 [q] Gen. 2:7; 3:19; 18:27 [r] [ch. 13:28]
20 [s] [Ps. 90:5, 6; Isai. 38:12] [t] [Isai. 42:25; 57:1]
21 [u] ch. 36:12; Prov. 5:23; 10:21; [Hos. 4:6]
Chapter 5
1 [v] ch. 15:15; Ps. 89:5, 7; Zech. 14:5
3 [w] Jer. 12:2, 3; [Ps. 37:35, 36; 73:18-20]
4 [x] [Ps. 119:15] [y] ch. 29:7; Ps. 127:5; Prov. 22:22; [Josh. 20:4; Amos 5:12]; See Ruth 4:1
7 [z] ch. 14:1; Gen. 3:17-19; Eccles. 2:23

1 Hebrew lacks *of God* 2 Or *more than*; twice in this verse 3 The meaning of the Hebrew is uncertain 4 Aquila, Symmachus, Syriac, Vulgate; Hebrew could be read as *snare* 5 Hebrew *their*

4:6 your fear of God. The fear you have of God, which is the Old Testament way of referring to true worship.

4:8 sow trouble reap the same. This is a wisdom truth that cannot be denied, but is Job guilty of this? That the innocent never perish (v. 7) is not true, nor has it ever been since the death of Abel (cf. Gen. 4:8–11).

4:16 A form. Eliphaz is not sure who it is or what it is, but he is sure it is a supernatural revelation.

4:17 in the right before God. The question is whether humans can be righteous at all in His sight. Even the angels are not pure in His sight (v. 18). It is possible that only v. 17 is the revelation from the Spirit, and that vv. 18–21 are Eliphaz's comment on these words. The quotation mark in that case would come after v. 17 instead of after v. 21.

4:21 die, and that without wisdom. That is, their death was without any purpose and therefore meaningless. They "perish forever" (v. 20) without there ever having been a purpose to their lives.

5:1 To which of the holy ones will you turn. None of the "sons of God," the holy angels, would dare to help Job.

5:7 man is born to trouble. Eliphaz's point is that trouble does not spring up spontaneously like a weed, but has to have been sown by those who reap it.

as the sparks fly upward. Lit. "the sons of Resheph fly upward." Resheph was the god of pestilence, lightning, and destruction. A similar idiom is used in Song 8:6, where love is described as "flashes of fire." In other places the idiom is used for bolts of lightning (Ps. 78:48) and of pestilence (Deut. 32:24; Hab. 3:5).

8 "As for me, I would seek God,
and to God would I commit
my cause,
9 who [a]does great things and
[b]unsearchable,
[c]marvelous things without number:
10 he gives [d]rain on the earth
and sends waters on the fields;
11 he [e]sets on high those who are lowly,
and those who mourn are lifted to
safety.
12 He [f]frustrates the devices of the crafty,
so that their hands achieve no
success.
13 He [g]catches the wise in their own
craftiness,
and the schemes of the wily are
brought to a quick end.
14 They meet with darkness in the
daytime
and [h]grope at noonday as in the
night.
15 But he [i]saves the needy from the
sword of their mouth
and from the hand of the mighty.
16 So the poor have hope,
and [j]injustice shuts her mouth.

17 "Behold, [k]blessed is the one whom
God reproves;
therefore [l]despise not the
discipline of the [m]Almighty.
18 For he wounds, but he [n]binds up;
he [o]shatters, but his hands heal.
19 He will [p]deliver you from six troubles;
in seven no [q]evil[1] shall touch you.
20 [r]In famine he will redeem you from
death,
and in war from the power of the
sword.
21 You shall be [s]hidden from the lash of
the tongue,
and shall not fear destruction
when it comes.
22 At destruction and famine you shall
laugh,
and shall not fear [t]the beasts of the
earth.
23 For you shall be in league with the
stones of the field,
and the beasts of the field shall be
at peace with you.
24 You shall know that your [u]tent is at
peace,
and you shall inspect your fold
and miss nothing.
25 You shall know also that your
[v]offspring shall be many,
and your descendants as [w]the grass
of the earth.
26 You shall come to your grave in [x]ripe
old age,
like a sheaf gathered up in its
season.
27 Behold, this we have [y]searched out;
it is true.
Hear, and know it for your good."[2]

Job Replies: My Complaint Is Just

6 Then Job answered and said:

2 "Oh that my vexation were weighed,
and all my calamity laid in the
balances!
3 For then it would be heavier than
[z]the sand of the sea;
therefore my words have been
rash.
4 For [a]the arrows of the Almighty are
in me;
my spirit drinks their poison;
the terrors of God are arrayed
against me.
5 Does the wild donkey bray when he
has grass,
or the ox low over his fodder?

[1] Or *disaster* [2] Hebrew *for yourself*

9 [a]ch. 9:10; [ch. 37:5; Ps. 40:5; 72:18; Rom. 11:33; Rev. 15:3] [b]ch. 9:10; 11:7; 34:24 [c][ch. 10:16]
10 [d]Ps. 65:9, 10; 147:8; Jer. 5:24; 14:22; Acts 14:17; [Ps. 104:10, 13; Matt. 5:45]
11 [e]1 Sam. 2:7; [Ps. 113:7]
12 [f][Ps. 33:10; Isai. 8:10]; [Neh. 4:15]
13 [g]Cited 1 Cor. 3:19; [Ps. 9:15, 16]
14 [h]ch. 12:25; Deut. 28:29; [Isai. 59:10]
15 [i]Ps. 35:10
16 [j]Ps. 107:42; [Ps. 63:11]
17 [k]Ps. 94:12; [James 1:12] [l]Prov. 3:11; Heb. 12:5; Rev. 3:19 [m]Gen. 17:1
18 [n]Isai. 30:26; 61:1; Hos. 6:1 [o][Deut. 32:39]
19 [p]Ps. 34:19; 91:3; 1 Cor. 10:13 [q]Ps. 91:10
20 [r]Ps. 33:19; 37:19
21 [s][Ps. 31:20]
22 [t][Isai. 11:8, 9; 35:9; 65:25; Ezek. 34:25; Hos. 2:18]
24 [u][ch. 21:9]
25 [v]ch. 21:8; Ps. 112:2 [w]Ps. 72:16
26 [x][Gen. 15:15; 25:8; 35:29; Prov. 9:11; 10:27]
27 [y][Ps. 111:2]
Chapter 6
3 [z][Prov. 27:3]
4 [a]Ps. 38:2

5:17–26 This reference to the disciplinary nature of human suffering is the only place in the speeches of the three counselors where the subject is even broached.

5:19 six . . . in seven. A poetic expression meaning "many."

5:23 in league with the stones of the field. Attempts to explain such a league as merely figurative language do not satisfy the context. Some read this, "in league with the offspring of the field," since the other side of the parallelism reads, "the beasts of the field shall be at peace with you." Since the wild animals often kill the domestic animals, this fits the entire context, for in v. 22 Eliphaz said that Job had no need to fear the beasts of the earth.

5:25 your offspring shall be many. Considering that Job has lost all his children, the statement is both unnecessary and cruel.

5:26 At this point neither Job nor Eliphaz could have imagined that this statement would come true for Job.

5:27 this we have searched out; it is true. This final verbal volley shows that Eliphaz was in error. He thought he understood what was happening to Job, but he did not. Such an assertion reveals spiritual arrogance.

6:1–7:21 Job upbraids Eliphaz for uttering presumptuous, insensitive, not to mention false, words about him (6:1–30), and then addresses his complaint to God.

6:3, 4 my words have been rash. For the arrows of the Almighty are in me. Job excuses his raging by fantasizing that God has become his enemy.

6 Can that which is tasteless be eaten
without salt,
or is there any taste in the juice of
the mallow?[1]
7 My appetite refuses to touch them;
they are as food that is loathsome
to me.[2]

8 "Oh that I might have my request,
and that God would fulfill my
hope,
9 that it would [b]please God to crush me,
that he would let loose his hand
and cut me off!
10 This would be my comfort;
I would even exult[3] in pain
[c]unsparing,
for I have not denied the words of
[d]the Holy One.
11 What is my strength, that I should
wait?
And what is my end, that I should
be patient?
12 Is my strength the strength of stones,
or is my flesh bronze?
13 Have I any help in me,
when resource is driven from me?

14 "He who [e]withholds[4] kindness from a
[f]friend
forsakes the fear of the Almighty.
15 My [g]brothers are [h]treacherous as a
torrent-bed,
as torrential [i]streams that pass away,
16 which are dark with ice,
and where the snow hides itself.
17 When they melt, they disappear;
when it is hot, they vanish from
their place.
18 The caravans turn aside from their
course;
they go up into [j]the waste and
perish.
19 The caravans of [k]Tema look,
the travelers of [l]Sheba hope.

9[b][Num. 11:15] 1 Kin. 19:4
10[c][Isai. 30:14] [d]Lev. 19:2; Isai. 57:15; Hos. 11:9
14[e][Deut. 20:8] [f][Prov. 17:17]
15[g][Ps. 38:11; 41:9] [h][1 Sam. 14:33] [i][Jer. 15:18]
18[j][Gen. 1:2; Jer. 4:23]
19[k]Gen. 25:15; 1 Chr. 1:30; Isai. 21:14; Jer. 25:23 [l]See 1 Kin. 10:1
20[m]Isai. 1:29; Jer. 14:3
23[n]ch. 15:20; 27:13
26[o]ch. 7:7; Isai. 41:29
27[p]Joel 3:3; Nah. 3:10
29[q]ch. 17:10
Chapter 7
1[r]ch. 14:14; Isai. 40:2 [s]ch. 14:5; Ps. 39:4

20 They are [m]ashamed because they
were confident;
they come there and are
[m]disappointed.
21 For you have now become nothing;
you see my calamity and are afraid.
22 Have I said, 'Make me a gift'?
Or, 'From your wealth offer a bribe
for me'?
23 Or, 'Deliver me from the adversary's
hand'?
Or, 'Redeem me from the hand of
[n]the ruthless'?

24 "Teach me, and I will be silent;
make me understand how I have
gone astray.
25 How forceful are upright words!
But what does reproof from you
reprove?
26 Do you think that you can reprove
words,
when the speech of a despairing
man is [o]wind?
27 You would even [p]cast lots over the
fatherless,
and bargain over your friend.

28 "But now, be pleased to look at me,
for I will not lie to your face.
29 [q]Please turn; let no injustice be done.
Turn now; my vindication is at
stake.
30 Is there any injustice on my tongue?
Cannot my palate discern the
cause of calamity?

Job Continues: My Life Has No Hope

7 "Has not man [r]a hard service on earth,
and are not his [s]days like the days
of a hired hand?

1 The meaning of the Hebrew word is uncertain 2 The meaning of the Hebrew is uncertain 3 The meaning of the Hebrew word is uncertain 4 Syriac, Vulgate (compare Targum); the meaning of the Hebrew word is uncertain

6:6, 7 tasteless . . . My appetite refuses. Eliphaz has offered him no real food (v. 5); i.e., words of comfort. What was supposed to be good food (words) made Job sick.

6:8 Oh that I might have my request. The only comfort left is the exquisite release from pain that death would bring him. He strongly affirms continued faith in the Lord. Note that this passage shows Job believes in a blissful afterlife.

6:25 How forceful are upright words. The difference between Job and his friends is summed up here. The speeches of the friends are formally correct but do not necessarily apply to Job. Indeed, the friends accuse Job falsely of having lived a sinful life. Job insists on speaking honest words about his life. He has not forsaken God or lived in a profligate way.

6:27 cast lots over the fatherless. Later, Job will speak of his own loving care for the fatherless (31:16–22). His own name possibly means "without a father."

6:29 is at stake. Lit. "is in it." The "it" is their insistence that he is suffering for his sins. Either he or they must be wrong.

6:30 my palate. In vv. 6, 7 Job had already spoken of their words as bad food. Here he pleads that they change the "stuff" they are feeding him.

7:1–21 Job now directs his words toward God. This is a prayer in the form of a complaint the psalmists often use.

7:1 hard service. The terminology often refers to military service.

2 Like a slave who longs for [t]the shadow,
and like [u]a hired hand who looks for his [v]wages,
3 so I am allotted months of [w]emptiness,
[x]and nights of misery are apportioned to me.
4 [y]When I lie down I say, 'When shall I arise?'
But the night is long,
and I am full of tossing till the dawn.
5 My flesh is clothed with [z]worms and [a]dirt;
my skin hardens, then [b]breaks out afresh.
6 My days are [c]swifter than [d]a weaver's shuttle
and come to their end without hope.

7 "Remember that my life is a [e]breath;
my eye will never again see good.
8 [f]The eye of him who sees me will behold me no more;
while your eyes are on me, [g]I shall be gone.
9 As [h]the cloud fades and vanishes,
so he who [i]goes down to Sheol does not come up;
10 he [j]returns no more to his house,
nor does his [k]place know him anymore.

11 "Therefore I will not [l]restrain my mouth;
I will speak in the anguish of my spirit;
I will [m]complain in [n]the bitterness of my soul.
12 Am I the sea, or [o]a sea monster,
that you set a guard over me?
13 [p]When I say, 'My bed will comfort me,
my couch will ease my complaint,'
14 then you scare me with dreams
and terrify me with visions,
15 so that I would choose strangling
and death rather than my [q]bones.
16 I [r]loathe my life; I would not live forever.
[s]Leave me alone, for my days are [t]a breath.
17 [u]What is man, that you make so much of him,
and that you set your heart on him,
18 [v]visit him every morning
and [w]test him every moment?
19 How long will you not [x]look away from me,
nor leave me alone till I swallow my spit?
20 If I sin, what do I do to you, you watcher of mankind?
Why have you made me [y]your mark?
Why have I become a burden to you?
21 Why do you not pardon my transgression
and take away my iniquity?
For now I shall lie in [z]the earth;
you will [a]seek me, [b]but I shall not be."

Bildad Speaks: Job Should Repent

8 Then [c]Bildad the Shuhite answered and said:

2 [t]S. of S. 2:17; 4:6; Jer. 6:4 [u]ch. 14:6 [v]Lev. 19:13
3 [w]ver. 16 [x][ch. 30:17]
4 [y]Deut. 28:67
5 [z]Isai. 14:11 [a][ch. 2:8] [b][ch. 2:7]
6 [c]ch. 9:25 [d][Isai. 38:12]
7 [e]ch. 6:26; Ps. 78:39
8 [f]ch. 20:9; [ch. 8:18; Ps. 37:36] [g][ver. 2]
9 [h]ch. 30:15 [i]See ch. 21:13
10 [j]ch. 10:21; 2 Sam. 12:23 [k]ch. 20:9; Ps. 103:16; [ch. 8:18]
11 [l]Ps. 40:9 [m]ch. 21:4; Ps. 77:3 [n]ch. 10:1; 21:25; 1 Sam. 1:10; Isai. 38:15; [ch. 3:20]
12 [o]Gen. 1:21
13 [p][ch. 9:27]
15 [q][ch. 19:20; 30:17]
16 [r][ch. 9:21; 10:1] [s]ch. 10:20; 14:6; Ex. 14:12; [Ps. 39:13] [t]ver. 3
17 [u]Ps. 8:4; 144:3; Heb. 2:6
18 [v]Ps. 17:3 [w]Ps 11:4, 5
19 [x]ch. 14:6
20 [y]ch. 16:12; Lam. 3:12
21 [z]Dan. 12:2 [a][ch. 8:5; 24:5; Prov. 1:28] [b][ver. 8]
Chapter 8
1 [c]ch. 2:11

7:5 Job's malady may have been a combination of diseases. Repellent symptoms, however, appeared all over his skin, his largest and most sensitive bodily organ.

7:7 never again see good. Worse than pain is the loss of hope for a return to health.

7:9 does not come up. This is the language of appearance. Job is not developing a doctrine, but merely stating what all observe. Later, Job will show he believes in the possibility of resurrection (14:12–15).

7:11 will not restrain my mouth. Like the psalmist, Job insists on complaining out of his "bitterness of soul"; but note that he complains to God, not to man here.

7:12 Am I the sea. The Hebrew uses "sea" as a proper name here without the definite article. This is poetic language for the boisterous Canaanite deity Yam (Sea). Job does not worship Yam, but he knows the story about him.

7:14 you scare me. Job imagines that God is actually doing all this. The reader knows from the prologue that He permitted Satan to do it. Yet that permission is within God's sovereign ordination.

7:15 I would choose . . . death. Job sees death as the way out, but Satan was not permitted to go that far, nor would death have served Satan's purpose of getting him to curse God to His face.

7:16 Leave me alone. Again, Job imagines that God is the one who torments him. We know from the prologue, however, that God has a high and holy purpose in permitting Satan to touch Job.

7:17 What is man, that you make so much of him. Cf. Ps. 8:4 and 144:3. The psalmist is not suffering, so his thoughts on this subject are positive. He marvels that God cares so much for the creature He has made to reflect His own image. But Job, in his distress, wishes that God would leave him alone.

7:20 you watcher of mankind. He thinks God is too faultfinding. For what sin is it that God is punishing him so severely?

7:21 and take away my iniquity. Though Job will stress his integrity (i.e., his honest commitment to godliness and righteousness) in his former life, he never denies that he was a sinner.

8:1–22 This reply presents Bildad as a blunt and unfeeling man. He had failed to hear Job's cry for compassion (6:13, 14, 26). His message to Job

2 “How long will you say these things,
and the words of your mouth be a
[d]great wind?
3 [e]Does God pervert justice?
Or does the Almighty pervert the
right?
4 If your [f]children have sinned against
him,
he has delivered them into the
hand of their transgression.
5 If you will seek God
and [g]plead with the Almighty for
mercy,
6 if you are pure and upright,
surely then he will [h]rouse himself
for you
and [i]restore your rightful
habitation.
7 And though your beginning was small,
[j]your latter days will be very great.

8 “For [k]inquire, please, of bygone ages,
and consider what [l]the fathers
have searched out.
9 For we are but of yesterday and
know nothing,
for our days on earth are [m]a shadow.
10 Will they not teach you and tell you
and utter words out of their
understanding?

11 “Can papyrus grow where there is no
marsh?
Can reeds flourish where there is
no water?
12 While yet in flower and not cut down,
they [n]wither before any other plant.
13 Such are the paths of all who [o]forget
God;
[p]the hope of [q]the godless shall
perish.
14 His confidence is severed,
and his trust is [r]a
spider’s web.[1]
15 He leans against his [s]house, but it
does not stand;
he lays hold of it, but it does not
endure.
16 He is a lush plant before the sun,
and his [t]shoots spread over his
garden.
17 His roots entwine the stone heap;
he looks upon a house
of stones.
18 If he is destroyed from his [u]place,
then it will deny him, saying, ‘I
have never [v]seen you.’
19 Behold, this is the joy of his way,
and out of [w]the soil others will
spring.

20 “Behold, God will not reject a
blameless man,
nor take the hand of evildoers.
21 He will yet [x]fill your mouth with
laughter,
and your lips with shouting.
22 Those who hate you will be [y]clothed
with shame,
and the tent of the wicked will be
no more.”

Job Replies: There Is No Arbiter

9 Then Job answered and said:

2 “Truly I know that it is so:
But how can a man be [z]in the right
before God?
3 If one wished to [a]contend with him,
one could not answer him once in
a thousand times.

2 [d]1 Kin. 19:11; [ch. 15:2]
3 [e]ch. 34:12; [Gen. 18:25; Deut. 32:4; 2 Chr. 19:7; Ezra 9:15; Dan. 9:14; Rom. 3:5]
4 [f]ch. 1:5, 18, 19
5 [g]ch. 9:15
6 [h]See Ps. 7:6 [i][Prov. 3:33]
7 [j][ch. 42:12; James 5:11]
8 [k]Deut. 4:32; 32:7; [ch. 15:18] [l]ch. 15:18
9 [m]ch. 14:2; 17:7; 1 Chr. 29:15; Ps. 102:11; 109:23; 144:4; Eccles. 6:12
12 [n][Ps. 37:2; 129:6]
13 [o]See Ps. 9:17 [p]Prov. 10:28; 11:7 [q]ch. 13:16; 15:34; 27:8
14 [r][Isai. 59:5, 6]
15 [s]ch. 27:18
16 [t]Ps. 80:11
18 [u]See ch. 7:10 [v]ch. 7:8
19 [w][ch. 36:24; 1 Sam. 2:7, 8; Ps. 103:16; 113:7]
21 [x]Ps. 126:2
22 [y]Ps. 35:26; 132:18; [Ps. 109:29]
Chapter 9
2 [z]ch. 4:17
3 [a][ch. 10:2; Ps. 143:2; Rom. 3:20]

1 Hebrew *house*

is forthright. He and his family have gotten what they deserve. If only now he will repent of the shameless deeds that brought on this disaster, he can be restored to even greater prosperity and happiness than he had before.

8:2 a great wind. This is a strong accusation. It is unlike the tone of Eliphaz who attempted a soft approach at first (4:2).

8:6 if you are pure and upright. In Bildad’s mind God has mercy only when human beings deserve it. Mercy, however, cannot ever be deserved. If it were deserved it would be justice.

8:8 inquire . . . bygone ages. Eliphaz had appealed to revelation as his authority, even though that revelation was somewhat enigmatic (4:12–17). Bildad appeals to human tradition.

8:13 the godless. Bildad draws on several illustrations from nature to describe the hopelessness of those whom he calls “the godless.” The Hebrew word refers to someone who is profane or defiled by sin. Obviously, Bildad sees Job as a case in point.

8:20 God will not reject a blameless man. This verse contains the heart of Bildad’s theology of suffering. As standard wisdom it was not wrong. Ps. 1:6 teaches that the Lord cares about the way of the righteous, but the way of the wicked shall perish. Bildad’s error consisted in assuming that because Job was suffering he had to be a godless person.

9:1–10:22 Job’s reply to Bildad in chs. 9; 10 starts with a discourse on God’s power and wisdom (9:1–13), but shifts to questioning His justice (9:14–35). In 9:30 he begins to direct his words to God, and this continues through ch. 10.

9:2 But how can a man be in the right before God. Job agrees with the view of Bildad that God punishes the wicked and cares for the righteous (Ps. 1:6), but is there anybody who is wholly righteous?

9:3 Job does not know yet that God Himself will be his cross-examiner (38:3; 40:7).

4 He is [b]wise in heart and mighty in
strength
—who has [c]hardened himself against
him, and succeeded?—
5 he who removes mountains, and they
know it not,
when he overturns them in his
anger,
6 who [d]shakes the earth out of its
place,
and [e]its pillars tremble;
7 who commands the sun, and it does
not rise;
who seals up the stars;
8 who alone [f]stretched out the heavens
and trampled the waves of the sea;
9 who [g]made [h]the Bear and [i]Orion,
the Pleiades [j]and the chambers of
the south;
10 who does [k]great things beyond
searching out,
and marvelous things beyond
number.
11 Behold, he passes by me, and I [l]see
him not;
he moves on, but I do not perceive
him.
12 Behold, he snatches away; [m]who can
turn him back?
[n]Who will say to him, 'What are
you doing?'
13 "God will not turn back his anger;
beneath him bowed the helpers of
[o]Rahab.
14 [p]How then can I [q]answer him,
choosing my words with him?
15 [r]Though I am in the right, I cannot
answer him;
I must [s]appeal for mercy to my
accuser.[1]
16 If I summoned him and he
answered me,
I would not believe that he was
listening to my voice.
17 For he crushes me with a tempest
and multiplies my wounds
[t]without cause;
18 he will not let me get my breath,
but fills me with bitterness.
19 If it is a contest of [u]strength, behold,
he is mighty!
If it is a matter of justice, who can
[v]summon him?[2]
20 Though I am in the right, [w]my own
mouth would condemn me;
though I am blameless, he would
prove me perverse.
21 I am [x]blameless; I regard not myself;
I [y]loathe my life.
22 It is all one; therefore I say,
He [z]destroys both the blameless
and the wicked.
23 When [a]disaster brings sudden death,
he mocks at the calamity[3] of the
innocent.
24 [b]The earth is given into the hand of
the wicked;
he [c]covers the faces of its judges—
[d]if it is not he, who then is it?
25 "My [e]days are swifter than [f]a runner;
they flee away; they see no good.
26 They go by like [g]skiffs of reed,
like [h]an eagle swooping on the
prey.
27 If I say, [i]'I will forget my complaint,
I will put off my sad face, and [j]be
of good cheer,'
28 I become [k]afraid of all my suffering,
for I know you will not [l]hold me
innocent.
29 I shall be [m]condemned;
why then do I labor in vain?
30 If I wash myself with snow
and [n]cleanse my hands with lye,
31 yet you will plunge me into a pit,
and my own clothes will [o]abhor me.

4 [b][ch. 12:13; 36:5] [c][Ex. 7:13; 32:9]
6 [d]Isai. 2:19, 21; 13:13; Hag. 2:6, 21; Heb. 12:26 [e]ch. 26:11; Ps. 75:3
8 [f]ch. 26:7; Ps. 104:2; Jer. 10:12; 51:15; Zech. 12:1
9 [g]Gen. 1:16 [h]ch. 38:32 [i]ch. 38:31; Amos 5:8 [j]ch. 37:9
10 [k]See ch. 5:9
11 [l]ch. 23:8, 9
12 [m]ch. 11:10; 23:13 [n]Isai. 45:9; [Jer. 18:6; Rom. 9:20]
13 [o]ch. 26:12; Ps. 40:4; 82:4; 89:10; Isai. 30:7; 51:9
14 [p]ch. 15:16 [q]ver. 3
15 [r]ch. 10:15 [s]ch. 8:5
17 [t]ch. 2:3; [ch. 34:6]
19 [u][ver. 4] [v]Jer. 49:19; 50:44
20 [w]ch. 15:6
21 [x]ch. 1:1 [y]ch. 7:16 (Heb.); [ch. 10:1]
22 [z]Eccles. 9:2, 3; Ezek. 21:3
23 [a]Isai. 10:26
24 [b][ch. 10:3] [c]See ch. 12:17 [d][ch. 24:25]
25 [e]ch. 7:6 [f][2 Chr. 30:6; Jer. 51:31]
26 [g][Isai. 18:2] [h]Hab. 1:8
27 [i][ch. 7:13] [j]Ps. 39:13
28 [k][Ps. 119:120] [l]ch. 10:14
29 [m][ch. 10:2]
30 [n]Isai. 1:25; Jer. 2:22; See ch. 22:30
31 [o]ch. 19:19; 30:10

1 Or *to my judge* 2 Compare Septuagint; Hebrew *me* 3 The meaning of the Hebrew word is uncertain

9:6 its pillars. The earth is described poetically as having subterranean architecture.

9:7 The reference is to an eclipse of the sun and the disappearance of certain stars over the seasons.

9:8 The poetic figures in this verse refer to God's creation and control of the forces of nature.

9:13 Rahab. Rahab is the Semitic sea monster after whom the prostitute in Josh. 2 was named. Cf. 26:12. In Is. 30:7 it is a symbol of Egypt.

9:15 Job desires an audience with God to prove his innocence, but thinks that his cause could be hopeless (vv. 14–20, 32–35).

9:21–24 These verses represent the lowest point of Job's speeches. As happens to many who suffer greatly over a long period, Job is tempted to be fatalistic. He wavers between hope and doubt and even accuses God.

9:24 if it is not he, who then is it. These sad but profound words reflect Job's belief in the absolute sovereignty of God. He would not have felt this perplexity if he thought God were limited.

9:25–31 Job finds himself caught in an impossible dilemma. He believes he is innocent, but according to the traditional view of suffering his experience proclaims that God thinks the contrary.

32 For he is not a man, as I am, that I
might answer him,
that we should [p]come to trial
together.
33 [q]There is no[1] arbiter between us,
who might lay his hand on us both.
34 [r]Let him take his [s]rod away from me,
and let [t]not dread of him terrify me.
35 Then I would speak without fear of
him,
for I am not so in myself.

Job Continues: A Plea to God

10 "I [u]loathe my life;
I will give free utterance to my
[v]complaint;
I will speak in [w]the bitterness of
my soul.
2 I will say to God, Do not
[x]condemn me;
let me know why you [y]contend
against me.
3 [z]Does it seem good to you to oppress,
to despise [a]the work of your hands
[b]and favor the designs of the wicked?
4 Have you [c]eyes of flesh?
[d]Do you see as man sees?
5 Are your days as the days of man,
or your [e]years as a man's years,
6 that you [f]seek out my iniquity
and search for my sin,
7 although you [g]know that I am not
guilty,
and there is [h]none to deliver out of
your hand?
8 [i]Your hands fashioned and made me,
and now you have destroyed me
altogether.
9 Remember that you have made me
like [j]clay;
and will you return me to the
[k]dust?
10 Did you not pour me out like milk
and curdle me like cheese?
11 You clothed me with skin and flesh,
and knit me together with bones
and sinews.
12 You have granted me life and
steadfast love,
and your care has preserved my
spirit.
13 Yet these things you hid in your
heart;
I know that [l]this was your
purpose.
14 If I sin, you [m]watch me
and do not [n]acquit me of my
iniquity.
15 [o]If I am guilty, woe to me!
If I am [p]in the right, I cannot lift
up my head,
for I am filled with disgrace
and [q]look on my affliction.
16 And were my head lifted up,[2] you
would hunt me like [r]a lion
and again work [s]wonders
against me.
17 You renew your [t]witnesses
against me
and increase your vexation
toward me;
you [u]bring fresh troops against me.
18 [v]"Why did you bring me out from the
womb?
Would that I had died before any
eye had seen me
19 [w]and were as though I had not been,
carried from the womb to the
grave.
20 [x]Are not my days few?
[y]Then cease, and leave me alone,
[z]that I may find a little cheer

32 [p]Eccles. 6:10; Rom. 9:20
33 [q]ver. 19; 1 Sam 2:25; [ch. 16:21]
34 [r][Ps. 39:10] [s]ch. 21:9; Ps. 89:32; Isai. 10:24 [t][ch. 13:21; 33:7]
Chapter 10
1 [u][ch. 7:16; 9:21; Num. 11:15; 1 Kin. 19:4] [v]ch. 21:4; 23:2 [w]See ch. 7:11
2 [x]ch. 9:29 [y]ch. 9:3
3 [z]ch. 13:9; Ps. 89:38 [a]ch. 14:15; Ps. 138:8; Isai. 64:8 [b][ch. 9:24]
4 [c][John 8:15] [d]1 Sam. 16:7
5 [e]ch. 36:26; Ps. 77:10; [Ps. 90:4; 2 Pet. 3:8]
6 [f][ch. 14:16]
7 [g][ch. 2:3, 9] [h]Deut. 32:39; Isai. 43:13
8 [i]Ps. 119:73
9 [j]See ch. 4:17 [k]ch. 34:15; Gen. 2:7; 3:19; Ps. 146:4; Eccles. 12:7
13 [l]ch. 23:14; 27:11
14 [m]ch. 13:27; 33:11; Ps. 130:3 [n]ch. 9:28
15 [o]Isai. 3:11 [p]ch. 9:15 [q][Ps. 25:18]
16 [r]ch. 28:8; Hos. 5:14; 13:7; [Isai. 38:13] [s][ch. 5:9]
17 [t][ch. 16:8; Ruth 1:21] [u][ch. 19:12]
18 [v]ch. 3:11; [ch. 3:3]
19 [w]Obad. 16
20 [x]See ch. 14:1 [y]See ch. 7:16 [z]ch. 9:27; Ps. 39:13

1 Or *Would that there were an* 2 Hebrew lacks *my head*

9:33 There is no arbiter. Eliphaz had taunted Job with the thought that no heavenly being would think of defending him (5:1). Here Job touches a profound truth, that sinful man needs an arbiter who can reach both God and man. Although not a direct prediction, this verse foresees the need of the "one mediator between God and men" (1 Tim. 2:5).

10:1 I loathe my life. Cf. 7:16; 9:21. Job is not only willing to die, but is seeking it as his only means of escape (6:8, 9). Nothing worse can happen, so he will complain freely.

10:2 let me know why you contend against me. He speaks on the assumption that the traditional view of suffering held by the counselors is correct. He has not been able to deliver himself from this view.

10:3 Does it seem good to you. Lit. "is it good?" Perhaps it should be translated, "is it right?"

favor the designs of the wicked. No wonder God would later accuse him of discrediting His justice (40:8).

10:4–7 Here is irony. Job knows God is omniscient. He does not have to search out sins like a human prosecutor. He knows Job is innocent; yet He has made Job His helpless victim.

10:8–12 Like the author of Ps. 139:13–16, Job understands that God fashioned him in the womb, gave him life, and blessed him. Now he cannot understand how the same good God can treat him so badly.

10:13 these things. What are the "things" Job refers to? Job seems to mean that his suffering is a divine punishment planned right from the beginning of his life. He does not understand that God's plan in his suffering is something other than punishment.

10:14, 15 All this is predicated on the mistaken assumption that his suffering is due to God's punitive wrath.

21 before I go—and [a]I shall not
return—
to the land of [b]darkness and [c]deep
shadow,
22 the land of gloom like thick
darkness,
like deep shadow without any
order,
where light is as thick darkness."

Zophar Speaks: You Deserve Worse

11 Then [d]Zophar the Naamathite answered and said:

2 "Should [e]a multitude of words go
unanswered,
and a man full of talk be judged
right?
3 Should your babble silence men,
and when you mock, shall no one
shame you?
4 For [f]you say, 'My [g]doctrine is pure,
and I am clean in God's[1] eyes.'
5 But oh, that God would speak
and open his lips to you,
6 and that he would tell you the
secrets of wisdom!
For he is manifold in
[h]understanding.[2]
Know then that God [i]exacts of you
less than your guilt deserves.

7 [j]"Can you find out the deep things of
God?
Can you find out the limit of the
Almighty?
8 It is [k]higher than heaven[3]—what can
you do?
Deeper than Sheol—what can you
know?
9 Its measure is longer than the earth
and broader than the sea.
10 If he [l]passes through and [m]imprisons
and summons the court, who can
[n]turn him back?
11 For he knows [o]worthless men;
when he sees iniquity, will he not
consider it?
12 But a stupid man will get
understanding
when [p]a wild donkey's colt is
[q]born a man!

13 "If you [r]prepare your heart,
you will [s]stretch out your hands
toward him.
14 If iniquity is in your hand, put it far
away,
and let not injustice dwell in your
tents.
15 Surely then you will [t]lift up your face
without [u]blemish;
you will be secure and will not fear.
16 You will [v]forget your misery;
you will remember it as waters that
have passed away.
17 And your life will be [w]brighter than
the noonday;
its darkness will be like the
morning.
18 And you will feel secure, because
there is hope;
you will look around and [x]take
your rest in security.
19 You will [x]lie down, and none will
make you afraid;
many will [y]court your favor.
20 But [z]the eyes of the wicked will fail;
all way of escape will be lost to
them,
and their hope is [a]to breathe their
last."

[1] Hebrew *your* [2] The meaning of the Hebrew is uncertain [3] Hebrew *the heights of heaven*

21 [a][ch. 16:22; 2 Sam. 12:23] [b]ch. 30:26; Ps. 88:12 [c]See ch. 3:5
Chapter 11
1 [d]ch. 2:11
2 [e]Prov. 10:19; Eccles. 5:3
4 [f]ch. 10:7 [g]Deut. 32:2; Prov. 4:2; Isai. 29:24
6 [h]ch. 5:12 (Heb.); [i][Ezra 9:13]
7 [j]ch. 5:9; Eccles. 3:11; 8:17; [Ps. 145:3; Rom. 11:33]
8 [k][ch. 22:12; Ps. 139:8]
10 [l]See ch. 9:11-16 [m]See ch. 12:14 [n]ch. 9:12; 23:13
11 [o]Ps. 26:4
12 [p][Ps. 73:22; Eccles. 3:18] [q]See ch. 39:5-8
13 [r]Ps. 78:8; See 1 Sam. 7:3 [s]Ps. 44:20; 88:9; 143:6
15 [t]ch. 22:26; [Gen. 4:5; Ps. 119:6; 1 John 3:21] [u]ch. 31:7; 2 Pet. 3:14
16 [v][Isai. 65:16]
17 [w][Ps. 37:6; Isai. 58:8, 10]
18 [x]Lev. 26:5, 6; Ps. 4:8; Prov. 3:24; Isai. 17:2; Zeph. 3:13
19 [x][See ver. 18 above] [y]Ps. 45:12
20 [z]ch. 17:5; 31:16 [a]Jer. 15:9

10:21 before I go . . . return. Notice the difference between Job's present description of that place as a land of darkness, while in 3:13–19 he looked on it as being a place of peace and rest. This proves that Job's emotional raging must not be used as a basis for constructing normative Old Testament or Christian theology. The rule of interpretation should be that when Job or the counselors are in agreement with normative theology we accept them. But in the dramatic flow of the book, neither he nor they can be relied on as a source of theological formulations.

11:1–20 Zophar, the most severe of Job's counselors, now speaks his mind on Job's plight, misapplying some truths about God.

11:1 the Naamathite. Possibly from Arabia. This is not the Naamah mentioned in Josh. 15:41, which was in the western foothills of Judah.

11:4 I am clean in God's eyes. This is not an exact quotation of Job, who has not said he was sinless. He has claimed not to have led the kind of sinful life that might deserve such severe suffering. He has admitted that no mortal can be righteous before God (9:2).

11:6 less than your guilt deserves. The words reflect Zophar's supposition of the enormity of Job's sin.

11:7–9 These words are an eloquent expression of the transcendence of God, which Zophar then misapplies.

11:13–20 This looks like good advice for a profligate sinner, but it does not properly apply to Job. Like Bildad, Zophar makes no allowance for mercy. Job has to become righteous before God will accept him.

11:14, 15 It is arrogance on the part of Zophar to think that he knows why Job is suffering. We know from the prologue that it was not because Job had sinned. Job was called by God to join that grand company of innocent sufferers for the glory of the Lord.

Job Replies: The LORD Has Done This

12 Then Job answered and said:
2 "No doubt you are the people,
and wisdom will die with you.
3 But I have [b]understanding as well as you;
I am not inferior to you.
Who does not know [c]such things as these?
4 I am [d]a laughingstock to my friends;
I, who [e]called to God and he answered me,
a just and blameless man, am a laughingstock.
5 In the thought of one who is [f]at ease
there is contempt for misfortune;
it is ready for those whose feet slip.
6 [g]The tents of robbers are at peace,
and those who provoke God are secure,
who bring their god in their hand.[1]

7 "But ask the beasts, and they will teach you;
the birds of the heavens, and they will tell you;
8 or the bushes of the earth,[2] and they will teach you;
and the fish of the sea will declare to you.
9 Who among all these does not know
that [h]the hand of the LORD has done this?
10 In [i]his hand is the life of every living thing
and the breath of all mankind.
11 Does not [j]the ear test words
as the palate tastes food?
12 Wisdom is with [k]the aged,
and understanding in length of days.

13 [l]"With God[3] are wisdom and might;
he has counsel and understanding.
14 If he tears down, none can rebuild;
if he [m]shuts a man in, none can open.
15 If he [n]withholds the waters, they dry up;
if he [o]sends them out, they overwhelm the land.
16 With him are strength and [p]sound wisdom;
the deceived and the deceiver are his.
17 He leads [q]counselors away stripped,
and [r]judges he makes fools.
18 He [s]looses the bonds of kings
and binds a waistcloth on their hips.
19 He leads priests away stripped
and overthrows the mighty.
20 He deprives of speech those who are trusted
[t]and takes away the discernment of the elders.
21 He [u]pours contempt on princes
and loosens the belt of the strong.
22 He [v]uncovers the deeps out of darkness
and brings [w]deep darkness to light.
23 He [x]makes nations great, and he destroys them;
he enlarges nations, and [y]leads them away.
24 He takes away understanding from the chiefs of the people of the earth
and [z]makes them wander in a pathless waste.
25 They [a]grope in the dark without light,
and he makes them [b]stagger like a drunken man.

Chapter 12
3 [b][ch. 13:2; 15:9] [c]ch. 16:2
4 [d]ch. 16:10; 17:2, 6; 21:3; 30:1 [e]Ps. 91:15
5 [f]ch. 3:18
6 [g]See ch. 21:7
9 [h]Isai. 41:20; [ch. 1:21]
10 [i]Num. 16:22; Dan. 5:23; Acts 17:28
11 [j]ch. 34:3
12 [k]ch. 32:7; [Ps. 119:100]
13 [l][ch. 9:4; 36:5]
14 [m]ch. 11:10; [Isai. 22:22; Rev. 3:7]
15 [n][Deut. 11:17; 1 Kin. 8:35; 17:1] [o][Gen. 7:11-24; Ps. 147:18; Amos 9:6]
16 [p][ch. 5:12]
17 [q][2 Sam. 17:23] [r]ch. 9:24; Isai. 40:23; [Isai. 29:14; 44:25; 1 Cor. 1:19]
18 [s]Ps. 116:16
20 [t][ch. 32:9]
21 [u]Ps. 107:40
22 [v]Dan. 2:22; 1 Cor. 4:5 [w]See ch. 3:5
23 [x]Isai. 9:3; 26:15 [y][2 Kin. 18:11]
24 [z]Ps. 107:40; [ch. 6:18]
25 [a]See ch. 5:14 [b]Ps. 107:27; Isai. 19:14

1 The meaning of the Hebrew is uncertain 2 Or *speak to the earth* 3 Hebrew *him*

12:1–14:22 Job's reply in this long speech starts with a blast of sarcasm against his counselors. He continues to speak to them through 13:19. Beginning in 13:20 Job turns to God, creating a major break in the speech. This inclination of Job to talk to God (to pray) is in notable contrast to the counselors, who never say a word to God. They only talk about Him.

12:4–6 Job agonizes over being made a laughingstock, even to his friends, while evildoers and idolaters live in ease and security.

12:7, 8 ask the beasts . . . the earth. Like Eliphaz who had called upon revelation and Bildad who had called upon tradition to support their arguments, Job calls on every creature in the universe to bear witness to his argument that the wicked prosper and the righteous suffer.

12:12 This verse can also be translated as a question: "Shouldn't wisdom be found among the aged?" The verse is irony aimed at the counselors who are old but have not become wise.

12:13–25 In this unit of poetry Job expounds the doctrine of God's sovereign freedom. Some have interpreted this as said tongue-in-cheek, a subtle criticism of God for mismanaging the universe. In this view God is limited, and needs to be "forgiven" by His creatures. But throughout this book, even when Job is raging over his suffering and suggesting doubts about God's justice, he always assumes that God is sovereign, and that man can make no effective objection to what He does. Job wrestles with a mystery, one too deep for the shallow counselors. This part of the speech may have been provoked by Zophar's question in 11:7, "Can you find out the deep things of God?" The poem may also be a reply to Eliphaz's hymn in 5:1–26, where only good things happen to good people, an idea proved false in this stanza.

Job Continues: Still I Will Hope in God

13 "Behold, my eye has seen all this,
my ear has heard and understood it.
2 [c]What you know, I also know;
I am not inferior to you.
3 [d]But I would speak to the Almighty,
and I desire to [e]argue my case with God.
4 As for you, [f]you whitewash with lies;
[g]worthless physicians are you all.
5 Oh that you would [h]keep silent,
and it would be your wisdom!
6 Hear now my argument
and listen to the pleadings of my lips.
7 Will you [i]speak falsely for God
and speak [j]deceitfully for him?
8 Will you show partiality toward him?
Will you [j]plead the case for God?
9 Will it be well with you when he [k]searches you out?
Or [l]can you deceive him, as one deceives a man?
10 He will surely rebuke you
if in secret you show partiality.
11 Will not his [m]majesty terrify you,
and the dread of him fall upon you?
12 Your maxims are proverbs of [n]ashes;
your defenses are defenses of clay.

13 "Let me have silence, and I will speak,
and let come on me what may.
14 Why should I take my flesh in my teeth
and [o]put my life in my hand?
15 [p]Though he slay me, I will [q]hope in him;[1]
yet I will [r]argue my ways to his face.
16 This will be my salvation,
that the godless shall not come before him.
17 [s]Keep listening to my words,
and let my declaration be in your ears.
18 Behold, I have [t]prepared my case;
I know that I shall be in the right.
19 [u]Who is there who will contend with me?
For then I would be silent and die.
20 Only grant me two things,
then I will not [v]hide myself from your face:
21 [w]withdraw your hand far from me,
and let not [x]dread of you terrify me.
22 [y]Then call, and I will answer;
or let me speak, and you reply to me.
23 How many are my iniquities and my sins?
[z]Make me know my transgression and my sin.
24 Why [a]do you hide your face
and [b]count me as your enemy?
25 Will you frighten [c]a driven leaf
and pursue dry [d]chaff?
26 For you [e]write bitter things against me
and make me inherit [f]the iniquities of my youth.
27 You put my feet in [g]the stocks
and [h]watch all my paths;
you set a limit for[2] the soles of my feet.
28 Man[3] wastes away like [i]a rotten thing,
like a garment that is [j]moth-eaten.

Job Continues: Death Comes Soon to All

14 "Man who is [k]born of a woman
is [l]few of days and [m]full of trouble.
2 He comes out like [n]a flower and [o]withers;
he flees like [p]a shadow and continues not.

1 Or *Behold, he will slay me; I have no hope* 2 Or *you marked* 3 Hebrew *He*

Chapter 13
2 [c][ch. 12:3; 15:9]
3 [d]ch. 23:4; 31:35 [e][ver. 15, 18]
4 [f]Ps. 119:69 [g][ch. 16:2]
5 [h]Prov. 17:28
7 [i]ch. 27:4
8 [j][Judg. 6:31]
9 [k]Prov. 28:11 [l]Gal. 6:7
11 [m]ch. 31:23
12 [n]Isai. 44:20
14 [o]See Judg. 12:3
15 [p][Prov. 14:32] [q]ch. 14:14 [r][ver. 3; ch. 27:5]
17 [s]ch. 21:2
18 [t]See ch. 33:5
19 [u]Isai. 50:8, 9
20 [v][Gen. 3:8]
21 [w]ch. 9:34; Ps. 39:10 [x]ch. 9:34; 33:7
22 [y]ch. 14:15
23 [z][Ps. 19:12]
24 [a]Deut. 32:20 [b]ch. 19:11; 33:10; [Lam. 2:5]
25 [c]Lev. 26:36 [d]ch. 21:18; Ps. 83:13
26 [e][Ps. 149:9] [f]Ps. 25:7
27 [g][ch. 20:11; 33:11] [h]See ch. 10:14
28 [i]Prov. 12:4; 14:30; Hab. 3:16 [j]ch. 4:19
Chapter 14
1 [k]ch. 15:14; 25:4; Matt. 11:11 [l]ch. 10:20; 16:22; Gen. 47:9; Ps. 39:5; 89:47 [m]See ch. 5:7
2 [n]Ps. 103:15; Isai. 40:6, 7; James 1:10; 1 Pet. 1:24 [o]Ps. 37:2; 90:6 [p]See ch. 8:9; 17:7; Ps. 109:23

13:13–27 Job returns to the thought suggested in v. 3. He has decided now that he must have an audience with God.

13:14 put my life in my hand. He is fearful that he might not survive such an audience.

13:15 Though he slay me, I will hope in him. This verse has often been quoted as the supreme expression of trust in the Lord. Job is confident that he will have an audience with God and that this will bring about his deliverance—"the godless shall not come before him." Moreover, v. 18 makes it clear that Job is positive about his being vindicated when he comes before the Lord. The words "in the right" imply that Job will be shown to be right in his claim that he is innocent of the false charges the counselors have been making against him.

13:23 How many are my iniquities and my sins. Job trusts that if his sins are discovered they will not include the sort of unbridled wickedness that might justify his terrible suffering. See notes 11:4 and 29:7–17.

13:24 and count me as your enemy. This is the delusive fantasy with which Job is struggling. God never considered Job His enemy.

13:28 This verse is probably the opening line of the poem in 14:1–6. In this poem Job imagines that God is constantly punishing human beings for their misdeeds.

3 And do you [q]open your eyes on such
a one
and [r]bring me into judgment with
you?
4 Who can bring [s]a clean thing out of
an unclean?
There is not one.
5 Since his [t]days are determined,
and [u]the number of his months is
with you,
and you have appointed his limits
that he cannot pass,
6 [v]look away from him and leave him
alone,[1]
that he may enjoy, like [w]a hired
hand, his day.

7 "For there is hope for a tree,
if it be cut down, that it will sprout
again,
and that its shoots will not cease.
8 Though its root grow old in the earth,
and [x]its stump die in the soil,
9 yet at the scent of water it will bud
and put out [y]branches like a young
plant.
10 But a man dies and is laid low;
man breathes his last, and [z]where
is he?
11 [a]As waters fail from a lake
and a river wastes away and
dries up,
12 so a man lies down and rises not again;
till [b]the heavens are no more he
will not awake
or be [c]roused out of his sleep.
13 Oh that you would [d]hide me in [e]Sheol,
that you would [d]conceal me [f]until
your wrath be past,
that you would appoint me a set
time, and remember me!
14 If a man dies, shall he live again?
All the days of my [g]service I would
[h]wait,
till my renewal[2] should come.
15 You would [i]call, and I would answer
you;
you would long for the [j]work of
your hands.
16 For then you would [k]number my
steps;
you would not keep [l]watch over
my sin;
17 my transgression would be [m]sealed
up in a bag,
and you would cover over my
iniquity.

18 "But the mountain falls and [n]crumbles
away,
and [o]the rock is removed from its
place;
19 the waters wear away the stones;
the torrents wash away the soil of
the earth;
so you destroy the hope of man.
20 You prevail forever against him, and
he passes;
you change his countenance, and
send him away.
21 His sons come to honor, and he
[p]does not know it;
they are brought low, and he
perceives it not.
22 He feels only the pain of his own
body,
and he mourns only for himself."

Eliphaz Accuses: Job Does Not Fear God

15 Then [q]Eliphaz the Temanite answered and said:

2 "Should [r]a wise man answer with
[s]windy knowledge,
and fill his [t]belly with [u]the east
wind?
3 Should he argue in unprofitable talk,
or in words with which he can do
no good?

1 Probable reading; Hebrew *that he may cease* 2 Or *relief*

3 [q][Ps. 8:4; 144:3] [r]ch. 22:4; Ps. 143:2 **4** [s]ch. 15:14; [Ps. 51:5; John 3:6] **5** [t][ch. 7:1; Ps. 39:4] [u]ch. 21:21 **6** [v]ch. 7:19 [w]ch. 7:1 **8** [x]Isai. 11:1 **9** [y][ch. 29:19] **10** [z]ch. 29:7 **11** [a]Isai. 19:5 **12** [b]Deut. 11:21; Ps. 89:29; [Ps. 72:5; Matt. 5:18] [c][John 11:11] **13** [d][Ps. 27:5; 31:20] [e]See ch. 21:13 [f][Isai. 26:20] **14** [g]ch. 7:1 [h]ch. 13:15 **15** [i]ch. 13:22 [j]See ch. 10:3 **16** [k]ch. 31:4; 34:21 [l][ch. 10:6] **17** [m]Deut. 32:34; [Hos. 13:12] **18** [n]Isai. 34:4 [o]ch. 18:4 **21** [p][Eccles. 9:5]
Chapter 15
1 [q]ch. 2:11 **2** [r][ch. 12:3] [s]ch. 16:3 [t]ver. 35 [u]ch. 6:26; 8:2; Hos. 12:1

14:7–22 Having concluded that death is the only escape from suffering, Job suggests that God let him die and then raise him up after His anger has cooled down. The reader, however, knows God was not angry to begin with. This chapter does not clearly teach a doctrine of resurrection, but it shows that the subject was in people's minds.

14:13 that you would hide me in Sheol. Job is doubtful that God will inflict a temporary death, and he concludes that He will not. But he believes in God's ability to do it.

14:14 I would wait. Here, and in succeeding verses, some translate "would" as "will."

renewal. A form of the word translated "sprout again" in v. 7.

14:18–22 Job finally concludes that the world will go on as it has in the past, and those suffering like him will continue to have little hope. He declares that God goes so far as to destroy man's hope (v. 19).

15:1–35 Eliphaz begins the second cycle of speeches (15:1–21:34), moving away from the tactful approach he used in chs. 4; 5.

15:3 words with which he can do no good. It is more than peer pressure that has moved Eliphaz. It was the additional raging that he heard coming from Job's lips.

4 But you are doing away with the fear
of God[1]
and hindering meditation before
God.
5 For your iniquity teaches your
mouth,
and you choose the tongue of the
crafty.
6 Your [v]own mouth condemns you,
and not I;
[w]your own lips testify against you.

7 [x]"Are you the first man who was born?
Or [y]were you brought forth [z]before
the hills?
8 Have you listened in [a]the council of
God?
And do you limit wisdom to
yourself?
9 [b]What do you know that we do not
know?
What do you understand that is
not clear to us?
10 [c]Both the gray-haired and the aged are
among us,
older than your father.
11 Are the comforts of God too small for
you,
or the word that deals gently with
you?
12 Why does your heart carry you away,
and why do your eyes flash,
13 that you turn your [d]spirit against
God
and bring such words out of your
mouth?
14 [e]What is man, [f]that he can be pure?
Or he who is [g]born of a woman,
that he can be righteous?
15 Behold, God[2] [h]puts no trust in his
[i]holy ones,
and the heavens are not pure in
his sight;
16 [j]how much less one who is
abominable and [k]corrupt,
a man who [l]drinks injustice like
water!

17 "I will show you; hear me,
and what I have seen I will declare
18 (what wise men have told,
without hiding it [m]from their
fathers,
19 to whom alone the land was given,
and no [n]stranger passed among
them).
20 The wicked man writhes in pain all
his days,
through all the [o]years that are laid
up for [p]the ruthless.
21 [q]Dreadful sounds are in his ears;
in [r]prosperity the destroyer will
come upon him.
22 He does not believe that he will
return out of darkness,
and he is marked for the sword.
23 He [s]wanders abroad for bread,
saying, 'Where is it?'
He knows that a day of darkness is
ready at his hand;
24 distress and anguish terrify him;
they [t]prevail against him, like a
king ready for battle.
25 Because he has stretched out his
hand against God
and defies the Almighty,
26 [u]running [v]stubbornly against him
with a thickly bossed shield;
27 because he has [w]covered his face
with his fat
and gathered fat upon his waist
28 and has lived in desolate cities,
in houses that none should inhabit,
which were ready to become heaps
of ruins;
29 he will not be rich, and his wealth
will not endure,
nor will his possessions spread
over the earth;[3]
30 he will not depart from darkness;
the flame will dry up his shoots,
and by [x]the breath of his mouth he
will depart.
31 Let him not [y]trust in emptiness,
deceiving himself,
for emptiness will be his payment.

6 [v]ch. 9:20; Luke 19:22 [w]2 Sam. 1:16
7 [x][ch. 38:21] [y]Prov. 8:25 [z]Ps. 90:2
8 [a]ch. 29:4; Jer. 23:18; Rom. 11:34; 1 Cor. 2:11; [Gen. 1:26; 3:22]
9 [b]ch. 12:3; 13:2
10 [c][ch. 12:12; 32:6, 7]
13 [d][ch. 21:4]
14 [e]For ver. 14-16, see ch. 25:4-6 [f][ch. 14:4; Ps. 14:3; Prov. 20:9; Eccles. 7:20; 1 John 1:8, 10] [g]See ch. 14:1
15 [h]ch. 4:18 [i]See ch. 5:1
16 [j]ch. 9:14 [k][Ps. 14:3; 53:1] [l]ch. 34:7; [Prov. 19:28; 26:6]
18 [m][ch. 8:8]; See Ps. 44:1
19 [n]Joel 3:17
20 [o][ch. 21:19; 24:1] [p]ch. 6:23; 27:13
21 [q]See ch. 18:11 [r][1 Thess. 5:3]
23 [s]Ps. 59:15; 109:10
24 [t]ch. 14:20
26 [u][ch. 16:14; Dan. 8:6] [v]Ps. 75:5
27 [w]See Ps. 17:10
30 [x]ch. 4:9
31 [y][Isai. 59:4]

[1] Hebrew lacks *of God* [2] Hebrew *he* [3] Or *nor will his produce bend down to the earth*

15:7, 8 This list of rhetorical questions drips with sarcasm. In v. 8 Eliphaz returns to Job the very sarcasm Job used on him in 12:2.

15:9 He continues to answer Job using Job's own words. Cf. 12:3; 13:2.

15:10 Job's irony in 12:12 is not lost on Eliphaz. He assures Job that all the elders are on their side, not his.

15:14, 15 Eliphaz harks back to the oracle he received in 4:17. Compare vv. 15, 16 with 4:18, 19.

15:30–35 A grim poetic description of what the counselors mean by perishing.

32 It will be paid in full [z]before his
time,
and his branch will not be green.
33 He will shake off his unripe grape
like the vine,
and cast off his blossom like the
olive tree.
34 For [a]the company of the godless is
barren,
and [b]fire consumes the tents of
bribery.
35 They [c]conceive trouble and give birth
to evil,
and their [d]womb prepares deceit."

Job Replies: Miserable Comforters Are You

16 Then Job answered and said:
2 "I have heard [e]many such things;
[f]miserable comforters are you all.
3 Shall [g]windy words have an end?
Or what provokes you that you
answer?
4 I also could speak as you do,
if you were in my place;
I could join words together against you
and [h]shake my head at you.
5 I could strengthen you with my
mouth,
and the solace of my lips would
assuage your pain.
6 "If I speak, my pain is not assuaged,
and if I forbear, how much of it
leaves me?
7 Surely now God has worn me out;
[i]he has[1] made desolate all my
company.
8 And he has[1] shriveled me up,
which is [j]a witness against me,
and my [k]leanness has risen up
against me;
it testifies to my face.
9 He has [l]torn me in his wrath [m]and
hated me;
he has [n]gnashed his teeth at me;
my adversary sharpens his eyes
against me.
10 Men have [o]gaped at me with their
mouth;
they have [p]struck me insolently on
the cheek;
they [q]mass themselves together
against me.
11 God gives me up to the ungodly
and casts me into the hands of the
wicked.
12 I was at ease, and he broke me apart;
he seized me by the neck and
dashed me to pieces;
he set me up as his [r]target;
13 his [s]archers surround me.
He slashes open my kidneys [t]and
does not spare;
he [u]pours out my gall on the
ground.
14 He breaks me with [v]breach upon
breach;
he [w]runs upon me like a warrior.
15 I have sewed [x]sackcloth upon my
skin
and have laid [y]my strength [z]in the
dust.
16 My face is red with weeping,
and on my eyelids is [a]deep darkness,
17 although there is no [b]violence in my
hands,
and my prayer is pure.
18 "O earth, [c]cover not my blood,
and let my [d]cry find no resting place.
19 Even now, behold, my [e]witness is in
heaven,
and he who testifies for me is [f]on
high.
20 My friends [g]scorn me;
my eye pours out tears to God,
21 that he would [h]argue the case of a
man with God,
as[2] a son of man does with his
neighbor.
22 For when a few years have come
I shall go the way [i]from which I
shall not return.

32 [z]ch. 22:16; Eccles. 7:17; [Ps. 55:23; 102:24]
34 [a]ch. 16:7 [b][ch. 20:26]
35 [c]Ps. 7:14; Isai. 59:4; [Hos. 10:13] [d]See ver. 2
Chapter 16
2 [e][ch. 12:3] [f][ch. 13:4]
3 [g][ch. 15:2]
4 [h]2 Kin. 19:21; Ps. 22:7; 109:25; Isai. 37:22; Jer. 18:16; Lam. 2:15; Matt. 27:39; Mark 15:29
7 [i][ch. 15:34]; See ch. 1:15-19
8 [j]ch. 10:17; [Ruth 1:21] [k]Ps. 109:24]
9 [l]ch. 18:4; Hos. 6:1; Amos 1:11 [m]ch. 30:21 [n]Ps. 35:16; 37:12; 112:10; Lam. 2:16; Acts 7:54
10 [o]Ps. 22:13 [p]Ps. 3:7; Isai. 50:6; Lam. 3:30; Mic. 5:1; [1 Kin. 22:24; Acts 23:2] [q]Ps. 35:15
12 [r]Lam. 3:12; [ch. 7:20]
13 [s]Jer. 50:29 [t]ch. 27:22 [u]ch. 20:25; [Lam. 2:11]
14 [v]ch. 30:14 [w]ch. 15:26
15 [x]See 2 Sam. 3:31 [y][Ps. 75:10] [z][Ps. 7:5]
16 [a]See ch. 3:5
17 [b]Isai. 53:9
18 [c]Isai. 26:21; Ezek. 24:7 [d][Gen. 4:10]
19 [e]Ps. 89:37; Rom. 1:9 [f][Ps. 148:1]
20 [g][ch. 12:5]
21 [h][ch. 31:35]
22 [i]See ch. 10:21

1 Hebrew *you have* 2 Hebrew *and*

16:1–17:16 Job dismisses Eliphaz's harangue as a sickening repetition of a defective perspective on suffering.

16:3 that you answer. Job has grown weary, not of the length of their speeches, but of their failure to say anything helpful.

16:8–14 Again Job imagines God as his adversary. In v. 9 the figure is that of a lion. In vv. 12–14 a graphic warrior figure is employed.

16:18 The earth is personified as a witness to Job's suffering.

16:19 Job believes he has a witness in heaven, a notion that was summarily dismissed by Eliphaz in 5:1. But now the thought has tremendous meaning for Job.

16:22 This verse goes better with ch. 17 (cf. 13:8 note). This is a reminder that the chapter divisions are not original. Job longs for death as a release from his constant pain (14:13), although he expects to live "a few years" longer.

Job Continues: Where Then Is My Hope?

17 My spirit is broken; my days are
[j]extinct;
[k]the graveyard is ready for me.
2 Surely there are mockers about me,
and my eye dwells on their
[l]provocation.
3 "Lay down a pledge for me with
yourself;
who is there who will put up
[m]security for me?
4 Since you have closed their hearts to
understanding,
therefore you will not let them
triumph.
5 He who informs against his friends to
get a share of their property—
the [n]eyes of his children will fail.
6 "He has made me [o]a byword of the
peoples,
and I am one before whom men
spit.
7 My [p]eye has grown dim from vexation,
and all my members are like [q]a
shadow.
8 The upright are [r]appalled at this,
and the innocent stirs himself up
against the godless.
9 Yet the righteous holds to his way,
and he who has [s]clean hands
grows stronger and stronger.
10 But you, [t]come on again, all of you,
and I shall not find a wise man
among you.
11 My [u]days are past; my plans are
broken off,
the desires of my heart.
12 They [v]make night into day;
'The light,' they say, 'is near to the
darkness.'[1]
13 If I hope for [w]Sheol as [x]my house,
if I make my bed in darkness,
14 if I say to the pit, 'You are my father,'
and to the worm, 'My mother,' or
'My sister,'
15 where then is my hope?
Who will see my hope?
16 Will it go down to the bars of
[w]Sheol?
Shall we [y]descend together [z]into
the dust?"

Bildad Speaks: God Punishes the Wicked

18 Then [a]Bildad the Shuhite answered
and said:
2 "How long will you [b]hunt for words?
Consider, and then we will speak.
3 Why are we counted as [c]cattle?
Why are we stupid in your sight?
4 You who [d]tear yourself in your
anger,
shall the earth be forsaken for you,
or [e]the rock be removed out of its
place?
5 "Indeed, [f]the light of the wicked is
put out,
and the flame of his fire does not
shine.
6 The light is [g]dark in his tent,
and his lamp above him is put out.
7 His strong steps are shortened,
and his [h]own schemes throw him
down.
8 For he is cast into a net by his own
feet,
and he walks on its mesh.
9 [i]A trap seizes him by the heel;
a snare lays hold of him.
10 A rope is hidden for him in the
ground,
a trap for him in the path.
11 [j]Terrors frighten him on every side,
and chase him at his heels.
12 His strength is famished,
and calamity is [k]ready for his
stumbling.
13 It consumes the parts of his skin;
[l]the firstborn of death consumes
his limbs.

Chapter 17
1 [j][ch. 18:5, 6] [k][Ps. 88:3, 4]
2 [l]1 Sam. 1:6, 7; [ch. 12:6]
3 [m]Ps. 119:122; Isai. 38:14; Heb. 7:22
5 [n][ch. 11:20; 31:16]
6 [o]ch. 30:9; Deut. 28:37; [Ps. 44:14; 69:11]
7 [p][Ps. 6:7; 31:9] [q]See ch. 14:2
8 [r]Isai. 52:14
9 [s]See ch. 22:30
10 [t]ch. 6:29
11 [u]ch. 7:6; 9:25
12 [v][ch. 11:17]
13 [w]See ch. 21:13 [x][Eccles. 12:5]
16 [w][See ver. 13 above] [y][ch. 3:17-19] [z]ch. 21:26; 40:13

Chapter 18
1 [a]ch. 2:11; 8:1
2 [b][Matt. 22:15; Mark 12:13; Luke 20:20]
3 [c]Ps. 73:22
4 [d]ch. 16:9 [e]ch. 14:18
5 [f]ch. 21:17; Prov. 13:9; 20:20; 24:20; See Ps. 18:28
6 [g]ch. 10:22
7 [h][ch. 5:13]
9 [i]Ps. 140:5
11 [j]ch. 15:21; 20:25; 27:20; 30:15; Jer. 6:25; 46:5; 49:29
12 [k]Ps. 38:17
13 [l]Isai. 14:30

[1] The meaning of the Hebrew is uncertain

17:3 Job wants God to vindicate him, i.e., to prove to the counselors that he is in the right.

17:4 their hearts. That is, the minds of the counselors.

17:6 Since God has not vindicated him, he continues to hold God responsible for his frightful condition. Cf. 30:10.

17:7 The symptoms of his disease included boils, other skin problems, and nightmares (2:7; 7:5, 14). Here and in 19:20 there is loss of weight; and in 19:17, bad breath; in 30:30, fever; and in 30:17, pain day and night.

17:12 Job appears to remember Zophar's words in 11:17.

18:1–21 Bildad accuses Job, impatiently repeating his earlier exposition on the destiny of the wicked (cf. 8:8–19).

18:2–4 Bildad opens his speech with a heartless rebuke of one who is suffering greatly. He has not changed his argument.

14 He is torn from the tent in which he
trusted
and is brought to [m]the king of
terrors.
15 In his tent dwells that which is none
of his;
[n]sulfur is scattered over his
habitation.
16 His [o]roots dry up beneath,
and his branches [p]wither above.
17 His [q]memory perishes from the earth,
and he has no name in the street.
18 [r]He is thrust from light into darkness,
and driven out of the world.
19 He has no [s]posterity or progeny
among his people,
and no survivor where he used to
live.
20 They of the west are appalled at his
[t]day,
and [u]horror seizes them of the east.
21 Surely such are the dwellings of the
unrighteous,
such is the place of him who
[v]knows not God."

Job Replies: My Redeemer Lives

19 Then Job answered and said:
2 "How long will you torment me
and break me in pieces with words?
3 These [w]ten times you have cast
reproach upon me;
are you not ashamed to wrong me?
4 And even if it be true that I have erred,
my error remains with myself.
5 If indeed you [x]magnify yourselves
against me
and make my disgrace an
argument against me,
6 know then that God has [y]put me in
the wrong
and closed his net about me.
7 Behold, I [z]cry out, 'Violence!' but I
am not answered;
I call for help, but there is no
justice.
8 He has [a]walled up my way, so that I
cannot pass,
and he has set darkness upon my
paths.
9 He has [b]stripped from me my glory
and taken the [c]crown from my
head.
10 He breaks me down on every side,
and I [d]am gone,
and my hope has he pulled up like
a tree.
11 He has kindled his wrath against me
and [e]counts me as his adversary.
12 His [f]troops come on together;
they have [g]cast up their siege
ramp[1] against me
and encamp around my tent.
13 "He has put my [h]brothers far from me,
and [i]those who knew me are
wholly estranged from me.
14 My relatives [j]have failed me,
my close [k]friends have
forgotten me.
15 The guests [l]in my house and my
maidservants count me as a
stranger;
I have become a foreigner in their
eyes.
16 I call to my servant, but he gives me
no answer;
I must plead with him with my
mouth for mercy.
17 My breath is strange to my [m]wife,
and I am a stench to the children
of [n]my own mother.
18 Even young [o]children despise me;
when I rise they talk against me.
19 All my [p]intimate friends abhor me,
and those whom I loved have
turned against me.
20 My [q]bones stick to my skin and to
my flesh,
and I have escaped by the skin of
my teeth.

14 [m][Rev. 9:11]
15 [n]See Ps. 11:6; Ezek. 38:22
16 [o]ch. 29:19; Hos. 9:16 [p]ch. 14:2
17 [q]Ps. 34:16; Prov. 10:7; [Ps. 109:13, 15]
18 [r]ch. 10:21, 22
19 [s]Isai. 14:22
20 [t]Ps. 37:13; Jer. 50:27; Ezek. 21:25, 29; Obad. 12; [1 Sam. 26:10] [u][ch. 21:6]
21 [v]Judg. 2:10; Jer. 9:3; 10:25; 1 Thess. 4:8; 2 Thess. 1:8
Chapter 19
3 [w]Gen. 31:7
5 [x]Ps. 35:26; 38:16; 55:12
6 [y][ch. 8:3; 34:12; Lam. 3:36]
7 [z]ch. 24:12; Hab. 1:2; [Lam. 3:8]
8 [a]Lam. 3:7, 9; Hos. 2:6; [ch. 3:23; 13:27]
9 [b]Ps. 89:44 [c]Ps. 89:39; Lam. 5:16; [ch. 29:14]
10 [d]ch. 27:21; [ch. 10:21; 14:20]
11 [e]See ch. 13:24
12 [f][ch. 10:17; 25:2] [g]ch. 30:12
13 [h]Ps. 69:8; [ch. 6:15] [i][Ps. 31:11; 88:8, 18]
14 [j]Ps. 38:11 [k]Ps. 55:13
15 [l][Gen. 17:27; Matt. 10:36]
17 [m]ch. 2:9 [n]ch. 3:10;
18 [o][2 Kin. 2:23]
19 [p][Ps. 41:9; 55:13, 14]
20 [q]Ps. 102:5; [Lam. 4:8]

1 Hebrew *their way*

18:14 the king of terrors. The Canaanites understood death as a god whose one lip touched the earth and the other the heavens, so that he swallowed up everything. According to Bildad, "the firstborn of death" following in the footsteps of his father, eats away the skin and devours the limbs of the wicked. According to Is. 25:8, the Lord will "swallow up death forever" (1 Cor. 15:54).

19:1–29 In ch. 19 Job accuses God of wronging him and not listening to his plea for justice (vv. 6, 7), of stripping him of honor and attacking him (vv. 9–12), and of alienating his kinsmen and friends (vv. 13–20). Job was wrong on all points. He was wrestling with God over the apparent meaninglessness of his suffering that was actually the work of the Adversary, but ordained by the Lord to accomplish a higher purpose. The counselors, on the other hand, had reduced God and His acts to an impersonal formula. They were incapable of empathy with the agony of Job's predicament or of showing him any mercy.

19:20 the skin of my teeth. This idiom has entered the English language through the Bible, but it is hard to see how the figure suggests a narrow escape. Some suggest that the phrase means "with only my skin or gums remaining." His teeth would be lost.

21 Have mercy on me, have mercy on
me, O you my friends,
for the hand of God has
[r]touched me!
22 Why do you, like God, [s]pursue me?
Why are you not satisfied with my
flesh?

23 "Oh that my words were written!
Oh that they were [t]inscribed in a
book!
24 Oh that with an iron [u]pen and lead
they were engraved in the rock
forever!
25 For I [v]know that my [w]Redeemer lives,
and at the last he will stand upon
the [x]earth.[1]
26 And after my skin has been thus
destroyed,
yet in[2] my flesh I shall [y]see God,
27 whom I shall see for myself,
and my eyes shall behold, and not
[z]another.
My heart [a]faints within me!
28 If you say, 'How we will [s]pursue
him!'
and, 'The root of the matter is
found in him,'
29 be afraid of the sword,
for wrath brings the punishment of
the sword,
that you may know there is [b]a
judgment."

Zophar Speaks: The Wicked Will Suffer

20 Then [c]Zophar the Naamathite answered and said:

2 "Therefore my [d]thoughts answer me,
because of my haste within me.
3 I hear censure that insults me,
and out of my understanding a
spirit answers me.
4 Do you not know this from of old,
[e]since man was placed on earth,
5 [f]that the exulting of the wicked is
short,
and the joy of the godless but for a
moment?
6 [g]Though his height mount up to the
heavens,
and his head reach to the clouds,
7 he will perish forever like his own
[h]dung;
those who have seen him will say,
[i]'Where is he?'
8 He will fly away like [j]a dream and
not be found;
he will be chased away like a
vision of the night.
9 [k]The eye that saw him will see him no
more,
nor will his place any more behold
him.
10 His children will seek the favor of the
poor,
and his hands will [l]give back his
wealth.
11 His bones are full of his [m]youthful
vigor,
but it will lie [n]down with him in
the dust.
12 "Though evil is sweet in his mouth,
though he hides it [o]under his
tongue,
13 though he is loath to let it go
and holds it in his mouth,
14 yet his food is turned in his stomach;
it is the venom of [p]cobras within
him.
15 He swallows down riches and vomits
them up again;
God casts them out of his belly.

1 Hebrew *dust* 2 Or *without*

21 [r]ch. 1:11; Isai. 53:4; (Heb.)
22 [s][Ps. 69:26]
23 [t]Isai. 30:8
24 [u]Jer. 17:1
25 [v]ch. 30:23 [w]Isai. 43:14; 44:6, 24; 49:7; [Gen. 48:16; Ps. 19:14; 103:4; 1 Thess. 1:10] [x]ch. 41:33
26 [y]Ps. 17:15; 1 Cor. 13:12; 1 John 3:2
27 [z][Prov. 27:2] [a][Ps. 73:26]
28 [s][See ver. 22 above]
29 [b]Eccles. 12:14; See Ps. 58:11
Chapter 20
1 [c]ch. 2:11
2 [d]ch. 4:13
4 [e][Deut. 4:32]
5 [f]Ps. 37:35, 36
6 [g][Isai. 14:13, 14; Obad. 3, 4]
7 [h]Ps. 83:10; Zeph. 1:17; [1 Kin. 14:10; 2 Kin. 9:37] [i]ch. 14:10
8 [j]Ps. 73:20; 90:5; Isai. 29:7, 8
9 [k]See ch. 7:8, 10
10 [l]ver. 18
11 [m][ch. 13:26; Ps. 25:7] [n]ch. 21:26
12 [o]Ps. 10:7
14 [p]Deut. 32:33; Ps. 140:3

19:21 Job needed heartfelt friendship (6:14), but nothing of the sort was possible from his counselors who only added to his misery.

19:23, 24 Job has an important message that he wants permanently inscribed for posterity. Through the inspiration of the Spirit his words are preserved for all time in the Bible (cf. Mark 14:9).

19:25 I know that my Redeemer lives. The Hebrew word translated "Redeemer" can also be rendered "Avenger," "Guarantor," "Vindicator," or "Kinsman-Redeemer" (Ruth 2:20 note). Job's words are clear, but from his perspective, who does he expect to help him? The prologue reveals that God was not Job's enemy. Indeed, God will become his vindicator (42:7). Job seems to be thinking of the Redeemer as a third party (16:19–21).

at the last he will stand upon the earth. In Job's mind this Vindicator will be both heavenly (16:19) and earthly (able to stand on the earth).

19:26 in my flesh. The meaning of the preposition "in" could be either "in" my flesh or "without" my flesh (see text note). Since the book does touch on the idea of resurrection in ch. 14, it seems likely that when death is spoken of in v. 26, resurrection is in mind here, and the translation should be "in" my flesh. What is certain is that Job believes he has a Redeemer who loves him and for whom his heart yearns (v. 27). The whole passage is strongly evocative of every sinner's need for the one Mediator who is both God and man (1 Tim. 2:5, 6).

20:1–29 Ch. 20 is another eloquent statement of the fate of the wicked. In it, Zophar expresses the truth of the moral governance of the world by God, but fails to make a correct application of it.

20:2 my haste within me. Job's closing words in 19:28, 29 have not been lost on Zophar.

16 He will suck the poison of cobras;
[q] the tongue of a viper will kill him.
17 He will not look upon [r] the rivers,
the streams flowing with [s] honey
and [t] curds.
18 He will [u] give back the fruit of his toil
and will not [v] swallow it down;
from the profit of his trading
he will get no enjoyment.
19 For he has crushed and abandoned
the poor;
he has seized a house that he did
not build.

20 "Because he [w] knew no [x] contentment
in his belly,
[y] he will not let anything in which
he delights escape him.
21 There was nothing left after he had
eaten;
therefore his prosperity will not
endure.
22 In the fullness of his sufficiency he
will be in distress;
the hand of everyone in misery will
come against him.
23 To fill his belly to the full
God[1] will send his burning anger
against him
and rain it upon him [z] into his
body.
24 [a] He will flee from an iron weapon;
[b] a bronze arrow will strike [c] him
through.
25 It [d] is drawn forth and comes out of
his body;
[e] the glittering point comes out of
his [f] gallbladder;
[g] terrors come upon him.
26 Utter darkness is laid up for his
treasures;
[h] a fire not fanned will devour him;
what is left in his tent will be
consumed.
27 [i] The heavens will reveal his iniquity,
and the earth will rise up against
him.
28 The possessions of his house will be
carried away,
dragged off in the day of God's[2]
wrath.
29 [j] This is the wicked man's portion
from God,
[j] the heritage decreed for him by
God."

Job Replies: The Wicked Do Prosper

21 Then Job answered and said:
2 [k] "Keep listening to my words,
and let this be your comfort.
3 Bear with me, and I will speak,
and after I have spoken, [l] mock on.
4 As for me, is my [m] complaint against
man?
Why should I not be impatient?
5 Look at me and be appalled,
and [n] lay your hand over your
mouth.
6 When I remember I am dismayed,
and shuddering seizes my flesh.
7 [o] Why do the wicked live,
reach old age, and grow mighty in
power?
8 Their [p] offspring are established in
their presence,
and their descendants before their
eyes.
9 Their houses are [q] safe from fear,
and [r] no rod of God is upon them.
10 Their bull breeds without fail;
their cow calves and [s] does not
miscarry.
11 They send out their [t] little boys like a
flock,
and their children dance.
12 They sing to [u] the tambourine and
[v] the lyre
and rejoice to the sound of [v] the
pipe.
13 They [w] spend their days in prosperity,
and in [x] peace they go down to
[y] Sheol.

1 Hebrew *he* 2 Hebrew *his*

16 [q] Isai. 59:5; [Prov. 23:32] **17** [r] [Ps. 36:8; Jer. 17:6] [s] Deut. 32:13, 14] [t] [ch. 29:6] **18** [u] ver. 10 [v] ver. 15 **20** [w] Isai. 59:8 [x] Prov. 17:1 [y] [Eccles. 5:13, 14] **23** [z] [Num. 11:33; Ps. 78:30, 31] **24** [a] [Isai. 24:18; Jer. 48:44; Amos 5:19] [b] 2 Sam. 22:35 [c] Judg. 5:26 **25** [d] Judg. 3:22 [e] Deut. 32:41 [f] ch. 16:13 [g] See ch. 18:11 **26** [h] [ch. 15:34; Ps. 21:9] **27** [i] [ch. 16:18, 19]

29 [j] ch. 27:13; [ch. 18:21; 31:2, 3]
Chapter 21
2 [k] ch. 13:17 **3** [l] [ch. 16:10, 20; 17:2] **4** [m] ch. 10:1; 23:2 **5** [n] ch. 29:9; 40:4; Judg. 18:19 **7** [o] ch. 12:6; Ps. 17:14; 37:1, 35; 73:3, 5; 92:7; Eccles. 8:14; Jer. 12:1, 2; Hab. 1:13, 16; Mal. 3:14, 15 **8** [p] [ch. 5:25] **9** [q] [ch. 5:24] [r] See ch. 9:34 **10** [s] Ex. 23:26 **11** [t] [Ps. 17:14] **12** [u] Ex. 15:20 [v] ch. 30:31; Gen. 4:21 **13** [w] ch. 36:11 [x] ch. 34:20; [ch. 24:19] [y] ch. 7:9; 14:13; 17:13; See Ps. 16:10

20:29 This is the wicked man's portion from God. What Zophar teaches will ultimately come to pass, but sadly, he has no word to say about God's mercy. Even in his earlier speech in 11:13–20, where he called on Job to change his ways, there is no mention of mercy. People get God's blessing, according to Zophar, only by earning it.

21:1–34 Job closes this second cycle with a firm rejection of the friends' arguments that the wicked always suffer. Note how he alludes to their very words. Cf. 20:11 with 21:7; 8:19 with 21:8; 18:5 with 21:17; 5:4 and 20:10 with 21:19; 20:5–7 with 21:28–30.

21:5 Look at me and be appalled, and lay your hand over your mouth. If they had any compassion, Job thinks that they would stop accusing him and lying about him.

21:7 Why do the wicked live. Job admits that he is perplexed. He has no answer. The counselors assumed they knew exactly what was going on (cf. John 9:41).

14 They say to God, [z]'Depart from us!
We do not desire the knowledge of your ways.
15 [a]What is the Almighty, that we should serve him?
And what [b]profit do we get if we pray to him?'
16 Behold, is not their prosperity in their hand?
[c]The counsel of the wicked is far from me.

17 "How often is it that [d]the lamp of the wicked is put out?
That their calamity comes upon them?
That God[1] distributes pains in his anger?
18 That they are like [e]straw before the wind,
and like [f]chaff that the storm carries away?
19 You say, 'God [g]stores up their iniquity for their [h]children.'
Let him pay it out to them, that they may [i]know it.
20 Let their own eyes see their destruction,
and let them [j]drink of the wrath of the Almighty.
21 For what do they care for their houses after them,
when [k]the number of their months is cut off?
22 [l]Will any teach God knowledge,
seeing that he [m]judges those who are on high?
23 One dies in his full vigor,
being wholly at ease and secure,
24 his pails[2] full of milk
and [n]the marrow of his bones moist.
25 Another dies in [o]bitterness of soul,
never having tasted of prosperity.
26 They [p]lie down alike in the dust,
and [q]the worms cover them.

27 "Behold, I know your thoughts
and your schemes to wrong me.
28 For you say, [r]'Where is the house of the prince?
Where is [s]the tent in which the wicked lived?'
29 Have you not asked those who travel the roads,
and do you not accept their testimony
30 that [t]the evil man is spared in the day of calamity,
that he is rescued in the day of wrath?
31 Who declares his way [u]to his face,
and who [v]repays him for what he has done?
32 When he is [w]carried to the grave,
watch is kept over his tomb.
33 [x]The clods of the valley are sweet to him;
[y]all mankind follows after him,
and those who go before him are innumerable.
34 How then will you comfort me with empty nothings?
There is nothing left of your answers but falsehood."

Eliphaz Speaks: Job's Wickedness Is Great

22 Then [z]Eliphaz the Temanite answered and said:
2 [a]"Can a man be profitable to God?
Surely he who is wise is profitable to himself.
3 Is it any pleasure to the Almighty if you are in the right,
or is it gain to him if you [b]make your ways blameless?
4 Is it for your fear of him that he reproves you
and [c]enters into judgment with you?
5 Is not your evil abundant?
There is no end to your iniquities.
6 For you have [d]exacted pledges of your brothers for nothing
[e]and stripped the naked of their clothing.

14[z]ch. 22:17
15[a][Ex. 5:2] [b]See ch. 34:9
16[c]ch. 22:18; [Ps. 1:1]
17[d]See ch. 18:5, 6
18[e]ch. 13:25; Ps. 83:13 [f]Ps. 1:4; 35:5; Isai. 17:13; 29:5
19[g]ch. 15:20 [h]Ex. 20:5 [i]Isai. 9:9; Ezek. 25:14; Hos. 9:7
20[j]Ps. 60:3; 75:8; Isai. 51:17, 22; Jer. 25:15; Obad. 16; Rev. 14:10
21[k]ch. 14:5
22[l]Isai. 40:14; Rom. 11:34; 1 Cor. 2:16 [m][ch. 4:18; 15:15]
24[n]Prov. 3:8; [Isai. 58:11; 66:14]
25[o]See ch. 7:11
26[p]ch. 20:11; [Eccles. 9:2] [q]Isai. 14:11
28[r][ch. 20:6, 7] [s][ch. 8:22; 15:34]
30[t][Prov. 16:4; 2 Pet. 2:9]
31[u]Deut. 7:10; Hos. 5:5; Gal. 2:11 [v]Deut. 7:10
32[w]ch. 10:19
33[x]ch. 38:38 [y][ch. 30:23; Heb. 9:27]
Chapter 22
1[z]ch. 2:11
2[a]See ch. 35:7
3[b]See Ps. 18:32
4[c]ch. 14:3; [Ps. 143:2]
6[d]ch. 24:3, 9; Ex. 22:26; Deut. 24:6, 17; Ezek. 18:12, 16 [e][ch. 31:16]

1 Hebrew *he* 2 The meaning of the Hebrew word is uncertain

21:22 Will any teach God knowledge. Job's high view of God only makes his problem more perplexing.

22:1–30 Eliphaz begins the third cycle of speeches (22:1–26:14) listing Job's sins and calling on him to repent.

22:2, 3 Eliphaz reacts to Job's statement that God allows wickedness to go unpunished, and he also says that human uprightness adds nothing to Him.

22:3 The sense may be, "Would it please God if you were vindicated?"

22:5 Eliphaz reached the conclusion Zophar and Bildad had already expressed—that Job's sins are endless.

22:6–11 Here is a direct personal attack on Job for specific sins, especially social sins against the poor and widows. Later Job will emphasize his social righteousness (chs. 29; 31).

7 You have given no water to the weary
to drink,
and you have [f]withheld bread from
the hungry.
8 [g]The man with power possessed the
land,
and [h]the favored man lived in it.
9 You have [i]sent widows away empty,
and [j]the arms of [k]the fatherless
were crushed.
10 Therefore [l]snares are all around you,
and sudden terror overwhelms you,
11 or [m]darkness, so that you cannot see,
and a [n]flood of [o]water covers you.

12 "Is not God high in the heavens?
See [p]the highest stars, how lofty
they are!
13 But you say, [q]'What does God know?
Can he judge through [r]the deep
darkness?
14 [s]Thick clouds veil him, so that he
does not see,
and he walks on the vault of heaven.'
15 Will you keep to the old way
that wicked men have trod?
16 They were snatched away [t]before
their time;
their foundation was washed away.
17 They said to God, [u]'Depart from us,'
and [v]'What can the Almighty do
to us?'[1]
18 Yet he filled their houses with good
things—
but [w]the counsel of the wicked is
far from me.
19 [x]The righteous see it and are glad;
the innocent one [y]mocks at them,
20 saying, 'Surely our adversaries are cut
off,
and what they left [z]the fire has
consumed.'

21 [a]"Agree with God, and [b]be at peace;
thereby good will come to you.
22 Receive instruction from [c]his mouth,
and [d]lay up his words in your heart.
23 If you [e]return to the Almighty you
will be [f]built up;
if you [g]remove injustice far from
your tents,
24 if you lay gold in [h]the dust,
and gold of [i]Ophir among the
stones of the torrent bed,
25 then the Almighty will be your gold
and your precious silver.
26 For then you [j]will delight yourself in
the Almighty
and [k]lift up your face to God.
27 You will [l]make your prayer to him,
and he will hear you,
and you will [m]pay your vows.
28 You will decide on a matter, and it
will be established for you,
and [n]light will shine on your ways.
29 For when they are humbled you say,
'It is because of pride';[2]
but he saves [o]the lowly.
30 He [p]delivers even the one who is not
innocent,[3]
who will be delivered through [q]the
cleanness of your hands."

7 [f][ch. 31:17; Isai. 58:7; Ezek. 18:7, 16; Matt. 25:42] 8 [g][ch. 35:9] [h]2 Kin. 5:1; Isai. 9:15 9 [i][Luke 1:53] [j][ch. 38:15] [k]ch. 31:21; Isai. 10:2; Ezek. 22:7 10 [l]ch. 18:8-10 11 [m][Ex. 10:22, 23] [n]ch. 38:34 [o][ch. 27:20; Ps. 69:1, 2, 14, 15; 124:5; Lam. 3:54; Jonah 2:3, 5] 12 [p][ch. 11:8] 13 [q]Ps. 73:11; [Ps. 10:11; 59:7; 64:5; 94:7; Isai. 29:15; Ezek. 8:12; 9:9] [r]ch. 38:9 14 [s][Ps. 139:11, 12]; [Prov. 8:27; Isai. 40:22] 16 [t]See ch. 15:32 17 [u]ch. 21:14 [v][Ps. 4:6] 18 [w]ch. 21:16 19 [x]Ps. 52:6; 58:10; 107:42; [Ps. 64:10] [y]Ps. 2:4 20 [z]ch. 1:16 21 [a]Ps. 139:3 [b][Prov. 3:2] 22 [c]Prov. 2:6; [Mal. 2:7] [d]Ps. 119:11 23 [e][ch. 8:5, 6; 11:13, 14; Mal. 3:7] [f]Jer. 24:6; 33:7 [g]ch. 11:14 24 [h]ch. 20:11; 21:26 [i]See 1 Kin. 9:28 26 [j]ch. 27:10; Ps. 37:4; Isai. 58:14 [k]See ch. 11:15 27 [l]ch. 33:26; Ps. 50:14, 15; Isai. 58:9 [m]Ps. 50:14 28 [n]Prov. 4:18 29 [o]Ps. 138:6; Prov. 3:34; 29:23; Matt. 23:12; Luke 1:52; James 4:6; 1 Pet. 5:5 30 [p][Gen. 18:26] [q]ch. 17:9; Ps. 18:20, 24; 24:4; 26:6; [ch. 9:30]

Job Replies: Where Is God?

23 Then Job answered and said:
2 "Today also my [r]complaint is
bitter;[4]
my [s]hand is heavy on account of
my groaning.
3 Oh, [t]that I knew where I might find
him,
that I might come even to his [u]seat!
4 I would [v]lay my case before him
and fill my mouth with
arguments.
5 I would know what he would
answer me
and understand what he would say
to me.
6 Would he [w]contend with me in the
greatness of his power?
No; he would pay attention to me.
7 There an upright man could argue
with him,
and I would be acquitted forever
by my judge.

Chapter 23 2 [r]ch. 10:1; 21:4 [s][Ps. 32:4] 3 [t][ch. 13:3; 16:21] [u][Ps. 9:7, 8; Isai. 57:15, 16] 4 [v]See ch. 33:5 6 [w][ch. 9:34; 13:21]

[1] Hebrew *them* [2] Or *you say, 'It is exaltation'* [3] Septuagint, Syriac, Vulgate; Hebrew *him that is not innocent* [4] Or *defiant*

22:12–14 Eliphaz attacks Job's complaint that God is absent (13:24). It is not unnatural for Job, in the midst of suffering, to complain that God is either too observant and intrusive to leave him alone (7:17–19; 10:8; 16:9), or too far away.

23:1–12 Job's thoughts vacillate. In ch. 9 he doubted God would give him a hearing. In ch. 13 he is convinced he will get a hearing and be vindicated. In 17:1 he is convinced only death awaits him, but also his counselors will not triumph and he will be vindicated (17:10–16). That conviction reaches its zenith in 19:25–27, and from then on he never again doubts it, as these verses and especially ch. 31 prove.

8 "Behold, [x]I go forward, but he is not
there,
and backward, but I do not
perceive him;
9 on the left hand when he is working,
I do not behold him;
he turns to the right hand, but I
do not see him.
10 But he [y]knows [z]the way that I [a]take;
when he has [b]tried me, I shall
come out as gold.
11 My foot [c]has held fast to his steps;
I have kept his way and have [d]not
turned aside.
12 I have not departed from the
commandment of his lips;
I have [e]treasured the words of his
mouth more than my [f]portion
of food.
13 But he is unchangeable,[1] and [g]who
can turn him back?
What he [h]desires, that he does.
14 For he will complete what he
[i]appoints for me,
and many such things are [j]in his
mind.
15 Therefore I am terrified at his
presence;
when I consider, I am in dread of
him.
16 God has made my [k]heart faint;
the Almighty has terrified me;
17 yet I am not silenced because of the
darkness,
nor because thick darkness covers
my face.

24 "Why are [l]not times of judgment
[m]kept by the Almighty,
and why do those who know him
never see his [n]days?
2 Some move [o]landmarks;
they seize flocks and pasture them.
3 They drive away the donkey of the
fatherless;
they [p]take the widow's ox for a
pledge.
4 They [q]thrust the poor off the road;
the poor of the earth [r]all hide
themselves.
5 Behold, like wild donkeys in the
desert
the poor[2] [s]go out to their toil,
[t]seeking game;
the wasteland yields food for their
children.
6 They gather their[3] fodder in the field,
and they glean the vineyard of the
wicked man.
7 They [u]lie all night naked, without
clothing,
and have no covering in the cold.
8 They are wet with the rain of the
mountains
and [v]cling to the rock for lack of
shelter.
9 (There are those who snatch the
fatherless child from the breast,
and they take a pledge against the
poor.)
10 They go about naked, without
clothing;
hungry, they [w]carry the sheaves;
11 among the olive rows of the wicked[4]
they make oil;
they tread the winepresses, but
suffer thirst.
12 From out of the city the dying groan,
and the soul of [x]the wounded cries
for help;
yet God charges no one with
[y]wrong.
13 "There are those who rebel [z]against
the light,
who are not acquainted with its
ways,
and do not stay in its paths.
14 The murderer rises before it is light,
that he [a]may kill the poor and
needy,
and in the night he is like a thief.
15 The eye of the adulterer also waits for
[b]the twilight,
saying, 'No [c]eye will see me';
and he veils his face.
16 In the dark they [d]dig through houses;
by day they shut themselves up;
they do not know the light.

8 [x]ch. 9:11; 35:14
10 [y]Ps. 139:1-3 [z]Ps. 139:24 [a][ch. 9:35] [b]Ps. 17:3; 26:2; 66:10; 139:23; Zech. 13:9; Mal. 3:3; 1 Pet. 1:7; Rev. 3:18; [James 1:12]
11 [c]Ps. 17:5; 44:18 [d]Ps. 125:5
12 [e][Ps. 119:11] [f][Ps. 119:103; John 4:32, 34]
13 [g][ch. 9:12; 12:14] [h]Ps. 115:3
14 [i][1 Thess. 3:3] [j][ch. 10:13; 27:11]
16 [k]Deut. 20:3; [Ps. 22:14]
Chapter 24
1 [l]Eccles. 9:12; Isai. 13:22; Jer. 27:7; Ezek. 22:3; 30:3 [m]ch. 15:20 [n]Isai. 2:12; 13:6, 9; Joel 1:15; 2:1; Amos 5:18; See ch. 18:20
2 [o]See Deut. 19:14
3 [p]See ch. 22:6
4 [q]Amos 2:7; 5:12; Mal. 3:5 [r]Prov. 28:28; [ch. 30:5, 6]
5 [s]Ps. 104:23 [t]Ps. 104:21
7 [u][Ex. 22:26, 27; Deut. 24:12, 13]
8 [v]Lam. 4:5
10 [w][2 Tim. 2:6; James 5:4]
12 [x]Jer. 51:52; Ezek. 30:24 [y]ch. 1:22
13 [z]John 3:19, 20
14 [a][Ps. 10:8]
15 [b]Prov. 7:9 [c]Ps. 10:11
16 [d]Ex. 22:2; Matt. 6:20; [ch. 31:9]

1 Or *one* 2 Hebrew *they* 3 Hebrew *his* 4 Hebrew *their olive rows*

23:8 Job's God is invisible but He has an all-seeing eye (v. 10).

24:1–25 Job has not yet learned the important lesson that justice does not operate mechanically in this world, but according to the divine will. If it were not so, the human race would have perished long ago. This chapter alternates between descriptions of the fortunate wicked and the sufferings of their victims, with emphasis on the sufferings. Job wants the wicked to be judged so that those who know God will see it and know that God is just. The chapter shows Job's hatred of wickedness.

17 For [e]deep darkness is morning to all
of them;
for they are friends with the terrors
of deep darkness.
18 "You say, [f]'Swift are they on the face
of the waters;
their portion is cursed in the
land;
no treader turns toward their
vineyards.
19 Drought and heat snatch away the
snow waters;
so does [g]Sheol those who have
sinned.
20 The womb forgets them;
the worm finds them sweet;
they are [h]no longer remembered,
so wickedness is broken like
[i]a tree.'
21 "They wrong the barren childless
woman,
and do no good to the widow.
22 Yet God[1] prolongs the life of the
mighty by his power;
they rise up when they despair of
life.
23 He gives them security, and they are
supported,
and his [j]eyes are upon their ways.
24 They are exalted [k]a little while, and
then [l]are gone;
they are brought low and gathered
up like all others;
they are [m]cut off like the heads of
grain.
25 If it is [n]not so, who will prove me a
liar
and show that there is nothing in
what I say?"

17 [e]See ch. 3:5
18 [f][ch. 9:26; Hos. 10:7]
19 [g]See ch. 21:13
20 [h][Prov. 10:7] [i][ch. 18:16]
23 [j]See Ps. 11:4; Prov. 15:3
24 [k]Ps. 37:10 [l][ch. 27:19] [m]ch. 14:2
25 [n][ch. 9:24]

Chapter 25
1 [o]ch. 2:11
3 [p]ch. 19:12; Ps. 103:21 [q]Matt. 5:45; James 1:17
4 [r]ch. 4:17-19; 9:2; 15:14-16; Ps. 130:3; 143:2 [s]See ch. 14:1 [t]ch. 14:4
6 [u]ch. 9:14; 15:16 [v]Ps. 22:6; Isai. 41:14 [w]ch. 35:8

Chapter 26
2 [x]Isai. 40:29 [y]Gen. 49:24; Hos. 7:15
3 [z]Ps. 73:24; James 1:5
4 [a]Gen. 2:7
5 [b]Ps. 88:10

Bildad Speaks: Man Cannot Be Righteous

25 Then [o]Bildad the Shuhite answered
and said:
2 "Dominion and fear are with God;[2]
he makes peace in his high heaven.
3 Is there any number to his [p]armies?
Upon whom does his [q]light not
arise?
4 How then can man be [r]in the right
before God?
How can he who is [s]born of
woman be [t]pure?
5 Behold, even the moon is not bright,
and the stars are not pure in his
eyes;
6 [u]how much less man, who is [v]a
maggot,
and [w]the son of man, who is a
worm!"

Job Replies: God's Majesty Is Unsearchable

26 Then Job answered and said:
2 "How you have [x]helped him who has
no power!
How you have saved [y]the arm that
has no strength!
3 How you have [z]counseled him who
has no wisdom,
and plentifully declared sound
knowledge!
4 With whose help have you uttered
words,
and whose breath [a]has come out
from you?
5 The [b]dead tremble
under the waters and their
inhabitants.

1 Hebrew *he* 2 Hebrew *him*

24:18–24 Some think these words are an unannounced quotation from the counselors since the views expressed here seem more consistent with their positions than Job's. Others think the whole chapter is an attempt by early editors to make Job sound more orthodox. But Job may have a reason for seeming to adopt the counselors' argument.

24:23, 24 These verses must be connected with v. 1 in order to understand the point of the chapter. Job is trying to show that, though the wicked are punished, it takes place little by little (vv. 23, 24), while what the righteous want to see is justice meted out completely. Job's thought anticipates the "day of the LORD" doctrine of the prophets, which looks for the final judgment day.

25:1–6 Bildad makes no new argument, but repeats what has already been said about God's dominion, power, and purity.

25:4 be in the right before God. Human impurity is a given, but what is missing here is a hint of grace. Paul, who developed the doctrine of the total depravity of man in Romans, did so as a background for God's marvelous grace. Bildad does not think in terms of grace.

25:5, 6 a maggot . . . a worm. Bildad risks overstating the depth of human worthlessness because he has a pessimistic view of man (cf. Eliphaz in 15:14–16). The doctrine of total depravity is not pessimistic. Even in sin human beings retain the image of God, giving each person dignity and value.

26:1–14 This chapter falls into distinct parts: vv. 1–4 and vv. 5–14. This has led some to say that only the opening verses are the words of Job. Notice the ironic use of rhetorical questions ending with the suggestion (v. 4) that his counselors represent some outside source.

26:5–14 These verses celebrate God's omnipotence. They are not unlike Job's words in 9:5–10, and need not be assigned, as they sometimes are, to one of the counselors.

26:5, 6 Unlike the Canaanite gods, who each had a restricted domain of power, the true God is Lord even of Sheol (Prov. 15:11), the supposed domain of Mot, the god of death.

6 Sheol is [c]naked before God,[1]
and [d]Abaddon has no covering.
7 He [e]stretches out the north over [f]the void
and hangs the earth on nothing.
8 He [g]binds up the waters in his thick clouds,
and the cloud is not split open under them.
9 He covers the face of the full moon[2]
and [h]spreads over it his cloud.
10 He has inscribed [i]a circle on the face of the waters
at the boundary between light and darkness.
11 [j]The pillars of heaven tremble
and are astounded at his [k]rebuke.
12 By his power he [l]stilled the sea;
by his understanding he shattered [m]Rahab.
13 [n]By his wind the heavens were made fair;
his hand pierced [o]the fleeing serpent.
14 Behold, these are but the outskirts of his [p]ways,
and how small [q]a whisper do we hear of him!
But the thunder of his power who can understand?"

Job Continues: I Will Maintain My Integrity

27 And Job again [r]took up his discourse, and said:
2 "As God lives, who has [s]taken away my right,
and the Almighty, who has [t]made my soul bitter,
3 as long as my breath is in me,
and [u]the spirit of God is in my nostrils,
4 my lips will not speak [v]falsehood,
and my tongue will not utter [v]deceit.
5 Far be it from me to say that you are right;
till I die I will not put away my [w]integrity from me.
6 I [x]hold fast my righteousness and will not let it go;
my heart does not [y]reproach me for any of my days.

7 "Let my enemy be as the wicked,
and let him who rises up against me be as the unrighteous.
8 [z]For what is the hope of the godless
[a]when God cuts him off,
when God takes away his life?
9 [b]Will God hear his cry
when distress comes upon him?
10 Will he [c]take delight in the Almighty?
Will he call upon God at all times?
11 I will teach you concerning the hand of God;
[d]what is with the Almighty I will not conceal.
12 Behold, all of you have seen it yourselves;
why then have you become altogether vain?

13 [e]"This is the portion of a wicked man with God,
and the heritage that [f]oppressors receive from the Almighty:
14 If his [g]children are multiplied, it is for [h]the sword,
and his descendants have not enough bread.
15 Those who survive him the pestilence buries,
and his [i]widows do not weep.
16 Though he [j]heap up silver like dust,
and pile up clothing like clay,
17 he may pile it up, but the righteous will wear it,
and [k]the innocent will divide the silver.

[1] Hebrew *him* [2] Or *his throne*

6 [c]Ps. 139:8; Prov. 15:11 [d]Rev. 9:11 **7** [e]See ch. 9:8 [f][Gen. 1:2] **8** [g]Prov. 30:4 **9** [h][ch. 36:29] **10** [i]Prov. 8:29; [ch. 38:8-11; Ps. 33:7; Jer. 5:22] **11** [j]ch. 9:6; Ps. 75:3 [k]Ps. 104:7 **12** [l]Isai. 51:15; Jer. 31:35 [m]See ch. 9:13 **13** [n][Ps. 33:6] [o]Isai. 27:1 **14** [p]ch. 40:19 [q]ch. 4:12
Chapter 27
1 [r]ch. 29:1; See Num. 23:7 **2** [s]ch. 34:5 [t][Ruth 1:20; 2 Kin. 4:27] **3** [u]ch. 33:4; [Gen. 2:7] **4** [v]ch. 13:7
5 [w]ch. 2:3, 9; [ch. 13:15] **6** [x]ch. 2:3 [y][Acts 23:1; 24:16; 1 Cor. 4:4] **8** [z]See ch. 8:13 [a]Matt. 16:26; [Luke 12:20] **9** [b]Ps. 18:41; Prov. 1:28; 15:29; Isai. 1:15; Jer. 11:11; 14:12; Ezek. 8:18; Mic. 3:4; Zech. 7:13; [ch. 35:12, 13]; See Ps. 66:18; **10** [c]See ch. 22:26 **11** [d]ch. 10:13; 23:14 **13** [e]ch. 20:29; [ch. 18:21; 31:2] [f]ch. 6:23; 15:20 **14** [g]Deut. 28:41; Hos. 9:13, 16 [h]Jer. 15:2 **15** [i]Ps. 78:64 **16** [j]Zech. 9:3 **17** [k][Prov. 13:22; Eccles. 2:26]

26:7, 8 Job's purpose here is not to teach the science of space or weather, but to glorify God through the mysteries of His work in nature.

26:11 The pillars of heaven. Here possibly is a reference to the mountains, that often reach into the clouds and appear to support the sky.

26:12 stilled the sea. God rules the supposed dominion of Yam, the Canaanite god of the sea. Jesus Christ showed He was the true God of His ancient people when He calmed the sea in Matt. 8:23–27.

Rahab. A mystical Canaanite monster of the deep, similar to Leviathan. This poetic imagery enriches the concept of God's great power over the boisterous sea (Ps. 89:9, 10).

27:1–12 These verses are directed at the counselors. With an oath founded on God's existence, Job denies their false accusations, and at the same time asserts his integrity.

27:7–10 Curses like these are found in the Psalms (Ps. 109:6–15; 139:19–22). See Introduction to Psalms.

27:13–23 Job turns to discuss the fate of the wicked, a topic overworked by the counselors. His comments show that he understands it as well as they do. But Job makes the counselors, and not himself, the implied objects of the destiny described.

18 He builds his [l]house like a moth's,
like [m]a booth that [n]a watchman
makes.
19 He goes to bed rich, but will [o]do so
no more;
he opens his eyes, and [p]his wealth
is gone.
20 [q]Terrors overtake him like [r]a flood;
in the night a whirlwind [s]carries
him off.
21 [t]The east wind lifts him up and he is
gone;
it [u]sweeps him out of his place.
22 It[1] hurls at him [v]without pity;
he flees from its[2] power in
headlong flight.
23 It [w]claps its hands at him
and [x]hisses at him from its place.

Job Continues: Where Is Wisdom?

28 "Surely there is a mine for
silver,
and a place for gold that they
[y]refine.
2 Iron is taken out of the earth,
and copper is smelted from the ore.
3 Man puts an end to darkness
and searches out to the farthest
limit
the ore in [z]gloom and [a]deep
darkness.
4 He opens shafts in a valley away
from where anyone lives;
they are forgotten by travelers;
they hang in the air, far away from
mankind; they swing to and fro.
5 As for the earth, [b]out of it comes
bread,
but underneath it is turned up as
by fire.
6 Its stones are the place of
[c]sapphires,[3]
and it has dust of gold.
7 "That path no bird of prey knows,
and the falcon's eye has not
seen it.
8 [d]The proud beasts have not
trodden it;
[e]the lion has not passed over it.
9 "Man puts his hand to [f]the flinty rock
and overturns mountains by the
roots.
10 He cuts out channels in the rocks,
and his eye sees every precious
thing.
11 He dams up the streams so that they
do not trickle,
and the thing that is hidden he
brings out to light.
12 [g]"But where shall wisdom be found?
And where is the place of
understanding?
13 Man does not know its worth,
and it is not found in [h]the land of
the living.
14 [i]The deep says, 'It is not in me,'
and the sea says, 'It is not
with me.'
15 It [j]cannot be bought for gold,
and silver cannot be weighed as its
price.
16 It cannot be valued in [k]the gold of
[l]Ophir,
in precious [m]onyx or [n]sapphire.
17 Gold and glass cannot equal it,
nor can it be exchanged for jewels
of fine gold.
18 No mention shall be made of [o]coral
or of crystal;
the price of wisdom is above
[o, p]pearls.
19 [q]The topaz of Ethiopia cannot
equal it,
nor can it be valued in pure gold.
20 "From where, then, does wisdom
come?
And where is the place of
understanding?
21 It is hidden from the eyes of [r]all
living
and concealed from the birds of
the air.
22 [s]Abaddon and Death say,
'We have heard a rumor of it with
our ears.'

18 [l]ch. 8:14, 15 [m]Isai. 1:8 [n]S. of S. 1:6; 8:11, 12 **19** [o]Jer. 8:2; Ezek. 29:5 [p]ch. 24:24 **20** [q]See ch. 18:11 [r]See ch. 22:11 [s]ch. 34:20, 25; 36:20 **21** [t][ch. 30:22] [u]ch. 8:18 **22** [v]ch. 16:13 **23** [w]Lam. 2:15; Ezek. 25:6; Nah. 3:19 [x][2 Chr. 29:8; Jer. 49:17; Lam. 2:15; Ezek. 27:36; Zeph. 2:15]
Chapter 28
1 [y][Mal. 3:3] **3** [z]ch. 10:22 [a]See ch. 3:5 **5** [b]Ps. 104:14 **6** [c]Ex. 24:10 **8** [d]ch. 41:34 [e]ch. 10:16 **9** [f]Deut. 8:15; 32:13; Ps. 114:8 **12** [g][Prov. 16:16; Eccles. 7:24] **13** [h]See Ps. 27:13 **14** [i]Gen. 49:25 **15** [j]Prov. 3:14; 8:10, 11, 19; 16:16 **16** [k]Ps. 45:9; Isai. 13:12 [l]See 1 Kin. 9:28 [m]Gen. 2:12 [n]Ex. 24:10 **18** [o]Ezek. 27:16 [p]Prov. 3:15; 8:11; 20:15; 31:10; Lam. 4:7 **19** [q]Ex. 28:17; 39:10; Ezek. 28:13 **21** [r]ch. 12:10; 30:23 **22** [s]See ch. 26:6

1 Or *He* (that is, God); also verse 23 2 Or *his*; also verse 23 3 Or *lapis lazuli*; also verse 16

28:1–28 The new form of ch. 28 indicates that the disputation or dialogue is over. Now a different type of wisdom literature is presented: the standard wisdom like that of the Book of Proverbs. The author of Job reflects on the lack of wisdom displayed so far in the dialogue. The subject is the elusiveness of true wisdom (cf. the refrain in vv. 12, 20). The poem ends (v. 28) with the answer to the question asked in the refrain, "Where shall wisdom be found?"

28:1–11 Man, the technologist, gathers treasure from the hidden recesses of the earth.

23 [t]"God understands the way to it,
and he knows its place.
24 For he [u]looks to the ends of the earth
and sees everything under the heavens.
25 When he [v]gave to the wind its weight
and apportioned the waters by measure,
26 when he made a decree for the rain
and [w]a way for the lightning of the thunder,
27 then he saw it and declared it;
he established it, and searched it out.
28 And he said to man,
'Behold, [x]the fear of the Lord, that is wisdom,
and to [y]turn away from evil is understanding.'"

Job's Summary Defense

29 And Job again [z]took up his discourse, and said:

2 "Oh, that I were as in the months of old,
as in the days when God watched over me,
3 when his [a]lamp shone upon my head,
and by his light I walked through darkness,
4 as I was in my prime,[1]
when the [b]friendship of God was upon my tent,
5 when the Almighty was yet with me,
when my [c]children were all around me,
6 when my steps were [d]washed with [e]butter,
and [f]the rock poured out for me streams of [g]oil!
7 When I went out to [h]the gate of the city,
when I prepared my seat in the square,
8 the young men saw me and withdrew,
and the aged rose and stood;
9 the princes refrained from talking
and [i]laid their hand on their mouth;
10 the voice of the nobles was hushed,
and their [j]tongue stuck to the roof of their mouth.
11 When the ear heard, it called me blessed,
and when the eye saw, it approved,
12 because I [k]delivered the poor who cried for help,
and the fatherless who had none to help him.
13 [l]The blessing of him who was [m]about to perish came upon me,
and I caused [n]the widow's heart to sing for joy.
14 I [o]put on righteousness, and it clothed me;
my justice was like a robe and [p]a turban.
15 I was [q]eyes to the blind
and feet to the lame.
16 I was a father to the needy,
and I searched out [r]the cause of him whom I did not know.
17 I [s]broke [t]the fangs of the unrighteous
and made him drop his prey from his teeth.
18 [u]Then I thought, 'I shall die in my [v]nest,
and I shall multiply my days as [w]the sand,
19 my [x]roots spread out to [y]the waters,
with the dew all night on my [z]branches,
20 my glory fresh with me,
and my [a]bow ever [b]new in my hand.'

23 [t]For ver. 23-28, see Prov. 8:22-31
24 [u][Prov. 15:3; Zech. 4:10]
25 [v][Ps. 135:7]
26 [w]ch. 38:25
28 [x]Deut. 4:6; Ps. 111:10; Prov. 1:7; [Eccles. 12:13] [y]Prov. 3:7; 14:16; 16:6
Chapter 29
1 [z]ch. 27:1; See Num. 23:7
3 [a]ch. 18:6; 2 Sam. 21:17; Ps. 18:28
4 [b]Ps. 25:14; Prov. 3:32; See ch. 15:8
5 [c]ch. 1:2; [Ps. 128:3]
6 [d][Gen. 49:11] [e]ch. 20:17 [f]Deut. 32:13, 14; Ps. 81:16 [g][Deut. 33:24]
7 [h]See ch. 5:4
9 [i]See ch. 21:5
10 [j]Ps. 22:15; 137:6; Lam. 4:4; Ezek. 3:26
12 [k]Ps. 72:12
13 [l]ch. 31:20 [m]Deut. 26:5; Prov. 31:6; Isai. 27:13 [n][Ruth 2:20]
14 [o]Ps. 132:9; Isai. 59:17; 61:10; [Isai. 11:5; Eph. 6:14; 1 Thess. 5:8] [p]Isai. 62:3; Zech. 3:5; [ch. 19:9]
15 [q]Num. 10:31
16 [r][Prov. 29:7]
17 [s]Ps. 3:7 [t]Ps. 58:6; Prov. 30:14
18 [u][Ps. 30:6] [v]Num. 24:21; See ch. 39:27 [w]Gen. 22:17
19 [x]ch. 18:16 [y]See Ps. 1:3 [z][ch. 14:9]
20 [a]Gen. 49:24 [b][Isai. 40:31; 41:1]

1 Hebrew *my autumn days*

28:28 The application of the poem that makes up ch. 28. We can learn God's wisdom through obedience to His revealed will (Deut. 4:5, 6; Prov. 8:4–9; 9:10). For the New Testament application, Col. 2:2, 3 and Eph. 3:8–10.

29:1–25 This chapter begins the first of three monologues (chs. 29–31 [Job]; chs. 32–37; chs. 38–41). First Job looks back at the days of blessing. In ch. 30, he laments his loss, especially the loss of God's friendship. In ch. 31 he defends himself and calls again for vindication.

29:2–6 Job bemoans the loss of God's favor on him and his house.

29:7–17 Job recalls the noble reputation he built as a practitioner of what James will call "pure and undefiled" religion (cf. vv. 12–16 with James 1:27).

29:14 righteousness . . . clothed me . . . justice was like a robe and a turban. This verse is the middle of the chapter, everything centering around it as an emphatic assertion of his main point, his call for vindication.

29:18–20 In light of his past deeds, Job had expected to be vigorous in the later years of his life.

21 "Men listened to me and waited
and kept silence for my counsel.
22 After I spoke they did not speak again,
and my word [c]dropped upon them.
23 They waited for me as for the rain,
and they [d]opened their mouths as for the [e]spring rain.
24 I smiled on them when they had no confidence,
and [f]the light of my [g]face they did not cast down.
25 I chose their way and sat as chief,
and I lived like [h]a king among his troops,
like one who comforts mourners.

30 "But now they [i]laugh at me,
men who are [j]younger than I,
whose fathers I would have disdained
to set with the dogs of my flock.
2 What could I gain from the strength of their hands,
[k]men whose [l]vigor is gone?
3 Through want and hard hunger
they [m]gnaw [n]the dry ground by night in [o]waste and desolation;
4 they pick saltwort and the leaves of bushes,
and the roots of the broom tree for their food.
5 [p]They are driven out from human company;
they shout after them as after a thief.
6 In the gullies of the torrents they must dwell,
in holes of the earth and of [q]the rocks.
7 Among the bushes they [r]bray;
under [s]the nettles they huddle together.
8 A senseless, a nameless brood,
they have been whipped out of the land.
9 "And now I have become their [t]song;
I am [u]a byword to them.
10 They [v]abhor me; they keep aloof from me;
they do not hesitate to [w]spit at the sight of me.
11 Because God has loosed my cord and humbled me,
they have cast off restraint[2] in my presence.
12 On my [x]right hand the rabble rise;
they push away my feet;
they [y]cast up against me their ways of destruction.
13 They break up my path;
they promote my [z]calamity;
they need no one to help them.
14 As through a wide [a]breach they come;
amid the crash they roll on.
15 [b]Terrors are turned upon me;
my honor is pursued as by the wind,
and my prosperity has passed away like [c]a cloud.

16 "And now my soul is [d]poured out within me;
days of affliction have taken hold of me.
17 [e]The night [f]racks my bones,
and the pain that [g]gnaws me takes no rest.
18 With great force my garment is [h]disfigured;
it binds me about like the collar of my tunic.
19 God[3] has cast me into the mire,
and I have become like [i]dust and ashes.
20 I cry to you for help and you do not answer me;
I stand, and you only look at me.
21 You have [j]turned cruel to me;
with the might of your hand you [k]persecute me.
22 [l]You lift me up on the wind; you make me ride on it,
and you toss me about in the roar of the storm.

22 [c][Deut. 32:2; 33:28] 23 [d]Ps. 119:131; [Isai. 5:14] [e]Prov. 16:15; Jer. 3:3; Zech. 10:1; [Deut. 11:14] 24 [f]Prov. 16:15 [g]Gen. 4:5 25 [h]ch. 15:24
Chapter 30
1 [i]See ch. 12:4 [j]ch. 32:6; [ch. 32:4] 2 [k]For ver. 2-8, see ch. 24:4-8 [l][ch. 5:26] 3 [m][ver. 17] [n]Jer. 2:6 [o]ch. 38:27; Zeph. 1:15 5 [p][1 Sam. 26:19] 6 [q]1 Sam. 13:6; Jer. 4:29 7 [r]ch. 6:5 [s]Prov. 24:31; Zeph. 2:9 9 [t]Ps. 69:12; Lam. 3:14, 63 [u]See ch. 17:6
10 [v]Ps. 88:8; [ch. 17:6] [w]Num. 12:14; Isai. 50:6; Matt. 26:67; 27:30 12 [x]Ps. 109:6 [y]ch. 19:12 13 [z]ch. 6:2 14 [a]ch. 16:14 15 [b]See ch. 18:11 [c]ch. 7:9; Isai. 44:22 16 [d]1 Sam. 1:15; [ch. 10:1] 17 [e][ch. 7:3] [f]ch. 33:19 [g]ver. 3 18 [h][1 Sam. 28:8; 1 Kin. 20:38] 19 [i]ch. 42:6; [Gen. 18:27] 21 [j]Lam. 4:3; [Isai. 63:10] [k]ch. 16:9 22 [l][ch. 27:21]

[1] Or *warmth* [2] Hebrew *the bridle* [3] Hebrew *He*

29:21–25 Job remembers his former dignity and honor.

30:1–31 Cf. ch. 30 with ch. 29. Here, point for point, Job laments how the blessings he enjoyed were taken away from him. In ch. 29 he dealt with honor from man, blessings from God, and his own benevolent deeds. Note how this chapter stresses the opposite.

30:1–15 Job bewails his dishonor from hoodlums (cf. 29:7–10, 21–25). These verses are a good example of the discursive style of the poet.

30:16–23 He has no blessing from God (cf. 29:2–6, 18–20).

30:18 my garment is disfigured. The Septuagint (ancient Greek translation) reads "He seizes my garment." Job is talking again as if God were his enemy.

23 [m] For I know that you will bring me to
death
and to the house appointed for [n] all
living.

24 "Yet does not one in a [o] heap of ruins
stretch out his hand,
and in his disaster cry for help?[1]
25 Did not I [p] weep for him whose day
was hard?
Was not my soul grieved for the
needy?
26 But [q] when I hoped for good, evil
came,
and when I waited for light,
[r] darkness came.
27 My inward parts are in turmoil and
never still;
days of affliction [s] come to
meet me.
28 I [t] go about darkened, but not by the
sun;
I stand up in [u] the assembly and
cry for help.
29 I am a brother of [v] jackals
and a companion of [w] ostriches.
30 My [x] skin turns black and falls
from me,
and my [y] bones burn with heat.
31 My [z] lyre is [a] turned to mourning,
and my [z] pipe to the voice of those
who weep.

Job's Final Appeal

31 "I have made a covenant with
my [b] eyes;
how then could I gaze at a
virgin?
2 What would be [c] my portion from
God above
and [c] my heritage from the
Almighty on high?
3 Is not calamity for the unrighteous,
and disaster for the workers of
iniquity?
4 [d] Does not he see my ways
and [e] number all my steps?

5 "If I have walked with falsehood
and my foot has hastened to
deceit;
6 (Let me be [f] weighed in a just
balance,
and let God know my integrity!)
7 if my step has turned aside from the
way
and [g] my heart has gone after my
eyes,
and if any [h] spot has stuck to my
hands,
8 then let me [i] sow, and another eat,
and let what grows for me[2] be
rooted out.

9 "If my heart has been enticed toward
a woman,
and I have [j] lain in wait at my
neighbor's door,
10 then let my wife [k] grind for another,
and let others [l] bow down on her.
11 For that would be a heinous crime;
that would be an iniquity [m] to be
punished by the judges;
12 for that would be a fire [n] that
consumes as far as Abaddon,
and it would burn to the root all
my increase.

13 "If I have rejected the cause of my
manservant or my maidservant,
when they brought a complaint
against me,
14 what then shall I do when God
rises up?
When he [o] makes inquiry, what
shall I answer him?
15 Did [p] not he who made me in the
womb make him?
And did not one fashion us in the
womb?

1 The meaning of the Hebrew is uncertain 2 Or *let my descendants*

23 [m] ch. 19:25 [n] ch. 28:21
24 [o] Ps. 79:1; Jer. 26:18; Mic. 1:6; 3:12
25 [p] Ps. 35:13, 14; Rom. 12:15
26 [q] Jer. 8:15; 14:19 [r] ch. 10:21, 22
27 [s] 2 Sam. 22:6; Ps. 18:5
28 [t] Ps. 38:6; 42:9; 43:2 [u] Prov. 26:26
29 [v] Mic. 1:8 [w] Isai. 13:21; 34:13; Jer. 50:39; Mic. 1:8
30 [x] [Ps. 119:83; Lam. 4:8; 5:10] [y] Ps. 102:3
31 [z] ch. 21:12 [a] Lam. 5:15
Chapter 31
1 [b] [Isai. 33:15; Matt. 5:28]
2 [c] See ch. 20:29
4 [d] ch. 14:16; 34:21; 2 Chr. 16:9; Prov. 5:21; 15:3; Jer. 16:17; 32:19; Zech. 4:10 [e] ch. 14:16
6 [f] Dan. 5:27
7 [g] Num. 15:39; Eccles. 11:9 [h] [ch. 11:15]
8 [i] Lev. 26:16; Deut. 28:30, 38; [John 4:37]
9 [j] [ch. 24:15]
10 [k] [Ex. 11:5; Isai. 47:2] [l] [2 Sam. 12:11; Jer. 8:10]
11 [m] ver. 28; [Lev. 20:10; Deut. 22:22]
12 [n] See Prov. 6:27-29
14 [o] Ps. 17:3
15 [p] ch. 34:19; Prov. 14:31; 22:2; [Eph. 6:9]

30:24–31 See 29:11–17. Job receives no benevolence from his friends. They forget his kindness without returning it.

31:1–40 The most important issue in Job's mind in ch. 31 is the false accusation that he was a man of exceptional wickedness, suffering no more than what he deserved. This chapter is based on an important theme in the legal procedure of Job's day. He appeals to God with an oath in the divine name and with a call for divine sanctions if he is lying. Although this is a protestation of innocence, it is not the self-righteousness of the Pharisee in Luke 18:11, 12. Like the psalmist, Job is the victim of false accusation, so vindication has become a passion with him.

31:1–4 Job explains that he determined not to sin with his eyes (1 John 2:16). He may be speaking of more than ordinary lust, that is of the worship of the fertility goddesses so popular in Old Testament times. The word translated "virgin" (v. 1) is used of the goddess of fertility in Canaanite writings. She was a kind of Venus and was called the "maiden Anat" in Ugarit.

31:5–8 Job clears himself of avarice with a sanction based on God's "just balance," His justice.

31:9–12 Job clears himself of adultery with God's fire as the sanction.

16 "If I have [q]withheld anything that the
poor desired,
or have [r]caused the eyes of the
widow to fail,
17 or have eaten my morsel alone,
and the fatherless has not eaten
of it
18 (for from my youth the fatherless[1]
grew up with me as with a
father,
and from my mother's womb I
guided the widow[2]),
19 if I have seen anyone [s]perish for [t]lack
of clothing,
or the needy without [t]covering,
20 if his body has not [u]blessed me,
and if he was not warmed with the
fleece of my sheep,
21 if I have raised my hand against [v]the
fatherless,
because I saw my help in [w]the
gate,
22 then let my shoulder blade fall from
my shoulder,
and let my arm be broken from its
socket.
23 For I was [x]in terror of calamity from
God,
and I could not have faced his
[x]majesty.

24 [y]"If I have made gold my [z]trust
or called [a]fine gold my confidence,
25 if I have [b]rejoiced because my wealth
was abundant
or because [c]my hand had found
much,
26 [d]if I have looked at the sun[3] when it
shone,
or [e]the moon moving in splendor,
27 and my heart has been secretly
enticed,
and my mouth has kissed my
hand,
28 this also would be [f]an iniquity to be
punished by the judges,
for I would have been false to God
above.

29 "If I have [g]rejoiced at the ruin of him
who hated me,
or exulted when evil overtook him
30 ([h]I have not let my mouth sin
by asking for his life with a curse),
31 if the men of my tent have not
said,
'Who is there that has not been
filled with his [i]meat?'
32 ([j]the sojourner has not lodged in the
street;
I have opened my doors to the
traveler),
33 if I [k]have concealed my
transgressions [l]as others do[4]
by hiding my iniquity in my
bosom,
34 because I stood in great fear of [m]the
multitude,
and the contempt of families
terrified me,
so that I kept silence, and did not
go out of doors—
35 Oh, that I had one to hear me!
(Here is my signature! Let the
Almighty [n]answer me!)
Oh, that I had [o]the indictment
written by my adversary!
36 Surely I would carry it on my
[p]shoulder;
I would [q]bind it on me as [r]a
crown;
37 I would give him an account of all
my steps;
like a prince I would approach
him.

38 "If my land has cried out against me
and its furrows have wept together,
39 [s]if I have eaten its yield without
payment
and made its owners [t]breathe their
last,
40 let [u]thorns grow instead of wheat,
and foul weeds instead of barley."

The words of Job are ended.

16 [q][ch. 22:7] [r]ch. 11:20; 17:5
19 [s]ch. 29:13 [t]ch. 24:7, 10
20 [u]ch. 29:13; Deut. 24:13
21 [v]ch. 22:9 [w]See ch. 5:4
23 [x]ch. 13:11
24 [y]Mark 10:24 [z]ch. 4:6 [a]ch. 28:16
25 [b]Ps. 62:10 [c]Deut. 8:17
26 [d]Deut. 4:19; [Deut. 17:3; 2 Kin. 23:5, 11; Ezek. 8:16] [e]See Jer. 44:17-19
28 [f]ver. 11
29 [g]Prov. 17:5
30 [h][Matt. 5:44; Rom. 12:14]
31 [i]Ex. 16:12; 1 Sam. 25:11
32 [j][Gen. 19:2, 3; Judg. 19:20, 21; Matt. 25:35; Heb. 13:2]
33 [k]Prov. 28:13 [l]Gen. 3:8, 12
34 [m][Ex. 23:2]
35 [n]ch. 13:22 [o][ch. 19:23]
36 [p]Isai. 9:6; 22:22 [q]Prov. 6:21 [r]Zech. 6:11
39 [s][ch. 22:6-9; Luke 10:7; 2 Tim. 2:6; James 5:4] [t][1 Kin. 21:16, 19]
40 [u]Gen. 3:18

[1] Hebrew *he* [2] Hebrew *her* [3] Hebrew *the light* [4] Or *as Adam did*

31:13–15 Job clears himself of injustice with reference to God's court as the sanction.

31:16–23 Job clears himself of neglect of the needy and abuse of the helpless with God's terror as the sanction.

31:24–27 Job clears himself of idolatry with regard to gold or the gods.

31:29–34 Job clears himself of hatred, selfishness, and hypocrisy. In these verses God's divine judgment is the sanction (v. 28).

31:35–37 The climax: Job attaches his binding signature ("Here is my signature," v. 35) and challenges for a specific indictment.

31:37 Job has already expressed confidence that God would accept him if he had an opportunity to present his case (13:14–16). In the end this is possible only through grace.

Elihu Rebukes Job's Three Friends

32 So these three men ceased to
answer Job, because he was [v]righ-
teous in his own eyes. 2 Then Elihu the son
of Barachel [w]the Buzite, of the family of
Ram, burned with anger. He burned with
anger at Job because he justified himself
[x]rather than God. 3 He burned with anger
also at Job's three friends because they had
found no answer, although they had [y]de-
clared Job to be in the wrong. 4 Now Elihu
had waited to speak to Job because they
were older than he. 5 And when Elihu saw
that there was no answer in the mouth of
these three men, he burned with anger.
6 And Elihu the son of Barachel the Buzite
answered and said:

"I am young in years,
and you are [z]aged;
therefore I was timid and afraid
to declare my opinion to you.
7 I said, 'Let days speak,
and many years teach wisdom.'
8 But it is [a]the spirit in man,
[b]the breath of the Almighty, that
makes him [c]understand.
9 [d]It is not the old[1] who are wise,
nor the aged who understand what
is right.
10 Therefore I say, 'Listen to me;
let me also declare my opinion.'
11 "Behold, I waited for your words,
I listened for your wise sayings,
while you searched out what to
say.
12 I gave you my attention,
and, behold, there was none
among you who refuted Job
or who answered his words.
13 Beware [e]lest you say, 'We have found
wisdom;
God may vanquish him, not a
man.'
14 He has not directed his words
against me,
and I will not answer him with
your speeches.
15 "They are dismayed; they answer no
more;
they have not a word to say.
16 And shall I wait, because they do not
speak,
because they stand there, and
answer no more?
17 I also will answer with my share;
I also will declare my opinion.
18 For I am full of words;
the spirit within me constrains me.
19 Behold, my belly is like wine that has
no vent;
like new [f]wineskins ready to burst.
20 [g]I must speak, that I may find [h]relief;
I must open my lips and answer.
21 I will not [i]show partiality to any
man
or use flattery toward any person.
22 For I do not know how to flatter,
else my Maker would soon take
me away.

Elihu Rebukes Job

33 "But now, hear my speech,
O Job,
and listen to all my words.
2 Behold, I [j]open my mouth;
the tongue in my mouth speaks.
3 My words declare the uprightness of
my heart,
and what my lips know they speak
sincerely.
4 [k]The Spirit of God has made me,
and [l]the breath of the Almighty
gives me life.
5 [m]Answer me, if you can;
[n]set your words in order before me;
take your stand.

Chapter 32
1 [v]See ch. 33:9
2 [w]Gen. 22:21; Jer. 25:23 [x]ch. 4:17; [ch. 34:5; 35:2; 40:8]
3 [y]ch. 8:6; 22:5;
6 [z]ch. 15:10
8 [a]ch. 33:4; 34:14 [b]ch. 33:4; Gen. 2:7 [c]ch. 35:11; 38:36; 39:17; 1 Kin. 3:12; 4:29; Prov. 2:6; Eccles. 2:26; Dan. 1:17; 2:21; James 1:5
9 [d]1 Cor. 1:26; [ch. 12:20; Matt. 11:25]
13 [e]Jer. 9:23
19 [f]Matt. 9:17; [Josh. 9:4]
20 [g][Ps. 39:3] [h]1 Sam. 16:23
21 [i]Lev. 19:15
Chapter 33
2 [j]ch. 3:1
4 [k]ch. 27:3 [l]ch. 32:8; Gen. 2:7; [Ezek. 37:9; Acts 17:25]
5 [m]ver. 32 [n]ch. 13:18; 23:4; [Ps. 5:3]

1 Hebrew *many* [in years]

31:40 The words of Job are ended. With his signature Job closes his case. The rest is now up to the Judge.

32:1–37:24 These chapters present the second monologue, that of the young man Elihu who, unlike the others, has a Hebrew name. Many critics see him as a self-important, know-it-all person. Others believe these chapters are additions to the original text. Both views are defective. Elihu is not mentioned in the Epilogue (ch. 42) but the reason is that he is not guilty of the same errors as the other three. Elihu's critique centers on Job's words uttered during the dispute. He quotes Job, but does not accuse him of having lived a wicked life. He stresses an issue neglected by the three friends: the disciplinary and redemptive role of suffering. Eliphaz alone had touched suffering as discipline (5:17). Elihu's wordiness, like that of Job and the counselors, was considered eloquent in their culture.

32:1–5 The narrator introduces Elihu's four speeches on Job's situation with an explanation for why he injected himself into the debate.

32:3 declared Job to be in the wrong. According to ancient Jewish tradition the original reading was "condemned Elohim," changed by pious convention to "condemned Job," so as to avoid writing a blasphemous thought.

32:6–33:7 It takes Elihu this entire section just to make his introduction

6 Behold, I am toward God as you are;
I too was pinched off from a piece of [o]clay.
7 Behold, no [p]fear of me need terrify you;
my [q]pressure will not be heavy upon you.

8 "Surely you have spoken in my ears,
and I have heard the sound of your words.
9 You say, 'I am [r]pure, without [s]transgression;
I am clean, and there is no iniquity in me.
10 Behold, he finds occasions against me,
he [t]counts me as his enemy,
11 he [u]puts my feet in the stocks
and [v]watches all my paths.'

12 "Behold, in this you are not right. I will answer you,
for God is greater than man.
13 Why do you [w]contend against him,
saying, 'He [x]will answer none of man's[1] words'?[2]
14 For God [y]speaks in one way,
[z]and in two, though man [a]does not perceive it.
15 In [b]a dream, in [c]a vision of [d]the night,
when [c]deep sleep falls on men,
while they slumber on their beds,
16 then he [e]opens the ears of men
and terrifies them with warnings,
17 that he may turn man aside from his [f]deed
and conceal pride from a man;
18 he keeps back his soul from the pit,
his life from [g]perishing by the sword.

19 "Man is also rebuked with pain on his bed
and with continual strife in his [h]bones,
20 so that his [i]life loathes bread,
and his appetite [j]the choicest food.
21 His flesh is so wasted away that it cannot be seen,
and his bones that were not seen [k]stick out.
22 His soul draws near [l]the pit,
and his life to [m]those who bring death.
23 If there be for him [n]an angel,
[o]a mediator, [p]one of the thousand,
to declare to man what is [q]right for him,
24 and he is merciful to him, and says,
'Deliver him from going down into the pit;
I have found [r]a ransom;
25 let his flesh [s]become fresh with youth;
let him return to the days of his youthful vigor';
26 then man[3] [t]prays to God, and he accepts him;
he [u]sees his face with a shout of joy,
and he [v]restores to man his righteousness.
27 He sings before men and says:
'I [w]sinned and perverted what was right,
and it was not repaid to me.
28 He has redeemed my [x]soul from going down [y]into the pit,
and my life shall [z]look upon the light.'

29 "Behold, God does all these things,
twice, [a]three times, with a man,
30 to bring back his soul from the pit,
that he may be lighted with [b]the light of life.
31 Pay attention, O Job, listen to me;
be silent, and I will speak.
32 If you have any words, [c]answer me;
[d]speak, for I desire to justify you.
33 If not, [e]listen to me;
be silent, and I will teach you wisdom."

1 Hebrew *his* 2 Or *He will not answer for any of his own words*
3 Hebrew *he*

6 [o]See ch. 4:19 **7** [p]ch. 9:34, 35; 13:21 [q][ch. 23:2] **9** [r]ch. 9:21; 10:7; 11:4; 12:4; 13:18; 16:17; 23:10, 11; 27:5; 29:14; 32:1; 34:5 [s]ch. 34:6 **10** [t]See ch. 13:24 **11** [u]ch. 13:27 [v]ch. 10:14; 14:16; 31:4 **13** [w]ch. 13:3; 16:21; 31:35; 40:2 [x]See ch. 9:12 **14** [y][ch. 40:5; Ps. 62:11] [z]ver. 29 [a][1 Sam. 3:4, 6] **15** [b]See Num. 12:6 [c]ch. 4:13 [d]Ps. 17:3 **16** [e]ch. 36:10, 15; Ps. 40:6; Isai. 50:5 **17** [f]ch. 36:9 **18** [g]ch. 36:12 **19** [h]ch. 30:17; **20** [i]Ps. 107:18 [j]Prov. 23:3

21 [k][Ps. 22:17] **22** [l]ver. 24, 28 [m]2 Sam. 24:16, 17; Ps. 78:49 **23** [n]Gen. 16:7; 22:11; 48:16; Ps. 34:7; Isai. 63:9; [Mal. 3:1] [o]Gen. 42:23; Isai. 43:27 [p]Eccles. 7:28; [S. of S. 5:10] [q][Prov. 14:2; Ezek. 18:21, 22] **24** [r]ch. 36:18; Ps. 49:7 **25** [s]2 Kin. 5:14; [Heb. 9:12] **26** [t]See ch. 22:27 [u]Ps. 17:15 [v][2 Sam. 12:13; Prov. 28:13; Luke 15:21-24; 1 John 1:9] **27** [w]Ps. 106:6; [Rom. 6:21] **28** [x]Isai. 38:17 [y]ver. 22, 24 [z][ch. 3:9] **29** [a]ver. 14 **30** [b]Ps. 56:13 **32** [c]ver. 5 [d]ch. 34:33 **33** [e]Ps. 34:11

and to give his reason for speaking. He appears to have a warmer personality than the counselors who never called Job by his name (cf. 33:1, 31).

33:8 your words. In quoting Job, Elihu is accurate (cf. 33:10, 11 with 13:24 and 27). Verbatim quotation was not the expected norm in ancient Eastern culture.

33:12–22 Elihu's appeal to God's transcendence repeats what the counselors have already said, but he handles the theme differently from them. His purpose is to show that, despite God's transcendence, He does speak to man: through revelation (dreams) and through suffering.

Elihu Asserts God's Justice

34 Then Elihu [f]answered and said:
2 "Hear my words, you wise men,
and give ear to me, you who know;
3 for [g]the ear tests words
as the palate tastes food.
4 Let us choose [h]what is right;
let us know among ourselves what
is good.
5 For Job has said, 'I am [i]in the right,
and [j]God has taken away my right;
6 in spite of my right I am counted a
liar;
my wound is incurable, though I
am [k]without transgression.'
7 What man is like Job,
who [l]drinks up scoffing like water,
8 who travels in company with evildoers
and walks [m]with wicked men?
9 For [n]he has said, 'It profits a man
nothing
that he should take delight in God.'
10 "Therefore, hear me, you men of
understanding:
far be it from God that he should
[o]do wickedness,
and from the Almighty that he
should do wrong.
11 For according to [p]the work of a man
he will repay him,
and [q]according to his ways he will
make it befall him.
12 Of a truth, God will not do wickedly,
and [r]the Almighty will not pervert
justice.
13 Who gave him charge over the earth,
and who [s]laid on him[1] the whole
world?
14 If he should [t]set his heart to it
and [u]gather to himself his [v]spirit
and his breath,
15 all flesh would perish together,
and man would [w]return to dust.
16 "If you have understanding, hear this;
listen to what I say.

Chapter 34
1 [f]ch. 3:2
3 [g]ch. 12:11
4 [h]1 Thess. 5:21, 22
5 [i]See ch. 33:9 [j]ch. 27:2
6 [k]ch. 33:9
7 [l]See ch. 15:16
8 [m][Ps. 1:1]
9 [n]ch. 9:22, 23, 30, 31; 21:7, 15; 24:1; [ch. 35:3; Mal. 3:14]
10 [o]ch. 36:23; Gen. 18:25; Deut. 32:4; 2 Chr. 19:7; Ps. 92:15; Rom. 9:14
11 [p]Ps. 62:12; Prov. 24:12; Matt. 16:27; Rom. 2:6; 2 Cor. 5:10; 1 Pet. 1:17; Rev. 22:12 [q]Jer. 17:10; 32:19; Ezek. 33:20
12 [r]See ch. 8:3
13 [s]See ch. 38:4-7
14 [t][ch. 2:3] [u]Ps. 104:29; [Ps. 146:4] [v]ch. 32:8
15 [w]See ch. 10:9

17 [x]Shall one who hates justice govern?
Will you condemn him who is
righteous and mighty,
18 who [y]says to a king, 'Worthless one,'
and to nobles, 'Wicked man,'
19 who [z]shows no partiality to princes,
nor regards the rich [a]more than
the poor,
for [b]they are all the work of his
hands?
20 In a moment [c]they die;
at [d]midnight the people are shaken
and pass away,
and the mighty are taken away by
[e]no human hand.
21 "For his eyes are on [f]the ways of a man,
and he sees all his [f]steps.
22 There is no [g]gloom or [h]deep darkness
where evildoers may hide
themselves.
23 For God[2] has no need to consider a
man further,
that he should go before God in
[i]judgment.
24 He [j]shatters the mighty [k]without
investigation
and sets [l]others in their place.
25 Thus, knowing their works,
he [m]overturns them in the night,
and they are crushed.
26 He strikes them for their wickedness
in a place for all to see,
27 because they turned aside from
[n]following him
and had no regard for any of his
ways,
28 so that they [o]caused the cry of the
poor to come to him,
and he [p]heard the cry of the
afflicted—
29 When he [q]is quiet, who can condemn?
When he hides his face, who can
behold him,
whether it be a nation or a man?—

17 [x][Gen. 18:25]
18 [y]Ex. 22:28
19 [z]Deut. 10:17; 2 Chr. 19:7; Acts 10:34; Rom. 2:11; Gal. 2:6; Eph. 6:9; Col. 3:25; 1 Pet. 1:17 [a][James 2:5] [b]See ch. 31:15
20 [c]ch. 21:13 [d]Ex. 11:4; [ch. 27:20; 36:20] [e]Dan. 8:25; [Lam. 4:6]
21 [f]ch. 14:16; See ch. 31:4
22 [g][Ps. 139:12; Amos 9:2, 3; Heb. 4:13] [h]See ch. 3:5
23 [i]ch. 14:3
24 [j]Ps. 2:9 [k]See ch. 5:9 [l]See ch. 8:19
25 [m]Prov. 12:7
27 [n]1 Sam. 15:11; Ps. 28:5; Isai. 5:12 28 [o]ch. 35:9; James 5:4; [Gen. 18:20, 21] [p]Ex. 3:7; 22:23; Isai. 32:17 29 [q]Ps. 94:13

1 Hebrew lacks *on him* 2 Hebrew *he*

33:23–30 Unlike the counselors who saw no place for grace or mediation (5:1), Elihu knows God provides both.

34:1–37 Following a pedantic introduction, Elihu quotes words from Job that are easy to refute (12:4; 13:18; 27:2, 6). His thesis is that no one is really innocent, so God denies no one justice (v. 5). The bulk of this second speech is a defense of God's goodness and justice (vv. 10–30). Elihu closes with another condemnation of Job's words and a call for repentance (vv. 31–37).

34:10 far be it from God that he should do wickedness. For the next twenty-one verses Elihu expounds this theme. In moments of extreme stress Job had said practically the opposite (10:3; 12:4–6; 21:7,8; 24:1–12).

34:14, 15 Elihu is right: God's continual common grace is necessary for any of His creatures to continue its existence.

30 that a godless man should not reign,
that he should not ensnare the people.
31 "For has anyone said to God,
'I have borne punishment; I will not offend any more;
32 [r]teach me what I do not see;
if I have done iniquity, I will do it no more'?
33 Will he then make repayment to suit you,
because you reject it?
For you must choose, and not I;
therefore [s]declare what you know.[1]
34 Men of understanding will say to me,
and the wise man who hears me will say:
35 'Job [t]speaks without knowledge;
his words are without insight.'
36 Would that Job were tried to the end,
because he answers like wicked men.
37 For he adds rebellion to his sin;
he [u]claps his hands among us
and multiplies his words against God."

Elihu Condemns Job

35 And Elihu answered and said:
2 "Do you think this to be just?
Do you say, [v]'It is my right before God,'
3 that you ask, [w]'What advantage have I?
How am I better off than if I had sinned?'
4 I will answer you
and [x]your friends with you.
5 [y]Look at the heavens, and see;
and behold the clouds, which are higher than you.
6 If you have sinned, [z]what do you accomplish against him?
And if your transgressions are multiplied, what do you do to him?

32 [r]ch. 35:11; 36:22; Ps. 19:12; 86:11 33 [s]ch. 33:32 35 [t]See ch. 35:16 37 [u]See ch. 27:23
Chapter 35 2 [v]See ch. 32:2 3 [w]See ch. 34:9 4 [x]ch. 34:8, 36 5 [y][ch. 22:12] 6 [z]Prov. 8:36; Jer. 7:19

7 [a]If you are righteous, what do you give to him?
Or what does he receive from your hand?
8 Your wickedness concerns a man like yourself,
and your righteousness [b]a son of man.
9 "Because of the multitude of [c]oppressions people [d]cry out;
they call for help because of the arm of [e]the mighty.[2]
10 But none says, 'Where is God my [f]Maker,
who gives [g]songs in the night,
11 who teaches us [h]more than the beasts of the earth
and makes us wiser than the birds of the heavens?'
12 There they [i]cry out, but he does not answer,
because of the pride of evil men.
13 Surely God does not hear an empty cry,
nor does the Almighty regard it.
14 How much less when you say that you [j]do not see him,
that the case is before him, and you are [k]waiting for him!
15 And now, because [l]his anger does not punish,
and he does not take much note of transgression,[3]
16 Job opens his mouth in empty talk;
he [m]multiplies words [n]without knowledge."

Elihu Extols God's Greatness

36 And Elihu continued, and said:
2 "Bear with me a little, and I will show you,
for I have yet something to say on God's behalf.

7 [a]ch. 22:2, 3; Prov. 9:12; Luke 17:10; [ch. 41:11; Rom. 11:35] 8 [b]ch. 25:6 9 [c]Amos 3:9 [d]Ex. 2:23; [ch. 34:28] [e][ch. 22:8] 10 [f]ch. 4:17; Deut. 32:6; Isai. 57:13 [g]Ps. 42:8; 77:6; 149:5; [Acts 16:25] 11 [h]ch. 36:22; Ps. 94:12; Isai. 28:26 12 [i]See ch. 27:9 14 [j]ch. 9:11; 23:8, 9 [k][ch. 13:15] 15 [l]Num. 16:29; Ps. 89:32 16 [m]ch. 34:37 [n]ch. 34:35; 36:12; 38:2; 42:3

1 The meaning of the Hebrew in verses 29-33 is uncertain 2 Or *the many* 3 Theodotion, Symmachus (compare Vulgate); the meaning of the Hebrew word is uncertain

34:16–20 Job had asked why the innocent do not see God's judgment of the wicked (24:1). Elihu's answer is that God is judging them all the time, though it is not always evident.

34:31 The Hebrew text of vv. 31–33 is difficult to understand.

35:3 This question resembles Eliphaz's words in 22:3, but may be extrapolated from Job's words in 9:14–31.

35:6, 7 Elihu does not say that God is beyond good and evil, but that God is not within the power of the creature. See Rom. 11:34, 35.

35:9–13 Job had complained in ch. 23 that God was indifferent to his condition. Elihu counters with some good advice (especially vv. 9–11). But some of it does not apply to Job (v. 12).

35:14–16 Elihu criticizes what Job has said and its effect on his relation to God.

36:1–37:24 Elihu's fourth speech focuses on Job's suffering from the per-

3 I will get my knowledge from [o]afar
and ascribe [p]righteousness to my
[q]Maker.
4 For truly my words are not false;
one who is [r]perfect in knowledge
is with you.

5 "Behold, God is mighty, and [s]does not
despise any;
he is [t]mighty in strength of
understanding.
6 He does not keep the wicked alive,
but gives [u]the afflicted their right.
7 He does not withdraw his [v]eyes from
the righteous,
but with [w]kings on the throne
he sets them forever, and they are
[x]exalted.
8 And if they are [y]bound in chains
and caught in the cords of affliction,
9 then he declares to them their work
and their transgressions, that they
are [z]behaving arrogantly.
10 He [a]opens their ears to instruction
and commands that they [b]return
from iniquity.
11 [c]If they listen and serve him,
they [d]complete their days in
prosperity,
and their years in pleasantness.
12 But if they do not listen, they [e]perish
by the sword
and die [f]without knowledge.

13 "The godless in heart [g]cherish anger;
they do not cry for help when he
[h]binds them.
14 They [i]die in youth,
and their life ends among the cult
prostitutes.
15 He delivers [j]the afflicted by their
affliction
and [k]opens their ear by adversity.
16 He also allured you out of distress
into [l]a broad place where there
was no cramping,
and what was set on your [m]table
was full of [n]fatness.

17 "But you are full of the judgment on
the wicked;
judgment and justice seize you.
18 Beware lest wrath entice you into
scoffing,
and let not the greatness of [o]the
ransom turn you aside.
19 Will your [p]cry for help avail to keep
you from distress,
or all the force of your strength?
20 Do not long for [q]the night,
when peoples vanish [r]in their place.
21 Take care; [s]do not turn to iniquity,
for this you have chosen rather
than affliction.
22 Behold, God is exalted in his power;
who is [t]a teacher like him?
23 Who has [u]prescribed for him his way,
or who can say, [v]'You have done
wrong'?

24 "Remember to [w]extol his work,
of which men have [x]sung.
25 All mankind has looked on it;
man beholds it from afar.
26 Behold, God is great, and we [y]know
him not;
the number of his [z]years is
unsearchable.
27 For he draws up the drops of water;
they distill his [a]mist in [b]rain,
28 which [c]the skies pour down
and drop on mankind abundantly.
29 Can anyone understand [d]the
spreading of the clouds,
the thunderings of his [e]pavilion?
30 Behold, he scatters his lightning
about him
and covers the roots of the sea.
31 For by these he [f]judges peoples;
he gives [g]food in abundance.
32 He covers his [h]hands with the
lightning
and commands it to strike the mark.
33 Its crashing declares his presence;[1]
the cattle also declare that he rises.

Chapter 36
3 [o][Ps. 78:2] [p][Rev. 15:3, 4; 16:5, 7; 19:1, 2] [q]ch. 35:10 **4** [r]ch. 37:16 **5** [s]ch. 8:20 (Heb.); [Ps. 138:6] [t]ch. 9:4; 12:13, 16 **6** [u]ver. 15; ch. 34:28 **7** [v][Ps. 33:18; 34:15] [w]Ps 132:12; [Ps. 113:8] [x]Ps. 75:10 **8** [y]ver. 13; Ps. 107:10 **9** [z]ch. 15:25 **10** [a]ch. 33:16 [b]Jer. 18:11 **11** [c]For ver. 11, 12, see Isai. 1:19, 20 [d]ch. 21:13 **12** [e]ch. 33:18 [f][ch. 4:21]; See ch. 35:16 **13** [g]Rom. 2:5 [h]ver. 8 **14** [i]ch. 15:32; 22:16; Ps. 55:23 **15** [j]ver. 6; See ch. 33:15-28 [k]ver. 10; [Ps. 119:67, 71] **16** [l][ch. 37:10; Ps. 4:1; 18:19; 31:8; 118:5] [m]Ps. 23:5 [n]Ps. 36:8

18 [o]ch. 33:24 **19** [p]Prov. 11:4 **20** [q]ch. 27:20; 34:20, 25 [r]ch. 40:12 **21** [s]Ps. 66:18 **22** [t]ch. 34:32; 35:11 **23** [u]ch. 34:13; [Isai. 40:13, 14; Rom. 11:34; 1 Cor. 2:16] [v][ch. 34:10] **24** [w]Luke 1:46; [Ps. 92:5; Rev. 15:3] [x][ch. 33:27; Ps. 104:33] **26** [y][ch. 37:5; 1 Cor. 13:12] [z]Ps. 90:2; 102:27 **27** [a]Gen. 2:6 (Heb.) [b]Ps. 147:8 **28** [c]Prov. 3:20; [Deut. 33:28] **29** [d][ch. 26:9] [e]Ps. 18:11; 105:39

31 [f]ch. 37:13 [g]Ps. 104:27, 28; 136:25; 145:15; 147:9; Acts 14:17 **32** [h]Hab. 3:4

[1] Hebrew *declares concerning him*

spective of God's perfect righteousness and absolute power.

36:1–4 Elihu opens the speech with an apology in which he reasserts his credentials.

36:5–15 Elihu struggles with Job's complaint about the wicked who prosper and the righteous who suffer (v. 6). With this in mind he dwells on God's power, goodness, justice, and mercy. But all this is in the context of the view of suffering where suffering is always in direct proportion to sins and righteousness is always blessed. Only the last judgment will reveal this; compare John 9:2, 3 with Rom. 2:6; 2 Cor. 5:10.

36:16–21 Elihu assures Job of God's good purpose in his suffering and sternly admonishes him to receive His divine discipline with its promise of deliverance from distress.

Elihu Proclaims God's Majesty

37 "At this also my heart trembles
and leaps out of its place.
2 Keep listening to the thunder of his voice
and the rumbling that comes from his mouth.
3 Under the whole heaven he lets it go,
and his [i]lightning to the [j]corners of the earth.
4 After it [k]his voice roars;
[l]he thunders with his majestic voice,
and he does not restrain the lightnings[1] when his voice is heard.
5 God thunders wondrously with his voice;
he does [m]great things that we cannot [n]comprehend.
6 For to [o]the snow he says, 'Fall on the earth,'
likewise to the downpour, his mighty downpour.
7 He [p]seals up the hand of every man,
that all men whom he made may [q]know it.
8 Then the beasts go into their [r]lairs,
and remain in their [s]dens.
9 From [t]its chamber [u]comes the whirlwind,
and [v]cold from the scattering winds.
10 By the breath of God [w]ice is given,
and [x]the broad waters are frozen fast.
11 He loads the thick cloud with moisture;
the clouds scatter his lightning.
12 They [y]turn around and around by his [z]guidance,
[z]to accomplish all that he commands them
on the face of [a]the habitable world.
13 Whether for [b]correction or for his [c]land
or for [d]love, he causes it to happen.

14 "Hear this, O Job;
stop and [e]consider the wondrous works of God.
15 Do you know how God lays his command upon them
and causes the lightning of his cloud to shine?
16 Do you know the balancings[2] of the clouds,
the wondrous works of him who is [f]perfect in knowledge,
17 you whose garments are hot
when the earth is still because of the south wind?
18 Can you, like him, [g]spread out the skies,
hard as a cast metal [h]mirror?
19 Teach us what we shall say to him;
we cannot draw up our case because of [i]darkness.
20 Shall it be told him that I would speak?
Did a man ever wish that he would be swallowed up?
21 "And now no one looks on the light
when it is bright in the skies,
when the wind has passed and cleared them.
22 Out of the north comes golden splendor;
God is clothed with [j]awesome majesty.
23 The Almighty—we [k]cannot find him;
he is [l]great in power;
[m]justice and abundant righteousness he will not [n]violate.
24 Therefore men [o]fear him;
he does not regard any who are [p]wise in their own conceit."[3]

The Lord Answers Job

38 Then the LORD [q]answered Job out of the whirlwind and said:

1 Hebrew *them* 2 Or *hovering* 3 Hebrew *in heart*

Chapter 37
3 [i]ch. 36:30, 32 [j]ch. 38:13; [Isai. 11:12; Ezek. 7:2]
4 [k]ch. 40:9; Ps. 68:33; See Ps. 29:3-9 [l]Ps. 18:13
5 [m]See ch. 5:9 [n]ch. 36:26
6 [o]Ps. 147:16, 17
7 [p]Dan. 12:9; [ch. 14:17] [q]Ps. 109:27
8 [r]ch. 38:40 [s]Ps. 104:22
9 [t]ch. 9:9 [u]Isai. 21:1; [ch. 1:19] [v]Ps. 147:17
10 [w]ch. 38:29, 30; Ps. 147:17 [x][ch. 36:16]
12 [y]Gen. 3:24 [z]Ps. 148:8 [a][Prov. 8:31]
13 [b]Ex. 9:18, 23; 1 Sam. 12:18, 19; Ezra 10:9; [ch. 36:31; 38:23] [c]ch. 38:26, 27 [d]1 Kin. 18:45
14 [e][Ps. 111:2]
16 [f]ch. 36:4; [1 Sam. 2:3]
18 [g]Isai. 42:5; 44:24; [Gen. 1:6] [h][Ex. 38:8]
19 [i]Isai. 60:2; [Eph. 4:18]
22 [j][Ps. 104:1]
23 [k]1 Tim. 6:16 [l]ch. 36:5 [m]Ps. 99:4 [n]Lam. 3:33
24 [o]Ps. 130:4; [Matt. 10:28] [p][Isai. 5:21; Matt. 11:25; 1 Cor. 1:26]
Chapter 38
1 [q]ch. 40:6; [ch. 13:22]

36:22–26 Elihu now returns to his opening thesis (v. 5) concerning the sovereignty of God, whose purpose is always good.

36:27–37:13 Elihu's graphic description of God's majesty displayed in the forces of nature is somewhat like the first speech by God (cf. ch. 38).

37:14–24 Here the link with the divine speeches (chs. 38–41) becomes more pronounced, as the young counselor begins to cross-examine Job about God's power and righteousness. His concluding words anticipate the appearance of God in the heavens (vv. 21, 22).

38:1–41:34 In His appearance to Job, God does not mention the subject of Job's suffering, much less give the reason for it. What the Lord says is far more important than Job's suffering, which the Lord knew He would shortly remove. Nor did Job receive the bill of indictment he wanted (31:35), because there was none. Job learns he must rest his case, including his desire for vindication, in the hands of a sovereign and good God, who is not his enemy (1 Pet. 4:19).

38:1–40:2 The Lord calls on Job to withdraw his accusations against the Almighty by exposing his weakness and foolishness.

2 "Who is this that [r]darkens counsel by
words [s]without knowledge?
3 [t]Dress for action[1] like a man;
I will question you, and you make
it known to me.

4 "Where were you when I [u]laid the
foundation of the earth?
Tell me, if you have
understanding.
5 Who determined its measurements—
surely you know!
Or who stretched the line upon it?
6 On what were its bases sunk,
or who laid its cornerstone,
7 when the morning stars [v]sang
together
and all [w]the sons of God [x]shouted
for joy?

8 "Or who [y]shut in the sea with doors
when it burst out from the
womb,
9 when I made clouds its garment
and [z]thick darkness its swaddling
band,
10 and prescribed [a]limits for it
and set bars and doors,
11 and said, 'Thus far shall you come,
and no farther,
and here shall your [b]proud waves
be stayed'?

12 "Have you [c]commanded the morning
since your days began,
and caused the dawn to know its
place,
13 that it might take hold of [d]the skirts
of the earth,
and the wicked be [e]shaken out
of it?
14 It is changed like clay under the
seal,
and its features stand out like a
garment.
15 From the wicked their [f]light is
withheld,
and [g]their uplifted arm is broken.

16 "Have you [h]entered into the springs of
the sea,
or walked in the recesses of the
deep?
17 Have [i]the gates of death been
revealed to you,
or have you seen the gates of [j]deep
darkness?
18 Have you comprehended the expanse
of the earth?
Declare, if you know all this.

19 "Where is the way to the dwelling of
light,
and where is the place of darkness,
20 that you may take it to its territory
and that you may discern [k]the
paths to its home?
21 You know, for [l]you were born then,
and the number of your days is
great!

22 "Have you entered [m]the storehouses
of the snow,
or have you seen [m]the storehouses
of the hail,
23 which I have reserved [n]for the time
of trouble,
[n]for the day of battle and war?
24 What is the way to the place where
the light is distributed,
or where the east wind is scattered
upon the earth?

25 "Who has cleft a channel for the
torrents of rain
and [o]a way for the thunderbolt,
26 to bring rain on [p]a land where no
man is,
on [q]the desert in which there is no
man,

2 [r]ch. 42:3 [s]See ch. 35:16
3 [t]1 Kin. 18:46
4 [u]Ps. 104:5; [Prov. 30:4; Isai. 40:12-14]; See Prov. 8:24-29
7 [v][Ps. 19:1-4] [w]See ch. 1:6 [x][Luke 2:13, 14]
8 [y]Gen. 1:9; Ps. 33:7; 104:8, 9; Jer. 5:22
9 [z]ch. 22:13
10 [a][ver. 33 (Heb.)]
11 [b][Ps. 65:7; 89:9; 93:4]
12 [c]Ps. 65:8; 74:16
13 [d]ch. 37:3 [e][Neh. 5:13]
15 [f]ch. 18:5; [Matt. 6:23]; See ch. 24:13-17 [g]Ps. 10:15; 37:17; Ezek. 30:21, 22
16 [h]Ps. 77:19
17 [i]Ps. 9:13; 107:18; [Isai. 38:10; Matt. 16:18] [j]See ch. 3:5
20 [k]ch. 24:13
21 [l][ch. 15:7]
22 [m][Ps. 135:7]
23 [n]Josh. 10:11; Isai. 28:17; 30:30; Ezek. 13:11, 13; 38:22; Rev. 16:21; [ch. 37:13]
25 [o]ch. 28:26
26 [p][ch. 37:13] [q]Ps. 107:35

[1] Hebrew *Gird up your loins*

38:1 the LORD. The divine covenant name is now used again, as in the prologue, showing that the author was an Israelite. Job and the counselors use other divine epithets, like "God," and "the Almighty." Job 12:9 is the only place where Job or the counselors use "Yahweh," and some manuscripts have "God" even there. Job was evidently not an Israelite.

38:4–39:30 In this cross-examination of Job, the Lord reveals Himself as sovereign over the natural world. He is Creator (38:4–14) of the earth (vv. 4–7), of the sea (vv. 8–11), and of day and night (vv. 12–15). He is Lord of inanimate nature (38:16–38) and of animate nature (38:39–39:30).

38:5 surely you know. The irony here and in vv. 18 and 21 is not sarcasm, but a reminder that God is the Creator.

38:7 For the personification of natural forces as God's angels see Ps. 104:4 and Heb. 1:7.

38:15 The light of the wicked is darkness (Is. 5:20; Luke 11:35).

38:17 the gates of death. The "gates" stand for dominion (Matt. 16:18). The Lord is sovereign over this invisible realm, which no living person has ever seen (17:16). According to the pagan religions of Canaan, the god Mot was ruler of the realm of the dead, but Job knew otherwise (cf. 26:6).

38:26 rain . . . the desert. In a world where rainwater was precious, God impresses on Job his sovereign freedom to do what perplexes those who don't appreciate the distinctions between the sovereign God and themselves.

27 to satisfy the waste and desolate
land,
and to make the ground sprout
with [r]grass?
28 "Has [s]the rain a father,
or who has begotten the drops of
dew?
29 From whose womb did [t]the ice come
forth,
and who has given birth to [t]the
frost of heaven?
30 The waters become hard like stone,
and the face of the deep is
[u]frozen.

31 "Can you bind the chains of [v]the
Pleiades
or loose the cords of [v]Orion?
32 Can you lead forth the Mazzaroth[1] in
their season,
or can you guide [v]the Bear with its
children?
33 Do you know [w]the ordinances of the
heavens?
Can you establish their rule on the
earth?

34 "Can you lift up your voice to the
clouds,
that [x]a flood of waters may cover
you?
35 Can you send forth lightnings, that
they may go
and say to you, 'Here we are'?
36 Who has [y]put wisdom in [z]the inward
parts[2]
or given understanding to the
mind?[3]
37 Who can number the clouds by
wisdom?
Or who can tilt the waterskins of
the heavens,
38 when the dust runs into a mass
and [a]the clods stick fast together?

39 "Can you hunt the prey for the lion,
or [b]satisfy the appetite of the
young lions,
40 when they crouch in their [c]dens
or lie in wait [d]in their thicket?
41 Who provides for [e]the raven its prey,
when its young ones cry to God for
help,
and wander about for lack of food?

39 "Do you know when [f]the mountain
goats give birth?
Do you observe [g]the calving of the
does?
2 Can you number the months that
they fulfill,
and do you know the time when
they give birth,
3 when they [h]crouch, bring forth their
offspring,
and are delivered of their young?
4 Their young ones become strong;
they grow up in the open;
they go out and [i]do not return to
them.

5 "Who has let the wild donkey go free?
Who has [j]loosed the bonds of the
swift donkey,
6 to whom I have given [k]the arid plain
for his home
and [l]the salt land for his dwelling
place?
7 He scorns the tumult of the city;
he hears not the shouts of the driver.
8 He ranges the mountains as his
pasture,
and he searches after every green
thing.

9 "Is [m]the wild ox willing to serve you?
Will he spend the night at your
[n]manger?
10 Can you bind [m]him in the furrow
with ropes,
or will he harrow the valleys after
you?
11 Will you depend on him because his
strength is great,
and will you leave to him your
labor?

27 [r]Gen. 1:11; 2 Sam. 23:4
28 [s]Ps. 147:8; Jer. 14:22
29 [t]Ps. 147:16, 17
30 [u][ch. 37:10]
31 [v]ch. 9:9; Amos 5:8
32 [v][See ver. 31 above]
33 [w]Jer. 31:35
34 [x]ch. 22:11
36 [y]See ch. 32:8 [z]Ps. 51:6
38 [a]ch. 21:33
39 [b][Ps. 104:21]
40 [c]ch. 37:8 [d]Ps. 17:12
41 [e]Ps. 147:9; Luke 12:24; [Matt. 6:26]
Chapter 39
1 [f]1 Sam. 24:2; Ps. 104:18 [g]Ps. 29:9
3 [h]1 Sam. 4:19
4 [i][Gen. 8:12]
5 [j][ch. 12:18; Ps. 116:16]
6 [k]ch. 24:5; Jer. 2:24 [l]Ps. 107:34; Jer. 17:6; [Deut. 29:23]
9 [m]Num. 23:22 [n]Prov. 14:4; Isai. 1:3
10 [m][See ver. 9 above]

[1] Probably the name of a constellation [2] Or *ibis* [3] Or *rooster*

38:31 bind . . . Pleiades . . . loose the cords of Orion. God alone has dominion over the cosmic forces that constrain the cluster of stars called Pleiades and those making up the belt of the hunter Orion.

38:36 the inward parts . . . the mind. The Hebrew word translated "mind" occurs only here, and its meaning has been in question since the ancient times. If one traditional translation is accepted, the verse asks who gave wisdom to "the ibis" and "the rooster," birds that were thought to announce the coming of the rain and the flooding of the Nile.

38:39 Here the questions shift from the inanimate to animate creation: a sampling of God's creatures great and small.

39:1, 2 Do you know . . . Do you observe . . . Can you number. God reminds Job of His creative, wise, and sustaining work even in the barren hills where man can scarcely live—and of Job's ignorance by contrast.

12 Do you have faith in him that he will
return your grain
and gather it to your threshing
floor?

13 "The wings of the ostrich wave
proudly,
but are they the pinions and
plumage of love?[1]

14 For she leaves her eggs to the earth
and lets them be warmed on the
ground,

15 forgetting that a foot may crush them
and that the wild beast may
trample them.

16 She [o]deals cruelly with her young, as
if they were not hers;
though her [p]labor be in vain, yet
she has no fear,

17 because God has made her forget
wisdom
and [q]given her no share in
understanding.

18 When she rouses herself to flee,[2]
she laughs at the horse and his
rider.

19 "Do you give the horse his might?
Do you clothe his neck with a
mane?

20 Do you make him leap like the
locust?
His majestic [r]snorting is terrifying.

21 He paws[3] in the valley and exults in
his strength;
he [s]goes out to meet the weapons.

22 He laughs at fear and is not dismayed;
he does not turn back from the
sword.

23 Upon him rattle the quiver,
the flashing spear and the javelin.

24 With fierceness and rage he swallows
the ground;
he cannot stand still at [t]the sound
of the trumpet.

25 When the trumpet sounds, he says
'Aha!'
He smells the battle from afar,
the thunder of the captains, and
the shouting.

26 "Is it by your understanding that the
hawk soars
and spreads his wings toward the
south?

27 Is it at your command that the eagle
mounts up
and makes his [u]nest on high?

28 On the rock he dwells and makes his
home,
on [v]the rocky crag and stronghold.

29 From there he spies out the prey;
his eyes behold it afar off.

30 His young ones suck up blood,
and [w]where the slain are, there
is he."

40 And the LORD [x]said to Job:

2 "Shall a faultfinder [y]contend with the
Almighty?
He who argues with God, let him
answer it."

Job Promises Silence

3 Then Job answered the LORD and said:

4 "Behold, I am [z]of small account; what
shall I answer you?
[a]I lay my hand on my mouth.

5 I have spoken [b]once, and I will not
answer;
[b]twice, but I will proceed no further."

The LORD Challenges Job

6 Then the LORD [c]answered Job out of the
whirlwind and said:

7 [d]"Dress for action[4] like a man;
[e]I will question you, and you make
it known to me.

16 [o][Lam. 4:3] [p]Isai. 49:4; 65:23
17 [q][ch. 35:11]
20 [r]Jer. 8:16
21 [s][Jer. 8:6]
24 [t]Jer. 4:19; Amos 3:6
27 [u][Num. 24:21; Jer. 49:16; Obad. 4; Hab. 2:9]
28 [v]1 Sam. 14:5
30 [w]Matt. 24:28; Luke 17:37
Chapter 40
1 [x]ch. 38:1
2 [y]See ch. 33:13
4 [z][ch. 42:6; Ezra 9:6] [a]ch. 21:5; 29:9; Judg. 18:19
5 [b]ch. 33:14; Ps. 62:11
6 [c]ch. 38:1
7 [d]ch. 38:3 [e]ch. 38:3; 42:4

1 The meaning of the Hebrew is uncertain 2 The meaning of the Hebrew is uncertain 3 Hebrew *They paw* 4 Hebrew *Gird up your loins*

39:5 Who has let the wild donkey go free. This wild creature was greatly admired for its freedom and its ability to live in "the arid plain" (v. 6).

39:9 Is the wild ox willing to serve you. This now extinct animal was already rare in Palestine in Job's day. They were hunted to extinction by the Egyptians and Assyrians.

39:18 she laughs at the horse and his rider. The ostrich is a bird that cannot fly yet runs faster than a horse. Job has complained of paradoxes in his life; God shows him natural paradoxes that are resolved only in the secret (or revealed) purposes of the self-existent God.

39:19 Do you give the horse his might. Probably this is the war-horse, by reputation the strongest and most intelligent animal.

39:29 his eyes behold it afar off. In addition to the mysterious migratory instinct of birds (v. 26), these words speak of the phenomenal eyesight of eagles.

40:1, 2 This conclusion of the first speech should be compared with its opening in 38:2. Both are directed toward Job's bold but erroneous utterances during his moments of doubt.

40:3–5 Job abandons his obsession with being vindicated. It is his turn to speak, but he has nothing to say. He is brought low before the Almighty.

8 Will you even put me in the wrong?
Will you condemn me that [f]you may be in the right?
9 Have you [g]an arm like God,
and can you thunder with [h]a voice like his?

10 "Adorn yourself with majesty and dignity;
[i]clothe yourself with glory and splendor.
11 Pour out the overflowings of your anger,
and look on everyone who is [j]proud and abase him.
12 Look on everyone who is proud and bring him low
and [k]tread down the wicked [l]where they stand.
13 [m]Hide them all in [n]the dust together;
bind their faces in the world below.[1]
14 Then will I also acknowledge to you
that your own [o]right hand can save you.

15 "Behold, Behemoth,[2]
which I made as I made you;
he eats [p]grass like an ox.
16 Behold, his strength in his loins,
and his power in the muscles of his belly.
17 He makes his tail stiff like a cedar;
the sinews of his thighs are knit together.
18 His bones are tubes of bronze,
his limbs like bars of iron.

19 "He is [q]the first of [r]the works[3] of God;
let him who made him bring near his sword!
20 For the mountains yield food for him
where all the wild beasts play.
21 Under the lotus plants he lies,
in the shelter of [s]the reeds and in the marsh.
22 For his shade the lotus trees cover him;
the willows of the brook surround him.
23 Behold, if the river is turbulent he is not frightened;
he is confident though Jordan rushes against his mouth.
24 Can one take him [t]by his eyes,[4]
or pierce his nose with a snare?

41

[5] "Can you draw out [u]Leviathan[6] with a fishhook
or press down his tongue with a cord?
2 Can you put [v]a rope in his nose
or pierce his jaw with [v]a hook?
3 Will he make many pleas to you?
Will he speak to you soft words?
4 Will he make a covenant with you
to take him for [w]your servant forever?
5 Will you play with him as with a bird,
or will you put him on a leash for your girls?
6 Will traders bargain over him?
Will they divide him up among the merchants?
7 Can you fill his skin with harpoons
or his head with fishing spears?
8 Lay your hands on him;
remember the battle—you will not do it again!
9 [7] Behold, the hope of a man is false;
he is laid low even at the sight of him.
10 No one is so fierce that he dares to stir him up.
Who then is he who can stand before me?
11 [x]Who has first given to me, that I should repay him?
[y]Whatever is under the whole heaven is mine.

8 [f]See ch. 32:2
9 [g]Ps. 89:13; Isai. 63:12 [h]See ch. 37:4
10 [i][Ps. 93:1; 104:1]
11 [j][Dan. 4:37]; See Isai. 2:11-17
12 [k]Isai. 63:3 [l][ch. 36:20]
13 [m]Isai. 2:10 [n]ch. 21:26
14 [o]Ps. 98:1; Isai. 59:16; 63:5
15 [p]Num. 22:4
19 [q][Prov. 8:22] [r]ch. 26:14
21 [s]Ps. 68:30
24 [t][Prov. 1:17]
Chapter 41
1 [u]ch. 3:8; Ps. 74:14; 104:26; Isai. 27:1
2 [v][2 Kin. 19:28; Isai. 37:29]
4 [w]Ex. 21:6; Deut. 15:17
11 [x]Rom. 11:35; [ch. 35:7] [y]See Ps. 24:1

1 Hebrew *in the hidden place* 2 A large animal, exact identity unknown 3 Hebrew *ways* 4 Or *in his sight* 5 Ch 40:25 in Hebrew 6 A large sea animal, exact identity unknown 7 Ch 41:1 in Hebrew

40:6–41:34 The Lord opens His second discourse (40:6, 7) as He did in 38:1–3, but here challenges Job with a new line of reasoning about Job's questioning whether God is just in judging the wicked. In His first speech God revealed Himself as Lord of nature, but here as the Lord of the moral realm.

40:8–14 This section emphasizes God's power over pride and wickedness (vv. 11, 12). The monsters in the verses following, Behemoth and Leviathan, probably represent such forces of evil that God can control but before which Job is helpless.

40:15 Behemoth. The Hebrew root is used for "cattle," but the form here implies the meaning "the beast beyond comparison." Parts of the description, especially v. 19, go beyond any natural creature like the hippopotamus or the crocodile. Canaanite literature describes the goddess Anat overcoming a terrible bull and a seven-headed "Leviathan." The Lord's speech indicates that whatever may be the forces suggested by such creatures, they are no more than playthings in comparison with His unfathomable power.

41:1 Leviathan. Possibly "Leviathan" and "Behemoth" form a poetic

12 "I will not keep silence concerning his
limbs,
or his mighty strength, or his
goodly frame.
13 Who can strip off his outer garment?
Who would come near him with a
bridle?
14 Who can open the doors of his face?
Around his teeth is terror.
15 His back is made of[1] rows of shields,
shut up closely as with a seal.
16 One is so near to another
that no air can come between them.
17 They are [z]joined one to another;
they clasp each other and cannot
be separated.
18 His sneezings flash forth light,
and his eyes are like [a]the eyelids of
the dawn.
19 Out of his mouth go flaming torches;
sparks of fire leap forth.
20 Out of his nostrils comes forth smoke,
as from a boiling pot and burning
rushes.
21 His breath [b]kindles coals,
and a flame comes forth from his
mouth.
22 In his neck abides strength,
and terror dances before him.
23 The folds of his flesh [c]stick together,
firmly cast on him and immovable.
24 His heart is hard as a stone,
hard as the lower millstone.
25 When he raises himself up the
mighty[2] are afraid;
at the crashing they are beside
themselves.
26 Though the sword reaches him, it
does not avail,
nor the spear, the dart, or the javelin.
27 He counts iron as straw,
and bronze as rotten wood.
28 The arrow cannot make him flee;
for him sling stones are turned to
stubble.

17 [z]ver. 23
18 [a]ch. 3:9
21 [b]2 Sam. 22:13; [Ps. 18:8]
23 [c]ver. 17

29 Clubs are counted as stubble;
he laughs at the rattle of javelins.
30 His underparts are like sharp
[d]potsherds;
he spreads himself like [e]a
threshing sledge on the mire.
31 He makes the deep boil like a pot;
he makes the sea like a pot of
ointment.
32 Behind him he leaves a shining wake;
one would think the deep to be
white-haired.
33 [f]On earth there is not his like,
a creature without fear.
34 He sees everything that is high;
he is king over all the [g]sons of
pride."

Job's Confession and Repentance

42 Then Job answered the LORD and
said:
2 "I know that you can [h]do all things,
and that no purpose of yours can
be thwarted.
3 [i]'Who is this that hides counsel
without knowledge?'
Therefore I have uttered what I did
not understand,
things [j]too wonderful for me,
which I did not know.
4 'Hear, and I will speak;
[k]I will question you, and you make
it known to me.'
5 I had heard of you by the hearing of
the ear,
but now my eye sees you;
6 therefore I despise myself,
and repent[3] in [l]dust and ashes."

The LORD Rebukes Job's Friends

7 After the LORD had spoken these words
to Job, the LORD said to Eliphaz [m]the
Temanite: "My anger burns against you

30 [d]ch. 2:8 [e]Isai. 28:27; 41:15
33 [f]ch. 19:25
34 [g]ch. 28:8
Chapter 42
2 [h]Gen. 18:14; Matt. 19:26
3 [i]ch. 38:2 [j]Ps. 40:5; 131:1; 139:6
4 [k]ch. 38:3; 40:7
6 [l][ch. 30:19; Gen. 18:27]; See ch. 2:8
7 [m]ch. 2:11; 1 Chr. 1:45

1 Or *His pride is in his* 2 Or *gods* 3 Or *and am comforted*

repetition, both referring to one creature. The poetic description in these lines is anchored in nature, but the creature or creatures described represent something more. Like Leviathan in Is. 27:1 and Ps. 74:14, they symbolize threatening powers in the heavenly and earthly realms (Rev. 12:7, 13:1).

41:34 This fits exactly the lines introducing Behemoth and Leviathan in 40:11, 12.

42:1–6 Appropriately, Job is now more than humbled: he must repent for his rash words doubting God's justice during his deepest suffering. Because of his experience, his repentance is unforced and sincere.

42:2 See "Omnipresence and Omnipotence" at Jer. 23:24.

42:5 but now my eye sees you. Job could not see physically through the whirlwind out of which God spoke (38:1; 40:6); he expresses a deeper meaning. He knew God with words, but he now experiences His living presence in his inner being. He meets Him as Savior and friend and, above all, God.

42:7–17 The drama introduced in the prologue now comes full circle.

42:7–9 God rebukes Job's counselors and accepts Job's prayers on their behalf.

and against your two friends, for you have
not spoken of me what is right, as my servant Job has. **8** Now therefore take [n]seven
bulls and seven rams and go to my servant
Job and [o]offer up a burnt offering for yourselves. And my servant Job shall [p]pray for
you, for I will accept his prayer not to deal
with you according to your folly. For you
have not spoken of me what is right, as
my servant Job has." **9** [q]So Eliphaz the
Temanite and Bildad the Shuhite and
Zophar the Naamathite went and did what
the LORD had told them, and the LORD
accepted Job's prayer.

The LORD Restores Job's Fortunes

10 And the LORD [r]restored the fortunes of
Job, when he had prayed for his friends.
And the LORD gave Job [s]twice as much as
he had before. **11** Then came to him all his
[t]brothers and sisters and all who had
[t]known him before, and ate bread with him
in his house. And they [u]showed him sympathy and comforted him for all the evil[1]
that the LORD had brought upon him. And
each of them gave him [v]a piece of money[2]
and [w]a ring of gold.
12 And the LORD blessed [x]the latter days of
Job more than his beginning. And he had
[y]14,000 sheep, 6,000 camels, 1,000 yoke of
oxen, and 1,000 female donkeys. **13** He had
also [z]seven sons and three daughters. **14** And
he called the name of the first daughter
Jemimah, and the name of the second
Keziah, and the name of the third Keren-
happuch. **15** And in all the land there were
no women so beautiful as Job's daughters.
And their father gave them an inheritance
[a]among their brothers. **16** And after this Job
lived 140 years, and [b]saw his sons, and his
sons' sons, four generations. **17** And Job
died, an old man, and [c]full of days.

8 [n]Num. 23:1; 1 Chr. 15:26 [o]ch. 1:5 [p]Gen. 20:7; 1 Sam. 12:23; James 5:16; 1 John 5:16
9 [q]ch. 2:11
10 [r]See Ps. 14:7 [s]Isai. 40:2; 61:7
11 [t]ch. 19:13 [u]ch. 2:11 [v]Gen. 33:19; Josh. 24:32 [w]Gen. 24:22
12 [x]ch. 8:7 [y][ver. 10; ch. 1:3]
13 [z]ch. 1:2
15 [a]See Num. 27:1-8
16 [b]Gen. 50:23; [Ps. 128:6; Isai. 53:10]
17 [c]See ch. 5:26

1 Or *disaster* 2 Hebrew *a qesitah*; a unit of money of unknown value

42:7 what is right. Since God has rebuked (and forgiven) Job for things he had said, why does He say here that Job said what was right while the counselors did not? Their words were often formally blameless. The counselors failed since without knowing why Job was suffering, they arrogantly assumed they did, and falsely accused Job of kinds of sins of which he was not guilty. That God accepted Job's prayer on their behalf indicates His gracious forgiveness of them also.

42:8 shall pray for you. We often assume that praying for one's detractors is a New Testament teaching, but it is here in Job. In this way Job foreshadows Christ, who when nailed to the cross prayed, "Father, forgive them, for they know not what they do" (Luke 23:34).

42:12 the LORD blessed. Job is restored, and those who refused to be near him in his dark hour (19:13–20) are forgiven. Commentators have objected to this restoration, since so many through the ages have suffered without being restored. But God had allowed Satan (the Adversary) to strike Job to prove that His servant would remain true. The reader knows that Satan was proved a liar: Job never cursed God (1:11; 2:5) and God was glorified. It was the good pleasure of God to reward His servant. The "steadfastness of Job" was known to God (James 5:11). Job's cry, "I will argue my ways to his face" (13:15), can be compared with Jacob's, "I will not let you go unless you bless me" (Gen. 32:26).

INTRODUCTION TO

Hebrew Poetry

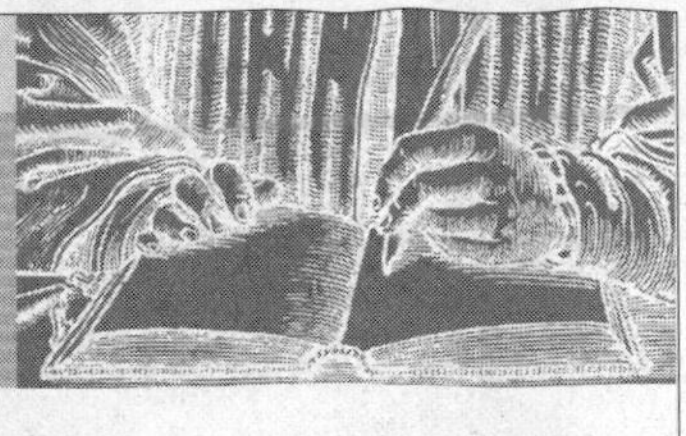

The most prominent distinguishing feature of Hebrew poetry is the repetition of ideas, called parallelism. An idea is stated and then immediately expressed again in different words, with the concepts of the two lines corresponding more or less closely. The types of parallelism were described by Lowth (1753) as belonging to three basic categories. These are: *synonymous*, in which the idea is repeated in a similar way; *antithetic*, in which the idea is stated by opposition; and *synthetic*, in which the second line develops or extends the thought of the first rather than merely repeating it. Other categories have also been distinguished. For example, in *emblematic* parallelism one line is a figure of speech and the other puts the same idea literally, explaining the figure. In *step*, *staircase*, or *climactic* parallelism, the succeeding lines carry the idea forward, each one adding a new element to what went before. Characteristic examples of the types mentioned are: (a) synonymous, Ps. 113:7; Ps. 147:10 (b) antithetic, Ps. 1:6; Prov. 10:1; (c) synthetic, Ps. 52:9; (d) emblematic, Prov. 25:4, 5; and (e) step, Judg. 5:30; Ps. 29:5, 6; 65:4.

The corresponding parts of parallel lines often help to explain each other. Two lines together may define an idea more clearly than one alone. More recently, it has been observed that even if the two lines are practically identical, there is still a special effect due to repetition alone. In this sense, all parallelisms are to some extent synthetic. However, the usual analysis has not lost its validity and is widely used in discussions of biblical poetry.

It is helpful to study the techniques of antithesis, figurative speech, and so on, in simple parallelisms, because the same techniques are combined in more complicated examples. Thus Ps. 92:12-15 has synonymous and emblematic elements that compare a flourishing tree with a righteous person, and define the righteous person as one who is planted, or remains, in God's house. The fruit of the tree is the praise of God's righteousness. Comparing and contrasting the balanced parts of parallel expressions is the basic key to understanding as well as enjoying biblical poetry.

The meter or rhythm of Hebrew poetry has been a subject of continuous debate. It seems established that there is at least one clearly defined meter, the *qinah* or lament, having three beats and then two in each line. But there is no general agreement about other proposed meters. In any case, while the parallelism of ideas can be carried over and appreciated even in translation, meter is much harder to replicate. The same is true of features like alliteration, rhyme, and other effects depending on the sound of words. In Hebrew poetry these are not nearly as important as parallelism.

Another formal feature, which is often indicated in the margins or notes of translations, is the acrostic. In this type of composition lines or stanzas begin with successive letters of the alphabet. This technique, like parallelism, would help in memorizing and teaching. It may also be a way of suggesting that the subject has been handled completely. The outstanding example is Ps. 119.

Poetry in general, and not just Hebrew poetry, is characterized by compression of ideas and economy of expression. This means that transitions are often left out and the relationship of ideas is left for the reader to determine. For example, in the Psalms there are many confusing changes of subject, and ideas that seem unrelated may nevertheless occur next to each other. But the difficulty and subtlety of poetic language can be regarded as a virtue. Good poetry rewards the effort required to understand it, as well as to memorize it.

THE BOOK OF

Psalms

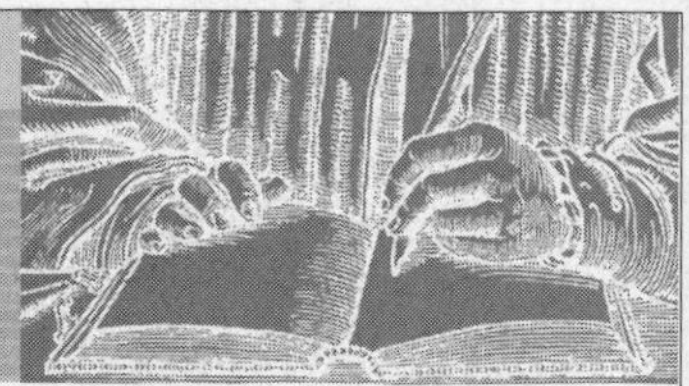

AUTHOR

Many of the psalms begin with a title linking the psalm with a particular individual or group, using a Hebrew preposition that could possibly indicate dedication ("to David"), subject matter ("about David"), or authorship ("by David"). However, one of the few psalm titles with an expanded context leaves no doubt that the title intends to identify the composer of the psalm (Ps. 18). David is by far the most frequently cited author, most of his psalms being in the first two books (see Structure), though there is a small collection of psalms by him at the very end (Ps. 138–145). The tradition that associates David with singing and psalm composition is so strong that there is little doubt that David wrote the psalms that bear his name (1 Sam. 16:14–23; 2 Sam. 1:17–27; 2 Sam. 22; 2 Sam. 23:1; 1 Chr. 6:31; 15:16; 16:7; Ps. 18; Amos 6:5).

Other authors appear in psalm titles: Moses (Ps. 90), Solomon (Ps. 72; 127), the sons of Korah (Ps. 42–49; 84; 85; 87; 88), Asaph (Ps. 50; 73–83), and Ethan the Ezrahite (Ps. 89). A number of psalms have no designated author (e.g. Ps. 1; 10).

DATE AND OCCASION

The titles of the psalms show that they were composed by individuals in response to a particular corporate or individual experience. The dates and occasions of the psalms (see introductory paragraphs to the psalms in the notes) range from the time of Moses (Ps. 90), to the experiences of David (Ps. 51), to the time after the exile of the Jews in Babylon (Ps. 126). Still, the psalms collected for use in public worship were never so specific that they could not be used in new situations.

Forming the collection took several centuries, arriving at its present form some time after the exile in Babylon. The name "Psalms" means "songs," and is taken from the Septuagint, the early Greek translation of the Old Testament. This is the name used in the New Testament (Luke 20:42; 24:44; Acts 1:20).

CHARACTERISTICS AND THEMES

Titles. The titles of individual psalms are usually not assigned a verse number in translations, giving the impression that they are separate from other verses. In the Hebrew Bible the titles are usually numbered as the first verse. The titles are either an original part of the psalms, or at least from extremely early tradition.

The titles may be divided into five basic types: authorship, historical, musical, genre (literary type), and instructions for use in worship.

1. Authorship Titles. See the discussion under "Author" above.

2. Historical Titles. There are fewer historical than authorship titles (Ps. 3; 7; 18; 30; 34; 51; 52; 54; 56; 57; 59; 60; 63; 142). The authenticity of the former has been disputed, although there is no textual evidence that they were added later. However, some believe that apparent disharmony between psalm and title (as in Ps. 30) or between the title and other books (Ps. 56 compared with 1 Sam. 21:10–15) indicates that those titles are late and artificial. Others argue that if historical titles were added later, whoever added them would have made sure they matched the content of the psalm. To give an example, why would a later editor connect Ps. 30 with the dedication of the temple when there was no mention of the temple in the psalm?

The historical titles may give us an indication of the origins of a psalm (see below), but they are of limited help in interpretation. That is, while psalms may have been written in reaction to particular historical events, the composers were careful not to be specific in the body of the poem.

The psalms were intended to express what others could share in formal and public worship, and were not private poems. However, the interpreter is not bound to reconstruct the historical background of all the psalms (a practice of many earlier psalm commentators).

3. Genre Titles. A number of the terms in the titles classify the psalms into genres, or literary types. It is difficult to know the precise meaning of the terms used. Some are found often: *mizmor* (a "song," e.g., Ps. 139) and *shir* ("song"), others rarely. In today's discussion literary types are determined from the content of the psalms and not from the titles.

4. Musical Notations. Some of the genre terms, as above, are also musical notations, notably *mizmor* (from a verbal root "to sing") and *shir* ("song"). Others are of less certain meaning. A few are probably names of tunes.

Selah is a word that occurs frequently in the body of the psalms. Its meaning is unknown, though it could be a musical term, like "rest" or "interlude."

5. Instructions for Use in Worship. Occasionally the titles indicate how the psalms were used in formal worship. Of these the best known are the "Songs of Ascents" (Ps. 120–134; see the introductory paragraph to Ps. 120).

Structure. The psalms are arranged in five books. Each book closes with a doxology and benediction (Ps. 1–41; 42–72; 73–89; 90–106; 107–150). Jewish tradition is that the number five was chosen to match the five books of Moses.

Psalms 1 and 2 are the entryway into the sanctuary of the Psalms, and Ps. 146–150 conclude the book with a long doxology. Ps. 1 transforms the prayers and praises originally offered in the temple into a book for meditation in meetings and at home.

The first two books celebrate Israel's golden age during the time of the united monarchy. Ps. 2 and 72 are prayers that the king will extend the rule of God to the ends of the earth. All the psalms in Book I are attributed to David, except Ps. 1, 2, and 33. Laments in the first two books always conclude with praise.

By contrast, Book III (Ps. 73–89) is dark. The first psalm of the section complains that the righteous suffer. The last psalm of the section laments that the Davidic covenant seems to have failed, with the king's crown rolling in the dust. Ps. 88 is as the only psalm without praise.

Book IV (Ps. 90–106) turns to God Himself who has been Israel's help in ages past. In this book Moses is mentioned seven times; he is mentioned only once before (Ps. 77). Psalms 93–99, called "enthronement psalms," look to God's reign on earth. The writer of Hebrews assigns the praise of God celebrated in Ps. 102:25–27 to Jesus Christ (Heb. 1:10–12).

Book V begins by thanking God for bringing Israel back from the exile. The book includes psalms holding up David as a model for piety (138–145) and psalms predicting the reign of Christ (110).

Genres. Distinguishing characteristics allow the psalms to be assigned to literary groups for the purpose of study. Following are the literary types commonly used.

1. Hymns of Praise. Hymns are easily recognized by their exuberant praise of the Lord. God is praised for who He is and for His power and mercy. For examples, see Ps. 8; 24; 29; 33; 47; 48.

2. Laments. Laments express an emotion opposite to that of praise. In the lament, the psalmist opens his heart honestly to God, a heart often filled with sadness, fear, or even anger. With few exceptions the laments turn to the Lord with confidence at the end. For examples, see Ps. 25; 39; 51; 86; 102; 120.

3. Thanksgiving Psalms. A psalm of thanksgiving is appropriate when the Lord answers a prayer of lament. The first three psalm types form a kind of triad. The psalmist sings hymns when he is right with the Lord, laments when he is out of harmony with Him, and gives thanks when the relationship is reestablished. For examples see Ps. 18; 66; 107; 118; 138.

4. Songs of Confidence (or trust). Some psalms have trust as their dominant mood. These are often short and contain a striking metaphor that captures the psalmist's trusting attitude. For examples, see Ps. 23; 121; 131.

5. Kingship Psalms. Since God, the King of the universe, is the subject of the Psalms and since David, the human king, is both singer and subject of many psalms, kingship is an important concept in the Psalter. However, a few psalms focus so intensely either on God's kingship (Ps. 24; 93) or on the human king (Ps. 20; 21; 45) that they stand out.

6. Wisdom Psalms. For biblical wisdom we commonly turn to books like Proverbs, Job, Song of Songs, and Ecclesiastes. In these books are practical directions for how God wants us to live our lives. The "wisdom psalms" make use of themes found in the wisdom books. For instance, the strong contrast between the righteous and the wicked found in the Book of Proverbs is found in Ps. 1. For other examples, see Ps. 37 and 49.

Poetic Style. No special knowledge is needed to recognize the poetic quality of the Psalter. Instead of sentences forming paragraphs, the psalms are composed of short poetic verses of nearly equal length. This characteristic is easily recognized on the printed page.

Poetry is deliberate communication that pays particular attention to its own form. The poetic language addresses not only the mind but the imagination and emotions. To say "The LORD is my shepherd" (Ps. 23:1) does more than inform. The metaphor of a shepherd evokes a picture and touches the emotions in a way that a didactic statement would not.

Parallelism is the most obvious poetic device in Old Testament poetry. Ps. 6:1 is a good example:

> O LORD, rebuke me not in your anger,
> nor discipline me in your wrath.

To interpret parallel lines, it is important to bear in mind that the second line continues and carries forward the thought of the first. In this verse, the first line asks the Lord not to punish in word, while the second part asks Him not to punish in deed.

Examples may be found of lines that are even more similar (Ps. 2:1) and of those where it is harder to recognize the connection (Ps. 2:6). But the general principle of interpretation is that the second half of a poetic verse carries forward the thought of the first half. See "Introduction to Hebrew Poetry."

Theology of the Psalms. Just as the Psalter was formed during the entire period of the Old Testament, so the theology of the psalms is as large as the Old Testament. Martin Luther called the Psalms "a little Bible, and the summary of the Old Testament."

Christian readers of the Psalms appreciate the relationship these ancient songs have to Jesus Christ. Jesus told His disciples after the Resurrection that "everything written about me in the Law of Moses and the Prophets and the Psalms must be fulfilled" (Luke 24:44). The Old Testament, including the Psalms, looked forward to Christ's coming, His suffering, and His glory. Jesus and the New Testament writers use psalm after psalm to express His suffering (Matt. 27:46) and His glorification (Matt. 22:41–46). In addition, Jesus was revealed as the object of the worship of the psalms. Since Christ is the Second Person of the Trinity, the hymns and laments of the psalms are directed to Him as to the Father and the Spirit. Jesus is both a singer of the psalms (Heb. 2:12) and the focus of their interest. We can sing to Him our praise, tell Him our complaints and petitions, and thank Him for His goodness. We extol Him as our King, rest our confidence in Him, and look to Him as the embodiment of God's wisdom.

The Curses of the Psalms. Some psalms cry out not only for the righteous to be vindicated, but also for God to punish the wicked (Ps. 69:22–28). Such prayers reflect the calling of Israel to holy war as God's instruments of judgment. With the coming of Christ to bear God's judgment, the warfare of God's people continues, directed now against "spiritual forces of evil in the heavenly places" (Eph. 6:12). In their present warfare, Christians are commanded not to curse, but to bless their personal enemies, overcoming evil with good (Rom. 12:17–21).

TITLE

"Psalms" means "songs" and is taken from the Septuagint, the early Greek translation of the Old Testament. The New Testament uses this name (Luke 20:42; 24:44; Acts 1:20). The corresponding Hebrew word *mizmor* occurs frequently in the psalms and means a vocal or instrumental song.

OUTLINE OF THE PSALMS

I. Book I, Psalms 1–41

II. Book II, Psalms 42–72

III. Book III, Psalms 73–89

IV. Book IV, Psalms 90–106

V. Book V, Psalms 107–150

BOOK ONE

The Way of the Righteous and the Wicked

1 Blessed is the man[1]
who [a]walks not in [b]the counsel
of the wicked,
nor stands in [c]the way of sinners,
nor [d]sits in [e]the seat of [f]scoffers;
2 but his [g]delight is in the law[2] of the
LORD,
and on his [h]law he meditates day
and night.

3 He is like [i]a tree
planted by [j]streams of water
that yields its fruit in its season,
and its [k]leaf does not wither.
[l]In all that he does, he prospers.
4 The wicked are not so,
but are like [m]chaff that the wind
drives away.

5 Therefore the wicked [n]will not stand
in the judgment,
nor sinners in [o]the congregation of
the righteous;
6 for the LORD [p]knows [q]the way of the
righteous,
but the way of the wicked will perish.

BOOK ONE
Psalm 1 1 [a]Prov. 4:14, 15 [b]Job 21:16 [c]Prov. 1:10 [d]Ps. 26:4; Jer. 15:17 [e][Ps. 107:32] [f]Prov. 1:22; 3:34; 19:29; 21:24; 29:8; [Isai. 28:14] 2 [g]Ps. 112:1; 119:35, 47, 92 [h]Ps. 119:1, 97; Josh. 1:8 3 [i]Jer. 17:8; Ezek. 19:10; [Num. 24:6; Job 29:19] [j]Ps. 46:4 [k]Ezek. 47:12; [Isai. 34:4] [l]Gen. 39:3, 23; [Ps. 128:2; Isai. 3:10] 4 [m]See Job 21:18 5 [n]Ps. 5:5; 76:7; Nah. 1:6; Luke 21:36; Eph. 6:13 [o][Ezek. 13:9] 6 [p]Ps. 31:7; 37:18; 144:3; Nah. 1:7; [John 10:14; 2 Tim. 2:19] [q]Ps. 37:5

The Reign of the LORD's Anointed

2 [r]Why do [s]the nations rage[3]
and the peoples plot in vain?
2 The kings of the earth set
themselves,
and the rulers take counsel
together,
against the LORD and against his
[t]anointed, saying,
3 "Let us [u]burst their bonds apart
and cast away their cords
from us."

4 He who [v]sits in the heavens
[w]laughs;
the Lord holds them in
derision.
5 Then he will speak to them in his
[x]wrath,
and terrify them in his fury,
saying,
6 "As for me, I have [y]set my King
on [z]Zion, my [a]holy hill."

Psalm 2 1 [r]Cited Acts 4:25, 26 [s][Ps. 46:6] 2 [t]Ps. 18:50; 20:6; 45:7; 89:20 3 [u]Jer. 5:5 4 [v]Ps. 11:4; 29:10; [Isai. 40:22] [w]Ps. 37:13; 59:8; Job 22:19; Prov. 1:26 5 [x]Rev. 6:16, 17 6 [y]Prov. 8:23 [z]2 Sam. 5:7; Ps. 110:2 [a]Ps. 3:4; 15:1; 43:3; 99:9

1 The singular Hebrew word for *man* (*ish*) is used here to portray a representative example of a godly person; see preface 2 Or *instruction* 3 Or *nations noisily assemble*

Ps. 1 Like the gateway to a sanctuary, one of the relatively few wisdom psalms introduces the whole collection. Before having close conversation with God, the reader's attitude toward the law of God has to be considered. The righteous person loves and studies it; the wicked person hates it.

1:1 Blessed. A stronger word than "happy"; to be "blessed" is to enjoy God's special favor and grace.

walks not . . . nor stands . . . nor sits. The righteous man is described by what he avoids. There is a downward progression in the verbs "walks," "stands," and "sits."

1:2 his delight. The righteous man is described as someone who loves the law of God. "Law" can refer to a specific command, but also to the whole Scripture. The righteous person grows by an obedient response to the Scriptures, which express the will of God.

1:3 like a tree. As Joseph prospered in Egypt, so will the righteous man. He is compared to a luxuriant tree, ever blooming because water is near.

1:4 The wicked are not so. The contrast is strong. The wicked are compared to dead and rootless plants. A puff of wind carries them away.

1:6 the LORD knows the way. The two ways of life are determined by one's relation to the Lord. The ideal of righteousness is fulfilled in Jesus Christ.

Ps. 2 The theme of kingship pervades this psalm. While most of the kingship psalms focus on either divine or human kingship, Ps. 2 masterfully integrates both, contrasting the divine King and His human counterpart with the hostile "kings of the earth." The psalm has no title, but the New Testament ascribes it to David (Acts 4:25). The New Testament frequently quotes and alludes to this psalm (Matt. 3:17; 17:5; Acts 4:25–27; 13:33; Rom. 1:4; Heb. 1:5; 5:5). Jesus Christ is the Son of David and the Son of God; the promises given to David come to fulfillment in Him.

2:2 kings. The nations are being organized by their political leaders.

his anointed. While the living Davidic king is undoubtedly in view for the psalmist, the ultimate reference of the song is to Christ, the King of Kings.

2:3 burst their bonds. A metaphor for rebellion.

2:4–6 The Lord answers His enemies with the installation of the King.

2:6 my King. The Lord counters the plotting of the kings by pointing to the establishment of His messianic King, prefigured in the temporal monarchy of Jerusalem.

Zion. Zion is a hill north of the Davidic city of Jerusalem. It is not important because of its size, but because it is the location of the temple. Jerusalem as a whole is sometimes called Zion. Earthly Zion was a token of the heavenly Zion. Much of the symbolism of the temple pointed to heavenly realities.

7 I will tell of the decree:
The LORD said to me, [b]"You are my Son;
today I have begotten you.
8 Ask of me, and I will make the nations your heritage,
and [c]the ends of the earth your possession.
9 You shall [d]break[1] them with [e]a rod of iron
and dash them in pieces like [f]a potter's vessel."
10 Now therefore, O kings, be wise;
be warned, O rulers of the earth.
11 [g]Serve the LORD with [h]fear,
and [i]rejoice with [g]trembling.
12 [j]Kiss [k]the Son,
lest he be angry, and you perish in the way,
for his [l]wrath is quickly kindled.
[m]Blessed are all who take refuge in him.

Save Me, O My God

3

A PSALM OF DAVID, [n]WHEN HE FLED FROM ABSALOM HIS SON.

1 O LORD, [o]how many are my foes!
Many are [p]rising against me;
2 many are saying of my soul,
[q]there is no salvation for him in God. *Selah*[2]
3 But you, O LORD, are [r]a shield [s]about me,
my glory, and [t]the lifter of my head.
4 I [u]cried aloud to the LORD,
and he [v]answered me from his [w]holy hill. *Selah*
5 I [x]lay down and slept;
I woke again, for the LORD sustained me.
6 I [y]will not be afraid of many thousands of people
who have [z]set themselves against me all around.
7 [a]Arise, O LORD!
Save me, O my God!
For you [b]strike all my enemies on the cheek;
you [c]break the teeth of the wicked.
8 [d]Salvation belongs to the LORD;
your blessing be on your people! *Selah*

Answer Me When I Call

4

TO THE [e]CHOIRMASTER: WITH [e]STRINGED INSTRUMENTS. A PSALM OF DAVID.

1 Answer me when I call, O God of my [f]righteousness!
You have [g]given me relief when I was in distress.
Be gracious to me and hear my prayer!
2 O men,[3] how long shall my honor be turned into shame?
How long will you love vain words
and seek after [h]lies? *Selah*

7 [b]Rom. 1:4; Cited Acts 13:33; Heb. 1:5; 5:5 **8** [c][Ps. 72:8; 89:27; Dan. 7:14] **9** [d]Ps. 89:23; Job 34:24 [e]Rev. 2:27; 12:5; 19:15 [f]Isai. 30:14; Jer. 19:11 **11** [g]Heb. 12:28 [h]Phil. 2:12 [i]Phil. 4:4 **12** [j]1 Sam. 10:1; 1 Kin. 19:18; [John 5:23] [k]Prov. 31:2 [l]ver. 5 [m]Ps. 34:8; 84:12; Prov. 16:20; Jer. 17:7; [Ps. 146:5; Isai. 30:18]
Psalm 3 [n]See 2 Sam. 15:14-17 **1** [o]2 Sam. 15:12 [p]2 Sam. 18:31, 32 **2** [q]Ps. 71:11; [2 Sam. 16:8] **3** [r]Ps. 28:7; 84:9; 119:114; Gen. 15:1 [s]Job 1:10 [t]Ps. 27:5, 6; [Job 10:15] **4** [u]Ps. 77:1; 142:1 [v]Ps. 34:4; 60:5; 108:6; [Ps. 6:8; 34:6] [w]See Ps. 2:6
5 [x]Ps. 4:8; [Lev. 26:6; Job 11:18, 19; Prov. 3:24] **6** [y][Ps. 23:4; 27:3] [z]Isai. 22:7; [1 Kin. 20:12]
7 [a]Ps. 7:6; 9:19; 10:12; Num. 10:35 [b]See Job 16:10 [c]Ps. 58:6; Job 29:17 **8** [d]Ps. 37:39; 62:7; Isai. 43:11; 45:21; Jer. 3:23; Hos. 13:4; Jonah 2:9; Rev. 7:10; 19:1
Psalm 4 [e]Ps. 61, title; Hab. 3:19 **1** [f]Isai. 54:17; Jer. 23:6 [g]See Job 36:16 **2** [h][Ps. 5:6, 7]

1 Revocalization yields (compare Septuagint) *You shall rule* 2 The meaning of the Hebrew word *Selah*, used frequently in the Psalms, is uncertain. It may be a musical or liturgical direction 3 Or *O men of rank*

2:7 You are my Son. The divine speech addressed to the divine Son (cf. Heb. 1:5), with David as witness, reflects the promise of 2 Sam. 7:14—the Davidic covenant, which had in view not merely David's earthly descendants, but the divine Son of whom David was also an ancestor.

2:9 See "God Reigns: Divine Sovereignty" at Dan. 4:34.

2:12 Kiss the Son. To kiss the Son is an act of submission (cf. 1 Sam. 10:1). The word "Son" is not the usual Hebrew term, but an unexpected Aramaic term.

Ps. 3 Surrounded by trouble and crying out to the Lord in distress, the psalmist expresses deep trust in God. The psalm was originally composed when David fled from Absalom and battled against revolt. The military terminology throughout the psalm may indicate that it continued to be used in warfare.

3:1 Many . . . rising. The number and nature of the foes betrays the royal origin of the psalm. The foes of the nation are also the king's foes.

3:3 lifter of my head. An expression of encouragement.

3:4 holy hill. That is, Zion (see note Ps. 2:6). God designated Zion as the place where His people could approach Him through sacrifice.

3:5 I lay down and slept. As in Ps. 91, the psalmist is able to sleep in the war camp, though the enemy surrounds him.

3:7 Arise. This expression is typical of psalms sung at the beginning of war. God fights for His people against their flesh and blood enemies.

Ps. 4 Like Ps. 3, this psalm was composed in distress, and the psalmist exhibits a deep confidence in God. Both psalms meditate on faith in the night (vv. 4, 8). The righteous have nothing to fear, because God hears their prayers and cares for them. The righteous are not without sin, but are in covenant relationship with God.

4:1 Answer me . . . my righteousness. The imperative verbs in this verse show the boldness of the psalmist in prayer. He can fearlessly call on God because he knows that God is his righteousness (Jer. 23:6).

4:2 my honor be turned into shame. It seems that the psalmist is angry at men who turn away from God to serve the false gods of the nations.

vain words. Lit. "empty things."

seek after lies. The idols of the nations are lies because they don't really exist; they are the figments of sinful imagination.

3 But know that the LORD has [i]set
apart [j]the godly for himself;
the LORD hears when I call to him.

4 [k]Be angry,[1] and do not sin;
[l]ponder in your own hearts [m]on
your beds, and be silent. *Selah*
5 Offer [n]right sacrifices,
and put your [o]trust in the LORD.

6 There are many who say, "Who will
show us some good?
[p]Lift up [q]the light of your face upon
us, O LORD!"
7 You have put [r]more joy in my heart
than they have when their grain
and wine abound.

8 In peace I will both [s]lie down and
sleep;
for you alone, O LORD, make me
[t]dwell in safety.

Lead Me in Your Righteousness

5

TO THE CHOIRMASTER: FOR THE FLUTES.
A PSALM OF DAVID.

1 Give ear to my words, O LORD;
consider my [u]groaning.
2 Give attention to the sound of my cry,
my [v]King and my God,
for [w]to you do I pray.
3 O LORD, in [x]the morning you hear
my voice;
in the morning I prepare a sacrifice
for you[2] and [y]watch.

4 For you are not a God who delights
in wickedness;
evil may not dwell with you.
5 The [z]boastful shall not [a]stand before
your eyes;
you [b]hate all evildoers.
6 You destroy those who speak [c]lies;
the LORD abhors [d]the bloodthirsty
and deceitful man.

7 But I, through the abundance of
your steadfast love,
will enter your house.
I will [e]bow down [f]toward your [g]holy
temple
in the fear of you.
8 [h]Lead me, O LORD, in your
righteousness
because of my enemies;
[i]make your way straight before me.

9 For there is no truth in their
mouth;
their inmost self is [j]destruction;
[k]their throat is [l]an open grave;
they [m]flatter with their tongue.
10 [n]Make them bear their guilt, O God;
let them [o]fall by their own
counsels;
because of the abundance of their
transgressions cast them out,
for they have rebelled against you.

11 But let all who [p]take refuge in you
[q]rejoice;
let them ever sing for joy,
and spread your protection over
them,
that those who love your name
may [r]exult in you.

1 Or *Be agitated* 2 Or *I direct my prayer to you*

3 [i][Ex. 11:7] [j][Ps. 50:5] **4** [k]Cited Eph. 4:26 [l]Ps. 77:6 [m]See Ps. 42:8 **5** [n]Ps. 51:19; Deut. 33:19 [o]Ps. 37:3; 62:8 **6** [p]Num. 6:26 [q]Ps. 89:15; [Ps. 31:16; 67:1; 80:3, 7, 19; 119:135] **7** [r][Isai. 9:3; 16:10; Jer. 48:38] **8** [s]See Ps. 3:5 [t]Ps. 16:9; Lev. 25:18, 19; 26:5; Deut. 33:28
Psalm 5
1 [u][Ps. 39:3] **2** [v]Ps. 84:3 [w]Ps. 65:2 **3** [x]Ps. 88:13; 119:147; 130:6 [y][Hab. 2:1] **5** [z]Ps. 73:3; 75:4; [Hab. 1:13] [a]See Ps. 1:5 [b]Ps. 11:5 **6** [c][Ps. 4:2]; Rev. 21:8; 22:15 [d]Ps. 55:23 **7** [e]Ps. 132:7 [f]1 Kin. 8:29, 30 [g]Ps. 11:4; 79:1 **8** [h][Ps. 23:3; 25:4, 5] [i][Ezra 8:21] **9** [j]Ps. 52:2 [k]Cited Rom. 3:13 [l]Jer. 5:16 [m]Ps. 12:2; Prov. 2:16; 7:5 **10** [n][Isai. 24:6] [o][2 Sam. 15:31; 17:14, 23] **11** [p]Ps. 2:12 [q]Ps. 33:21 [r][Ps. 9:2; 1 Sam. 2:1]

4:3 godly. Those who are in covenant with God, the recipients of God's lovingkindness.

4:4 Be angry, and do not sin. Compare with Eph. 4:26. These are the sacrifices prescribed in Lev. 1–7, offered with a righteous attitude without which all sacrifice or worship is unacceptable (Ps. 40:6–8).

4:6 good. The skeptics taunt that there is nothing good. The psalmist responds to their doubts with an appeal that God would reveal Himself.

light of your face. The phrase resembles the priestly blessing found in Num. 6:25, 26.

4:8 In peace I will . . . lie down. God's intimate presence allows the psalmist to sleep peacefully and with full confidence. His heart is filled with spiritual blessing.

Ps. 5 This lament petitions the Lord in the midst of distress. However, the psalmist also expresses trust in the Lord's protection. The psalmist's distress is caused by the evil speech of the wicked.

5:1 groaning. The Hebrew word implies a kind of muttering or scarcely audible speech, as would accompany memorizing and reflection (1:2).

5:2 King. David, Israel's king, addresses God as his King. He knows that his own kingship is a pale reflection of God's.

5:4 not a God who delights in wickedness. This is a poetic understatement. God hates sin (v. 5; 11:5).

evil may not dwell. God is holy, "set apart" from all evil. Sinful people may not come into His presence without a substitutionary sacrifice.

5:7 abundance of your steadfast love. The writer knows that he is different from the wicked only because of God's grace. His own sin would destroy him if God did not have compassion on him as he approached God's presence.

will enter your house. The psalmist protests his innocence by stating his desire to worship the Lord. "your house" and "your holy temple" may refer to the site where the temple would be built, or perhaps the tabernacle of the psalmist's own time (1 Sam. 1:9).

5:8 your way. The path of safety that God opens is also the path of obedience to His will.

5:9 destruction . . . open grave. Note how evil speech brings death.

5:10 let them fall by their own counsels. The psalmist calls upon God to punish the wicked because they are guilty. Sin often brings its own retributive consequences.

12 For you [s]bless the righteous, O LORD;
you [t]cover him with favor as with
[u]a shield.

O LORD, Deliver My Life

6

TO THE CHOIRMASTER: WITH STRINGED INSTRUMENTS; ACCORDING TO [v]THE SHEMINITH.[1] A PSALM OF DAVID.

1 O LORD, [w]rebuke me not in your anger,
nor [x]discipline me in your wrath.
2 Be gracious to me, O LORD, for I am languishing;
[y]heal me, O LORD, [z]for my bones are troubled.
3 My [a]soul also is greatly troubled.
But you, O LORD—[b]how long?

4 Turn, O LORD, deliver my life;
save me for the sake of your steadfast love.
5 For in [c]death there is no remembrance of you;
in Sheol who will give you praise?

6 I am [d]weary with my [e]moaning;
every night I flood my bed with tears;
I drench my couch with my weeping.
7 My [f]eye wastes away because of grief;
it grows weak because of all my foes.

8 [g]Depart from me, all you [h]workers of evil,
for the LORD [i]has heard the sound of my weeping.
9 The LORD has heard my [j]plea;
the LORD accepts my prayer.
10 All my enemies shall be ashamed and greatly troubled;
they shall [k]turn back and be put to shame in a moment.

In You Do I Take Refuge

7

A [l]SHIGGAION[2] OF DAVID, WHICH HE SANG TO THE LORD CONCERNING THE WORDS OF CUSH, A BENJAMINITE.

1 O LORD my God, in you do I [m]take refuge;
[n]save me from all my pursuers and deliver me,
2 lest like [o]a lion they tear my soul apart,
rending it in pieces, with [p]none to deliver.

3 O LORD my God, [q]if I have done this,
if there is [r]wrong in my hands,
4 if I have repaid [s]my friend[3] with evil
or [t]plundered my enemy without cause,
5 let the enemy pursue my soul and overtake it,
and let him [u]trample my life to the ground
and lay my glory in the dust. *Selah*

6 [v]Arise, O LORD, in your anger;
[w]lift yourself up against the fury of my enemies;
[x]awake for me; you have appointed a judgment.

12 [s]Ps. 115:13 [t][Ps. 103:4] [u][Ps. 35:2] **Psalm 6** [v]1 Chr. 15:21 **1** [w]Ps. 38:1 [x][Ps. 94:12; 118:18; Prov. 3:11, 12; Jer. 30:11; 46:28]; See Heb. 12:3-11 **2** [y]Ps. 30:2; 41:4; 103:3 [z]See Ps. 31:10 **3** [a][John 12:27] [b]Ps. 90:13 **5** [c]Ps. 30:9; 88:10-12; 115:17; Isai. 38:18 **6** [d]Ps. 69:3 [e]Ps. 38:9 **7** [f]Ps. 31:9; 88:9; [Ps. 38:10; Job 17:7; Lam. 2:11; 5:17] **8** [g]Ps. 119:115; 139:19; Matt. 7:23; 25:41; Luke 13:27 [h]Ps. 94:4 [i][Ps. 3:4] **9** [j]Ps. 55:1; 1 Kin. 8:38 **10** [k]Ps. 40:14; 56:9 **Psalm 7** [l]Hab. 3:1 **1** [m]See Ps. 11:1 [n]Ps. 31:15 **2** [o]See Job 10:16 [p]Ps. 50:22 **3** [q][2 Sam. 16:7, 8] [r]1 Sam. 24:11; 26:18; [Ps. 59:3] **4** [s]Ps. 55:20 [t]1 Sam. 24:7; 26:9 **5** [u]Dan. 8:7; [Ps. 89:39]

6 [v]See Ps. 3:7 [w]Ps. 94:2; Isai. 33:10 [x]Ps. 35:23; 44:23; 59:4; Job 8:6

1 Probably a musical or liturgical term 2 Probably a musical or liturgical term 3 Hebrew *the one at peace with me*

Ps. 6 The psalm is an individual lament. As with many laments, the psalmist expresses his trust in the Lord at the end of the psalm. The occasion of the psalm appears to be a severe illness (vv. 2, 5). This psalm is one of seven "penitential psalms" (along with 32; 38; 51; 102; 130; 143).

6:1 rebuke . . . discipline. The psalmist begs the Lord to refrain from verbal and physical punishment. Though God disciplines His people (Heb. 12:1–13), it is for correction and not destruction.

6:2 I am languishing . . . my bones are troubled. The psalmist experiences suffering, probably a serious illness. Some take the language as figurative for spiritual distress.

6:3 how long. The psalmist boldly asks how long God will permit his suffering to continue. He desperately seeks relief from the One who is able to give it.

6:4 Turn, O LORD. The psalmist thinks that God has turned away from him.

the sake of your steadfast love. The word translated "steadfast love" indicates how devotedly God binds Himself to His people by His covenant.

6:5 no remembrance. A similar statement is expressed in 30:9. The doctrine of resurrection, like the doctrine of the Trinity, is implicit in the Old Testament, but not developed fully until the New Testament. The living observe that the dead are silent and do not take part in worship.

Sheol. This word is found most often in poetic passages that reveal the thoughts and fears of the living, but are not presentations of a doctrine of resurrection or of the intermediate state. See Is. 14:9–11 note.

6:8 all you workers of evil. This reference, along with the reference to "foes" in the preceding verse, is abrupt. It is possible that the foes are people, like the "friends" of Job, who blamed the patient's sickness on his sin.

Ps. 7 A lament and psalm of refuge by an innocent person beset by enemies. As one falsely accused of murder could find sanctuary in the house of God and appeal his case to God's judgment, so the psalmist commits his case to God. His protestations of innocence refer to specific charges and are not a claim to be sinless. See Ps. 11; 17; 26; 27; 31; 71.

7:2 like a lion. Though not found in Israel today, lions were plentiful there in ancient times. The lion often symbolized power, cruelty, and ruthlessness (Is. 5:29; Nah. 2:11, 12).

7:5 let the enemy. He is not afraid to invoke a curse on himself, since he knows he is innocent.

7:6 Arise. See 3:7 note.

7 Let the assembly of the peoples be
gathered about you;
over it return on high.

8 The LORD [y]judges the peoples;
[z]judge me, O LORD, according to
my righteousness
and according to the integrity that
is in me.
9 Oh, let the evil of the wicked come
to an end,
and may you establish the
righteous—
you who [a]test [b]the minds and
hearts,[1]
O righteous God!
10 My shield is [c]with God,
who saves [d]the upright in heart.
11 God is [e]a righteous judge,
and a God who feels [f]indignation
every day.

12 If a man[2] does not repent, God[3] will
[g]whet his sword;
he has [h]bent and [i]readied
his bow;
13 he has prepared for him his deadly
weapons,
making his [j]arrows [k]fiery shafts.
14 Behold, the wicked man [l]conceives
evil
and is [l]pregnant with mischief
and gives birth to lies.
15 He makes [m]a pit, digging it out,
and falls into the hole that he has
made.
16 His [n]mischief returns upon his own
head,
and on his own skull his violence
descends.

8 [y]See Ps. 58:11 [z]Ps. 26:1; 35:24; 43:1; [Ps. 18:20]
9 [a]Ps. 11:5; Job 23:10; [Ps. 139:1; 1 Sam. 16:7; 1 Chr. 28:9] [b]Ps. 26:2; Jer. 11:20; 17:10; 20:12 Rev. 2:23
10 [c][Ps. 62:8] [d]2 Chr. 29:34
11 [e][Job 8:3] [f]Nah. 1:2, 6
12 [g]Deut. 32:41 [h]Ps. 11:2; 37:14 [i]Ps. 21:12
13 [j]See Ps. 18:14 [k][Eph. 6:16]
14 [l]Job 15:35; Isai. 59:4; [Isai. 33:11; James 1:15]
15 [m]Ps. 9:15; 57:6; 119:85; Prov. 26:27; 28:10; Eccles. 10:8
16 [n][Ps. 94:23; 141:10; Judg. 9:24; 1 Kin. 2:32; Esth. 7:10; 9:25; Prov. 5:22]
17 [o]Ps. 9:2
Psalm 8
[p]Ps. 81, title; 84, title
1 [q]Ps. 148:13; Isai. 12:4; [Ex. 34:5] [r]Ps. 113:4
2 [s]Cited Matt. 21:16; [Matt. 11:25; 1 Cor. 1:27] [t]Jer. 16:19 [u]Ps. 44:16
3 [v][Ps. 111:2] [w]Ex. 8:19; 31:18 [x]Gen. 1:16

17 I will give to the LORD the thanks due
to his righteousness,
and I will [o]sing praise to the name
of the LORD, the Most High.

How Majestic Is Your Name

8 TO THE CHOIRMASTER: ACCORDING TO THE [p]GITTITH.[4] A PSALM OF DAVID.

1 O LORD, our Lord,
how majestic is your [q]name in all
the earth!
You have set your [r]glory above the
heavens.
2 [s]Out of the mouth of babes and
infants,
you have established [t]strength
because of your foes,
to still [u]the enemy and the avenger.

3 When I [v]look at your heavens, the
work of your [w]fingers,
the moon and the stars, [x]which
you have set in place,
4 [y]what is man that you are [z]mindful of
him,
and [a]the son of man that you [b]care
for him?

5 Yet you have made him a little lower
than [c]the heavenly beings[5]
and crowned him with [d]glory and
honor.
6 You have given him [e]dominion over
the works of your hands;
[f]you have put all things under his
feet,

4 [y]Cited Heb. 2:6-8; [Ps. 144:3; Job 7:17; 25:6] [z][Gen. 8:1] [a]Ps. 80:17 [b]Ps. 65:9; Gen. 21:1; 50:24 **5** [c][Gen. 1:26] [d]Ps. 21:5 **6** [e]Gen. 1:26, 28 [f]Cited 1 Cor. 15:27; [Matt. 28:18]

1 Hebrew *the hearts and kidneys* 2 Hebrew *he* 3 Hebrew *he*
4 Probably a musical or liturgical term 5 Or *than God*; Septuagint *than the angels*

7:8 judge. There is a judicial setting in this psalm of refuge. God must judge between the psalmist and his opponents.

7:14, 15 conceives evil . . . makes a pit. These terms express the conviction that a sinner reaps what he sows. Sin brings its own retribution.

Ps. 8 The subject of this hymn is the excellence of God in His works of creation, a major theme of the wisdom literature. The psalm can be called a wisdom poem. It ponders God's exaltation of lowly humanity in giving them dominion over creation (Gen. 1:28).

8:1 LORD. The personal, or covenantal, name of God revealed to Moses at the burning bush (Ex. 3).

our Lord. A title, which can also be translated "governor" or "master." He is *our* Lord because He has established His covenant with His people.

how majestic is your name. The repetition of this line at the end enhances the high note of reverence that pervades the psalm. "Name" signifies the character or reputation of God.

8:2 babes . . . foes. Note the contrast between the weak and the strong. However, because of God whose praise they sing, the weak silence the powerful. See Matt. 21:16.

8:3 the work of your fingers. The almost limitless universe is described as the work of God's fingers, emphasizing the power of God.

8:4–6 This passage is applied to Jesus in Heb. 2:6–8. He was perfect Man as well as God. Jesus is the model of redeemed humanity and restored human dominion over creation (Gen. 1:28). See also 1 Cor. 15:27 and Eph. 1:22.

8:4 what is man. See Job 7:17; 25:6; Ps. 144:3. In the vastness of the universe and against the greatness of God's power, man is little.

8:5 heavenly beings. The Hebrew word *'elohim,* here translated "heavenly beings," usually means "God," but it can mean "divine beings" (see text note). If God were in view one would have expected, "You have made him a little lower than Yourself."

8:6 dominion. The "cultural mandate" of Gen. 1:28 divinely confers on humanity the authority and responsibility for governing earthly life.

7 all sheep and oxen,
and also the beasts of the field,
8 the birds of the heavens, and the fish
of the sea,
whatever passes along the paths of
the seas.

9 O LORD, our Lord,
how majestic is your name in all
the earth!

I Will Recount Your Wonderful Deeds

9 [1] TO THE CHOIRMASTER: ACCORDING TO MUTH-LABBEN.[2] A PSALM OF DAVID.

1 I will give thanks to the LORD with
my whole heart;
I will recount all of your
[g]wonderful deeds.
2 I will be glad and [h]exult in you;
I will [i]sing praise to your name,
[j]O Most High.

3 When my enemies turn back,
they stumble and perish before[3]
your presence.
4 For you have [k]maintained my just
cause;
you have [l]sat on the throne, giving
righteous judgment.

5 You have [m]rebuked the nations; you
have made the wicked perish;
you have [n]blotted out their name
forever and ever.
6 The enemy came to an end in
everlasting ruins;
their cities you rooted out;
the very memory of them has
perished.

7 But the LORD sits enthroned
forever;
he has established his throne for
justice,
8 and he [o]judges the world with
righteousness;
he [p]judges the peoples with
uprightness.

9 The LORD is [q]a stronghold for [r]the
oppressed,
a stronghold in [s]times of trouble.
10 And those who [t]know your name put
their trust in you,
for you, O LORD, have not forsaken
those who seek you.

11 Sing praises to the LORD, who [u]sits
enthroned in Zion!
Tell among the peoples his
[v]deeds!
12 For he who [w]avenges blood is
mindful of them;
he [x]does not forget the cry of the
afflicted.

13 [y]Be gracious to me, O LORD!
See my affliction from those who
hate me,
O you who lift me up from [z]the
gates of death,
14 that I may recount all your praises,
that in the gates of [a]the daughter
of Zion
I may [b]rejoice in your salvation.

15 The nations have sunk in [c]the pit
that they made;
in [d]the net that they hid their own
foot has been caught.
16 The LORD has made himself [e]known;
he has executed judgment;
the wicked are snared in the work
of their own hands.
Higgaion.[4] *Selah*

Psalm 9
1 [g]Ps. 26:7; 40:5; 96:3; 105:5
2 [h]Ps. 5:11 [i]Ps. 7:17 [j]See Ps. 83:18
4 [k]Ps. 140:12 [l]Ps. 29:10
5 [m]Ps. 68:30 [n]Deut. 9:14; 29:20; [Prov. 10:7]
8 [o]Ps. 58:11; 96:13; 98:9 [p]Ps. 96:10
9 [q]2 Sam. 22:3; [Prov. 18:10] [r]Ps. 10:18; 74:21 [s]Ps. 10:1
10 [t]Ps. 91:14
11 [u]Ps. 76:2 [v]Ps. 77:12; [Ps. 107:22]
12 [w]Gen. 9:5; [Ps. 10:13]; See 1 Kin. 21:17-19 [x]ver. 18; Ps. 10:12; [Ps. 12:5]
13 [y]Ps. 4:1 [z]See Job 38:17
14 [a]2 Kin. 19:21; Isai. 37:22 [b]Ps. 13:5; 20:5; 21:1; 35:9; 1 Sam. 2:1
15 [c]See Ps. 7:15 [d]See Job 18:8
16 [e]Ex. 7:5; 14:4
17 [f][Gen.

1 Psalms 9 and 10 together follow an acrostic pattern, each stanza beginning with the successive letters of the Hebrew alphabet. In the Septuagint they form one psalm 2 Probably a musical or liturgical term 3 Or *because of* 4 Probably a musical or liturgical term

Ps. 9 This lament begins like a thanksgiving, but in v. 13 the psalmist turns to the Lord with new petitions, and the psalm concludes on this note. Probably Ps. 9 and 10 were originally a single psalm. Together they form a single acrostic (see Introduction to Hebrew Poetry).

9:1 wonderful deeds. The Hebrew word refers to the great acts of God, His intervention in human affairs, as at the Exodus from Egypt.

9:3 When my enemies turn back. This is a statement of future hope, not past reality.

9:4 throne, giving righteous judgment. The psalmist is not confident in himself, but in God's character as the righteous Judge.

9:5 blotted out their name. To be remembered no more, contrasted with God's name (v. 2), which will be praised forever.

9:11 enthroned in Zion. See 2:6 note. The afflicted should know that God is present with them in the world.

9:12 avenges blood. Lit. "seeks blood." God does not let wickedness go unpunished (Gen. 9:6; Nah. 1:2–6).

9:13 gates of death. See Prov. 1:12 note. This verse is the first sign of the psalmist's present distress.

9:14 the gates of the daughter of Zion. Contrasted with "gates of death" in the previous verse. The psalmist will praise God for answered prayer in the most public places in Jerusalem, the "daughter of Zion."

9:15 have sunk in the pit that they made. See Ps. 7:14–16. The wickedness of such enemies will come back to haunt them.

17 The wicked shall [f]return to Sheol,
all the nations that [g]forget God.
18 For the needy shall not always be forgotten,
and [h]the hope of the poor shall not perish forever.
19 [i]Arise, O LORD! Let not [j]man prevail;
let the nations be judged before you!
20 Put them in fear, O LORD!
Let the nations know that they are but [j]men! *Selah*

Why Do You Hide Yourself?

10 Why, O LORD, do you stand [k]afar off?
Why [l]do you hide yourself in [m]times of trouble?
2 In arrogance the wicked hotly pursue the poor;
let them [n]be caught in the schemes that they have devised.
3 For the wicked [o]boasts of the desires of his soul,
and the one greedy for gain [p]curses[1] and [q]renounces the LORD.
4 In the pride of his face[2] the wicked does not [q]seek him;[3]
all his thoughts are, [r]"There is no God."
5 His ways prosper at all times;
your judgments are on high, [s]out of his sight;
as for all his foes, he [t]puffs at them.
6 He [u]says in his heart, "I shall not be moved;
throughout all generations I [v]shall not meet adversity."
7 [w]His mouth is filled with cursing and [x]deceit and [y]oppression;
[z]under his tongue are [a]mischief and [b]iniquity.
8 He sits in ambush in the villages;
in [c]hiding places he murders the innocent.
His eyes stealthily watch for the helpless;
9 he lurks in ambush like [d]a lion in his [e]thicket;
he [f]lurks that he may seize the poor;
he seizes the poor when he draws him into his [g]net.
10 The helpless are crushed, sink down,
and fall by his might.
11 He says in his heart, "God has forgotten,
he has [h]hidden his face, he [i]will never see it."
12 [j]Arise, O LORD; O God, [k]lift up your hand;
[l]forget not the afflicted.
13 Why does the wicked [m]renounce God
and say in his heart, "You will not [n]call to account"?

[1] Or *he blesses the one greedy for gain* [2] Or *of his anger* [3] Or *the wicked says, "He will not call to account"*

3:19] [g]Ps. 50:22; Job 8:13; Isai. 51:13
18 [h][Prov. 23:18; 24:14]
19 [i]See Ps. 3:7 [j][Ps. 10:18]
20 [j][See ver. 19 above]
Psalm 10
1 [k]Ps. 22:1, 11, 19; 35:22; 38:21 [l]Ps. 13:1 [m]Ps. 9:9
2 [n][Ps. 7:15, 16]
3 [o]Ps. 94:4; [Isai. 3:9] [p]ver. 13 [q]Job 1:5, 11
4 [q][See ver. 3 above] [r]Ps. 14:1; 53:1
5 [s][Isai. 26:11] [t]Ps. 12:5
6 [u]ver. 11, 13 [v][Rev. 18:7]
7 [w]Cited Rom. 3:14 [x]Ps. 36:3 [y]Ps. 55:11; 72:14 [z]Job 20:12; [Ps. 140:3; S. of S. 4, 11] [a]Ps. 7:14 [b]Ps. 5:5; 6:8
8 [c]Ps. 17:12; 64:4; [Hab. 3:14]
9 [d]Ps. 17:12 [e]Job 38:40 [f]Ps. 59:3; Mic. 7:2 [g]Ps. 9:15
11 [h][Ps. 73:11]; Job 22:13 [i]Ps. 94:7; Ezek. 8:12; 9:9; [Zeph. 1:12]
12 [j]See Ps. 3:7 [k]Mic. 5:9 [l]Ps. 9:12, 18
13 [m]ver. 3 [n]Ps. 9:12
14 [o]Ps. 33:13

9:17 wicked. Further defined in the second half of the verse as "all the nations that forget God."

Sheol. See Prov. 1:12 note.

9:18 the needy . . . the poor. The phrase "the poor and needy" (35:10; 74:21; Prov. 31:9; Ezek. 18:12) is a fixed expression in the Old Testament, and the words also appear frequently in parallel (72:12; Job 24:4; Is. 32:7; Amos 8:4). The meaning is frequently literal poverty, but the words may also be used figuratively to express total dependence on God (40:17; 86:1; 109:22; also Matt. 5:3 and Luke 6:20). Poverty is not itself meritorious, but God gives special attention to the cries of the oppressed (12:5; 72:4 note). Jeremiah equates bringing "justice and righteousness" to the "poor and needy" with knowing God (Jer. 22:15, 16). This was an explicit responsibility of those in power.

9:19 Arise. See Ps. 3:7 note.

Ps. 10 This psalm has no title. In its original form, it was likely combined with Ps. 9 (see above on Ps. 9). Taken separately the psalm would be an individual lament, bemoaning the wicked who victimize the righteous and calling on God to restore justice.

10:1 Why . . . do you stand afar off. The psalmist is more troubled by the apparent absence of God than by the presence of enemies.

10:3 boasts . . . renounces. The wicked person's ethical judgments are upside-down. He should bless the Lord and reject the greedy.

10:5 prosper at all times. From the perspective of the oppressed, it appears that the oppressor has no troubles (Ps. 73:12).

10:6 I shall not be moved. This attitude of self-trust brought trouble to the psalmist himself (Ps. 30:6). Confidence must be in God, not in one's own ability.

10:7 mouth . . . tongue. Sins of speech are the focus of attention. Rom. 3:14 alludes to this verse.

10:8 sits in ambush. The metaphor of the wicked in ambush is well known from Proverbs (Prov. 1:11).

stealthily. The wicked prefer to work in darkness, not in the light (John 3:19).

10:9 into his net. The wicked is a hunter of the helpless.

10:12 Arise, O LORD. See note 3:7.

lift up your hand. The metaphor refers to God's active intervention on behalf of the psalmist.

14 But you do see, for you [o]note
mischief and vexation,
that you may take it into your
hands;
to you the helpless [p]commits
himself;
you have been [q]the helper of the
fatherless.
15 [r]Break the arm of the wicked and
evildoer;
[s]call his wickedness to account till
you find none.
16 [t]The LORD is king forever and ever;
the [u]nations perish from his land.
17 O LORD, you hear the desire of the
afflicted;
you will [v]strengthen their heart;
you will incline your ear
18 to [w]do justice to the fatherless and
[x]the oppressed,
so that [y]man who is of the earth
may strike terror no more.

The LORD Is in His Holy Temple

11 TO THE CHOIRMASTER. OF DAVID.
In the LORD I take refuge;
how can you say to my soul,
[z]"Flee like a bird to your mountain,
2 for behold, the wicked [a]bend the
bow;
[b]they have fitted their arrow to the
string
to shoot in the dark at the upright
in heart;
3 if [c]the foundations are destroyed,
what can the righteous do?"[1]
4 [d]The LORD is in his holy temple;
the LORD's [e]throne is in heaven;
his eyes see, his eyelids [f]test, the
children of man.
5 The LORD [g]tests the righteous,
but [h]his soul hates the wicked and
the one who loves violence.
6 Let him rain coals on the wicked;
[i]fire and sulfur and a scorching
wind shall be [j]the portion of
their cup.
7 For the LORD is righteous;
he [k]loves righteous deeds;
[l]the upright shall behold his face.

The Faithful Have Vanished

12 TO THE CHOIRMASTER: ACCORDING TO
THE SHEMINITH.[2] A PSALM OF DAVID.
1 Save, O LORD, for [m]the godly one is
gone;
for the faithful have vanished from
among the children of man.
2 Everyone [n]utters lies to his neighbor;
with [o]flattering lips and [p]a double
heart they speak.
3 May the LORD cut off all [o]flattering lips,
the tongue that makes [q]great boasts,
4 those who say, "With our tongue we
will prevail,
our lips are with us; who is master
over us?"

[p]2 Tim. 1:12; 1 Pet. 4:19 [q]Ps. 68:5; 146:9; Hos. 14:3
15 [r]See Ps. 37:17 [s][Ps. 37:36; Isai. 41:12]
16 [t]Ps. 29:10; Ex. 15:18; Jer. 10:10; Lam. 5:19; Dan. 4:34; 6:26; 1 Tim. 1:17; Rev. 11:15 [u]Deut. 8:20
17 [v]1 Chr. 29:18
18 [w]Ps. 82:3; [Isai. 1:17; 11:4] [x]Ps. 9:9; 74:21 [y]Ps. 9:19, 20; 17:14
Psalm 11
1 [z][1 Sam. 23:14, 19; 24:2; 26:19, 20]
2 [a]Ps. 7:12; 64:4; [Jer. 9:3] [b]Ps. 21:12; 58:7; See Ps. 7:10
3 [c]Ps. 82:5; Ezek. 30:4
4 [d]Ps. 18:6; Hab. 2:20; Mic. 1:2 [e]Ps. 2:4; Isai. 66:1; Matt. 5:34; 23:22; Acts 7:49 [f]See Job 23:10
5 [g]Gen. 22:1; James 1:12 [h]Ps. 5:5
6 [i]Gen. 19:24; Job 18:15; Ezek. 38:22 [j]Ps. 75:8; [Job 21:20]
7 [k]See Ps. 33:5 [l][Ps. 17:15; 140:13; 1 John 3:2; Rev. 22:4]
Psalm 12 **1** [m]Isai. 57:1; Mic. 7:2 **2** [n]Ps. 41:6; 144:8 [o]Ps. 5:9; Jer. 9:8; Rom. 16:18 [p]1 Chr. 12:33; James 1:8 **3** [o][See ver. 2 above] [q]Dan. 7:8; Rev. 13:5; [Ps. 17:10]

1 *Or for the foundations will be destroyed; what has the righteous done?*
2 Probably a musical or liturgical term

10:14 fatherless. In the ancient Near East the fatherless and the widow were extreme examples of helplessness, since they had no kinship protection.

10:16 king. God is covenant LORD; see Introduction: Characteristics and Themes.

nations. Those who worship other gods and persecute God's people.

10:17, 18 justice to the fatherless. The lament concludes with a strong statement of trust in God, who delivers the weak from oppression. Men terrify, but God overrules the wickedness in men.

Ps. 11 Another psalm of refuge. Threatened by his enemies, the psalmist puts his confidence in God.

11:1 to your mountain. Possibly, "from your mountain." If it is "to your mountain," then the advice is to flee the city for a mountain fortress. If it is "from your mountain," the reference is to Zion. In either case David is being advised by others to find salvation elsewhere than in God.

11:2 bow . . . arrow. While the psalm may have had an original military setting, and would find an appropriate use during periods of war, the image could also refer to other types of affliction as well.

11:3 foundations. That is, of the kingdom conceived as a political entity; including its economy, military, and the like.

righteous. Or perhaps this is a reference to God: "Righteous One." The next few verses go on to describe what God is doing.

11:4 throne. As King of the universe, God is in control. Nothing escapes His notice. Not even the actions of the wicked are beyond His purview.

11:6 fire and sulfur. Reminiscent of the judgment on Sodom and Gomorrah (Gen. 19:24). Evil will be completely burned up.

the portion of their cup. There is a cup of God's blessing (Ps. 23:5) as well as a cup of His wrath. The wicked will drink wrath to its dregs (75:8). Jesus Christ took His people's punishment upon Himself by drinking the cup of God's judgment.

11:7 his face. God will make His presence known to His people in the darkness. In the resurrection of the just this hope will be realized.

12:1 the godly one is gone. Like Elijah in 1 Kin. 19:14, the psalmist feels alone in his devotion to the Lord.

12:2 Everyone utters lies. Lit. "they speak lies," or "emptiness," including outright falsehoods, but also insincere and irresponsible talk, which cheapens and corrodes all human communication.

12:3 cut off. To be "cut off" usually means to be excluded from the community, but occasionally may mean death.

5 “Because [r]the poor are plundered,
because the needy groan,
[s]I will now arise,” says the LORD;
“I will place him in the safety for which he [t]longs.”
6 [u]The words of the LORD are pure words,
like silver [u]refined in a furnace on the ground,
purified seven times.
7 You, O LORD, will keep them;
you will guard us[1] from this generation forever.
8 On every side the wicked prowl,
as vileness is exalted among the children of man.

How Long, O LORD?

13 TO THE CHOIRMASTER. A PSALM OF DAVID.

1 [v]How long, O LORD? Will you [w]forget me forever?
How long will you [x]hide your face from me?
2 How long must I take [y]counsel in my soul
and have sorrow in my heart all the day?
How long shall my enemy be exalted over me?
3 [z]Consider and answer me, O LORD my God;
[a]light up my eyes, lest [b]I sleep the sleep of death,
4 [c]lest my enemy say, “I have prevailed over him,”
lest my foes rejoice because I am [d]shaken.
5 But I have [e]trusted in your steadfast love;
my heart shall [f]rejoice in your salvation.
6 I will sing to the LORD,
because he has dealt bountifully with me.

The Fool Says, There Is No God

14 TO THE CHOIRMASTER. OF DAVID.
[g]The [h]fool says in his heart,
[i]“There is no God.”
They are [j]corrupt, they do abominable deeds,
[k]there is none who does good.
2 The LORD [l]looks down from heaven on the children of man,
to see if there are any who understand,[2]
who [m]seek after God.
3 They have all turned aside; together they have become [n]corrupt;
there is none who does good,
not even one.
4 Have they no [o]knowledge, all the evildoers
who [p]eat up my people as they eat bread
and [q]do not call upon the LORD?
5 There they are in great terror,
for God is with [r]the generation of the righteous.
6 You would shame the plans of the poor,
but[3] the LORD is his [s]refuge.

5 [r]Ps. 9:12 [s]Isai. 33:10; [Ps. 82:8] [t]Ps. 10:5
6 [u]Ps. 18:30; 119:140; Prov. 30:5; [Ps. 19:8]
Psalm 13
1 [v]Ps. 79:5; 89:46; [Rev. 6:10] [w]Ps. 10:12; 44:24; 74:19, 23; Lam. 5:20 [x]See Job 13:24
2 [y][Ps. 77:6]
3 [z]Ps. 5:1; 119:153 [a]Ps. 19:8; Ezra 9:8; Prov. 29:13; Eph. 1:18; [1 Sam. 14:27] [b][Jer. 51:39]
4 [c]Deut. 32:27 [d]See Ps. 10:6
5 [e]See Ps. 11:1 [f]See Ps. 9:14
Psalm 14
1 [g]For ver. 1-7, see Ps. 53:1-6 [h]Ps. 74:18, 22; Job 2:10 [i]Ps. 10:4 [j]Gen. 6:5, 11, 12 [k]Cited Rom. 3:10-12
2 [l]Ps. 102:19; [Ps. 11:4] [m]2 Chr. 15:2; 19:3
3 [n]Job 15:16
4 [o]Ps. 82:5; [Isai. 1:3; Jer. 4:22] [p]Prov. 30:14; Jer. 10:25; Hos. 7:7; [Ps. 27:2; Amos 8:4; Mic. 3:3] [q]Ps. 79:6; Jer. 10:25; Hos. 7:7; [Isai. 64:7]
5 [r]Ps. 24:6; 73:15
6 [s]Ps. 46:1; 61:3; 62:7, 8; 91:2; 142:5

1 Or *guard him* 2 Or *that act wisely* 3 Or *for*

12:5 arise. See Ps. 3:7 note.

Ps. 13 A lament expressed from the perspective of an individual. The situation of distress is not clearly defined, allowing multiple applications. If “enemy” is taken literally, warfare is in view. Or the psalmist may be ill and near death (v. 3).

13:1 How long. See note Ps. 6:3. The fourfold repetition expresses his anguish.

13:5 steadfast love. A covenant term, specifically, gracious devotion, the love by which God has bound Himself to His people.

shall rejoice. Contrast v. 4. The enemy rejoices in the fall (death) of the psalmist; God, in his salvation.

Ps. 14 This psalm has an attitude of quiet meditation while focusing on human evil. See Ps. 53, which has a similar opening.

14:1 fool. The fool may be highly intelligent by the world’s standards, but is oblivious to the true nature of reality (Eccl. 2:14). To be called a fool is a moral judgment.

There is no God. The fool denies the existence of God as a matter of human concern. This is practical atheism. God is held to be unconcerned about the affairs of the world and especially the affairs of the individual. See “Mankind’s Guilty Knowledge of God” at Rom. 1:19.

corrupt. Note the use of this psalm by Paul in Rom. 3:10–18. Foolishness points to lack of morality, not absence of native intellect.

14:2 who seek after God. Fallen man does not actively seek God.

14:4 as they eat bread. The wicked exploit people frequently and without feeling guilt. It is as natural to them as eating bread.

14:6 his refuge. God can overrule the wicked plans of evildoers for the good of the afflicted. This principle is stated by Joseph (Gen. 50:20), and is applied to the Crucifixion in Acts 2:22–24.

7 Oh, that salvation for Israel would
come out of Zion!
When the LORD [t]restores the
fortunes of his people,
let Jacob rejoice, let Israel be glad.

Who Shall Dwell on Your Holy Hill?

15 A PSALM OF DAVID.
O LORD, [u]who shall sojourn in
your [v]tent?
Who shall dwell on your [w]holy hill?

2 He who [x]walks blamelessly and [y]does
what is right
and [z]speaks truth in his heart;
3 who [a]does not slander with his tongue
and does no evil to his neighbor,
nor [b]takes up a reproach against
his friend;
4 [c]in whose eyes a vile person is despised,
but who honors those who fear the
LORD;
who [d]swears to his own hurt and
does not change;
5 who [e]does not put out his money at
interest
and [f]does not take a bribe against
the innocent.
He who does these things shall never
be [g]moved.

You Will Not Abandon My Soul

16 A [h]MIKTAM[1] OF DAVID.
Preserve me, O God, for in you I
[i]take refuge.
2 I say to the LORD, "You are my Lord;
[j]I have no good apart from you."

3 As for [k]the saints in the land, they
are the excellent ones,
in whom is all my delight.[2]
4 The sorrows of those who run after[3]
another god shall multiply;
their drink offerings of blood I will
not pour out
or [l]take their names on my lips.
5 The LORD is [m]my chosen portion and
my [n]cup;
you hold my [o]lot.
6 [p]The lines have fallen for me in
pleasant places;
indeed, I have a beautiful
inheritance.
7 I bless the LORD who [q]gives me counsel;
in [r]the night also my [s]heart
instructs me.[4]
8 [t]I have [u]set the LORD always before me;
because he is at my [v]right hand, I
shall not be [w]shaken.
9 Therefore my heart is glad, and my
[x]whole being[5] rejoices;
my flesh also dwells secure.
10 For you will not abandon my soul to
[y]Sheol,
[z]or let your [a]holy one see
[b]corruption.[6]

7 [t]Ps. 85:1; 126:1; Job 42:10; Jer. 30:18; Ezek. 16:53; 39:25; Hos. 6:11; Joel 3:1
Psalm 15
1 [u]For ver. 1-5, see Ps. 24:3-5; Isai. 33:14-16 [v]Ps. 61:4 [w]See Ps. 2:6
2 [x]Prov. 28:18 [y]Ps. 106:3; [Matt. 6:1] [z]Zech. 8:16; Eph. 4:25; [John 1:47; Col. 3:9]
3 [a]Lev. 19:16; [Ps. 34:13] [b]Ex. 23:1
4 [c][Esth. 3:2] [d][Judg. 11:35]
5 [e]Ex. 22:25; Lev. 25:36; Deut. 23:19; Ezek. 18:8; 22:12 [f]Ex. 23:8; Deut. 16:19 [g]See Ps. 10:6
Psalm 16
[h][Ps. 56, title; 57, title; 60, title]
1 [i]See Ps. 11:1
2 [j][Ps. 73:25]
3 [k][Ex. 19:6; Deut. 7:6; 1 Pet. 2:9]
4 [l]Ex. 23:13; Josh. 23:7
5 [m]Ps. 73:26; 119:57; 142:5 Num. 18:20; Lam. 3:24; [Deut. 32:9; Jer. 10:16; 51:19] [n]Ps. 23:5; 116:13 [o]Ps. 125:3
6 [p]Mic. 2:5

7 [q]See 1 Sam. 23:9-12; 2 Sam. 5:18, 19 [r]Ps. 17:3; See Ps. 42:8 [s]Ps. 7:9 8 [t]Cited Acts 2:25-28 [u]Ps. 119:30 [v]Ps. 109:31; 110:5; 121:5 [w]Ps. 10:6; 15:5 9 [x]Ps. 30:12; 57:8; 108:1; Gen. 49:6 10 [y]See Job 21:13 [z]Cited Acts 13:35 [a]Ps. 89:18; [Mark 1:24] [b]Ps. 49:9; 103:4

1 Probably a musical or liturgical term 2 Or *To the saints in the land, the excellent in whom is all my delight, I say:* 3 Or *who acquire* 4 Hebrew *my kidneys instruct me* 5 Hebrew *my glory* 6 Or *see the pit*

14:7 out of Zion. The place where God most personally and directly revealed His presence.

Ps. 15 This psalm, reminiscent of Ps. 1, focuses on the requirements for approaching God's presence at the sanctuary. It is similar to Ps. 24:3–6. The two passages (cf. also Is. 33:14–16) have been called "entrance liturgies," since they answer the question, "Who can enter the holy place of God?"

15:1 tent. Before the temple was built, the symbol of God's dwelling with His people was a tent.

holy hill. Mount Zion, where the temple was located.

15:2–5 The ten requirements for entrance are ethical, not formal or liturgical.

15:4 to his own hurt. Alternatively, "and does not falter." The point is the same: when he promises, the righteous person fulfills his word.

15:5 not . . . at interest. See Deut. 23:19, 20. A foreigner could be charged interest, but not a fellow Israelite. Loans were intended to relieve extreme need, and such interest was a form of exploitation.

Ps. 16 This psalm expresses confidence in the Lord, though it is difficult to tell whether the crisis is past or present to the psalmist. Death may be imminent for him (v. 10).

16:1 An invocation of the Lord and a plea for help. This line indicates that the crisis is still present to the psalmist.

16:3 saints. Lit. "those who are set apart," God's elect people.

16:4 another god. The danger of worshiping other gods was always present in Israel (cf. 1 Kin. 18). The psalms emphasize that the powers and epithets ascribed to the pagan gods really belong to Yahweh (Ps. 29).

offerings of blood . . . names. That is, of foreign gods. These are two examples of ways that the religious systems of the surrounding nations tried to compel their gods to help them.

16:5 portion . . . cup . . . lot. Three metaphors that describe life as a gift of God.

16:6 lines. Once again, probably metaphoric for the psalmist's quality of life. Not only is the life that God has given him secure (v. 5), it is also "pleasant."

16:7 heart. Lit. "kidneys" (text note). Like "heart," it stands for the core of a person's being.

16:10 you will not abandon my soul to Sheol. The immediate application of this psalm is to David and to the Old Testament saints. It refers to deliverance from the immediate threat of death, but it points prophetically to the Son of David whom the historical David reflected and anticipated. Both Peter and Paul recognized that Jesus was the ultimate fulfillment of this psalm (Acts 2:25–28; 13:35).

11 You make known to me [c]the path of
life;
in your presence there is [d]fullness
of joy;
at your right hand are [e]pleasures
forevermore.

In the Shadow of Your Wings

17 A [f]Prayer of David.
Hear a just cause, O Lord;
[g]attend to my cry!
Give ear to my prayer from lips
free of deceit!
2 From your presence [h]let my
vindication come!
Let your eyes behold the right!
3 You have [i]tried my heart, you have
[j]visited me by [k]night,
you have [l]tested me, and you will
find nothing;
I have purposed that my mouth
will not transgress.
4 With regard to the works of man, by
the word of your lips
I have avoided the ways of the
violent.
5 My steps have [m]held fast to your
paths;
my feet have not slipped.
6 I [n]call upon you, for you will answer
me, O God;
[o]incline your ear to me; hear my
words.
7 [p]Wondrously show[1] your steadfast
love,
O Savior of those who seek
refuge
from [q]their adversaries at your
right hand.
8 Keep me as [r]the apple of
your eye;
hide me in [s]the shadow of your
wings,
9 from the wicked who do me
violence,
my deadly enemies who
[t]surround me.
10 They close their [u]hearts to pity;
with their mouths they [v]speak
arrogantly.
11 They have now surrounded our
[w]steps;
they set their eyes to [x]cast us to
the ground.
12 He is like a lion eager to tear,
as a young lion [y]lurking in
ambush.
13 Arise, O Lord! Confront him,
subdue him!
Deliver my soul from the wicked
by your sword,
14 from men by your hand,
O Lord,
from [z]men of the world whose
[a]portion is in this life.[2]
You fill their womb with
treasure;[3]
they are satisfied with
[b]children,
and they leave their abundance to
their infants.
15 As for me, I shall [c]behold your face
in righteousness;
when I [d]awake, I shall be [e]satisfied
with your likeness.

11 [c]Matt. 7:14 [d]Ps. 17:15; 21:6; 36:8; 65:4 [e]Ps. 36:8
Psalm 17
[f][Ps. 86, title; Ps. 142, title]
1 [g]Ps. 142:6; [Ps. 61:1; Jer. 7:16]
2 [h][Ps. 26:1]
3 [i]See Job 23:10 [j]Job 31:14 [k]Ps. 16:7; [Job 33:15] [l]Judg. 7:4; Zech. 13:9; 1 Pet. 1:7; [Ps. 139:1; Mal. 3:2, 3]
5 [m]Job 23:11; [Ps. 44:18]
6 [n]Ps. 86:6, 7; 116:1, 2 [o]See Ps. 31:2
7 [p]Ps. 31:21 [q]Ps. 44:5; 59:1; 139:21
8 [r]Deut. 32:10; Zech. 2:8 [s]Ps. 36:7; 57:1; 63:7; 91:4; [Matt. 23:37; Luke 13:34]; See Ruth 2:12
9 [t][1 Sam. 23:26]
10 [u]Ps. 73:7; 119:70; Job 15:27; Isai. 6:10; [Deut. 32:15] [v]Ps. 31:18; 1 Sam. 2:3
11 [w][Ps. 89:51] [x]Ps. 62:4
12 [y][Ps. 10:8, 9]
14 [z][Ps. 10:18; Luke 16:8; 20:34] [a]Matt. 6:2, 5, 16; Luke 16:25 [b][Job 21:11]
15 [c]Job 33:26; 1 John 3:2; [Ps. 11:7] [d]Isai. 26:19; Dan. 12:2 [e][Ps. 16:11]

1 Or *Distinguish me by* 2 Or *from men whose portion in life is of the world* 3 Or *As for your treasured ones, you fill their womb*

Ps. 17 A psalm of refuge whose title is "Prayer." The Book of Psalms is a prayer book as well as a collection of hymns.

17:1 my prayer. The psalmist is not denying that he is a sinner. He is denying specific charges made against him.

17:2 vindication. Lit. "judgment." The psalmist appeals his case to God.

17:3 tried my heart. Here, the "heart" is the hidden center of a person's being, but God can read the heart.

17:4 word of your lips. God's will, disclosed in the law of God.

17:5 your paths. These ways, as spelled out in God's Word, are to be contrasted with the "ways of the violent" (v. 4).

17:7 steadfast love. The Hebrew word denotes God's love toward those with whom He is in covenant relationship.

Savior. The psalmist could look back over the history of Israel and see how many times God saved His people in distress. The Exodus from Egypt is the prime example of God's saving love.

17:8 apple. The pupil, one of the most sensitive parts of the body (Deut. 32:10).

17:10 their hearts. An alternative translation is "their fat," a caricature of their physical appearance.

17:11 surrounded our steps. The enemy has taken the initiative to destroy the psalmist.

17:12 lion. Commonly known for its ruthlessness and cruelty. Cf. Ps. 7:2; 10:9; 22:13.

17:13 Arise. Ps. 3:7 note.

17:14 You fill their womb. This verse expresses the general truth that the righteous will not want.

17:15 shall behold your face. The psalmist will know God's presence, hinting at his resurrection in the "likeness" of God (1 John 3:2).

The LORD Is My Rock and My Fortress

18 TO THE CHOIRMASTER. A PSALM OF DAVID, [f]THE SERVANT OF THE LORD, [g]WHO ADDRESSED THE WORDS OF THIS [h]SONG TO THE LORD ON THE DAY WHEN THE LORD RESCUED HIM FROM THE HAND OF ALL HIS ENEMIES, AND FROM THE HAND OF SAUL. HE SAID:

1 I love you, O LORD, my strength.
2 The LORD is my [i]rock and my
[j]fortress and my deliverer,
my God, my [i]rock, in [k]whom I
take refuge,
my [l]shield, and [m]the horn of my
salvation, my [n]stronghold.
3 I call upon the LORD, who is [o]worthy
to be praised,
and I am saved from my enemies.

4 [p]The cords of death encompassed me;
[q]the torrents of destruction
assailed me;[1]
5 [p]the cords of Sheol entangled me;
the snares of death confronted me.

6 [r]In my distress I called upon the
LORD;
to my God I cried for help.
From his [s]temple he heard my voice,
and my cry to him reached his
ears.

7 Then the earth [t]reeled and rocked;
the foundations also of the
mountains trembled
and quaked, because he was
angry.
8 Smoke went up from his nostrils,[2]
and devouring [u]fire from his
mouth;
glowing coals flamed forth from
him.
9 He [v]bowed the heavens and [w]came
down;
[x]thick darkness was under his feet.
10 He rode on a cherub and flew;
he [y]came swiftly on [z]the wings of
the wind.
11 He made darkness his covering, his
[a]canopy around him,
thick clouds [b]dark with water.
12 Out of the brightness before him
[c]hailstones and coals of fire broke
through his clouds.

13 The LORD also [d]thundered in the
heavens,
and the Most High uttered his
[e]voice,
hailstones and coals of fire.
14 And he sent out his [f]arrows and
scattered them;
he flashed forth lightnings and
[g]routed them.
15 Then [h]the channels of the sea were
seen,
and the foundations of the world
were laid bare
at your [i]rebuke, O LORD,
at the blast of [j]the breath of your
nostrils.

Psalm 18 [f]Ps. 36, title; 89:3, 20; [2 Sam. 3:18; 7:5] [g]See 2 Sam. ch. 22 [h]Ex. 15:1; Deut. 31:30 **2** [i]ver. 31, 46; Ps. 19:14; 31:3 [j]Ps. 91:2; 144:2 [k]Cited Heb. 2:13 [l]ver. 30; Gen. 15:1 [m]Ps. 112:9; Luke 1:69 [n]See Ps. 9:9 **3** [o]Ps. 48:1; 96:4; 113:3; 145:3 **4** [p]Ps. 116:3; [Ps. 119:61] [q]See Ps. 32:6 **5** [p][See ver. 4 above] **6** [r]Ps. 66:14; 102:2; 120:1; [Jonah 2:2] [s]See Ps. 11:4 **7** [t][Judg. 5:4; Acts 4:31; 16:26] **8** [u]See Ps. 21:9 **9** [v]Ps. 144:5 [w]Isai. 64:1 [x]See Ex. 20:21 **10** [y]Deut. 28:49 [z]Ps. 104:3 **11** [a]Job 36:29; [Ps. 97:2] [b][Ps. 29:3] **12** [c][Ps. 148:8; Josh. 10:11] **13** [d]1 Sam. 2:10; 7:10; See Job 37:4 [e]Isai. 30:30; See Ps. 29:3-9

14 [f]Ps. 7:13; 64:7; 77:17; 144:6; Deut. 32:23, 42; Hab. 3:11 [g]Ex. 14:24; Josh. 10:10 **15** [h]Ps. 42:1; Joel 1:20 (Heb.); [Job 36:30] [i]Ps. 106:9; Nah. 1:4 [j][Ex. 15:8]

1 Or *terrified me* 2 Or *in his wrath*

Ps. 18 The psalm thanks the Lord for a great deliverance. The same psalm appears in 2 Sam. 22 with minor differences.

18:title See Introduction: Author; Characteristics and Themes. The title unambiguously attributes this psalm to David.

18:1 love. Not the usual Hebrew word for love, it emphasizes intimacy, expressing David's personal devotion.

18:2 rock. This term connotes protection. When David fled from Saul, he could find refuge in the caves and cliffs of the dry streambeds.

18:4 cords of death. The tentacles of death rise up from Sheol, the underworld, to drag the psalmist down.

torrents of destruction. The powers of evil and death are frequently likened to an overwhelming flood (Is. 28:15, 17, 18; Matt. 16:18; Ps. 46:2 note; 69:1, 2 notes).

18:6 From his temple. The place of God's special presence. At the dedication of the temple Solomon indicated that this was the proper response to trouble (1 Kin. 8).

18:7 the earth . . . rocked. When God reveals Himself as a warrior, nature convulses (Is. 24:4–13; Nah. 1:5).

mountains. The hills symbolize all that is firm and established in the world, but they shake before the might of God.

18:8 nostrils . . . mouth. The nostrils and mouth are standard figures of speech for anger (see text note). Smoke and fire often accompany a theophany (a visual self-revelation of God; Gen. 15:17; Ex. 19:18; Nah. 1:6).

18:9 darkness was under his feet. God is pictured as coming with the storm clouds into battle. This portrayal is frequent in the Bible (Ps. 68:4; 104:3; Nah. 1:3; Dan. 7:13). In the New Testament, Christ is portrayed as coming in the clouds (Mark 13:26; Rev. 1:7).

18:10 cherub. Angelic beings first mentioned in Gen. 3:24. Their role in Gen. 3 and their symbolic representation at key places in the tabernacle (Ex. 26:1, 31) indicate that they are guardians of God's holiness (cf. Ezek. 1 and 10).

18:13 voice. Thunder; cf. Ps. 29:3–9.

18:14 his arrows. Lightning.

18:15 were seen . . . laid bare. When God appears as a defender of His people, the waters representing chaos and evil shrink back. Compare 77:16–19 (reflecting on the Exodus from Egypt); Nah. 1:4; Rev. 21:1.

rebuke. God controls the chaotic waters of the sea (Ps. 106:9). Jesus shows Himself to be the Second Person of the Trinity by silencing the chaotic waters with His rebuke (Luke 8:22–25).

16 He [k]sent from on high, he took me;
he [l]drew me out of [m]many waters.
17 He rescued me from my strong enemy
and from those who hated me,
for they were [n]too mighty for me.
18 They confronted me in the day of my
calamity,
but the LORD was my support.
19 He brought me out into [o]a broad
place;
he rescued me, because he
[p]delighted in me.

20 The LORD dealt with me [q]according
to my righteousness;
according to [r]the cleanness of my
hands he rewarded me.
21 For I have [s]kept the ways of the
LORD,
and have not wickedly departed
from my God.
22 For [t]all his rules were before me,
and his statutes I did not put away
from me.
23 I was [u]blameless before him,
and I kept myself from my guilt.
24 So the LORD has rewarded me
according to my righteousness,
according to the cleanness of my
hands in his sight.

25 With [v]the merciful you show yourself
merciful;
with the blameless man you show
yourself blameless;
26 with the purified you show yourself
pure;
and with [w]the crooked you make
yourself seem tortuous.
27 For you save [x]a humble people,
but [y]the haughty eyes you bring
down.

16k[Ps. 144:7] l[Ex. 2:10] mSee Ps. 32:6; Job 22:11
17nPs. 142:6
19oPs. 31:8; 118:5; [ver. 36] pPs. 22:8; 2 Sam. 15:26
20qPs. 7:8; 1 Sam. 24:19; 26:23; 1 Kin. 8:32 rSee Job 22:30
21s[Gen. 18:19; Prov. 8:32]
22tPs. 119:30, 102
23uGen. 17:1; [1 Kin. 14:8]
25vMatt. 5:7
26wPs. 81:12; Lev. 26:23, 24; Prov. 3:34; Acts 7:42; Rom. 1:28
27x[Ex. 3:7] ySee Ps. 101:5

28zPs. 132:17; 1 Kin. 11:36; 15:4; 2 Kin. 8:19; [2 Sam. 21:17]; See Job 18:5, 6
29a[Isai. 35:6] bSee 2 Sam. 5:6-9
30cDeut. 32:4; Dan. 4:37; Matt. 5:48; [Rev. 15:3] dSee Ps. 12:6 ever. 2 fPs. 17:7
31g[Ps. 86:8] hSee ver. 2
32i1 Sam. 2:4; Isai. 45:5 jPs. 101:2, 6; 119:1; Job 22:3
33kHab. 3:19 lDeut. 32:13; Isai. 58:14
34mPs. 144:1
35nPs. 20:2 o[Isai. 63:9]
36pPs. 31:8; Prov. 4:12; [ver. 19]

28 For it is you who light my [z]lamp;
the LORD my God lightens my
darkness.
29 For by you I can run against a
troop,
and by my God I can [a]leap over [b]a
wall.
30 This God—his way is [c]perfect;[1]
the word of the LORD [d]proves true;
he is [e]a shield for all those who
[f]take refuge in him.

31 For [g]who is God, but the LORD?
And who is [h]a rock, except our
God?—
32 the God who [i]equipped me with
strength
and made my way [j]blameless.
33 He made my feet like the feet of a
[k]deer
and set me secure on [l]the heights.
34 He [m]trains my hands for war,
so that my arms can bend a bow
of bronze.
35 You have given me the shield of your
salvation,
and your right hand
[n]supported me,
and your [o]gentleness made me
great.
36 You [p]gave a wide place for my steps
under me,
and my feet did not slip.
37 I pursued my enemies and overtook
them,
and did not turn back till they
were consumed.
38 I thrust them through, so that they
were not able to rise;
they fell under my feet.

1 Or *blameless*

18:16 many waters. Symbolic of trouble and distress (Ps. 69:2).

18:19 broad place. This may be an allusion to the Exodus and the conquest of Canaan. God delivered Israel from many waters (Red Sea) and brought them to a broad place (the Promised Land). The broad place contrasts with a narrow one, from which it would be hard or impossible to escape from an enemy.

18:21 ways of the LORD. God's covenant law.

18:25 merciful . . . show yourself merciful. The term translated "merciful" has reference to God's special lovingkindness toward those with whom He is in covenant relationship.

18:27 you save a humble people. A constant teaching of the Old Testament and the Psalms, most notably Ps. 113:7–9.

18:29 against a troop. A glimpse at the original inspiration of the verse. It appears as if the psalmist is waging war.

18:30 the word of the LORD. His revelation to His people. Since this is a psalm of David in a warfare setting, perhaps the reference is more specifically to 2 Sam. 7, the Davidic covenant, where God promises to be David's Father and God.

18:31 but the LORD. The use of these rhetorical questions is emphatic: there is no one like the Lord (Ex. 15:11).

18:34 bow of bronze. Bows were constructed primarily of wood, at times reinforced with metal. The bronze bow is meant to suggest the psalmist's God-given strength.

18:36 my feet did not slip. Paths are narrow and rocky in Israel permitting slipping and injury to a soldier. The divinely enabled, steadfast faith of David is illustrated.

18:38–40 under my feet . . . turn their backs to me. See text note. Ancient Near Eastern tablets and stone memorials show enemies under the feet of conquerors and bowing before their captors.

39 For you equipped me with strength
for the battle;
you made those who rise against
me sink under me.
40 You made my enemies [q]turn their
backs to me,[1]
and those who hated me I
destroyed.
41 [r]They cried for help, but there was
none to save;
they cried to the LORD, but he did
not answer them.
42 I beat them fine as [s]dust before the
wind;
I cast them out like [t]the mire of
the streets.
43 You delivered me from [u]strife with
the people;
you made me [v]the head of the
nations;
[w]people whom I had not known
served me.
44 As soon as they heard of me they
obeyed me;
[x]foreigners [y]came cringing to me.
45 [x]Foreigners lost heart
and [z]came trembling out of their
fortresses.
46 The LORD lives, and blessed be my
rock,
and exalted be the God of my
salvation—
47 the God who gave me vengeance
and [a]subdued peoples under me,
48 who delivered me from my enemies;
yes, you [b]exalted me above those
who rose against me;
you rescued me from [c]the man of
violence.

40 [q]Ex 23:27; [Ps. 21:12] **41** [r]See Job 27:9 **42** [s]2 Kin. 13:7 [t]Isai. 10:6; Mic. 7:10; Zech. 10:5 **43** [u][2 Sam. 3:1; 19:9, 43; 20:1] [v][Ps. 2:8]; See 2 Sam. 8:1-14 [w]Isai. 55:5; [Ps. 22:27] **44** [x]Ps. 144:7 [y]Ps. 66:3; 81:15; Deut. 33:29 **45** [x][See ver. 44 above] [z]Mic. 7:17 **47** [a]Ps. 47:3; 144:2; [Isai. 45:1] **48** [b]Ps. 59:1 [c]Ps. 140:1

49 [d]Cited Rom. 15:9 [e]Ps. 66:4 **50** [f]Ps. 144:10 [g]See Ps. 2:2 [h][Ps. 89:29; 2 Sam 7:12, 13, 29]
Psalm 19
1 [i]Ps. 50:6; [Rom. 1:19, 20] **4** [j]Cited Rom. 10:18 [k][Isai. 28:10] [l][Eccles. 1:5] **5** [m][Judg. 5:31] [n]Joel 2:16

49 [d]For this I will praise you, O LORD,
among the nations,
and [e]sing to your name.
50 Great [f]salvation he brings to his
king,
and shows steadfast love to his
[g]anointed,
to [h]David and his offspring forever.

The Law of the LORD Is Perfect

19

TO THE CHOIRMASTER. A PSALM OF DAVID.

1 [i]The heavens declare the glory of
God,
and the sky above[2] proclaims his
handiwork.
2 Day to day pours out speech,
and night to night reveals
knowledge.
3 There is no speech, nor are there
words,
whose voice is not heard.
4 [j]Their [k]measuring line[3] goes out
through all the earth,
and their words to the end of the
world.
In them he has set a tent for [l]the
sun,
5 [m]which comes out like [n]a
bridegroom leaving his
chamber,
and, like a strong man, runs its
course with joy.
6 Its rising is from the end of the
heavens,
and its circuit to the end of them,
and there is nothing hidden from
its heat.

1 Or *You gave me my enemies' necks* 2 Hebrew *expanse*; see Genesis 1:6-8
3 Hebrew; Septuagint, Jerome (compare Syriac) *Their voice*

18:41 They cried . . . to the LORD. This indicates that the psalmist was battling fellow Israelites.

18:43 me. David's personal imprint is strong here. God granted him victories over neighboring nations that were brought under his rule (2 Sam. 8:1–14).

18:49 among the nations. Quoted by Paul in Rom. 15:9 as fulfilled in Christ, who brings the Gentiles to join in His praise of God the Father.

18:50 anointed. At his coronation, the king was anointed with oil by the priest. Jesus Christ, David's Lord and descendant, fulfills this psalm.

Ps. 19 The psalm praises the Lord for His two great gifts to humanity: creation and the law. To use modern terminology, the psalm speaks of God's general revelation in nature and His special revelation in Scripture.

19:1–6 God is revealed in His creation, but people resist what they see (Rom. 1:18–20).

19:1 heavens. The psalmist uses creation language here; compare Gen. 1:1–8, where this word has been translated "expanse." See theological note "General Revelation."

19:2 pours out speech. This metaphor claims that the creation, specifically the heavens, constantly attests God's power and goodness.

19:4 all the earth. God's revelation in creation is open to all who do not suppress it. Paul applies this verse to gospel proclamation (Rom. 10:18).

set a tent. The sun is personified throughout this section, but not deified as in other ancient Near Eastern religions. The context indicates that the reference to the tent is probably an allusion to its absence from the nighttime sky.

19:5 like a strong man. Robust and strong as it courses across the sky, the sun is God's creation. If it is powerful, how much more is God.

19:6 nothing. Nothing escapes the heat of the sun, and nothing can hide from the Creator.

7 [o] The law of the LORD is perfect,[1]
[p] reviving the soul;
[q] the testimony of the LORD is [r] sure,
[s] making wise [t] the simple;
8 [u] the precepts of the LORD are right,
rejoicing the heart;
the commandment of the LORD is
[v] pure,
[w] enlightening the eyes;
9 the fear of the LORD is clean,
enduring forever;
the rules of the LORD are [x] true,
and righteous altogether.
10 More to be desired are they than
[y] gold,
even much [z] fine gold;
[a] sweeter also than honey
and drippings of [b] the honeycomb.
11 Moreover, by them is your servant
warned;
[c] in keeping them there is great
reward.
12 [d] Who can discern his errors?
[e] Declare me innocent from [f] hidden
faults.
13 [g] Keep back your servant also from
[h] presumptuous sins;
let them not have [i] dominion
over me!
Then I shall be blameless,
and innocent of great
transgression.
14 Let the words of my mouth and the
meditation of my heart
be acceptable in your sight,
O LORD, my [j] rock and my [k] redeemer.

7 [o] Rom. 7:12 [p] Ps. 23:3; [2 Tim. 3:16] [q] Ex. 25:16; See Ps. 78:5 [r] Ps. 111:7 [s] [Matt. 11:25; 1 Cor. 1:27; 2 Tim. 3:15] [t] Ps. 119:130; Prov. 1:4 **8** [u] Ps. 103:18; 111:7; 119:4, 27 [v] [Ps. 12:6] [w] See Ps. 13:3 **9** [x] Ps. 119:142, 151, 160 **10** [y] Ps. 119:72, 127; Prov. 8:10 [z] Job 28:17; Prov. 8:19 [a] Ps. 119:103 [b] Prov. 16:24 **11** [c] [Prov. 29:18] **12** [d] Ps. 40:12; [1 Cor. 4:4] [e] [Lev. 4:2; Num. 15:27] [f] Ps. 90:8; See Job 34:32 **13** [g] Gen. 20:6; 1 Sam. 25:33, 34, 39 [h] [Num. 15:30] [i] Ps. 119:133; Rom. 6:12, 14

Trust in the Name of the LORD Our God

20

TO THE CHOIRMASTER. A PSALM OF DAVID.

1 May the LORD [l] answer you in the day
of trouble!
May [m] the name of the God of
Jacob [n] protect you!
2 May he send you help from [o] the
sanctuary
and give you support from [p] Zion!

14 [j] See Ps. 18:2 [k] See Job 19:25
Psalm 20 **1** [l] [Gen. 35:3] [m] Prov. 18:10 [n] Ps. 59:1; 69:29 **2** [o] Ps. 73:17; 2 Chr. 20:8 [p] Ps. 128:5

[1] Or *blameless*

General Revelation

God's world is not a veil hiding the Creator's power and majesty; "The heavens declare the glory of God, and the sky above proclaims his handiwork" (Ps. 19:1). The natural order proves that there is a mighty and majestic Creator. Paul says the same in Rom. 1:19–21, and in Acts 17:28 calls Aratus, a Greek poet, to witness that every living person was created by the same God. Paul also affirms that the goodness of the Creator is evident from kindly providences (Acts 14:17; cf. Rom. 2:4), and that some at least of the demands of His law are apparent to every human conscience (Rom. 2:14, 15), along with the uncomfortable certainty of eventual judgment (Rom. 1:32). These evident certainties are the content of general revelation.

General revelation is so called because it comes to everyone, just through their being alive in God's world. God has revealed Himself this way from the start of human history. He actively discloses these aspects of Himself to everyone, so that failure to thank and serve the Creator is always a sin against knowledge. In the end no denial of having received this knowledge will be admitted. Paul uses God's universal revelation of His power and goodness as the basis for his indictment of the whole human race as sinful and guilty before God for our failure to serve Him as we should (Rom. 1:18–3:19).

God has added to general revelation the further revelation of Himself as the Savior of sinners through Jesus Christ. This revelation, accomplished in history and written in Scripture, is called "special revelation." It includes explicit verbal statement of all that general revelation tells us about God.

19:7–11 The law, God's special revelation, reflects the character of its author. Different names are used for the law, synonyms that point to the whole of God's special revelation to humanity.

19:7 law. Torah, the most general term for the law.

reviving the soul. God's Word transforms the lives of those subject to that Word.

making wise. Wisdom is not superior intellectual power. God's Word instills reverence for God.

19:12, 13 hidden faults . . . presumptuous sins. The psalmist knows that he sins consciously and unconsciously, in ignorance of what God requires. He prays against both faults.

I shall be blameless. Only by God's grace.

20:1 you. The king. The congregation calls upon the Lord to bless the king as he sets out for war. The blessings in these verses are also properly applied to New Testament believers in their battle of faith.

20:2 from the sanctuary. Cf. 1 Kin. 8:44, 45.

3 May he [q]remember all your
offerings
and regard with favor your burnt
sacrifices! *Selah*
4 May he [r]grant you your heart's
desire
and fulfill all your plans!
5 May we shout for joy over [s]your
salvation,
and in the name of our God set up
our [t]banners!
May the LORD fulfill all your
petitions!
6 Now I know that the LORD saves his
anointed;
he will answer him from his holy
heaven
with [u]the saving might of his right
hand.
7 Some trust in [v]chariots and some in
[w]horses,
[x]but we trust in the name of the
LORD our God.
8 They collapse and fall,
but we rise and stand upright.
9 O LORD, save the king!
May [y]he answer us when we
call.

The King Rejoices in the LORD's Strength

21 TO THE CHOIRMASTER. A PSALM OF DAVID.

1 O LORD, in your [z]strength the king
rejoices,
and in your [a]salvation how greatly
he exults!
2 You have [b]given him his heart's
desire
and have not withheld the request
of his lips. *Selah*
3 For you [c]meet him with rich
blessings;
you set [d]a crown of [e]fine gold
upon his head.
4 He asked life of you; you [f]gave it
to him,
[g]length of days forever and ever.
5 His [h]glory is great through your
salvation;
[i]splendor and majesty you bestow
on him.
6 For you make him most blessed
forever;[1]
you make him glad with the [j]joy
of your presence.
7 For the king trusts in the
LORD,
and through the steadfast love of
the Most High he shall not be
[k]moved.
8 Your hand will [l]find out all your
enemies;
your right hand will find out
those who hate you.
9 You will make them as [m]a blazing
oven
when you appear.
The LORD will [n]swallow them up in
his wrath,
and [o]fire will consume them.
10 You [p]will destroy their
[q]descendants from the earth,
and their offspring from among
the children of man.
11 Though they plan evil
against you,
though they [r]devise mischief, they
will not succeed.
12 For you will put them [s]to
flight;
you will [t]aim at their faces with
your bows.
13 Be exalted, O LORD, in your
strength!
We will sing and praise your
power.

3 [q][Acts 10:4]
4 [r]Ps. 21:2
5 [s]Ps. 9:14 [t]Ps. 60:4; S. of S. 6:4, 10
6 [u][Ps. 28:8]
7 [v]Isai. 31:1; 36:9 [w]Prov. 21:31 [x][1 Sam. 17:45; 2 Chr. 32:8]
9 [y]Ps. 48:2
Psalm 21
1 [z]Ps. 8:2; 28:7, 8 [a]Ps. 9:14
2 [b]Ps. 20:4, 5
3 [c]Ps. 59:10 [d][2 Sam. 12:30; 1 Chr. 20:2] [e]Ps. 19:10
4 [f]Ps. 61:6; [2 Sam. 7:19] [g]Ps. 91:16; [1 Kin. 1:31; Neh. 2:3]
5 [h]Ps. 8:5 [i]Ps. 45:3; 96:6
6 [j]Ps. 45:7; See Ps. 16:11
7 [k]Ps. 10:6; 16:8
8 [l][Isai. 10:10]
9 [m]Mal. 4:1; [Ps. 83:14] [n]Ps. 56:1, 2; 57:3 [o]Ps. 18:8; 50:3; 97:3; Isai. 26:11; [Job 20:26; Dan. 7:10; Hab. 3:5]
10 [p]Ps. 34:16; 1 Kin. 13:34 [q]Ps. 37:28; 109:13; Job 18:16, 17, 19; Isai. 14:20
11 [r]Ps. 2:1; 10:2
12 [s]Ps. 18:40 [t]Ps. 7:12; 11:2

[1] Or *make him a source of blessing forever*

20:5 shout for joy over your salvation. The psalms contain hymns of praise sung to God after victories. Two examples are Ps. 24 and 98.

20:6–8 Israel will win the battle because of the Lord's presence. Israel's trust is rooted in God's promise to protect His people in warfare when they are obedient to His commands (Deut. 7 and 20).

20:6 anointed. The Davidic king, anticipating the Son of David who reigns forever, Jesus Christ.

20:7 we trust in the name. The believer's rescue from sin and Satan, like Israel's deliverance from enemies, is grounded in God's trustworthiness.

21:2 his heart's desire. Similar language is used in 20:4, though it is uncertain whether the same occasion inspired both psalms. The first part of Ps. 21 sounds like the answer to the prayer in Ps. 20.

21:3 set a crown . . . upon his head. While some think this verse is about a coronation, it probably refers to the king's transition from a war leader (who does not wear his crown) to a king sitting on his throne.

21:4 asked life of you . . . forever and ever. The king prays that his life will be spared during battle—and was also given life eternal, as is the believer of today.

Why Have You Forsaken Me?

22 To the choirmaster: according to The Doe of the Dawn. A Psalm of David.

1 [u]My God, my God, why have you
forsaken me?
Why are you so [v]far from saving
me, from the words of my
[w]groaning?
2 O my God, I cry by [x]day, but you do
not answer,
and by night, but I find no rest.

3 Yet you are [y]holy,
[z]enthroned on [a]the praises[1] of
Israel.
4 In you our fathers trusted;
they trusted, and you delivered
them.
5 To you they [b]cried and were
rescued;
in you they [c]trusted and were not
put to shame.

6 But I am [d]a worm and not a man,
[e]scorned by mankind and [f]despised
by the people.
7 All who see me [g]mock me;
they make mouths at me; they
[h]wag their heads;
8 [i]"He trusts in the LORD; let him
[j]deliver him;
let him rescue him, for he [k]delights
in him!"

9 Yet you are he who [l]took me from
the womb;
you made me trust you at my
mother's breasts.
10 On you was I cast from my birth,
and from [m]my mother's womb you
have been my God.
11 Be not [n]far from me,
for trouble is near,
and there is [o]none to help.

12 Many bulls encompass me;
[p]strong bulls of [q]Bashan surround me;
13 they [r]open wide their mouths at me,
like a ravening and roaring lion.

14 I am [s]poured out like water,
and all my bones are [t]out of joint;
my [u]heart is like [v]wax;
it is melted within my breast;
15 my strength is [w]dried up like a
potsherd,
and my [x]tongue sticks to my jaws;
you lay me in the dust of death.

16 For [y]dogs encompass me;
a company of evildoers
[z]encircles me;
they have [a]pierced my hands and
feet[2]—
17 I can count all my bones—
they [b]stare and gloat over me;
18 [c]they divide my garments among them,
and for my clothing they cast lots.

19 But you, O LORD, [n]do not be far off!
O you my help, [d]come quickly to
my aid!

Psalm 22
1 [u]Cited Matt. 27:46; Mark 15:34 [v]ver. 11 [w]Ps. 32:3; 38:8; Job 3:24; Isai. 59:11; [Heb. 5:7]
2 [x]Ps. 88:1
3 [y]Lev. 19:2 [z][Ps. 80:1; 99:1] [a][Ps. 9:11, 14; 65:1; 102:21; 147:12]
5 [b]See Judg. 3:9 [c]Ps. 25:2; 31:1; 71:1; Isai. 49:23; Rom. 9:33
6 [d]Job 25:6; Isai. 41:14 [e]Ps. 69:19; 109:25 [f]Isai. 49:7; 53:3
7 [g]See Matt. 27:39-43; Mark 15:29-32; Luke 23:35, 36 [h]Ps. 109:25; [Ps. 44:14; 2 Kin. 19:21; Lam. 2:15; Isai. 37:22]
8 [i][Ps. 37:5; Prov. 16:3] [j]Ps. 91:14 [k]Ps. 18:19; Matt. 3:17; Mark 1:11; Luke 3:22
9 [l]Ps. 71:6
10 [m]Isai. 46:3; 49:1; Gal. 1:15
11 [n]See ver. 1; Ps. 10:1 [o]Ps. 107:12; 2 Kin. 14:26; Isai. 63:5
12 [p][Ps. 68:30 (Heb.)] [q]Amos 4:1
13 [r]Ps. 35:21; Job 16:10; Lam. 2:16; 3:46

14 [s][Lam. 2:11] [t][Dan. 5:6] [u][Job 23:16; Nah. 2:10]; See Josh. 2:11 [v]See Ps. 68:2 **15** [w]Prov. 17:22 [x][John 19:28; See Job 29:10] **16** [y][Phil. 3:2; Rev. 22:15] [z]Ps. 88:17 [a]Matt. 27:35; Mark 15:24; Luke 23:33; 24:40; John 19:23, 37; 20:25; Zech. 12:10] **17** [b]Luke 23:35 **18** [c]Cited John 19:24; [Matt. 27:35; Luke 23:34] **19** [n][See ver. 11 above] [d]Ps. 38:22

1 Or *dwelling in the praises* 2 Some Hebrew manuscripts, Septuagint, Vulgate, Syriac; most Hebrew manuscripts *like a lion* [they are at] *my hands and feet*

Ps. 22 This psalm is well known for its many citations and allusions in the New Testament (Matt. 27:35, 39, 43, 46; John 19:23, 24, 28; Heb. 2:12). The psalm, like Ps. 69, expresses the suffering of Christ, the Son of David, dying at the hands of wicked men.

22:1 why have you forsaken me. The psalmist cries in anguish the "why?" of the righteous sufferer. Where is the presence God has promised (Josh. 1:5)? The cry is taken up by Jesus, who knew the reality of a total abandonment that was only partial with David. In the place of David and all the people of God, Jesus bore the dreadful curse that sin deserves.

22:3 enthroned on the praises. God's kingship exists before any human acclamation, but His reign becomes manifest to worshipers through their praises.

22:4, 5 our fathers. David could think of the time that Abraham was delivered from the five kings (Gen. 14), Joseph from the Egyptian prison (Gen. 41), and most of all Moses and Israel from the land of Egypt (Ex. 1–15).

22:7 mock. His enemies ridicule his trust in God. This experience is alluded to in Matt. 27:41–44, as Christ had to endure the ridicule of hypocritical priests and criminals.

22:9 from the womb. He affirms a long-standing trust in God's ability to save him. He has had confidence in God as far back as he can remember.

22:12 bulls of Bashan. These bulls were noted for their power and size (Amos 4:1).

22:13 roaring lion. Often representing power, ferocity, and ruthlessness in the Bible and the ancient Near East (Nah. 2:14; Zeph. 3:3).

22:14 my bones . . . my heart. Outward attack is matched by inward agony. The figures, as used by David, reflect the inward turmoil induced by the encircling threat of his enemies. As fulfilled in Christ, the prophetic words describe the agony of the crucified One.

22:16 pierced. The traditional Hebrew reading may reflect a copyist's error, for it reads (lit.) "like a lion" (text note). The Septuagint (the ancient Greek translation of the Old Testament) suggests that the correct reading is "pierced."

22:19–21 After the laments and confessions of trust comes the climax, an appeal to the Lord. Notice that the enemies are named in reverse: humans, dogs, lions, and oxen.

20 Deliver my soul from the sword,
my precious life from the power of
[e]the dog!
21 Save me from [f]the mouth of the
lion!
You have rescued[1] me from the
horns of [g]the wild oxen!

22 [h]I will tell of your name to my
[i]brothers;
in the midst of the congregation I
will praise you:
23 You who [j]fear the LORD, praise him!
All you offspring of Jacob, [k]glorify
him,
and stand in awe of him, all you
offspring of Israel!
24 For he has not despised or abhorred
the affliction of [l]the afflicted,
and he has not [m]hidden his face
from him,
but has heard, when he [n]cried
to him.

25 From you comes my praise in the
great [o]congregation;
my [p]vows I will [q]perform before
those who fear him.
26 [r]The afflicted[2] shall [s]eat and be
satisfied;
those who seek him shall praise
the LORD!
May your hearts [t]live forever!

27 All [u]the ends of the earth shall
remember
and turn to the LORD,
and all [v]the families of the nations
shall worship before you.
28 For [w]kingship belongs to the LORD,
and he rules over the nations.
29 All [x]the prosperous of the earth eat
and worship;
before him shall [y]bow all who go
down to the dust,
even the one who could not [z]keep
himself alive.
30 Posterity shall serve him;
it shall be told of the Lord to the
coming [a]generation;
31 they shall [b]come and proclaim his
righteousness to a people yet
[c]unborn,
that he has done it.

20 [e][Phil. 3:2; Rev. 22:15]
21 [f]2 Tim. 4:17 [g]See Num. 23:22
22 [h]Cited Heb. 2:12; [Ps. 102:21; John 17:6] [i]Matt. 28:10; John 20:17; Rom. 8:29
23 [j]Ps. 135:20 [k]Ps. 50:15, 23
24 [l][Isai. 53:4, 7] [m]Ps. 10:1; 13:1; See Job 13:24 [n]Heb. 5:7
25 [o]Ps. 35:18; 40:9, 10; 111:1 [p]Lev. 7:16 [q]Ps. 66:13; Jonah 2:9; See Ps. 50:14
26 [r]Ps. 69:32 [s]Isai. 25:6; 65:13 [t]John 6:51
27 [u]Ps. 2:8; 67:7 [v]Ps. 96:7
28 [w]Obad. 21; [Ps. 47:8; Zech. 14:9]
29 [x][Ps. 45:12] [y]Ps. 72:9; [Phil. 2:10] [z]Ezek. 18:27
30 [a]Ps. 48:13; 71:18
31 [b]Ps. 86:9; [Isai. 60:3] [c]Ps. 78:6; 102:18

The LORD Is My Shepherd

23 A PSALM OF DAVID.
The LORD is my [d]shepherd; I shall
not [e]want.
2 He makes me lie down in green
[f]pastures.
He leads me beside still waters.[3]
3 He [g]restores my soul.
He [h]leads me in [i]paths of
righteousness[4]
for his [j]name's sake.

4 Even though I [k]walk through the
valley of [l]the shadow of death,[5]
I will [m]fear no evil,
for [n]you are with me;
your [o]rod and your staff,
they comfort me.

Psalm 23
1 [d]Ps. 78:52; 80:1; Isai. 40:11; Jer. 31:10; Ezek. 34:11, 12, 23; John 10:11; Heb. 13:20; 1 Pet. 2:25; 5:4 [e]Ps. 34:9, 10; [Matt. 6:33]
2 [f]Ezek. 34:14; John 10:9
3 [g]Ps. 19:7 [h]Ps. 5:8; 31:3; 139:10, 24; 143:10; Isai. 40:11; 49:10 [i]Prov. 4:11; 8:20 [j]Ps. 25:11; 31:3; 79:9; 109:21; Ezek. 20:9, 14
4 [k]Ps. 138:7 [l]See Job 3:5 [m]Ps. 3:6; 27:1, 3; 118:6 [n]Ex. 3:12; Isai. 43:2 [o]Mic. 7:14

1 Hebrew *answered* 2 Or *The meek* 3 Hebrew *beside waters of rest*
4 Or *in right paths* 5 Or *the valley of deep darkness*

22:21 You have rescued. The assurance of being heard is also present in other psalms of lament (3:4; 28:6; cf. 27:13; 34:4, 6; 38:15; 118:5, 21).

22:22 I will tell. The thankful praise of the psalmist will be offered as the payment of his vows (v. 25). In Heb. 2:12 this verse is applied to Christ, who leads the praise of the great congregation.

22:24 he has not hidden his face. Christ's enemies despised Him, but God did not.

22:25 my vows I will perform. Mention of vows is common in psalms of lament (13:6; 27:6; 35:18; 54:6; 69:30, 31; cf. 51:16; 116:13, 14). The sufferer promises to bring a thanksgiving when his prayer is answered (Lev. 7:16; 22:23; Deut. 12:6, 7).

22:26 shall eat and be satisfied. Perhaps a reference to the sacrificial meal of the Old Testament peace offering, when the vow is paid and the worshipers are included.

22:27 All the ends of the earth. The scope of praise expands, showing the prophetic reference to Christ and the New Testament church.

22:31 that he has done it. The final victory of salvation is accomplished by Christ (John 19:30).

Ps. 23 This psalm is perhaps the best known example of a psalm of confidence (Introduction: Characteristics and Themes). It is a literary unity, with two governing metaphors expressing God's care and goodness: the shepherd and the banquet table.

23:1 shepherd. The image of God as shepherd is inexhaustibly rich. The shepherd stays with the flock (Is. 40:11; 63:9–12). His sheep are totally dependent upon him for food, water, and protection from wild animals. In the New Testament, Jesus is revealed as the shepherd of His people (John 10:11, 14), fulfilling the prophecy that God will come to shepherd His people (Ezek. 34:7–16, 23).

23:2, 3 makes me lie down . . . leads me . . . restores . . . leads me. These verses extend the metaphor of the shepherd's care for the sheep. The Lord lovingly cares for His people.

23:4 valley of the shadow of death. See Job 10:21, 22.

rod . . . staff. The rod was used to fight wild animals and the staff to direct the flock.

5 You [p]prepare a table before me
in [q]the presence of my enemies;
you [r]anoint my head with oil;
my [s]cup overflows.
6 Surely[1] goodness and mercy[2] shall
follow me
all the days of my life,
and I shall [t]dwell[3] in the house of
the LORD
[u]forever.[4]

The King of Glory

24 A PSALM OF DAVID.
[v]The earth is the LORD's and the
fullness thereof,[5]
the world and those who dwell
therein,
2 for he has [w]founded it upon [x]the seas
and established it upon the rivers.

3 [y]Who shall ascend the hill of the LORD?
And who shall stand in his [z]holy
place?
4 [a]He who has [b]clean hands and [c]a pure
heart,
who does not [d]lift up his soul to
[e]what is false
and does not swear deceitfully.
5 He will receive [f]blessing from the
LORD
and [g]righteousness from [h]the God
of his salvation.
6 Such is [i]the generation of those who
seek him,
who [j]seek the face of the God of
Jacob.[6] *Selah*

7 [k]Lift up your heads, O gates!
And be lifted up, O ancient doors,
that [l]the King of glory may come in.

5 [p]Ps. 78:19; [John 6:51; See 2 Sam. 17:27-29; Prov. 9:2] [q][Ps. 31:19] [r]Ps. 45:7; 133:2; Luke 7:46; [Ps. 92:10] [s]Ps. 16:5
6 [t]Ps. 27:4 [u]Ps. 21:4
Psalm 24
1 [v]Ps. 50:12; 89:11; Ex. 9:29; 19:5; Deut. 10:14; Job 41:11; Cited 1 Cor. 10:26
2 [w]Ps. 104:5; Job 38:6; Prov. 8:29 [x]Ps. 136:6; Gen. 1:9
3 [y]For ver. 3-5, see Ps. 15:1-5 [z]Ps. 2:6
4 [a][Deut. 10:12; Isai. 33:15, 16; Mic. 6:8] [b]See Job 22:30 [c]Ps. 73:1; Matt. 5:8 [d][Ezek. 18:6] [e]Ps. 31:6; 119:37
5 [f][Gen. 22:17, 18] [g]Isai. 46:13; 56:1 [h]Ps. 27:9; 38:22; 51:14; 88:1
6 [i]Ps. 14:5 [j]Ps. 27:8; 105:4
7 [k][Ps. 118:19, 20; Isai. 26:2] [l][1 Cor. 2:8]
8 [m][Ex. 15:3]
10 [n]Mal. 1:14
Psalm 25
1 [o]Ps. 86:4; 143:8; Lam. 3:41; [Ps. 24:4]
2 [p]See Ps. 11:1 [q]ver. 20; Ps. 31:1, 17; 71:1 [r][Ps. 13:4]

8 Who is this King of glory?
The LORD, strong and mighty,
the LORD, [m]mighty in battle!
9 Lift up your heads, O gates!
And lift them up, O ancient doors,
that the King of glory may
come in.
10 Who is this King of glory?
[n]The LORD of hosts,
he is the King of glory! *Selah*

Teach Me Your Paths

25 [7]OF DAVID.
To you, O LORD, I [o]lift up my soul.
2 O my God, in you I [p]trust;
[q]let me not be put to shame;
[r]let not my enemies exult over me.
3 Indeed, [s]none who wait for you shall
be put to shame;
they shall be ashamed who are
[t]wantonly [u]treacherous.

4 [v]Make me to know your ways,
O LORD;
teach me your paths.
5 Lead me in your [w]truth and
teach me,
for you are the God of my
salvation;
for you I wait all the day long.

6 Remember your [x]mercy, O LORD, and
your steadfast love,
[y]for they have been from of old.

3 [s]Isai. 49:23; [Rom. 5:5; Phil. 1:20] [t][Ps. 59:3, 4] [u][Jer. 3:20] 4 [v]Ps. 27:11; 86:11; 143:8, 10; Ex. 33:13; [Ps. 5:8; 119:35] 5 [w]Ps. 26:3; 86:11 6 [x]Ps. 51:1; [Ps. 103:17; Isai. 63:15] [y][Gen. 8:1; 9:15; 19:29]

1 Or *Only* 2 Or *steadfast love* 3 Or *shall return to dwell* 4 Hebrew *for length of days* 5 Or *and all that fills it* 6 Septuagint, Syriac, and two Hebrew manuscripts; Masoretic Text *Jacob, who seek your face* 7 This psalm is an acrostic poem, each verse beginning with the successive letters of the Hebrew alphabet

23:5, 6 The Lord treats the psalmist as an honored guest.

23:5 table. The image shifts to that of a banquet, a victory celebration.

anoint. Guests were anointed at feasts (Ps. 104:15; Luke 7:46).

23:6 I shall dwell. Like the sheep with its shepherd, the psalmist quiets himself in God's assurance of an eternal home with Him. See John 14:23; "God Is Love: Divine Goodness and Faithfulness" at Ps. 136:1.

Ps. 24 Jesus alone is qualified to ascend to heaven (vv. 3, 4), and He is the victorious Lord, for whom the gates of glory open (vv. 7–10).

24:1 The earth is the LORD's. God created and sustains the whole earth; it belongs to Him. Paul cites this verse to establish the principle that there is no food, even things offered to pagan idols, which is unlawful for Christians to eat (1 Cor. 10:25, 26).

24:2 he has founded it upon the seas. This section reflects the creation account in Gen. 1. However, the sea is also a poetic image for evil. Throughout the psalms and the prophets, God is pictured as winning a victory over the sea (Ps. 29:10, 11; 77:16–20; 104:5–9; Nah. 1:4; Dan. 7).

24:3 See "God's Pattern for Worship" at 1 Chr. 16:29.

24:4 clean hands. Righteous action.

pure heart. Righteous thoughts and motives.

deceitfully. By the names of false gods.

24:7–9 heads. The city or temple gates are personified.

may come in. The return of the King of glory implies that He has gone out to battle and returns in victory.

Ps. 25 This acrostic psalm is primarily the lament of an individual (vv. 16–21), but the last verse applies it to the community. Covenantal (v. 10) and wisdom (vv. 4, 5) language pervade the poem.

25:5 See "Understanding the Word of God" at 119:34.

25:6, 7 Remember . . . mercy . . . steadfast love. These words are all closely connected with God's covenant, which is the basis of the psalmist's trust.

7 Remember not [z]the sins of my youth
or my transgressions;
according to your [a]steadfast love
remember me,
for the sake of your goodness,
O LORD!

8 [b]Good and upright is the LORD;
therefore he [c]instructs sinners in
the way.
9 He leads the humble in what is right,
and teaches the humble his way.
10 All the paths of the LORD are
[d]steadfast love and faithfulness,
for those who keep his covenant
and his testimonies.

11 For your [e]name's sake, O LORD,
pardon my guilt, for it is [f]great.
12 Who is the man who fears the LORD?
Him [c]will he instruct in the way
that he should choose.
13 His soul shall [g]abide in well-being,
and his [h]offspring [i]shall inherit the
land.
14 [j]The friendship[1] of the LORD is for
those who fear him,
and he makes known to them his
covenant.
15 My [k]eyes are ever toward the LORD,
for he will [l]pluck my feet out of
the net.

16 [m]Turn to me and be gracious to me,
for I am lonely and afflicted.
17 The troubles of my heart are
enlarged;
bring me out of my distresses.
18 [n]Consider my affliction and my
trouble,
and forgive all my sins.

19 Consider how many are my foes,
and with what violent hatred they
hate me.

7 [z]Job 13:26; 20:11; Jer. 3:25 [a]Ps. 51:1
8 [b]Ps. 100:5 [c]Ps. 32:8
10 [d][John 1:17]
11 [e]See Ps. 23:3 [f][Rom. 5:20]
12 [c][See ver. 9 above]
13 [g][Prov. 1:33; 19:23] [h]Ps. 112:2 [i]See Ps. 37:9
14 [j][Amos 3:7; See Job 29:4]
15 [k]Ps. 123:1, 2; 141:8; [2 Chr. 20:12] [l]Ps. 31:4
16 [m]Ps. 69:16; 86:16; 119:132
18 [n][Job 10:15]
20 [o]See ver. 2
22 [p]Ps. 34:22; 71:23; 130:8; Lam. 3:58; [2 Sam. 4:9]
Psalm 26
1 [q]See Ps. 7:8 [r]ver. 11 [s]See Ps. 11:1
2 [t]See Ps. 7:9; 17:3; 139:23 [u]Ps. 7:9
3 [v][Ps. 25:10] [w]2 Kin. 20:3; [Ps. 86:11]
4 [x]See Ps. 1:1 [y]Job 11:11
5 [z]Ps. 31:6; 139:21, 22
6 [a]Ps. 73:13; [Ex. 30:19, 20; Deut. 21:6]
7 [b]See Ps. 9:1
8 [c][Ps. 27:4]
9 [d][Ps. 28:3]
10 [e]Ex. 23:8; Deut. 16:19

20 Oh, guard my soul, and deliver me!
[o]Let me not be put to shame, for I
take refuge in you.
21 May integrity and uprightness
preserve me,
for I wait for you.

22 [p]Redeem Israel, O God,
out of all his troubles.

I Will Bless the LORD

26

OF DAVID.
[q]Vindicate me, O LORD,
for I have [r]walked in my integrity,
and I have [s]trusted in the LORD
without wavering.
2 [t]Prove me, O LORD, and try me;
test my heart and [u]my mind.[2]
3 For your [v]steadfast love is before my
eyes,
and I [w]walk in your [v]faithfulness.

4 I do not [x]sit with men of [y]falsehood,
nor do I consort with hypocrites.
5 I [z]hate the assembly of evildoers,
and I will not sit with the wicked.

6 I [a]wash my hands in innocence
and go around your altar,
O LORD,
7 proclaiming thanksgiving aloud,
and telling all your [b]wondrous
deeds.

8 O LORD, I [c]love the habitation of
your house
and the place where your glory
dwells.
9 [d]Do not sweep my soul away with
sinners,
nor my life with bloodthirsty men,
10 in whose hands are evil devices,
and whose right hands are full of
[e]bribes.

1 Or *The secret counsel* 2 Hebrew *test my kidneys and my heart*

25:10 his covenant and his testimonies. His revealed will for our lives; that is, the law.

25:12 fears the LORD. Cf. Prov. 1:7 and Eccl. 12:13. The fear of the Lord is reverence and awe toward God, not life-disrupting anxiety. Also, see note Ps. 111:10.

25:13 inherit the land. The blessings and curses of Deut. 27; 28 make it clear that Israel will keep the land given them by God if they remain faithful to the conditions of the covenant (cf. v. 10).

25:14 makes known to them his covenant. Each time Abraham doubted God's ability to fulfill the promises of Gen. 12:1–3, God appeared to him and renewed the covenant (Gen. 15 and 17).

25:18, 19 my sins . . . my foes. He recognizes that his troubles are caused by both his own sins and the attacks of outside forces (the "foes").

26:1 in my integrity. David identifies himself in motive and action with the righteous rather than the wicked. He invites God to test the truth of this claim (v. 2). David has no illusions of being sinless (53:5) or of having no need for mercy (v. 11; 130:3).

26:4 I do not sit. Cf. Ps. 1:1.

26:6 your altar. The language fits a prayer for admission to the sanctuary.

26:9 sinners. He wants to distance himself from the wicked, for if they enter the sanctuary precincts (vv. 6–8), they will be quickly destroyed. David asks to be spared this judgment.

11 But as for me, I shall walk in my
integrity;
redeem me, and be gracious to me.
12 My foot stands on [f]level ground;
in [g]the great assembly I will bless
the LORD.

The LORD Is My Light and My Salvation

27 OF DAVID.
The LORD is my [h] light and my
[i] salvation;
[j] whom shall I fear?
The LORD is the stronghold[1] of my life;
of whom shall I be afraid?

2 When evildoers assail me
to [k]eat up my flesh,
my adversaries and foes,
it is they who stumble and fall.

3 [l]Though an army encamp against me,
my heart shall not fear;
though war arise against me,
yet[2] I will be confident.

4 [m] One thing have I asked of the LORD,
that will I seek after:
that I may [n]dwell in the house of the
LORD
all the days of my life,
to gaze upon [o]the beauty of the LORD
and to inquire[3] in his temple.

5 For he will [p]hide me in his shelter
in the day of trouble;
he will conceal me under the cover of
his tent;
he will [q]lift me high upon a rock.

6 And now my [r]head shall be lifted up
above my enemies all around me,
and I will offer in his tent
sacrifices with shouts of [s]joy;
[t]I will sing and make melody to the
LORD.

7 [u]Hear, O LORD, when I cry aloud;
be gracious to me and
answer me!
8 You have said, [v]"Seek[4] my face."
My heart says to you,
"Your face, LORD, do I seek."[5]
9 [w]Hide not your face from me.
Turn not your servant away
in anger,
O you who have been my help.
Cast me not off; forsake me not,
[x]O God of my salvation!
10 For [y]my father and my mother have
forsaken me,
but the LORD will [z]take me in.

11 [a]Teach me your way, O LORD,
and lead me on [b]a level path
because of my enemies.
12 [c]Give me not up to the will of my
adversaries;
for [d]false witnesses have risen
against me,
and they [e]breathe out violence.

13 I believe[6] that I shall look upon [f]the
goodness of the LORD
in [g]the land of the living!
14 [h]Wait for the LORD;
[i]be strong, and let your heart take
courage;
wait for the LORD!

The LORD Is My Strength and My Shield

28 OF DAVID.
To you, O LORD, I call;
[j]my rock, be not deaf to me,
lest, if you [k]be silent to me,
I become like those who [l]go down
to the pit.

12 [f]See Ps. 27:11 [g]Ps. 22:25
Psalm 27
1 [h]Isai. 60:20; Mic. 7:8; [Ps. 84:11] [i]Ps. 118:14; Ex. 15:2; Isai. 12:2; 62:11 [j]See Ps. 23:4
2 [k]Ps. 14:4
3 [l]Ps. 3:6
4 [m][Ps. 26:8; 84:1, 2] [n]Ps. 23:6; 65:4; [Luke 2:37] [o]Ps. 90:17
5 [p]Ps. 31:20; [Ps. 91:1; Job 5:21; Isai. 4:6] [q]Ps. 40:2
6 [r]Ps. 3:3 [s][Num. 10:10] [t]Eph. 5:19; Col. 3:16
7 [u]Ps. 30:10
8 [v]Ps. 24:6; 105:4
9 [w]Ps. 69:17; 102:2; 143:7 [x]See Ps. 24:5
10 [y][Isai. 49:15; 63:16] [z][Isai. 40:11]
11 [a]See Ps. 25:4 [b][Ps. 5:8]
12 [c]Ps. 41:2 [d]Ps. 35:11; [1 Kin. 21:13; Matt. 26:59, 60; Mark 14:55, 56] [e]Acts 9:1
13 [f]Ex. 33:19 [g]Ps. 52:5; 116:9; 142:5; Job 28:13
14 [h]Ps. 37:34; 62:5; Prov. 20:22 [i]Ps. 31:24; Deut. 31:7; Josh. 1:6, 9, 18
Psalm 28
1 [j]See Ps. 18:2 [k]Ps. 35:22; 39:12; 83:1; 109:1 [l]Ps. 88:4; 143:7

1 Or *refuge* 2 Or *in this* 3 Or *meditate* 4 The command (*seek*) is addressed to more than one person 5 The meaning of the Hebrew verse is uncertain 6 Other Hebrew manuscripts *Oh! Had I not believed*

26:12 on level ground. A metaphor for personal stability and right relationship with the Lord.

27:1 light. God brings clarity, order, and understanding, while darkness is evil and chaotic. See Nah. 1:8, where the defeat of the enemy is shown by their being pursued into darkness. Also see "God Is Light: Divine Holiness and Justice" at Lev. 11:44.

27:2 eat up my flesh. The enemy seeks the physical harm of the psalmist. The expression also has a figurative meaning, "to slander me."

27:4 house of the LORD. The place where God's presence is manifest is a place of sanctuary from the enemy.

27:5 lift me high. Above all trouble.

27:6 sacrifices with shouts of joy. He shouts for victory because the Lord has saved him.

27:8 face. To seek God's face is to seek intimate fellowship with Him.

27:9 Hide not your face. The psalmist recognizes that, however great his desire, he can only see God's face if God reveals it.

27:13 goodness of the LORD. He is confident of God's vindication while he is still alive.

27:14 Wait for the LORD. His counsel is, "In the midst of present trouble, do not give up; give God time to answer."

28:1 my rock. Using this familiar name the psalmist remembers God as his source of protection and strength (Deut. 32:4, 18, 31; Ps. 78:35).

go down to the pit. That is, to die. The pit stands for Sheol, the grave (6:5 note).

2 [m] Hear the voice of my pleas for mercy,
when I cry to you for help,
when I [n] lift up my hands
[o] toward your most holy sanctuary.[1]
3 Do not [p] drag me off with the wicked,
with the workers of evil,
[q] who speak peace with their neighbors
while evil is in their hearts.
4 [r] Give to them according to their work
and according to the evil of their deeds;
give to them according to the work of their hands;
[s] render them their due reward.
5 Because they [t] do not regard the works of the LORD
or the work of his hands,
he will tear them down and build them up no more.
6 Blessed be the LORD!
for he has [u] heard the voice of my pleas for mercy.
7 The LORD is my strength and [v] my shield;
in him my heart [w] trusts, and I am helped;
my heart exults,
and with my [x] song I give thanks to him.
8 The LORD is the strength of his people;[2]
he is [y] the saving refuge of his anointed.
9 Oh, save your people and bless [z] your heritage!
[a] Be their shepherd and [b] carry them forever.

2 [m] Ps. 140:6; Prov. 1:12 [n] Ps. 134:2; 141:2; Lam. 2:19; 1 Tim. 2:8; [Ps. 119:48] [o] Ps. 5:7; 138:2; [1 Kin. 8:29]
3 [p] [Ps. 26:9; Ezek. 32:20] [q] Jer. 9:8; [Ps. 5:9; 12:2; 55:21; 62:4]
4 [r] Jer. 50:15, 29; Rev. 18:6; [2 Tim. 4:14] [s] [Ps. 137:8]
5 [t] Isai. 5:12; [Job 34:27]
6 [u] ver. 2
7 [v] See Ps. 3:3 [w] See Ps. 11:1 [x] Ps. 69:30
8 [y] Ps. 140:7; [Ps. 20:6]
9 [z] Deut 9:29; 32:9 [a] Ps. 78:71, 72 [b] Isai. 40:11; 46:3; 63:9

Psalm 29
1 [c] Ps. 96:7, 8; 1 Chr. 16:28, 29; [Ps. 68:34]
2 [d] Ps. 110:3; 1 Chr. 16:29; [Ex. 28:2]
3 [e] [Ps. 18:11]
3 [f] Job 37:4, 5
4 [g] Ps. 68:33
5 [h] Ps. 104:16; Judg. 9:15
6 [i] Ps. 114:4, 6 [j] Deut. 3:9 [k] Num. 23:22
8 [l] Num. 13:26
9 [m] [Job 39:1-3]

Ascribe to the LORD Glory

29 A PSALM OF DAVID.
Ascribe to the LORD, O heavenly beings,[3]
[c] ascribe to the LORD glory and strength.
2 Ascribe to the LORD the glory due his name;
worship the LORD in [d] the splendor of holiness.[4]

3 The voice of the LORD is over [e] the waters;
the God of glory [f] thunders,
the LORD, over many waters.
4 The voice of the LORD is [g] powerful;
the voice of the LORD is full of majesty.

5 The voice of the LORD breaks the cedars;
the LORD breaks [h] the cedars of Lebanon.
6 He makes Lebanon to [i] skip like a calf,
and [j] Sirion like a young [k] wild ox.

7 The voice of the LORD flashes forth flames of fire.
8 The voice of the LORD shakes the wilderness;
the LORD shakes the wilderness of [l] Kadesh.

9 The voice of the LORD makes [m] the deer give birth[5]
and strips the forests bare,
and in his temple all cry, "Glory!"

1 Hebrew *your innermost sanctuary* 2 Some Hebrew manuscripts, Septuagint, Syriac; most Hebrew manuscripts *is their strength*
3 Hebrew *sons of God*, or *sons of might* 4 Or *in holy attire*
5 Revocalization yields *makes the oaks to shake*

28:2 holy sanctuary. The Most Holy Place, the inner room in the tabernacle or temple where the ark of the covenant stood.

28:3 speak peace. The psalmist knows the hypocrisy of his enemies.

28:4 render them. An imprecation, that is, a prayer that God would punish the enemy.

28:5 he will tear them down. The previous verse appealed for judgment and this one pronounces it.

28:9 your people. The psalmist broadens his appeal to the Lord to include the whole nation.

Be their shepherd. See note Ps. 23:1.

Ps. 29 A song of praise to God the King. The psalm uses themes that were current in the religions of the surrounding nations: the power behind storms (vv. 3–9) and the victor over floodwaters (vv. 10, 11). The psalmist attacks these religions by taking the praises they claimed for their false gods and ascribing them to the Lord. The picture of God as King, enthroned over the vanquished floodwaters, is one of many indications that the psalm was used to celebrate a divinely given victory in battle.

29:1 heavenly beings. Lit. "sons of gods" (see text note). This phrase is used in the religious texts of the Canaanites and refers to the gods of their pantheon. In the Bible it would refer to spiritual beings such as the cherubim and the angels.

29:2 name. This is His reputation achieved through His acts in history.

29:3–9 The Canaanites believed that Baal provided rain and fertility, and that his power was seen in the storm. They called him "cloud rider" in their religious texts. But the Lord controls nature (1 Kin. 18).

29:3 voice of the LORD. Thunder.

waters . . . many waters. In the religions of the Near East, as in the Bible, the sea represents forces of chaos and evil. See 18:4; 46:2; 69:1, 2 and notes.

29:6 Lebanon . . . Sirion. These are regions of mountains that will shake before the power of God. See Ps. 46:2.

29:8 wilderness of Kadesh. This could be translated (lit.) "holy desert." Its location is uncertain.

10 The LORD sits enthroned over [n]the
flood;
the LORD sits enthroned [o]as king
forever.
11 May the LORD give [p]strength to his
people!
May the LORD bless[1] his people
with [q]peace!

Joy Comes in the Morning

30 A PSALM OF DAVID. A SONG AT THE DEDICATION OF [r]THE TEMPLE.

1 I will [s]extol you, O LORD, for you
have drawn me up
and have not let my foes [t]rejoice
over me.
2 O LORD my God, I [u]cried to you for
help,
and you have [v]healed me.
3 O LORD, you have brought up my
soul from [w]Sheol;
you restored me to life from
among those who [x]go down to
the pit.[2]

4 Sing praises to the LORD, O you [y]his
saints,
and [z]give thanks to his holy name.[3]
5 [a]For his anger is but for a moment,
and [b]his favor is for a lifetime.[4]
[c]Weeping may tarry for the night,
but [d]joy comes with the morning.

6 As for me, I said in my [e]prosperity,
"I shall never be [f]moved."
7 By your favor, O LORD,
you made my [g]mountain stand
strong;
you [h]hid your face;
I was [i]dismayed.

8 To you, O LORD, I cry,
and [j]to the Lord I plead for mercy:
9 "What profit is there in my death,[5]
if I go down to the pit?[6]
Will [k]the dust praise you?
Will it tell of your faithfulness?
10 [l]Hear, O LORD, and be merciful to me!
O LORD, be my helper!"

11 You have turned for me my
mourning into [m]dancing;
you have loosed my sackcloth
and clothed me with gladness,
12 that my [n]glory may sing your praise
and not be silent.
O LORD my God, I will give thanks
to you forever!

Into Your Hand I Commit My Spirit

31 TO THE CHOIRMASTER. A PSALM OF DAVID.

1 [o]In you, O LORD, do I [p]take refuge;
[q]let me never be put to shame;
in your [r]righteousness deliver me!
2 Incline your ear to me;
rescue me speedily!
Be [s]a rock of [t]refuge for me,
a strong fortress to save me!

3 For you are my rock and my fortress;
and for your [u]name's sake you lead
me and guide me;
4 you [v]take me out of [w]the net they
have hidden for me,
for you are my [x]refuge.
5 [y]Into your hand I commit my spirit;
you have redeemed me, O LORD,
[z]faithful God.

10 [n][Gen. 6:17] [o]Ps. 10:16
11 [p]Ps. 68:35; [Isai. 40:29] [q]Phil. 4:7
Psalm 30 [r]2 Sam. 5:11; 1 Chr. 22:1
1 [s]Ps. 107:32 [t]Ps. 25:2; 35:19, 24; [Ps. 13:4]
2 [u]Ps. 88:13 [v]See Ps. 6:2
3 [w]See Ps. 16:10 [x]Ps. 28:1
4 [y]Ps. 50:5 [z]Ps. 97:12; [1 Chr. 16:4]
5 [a][Ps. 103:9; Job 33:26; Isai. 26:20; 54:7, 8] [b]Ps. 63:3 [c][2 Cor. 4:17, 18] [d]Ps. 126:5 (Heb.)
6 [e][Job 29:18; Prov. 1:32] [f]Ps. 10:6
7 [g][2 Sam. 5:9] [h]Ps. 104:29; [Deut. 31:17] [i][2 Sam. 24:10]
8 [j]Ps. 142:1
9 [k]See Ps. 6:5
10 [l]Ps. 27:7
11 [m]Ex. 15:20; 2 Sam. 6:14; Jer. 31:4, 13; [Ps. 149:3; 150:4; Lam. 5:15]
12 [n]See Ps. 16:9
Psalm 31
1 [o]For ver. 1-3, see Ps. 71:1-3 [p]See Ps. 11:1 [q]ver. 17 [r]Ps. 143:1
2 [s]See Ps. 18:2 [t][Ps. 91:2]
3 [u]See Ps. 23:3
4 [v]Ps. 25:15 [w]See Job 18:8 [x]Ps. 43:2
5 [y]Cited Luke 23:46; [Acts 7:59] [z]Deut. 32:4

[1] Or *The LORD will give . . . The LORD will bless* [2] Or *to life, that I should not go down to the pit* [3] Hebrew *to the memorial of his holiness* (see Exodus 3:15) [4] Or *and in his favor is life* [5] Hebrew *in my blood* [6] Or *to corruption*

29:10 flood. See v. 3.

Ps. 30 The title indicates that the psalm was written for the dedication of the temple. In David's time the temple had not yet been built, but he could have prepared for its dedication much as he prepared for building it by gathering supplies (1 Chr. 22). A greater difficulty is the lack of any mention of the temple in the body of the psalm (Introduction: Characteristics and Themes). Attempts to link the psalm with the plague recorded in 1 Chr. 21:1–22:1 fail to take into account that David himself was not afflicted.

30:1 drawn me up. The Hebrew verb is used of drawing a bucket out of a well, an appropriate portrayal of saving someone from Sheol (i.e., the grave), which is often pictured as a wet and muddy pit.

30:2 healed me. An indication that the psalm is a thanksgiving in response to physical healing.

30:3 soul. See "Body and Soul, Male and Female" at Gen. 2:7.

30:4 saints. The word is related to covenant lovingkindness and specifies those in covenant relationship with God.

30:5 for a moment. God's mercy is sure. See Rom. 8:18; 2 Cor. 4:17.

morning. Cf. Ps. 90:14.

30:7 my mountain. Mountains, as opposed to the sea, are a symbol of stability and often represent security in the protection of God (Ps. 46:2).

30:9 profit. The psalmist bargains with God for his life (Gen. 18) by pointing out that God would gain a voice of praise if He healed him. This is not a developed treatment of the afterlife. The point is that death would bring to a conclusion David's desire to glorify God in this world.

31:1 in your righteousness. The psalmist appeals to the Lord's righteousness in his distress caused by the wickedness of the enemy. "Your righteousness" indicates God's commitment to save those who are in covenant relationship with Him.

31:5 I commit my spirit. Jesus quoted these words on the cross (Luke 23:46). The desperate cries of lament found in the psalms often express Christ's own anguish as He faced the rejection of the world (Ps. 22 and 69).

6 I [a]hate[1] those who pay [b]regard to
worthless [c]idols,
but I trust in the LORD.
7 I will rejoice and be glad in your
steadfast love,
because you have seen my affliction;
you have [d]known the distress of
my soul,
8 and you have not [e]delivered me into
the hand of the enemy;
you have set my feet in [f]a broad
place.

9 Be gracious to me, O LORD, for I am
[g]in distress;
[h]my eye is wasted from grief;
my soul and my body also.
10 For my life is spent with sorrow,
and my years with sighing;
my strength fails because of my
iniquity,
and [i]my bones waste away.

11 Because of all my adversaries I have
become [j]a reproach,
especially to my [k]neighbors,
and an object of dread to my
acquaintances;
those who see me in the street [l]flee
from me.
12 I have been [m]forgotten like one who
is dead;
I have become like [n]a broken vessel.
13 For I [o]hear the whispering of many—
terror on every side!—
[p]as they scheme together against me,
as they plot to take my life.

14 But I [q]trust in you, O LORD;
I say, "You are my God."
15 My [r]times are in your hand;
[s]rescue me from the hand of my
enemies and from my
persecutors!

6 [a]Ps. 26:5 [b]Jonah 2:8 [c]Deut. 32:21; Jer. 8:19; 14:22
7 [d]See Ps. 1:6
8 [e][Deut. 32:30] [f]See Job 36:16
9 [g]Ps. 66:14 [h]See Ps. 6:7
10 [i]Ps. 6:2; 32:3; 38:3; 102:3
11 [j][Ps. 41:7, 8; Isai. 53:3] [k]See Job 19:13, 14 [l][Matt. 26:56; Mark 14:50]
12 [m]Ps. 88:5; Eccles. 9:5 [n]Isai. 30:14
13 [o]Jer. 20:10 [p][Matt. 27:1]; See 2 Sam. 17:1-4
14 [q]ver. 1, 6
15 [r]1 Chr. 29:30; Job 24:1 [s]Ps. 7:1
16 [t]See Ps. 4:6
17 [u]ver. 1 [v]1 Sam. 2:9; [Ps. 94:17; 115:17]
18 [w][Jude 15] [x]Ps. 17:10
19 [y]Ps. 23:5
20 [z]See Ps. 32:7 [a]See Ps. 27:5
21 [b]Ps. 17:7 [c][1 Sam. 23:7]
22 [d]Ps. 116:11; [2 Sam. 15:14] [e]Isai. 38:11, 12; Lam. 3:54 [f]Jonah 2:4
23 [g]Ps. 30:4 [h]Deut. 32:41
24 [i]See Ps. 27:14

16 [t]Make your face shine on your servant;
save me in your steadfast love!
17 O LORD, [u]let me not be put to shame,
for I call upon you;
let the wicked be put to shame;
let them go [v]silently to Sheol.
18 Let the lying lips be mute,
which [w]speak [x]insolently against
the righteous
in pride and contempt.

19 Oh, how abundant is your goodness,
which you have stored up for those
who fear you
and worked for those who take
refuge in you,
[y]in the sight of the children of
mankind!
20 In [z]the cover of your presence you
hide them
from the plots of men;
you [a]store them in your shelter
from the strife of tongues.

21 Blessed be the LORD,
for he has wondrously [b]shown his
steadfast love to me
when I was in [c]a besieged city.
22 I had said in my [d]alarm,[2]
"I am [e]cut off from [f]your sight."
But you heard the voice of my pleas
for mercy
when I cried to you for help.

23 Love the LORD, all you his [g]saints!
The LORD preserves the faithful
but abundantly [h]repays the one
who acts in pride.
24 [i]Be strong, and let your heart take
courage,
all you who wait for the LORD!

1 Masoretic Text; one Hebrew manuscript, Septuagint, Syriac, Jerome *You hate* 2 Or *in my haste*

31:6 worthless idols. They are worthless because they are the figments of their worshipers' imaginations. The psalmist trusts the Lord, who is "faithful" (v. 5).

31:7 steadfast love. Specifically, the love between covenant partners (God and David), which moves God to respond to the psalmist's distress.

31:10 iniquity. Several ancient translations read, "affliction," which draws support from the psalm's general theme of distress from outside forces rather than from the psalmist's guilt.

31:12 broken vessel. A metaphor for serious illness, even death (Eccl. 12:6).

31:14 You are my God. A simple and foundational confession that David is in covenant with God.

31:15 My times. The psalmist knows that God controls history in general and his life in particular. This comforts him in his distress.

31:16 face shine. See the priestly blessing of Num. 6:25. The metaphor of God's face represents His loving presence that will bring salvation to the psalmist.

31:21 besieged city. This phrase is difficult to understand. The psalmist could be remembering a particular incident. It may be that the original reading was "in a difficult time," a rendering that fits the context well. A copyist's error in one letter would account for the difference of reading.

31:23 his saints. The word is formed from the same Hebrew root (*ḥesed*) as "steadfast love," understood as God's lovingkindness toward those in a covenant relationship with Him.

Blessed Are the Forgiven

32 A MASKIL[1] OF DAVID.
[j] Blessed is the one whose
[k] transgression is forgiven,
whose sin is covered.
2 Blessed is the man against whom the
LORD [l] counts no iniquity,
and in whose spirit [m] there is no
deceit.

3 For when I kept silent, my [n] bones
wasted away
through my [o] groaning all
day long.
4 For day and night your [p] hand was
heavy upon me;
my strength was dried up[2] as by
the heat of summer. *Selah*

5 I [q] acknowledged my sin to you,
and I did not cover my iniquity;
I said, "I [r] will confess my
transgressions to the LORD,"
and you forgave the iniquity of my
sin. *Selah*

6 Therefore let everyone who is
[s] godly
offer prayer to you at a time when
you [t] may be found;
surely in the rush of [u] great waters,
they shall not reach him.
7 You are a [v] hiding place for me;
you preserve me from [w] trouble;
you surround me with [x] shouts of
deliverance. *Selah*

8 I will [y] instruct you and teach you in
the way you should go;
I will [z] counsel you with my eye
upon you.
9 [a] Be not like a horse or a mule,
without understanding,
which must be curbed with [b] bit
and bridle,
or it will not stay near you.

10 [c] Many are the sorrows of the wicked,
but steadfast love surrounds the
one who [d] trusts in the LORD.
11 [e] Be glad in the LORD, and rejoice,
O righteous,
and [f] shout for joy, all you [g] upright
in heart!

The Steadfast Love of the LORD

33 [h] Shout for joy in the LORD, O you
righteous!
[i] Praise befits the upright.
2 Give thanks to the LORD with the
[j] lyre;
make melody to him with [j] the
harp of [k] ten strings!
3 Sing to him [l] a new song;
play skillfully on the strings, with
loud shouts.

4 For the word of the LORD is upright,
and all his work is done in
[m] faithfulness.
5 He [n] loves righteousness and justice;
[o] the earth is full of the steadfast
love of the LORD.

6 By [p] the word of the LORD the
heavens were made,
and by [q] the breath of his mouth all
[r] their host.

Psalm 32
1 [j] Cited Rom. 4:7, 8; [Ps. 85:2] [k] [Ex. 34:7; John 1:29]
2 [l] [2 Cor. 5:19] [m] John 1:47
3 [n] See Ps. 31:10 [o] See Ps. 22:1
4 [p] 1 Sam. 5:6, 11; [Ps. 38:2]
5 [q] Ps. 51:3 [r] Ps. 38:18; Job 33:27; Prov. 28:13; [Luke 15:18, 21; 1 John 1:9]
6 [s] Ps. 30:4 [t] See Ps. 69:13 [u] [Ps. 18:4, 16; 42:7; 69:1; 144:7]; See Job 22:11
7 [v] Ps. 91:1; 119:114; [Ps. 27:5; 31:20] [w] Ps. 9:9 [x] [Ps. 18, title]; See Ex. 15:1-18; Judg. 5:1-31; Ex. 15:1
8 [y] Ps. 25:8, 12 [z] Ps. 73:24
9 [a] Prov. 26:3; [Job 35:11] [b] James 3:3
10 [c] [Prov. 13:21; Rom. 2:9] [d] Ps. 34:8; 84:12; Prov. 16:20; Jer. 17:7
11 [e] Ps. 64:10; 68:3; 97:12; [Ps. 33:1] [f] Deut. 32:43 [g] See Ps. 7:10

Psalm 33
1 [h] [Ps. 32:11] [i] Ps. 147:1
2 [j] Ps. 71:22 [k] Ps. 92:3; 144:9
3 [l] Ps. 40:3; 96:1; Isai. 42:10
4 [m] Ps. 119:75
5 [n] Ps. 11:7; 36:5, 6; 45:7; 89:14 [o] Ps. 119:64 6 [p] Gen. 1:6, 7; Heb. 11:3; 2 Pet. 3:5; [John 1:3] [q] [Job 26:13; Isai. 11:4] [r] Gen. 2:1

1 Probably a musical or liturgical term 2 Hebrew *my vitality was changed*

Ps. 32 A penitential psalm containing some distinctive wisdom language (vv. 1, 2, 8–10).

32:2 iniquity. Three different words for sin are used in the first two verses to bring out the many aspects of man's rebellion against God. Paul cites the first two verses of this psalm in Rom. 4:6–8 in describing the grace of God's forgiveness.

32:3 my bones wasted away. The psalmist perceives sin's consequences in his body. This is not merely poetic language, although sin does not always have immediate physical consequences.

32:4 my strength was . . . heat. Guilt immobilized and enervated the psalmist.

32:5 I acknowledged my sin to you. He praises God's willingness and authority to forgive.

32:6 godly. Or "saints"; see Ps. 31:23 note.

great waters. Elsewhere translated "many waters." See notes Ps. 18:4, 16; 29:3, 10; 46:2; 69:1, 2; 144:7.

32:8 I will instruct you. Using language found in wisdom sections of the Old Testament (e.g., Ps. 1 and Prov. 1–9), God promises to direct the psalmist in the way of the covenant, in the way of righteousness.

32:9 like a horse. Horses and mules do the will of their masters only under compulsion (Prov. 26:3). The righteous should obey out of love and gratitude to their God.

Ps. 33 There are twenty-two verses in the psalm, the same as the number of letters in the Hebrew alphabet, but the psalm is not an acrostic (see Introduction to Hebrew Poetry).

33:3 new song. Often such "new" psalms are found in contexts of victorious war and can be seen as shouts of victory. Cf. Ps. 96; 98; 144; 149; Is. 42:10; Rev. 5:9; 14:3).

33:4 the word of the LORD is upright. God's speech to men reflects His character. He does not deceive His people, but leads them into the truth. The Bible, as God's written Word, does the same.

33:6 all their host. Literally, this word is simply "hosts" and may refer not merely to the innumerable stars of heaven, but also to the angelic armies.

7 He gathers the waters of the sea as [s]a heap;
he [t]puts the deeps in storehouses.

8 Let all the earth fear the LORD;
let all the inhabitants of the world stand in awe of him!
9 For [u]he spoke, and it came to be;
he commanded, and it stood firm.

10 The LORD [v]brings the counsel of the nations to nothing;
he frustrates the plans of the peoples.
11 [w]The counsel of the LORD stands forever,
the plans of his heart to all generations.
12 [x]Blessed is the nation whose God is the LORD,
the people whom he has [y]chosen as his heritage!

13 The LORD [z]looks down from heaven;
he sees all the children of man;
14 from [a]where he sits enthroned he [b]looks out
on all the inhabitants of the earth,
15 he who fashions the hearts of them all
and observes all their deeds.
16 [c]The king is not saved by his great army;
a warrior is not delivered by his great strength.
17 [d]The war horse is a false hope for salvation,
and by its great might it cannot rescue.

18 Behold, [e]the eye of the LORD is on those who fear him,
[f]on those who hope in his steadfast love,
19 that he may [g]deliver their soul from death
and keep them alive in [h]famine.

20 Our soul [i]waits for the LORD;
he is our [j]help and [k]our shield.
21 For our heart is [l]glad in him,
because we [m]trust in his holy name.
22 Let your steadfast love, O LORD, be upon us,
even as we hope in you.

7 [s]Ps. 78:13; Ex. 15:8; Josh. 3:13, 16 [t]See Job 38:8
9 [u]Ps. 148:5, 6; Gen. 1:3; [Ps. 147:15, 18]
10 [v]Isai. 19:3; Luke 1:51; [2 Sam. 15:34; 17:14; Neh. 4:15; Job 5:12; Isai. 8:10]
11 [w]Prov. 19:21; Isai. 46:10
12 [x]Ps. 144:15; Deut. 33:29 [y]Ps. 65:4; Deut. 7:6; [Ex. 19:5]
13 [z]Job 28:24; See Ps. 11:4
14 [a]1 Kin. 8:39, 43, 49 [b][Prov. 15:3; Jer. 32:19]
16 [c][Ps. 44:6]
17 [d]Ps. 20:7; 147:10; Prov. 21:31; Hos. 1:7
18 [e]Ps. 34:15; Job 36:7; 1 Pet. 3:12 [f]Ps. 147:11
19 [g][Acts 12:11] [h]Ps. 37:19; Job 5:20
20 [i]Ps. 62:1, 5; 130:6; Isai. 8:17 [j]Ps. 115:9-11 [k]See Ps. 3:3
21 [l]Zech. 10:7; See Ps. 9:14 [m]See Ps. 11:1
Psalm 34 [n]1 Sam. 21:13 [o][1 Sam. 21:10, 11, 12, 14]
1 [p][Eph. 5:20; 1 Thess. 5:18]
2 [q]Ps. 44:8; 1 Sam. 2:1; Jer. 9:24 [r]Ps. 119:74

Taste and See That the LORD Is Good

34 [1] OF DAVID, WHEN HE [n]CHANGED HIS BEHAVIOR BEFORE [o]ABIMELECH, SO THAT HE DROVE HIM OUT, AND HE WENT AWAY.

1 I will bless the LORD [p]at all times;
his praise shall continually be in my mouth.
2 My soul [q]makes its boast in the LORD;
let the humble hear and [r]be glad.
3 Oh, [s]magnify the LORD with me,
and let us exalt his name together!

4 I [t]sought the LORD, and he answered me
and delivered me from all my fears.
5 Those who look to him are [u]radiant,
and their faces shall never be ashamed.
6 [v]This poor man cried, and the LORD heard him
and [w]saved him out of all his troubles.

3 [s]Ps. 35:27; 40:16; 69:30; 70:4; Luke 1:46 **4** [t]2 Chr. 15:2; [Matt. 7:7] **5** [u]Isai. 60:5; [Ps. 4:6] **6** [v]ver. 15, 17 [w]ver. 17, 19; 2 Sam. 22:1

1 This psalm is an acrostic poem, each verse beginning with the successive letters of the Hebrew alphabet

33:7 the waters of the sea. The creator is pictured poetically as exercising command over the waters of chaos (Ps. 18:16 note). There may also be a poetical allusion to the song of Moses and Israel at the Red Sea (Ex. 15).

33:8 fear the LORD. To honor, love, and obey Him.

33:10 nations. Godless nations who seek their own will and not God's.

33:11 The counsel of the LORD stands forever. Nothing can subvert God's purposes. He is in absolute control of history.

33:12 the people whom he has chosen. God is the One who initiated the relationship with Israel, the nation He chose (Deut. 7:7–11).

33:13 heaven. See "Heaven" at Rev. 21:1.

33:15 God not only sees all, He forms the hearts of all.

Ps. 34 The psalm has a historical title (see below), but the verses themselves are written in a general style, lending the poem to use by different people in different situations. The psalm is an acrostic (Introduction: Characteristics and Themes), although there is no line for the sixth Hebrew letter (*waw*), and the line for the seventeenth letter is out of order, coming last.

34:title See 1 Sam. 21:10–15 for the historical situation of the title. Abimelech is probably a royal title for the king of the Philistines, not the proper name of the king (Achish, in the time of Samuel).

34:2 boast in the LORD. While boasting in oneself is the height of pride and godlessness (Rom. 1:30), to boast in God is right (Jer. 9:24; 2 Cor. 10:17).

34:3 his name. That is, His reputation. The congregation is exhorted to witness to God's great acts in history and in our lives.

34:4 he answered me. One of the most frequent themes of the psalms is stated boldly: God hears and answers the prayers of His people.

34:5 are radiant. They reflect the Lord's shining upon them (Ps. 31:16 note). Radiance reflects the joy of God's revealed presence, while the sense of God's withdrawal from us brings the darkness of shame.

34:6 This poor man. The psalmist, who had no power to save himself.

7 [x]The angel of the LORD [y]encamps
around those who fear him, and
delivers them.
8 Oh, [z]taste and see that [a]the LORD is
good!
[b]Blessed is the man who takes
refuge in him!
9 Oh, fear the LORD, you his saints,
for those who fear him have no
lack!
10 [c]The young lions suffer want and
hunger;
but those who [d]seek the LORD lack
no good thing.
11 [e]Come, O children, listen to me;
[f]I will teach you the fear of the
LORD.
12 [g]What man is there who desires life
and loves many days, that he may
[h]see good?
13 [i]Keep your tongue from evil
and your lips from [j]speaking
deceit.
14 [k]Turn away from evil and do good;
seek peace and [l]pursue it.
15 [m]The eyes of the LORD are toward the
righteous
[n]and his ears toward their cry.
16 [o]The face of the LORD is against those
who do evil,
to [p]cut off the memory of them
from the earth.
17 [n]When the righteous cry for help, the
LORD hears
and delivers them out of all their
troubles.
18 The LORD is near to [q]the
brokenhearted
and saves [r]the crushed in spirit.
19 [s]Many are the afflictions of the
righteous,
[t]but the LORD delivers him out of
them all.
20 He keeps all his bones;
[u]not one of them is broken.
21 [v]Affliction will slay the wicked,
and those who hate the righteous
will be condemned.
22 The LORD [w]redeems the life of his
servants;
none of those who take refuge in
him will be [x]condemned.

7[x]Dan. 6:22; Heb. 1:14 [y][Gen. 32:1, 2; 2 Kin. 6:17] **8**[z]Heb. 6:5; 1 Pet. 2:3 [a]Ps. 100:5 [b]See Ps. 2:12 **10**[c]Job 4:10, 11 [d][Ps. 84:11] **11**[e]Ps. 66:16 [f][Ps. 32:8] **12**[g]Cited 1 Pet. 3:10-12 [h]Eccles. 3:13; 6:6 **13**[i]Ps. 15:3; 39:1; 141:3; Prov. 13:3; 21:23; James 1:26; 3:2; 1 Pet. 2:1, 22 [j]John 1:47; Rev. 14:5 **14**[k]Ps. 37:27; Isai. 1:16, 17; [Job 28:28] [l]Rom. 14:19; Heb. 12:14; [Rom. 12:18] **15**[m]See Ps. 33:18 [n]ver. 6, 8; Ps. 145:18; [John 9:31] **16**[o]Jer. 44:11; Amos 9:4 [p]See Ps. 21:10 **17**[n][See ver. 15 above] **18**[q]Ps. 51:17; 147:3; Isai. 61:1 [r]Isai. 57:15; 66:2; See Luke 15:17-24
19[s]2 Tim. 3:11, 12 [t]ver. 6, 17, 22; [Acts 12:11] **20**[u]John 19:36 **21**[v]Ps. 94:23; Prov. 24:16; [Ps. 7:15, 16] **22**[w]See Ps. 25:22 [x][Rom. 8:33, 34] **Psalm 35** **1**[y]Isai. 49:25 [z][Ex. 14:25; Isai. 42:13] **2**[a]Ps. 91:4; [Ps. 5:12]

Great Is the LORD

35

OF DAVID.
1 Contend, O LORD, with those who
[y]contend with me;
[z]fight against those who fight
against me!
2 Take hold of [a]shield and buckler
and rise for my help!
3 Draw the spear and javelin[1]
against my pursuers!
Say to my soul,
"I am your salvation!"
4 [b]Let them be [c]put to shame and
dishonor
who seek after my life!
Let them be [d]turned back and
disappointed
who devise evil against me!
5 Let them be like [e]chaff before the wind,
with the angel of the LORD driving
them away!
6 Let their way be dark and [f]slippery,
with the angel of the LORD
pursuing them!

4[b]For ver. 4-8, see Ps. 69:22-28; 109:6-15 [c]ver. 26; Ps. 40:14; 70:2; 71:13; 83:17 [d]Ps. 129:5 **5**[e]See Job 21:18 **6**[f]Ps. 73:18; Jer. 23:12

1 Or *and close the way*

34:7 The angel of the LORD. One of God's heavenly troops. See "Angels" at Zech. 1:9.

those who fear him. Those who are in a right relationship with Him. Gehazi learned the truth of this verse when Elisha prayed for his eyes to be opened and showed him the army of the Lord (2 Kin. 6:8–23).

34:8 taste. The psalmist describes his personal experience of God's goodness. After tasting God's goodness in Christ, Peter alludes to this passage (1 Pet. 2:3).

34:10 The young lions. The strong and ruthless do not always get what they want, but God's people lack nothing that is good for them.

34:11 children. A common and poetic form of address to all ages.

34:20 not one of them is broken. John 19:36 applies this verse to Christ, the only perfect righteous Man.

Ps. 35 The psalm is a lament by one whose life is threatened. The psalm uses the language of warfare (vv. 1–3) as well as legal language (vv. 11, 23, 24). Twice the psalm comes to a climax with the figure of the offering of a vow in praise (vv. 18, 28).

35:1 Contend. The word is a legal term that means "bring a case against someone." Such language runs through the psalm (vv. 11–16, 23, 24), as David commits his case to God.

fight. The psalmist calls upon the Lord to wage war on his behalf.

35:2 rise. A request that occurs in many of the psalms in the setting of warfare (cf. 3:7; 7:6; 12:5).

35:3 your salvation. In the particular context, this phrase indicates victory in battle.

35:5 like chaff. Easily scattered and unable to stand. See Ps. 1:4.

7 For [g]without cause [h]they hid their
net for me;
without cause they dug [i]a pit for
my life.[1]
8 Let [j]destruction come upon him
[k]when he does not know it!
And let the net that he hid ensnare
him;
let him fall into it—to his
destruction!
9 Then my soul will rejoice in the LORD,
[l]exulting in his salvation.
10 All my [m]bones shall say,
"O LORD, [n]who is like you,
delivering the poor
from him who is too strong for
him,
the poor and needy from him who
robs him?"
11 [o]Malicious[2] witnesses rise up;
they ask me of things that I do not
know.
12 [p]They repay me evil for good;
my soul is bereft.[3]
13 But I, [q]when they were sick—
I [r]wore sackcloth;
I [s]afflicted myself with fasting;
I prayed [t]with head bowed[4] on my
chest.
14 I went about as though I grieved
for my friend or my brother;
as one who laments his mother,
I [u]bowed down in mourning.
15 But at my stumbling they rejoiced
and gathered;
they gathered together against me;
[v]wretches whom I did not know
tore at me without ceasing;
16 like profane mockers at a feast,[5]
they [w]gnash at me with their teeth.
17 How long, O Lord, will you [x]look on?
Rescue me from their destruction,
[y]my precious life from the lions!

7 [g]See Ps. 69:4 [h]See Job 18:8 [i]See Ps. 7:15
8 [j][1 Thess. 5:3] [k]Isai. 47:11
9 [l]Luke 1:47; See Ps. 9:14
10 [m]Ps. 51:8 [n]Ps. 71:19; 86:8; 89:6, 8; 113:5; Ex. 15:11
11 [o]See Ps. 27:12
12 [p]Ps. 38:20; 109:4; Jer. 18:20; [John 10:32]
13 [q][Job 30:25] [r]Ps. 69:11; [1 Kin. 20:31] [s]Ps. 69:10; Num. 29:7 [t][Matt. 10:13]; Luke 10:6
14 [u]See Ps. 38:6
15 [v]Job 30:1, 8, 12
16 [w]Ps. 37:12; Job 16:9; Lam. 2:16
17 [x]Hab. 1:13 [y]Ps. 22:20
18 [z]Ps. 22:25
19 [a]ver. 24; See Ps. 13:4 [b]Ps. 38:19; 69:4; 119:78, 86 [c]Prov. 6:13; 10:10 [d]Ps. 69:4; Cited John 15:25 [e]ver. 7
21 [f]See Ps. 22:13 [g]ver. 25; Ps. 40:15; 70:3
22 [h][Ex. 3:7] [i]Ps. 28:1 [j]See Ps. 10:1
23 [k]Ps. 44:23; 59:4; 80:2 [l]Ps. 7:6
24 [m]Ps. 7:8 [n]ver. 19
25 [o]ver. 21 [p]2 Sam. 17:16; Lam. 2:16
26 [q]See ver. 4 [r]See Job 8:22 [s]See Job 19:5

18 I will thank you in [z]the great
congregation;
in the mighty throng I will
praise you.
19 [a]Let not those rejoice over me
who are [b]wrongfully my foes,
and let not those [c]wink the eye
who [d]hate me [e]without
cause.
20 For they do not speak peace,
but against those who are quiet
in the land
they devise words of deceit.
21 They [f]open wide their mouths
against me;
they say, [g]"Aha, Aha!
our eyes have seen it!"
22 [h]You have seen, O LORD; [i]be not
silent!
O Lord, [j]be not far from me!
23 Awake and [k]rouse yourself for [l]my
vindication,
for my cause, my God and my
Lord!
24 [m]Vindicate me, O LORD, my God,
according to your
righteousness,
and [n]let them not rejoice
over me!
25 Let them not say in their hearts,
[o]"Aha, our heart's desire!"
Let them not say, [p]"We have
swallowed him up."
26 Let them be [q]put to shame and
disappointed altogether
who rejoice at my calamity!
Let them be [r]clothed with shame
and dishonor
who [s]magnify themselves
against me!

1 The word *pit* is transposed from the preceding line; Hebrew *For without cause they hid the pit of their net for me; without cause they dug for my life* 2 Or *Violent* 3 Hebrew *it is bereavement to my soul* 4 Or *My prayer shall turn back* 5 The meaning of the Hebrew phrase is uncertain

35:7 without cause. The Lord's righteous servant has done no evil to his enemies.

35:8 Let destruction come upon him. The enemies' evil intentions turn back on themselves. Their evil becomes their own judgment, a frequent theme in the prophets. If they dig a pit for someone they will fall into it themselves. See Ps. 7:14–16; 34:21.

35:10 LORD, who is like you. Compare Ex. 15:11, in another divine warrior psalm. Vv. 9, 10 anticipate the sure victory of God.

35:11 Malicious witnesses. The law condemns circulating false reports (Ex. 23:1). "Malicious" indicates the cruelty of such witnesses who want to harm the defendant.

35:12 evil for good. The height of injustice; cf. Gen. 44:4; 1 Sam. 25:21; Ps. 38:20; 109:5; Prov. 17:13.

35:13, 14 The psalmist did no evil to those who now attack him; he actively and sacrificially pursued their well-being.

35:19 wink the eye. Taunting the psalmist.

35:20 do not speak peace. A technical term in ancient treaties. They are breaking their covenant agreement.

27 Let those who delight in my
righteousness
shout for joy and be glad
[t] and say evermore,
[u] "Great is the LORD,
who [v] delights in the welfare of his
servant!"
28 Then my [w] tongue shall tell of your
righteousness
and of your praise all the day long.

How Precious Is Your Steadfast Love

36 TO THE CHOIRMASTER. OF DAVID, THE [x] SERVANT OF THE LORD.

1 Transgression speaks to the wicked
deep in his heart;[1]
[y] there is no fear of God
before his eyes.
2 [z] For he flatters himself in his own
eyes
that his iniquity cannot be found
out and hated.
3 The words of his mouth are [a] trouble
and deceit;
[b] he has ceased to act wisely and do
good.
4 He [c] plots [d] trouble while on his bed;
he sets himself in [e] a way that is
not good;
[f] he does not reject evil.

5 Your steadfast love, O LORD, extends
to the heavens,
your faithfulness to the clouds.
6 [g] Your righteousness is like the
mountains of God;
[h] your judgments are like the great
deep;
man and beast you [i] save, O LORD.

7 [j] How precious is your steadfast love,
O God!
The children of mankind take
refuge [k] in the shadow of your
wings.
8 They feast on [l] the abundance of your
house,
and you give them drink from
[m] the river of [n] your delights.
9 For with you is [o] the fountain of life;
[p] in your light do we see light.

10 Oh, continue your steadfast love to
those who [q] know you,
and your righteousness to [r] the
upright of heart!
11 Let not the foot of arrogance come
upon me,
nor the hand of the wicked drive
me away.
12 There [s] the evildoers lie fallen;
they are thrust down, [t] unable to
rise.

He Will Not Forsake His Saints

37[2] OF DAVID.
[u] Fret not yourself because of
evildoers;
be not [v] envious of wrongdoers!
2 For they will soon [w] fade like [x] the
grass
and wither [y] like the green herb.

3 [z] Trust in the LORD, and do good;
[a] dwell in the land and befriend
faithfulness.[3]

3 [z] Ps. 62:8; 115:9-11; Prov. 3:5; Isai. 26:4 [a] Lev. 26:5; Prov. 2:21

1 Some Hebrew manuscripts, Syriac, Jerome (compare Septuagint) most Hebrew manuscripts *in my heart* 2 This psalm is an acrostic poem, each stanza beginning with the successive letters of the Hebrew alphabet 3 Or *and feed on faithfulness*, or *and find safe pasture*

27 [t] Ps. 40:16; 70:4 [u] Ps. 34:3 [v] Ps. 149:4
28 [w] Ps. 51:14; 71:8, 15, 24
Psalm 36
[x] See Ps. 18, title
1 [y] Cited Rom. 3:18
2 [z] Deut. 29:19; [Ps. 10:3; 49:18]
3 [a] [Ps. 12:2] [b] [Jer. 4:22]
4 [c] Mic. 2:1; [Prov. 4:16] [d] Ps. 10:7 [e] Isai. 65:2 [f] [Ps. 97:10]
6 [g] [Ps. 71:19] [h] Ps. 92:5; Rom. 11:33 [i] Ps. 104:14, 15; 145:9, 15, 16; Neh. 9:6
7 [j] [Ps. 31:19] [k] See Ruth 2:12
8 [l] Ps. 23:5; 27:4; 65:4; Isai. 25:6; See Jer. 31:12-14 [m] Ps. 46:4; Rev. 22:1 [n] Ps. 16:11
9 [o] Jer. 2:13; John 4:10, 14; 5:26 [p] John 1:9; Acts 26:18; 1 Pet. 2:9
10 [q] Jer. 22:16; Gal. 4:9; [Ps. 79:6] [r] See Ps. 7:10
12 [s] Ps. 94:4 [t] See Ps. 1:5
Psalm 37
1 [u] ver. 7, 8; Prov. 24:19 [v] Ps. 73:3; Prov. 3:31; 23:17; 24:1, 19
2 [w] Job 14:2; See Job 27:13-23 [x] Ps. 90:5, 6 [y] Ps. 129:6

35:28 my tongue shall tell. The deliverance has not yet come, but the psalmist is singing with praises.

36:1 no fear of God. The psalmist identifies the root of all evil, just as Prov. 1:7 cites the fear of God as the beginning of all knowledge. The fear of God that springs from faith is a special response to revelation, the reverential awe that recognizes total dependence upon the Lord. In the absence of reverence a different type of fear of the Lord will be experienced, namely dread.

36:3 trouble . . . wisely. Wisdom has an ethical side: to be wise is to do good.

36:4 on his bed. Wickedness is a full-time occupation for the wicked. Even at night, when they should be praying before sleep, wicked people plot and scheme.

36:5 steadfast love. A special word in Hebrew, signifying the loving devotion in which God binds Himself to His people. It indicates His lovingkindness toward those with whom He is in covenant relationship. This word recurs throughout Psalms, showing that it is a book of covenantal prayers.

36:6 mountains. See notes Ps. 29:6; 30:7; 46:2.

36:7 wings. This seems to refer to the wings of the cherubim of God's throne, as represented by the beings depicted as covering the ark of the covenant with their wings. Otherwise God is perceived as the protector of His people, like a mother bird who protects her young brood.

36:8 feast on the abundance. The psalmist pictures God as a rich and generous host.

36:9 fountain of life. God is the source of all life. The doctrine of eternal life is more fully revealed in the New Testament (e.g., Matt. 22:31, 32; Luke 23:42, 43; John 3:16; Rev. 21:3–7; 22:3–5). See "Resurrection and Glorification" at 1 Cor. 15:21.

Ps. 37 An acrostic (Introduction: Characteristics and Themes), and like most acrostics, a wisdom meditation.

37:2 grass. The metaphor is apt. In Israel the grass comes up and flourishes in the winter, but in the summer is withered by the sun.

4 [b]Delight yourself in the LORD,
and he will [c]give you the desires of your heart.
5 [z]Commit your way to the LORD;
[d]trust in him, and he will act.
6 [e]He will bring forth your righteousness as the light,
and your justice as [f]the noonday.

7 [g]Be still before the LORD and wait patiently for him;
[h]fret not yourself over the one who [i]prospers in his way,
over the man who carries out evil devices!

8 [j]Refrain from anger, and forsake wrath!
[h]Fret not yourself; it tends only to evil.
9 [k]For the evildoers shall be cut off,
but those who wait for the LORD shall [l]inherit the land.

10 In [m]just a little while, the wicked will be no more;
though you look carefully at [n]his place, he will not be there.
11 But [o]the meek shall inherit the land
and delight themselves in [p]abundant peace.

12 The wicked [q]plots against the righteous
and [r]gnashes his teeth at him,
13 but the Lord [s]laughs at the wicked,
for he sees that his [t]day is coming.

14 The wicked draw the sword and [u]bend their bows
to bring down the poor and needy,
to slay those whose [v]way is upright;
15 their sword shall enter their own heart,
and their [w]bows shall be broken.

4[b]Job 22:26; Isai. 58:14; [Phil. 3:1; 4:4] [c]Matt. 6:33
5[z][See ver. 3 above] [d]Ps. 22:8; 55:22; Prov. 16:3; 1 Pet. 5:7
6[e]Isai. 58:8, 10; Mic. 7:9 [f]Job 11:17
7[g][Ps. 62:1; Isai. 30:15; Lam. 3:26] [h]ver. 1 [i]Jer. 12:1
8[j][Eph. 4:26] [h][See ver. 7 above]
9[k]ver. 2, 22 [l]Ps. 25:13; Prov. 2:21; Isai. 57:13; 60:21
10[m]Job 24:24 [n]Job 7:10
11[o]Cited Matt. 5:5 [p]Ps. 119:165; [Isai. 32:17]
12[q]Ps. 31:13 [r]See Ps. 35:16
13[s]See Ps. 2:4 [t]See Job 18:20
14[u]Ps. 7:12 [v]See Ps. 7:10
15[w]See 1 Sam. 2:4
16[x]Prov. 15:16; 16:8; [1 Tim. 6:6]
17[y]Ps. 10:15; Job 38:15; Ezek. 30:21, 22 [z]ver. 24
18[a]See Ps. 1:6 [b]ver. 9
19[c]Ps. 33:19; Job 5:20
20[d][Matt. 6:30; James 1:11] [e]Ps. 68:2; 102:3; Hos. 13:3
21[f]ver. 26
22[g]See ver. 9 [h]ver. 2
23[i]Ps. 25:12; 1 Sam. 2:9 [j]Ps. 40:2; 119:5
24[k]Prov. 24:16; Mic. 7:8; 2 Cor. 4:9 [l]ver. 17
25[m][Ps. 109:10; Job 15:23]

16 [x]Better is the little that the righteous has
than the abundance of many wicked.
17 For [y]the arms of the wicked shall be broken,
but the LORD [z]upholds the righteous.

18 The LORD [a]knows the days of the blameless,
and their [b]heritage will remain forever;
19 they are not put to shame in evil times;
in [c]the days of famine they have abundance.

20 But the wicked will perish;
the enemies of the LORD are like [d]the glory of the pastures;
they vanish—like [e]smoke they vanish away.

21 The wicked borrows but does not pay back,
but the righteous [f]is generous and gives;
22 for those blessed by the LORD[1] shall [g]inherit the land,
but those cursed by him [h]shall be cut off.

23 The [i]steps of a man are [j]established by the LORD,
when he delights in his way;
24 [k]though he fall, he shall not be cast headlong,
for the LORD [l]upholds his hand.

25 I have been young, and now am old,
yet I have not seen the righteous forsaken
or his children [m]begging for bread.

1 Hebrew *by him*

37:8 anger. Probably anger against God.

tends only to evil. Anger is a dangerous force (James 1:20).

37:9 cut off. A technical term meaning to be exiled, to be excommunicated from society, or even to be executed (Gen. 17:14; Lev. 17:14).

37:11 the meek shall inherit the land. Land and its cultivation is the basis of physical life. This verse is used in Matt. 5:5.

37:13 the Lord laughs at the wicked. See Ps. 2:4. Vivid human language describes the folly of rebellion against the Almighty. God is not threatened, nor is His judgment avoided.

37:15 their sword shall enter their own heart. The consequences of sin are frequently the result of its own outworking. See 7:14–16; 34:21; 35:8.

37:21 borrows but does not pay back. The wicked break the eighth commandment, against stealing, by not repaying their debts. The righteous pay their debts and give money generously. Those who give mercifully in God's cause prosper at last.

37:24 fall. The wise man is not perfect—he may fall in the way. But God guides and protects him even when he sins and encounters obstacles.

37:25, 26 Confirming the truth of v. 24, the psalmist draws on the experience of his own long life to assure the upright that God will abandon neither them nor their children. The righteous are known by their deeds of mercy and generosity.

26 He is ever [n]lending generously,
and his children become a blessing.
27 [o]Turn away from evil and do good;
so shall you [p]dwell forever.
28 For the LORD [q]loves justice;
he will not forsake his [r]saints.
They are preserved forever,
but the children of the wicked
shall be [s]cut off.
29 The righteous shall inherit the land
and [p]dwell upon it forever.

30 The mouth of the righteous utters
wisdom,
and his tongue speaks justice.
31 [t]The law of his God is in his heart;
his [u]steps do not slip.
32 The wicked [v]watches for the righteous
and seeks to put him to death.
33 The LORD will not [w]abandon him to
his power
or let him [x]be condemned when
he is brought to trial.

34 [y]Wait for the LORD and keep his way,
and he will exalt you to inherit the
land;
you will look on [z]when the wicked
are cut off.
35 [a]I have seen a wicked, ruthless man,
spreading himself like [b]a green
laurel tree.[1]
36 But he passed away,[2] and behold,
[c]he was no more;
though I sought him, he could not
be found.
37 Mark the blameless and behold the
upright,
for there is a future for the man of
[d]peace.
38 But [e]transgressors shall be altogether
destroyed;
the future of the wicked [f]shall be
cut off.
39 [g]The salvation of the righteous is from
the LORD;
he is their stronghold in [h]the time
of trouble.
40 The LORD helps them and [i]delivers
them;
[j]he delivers them from the wicked
and saves them,
because they [k]take refuge in him.

26 [n]Ps. 112:5, 9; Deut. 15:8, 10; Matt. 5:42; Luke 6:35
27 [o]See Ps. 34:14 [p][Ps. 102:28]
28 [q]See Ps. 11:7 [r]See Ps. 16:10 [s]ver. 2, 9; Ps. 21:10; Prov. 2:22; Isai. 14:20
29 [p][See ver. 27 above]
31 [t]Ps. 40:8; 119:11; Deut. 6:6; Isai. 51:7; Jer. 31:33; [Rom. 7:22] [u][Ps. 73:2]
32 [v]Ps. 10:8
33 [w][2 Pet. 2:9] [x]Ps. 109:31
34 [y]ver. 9; See Ps. 27:14 [z]Ps. 52:5, 6; 91:8
35 [a]See Job 5:3 [b][Ps. 52:8]
36 [c]ver. 10; Job 20:5
37 [d]ver. 11; Ps. 119:165; Isai. 57:2
38 [e][Ps. 52:5; 104:35; Prov. 2:22] [f]Ps. 73:17; Job 18:17
39 [g]See Ps. 3:8 [h]Ps. 9:9
40 [i][Isai. 31:5; Acts 12:11] [j][1 Chr. 5:20; Dan. 3:17, 28; 6:23] [k]See Ps. 11:1
Psalm 38 [l]Ps. 70, title; [1 Chr. 16:4]
1 [m]Ps. 6:1
2 [n]Job 6:4 [o]See Ps. 32:4
3 [p]Isai. 1:6 [q]See Ps. 31:10
4 [r]Ps. 40:12; Ezra 9:6
6 [s]Ps. 35:14; 42:5, 6, 11; 43:5 [t]Isai. 21:3 [u][Job 30:28]

Do Not Forsake Me, O LORD

38

A PSALM OF DAVID, [l]FOR THE MEMORIAL OFFERING.

1 O LORD, [m]rebuke me not in your
anger,
nor discipline me in your wrath!
2 For your [n]arrows have sunk into me,
and your hand [o]has come down
on me.

3 There is [p]no soundness in my flesh
because of your indignation;
there is no health in my [q]bones
because of my sin.
4 For my [r]iniquities have gone over my
head;
like a heavy burden, they are too
heavy for me.

5 My wounds stink and fester
because of my foolishness,
6 I am [s]utterly bowed down and
[t]prostrate;
all the day I [u]go about
mourning.

1 The identity of this tree is uncertain 2 Or *But one passed by*

37:30, 31 Governed inwardly by God's law, both the speech and actions of the righteous person are wise and just. In Hebrew, "heart" is the normal way of referring to the inner principle that governs outward performance (Prov. 4:23).

37:33 brought to trial. The Lord will not allow the accusations of the wicked to destroy those He deems righteous. At His own bar of justice God will pronounce them innocent.

37:35 green laurel tree. It commonly happens that the wicked prosper in the business of this world (Luke 16:8). Far from being envied they should be mourned, since their temporary success is but a prelude to eternal loss.

37:37 future. Or "posterity." Either the individual's later life or his children are meant here, but in the ultimate sense this promise speaks of the eternal peace enjoyed in God's presence.

Ps. 38 In this penitential psalm the writer attributes his illness to sin and guilt. He calls on the Lord for help in the midst of intense pain.

38:2 your arrows. God usually fights for the psalmist and against the enemy (Ps. 18:14), but here is a quite different case. The psalmist confesses the sin that has brought God's anger upon him.

38:3 because of your indignation . . . because of my sin. These two phrases are parallel and show a dual (divine and human) reason for the psalmist's illness.

no health. The psalmist's sin had serious effects on his health. In some cases sin and guilt are the cause of illness, but sickness is not always the result of sins committed by the person who suffers (Book of Job; John 9:1-12).

38:5 wounds. Implies some kind of physical abuse by others. The symptoms cannot all be related to a specific disease or condition. It has been suggested that the symptoms are actually a catalog of distresses experienced over a period of time.

7 For my sides are filled with burning,
and there is [p]no soundness in my flesh.
8 I am feeble and crushed;
I [v]groan because of the tumult of my heart.

9 O Lord, all my longing is before you;
my [w]sighing is not hidden from you.
10 My heart throbs; my strength fails me,
and [x]the light of my eyes—it also has gone from me.
11 My [y]friends and companions [z]stand aloof from my [a]plague,
and my nearest kin [b]stand far off.

12 Those who seek my life [c]lay their snares;
those who seek my hurt [d]speak of ruin
and meditate [e]treachery all day long.

13 But I am like a deaf man; I do not hear,
like [f]a mute man who does not open his mouth.
14 I have become like a man who does not hear,
and in whose mouth are no [g]rebukes.

15 But for [h]you, O LORD, do I wait;
it is you, O Lord my God, who will answer.
16 For I said, "Only [i]let them not rejoice over me,
who [j]boast against me when my [k]foot slips!"

17 For I am [l]ready to fall,
and my pain is ever before me.
18 I [m]confess my iniquity;
I am [n]sorry for my sin.
19 But my foes are vigorous, they are mighty,
and many are those who hate me [o]wrongfully.
20 Those who [p]render me evil for good
[q]accuse me because I [r]follow after good.

21 Do not forsake me, O LORD!
O my God, be not [s]far from me!
22 [t]Make haste to help me,
O Lord, my [u]salvation!

What Is the Measure of My Days?

39

TO THE CHOIRMASTER: TO [v]JEDUTHUN.[1] A PSALM OF DAVID.

1 I said, "I will [w]guard my ways,
that I [x]may not sin with my tongue;
I will [y]guard my mouth with a muzzle,
so long as the wicked are in my presence."
2 I was [z]mute and silent;
I held my peace to no avail,
and my distress grew worse.
3 My [a]heart became hot within me.
As I mused, the fire burned;
then I spoke with my tongue:

4 "O LORD, [b]make me know my end
and what is the measure of my days;
let me know how fleeting I am!
5 Behold, you have made my days a few handbreadths,
and [c]my lifetime is as nothing before you.
Surely [d]all mankind stands as a mere breath! *Selah*
6 Surely a man [e]goes about as a shadow!
Surely for nothing[2] they are in turmoil;
man [f]heaps up wealth and does not know who will gather!

7[p][See ver. 3 above] **8**[v]See Ps. 22:1 **9**[w]Ps. 6:6 **10**[x]See Ps. 6:7 **11**[y]Ps. 88:18; See Job 19:13-20 [z][Luke 10:31, 32] [a]Ps. 39:10; Isai. 53:4, 8 [b][Matt. 27:55; Mark 15:40; Luke 23:49] **12**[c][Matt. 22:15]; Mark 12:13; Luke 20:20; See 2 Sam. 17:1-3 [d][2 Sam. 16:7, 8] [e]Ps. 35:20 **13**[f]Ps. 39:2, 9; Isai. 53:7; 1 Pet. 2:23 **14**[g][Job 23:4] **15**[h]Ps. 39:7; [2 Sam. 16:12] **16**[i][Ps. 13:4] [j]See Job 19:5 [k]Ps. 94:18 **17**[l]Ps. 35:15; Jer. 20:10 **18**[m]See Ps. 32:5 [n][2 Cor. 7:9, 10] **19**[o]Ps. 35:19

20[p]See Ps. 35:12 [q]Ps. 109:4 [r][3 John 11] **21**[s]See Ps. 10:1 **22**[t]See Ps. 40:13 [u]See Ps. 27:1 **Psalm 39** [v]Ps. 62, title; 77, title; 1 Chr. 16:41; 25:1 **1**[w]1 Kin. 2:4; 2 Kin. 10:31 [x]Job 2:10 [y]See Ps. 34:13 **2**[z]ver. 9; Job 40:4, 5; See Ps. 38:13 **3**[a]Jer. 20:9; Luke 24:32; [Job 32:18, 19] **4**[b]Ps. 90:12

5[c]Ps. 89:47; 90:4 [d]ver. 11; [Job 14:2] **6**[e][1 Cor. 7:31; James 4:14] [f]Ps. 49:10; Job 27:16, 17; Luke 12:20; [Eccles. 2:18, 21, 26; Jer. 17:11]

1 Probably a musical or liturgical term 2 Hebrew *Surely as a breath*

38:11 My friends . . . stand aloof. Friends are of no help to the psalmist because they are afraid or repulsed by the intensity of his suffering. Here, as elsewhere in the psalm, we are reminded of Job's experience (v. 3).

38:12 lay their snares. While friends stay away, his enemies draw near to hurry his downfall.

38:13 deaf man . . . mute. The psalmist is totally unable to do anything to help himself.

38:15 for you . . . I wait. This verse strikes the most positive note of confidence in the psalm.

38:16 let them not rejoice over me. He mentions to God the shame he will suffer when the enemy rejoices at the downfall of one of God's children.

Ps. 39 This lament is more personal and autobiographical than most. The author seems to have been an older, reflective person, like the writer of Ecclesiastes. His anger (vv. 2, 3) is not unlike Job's.

39:1 that I may not sin with my tongue. The psalmist may have been questioning the prosperity of the wicked, and feared that if he spoke in his anger and frustration he might say something offensive to God.

muzzle. He desires to speak out and has to force himself to be quiet.

39:2 my distress. The psalmist repressed his feelings but could not do away with them. Finally, he spoke.

39:4 measure of my days. Their own short, hard lives tempted the faithful as they compared them to the prosperity of the wicked and questioned God's wisdom and justice. See note Ps. 88:5.

39:6 for nothing. The same Hebrew word is translated "mere breath" in v. 5. The sentiment is similar to that found in the Book of Ecclesiastes (5:8–20).

7 "And now, O Lord, for what do I
wait?
[g] My hope is in you.
8 Deliver me from all my transgressions.
[h] Do not make me the scorn of the
fool!
9 [i] I am mute; I do not open my mouth,
[j] for it is you who have done it.
10 [k] Remove your stroke from me;
I am spent by the hostility of your
hand.
11 When you discipline a man
with [l] rebukes for sin,
you consume like a [m] moth [n] what is
dear to him;
[o] surely all mankind is a mere
breath! *Selah*

12 [p] "Hear my prayer, O LORD,
and give ear to my cry;
hold not your peace at my tears!
For I am [q] a sojourner with you,
[q] a guest, like all my fathers.
13 [r] Look away from me, that I may smile
again,
[s] before I depart and [t] am no more!"

My Help and My Deliverer

40

TO THE CHOIRMASTER. A PSALM OF DAVID.

1 I [u] waited patiently for the LORD;
he inclined to me and [v] heard
my cry.
2 He drew me up from [w] the pit of
destruction,
out of [x] the miry bog,
and [y] set my feet upon a rock,
[z] making my steps secure.
3 He put [a] a new song in my mouth,
a song of praise to our God.
Many will [b] see and fear,
and put their trust in the LORD.

4 Blessed is the man who [c] makes
the LORD his trust,
who does not turn to the proud,
to those who [d] go astray after a lie!
5 You have multiplied, O LORD my
God,
your [e] wondrous deeds and your
[f] thoughts toward us;
none can compare with you!
I will proclaim and tell of them,
yet they are [g] more than can be
told.

6 [h] Sacrifice and offering you have not
desired,
but you have given me an open
[i] ear.[1]
Burnt offering and sin offering
you have not required.
7 Then I said, "Behold, I have come;
in the scroll of the book it is
written [j] of me:
8 [k] I desire to do your will, O my God;
your law is [l] within my heart."

9 I have told the glad news of
deliverance[2]
in [m] the great congregation;
behold, I have not [n] restrained my
lips,
[o] as you know, O LORD.

7 [g] Ps. 38:15 8 [h] See Ps. 44:13 9 [i] ver. 2 [j] 2 Sam. 16:10; Job 2:10 10 [k] Job 9:34; 13:21 11 [l] Ps. 80:16 [m] Job 13:28; Isai. 50:9 [n] Ps. 49:14 [o] See ver. 5 12 [p] Ps. 102:1 [q] Ps. 119:19; Lev. 25:23; 1 Chr. 29:15; Heb. 11:13; 1 Pet. 2:11; [Gen. 47:9] 13 [r] Job 7:19 [s] Job 10:21 [t] Job 7:8; 14:10-12; 20:9
Psalm 40
1 [u] Ps. 27:14; 37:7 [v] Ps. 39:12 2 [w] [Jer. 38:6] [x] Ps. 69:2, 14 [y] Ps. 27:5 [z] Ps. 37:23 3 [a] See Ps. 33:3 [b] Ps. 52:6; 64:8, 9; Deut. 13:11 4 [c] See Ps. 2:12 [d] Ps. 101:3; 125:5; Lev. 19:4; Deut. 29:18; Job 23:11; Hos. 3:1 5 [e] Ps. 9:1; Ex. 15:11 [f] Ps. 92:5; 139:17; Isai. 55:8 [g] Ps. 71:15; 139:18 6 [h] Ps. 51:16; 1 Sam. 15:22; Cited Heb. 10:5-7; See Prov. 21:3 [i] See Job 33:16 7 [j] Luke 24:44 8 [k] Ps. 119:16, 24, 35, 92; [John 4:34] [l] See Ps. 37:31
9 [m] See Ps. 22:25 [n] Ps. 119:13; [Acts 20:20, 27] [o] Josh. 22:22

1 Hebrew *ears you have dug for me* 2 Hebrew *righteousness*; also verse 10

39:10 your stroke. This could be sickness, but it could include depression and other setbacks in life.

39:12 The psalmist has passed from anger to weeping. The strong emotion of the psalm makes its final prayer especially vivid.

Ps. 40 This psalm has two sections joined together with vv. 9–10 as an appropriate transition. God has answered an earlier prayer of the psalmist, but he still has problems to bring before God. He looks to God in a time of new crisis.

40:2 pit of destruction . . . rock. A miry pit is contrasted with the sure footing of a rock. Sheol, the grave, is often pictured as a pit (6:5 and notes; 30:3). Perhaps the psalmist was ill and threatened with death; or, since the psalm is probably royal, he may have felt the threat of death in battle.

40:3 new song. See Ps. 33:3 note.

40:4 Blessed. See Ps. 1:1 note.

proud. A rare word used of Egypt in Ps. 87:4 and there simply translated "Rahab." Here it probably refers to the false idols of the surrounding nations.

40:6 you have not desired. The psalmist knows that the animal sacrifices of the Old Testament were mandated by God. But if they were offered without genuine repentance and faith, God did not want them.

you have given me an open ear. This difficult phrase may be idiomatic. The Hebrew more literally translated would be "ears you have dug for me" (see text note). This would mean that God gave the psalmist ears to hear and obey. The phrase is important because it is cited in Heb. 10:5–7. Hebrews uses the Septuagint (Greek Old Testament) translation, "a body have you prepared for me." The meaning is the same; the "ears" are to the "body" as the part to the whole. The obedience of Jesus in the body is to offer Himself once and for all, replacing the animal sacrifices of the Old Testament.

40:7 in the scroll of the book it is written of me. The reference may refer to the commandment recorded for kings in Deut. 17.

40:8 I desire to do your will. This verse comes to the heart of the matter. The psalmist offers what God requires—heartfelt obedience.

40:9 great congregation. Either the assembled worshipers or the whole nation.

10 I have not hidden your deliverance
within my heart;
I have spoken of your faithfulness
and your salvation;
I have not concealed your steadfast
love and your faithfulness
from the great congregation.

11 As for you, O LORD, you will not
restrain
your mercy from me;
your [p]steadfast love and your
faithfulness will
ever preserve me!
12 For evils have [q]encompassed me
beyond number;
my [r]iniquities have overtaken me,
and I cannot [s]see;
they are [t]more than the hairs of my
head;
my heart [u]fails me.

13 [v]Be pleased, O LORD, to [w]deliver me!
O LORD, [x]make haste to help me!
14 [y]Let those be put to shame and
disappointed altogether
who seek to snatch away my life;
let those be [z]turned back and
brought to dishonor
who desire my hurt!
15 Let those be appalled because of
their shame
who [a]say to me, "Aha, Aha!"

16 But may all who seek you
rejoice and be glad in you;
may those who love your salvation
[b]say continually, "Great is the
LORD!"
17 As for me, I am [c]poor and needy,
but [d]the Lord takes thought for me.
You are my help and my deliverer;
do not delay, O my God!

11 [p]Ps. 57:3; 61:7; Prov. 20:28; See Ps. 36:5
12 [q]Ps. 116:3 [r]Ps. 38:4 [s][Ps. 38:10] [t]Ps. 69:4 [u]Ps. 73:26
13 [v]For ver. 13-17, see Ps. 70:1-5 [w]Ps. 22:20 [x]Ps. 22:19; 38:22; 71:12; 141:1
14 [y]Ps. 35:4, 26; 71:13 [z]Ps. 6:10
15 [a]Ps. 35:21, 25; 70:3
16 [b]Ps. 35:27
17 [c]Ps. 86:1; 109:22 [d][1 Pet. 5:7]

Psalm 41
1 [e]Prov. 14:21 [f]Ps. 37:19
2 [g]Ps. 27:12
4 [h]Ps. 4:1 [i]Ps. 6:2; 147:3; 2 Chr. 30:20
6 [j]Ps. 12:2; 144:8
9 [k]Ps. 55:12, 13, 20; Job 19:13, 14, 19; Jer. 9:4; 20:10; Mic. 7:5; [2 Sam. 15:12] [l]Cited John 13:18

O LORD, Be Gracious to Me

41 TO THE CHOIRMASTER. A PSALM OF DAVID.

1 [e]Blessed is the one who considers the
poor![1]
[f]In the day of trouble the LORD
delivers him;
2 the LORD protects him and keeps him
alive;
he is called blessed in the land;
you [g]do not give him up to the will
of his enemies.
3 The LORD sustains him on his sickbed;
in his illness you restore him to
full health.[2]

4 As for me, I said, "O LORD, [h]be
gracious to me;
[i]heal me,[3] for I have sinned against
you!"
5 My enemies say of me in malice,
"When will he die and his name
perish?"
6 And when one comes to see me, [j]he
utters empty words,
while his heart gathers iniquity;
when he goes out, he tells it
abroad.
7 All who hate me whisper together
about me;
they imagine the worst for me.[4]

8 They say, "A deadly thing is poured
out[5] on him;
he will not rise again from where
he lies."
9 Even my [k]close friend in whom I
trusted,
who [l]ate my bread, has lifted his
heel against me.

1 Or *weak* 2 Hebrew *you turn all his bed* 3 Hebrew *my soul* 4 Or *they devise evil against me* 5 Or *has fastened*

40:12 evils . . . iniquities. The psalmist identifies the source of his troubles as both external (enemies seeking to thwart him) and internal (his own sin).

40:13–17 See notes Ps. 70.

Ps. 41 The psalm begins with the atmosphere of the wisdom tradition, shifting in v. 4 to lament and prayer.

41:1 Blessed. See note Ps. 1:1.

considers the poor. Understands or empathizes with those who are helpless and unable to take care of themselves. The psalmist is in this condition due to his debilitating sickness. Accordingly, the first three verses here may have been spoken to him by another person, perhaps a priest.

the LORD delivers him. Those strong in self-confidence do not turn to the Lord, because they think they have no need for Him. Those not so deluded, realizing their weakness, have nowhere else to turn.

41:2 in the land. The Lord preserves the life of His people, but He will also prosper them in the land. This applies the promise of the land found in the Abrahamic covenant (Gen. 12:1–3).

41:6 he utters empty words. The psalmist's enemies visited him while he was ill, speaking words of comfort, but afterward spreading malicious lies about him.

41:9 lifted his heel. For this idiom see Gen. 25:19–26, where the noun "heel" is connected with the verb "to deceive." The point is that the psalmist's close friend has betrayed him in his moment of need. He is abandoned by everyone. Jesus applied this verse specifically to Judas Iscariot (John 13:18).

10 But you, O LORD, be gracious to me,
and raise me up, that I may repay them!
11 By this I know that [m]you delight in me:
my enemy will not shout in triumph over me.
12 But [n]you have upheld me because of [o]my integrity,
and [p]set me in your presence [q]forever.

13 [r]Blessed be the LORD, the God of Israel,
from everlasting to everlasting!
Amen and Amen.

BOOK TWO

Why Are You Cast Down, O My Soul?

42 TO THE CHOIRMASTER. A MASKIL[1] OF [s]THE SONS OF KORAH.

1 [t]As a deer pants for flowing streams,
so pants my soul for you, O God.
2 [u]My soul thirsts for God,
for [v]the living God.
When shall I come and [w]appear before God?[2]
3 [x]My tears have been my food
day and night,
[y]while they say to me continually,
"Where is your God?"
4 These things I remember,
as I [z]pour out my soul:
[a]how I would go [b]with the throng
and lead them in procession to the house of God
with glad shouts and songs of praise,
[c]a multitude keeping festival.

5 [d]Why are you cast down, O my soul,
and why are you [e]in turmoil within me?
[f]Hope in God; for I shall again praise him,
my salvation[3] 6 and my God.

My soul is cast down within me;
therefore I [g]remember you
[h]from the land of Jordan and of [i]Hermon,
from Mount Mizar.
7 Deep calls to deep
at the roar of your waterfalls;
[j]all your breakers and your [k]waves
have gone over me.
8 By day the LORD [l]commands his steadfast love,
and at [m]night his song is with me,
a prayer to the God of my life.

9 I say to God, "[n]my rock:
"Why have you forgotten me?
[o]Why do I go mourning
because of the oppression of the enemy?"
10 As with a deadly wound in my bones,
my adversaries taunt me,
[p]while they say to me continually,
"Where is your God?"

11 [q]Why are you cast down, O my soul,
and why are you in turmoil within me?
Hope in God; for I shall again praise him,
my salvation and my God.

11 [m][2 Sam. 15:25, 26]
12 [n]Ps. 63:8 [o]Ps. 26:1 [p]Job 36:7 [q]Ps. 23:6
13 [r]Luke 1:68; [Ps. 72:18, 19; 89:52; 106:48; 150:6]
BOOK TWO
Psalm 42
[s]1 Chr. 6:33; 37
1 [t][Joel 1:20]
2 [u]Ps. 63:1; John 7:37; [Isai. 41:17; 55:1]; See Ps. 84:2 [v]Ps. 84:2; Josh. 3:10; Dan. 6:26 [w]Ps. 84:7; [Ex. 23:17]
3 [x]Ps. 80:5; 102:9 [y]ver. 10; Ps. 79:10; 115:2; Joel 2:17; Mic. 7:10
4 [z]Ps. 62:8; 1 Sam. 1:15; Job 30:16; Lam. 2:19 [a][Isai. 30:29] [b]Ps. 55:14 [c][2 Sam. 6:15]
5 [d]ver. 11; Ps. 43:5; [Matt. 26:38; John 12:27] [e]Ps. 77:3 [f]Lam. 3:24
6 [g]Jonah 2:7 [h]2 Sam. 17:22, 24 [i]Deut. 3:9
7 [j]Jonah 2:3 [k]Ps. 88:7; See Ps. 32:6
8 [l]Ps. 44:4; 68:28; 71:3; 133:3 [m]Job 35:10; [Ps. 4:4; 16:7; 63:6; 77:6; 119:55, 62, 148; 149:5]
9 [n]See Ps. 18:2; 2 Sam. 22:2 [o]Ps. 38:6; 43:2 10 [p]See ver. 3 11 [q]See ver. 5

1 Probably a musical or liturgical term 2 Revocalization yields *and see the face of God* 3 Hebrew *the salvation of my face*; also verse 11 and 43:5

41:13 Blessed be. After a note of confidence (vv. 11, 12), a doxology concludes the final psalm of Book I of the Psalter (Introduction: Characteristics and Themes).

Ps. 42 This psalm and Ps. 43 are actually two halves of a single psalm. A number of early Hebrew manuscripts put them together, and a common refrain unites them (42:5, 11; 43:5). Ps. 43 is without a title in a part of the Psalter where almost every psalm is titled. The two psalms are a single lament in three parts, each concluding with the same refrain (42:1–5, 6–11; Ps. 43:5). For some reason the psalmist is forced to be separated from Jerusalem, the place God has chosen to make His throne. His distance from the Lord and the presence of his enemies causes him to cry out to the Lord for help.

42:1 As a deer pants for flowing streams. A powerful description of deep desire for God's presence.

42:2 appear before God. Due to Jesus' redemptive work on the cross, the Christian has ready access to the Lord in prayer. The psalmist suffers because he is separated from the temple, the place God specifically set apart for worship during the period between David and Jesus. The psalmist desires to return to the temple and the assurance of God's life-giving presence.

42:4 These things I remember. During this time of depression and separation from God, the psalmist recalls the past when his relationship with God was good and he rejoiced in participating in the worship processions in Jerusalem. The Songs of Ascents (Ps. 120–134) were sung at these celebrations.

42:5 Why are you cast down, O my soul. This verse occurs twice more as a refrain (v. 11 and 43:5). In dialogue with himself, the psalmist takes fresh hold on God.

42:6 I remember you. Ps. 77 is another lament where the remembrance of God's grace provides a bulwark against depression in the present.

land of Jordan . . . Hermon, . . . Mizar. Hermon is the mountain range at the far north of Israel's boundaries, near the source of the Jordan River. Mizar is of unknown location.

42:7 have gone over me. The overwhelming waters of chaos are a well-known image of despair and trouble in the Bible. Cf. Ps. 18:4; 32:6; 46:2, 3; 69:1, 2; 114:3.

42:8 steadfast love. Specifically, God's lovingkindness toward those in covenant with Him, who acknowledge His rule over them, and to whom He has given promises.

Send Out Your Light and Your Truth

43

[r]Vindicate me, O God, and [s]defend
my cause
against an ungodly people,
from [t]the deceitful and unjust man
deliver me!
2 For you are [u]the God in whom I take
refuge;
why have you [v]rejected me?
Why do I [w]go about mourning
because of the oppression of the
enemy?

3 [x]Send out your light and your truth;
let them lead me;
let them bring me to your [y]holy
hill
and to your [z]dwelling!
4 Then I will go to the altar of God,
to God my exceeding joy,
and I will praise you with the lyre,
O God, my God.

5 [a]Why are you cast down, O my
soul,
and why are you in turmoil
within me?
[b]Hope in God; for I shall again
praise him,
my salvation and my God.

Come to Our Help

44

To the choirmaster. [c]A Maskil[1]
of the Sons of Korah.

1 O God, we have heard with
our ears,
[d]our fathers have told us,
what deeds you performed in their
days,
[e]in the days of old:
2 you with your own hand [f]drove out
the nations,
but [g]them you planted;
you afflicted the peoples,
but [h]them you set free;
3 for not [i]by their own sword did they
win the land,
nor did their own arm save them,
but your right hand and your arm,
and [j]the light of your face,
[k]for you delighted in them.

4 [l]You are my King, O God;
[m]ordain salvation for Jacob!
5 Through you we [n]push down our foes;
through your name we [o]tread
down those who rise up
against us.
6 For not in [p]my bow do I trust,
nor can my sword save me.
7 But you have saved us from our foes
and have [q]put to shame those who
hate us.
8 [r]In God we have boasted continually,
and we will give thanks to your
name forever. *Selah*

9 But you have [s]rejected us and
disgraced us
and [t]have not gone out with our
armies.
10 You have made us [u]turn back from
the foe,
and those who hate us have gotten
spoil.
11 You have made us like [v]sheep for
slaughter
and have [w]scattered us among the
nations.

Psalm 43
1 [r]Ps. 7:8; 26:1 [s]See 1 Sam. 24:15 [t]Ps. 5:6
2 [u]Ps. 31:4 [v]See Ps. 44:9 [w]Ps. 42:9
3 [x]Ps. 40:11; 57:3
3 [y]See Ps. 2:6; 46:4 [z]Ps. 84:1
5 [a]See Ps. 42:5 [b]Ps. 42:5, 11

Psalm 44
[c]Ps. 42, title
1 [d]Ps. 78:3; Ex. 10:2; 12:26, 27; 13:8, 14, 15; Judg. 6:13; See Deut. 6:20-23 [e]See Ps. 77:5
2 [f]Ps. 78:55; 80:8; Josh. 3:10 [g]Ex. 15:17; 2 Sam. 7:10 [h]Ps. 80:9-11; [Jer. 17:8]
3 [i]Josh. 24:12; Hos. 1:7 [j]See Ps. 4:6 [k]Deut. 4:37; 7:7, 8; 10:15
4 [l]Ps. 74:12 [m]See Ps. 42:8
5 [n][Deut. 33:17; Dan. 8:4] [o]Ps. 60:12
6 [p][Ps. 33:16; 1 Sam. 17:47]
7 [q]See Ps. 35:4
8 [r]See Ps. 34:2
9 [s]ver. 23; Ps. 43:2; 60:1, 10; 74:1; 108:11; See Ps. 89:38-45 [t][Judg. 4:14; 2 Sam. 5:24]
10 [u]Lev. 26:17; Deut. 28:25; Josh. 7:8, 12
11 [v][ver. 22] [w]Ps. 106:27; Lev. 26:33; Deut. 4:27; 28:64; Isai. 52:3; Ezek. 20:23; [John 7:35; 1 Pet. 1:1]

[1] Probably a musical or liturgical term

Ps. 43 See introduction to Ps. 42. The two psalms were originally one.

43:1 Vindicate me . . . defend my cause. These words are technical legal terms that give the psalm a judicial setting.

ungodly. Literally, those who are without covenant lovingkindness. These are nations or people who do not enjoy a covenant relationship with God, who do not honor His laws, and therefore do not share in His covenant promises.

43:3 your holy hill. This is Mount Zion in Jerusalem, where the temple was located. God's firm mountain is to be contrasted with the turbulent waters of chaos (46:2, 3).

43:5 Why are you cast down. See note 42:5.

Ps. 44 In this psalm an alternation between "I" and "we" suggests that the psalmist is the king of Israel. It is not possible to identify a special occasion for the writing of the psalm, and it can be applied to many different occasions.

44:1 deeds you performed in their days. Memory plays a key role in the psalms (Ps. 77). When in distress, it brings healing to remember God's gracious acts in the past. In this psalm, however, past deliverance throws a question mark over the present. Why doesn't God work now as He did for our fathers in the past?

44:2 them you planted. The reference is to the conquest and settlement of the land as recorded in the Book of Joshua.

44:3 your right hand. Israel did not take possession of the land by their own might or strategy, but through God's power. God fought for them like a warrior in their midst (Josh. 6; Deut. 7).

44:4 Jacob. Another name for Israel.

44:6 nor can my sword save me. God's people must fight, but they do not trust in the size of their army nor in their weapons.

44:9 you have rejected us and disgraced us. God was with Israel at Jericho, but now He does not bless the army with His leadership. This resulted in their easy defeat.

12 [x] You have sold your people for a trifle,
demanding no high price for them.
13 You have made us [y] the taunt of our neighbors,
the derision and [z] scorn of those around us.
14 You have made us [a] a byword among the nations,
[b] a laughingstock[1] among the peoples.
15 All day long my disgrace is before me,
and [c] shame has covered my face
16 at the sound of the taunter and reviler,
at the sight of [d] the enemy and the avenger.

17 [e] All this has come upon us,
though we have not forgotten you,
and we have not been false to your covenant.
18 Our heart has not turned back,
nor have our [f] steps [g] departed from your way;
19 yet you have [h] broken us in the place of [i] jackals
and covered us with [j] the shadow of death.
20 If we had forgotten the name of our God
or [k] spread out our hands to [l] a foreign god,
21 [m] would not God discover this?
[n] For he knows the secrets of the heart.
22 Yet [o] for your sake we are killed all the day long;
we are regarded as sheep to be slaughtered.

12 [x] [Deut. 32:30; Judg. 2:14; 3:8; Jer. 15:13]
13 [y] Ps. 39:8; 79:4; 89:41; 119:22; [Neh. 2:17] [z] [Ps. 80:6]
14 [a] Jer. 24:9; See Job 17:6 [b] See Job 16:4
15 [c] 2 Chr. 32:21
16 [d] Ps. 8:2
17 [e] Dan. 9:13
18 [f] Ps. 37:31 [g] Ps. 119:51, 157; Job 23:11
19 [h] Ps. 51:8 [i] See Job 30:29 [j] See Job 3:5
20 [k] Ps. 68:31; Job 11:13 [l] See Ps. 81:9
21 [m] Ps. 139:1; Jer. 17:10 [n] [John 2:25; Heb. 4:13]
22 [o] ver. 11; Cited Rom. 8:36
23 [p] See Ps. 35:23 [q] ver. 9
24 [r] See Job 13:24
25 [s] Ps. 119:25
26 [t] Ps. 63:7 [u] See Ps. 25:22
Psalm 45 [v] Ps. 42, title
1 [w] [Ezra 7:6
2 [x] [Isai. 33:17] [y] [Luke 4:22; See Isai. 61:1-3]
3 [z] Ex. 32:27 [a] [Isai. 49:2; Heb. 4:12; Rev. 1:16; 19:15] [b] [Ps. 24:8; Isai. 9:6] [c] Ps. 21:5; 96:6, 7
4 [d] [Rev. 16:2] [e] See Ps. 65:5

23 [p] Awake! Why are you sleeping, O Lord?
Rouse yourself! [q] Do not reject us forever!
24 Why [r] do you hide your face?
Why do you forget our affliction and oppression?
25 For our [s] soul is bowed down to the dust;
our belly clings to the ground.
26 Rise up; [t] come to our help!
[u] Redeem us for the sake of your steadfast love!

Your Throne, O God, Is Forever

45 TO THE CHOIRMASTER: ACCORDING TO LILIES. A MASKIL[2] OF [v] THE SONS OF KORAH; A LOVE SONG.

1 My heart overflows with a pleasing theme;
I address my verses to the king;
my tongue is like the pen of [w] a ready scribe.

2 You are [x] the most handsome of the sons of men;
[y] grace is poured upon your lips;
therefore God has blessed you forever.
3 [z] Gird your [a] sword on your thigh,
O [b] mighty one,
in [c] your splendor and majesty!

4 In your majesty [d] ride out victoriously
for the cause of truth and meekness and righteousness;
let your right hand teach you
[e] awesome deeds!

1 Hebrew *a shaking of the head* 2 Probably a musical or liturgical term

44:12 You have sold your people for a trifle. These are bold words, a striking example of the honesty of the psalmist's approach to God in prayer.

44:19 shadow of death. Normally reserved for God's enemies (Nah. 1:8).

44:22 for your sake. The world seems utterly turned around. The people have not forgotten God, yet they suffer for His sake. Paul quotes this verse in Rom. 8:36.

44:23 Awake. The psalmist prays as if God were asleep and unaware of Israel's plight. This daring language reflects the writer's frustration. The usual cry to God before battle is "Arise" (Ps. 7:6).

44:26 for the sake of your steadfast love. Specifically, God's loving-kindness to those with whom He is in covenantal relationship (e.g., Abraham, Gen. 17:1–9).

Ps. 45 As the title indicates, Ps. 45 is a wedding song. There are no other examples in the Psalter. The closest parallels are the love poems found in the Song of Solomon. This song is appropriate for a royal wedding, and was probably used in many royal weddings throughout the history of Israel. Since the Davidic kingship reflects God's ultimate kingship and anticipates Christ as King, the psalm has a second application to Christ, the King and Bridegroom, and the church as His bride (Eph. 5:25–32). Ps. 45 is applied to Jesus Christ in Heb. 1:8, 9.

45:1 pleasing theme . . . the king. The messianic King is described.

tongue. This word could mean that this psalm and others were composed orally and written down later.

45:2 most handsome. The poet takes the bride's part in extolling the beauty of her lover.

blessed you forever. This language reflects the promises of the Davidic covenant in 2 Sam. 7. David would have a descendant on the throne forever, a promise fulfilled in Jesus Christ, who as the Son of David rules from heaven as King.

45:4 your right hand. The Davidic king was the head of the military forces of Israel, ordained by God to fight for the people. In this role the king reflects God's glory, since the Lord fought on behalf of Israel. Likewise, Jesus Christ leads the church against demonic forces (Eph. 6:10–20) and will return again to destroy all evil (Rev. 19:11–16).

5 Your arrows are sharp
in the heart of the king's enemies;
the peoples fall under you.

6 [f]Your throne, O God, is forever and ever.
The [g]scepter of your kingdom is a scepter of uprightness;
7 [h]you have loved righteousness and hated wickedness.
Therefore [i]God, your God, has [j]anointed you
with the oil of [k]gladness [l]beyond your companions;
8 your robes are all fragrant with [m]myrrh and aloes and cassia.
From ivory palaces [n]stringed instruments make you glad;
9 daughters of kings are among your ladies of honor;
[o]at your right hand stands the queen in [p]gold of Ophir.

10 Hear, O daughter, and consider, and incline your ear:
forget your people and your father's house,
11 and the king will desire your beauty.
Since he is your [q]lord, [r]bow to him.
12 The people[1] of Tyre will [s]seek your favor with [t]gifts,
[u]the richest of the people.[2]

13 All glorious is [v]the princess in her chamber, with robes interwoven with gold.
14 [w]In many-colored robes [x]she is led to the king,
with her virgin companions following behind her.

6[f][Ps. 93:2; 110:2; Cited Heb. 1:8, 9 [g][Ps. 67:4; 96:10]
7[h]See Ps. 11:7 [i]Isai. 61:1 [j]Ps. 2:2; 1 Kin. 1:39; [Acts 10:38] [k][Ps. 21:6] [l][1 Kin. 3:13]
8[m]John 19:39; [Matt. 2:11] [n]Ps. 150:4
9[o][1 Kin. 2:19; Neh. 2:6] [p]See Job 28:16
11[q]Isai. 54:5 [r]Ps. 95:6
12[s][Job 11:19] [t]Ps. 96:8 [u]Ps. 22:29; 68:29; 72:10; Isai. 49:7
13[v][Rev. 19:7, 8]
14[w][Judg. 5:30; Ezek. 16:18; 26:16] [x][S. of S. 1:4]
16[y]1 Pet. 2:9; Rev. 1:6; 5:10; 20:6; 22:5
17[z][Mal. 1:11]
Psalm 46 [a]Ps. 42, title [b]1 Chr. 15:20
1[c]See Ps. 14:6 [d]Ps. 145:18; Deut. 4:7 [e]Ps. 9:9
2[f][Ps. 18:7] [g]Ezek. 27:26
3[h][Ps. 93:3, 4; Jer. 5:22]
4[i]Ps. 36:8; 65:9; [Isai. 8:6; 33:21; Rev. 22:1, 2] [j]Ps. 48:1; 87:3; [Isai. 60:14] [k]Ps. 43:3; 84:1

15 With joy and gladness they are led along
as they enter the palace of the king.

16 In place of your fathers shall be your sons;
you will make them [y]princes in all the earth.
17 [z]I will cause your name to be remembered in all generations;
therefore nations will praise you forever and ever.

God Is Our Fortress

46 To the choirmaster. Of [a]the Sons of Korah. According to [b]Alamoth.[3] A Song.

1 God is our [c]refuge and strength,
a very [d]present[4] help in [e]trouble.
2 Therefore we will not fear [f]though the earth gives way,
though the mountains be moved into [g]the heart of the sea,
3 though [h]its waters roar and foam,
though the mountains tremble at its swelling. *Selah*

4 There is [i]a river whose streams make glad [j]the city of God,
the holy [k]habitation of the Most High.
5 [l]God is in the midst of her; she shall not be moved;
God will help her when morning dawns.

5[l]Lev. 26:12; Deut. 23:14; Isai. 12:6; Ezek. 43:7, 9; Hos. 11:9; Joel 2:27; Zeph. 3:15; Zech. 2:5, 10, 11; 8:3

1 Hebrew *daughter* 2 Or *The daughter of Tyre is here with gifts, the richest of people seek your favor* 3 Probably a musical or liturgical term 4 Or *well proved*

45:6 O God. Here is a clear identification of the divine King in this psalm, that is, Christ.

45:7 anointed you. Davidic kings were anointed at their inauguration (1 Sam. 16:13), which was a temporal prefiguration of the Christ as the anointed King of glory.

45:8 myrrh and aloes and cassia. A description of the king on his wedding day.

45:10 forget your people. Just as the bride is exhorted to leave her former family, so the Christian believer breaks every tie to be joined to Christ (Gen. 2:24; Matt. 10:37, 38).

45:16 your sons. The Redeemer-King is the divine Agent by whom many sons are brought forth to glory (Heb. 2:10).

45:17 nations will praise you forever. Eternal praises belong to the King of this psalm, the Messiah.

Ps. 46 This psalm has some affinities with Ps. 48; 76; 84; and 87, which are called "Zion Songs." Though Zion is not specifically mentioned, it is alluded to in vv. 4, 5. Martin Luther was moved by this psalm to write the famous hymn, "A Mighty Fortress Is Our God."

46:1 strength. See "Omnipresence and Omnipotence" at Jer. 23:24.

46:2 the mountains . . . the sea. A violent earthquake is described; there may be ancient Near Eastern portrayals of cosmic violence employed here. God overcomes the sea to accomplish His purposes (cf. Ps. 18; 74; 77; Nah. 1).

46:4 a river. Ancient and present Jerusalem have no river. There was a river in Eden (Gen. 2:10), as well as a "river . . . of life" that flows from the throne of God in the New Jerusalem (Rev. 22:1, 2).

the holy habitation. As the Israelites looked to the temple, they felt secure in the symbol of God's protection. Later in their history the people regarded the temple as a kind of idol that would save them from the Babylonians (Jer. 7). In this psalm, however, their trust is faithful and obedient, prefiguring the security enjoyed by God's people in the eternal city that is to come (Rev. 22:3).

46:5 she shall not be moved. Ancient Jerusalem indeed fell to the Babylonians in 586 B.C. The New Jerusalem will stand "forever and ever" (Rev. 22:5).

when morning dawns. In military campaigns, fighting commenced at first light. God's help will not be slow.

6 [m] The nations rage, the kingdoms totter;
he [n] utters his voice, the earth [o] melts.
7 [p] The LORD of hosts is with us;
the God of Jacob is our fortress. *Selah*
8 [q] Come, behold the works of the LORD,
how he has brought desolations on the earth.
9 [r] He makes wars cease to the end of the earth;
he [s] breaks the bow and shatters the spear;
[t] he burns the chariots with fire.
10 [u] "Be still, and know that I am God.
[v] I will be exalted among the nations,
I will be exalted in the earth!"
11 [p] The LORD of hosts is with us;
the God of Jacob is our fortress. *Selah*

God Is King over All the Earth

47 TO THE CHOIRMASTER. A PSALM OF [w] THE SONS OF KORAH.

1 [x] Clap your hands, all peoples!
[y] Shout to God with loud songs of joy!
2 For the LORD, the Most High, [z] is to be feared,
[a] a great king over all the earth.
3 He [b] subdued peoples under us,
and nations under our feet.
4 He chose our [c] heritage for us,
[d] the pride of Jacob whom he loves. *Selah*
5 God [e] has gone up with a shout,
the LORD with the sound of a trumpet.
6 Sing praises to God, sing praises!
Sing praises to our King, sing praises!
7 For God is [f] the King of all the earth;
sing praises [g] with a psalm![1]
8 God [h] reigns over the nations;
God sits on his holy throne.
9 [i] The princes of the peoples gather
as the people of the God of Abraham.
For [j] the shields of the earth belong to God;
he is highly exalted!

6 [m] Ps. 2:1 [n] Ps. 18:13; 68:33; 76:8; Jer. 25:30; Joel 2:11; 3:16; Amos 1:2 [o] Ex. 15:15; Josh. 2:9, 24; Amos 9:5 **7** [p] ver. 11; 2 Chr. 13:12; 20:17; [Num. 14:9] **8** [q] Ps. 66:5 **9** [r] Isai. 2:4; Mic. 4:3 [s] Ps. 76:3; 1 Sam. 2:4 [t] Ezek. 39:9 **10** [u] [Ex. 14:13] [v] Isai. 2:11, 17; 33:10 **11** [p] [See ver. 7 above]
Psalm 47 [w] Ps. 42, title **1** [x] 2 Kin. 11:12; Isai. 55:12; Nah. 3:19 [y] Ps. 95:1; [1 Sam. 10:24] **2** [z] Ps. 66:3, 5; 68:35; Deut. 7:21 [a] Mal. 1:14 **3** [b] See Ps. 18:47 **4** [c] Ps. 2:8; [1 Pet. 1:4] [d] Amos 6:8; 8:7; Nah. 2:2 **5** [e] 2 Sam. 6:15; [Ps. 68:18] **7** [f] Zech. 14:9 [g] 1 Cor. 14:15 **8** [h] Ps. 22:28; 1 Chr. 16:31 **9** [i] [Ps. 72:11; Isai. 49:7, 23] [j] Ps. 89:18

Zion, the City of Our God

48 A SONG. A PSALM OF [k] THE SONS OF KORAH.

1 [l] Great is the LORD and greatly to be praised
in [m] the city of our God!
His [n] holy mountain, 2 [o] beautiful in elevation,
is [p] the joy of all the earth,
Mount Zion, in the far north,
[q] the city of the great King.
3 Within her citadels God
has made himself known as a fortress.

Psalm 48 [k] Ps. 42, title; 46, title **1** [l] Ps. 96:4; 145:3 [m] See Ps. 46:4 [n] Ps. 2:6; 87:1; Zech. 8:3; [Isai. 2:3; Mic. 4:1] **2** [o] See Ps. 50:2 [p] Lam. 2:15; [Ezek. 20:6] [q] Matt. 5:35

[1] Hebrew *maskil*

46:6 the earth melts. At the voice of God the tumult of the rebellious is stilled forever.

46:7 with us. The refrain (again in v. 11) reflects the consolation of God's people enjoying His protection.

46:10 Be still. In the true knowledge of God and His deliverance there is peace, in contrast with the troubled "nations" (v. 6).

Ps. 47 Along with Ps. 93 and 95–99, this psalm can be classified as a kingship psalm. The image of God's enthronement is at the heart of the psalm. The occasion is a great military victory, and God is King, not only of Israel, but of the universe. This prayer also properly celebrates the ascension and rule of Jesus Christ. Jesus is both King and Warrior (Luke 19:38; 23:38; John 1:49).

47:1 all peoples. Since God is King of all the earth, and not just Israel, all the nations are called to join in the praise.

47:2 king over all the earth. See "God Reigns: Divine Sovereignty" at Dan. 4:34.

47:3 He subdued peoples. God won innumerable victories for His people throughout their history, beginning with the great victory at the Red Sea (Ex. 15).

47:4 our heritage. This refers to the conquest and allotment of the Promised Land. Deut. 7:1–11 explains that it is only through God's grace that Israel possessed the land.

47:5 has gone up. This is an enthronement. God has been King from all eternity (Ps. 93:2), but after the victory His kingship is celebrated anew.

47:9 The princes. These leaders should gather today; they will gather tomorrow when Christ returns.

Ps. 48 Ps. 48 is similar to Ps. 46, and it may also be compared with Ps. 76; 84; 87; 122. After the Fall (Gen. 3) sinful human beings lost their access to God. His holiness could not tolerate their unatoned sin. The patriarchs worshiped God at altars of sacrifice. After the Exodus, sacrifices were offered at the tabernacle and then at the temple appointed by God to be in Jerusalem. The whole city derived its sanctity from God's house. Jesus Christ replaced the symbolism of the temple with the reality of His incarnation (John 1:14). Through His Spirit, the people of God are His temple (1 Cor. 3:16; 6:19; Eph. 2:21; 1 Pet. 2:5). The true Mount Zion is a heavenly reality that is known in the earthly assembly of the saints (Gal. 4:26; Heb. 12:18–28).

48:1 His holy mountain. Mount Zion, the location of the temple in Jerusalem. See "The Greatness of God" at 1 Chr. 29:11.

48:2 joy of all the earth. Although the nations did not acknowledge Him, God is King of the universe and not only of Israel.

the far north. Lit. "beyond Zaphon." This is not a reference to Jerusalem but to a mountain often described in Canaanite texts as the dwelling place of their gods (Is. 14:13 and notes). Yahweh is described with terms used by the neighboring religions to show that all praise really belongs to the true God. Praise to other gods is in vain because they do not exist (Is. 44:6; 1 Cor. 8:4).

4 For behold, [r]the kings assembled;
they came on together.
5 As soon as they saw it, they were
astounded;
they were in panic; they took to
flight.
6 [s]Trembling took hold of them
there,
anguish [t]as of a woman in labor.
7 By [u]the east wind you [v]shattered
the ships of [w]Tarshish.
8 As we have heard, so have we seen
in the city of the LORD of hosts,
in [m]the city of our God,
which God will [x]establish
forever. *Selah*
9 We have thought on your [y]steadfast
love, O God,
in the midst of your temple.
10 As your [z]name, O God,
so your praise reaches to [a]the ends
of the earth.
Your right hand is filled with
righteousness.
11 Let Mount [b]Zion be glad!
Let [b]the daughters of Judah rejoice
because of your judgments!
12 Walk about Zion, go around her,
number her towers,
13 consider well her [c]ramparts,
go through her citadels,
[d]that you may tell the next
generation
14 that this is God,
our God forever and ever.
He will [e]guide us forever.[1]

4 [r]See 2 Sam. 10:6-19
6 [s][Ex. 15:15] [t]Isai. 13:8; Hos. 13:13
7 [u]Jer. 18:17 [v]1 Kin. 22:48; Ezek. 27:26 [w]1 Kin. 10:22
8 [m][See ver. 1 above] [x]Ps. 87:5; Isai. 2:2; Mic. 4:1
9 [y]Ps. 26:3; 40:10
10 [z]Ps. 113:3; [Ex. 34:5, 6; Deut. 28:58; Mal. 1:11, 14] [a]See Ps. 22:27
11 [b]Ps. 97:8
13 [c]Ps. 122:7 [d][Ps. 78:4-6]
14 [e]Ps. 23:3, 4
Psalm 49
[f]Ps. 42, title
1 [g]Ps. 78:1; Isai. 1:2; Mic. 1:2
2 [h]Ps. 62:9
3 [i]Prov. 1:20; 9:1
4 [j]Ps. 78:2; Num. 21:27; Matt. 13:35 [k]Num. 12:8; Prov. 1:6
5 [l][Ps. 37:1] [m]Ps. 94:13
6 [n]Ps. 52:7; Prov. 11:28; Mark 10:24; [Job 31:24]
7 [o][Matt. 25:9] [p][Matt. 16:26] [q]See Job 33:24
8 [r]Job 36:18, 19
9 [s]Ps. 16:10; [Ps. 89:48]
10 [t]Eccles. 2:16 [u]Ps. 73:22; 92:6; 94:8; Prov. 30:2 [v]See Ps. 39:6
11 [w]Ps. 5:9; 64:6 [x]Ps. 10:6 [y][Gen. 4:17]

Why Should I Fear in Times of Trouble?

49

TO THE CHOIRMASTER. A PSALM OF [f]THE SONS OF KORAH.

1 [g]Hear this, all peoples!
Give ear, all inhabitants of the world,
2 [h]both low and high,
rich and poor together!
3 My mouth shall speak [i]wisdom;
the meditation of my heart shall be
understanding.
4 I will incline my ear to [j]a proverb;
I will solve my [k]riddle to the music
of the lyre.
5 [l]Why should I fear in [m]times of trouble,
when the iniquity of those who
cheat me surrounds me,
6 those who [n]trust in their wealth
and boast of the abundance of
their riches?
7 Truly no man [o]can ransom another,
or [p]give to God [q]the price of his life,
8 for [r]the ransom of their life is costly
and can never suffice,
9 that he should live on forever
and [s]never see the pit.
10 For he sees [t]that even the wise die;
[u]the fool and the stupid alike must
perish
and [v]leave their wealth to others.
11 Their [w]graves are their homes forever,[2]
their dwelling places [x]to all
generations,
though they [y]called lands by their
own names.

1 Septuagint; another reading is (compare Jerome, Syriac) *He will guide us beyond death* 2 Septuagint, Syriac, Targum; Hebrew *Their inward thought was that their homes were forever*

48:4 the kings assembled. The language is similar to Ps. 2:1–3.

48:5 were in panic. Their fear is due to God's power, which He exercised in Jerusalem, because He had chosen that city as His dwelling place.

48:7 ships of Tarshish. Seagoing merchant ships.

48:8 LORD of hosts. A military title identifying God as the One who leads His heavenly army into battle for the protection of His people.

48:9 steadfast love. Specifically, God's love for those in covenant relationship with Him.

48:14 He will guide. Israel's fate was not a matter of chance or human striving. God is in control and His sovereignty is not limited by death.

Ps. 49 This psalm is in the wisdom tradition (vv. 3, 4), treating issues typical of the wisdom books. The psalmist wrestles with two problems: death and the prosperity of the rich. The psalm is one of the most difficult to translate and interpret correctly. Few places in the Old Testament express so directly the hope for the resurrection of the dead. The full doctrine of the resurrection was not revealed until Jesus rose from the grave and ascended to the right hand of God.

49:1 all peoples. The psalm applies not only to people in redemptive relationship with God, but to all people everywhere.

49:2 rich and poor. The psalmist is disturbed by the complacency of the rich.

49:3 speak wisdom. The psalm will provide practical insight on the problem at hand. The psalmist identifies himself with the sages of Israel.

49:4 proverb . . . riddle. These words locate the psalm in the wisdom tradition.

49:5 times of trouble. These are the days approaching one's death (cf. Eccl. 12:1).

49:6 trust in their wealth. Rather than trusting God.

49:7 no man can ransom another. No amount of money can prevent death, and no one can escape his or her obligation to die.

49:10 the wise die; the fool. The thought is reminiscent of Eccl. 2:12–16. The psalmist classifies the rich oppressor with the fools and the senseless.

49:11 their dwelling places to all generations. The rich spend much of their lifetime building earthly homes and amassing wealth. But all these things soon pass away.

12 Man in his pomp [z]will not remain;
[a]he is like the beasts that perish.
13 This is the path of those who have
[b]foolish confidence;
yet after them people approve of
their boasts.[1] *Selah*
14 Like sheep they are appointed for
Sheol;
Death shall be their shepherd,
and the upright [c]shall rule over them
in the morning.
[d]Their form shall be consumed [e]in
Sheol, with no place to dwell.
15 But God will [f]ransom my soul from
the power of Sheol,
for he will [g]receive me. *Selah*
16 Be not afraid when a man becomes
rich,
when the glory of his house
increases.
17 [h]For when he dies he will [i]carry
nothing away;
his glory will not go down after
him.
18 For though, while he lives, he counts
himself [j]blessed,
—and though you get praise when
you do well for yourself—
19 his soul will [k]go to the generation of
his fathers,
who will never again [l]see light.
20 [m]Man in his pomp yet without
understanding is like the
beasts that perish.

12 [z]ver. 20; [Ps. 39:5; 82:7] [a]ver. 20; Eccles. 3:19 **13** [b][Luke 12:20] **14** [c][Dan. 7:22; Mal. 4:3; Luke 22:30; 1 Cor. 6:2; Rev 2:26; 20:4] [d]Ps. 39:11 [e]Job 24:19, 20 **15** [f]Hos. 13:14; [Dan. 12:2] [g]Ps. 16:11; 17:15; 73:24; [Gen. 5:24] **17** [h][Job 27:19] [i]1 Tim. 6:7 **18** [j]Ps. 10:3; 36:2; Deut. 29:19; Luke 12:19 **19** [k]Gen. 15:15 [l]Ps. 56:13; Job 33:30 **20** [m]ver. 12

Psalm 50 [n]1 Chr. 6:39; 15:17; 16:5, 7; 25:2; 2 Chr. 29:30 **1** [o]Josh. 22:22 [p]Ps. 113:3 **2** [q][Lam. 2:15]; See Ps. 48:2 [r]Ps. 80:1; 94:1; Deut. 33:2 **3** [s][Ex. 19:16] [t]Ps. 21:9; 97:3; Lev. 10:2; Num. 16:35; Dan. 7:10 **4** [u]Deut. 4:26; 31:28; 32:1; Isai. 1:2; Mic. 6:1, 2

God Himself Is Judge

50 A PSALM OF [n]ASAPH.
[o]The Mighty One, God the LORD,
speaks and summons the earth
[p]from the rising of the sun to its
setting.
2 Out of Zion, [q]the perfection of
beauty,
[r]God shines forth.
3 Our God comes; he [s]does not keep
silence;[2]
before him is a devouring [t]fire,
around him a mighty tempest.
4 [u]He calls to the heavens above
and to the earth, that he may
judge his people:
5 "Gather to me my faithful ones,
who made [v]a covenant with me by
sacrifice!"
6 [w]The heavens declare his
righteousness,
for [x]God himself is
judge! *Selah*
7 [y]"Hear, O my people, and I will speak;
O Israel, I will testify against you.
[z]I am God, your God.
8 Not for your sacrifices [a]do I
rebuke you;
your burnt offerings are
continually before me.

5 [v]Ex. 24:7, 8; See Gen. 15:9-18 **6** [w]Ps. 89:5; 97:6; [Rev. 16:5, 7; 19:2] [x]Ps. 58:11; 75:7 **7** [y]Ps. 81:8; [Ps. 49:1] [z]Ex. 20:2 **8** [a]See Ps. 40:6

[1] *Or and of those after them who approve of their boasts* [2] *Or May our God come, and not keep silence*

49:12 he is like the beasts that perish. In comparing this experience of both humans and animals, the psalmist parallels the thought of Eccl. 3:18–21.

49:14 Like sheep. Unaware, the self-trusting rich are on the road to slaughter.

49:15 God will ransom my soul from . . . Sheol. While God does not accept a ransom for death (v. 7), He provides one for the psalmist. The key to this Old Testament awareness of redemption from death is recognition of the eternity of God and of His eternal relationship with His people: "he will receive me." See Mark 12:26, 27.

49:16–20 The wicked rich cannot carry their wealth into the dark, joyless eternity to which they are appointed.

Ps. 50 This psalm has a prophetic cast since a large part of it is composed of two oracles of the Lord, one spoken to the righteous, and the other against the wicked. The psalm places special focus on the need to give thanks (vv. 14, 15, 22, 23). With regard to its title, see Introduction: Author.

50:1 The Mighty One, God the LORD. The psalm opens impressively with three divine names. The third is God's covenant name, conventionally translated with the word "LORD" in small capitals. In Hebrew it is four consonants, called the "Tetragrammaton," and probably pronounced "Yahweh." "Jehovah" uses the vowels of a different word in a way suggested by the Jewish custom of not pronouncing God's sacred name. See Ex. 3:13–15 and notes.

from the rising of the sun to its setting. From east to west, God addresses the whole earth.

50:2 Zion. The location of the temple, the place God has chosen to make His presence known. See Ps. 2:6.

shines forth. The language indicates a "theophany," a visual self-revelation of God. God's presence is manifest at His temple in Jerusalem. See Deut. 33:2.

50:3 before him is a devouring fire. God's theophany (v. 2 note) is often accompanied by powerful and dangerous forces, especially when He speaks in judgment (Ex. 19; Is. 24; Nah. 1).

50:5 a covenant with me by sacrifice. A covenant is a solemn agreement between persons. Here, as in most places, it signifies the bond between God and His people. However, since man is sinful, this relationship must be accompanied by sacrifice, representing the punishment for sin.

50:6 heavens. Possibly a poetic way of referring to the inhabitants of heaven, the angels; otherwise, the glory of the inanimate, created heavens.

50:7 testify. This legal terminology is used because covenants were legal instruments, like contracts or treaties. When there was some disruption in the people's faithfulness, they were often put on trial by the Lord or by one of His prophets (Mic. 6:1–8).

50:8 Not for your sacrifices do I rebuke you. This verse indicates that the people's problem was not observance of the sacrificial rites. They were faithful to do them, but they apparently misunderstood their significance.

9 I will not accept a bull from your
house
or goats from your folds.
10 For every beast of the forest is mine,
the cattle on a thousand hills.
11 [b] I know all the birds of the hills,
and all that moves in the field is
mine.

12 "If I were hungry, I would not tell
you,
[c] for the world and its fullness are
mine.
13 Do I eat the flesh of bulls
or drink the blood of goats?
14 [d] Offer to God a sacrifice of
thanksgiving,[1]
and [e] perform your vows to the
Most High,
15 and [f] call upon me in the day of
trouble;
I will [g] deliver you, and you shall
[h] glorify me."

16 But to the wicked God says:
"What right have you to recite my
statutes
or take my covenant on your lips?
17 [i] For you hate discipline,
[j] and you cast my words behind
you.
18 If you see a thief, [k] you are pleased
with him,
[l] and you keep company with
adulterers.

19 "You give your mouth free rein for
evil,
[m] and your tongue frames deceit.

20 You sit and speak against your brother;
you slander your own mother's son.
21 These things you have done, and I
[n] have been silent;
you thought that I[2] was one like
yourself.
But now I [o] rebuke you and [p] lay the
charge before you.

22 "Mark this, then, you who [q] forget God,
lest I tear you apart, and there be
[r] none to deliver!
23 The one who [s] offers thanksgiving as
his sacrifice glorifies me;
to one who [t] orders his way rightly
I will show the [u] salvation of God!"

11 [b] [Matt. 10:29] 12 [c] See Ps. 24:1 14 [d] ver. 23; Ps. 27:6; 69:30; 107:22; Heb. 13:15; [Hos. 14:2; Rom. 12:1] [e] Ps. 22:25; 61:8; 65:1; 76:11; 116:14, 18; Num. 30:2; Deut. 23:21; Job 22:27; Eccles. 5:4, 5 15 [f] Ps. 81:7; Zech. 13:9; [Ps. 107:6] [g] Ps. 91:15 [h] ver. 23; Ps. 22:23 17 [i] [Rom. 2:21, 22] [j] 1 Kin. 14:9; Neh. 9:26 18 [k] Rom. 1:32 [l] [1 Tim. 5:22] 19 [m] [Ps. 52:2]
21 [n] Eccles. 8:11; Isai. 57:11 [o] Ps. 90:8; 2 Kin. 19:4 [p] Job 13:18; 23:4 22 [q] See Ps. 9:17 [r] Ps. 7:2 23 [s] ver. 14, 15 [t] [Gal. 6:16] [u] Ps. 91:16

Create in Me a Clean Heart, O God

51 To the choirmaster. A Psalm of David, when [v] Nathan the prophet went to him, after he had gone in to Bathsheba.

1 [w] Have mercy on me,[3] O God,
according to your steadfast love;
according to your [x] abundant mercy
[y] blot out my transgressions.
2 [z] Wash me thoroughly from my iniquity,
and [a] cleanse me from my sin!

3 [b] For I know my transgressions,
and my sin is ever before me.
4 [c] Against you, you only, have I sinned
and done what is evil [d] in your sight,
[e] so that you may be justified in your
words
and blameless in your judgment.

Psalm 51 [v] 2 Sam. 12:1 1 [w] See Ps. 4:1 [x] See Ps. 106:45 [y] ver. 9; Isai. 43:25; 44:22; Acts 3:19; Col. 2:14 2 [z] ver. 7; Isai. 1:16; Jer. 4:14; Mal. 3:3; Acts 22:16 [a] Heb. 9:14; 1 John 1:7, 9; [Lev. 13:6] 3 [b] Ps. 32:5; [Prov. 28:13]
4 [c] Gen. 20:6; 39:9; 2 Sam. 12:13; [1 Cor. 8:12] [d] Luke 15:18, 21 [e] Cited Rom. 3:4

[1] Or *Make thanksgiving your sacrifice to God* [2] Or *that the* I AM [3] Or *Be gracious to me*

50:9 will not accept. The people of the surrounding nations thought that their gods ate the sacrifices offered to them and grew hungry when deprived. In the Gilgamesh Epic, the goddess Ishtar bemoans the lack of sacrifices that resulted in her god-sized hunger.

50:10 every beast of the forest is mine. God affirms that He created and owns all the creatures of the world.

50:13, 14 Do I eat the flesh of bulls. This rhetorical question makes it clear that the Lord neither eats the sacrifices, nor is He satisfied with them apart from sincere commitment and thanksgiving.

50:16 wicked. Probably the wicked people within the professing covenant community, since they know God's law.

recite. This may be a reference to a covenant renewal ceremony in which the covenant community together recites the law and reaffirms its intention to keep it (Deut. 31:9–11).

50:17 hate discipline. A sure sign of a fool (Prov. 1:7).

50:18, 19 The psalmist cites the seventh, eighth, and ninth commandments.

50:21 I have been silent. God's silence was frequently taken by the wicked as a sign that He didn't care if they sinned.

50:22 lest I tear you apart. God insists on obedience from the wicked hypocrites, or they will meet a fearful end.

Ps. 51 Ps. 51 is a uniquely powerful statement of the depths of sin and repentance. It is the most striking of the "prayers of penitence" (introduction to Ps. 6), a type of lament.

51:1 according to your steadfast love. David had been guilty of a great sin in the matter of Uriah, husband of Bathsheba (2 Sam. 11). David pleads for God's mercy, in keeping with His promised love for His people.

mercy. God's forgiveness of sinners is the result of His mercy. Sinners deserve death, but He gives life.

51:2 Wash. The word means specifically to "wash clothes." The psalmist's iniquity is like filthy clothes that need to be laundered.

51:4 you only. David committed adultery with Bathsheba and sent her husband to his death. How can he say he sinned against God only? Rebellion against God was the root of his sin, and his crime injured people who belonged to God and transgressed a social order created by God.

5 Behold,[f] I was brought forth in iniquity,
and in sin did my mother
conceive me.
6 Behold, you delight in truth in [g] the
inward being,
and you teach me wisdom in the
secret heart.

7 Purge me [h] with hyssop, and I shall
be clean;
[z] wash me, and I shall be [i] whiter
than snow.

5 [f] Rom. 5:12, 19; Eph. 2:3; See Job 14:4; 15:14
6 [g] Job 38:36
7 [h] Ex. 12:22; Lev. 14:4; Num. 19:18; Heb. 9:19 [z] [See ver. 2 above] [i] Isai. 1:18
8 [j] Ps. 35:10 [k] Ps. 44:19; Isai. 38:13
9 [l] Jer. 16:17 [y] [See ver. 1 above]

8 Let me hear joy and gladness;
[j] let the bones [k] that you have
broken rejoice.
9 [l] Hide your face from my sins,
and [y] blot out all my iniquities.
10 [m] Create in me a [n] clean heart,
O God,
and [o] renew a right[1] spirit
within me.

10 [m] 1 Sam. 10:9; Jer. 24:7; Ezek. 11:19; 36:26; Eph. 4:23, 24 [n] Ps. 24:4; Matt. 5:8; Acts 15:9 [o] Lam. 5:21

1 Or *steadfast*

Original Sin and Total Depravity

Scripture diagnoses sin as a universal deformity of human nature, found at every point in every person (1 Kin. 8:46; Rom. 3:9–23; 7:18; 1 John 1:8–10). Both Testaments describe sin as rebellion against God's rule, missing the mark God set for us to aim at, transgressing God's law, offending God's purity by defiling oneself, and incurring guilt before God the Judge. The moral deformity is dynamic: sin is an energy of irrational, negative, and rebellious reaction to God. It is a spirit of fighting God in order to play God. The root of sin is pride and enmity against God, the spirit seen in Adam's first transgression, and sinful acts always have behind them thoughts and desires that one way or another express the willful opposition of the fallen heart to God's claims on our lives.

Sin may be defined as breaking the law of God, or failing to conform to it, in any aspect of life, whether thought, word, or deed. Scriptures illustrating different aspects of sin include Jer. 17:9; Matt. 12:30–37; Mark 7:20–23; Rom. 1:18–3:20; 7:7–25; 8:5–8; 14:23 (Luther said that Paul wrote Romans to "magnify sin"); Gal. 5:16–21; Eph. 2:1–3; 4:17–19; Heb. 3:12; James 2:10–11; 1 John 3:4; 5:17.

"Original sin," meaning sin derived from our origin, is not a biblical phrase (it comes from Augustine), but it does bring into focus the reality of sin in our spiritual system. Original sin does not mean that sin belongs to human nature as such; "God made man upright" (Eccl. 7:29). Nor does it mean that the processes of reproduction and birth are sinful; the uncleanness associated with sexuality in the Law (Lev. 12; 15) was typical and ceremonial, not moral. Rather, "original sin" means that sinfulness marks everyone from birth, in the form of a heart inclined toward sin, prior to any actual sins; this inner sinfulness is the root and source of all actual sins; it is transmitted to us from Adam, our first representative before God. The doctrine of original sin makes the point that we are not sinners because we sin, but we sin because we are sinners, born with a nature enslaved to sin.

The phrase "total depravity" is commonly used to make explicit the implications of original sin. It signifies a corruption of our moral and spiritual nature that is total in principle, although not in degree (for no one is as bad as he or she might be). No part of us is untouched by sin, and no action of ours is as good as it should be. Consequently, nothing we do is ever meritorious in God's eyes. We cannot earn God's favor, no matter what we do; unless grace saves us, we are lost.

Total depravity includes total inability, that is, being without power to believe in God or His word (John 6:44; Rom. 8:7, 8). Paul calls this universal unresponsiveness a form of death; the fallen heart is "dead" (Eph. 2:1, 5; Col. 2:13). As the *Westminster Confession* (IX. 3) explains, "Man by his fall into a state of sin, hath wholly lost all ability of will to any spiritual good accompanying salvation; so as a natural man, being altogether averse from that good, and dead in sin, is not able by his own strength to convert himself, or to prepare himself thereunto." To this darkness the word of God alone brings light (Luke 18:27; 2 Cor. 4:6).

justified . . . blameless. David recognized that God's anger against him was just. This verse is cited by Paul in Rom. 3:4.

51:5 brought forth in iniquity. The Bible clearly teaches that children are sinners. They are not born innocent and only later become sinners. Children, too, need God's salvation. See theological note "Original Sin and Total Depravity."

51:6 the inward being . . . the secret heart. That is, truth and wisdom at the center of one's being.

51:7 with hyssop. The allusion is to Lev. 14:6, 7, where the cleansing of a leper is described.

wash me. This may be an allusion to Num. 19:19, where instructions are given for ritual washing after contact with a dead person. On the need for washing the heart, see "Legalism" at Matt. 23:4.

51:10 Create. The verb is the same used at Gen. 1:1 for the creation of the world. The psalmist knows that the redirection of his desires and thoughts can only come about through the intervention of God. See "Repentance" at Acts 26:20.

11 [p]Cast me not away from your
presence,
and take not [q]your Holy Spirit
from me.
12 Restore to me the joy of your
salvation,
and uphold me with a willing spirit.

13 Then I will teach transgressors your
ways,
and sinners will [r]return to you.
14 Deliver me from [s]bloodguiltiness,
O God,
O [t]God of my salvation,
and [u]my tongue will sing aloud of
your [v]righteousness.
15 O Lord, open my lips,
and my mouth will declare your
praise.
16 [w]For you will not delight in sacrifice,
or I would give it;
you will not be pleased with a
burnt offering.
17 The sacrifices of God are [x]a broken
spirit;
a broken and contrite heart,
O God, you will not despise.

18 [y]Do good to Zion in your good
pleasure;
[z]build up the walls of Jerusalem;
19 then will you delight in [a]right
sacrifices,
in burnt offerings and [b]whole
burnt offerings;
then bulls will be offered on your
altar.

11 [p]Ps. 102:10; 2 Kin. 13:23; 17:20; 24:20; Jer. 7:15 [q]Rom. 8:9; Eph. 4:30
13 [r][Luke 22:32]
14 [s]2 Sam. 11:17; 12:9 [t]Ps. 24:5 [u]Ps. 35:28; 71:8, 15, 24 [v][1 John 1:9]
16 [w]See Ps. 40:6
17 [x]See Ps. 34:18
18 [y][Ps. 69:35; 122:6] [z]Ps. 147:2
19 [a]Ps. 4:5; [Mal. 3:3] [b]Deut. 33:10

Psalm 52
[c]1 Sam. 22:9
2 [d]Ps. 50:19 [e][Ps. 57:4] [f]Ps. 101:7
3 [g][Jer. 9:4, 5]
5 [h]Prov. 2:22 [i]See Ps. 27:13
6 [j]See Ps. 40:3 [k]See Ps. 2:4
7 [l]See Ps. 49:6
8 [m]Jer. 11:16; [Ps. 1:3; 37:35; 92:12, 13; 128:3; 144:12; Hos. 14:6]

The Steadfast Love of God Endures

52 To the choirmaster. A Maskil[1] of David, when [c]Doeg, the Edomite, came and told Saul, "David has come to the house of Ahimelech."

1 Why do you boast of evil, O mighty
man?
The steadfast love of God endures
all the day.
2 Your [d]tongue plots destruction,
like [e]a sharp razor, you [f]worker of
deceit.
3 You love evil more than good,
and [g]lying more than speaking
what is right. *Selah*
4 You love all words that devour,
O deceitful tongue.

5 But God will break you down forever;
he will snatch and [h]tear you from
your tent;
he will uproot you from [i]the land
of the living. *Selah*
6 The righteous shall [j]see and fear,
and shall [k]laugh at him, saying,
7 "See the man who would not make
God his refuge,
but [l]trusted in the abundance of his
riches
and sought refuge in his own
destruction!"[2]

8 But I am like [m]a green olive tree
in the house of God.
I trust in the steadfast love of God
forever and ever.

[1] Probably a musical or liturgical term [2] Or *in his work of destruction*

51:11 Holy Spirit. The Old Testament does not make a full disclosure of the personhood of the Holy Spirit. David understands that his spiritual well-being depends on God's presence with him. He fears that the Spirit may be taken away, because the Spirit is holy and David is sinful. See "The Holy Spirit" at John 14:26.

51:12 joy of your salvation. David had suffered from a spiritual dullness that led to moral bankruptcy. To prevent such disaster in the future, he prays for joy.

51:13 I will teach transgressors your ways. If forgiven, the psalmist promises to use his life to help others find forgiveness.

51:14 sing aloud of your righteousness. David has previously spoken of God's justice in condemning sin (v. 4). Now, the same justice overcomes sin and condemnation through grace, as explained in Rom. 3:21–26 and epitomized in 1 John 1:9.

51:16 you will not be pleased with a burnt offering. The Bible values heartfelt obedience above outward religious conformity (40:6–8; Mic. 6:6–8). As v. 19 shows, this did not condemn sacrifices as such.

51:18, 19 The restoration of the king leads to blessing for the people.

Ps. 52 This psalm expresses confidence in the Lord like a psalm of trust, pronounces judgment on the wicked like a lament, and uses wisdom language.

52:title The historical title refers to the event recorded in 1 Sam. 22:6–23. In effect, the title identifies Doeg with the boastful, wicked man, and David with the righteous psalmist. However, the psalm itself is not so specific and continues to be immediately relevant to the people of God.

52:1 mighty man. A soldier or warrior.

52:4 devour. More exactly, "confused." The wisdom literature consistently teaches that confusion is on the side of the wicked and order on the side of righteousness.

52:6 fear. This verb may seem strange as associated with laughter. The meaning, however, is not fear in the sense of dread, but rather of reverence and awe. The righteous see the justice of God's judgment against the wicked.

52:7 who would not make God his refuge. This man is the opposite of everything the psalms stand for. Throughout the psalms people are urged to make God their stronghold and to put no trust in themselves. God is the power behind His people in all their victories.

52:8 olive tree. Reminiscent of Ps. 1. Olive trees can live for hundreds of years.

9 I will thank you forever,
because you have done it.
I will wait for your name, [n]for it is
good,
in the presence of the [o]godly.

There Is None That Does Good

53 To the choirmaster: according to [p]Mahalath. A Maskil[1] of David.

1 [q]The fool says in his heart, "There is
no God."
They are corrupt, doing
abominable iniquity;
there is none who does good.

2 God looks down from heaven
on the children of man
to see if there are any who
understand,[2]
who seek after God.

3 They have all fallen away;
together they have become corrupt;
there is none who does good,
not even one.

4 Have those who work evil no
knowledge,
who eat up my people as they eat
bread,
and do not call upon God?

5 There they are, in great terror,
[r]where there is no terror!
For God [s]scatters the bones of him
who encamps against you;
you put them to shame, for God
has rejected them.

6 Oh, that salvation for Israel would
come out of Zion!
When God restores the fortunes of
his people,
Let Jacob rejoice, let Israel be glad.

9 [n]Ps. 54:6 [o]See Ps. 50:5
Psalm 53 [p] Ps. 88, title
1 [q]For ver. 1-6, see Ps. 14:1-7
5 [r][Lev. 26:17, 36; Prov. 28:1] [s]Ps. 89:10; 141:7; Jer. 8:1, 2; Ezek. 6:5

Psalm 54 [t]Ps. 4, title [u]1 Sam. 23:19; 26:1
1 [v]Ps. 5:11; 52:9
2 [w]See Ps. 55:1
3 [x]Ps. 86:14 [y]Ps. 18:44; 144:7; Isai. 25:5 [z][1 Sam. 23:15]
4 [a]Ps. 118:7
5 [b][Ps. 89:49] [c]Ps. 143:12
6 [d]Ps. 52:9
7 [e]Ps. 59:10; 92:11; 112:8; 118:7
Psalm 55 [f] Ps. 4, title
1 [g]Ps. 54:2; 61:1; 86:6

The Lord Upholds My Life

54 To the choirmaster: with [t]stringed instruments. A Maskil[3] of David, [u]when the Ziphites went and told Saul, "Is not David hiding among us?"

1 O God, save me, by your [v]name,
and vindicate me by your might.
2 O God, [w]hear my prayer;
give ear to the words of my mouth.

3 [x]For [y]strangers[4] have risen against me;
ruthless men [z]seek my life;
they do not set God before
themselves. *Selah*

4 Behold, [a]God is my helper;
the Lord is the upholder of my life.
5 He will return the evil to my enemies;
in your [b]faithfulness [c]put an end to
them.

6 With a freewill offering I will sacrifice
to you;
I will give thanks to your name,
O Lord, [d]for it is good.
7 For he has delivered me from every
trouble,
and my eye has [e]looked in triumph
on my enemies.

Cast Your Burden on the Lord

55 To the choirmaster: with [f]stringed instruments. A Maskil[5] of David.

1 [g]Give ear to my prayer, O God,
and hide not yourself from my plea
for mercy!

1 Probably musical or liturgical terms 2 Or *that act wisely* 3 Probably a musical or liturgical term 4 Some Hebrew manuscripts and Targum *insolent men* (compare Psalm 86:14) 5 Probably a musical or liturgical term

52:9 in the presence of the godly. The assurance of the psalmist leads to praise in public worship. See note 22:22.

Ps. 53 Cf. Ps. 14. A meditation on the wickedness of the fool. God will destroy the fool and restore Israel's fortunes. Ps. 53, in contrast to Ps. 14, uses "God" rather than the more specific, covenant "Lord" to refer to the deity. This variation fits the broader context, since Ps. 53 is in Book II of the Psalter, which uses the broader term rather than the covenant name.

53:1–4 See notes Ps. 14:1–4.

53:5 scatters the bones. In the Old Testament God often fights for His people against their flesh-and-blood enemies. With New Testament revelation the underlying spiritual conflict to save His people from sin becomes the dominant theme, although the real conflict has been at this level from the beginning (Gen. 3:4, 5).

53:6 salvation for Israel. An expression of hope for deliverance from evil.

54:title The historical title locates the inspiration of the psalm in David's premonarchical days. He wrote the psalm after being betrayed by the Ziphites (1 Sam. 23:19; 26:11).

54:1 vindicate me. The word identifies his complaint as a judicial one. David had been unjustly betrayed by the Ziphites, his countrymen from Judah.

54:3 strangers. Though they are countrymen, he does not know them personally.

54:6, 7 A vow to sacrifice to the Lord as thanks for being rescued from trouble. See 22:22 and note.

Ps. 55 Like many laments, this psalm bemoans the attack of enemies. Most unusual is the sorrow over betrayal by a friend. The psalm descends to the pits of despair, but turns at the end toward the Lord with hope. The psalm anticipates the suffering of Christ, who was betrayed by Judas, a disciple of His inner circle (Matt. 26:47–56).

2 Attend to me, and answer me;
I am restless [h]in my complaint and
I [i]moan,
3 because of the noise of the enemy,
because of the oppression of the
wicked.
For they [j]drop trouble upon me,
and in anger they bear a grudge
against me.

4 My heart is in anguish within me;
[k]the terrors of death have fallen
upon me.
5 Fear and trembling come upon me,
and [l]horror [m]overwhelms me.
6 And I say, "Oh, that I had wings like
a dove!
I would fly away and be at rest;
7 [n]yes, I would wander far away;
I would lodge in the
wilderness; *Selah*
8 I would hurry to find a shelter
from [o]the raging wind and tempest."

9 Destroy, O Lord, [p]divide their tongues;
for I see [q]violence and strife in the
city.
10 Day and night they go around it
on its walls,
and [r]iniquity and trouble are within it;
11 ruin is in its midst;
[s]oppression and fraud
do not depart from its marketplace.

12 For it is not an enemy who
taunts me—
then I could bear it;
it is not an adversary who [t]deals
insolently with me—
then I could hide from him.
13 [u]But it is you, a man, my equal,
my companion, my familiar friend.
14 We used to take sweet counsel
together;
within God's house we walked in
[v]the throng.
15 Let death steal over them;
let them go down to Sheol [w]alive;
for evil is in their dwelling place
and in their heart.

16 But I call to God,
and the LORD will save me.
17 [x]Evening and [y]morning and
at [z]noon
I [a]utter my complaint and moan,
and he hears my voice.
18 He redeems my soul in safety
from the battle that I wage,
for [b]many are arrayed against me.
19 God will give ear and humble them,
he who is [c]enthroned from
of old, *Selah*
because they do not [d]change
and do not fear God.

20 My companion[1] [e]stretched out his
hand against his friends;
he violated his covenant.
21 His [f]speech was [g]smooth as butter,
yet war was in his heart;
his words were softer than oil,
yet they were [h]drawn swords.

22 [i]Cast your burden on the LORD,
and he will sustain you;
[j]he will never permit
the righteous to be moved.

1 Hebrew *He*

2 [h]ver. 17; Ps. 64:1 [i][Isai. 38:14; 59:11]
3 [j][2 Sam. 16:7, 8]
4 [k]Ps. 116:3
5 [l]Job 21:6; Isai. 21:4; Ezek. 7:18 [m]Ps. 78:53
7 [n][Jer. 9:2]
8 [o]Ps. 83:15
9 [p][Gen. 11:9] [q]Jer. 6:7
10 [r]Ps. 5:9
11 [s][Ps. 10:7]
12 [t]Job 19:5
13 [u][2 Sam. 15:12; 16:23]; See Ps. 41:9
14 [v]Ps. 42:4
15 [w]Num. 16:30, 33; Prov. 1:12; [Ps. 124:3]
17 [x]Ps. 141:2; Acts 3:1; 10:3, 30 [y]Ps. 5:3; 88:13; 92:2 [z]Acts 10:9; [Dan. 6:10] [a]ver. 2
18 [b][Ps. 56:2]
19 [c]Deut. 33:27 [d]Job 10:17; See Job 21:7-15
20 [e]Acts 12:1
21 [f]See Ps. 28:3 [g]Prov. 5:3, 4
21 [h]See Ps. 57:4
22 [i]See Ps. 37:5 [j]Ps. 10:6

55:3 enemy. The psalmist refers to enemies in general terms because he knows that his song will be used by other people in other situations (v. 22).

55:6 I would fly away. The writer has the urge to escape the source of his distress, but is unable to do so.

55:9 divide their tongues. The psalmist alludes to the judgment the Lord brought upon the wicked generation who built the tower of Babel (Gen. 11:1–9).

55:10 go around it on its walls. Lawless men are loose and active on the walls, the main defense of the city.

55:11 its marketplace. This description of an ancient city of Israel, presumably Jerusalem during David's reign, could be applied to today's lawless cities.

55:13 The terms become increasingly intimate, from "a man, my equal" to "my companion" to the climax, "my familiar friend."

55:14 sweet counsel together. The worst hurt of all is that the close friend was a fellow worshiper in the house of God.

55:15 down to Sheol alive. That is, into Sheol, the grave.

55:18 the battle. While the psalm could conceivably have had its origin in battle, it is more likely that the battle is a metaphor for the struggles that the psalmist feels with his enemies and friends who surround him.

55:19 enthroned from of old. God hears the psalmist's prayers from His kingly throne in heaven.

55:20 his covenant. The psalmist describes the willful breaking of a formal agreement between friends. A covenant is a solemn agreement under sanctions.

55:21 smooth as butter . . . softer than oil. A powerful poetic description of hypocrisy and deceit.

55:22 he will never permit the righteous to be moved. The context of the psalm shows that there is no unqualified promise that the righteous will always be happy and prosperous. The psalmist sings this lament to the Lord because he is in despair. The verse must mean that God will not leave the righteous in the fallen position forever, but will vindicate them in the end.

23 But you, O God, [k]will cast them
down
into [l]the pit of destruction;
men of [m]blood and treachery
shall not [n]live out half their
days.
But I will [o]trust in you.

In God I Trust

56

To the choirmaster: according to The Dove on Far-off Terebinths. A [p] Miktam[1] of David, when the [q] Philistines seized him in Gath.

1 [r]Be gracious to me, O God, for man
[s]tramples on me;
all day long an attacker
oppresses me;
2 my enemies trample on me all day
long,
for many attack me proudly.
3 When I am afraid,
I [t]put my trust in you.
4 In God, whose word I praise,
in God I trust; [u]I shall not be
afraid.
What can flesh do to me?

5 All day long they injure my cause;[2]
all their thoughts are against me
for evil.
6 They [v]stir up strife, they [w]lurk;
they [x]watch my steps,
as they have waited for my life.
7 For their crime will they escape?
[y]In wrath [z]cast down the peoples,
O God!

8 You have kept count of my
tossings;[3]
[a]put my tears in your bottle.
[b]Are they not in your book?
9 Then my enemies will turn back
[c]in the day when I call.
This I know, that[4] [d]God is for me.
10 In God, whose word I praise,
in the Lord, whose word I praise,
11 in God I trust; [u]I shall not be afraid.
What can man do to me?

12 I must perform my [e]vows to you,
O God;
I will [e]render thank offerings to you.
13 [f]For you have delivered my soul from
death,
yes, my feet from falling,
[g]that I may walk before God
[h]in the light of life.

Let Your Glory Be over All the Earth

57

To the choirmaster: according to [i] Do Not Destroy. A [j] Miktam[5] of David, when he fled from Saul, in [k] the cave.

1 [l]Be merciful to me, O God, be
merciful to me,
for in you my soul [m]takes refuge;
in [n]the shadow of your wings I will
take refuge,
[o]till the storms of destruction
pass by.
2 I cry out to God Most High,
to God who [p]fulfills his purpose
for me.
3 [q]He will send from heaven and
save me;
he will put to shame [r]him who
tramples on me. *Selah*
[s]God will send out [t]his steadfast love
and his faithfulness!

23[k]ver. 15; Ps. 56:7; 59:11 [l]Ps. 69:15; 94:13 [m]Ps. 5:6 [n]Prov. 10:27; See Job 15:32 [o]See Ps. 11:1
Psalm 56 [p]Ps. 16, title; 57, title [q][1 Sam. 21:10, 11; 22:1]
1[r]Ps. 57:1; See Ps. 4:1 [s]Ps. 57:3; 124:3; Num. 16:30; Prov. 1:12
3[t]See Ps. 11:1
4[u]Ps. 27:1; 118:6; Isai. 51:12; Heb. 13:6
6[v]Ps. 59:3; 140:2; Isai. 54:15 [w]Ps. 10:8 [x]Ps. 71:10
7[y]Ps. 7:6; 59:5 [z]See Ps. 55:23
8[a][Ps. 39:12; 2 Kin. 20:5] [b][Mal. 3:16]
9[c]Ps. 102:2 [d]Ps. 118:6; [Rom. 8:31]
11[u][See ver. 4 above]
12[e]See Ps. 50:14
13[f]Ps. 49:15; 116:8 [g]Ps. 116:9 [h][Ps. 49:19]
Psalm 57 [i][Ps. 58, title; 59, title; 75, title] [j]Ps. 16, title; 56, title [k]1 Sam. 22:1; 24:1-3; [Ps. 142, title]
1[l]Ps. 56:1; See Ps. 4:1 [m]Ps. 91:4 [n]See Ps. 17:8 [o]Isai. 26:20
2[p]Ps. 138:8
3[q]Ps. 144:5, 7; [Ps. 18:16] [r]See Ps. 56:1 [s]Ps. 43:3 [t]See Ps. 36:5; 40:11

1 Probably a musical or liturgical term 2 Or *they twist my words* 3 Or *wanderings* 4 Or *because* 5 Probably a musical or liturgical term

55:23 the pit of destruction. The grave.

56:title The title is difficult to fit into David's life as it is known from the historical books. The closest parallel is 1 Sam. 21:10–15, when David was feigning madness before the king of Gath in order to escape him.

56:2 trample on me. The enemies, like ruthless animals, treat the psalmist as their prey.

56:5 injure my cause. They change the meanings of his words (see text note) to put him in a bad light.

56:7 cast down the peoples. The parallelism of this verse suggests that the enemies are the foreign nations that surround Israel.

56:8 kept count. The psalmist is calling upon God to hear and remember his prayer.

56:9 This I know. The psalmist remembers God's covenant promises, such as Deut. 28:7, a promise that God will scatter the enemies of His people.

56:12 render thank offerings. When the psalmist's prayer is answered, he promises to return to offer his thanks. He would do this by offering sacrifices and singing thanksgiving songs similar to Ps. 34. See Ps. 22:22 and note.

Ps. 57 The psalm was composed before David was king, when he was hiding from Saul in a cave. Many scholars relate the psalm to 1 Sam. 24, but a closer parallel is 1 Sam. 22:1–5, when David fled to the cave of Adullam. This song ends with an intense concluding statement that is close in wording to Ps. 108:1–5.

57:1 in the shadow of your wings. The image of God as a protective mother bird protecting her young from trouble communicates God's compassion for His people. See note on maternal representations of God at Ps. 131:2.

57:2 who fulfills his purpose for me. This Hebrew phrase might be rendered "who avenges me," and indicates that God judges His people's enemies.

4 My soul is in the midst of [u]lions;
I lie down amid fiery beasts—
the children of man, whose [v]teeth are spears and arrows,
whose [w]tongues are sharp swords.
5 [x]Be exalted, O God, above the heavens!
Let your glory be over all the earth!
6 They set [y]a net for my steps;
my soul was [z]bowed down.
They [a]dug a pit in my way,
but they have fallen into it themselves. *Selah*
7 [b]My heart is [c]steadfast, O God,
my heart is steadfast!
I will sing and make melody!
8 [d]Awake, [e]my glory![1]
Awake, [f]O harp and lyre!
I will awake the dawn!
9 I will give thanks to you, O Lord, among the peoples;
I will sing praises to you among the nations.
10 For your [g]steadfast love is great to the heavens,
your faithfulness to the clouds.
11 [x]Be exalted, O God, above the heavens!
Let your glory be over all the earth!

God Who Judges the Earth

58 TO THE CHOIRMASTER: ACCORDING TO [h]DO NOT DESTROY. A [i]MIKTAM[2] OF DAVID.

1 Do you indeed decree what is right, you gods?[3]
Do you judge the children of man uprightly?
2 No, in your hearts you devise wrongs;
your hands [j]deal out violence on earth.
3 The wicked are [k]estranged from the womb;
they go astray from birth, speaking lies.
4 [l]They have venom like the venom of a serpent,
like the deaf adder that stops its ear,
5 so that it [m]does not hear the voice of charmers
or of the cunning enchanter.
6 O God, [n]break the teeth in their mouths;
tear out the fangs of the young lions, O LORD!
7 Let them [o]vanish like water that runs away;
when he [p]aims his arrows, let them be blunted.
8 Let them be like the snail [o]that dissolves into slime,
like [q]the stillborn child who never sees the sun.
9 Sooner than your pots can feel the heat of [r]thorns,
whether green or ablaze, may he [s]sweep them away![4]
10 [t]The righteous will rejoice when he sees the vengeance;
he will [u]bathe his feet in the blood of the wicked.

1 Or *my whole being* 2 Probably a musical or liturgical term 3 Or *mighty lords* (by revocalization; Hebrew *in silence*) 4 The meaning of the Hebrew verse is uncertain

4 [u]Ps. 58:6 [v]Prov. 30:14 [w]Ps. 55:21; 59:7; 64:3; Prov. 12:18; [Ps. 52:2; Jer. 9:8] 5 [x]Ps. 108:5; [Ps. 113:4] 6 [y]See Job 18:8 [z]Ps. 145:14; 146:8 [a]See Ps. 7:15 7 [b]For ver. 7-11, see Ps. 108:1-5 [c]Ps. 112:7 8 [d]Judg. 5:12 [e]See Ps. 16:9 [f]1 Chr. 15:16 10 [g]See Ps. 36:5 11 [x][See ver. 5 above] **Psalm 58** [h]See Ps. 57, title [i]See Ps. 16, title

2 [j][Ps. 94:20] 3 [k]Ps. 51:5; Isai. 48:8 4 [l]Ps. 140:3; [Deut. 32:33] 5 [m]Jer. 8:17 6 [n]Ps. 3:7; Job 4:10; 29:17 7 [o]Ps. 112:10; Josh. 7:5 [p]Ps. 64:3 8 [o][See ver. 7 above] [q]See Job 3:16 9 [r]Ps. 118:12; Eccles. 7:6 [s][Job 27:21; See Prov. 10:25] 10 [t]Deut. 32:43; See Job 22:19 [u]Ps. 68:23

57:4 lions. Lions were numerous in the ancient Near East and in Palestine. They often symbolized power and ruthlessness.

57:5 above the heavens. God is so great that not even the heavens can hold Him (1 Kin. 8:27). He is transcendent, but in His compassion He dwells with men.

57:6 a net . . . a pit. Like a hunter, the enemy sets snares and traps for the psalmist. The principle that evil people are ultimately caught by their own wicked schemes is a theme that runs through the psalms and the prophets. See Ps. 7:14–16; 34:21; 35:8; 37:15.

57:7 steadfast. Nothing can swerve the psalmist from his faithful intention to offer up his hymn of praise.

57:8 I will awake the dawn. He will praise the Lord through the night, until dawn arises.

57:9 among the peoples. God is more than the God of Israel. He is King of the universe, and the psalmist will praise God's great deeds throughout the universe.

Ps. 58 Psalms of lament often contain sections that are curses directed against the evil and unjust. The objects of the psalmist's scorn seem to be human rulers (v. 1 note), especially unjust judges. Early Christian tradition associated this psalm with the high priest and the Sanhedrin as they condemned Jesus (Matt. 26:57–68).

58:1 you gods. The word "gods" could be used for the corrupt judges of this verse, according to the example in Ps. 82:1 (see text note).

58:3 from the womb. David recognized this of himself in Ps. 51:5. All are born with a nature that rebels against God—this is the meaning of the doctrine of original sin. David means that the wickedness of the evil judges in particular extends back to the beginning of their lives.

58:4, 5 venom of a serpent. The psalmist likens the wicked rulers to snakes. The story of the Fall (Gen. 3), initiated by the serpent, sharpens the image. The rulers' words are as distinctive as the venom of the serpent, and they turn a deaf ear to logical arguments and even divine judgments that may be addressed to them.

58:7 when he aims his arrows . . . blunted. Bring to nothing their evil schemes that seek violence against the innocent.

58:10 The righteous will rejoice. Eternity will show that God's judgment of the wicked is just. This judgment will cause rejoicing since the alternative would be unthinkable: heaven populated with God's enemies (Rev. 16:5, 6; 19:1–3; 21:27).

11 Mankind will say, "Surely there is [v]a
reward for the righteous;
surely there is a God who [w]judges
on earth."

Deliver Me from My Enemies

59 To the choirmaster: according to
[x]Do Not Destroy. A [y]Miktam [1] of
David, [z]when Saul sent men to
watch his house in order to kill
him.

1 [a]Deliver me from my enemies, O my
God;
[b]protect me from those who [c]rise
up against me;
2 deliver me from [d]those who work evil,
and save me from [e]bloodthirsty
men.
3 For behold, they [f]lie in wait for my life;
fierce men [g]stir up strife against me.
[h]For no transgression or sin of mine,
O Lord,
4 for no fault of mine, they run and
make ready.
[i]Awake, come to meet me, and see!
5 You, [j]Lord God of hosts, are God
of Israel.
Rouse yourself to punish all the
nations;
spare none of those who
treacherously plot evil. *Selah*
6 Each evening they [k]come back,
howling like dogs
and prowling about the city.
7 There they are, [l]bellowing with their
mouths
with [m]swords in their lips—
for [n]"Who," they think,[2] "will
hear us?"

8 But you, O Lord, [o]laugh at them;
you hold all the nations in
derision.
9 O my Strength, I will watch for you,
for you, O God, are [p]my fortress.
10 [q]My God in his steadfast love[3] [r]will
meet me;
God will let me [s]look in triumph
on my enemies.
11 Kill them not, lest my people forget;
make them totter[4] by your power
and [t]bring them down,
O Lord, our [u]shield!
12 For [v]the sin of their mouths, the
words of their lips,
let them be trapped in their pride.
For the cursing and lies that they
utter,
13 [w]consume them in wrath;
consume them till they are no
more,
that they may [x]know that God rules
over Jacob
to [y]the ends of the earth. *Selah*
14 [z]Each evening they come back,
howling like dogs
and prowling about the city.
15 They [a]wander about for food
and growl if they do not get their
fill.
16 But I will sing of your strength;
I will sing aloud of your steadfast
love in the morning.
For you have been to me [b]a fortress
and [c]a refuge in [d]the day of my
distress.

11 [v]Isai. 3:10 [w]Ps. 67:4; 94:2; Gen. 18:25; Job 19:20; Eccles. 12:14
Psalm 59 [x]Ps. 57, title [y]Ps. 16, title [z][1 Sam. 19:11]
1 [a]Ps. 143:9; [Ps. 18:48] [b]See Ps. 20:1 [c]See Ps. 17:7
2 [d]Ps. 94:4 [e]Ps. 5:6
3 [f]Ps. 10:9 [g]See Ps. 56:6 [h]1 Sam. 24:11; [Ps. 7:3; 69:4]
4 [i]See Ps. 35:23
5 [j]Ps. 80:4; 84:8
6 [k][Ps. 22:16]
7 [l]Prov. 15:2, 28; [Ps. 94:4] [m]See Ps. 57:4 [n]See Job 22:13
8 [o]See Ps. 2:4
9 [p]ver. 16, 17; See Ps. 9:9
10 [q]ver. 17 [r]Ps. 21:3 [s]See Ps. 54:7
11 [t]See Ps. 55:23 [u]See Ps. 3:3
12 [v]See Prov. 12:13
13 [w][Ps. 7:9] [x]Ps. 83:18 [y]Ps. 22:27
14 [z][Ps. 22:16]
15 [a]Ps. 109:10; Job 15:23
16 [b]ver. 9 [c]2 Sam. 22:3 [d]Ps. 18:6

1 Probably a musical or liturgical term 2 Hebrew lacks *they think* 3 Or *The God who shows me steadfast love* 4 Or *wander*

58:11 there is a reward. When the wicked prosper or the righteous suffer, faith is shaken. The covenant promises of Deut. 28 provide for curses on the wicked and blessings for the righteous. The last judgment will set things right again.

Ps. 59 The psalm comes from the period before David became king. Saul set a watch over David's house, hoping to kill him; but David's wife Michal, the daughter of Saul, helped David escape (1 Sam. 19:11–17).

59:3 For no transgression or sin of mine. The psalmist is not saying that he is without sin; he is asserting that the enemy has no cause against him. This was true of the original situation, where David had committed no aggression against Saul's kingship. See Ps. 26.

59:5 God of hosts. This divine title indicates that God has heavenly armies at His command.

nations . . . plot evil. The enemies come from the nations outside of Israel, but also from within.

59:6 like dogs. The enemies are like a pack of dogs who roam the streets of the city and make them unsafe. Dogs were not valued in the ancient Near East.

59:7 Who . . . will hear us. See 64:5 and note.

59:10 God . . . will meet me. God will lead the way in the fight against the enemy. In the time of Joshua, the ark, symbolic of God's presence, led Israel into the Promised Land.

look in triumph. For now, the enemy gloats over the psalmist, but the psalmist expects a reversal.

59:11 Kill them not. The psalmist desires to prolong the suffering of the enemy. This will make them an example to the rest of Israel that evil doesn't pay.

59:12 sin of their mouths. Words are powerful, and can bring either great blessing or tremendous harm.

59:13 that they may know. The ultimate goal of the destruction of the enemy is that the glory of God's justice may be seen.

17 O my Strength, I will sing praises to
you,
for you, O God, [b]are my fortress,
[e]the God who shows me steadfast
love.

He Will Tread Down Our Foes

60 TO THE CHOIRMASTER: ACCORDING TO [f]SHUSHAN EDUTH. A [g]MIKTAM[1] OF DAVID; [h]FOR INSTRUCTION; WHEN HE [i]STROVE WITH ARAM-NAHARAIM AND WITH ARAM-ZOBAH, AND WHEN JOAB ON HIS RETURN STRUCK DOWN TWELVE THOUSAND OF EDOM IN THE VALLEY OF SALT.

1 O God, [j]you have rejected us,
[k]broken our defenses;
you have been angry; [l]oh, restore us.
2 You have made the land to quake;
you have torn it open;
[m]repair its breaches, for it totters.
3 [n]You have made your people see hard
things;
[o]you have given us [p]wine to drink
that made us stagger.

4 You have set up [q]a banner for those
who fear you,
that they may flee to it [r]from the
bow.[2] *Selah*
5 [s]That your [t]beloved ones may be
delivered,
give salvation by your right hand
and answer us!

6 God has spoken [u]in his holiness:[3]
"With exultation [v]I will divide up
[w]Shechem
and portion out the Vale of
[x]Succoth.
7 [y]Gilead is mine; Manasseh is mine;
[z]Ephraim is [a]my helmet;
Judah is my [b]scepter.
8 [c]Moab is my washbasin;
upon Edom I [d]cast my shoe;
over [e]Philistia I shout in
triumph."[4]

9 Who will bring me to the fortified city?
[f]Who will lead me to Edom?
10 Have you not [g]rejected us,
O God?
You [h]do not go forth, O God,
with our armies.
11 Oh, grant us help against the foe,
for [i]vain is the salvation of man!
12 With God we shall [j]do valiantly;
it is he who will [k]tread down our
foes.

Lead Me to the Rock

61 TO THE CHOIRMASTER: WITH [l]STRINGED INSTRUMENTS. OF DAVID.

1 Hear my cry, O God,
[m]listen to my prayer;

17 [b][See ver. 16 above] [e]ver. 10 **Psalm 60** [f]Ps. 80, title [g]See Ps. 16, title [h]Deut. 31:19 [i][2 Sam. 8:3, 13, 14; 10:16]; 1 Chr. 18:3, 12 **1** [j]ver. 10; See Ps. 44:9 [k][2 Sam. 5:20] [l]See Ps. 80:3 **2** [m]2 Chr. 7:14 **3** [n]Ps. 71:20 [o]Job 21:20 [p]Isai. 51:17, 22 **4** [q]Isai. 5:26; 11:12; 13:2; [Ps. 20:5] [r]Prov. 22:21 **5** [s]For ver. 5-12, see Ps. 108:6-13 [t]Deut. 33:12; Jer. 11:15 **6** [u]Ps. 89:35; Amos 4:2 [v][Josh. 1:6] [w]Gen. 12:6; 33:18; Josh. 17:7 [x]Gen. 33:17; Josh. 13:27 **7** [y]Josh 13:31 [z]Deut. 33:17 [a]Ps. 140:7 [b]Gen. 49:10 **8** [c][2 Sam. 8:2] [d][Matt. 3:11] [e][2 Sam. 8:1] **9** [f][2 Sam. 8:14] **10** [g]ver. 1 [h]See Ps. 44:9 **11** [i][Ps. 146:3] **12** [j]Ps. 118:15, 16; Num. 24:18 [k]Ps. 44:5; Isai. 63:3

Psalm 61 [l]Ps. 4, title **1** [m]Ps. 55:1, 2

1 Probably musical or liturgical terms 2 Or *that it may be displayed because of truth* 3 Or *sanctuary* 4 Revocalization (compare Psalm 108:10); Masoretic Text *over me, O Philistia, shout in triumph*

Ps. 60 The psalm laments a military defeat and asks God why He has rejected the people. For the most part, the community voice dominates and the psalm addresses God with the first person plural.

60:title This psalm has the longest title in the Psalter, referring to the events recorded in 2 Sam. 8 and 1 Chr. 18. The historical books, however, tell only of the conclusion of the battle's victory. The title and the psalm suggest that David experienced setbacks on the way to victory. The historical books and the psalm differ on the number of Edomites killed in the Valley of Salt, probably through a copyist's error. The psalm associates Joab with the victory, while 2 Sam. 8:13 names David, and 1 Chr. 18:12 lists Abishai. All three were high commanders in the army and could be credited with the victory.

60:1 rejected us. When God rejects His people, He abandons them and leaves them to the mercy of the enemy. It is only with God's approval that the people of Israel have any reason for confidence.

60:3 wine to drink . . . stagger. The image is a frequent one in the prophets. The cup that makes a nation stagger is the cup of judgment (Jer. 25:15–38; Nah. 3:11). Jesus drank the cup of wrath to its dregs on behalf of His people (Matt. 26:39 and parallels).

60:4 those who fear you. The verse is a token of hope for the faithful. God gives protection to His people from the weapons of the enemy.

60:6 God has spoken in his holiness. The divine oracle was probably spoken through a prophet associated with the temple (see text note). The gist of his message is that victory will be forthcoming, a message borne out by the report in 2 Sam. 8.

I will divide. The following verses exult in the inheritance of the Promised Land.

Shechem . . . Succoth. These names are the first two places that Jacob occupied after returning from his encounter with Esau (Gen. 33:17–20). They are on opposite sides of the Jordan River.

60:7 Gilead . . . Manasseh. Both these areas are located, at least in part, in the region of the Transjordan.

Ephraim . . . Judah. These were the two most powerful tribes in Israel. They were frequently rivals, but here they are united as parts of God's army.

60:8 Moab . . . Edom . . . Philistia. Moab and Edom were east of Judah, and Philistia was west of Judah on the Mediterranean coast. These countries were traditional enemies of Israel, but in this song God exults in His power and authority over them.

cast my shoe. A gesture of contempt, or possibly a claim to ownership (Ruth 4:7).

60:9 me. Likely the king, who speaks on behalf of the nation.

60:12 we shall do valiantly. The psalmist confesses that it is only through God's power that they will win the victory. This is the primary attitude that motivates Israel's wars in the Old Testament.

Ps. 61 Elements of lament, thanksgiving, and petition are combined in this memorable psalm.

2 from the end of the earth I call to
you
when my heart is [n]faint.
Lead me to [o]the rock
that is higher than I,
3 for you have been [p]my refuge,
a strong [q]tower against the enemy.

4 Let me [r]dwell in your tent forever!
Let me take refuge under [s]the
shelter of your wings! *Selah*
5 For you, O God, have heard my
vows;
you have given me the heritage of
those who fear your name.

6 [t]Prolong [u]the life of the king;
may his years endure to all
generations!
7 May he be enthroned forever before
God;
appoint [v]steadfast love and
faithfulness to watch over him!

8 So will I ever sing praises to your
name,
as I [w]perform my vows day after
day.

My Soul Waits for God Alone

62 TO THE CHOIRMASTER: ACCORDING TO [x]JEDUTHUN. [1] A PSALM OF DAVID.

1 For God alone [y]my soul [z]waits in
silence;
from him comes my salvation.

2 [a]He only is my rock and my salvation,
my [b]fortress; [c]I shall not be greatly
shaken.

3 How long will all of you attack a man
to batter him,
like [d]a leaning wall, a tottering
fence?
4 They only plan to thrust him down
from his [e]high position.
They take pleasure in falsehood.
[f]They bless with their mouths,
but inwardly they curse. *Selah*

5 For God alone, O [y]my soul, wait in
silence,
for my hope is from him.
6 [a]He only is my rock and my
salvation,
my fortress; I shall not be shaken.
7 On God rests my [g]salvation and my
glory;
my mighty rock, [h]my refuge is
God.

8 [i]Trust in him at all times, O people;
[j]pour out your heart before him;
God is [h]a refuge for us. *Selah*
9 [k]Those of low estate [l]are but a breath;
those of high estate [l]are a
delusion;
in the balances they go up;
[l]they are together lighter than a
breath.

2 [n]Ps. 77:3 [o][Ps. 18:2] 3 [p]See Ps. 14:6 [q]Prov. 18:10 4 [r]See Ps. 15:1; 27:4 [s]See Ps. 17:8 6 [t]See Ps. 21:4 [u]Ps. 63:11 7 [v]See Ps. 40:11 8 [w]See Ps. 50:14 **Psalm 62** [x]See Ps. 39, title 1 [y]See Ps. 33:20 [z]Ps. 65:1; [Ps. 37:7]

2 [a]Ps. 18:2 [b]See Ps. 9:9 [c]See Ps. 10:6 3 [d][Isai. 30:13] 4 [e]Job 13:11 [f]See Ps. 28:3 5 [y][See ver. 1 above] 6 [a][See ver. 2 above] 7 [g]See Ps. 3:8 [h]See Ps. 14:6 8 [i]See Ps. 37:3 [j]See Ps. 42:4 [h][See ver. 7 above] 9 [k]Ps. 39:5; [Isai. 40:17] [l][Ps. 116:11]

[1] Probably a musical or liturgical term

61:2 from the end of the earth. The psalmist means that he is at a distance from the sanctuary on Mount Zion, and feels himself to be far from God.

rock. He comes to the critical recognition that he does not have the strength to rescue himself; he can only turn to God in trust.

61:3 against the enemy. God has protected the writer in the past against his enemies. This phrase leads us to believe that the psalmist is not only physically distant from the temple, but is engaged in a military action for which he needs God's help.

61:4 The psalmist yearns for God's fellowship. See v. 2.

under the shelter of your wings. Some see here a metaphor for God's compassion, as in the protection of the mother bird for her young. On the other hand, David's reference to the familiar wings of the cherubim portrayed on the ark of the covenant seems more likely.

61:5 my vows. In the process of petitioning the Lord, the psalmist has made promises of obedience to the Lord. See 22:22 and 1 Sam. 1:11.

heritage. As a member of God's community, he receives the promises of the covenant, including the land of Israel and the promise of God's protection.

61:6 the life of the king. Israel's king was the center of the social order in Israel. The stability of that office affected the stability of the society as a whole. The earthly king was a symbol of the divine King. When Christ came, His gospel announced the "kingdom of heaven."

61:7 be enthroned forever. Jesus Christ, David's greater Son, fulfilled this verse beyond the expectation of the psalmist.

steadfast love. Specifically, lovingkindness toward those with whom God is in covenantal relationship.

62:1 waits in silence. Lit. "is silent." True contentment can be found only in a right relationship with God.

62:2 my rock . . . my fortress. Portrayals of God's protection from the dangers of life. See note Ps. 28:1.

62:3 leaning wall, a tottering fence. The modern idiom is to "kick a man when he's down." The wicked continue to take advantage of the weak.

62:4 They bless. The wicked add hypocrisy to violence.

62:5 my hope. His hope to be saved from the enemy.

62:8 O people. The psalmist turns to the faithful in the congregation and encourages them to put their trust in God alone.

62:9 breath . . . breath. The word may be translated variously. It is the most characteristic word of Ecclesiastes, where it is often translated "vanity" or "meaningless." The point is that people are meaningless and without consequence *in and of themselves.* The psalmist takes comfort in this; his persecutors, in reality, are not significant.

10 Put no trust in extortion;
[m] set no vain hopes on robbery;
[n] if riches increase, set not your
heart on them.
11 [o] Once God has spoken;
[o] twice have I heard this:
that [p] power belongs to God,
12 and that to you, O Lord, [q] belongs
steadfast love.
For you will [r] render to a man
according to his work.

My Soul Thirsts for You

63 A PSALM OF DAVID, [s] WHEN HE WAS IN THE WILDERNESS OF JUDAH.

1 O God, you are my God; [t] earnestly I
seek you;
[u] my soul thirsts for you;
my flesh faints for you,
as in [v] a dry and weary land where
there is no water.
2 So I have looked upon you in the
sanctuary,
beholding [w] your power and
glory.
3 Because your [x] steadfast love is better
than life,
my lips will praise you.
4 So I will bless you [y] as long as I live;
in your [z] name I will [a] lift up my
hands.
5 My soul will be [b] satisfied as with fat
and rich food,
and my mouth will praise you with
joyful lips,
6 when I remember you [c] upon my bed,
and meditate on you in [c] the
watches of the night;
7 for you have been my help,
and in [d] the shadow of your wings I
will sing for joy.
8 My soul [e] clings to you;
your right hand [f] upholds me.
9 But those who seek to destroy my life
[g] shall go down into [h] the depths of
the earth;
10 they shall be given over to the power
of the sword;
they shall be a portion for jackals.
11 But [i] the king shall rejoice in God;
all who [j] swear by him shall exult,
[k] for the mouths of [l] liars will be
stopped.

Hide Me from the Wicked

64 TO THE CHOIRMASTER. A PSALM OF DAVID.

1 Hear my voice, O God, in my
[m] complaint;
preserve my life from dread of the
enemy.
2 Hide me from [n] the secret plots of the
wicked,
from the throng of evildoers,
3 who [o] whet their tongues like swords,
who [p] aim bitter words like arrows,
4 shooting from [q] ambush at the
blameless,
shooting at him suddenly and
[r] without fear.

10 [m] [Jer. 2:3]; See Prov. 1:10-19 [n] Luke 12:15; See Ps. 49:6
11 [o] Job 33:14; 40:5 [p] Rev. 19:1; [Ps. 59:9, 17]
12 [q] Ps. 86:5, 15; 103:8; Dan. 9:9 [r] See Job 34:11
Psalm 63 [s] [2 Sam. 16:14; 17:2, 29]
1 [t] Ps. 78:34; Isai. 26:9 [u] See Ps. 84:2 [v] Ps. 143:6; Isai. 32:2
2 [w] Ps. 78:61; [Ps. 27:4]
3 [x] [Ps. 69:16]
4 [y] Ps. 104:33; 146:2 [z] Ps. 20:1, 5 [a] See Ps. 28:2
5 [b] See Ps. 36:8
6 [c] See Ps. 42:8
7 [d] See Ps. 17:8
8 [e] [Num. 14:24] [f] See Ps. 41:12
9 [g] Ps. 9:17; 55:15 [h] Ezek. 26:20; 31:14 Eph. 4:9
11 [i] Ps. 61:6 [j] Deut. 6:13; Isai. 45:23; 65:16 [k] Ps. 107:42; Job 5:16; [Rom. 3:19] [l] Ps. 38:12; 41:5-8
Psalm 64 1 [m] Ps. 55:2
2 [n] [Ps. 55:14]
3 [o] See Ps. 57:4 [p] See Ps. 11:2
4 [q] [Ps. 10:8] [r] Ps. 55:19

62:10 riches increase. Doubt arises when people become rich through evil means (Ps. 73). In this psalm, the author clearly sees that such riches are transitory.

62:12 steadfast love. God is not only able to save the psalmist; He desires to do so.

render . . . according to his work. The psalmist has a long-range perspective here, since at present the righteous are often at the mercy of the wicked. From the New Testament we understand that there will be many unresolved injustices in the present life until Christ returns.

Ps. 63 This beautiful psalm expresses quiet confidence in God's ability to protect the psalmist.

63:title The setting of the psalm is the desert of Judah.

63:1 thirsts. Cf. Ps. 42.

my flesh. The Book of Psalms permits no false spiritualization. The whole person yearns for God, not merely a non-physical aspect of the person.

63:2 in the sanctuary. The psalmist remembers the place of God's appointment, and the vision of God's "power" and "glory" entrusted to him there.

63:3 your steadfast love. That is, the unchanging love God shows toward those joined to Him by His covenant.

63:5 will be satisfied. Only in praise to God, in intimate communion with Him, will the psalmist feel spiritually content.

63:6 watches of the night. The psalmist has confidence in the Lord when he is most vulnerable to fear and attack.

63:7 your wings. God may be compared to a mother bird who protects her young, but see second note on 61:4.

63:8 My soul clings to you. Though far removed from the sanctuary, the place where he has experienced God's presence, the psalmist still enjoys intimate communion with Him. Clinging to the Lord means finding in Him one's only hope (Deut. 10:20; 11:22).

63:9 seek to destroy my life. This verse is the first indication of distress or danger in the poem of the psalmist's distress.

63:11 who swear by him shall exult. God's justice wins out. Those who love God will continue to praise Him, while the wicked will be stifled.

64:1 dread of the enemy. Because unnamed, the "enemy" can apply to any adversary.

64:3 like swords . . . bitter words like arrows. The Bible consistently teaches that words are powerful and can be used for good (Prov. 25:15) or evil (Prov. 12:18; 25:18).

5 They [s]hold fast to their evil purpose;
they talk of [t]laying snares secretly,
thinking, [u]"who can see them?
6 They search out injustice,
saying, "We have accomplished a
diligent search."
For [v]the inward mind and heart of
a man are deep!
7 [w]But God shoots his arrow at them;
they are wounded suddenly.
8 They are brought to ruin, with their
own [x]tongues turned against
them;
all who [y]see them will [z]wag their
heads.
9 Then all mankind [y]fears;
they [a]tell what God has brought
about
and ponder what he has done.
10 Let [b]the righteous one rejoice in the
LORD
and [c]take refuge in him!
Let all [d]the upright in heart exult!

O God of Our Salvation

65 TO THE CHOIRMASTER. A PSALM OF DAVID. A SONG.

1 Praise [e]is due to you,[1] O God, in Zion,
and to you shall [f]vows be
performed.
2 O you who [g]hears prayer,
to you [h]shall all flesh come.

5 [s]Jer. 23:14; Ezek. 13:22 [t]See Ps. 140:5 [u]See Job 22:13
6 [v]Ps. 49:11
7 [w]Ps. 7:12, 13; [Ps. 58:7]
8 [x]See Prov. 12:13; 18:7 [y]See Ps. 40:3 [z]Jer. 18:16; 48:27; See Ps. 22:7
9 [y][See ver. 8 above] [a]Jer. 50:28; 51:10
10 [b]See Ps. 32:11; Job 22:19 [c]See Ps. 11:1 [d]See Ps. 7:10
Psalm 65
1 [e]Ps. 62:1 [f]See Ps. 50:14
2 [g]2 Kin. 19:20 [h]See Ps. 86:9
3 [i]See Ps. 38:4 [j]Ps. 79:9; Isai. 6:7; See Ps. 51:2
4 [k][Ps. 38:12] [l]Ps. 84:4; See Ps. 27:4 [m]See Ps. 16:11
5 [n]Ps. 45:4; 106:22; Deut. 10:21; 2 Sam. 7:23; [Rev. 15:3] [o]See Ps. 22:27
6 [p]Ps. 93:1
7 [q]Ps. 89:9; 93:3, 4; 107:29; Matt. 8:26; [Jer. 5:22] [r]Ps. 74:23; Isai. 17:12, 13

3 When [i]iniquities prevail against me,
you [j]atone for our transgressions.
4 [k]Blessed is the one you choose and
bring near,
to [l]dwell in your courts!
We shall be [m]satisfied with the
goodness of your house,
the holiness of your temple!

5 By [n]awesome deeds you answer us
with righteousness,
O God of our salvation,
the hope of all [o]the ends of the earth
and of the farthest seas;
6 the one who by his strength
established the mountains,
being [p]girded with might;
7 who [q]stills the roaring of the seas,
the roaring of their waves,
[r]the tumult of the peoples,
8 so that those who dwell at the ends
of the earth are in awe at your
signs.
You make the going out of the
morning and the evening to
shout for joy.

9 You visit the earth and [s]water it;[2]
you greatly enrich it;
[t]the river of God is full of water;
[u]you provide their grain,
for so you have prepared it.

9 [s]Ps. 68:9; 72:6; Lev. 26:4; See Job 5:10 [t][Ps. 46:4] [u][Ps. 147:14]

[1] Or *Praise waits for you in silence* [2] Or *and make it overflow*

64:5 who can see them. They do not fear men, and by their question they show they do not fear God. They think their acts go unnoticed, forgetting that there is a just God in heaven who watches their every move (Ps. 2).

64:6 accomplished a diligent search. To their other crimes, these evildoers add the sin of pride.

64:7 shoots his arrow at them. This verse should be contrasted with v. 4. Some of the same words are used to highlight the reversal. The wicked who try to shoot the righteous are themselves struck by the arrows of God.

64:8 their own tongues. Contrast with v. 3. God reverses the effects of their tongues. They wanted to use their tongues against the psalmist; they finally incriminated themselves.

64:9 fears. Seeing God's justice, the world will be startled by the judgment of the wicked. People of the world will reconsider their own acts in the light of God's dealings with the wicked.

Ps. 65 Israel's agricultural economy depended on rainfall, which was commonly variable. This psalm thanks God for sending rain in answer to prayer.

65:1 in Zion. The location chosen by God for the temple, and the place toward which praise is directed. See notes Ps. 50:2; 128:5; 129:5, and especially 2:6.

vows. When Israel brought petitions before the Lord, they frequently promised to offer sacrifices in response to answered prayer.

65:3 our transgressions. From the perspective of the sinner, there is no hope. God in His grace, however, forgives the sinner; this is a source of great joy to the psalmist.

65:4 Blessed. See Ps. 1:1.

you choose. God's free grace is the source of blessing, and the highest blessing of all is to enjoy His fellowship (Ps. 16:11).

65:5 awesome deeds. God is not a distant deity who has nothing to do with His creation. He answers prayer by intervening in history and in the lives of His people.

ends of the earth. In the theologies of the surrounding lands, it was thought that there were different gods for different localities; e.g., Marduk of Babylon and Baal of Ugarit. The psalmist knows that the Lord is not simply another god among many; He is the God of the universe.

65:6 the mountains. A symbol of firmness and strength. God's creation of them shows His power and greatness (Ps. 46:2, 3 and notes).

girded with might. God is clothed with power as a divine warrior who conquers the enemies of Israel (Ex. 15; Josh. 5:13–15; Judg. 5).

65:7 the roaring of their waves. The seas represent chaos and evil (Ps. 77:16–19 and notes), often the chaos and evil of surrounding nations who attack Israel (Dan. 7).

65:8 dwell at the ends of the earth. A deeper meaning of this verse was brought to light in the coming of Christ and the preaching of the gospel throughout the world.

65:9 water it. Compare 1 Kin. 17–19, the time of Elijah, when God cursed His rebellious people by withholding the rain.

10 You water its furrows abundantly,
settling its ridges,
softening it with [v]showers,
and blessing its growth.
11 You crown the year with your bounty;
your wagon tracks [w]overflow with abundance.
12 [x]The pastures of the wilderness overflow,
the hills [y]gird themselves with joy,
13 [z]the meadows clothe themselves with flocks,
the valleys deck themselves with grain,
they [a]shout and sing together for joy.

How Awesome Are Your Deeds

66 TO THE CHOIRMASTER. A SONG. A PSALM.

1 [b]Shout for joy to God, all the earth;
2 sing the glory of his name;
[c]give to him glorious praise!
3 Say to God, [d]"How awesome are your deeds!
So great is your power that your enemies [e]come cringing to you.
4 [f]All the earth worships you
and sings praises to you;
they sing praises to your name." *Selah*
5 [g]Come and see what God has done:
[d]he is awesome in his deeds toward the children of man.
6 He [h]turned the sea into dry land;
they [i]passed through the river on foot.
There did we rejoice in him,
7 who rules by his might forever,
whose [j]eyes keep watch on the nations—
let not the rebellious exalt themselves. *Selah*

8 Bless our God, O peoples;
let the sound of his praise be heard,
9 who has kept our soul among the living
and [k]has not let our feet slip.
10 For you, O God, have [l]tested us;
you have tried us as silver is tried.
11 You brought us into [m]the net;
you laid a crushing burden on our backs;
12 you let men [n]ride over our heads;
we went through fire and through [o]water;
yet you have brought us out to a place of abundance.

13 I will come into your house with burnt offerings;
I will [p]perform my vows to you,
14 that which my lips uttered
and my mouth promised [q]when I was in trouble.
15 I will offer to you burnt offerings of fattened animals,
with the smoke of the sacrifice of rams;
I will make an offering of bulls and goats. *Selah*

16 [r]Come and hear, all you who fear God,
and I will tell what he has done for my soul.
17 I cried to him with my mouth,
and high praise was on[1] my tongue.[2]

10 [v]Deut. 32:2
11 [w]Job 36:28
12 [x]Joel 2:22; [Job 38:26, 27] [y]Isai. 55:12
13 [z]Isai. 30:23 [a]Ps. 98:8; [Isai. 44:23]
Psalm 66
1 [b]Ps. 81:1; 95:1; 98:4; 100:1
2 [c][Josh. 7:19]; Isai. 42:12
3 [d]See Ps. 47:2; 65:5 [e]See Ps. 18:44
4 [f]See Ps. 22:27
5 [g]ver. 16; Ps. 46:8 [d][See ver. 3 above]
6 [h][Ex. 14:21] [i]Ps. 74:15; See Josh. 3:14-17
7 [j]See Ps. 11:4
9 [k]See Ps. 121:3
10 [l]See Job 23:10
11 [m]Lam. 1:13; Ezek. 12:13
12 [n]Isai. 51:23 [o]Isai. 43:2
13 [p]See Ps. 50:14
14 [q]See Ps. 18:6
16 [r]ver. 5; Ps. 34:11

1 Hebrew *under* 2 Or *and he was exalted with my tongue*

66:3 awesome. Great and fearful.

cringing. When God appears as a warrior, the enemies have reason to fear they will be destroyed (Josh. 2:11).

66:5 Come and see. The psalmist invites the hearer to remember God's great acts in history (Ps. 46:8).

66:6 sea . . . river. The first phrase of this verse refers to crossing the Red Sea (Ex. 14; 15). The second refers to crossing the Jordan forty years later (Josh. 3). These great acts demonstrated God's power to His people.

66:9 kept our soul. This is a general truth, but there may be an allusion to the Exodus. A context of Israel's more recent testing may also be possible.

66:10 tested us. God occasionally laid difficult decisions before His people to see whether they would be obedient to Him in spite of their suffering (Ex. 15:25).

as silver. When silver is refined, it is purified; the dross is taken away. When God tests His people, those who are not obedient are taken away, while the faithful remain steadfast.

66:11 into the net. The Lord has brought the psalmist and the faithful through a period of affliction.

66:12 to a place of abundance. A possible reference to recent salvation from distress, but there may also be an allusion to Israel's conquest of Canaan.

66:13 perform my vows. The psalmist expresses his individual thanks. Apparently, God has recently saved him from some distress. While he was suffering, he promised to worship God with sacrifices if God heard his prayer (22:22 note).

66:16 Come and hear. Often, the fulfilling of the vow leads to public praise, witnessing to God's salvation.

18 If I had [s]cherished iniquity in my
heart,
[t]the Lord would not have listened.
19 But truly [u]God has listened;
he has attended to the voice of my
prayer.

20 Blessed be God,
because he has not rejected my
prayer
or removed his steadfast love
from me!

Make Your Face Shine upon Us

67 To the choirmaster: with [v]stringed instruments. A Psalm. A Song.

1 May God [w]be gracious to us and
bless us
and make his face to [x]shine
upon us, *Selah*
2 that [y]your way may be known on
earth,
your [z]saving power among all
nations.
3 [a]Let the peoples praise you, O God;
let all the peoples praise you!

4 Let the nations be glad and sing for
joy,
for you [b]judge the peoples with
equity
and guide the nations upon
earth. *Selah*
5 [a]Let the peoples praise you,
O God;
let all the peoples praise you!

6 The earth has [c]yielded its increase;
God, our God, shall bless us.

18 [s]Job 36:21 [t][Prov. 28:9; Isai. 59:2; John 9:31; James 4:3; See Job 27:9]
19 [u]Ps. 116:1, 2
Psalm 67 [v]Ps. 4, title
1 [w]Num. 6:25 [x]See Ps. 4:6
2 [y][Acts 18:25] [z]Ps. 98:3; Luke 2:30; Tit. 2:11
3 [a]See Ps. 22:27
4 [b]See Ps. 58:11
5 [a][See ver. 3 above]
6 [c]Ps. 85:12; Lev. 26:4; Ezek. 34:27; [Hos. 2:22]
7 [d]See Ps. 22:27
Psalm 68
1 [e]Num. 10:35; Isai. 33:3 [f][Ps. 89:10; 92:9]
2 [g]See Ps. 37:20 [h]Ps. 22:14; 97:5; Mic. 1:4
3 [i]See Ps. 32:11
4 [j]Ps. 66:4 [k]Isai. 57:14; 62:10 [l]ver. 33; [Ps. 18:10] [m]Isai. 40:3 [n]Ps. 89:8
5 [o]See Ps. 10:14 [p]Deut. 10:18
6 [q]Ps. 113:9; 1 Sam. 2:5 [r]Ps. 69:33; 107:10, 14; 146:7; Acts 12:7; 16:26 [s]ver. 18 [t][Ps. 107:33, 40]
7 [u]Ex. 13:21; Judg. 4:14; Hab. 3:13; Zech. 14:3 [v]Judg. 5:4 [w]Ps. 78:40

7 God shall bless us;
let [d]all the ends of the earth fear
him!

God Shall Scatter His Enemies

68 To the choirmaster. A Psalm of David. A Song.

1 [e]God shall arise, his enemies shall be
[f]scattered;
and those who hate him shall flee
before him!
2 As [g]smoke is driven away, so you
shall drive them away;
[h]as wax melts before fire,
so the wicked shall perish before
God!
3 But [i]the righteous shall be glad;
they shall exult before God;
they shall be jubilant with joy!

4 Sing to God, [j]sing praises to his
name;
[k]lift up a song to him who [l]rides
through [m]the deserts;
his name is [n]the LORD;
exult before him!
5 [o]Father of the fatherless and
[p]protector of widows
is God in his holy habitation.
6 God [q]settles the solitary in a
home;
he [r]leads out the prisoners to
prosperity,
but [s]the rebellious dwell in [t]a
parched land.

7 O God, when you [u]went out before
your people,
[v]when you marched through [w]the
wilderness, *Selah*

Ps. 67 The universal scope of this psalm is striking, even in the Book of Psalms where such far-reaching vision is not rare.

67:1 make his face to shine upon us. The psalmist picks up the standard priestly blessing found in Num. 6:25. The thing promised in the blessing is that God will be present.

67:2 all nations. God is sovereign over all, not merely of a particular country.

67:3 Let the peoples. The psalmist's desire to see peoples from many different nations praise the Lord was begun in a new way when the crucifixion and resurrection of Christ broke down "the dividing wall of hostility" (Eph. 2:14).

67:6 increase. The psalm may have been sung at one of the agricultural festivals, such as the Feast of Ingathering (Ex. 23:14–17).

Ps. 68 This psalm has an enigmatic quality. Some have found it so disconnected as to suggest that it was a collection of first lines of other poems. Yet there are common themes and attitudes in the psalm. It has a hymn-like mood of joy with frequent allusions to community worship. God appears as a warrior at its center. His victory over His enemies as expressed here became the background for Jesus' victory over the forces of Satan at the Ascension (Eph. 4:7–13).

68:1 God shall arise. See Num. 10:35. These were the first words Moses spoke each day before Israel marched during the wilderness period. As he spoke, the ark of the covenant would be raised to lead the procession.

68:2 smoke . . . wax. The two images call on God to deal with the enemy quickly.

68:5 fatherless . . . widows. Widows and orphans were particularly vulnerable in ancient society. God commanded Israel to care for them (Ex. 22:22; Deut. 10:18; Ruth 4:14, 15).

68:6 the solitary. Since the family was the center of Israelite society, those outside of its structure were alone and often needy.

68:7 through the wilderness. The reference is to the forty years of wilderness wanderings.

8 [x]the earth quaked, the heavens
poured down rain,
before God, the One of Sinai,
before God, the God of Israel.
9 [y]Rain in abundance, O God, you shed
abroad;
you restored your inheritance as it
languished;
10 your flock[1] found a dwelling in it;
in your goodness, O God, you
[z]provided for the needy.

11 The Lord gives [a]the word;
[b]the women who announce the
news are a great host:
12 [c]"The kings of the armies—they flee,
they flee!"
The women at home [d]divide the
spoil—
13 though you men lie among [e]the
sheepfolds—
the wings of a dove covered with
silver,
its pinions with shimmering gold.
14 When the Almighty scatters kings
there,
let snow fall on [f]Zalmon.

15 O mountain of God, mountain of
Bashan;
O many-peaked[2] mountain,
mountain of Bashan!
16 Why do you look with hatred,
O many-peaked mountain,
at the mount that God [g]desired for
his abode,
yes, where the LORD will dwell
forever?

17 [h]The chariots of God are twice ten
thousand,
thousands upon thousands;
the Lord is among them; Sinai is
now in the sanctuary.
18 [i]You ascended on high,
[j]leading a host of captives in your
train
and [k]receiving gifts among men,
even among [l]the rebellious, [m]that the
LORD God may dwell there.

19 Blessed be the Lord,
who daily [n]bears us up;
God is our salvation. *Selah*
20 Our God is a God of salvation,
[o]and to GOD, the Lord, belong
deliverances from death.
21 [p]But God will strike the heads of his
enemies,
the hairy crown of him who walks
in his guilty ways.

22 The Lord said,
"I will bring them back [q]from
Bashan,
[r]I will bring them back from the
depths of the sea,
23 that you may [s]strike your feet in their
blood,
that [t]the tongues of your dogs may
have their portion from the foe."

24 Your procession is[3] seen, O God,
the procession of my God, my
King, into the sanctuary—
25 [u]the singers in front, [v]the musicians
last,
between them [w]virgins playing
tambourines:
26 [x]"Bless God in the great congregation,
the LORD, O you[4] who are of
[y]Israel's fountain!"
27 There is [z]Benjamin, the least of
them, in the lead,
the princes of Judah in their throng,
the princes of [a]Zebulun, the
princes of Naphtali.

8 [x]Ex. 19:18; Judg. 5:4
9 [y]See Ps. 65:9, 10
10 [z]Ps. 65:9; 78:20
11 [a][Ps. 33:9] [b][Ex. 15:20; 1 Sam. 18:6]
12 [c]Ps. 110:5; [Num. 31:8; Josh. 10:16; Judg. 5:19]; See Josh. 12:7-24 [d]Judg. 5:30
13 [e][Gen. 49:14; Judg. 5:16]
14 [f]Judg. 9:48
16 [g]Ps. 132:13, 14; [Ps. 78:54; 87:1, 2; Deut. 12:5]
17 [h]2 Kin. 6:17; Hab. 3:8
18 [i]Ps. 7:7; 47:5; Cited Eph. 4:8; [Acts 1:9] [j]Judg. 5:12 [k][Acts 2:4, 33] [l][Rom. 5:8; 1 Tim. 1:13] [m]Ps. 78:60; Ex. 29:45; Rev. 21:3; [John 14:23]
19 [n][Isai. 46:4]
20 [o]Deut. 32:39; Eccles. 7:18; Rev. 1:18
21 [p]Ps. 110:6; Hab. 3:13
22 [q]Num. 21:33 [r]See Amos 9:2-4
23 [s]Ps. 58:10 [t][1 Kin. 21:19; 22:38]
25 [u]Ps. 47:5; 1 Chr. 13:8; 15:16 [v]See Ps. 33:3 [w]Ex. 15:20 Judg. 11:34
26 [x]Ps. 22:25; 26:12 [y]Deut. 33:28; Isai. 48:1; [Isai. 51:1]
27 [z][1 Sam. 9:21] [a][Judg. 5:18]

1 Or *your congregation* 2 Or *hunch-backed*; also verse 16 3 Or *has been*
4 The Hebrew for *you* is plural here

68:8 the earth quaked. God made the earth shake at Sinai (Ex. 19:18, 19).

68:9 Rain in abundance. An essential blessing in a land not known for rainfall. Long droughts had devastating effects (1 Kin. 17–19).

68:11 great host. The word is a military term.

68:12 divide the spoil. See Judg. 5:30.

68:16 the mount that God desired for his abode. Though the Bashan mountains are physically majestic, far more imposing than Zion, the latter is surpassing because Zion's majesty is spiritual, not physical.

68:18 receiving gifts. In Eph. 4:8 Paul writes "gave gifts." In a procession of triumph, the victor would receive and distribute gifts.

68:19 who daily bears us up. God cares for His people and is constantly in touch with their needs. This passage may be contrasted with Is. 46:1–4, where the prophet decries the inability of the idols to care for their worshipers.

68:20 God of salvation. The Lord saves His people from illness and from death in battle. In Jesus Christ His people learn that He, by His resurrection, delivers from death by obtaining eternal life for them.

68:22 from Bashan. Likely a reference to the defeat of Og, king of Bashan in the period before the conquest of the land (Deut. 3).

from the depths of the sea. God delivered Israel from death at the Red Sea (Ex. 14).

68:24 Your procession. After being led by God in battle, the army would return to the city of Jerusalem, carrying the ark with them (Ps. 24). Worshiping crowds would accompany it to the temple.

28 [b] Summon your power, O God,[1]
the power, O God, by which you
have worked for us.
29 Because of your temple at Jerusalem
kings shall [c] bear gifts to you.
30 Rebuke [d] the beasts that dwell among
the reeds,
the herd of [e] bulls with the calves
of the peoples.
[f] Trample underfoot those who lust
after tribute;
scatter the peoples who delight in
war.[2]
31 Nobles shall come from [g] Egypt;
[h] Cush shall hasten to [i] stretch out
her hands to God.
32 [j] O kingdoms of the earth, sing to
God;
sing praises to the Lord, *Selah*
33 to him [k] who rides in [l] the heavens,
the ancient heavens;
behold, he [m] sends out his voice,
his mighty voice.
34 [n] Ascribe power to God,
whose majesty is over Israel,
and whose [o] power is in [p] the skies.
35 [q] Awesome is God from his[3]
[r] sanctuary;
the God of Israel—he is the one
who gives [s] power and strength
to his people.
Blessed be God!

Save Me, O God

69 To the choirmaster: according to [t] Lilies. Of David.

1 Save me, O God!
For [u] the waters have come up to
my neck.[4]
2 I sink in deep [v] mire,
where there is no foothold;
I have come into deep waters,
and the flood [w] sweeps over me.
3 [x] I am weary with my crying out;
[y] my throat is parched.
[z] My eyes grow dim
with [a] waiting for my God.
4 [b] More in number than the hairs of
my head
are [c] those who hate me [d] without
cause;
mighty are those who would
destroy me,
[e] those who attack me with lies.
What I did not steal
must I now restore?
5 O God, you know my folly;
the wrongs I have done are not
hidden from you.
6 Let not those who hope in you [f] be
put to shame through me,
O Lord God of hosts;
let not those who seek you be
brought to dishonor through me,
O God of Israel.
7 For it is [g] for your sake that I have
borne reproach,
that dishonor has covered my face.
8 I have become [h] a stranger to my
brothers,
an alien to my mother's sons.
9 For [i] zeal for your house has
consumed me,
and [j] the reproaches of those who
reproach you have fallen on me.

28 [b] See Ps. 42:8 **29** [c] Ps. 45:12; 76:11; 1 Kin. 10:10, 25; 2 Chr. 32:23; Isai. 18:7 **30** [d] Job 40:21; Isai. 19:6; Ezek. 29:3, 4; [Ezek. 32:2] [e] Ps. 22:12 [f] [2 Sam. 8:2, 6] **31** [g] Isai. 19:19, 21 [h] Ps. 87:4; Isai. 45:14; Zeph. 3:10 [i] Ps. 44:20 **32** [j] Ps. 102:22 **33** [k] Ps. 18:10; 104:3; Deut. 33:26 [l] Deut. 10:14; 1 Kin. 8:27 [m] Ps. 29:4; See Ps. 46:6 **34** [n] Ps. 29:1 [o] Ps. 150:1 [p] Ps. 36:5; 57:10; 108:4 **35** [q] [Ps. 65:5]; See Ps. 47:2 [r] [Ps. 110:2] [s] Isai. 40:29; See Ps. 29:11 **Psalm 69** [t] Ps. 45, title **1** [u] ver. 14, 15; See Ps. 32:6; 130:1; Job 22:11 **2** [v] ver. 14; Ps. 40:2 [w] Ps. 124:4 **3** [x] Ps. 6:6 [y] [Ps. 22:15] [z] Ps. 119:82, 123; Deut. 28:32; Isai. 38:14 [a] See Ps. 31:24 **4** [b] Ps. 40:12 [c] Cited John 15:25 [d] [Ps. 35:7; 59:3, 4; 109:3; 119:161] [e] Ps. 35:19; 38:19 **6** [f] See Ps. 25:2 **7** [g] Jer. 15:15; [Ps. 44:22] **8** [h] [Ps. 31:11; 38:11; Job 19:13; John 1:11] **9** [i] Cited John 2:17; [Ps. 119:139]; See Ps. 132:1-5 [j] Cited Rom. 15:3; [Ps. 89:41, 50]

[1] Hebrew *Your God has summoned your power* [2] The meaning of the Hebrew verse is uncertain [3] Septuagint; Hebrew *your* [4] Or *waters threaten my life*

68:29 Because of your temple. Jerusalem's prestige has a single, spiritual cause: God has for that time chosen it as a special place of His dwelling (Deut. 12; 2 Sam. 7; cf. Is. 22:1, 2).

68:30 Rebuke. More than a verbal assault, to "rebuke" a nation is to destroy it.

the beasts . . . reeds. Either the crocodile or the hippopotamus, both symbols of Egypt.

68:31 Cush. A traditional ally of Egypt (Nah. 3:9). Cush is the remote land south of Egypt, including parts of modern Eritrea, Ethiopia, and Sudan.

68:33 rides in the heavens. The psalmist poetically alludes to the heavens as God's war chariot.

Ps. 69 This psalm is well known because of its application in the New Testament to the anguish of Jesus, God's righteous Servant, as He sought His Father's will during His earthly ministry.

69:1 the waters. The psalmist pictures his distress as one slowly sinking down in a river. The raging waters are a frequent biblical illustration of social or personal chaos. See notes Ps. 18:4; 46:2, 3.

69:2 the flood sweeps over me. The poetic language in this section can be compared to a water ordeal, in which a person suspected of a crime might be cast into a river. The river would be expected to overwhelm and carry away the guilty one, but to release the innocent.

69:5 the wrongs I have done. Although the psalmist is innocent of the charges alluded to in v. 4, he does not claim to be without sin.

69:6 those who seek you. The psalmist is concerned not for himself only, but for others in Israel who might be injured in some way through his sins. The possibility that his sins would affect others is enhanced by his power and prominence in society.

69:9 for your house. This verse is applied to Jesus as He cleared the temple of money changers (John 2:17), and through doing good attracted the hatred of the wicked. Enmity directed toward God may cause suffering for those who are like God (Rom. 15:3).

10 When I wept and humbled[1] my soul
with fasting,
it became my reproach.
11 When I made [k]sackcloth my
clothing,
I became [l]a byword to them.
12 I am the talk of those who [m]sit in the
gate,
and the drunkards make [n]songs
about me.

13 But as for me, my [o]prayer is to you,
O LORD.
At [p]an acceptable time, O God,
in the abundance of your steadfast
love answer me in your saving
faithfulness.
14 Deliver me
from sinking in [q]the mire;
[r]let me be delivered from my enemies
and from [s]the deep waters.
15 Let not the flood sweep over me,
or the deep swallow me up,
or [t]the pit close [u]its mouth
over me.

16 Answer me, O LORD, for your
[v]steadfast love is good;
according to your abundant
[w]mercy, [x]turn to me.
17 [y]Hide not your face from your servant;
[z]for I am in distress; [a]make haste to
answer me.
18 Draw near to my soul, redeem me;
ransom me because of my enemies!

19 You know my [b]reproach,
and my shame and my dishonor;
my foes are all known to you.
20 [b]Reproaches have broken my heart,
so that I am in [c]despair.
I [d]looked for [e]pity, but there was
none,
and for [f]comforters, but I found
none.
21 They gave me [g]poison for food,
and for my thirst they gave me
[h]sour wine to drink.

22 [i]Let their own [j]table before them
become a snare;
[k]and when they are at peace, let it
become a trap.[2]
23 [l]Let their eyes be darkened, so that
they cannot see,
[m]and make their loins tremble
continually.
24 Pour out your indignation upon
them,
and let your burning anger
overtake them.
25 [n]May their camp be a desolation;
let no one dwell in their tents.
26 For they [o]persecute him whom [p]you
have struck down,
and they recount the pain of
[q]those you have wounded.
27 [r]Add to them punishment upon
punishment;
may they have no acquittal from
you.[3]
28 Let them be [s]blotted out of the book
of the living;
let them not be [t]enrolled among
the righteous.

29 But I am afflicted and in pain;
let your salvation, O God, [u]set me
on high!

30 I will [v]praise the name of God with a
song;
I will [w]magnify him with
[x]thanksgiving.
31 This will [y]please the LORD more than
an ox
or a bull [z]with horns and hoofs.

11 [k]See Ps. 35:13 [l]See Job 17:6 **12** [m][Gen. 19:1; Esth. 2:19] [n]See Job 30:9 **13** [o]Ps. 109:4 [p]Isai. 49:8; 2 Cor. 6:2; [Ps. 32:6] **14** [q]ver. 2 [r]Ps. 144:7 [s]ver. 1, 2 **15** [t]Ps. 55:23 [u]Num. 16:33 **16** [v]Ps. 63:3; 109:21 [w]Ps. 106:45 [x]See Ps. 25:16 **17** [y]See Ps. 27:9 [z]See Ps. 18:6 [a]Ps. 102:2; 143:7 **19** [b]ver. 10, 11; [Heb. 12:2]; See Ps. 22:6 **20** [b][See ver. 19 above] [c][Matt. 26:37] [d]Ps. 142:4; [Isai. 63:5] [e]Jer. 15:5 [f]Job 16:2 **21** [g]Deut. 29:18; Matt. 27:34 [h]Matt. 27:48; Luke 23:36; John 19:29; [Mark 15:23] **22** [i]Cited Rom. 11:9, 10; See Ps. 35:4-8; 109:6-15 [j]Ps. 23:5 [k][1 Thess. 5:3] **23** [l]Isai. 6:10; [Matt. 13:14] [m]Dan. 5:6; Nah. 2:10 **25** [n]Cited Acts 1:20; [Matt. 23:38; Luke 13:35] **26** [o][Zech. 1:15] [p]Isai. 53:4 [q][Job 19:21] **27** [r]Neh. 4:5 **28** [s]Ex. 32:32; Rev. 3:5; [Phil. 4:3] [t][Ezek. 13:9; Luke 10:20; Heb. 12:23] **29** [u]Ps. 20:1 **30** [v]Ps. 28:7 [w]See Ps. 34:3 [x]See Ps. 50:14, 23 **31** [y]Ps. 50:13 [z]Lev. 11:3

1 Hebrew lacks *and humbled* 2 Hebrew; a slight revocalization yields (compare Septuagint, Syriac, Jerome) *a snare, and retribution and a trap* 3 Hebrew *may they not come into your righteousness*

69:11 made sackcloth my clothing. When the psalmist performs religious acts like fasting, he must bear the brunt of ridicule from rich and poor alike (v. 12).

69:15 the pit. See Prov. 1:12; Is. 5:14 and notes.

69:21 poison . . . sour wine. The bitterness of gall is proverbial. When the psalmist suffers such maltreatment, he responds with a curse (vv. 22–29). The metaphor became a reality when Jesus Christ was offered vinegar at His crucifixion (John 19:29). He responded with compassion for those who tormented Him.

69:25 May their camp be a desolation. The psalmist asks for the death of the wicked (v. 28). Peter cites this verse in connection with the death of Judas Iscariot and the void he left among the disciples (Acts 1:20).

69:26 they persecute him whom you have struck down. The enemy furthers the pain of the afflicted. If God chastises someone, this is no excuse for others to increase his pain.

69:30 I will praise. The transition from pain and the call for judgment to resolute praise is abrupt. Such compression of thought is not unusual in biblical poetry.

69:31 more than an ox. An ox was the most expensive sacrifice. God is concerned with genuine praise, not wealth (50:12–14, 23; Hos. 14:2; Rom. 15:6; Heb. 13:15).

32 When [a]the humble see it they will be glad;
you who seek God, [a]let your hearts revive.
33 For the LORD hears the needy
and [b]does not despise his own people who are prisoners.
34 Let [c]heaven and earth praise him,
the seas and everything that moves in them.
35 For [d]God will save Zion
and build up the cities of Judah,
and people shall dwell there and possess it;
36 [e]the offspring of his servants shall inherit it,
and those who love his name shall dwell in it.

O LORD, Do Not Delay

70 TO THE CHOIRMASTER. OF DAVID, [f]FOR THE MEMORIAL OFFERING.

1 [g]Make haste, O God, to deliver me!
O LORD, make haste to help me!
2 Let them be put to shame and confusion
who seek my life!
Let them be turned back and brought to dishonor
who desire my hurt!
3 Let them turn back because of their shame
who say, "Aha, Aha!"
4 May all who seek you
rejoice and be glad in you!
May those who love your salvation
say evermore, "God is great!"
5 But I am poor and needy;
[h]hasten to me, O God!
You are my help and my deliverer;
O LORD, do not delay!

32 [a]Ps. 22:26; 34:2
33 [b][Ps. 68:6]
34 [c]Ps. 96:11; 98:7; Isai. 44:23; 49:13; See Ps. 148:1-12
35 [d]See Ps. 51:18; [Isai. 44:26]
36 [e]Ps. 102:28; Isai. 65:9; [Ps. 37:29]
Psalm 70 [f]Ps. 38, title; [1 Chr. 16:4]
1 [g]For ver. 1-5, see Ps. 40:13-17
5 [h]Ps. 141:1
Psalm 71
1 [i]For ver. 1-3, see Ps. 31:1-3
3 [j][Ps. 90:1; 91:9; Deut. 33:27] [k]See Ps. 42:8 [l]See Ps. 18:2
4 [m]Ps. 140:1, 4
5 [n]Jer. 14:8; 17:13; 50:7; 1 Tim. 1:1
6 [o]See Ps. 22:10 [p]Ps. 22:9
7 [q]Isai. 8:18; [1 Cor. 4:9]
8 [r]ver. 24
9 [s]ver. 18
10 [t]Ps. 56:6 [u]Ps. 83:5; [Ps. 41:7, 8]

Forsake Me Not When My Strength Is Gone

71 [i]In you, O LORD, do I take refuge;
let me never be put to shame!
2 In your righteousness deliver me and rescue me;
incline your ear to me, and save me!
3 Be to me a rock of [j]refuge,
to which I may continually come;
you have [k]given the command to save me,
for you are my [l]rock and my fortress.
4 [m]Rescue me, O my God, from the hand of the wicked,
from the grasp of the unjust and cruel man.
5 For you, O Lord, are my [n]hope,
my trust, O LORD, from my youth.
6 Upon you I have leaned [o]from before my birth;
you are he who [p]took me from my mother's womb.
My praise is continually of you.
7 I have been as [q]a portent to many,
but you are my strong refuge.
8 My [r]mouth is filled with your praise,
and with your glory all the day.
9 [s]Do not cast me off in the time of old age;
forsake me not when my strength is spent.
10 For my enemies speak concerning me;
those who [t]watch for my life
[u]consult together
11 and say, "God has forsaken him;
pursue and seize him,
for there is none to deliver him."

69:32, 33 the humble . . . the needy. The way to God is open to the humble poor.

69:35 build up the cities of Judah. The last verses were probably added later than David, during or shortly after the exile of the Jews to Babylon in the sixth century B.C.

Ps. 70 This psalm is nearly identical with Ps. 40:13–17.

70:title FOR THE MEMORIAL OFFERING. This title is used elsewhere only for Ps. 38.

70:1 Make haste . . . to deliver me. In his desperate plight, the psalmist boldly asks the Lord to come to his rescue.

70:2 be turned back and brought to dishonor. He wants the Lord to turn the tables on the enemy. They seek the psalmist's ruin and his life; he asks God to ruin them.

70:5 poor and needy. See 9:18 note.

Ps. 71 A psalm of lament uttered by an older man (v. 9). This psalm is one of the few in the first two books of the Psalms without a title.

71:2 In your righteousness. See note Ps. 31:1.

71:3 my rock and my fortress. God is the psalmist's only place of protection. See note Ps. 61:2.

71:5 from my youth. The language of the psalmist shows that he is now an older man. He is in a position where he can look back over his life and ponder his relationship with God.

71:6 from my mother's womb. The psalmist confesses that God created him for a gracious purpose.

71:11 God has forsaken him. Like Job's friends, the psalmist's enemies have come to the wrong conclusion about his suffering.

12 O God, be not [v]far from me;
O my God, [w]make haste to help me!
13 May my accusers be [x]put to shame
and consumed;
[y]with scorn and disgrace may they
be covered
who [z]seek my hurt.
14 But I will [a]hope continually
and will [b]praise you yet more and
more.
15 My [c]mouth will tell of your righteous
acts,
of your deeds of salvation all the day,
for [d]their number is past my
knowledge.
16 With the mighty deeds of the Lord
GOD I will come;
I will remind them of your
righteousness, yours alone.

17 O God, from my youth you have
taught me,
and I still proclaim your wondrous
deeds.
18 So even to [e]old age and gray hairs,
O God, [f]do not forsake me,
until I proclaim your might to
another generation,
your power to all those to come.
19 Your [g]righteousness, O God,
reaches the high heavens.
You who have done [h]great things,
O God, [i]who is like you?
20 You who have [j]made me see many
troubles and calamities
will [k]revive me again;
from the depths of the earth
you will bring me up again.
21 You will increase my greatness
and comfort me again.
22 I will also praise you with [l]the harp
for your faithfulness,
O my God;
I will sing praises to you with the
lyre,
O [m]Holy One of Israel.
23 My lips will shout for joy,
when I sing praises to you;
my soul also, which you have
[n]redeemed.
24 And my [o]tongue will talk of your
righteous help all the
day long,
for they have been [p]put to shame
and disappointed
who sought to do me hurt.

Give the King Your Justice

72 OF [q] SOLOMON.
Give the king your [r] justice, O God,
and your righteousness to the royal
son!
2 May he [s]judge your people with
righteousness,
and your poor with justice!
3 Let the mountains bear [t]prosperity
for the people,
and the hills, in righteousness!
4 May he defend the cause of the poor
of the people,
give deliverance to the children of
the needy,
and crush the oppressor!

5 May they fear you[1] while [u]the sun
endures,
and as long as the moon,
[v]throughout all generations!

12 [v]See Ps. 10:1 [w]Ps. 70:5; See Ps. 40:13
13 [x]ver. 24; See Ps. 35:4, 26 [y]Ps. 109:29 [z]ver. 24; Esth. 9:2; [Ps. 70:2]
14 [a]ver. 5 [b]ver. 22
15 [c]ver. 8, 24 [d]See Ps. 40:5
18 [e]Isai. 46:4 [f]ver. 9
19 [g]Ps. 36:5 [h]Ps. 126:2; 1 Sam. 12:24; Luke 1:49 [i]Ps. 35:10
20 [j]Ps. 60:3 [k]Ps. 80:18; 85:6; 119:25; 138:7; 143:11; Hos. 6:2
22 [l]Ps. 33:2 [m]Ps. 78:41; 89:18; 2 Kin. 19:22; Isai. 60:9
23 [n]Ps. 34:22
24 [o][ver. 8, 15]; See Ps. 35:28 [p][ver. 13]
Psalm 72 [q]Ps. 127, title
1 [r][1 Chr. 22:12]
2 [s]Isai. 9:7; 11:2-4; 32:1; See Ps. 122:5
3 [t][Ps. 85:10; Isai. 32:17; 52:7]
5 [u]ver. 7, 17; Ps. 89:36, 37; Jer. 31:35, 36; [Jer. 33:20, 25] [v]Ps. 89:4; [Luke 1:33]

1 Septuagint *He shall endure*

71:14 I will hope continually. He can look back over his long life and see how God has saved him in the past. His memory serves as a bulwark of devotion.

71:15 their number is past my knowledge. Uninterrupted praise cannot adequately express God's mercy; His salvation is beyond comprehension.

71:18 to another generation. It is the duty of the older members of God's community to teach the young what God has done in their elder's lives.

71:19 reaches the high heavens. God's righteousness is so great it cannot be contained. It is without limit.

who is like you. To ask this rhetorical question is to answer it.

71:20 You . . . made me see . . . troubles. The psalmist knows that life is hard and that God has not sheltered him from every difficulty. Nonetheless, he has confidence that God will deliver him.

71:21 comfort me again. Job is an example of a person who was restored after a time of intense suffering. But this kind of restoration does not always happen during earthly existence (Luke 16:25; Rom. 8:18; 2 Cor. 4:17).

Ps. 72 The second part of Psalms concludes with a royal psalm asking God to bless the just king. Some of the language goes beyond what applies to the earthly king, anticipating the Messiah.

72:title See Introduction: Author. The Septuagint (ancient Greek translation of the Old Testament) understands the title to name Solomon as the subject matter and not as the author of the psalm. The traditional understanding of the Hebrew is to indicate authorship.

72:1 your justice . . . your righteousness. God, the divine King, is the source of all justice and righteousness. If the human king is to have such qualities, he must receive them from God.

72:2 your people. The human king receives his calling from the divine King.

72:3 prosperity. See note 122:6.

72:4 poor . . . needy. The king had a special responsibility to the vulnerable in society. God has a special concern and love for the poor, and the earthly king must take special care of them. See 9:18 note.

72:5 while the sun endures. As applied to an earthly king, this is a poetic overstatement. The language looks forward to the one King who will live forever (Luke 1:33; Heb. 7:16; Rev. 11:15).

6 May he be like [w]rain that falls on
[x]the mown grass,
like [y]showers that water the earth!
7 In his days may [z]the righteous
flourish,
and [a]peace abound, till the moon
be no more!
8 May he have dominion from [b]sea to
sea,
and from [b]the River[1] to the [c]ends
of the earth!
9 May desert tribes [d]bow down before
him
and his enemies [e]lick the dust!
10 May the kings of [f]Tarshish and of
[g]the coastlands
render him [h]tribute;
may the kings of [i]Sheba and [j]Seba
bring gifts!
11 May all kings [k]fall down before him,
all nations serve him!
12 For he delivers [l]the needy when he
calls,
the poor and him who has no
helper.
13 He has pity on the weak and the
needy,
and saves the lives of the
needy.
14 From oppression and violence he
redeems their life,
and [m]precious is their blood in his
sight.
15 Long may he live;
may [n]gold of Sheba be given to
him!
May prayer be made [o]for him
continually,
and blessings invoked for him all
the day!

6 [w]2 Sam. 23:4; Hos. 6:3 [x]Amos 7:1 [y]Deut. 32:2; [Ps. 65:10; Job 5:10] 7 [z]See Ps. 92:12 [a]Isai. 2:4; [Eph. 2:14] 8 [b]Ex. 23:31; 1 Kin. 4:21, 24; Zech. 9:10; [Ps. 80:11; 89:25] [c]See Ps. 2:8 9 [d]Ps. 22:29 [e]Isai. 49:23; Mic. 7:17 10 [f]1 Kin. 10:22 [g]Isai. 42:10, 12; 51:5; 60:9 [h]See Ps. 68:29; 1 Sam. 10:27 [i]See 1 Kin. 10:1 [j]Gen. 10:7; Isai. 43:3; 45:14 11 [k]Isai. 49:7, 23 12 [l]See Job 29:12-17 14 [m]Ps. 116:15; 2 Kin. 1:13 15 [n]1 Kin. 10:10 [o]Deut. 9:20

16 [p]Ps. 92:7 [q]Job 5:25 17 [r]Ps. 104:31; [Ps. 89:36] [s]Gen. 12:3; 18:18; 22:18; 26:4 [t]Luke 1:48 18 [u]See Ps. 41:13 [v]Ps. 77:14; 86:10; 136:4; Ex. 15:11; See Job 5:9 19 [w]Neh. 9:5 [x]Num. 14:21 [y]Ps. 41:13 20 [z]Ps. 17, title; 55:1; 86, title [a]2 Sam. 23:1

BOOK THREE Psalm 73 [b]See Ps. 50, title 1 [c]John 1:47 [d]See Ps. 24:4

16 May there be abundance of grain in
the land;
on the tops of the mountains may
it wave;
may its fruit be like Lebanon;
and may people [p]blossom in the
cities
like the [q]grass of the field!
17 [r]May his name endure forever,
his fame continue as long as the
sun!
[s]May people be blessed in him,
[t]all nations call him blessed!

18 [u]Blessed be the LORD, the God of Israel,
who alone does [v]wondrous things.
19 Blessed be his [w]glorious name forever;
may [x]the whole earth be filled with
his glory!
[y]Amen and Amen!

20 [z]The prayers of [a]David, the son of
Jesse, are ended.

BOOK THREE

God Is My Strength and Portion Forever

73 A PSALM OF [b]ASAPH.
Truly God is good to [c]Israel,
to those who are [d]pure in heart.
2 But as for me, my feet had almost
stumbled,
my steps had nearly slipped.
3 [e]For I was [f]envious of the arrogant
when I saw the prosperity of the
wicked.

4 For they have no [g]pangs until death;
their bodies are fat and sleek.
5 They are not in trouble as others are;
they are not [h]stricken like the rest
of mankind.

3 [e]See Job 21:7 [f]Ps. 37:1; Prov. 23:17 4 [g]Isai. 58:6 5 [h][Isai. 53:4]

[1] That is, the Euphrates

72:8 from sea to sea. There is an allusion here to the promised boundaries of Ex. 23:31, but the language far exceeds any achievement of an earthly king of Israel, and so looks forward to the Messiah's reign.

72:9 desert tribes. He will subdue the rebellious tribes of the desert.

72:10 Tarshish . . . Sheba . . . Seba. These places were considered to be remote. Tarshish is usually associated with Tartessus in Spain. Sheba and probably Seba are in southern Arabia.

72:17 May his name endure forever. The verse recalls the Abrahamic promises of Gen. 12:2, 3. The king is a focal point for the society of God's people. He represents the people and is the heir of the promises; in Jesus Christ these promises come to fulfillment.

72:18, 19 Each of the five books of the Psalms concludes with a doxology praising the name of the Lord.

72:20 At some point in the process of collecting the psalms, all of the psalms of David were grouped together in the first two books. This unity was not preserved as the book continued, and this verse cannot be applied strictly to Ps. 1–72.

Ps. 73 The psalm begins with an assertion that God is good, a belief won only after long struggle with what is observed in the world, especially the prosperity of the wicked. This important theme is also treated in Ps. 37; 49; and the Book of Job.

73:1 God is good. What clouded the psalmist's heart and troubled his relationship with the Lord has been resolved.

73:2 my feet had almost stumbled. An obedient life is often compared to a walk along a straight path (Prov. 1–9). The psalmist describes doubt and skepticism with the image of falling off a path.

6 Therefore pride is [i]their necklace;
violence covers them as [j]a garment.
7 Their [k]eyes swell out through fatness;
their hearts overflow with follies.
8 They scoff and [l]speak with malice;
loftily they threaten oppression.
9 They set their mouths against the heavens,
and their tongue struts through the earth.
10 Therefore his people turn back to them,
and find [m]no fault in them.[1]
11 And they say, [n]"How can God know?
Is there knowledge in the Most High?"
12 Behold, these are the wicked;
always at ease, they [o]increase in riches.
13 All in vain have I [p]kept my heart clean
and [q]washed my hands in innocence.
14 For all the day long I have been [h]stricken
and [r]rebuked [s]every morning.
15 If I had said, "I will speak thus,"
I would have betrayed [t]the generation of your children.

16 But when I thought how to understand this,
it seemed to me [u]a wearisome task,
17 until I went into [v]the sanctuary of God;
then I discerned their [w]end.

18 Truly you set them in [x]slippery places;
you make them fall to ruin.
19 How they are destroyed [y]in a moment,
swept away utterly by [z]terrors!
20 Like [a]a dream when one awakes,
O Lord, when [b]you rouse yourself, you despise them as phantoms.
21 When my soul was embittered,
when I was pricked in heart,
22 I was [c]brutish and ignorant;
I was like [d]a beast toward you.

23 Nevertheless, I am continually with you;
you [e]hold my right hand.
24 You [f]guide me with your counsel,
and afterward you will [g]receive me to glory.
25 [h]Whom have I in heaven but you?
And there is nothing on earth that I desire besides you.
26 [i]My flesh and my heart may fail,
but God is [j]the strength[2] of my heart and my [k]portion [l]forever.

27 For behold, those who are [m]far from you shall perish;
you put an end to everyone who is [n]unfaithful to you.
28 But for me it is good to [o]be near God;
I have made the Lord GOD my [p]refuge,
that I may [q]tell of all your works.

6 [i][Judg. 8:26] [j][Ps. 109:18] 7 [k]See Job 15:27 8 [l][2 Pet. 2:18; Jude 16] 10 [m][Job 15:16] 11 [n]See Job 22:13 12 [o][ver. 3] 13 [p][ver. 1]; See Job 34:9 [q]See Ps. 26:6 14 [h][See ver. 5 above] [r]Rev. 3:19 [s][Ps. 101:8] 15 [t][Ps. 14:5] 16 [u]Eccles. 8:17 17 [v]Ps. 20:2 [w]Ps. 37:38
18 [x]Ps. 35:6 19 [y][Num. 16:21] [z]See Job 18:11 20 [a]See Job 20:8 [b]Ps. 78:65 22 [c]See Ps. 49:10 [d]Job 18:3; [Job 11:12] 23 [e]Ps. 63:8; [Ps. 41:12] 24 [f]Ps. 32:8 [g]See Ps. 49:15 25 [h]Ps. 16:2; [Phil. 3:8] 26 [i]Ps. 40:12; See Ps. 84:2 [j]Ps. 18:2 [k]See Ps. 16:5 [l][Dan. 12:3] 27 [m]Ps. 119:155 [n]Ps. 106:39; Ex. 34:15; Num. 15:39; James 4:4 28 [o]James 4:8; [Heb. 10:22] [p]See Ps. 14:6 [q]See Ps. 118:17

1 Probable reading; Hebrew *the waters of a full cup are drained by them*
2 Hebrew *rock*

73:6 pride is their necklace. The prosperity of the wicked leads to the deeper sins of pride and violence.

73:7 eyes swell out. A figure for a heart made insensitive by overindulgence (1 John 2:16).

73:9 against the heavens. The proud are not afraid to talk as if they had created the world themselves, leaving God behind (Acts 20:22).

73:13 in vain. These verses show the poet's attitude before he resolved the issue in his mind.

73:15 If I had said. If he had broadcast his doubts and complaints before coming to a solution, he would have instilled doubt in the community of God.

73:16 this. That is, the prosperity of the wicked and the suffering of the righteous.

73:17 into the sanctuary. The change came for him when he entered the presence of God revealed in the temple.

their end. Though the wicked may prosper for a time, their final lot is destruction. See "The Final Judgment" at Matt. 25:41.

73:20 Like a dream. God will come in judgment against the wicked. When He does, their prosperity will seem like a dream.

73:22 brutish and ignorant. His negative emotions blocked clear thinking about God and His ways.

73:23 you hold my right hand. God is close to the worshiper to counsel and guide him.

73:24 to glory. While some take this to refer to earthly fame and reputation, it is more likely a reference to eternal glory. Nothing will break the intimate fellowship the psalmist enjoys with God (Rom. 8:38, 39).

Arise, O God, Defend Your Cause

74 A MASKIL[1] OF [r] ASAPH.
1 O God, why do you [s] cast us off
forever?
Why does your anger [t] smoke
against [u] the sheep of your
pasture?
2 [v] Remember your congregation, which
you have [w] purchased of old,
which you have [x] redeemed to be
[y] the tribe of your heritage!
Remember Mount Zion, [z] where
you have dwelt.
3 Direct your steps to [a] the perpetual
ruins;
the enemy has destroyed
everything in the sanctuary!

4 Your foes have [b] roared in the midst
of your meeting place;
[c] they set up their [d] own signs for
[e] signs.
5 They were like those who swing [f] axes
in a forest of trees.[2]
6 And all its [g] carved wood
they broke down with hatchets
and hammers.
7 They [h] set your sanctuary on fire;
they [i] profaned [j] the dwelling place
of your name,
bringing it down to the ground.
8 They [k] said to themselves, "We will
utterly subdue them";
they burned all the meeting places
of God in the land.

9 We do not see our [l] signs;
[m] there is no longer any prophet,
and there is none among us who
knows how long.
10 How long, O God, [n] is the foe to scoff?
Is the enemy to revile your name
forever?
11 Why [o] do you hold back your hand,
your right hand?
Take it from the fold of your
garment[3] and destroy them!

12 Yet [p] God my King is from of old,
working salvation in the midst of
the earth.
13 You [q] divided the sea by your might;
you [r] broke the heads of [s] the sea
monsters[4] on the waters.
14 You crushed the heads of [t] Leviathan;
you gave him as food for the
creatures of the wilderness.
15 You [u] split open springs and brooks;
you [v] dried up ever-flowing streams.
16 Yours is the day, yours also the
night;
you have established [w] the heavenly
lights and the sun.
17 You have [x] fixed all the boundaries of
the earth;
you have made [y] summer and winter.

18 [z] Remember this, O LORD, how the
enemy scoffs,
and [a] a foolish people reviles your
name.
19 Do not deliver the soul of your [b] dove
to the wild beasts;
[c] do not forget the life of your poor
forever.

Psalm 74 [r] See Ps. 50, title **1** [s] See Ps. 44:9 [t] Deut. 29:20; [Ps. 18:8] [u] Ps. 79:13; 100:3; Jer. 23:1; Ezek. 34:31; [Ps. 95:7] **2** [v] ver. 18, 22 [w] Ex. 15:16; Deut. 32:6; [Ps. 78:54] [x] Ps. 77:15; Isai. 63:9 [y] Isai. 63:17; Jer. 10:16; 51:19 [z] Ps. 9:11 **3** [a] [Isai. 61:4] **4** [b] Lam. 2:6, 7 [c] [Matt. 24:15] [d] Num. 2:2 [e] [ver. 9] **5** [f] [Jer. 46:22] **6** [g] [1 Kin. 6:18, 29, 32, 35] **7** [h] 2 Kin. 25:9; [Ps. 79:1] [i] Ps. 89:39; [Lam. 2:2] [j] [Ps. 26:8] **8** [k] Ps. 83:4 **9** [l] [ver. 4] [m] [1 Sam. 3:1; Lam. 2:9; Ezek. 7:26; Amos 8:11]

10 [n] ver. 18, 22; Ps. 79:12; 89:51 **11** [o] Lam. 2:3 **12** [p] Ps. 44:4 **13** [q] Ex. 14:21 [r] Isai. 51:9 [s] Isai. 27:1 **14** [t] See Job 41:1 **15** [u] Ps. 78:15; 105:41; Ex. 17:5, 6; Num. 20:11; Isai. 48:21 [v] Josh. 2:10; 4:23; Isai. 51:10; [Ps. 66:6]; See Ex. 14:21-25; Josh. 3:13-17

16 [w] Ps. 104:19; See Gen. 1:14-16 **17** [x] Deut. 32:8; [Acts 17:26] [y] Gen. 8:22 **18** [z] ver. 2, 22; Ps. 89:50; Rev. 16:19; 18:5 [a] Ps. 39:8; Deut. 32:6 **19** [b] S. of S. 2:14 [c] [Ps. 68:10]

1 Probably a musical or liturgical term 2 The meaning of the Hebrew is uncertain 3 Hebrew *from your bosom* 4 Or *the great sea creatures*

Ps. 74 This lament for the destruction of the temple in 586 B.C. is comparable to the mournful poems of Lamentations.

74:1 cast us off. Israel's defeat at the hands of the Babylonians indicated that God had abandoned His chosen people and would protect them no longer. The prophets (Ezek. 9–11) describe God's abandonment of His temple, blaming it on Israel's sin and unbelief. See note Ps. 22:1.

the sheep. The writer appeals to this metaphor of intimate relationship between God and His people in order to plead for restoration. See Ps. 23:1.

74:2 Remember. The psalmist means more than mental recall here; he wants God to act on His ancient covenant promise to save His people.

Mount Zion. The location of the temple and the place where God made His presence known in a special way. See Ps. 2:6; 50:2; 128:5; 129:5.

74:3 Direct your steps. The psalmist asks God to survey and to react to the damage the enemy has inflicted on His possessions. When Nebuchadnezzar took Jerusalem in 586 B.C. he ordered the sanctuary to be demolished.

74:9 do not see our signs . . . any prophet. The worst fear of all is that God will be silent in the face of destruction. This psalm was likely written soon after the event, since a number of prophets were active during the period of restoration.

74:10 revile your name. The psalmist tries to persuade God by arguing that His own reputation is in danger. Asaph is distressed by God's apparent inactivity.

74:13 the sea. In the next few verses the poet alludes to a popular concept of creation and applies it to the Lord. For the defeat of the "Sea," see Ezek. 28:2 and note. In using these figures, the psalmist is not endorsing the popular myths, but using them to say that the God of Israel is the Creator of all. The gods of the Near East are nothing because they do not exist. See Ps. 18:4; 29:3, 10; 46:2, 3; 69:1, 2; Jer. 14:22; 1 Cor. 8:4.

74:14 heads of Leviathan. The psalmist borrows the language of popular mythology, related in texts discovered at ancient Ugarit in Syria. In those texts "Leviathan" (or "Lothan") is a seven-headed sea monster defeated by Baal at the time of creation.

20 Have regard for [d]the covenant,
for [e]the dark places of the land are
full of the habitations of violence.
21 Let not [f]the downtrodden [g]turn back
in shame;
let [h]the poor and needy praise your
name.

22 Arise, O God, [i]defend your cause;
[j]remember how the foolish scoff at
you all the day!
23 Do not forget the clamor of your foes,
[k]the uproar of those who rise
against you, which goes up
continually!

God Will Judge with Equity

75 To the choirmaster: according to [l]Do Not Destroy. [m]A Psalm of Asaph. A Song.

1 We give thanks to you, O God;
we give thanks, for your name is
[n]near.
We[1] recount your wondrous deeds.
2 "At [o]the set time that I appoint
I will judge [p]with equity.
3 When the earth [q]totters, and all its
inhabitants,
it is I who keep steady its
[r]pillars. *Selah*
4 I say to the boastful, 'Do not boast,'
and to the wicked, [s]'Do not lift up
your horn;
5 do not lift up your horn on high,
or speak with haughty neck.'"

6 For not from the east or from the west
and not from the wilderness comes
[t]lifting up,
7 but it is [u]God who executes
judgment,
[v]putting down one and lifting up
another.
8 [w]For in the hand of the Lord there is
[x]a cup
with foaming wine, [y]well
mixed,
and he pours out from it,
and all the wicked of the earth
shall [z]drain it down to
the dregs.

9 But I will declare it forever;
I will sing praises to the God of
Jacob.
10 [a]All the horns of the wicked I will
cut off,
[b]but the horns of the righteous
shall be lifted up.

Who Can Stand Before You?

76 To the choirmaster: with [c]stringed instruments. A Psalm of [d]Asaph. A Song.

1 In Judah God is [e]known;
his name is great in Israel.
2 His [f]abode has been established in
[g]Salem,
his [h]dwelling place in Zion.
3 There he [i]broke the flashing
arrows,
the shield, the sword, and the
weapons of war. *Selah*

4 Glorious are you, more majestic
[j]than the mountains of [k]prey.

1 Hebrew *They*

20[d]Ps. 106:45; Gen. 17:7, 8; Lev. 26:44, 45; Jer. 33:21 [e][Ps. 10:8]
21[f]Ps. 9:9; 10:18 [g][Ps. 6:10] [h]Ps. 86:1
22[i][1 Sam. 24:15] [j]ver. 2, 18
23[k]See Ps. 65:7
Psalm 75
[l]See Ps. 57, title [m]See Ps. 50, title
1[n]Ps. 145:18
2[o]Dan. 8:19; Hab. 2:3; See Ps. 102:13 [p]Ps. 17:2
3[q]Isai. 24:19 [r]1 Sam. 2:8
4[s]ver. 10; Zech. 1:21
6[t]See Ps. 3:3
7[u]See Ps. 50:6 [v]1 Sam. 2:7; Dan. 2:21
8[w]See Job 21:20 [x]Ps. 11:6 [y]Prov. 23:30 [z]Ps. 73:10
10[a]Jer. 48:25 [b]ver. 4; Ps. 89:17; 112:9; 1 Sam. 2:1
Psalm 76
[c]Ps. 4, title [d]See Ps. 50, title
1[e]Ps. 48:3
2[f]Ps. 27:5; Lam. 2:6 [g]Gen. 14:18 [h]Ps. 9:11; 74:2
3[i]Ps. 46:9; [Ezek. 39:9]
4[j][Isai. 14:25; Ezek. 39:4] [k]Nah. 2:13

74:20 the covenant. The writer appeals to God's covenant, knowing that His patience is not exhausted despite the disobedience that led to the fall of the northern kingdom in the eighth century B.C.

74:22 Arise. See note Ps. 7:6.

Ps. 75 The theme of casting down the wicked and lifting up the righteous is also found in Hannah's song (1 Sam. 2:1–10) and Mary's words of praise (Luke 1:46–55).

75:1 We. The psalm begins as a communal thanksgiving, though at the end an individual speaks for the community.

name. See Ps. 8:1.

your wondrous deeds. God's great acts in history (Rev. 15:3, 4).

75:2 judge with equity. God's judgments are always just, and He knows the secrets of the heart.

75:3 keep steady its pillars. God provides the underlying stability of the world order.

75:4 horn. This common metaphor is one of a powerful horned beast proudly lifting up its head in defiance and anger. God warns the wicked not to act in this way against Him.

75:7 it is God who executes judgment. God and not any person in the east, west, or south determines what shall stand.

75:8 a cup. See note Ps. 11:6.

Ps. 76 The psalm celebrates a great victory over Israel's enemies. From the New Testament perspective, this song praises God for His victory at the cross and looks forward to the great final victory over evil at the end of the age (Rev. 19:11–21).

76:2 in Salem . . . his dwelling place. Salem is the ancient name for Jerusalem. God's tabernacle is His sanctuary. The tabernacle was a tent, but the temple that replaced it could still be called a tent poetically.

Zion. The mountain where the temple was situated (Ps. 2:6).

76:3 he broke. God defeated the enemy at Jerusalem. A good example of such a battle would be the siege by Sennacherib in 701 B.C. (2 Kin. 19; Is. 37).

76:4 Glorious. See John 1:4–9.

5 [l]The stouthearted were stripped of their spoil;
[m]they sank into sleep;
all the men of war
were unable to use their hands.
6 At your rebuke, O God of Jacob,
both [n]rider and horse lay stunned.

7 [o]But you, you are to be feared!
Who can [p]stand before you
when once your anger is roused?
8 From the heavens you uttered judgment;
[q]the earth feared and was still,
9 when God [r]arose to establish judgment,
to save all the humble of the earth. *Selah*

10 Surely [s]the wrath of man shall praise you;
the remnant[1] of wrath you will put on like a belt.
11 [t]Make your vows to the LORD your God and perform them;
let all around him [u]bring gifts
to him who [v]is to be feared,
12 who [w]cuts off the spirit of princes,
who [x]is to be feared by the kings of the earth.

In the Day of Trouble I Seek the Lord

77 TO THE CHOIRMASTER: ACCORDING TO [y]JEDUTHUN. [2] A PSALM OF [z]ASAPH.

1 I [a]cry aloud to God,
aloud to God, and he will hear me.
2 [b]In the day of my trouble I seek the Lord;
in [c]the night my [d]hand is stretched out without wearying;
my soul [e]refuses to be comforted.
3 When I remember God, I [f]moan;
when I meditate, my spirit faints. *Selah*

4 You hold my eyelids open;
I am so [g]troubled that I cannot speak.
5 I consider [h]the days of old,
the years long ago.
6 I said,[3] "Let me remember my [i]song in the night;
let me [j]meditate in my heart."
Then my spirit made a diligent search:
7 "Will the Lord [k]spurn forever,
and never again [l]be favorable?
8 Has his steadfast love forever ceased?
Are his [m]promises at an end for all time?
9 [n]Has God forgotten to be gracious?
[o]Has he in anger shut up his compassion?" *Selah*

10 Then I said, [p]"I will appeal to this,
to the years of the right hand of the Most High."[4]

11 I will remember the deeds of the LORD;
yes, I will [q]remember your wonders of old.
12 I will ponder all your [r]work,
and meditate on your [s]mighty deeds.
13 Your way, O God, is [t]holy.
[u]What god is great like our God?
14 You are the God who [v]works wonders;
you have [w]made known your might among the peoples.

5 [l]Isai. 46:12 [m]Ps. 13:3; 2 Kin. 19:35; Jer. 51:39; Nah. 3:18 **6** [n]Ex. 15:1, 21 **7** [o]Ps. 47:2 [p]Ps. 130:3 **8** [q]2 Chr. 20:29, 30; [Hab. 2:20] **9** [r][Ps. 9:7, 8] **10** [s][Ex. 9:16] **11** [t]See Ps. 50:14 [u]See Ps. 68:29 [v]Ps. 89:7; Gen. 31:42, 53; Isai. 8:13 **12** [w][Isai. 18:5] [x]See Ps. 47:2
Psalm 77 [y]Ps. 39, title [z]Ps. 50, title **1** [a]See Ps. 3:4 **2** [b]Ps. 86:7; [Ps. 20:1; 50:15; Isai. 26:16] [c]Ps. 63:6; Isai. 26:9 [d][Ps. 143:6] [e]Gen. 37:35
3 [f]Ps. 42:5, 11; 43:5 **4** [g][Gen. 41:8] **5** [h]ver. 10, 11; Ps. 44:1; 143:5; Deut. 32:7; Isai. 51:9 **6** [i]See Ps. 42:8 [j]Ps. 4:4 **7** [k]See Ps. 44:9 [l]Ps. 85:1 **8** [m][Rom. 9:6] **9** [n][Isai. 49:15] [o][Hab. 3:2] **10** [p][Ps. 109:2] **11** [q]ver. 5; Ps. 105:5 **12** [r]Ps. 90:16 [s]Ps. 9:11 **13** [t]Ps. 73:17 [u]See Ps. 35:10 **14** [v]See Ps. 72:18 [w]Ps. 106:8

[1] Or *extremity* [2] Probably a musical or liturgical term [3] Hebrew lacks *I said* [4] Or *This is my grief: that the right hand of the Most High has changed*

76:5 stouthearted were stripped of their spoil. God has destroyed powerful soldiers; they are no match for Him.

76:6 rebuke. God's rebuke is the word of His powerful judgment. At His rebuke the forces of chaos and evil flee before Him and peace reigns (Nah. 1:4; Matt. 8:23–27; 17:18).

76:10 the wrath . . . shall praise you. God's wrath brings praise because it is directed against the wicked and unjust, who afflict the poor and vulnerable (9:18 note).

76:11 vows. See Lev. 27.

Ps. 77 An individual prays on behalf of the community (vv. 7–9). A deep lament is followed by eloquent memory of the Exodus.

77:2 my hand is stretched out. A common gesture of prayer was reaching out toward heaven.

77:5 the days of old. The days when God was near and acted to save Israel from its distress.

77:7 spurn. The Lord's promise to be with His people required their obedience. Though God was longsuffering, at times His patience would run out (1 Sam. 4; Ezek. 9–11; Lamentations).

77:9 Has God forgotten to be gracious. It is impossible that God should cease to be merciful, but the distress of life elicit these questions in the psalmist.

77:10 I will appeal to this. This verse provides a crucial transition in the psalm. By remembering God's great acts in the past, the poet builds confidence in the present and for the future.

years of the right hand. When God's power was seen to act for them (Ex. 15:6).

77:13 great. As the writer remembers God's great acts in the past, he is reminded of God's attributes: His holiness and His unique power.

15 You [x]with your arm redeemed your people,
the children of Jacob and Joseph. *Selah*
16 When [y]the waters saw you, O God,
when the waters saw you, they were afraid;
indeed, the deep trembled.
17 The clouds poured out water;
the skies [z]gave forth thunder;
your [a]arrows flashed on every side.
18 [b]The crash of your thunder was in the whirlwind;
[c]your lightnings lighted up the world;
the earth [d]trembled and shook.
19 Your [e]way was through the sea,
your path through the great waters;
yet your footprints [f]were unseen.[1]
20 You [g]led your people like a flock
by the hand of Moses and Aaron.

Tell the Coming Generation

78 A MASKIL[2] OF [h] ASAPH.
[i] Give ear, O my people, to my teaching;
incline your ears to the words of my mouth!
2 [j]I will open my mouth [k]in a parable;
I will utter dark sayings from of old,
3 things that we have heard and known,
that our [l]fathers have told us.
4 We will not [m]hide them from their children,
but [n]tell to the coming generation
the glorious deeds of the LORD, and his might,
and [o]the wonders that he has done.
5 He established [p]a testimony in [q]Jacob
and appointed a law in [q]Israel,
which he commanded our fathers
to teach to their children,
6 that [r]the next generation might know them,
the children yet unborn,
and arise and tell them to their children,
7 so that they should set their hope in God
and not forget [s]the works of God,
but [t]keep his commandments;
8 and that they should not be [u]like their fathers,
[v]a stubborn and rebellious generation,
a generation [w]whose heart was not steadfast,
whose spirit was not faithful to God.
9 The Ephraimites, armed with[3] the bow,
[x]turned back on the day of battle.
10 They [y]did not keep God's covenant,
but refused to walk according to his law.
11 They [z]forgot his works
and [a]the wonders that he had shown them.
12 In the sight of their fathers [b]he performed wonders
in the land of Egypt, in [c]the fields of Zoan.

15 [x][Ps. 74:2; Ex. 6:6; Deut. 9:29] 16 [y]Ps. 114:3; Ex. 14:21; Josh. 3:15, 16; Hab. 3:10 17 [z][Ps. 68:33] [a]See Ps. 18:14 18 [b]Ps. 104:7 [c]Ps. 97:4 [d]See Ps. 18:7 19 [e]Hab. 3:15 [f]Ps. 36:6 20 [g]Ps. 78:52, 53; 80:1; Ex. 13:21; 14:19; Isai. 63:11, 12
Psalm 78
1 [h] Ps. 50, title [i][Isai. 51:4]; See Ps. 49:1; 50:7 2 [j]Cited Matt. 13:35; See Ps. 49:4 [k][Num. 21:27] 3 [l]See Ps. 44:1 4 [m]Job 15:18 [n][Ex. 12:26, 27; 13:8, 14; Deut. 11:19; Josh. 4:6, 7; Joel 1:3] [o]ver. 11, 32
5 [p]Ps. 19:7; [Ps. 81:5] [q]Ps. 147:19 6 [r]ver. 4; Ps. 102:18 7 [s]Ps. 77:12 [t]Ps. 105:45 8 [u]2 Kin. 17:14; 2 Chr. 30:7; Ezek. 20:18 [v]Ex. 32:9; 33:3; Deut. 9:7, 24; 31:27; Jer. 5:23 [w]ver. 37; Job 11:13 9 [x]ver. 57 10 [y][2 Kin. 17:15] 11 [z]See Ps. 106:13 [a]ver. 4 12 [b]ver. 43; See Ex. 7-12; Ps. 72:18 [c]ver. 43; Num. 13:22; Isai. 19:11, 13; Ezek. 30:14

1 Hebrew *unknown* 2 Probably a musical or liturgical term 3 Hebrew *armed and shooting*

77:15 redeemed your people. The context shows that the psalmist has in mind the deliverance of Israel from Egypt.

77:16 waters. In this poetic remembrance of the Exodus, the waters of the Red Sea are personified. In this way the crossing of the Red Sea is pictured as a battle against the waters of chaos (18:4; 29:3, 10; 46:2, 3 and notes).

77:19 your footprints were unseen. God's action was from above, not controlled by the constraints of earthly conditions.

77:20 You led your people like a flock. The crossing of the Red Sea was a violent conflict; in this verse, the mood is calm as the Shepherd of Israel leads His people through the desert.

78:2 in a parable. The writer means that he will recount the events of the past in a poetic way designed to instruct the hearts of distant generations.

78:3 told us. Instruction was disseminated in his family from generation to generation (Deut. 6:4–9; 32:7).

78:5 testimony . . . law. God established a relationship with His people based on grace alone. In this context He gave them laws to live by and to show their gratefulness to Him. These laws are summarized in the Ten Commandments (Ex. 20; Deut. 5).

78:6 tell them to their children. See note on v. 3.

78:7 keep his commandments. The object of the history lesson is not merely antiquarian, but to deepen the faith and obedience of God's people.

78:9 Ephraimites. This verse should be compared to vv. 67, 68, where the choice of Judah is coupled with the rejection of Ephraim.

78:10 God's covenant. God promised to protect His people if they obeyed the terms of His covenant, but to destroy them if they disobeyed (Deut. 27:9–28:68).

13 He [d]divided the sea and let them
pass through it,
and made the waters [e]stand like a
heap.
14 [f]In the daytime he led them with a
cloud,
and all the night with a fiery light.
15 He [g]split rocks in the wilderness
and gave them drink abundantly as
from the deep.
16 He made streams come out of [h]the
rock
and caused waters to flow down
like rivers.
17 Yet they sinned still more against him,
[i]rebelling against the Most High in
the desert.
18 They [j]tested God in their heart
by demanding the food they
craved.
19 They spoke against God, saying,
[k]"Can God [l]spread a table in the
wilderness?
20 [m]He struck the rock so that water
gushed out
and streams overflowed.
Can he also give bread
or provide meat for his people?"
21 Therefore, when the LORD heard, he
was full of wrath;
[n]a fire was kindled against Jacob;
his anger rose against Israel,
22 because they [o]did not believe in God
and did not trust his saving power.
23 Yet he commanded the skies above
and [p]opened the doors of heaven,
24 and he [q]rained down on them manna
to eat
and gave them [r]the grain of
heaven.
25 Man ate of the bread of [s]the angels;
he sent them food [t]in abundance.
26 He [u]caused the east wind to blow in
the heavens,
and by his power he led out the
south wind;
27 he rained meat on them like [v]dust,
winged birds like [w]the sand of the
seas;
28 he [x]let them fall in the midst of their
camp,
all around their dwellings.
29 And they [y]ate and were well filled,
for he gave them what they [z]craved.
30 But before they had satisfied their
craving,
[a]while the food was still in their
mouths,
31 the anger of God rose against them,
and he killed [b]the strongest of them
and laid low [c]the young men of
Israel.
32 In spite of all this, they [d]still sinned;
[e]despite his wonders, they did not
believe.
33 So he made [f]their days [g]vanish like[1]
a breath,[2]
and their years in terror.
34 When he killed them, they [h]sought
him;
they repented and sought God
earnestly.
35 They remembered that God was their
[i]rock,
the Most High God their
[j]redeemer.
36 But they [k]flattered him with their
mouths;
they [l]lied to him with their tongues.
37 Their [m]heart was not [n]steadfast
toward him;
they were not faithful to his
covenant.

13 [d]Ps. 136:13; Ex. 14:21 [e]Ex. 15:8
14 [f]See Ps. 105:39
15 [g]ver. 20; Ps. 105:41; 114:8; Ex. 17:6; Isai. 48:21
16 [h]Num. 20:8, 10, 11
17 [i]ver. 40, 56; Deut. 9:22; Isai. 63:10
18 [j]ver. 41, 56; Ps. 95:9; 106:14; Deut. 6:16; 1 Cor. 10:9
19 [k][Ex. 16:3; Num. 11:4; 20:3; 21:5] [l]See Ps. 23:5
20 [m]ver. 15, 16
21 [n]Num. 11:1
22 [o]ver. 8, 32, 37
23 [p]Gen. 7:11; [Mal. 3:10]
24 [q]Ex. 16:4 [r]Ps. 105:40; [John 6:31]
25 [s]Ps. 103:20 [t][ver. 29]
26 [u]Num. 11:31
27 [v][Gen. 13:16] [w][Gen. 22:17]
28 [x]Ex. 16:13; Num. 11:31
29 [y]Num. 11:19, 20 [z]Num. 11:4, 34
30 [a]Num. 11:33; [Job 20:23]
31 [b]Isai. 10:16 [c]ver. 63
32 [d]See Num. ch. 14; 16; 17 [e]ver. 22; Num. 14:11
33 [f]Num. 14:29, 35; 26:64, 65 [g]Ps. 39:5
34 [h]Hos. 5:15
35 [i]Deut. 32:4, 15, 31 [j]Ex. 15:13; See Ps. 74:2
36 [k]Isai. 29:13; Ezek. 33:31 [l]Isai. 57:11
37 [m]ver. 8 [n]Ps. 51:10

1 Hebrew *in* 2 Or *vapor*

78:13 He divided the sea. Chief among the great acts of God was the deliverance from Egypt by which God rescued His people from slavery and brought them into their own land. The Red Sea crossing was the greatest demonstration of God's power in the past and, accordingly, was often called to memory by psalmists and prophets.

78:18 tested God. Time and time again Israel grumbled about the food in the wilderness, and God provided for their needs (Ex. 16).

78:20 Can he also give bread. God's provision of water in the wilderness should have led to faith and trust. Instead the Israelites tested the Lord by asking for food (cf. John 6:25–58).

78:21 full of wrath. Rebellion against the Lord led to His judgment (Num. 11:1–3). After judging the people, He returned with His grace (vv. 23–39), but grace led only to further rebellion (vv. 40, 41). This is the story of Israel throughout the Old Testament, perhaps best represented in the Book of Judges (see Judg. 2:6–23). Heb. 12:1–12 reminds us that God chastises those He loves.

78:33 like a breath. This word is the same as found in the opening words of Ecclesiastes: "vanity" (Eccl. 1:2). It describes the world apart from God and under the curse of the Fall. Apart from God we have nothing: only the fear of death and the void.

78:37 faithful to his covenant. See v. 10. God initiated a relationship with Israel through His grace, and then revealed His will to them through His law, including the curses and blessings of the covenant. The people disobeyed the law and brought on themselves God's judgment.

38 Yet he, being [o]compassionate,
[p]atoned for their iniquity
and did not destroy them;
he restrained his anger often
and did not stir up all his wrath.
39 He [q]remembered that they were but
[r]flesh,
[s]a wind that passes and comes not
again.
40 How often they [t]rebelled against him
in the wilderness
and [u]grieved him in [v]the desert!
41 They [w]tested God again and again
and provoked [x]the Holy One of
Israel.
42 They [y]did not remember his power[1]
or the day when he redeemed
them from the foe,
43 [z]when he performed his [a]signs in
Egypt
and his [b]marvels in [c]the fields of
Zoan.
44 He [d]turned their rivers to blood,
so that they could not drink of
their streams.
45 He sent among them swarms of
[e]flies, which devoured them,
and [f]frogs, which destroyed them.
46 He gave their crops to [g]the
destroying locust
and the fruit of their labor to the
locust.
47 He destroyed their vines with [h]hail
and their sycamores with frost.
48 He gave over their [i]cattle to the hail
and their flocks to thunderbolts.
49 He let loose on them his burning
anger,
wrath, indignation, and distress,
a company of [j]destroying angels.
50 He made a path for his anger;
he did not spare them from death,
but gave their lives over to the
plague.

38 [o]Ex. 34:6 [p]Num. 14:20 **39** [q][Ps. 103:14; Job. 10:9] [r]Gen. 6:3 [s]Job 7:7 **40** [t]ver. 17, 56; Ps. 107:11 [u][Eph. 4:30] [v]Ps. 106:14 **41** [w]See ver. 18 [x]See Ps. 71:22 **42** [y]Judg. 8:34 **43** [z]For ver. 43-51, see Ps. 105:27-36 [a]Ex. 7:3; [Ps. 106:22]; Acts 7:36 [b]Ex. 4:21; 11:9, 10 [c]See ver. 12 **44** [d]See Ex. 7:17-24 **45** [e]See Ex. 8:21-24 [f]See Ex. 8:2-14 **46** [g]See Ex. 10:12-15 **47** [h]See Ex. 9:23-25 **48** [i]See Ex. 9:19-21 **49** [j]Ex. 12:13, 23; [2 Sam. 24:16]

51 [k]Ex. 12:29; [Ps. 105:36; 135:8; 136:10] [l]Ps. 105:23, 27; 106:22 **52** [m]See Ps. 77:20 **53** [n][Ex. 14:19, 20] [o][Ex. 14:13] [p]Ex. 14:27, 28; 15:10 **54** [q]Ex. 15:17 [r]Isai. 11:9; 57:13; [Ps. 68:16] [s]Ps. 74:2 **55** [t]See Ps. 44:2 [u]Josh. 23:4; [Ps. 135:12; 136:21, 22; Acts 13:19] **56** [v]ver. 18; Judg. 2:11, 12 [w]ver. 40 **57** [x]Hos. 7:16; [ver. 9]

51 He struck down every [k]firstborn in
Egypt,
the firstfruits of their strength in
the tents of [l]Ham.
52 Then he led out his people [m]like sheep
and guided them in the wilderness
like a flock.
53 [n]He led them in safety, so that they
[o]were not afraid,
but [p]the sea overwhelmed their
enemies.
54 And he brought them to his [q]holy
land,
[r]to the mountain which his right
hand had [s]won.
55 He [t]drove out nations before them;
he [u]apportioned them for a
possession
and settled the tribes of Israel in
their tents.
56 Yet they [v]tested and [w]rebelled against
the Most High God
and did not keep his testimonies,
57 but turned away and acted
treacherously like their fathers;
they twisted like [x]a deceitful bow.
58 For they [y]provoked him to anger
with their [z]high places;
they [a]moved him to jealousy with
their [b]idols.
59 When God heard, he was full of [c]wrath,
and he utterly rejected Israel.
60 He [d]forsook his dwelling at [e]Shiloh,
the tent where he dwelt among
mankind,
61 and delivered his [f]power to captivity,
his [g]glory to the hand of the foe.
62 He [h]gave his people over to the sword
and [i]vented his wrath on his
heritage.

58 [y]Deut. 31:29 [z]Lev. 26:30; Deut. 12:2; 1 Kin. 11:7; 12:31; Ezek. 20:28 [a]Num. 25:11; Deut. 32:16, 21; Judg. 2:12 [b]Deut. 7:5, 25; 12:3 **59** [c]ver. 62; Ps. 106:40; Deut. 3:26 **60** [d]1 Sam. 4:11; Jer. 7:12, 14; 26:6 [e]Josh. 18:1 **61** [f]Ps. 132:8; [Ps. 63:2; 96:6] [g][1 Sam. 4:21] **62** [h][1 Sam. 4:10] [i]ver. 59

1 Hebrew *hand*

78:40 often they rebelled. Examples include Num. 11; 14; 16.

78:44–51 He lists six of the plagues of Egypt.

78:52 like a flock. See Ps. 77:20.

78:54–64 God blessed them with the Promised Land, but they quickly forgot Him.

78:55 He drove out nations. Israel fought, but the faithful knew that it was God, the Divine Warrior, who actually won the victories against the enemies. The story of the defeat of Jericho is a model for the battles of the conquest under Joshua (Josh. 5:13–6:27).

78:56 tested and rebelled against the Most High God. They did not keep His law in the desert, nor did they keep it in the Promised Land. See Judg. 2:10–15.

78:58 with their idols. The height of their rebellion was to worship false gods.

78:60 dwelling at Shiloh. Soon after entering the Promised Land, the tabernacle was set up in Shiloh (Josh. 18:1), twenty miles northeast of Jerusalem, in the tribal territory of Ephraim.

78:61 his power to captivity. During Samuel's youth, God punished Israel and its leaders, particularly Eli's sons, by abandoning Israel in battle and allowing the Philistines to capture the ark (1 Sam. 4; 5).

63 [j] Fire devoured their young men,
and their young women had no
[k] marriage song.
64 Their [l] priests fell by the sword,
and their [m] widows made no
lamentation.
65 Then the Lord [n] awoke as from sleep,
like a strong man shouting because
of wine.
66 And he [o] put his adversaries to rout;
he put them to everlasting shame.

67 He rejected the tent of [p] Joseph;
he did not choose the tribe of
Ephraim,
68 but he chose the tribe of Judah,
Mount Zion, which he [q] loves.
69 He [r] built his sanctuary like the high
heavens,
like the earth, which he has
founded forever.
70 He [s] chose David his servant
and took him from the sheepfolds;
71 from [t] following the nursing ewes he
brought him
to [u] shepherd Jacob his people,
Israel his [v] inheritance.
72 With [w] upright heart he shepherded
them
and [x] guided them with his skillful
hand.

How Long, O Lord?

79 A Psalm of [y] Asaph.
O God, [z] the nations have come
into your [a] inheritance;
they have defiled your [b] holy
temple;
they have [c] laid Jerusalem in ruins.
2 They have given [d] the bodies of your
servants
to the birds of the heavens for
food,
the flesh of your [e] faithful to [f] the
beasts of the earth.
3 They have poured out their blood
like water
all around Jerusalem,
and there was [g] no one to bury
them.
4 We have become [h] a taunt to our
neighbors,
[h] mocked and derided by those
around us.

5 [i] How long, O Lord? Will you be
angry [j] forever?
Will your [k] jealousy [l] burn like
fire?
6 [m] Pour out your anger on the
nations
that [n] do not know you,
and on the kingdoms
that [o] do not call upon your
name!
7 For they have devoured Jacob
and laid waste his
habitation.

8 [p] Do not remember against us [q] our
former iniquities;[1]
let your compassion come
speedily to meet us,
for we are [r] brought very low.
9 [s] Help us, O God of our salvation,
for the glory of your name;
deliver us, and [t] atone for our sins,
for your [u] name's sake!

1 Or *the iniquities of former generations*

63 [j] [Ps. 79:5; 89:46] [k] [Jer. 7:34]
64 [l] 1 Sam. 4:11 [m] Job 27:15
65 [n] Ps. 73:20; See Ps. 35:23
66 [o] [Ps. 40:14]
67 [p] Ps. 80:1; 81:5
68 [q] Ps. 87:2
69 [r] See 1 Kin. 6
70 [s] 1 Sam. 16:12, 13
71 [t] 2 Sam. 7:8 [u] 2 Sam. 5:2; [Ps. 28:9] [v] 1 Sam. 10:1
72 [w] Ps. 101:2; 1 Kin. 9:4 [x] [Ps. 77:20]
Psalm 79 [y] Ps. 50, title
1 [z] Lam. 1:10 [a] Ex. 15:17; See Ps. 74:2 [b] [Ps. 74:7] [c] Jer. 26:18; Mic. 3:12; [2 Kin. 25:9, 10]; 2 Chr. 36:19
2 [d] Deut. 28:26; Jer. 7:33; 16:4; 19:7; 34:20 [e] See Ps. 50:5 [f] Ps. 74:19
3 [g] Jer. 14:16; [2 Kin. 9:10]
4 [h] Dan. 9:16; See Ps. 44:13
5 [i] [Ps. 74:10; 80:4] [j] [Ps. 74:1; 85:5]; See Ps. 13:1 [k] Ps. 78:58 [l] Ps. 78:21; 89:46
6 [m] Cited Jer. 10:25; [Zeph. 3:8] [n] 2 Thess. 1:8 [o] See Ps. 14:4
8 [p] Isai. 64:9 [q] Jer. 11:10 [r] Ps. 116:6; 142:6
9 [s] 2 Chr. 14:11 [t] See Ps. 65:3 [u] Jer. 14:7, 21; See Ps. 23:3

78:65 as from sleep. God had left Israel temporarily and seemed to be asleep. An unusual figure of speech explains how He began to act.

78:67 He rejected. The rejection of the tribe of Ephraim refers to the abandonment of the Shiloh sanctuary, and perhaps also the rejection of Saul's monarchy.

78:68 but he chose the tribe of Judah. Jerusalem succeeded Shiloh as the designated location for the worship of God.

Mount Zion. See note Ps. 2:6.

78:70 sheepfolds. This verse recalls David's humble origins (1 Sam. 16:11–13).

78:72 upright heart. The psalm climaxes on a positive note with a faithful king in Jerusalem, the place of God's special presence.

Ps. 79 The destruction of the temple (v. 1) dates this psalm to the period after the Babylonian defeat of Jerusalem in 586 B.C.

79:1 the nations have come into your inheritance. Because the people disobeyed God's covenant, He did what He had warned them He would do (Deut. 28:15–68), sending a foreign nation against them. Both city and temple were destroyed at this time (2 Kin. 25; 2 Chr. 36:15–23; Lamentations).

79:2 your servants . . . your faithful. The faithful also suffered at the hands of the Babylonians. The psalmist singles out the death of the faithful as he appeals to God for restoration.

79:5 How long, O Lord. This is a prayer to God to change a hard situation.

jealousy. A synonym for anger.

79:6 Pour out your anger on the nations. The poet calls for a reversal, asking God to turn His wrath from Israel to the nations God was using to punish them. In the end the Lord answered the psalmist's prayer, restoring Israel and destroying Babylon.

79:8 former iniquities. This psalm may have been written some time after the destruction of Jerusalem. The chief sin was idolatry, turning to false gods.

10 [v]Why should the nations say,
"Where is their God?"
Let [w]the avenging of the outpoured
blood of your servants
be known among the nations
before our eyes!
11 Let [x]the groans of the prisoners come
before you;
according to your great power,
preserve those [y]doomed to die!
12 Return [z]sevenfold into the [a]lap of our
neighbors
the [b]taunts with which they have
taunted you, O Lord!
13 But we your people, the [c]sheep of
your pasture,
will [d]give thanks to you forever;
from generation to generation we
will recount your praise.

Restore Us, O God

80 To the choirmaster: according to [e]Lilies. A Testimony. Of [f]Asaph, a Psalm.

1 Give ear, O Shepherd of Israel,
you who lead [g]Joseph like
[h]a flock!
You who are [i]enthroned upon the
cherubim, [j]shine forth.
2 Before [k]Ephraim and Benjamin
and Manasseh,
[l]stir up your might
and [m]come to save us!
3 [n]Restore us,[1] O God;
[o]let your face shine, that we may be
saved!
4 O [p]Lord God of hosts,
[q]how long will you be angry with
your people's prayers?
5 You have fed them with [r]the bread of
tears
and given them tears to drink in
full measure.
6 [s]You make us an object of contention
for our [s]neighbors,
and our enemies laugh among
themselves.
7 [n]Restore us, O God of hosts;
let your face shine, that we may be
saved!
8 You brought [t]a vine out of Egypt;
you [u]drove out the nations and
planted it.
9 You [v]cleared the ground for it;
it took deep root and filled the
land.
10 The mountains were covered with its
shade,
the mighty cedars with its
branches.
11 It sent out its branches to [w]the sea
and its shoots to [w]the River.[2]
12 Why then have you [x]broken down its
walls,
so that all who pass along the way
pluck its fruit?
13 [y]The boar from the forest
ravages it,
and all that move in the field feed
on it.
14 Turn again, O God of hosts!
[z]Look down from heaven, and see;
have regard for this vine,
15 the stock that your right hand
planted,
and for the son whom you made
strong for yourself.

10 [v]See Ps. 42:3 [w]See Ps. 94:1
11 [x]Ps. 102:20 [y][1 Sam. 20:31]
12 [z]Gen. 4:15, 24; Lev. 26:21, 28; Prov. 6:31 [a]Ps. 35:13; Isai. 65:6, 7; Jer. 32:18 [b]See Ps. 74:10
13 [c]See Ps. 74:1 [d]Isai. 43:21
Psalm 80 [e]Ps. 60, title [f]Ps. 50, title
1 [g]Ps. 78:67; 81:5 [h][Ps. 95:7]; See Ps. 77:20 [i]Ps. 99:1; Ex. 25:22; 1 Sam. 4:4; 2 Sam. 6:2 [j]See Ps. 50:2
2 [k]See Num. 2:18-24 [l]See Ps. 35:23 [m][Ps. 118:14, 21]
3 [n]ver. 19; Ps. 60:1; 85:4; Lam. 5:21 [o]Num. 6:25; See Ps. 4:6
4 [p]See Ps. 59:5 [q][Ps. 74:10; 79:5]
5 [r]Ps. 42:3; 102:9; [1 Kin. 22:27; Isai. 30:20]
6 [s]See Ps. 44:13
7 [n][See ver. 3 above]
8 [t]Isai. 5:1; 27:2; Jer. 2:21; 12:10; Ezek. 17:6; Matt. 21:33; Mark 12:1; Luke 20:9 [u]See Ps. 44:2
9 [v][Josh. 24:12]
11 [w]See Ps. 72:8
12 [x]Ps. 89:40; Isai. 5:5
13 [y][Jer. 5:6]
14 [z][Isai. 63:15]

[1] Or *Turn us again*; also verses 7, 19 [2] That is, the Euphrates

79:11 the prisoners. The writer knows that God has a special place in His heart for the oppressed and vulnerable, so he reminds Him of those who need Him (9:18 note).

80:1 O Shepherd. God is Israel's Shepherd (Ps. 23) because He guides them and provides for them (77:20; 78:52, 71, 72; 79:13). In the ancient Near East, "shepherd" is not an unusual title for kings.

upon the cherubim. Above the ark of the covenant, in the Most Holy Place of the temple, the wings of the cherubim stretched out over God's throne (Ex. 25:22; Num. 7:89).

shine forth. Note the allusion to the priestly benediction in Num. 6:24–26. The psalmist is calling upon God to reveal His gracious presence to them.

80:2 Ephraim and Benjamin and Manasseh. The mention of these chief tribes of the northern kingdom may indicate that the psalm was composed in the last days of that kingdom.

80:5 bread of tears. Their mourning is so continuous that it is like their daily food and drink.

80:8 vine. Israel is the vine God transplanted from slavery in Egypt to the fruitful soil of Palestine (Is. 5:1–7; John 15:1, 2).

80:10 covered with its shade. The lowly vine became so great through the blessing of God that the mountains and the giant cedars were covered with its shadow (Luke 13:19).

80:11 sea . . . River. See text note. The language is reminiscent of the promises made to Abraham.

80:12 Why then have you. The psalmist knows that no matter what human army actually defeated Israel, God had allowed it. God seemed to be turning His back on the people He had created.

16 They have [a]burned it with fire; they
have [a]cut it down;
may they perish at [b]the rebuke of
your face!
17 But [c]let your hand be on the man of
your right hand,
the son of man whom you have
made strong for yourself!
18 Then we shall not turn back from you;
[d]give us life, and we will call upon
your name!
19 [e]Restore us, O LORD God of hosts!
let your face shine, that we may be
saved!

Oh, That My People Would Listen to Me

81 TO THE CHOIRMASTER: ACCORDING TO [f]THE GITTITH.[1] OF [g]ASAPH.

1 [h]Sing aloud to God our strength;
[i]shout for joy to the God of Jacob!
2 Raise a song; sound [j]the
tambourine,
[k]the sweet lyre with [k]the harp.
3 Blow the trumpet at [l]the new moon,
at the full moon, on our
feast day.
4 For it is a statute for Israel,
a rule of the God of Jacob.
5 He made it [m]a decree in [n]Joseph
when he [o]went out over[2] the land
of Egypt.
[p]I hear a language [q]I had not known:
6 "I [r]relieved your[3] shoulder of [s]the
burden;
your hands were freed from the
basket.
7 In distress you [t]called, and I
delivered you;
I [u]answered you in the secret place
of thunder;
I [v]tested you at the waters of
Meribah. *Selah*
8 [w]Hear, O my people, while I
admonish you!
O Israel, if you would but listen
to me!
9 There shall be no [x]strange god
among you;
you shall not bow down to a
[y]foreign god.
10 [z]I am the LORD your God,
who brought you up out of the
land of Egypt.
[a]Open your mouth wide, and I will
fill it.
11 "But my people did not listen to my
voice;
Israel [b]would not submit to me.
12 So I [c]gave them over to their
[d]stubborn hearts,
to follow their own [e]counsels.
13 [f]Oh, that my people would listen
to me,
that Israel would [g]walk in my
ways!
14 I would soon subdue their enemies
and [h]turn my hand against their
foes.
15 Those who hate the LORD would
[i]cringe toward him,
and their fate would last forever.

1 Probably a musical or liturgical term 2 Or *against* 3 Hebrew *his*; also next line

16[a]Isai. 33:12 [b]Ps. 76:6; [Ps. 39:11]
17[c]Ps. 89:21
18[d]See Ps. 71:20
19[e]ver. 3, 7
Psalm 81 [f]Ps. 8, title; 84, title [g]Ps. 50, title
1[h][Deut. 32:43] [i]See Ps. 66:1
2[j]Ex. 15:20 [k]Ps. 71:22
3[l]Lev. 23:24; Num. 10:10; 29:1
5[m]Ps. 122:4; [Ps. 78:5] [n]Ps. 77:15; 78:67; 80:1 [o]Ex. 11:4 [p]Ps. 114:1 [q][Deut. 28:49; Jer. 5:15]
6[r]Isai. 9:4; 10:27 [s]Ex. 1:11
7[t]Ps. 50:15; [Ex. 2:23; 14:10] [u]Ex. 19:19; See Ps. 18:11-14 [v]Ex. 17:7; Num. 20:13
8[w]See Ps. 50:7
9[x]Ps. 44:20; Isai. 43:12; [Ex. 20:3] [y]Deut. 32:12
10[z]Ex. 20:2 [a][Ps. 37:3, 4]
11[b]Ex. 32:1; Deut. 32:15, 18; Prov. 1:25, 30
12[c]Job 8:4; [Acts 7:42; 14:16; Rom. 1:24, 26] [d][Deut. 29:19] [e]Ps. 106:43; Jer. 7:24; Mic. 6:16
13[f]Deut. 5:29; 32:29; Isai. 48:18 [g]Deut. 5:33
14[h]Amos 1:8
15[i]Ps. 18:44

80:17 the son of man. Though the reference might be to Israel, it is more likely to the Davidic king, and ultimately to the Messiah.

Ps. 81 This psalm begins like a hymn, but most of it is a divine pronouncement in which God reminds Israel of the Exodus and the nation's subsequent apostasy. The original setting of the psalm was clearly the Feast of Booths (v. 3).

81:2 Raise a song. The psalms teach us by example to worship with exuberance.

81:3 new moon. The Bible occasionally mentions a special celebration that took place at the time of the new moon (1 Sam. 20:5, 18; 2 Kin. 4:23; Is. 66:23; Ezek. 46:1, 6; Amos 8:5). Frequently, the New Moon festival is mentioned along with regular Sabbath observance; see also Col. 2:16, 17.

81:5 a language I had not known. The language may be Egyptian. Another translation is "a voice we did not know," to refer to the verses following.

81:6 I relieved . . . the burden. With specific language God reminds Israel of their slavery in Egypt.

81:7 secret place of thunder. This may refer to God's appearance at Mount Sinai (Ex. 19:16–25), although thunder and lightning were frequent signs of His presence.

Meribah. See Ex. 17:1–7; Num. 20:1–13.

81:9 you shall not bow down to a foreign god. The warning implies that Israel was not observing this basic commandment (Ex. 20:3).

81:10 I am the LORD your God. Strongly reminiscent of the preamble to the Ten Commandments (Ex. 20:2). The relationship of grace came before revelation of the law.

I will fill it. Much of Israel's history, as recorded in Joshua through Chronicles, is the story of God's people looking for satisfaction without God. If they were worried about rain, they turned to Baal (1 Kin. 18). If they were worried about enemies, they wanted a strong king (1 Sam. 8). They kept forgetting they had a God who could and would fulfill all their needs easily.

81:12 I gave them over. See Rom. 1:24.

81:13 Oh, that my people. God's compassion for Israel is clearly seen in this verse.

16 But he would feed you[1] with [j]the
finest of the wheat,
and with [k]honey from the rock I
would satisfy you."

Rescue the Weak and Needy

82 A PSALM OF [l]ASAPH.
[m]God [n]has taken his place in
[o]the divine council;
in the midst of [p]the gods he [q]holds
judgment:
2 "How long will you judge unjustly
and [r]show partiality to [s]the
wicked? *Selah*
3 [t]Give justice to [u]the weak and the
fatherless;
[v]maintain the right of the afflicted
and the destitute.
4 [w]Rescue the weak and the needy;
[x]deliver them from the hand of the
wicked."

5 [y]They have neither knowledge nor
understanding,
[z]they walk about in darkness;
[a]all the foundations of the earth are
[b]shaken.

6 [c]I said, "You are gods,
sons of the Most High, all of you;
7 nevertheless, like men [d]you shall die,
and fall like any prince."[2]
8 [e]Arise, O God, judge the earth;
for you shall [f]inherit all the nations!

O God, Do Not Keep Silence

83 A SONG. A PSALM OF [g]ASAPH.
O God, do not keep silence;
[h]do not hold your peace or be still,
O God!

2 For behold, your enemies [i]make an
uproar;
those who hate you have [j]raised
their heads.
3 They lay [k]crafty plans against your
people;
they consult together against your
[l]treasured ones.
4 They say, "Come, [m]let us wipe them
out as a nation;
let the name of Israel be
remembered no more!"
5 For they conspire with one accord;
against you they make a
covenant—
6 the tents of [n]Edom and [o]the
Ishmaelites,
[p]Moab and [q]the Hagrites,
7 [r]Gebal and [p]Ammon and [s]Amalek,
[t]Philistia with the inhabitants of
[u]Tyre;
8 [v]Asshur also has joined them;
they are the strong arm of [w]the
children of Lot. *Selah*

9 Do to them as you did to [x]Midian,
as to [y]Sisera and Jabin at [z]the river
Kishon,
10 who were destroyed at [a]En-dor,
who became [b]dung for the
ground.
11 Make their nobles like [c]Oreb and
Zeeb,
all their princes like [d]Zebah and
Zalmunna,

16 [j]Ps. 147:14; Deut. 32:14 [k]Deut. 32:13; [Job 29:6; Ezek. 16:19] **Psalm 82** [l]See Ps. 50, title **1** [m][2 Chr. 19:5, 6; Eccles. 5:8] [n]Isai. 3:13 [o][Josh. 22:16, 17] [p][1 Sam. 28:13] [q]See Ps. 58:11 **2** [r]Deut. 1:17 [s]Prov. 18:5 **3** [t]Ps. 10:18 [u]Ps. 41:1 [v]Jer. 22:3 **4** [w]Job 29:12 [x]Prov. 24:11 **5** [y][Mic. 3:1]; See Ps. 14:4 [z]Prov. 2:13 [a]See Ps. 11:3 [b]Ps. 10:6 **6** [c]ver. 1; Cited John 10:34 **7** [d]Ps. 49:12; Job 21:32; Ezek. 31:14; See Ezek. 28:2-10 **8** [e]See Ps. 12:5 [f]Ps. 2:8; [Rev. 11:15] **Psalm 83** [g]See Ps. 50, title **1** [h]See Ps. 28:1

2 [i][Ps. 2:1] [j]Judg. 8:28 **3** [k][Neh. 4:8] [l]See Ps. 27:5; 31:20 **4** [m]Jer. 48:2; [Ps. 74:8; Esth. 3:6] **6** [n]Ps. 137:7; See 2 Chr. 20:10 [o]See Gen. 25:12-16 [p]2 Chr. 20:10 [q]1 Chr. 5:10

7 [r]Josh. 13:5 [p][See ver. 6 above] [s]1 Sam. 15:2 [t]1 Sam. 4:1; [Amos 1:6] [u]Ezek. 27:3; [Amos 1:9] **8** [v]2 Kin. 15:19 [w]Deut. 2:9, 19 **9** [x]Num. 31:7; See Isai. 9:4 [y]Judg. 4:15, 24 [z]Judg. 4:7; 5:21 **10** [a]Josh. 17:11; 1 Sam. 28:7 [b]See Job 20:7 **11** [c]Judg. 7:25; 8:3 [d]See Judg. 8:5-21

[1] That is, Israel; Hebrew *him* [2] Or *fall as one man, O princes*

Ps. 82 This short psalm presents some difficult problems. Chief among them is the "gods" mentioned in vv. 1 and 6. A number of scholars take this as a reference to angelic powers, lesser spiritual beings who make up God's heavenly council. A second interpretation understands "gods" literally, as deities made subordinate to Yahweh. The most probable interpretation is that the "gods" are human judges. The Hebrew word *'elohim* ("gods") is used of human judges in Ex. 21:6; 22:8, 9. Within Ps. 82, the human nature of these "gods" is indicated by vv. 6, 7. A rough paraphrase would be, "As judges, people may call you 'lord,' but you are as mortal as anyone else."

82:1 the divine council. The exact scope of this congregation is unclear. It may be the heavenly assembly (including only spiritual powers), or it may include earthly kings.

82:3 the weak. See Ps. 9:18 note.

82:8 judge the earth. Since the human judges were failing to reflect His justice, God Himself would have to do it.

Ps. 83 The psalm is a model prayer for the Christian's spiritual warfare. Instead of calling upon the Lord to destroy our flesh-and-blood enemies, we call upon Him to vanquish the spiritual forces of evil.

83:1 do not keep silence; do not hold your peace. The heart of the covenant is the promise that God will be present with His people. To the psalmist's eyes God is absent from His people if they are defeated before the enemy.

83:5 they. The nations involved in the plot against Israel are listed in vv. 6–8. Attempts have been made to identify the historical situation behind the psalm, but no time period is known in which all of these enemies were actively hostile toward Israel at the same time. The closest is Jehoshaphat's war recorded in 2 Chr. 20, but there is no mention of Assyria there.

83:8 children. That is, Moab and Ammon (Gen. 19:30–38).

83:9 Midian. God enabled Gideon to destroy the Midianites (Judg. 7).

Sisera . . . Jabin. Jabin was a king of Canaan and Sisera was his general early in the period of the judges. God delivered the Israelites from them through the work of Deborah (Judg. 4; 5).

83:11 Oreb . . . Zeeb. Two leaders who were destroyed by Ephraimites during Gideon's battle against the Midianites (Judg. 7:25–8:3).

Zebah and Zalmunna. Midianite kings who were captured and executed by Gideon (Judg. 8:4–21).

12 who said, [e]"Let us take possession
for ourselves
of the pastures of God."
13 O my God, make them like [f]whirling
dust,[1]
like [g]chaff before the wind.
14 As [h]fire consumes the forest,
as the flame [i]sets the mountains
ablaze,
15 so may you pursue them [j]with your
tempest
and terrify them with your
hurricane!
16 [k]Fill their faces with shame,
that they may seek your name,
O LORD.
17 Let them be [l]put to shame and
dismayed forever;
let them perish in disgrace,
18 that they may [m]know that you alone,
[n]whose name is the LORD,
are [o]the Most High over all the earth.

12[e][2 Chr. 20:11]
13[f]Isai. 17:13 [g]Job 13:25; 21:18; [Ps. 1:4]
14[h][Isai. 9:18]; See Isai. 10:16-19 [i]Deut. 32:22
15[j]Job 9:17
16[k][Ps. 35:4, 26; Job 10:15]
17[l]Ps. 35:4
18[m]Ps. 59:13 [n]Ex. 6:3 [o]Ps. 9:2; 18:13; 97:9

My Soul Longs for the Courts of the LORD

84

TO THE CHOIRMASTER: ACCORDING TO [p]THE GITTITH.[2] A PSALM OF [q]THE SONS OF KORAH.

1 How [r]lovely is your [s]dwelling place,
O LORD of hosts!
2 My soul [t]longs, yes, [u]faints
for the courts of the LORD;
my heart and flesh sing for joy
to [v]the living God.
3 Even the sparrow finds a home,
and the swallow a nest for herself,
where she may lay her young,
at your altars, O LORD of hosts,
[w]my King and my God.
4 [x]Blessed are those who dwell in your
house,
ever [y]singing your praise! *Selah*
5 Blessed are those whose strength is
in you,
[z]in whose heart are the highways to
Zion.[3]
6 As they go through the Valley of Baca
they make it a place of springs;
[a]the early rain also covers it with
[b]pools.
7 They go [c]from strength to strength;
each one [d]appears before God in
Zion.
8 O [e]LORD God of hosts, hear my
prayer;
give ear, O God of Jacob! *Selah*
9 [f]Behold our [g]shield, O God;
look on the face of your anointed!
10 For a day [h]in your courts is better
than a thousand elsewhere.
I would rather be [i]a doorkeeper in
the house of my God
than dwell in the tents of
wickedness.

Psalm 84 [p]Ps. 8, title; 81, title [q]Ps. 42, title
1[r][Ps. 27:4] [s]Ps. 43:3; 132:5
2[t][Ps. 42:1, 2; 63:1] [u][Ps. 73:26; 119:81; 143:6; Job 19:27] [v]See Ps. 42:2
3[w]Ps. 5:2
4[x]See Ps. 65:4 [y]Ps. 42:5, 11; 43:5
5[z][Ps. 122:1]
6[a]Joel 2:23 [b]Ezek. 34:26
7[c]Prov. 4:18; Isai. 40:31; [John 1:16; 2 Cor. 3:18] [d]See Ps. 42:2
8[e]See Ps. 59:5
9[f]Ps. 80:14 [g]See Ps. 3:3
10[h]ver. 2 [i]1 Chr. 26:19

1 Or *like a tumbleweed* 2 Probably a musical or liturgical term
3 Hebrew lacks *to Zion*

83:12 the pastures of God. The land of Israel, where the Shepherd-God settled His sheep, the people of Israel. The quote is ascribed to Israel's enemies in order to highlight the blasphemous nature of their plots against Israel.

83:15 your tempest . . . your hurricane. God's wrath is often compared to a violent storm (Ps. 18:7–15; Nah. 1:3).

83:16 seek your name. The psalm supplies a redemptive reason behind the judgment. As God judges the wickedness of the attackers, they will see their folly and turn to Him.

83:18 Most High. The Hebrew words used sound similar to the most common title of the Canaanite god Baal. The poet is asking God to judge the nations so that they will see that Yahweh, not Baal, is the only God.

Ps. 84 This psalm expresses the author's deep longing for the presence of God. While Christians do not have to travel to a special location to enjoy God's presence (John 4:21–24), the psalm gives voice to the yearning and happiness experienced in Christ's nearness.

84:1 your dwelling place. The temple, the place which God chose to reveal His presence to the people (Deut. 12; 1 Kin. 8).

84:2 living God. The true object of the psalmist's devotion is not the temple building itself, but the God who revealed Himself there. Israel was often tempted to forget God and rely on the external trappings of religion (Jer. 7).

84:3 sparrow . . . swallow. Note the playful envy expressed by the psalmist. He is jealous of the birds who are able to build their homes near the altar. In this way he expresses his deepest longings to be as close as possible to God.

84:4 Blessed. See note Ps. 1:1.

your house. The temple, being the place of God's appointment on earth, is like heaven on earth. From a New Testament perspective, this verse gives a glimpse of the unending happiness of heaven.

84:5 Blessed. See note Ps. 1:1.

whose strength is in you. Their vitality in life is found in God's power, not in their own.

the highways. People living outside of Jerusalem made special trips to the temple to enjoy God's presence in worship. The Songs of Ascents (120–134) were probably used during these journeys (120:title).

84:6 Valley of Baca. The name of a valley otherwise unknown. There is a similar sounding Hebrew verb meaning "to weep." Others identify the noun as a certain kind of tree that flourishes in dry places, like the balsam or aspen. The context indicates that the valley is arid but transformed by the presence of the joyful pilgrims.

84:7 in Zion. The location of the temple, the ultimate goal of their pilgrimage. See notes Ps. 2:6; 50:2; 74:2; 137:1.

84:9 our shield . . . your anointed. The king is not only the political leader of Israel, but also the reflection of God's kingship on earth.

11 For the LORD God is [j]a sun and
[g]shield;
the LORD bestows favor and
honor.
[k]No good thing does he withhold
from those who [l]walk uprightly.
12 O LORD of hosts,
[m]blessed is the one who trusts in
you!

Revive Us Again

85 TO THE CHOIRMASTER. A PSALM OF [n]THE SONS OF KORAH.

1 LORD, you were [o]favorable to your
land;
you [p]restored the fortunes of
Jacob.
2 You [q]forgave the iniquity of your
people;
you [q]covered all their sin. *Selah*
3 You withdrew all your wrath;
you [r]turned from your hot
anger.
4 [s]Restore us again, O God of our
salvation,
and put away your indignation
toward us!
5 [t]Will you be angry with us forever?
Will you prolong your anger to all
generations?
6 Will you not [u]revive us again,
that your people may [v]rejoice in
you?
7 Show us your steadfast love,
O LORD,
and grant us your salvation.
8 [w]Let me hear what God the LORD will
speak,
for he will [x]speak peace to his
people, to his [y]saints;
but let them not [z]turn back to
[a]folly.
9 Surely his [b]salvation is near to those
who fear him,
that [c]glory may dwell in
our land.
10 [d]Steadfast love and faithfulness meet;
[e]righteousness and peace kiss each
other.
11 Faithfulness springs up from the
ground,
and righteousness looks down
from the sky.
12 Yes, [f]the LORD will give what is good,
and our land [g]will yield its
increase.
13 [h]Righteousness will go before him
and make his footsteps a way.

Great Is Your Steadfast Love

86 [i]A PRAYER OF DAVID.

[j]Incline your ear, O LORD,
and answer me,
for I am [k]poor and needy.
2 Preserve my life, for I am [l]godly;
save your servant, who [m]trusts in
you—you are my God.
3 [n]Be gracious to me, O Lord,
for to you do I cry all the day.
4 Gladden the soul of your
servant,
for [o]to you, O Lord, do I lift up
my soul.

11 [j]Isai. 60:19, 20; See Ps. 27:1; Mal. 4:2; Rev. 21:23 [g][See ver. 9 above] [k]Ps. 85:12; [Ps. 34:9, 10; Matt. 6:33; 7:11] [l]Ps. 15:2; Prov. 2:7
12 [m]See Ps. 2:12
Psalm 85 [n]Ps. 42, title
1 [o]Ps. 77:7 [p]Ps. 14:7
2 [q]Ps. 32:1
3 [r]Ps. 78:38; 106:23; Ex. 32:12; Deut. 13:17; Jonah 3:9
4 [s]See Ps. 80:3
5 [t][Ps. 79:5]
6 [u]Ps. 71:20 [v]Ps. 90:14; 149:2
8 [w][Hab. 2:1] [x]Zech. 9:10; [Hag. 2:9] [y]See Ps. 50:5 [z][2 Pet. 2:21] [a][Ps. 49:13]
9 [b]Isai. 46:13 [c]Zech. 2:5; [John 1:14]
10 [d]Ps. 89:14; See Ps. 40:11 [e][Isai. 45:8]; See Ps. 72:3
12 [f]Ps. 84:11; [James 1:17] [g]See Ps. 67:6
13 [h]Ps. 89:14; Isai. 58:8
Psalm 86 [i][Ps. 72:20]
1 [j]See Ps. 31:2 [k]Ps. 40:17
2 [l]See Ps. 50:5 [m]See Ps. 11:1
3 [n]ver. 16; Ps. 56:1; 57:1; See Ps. 4:1
4 [o]See Ps. 25:1

84:11 sun. The metaphor comparing God to the sun praises Him as the source of light and energy. The burning rays of the sun in the dry country east of the Mediterranean make it a suitable portrayal of God's power.

No good thing does he withhold. See Rom. 8:28–39, especially v. 32.

85:1 favorable to your land. A number of occasions in biblical history are illustrative for the psalm. Perhaps most appropriate, though the psalm could have already been in existence for many years, was Judah's return from Babylonian captivity in the sixth century B.C.

85:2 forgave the iniquity. The people's misfortunes came from their sin before God. Forgiveness of sins means that God's wrath will be stilled. The necessary repentance is also the gift of God's grace.

85:8 me. The community has been speaking as a unit up to this point ("us"), but now an individual steps forward. Whoever he is (priest or prophet), he speaks on behalf of God.

he will speak peace. The word for "peace" (Hebrew *shalom*) indicates health and wholeness, and like "steadfast love," (v. 7) is a word intimately associated with the covenant. God promises the restoration of intimate relationship with His people.

his saints. This word is formed from the same root as "steadfast love" (v. 7), and denotes those who are the objects of God's covenant love.

85:10 meet . . . kiss each other. This verse has long been interpreted to refer to the reconciliation that Jesus Christ effected between God's justice, that cannot tolerate sin, and His mercy, that does not rejoice in the death of the wicked (Ezek. 33:11; 2 Pet. 3:9). Justice and mercy came together in the cross of Christ. See "God Is Light: Divine Holiness and Justice" at Lev. 11:44.

85:11 up from the ground . . . down from the sky. The future restored relationship with God will join God's blessing from heaven with the faithfulness of His people on earth.

85:12 yield its increase. Fertility of land in an arid climate is an indication of God's care and love for His people.

85:13 Righteousness will go before him. This attribute of God is personified as a herald who proclaims God's way before Him (cf. Ps. 23:6).

86:title PRAYER. See introduction to Ps. 17.

86:2 who trusts in you. The psalmist recognizes his own inability, but he knows where true strength lies.

86:3 Be gracious to me. The poet knows that God's answer to his prayer is a manifestation of His unmerited grace. God owes him nothing.

5 For you, O Lord, are good and
[p]forgiving,
[q]abounding in steadfast love to all
who call upon you.
6 [r]Give ear, O LORD, to my prayer;
listen to my plea for grace.
7 In [s]the day of my trouble I call upon
you,
[t]for you answer me.

8 There is [u]none like you among the
gods, O Lord,
[v]nor are there any works like yours.
9 [w]All the nations you have made shall
come
and worship before you, O Lord,
and shall glorify your name.
10 For [x]you are great and [y]do wondrous
things;
[z]you alone are God.
11 [a]Teach me your way, O LORD,
that I may [b]walk in your truth;
[c]unite my heart to fear your name.
12 I give thanks to you, O Lord my
God, with my whole heart,
and I will glorify your name forever.
13 [d]For great is your steadfast love
toward me;
you have [e]delivered my soul from
the depths of Sheol.

14 O God, insolent men have [f]risen up
against me;
a band of ruthless men seek my life,
and they do not set you before them.

5[p]Ps. 130:4 [q]ver. 15; Ps. 103:8; 145:8, 9; Ex. 34:6; Joel 2:13
6[r]Ps. 55:1, 2
7[s]See Ps. 77:2 [t]Ps. 17:6
8[u][Ps. 89:6; Ex. 15:11] [v]Deut. 3:24
9[w]Ps. 66:4; [Ps. 22:31; 65:2; Isai. 66:23; Zech. 14:18; Rev. 15:4]
10[x]Ps. 77:13 [y]See Ps. 72:18 [z]Deut. 6:4; Isai. 37:16; 44:6, 8; 1 Cor. 8:4, 6
11[a]See Ps. 25:4 [b]Ps. 26:3 [c][Jer. 32:39]
13[d][ver. 5] [e]Ps. 30:3; [Ps. 88:6; Ezek. 26:20]
14[f]Ps. 54:3
15[g]ver. 5; Ps. 111:4; 112:4; Num. 14:18; Neh. 9:17; Jonah 4:2; See Ps. 62:12
16[h]See Ps. 25:16 [i]See Ps. 116:16
17[j][Judg. 6:17] [k]Neh. 5:19; 13:31
Psalm 87 [l]Ps. 42, title
1[m]See Ps. 48:1 [n]Isai. 28:16
2[o]Ps. 78:67, 68

15 But you, O Lord, are a God [g]merciful
and gracious,
slow to anger and abounding in
steadfast love and faithfulness.
16 [h]Turn to me and be gracious to me;
give your strength to [i]your servant,
and save [i]the son of your
maidservant.
17 [j]Show me a sign of your [k]favor,
that those who hate me may see
and be put to shame
because you, LORD, have helped
me and comforted me.

Glorious Things of You Are Spoken

87 A PSALM OF [l]THE SONS OF KORAH.
A SONG.

1 On [m]the holy mount [n]stands the
city he founded;
2 the LORD [o]loves the gates of Zion
more than all the dwelling places
of Jacob.
3 [p]Glorious things of you are spoken,
O [q]city of God. *Selah*
4 Among those who [r]know me I
mention [s]Rahab and Babylon;
behold, Philistia and Tyre, with
[t]Cush[1]—
"This one was born there," they say.

3[p][Isai. 60:1]; See Isai. 54:1-3 [q]Ps. 46:4 4[r]Ps. 36:10; [John 10:14] [s]See Job 9:13; See Isai. 19:22-25 [t]See Ps. 68:31

1 Probably *Nubia*

86:5 steadfast love. The special love of God toward those in covenant with Him.

to all who call upon you. God does not forgive all people indiscriminately; He waits until they turn to Him with prayers of repentance.

86:8 There is none like you. The psalmist sees that no god of the surrounding nations can be compared with the Lord in what He is or what He does. This confession of God's uniqueness is not a tacit admission that other gods exist (see v. 10). The psalmist is comparing the foreigners' vain imaginations with the reality of Yahweh.

86:9 All the nations you have made. Yahweh is the God of all the nations, even though they may not recognize Him. God gives them their existence and whatever blessings they have.

86:11 unite my heart. Such a united heart is one totally set on God.

86:13 steadfast love. The lovingkindness freely offered and promised in the gospel.

Ps. 87 The object of this psalm is to glorify Jerusalem, or Zion, the seat of God's special presence; see Ps. 46; 48; 76. The unique contribution of Ps. 87 is to give a glimpse of the universal character of God's worship. Its universalistic language brings to mind the future day when the Gentiles should be "fellow heirs" in the gospel (Eph. 3:6).

87:1 holy mount. God is omnipresent: He is everywhere. Nevertheless, God met His people in an intimate and special way at Zion. See notes Ps. 2:6; 29:6; 46:2.

he founded. This refers to the building of the temple on Mount Zion, north of the city of David and towering over it.

87:2 loves . . . more than. The point is not that God hated other parts of Israel, but that He blessed Jerusalem with His presence. After the temple was built, there was only one designated place for the official worship of God—at Jerusalem (Deut. 12).

87:3 of you are spoken. Referring to the divine pronouncement to follow in the next few verses.

87:4 those who know me. There were occasional foreigners, like Rahab and Naaman, who worshiped the Lord during the Old Testament period (cf. Ex. 12:38). This amazing verse looks forward to whole foreign nations bowing down to God.

mention. This formal introduction to the divine pronouncement uses the idea of the "book of the living" (Ps. 69:28; cf. Ex. 32:32; Ps. 139:16; Is. 4:3; Rev. 21:24–27).

Rahab and Babylon. Rahab is a name for Egypt (Is. 30:7). Egypt and Babylon were the two superpowers who continually fought against Israel.

Philistia. Israel's traditional enemy on the Mediterranean coast west of Judah.

Tyre. An affluent sea power north of Israel.

Cush. Biblical Cush is the remote region south of Egypt, including parts of modern Eritrea, Ethiopia, and Sudan.

5 And of Zion it shall be said,
"This one and that one were born
in her";
for the Most High himself will
[u]establish her.
6 The LORD records as he [v]registers the
peoples,
"This one was born there." *Selah*
7 [w]Singers and [x]dancers alike say,
"All my [y]springs are in you."

I Cry Out Day and Night Before You

88 A SONG. A PSALM OF [z]THE SONS OF KORAH. TO THE CHOIRMASTER: ACCORDING TO [a]MAHALATH LEANNOTH. A MASKIL[1] OF [b]HEMAN THE EZRAHITE.

1 O LORD, [c]God of my salvation;
I [d]cry out day and night before
you.
2 Let my prayer come before you;
[e]incline your ear to my cry!
3 For my soul is full of troubles,
and [f]my life draws near to [g]Sheol.
4 I am counted among those who [h]go
down to the pit;
I am a man who has no strength,
5 like one set loose among the dead,
like the slain that lie in the grave,
like those whom [i]you remember no
more,
for they are [j]cut off from your
hand.
6 You have put me in [k]the depths of
the pit,
in the [l]regions dark and [m]deep.
7 Your wrath [n]lies heavy upon me,
and you overwhelm me with [o]all
your waves. *Selah*
8 You have caused [p]my companions to
shun me;
you have made me [q]a horror[2] to
them.
I am [r]shut in so that I cannot escape;
9 [s]my eye grows dim through sorrow.
Every day I call upon you, O LORD;
I [t]spread out my hands to you.
10 Do you work wonders for the dead?
[u]Do the departed rise up to praise
you? *Selah*
11 Is your steadfast love declared in the
grave,
or your faithfulness in Abaddon?
12 Are your [v]wonders known in [w]the
darkness,
or your righteousness in the land
of [x]forgetfulness?
13 But I, O LORD, cry [y]to you;
[z]in the morning my prayer comes
before you.
14 O LORD, why [a]do you cast my soul
away?
Why [b]do you hide your face
from me?
15 Afflicted and close to death from my
youth up,
I suffer your terrors; I am
helpless.[3]
16 Your wrath has swept over me;
your [c]dreadful assaults destroy me.
17 They [d]surround me like a flood [e]all
day long;
they [f]close in on me together.
18 You have caused [g]my beloved and
my friend to shun me;
my companions have become
darkness.[4]

5 [u]Ps. 48:8
6 [v]See Ps. 69:28
7 [w]Ps. 68:25 [x]2 Sam. 6:14 [y]Ps. 36:9; Isai. 12:3; Rev. 21:6
Psalm 88 [z]Ps. 42, title [a]Ps. 53, title [b]1 Kin. 4:31; 1 Chr. 2:6
1 [c]See Ps. 24:5 [d]Ps. 22:2; Luke 18:7
2 [e]See Ps. 31:2
3 [f][Ps. 107:18] [g]See Ps. 16:10
4 [h]See Ps. 28:1
5 [i][Ps. 31:12] [j]Isai. 53:8
6 [k][Ps. 63:9] [l]ver. 12, 18; Ps. 143:3; Lam. 3:6 [m]Ps. 69:15
7 [n][Ps. 32:4] [o]Ps. 42:7
8 [p]ver. 18; Ps. 142:4; See Job 19:13 [q]Job 30:10 [r]Jer. 32:2
9 [s][Ps. 6:7] [t]See Job 11:13
10 [u][Ps. 6:5]
12 [v]Ps. 89:5 [w]ver. 6; Job 10:21 [x][Eccles. 9:5]
13 [y]Ps. 30:2 [z]See Ps. 5:3
14 [a]See Ps. 44:9 [b]See Job 13:24
16 [c]Job 6:4; 9:34
17 [d]See Ps. 118:10-12 [e]Ps. 86:3 [f]Ps. 18:4; 22:16; [Ps. 118:10]
18 [g]See Job 19:13, 14

[1] Probably musical or liturgical terms [2] Or *an abomination* [3] The meaning of the Hebrew word is uncertain [4] Or *darkness has become my only companion*

87:5 were born in her. The verse refers metaphorically to a spiritual birth in Zion. Zion is mother to the spiritual birth of peoples from all over the world.

87:6 registers the peoples. See v. 4, note on "mention" ("book of the living.")

87:7 my springs. Physical thirst stands for spiritual thirst (Ps. 42:1, 2), that can only be satisfied in Jerusalem, God's chosen place.

Ps. 88 This psalm is the most depressed of all the laments in the Psalter. The writer's distress can be heard from beginning to end, because his pain has lasted from his youth (v. 15) until the present. Most laments turn to confidence and praise at the end, but in this one the only glimmer of hope is that the psalmist is concerned to pray at all. He refers to God as "my salvation" (v. 1). A Christian is not, as such, free from the suffering of this world. Contrariwise, the Christian lot commonly is suffering and pain. We cannot hope to escape all suffering, but we find solace in the suffering and resurrection of Christ (Phil. 3:10).

88:3 Sheol. See 6:5 note.

88:5 set loose among the dead. His condition is so bad that people treat him as if he were already dead.

88:8 a horror. The psalmist's unhappiness is reminiscent of the suffering of Job.

88:9 spread out my hands. An attitude of prayer. Though God afflicts him, or perhaps, because God afflicts him, the psalmist knows there is only one refuge for him—God.

88:10 work wonders for the dead. See 6:5; 30:9 and notes.

88:17 like a flood. For water as a figure of trouble, see notes 18:4, 15.

88:18 my companions have become darkness. His closest friends have abandoned him (v. 8), and God is distant (v. 14), leaving only darkness nearby. This is the only psalm that ends on such a downcast note (introduction to Ps. 88).

I Will Sing of the Steadfast Love of the LORD

89 A MASKIL[1] OF [h] ETHAN THE EZRAHITE.
[i] I will sing of [j] the steadfast love of
the LORD, forever;
with my mouth I will make known
your [k] faithfulness to all
generations.
2 For I said, [j] "Steadfast love will be
built up forever;
in the heavens [l] you will establish
your [k] faithfulness."
3 You have said, "I have made [m] a
covenant with my [n] chosen one;
I have [o] sworn to David my servant:
4 'I will establish your [p] offspring forever,
and build your [q] throne for all
generations.'" *Selah*
5 Let [r] the heavens praise your
[s] wonders, O LORD,
your faithfulness in the assembly
of [t] the holy ones!
6 For [u] who in the skies can be
compared to the LORD?
[u] Who among the heavenly beings[2]
is like the LORD,
7 a God greatly [v] to be feared in the
council of [t] the holy ones,
and awesome above all [w] who are
around him?
8 O LORD God of hosts,
[x] who is mighty as you are, O [y] LORD,
with your faithfulness all around
you?
9 You rule the raging of the sea;
when its waves rise, you [z] still them.
10 You [a] crushed [b] Rahab like a carcass;
you [c] scattered your enemies with
your mighty arm.
11 [d] The heavens are yours; the earth also
is yours;
[e] the world and all that is in it, you
have [f] founded them.
12 [g] The north and the south, you have
created them;
[h] Tabor and [i] Hermon [j] joyously
praise your name.
13 You have a mighty arm;
strong is your hand, high your
right hand.
14 [k] Righteousness and justice are the
foundation of your throne;
[l] steadfast love and faithfulness go
before you.
15 Blessed are the people who know
[m] the festal shout,
who walk, O LORD, in [n] the light of
your face,
16 who exult in your [o] name all the day
and in your righteousness are
[p] exalted.
17 For you are [q] the glory of their strength;
by your favor our [r] horn is exalted.

Psalm 89 [h] 1 Kin. 4:31; 1 Chr. 2:6
1 [i] Ps. 101:1 [j] ver. 1, 14, 24, 28, 33, 49; [Isai. 55:3] [k] ver. 1, 5, 8, 24, 33, 49; Ps. 88:11; 119:90
2 [j] [See ver. 1 above] [l] See Ps. 36:5 [k] [See ver. 1 above]
3 [m] ver. 28, 34, 39 [n] ver. 19; 1 Kin. 8:16; Isai. 42:1 [o] ver. 35, 49; Ps. 132:11; See 2 Sam. 7:8-16; 1 Chr. 17:7-14; Jer. 33:17-21
4 [p] ver. 29, 36; John 12:34 [q] ver. 29, 36; [Isai. 9:7; Luke 1:32, 33]
5 [r] Ps. 19:1; 50:6; 97:6; See Rev. 7:10-12 [s] Ps. 88:12 [t] ver. 7; Job 5:1; 15:15; [Job 1:6]
6 [u] ver. 8; [Ps. 86:8]
7 [v] See Ps. 47:2 [t] [See ver. 5 above] [w] [Ps. 103:20, 21]
8 [x] [1 Sam. 2:2]; See Ps. 35:10 [y] See Ps. 68:4
9 [z] Ps. 65:7; Job 38:11
10 [a] [Ex. 14:30] [b] See Job 9:13 [c] See Ps. 53:5 11 [d] Gen. 1:1; 1 Chr. 29:11 [e] See Ps. 24:1 [f] See Ps. 104:5 12 [g] Job 26:7 [h] Jer. 46:18 [i] Deut. 3:9 [j] Ps. 98:8 14 [k] Ps. 97:2 [l] ver. 2; [Ps. 85:13] 15 [m] See Ps. 66:1 [n] See Ps. 4:6 16 [o] [Ps. 20:5, 7] [p] [Job 36:7] 17 [q] [Ps. 78:61] [r] ver. 24; See Ps. 75:10

1 Probably a musical or liturgical term 2 Hebrew *the sons of God*, or *the sons of might*

Ps. 89 The psalm opens joyfully, but is finally a lament. The issue at the heart of the psalm is the Davidic covenant. In 2 Sam. 7:4–17 (cf. 1 Chr. 17:1–15) God established a covenant with David in which He promised that the special relationship would pass on to David's obedient sons (32:11). God's language was bold; the covenant was to last "forever" (2 Sam. 7:13).

But this promise was not without conditions upon the recipients. If they sinned they would be punished (1 Kin. 8:25; 2 Sam. 7:14). David's own son Solomon began his slide into apostasy by admitting the religious cults of his foreign wives (1 Kin. 11). The continuing disobedience of the Davidic kings resulted in the Babylonian exile and an end to that period of Israel's monarchy in the sixth century b.c. But the spiritual substance of the promise was not canceled; Christ came to take the throne of David forever (Is. 9:7; Luke 1:32; 22:30).

89:1 steadfast love. The wonders of God's devotion to His people in the love of His covenant with them.

faithfulness. God is not fickle or capricious, but will keep the promises He makes. Hope in the fulfillment of God's promise to David is what will motivate the lament at the end of the psalm (vv. 38–51).

89:5 heavens. The heavens are here personified; the reference is to the beings in heaven, such as the cherubim and the angels. God is so great that even these powerful spiritual entities fall to their knees in adoration.

assembly. The angels and other spiritual beings in heaven are God's divine assembly through whom He works His will.

89:6 in the skies. Having mentioned spiritual beings, the psalmist is quick to point out the uniqueness of God. The writings of the Canaanites and Mesopotamians also mention an "assembly of the holy ones," but this was an assembly made up of different gods. The God of Israel is not the best of such gods but wholly different from them. The Old Testament expresses His transcendence in numerous places (Is. 44:6).

89:10 Rahab. Like Leviathan, Rahab is here a sea monster of Near Eastern mythology, standing for forces of evil and chaos (Job 9:13; Ezek. 29:3 and note). Frequently the name Rahab is applied to Egypt (Ps. 87:4 and note).

89:11 you have founded them. Unlike the heathen gods, the Lord is the Creator of the world.

89:12 Tabor and Hermon. Hermon in the far north is the highest peak in Israel. Tabor is a mountain of distinctive shape standing in the Megiddo plain, a landmark of the boundary of three tribes.

89:14 Righteousness and justice. As King, God is responsible for the administration of law in the land. He does not judge arbitrarily.

go before you. See Ps. 85:13.

89:17 our horn. The king. The metaphor of the horn is associated with that of the bull, which stands for strength. God is the One who endows the human king with power. This thought is specified in the next line.

18 For our [s]shield belongs to the LORD,
our king to [t]the Holy One of Israel.

19 [u]Of old you spoke in a vision to your
godly one,[1] and said:
"I have [v]granted help to one who is
[w]mighty;
I have exalted one [x]chosen from
the people.
20 [y]I have found David, my servant;
with my holy oil I have [z]anointed
him,
21 so that my [a]hand shall be established
with him;
my arm also shall strengthen him.
22 The enemy shall not outwit him;
[b]the wicked shall not humble him.
23 I will [c]crush his foes before him
and strike down those who hate
him.
24 My [d]faithfulness and my [d]steadfast
love shall be with him,
and in my name shall his [e]horn be
exalted.
25 I will set his hand on [f]the sea
and his right hand on [f]the rivers.
26 He shall cry to me, 'You are my
[g]Father,
my God, and [h]the Rock of my
salvation.'
27 And I will make him the [i]firstborn,
[j]the highest of the kings of the earth.
28 My steadfast love I will keep for him
forever,
and my [k]covenant will stand firm[2]
for him.
29 I will establish his [l]offspring forever
and his [l]throne as [m]the days of the
heavens.
30 [n]If his children forsake my law
and do not walk according to my
rules,
31 if they violate my statutes
and do not keep my
commandments,
32 then I will punish their
transgression with [o]the rod
and their iniquity with stripes,
33 but I will not remove from him my
steadfast love
or be false to my faithfulness.
34 I will not violate my [k]covenant
or alter the word that went forth
from my lips.
35 Once for all I have sworn [p]by my
holiness;
I will not [q]lie to David.
36 His [l]offspring shall endure
forever,
[r]his [l]throne as long as [s]the sun
before me.
37 Like [s]the moon it shall be
established forever,
[t]a faithful witness in the
skies." *Selah*
38 But now you have [u]cast off and
rejected;
you are full of wrath against your
[v]anointed.
39 You have [w]renounced [x]the covenant
with your servant;
you have [y]defiled his [z]crown in the
dust.
40 You have [a]breached all his walls;
you have laid his strongholds in
ruins.

18 [s]Ps. 47:9 [t]See Ps. 71:22
19 [u][ver. 3, 4] [v][Ps. 21:5] [w]2 Sam. 17:10 [x]See ver. 3
20 [y]Cited Acts 13:22 [z]1 Sam. 16:13
21 [a]Ps. 80:17
22 [b][2 Sam. 7:10]
23 [c][2 Sam. 7:9]; See Ps. 2:9
24 [d]ver. 1 [e]ver. 17
25 [f]See Ps. 72:8
26 [g][2 Sam. 7:14]
26 [h][Ps. 18:2]
27 [i]Ex. 4:22; [Rom. 8:29; Col. 1:15, 18; Heb. 1:5] [j]Num. 24:7; [Rev. 19:16]
28 [k]See ver. 3
29 [l]See ver. 4 [m]See Job 14:12
30 [n]2 Sam. 7:14; 1 Kin. 2:4
32 [o]See Job 9:34
34 [k][See ver. 28 above]
35 [p]See Ps. 60:6 [q][Heb. 6:18]
36 [l][See ver. 29 above] [r]See ver. 4 [s]See Ps. 72:5
37 [s][See ver. 36 above] [t]See Job 16:19
38 [u]See Ps. 44:9 [v]ver. 20, 51
39 [w]Lam. 2:7 [x]See ver. 3 [y]See Ps. 74:7 [z]Job 19:9
40 [a]See Ps. 80:12

1 Some Hebrew manuscripts *godly ones* 2 Or *will remain faithful*

89:19 in a vision. The exact words of this vision are not found elsewhere in Scripture, but the allusion is probably to the prophetic insight of Nathan in 2 Sam. 7, if not to the initial divine word given to Samuel concerning David's kingship (1 Sam. 6).

89:21 shall strengthen him. The king had sacred responsibilities, both political and religious. God promises to give David the strength he needs to carry out his divinely given tasks.

89:24 My faithfulness and my steadfast love. These two key words reverberate throughout the psalm, beginning in v. 1; see note on v. 1.

89:26 You are my Father. A reference to the intimate relationship established between God and David in 2 Sam. 7:14. The king played an important role as mediator of the Davidic covenant between God and His people. This special function made the apostasy of later kings especially heinous.

89:27 the firstborn. Calling David the "firstborn" means that he was first in rank in the covenant community, the head of a household (Gen. 4:4; 25:31 and notes). David in particular foreshadows Christ, uniquely the Son of God and Head of the church (Eph. 1:22; Heb. 3:6).

89:29 forever. The dynasty of David as an earthly political enterprise was long-lived, but not eternal. It fell because of the sins of David's successors. Superseding it, as the reality casting a shadow, was the eternal kingdom of Jesus Christ.

89:31 my statutes. God's will as summarized in the first five books of the Old Testament. Deut. 17:19 commands the king to be well versed in God's law and obedient to it.

89:34 I will not violate. God's promises stand forever. The Davidic covenant has a conditional element, as this psalm points out in v. 32, but its ultimate fulfillment does not depend on human response. David and the psalmist knew that it would be fulfilled, but could not know everything about how that would occur (Acts 2:29–31; 1 Pet. 1:10, 11).

89:38 you have cast off. The focus of the psalm shifts to the present and the great rift in the relationship between God and the king.

your anointed. An unspecified Davidic successor to the throne.

89:39 renounced. The psalmist is outspoken, speaking boldly in his appeal to break God's silence.

41 [a] All who pass by plunder him;
he has become [b] the scorn of his neighbors.
42 You have exalted the right hand of his foes;
you have made all his enemies rejoice.
43 You have also turned back the edge of his sword,
and you have not made him stand in battle.
44 You have made his splendor to cease
and cast his throne to the ground.
45 You have cut short [c] the days of his youth;
you have [d] covered him with shame. *Selah*
46 [e] How long, O LORD? Will you hide yourself forever?
How long will your wrath [f] burn like fire?
47 [g] Remember [h] how short my [i] time is!
For what vanity you have created all the children of man!
48 [j] What man can live and never [k] see death?
Who can deliver his soul from the power of [l] Sheol? *Selah*
49 Lord, where is your [m] steadfast love of old,
which by your [m] faithfulness you swore to David?
50 [n] Remember, O Lord, how your servants are mocked,
and how I bear in my [o] heart the insults[1] of all the many nations,
51 with which your enemies mock, O LORD,
with which they mock [p] the footsteps of your [q] anointed.

41 [a] [See ver. 40 above] [b] [ver. 50]; See Ps. 44:13; 69:9, 19
45 [c] Ps. 102:23 [d] Ps. 71:13; 109:29
46 [e] See Ps. 13:1 [f] Ps. 78:63; 79:5
47 [g] Job 7:7; 10:9 [h] [Job 14:1] [i] Ps. 39:5
48 [j] [Ps. 49:9] [k] [Luke 2:26; Heb. 11:5] [l] See Ps. 16:10
49 [m] [ver. 1, 2]
50 [n] [ver. 41]; See Ps. 74:18, 22 [o] Ps. 79:12
51 [p] [Ps. 17:11; 49:5; 56:6] [q] ver. 20, 38
52 [r] See Ps. 41:13
BOOK FOUR
Psalm 90 [s] Ps. 17, title; 55:1 [t] Deut. 33:1; Josh. 14:6; Ezra 3:2
1 [u] See Ps. 71:3
2 [v] Prov. 8:25 [w] [Deut. 33:15; Job 15:7] [x] See Job 36:26
3 [y] Gen. 3:19 [z] Eccles. 12:7
4 [a] 2 Pet. 3:8 [b] [Ps. 39:5] [c] Ex. 14:24 [d] Judg. 7:19
5 [e] See Job 20:8 [f] Ps. 37:2 [g] Ps. 103:15; 2 Kin. 19:26 [h] Isai. 40:6-8; 1 Pet. 1:24
6 [i] See Job 4:20 [j] Job 14:2; [Ps. 92:7] [k] James 1:11
8 [l] Jer. 16:17; Heb. 4:13 [m] Ps. 19:12

52 [r] Blessed be the LORD forever!
Amen and Amen.

BOOK FOUR

From Everlasting to Everlasting

90 A [s] PRAYER OF MOSES, THE [t] MAN OF GOD.

1 Lord, you have been our [u] dwelling place[2]
in all generations.
2 [v] Before the [w] mountains were brought forth,
or ever you had formed the earth and the world,
[x] from everlasting to everlasting you are God.

3 You return man to dust
and say, [y] "Return, [z] O children of man!"[3]
4 For [a] a thousand years in your sight
are but as [b] yesterday when it is past,
or as [c, d] a watch in the night.

5 You sweep them away as with a flood; they are like [e] a dream,
like [f] grass that is [g] renewed in the [h] morning:
6 in [i] the morning it flourishes and is renewed;
in the evening it [j] fades and [k] withers.

7 For we are brought to an end by your anger;
by your wrath we are dismayed.
8 You have [l] set our iniquities before you,
our [m] secret sins in the light of your presence.

1 Hebrew lacks *the insults* 2 Some Hebrew manuscripts (compare Septuagint) *our refuge* 3 Or *of Adam*

89:41 All . . . plunder him. God's absence is experienced through the victory of their enemies.

89:49 your steadfast love of old. God's lovingkindness is the love by which God binds Himself to His people in covenant devotion.

89:52 A doxology concludes Book III of the Psalter (Introduction: Characteristics and Themes).

Ps. 90 This psalm, the only one ascribed to Moses, contrasts God's eternity and human mortality. Moses seems to pray for God's blessing on his own generation, doomed to wander in the wilderness.

90:2 from everlasting to everlasting you are God. The psalmist affirms the eternal existence of God. God's work of creation (Gen. 1) brought the whole universe into existence; God Himself had always been there. See theological note "The Self-Existence of God" on next page.

90:3 to dust. God's judgment returns the descendants of Adam to the dust in death.

90:4 as yesterday. God is not subject to time, but is its Creator. See "God the Creator" at 148:5.

90:5 The brevity of human life—like a sleep—contrasts with God's eternity.

90:8 our secret sins. People commit sins they think they can hide, like envy, hatred, and lust. But before God there are no secrets (Heb. 4:12, 13).

9 For all our days pass away under
your wrath;
we bring our years to an end like a
sigh.
10 The years of our life are seventy,
or even by reason of strength
eighty;
yet their span[1] is but toil and
trouble;
they are soon gone, and we fly
away.
11 Who considers the power of your
anger,
and your wrath according to the
fear of you?

12 [n] So teach us to number our days
that we may get a heart of wisdom.
13 [o] Return, O LORD! [p] How long?
Have [q] pity on your [r] servants!
14 Satisfy us in the [s] morning with your
steadfast love,
that we may [t] rejoice and be glad
all our days.
15 Make us glad for as many days as
you have [u] afflicted us,
and for as many years as we have
seen evil.
16 Let your [v] work be shown to your
[w] servants,
and your glorious power to their
children.
17 Let the [x] favor[2] of the Lord our God
be upon us,
and establish [y] the work of our
hands upon us;
yes, establish the work of our
[z] hands!

12 [n] Ps. 39:4
13 [o] Ps. 6:4 [p] See Ps. 74:9, 10 [q] Ps. 106:45; 135:14; Ex. 32:12; Deut. 32:36 [r] Judg. 2:18; Jonah 3:10; See Gen. 6:6
14 [s] See Ps. 46:5 [t] See Ps. 85:6
15 [u] [Deut. 8:2]
16 [v] Ps. 77:12; 92:4; 95:9 [w] Deut. 32:4; Hab. 3:2
17 [x] Ps. 27:4 [y] [Ps. 128:2] [z] [Isai. 26:12]
Psalm 91
1 [a] See Ps. 32:7 [b] Ps. 121:5; [Isai. 25:4; 32:2]
2 [c] ver. 9; See Ps. 14:6 [d] See Ps. 18:2 [e] See Ps. 11:1

My Refuge and My Fortress

91

1 He who dwells in [a] the shelter of
the Most High
will abide in [b] the shadow of the
Almighty.
2 I will say[3] to the LORD, "My [c] refuge
and my [d] fortress,
my God, in whom I [e] trust."

[1] Or *pride* [2] Or *beauty* [3] Septuagint *He will say*

The Self-Existence of God

Children sometimes ask, "Who made God?" The clearest answer is that God never needed to be made, because He was always there. He exists in a different way from us: we exist in a derived, finite, and fragile way, but our Creator exists as eternal, self-sustaining, and necessary. His existence is necessary in the sense that there is no possibility in Him of ceasing to exist.

God's self-existence is a basic truth. In his presentation of the "unknown God" to the Athenians, Paul explained that the Creator of the world is not "served by human hands, as though he needed anything, since he himself gives to all mankind life and breath and everything" (Acts 17:25). The Creator has life in Himself and draws His unending energy from Himself, needing nothing. The independent self-existence of God is a truth stated clearly in the Bible (Ps. 90:1–4; 102:25–27; Is. 40:28–31; John 5:26; Rev. 4:10).

In theology, many errors result from supposing that the conditions and limits of our own finite existence apply to God. In the life of faith we can too easily impoverish ourselves by embracing an idea of God that is limited and small. The doctrine of His self-existence is a bulwark and defense against such mistakes. The principle that God exists from Himself alone distinguishes Him from every creature and is a foundation of our thinking about Him. Knowing that God's existence is independent protects our understanding of His greatness, and so has clear practical value for our spiritual health.

90:10 seventy. To a young person, seventy years seems like a long time. But before God's eternity, and in human retrospect, it is brief.

90:11 Who considers. Only Jesus Christ, who drank the full cup of God's wrath for sinners, knows the full power of death.

90:13 How long. See note Ps. 6:3.

90:16 your work. God must act to redeem and restore.

their children. Moses contemplates a generation entering the Promised Land.

90:17 the favor of the LORD our God. In the midst of life in the wilderness, only the blessing of God's own presence can give meaning and joy.

establish the work of our hands. Wanderers in the wilderness may leave no monuments, but God can give eternal significance to the deeds of hands that serve Him.

Ps. 91 The original setting of this poem appears to be warfare with its threats of battle and plague among the soldiers (vv. 3–8). In the face of the hard realities of war, God is portrayed as a compassionate mother bird protecting her young (v. 4).

91:1 He who dwells . . . will abide. The verse states the theme of the whole psalm. Those who draw near to God can have peace in Him, however difficult their circumstances.

3 For he will deliver you from [f]the
snare of the fowler
and from the deadly pestilence.
4 He will [g]cover you with his pinions,
and under his [h]wings you will [i]find
refuge;
his [j]faithfulness is [k]a shield and
buckler.
5 [l]You will not fear [m]the terror of the
night,
nor the arrow that flies by day,
6 nor the pestilence that stalks in
darkness,
nor the destruction that wastes at
noonday.

7 A thousand may fall at your side,
ten thousand at your right hand,
but it will not come near you.
8 You will only look with your eyes
and [n]see the recompense of the
wicked.

9 Because you have made the LORD
your [o]dwelling place—
the Most High, who is my [c]refuge[1]—
10 [p]no evil shall be allowed to befall you,
[q]no plague come near your tent.

11 [r]For he will command his [s]angels
concerning you
to [t]guard you in all your ways.
12 On their hands they will bear you up,
lest you [u]strike your foot against a
stone.
13 You will tread on [v]the lion and the
[w]adder;
the young lion and [x]the serpent
you will [y]trample underfoot.

14 "Because he [z]holds fast to me in love,
I will deliver him;
I will protect him, because he
[a]knows my name.
15 When he [b]calls to me, I will answer
him;
I will be with him in trouble;
I will rescue him and [c]honor him.
16 With [d]long life I will satisfy him
and [e]show him my salvation."

3 [f]Ps. 124:7; 140:5; 141:9; Prov. 6:5 4 [g][1 Kin. 8:7] [h]See Ps. 17:8 [i]Ps. 57:1 [j]See Ps. 36:5 [k]See Ps. 35:2 5 [l]Prov. 3:23; Isai. 43:1; See Job 5:19-23 [m]S. of S. 3:8 8 [n]See Ps. 37:34 9 [o]See Ps. 71:3 [c][See ver. 2 above] 10 [p][ver. 5]; See Prov. 12:21 [q]Ps. 38:11 11 [r]Cited Matt. 4:6; Luke 4:10, 11 [s]See Ps. 34:7 [t]Ex. 23:20 12 [u]Prov. 3:23; [Ps. 37:24] 13 [v][Dan. 6:23] [w][Acts 28:5] [x]See Ps. 74:13 [y]Luke 10:19; [Mark 16:18]

14 [z]Deut. 7:7; 10:15 [a]Ps. 9:10 15 [b]Job 12:4; See Ps. 50:15 [c]1 Sam. 2:30; John 12:26 16 [d]Ps. 21:4; Deut. 6:2; 1 Kin. 3:14; Prov. 3:2, 16 [e]Ps. 50:23; [Ps. 118:14, 21]

Psalm 92 1 [f]Ps. 147:1; [Ps. 71:22] [g][Gen. 14:19, 20] 2 [h]See Ps. 36:5 [i][Ps. 119:147, 148] 3 [j]See Ps. 33:2 4 [k]See Ps. 90:16 [l]Ps. 8:6

How Great Are Your Works

92 A PSALM. A SONG FOR THE SABBATH.
[f]It is good to give thanks to
the LORD,
to sing praises to your name,
[g]O Most High;
2 to declare your [h]steadfast love in [i]the
morning,
and your [h]faithfulness by [i]night,
3 to the music of [j]the lute and [j]the harp,
to the melody of [j]the lyre.
4 For you, O LORD, have made me glad
by your [k]work;
at [l]the works of your hands I sing
for joy.

5 How [m]great are your works, O LORD!
Your [n]thoughts are very [o]deep!
6 The stupid man cannot know;
the fool cannot understand this:
7 that though [p]the wicked sprout like
grass
and all [q]evildoers flourish,
they are doomed to destruction forever;

5 [m]Ps. 111:2; Rev. 15:3 [n]Ps. 40:5; 139:17 [o][Rom. 11:33]; See Ps. 36:6 7 [p]See Job 21:7 [q]Ps. 94:4; 125:5

1 Or *For you, O LORD, are my refuge! You have made the Most High your dwelling place*

91:3 he will deliver you. God is present and able to deliver His people. See "Omnipresence and Omnipotence" at Jer. 23:24.

91:4 with his pinions. Psalms of confidence often have a metaphor for God's compassion at their core. God is likened to a mother bird who protects her young.

his faithfulness. God's steadfast love and the certainty that He will keep His promises sustain the psalmist.

91:5 the terror of the night. Perhaps a reference to plagues that could sweep through an encampment.

arrow. The literal setting of battle can be taken figuratively for the struggles of life.

91:11, 12 his angels. God often works His will through His spiritual attendants, the angels.

91:12 they will bear you up. Satan quoted this passage to Jesus in the wilderness (Matt. 4:6) tempting Him to jump from the top of the temple. Satan's aim was to turn faith into presumption.

91:14 Because he holds fast to me in love. God's promise of protection comes to those who have faith in Him.

92:1 Most High. This title is similar to one commonly given to Baal in Canaanite religious texts. Applying it to the God of Israel is a kind of taunt directed toward anyone tempted to worship Baal (83:18).

92:2 your steadfast love . . . your faithfulness. In His covenant with His people, God pledges Himself to love them faithfully. He is the author of the terms of the covenant binding Him and His people together (136:1 and note).

92:4 your work . . . the works of your hands. The psalmist concentrates on God's acts in time and space. God is not out of touch with created reality, but works through such reality to demonstrate His love for His people.

92:5 How great . . . thoughts are very deep. God's acts and thoughts overwhelm us as we contemplate them. They draw us on to reverent fascination and humble devotion that exceeds our poor grasp.

92:7 the wicked sprout like grass. The psalmist does not deny that the wicked appear to prosper in this world.

8 but you, O LORD, are [r]on high
forever.
9 For behold, your enemies, O LORD,
for behold, your enemies shall
perish;
all evildoers shall be [s]scattered.

10 But you have exalted my [t]horn like
that of [u]the wild ox;
you have [v]poured over me[1] fresh oil.
11 My [w]eyes have seen the downfall of
my enemies;
my ears have heard the doom of
my evil assailants.

12 [x]The righteous flourish like the palm
tree
and grow like a cedar in Lebanon.
13 They are planted in the house of the
LORD;
they flourish in [y]the courts of our
God.
14 They still bear fruit in old age;
they are ever full of sap and green,
15 [z]to declare that the LORD is upright;
he is my [a]rock, and there is [b]no
unrighteousness in him.

The LORD Reigns

93 [c]The LORD reigns; he is [d]robed in
majesty;
the LORD is [e]robed; he has [f]put on
strength as his belt.
[g]Yes, the world is established; [h]it shall
never be moved.
2 [i]Your throne is established from of old;
[j]you are from everlasting.

8 [r]Ps. 93:4
9 [s]See Ps. 68:1
10 [t]See Ps. 75:10; 1 Sam. 2:1 [u]Num. 23:22 [v]See Ps. 23:5
11 [w]See Ps. 37:34; 54:7
12 [x]Ps. 1:3; 52:8; 72:7; Prov. 11:28; [Num. 24:6; Isai. 61:3]; See Hos. 14:5-8
13 [y]Ps. 100:4; 116:19; 135:2
15 [z][Ps. 58:11] [a]See Ps. 18:2 [b]See Job 34:10
Psalm 93
1 [c]Ps. 96:10; See 1 Chr. 16:31 [d]Ps. 104:1 [e]Isai. 51:9 [f]Ps. 65:6 [g]Ps. 96:10; [Ps. 46:5] [h]See Ps. 125:1
2 [i][Ps. 45:6] [j]Ps. 90:2
3 [k][Ps. 98:7, 8; Hab. 3:10]
4 [l]See Ps. 65:6, 7 [m]Ps. 92:8
5 [n][Ps. 89:28, 37] [o]See Ps. 29:2
Psalm 94
1 [p]Deut. 32:35, 41, 43; Isai. 35:4; Jer. 51:56; Nah. 1:2; Rom. 12:19 [q]See Ps. 50:2
2 [r]See Ps. 7:6 [s]See Ps. 58:11 [t]Luke 1:51
3 [u]Rev. 6:10; See Ps. 74:10 [v][Job 20:5]

3 [k]The floods have lifted up, O LORD,
the floods have lifted up their voice;
the floods lift up their roaring.
4 Mightier than the thunders of many
waters,
mightier than the waves of the sea,
[l]the LORD [m]on high is mighty!

5 Your [n]decrees are very trustworthy;
[o]holiness befits your house,
O LORD, forevermore.

The LORD Will Not Forsake His People

94 O LORD, God of [p]vengeance,
O God of vengeance, [q]shine
forth!
2 [r]Rise up, O [s]judge of the earth;
repay to the [t]proud what they
deserve!
3 O LORD, [u]how long shall the
wicked,
how long shall [v]the wicked exult?
4 They pour out their [w]arrogant
words;
all [x]the evildoers boast.
5 They [y]crush your people, O LORD,
and afflict your heritage.
6 They kill [z]the widow and the
sojourner,
and murder [z]the fatherless;
7 [a]and they say, "The LORD does not
see;
the God of Jacob does not
perceive."

4 [w]Ps. 31:18; 1 Sam. 2:3; [Jude 15] [x]Ps. 92:7, 9; 125:5 5 [y][Prov. 22:22; Isai. 3:15] 6 [z][Isai. 10:2] 7 [a]See Job 22:13

1 Compare Syriac; the meaning of the Hebrew is uncertain

92:9 your enemies shall perish. As the psalmist meditates on the greatness and justice of God, he comes to the sure conclusion that the wicked will be destroyed.

92:10 you have exalted my horn. The horn of an animal is used in the Bible as a symbol of power. The wild ox raises its horn with pride and confidence. See 75:4; 89:17; 132:17; 148:14 and notes.

92:12 like the palm tree . . . like a cedar. A strong contrast is drawn between the flourishing of the righteous and the destruction of the wicked (v. 7). The wicked are like fragile grass, whereas the righteous are strong, vital, and productive trees. A similar type of contrast is found in Ps. 1.

92:13 planted in the house of the LORD. The source of the vitality of the righteous is not themselves, but God.

Ps. 93 This short poem stands at the head of a group of psalms that praise God as King (93; 95–100). Comparison may also be made with Ps. 24 and 46.

93:1 The LORD reigns. This phrase and its slight variants may be found throughout this section of the Psalter (Ps. 96:10; 97:1; 98:6; 99:1). God is King, with omnipotent power and sovereign control over the world. See "God Reigns: Divine Sovereignty" at Dan. 4:34.

the world is established. This word of assurance is based on the fact that the King has created and maintains the world. The forces of evil, disorder, and chaos (vv. 3, 4) will not overwhelm the world.

93:2 you are from everlasting. God has no beginning; He is uncreated. This conception of the eternal kingship of God stands in stark contrast with the theology of Mesopotamia and Canaan. In these neighboring regions, the power of the gods varied according to changes in the political arena.

93:3 The floods. An ancient symbol of the forces of chaos and evil. See notes 18:4, 15.

93:5 Your decrees. The stability and order that exists because of God's eternal kingship is shared with humanity through the revealed law.

Ps. 94 The psalmist calls on the Lord as Judge to bring justice to arrogant evildoers, those who disobey Him.

94:2 Rise up, O judge. See notes 3:7 and 7:6; "God Is Light: Divine Holiness and Justice" at Lev. 11:44.

94:3 how long. See note Ps. 6:3.

94:4 arrogant words. They should be ashamed and silent, but instead they shout their evil accomplishments from the rooftops.

94:6 widow . . . sojourner . . . fatherless. See 9:18 note.

94:7 The LORD does not see. The wicked in their prosperity believe that God does not care what they do.

8 [b] Understand, O dullest of the people!
Fools, when will you be wise?
9 [c] He who planted the ear, does he not hear?
He who formed the eye, does he not see?
10 He who [d] disciplines the nations, does he not rebuke?
He who [e] teaches man knowledge—
11 [f] the LORD—knows the thoughts of man,
that they are [g] but a breath.[1]
12 [h] Blessed is the man whom you [i] discipline, O LORD,
and whom you teach out of your law,
13 to give him [j] rest from [k] days of trouble,
until [l] a pit is dug for the wicked.
14 [m] For the LORD will not forsake his [n] people;
he will not abandon his [n] heritage;
15 for [o] justice will return to the righteous,
and all the upright in heart will [p] follow it.
16 [q] Who rises up for me against the wicked?
Who stands up for me against evildoers?
17 [r] If the LORD had not been my help,
my soul would soon have lived in the land of [s] silence.
18 When I thought, [t] "My foot slips,"
your steadfast love, O LORD, [u] held me up.
19 When the [v] cares of my heart are many,
your consolations cheer my soul.
20 Can [w] wicked rulers be allied with you,
those who frame injustice by [x] statute?
21 They [y] band together against the life of the righteous
and condemn [z] the innocent to death.[2]
22 But the LORD has become my [a] stronghold,
and my God [b] the rock of my [c] refuge.
23 He will bring back on them [d] their iniquity
and [e] wipe them out for their wickedness;
the LORD our God will wipe them out.

Let Us Sing Songs of Praise

95 Oh come, let us sing to the LORD;
let us [f] make a joyful noise to [g] the rock of our salvation!
2 Let us [h] come into his presence with thanksgiving;
let us [f] make a joyful noise to him with songs of praise!
3 For the LORD is [i] a great God,
and a great King [j] above all gods.
4 In his hand are the depths of the earth;
the heights of the mountains are his also.
5 The sea is his, for [k] he made it,
and his hands formed [k] the dry land.
6 Oh come, let us worship and bow down;
let us [l] kneel before the LORD, our [m] Maker!

8 [b] See Ps. 49:10 9 [c] [Ex. 4:11; Prov. 20:12] 10 [d] [Job 12:28] [e] See Job 35:11 11 [f] Cited 1 Cor. 3:20 [g] [Ps. 30:5, 11] 12 [h] Prov. 3:11, 12; Heb. 12:5, 6; See Job 5:17 [i] Deut. 8:5; 1 Cor. 11:32 13 [j] Job 34:29 [k] Ps. 49:5 [l] Ps. 55:23 14 [m] 1 Sam. 12:22; Rom. 11:2 [n] Deut. 32:9 15 [o] [Isai. 42:3] [p] 1 Sam. 12:14; 1 Kin. 14:8 16 [q] See Ps. 12:5 17 [r] Ps. 124:1, 2 [s] See Ps. 31:17 18 [t] Ps. 38:16; [Ps. 73:2] [u] [Ps. 20:2] 19 [v] [Job 4:13] 20 [w] [Amos 6:3] [x] Ps. 50:16; 58:2; Isai. 10:1 21 [y] Matt. 27:1 [z] Matt. 27:4 22 [a] See Ps. 9:9 [b] See Ps. 18:2 [c] See Ps. 14:6 23 [d] See Ps. 7:16; 34:21; [Prov. 2:22] [e] [Ps. 92:9]
Psalm 95 1 [f] See Ps. 66:1 [g] Ps. 89:26; [Ps. 94:22] 2 [h] Mic. 6:6 [f] [See ver. 1 above] 3 [i] Ps. 93:4; 135:5 [j] Ps. 86:8; 96:4; 97:9; 2 Chr. 2:5 5 [k] Gen. 1:9, 10; Jonah 1:9 6 [l] 2 Chr. 6:13; Dan. 6:10 [m] Ps. 100:3; 149:2; Deut. 32:6, 15, 18

[1] Septuagint *they are futile* [2] Hebrew *condemn innocent blood*

94:8 be wise. The wicked will be wise when they shed the illusion that God does not know their evil schemes, or that He is unable to do anything about them.

94:11 knows the thoughts of man. The Lord knows even the secret thoughts hidden away in the heart (Ps. 90:8).

94:13 until a pit is dug. The psalmist recognizes that there is often a delay between a wicked act and its punishment. The unrighteous may prosper for a time. However, that they will pay for their crimes is a certainty.

94:14 will not forsake his people. God may discipline the righteous (v. 12), to return them to conformity to His will, but He will never leave them.

94:16 for me. The psalm takes on a personal note as the author prepares to mention how God delivered him.

94:18 your steadfast love. Specifically, God's love for those in covenant with Him.

94:20 wicked rulers. A king who perverts justice. A king of Israel was to reflect the kingship of God, particularly God's justice and compassion. The psalmist refers to an Israelite king who did not seek the will of God. There are many such examples from the history of the divided kingdoms of Israel and Judah.

Ps. 95 The psalm opens with an exuberant hymn and ends with God's warning to listen to His voice and obey Him.

95:1 let us. A worship leader, such as a priest, calls on the congregation to worship the Lord together with him.

95:3 a great King above all gods. As the supreme God of the universe all sovereignty is His. The reference is to popular Near Eastern mythology, not the actual existence of such gods (48:2; 74:13 and notes).

95:5 The sea . . . the dry land. As in v. 4, complementary terms are used to indicate the whole earth.

95:6 our Maker. We worship our Creator.

7 For he is our [n]God,
and we are the people of his
[o]pasture,
and the sheep of his hand.
[p]Today, if you [q]hear his voice,
8 [r]do not harden your hearts, as at
[s]Meribah,
as on the day at [t]Massah in the
wilderness,
9 when your fathers put me to the [u]test
and put me to the proof, though
they had seen my [v]work.
10 [w]For forty years I loathed that
generation
and said, "They are a people who
go astray in their heart,
and they have not known [x]my ways."
11 Therefore I [y]swore in my wrath,
"They shall not enter [z]my rest."

Worship in the Splendor of Holiness

96 [a]Oh sing to the LORD [b]a new
song;
sing to the LORD, all the earth!
2 Sing to the LORD, bless his name;
[c]tell of his salvation from day to
day.
3 Declare his glory among the nations,
his marvelous works among all the
peoples!
4 For [d]great is the LORD, and [e]greatly to
be praised;
he is to be feared above [f]all gods.
5 For all the gods of the peoples are
worthless idols,
but the LORD [g]made the heavens.
6 Splendor and majesty are before him;
[h]strength and beauty are in his
sanctuary.

7[n]Ps. 48:14 [o]See Ps. 74:1 [p]Cited Heb. 3:7-11, 15; 4:7 [q]Num. 14:22 **8**[r]Ex. 9:34; 1 Sam. 6:6; 2 Chr. 36:13; Prov. 28:14 [s]Ex. 17:7; Num. 20:13 [t]Ex. 17:7; Deut. 6:16 **9**[u]1 Cor. 10:9; [Ps. 78:18, 41, 56] [v]See Ps. 90:16; [Num. 14:22] **10**[w]Acts 7:36; 13:18; Heb. 3:17; [Deut. 9:7] [x][Ps. 81:13] **11**[y]Num. 14:23, 28, 30; Deut. 1:35; Cited Heb. 3:11; 4:3, 5 [z]Deut. 12:9
Psalm 96 **1**[a]For ver. 1-13, see 1 Chr. 16:23-33 [b]Ps. 98:1; See Ps. 33:3 **2**[c][Isai. 52:7; 60:6] **4**[d]See Ps. 48:1 [e]Ps. 18:3 [f]See Ps. 95:3 **5**[g]Ps. 115:15; Isai. 42:5; 44:24; Jer. 10:12 **6**[h][Ps. 78:61]
7[i]Ps. 22:27 [j]See Ps. 29:1 **8**[k]Ps. 29:2 [l][Ps. 45:12]; See Ps. 68:29; 72:10 [m]Ps. 100:4 **9**[n]See Ps. 29:2 [o]Ps. 114:7 **10**[p]See Ps. 93:1 [q]ver. 13; See Ps. 9:8; 58:11

7 Ascribe to the LORD, O [i]families of
the peoples,
[j]ascribe to the LORD glory and
strength!
8 Ascribe to the LORD [k]the glory due
his name;
bring [l]an offering, and [m]come into
his courts!
9 Worship the LORD in [n]the splendor
of holiness;[1]
[o]tremble before him, all the earth!
10 Say among the nations, [p]"The LORD
reigns!
Yes, the world is established; it
shall never be moved;
he will [q]judge the peoples with
equity."
11 Let [r]the heavens be glad, and let [s]the
earth rejoice;
let [t]the sea roar, and all that fills it;
12 let [u]the field exult, and everything
in it!
Then shall all [v]the trees of the forest
sing for joy
13 before the LORD, for he comes,
for he comes [w]to judge the earth.
He will judge the world in
righteousness,
and the peoples in his faithfulness.

The LORD Reigns

97 [x]The LORD reigns, [y]let the earth
rejoice;
let the many [z]coastlands be glad!

11[r]See Ps. 69:34 [s]Ps. 97:1 [t]Ps. 98:7 **12**[u][Isai. 35:1] [v][Isai. 55:12] **13**[w]See Isai. 11:1-9
Psalm 97 **1**[x]See Ps. 93:1 [y]Ps. 96:11 [z]See Ps. 72:10

1 Or *in holy attire*

95:7 Today. This is an ever-present day.

95:8 Meribah . . . Massah. These place-names may be translated "quarreling" and "testing." They sum up Israel's attitude toward God during the forty years of wandering in the wilderness. For the history see Ex. 17:1–7 and notes; Num. 20:1–13.

95:11 They shall not enter my rest. Those who rebelled against the Lord in the wilderness never entered the Promised Land. Heb. 3:7–4:7 cites this passage and applies it to the Christian's life. Professing Christians must heed God's Word, or they will not enter God's eternal rest.

Ps. 96 The psalmist calls on all nations to proclaim God as their King. The psalm contrasts God with the lifeless idols of the nations (vv. 4–6). The theme of God's universal kingship is similar to that seen in Ps. 47; 93; 97; 99, and particularly Ps. 98. 1 Chr. 16:8–36 records the thanksgiving song of David when he brought the ark to Jerusalem, a song composed from Ps. 96 and 105. See especially 1 Chr. 16:23–33 for Ps. 96.

96:1 a new song. See note Ps. 33:3.

all the earth. Since God is King of the whole earth, and not merely of Israel, the writer calls on all His subjects to praise Him. It is not until Christ returns that substantial numbers from the nations join in the universal chorus of praise.

96:3 his marvelous works. God's acts in history provide marvelous events for which to praise Him, e.g., He "made the heavens" (v. 5).

96:8 an offering. See Lev. 2. The word is also used for the tribute due a king (2 Kin. 17:4).

96:10 The LORD reigns. The psalmist proclaims God's kingship among the nations.

it shall never be moved. God created the world, and He will hold the forces of chaos in check.

judge . . . with equity. God does not rule according to whim, but according to justice and righteousness. As there is stability in creation, so there is stability in justice.

97:1 The LORD reigns. For God as King, see note Ps. 93:1.

the earth. The psalm calls on all the earth to praise God. This call to the nations has taken on a whole new meaning after the death and resurrection of Jesus Christ.

2 [a] Clouds and thick darkness are all
around him;
[b] righteousness and justice are the
foundation of his throne.
3 [c] Fire goes before him
and burns up his adversaries all
around.
4 His [d] lightnings light up the world;
the earth sees and [e] trembles.
5 The mountains [f] melt like [g] wax before
the LORD,
before [h] the Lord of all the earth.
6 [i] The heavens proclaim his
righteousness,
and all [j] the peoples see his glory.
7 All worshipers of images are [k] put to
shame,
who make their boast in [l] worthless
idols;
[m] worship him, all you gods!
8 Zion hears and [n] is glad,
and the daughters of Judah
rejoice,
because of your judgments,
O LORD.
9 For you, O LORD, are [o] most high over
all the earth;
you are exalted far above [p] all gods.
10 O you who love the LORD, [q] hate evil!
He [r] preserves the lives of his
[s] saints;
he [t] delivers them from the hand of
the wicked.
11 [u] Light [v] is sown[1] for the righteous,
and joy for the upright in heart.
12 [w] Rejoice in the LORD, O you
righteous,
and [x] give thanks to his holy
name!

2 [a] Ex. 19:9; Deut. 4:11; 5:22; 1 Kin. 8:12; See Ps. 18:11 [b] Ps. 89:14
3 [c] See Ps. 21:9; 50:3
4 [d] Ps. 77:18 [e] [Ps. 96:9]
5 [f] Nah. 1:5; [Judg. 5:5] [g] See Ps. 68:2 [h] Josh. 3:11
6 [i] See Ps. 50:6 [j] Isai. 40:5; 66:18; [Ps. 96:3]
7 [k] Isai. 42:17; 44:9 [l] Ps. 96:5 [m] Heb. 1:6
8 [n] Ps. 48:11
9 [o] See Ps. 83:18 [p] See Ps. 95:3
10 [q] Prov. 8:13; Amos 5:15; Rom. 12:9; See Ps. 34:14 [r] Ps. 31:23; 37:28; 121:4; 145:20; Prov. 2:8 [s] See Ps. 30:4 [t] Dan. 3:28; 6:27; Acts 12:11
11 [u] Ps. 112:4; 118:27; Prov. 4:18 [v] [Prov. 11:18; Hos. 10:12; James 3:18]
12 [w] See Ps. 32:11 [x] See Ps. 30:4

Psalm 98
1 [y] See Ps. 33:3 [z] [Ps. 96:3]; Ps. 72:18 [a] [Ex. 15:6; Luke 1:51]; See Job 40:14
2 [b] Isai. 49:6; 52:10; Luke 2:30, 31; [Isai. 59:16; 63:5] [c] Isai. 62:2; Rom. 3:25, 26 [d] Ps. 96:2, 3
3 [e] Luke 1:54, 72 [f] See Ps. 36:5 [g] Ps. 22:27 [h] ver. 2

Make a Joyful Noise to the LORD

98 A PSALM.
Oh sing to the LORD [y] a new
song,
for he has done [z] marvelous things!
His [a] right hand and his holy arm
have worked salvation for him.
2 The LORD has [b] made known his
salvation;
he has [c] revealed his righteousness
in [d] the sight of the nations.
3 He has [e] remembered his [f] steadfast
love and faithfulness
to the house of Israel.
All [g] the ends of the earth have seen
[h] the salvation of our God.
4 [i] Make a joyful noise to the LORD, all
the earth;
[j] break forth into joyous song and
sing praises!
5 Sing praises to the LORD with the lyre,
with the lyre and the [k] sound of
melody!
6 With [l] trumpets and the sound of
[m] the horn
[i] make a joyful noise before the
King, the LORD!
7 [n] Let the sea roar, and [o] all that fills it;
[o] the world and those who dwell in it!
8 Let the rivers [p] clap their hands;
let [q] the hills sing for joy together
9 before the LORD, for he comes
to [r] judge the earth.
He will judge the world with
righteousness,
and the peoples with equity.

4 [i] See Ps. 66:1 [j] Isai. 44:23 5 [k] Isai. 51:3 6 [l] Num. 10:10; 1 Chr. 15:24 [m] 2 Chr. 15:14 [i] [See ver. 4 above] 7 [n] Ps. 96:11; [o] Ps. 24:1 8 [p] Isai. 55:12; [Ps. 93:3] [q] Ps. 89:12 9 [r] Ps. 96:13; See Ps. 58:11

1 Most Hebrew manuscripts; one Hebrew manuscript, Septuagint, Syriac, Jerome *Light dawns*

97:2, 3 Clouds . . . darkness . . . fire. See Ps. 18 and 29. The visible revelation of God (i.e., in theophany) was sometimes in the context of a storm-like event. Such a manifestation helped God's people to appreciate His awesome power.

97:5 mountains. See note Ps. 46:2, 3.

97:7 who make their boast . . . idols. See Ps. 96:4–6.

97:8 because of your judgments. The people of God know that the judgments of God will remove the wicked and so bring about their own liberation.

Ps. 98 A royal psalm, like Ps. 47; 93; 95; 96; 97; 99. The theme of deliverance is divided into past (vv. 1–3), present (vv. 4–6), and future (vv. 7–9).

98:1 a new song. See "Music in the Church" at Col. 3:16.

marvelous things. This phrase translated "wonderful deeds" in Ps. 9:1 (see note there).

worked salvation. In its Old Testament context the reference is to a military victory. It is appropriate today to apply the verse to a spiritual victory, since it is a great victory by God over "the cosmic powers" (Eph. 6:12).

98:3 has remembered. More than mere memory, God's remembrance includes His favorable action.

98:4 Make a joyful noise. This section demonstrates the enthusiastic worship of a people who have deep love for God. Their worship is active and noisy.

98:7 the sea. Nature is here personified as praising the Lord. He is Creator of all, animate and inanimate (Ps. 95:5).

98:8 the rivers . . . the hills. See note on v. 7 and on Ps. 46:2, 3.

98:9 judge . . . with equity. See note Ps. 96:10.

The LORD Our God Is Holy

99 [s]The LORD reigns; [t]let the peoples
tremble!
He [u]sits enthroned upon the
cherubim; [v]let the earth
quake!
2 The LORD is [w]great in Zion;
he is [x]exalted over all the peoples.
3 Let them praise your [y]great and
awesome name!
[z]Holy is he!
4 [a]The King in his might [b]loves
justice.[1]
You have established equity;
you have executed justice
and righteousness in Jacob.
5 [c]Exalt the LORD our God;
[d]worship at his [e]footstool!
[z]Holy is he!
6 [f]Moses and Aaron were among his
[g]priests,
Samuel also was among those who
[h]called upon his name.
They [i]called to the LORD, and he
answered them.
7 In [j]the pillar of the cloud he spoke to
them;
they [k]kept his testimonies
and the statute that he gave them.
8 O LORD our God, you answered
them;
you were [l]a forgiving God to them,
but [m]an avenger of their
wrongdoings.
9 Exalt the LORD our God,
and worship at his [n]holy
mountain;
for the LORD our God
is holy!

Psalm 99
1 [s]Ps. 93:1; See 1 Chr. 16:31 [t][Ps. 96:9] [u]See Ps. 80:1 [v][Isai. 24:19, 20]
2 [w][Isai. 24:23] [x]Ps. 113:4; [Ps. 92:8; 93:4]
3 [y][Ps. 111:9; Deut. 28:58] [z]Josh. 24:19; Isai. 6:3; Rev. 15:4
4 [a][ver. 1] [b]Ps. 11:7; Isai. 61:8; [Job 36:5-7]
5 [c]Ps. 107:32; 118:28; Ex. 15:2; Isai. 25:1 [d]Ps. 132:7; 1 Chr. 28:2 [e]Isai. 60:13; Lam. 2:1; Ezek. 43:7 [z][See ver. 3 above]
6 [f][Jer. 15:1] [g]See Ex. 24:6-8; 40:22-27; Lev. 8:1-30 [h]1 Sam. 7:9; 12:18; See Ps. 105:1 [i]Ps. 106:23; Ex. 14:15; 17:11, 12; 32:30; Num. 12:13; 16:48; Deut. 9:18
7 [j]Ex. 33:9; Num. 12:5 [k][Ps. 105:28]
8 [l]Num. 14:20 [m]Ex. 32:35; Num. 20:12; Deut. 9:20; [Jer. 46:28]
9 [n]See Ps. 2:6

His Steadfast Love Endures Forever

100 A PSALM FOR [o]GIVING THANKS.
[p]Make a joyful noise to the
LORD, all the earth!
2 [q]Serve the LORD with
gladness!
[r]Come into his presence with
singing!
3 Know that [s]the LORD, he
is God!
It is he who [t]made us, and
[u]we are his;[2]
we are his [v]people, and [w]the
sheep of his pasture.
4 [x]Enter his gates with
thanksgiving,
and his [y]courts with praise!
Give thanks to him; [z]bless his
name!
5 [a]For the LORD is good;
his steadfast love endures
forever,
and his [b]faithfulness to all
generations.

Psalm 100 [o][Ps. 50:14] **1** [p]See Ps. 66:1 **2** [q][Ps. 2:11] [r][Ps. 95:2] **3** [s]1 Kin. 18:39 [t]See Ps. 95:6; Job 10:3, 8 [u]Isai. 43:1 [v]Ezek. 34:30 [w]See Ps. 74:1 **4** [x][Ps. 66:13] [y]Ps. 96:8 [z]Ps. 96:2 **5** [a]Ps. 25:8; 106:1; 119:68; 2 Chr. 5:13; Ezra 3:11; Jer. 33:11; Nah. 1:7 [b]See Ps. 36:5

1 Or *The might of the King loves justice* 2 Or *and not we ourselves*

Ps. 99 A royal psalm (Ps. 93 note). The psalm may be divided into three uneven stanzas based on a refrain that is repeated three times with some variation (vv. 3, 5, 9).

99:1 The LORD reigns. See notes Ps. 5:2 and 93:1.

upon the cherubim. Cherubim are spiritual beings who dwell in heaven with God. They are guardians of God's holiness, as witnessed by their role in protecting the post-Fall garden (Gen. 3:24). Cherubim were symbolically represented in the tabernacle, both in the innermost curtain (Ex. 36:35), and in the Most Holy Place (Ex. 37:1–9). The psalm refers to the cherubim of God's throne with their outstretched wings above the ark of the covenant.

let the earth quake. At God's special self-revelations (theophanies) reverberations, like those of a natural earthquake were sometimes felt throughout the earth. See "The Greatness of God" at 1 Chr. 29:11.

99:2 in Zion. The location of the temple. See note Ps. 3:4.

99:3 name. See note Ps. 8:1.

Holy is he. This is the refrain of the song (vv. 5, 9); God is set apart from all His creatures. This is evident from His uncreated nature, His power, and His moral perfection.

99:4 executed justice. See note Ps. 96:10.

99:6 Moses . . . Aaron . . . Samuel. Three of the most prominent leaders of Israel in the period before the monarchy. All three served as mediators between God and His people.

called upon his name. The emphasis in this section of the psalm is that God speaks to His people when they turn to Him for help in prayer.

99:7 the pillar of the cloud. See Ex. 13:21, 22; 40:34–38.

99:8 an avenger of their wrongdoings. For their own good, and to preserve His holiness, God may punish His people for the sins they commit. Israel knew this because God gave foreign enemies power over them when they persisted in unbelief. This reflects God's corrective punishment.

99:9 God is holy. See note on v. 3.

Ps. 100 See 95:1 note.

100:1 all the earth. As in the royal psalms preceding, the call goes out beyond the chosen people to all the peoples of the earth. God is their King too, whether they are aware of it or not.

100:2 with gladness. God is not a despotic king who forces his people to serve him. Loving service is grateful response to the grace of God.

100:3 the sheep of his pasture. See Ps. 23:1 for note on royal overtones of the portrayal of God as a shepherd.

100:4 his gates . . . his courts. Those of the temple. This psalm may have been sung during a festive entry into the temple precincts.

100:5 his steadfast love. God's lovingkindness to people who are in covenant with Him.

I Will Walk with Integrity

101 A Psalm of David.
I will sing of [c] steadfast love and
justice;
to you, O LORD, I will make music.
2 I will [d] ponder the way [e] that is
blameless.
Oh when will you [f] come to me?
I will [g] walk with [h] integrity of heart
within my house;
3 I will not set before my eyes
anything [i] that is worthless.
I hate the work of those who [j] fall away;
it shall not cling to me.
4 [k] A perverse heart shall be far from me;
I will [l] know nothing of evil.
5 Whoever slanders his neighbor
[m] secretly
I will [n] destroy.
Whoever has a [o] haughty look and an
[p] arrogant heart
I will not endure.
6 I will look with favor on the faithful
in the land,
that they may dwell with me;
he who walks in [q] the way that is
blameless
shall minister to me.
7 No one who [r] practices deceit
shall dwell in my house;
no one who utters lies
shall [s] continue before my eyes.
8 [t] Morning by morning I will destroy
all the wicked in the land,
[u] cutting off all [v] the evildoers
from [w] the city of the LORD.

Psalm 101
1 [c] [Ex. 34:7]
2 [d] 1 Sam. 18:5 [e] Ps. 119:1; Prov. 11:20; [Matt. 5:48] [f] [Ex. 20:24; John 14:23]
[g] 1 Kin. 9:4
[h] Ps. 78:72
3 [i] Deut. 15:9
[j] See Ps. 40:4
4 [k] Prov. 11:20; 17:20
[l] [1 Cor. 5:11]
5 [m] Ps. 15:3
[n] ver. 8 [o] Ps. 18:27; 131:1; Prov. 6:17; 21:4; 30:13
[p] Prov. 16:5
6 [q] Ps. 119:1; Prov. 11:20; [Matt. 5:48]
7 [r] Ps. 52:2 [s] Ps. 102:28
8 [t] [Ps. 73:14]
[u] Ps. 75:10
[v] Ps. 94:4 [w] Ps. 48:1, 8; [Isai. 52:1]

Psalm 102
[x] Ps. 61:2 [y] Ps. 142:2
1 [z] Ps. 39:12
[a] Ps. 18:6; Ex. 2:23; 1 Sam. 9:16
2 [b] See Ps. 27:9 [c] See Ps. 18:6 [d] See Ps. 31:2 [e] Ps. 56:9
[f] See Ps. 69:17
3 [g] [James 4:14]; See Ps. 37:20 [h] Job 30:30; Lam. 1:13; See Ps. 31:10
4 [i] Ps. 121:6
[j] Ps. 37:2; Isai. 40:7; [James 1:10, 11]
[k] 1 Sam. 1:7; 2 Sam. 12:17; 1 Kin. 21:4; Job 33:20]

Do Not Hide Your Face from Me

102 A Prayer of one afflicted,
when he is [x] faint and [y] pours
out his complaint before the
Lord.
1 [z] Hear my prayer, O LORD;
let my cry [a] come to you!
2 [b] Do not hide your face from me
in [c] the day of my distress!
[d] Incline your ear to me;
[e] answer me speedily [f] in the day
when I call!
3 For my days [g] pass away like smoke,
and my [h] bones burn like a furnace.
4 My heart is [i] struck down like grass
and [j] has withered;
I [k] forget to eat my bread.
5 Because of my loud groaning
my [l] bones cling to my flesh.
6 I am like [m] a desert owl of the
wilderness,
like an owl[1] of the waste places;
7 I [n] lie awake;
I am like a lonely sparrow on the
housetop.
8 All the day my enemies taunt me;
those who [o] deride me [p] use my
name for a curse.
9 For I eat ashes like bread
and [q] mingle tears with my drink,
10 because of your indignation and anger;
for you have [r] taken me up and
[s] thrown me down.

5 [l] See Job 19:20 6 [m] Isai. 34:11; Zeph. 2:14; [Job 30:29] 7 [n] Ps. 77:4 8 [o] [Acts 26:11] [p] Isai. 65:15; Jer. 29:22 9 [q] See Ps. 42:3 10 [r] Ezek. 3:12, 14 [s] Ps. 51:11

1 The precise identity of these birds is uncertain

Ps. 101 In this psalm the king promises to live a life of obedience, pursuing holiness in his own life and seeking to root out evil from his kingdom. David could not live up to his own ideals. He failed time after time, though he lived a life of repentance. Many believe that Psalm 101 was written by David and later used as a coronation psalm, beginning with Solomon. If so, high ideals at the beginning of his reign degenerated into disobedience and, in the case of Solomon, open apostasy. Christ alone could offer perfect obedience in the flesh.

101:1 justice. The reference is to God's judgments. The psalmist praises the Lord for them because they are consistent and righteous, not arbitrary.

101:2 the way that is blameless. As defined by the law of God. See Mic. 6:8 for the classic description.

101:3 I hate. The psalmist strongly repudiates wicked deeds. He will not tolerate them in his presence. In this he seeks to emulate God, who will not tolerate an unrepentant sinner in His presence.

101:5 I will destroy . . . I will not endure. The psalmist will actively oppose unrighteousness in his area of authority.

haughty look . . . arrogant heart. The heart is the foundation of a person's being and character. The "look" refers to demeanor. See Ps. 131:1.

102:title The title is unusual in that it gives, not a specific historical occasion, but the situation (affliction) in which the psalm finds appropriate use.

102:2 hide your face. The psalmist wonders at the withdrawal of God's friendship. He knows it is a sign of God's wrath, since He promised to be with His obedient covenant people.

102:3 like a furnace. Points to the pain and suffering of life or more specifically to a raging fever.

102:5 bones cling to my flesh. His suffering is not only spiritual and psychological, but physical as well.

102:6 like a desert owl of the wilderness. He is silent in his affliction, and without friends or supporters.

102:8 my enemies. As is typical in a lament, unnamed but real enemies are a source of distress to the psalmist. Because the enemies are unnamed, the psalm has timeless application to all generations.

102:10 your indignation and anger. The psalmist knows the ultimate cause of his suffering: God's anger. He never disputes the justice of that anger, but he turns to God for relief.

11 My days are like [t]an evening shadow;
I [j]wither away like grass.
12 But you, O LORD, are [u]enthroned forever;
you [v]are remembered throughout all generations.
13 You will [w]arise and have [x]pity on Zion;
it is the time to favor her;
[y]the appointed time has come.
14 For your servants hold her [z]stones dear
and have pity on her dust.
15 Nations will [a]fear the name of the LORD,
and all [b]the kings of the earth will fear your glory.
16 For the LORD [c]builds up Zion;
he [d]appears in his glory;
17 he [e]regards the prayer of the destitute
and does not despise their prayer.
18 Let this be [f]recorded for [g]a generation to come,
so that [h]a people yet to be created may praise the LORD:
19 that he [i]looked down from his holy height;
from heaven the LORD looked at the earth,
20 to hear [j]the groans of the prisoners,
to set free [k]those who were doomed to die,
21 that they may [l]declare in Zion the name of the LORD,
and in Jerusalem his praise,
22 when [m]peoples gather together,
and kingdoms, to worship the LORD.

23 He has broken my strength in midcourse;
he [n]has shortened my days.
24 "O my God," [o]I say, "take me not away
in the midst of my days—
[p]you whose years endure throughout all generations!"
25 [q]Of old you laid the foundation of the earth,
and [r]the heavens are the work of your hands.
26 [s]They will perish, but [t]you will remain;
they will all wear out like a garment.
You will change them like a robe,
and they will pass away,
27 but [u]you are the same, and your years have no end.
28 [v]The children of your servants [w]shall dwell secure;
[x]their offspring shall be established before you.

Bless the LORD, O My Soul

103

OF DAVID.
[y]Bless the LORD, O my soul,
and all that is within me,
bless his holy name!
2 [y]Bless the LORD, O my soul,
and [z]forget not all his benefits,
3 who [a]forgives all your iniquity,
who [b]heals all your diseases,
4 who [c]redeems your life from the pit,
who [d]crowns you with steadfast love and mercy,

11 [t]Ps. 109:23; 144:4; Job 8:9 [j][See ver. 4 above] **12** [u]ver. 26; See Ps. 9:7 [v]Ps. 135:13; Ex. 3:15 **13** [w]Ps. 68:1 [x]Isai. 60:10; Zech. 1:12 [y]Ps. 75:2; Jer. 29:10; Dan. 9:2; [Isai. 40:2] **14** [z]Neh. 4:2; [Lam. 4:1] **15** [a]1 Kin. 8:43; Isai. 59:19 [b]Ps. 138:4; Isai. 60:3 **16** [c]Ps. 147:2 [d]Isai. 60:1,2 **17** [e]Neh. 1:6, 11 **18** [f][Deut. 31:19; Rom. 15:4; 1 Cor. 10:1] [g]Ps. 48:13; See Ps. 78:4, 6 [h]See Ps. 22:31; [Isai. 43:21] **19** [i]See Ps. 11:4 **20** [j]Ps. 79:11 [k]Ps. 79:11 **21** [l]See Ps. 22:22 **22** [m][Isai. 45:14]; See Ps. 22:27
23 [n]Ps. 89:45 **24** [o][Isai. 38:10] [p]Ps. 90:2; Job 36:26; Hab. 1:12 **25** [q]Gen. 1:1; 2:1; Cited Heb. 1:10 [r]See Ps. 96:5 **26** [s]Isai. 34:4; 51:6; Matt. 24:35; 2 Pet. 3:7, 10, 12; Rev. 20:11; 21:1; Cited Heb. 1:11, 12 [t]ver. 12

27 [u]Isai. 41:4; 48:12; Mal. 3:6; [Heb. 13:8; James 1:17] **28** [v]See Ps. 69:36 [w]Ps. 37:29 [x]Ps. 112:2
Psalm 103 **1** [y]ver. 22; Ps. 104:1 **2** [y][See ver. 1 above] [z]Deut. 6:12; 8:11 **3** [a]Ex. 34:7; Isai. 33:24; Matt. 9:2; Mark 2:5; [Luke 7:47] [b]Ps. 107:20; 147:3; Ex.15:26; [Matt. 8:17] **4** [c]See Ps. 56:13 [d][Ps. 5:12]

102:12 forever. Over against the fragility of the psalmist's life stands the constancy and eternity of the Lord.

102:13 arise. See notes Ps. 3:7 and 7:6.

on Zion. See Ps. 2:6; 3:3. The references to the destruction of Zion have led many commentators to place the psalm just after the Babylonian captivity.

102:15 Nations will fear. As Jerusalem rises up from destruction, all who see it will praise the Lord.

102:20 to hear . . . to set free. Though God is above heaven, He enters the world to help the afflicted (9:18; 72:4 and notes).

102:23 shortened my days. Through the sickness that now threatens the psalmist's life.

102:25 Of old. God existed before His work of creation. The author of Hebrews applies vv. 25–27 to Christ (Heb. 1:10–12). There the argument is that however great the angels are considered, they are created, and not eternal. But Christ, the Second Person of the Trinity, exists through all eternity.

102:27 you are the same. See "The Self-Existence of God" at 90:2.

102:28 The children of your servants. The poet's hope is with the future generations. Though he suffers now in the present, he sees a brighter future.

103:1 O my soul. The psalmist carries on a public dialogue with himself. He encourages himself to praise, and so encourages others who see his example.

103:3 forgives all your iniquity. The primary benefit of grace is the forgiveness of sins (Acts 13:38). God is compassionate toward His repentant people.

103:4 from the pit. That is, from death.

steadfast love. See 92:2 note.

5 who [e]satisfies you with good
so that your youth is renewed like
[f]the eagle's.

6 The LORD works [g]righteousness
and justice for all who are
oppressed.
7 He made known his [h]ways to Moses,
his [i]acts to the people of Israel.
8 The LORD is [j]merciful and gracious,
slow to anger and abounding in
steadfast love.
9 [k]He will not always chide,
nor will he [l]keep his anger forever.
10 He does not deal with us [m]according
to our sins,
nor repay us according to our
iniquities.
11 For [n]as high as the heavens are above
the earth,
so great is his [o]steadfast love
toward [p]those who fear him;
12 as far as the east is from the west,
so far does he [q]remove our
transgressions from us.
13 As [r]a father shows compassion to his
children,
so the LORD shows compassion [p]to
those who fear him.
14 For he knows our frame;[1]
he [s]remembers that we are dust.
15 As for man, his days are like [t]grass;
he flourishes like [u]a flower of the
field;
16 for [v]the wind passes over it, and [w]it
is gone,
and [x]its place knows it no more.
17 But [y]the steadfast love of the LORD is
from everlasting to everlasting
on [p]those who fear him,
and his righteousness to
[z]children's children,
18 to those who [a]keep his covenant
and [b]remember to do his
commandments.
19 The LORD has [c]established his throne
in the heavens,
and his [d]kingdom rules over all.
20 Bless the LORD, O you [e]his angels,
you [f]mighty ones who [g]do his word,
obeying the voice of his word!
21 Bless the LORD, all his [h]hosts,
his [i]ministers, who do his will!
22 [j]Bless the LORD, all his works,
in all places of his dominion.
[k]Bless the LORD, O my soul!

O LORD My God, You Are Very Great

104 [l]Bless the LORD, O my soul!
O LORD my God, you are [m]very
great!
[n]You are clothed with splendor and
majesty,
2 covering yourself with light as with
a garment,
[o]stretching out the heavens [p]like a
tent.
3 He [q]lays the beams of his [r]chambers
on the waters;
he makes [s]the clouds his chariot;
he rides on [t]the wings of the wind;

5 [e]Ps. 107:9 [f]Isai. 40:31 6 [g]Ps. 146:7 7 [h]Ex. 33:13; [Ps. 25:4] [i][Ps. 78:11; Ex. 34:10] 8 [j]See Ps. 86:15 9 [k]Isai. 57:16 [l]Ps. 30:5; Jer. 3:5, 12; Mic. 7:18 10 [m]Ezra 9:13 11 [n]See Ps. 36:5 [o]Ps. 117:2 [p]ver. 13, 17; Luke 1:50 12 [q][Isai. 38:17; 43:25; Mic. 7:19] 13 [r]Mal. 3:17 [p][See ver. 11 above] 14 [s]Ps. 78:39 15 [t]Ps. 90:5 [u]See Job 14:2 16 [v]Isai. 40:7 [w]Ps. 37:36 [x]See Job 7:10 17 [y]Ps. 25:6 [p][See ver. 11 above] [z]Ex. 20:5, 6 18 [a]Deut. 7:9 [b]Ps. 19:8 19 [c]Ps. 11:4; 93:2 [d]Ps. 47:2; Dan. 4:17 20 [e]Ps. 148:2; [Luke 2:13] [f]Ps. 78:25 [g]Matt. 6:10 21 [h]Gen. 32:2; Josh. 5:14; 1 Kin. 22:19 [i]Ps. 104:4; Dan. 7:10; Heb. 1:14 22 [j]Ps. 145:10 [k]ver. 1, 2

Psalm 104 1 [l]Ps. 103:1, 2, 22 [m]See 2 Sam. 7:22 [n]Ps. 93:1; Job 40:10; [Job 37:22] 2 [o]See Job 9:8 [p]Isai. 40:22 3 [q]Amos 9:6 [r]ver. 13; [s]Isai. 19:1; [t]Ps. 18:10; 2 Sam. 22:11

1 Or *knows how we are formed*

103:5 with good. God provides everything that is constructive and wholesome for His people.

103:6 for all who are oppressed. See 102:2 note.

103:7 to Moses. By referring to Moses, the psalmist calls to mind all of God's blessings associated with the Exodus, the wilderness wanderings, and even the conquest of the Promised Land.

103:12 as far as the east is from the west. When God forgives sins, He completely removes them. The height and breadth of His mercy are vast.

103:13 As a father. The comparison of God to a compassionate and loving father is developed in Rom. 8:12–17. See Ex. 4:22, 23; Hos. 11:1, 8, 9.

103:14 For he knows. God knows us better than we know ourselves.

we are dust. According to Gen. 2:7, God formed Adam from the dust of the ground. The consequence of sin is that humans die as surely as the animals (Eccl. 3:19). Yet God has mercy on us. See "Body and Soul, Male and Female" at Gen. 2:7.

103:17 steadfast love . . . on those who fear him. There is a reciprocal relationship between divine initiative and human response. God first loves us, then we love Him in return as shown in the faithful obedience of our lives (Rom. 5:8; 1 John 4:10).

103:18 those who keep his covenant. The obedience of those who keep God's covenant shows the reality of His mercy. They walk in devoted fellowship with the Lord who loved them in His covenant of grace.

103:19 rules over all. See "Providence" at Prov. 16:33.

103:21 his hosts. A reference to the divine army. It would include the angels, the cherubim, and other heavenly creatures. See "Angels" at Zech. 1:9.

Ps. 104 God's great act of creation is emphasized, reflecting the teaching and vocabulary of Gen. 1. Parallels may be observed between this song and an Egyptian hymn of Amenhotep IV (Akhenaton) to the sun. But the psalm affirms that the Creator alone, and not any aspect of creation, such as the sun, should be worshiped.

104:1 O my soul. See comment on Ps. 103:1.

You are clothed. This section develops the metaphor of the creation as God's garment. This emphasizes the distinction between the Creator and the creation and implicitly disparages worship of any aspect of the creation, however glorious it may seem (Rom. 1:22).

104:2 with light. A reference to the first day of creation (Gen. 1:3).

the heavens. The second day of creation (Gen. 1:6–8).

104:3 the wings of the wind. See 18:9 and note.

4 he [u]makes his messengers winds,
his [v]ministers [w]a flaming fire.
5 He [x]set the earth on its foundations,
so that it should never be moved.
6 You [y]covered it with the deep as with a garment;
the waters stood above the mountains.
7 At [z]your rebuke they fled;
at [a]the sound of your thunder they [b]took to flight.
8 The mountains rose, the valleys sank down
to the place that you [c]appointed for them.
9 You set [d]a boundary that they may not pass,
so that they [e]might not again cover the earth.

10 You make springs gush forth in the valleys;
they flow between the hills;
11 they [f]give drink to every beast of the field;
the wild donkeys quench their thirst.
12 Beside them the birds of the heavens dwell;
they sing among the branches.
13 [g]From your lofty abode you [h]water the mountains;
the earth is satisfied with the fruit of your work.
14 You cause [i]the grass to grow for the livestock
and [j]plants for man to cultivate,
that he may bring forth [k]food from the earth
15 and [l]wine to gladden the heart of man,
[m]oil to make his face shine
and bread to [n]strengthen man's heart.
16 The trees of the LORD are watered abundantly,
[o]the cedars of Lebanon [p]that he planted.
17 In them the birds build their nests;
the stork has her home in the fir trees.
18 The high mountains are for [q]the wild goats;
the rocks are a refuge for [r]the rock badgers.

19 He made the moon to mark the [s]seasons;[1]
the sun knows its time for setting.
20 [t]You make darkness, and it is night,
when all the beasts of the forest creep about.
21 [u]The young lions roar for their prey,
seeking their food from God.
22 When the sun rises, they steal away
and lie down in their [v]dens.
23 [w]Man goes out to his work
and to his labor until the evening.

24 O LORD, how manifold are your works!
In [x]wisdom have you made them all;
the earth is full of your creatures.
25 Here is the sea, great and wide,
[y]which teems with creatures innumerable,
living things both small and great.
26 There go the ships,
and [z]Leviathan, which you formed
to [a]play in it.[2]

1 Or *the appointed times* (compare Genesis 1:14) 2 Or *you formed to play with*

4 [u]Cited Heb.1:7; [Ps. 148:8] [v]Ps. 103:21 [w][2 Kin. 1:10; 2:11] 5 [x]Ps. 24:2; 89:11; 136:3; See Job 38:4 6 [y]Gen. 7:19 7 [z]Ps. 18:15; [Ps. 106:9; Gen. 1:9; 8:1, 5; Matt. 8:26] [a]Ps. 77:18 [b]Ps. 48:5 8 [c][Job 38:8, 10, 11] 9 [d]See Job 26:10 [e]See Gen. 9:11-16 11 [f][ver.18] 13 [g]ver. 3 [h][Ps. 65:9; 147:8; Deut. 11:11; Job 5:10; Jer. 10:13; 14:22] 14 [i]Ps. 147; .8, 9 [j]Gen.1:11, 29, 30; 3:18; 9:3 [k]Job 28:5; [Ps. 136:25; 147:9]

15 [l]Judg. 9:13; Eccles. 10:19; [Prov. 31:6, 7] [m][Ps. 23:5; Judg. 9:9] [n][Gen. 18:5] 16 [o]See Judg. 9:15 [p][Num. 24:6] 18 [q]See Job 39:1 [r]Lev. 11:5; Prov. 30:26 19 [s]Gen. 1:14; Lev. 23:4 20 [t]Isai. 45:7 21 [u]Job 38:39 22 [v]Job 37:8 23 [w][Gen. 3:19] 24 [x]Prov. 3:19 25 [y]Ps. 69:34 26 [z]See Job 41:1 [a][Job 40:20]

104:4 a flaming fire. God's heavenly servants have an awesome appearance. How much more powerful must God, their Creator, be. This verse may be a polemic against Baal worship, since Canaanite mythological texts describe the servants of their god as flames of fire.

104:5 should never be moved. The world is stable and ordered, not chaotic. God's control of the world is comforting to those who recognize it. See "God the Creator" at 148:5.

104:6 the waters. God created the waters and ordered them in rivers, lakes, and oceans. In the religions of the surrounding nations, the sea is a symbol of chaos and disorder. Their pantheistic theology deifies the sea and sets it against the gods of order. The Bible uses this imagery, but disallows the polytheistic theology (Ps. 18:4; 46:2, 3; 74:13–15; Nah. 1).

104:9 might not again cover. A reference to the promise God made to Noah after the Flood (Gen. 9:11).

104:14 You cause the grass to grow. A reflection of the third day of creation (Gen. 1:9–13).

104:15 wine to gladden the heart of man. God's kindness is exhibited in His provisions for daily life (Acts 14:17; 1 Tim. 4:3, 4).

104:19 the moon . . . the sun. See Gen. 1:14–19—the fourth day of creation.

104:21 from God. What appears to be purely natural—lions seeking their prey—is an act of providence.

104:23 Man goes out. God has given His creation a wonderfully ordered rhythm.

104:24 In wisdom. See notes Prov. 8:22–31. The divine answer to Job (Job 38–41) contains many examples of God's wisdom in creation. See "The Wisdom and Will of God" at Dan. 2:20.

104:25 sea . . . creatures innumerable. The fifth day of creation (Gen. 1:20–23).

104:26 the ships . . . Leviathan. The psalmist's imagination is caught up with God's mysterious sea. On its surface ships glide to and fro from distant ports, while underneath lurks the monster Leviathan, here, a poetic symbol of God's creative power (Job 41).

27 These [b]all look to you,
to [c]give them their food in due season.
28 When you give it to them, they gather it up;
when you [d]open your hand,
they are filled with good things.
29 When you [e]hide your face, they are [f]dismayed;
when you [g]take away their breath,
they die
and [h]return to their dust.
30 When you [i]send forth your Spirit,[1]
they are created,
and you [j]renew the face of the ground.

31 May the glory of the LORD [k]endure forever;
may the LORD [l]rejoice in his works,
32 who looks on the earth and it [m]trembles,
who [n]touches the mountains and they smoke!
33 I will sing to the LORD [o]as long as I live;
I will sing praise to my God while I have being.
34 May my [p]meditation be pleasing to him,
for I rejoice in the LORD.
35 Let [q]sinners be consumed from the earth,
and let the wicked be no more!
[r]Bless the LORD, O my soul!
[s]Praise the LORD!

27 [b]Ps. 145:15 [c][ver. 14]; See Job 36:31
28 [d]Ps. 145:16
29 [e]Ps. 30:7; [Deut. 31:17] [f]Job 23:15 [g]See Job 34:14 [h]See Job 10:9
30 [i]See Job 33:4 [j][Rev. 21:5]
31 [k]Ps. 72:17 [l][Gen. 1:31; Prov. 8:31]
32 [m][Hab. 3:10] [n]Ps. 144:5; Ex. 19:18; [Amos 9:5]
33 [o]See Ps. 63:4
34 [p]Job 15:4
35 [q]See Ps. 37:38 [r]See ver. 1 [s]Ps. 105:45; 106:48; 113:9; 150:6

Tell of All His Wonderful Works

105 [t]Oh give thanks to the LORD;
[u]call upon his name;
[v]make known his deeds among the peoples!
2 Sing to him, sing praises to him;
[w]tell of all his wondrous works!
3 Glory in his holy name;
let the hearts of those who seek the LORD rejoice!
4 Seek the LORD and his [x]strength;
[y]seek his presence continually!
5 Remember the [z]wondrous works that he has done,
his miracles, and [a]the judgments he uttered,
6 O offspring of [b]Abraham, his servant,
children of Jacob, his [c]chosen ones!

7 He is the LORD our God;
his [d]judgments are in all the earth.
8 He [e]remembers his covenant forever,
the word that he commanded, for [f]a thousand generations,
9 [g]the covenant that he made with Abraham,
his [h]sworn promise to Isaac,
10 which he confirmed to [i]Jacob as a statute,
to Israel as an everlasting covenant,
11 saying, [j]"To you I will give the land of Canaan
as [k]your portion for an inheritance."

Psalm 105
1 [t]Ps. 106:1; 1 Chr. 16:34; Isai. 12:4; For ver. 1-15, see 1 Chr. 16:8-22 [u]Ps. 99:6; 116:13, 17; [Gen. 4:26] [v]Ps. 145:4, 5, 11, 12
2 [w]Ps. 77:12
4 [x]See Ps. 78:61 [y][Ps. 27:8]
5 [z]Ps. 77:11; See Ps. 72:18 [a]Ex. 6:6; 7:4
6 [b]ver. 42 [c]ver. 43; Ps. 106:5; [Ps. 135:4]
7 [d]Isai. 26:9
8 [e]ver. 42; Ps. 106:45; 111:5; Luke 1:72 [f]Deut. 7:9
9 [g]Gen. 17:2; See Gen. 22:15-18 [h]Gen. 26:3
10 [i]Gen. 28:13, 14; 35:11, 12
11 [j]Gen. 13:15; 15:18 [k]Ps. 78:55

[1] Or *breath*

104:29 hide your face. God is omnipresent: He is everywhere (Ps. 139). However, in His anger God withdraws covenant blessings and this is experienced as divine absence.

104:30 your Spirit. This alludes to Gen. 2:4–8, the creation of man on the sixth day.

104:32 the mountains . . . smoke. Hills are the symbol of stability and firmness (Ps. 46:2, 3), but God's mere touch sets them aflame.

104:35 Let sinners be consumed from the earth. The psalmist would like to see the removal of everything that opposes the godly order he has so eloquently described.

Ps. 105 While Ps. 104 praises God's acts in creating the world, this song meditates on His acts in the world's continuing history. The first fifteen verses are quoted (along with Ps. 96 and part of 106) in 1 Chr. 16, perhaps indicating use of the psalm in worship.

105:1 among the peoples. Israel cannot hide its light "under a basket" (Matt. 5:15). True people of God gladly bear witness to God's grace throughout the world.

105:2 his wondrous works. Those acts of grace and judgment that God performs in history. God enters history and acts graciously on behalf of His people, remarkably so in the life, death, resurrection and ascension of His only begotten Son.

105:4 seek his presence. Seek to live in His presence. The psalmist often testifies of the horror associated with the withdrawal of God's friendship (Ps. 22:1; 28:1).

105:5 Remember. "Remembering" God's works is more than recalling what they were; it means reacting with faith and obedience to what they mean.

105:8 He remembers. Once again (as in v. 5) remembrance involves doing as well as knowing. In this case, God acts in the present based on the promises given to Abraham.

his covenant. The specific covenant here is the Abrahamic covenant (Gen. 12:1–3; 15; 17).

105:9, 10 to Isaac . . . to Jacob. God reaffirmed His covenant relationship with the descendants of Abraham. See Gen. 26:3.

105:11 I will give the land of Canaan. See Gen. 15:17–20.

12 When they were [l]few in number,
of little account, and [m]sojourners
in it,
13 wandering from nation to nation,
from one kingdom to another
people,
14 he [n]allowed no one to oppress them;
he [o]rebuked kings on their
account,
15 saying, [p]"Touch not my anointed
ones,
do my prophets no harm!"

16 When he [q]summoned a famine on
the land
and [r]broke all supply[1] of bread,
17 he had [s]sent a man ahead of them,
Joseph, who was [t]sold as a slave.
18 His [u]feet were hurt with fetters;
his neck was put in a collar of
iron;
19 until [v]what he had said came to pass,
the word of the LORD [w]tested him.
20 [x]The king sent and [y]released him;
the ruler of the peoples set him
free;
21 he [z]made him lord of his house
and ruler of all his possessions,
22 to bind[2] his princes at his pleasure
and to teach his elders wisdom.

23 Then [a]Israel came to Egypt;
Jacob [b]sojourned in [c]the land of
Ham.
24 And the LORD [d]made his people very
fruitful
and made them stronger than their
foes.
25 He [e]turned their hearts to hate his
people,
to [f]deal craftily with his servants.

26 He [g]sent Moses, his servant,
and Aaron, [h]whom he had chosen.

12 [l]Gen. 34:30; Deut. 7:7; 26:5 [m]Heb. 11:9
14 [n][Gen. 35:5] [o]Gen. 12:17; 20:3
15 [p]Gen. 20:6, 7; [Gen. 26:11]
16 [q]Gen. 41:54; [2 Kin. 8:1; Hag. 1:1] [r]Lev. 26:26; Isai. 3:1; Ezek. 4:16; [Ps. 104:15]
17 [s]Gen. 45:5; 50:20 [t]Gen. 37:28, 36; Acts 7:9
18 [u][Gen. 39:20]
19 [v]Gen. 40:20, 21; 41:53, 54 [w][Judg. 7:4]
20 [x]Gen. 41:14 [y]Ps. 146:7
21 [z]Gen. 41:40
23 [a]Gen. 46:6; Acts 7:15 [b]Acts 13:17 [c]Ps. 106:22; [Ps. 78:51]
24 [d]Ex. 1:7; Deut. 26:5
25 [e][Ex. 9:12; Rom. 11:8]; See Ex.1:8-14 [f]Ex. 1:10; Acts 7:19
26 [g]Ex. 3:10; 4:12 [h]Num. 16:5; 17:5
27 [i]For ver. 27-36, see Ps. 78:43-51 [c][See ver. 23 above]
28 [j]Ex. 10:21-23 [k]Ps. 99:7
29 [l]Ex. 7:21
30 [m]Ex. 8:3
31 [n]Ex. 8:21 [o]Ex. 8:16
32 [p]Ex. 9:23
33 [q]Ex. 9:25
34 [r]See Ex. 10:12-15
36 [s]See Ps. 78:51
37 [t]Ex. 12:35, 36
38 [u]Ex. 12:23 [v]Ex. 15:16

27 [i]They performed his signs among
them
and miracles in [c]the land of Ham.
28 He [j]sent darkness, and made the
land dark;
they [k]did not rebel[3] against his
words.
29 He turned their waters into blood
and [l]caused their fish to die.
30 Their land swarmed with frogs,
even in [m]the chambers of their
kings.
31 He spoke, and there came [n]swarms
of flies,
[o]and gnats throughout their
country.
32 He gave them hail for rain,
and fiery [p]lightning bolts through
their land.
33 He struck down their vines and fig
trees,
and [q]shattered the trees of their
country.
34 He spoke, and the [r]locusts came,
young locusts without number,
35 which devoured all the vegetation in
their land
and ate up the fruit of their
ground.
36 He [s]struck down all the firstborn in
their land,
[s]the firstfruits of all their strength.

37 Then he brought out Israel with
[t]silver and gold,
and there was none among his
tribes who stumbled.
38 [u]Egypt was glad when they departed,
for [v]dread of them had fallen
upon it.

1 Hebrew *staff* 2 Septuagint, Syriac, Jerome *instruct* 3 Septuagint, Syriac omit *not*

105:12 sojourners. Abraham, Isaac, and Jacob lived in the Promised Land as resident aliens. They wandered from place to place in Canaan.

105:14 he rebuked kings. See Gen. 12:10–20; 26.

105:15 my prophets. Abraham is referred to as a prophet in Gen. 20:7.

105:16–22 God promoted Joseph to a position of power in Egypt.

105:16 he summoned. God directed the events in Egypt so that when famine threatened that country Joseph was in power and able to save many people (Gen. 50:20).

105:23 Israel came to Egypt. See Gen. 46.

the land of Ham. Another name for Egypt.

105:28 He sent darkness. The psalmist emphasizes the ninth plague by naming it first.

105:31 flies, and gnats. These are the third and fourth plagues in reverse order of their actual occurrence in Egypt.

105:32 hail. The fifth and sixth plagues are unmentioned by the psalmist. The plague of hail was the seventh.

105:36 the firstborn. The tenth and final plague, after which Egypt allowed Israel to leave Goshen.

105:37 with silver and gold. God's great mercy and generosity may be seen here. As a slave nation in Egypt, Israel had little to call their own. Through the plagues, however, God struck fear into the hearts of the Egyptians so that they not only let Israel go, but were willing to hand over their valuables to encourage Israel's exodus (Ex. 12:33–36).

39 He [w]spread a cloud for a covering,
and fire to give light by night.
40 [x]They asked, and he [y]brought quail,
and gave them [z]bread from heaven
in abundance.
41 He opened the rock, and [a]water
gushed out;
it flowed through [b]the desert like a
river.
42 For he [c]remembered his holy
promise,
and [d]Abraham, his servant.
43 So he brought his people out with
joy,
his [d]chosen ones with [e]singing.
44 And he [f]gave them the lands of the
nations,
and they took possession of the
fruit of the peoples' toil,
45 that they might [g]keep his statutes
and [h]observe his laws.
[i]Praise the LORD!

Give Thanks to the LORD, for He Is Good

106 [i]Praise the LORD!
[j]Oh give thanks to the LORD,
[k]for he is good,
[l]for his steadfast love endures
forever!
2 Who can utter the mighty deeds of
the LORD,
or declare all his praise?
3 Blessed are they who observe justice,
who [m]do righteousness at all
times!
4 [n]Remember me, O LORD, when you
show favor to your people;
help me when you save them,[1]
5 that I may look upon the prosperity
of your [o]chosen ones,
that I may rejoice in the gladness
of your nation,
that I may glory with your
inheritance.
6 [p]Both we and [q]our fathers have sinned;
we have committed iniquity; we
have done wickedness.
7 Our fathers, when they were in Egypt,
did not consider your wondrous
works;
they [r]did not remember the
abundance of your steadfast
love,
but [s]rebelled by the Sea, at the Red
Sea.
8 Yet he saved them [t]for his name's sake,
[u]that he might make known his
mighty power.
9 He [v]rebuked the Red Sea, and it
[w]became dry,
and he [x]led them through the deep
as through a desert.
10 So he [y]saved them from the hand of
the foe
and [z]redeemed them from the
power of the enemy.
11 And [a]the waters covered their
adversaries;
not one of them was left.
12 Then [b]they believed his words;
they [c]sang his praise.
13 But they soon [d]forgot his works;
they did not wait for [e]his counsel.

39 [w][Job 36:20; Isai. 4:5]; See Ex. 13:21 **40** [x]Ps. 78:18, 27 [y]Ex. 16:13 [z]Ps. 78:24, 25; [John 6:31] **41** [a]See Ps. 78:15 [b]See Ps. 63:1 **42** [c]ver. 8, 9; Ex. 2:24 [d][Gen. 15:14]; See ver. 6 **43** [d][See ver. 42 above] [e][Isai. 35:10]; See Ex. 15:1-21 **44** [f]Josh. 24:13; [Ps. 78:55] **45** [g]Deut. 4:1, 40 [h]Ps. 78:7 [i]See Ps. 104:35
Psalm 106
1 [i][See Ps. 105:45 above] [j]See Ps. 105:1 [k]See Ps. 100:5 [l]See 1 Chr. 16:34, 41 **3** [m][Ps. 15:2] **4** [n][Ps. 119:132] **5** [o]Ps. 105:6, 43 **6** [p]1 Kin. 8:47; Ezra 9:6; Neh. 1:6, 7; 9:16; Jer. 3:25; 14:20; Dan. 9:5 [q]Ps. 79:8; Lev. 26:40 **7** [r][ver. 13, 21] [s]Ex. 14:11, 12 **8** [t]Ezek. 20:9, 14 [u]Ex. 9:16 **9** [v][Ps. 18:15; 104:7] [w]Ex. 14:21; [Isai. 50:2; 51:10] [x]Isai. 63:13 **10** [y]Ex. 14:30 [z]Ps. 107:2 **11** [a]Ex. 14:28; 15:5 **12** [b]Ex. 14:31 [c]See Ex. 15:1-21 **13** [d]Ps. 78:11; [Ex. 15:24; 16:2; 17:2]; [e][Ps. 107:11]

[1] Or *Remember me, O LORD, with the favor you show to your people; help me with your salvation*

105:40 bread from heaven. The manna. God's providential mercy went beyond bringing them out of Egypt—He provided for them in the wilderness by giving them food and drink.

105:42 his holy promise. The Abrahamic covenant included the promise that God would make Israel "a great nation" (Gen. 12:2).

105:45 observe his laws. The covenant relationship between God and His people is established and maintained by God alone as His work of grace. His people (indeed, all humanity) are responsible to reciprocate, not merely in the formal observance of particular commands, but appropriately with all of their being (Mark 12:29–34; cf. 10:20–22).

Ps. 106 While Ps. 105 is mainly concerned with God's redemptive acts, this psalm focuses on human sin.

106:1 Praise the LORD. In Hebrew *Hallu yah,* "You (plural) praise Yah."

for he is good. Though the writer is concerned about Israel's suffering, he knows that its source is in Israel's sin and not in God's character.

106:4 me. The psalmist has no doubt that God will come to aid His chosen people, but he does not assume that he will personally enjoy God's blessing. He turns to God in prayer for this.

106:6 we . . . have sinned. This verse is an introductory statement that gives the theme for the body of the psalm down through v. 39. Israel has deliberately and constantly rebelled against the Lord.

106:7 rebelled by the Sea. The poet stands amazed at the stubbornness of his people. He remembers that a previous generation had doubted God's power—even though they had just witnessed the ten plagues—when they were caught between the Egyptian army and the Red Sea (Ex. 14).

106:9 He rebuked the Red Sea. By personifying the Red Sea, the psalmist makes it a part of God's defeat of the powers of chaos.

he led them through. In spite of their sin, God saved them. God's persevering love in the face of rejection is a major theme here, and indeed throughout the Bible.

106:13 they soon forgot. The people's faith and thanks were short-lived. As remembrance (Ps. 105:5 note) includes obedience, so forgetting leads to disobedience.

14 But they had [f]a wanton craving in
the wilderness,
and [g]put God to the test in the
desert;
15 he [h]gave them what they asked,
but sent [i]a wasting disease among
them.
16 When men in the camp [j]were jealous
of Moses
and Aaron, [k]the holy one of the
LORD,
17 [l]the earth opened and swallowed up
Dathan,
and covered the company of
Abiram.
18 [m]Fire also broke out in their company;
the flame burned up the wicked.
19 They [n]made a calf in Horeb
and worshiped a metal image.
20 They [o]exchanged the glory of God
for the image of an ox that eats
grass.
21 They [p]forgot God, their Savior,
who had done great things in
Egypt,
22 wondrous works in [q]the land of Ham,
and awesome deeds by the Red
Sea.
23 Therefore [r]he said he would destroy
them—
had not Moses, his [s]chosen one,
[t]stood in the breach before him,
to turn away his wrath from
destroying them.
24 Then they [u]despised [v]the pleasant
land,
having [w]no faith in his promise.
25 They [x]murmured in their tents,
and did not obey the voice of the
LORD.
26 Therefore he [y]raised his hand and
swore to them
that he would make them fall in
the wilderness,
27 and would make their offspring fall
among the nations,
[z]scattering them among the lands.
28 Then they [a]yoked themselves to the
[a]Baal of Peor,
and ate sacrifices offered to [b]the
dead;
29 they provoked the LORD to anger
with their deeds,
and a plague broke out among them.
30 Then [c]Phinehas stood up and
intervened,
and the plague was stayed.
31 And that was [d]counted to him as
righteousness
from generation to generation
forever.
32 They [e]angered him at the waters of
Meribah,
and it went ill with Moses on their
account,
33 for they [f]made his spirit bitter,[1]
and he [g]spoke rashly with his lips.
34 They did not [h]destroy the peoples,
[i]as the LORD commanded them,
35 but they [j]mixed with the nations
and learned to do as they did.

14 [f]Num. 11:4; 1 Cor. 10:6; [Ps. 78:18] [g]Ex. 17:2; 1 Cor. 10:9 **15** [h]Ps. 78:29 [i]Isai. 10:16 **16** [j]See Num. 16:1-3 [k]Deut. 33:2; Zech. 14:5; Jude 14 **17** [l]Num. 16:31, 32; Deut. 11:6 **18** [m]Num. 16:35 **19** [n]Ex. 32:4; Deut. 9:8; Acts 7:41 **20** [o]Jer. 2:11; [Rom. 1:23] **21** [p]ver. 7, 13; Ps. 78:11; Deut. 32:18 **22** [q]Ps. 105:23, 27; [Ps. 78:51] **23** [r]Ex. 32:10; Deut. 9:14; Ezek. 20:8 [s]Ps. 105:6 [t]Ezek. 22:30 **24** [u]Num. 14:31 [v]Zech. 7:14 [w]Deut. 1:32; 9:23 **25** [x]Num 14:2; Deut.1:27 **26** [y]Ex. 6:8; Num. 14:30; Deut. 32:40; Ezek. 20:6, 15, 23; [Ps. 95:11] **27** [z]See Ps. 44:11 **28** [a]Num. 25:3; Hos. 9:10 [b]Isai. 8:19 **30** [c]Num. 25:7, 8 **31** [d][Gen. 15:6]; See Num. 25:10-13 **32** [e]See Num. 20:2-13; Deut. 1:37

33 [f]Ps. 107:11; [Ps. 78:40; Isai. 63:10] [g]Num. 20:10 **34** [h]See Judg. 1:21, 27-36 [i]Deut. 7:2, 16; Judg. 2:2 **35** [j]Judg. 3:5, 6; [Ezra 9:2]

1 Or *they rebelled against God's Spirit*

106:17 Dathan . . . Abiram. See Num. 16.

106:20 exchanged the glory. They put a metal idol in the place of God and worshiped it. As Paul points out (Rom. 1:21–23), idolatry consists in worshiping any part or aspect of creation as God.

106:22 wondrous works in the land of Ham. Ham is another name for Egypt, and the works are preeminently the ten plagues.

106:23 Moses . . . stood in the breach before him. See Ex. 32:11–14. Moses interceded on behalf of the people and saved them from the wrath of God. In this, he foreshadowed the work of Jesus Christ, who not only prayed for His people but died to save them.

106:24 they despised the pleasant land. They despised the Promised Land by not having faith that God could give it to them (Num. 13; 14).

106:26 raised his hand. This gesture accompanies a formal oath, showing God's determination to judge the sons of Israel.

106:28 yoked themselves. The language is derogatory; worshiping a foreign idol is like becoming a beast of burden.

Baal of Peor. Baal was a god of the eastern Mediterranean region at the time Israel was entering the Promised Land. Baal took slightly different characteristics in each local worship site and so is often identified by the region.

sacrifices offered to the dead. This could refer to funeral rituals of some sort. Canaanite funeral rituals involved heavy drinking, feasting, and obscene lust. The whole incident, initiated by Balaam, is reported in Num. 25.

106:31 counted to him as righteousness. When Israel took the fateful steps toward idolatry, Phinehas took a violent step to bring Israel back to the way of God. As a result, God made a covenant with his family to give them the priesthood. Similar language is used in connection with the covenant promises given to Abraham (Gen. 15:6) and inherited by the church (Rom. 4:3).

106:32 waters of Meribah. See Num. 20:1–13.

106:33 they made his spirit bitter. By not trusting God to provide for their survival in the wilderness.

36 They served their idols,
which became [k]a snare to them.
37 They [l]sacrificed their sons
and their daughters to [m]the demons;
38 they poured out innocent blood,
the blood of their sons and daughters,
whom they sacrificed to the idols of Canaan,
and the land was [n]polluted with blood.
39 Thus they [o]became unclean by their acts,
and [p]played the whore in their deeds.

40 Then [q]the anger of the LORD was kindled against [r]his people,
and he abhorred his [r]heritage;
41 he [s]gave them into the hand of the nations,
so that those who hated them ruled over them.
42 Their enemies [t]oppressed them,
and they were brought into subjection under their power.
43 [u]Many times he delivered them,
but they were rebellious in their [v]purposes
and were [w]brought low through their iniquity.

44 Nevertheless, he looked upon their distress,
when he [x]heard their cry.
45 For their sake he [y]remembered his covenant,
and [z]relented according to [a]the abundance of his steadfast love.
46 He caused them to be [b]pitied
by all those who held them captive.

36 [k]Ex. 23:33; Deut. 7:16; Judg. 2:3 37 [l]2 Kin. 16:3; Isai. 57:5; Ezek. 16:20; 20:26 [m]Deut. 32:17; [1 Cor. 10:20] 38 [n]Isai. 24:5 39 [o]Ezek. 20:18, 30, 31 [p]See Ps. 73:27 40 [q]Ps. 78:59, 62; Judg. 2:14 [r]See Ps. 28:9 41 [s]Neh. 9:27 42 [t]Judg. 4:3; 10:12 43 [u]Judg. 2:16 [v]See Ps. 81:12 [w]Lev. 26:39 44 [x]Judg. 3:9; 4:3; 6:7; 10:10 45 [y]Ps. 105:8; Lev. 26:42 [z]See Ps. 90:13 [a]ver. 7; Ps. 51:1; 69:16; Isai. 63:7; Lam. 3:32 46 [b]1 Kin. 8:50; 2 Chr. 30:9; Ezra 9:9; Neh. 1:11; Jer. 42:12

47 [c]For ver. 47, 48, see 1 Chr. 16:35, 36 [d]See Ps. 107:3 48 [e]See Ps. 41:13 [f]See Ps. 104:35

BOOK FIVE
Psalm 107 1 [g]See Ps. 105:1 [h]See Ps. 100:5 2 [i]Ps. 106:10 [j]Isai. 62:12; 63:4 3 [k]Ps. 106:47; Deut. 30:3; Isai. 11:12; 43:5; 56:8; Jer. 29:14; 31:8, 10; Ezek. 20:34, 41; 39:27 4 [l]ver. 40; [Deut. 32:10] [m]ver. 36 5 [n]Ps. 77:3 6 [o]ver. 13, 19, 28; Ps. 106:44

47 [c]Save us, O LORD our God,
and [d]gather us from among the nations,
that we may give thanks to your holy name
and glory in your praise.
48 [e]Blessed be the LORD, the God of Israel,
from everlasting to everlasting!
[e]And let all the people say, "Amen!"
[f]Praise the LORD!

BOOK FIVE

Let the Redeemed of the LORD Say So

107 [g]Oh give thanks to the LORD,
[h]for he is good,
for his steadfast love endures forever!
2 Let [i]the redeemed of the LORD say so,
whom he has [j]redeemed from trouble[1]
3 and [k]gathered in from the lands,
from the east and from the west,
from the north and from the south.

4 Some [l]wandered in desert wastes,
finding no way [m]to a city to dwell in;
5 hungry and thirsty,
their soul [n]fainted within them.
6 Then they [o]cried to the LORD in their trouble,
and he delivered them from their distress.
7 He led them by [p]a straight way
till they reached [m]a city to dwell in.
8 [q]Let them thank the LORD for his steadfast love,
for his wondrous works to the children of men!

7 [p]Ezra 8:21 [m][See ver. 4 above] 8 [q]ver. 15, 21, 31

[1] Or *from the hand of the foe*

106:37 to the demons. The spiritual reality behind the lifeless idols is demonic, a world of hostility to the one God.

106:39 they . . . played the whore. Joining themselves to a false god is spiritual adultery.

106:45 he remembered his covenant. God's promises express the commitment that causes Him to continue with His people even though they turned their backs on Him. On remembrance, see Ps. 105:5.

Ps. 107 This community thanksgiving accompanied the offering of sacrifices (v. 22). The date of its original composition is not certain.

107:1 he is good. See vv. 1, 8, 15, 21, 31, 43.

his steadfast love. God's covenant devotion, by which He binds Himself to His people.

107:3 gathered. The situation after the Babylonian exile seems to be in view here.

107:4–9 God guides those wandering in the wilderness to a city.

107:6 they cried . . . he delivered them. This section is the first of four that illustrate God's readiness to answer the prayers of His people.

9 For he [r]satisfies the longing soul,
[s]and the hungry soul he fills with good things.
10 [t]Some sat in darkness and in [u]the shadow of death,
prisoners in [v]affliction and in irons,
11 for they [w]had rebelled against the words of God,
and [x]spurned the counsel of the Most High.
12 So he bowed their hearts down with hard labor;
they fell down, [y]with none to help.
13 [z]Then they cried to the LORD in their trouble,
and he delivered them from their distress.
14 He brought them out of [a]darkness and the shadow of death,
and [b]burst their bonds apart.
15 [c]Let them thank the LORD for his steadfast love,
for his wondrous works to the children of men!
16 For he [d]shatters the doors of bronze
and cuts in two the bars of iron.

17 Some were [e]fools through their sinful ways,
and because of their iniquities suffered affliction;
18 [f]they loathed any kind of food,
and they [g]drew near to [h]the gates of death.
19 [i]Then they cried to the LORD in their trouble,
and he delivered them from their distress.
20 He [j]sent out his word and [k]healed them,
and [l]delivered them from their destruction.
21 [m]Let them thank the LORD for his steadfast love,
for his wondrous works to the children of men!
22 And let them [n]offer sacrifices of thanksgiving,
and [o]tell of his deeds in [p]songs of joy!

23 Some [q]went down to the sea in ships,
doing business on the great waters;
24 they saw the deeds of the LORD,
his wondrous works in the deep.
25 For he [r]commanded and [s]raised the stormy wind,
which lifted up the waves of the sea.
26 They mounted up to heaven; they went down to the depths;
their courage [t]melted away in their evil plight;
27 they reeled and [u]staggered like drunken men
and [v]were at their wits' end.[1]
28 [w]Then they cried to the LORD in their trouble,
and he delivered them from their distress.
29 He [x]made the storm be still,
and the waves of the sea were hushed.
30 Then they were glad that the waters[2] were quiet,
and he brought them to their desired haven.
31 [y]Let them thank the LORD for his steadfast love,
for his wondrous works to the children of men!

9 [r][Ps. 34:10; 146:7] [s]Luke 1:53
10 [t]Luke 1:79; [Isai. 42:7; 49:9; Mic. 7:8] [u]ver. 14; Job 10:21 [v][Job 36:8]
11 [w]Ps. 106:7, 33, 43; See Ps. 78:40 [x]Prov. 1:30; 5:12; 15:5; [Deut. 31:20; Luke 7:30]
12 [y]See Ps. 22:11
13 [z]ver. 6, 19, 28
14 [a]See ver. 10 [b][Ps. 2:3]
15 [c]ver. 8, 21, 31
16 [d]Isai. 45:2
17 [e]Prov. 1:7; 14:9
18 [f]Job 33:20 [g]Ps. 88:3; Job 33:22 [h]See Job 38:17
19 [i]ver. 6, 13, 28
20 [j]Ps. 147:15, 18; [Matt. 8:8] [k]Ps. 30:2, 3; 2 Kin. 20:5; Job 33:29, 30 [l]Ps. 103:4
21 [m]ver. 8, 15, 31
22 [n]See Ps. 50:14 [o]Ps. 9:11; See Ps. 118:17 [p]Ps. 105:43
23 [q]Isai. 42:10
25 [r]Ps. 105:31, 34 [s]Ps. 148:8; Jonah 1:4
26 [t]Ps. 119:28; See Ps. 22:14
27 [u]Isai. 24:20; 29:9; See Job 12:25 [v]Isai. 19:3
28 [w]ver. 6, 13, 19
29 [x]See Ps. 65:7
31 [y]ver. 8, 15, 21

1 Hebrew *and all their wisdom was swallowed up* 2 Hebrew *they*

107:10–16 God delivers His imprisoned people to freedom.

107:12 he bowed their hearts down. God chastises His wayward people in order to elicit their repentance. See Heb. 12:1–13.

107:13 they cried to the LORD . . . he delivered them. See v. 6.

107:17–22 God saves foolish rebels when they call on Him.

107:17 fools. Not because they were without natural intelligence, but because they refused to face the reality that the Lord is God. "Foolishness" is an ethical-spiritual category, not an academic one.

107:18 loathed any kind of food. It seems that a physical malady, some kind of sickness, is in view here.

107:20 his word. We learn as early as the creation account (Gen. 1:3) that God's word is powerful and effective.

107:22 sacrifices of thanksgiving. This verse points to public worship in the temple.

107:23–32 God rescues those in trouble on the seas.

107:24 the deeds of the LORD. The mystery, power, and beauty of the sea, with everything that lives in it, testifies eloquently to God's wisdom (Gen. 1:9, 10, 21).

107:26 They mounted up . . . went down. The ship as it rises and falls on the waves.

107:28 they cried to the LORD . . . he delivered them. See vv. 6, 13, and 19.

107:29 He made the storm be still. God shows His divine power and might by controlling the chaotic sea. See notes Ps. 18:4, 15. Christ demonstrated His power from on high when He stilled the waters (Mark 4:35–41).

32 Let them [z]extol him in [a]the
congregation of the people,
and praise him in the assembly of
the elders.

33 He [b]turns rivers into a desert,
springs of water into thirsty
ground,
34 [c]a fruitful land into a salty waste,
because of the evil of its
inhabitants.
35 He [d]turns a desert into pools of water,
[e]a parched land into springs of
water.
36 And there he lets the hungry dwell,
and they establish [f]a city to live in;
37 they sow fields and plant vineyards
and get a fruitful yield.
38 [g]By his blessing they multiply greatly,
and he does not let their livestock
diminish.

39 When they are diminished and
brought low
through oppression, evil, and
sorrow,
40 [h]he pours contempt on princes
and [i]makes them wander [j]in
trackless wastes;
41 but [k]he raises up the needy out of
affliction
and [l]makes their families like
flocks.
42 [m]The upright see it and are glad,
and [n]all wickedness shuts its
mouth.

43 [o]Whoever is wise, let him attend to
these things;
let them consider the steadfast love
of the LORD.

With God We Shall Do Valiantly

108 A SONG. A PSALM OF DAVID.
[p]My heart is steadfast, O God!
I will sing and make melody with
all my being![1]
2 Awake, O harp and lyre!
I will awake the dawn!
3 I will give thanks to you, O LORD,
among the peoples;
I will sing praises to you among
the nations.
4 For your steadfast love is great
[q]above the heavens;
your faithfulness reaches to the
clouds.
5 Be exalted, O God, above the heavens!
Let your glory be over all the earth!
6 [r]That your beloved ones may be
delivered,
give salvation by your right hand
and answer me!

7 God has promised in his holiness:[2]
"With exultation I will divide up
Shechem
and portion out the Valley of
Succoth.
8 Gilead is mine; Manasseh is mine;
Ephraim is my helmet,
Judah my scepter.

[1] Hebrew *with my glory* [2] Or *sanctuary*

32 [z]See Ps. 99:5 [a]Ps. 22:22, 25
33 [b]Isai. 50:2; [Isai. 42:15]
34 [c][Gen. 13:10; 14:3; Deut. 29:23]; See Gen. 19:24-28
35 [d]Ps. 114:8; Isai. 41:18; [Isai. 35:6, 7; 43:19, 20] [e]Job 38:26, 27
36 [f]ver. 4, 7
38 [g]Gen. 12:2; 17:20; Ex. 1:7
40 [h]Job 12:21 [i]Job 12:24 [j][Deut. 32:10]
41 [k]Ps. 113:7, 8; 1 Sam. 2:8 [l]Job 21:11
42 [m]See Job 22:19 [n]See Ps. 63:11
43 [o][Ps. 64:9; Jer. 9:12; Hos. 14:9]
Psalm 108
1 [p]For ver. 1-5, see Ps. 57:7-11
4 [q][Ps. 113:4]
6 [r]For ver. 6-13, see Ps. 60:5-12

107:33–38 God turns fertility into waste, and waste into fertility. He controls all things.

107:34 because of the evil. God does not arbitrarily bring destruction upon His people. Here the reason is identified as the people's sin. A historical example of this verse may be found in 1 Kin. 17, where God determined to withhold rain and dew from Israel because Ahab and Jezebel had turned the nation toward Baal.

107:36 establish a city. The ultimate reference is to the conquest in which God gave the land of Canaan to Israel. They passed from the hard conditions of the wilderness wanderings into the pleasant land of Palestine.

107:39–42 God punishes and blesses His people.

107:40 trackless wastes. Perhaps a reference to the Babylonian exile.

Ps. 108 This psalm is composed of two previous psalms. The first five verses are from Ps. 57:7–11, and vv. 6–13 are from Ps. 60:5–12. There are only minor changes of wording, but the overall effect of the psalm is quite different. Ps. 57 and 60 include elements of complaint; this psalm is a statement of assurance.

108:1 steadfast. The psalmist has resolved to praise the Lord, and nothing can cause him to swerve from his resolve to offer up his hymn of praise.

108:2 I will awake the dawn. See note 57:8.

108:3 among the peoples. The psalmist realizes that God is more than the God of Israel. He is the King of the universe, and as a result He will witness to God's great deeds throughout the universe.

108:4 your steadfast love. Specifically, the mercy God has for the people who are in covenant relationship with Him.

108:5 above the heavens. God is so great that not even the heavens can contain Him (1 Kin. 8:27). He is transcendent, yet in special ways (presently by the Holy Spirit), He is also immanent in that He compassionately condescends to dwell with His people.

108:7 God has promised in his holiness. The divine oracle was probably spoken through a prophet associated with the temple. The sense of His message is that victory will be forthcoming.

Shechem . . . Succoth. These two places are associated with Jacob in Gen. 33:17–20 as the first two places the patriarch occupied after returning from his encounter with Esau. They are on opposite sides of the Jordan River.

108:8 Gilead . . . Manasseh. Both these areas are located, at least in part, east of the Jordan River.

Ephraim . . . Judah. The two most powerful tribes in Israel. They were frequently rivals, but here they are united as parts of God's army.

scepter. See Gen. 49:10.

9 Moab is my washbasin;
upon Edom I cast my shoe;
[s]over Philistia I shout in triumph."
10 Who will bring me to the fortified city?
Who will lead me to Edom?
11 Have you not rejected us, O God?
You do not go out, O God, with
our armies.
12 Oh grant us help against the foe,
for vain is the salvation of man!
13 With God we shall do valiantly;
it is he who will tread down our
foes.

Help Me, O Lord My God

109 To the choirmaster. A Psalm of David.

1 [t]Be not silent, O [u]God of my praise!
2 For wicked and [v]deceitful mouths are
opened against me,
speaking against me with lying
tongues.
3 They encircle me with words of hate,
and attack me [w]without cause.
4 In return for my love they [x]accuse me,
but I [y]give myself to prayer.[1]
5 So they [z]reward me evil for good,
and hatred for my love.

6 [a]Appoint a wicked man [b]against him;
let an accuser stand [c]at his right
hand.
7 When he is tried, let him come forth
guilty;
let his [d]prayer be counted as sin!
8 May his [e]days be few;
may [f]another take his [g]office!
9 May his [h]children be fatherless
and his wife a widow!
10 May his children [i]wander about and
beg,
[j]seeking food far from the ruins
they inhabit!
11 May [k]the creditor seize all that he has;
may [k]strangers plunder the fruits
of his toil!
12 Let there be none to [l]extend
kindness to him,
nor any to [m]pity his fatherless
children!
13 May his [n]posterity be cut off;
may his [o]name be blotted out in
the second generation!
14 May [p]the iniquity of his fathers be
remembered before the Lord,
and let not the sin of his mother
be [q]blotted out!
15 [r]Let them be before the Lord
continually,
that he may [s]cut off the memory of
them from the earth!

16 For he did not remember to show
kindness,
but pursued [t]the poor and needy
and [u]the brokenhearted, to put
them to death.
17 [v]He loved to curse; let curses come[2]
upon him!
He did not delight in blessing; may
it be far[3] from him!
18 He [w]clothed himself with cursing as
his coat;
may it [x]soak[4] into his body like
water,
like oil into his bones!

9 [s][Ps. 60:8]
Psalm 109
1 [t]See Ps. 28:1 [u]Deut. 10:21; [Ps. 71:6; Jer. 17:14]
2 [v]Ps. 52:4
3 [w]See Ps. 69:4
4 [x]Ps. 38:20 [y][Ps. 69:13]
5 [z]See Ps. 35:12
6 [a]For ver. 6-15, see Ps. 35:4-8; 69:22-28 [b][1 Chr. 21:1; Zech. 3:1] [c]Job 30:12
7 [d]Prov. 28:9; [Prov. 15:8; 21:27]
8 [e][Ps. 55:23] [f]Cited Acts 1:20; [John 17:12] [g]Num. 4:16; [1 Chr. 24:3]
9 [h]Ex. 22:24
10 [i][Gen. 4:12]; See Ps. 59:15 [j][Ps. 37:25]
11 [k][Deut. 28:43, 44]
12 [l][Ps. 36:10] [m][Job 5:4]
13 [n]See Ps. 21:10 [o]Prov. 10:7
14 [p]Ex. 20:5 [q]Neh. 4:5; Jer. 18:23
15 [r][Ps. 90:8] [s]Ps. 34:16
16 [t]ver. 22; Ps. 40:17 [u]See Ps. 34:18
17 [v][Prov. 14:14; Ezek. 35:6]
18 [w][ver. 29; Ps. 73:6] [x][Num. 5:22]

1 Hebrew *but I am prayer* 2 Revocalization; Masoretic Text *curses have come* 3 Revocalization; Masoretic Text *it is far* 4 Revocalization; Masoretic Text *it has soaked*

108:9 On this verse see 60:8 and notes.

108:10 me. Likely the king, who speaks on behalf of the nation.

108:13 With God. The writer confesses that it is only through God's power that they will be victorious.

Ps. 109 The psalmist stands before a corrupt court, falsely accused of a crime. In his distress, he turns to God for help, asking Him to reverse the roles and allow him to judge the court, and one person in particular (either the judge or the accuser). The poet does not conceal his strong feelings against his enemies (Introduction: Characteristics and Themes).

109:1 Be not silent. See note Ps. 83:1.

109:4 they accuse me. The legal language here and elsewhere in the psalm reveals that the psalmist is a defendant in a courtroom setting.

109:5 evil for good. See note Ps. 35:12.

for my love. What makes the writer's plight so poignant is that his attackers were once friends but have turned treacherously against him.

109:6 a wicked man . . . an accuser. The penalty for accusing someone of a certain crime falsely was the penalty corresponding to that crime (Deut. 19:16–21).

109:8 may another take his office. As this accuser brought false charges against the psalmist, so Judas Iscariot sought Christ's death by turning Him over to the Jewish authorities. Afterwards Judas killed himself in remorse. Peter understood that this psalm was about that situation and cited it as a replacement was sought for Judas among the disciples (Acts 1:20).

109:9 fatherless . . . widow. Among people who depended heavily on their relatives for social support, this verse was a hard-hitting curse, calling for punishment on the accuser and on his family as well.

109:13 his name be blotted out. The curses focus on eradicating the accuser's family line. To have descendants stretching into the distant future was considered extremely important in ancient Israel.

109:17 let curses come upon him. Once again the psalmist invokes the principle that the unrighteous will receive the penalty they are trying to call down upon another. See note on v. 6.

19 May it be like a garment that he
wraps around him,
like a belt that he puts on every day!
20 May this be the reward of my
[y]accusers from the LORD,
of those who speak evil against my
life!

21 But you, O GOD my Lord,
deal on my behalf [z]for your name's
sake;
because your [a]steadfast love is
good, deliver me!
22 For I am [b]poor and needy,
and my heart is stricken within me.
23 I am gone like [c]a shadow at evening;
I am [d]shaken off like a locust.
24 My knees are weak [e]through fasting;
my [f]body has become gaunt, with
no fat.
25 I am [g]an object of scorn to my
accusers;
when they see me, they [h]wag their
heads.

26 [i]Help me, O LORD my God!
Save me according to your
steadfast love!
27 Let them [j]know that this is your hand;
you, O LORD, have done it!
28 [k]Let them curse, but you will bless!
They arise and are put to shame,
but [l]your servant will be glad!
29 May my accusers be [m]clothed with
dishonor;
may they [n]be wrapped in their own
shame as in a cloak!

30 With my mouth I will give great
thanks to the LORD;
I will [o]praise him in the midst of
the throng.
31 For he stands [p]at the right hand of
the needy,
to save him from those who
condemn his soul to death.

Sit at My Right Hand

110 A PSALM OF DAVID.
[q]The LORD says to my Lord:
[r]"Sit at my right hand,
[s]until I make your enemies your
[t]footstool."

2 The LORD sends forth [u]from Zion
[v]your mighty scepter.
[w]Rule in the midst of your enemies!
3 [x]Your people will [y]offer themselves
freely
on the day of your [z]power,[1]
in [a]holy garments;[2]
from the womb of the morning,
the dew of your youth will be yours.[3]

20 [y]ver. 6, 29
21 [z][Jer. 14:7]; See Ps. 23:3 [a]Ps. 69:16; [Ps. 63:3]
22 [b]ver. 16
23 [c]See Ps. 102:11 [d]Ex. 10:19; [Neh. 5:13; Job 38:13]
24 [e]Ps. 35:13 [f][Job 16:8]
25 [g]Ps. 22:6; 69:19 [h]See Ps. 22:7
26 [i]Ps. 119:86
27 [j][Job 37:7]
28 [k][2 Sam. 16:12] [l][Isai. 65:14]
29 [m]ver. 18; See Job 8:22 [n]Ps. 71:13; [Ps. 35:26]
30 [o][Ps. 22:25]
31 [p]ver. 6; See Ps. 16:8

Psalm 110
1 [q]Cited Matt. 22:44; Mark 12:36; Luke 20:42, 43; Acts 2:34, 35 [r]Cited Heb. 1:13; [Matt. 26:64; Eph. 1:20; Col. 3:1; Heb. 1:3; 8:1; 10:12; 12:2] [s]Heb. 10:13; [1 Cor. 15:25; Eph. 1:22; Heb. 2:8; 1 Pet. 3:22] [t][Ps. 8:6; 18:38; Josh. 10:24]
2 [u][Ps. 68:35] [v]Jer. 48:17; Ezek. 19:14; [Ps. 45:6] [w]Ps. 72:8; [Dan. 7:13, 14]
3 [x]Judg. 5:2; Neh. 11:2 [y][Ex. 35:29] [z][Isai. 13:3, 4] [a][Rev. 19:14]; See 1 Chr. 16:29

1 Or *on the day you lead your forces* 2 Masoretic Text; some Hebrew manuscripts and Jerome *on the holy mountains* 3 The meaning of the Hebrew is uncertain

109:21 for your name's sake. The psalmist appeals to God's reputation (Ps. 8:1). He belongs to God, and if he should die at the hand of the wicked, it will appear as if God can do nothing about evil.

109:25 wag their heads. In disgust.

109:26 according to your steadfast love. The Hebrew word for "steadfast love" refers salvation to God's covenant faithfulness.

109:31 stands at the right hand. Instead of finding an accuser at his right hand, the psalmist finds his support in God.

Ps. 110 There can be no doubt that this psalm looks forward to Christ. Jesus Himself cites it to show that David knew that its ultimate fulfillment would come with One who is greater than he (Mark 12:35–37 and parallels). Even before Christ's coming, a prophetic-messianic interpretation of the psalm was well known among Jewish interpreters.

Nevertheless, like all other royal psalms, Ps. 110 does address the time in which it was first composed. It is likely that it was sung at the time of the coronation of the king. The composition seems to have been written after David defeated Jebus (Jerusalem), and celebrates his victory and enthronement in that city, explaining why he also inherits the royal priesthood of Melchizedek.

Focusing on two divine oracles, the first (v. 1) shows the close, but subordinate, relationship that the human king bears to the divine King. The New Testament writers cite this oracle to demonstrate Jesus' post-resurrection glory and to point to the struggle between God and the spiritual powers of evil (Acts 2:34, 35; 1 Cor. 15:25; Eph. 1:20; Col. 3:1; Heb. 1:13; 1 Pet. 3:22).

The second oracle appointed the king as a priest, but as a special type of priest. As opposed to the hereditary Aaronic priesthood, this priesthood is descended from Melchizedek (Gen. 14:18–23), whose mysterious origins are related to Jesus Christ, the great High Priest (Heb. 5:6; 7:17; 8:1; 10:12–14).

110:title The truth of the authorship title of this psalm is critical for its interpretation in the New Testament (Mark 12:35–37).

110:1 LORD. As the translators indicate with the use of small capital letters, this is God's name, Yahweh.

Lord. This title is often used for God but can also be addressed to a king or other respected person. The New Testament makes it clear that King David refers to his Son as his "Lord" (Mark 12:35–37). The promised Messiah descended from David but is greater than David. See "Jesus' Heavenly Reign" at Acts 7:55.

at my right hand. The place of honor. After His resurrection, Jesus was exalted to the right hand of God in heaven.

your enemies. In the Old Testament they were physical flesh and blood enemies of Israel. In the New Testament the battle is intensified, as Jesus fights against the invisible, cosmic powers of evil.

footstool. A place of disgrace, symbolizing subjugation. After a victory, Near Eastern leaders would humiliate their defeated enemies by stepping on their heads or necks (Josh. 10:24–26).

110:2 sends forth. God will enlarge the King's authority.

from Zion. See note Ps. 2:6.

scepter. A common symbol of governmental power and authority.

110:3 the dew of your youth. A difficult phrase in the Hebrew. The image compares the dew, that appears suddenly during the night and is present in the morning, with the eager and mysterious appearance of the king's troops.

4 [b]The LORD has [c]sworn
and will [d]not change his mind,
[e]"You are [f]a priest [g]forever
after the order of [h]Melchizedek."

5 The Lord is at your [i]right hand;
he will [j]shatter kings on [k]the day
of his wrath.
6 He will [l]execute judgment among the
nations,
[m]filling them with corpses;
he will [n]shatter chiefs[1]
over the wide earth.
7 He will [o]drink from the brook by the
way;
therefore he will lift up his head.

Great Are the LORD's Works

111 [2] [p]Praise the LORD!
I [q]will give thanks to the LORD
with my whole heart,
in the company of [r]the upright, in
the congregation.
2 [s]Great are the works of the LORD,
[t]studied by all who delight in them.
3 [u]Full of splendor and majesty is his
work,
and his [v]righteousness endures
forever.
4 He has [w]caused his wondrous works
to be remembered;
the LORD is gracious and
merciful.
5 He provides food for those who fear
him;
he [x]remembers his covenant forever.
6 He has shown his people the power
of his works,
in giving them the inheritance of
the nations.
7 The works of his hands are faithful
and just;
all his precepts are [y]trustworthy;
8 they are [z]established forever and ever,
to be performed with [a]faithfulness
and uprightness.
9 He sent [b]redemption to his people;
he has [c]commanded his covenant
forever.
[d]Holy and awesome is his name!
10 [e]The fear of the LORD is the
beginning of wisdom;
all those who practice it have [f]a
good understanding.
His [g]praise endures forever!

The Righteous Will Never Be Moved

112 [3] [h]Praise the LORD!
[i]Blessed is the man who fears
the LORD,
who [j]greatly delights in his
commandments!

4 [b]Cited Heb. 7:21 [c]Ps. 132:11; Heb. 6:17, 18 [d]Num. 23:19 [e]Cited Heb. 5:6; 7:17, 21; [Heb. 6:20] [f]Zech. 6:13 [g]Heb. 7:24, 28; [John 12:34] [h]Gen. 14:18
5 [i]See Ps. 16:8 [j][Ps. 68:14] [k]Rom. 2:5; Rev. 6:17; [Ps. 2:5, 12]
6 [l]Isai. 2:4; Joel 3:12; Mic. 4:3 [m]See Ezek. 39:17-19; Rev. 19:17, 18 [n][Ps. 68:21]
7 [o][Judg. 7:5, 6]
Psalm 111 1 [p]See Ps. 104:36 [q]Ps. 138:1 [r][Ps. 149:1]
2 [s]Ps. 92:5; Rev. 3:2; [Ps. 139:14] [t]Ps. 119:45, 94, 155; [Ps. 112:1; 143:5]
3 [u]Ps. 145:5 [v]Ps. 112:3, 9
4 [w][Ps. 78:4]
5 [x]See Ps. 105:8
7 [y]Ps. 93:5; [Ps. 19:7]
8 [z]Isai. 40:8; Matt. 5:18 [a]Ps. 19:9; Rev. 15:3
9 [b][Matt. 1:21]; Luke 1:68 [c][Ps. 133:3] [d]Ps. 99:3; Luke 1:49; [Ps. 8:1]
10 [e]Prov. 9:10; See Prov. 1:7 [f][Prov. 3:4; 13:15; John 7:17] [g][Ps. 44:8]
Psalm 112 1 [h]See Ps. 104:35 [i]Ps. 128:1, 4; [Ps. 111:10; 115:13] [j]See Ps. 1:2

[1] Or *the head* [2] This psalm is an acrostic poem, each line beginning with the successive letters of the Hebrew alphabet [3] This psalm is an acrostic poem, each line beginning with the successive letters of the Hebrew alphabet

110:4 the order of Melchizedek. The regular priesthood of Israel was from Aaron, and their duties were limited to religious worship. Little is known about Melchizedek (Gen. 14:18–20), but it appears that he combined the functions of king and priest. David also combined these functions to an extent. Jesus Christ is both King and Priest, though not descended from the line of Aaron (Heb. 5:6; 7:17; 8:1; 10:12–14).

110:5 Lord. A title of respect (v. 1 note).

110:6 judgment among the nations. God often used the human king to bring His judgment upon the nations through warfare. As applied to Jesus, this verse anticipates the Last Judgment that will take place at the end of time.

110:7 He will drink. This verse is difficult in Hebrew. The king finds refreshment during the battle and can carry on God's work of judgment.

Ps. 111 This psalm of praise recalls the Exodus, wilderness wanderings, and conquest of the Promised Land. The psalm is an acrostic (see introduction to Ps. 112; 119), a trait common among wisdom poems, and it ends on a note that could be called the "motto" of the Book of Proverbs (v. 10).

111:1 in the company. The holy congregation as they gather to praise the Lord in the sanctuary.

111:2 the works of the LORD. The psalmist has in mind the great acts of redemption that God performed in their past. The preeminent example would be the Exodus, when God rescued His people from their oppressors in Egypt.

111:3 his righteousness. God acts in history in conformity to His character and law. Through His great historical acts, people can recognize His righteousness.

111:4 to be remembered. Remembrance involves more than an act of the memory; it also involves devotion and obedience. See Ps. 44:1.

gracious and merciful. Israel, due to sin, could not deserve God's salvation; it springs from God's love for His people. See Ex. 34:6.

111:5 provides food. This may allude to the wilderness wanderings when God miraculously provided food for Israel (e.g., Num. 11).

his covenant. When God acts to save His people, He does so because of the relationship He has already established with them.

forever. God is not fickle. His people may depend on Him.

111:6 giving them the inheritance of the nations. God gave to Israel the land of a number of peoples when He gave them the Promised Land (Deut. 7:1–6).

111:10 fear of the LORD. This well-known phrase captures the right way to approach the Lord. The Lord is God, inspiring reverence and awe. He will make good His threats against the wicked. See notes Ps. 34:7; 36:1; 128:1; 130:4.

Ps. 112 Ps. 112 is in the center of three psalms that begin with the expression "Praise the LORD" (Hebrew *hallu yah*). Both Ps. 111 and 112 are acrostics, each half-line beginning with successive letters of the Hebrew alphabet, and they complement each other in content. Ps. 111 tells about God and His deeds, while Ps. 112 describes the happiness of the person who serves God.

112:1 in his commandments. The righteous person receives the law as a testimony of God; they are a joy, to be kept in love and gratitude for His great salvation.

2 His [k]offspring will be mighty in the
land;
[l]the generation of the upright will
be blessed.
3 [m]Wealth and riches are in his house,
and his [n]righteousness endures
forever.
4 Light dawns in the darkness [o]for the
upright;
he is gracious, merciful, and
[p]righteous.
5 It is well with the man who [q]deals
generously and lends;
who conducts his affairs with
justice.
6 For the righteous will [r]never be
moved;
[s]he will be remembered forever.
7 He is not [t]afraid of bad news;
his [u]heart is firm, [v]trusting in the
LORD.
8 His heart is steady; he will not be
afraid,
until he looks in triumph on his
adversaries.
9 He has [w]distributed freely; he has
given to the poor;
his righteousness endures
forever;
his [x]horn is exalted in honor.
10 The wicked man sees it and is
angry;
he [y]gnashes his teeth and [z]melts
away;
[a]the desire of the wicked will
perish!

2 [k][Ps. 25:12; 102:28; Prov. 11:21; 20:7] [l]Ps. 37:26
3 [m]See Prov. 3:16 [n][Ps. 111:3]
4 [o][Job 11:17]; See Ps. 97:11 [p][Matt. 1:19]
5 [q]See Ps. 37:26
6 [r]Ps. 55:22 [s][Prov. 10:7]
7 [t]Prov. 1:33 [u]Ps. 57:7 [v]Ps. 11:1; 64:10
9 [w]Cited 2 Cor. 9:9 [x]See Ps. 75:10
10 [y][Matt. 8:12; Luke 13:28]; See Job 16:9 [z][Ps. 58:8] [a]See Job 8:13

Psalm 113
1 [b]See Ps. 104:35 [c]Ps. 135:1 [d]Ps. 34:22; 69:36; 102:28
2 [e]Ps. 115:18; See Job 1:21
3 [f]Ps. 50:1; Isai. 59:19; Mal. 1:11 [g]See Ps. 48:10 [h]See Ps. 18:3
4 [i]Ps. 99:2 [j]Ps. 8:1; 57:5, 11; 148:13
5 [k]See Ps. 35:10
6 [l]See Ps. 11:4; [Ps. 138:6]
7 [m][Ps. 136:23]; See Ps. 107:41
8 [n][Job 36:7]
9 [o]Ps. 68:6; 1 Sam. 2:5; [Ex. 1:21; Isai. 54:1] [b][See ver. 1 above]

Who Is like the LORD Our God?

113 [b]Praise the LORD!
[c]Praise, O [d]servants of the
LORD,
praise the name of the LORD!
2 [e]Blessed be the name of the LORD
from this time forth and
forevermore!
3 [f]From the rising of the sun to its
setting,
[g]the name of the LORD is [h]to be
praised!
4 The LORD is [i]high above all nations,
and his [j]glory above the
heavens!
5 [k]Who is like the LORD our God,
who is seated on high,
6 who [l]looks far down
on the heavens and the earth?
7 He [m]raises the poor from the dust
and lifts the needy from the ash
heap,
8 to make them [n]sit with princes,
with the princes of his people.
9 He [o]gives the barren woman a home,
making her the joyous mother of
children.
[b]Praise the LORD!

Tremble at the Presence of the LORD

114 When [p]Israel went out from
Egypt,
the house of Jacob from [q]a people
of strange language,

Psalm 114 1 [p]Ex. 12:37 [q]Ps. 81:5; [Gen. 42:23]

112:4 in the darkness. Darkness is a metaphor for troubled times. The psalmist knows that there are hard times, but he also knows that "for those who love God all things work together for good" (Rom. 8:28).

gracious, merciful, and righteous. The godly man reflects the attributes of his Lord; see 111:4.

112:7 not afraid of bad news. The righteous man does not fear trouble or distress, because he knows that God is able to bring him through it.

112:9 has distributed freely. Generosity is a basic characteristic of a servant of God. Paul quotes this verse in 2 Cor. 9:9 in a context that encourages generosity.

Ps. 113 God is both transcendent (vv. 4–6) and immanent (vv. 7–9); above creation but present with His people. Ps. 113 is the first of several psalms used to celebrate the great annual festivals of Passover, Weeks, Tabernacles, New Moon, and the Dedication of the temple. Ps. 113–118 were sung during the Passover, so it is likely that Jesus and His disciples sang them during their last evening together (Matt. 26:30; Mark 14:26). Ps. 113 (see v. 9) should be compared with the songs of Hannah (1 Sam. 2, especially vv. 5, 8) and Mary (Luke 1:46–55).

113:1 O servants of the LORD. A priest leads the faithful in worship.

113:3 From the rising of the sun to its setting. That is, from east to west, everywhere.

113:4 high above all nations. In the ancient Near East each nation had its imagined national gods. Only the God of Israel could proclaim Himself the true God of all nations.

113:5 Who is like. Yahweh is incomparable.

113:6 who looks far down. Part of God's greatness is His condescension, as at Bethlehem (Luke 2:4–7; Phil. 2:5–11).

on the heavens. Often the heavens are spoken of as the dwelling place of God, but strictly speaking, God's infinite transcendence is such that even the heavens are unable to contain Him (1 Kin. 8:27).

Ps. 114 Jewish tradition assigned this psalm to the eighth day of Passover. In eight short verses, and with virtually unrivaled poetic subtlety, the psalmist describes the tremendous power of God's visual self-revelation (theophany) at the time of Israel's salvation from Egypt and entry into Canaan (Ex. 13:21).

114:1 went out from Egypt. The Exodus was the most tremendous display of God's redemptive power during the Old Testament period. It was constantly remembered and became a source of encouragement for later generations, including Christians who perceive themselves as "strangers and exiles" in search of their true "homeland" (Heb. 11:13, 14).

2 Judah became his [r]sanctuary,
Israel his dominion.

3 [s]The sea looked and fled;
[t]Jordan turned back.
4 [u]The mountains skipped like rams,
the hills like lambs.

5 What [v]ails you, O sea, that
you flee?
O Jordan, that you turn back?
6 O mountains, that you skip like
rams?
O hills, like lambs?

7 [w]Tremble, O earth, at the presence of
the Lord,
at the presence of the God of
Jacob,
8 who turns [x]the rock into [y]a pool of
water,
[z]the flint into a spring of water.

To Your Name Give Glory

115

1 [a]Not to us, O LORD, not to us,
but to your name give glory,
[b]for the sake of your steadfast love
and your faithfulness!

2 Why should the nations say,
[c]"Where is their God?"
3 [d]Our God is in the heavens;
[e]he does all that he pleases.
4 [f]Their idols are silver and gold,
[g]the work of human hands.
5 They have mouths, [h]but do not
speak;
eyes, but do not see.

2 [r]Ps. 78:68, 69; [Ex. 15:17; 25:8] **3** [s]See Ps. 77:16 [t]See Josh. 3:13-16 **4** [u][Ps. 18:7; 29:6; Ex. 19:18] **5** [v][Hab. 3:8] **7** [w]Ps. 96:9 **8** [x]Num. 20:11; See Ps. 78:15 [y]See Ps. 107:35 [z]Deut. 8:15 **Psalm 115** **1** [a][Isai. 48:11; Ezek. 36:22; Dan. 9:18, 19] [b]See Ps. 36:5 **2** [c][Ex. 32:12; Num. 14:13, 14]; See Ps. 42:3 **3** [d]See Ps. 11:4 [e]Ps. 135:6; Dan. 4:35 **4** [f]For ver. 4-8, see Ps. 135:15-18 [g]Deut. 4:28; 2 Kin. 19:18; Isai. 37:19; Acts 19:26; See Isai. 44:10-20; Jer. 10:3-5 **5** [h][Isai. 46:7; Hab. 2:18] **8** [i][Isai. 44:9] **9** [j][Ps. 118:2-4; 135:19, 20] [k]Ps. 37:3; 62:8 [l]Ps. 33:20 **10** [j][See ver. 9 above] [m]See Ps. 3:3 **11** [n]Ps. 22:23; 103:11, 13, 17 **12** [o][Ps. 118:2-4; 135:19, 20]

6 They have ears, but do not hear;
noses, but do not smell.
7 They have hands, but do not feel;
feet, but do not walk;
and they do not make a sound in
their throat.
8 [i]Those who make them become like
them;
so do all who trust in them.

9 O [j]Israel,[1] [k]trust in the LORD!
He is their [l]help and their
shield.
10 O [j]house of Aaron, trust in
the LORD!
He is their help and [m]their
shield.
11 You [n]who fear the LORD, trust in the
LORD!
He is their help and their
shield.

12 The LORD has remembered us; he
will bless us;
he will bless [o]the house of Israel;
he will bless [o]the house of Aaron;
13 he will [p]bless those who fear the
LORD,
[q]both the small and the great.

14 May the LORD [r]give you increase,
you and your children!
15 May [s]you be blessed by the LORD,
[t]who made heaven and earth!

13 [p]See Ps. 112:1 [q]Jer. 16:6; 31:34 **14** [r]Deut. 1:11 **15** [s]See Ruth 2:20 [t]Ps. 121:2; 124:8; 134:3; 146:6; Acts 14:15; Rev. 14:7; [Gen. 1:1; 14:19; Jer. 10:11]

[1] Masoretic Text; many Hebrew manuscripts, Septuagint, Syriac *O house of Israel*

114:2 his sanctuary. The people and their country were God's sanctuary because God chose to be present with them. The tabernacle, and then the temple, were symbols of His presence.

114:3 The sea looked. The Red Sea is personified (Ex. 14; 15), poetically describing the crossing of the sea as a conflict between it and the Lord.

114:4 The mountains. The mountains were symbols of power, firmness, and endurance (Ps. 46). God's appearance shakes them like frightened rams.

114:5 What ails you. The psalmist questions the poetically personified sea and mountains making explicit what was implicit in the first two stanzas of the poem.

114:7 Tremble. When God comes in judgment and with power, the inhabitants of the earth should fear because they will be objects of His judgment. Nothing can stand in His way.

114:8 turns the rock into a pool. God's provision at Kadesh (Num. 20:1–13) demonstrates His power and compassion.

Ps. 115 This psalm is a liturgy for public worship, declaring Israel's faith in the Lord over against the worthless idols of the nations.

115:1 your steadfast love. God's covenantal affection for His people.

115:2 the nations. The nations that surrounded Israel at different times: Canaan, Babylonia, Assyria, Persia, and Egypt.

Where is their God. As the nations observed Israel struggling, they would say that Israel's God was unable or unwilling to act.

115:3 all that he pleases. A notable expression of God's sovereignty.

115:4 Their idols. The psalmist draws a sharp contrast between the living God of Israel and the man-made deities of the Near East. See Is. 44:6–23; Rom. 1:21–23; "Syncretism and Idolatry" at Hos. 2:13.

115:8 like them. When people construct their own gods, they make them in their own image. As they worship these gods, they are more and more conformed to their likeness. See 2 Kin. 17:15.

115:9 O Israel. A reference to all the people of God.

115:10 house of Aaron. The speaker addresses the priests of Israel.

115:11 You who fear the LORD. Finally, the psalmist singles out those who tremble before the Lord. These are the faithful within Israel or, as later usage suggests, also proselytes.

115:12 remembered. See Ps. 44:1.

115:15 who made heaven and earth. As the Creator of all, God is able to provide for His people the material blessings they need.

16 The heavens are the LORD's heavens,
but the earth he has given to the
children of man.
17 [u]The dead do not praise the LORD,
nor do any who go down into
[v]silence.
18 But [w]we will bless the LORD
from this time forth and
forevermore.
[x]Praise the LORD!

I Love the LORD

116 I [y]love the LORD, because he has
[z]heard
my voice and my pleas for mercy.
2 Because he [a]inclined his ear to me,
therefore I will call on him as long
as I live.
3 [b]The snares of death
encompassed me;
the pangs of Sheol laid hold
on me;
I suffered distress and anguish.
4 Then [c]I called on the name of the
LORD:
"O LORD, I pray, deliver my soul!"
5 [d]Gracious is the LORD, and [e]righteous;
our God is [f]merciful.
6 The LORD preserves [g]the simple;
when [h]I was brought low, he
saved me.
7 Return, O my soul, to your [i]rest;
for the LORD has [j]dealt bountifully
with you.
8 For [k]you have delivered my soul from
death,
my eyes from tears,
my feet from stumbling;
9 I will walk before the LORD
[l]in the land of the living.
10 [m]I believed, [n]even when[1] I spoke,
"I am greatly afflicted";
11 [o]I said in my alarm,
[p]"All mankind are liars."
12 What shall I [q]render to the LORD
for all his benefits to me?
13 I will lift up [r]the cup of salvation
and [s]call on the name of
the LORD,
14 I will [t]pay my vows to the LORD
in the presence of all his
people.
15 [u]Precious in the sight of the LORD
is the death of his [v]saints.
16 O LORD, I am your [w]servant;
I am your servant, [x]the son of your
maidservant.
You have [y]loosed my bonds.
17 I will [z]offer to you the sacrifice of
thanksgiving
and [s]call on the name of
the LORD.
18 I will [t]pay my vows to the LORD
in the presence of all his
people,
19 in [a]the courts of the house of the
LORD,
in your midst, O Jerusalem.
[b]Praise the LORD!

The LORD's Faithfulness Endures Forever

117 [c]Praise the LORD, all nations!
Extol him, all peoples!

17[u]See Ps. 6:5 [v]See Ps. 31:17
18[w]Ps. 113:2 [x]See Ps. 104:35
Psalm 116
1[y]Ps. 18:1 [z]Ps. 66:19; 118:21
2[a][Ps. 31:2]
3[b]See Ps. 18:4
4[c]Ps. 118:5; See Ps. 18:6
5[d]See Ps. 86:15 [e]Ps. 7:9; 119:137; 145:17; Ezra 9:15; Neh. 9:8; Jer. 12:1; Dan. 9:7 [f]See Ps. 62:12
6[g]See Ps. 19:7 [h]Ps. 79:8; 142:6
7[i]Jer. 6:16; [Matt. 11:23] [j]See Ps. 13:6
8[k]Ps. 49:15; 56:13; [Ps. 86:13]
9[l]See Ps. 27:13
10[m]Cited 2 Cor. 4:13 [n][Ps. 39:3]
11[o]Ps. 31:22 [p][Ps. 62:9]
12[q]2 Chr. 32:25
13[r][Ps. 16:5] [s]See Ps. 99:6; 105:1
14[t]See Ps. 50:14
15[u]See Ps. 72:14 [v]See 50:5
16[w]Ps. 119:125; 143:12; [Ps. 113:1] [x]Ps. 86:16 [y][Job 12:18]
17[z]See Ps. 50:14 [s][See ver. 13 above]
18[t][See ver. 14 above]
19[a]See Ps. 92:13 [b]See Ps. 104:35

Psalm 117 1[c]Cited Rom. 15:11

[1] Or *believed, indeed*; Septuagint *believed, therefore*

115:16 the earth he has given to the children of man. God created the earth and it belongs to Him. Along with the gift of the earth comes the responsibility to work and serve God faithfully.

115:17 The dead. See note Ps. 88:5.

Ps. 116 An exuberant thanksgiving to the Lord for delivering the psalmist from death. It is impossible to be precise about the threat that hung over the psalmist (perhaps sickness), but he looks back to his cry of distress to the Lord and proclaims with gladness that God heard him. As a result, he determines to offer sacrifices to the Lord. For the use of this psalm at a feast, see introduction to Ps. 113.

116:1 I love the LORD. The psalmist expresses his deep affection for the Lord, grounding it in God's own love toward him. God showed His love for the psalmist by hearing his prayer.

116:3 The snares of death. It was as if ropes came out of a grave, pulling the psalmist into the ground.

116:5 Gracious . . . righteous . . . merciful. God reveals His kindness in His answer to the psalmist's request. He does not stand at a distance when His people suffer.

116:10 when I spoke. It was the psalmist's faith in God that led him (see text note) to pray to Him in the beginning.

116:11 "All mankind are liars." He remembers his complaint; he apparently had been the object of a false accusation.

116:13 the cup of salvation. This may be a reference to a drink offering (Num. 15:10), but it is more likely a metaphor, contrasting with the more common "cup" of God's wrath (Ps. 75:8).

116:14 in the presence of all his people. The psalmist promises to proclaim publicly God's great acts (Ps. 22:22 note).

116:15 Precious. Their deaths, like their lives, are significant and important to God. See "Death and the Intermediate State" at Phil. 1:23.

116:19 the courts of the house of the LORD. The temple in Jerusalem.

Ps. 117 This is the shortest chapter in the Bible, but the song's exuberant praise reaches to all the nations. Paul uses the psalm to show that the nations share in the promises to the patriarchs (Rom. 15:7–11).

117:1 all nations. The call to praise goes beyond Israel to all nations.

2 For [d] great is his steadfast love
toward us,
and [e] the faithfulness of the LORD
endures forever.
[b] Praise the LORD!

His Steadfast Love Endures Forever

118 [f] Oh give thanks to the LORD, for
he is good;
for his steadfast love endures forever!
2 [g] Let Israel say,
"His steadfast love endures forever."
3 [g] Let the house of Aaron say,
"His steadfast love endures forever."
4 [h] Let those who fear the LORD say,
"His steadfast love endures forever."
5 Out of my distress I [i] called on the
LORD;
the LORD answered me and set me
[j] free.
6 [k] The LORD is on my side; [l] I will not
fear.
What can man do to me?
7 [m] The LORD is on my side as my helper;
I shall [n] look in triumph on those
who hate me.
8 [o] It is better to take refuge in the LORD
[p] than to trust in man.
9 It is better to take refuge in the LORD
[p] than to trust in princes.
10 [q] All nations surrounded me;
in the name of the LORD I cut
them off!
11 They surrounded me, surrounded me
on every side;
in the name of the LORD I cut
them off!
12 [r] They surrounded me like bees;
they went out like [s] a fire among
thorns;
in the name of the LORD I cut
them off!
13 I was [t] pushed hard,[1] so that I was
falling,
but the LORD helped me.
14 The LORD is my strength and my
song;
[u] he has become my salvation.
15 Glad songs of salvation
are in the tents of the
righteous:
[v] "The right hand of the LORD [w] does
valiantly,
16 the right hand of the LORD exalts,
the right hand of the LORD [w] does
valiantly!"
17 [x] I shall not die, but I shall live,
and [y] recount the deeds of the
LORD.
18 The LORD has [z] disciplined me
severely,
but he has not given me over to
death.
19 [a] Open to me the gates of
righteousness,
that I may enter through them
and give thanks to the LORD.
20 This is the gate of the LORD;
[b] the righteous shall enter
through it.
21 I thank you that [c] you have
answered me
[u] and have become my salvation.

2 [d] Ps. 103:11; [Ps. 116:5] [e] [Ps. 100:5] [b] [See Ps. 116:19 above]
Psalm 118
1 [f] ver. 29; See Ps. 100:5
2 [g] [Ps. 115:9, 10, 11]
3 [g] [See ver. 2 above]
4 [h] [Ps. 115:9, 10, 11]
5 [i] [Ps. 116:4] [j] See Ps. 18:19
6 [k] Ps. 56:9; Cited Heb. 13:6 [l] See Ps. 23:4; 56:4, 11
7 [m] Ps. 54:4 [n] See Ps. 54:7
8 [o] [Ps. 40:4; 62:8] [p] Ps. 146:3
9 [p] [See ver. 8 above]
10 [q] [Ps. 88:17]
12 [r] Deut. 1:44 [s] [Ps. 58:9]
13 [t] [Ps. 140:4]
14 [u] See Ps. 27:1
15 [v] Ex. 15:6; Luke 1:51 [w] Ps. 60:12
16 [w] [See ver. 15 above]
17 [x] [Hab. 1:12] [y] Ps. 73:28; 107:22; [Ps. 6:5]
18 [z] [Jer. 30:11; 2 Cor. 6:9]
19 [a] Isai. 26:2; [Ps. 24:7, 9]
20 [b] Rev. 21:27; 22:14; [Isai. 35:8]
21 [c] Ps. 116:1 [u] [See ver. 14 above]

1 Hebrew *You* (that is, the enemy) *pushed me hard*

117:2 his steadfast love. Specifically, the love connected with His covenant. This verse, though using different vocabulary, may be seen as a meditation on the truth expressed in Ex. 34:6. It celebrates God's covenant relationship with His people.

Ps. 118 This psalm concludes the section associated with the celebration of Passover (113–118). As the last song of the group, it may have been the final psalm in the mind of Jesus as He celebrated Passover with His disciples (Mark 14:26). Jesus quoted vv. 22, 23 about Himself (Mark 12:10, 11; Matt. 23:29; Luke 13:35; cf. Acts 4:11). The people greeted Jesus' triumphal entry with shouts of joy taken from this psalm (Mark 11:9, 10; Luke 19:38; John 12:13). The main speaker is likely the king (vv. 5–21), but the psalm as a whole is a liturgy with other speakers as well (vv. 21–27). The references to altar, temple, and procession (vv. 19, 20, 27) show that it was used in corporate worship.

118:1 his steadfast love endures forever. A refrain of this psalm and Ps. 136.

118:5 I. The king.

118:6 The LORD is on my side. This is the heart of the covenant of grace: God siding with His redeemed. The implication for the psalmist is that he has nothing to fear from anyone because God is in control. Victory is not guaranteed by superior forces or weapons; it is a gift from God.

118:12 a fire among thorns. The simile has two sides: Thorns, with their sharp points are apt descriptions of an enemy; they also burn quickly, like an enemy running away.

118:14 my salvation. For the psalmist the "salvation" in view is victory in battle.

118:15 Glad songs of salvation. Israel responds to God's help by singing victory songs that rejoice in God's salvation.

The right hand. This is the arm that is used to wield the sword in battle (v. 16; cf. Ex. 15:6, 12).

118:19 the gates of righteousness. The entrance to the sanctuary, leading to the presence of God, where the psalmist will offer thanks. The gates are righteous because the One who dwells behind them is righteous, and those who enter must be righteous as well (Ps. 15 and 24).

118:21 my salvation. See note on v. 14.

22 [d]The stone that the builders
rejected
has become the
cornerstone.[1]
23 This is the LORD's doing;
it is marvelous in our eyes.
24 This is the day that the LORD has
made;
let us rejoice and be glad in it.

25 Save us, we pray, O LORD!
O LORD, we pray, give us
success!

26 [e]Blessed is he who comes in the
name of the LORD!
We [f]bless you from the house of
the LORD.
27 The LORD is God,
and he has made [g]his light to
shine upon us.
Bind the festal sacrifice with cords,
up to [h]the horns of the altar!

28 You are my God, and I will give
thanks to you;
you are my God; I will [i]extol you.
29 [j]Oh give thanks to the LORD, for
he is good;
for his steadfast love endures
forever!

22 [d]Cited Matt. 21:42; Mark 12:10, 11; Luke 20:17; [Isai. 28:16]; Acts 4:11; Eph. 2:20; 1 Pet. 2:4-7 26 [e]Matt. 21:9; 23:39; Mark 11:9; Luke 13:35; 19:38 [f]Ps. 129:8 27 [g]Ps. 18:28; 97:11; [Esth. 8:16; 1 Pet. 2:9] [h]See Ex. 27:2 28 [i]See Ps. 99:5 29 [j]ver. 1

Psalm 119
1 [k]Prov. 11:20; 13:6 [Ps. 101:2, 6] [l]Ps. 128:1; [Gen. 17:1] 2 [m][ver. 22] [n][Ps. 78:5] [o][ver. 10; 2 Chr. 15:2] 3 [p]1 John 3:9; 5:18 4 [q]Ps. 19:8 5 [r]Ps. 37:23; [Prov. 16:9; Jer. 10:23] 6 [s]ver. 80; [1 John 2:28] 7 [t]ver. 62, 106; Ex. 24:3 8 [u]Ps. 38:21; 71:9, 18 9 [v][Ps. 25:7]

Your Word Is a Lamp to My Feet

ALEPH

119 [2]Blessed are those whose [k]way is
blameless,
who [l]walk in the law of the LORD!
2 Blessed are those who [m]keep his
[n]testimonies,
who [o]seek him with their whole
heart,
3 who also [p]do no wrong,
but walk in his ways!
4 You have commanded your [q]precepts
to be kept diligently.
5 Oh that my ways may [r]be steadfast
in keeping your statutes!
6 [s]Then I shall not be put to shame,
having my eyes fixed on all your
commandments.
7 I will praise you with an upright heart,
when I learn [t]your righteous rules.
8 I will keep your statutes;
[u]do not utterly forsake me!

BETH

9 How can [v]a young man keep his way
pure?
By guarding it according to your
word.

1 Hebrew *the head of the corner* 2 This psalm is an acrostic poem of twenty-two stanzas, following the letters of the Hebrew alphabet; within a stanza, each verse begins with the same Hebrew letter

118:22 The stone that the builders rejected. The metaphor would likely refer originally to the king, who represented his people. The stone was cast off in despair when defeat seemed inevitable, and victory was no longer a realistic hope (but see following note).

the cornerstone. The low and insignificant, despite having been rejected, is exalted to the chief place. Jesus later applies this passage to Himself (Matt. 21:42; Mark 12:10; Luke 20:17; Acts 4:11 and 1 Pet. 2:7). Jesus is the cornerstone (Eph. 2:20), cast away by the earthly rulers of His day, but exalted to the right hand of the Father. To some this is a cause for stumbling (Is. 8:14; 1 Pet. 2), but to others the basis of hope.

118:24 the day that the LORD has made. Because of God's victory, His people will turn the day of despair into a day of worship before the Lord.

118:26 Blessed is he who comes in the name of the LORD. Later, this cry is lifted up by the crowds as they welcome the true King, Christ Jesus, into Jerusalem (Matt. 21:9). In a way still beyond their understanding, Jesus was about to defeat sin and death on the cross.

118:27 the festal sacrifice. The sacrifice was performed in public worship before the Lord.

118:29 Oh give thanks to the LORD. The psalm ends as it began.

Ps. 119 As Ps. 117 has the distinction of being the shortest chapter in the Bible, so Ps. 119 is the longest. The psalm is an acrostic of twenty-two stanzas, one for each letter of the Hebrew alphabet. The eight poetic lines of each stanza begin with the same Hebrew letter.

The number eight may be connected with eight Hebrew words that appear throughout the psalm concerning its main theme. The words are translated variously as "law," "testimonies," "precepts," "statutes," "commandments," "rules," and "word." In five stanzas all eight Hebrew words occur, and every stanza has at least six of the eight.

While the psalmist expresses his love for the law and his desire to obey it, he also recognizes his failures. Elements of lament and petition are intertwined with expressions of confidence and innocence.

The law is a faithful expression of God's character. God sent His Son to keep the law for us. The law no longer condemns us, setting us free to accept it as our own guide for pleasing the One who died in our place.

119:1 Blessed. See Ps. 1:1.

who walk. A metaphor for the activities of daily life.

the law of the LORD. The law, or Torah, refers to the first five books of the Bible as a unit, or to the legal sections of those books. Here the latter is meant: the Ten Commandments and the other laws of the Pentateuch.

119:2 with their whole heart. The psalmist is not speaking of a mere external adherence to the law. He calls for obedience that comes from a deep-seated faith in the Lord.

119:4 You have commanded your precepts. God entered into a covenant relationship with Israel freely out of grace, and within that relationship God gave them His law to obey. He was not asking them to earn His favor, or pay for their redemption. It was the way of thankful obedience for those in covenant with Him.

119:5 Oh. The psalmist does not think of himself as an example of perfect obedience.

119:7 when I learn. Worship and obedience requires knowledge of the Scripture.

119:8 I will. The psalmist decides to follow God's law.

119:9–16 The psalmist seeks to keep his way pure by meditating on God's law.

119:9 according to your word. God does not hide from us what pleases Him. He states it clearly in His Word, the Bible.

10 [w] With my whole heart I seek you;
let me not [x] wander from your commandments!
11 I have [y] stored up your word in my heart,
that I might not sin against you.
12 Blessed are you, O LORD;
[z] teach me your statutes!
13 With my lips I [a] declare
all the rules of your mouth.
14 In the way of your testimonies I [b] delight
as much as in all [c] riches.
15 I will [d] meditate on your precepts
and fix my eyes on your [e] ways.
16 I will [f] delight in your statutes;
I will not forget your word.

GIMEL

17 [g] Deal bountifully with your servant,
[h] that I may live and keep your word.

10 [w] [ver. 10; 2 Chr. 15:2] [x] [ver. 21, 118] 11 [y] Luke 2:19, 51; See Ps. 37:31 12 [z] ver. 26, 64, 68, 108, 124, 135, 171; See Ps. 25:4 13 [a] Ps. 40:9; [Deut. 6:7] 14 [b] ver. 111, 162 [c] See Prov. 3:13-15; 8:10, 11, 18, 19

15 [d] ver. 23, 78, 97 [e] Ps. 25:4 16 [f] ver. 24, 47, 70, 77, 92, 143, 174 17 [g] See Ps. 13:6 [h] ver. 144

Understanding the Word of God

All Christians have a right and duty, not only to learn from the church's heritage of faith, but also to interpret Scripture for themselves. The church of Rome at one time forbid this, alleging that individuals easily misinterpret the Scriptures. The *Westminster Confession of Faith* agrees that "All things in Scripture are not alike in plain in themselves, nor alike clear unto all," but it also states clearly the authority of individual believers to read the Bible for themselves: "not only the learned, but the unlearned, in a due use of the ordinary means, may attain unto a sufficient understanding" of the Scriptures. The "ordinary means" include principles of interpretation such as the following.

The Bible is inspired by God, and its words continue to be God's words, but the Bible is also the product of human writers. Realizing this is essential. No allegorizing or other fanciful method that ignores the original writer's expressed meaning can be appropriate.

Each book was written, not in code, but in a way that could be understood by the readers to whom it was addressed. This is true even of such books as Daniel, Zechariah, and Revelation, that primarily use symbolism; the main thrust is always clear, even if details are clouded. So when we understand the words used, the historical background, and the cultural conventions of the writer and his readers, we are well on the way to grasping the thoughts that are being conveyed. But a spiritual understanding—that is, discerning the reality of God, His ways with His people, His present will, and one's own relationship to Him—will not reach us from the text until the veil is removed from our hearts and we are able to share the writer's own passion for God (1 Cor. 2:14; 2 Cor. 3:16). We should pray that God's Spirit would generate this passion in us and show us God in the text. See Ps. 119:18, 19, 26, 27, 33, 34, 73, 125, 144, 169; Eph. 1:17–19; 3:16–19.

Each book took its form at a particular time in the process of God's revelation of grace. That place must be considered when interpreting the text. The psalms, for instance, model the godly heart in every age, but they express its prayers and praises in terms of the realities of the life of grace before the coming of Christ—such as the ceremonial law, the sacrificial system, and the special role of Israel as a theocratic kingdom.

Each book proceeded from the same divine mind, so the teaching of the Bible's sixty-six books is complementary and consistent. If we cannot yet see this, the fault is in us, not in Scripture. Scripture nowhere contradicts Scripture; rather, one passage explains another. This sound principle of interpreting Scripture by Scripture is sometimes called the analogy of Scripture, or the analogy of faith.

Each book exhibits unchanging truth about God, the world, and His will for people, applied to and illustrated by particular situations. The final stage in biblical interpretation is to reapply these truths to our own life-situations; this is the way to discern what God in Scripture is saying to us at this moment. Examples of such reapplication are Josiah's realization of God's wrath at Judah's failure to observe His law (2 Kin. 22:8–13), Jesus' reasoning from Gen. 2:24 (Matt. 19:4–6), and Paul's use of Gen. 15:6 and Ps. 32:1, 2 to show the reality of present righteousness by faith (Rom. 4:1–8).

No meaning may be read into or imposed on Scripture that cannot with certainty be read out of Scripture—shown, that is, to be unambiguously expressed by one or more of the human writers.

Careful and prayerful observance of these rules is a mark of every Christian who is "rightly handling the word of truth" (2 Tim. 2:15).

119:10 I seek . . . let me not wander. There is a deep connection between striving after moral perfection and the realization that the quest is itself impossible without God's help.

119:15 I will meditate. God's law requires more than surface reading or rote memorization; it demands careful reflection.

119:17 that I may live. The psalmist's life depends on grace.

18 Open my eyes, that I may behold
wondrous things out of your law.
19 I am [i]a sojourner on the earth;
[j]hide not your commandments
from me!
20 My soul is consumed with [k]longing
for your rules at all times.
21 You rebuke [l]the insolent, [m]accursed
ones,
who [n]wander from your
commandments.
22 Take away from me [o]scorn and
contempt,
[p]for I have kept your testimonies.
23 Even though [q]princes sit plotting
against me,
your servant will [r]meditate on your
statutes.
24 Your testimonies are my [s]delight;
they are my [t]counselors.

DALETH

25 [u]My soul clings to the dust;
[v]give me life [w]according to your
word!
26 When [x]I told of my ways, you
answered me;
[y]teach me your statutes!
27 [z]Make me understand the way of your
precepts,
and I will [a]meditate on your
wondrous works.
28 [b]My soul melts away for sorrow;
strengthen me according to your
word!
29 Put false ways far from me
and graciously [c]teach me your law!
30 I have chosen the way of
faithfulness;
I [d]set your rules before me.
31 I cling to your testimonies, O LORD;
[e]let me not be put to shame!

19 [i]See Ps. 39:12 [j][Isai. 6:9, 10]
20 [k]ver. 40, 131, 174; [Ps. 42:1, 2]
21 [l]See ver. 51 [m]Deut. 27:26 [n][ver. 10]
22 [o]See Ps. 44:13 [p][ver. 2]
23 [q]ver. 161; [Dan. 6:4] [r]ver. 15, 27, 28
24 [s][Rom. 7:22]; See ver. 16 [t][ver. 104]
25 [u]Ps. 44:25 [v]ver. 37, 40, 88, 107, 149, 154, 156, 159; See Ps. 71:20 [w]ver. 65
26 [x][Ps. 37:5] [y]ver. 12
27 [z]ver. 18, 34, 73, 125, 144, 169; [Job 32:8] [a]ver. 15, 23, 78
28 [b]See Ps. 22:14
29 [c][ver. 27]
30 [d][Ps. 16:8]
31 [e]ver. 116
32 [f]1 Kin. 4:29; Isai. 60:5; 2 Cor. 6:11, 13
33 [g]ver. 12, 26 [h]ver. 112; [Matt. 10:22; Heb. 3:6; Rev. 2:26]
34 [i]ver. 27; Prov. 2:6; James 1:5
35 [j]See Ps. 25:4, 5 [k]ver. 16; See Ps. 1:2
36 [l]ver. 112; 1 Kin. 8:58; [Ps. 141:4] [m][Luke 12:15; 1 Tim. 6:10; Heb. 13:5]
37 [n][Prov. 23:5; Isai. 33:15] [o]ver. 25

32 I will run in the way of your
commandments
when you [f]enlarge my heart![1]

HE

33 [g]Teach me, O LORD, the way of your
statutes;
and I will keep it [h]to the end.[2]
34 [i]Give me understanding, that I may
keep your law
and observe it with my whole
heart.
35 [j]Lead me in the path of your
commandments,
for I [k]delight in it.
36 [l]Incline my heart to your testimonies,
and not to [m]selfish gain!
37 [n]Turn my eyes from looking at
worthless things;
and [o]give me life in your ways.
38 [p]Confirm to your servant your
promise,
[q]that you may be feared.
39 Turn away the [r]reproach that I dread,
for your rules are good.
40 Behold, I [s]long for your precepts;
[t]in your righteousness give me life!

WAW

41 Let your [u]steadfast love come to me,
O LORD,
your salvation [v]according to your
promise;
42 then [w]shall I have an answer for him
[r]who taunts me,
for I trust in your word.
43 And take not the word of truth
utterly out of my mouth,
for my [x]hope is in your rules.

38 [p]2 Sam. 7:25 [q][Ps. 25:10; 112:1; 128:1; 130:4] **39** [r]ver. 22 **40** [s]ver. 20 [t][ver. 149, 156] **41** [u]ver. 77; [Ps. 106:4] [v]ver. 58, 65, 76, 116, 170 **42** [w]Prov. 27:11 [r][See ver. 39 above] **43** [x]ver. 49, 74, 81, 114, 147; [Ps. 31:24]

[1] Or *for you set my heart free* [2] Or *keep it as my reward*

119:18 Open my eyes. We need God's grace to illumine His word. He must guide our understanding.

119:19 sojourner. See Heb. 11:13. His true home is not on the earth, but with God.

119:22 Take away from me. The psalm goes beyond praise of the law to petition for God's grace in distress.

119:23 princes sit plotting against me. Perhaps indicating the royal status of the psalmist.

119:29 Put false ways far from me. The psalmist sees that, if left to himself, he would be walking in ways contrary to God's law.

119:33–40 The psalmist beseeches the Lord for instruction in His law.

119:34 with my whole heart. He resolves with his whole mind, strength, and will. The psalmist expresses his deep devotion to the Lord. He loves the Lord and wants to be obedient. Jesus told His disciples, "If you love me, you will keep my commandments" (John 14:15). See theological note "Understanding the Word of God."

119:36 Incline my heart. He realizes that his love for the Lord has its source in God Himself.

119:37 Turn my eyes from . . . worthless things. Matching his positive desire to move closer to God's law, there is a corresponding negative desire to turn away from worthless things, particularly idols. For the same word, see note Ps. 31:6.

119:38 your promise. Likely referring to God's covenant promise of blessing.

119:41 your steadfast love. God's love or devotion to those in covenant with Him.

44 I will keep your law continually,
forever and ever,
45 and I shall walk [y]in a wide place,
for I have [z]sought your precepts.
46 I will also speak of your testimonies
[a]before kings
and shall not be put to shame,
47 for I [b]find my delight in your
commandments,
which I love.
48 I will [c]lift up my hands toward your
commandments, which I love,
and I will [d]meditate on your
statutes.

Zayin

49 Remember [e]your word to your
servant,
in which you have made me [f]hope.
50 This is [g]my comfort in my affliction,
that your promise [h]gives me life.
51 [i]The insolent utterly deride me,
but I do not [j]turn away from your
law.
52 When I think of your rules from of
old,
I take comfort, O LORD.
53 [k]Hot indignation seizes me because of
the wicked,
who forsake your law.
54 Your statutes have been my songs
in the house of my [l]sojourning.
55 I [m]remember your name in the night,
O LORD,
and keep your law.
56 This blessing has fallen to me,
that [n]I have kept your precepts.

Heth

57 [o]The LORD is my portion;
I promise to keep your words.
58 I [p]entreat your favor with all my heart;
be gracious to me [q]according to
your promise.
59 When I [r]think on my ways,
I turn my feet to your testimonies;
60 I hasten and do not delay
to keep your commandments.
61 Though [s]the cords of the wicked
ensnare me,
I do not [t]forget your law.
62 At [u]midnight I rise to praise you,
because of your [v]righteous rules.
63 [w]I am a companion of all who fear
you,
of those who keep your precepts.
64 [x]The earth, O LORD, is full of your
steadfast love;
[y]teach me your statutes!

Teth

65 You have dealt well with your
servant,
O LORD, [z]according to your word.
66 Teach me [a]good judgment and
knowledge,
for I believe in your
commandments.
67 [b]Before I was afflicted I went astray,
but now I keep your word.
68 [c]You are good and do good;
[d]teach me your statutes.
69 [e]The insolent [f]smear me with lies,
but with my whole heart I [g]keep
your precepts;
70 their heart is unfeeling [h]like fat,
but I [i]delight in your law.
71 It is [j]good for me that I was afflicted,
that I might learn your statutes.
72 [k]The law of your mouth is better to me
than thousands of gold and silver
pieces.

Yodh

73 [l]Your hands have made and
fashioned me;
[m]give me understanding that I may
learn your commandments.

45[y]Prov. 4:12 [z]ver. 94, 155
46[a][Matt. 10:18; Acts 26:1, 2]
47[b]ver. 16
48[c]See Ps. 28:2 [d]ver. 13
49[e]ver. 41, 42, 43 [f]ver. 43
50[g][Rom. 15:4] [h]ver. 25; See Ps. 71:20
51[i]ver. 69, 78, 85, 122; Jer. 20:7; [Ps. 42:3; 123:4] [j]ver. 157; Ps. 44:18; Job 23:11
53[k][Neh. 13:25]
54[l]See Ps. 39:12
55[m]See Ps. 42:8
56[n]ver. 22, 69, 100
57[o]See Ps. 16:5
58[p]Ps. 45:12 [q]ver. 41
59[r][Luke 13:17]
61[s]ver. 110 [t]ver. 83
62[u][Acts 16:25] [v]ver. 7
63[w][Ps. 101:6]
64[x]Ps. 33:5 [y]ver. 12
65[z][ver. 41]
66[a] Phil. 1:9; [James 1:5]
67[b]ver. 71, 75; Jer. 31:18, 19; See Heb. 12:5-11
68[c]Ps. 106:1 [d]ver. 12
69[e]ver. 51 [f]Job 13:4; [Ps. 109:2] [g]ver. 56
70[h]Isai. 6:10; See Ps. 17:10 [i]ver. 16
71[j][ver. 67]
72[k]ver. 127; Ps. 19:10; Prov. 8:10
73[l]Job 10:8; See Ps. 95:6; Job 31:15 [m]ver. 27

119:45 in a wide place. By keeping God's laws the writer will be liberated from slavery to sin.

119:49 Remember. See Ps. 44:1.

119:52 your rules from of old. Given through Moses and contained in the books of Exodus, Leviticus, and Deuteronomy.

119:54 Your statutes . . . my songs. The law was not simply a matter of obedience for the psalmist, but of worship.

119:55 name. See Ps. 8:1.

119:57 my portion. The poet's portion is not an inheritance in the land, but the Lord Himself (Num. 18:20).

119:63 a companion. Obedience to the Lord takes place in community with other believers who also serve the Lord.

who fear you. See Ps. 34:7.

119:65–72 The psalmist found that affliction brought him back from wandering away from God.

119:67 I went astray. God uses distress and suffering in our lives to bring us back to Him (Ps. 31; Heb. 12:1–13).

119:70 like fat. Cf. 1 Tim. 4:2.

119:71 It is good for me . . . afflicted. In retrospect the writer is thankful for his suffering because it has led to a new intimacy with the Lord.

74 Those who fear you shall see me and
[n]rejoice,
because I have [o]hoped in your
word.
75 I know, O LORD, that your rules are
[p]righteous,
and that in [q]faithfulness you have
afflicted me.
76 Let your steadfast love comfort me
according to your promise to your
servant.
77 Let your [r]mercy come to me, that I
may live;
for your law is my [s]delight.
78 Let [t]the insolent be put to [u]shame,
because they have [v]wronged me
with falsehood;
as for me, I will [w]meditate on your
precepts.
79 Let those who fear you [x]turn to me,
that they may know your
testimonies.
80 May my heart be [y]blameless in your
statutes,
[z]that I may not be put to shame!

KAPH

81 My soul [a]longs for your salvation;
I [b]hope in your word.
82 My [c]eyes long for your promise;
I ask, [d]"When will you
comfort me?"
83 For I have [e]become like a [f]wineskin
in the smoke,
yet I have not forgotten your
statutes.
84 [g]How long must your servant
endure?[1]
[h]When will you judge those who
persecute me?
85 [i]The insolent have [j]dug pitfalls
for me;
they do not live according to your
law.
86 All your commandments are [k]sure;
they persecute me [l]with falsehood;
[m]help me!
87 They have almost made an end of me
on earth,
but I have not forsaken your
precepts.
88 In your steadfast love [n]give me life,
that I may keep the testimonies of
your mouth.

LAMEDH

89 Forever, O LORD, your [o]word
is firmly fixed in the heavens.
90 Your [p]faithfulness endures to all
generations;
you have [q]established the earth,
and it [r]stands fast.
91 By your [s]appointment they stand this
day,
for all things are your servants.
92 If your law had not been my
[t]delight,
I would have perished in my
affliction.
93 I will never forget your precepts,
for by them you have [u]given me
life.
94 I am yours; save me,
[v]for I have sought your precepts.
95 The wicked lie in wait to
destroy me,
but I consider your testimonies.
96 I have seen a limit to all perfection,
but your commandment is
exceedingly [w]broad.

MEM

97 Oh how [x]I love your law!
It is my [y]meditation all the day.
98 Your commandment makes me
[z]wiser than my enemies,
for it is ever with me.

74 [n]Ps. 34:2; 35:27; 107:42 [o]ver. 43; Ps. 130:5
75 [p]ver. 138 [q]Ps. 33:4; See ver. 67
77 [r]ver. 41 [s]ver. 24, 47, 174
78 [t]See ver. 51 [u]Ps. 25:3 [v]ver. 86 [w]ver. 15, 23
79 [x][Jer. 15:19]
80 [y]ver. 1 [z]ver. 6
81 [a]See Ps. 84:2 [b]ver. 74, 114
82 [c]See Ps. 69:3 [d][Ps. 101:2]
83 [e][Job 30:30] [f][Matt. 9:17; Mark 2:22]
84 [g][Ps. 39:4] [h]Rev. 6:10; [Zech. 1:12]
85 [i]ver. 51 [j]See Ps. 7:15
86 [k]ver. 138 [l]ver. 78; Ps. 35:19 [m]Ps. 109:26
88 [n]ver. 25; See Ps. 71:20
89 [o]ver. 152; [Matt. 24:35; 1 Pet. 1:25]; [Jer. 31:35-37]
90 [p]See Ps. 36:5 [q][Ps. 148:6] [r]Eccles. 1:4
91 [s]Jer. 33:25
92 [t]ver. 77
93 [u]ver. 25; See Ps. 71:20
94 [v]ver. 45
96 [w][Ps. 18:19]
97 [x]ver. 113, 163, 165; [Ps. 1:2] [y]ver. 15
98 [z][Deut. 4:6]

1 Hebrew *How many are the days of your servant?*

119:74 shall see me. As others who share the psalmist's deep commitment to the Lord see his happiness, they will be encouraged.

119:75 you have afflicted me. See vv. 67 and 71.

119:82 My eyes long for. Because he has been looking so long in expectation.

119:83 a wineskin in the smoke. A striking metaphor, unparalleled elsewhere. The smoke damages the wineskin; this is comparable to the harm the writer has suffered at the hand of his enemies.

119:84 When will you judge. The poet expects God to come to his aid and punish those who persecute him unjustly. God's seeming delay is a trial for him.

119:86 with falsehood. See Ps. 38:19.

119:87 but I have not forsaken your precepts. The psalmist would not allow his obedience to depend on his situation.

119:89 Forever. As God is eternal, so is His word. It is forever valid. It speaks to all people and for all time.

119:93 forget. To forget something, in the psalms, implies disobedience.

119:97 I love your law. The psalmist loves the law because it comes from his God and Savior. See "The Law of God" at Ex. 20:1.

119:98 wiser than my enemies. His enemies rebel against God and reject the law, refusing the insight that God their Creator can give them.

99 I have more understanding than all
my teachers,
for [a]your testimonies are my
meditation.
100 I understand more than [b]the aged,[1]
for I [c]keep your precepts.
101 I [d]hold back my feet from every evil
way,
in order to keep your word.
102 I do not turn aside from your rules,
for you have taught me.
103 How [e]sweet are your words to my
taste,
sweeter than honey to my mouth!
104 Through your precepts I get
understanding;
therefore [f]I hate every false way.

NUN

105 [g]Your word is a lamp to my feet
and a light to my path.
106 I have [h]sworn an oath and
confirmed it,
to keep your [i]righteous rules.
107 I am severely [j]afflicted;
[k]give me life, O LORD, according to
your word!
108 Accept [l]my freewill offerings of
praise, O LORD,
and [m]teach me your rules.
109 I hold my life [n]in my hand
continually,
but I do not [o]forget your law.
110 The wicked have laid [p]a snare for me,
but [q]I do not stray from your
precepts.
111 Your testimonies are [r]my heritage
forever,
for they are [s]the joy of my heart.
112 I [t]incline my heart to perform your
statutes
forever, [u]to the end.[2]

SAMEKH

113 I hate [v]the double-minded,
but I love [w]your law.
114 You are my [x]hiding place and my
[y]shield;
I [z]hope in your word.
115 [a]Depart from me, you evildoers,
that I may [b]keep the
commandments of my God.
116 Uphold me [c]according to your
promise, that I may live,
and let me not be [d]put to shame in
my [e]hope!
117 [f]Hold me up, that I may be safe
and have regard for your statutes
continually!
118 You [g]spurn all who [h]go astray from
your statutes,
for their cunning is in vain.
119 All the wicked of the earth you
discard like [i]dross,
therefore [j]I love your testimonies.
120 My flesh [k]trembles for fear of you,
and I am afraid of your judgments.

AYIN

121 I have done what is just and right;
do not leave me to my oppressors.
122 Give your servant [l]a pledge of good;
let not [m]the insolent oppress me.
123 My [n]eyes long for your salvation
and for the fulfillment of your
righteous promise.
124 Deal with your servant according to
your steadfast love,
and [o]teach me your statutes.
125 I am your [p]servant; [q]give me
understanding,
that I may know your testimonies!
126 It is time for the LORD to act,
for your law has been broken.

99 [a][2 Tim. 3:15] **100** [b]See Job 32:7-9 [c]ver. 56, 69 **101** [d]Prov. 1:15 **103** [e]Ps. 19:10 **104** [f]ver. 128 **105** [g]Prov. 6:23 **106** [h]Neh. 10:29 [i]ver. 7 **107** [j][ver. 25, 50] [k]ver. 88; See Ps. 71:20 **108** [l][Hos. 14:2] [m]ver. 12 **109** [n]See Judg. 12:3 [o]ver. 83 **110** [p]See Ps. 91:3 [q]ver. 10 **111** [r]Deut. 33:4 [s]ver. 14, 162 **112** [t]ver. 36 [u]See ver. 33

113 [v][1 Kin. 18:21; James 1:8; 4:8] [w]ver. 97 **114** [x]See Ps. 32:7 [y]See Ps. 3:3 [z]ver. 74 **115** [a]See Ps. 6:8 [b][ver. 22] **116** [c]ver. 41 [d]ver. 31; See Ps. 25:2 [e]Ps. 146:5 **117** [f][Ps. 20:2] **118** [g]Lam. 1:15 [h]ver. 10, 21, 110 **119** [i]Isai. 1:25; [Ezek. 22:18; Mal. 3:2, 3] [j]ver. 97 **120** [k][Job 4:14; Hab. 3:16] **122** [l]See Job 17:3 [m]ver. 51 **123** [n]ver. 82 **124** [o]ver. 12 **125** [p]See Ps. 116:16 [q]ver. 27

1 Or *the elders* 2 Or *statutes; the reward is eternal*

119:99 more understanding than all my teachers. The psalmist does not mean this as a boast but as an emphatic expression of his devotion to God's law.

119:102 you have taught me. The psalmist does not claim to study with superior intelligence, or even superior determination; he attributes everything to God.

119:105 a lamp to my feet. God's revelation provides the insight to guide His servant. He will not trip in the darkness.

119:109 my life in my hand continually. The psalmist's obedience is not risk-free, for it exposes him to the wiles of his enemies. He could wish to be free of the danger, but is more concerned to live a godly life in spite of it.

119:113 double-minded. The poet is of a single mind; he loves God and His law. Consequently, he is stable, unlike the double-minded man (James 1:8).

119:119 dross. The waste that results when metal is smelted. When the wicked are similarly cast off, the righteous remain as refined silver. Cf. Prov. 25:3–5; Is. 1:22, 25.

119:120 The fear of the Lord is vividly described.

119:123 My eyes long. See v. 82.

119:124 according to your steadfast love. The devotion that God shows toward His covenant people, demonstrating His mercy and compassion.

119:126 It is time for the LORD to act. With the direct honesty characteristic of the psalmist, he tells God that He has delayed His judgment long enough. The wicked deserve the punishment they are about to receive.

127 Therefore I [r]love your commandments
above gold, above fine gold.
128 Therefore I consider all your precepts
to be right;
I hate every [s]false way.

Pe

129 Your testimonies are [t]wonderful;
therefore my soul [u]keeps them.
130 The unfolding of your words gives
light;
it imparts [v]understanding to the
simple.
131 I [w]open my mouth and [x]pant,
because I [y]long for your
commandments.
132 [z]Turn to me and be gracious to me,
as is your way with those who love
your name.
133 [a]Keep steady my steps according to
your promise,
and let no iniquity [b]get dominion
over me.
134 [c]Redeem me from man's oppression,
that I may keep your precepts.
135 [d]Make your face shine upon your
servant,
and [e]teach me your statutes.
136 My eyes [f]shed streams of tears,
because people [g]do not keep your
law.

Tsadhe

137 [h]Righteous are you, O Lord,
and right are your rules.
138 You have appointed your testimonies
in [i]righteousness
and in all [j]faithfulness.
139 My [k]zeal consumes me,
because my foes forget your words.
140 Your promise is well [l]tried,
and your servant [m]loves it.

127 [r]ver. 72; Ps. 19:10 128 [s]ver. 104 129 [t]ver. 18, 27 [u]ver. 22 130 [v]See Ps. 19:7 131 [w]Ps. 81:10; Job 29:23 [x]Ps. 42:1 [y]ver. 20 132 [z]See Ps. 25:16 133 [a][Ps. 17:5] [b]Ps. 19:13 134 [c][Luke 1:74] 135 [d]See Ps. 4:6 [e]ver. 12 136 [f]Jer. 9:1, 18; 14:17; Lam. 3:48; [Ezek. 9:4; Phil. 3:18] [g]ver. 158 137 [h]See Ps. 116:5 138 [i]ver. 75, 172; See Ps. 19:7-9 [j]ver. 86 139 [k]See Ps. 69:9 140 [l]See Ps. 12:6 [m]ver. 97

141 [n]ver. 83 142 [o]ver. 151, 160; John 17:17; [Ps. 19:2] 143 [p]ver. 24 144 [q]ver. 27 [r]ver. 17 145 [s]ver. 2, 10 [t]ver. 22, 33 147 [u]See Ps. 5:3 [v]ver. 74 148 [w]See Ps. 42:8 149 [x]ver. 156; [ver. 40] [y]ver. 25; See Ps. 71:20 151 [z]See Ps. 145:18 [a]See ver. 142 152 [b]ver. 89, 160; [Matt. 5:18] 153 [c]Job 36:15 [d]ver. 83

141 I am small and despised,
yet I do not [n]forget your precepts.
142 Your righteousness is righteous
forever,
and your law is [o]true.
143 Trouble and anguish have found me
out,
but your commandments are my
[p]delight.
144 Your testimonies are righteous forever;
[q]give me understanding that I may
[r]live.

Qoph

145 With my [s]whole heart I cry; answer
me, O Lord!
I will [t]keep your statutes.
146 I call to you; save me,
that I may observe your testimonies.
147 I rise before [u]dawn and cry for help;
I [v]hope in your words.
148 My eyes are awake before [w]the
watches of the night,
that I may meditate on your
promise.
149 Hear my voice according to your
steadfast love;
O Lord, [x]according to your justice
[y]give me life.
150 They draw near who persecute me
with evil purpose;
they are far from your law.
151 But [z]you are near, O Lord,
and all your commandments are
[a]true.
152 Long have I known from your
testimonies
that you have [b]founded them forever.

Resh

153 Look on my [c]affliction and deliver me,
for [d]I do not forget your law.

119:130 The unfolding of your words. It is not clear whether the writer refers to the initial act of revelation, the process of interpreting God's word, or applying the law to his heart. Perhaps all three are intended as a single process bringing light, hope, and understanding to the dark soul.

119:131 pant. The concept is the same as Ps. 42:1, 2.

119:132 with those who love your name. Cf. Rom. 8:28.

119:133 Keep steady my steps. The psalmist wants the Lord to guide him through life. He realizes that one is within the will of God while seeking to obey His revealed word. But he also knows that obedience is impossible unless God supplies the grace to do so.

119:135 Make your face shine upon your servant. The psalmist asks for God to come and be with him. He wants to live in the consciousness of God's favor. Compare the priestly blessing in Num. 6:22–27.

119:137 Righteous are you. God acts according to His nature; there is nothing arbitrary or inconsistent about Him.

119:145 With my whole heart. The psalmist is a model of fervent and honest prayer to God.

119:147 I rise before dawn. The poet's first thought as he awakens is the Lord. His prayer is frequent as well as fervent.

119:149 according to your steadfast love . . . according to your justice. God's love and devotion toward His people is not incompatible with His law.

119:151 you are near, O Lord. God's covenantal presence nullifies the negative effects of the presence of the enemy (v. 150).

119:153 for I do not forget your law. The psalmist expects that God will bless him because he is obedient. Such an attitude could be presumptuous, a sin the Book of Job guards against, but it could also arise from faith.

154 [e] Plead my cause and redeem me;
[f] give me life according to your
promise!
155 [g] Salvation is far from the wicked,
[h] for they do not seek your statutes.
156 [i] Great is your mercy, O LORD;
[f] give me life according to your
rules.
157 [j] Many are my persecutors and my
adversaries,
but I do not [k] swerve from your
testimonies.
158 I look at [l] the faithless with [m] disgust,
because they do not keep your
commands.
159 Consider how I [n] love your precepts!
[f] Give me life according to your
steadfast love.
160 [o] The sum of your word is [p] truth,
and every one of your [q] righteous
rules endures forever.

SIN AND SHIN

161 [r] Princes persecute me [s] without cause,
but my heart [t] stands in awe of
your words.
162 I [t] rejoice at your word
like one who [u] finds great spoil.
163 I hate and abhor falsehood,
but I love [v] your law.
164 Seven times a day I praise you
for your [q] righteous rules.
165 Great [w] peace have those who love
your law;
[x] nothing can make them stumble.
166 I [y] hope for your salvation, O LORD,
and I do your commandments.
167 My soul keeps your testimonies;
I [v] love them exceedingly.
168 I keep your precepts and testimonies,
[z] for all my ways are before you.

TAW

169 Let my [a] cry come before you,
O LORD;
[b] give me understanding [c] according
to your word!
170 Let my plea come before you;
[d] deliver me according to your
word.
171 My lips will [e] pour forth praise,
for you [f] teach me your statutes.
172 My tongue will sing of your word,
for [g] all your commandments are
right.
173 Let your hand be ready to help me,
for I have [h] chosen your
precepts.
174 I [i] long for your salvation, O LORD,
and your law is my [j] delight.
175 Let my soul live and praise you,
and let your rules help me.
176 I have [k] gone astray like a lost
sheep; seek your servant,
for I do not [l] forget your
commandments.

Deliver Me, O LORD

120 A SONG OF [m] ASCENTS.
In my distress I called to the
LORD,
and he answered me.
2 Deliver me, O LORD,
from lying lips,
from a deceitful tongue.

3 What shall be given to you,
[n] and what more shall be done to you,
you deceitful tongue?
4 [o] A warrior's [p] sharp arrows,
with glowing [q] coals of the
broom tree!

154 [e] Ps. 35:1 [f] ver. 25
155 [g] Job 5:4 [h] [ver. 150]
156 [i] 2 Sam. 24:14 [f] [See ver. 154 above]
157 [j] Ps. 3:1, 2 [k] See ver. 51
158 [l] [Jer. 3:20] [m] Ps. 139:21; [ver. 136]
159 [n] ver. 97 [f] [See ver. 154 above]
160 [o] Ps. 139:17 [p] [ver. 142, 172] [q] ver. 7
161 [r] ver. 23; [1 Sam. 24:11; 26:18] [s] See Ps. 69:4 [t] [Ps. 2:11]
162 [t] [See ver. 161 above] [u] 1 Sam. 30:16; Isai. 9:3; [Matt. 13:44]
163 [v] ver. 97 [q] [See ver. 160 above]
165 [w] Ps. 37:11, 37; [Prov. 3:2] [x] Prov. 3:23; 1 John 2:10; [Matt. 13:41]
166 [y] ver. 174; Gen. 49:18
167 [v] [See ver. 163 above]
168 [z] Ps. 139:3; Prov. 5:21
169 [a] [ver. 145] [b] See ver. 34 [c] ver. 65
170 [d] ver. 41
171 [e] Ps. 145:7 [f] ver. 12
172 [g] [ver. 160]
173 [h] Josh. 24:22; [Prov.1:29]
174 [i] ver. 20 [j] ver. 24
176 [k] Isai. 53:6; 1 Pet. 2:25; [Matt. 18:12; Luke 15:4] [l] ver. 83

Psalm 120 [m] Ex. 34:24; 1 Kin. 12:27; Isai. 30:29 **3** [n] [1 Sam. 3:17] **4** [o] Ps. 127:4; Jer. 50:9 [p] Ps. 45:5 [q] Ps. 140:10; Prov. 25:22

119:154 Plead my cause. This phrase comes from the courtroom. The psalmist asks the Lord to intercede for him before his enemies.

119:156 Great is your mercy. See Lam. 3:23.

119:161 Princes persecute me. The opposition of princes indicate that the psalmist is probably a powerful person, perhaps the king of Israel.

without cause. See Ps. 38:19.

119:167 I love them exceedingly. Obedience is not an onerous task for the psalmist; he follows God's law because he wants to.

119:169 give me understanding. This line sums up one of the major themes of the psalm: the desire for insight into God's will so that the writer may act in obedience.

119:170 deliver me. Another major theme of the psalm is summed up: the psalmist's need for deliverance.

119:175 Let my soul live. Once again, an indication that the poet was in the midst of trouble at the time he composed his song.

119:176 seek your servant. The psalmist concludes by invoking God as his Shepherd (Ps. 23; John 10); he begs Him to bring him back into the flock.

Ps. 120 This psalm is the first of the fifteen "Songs of Ascents" (120–134). As tradition suggests, they were sung by pilgrims traveling to the mountain of God (Zion) to worship. Ps. 120 opens the group appropriately with the song of a faithful worshiper who is far away from the temple among pagan people (v. 5 note).

120:2 lying lips . . . deceitful tongue. The psalmist's enemies slander him unmercifully.

120:3 to you. The enemy whose lies trouble the psalmist.

120:4 warrior's sharp arrows. The liars will be repaid in kind.

5 Woe to me, that I sojourn in
[r]Meshech,
that I dwell among [s]the tents of
[t]Kedar!
6 Too long have I had my dwelling
among those who hate peace.
7 [u]I am for peace,
but when I speak, they are for war!

My Help Comes from the LORD

121 A SONG OF [m]ASCENTS.
I [v]lift up my eyes to [w]the hills.
From where does my help come?
2 [x]My help comes from the LORD,
who [y]made heaven and earth.

3 He will not [z]let your foot be moved;
he who [a]keeps you will not
slumber.
4 Behold, he who keeps Israel
will neither slumber nor sleep.

5 The LORD is your keeper;
the LORD is your [b]shade on your
[c]right hand.
6 [d]The sun shall not [e]strike you by day,
nor the moon by night.

7 The LORD will [a]keep you from all evil;
he will [a]keep your life.
8 The LORD will keep
your [f]going out and your coming in
from this time forth and
forevermore.

5 [r]Gen. 10:2; Ezek. 27:13; 38:2, 3; 39:1 [s]S. of S. 1:5 [t]Gen. 25:13; Isai. 60:7; Jer. 49:28; Ezek. 27:21
7 [u][Ps. 109:4]
Psalm 121 [m][See Ps. 120, title]
1 [v]See Ps. 123:1 [w]Ps. 87:1; 133:3; Jer. 3:23; [Ps. 48:1]
2 [x]Ps. 124:8; [Ps. 20:2] [y]See Ps. 115:15
3 [z]Ps. 66:9; Prov. 3:23, 26; [1 Sam. 2:9] [a]Ps. 41:2; 127:1; [Isai. 27:3]; See Ps. 97:10
5 [b]Ps. 91:1 [c]See Ps. 16:8
6 [d]Isai. 49:10; Rev. 7:16 [e]2 Kin. 4:19; Jonah 4:8
7 [a][See ver. 3 above]
8 [f]Deut. 28:6; 31:2; [Num. 27:17; 1 Sam. 29:6; 1 Kin. 3:7; Acts 1:21]
Psalm 122 [m][See Ps. 120, title]
1 [g]Isai. 2:3; Mic. 4:2; Zech. 8:21
3 [h]Ps. 147:2 [i]Neh. 4:6
4 [j]Deut. 16:16 [k]Ps. 78:5

Let Us Go to the House of the LORD

122 A SONG OF [m]ASCENTS. OF DAVID.
I was glad when they said
to me,
[g]"Let us go to the house of the
LORD!"
2 Our feet have been standing
within your gates, O Jerusalem!

3 Jerusalem—[h]built as a city
that is [i]bound firmly together,
4 to which the tribes [j]go up,
the tribes of the LORD,
as was [k]decreed for[1] Israel,
to give thanks to the name of the
LORD.
5 There [l]thrones for judgment
were set,
the thrones of the house of
David.

6 [m]Pray for the peace of Jerusalem!
"May they be secure who love you!
7 Peace be within your [n]walls
and security within your [n]towers!"
8 For my brothers and companions'
sake
I will say, [o]"Peace be within you!"
9 For the sake of the house of the LORD
our God,
I will [p]seek your good.

5 [l]Deut. 17:8; 2 Sam. 15:2; 1Kin. 3:16; 7:7; 2 Chr. 19:8 6 [m][Ps. 51:18; Jer. 27:7] 7 [n]Ps. 48:13 8 [o][1 Sam. 25:6; Ps. 85:8] 9 [p]Neh. 2:10; Esth. 10:3

[1] *Or as a testimony for*

120:5 Meshech . . . Kedar. The writer may be speaking figuratively, comparing the treatment he receives from God's people to what he might expect from barbarians. The literal places are far from Israel and also from each other. Meshech was in Asia Minor (Gen. 10:2; Ezek. 38:2) and Kedar was in Arabia (Is. 21:16; Ezek. 7:21).

Ps. 121 The first verse suggests why this psalm was included among the "Songs of Ascents" (Ps. 120 note). The psalmist's vision is set firmly on the final goal, Jerusalem, and Zion, the hill of God. The pronoun shift from "I" to "you" could represent an internal dialogue (similar to Ps. 42; 43 or Ps. 103), or more likely the words of the pilgrim who begins the psalm followed by the assurance spoken by a priest or other person.

121:1 to the hills. Jerusalem was in the hill country; the temple was also built on a hill—Zion.

121:3 He will not let your foot be moved. A particularly apt image of God's careful protection; Israel is notorious for its rocky and slippery terrain.

121:4 will neither slumber nor sleep. God never sleeps, and there is no danger that the psalmist will be forgotten. Elijah ridiculed the prophets of Baal by sarcastically suggesting their god was asleep when they needed him (1 Kin. 18:27).

121:5 your shade. As a person's shadow is always with him, so is God with His people. The metaphor comes from ancient treaty language and has covenantal overtones.

Ps. 122 This "Song of Ascents" records the decision of the poet to accompany a group on a visit to Jerusalem. The psalm describes the glories of Jerusalem, where God is worshiped and where the dynasty of David rules (2 Sam. 7), asking God to protect the city and its inhabitants.

This psalm is similar to the "Zion" songs which extol the city of Jerusalem (46; 48; 76). Jerusalem was prized above other cities because God chose to reveal Himself there to His people. Since Christ has come, God's people can meet Him in Christ anywhere on the face of the earth (John 4:19–23). Jerusalem represents all believers (Gal. 4:26), and it typifies the coming New Jerusalem (Rev. 21:9–27).

122:1 I. David is the speaker, although the circumstances of composition are not revealed. Later the psalm would be appropriate for pilgrims going to Jerusalem, as for one of the major festivals (Ex. 23:14–19).

122:4 as was decreed for Israel. Perhaps a reference to the law of centralization of worship (Deut. 12), or to laws connected with the annual festivals.

122:5 thrones for judgment. The king was the paramount judge in the land, and Jerusalem was the political as well as religious capital of Israel.

122:6 peace. The well-known Hebrew term *shalom,* which denotes wholeness and health. The prayer is for absence of war and for prosperity and growth.

122:8 For my brothers and companions' sake. The psalm promotes a sense of community among the people of God. Ultimately, Jerusalem is not bricks and mortar, but people in relationship with one another and with God.

122:9 the house of the LORD our God. The temple building stands for the presence of God in the midst of the people of God.

Our Eyes Look to the LORD Our God

123 A SONG OF [m] ASCENTS.
To you I [q] lift up my eyes,
O you who are [r] enthroned in the heavens!
2 Behold, as the eyes of servants
look to the hand of their master,
as the eyes of a maidservant
to the hand of her mistress,
so our eyes look to the LORD our God,
till he has mercy upon us.

3 [s] Have mercy upon us, O LORD, have mercy upon us,
for we have had more than enough of [t] contempt.
4 Our soul has had more than enough
of [u] the scorn of [v] those who are at ease,
of the contempt of [w] the proud.

Our Help Is in the Name of the LORD

124 A SONG OF [m] ASCENTS. OF DAVID.
[x] If it had not been the LORD
who was on our side—
[y] let Israel now say—
2 if it had not been the LORD who was on our side
when people rose up against us,
3 then they would have [z] swallowed us up alive,
when their anger was kindled against us;
4 then [a] the flood would have [b] swept us away,
the torrent would have gone [c] over us;
5 then over us would have gone
the raging waters.

6 Blessed be the LORD,
who has not given us
as prey to their teeth!
7 We have escaped like a bird
from [d] the snare of the fowlers;
the snare is broken,
and we have escaped!

8 [e] Our help is in the name of the LORD,
who made heaven and earth.

The LORD Surrounds His People

125 A SONG OF [m] ASCENTS.
Those who [f] trust in the LORD are like Mount Zion,
which [g] cannot be moved, but abides forever.
2 As the mountains surround Jerusalem,
so [h] the LORD surrounds his people,
from this time forth and forevermore.
3 For [i] the scepter of wickedness shall not [j] rest
on [k] the land allotted to the righteous,
lest the righteous [l] stretch out their hands to do wrong.
4 [m] Do good, O LORD, to those who are good,
and to those who are [n] upright in their hearts!
5 But those who [o] turn aside to their [p] crooked ways
the LORD will lead away with [q] evildoers!
[r] Peace be upon Israel!

Psalm 123 [m][See Ps. 120, title] **1** [q]Ps. 121:1; [Ps. 141:8]; See Ps. 25:15 [r]See Ps. 2:4 **3** [s]Ps. 4:1 [t][Neh. 4:4] **4** [u][Neh. 2:19] [v]Isai. 32:9, 11; Amos 6:1 [w]See Ps. 119:51
Psalm 124 [m][See Ps. 120, title] **1** [x]Ps. 94:17 [y]Ps. 129:1 **3** [z]See Ps. 56:1 **4** [a]See Ps. 32:6; Job 22:11 [b]Ps. 69:2; Isai. 8:8 [c]Ps. 69:1 **7** [d]See Ps. 91:3 **8** [e]Ps. 121:2
Psalm 125 [m][See Ps. 120, title] **1** [f]Ps. 25:2, 3 [g]Ps. 93:1; 104:5; [Prov. 10:30] **2** [h][2 Kin. 6:17; Zech. 2:5] **3** [i]Isai. 14:5 [j]Isai. 30:30 [k]See Ps. 16:5 [l]Gen. 3:22; Ex. 22:8 **4** [m]Ps. 119:68 [n]See Ps. 7:10 **5** [o]See Ps. 40:4 [p]Prov. 2:15 [q]Ps. 92:7, 9; 94:4 [r]Ps. 128:6; Gal. 6:16

Ps. 123 The last two verses (vv. 3, 4) show that this prayer arises from a situation of distress and persecution.

123:1 I lift up my eyes. See Ps. 121:1.

who are enthroned in the heavens. The ark and the cherubim in the Most Holy Place were in a representative sense God's earthly throne, but the psalmist, like Solomon, knew that "heaven and the highest heaven cannot contain you" (1 Kin. 8:27).

123:2 so our eyes look to the LORD our God. A servant watches the employer's hand for a variety of reasons: to receive orders, to hear instruction, to receive salary or provisions. The verse teaches that God's people are utterly dependent upon Him for every aspect of their well-being.

123:3 more than enough of contempt. The strong wording has led some to date the psalm to the period following the Babylonian exile of the sixth century B.C.

Ps. 124 In this psalm of thanksgiving the people praise the Lord for delivering them from a dangerous confrontation with their enemies. The psalm is included in the "Songs of Ascents" indicating its use during festal pilgrimages. The deliverance described would not necessarily be recent, but could be the exodus from Egypt. Today the psalm appeals to the Lord as the One who is able to protect His church from the attacks of principalities and powers in the spiritual realm (Eph. 6:10–20).

124:1 who was on our side. See 118:6 note.

let Israel now say. These words would be spoken by a priest leading the congregation in corporate thanksgiving.

124:3 they would have swallowed us up alive. The enemies would have killed them. See Prov. 1:12 note.

124:4 the flood. See 18:4, 15 and notes.

124:6 to their teeth. The enemy is compared to a lion (Ps. 34:10; 58:6) or a dog (Ps. 59:6, 14).

124:8 who made heaven and earth. Israel has nothing to fear while God fights for them.

Ps. 125 The sixth of the "Songs of Ascents" begins like a confident Zion hymn (cf. Ps. 46; 48; 76). From the temple on Mount Zion the Lord provides protection for His people.

125:2 As the mountains surround Jerusalem. The surrounding mountains were important in the defense of the city and picture God's protective presence (12:1; 2 Kin. 6:17).

125:3 the scepter of wickedness. The scepter is a symbol of political and military rule, in this case pointing to the oppression of the people of God by a wicked, possibly foreign force.

stretch out their hands. By way of imitation, or under the pressures of a corrupt government and society.

125:4, 5 See 18:25, 26.

Restore Our Fortunes, O LORD

126 A SONG OF [m] ASCENTS.
When the LORD [s] restored the
fortunes of Zion,
we were like those who [t] dream.
2 Then our [u] mouth was filled with
laughter,
and our tongue with shouts of joy;
then they said among the nations,
[v] "The LORD has done great things for
them."
3 The LORD has done great things for us;
we are glad.

4 Restore our fortunes, O LORD,
like streams in the Negeb!
5 [w] Those who sow in tears
shall reap with shouts of joy!
6 He who goes out weeping,
bearing the seed for sowing,
shall come home with shouts of joy,
bringing his sheaves with him.

Unless the LORD Builds the House

127 A SONG OF [m] ASCENTS. OF
SOLOMON.

1 Unless the LORD builds the house,
those who build it labor in vain.
Unless the LORD [x] watches over the city,
the watchman stays awake in vain.
2 It is in vain that you rise up early
and go late to rest,
eating the bread of anxious [y] toil;
for he gives to his [z] beloved [a] sleep.
3 Behold, [b] children are a heritage
from the LORD,
[c] the fruit of the womb a
reward.
4 Like arrows in the hand of [d] a
warrior
are the children[1] of one's
youth.
5 Blessed is the man
who fills his quiver with them!
He shall not be put to shame
when he speaks with his enemies
[e] in the gate.[2]

Blessed Is Everyone Who Fears the LORD

128 A SONG OF [m] ASCENTS.
[f] Blessed is everyone who fears
the LORD,
who [g] walks in his ways!
2 You [h] shall eat the fruit of the labor
of your hands;
you shall be blessed, and it shall
be well with you.

3 Your wife will be like [i] a fruitful vine
within your house;
your children will be like [j] olive
shoots
around your table.
4 Behold, thus shall the man be
blessed
who fears the LORD.

Psalm 126
[m] [See Ps. 120, title]
1 [s] See Ps. 14:7 [t] [Acts 12:9]
2 [u] Job 8:21 [v] See Ps. 71:19
5 [w] [Jer. 31:9; Ezra 6:22; Neh. 12:43; Gal. 6:9]; see Hag. 2:3-9
Psalm 127
[m] [See Ps. 120, title]
1 [x] See Ps. 121:4
2 [y] Gen. 3:17, 19 [z] Ps. 60:5 [a] [Mark 4:26, 27]
3 [b] [Gen. 33:5] [c] Deut. 28:4; [Ps. 132:11]
4 [d] Ps. 120:4
5 [e] See Job 5:4
Psalm 128
[m] [See Ps. 120, title]
1 [f] See Ps. 112:1 [g] Ps. 119:1; [Prov. 8:32]
2 [h] Isai. 3:10; [Ps. 109:11]
3 [i] Ezek. 19:10; [Gen. 49:22] [j] See Ps. 52:8

[1] Or *sons* [2] Or *They shall not be put to shame when they speak with their enemies in the gate*

126:1 When the LORD restored the fortunes of Zion. The allusion is to the return from Babylonian exile in the sixth century B.C., when the captive people of Israel were permitted to return to their country (see books of Ezra, Nehemiah). Cyrus's decision to allow the return was not the mere result of political policy, but of God's intervention.

126:4 Restore our fortunes. Restoration from captivity meant more than a physical return to the land. God's covenantal presence was still needed.

like streams in the Negeb. The south of Israel is dry, and in a rainstorm the wadi (seasonal streambeds) become dangerous floods.

126:5 shall reap with shouts of joy. God reverses the fortunes of His people. He overrules evil with good, suffering with blessing (Ps. 30:11, 12; John 16:20).

Ps. 127 This wise prayer falls into two related parts. The first stanza (vv. 1, 2) expresses the belief that human effort is useless apart from God (paralleling the message of Ecclesiastes), whether for building a house, defending a city, or earning a living. The second stanza (vv. 3–5) focuses on another meaning of building, that of raising children. Children are a gift from God.

A father could be supported during his old age by strong, young sons. Children were a fulfillment of the promise to Abraham that the chosen people would become a great and numerous nation (Gen. 12:1–3). The ultimate focus of the Abrahamic promise of many descendants is on Jesus Christ. In the present day the psalm expresses the joy of Christian parents as they reflect on God's gift of children and His promise to them (Acts 2:39).

127:1 builds the house. The primary reference is to the actual building of a residence, but as a "Song of Ascents" written by Solomon, it is natural to think specifically of the temple. Furthermore, in the light of the second half of the psalm, the house refers to the family as well as to a physical structure.

watches over the city. A city is not secured by its defenses, but by the protection of the Lord. The psalm would remind pilgrims that Jerusalem was not a place of magical protection and security, but that all depended on the Lord.

127:3 children. Lit. "the fruit of the womb." The psalm concentrates on sons, who had the power to provide for their father in his old age, but the second part of this verse includes all children, male and female alike.

127:5 in the gate. Formal court proceedings were held in the vicinity of the city gates.

128:1 fears the LORD. See notes Ps. 34:7; 36:1; 119:63.

walks in his ways. Those who obey God's will for their lives as manifested in His law.

128:2 the labor of your hands. One result of the Fall was that Adam would have to work hard to get food on the table (Gen. 3:17–19). The Preacher of Ecclesiastes was driven to despair because some people labored while others, less deserving, enjoyed the benefits of their labor (Eccl. 5:8–6:12; Is. 65:22). The psalmist envisions the righteous prospering from their own labor, a just situation.

128:3 a fruitful vine. The vine produced the grapes for wine, a source of joy to the Israelites (Ps. 104:15). The blessing that the fruitful wife brings includes children around the table.

olive shoots. Olives and olive oil were valued staple commodities in the nation's life.

5 [k]The LORD bless you [l]from Zion!
May you see [m]the prosperity of
Jerusalem
all the days of your life!
6 May you see your [n]children's children!
[o]Peace be upon Israel!

They Have Afflicted Me from My Youth

129 A SONG OF [m]ASCENTS.
"Greatly [1] have they [p]afflicted
me [q]from my youth"—
[r]let Israel now say—
2 "Greatly have they [p]afflicted me [q]from
my youth,
[s]yet they have not prevailed
against me.
3 [t]The plowers plowed [u]upon my back;
they made long their furrows."
4 The LORD is righteous;
he has cut [v]the cords of the
wicked.
5 May all who hate Zion
be [w]put to shame and turned
backward!
6 Let them be like [x]the grass on the
housetops,
which [y]withers before it grows up,
7 with which the reaper does not fill
his hand
nor the binder of sheaves his
[z]arms,
8 nor do those who pass by say,
[a]"The blessing of the LORD be upon
you!
We [b]bless you in the name of the
LORD!"

5 [k]Ps. 134:3 [l]Ps. 20:2; 135:21 [m][Ps. 122:9] **6** [n]Prov. 17:6; See Job 42:16 [o]Ps. 125:5
Psalm 129 [m][See Ps. 120, title] **1** [p][Ex. 1:14; Judg. 3:8, 14; 4:3; 6:2; 10:8] [q]Isai. 47:12; Jer. 2:2; 22:2; Hos. 2:15 [r]Ps. 124:1 **2** [p][See ver. 1 above] [q][See ver. 1 above] [s][2 Cor. 4:8-10] **3** [t]Mic. 3:12 [u][Isai. 50:6; 51:23] **4** [v]Ps. 2:3 **5** [w]See Ps. 35:4 **6** [x]2 Kin. 19:26; Isai. 37:27 [y]Ps. 37:2; Job 8:12 **7** [z]See Ps. 79:12 **8** [a]Ruth 2:4 [b]Ps. 118:26
Psalm 130 [m][See Ps. 120, title] **1** [c]Ps. 69:2, 14; Lam. 3:55; Jonah 2:2 **2** [d]Ps. 86:6; 2 Chr. 6:40 [e]Ps. 140:6 **3** [f][Ps. 90:8]; See Job 10:14 [g]Ps. 76:7; Amos 2:15; Nah. 1:6; Mal. 3:2; Eph. 6:13; Rev. 6:17; [Ps. 143:2]

My Soul Waits for the LORD

130 A SONG OF [m]ASCENTS.
Out of [c]the depths I cry to you,
O LORD!
2 O Lord, hear my voice!
[d]Let your ears be attentive
to [e]the voice of my pleas for
mercy!
3 If you, O LORD, should [f]mark
iniquities,
O Lord, who could [g]stand?
4 But with you there is
[h]forgiveness,
[i]that you may be feared.
5 I [j]wait for the LORD, [k]my soul
waits,
and [l]in his word I hope;
6 my soul [m]waits for
the Lord
more than [n]watchmen for [o]the
morning,
more than watchmen for the
morning.
7 O Israel, [p]hope in the LORD!
For [q]with the LORD there is
steadfast love,
and with him is plentiful
redemption.
8 And he will [r]redeem Israel
from all his iniquities.

4 [h]ver. 7; Isai. 55:7; Dan. 9:9; See Ps. 86:5, 15 [i]1 Kin. 8:39, 40; Jer. 33:8, 9; [Rom. 2:4] **5** [j]Ps. 40:1; Isai. 8:17; 26:8 [k]See Ps. 33:20 [l]Ps. 119:74, 81 **6** [m][Ps. 123:2] [n][Ps. 63:6; 119:147] [o]See Ps. 5:3 **7** [p]Ps. 131:3 [q]ver. 4 **8** [r]Ps. 111:9; Luke 1:68; Tit. 2:14; [Matt. 1:21]; See Ps. 25:22

[1] Or *Often*; also verse 2

128:5 from Zion. That is, from the temple (Ps. 2:6; 50:2).

128:6 your children's children. Long life and large families were a blessing in ancient Israel, particularly in the light of the Abrahamic covenant (Gen. 12:1–3).

Peace. See 122:6 note.

Ps. 129 The purpose of this psalm is to curse Israel's enemies (vv. 5–8). The introduction (vv. 1–4) confidently asserts that the Lord has overturned evil plans against His people frequently in the past.

129:1 afflicted me. The history of Israel is often a history of suffering and oppression, beginning with slavery in Egypt and continuing through the Babylonian captivity.

from my youth. From Israel's beginning as a nation. The nation is personified, speaking of itself as "me" and "my."

129:2 they have not prevailed against me. Slavery in Egypt ended in the Exodus; the Babylonian exile ended with the return and restoration of Judah.

129:3 plowed upon my back. The metaphor describes the horrors of Israel's past suffering.

129:4 he has cut the cords. It was as if the wicked held Israel a prisoner bound by strong ropes, but their Savior set them free.

129:5 Zion. See notes Ps. 2:6; 50:2; 128:5.

129:6 grass on the housetops. Grass is a common metaphor for the brevity of life (37:2; 90:5, 6; 92:7). On the housetop the shallow roots and hot sun make the grass more fragile still.

Ps. 130 The psalm is a complaint of a special kind, since the author does not ask for the destruction of the enemy, but meekly turns to God for forgiveness of his own sins.

130:1 Out of the depths. The allusion is to the deep waters of sorrow that overwhelm the psalmist (18:14 and notes).

130:3 who could stand. The psalmist is well aware that there is no one without sin (Ps. 53:1–3; Rom. 3:9–20).

130:4 there is forgiveness. See 103:3; Ex. 34:7; Luke 7:49; Eph. 2:4, 5. The perception of God's mercy helps the heart to rightly cultivate the fear of the Lord.

130:6 watchmen for the morning. The phrase expresses not only the intense yearning of the poet, but also the certainty of his hope.

130:7 O Israel. The writer now calls upon the whole nation to share his penitence and hope.

I Have Calmed and Quieted My Soul

131 A SONG OF [m] ASCENTS. OF DAVID.
O LORD, my heart is not
[s] lifted up;
my eyes are not [t] raised too high;
I do not [u] occupy myself with things
too great and [v] too marvelous for me.
2 But I have calmed and quieted my
soul,
like a weaned [w] child with its mother;
like a weaned child is my soul
within me.

3 [x] O Israel, hope in the LORD
from this time forth and
forevermore.

The LORD Has Chosen Zion

132 A SONG OF [m] ASCENTS.
Remember, O LORD, in David's
favor,
all [y] the hardships he endured,
2 how he swore to the LORD
and [z] vowed to [a] the Mighty One of
Jacob,
3 "I will not enter my house
or get into my bed,
4 I will not [b] give sleep to my eyes
or slumber to my eyelids,
5 until I [c] find a place for the LORD,
a dwelling place for [a] the Mighty
One of Jacob."

6 Behold, we heard of it in
[d] Ephrathah;
we found it in [e] the fields of Jaar.
7 "Let us go to his dwelling place;
let us [f] worship at his
[g] footstool!"

8 [h] Arise, O LORD, and go to your
[i] resting place,
you and the ark of your [j] might.
9 Let your [k] priests be [l] clothed with
righteousness,
and let your [m] saints shout for joy.
10 For the sake of your servant David,
[n] do not turn away the face of [o] your
anointed one.

11 [p] The LORD swore to David a
sure oath
[q] from which he will not turn back:
[r] "One of the sons of your body[1]
I will set on your throne.
12 If your sons keep my covenant
and my testimonies that I shall
teach them,
their sons also forever
shall [s] sit on your throne."

13 For the LORD has [t] chosen Zion;
he has [u] desired it for his
dwelling place:

Psalm 131 [m][See Ps. 120, title] 1 [s][Ps. 138:6; Isai. 57:15] [t]See Ps. 101:5 [u][Jer. 45:5; Rom. 12:16] [v]See Job 42:3 2 [w][Matt. 18:3; 1 Cor. 14:20] 3 [x]Ps. 130:7
Psalm 132 [m][See Ps. 120, title] 1 [y]1 Chr. 22:14 2 [z]Ps. 50:14 [a]ver. 5; Gen. 49:24; Isai. 49:26; 60:16 4 [b]Prov. 6:4 5 [c]1 Chr. 22:7; Acts 7:46 [a][See ver. 2 above]
6 [d]1 Sam. 17:12; [Gen. 35:19] [e][1 Sam. 7:1] 7 [f]Ps. 5:7 [g]See Ps. 99:5 8 [h]Ps. 68:1; 2 Chr. 6:41, 42 [i]ver. 14 [j]Ps. 78:61 9 [k]ver. 16 [l]See Job 29:14 [m][Ps. 149:5] 10 [n][2 Kin. 18:24] [o]ver. 17; [1 Kin. 1:39] 11 [p]Ps. 89:3, 34 [q]Ps. 110:4 [r]2 Sam. 7:12; 2 Chr. 6:16; Luke 1:32; Acts 2:30
12 [s]1 Kin. 8:25; [Job 36:7] 13 [t]Ps. 78:68; [Ps. 135:21] [u]See Ps. 68:16

[1] Hebrew *of your fruit of the womb*

Ps. 131 David expresses his deeply felt confidence in the Lord with this simple, clear, yet profound prayer. It voices the trust of a close, personal relationship with God.

131:1 heart . . . eyes . . . things too great. The first verse has a threefold denial of pride: in the heart, in the eyes, and in actions.

131:2 like a weaned child. The psalmist draws a beautiful picture of the perfect contentment and confidence he enjoys in God. He is not like an unweaned child, easily disturbed by hunger.

with its mother. God is the Creator of both men and women. The care and protection that is the strength of the mother is a reflection of an aspect of God's own character (Prov. 8; Is. 66:12, 13).

131:3 O Israel. Like Ps. 130, this intensely personal prayer becomes corporate at the end.

Ps. 132 Here is a lament asking God to save the king (vv. 1, 6–9). The psalm grounds the petition in God's covenant with David (vv. 10–12; cf. 2 Sam. 7 and Ps. 89) and in the choice of Zion as a revelation of God's earthly presence (see Ps. 46; 48; 76). Since vv. 8–10 are quoted in Solomon's prayer (2 Chr. 6:41, 42), it is likely that this is the time of its composition. After the period of the Hebrew monarchy, the psalm's reference to the Messiah became increasingly clear.

132:1 hardships. The historical books record the troubles David endured as he sought to serve the Lord faithfully. In his young manhood he had to run away from Saul; in his maturity he dealt with troubles in his realm, notably Absalom's revolt.

132:2 vowed. David's vow gives the temple and its worship the highest priority. Fulfillment of the vow is implied in vv. 6–9, when David ordered that the ark be removed from Kiriath-jearim and brought to Jerusalem (1 Chr. 13:6).

132:3 I will not enter my house. Similar to his sentiment recorded in 2 Sam. 7, David felt uneasy that he had a comfortable dwelling place while the ark of the covenant, the primary symbol of God's presence, was still housed in the tabernacle.

132:6–9 The ark comes to its proper place.

132:6 Ephrathah. Bethlehem.

the fields of Jaar. Kiriath-jearim (1 Chr. 13:1–14).

132:7 at his footstool. A common way to refer to the ark of the covenant. The Lord revealed Himself as enthroned over the ark, resting His feet on it.

132:8 Arise, O LORD. See Ps. 3:7; 7:6.

132:10 For the sake of your servant David. The climax of the psalm is an appeal to the Lord to bless the descendant of David who is ruling on the throne. God had promised David that his descendants would rule after him (2 Sam. 7:11–16). Although the line of David was interrupted, God's promises were not thwarted. Jesus, David's greater Son, fulfills the Davidic covenant, and so it is no surprise that the psalm was understood messianically in the early church (cf. Luke 1:32; Acts 2:30).

132:11 I will set on your throne. An allusion to 2 Sam. 7:11–16.

132:12 If your sons keep my covenant. There was a conditional element in the Davidic covenant. His physical descendants would only rule successfully in Jerusalem if they were obedient to the covenant.

132:13 Zion. See notes Ps. 2:6; 50:2.

14 "This is my [v]resting place forever;
here I will [w]dwell, for I have
desired it.
15 I will abundantly [x]bless her provisions;
I will [y]satisfy her poor with bread.
16 Her [z]priests I will clothe with
salvation,
and her [z]saints will shout for joy.
17 There I will make [a]a horn to sprout
for David;
I have prepared [b]a lamp for [c]my
anointed.
18 His enemies I will [d]clothe with
shame,
but on him his crown will shine."

When Brothers Dwell in Unity

133

A SONG OF [m]ASCENTS. OF DAVID.
Behold, how good and pleasant
it is
when [e]brothers dwell in unity![1]
2 It is like the precious [f]oil on [g]the
head,
running down on the beard,
on the beard of Aaron,
running down on [h]the collar of his
robes!
3 It is like [i]the dew of [j]Hermon,
which falls on [k]the mountains of
Zion!
For there the LORD [l]has commanded
the blessing,
life forevermore.

14 [v]ver. 8 [w]Matt. 23:21
15 [x]Ps. 147:14 [y]Ruth 1:6
16 [z]ver. 9
17 [a]Ezek. 29:21; [Luke 1:69] [b]1 Kin. 11:36; 15:4; 2 Kin. 8:19; 2 Chr. 21:7 [c]ver. 10
18 [d]See Job 8:22
Psalm 133 [m][See Ps. 120, title]
1 [e][Gen. 13:8; Heb. 13:1]
2 [f]Ex. 30:25, 30 [g]Ex. 29:7; Lev. 8:12 [h]Ex. 28:33; 38:24; [Ex. 28:32; 39:23; Job 30:18]
3 [i]Prov. 19:12; Mic. 5:7 [j]Deut. 3:9; 4:48 [k]See Ps. 48:1 [l]Lev. 25:21; Deut. 28:8; See Ps. 42:8

Psalm 134 [m][See Ps. 120, title]
1 [m]Ps. 135:1 [n]1 Chr. 9:33; [Lev. 8:35] [o]Deut. 10:8; 18:7; 1 Chr. 23:30; 2 Chr. 29:11; 35:5
2 [p]See Ps. 28:2 [q]Ps. 63:2
3 [r]Num. 6:24 [s]Ps. 128:5 [t]See Ps. 115:15

Come, Bless the LORD

134

A SONG OF [m] ASCENTS.
Come, bless the LORD, all you
[m] servants of the LORD,
who [n]stand [o]by night in the house
of the LORD!
2 [p]Lift up your hands to [q]the holy place
and bless the LORD!

3 May the LORD [r]bless you [s]from
Zion,
he who [t]made heaven and
earth!

Your Name, O LORD, Endures Forever

135

[u]Praise the LORD!
Praise the name of the LORD,
give praise, O [v]servants of the
LORD,
2 who [n]stand in the house of the
LORD,
in [w]the courts of the house of our
God!
3 Praise the LORD, for [x]the LORD is
good;
sing to his name, [y]for it is
pleasant![2]
4 For the LORD has [z]chosen Jacob for
himself,
Israel as his [a]own possession.

Psalm 135 1 [u]See Ps. 104:35 [v]See Ps. 113:1 2 [n][See Ps. 134:1 above] [w]Ps. 92:13 3 [x]See Ps. 100:5 [y]Ps. 147:1; [Ps. 52:9] 4 [z]Deut. 7:6, 7; 10:15; See Ps. 105:6 [a]Ex. 19:5

1 Or *dwell together* 2 Or *for he is beautiful*

132:14 here I will dwell. God chose Zion and had the temple built as the earthly reflection of His heavenly residence. In this sense the temple is His palace from which He rules the world.

132:15 I will . . . bless her. As a generous king, the Lord will tend His subject people Israel with a special eye on the destitute (9:18 note; Deut. 28:1–14).

132:17 horn. A symbol for political strength (92:10 note).

a lamp. See 1 Kin. 11:36.

Ps. 133 In this "Song of Ascents," dwelling "in unity" refers to the relationship among believers as they worship the Lord at Mount Zion. Through Jesus Christ, the New Testament includes with them peoples from all over the world (John 10:16; Rom. 1:5; 15:16; Eph. 2:11–22).

133:title OF DAVID. David's own sons did not live in unity, but fought each other bitterly—Amnon against Absalom, and Adonijah against Solomon.

133:1 brothers. This term could refer to family members, but here probably refers to tribal and national comrades as they unite in worship.

133:2 like the precious oil. The first simile refers to the anointing of Aaron, the high priest. The special and exclusive blend of oil (Ex. 30:22–33) was poured out extravagantly, running down his beard and onto his sacred robes. In the same way the unity of the people of God is a rich perfume making their worship pleasing to Him (Rom. 15:6).

133:3 the dew of Hermon . . . mountains of Zion. Hermon is a majestic mountain on the northern boundaries of Israel, known for a heavy precipitation of refreshing dew. The downward flow of the liquid signifies that God gives the blessing of unity—through the gift of the Holy Spirit.

there. In the place where unity is found.

Ps. 134 This brief conclusion to the "Songs of Ascents" is composed of a call to worship (vv. 1, 2) followed by a blessing (v. 3). Many take the first two verses as an exhortation from the departing worshipers to the priests who tend the temple precincts at night. In response the priests bless the congregation. The psalm is a reminder that God's praise is a continual, not momentary, activity (cf. 1 Thess. 5:16, 17).

134:1 servants of the LORD. Priests or Levites who tend the temple at night.

house of the LORD. The temple. See note Ps. 2:6.

134:3 from Zion. The mountain where God's temple was.

135:1 Praise the LORD. Hebrew *hallu yah*. The phrase opens and closes (v. 21) the psalm with praise.

name. See Ps. 8:1.

servants. The reference is probably to the priests and Levites who serve in the temple area. While some have said that "servants" is never used in such a restricted manner, the next two phrases seem to limit the reference to the temple personnel.

135:4 chosen . . . for himself. The Lord chose Israel for Himself out of His unconditional love, not because of any merit in Israel (Deut. 7:7–11).

possession. God has lifted the lowly and made them great in His eyes.

5 For I know that [b]the LORD is great,
and that our Lord is above all
gods.
6 [c]Whatever the LORD pleases, he does,
in heaven and on earth,
in the seas and all deeps.
7 [d]He it is who makes the clouds rise at
the end of the earth,
who [e]makes lightnings for the rain
and brings forth the wind from his
[f]storehouses.

8 He it was who [g]struck down the
firstborn of Egypt,
both of man and of beast;
9 who in your midst, O Egypt,
sent [h]signs and wonders
against Pharaoh and all his
servants;
10 [i]who struck down many nations
and killed mighty kings,
11 [j]Sihon, king of the Amorites,
and [k]Og, king of Bashan,
and [l]all the kingdoms of Canaan,
12 and [m]gave their land as a heritage,
a heritage to his people Israel.

13 [n]Your name, O LORD, endures forever,
[o]your renown,[1] O LORD, throughout
all ages.
14 [p]For the LORD will vindicate his
people
and [q]have compassion on his
servants.

15 [r]The idols of the nations are silver
and gold,
the work of human hands.
16 They have mouths, but do not speak;
they have eyes, but do not see;
17 they have ears, but do not hear,
nor is there any breath in their
mouths.
18 Those who make them become like
them,
so do all who trust in them!

19 [s]O house of Israel, bless the LORD!
O house of Aaron, bless the
LORD!
20 O house of Levi, bless the LORD!
You who fear the LORD, bless the
LORD!
21 Blessed be the LORD [t]from Zion,
he who [u]dwells in
Jerusalem!
[v]Praise the LORD!

5 [b]Ps. 95:3
6 [c]Ps. 115:3
7 [d]Jer. 10:13; 51:16 [e][Job 28:25, 26; 38:25; Zech. 10:1] [f]Job 38:22
8 [g]See Ps. 78:51
9 [h]Deut. 6:22
10 [i]For ver. 10-12, see Ps. 136:17-22
11 [j]Deut. 29:7; See Num. 21:21-26 [k]See Num. 21:33-35 [l]See Josh. 12:7-24
12 [m]Deut. 29:8; See Ps. 78:55
13 [n]Ex. 3:15 [o]Ps. 102:12
14 [p]Deut. 32:36 [q]See Ps. 90:13
15 [r]For ver. 15-18, see Ps. 115:4-8
19 [s]See Ps. 115:9
21 [t]Ps. 128:5 [u]Ps. 132:13, 14 [v]ver. 1

His Steadfast Love Endures Forever

136 [w]Give thanks to the LORD,
for he is good,
[x]for his steadfast love endures
forever.
2 Give thanks to [y]the God of gods,
for his steadfast love endures
forever.
3 Give thanks to [y]the Lord of lords,
for his steadfast love endures
forever;
4 to him who alone [z]does great
wonders,
for his steadfast love endures
forever;
5 to him who [a]by understanding
[b]made the heavens,
for his steadfast love endures
forever;

Psalm 136
1 [w]Ps. 106:1; 107:1; 118:1 [x]See 1 Chr. 16:41
2 [y]Deut. 10:17
3 [y][See ver. 2 above]
4 [z]See Ps. 72:18
5 [a]Prov. 3:19; Jer. 10:12; 51:15 [b]See Gen. 1:1

[1] Or *remembrance*

135:5 is above all gods. The foreign nations could not imagine a god like the Lord (113:4 note).

135:6 in the seas. Special reference is made to the seas, since the seas culturally represented the forces of chaos in the ancient Near East (18:4, 15 and notes). But it is God Himself who controls the seas.

135:7 lightnings for the rain. God's control over the storm may be a reply to Canaanites or Israelites who dared to attribute the power of the storm to Baal (Ps. 29 and notes).

135:8 the firstborn of Egypt. The culmination of the ten plagues God used to win freedom for His people (Ex. 11).

135:11 Sihon . . . Og. Kings opposing Israel during their time in the wilderness under Moses (Num. 21:21–35).

135:15 The idols of the nations. The surrounding nations worshiped their gods by statues of wood and precious metals. The psalmist, like Isaiah (Is. 44), ridicules this practice. It is a crude and absurd example of taking a piece of creation and exalting it above the Creator (Rom. 1:21–23).

135:18 like them. The pagans made their gods in their own image. Those who serve such gods will become like them, powerless and contemptible. See Is. 44:9–20; Rom. 1:22–25.

135:19 house of Aaron. The priests. See Ps. 115:9–11 for a similar progression.

Ps. 136 This psalm is an antiphonal liturgy with the memorable refrain, "his steadfast love endures forever." A priest or soloist would chant the first part of a verse, and the congregation would respond with the refrain. Performance of the liturgy must have been powerful and moving, as the priest added example to example of God's praise.

136:1 his steadfast love endures forever. God's mercy is His devotion to His people, to whom He is freely bound by the pledge of His own grace in His covenant. See theological note "God Is Love: Divine Goodness and Faithfulness" on next page.

136:5 by understanding. God's wisdom is associated often with the creation (Prov. 8).

made the heavens. This section meditates on God's creation as described in Gen. 1.

6 to him who [c]spread out the earth
[d]above the waters,
for his steadfast love endures
forever;
7 to him who [e]made the great lights,
for his steadfast love endures
forever;
8 the sun to rule over the day,
for his steadfast love endures
forever;
9 the moon and stars to rule over the
night,
for his steadfast love endures forever;
10 to him who [f]struck down the
firstborn of Egypt,
for his steadfast love endures
forever;
11 and [g]brought Israel out from among
them,
for his steadfast love endures
forever;
12 with [h]a strong hand and an
outstretched arm,
for his steadfast love endures
forever;
13 to him who [i]divided the Red Sea in
two,
for his steadfast love endures
forever;
14 [j]and made Israel pass through the
midst of it,
for his steadfast love endures
forever;
15 but [k]overthrew[1] Pharaoh and his
host in the Red Sea,
for his steadfast love endures
forever;
16 to him who [l]led his people through
the wilderness,
for his steadfast love endures
forever;

6 [c]Isai. 42:5; 44:24 [d]Ps. 24:2
7 [e]Gen. 1:16
10 [f]See Ps. 78:51
11 [g]Ex. 12:51; 13:3
12 [h]Deut. 4:34
13 [i]See Ps. 78:13
14 [j]Ex. 14:21, 22
15 [k]Ex. 14:27; [Ps. 78:53]
16 [l]Ex. 15:22; Deut. 8:15; See Ps. 77:20

1 Hebrew *shook off*

God Is Love: Divine Goodness and Faithfulness

The statement, "God is love," is often explained in terms of the revelation, given through the life and teaching of Christ, of the endless life of the triune God as one of mutual affection and honor (Matt. 3:17; 17:5; John 3:35; 14:31; 16:13, 14; 17:1–5, 22–26). With this idea is linked the recognition that God made angels and men to glorify Him in sharing the joyful give-and-take of this divine life according to their own creaturely mode. But when John says "God is love" (1 John 4:8), he means, as he goes on to explain, that God through Christ has saved sinners. "In this the love of God was made manifest among us, that God sent his only Son into the world, so that we might live through him. In this is love, not that we have loved God but that he loved us and sent his Son to be the propitiation for our sins" (1 John 4:9, 10).

As always in the New Testament, "we" or "us" as the objects and beneficiaries of redeeming love means "us who believe." "We" or "us" does not refer to every individual belonging to the human race. When "the world" is said to be loved and redeemed (John 3:16, 17; 2 Cor. 5:19; 1 John 2:2), that "world" is the great number of God's elect scattered worldwide, in every nation (cf. John 10:16; 11:52). The redeemed "world" is not each and every person who ever did or will exist.

Sovereign redemptive love is one facet of the quality Scripture calls God's goodness (Ps. 100:5; Mark 10:18), that is, the glorious kindness and generosity that touches all His creatures (Ps. 145:9, 15, 16) and that ought to lead all sinners to repentance (Rom. 2:4). Other aspects of this goodness are the pity that shows kindness to people in distress and rescues them from trouble (Ps. 107; 136), and the patience that does not cut off God's kindness from people who continue in sin (Ex. 34:6; Ps. 78:38; Jon. 3:10–4:11; Rom. 9:22; 2 Pet. 3:9). The supreme expression of God's goodness is the love that saves sinners who deserve only condemnation: saving them, moreover, at the cost of Christ's death on Calvary (Rom. 3:22–24; 5:5–8; 8:32–39; Eph. 2:1–10; 3:14–18; 5:25–27).

God's faithfulness is another aspect of His goodness and praiseworthiness. People lie, and break their word; God will do neither. In the worst of times it can be affirmed: "his mercies never come to an end . . . great is your faithfulness" (Lam. 3:22, 23; Ps. 36:5; cf. Ps. 89, especially vv. 1, 2, 14, 24, 33, 37, 49). Even when circumstances are unexpected and bewildering, and threaten to hide His faithfulness, still we know that God keeps His promises to us who believe: "All have come to pass for you; not one . . . has failed" (Josh. 23:14).

136:7 great lights. The sun and the moon (vv. 8, 9).

136:10 the firstborn of Egypt. The tenth and most terrible plague preceding the Exodus (Ex. 11).

136:13 who divided the Red Sea in two. Ex. 14; 15.

17 to him [m]who struck down great kings,
for his steadfast love endures
forever;
18 and killed mighty kings,
for his steadfast love endures
forever;
19 Sihon, king of the Amorites,
for his steadfast love endures
forever;
20 and Og, king of Bashan,
for his steadfast love endures
forever;
21 and gave their land as a heritage,
for his steadfast love endures
forever;
22 a heritage to Israel his [n]servant,
for his steadfast love endures
forever.

23 It is he who [o]remembered us in our
low estate,
for his steadfast love endures
forever;
24 and [p]rescued us from our foes,
for his steadfast love endures
forever;
25 he who [q]gives food to all flesh,
for his steadfast love endures
forever.

26 Give thanks to [r]the God of
heaven,
for his steadfast love endures forever.

17 [m]For ver. 17-22, see Ps. 135:10-12 **22** [n]Ps. 105:6, 26 **23** [o]Gen. 8:1; [Deut. 32:36] **24** [p]Ps. 107:2 **25** [q]Ps. 104:27; See Job 36:31 **26** [r]Ezra 5:12; Neh. 1:4; Dan. 2:18

How Shall We Sing the LORD's Song?

137 By the waters of Babylon,
there we sat down and wept,
when we remembered Zion.
2 On the willows[1] there
we hung up our lyres.
3 For there our captors
required of us songs,
and our tormentors, mirth,
saying,
"Sing us one of the songs of
Zion!"

4 [s]How shall we sing the LORD's song
in a foreign land?
5 If I forget you,
O Jerusalem,
[t]let my right hand forget its
skill!
6 Let my [u]tongue stick to the roof of
my mouth,
if I do not remember you,
if I do not set Jerusalem
above my highest joy!

7 Remember, O LORD, against the
[v]Edomites
[w]the day of Jerusalem,
how they said, [x]"Lay it bare, lay it
bare,
down to its foundations!"
8 O daughter of Babylon, [y]doomed
to be destroyed,
blessed shall he be who [z]repays
you
with what you have done
to us!
9 Blessed shall he be who takes your
little ones
and [a]dashes them against the
rock!

[1] Or *poplars*

Psalm 137 **4** [s][Neh. 2:3] **5** [t][Ps. 76:5] **6** [u]Job 29:10; Ezek. 3:26 **7** [v]Isai. 34:5, 6; Lam. 4:21, 22; Ezek. 35:2; [Amos 1:11, 12]; See Jer. 49:7-22; Ezek. 25:12-14; Obad. 8-14 [w]See Job 18:20 [x]Hab. 3:13; Zeph. 2:14 **8** [y]Isai. 21:9; 47:1-15; Jer. 25:12; 50:1-46; 51:1-64; See Isai. 13:1-22 [z]Jer. 51:24, 56; [Ps. 28:4] **9** [a]2 Kin. 8:12; Isai. 13:16; Hos. 10:14; Nah. 3:10

136:19, 20 Sihon . . . Og. See 135:11 and note.

136:23 remembered us. The psalm becomes personal, applying God's salvation to the present. God continues to work as He has worked in the past to save His people from distress.

136:24 our foes. The enemies are not specified, permitting the easy application of the psalm to all generations.

Ps. 137 Of all the psalms this is probably the most clearly related to a historical event, the Exile of Judah to Babylon in the sixth century B.C. There is conflicting evidence about whether the psalm was composed during the Exile or immediately afterward (v. 1 note). The despair experienced in the Exile is eloquently expressed along with anger toward the enemy (vv. 7–9).

137:1 the waters of Babylon. The Tigris and Euphrates as well as numerous canals flowed near Babylon, far from Zion and the temple.

we sat down and wept. These words express the deep despair caused by deportation and exile.

Zion. See Ps. 2:6; 50:2; 65:1; 74:2; 128:5; 129:5.

137:2 lyres. Instruments of joy. After a victory Israel responded with songs (Ex. 15; Judg. 5). In defeat, the music ceases and there is silence (Is. 24:8, 9).

137:3 our captors. The Babylonians.

one of the songs of Zion. These are songs such as Ps. 46 and 48, about the greatness of Zion and Jerusalem. With Jerusalem destroyed, the Babylonians ridiculed their captives.

137:5 my right hand forget. How to play the harp. If he cannot sing of Jerusalem, he will not sing at all.

137:6 my highest joy. Now that Christ has come, there are no special holy places, but during the period of the Psalms there was but one—Zion. Jerusalem symbolically represented the City of God, composed of all believers (Gal. 4:26; Rev. 21:9–27). For the exiles, not only religious but political and cultural feelings were evoked by thoughts of their homeland.

137:7 Remember . . . the Edomites. Obadiah testifies to the callousness and hostility of the Edomites when Jerusalem fell to the Babylonians.

137:8 daughter of Babylon. A personification of the nation of Babylon.

137:9 dashes . . . against the rock. See Is. 13:16; Hos. 13:16; Nah. 3:10. On this cry for retributive justice see Introduction: The Curses of the Psalms.

Give Thanks to the LORD

138 OF DAVID.
[b]I give you thanks, O LORD,
with my whole heart;
before [c]the gods I sing your
praise;
2 I bow down [d]toward your [e]holy
temple
and give thanks to your name for
your steadfast love and your
faithfulness,
for you have exalted above all things
your name and your word.[1]
3 On the day I called, you
answered me;
my strength of soul you
increased.[2]
4 [f]All the kings of the earth shall give
you thanks, O LORD,
for they have heard the words of
your mouth,
5 and they shall sing of [g]the ways of
the LORD,
for great is the glory of the LORD.
6 [h]For though the LORD is high, he
regards the lowly,
but the haughty he knows from
afar.
7 [i]Though I walk in the midst of
trouble,
you [j]preserve my life;
you [k]stretch out your hand against
the wrath of my enemies,
and your [l]right hand
delivers me.
8 The LORD will [m]fulfill his purpose
for me;
[n]your steadfast love, O LORD,
endures forever.
Do not forsake [o]the work of your
hands.

Search Me, O God, and Know My Heart

139 TO THE CHOIRMASTER. A PSALM OF DAVID.
1 O LORD, you have [p]searched me and
known me!
2 You [q]know when I sit down and
when I rise up;
you [r]discern my thoughts from
afar.
3 You search out my path and my lying
down
and are acquainted with all my ways.
4 Even before a word is on my tongue,
behold, O LORD, [s]you know it
altogether.
5 You [t]hem me in, behind and before,
and [u]lay your hand upon me.
6 [v]Such knowledge is [w]too wonderful
for me;
it is high; I cannot attain it.
7 [x]Where shall I go from your Spirit?
Or where [y]shall I flee from your
presence?
8 [z]If I ascend to heaven, you are there!
[a]If I make my bed in Sheol, you are
there!

Psalm 138
1 [b]Ps. 111:1 [c]Ps. 95:3; 96:5
2 [d]Ps. 28:2; 1 Kin. 8:29 [e]Ps. 5:7
4 [f]See Ps. 102:15
5 [g]Ps. 103:7
6 [h][Ps. 131:1; Prov. 3:34; Luke 1:48; James 4:6]; See Ps. 113:5, 6
7 [i][Ps. 23:4] [j]See Ps. 71:20 [k][1 Sam. 24:6; Job 1:12] [l]Ps. 60:5
8 [m]Ps. 57:2; [Phil. 1:6] [n]Ps. 136:1; See 1 Chr. 16:41 [o]See Ps. 100:3

Psalm 139
1 [p]Jer. 12:3; See Ps. 7:9; 17:3; 44:21
2 [q]2 Kin. 19:27; Lam. 3:63 [r][Job 14:16; 31:4; Matt. 9:4; John 2:24, 25]
4 [s]Heb. 4:13
5 [t]Job 19:8 [u]Job 9:33
6 [v]Rom. 11:33 [w]Job 42:3
7 [x][Jer. 23:24] [y]Jonah 1:3
8 [z][Amos 9:2] [a][Job 26:6]

1 *Or you have exalted your word above all your name* 2 *Hebrew you made me bold in my soul with strength*

Ps. 138 The next eight psalms are assigned to David.

138:1 before the gods. See introduction to Ps. 82.

138:3 I called, you answered me. The motivating force behind David's thanksgiving. God answers prayer.

138:4 All the kings of the earth. David knows that his individual praise is unworthy of the greatness of God. He envisions all the rulers of the world calling upon the Lord. This never happened during the period of the Old Testament; if anything, the kings of the earth were opposed to God (Ps. 2; 48). After the coming of Christ, the gospel was extended to the nations (note on 133:title). In the end, all the kings of the earth will bring their glory into the New Jerusalem (Rev. 21:24).

138:6 he regards. He cares for them and meets them in their need.

138:7 in the midst of trouble. The trouble is general, enabling later worshipers to readily apply this thought to their own condition.

your right hand. See Ps. 74:11.

138:8 your steadfast love. See v. 2.

Ps. 139 This psalm is the prayer of a person who calls on God, announcing that he is innocent of all charges. With this purpose in mind he meditates on the character of God, exploring God's wisdom, His omniscience, and His greatness as the Creator.

139:1 you have searched me and known me. Compare the appeal in vv. 23, 24. He is the all-knowing God who has an intimate understanding of the psalmist, as of all His creation.

139:2 you discern my thoughts. God is omniscient. Thoughts may be the most private areas of life, but they cannot be hidden from the Lord (1 Chr. 28:9; Jer. 17:10; John 2:25).

139:4 before a word is on my tongue. God knows David's thought before it is spoken. This is why we can pray to God silently in our thoughts. See "God Sees and Knows: Divine Omniscience" at Prov. 15:3.

139:5 You hem me in. The Lord sets His limits around the psalmist's actions.

lay your hand. To guide him in life.

139:7 your Spirit . . . your presence. God's personal presence is everywhere throughout His creation. The thought of these rhetorical questions is that there is nowhere the psalmist can go that is beyond God's view. Jonah learned this lesson when he tried to flee God's commission to preach to the Ninevites. See "The Spiritual Nature of God" at Is. 66:1.

139:8 to heaven . . . in Sheol. The psalmist expresses God's omnipresence through a series of contrasts. The first contrast is spatial—God is in heaven; His presence reaches even to Sheol. Yet the hope of life beyond the grave shines through in the psalm (v. 10).

9 If I take the wings of the morning
and dwell in the uttermost parts of
the sea,
10 even there your hand shall [b]lead me,
and your right hand shall
hold me.
11 If I say, [c]"Surely the darkness shall
cover me,
and the light about me be night,"
12 [d]even the darkness is not dark to you;
the night is bright as the day,
for darkness is as light with you.

13 For you [e]formed my inward parts;
you [f]knitted me together in my
mother's womb.
14 I praise you, for I am fearfully and
wonderfully made.[1]
[g]Wonderful are your works;
my soul knows it very well.
15 [h]My frame was not hidden
from you,
when I was being made in secret,
intricately woven in [i]the depths of
the earth.
16 Your eyes saw my unformed
substance;
in your [j]book were written, every one
of them,
the days that were formed for me,
when as yet there were none of
them.

17 How precious to me are your
[k]thoughts, O God!
How vast is the sum of them!
18 [l]If I would count them, they are more
than [m]the sand.
I awake, and I am still with you.

10 [b]ver. 24; Ps. 23:3 11 [c][Job 22:14] 12 [d]Job. 34:22; [Dan. 2:22] 13 [e]Deut. 32:6 [f][Job 10:11] 14 [g]See Ps. 72:18 15 [h][Job 10:8-10; Eccles. 11:5] [i]Ps. 63:9 16 [j]Ps. 56:8 17 [k]Ps. 92:5 18 [l]Ps. 40:5 [m]Gen. 22:17

19 [n]Isai. 11:4; [Ps. 9:17] [o]Ps. 5:6 [p]See Ps. 6:8 20 [q][Jude 15] [r]Ex. 20:7 21 [s]See Ps. 26:5 [t]Ps. 119:158 [u]Ps. 59:1 23 [v]Ps. 26:2 24 [w]ver. 10 [x][Jer. 6:16; 18:15]
Psalm 140 1 [y]Ps. 71:4; 119:153, 170 [z]Ps. 18:48; Prov. 3:31 2 [a]See Ps. 56:6 3 [b][Ps. 52:2] [c]Ps. 58:4 [d]Ps. 10:7 [e]Cited Rom.3:13 4 [z][See ver. 1 above]

19 Oh that you would [n]slay the wicked,
O God!
O [o]men of blood, [p]depart from me!
20 They [q]speak against you with
malicious intent;
your enemies [r]take your name in
vain![2]
21 [s]Do I not hate those who hate you,
O LORD?
And do I not [t]loathe those who
[u]rise up against you?
22 I hate them with complete hatred;
I count them my enemies.

23 Search me, O God, and know my
heart!
[v]Try me and know my thoughts![3]
24 And see if there be any grievous way
in me,
and [w]lead me in [x]the way
everlasting![4]

Deliver Me, O LORD, from Evil Men

140 TO THE CHOIRMASTER. A PSALM OF DAVID.

1 [y]Deliver me, O LORD, from evil men;
preserve me from [z]violent men,
2 who plan evil things in their heart
and [a]stir up wars continually.
3 They make [b]their tongue sharp as [c]a
serpent's,
and [d]under their lips is the [e]venom
of asps. *Selah*

4 Guard me, O LORD, from the hands
of the wicked;
preserve me from [z]violent men,
who have planned to trip up my feet.

1 Or *for I am fearfully set apart* 2 Hebrew lacks *your name* 3 Or *cares*
4 Or *in the ancient way* (compare Jeremiah 6:16)

139:9 the wings of the morning . . . uttermost parts of the sea. A poetic expression meaning from the east to the west, anywhere on earth.

139:10 shall lead me. It is not merely that God will see the psalmist wherever he is: He will be there to guide and support him as well. See "Omnipresence and Omnipotence" at Jer. 23:24.

your right hand. See Ps. 73:23–26; 74:11; 138:7.

139:13 you formed my inward parts. God's knowledge of the writer goes back even before his birth, to his conception, when the Lord created the psalmist's personal existence.

139:14 Wonderful are your works. Such works include creating the writer and every other human being. The wonder of the developing child in the womb gives praise to the Creator.

139:15 in secret. In his mother's womb.

depths of the earth. Here a metaphor for the womb.

139:16 the days that were formed for me. God's preparation of the poet's days does not wait for time. He rejoices in God's predetermined course for his life.

139:17 precious to me. The incomprehensible greatness of God's knowledge overwhelms the psalmist. To know that One so great knows him so intimately is a source of consolation to David.

139:19 depart from me. The psalmist wants to distance himself from the wicked, because he is allied with God.

139:23 Search . . . know . . . Try. The psalmist trusts God and invites Him to probe his innermost thoughts and feelings (v. 1). He submits himself to God's correction and direction.

Ps. 140 This psalm is a complaint, which characteristically turns to the Lord at the end with confidence (vv. 12, 13).

140:2 stir up wars. Taken literally, this language suggests that the original setting of the psalm was war. Probably the language is figurative, like the reference to hunting in v. 5.

140:3 venom of asps. The enemy, through gossip and slander, has carefully planned the writer's destruction.

5 The arrogant have [f]hidden a trap
for me,
and with cords they have spread
[g]a net;[1]
beside the way they have set
[h]snares for me. *Selah*

6 [i]I say to the LORD, You are my God;
give ear to [j]the voice of my pleas
for mercy, O LORD!
7 O LORD, my Lord, [k]the strength of
my salvation,
you have covered my head in the
day of battle.
8 [l]Grant not, O LORD, the desires of the
wicked;
do not further their[2] evil plot or
[m]they will be exalted! *Selah*

9 As for the head of those who
surround me,
let [n]the mischief of their lips
overwhelm them!
10 Let [o]burning coals fall upon them!
Let them be cast into fire,
into miry pits, no more to rise!
11 Let not the slanderer be established
in the land;
let evil hunt down the violent man
speedily!
12 I know that the LORD will [p]maintain
the cause of the afflicted,
and [q]will execute justice for the
needy.
13 Surely [r]the righteous shall give
thanks to your name;
[s]the upright shall dwell in your
presence.

Give Ear to My Voice

141

A PSALM OF DAVID.
O LORD, I call upon you; [t]hasten
to me!
Give ear to my voice when I call to
you!
2 Let [u]my prayer be counted as incense
before you,
and [v]the lifting up of my hands as
[w]the evening sacrifice!

3 [x]Set a guard, O LORD, over my mouth;
[y]keep watch over the door of my
lips!
4 [z]Do not let my heart incline to any
evil,
to busy myself with wicked deeds
in company with men who [a]work
iniquity,
and [b]let me not eat of their
delicacies!

5 [c]Let a righteous man strike me—it is
a kindness;
let him rebuke me—it is oil for
my head;
let my head not refuse it.
Yet [d]my prayer is continually against
their evil deeds.
6 When their judges are [e]thrown over
the cliff,[3]
then they shall hear my words,
for they are pleasant.
7 As when one plows and breaks up
the earth,
so shall our bones [f]be scattered at
the mouth of Sheol.[4]

8 But [g]my eyes are toward you,
O GOD, my Lord;
[h]in you I seek refuge; leave me not
defenseless![5]
9 Keep me from [i]the trap that they
have laid for me
and from the snares of
evildoers!
10 Let the wicked [j]fall into their own nets,
while I pass by safely.

140:5 [f]Ps. 35:7; 141:9; 142:3; Jer. 18:22 [g]Job 18:8-10 [h]Ps. 64:5
6 [i]Ps. 142:5 [j]Ps. 28:2; 31:22; 130:2
7 [k]Ps. 28:8
8 [l][Ps. 35:25] [m]Isai. 14:21
9 [n][Prov. 12:13; 18:7]; See Ps. 7:16
10 [o][Ps. 11:6; 18:13]
12 [p]Ps. 9:4 [q]1 Kin. 8:45, 49, 59
13 [r][Ps. 64:10] [s][Ps. 11:7]
Psalm 141
1 [t]Ps. 40:13; 70:5
2 [u]Luke 1:10; Rev. 5:8; 8:3, 4 [v]See Ps. 28:2 [w]See Ex. 29:41
3 [x]Ps. 34:13 [y]Mic. 7:5
4 [z]Ps. 119:36 [a]ver. 9; Ps. 94:4 [b]Prov. 23:6
5 [c][Prov. 9:8; 19:25; 25:12; 27:6; Eccles. 7:5] [d][Ps. 109:4]
6 [e]2 Chr. 25:12; [Luke 4:29]
7 [f]Ps. 53:5; [Ezek. 37:1]
8 [g]Ps. 25:15 [h]See Ps. 11:1
9 [i]See Ps. 140:5
10 [j][Ps. 7:15]

[1] Or *they have spread cords as a net* [2] Hebrew *his* [3] Or *When their judges fall into the hands of the Rock* [4] The meaning of the Hebrew in verses 6, 7 is uncertain [5] Hebrew *refuge; do not pour out my life!*

140:7 in the day of battle. See v. 2 note. The psalmist reminds God that He has been his protector.

140:9 mischief of their lips. He asks God to turn back on his persecutors the evil they meant for him (7:14–16 notes).

140:10 Let them be cast into fire. See Introduction: Characteristics and Themes.

140:12 will maintain the cause of the afflicted. See 9:18 note; 72:4.

141:2 as incense . . . as the evening sacrifice. This simile comes from the sacrificial worship of ancient Israel and suggests that the psalm was set in that context. The incense was valuable and pleasing to the Lord (Ex. 30:34–38), and the psalmist asks for his prayers to be received favorably also. In Rev. 8:3–5, an angel carries the prayers of the saints, together with incense, to the throne of God.

141:3 Set a guard . . . over my mouth. The writer foresees that he will be tempted to speak unwisely, and so shows forthright humility in asking God to deter him.

141:4 to any evil. Indicating any compromise.

141:5 Let a righteous man strike me. A wise person accepts correction; the person who refuses to listen will finally be destroyed (Prov. 29:1; Heb. 12:1–13).

141:9 the snares. A hunting image; see note Ps. 140:5.

141:10 into their own nets. See 7:14, 15 and note.

You Are My Refuge

142 A MASKIL[1] OF DAVID, WHEN HE WAS IN [k] THE CAVE. A PRAYER.

1 With my voice I [l]cry out to the LORD;
with my voice I [m]plead for mercy
to the LORD.
2 I [n]pour out my complaint before him;
I tell my trouble before him.

3 When my spirit [o]faints within me,
you know my way!
In the path where I walk
they have [p]hidden a trap for me.
4 [q]Look to the [r]right and see:
[s]there is none who takes notice of me;
[t]no refuge remains to me;
no one cares for my soul.

5 I cry to you, O LORD;
I say, "You are my [u]refuge,
my [v]portion in [w]the land of the
living."
6 [x]Attend to my cry,
for [y]I am brought very low!
Deliver me from my persecutors,
[z]for they are too strong for me!
7 [a]Bring me out of prison,
that I may give thanks to your
name!
The righteous will surround me,
for you will [b]deal bountifully
with me.

My Soul Thirsts for You

143 A PSALM OF DAVID.
Hear my prayer, O LORD;
[c]give ear to my pleas for mercy!
In your [d]faithfulness answer me, in
your [d]righteousness!

2 [e]Enter not into judgment with your
servant,
for no one living is righteous
[f]before you.
3 For the enemy has pursued my soul;
[g]he has crushed my life to the
ground;
[h]he has made me sit in darkness
like those long dead.
4 Therefore my spirit [i]faints within me;
my heart within me is appalled.

5 [j]I remember the days of old;
[k]I meditate on all that you have
done;
I ponder the work of your hands.
6 [l]I stretch out my hands to you;
[m]my soul thirsts for you like [n]a
parched land. *Selah*

7 [o]Answer me quickly, O LORD!
[p]My spirit fails!
[q]Hide not your face from me,
[r]lest I be like those who go down to
the pit.
8 [s]Let me hear in the morning of your
steadfast love,
for in you I [t]trust.
[u]Make me know the way I should go,
[v]for to you I lift up my soul.

9 [w]Deliver me from my enemies, O LORD!
I have fled to you for refuge![2]
10 [x]Teach me to do your will,
for you are my God!
[y]Let your good Spirit [z]lead me
on [a]level ground!

Psalm 142
[k]Ps. 57, title
1 [l]Ps. 3:4 [m]Ps. 30:8
2 [n][Isai. 26:16]; See Ps. 102, title
3 [o]See Ps. 77:3 [p]Ps. 140:5
4 [q]Ps. 69:20 [r]Ps. 16:8 [s][Ps. 31:11] [t]Job 11:20; Jer. 25:35
5 [u]See Ps. 14:6 [v]Ps. 16:5 [w]Ps. 27:13
6 [x]Ps. 17:1 [y]Ps. 79:8 [z]Ps. 18:17
7 [a]Isai. 42:7; [Ps. 143:11] [b]Ps. 13:6
Psalm 143
1 [c]Ps. 140:6 [d]1 John 1:9; [Ps. 31:1]
2 [e][Job 14:3] [f]Ps. 130:3; 1 Kin. 8:46; Job 9:2; 15:14; 25:4; Eccles. 7:20; Rom. 3:23; 1 Cor. 4:4
3 [g]See Ps. 88:3-6 [h]Lam. 3:6
4 [i]See Ps. 77:3
5 [j]Ps. 77:5, 11 [k]Ps. 77:12; 111:2
6 [l]See Job 11:13 [m]Ps. 42:2 [n][Ps. 63:1]
7 [o]Ps. 69:17; 102:2 [p][Ps. 84:2] [q]Ps. 27:9 [r]Ps. 28:1; 88:4
8 [s][Ps. 90:14] [t]Ps. 11:1; 25:2 [u]Ps. 25:4 [v]Ps. 25:1
9 [w]Ps. 59:1; 142:6
10 [x][Ps.119:12] [y]Neh. 9:20 [z]See Ps. 23:3 [a]Isai. 26:10; [Ps. 27:11]

1 Probably a musical or liturgical term 2 One Hebrew manuscript, Septuagint; most Hebrew manuscripts *To you I have covered*

Ps. 142 The psalm is the complaint of someone at the end of his resources.

142:title WHEN HE WAS IN THE CAVE. Except for this instance, historical titles for psalms are found only in the first two books of the Psalter.

142:3 my spirit faints within me. The psalmist was exhausted from persecution.

142:4 to the right. The place where one would expect to find a helper for him; he wants God to see that there is no one on his side (16:8; 110:5; 121:5).

142:7 out of prison. According to the title, the reference is to the cave where David hid (57:title). In later use, the prison could be any situation that holds a person captive, including a literal prison.

The righteous will surround me. David looks forward to a time when God will be with him and he will not be alone.

Ps. 143 This song is the last of the "penitential psalms" (introduction to Ps. 6). The note of penitence is seen in v. 2, which may be alluded to by Paul (Rom. 3:20; Gal. 2:16). Ps. 142 and 143 are both appeals to God for help in the midst of trouble when there are no resources to depend on.

143:1 In your faithfulness . . . righteousness. The psalmist appeals to God's nature and character.

143:2 no one living is righteous. David has measured his own heart in the sight of God and has learned that no one can pretend to be righteous at the bar of God's judgment.

143:4 my spirit faints within me. See note Ps. 142:3.

143:5 I remember. See note Ps. 44:1; cf. Ps. 77:3, 11; 111:4.

143:7 who go down to the pit. He will die (Ezek. 26:20).

143:8 the morning. The psalmist utters his prayer at night or in the very early morning, hoping that God's answer will greet him at dawn.

steadfast love. The love of God's covenant devotion to His people.

Make me. The psalmist not only desires deliverance—he wants God's guidance. He knows that it is only as he walks in the way of the Lord that he will live safely.

11 [b]For your name's sake, O LORD,
[c]preserve my life!
In your righteousness [d]bring my
soul out of trouble!
12 And in your steadfast love you will
[e]cut off my enemies,
and you will destroy all the
adversaries of my soul,
for I am your [f]servant.

My Rock and My Fortress

144

OF DAVID.
1 Blessed be the LORD, my [g]rock,
[h]who trains my hands for war,
and my fingers for battle;
2 he is my [i]steadfast love and my
[j]fortress,
my [k]stronghold and my deliverer,
my [l]shield and he in whom I take
refuge,
who [m]subdues peoples[1] under me.

3 O LORD, [n]what is man that you
[o]regard him,
or the son of man that you think
of him?
4 [p]Man is like a breath;
his days are like [q]a passing
[r]shadow.

5 [s]Bow your heavens, O LORD, and
come down!
[t]Touch the mountains so that they
smoke!
6 [u]Flash forth the lightning and scatter
them;
[u]send out your arrows and rout them!
7 [v]Stretch out your hand from
on high;
[w]rescue me and deliver me from
the many waters,
from the hand [x]of foreigners,
8 whose mouths speak [y]lies
and whose right hand is [z]a right
hand of falsehood.

9 I will sing [a]a new song to you,
O God;
upon [a]a ten-stringed harp I will
play to you,
10 who gives victory to kings,
who [b]rescues David his servant
from the cruel sword.
11 Rescue me and deliver me
from the hand [x]of foreigners,
whose mouths speak [y]lies
and whose right hand is a right
hand of falsehood.

12 May our sons in their youth
be like [c]plants full grown,
our daughters like [d]corner pillars
cut for the structure of a
palace;
13 may our granaries be full,
providing all kinds of produce;
may our sheep bring forth
thousands
and ten thousands in our
fields;
14 may our cattle be heavy with
young,
suffering no [e]mishap or failure in
[f]bearing;[2]
may there be no [g]cry of distress in
our streets!
15 [h]Blessed are the people to whom
such blessings fall!
[i]Blessed are the people whose God
is the LORD!

11 [b]Ps. 23:3; 25:11 [c]See Ps. 71:20 [d]Ps. 142:7
12 [e]Ps. 54:5 [f]See Ps. 116:16
Psalm 144
1 [g]See Ps. 18:2, 31, 46 [h]Ps. 18:34
2 [i][Ps. 59:10, 17; Jonah 2:8] [j]Ps. 18:2; 91:2 [k]Ps. 18:2; 59:9 [l]Ps. 7:10; 18:2 [m]Ps. 18:47
3 [n]See Ps. 8:4 [o]See Ps. 31:7
4 [p]Ps. 39:5 [q]Ps. 102:11; 109:23 [r]Job 8:9
5 [s]Ps. 18:9; [Isai. 64:1] [t]See Ps. 104:32
6 [u]See Ps. 18:14
7 [v]Ps. 18:16 [w]Ps. 69:14 [x]Ps. 18:44, 45
8 [y]Ps. 12:2; 41:6 [z][Ps. 106:26; Gen. 14:22; Deut. 32:40; Isai. 62:8]
9 [a]Ps. 33:2, 3
10 [b]Ps. 18:50
11 [x][See ver. 7 above] [y][See ver. 8 above]
12 [c][Ps. 128:3] [d][Zech. 9:15]
14 [e][Amos 4:3] [f][Jer. 29:16] [g][Isai. 24:11; Jer. 14:2; 46:12]
15 [h]Deut. 33:29 [i]Ps. 33:12; 146:5

1 Many Hebrew manuscripts, Dead Sea Scroll, Jerome, Syriac, Aquila; most Hebrew manuscripts *subdues my people* 2 Hebrew *with no breaking in or going out*

143:11 your name's sake. See Ps. 8:1.

Ps. 144 This psalm is set in the midst of conflict (v. 11), but the speaker does not panic as he calls upon the Lord to appear. The language of God's appearance is similar to Ps. 18, also by David. The language of battle applies figuratively to the spiritual warfare that Christians wage against the "spiritual forces of evil" (Eph. 6:10–20).

144:1 my rock. See notes Ps. 62:2; cf. Ps. 28:7; Deut. 32:18; Ex. 17:6.

who trains my hands for war. The association of God with warfare can be a stumbling block in appreciating the Old Testament. There is no conflict between the Old and New Testaments on this point. The warfare of God's people has been heightened and intensified for Christians, whose war is against unseen spiritual enemies arrayed against God and themselves for His sake (Eph. 6:10–20).

144:2 steadfast love . . . fortress. The Bible presents no conflict between God's love and His warfare.

under me. David and later faithful kings.

144:3 what is man. See Ps. 8:4.

144:4 like a breath. Ephemeral and short-lived. The word is translated "vanity" in Eccl. 1:2. The poet is amazed that God cares for him.

144:5 so that they smoke. When God appears, nature trembles before Him (Ex. 19:16–19).

144:7 many waters. The enemies are compared to the Near Eastern popular conception of the cosmic waters of chaos (18:4, 14 and notes).

144:9 a new song. See note Ps. 33:3.

144:11 from the hand of foreigners. The threat is from outside Israel.

144:12 our sons . . . our daughters. When the oppressive foreigners have been thrown back, the next generation will flourish.

144:14 no mishap. The poet envisions complete security from outside military threats (see text note).

Great Is the Lord

145 [1] A Song of Praise. Of David.
[j] I will extol you, my God and [k] King,
and bless your name forever and ever.
2 Every day I will bless you
[l] and praise your name forever and ever.
3 [m] Great is the Lord, and greatly to be praised,
and his [n] greatness is unsearchable.

4 [o] One generation shall commend your works to another,
and shall declare your mighty acts.
5 On [p] the glorious splendor of your majesty,
and on your wondrous works, I will meditate.
6 They shall speak of [q] the might of your awesome deeds,
and I will declare your greatness.
7 They shall pour forth the fame of your [r] abundant goodness
and shall sing aloud of your righteousness.

8 The Lord is [s] gracious and merciful,
slow to anger and abounding in steadfast love.
9 The Lord is [t] good to all,
and his mercy is over all that he has made.

10 [u] All your works shall give thanks to you, O Lord,
and all your [v] saints shall bless you!
11 They shall speak of the glory of your kingdom
and tell of your power,
12 to [w] make known to the children of man your[2] [x] mighty deeds,
and [y] the glorious splendor of your kingdom.
13 [z] Your kingdom is an everlasting kingdom,
and your dominion endures throughout all generations.

[The Lord is faithful in all his words
and kind in all his works.][3]
14 The Lord [a] upholds all who are falling
and [b] raises up all who are bowed down.
15 The eyes of all [c] look to you,
and you give them their food in due season.
16 You [d] open your hand;
you [e] satisfy the desire of every living thing.
17 The Lord is [f] righteous in all his ways
and [g] kind in all his works.
18 The Lord is [h] near to all who call on him,
to all who call on him [i] in truth.
19 He [j] fulfills the desire of those who fear him;
he also [k] hears their cry and saves them.
20 The Lord [l] preserves all who love him,
but all the wicked he will destroy.

21 My mouth will speak the praise of the Lord,
and [m] let all flesh bless his holy name forever and ever.

Psalm 145
1 [j] Ps. 99:5, 9 [k] Ps. 98:6
2 [l] [Ps. 146:2]
3 [m] Ps. 48:1 [n] Job 5:9; [Isai. 40:28]
4 [o] Isai. 33:19
5 [p] ver. 12
6 [q] [Ps. 78:4]
7 [r] Isai. 63:7
8 [s] See Ps. 86:5, 15
9 [t] See Ps. 100:5
10 [u] [Ps. 19:1; 103:22] [v] [Ps. 132:9, 16]
12 [w] Ps. 105:1 [x] ver. 4; Ps. 150:2; Deut. 3:24 [y] ver. 5
13 [z] See Ps. 10:16
14 [a] [Ps. 37:17, 24] [b] Ps. 146:8
15 [c] Ps. 104:27
16 [d] Ps. 104:28 [e] [Ps. 104:21; 147:8]
17 [f] See Ps. 116:5 [g] Ps. 18:25; Jer. 3:12
18 [h] [Ps. 34:18; 119:151; Deut. 4:7] [i] John 4:23, 24
19 [j] Prov. 10:24; [John 9:31] [k] Ps. 31:22
20 [l] See Ps. 97:10
21 [m] [Ps. 150:6]

1 This psalm is an acrostic poem, each verse beginning with the successive letters of the Hebrew alphabet 2 Hebrew *his*; also next line 3 These two lines are supplied by one Hebrew manuscript, Septuagint, Syriac (compare Dead Sea Scroll)

Ps. 145 The psalmist leads Israel in praise of the Lord. This poem is the first of six hymns that close the Psalter like a display of fireworks. The psalm is an acrostic, each parallel line beginning with a consecutive letter of the alphabet. One letter (*nun*) is missing, here, possibly a copyist's error.

145:1 my God and King. See note Ps. 93:1.

145:3 unsearchable. God's power and might are so great that finite human minds are unable to comprehend them fully. This verse teaches the doctrine of the incomprehensibility of God. People can have a true understanding of God, but never a complete or exhaustive one.

145:4 One generation . . . to another. See Ps. 78:4. Parents had the duty of instructing their children in the ways of the Lord (Deut. 6:20–25).

145:5 your majesty . . . your wondrous works. God is great in what He is and what He does.

145:8 The Lord is gracious. The wording of this verse occurs a number of times throughout Scripture, beginning at Ex. 34:6.

merciful. That God allows people to live in spite of their deep sin is a sign of His mercy.

steadfast love. The love of God's covenant devotion to His people.

145:10 All your works. See "General Revelation" at 19:1.

145:11 your kingdom. The revelation of God as the King who rules His kingdom emphasizes His sovereign power and control over His creation.

145:13 an everlasting kingdom. God is eternal, and His kingdom will never be destroyed. See Nebuchadnezzar's confession in Dan. 4:34.

145:14 upholds all who are falling. God is compassionate toward the weak and restores the erring (9:18 note; 72:4).

145:16 of every living thing. God gives gifts to all His creatures, people and animals, saints and sinners.

145:18 to all who call on him. While God is kind to all creation, the psalm goes on to specify those who love Him and turn to Him.

145:19 those who fear him. See notes Ps. 34:7; 36:1.

Do Not Put Your Trust in Princes

146 [n]Praise the LORD!
Praise the LORD, O my soul!
2 I will praise the LORD [o]as long as I live;
[p]I will sing praises to my God while
I have my being.
3 [q]Put not your trust in princes,
[r]in a son of man, in whom there is
[s]no salvation.
4 When [t]his breath departs he returns
to the earth;
on that very day his plans perish.
5 [u]Blessed is he whose help is the God
of Jacob,
whose [v]hope is in the LORD his God,
6 [w]who made heaven and earth,
the sea, and all that is in them,
[x]who keeps faith forever;
7 [y]who executes justice for the
oppressed,
[z]who gives food to the hungry.
[a]The LORD sets the prisoners free;
8 [b]the LORD opens the eyes of the
blind.
[c]The LORD lifts up those who are
bowed down;
[d]the LORD loves the righteous.
9 [e]The LORD watches over the sojourners;
[f]he upholds the widow and the
fatherless,
but [g]the way of the wicked he
brings to ruin.
10 [h]The LORD will reign forever,
your God, O Zion, to all generations.
[n]Praise the LORD!

Psalm 146
1 [n]See Ps. 135:1
2 [o]Ps. 63:4; [Ps. 145:2] [p]Ps. 104:33
3 [q]Ps. 118:9 [r]Ps. 118:8; [Isai. 2:22; Jer. 17:5] [s]Ps. 60:11; 108:12
4 [t]Ps. 104:29; [Eccles. 12:7]; See Job 10:9; 34:14, 15
5 [u][Ps. 144:15] [v]Ps. 119:116; See Ps. 2:12
6 [w]See Ps. 115:15 [x][Ps. 100:5; 117:2]
7 [y]Ps. 103:6 [z]Ps. 107:9; 145:15 [a]Ps. 105:20; Isai. 61:1; [Ps. 68:6]
8 [b]Matt. 9:30; John 9:7 [c]Ps. 145:14; [Ps. 147:6] [d]Ps. 11:7
9 [e][Ex. 22:21] [f]Deut. 10:18; [Ex. 22:22]; See Ps. 10:14 [g][Ps. 147:6]
10 [h]See Ps. 10:16 [n]See Ps. 135:1

Psalm 147
1 [i]See Ps. 135:1 [j]Ps. 92:1 [k]Ps. 135:3 [l]Ps. 33:1
2 [m]Ps. 51:18; 102:16 [n]Deut. 30:3; Isai. 11:12; 27:13; 56:8; Ezek. 39:28
3 [o]Ps. 34:18 [p]Ezek. 34:16
4 [q][Gen. 15:5] [r]Isai. 40:26

He Heals the Brokenhearted

147 [i]Praise the LORD!
For [j]it is good to sing praises to
our God;
for [k]it is pleasant,[1] and [l]a song of
praise is fitting.
2 The LORD [m]builds up Jerusalem;
he [n]gathers the outcasts of Israel.
3 He heals [o]the brokenhearted
and [p]binds up their wounds.
4 He [q]determines the number of the
stars;
he [r]gives to all of them their names.
5 [s]Great is our Lord, and [t]abundant in
power;
[u]his understanding is beyond
measure.
6 The LORD [v]lifts up the humble;[2]
he casts the wicked to the
ground.
7 [w]Sing to the LORD with thanksgiving;
make melody to our God on [x]the
lyre!
8 He covers the heavens with clouds;
he prepares [y]rain for the earth;
he makes [z]grass grow on the hills.
9 He [a]gives to the beasts their food,
and to [b]the young ravens that cry.
10 His delight is not in [c]the strength of
the horse,
nor his pleasure in the legs of a
man,

5 [s]Ps. 48:1 [t]Nah. 1:3 [u]Isai. 40:28; [Job 5:9] 6 [v][Ps. 146:8, 9] 7 [w]Ex. 15:21; [Ps. 95:1, 2] [x]See 1 Chr. 15:16 8 [y]See Job 5:10 [z]Ps. 104:14; Job 38:27 9 [a]Ps. 104:27, 28 [b]See Job 38:41 10 [c]Ps. 33:17

1 Or *for he is beautiful* 2 Or *afflicted*

Ps. 146 The last five psalms are hymns marked by opening and closing cries of "Praise the LORD," characterizing their pervasive mood.

146:1 O my soul. See note Ps. 103:1.

146:3 in princes. Some believe that this reference is to foreign kings who rule over Judah after the nation's Babylonian exile of the sixth century B.C. However, there were earlier times when the children of Israel misplaced their trust in native rulers (1 Sam. 8).

146:5 Blessed. See Ps. 1:1.

whose help. God is the only One capable of helping those in distress. This verse provides the theme of the psalm, and the following verses describe His power and compassion.

146:6 who made. God's role as Creator is highlighted to emphasize His power.

the sea. See Ps. 24:2.

146:7 the oppressed . . . the hungry. See 9:18 note; 72:4.

146:9 the wicked he brings to ruin. While God promotes the cause of the weak, He resists the proud and abusive.

146:10 reign forever. See Ps. 93:1.

O Zion. See 2:6 note; 50:2; 74:2; 84:7; 128:5; 129:5; 137:6.

Praise the LORD. See v. 1.

Ps. 147 This is part of the great doxology that concludes the Psalter. It praises the Lord for rebuilding Jerusalem and was probably composed during the period of Judah's restoration following its Babylonian captivity in the sixth century B.C. (Neh. 12:27–47). As in Ps. 146, God's power is radically contrasted with human might.

147:1 it is good. In this way the poet encourages the congregation to praise the Lord.

147:2 gathers the outcasts. See introduction to this psalm. This verse probably refers to the return of Judeans to the Promised Land following Cyrus's decree (2 Chr. 36:22, 23) that ended the Babylonian exile.

147:4 the number of the stars. The number of stars seems infinite. Cf. Gen. 15:5.

147:5 his understanding is beyond measure. God is above and beyond human intelligence. There is no scale that can measure infinity.

147:8, 9 clouds . . . rain . . . grass . . . food. God regulates all the processes that provide food for His creatures.

147:10 the legs of a man. God does not judge people by their physical strength or appearance, but according to their heart's attitude toward Him (1 Sam. 16:7). Strong legs, like good horses, were important for soldiers.

11 but the LORD [d]takes pleasure in those
who fear him,
in those who [e]hope in his
steadfast love.

12 Praise the LORD, O Jerusalem!
Praise your God, O Zion!
13 For he strengthens [f]the bars of your
gates;
he blesses your children within
you.
14 He [g]makes peace in your borders;
he [h]fills you with the [i]finest of the
wheat.
15 He [j]sends out his command to the
earth;
his word runs swiftly.
16 He gives [k]snow like wool;
he scatters [l]hoarfrost like ashes.
17 He hurls down his crystals of [m]ice
like crumbs;
who can stand before his
[n]cold?
18 He [o]sends out his word, and melts
them;
he makes his wind blow and the
waters flow.
19 He declares his word to Jacob,
his [p]statutes and rules to
Israel.
20 He [q]has not dealt thus with any
other nation;
they do not know his rules.
[r]Praise the LORD!

Praise the Name of the LORD

148 [r]Praise the LORD!
Praise the LORD [s]from the
heavens;
praise him [t]in the heights!
2 Praise him, all his angels;
praise him, all his [u]hosts!

3 Praise him, sun and moon,
praise him, all you shining stars!
4 Praise him, you [v]highest heavens,
and you [w]waters above the
heavens!

5 [x]Let them praise the name of the
LORD!
For [y]he commanded and they
were created.
6 And he [z]established them forever
and ever;
he gave [a]a decree, and it shall not
[b]pass away.[1]

7 Praise the LORD [c]from the earth,
you [d]great sea creatures and all
deeps,
8 [e]fire and hail, [f]snow and mist,
[g]stormy wind [h]fulfilling his word!

9 [i]Mountains and all hills,
[j]fruit trees and all [k]cedars!
10 [l]Beasts and all livestock,
creeping things and [m]flying birds!

11 Kings of the earth and [n]all peoples,
princes and all rulers of
the earth!
12 Young men and maidens together,
old men and children!

13 [o]Let them praise the name of the LORD,
for [p]his name alone is exalted;
[q]his majesty is above earth and
heaven.

11 [d]Ps. 149:4 [e]Ps. 33:18
13 [f]Neh. 7:3
14 [g]Ex. 34:24; Prov. 16:7; Isai. 60:17, 18 [h]Ps. 132:15 [i]Ps. 81:16; Deut. 32:14
15 [j][Ps. 148:8]
16 [k]Job 37:6 [l][Job 38:29]
17 [m]Job 37:10 [n]Job 37:9
18 [o]ver. 15; [Job 37:12]; See Ps. 33:9; 107:20
19 [p]Mal. 4:4; [Ps. 78:5]; See Deut. 33:2-4
20 [q]Deut. 4:7; See Deut. 4:32-34 [r]See Ps. 135:1
Psalm 148
1 [r][See Ps. 147:20 above] [s][ver.7]; See Ps. 69:34 [t]Matt. 21:9
2 [u]See Ps. 103:20, 21
4 [v]Ps. 68:33; Deut. 10:14; Neh. 9:6; See 1 Kin. 8:27 [w]Gen. 1:7
5 [x]ver. 13 [y]See Ps. 33:6, 9
6 [z]Ps. 119:90, 91 [a][Job 28:26; Jer. 31:36, 36; 33:25] [b][Ps. 104:9; Esth. 1:19; Job 14:5]
7 [c][ver. 1] [d][Gen. 1:21]; See Ps. 74:13
8 [e]Ps. 18:12; 105:32 [f]Ps. 147:16 [g]Ps. 107:25 [h]Ps. 103:20; See Ps. 147:15-18
9 [i]Isai. 44:23; 49:13; 55:12 [j]Gen. 1:11 [k]Ps. 104:16
10 [l]Gen. 1:24 [m]Gen. 1:20, 21 11 [n][Rev. 7:9] 13 [o]ver. 5 [p]Ps. 8:1 [q]See Ps. 113:4

1 Or *it shall not be transgressed*

147:11 who fear him. See notes Ps. 34:7 and 36:1.

steadfast love. God's covenant love for His people.

147:13 the bars of your gates. The gates provide security for the city; note what happens when they are weak (Nah. 3:13).

147:14 the finest of the wheat. Representative of fertility and provision.

147:15 his word runs swiftly. It accomplishes its purpose quickly.

147:19 his statutes and rules. He guides Israel in the proper way of corporate behavior.

147:20 Praise the LORD. See v. 1.

Ps. 148 The summons to praise takes prominence over the reasons for praise in this psalm. The initial exhortation is toward heaven (vv. 1–6), the second to the earth (vv. 7–12), and the last to the chosen people of God (vv. 13, 14).

148:1 the heavens. The heavens are normally described as containing different levels, though the details are never spelled out in the Bible (cf. 2 Cor. 12:2). The highest heavens cannot contain God (1 Kin. 8:27), showing that His transcendence cannot be measured.

148:4 waters above the heavens. See Gen. 1:7.

148:5 they were created. See the six days of creation in Gen. 1; theological note "God the Creator" on next page.

148:7 from the earth. This idea is elaborated in the following verses as different parts of creation are called to praise God.

sea creatures. The sea was a source of special fascination and fear to the Israelites. Often, the sea represents everything opposed to God and His created order (18:4, 15 notes). God's greatness is demonstrated as He requires their praise.

148:11 Kings of the earth. The psalm proclaims that universal praise is due to the Lord (138:4 note).

148:13 the name of the LORD. See Ps. 8:1.

14 He has [r]raised up a horn for his
people,
[s]praise for all his saints,
for the people of Israel who are
[t]near to him.
[u]Praise the LORD!

Sing to the LORD a New Song

149 [u]Praise the LORD!
Sing to the LORD [v]a new song,
his praise in [w]the assembly of the
godly!
2 Let Israel [x]be glad in [y]his Maker;
let the children of Zion rejoice in
their [z]King!
3 Let them praise his name with
[a]dancing,
making melody to him with
[b]tambourine and [c]lyre!
4 For the LORD [d]takes pleasure in his
people;
he [e]adorns the humble with
salvation.
5 Let the godly exult in glory;
let them [f]sing for joy on their
[g]beds.
6 Let [h]the high praises of God be in
their throats
and [i]two-edged swords in their
hands,
7 to execute vengeance on the
nations
and punishments on the peoples,
8 to bind their kings with [j]chains
and their nobles with fetters of
iron,

14 [r]See 1 Sam. 2:1 [s][Deut. 10:21; Jer. 17:14] [t]Deut. 4:7; Eph. 2:17 [u]See Ps. 135:1
Psalm 149
1 [u][See Ps. 148:14 above] [v]See Ps. 33:3 [w]Ps. 89:5, 7
2 [x]Ps. 85:6 [y]See Ps. 95:6; Job 35:10 [z]1 Sam. 12:12; Zech. 9:9
3 [a]Ps. 150:4; [Ps. 30:11] [b]Ps. 150:4 Ex. 15:20 [c]Ps. 150:3
4 [d]Ps. 35:27; 147:11 [e][Isai. 61:3]
5 [f]See Job 35:10 [g]Ps. 4:4; 63:6; [Hos. 7:14] **6** [h][Ps. 66:17] [i]Heb. 4:12; Rev. 1:16; 2:12; [Prov. 5:4] **8** [j][Job 36:8]

God the Creator

"In the beginning, God created the heavens and the earth" (Gen. 1:1). There was no preexisting material; God created from nothing, by fiat. He decided that things should exist and called them into being with His word ("Let there be . . ."). God gave the creation an existence dependent on His own existence yet distinct from it. In the work of creation, Father, Son, and Holy Spirit acted together (Gen. 1:2; Ps. 33:6, 9; 148:5; John 1:1–3; Col. 1:15, 16; Heb. 1:2; 11:3).

The act of creation is a mystery to us; there is more in it than we can understand. We cannot create by a mere act of the will, and we do not know how God could. To say that He created "out of nothing" is to confess the mystery, not explain it. In particular, we cannot conceive how a dependent existence can be distinct, or how angels and people in their dependent existence can make free decisions and be morally accountable to their Maker. Yet Scripture everywhere teaches us this truth.

As the world-order is not self-created, so also it is not self-sustaining, as God is. The universe is constantly upheld by God; without this activity of the divine Son (Col. 1:17; Heb. 1:3), every creature of every kind, including ourselves, would cease to be. As Paul told the Athenians, He "gives to all mankind life and breath and everything . . . In him we live and move and have our being" (Acts 17:25, 28).

God is not "in" space or time; space and time are dimensions of the created order, and God is not bound by them as we are. He is able to act in the created order in ways that are not accessible to our understanding.

Knowing that God created us and the world around us is basic to true religion. God is to be praised as the Creator, known from the marvelous order and beauty of His works (see, for example, Ps. 104). God is a sovereign Lord, whose eternal plan covers all events and destinies without exception. He has power to redeem, recreate, and renew. Realizing that we depend on God for our moment-by-moment existence calls us to live lives of devotion, gratitude, and loyalty towards Him.

148:14 a horn. The horn symbolizes the strength and vigor of the nation as a whole or the king in particular. See 92:10 note.

near to him. See Deut. 7:7–11.

Ps. 149 Reference to a "new song" (v. 1) and the martial language of vv. 6–9 suggest that the song was sung in celebration of a victory in battle. On war, see 144:1 note.

149:1 Praise the LORD. See note Ps. 146:1. Note the parallel phrase at v. 9.

new song. See note Ps. 33:3.

149:2 his Maker . . . their King. God brought Israel into being as a nation in the Exodus and at Sinai, and now He rules over them. These events provide ample reasons to worship Him.

children of Zion. See note Ps. 2:6.

149:3 with dancing . . . with tambourine and lyre. The psalmist calls on Israel to celebrate the Lord actively, with enthusiasm and joy.

149:5 on their beds. They may worship God at all times, in public and private.

149:7 execute vengeance on the nations. God uses His people to bring judgment on the nations. The most notable example from biblical history is the judgment brought upon the Canaanites in the time of Joshua.

9 to execute on them the judgment
[k]written!
[l]This is honor for all his godly
ones.
[u]Praise the LORD!

Let Everything Praise the LORD

150 [u]Praise the LORD!
Praise God in his [m]sanctuary;
praise him in [n]his mighty
heavens![1]
2 Praise him for his [o]mighty deeds;
praise him according to his
excellent [p]greatness!
3 Praise him with [q]trumpet sound;
praise him with [r]lute and [r]harp!
4 Praise him with [s]tambourine and
[s]dance;
praise him with [t]strings and [u]pipe!
5 Praise him with sounding [v]cymbals;
praise him with loud clashing
cymbals!
6 Let [w]everything that has breath praise
the LORD!
[x]Praise the LORD!

9 [k]Isai. 65:6; [Job 13:26] [l][Ps. 148:14] [u][See Ps. 148:14 above]
Psalm 150
1 [u][See Ps. 148:14 above] [m][Ps. 11:4; 134:2] [n][Ps. 68:34]
2 [o]Ps. 145:12 [p]Deut. 3:24
3 [q]Ps. 98:6 [r]Ps. 33:2; 71:22
4 [s]Ps. 149:3 [t]Ps. 45:8; [Isai. 38:20] [u]Job 21:12
5 [v]2 Sam. 6:5; 1 Chr. 15:16, 19, 28; 25:1, 6 6 [w][Ps. 145:21] [x]ver. 1

[1] Hebrew *expanse* (compare Genesis 1:6-8)

149:9 Praise the LORD. See v. 1.

150:1 Praise the LORD. See Ps. 146:1. Note the parallel closing at v. 6.

in his sanctuary . . . in his mighty heavens. These are the locations where worship was focused.

150:2 his mighty deeds . . . his excellent greatness. This verse gives reasons why God should be worshiped.

150:3–5 trumpet . . . lute and harp . . . tambourine and dance . . . strings and pipe . . . cymbals. A wonderful array of instruments for the praises of God. See "Music in the Church" at Col. 3:16.

150:6 everything that has breath. See Gen. 2:7. Life is represented in the breath. The breath is also the means of speech, for prayer, and for praise.

Praise the LORD. See v. 1.

INTRODUCTION TO THE

Wisdom Literature

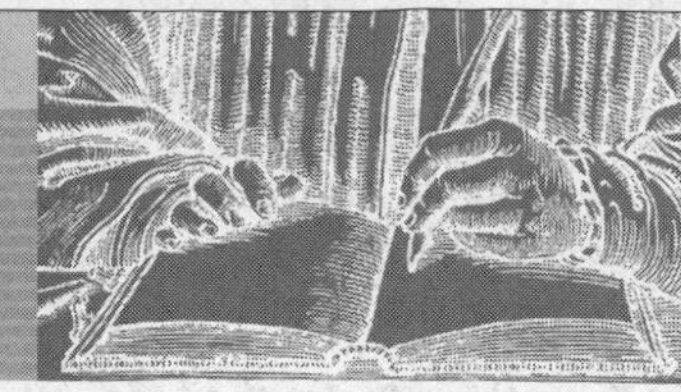

Job, Proverbs, and Ecclesiastes make up the wisdom literature of the Bible. Wisdom literature has a recognizable approach as well as a distinctive range of subject matter that makes it a separate department of study. In these books the term "wisdom" and its synonyms, such as "understanding," are used noticeably more often than in other parts of the Bible. These books can be distinguished from the Prophets and the histories of the Old Testament by the way truth is revealed in them. Like the historians, the wisdom writers rely on observation and study. But they make greater use of introspection and meditation than the historians. Unlike the historians, the sages do not discuss Israel's history. They say little or nothing about Moses, the Law, the kings, geography, or politics. Instead, the wisdom writers speak of the human condition as such, in its enduring aspects. They bring to it the perspective of the divine majesty and superintending providence, pondering the question of how the creature should think about the Creator. They give special attention to the problem of human suffering.

Wisdom literature resembles prophecy in the use of poetry and the expression of profound truths. But, in their role as messengers of God, the prophets transmit divine messages directed to specific situations. They also predict the future. The sages observed the world around them, and under the guidance of the Spirit drew conclusions about human nature and living a life that is pleasing to God.

Other poetic sections of the Bible, like the Psalms (Ps. 8:3, 4), may deal with themes similar to those found in wisdom literature, and such sections are commonly regarded as showing the presence or influence of the wisdom tradition. Indeed, wisdom is a kind of human tradition or culture. It is found not only in Israel but in other civilizations as well. A constituent part of all wisdom, in addition to its philosophy, is practical advice and teaching on how to live. Yet the wisdom of the Bible is distinctive, because in all its ways through the heights and depths of human experience it relies on the God of Abraham, the Father of Jesus Christ. Wisdom has its source and beginning in "the fear of the LORD" (Prov. 9:10), both in its ideas and equally in its methods and morals.

In His revelation through the sages, the Spirit of God ranges from direct and homely proverbs, to the puzzling, often difficult words of Ecclesiastes, and to the mysterious and sublime words of Job. It is often said that the parables of Jesus are allied to the wisdom tradition. This association shows that the proverbial, humble, and seemingly human origin of much wisdom literature is not an obstacle to perceiving its divine inspiration. On the contrary, it is the many-sided wisdom of God that is revealed in wisdom literature.

THE BOOK OF

Proverbs

AUTHOR

Proverbs is a collection of wise sayings from a number of authors. Solomon's name appears in 1:1; 10:1; 25:1. Chapter 30 is attributed to Agur, and ch. 31 to Lemuel. That Solomon was a key figure in the wisdom movement and wrote many proverbs is clear from 1 Kin. 4:29–34. Solomon's general influence upon the Book of Proverbs is considerable, and his direct authorship of much of the material need not be doubted. The statement in 1:1 ("The proverbs of Solomon") need not be taken, however, to assert more than the leading role of the king in the compilation. The Solomonic title may refer as much to the stamp of Solomon's character on the wisdom literature as to its direct authorship. While it is obvious that he did not write the whole book as we have it, 1:1–7 indicates that this is no haphazard collection, but a purposeful construction with certain aims.

DATE AND OCCASION

Nothing in the literary forms or content of Proverbs demands a dating later than the fall of Jerusalem and the Babylonian exile of the sixth century B.C. The whole work is consonant with that period, although when the book reached its present form is impossible to say. Parts of it are from the time of King Hezekiah (25:1).

CHARACTERISTICS AND THEMES

The Book of Proverbs displays two major forms of wisdom writing. In chs. 1–9 there are a number of longer constructions that are similar to the "instruction" of some early Egyptian literature. Some dependence in form and content should not surprise us, given the common concerns of wisdom in all cultures. Whether the form developed in schools for the elite (as in Egypt) or in the home (as was probably the case in Israel), the content is wisdom for life as it was taught to the youth by an elder. The instruction generally begins with an address ("My son"), followed by exhortations and commands with supporting explanations and encouragements.

The other major form in Proverbs is a one-sentence proverbial saying, found mainly in 10:1–22:16 and 25:1–29:27. These sayings are frequently given in a parallel form, in which the second line makes a direct contrast with the first, or in which the second line carries forward the idea contained in the first. The contrasting parallel is typically used to compare wisdom with folly and righteousness with wickedness.

Another prominent form is the numerical saying (6:16–19; 30:15, 16, 18, 19), which, particularly with the one-sentence sayings, appears to promote the perception of order in the complex issues and experiences of life. By groupings and comparisons of these the task of gaining and assessing knowledge proceeds so that we learn what the good life is and how to pursue it.

For additional discussion of the characteristics, themes, and poetic forms of Proverbs, see introductions to the Wisdom Literature and to Hebrew Poetry. Proverbs, like the Law of Moses, bears witness to Christ by portraying His person and work. The Law presents the righteousness and holiness of Christ, the great descendant of Abraham who would inherit God's covenant blessings and mediate them to all nations (Gal. 3:14). Proverbs and the other wisdom books display the wisdom and discernment of Christ. According to the New Testament, Jesus Christ is the wisdom of God incarnate (1 Cor. 1:24, 30; Col. 2:2, 3).

The Book of Proverbs does not touch on several of the more prominent religious themes in the Old Testament. But through dealing with what are often considered the more mundane areas of life, Proverbs teaches us that all of life is to be lived to the glory of the sovereign Creator. There is a moral order to all of creation, and violations of that order only lead to adverse consequences.

OUTLINE OF PROVERBS

- **I. Prologue: the Purpose of the Book (1:1–7)**
- **II. Wisdom's Instructions (1:8–9:18)**
  - A. *Recommendation of Wisdom (1:8, 9)*
  - B. *Warning Against Violence (1:10–19)*
  - C. *Rewards of Wisdom (1:20–33)*
  - D. *Wisdom as a Divine Gift and Human Task (ch. 2)*
  - E. *The Lord's Discipline (3:1–12)*
  - F. *Hymn to Wisdom (3:13–20)*
  - G. *Guidance in Life's Way (3:21–26)*
  - H. *Precepts on Human Relationships (3:27–35)*
  - I. *Commendations of Wisdom (ch. 4)*
  - J. *Warning Against Adultery (ch. 5)*
  - K. *Cautionary Instructions (6:1–19)*
  - L. *More Warnings Against Adultery (6:20–7:27)*
  - M. *Wisdom's Call and Self-commendation (ch. 8)*
  - N. *Competing Calls of Wisdom and Folly (ch. 9)*
- **III. Proverbs of Solomon (10:1–22:16)**
- **IV. Instructions of the Wise Men (22:17–24:22)**
- **V. More Sayings of the Wise Men (24:23–34)**
- **VI. More Proverbs of Solomon, Copied by Hezekiah's Men (chs. 25–29)**
- **VII. The Words of Agur (ch. 30)**
- **VIII. The Words of King Lemuel (ch. 31)**
  - A. *The Good King (31:1–9)*
  - B. *The Good Wife (31:10–31)*

The Beginning of Knowledge

1 [a]The proverbs of Solomon, son of David, king of Israel:

2 To know wisdom and instruction,
to understand words of insight,
3 to receive instruction in wise dealing,
in [b]righteousness, justice, and equity;
4 to give prudence to [c]the simple,
knowledge and [d]discretion to the youth—
5 Let the wise hear and [e]increase in learning,
and the one who understands obtain guidance,
6 to understand a proverb and a saying,
[f]the words of the wise and their [g]riddles.

Chapter 1
1 [a]ch. 10:1; 25:1; 1 Kin. 4:32; Eccles. 12:9
3 [b]ch. 2:9
4 [c]ch. 8:5; 14:15, 18 [d]ch. 2:11; 3:21
5 [e]ch. 9:9
6 [f]ch. 22:17; 26:23 [g]Judg. 14:12; Ps. 78:2

1:1 proverbs. The Hebrew word has a range of meanings, but is usually applied to an aphorism or maxim in a wisdom context. The prologue (1:1–7) applies to the whole book and the variety of wisdom sayings it contains, all broadly classified as "proverbs."

Solomon. Although Solomon wrote many proverbs (1 Kin. 4:32), the words of sages other than Solomon are apparently included under this heading (e.g., Agur, 30:1; and Lemuel, 31:1). Even in the materials attributed to Solomon, something other than direct authorship may be involved. The roots of proverbial traditions in folk experience make it unlikely that Solomon was the exclusive originator of all the proverbs that he wrote down (Introduction: Author).

1:2–4 Explicit reference to the purpose behind this collection suggests that some kind of formal educational use was being made of such material, although evidence for wisdom schools in Israel is not strong.

1:2 wisdom. The purpose of Proverbs is to guide the reader into wisdom, a word with many nuances. It is related to the intellect and the control of human behavior. It is a way of thinking about reality that enables one to pursue what is good in life. Through wisdom, God reveals what the values of life are and how they may be achieved.

instruction. The word suggests moral and intellectual discipline. It often means the learning of wisdom.

insight. Or discernment, the ability to read between the lines and make correct distinctions.

1:3 righteousness, justice, and equity. These words can be used in religious and ethical contexts as well as in temporal affairs. At times, biblical wisdom seems to concern itself with worldly matters, but it always does so within the framework of divine design in the created order.

1:4 prudence. That is, shrewdness.

simple. The word is paralleled in this verse by "youth"; it refers to the untutored and inexperienced, not those lacking intellectual powers. Wisdom is a matter of practical godliness.

discretion. The word suggests making right decisions with understanding.

1:5 increase. Wisdom was institutionalized in the ancient culture in that the wise called upon people to improve their wisdom. Succeeding generations were to learn from those who went before (v. 8). Note the typical parallel structure of this verse in which almost synonymous phrases are joined.

guidance. This Hebrew word, used only in Proverbs and Job, means to guide, steer, or direct. It highlights the importance of right thinking and experience in decision making.

1:6 These different words may be used synonymously, as in Hab. 2:6, but probably here they are distinct forms of wisdom sayings, having as a common characteristic an enigma that challenges the intellect (1:1 note).

saying. Sometimes rendered "parable." Actually the parables of Jesus are somewhat different from what is found in Proverbs, although they show the influence of wisdom literature.

riddles. These are probably a broad but identifiable type of wisdom literature. The word is used of Samson's riddle (Judg. 14:12–19), of an allegory (Ezek. 17:2), and of the sayings used to test Solomon (1 Kin. 10:1).

7 [h]The fear of the LORD is the beginning
of knowledge;
fools despise wisdom and
instruction.

The Enticement of Sinners

8 [i]Hear, my son, your father's
instruction,
and forsake not your mother's
teaching,
9 for they are [j]a graceful garland for
your head
and [k]pendants for your neck.
10 My son, if sinners [l]entice you,
do not consent.
11 If they say, "Come with us, [m]let us
lie in wait for blood;
[n]let us ambush the innocent
without reason;
12 like Sheol let us [o]swallow them alive,
and whole, like [p]those who go
down to the pit;
13 we shall find all precious goods,
we shall fill our houses with
plunder;
14 throw in your lot among us;
we will all have one purse"—
15 my son, [q]do not walk in the way
with them;
[r]hold back your foot from their
paths,
16 for [s]their feet run to evil,
and they make haste to shed
blood.
17 [t]For in vain is a net spread
in the sight of any bird,
18 but these men [u]lie in wait for their
own blood;
they [u]set an ambush for their own
lives.
19 [v]Such are the ways of everyone who is
[w]greedy for unjust gain;
[x]it takes away the life of its
possessors.

The Call of Wisdom

20 [y]Wisdom cries aloud in the
street,
in the markets she raises her
voice;
21 at the head of the noisy streets she
cries out;
at [z]the entrance of the city gates
she speaks:

7 [h]ch. 9:10; [ch. 15:33]; See Job 28:28
8 [i]ch. 6:20; [Ps. 34:11; Eph. 6:1, 2]
9 [j]ch. 4:9; [ch. 3:22] [k][Gen. 41:42; Dan. 5:29]
10 [l]ch. 16:29
11 [m]ver. 18; ch. 12:6; Jer. 5:26 [n]ver. 18; Ps. 10:8; 64:5
12 [o]Ps. 56:1; 124:3; [Num. 16:32, 33] [p]Ps. 28:1
15 [q]ch. 4:14; 24:1; Ps. 1:1 [r][Ps. 119:101]
16 [s]ch. 6:18; Isai. 59:7; [Rom. 3:15]
17 [t][Job 40:24]
18 [u]ver. 11
19 [v][Job 8:13] [w]ch. 15:27 [x][1 Tim. 6:10]
20 [y]ch. 8:1; 9:3; [John 7:37]
21 [z]ch. 8:3

1:7 The fear of the LORD. This idea is the controlling principle of Proverbs, and is ancient Israel's decisive contribution to the human quest for knowledge and understanding. The fear of the Lord is the only basis of true knowledge. This "fear" is not distrustful terror of God, but rather the reverent awe and worshipful response of faith to the God who reveals Himself as Creator, Savior, and Judge.

Although Israel's covenant relationship with God receives little overt attention in Proverbs, the use of the divine name most closely associated with the covenant, the LORD (Hebrew *Yahweh*, Ex. 3:15; 6:3 and notes), is significant. It indicates that God's redemptive covenant with His people and the special revelation that accompany it are foundational for true wisdom. In Deuteronomy, "fear the LORD" means living by the stipulations of the covenant in grateful response to God's redemptive grace (Deut. 6:2, 24). The temple built by Solomon later became the visible expression of Israel's covenant relationship with the Lord, which again is described as the "fear" of the Lord (1 Kin. 8:40, 43). There is an important link through Solomon and the temple between biblical wisdom and the covenant theology found elsewhere in the Old Testament.

is the beginning of knowledge. See also 2:4–6; 9:10; 15:33; Job 28:28; Ps. 111:10. The Hebrew means either the starting point of knowledge, or its basic, ruling principle. The latter is in view here. While in His common grace God enables unbelievers to know much about the world, only the fear of the Lord enables one to know what anything means ultimately. Relying on this light, wisdom pursues the task of reflecting on human experience. See "The Wisdom and Will of God" at Dan. 2:20.

1:8, 9 The instruction form of ancient Near Eastern wisdom literature typically begins with a call for attentiveness. Father and mother were both involved in home instruction.

1:8 instruction. See note 3:1.

1:9 graceful garland . . . pendants. These metaphors portray the effect of wisdom in beautifying one's life.

1:10–19 These verses make up another unit in the instruction form. Possibly this form was a teaching tool in more formal education outside the home as wise men taught their pupils. The conditional "if" clauses (vv. 10, 11) indicate the situations to which this wisdom applies. The command in v. 15 is supported by the reasons for it in vv. 16–19.

1:12 Sheol. The realm of death is here depicted as ready to swallow its victims. Elsewhere this poetic term denotes a realm where corruption is father and the worm is mother (Job 17:13, 14), a domain with gates (Is. 38:10). It is a land of no return (Job 7:9), silence (Ps. 94:17), darkness (Ps. 143:3), and forgetfulness (Ps. 88:11, 12). See 9:18 note; Is. 14:9–11 note.

1:13 precious goods. Proverbs does not forbid or discourage wealth—only the use of evil to get it. However, the ultimate wealth is wisdom itself (2:4; 3:13–16; Job 28:12–19).

1:15 my son. After the extended conditional clause (vv. 10–14) the address is repeated to reinforce the command to avoid evil people.

1:16 This verse is almost identical with Is. 59:7 and is partly quoted in Rom. 3:15.

1:17 in vain . . . bird. This saying is introduced to strengthen the reasons for the author's counsel. The apparent meaning is that even a bird will avoid a trap once it has knowledge of it. Those who are tempted should do the same.

1:19 Such folly is contrary to the true order of the world which, though fallen, is still under God's sovereign rule. This expression of inevitable retribution is based on the observable order of causes and consequence. Apparent interruptions in this pattern prompted other biblical writers to address the problem of the prosperous wicked and the suffering righteous (Job; Ps. 73).

1:20 Wisdom is portrayed as an open-air preacher similar to the caller in Is. 55. Personified as a woman, she calls on the simple to repent of folly and to seek wisdom before it is too late. Personification of wisdom is found also in 3:14–18; 8:1–36; 9:1–12.

1:21 gates. The town gate was the public forum for counsel and judgment (Deut. 22:15; 25:7; Ruth 4:1, 11; 2 Sam. 19:8). This is the fitting location for the figure of wisdom to call people to heed her counsel.

22 "How long, O [a]simple ones, will you
love being simple?
How long will [b]scoffers delight in
their scoffing
and fools [c]hate knowledge?
23 If you turn at my reproof,[1]
behold, I will [d]pour out my spirit to
you;
I will make my words known to
you.
24 [e]Because I have called and [f]you
refused to listen,
have [g]stretched out my hand and
no one has heeded,
25 because you have [h]ignored all my
counsel
and [i]would have none of my
reproof,
26 I also [j]will laugh at your calamity;
I will mock when [k]terror strikes
you,
27 when terror strikes you like [l]a
storm
and your calamity comes like a
whirlwind,
when distress and anguish come
upon you.
28 [m]Then they will call upon me, but I
will not answer;
they will seek me diligently but
will not find me.
29 Because they [c]hated knowledge
and [n]did not choose the fear of the
LORD,
30 [h]would have none of my counsel
and [i]despised all my reproof,
31 therefore they shall eat [o]the fruit of
their way,
and have [p]their fill of their own
devices.
32 For the simple are killed by [q]their
turning away,
and [r]the complacency of fools
destroys them;
33 but [s]whoever listens to me will dwell
secure
and will be [t]at ease, without dread
of disaster."

The Value of Wisdom

2 [u]My son, [v]if you receive my words
and treasure up my commandments
with you,
2 making your ear attentive to wisdom
and inclining your heart to
understanding;
3 yes, if you call out for insight
and raise your voice [w]for
understanding,
4 if you seek it like [x]silver
and search for it as for [y]hidden
treasures,

22 [a]See ver. 4 [b]See Ps. 1:1 [c]ver. 29; ch. 5:12; [Job 21:14]
23 [d]Joel 2:28; Acts 2:17
24 [e]Isai. 65:12; 66:4; Jer. 7:13 [f]Zech. 7:11 [g]Rom. 10:21
25 [h]See Ps. 107:11 [i][Ps. 81:11; Luke 7:30]
26 [j]See Ps. 2:4 [k]ch. 10:24; Jer. 48:43; 49:5
27 [l][Zeph. 1:15]
28 [m]See 1 Sam. 8:18; Job 27:9
29 [c][See ver. 22 above] [n][Job 21:14]
30 [h][See ver. 25 above] [i][See ver. 25 above]
31 [o]Jer. 6:19 [p]ch. 14:14; Isai. 3:11; [Job 4:8]
32 [q]Jer. 2:19 [r][Ps. 73:18, 19]
33 [s][Ps. 25:12, 13] [t]Ps. 112:7, 8
Chapter 2
1 [u]See ch. 1:8 [v][ch. 4:1, 10, 20; 7:1]
3 [w]ch. 4:1, 5, 7
4 [x]ch. 3:14 [y]Job 3:21; [Matt. 13:44]

[1] Or *Will you turn away at my reproof?*

1:22 simple ones. See v. 4 and note. There has been a development of thought. At issue is not merely gaining more insight, but a deliberate choice between two ways. Wisdom and folly, righteousness and wickedness, are constantly opposed in Proverbs as the only two options for life (cf. Matt. 7:24–27).

scoffers. The precise meaning of this word, used mostly in Proverbs, is difficult to determine. The mocker, or scoffer, is a person who resists the discipline of the wise (9:7, 8; 13:1; 14:6; 21:11).

fools. Thick, unteachable people.

knowledge. See 1:7. In wisdom literature, "knowledge" is often a synonym for wisdom.

1:23 my spirit. Proverbs recognizes wisdom as both a divine gift and a human task. The former is seen in 1:7, where the fear of the Lord grows from the grace of God in redemption. Redemption involves renewal of the mind as well as regeneration of the soul (Rom. 12:1, 2; 1 Cor. 1:18–2:6).

1:24 you refused. The rejection of wisdom's evangel has its parallels in the rejection of God's grace by Israel.

1:25 counsel. Here wisdom speaks with full authority. As God's counsel, her counsel and advice is not open to debate (2:6; 8:14).

1:28 I will not answer. True wisdom is an aspect of God's saving grace, and there comes a point of no return for those who reject it. This truth reinforces the urgency of the message. No one can expect God's favor and at the same time scorn the gifts He offers (Deut. 1:45; 1 Sam. 28:6; Ps. 18:41).

1:29 knowledge. This word is a synonym for wisdom, and is explained here by the phrase parallel with it, "the fear of the LORD." Wisdom comes from above (James 3:17), as God's gift in redemptive revelation. This is true even when it must be desired and strived for (2:4–6; Heb. 5:7, 8; James 1:5).

1:31 fruit. The relationship between deed and outcome is observable in natural cause and effect. Here the image is not one of pleasure after a full meal, but disgust at being glutted.

1:32 turning away. Indifference or willful neglect.

complacency of fools. The ignorant self-satisfaction of the willfully unteachable, who see no need to learn anything from anyone.

1:33 This verse stands in direct contrast with v. 32. Wisdom brings life and security. To reject wisdom is to reject all that promotes life.

2:1–22 Although this instruction lacks the usual imperatives, the emphatic force is indicated by the subject matter—wisdom that delivers from death. The consequences of accepting wisdom are knowing God and the blessings of life (vv. 5, 9, 21). The two aspects of wisdom—divine gift and human task—are clearly seen (e.g., vv. 4, 6).

2:2 heart. The seat of reason and the will. Today's popular distinction between heart knowledge and head knowledge does not apply here. The usual Old Testament contrast is between a formal or outward compliance lacking true assent of will, and willing, whole-hearted compliance.

2:3 call out . . . raise your voice. In contrast with the lack of response to wisdom's call in 1:20–23.

2:4 hidden treasures. Note the similar image used by Jesus in Matt. 13:44.

5 then [z]you will understand the fear of
the LORD
and find the knowledge of God.
6 For [a]the LORD gives wisdom;
from his mouth come knowledge
and understanding;
7 he stores up sound wisdom for the
upright;
he is [b]a shield to those who [c]walk
in integrity,
8 guarding the paths of justice
and [d]watching over the way of his
[e]saints.
9 [f]Then you will understand
[g]righteousness and justice
and equity, every good path;
10 for wisdom will come into your
heart,
and knowledge will be pleasant to
your soul;
11 [h]discretion will [i]watch over you,
understanding will guard you,
12 delivering you from the way
of evil,
from men of perverted speech,
13 who forsake the paths of
uprightness
to [j]walk in the ways of darkness,
14 who [k]rejoice in doing evil
and [l]delight in the perverseness of
evil,
15 men whose [m]paths are crooked,
[n]and who are [o]devious in their
ways.
16 So [p]you will be delivered from the
forbidden[1] woman,
from [q]the adulteress[2] with [r]her
smooth words,
17 who forsakes [s]the companion of her
youth
and forgets [t]the covenant of her
God;
18 [u]for her house sinks down to
death,
and her paths to the departed;[3]
19 none who go to her come back,
nor do they regain the paths
of life.
20 So you will walk in the way of the
good
and keep to the paths of the
righteous.
21 For the upright [v]will inhabit the
land,
and those with integrity will
remain in it,
22 but the wicked will be [w]cut off from
the land,
and the treacherous will be [x]rooted
out of it.

5 [z][Ps. 25:14; John 7:17; 14:21]
6 [a]Job 32:8
7 [b]ch. 30:5; See Ps. 3:3 [c]Ps. 84:11
8 [d]1 Sam. 2:9; Ps. 66:9; 97:10 [e]See Ps. 30:4
9 [f][ver. 5] [g]ch. 1:3
11 [h]ch. 1:4 [i]ch. 6:22
13 [j]Ps. 82:5; [John 3:19, 20]
14 [k]Jer. 11:15; [ch. 10:23] [l][Ps. 50:18; Rom. 1:32]
15 [m]Ps. 125:5; [ch. 21:8] [n]ch. 14:2 [o]ch. 3:32
16 [p]ch. 7:5 [q]ch. 6:24; 23:27 [r]ch. 6:24; Ps. 5:9
17 [s]Jer. 3:4; [Ps. 55:13] [t][Mal. 2:14, 15]
18 [u]ch. 7:27
21 [v]ch. 10:30
22 [w]See Ps. 37:38 [x]ch. 15:25; Deut. 28:63; Ps. 52:5

[1] Hebrew *strange* [2] Hebrew *foreign woman* [3] Hebrew *to the Rephaim*

2:5 you will understand . . . LORD. In 1:7 the fear of the Lord is the beginning of knowledge, and here it is the goal. There is no discrepancy, since wisdom is both a gift and a task. God gives knowledge of Himself in redemptive revelation. Starting here, the wise person takes up the task of learning more wisdom and of knowing God, always moving toward the goal of knowing Him more perfectly and being conformed to the image of His Son.

2:6 the LORD gives wisdom. No matter how much we are engaged in the task of searching for knowledge through our human experience in the world, the source of all truth is God. He must provide the wisdom necessary for the proper interpretation of reality (3:5).

from his mouth. Although their emphasis is different, both Deuteronomy and Proverbs recognize that the underlying foundation of knowledge is the Word of God (Deut. 8:3). Even before sin had entered the world, Adam and Eve needed God's Word in order to know themselves and their relationship to creation (Gen. 1:28–30).

2:7 The character of God, which the wise come to know (v. 5), is the basis of morality. Standards of integrity and righteousness are expressions of wisdom.

2:8 his saints. These are people who show that they possess the fear of the Lord by imitating His covenant love.

2:9 every good path. The wisdom literature is important to our understanding of God's guidance of our lives. It points to the task of gaining wisdom so that we can make decisions that are responsible and consistent with our covenant status as God's people (1 Pet. 2:9).

2:11 discretion. Or, "resourcefulness."

2:12 Right moral discernment will save us from those who scorn wisdom.

perverted speech. Words of rebellion that overturn truth.

2:16 forbidden woman. Adultery is a radical departure from God's order for human relationships (5:1–23; 6:20–29; 7:1–27). The Hebrew term is "foreign" or "strange" woman. In this context it means a woman who is foreign to the proper marital relationship, a harlot or adulteress.

2:17 companion. That is, her husband.

covenant of her God. If the "forbidden woman" is a non-Israelite (v. 16 note), "covenant" may refer to a marriage witnessed to by some foreign god. More likely, the woman is an Israelite who transgresses the requirements of the covenant given at Sinai, particularly the commandment against adultery (Ex. 20:14).

2:18 death. In wisdom literature, "life" is not mere existence, but a way characterized by true relationships that conform to God's design. "Death" is not only the end of physical life, but an irreversible descent into the disorder of moral perversity (cf. 5:23, where "dies" is parallel with "led astray").

2:19 none . . . come back. This note of finality highlights the seriousness of breaching standards that are not merely social customs, but creation ordinances of God.

2:20–22 The promise of land was a basic part of the covenant God made with Abraham, Moses, and the people (Gen. 13:15 and note; Ex. 20:12; Deut. 1:8; 26:1–9). These promises foreshadow the promise of eternal life (Heb. 11:16). The conditional aspect of the covenant is reflected here (Gen. 17:2 note)—the upright and the wise inherit the land, but the wicked are removed (Deut. 28).

Trust in the Lord with All Your Heart

3 [y]My son, do not forget my teaching,
[z]but let your heart keep my
commandments,
2 for [a]length of days and years of life
and [b]peace they will add to you.

3 Let not [c]steadfast love and
[d]faithfulness forsake you;
[e]bind them around your neck;
[f]write them on the tablet of your
heart.
4 So you will [g]find favor and [h]good
success[1]
in the sight of God and man.

5 [i]Trust in the Lord with all your
heart,
and [j]do not lean on your own
understanding.
6 In all your ways [k]acknowledge him,
and he [l]will make straight your
paths.
7 [m]Be not wise in your own eyes;
[n]fear the Lord, and turn away from
evil.
8 It will be [o]healing to your flesh[2]
and [p]refreshment[3] to your bones.

9 Honor the Lord with your wealth
and with [q]the firstfruits of all your
produce;
10 then your [r]barns will be filled with
plenty,
and your vats will be bursting with
wine.

11 [s]My son, do not despise the Lord's
discipline
or be weary of his reproof,
12 for the Lord reproves him whom he
loves,
as [t]a father the son in whom he
delights.

Blessed Is the One Who Finds Wisdom

13 [u]Blessed is the one who finds wisdom,
and the one who gets understanding,
14 [v]for the gain from her is better than
gain from silver
and her profit better than [w]gold.

Chapter 3
1 [y]See ch. 1:8 [z]Deut. 8:1; 30:16, 20
2 [a]ver. 16; ch. 4:10; 9:11; 10:27; See Ps. 91:16 [b]ch. 1:33; Ps. 119:165
3 [c][Ps. 85:10] [d][ch. 20:28; Isai. 59:14] [e][ch. 1:9; 6:21; 7:3] [f]ch. 7:3; [Jer. 17:1; 2 Cor. 3:3]
4 [g][1 Sam. 2:26; Luke 2:52; Rom. 14:18] [h]See Ps. 111:10
5 [i]Ps. 37:3, 5 [j][Jer. 9:23]
6 [k]1 Chr. 28:9 [l][Ps. 73:24]
7 [m][Rom. 12:16]; See ch. 12:15 [n]Job 1:1; 28:28
8 [o][ch. 4:22] [p]See Job 21:24
9 [q]Ex. 23:19; 34:26; Deut. 26:2
10 [r]Deut. 28:8
11 [s]Cited Heb. 12:5, 6; See Job 5:17
12 [t]Deut. 8:5; [1 Cor. 11:32]
13 [u]ch. 8:34, 35 **14** [v]See Job 28:15-19 [w]ch. 8:10, 19; 16:16; Ps. 19:10

[1] Or *repute* [2] Hebrew *navel* [3] Or *medicine*

3:1–12 These verses are probably a single unit of instruction, with the typical "my son" address repeated in v. 11. The unit contains the usual imperatives (vv. 1, 3, 5–7, 9, 11) and motivating clauses (vv. 2, 4, 8, 10). Verse 12 explains the purpose of the Lord's discipline, encouraging the wise to follow the precept of v. 11.

3:1 teaching. The Hebrew word for "teaching," *torah*, has the basic meaning of "instruction" and in Jewish tradition designates the Pentateuch. Wisdom's instruction, while not to be confused with the precepts of the Law of Moses, is likewise authoritative.

commandments. This word is also found in the law. As is typical of the parallel phrases of Hebrew poetry, the second half of the verse repeats the idea of the first half, clarifying it or expanding on it. Essentially, this verse means to memorize the commands and then put them into practice.

3:2 length of days. The normal expectation is that wisdom will lead to a long, prosperous life, which is the blessing of God (Ex. 20:12).

peace. Hebrew *shalom*. The term denotes general well-being, a harmony of relationships, wholeness, and health (v. 8). In the Old Testament, the blessings of God are seen primarily in terms of this present life. It was not easy to reconcile this perspective with the suffering of the righteous or the prosperity of the wicked. The revelation that was to come with Christ and especially His resurrection from the dead was still far in the future.

3:3 steadfast love and faithfulness. The Hebrew phrase indicates clearly that wisdom is being advanced in a covenantal framework. The instruction (v. 1) is practical teaching for life based on the character of God revealed in His Word.

bind . . . neck. This metaphor indicates that wisdom will beautify one's life.
write . . . heart. The sense is the same as v. 1. Make them part of you by committing them to memory and then conforming your will to them.

3:5 Trust in the Lord. Rely entirely upon the Lord's Word and promises as revealed through the sage (2:6; 16:20). See note 1:7.

lean . . . understanding. The contrast is between the perception of reality that submits to God's revealed Word as the authority for all truth, and a perception that assumes human conjecture to have that authority.

3:6 acknowledge him. This is the practical expression of the mind that submits to God and knows Him.

he will make straight your paths. The Lord will guide you to the final goal of life. God gives wisdom and with it the task of making wise decisions; these are the two aspects of guidance in wisdom teaching. There is no hint of guidance that bypasses the duty of making decisions. But human decisions do not overrule the protection of God's providence (Gen. 50:20, 21; Ps. 103:14).

3:7 wise in your own eyes. The phrase summarizes the idea that the human mind with its intellect and reason is independently capable of reaching a true understanding of reality, without any dependence upon God's revelation.

3:8 True wisdom is life-affirming in the most practical ways.

3:9, 10 Honoring God with the right use of material things expresses gratitude for His favor and recognizes that He controls the natural order and its processes.

3:9 firstfruits. This first part of the annual harvest was given to the priests (Lev. 23:10; Num. 18:12, 13).

3:11 discipline. Although the instruction of God will require chastisement, this correction is not calculated to harm or anger His children. But because chastisement is suffering, specific encouragement not to rebel against it is necessary.

3:12 Heb. 12:3–11 explains that God's correction is better than that of an earthly father; for the comparison, see Luke 11:11–13. Chastisement is not the main content of God's fatherly teaching; the instruction of Proverbs is designed for people who want to hear it (2:3–5; 4:5–9; 8:11, 17).

3:13–20 This section is formed more as a hymn in praise of wisdom than as a piece of instruction (cf. Ps. 1). But see 8:32–36 for a practical conclusion.

3:13 Blessed. The word does not mean merely a subjective feeling. It is found almost exclusively in the Psalms and the wisdom literature, describing the life that enjoys God's grace and favor.

3:14, 15 Job 28 describes wisdom as a treasure. Psalm 19:10 refers specifically to the revealed law.

15 She is more precious than [x]jewels,
and [y]nothing you desire can
compare with her.
16 [z]Long life is in her right hand;
in her left hand are [a]riches and
honor.
17 Her [b]ways are ways of pleasantness,
and all her paths are peace.
18 She is [c]a tree of life to those who [d]lay
hold of her;
those who hold her fast are called
blessed.

19 [e]The LORD by wisdom founded the earth;
by understanding [e]he established
the heavens;
20 by his knowledge [f]the deeps broke
open,
and [g]the clouds drop down the dew.

21 My son, [h]do not lose sight of these—
keep sound wisdom and discretion,
22 and they will be [i]life for your soul
and [j]adornment for your neck.
23 [k]Then you will walk on your way
securely,
[l]and your foot will not stumble.
24 [m]If you lie down, you will not be afraid;
when you lie down, [n]your sleep
will be sweet.
25 [o]Do not be afraid of sudden terror
or of [p]the ruin[1] of the wicked,
when it comes,
26 for the LORD will be your confidence
and will [q]keep your foot from
being caught.

27 [r]Do not withhold good from those to
whom it is due,[2]
when it is in your power to do it.
28 [s]Do not say to your neighbor, "Go,
and come again,
tomorrow I will give it"—when
you have it with you.
29 [t]Do not plan evil against your neighbor,
who [u]dwells trustingly beside you.
30 [v]Do not contend with a man for no
reason,
when he has done you no harm.
31 [w]Do not envy [x]a man of violence
and do not choose any of his ways,
32 for [y]the devious person is an
abomination to the LORD,
but the upright are [z]in his
confidence.
33 [a]The LORD's curse is on the house of
the wicked,
but he [b]blesses the dwelling of the
righteous.
34 Toward the [c]scorners he [d]is scornful,
[e]but to the humble he gives favor.[3]
35 The wise will inherit honor,
but fools get[4] disgrace.

A Father's Wise Instruction

4 [f]Hear, O sons, a father's instruction,
and be attentive, that you may [g]gain[5]
insight,

15 [x]Job 28:18 [y]ch. 8:11
16 [z]ver. 2 [a]ch. 8:18; 22:4
17 [b][Matt. 11:29, 30]
18 [c]ch. 11:30; 13:12; 15:4; Gen. 2:9; 3:22; Rev. 2:7; 22:2 [d]ch. 4:13
19 [e]ch. 8:27; Ps. 104:5, 24; 136:5
20 [f]Gen. 7:11; [Job 38:8] [g]Job 36:28
21 [h]ch. 4:21
22 [i]See ch. 4:22 [j][ch. 1:9]
23 [k]ch. 10:9; [ch. 28:18; Ps. 91:11] [l]ch. 4:12; Ps. 91:12
24 [m][ch. 6:22; Ps. 3:5; 4:8]; See Job 11:19 [n]Jer. 31:26
25 [o][1 Pet. 3:14]; See Ps. 91:5 [p][Job 5:21]
26 [q]See 1 Sam. 2:9
27 [r]Gal. 6:10
28 [s][Lev. 19:13; Deut. 24:15]
29 [t]ch. 6:14; 12:20; 14:22 [u][Judg. 18:7, 27]
30 [v][Rom. 12:18]
31 [w]See Ps. 37:1 [x]Ps. 18:48; 140:1
32 [y]ch. 2:15 [z]See Job 29:4
33 [a]Ps. 37:22; Zech. 5:4; Mal. 2:2; See Lev. 26:14-39 [b][Job 8:6]
34 [c]See Ps. 1:1 [d][Ps. 18:26; James 4:6; 1 Pet. 5:5; See Ps. 138:6 [e][Ps. 18:26; James 4:6; 1 Pet. 5:5]; See Ps. 138:6
Chapter 4 1 [f]ch. 1:8; [ch. 5:7; 7:24; 8:33; Ps. 34:11] [g]ch. 2:2

1 Hebrew *storm* 2 Hebrew *Do not withhold good from its owners* 3 Or *grace* 4 The meaning of the Hebrew word is uncertain 5 Hebrew *know*

3:16, 17 See v. 2 and notes.

3:18 tree of life. This is probably not a specific allusion to the tree of life in Gen. 2:9, though the author would have known of it. The flourishing tree was a common figure in the literature of the time for continuing blessings. The metaphor is used again in 11:30; 13:12; 15:4. More important is the theme of "life" in Proverbs. "Life" in the Bible is essentially linked to our relationship with God. Disruption of the proper relationship with God, the source of life, leads to death (Gen. 2:17). Wisdom is concerned with proper relationships with God, other people, and with nature.

3:19, 20 Wisdom, understanding, and knowledge belong to God and find expression in the act of creation (8:22–31). The writer points to the purposefulness and design of creation. The order of creation is not totally destroyed by sin, and the theology of creation is an important part of wisdom literature.

3:21–26 This collection of sayings centers on the theme of guidance in life's way.

3:21 See note 1:4.

3:22 See notes on vv. 2, 3.

3:23 Again guidance is seen in terms of making wise decisions.

3:24 Part of wisdom is the avoidance of life-threatening situations, not by refusing to face danger when necessary, but by pursuing right relationships and an orderly existence.

3:27–35 The section begins with a series of commandments about certain abuses in human relationships (vv. 27–31). These are followed by clauses explaining the Lord's direct interest in the morality of these precepts (vv. 32–35).

3:32 Devious persons are alienated from God, but those who are righteous enjoy intimacy with the Lord.

3:33 Here the typical proverbial contrast between the righteous and the wicked (cf. 10:2, 3, 6, 7, 11, 16) is related to God's blessings and curses. This parallels the covenant theology of Deuteronomy, in which faithfulness is rewarded by the blessings of God (Deut. 11:26–29; 28:1–19).

4:1–27 This chapter most naturally divides into three instructional sayings, each beginning with the usual address of father to son (vv. 1, 10, 20). The first saying sees wisdom as a most precious acquisition (vv. 1–9), the second as the path to true life (vv. 10–19), and the third as the way of uprightness (vv. 20–27). There is no direct reference to religion.

Wisdom traditions are shared by peoples of different cultures and religions. See notes 22:17–24:22. Solomon discussed wisdom with people from other nations (1 Kin. 4:29–34; 10:1–7), showing how certain features of wisdom were shared across national and religious boundaries. In Israel, the insights of empirical wisdom were used in the framework of the covenant relationship and cannot be separated from special revelation (1:7 and notes).

2 for I give you good [h]precepts;
do not forsake my teaching.
3 When I was a son with my father,
[i]tender, [j]the only one in the sight
of my mother,
4 he [k]taught me and said to me,
[l]"Let your heart hold fast my words;
[m]keep my commandments, and live.
5 [n]Get wisdom; get [g]insight;
do not forget, and do not turn
away from the words of my
mouth.
6 Do not forsake her, and she will
keep you;
[o]love her, and she will guard you.
7 [p]The beginning of wisdom is this: Get
wisdom,
and whatever you get, get [g]insight.
8 Prize her highly, and she will exalt you;
she will [q]honor you [r]if you
embrace her.
9 She will place on your head [s]a
graceful garland;
she will bestow on you a beautiful
crown."

10 [f]Hear, [t]my son, and accept my words,
that [u]the years of your life may be
many.
11 I have [v]taught you the way of wisdom;
I have led you in the paths of
uprightness.
12 When you walk, [w]your step will not
be hampered,
and [x]if you run, you will not
stumble.

2 [h]Job 11:4
3 [i]See 1 Chr. 22:5 [j]Zech. 12:10
4 [k]1 Chr. 28:9; [Eph. 6:4] [l][ch. 3:1] [m]ch. 7:2; Lev. 18:5; Isai. 55:3
5 [n]ch. 2:2 [g][See ver. 1 above]
6 [o][2 Thess. 2:10]
7 [p][ch. 1:7] [g][See ver. 1 above]
8 [q]1 Sam. 2:30 [r][S. of S. 2:6]
9 [s]ch. 1:9
10 [f][See ver. 1 above] [t]ch. 2:1 [u]See ch. 3:2
11 [v]See 1 Sam. 12:23
12 [w][Job 18:7; Ps. 18:36; 119:45] [x]ch. 3:23
13 [y]ch. 3:18 [z]ver. 22; [John 1:4; 1 John 5:12]
14 [a]ch. 1:15; Ps. 1:1
16 [b][Ps. 36:4]
17 [c][Amos 2:8]
18 [d]Job 11:17; 22:28; Isai. 60:3; 62:1, 2; Dan. 12:3 [e]2 Sam. 23:4; See Ps. 97:11 [f][Ps. 84:7] [g][1 John 3:2]
19 [h]1 Sam. 2:9; Isai. 59:9,10; Jer. 23:12; John 12:35; [Job 18:5] [i][Matt. 6:23] [j][John 11:10; 1 John 2:10]

13 [y]Keep hold of instruction; do not
let go;
guard her, for she is your [z]life.
14 [a]Do not enter the path of the wicked,
and do not walk in the way of the
evil.
15 Avoid it; do not go on it;
turn away from it and pass on.
16 For they [b]cannot sleep unless they
have done wrong;
they are robbed of sleep unless
they have made someone
stumble.
17 For they eat the bread of
wickedness
[c]and drink the wine of violence.
18 But [d]the path of the righteous is like
[e]the light of dawn,
which shines [f]brighter and brighter
until [g]full day.
19 [h]The way of the wicked is like deep
[i]darkness;
they do not know over what they
[j]stumble.

20 [k]My son, be attentive to my words;
incline your ear to my sayings.
21 [l]Let them not escape from your
sight;
[m]keep them within your heart.
22 For they are [n]life to those who find
them,
and healing to all their[1] flesh.

20 [k]ver.10 21 [l]ch. 3:21 [m][ch. 2:1] 22 [n]ver. 13; ch. 8:35; 21:21; Deut. 32:47; [1 Tim. 4:8]

1 Hebrew *his*

4:2 precepts. Or "teaching." The Hebrew term emphasizes the receptive activity of the learner.

4:3, 4 The wise continue the tradition of wisdom by passing on to succeeding generations the wisdom they learned from their parents. Age and experience are not absolute authorities, but they are important and must be highly regarded (Lev. 19:32).

4:4 live. See notes 2:18 and 3:2.

4:6 Note the parallel structure in this verse, where the second line says almost the same as the first, yet with some development of thought. "Do not forsake" becomes the positive injunction to "love." Wisdom is far more than an accumulation of facts. It involves trust and commitment.

4:7 The beginning of wisdom. As translated the verse means, "Wisdom is of the first importance, do not neglect it." Another possible sense is that "Wisdom is first in line" for the learner. Wisdom is ready, and the one who wishes to learn may begin immediately.

whatever you get. Jesus used a similar saying about how one should seek the kingdom of God (Matt. 13:45, 46).

4:9 See note 1:9.

4:10 See note 3:2.

4:11 The metaphor of life as a way or path is common in Israelite wisdom.

4:13 she is your life. Life cannot exist without wisdom. In the New Testament, Christ is called our wisdom (1 Cor. 1:30) and our life (Col. 3:4).

4:14 path of the wicked. Wisdom typically contrasts opposing ways and ideas (especially in the concise proverbs of chs. 10–22). This teaching device accentuates the path of wisdom by opposing various aspects of it to the path of folly and evil. Here vv. 11–13 contrast with vv. 14–17, and v. 18 with v. 19.

4:16 cannot sleep. Evil is like an addictive drug. Those who embrace it find that without their daily dose they are unable to sleep.

4:17 eat . . . drink. Wickedness and violence become their staple food.

4:18, 19 These verses use imagery of an ever-increasing light to characterize righteousness, and an impenetrable gloom for wickedness (John 8:12; Eph. 5:8–13).

4:20–27 This instruction contrasts the two ways of wisdom and folly without using those terms. The emphasis is on concentration of mind and attention to the wisdom teaching, which leads to life.

4:21 heart. Or, the mind (2:2 note).

4:22 healing. Wholeness and soundness that includes the body (3:8).

23 Keep your heart with all vigilance,
for [o]from it flow [p]the springs
of life.
24 Put away from you [q]crooked speech,
and put [r]devious talk far from you.
25 [s]Let your eyes look directly forward,
and your gaze be straight before you.
26 [t]Ponder[1] the path of your feet;
[u]then all your ways will be sure.
27 [v]Do not swerve to the right or to the
left;
turn your foot away from evil.

Warning Against Adultery

5 [w]My son, be attentive to my
wisdom;
[x]incline your ear to my
understanding,
2 that you may keep [y]discretion,
and your lips may [z]guard knowledge.
3 For the lips of [a]a forbidden[2] woman
drip honey,
and her speech[3] is [b]smoother
than oil,
4 but in the end she is [c]bitter as
[d]wormwood,
[e]sharp as [f]a two-edged sword.
5 Her feet [g]go down to death;
her steps follow the path to[4] Sheol;
6 she [h]does not ponder the path of life;
her ways wander, and she does not
know it.

7 And [i]now, O sons, listen to me,
and do not depart from the words
of my mouth.
8 Keep your way far from her,
and do not go near the door of
her house,
9 lest you give your honor to others
and your years to the
merciless,
10 lest strangers take their fill of your
strength,
and your [j]labors go to the house
of a foreigner,
11 and at the end of your life you
[k]groan,
when your flesh and body are
consumed,
12 and you say, [l]"How I hated
discipline,
and my heart [m]despised reproof!
13 I did not listen to the voice of my
teachers
or incline my ear to my
instructors.
14 [n]I am at the brink of utter ruin
in the assembled congregation."

15 Drink [o]water from your own
cistern,
flowing water from your
own well.

23 [o][Matt. 12:35] [p][Ps. 68:20]
24 [q]ch. 6:12 [r]ch. 2:15
25 [s][Heb. 12:2]
26 [t]ch. 5:6, 21; [Heb. 12:13] [u][Ps. 119:5]
27 [v]Deut. 5:32; 28:14; Josh. 1:7; 1 Kin. 15:5
Chapter 5
1 [w]ch. 4:20; [ch. 2:1, 2] [x]ch. 22:17
2 [y]ch. 1:4 [z]Mal. 2:7
3 [a]See ch. 2:16 [b]Ps. 55:21
4 [c][Eccles. 7:26] [d]Deut. 29:18; Jer. 9:15; Lam. 3:15, 19; Rev. 8:11 [e]Ps. 57:4; [Ps. 55:21] [f]See Ps. 149:6
5 [g]See ch. 7:27
6 [h]ver. 21; ch. 4:26
7 [i]See ch. 4:1
10 [j]Ps. 127:2
11 [k]Ezek. 24:23
12 [l]ch. 1:22, 29; See ch. 12:1 [m]ch. 1:25; See Ps. 107:11
14 [n][Ps. 94:17]
15 [o]ver. 18; [ch. 9:17; S. of S. 4:12, 15; Jer. 2:13]

[1] Or *Make level* [2] Hebrew *strange*; also verse 20 [3] Hebrew *palate* [4] Hebrew *lay hold of*

4:23 from it . . . life. Our thoughts in turn shape the way we speak and live. See Matt. 12:35; Mark 7:21; Rom. 2:29.

4:25–27 Wisdom enables one to keep to life's path without swerving into the mire.

5:1–23 This passage is best taken as a single unit. While vv. 15–23 are conceivably a distinct composition, the theme is a logical development of what goes before. Wisdom urges us to avoid the life-destroying adulteress and to find sexual and emotional satisfaction in faithfulness to the marriage bond.

5:1–6 These verses describe the character of the seducing adulteress. On the surface she is all sweetness and light, but underneath is the stench of death.

5:2 lips may guard knowledge. The sense may be that one should learn to maintain discreet silence when necessary, or possibly, that one should have something of substance to say (Mal. 2:7).

5:3 In contrast with v. 2, the seducer begins with deceptive words of charm. Cf. the sweetness of true love in Song 4:11.

5:4 in the end. The phrase speaks of the end result for the victim of seduction.

bitter as wormwood. A plant especially bitter to the taste, wormwood is used as a metaphor for the experience of affliction (Deut. 29:18).

two-edged sword. The smoothness of her words is deceptive (v. 3), and the liaison leads only to injury.

5:5 death. Not merely a matter of an early demise brought about by dissolute living, "death" in this context is all that does not promote "life" as defined by God.

Sheol. The place of the dead. Disorderly life leads to physical death. See Is. 14:9–11 note.

5:6 her ways wander. The moral censure here is inseparable from the wisdom idea that folly and wickedness involve a rejection of God's order and plan for things.

5:7–14 These verses provide a more detailed description of the fruit of immorality and the price it exacts.

5:8 Keep . . . far from her. The wise will make a conscious choice to avoid any contact with immorality and keep out of the way of temptation.

5:9–11 Those who foolishly engage in immorality pay a high price for it.

5:9 the merciless. Perhaps the outraged husband of the adulteress (6:34, 35).

5:10 This verse may refer literally to the high cost of keeping a mistress (a "foreigner"). Or the warning may be that immorality takes away wealth and strength.

5:11 Such dissipation leads to regret as one reflects on the waste and futility of the life that has been lived.

5:12, 13 Sexual immorality epitomizes the way of folly that rejects the discipline of wise instruction.

5:14 congregation. In view here is either public disgrace or punishment by the covenant community.

5:15 Drink water . . . cistern. The context suggests that this is a metaphor for marital relations with one's wife.

16 Should your [p] springs be scattered
abroad,
streams of water [q] in the streets?
17 [r] Let them be for yourself alone,
and not for strangers with you.
18 Let your [o] fountain be blessed,
and [s] rejoice in [t] the wife of your
youth,
19 a lovely [u] deer, a graceful doe.
Let her breasts [v] fill you at all times
with delight;
be intoxicated[1] always in her love.
20 Why should you be intoxicated, my
son, with [w] a forbidden
woman
and embrace the bosom of [w] an
adulteress?[2]
21 For [x] a man's ways are [y] before the
eyes of the LORD,
and he [z] ponders[3] all his paths.
22 The [a] iniquities of the wicked
[b] ensnare him,
and he is held fast in the cords of
his sin.
23 [c] He dies for lack of discipline,
and because of his great folly he is
[d] led astray.

Practical Warnings

6 My son, if you have put up [e] security
for your neighbor,
have [e] given your pledge for a
stranger,
2 if you are [f] snared in the words of
your mouth,
caught in the words of your mouth,
3 then do this, my son, and save
yourself,
for you have come into the hand of
your neighbor:
go, hasten,[4] and [g] plead urgently
with your neighbor.
4 [h] Give your eyes no sleep
and your eyelids no slumber;
5 save yourself like a gazelle from the
hand of the hunter,[5]
[i] like a bird from the hand of the
fowler.
6 [j] Go to [k] the ant, O [l] sluggard;
consider her ways, and [m] be wise.
7 [n] Without having any chief,
[o] officer, or ruler,
8 she prepares her bread [p] in summer
and [q] gathers her food in harvest.
9 [r] How long will you lie there,
[l] O sluggard?
When will you arise from your
sleep?
10 [s] A little sleep, a little slumber,
[t] a little [s] folding of the hands to rest,
11 [u] and poverty will come upon you like
a robber,
and want like an armed man.

16 [p] See Ps. 68:26 [q] [Jer. 9:21; Zech. 8:5]
17 [r] [ch. 14:10]
18 [o] [See ver. 15 above] [s] Deut. 24:5 [t] Mal. 2:14
19 [u] S. of S. 2:9, 17; 8:14 [v] [Jer. 31:14]
20 [w] See ch. 2:16
21 [x] Ps. 119:168 [y] Hos. 7:2; Heb. 4:13; See Job 14:16; Ps. 11:4 [z] ver. 6
22 [a] See Ps. 7:15, 16 [b] ch. 6:2
23 [c] See Job 4:21 [d] [Job 12:24]
Chapter 6
1 [e] See Job 17:3
2 [f] [ch. 5:22]
3 [g] [Luke 11:8; 18:5]
4 [h] ch. 20:13; Ps. 132:4
5 [i] See Ps. 91:3
6 [j] [Job 12:7] [k] ch. 30:25 [l] ch. 10:26 [m] ch. 23:19; 27:11
7 [n] [ch. 30:27] [o] Ex. 5:6, 15
8 [p] [ch. 10:5] [q] [ch. 10:5]
9 [r] [Jonah 1:6] [l] [See ver. 6 above]
10 [s] ch. 24:33 [t] Eccles. 4:5
11 [u] ch. 24:34

1 Hebrew *be led astray*; also verse 20 2 Hebrew *a foreign woman* 3 Or *makes level* 4 Or *humble yourself* 5 Hebrew lacks *of the hunter*

5:16 springs . . . streams. The imagery suggests the wastefulness of a promiscuous life.

5:18 fountain. Another metaphor for the wife, perhaps indicating the bearing of many children.

wife of your youth. The wife taken when you were young.

5:19 The poetic language of this verse is like that of the Song of Solomon. The imagery of a graceful animal of rare beauty emphasizes physical pleasure as integral to marital relations. See Song 1:2, 3; 4:1–7.

5:21–23 Up to this point, the warnings against adultery have not been referred to God's law. Similar warnings can be found in other wisdom traditions. Now the writer explains that the natural consequences of folly, and especially sexual folly, are punishments ordained by God.

5:21 ponders. Or "takes note of." Our behavior is under constant scrutiny. The text does not say that every sin is visited with an immediate penalty. Rather, God oversees the created order so that sinners are captured by their own folly (vv. 22, 23).

5:23 dies. See notes on v. 5 and 2:18.

6:1 pledge for a stranger. Such an agreement to guarantee another's debt is unwise because it involves matters quite beyond the guarantor's control (11:15; 17:18; 22:26).

6:2 snared. Borrowing money is one thing, but to provide security for another is to walk into a trap of one's own making.

6:3 into the hand. By accepting responsibility for another's debts you allow another to take control of your life.

hasten. See text note. This is not the time for pride.

6:4 Give your eyes no sleep. There must be an unremitting effort to have the contract annulled.

6:5 The imagery of creatures hunted and trapped heightens the sense of urgency.

6:6–11 These verses are an object lesson based on the industry of the ant. The underlying assumption is not only that the universe is orderly, but that there are points of analogy between even the lowly insect world and humans. Solomon's nature proverbs may have drawn other such analogies (1 Kin. 4:33).

6:6 ant. See 30:25. The ant's industry gives the appearance of prudent activity.

sluggard. The word suggests a lazy person whose inactivity expresses an attitude of folly (10:26; 13:4; 15:19; 19:24; 20:4; 26:16).

6:10, 11 This proverbial saying has been linked with the previous saying (vv. 6–9) to provide an application of it. The same saying is later linked with a different object lesson (24:33, 34).

6:11 poverty. Proverbs warns against attitudes and behavior that produce poverty. Laziness is one of these (10:4, 5; 19:15; 20:13). While diligence and industry are normally associated with prosperity (12:11; 13:4; 14:23), it must not be said that all poverty is the result of folly (14:31; 17:5; 19:1, 17, 22; 21:12; 22:22; 28:3, 11).

like a robber . . . an armed man. The comparison is not so much to a sneaky thief who comes at night, as to a robber who overpowers his victim.

12 [v]A worthless person, a wicked man,
goes about with [w]crooked speech,
13 [x]winks with his eyes, signals[1] with his feet,
points with his finger,
14 with [y]perverted heart [z]devises evil,
continually [a]sowing discord;
15 therefore calamity will come upon him suddenly;
[b]in a moment he will be broken
[c]beyond healing.

16 There are [d]six things that the LORD hates,
[d]seven that are an abomination to him:
17 [e]haughty eyes, [f]a lying tongue,
and [g]hands that shed innocent blood,
18 [h]a heart that devises wicked plans,
[i]feet that make haste to run to evil,
19 [j]a false witness who [k]breathes out lies,
and one who [a]sows discord among brothers.

Warnings Against Adultery

20 [l]My son, keep your father's commandment,
[l]and forsake not your mother's teaching.
21 [m]Bind them on your heart always;
[n]tie them around your neck.
22 [o]When you walk, they[2] will lead you;
[o]when you lie down, they will
[p]watch over you;
and when you awake, they will talk with you.
23 For the commandment is [q]a lamp
and the teaching a light,
and the [r]reproofs of discipline are the way of life,
24 to preserve you from the evil woman,[3]
from the smooth tongue of [s]the adulteress.[4]
25 [t]Do not desire her beauty in your heart,
and do not let her capture you
with her [u]eyelashes;
26 for [v]the price of a prostitute is only
[w]a loaf of bread,[5]
but a married woman[6] [x]hunts
down a precious life.

12[v]ch. 16:27 [w]ch. 4:24 **13**[x]ch. 10:10; Ps. 35:19 **14**[y]See ch. 2:12 [z][Mic. 2:1]; See ch. 3:29 [a][ch. 16:28] **15**[b]Isai. 30:13, 14; Jer. 19:11 [c]ch. 29:1; 2 Chr. 36:16 **16**[d]See Job 5:19 **17**[e][ch. 8:13; 16:5; 21:4]; See Ps. 101:5 [f]ch. 12:22; 17:7; Ps. 31:18; 120:2 [g]Deut. 19:10; Isai. 1:15; 59:3, 7 **18**[h]Gen. 6:5 [i]See ch. 1:16 **19**[j]See Ps. 27:12 [k]ch. 12:17; 14:5, 25; 19:5, 9 [a][See ver. 14 above] **20**[l]See ch. 1:8

21[m]See ch. 3:3 [n][Job 31:36] **22**[o]See ch. 3:23, 24 [p]ch. 2:11 **23**[q]Ps. 119:105; [Ps. 13:3] [r][ch. 10:17] **24**[s]See ch. 2:16

25[t][Matt. 5:28] [u][2 Kin. 9:30] **26**[v][ch. 29:3] [w]ch. 28:21; 1 Sam. 2:36 [x]Ezek. 13:18

1 Hebrew *scrapes* 2 Hebrew *it*; three times in this verse
3 Revocalization (compare Septuagint) yields *from the wife of a neighbor* 4 Hebrew *the foreign woman* 5 Or (compare Septuagint, Syriac, Vulgate) *for a prostitute leaves a man with nothing but a loaf of bread* 6 Hebrew *a man's wife*

6:12–15 The form suggests a proverbial saying that has been expanded to apply to a specific situation. A string of descriptive clauses is added to the main thought, that the worthless person stirs up discord.

6:12 worthless person. Lit. "man of Belial," a phrase of uncertain origin and meaning. It probably indicates a base and worthless person, with an element of active malevolence.

6:13 winks . . . signals . . . points. The wicked will not speak plainly and openly, but make veiled suggestions and signs that sow seeds of distrust and dissension.

6:15 Such people, in time, bring destruction upon themselves. The Old Testament reveals that ultimately God will punish the wicked (24:19, 20) and reward the righteous (23:17, 18; 24:15, 16), but it does not present a fully developed doctrine of punishment in the afterlife. The prosperity of the wicked was a continuing problem (Ps. 37:7; 73:3–14). The New Testament clearly indicates that the righteous judgment of God falls on the wicked, whether in this life or the next (Luke 16:23, 24; Rev. 14:10–12; 20:15).

6:16–19 These verses are the first of the numerical sayings in Proverbs (cf. 30:15–31). The form of these sayings suggests a kind of riddle with an answer provided, not to dispose of the question, but to invite further appropriate answers. Wisdom literature often lists things together that are perceived to have something in common. Relationships are established in surprising ways, and the process of discerning orderly relationships in the universe increases wisdom. This unit is quite distinct from the previous one (vv. 12–15), but is probably placed next to it for development of the theme. Whereas v. 15 expresses the perspective of an unspecified natural retribution, this saying implies that the Lord renders judgment (5:21–23 note).

6:16 six . . . seven. The use of successive numbers is a common device in Hebrew poetry (Job 5:19; Amos 1:3).

6:20–35 Another warning against adultery (chs. 5; 7; 30:20). The form of this section is essentially that of the instruction, but with considerable variation. Some quite elaborate word-pictures are used to heighten the urgency of the warnings (vv. 23, 26, 27, 28, 30, 31). Verses 21 and 23 depend on Deut. 6:8 and Ps. 119:105, which refer to the Law. The Law provides a clear framework for revelation, showing Israel the proper response to God's covenant relationship with her. Wisdom works within that framework to describe the bounds of human responsibility. The Law condemns adultery and prescribes a penalty for it (Ex. 20:14; Lev. 20:10). Wisdom shares this opposition to adultery—the sages were all men of the covenant—and it adds its warnings about the inevitable disaster that such folly brings.

6:20 See 1:8.

commandment. See note 3:1.

6:21 See 3:3 and Deut. 6:6, 8.

6:22 See notes 3:23, 24; cf. Deut. 6:7. Wisdom is comprehensive in its effects on one's life.

they will lead you. See notes 1:5; 2:9; 3:6.

6:23 In Ps. 119:105 the same metaphor is applied to the law as such. The wise person accepts the revealed law, and depending on it, examines nature and the experiences of life. In this way, wisdom supplements the law from its own perspective.

6:24 See notes 2:16 and 5:3.

6:25 Do not desire. The lustful desire of the heart is the start of the progression of folly. The connection between the desire and the act is not as starkly put as in Matt. 5:28, but it is present.

6:26 loaf of bread. Although consorting with prostitutes is self-destructive, adultery is worse. It is not only a violation of marriage, but a direct attack on it.

27 Can a man carry [y]fire next to his
[z]chest
and his clothes not be burned?
28 Or can one [a]walk on hot coals
and his feet not be scorched?
29 So is he who goes in to his
neighbor's wife;
none who touches her [b]will go
unpunished.
30 People do not despise a thief if he
steals
to [c]satisfy his appetite when he is
hungry,
31 but [d]if he is caught, he will pay
[e]sevenfold;
he will give all the goods of his
house.
32 He who commits adultery lacks
sense;
he who does it destroys himself.
33 Wounds and dishonor will he get,
and his disgrace will not be wiped
away.
34 For [f]jealousy makes a man furious,
and he will not spare when [g]he
takes revenge.
35 He will accept no compensation;
he will refuse though you multiply
gifts.

Warning Against the Adulteress

7 [h]My son, keep my words
and [h]treasure up my commandments
with you;
2 [i]keep my commandments and live;
keep my teaching as [j]the apple of
your eye;
3 [k]bind them on your fingers;
[k]write them on the tablet of your
heart.
4 Say to wisdom, "You are my sister,"
and call insight your intimate
friend,
5 to keep you from [l]the forbidden[1]
woman,
from [l]the adulteress[2] with her
smooth words.

6 For at [m]the window of my house
I have looked out through my
lattice,
7 and I have seen among [n]the simple,
I have perceived among the youths,
a young man [o]lacking sense,
8 passing along the street [p]near her
corner,
taking the road to her house
9 in [q]the twilight, in the evening,
at [r]the time of night and darkness.

10 And behold, the woman meets him,
[s]dressed as a prostitute, wily of
heart.[3]
11 She is [t]loud and [u]wayward;
[v]her feet do not stay at home;
12 now in the street, now in the market,
and [w]at every corner she [x]lies in
wait.
13 She seizes him and kisses him,
and with [y]bold face she says to him,
14 "I had to [z]offer sacrifices,[4]
and today I have [a]paid my vows;

27 [y]Job 31:12 [z]Ps. 79:12
28 [a]Isai. 43:2
29 [b]ch. 16:5
30 [c]Job 38:39
31 [d][Ex. 22:4] [e]See Ps. 79:12
34 [f]ch. 27:4; S. of S. 8:6 [g][Lev. 20:10]
Chapter 7
1 [h]See ch. 2:1
2 [i]See ch. 4:4 [j]Deut. 32:10
3 [k]See ch. 3:3
5 [l]See ch. 2:16
6 [m]Judg. 5:28
7 [n]See ch. 1:4 [o]See ch. 6:32
8 [p]ver. 12
9 [q]Job 24:15 [r]ch. 20:20
10 [s][Gen. 38:14]
11 [t]ch. 9:13 [u][Hos. 4:16] [v]1 Tim. 5:13; [Tit. 2:5]
12 [w]ver. 8 [x]ch. 23:28
13 [y]ch. 21:29
14 [z]Lev. 7:11 [a]See Ps. 50:14

1 Hebrew *strange* 2 Hebrew *the foreign woman* 3 Hebrew *guarded in heart* 4 Hebrew *peace offerings*

6:27–29 The vivid and transparent metaphors emphasize the folly of adultery.

6:29 unpunished. Wisdom in Proverbs emphasizes the expected results of folly, but also, from time to time, goes behind the natural cause-and-effect chain to the overarching purpose and judgment of God.

6:30–33 The person driven by hunger to steal is still subject to the law, but people can understand such need. By contrast, adultery has no such extenuating factor and brings utter disgrace. The law required restoration of four times the theft; "sevenfold" exaggerates this for emphasis (Ex. 22:1).

6:34, 35 The offended husband's jealousy leads to fury and to a merciless revenge that no offer of compensation can avert. The forces that drive human relationships are often at the center of wisdom thinking.

7:1–27 This chapter is made up of three, possibly independent, parts, linked by the common theme of adultery. The first (vv. 1–5) and third (vv. 24–27) are in the form of instructions, and both warn about involvement with the adulteress. The middle section (vv. 6–23) appears as a dramatic narrative that functions as an imaginative reinforcement of the instruction.

7:1 commandments. See note 3:1.

7:2 live. See notes 2:18 and 3:2.

apple of your eye. Lit. "the little man of your eye," a reference to the pupil, in which the image of the observer is reflected. The pupil admits light to the eye and must be protected from all harm (cf. Deut. 32:10; Ps. 17:8; Zech. 2:8).

7:3 See 3:3 and notes. The procedures outlined in vv. 1–3 are an aspect of wisdom's method. The traditions are handed down in order to mold life and character.

7:4 sister . . . intimate friend. One should think of wisdom and understanding as one's close relatives. This is probably intended to depict the desired intimacy with wisdom, rather than to contrast with the adulteress of v. 5.

7:7 simple . . . lacking sense. See note 1:4. The lad is naive and unskilled in the art of living. The teaching of wisdom is aimed at such an impressionable type (1:2–4).

7:10 Seduction involves a deceitful show that attracts the victim while at the same time concealing the real intent.

7:14 sacrifices. The food from these religious offerings provided opportunity for gluttony (Lev. 7:12–18). See 17:1; 21:27.

15 so now I have come out to meet you,
to seek you eagerly, and I have
found you.
16 I have spread my couch with
[b]coverings,
colored linens from [c]Egyptian linen;
17 I have perfumed my bed with
[d]myrrh,
aloes, and [e]cinnamon.
18 Come, let us take our fill of love till
morning;
let us delight ourselves with love.
19 For [f]my husband is not at home;
he has gone on a long journey;
20 he took a bag of money with him;
at full moon he will come home."

21 With much seductive speech she
persuades him;
with [g]her smooth talk she compels
him.
22 All at once he follows her,
as an ox goes to the slaughter,
or as a stag is caught fast[1]
23 till an arrow pierces its liver;
as [h]a bird rushes into a snare;
he does not know that it will cost
him his life.

24 And [i]now, O sons, listen to me,
and be attentive to the words of
my mouth.
25 Let not your heart turn aside to her
ways;
do not stray into her paths,
26 for many a victim has she laid low,
and all her slain are [j]a mighty throng.
27 Her house is [k]the way to Sheol,
going down to the chambers of
death.

The Blessings of Wisdom

8 Does not [l]wisdom call?
Does not [m]understanding raise
her voice?
2 On [n]the heights beside the way,
at the crossroads she takes her stand;
3 beside [o]the gates in front of [p]the town,
at the entrance of the portals she
cries aloud:
4 "To you, O [q]men, I call,
and my cry is to [q]the children of
man.
5 O [r]simple ones, learn [s]prudence;
O [t]fools, learn sense.
6 Hear, for I will speak [u]noble things,
and from my lips will come [v]what
is right,
7 for my [w]mouth will utter truth;
wickedness is an abomination to
my lips.

1 Probable reading (compare Septuagint, Vulgate, Syriac); Hebrew *as an anklet for the discipline of a fool*

16 [b]ch. 31:22 [c][Isai. 19:9] 17 [d]Ps. 45:8 [e]Ex. 30:23 19 [f]Matt. 20:11 21 [g]ch. 5:3; 6:24; See Ps. 12:2 23 [h]Eccles. 9:12 24 [i]See ch. 4:1
26 [j][Neh. 13:26]; See Judg. 16:1-5 27 [k][ch. 2:18; 5:5; 9:18]
Chapter 8
1 [l]See ch. 1:20 [m]Job 28:12 2 [n]ch. 9:3, 14 3 [o]ch. 1:21 [p]Job 29:7 4 [q][Ps. 49:1, 2] 5 [r]See ch. 1:4 [s]ver. 12 [t][ch. 1:22] 6 [u][ch. 22:20] [v]ch. 23:16 7 [w]Ps. 37:30

7:15 The words are flattery, assuring the young man that he was specially chosen for this treat.

7:17 myrrh, aloes, and cinnamon. Aromatic spices used for perfuming garments and beds.

7:18 take our fill of love. This is the most fraudulent proposition of all. To suggest that casual and illicit sex can satisfy deep longings for mutual, loving commitment is a destructive lie.

7:19, 20 The woman is aware that this illicit relationship involves them in deceit. They vainly hope to avoid the jealous husband's rage (6:33–35).

7:21 The seductive power of words is a constant theme (2:16; 5:3; 6:24; 9:16, 17). Over against this is contrasted the healing power of wisdom's words (2:1–6; 3:1, 2; 5:1, 2; 7:24, 25).

7:22 as an ox goes to the slaughter. The dumb animal is unaware of its fate and allows itself to be led.

as a stag is caught fast. See text note. The uncertainty of this line does not obscure the overall sense of the verse: the young man has walked into a trap.

7:23 arrow pierces its liver. A mortal wound.

7:25 heart. See note 2:2.

do not stray into her paths. The wise man's prescription is to keep one's thoughts (heart) from adultery, and to stay away from places where there is temptation.

7:26, 27 A motive for prudence is to avoid the carnage that results from folly.

7:27 Sheol . . . death. See 1:12; 2:18; 5:5 and notes.

8:1–36 In chs. 1–7, the mouthpiece of wisdom is a teacher or sage. In this majestic poem, wisdom is personified as the supreme teacher who teaches on her own authority. The personification is most probably a poetic device to express more vividly the authority of wisdom. Although it is premature to see personified wisdom (especially in vv. 22–31) as a direct portrayal of a divine being, there is no doubt that the revelation of Jesus Christ as the wisdom of God shows us the significance of a wisdom that is its own absolute authority (1 Cor. 1:24, 30; Heb. 1:1–4; Col. 1:15, 16; John 1:1–18). The poem progresses from a consideration of the human task of learning wisdom (vv. 1–11) to the powerful effects of wisdom in the world (vv. 12–21)—and then to the divine origin of wisdom and its place in the totality of creation (vv. 22–31). A final appeal equates wisdom with life (vv. 32–36). Behind human wisdom is the original, uncreated wisdom of God, by which He established all created things in their proper relationships to God and to one another. This means that human wisdom is valid and life-affirming insofar as it proceeds within the context provided by divine special revelation (ch. 4 note).

8:1–3 See notes 1:20–33.

8:4 men. The Hebrew word usually applies to males, but may extend to all humanity. Wisdom, in the role of the instructor, addresses not sons or pupils, but all people. There is no elite class in the matter of learning wisdom; it is for all.

8:5 See notes 1:4, 22.

8:6 noble things. Princely or valuable things.

what is right. The moral element is implied.

8:7 truth. The word denotes what is utterly reliable. It is the opposite of wickedness. Proverbs relates truth to wisdom in several places, and here the word of wisdom is described in a way suggestive of divine origin.

8 All the words of my mouth are righteous;
there is nothing [x]twisted or crooked in them.
9 They are all [y]straight to him who understands,
and right to those who find knowledge.
10 [z]Take my instruction instead of silver,
and knowledge rather than choice gold,
11 [a]for wisdom is better than jewels,
and [b]all that you may desire cannot compare with her.

12 "I, wisdom, dwell with prudence,
and I find knowledge and [c]discretion.
13 [d]The fear of the LORD is [e]hatred of evil.
[f]Pride and arrogance and the way of evil
and [g]perverted speech I hate.
14 I have [h]counsel and [i]sound wisdom;
I have insight; [j]I have strength.
15 By me [k]kings reign,
and rulers decree what is just;
16 by me princes rule,
and nobles, all who govern justly.[1]
17 [l]I love those who love me,
and [m]those who seek me diligently find me.
18 [n]Riches and honor are with me,
[o]enduring wealth and [o]righteousness.
19 My fruit is [p]better than [q]gold, even fine gold,
and my yield than [r]choice silver.
20 I walk in the way of righteousness,
in the paths of justice,
21 granting an inheritance to those who love me,
and filling their treasuries.

22 [s]"The LORD [t]possessed[2] me at the beginning of his work,[3]
the first of his acts [u]of old.
23 Ages ago I was [v]set up,
at the first, [w]before the beginning of the earth.

8 [x]Deut. 32:5 **9** [y][ch. 14:6; 1 Cor. 2:10] **10** [z]ver. 19; ch. 3:14; Ps. 119:72, 127 **11** [a][ch. 16:16]; See Job 28:12-19 [b]ch. 3:15 **12** [c]ch. 1:4 **13** [d][ch. 16:6] [e]See Ps. 97:10 [f][ch. 6:17; 16:5] [g]ch. 2:12; 4:24 **14** [h]Isai. 11:2; [Isai. 9:6] [i][ch. 2:7] [j]Eccles. 7:19; [Ps. 89:19] **15** [k][Dan. 2:21; Rom. 13:1; Rev. 19:16] **17** [l]Ps. 91:14; John 14:21; [1 Sam. 2:30] [m]James 1:5; [ch. 1:28] **18** [n]ch. 3:16 [o]Ps. 112:3; [Matt. 6:33; Luke 16:11; Eph. 3:8] **19** [p]ch. 3:14 [q]ver. 10 [r]ch. 10:20 **22** [s]See Job 28:25-28 [t]Gen. 14:19, 22; [Ps. 104:24; 136:5] [u]Ps. 93:2 **23** [v]Ps. 2:6 [w][John 17:5]

1 Most Hebrew manuscripts; many Hebrew manuscripts, Septuagint *govern the earth* 2 Or *fathered*; Septuagint *created* 3 Hebrew *way*

8:8 righteous. See note on v. 18.

8:9 Wisdom is a self-consistent reality. One must be attuned to it in order to learn it. This is another way of saying that all truth is God's truth and without the knowledge of God we cannot know the absolute truth. Cf. the wisdom of Jesus in Matt. 13:10–16; Luke 11:52.

8:10, 11 The comparison of wisdom to the most desirable emblems of wealth is a way of emphasizing its value (2:4; 3:14, 15; 8:19–21; Job 28:17). The warning against crass materialism is obvious.

8:12 See 1:4 and note.

8:13 The fear of the LORD. See 1:7; 2:5; 3:7; 9:10 and notes. Wisdom reminds us that the search for an ethic based solely on experience is futile. Education and experience must build on the basis of the faithfulness and hope provided by God's covenant promises. Ethical systems without the absolute standard of right, goodness, and truth revealed in the Scriptures cannot survive (Ps. 36:9).

Pride . . . I hate. Wisdom echoes the hatred that God has for evil (6:16; Deut. 12:31; 16:22; Ps. 5:5; Is. 61:8; Jer. 44:4).

8:14 counsel. The word means advice derived from wisdom and experience, and also, plans made by joint deliberation on a course of action. The same word is used for the mind of God concerning His own plans and purposes (Is. 5:19; 19:17; 25:1; 28:29). Wisdom has access to this counsel.

8:15, 16 The proper function of human rulers is defined by the order of God's creation as revealed in the Word of God (Gen. 1:26–28). Wise rulership begins with the fear of the Lord (Deut. 17:18–20; 1 Kin. 3:6–9; 4:29–34). The Messiah will rule by perfect wisdom (Is. 11:1–3). See "Christians and Civil Government" at Rom. 13:1.

8:17 I love those who love me. The statements contrast with wisdom being hidden from fools (1:28, 29). Wisdom cares for her own (4:6, 8, 9).

those who seek me . . . find me. See 2:4, 5; 3:13–15. This suggests a relationship between wisdom and the grace of God that causes Him to draw near to us (Is. 55:6). Jesus, Himself the final revelation of divine wisdom (1 Cor. 1:24, 30; Col. 2:2, 3), possibly alludes to this verse in Matt. 7:7.

8:18 Riches and honor. See 3:2, 16. Solomon's early reign was an example of the material and social benefits of wisdom (1 Kin. 10:1–9).

righteousness. This means obedience to God's law, extending to the cultivation of right relationships between God, people, and creation. See Rom. 12:18; 1 Tim. 2:1–4.

8:19 See note on vv. 10, 11.

8:22–31 This hymn-like section presents wisdom as the basis of design in the universe. The focus is unusual, but this view of wisdom does not go against the theology of the covenant and God's saving acts in Israel. The sages were also men of the covenant (1:7; 2:20–22 and notes). The method of wisdom is to emphasize the biblical theology of creation as the basis for understanding our lives as redeemed people of God.

8:22 The LORD. The proper name of God as the Redeemer and the Author of the covenant (Ex. 3:15 and notes). God's redemptive covenant with Israel underscores His commitment to creation, for the covenant promises culminate in Jesus Christ—the great Seed of Abraham (Gen. 12:7; cf. Gal. 3:16) and Son of David (2 Sam. 7:16; cf. Luke 1:32)—through whom the broken and fallen creation is redeemed (Rom. 8:20–22; 2 Cor. 5:17 note; Col. 1:15–20; Rev. 21:1).

possessed me. Wisdom is not a fourth divine person, but an attribute of God that is given expression in creation as well as redemption. In this chapter, wisdom is personified for poetic effect. The attributes of God are eternal, so the figure of wisdom is said to be from "the beginning."

at the beginning of his work. Wisdom is the prior counsel of God's will (Eph. 1:11), the eternal decree that establishes all things in their relationships and determines the course of history.

the first of his acts of old. Wisdom existed prior to God's self-revelation in His covenant and saving acts.

8:23 Wisdom was also prior to the creation of the universe.

24 When there were no [x]depths I was
[y]brought forth,
when there were no springs
abounding with water.
25 Before the mountains [z]had been
shaped,
[a]before the hills, I was brought
forth,
26 before he had made the earth with its
fields,
or the first of the dust of the
world.
27 When he [b]established the heavens, I
was there;
when he drew [c]a circle on the face
of the deep,
28 when he [d]made firm the skies above,
when he established[1] the fountains
of the deep,
29 when he [e]assigned to the sea its
[f]limit,
so that the waters might not
transgress his command,
when he marked out [g]the
foundations of the earth,
30 then [h]I was beside him, like a
master workman,
and I was daily his[2] [i]delight,
rejoicing before him always,
31 [j]rejoicing in his [k]inhabited world
and delighting in the children of
man.

32 "And now, [l]O sons, listen to me:
[m]blessed are those who keep my
ways.
33 [n]Hear instruction and be wise,
and do not neglect it.
34 [o]Blessed is the one who listens
to me,
watching daily at my gates,
waiting beside my doors.
35 For [p]whoever finds me [q]finds life
and [r]obtains favor from the
LORD,
36 but he who fails to find me [s]injures
himself;
all who [t]hate me [u]love death."

The Way of Wisdom

9 [v]Wisdom has built her house;
she has hewn her [w]seven [x]pillars.
2 She has [y]slaughtered her beasts; she
has [z]mixed her wine;
she has also [a]set her table.
3 She has [b]sent out her young women
to [c]call
from [d]the highest places in the
town,
4 [e]"Whoever is simple, let him turn in
here!"
[f]To him who lacks sense she says,

24 [x]ver. 27, 28; ch. 3:20; Gen. 1:2 [y]Job 15:7; Ps. 51:5
25 [z]Job 38:6 (Heb.) [a]Ps. 90:2
27 [b]ch. 3:19 [c]Job 22:14
28 [d]Gen. 1:6
29 [e]Gen. 1:9, 10 [f]See Job 26:10 [g]See Ps. 104:5
30 [h]Zech. 13:7; [John 1:1, 2] [i]Ps. 16:3; [Matt. 3:17]
31 [j][Gen. 1:31; Ps. 104:31] [k]Isai. 45:18
32 [l]ch. 5:7; 7:24; [1 John 3:1] [m]Ps. 119:1, 2; 128:1, 2; [Luke 11:28]
33 [n]See ch. 4:1
34 [o][ch. 3:13]
35 [p]ch. 3:18; See ch. 4:22 [q]John 1:4; 17:3 [r]ch. 12:2; 18:22
36 [s][ch. 15:32; 20:2; 29:24] [t]ch. 12:1 [u]ch. 21:6
Chapter 9
1 [v][Matt. 16:18; 1 Pet. 2:5]; See Eph. 2:20-22 [w][Rev. 1:4] [x][1 Tim. 3:15]

2 [y][Matt. 22:4] [z]ch. 23:30; S. of S. 8:2 [a]Ps. 23:5; [Luke 14:17] 3 [b][Ps. 68:11; Matt. 22:3; 23:34] [c]ch. 8:1, 2 [d]ver. 14; ch. 8:2; [Matt. 10:27] 4 [e]ver. 16; [Matt. 11:25; 1 Cor. 1:26] [f]ch. 6:32

1 The meaning of the Hebrew is uncertain 2 Or *daily filled with*

8:24–31 Job reminds us that creation wisdom ultimately belongs to God alone (Job 38; 39). The "cultural mandate," assigning to humans the task of understanding creation and exercising dominion over it (Gen. 1:26–28), is the basis for wisdom's interest in knowing the world of nature (1 Kin. 4:29, 33). This is pursued within the framework established by special revelation (the Scripture) and in the fear of the Lord (1:7 note; 8:1–36 note; 9:10).

8:24 I was brought forth. The wise plan of God precedes His action. Reference to being "brought forth" suggests that wisdom is uniquely the child of God, but this is still a poetic device and does not refer to a new divine being.

8:27 I was there. Wisdom was prior to creation and a participant in it. Creation is the first great demonstration of the wisdom of God.

8:28 fountains of the deep. See Gen. 7:11; 8:2.

8:30 a master workman. Wisdom is now described as the agent of creation. Skilled craftsmanship is an aspect of wisdom (cf. Ex. 31:3), which points to the practical nature of wisdom. See 1:2 and note.

8:31 rejoicing . . . delighting. Wisdom reflects the satisfaction expressed in the divine declaration that creation is very good (Gen. 1:31).

8:32 blessed. See note 3:13. The blessings of God on obedience are a feature of covenant theology (Deut. 28:1–14; see "God's Covenant of Grace" at Gen. 12:1). Here the word describes the rewards of wisdom (3:13–18).

8:34 watching daily at my gates. The pupil attends at the house of the teacher, eager to learn whatever wisdom will impart.

8:35 The benefits of wisdom are equated with life itself. To be truly alive is to be rightly related to God, other people, and the created order. See notes 3:2, 18.

favor from the LORD. That is, acceptance and goodwill. The sage is not describing an alternative way of gaining acceptance other than that provided in the covenant community and sacrifices. Rather, he describes the richness of the believers' fellowship with the Lord as their lives are molded by true wisdom (12:2).

8:36 hate. To hate wisdom is to hate life, and therefore to love death.

9:1–18 This section consists of two competing invitations, one from wisdom and the other from folly. Both are portrayed as women calling people to enter their houses. Wisdom invites the simple to eat of her life-giving food (vv. 1–12). Folly offers food that leads to death (vv. 13–18).

9:1 her seven pillars. The significance of "seven pillars" is not clear. It may simply indicate the architectural splendor of the house. However, "seven" often symbolizes perfection or completeness, and so may here represent the perfection of divine wisdom.

9:2 mixed her wine. The mixture was probably of wine and spices (Song 8:2).

9:3 her young women. Wisdom's servants are sent out to summon any who will hear her invitation to life.

from the highest places. The invitation is open and universal (Is. 52:7).

9:4 simple. See 1:4 and note. Note the competing call of folly in v. 16.

lacks sense. Lit. "lacks heart," the will to think and act rightly.

5 "Come, [g]eat of my bread
and [h]drink of [z]the wine I have
mixed.
6 Leave [i]your simple ways,[1] and [j]live,
[k]and walk in the way of insight."
7 Whoever corrects a scoffer gets
himself abuse,
and he who reproves a wicked
man incurs injury.
8 [l]Do not reprove a scoffer, or he will
hate you;
[m]reprove a wise man, and he will
love you.
9 Give instruction[2] to a wise man, and
he will be [n]still wiser;
teach a righteous man, and he will
[o]increase in learning.
10 [p]The fear of the LORD is the beginning
of wisdom,
and [q]the knowledge of the Holy
One is insight.
11 For by me [r]your days will be
multiplied,
and years will be added to your
life.
12 [s]If you are wise, you are wise for
yourself;
if you scoff, you alone will bear it.

The Way of Folly

13 [t]The woman Folly is [u]loud;
she is seductive[3] and [v]knows
nothing.
14 She sits at the door of her house;
she takes a seat on [w]the highest
places of the town,
15 calling to those who pass by,
who are [x]going straight on their way,
16 [y]"Whoever is simple, let him turn in
here!"
And to him who lacks sense she
says,
17 [z]"Stolen water is sweet,
and [a]bread eaten in secret is
pleasant."
18 But he does not know [b]that the
dead[4] are there,
that her guests are in the depths of
Sheol.

The Proverbs of Solomon

10 [c]The proverbs of Solomon.

[d]A wise son makes a glad father,
[e]but a foolish son is a sorrow to his
mother.

5 [g][S. of S. 5:1; Isai. 55:1; John 6:27] [h][John 7:37] [z][See ver. 2 above]
6 [i]See ch. 1:4 [j][ver. 11] [k][ch. 23:19]
8 [l][Matt. 7:6] [m]See Ps. 141:5
9 [n][Matt. 13:12] [o]ch. 1:5
10 [p]See ch. 1:7 [q]ch. 30:3
11 [r][ch. 10:27]; See ch. 3:2
12 [s][Job 22:2, 3; 1 Cor. 3:8; Gal. 6:5]
13 [t]For ver. 13-18, see ch. 7:7-27 [u]ch. 7:11 [v]ch. 5:6
14 [w]ver. 3
15 [x][ver. 6]
16 [y]ver. 4
17 [z][ch. 5:15] [a][ch. 20:17; 30:20]
18 [b]See ch. 7:27
Chapter 10
1 [c]See ch. 1:1 [d]See ch. 29:3 [e]ch. 17:25; 29:15

1 Or *Leave the company of the simple* 2 Hebrew lacks *instruction* 3 Or *full of simpleness* 4 Hebrew *Rephaim*

9:5 Come, eat. A banquet is the right setting for the food distributed by wisdom. The banquet motif is later used to portray the blessings of the redeemed (Is. 55:1, 2; Matt. 22:1–13; 26:29; Rev. 19).

9:6 Leave your simple ways, and live. See 1:4, 22; 2:19; 3:2, 18; 8:35 and notes.

9:7–12 These verses contrast the wise and the fool, not only at the point of decision to enter the houses of wisdom or folly, but in the kind of lives that result from those decisions.

9:7 scoffer. The scoffer has gone beyond a simple lack of judgment, and has made a conscious decision for evil.

gets himself abuse. The effort to correct such a person will fail and may backfire.

he who reproves. This parallel phrase is synonymous in meaning to the first part of the verse.

9:8 Here the parallel structure is antithetic (i.e., the two parts are contrasted opposites).

reprove a wise man. While a fool shuts out wisdom, a wise person is glad for the opportunity to shut out folly. Wisdom perceives the positive side of correction; wisdom is not defensive and easily offended, but humble and responsive.

9:9 Wisdom recognizes an important principle of human nature: there is no standing still; we progress in the direction of our choice. Wisdom accumulates more wisdom (cf. Matt. 13:12).

9:10 The fear of the LORD. See 1:7 and note; "The Wisdom and Will of God" at Dan. 2:20.

Holy One. Lit. "holy ones" or "saints." The translation here is based on the parallel with "the LORD" in the previous line (cf. 30:3, where the same plural form is used).

9:11 See 3:2 and note.

9:12 you are wise for yourself. That is, you will benefit (3:13–18; 4:9–13; 8:34, 35).

9:13–18 The description of folly is directly opposed to that of wisdom in vv. 1–6.

9:13 loud. See 7:11, 12.

seductive and knows nothing. The sensuous appeal of folly contrasts with wisdom as the teacher.

9:14 on the highest places of the town. Folly counterfeits the actions of wisdom so as to appear wise (cf. v. 3).

9:15, 16 Folly's entreaties further imitate those of wisdom (cf. v. 4).

9:17 Stolen water. Anything that is forbidden, especially illicit sex (5:3, 15; 7:16–18).

bread eaten in secret. Because it is stolen or forbidden. There is a perversity in human nature that is stirred up by prohibition and the law (Rom. 7:7–11).

9:18 the dead. Hebrew *rephaim*, of uncertain derivation. The word is used eight times in the Bible, all in Hebrew poetry, referring to the spirits of the departed.

Sheol. Lit. "the grave." See 1:12; 5:5; 7:27 and notes. In Proverbs, Sheol is the fitting destination of fools not because it is a place of torment, as Hell is later described (Rev. 14:9–11), but simply because those who go there have lost the possibility of relationship with the living God. See also 2:18 and note.

10:1–22:16 This section consists mainly of single-sentence proverbs. There is no evidence that these are a form of wisdom writing from a different time than the longer instructions of chs. 1–9. They are simply different forms, and function in different ways. Aphorisms are often stated categorically, without the qualifications that might allow them to cover every conceivable situation.

2 [f] Treasures gained by wickedness do
not profit,
[g] but righteousness delivers from
death.
3 [h] The LORD does not let the righteous
go hungry,
[i] but he thwarts the craving of the
wicked.
4 A slack hand [j] causes poverty,
[k] but the hand of the diligent makes
rich.
5 He who [l] gathers in summer is a
prudent son,
but he who sleeps in harvest is
[m] a son who brings shame.
6 Blessings are on the head of the
righteous,
but [n] the mouth of the wicked
conceals violence.
7 [o] The memory of the righteous is a
blessing,
but [p] the name of the wicked will rot.
8 [q] The wise of heart will receive
commandments,
but a babbling fool will come to
ruin.
9 [r] Whoever walks in integrity walks
securely,
but he who makes his ways
crooked [s] will be
found out.
10 Whoever [t] winks the eye causes
trouble,
but a babbling fool will come to
ruin.
11 [u] The mouth of the righteous is [v] a
fountain of life,
but the mouth of the wicked
[n] conceals violence.
12 Hatred stirs up
strife,
but [w] love covers all
offenses.
13 On the lips of him who has
understanding, wisdom is
found,
but [x] a rod is for the back of him
who [y] lacks sense.
14 The wise [z] lay up
knowledge,
but [a] the mouth of a fool brings
ruin near.

2 [f] [ch. 21:6; Ezek. 7:19; Luke 12:19, 20] [g] ch. 11:4, 6
3 [h] Ps. 34:9, 10; 37:25; [Matt. 6:33] [i] [Ps. 112:10; James 4:3]
4 [j] [ch. 6:11; 12:24; 13:4] [k] ch. 21:5
5 [l] [ch. 6:8] [m] ch. 17:2; 19:26
6 [n] [Ps. 69:7; Obad. 10]
7 [o] Ps. 112:6 [p] [Ps. 9:5]
8 [q] [Matt. 7:24, 25]
9 [r] ch. 3:23; 28:18; Ps. 23:4; Isai. 33:15, 16 [s] [Matt. 10:26; 1 Tim. 5:25]
10 [t] ch. 6:13
11 [u] Ps. 37:30 [v] ch. 13:14; Ps. 36:9 [n] [See ver. 6 above]
12 [w] 1 Pet. 4:8; [James 5:20]
13 [x] ch. 19:29; 26:3 [y] See ch. 6:32
14 [z] [ver. 8; ch. 12:23] [a] ch. 18:7

The wisdom of Proverbs presupposes and builds upon the special revelation of God in the Law (1:7 and notes). The Hebrew sages assumed that, given human intelligence and the gift of God's wisdom in His self-revelation, God's people learn to discern the order and relationships that make for a meaningful and productive life. The wisdom of Proverbs gives the fruit of experience and reflection, stressing the need to think through and to apply human knowledge and the Word of God to all the affairs of life in a responsible way.

10:1–32 As is often the case in the Bible, the chapter divisions are rather arbitrary and do not aid the analysis of the text. The individual sentences can be classified according to their literary structures and their themes. Chapters 10–15 consist mainly of contrasts between opposites, as indicated by the conjunction "but" introducing the second line of most of these proverbs. This common literary device uses contrasting pairs such as "righteous" versus "wicked" and "wise" versus "fool." Occasional grouping of sentences according to theme and form is evident in the book, a method that aids memorization but does not assist the interpretation of the mostly independent sayings. Each sentence has its own social setting and special aim. Much like folk sayings in our Western societies, some of the sayings have been separated from their contexts in order to provide concise, practical guidelines for living.

10:1 The proverbs of Solomon. See Introduction: Author.

10:2 righteousness. See note 8:18. In this chapter, about half the verses contain a contrast between the righteous and the wicked.

delivers from death. See 2:18; 3:18 and notes.

10:3 does not let . . . go hungry. There is a correlation between righteousness and life both in the covenant promises of God and in general life experience. The suffering of the righteous is not in view, however (cf. 1:19 note).

10:4, 5 See 6:6–11; 13:4; 15:19; 24:30–34. A frequently used wisdom theme, poverty itself is no shame, but poverty due to laziness is.

10:5 prudent son. Family relationships and obligations are primary concerns in wisdom literature.

10:6 Blessings. The unspecified blessings leave the application open to a range of situations, but, as in v. 22, the goodness of the Lord is experienced.

10:7 memory. How the righteous person is remembered after death.

10:8 receive commandments. The wise person is teachable and receives the commands of wisdom (2:1; 3:1 note).

babbling fool. Fools do not know when to be silent and listen. They lack the discipline of wisdom and promote their own downfall (v. 14 note).

10:9 will be found out. The one who attempts to pervert the truth will be exposed and disciplined by God.

10:10 winks the eye. See 6:13 and note.

babbling fool. See v. 8 and note. This phrase does not seem to correspond to the first line, either as a parallel or a contrast. The Septuagint (Greek Old Testament) reads, "but the one who boldly reproves makes peace."

10:11 fountain of life. The image is similar to "tree of life" (3:18 note). The words of the wise, like a well, are a source of life (Ezek. 47:1–12; Rev. 22:1–3).

10:12 Hatred. The word suggests the rejection of the good order, indeed the dissolution (cf. 1 John 3:15) of human relationships. Such hatred causes the fragmentation of society.

love. The word suggests seeking the best for others. Love is the greatest expression of ordered relationships.

covers. In order to promote harmony of relationships, love covers over those matters that cause friction. This verse is alluded to in James 5:20 and 1 Pet. 4:8.

10:13 Those who are perceptive reveal their character in the wisdom of their words. Those who lack sense simply involve themselves in strife. The parallel suggests that foolish talk is the cause of their problems.

10:14 lay up knowledge. The wise person, though no longer the pupil, will continue to learn. Only a fool claims to know everything.

mouth of a fool. Note how often the fool is portrayed as a babbler (vv. 6, 8, 13, 18, 19, 31, 32). The Book of James, the "Proverbs" of the New Testament, also explores this theme (James 1:26; 3:1–12). Knowing when to speak and when to keep silent is a prominent wisdom theme (11:12 note; 26:4–5; Job 38:2; 42:1–6).

15 [b]A rich man's wealth is his strong
city;
the poverty of the poor is their ruin.
16 The wage of the righteous leads [c]to
life,
the gain of the wicked to sin.
17 Whoever heeds instruction is on [d]the
path to life,
but he who rejects reproof leads
others astray.
18 The one who conceals hatred has
lying lips,
and whoever utters slander is a
fool.
19 [e]When words are many, transgression
is not lacking,
[f]but whoever restrains his lips is
prudent.
20 The tongue of the righteous is
[g]choice silver;
the heart of the wicked is of little
worth.
21 The lips of the righteous feed many,
but fools die for [h]lack of sense.
22 [i]The blessing of the LORD makes rich,
and he adds no sorrow with it.[1]
23 Doing wrong is [j]like a joke to a fool,
but [k]wisdom is pleasure to a man
of understanding.
24 [l]What the wicked dreads [m]will come
upon him,
but [n]the desire of the righteous
will be granted.
25 When [o]the tempest passes, the
wicked is no more,
but [p]the righteous is established
forever.
26 Like vinegar to the teeth and smoke
to the eyes,
so is the sluggard to those who
send him.
27 [q]The fear of the LORD prolongs
life,
[r]but the years of the wicked
will be short.
28 [s]The hope of the righteous
brings joy,
[t]but the expectation of the wicked
will perish.
29 [u]The way of the LORD is a stronghold
to the blameless,
but destruction to
evildoers.
30 [v]The righteous will never be
removed,
but [w]the wicked will not dwell in
the land.
31 [x]The mouth of the righteous brings
forth wisdom,
but the perverse tongue will be
cut off.
32 The lips of the righteous [y]know what
is acceptable,
but the mouth of the wicked,
[z]what is perverse.

15 [b]ch. 18:11; [Ps. 52:7; Mark 10:24] **16** [c]ch. 11:19; 19:23 **17** [d][ch. 6:23] **19** [e][Matt. 12:36, 37] [f]ch. 17:27; [James 3:2] **20** [g]ch. 8:19; 16:16 **21** [h][Hos. 4:6] **22** [i][Gen. 24:35; 26:12; Deut. 8:18] **23** [j]ch. 2:14; 15:21 [k][ch. 8:30] **24** [l]Isai. 66:4; Heb. 10:27; [Job 15:21] [m]Job 3:25 [n]Ps. 145:19; Matt. 5:6; 1 John 5:14, 15 **25** [o][Job 21:18; Ps. 58:9]; See Matt. 7:26, 27 [p]ch. 12:3; Ps. 15:5; [Matt. 7:24, 25] **27** [q]See ch. 3:2 [r]See Job 15:32, 33 **28** [s][Luke 21:28] [t]See Job 8:13 **29** [u][Ps. 25:12; Matt. 22:16; Acts 9:2] **30** [v]ver. 25; Ps. 37:22, 29; 125:1 [w]ch. 2:21, 22 **31** [x]Ps. 37:30 **32** [y][Eccles. 10:12] [z]ch. 2:12

[1] Or *and toil adds nothing to it*

10:15 strong city. The image is that of security against the uncertainties of life.

poverty of the poor. The poor do not have much defense against the unexpected. This circumstance is observed without comment on its rightness or wrongness (cf. Matt. 26:11). In the final analysis, however, the rich, whose confidence is in themselves (28:11), will find that their monetary security is illusory (11:4, 28; 18:10, 11; 23:4, 5). Only the Lord is a sure defense (3:5, 6).

10:16 wage. The outcome or reward of righteousness is life (3:2, 18 and notes; cf. Rom. 6:23).

sin. "Sin," or its consequence, punishment, is opposed to life.

10:18 The form of this verse differs from the parallel of opposites (antithetic parallelism) found in much of this chapter. Again the subject is foolish speech (lying or slander), and the one who engages in such action is either malicious or foolish (v. 14 note). Such foolishness is not lightly regarded, because this folly is actually sin (Ex. 20:16).

10:20 heart. Here the word is parallel with tongue. The mind, will, and inner character of the wicked are the source of futile words (Matt. 15:18, 19).

10:21 See vv. 11 and 17. The wisdom of the righteous has good effects upon others, but fools cannot even sustain themselves.

10:22 rich. In the Old Testament context this would be material wealth, a result of Solomon's wisdom (1 Kin. 4:22–28; 10:4–13). Wealth is not wisdom's goal, but is often wisdom's reward (v. 2).

10:24 What the wicked dreads. The wicked's fear of punishment. The meaning seems to be that God's righteous judgment is inevitable.

10:26 The form of this proverb differs from the parallel of opposites (antithetic parallelism) usual in this chapter. The comparison turns on what is common to the three pairs (synonymous parallelism; see "Introduction to Hebrew Poetry"). The lazy person is a distasteful irritant to his employer.

10:27 The fear of the LORD. See 1:7; 9:10 and notes. Harmony with God, here recognized as coming through the provisions of the covenant, means harmony with life. As in the fifth commandment, the blessings of God are seen in terms of a lengthy and fruitful life in the Promised Land (Ex. 20:12; Deut. 5:16 note). See 2:20–22; 3:2 and note.

10:29 This proverb states a basic principle of covenant theology rather than an observation on human life. The wisdom writers remind us that the source of all true knowledge and wisdom is the self-revelation of God in His creative, providential, and saving works, and especially in the Scriptures.

10:30 See v. 27. Here is another proverb grounded in God's covenant with Israel. The "land" is that promised to Israel, and its possession is basic to life. Possession of the land was conditional upon the response of faith to the covenant promises.

10:31, 32 See note on v. 14.

10:31 perverse. The word suggests that which speaks dishonestly and seeks to prevent sound judgment in others.

11 [a]A false balance is an abomination
to the LORD,
[b]but a just weight is his delight.
2 [c]When pride comes, then comes
disgrace,
but with [d]the humble is wisdom.
3 [e]The integrity of the upright guides
them,
[f]but the crookedness of the
treacherous destroys them.
4 [g]Riches do not profit in the day of
wrath,
[h]but righteousness delivers from
death.
5 The righteousness of the blameless
[i]keeps his way straight,
but the wicked falls by his own
wickedness.
6 [h]The righteousness of the upright
delivers them,
but the treacherous [j]are taken
captive by their lust.
7 When the wicked dies, his [k]hope will
perish,
and [l]the expectation of wealth[1]
perishes too.
8 [m]The righteous is delivered from
trouble,
and the wicked walks into it
instead.

Chapter 11
1 [a]ch. 16:11; 20:10, 23; See Lev. 19:35, 36 [b][ch. 12:22]
2 [c]ch. 16:18; 18:12; 29:23; [Dan. 4:30, 31] [d]Mic. 6:8
3 [e]ch. 13:6 [f]ch. 19:3
4 [g]Zeph. 1:18; See ch. 10:2 [h][Gen. 7:1]
5 [i]ch. 3:6
6 [h][See ver. 4 above] [j]See Ps. 7:15, 16
7 [k]ch. 10:28 [l]See Job 8:13, 14
8 [m]ver. 6; [ch. 21:18]
10 [n][ch. 28:12; Esth. 8:15]
11 [o]Ps. 10:7 [p][ch. 14:1; 29:8]
12 [q]ch. 14:21; [Matt. 7:1]
13 [r]ch. 20:19; Lev. 19:16
14 [s]ch. 15:22; 20:18; 24:6
15 [t][ch. 6:1; Job 17:3]

9 With his mouth the godless man
would destroy his neighbor,
but by knowledge the righteous are
delivered.
10 [n]When it goes well with the righteous,
the city rejoices,
and when the wicked perish there
are shouts of gladness.
11 By the blessing of the upright a city
is exalted,
but [o]by the mouth of the wicked
[p]it is overthrown.
12 Whoever [q]belittles his neighbor lacks
sense,
but a man of understanding
remains silent.
13 Whoever [r]goes about slandering
reveals secrets,
but he who is trustworthy in spirit
keeps a thing covered.
14 Where there is [s]no guidance, a
people falls,
[s]but in an abundance of counselors
there is safety.
15 [t]Whoever puts up security for a
stranger will surely suffer
harm,
but he who hates striking hands in
pledge is secure.

1 Or *of his strength*, or *of iniquity*

11:1–31 As in ch. 10, many sayings in this chapter contrast the ways of righteousness and wickedness. Other sentences not explicitly naming these two opposites nevertheless compare specific examples of them.

11:1 false balance. Honesty and fair dealing are basic to covenant ethics. Reference to the Lord indicates that covenant relationships are in view.

11:2 pride . . . disgrace. Wisdom recognizes the importance of self-control. Arrogance and pride are easily recognized by others who will then withhold honor.

with the humble is wisdom. Because humility involves the realistic appraisal of one's place in relationship to others, it promotes a wise sense of the true order of things.

11:3 integrity. From a Hebrew root meaning "complete," this word indicates ethical straightness and perfection. Guidance in living is put in its ethical framework. A right relationship to the Lord leads to a right course in life.

crookedness. This lifestyle destroys a person because God's order cannot ultimately be resisted.

11:4 day of wrath. The saying anticipates not merely natural and impersonal retribution in life, but a personal Judge and His wrath. Wealth cannot secure anyone from God's wrath (Luke 12:13–21).

righteousness. See note 8:18.

11:5, 6 The sense is almost identical with v. 3.

11:8 delivered. An apparent reference to God's providential intervention. Proverbial sayings often state what is generally true, but not without exceptions. The suffering of the righteous (e.g., Job) shows that while a degree of order is perceptible in human experience, such order is not invariable since God is sovereign and pursues His own eternal purposes. Only trust in God's goodness, even when His goodness is not immediately seen, addresses the problem of the righteous sufferer. See note 10:1–22:16; and "Introduction to Hebrew Poetry."

11:9 With his mouth. See 10:13, 14, 18 and notes.

knowledge. Wisdom and knowledge as the way to life enable one to escape the ways of the godless (vv. 4, 6, 8).

11:10 A viable society must have some recognition of right and wrong and of reward and retribution. Without descending to vindictive revenge, there is a proper rejoicing when the perpetrators of evil, corruption, and human misery are destroyed.

11:11 The corporate implications of behavior are apparent: righteous lives strengthen the community, while the wicked corrupt and overthrow it.

11:12 See note 10:14. Gossip and derision easily destroy another's reputation, but they do not advance the reputation of the gossiper. The wise know when to keep silent (v. 13; 12:23; 13:3; 17:28; 18:2, 6–8; Eccl. 3:7).

11:13 A variation on v. 12, this verse notes that maintaining confidences strengthens relationships, while a fool's gossip destroys them (10:14 and note).

11:14 guidance . . . counselors. See 15:22; 20:18; 24:6. Counsel or advice was a feature of the emergence of wisdom in political life during the reign of David (2 Sam. 15:30–17:23).

11:15 See 6:1 and note.

16 [u] A gracious woman gets honor,
and [v] violent men get riches.
17 [w] A man who is kind benefits
himself,
but a cruel man hurts himself.
18 The wicked earns deceptive wages,
but one who [x] sows righteousness
gets a sure reward.
19 Whoever is steadfast in righteousness
[y] will live,
but [z] he who pursues evil will die.
20 Those of [a] crooked heart are [b] an
abomination to the LORD,
but those of [c] blameless ways are
[d] his delight.
21 [e] Be assured, [f] an evil person will not
go unpunished,
but [g] the offspring of the righteous
will be delivered.
22 Like [h] a gold ring in a pig's snout
is a beautiful woman without
discretion.
23 The desire of the righteous ends only
in good;
[i] the expectation of the wicked in
wrath.
24 [j] One gives [k] freely, yet grows all the
richer;
another withholds what he should
give, and only suffers want.

16 [u] [ch. 31:30] [v] [Luke 11:21]
17 [w] [Matt. 5:7]; See Matt. 25:34-40
18 [x] Hos. 10:12; Gal. 6:8, 9; [James 3:18]
19 [y] ch. 10:16; 19:23 [z] [Rom. 6:23; Gal. 6:8]
20 [a] [ch. 17:20] [b] ch. 12:22; 16:5 [c] ch. 13:6; Ps. 119:1 [d] 1 Chr. 29:17
21 [e] ch. 16:5 [f] ch. 12:7; [Ps. 37:2, 9]; See Isai. 28:15-18 [g] See Ps. 112:2
22 [h] [Gen. 24:47; Isai.3:21; Ezek. 16:12]
23 [i] Rom. 2:8, 9
24 [j] ch. 13:7 [k] Ps. 37:21; 112:9; [ch. 19:17]
25 [l] See 2 Cor. 9:6-11 [m] ch. 13:4; 28:25 [n] [Matt. 7:2]
26 [o] ch. 24:24 [p] [Job 29:13] [q] [Gen. 42:6]
27 [r] See Ps. 7:16
28 [s] See Ps. 49:6 [t] Jer. 17:8; See Ps. 92:12

25 [l] Whoever brings blessing [m] will be
enriched,
and [n] one who waters will himself
be watered.
26 [o] The people curse him who holds
back grain,
but [p] a blessing is on the head of
him who [q] sells it.
27 Whoever diligently seeks good seeks
favor,[1]
but evil comes to [r] him who
searches for it.
28 Whoever [s] trusts in his riches
will fall,
but the righteous will [t] flourish like
a green leaf.
29 Whoever [u] troubles his own
household will [v] inherit
the wind,
and the fool will be servant to the
wise of heart.
30 The fruit of the righteous is [w] a tree
of life,
and whoever [x] captures souls
is wise.
31 If [y] the righteous is repaid on earth,
how much more the wicked and
the sinner!

29 [u] ch. 15:27 [v] [Eccles. 5:16] 30 [w] See ch. 3:18 [x] Dan. 12:3; James 5:20; See 1 Cor. 9:19-22 31 [y] [Jer. 25:29; 1 Pet. 4:18]

[1] Or *acceptance*

11:16 These opposed parallel thoughts (antithetic parallelism) perhaps teach the desirability of respect over mere wealth (22:1; cf. Eccl. 7:1). Alternatively, the sense may be that the gracious woman retains honor as surely as the ruthless acquire riches.

11:17 kind. The word describes one who behaves rightly toward others. There is a legitimate self-interest expressed in "love your neighbor as yourself" (Lev. 19:18). What is best for others is best for us.

11:18 See 10:2, 16; cf. 1 Cor. 9:6–11. The reward may be material or spiritual. The principle is the lasting value of the rewards of righteousness.

11:19 The ways of righteousness and evil, worked out in specific detail in many sayings in the chapter, are here stated in the broadest terms. The underlying principle is explained in Deut. 30:15–20. In this verse, "righteousness" and "evil" are used broadly, to include the God-given order in existence that experience discerns (8:18 note).

11:21 will not go unpunished. The legal terminology indicates that the judgment of God, and not merely natural retribution, is involved. In the same way, there is a judicial act of God involved in the escape of the righteous from judgment.

11:23 See 10:24, 25, 28–30. The contrast of the righteous and the wicked is seen in their destinies.

11:24–26 These verses make the general point that the generous person is blessed, while miserliness leads to ruin (v. 17 note).

11:26 The generosity of v. 25 is illustrated by the community-minded merchant who puts the needs of others ahead of his own interests.

11:27 See v. 17 and note. The one who "seeks good" is either the benefactor of society who receives community approval in return, or the seeker of righteousness who receives the approval of God (cf. Matt. 5:6).

11:28 Whoever trusts in his riches will fall. See v. 4 and note. When possessions are seen to ensure life, God is excluded, as are right relations with others. The result is a life of diminished quality.

11:29 The parallel thoughts of this verse are not obvious unless we understand the first line to mean a reckless use of the family wealth that brings ruin on the household. The fool inherits nothing (wind) and must be the servant of the one who has managed his finances well.

11:30 fruit . . . tree of life. The metaphor is curiously mixed. The result of righteousness is life. See 3:18 and note, 13:12; 15:4.

captures souls. Lit. "takes souls" or "takes lives." The usual meaning of the phrase is to kill, or take away life. To accommodate this, the Septuagint (Greek Old Testament) renders the clause, "But the souls of the lawless are taken away before their time." The translation is uncertain.

11:31 The form of this proverb, using intensification ("how much more") is typical of wisdom (15:11; 17:7; 19:7, 10; 21:27).

the righteous is repaid. Not even the righteous escape the scrutiny of judgment. The Septuagint (Greek Old Testament) translation reads, "If the righteous one is scarcely saved" (as quoted in 1 Pet. 4:18).

on earth. Or, "in the land" (2:20–22 note).

how much more the wicked. If the sins of the righteous are judged, obviously those of the ungodly are judged as well. The principle of human responsibility is clear: even the righteous must accept responsibility for their folly.

12

Whoever loves discipline loves
knowledge,
but he who [z]hates reproof is [a]stupid.
2 A good man [b]obtains favor from the
LORD,
but a man of evil devices he
condemns.
3 No one is established by wickedness,
but the root of [c]the righteous will
never be moved.
4 [d]An excellent wife is [e]the crown of her
husband,
but she who [f]brings shame is like
[g]rottenness in his bones.
5 [h]The thoughts of the righteous are just;
the counsels of the wicked are
deceitful.
6 The words of the wicked [i]lie in wait
for blood,
but [j]the mouth of the upright
delivers them.
7 [k]The wicked are [l]overthrown and are
no more,
[m]but the house of the righteous will
stand.
8 A man is commended according to
his good sense,
but one of twisted mind is
[n]despised.
9 Better to be lowly and have a servant
than to play the great man and
lack bread.
10 [o]Whoever is righteous has regard for
the life of his beast,
but the mercy of the wicked is
cruel.
11 [p]Whoever works his land [q]will have
plenty of bread,
[r]but he who follows [s]worthless
pursuits lacks sense.
12 Whoever is wicked covets [t]the spoil
of evildoers,
but the root of the righteous bears
fruit.
13 An evil man is ensnared [u]by the
transgression of his lips,
[v]but the righteous escapes from
trouble.
14 From the fruit of his mouth [w]a man
is satisfied with good,
[x]and the work of a man's hand
comes back to him.
15 [y]The way of a fool is right in his own
eyes,
but a wise man listens to advice.
16 [z]The vexation of a fool is known at
once,
but the prudent ignores an insult.
17 [a]Whoever speaks[1] the truth gives
honest evidence,
but [b]a false witness utters
deceit.

Chapter 12
1 [z]ch. 5:12; 15:10 [a]Ps. 49:10
2 [b]ch. 8:35
3 [c]See ch. 10:25
4 [d]See ch. 31:10 [e]S. of S. 3:11 [f]ch. 10:5 [g]ch. 14:30
5 [h][Matt. 12:35]
6 [i]See ch. 1:11 [j]ch. 14:3
7 [k]See ch. 11:21 [l]Job 34:25 [m][ch. 10:25, 30]
8 [n][1 Sam. 20:30]
10 [o][Deut. 25:4]
11 [p]ch. 28:19 [q]ch. 20:13 [r]ch. 28:19 [s]Judg. 9:4
12 [t][Ps. 10:9]
13 [u]ch. 18:7; [Ps. 64:8; Matt. 12:37] [v]ch. 21:23
14 [w]ch. 13:2; 14:14; 18:20 [x]ch. 19:17; Isai. 3:10, 11; [Judg. 9:16, 56]
15 [y]ch. 3:7; 16:2; 21:2; 26:12; [ch. 14:12; 16:25]
16 [z][ch. 14:33; 29:11]
17 [a]ch. 14:5 [b]See ch. 6:19

1 Hebrew *breathes out*

12:1 Whoever loves discipline loves knowledge. Lit. "loving discipline, loving knowledge." The form of this proverb, like 13:3 and 14:2, groups things that belong together without explicitly stating the relationship. These are then contrasted with their opposites. The wise person accepts correction and consequently grows wiser, but the one who cannot accept criticism goes nowhere.

12:2 favor. See note 8:35.

LORD. See note 1:7.

12:4 See the extended appraisal of the virtuous wife at 31:10–31.

12:5 The character of a person establishes principles for action. There is an implicit warning against trusting people on the basis of appearances.

12:6 See 1:11. This verse stresses the power of words for good or evil.

delivers them. That is, they will rescue the victims of the wicked.

12:7 See 10:25 and note.

12:8 good sense. The display of mastery in life wins praise.

twisted mind. The phrase suggests an inability to think straight; more muddled than evil.

12:9 A number of proverbs have this form of direct comparison using the "better . . . than" formula (15:16, 17; 16:8, 19, 32; 17:1, 12; 19:1).

to be lowly. A person of no social standing or reputation.

have a servant. The Septuagint (Greek Old Testament) renders this phrase, "who works for himself." The meaning is either, "Better humble prosperity than poverty concealed by pretense," or, "Better to work without esteem than to go hungry while dreaming of affluence."

12:10 God takes account of our treatment of animals (1 Kin. 4:33). This is consistent with concern for the right order of things in the world.

righteous. See note 8:18.

mercy . . . is cruel. The wicked person is incapable of kindness even towards his livestock.

12:11 A variation of v. 9, this verse contrasts the benefits of honest hard work with fantasies that produce nothing. See 6:6–11; 20:4; 24:30–34; 28:19.

12:12 Although the Hebrew of this verse is difficult, the basic contrast—the benefits of righteousness against the effects of wickedness—is plain.

12:13 See 10:11, 14, 31.

12:14 The principle of rewards, expressed for example in v. 21, is focused on wise speech. Such speech creates good relationships and shows care for the life-enhancing order of things. Its rewards are as tangible as those of physical labor.

12:15 The fool thinks he knows better than others. The wise person is humble enough to learn from the experience of others and has the ability to discern what is good counsel (v. 1).

12:16 Self-control is characteristic of the wise. The fool reacts too strongly and too soon, destroying relationships. The wise person leaves the way open for reconciliation.

12:17 On first sight this proverb expresses what should be self-evident, but it effectively illustrates the inevitable relationship between character and deeds (v. 5 note).

18 [c]There is one whose rash words are
like sword thrusts,
but the tongue of the wise brings
[d]healing.
19 Truthful lips endure forever,
but [e]a lying tongue is but for a
moment.
20 Deceit is in the heart of [f]those who
devise evil,
but those who plan peace have joy.
21 [g]No ill befalls the righteous,
but the wicked are filled with
trouble.
22 [h]Lying lips are [i]an abomination to the
LORD,
[j]but those who act faithfully are his
delight.
23 [k]A prudent man conceals knowledge,
[k]but the heart of fools proclaims
folly.
24 [l]The hand of the diligent will rule,
while the slothful will be [m]put to
forced labor.
25 [n]Anxiety in a man's heart weighs him
down,
but a good word makes him glad.
26 One who is righteous is a guide to
his neighbor,[1]
but the way of the wicked leads
them astray.

18 [c]See Ps. 57:4 [d]See ch. 4:22
19 [e]ch. 19:9; [Ps. 52:4, 5]
20 [f]ch. 3:29
21 [g]Ps. 91:10; [1 Pet. 3:13; 2 Pet. 2:9]
22 [h][Rev. 22:15]; See ch. 6:17 [i]ch. 11:20 [j][ch. 11:1]
23 [k][ch. 13:16; 15:2]
24 [l][ch. 10:4; 13:4] [m][Gen. 49:15; 1 Kin. 9:21]
25 [n]ch. 15:13; [ch. 17:22]
27 [o][ver. 24]
28 [p]See ch. 10:2
Chapter 13
1 [q]ch. 1:22; See Ps. 1:1
2 [r]ch. 12:14 [s][ch. 1:31; 26:6]
3 [t]ch. 21:23; [ch. 12:13; 18:21; James 3:2] [u]ch. 20:19 [v]ch. 18:7
4 [w]See ch. 6:9-11 [x]ch. 11:25
6 [y]ch. 11:3, 5, 6 [z]ch. 11:20

27 [o]Whoever is slothful will not roast his
game,
but the diligent man will get
precious wealth.[2]
28 [p]In the path of righteousness is life,
and in its pathway there is no
death.

13 A wise son hears his father's
instruction,
but [q]a scoffer does not listen to
rebuke.
2 From the fruit of his mouth a man
[r]eats what is good,
but the desire of the treacherous
[s]is for violence.
3 [t]Whoever guards his mouth preserves
his life;
[u]he who opens wide his lips [v]comes
to ruin.
4 [w]The soul of the sluggard craves and
gets nothing,
while the soul of the diligent [x]is
richly supplied.
5 The righteous hates falsehood,
but the wicked brings shame[3] and
disgrace.
6 [y]Righteousness guards him whose
[z]way is blameless,
but sin overthrows the wicked.

1 Or *The righteous chooses his friends carefully* 2 Or *but diligence is precious wealth* 3 Or *stench*

12:18, 19 These two proverbs may have been placed with v. 17 because they enlarge on the same theme. Verse 18 considers the effects of words on our relationships with others, while v. 19 considers the strength of truth compared with the weakness of lies that inevitably give themselves away (cf. v. 13).

12:20 Deceit. The contrast with "joy" seems to require that this means deceiving oneself.

peace. This word (Hebrew *shalom*) refers to wholeness; it is a term addressing relationships rather than a reference to the private experience of tranquility.

12:21 No ill. This basic condition of the righteous refers both to natural calamity and the judgment of God. See note 11:8.

12:22 The Lord's self-revealed character and attitudes provide a strong motive for truth.

12:23 conceals knowledge. Not out of selfishness but so that he does not parade his knowledge. Wisdom knows when it is right to keep silent and when to speak (26:4, 5; Eccl. 3:7; James 3:17, 18).

proclaims folly. The fool not only has an inflated assessment of his own cleverness (v. 15), but cannot resist showing it off. Such posturing betrays his real foolishness.

12:25 The ministry of encouragement is more than a superficial word (James 2:15, 16), but the spoken word is still an important aspect of caring for one another. God acts towards us with deeds interpreted by His Word.

12:27 roast. It is difficult to tell whether the translation should be that the man is too lazy to roast his prey, or too lazy to catch it in the first place. The second line praises diligence without continuing the metaphor of the hunt.

12:28 life. See 3:2, 18 and notes.

no death. Hebrew "not death." See 2:18 and note, also 3:2. The Hebrew consonants translated as "no" can also mean "to"; in contrast to the "path of righteousness" leading to life, "there is a path that leads to death."

13:1 The teachability of the child or pupil contrasts with the fool's propensity to scoff and to refuse correction (1:8, 22 and notes).

13:2 fruit of his mouth. The power of words is a frequent wisdom theme. See 10:11, 13, 19; 12:14 and notes. Wise words are constructive, and the speaker personally benefits from them.

treacherous. The word suggests treacherous deceivers whose social conscience is warped.

13:3 guards his mouth. Having control over one's speech so that what is said is carefully considered for its possible effects.

opens wide his lips. Blurts out words, either hastily or maliciously, without concern for the consequences.

13:4 sluggard. See 6:6–11 and notes. Human responsibility cannot be avoided. Neither the world nor God owes us a living.

diligent. Rightly understanding the rewards of honest labor, the industrious person is sustained.

13:5 righteous. See note 8:18.

13:6 See 10:9; 11:3–9.

7 [a] One pretends to be rich, yet has
nothing;
[b] another pretends to be poor, yet
has great wealth.
8 The ransom of a man's life is his
wealth,
but a poor man [c] hears no threat.
9 [d] The light of the righteous rejoices,
but [e] the lamp of the wicked will be
put out.
10 [f] By insolence comes nothing but
strife,
but with those who take advice is
wisdom.
11 [g] Wealth gained hastily[1] will
dwindle,
but whoever gathers little by little
will increase it.
12 Hope deferred makes the heart sick,
[h] but a desire fulfilled is [i] a tree of
life.
13 Whoever [j] despises [k] the word
brings destruction on himself,
but he who reveres the
commandment will be
[l] rewarded.
14 The teaching of the wise is [m] a
fountain of life,
that one may [n] turn away from the
snares of death.
15 [o] Good sense wins [p] favor,
but the way of the treacherous is
their ruin.[2]
16 [q] In everything the prudent acts with
knowledge,
[r] but a fool flaunts his
folly.
17 A wicked messenger falls into
trouble,
but [s] a faithful envoy brings
healing.
18 Poverty and disgrace come to him
who [t] ignores instruction,
[u] but whoever [v] heeds reproof is
honored.
19 [w] A desire fulfilled is sweet to
the soul,
but to turn away from evil is an
abomination to fools.
20 Whoever walks with the wise
becomes wise,
but the companion of fools will
suffer harm.
21 [x] Disaster[3] pursues sinners,
[y] but the righteous are rewarded
with good.
22 [z] A good man leaves an inheritance to
his children's children,
but [a] the sinner's wealth is laid up
for the righteous.
23 The fallow ground of the poor would
yield much food,
but it is swept away through
[b] injustice.

7 [a] ch. 11:24; [Luke 12:21; Rev. 3:17] [b] [Luke 12:33; 2 Cor. 6:10; James 2:5]
8 [c] [ver. 1]
9 [d] [Job 29:3] [e] See Job 18:5
10 [f] [ch. 28:25]
11 [g] [ch. 10:2; 20:21; 21:6; 28:20, 22]
12 [h] [ver. 19] [i] See ch. 3:18
13 [j] [ch. 19:16; Num. 15:31; 2 Chr. 36:16] [k] ch. 16:20; Deut. 30:14 [l] [ver. 21]
14 [m] See ch. 10:11 [n] ch. 14:27; [Ps. 18:5; 2 Tim. 2:26]
15 [o] [Luke 2:52]; See Ps. 111:10 [p] ch. 3:4; 22:1
16 [q] [ch. 12:23; 15:2] [r] [ch. 18:2; Eccles. 10:3]
17 [s] ch. 25:13; [ch. 14:5]
18 [t] [ch. 15:5, 31, 32] [u] [ch. 15:5] [v] [ch. 15:31]
19 [w] [ver. 12]
21 [x] [Ps. 11:6; 32:10] [y] [ver. 13; Luke 6:38]
22 [z] [Ezra 9:12; Ps. 37:25] [a] ch. 28:8; See Job 27:16, 17
23 [b] [ch. 16:8]

[1] Or *by fraud* [2] Probable reading (compare Septuagint, Syriac, Vulgate); Hebrew *is rugged*, or *is an enduring rut* [3] Or *Evil*

13:7 pretends to be. Though the disparity of possessions is noted, the point of the proverb seems to be the similarity of pretense. Each misrepresents the facts about himself.

13:8 The rich may be kidnapped for ransom, but such threats do not concern the poor. Behind each situation is the principle that the security of riches can be illusory while the insecurity of poverty has its advantages.

13:9 rejoices. The metaphor presents two kinds of houses: one brightly lit and happy, the other dark and deserted. These houses symbolize human lives: one person prospers and lives long while another is cut short (10:27 note).

13:11 The wisdom of honest hard work is contrasted with the folly of dishonest gain.

13:12 A common human experience: frustrated expectations cause a loss of morale and a sense of hopelessness. This does not imply that instant gratification is good, but rather that we should honestly strive for desirable goals in life.

tree of life. See 3:18 and note.

13:13 word. The word of wise instruction.

commandment. See 3:1 and note. The opposite effects of obedience and disobedience are constant themes.

13:15 treacherous. See v. 2 and note.

13:16 The truth of this proverb seems to be self-evident, but see 12:17 and note.

13:17 wicked messenger. One who brings a deceitful message.

trouble. Or, "misfortune." Such a messenger was the Amalekite who, hoping to win favor from David, falsely claimed to have killed Saul, but was executed for his trouble (2 Sam. 1:1–16). The parallel statements of this proverb suggest that the faithful messenger, perhaps an envoy, promotes the welfare of others.

13:19 See v. 12 and note. The achievement of a worthwhile goal has benefits for one's life. Fools will not turn from evil to pursue such goals.

13:20 The simple lesson is that we become like those whose company we keep.

13:21 Hebrew wisdom, with its focus on the lessons from human experience (ch. 4 note), stresses the general cause-and-effect relation between lifestyles and their outcome. While this can be thought of as natural retribution because of the observed patterns of human experience, there is an underlying assumption that the order in the world is a consequence of God's rule.

13:22 leaves an inheritance. Wisdom in life has lasting effects, especially in one's own family.

laid up for the righteous. The wealth of the wicked may be taken away and given to those more deserving (28:8; Job 27:13–19). This verse may point to the irresponsible dissipation of wealth due to folly, or to divine retribution on the wicked wealthy for other sins (cf. James 5:1–3).

13:23 The natural relationship between diligence and sufficiency (vv. 4, 11 notes) is broken by oppression and injustice.

24 [c] Whoever spares the rod hates his son,
but he who loves him is diligent to discipline him.[1]
25 [d] The righteous has enough to satisfy his appetite,
but the belly of the wicked suffers want.

14

[e] The wisest of women [f] builds her house,
but folly with her own hands [g] tears it down.
2 Whoever [h] walks in uprightness fears the LORD,
but he who is [i] devious in his ways despises him.
3 By the mouth of a fool comes [j] a rod for his back,[2]
[k] but the lips of the wise will preserve them.
4 Where there are no oxen, the manger is clean,
but abundant crops come by the strength of the ox.
5 [l] A faithful witness does not lie,
but [m] a false witness breathes out lies.
6 [n] A scoffer seeks wisdom [o] in vain,
but [p] knowledge is easy for a man of understanding.
7 Leave the presence of a fool,
for there you do not meet words of knowledge.
8 The wisdom of the prudent is to discern his way,
but the folly of fools is deceiving.
9 [q] Fools mock at the guilt offering,
but the upright enjoy acceptance.[3]
10 The heart knows its own [r] bitterness,
and no stranger shares its joy.
11 [s] The house of the wicked will be destroyed,
but the tent of the upright will flourish.
12 [t] There is a way that seems right to a man,
but [u] its end is the way to death.[4]
13 Even in laughter the heart may ache,
and [v] the end of joy may be [w] grief.
14 The backslider in heart will be [x] filled with the fruit of his ways,
and [y] a good man will be filled with the fruit of his ways.
15 [z] The simple believes everything,
but the prudent gives thought to his steps.
16 [a] One who is wise is cautious[5] and [b] turns away from evil,
but a fool is reckless and careless.

24[c]ch. 19:18; 22:15; 23:13, 14; 29:15, 17]
25[d]See ch. 10:3
Chapter 14
1[e][ch. 9:1; 24:3] [f]Deut. 25:9; Ruth 4:11 [g][ch. 11:11]
2[h]ch. 19:1; 28:6 [i]ch. 2:15
3[j][Jer. 18:18] [k]ch. 12:6
5[l][Ex. 23:1] [m]See ch. 6:19
6[n][ch. 24:7] [o][Ps. 25:9; 1 Pet. 5:5] [p][ch. 8:9; 15:14; 17:24]
9[q][ch. 10:23]
10[r][1 Sam. 1:10]; See Job 3:20
11[s][ch. 3:33; 15:25; Job 8:15; 21:28]
12[t]ch. 16:25; See ch. 12:15 [u][ch. 5:5; Rom. 6:21]; See ch. 7:27
13[v][Eccles. 2:2; Luke 6:25] [w]ch. 10:1
14[x][ch. 1:31; Matt. 6:2, 5] [y]ch. 12:14; Isai. 3:10
15[z]See ch. 1:4
16[a][ch. 22:3; 27:12] [b][ch. 3:7]; See Job 28:28; Ps. 34:14

1 Or *who loves him disciplines him early* 2 Or *In the mouth of a fool is a rod of pride* 3 Hebrew *but among the upright is acceptance* 4 Hebrew *ways of death* 5 Or *fears* [the LORD]

13:24 rod. Although the word may symbolize any kind of disciplinary correction, there is little doubt that corporal punishment was approved in some situations (10:13; 22:15; 23:13, 14; 29:15). Discipline with love prevents the rod from being destructive (3:11, 12 and notes).

13:25 See vv. 13, 18, 21 and notes.

14:1 wisest of women builds her house. Note the verbal parallels with the personification of wisdom as a woman who builds her house in 9:1.

14:2 uprightness. A contrast with "devious," the word means "straight," "honest."

fears the LORD. See 1:7 and note.

14:3 See 10:13 and note.

14:4 clean. It is unclear whether the Hebrew means that the trough is "clean," or full of "grain," as a result of being unused. In either case, the minor benefit of the unused trough must be weighed against the nothing that is produced when no oxen are working. Expenses must be accepted if anything is to be accomplished.

14:5 A fact and a warning that emphasize the consistency of character with action (12:5, 17 and notes).

14:6 scoffer. See 1:22 and note.

seeks wisdom. This kind of person may recognize the value of wisdom, but does not have the teachability to succeed.

14:8 prudent. In the context of wisdom, the term indicates one who is shrewd, who acts with real discernment in a way that promotes life. See 12:16, 23; 13:16 and notes.

deceiving. Perhaps self-deception (cf. 12:20 and note), although the deception of others may be involved.

14:9 mock at the guilt offering. This may mean that they mock at the suggestion of presenting the sacrificial guilt offering to God, or of making restitution to the person wronged (Lev. 6:1–7).

acceptance. The second line of the verse contrasts with the first, and the sense of the word is either acceptance with God or restored fellowship with others.

14:10 While much biblical wisdom literature reflects on interpersonal relationships, there is also a concern for those aspects of life that are personal and private. Some things cannot be communicated and one must learn to know what they are.

14:12 See 2:18, 20–22; 3:18 and notes.

seems right. The saying implies that the way is not right and that the person in question is rash, undiscerning, or ignorant.

14:13 Cf. v. 10 and note. Outward joy and hidden grief may coexist, but grief may be the truth to be faced in the end.

14:14 The Hebrew in the second line of this verse is difficult, but the basic contrast between the rewards for good and evil behavior is apparent.

14:15 simple. See note 1:4. The "simple" person is unskilled in the use of critical judgment.

prudent. See note on v. 8.

17 A man of [c]quick temper acts foolishly,
and a man of evil devices is hated.
18 The simple inherit folly,
but the prudent are crowned with knowledge.
19 [d]The evil bow down before the good,
the wicked at the gates of the righteous.
20 [e]The poor is disliked even by his neighbor,
[f]but the rich has many friends.
21 Whoever [g]despises his neighbor is a sinner,
but [h]blessed is he who is generous to the poor.
22 Do they not go astray who [i]devise evil?
Those who devise good meet[1]
[j]steadfast love and faithfulness.
23 In all toil there is profit,
but mere talk [k]tends only to poverty.
24 The crown of the wise is their wealth,
but the folly of fools brings folly.
25 A truthful witness saves lives,
but one who [l]breathes out lies is deceitful.
26 In the fear of the LORD one has [m]strong confidence,
and [n]his children will have [o]a refuge.
27 The fear of the LORD is [p]a fountain of life,
that one may [q]turn away from the snares of death.
28 In [r]a multitude of people is the glory of a king,
but without people a prince is ruined.
29 Whoever is [s]slow to anger has great understanding,
but he who has a hasty temper exalts folly.
30 A tranquil[2] heart gives [t]life to the flesh,
but [u]envy[3] makes [v]the bones rot.
31 Whoever oppresses a poor man [w]insults his [x]Maker,
[y]but he who is generous to the needy honors him.
32 [z]The wicked is overthrown through his evildoing,
but [a]the righteous finds refuge in his death.
33 Wisdom [b]rests in the heart of a man of understanding,
but it makes itself known even in the midst of fools.[4]
34 Righteousness exalts a nation,
but sin is a reproach to any people.
35 A servant who deals wisely has [c]the king's favor,
but his wrath falls on one who acts shamefully.

1 Or *show* 2 Or *healing* 3 Or *jealousy* 4 Or *Wisdom rests quietly in the heart of a man of understanding, but makes itself known in the midst of fools*

17 [c][ver. 29]
19 [d][Gen. 42:6; 1 Sam. 2:36]
20 [e]ch. 19:7 [f]ch. 19:4
21 [g]ch. 11:12 [h]Ps. 41:1
22 [i]See ch. 3:29 [j]ch. 3:3
23 [k][ch. 11:24; 21:5; 22:16]
25 [l]ver. 5
26 [m][ch. 1:33] [n][Ps. 73:15] [o]See Ps. 14:6
27 [p]See ch. 10:11 [q]See ch. 13:14
28 [r][1 Kin. 4:20]
29 [s]ch. 16:32; 19:11; [ver. 17; Eccles. 7:9; James 1:19]
30 [t]See ch. 4:22 [u][Ps. 112:10] [v]ch. 12:4
31 [w]ch. 17:5; [Matt. 25:40, 45] [x]ch. 22:2; See Job 35:10 [y]ch. 28:8
32 [z]ch. 24:16 [a]Gen. 49:18; Ps. 16:11; 17:15; 23:4; 2 Cor. 1:9; 5:8; 2 Tim. 4:18; [Num. 23:10]; See Job 19:25-27
33 [b]Eccles. 7:9; ch. 12:16; 29:11
35 [c][ch. 16:13; 22:11]; See Matt. 24:45-47

14:17 quick temper. See v. 29; 16:32; 19:11 and notes.

of evil devices. The Hebrew word usually signifies "discretion," a positive virtue (1:4; 2:11; 3:21; 5:2; 8:12). A following line of opposite meaning (antithetic parallelism), as found in most of the proverbs in this chapter, would suggest the opposite of quick-tempered.

14:18 knowledge. See 1:7 and note.

14:19 Even in this life, evil people are sometimes compelled to give grudging respect to the good. But the justice of God may be intended, in which the righteous are finally vindicated and the wicked made to bow before them at the last judgment.

14:20 Although originally an independent saying regarding friends who can assist in times of trouble (cf. Luke 16:9), its placement immediately before the proverb of v. 21 gives it an additional application. Even with the best of intentions, people grow tired of a friendship that always makes demands. Friendship is easy when it makes no demands or brings gains.

14:21 God's law commands kindness and care for one's neighbor as a reflection of the Lord's own character (Lev. 19:10–18). This principle has even greater clarity in the New Testament, which requires that we treat each other in a way that reflects God's gracious treatment of us through Christ (1 John 4:7–11).

14:22 steadfast love and faithfulness. This phrase, used of God's loving compassion for His covenant people (Ps. 86:15), is here applied to the highest human love and loyalty.

14:23 See 10:4; 12:11; 13:4 and notes.

14:24 As it stands, this verse is similar to v. 23. The self-evident truth in the second line emphasizes the futility of folly.

14:25 See v. 5. The first line expresses the results of truthful witness in a legal dispute. The second line does not express the opposite of the thought in the first line (as is usually the case in antithetic parallelism), but simply indicates the nature of false witness as it obscures the truth.

14:26 fear of the LORD. See 1:7 and note.

14:27 fountain of life. See 3:18; 10:11; 11:30; 13:14 and notes.

14:29 See v. 17.

14:30 heart. See note 2:2. The ancients recognized the link between mental and spiritual tranquility and physical health (3:7, 8).

14:32 death. The Septuagint (Greek Old Testament) reads "piety," making a more direct contrast with "wickedness." The Hebrew text does not speak explicitly of resurrection from death, but it does suggest confidence that God vindicates the righteous (23:18 and note).

14:33 makes itself known. The meaning of this line is uncertain. Either the fool readily flaunts what he imagines to be his wisdom, or even the fool manifests an occasional bit of wisdom.

14:34 exalts. Either morally, or as a consequence of divine material blessings (Deut. 28:1–14; 1 Kin. 4:20–28).

14:35 The wisdom of the royal court provides this warning against the incompetent fool.

15 [d]A soft answer turns away wrath,
but [e]a harsh word stirs up anger.
2 The tongue of the wise commends knowledge,
but [f]the mouths of fools pour out folly.
3 [g]The eyes of the LORD are in every place,
keeping watch on the evil and the good.
4 [h]A gentle[1] tongue is [i]a tree of life,
but [j]perverseness in it breaks the spirit.
5 [k]A fool [l]despises his father's instruction,
but [m]whoever heeds reproof is prudent.
6 In the house of the righteous there is much treasure,
but trouble befalls the income of the wicked.
7 [n]The lips of the wise spread knowledge;
[n]not so the hearts of fools.[2]
8 [o]The sacrifice of the wicked is an abomination to the LORD,
but [p]the prayer of the upright is acceptable to him.
9 The way of the wicked is an abomination to the LORD,
but he loves him [q]who pursues righteousness.
10 There is [r]severe discipline for him who forsakes the way;
[s]whoever hates reproof will die.
11 Sheol and Abaddon lie open before the LORD;
how much more [t]the hearts of the children of man!

Chapter 15
1 [d][ch. 25:15]; See Judg. 8:1-3 [e]See 1 Sam. 25:10-13; 1 Kin. 12:13-16
2 [f][ver. 28; ch. 12:23; 13:16; 18:2]
3 [g]See Job 31:4
4 [h][ch. 12:18] [i]See ch. 3:18 [j]ch. 11:3
5 [k][ch. 10:1] [l][Ps. 107:11] [m][ch. 13:18]
7 [n][Matt. 12:34, 35]
8 [o]ch. 21:27; Eccles. 5:1; Isai. 1:11, 15 [p][ver. 29]
9 [q]ch. 21:21; 1 Tim. 6:11; [ch. 11:19]
10 [r][Isai. 1:5] [s]See ch. 12:1
11 [t]2 Chr. 6:30; Ps. 44:21; John 2:24; See 1 Sam. 16:7

1 Or *healing* 2 Or *the hearts of fools are not steadfast*

God Sees and Knows: Divine Omniscience

"Omniscient" means "knowing everything." God's eyes run everywhere (Job 24:23; Ps. 33:13–15; 139:13–16; Prov. 15:3; Jer. 16:17; Heb. 4:13), and He searches all hearts, as well as observing everyone's ways (1 Sam. 16:7; 1 Kin. 8:39; 1 Chr. 28:9; Ps. 139:1–6, 23; Jer. 17:10; Luke 16:15; Rom. 8:27; Rev. 2:23)—in other words, He knows everything about everything and everybody all the time. He knows the future no less than the past and present, and possible events that never happen no less than the actual events that do (1 Sam. 23:9–13; 2 Kin. 13:19; Ps. 81:14, 15; Is. 48:18). Nor does He have to search for information about things, as a computer might retrieve a file; all His knowledge is immediately and directly before Him. Bible writers stand in awe of the capacity of God's mind in this regard (Ps. 139:1–6; 147:5; Is. 40:13, 14, 28; cf. Rom. 11:33–36).

God's knowledge is linked with His sovereignty: He knows each thing because He created it, sustains it, and now makes it function every moment according to His plan (Eph. 1:11). The idea that God could know, and foreknow, everything without controlling everything is not only unscriptural but illogical.

Believers are encouraged by God's omniscience because it assures them that everything about them is known to One who loves them, and who will overlook nothing at all that concerns them (Is. 40:27–31; Matt. 6:8). To the unbeliever, the truth of God's universal knowledge must bring dread, for it comes as a reminder that one cannot hide either oneself or one's sins from God (Ps. 94:1–11; 139:7–12; Jon. 1:1–12).

15:1 The power of words to build up or to destroy relationships is stressed here and in vv. 2, 4, 7, 14, and 23.

15:2 See 6:17, 24; 10:20, 31; 12:17–19.

15:3 eyes of the LORD. See 2 Chr. 16:9; Ps. 33:13–15. The sages sometimes looked beyond the observable events and natural retribution to remind themselves of the reality of divine justice. See theological note "God Sees and Knows: Divine Omniscience."

15:4 gentle. See text note. A conciliatory tongue mends relationships (v. 2; 12:18).

tree of life. See 3:18 and note.

perverseness. See note 11:3.

breaks the spirit. Destroys morale and self-esteem.

15:5 See 1:8; 6:20; 12:15; 13:1, 13, 18. Humble teachability is the mark of the wise.

15:6 treasure. Either material riches, or perhaps a metaphor for wisdom itself (cf. 8:18–21).

trouble. Or, "will be destroyed," as in the Septuagint (Greek Old Testament translation).

15:7 See v. 2 and note.

15:8 See Is. 1:12–15; Amos 5:21–24. The sage here draws on Israel's religious life, illustrating the covenantal framework within which biblical wisdom operates.

15:10 the way. The way of divine wisdom (2:12–20). Discipline will be needed to bring this one back to God's path (v. 5; 12:1).

hates reproof will die. See 2:18 and note.

15:11 Abaddon. Death is here portrayed as a kind of destruction from the Lord. The Lord penetrates the secrets of the grave; how much easier is it for Him to know our minds (Ps. 139:23, 24).

12 [u] A scoffer [v] does not like to be reproved;
he will not go to the wise.
13 [w] A glad heart makes a cheerful face,
but by [x] sorrow of heart the spirit is [y] crushed.
14 [z] The heart of him who has understanding seeks knowledge,
but the mouths of fools feed on folly.
15 All the days of the afflicted are evil,
but [a] the cheerful of heart has a continual feast.
16 [b] Better is a little with the fear of the LORD
than great treasure and trouble with it.
17 [c] Better is a dinner of herbs where love is
than [d] a fattened ox and hatred with it.
18 [e] A hot-tempered man [f] stirs up strife,
but he who is [g] slow to anger quiets contention.
19 The way of [h] a sluggard is like a hedge of [i] thorns,
but the path of the upright is [j] a level highway.
20 [k] A wise son makes a glad father,
but a foolish man despises his mother.
21 [l] Folly is a joy to him who lacks sense,
but a man of understanding [m] walks straight ahead.

12 [u] See Ps. 1:1 [v] Amos 5:10
13 [w] [ver. 15; ch. 17:22] [x] See ch. 12:25 [y] ch. 18:14
14 [z] ch. 14:6; 19:24
15 [a] ver. 13
16 [b] ch. 16:8; Ps. 37:16; [1 Tim. 6:6]
17 [c] ch. 17:1 [d] [Matt. 22:4; Luke 15:23]
18 [e] ch. 29:22; [ch. 16:28; 26:21] [f] ch. 28:25 [g] See ch. 14:29
19 [h] ch. 19:24; 22:13 [i] ch. 22:5 [j] Jer. 18:15
20 [k] See ch. 29:3
21 [l] ch. 10:23 [m] [Eph. 5:15]
22 [n] ch. 11:14; [ch. 20:18]
23 [o] ch. 25:11; [Isai. 50:4]
24 [p] Col. 3:1, 2; [ch. 2:18, 19; Phil. 3:20]
25 [q] [ch. 29:23] [r] [ch. 23:10] [s] [Ps. 68:5; 146:9]
26 [t] ch. 6:16, 18 [u] ch. 16:24
27 [v] ch. 1:19; [Isai. 5:8; Jer. 17:11] [w] ch. 11:29; [Josh. 7:25] [x] ch. 17:23
28 [y] Ps. 37:30 [z] [1 Pet. 3:15]; See ver. 2
29 [a] [Ps. 18:41; 34:16] [b] Ps. 145:18, 19; [ver. 8]
30 [c] Ps. 38:10 [d] [ch. 25:25]

22 [n] Without counsel plans fail,
but with many advisers they succeed.
23 To make an apt answer is a joy to a man,
and [o] a word in season, how good it is!
24 The path of life leads upward [p] for the prudent,
that he may turn away from Sheol beneath.
25 The LORD tears down the house of [q] the proud
but [r] maintains [s] the widow's boundaries.
26 [t] The thoughts of the wicked are an abomination to the LORD,
but [u] gracious words are pure.
27 Whoever is [v] greedy for unjust gain [w] troubles his own household,
but he who hates [x] bribes will live.
28 The heart of the righteous [y] ponders how to answer,
but [z] the mouth of the wicked pours out evil things.
29 The LORD is [a] far from the wicked,
but he [b] hears the prayer of the righteous.
30 [c] The light of the eyes rejoices the heart,
and [d] good news refreshes [1] the bones.

1 Hebrew *makes fat*

15:12 scoffer. See note 1:22.

15:13 See note 14:30.

15:15 feast. A metaphor for joy.

15:16 For examples of the "better . . . than" comparison form, see note 12:9. The fear of the Lord brings its own riches (v. 6 note).

treasure and trouble. See 10:2. Riches that do not accrue from a wise life carry their own seeds of destruction (Mark 10:25).

15:17 The contrast is indicative of poverty and wealth. The quality of family relationships is not tied to wealth; the quality of hospitality is based on relationships, not on the food provided.

15:18 See 14:17, 29; 15:1. The disposition of people calms or inflames a quarrel. We can disagree without being disagreeable.

15:19 See 6:6–11; 10:4; 13:4.

upright. The word is used here as the opposite of "lazy." There is an implied link between sloth and unrighteousness, diligence and virtue.

15:23 The wise receive great satisfaction from being able to give the proper word at the right time.

15:24 See 2:18–22 and notes.

Sheol. See note 1:12.

15:25 A recognition of ultimate divine retribution.

house of the proud. See 14:11.

the widow's boundaries. See note Deut. 19:14. Since the oppression of widows did take place (e.g., Is. 1:17, 23; 10:2), this proverb must be seen as a statement of confidence that God's righteousness is finally realized.

15:26 As with vv. 8, 9, to maintain a right relationship with the Lord is the ultimate wisdom.

15:27 greedy . . . bribes. These parallel lines suggest one whose riches are ill-gotten. Our folly usually has repercussions on those closest to us (1:19).

will live. See 2:20–22 and notes.

15:28 The wise and righteous recognize the need to weigh matters carefully before giving advice.

15:29 See note on v. 8.

15:30 The light of the eyes. The idea seems to be that a cheerful, radiant person, or a beautiful scene, affects one's mind in the same way that good news promotes our general well-being. See note 14:30.

31 [e] The ear that listens to [f] life-giving
reproof
will dwell among the wise.
32 Whoever [g] ignores instruction
[h] despises himself,
but he who listens to reproof
[i] gains intelligence.
33 [j] The fear of the LORD is instruction in
wisdom,
and [k] humility comes before honor.

16 The plans of the heart belong to
man,
but [l] the answer of the tongue is
from the LORD.
2 [m] All the ways of a man are pure in his
own eyes,
but the LORD [n] weighs the spirit.
3 [o] Commit your work to the LORD,
and your plans will be
established.
4 [p] The LORD has made everything for its
purpose,
even [q] the wicked for the day of
trouble.
5 Everyone who is arrogant in heart is
[r] an abomination to the
LORD;
[s] be assured, he will not go
unpunished.
6 By [t] steadfast love and faithfulness
iniquity is atoned for,
and by [u] the fear of the LORD one
[v] turns away from evil.
7 When a man's ways please the LORD,
[w] he makes even his enemies to be
at peace with him.
8 [x] Better is a little with righteousness
than great revenues with injustice.
9 [y] The heart of man plans his way,
but [z] the LORD establishes his steps.
10 [a] An oracle is on the lips of a king;
his mouth does not sin in
judgment.
11 [b] A just balance and scales are the
LORD's;
all the weights in the bag are his
work.
12 It is an abomination to kings to do
evil,
for [c] the throne is established by
righteousness.
13 [d] Righteous lips are the delight of a
king,
and he loves him who speaks what
is right.
14 [e] A king's wrath is a messenger of death,
and a wise man will [f] appease it.
15 [g] In the light of a king's face there is
life,
and his [d] favor is like [h] the clouds
that bring the spring rain.
16 [i] How much better to get wisdom than
[j] gold!
To get understanding is to be
chosen rather than [k] silver.

31 [e] ver. 5; ch. 20:12; 25:12 [f] [ch. 6:23] **32** [g] [ch. 8:33] [h] See ch. 8:36 [i] [ch. 19:8] **33** [j] See ch. 1:7 [k] ch. 18:12
Chapter 16
1 [l] [Matt. 10:19, 20] **2** [m] ch. 21:2; [ch. 12:15]; See ch. 30:12; [n] ch. 24:12; See 1 Sam. 16:7 **3** [o] See Ps. 37:5 **4** [p] Rom. 11:36 [q] Job 21:30; [Ex. 9:16] **5** [r] ch. 6:16, 17; 8:13; Luke 16:15 [s] ch. 11:21; [ch. 28:20] **6** [t] Dan. 4:27; Luke 11:41 [u] ch. 14:16 [v] ver. 17; Job 28:28 **7** [w] [Gen. 26:28; 2 Chr. 17:10] **8** [x] See ch. 15:16 **9** [y] [ver. 1; ch. 19:21] [z] ch. 20:24; [Ps. 37:23; Jer. 10:23] **10** [a] [1 Kin. 3:28] **11** [b] See ch. 11:1 **12** [c] ch. 25:5; [ch. 20:28; 29:14; Isai. 16:5] **13** [d] [ch. 14:35; 22:11] **14** [e] ch. 19:12; 20:2 [f] [ch. 25:15]
15 [g] [Job 29:24] [d] [See ver. 13 above] [h] [Ps. 72:6]; See Job 29:23 **16** [i] ch. 8:10, 11, 19 [j] See ch. 3:14 [k] ch. 10:20

15:32 despises himself. Folly is self-destructive.

15:33 See 1:7; 11:2 and notes.

16:1 The sages occasionally remind us that human responsibility to reason and act does not contradict God's sovereignty (vv. 2, 9).

answer . . . from the LORD. The phrase means either that God enables us to give that apt answer and carry through plans, or that God's answer (His word of decision) is the real power that shapes events (19:21; cf. Phil. 2:12, 13).

16:2 spirit. People are able to rationalize almost any kind of behavior as they strive to justify themselves (12:15; 30:12). God's knowledge is a warning against such self-deception (Heb. 4:12; cf. 1 Cor. 4:3–5).

16:3 Commit. Hebrew "roll." The expression is unusual. It may mean that our plans should be entrusted to the Lord (Ps. 37:5), or devised with conscious application of the principles of God's Word.

16:4 for its purpose. Lit. "for His answer" or "for its answer." All of creation, even the wicked and their actions, stand under God's sovereignty and serve His purposes (cf. Rom. 9:17–23).

16:5 See 11:20, 21.

16:6 steadfast love and faithfulness. The phrase summarizes the attitude of the wise to the Lord (3:3; 14:22; 20:28). The saying is a rebuke to formal religion without true faith.

16:7 please the LORD. Following God's way has reconciling and healing effects on personal relationships.

16:8 See 15:16, 17 and notes.

16:9 See vv. 1, 2 and notes.

16:10 An oracle. The king's word was law, and he was entitled to seek divine guidance for his judgments. David spoke as a messenger of God (2 Sam. 14:17, 20) and Solomon desired a discerning heart (1 Kin. 3:9). The gift of God's wisdom to the king did not relieve him of the responsibility to seek wisdom and to act according to justice.

16:11 See 11:1; 20:10, 23; Amos 8:5. Behind this statement is wisdom's view of God as the One who establishes and maintains the righteous order that makes life meaningful. For the law against false weights, see Lev. 19:35, 36; Deut. 25:13–16.

16:12–15 Wisdom concerning kingship not only reflects the ideal of Solomon and his wise rule, but also expresses the power of the king to establish righteous order in his realm.

16:15 clouds that bring the spring rain. See note Amos 4:7, 8. The king's favor can cause one's life to flourish like crops in spring.

16:16 The "better . . . than" comparisons unambiguously state the superiority of the one thing over another, but without saying why (12:9 note). That wisdom is better than material riches is a common wisdom theme (3:13–15; 8:10, 11, 19). This does not mean that riches are in themselves undesirable (3:9, 10; 1 Kin. 3:10–13; 10:7–9), but only that they must be acquired as the fruit of wisdom.

17 The highway of the upright [l] turns
aside from evil;
whoever guards his way preserves
his life.
18 [m] Pride goes before destruction,
and a haughty spirit before a fall.
19 [n] It is better to be of a lowly spirit with
the poor
than to [o] divide the spoil with the
proud.
20 Whoever gives thought to the word [1]
[p] will discover good,
and blessed is he [q] who trusts in
the LORD.
21 The wise of heart is called discerning,
and sweetness of speech [r] increases
persuasiveness.
22 Good sense is [s] a fountain of life to
him who has it,
but the instruction of fools is folly.
23 [t] The heart of the wise makes his
speech judicious
and adds persuasiveness to his
lips.
24 [u] Gracious words are like [v] a
honeycomb,
sweetness to the soul and [w] health
to the body.
25 There is a way that seems right to a
man,
but its end is the way to death. [2]
26 A worker's appetite works for him;
his [x] mouth urges him on.
27 [y] A worthless man plots evil,
and his speech [3] is like [z] a
scorching fire.
28 [a] A dishonest man spreads strife,
and [b] a whisperer [c] separates close
friends.
29 A man of violence [d] entices his
neighbor
and leads him in a way that is not
good.
30 Whoever winks his eyes plans [4]
[e] dishonest things;
he who [f] purses his lips brings evil
to pass.
31 [g] Gray hair is [h] a crown of glory;
it [i] is gained in a righteous life.
32 [j] Whoever is slow to anger is better
than the mighty,
and he who rules his spirit than he
who takes a city.
33 [k] The lot is cast into the lap,
but its every decision is [l] from the
LORD.

17

1 [m] Better is a dry morsel with quiet
than a house full of feasting [5] with
strife.
2 A servant who deals wisely will rule
over [n] a son who acts
shamefully
and [o] will share the inheritance as
one of the brothers.
3 [p] The crucible is for silver, and the
furnace is for gold,
[q] and the LORD tests hearts.
4 An evildoer listens to wicked lips,
and a liar gives ear to a
mischievous tongue.

1 Or *to a matter* 2 Hebrew *ways of death* 3 Hebrew *what is on his lips* 4 Hebrew *to plan* 5 Hebrew *sacrifices*

17 [l] ver. 6 **18** [m] See ch. 11:2 **19** [n] ch. 29:23; Isai. 57:15 [o] See Ex. 15:9 **20** [p] ch. 19:8 [q] See Ps. 2:12 **21** [r] ver. 23 **22** [s] See ch. 10:11 **23** [t] [Ps. 37:30; Matt. 12:34] **24** [u] ch. 15:26 [v] Ps. 19:10 [w] See ch. 4:22 **26** [x] [Eccles. 6:7] **27** [y] [ch. 6:12, 14, 19] [z] James 3:6 **28** [a] See ch. 15:18 [b] [ch. 18:8; 26:20, 22] [c] ch. 17:9 **29** [d] ch. 1:10 **30** [e] See ch. 2:12 [f] [ch. 6:13] **31** [g] ch. 20:29 [h] ch. 17:6 [i] See ch. 3:1, 2 **32** [j] ch. 14:29; [ch. 19:11; 25:28] **33** [k] [Acts 1:26] [l] ch. 29:26
Chapter 17 **1** [m] ch. 15:17 **2** [n] ver. 21, 25; ch. 10:5; 19:26 [o] [2 Sam. 16:4] **3** [p] ch. 27:21 [q] 1 Chr. 29:17; Ps. 26:2; Jer. 17:10; Mal. 3:3

16:18 See 11:2 and note. The proud are unteachable and, therefore, headed for destruction.

16:19 See v. 16; 15:16 and notes.

16:21 sweetness of speech. "Honeyed words"; words that reflect an aptitude for communication.

16:22 fountain of life. See 10:11 and note.

instruction of fools is folly. That is, it is senseless to correct fools because they will not listen. The Hebrew could also mean that their own foolishness becomes an adequate punishment for fools.

16:23 heart. See note 2:2. The wise person speaks out of a mind informed by the truth.

16:24 Gracious words. See note on v. 21. Such words have healing value for human relationships and for personal well-being.

16:26 mouth. The most basic incentive against idleness is the threat of hunger (2 Thess. 3:10–12).

16:27 worthless man. See note on 6:12.

a scorching fire. The metaphor emphasizes the destructive power of vindictive and slanderous words.

16:30 winks. See note 6:13.

16:31 it is gained. Or, "It is found." The righteous life is the wise life that promotes longevity (3:2 note). The elderly are honored for their wisdom, learning, and experience.

16:32 slow to anger. Such a person brings calm and sound judgment to a crisis (James 1:19, 20).

16:33 The lot. See note Jon. 1:7; theological note "Providence" on next page.

every decision is from the LORD. When the lot was properly used the answer was not a matter of chance, but came from God.

17:1 feasting with strife. Lit. "sacrifices of strife" (see text note), perhaps a contrast with the peace or fellowship offering (Deut. 27:7). Harmony can exist without lavish provision.

17:2 Inherited privilege can easily be forfeited to those who by diligence show themselves worthy to enjoy it (11:29).

17:3 the LORD tests hearts. The comparisons indicate that the Lord uses our experiences to improve us. The fiery test is not to destroy, but to refine.

17:4 The sin is not simply in the listening, but in the implied perverse desire to use for evil what is heard (cf. 16:27).

5 Whoever mocks the poor [r]insults his Maker;
he who is [s]glad at calamity will not go [t]unpunished.
6 [u]Grandchildren are [v]the crown of the aged,
and the glory of children is their fathers.

5 [r]ch. 14:31; [Matt. 25:40, 45] [s]Job 31:29; Obad. 12; [ch. 24:17] [t]ch. 16:5
6 [u]Ps. 128:6; [Ps. 127:3, 4] [v]ch. 16:31
7 [w][ch. 19:10; 26:1] [x]ch. 6:17

7 Fine speech is not [w]becoming to a fool;
still less is [x]false speech to a prince.
8 [y]A bribe is like a magic stone in the eyes of the one who gives it;
wherever he turns he prospers.

8 [y]ver. 23; ch. 18:16; 19:6; 21:14; [Ex. 23:8; Isai. 1:23; Amos 5:12]

Providence

"God's works of providence are, His most holy, wise, and powerful preserving and governing all His creatures, and all their actions" (*Westminster Shorter Catechism*, Q. 11). If creation was a unique exercise of divine energy causing the world to be, providence is a continued exercise of the same energy. By it the Creator, according to His own will, keeps all creatures in being, involves Himself in all events, and directs all things to their appointed end. God is completely in charge of His world. His hand may be hidden, but His perfect rule extends to all things.

It is sometimes supposed that God knows the future but does not control it; that He upholds the world, but does not intervene in it; or that He gives general direction, but is not concerned with details. The Bible emphatically rules out all such limitations of His providence.

> The Bible clearly teaches God's providential control (1) over the universe at large, Ps. 103:19; Dan. 4:35; Eph. 1:11; (2) over the physical world, Job 37; Ps. 104:14; 135:6; Mt. 5:45; (3) over the brute creation, Ps. 104:21, 28; Mt. 6:26; 10:29; (4) over the affairs of nations, Job 12:23; Ps. 22:28; 66:7; Acts 17:26; (5) over man's birth and lot in life, 1 Sam. 16:1; Ps. 139:16; Is. 45:5; Gal. 1:15, 16; (6) over the outward successes and failures of men's lives, Ps. 75:6, 7; Lk. 1:52; (7) over things seemingly accidental or insignificant, Pr. 16:33; Mt. 10:30; (8) in the protection of the righteous, Ps. 4:8; 5:12; 63:8; 121:3; Rom. 8:28; (9) in supplying the wants of God's people, Gn. 22:8, 14; Dt. 8:3; Phil. 4:19; (10) in giving answers to prayer, 1 Sam. 1:19; Is. 20:5, 6; 2 Chr. 33:13; Ps. 65:2; Mt. 7:7; Lk. 18:7, 8; and (11) in the exposure and punishment of the wicked, Ps. 7:12, 13; 11:6. (L. Berkhof, *Systematic Theology* 2d rev. ed. [Grand Rapids: Wm. B. Eerdmans Publishing Co., 1941], p. 168.).

Describing God's involvement in the world and in the acts of rational creatures requires complementary statements. For example, a person wills an action, an event is triggered by natural causes, or Satan shows his hand—yet God overrules. Again, people may go against God's will of command—yet they fulfill His will of events. People's motives may be evil—yet God uses their actions for good (Gen. 50:20; Acts 2:23). Although human sin is under God's decree, God is not the author of sin (James 1:13–17).

God's "concurrent" or "confluent" involvement in all that occurs does not violate the natural order, ongoing causal processes, or the free, responsible agency of human beings. God's sovereign control does not take away the responsibility and power of second causes; on the contrary, they are created and have their roles by His appointment.

Of the evils that infect God's world (spiritual, moral, and physical) the Bible says: God permits evil (Acts 14:16); He uses evil as a punishment (Ps. 81:11–12; Rom. 1:26–32); He brings good out of evil (Gen. 50:20; Acts 2:23; 4:27–28; 13:27; 1 Cor. 2:7–8); He uses evil to test and discipline those He loves (Matt. 4:1–11; Heb. 12:4–14); but one day He will redeem His people from the power and presence of evil altogether (Rev. 21:27; 22:14–15).

The doctrine of providence teaches Christians that they are never in the grip of blind fortune, chance, luck, or fate. All that happens to them is divinely planned, and each event comes as a new summons to trust, obey, and rejoice, knowing that all is for one's spiritual and eternal good (Rom. 8:28).

17:5 See 14:21 and note.

17:6 Grandchildren. The natural desire of all parents to have grandchildren was intensified in Israel, where the full blessings of the covenant, which lay in the future, were to be possessed by one's descendants (Ps. 127:3; 128:1–6).

glory of children is their fathers. See Ex. 20:12. The parents are the guardians and most influential teachers of divine truth to their children.

17:7 false speech to a prince. See 8:15, 16; 16:10, 12, 13 and notes.

17:8 bribe. Bribery is often effective. This observation of corrupt human behavior is made without passing moral judgment (cf. the unjust steward in Luke 16:1–9). Bribery is condemned in 15:27. Wisdom rejects pragmatism in favor of obedience to God's law.

9 Whoever [z]covers an offense seeks
love,
but he who repeats a matter
[a]separates close friends.
10 A rebuke goes deeper into a man of
understanding
than a hundred blows into a fool.
11 An evil man seeks only rebellion,
and [b]a cruel messenger will be sent
against him.
12 Let a man meet [c]a she-bear robbed of
her cubs
[d]rather than a fool in his folly.
13 If anyone [e]returns evil for good,
[f]evil will not depart from his
house.
14 The beginning of strife is like letting
out water,
so [g]quit before the quarrel breaks
out.
15 He who [h]justifies the wicked and he
who [i]condemns the righteous
are both alike an abomination to
the LORD.
16 Why should a fool have money in his
hand [j]to buy wisdom
when he has no sense?
17 [k]A friend loves at all times,
and a brother is born for adversity.
18 One who lacks sense gives a pledge
and puts up security in the
presence of his neighbor.
19 Whoever loves transgression loves
strife;
he who [l]makes his door high seeks
destruction.
20 [m]A man of crooked heart does not
discover good,
and one with a dishonest tongue
falls into calamity.
21 He who [n]sires a fool gets himself
sorrow,
and the father of a fool has no joy.
22 [o]A joyful heart is good medicine,
but a crushed spirit [p]dries up the
bones.
23 The wicked accepts [q]a bribe in secret[1]
to [r]pervert the ways of justice.
24 [s]The discerning sets his face toward
wisdom,
but the eyes of a fool are on the
ends of the earth.
25 [n]A foolish son is a grief to his father
[t]and bitterness to [u]her who bore him.
26 [v]To impose a fine on a righteous man
is not good,
nor to strike the noble for their
uprightness.
27 Whoever [w]restrains his words has
knowledge,
and he who has a cool spirit is a
man of understanding.
28 Even a fool [x]who keeps silent is
considered wise;
when he closes his lips, he is
deemed intelligent.

18 Whoever [y]isolates himself seeks
his own desire;
he breaks out against all sound
judgment.
2 A fool takes no pleasure in
understanding,
but only [z]in expressing his opinion.
3 When wickedness comes, contempt
comes also,
and with dishonor comes disgrace.
4 The words of a man's mouth are
[a]deep waters;
the fountain of wisdom is a
bubbling brook.

1 Hebrew *a bribe from the bosom*

9 [z]ch. 10:12 [a]ch. 16:28
11 [b][1 Kin. 2:29]
12 [c]2 Sam. 17:8; Hos. 13:8 [d][ch. 27:3]
13 [e]Ps. 35:12; 109:4, 5; [ch. 20:22; Matt. 5:39] [f][2 Sam. 12:10]
14 [g]ch. 20:3; 25:8
15 [h]ch. 24:24; Ex. 23:7; Isai. 5:23 [i]Job 34:17; Ps. 94:21; [ver. 26; ch. 18:5]
16 [j][ch. 23:23]
17 [k]ch. 18:24; 27:10; [Ruth 1:16; Job 6:14]
19 [l][ch. 11:2; 29:23]
20 [m][ch. 11:20]
21 [n]ch. 10:1; 19:13
22 [o]See ch. 15:13 [p]Ps. 22:15; [ch. 12:25]
23 [q]See ver. 8 [r][Mic. 3:11; 7:3]
24 [s][ch. 14:6; 15:14; Eccles. 2:14]; See Deut. 30:11-14
25 [n][See ver. 21 above] [t]ch. 10:1 [u]ch. 23:25
26 [v][ver. 15]
27 [w]ch. 10:19; [James 1:19]
28 [x]Job 13:5
Chapter 18
1 [y][Jude 19]
2 [z]ch. 13:16; [Eccles. 10:3]
4 [a]ch. 20:5

17:10 A frequent wisdom theme: wise people are teachable. By contrast, the fool will not learn at all (9:7–9).

17:11 Government is given by God for the preservation of order in society (Rom. 13:1–5). Rebellion invites official retribution against the attempt to destroy social order.

17:16 buy wisdom. The fool cannot overcome lack of wisdom by buying an education.

17:18 See 6:1–3 and notes.

17:19 The parallel lines of this proverb relate pride and wrongdoing with fighting and destruction, giving the reader material for reflection.

17:21 See 10:1; 15:20; 17:25.

17:22 See 14:30; 15:13, 30 and notes.

17:23 See v. 8 and note.

17:24 The contrast is between concentration on the task of learning wisdom and day dreaming (12:11 note).

17:25 See v. 21 and note.

17:27 restrains. That is, restrains his speech. This proverb contrasts with 16:27, 28. The wise know how to control their tongues.

17:28 The proverb is a hypothetical extension of v. 27. Ironically, the fool who has the wit to keep silent shows at least some potential for wisdom.

18:1 The Hebrew is difficult. The first line suggests that the unfriendly person (Hebrew "estranged") is self-seeking.

18:3 The social consequences of folly and wickedness are loss of honor and esteem.

18:4 The words of a man's mouth are deep waters. The sense of the clause is either that a common person's words are obscure, or a wise person's words are profound. If the former meaning is taken, then line two contrasts such obscurity with the clarity of wisdom. If the wise are in view, line two develops the theme. The ambiguity may be deliberate, leaving the application open.

5 It is not good to [b]be partial to[1] the
wicked
or to [c]deprive the righteous of
justice.
6 A fool's lips walk into a fight,
and his mouth invites [d]a beating.
7 [e]A fool's mouth is his ruin,
and his lips are a snare to
his soul.
8 [f]The words of a whisperer are like
delicious morsels;
they go down into [g]the inner parts
of the body.
9 Whoever is slack in his work
is a [h]brother to him who destroys.
10 [i]The name of the LORD is [j]a strong
tower;
the righteous man runs into it and
[k]is safe.
11 [l]A rich man's wealth is his strong
city,
and like a high wall in his
imagination.
12 [m]Before destruction a man's heart is
haughty,
but [n]humility comes before honor.
13 If one gives an answer [o]before he
hears,
it is his folly and shame.
14 A man's spirit will endure sickness,
but [p]a crushed spirit who can
bear?
15 An intelligent heart acquires
knowledge,
and the ear of the wise seeks
knowledge.
16 A man's [q]gift makes room
for him
and brings him before the great.
17 The one who states his case first
seems right,
until the other comes and
examines him.
18 [r]The lot puts an end to quarrels
and decides between powerful
contenders.
19 A brother offended is more
unyielding than a strong city,
and quarreling is like the bars of a
castle.
20 [s]From the fruit of a man's mouth his
stomach is satisfied;
he is satisfied by the yield of his
lips.
21 [t]Death and life are in the power of the
tongue,
and those who love it will eat its
fruits.
22 He who finds [u]a wife finds [v]a good
thing
and [w]obtains favor [x]from the LORD.
23 The poor use entreaties,
but [y]the rich answer roughly.
24 A man of many companions may
come to ruin,
but [z]there is a friend who sticks
closer than a brother.

19 [a]Better is a poor person who
[b]walks in his integrity
than one who is crooked in speech
and is a fool.

1 Hebrew *to lift the face of*

5 [b]ch. 24:23; 28:21; Lev. 19:15; Deut. 1:17; Ps. 82:2 [c]See ch. 17:15
6 [d]See ch. 19:29
7 [e]ch. 10:14; 12:13; 13:3; Ps. 64:8; 140:9; Eccles. 10:12
8 [f]ch. 26:22; [ch. 16:28] [g]ch. 20:27
9 [h][ch. 28:24]
10 [i]See Ex. 34:5-7 [j]Ps. 61:3; [Ps. 18:2]; See 2 Sam. 22:3 [k][Ps. 20:1]
11 [l]See ch. 10:15
12 [m]See ch. 11:2 [n]ch. 15:33
13 [o][John 7:51]
14 [p]ch. 15:13
16 [q][Gen. 32:20; 1 Sam. 25:27]; See ch. 17:8
18 [r][ch. 16:33]
20 [s]See ch. 12:14
21 [t]Matt. 12:36, 37; [ch. 4:23; 12:13]
22 [u]ch. 12:4; 19:14; See ch. 31:10-31 [v][Gen. 2:18] [w]ch. 8:35 [x]ch. 19:14
23 [y][James 2:3, 6]
24 [z]See ch. 17:17
Chapter 19
1 [a]ch. 28:6 [b]ch. 14:2; 20:7; Ps. 26:1, 11

18:6, 7 See 6:2; 10:11, 14; 13:3; 14:3 and notes.

18:7 his soul. Or, "of his life."

18:8 It is part of our sinful human nature to have an appetite for gossip.

18:9 See 6:9–11.

18:10 The name of the LORD. In Hebrew culture, a name was not a mere label, but usually an expression of the character of a person. God's covenant name, "LORD," is associated with His character as Savior of His people (Ex. 3:13–15; 15:1–3 and notes).

a strong tower. The security of the righteous is based on God's character as a faithful Savior.

18:11 This verse is a clear contrast with v. 10 (cf. 10:15). The implicit warning is against trusting only wealth (Luke 12:13–21).

18:13 Fools blurt out opinions on matters that they have not taken the trouble to hear carefully. One should listen well before speaking.

18:14 See 14:30 and note.

18:16 Here the gift is not necessarily a bribe, but the practical effects of a gift are noted (17:8 note).

18:17 An argument in a dispute may be persuasive until it is challenged by the other side. This piece of practical wisdom stresses the importance of getting to the truth.

18:18 The lot. If the decision comes from without, the contending parties can both rest.

18:19 A brother offended. The precise meaning of this verse is uncertain. The apparent intent is that reconciliation is difficult.

18:20 the fruit of a man's mouth. See 12:14; 13:2 and notes.

he is satisfied. Probably a metaphor for the constructive results of wise speech that promotes life-giving relationships.

18:21 Speech can do good or harm. The person who is fond of talk should note which way its effects go.

18:22 a wife. The assumption is that she is a good wife, such as the one described in 31:10–31 (12:4; 19:14 and notes).

favor from the LORD. See note 8:35.

18:23 The proverb is a matter-of-fact observation of the harsh reality of life's inequalities due to the effects of sin.

18:24 A man . . . come to ruin. The contrast seems to be between two kinds of companions: those whose friendship is superficial and who cause trouble, and the rare friend who is as loyal as a brother (17:17).

2 Desire[1] without knowledge is not
good,
and whoever [c]makes haste with his
feet misses his way.
3 When a man's folly [d]brings his way
to ruin,
his heart [e]rages against the LORD.
4 [f]Wealth brings many new friends,
[f]but a poor man is deserted by his
friend.
5 [g]A false witness will not go
unpunished,
and he who [h]breathes out lies will
not escape.
6 Many seek the favor of a generous
man,[2]
and everyone is a friend to a man
who gives [i]gifts.
7 [j]All a poor man's brothers hate him;
[k]how much more do his friends go
far from him!
He pursues them with words, but
does not have them.[3]
8 [l]Whoever gets sense loves his own
soul;
he who keeps understanding will
[m]discover good.
9 [g]A false witness will not go
unpunished,
and he who [h]breathes out lies will
perish.
10 [n]It is not fitting for a fool to live in
luxury,
much less for [o]a slave to rule over
princes.

2 [c][ch. 21:5; 28:20; 29:20] **3** [d][ch. 11:3] [e][Ps. 37:7; Isai. 8:21; Rev. 16:11] **4** [f]ch. 14:20 **5** [g][ch. 12:19; 21:28]; See Deut. 19:16-19 [h]See ch. 6:19 **6** [i]See ch. 17:8 **7** [j][ver. 4] [k][Ps. 38:11] **8** [l][ch. 15:32] [m]ch. 16:20 **9** [g][See ver. 5 above] [h][See ver. 5 above] **10** [n][ch. 17:7; 26:1] [o]ch. 30:22; Eccles. 10:6, 7

11 [p]See ch. 14:29 **12** [q]ch. 20:2; [ch. 16:14, 15; 28:15] [r]ch. 14:35 [s]Ps. 133:3; Hos. 14:5; Mic. 5:7 **13** [t]ch. 10:1; 17:21 [u]See ch. 21:9 [v]ch. 27:15 **14** [w][2 Cor. 12:14] [x]ch. 18:22 **15** [y]See ch. 6:9-11 [z]Job 4:13 [a][ch. 10:4; 20:4, 13; 23:21] **16** [b][ch. 13:13; Luke 10:28]

11 [p]Good sense makes one slow to anger,
and it is his glory to overlook an
offense.
12 A king's wrath is like [q]the growling
of a lion,
but his [r]favor is like [s]dew on the
grass.
13 [t]A foolish son is ruin to his father,
and [u]a wife's quarreling is [v]a
continual dripping of rain.
14 [w]House and wealth are inherited from
fathers,
but a prudent wife is [x]from the
LORD.
15 [y]Slothfulness casts into [z]a deep sleep,
and [a]an idle person will suffer
hunger.
16 Whoever [b]keeps the commandment
keeps his life;
he who despises his ways will die.
17 [c]Whoever is generous to the poor
lends to the LORD,
and he [d]will repay him for his [e]deed.
18 [f]Discipline your son, for there is hope;
do not set your heart on [g]putting
him to death.
19 A man of great wrath will pay the
penalty,
for if you deliver him, you will only
have to do it again.

17 [c][ch. 22:9; 28:27; Eccles. 11:1; Matt. 10:42; Heb. 6:10]; See Deut. 15:7-10; Matt. 25:40; 2 Cor. 9:6-8 [d][Luke 6:38] [e]See ch. 12:14 **18** [f]See ch. 13:24 [g][ch. 23:13]; See Deut. 21:18-21

[1] Or *A soul* [2] Or *of a noble* [3] The meaning of the Hebrew sentence is uncertain

19:2 Desire without knowledge . . . whoever makes haste. That is, one who rushes on without proper planning. Sincerity and energy by themselves miss the mark (Rom. 10:2).

19:3 Sinners bring their own misfortune, but they blame God for it.

19:4 A common fact of life, stated without moral judgment (vv. 6, 7; 18:23), although the sinful partiality is obvious (James 2:1–4).

19:5 See v. 9. In an ordered society, perjury is a serious crime severely punished (cf. Ex. 20:16). Divine retribution is not in view here, but rather the demands of normal social order.

19:6, 7 See v. 4 and note.

19:8 loves his own soul. Or, "loves life." Wisdom promotes relationships that are essential for the good life.

19:9 See v. 5 and note.

19:10 fool . . . luxury. A fool cannot handle the responsibility of riches. Possibly the verse refers to a fool in a position of administrative power rather than of wealth.

a slave to rule over princes. The situation is unfitting, not so much because the oppressed become the new oppressors, but because it is incongruous for those not socially and intellectually prepared to govern society. But compare 2 Sam. 7:8 for the exception.

19:11 slow to anger. See 14:17, 29; 16:32 and notes. Discipline is a mark of the wise man. A proper self-evaluation prevents him from taking offense at every little insult.

19:13 See 10:1; 17:21.

quarreling. Or "nagging." Closer relationships have potential for greater destructiveness.

continual dripping. Like the leaking roof that makes a house uninhabitable during rain (27:15).

19:14 This proverb does not imply that the Lord is not ultimately in control of the inheritance of wealth. It emphasizes rather that the outcome of one's choice of spouse is not so easy to predict or control. A happy marriage is indeed cause to thank God.

19:15 See 6:10, 11; 10:4 and notes.

19:16 commandment. See note 3:1.

will die. See 2:18 and note.

19:17 The Lord rewards those who show compassion to the poor.

19:18 Discipline. See 3:11 and note.

hope. That is, reason to expect a desired result.

set your heart on putting him to death. That is, contribute to his untimely death by failure to discipline and correct him.

20 Listen to advice and accept instruction,
that you may gain wisdom in [h]the future.
21 [i]Many are the plans in the mind of a man,
but [j]it is the purpose of the LORD [k]that will stand.
22 What is desired in a man is steadfast love,
and a poor man is better than a liar.
23 The fear of the LORD [l]leads to life,
and whoever has it rests [m]satisfied;
he will [n]not be visited by harm.
24 [o]The sluggard buries his hand in [p]the dish
and will not even bring it back to his mouth.
25 [q]Strike [r]a scoffer, and the simple will [s]learn prudence;
[t]reprove a man of understanding,
and he will gain knowledge.
26 He who does violence to his father
and chases away his mother
is [u]a son who brings shame and reproach.
27 Cease to hear instruction, my son,
[v]and you will stray from the words of knowledge.
28 A worthless witness mocks at justice,
and the mouth of the wicked [w]devours iniquity.
29 Condemnation is ready for [r]scoffers,
and [x]beating for the backs of fools.

20[h]Ps. 37:37
21[i]Ps. 33:10, 11 [j]Job 23:13; Isai. 14:26, 27 [k]Isai. 46:10
23[l]ch. 10:16; 11:19; [Isai. 38:5; Mark 10:30] [m][Ps. 25:13] [n][Lev. 26:6]
24[o]ch. 26:15; [ch. 15:19; 20:4] [p][Matt. 26:23; Mark 14:20]
25[q]ch. 21:11 [r]See Ps. 1:1 [s]See Deut. 13:6-11 [t][ch. 9:8]
26[u]ch. 10:5; 17:2
27[v][2 Pet. 2:21]
28[w]Job 15:16; [ch. 18:8; Job 34:7]
29[r][See ver. 25 above] [x]ch. 10:13; 18:6; 26:3

Chapter 20
1[y][Gen. 9:21]; See ch. 23:29-32 [z]ch. 31:4 [a]Isai. 28:7; [Hos. 4:11]
2[b]See ch. 19:12 [c]Num. 16:38; Hab. 2:10; See ch. 8:36
3[d][ch. 17:14]
4[e][ch. 19:24] [f]ch. 19:15; [ch. 6:11]
5[g]ch. 18:4
6[h][ch. 25:14; Matt. 6:2; Luke 18:11] [i][Ps. 12:1]

20

[y]Wine is a mocker, [z]strong drink a brawler,
and whoever [a]is led astray by it is not wise.[1]
2 The terror of a king is like [b]the growling of a lion;
whoever provokes him to anger [c]forfeits his life.
3 It is an honor for a man to [d]keep aloof from strife,
but every fool will be quarreling.
4 [e]The sluggard does not plow in the autumn;
[f]he will seek at harvest and have nothing.
5 The purpose in a man's heart is like [g]deep water,
but a man of understanding will draw it out.
6 Many a man [h]proclaims his own steadfast love,
but [i]a faithful man who can find?
7 The righteous who [j]walks in his integrity—
[k]blessed are his children after him!
8 [l]A king who sits on the throne of judgment
[m]winnows all evil with his eyes.
9 [n]Who can say, "I have made my heart pure;
I am clean from my sin"?

7[j]See ch. 19:1 [k][1 Kin. 15:4; Ps. 37:26; 112:2; Jer. 33:20, 21] 8[l][ch. 16:10] [m][ver. 26; ch. 25:5; Ps. 101:5] 9[n]See 1 Kin. 8:46

1 Or *will not become wise*

19:21 See 16:1, 9 and notes.

19:22 steadfast love. Or, "loyalty."

better than a liar. A loyal friend, though poor, is better than a treacherous friend.

19:23 The fear of the LORD. See 1:7; 2:5 and notes. "The fear of the LORD" here is probably a synonym for the wisdom of which the Lord is the wise Author (James 3:17).

leads to life. See 3:18 and note.

rests satisfied. Or, "sleep secure" in the care of the Lord.

19:24 The proverb is a humorous comment on the sluggard (6:6 note). The picture of a person too lazy to feed himself reflects the situation of 6:10, 11. Such a one does not have the will for self-preservation.

19:25 scoffer. See note 9:7.

simple will learn prudence. See 1:4 and note. The mocker deserves the punishment, and the teachable mind of the untutored observes it and learns, and so is deterred from similar folly.

19:26 The meaning is clear, especially viewed against the background of God's purposes for family relationship (17:6; Ex. 20:12).

19:28 worthless. See note on 6:12.

19:29 See v. 25; 10:13; 14:3. Even if the punishment will not deter them, it is deserved.

20:1 mocker. Wine mocks the person who comes under its spell, or, more likely, it makes one become a mocker (9:7 note).

is not wise. Either that it is folly to get drunk, or that the intoxicated person cannot act wisely.

20:2 See 16:14.

20:3 See 15:18; 17:14.

20:4 See 6:6–11.

20:5 will draw it out. If "deep water" refers to truth deeply hidden in the "heart," the wise person is seen as one who can draw such wisdom to the surface and bring it to expression (18:4 and note).

20:6 Many profess such mercy, but few practice it in their relationships with others.

20:7 See 13:22 and note; 14:11.

righteous. See 8:18 and note.

20:8 See v. 26. The wise king can discriminate between the wheat and the chaff, between good and evil.

20:9 See 16:2 and note. The answer to this question must be simply, "No one" (1 John 1:8).

10 [o] Unequal[1] weights and unequal
measures
are both alike an abomination to
the LORD.
11 Even a child [p] makes himself known
by his acts,[2]
by whether his conduct is pure
and upright.
12 [q] The hearing ear and the seeing eye,
[r] the LORD has made them both.
13 [s] Love not sleep, lest you [t] come to
poverty;
open your eyes, and you will have
[u] plenty of bread.
14 "Bad, Bad," says the buyer,
but when he goes away, then he
boasts.
15 There is gold and abundance of
[v] costly stones,
[w] but the lips of knowledge are a
precious jewel.
16 [x] Take a man's garment when he has
put up security for a stranger,
and [y] hold it in pledge when he
puts up security for foreigners.[3]
17 [z] Bread gained by deceit is sweet to a
man,
but afterward his mouth will be
full of [a] gravel.
18 [b] Plans are established by counsel;
by [c] wise guidance [d] wage war.
19 Whoever [e] goes about slandering
reveals secrets;
therefore do not associate with [f] a
simple babbler.[4]

20 [g] If one curses his father or his mother,
[h] his lamp will be put out in utter
darkness.
21 [i] An inheritance gained hastily in the
beginning
will not be blessed in the end.
22 Do not say, [j] "I will repay evil";
[k] wait for the LORD, and he will
deliver you.
23 [l] Unequal weights are an abomination
to the LORD,
and [m] false scales are not good.
24 A man's [n] steps are from the LORD;
how then can man understand
his way?
25 It is a snare to say rashly, "It is holy,"
and to reflect only [o] after making
vows.
26 A wise king [p] winnows the wicked
and drives [q] the wheel over them.
27 [r] The spirit[5] of man is the lamp of the
LORD,
[s] searching all [t] his innermost parts.
28 [u] Steadfast love and faithfulness
preserve the king,
and by steadfast love his [v] throne is
upheld.
29 The glory of young men is their
strength,
but [w] the splendor of old men is
their gray hair.

10 [o] ver. 23; See ch. 11:1 **11** [p] [Matt. 7:16] **12** [q] ch. 15:31; 25:12 [r] Ex. 4:11; Ps. 94:9 **13** [s] [ch. 6:4; 19:15; 31:15; Rom. 12:11] [t] [ver. 4] [u] ch. 12:11 **15** [v] Job 28:18 [w] [ch. 3:14, 15] **16** [x] ch. 27:13; [ch. 6:1; 22:26] [y] See Job 22:6 **17** [z] [ch. 9:17] [a] [Lam. 3:16] **18** [b] [ch. 11:14; 15:22] [c] ch. 24:6 [d] Luke 14:31 **19** [e] ch. 11:13 [f] ch. 13:3; [Rom. 16:18] **20** [g] ch. 30:11, 17; See Ex. 21:17 [h] See 2 Sam. 21:17; Job 18:5 **21** [i] See ch. 13:11 **22** [j] ch. 24:29; [ch. 17:13; Matt. 5:39; Rom. 12:17, 19; 1 Thess. 5:15; 1 Pet. 3:9] [k] Ps. 27:14 **23** [l] ver. 10 [m] See ch. 11:1 **24** [n] See ch. 16:9 **25** [o] [Eccles. 5:4, 5] **26** [p] [Matt. 3:12] [q] Isai. 28:27 **27** [r] [1 Cor. 2:11] [s] [Zeph. 1:12] [t] ch. 18:8

28 [u] ch. 3:3 [v] See ch. 16:12 **29** [w] ch. 16:31

[1] Or *Two kinds of*; also verse 23 [2] Or *Even a child can dissemble in his actions* [3] Or *for an adulteress* (compare 27:13) [4] Hebrew *with one who is simple in his lips* [5] Hebrew *breath*

20:10 See 11:1 and note.

20:11 child. The Hebrew word covers a wide age range, from infancy to early adulthood.

20:12 Two of the principal means of gaining knowledge are God-given and therefore reliable. There may be an implied warning against the wrong use of them.

20:13 See 6:6–11; 10:4; 19:15 and notes.

20:14 A humorous comment on customs of the marketplace where bargaining is a well-established social ritual.

20:15 See 3:13–15; 8:10, 11; 16:16. Wealth is not condemned, but wisdom is more desirable.

20:16 Take a man's garment. The garment is security taken for a loan (Deut. 24:6 note). The verse is probably a warning to be careful with money in dealing with people who take risks or who are unreliable.

20:17 Bread. This is a metaphor for wealth, which, when pursued dishonestly does not satisfy.

20:18 Count the cost and leave nothing to chance (1:5; 15:22; cf. Luke 14:28–32).

20:20 his lamp will be put out. See 13:9 and note. Death will come, either by society executing the law, by divine retribution, or by indirect consequences of such enormous sin.

20:21 gained hastily in the beginning. That is, prematurely, before gaining the wisdom to handle it, or by the wrong means.

20:22 This directive parallels the principle in Deut. 32:35 and Rom. 12:19, warning against taking the law into one's own hands and undermining the order of society. The deliverance is not national (Deut. 32:35, 36) but individual, possibly by means of due legal process, but ultimately with the Lord Himself as its source.

20:23 See v. 10 and note.

20:24 See 16:1, 9 and notes; 19:21. Such passages point to the limitations of knowledge obtained from observation. God's sovereign purposes alone are certain.

20:25 It is holy. A rash vow that cannot be honored is worse than no vow at all (Eccl. 5:4–7).

20:26 See v. 8 and note. The wise king has the ability to discern.

20:27 the lamp of the LORD. A metaphor for the searching eye of God that knows our inmost thoughts (cf. v. 24).

20:28 Steadfast love and faithfulness. This may refer to the king's attitude toward his people, which establishes a stable society and a secure throne (3:3; 14:22 and notes). However, it is probable that the phrase is used here of God's covenant with the dynasty of David (2 Sam. 7:11–15).

20:29 See 16:31 and note. While physical strength decreases with age, wisdom should increase.

30 [x]Blows that wound cleanse away evil;
strokes make clean [r]the innermost parts.

21

The king's heart is a stream of water in the hand of the LORD;
he [y]turns it wherever he will.
2 [z]Every way of a man is right in his own eyes,
but the LORD [a]weighs the heart.
3 [b]To do righteousness and justice
is more acceptable to the LORD than sacrifice.
4 [c]Haughty eyes and a proud heart,
[d]the lamp[1] of the wicked, are sin.
5 The plans of [e]the diligent lead surely to abundance,
but everyone who is [f]hasty comes
[g]only to poverty.
6 [h]The getting of treasures by a lying tongue
is a [i]fleeting [j]vapor and a [k]snare of death.[2]
7 The violence of the wicked will
[l]sweep them away,
because they refuse to do what is just.
8 The way of the guilty [m]is crooked,
but the conduct of the pure is upright.
9 It is [n]better to live in a corner of the housetop
than in a house shared with a quarrelsome wife.

30 [x][Isai. 53:5] [r][See ver. 27 above]
Chapter 21
1 [y][Ezra 6:22]
2 [z]ch. 16:2; [ch. 12:15] [a]ch. 24:12; [Luke 16:15; 1 Cor. 4:4]; See 1 Sam. 16:7
3 [b]See ch. 15:8; 1 Sam. 15:22
4 [c]See ch. 6:17; Ps. 101:5 [d]1 Kin. 11:36
5 [e]ch. 10:4 [f][ch. 19:2] [g][ch. 11:24; 14:23; 22:16]
6 [h]ch. 20:21; See ch. 10:2 [i][ch. 13:11] [j]Job 13:25 [k][ch. 8:36]
7 [l][Jer. 30:23]
8 [m][ch. 2:15]
9 [n]ch. 25:24; [ver. 19; ch. 19:13; 27:15]
11 [o]ch. 19:25; See Ps. 1:1
12 [p]Ps. 37:35, 36
13 [q][James 2:13]; See Matt. 18:30-34
14 [r][ch. 17:8; 18:16]
15 [s][ch. 10:29]
16 [t][Ps. 49:14]
18 [u][ch. 11:8] [v]Isai. 43:3

10 The soul of the wicked desires evil;
his neighbor finds no mercy in his eyes.
11 When [o]a scoffer is punished, the simple becomes wise;
when a wise man is instructed, he gains knowledge.
12 The Righteous One [p]observes the house of the wicked;
he throws the wicked down to ruin.
13 [q]Whoever closes his ear to the cry of the poor
will himself call out and not be answered.
14 [r]A gift in secret averts anger,
and a concealed bribe,[3] strong wrath.
15 When justice is done, it is a joy to the righteous
[s]but terror to evildoers.
16 One who wanders from the way of good sense
[t]will rest in the assembly of the dead.
17 Whoever loves pleasure will be a poor man;
he who loves wine and oil will not be rich.
18 [u]The wicked is a [v]ransom for the righteous,
and the traitor for the upright.

1 Or *the plowing* 2 Some Hebrew manuscripts, Septuagint, Latin; most Hebrew manuscripts *vapor for those who seek death* 3 Hebrew *a bribe in the bosom*

20:30 Corporal punishment has a place in prodding the conscience, but it takes wisdom to know when and how to apply it.

21:1 The king's heart . . . LORD. Possibly a reference to the sovereignty of God even over pagan kings who unwittingly do His will (e.g., Cyrus in Is. 45:1), or to the king of Israel, who, like Solomon, received a special endowment of the wisdom of God (16:10 and note). See "God Reigns: Divine Sovereignty" at Dan. 4:34.

21:3 See v. 27. Prophetic themes such as this (1 Sam. 15:22; Is. 1:11–17) are rarely found in wisdom literature (15:8 note).

21:4 Haughty eyes. See 6:17. This expression describes pride and arrogance, similar to "a proud heart."

the lamp of the wicked. The meaning of this metaphor is uncertain.

21:5 In v. 25 and 19:15 poverty is brought on by laziness. Here it results from rash and unwise action.

21:6 The Hebrew is difficult (see text note). The meaning of the proverb is probably similar to that of 20:17 (note).

21:7 will sweep them away. Or, "snare them." See 1:17, 19 and notes; 12:13.

21:8 upright. See note 14:2.

21:9 corner of the housetop. The reference is probably to a small attic room built on the customarily flat housetop.

quarrelsome wife. See v. 19; 19:13 and note. This wife is the opposite of the prudent wife in 19:14.

21:10 evil. That which is destructive of human relationships.

21:12 The Righteous One. The Hebrew can be translated "righteous person," but it makes more sense as a reference to God. The divine retribution is then affirmed on the basis of divine righteousness rather than human observation.

21:14 See 17:8; 18:16 and notes.

21:15 Maintaining true order (justice) establishes the well-being of those who live according to it. Those who transgress it will be undone. The wise discern this divine, providential order which, though marred by sin, is to some degree maintained in the world. God preserves such an order, and it is our task to perceive His order and live in harmony with it. At its center are God's Word and our faithful obedience to it. Such obedience is what is meant by "the fear of the LORD."

21:16 This proverb contrasts the ways of life and death (2:18; 3:18 and notes). To forsake wisdom is to forsake life itself and to end up with the dead.

21:17 wine and oil. The words suggest extravagance, especially in feasting.

21:18 See 11:8 and note. A ransom is a sum paid to release someone. However, this proverb does not depend on this precise sense, but points in general terms to the Last Judgment, when the righteous will be vindicated and the wicked defeated.

19 It is [w]better to live in a desert land
than with a quarrelsome and
fretful woman.
20 [x]Precious treasure and oil are in a
wise man's dwelling,
but a foolish man [y]devours it.
21 Whoever [z]pursues righteousness and
kindness
will find [a]life, righteousness, and
honor.
22 [b]A wise man scales the city of the
mighty
and brings down the stronghold in
which they trust.
23 [c]Whoever keeps his mouth and his
tongue
[d]keeps himself out of [e]trouble.
24 [f]"Scoffer" is the name of the arrogant,
haughty man
who acts with arrogant pride.
25 The desire of [g]the sluggard
kills him,
for his hands refuse to labor.
26 All day long he craves and craves,
but the righteous [h]gives and does
not hold back.
27 [i]The sacrifice of the wicked is an
abomination;
how much more [j]when he brings it
with evil intent.
28 [k]A false witness will perish,
but the word of a man who hears
will endure.
29 A wicked man puts on a bold face,
but the upright [l]gives thought to[1]
his ways.
30 [m]No wisdom, no understanding, no
counsel
can avail against the LORD.
31 [n]The horse is made ready for the day
of battle,
but [o]the victory belongs to the
LORD.

22 [p]A good name is to be chosen
rather than great riches,
and favor is better than silver or
gold.
2 [q]The rich and the poor meet together;
the LORD is [r]the maker of them all.
3 [s]The prudent sees danger and hides
himself,
but the simple go on and suffer
for it.
4 The reward for humility and fear of
the LORD
is [t]riches and honor and life.[2]
5 [u]Thorns and snares are in the way of
the crooked;
whoever [v]guards his soul will keep
far from them.
6 [w]Train up a child in the way he
should go;
even when he is old he will not
depart from it.

19 [w][ver. 9] 20 [x][Ps. 112:3] [y][Job 20:15, 18] 21 [z]ch. 15:9; Matt. 5:6; [ch. 3:3] [a]ch. 3:16; 1 Kin. 3:11; Matt. 6:33; See ch. 4:22 22 [b][ch. 24:5; Eccles. 7:19]; See 2 Sam. 5:6-9; Eccles. 9:14-18 23 [c]See ch. 13:3 [d]ch. 22:5 [e]ch. 12:13 24 [f]ch. 1:22; See Ps. 1:1 25 [g][ch. 13:4] 26 [h]See Ps. 37:26 27 [i]Isai. 66:3; See ch. 15:8 [j][ch. 24:9] 28 [k]ch. 19:5, 9

29 [l]Ps. 119:5 30 [m]Isai. 8:9, 10; 1 Cor. 3:19, 20; [ch. 19:21] 31 [n][Ps. 20:7; 33:17; Isai. 31:1 [o]Jer. 3:23

Chapter 22
1 [p][Eccles. 7:1] 2 [q][ch. 29:13] [r]ch. 14:31; Job 31:15 3 [s]ch. 27:12; [ch. 14:16] 4 [t][ch. 21:20, 21] 5 [u]ch. 15:19 [v]ch. 21:23; [1 John 5:18] 6 [w]Eph. 6:4; 2 Tim. 3:15

1 Or *establishes* 2 Or *The reward for humility is the fear of the LORD, riches and honor and life*

21:19 See 19:13; 21:9 and notes.

21:21 Those who cultivate right relationships and loyalty find lasting benefits in life (v. 16 and note).

21:22 See 16:32 and note. Force is no match for wisdom. A similar image is applied to spiritual warfare in 2 Cor. 10:4.

21:23 See 13:3; 15:23; 18:13 and notes.

21:24 Scoffer. See 9:7 and note; 19:25.

21:25 desire. This desire does not connect him to the real world where work would bring its rewards (13:4; 19:24 and notes).

21:26 The proverb seems to be a continuation of v. 25. If not, it is a contrast between greed and self-giving.

21:27 See v. 3; 15:8 and notes.

21:28 See 14:25; 19:5, 9 and notes.

21:29 puts on a bold face. The wicked man resorts to arrogant bluffing in his dealings with others.

gives thought to his ways. The Septuagint (Greek Old Testament) renders this "considers his ways," indicating that the righteous person is concerned to live by truth and its consequences.

21:30 The limits of human understanding must be acknowledged in the light of God's wisdom and sovereignty. The fear of the Lord (1:7 note) puts us in touch with the revealed wisdom of God. But God is wise beyond what He reveals, and this unrevealed wisdom is not comprehended by us.

21:31 The verse takes for granted that people will make suitable preparations to reach their goals, while recognizing that the result depends on God.

22:1 A good name. A choice reputation is one of the social consequences of wisdom.

rather than great riches. Riches are not discouraged but put into right perspective (16:16 note).

22:2 meet together. Despite the inequalities of this life, both rich and poor stand under God as their Creator and Judge.

22:3 prudent . . . simple. See 1:4 and note.

22:4 humility and fear of the LORD. See 1:7; 15:33 and notes.

riches and honor and life. A life governed by wisdom tends to prosperity. Israel's sages emphasized that a right relationship with the Lord is the ultimate wisdom that enhances life (3:2, 18; 8:18 and notes).

22:5 Thorns and snares. These are metaphors for the misfortunes of life that stem from a breakdown of the true life-giving order (cf. 15:19).

guards his soul. That is, by establishing his life on the wisdom of God.

22:6 Train up a child. The Hebrew expression includes the idea of inauguration, or starting a child's life along a particular way. That way is the way of wisdom (1:22 note). True wisdom maintains itself because it has the humility to continue learning in the way. See "The Christian Family" at Eph. 5:22.

7 [x]The rich rules over the poor,
and the borrower is the slave of the lender.
8 Whoever [y]sows injustice will reap calamity,
and [z]the rod of his fury will fail.
9 [a]Whoever has a bountiful[1] eye will be blessed,
for he [b]shares his bread with the poor.
10 [c]Drive out a scoffer, [d]and strife will go out,
and [e]quarreling and abuse will cease.
11 He who [f]loves purity of heart,
and whose [g]speech is gracious,
[h]will have the king as his friend.
12 The eyes of the LORD keep watch over knowledge,
but he [i]overthrows the words of the traitor.
13 [j]The sluggard says, "There is a lion outside!
I shall be killed in the streets!"
14 The mouth of [k]forbidden[2] women is [l]a deep pit;
[m]he with whom the LORD is angry will fall into it.
15 Folly is bound up in the heart of a child,
but [n]the rod of discipline drives it far from him.
16 Whoever oppresses the poor to increase his own wealth,
or gives to the rich, [o]will only come to poverty.

Words of the Wise

17 [p]Incline your ear, and hear [q]the words of the wise,
[r]and apply your heart to my knowledge,
18 for it will be pleasant if you keep them within you,
if all of them are ready on your lips.
19 That your trust may be in the LORD,
I have made them known to you today, even to you.
20 Have I not written for you [s]thirty sayings
of counsel and knowledge,
21 to [t]make you know what is right and true,
that you may give a true answer to those who sent you?
22 [u]Do not rob the poor, because he is poor,
or [v]crush the afflicted at [w]the gate,
23 for [x]the LORD will plead their cause
and rob of life those who rob them.
24 Make no friendship with a man given to anger,
nor go with a wrathful man,

7 [x]James 2:6
8 [y]Job 4:8; [Hos. 10:13] [z][Isai. 14:6; 30:31]
9 [a][ch. 19:17; 2 Cor. 9:6] [b][ch. 19:17; Luke 14:13, 14]
10 [c][Gen. 21:9, 10] [d][ch. 26:20] [e]ch. 26:20
11 [f][ch. 16:13; Ps. 101:6] [g][Eccles. 10:12] [h][ch. 14:35]
12 [i]ch. 21:12; [ch. 11:3]
13 [j]ch. 26:13
14 [k]See ch. 2:16 [l][ch. 23:27] [m]Eccles. 7:26
15 [n]See ch. 13:24
16 [o]ch. 28:22
17 [p]ch. 5:1 [q]ch. 1:6; 24:23 [r][ch. 22:17]
20 [s]ch. 8:6
21 [t][Luke 1:3, 4]
22 [u][Ex. 23:6; Zech. 7:10; Mal. 3:5] [v]See Job 5:4 [w]Job 31:21
23 [x]ch. 23:11; 1 Sam. 25:39; Ps. 12:5; 35:10; 68:5; 140:12; Jer. 51:36

[1] Hebrew *good* [2] Hebrew *strange*

22:7 A simple observation of present reality: in this world, wealth is power (10:15 and note).

22:8 Folly transgresses the divine order, inviting the punishments of sorrow and dissolution (Hos. 8:7; Gal. 6:7–9).

22:9 Whoever has a bountiful eye. One who is willingly disposed to the needy. Our own well-being is bound up with that of others, so that what we do for their good benefits ourselves as well (19:17).

22:10 scoffer. See 9:7 and note. Social harmony cannot exist with such a person stirring up strife.

22:11 king. See 8:15, 16; 14:35; 16:12, 13; 20:26 and notes.

22:12 The eyes of the LORD. See 15:3; 20:8, 27 and notes. The Lord is the guardian of truth.

22:13 sluggard. See 6:6 and note. With humor and irony the proverb mocks the sluggard's excuses for avoiding work.

22:14 See 5:3–5; 6:24; 7:5, 14–21. Here the fool's downfall is seen as due to the wrath of God.

22:15 Folly is bound up in the heart of a child. The inborn propensity of fallen human nature is toward folly.

the rod of discipline. The rod may apply to a wide range of disciplinary choices, including corporal punishment (13:24; 29:15). Discipline is an educational task of wisdom, and is necessary until the child learns self-discipline.

22:16 The Hebrew is difficult to translate. As rendered here, both oppression of the poor and currying favor with the rich lead one into poverty.

22:17–24:22 This section is a collection of wisdom sayings mainly in the form of instructions (Introduction: Characteristics and Themes). There is evidence that the first part (22:17–23:11) has drawn upon the Egyptian wisdom of Amenemope (cf. 4:1–27 note). If so, these insights have been consciously appropriated as admonitions that assist one in meeting covenant obligations to "trust . . . in the LORD" (22:19). The author of Proverbs, like the historians of the Bible, was not prevented in principle from using existing materials in the course of writing what God inspired.

22:17–21 This introductory section exhorts the hearer to pay attention and listen, and also indicates some of the benefits of such learning.

22:17 apply your heart. Think carefully (2:2 and note).

22:18 on your lips. The internalized sayings are ready for use.

22:19 This saying expresses the biblical view of wisdom (3:5 note).

22:20 thirty sayings. Section 22:17–24:22 divides into roughly thirty parts, which is formally similar to Amenemope's thirty-chapter arrangement (22:17–24:22 note).

22:22, 23 A short instruction highlighting the threat of divine retribution. The Lord is pictured as the legal advocate of the poor (Ps. 9:18 note).

22:24, 25 The danger of unwise friendships is expounded in 1:10–19; 12:26.

22:24 a man given to anger. The person is quick to lose self-control (14:17; 15:18 and notes).

25 lest you learn his ways
and entangle yourself in a snare.
26 Be not one of those who [y]give pledges,
who put up security for debts.
27 If you have nothing with which to pay,
why should [z]your bed be taken
from under you?
28 Do not move the ancient [a]landmark
that your fathers have set.
29 Do you see a man skillful in his work?
He will [b]stand before kings;
he will not stand before obscure
men.

23 When you sit down to eat with a
ruler,
observe carefully what[1] is before you,
2 and put a knife to your throat
if you are given to appetite.
3 [c]Do not desire his delicacies,
for they are deceptive food.
4 [d]Do not toil to acquire wealth;
[e]be discerning enough to desist.
5 When your eyes light on it, it is
gone,
[f]for suddenly it sprouts wings,
flying like an eagle toward heaven.
6 [g]Do not eat the bread of a man who is
[h]stingy;[2]
[i]do not desire his delicacies,
7 for he is like one who is inwardly
calculating.[3]
"Eat and drink!" he says to you,
but his [j]heart is not with you.
8 You will vomit up the morsels that
you have eaten,
and waste your pleasant words.
9 Do not speak in the hearing of
a fool,
for he will despise the good sense
of your words.
10 [k]Do not move an ancient landmark
or enter the fields of the
fatherless,
11 for their [l]Redeemer is strong;
he will [m]plead their cause against
you.
12 Apply your heart to instruction
and your ear to words of
knowledge.
13 Do not withhold [n]discipline from a
child;
[o]if you strike him with a rod, he
will not die.
14 If you strike him with the rod,
you will [p]save his soul from Sheol.
15 [q]My son, if your heart is wise,
my heart too will be glad.
16 My [r]inmost being[4] will exult
when your lips speak [s]what is
right.
17 Let not your heart [t]envy sinners,
but continue in [u]the fear of the
LORD all the day.
18 Surely [v]there is a future,
and your [w]hope will not be cut off.

26 [y]See Job 17:3
27 [z][ch. 20:16; Ex. 22:26]
28 [a]ch. 23:10; Deut. 19:14; 27:17; Job 24:2; Hos. 5:10
29 [b]1 Kin. 10:8; See Gen. 41:46
Chapter 23
3 [c]ver. 6
4 [d]ch. 15:27; 28:20; Matt. 6:19; 1 Tim. 6:9, 10; Heb. 13:5 [e][ch. 3:5, 7; 26:12; Isai. 5:21; Rom. 12:16]
5 [f]ch. 27:24
6 [g][Ps. 141:4] [h]ch. 28:22; Deut. 15:9; Matt. 6:23 [i]ver. 3
7 [j][Ps. 12:2]
10 [k]See ch. 22:28
11 [l][Ex. 6:6]; See Job 19:25 [m]See ch. 22:23
13 [n]See ch. 13:24 [o][ch. 19:18]
14 [p][1 Cor. 5:5]
15 [q]ver. 24, 25; See ch. 29:3
16 [r]Ps. 7:9; 73:21 [s][ch. 8:6]
17 [t]See Ps. 37:1 [u][ch. 28:14]
18 [v]ch. 24:14, 20 [w]Ps. 9:18

1 Or *who* 2 Hebrew *whose eye is evil* 3 Or *for as he calculates in his soul, so is he* 4 Hebrew *My kidneys*

22:26, 27 See 6:1–5 and notes.

22:28 See 15:25 and notes. In 23:10, 11 the command is given against the background of God's determination to defend the oppressed.

22:29 a man skillful. Hebrew "who is quick." Such speed in work comes from well-learned skills rather than from taking shortcuts.

He will stand before kings. The words are an indirect exhortation to excellence, which, as in the Egyptian schools of the wise, was the way of promotion to higher service (22:17–24:22 note).

23:1–3 The verses are a warning, possibly to a diplomat, against over-indulgence in the pleasures of the table with a ruler.

23:1 what is before you. Or, "who is before you." The sense is either, "Do not allow the feast to excite you with greed," or, "Be attentive to the great ruler, and not to the food."

23:3 deceptive food. Gluttony may undermine human relationships and their advantages.

23:4, 5 It is not worth ruining one's health for riches that have the habit of elusively disappearing.

23:6 a man who is stingy. The meaning is uncertain, but the context suggests a person whose hospitality is insincere, presumably with hidden motives.

23:8 vomit. A metaphor for the spoiled relationship and the feeling of disgust at the host's insincerity.

23:9 This short instruction repeats the meaning of proverbs such as 9:7 that indicate that the fool is unteachable (cf. Matt. 7:6).

23:10, 11 See 22:28 and note.

23:11 Redeemer. In ancient Israelite society, the redeemer (Hebrew *goel*) helped another family member in great need (Ruth 2:20 note). The term is frequently applied to God in His saving action for His people (e.g., Job 19:25; Ps. 19:14; Is. 41:14; 43:14; 44:24), as it is here.

23:13, 14 See 13:24; 19:18; 22:6, 15 and notes.

23:13 he will not die. The meaning is either that such corporal punishment will not unduly hurt him, or that by the discipline he will avoid death (the meaning of v. 14).

23:14 Sheol. See 9:18 note.

23:17, 18 This instruction reflects Israel's covenant relationship and the promises of God (1:7 note). It goes beyond the practical and immediate concerns of wisdom to the revelation that sustains the suffering righteous. See notes 1:19; 11:8.

23:17 the fear of the LORD. See 1:7 and note.

23:18 a future . . . your hope. The word "future" may be a reference to a hope for life and vindication after death. More likely, however, it refers to a long and full life.

19 Hear, my son, and [x]be wise,
and [y]direct your heart in the way.
20 Be not among [z]drunkards[1]
or among [a]gluttonous eaters of meat,
21 for the drunkard and the glutton will
come to poverty,
and [b]slumber will clothe them
with rags.

22 [c]Listen to your father who gave you life,
[d]and do not despise your mother
when she is old.
23 [e]Buy truth, and do not sell it;
buy wisdom, instruction, and
understanding.
24 [f]The father of the righteous will
greatly rejoice;
he who fathers a wise son will be
glad in him.
25 [f]Let your father and mother be glad;
let [g]her who bore you rejoice.

26 My son, give me your heart,
and let your eyes observe[2] my ways.
27 For a prostitute is [h]a deep pit;
[i]an adulteress[3] is a narrow [j]well.
28 [k]She lies in wait like a robber
and increases the traitors among
mankind.

29 [l]Who has woe? Who has sorrow?
Who has strife? Who has
complaining?
Who has [m]wounds without cause?
Who has [n]redness of eyes?
30 Those who [o]tarry long over wine;
those who go to try [p]mixed
wine.
31 Do not look at wine when it
is red,
when it sparkles in the cup
and goes down smoothly.
32 In the end it [q]bites like a serpent
and stings like an adder.
33 Your eyes will see strange things,
and your heart utter [r]perverse
things.
34 You will be like one who lies down
in the midst of the sea,
like one who lies on the top of a
mast.[4]
35 "They [s]struck me," you will say,[5]
"but I was not hurt;
they beat me, but I did not feel it.
When shall I awake?
I [t]must have another drink."

24 Be not [u]envious of evil men,
nor desire to be [v]with them,
2 for their hearts [w]devise violence,
and their lips [x]talk of trouble.

3 By [y]wisdom a house is built,
and by understanding it is
established;
4 by knowledge the rooms are filled
with all [z]precious and pleasant
riches.

19 [x]ch. 6:6 [y][ch. 9:6]
20 [z][ver. 29, 30; Isai. 5:11, 22; Matt. 24:49; Luke 21:34; Rom. 13:13; Eph. 5:18] [a]ch. 28:7
21 [b][ch. 6:10, 11]
22 [c]See ch. 1:8 [d][ch. 30:17]
23 [e][ch. 4:5, 7; 18:15; Matt. 13:44]
24 [f]ver. 15; See ch. 29:3
25 [f][See ver. 24 above] [g]ch. 17:25
27 [h][ch. 22:14] [i]See ch. 2:16 [j]Ps. 55:23
28 [k]ch. 7:12; [Eccles. 7:26]
29 [l][ver. 20, 21] [m][ver. 35] [n]Gen. 49:12
30 [o]Isai. 5:11; [p]ch. 9:2, 5; Ps. 75:8; Isai. 5:22; 65:11
32 [q]Job 20:16
33 [r]See ch. 2:12
35 [s]Jer. 5:3; [ver. 29] [t]Isai. 56:12
Chapter 24
1 [u]ver. 19; See Ps. 37:1 [v]See ch. 1:15
2 [w][Isai. 59:13] [x]Ps. 10:7
3 [y][ch. 14:1]
4 [z][ch. 23:23; Luke 16:11]

1 Hebrew *those who drink too much wine* 2 Or *delight in* 3 Hebrew *a foreign woman* 4 Or *of the rigging* 5 Hebrew lacks *you will say*

23:19–21 Poor company, drunkenness, and gluttony are examples of the foolish life that easily overtakes one.

23:22–25 Instructions to children on right family relationships. These principles are derived from the fifth commandment (Ex. 20:12) and testified to by the sages' discerning observation of harmonious and joyful human relationships.

23:26–28 A warning against immoral women (2:16–19; 5:1–20).

23:26 give me your heart. That is, pay attention (2:2 note). The wisdom teachers call for undivided attention and trust in their teaching.

23:27 deep pit. The image is of a pit for trapping wild animals.

adulteress. Lit. "a foreign woman," a term used for immoral or adulterous persons (2:16 note).

narrow well. Impossible to escape from (Jer. 38:6).

23:28 traitors. Lit. "treacherous," here signifying unfaithfulness in marriage.

23:29–35 The perils of drunkenness are put in the form of a riddle. The effects are seen objectively (v. 29) and subjectively (vv. 33–35). The values of biblical wisdom are opposite: self-control, clear perception of reality, and positive relationships.

23:30 mixed wine. See 9:2 and note.

23:31 look at wine when it is red. The occasions when wine seems especially desirable call for deliberate caution in its use.

23:32 bites like a serpent. The hangover, which is the natural consequence of drunkenness, is like a snakebite.

23:33 strange things . . . perverse things. The words suggest hallucinations and confused thinking.

23:34 midst of the sea . . . top of a mast. Two nautical metaphors express the feeling of dizziness that drunkenness produces.

23:35 I was not hurt. Numbed by drink, the drunk does not notice injuries.

another drink. The alcoholic craves more despite the pain it brings.

24:1, 2 See v. 19.

24:2 their hearts devise violence. These are deliberately evil people who use all their intellect and determination to harm others.

24:3, 4 wisdom . . . understanding . . . knowledge. These words are used synonymously of the perception and harnessing of right relationships. True wisdom applies to the craftsman's skill in construction (as in Ex. 36:1), to human relationships, and to the legitimate achievement of prosperity.

24:3 a house is built. "House" refers either literally to a building to live in, or is a metaphor for a family, or even a dynasty (2 Sam. 7:11, 12).

24:4 riches. Either material wealth (e.g., Solomon's wealth), or metaphorically, the beauty of good family relationships.

5 [a] A wise man is full of strength,
and a man of knowledge enhances his might,
6 for by [b] wise guidance you can wage your war,
and in [c] abundance of counselors there is victory.
7 Wisdom is [d] too high for a fool;
in [e] the gate he does not open his mouth.

8 Whoever [f] plans to do evil
will be called a schemer.
9 [g] The devising[1] of folly is sin,
and [h] the scoffer is an abomination to mankind.

10 If you [i] faint in the day of adversity,
your strength is small.
11 [j] Rescue those who are being taken away to death;
hold back those who are stumbling to the slaughter.
12 If you say, "Behold, we did not know this,"
[k] does not he who [l] weighs the heart perceive it?
Does not he who [m] keeps watch over your soul know it,
and will he not repay man
[n] according to his work?

13 My son, [o] eat honey, for it is good,
and [p] the drippings of the honeycomb are sweet to your taste.
14 Know that wisdom is such to your soul;
if you find it, there will be [q] a future,
and your hope will not be cut off.

15 [r] Lie not in wait as a wicked man against the dwelling of the righteous;
do no violence to his home;
16 [s] for the righteous falls [t] seven times and rises again,
but [u] the wicked stumble in times of calamity.

17 [v] Do not rejoice when your enemy falls,
and let not your heart be glad when he stumbles,
18 lest the LORD see it and be displeased,
and turn away his anger from him.

19 [w] Fret not yourself because of evildoers,
and be not [x] envious of the wicked,
20 for the evil man has no [q] future;
[y] the lamp of the wicked will be put out.

21 My son, [z] fear the LORD and the king,
and do not join with those who do otherwise,
22 for disaster from them will rise suddenly,
and who knows the ruin that will come from them both?

5 [a] [ch. 21:22] 6 [b] ch. 20:18 [c] See ch. 11:14 7 [d] [ch. 14:6] [e] See Job 5:4 8 [f] Rom. 1:30 9 [g] [ch. 21:27] [h] See Ps. 1:1 10 [i] [Heb. 12:3] 11 [j] Ps. 82:4; [Isai. 58:6, 7] 12 [k] [Eccles. 5:8] [l] ch. 16:2; See 1 Sam. 16:7 [m] [Ps. 91:11] [n] See Job 34:11 13 [o] [Ps. 19:10; 119:103; S. of S. 5:1; Isai. 7:15] [p] S. of S. 4:11 14 [q] See ch. 23:18 15 [r] Ps. 10:9, 10 16 [s] See Ps. 37:24 [t] See Job 5:19 [u] ch. 14:32 17 [v] Ps. 35:15, 19; [Mic. 7:8]; See ch. 17:5 19 [w] [Jer. 12:1]; See Ps. 37:1 [x] ver. 1 20 [q] [See ver. 14 above] [y] ch. 13:9; See Job 18:5 21 [z] 1 Pet. 2:17; [Rom. 13:7]

[1] Or *scheming*

24:5, 6 See 11:14; 21:22 and notes.

24:7 too high. Fools are out of their depth since they are unteachable.

the gate. The traditional meeting place for counsel and judgment was the town gate.

24:8 will be called a schemer. In a well-ordered society, social values act beneficially to suppress evil. Here the one who schemes is shamed.

24:9 The devising of folly is sin. See v. 2 and note. Folly is not lack of intellect, but active rebellion against truth and the order derived from it.

an abomination to mankind. See v. 8 and note.

24:10 A person's moral strength is only seen when it is truly tested.

24:11, 12 These two verses are best taken together. One cannot use the excuse of ignorance to avoid the responsibility to help another in need.

24:12 he who weighs the heart. One's accountability to God is stressed. Here the eternal rather than the merely social consequences of failing to help others are considered.

24:13 eat honey. This mention of honey is not merely a metaphor. Good food, a part of the prosperous life, is a concern of wisdom (25:16; Eccl. 9:7, 8; Song 5:1).

24:14 wisdom. Wisdom sustains our inner life as honey sustains the body.

future. That is, hope for the future (see also 23:18 and note).

24:15, 16 The assumption is that God does not allow the unrighteous to prosper permanently. On the other hand, the righteous may suffer many adversities, yet God finally vindicates them.

24:17 Do not rejoice. On its own, this verse would make perfect sense as implying that compassion should not be entirely withdrawn from any other human being. While the motive cited in v. 18 may initially appear vindictive, it seems to teach that when we are devoid of kindness to our enemy, we deserve God's wrath more than the enemy does.

24:19 Fret. Lit. "become hot," i.e., become agitated or vexed.

be not envious. See v. 1.

24:20 future. Or, "future . . . hope" (v. 14; 23:18 and note).

24:21 fear the LORD. See 1:7 and note.

the king. In Israel's covenant-based society, the king became the exemplar of wisdom and the agent of God's rule (cf. Deut. 17:14–20 and notes).

24:22 the ruin. That is, righteous retribution from God and the king.

More Sayings of the Wise

23 These also are sayings of [a]the wise.

[b]Partiality in judging is not good.
24 Whoever [c]says to the wicked, "You
are in the right,"
[d]will be cursed by peoples,
abhorred by nations,
25 but those who rebuke the wicked
will have delight,
and a good blessing will come
upon them.
26 Whoever gives an honest answer
kisses the lips.

27 [e]Prepare your work outside;
get everything ready for yourself in
the field,
and after that build your house.

28 [f]Be not a witness against your
neighbor without cause,
and do not deceive with your lips.
29 Do not say, [g]"I will do to him as he
has done to me;
I will pay the man back for what
he has done."

30 [h]I passed by the field of a sluggard,
by the vineyard of a man [i]lacking
sense,
31 and behold, it was all overgrown
with thorns;
the ground was covered with
nettles,
and its stone [j]wall was broken
down.
32 Then I saw and [k]considered it;
I looked and received instruction.
33 [l]A little sleep, a little slumber,
a little folding of the hands to rest,
34 and poverty will come upon you like
a robber,
and want like an armed man.

More Proverbs of Solomon

25 These also are [m]proverbs of Solomon which the men of Hezekiah king of Judah copied.

2 It is the glory of God to [n]conceal
things,
but the glory of kings is to [o]search
things out.
3 As the heavens for height, and the
earth for depth,
so the heart of kings is
[p]unsearchable.
4 Take away [q]the dross from the silver,
and [r]the smith has material for a
vessel;
5 take away [s]the wicked from the
presence of the king,
and his [t]throne will be established
in righteousness.
6 Do not put yourself forward in the
king's presence
or stand in the place of the great,
7 for [u]it is better to be told, "Come up
here,"
than to be put lower in the
presence of a noble.
What [v]your eyes have seen

23 [a]ch. 1:6; 22:17 [b]See ch. 18:5
24 [c]See ch. 17:15 [d]ch. 11:26
27 [e][Luke 14:28]
28 [f][ch. 25:18]
29 [g]See ch. 20:22
30 [h][Job 5:3] [i]See ch. 6:32
31 [j]Isai. 5:5
32 [k][ch. 22:17]
33 [l]For ver. 33, 34, see ch. 6:10, 11
Chapter 25
1 [m]See ch. 1:1
2 [n][Deut. 29:29; Rom. 11:33] [o]Job 29:16
3 [p][Ps. 145:3]
4 [q][ch. 26:23; Ezek. 22:18; 2 Tim. 2:20, 21] [r][Mal. 3:2, 3]
5 [s][ch. 20:8] [t]See ch. 16:12
7 [u]See Luke 14:8-11 [v][2 Kin. 25:19; Jer. 52:25; Esth. 1:14]

24:23–25 Justice is essential. A well-ordered society is one in which justice is done and is seen to be done. This complements the directive given in vv. 21, 22.

24:26 kisses the lips. This comparison to the most intimate expression of friendship highlights the value of a just and right answer (cf. 27:6).

24:27 build your house. Either the physical structure, or the family (v. 3 note). Both need a firm economic basis, such as is provided by the proceeds of one's crops, before they can be built.

24:28, 29 If, as seems likely, these two verses belong together, there is even more at stake than the need to avoid giving false witness (6:16, 19). Revenge is born out of anger and the heat of passion. The loss of control depicted in v. 29 is the opposite of the self-restraint called for by biblical wisdom.

24:30–34 See 6:6–11 and notes.

25:1 proverbs of Solomon. See Introduction: Author; note on 1:1.

Hezekiah. He was king of Judah at the time of the destruction of the northern kingdom of Israel. Hezekiah vigorously carried out reforms of Judah's corrupt religious practices. This introduction to a new section of the Book of Proverbs shows that Hezekiah not only promoted a return to the Law of Moses, but also encouraged the wisdom movement by literary activity.

copied. The development of a scribal class in Israel was dictated by the religious and administrative needs of the nation. The Hebrew word used here indicates transmission and may mean committing oral tradition to writing, or transcribing something already written.

25:2 It can already be seen from creation that the wisdom of God is beyond all human knowing (Ps. 92:5; 147:5; Is. 40:12–17; Rom. 1:20). The king as God's servant makes probing inquiry into the questions that concern his rule, and he is to be admired for his success in uncovering what he has to know (16:12–15; 20:8, 26; 25:3, 5 and notes).

25:3 unsearchable. The same verb as in v. 2 is used here in the negative. The knowledge that the king has acquired through effort and the royal decisions based on it are reflections of God's rule based on His wisdom. The king is understood to rule through God's appointment (cf. Rom. 13:4).

25:4, 5 No matter how skilled the craftsman, he must have good materials to work with. In the same way, the king needs a society purged of evil elements if he is to establish a righteous rule. Good order in society cannot simply be commanded from the throne.

25:6, 7 Wisdom of the royal court observes an unspoken protocol. It rebukes conceit and self-seeking that overreaches itself and leads to humiliation. It is better to start out with humility and then be exalted. Jesus adapted this instruction to speak of our place in the kingdom of God (Luke 14:7–11).

8 [w] do not hastily bring into court,
for[1] what will you do in the end,
when your neighbor puts you to shame?
9 [x] Argue your case with your neighbor himself,
and do not reveal another's secret,
10 lest he who hears you bring shame upon you,
and your ill repute have no end.
11 [y] A word fitly spoken
is like apples of gold in a setting of silver.
12 Like [z] a gold ring or an ornament of gold
is a wise reprover to [a] a listening ear.
13 Like the cold of snow in the time of harvest
is [b] a faithful messenger to those who send him;
he refreshes the soul of his masters.
14 Like [c] clouds and wind without rain
is a man who [d] boasts of a gift he does not give.
15 With [e] patience a ruler may be persuaded,
and a soft tongue will break a bone.
16 If you have [f] found honey, eat [g] only enough for you,
lest you have your fill of it and vomit it.
17 Let your foot be seldom in your neighbor's house,
lest he have his fill of you and hate you.
18 A man who [h] bears false witness against his neighbor
is like a war club, or [i] a sword, or a sharp arrow.
19 Trusting in a treacherous man in time of trouble
is like a bad tooth or a foot that slips.
20 Whoever [j] sings songs to a heavy heart
is like one who takes off a garment on a cold day,
and like vinegar on soda.
21 [k] If your enemy is hungry, give him bread to eat,
and if he is thirsty, give him water to drink,
22 for you will heap [l] burning coals on his head,
and the LORD will reward you.
23 The north wind brings forth rain,
and a backbiting tongue, angry looks.

8 [w] Matt. 5:25; Luke 12:58; [ch. 17:14] 9 [x] Matt. 18:15 11 [y] ch. 15:23; [Isai. 50:4] 12 [z] [Gen. 24:22] [a] ch. 15:31; 20:12 13 [b] ch. 13:17 14 [c] Jude 12 [d] ch. 20:6 15 [e] ch. 15:1; 16:14; [Eccles. 10:4] 16 [f] [Judg. 14:8; 1 Sam. 14:25] [g] [ver. 27] 18 [h] [ch. 24:28] [i] ch. 12:18; See Ps. 57:4 20 [j] [Rom. 12:15] 21 [k] Cited Rom. 12:20; [2 Kin. 6:22; 2 Chr. 28:15]; See Ex. 23:4, 5 22 [l] Ps. 140:10

1 Hebrew *or else*

25:8 court. The principle can apply more widely to the need for prudence in speech that reflects on the character of others.

25:9 do not reveal another's secret. Do not involve others in a dispute.

25:10 your ill repute have no end. Betrayal of confidences will lead to a reputation for disloyalty.

25:11 Lit. "Apples of gold in settings of silver, a word fitly spoken." This kind of proverbial comparison simply places two or more things side by side (cf. v. 18), leaving the reader to work out the nature of the comparison. The importance of well-chosen words, a common wisdom theme, is highlighted by their comparison with objects of fine craftsmanship.

25:12 A similar comparison of ideas is found in v. 11. Two pieces of jewelry are set alongside a good relationship between the wise teacher's rebuke and the receptive pupil. The implied comparison says either that a rebuke is as valuable as fine gold jewelry, or that a wise rebuke and a receptive ear go together like matched jewelry.

25:13 Like the cold of snow. The imagery is not of an unseasonable snowfall, which would be disastrous for the harvest, but of refreshment (cf. v. 25).

25:14 Inhabitants of Palestine often experienced clouds that promised rain but proved to be dry (Jude 12). Such a proverb today might be applied to those who seek power and influence, whether political or personal, by promises that are not fulfilled.

25:15 With patience. That is, by being slow to anger and resisting provocation.

break a bone. By gentle diplomacy strong resistance is broken.

25:16, 17 What were probably separate sayings are here joined to reinforce the message they have in common: Know when to stop; honey is good for you, but too much makes you sick; neighborly friendship is good, but excessive familiarity can abuse another's privacy. Relationships need to be wisely defined.

25:18 False testimony belongs to the same group as weapons of war because they all are lethal instruments used to assault another's well-being.

25:20 vinegar on soda. The application of vinegar to "soda" (a cleansing agent such as baking soda) renders the latter useless. Another possible translation is, "like vinegar on a wound." Just as taking away someone's coat or pouring vinegar on wounds causes pain, so also does frivolity in the presence of sorrow (Ps. 137:3, 4; Rom. 12:15).

25:22 you will heap burning coals on his head. The meaning of this metaphor must be determined from its context (see v. 21). The apostle Paul (Rom. 12:20) uses it, as here, as an image of overcoming evil with good. Ps. 140:10 uses the phrase as a description of punishment. The most likely meaning is penitence through a burning sense of shame. Some associate the image with an Egyptian penitential rite in which coals were carried on the head to show contrition. But the proverb comments on divine recompense: "the LORD will reward you." See note 1:7.

Apart from Ex. 23:4, 5, Israel was rarely ordered to show kindness to enemies. This is probably because of the significance of the enemies as those who not only oppose God's kingdom but also threaten Israel's survival as the messianic people. Jesus developed the implications of the gospel for the treatment of personal enemies in Matt. 5:43–48.

25:23 Note the inevitable cause and effect relationship expressed in both lines.

24 [m] It is better to live in a corner of the
housetop
than in a house shared with a
quarrelsome wife.
25 Like cold water to [n] a thirsty soul,
so is [o] good news from a far country.
26 Like [p] a muddied spring or a polluted
fountain
is a righteous man who gives way
before the wicked.
27 It is [q] not good to eat much honey,
nor is it glorious to [r] seek one's
own glory.[1]
28 A man [s] without self-control
is like [t] a city broken into and left
without walls.

26

1 Like snow in summer or [u] rain in
harvest,
so [v] honor is [w] not fitting for a fool.
2 Like [x] a sparrow in its flitting, like a
swallow in its flying,
[y] a curse that is causeless does not
alight.
3 [z] A whip for the horse, a bridle for the
donkey,
and [a] a rod for the back of fools.
4 [b] Answer not a fool according to his
folly,
lest you be like him yourself.
5 [c] Answer a fool according to his folly,
lest he be [d] wise in his own eyes.
6 Whoever sends a message by the
hand of a fool
cuts off his own feet and [e] drinks
violence.
7 Like a lame man's legs, which hang
useless,
is a proverb in the mouth of fools.
8 Like one who binds the stone in the
sling
is [f] one who gives honor to a fool.
9 Like [g] a thorn that goes up into the
hand of a drunkard
is a proverb in the mouth of fools.
10 Like an archer who wounds everyone
is one who hires a passing fool or
drunkard.[2]
11 Like [h] a dog that returns to his vomit
is [i] a fool who repeats his folly.
12 Do you see a man who is [j] wise in his
own eyes?
[k] There is more hope for a fool than
for him.
13 [l] The sluggard says, "There is a lion in
the road!
There is a lion in the streets!"
14 As a door turns on its hinges,
so does a sluggard on his bed.
15 [m] The sluggard buries his hand in the
dish;
it wears him out to bring it back to
his mouth.
16 The sluggard is [j] wiser in his own eyes
[n] than seven men who can answer
sensibly.
17 Whoever meddles in a quarrel not
his own
is like one who takes a passing dog
by the ears.

24 [m] ch. 21:9
25 [n] [Ps. 42:2] [o] ch. 15:30
26 [p] [Ezek. 32:2; 34:18, 19]
27 [q] [ver. 16] [r] [ch. 27:2]
28 [s] [ch. 16:32] [t] [2 Chr. 32:5; 36:19; Neh. 1:3]
Chapter 26
1 [u] [1 Sam. 12:17] [v] [ver. 8] [w] ch. 17:7; 19:10
2 [x] ch. 27:8; Ps. 84:3 [y] [Num. 23:8; Deut. 23:5; 2 Sam. 16:12]
3 [z] [Ps. 32:9] [a] See ch. 19:29
4 [b] [2 Sam. 16:11; 2 Kin. 18:36; Luke 23:9]
5 [c] See Matt. 16:1-4; 21:24-27 [d] ch. 28:11; [Rom. 12:16]
6 [e] [ch. 13:2; Job 15:16]
8 [f] [ver. 1]
9 [g] [ch. 23:35]
11 [h] Cited 2 Pet. 2:22 [i] [Ex. 8:15]
12 [j] ch. 28:11; [Rom. 12:16] [k] ch. 29:20
13 [l] ch. 22:13
15 [m] ch. 19:24
16 [j] [See ver. 12 above] [n] [ver. 25; ch. 6:16]; See Job 5:19

1 The meaning of the Hebrew line is uncertain 2 Or *hires a fool or passersby*

25:24 See 21:9 and note.

25:25 For the form of this proverb, see note on v. 11.

25:26 righteous man. See note 8:18.

25:28 This comparison (see v. 11 note) illustrates the vulnerability of the person who lacks self-control.

26:1 The comparison is explicit ("Like . . . so"). The perceptible orderliness of nature should be paralleled in society's estimation of human character.

26:2 The form is the same as in v. 1. Curses have no power to afflict someone who is innocent. Such a curse has meaning only as an expression of divine retribution.

26:4, 5 Taken together these verses illustrate the point that no proverb is intended to cover every possible situation. The apparent contradiction in the two proverbs indicates that proverbs must be appropriately applied. One situation demands that we avoid playing the fool's game by giving an answer, while another demands that we expose the folly so that the fool is not considered wise.

26:6 drinks violence. Or, "suffers violence." Sending a fool on an errand is asking for trouble.

26:7 A wisdom saying uttered by a fool is so incongruous with his character that it loses power.

26:8 The absurdity of preventing a stone from leaving the sling illustrates the absurdity of honoring the fool.

26:9 Like a thorn . . . a proverb. This saying apparently refers to a thorn piercing the hand of a person too drunk to sense it. Either the fool is too simple to perceive the significance of the proverb, or, as the thorn injures the drunkard's hand, so fools will use the proverb to their own hurt.

26:11 Fools will not learn from their mistakes but rather return, like a dog to its vomit, to repeat them.

26:12 There are degrees of folly, and the highest is found in fools who think they are wise. An extreme example is seen in the worldly wisdom that regards God's wisdom as folly (1 Cor. 1:18–2:5).

26:13–16 Four proverbs reflect on laziness that works against well-ordered human existence and against life itself. See 6:6–11; 24:30–34 and notes.

26:13 See 22:13 and note.

26:14 Just like a door on its hinges, so lazy persons turn restlessly on their beds.

26:16 seven men. The precise number, although often symbolizing completeness, is not important in this instance; it serves only to highlight the self-delusion of the fool.

26:17 Wisdom includes knowing when not to interfere in others' disputes.

18 Like a madman who throws
[o]firebrands, arrows, and death
19 is the man who deceives his neighbor
and says, "I am only joking!"
20 For lack of wood the fire goes out,
and where there is no [p]whisperer,
[q]quarreling ceases.
21 As charcoal to hot embers and wood
to fire,
so is [r]a quarrelsome man for
kindling strife.
22 [s]The words of [p]a whisperer are like
delicious morsels;
they go down into the inner parts
of the body.
23 [t]Like the [u]glaze[1] covering an earthen
vessel
are fervent lips with an evil heart.
24 Whoever hates disguises himself with
his lips
and harbors deceit in his heart;
25 [v]when he speaks graciously, believe
him not,
for there are [w]seven abominations
in his heart;
26 though his hatred be covered with
deception,
his wickedness will be exposed in
the assembly.
27 [x]Whoever digs a pit will fall into it,
and a stone will come back on him
who starts it rolling.
28 A lying tongue hates its victims,
and a flattering mouth works ruin.

27

Do not boast about tomorrow,
[y]for you do not know what a day
may bring.

18 [o][Isai. 50:11] 20 [p]ch. 16:28 [q]ch. 22:10 21 [r]See ch. 15:18 22 [s]ch. 18:8 [p][See ver. 20 above] 23 [t][Matt. 23:27; Luke 11:39] [u]See ch. 25:4 25 [v]See Ps. 28:3 [w][ver. 16] 27 [x][ch. 28:10]; See Ps. 7:15
Chapter 27
1 [y]Luke 12:19, 20 James 4:13, 14
2 [z]2 Cor. 10:12, 18; [ch. 25:27; 2 Cor. 12:11] 3 [a][ch. 12:16; 17:12] 4 [b]ch. 6:34 5 [c][ch. 28:23] 6 [d]Ps. 141:5 7 [e][ch. 25:16] 8 [f]ch. 26:2 9 [g][Ps. 23:5] 10 [h]See 1 Kin. 12:6-8; 2 Chr. 10:6-8 [i]See ch. 17:17

2 Let [z]another praise you, and not your
own mouth;
a stranger, and not your own lips.
3 A stone is heavy, and sand is
weighty,
but [a]a fool's provocation is heavier
than both.
4 Wrath is cruel, anger is
overwhelming,
but who can stand before
[b]jealousy?
5 [c]Better is open rebuke
than hidden love.
6 Faithful are [d]the wounds of a
friend;
profuse are the kisses of an
enemy.
7 One who is full loathes [e]honey,
but to one who is hungry
everything bitter is sweet.
8 Like [f]a bird that strays from its nest
is a man who strays from his
home.
9 [g]Oil and perfume make the heart
glad,
and the sweetness of a friend
comes from his earnest
counsel.[2]
10 Do not forsake your friend and [h]your
father's friend,
and do not go to your brother's
house in the day of your
calamity.
[i]Better is a neighbor who is near
than a brother who is far away.

1 By revocalization; Hebrew *silver of dross* 2 Or *and so does the sweetness of a friend that comes from his earnest counsel*

26:18, 19 The common element is the potential for destruction: to property and persons (v. 18), and to personal relationships (v. 19).

26:20 whisperer. A gossip, a purveyor of malicious murmuring with little concern for the truth.

26:21 quarrelsome man. Such people are not happy unless they are actively undermining personal relationships.

26:22 See 18:8 and note.

26:23 Although the Hebrew text is difficult, the apparent meaning is like that of vv. 24–26: a pleasing veneer can hide an opposite nature beneath.

26:25, 26 The person of v. 24 must be avoided. In time, people will see through such deceptions (5:14 and note).

26:27 Troublemakers often make trouble for themselves (cf. Gal. 6:7). The theme of retribution is probably intended to be linked with vv. 23–26. Here the emphasis is not on direct divine judgment, but on the providentially self-destructive nature of folly aimed at destroying others.

26:28 Hatred is the ultimate breakdown in human relationships (1 John 3:15). Human speech has enormous potential for evil, and its misuse cannot be lightly excused (James 3:5–10).

27:1 Though wisdom is concerned with taking hold on life, people do not have complete control over their future. Fools think they have, but they do not reckon with the sovereign will of God (21:30 note; Luke 12:19, 20).

27:2 Wisdom is humble (cf. 1 Cor. 13:4, 5).

27:3, 4 Two comparisons emphasize the destructiveness of folly.

27:5 open rebuke. A salutary word aimed at correction for one's good.

hidden love. This love, though genuine, lacks the moral strength to risk giving a rebuke.

27:6 wounds of a friend. The meaning is similar to "open rebuke" in v. 5.

27:7 See 25:16, 17, 27 and notes. The meaning of the proverb is not limited to food, but applies to anything for which we have an appetite.

27:8 Rootlessness hurts both the wanderer and those with whom he should be relating. Human beings need personal relationships.

27:10 The point of this instruction seems to be that one should develop relationships beyond the immediate family, for relatives are sometimes unwilling or unable to come to our aid.

11 [j] Be wise, [k] my son, and [l] make my
heart glad,
that I may [m] answer him who
reproaches me.
12 [n] The prudent sees danger and hides
himself,
but [o] the simple go on and suffer
for it.
13 [p] Take a man's garment when he has
put up security for a stranger,
and hold it in pledge when he puts
up security for an adulteress.[1]
14 Whoever blesses his neighbor with a
loud voice,
rising early in the morning,
will be counted as cursing.
15 [q] A continual dripping on a rainy day
and a quarrelsome wife are alike;
16 to restrain her is to restrain the wind
or to grasp[2] oil in one's right
hand.
17 Iron sharpens iron,
and one man sharpens another.[3]
18 [r] Whoever tends a fig tree will eat its
fruit,
and he who [s] guards his master will
be honored.
19 As in water face reflects face,
so the heart of man reflects the
man.
20 [t] Sheol and Abaddon are [u] never
satisfied,
and [v] never satisfied are the eyes of
man.
21 [w] The crucible is for silver, and the
furnace is for gold,
and a man is tested by his praise.

11 [j] ch. 6:6 [k] ch. 10:1; 23:15, 24 [l] See ch. 29:3 [m] Ps. 119:42; [Ps. 127:5]
12 [n] ch. 22:3 [o] See ch. 1:4
13 [p] See ch. 20:16
15 [q] ch. 19:13
18 [r] S. of S. 8:12; 1 Cor. 3:8; 9:7; 2 Tim. 2:6 [s] [Matt. 25:21]
20 [t] ch. 15:11; See Job 26:6 [u] ch. 30:15, 16; Hab. 2:5; [ch. 1:12] [v] Eccles. 1:8; 4:8
21 [w] ch. 17:3
22 [x] [ch. 23:35; Isai. 1:5; Jer. 5:3]
23 [y] [John 10:3, 14; Acts 20:28; 1 Pet. 5:2, 4]
24 [z] ch. 23:5
25 [a] Ps. 37:2; 90:5, 6
26 [b] [1 Tim. 6:8]
27 [b] [See ver. 26 above]
Chapter 28
1 [c] Lev. 26:17; Ps. 53:5 [d] Lev. 26:8; 1 Sam. 17:32
2 [e] [1 Kin. 15:27]; See 1 Kin. 16:8-28; 2 Kin. 15:8-15
3 [f] [Matt. 18:28]

22 [x] Crush a fool in a mortar with a pestle
along with crushed grain,
yet his folly will not depart from
him.
23 [y] Know well the condition of your
flocks,
and [y] give attention to your herds,
24 for [z] riches do not last forever;
and does a crown endure to all
generations?
25 [a] When the grass is gone and the new
growth appears
and the vegetation of the
mountains is gathered,
26 [b] the lambs will provide your
clothing,
and the goats the price of a field.
27 [b] There will be enough goats' milk for
your food,
for the food of your
household
and maintenance for your girls.

28

[c] The wicked flee when no one
pursues,
but [d] the righteous are bold as a
lion.
2 When a land transgresses, [e] it has
many rulers,
but with a man of understanding
and knowledge,
its stability will long continue.
3 [f] A poor man who oppresses the poor
is a beating rain that leaves no
food.

[1] Hebrew *a foreign woman*; slight emendation yields (compare Vulgate; see also 20:16) *for foreigners* [2] Hebrew *to meet with* [3] Hebrew *sharpens the face of another*

27:11 Parents are vindicated before others by their success in passing wisdom on to their children (10:1).

27:12 prudent . . . simple. See 1:4; 12:16 and notes.

27:13 See 20:16 and note.

27:14 The reference is probably to false and inappropriately timed protestations of friendship that cloak an evil intent (26:18, 19, 24–26).

27:17 This saying probably refers to the positive effect of interaction with others on one's character.

27:18 Diligent work and honest service are rewarded (22:29).

27:19 Just as water reflects our outward appearance, so the thoughts of our "hearts" reveal our inner nature and character.

27:20 Sheol and Abaddon. See notes 15:11. The parallel with destruction implies that the insatiability of the eyes involves endless desires that become destructive.

27:21 The sense is either that public praise tests character (here one's resistance to the temptation of pride), or that public esteem is generally a reliable indication of one's character (but cf. Matt. 5:11).

27:22 mortar . . . pestle. A bowl and a rod used to grind things in it. The fool is unteachable even when the most drastic measures are taken.

27:23–27 Economic resources of a renewable sort (flocks, crops) are preferable to riches that cannot be replaced. Careful attention to the providential order of nature generally ensures lasting provision for our needs. The ecological implications of this passage are even more obvious in the modern context.

28:1–28 This chapter contains a heavier concentration of theological reflection than earlier chapters of proverbial sentences. Sometimes this is explicit, with references to God or to the law and righteousness. In other sentences it is more implicit, as in the contrast of the righteous and the wicked, which seems to assume the underlying providential order and judgment of God.

28:2 Although the Hebrew is difficult, the meaning seems to be that unrighteousness and political instability (as occurred in the northern kingdom of Israel) go hand in hand, while a wise or righteous person helps maintain social order.

28:3 A poor man . . . the poor. The change of a Hebrew vowel produces the reading, "A ruler who oppresses the poor." Both excessive rainfall and a wicked ruler can do great harm.

4 Those who forsake the law [g]praise
the wicked,
but those who keep the law [h]strive
against them.
5 Evil men [i]do not understand
justice,
but those who seek the LORD
[j]understand it completely.
6 [k]Better is a poor man who [l]walks in
his integrity
than a rich man who is [l]crooked in
his ways.
7 The one who keeps the law is a son
with understanding,
but [m]a companion of gluttons
shames his father.
8 Whoever multiplies his wealth [n]by
interest and profit[1]
[o]gathers it for him who is [p]generous
to the poor.
9 If one turns away his ear from
hearing the law,
even his [q]prayer is an
abomination.
10 Whoever misleads the upright into
an evil way
[r]will fall into his own pit,
but the blameless [s]will have a
goodly inheritance.
11 A rich man is wise in his [t]own eyes,
but a poor man who has
understanding [u]will find
him out.

4 [g]Ps. 10:3; Rom. 1:32 [h][1 Kin. 18:18, 21; Neh. 13:11, 15; Matt. 3:7; 14:4; Eph. 5:11]
5 [i]Ps. 92:6; [John 12:39, 40] [j]Ps. 119:100; [John 7:17; 1 Cor. 2:15; James 1:5; 1 John 2:20, 27]
6 [k]ch. 19:1 [l]ver. 18
7 [m][ch. 23:20; 29:3]
8 [n]Ex. 22:25; Lev. 25:36 [o]See Job 27:17 [p]ch. 14:31
9 [q][Ps. 109:7]; See ch. 15:8
10 [r]See Ps. 7:15 [s][Matt. 6:33]
11 [t]ch. 26:5, 16 [u]Job 13:9
12 [v]ch. 11:10 [w]ver. 28; [ch. 29:2; Eccles. 10:5, 6]
13 [x][Job 31:33; Ps. 32:3]; See 1 John 1:8-10 [y]Ps. 32:5; 1 John 1:9
14 [z]ch. 23:17; Isai. 66:2; Phil. 2:12 [a]See Ps. 95:8
15 [b]ch. 19:12; 1 Pet. 5:8 [c][2 Kin. 2:24] [d][Ex. 1:14, 16, 22; Matt. 2:16]
16 [e]See ch. 6:32

12 When [v]the righteous triumph, there
is great glory,
but when [w]the wicked rise, people
hide themselves.
13 Whoever [x]conceals his transgressions
will not prosper,
but he who [y]confesses and forsakes
them will obtain mercy.
14 Blessed is the one who [z]fears the
LORD always,
but whoever [a]hardens his heart
will fall into calamity.
15 Like [b]a roaring lion or [c]a charging bear
is [d]a wicked ruler over a poor people.
16 A ruler who [e]lacks understanding is a
cruel oppressor,
but he who hates unjust gain will
prolong his days.
17 If one is burdened with [f]the blood of
another,
he will be a fugitive until death;[2]
let no one help him.
18 [g]Whoever [h]walks in integrity will be
delivered,
but he who is crooked in his ways
will suddenly fall.
19 [i]Whoever works his land will have
plenty of bread,
but he who follows worthless
pursuits will have plenty of
poverty.

17 [f][Gen. 9:6] 18 [g][ch. 3:23; 10:9] [h]ver. 6 19 [i]ch. 12:11

1 That is, profit that comes from charging interest to the poor
2 Hebrew *until the pit*

28:4 the law. Probably the Law of Moses, although wisdom instruction may be in view (3:1 note). Although wisdom literature often seems to reflect more on human experience in the created order than on God's revelation in Scripture, the Hebrew sages were men of God who knew the law and its demands (1:7 note).

28:5 justice. The word refers either to God's moral rule of the universe, or to the good order of things, of which God's rule is the basis.

those who seek the LORD. Those whose faith recognizes that the purpose of life is to serve God.

understand it completely. The phrase does not imply total knowledge or infallibility, but a renewed mind that knows things truly because it knows them as they are interpreted by God's revelation in Scripture (1:7 note).

28:6 in his integrity. Integrity in one's relationships with God and others is more important than riches.

28:7 law. See v. 4 and note.

companion of gluttons shames. See 23:19–25 and notes.

28:8 interest and profit. In Lev. 25:35–38, the grace of God establishes the principle of helping others freely and not for gain (Deut. 23:19, 20).

gathers it for him. The justice of God will not allow the greedy rich to retain their wealth (13:22; 22:16; Job 27:13–19), but will instead give it to those who generously aid others (19:17).

28:9 See 15:8, 29.

28:10 misleads the upright into an evil way. The justice of God seems to be implied here; there is a special judgment on those who seek to seduce God's people (Matt. 5:19; 18:6).

28:11 While riches do not necessarily correlate with unrighteousness, nor poverty with wisdom and righteousness, there is that tendency nevertheless (vv. 6, 8, 20, 22, 25, 27).

wise in his own eyes. See 26:5, 16. There are no greater fools than those who see their folly as wisdom (cf. 1 Cor. 1:18–25).

28:12 Righteousness leads to social order and happiness, while unrighteousness destroys and alienates (v. 28 and 29:2).

28:13 The orderliness and well-being in one's life is linked to an intensely personal relationship with God. Unconfessed sin is the ultimate disorder in life. Confession and repentance lead to a restoration of a right relationship with God, based on mercy (Ps. 32:1–4; 1 John 1:6–9). All other relationships depend on this.

28:14 Blessed. See 3:13 and note.

whoever hardens his heart. One who sets his will against the Lord (Ex. 7:3, 13).

28:15 See vv. 3, 16.

28:16 Tyranny is so contrary to wisdom that it demonstrates a lack of discernment. The second line implies that the greedy tyrant brings about his own destruction.

28:18 Whoever . . . will be delivered. See notes 1:19; 10:3; 11:8.

20 A faithful man will abound with
blessings,
but whoever hastens to be rich
[j]will not go unpunished.
21 To show [k]partiality is not good,
but for [l]a piece of bread a man will
do wrong.
22 A [m]stingy man[1] [n]hastens after
wealth
and does not know that [o]poverty
will come upon him.
23 Whoever [p]rebukes a man will
afterward find more favor
than [q]he who flatters with his
tongue.
24 Whoever robs his father or his
mother
and says, "That is no
transgression,"
is [r]a companion to a man who
destroys.
25 A greedy man [s]stirs up strife,
but the one who trusts in the LORD
will [t]be enriched.
26 Whoever [u]trusts in his own mind is a
fool,
but he who walks in wisdom will
be delivered.
27 Whoever [v]gives to the poor will not
want,
but he who [w]hides his eyes will get
many a curse.
28 When [x]the wicked rise, [y]people hide
themselves,
but when they perish, the
righteous increase.

29

1 [z]He who is often reproved, yet
stiffens his neck,
will suddenly be [a]broken [b]beyond
healing.
2 When [c]the righteous increase, the
people rejoice,
but when [d]the wicked rule, the
people groan.
3 He who [e]loves wisdom makes his
father glad,
but [f]a companion of prostitutes
[g]squanders his wealth.
4 By justice a king [h]builds up the land,
but he who exacts gifts[2] tears it
down.
5 [i]A man who flatters his neighbor
spreads [j]a net for his feet.
6 An evil man is [k]ensnared in his
transgression,
but a righteous man [l]sings and
rejoices.
7 A righteous man [m]knows the rights
of the poor;
a wicked man does not
[n]understand such knowledge.
8 [o]Scoffers set a city aflame,
but the wise turn away wrath.
9 If a wise man has an argument with a
fool,
the fool only rages and laughs, and
there is [p]no quiet.
10 Bloodthirsty men [q]hate one who is
blameless
and seek the life of the upright.[3]

20[j]ch. 16:5 **21**[k]See ch. 18:5 [l]Ezek. 13:19 **22**[m]See ch. 23:6 [n][ver. 20] [o]ch. 22:16 **23**[p]ch. 27:5, 6 [q]ch. 29:5 **24**[r][ch. 18:9] **25**[s]See ch. 15:18 [t]ch. 11:25; 13:4 **26**[u][1 Cor. 3:18] **27**[v][ch. 11:24]; See ch. 19:17 [w][ch. 29:7] **28**[x]See ver. 12 [y]Job 24:4

Chapter 29
1[z][1 Sam. 2:25]; See ch. 1:24-27 [a][Isai. 30:14; Jer. 19:11] [b]ch. 6:15 **2**[c]ch. 11:10; 28:12, 28; [Esth. 8:15] [d][Esth. 3:15] **3**[e][ch. 10:1; 15:20; 27:11; 28:7] [f][ch. 5:9, 10; 6:26] [g]Luke 15:13, 30 **4**[h][ver. 14; 2 Chr. 9:8] **5**[i]ch. 28:23 [j][Ps. 9:15] **6**[k][Eccles. 9:12] [l][Ex. 15:1, 21; Ps. 35:27] **7**[m]Job 29:16; Ps. 41:1 [n][ch. 28:27] **8**[o][ch. 11:11] **9**[p][Eccles. 4:6] **10**[q][Gen. 4:5, 8; 1 John 3:12]

1 Hebrew *A man whose eye is evil* 2 Or *who taxes heavily* 3 Or *but the upright seek his soul*

28:20 Faith and wisdom may lead to riches, but to give priority to riches is serious error.

28:21 See 18:5; 24:23, 24. Even a small bribe can have disastrous results in the maintenance of order and justice in society.

28:22 A stingy man. A miser (23:6 note and text note).

poverty will come. The meaning is either that the miser lacks the wisdom to gain and keep wealth, or that God's justice will not allow such a one to be rich (v. 20).

28:23 A needed rebuke ultimately has a positive effect on personal relationships (27:5), while flattery only undermines them.

28:24 See 19:26 and note.

That is no transgression. Family relationships are at the hub of all human ties. To plunder one's parents without shame shows moral depravity that undermines all relationships.

28:25 trusts in the LORD. Reliance and faith are included in the fear of the Lord (1:7 note).

28:26 trusts in his own mind. See 3:5, 6 and notes. Trust in self is the destructive opposite of trusting the Lord.

walks in wisdom. The way of wisdom and the fear of the Lord are correlated in vv. 25, 26 (1:7 note).

28:27 See 11:24–26; 14:21; 22:9 and notes.

28:28 See v. 12 and note; 29:2.

29:1 often reproved. See 1:30; 5:12; 9:7, 8; 10:17; 12:1 and notes.

stiffens his neck. That is, becomes self-willed and unteachable (28:14).

29:3 makes his father glad. See 10:1; 28:7.

squanders his wealth. The parallelism implies that such behavior is a disgrace and a sorrow to one's father (6:26).

29:4 See 8:15, 16; 20:8, 26 and notes.

29:5 See 28:23.

29:7 knows the rights. Lit. "knows the judgment." They know and do what God requires for the poor.

29:8 Scoffers. See 1:22 and note.

set a city aflame. The unwise, by nature, tend to undermine harmony in society.

29:9 If at all possible, the wise should avoid disputing with fools. Fools are incapable of rational argument, and even when right judgment is given they cannot be reconciled. See note 26:4, 5.

11 A fool gives full vent to his spirit,
but a wise man quietly holds it back.
12 If a ruler listens to falsehood,
all his officials will be wicked.
13 The poor man and the oppressor [r]meet together;
the LORD [s]gives light to the eyes of both.
14 If a king [t]faithfully judges the poor,
his throne will [u]be established forever.
15 [v]The rod and reproof give wisdom,
but a child left to himself [w]brings shame to his mother.
16 When the wicked increase,
transgression increases,
but [x]the righteous will look upon their downfall.
17 [y]Discipline your son, and he will give you rest;
he will give delight to your heart.
18 Where [z]there is no prophetic vision
the people [a]cast off restraint,[1]
but blessed is he who [b]keeps the law.
19 By mere words a servant is not disciplined,
for though he understands, he will not respond.
20 Do you see a man who is hasty in his words?
[c]There is more hope for a fool than for him.
21 Whoever pampers his servant from childhood
will in the end find him his heir.[2]
22 [d]A man of wrath stirs up strife,
and one given to anger causes much transgression.
23 [e]One's pride will bring him low,
[f]but he who is lowly in spirit will obtain honor.
24 The partner of a thief [g]hates his own life;
[h]he hears the curse, but discloses nothing.
25 [i]The fear of man lays a snare,
but whoever trusts in the LORD is safe.
26 Many [j]seek the face of a ruler,
but it is from the LORD that a man [k]gets justice.
27 [l]An unjust man is an abomination to the righteous,
but one whose way is straight is an abomination to the wicked.

The Words of Agur

30 The words of Agur son of Jakeh. The oracle.[3]

The man declares, I am weary, O God;
I am weary, O God, and worn out.[4]
2 Surely I am too [m]stupid to be a man.
I have not the understanding of a man.

13 [r][ch. 22:2] [s]Ps. 13:3; See Job 25:3 **14** [t][Ps. 72:4] [u][ver. 4]; See ch. 16:12 **15** [v]See ver. 17 [w]ch. 10:1; 17:25 **16** [x]Ps. 37:34, 36; 58:10; 91:8; 92:11 **17** [y]See ch. 13:24 **18** [z]1 Sam. 3:1; [2 Chr. 15:3; Ps. 74:9; Amos 8:11, 12] [a]Ex. 32:25 [b]Luke 11:28; John 13:17; James 1:25 **20** [c]ch. 26:12 **22** [d]See ch. 15:18 **23** [e]ch. 17:19; 2 Sam. 22:28; Matt. 23:12; James 4:6; See ch. 11:2 [f]ch. 15:33; 18:12 **24** [g]See ch. 8:36 [h]See Lev. 5:1 **25** [i]Luke 12:4; [Gen. 12:12, 13; 20:2, 11; 26:7; John 12:42, 43] **26** [j]ch. 19:6 [k]Isai. 49:4; 1 Cor. 4:4, 5 **27** [l][2 Cor. 6:14] **Chapter 30** **2** [m]See Ps. 49:10

[1] Or *the people are discouraged* [2] The meaning of the Hebrew word rendered *his heir* is uncertain [3] Or *Jakeh, the man of Massa* [4] Revocalization; Hebrew *The man declares to Ithiel, to Ithiel and Ucal*

29:12 Corruption in society tends to start at the top. The dishonest ruler not only attracts evil officials, but encourages subordinates to become corrupt.

29:13 gives light to the eyes of both. God has created both rich and poor (22:2 and note).

29:14 See v. 4; 16:12–15 and notes.

29:15 See 13:24; 22:15; 23:13, 14 and notes.

29:16 This proverb implicitly expresses confidence in the ultimate establishment of a just order under the rule of God.

29:17 Discipline. Not only chastening (v. 15) is in view, but also active and positive instruction in wisdom. In the covenantal context of Israel's faith, discipline and instruction come from the revelation of God in His word and acts.

29:18 prophetic vision. Either there is no word (1 Sam. 3:1), or there is an inability to hear the word (Amos 8:11, 12).

29:19 An observation of conditions in Hebrew society rather than a constant attitude of all workers (cf. 18:23 and note). The educational applications of wisdom are in view here, with the recognition that not all dispositions can be changed by words or reason alone.

29:21 will in the end. In what is perhaps a better reading, the Septuagint (Greek Old Testament) translates this, "in the end he will come to grief." Servants who are not corrected and disciplined will be a source of grief (v. 19).

29:22 stirs up strife. See 15:18 and note.

29:23 See 15:33; also 16:18, 19 and notes. The sin of pride does not allow the fool to benefit from another's wisdom.

29:24 This verse depicts the predicament of accomplices to a crime. They are obliged to be witnesses (Lev. 5:1), but if they do testify they incriminate themselves.

29:26 Wisdom recognizes the special function of rulers to maintain godly order, and thus to be agents of God's rule (21:1 note). It also recognizes the weakness of human rulers. Here the supplicant seeks special treatment that would involve injustice. The only sure way to justice is to seek it from the Lord.

30:1 Agur son of Jakeh. His identity is unknown, but many consider him to be a foreigner. See note 22:17–24:22; and Introduction: Author.

The oracle. It is possible that the Hebrew word is a place-name, "Massa" (also in 31:1), and that both Agur and Lemuel were Ishmaelites from Massa, thought to be in Arabia (Gen. 25:14).

30:2, 3 This statement is not mere modesty or humility, but a recognition of the mystery of the being and ways of God such as is found in Job and Ecclesiastes. The writer is acutely conscious of the bounds of human knowledge and wisdom. God is not an object for our investigation or speculation, but the infinite and personal Creator in whom we must trust. There may be a note of irony in the profession of ignorance here, but v. 4 indicates the meaning.

3 I have not learned wisdom,
nor have I knowledge of [n]the Holy One.
4 Who has [o]ascended to heaven and come down?
Who has [p]gathered the wind in his fists?
Who has [q]wrapped up the waters in a garment?
Who has established all [r]the ends of the earth?
[s]What is his name, and what is his son's name?
Surely you know!

5 [t]Every word of God proves true;
he is [u]a shield to those who take refuge in him.
6 [v]Do not add to his words,
lest he rebuke you and you be found a liar.

7 Two things I ask of you;
deny them not to me [w]before I die:
8 Remove far from me falsehood and lying;
give me neither poverty nor riches;
feed me with the food that is [x]needful for me,
9 lest I be [y]full and [z]deny you
and say, [a]"Who is the LORD?"
or lest I be poor and steal
[b]and profane the name of my God.

10 [c]Do not slander a servant to his master,
[d]lest he curse you and you be held guilty.

11 There are those[1] who [e]curse their fathers
and do not bless their mothers.
12 There are those who are [f]clean in their own eyes
but are not washed of their filth.
13 There are those—how [g]lofty are their eyes,
how high their eyelids lift!
14 There are those whose teeth are [h]swords,
whose [i]fangs are knives,
to [j]devour the poor from off the earth,
the needy from among mankind.

15 The leech has two daughters;
"Give" and "Give," they cry.[2]
[k]Three things are never satisfied;
[k]four never say, "Enough":
16 [l]Sheol, [m]the barren womb,
the land never satisfied with water,
and the fire that never says, "Enough."

17 The eye that [n]mocks a father
and [o]scorns to obey a mother
will [p]be picked out by [q]the ravens of the valley
and eaten by the vultures.

18 [k]Three things are [r]too wonderful for me;
[k]four I do not understand:
19 the way of an eagle in the sky,
the way of a serpent on a rock,
the way of a ship on the high seas,
and the way of a man with a virgin.

3 [n]ch. 9:10
4 [o]John 3:13 [p][Isai. 40:12]; See Job 38:4-11; Ps. 104:3-6 [q]Job 26:8 [r]Ps. 22:27 [s][Rev. 19:12]
5 [t]Ps. 12:6; 18:30 [u]See Ps. 3:3
6 [v]Deut. 4:2; 12:32; [Rev. 22:18]
7 [w]Gen. 45:28
8 [x]Job 23:12; Matt. 6:11; Luke 11:3
9 [y]Deut. 8:12; 31:20; 32:15; Neh. 9:25; [ver. 22] [z]Josh. 24:27 [a]Ex. 5:2 [b][Job 21:14, 15]; See Ex. 20:7
10 [c][Ps. 15:3; 101:5] [d]Eccles. 7:21
11 [e]ch. 20:20; [ver. 17]; See Ex. 21:17
12 [f]ch. 16:2; [Luke 18:11; Rev. 3:17]
13 [g]See Ps. 101:5
14 [h]See Ps. 57:4 [i]Job 29:17 [j]See Ps. 14:4
15 [k]ver. 18, 21, 29; [ch. 6:16]
16 [l]See ch. 27:20 [m][Gen. 30:1]
17 [n][ver. 11; Gen. 9:22] [o][ch. 23:22] [p][Num. 16:14] [q][Jer. 16:4]
18 [k][See ver. 15 above] [r]See Job 42:3

1 Hebrew *There is a generation*; also verses 12, 13, 14 2 Or *"Give, give," they cry*

30:4 These questions express the conviction that knowledge based solely on observation of creation can never fully comprehend God. In Job 38, the same point is made in the course of God's answer to Job.

30:5, 6 With these words Agur gives an assessment of God's Word within the framework of Israel's law and prophetic writings. He quotes Ps. 18:30 and echoes Deut. 4:2. The full knowledge of God comes through special revelation and is received by faith (1:7 note).

30:5 proves true. That is, tried and found to be utterly reliable.

30:6 Do not add to his words. To add to God's words is to sit in judgment on them and to find them wanting by human standards. This shifts the basis of knowledge and truth from God to ourselves. This pride of the creature is a mainspring of sin (Gen. 2:9 note).

30:7–9 This prayer reflects a desire to learn from the kind of wisdom that is in Proverbs.

30:8 the food that is needful for me. The request is for a sufficiency that avoids both extremes of poverty and unnecessary riches.

30:9 Who is the LORD. People who have an excess of material possessions soon forget their dependence on the Lord (Deut. 8:10–18; Luke 12:16–21).

30:10 This saying is only superficially connected with what precedes or follows. The point is that interference in another's domestic affairs may backfire.

30:12 clean in their own eyes. See 16:2; 21:2.

30:15–31 On the form of these numerical sayings, see notes 6:16–19.

30:15 The leech . . . "Give" and "Give." The two ends of the leech look the same, and the animal seems to have no function except to devour. The following numerical sayings share the theme of greed.

30:17 The eye that mocks. The contemptuous look can be as poisonous as words. Dishonor toward parents, evidence of breakdown in the most basic human relationship, deserves the ultimate curse.

picked . . . ravens. The words portray the fate of the corpse that lies unburied, with special attention to the offending eye.

30:18, 19 The four ways cannot be understood, either because they leave no traces or because they are so easily, yet mysteriously, mastered. Some suggest that the emphasis is on the fourth way, human sexual relations, of which the other three may be metaphors.

20 This is the way of an adulteress:
she eats and wipes her mouth
and says, "I have done no wrong."
21 Under [k]three things [s]the earth trembles;
under [k]four it cannot bear up:
22 [t]a slave when he becomes king,
and a fool when he is [u]filled with food;
23 [v]an unloved woman when she [w]gets a husband,
and a maidservant when she displaces her mistress.
24 [k]Four things on earth are small,
but they are exceedingly wise:
25 [x]the ants are a people not strong,
yet they provide their food in the summer;
26 [y]the rock badgers are a people not mighty,
yet they make their homes in the cliffs;
27 the locusts have no [z]king,
yet all of them march in [a]rank;
28 the lizard you can take in your hands,
yet it is in kings' palaces.
29 [b]Three things are stately in their tread;
[b]four are stately in their stride:
30 the lion, which is mightiest among beasts
and [c]does not turn back before any;
31 the [d]strutting rooster,[1] the he-goat,
and a king whose army is with him.[2]
32 If you have been foolish, exalting yourself,
or if you have been devising evil,
[e]put your hand on your mouth.
33 For pressing milk produces curds,
pressing the nose produces blood,
and pressing anger produces strife.

The Words of King Lemuel

31 The words of King Lemuel. An oracle that his mother taught him:

2 What are you doing, my son?[3] What are you doing, [f]son of my womb?
What are you doing, [g]son of my vows?
3 Do [h]not give your strength to women,
your ways to those [i]who destroy kings.
4 [j]It is not for kings, O Lemuel,
it is not for kings [k]to drink wine,
or for rulers to take [l]strong drink,
5 lest they drink and forget what has been decreed
and [m]pervert the rights of all the afflicted.
6 Give strong drink to the one who [n]is perishing,
and wine to [o]those in bitter distress;[4]
7 [p]let them drink and forget their poverty
and remember their misery no more.

1 Or *the magpie*, or *the greyhound*; Hebrew *girt-of-loins* 2 Or *against whom there is no rising up* 3 Hebrew *What, my son?* 4 Hebrew *those bitter in soul*

21 [k][See ver. 15 above] [s]Joel 2:10; Amos 8:8
22 [t]ch. 19:10 [u][ver. 9]
23 [v]Deut. 21:15 [w][Isai. 54:1; 62:4]
24 [k][See ver. 15 above]
25 [x]ch. 6:6-8
26 [y]Lev. 11:5; Ps. 104:18
27 [z][ch. 6:7] [a][Joel 2:7, 8, 25]
29 [b]ver. 18, 21, 29; [ch. 6:16]
30 [c][Job 39:22]
31 [d][Job 40:16]
32 [e]Mic. 7:16; See Job 21:5
Chapter 31
2 [f]Isai. 49:15 [g][1 Sam. 1:27]
3 [h][ch. 5:9] [i][ch. 7:26; Deut. 17:17; 1 Kin. 11:1; Neh. 13:26]
4 [j]Eccles. 10:17; [1 Kin. 16:9; 20:16] [k][Hos. 4:11] [l]ch. 20:1
5 [m][Isai. 5:22, 23]
6 [n]Job 29:13 [o]Job 3:20
7 [p][Ps. 104:15]

30:20 eats and wipes her mouth. The expression is a metaphor for sexual intercourse (7:18; 9:17)—her adultery has become as natural to her as eating. This verse is not part of the previous saying.

30:21 the earth trembles. The four items in vv. 22, 23 hardly seem able to produce such dire consequences in the natural order. This is likely a figure of speech for an intolerable state of affairs.

30:24–28 If this saying went no farther than natural history, it would still fulfill a purpose of wisdom: the perception of order and of how things work together. Many proverbs show an interest in nature as a parable on human life (e.g., 6:6–11). The fact that wisdom is ascribed to these creatures implies some unity with human existence. The creatures are wise because they are able to surmount some serious inherent weakness, and so to survive well. These gifts of wisdom, to each according to its kind, are given by the Creator of all.

30:29–31 The inclusion of a king with the animals suggests a human parallel with nature and the underlying coherence of all creation. The observation of rule and order in both animal and human society indicates that both are products of the same Creator's genius.

30:32 put your hand on your mouth. That is, stop talking; cease your scheming and provocation.

30:33 pressing . . . pressing . . . pressing. The repetition emphasizes the parallel in each situation. In this proverb we have a warning that provocation leads to strife.

31:1 The words of King Lemuel. See note 30:1. Lemuel was not an Israelite king. The nature of this section (vv. 1–9) suggests an Egyptian or perhaps a Babylonian origin. Its intention is apparently vocational, the equipping of the ruler for his task. The form is similar to the instructions of chs. 1–9 (Introduction: Characteristics and Themes). In this case, the teaching is given by the mother (1:8; 4:1, 3). While the father may have been the principal teacher of the children, godly women also took that role (cf. 14:1 note), and there were in Israel noteworthy wise women (2 Sam. 14:2; 20:16).

31:2 son of my vows. The expression may refer to a vow made in anticipation of the birth (cf. 1 Sam. 1:11).

31:3 those who destroy kings. The parallel indicates that fornication is perhaps in view.

31:4 not for kings to drink wine. The king's responsibilities give him no leisure to be confused by wine.

31:6 Give strong drink . . . wine. While the king must avoid using strong drink as a means of escape from the concerns of high office, it may be given to those whose suffering is too much to bear.

8 [q] Open your mouth for the mute,
for the rights of all who are destitute.[1]
9 Open your mouth, [r] judge righteously,
[s] defend the rights of [t] the poor and needy.

The Woman Who Fears the LORD

10[2] [u] An excellent wife who can find?
She is far more precious than [v] jewels.
11 The heart of her husband trusts in her,
and he will have no lack of gain.
12 She does him good, and not harm,
all the days of her life.
13 She [w] seeks wool and flax,
and works with willing hands.
14 She is like the ships of the merchant;
she brings her food from afar.
15 She [x] rises while it is yet night
and [y] provides food for her household
and portions for her maidens.
16 She considers a field and buys it;
with the fruit of her hands she plants a vineyard.
17 She [z] dresses herself[3] with strength
and makes her arms strong.
18 She perceives that her merchandise is profitable.
Her lamp does not go out at night.
19 She puts her hands to the distaff,
and her hands hold the spindle.
20 She [a] opens her hand to [b] the poor
and reaches out her hands to [b] the needy.
21 She is not afraid of snow for her household,
for all her household are clothed in [c] scarlet.[4]
22 She makes [d] bed coverings for herself;
her clothing is [e] fine linen and [f] purple.
23 Her husband is known in [g] the gates
when he sits among the elders of the land.
24 She makes [h] linen garments and sells them;
she delivers sashes to the merchant.
25 [i] Strength and dignity are her clothing,
and she laughs at the time to come.
26 She opens her mouth with wisdom,
and the teaching of kindness is on her tongue.
27 She looks well to the ways of her household
and does not eat the bread of idleness.
28 Her children rise up and call her blessed;
her husband also, and he praises her:
29 "Many [j] women have done [k] excellently,
but you surpass them all."
30 [l] Charm is deceitful, and beauty is vain,
but a woman who fears the LORD is to be praised.
31 Give her of the fruit of her hands,
and let her works praise her in the gates.

8 [q] Job 29:12, 15, 16; [Isai. 1:17]
9 [r] Lev. 19:15; Deut. 1:16 [s] Jer. 22:16; [Isai. 1:17] [t] ver. 20; Ps. 40:17; 86:1
10 [u] ch. 12:4; Ruth 3:11; [ch. 18:22; 19:14] [v] Job 28:18
13 [w] [ver. 21, 22, 24]
15 [x] [ch. 20:13] [y] Luke 12:42; [Ps. 111:5]
17 [z] [ver. 25]
20 [a] [Rom. 12:13; Eph. 4:28] [b] [ver. 9]
21 [c] 2 Sam. 1:24
22 [d] ch. 7:16 [e] Gen. 41:42; Rev. 19:8, 14 [f] Judg. 8:26
23 [g] See Ruth 4:1, 2
24 [h] Judg. 14:12; Isai. 3:23
25 [i] [ver. 17]
29 [j] S. of S. 6:9 [k] [ver. 10]
30 [l] [ch. 11:16]

1 Hebrew *are sons of passing away* 2 Verses 10-31 are an acrostic poem, each verse beginning with the successive letters of the Hebrew alphabet 3 Hebrew *She girds her loins* 4 Or *in double thickness*

31:8, 9 The king's task is to uphold righteousness in society. In Israel, this task was viewed in the context of the covenant with the Lord (Deut. 17:14–20).

31:10–31 This section is an acrostic poem extolling the virtues of a wife who exemplifies the principles of wisdom, both practically and spiritually. The sequence of virtues is governed more by the demands of the acrostic (the first word in each verse beginning with successive letters of the alphabet) than by logic. Yet the overall effect is of a coherent description of a woman beautified by her virtues of practical wisdom and charity. That the household described is well-to-do does not detract from the universal applicability of the principles of wifely wisdom.

31:10 who can find. Such a wife is not an impossible dream, but may be hard to find.

31:11 no lack of gain. This state of affairs results from the wife's astuteness in household affairs.

31:12 See 18:22 and notes.

31:14 like the ships of the merchant. As vv. 16, 18 indicate, she engages in commerce.

31:15 portions. Either food or duties.

31:16 She is able in business and reinvests her earnings.

31:18 Her lamp does not go out. This is either a metaphor for prosperity (13:9), or a reference to her diligence in using the hours of dark for work.

31:19 distaff. The meaning is uncertain. The context indicates ability to make her own thread.

31:21 scarlet. If "scarlet" is the correct reading, it probably indicates high quality cloth that is very warm.

31:22 fine linen and purple. As in v. 21, high quality articles are in view.

31:23 The implication is that the wife's skill and diligence in home affairs remove all concerns about them from her husband. He is free to pursue his place as a respected elder in public life.

in the gates. See 1:21 and note.

31:25 Strength and dignity are her clothing. The words refer either to her character, or, as is more likely in view of the second line, to the esteem earned by her economic prowess. She has no worry about the future. Both interpretations are consistent with wisdom.

31:28, 29 The result of her skill and wisdom is the cementing of family relationships. The praise of husband and children is her great reward.

31:30, 31 who fears the LORD. Up to this point the poem concentrates on practical wisdom. Now the basis of all true wisdom is emphasized. The Book of Proverbs ends as it begins: observation of the created order can provide some wisdom and knowledge of God (Rom. 1:20–23), but only the self-revelation of the Creator enables us to know and appreciate the God-centered meaning of reality. True wisdom is seen as the life lived in wholehearted obedience to God's revelation in His Word, which is "the fear of the LORD" (1:7 and note). This trust is the foundation and continuing path of wisdom as it brings us to final perfection in Christ.

THE BOOK OF

Ecclesiastes

AUTHOR

To many interpreters of Ecclesiastes, the lineage (1:1), kingship in Jerusalem (1:12), unsurpassed wisdom (1:16), and unrivaled wealth (2:4–9) of the author indicate that Solomon (1 Kin. 3; 4:21–34; 10), calling himself "the Preacher" (1:12), is the author of Ecclesiastes. There is a concluding tribute to the book (12:9–14), praising Solomon's wisdom and summarizing with the central admonition to "Fear God and keep his commandments" (12:13).

Some interpreters, however, believe that the type of Hebrew language used in the book, as well as the negative view of rulers suggested in it (4:13; 7:19; 8:2–4; 10:4–7), indicate that the work was written after Solomon's time and presented as a legitimate voice of the wisdom tradition that has Solomon as its most famous exponent, therefore going by his name.

It is notable that Ecclesiastes is not a summary of other wisdom teaching, but a particular statement of wisdom teaching that deepens it while adding to its broad appeal.

DATE AND OCCASION

Those who see the book as coming from a writer later than Solomon generally date Ecclesiastes after the Jewish exile in Babylon, which occurred in the sixth century B.C. If it is assumed that Solomon was the author, the book is to be dated from the tenth century B.C.

Ecclesiastes has been understood as an apologetic work, that is, an attempt to recommend faith in God by way of answering negative arguments. As such an attempt, the book often seems to express a secular point of view, arguing that life is meaningless. In the face of such arguments the writer comes to the conclusion that faith in God is the only avenue to satisfaction in life. While the book's teaching may be used in evangelism, most Jewish and Christian interpreters have understood Ecclesiastes to be addressed to God's people, rather than to those who are ignorant of God or in rebellion against Him. The book is God's wise counsel to those who know His ways but have found them perplexing and troubling.

CHARACTERISTICS AND THEMES

Ecclesiastes searches for an answer to the question, What is the advantage of humanity's work and wisdom? Work and wisdom comprise two main themes of the book. The word "profit" and its related words such as "advantage" (6:8) occur eighteen times. Another important word, "vanity," which conveys the notion of uselessness, occurs 38 times. This key term is used in the motto that frames the book (1:2; 12:8), which in each case is accompanied by a poem related to the motto (1:3–11; 1:7–12:7). Apart from these obvious literary structures, no consensus has been reached about the book's structure. Its cross-currents of optimism and pessimism make the overall intention of the book difficult to discern. Nevertheless, the blocks of material that comprise the book mostly relate to these two themes. A helpful outline arranges these blocks into three cycles (1:3–3:8; 3:9–6:7; 6:8–12:7), each, though formulated differently, beginning with the crucial question "what does man gain?" The question is raised also at the end of both 5:16 and 6:11.

The first cycle contains three pairs of sections about work and wisdom (1:12–15 and 1:16–18; 2:1–11 and 2:12–17; 2:18–26 and 3:1–8) presenting the conclusion that although the employment of human labor and understanding provides satisfaction of accomplishment, the profit achieved by a person is canceled by death.

The second cycle (3:9–6:7) treats the theme of humanity's labor, contrasting it with God's perfect enduring works and counseling enjoyment of the simple blessings God provides in this life, even in the face of human oppression. The third cycle (6:8–12:7) elaborates the theme of human wisdom, contrasting it with the inscrutability of God's ways.

Solomon's conclusion that death makes vain all human labor and wisdom on earth ("under the sun"; 1:14, 17: 2:11, 17) does not mean that people should abandon society and culture to lead an ascetic life. Neither does the Christian priority of proclaiming the gospel for the conversion of sinners (a "labor . . . not in vain," 1 Cor. 15:58) mean Christians should abdicate their cultural responsibilities. On the contrary, Solomon commands (9:7–10) God's people to enjoy life, despite its futility, harsh realities, and uncertainties, and to work with full vigor. This practical approach to life is neither a version of Greek stoicism nor a product of human effort: it is a gift of God (3:13; 5:19) for those who fear Him and keep His commands (5:1–7; 12:13, 14). Ecclesiastes teaches both the human responsibility to obey God joyfully, and God's sovereign provision of the ability to obey.

Ecclesiastes grapples with the question of how people should live (6:12) in a world where the good Creator (3:11, 14) and just Judge (3:17) sovereignly ordains that "bad" things happen to the righteous (7:13, 14) as well as to the wicked, and not according to what they deserve (8:14; 9:1). The gift of contentment is to be exercised not only in the face of human oppression (3:22–4:3) but under the futility and death (9:7–10) that God imposed upon the human race because of sin.

Relating the book to Christ and the New Testament, we would make the following points. If the divine verdict of righteous or unrighteous is not rendered in this life, it will be given after death, at the Judgment (3:17; 12:14). Ecclesiastes teaches existence after death (9:10; 12:7), but the resurrection of the body is not mentioned; the resurrection of Christ, which guarantees the resurrection of believers to eternal life (1 Cor. 15), was still in the future.

The sphere of creation discussed in Ecclesiastes is indicated by the synonymous phrases "under the sun," "under heaven," and "on earth." Solomon's determination that everything is futile is not applied to transcendent heavenly reality; there is no contradiction between Solomon and Paul. Whatever earthly treasures are gathered by Adam's descendants will be taken away, but heavenly labors performed through the Second Adam who conquered death are never in vain (1 Cor. 15:58).

In summary, Ecclesiastes teaches how God's elect (1 Pet. 1:1), pilgrims in this world "under the sun," but also citizens of heaven (Phil. 3:20), should live amid the profound frustrations and tensions of the present evil age (Rom. 8:18–23).

TITLE

"Ecclesiastes" is a translation of the Hebrew word *qoheleth*, meaning "assembler of the covenant community" and conventionally translated "preacher." The term "Ecclesiastes" was used by the Septuagint (Greek) translation of the Bible and by the Vulgate (Latin) translation.

OUTLINE OF ECCLESIASTES

I. Introduction (1:1)

II. Motto (1:2)

III. Limitations of Work and Wisdom (1:3–3:8)
- A. *Cycles in Creation (1:3–11)*
- B. *Futility of Work and Wisdom (1:12–18)*
- C. *Ephemeral Rewards of Work and Wisdom (2:1–17)*
- D. *Enigmas of Work and Wisdom (2:18–3:8)*

IV. Work in Fear Before God Whose Work Endures (3:9–6:7)
- A. *God as Creator and Judge (3:9–21)*
- B. *Contentment or Envy (3:22–4:16)*
- C. *Sincere Commitment to God (5:1–7)*
- D. *Dissatisfaction in Work (5:8–6:7)*

V. Wisdom in Humility Before a Judging God Whose Wisdom Is Unfathomable (6:8–12:7)
- A. *The Futility of Contending with God (6:8–12)*
- B. *What Is Good for Man (7:1–18)*
- C. *Wisdom's Power (7:19–8:8)*
- D. *Unfulfilled Judgment (8:9–9:10)*
- E. *Folly's Power (9:11–10:7)*
- F. *Advice for Wise Living (10:8–12:7)*

VI. Motto (12:8)

VII. Conclusion (12:9–14)

All Is Vanity

1 The words of [a]the Preacher,[1] the son of
David, [b]king in Jerusalem.

2 [c]Vanity[2] of vanities, says [a]the Preacher,
[c]vanity of vanities! [d]All is vanity.
3 [e]What [f]does man gain by all the toil
at which he toils under the sun?
4 A generation goes, and a generation
comes,
but [g]the earth remains forever.
5 [h]The sun rises, and the sun goes down,
and hastens[3] to the place where it
rises.
6 [i]The wind blows to the south
and goes around to the north;
around and around goes the wind,
and on its circuits the wind returns.
7 All [j]streams run to the sea,
but the sea is not full;
to the place where the streams flow,
there they flow again.
8 All things are full of weariness;
a man cannot utter it;
[k]the eye is not satisfied with seeing,
nor the ear filled with hearing.
9 [l]What has been is what will be,
and what has been done is what
will be done,
and there is nothing new under
the sun.

Chapter 1
1 [a]ver. 12; ch. 7:27; 12:8-10 [b]ver. 12
2 [c]ch. 12:8 [a][See ver. 1 above] [d][Rom. 8:20]
3 [e]ver. 14; Ps. 144:4; See Job 7:16; Ps. 39:5 [f]ch. 2:11, 22; 3:9; 5:16
4 [g]Ps. 104:5; 119:90
5 [h][Ps. 19:4-6]
6 [i][ch. 11:5; John 3:8]
7 [j]Ps. 104:8, 9
8 [k]ch. 4:8; Prov. 27:20
9 [l]ch. 3:15; 6:10; [ch. 2:12]
10 [m]ch. 3:15
11 [n]ch. 2:16; See ch. 9:5
12 [o]ver. 1
13 [p]ver. 17; [1 Kin. 4:33] [q]ch. 2:23, 26; 3:10; [Gen. 3:19]
14 [r]ver. 2; ch. 2:11, 17, 26; 4:4; 6:9
15 [s]See ch. 7:13
16 [t]ch. 2:9; [1 Kin. 3:12, 13; 4:30; 10:7, 23]

10 Is there a thing of which it is said,
"See, this is new"?
It has been [m]already
in the ages before us.
11 There is no [n]remembrance of former
things,[4]
nor will there be any remembrance
of later things[5] yet to be
among those who come after.

The Vanity of Wisdom

12 I [o]the Preacher have been king over
Israel in Jerusalem. 13 And I [p]applied my
heart[6] to seek and to search out by wisdom
all that is done under heaven. It is an
unhappy [q]business that God has given to
the children of man to be busy with. 14 I
have seen everything that is done under the
sun, and behold, all is [r]vanity and a striving after wind.[7]
15 [s]What is crooked cannot be made
straight,
and what is lacking cannot be
counted.

16 I said in my heart, "I have acquired
great [t]wisdom, surpassing all who were

[1] Or *Convener*, or *Collector*; Hebrew *Qoheleth* (so throughout Ecclesiastes) [2] Hebrew *vapor* (so throughout Ecclesiastes) [3] Or *and returns panting* [4] Or *former people* [5] Or *later people* [6] The Hebrew term denotes the center of one's inner life, including mind, will, and emotions [7] Or *a feeding on wind*; compare Hosea 12:1 (so throughout Ecclesiastes)

1:1 Preacher. The Hebrew emphasizes Solomon's function as convener of the covenant community to witness and to celebrate the glory of the King of heaven that fills His earthly temple (1 Kin. 8). Solomon's words are directed to God's people, not to agnostics.

son of David. See Introduction: Author.

1:2 Vanity. The Hebrew word means "breath" or "vapor," and hence what is "insubstantial," "useless," or "futile." Human death makes the deeds and desires of people who build earthly culture ("under the sun") useless.

All. This word is qualified by the phrase "under the sun" (v. 3) and means everything people experience with their senses (v. 8).

1:3–11 The phrase, "What does man gain," provides the theme of this opening poem, focusing the reader's attention on the apparent futility of work and study. Although these offer some satisfaction in accomplishment, death seems to make them meaningless.

1:3–8 Because of death, people must continuously begin cultural labors again. They are never completely satisfied with the results and are driven to repeat previous efforts.

1:3 gain. The idea that life's labor is unprofitable, presented here as a rhetorical question, is stated directly in 2:11.

under the sun. This phrase is synonymous with "under heaven" and "on earth." Paul's equivalent is "the present evil age" (Gal. 1:4). The energies poured into earthly kingdoms are often of no value to the kingdom of heaven (Mark 8:36). By contrast, the work of the Lord is not in vain (John 6:27–29; 1 Cor. 15:58).

1:4 goes . . . comes. People are constantly starting over (like the sun in v. 5), while by contrast the earth (to which every person returns) abides.

1:6 around and around. This phrase is the focal point of the poem in 1:4–8, an image for Solomon's recurrent refrain "striving after wind."

1:7 is not full. People's experiences commonly never fill or satisfy them, just as waters never fill the sea.

1:9–11 Cultural endeavors cannot reverse the futile process of repeating what has already been done, for all die and their works are forgotten.

1:12–15 Solomon's personal investigation concludes that human culture is misdirected and incomplete.

1:12 king . . . in Jerusalem. See Introduction: Author.

1:13 by wisdom. The endeavors of this world performed under the curse of God (Gen. 3:16–19) are futile and frustrating.

unhappy business. Human existence includes divinely imposed burdens (Gen. 3:16–19; Rom. 8:22, 23). Jesus makes them bearable (Matt. 11:28–30).

God. God's personal covenant name "Yahweh" (conventionally translated LORD, with small capitals) is not used in this book.

1:13, 14 under heaven . . . under the sun. See 1:3 note.

1:14 I have seen everything. Solomon had an accurate perspective on the present, because of God's gift (1 Kin. 3), as well as on the past, because he meditated on God's revealed Word.

1:15 crooked . . . lacking. This is the result not only of human evil, but also of the divine curse (7:13; Gen. 3:16–19).

1:16 wisdom. An increase in true wisdom heightens one's sensitivity to the unhappy effects of sin, not all of which are immediately visible.

all who were over Jerusalem. From Solomon's perspective these would refer to ancient pre-Israelite kings (Gen. 14:18; Josh. 10:1).

over Jerusalem before me, and my heart
has had great experience of wisdom and
knowledge." 17 And I [u]applied my heart to
know wisdom and to know [v]madness and
folly. I perceived that this also is but [r]a
striving after wind.

18 For [w]in much wisdom is much
vexation,
and he who increases knowledge
increases sorrow.

The Vanity of Self-Indulgence

2 I [x]said in my heart, "Come now, I will
test you with pleasure; enjoy yourself."
But behold, this also was vanity. 2 I [y]said of
laughter, "It is mad," and of pleasure,
"What use is it?" 3 I [z]searched with my
heart how to cheer my body with wine—
my heart still guiding me with wisdom—
and how to lay hold on [a]folly, till I might
see what was good for the children of man
to do under heaven during the few days of
their life. 4 I made great works. I [b]built
houses and planted [c]vineyards for myself.
5 I made myself [d]gardens and parks, and
planted in them all kinds of fruit trees. 6 I
made myself pools from which to water the
forest of growing trees. 7 I bought male and
female slaves, and had [e]slaves who were
born in my house. I had also great possessions of [f]herds and flocks, more than any
who had been before me in Jerusalem. 8 I
also gathered for myself silver and [g]gold
and the treasure of [h]kings and [i]provinces. I
got [j]singers, both men and women, and
many [k]concubines,[1] the delight of the children of man.

9 So I became great and [l]surpassed all
who were before me in Jerusalem. Also my
[l]wisdom remained with me. 10 And whatever my eyes desired I did not keep from
them. I kept my heart from no pleasure, for
my heart [m]found pleasure in all my toil,
and this was my [n]reward for all my toil.
11 Then I considered all that my hands had
done and the toil I had expended in doing
it, and behold, all was [o]vanity and a striving after wind, and there was nothing [p]to
be gained under the sun.

The Vanity of Living Wisely

12 [q]So I turned to consider [r]wisdom and
madness and folly. For what can the man
do who comes after the king? Only [s]what
has already been done. 13 Then I saw that
there is more gain in wisdom than in folly,
as there is more gain in light than in darkness. 14 [t]The wise person has his eyes in his
head, but the fool walks in darkness. And
yet I perceived that the [u]same event happens to all of them. 15 Then I said in my
heart, [v]"What happens to the fool will happen to me also. Why then have I been so
very wise?" And I said in my heart that this
also is vanity. 16 For of the wise as of the fool
there is [w]no enduring remembrance, seeing
that in the days to come all will have been
long forgotten. [x]How the wise dies just like
the fool! 17 So I hated life, because what is
done under the sun was grievous to me, for
[o]all is vanity and a striving after wind.

The Vanity of Toil

18 I hated [y]all my toil in which I toil under
the sun, seeing that I must [z]leave it to the
man who will come after me, 19 and who
knows whether he will be wise or a fool?
Yet he will be master of all for which I
toiled and used my wisdom under the sun.
This also is vanity. 20 So I [a]turned about and
gave my heart up to despair [b]over all the
toil of my labors under the sun, 21 because
sometimes a person who has toiled with
wisdom and knowledge and skill must
leave everything to be enjoyed by someone

17 [u]ver. 13; [ch. 2:3, 12; 7:23, 25] [v]ch. 9:3 [r][See ver. 14 above]
18 [w][ch. 12:12]
Chapter 2
1 [x]Luke 12:19
2 [y][Prov. 14:13]
3 [z][ch. 1:17] [a]ch. 7:25
4 [b]See 1 Kin. 7:1-12 [c]S. of S. 8:11
5 [d]S. of S. 4:16; 5:16
7 [e]Gen. 14:14; 15:3 [f][1 Kin. 4:23]
8 [g]1 Kin. 9:28; 10:10, 14, 21 [h][1 Kin. 4:21; 10:15] [i]1 Kin. 20:14; Ezek. 19:8 [j]2 Sam. 19:35; 2 Chr. 35:25 [k]1 Kin. 11:3
9 [l]1 Chr. 29:25; See ch. 1:16
10 [m][Prov. 8:31] [n]ch. 3:22; 5:18; 9:9
11 [o]See ch. 1:14 [p]See ch. 1:3
12 [q]ch. 7:25 [r]See ch. 1:17 [s]ch. 1:9, 10
14 [t][Prov. 17:24] [u]ch. 3:19; 9:2, 3; Ps. 49:10
15 [v][ver. 16; ch. 6:8]
16 [w]ch. 1:11; See ch. 9:5 [x]See ver. 14
17 [o][see ver. 11 above]
18 [y]ch. 1:3 [z]Ps. 39:6; 49:10
20 [a]ch. 7:25 [b]ch. 1:3

[1] The meaning of the Hebrew word is uncertain

2:1–11 The joys of earthly accomplishments are unsatisfying, for Solomon in particular (1 Kin. 4–11).

2:1 pleasure. A reference to self-indulgence.

2:3 my heart still guiding me. See v. 9. To determine what was good for people to do, Solomon investigated life without forgetting the protective guidance of God's word.

2:4–9 great . . . surpassed. The world's wealth flowed into Jerusalem for Solomon's disposition.

2:10, 11 found pleasure . . . reward . . . under the sun. Solomon experienced joy in doing work, but failed to achieve the satisfaction of producing anything of final heavenly value.

2:12–17 The earthly advantage of wisdom over folly is canceled by death.

2:12, 13 wisdom. Not secular wisdom or shrewdness, but unmatched, God-given wisdom.

2:15 wise. Wisdom's value appears to be compromised because it cannot keep the wise any more than the fool from the abyss of death.

2:17 hated. Concluding that the curse of death erases the profit of wise labor, Solomon comes to hate life in this present evil age.

2:18–26 Solomon reflects on the frustrations associated with work. Death takes labor's profit from its producer. The situation is made harder to bear by not knowing whether in the future the property will be dissipated by a fool (vv. 18, 19) or given to an heir who will not appreciate it (vv. 20, 21).

who did not toil for it. This also is vanity
and a great evil. 22 What has a man from [c]all
the toil and striving of heart with which he
toils beneath the sun? 23 For [d]all his days
are full of sorrow, and his [e]work is a vexation. Even in the night his heart does not
rest. This also is vanity.

24 [f]There is nothing better for a person
than that he should [g]eat and drink and find
enjoyment[1] in his toil. This also, I saw, is
[h]from the hand of God, 25 for apart from
him[2] who can eat or who can have enjoyment? 26 For to the one who pleases him
[i]God has given wisdom and knowledge
and joy, but to the sinner he has given [e]the
business of gathering and collecting, [j]only
to give to one who pleases God. [k]This also
is vanity and a striving after wind.

A Time for Everything

3 For everything there is a season, and [l]a
time for every matter under heaven:

2 a time to be born, and a time to
[m]die;
a time to plant, and a time to pluck
up what is planted;
3 a time to kill, and a time to heal;
a time to break down, and a time to
build up;
4 a time to [n]weep, and a time to laugh;
a time to mourn, and a time to
[o]dance;
5 a time to [p]cast away stones, and a
time to [q]gather stones
together;
a time to embrace, and a time to
[r]refrain from embracing;
6 a time to seek, and a time to [s]lose;
a time to keep, and a time to [t]cast
away;
7 a time to [u]tear, and a time to sew;
a time to [v]keep silence, and a time to
speak;
8 a time to love, and a time to [w]hate;
a time for war, and a time for peace.

The God-Given Task

9 What [x]gain has the worker from his toil?
10 I have seen [y]the business that [z]God has
given to the children of man to be busy
with. 11 He has [a]made everything beautiful
in its time. Also, he has put eternity into
man's heart, yet so that he cannot [b]find out
what God has done from the beginning to
the end. 12 I perceived that there is [c]nothing
better for them than to be joyful and to [d]do
good as long as they live; 13 also [e]that everyone should eat and drink and take pleasure
in all his toil—this is [f]God's gift to man.
14 I perceived that whatever God does
endures forever; [g]nothing can be added to
it, nor anything taken from it. God has
done it, so that people fear before him.
15 That which is, [h]already has been; that
which is to be, already has been; and God
[i]seeks what has been driven away.[3]

From Dust to Dust

16 Moreover, [j]I saw under the sun that in
the place of justice, even [k]there was
wickedness, and in the place of righteousness, even there was wickedness. 17 I said in
my heart, [l]God will judge the righteous and
the wicked, for there is [m]a time for every
matter and for every work. 18 I said in my
heart with regard to the children of man
that God is testing them that they may see
that they themselves are but [n]beasts. 19 [o]For
what happens to the children of man and

22 [c]See ch. 1:3
23 [d]Job 5:7; 14:1 [e]See ch. 1:13
24 [f]ch. 3:12, 13, 22; 5:18; 8:15; [1 Tim. 6:17] [g][ch. 9:7; Luke 12:19; 1 Cor. 15:32] [h][ch. 3:13; 5:19]
26 [i]Job 32:8 [e][See ver. 7 above] [j][Job 27:16, 17; Prov. 13:22] [k]See ch. 1:14
Chapter 3
1 [l]ver. 17; ch. 8:6
2 [m]Heb. 9:27
4 [n][Rom. 12:15] [o][2 Sam. 6:14]; See Ex. 15:20
5 [p][2 Kin. 3:25] [q][Isai. 5:2] [r][Joel 2:16]
6 [s][Matt. 10:39] [t][Prov. 11:24]
7 [u]See Gen. 37:29 [v]Amos 5:13
8 [w][Luke 14:26]
9 [x]See ch. 1:3
10 [y]See ch. 1:13 [z]See Gen. 3:17-19
11 [a][Gen. 1:31] [b]ch. 8:17; [Job 5:9; Rom. 11:33]
12 [c][ver. 22] [d]Ps. 34:14; 37:3
13 [e]See ch. 2:24 [f][ch. 2:24; 5:19]
14 [g][James 1:17]
15 [h][ch. 1:9] [i][ch. 12:14]
16 [j]ch. 4:1 [k]ch. 5:8; [ch. 4:1]
17 [l]Matt. 16:27; 2 Cor. 5:10; See Rom. 2:6-11; 2 Thess. 1:6-10 [m]ver. 1; ch. 8:6
18 [n]Ps. 49:12, 20; 73:22 19 [o]See ch. 2:14

1 Or *and make his soul see good* 2 Some Hebrew manuscripts, Septuagint, Syriac; most Hebrew manuscripts *apart from me* 3 Hebrew *what has been pursued*

2:23 does not rest. The ever-present, painful burdens of life undermine even the legitimate pleasures of work (v. 10) and can deprive the laborer of sleep.

2:24 better. In his conclusion about what is good (v. 3) Solomon observes that the common pleasures of life and work are also from God.

2:26 to the one who pleases him . . . sinner. However great the temporary prosperity of the wicked, it is the righteous "who please God" who are at last the beneficiaries of God's blessings.

vanity. The point seems to be the futility of the work of one person being transferred to another, as in vv. 20, 21.

3:1 time. The truly wise know that all their "times" are in God's hand (Ps. 31:15) and that there is an appropriate time for every human activity.

3:11 eternity. This is the Hebrew term translated "forever" in v. 14 and explained in v. 11 as "from the beginning to the end." The heart knows that history is not meaningless, but is frustrated in its efforts to discern the pattern of events.

3:12 nothing better. The author's major application is his repeated advice (2:24–26; 3:12, 22; 5:18–20; 8:15) and command (9:7–10) to be content with what God has ordained for one's life (1 Cor. 7:20; 1 Tim. 6:8).

3:14 fear. The term means to give God the honor corresponding to what He is (Ex. 34:8; Is. 6:5; Luke 5:8; Rev. 1:17).

3:15–21 God the Judge is in view.

3:17 the righteous and the wicked. As punishment for sin, people, like animals (vv. 18–20), must die (Gen. 3:19). Nevertheless the distinction between the righteous and the wicked is not removed by death, but will be revealed at God's judgment.

time. God ordains whatever occurs on earth (vv. 1–8). He has also appointed a day for judging the deeds of all (the "day of the LORD"; Joel 3).

what happens to the beasts is the same; as
one dies, so dies the other. They all have
the same breath, and man has no advantage over the beasts, for all is vanity. 20 All
go to one place. All are from [p]the dust, and
to dust all return. 21 Who knows whether
[q]the spirit of man goes upward and the
spirit of the beast goes down into the
earth? 22 So I saw that there is [r]nothing better than that a man should rejoice in his
work, for [s]that is his lot. Who can bring
him to see [t]what will be after him?

Evil Under the Sun

4 [u]Again I [v]saw all [w]the oppressions that
are done under the sun. And behold,
the tears of the oppressed, and they had
[x]no one to comfort them! On the side of
their oppressors there was power, and
there was no one to comfort them. 2 And I
[y]thought the dead who are already dead
more fortunate than the living who are still
alive. 3 But [z]better than both is he who has
not yet been and has not seen the evil
deeds that are done under the sun.

4 Then I saw that all toil and all skill in
work come from a man's envy of his neighbor. This also is [a]vanity and a striving after
wind.

5 The fool [b]folds his hands and [c]eats his
own flesh.

6 [u]Better is a handful of [d]quietness than
two hands full of toil and a striving after
wind.

7 [e]Again, I saw vanity under the sun:
8 one person who has no other, either son
or brother, yet there is no end to all his
toil, and his [f]eyes are never satisfied with
riches, so that he never asks, [g]"For whom
am I toiling and depriving myself of pleasure?" This also is vanity and an unhappy
[h]business.

9 Two are better than one, because they
have a good reward for their toil. 10 For if
they fall, one will lift up his fellow. But woe
to him who is alone when he falls and has
not another to lift him up! 11 Again, if two
lie together, they keep warm, [i]but how can
one keep warm alone? 12 And though a man
might prevail against one who is alone, two
will withstand him—a threefold cord is not
quickly broken.

13 Better was [j]a poor and wise youth than
an old and foolish king who no longer
knew how [k]to take advice. 14 For he went
[l]from prison to the throne, though in his
own kingdom he had been born poor. 15 I
saw all the living who move about under
the sun, along with that[1] youth who was to
stand in the king's[2] place. 16 There was no
end of all the people, all of whom he led.
Yet those who come later will not rejoice in
him. Surely this also is [m]vanity and a striving after wind.

Fear God

5 [3] [n]Guard your steps when you go to
[o]the house of God. To draw near to listen is better than to [p]offer the sacrifice of
fools, for they do not know that they are
doing evil. 2 [4]Be not rash with your mouth,
nor let your heart be hasty to utter a word
before God, for God is in heaven and you
are on earth. Therefore [q]let your words be
few. 3 For a dream comes with much business, and a fool's voice with [r]many words.

4 When [s]you vow a vow to God, [t]do not
delay paying it, for he has no pleasure in
fools. [u]Pay what you vow. 5 [v]It is better that
you should not vow than that you should
vow and not pay. 6 Let not your mouth lead
you[5] into sin, and do not say before [w]the

20 [p]ch. 12:7; Gen. 3:19
21 [q][ch. 12:7]
22 [r]See ch. 2:24 [s]See ch. 2:10 [t]ch. 2:19; 6:12; 8:7; 10:14
Chapter 4
1 [u]ch. 9:11 [v]ch. 3:16 [w]ch. 5:8; Job 35:9 [x]Lam. 1:2
2 [y]See Job 3:11-26
3 [z]ch. 6:3
4 [a]See ch. 1:14
5 [b]Prov. 6:10; 24:33 [c][Isai. 9:20]
6 [u][see ver. 1 above] [d]See Prov. 15:16
7 [e]ch. 6:5
8 [f]ch. 1:8; [Prov. 27:20; 1 John 2:16] [g]ch. 2:18; Ps. 39:6 [h]See ch. 1:13
11 [i]See 1 Kin. 1:1-4
13 [j][ch. 9:15, 16] [k][ch. 12:12]
14 [l]See Gen. 41:14, 41-43
16 [m]See ch. 1:14
Chapter 5
1 [n][Ex. 3:5; Isai. 1:12] [o][Gen. 28:17] [p]Prov. 15:8; See 1 Sam. 15:22
2 [q][Matt. 6:7]
3 [r]Prov. 10:19; [Job 11:2]
4 [s]Num. 30:2 [t]Deut. 23:21; Ps. 50:14; 76:11 [u][Ps. 66:13, 14]
5 [v][Prov. 20:25; Acts 5:1]
6 [w][1 Cor. 11:10]

1 Hebrew *the second* 2 Hebrew *his* 3 Ch 4:17 in Hebrew 4 Ch 5:1 in Hebrew 5 Hebrew *your flesh*

3:21 Who knows whether the spirit of man. Elsewhere Solomon observes that though the physical body returns to dust, the spirit returns to God (12:7).

4:1–3 the oppressions . . . more fortunate. Viewing the plight of the oppressed, Solomon speculates that the dead and unborn are better off.

4:4–16 Envy and lack of contentment fuel the futile drive for earthly satisfaction.

4:5, 6 quietness. Notwithstanding his previous dark thoughts, Solomon does conclude that sufficiency with contentment is better than need resulting from laziness (v. 5) or excess accompanied by restless toil (vv. 6, 8).

4:9–12 Two. Cooperation, rather than strife rooted in envy, produces success and provides protection from the covetous.

4:13–16 A characteristically discontented people does not appreciate good leaders, a thought that brings Solomon back to his theme of the apparent futility of life.

5:1–7 The summary of the book (12:13) enlarges on the exhortation to fear God (v. 7), the principle here emphasized by Solomon.

5:2 mouth. The thoughts of the heart are expressed in the words of the mouth. God will judge them (Matt. 12:34–37).

5:4, 5 vow. A particular promise made to God (Deut. 23:21–23). See "Honest Speech, Oaths, and Vows" at Neh. 5:12.

5:6 mouth. See note on v. 2.

messenger. This Hebrew word can also be translated "angel." It could refer to a priest serving in the temple (Mal. 2:7).

messenger[1] that it was [x]a mistake. Why
should God be angry at your voice and
destroy the work of your hands? 7 For when
dreams increase and words grow many, there
is vanity;[2] but [y]God is the one you must fear.

The Vanity of Wealth and Honor

8 [z]If you see in a province the oppression
of the poor and the violation of justice and
righteousness, [a]do not be amazed at the
matter, [b]for the high official is watched by
a higher, and there are yet higher ones over
them. 9 But this is gain for a land in every
way: a king committed to cultivated fields.[3]

10 He who loves money will not be satisfied with money, nor he who loves wealth
with his income; this also is vanity.
11 When goods increase, they increase who
eat them, and what advantage has their
owner but to see them with his eyes?
12 Sweet is the sleep of a laborer, whether
he eats little or much, but the full stomach
of the rich will not let him sleep.

13 [c]There is a grievous evil that I have seen
under the sun: riches were kept by their
owner to his hurt, 14 and those riches were
lost in a bad venture. And he is father of a
son, but he has nothing in his hand. 15 [d]As
he came from his mother's womb he shall
go again, naked as he came, and shall take
nothing for his toil that he may carry away
in his hand. 16 This also is a grievous evil:
just as he came, so shall he go, and what
[e]gain is there to him who [f]toils for the wind?
17 Moreover, all his days he [g]eats in darkness
in much vexation and sickness and anger.

18 Behold, what I have seen to be [h]good and
fitting is to eat and drink and find enjoyment[4]
in all the toil with which one toils under the
sun the few days of his life that God has given
him, for this is his [i]lot. 19 Everyone also to
whom [j]God has given [k]wealth and possessions [l]and power to enjoy them, and to
accept his lot and rejoice in his toil—this is
[m]the gift of God. 20 For he will not much
remember the days of his life because God
keeps him occupied with joy in his heart.

6 [n]There is an evil that I have seen under
the sun, and it lies heavy on mankind:
2 a man [o]to whom [p]God gives wealth, possessions, and honor, so that he [q]lacks nothing of all that he desires, yet God [r]does not
give him power to enjoy them, but a stranger
enjoys them. This is vanity; it is a grievous
evil. 3 If a man fathers a hundred children
and lives many years, so that [s]the days of his
years are many, but his soul is not satisfied
with life's [t]good things, and he also has no
[u]burial, I say that [v]a stillborn child is better
off than he. 4 For it comes in vanity and goes
in darkness, and in darkness its name is covered. 5 Moreover, it has not [w]seen the sun or
known anything, yet it finds [x]rest rather than
he. 6 Even though he should live a thousand
years twice over, yet enjoy[5] no good—do not
all go to the one place?

7 [y]All the toil of man is for his mouth, yet
his appetite is not satisfied.[6] 8 For what
advantage has the wise man [z]over the fool?
And what does the poor man have who
knows how to conduct himself before the
living? 9 Better [a]is the sight of the eyes than
the wandering of the appetite: this also is
[b]vanity and a striving after wind.

10 Whatever has come to be has [c]already
been named, and it is known what man is,
and that he is not able to [d]dispute with one

6 [x]ch. 10:5; Num. 15:25, 26
7 [y]ch. 12:13
8 [z]ch. 3:16; 4:1 [a][1 Pet. 4:12] [b][Ps. 12:5; 58:11; 82:1]
13 [c]ch. 6:1
15 [d]See Job 1:21
16 [e]See ch. 1:3 [f][Prov. 11:29]
17 [g][Ps. 127:2]
18 [h]See ch. 2:24
[i]See ch. 2:10
19 [j]ch. 6:2; [ch. 2:24] [k]2 Chr. 1:11 [l][ch. 6:2] [m]See ch. 3:13

Chapter 6
1 [n]ch. 5:13
2 [o]ch. 5:19 [p][1 Kin. 3:13] [q]Ps. 17:14; 73:7; See Job 21:7-13 [r][ch. 5:19; Luke 12:20]
3 [s]Gen. 47:8, 9 [t][ver. 6] [u]Isai. 14:20; Jer. 8:2; 22:19; [2 Kin. 9:35] [v]ch. 4:3; Job 3:16
5 [w]ch. 7:11; 11:7 [x]ch. 4:6
7 [y][Prov. 16:26]
8 [z][ch. 2:15]
9 [a]ch. 11:9 [b]See ch. 1:14
10 [c]ch. 1:10; 3:15 [d]Job 9:32; Isai. 45:9; [1 Cor. 10:22]

1 Or *angel* 2 Or *For when dreams and vanities increase, words also grow many* 3 The meaning of the Hebrew verse is uncertain 4 Or *and see good* 5 Or *see* 6 Hebrew *filled*

5:8–17 Greed is responsible for many of the detrimental aspects of wealth.

5:8 do not be amazed. Oppression and injustice are inevitable (4:1–3).

5:10–12 loves money. Greed is insatiable and robs one of sleep; contentment provides rest (1 Tim. 6:6–10).

5:13–17 Solomon ponders the tragedies of unused and lost wealth. Whatever is not lost "in a bad venture" must be left behind at death. Earthly labor appears to be in vain.

5:18–6:7 God sovereignly distributes wealth.

5:18 good. God intends that people should enjoy the benefits of their work as a due reward of their labor.

5:19 gift of God. The ability to enjoy earthly labor comes not from stoic human strength, but from God-given grace, granted to rich and poor (v. 12) alike.

6:2 God. Riches and poverty, as well as the ability or inability to enjoy one's resources, are decreed by God.

power to enjoy. This involves control over the management of wealth, not merely pleasure derived from spending it.

6:3 his soul is not satisfied with life's good things. To be discontented with God's abundant provision is a great tragedy.

6:6 one place. The case of those who live long in discontent is more pathetic than that of a stillborn child. The stillborn, at least, does not spend long years in the self-inflicted misery of ingratitude.

6:7 appetite is not satisfied. Again, earthly labor by itself does not fill the emptiness of the soul (1:8).

6:8 what does the poor man have. Those, though poor, who know how to live effectively in the world avoid the discontentment of wandering, unsatisfied desires.

6:10 named . . . known. God identifies every person as a sinner (7:20).

dispute. No one, apart from Christ, has a defense against God.

stronger than he. 11 The more words, the
more vanity, and what is the advantage to
man? 12 For who knows what is good for
man while he lives the few days of his [e]vain
life, which he passes like [f]a shadow? For
who can tell man what will be [g]after him
under the sun?

The Contrast of Wisdom and Folly

7 [h]A good name is better than precious ointment,
and [i]the day of death than the day of birth.
2 It is better to go to the house of mourning
than to go to the house of feasting,
for this is the end of all mankind,
and the living will [j]lay it to heart.
3 Sorrow is better than laughter,
[k]for by sadness of face the heart is made glad.
4 The heart of the wise is in the house of mourning,
but the heart of fools is in the house of mirth.
5 It is [l]better for a man to hear the rebuke of the wise
than to hear the song of fools.
6 [m]For as the crackling of [n]thorns under a pot,
so is the laughter of the fools;
this also is vanity.
7 Surely [o]oppression drives the wise into madness,
and [p]a bribe corrupts the heart.
8 Better is the end of a thing than its beginning,
and [q]the patient in spirit is better than the proud in spirit.

12 [e][ch. 7:15; 9:9] [f]ch. 8:13; See Job 14:2 [g][ch. 2:18; 3:22]
Chapter 7
1 [h]Prov. 22:1; [S. of S. 1:3] [i]ch. 4:2
2 [j][Ps. 90:12]
3 [k][2 Cor. 7:10]
5 [l]Prov. 13:18; 15:31, 32; [Ps. 141:5]
6 [m][Joel 2:5] [n][Ps. 58:9; 118:12]
7 [o][ch. 4:1] [p]Deut. 16:19; See Prov. 17:8
8 [q]See Prov. 14:29
9 [r][Prov. 14:17; 16:32; James 1:19] [s][Eph. 4:26]
11 [t]ch. 6:5; 11:7
12 [u][ch. 10:19] [v]Prov. 3:18
13 [w][ch. 3:11] [x][ch. 1:15; Job 12:14; Isai. 14:27]
14 [y][ch. 3:4, 22; Deut. 28:47] [z][ch. 3:18; 6:12]
15 [a]ch. 6:12; 9:9 [b]See ch. 8:14 [c]ch. 8:12, 13
16 [d][Rom. 12:3]
17 [e][Prov. 10:27]; See Job 22:16
18 [f][ver. 17] [g][ver. 16] [h]ch. 11:6
19 [i]ch. 9:16, 18 Prov. 21:22; 24:5
20 [j]See 1 Kin. 8:46

9 [r]Be not quick in your spirit to become angry,
[s]for anger lodges in the bosom of fools.
10 Say not, "Why were the former days better than these?"
For it is not from wisdom that you ask this.
11 Wisdom is good with an inheritance,
an advantage to those who [t]see the sun.
12 For the protection of wisdom is like
[u]the protection of money,
and the advantage of knowledge is
that [v]wisdom preserves the life of him who has it.
13 Consider [w]the work of God:
[x]who can make straight what he has made crooked?

14 [y]In the day of prosperity be joyful, and
in the day of adversity consider: God has
made the one as well as the other, [z]so that
man may not find out anything that will be
after him.
15 In my [a]vain life I have seen everything.
There is [b]a righteous man who perishes in
his righteousness, and there is a wicked
man who [c]prolongs his life in his evildoing.
16 Be not overly righteous, and do not [d]make
yourself too wise. Why should you destroy
yourself? 17 Be not overly wicked, neither be
a fool. [e]Why should you die before your
time? 18 It is good that you should take hold
of [f]this, and from [g]that [h]withhold not your
hand, for the one who fears God shall come
out from both of them.
19 [i]Wisdom gives strength to the wise
man more than ten rulers who are in a city.
20 Surely [j]there is not a righteous man on
earth who does good and never sins.

7:1 day of death. For the godly, death is "far better" (Phil. 1:23) because they are with Christ.

7:2, 4 house of mourning. A funeral provides an indispensable perspective on the universally terminal condition.

7:7 oppression . . . a bribe. These common experiences may threaten to destabilize an otherwise good spiritual condition (4:1–3).

7:9 anger lodges. If unquenched, the anger ignited by life's frustrations leads to folly.

7:11, 12 Wisdom . . . preserves the life. True wisdom gives benefits in this life (contrast 8:8) and that to come. Christ is the redemptive wisdom of God (1 Cor. 1:30), making wisdom accessible to sinners.

7:13–18 Both human illusions of perfection in this life and the abandonment of oneself to wickedness have God for an adversary.

7:13 who can make straight. God's decrees cannot be reversed. The curse of Gen. 3 will not be annulled until the consummation.

7:14 prosperity . . . adversity. God decrees the one as the other.

man may not find out anything. The future is unknown.

7:15 righteous . . . wicked. The question implied by this observation is formulated in Jer. 12:1 ("Why does the way of the wicked prosper?") and handled at more length in Ps. 37 and 73.

7:16, 17 Be not overly righteous . . . overly wicked. Pride can masquerade as righteousness, even in small things; on the other hand, there is an impulse to lawlessness that goes beyond everyday standards of life.

7:18 this . . . from that. Right knowledge of God delivers those who possess it from destructive excesses of self-righteousness and wickedness.

7:19 gives strength to the wise. Wisdom is powerful and encouraging.

7:20 not a righteous man. All are guilty before God (Ps. 14:3; 53:3).

21 Do not take to heart all the things that
people say, lest you hear [k]your servant cursing you. 22 Your heart knows that [l]many
times you have yourself cursed others.
23 All this I have tested by wisdom. [m]I
said, "I will be wise," but it was far from
me. 24 That which has been is far off, and
[n]deep, very deep; [o]who can find it out?
25 [p]I turned my heart to know and to
search out and to seek wisdom and the
scheme of things, and to know the wickedness of folly and the foolishness that is
madness. 26 And I find something more
[q]bitter than death: [r]the woman whose
heart is [s]snares and nets, and whose hands
are fetters. He who pleases God escapes
her, but [t]the sinner is taken by her.
27 Behold, this is what I found, says [u]the
Preacher, while adding one thing to another to find the scheme of things— 28 which
my soul has sought repeatedly, but I have
not found. [v]One man among a thousand I
found, but [w]a woman among all these I
have not found. 29 See, this alone I found,
that [x]God made man upright, but [y]they
have sought out many schemes.

Keep the King's Command

8 Who is like the wise?
And who knows the interpretation of
a thing?
[z]A man's wisdom makes his face shine,
and [a]the hardness of his face is
changed.

2 I say:[1] Keep the king's command,
because of [b]God's oath to him.[2] 3 Be not
hasty to [c]go from his presence. Do not take
your stand in an evil cause, for he does
whatever he pleases. 4 For the word of the
king is supreme, and [d]who may say to him,
"What are you doing?" 5 Whoever keeps a
command will know no evil thing, and the
wise heart will know the proper time and
the just way. 6 For there is a time and a way
[e]for everything, although man's trouble[3]
lies heavy on him. 7 For he [f]does not know
what is to be, for [g]who can tell him how it
will be? 8 No man has power to [h]retain the
spirit, [i]or power over the day of death.
There is no [j]discharge from war, nor will
wickedness deliver those who are given to
it. 9 [k]All this I observed while applying my
heart to all that is done under the sun,
when man had power over man to his hurt.

Those Who Fear God Will Do Well

10 Then I saw the wicked buried. They
used to go in and out of [l]the holy place and
were [m]praised[4] in the city where they had
done such things. This also is vanity.
11 Because [n]the sentence against an evil
deed is not executed speedily, [o]the heart of
the children of man is fully set to do evil.
12 Though a sinner does evil a hundred
times and [p]prolongs his life, yet I know
that [q]it will be well with [r]those who fear
God, because they fear before him. 13 But it
will [s]not be well with the wicked, neither
will he prolong his days like [t]a shadow,
because he does not fear before God.

Man Cannot Know God's Ways

14 There is a vanity that takes place on
earth, that there are righteous people [u]to
whom it happens according to the deeds of
the wicked, and there are wicked people
[v]to whom it happens according to the
deeds of the righteous. I said that this also
is vanity. 15 And I commend joy, for man
[w]has no good thing under the sun but to
[x]eat and drink and be joyful, for this will go
with him in his toil through the days of his
life that God has given him under the sun.
16 When I applied my heart to know wisdom, and to see [y]the business that is done

21 [k]Prov. 30:10 **22** [l][Gal. 6:1] **23** [m][Rom. 1:22] **24** [n][Rom. 11:33] [o]Job 28:12, 20; [1 Tim. 6:16] **25** [p]See ch. 1:17 **26** [q]Prov. 5:4 [r]See Prov. 2:16 [s]Prov. 12:12; [Prov. 23:28] [t]Prov. 22:14 **27** [u]See ch. 1:1 **28** [v]Job 33:23; [ver. 20] [w][1 Kin. 11:3] **29** [x][Gen. 1:27] [y][Gen. 3:6, 7]
Chapter 8
1 [z]Prov. 4:8, 9; [Acts 6:15] [a]Prov. 21:29; [Deut. 28:50] **2** [b]Ex. 22:11; 2 Sam. 21:7; 1 Kin. 2:43; [2 Chr. 36:13; Ezek. 17:18] **3** [c][ch. 10:4] **4** [d]Dan. 4:35; See Job 9:12
6 [e]ch. 3:1, 17 **7** [f][Prov. 24:22] [g]ch. 3:22; 6:12; 9:12; 10:14 **8** [h][Job 14:5] [i][ch. 3:19; 9:11] [j]See Deut. 20:5-8 **9** [k][ch. 1:13] **10** [l][Neh. 11:1; Matt. 24:15] [m][ch. 9:5; Prov. 10:7] **11** [n][Ps. 10:6; 50:21; Isai. 26:10; Rom. 2:4, 5; 2 Pet. 3:9] [o][Esth. 7:5; Acts 5:3] **12** [p]ch. 7:15; Isai. 65:20 [q][Deut. 12:25; Isai. 3:10] [r][Ps. 37:11, 18, 19; Prov. 1:33; Matt. 25:34] **13** [s]Isai. 3:11 [t]ch. 6:12; See Job 14:2
14 [u]ch. 7:15; [Ps. 73:3]; See ch. 2:14 [v][Job 21:7; Ps. 17:9, 10; 73:12; Jer. 12:1] **15** [w]See ch. 2:24 [x]1 Kin. 4:20 **16** [y]ch. 1:13; 3:10

[1] Hebrew lacks *say* [2] Or *because of your oath to God* [3] Or *evil* [4] Some Hebrew manuscripts, Septuagint, Vulgate; most Hebrew manuscripts *forgotten*

7:22 many times. We are all multiple offenders in God's sight.

7:24 who can find it out. No one can fully comprehend God's understanding; it is qualitatively different from human knowledge (8:16, 17; 1 Cor. 2:11).

7:29 made man upright. God created Adam morally good (Gen. 1:31), but all sin (Rom. 3:23; 5:12). See "The Fall" at Gen. 3:6.

8:5, 6 proper time and the just way. The truly wise seek and commonly find the proper time for every action (3:1–8).

8:8 power. We cannot control death or evil, but Christ has this power (John 10:18; Rev. 1:18).

8:9 to his hurt. Probably this means to hurt the one ruled. Solomon has seen how the irresponsible use of God-given authority injures people (Rom. 13:3, 4).

8:10–13 Though inequities abound in human societies, as experienced in civil disorders of our own time, God will nevertheless settle all accounts justly.

8:14 on earth. In this life the righteous and wicked do not necessarily get what they deserve.

8:15 commend. In the face of injustice, people are nevertheless to rejoice in this life. Solomon's mode of expression is pessimistic, but in the immediate context he mentions that life is the gift of God.

on earth, how neither [z]day nor night do
one's eyes see sleep, 17 then I saw all the
work of God, that [a]man cannot find out
the work that is done under the sun.
However much man may toil in seeking, he
will not find it out. Even though a wise
man claims to know, [b]he cannot find it out.

Death Comes to All

9 But all this I laid to heart, examining it
all, [c]how the righteous and the wise
and their deeds are [d]in the hand of God.
Whether it is love or hate, man does not
know; both are before him. 2 [e]It is the same
for all, since [f]the same event happens to
the righteous and the wicked, to the good
and the evil,[1] to the clean and the unclean,
to him who sacrifices and him who does
not sacrifice. As is the good, so is the sinner, and he who [g]swears is as he who
shuns an oath. 3 This is an evil in all that is
done under the sun, that [e]the same event
happens to all. Also, the hearts of the children of man are full of evil, and [h]madness
is in their hearts while they live, and after
that they go to the dead. 4 But he who is
joined with all the living has hope, for a living dog is better than a dead lion. 5 For the
living know that they will die, but [i]the dead
know nothing, and they have no more
reward, for [j]the memory of them is forgotten. 6 Their love and their hate and their
envy have already perished, and forever
they have no more share in all that is done
under the sun.

Enjoy Life with the One You Love

7 Go, [k]eat your bread in joy, and drink
your wine with a merry heart, for God has
already approved what you do.
8 [l]Let your garments be always white. Let
not [m]oil be lacking on your head.
9 Enjoy life with the wife whom you love,
all the days of your [n]vain life that he has
given you under the sun, because that is
your [o]portion in life and in your toil at
which you toil under the sun. 10 Whatever
your hand finds to do, [p]do it with your
might,[2] [q]for there is no work or thought or
knowledge or wisdom in Sheol, to which
you are going.

Wisdom Better than Folly

11 [r]Again I saw that under the sun [s]the
race is not to the swift, nor [t]the battle to the
strong, nor bread to the wise, nor riches to
the intelligent, nor favor to those with
knowledge, but time and [u]chance [v]happen
to them all. 12 For man [w]does not know his
time. Like fish that are taken in an evil net,
and [x]like birds that are caught in a snare, so
the children of man are [y]snared at an evil
time, when it suddenly falls upon them.
13 I have also seen this example of wisdom
under the sun, and it seemed great to me.
14 There was a little city with few men in it,
and a great king came against it and besieged
it, building great siegeworks against it.
15 But there was found in it [z]a poor, wise
man, and he by his [a]wisdom delivered the
city. Yet no one remembered that poor
man. 16 But I say that [b]wisdom is better than
might, though [c]the poor man's wisdom is
despised and his words are not heard.
17 The words of the wise heard in [d]quiet are
better than the shouting of a ruler among
fools. 18 [e]Wisdom is better than weapons of
war, but [f]one sinner destroys much good.

10 Dead flies make [g]the perfumer's
ointment give off a stench;
so a little folly outweighs wisdom
and honor.
2 [h]A wise man's heart inclines him to
the right,
but a fool's heart to the left.

[1] Septuagint, Syriac, Vulgate; Hebrew lacks *and the evil* [2] Or *finds to do with your might, do it*

16 [z][Ps. 127:2] **17** [a][Prov. 25:2]; See ch. 3:11 [b][Ps. 73:16]
Chapter 9
1 [c][ch. 8:14] [d]Deut. 33:3
2 [e]Job 9:22 [f]See ch. 2:14 [g]Zech. 5:3; [Mal. 3:5]
3 [e][see ver. 2 above] [h]ch. 1:17
5 [i]Job 14:21 [j]ch. 1:11; 8:10; Ps. 31:12; 88:5, 12; Isai. 26:14
7 [k]See ch. 2:24
8 [l][Rev. 3:4] [m]Ps. 23:5
9 [n]ch. 6:12; 7:15
[o]See ch. 2:10
10 [p]Rom. 12:11; Col. 3:23 [q][ver. 5]
11 [r]ch. 4:1, 7 [s]Amos 2:14, 15; [Rom. 9:16] [t][2 Chr. 20:15; Jer. 9:23] [u][1 Kin. 22:34] [v]See ch. 2:14
12 [w][ch. 8:7] [x]Prov. 7:23 [y][Prov. 29:6; Ezek. 12:13; Hos. 7:12; Luke 21:34, 35; 1 Thess. 5:3]
15 [z][ch. 4:13] [a]ver. 18; [2 Sam. 20:22]
16 [b]See ch. 7:19 [c][Mark 6:2, 3]
17 [d]ch. 4:6
18 [e]ver. 16 [f][Josh. 7:1]
Chapter 10
1 [g]Ex. 30:25
2 [h][ch. 2:14]

8:17 all the work of God. See 7:13; 11:5.
cannot find out. God's work cannot be fathomed.

9:1–10 Solomon commands the enjoyment of life, despite the reality of death.

9:1 in the hand of God. God sovereignly controls the affairs of both the righteous and wicked.

love or hate. Presently both "good" and "bad" things happen to righteous and wicked people according to God's inscrutable design (Matt. 5:44, 45; Luke 13:1–5).

9:3 full of evil. People are totally depraved, that is, corrupt in every aspect (Gen. 6:5).

9:10 with your might. Like v. 4, this verse emphasizes the necessity of dealing with life as we find it.

9:11, 12 chance. Solomon describes people as victims of inscrutable or even cruel chance. Nevertheless, the believer understands that God orders events in unexpected ways.

9:16 despised. Solomon sees that wisdom is indeed better than might—but that the wise are not appreciated.

10:2 right . . . left. These had the conventional meanings of good and bad, or blessing and cursing, in the ancient world.

3 Even when the fool walks on the
road, he lacks sense,
and he [i]says to everyone that he is
a fool.
4 If the anger of the ruler rises against
you, [j]do not leave your place,
[k]for calmness[1] will lay great
offenses to rest.

5 There is an evil that I have seen under
the sun, as it were [l]an error proceeding
from the ruler: 6 [m]folly is set in many high
places, and the rich sit in a low place. 7 [n]I
have seen slaves [o]on horses, and princes
walking on the ground like slaves.

8 He who [p]digs a pit will fall into it,
and [q]a serpent will bite him who
breaks through a wall.
9 [r]He who quarries stones is hurt by
them,
and he who [s]splits logs is
endangered by them.
10 If the iron is blunt, and one does not
sharpen the edge,
he must use more strength,
but wisdom helps one to succeed.[2]
11 If the serpent bites before it is
[t]charmed,
there is no advantage to the
charmer.
12 The words of a wise man's mouth
[u]win him favor,[3]
but [v]the lips of a fool consume him.
13 The beginning of the words of his
mouth is foolishness,
and the end of his talk is evil
madness.
14 [w]A fool multiplies words,
though no man knows what is to be,
and who can tell him [x]what will be
after him?
15 The toil of a fool wearies him,
for he does not know [y]the way to
the city.

16 [z]Woe to you, O land, when your king
is a child,
and your princes feast in the
morning!
17 Happy are you, O land, when your
king is the son of the nobility,
and your princes feast at the
proper time,
for strength, and not for
[a]drunkenness!
18 Through sloth the roof sinks in,
and through indolence the house
leaks.
19 Bread is made for laughter,
and [b]wine gladdens life,
and [c]money answers everything.
20 Even in your thought, [d]do not curse
the king,
nor in your [e]bedroom curse the rich,
for a bird of the air will carry your voice,
or some winged creature tell the
matter.

Cast Your Bread upon the Waters

11 [f]Cast your bread upon the waters,
[g]for you will find it after many days.
2 [h]Give a portion to [i]seven, or even to
eight,
[j]for you know not what disaster
may happen on earth.
3 If the clouds are full of rain,
they empty themselves on the earth,
and if a tree falls to the south or to
the north,
in the place where the tree falls,
there it will lie.
4 He who observes the wind will not sow,
and he who regards the clouds will
not reap.

5 As you do not know the way [k]the spirit
comes to [l]the bones in the womb[4] of a
woman with child, so you do not know the
work of God who makes everything.

3 [i][Prov. 13:16; 18:2]
4 [j][ch. 8:3] [k][1 Sam. 25:24, 32, 33]; See Prov. 25:15
5 [l]ch. 5:6
6 [m][Esth. 3:1; Prov. 28:12; 29:2]
7 [n]Prov. 19:10; [Prov. 30:22] [o][Esth. 6:8]
8 [p]See Ps. 7:15 [q]Amos 5:19
9 [r][1 Chr. 22:2] [s][Deut. 19:5]
11 [t][Jer. 8:17]
12 [u]Prov. 10:32; 22:11; [Luke 4:22] [v]See Prov. 18:7
14 [w]See Prov. 15:2 [x]See ch. 3:22
15 [y][Isai. 35:8]
16 [z]Isai. 3:4, 12; [2 Chr. 13:7]
17 [a][Isai. 5:11; Prov. 31:4]
19 [b]See Ps. 104:15 [c][ch. 7:12]
20 [d]Ex. 22:28 [e]See 2 Kin. 6:12; Luke 12:3
Chapter 11
1 [f][Isai. 32:20] [g][Deut. 15:10; Prov. 19:17; Matt. 10:42; Luke 14:14; 2 Cor. 9:8; Gal. 6:9, 10; Heb. 6:10]
2 [h][Ps. 112:9; Matt. 5:42; Luke 6:30; 1 Tim. 6:18, 19] [i]Mic. 5:5; See Job 5:19; Prov. 6:16 [j][Luke 16:9; Eph. 5:16]
5 [k][ch. 1:6; John 3:8] [l]See Ps. 139:13-16

1 Hebrew *healing* 2 Or *wisdom is an advantage for success* 3 Or *are gracious* 4 Some Hebrew manuscripts, Targum; most Hebrew manuscripts *As you do not know the way of the wind, or how the bones grow in the womb*

10:5 error. Rulers often govern inappropriately.

10:10 sharpen the edge. Overcome the obstacles to effective work by being properly prepared with the wisdom or skill needed for the task.

10:12–14 words. Words reveal a person's heart, and what is spoken can have serious consequences (Matt. 12:34–37).

10:19 everything. This can mean that money is needed for both food and wine, or that money provides life's needs (cf. 7:12).

10:20 bird. A figure of speech meaning a spy or an informer.

11:1 bread upon the waters. Possibly a reference to Solomon's grain trade by sea.

11:2 seven . . . eight. An admonition to spread the risks you take (v. 6).

you know not. Uncertainty is a reason for diversity in financial management. See v. 6.

11:3, 4 clouds. Do not use uncertainty as an excuse for laziness.

11:5 work of God. Here again is an affirmation of God's incomprehensible, secret counsel (8:17 note).

6 In the morning sow your seed, and at
evening [m]withhold not your hand, for you
do not know which will prosper, this or
that, or whether both alike will be good.
7 Light is sweet, and it is pleasant for the
eyes to [n]see the sun.
8 So if a person lives many years, let him
rejoice in them all; but let him remember
[o]that the days of darkness will be many. All
that comes is [p]vanity.
9 [q]Rejoice, O young man, in your youth,
and let your heart cheer you in the days of
your youth. [r]Walk in the ways of your heart
and [s]the sight of your eyes. But know that
for all these things [t]God will bring you into
judgment.
10 Remove vexation from your heart, and
[u]put away pain[1] from your body, for youth
and the dawn of life are vanity.

Remember Your Creator in Your Youth

12 Remember also your Creator in
[v]the days of your youth, before [w]the
evil days come and the years draw near of
which [x]you will say, "I have no pleasure
in them"; 2 before [y]the sun and the light
and the moon and the stars are darkened
and the clouds return after the rain, 3 in
the day when the keepers of the house
tremble, and the strong men are bent, and
the grinders cease because they are few,
and [z]those who look through the windows
are dimmed, 4 and [a]the doors on the street
are shut—when [b]the sound of the grinding
is low, and one rises up at the sound of
a bird, and all [c]the daughters of song are
brought low—5 they are afraid also of what
is high, and [d]terrors are in the way; the
almond tree blossoms, the grasshopper
drags itself along,[2] and desire fails,
because man is going to his [e]eternal
[f]home, and the [g]mourners go about the
streets—6 before the silver cord is
snapped, or [h]the golden bowl is broken, or
the pitcher is [i]shattered at the fountain, or
the wheel broken at the cistern, 7 and [j]the
dust returns to the earth as it was, and
[k]the spirit returns to God [l]who gave it.
8 [m]Vanity of vanities, says [n]the Preacher; all
is vanity.

Fear God and Keep His Commandments

9 Besides being wise, [n]the Preacher also
taught the people knowledge, weighing
and studying and arranging [o]many
proverbs with great care. 10 [n]The Preacher
sought to find words of delight, and
uprightly he wrote words of truth.
11 [p]The words of the wise are like goads,
and like [q]nails firmly fixed are the collected
sayings; they are [r]given by [s]one Shepherd.
12 My son, [t]beware of anything beyond
these. Of making [u]many books there is no
end, and [v]much study is a weariness of the
flesh.
13 The end of the matter; all has been
heard. [w]Fear God and keep his commandments, for this is the whole duty of man.[3]
14 For [x]God will bring every deed into judgment, with[4] every secret thing, whether
good or evil.

6 [m]ch. 7:18 **7** [n]ch. 6:5; 7:11 **8** [o][ch. 12:1, 2] [p]ch. 2:23; See ch. 1:2 **9** [q][ch. 2:10; 9:7] [r][Num. 15:39; Job 31:7] [s]ch. 6:9 [t]See ch. 12:14 **10** [u]2 Cor. 7:1; 2 Tim. 2:22
Chapter 12
1 [v][Lam. 3:27] [w][ch. 11:8] [x][2 Sam. 19:35] **2** [y][Job 3:9; Isai. 5:30; Ezek. 32:7, 8] **3** [z][Gen. 27:1; 48:10; 1 Sam. 3:2] **4** [a][Ps. 141:3] [b][Jer. 25:10; Rev. 18:22] [c][ch. 2:8] **5** [d][Prov. 26:13]
[e][Ps. 143:3] [f][Job 17:13; 30:23; Isai. 14:18] [g][2 Chr. 35:25; Jer. 9:17; Matt. 9:23] **6** [h][Zech. 4:2, 3] [i][Isai. 30:14] **7** [j]Ps. 90:3; 103:14; See ch. 3:20; Job 34:15 [k][ch. 3:21] [l][Job 34:14; Isai. 57:16; Zech. 12:1]; See Gen. 2:7 **8** [m]ch. 1:2 [n]See ch. 1:1 **9** [n][See ver. 8 above] [o]See Prov. 1:1 **10** [n][See ver. 8 above]
11 [p]Prov. 22:17 [q]Ezra 9:8; Isai. 22:23 [r]Prov. 1:6; 2:6 [s]Ps. 80:1; Ezek. 34:23; John 10:11, 16 **12** [t][ch. 4:13] [u][1 Kin. 4:32, 33] [v][ch. 1:18] **13** [w]ch. 5:7; Deut. 6:2; 10:12 **14** [x]ch. 11:9; Job 19:29; Matt. 12:36; Acts 17:31; Rom. 2:16; 14:10, 12; 1 Cor. 4:5; [ch. 3:15, 17; Gen. 18:25; Ps. 58:11]

[1] Or *evil* [2] Or *is a burden* [3] Or *the duty of all mankind* [4] Or *into the judgment on*

11:6 do not know. See note on v. 2.

11:7–12:7 Natural, youthful life is to be governed with discretion, because this present life will be followed by a certain meeting with God (12:8).

11:8 rejoice . . . remember. The joys of present life should be held loosely, in the awareness that such joy is temporary.

11:9 judgment. Solomon does not encourage mindless self-indulgence, but gives a sober warning that God will bring everything into judgment (Matt. 12:36).

12:1 evil days. If pleasure is unrestrained in youth, both pleasure and the Creator will be unknown in later years.

12:2–7 Solomon comments on aging and death, using the extended metaphor of a house that is falling down. He contrasts the deterioration of the house with the permanence of nature. It is best to take the metaphors here for their overall effect, rather than speculate on the meaning of each individual figure. As the following notes indicate, some associations are clearer than others.

12:3 keepers of the house. The phrases here probably refer to parts of the body as members of a household.

12:5 the almond tree blossoms. Their white color is associated with the hair of the aged.

eternal home. The words refer not just to the grave, but to the presence of one's Creator and Judge (v. 7).

12:6 golden bowl. These words describe a lamp broken in the fall caused by a break in a silver chain. Broken vessels and severed cords suggest the frailty that comes with aging.

12:7 the spirit returns. Human existence continues beyond death.

12:8 Vanity. A final reiteration of the Preacher's refrain.

12:9–14 The book concludes with a tribute to Solomon's wisdom, providing the keys to interpreting the book.

12:11 given by one Shepherd. The words of Ecclesiastes are God-breathed (2 Tim. 3:16).

12:13 end of the matter. Loyal submission to the rule of God is the central and summary admonition of wisdom literature (5:7; Job 28:28; Prov. 1:7; 9:10).

12:14 judgment. God's judgment of thoughts and deeds is a dominant theme that emerges throughout the book (3:17; 8:12, 13; 11:9; 2 Cor. 5:10).

THE

Song of Solomon

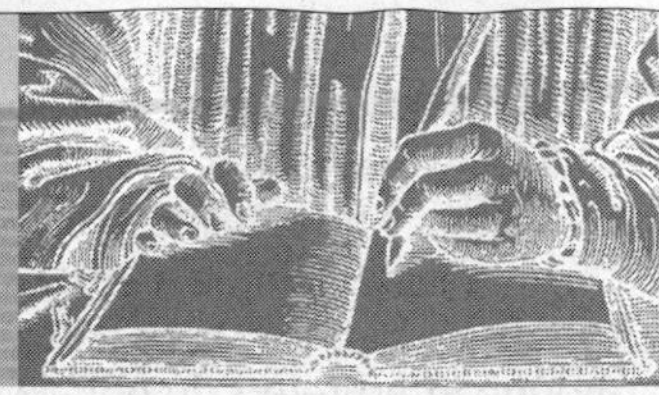

AUTHOR

According to the title, the Song belongs to Solomon. The Hebrew phrase "which is Solomon's" (1:1) can be translated "by" Solomon (as its author), or "for" Solomon (as the person to whom it is dedicated). The traditional view among Jews and Christians is that Solomon was the author (cf. 1 Kin. 4:32).

DATE AND OCCASION

If the Song was written by Solomon, it would have been composed in the mid-tenth century B.C. Dedication of the Song to Solomon might also favor this date, as do certain other features of the book (cf. 6:4 note).

Many interpreters, both Jewish and Christian, have regarded the Song as an allegory of God's love for Israel or the Church. The association of the book with Solomon, however, points us in the direction of the wisdom literature of the Old Testament. Wisdom literature is distinguished, among other things, by its focus on the common sphere of human relationships. The Book of Proverbs uses language similar to that of the Song of Solomon in talking about marital love (Prov. 5:15–19), the subject of the Song. This love must finally be seen in the context of the even greater love of God that the Bible as a whole reveals. The beauty and worth of sexual love is affirmed at the beginning of the Bible, where the difference and relationship of the sexes is associated with the creation of humanity in God's image (Gen. 1:27; cf. 2:19–25). If sexual love were evil in itself, it would be inappropriate as an allegory of Christ's love for His church.

The Song of Solomon reveals three qualities of love between a man and a woman: self-giving, desire, and commitment. In all these ways love reflects the greater love of God our Creator. God delights in us and gives Himself to us. God desires us wholly for Himself. God feels deeply both the pain and pleasure of His relationship with us. Although it is not proper to attribute sexuality to God, there is an analogy between the love we experience in marriage and the love that God has for us. The Old Testament prophets compare the love of God for His people to the love of a bridegroom for the bride (e.g., Jer. 2:2; Hos. 2:14–20). Christian marriage, according to Paul, should be modeled on the most perfect expression of such love, the self-giving love of Christ for His church and its willing response (Eph. 5:22, 33). The climax of the Song of Solomon is the praise of vehement and faithful love (8:6, 7).

The Song of Solomon shows us love outside Eden, not free from sorrow, but still beautiful and a reflection of God's own love for us. It looks back to the gift of love in creation, and forward to the perfection of love in One greater than Solomon, the Lord Jesus Christ.

CHARACTERISTICS AND THEMES

The Song is written in verse, as love poetry. The lines are short and rhythmical, the language rich in imagery and highly sensual. The poem deals more with emotions than with rational ideas, requiring a special sensitivity in the reader. It is irrelevant, for example, whether the woman who is described in 6:9 is really "perfect" in any way that could be proven. The word is an expression of her beloved's deep affection for her, and that is all that the images are intended to be. The Song is a rhapsody of love: an outpouring of the words and feelings of people who are experiencing human, sexual love with all its pains and pleasures. It is a book for those who want to know, or to remember, what it is like to be in love.

Although not a formal drama, there are

nevertheless exchanges between the characters within the poem. It is possible to identify the characters who speak certain lines based on clues provided by the gender, number, and person of the Hebrew verbs and pronouns, even though interpreters do not always agree on the precise divisions and identifications. The speakers have been identified by capitalized headings inserted in the translation (no such headings appear in the Hebrew text). The most important characters are the Shulammite (6:13), a young country girl (SHE); the beloved, (HE), her shepherd lover (1:7; 6:3); and the daughters of Jerusalem, (OTHERS), who function much like the chorus in a drama (2:7). There are numerous minor figures—Solomon himself is mentioned (1:5; 3:7, 9, 11; 8:11, 12), as are the mothers of the young lovers (6:9; 8:5), her brothers (cf. 8:8, 9), their friends (5:1), and the city watchmen (3:3; 5:7).

The presence of these characters has led many commentators to propose that the book is about a relationship between the girl and the shepherd, with Solomon as an intruder. But it is hard to see how Solomon could appear so unfavorably in a book that was either written by him or dedicated to him. It has proved difficult to identify a clear story line of the interactions between these three characters, or even to decide which words are Solomon's and which the shepherd's. Because of such problems, many writers have argued that the book is an anthology of love poems with common themes rather than a unified work. But such a division of the book into separate poems is unhelpful and unnecessary.

The poem is perhaps best understood as expressing the depth of love between the Shulammite girl and her beloved shepherd in the language of romantic fantasy. She envisions him as a dashing king, the prince of her dreams. In this interpretation Solomon is the archetypal lover, not an intruder. Yet he is not presented as one who must be envied. The Song shows us a world in which a country girl and a shepherd can be as happy and fulfilled as a king on his throne (8:11, 12).

A refrain is found at three points in the Song (2:7; 3:5; 8:4), addressed to the "daughters of Jerusalem." Its essence is: "Do not try to force the situation. Let love take its natural course and its own time." This refrain creates movement and suspense. The lovers experience separation, hostility, and interference, but the refrain anticipates that the relationship is nevertheless moving forward. There is a sense of fulfillment at the end of the book, when the lovers, together at last and at ease in public, walk arm-in-arm to the home of the parents, the place where their relationship began (8:5). The following two verses praise the excellence of love (8:6, 7). This is the climax of the Song, but not quite the end. It concludes by quietly echoing some of the key elements of the work (8:8–14).

Between the expressions of longing at the beginning and the consummation at the end, there is what seems to be a dream sequence in chs. 3–6 (3:1; 5:2). In this section the girl dreams about her wedding and the lovemaking that will follow. There is everything that we might expect here: erotic reveries, nightmares, fears of losing her lover, and romantic experiences that transform him into a prince. In her dreams, the girl's wedding becomes a splendid, royal occasion, and the lover is identified with Solomon himself.

Despite the romantic images and fantasies in this book, there is realism in it. The author knows about erotic desire, meddling relatives, and the struggle to establish a relationship in the face of separation and hostility. He understands that we no longer live in the Garden of Eden, but in a fallen world, where love, too, has its pain. But there remains also idealism. The overwhelming impression that the book leaves with the reader is that love is beautiful, and can provide deep satisfaction and contentment.

TITLE

The title has been translated "The Song of Solomon," "Song of Songs," and "Canticles" (from the Latin word for "song"). The word "song" in the title is the common Hebrew word for a happy song, with no special religious connotation. The whole phrase "song of songs" is a superlative expression meaning "the greatest song," announcing that the book is a single song of outstanding quality.

OUTLINE OF SONG OF SOLOMON

I. Desire for Love (1:1–2:17)
- A. *Title (1:1)*
- B. *Mutual Praise and Longing (1:2–2:7)*
- C. *Visit of the Beloved (2:8–17)*

II. The Bride's Reverie (3:1–6:3)
- A. *Dream of Separation (3:1–5)*
- B. *Wedding Procession (3:6–11)*
- C. *Praise of the Shulammite (4:1–5:1)*
- D. *Anxiety in Love (5:2–6:3)*

III. Mutual Praise and Longing (6:4–8:4)
- A. *Praise of the Shulammite (6:4–10)*
- B. *Union of the Shulammite and Her Beloved (6:11–8:4)*

IV. The Value of Love in Union (8:5–14)
- A. *In Praise of Love (8:5–7)*
- B. *Conclusion (8:8–14)*

1 The Song of [a]Songs, which is Solomon's.

The Bride Confesses Her Love

SHE[1]

2 Let him kiss me with the kisses of
his mouth!
For your [b]love is better than
wine;
3 your [c]anointing oils are
fragrant;
your [d]name is oil poured out;
therefore virgins love you.
4 [e]Draw me after you; [f]let us run.
[g]The king has brought me into
his chambers.

OTHERS

We will [h]exult and rejoice in you;
we will extol [b]your love more than
wine;
rightly do they love you.

SHE

5 I am very dark, but [i]lovely,
O [j]daughters of Jerusalem,
like [k]the tents of [l]Kedar,
like the curtains of
Solomon.
6 Do not gaze at me because I am
dark,
because the sun has looked
upon me.
My [m]mother's sons were angry
with me;
they made me [n]keeper of [o]the
vineyards,
but [p]my own vineyard I have not
kept!
7 Tell me, you [q]whom my soul loves,
where you [r]pasture your flock,
where you make it [s]lie down at
noon;
for why should I be like one who
veils herself
beside the flocks of your
[t]companions?

Solomon and His Bride Delight in Each Other

HE

8 If you do not know,
O [u]most beautiful among
women,
follow in the tracks of the flock,
and pasture your young goats
beside the shepherds' tents.

Chapter 1
1 [a]1 Kin. 4:32
2 [b]ch. 4:10
3 [c][Luke 7:46; John 12:3] [d]Eccles. 7:1
4 [e][Hos. 11:4; John 6:44; 12:32] [f]Ps. 119:32; See Phil. 3:12-14 [g]Ps. 45:14, 15; [ch. 2:4; John 14:2; Eph. 2:6] [h]Ps. 9:2; 45:15 [b][See ver. 2 above]
5 [i]ch. 2:14; 4:3; 6:4 [j]ch. 2:7; 3:5, 10, 11; 5:8, 16; 8:4; Luke 23:28 [k]Ps. 120:5 [l]Isai. 60:7
6 [m][Ps. 69:8] [n]Job 27:18; Prov. 27:18 [o]ch. 8:11, 12 [p][1 Cor. 9:27]
7 [q]See ch. 3:1-4 [r]ch. 2:16; 6:3; [Ps. 23:1-3; Ezek. 34:14, 15;] [s][Isai. 13:20; Jer. 33:12] [t]ch. 8:13
8 [u]ch. 5:9; 6:1

[1] The translators have added speaker identifications based on the gender and number of the Hebrew words

1:1 See Introduction: Author; Title.

1:2–4 Third person expressions in 1:2 and 1:4 ("Let him kiss me . . . The king has brought me") open and close the paragraph, which is otherwise in the second person ("your love . . . your name"). The girl oscillates between thinking about her absent lover and addressing him as though he were present.

1:4 The king has brought me. This is the first of five occurrences of the word "king" (1:4, 12; 3:9, 11; 7:5). Here in v. 4 there are two possibilities: either the king is Solomon, who has tried unsuccessfully to win the girl's affections, or he is her lover, whom she romantically fantasizes as her king. The latter interpretation is to be preferred (see Introduction: Characteristics and Themes). The paragraph ends, as it began, with the girl referring to her absent lover in the third person (vv. 2–4 note).

We will exult and rejoice in you. The "daughters of Jerusalem" (v. 5) agree with the girl that the love of her lover is better than wine (v. 2).

1:5, 6 The girl responds to criticism of her complexion (v. 5, "I am very dark") by the daughters of Jerusalem (5:10–16 note). She is deeply tanned because her brothers have made her work in the vineyards, and consequently she has not been able to care properly for her "own vineyard" (her body, v. 6).

tents of Kedar. The Bedouin tribes living on the edge of the deserts east of Israel made their tents of dark goat hair.

1:7 like one who veils herself. The word "veils" has the same negative connotations here as it does in Gen. 38:14, 15. The girl does not want to be mistaken for a prostitute.

1:8 most beautiful among women. Elsewhere in the Song this form of address is used only by the daughters of Jerusalem (5:9; 6:1).

9 I compare you, [v]my love,
to [w]a mare among Pharaoh's
chariots.
10 [x]Your cheeks are lovely with ornaments,
your neck with strings of jewels.

OTHERS

11 We will make for you[1] ornaments of
gold,
studded with silver.

SHE

12 While [y]the king was on his couch,
my [z]nard gave forth its fragrance.
13 My beloved is to me a sachet of [a]myrrh
that lies between my breasts.
14 My beloved is to me a cluster of
[b]henna blossoms
in the vineyards of [c]Engedi.

HE

15 [d]Behold, [e]you are beautiful, [f]my love;
behold, you are beautiful;
your [g]eyes are doves.

SHE

16 Behold, you are beautiful, [h]my
beloved, truly [i]delightful.
Our couch is green;
17 the beams of our house are [j]cedar;
our rafters are [j]pine.

2 I am a rose[2] of Sharon,
[k]a lily of the valleys.

HE

2 As a lily among brambles,
so is [l]my love among the young
women.

SHE

3 As an apple tree among the trees of
the forest,
so is my [m]beloved among the
young men.
With great delight I sat [n]in his shadow,
and his [o]fruit was sweet to my taste.
4 He [p]brought me to the banqueting
house,[3]
and his [q]banner over me was love.
5 Sustain me with [r]raisins;
refresh me with apples,
[s]for I am sick with love.
6 His [t]left hand is under my head,
and his right hand [u]embraces me!
7 I [v]adjure you,[4] O [w]daughters of
Jerusalem,
by [x]the gazelles or the does of the
field,
that you not stir up or awaken love
until it pleases.

The Bride Adores Her Beloved

8 The voice of my beloved!
Behold, he comes,
leaping [y]over the mountains,
bounding over the hills.

9 [v]See ver. 15 [w][2 Chr. 1:16, 17] **10** [x][ch. 5:13]; See Ezek. 16:11-14 **12** [y][ver. 4] [z]ch. 4:13, 14; [Mark 14:3; John 12:3] **13** [a]Ps. 45:8; [John 19:39] **14** [b]ch. 4:13 [c]1 Sam. 23:29 **15** [d]ch. 4:1 [e][Ezek. 16:13] [f]ver. 9; ch. 2:2, 10, 13; 4:1, 7; 5:2; 6:4 [g]ch. 4:1; 5:12 **16** [h]ch. 2:3 [i][2 Sam. 1:23, 26] **17** [j]Isai. 37:24; 60:13; Ezek. 31:8
Chapter 2
1 [k]Hos. 14:5; [ch. 5:13] **2** [l]See ch. 1:15 **3** [m]ch. 1:16 [n]Isai. 25:4; 32:2 [o][Rev. 22:2] **4** [p]ch. 1:4 [q][Ps. 20:5] **5** [r]2 Sam. 6:19; 1 Chr. 16:3; Hos. 3:1 [s]ch. 5:8 **6** [t]ch. 8:3; [Deut. 33:27] [u][Prov. 4:8] **7** [v]ch. 3:5; 5:8, 9; 8:4 [w]See ch. 1:5 [x]See ver. 9 **8** [y][Isai. 52:7]

1 The Hebrew for *you* is feminine singular 2 Probably a bulb, such as a crocus, asphodel, or narcissus 3 Hebrew *the house of wine* 4 That is, I put you on oath; so throughout the Song

1:9 a mare among Pharaoh's chariots. Solomon began his reign by making a marriage alliance with Pharaoh (1 Kin. 3:1). He also traded in horses from Egypt (1 Kin. 10:28), and Pharaoh's chariots with their twin stallions would be well-known and much admired in Israel. What is envisaged here would have been exceptional: a bejewelled mare among the stallions, causing wonder and excitement.

1:11 We. In v. 4 the "daughters of Jerusalem" echo the girl's praise of her lover; here they respond similarly to his praise of her. The plural subject "we" goes against taking this verse as a speech of the girl's lover using courtly language. The so-called "royal we" is not used in ancient Near Eastern literature.

1:12 the king. The girl's lover is again presented as a king, as indicated by the following verse.

on his couch. The Hebrew here is an unusual expression, lit. "in his surroundings." The surroundings are not a couch, but grass and trees (vv. 16, 17). The girl is thinking of the times she and her lover spend alone in the woods.

1:14 Engedi. This lush oasis is halfway down the western shore of the Dead Sea.

1:15 your eyes are doves. The point of the comparison is not stated. Perhaps it is the gentleness of her gaze. The girl returns the compliment indirectly in 5:12.

2:1 rose. The Hebrew indicates a plant of the bulb family, like a crocus or daffodil (text note).

Sharon. This plain extends south from Mount Carmel along the Mediterranean coast. In this verse the girl modestly compares herself to some familiar wildflowers.

2:4 banqueting house. Lit. "house of wine" (text note). The setting is outdoors (1:12 note). The lovers' "house" to this point has been the forest (1:16, 17). Now they move to a different "house," namely, the young man's vineyard, his "house" of wine. The expression continues the royal imagery of 1:4, 12 (the shepherd is a king), and the comparison of love and wine in 1:2.

his banner. Banners commonly adorned royal banquet halls, but this banquet hall, or "house of wine," is different. It has only one banner, love, and that is also the only "wine" that will be consumed at the banquet.

2:5 raisins . . . apples. Raisins or "raisin cakes" are associated elsewhere in the Old Testament with religious rites, sometimes even in a pagan context (2 Sam. 6:19; Hos. 3:1). This has led some commentators to suppose that the Song of Solomon originated as the script of a pagan fertility rite involving ritual sex (cf. Hos. 4:11–14). But the lovemaking in the Song has no obvious religious dimension. The raisins here, like the apples, are simple aphrodisiacs. The girl calls for raisins and apples to renew her strength.

2:7 For comments on this refrain, which occurs also at 3:5 and 8:4, see Introduction: Characteristics and Themes. Here the refrain is a reminder that the lovemaking so far has been imagined rather than actual, despite the vivid language.

2:8–17 The image of the shepherd-lover as a gazelle or a young stag on the hills introduces and concludes this section, another imagined rendezvous between the two lovers. After her brief address to the daughters of Jerusalem in v. 7, the girl has returned to her musings.

9 My beloved is like [z]a gazelle
or a young stag.
Behold, there he stands
behind our wall,
gazing through the windows,
looking through the lattice.
10 My beloved speaks and says to me:
[a]"Arise, my love, my beautiful one,
and come away,
11 for behold, the winter is past;
[b]the rain is over and gone.
12 [c]The flowers appear on the earth,
the time of singing[1] has come,
and the voice of [d]the turtledove
is heard in our land.
13 [e]The fig tree ripens its figs,
and [f]the vines are in blossom;
they give forth fragrance.
[g]Arise, my love, my beautiful one,
and come away.
14 O my [h]dove, in the [i]clefts of the
rock,
in the crannies of the cliff,
let me see your face,
let me [j]hear your voice,
for your voice is sweet,
and your face is [k]lovely.
15 Catch [l]the foxes[2] for us,
the little foxes
that spoil the vineyards,
[f]for our vineyards are in blossom."
16 [m]My beloved is mine, and I am his;
he [n]grazes[3] among the lilies.
17 Until [o]the day breathes
and [p]the shadows flee,
turn, my beloved, be like [q]a gazelle
or a young stag on cleft
mountains.[4]

9 [z]ch. 4:5; 7:3; 8:14; 2 Sam. 2:18; 1 Chr. 12:8; [Ps. 18:33; Hab. 3:19]
10 [a]ver. 13
11 [b][Joel 2:23]
12 [c][2 Sam. 23:4] [d][Jer. 8:7]
13 [e][Matt. 24:32] [f]ch. 7:12 [g]ver. 10
14 [h]ch. 5:2; 6:9; [ch. 1:15] [i]Jer. 48:28; 49:16; Obad. 3 [j]ch. 8:13 [k]ch. 1:5; 4:3
15 [l][Ezek. 13:4] [f][See ver. 13 above]
16 [m]ch. 6:3; 7:10 [n]ch. 4:5; 6:3
17 [o]ch. 4:6; [Gen. 3:8] [p]Jer. 6:4 [q]See ver. 9

Chapter 3
1 [r]Isai. 26:9 [s]ch. 1:7 [t]ch. 5:6; [John 7:34]
2 [u]Jer. 5:1 [s][See ver. 1 above]
3 [v]ch. 5:7
4 [s][See ver. 1 above] [w][Job 27:6] [x]ch. 8:2 [y][Hos. 2:5]
5 [z]See ch. 2:7 [a]See ch. 1:5 [b]See ch. 2:9
6 [c]ch. 8:5; [ch. 6:10; Isai. 60:8] [d]Ex. 13:21; Joel 2:30 [e]ch. 4:6, 14; Matt. 2:11; John 19:39

The Bride's Dream

3 On my bed [r]by night
I sought [s]him whom my soul loves;
[t]I sought him, but found him not.
2 I will rise now and go about the city,
in [u]the streets and in the squares;
I will seek [s]him whom my soul loves.
I sought him, but found him not.
3 [v]The watchmen found me
as they went about in the city.
"Have you seen him whom my soul
loves?"
4 Scarcely had I passed them
when I found [s]him whom my soul
loves.
I [w]held him, and would not let
him go
until I had [x]brought him into my
mother's house,
and into the chamber of [y]her who
conceived me.
5 [z]I adjure you, [a]O daughters of
Jerusalem,
[b]by the gazelles or the does of the
field,
that you not stir up or awaken love
until it pleases.

Solomon Arrives for the Wedding

6 [c]What is that coming up from the
wilderness
like [d]columns of smoke,
perfumed with [e]myrrh and
frankincense,
with all the fragrant powders of a
merchant?

[1] Or *pruning* [2] Or *jackals* [3] Or *he pastures his flock* [4] Or *mountains of Bether*

2:14 let me see your face. The switch to the feminine form of the possessive pronoun "your" suggests that this verse and the following one should be assigned to the shepherd, "HE."

2:15 the little foxes that spoil the vineyards. The foxes are the one negative element in the otherwise ideal spring setting of vv. 10–15. The imperative with no specific subject is like a passive ("May the foxes be caught"), and the whole verse is a wish by the lovers that nothing should be allowed to interfere with their lovemaking.

2:16 he grazes among the lilies. In view of the context, this is most likely a metaphor for lovemaking. See note on v. 15 and 6:2.

2:17 Until the day breathes and the shadows flee. Traditionally, these lines have been taken with what follows, but they may make better sense if read with v. 16. The lovers have been together through the night, and when day breaks they must part. The young man's return to the hills marks the end of the unit that opened in v. 8 (see 2:8–17 note).

3:1 On my bed by night. The girl is not yet with her lover, but alone on her bed, imagining various encounters with him. A more explicit indication that she is dreaming is given in 5:2. It is not clear where the dream begins or ends, but it is certainly a major feature of the book (Introduction: Characteristics and Themes).

3:2–4 This search for her lover either follows the girl's night of dreaming, or is itself one of her dreams. The presence of watchmen patrolling the city streets indicates that it is night, and that this is probably a dream. The parallel in 5:2–8 is a dream (5:2). Both dreams have a nightmarish quality, the one in ch. 5 more obviously than this one (see especially 5:7).

3:4 my mother's house. This is presumably where the unmarried girl lies sleeping (v. 1). In her dream she brings her beloved home.

3:5 This second occurrence of the refrain confirms that the lovemaking at this stage is imagined rather than real. The consummation remains future (2:7 note).

3:6–11 Placed as it is between the two indications that the girl is at home in bed (3:1; 5:2), this wedding scene is best taken as part of her dreaming. Nightmare gives way to fantasy. She dreams of her wedding day, transformed into a royal occasion, with her lover as a king, the magnificent Solomon. It is not the first time she has pictured her lover as a king (1:4, 12; 2:4).

7 Behold, it is the litter[1] of Solomon!
Around it are [f]sixty [g]mighty men,
some of the mighty men of Israel,
8 all of them wearing swords
and expert in war,
each with his [h]sword at his thigh,
against [i]terror by night.
9 King Solomon made himself a carriage[2]
from the wood of Lebanon.
10 He made its posts of silver,
its back of gold, its seat of purple;
its interior was inlaid with love
by [j]the daughters of Jerusalem.
11 Go out, O [k]daughters of Zion,
and look upon King Solomon,
with the crown with which his
mother crowned him
on [l]the day of his wedding,
on the day of the gladness of his
heart.

Solomon Admires His Bride's Beauty

HE

4 Behold, [m]you are beautiful, my love,
behold, you are beautiful!
[n]Your eyes are doves
[o]behind your veil.
[p]Your hair is like a flock of goats
leaping down [q]the slopes of Gilead.
2 Your [r]teeth are like a flock of shorn
ewes
that have come up from the washing,
all of which bear twins,
and not one among them has lost
its young.
3 Your lips are like [s]a scarlet thread,
and your mouth is [t]lovely.
Your [u]cheeks are like halves of a
pomegranate
[o]behind your veil.
4 Your [v]neck is like the tower of David,
built in [w]rows of stone;[3]
on it [x]hang a thousand shields,
all of [y]them shields of warriors.
5 Your [z]two breasts are like two
[a]fawns,
twins of a gazelle,
that [b]graze among the lilies.
6 [c]Until the day breathes
and the shadows flee,
I will go away to the mountain of
[d]myrrh
and the hill of [d]frankincense.
7 [e]You are altogether beautiful, my love;
there is no [f]flaw in you.
8 [g]Come with me from [h]Lebanon, my
[i]bride;
come with me from [h]Lebanon.
Depart[4] from the peak of Amana,
from the peak of [j]Senir and
[k]Hermon,
from the dens of lions,
from the mountains of leopards.
9 You have captivated my heart, my
[l]sister, my bride;
you have captivated my heart with
one glance of your eyes,
with one [m]jewel of your necklace.

7 [f]ch. 6:8 [g]2 Sam. 23:8; 1 Chr. 11:10
8 [h]Ps. 45:3 [i]Ps. 91:5
10 [j]See ch. 1:5
11 [k]Isai. 3:16, 17; 4:4 [l][Isai. 62:5]
Chapter 4
1 [m]See ch. 1:15 [n]ch. 1:15; 5:12 [o]ch. 6:7 [p]ch. 6:5; [ch. 7:5] [q]Mic. 7:14
2 [r]ch. 6:6
3 [s][Josh. 2:18] [t]ch. 1:5; 2:14 [u]ch. 6:7 [o][See ver. 1 above]
4 [v][ch. 7:4] [w]Neh. 3:19 [x][Ezek. 27:10, 11] [y][2 Sam. 1:21]
5 [z]ch. 7:3; [ch. 8:10; Prov. 5:19] [a]See ch. 2:9 [b]ch. 2:16; 6:3
6 [c]ch. 2:17 [d]ver. 14; [ch. 3:6]
7 [e]See ch. 1:15 [f]ch. 5:2; [Eph. 5:27]
8 [g][Ps. 45:10, 11] [h]ch. 7:4; See 1 Kin. 4:33 [i][Isai. 62:5] [j]Deut. 3:9; 1 Chr. 5:23 [k]Ps. 89:12
9 [l]ch. 5:1,2 [m][Judg. 8:26]

1 That is, the couch on which servants carry a king 2 Or *sedan chair*
3 The meaning of the Hebrew word is uncertain 4 Or *Look*

3:8 against terror by night. Solomon's men would form a bodyguard for protection from marauders, especially as weddings were celebrated at nightfall. But the verse has a double reference. There is also the "night" introduced in 3:1, which was spoiled by the girl's own "terror by night." These fears are banished, at least for a time, by the splendid vision of Solomon with his fighting men (vv. 2–4 note).

3:11 Zion. An alternative name for Jerusalem (e.g., Is. 40:9).

the crown. This is not the king's crown, but the sort of crown worn by brides and grooms at Jewish weddings. The custom was abandoned by the Jews in their sorrow caused by the tragic war with Rome and the loss of Jerusalem (A.D. 70). A rabbinic proverb states that "a bridegroom resembles a king."

his mother. The family structure reflected in the Song appears to be matriarchal (1:6; 3:4; 6:9; 8:1, 2, 5). There is no reference to a father, and within the relationship between the lovers there appears to be mutuality. But there are nonetheless elements of male dominance in the Song, notably the roles played by the girl's brothers (1:6; 8:8, 9) and the watchmen (5:7).

the day of his wedding. The real Solomon had many weddings (1 Kin. 11:3). The one day in view here is a romantic ideal (vv. 6–11 note).

4:1–5:1 In this single unit the man praises the Shulammite (4:1–15); she responds with an invitation (4:16); and he accepts (5:1).

4:1 Gilead. A high plateau east of the Jordan River.

4:4 the tower of David. The location of this tower is unknown. It is not the present-day tower of David just inside the Jaffa gate of Jerusalem, since that tower is no older than the time of Herod the Great. The girl's neck is adorned with jewelry as the famous tower was adorned with shields.

4:6 Until the day breathes. The time when the lovers must part is approaching (2:17 note).

the mountain of myrrh . . . the hill of frankincense. Frankincense, like myrrh, was an imported aromatic spice (cf. Matt. 2:11). Despite the exotic language, the reference is probably to the local hill country, fragrant with spring blossoms (cf. 1:13–17).

4:8 Lebanon . . . Amana . . . Senir . . . Hermon. All these sites are in the remote north of Palestine. We are not meant to think of the girl as living on the summit of Mount Hermon. Rather, the place names are symbols of the inaccessibility that the wooing is meant to overcome.

my bride. The word is not used literally, but as a term of affection, in anticipation of marriage.

4:9 my sister. In ancient Near Eastern languages "sister" is commonly used by lovers as a term of endearment. It expresses a closeness between persons who are not members of the same family.

10 How beautiful is your love, my
[l]sister, my bride!
How much [n]better is your love
than wine,
and [o]the fragrance of your oils than
any spice!
11 Your [p]lips drip nectar, my bride;
[q]honey and milk are under your
tongue;
the fragrance of your garments is
[r]like the fragrance of
[h]Lebanon.
12 A garden locked is my [l]sister, my
bride,
a spring locked, [s]a fountain
[t]sealed.
13 Your shoots are [u]an orchard of
pomegranates
with all [v]choicest fruits,
[w]henna with [x]nard,
14 nard and saffron, [y]calamus and
[y]cinnamon,
with all trees of [z]frankincense,
[a]myrrh and [b]aloes,
with all [y]chief spices—
15 a garden fountain, a well of [c]living
water,
and flowing streams from
[h]Lebanon.

16 Awake, O north wind,
and come, O south wind!
Blow upon my [d]garden,
let its spices flow.

Together in the Garden of Love

SHE

[e]Let my beloved come to his [f]garden,
and eat its [v]choicest fruits.

10 [l][See ver. 9 above] [n]ch. 1:2, 4 [o][ch. 1:3]
11 [p][Prov. 5:3] [q]Prov. 24:13 [r]Hos. 14:6; [Gen. 27:27] [h][See ver. 8 above]
12 [l][See ver. 9 above] [s][Gen. 29:3]; Dan. 6:17 [t][Prov. 5:15]
13 [u]Eccles. 2:5 [v]ch. 7:13 [w]ch. 1:14 [x]See ch. 1:12
14 [y]Ex. 30:23 [z]ver. 6 [a]See ch. 3:6 [b]John 19:39
15 [c]Jer. 2:13; [John 4:10; 7:38] [h][See ver. 8 above]
16 [d][ch. 5:1; 6:2] [e][ch. 6:2] [f]ch. 6:2 [v][See ver. 13 above]

Chapter 5
1 [g][ch. 4:16; 6:2] [h]ch. 4:9, 10, 12 [i]ver. 5, 13; ch. 4:14 [j]ch. 4:11 [k][Prov. 9:5] [l][John 15:14, 15]
2 [m][Rev. 3:20] [n]ch. 4:9, 10, 12 [o]See ch. 1:15 [p]See ch. 2:14 [q]ch. 6:9; [ch. 4:7] [r]ver. 11
3 [s][Luke 11:7] [t]See Gen. 18:4
5 [u]ver. 13
6 [v][ver. 2] [w]ch. 3:1 [x][Prov. 1:28]

HE

5 I [g]came to my garden, my [h]sister,
my bride,
I gathered my [i]myrrh with my
spice,
I ate my [j]honeycomb with my
honey,
I [k]drank my wine with my milk.

OTHERS

Eat, [l]friends, drink,
and be drunk with love!

The Bride Searches for Her Beloved

SHE

2 I slept, but my heart was awake.
A sound! My beloved is [m]knocking.
"Open to me, my [n]sister, my [o]love,
my [p]dove, my [q]perfect one,
for my head is wet with dew,
my [r]locks with the drops of the
night."
3 [s]I had put off my garment;
how could I put it on?
I had [t]bathed my feet;
how could I soil them?
4 My beloved put his hand to the latch,
and my heart was thrilled within me.
5 I arose to open to my beloved,
and my hands dripped with myrrh,
my fingers with [u]liquid myrrh,
on the handles of the bolt.
6 I opened to my beloved,
but my beloved had turned and
gone.
My soul failed me when he [v]spoke.
[w]I sought him, but found him not;
[x]I called him, but he gave no
answer.

4:10 better . . . than wine. The compliment of 1:2 is returned.

4:12 A garden locked . . . a spring locked. These are images of virginity. **spring . . . fountain.** Her beloved longs for her as a thirsty traveller longs for refreshing water (Prov. 5:15–20).

4:13, 14 Your shoots. The image of the enclosed garden is further developed (v. 12 note). "Shoots" alludes to the anticipated delights of lovemaking.

4:15 a well of living water. This image expresses how the young man would like his lover to be: no longer a sealed fountain (v. 12 and note). There is an implicit invitation to sexual surrender.

4:16 Let my beloved come to his garden. The girl unlocks the "garden" of her virginity to her beloved (v. 12 note).

5:1 came to my garden. The lover accepts his beloved's invitation. **my sister, my bride.** The girl's inaccessibility has finally been overcome (4:8 note).

Eat . . . drunk with love. The speakers are not specified, but they echo the language used by the shepherd in the previous two lines ("I ate . . . I drank"). Eating and drinking are often figurative for lovemaking. The girl dreams of the time when her relationship with her beloved will not only be consummated, but have the approval of family and friends.

5:2 slept . . . awake. See notes 3:1 and 3:2–4.

5:5 liquid myrrh. Myrrh in its virgin, liquid state, exactly as it flows from the tree, was a rare and precious substance (cf. Ex. 30:23). It is not clear from the Hebrew whether the girl has applied it liberally to herself before going to the door, or whether her disappointed lover has left it on the door latch as a token of his love. The repetition of the exact expression in v. 13 marginally favors the latter.

5:6 my beloved had turned and gone. At this point the dream becomes a nightmare as the girl's fears rise up to confront her. First is the fear of losing her lover.

7 [y] The watchmen found me
as they went about in the city;
they beat me, they bruised me,
they took away my veil,
those watchmen of the walls.
8 I [z] adjure you, O [a] daughters of
Jerusalem,
if you find my beloved,
that you tell him
[b] I am sick with love.

OTHERS

9 What is your beloved more than
another beloved,
O [c] most beautiful among women?
What is your beloved more than
another beloved,
that you thus [z] adjure us?

The Bride Praises Her Beloved

SHE

10 My beloved is radiant and [d] ruddy,
[e] distinguished among ten thousand.
11 His head is the finest gold;
[f] his locks are wavy,
black as a raven.
12 His [g] eyes are like doves
beside streams of water,
bathed in milk,
[h] sitting beside a full pool.[1]
13 His [i] cheeks are like [j] beds of spices,
mounds of sweet-smelling herbs.
His lips are [k] lilies,
dripping [u] liquid myrrh.
14 His arms are rods of gold,
set with [l] jewels.
His body is polished ivory,[2]
bedecked with [m] sapphires.[3]
15 His legs are alabaster columns,
set on bases of gold.
His [n] appearance is like [o] Lebanon,
choice as the cedars.
16 His [p] mouth[4] is most sweet,
and he is altogether desirable.
This is my beloved and this is my
friend,
O [a] daughters of Jerusalem.

OTHERS

6 Where has your beloved gone,
O [c] most beautiful among women?
Where has your beloved turned,
that we may seek him with you?

Together in the Garden of Love

SHE

2 My beloved has gone down to his
[q] garden
to [r] the beds of spices,
to [s] graze[5] in the gardens
and to gather [t] lilies.
3 [u] I am my beloved's and my beloved is
mine;
he grazes among the lilies.

Solomon and His Bride Delight in Each Other

HE

4 You are beautiful as [v] Tirzah, [w] my love,
[x] lovely as [y] Jerusalem,
[z] awesome as an army with banners.

7 [y] ch. 3:3
8 [z] See ch. 2:7 [a] See ch. 1:5 [b] ch. 2:5
9 [c] ch. 1:8; 6:1 [z] [See ver. 8 above]
10 [d] [1 Sam. 16:12] [e] [Ps. 45:2]
11 [f] ver. 2
12 [g] ch. 1:15; 4:1 [h] [Ex. 25:7; 35:9]
13 [i] [ch. 1:10] [j] ch. 6:2 [k] [ch. 2:1] [u] [See ver. 5 above]
14 [l] Ex. 28:20; 39:13; Ezek. 1:16
[m] Ex. 24:10; Ezek. 1:26; 10:1
15 [n] [ch. 7:5] [o] See 1 Kin. 4:33
16 [p] [ch. 7:9] [a] [See ver. 8 above]
Chapter 6
1 [c] [See ch. 5:9 above]
2 [q] ch. 4:16; 5:1 [r] ch. 5:13 [s] ch. 1:7 [t] [ch. 2:1]
3 [u] ch. 2:16; 7:10
4 [v] See 1 Kin. 14:17 [w] See ch. 1:15 [x] ch. 1:5 [y] Ps. 48:2; 50:2; Lam. 2:15; [Rev. 21:2] [z] ver. 10

1 The meaning of the Hebrew is uncertain 2 The meaning of the Hebrew word is uncertain 3 Hebrew *lapis lazuli* 4 Hebrew *palate* 5 Or *to pasture his flock*; also verse 3

5:7 beat me . . . bruised me . . . took away my veil. The nightmare continues, as the girl now dreams of being attacked (v. 6 note). The bride-to-be both longs for and fears love, and the dream combines these longings and fears.

5:10–16 In response to an implied devaluation of her beloved by the daughters of Jerusalem (v. 9), the girl praises him in elaborate terms. The situation parallels 1:5, 6, where the girl responds to an implied criticism of her own complexion by the same group of women.

5:12 His eyes are like doves. The compliment of 1:15 and 4:1 is returned (1:15 note). The contrast with "locks . . . black as a raven" in the previous line is striking. Her description suggests that her beloved displays both strength and gentleness.

bathed in milk. This image probably refers to the whites of the eyes. The description of the eyes in this verse is an example of mixed metaphor.

5:13 dripping liquid myrrh. Lit. "dripping flowing myrrh." See note on v. 5.

5:14 jewels. The exact stone referred to cannot be determined. In Ex. 28:20 the same type of stone is set in gold on the breastpiece worn by the high priest.

5:16 my beloved . . . my friend. The relationship between man and woman in the Song is broader than lovemaking, although that is central to it. It involves companionship as well.

6:1 seek him. The girl's spirited praise of her lover seems to have convinced the daughters of Jerusalem that he is worth looking for (cf. 5:9). But whether they want to find him for their friend's sake or for their own is not clear.

6:2, 3 The language of these two verses is taken from two earlier passages dealing with imagined encounters between the girl and her beloved, 5:1 and 2:16. Most likely because she suspects their motives (v. 1 note), the girl has in effect rejected the offer of the daughters of Jerusalem to help her search for her beloved, and has returned to musing about her times of intimacy with him.

6:4 Tirzah. This city six miles northeast of Shechem in central Palestine is in a setting of great natural beauty. It was the capital of the breakaway northern kingdom for approximately fifty years following Solomon's death. It continued to be a place of political intrigue until it was destroyed in the seventh century B.C. (1 Kin. 14:17; 15:21; 16:8–18; 2 Kin. 15:14–16). The positive reference to Tirzah here, particularly in parallel with Jerusalem, supports the traditional view that the Song originated in the time of Solomon, before hostility between the northern and southern tribes led to the division into two separate kingdoms.

5 Turn away your eyes from me,
for they overwhelm me—
[a] Your hair is like a flock of goats
leaping down the slopes of Gilead.
6 [b] Your teeth are like a flock of ewes
that have come up from the washing;
all of them bear twins;
not one among them has lost its
young.
7 [c] Your cheeks are like halves of a
pomegranate
behind your veil.
8 There are [d] sixty [e] queens and eighty
[e] concubines,
and [f] virgins without number.
9 My [g] dove, my [h] perfect one, is the
only one,
the only one of her mother,
pure to [i] her who bore her.
[j] The young women saw her and
called her blessed;
[e] the queens and [e] concubines also,
and they praised her.
10 [k] "Who is this who looks down like the
dawn,
beautiful as the moon, bright as
the sun,
[l] awesome as an army with banners?"

SHE

11 I went down to the nut orchard
to look at [m] the blossoms of the valley,
[n] to see whether the vines had budded,
whether the pomegranates were in
bloom.
12 [o] Before I was aware, my desire set me
among [p] the chariots of my
kinsman, a prince.[1]

OTHERS

13[2] Return, return, O [q] Shulammite,
return, return, that we may look
upon you.

HE

Why should you look upon [q] the
Shulammite,
as upon [r] a dance before [s] two armies?[3]

7 How beautiful are your feet in sandals,
O [t] noble daughter!
Your rounded thighs are like [u] jewels,
the work of [v] a master hand.
2 Your navel is a rounded bowl
that never lacks mixed wine.
Your belly is a heap of wheat,
encircled with [w] lilies.
3 [x] Your two breasts are like two fawns,
twins of a gazelle.
4 Your [y] neck is like an ivory tower.
Your [z] eyes are pools in [a] Heshbon,
by the gate of Bath-rabbim.
Your nose is like a tower of [b] Lebanon,
which looks toward [c] Damascus.

5 [a] ch. 4:1
6 [b] ch. 4:2
7 [c] ch. 4:3
8 [d] [ch. 3:7] [e] [1 Kin. 11:3] [f] Ps. 45:9, 14
9 [g] See ch. 2:14 [h] ch. 5:2 [i] Prov. 17:25 [j] [Gen. 30:13] [e] [See ver. 8 above]
10 [k] See ch. 3:6 [l] ver. 4
11 [m] [Job 8:11, 12] [n] ch. 7:12
12 [o] [Ps. 35:8; Prov. 5:6] [p] [2 Kin. 2:12; 13:14]
13 [q] [1Kin. 1:3; 2 Kin. 4:12] [r] [Judg. 21:21] [s] Gen. 32:2; 2 Sam. 17:24

Chapter 7

1 [t] Ps. 45:13 [u] Prov. 25:12 [v] [Prov. 8:30]
2 [w] ch. 2:1
3 [x] ch. 4:5
4 [y] [ch. 4:4] [z] [ch. 5:12] [a] Num. 21:26 [b] ch. 4:8; See 1 Kin. 4:33 [c] 1 Kin. 11:24; 2 Kin. 5:12

[1] Or *chariots of Ammi-Nadib* [2] Ch 7:1 in Hebrew [3] Or *dance of Mahanaim*

6:5 Gilead. See note 4:1.

6:8, 9 The two references to queens and concubines indicate that vv. 8 and 9 belong together. In her beloved's eyes the girl is more beautiful than all the women of Solomon's harem (8:11, 12 and notes).

6:8 sixty . . . eighty. At its peak Solomon's harem contained many more wives and concubines than this (1 Kin. 11:13), and there is already a suggestion of its future growth in the expression "virgins without number."

concubines. A concubine was not an illicit or casual partner, but a wife of secondary status (Gen. 25:6; 36:12; Judg. 20:4).

6:9 My dove, my perfect one. In her dreams the girl's mind returns again and again to her beloved's terms of endearment (5:2).

the only one of her mother. The close relationship between the daughter and her mother is apparent throughout the book (3:11 note), but there is no sign of possessiveness on the mother's part.

6:10 Who is this. It is the girl who is praised here.

dawn . . . moon . . . sun. The girl is described almost as a goddess.

awesome as an army with banners. The phrase is an exact repetition of the last line of v. 4. The praise given here is that of the girl's beloved, and rounds off the unit (vv. 4–10).

6:12 The Hebrew of this verse is difficult. At the least the verse indicates that the girl is still dreaming or daydreaming that she is a princess and her beloved is a prince or king. See note 3:6–11.

6:13 Return. The speakers are most likely male, as indicated by the response of the girl here: "why should you (masculine plural) look . . . ?" They are possibly the watchmen of 5:7 from whom she has presumably fled. This identification would explain the suggestions of lust in their call. If so, she is still dreaming. A nightmarish quality returns briefly in this verse, only to be dispelled by the timely appearance of the girl's beloved.

Shulammite. The designation probably refers to the girl's hometown, as a variant spelling of "Shunammite" (1 Kin. 1:3, 15; 2:17–22).

two armies. See text note. Mahanaim is the name of a town east of the Jordan River (Gen. 32:2). The nature of the "dance before two armies" is unknown, but the word "look" suggests that the girl's honor would have been compromised by performing it, causing her beloved to intervene as he does.

7:1 noble daughter. "Noble" here is the same word found in 6:12. There the girl imagined herself to be a princess; here she imagines her beloved addressing her as such. In everyday life she is a country maiden (1:5, 6).

7:4 Heshbon. This city east of the Jordan River opposite Jerusalem was captured by the Israelites in the time of Moses (Num. 21:25, 26). Excavations have revealed large reservoirs near the city, perhaps the pools mentioned here.

gate of Bath-rabbim. *Bath-rabbim* ("daughter of many") is probably the name of the gate, possibly one of the gates of Heshbon.

tower of Lebanon. The identity of this tower is not known. The great height suggested by "looks toward" or over Damascus has led some to take it as referring to the Lebanon mountains (cf. v. 5).

5 [d]Your head crowns you like [e]Carmel,
and your [f]flowing locks are like purple;
a king is held captive in the tresses.
6 [g]How beautiful and [h]pleasant you are,
O loved one, with all your delights![1]
7 Your stature is like a palm tree,
and your breasts are like its clusters.
8 I say I will climb the palm tree
and lay hold of its fruit.
Oh may your breasts be like [i]clusters of the vine,
and the scent of your breath like apples,
9 and your [j]mouth[2] like the best wine.

SHE

It goes down smoothly for my beloved,
gliding over lips and teeth.[3]
10 [k]I am my beloved's,
[l]and his desire is for me.

The Bride Gives Her Love

11 [m]Come, my beloved,
let us go out into the fields
and lodge in the villages;[4]
12 let us go out early to the vineyards
[n]and see whether the vines have budded,
whether [o]the grape blossoms have opened
and the pomegranates are in bloom.
There I will give you my love.
13 [p]The mandrakes give forth fragrance,
and beside our doors are all choice fruits,
[q]new as well as old,
which I have laid up for you, O my beloved.

Longing for Her Beloved

8 Oh that you were like a brother to me
who nursed at my mother's breasts!
If I found you outside, I would kiss you,
and none would despise me.
2 I would lead you and [r]bring you
into the house of my mother—
she who used to teach me.
I would give you [s]spiced wine to drink,
the juice of my pomegranate.
3 [t]His left hand is under my head,
and his right hand embraces me!
4 I [u]adjure you, O [v]daughters of Jerusalem,
[w]that you not stir up or awaken love
until it pleases.
5 [x]Who is that coming up from the wilderness,
leaning on her beloved?

Under the apple tree I awakened you.
There your mother was in labor with you;
there she who bore you was in labor.

5 [d][ch. 5:15] [e]See Josh. 19:26 [f][ch. 4:1] 6 [g][ch. 1:15, 16] [h]2 Sam. 1:23, 26 8 [i][ch. 1:14; Mic. 7:1] 9 [j][ch. 5:16] 10 [k]ch. 2:16; 6:3 [l][Ps. 45:11] 11 [m][ch. 2:10; 4:8] 12 [n]ch. 6:11 [o]ch. 2:13, 15 13 [p]Gen. 30:14; ch. 4:13 [q][Matt. 13:52] Chapter 8 2 [r]ch. 3:4 [s][Prov. 9:2, 5] 3 [t]ch. 2:6, 7 4 [u]See ch. 2:7 [v]See ch. 1:5 [w][ch. 2:7] 5 [x]See ch. 3:6

1 Or *among delights* 2 Hebrew *palate* 3 Septuagint, Syriac, Vulgate; Hebrew *causing the lips of sleepers to speak* 4 Or *among the henna plants*

7:5 like Carmel. There are two places with this name in the Old Testament. One is in the relatively arid south, in the hills west of the Dead Sea (1 Sam. 15:12). The other is the famous mountain where Elijah confronted the prophets of Baal (1 Kin. 18), in the lush north. This is probably the one used here as a favorable comparison. Mount Carmel is on the Mediterranean coast, due west of the Sea of Chinnereth (Galilee).

a king. The man fancies himself a king, enchanted by the beauty of his princess (v. 1; cf. 1:4, 12; 6:12).

7:8 I will climb . . . lay hold. These are images of lovemaking (v. 7; cf. 5:1).

7:9–13 Here as in 4:16 the woman responds to her beloved's wooing with happy surrender.

7:13 mandrakes. This plant has purple flowers and an orange, tomato-like fruit, and was believed to be an aphrodisiac (Gen. 30:14–16).

our doors. The imagined meeting place of the lovers is outdoors (v. 12); "beside our doors" simply means "ready at hand." Note the figurative use of "house" in 1:17.

8:1 like a brother. The key word here is "like." She does not, of course, wish that her lover were actually her brother, but only that she had the freedom to kiss him in public and to go with him anywhere without attracting comment.

8:2 house of my mother. See note 3:4.

she who used to teach me. The Hebrew can also mean "you (the man) would teach me," and the context seems to favor this translation. The man would lead the woman in the art of lovemaking.

8:3 This verse is identical to 2:6. In both cases the girl is dreaming of being in her beloved's embrace.

8:4 Occurring for the third and last time, the refrain points to the consummation that is yet to be (2:7; 3:5; Introduction: Characteristics and Themes).

8:5 Who is that coming up from the wilderness. This clause is an exact repetition of 3:6, where it introduces the wedding segment of the girl's dream (3:6–11 note). Now the dream has given way to reality. The happy pair, married at last, no longer have to conceal their relationship, but can walk in public arm in arm (contrast v. 1 and note).

leaning on her beloved. This simple statement captures an intimate and typical pose of man and woman.

I awakened you. That is, "began to woo you." The Hebrew text itself does not make clear whether it is the girl or her beloved who speaks here and in the next three lines. Tradition, as indicated by the vowel marks added later, makes the girl the speaker. The content of the lines suggests that it is the man who is speaking, at least to the end of v. 5. Either way, the passage indicates that the consummation has been reached, and the lovers reminisce about how it all began.

There. Presumably this does not refer to "apple tree" but to her parents' home that they are now approaching. The girl had dreamed about bringing her beloved home (3:4; 8:2); now she does so.

6 Set me as a seal upon your heart,
as [y]a seal upon your arm,
for [z]love is strong as death,
[a]jealousy[1] is fierce as the grave.[2]
Its flashes are flashes of fire,
the very [b]flame of the LORD.
7 Many waters cannot quench love,
neither can floods drown it.
If a man offered for love
all the wealth of his [c]house,
he[3] would be utterly despised.

Final Advice

OTHERS

8 We have a little sister,
and she [d]has no breasts.
What shall we do for our sister
on the day when she is spoken for?
9 If she is a wall,
we will build on her a battlement
of silver,
but if she is a door,
we will enclose her with [e]boards of
cedar.

SHE

10 [f]I was a wall,
and my [g]breasts were like towers;

6 [y]Isai. 49:16; Jer. 22:24; Hag. 2:23 [z][Rom. 8:35] [a][Ex. 34:14]; Deut. 4:24 [b][Job 1:16] **7** [c]Prov. 6:35 **8** [d][Ezek. 16:7] **9** [e]1 Kin. 6:15] **10** [f][ch. 4:12, 13] [g][ch. 4:5; 7:3]

11 [h]Eccles. 2:4 [i][Matt. 21:33] [j]ch. 1:6 [k][Isai. 7:23] **12** [l]See Prov. 27:18 **13** [m][ch. 5:1] [n]ch. 1:7 [o]ch. 2:14 **14** [p][Rev. 22:17, 20] [q]See ch. 2:9 [r][ch. 4:6]

then I was in his eyes
as one who finds[4] peace.

11 Solomon had [h]a vineyard at
Baal-hamon;
he [i]let out the vineyard to
[j]keepers;
each one was to bring for its
fruit [k]a thousand pieces of
silver.
12 My vineyard, my very own, is
before me;
you, O Solomon, may have the
thousand,
and [l]the keepers of the fruit two
hundred.

HE

13 [m]O you who dwell in the gardens,
with [n]companions listening for
your voice;
[o]let me hear it.

SHE

14 [p]Make haste, my beloved,
and be [q]like a gazelle
or a young stag
on [r]the mountains of spices.

1 Or *ardor* 2 Hebrew *as Sheol* 3 Or *it* 4 Or *brings out*

8:6 seal. This "seal" is a signet made of metal or stone and worn on a necklace over the heart or on an arm band (Gen. 38:18).

strong as death. Love is as strong as the most powerful, negative human experience. This phrase marks the beginning of a short "hymn to love" spoken by the bride.

jealousy. In parallel with "love" here, "jealousy" is positive zeal, like the jealousy of God (Ex. 20:5; John 2:17). Like God's love, the love being celebrated tolerates no rivals.

8:8–10 The climax of the Song has been reached and passed (see Introduction: Characteristics and Themes), but there is still room for a few memories. In this unit, the daughters of Jerusalem remember how possessive and protective the bride's brothers were when she was too young to marry (1:6).

8:8 spoken for. That is, asked for as a prospective bride.

8:9 If she is a wall. That is, if she is firm in her refusal of the marriage proposal. The brothers' response to this answer will be to "build on her a battlement of silver"; that is, they will confirm her refusal and honor her for it.

if she is a door. That is, if she accepts the proposal. Then the brothers will "enclose her with boards of cedar"; that is, they will refuse her permission to marry.

8:10 I was a wall, and my breasts were like towers. The girl affirms the strength of her moral integrity, but also her sexual maturity (contrast v. 8).

peace. Complete well-being, the Hebrew *shalom*. By implication, the Song points to the marriage relationship as the place where such fulfillment is to be found.

8:11 a vineyard at Baal-hamon. Some interpreters have regarded this "vineyard" as a metaphor for Solomon's harem, but the designation of a specific place suggests otherwise. The location of Baal-hamon is unknown.

for its fruit. The keepers would bring what came in from selling the fruit.

8:12 The expression "My vineyard" suggests that this verse is spoken by the woman. Here as in 1:8 the literal use of "vineyard" is followed by a metaphorical use. The girl's "vineyard" is her body, with its natural, rustic beauty. She is content with this treasure to share with the one she loves. Solomon can keep his wealth.

8:13 companions. Probably these are wedding guests.

let me hear it. The bridegroom is eager to be alone with his bride.

8:14 Make haste, my beloved. The desire is mutual. She invites him to come with her in language reminiscent of the lovemaking of her dreams (2:8, 9; 4:6).

INTRODUCTION TO THE

Prophets

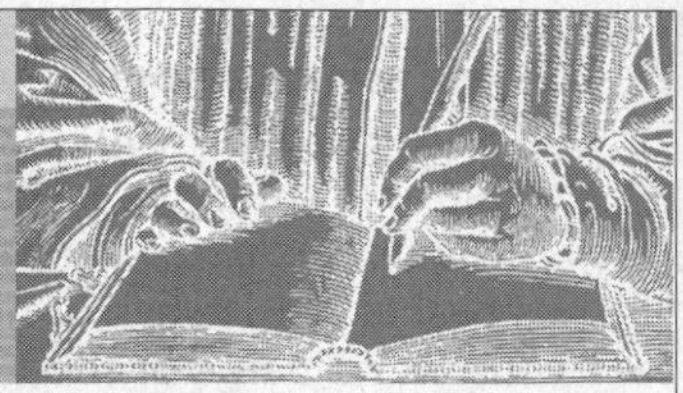

The idea of prophecy is introduced in the Old Testament by the relationship between Moses and Aaron. Since Moses declined to speak on his own, Aaron was appointed by God to serve as Moses' "mouth" (Ex. 4:12-16) to speak for him. Aaron's role is later described as being Moses' "prophet" (Ex. 7:1, 2). Likewise, the prophet of God is one who transmits the words of God. While God is not unable to speak—as the burning bush, the bringing of the Law, and the still small voice heard by Elijah show—His choice is to speak His words to His people through the voice of human beings, who are His agents of revelation.

According to Heb. 1:1, the revelation of the Old Testament period was given in "many ways." The phenomena of Old Testament prophecy illustrate this point. There are visions, trances, enigmatic actions, inner compulsion, signs, and wonders. It is difficult to summarize these aspects of an institution that covered many times and situations, although it should be observed that the message of prophecy is in the words of the prophets, and their actions can hardly be interpreted on their own. Old Testament prophecy is not dark or chaotic, and does not lead people into selfish, occult, and self-destructive paths. As God's voice, the prophets exhorted, threatened, and encouraged the public. To the continual sin of the human heart they opposed the contrary word of God.

The history of Old Testament prophecy is generally divided into three main periods. The prophets who ministered during the early years of the monarchy in Israel and Judah are known to us only from what is recorded about them in the historical books. Such important prophets in Israel's history as Samuel, Nathan, Elijah, and Elisha belong to this "preclassical" period of Israelite prophecy. Since they did not write down their prophecies in separate books, these prophets are often better remembered for what they did than for what they said. The "classical" period of Israelite prophecy in the eighth and seventh centuries B.C. saw the first collections of written oracles. The prophets during this period appear to cluster around two great crises: the fall of Israel to the Assyrians (Amos and Hosea in Israel, Isaiah and Micah in Judah), and the fall of Judah to the Babylonians (Zephaniah, Nahum, Habakkuk, and Jeremiah). Finally, the "exilic and postexilic" prophets spoke God's word to the people during the dark years of the Babylonian exile (Ezekiel and Daniel) and the period of Judah's restoration in Palestine (Haggai, Zechariah, and Malachi).

The content of the Protestant canon of Scripture indicates that the prophetic ministry as the precursor of the kingdom of God fell into silence between Malachi and John the Baptist. Malachi predicted that the Messiah would be preceded by a reappearance of Elijah (Mal. 4:5, 6). Elijah was not reincarnated, but his authority was heard again in John the Baptist. The character and message of John the Baptist form a kind of summary description of his prophetic predecessors. John was a person separated from society, but whose message could compel them to listen. He appeared before kings and suffered persecution from them. His message called people to change their ways and return to God. He predicted the coming and the greatness of Jesus Christ. In all these ways he resembles the Old Testament prophets.

Just as John the Baptist had disciples (Luke 7:19; John 1:35-37; cf. Acts 19:1-5), so the Old Testament prophets were assisted by servants (1 Kin. 19:19-21; 2 Kin. 5:20) and accompanied by prophetic guilds known as "the sons of the prophets" (2 Kin. 2:3-7, 15; 4:38; 6:1-3; cf. 1 Sam. 10:10-12). Based on the evidence of Baruch's relationship with Jeremiah (Jer. 36:4, 14-18, 32), it seems that these prophetic guilds played an important part in writing down the oracles delivered by the prophets and preserving the books that bear their names. A noticeable feature of the prophetic books is that they often bring short passages together whose only connection is that they came from the same prophet. There is little narrative or connective writing, and the original historical reference may be impossible to recover.

The prophetic books were originally written on separate scrolls, long before the production of long books in one physical unit was possible. Not surprisingly, then, the order of the prophetic books in the finished canon of Scripture shows some variation. The Old Testament received by the Protestant churches is identical in content with the Hebrew Bible, despite the differences in the order of the books. In general, like the New Testament books, the order of the prophetic books is a compromise of overlapping considerations of length, date, and authorship. Isaiah, Jeremiah, and Ezekiel, self-evidently "major prophets," are arranged chronologically at the head of the collection. The relatively short books of the twelve "minor prophets" (counted together as one book in the Hebrew Bible) then follow in roughly chronological order. In the Hebrew Bible, Lamentations and Daniel (the last of the "major prophets" in the Protestant canon) are included in "the Writings," with Job, Psalms, and other books, notably Ezra and Nehemiah, which deal with the same period of history.

The words of the prophets are the message of God to the people of God. Although they contain a wide range of subjects and styles, there are some recurrent themes that are useful to review.

1. The figure of marriage often occurs, as the Lord impresses on His people the closeness of His relationship with them and its foundation in His solemn commitment to them (Ezek. 16:8-14; Hos. 2:14-20).

2. The covenant lawsuit (Hebrew *rib*) is a form in which God brings against the people the complaint that they have broken their covenant with Him (Hos. 12:3; Mic. 6:1-3). The features of a courtroom, such as witnesses and a formal accusation, identify this form. Often the prophets indicted the rich, the powerful, and the religious elite for oppressing the poor. The prophets criticized the nation as a whole with the charge that there was no "knowledge of God in the land" (Hos. 4:1). The people knew *about* God, but they had not maintained a faithful and trusting relationship with Him.

3. The oracles against the nations are speeches denouncing the enemies of God's people and condemning anyone who commits the sins described (Jer. 46-51; Ezek. 25-32). Israel is not always held up as more righteous than its neighbors.

4. The moral teaching of the prophets includes decisive pronouncements that defy the will of sinners. The prophets condemn dishonesty, cruelty, pride, and sensuality. They denounce false religion, but also the distortion of true religion, especially any ritual that conceals an empty heart.

5. The tension between true and false prophecy can emerge in conflicts between God's prophets and either the prophets of false gods (the prophets of Baal, 1 Kin. 18:22) or prophets who claim falsely to speak in God's name (Hananiah, Jer. 28). The proof that a prophet comes from God and is not an impostor follows from the prophetic commission to transmit the divine word (Deut. 18:20-22). The prophecies must be true, including prophecies that foretell future events. The life of a prophet must be agreeable to God's word. Finally, the prophet's message must be consistent with the character and teaching of God.

6. Many prophecies refer to the Messiah. In the course of His life on earth, Jesus fulfilled numerous predictions. Together these prophecies are a persuasive witness to the unique status of Jesus, the focus of the prophetic word. The New Testament says that "the testimony of Jesus is the spirit of prophecy" (Rev. 19:10), and that "all the promises of God" are "Yes" and "Amen" in Him (2 Cor. 1:20).

The prophets often write in poetry. This, together with their reference to historical situations long past, can make translating and interpreting their words extremely difficult. Consequently, it is necessary to give particular attention to the original context of the prophecy to provide the right foundation for hearing its enduring message. The prophets brought instruction and rebuke to people at all levels of society, denouncing every kind of sin. Religiously, they are "ethical monotheists"; socially, they are the unquenchable conscience of the just; spiritually, they are the precursors of the kingdom of God, announcing Jesus Christ to the world.

The distinctive ministry of the Old Testament prophets ended with the coming of Jesus as the last and greatest Prophet, as He Himself suggests (Luke 7:24-28). All the prophets before Him pointed to Him; when He was present, the future orientation of prophecy had to undergo a permanent change. At the Day of Pentecost, all the Lord's people received the Spirit (Acts 2:17; cf. Num. 11:29), and the gift of prophecy continued with the "prophets" of the early church (Acts 21:10, 11; Rom. 12:6; 1 Tim. 4:14; Rev. 1:3). Their new authority and inspiration should be distinguished from that of the Old Testament prophets.

The ministry of the Word was committed to the apostles, and then to the church founded on their testimony. The gospel is no longer proclaimed in the "many ways" that characterized the Old Testament prophets (Heb. 1:1). Yet the prophets of ancient Israel are the common property of the church of all ages, and after the passing of centuries, continue to be God's voice to His people.

THE BOOK OF

Isaiah

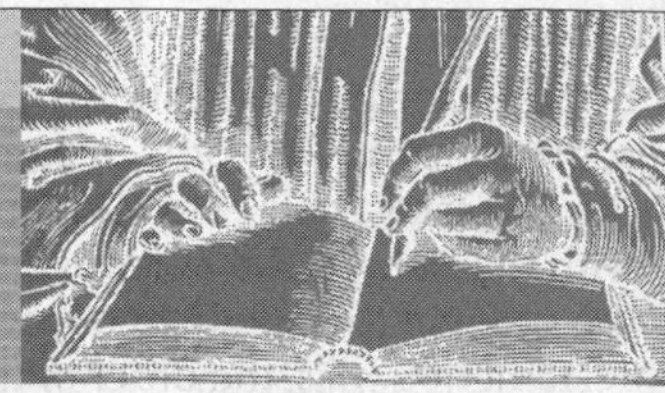

AUTHOR

Isaiah was an aristocrat by birth, well-educated, and by calling a preacher of God's oracles. He was God's appointed instrument in Jerusalem. Isaiah was married, and two of his children are named in the book: Shear-jashub and Maher-shalal-hash-baz (7:3; 8:3). According to tradition, Isaiah was martyred by being sawn in two (cf. Heb. 11:37).

DATE AND OCCASION

Isaiah ministered for a period of more than forty years, from 740 until after 701 B.C. The opening sentence of Isaiah names the kings who ruled in Judah during that time: Uzziah (died 740 B.C.), Jotham (750–731 B.C.), Ahaz (735–715 B.C.), and Hezekiah (729–686 B.C.). It was an era of great political turmoil due to Assyrian imperialism.

In Jotham's reign there was a war between Judah and the united kingdoms of Israel and Syria (the Syro-Ephraimite crisis of 734–732 B.C.; Isaiah 7–9). In this war Ahaz, the King of Judah, was opposed by a coalition of forces from Pekah, King of Israel, and Rezin, King of Aram or Syria. Ahaz responded with fear and unbelief. He refused God's sign (7:10) and tried to find a political solution.

During the reign of Hezekiah, Judah and several other nations fought against Assyria under Sennacherib (705–681 B.C.). Sennacherib's response was to devastate the countryside of Judah and lay siege to Jerusalem itself. But unlike Ahaz, Hezekiah trusted in the Lord. He poured out his burden before God in prayer and trusted God's word through Isaiah (37:14–35).

During the second half of the eighth century the prophet railed against the leaders for their hypocrisy (1:10–15), greed (5:8), self-indulgence (5:11), and cynicism (5:19). With these sins they were bringing the nation to moral ruin. God raised up Isaiah to announce their fate (6:11–13). As Isaiah predicted, Israel was exiled in 722 B.C., and Hezekiah barely escaped the Assyrian destruction (36:1–37:37).

The exile of Israel in Babylon is the context of Isaiah's ministry of encouragement to the afflicted. In a brilliant series of wide-ranging, yet specific prophecies, Isaiah predicts the fall of pagan Babylon (46:1–47:15) and the salvation of Israel's remnant. He names Cyrus, the Persian, as God's anointed agent to restore the remnant to the land more than a century before he came to power (44:24–45:13). He urges the remnant to flee from Babylon (48:20, 21). He challenges the people to renew their loyalty to the Lord when they return to the land (56:1–8) and to avoid falling back into acts of treachery (57:3–13).

Beyond this immediate salvation Isaiah predicted the coming of a Servant and Savior much greater than Cyrus. This anonymous Servant would bring justice to the nations (42:1–4), establish Israel in a new covenant with the Lord (42:5–7), become a light to the Gentiles (49:1–7), and take away the sins of His people (52:13–53:12). The Servant would suffer willingly to achieve these victories, and God would reward and vindicate Him (50:4–11). The New Testament identifies the Servant as Jesus Christ, the incarnate Lord.

INTERPRETIVE DIFFICULTIES

For over two centuries scholars have disputed the unity of Isaiah. They have raised historical, philosophical, and linguistic issues to argue that the book is the result of a complex transmission through many hands. Briefly, they divide the book into three sections, assigning these to Isaiah of Jerusalem (chs. 1–39); to a prophet of the time of the Exile (second, or "Deutero-Isaiah," chs. 40–55); and to a post-exilic prophet (the "Third Isaiah," chs. 56–66).

Variations in language between the proposed divisions of the book may be due to differences in subject matter, changed perspectives, or the prophet's personal growth. The similarities among the three sections have led many critics to conclude that a final hand unified the work. These unifying features include the repetition of theological themes (Zion, the advent of God, the Davidic representative, and the outworking of the Lord's sovereign plan), the names for God ("the Holy One of Israel," 1:4 and note), and the unified message of judgment and salvation. Conservative scholars defend the traditional understanding that the book is all the work of one prophet, Isaiah. The book was published under his name (1:1), and he is frequently mentioned in it (2:1; 7:3; 13:1; etc.).

Other books of the Old Testament that have multiple authors, such as Psalms and Proverbs, name them. Nothing in what this book says about its own authorship indicates more than one writer. In the New Testament, the apostle John attributes prophecies from Is. 6:10 and 53:10, allegedly from "Proto-Isaiah" and "Deutero-Isaiah," simply to Isaiah (John 12:38–41).

Modern critics assume that a prophet addresses only his contemporaries. They argue that since chs. 1–39 are addressed to the nation during the Assyrian invasions (ca. 740–700 B.C.), chs. 40–55 to the exiles in Babylon (600–539 B.C.), and chs. 56–66 to the community after its return to the land (c. 539–500 B.C.), more than one prophet must have spoken. But prophets often ask one generation to participate by faith in a salvation that lies in the distant future. For example, even though Israel's prosperity still lay in a remote future, Isaiah commanded the dispirited people to "Enlarge the place of your tent" (54:2).

The Old Testament views the covenant community as a historical unity. Every part of Israel participates in its past and future history. Moses addressed the generation born after their ancestors had entered into covenant with the Lord at Sinai as though they had been there (Deut. 5:3).

The critics assume that miraculous prophecy, such as naming Cyrus more than a century beforehand and predicting the birth of Jesus from the Virgin Mary, is impossible. But the Bible reproves philosophical naturalism. In fact, Isaiah reproaches Ahaz for this kind of unbelief (7:10–13). In chs. 40–55 the Lord validates His sovereign rule over the nations precisely by the powers of His prophets. Pagan prophets were deceived by their idols. They could not meet the Lord's challenge of showing that their past prophecies had been fulfilled, nor could they give any reliable prophecies of what was to come (41:21–29). By contrast, Israel's God fulfilled Isaiah's former prophecies about Assyria. He also predicted the future, mentioning Cyrus by name. Isaiah delivered these supernatural prophecies (41:21–29; 44:24–45:8) to leave unbelievers without excuse (48:3–5). Isaiah's remarkable prophecies about Christ's suffering and death put the case for supernatural prophecy beyond reasonable doubt.

CHARACTERISTICS AND THEMES

Isaiah served God in the role of covenant prosecutor. His message consists of charges, condemnation, and judgments, as he declares God's curse on Israel, Judah, and the nations (1:2–31; 13–23; 56; 57; 65). Isaiah's autobiographical account of his call to become a messenger from the Lord's heavenly court is recounted in ch. 6. When Isaiah was summoned to represent the heavenly court in Jerusalem's earthly court, he discovered to his dismay that God was not sending him to save Israel but to harden their impenitent hearts (6:9, 10). Isaiah was to present to the people the Lord's complaint that they were faithless and rebellious (1:2, 3; 31:1–3; 57:3–10). God's people had become like the nations in their pride, sarcasm, and selfishness. They had lost the vision of God's kingdom of righteousness, love, and peace and had tried to establish their own kingdom. The prophet also serves as an advocate. He calls on the godly to seek the Lord, to hope for God's kingdom, to experience God's peace within, and to respond with faith to God's new acts of redemption. The Lord's covenant ends with blessings on Israel, not curses (Deut. 30:1–10). In the end, a godly remnant will survive the judgment.

The first part of the book, chs. 1–35, focuses on God's judgment on Israel by Assyria; the second, chs. 40–66, on the remnant's return from Babylon and their ultimate deliverance in the remote future (see the note on 36:1–39:8 for a bridge between these sections). The second part like the first begins with a vision of the heavenly court. Isaiah overhears God sending messengers to announce that Israel's punishment has been paid for and will come to an end (40:1–8). Isaiah's vision of God's kingdom is great, because it includes the history of redemption from his day until the fullness of redemption. It embraces the exile, the return of the Jews from exile, the mission, ministry, and kingdom of Jesus Christ, the mission and hope of the church, Jesus' present rule over this world, and the restoration of all things in holiness and righteousness.

Isaiah was a master of his language, using a rich vocabulary and imagery. Many of his words and expressions are used nowhere else in the Old Testament. His imagery reveals that he knew the tragedies of war (63:1–6), the injustices of high society (3:1–17), and the disappointments of agriculture (5:1–7).

Isaiah was a gifted preacher. Through his poetic imagination and rhetorical style he exposed the folly of relying on human structures as over against the wisdom of trusting in God's kingdom. Although the ungodly harden themselves against the Lord (6:10), Isaiah's prophetic oracles move the godly to respond with awe and worship of God.

OUTLINE OF ISAIAH

I. The Lord Is the Holy One of Israel (chs. 1–12)

- A. *Oracles of Judgment and Hope (chs. 1–5)*
- B. *The Prophetic Call and Revelation of God's Holiness (ch. 6)*
- C. *Oracles of Judgment and Hope During the War with Israel and Syria (chs. 7–11)*
- D. *The Hymn of the Redeemed (ch. 12)*

II. The Day of the Lord in All Creation (chs. 13–23)

- A. *Babylon and Assyria (13:1–14:27)*
- B. *Philistia (14:28–32)*
- C. *Moab (chs. 15; 16)*
- D. *Damascus and Ethiopia (chs. 17; 18)*
- E. *Egypt (chs. 19; 20)*
- F. *Babylon (21:1–10)*
- G. *Edom (21:11, 12)*
- H. *Arabia (21:13–17)*
- I. *Jerusalem (ch. 22)*
- J. *Tyre (ch. 23)*

III. The Little Apocalypse (chs. 24–27)

- A. *The Immanence of the Day of the Lord (ch. 24)*
- B. *Joy in Transformation (ch. 25)*
- C. *The Relationship Between God and His People (26:1–27:1)*
- D. *Transformation (27:2–13)*

IV. Judgment and Salvation (chs. 28–35)

- A. *The Kingdoms of This World (chs. 28–33)*
- B. *The Day of Vengeance and Favor (chs. 34; 35)*

V. Isaiah and Hezekiah (chs. 36–39)

- A. *Sennacherib and Jerusalem (chs. 36; 37)*
- B. *Hezekiah's Illness (ch. 38)*
- C. *Hezekiah's Self-confidence and the Future Exile of Judah (ch. 39)*

VI. The Glorious Kingdom of God (chs. 40–48)

- A. *The Proclamation of Restoration (ch. 40)*
- B. *The Lord's Plan of Restoration (ch. 41)*
- C. *The People, Witnesses to the Lord's Redemption (42:1–13)*
- D. *The Restoration of Israel (42:14–44:23)*
- E. *The Lord's Use of Cyrus (44:24–45:25)*
- F. *The Fall of Babylon (chs. 46; 47)*
- G. *An Invitation to Return to the Lord and to Escape His Judgment on Babylon (ch. 48)*

VII. The Ministry of Restoration (chs. 49–55)

- A. *The Servant of God and the Renewal of the Promises (chs. 49; 50)*
- B. *Encouragement to the Godly (51:1–52:12)*
- C. *The Suffering Servant (52:13–53:12)*
- D. *The Renewal of the Covenant (chs. 54; 55)*

VIII. Responsibility Toward and Certainty of the Glorious Kingdom (chs. 56–66)

- A. *The Pursuit of Justice and Promise of God's Presence (chs. 56; 57)*
- B. *Call to Repentance Because of God's Covenant (chs. 58; 59)*
- C. *The Nature of the Glorious Salvation (ch. 60)*
- D. *The Grandeur of the Lord's Favor and the Glory of Zion (61:1–63:6)*
- E. *The Prayer for the Lord's Deliverance (63:7–64:12)*
- F. *The Benefits of God's Salvation and the Severity of His Judgment (chs. 65; 66)*

1

The [a]vision of Isaiah the son of Amoz, which he saw concerning Judah and Jerusalem [b]in the days of [c]Uzziah, [d]Jotham, [e]Ahaz, and [f]Hezekiah, kings of Judah.

The Wickedness of Judah

2 [g]Hear, O heavens, and give ear, O [h]earth;
for the LORD has spoken:
"Children[1] [i]have I reared and
brought up,
but they have rebelled against me.
3 The ox [j]knows its owner,
and the donkey its master's crib,
but Israel does [j]not know,
my people do not understand."

4 Ah, sinful nation,
a people laden with iniquity,
[k]offspring of evildoers,
children who deal corruptly!
They have forsaken the LORD,
they have [l]despised [m]the Holy One
of Israel,
they are utterly [n]estranged.

5 Why will you still be [o]struck down?
Why will you [p]continue to rebel?
The whole head is sick,
and the whole heart faint.
6 [q]From the sole of the foot even to the
head,
there is no soundness in it,
but bruises and sores
and raw wounds;
they are [r]not pressed out or bound up
or softened with oil.

7 [s]Your country lies desolate;
your cities are burned with fire;
in your very presence
foreigners devour your land;
it is desolate, as overthrown by
foreigners.
8 And [t]the daughter of Zion is left
like a [u]booth in a vineyard,
like a lodge in a cucumber field,
like a besieged city.

9 [v]If the LORD of hosts
had not left us [w]a few survivors,
we should have been like [x]Sodom,
and become like [x]Gomorrah.

10 Hear the word of the LORD,
you rulers of [y]Sodom!
Give ear to the teaching[2] of our God,
you people of [z]Gomorrah!
11 [a]"What to me is the multitude of your
sacrifices?
says the LORD;
I have had enough of burnt offerings
of rams

Chapter 1
1 [a]ch. 6:1 [b]Hos. 1:1; Mic. 1:1 [c][2 Kin. 15:1, 7]; See 2 Chr. ch. 26 [d]See 2 Kin. 15:32-38; 2 Chr. ch. 27 [e]ch. 7:1, 3, 10, 12; 14:28; See 2 Kin. ch. 16; 2 Chr. ch. 28 [f]See ch. 37:2–39:8; 2 Kin. ch. 18–20; 2 Chr. ch. 29–32
2 [g]Deut. 32:1; [Deut. 4:26] [h]Mic. 1:2; 6:2 [i][Deut. 32:6, 10, 15]
3 [j][Jer. 8:7]
4 [k][Matt. 3:7] [l]ch. 5:24 [m]See ch. 31:1 [n]Ezek. 14:5
5 [o]Jer. 5:3; [ch. 9:13] [p]ch. 31:6
6 [q]Ps. 38:3 [r][Jer. 8:22]
7 [s]ch. 5:5; 6:11, 12; Deut. 28:51, 52
8 [t]ch. 10:32; 37:22; Zech. 2:10; 9:9 [u]Job 27:18
9 [v]Lam. 3:22 [w]ch. 10:21, 22; Cited Rom. 9:29 [x]ch. 13:19; Gen. 19:24, 25
10 [y]Ezek. 16:46, 48, 49, 55; [ch. 3:9; Rev. 11:8] [z][Deut. 32:32] **11** [a]Prov. 15:8; Jer. 6:20; Mal. 1:10; [ch. 66:3]; See 1 Sam. 15:22

[1] Or *Sons*; also verse 4 [2] Or *law*

1:1 vision . . . Isaiah. The superscription refers to the entire Book of Isaiah. "Vision" means that the book is a revelation from God.

Isaiah. "The Lord saves."

kings of Judah. See Introduction: Date and Occasion.

1:2 heavens . . . earth. The whole of creation will bear witness against Israel that the Lord had warned them they would be judged if they broke their covenant with Him (Deut. 30:19; 32:1).

LORD. This name signifies the personal revelation of God to Israel and His solemn promise to be their God (Ex. 3:15).

Children. They were children by creation, by election, and by covenant (45:11; 49:7; 64:8; Deut. 32:6, 18; Mal. 2:10).

rebelled. Rebellion is willful transgression against the Lord's sovereign and gracious rule (1:28; 43:27; 48:8; 59:13).

1:4 Ah. This is an emphatic particle used in contexts of lament (1:4), but more often in threats ("woe," 3:9, 11; 5:11, 18, 20, 21). The staccato lament decries the folly and evil of God's children.

the Holy One of Israel. With his special designation for the Lord, Isaiah calls attention to the unique and awe-inspiring splendor of the Lord. The phrase occurs twenty-six times in Isaiah (e.g., 5:19, 24; 41:14, 16, 20; 60:9, 14). See also "the Holy One of Jacob" (29:23), "Holy One" (10:17; 40:25), and "your Holy One" (43:15).

1:5 Why. Further preaching only hardens impenitent sinners.

1:5, 6 struck . . . wounds. The people were unable to recover from God's chastisement. The imagery of the suffering nation has its counterpart in the suffering of God's Servant (53:4, 5), who endured the judgment of God in His own body vicariously (that is, as a substitute for others).

1:8 daughter of Zion. This Hebrew idiom is a personification of Jerusalem. Zion was the hill captured by David (2 Sam. 5:7), but the term often stands for all of Jerusalem or even all of Judah and Israel.

booth. A temporary shelter used by watchmen during harvest. See 4:6 note.

1:9 LORD of hosts. This designation of God presents Him as a divine warrior (13:4; 30:27; 40:10; 42:13, 25; 59:17; 66:15, 16), the commander over all troops whether in heaven or on earth. Israel's survival ultimately is not due to the enemy's weakness, but to God's sovereign power.

a few survivors. The Lord will not overturn His promise. Even in the midst of judgment He will preserve a remnant. Paul quotes this verse in Rom. 9:29, presenting the idea of a remnant taken out of a larger group as an expression of the electing grace of God. In Rom. 9:27 he quotes from Isaiah's teaching about the remnant at 10:20–23. See also Is. 4:3; 7:3 and note; 11:11, 12, 16; 28:5; 37:31, 32; 46:3.

Sodom . . . Gomorrah. God's people have become like the wicked inhabitants of Canaan, whose cities were destroyed (1:10; Gen. 18:20, 21; 19:24, 25). The fate of Sodom and Gomorrah typifies the terrible judgment of God on the kingdoms of this world (3:9; 13:19; Luke 17:28, 29; 2 Pet. 2:6–10; Jude 7; Rev. 11:8).

1:11 sacrifices. These were the central visible observances of Old Testament religion. Although God had ordered them to be performed, they were of no value without obedience from the heart (vv. 16, 17; 1 Sam. 15:22, 23; Ps. 51:16, 17; Mic. 6:6–8; Matt. 23:23).

and the fat of well-fed beasts;
I do not delight in the blood of bulls,
or of lambs, or of goats.
12 "When you come to [b]appear before me,
who has required of you
this trampling of my courts?
13 Bring no more vain offerings;
incense is an abomination to me.
[c]New moon and Sabbath and the
[d]calling of convocations—
I cannot endure [e]iniquity and
[f]solemn assembly.
14 Your [c]new moons and your
appointed feasts
my soul hates;
they have become a burden to me;
I am weary of bearing them.
15 When you [g]spread out your hands,
I will hide my eyes from you;
[h]even though you make many prayers,
I will not listen;
[i]your hands are full of blood.
16 [j]Wash yourselves; make yourselves clean;
remove the evil of your deeds from
before my eyes;
[k]cease to do evil,
17 learn to do good;
[l]seek justice,
correct oppression;
[m]bring justice to the fatherless,
plead the widow's cause.
18 "Come now, [n]let us reason[1] together,
says the LORD:
though your sins are like scarlet,
they shall be as [o]white as snow;
though they are red like crimson,
they shall become like wool.

19 [p]If you are willing and obedient,
you shall eat the good of the land;
20 but if you refuse and rebel,
you shall be eaten by the sword;
[q]for the mouth of the LORD has
spoken."

The Unfaithful City

21 How the faithful city
[r]has become a whore,[2]
[s]she who was full of justice!
Righteousness lodged in her,
but now murderers.
22 [t]Your silver has become dross,
your best wine mixed with water.
23 Your princes are rebels
and companions of thieves.
Everyone [u]loves a bribe
and runs after gifts.
[v]They do not bring justice to the
fatherless,
and the widow's cause does not
come to them.

24 Therefore the [w]Lord declares,
the LORD of hosts,
the [x]Mighty One of Israel:
"Ah, I will get relief from my
enemies
[y]and avenge myself on my foes.
25 [z]I will turn my hand against you
and will smelt away your [a]dross as
with lye
and remove all your alloy.
26 And I will restore your judges [b]as at
the first,
and your counselors as at the
beginning.

12 [b]Ex. 23:17; 34:23 **13** [c]Num. 28:11; 1 Chr. 23:31 [d]Ex. 12:16; Lev. 23:36 [e][Jer. 7:9, 10] [f]See Joel 2:15-17 **14** [c][See ver. 13 above] **15** [g]1 Kin. 8:22 [h]Prov. 1:28; Mic. 3:4 [i]ch. 59:3 **16** [j][Jer. 2:22] [k][1 Pet. 3:11] **17** [l]Jer. 22:3 [m][ver. 23; James 1:27] **18** [n]Mic. 6:2; [ch. 43:26] [o]Ps. 51:7; [Rev. 7:14] **19** [p]Deut. 30:15, 16 **20** [q]ver. 2; ch. 24:3; 40:5; 58:14; Mic. 4:4; [Num. 23:19] **21** [r]Jer. 2:20; [Ex. 34:15] [s][Jer. 31:23] **22** [t][Jer. 6:30; Ezek. 22:18] **23** [u]Mic. 7:3; [Ex. 23:8] [v]Jer. 5:28; Zech. 7:10; [ver. 17] **24** [w]ch. 3:1; 10:33 [x]Ps. 132:2 [y][Deut. 32:41] **25** [z]Ps. 81:14; Amos 1:8; [ch. 5:25] [a][Ezek. 22:20; Mal. 3:3] **26** [b]Jer. 33:7, 11

[1] Or *dispute* [2] Or *become unchaste*

do not delight. The Lord's distaste for sacrifices offered by those who do evil (v. 16) is expressed with increasing sharpness: "I cannot endure" (v. 13); "my soul hates" (v. 14).

1:17 the fatherless . . . the widow's cause. Concern for the needy is a practical demonstration of true godliness (v. 23; 58:7; Ps. 9:18 note; Jer. 22:16; James 1:27).

1:18 scarlet. The color depicts hands "full of blood" (v. 15).

white as snow. God can take away the stain of sin without compromising His righteousness because Jesus Christ bore God's punishment for sinners (53:4–6; Rom. 3:21–26).

1:19, 20 The gospel is a two-edged sword: eternal life (v. 19) or eternal death (v. 20; 66:24).

1:21 faithful. Godliness is demonstrated by perseverance, stability, and consistency in doing God's will. Through the purifying process, the Lord will renew a remnant who will again constitute a "faithful city" (v. 26), because He is faithful (49:7; 55:3).

whore. A "whore" in religion is an idolater, someone who has forsaken God to serve idols (Jer. 2:20; 3:1; Hos. 2:2; 3:1; Ezek. 16:23–30). The sins listed (vv. 21–23) are all evidence that God's people had forsaken Him.

justice . . . Righteousness. Justice means right relations between people. It is violated by murder, rebellion, stealing, and bribery (vv. 21–23). True justice will defend the cause of orphans and widows as much as the cause of those who can pay bribes and give rewards. The enemies of justice may even pass laws that facilitate their wrongdoing (10:1). Despite all such obstacles, God promises to restore righteousness to the earth (v. 26; 32:1; 33:5, 6; 42:1–4).

1:22 silver . . . wine. These are figures for Jerusalem's unjust rulers (v. 23).

1:23 bribe. The practice of bribery is strongly condemned in God's law, since it fosters injustice and discrimination (cf. Is. 5:23; Ex. 23:8; Deut. 16:19).

1:24 the Lord. That is, the Master. God, the Sovereign, will restore justice by removing His enemies, the unrighteous leaders of Jerusalem.

1:26 as at the first. The new age will be a restoration, bringing miraculous continuation and renewal to the covenant community. Leadership and people will live in harmony with God's will (24:23; 32:1).

city of righteousness. The new community is composed of men and women who practice righteousness and demonstrate a commitment to God and to other human beings (1:21 note).

Afterward [c]you shall be called the
city of righteousness,
the faithful city."

27 [d]Zion shall be redeemed by justice,
and those in her who repent, by
righteousness.

28 [e]But rebels and sinners shall be
broken together,
and those who forsake the LORD
shall be consumed.

29 [f]For they[1] shall be ashamed of [g]the oaks
that you desired;
and you shall blush for [h]the gardens
that you have chosen.

30 For you shall be [i]like an oak
whose leaf withers,
and like a garden without water.

31 And the strong shall become [j]tinder,
and his work a spark,
and both of them shall burn together,
with [k]none to quench them.

26 [c][Zech. 8:3]
27 [d]Jer. 22:3, 4
28 [e]Job 31:3; Ps. 1:6
29 [f]Hos. 4:19 [g]ch. 57:5; Hos. 4:13 [h]ch. 65:3; 66:17
30 [i][Jer. 17:8]
31 [j]Judg. 16:9 [k]ch. 66:24

The Mountain of the LORD

2 The word that Isaiah the son of Amoz saw concerning Judah and Jerusalem.

2 [l]It shall come to pass in the latter days
that [m]the mountain of the house of
the LORD
shall be established as the highest of
the mountains,
and shall be lifted up above the hills;
and [n]all the nations shall flow to it,

3 and [o]many peoples shall come,
and say:
"Come, let us go up to the mountain
of the LORD,
to the house of the God of Jacob,
that he may teach us his ways
and that we may walk in his paths."
For [p]out of Zion shall go the law,[2]
and the word of the LORD from
Jerusalem.

4 He shall judge between the nations,
and shall decide disputes for many
peoples;
[q]and they shall beat their swords into
plowshares,
and their spears into pruning hooks;
[r]nation shall not lift up sword against
nation,
neither shall they learn war anymore.

5 O house of Jacob,
come, let us walk
in [s]the light of the LORD.

Chapter 2
2 [l]For ver. 2-4, see Mic. 4:1-3 [m]ch. 14:13; 25:6 [n][ch. 56:7]
3 [o]See Zech. 8:20-23 [p][Luke 24:47; John 4:22]
4 [q][Joel 3:10] [r]ch. 9:7; Ps. 72:3, 7; Hos. 2:18; Zech. 9:10
5 [s]ch. 60:1, 2; [Eph. 5:8]
6 [t][2 Kin. 16:10, 11] [u]Mic. 5:12 [v]2 Kin. 1:2 [w][2 Kin. 16:7, 8]

The Day of the LORD

6 For you have rejected your people,
the house of Jacob,
because they are full of things [t]from
the east
and [u]of fortune-tellers [v]like the
Philistines,
and they [w]strike hands with the
children of foreigners.

1 Some Hebrew manuscripts *you* 2 Or *teaching*

1:27 redeemed. The term means "ransomed," transferred or freed from ownership by another through the payment of a price. The penitent, who turn their backs on idolatry and injustice, find freedom from Satan, sin, and death through the righteousness of Christ imputed to them and applied to their hearts by the Holy Spirit.

1:29 ashamed . . . blush. What people hold in honor will be exposed as worthless. Sinners will see how wrong they have been when they come to ruin (26:11; 44:9, 11; 65:13; 66:5).

oaks . . . gardens. These were places of fertility rites and pagan worship that the people had chosen in preference to serving God (65:3 and note; 66:17).

1:30 without water. Drought and fire are metaphors for judgment. Water in Isaiah signifies free, gracious, and bountiful salvation (11:9; 32:2; 41:18; 55:1; 58:11). The absence of water signifies separation from God's blessings (3:1; 50:2).

1:31 burn. See note 4:4.

2:2 in the latter days. This reference to "the latter days" is indefinite and may include a lengthy process of fulfillment, including the reigns of Hezekiah and Josiah, the period of restoration after the Exile, the First Advent of our Lord, the present age, and the glorious consummation (Jer. 23:20; 30:24; Ezek. 38:8, 16; Hos. 3:5). The term designates a new epoch that for the prophet lies in the hidden future. The new epoch alters history in every dimension and is the goal toward which events are striving. The apostle Peter relates this time to the new age begun at Pentecost by using the phrase for an introduction to his citation of Joel 2:28–32 (Acts 2:17).

mountain. The prophet spoke of the temple mount as a metaphor for the Lord's kingdom that will be exalted above all other kingdoms (cf. 11:9; 65:25; 66:20). Mount Zion and the temple on it were symbols of heaven and the heavenly sanctuary (Heb. 9:24). These earthly representations have passed away (Heb. 8:13); through the priesthood of the ascended Lord, the church comes directly to the heavenly reality (Heb. 12:22–24).

highest of the mountains. Pagans worshiped their gods at mountain shrines. Israel's God, who is worshiped on Mount Zion, will establish Himself in the eyes of all races and nations as the only true and living God, even as He is worshiped today.

2:3 let us go. They encourage one another to worship God from regenerate hearts (John 3:3–8).

out of Zion. The prophet proclaims the new era in which Jews and Gentiles will serve one King (11:10–12; 27:13; 56:3–8; 66:19–23). Zion, or Jerusalem, stands for God's throne (1:8 note).

2:4 swords into plowshares. Compare Joel 3:10.

2:5 light. Light stands for God's blessings, presence, and revelation (9:2; 30:26; 42:6, 16; 60:1–3). The Lord is the light in blessing and in judgment (10:17; 60:19, 20; cf. John 1:4; 8:12). People who exchange His light for the darkness of their corrupt minds (5:20; 8:20), will experience His judgment and live in the darkness of separation from God (5:30; 13:10; 59:9; cf. John 3:19, 20).

2:6–9 Isaiah condemns syncretism, the mixture of religions. These verses contrast the light with all the things the people adopted from the nations: magic, greed, warfare, and idolatry.

2:6 things from the east . . . Philistines. This refers to the pagan cultures on either side of Judah; Philistia was to the west. The law condemns all forms of magic and divination (Lev. 19:26; Deut. 18:10, 11).

7 Their land is [x]filled with silver and gold,
and there is no end to their treasures;
their land is [y]filled with horses,
and there is no end to their chariots.
8 Their land is [z]filled with idols;
they bow down to [a]the work of their hands,
to what their own fingers have made.
9 So man [b]is humbled,
and each one [b]is brought low—
do not forgive them!
10 [c]Enter into the rock
and hide in the dust
[d]from before the terror of the LORD,
and from the splendor of his majesty.
11 [e]The haughty looks of man shall be brought low,
and the lofty pride of men shall be humbled,
and the LORD alone will be exalted in that day.
12 [f]For the LORD of hosts has a day
against all that is proud and lofty,
against all that is lifted up—and it shall be brought low;
13 against all the [g]cedars of Lebanon,
lofty and lifted up;
and against all the [h]oaks of Bashan;
14 against all [i]the lofty mountains,
and against all the uplifted hills;
15 against every high tower,
and against every fortified wall;
16 against all [j]the ships of Tarshish,
and against all the beautiful craft.

7 [x]ch. 39:2; [ch. 22:8, 11; Deut. 17:17] [y]ch. 30:16; [Deut. 17:16; Mic. 5:10]
8 [z]ver. 18, 20; ch. 10:10, 11; Jer. 2:28 [a]See ch. 44:9-17
9 [b]ch. 5:15
10 [c]ver. 19, 21; [Rev. 6:15, 16] [d]Cited 2 Thess. 1:9
11 [e]ver. 17; Ps. 18:27; [Mic. 2:3; 2 Cor. 10:5]
12 [f][Job 40:11, 12; Mal. 4:1]
13 [g]ch. 14:8; See Judg. 9:15 [h]Ezek. 27:6; Zech. 11:2
14 [i][ch. 30:25]
16 [j]ch. 60:9; 1 Kin. 10:22
17 [k]ver. 17; Ps. 18:27; [Mic. 2:3; 2 Cor. 10:5]
18 [l]ver. 8
19 [m]ver. 10; Hos. 10:8; Luke 23:30; Rev. 6:16 [n][Ps. 76:8, 9; Hab. 3:6]
20 [o]ch. 30:22; 31:7 [p]Lev. 11:19; Deut. 14:18
21 [m][See ver. 19 above] [n][See ver. 19 above]
22 [q]Ps. 146:3 [r]Job 27:3; [James. 4:14]
Chapter 3
1 [s]ch. 1:24 [t]Lev. 26:26; Ezek. 4:16
2 [u]2 Kin. 24:14; Ezek. 17:13, 14

17 [k]And the haughtiness of man shall be humbled,
and the lofty pride of men shall be brought low,
and the LORD alone will be exalted in that day.
18 [l]And the idols shall utterly pass away.
19 [m]And people shall enter the caves of the rocks
and the holes of the ground,[1]
from before the terror of the LORD,
and from the splendor of his majesty,
[n]when he rises to terrify the earth.
20 In that day [o]mankind will cast away
their idols of silver and their idols of gold,
which they made for themselves to worship,
to the moles and to the [p]bats,
21 [m]to enter the caverns of the rocks
and the clefts of the cliffs,
from before the terror of the LORD,
and from the splendor of his majesty,
[n]when he rises to terrify the earth.
22 [q]Stop regarding man
[r]in whose nostrils is breath,
for of what account is he?

Judgment on Judah and Jerusalem

3 For behold, the [s]Lord GOD of hosts
is taking away from Jerusalem and from Judah
support and supply,[2]
all [t]support of bread,
and all support of water;
2 [u]the mighty man and the soldier,
the judge and the prophet,
the diviner and the elder,

1 Hebrew *dust* 2 Hebrew *staff*

2:7 horses . . . chariots. They relied on their own strength (30:16; 31:1, 3), rather than on the Lord (Ps. 20:7).

2:10 rock. At God's judgment people may seek shelter, but no one can hide from Him (Rev. 6:16).

2:11 in that day. The day of the Lord brings judgment on the godless, but blessing and salvation to the godly (Joel 2:31; Zeph. 1:7; 2:13–18). Isaiah's reference encompasses historical events (the fall of Israel, Assyria, Judah) and the coming judgment and salvation (3:7; 7:18–25; 11:10, 11; 24:21; 27:1).

2:13 cedars of Lebanon . . . oaks of Bashan. These were large, impressive trees with valuable wood (Ezek. 27:5, 6). Like the forests of the American Northwest, they symbolized the permanence and splendor of nature. But even they were subject to God's judgment.

2:16 ships . . . craft. These symbolize pride at being first in trade and commerce (23:1, 8).

2:17 in that day. See 2:11 note.

2:22 man . . . breath. One must trust God, who gives breath, not those who are dependent on Him.

3:1 bread . . . water. The chaotic conditions result in lack of food and water. See note 1:30.

3:2, 3 mighty man . . . expert in charms. The Lord will remove every kind of leader that the people were trusting to secure their society: warriors, sages, magicians, and other prominent people. See 11:2 note.

3 the captain of fifty
and the man of rank,
the counselor and the skillful
magician
and the expert in charms.
4 [v]And I will make boys their princes,
and infants[1] shall rule over them.
5 [w]And the people will oppress one
another,
every one his fellow
and every one his neighbor;
the youth will be insolent to the elder,
and the despised to the honorable.
6 For [x]a man will take hold of his
brother
in the house of his father, saying:
"You have a cloak;
you shall be our leader,
and this heap of ruins
shall be under your rule";
7 in that day he will speak out, saying:
"I will not be a [y]healer;[2]
in my house there is neither bread
nor cloak;
you shall not make me
leader of the people."
8 For Jerusalem has stumbled,
and Judah has fallen,
because their [z]speech and their
deeds are against the LORD,
[a]defying his glorious presence.[3]
9 For the look on their faces bears
witness against them;
they proclaim their sin [b]like
Sodom;
they do not hide it.
Woe to them!
[c]For they have brought evil on
themselves.
10 [d]Tell the righteous that it shall be well
with them,
[e]for they shall eat the fruit of their
deeds.

4 [v]ver. 12; Eccles. 10:16
5 [w]See Mic. 7:3-6
6 [x]ch. 4:1
7 [y][ch. 1:6]
8 [z]See Ps. 73:9-11 [a]ch. 65:3
9 [b]Gen. 13:13; 18:20; Ezek. 16:46, 48, 49 [c][Rom. 6:23]
10 [d]Eccles. 8:12; See Deut. 28:1-14 [e]Ps. 128:2
11 [f]Eccles. 8:13; See Deut. 28:15-68
12 [g]ver. 4 [h]See ch. 28:14-22
13 [i]Ps. 7:6; Hos. 4:1
14 [j]Mic. 3:1 [k]Ps. 14:4 [l]Amos 3:10
15 [m][Ps. 94:5]
16 [n]See ch. 32:9-11 [o]ch. 4:4; S. of S. 3:11 [p]ver. 18
17 [q][Deut. 28:60] [o][See ver. 16 above]
18 [r]ver. 16 [s][1 Pet. 3:3]

11 [f]Woe to the wicked! It shall be ill
with him,
for what his hands have dealt out
shall be done to him.
12 My people—[g]infants are their
oppressors,
and women rule over them.
O my people, [h]your guides mislead
you
and they have swallowed up[4] the
course of your paths.
13 The LORD [i]has taken his place to
contend;
he stands to judge peoples.
14 The LORD will enter into judgment
with the [j]elders and princes of his
people:
"It is you who [k]have devoured[5] the
vineyard,
[l]the spoil of the poor is in your
houses.
15 What do you mean by [m]crushing my
people,
by grinding the face of the poor?"
declares the Lord GOD of hosts.
16 The LORD said:
[n]Because [o]the daughters of Zion are
haughty
and walk with outstretched necks,
glancing wantonly with their eyes,
mincing along as they go,
[p]tinkling with their feet,
17 therefore the Lord [q]will strike with a
scab
the heads of [o]the daughters of
Zion,
and the LORD will lay bare their
secret parts.

18 In that day the Lord will take away [r]the
finery of the anklets, the [s]headbands, and

1 Or *caprice* 2 Hebrew *binder of wounds* 3 Hebrew *the eyes of his glory*
4 Or *they have confused* 5 Or *grazed over;* compare Exodus 22:5

3:4 boys . . . infants. The nation will be ruled by people without experience and unable to govern wisely.

3:5 every one his neighbor. The collapse of civilization comes with social strife: rich against poor, young against old.

3:6 cloak. In a collapsing society, someone who has as little as a decent suit of clothes will seem prosperous enough to be made a ruler. But when the people try to draft such a person, he will reply that his wealth is only an illusion; he has no better answers than they have.

3:8 Jerusalem . . . Judah. The fall of Jerusalem (586 B.C.) was a partial fulfillment of this prophecy, as was the devastation caused by Sennacherib's siege of the city in 701 B.C.

3:9 Sodom. Israel has no sense of shame, defying God and acting as if the covenant did not exist. See 1:9, 10.

3:12 O my people. See note 40:1. On the lack of leadership and its consequences, see 3:4–7 and notes.

3:15 crushing my people. Compare the actions of these rulers with those of the ideal Davidic king in 11:3–5.

3:16 daughters of Zion. They live to the fullest at the expense of others. The ornaments are meant to impress others, to provide cash in case of an emergency, and to supply magical protection from sudden disaster. This outward adornment reflects an inner attitude of pride (1 Pet. 3:3, 4).

the [t]crescents; 19 the pendants, the bracelets,
and the scarves; 20 the [u]headdresses, the
armlets, the sashes, the perfume boxes, and
the amulets; 21 the signet rings and [v]nose
rings; 22 the [w]festal robes, the mantles, the
cloaks, and the handbags; 23 the mirrors, the
linen garments, the turbans, and the veils.

24 Instead of [x]perfume there will be
rottenness;
and instead of a [y]belt, a rope;
and instead of [z]well-set hair, [a]baldness;
and instead of a rich robe, a [b]skirt
of sackcloth;
and [c]branding instead of beauty.
25 Your men shall fall by the sword
and your mighty men in battle.
26 And [d]her gates shall lament and
mourn;
empty, she shall [e]sit on the ground.

4 [f]And seven women [g]shall take hold of
[f]one man in that day, saying, "We will
eat our own bread and wear our own
clothes, only let us be called by your name;
[h]take away our reproach."

The Branch of the LORD Glorified

2 In that day [i]the branch of the LORD shall
be beautiful and glorious, and [j]the fruit of
the land shall be the pride and honor of the
survivors of Israel. 3 [k]And he who is left in
Zion and remains in Jerusalem will be called
[l]holy, everyone who has [m]been recorded for
life in Jerusalem, 4 when [n]the Lord shall have
washed away the filth of [o]the daughters of
Zion and cleansed the bloodstains of
Jerusalem from its midst by a spirit of judgment and by [p]a spirit of burning.[1] 5 Then the
LORD will create over the whole site of Mount
Zion and over her assemblies [q]a cloud by
day, and smoke and the shining of a flaming
fire by night; for over all the glory there will
be [r]a canopy. 6 [s]There will be a [t]booth for
shade by day from the heat, and [u]for a refuge
and a shelter from the storm and rain.

18 [t]Judg. 8:21, 26
20 [u]Ex. 39:28; Ezek. 24:17
21 [v]Gen. 24:47; Ezek. 16:12
22 [w][Luke 15:22]
24 [x][Esth. 2:12] [y]Prov. 31:24 [z]1 Pet. 3:3 [a]ch. 15:2; 22:12; Ezek. 27:31; Amos 8:10; Mic. 1:16 [b]ch. 15:3; Gen. 37:34; Lam. 2:10 [c]Lev. 19:28
26 [d]Jer. 14:2; Lam. 1:4 [e]Job 2:13; Lam. 2:10
Chapter 4
1 [f][ch. 13:12] [g]ch. 3:6 [h]See Gen. 30:23
2 [i]Jer. 23:5; 33:15; Zech. 3:8; 6:12 [j][ch. 27:6]
3 [k]ch. 6:13; 10:20 [l]Obad. 17 [m]Ex. 32:32; Luke 10:20; Heb. 12:23; [Ps. 69:28]
4 [n]Ezek. 36:25 [o]ch. 3:16 [p]ch. 33:14; Mal. 3:2; Matt. 3:11; Luke 3:17
5 [q]Ex. 13:21 [r][Rev. 7:15]
6 [s]ch. 25:4 [t]See Ps. 27:5 [u]ch. 25:4

The Vineyard of the LORD Destroyed

5 Let me sing for my beloved
my love song concerning his vineyard:
My beloved had [v]a vineyard
on a very fertile hill.
2 He dug it and cleared it of stones,
and planted it with [w]choice vines;
he built a watchtower in the midst
of it,
and hewed out a wine vat in it;
and [x]he looked for it to yield grapes,
but it yielded wild grapes.

3 And now, O inhabitants of Jerusalem
and men of Judah,
judge between me and my vineyard.
4 [y]What more was there to do for my
vineyard,
that I have not done in it?
[x]When I looked for it to yield
grapes,
why did it yield wild grapes?

Chapter 5 1 [v]Ps. 80:8; Matt. 21:33; Mark 12:1; Luke 20:9; [Hos. 9:10] 2 [w]Jer. 2:21 [x][Matt. 21:19; Mark 11:13; Luke 13:6] 4 [y][Mic. 6:3, 4] [x][See ver. 2 above]

[1] Or *purging*

3:24–4:1 rottenness . . . reproach. The destitution threatened by the day of the Lord is expressed with words associated with bloodshed, war, and captivity.

3:26 gates. Jerusalem is personified and joins in the lament.

4:1 in that day. See note 2:11.

4:2 branch. The term has two possible senses: one is literal, corresponding to the parallel phrase "fruit of the land," and the other is as a messianic title for Jesus Christ, who yields spiritual fruit (11:1–5; Jer. 23:5; Zech. 3:8; John 15:1–8). The remnant find life in Him (6:13). Because Jesus humbled Himself, He is crowned with glory (52:13; 53:12; Phil. 2:9–11).

glorious. This means displaying the splendor and brightness of God. The glory of God is revealed in all His works, but especially in the Messiah (Ps. 19:1; John 1:18).

the survivors. That is, a remnant (1:9 note).

4:3 Zion. See note 1:8.

holy. Consecrated to God, the Holy One of Israel (1:4 note; 62:12).

recorded. Their names are written in the "book" of life (Ex. 32:32, 33; Ps. 69:28; Dan. 12:1; Rev. 20:12).

4:4 spirit. Possibly this is the Holy Spirit, but more likely it refers to the process of purification (cf. 28:6).

burning. This metaphor signifies judgment (1:31; 10:17; 30:27; 42:25). Through the process of refining fire, consuming the faithless and purifying the faithful, God will produce a holy Zion.

4:5 create. In the new act of redemption, the Creator of heaven and earth (40:26; 42:5; 45:12, 18) will renew everything for the sake of His people. The glory of the messianic age is given by God, and does not come from human effort or skill (Jon. 2:9; Eph. 2:4–10).

cloud . . . smoke . . . shining of a flaming fire. Unlike the burning of the fire of judgment in v. 4, this cloud and fire signals God's protective presence, as at the Red Sea (Ex. 13:20–22), over the tabernacle (Ex. 40:34–38), and in the wilderness (Num. 9:15–23). Here His presence covers a restored and sanctified Mount Zion (2:2 note).

4:6 shade. See note 30:2.

refuge. In contrast to human deceptions (28:15, 17), the Lord provides effective shelter from the storm (25:4; cf. Ps. 14:6; 46:1; 62:7; 94:22).

5:1–7 The owner and the vineyard stand for God and His people. The song is fulfilled in Jesus Christ, who replaces sour grapes with new fruit (Matt. 21:33–44; John 15:1–6).

5:2 watchtower . . . grapes. These images reinforce the expectation of an abundant harvest.

wild grapes. The Hebrew means "stinking things."

5 And now I will tell you
what I will do to my vineyard.
I will remove [z]its hedge,
and it shall be devoured;[1]
[a]I will break down its wall,
and it shall be trampled down.
6 I will make it a waste;
it shall not be pruned or hoed,
and [b]briers and thorns shall grow up;
[c]I will also command the clouds
that they rain no rain upon it.

7 [d]For the vineyard of the LORD of hosts
is the house of Israel,
and the men of Judah
are his pleasant planting;
and he looked for justice,
but behold, bloodshed;[2]
for righteousness,
but behold, an outcry![3]

Woe to the Wicked

8 Woe to those who [e]join house to house,
who add field to field,
until there is no more room,
and you are made to dwell alone
in the midst of the land.
9 The LORD of hosts has sworn in my hearing:
[f]"Surely many houses shall be desolate,
large and beautiful houses, without inhabitant.
10 [g]For ten acres[4] of vineyard shall yield
but one bath,
and a [h]homer of seed shall yield
but an ephah."[5]

11 Woe to those who [i]rise early in the morning,
that they may run after strong drink,
who tarry late into the evening
as wine inflames them!
12 [j]They have lyre and harp,
tambourine and flute and wine at their feasts,
[k]but they do not regard the deeds of the LORD,
or see the work of his hands.

13 Therefore my people go into exile
[l]for lack of knowledge;[6]
their [m]honored men go hungry,[7]
and their multitude is parched with thirst.
14 Therefore Sheol has [n]enlarged its appetite
and opened [o]its mouth beyond measure,
and the nobility of Jerusalem[8] and her multitude will go down,
her revelers and he who [p]exults in her.
15 [q]Man is humbled, and each one is brought low,
and the eyes of the haughty[9] are brought low.
16 [r]But the LORD of hosts is exalted[10] in justice,
and the Holy God shows himself holy in righteousness.

5 [z][Jer. 5:10] [a]Ps. 80:12; [Prov. 24:31]
6 [b]See ch. 7:23-25 [c][1 Kin. 17:1; Jer. 14:1, 22]
7 [d][ch. 3:14]; See Ps. 80:8-11
8 [e]Mic. 2:2
9 [f]ch. 6:12
10 [g][Lev. 26:26; Hag. 1:6; 2:16] [h]Ezek. 45:11
11 [i]ver. 22; [Prov. 23:29, 30; Eccles. 10:16, 17]
12 [j]Amos 6:5, 6 [k]ch. 26:11
13 [l]ch. 1:3; Hos. 4:6 [m][Lam. 4:2, 7, 8]
14 [n]Hab. 2:5 [o]Ps. 141:7 [p][ver. 12; Job 1:18, 19]
15 [q]ch. 2:9
16 [r]ch. 2:11, 17

1 Or *grazed over*; compare Exodus 22:5 2 The Hebrew words for *justice* and *bloodshed* sound alike 3 The Hebrew words for *righteous* and *outcry* sound alike 4 Hebrew *ten yoke*, the area ten yoke of oxen can plow in a day 5 A *bath* was about 6 gallons or 22 liters; a *homer* was about 6 bushels or 220 liters; an *ephah* was about 3/5 bushel or 22 liters 6 Or *without their knowledge* 7 Or *die of hunger* 8 Hebrew *her nobility* 9 Hebrew *high* 10 Hebrew *high*

5:5 devoured . . . trampled. God decrees desolation.

5:6 briers and thorns. The weeds represent God's curse (7:23–25; 32:13), that is, the anarchy following war (3:4, 5). God can also turn curse into blessing, replacing the briers and thorns with the pine tree and myrtle (55:13).

5:7 LORD of hosts. See note 1:9.

5:8 This is the first of six exclamations of woe, proclaiming God's displeasure on greed, drunkenness, and other sins. The first woe condemns greed.

add field to field. The land belonged to God (Lev. 25:23), had been allotted to specific families by patrimony (Num. 33:54), and was the basis of livelihood. Deprived of their land, small farmers in Israel became day laborers or slaves.

5:9 houses. God's judgment targets the rich in their self-indulgence. Mansions provide no protection from his eye (24:10 note).

5:10 bath . . . homer . . . ephah. The bath was a liquid measure of about six gallons. For its size, the vineyard would produce practically nothing. Likewise, a homer of seed planted would yield only an ephah of produce. Six bushels of seed would yield about a half bushel at harvest. The land would be cursed (Deut. 28:38, 39).

5:11 wine. The second woe condemns drunkenness. See note 24:11. Overindulgence in drink is a characteristic of social corruption and moral laxity (chs. 22, 28; Amos 4:1–3; 6:6, 7).

5:13 my people. See note 40:1.

exile. The exile with all its miseries is threatened as a judgment on the people, who have shown no knowledge of the right way to behave.

5:14 Sheol. This is the Hebrew word for "the grave," used almost exclusively in poetry. See Prov. 9:18 and notes. Isaiah portrays death as a terrible beast that devours anyone without regard to social class, both the "honored" and the "multitude" (v. 13).

5:16 righteousness. See 1:21 note.

17 Then shall the lambs graze [s]as in
their pasture,
and [t]nomads shall eat among the
ruins of the rich.

18 Woe to those who draw iniquity with
[u]cords of falsehood,
who draw sin as with cart ropes,
19 who say: [v]"Let him be quick,
let him speed his work
that we may see it;
let the counsel of the Holy One of
Israel draw near,
and let it come, that we may
know it!"
20 Woe to [w]those who call evil good
and good evil,
[x]who put darkness for light
and light for darkness,
who put bitter for sweet
and sweet for bitter!
21 Woe to those who are [y]wise in their
own eyes,
and shrewd in their own sight!
22 Woe to those who are [z]heroes at
drinking wine,
and valiant men in mixing strong
drink,
23 who [a]acquit the guilty for a bribe,
and deprive the innocent of his right!
24 Therefore, [b]as the tongue of fire
devours the stubble,
and as dry grass sinks down in the
flame,
so [c]their root will be [d]as rottenness,
and their blossom go up like dust;
for they have [e]rejected the law of the
LORD of hosts,
and have [f]despised the word of the
Holy One of Israel.
25 Therefore [g]the anger of the LORD was
kindled against his people,
and he stretched out his hand
against them and struck them,
and [h]the mountains quaked;
and their corpses were [i]as refuse
in the midst of the streets.
[j]For all this his anger has not turned
away,
and his hand is stretched out still.

26 He will [k]raise a signal for nations
afar off,
and [l]whistle for them [m]from the
ends of the earth;
and behold, quickly, speedily they come!
27 [n]None is weary, none stumbles,
none slumbers or sleeps,
not a waistband is loose,
not a sandal strap broken;
28 [o]their arrows are sharp,
all their bows bent,
their horses' hoofs seem like flint,
and their wheels [p]like the whirlwind.
29 Their roaring is like a lion,
like young lions they roar;
they growl and [q]seize their prey;
they carry it off, and none can rescue.
30 They will growl over it on that day,
like the growling of the sea.
And if one looks to the land,
behold, [r]darkness and distress;
and the light is darkened by its clouds.

17 [s]Mic. 2:12 [t][Judg. 6:3] **18** [u]Prov. 5:22 **19** [v][Ezek. 12:22; 2 Pet. 3:4] **20** [w][Amos 5:7] [x][Job 17:12; Matt. 6:22, 23; Luke 11:34, 35] **21** [y]Prov. 3:7; Rom. 12:16 **22** [z]ver. 11 **23** [a]Ex. 23:8; Prov. 17:15 **24** [b]ch. 47:14; Joel 2:5; [Ex. 15:7] [c]Job 18:16 [d]Hos. 5:12 [e]ch. 30:9 [f]ch. 1:4 **25** [g]2 Kin. 22:13, 17 [h]Jer. 4:24; [Ps. 97:5; Hab. 3:6] [i][2 Kin. 9:37; Jer. 36:30] [j]ch. 9:12, 17, 21; 10:4 **26** [k]ch. 11:12; 13:2; 18:3 [l]ch. 7:18; Zech. 10:8 [m]ch. 10:3; Deut. 28:49 **27** [n]See ch. 10:28-31 **28** [o]Ps. 7:12, 13 [p]ch. 21:1 **29** [q]See 2 Kin. 18:13-16 **30** [r]ch. 8:22

5:18 The third woe condemns those who mock God as they sin.

5:19 the Holy One of Israel. See 1:4 note.

5:20 The fourth woe condemns moral corruption.

darkness . . . light. See notes 2:5 and 5:30.

5:21 The fifth woe condemns pride and self-righteousness.

wise in their own eyes. This is an expression for irrational, arrogant autonomy. A revelation from God, who alone knows all things, is the only firm foundation for knowledge.

5:22 The sixth woe condemns those who pervert justice.

mixing strong drink. This refers to wine and beer with spices added. Once again, as in 5:11, Isaiah speaks of overindulgence.

5:23 bribe. See note 1:23. Bribery involves injustice and greed, as in 5:8.

5:24 fire. See note on "burning" at 4:4.

5:25 the mountains quaked. At the revelation of God's anger, nature quakes (2:19; 13:13; 24:18, 19; Ezek. 32:6–8 note). For a contrasting image of redemption, see 54:10.

streets. See note 24:11.

his anger has not turned away. God is not reconciled, and His wrath hangs over the disobedient (9:12, 17, 21; 10:4; 31:3).

5:26–30 This description of the Assyrian army closely matches its portrayal on ancient Assyrian reliefs; perhaps the poet had seen such troops with his own eyes.

5:26 signal. This is a signal flag (11:10, 12; 18:3; 49:22; 62:10). Like a commander in battle, the Lord summons the nations to execute His judgment (10:5).

nations afar off. These would be Syria, Assyria, Babylon, etc. The imperial Assyrian army was composed of mercenaries hired from all over the Assyrian Empire.

5:30 on that day. See note 2:11.

darkness. This metaphor for depression, alienation, and judgment (8:22; 42:7; 47:5; 60:2) teaches that all who twist justice by living in darkness (5:20; 29:15) will suffer the darkness of God's judgment. By contrast, the light of God will dawn on the needy (9:2; 29:18; 42:7; 49:9; 58:10; 60:1, 2). The Lord is sovereign over darkness and light (45:7).

distress. The Hebrew word means "sorrow," "narrowness." God delivers His own from such confinement (25:4; 63:9).

Isaiah's Vision of the LORD

6 In the year that [s]King Uzziah died I
[t]saw the Lord sitting upon a throne,
high and lifted up; and the train[1] of his
robe filled the temple. 2 Above him stood
the seraphim. Each had [u]six wings: with
two he covered his face, and with two he
covered his feet, and with two he flew.
3 And one called to another and said:

[u]"Holy, holy, holy is the LORD of hosts;
[v]the whole earth is full of his glory!"[2]

4 And [w]the foundations of the thresholds
shook at the voice of him who called, and
[x]the house was filled with smoke. 5 And I
said: "Woe is me! [y]For I am lost; [z]for I am
a man of unclean lips, and I dwell in the
midst of a people of unclean lips; for my
eyes have seen the [a]King, the LORD of
hosts!"
6 Then one of the seraphim flew to me,
having in his hand a burning coal that he
had taken with tongs from the altar. 7 And
he [b]touched my mouth and said: "Behold,
this has touched your lips; your guilt is
taken away, and your sin atoned for.

Isaiah's Commission from the Lord

8 And I heard the voice of the Lord saying,
"Whom shall I send, and who will go for
[c]us?" Then I said, "Here am I! Send me."
9 And he said, "Go, and say to this people:

[d]"'Keep on hearing,[3] but do not
understand;
keep on seeing,[4] but do not
perceive.'
10 [e]Make the heart of this people
[f]dull,[5]
and their ears heavy,
and blind their eyes;
[g]lest they see with their eyes,
and hear with their ears,
and understand with their hearts,
and turn and be healed."
11 Then I said, [h]"How long,
O Lord?"
And he said:
"Until [i]cities lie waste
without inhabitant,
and houses without people,
and the land is a desolate
waste,
12 and the LORD removes people far
away,
and the forsaken places are many
in the midst of the land.
13 [j]And though a tenth remain in it,
it will be burned[6] again,
like a terebinth or an oak,
whose stump [k]remains
when it is felled."
[l]The holy seed[7] is its stump.

Chapter 6
1 [s]ch. 1:1; 2 Chr. 26:16-21 [t][John 12:41]
2 [u]Rev. 4:8
3 [u][See ver. 2 above] [v]Ps. 72:19
4 [w]Amos 9:1 [x]1 Kin. 8:10, 11; Rev. 15:8; [Ex. 19:18]
5 [y][Judg. 13:22] [z][Luke 5:8] [a]ch. 33:17; Jer. 10:10; [1 Sam. 12:12]
7 [b]Jer. 1:9; Dan. 10:16
8 [c]See Gen. 1:26
9 [d]Cited Matt. 13:14, 15; Acts 28:26, 27; [Mark 4:12; Luke 8:10; Rom. 11:8]
10 [e]Cited John 12:40 [f]Ps. 119:70 [g][Jer. 5:21]
11 [h]Ps. 79:5; 89:46 [i][ch. 1:7; 27:10]
13 [j][ch. 10:22] [k][Job 14:7] [l]Ezra 9:2

1 Or *hem* 2 Or *may his glory fill the whole earth* 3 Or *Hear indeed* 4 Or *see indeed* 5 Hebrew *fat* 6 Or *purged* 7 Or *offspring*

6:1 Uzziah. He died in 740 B.C., having suffered from leprosy (2 Chr. 26:16–21).

I saw. Isaiah describes a "theophany," a visible manifestation of God. God's coming is often attended by such phenomena as earthquakes, smoke, fire, and lightning (13:3 note; 29:6; 30:27–31; Ex. 19:18, 19; Ps. 18:7–15; 50:3; 97:2; Mic. 1:3, 4; Nah. 1:3–8; Hab. 3:3–15).

the Lord. *Adonai* in Hebrew, meaning "Sovereign."

throne. The Lord rules heaven and earth from His throne. The choir of seraphim (6:2 note) and the splendor of God's holiness inspired the prophet throughout his ministry.

the temple. In his vision he saw not the temple in Jerusalem, but the heavenly temple (cf. Rev. 4:1–8).

6:2 seraphim. This is a Hebrew word probably meaning "burning ones" (cf. the fiery serpents in Num. 21:6). Representations of angelic creatures with six wings have been discovered in the Near East by archaeologists.

covered his face. The seraphim have no glory to compare with God's and they cannot look on Him directly.

covered his feet. This may be an indication of modesty.

flew. The seraph does the Sovereign's will. Here it is to praise Him.

6:3 Holy, holy, holy. A three-fold repetition is the strongest sort of superlative. Nothing is as holy as God. See note 1:4.

LORD of hosts. See note 1:9.

whole earth. This announcement explains the cosmic perspective of the prophet. God is King of the world, and His salvation and judgment extend to all nations (11:4, 9, 12; 42:1, 4, 5; 65:17; 66:1; cf. Luke 2:14).

glory. See note 4:2, "glorious."

6:5 Woe is me. Isaiah was astonished by the glory of God; like Peter he became afraid (Luke 5:8). He pronounces an oracular curse upon himself.

6:6 altar. The altar from which the live coal was taken is not described. The stress is on the purification necessary for approaching God. The altar symbolizes purification by blood, and the fire, purification by the Spirit. The blood of Christ and the ministry of the Holy Spirit sanctify believers today.

6:7 my mouth . . . your lips. The purification makes the prophet acceptable as a minister of God's words (Jer. 1:9).

6:8 who will go for us. The Lord invited Isaiah to listen in on the sessions of the royal, heavenly court. From this moment on Isaiah is a servant of God's court and proclaims God's message to kings and people alike (cf. 1 Kin. 22:19, 20; Jer. 23:18, 22).

6:9 Go. Isaiah's mission is paradoxical in its effect, as is the proclamation of the word of God (Matt. 13:13–15; Rom. 11:7–10, 25). The prophetic word closes the way of God to those who are rebellious, proud and hypocritical (29:13–16; 65:1–7), but opens it to the deaf, the blind, the humble, and the poor (29:18, 19).

6:13 a tenth. The land will be laid waste, but a remnant will be saved and purified (1:9 note).

stump. The Middle Eastern terebinth and oak trees can produce new shoots even when they appear to have been cut or damaged beyond all hope.

Isaiah Sent to King Ahaz

7 In the days of [m]Ahaz the son of
Jotham, son of Uzziah, king of Judah,
[n]Rezin the king of Syria and [n]Pekah the
son of Remaliah the king of Israel came up
to Jerusalem to wage war against it, but
could not yet mount an attack against it.
2 When the house of David was told,
[o]"Syria is in league with[1] [p]Ephraim," the
heart of Ahaz[2] and the heart of his people
shook as the trees of the forest shake
before the wind.
3 And the LORD said to Isaiah, "Go out to
meet Ahaz, you and [q]Shear-jashub[3] your
son, at the end of [r]the conduit of the upper
pool on the highway to the Washer's Field.
4 And say to him, [s]'Be careful, [t]be quiet,
do not fear, and do not let your heart be
faint because of these two [u]smoldering
stumps of firebrands, at the fierce anger of
Rezin and Syria and [v]the son of Remaliah.
5 Because Syria, with Ephraim and [v]the son
of Remaliah, has devised evil against you,
saying, 6 "Let us go up against Judah and
terrify it, and let us conquer it[4] for ourselves, and set up the son of Tabeel as king
in the midst of it," 7 thus says the Lord
GOD:

[w]" 'It shall not stand,
and it shall not come to pass.
8 For the head of Syria is [x]Damascus,
and the head of Damascus is Rezin.
(Within sixty-five years Ephraim will be
broken to pieces so that it will no longer be
a people.)
9 " 'And the head of Ephraim is Samaria,
and the head of Samaria is [y]the
son of Remaliah.
[z]If you[5] are not firm in faith,
you will not be firm at all.' "

The Sign of Immanuel

10 Again the LORD spoke to Ahaz, 11 "Ask
[a]a sign of the LORD your[6] God; let it
be deep as Sheol or high as heaven."
12 But Ahaz said, "I will not ask, and I will
not put the LORD to the test." 13 And he[7]
said, "Hear then, O house of David! Is
it too little for you to weary men, that
you [b]weary my God also? 14 Therefore the
[c]Lord himself will give you a sign. [d]Behold,
the [e]virgin shall conceive and bear a
son, and shall call his name [f]Immanuel.[8]

1 Hebrew *Syria has rested upon* 2 Hebrew *his heart* 3 *Shear-jashub* means *A remnant shall return* 4 Hebrew *let us split it open* 5 The Hebrew for *you* is plural in verses 9, 13, 14 6 The Hebrew for *you* and *your* is singular in verses 11, 16, 17 7 That is, Isaiah 8 *Immanuel* means *God is with us*

Chapter 7
1 [m]ch. 1:1 [n]2 Kin. 15:37; 16:5
2 [o][ch. 8:12] [p]ch. 9:9
3 [q][ch. 8:3, 18] [r]ch. 36:2; 2 Kin. 18:17
4 [s][ch. 8:12] [t][Ex. 14:13] [u][Amos 4:11; Zech. 3:2] [v]ver. 1
5 [v][See ver. 4 above]
7 [w]ch. 8:10
8 [x]Gen. 14:15
9 [y]ver. 1 [z][2 Chr. 20:20]
11 [a]See 2 Kin. 19:29
13 [b]ch. 43:24
14 [c]ch. 37:30; 38:7, 8 [d]ch. 9:6; Cited Matt. 1:23; [Luke 1:31, 34] [e]Gen. 24:43 (Heb.); Ex. 2:8 (Heb.); Ps. 68:25 (Heb.); Prov. 30:19 (Heb.) [f]ch. 8:8, 10

7:1–11:16 These oracles of judgment and hope are associated with the war between Judah and a coalition of Israel and Syria (734–732 B.C.). Ahaz, king of Judah, was seriously threatened by the alliance of Pekah, king of Israel, with Rezin, king of Syria (2 Kin. 16:5–18; 2 Chr. 28:16–21). They threatened to invade Judah if Ahaz would not help them against Assyria.

7:2 the house of David. This expression means the current head of the house, Ahaz. It recalls the Lord's covenant with David, granting him an eternal offspring and kingdom (2 Sam. 7:12–16). The attempt to replace his dynasty with another ("the son of Tabeel," v. 6) cannot succeed because God's promises are at stake.

shook. Ahaz, the proud king, was unable to calm his people. The response of the leader created panic among the people (22:3 note).

7:3 Shear-jashub. The name means "a remnant shall return" (10:20–22). It is a promise of salvation and life for the faithful beyond the imminent doom of the unfaithful. Judah may suffer, but a remnant will remain.

7:4 two smoldering stumps. Two kingdoms were about to be destroyed: Damascus in 732 B.C. by Tiglath-pileser III, and Samaria in 722 B.C. by Sargon II.

7:7 Lord GOD. See note 25:8. The Lord voids the counsel of kings (8:9, 10; 40:23; Ps. 33:10, 11).

7:8 sixty-five years. God will fulfill His promises after Ahaz's death (2 Kin. 17:24–41).

7:9 firm . . . firm. This is a play on different meanings of the same Hebrew word. Faith means knowing God's promise, assenting to it intellectually, and trusting Him to keep it.

7:11 a sign. A sign would authenticate the prophetic message concerning the future.

deep . . . high. Nothing is outside Yahweh's sovereignty (Deut. 10:14; Ps. 139:8; Rom. 8:39).

7:13 house of David. See note 7:2.

7:14 virgin. The Hebrew word occurs seven times in the Old Testament. It means a young woman of marriageable age, normally a virgin (Gen. 24:43). The Septuagint (the Greek translation of the Old Testament made about 150 B.C.) translated with a word more specifically meaning "virgin." The New Testament understands Isaiah to be designating the Virgin Mary (Matt. 1:23). See "The Virgin Birth of Jesus" at Luke 1:27.

Immanuel. "God with us." The name conveys God's promise to save, bless, and protect His children. The identity of the virgin and the child has been the subject of considerable discussion. Three major views have been proposed. First, some, especially Jews of the second century A.D., understood the prophecy to mean Ahaz's wife and her child, Hezekiah (2 Kin. 18:2). But as Jerome (c. 400 A.D.) pointed out, Hezekiah was already born. Second, others identify the woman as Isaiah's wife or a woman betrothed to him (8:3). The child is then Isaiah's son, Maher-shalal-hash-baz. This interpretation is questionable. The Hebrew term translated "virgin" would not normally be used for a woman who was already a mother (of Shear-jashub, 7:3). If someone engaged to the prophet is meant, it becomes necessary to assume that his first wife had died. Also, the interpretation requires that the child have contradictory names: "God Is With Us" (Immanuel) and "The Spoil Speeds, the Prey Hastens" (Maher-shalal-hash-baz). Though not impossible, it seems unlikely. Finally, the child's diet of "curds and honey" suggests that He would grow up after Judah's destruction (v. 15 note). Tradition suggests a third interpretation, identifying the child as the Messiah, a divine personage whose birth is above nature. It equates the Child named "Immanuel" with the Child possessing God's titles in 9:6, and with the "Branch" of ch. 11. According to Matthew, the virgin is Mary and the Child is Jesus Christ (Matt. 1:22, 23). In v. 16, the birth seems nevertheless to be imminent. Perhaps the prophecy has a partial fulfillment in the birth of Isaiah's son Maher-shalal-hash-baz (8:1–3), while the definitive fulfillment waits for the birth of Jesus Christ, who secures God's throne forever.

15 He shall eat [g]curds and honey when he
knows how to refuse the evil and choose
the good. 16 [h]For before the boy knows
how to refuse the evil and choose the
good, the land whose two kings you
dread will be [i]deserted. 17 [j]The LORD will
bring upon you and upon your people
and upon your father's house such days
as have not come since the day that
[k]Ephraim departed from Judah—the king
of Assyria."
18 In that day the LORD will [l]whistle for
the fly that is at the end of the streams of
Egypt, and for the bee that is in the land of
Assyria. 19 And they will all come and settle
in the steep ravines, and [m]in the clefts of
the rocks, and on all the thornbushes, and
on all the pastures.[1]
20 In that day [n]the Lord will [o]shave with a
razor that is [p]hired beyond [q]the River—
with the king of Assyria—the head and the
hair of the feet, and it will sweep away the
beard also.
21 [r]In that day a man will keep alive a
young cow and two sheep, 22 and because
of the abundance of milk that they give, he
will eat curds, for everyone who is left in
the land will eat [s]curds and honey.
23 In that day every place where there
used to be a thousand vines, worth a
thousand shekels[2] of silver, will become
[t]briers and thorns. 24 [u]With bow and
arrows a man will come there, for all the

15 [g]ver. 22
16 [h][ch. 8:4] [i]ch. 6:12
17 [j]ch. 8:7; [2 Chr. 28:20] [k]1 Kin. 12:16
18 [l]ch. 5:26
19 [m]ch. 2:19; Jer. 13:4; 16:16
20 [n]ch. 24:1; See 2 Kin. 18:13-16 [o]Ezek 5:1 [p][ch. 10:5, 15] [q]ch. 8:7; 11:15
21 [r][ch. 5:17]
22 [s]ver. 15
23 [t]ch. 5:6
24 [u][Judg. 5:11]
25 [v]ch. 32:13, 14 [t][See ver. 23 above]
Chapter 8
1 [w]ch. 30:8
2 [x][ch. 43:10] [y]2 Kin. 16:10, 11, 15, 16
3 [z][Hos. 1:4]
4 [a][ch. 7:16] [b]See ch. 7:8, 9
6 [c][Neh. 3:15; John 9:7, 11] [d]See ch. 7:1, 4
7 [e][ch. 17:12, 13] [f]See ch. 7:20 [g][Jer. 46:8]

land will be briers and thorns. 25 [v]And as
for all the hills that used to be hoed with
a hoe, you will not come there for fear [t]of
briers and thorns, but they will become a
place where cattle are let loose and where
sheep tread.

The Coming Assyrian Invasion

8 Then the LORD said to me, "Take a
large tablet [w]and write on it in common characters,[3] 'Belonging to Maher-
shalal-hash-baz.'[4] 2 And [x]I will get reliable
witnesses, [y]Uriah the priest and Zechariah
the son of Jeberechiah, to attest for me."
3 And I went to the prophetess, and she
conceived and bore a son. Then the LORD
said to me, [z]"Call his name Maher-shalal-
hash-baz; 4 [a]for before the boy knows how
to cry 'My father' or 'My mother,' the
[a]wealth of [b]Damascus and the spoil of
[b]Samaria will be carried away before the
king of Assyria."
5 The LORD spoke to me again: 6 "Because
this people have refused the waters of
[c]Shiloah that flow gently, and rejoice over
[d]Rezin and the son of Remaliah, 7 therefore,
behold, the Lord is bringing up against
them [e]the waters of [f]the River, mighty and
many, the king of Assyria and all his glory.
And it [g]will rise over all its channels and go

1 Or *watering holes*, or *brambles* 2 A *shekel* was about 2/5 ounce or 11 grams 3 Hebrew *with a man's stylus* 4 *Maher-shalal-hash-baz* means *The spoil speeds, the prey hastens*

7:15 curds and honey. This is not a typical food for infants, but points to a time when people will have to live off unworked fields (v. 22). The Child is identified with the remnant.

when he knows how to refuse the evil. Self-indulgence made the failed leadership of Israel insensitive to social and spiritual values (5:11–23), but this diet will sensitize Christ to the work of the Lord (42:1–4).

7:16 For before. The verse seems to mean that before the time required for a child to become accountable—twelve years—Pekah and Remaliah will both be defeated. In this understanding, "child" will point primarily to Isaiah's son, and secondarily to Christ.

7:18 In that day. See note 2:11. The fall of Damascus, of Samaria, and the devastation of Judah are foretastes of the events of the Last Judgment.

fly . . . bee. These insects swarm in great numbers, like the hordes of invaders.

7:19 steep ravines . . . clefts. Traditional hiding places will provide no escape (2:19).

7:20 razor that is hired. Shaving the head is a sign of mourning (15:2) and a way of humiliating conquered enemies (2 Sam. 10:4, 5). Ahaz had hired Assyria to help him against Syria and Samaria, but the Lord would use Assyria to humiliate Israel instead (v. 17).

7:22 abundance. The land will be so depopulated that this limited food will seem abundant.

curds and honey. See note on v. 15. The remnant will have something to eat.

7:23–25 In that day. The cultivated land will return to weeds, barely fit for grazing.

8:1 tablet. Probably a polished piece of wood like a signboard. The meaning of the name is given in the text note and explained in v. 4.

8:2 witnesses. The apostate king, Ahaz, was forced to take part in the sign of Immanuel's birth (7:10–14). Now an apostate priest, Uriah (2 Kin. 16:10, 11), and a presumably false prophet, Zechariah, are forced to become parties to this prophecy.

8:3 prophetess. Isaiah refers to his wife in this way, perhaps because of her association with him as a prophet, or perhaps because she was a prophet in her own right (Judg. 4:4; 2 Kin. 22:14).

Maher-shalal-hash-baz. See text note on v. 1. The name signifies the rapid devastation of Syria, Israel, and Judah, but also the presence of God with the remnant and the impending fulfillment of God's word.

8:6 this people. That is, Judah.

waters of Shiloah. Perhaps this refers to a stream flowing from the Gihon Spring (2 Chr. 32:30). It is a symbol of the Lord's provision, which the people despised (cf. 1:30 note; Jer. 2:13; Zech. 4:10).

rejoice. The people may have looked forward to the fall of Rezin, king of Syria, without considering that the word of judgment applied to Judah as well.

8:7 the River. The River Euphrates, standing for the Assyrian invaders. The Euphrates contrasts with the soft waters of Shiloah (v. 6).

over all its banks, 8 and it will sweep on into
Judah, it will overflow and pass on, [h]reach-
ing even to the neck, and its [i]outspread
wings will fill the breadth of your land,
[j]O Immanuel."

9 Be broken,[1] you peoples, and [k]be
shattered;[2]
give ear, all you far countries;
strap on your armor and be
shattered;
strap on your armor and be
shattered.
10 Take counsel together, but it will
come to nothing;
speak a word, [l]but it will not
stand,
for God [m]is with us.[3]

Fear God, Wait for the LORD

11 For the LORD spoke thus to me with his
strong hand upon me, and [n]warned me not
to walk in the way of this people, saying:
12 "Do not call [o]conspiracy all that this people calls conspiracy, and [p]do not fear what
they fear, nor be in dread. 13 But the LORD
of hosts, [q]him you shall regard as holy. Let
him be your fear, and let him be your
dread. 14 And he will become a [r]sanctuary
and [s]a stone of offense and a rock of stumbling to both houses of Israel, a trap and a
snare to the inhabitants of Jerusalem.
15 And many [t]shall stumble on it. They shall
fall and be broken; they shall be snared
and taken."

16 Bind up [u]the testimony; [v]seal the
teaching[4] among my disciples. 17 I will
[w]wait for the LORD, who is [x]hiding his face
from the house of Jacob, and I will hope in
him. 18 [y]Behold, I and [z]the children whom
the LORD has given me are signs and por-
tents in Israel from the LORD of hosts, who
dwells on Mount Zion. 19 And when they
say to you, "Inquire of the [a]mediums and
the necromancers who chirp and mutter,"
should not a people inquire of their God?
Should they inquire of [b]the dead on behalf
of the living? 20 [c]To the teaching and to the
testimony! If they will not speak according
to this word, it is because they have no
[d]dawn. 21 They will pass through the land,[5]
greatly distressed and hungry. And when
they are hungry, they will be enraged and
will speak contemptuously against[6] their
king and their God, and turn their faces
upward. 22 [e]And they will look to the earth,
but behold, distress and darkness, the
gloom of anguish. And they will be thrust
into [f]thick darkness.

For to Us a Child Is Born

9 [7] But there will be no [g]gloom for her
who was in anguish. In the former
time he [h]brought into contempt the land of
[i]Zebulun and the land of Naphtali, but in
the latter time he [j]has made glorious the
way of the sea, the land beyond the Jordan,
Galilee of the nations.[8]

8 [h]ch. 30:28 [i][ch. 36:1] [j]ch. 7:14
9 [k][Dan. 2:34, 35]
10 [l]ch. 7:7 [m][ver. 8; Rom. 8:31]
11 [n][Ezek. 2:8]
12 [o][ch. 7:2] [p]Cited 1 Pet. 3:14, 15
13 [q]See Num. 20:12
14 [r]Ezek. 11:16 [s]Cited Rom. 9:33; 1 Pet. 2:8; [ch. 28:16]
15 [t][ch. 28:13; Matt. 21:44; Luke 20:18]
16 [u]ver. 1, 2 [v]Dan. 12:4
17 [w]Ps. 27:14; 33:20; Hab. 2:3 [x]ch. 1:15; 54:8; Deut. 31:17
18 [y]Cited Heb. 2:13 [z][ch. 7:3]
19 [a]ch. 19:3; 2 Kin. 21:6; 23:24; 2 Chr. 33:6; See Lev. 19:31 [b][Ps. 106:28]; See 1 Sam. 28:11-14
20 [c][Luke 16:29] [d][ch. 60:1]
22 [e]ch. 5:30 [f]Nah. 1:8
Chapter 9
1 [g][ch. 8:22] [h][2 Kin. 15:29; 2 Chr. 16:4] [i]Cited Matt. 4:15, 16 [j]ch. 26:15

[1] Or *Be evil* [2] Or *dismayed* [3] The Hebrew for *God is with us* is *Immanuel* [4] Or *law*; also verse 20 [5] Hebrew *it* [6] Or *speak contemptuously by* [7] Ch 8:23 in Hebrew [8] Or *of the Gentiles*

8:8 the neck. The implication is that Assyria will almost, but not quite, annihilate Judah. At the height of the Assyrian invasion in 701 B.C., Jerusalem did escape.

O Immanuel. See v. 10; 7:14 note. Isaiah bestows the name of the virgin's Child on Judah as the object of God's care.

8:9 you peoples. Syria and Israel.

8:10 Take counsel together. See note 11:2.

God is with us. In Hebrew, "Immanuel." God is with the remnant of Judah, which will not be destroyed (v. 8, notes; 7:14 note).

8:11 with his strong hand. Isaiah had an experience of inner compulsion from the Spirit of God (Ezek. 1:3; 3:14).

8:12 conspiracy. The people considered Isaiah a traitor because he said that Ahab and his administration were wrong to rely on Assyria.

8:13 fear . . . dread. It is not people (v. 12), but the Lord who is the object of fear. He is the ultimate authority to whom all must submit, in whom all may trust, and to whom everyone must render an account (12:2; 33:6; 50:10; 59:19; Ps. 25:12–15; 34:11–14).

8:14 sanctuary. A place of refuge.

both houses. Judah and Israel.

8:16 testimony . . . teaching. This could refer to the revelation of God (1:10) to Moses (Deut. 4:44, 45), to Isaiah, or to both.

disciples. Isaiah's followers wrote down and sealed his prophecy like a law so that it could be known whether it failed or was fulfilled by events (vv. 1, 2, 20). This is the test of a true prophet (Deut. 18:21, 22; Jer. 28:9), through whom God is known and trusted.

8:17 wait . . . hope. See 25:9; 26:8; 30:18; 33:2; 40:31; 49:23; 64:4.

hiding his face. The covenant God is free in bestowing grace (54:8; 64:7; Deut. 31:18; 32:20).

8:18 I and the children . . . signs. The children's names were significant (7:3; 8:1, 3 and notes).

8:19 mediums and the necromancers. Diviners were prohibited by God's law (Is. 2:6 note).

chirp and mutter. The mediums promised contact with the dead, who in the popular understanding were insubstantial and weak-voiced. Isaiah regards calling on them as contemptible.

8:20 teaching . . . testimony. See note 8:16.

dawn. See note 2:5.

8:22 darkness. This is a figure for despair (5:30 note; 50:10).

9:1 Zebulun . . . Naphtali. These regions in Galilee were the first to suffer from the Assyrian invasion of 732 B.C. (2 Kin. 15:29).

2[1] [i]The people [k]who walked in darkness
have seen a great light;
those who dwelt in a land of [l]deep
darkness,
on them has light shined.
3 [m]You have multiplied the nation;
you have increased its joy;
they rejoice before you
as with [n]joy at the harvest,
as they [o]are glad [p]when they divide
the spoil.
4 [q]For the yoke of his burden,
[r]and the staff for his shoulder,
the rod of his oppressor,
you have broken as [s]on the day of
Midian.
5 [t]For every boot of the tramping
warrior in battle tumult
and every garment rolled in blood
will be burned as fuel for the fire.
6 [u]For to us a child is born,
to us [v]a son is given;
[w]and the government shall be [x]upon[2]
his shoulder,
and his name shall be called[3]
Wonderful [y]Counselor, [z]Mighty
God,
[a]Everlasting [b]Father, Prince of
[c]Peace.
7 Of the increase of his government
and of peace
[d]there will be no end,
on the throne of David and over his
kingdom,
to establish it and to uphold it
[e]with justice and with righteousness
from this time forth and
forevermore.
[f]The zeal of the LORD of hosts will do
this.

Judgment on Arrogance and Oppression

8 The Lord has sent a word against
Jacob,
and it will fall on Israel;
9 and all the people will know,
[g]Ephraim and the inhabitants of
Samaria,
who say in pride and in arrogance
of heart:
10 "The bricks have fallen,
but we will build with dressed
stones;
the sycamores have been cut down,
but we will put cedars in their
place."
11 But the LORD raises the adversaries of
Rezin against him,
and stirs up his enemies.
12 [h]The Syrians on the east and [i]the
Philistines on the west
devour Israel with open mouth.
[j]For all this his anger has not turned
away,
and his hand is stretched out still.
13 The people [k]did not turn to him who
struck them,
nor inquire of the LORD of hosts.

2 [i][See ver. 1 above] [k][Luke 1:79; Eph. 5:8, 14] [l]See Job 3:5
3 [m]ch. 26:15 [n]Ps. 4:7; [John 4:36] [o]Ps. 119:162; [1 Sam. 30:16] [p][Judg. 5:30]
4 [q]ch. 10:27; 14:25; Nah. 1:13; [Matt. 11:29] [r]ch. 10:5, 24; 14:5 [s]ch. 10:26; Ps. 83:9; See Judg. 7:19-25; 8:10-21
5 [t]Ezek. 39:9
6 [u]Luke 2:11; [John 3:16] [v]ch. 7:14 [w][Matt. 28:18; 1 Cor. 15:25] [x]ch. 22:22 [y][ch. 28:29] [z]ch. 10:21; Deut. 10:17; Neh. 9:32; Jer. 32:18; [Ps. 45:3] [a]Ps. 72:17 [b]ch. 63:16; [John 14:18] [c]Ps. 72:7; [Eph. 2:14]; See ch. 11:6-9
7 [d]Ps. 89:4; Luke 1:32, 33
[e]Jer. 23:5 [f]ch. 37:32; 2 Kin. 19:31; [Zech. 1:14]
9 [g]ch. 7:2, 5, 8, 9, 17
12 [h][2 Kin. 16:6] [i][2 Chr. 28:18] [j]ver. 17, 21; ch. 5:25; 10:4
13 [k][ch. 1:5; Hos. 7:10]

1 Ch 9:1 in Hebrew 2 Or *is upon* 3 Or *is called*

9:2 light. See note 2:5.

deep darkness. The Assyrians cast their terrible shadow over the land and the people (cf. Ps. 23:4; 44:19; 107:10). Yet there is hope.

9:3 joy. God opens up a new future for the humble (29:19) where gloom had previously existed (35:10; 51:3; 61:7). This new joy finds expression in the metaphors of harvest and of victory. Contrast 5:10; 8:4.

9:4 yoke . . . staff. These are figures of oppression (10:27; 14:25; 47:6; contrast at Matt. 11:29, 30).

day of Midian. A reference to Gideon's defeat of the Midianites (10:26, 27; Judg. 6:7; 7:22–25).

9:5 The debris left from battle can be removed and burned when the fighting stops. God will bring an end to war (2:4; Ps. 46:9, 10; 2 Cor. 10:4).

9:6 child . . . son. The good news is the birth of Jesus Christ. The four royal names express His divine and human qualities, giving assurance that He is indeed "Immanuel" (7:14).

born . . . given. The verbs are consistent with His humanity and deity respectively.

Mighty God. As a warrior, God protects His people (10:21; Deut. 10:17; Jer. 32:18).

Everlasting Father. The Father and King cares for His subjects (40:9–11; 65:17–25; Matt. 18:12–14; 23:9–12; Rom. 8:15–17).

Prince of Peace. His government brings peace (2:4; 11:6–9; Ps. 72:7; Zech. 9:10; Luke 2:14).

9:7 throne of David. He is a descendant of David (11:1 note), who will establish the kingdom of God in "justice and with righteousness" (1:21 note).

zeal. God guarantees that this will be fulfilled (37:32; 42:13; Zech. 1:14).

9:8–10:4 The Lord will judge Israel (the northern kingdom) and its capital Samaria. The northern kingdom is also sometimes called Ephraim. (Judah is the southern kingdom, with Jerusalem as its capital.)

9:9 in pride and in arrogance. Their motivation was to preserve and glorify themselves. Compare also their words "we will . . . we will" in v. 10 (Gen. 11:3, 4; Is. 5:21).

9:10 dressed stones . . . cedars. The people thought they were going to start rebuilding with the best materials, when in reality there was destruction ahead.

9:11, 12 adversaries of Rezin. Foes. The Assyrians (7:1 note; 7:20 note; 8:7 note) will attack from the north and the Philistines from the south. The Lord will raise up many enemies.

9:12 his anger has not turned away. This refrain is also found in 9:17, 21; 10:4 (cf. 31:3). See note 5:25.

9:13 did not turn. They were unresponsive to divine discipline (Amos 4:6, 8–11). They did not depend wholly on the Lord or seek Him with diligence (8:19; 11:10; 31:1; 55:6; 58:2; 65:10).

14 So the LORD cut off from Israel [l]head
and tail,
palm branch and reed in one
day—
15 [m]the elder and honored man is the
head,
and [n]the prophet who teaches lies
is the tail;
16 for those who guide this people have
been leading them astray,
and those who are guided by them
are swallowed up.
17 Therefore the Lord does not [o]rejoice
over their young men,
and has no compassion on their
fatherless and widows;
for everyone is [p]godless and an
evildoer,
and every mouth speaks [q]folly.[1]
[j]For all this his anger has not turned
away,
and his hand is stretched out
still.

18 For wickedness burns like [r]a fire;
it consumes briers and thorns;
it kindles the thickets of the
forest,
and they roll upward in a column
of smoke.
19 Through the wrath of the LORD of
hosts
the land is scorched,
and [s]the people are like fuel for
the fire;
[t]no one spares another.
20 [u]They slice meat on the right, but are
still hungry,
and they devour on the left, but
are not satisfied;
[v]each devours the flesh of his
own arm,
21 Manasseh devours Ephraim, and
Ephraim devours Manasseh;
together they are [w]against Judah.
[x]For all this his anger has not turned
away,
and his hand is stretched out still.

10 Woe to those who [y]decree
iniquitous decrees,
and the writers who [z]keep writing
oppression,
2 to turn aside the needy from justice
and [a]to rob the poor of my people
of their right,
that widows may be their spoil,
and that they may make the
fatherless their prey!
3 What will you do on [b]the day of
punishment,
in the ruin that will come [c]from
afar?
To whom will you flee for help,
and where will you leave your
wealth?
4 Nothing remains but to crouch
among the prisoners
or fall among the slain.
[d]For all this his anger has not turned
away,
and his hand is stretched out still.

Judgment on Arrogant Assyria

5 Ah, Assyria, [e]the rod of my anger;
the staff in their hands is my
fury!
6 Against a [f]godless nation I send him,
and against the people of my wrath
I command him,
to take [g]spoil and seize plunder,
and to [h]tread them down like the
mire of the streets.

1 Or *speaks disgraceful things*

14 [l]ch. 19:15; Deut. 28:13
15 [m]ch. 3:2, 3 [n][ch. 28:7; Mic. 3:5]
17 [o]Ps. 147:10, 11 [p]ch. 10:6 [q]Gen. 34:7 [j][See ver. 12 above]
18 [r]Ps. 83:14; [James 3:5]
19 [s]ch. 24:6 [t][Mic. 7:2]
20 [u]ch. 8:21 [v]ch. 49:26; See Deut. 28:53-57
21 [w][ch. 11:13]; See 2 Chr. 28:6-9 [x]See ver. 12
Chapter 10
1 [y][Ps. 94:20] [z]Jer. 8:8
2 [a]ch. 5:23
3 [b]Jer. 5:29; Hos. 9:7; [Luke 19:44] [c]ch. 5:26
4 [d]See ch. 9:12
5 [e]ver. 24; ch. 9:4; [Mic. 5:1; 6:9]
6 [f]ch. 9:17 [g]See 2 Kin. 18:14-16 [h]ch. 5:5

9:14 head and tail. These figures represent the civil and religious leadership, as explained in v. 15 (cf. 3:1–3; 30:10 note). The same figures, including the "palm branch and reed," are used of Egyptian leaders in 19:15.

9:17 fatherless and widows. See note 1:16–18. The gravity of God's anger is vividly expressed when it is said that He will have no mercy on the fatherless.

everyone is godless and an evildoer. Sin is found in every person, even the fatherless and widow, and it corrupts both their thoughts and their deeds (Gen. 6:5; 8:21).

9:20, 21 devour . . . devours. Pride, narcissism, and greed destroy the fiber of society, especially the covenant relationship among the tribes. Historically, Manasseh had fought Ephraim (Judg. 12:4), and together they battled Judah during the war with Israel and Syria.

10:1–4 The principle of retribution is an important biblical teaching. People reap what they sow, whether to destruction or benefit (Gal. 6:7, 8).

10:2 justice. See note 1:21. On social injustice, see 1:23.

poor . . . fatherless. See 1:16–18; 11:4; Ps. 9:18 and notes.

my people. See note 40:1.

10:3 day of punishment. The day of the Lord (2:11 note).

from afar. The desolation brought by the Assyrians.

10:5 rod of my anger. God makes the nations serve Him as instruments of His will, but they continue to be responsible for their acts (5:25; 7:20 and notes). God's anger is against those who administer His kingdom on earth corruptly, both rulers and people (9:12, 17, 21; 10:4, 25).

10:6 godless nation. This includes Israel and Judah (v. 11).

7 But he [i]does not so intend,
and his heart does not so think;
but it is in his heart to destroy,
and to cut off nations not a few;
8 for he says:
[j]"Are not my commanders all kings?
9 [k]Is not [l]Calno like [m]Carchemish?
Is not [n]Hamath like [o]Arpad?
[p]Is not [q]Samaria like
Damascus?
10 As my hand has reached to [r]the
kingdoms of the idols,
whose carved images were greater
than those of Jerusalem and
Samaria,
11 shall I not do to Jerusalem and [s]her
idols
[t]as I have done to Samaria and her
images?"

12 [u]When the Lord has finished all his
work on Mount Zion and on Jerusalem,
[v]he[1] will punish the speech of the arrogant
heart of the king of Assyria and the boastful look in his eyes. 13 [w]For he says:

"By the strength of my hand I have
done it,
and by my wisdom, for I have
understanding;
I remove the boundaries of
peoples,
and plunder their treasures;
like a bull I bring down those who
sit on thrones.
14 My hand has found like a nest
the wealth of the peoples;
and as one gathers eggs that have
been forsaken,
so I have gathered all the earth;
and there was none that moved a
wing
or opened the mouth or
chirped."

7 [i][Mic. 4:12] 8 [j][2 Kin. 18:24] 9 [k]2 Kin. 19:12, 13 [l][Gen. 10:10; Amos 6:2] [m]2 Chr. 35:20; Jer. 46:2 [n]ch. 11:11; Amos 6:2; Zech. 9:2 [o]2 Kin. 18:34 [p][2 Kin. 16:9; 17:6] [q]ch. 7:9 10 [r][2 Kin. 19:17, 18] 11 [s]2 Kin. 18:34 [t]ch. 2:8 12 [u][ch. 29:4, 5; 30:18; 2 Kin. 19:31] [v]See 2 Kin. 19:35-37 13 [w]ch. 37:23-25; 2 Kin. 19:22-24

15 [x][ver. 5; ch. 29:16; 45:9; Rom. 9:17] 16 [y]Ps. 78:31 [z][ch. 30:33] 17 [a][Obad. 18] [b]ch. 37:23 [c]ch. 27:4; [ch. 9:18; Nah. 1:10] [d][ch. 9:14; 2 Kin. 19:35] 18 [e]ver. 33; [ch. 2:13] [f][Ex. 17:11] 20 [g]ver. 27; ch. 2:11 [h]ch. 4:2 [i][2 Kin. 16:7; 2 Chr. 28:20, 21] [j]2 Kin. 19:14 21 [k]ch. 9:6 22 [l]Cited Rom. 9:27, 28 [m][ch. 6:13] [n]ch. 28:22

15 Shall [x]the axe boast over him who
hews with it,
or the saw magnify itself against
him who wields it?
As if a rod should wield him who
lifts it,
or as if a staff should lift him who
is not wood!
16 Therefore the Lord GOD of hosts
will send wasting sickness among
his [y]stout warriors,
and under his glory [z]a burning will
be kindled,
like the burning of fire.
17 [a]The light of Israel will become a fire,
and [b]his Holy One a flame,
and [c]it will burn and devour
his thorns and briers [d]in one day.
18 The glory of [e]his forest and of his
fruitful land
the LORD will destroy, both soul
and body,
and it will be as when [f]a sick man
wastes away.
19 The remnant of the trees of his forest
will be so few
that a child can write them down.

The Remnant of Israel Will Return

20 [g]In that day [h]the remnant of Israel
and the survivors of the house of Jacob
will no more [i]lean on him who struck
them, but [j]will lean on the LORD, the
Holy One of Israel, in truth. 21 [k]A remnant
will return, the remnant of Jacob, [k]to the
mighty God. 22 [l]For though your people
Israel be as the sand of the sea, [m]only a
remnant of them will return. [n]De-
struction is decreed, overflowing with
righteousness. 23 For the Lord GOD of
hosts will make a full end, as decreed, in
the midst of all the earth.

1 Hebrew *I*

10:9 Calno . . . Damascus. These cities were conquered by Assyria: Calno (Calneh, Amos 6:2) in 738 B.C.; Carchemish in 717 B.C.; Hamath in 738 and 720 B.C.; Arpad in 740 B.C.; Samaria in 722 B.C.; and Damascus in 732 B.C. See also 36:19; 37:12, 13.

10:10 my hand. Assyria boasts of its power (cf. Dan. 4:30; Luke 12:18–20).

kingdoms. See note 13:4.

10:12 Zion. See note 1:8.

10:13, 14 These verses are a restatement of vv. 5–11. For similar expressions of pride, see 14:13, 14; Ezek. 28:2–5.

10:15 axe . . . staff. See note on v. 5.

10:17 light. See note 2:5.

10:18 glory. See note 4:2. What men think should be honored or despised means little before God's fiery judgment.

forest . . . fruitful land. The Assyrian pride will end quickly like thorns in a fire. Little will remain (v. 19).

10:20 In that day. See note 2:11.

remnant. See note 1:8.

10:22 sand of the sea. This phrase recalls God's promise to Abraham (Gen. 22:17; cf. 1 Kin. 4:20).

decreed. God is determined in His judgment (v. 23; 28:22).

10:23 the Lord GOD of hosts. See notes 1:9, 24.

24 Therefore thus says the Lord GOD of
hosts: "O my people, [o]who dwell in Zion,
[p]be not afraid of the Assyrians when they
strike with the rod and lift up their staff
against you as [q]the Egyptians did. 25 For [r]in
a very little while my fury will come to an
end, and my anger will be directed to their
destruction. 26 And [s]the LORD of hosts will
wield against them a whip, as when he
struck [t]Midian [u]at the rock of Oreb. And
his staff will be over the sea, and he will lift
it [v]as he did in Egypt. 27 And in that day
[w]his burden will depart from your shoulder,
and [x]his yoke from your neck; and the
yoke will be broken because of the fat."[1]

28 He has come to Aiath;
he has passed through [y]Migron;
at Michmash he stores [z]his baggage;
29 they have crossed over [a]the pass;
at [b]Geba they lodge for the night;
[c]Ramah trembles;
[d]Gibeah of Saul has fled.
30 Cry aloud, O daughter of [e]Gallim!
Give attention, O Laishah!
O Poor [f]Anathoth!
31 Madmenah is in flight;
the inhabitants of Gebim flee for
safety.
32 This very day he will halt at [g]Nob;
he will shake his fist
at the mount of [h]the daughter of
Zion,
the hill of Jerusalem.

24 [o][ch. 31:5] [p]2 Kin. 19:6 [q]Ex. 2:23
25 [r][ch. 17:14]
26 [s]2 Kin. 19:35 [t]ch. 9:4 [u]Judg. 7:25; [ch. 9:4] [v][Ex. 14:30]
27 [w]2 Kin. 18:14 [x][ch. 9:4; Nah. 1:13]
28 [y]1 Sam. 14:2 [z]Judg. 18:21; 1 Sam. 17:22; Acts 21:15; [ch. 46:1]
29 [a]1 Sam. 13:23 [b]1 Sam. 13:16 [c]1 Sam. 7:17 [d]1 Sam. 11:4
30 [e]1 Sam. 25:44 [f]Jer. 1:1
32 [g]1 Sam. 21:1; 22:19 [h]ch. 1:8; 37:22
33 [i][Nah. 1:12] [j]ver. 18
34 [j][See ver. 33 above] [k][Ezek. 31:3; Amos 2:9]
Chapter 11
1 [l]ver. 10; Acts 13:23
2 [m]ch. 61:1; Matt. 3:16; Mark 1:10; Luke 3:22
3 [n][John 7:24] [o][Eccles. 1:8]

33 Behold, the Lord GOD of
hosts
[i]will lop [j]the boughs with terrifying
power;
the great in height will be hewn
down,
and the lofty will be brought
low.
34 He will cut down [j]the thickets of the
forest with an axe,
and [k]Lebanon will fall by the
Majestic One.

The Righteous Reign of the Branch

11 There shall come forth a shoot
from the stump of [l]Jesse,
and a branch from his roots shall
bear fruit.
2 And [m]the Spirit of the LORD shall rest
upon him,
the Spirit of wisdom and
understanding,
the Spirit of counsel and
might,
the Spirit of knowledge and the
fear of the LORD.
3 And his delight shall be in the fear of
the LORD.
[n]He shall not judge by [o]what his eyes
see,
or decide disputes by [o]what his
ears hear,

1 The meaning of the Hebrew is uncertain

10:24 be not afraid. A word of encouragement for the remnant in Judah (37:6; 41:10, 13; 43:1). See note 35:4.

10:25 destruction. The instruments of destruction will themselves be destroyed.

10:26 Midian . . . Oreb . . . Egypt. Two examples are taken from the history of redemption: the defeat of Midian at the rock of Oreb (a Midianite leader; Judg. 7:25), and the victory over Egypt at the Red Sea (Ex. 14:26–28).

10:28–32 Aiath . . . Zion. These verses describe a march to Judah from north to south through the cities mentioned. The last, Nob, is within sight of Zion. For a similar portrayal of Assyria's invasion, but from the southwest, see Mic. 1:10–16.

10:33 The Assyrians may inspire Judah with terror, but the Lord will intervene.

10:34 cut down . . . the forest. The Assyrians are portrayed as a forest that the Lord is going to cut down (v. 18 note).

Majestic One. See 33:21.

11:1 stump. All that is left of the Davidic dynasty is a stump. The privileged sons of David no less than Assyria are like trees that have been chopped down (10:33, 34). But in spite of this judgment on Judah, the Lord will raise up new leadership from the dynasty of David (Matt. 1:1).

Jesse. The father of David (1 Sam. 16:10–13). David inaugurated a great kingdom, but the greater David (Ezek. 34:23–25; Zech. 12:7–10), now only a tender plant (53:2), will rule an incomparably greater kingdom.

branch. See note 4:2.

11:2 Spirit of the LORD. As the fourfold repetition emphasizes, the same God-given endowment of the Spirit that brought David his successes (1 Sam. 16:13; Ps. 51:11) will empower the Messiah (42:1; Luke 3:22). The Spirit is the creative agent for establishing God's kingdom (Gen. 1:2; Judg. 3:10; 6:34; 1 Sam. 10:6 and notes).

rest upon him. The Spirit came in a powerful way on saints in the Old Testament: Moses (Num. 11:17); certain elders (Num. 11:25, 26); Joshua (Deut. 34:9); the judges (Judg. 3:10; 11:29; 13:25); kings (1 Sam. 11:6); and prophets (1 Sam. 10:10; 2 Sam. 23:2; 1 Kin. 22:24; 2 Kin. 2:15; Mic. 3:8). The Spirit is the divine agent of restoration (32:15; Joel 2:28–32).

wisdom. Solomon prayed for wisdom and understanding (1 Kin. 3:9), the administrative skill to govern the people in righteousness and justice. See Introduction to the Wisdom Literature.

counsel. Authoritative plans and decisions are in view here. Human counsel may or may not be in accord with God's plan (30:1), but the Messiah's counsel is by "the Spirit."

knowledge. This refers to wise and submissive living in accordance with the will of God (33:6; 53:11). It is a perfection of God (40:14).

fear of the LORD. Fearing God includes obeying His commandments because of faith that the Lord will keep His threats against transgressors (Prov. 1:7 note).

11:3 judge. See note 2:4.

4 but [p]with righteousness he shall
judge the poor,
and decide with equity for the
meek of the earth;
and he shall [q]strike the earth with
the rod of his mouth,
and [r]with the breath of his lips [s]he
shall kill the wicked.
5 Righteousness shall be the belt of his
waist,
and [t]faithfulness the belt of his
loins.

6 [u]The wolf shall dwell with the lamb,
and the leopard shall lie down
with the young goat,
and the calf and the lion and the
fattened calf together;
and a little child shall lead them.
7 The cow and the bear shall graze;
their young shall lie down together;
and the lion shall eat straw like
the ox.
8 The nursing child shall play over the
hole of the cobra,
and the weaned child shall put his
hand on the adder's den.
9 [u]They shall not hurt or destroy
in all [v]my holy mountain;
[w]for the earth shall be full of the
knowledge of the LORD
as the waters cover the sea.

10 In that day [x]the root of [y]Jesse, who
shall stand as [z]a signal for the peoples—of
him shall the nations inquire, and his resting place shall be glorious.

11 [a]In that day the Lord will extend his hand
yet a second time to recover the remnant
that remains of his people, [b]from Assyria,
[b]from Egypt, from [c]Pathros, from [d]Cush,[1]
from [e]Elam, from [f]Shinar, from [g]Hamath,
and from [h]the coastlands of the sea.

12 He will raise [z]a signal for the nations
and will assemble [i]the banished of
Israel,
and gather the dispersed of Judah
from the four corners of the earth.
13 [j]The jealousy of Ephraim shall depart,
and those who harass Judah shall
be cut off;
Ephraim shall not be jealous of
Judah,
and Judah shall not harass
Ephraim.
14 [k]But they shall swoop down on the
shoulder of the Philistines in
the west,
and together they shall plunder
[l]the people of the east.
They shall put out their hand
[m]against [n]Edom and [o]Moab,
and [p]the Ammonites shall obey
them.
15 And the LORD will utterly destroy[2]
[q]the tongue of the Sea of Egypt,
and will wave his hand over [r]the
River
with his scorching breath,[3]
and strike it into seven channels,
and he will lead people across in
sandals.

4 [p]Ps. 72:2, 4 [q]Ps. 2:9; [Mal. 4:6] [r]Job 4:9; 2 Thess. 2:8 [s]Ps. 139:19
5 [t][Eph. 6:14]
6 [u]ch. 65:25; [Hos. 2:18]
9 [u][See ver. 6 above] [v]Ps. 78:54 [w]Hab. 2:14
10 [x]Cited Rom. 15:12 [y]ver. 1 [z]ch. 49:22; [Ex. 17:15]
11 [a]ch. 10:20 [b]ch. 27:13; Mic. 7:12; Zech. 10:10 [c]Jer. 44:1, 15; Ezek. 29:14; 30:14 [d]See Gen. 10:6-12 [e]Gen. 10:22; 14:1, 9; Jer. 25:25; See Jer. 49:34-39 [f]Gen. 11:2 [g]See ch. 10:9 [h]Esth. 10:1
12 [z][See ver. 10 above] [i]ch. 56:8; [Zech. 10:6]
13 [j]Ezek. 37:16, 17; [ch. 9:21; Zech. 11:14]
14 [k][2 Sam. 8:1; 2 Kin. 18:8] [l]Judg. 6:3; See Jer. 49:28 [m]Ps. 60:8 [n][2 Sam. 8:14] [o][2 Sam. 8:2] [p]See 2 Sam. 12:26-31
15 [q][Zech. 10:11] [r]See ch. 7:20

1 Probably *Nubia* 2 Hebrew *devote to destruction* 3 Or *wind*

11:4 righteousness. See note 1:21.

poor . . . meek. That is, those who long for divine righteousness and justice (25:4) because of oppression by the rulers of this earth (3:15; 10:2; 32:7; 61:1). They are the afflicted, oppressed, and humble, whom Jesus also blessed (Matt. 5:3–10; Ps. 19:8 note).

equity. The Hebrew word also means "level" or "straight" (40:4). God's judgment is balanced and fair.

rod . . . breath. With great power and authority (Ps. 2:9; 82:8; Rev. 6:15–17; 20:11–12) the Messiah will conquer by His word (49:2; 61:1; Heb. 4:12; Rev. 19:15).

11:5 faithfulness. See note 1:21; cf. 25:1; 33:6.

11:6–9 Carnivorous animals, now remade with natures that protect what they formerly devoured, effectively portray the wonderful peace on earth in the new age ruled by the Messiah. The vision corresponds to reconciling love in the church (Eph. 2:14–18) and will be consummated in the new heavens and new earth (Rev. 21:4, 24–27).

11:10 In that day. See note 2:11.

root of Jesse. See note on v. 1 (Rev. 22:16).

signal. Here the signal is a sign of hope (cf. John 12:32), in contrast to 5:26 (see note).

glorious. See note 4:2.

11:11 a second time. The first time God reclaimed a people was from Egypt through the Exodus; the second time is from the Exile (51:9–11).

remnant. See note 1:8. The Lord will lead His children from wherever they are distressed.

11:12 four corners. The remnant will come from all the known world, described as the four corners of the earth (24:15; 42:4, 10; 51:5; 59:18, 19; cf. Matt. 24:31).

11:13 Ephraim . . . Judah. The era of restoration will witness a reconciliation of the disunited tribes. When the remnant returned to the land after the Exile, they offered sacrifices on behalf of all twelve tribes (Ezra 6:17; 8:35).

11:14 Philistines . . . Ammonites. This is a figure for freedom from the oppression, subjugation, and harassment that had characterized Israel's experience in the land (cf. 54:3; Mic. 5:6 note for a similar use of Assyria).

11:15 destroy . . . the River. The second Exodus will come by another miracle similar to the parting of the Red Sea (vv. 11, 12).

scorching breath. See Ex. 14:24–27.

16 And there will be [s]a highway from
Assyria
for the remnant that remains of his
people,
[t]as there was for Israel
when they came up from the land
of Egypt.

The LORD Is My Strength and My Song

12 You[1] will say [u]"in that day:
"I will give thanks to you, O LORD,
for though you were angry with me,
[v]your anger turned away,
that you might comfort me.

2 "Behold, God is my salvation;
I will trust, and will not be afraid;
for [w]the LORD GOD[2] is my strength
and my song,
and he has become my salvation."

3 [x]With joy you[3] will draw water from the
wells of salvation. 4 [y]And you will say in
that day:

[z]"Give thanks to the LORD,
call upon his name,
[a]make known his deeds among the
peoples,
proclaim [b]that his name is exalted.
5 [c]"Sing praises to the LORD, for he has
done gloriously;
let this be made known[4] in all the
earth.
6 Shout, and sing for joy, O inhabitant
of Zion,
for great [d]in your[5] midst is [e]the
Holy One of Israel."

The Judgment of Babylon

13 The oracle concerning [f]Babylon
which [g]Isaiah the son of Amoz saw.

2 On a bare hill [h]raise a signal;
cry aloud to them;
wave the hand for [i]them to enter
the gates of the nobles.
3 I myself have commanded my
consecrated ones,
and have summoned my mighty
men to execute my anger,
my proudly exulting ones.[6]

4 The sound [j]of a tumult is on the
mountains
as of a great multitude!
The sound of an uproar of kingdoms,
of nations gathering together!
[k]The LORD of hosts is mustering
a host for battle.
5 [l]They come from a distant land,
from the end of the heavens,
the LORD and the weapons of his
indignation,
to destroy the whole land.[7]

16 [s]ch. 19:23; [ch. 35:8] [t]Ex. 14:29
Chapter 12
1 [u]ch. 11:11 [v][ch. 10:4]
2 [w]Ex. 15:2; Ps. 118:14
3 [x][John 4:13, 14; 7:37, 38]
4 [y]ch. 11:11 [z]Ps. 105:1 [a][Ps. 145:4-6] [b]Ps. 148:13
5 [c]Ex. 15:1; Ps. 98:1
6 [d]ch. 5:24; 41:14, 16 [e]Ps. 46:5; Hos. 11:9
Chapter 13
1 [f]ver. 19; ch. 14:4; 21:9; 47:1; See Jer. ch. 51, 52 [g]ch. 1:1
2 [h]ch. 5:26 [i][ch. 41:25]
4 [j][ch. 22:5] [k][Josh. 5:13, 14]
5 [l][ch. 46:11]

1 The Hebrew for *you* is singular in verse 1 2 Hebrew *for Yah, the LORD* 3 The Hebrew for *you* is plural in verses 3, 4 4 Or *this is made known* 5 The Hebrew for *your* in verse 6 is singular, referring to the *inhabitant of Zion* 6 Or *those who exult in my majesty* 7 Or *earth*; also verse 9

11:16 highway. A level way is prepared by the Lord, a figure for the certainty of His salvation (35:8, 9; 40:3–5; 57:14; 62:10).

12:1–6 Isaiah's new hymn at the second Exodus corresponds to that of Moses at the first (Ex. 15).

12:1 in that day. See note 2:11.

I will give thanks. The prophet speaks as a representative of the people of God. The reason for praise is God Himself.

12:2 God is my salvation. See Ex. 15:2. He is the source and the initiator of salvation (49:6, 8; 51:6, 8; 56:1; 62:1).

the LORD GOD. The double reference to the name of the LORD is a poetic emphasis on the certainty of salvation provided by Yahweh, the covenant God (Ex. 3:15).

12:3 joy . . . salvation. The salvation of the Lord always brings joy (35:10; 51:3, 11; 61:3), as God removes the causes for sorrow and anxiety.

water . . . wells. Salvation is compared to an abundance of water (Ps. 1:3; 65:9; 104:10–13; 107:35) coming "from the wells of salvation" (41:18; cf. John 4:14).

12:4 exalted. See 2:11, 17; 33:5.

12:5 done gloriously. This is an allusion to "triumphed gloriously" (Ex. 15:1) and a synonym for "exalted" (v. 4).

13:1–23:18 Isaiah prophesies concerning the day of the Lord and what it means for the nations. Babylon and Assyria are treated together in the first oracle (13:1–14:27) because Babylon became the crown jewel of the Assyrian Empire. Assyrian kings had themselves crowned as kings of this renowned city. Babylon was regarded as an epitome of religion and culture, and as such Babylon represents the kingdoms of this world. Peter and John continue to use Babylon as a symbol for ungodly nations (1 Pet. 5:13; Rev. 14:8; 16:19; 17:1–18:24).

13:1 oracle. The Hebrew word can mean a literal weight, corresponding to the idea that the prophetic word is a heavy responsibility for the prophet who must deliver it. On the other hand, the word can mean simply a message or oracle, without the suggestion of weight.

13:2 signal. See 5:26 note.

gates of the nobles. It is implied that the city is proud.

13:3 consecrated ones . . . mighty men. These are the armies used by God as instruments of judgment.

13:4 sound. The great noise indicates the exercise of God's power (30:30, 31; 33:3; Ps. 29:5–9).

kingdoms, of nations. The Lord is the commander of human kingdoms. Babylon thought of herself as "the glory of kingdoms" (13:19) or the "mistress of kingdoms" (47:5) and ruled over others with great force (14:16).

13:5 distant land . . . end of the heavens. Yahweh's kingdom is universal.

weapons of his indignation. See note 10:5.

6 [m] Wail, for [n] the day of the LORD is near;
as destruction from the Almighty[1]
it will come!
7 Therefore all hands will be feeble,
and every human heart [o] will melt.
8 They will be dismayed:
[p] pangs and agony will seize them;
[q] they will be in anguish like a
woman in labor.
They will look aghast at one another;
their faces will be aflame.

9 Behold, [n] the day of the LORD comes,
cruel, with wrath and fierce anger,
to make the land a desolation
and [r] to destroy its sinners from it.
10 [s] For the stars of the heavens and their
constellations
will not give their light;
[t] the sun will be dark at its rising,
and the moon will not shed its
light.
11 I will punish [u] the world for its evil,
and the wicked for their iniquity;
I will [v] put an end to the pomp of the
arrogant,
[w] and lay low the pompous pride of
the ruthless.
12 I will make [x] people more rare than
fine gold,
and mankind than the [y] gold of
Ophir.
13 Therefore [z] I will make the heavens
tremble,
and the earth will be shaken out of
its place,
at the wrath of the LORD of hosts
in the day of his fierce anger.

6 [m] ch. 14:31; 15:2, 3, 8; 16:7; Jer. 51:8; Ezek. 30:2 [n] ch. 2:12; Joel 1:15; Zeph. 1:7
7 [o] See Josh. 2:11
8 [p] [Nah. 2:10] [q] ch. 26:17; Jer. 4:31; 6:24; Mic. 4:9, 10; John 16:21
9 [n] [See ver. 6 above] [r] [Ps. 104:35]
10 [s] [ch. 34:4] [t] Ezek. 32:7; Joel 2:31; 3:15; Matt. 24:29; Mark 13:24; Luke 21:25
11 [u] ch. 24:21 [v] [ch. 24:4] [w] [ch. 2:11, 17]
12 [x] ch. 24:6 [y] 1 Kin. 10:11; Job 28:16
13 [z] Hag. 2:6
14 [a] Jer. 50:16; 51:9; [1 Kin. 22:36]
16 [b] Ps. 137:9; Nah. 3:10
17 [c] ch. 21:2; Jer. 51:11, 28; Dan. 5:28, 31
18 [d] Jer. 50:14, 29; 51:3
19 [e] [ch. 47:5] [f] ch. 1:9; Gen. 19:24; Jer. 50:40; Amos 4:11
20 [g] Jer. 51:37, 43 [h] Jer. 3:2 [i] Jer. 33:12

14 And like a hunted gazelle,
or like sheep with none to gather
them,
[a] each will turn to his own people,
and each will flee to his own
land.
15 Whoever is found will be thrust
through,
and whoever is caught will fall by
the sword.
16 [b] Their infants will be dashed in
pieces
before their eyes;
their houses will be plundered
and their wives ravished.

17 Behold, [c] I am stirring up the Medes
against them,
who have no regard for silver
and do not delight in gold.
18 [d] Their bows will slaughter[2] the young
men;
they will have no mercy on the
fruit of the womb;
their eyes will not pity children.
19 And Babylon, [e] the glory of
kingdoms,
the splendor and pomp of the
Chaldeans,
will be [f] like Sodom and Gomorrah
when God overthrew them.
20 [g] It will never be inhabited
or lived in for all generations;
no [h] Arab will pitch his tent there;
no [i] shepherds will make their
flocks lie down there.

1 The Hebrew words for *destruction* and *almighty* sound alike
2 Hebrew *dash in pieces*

13:6–22 The terror of the day of the Lord is described.

13:6 the day of the LORD. This is also called "the day" (v. 13); see note 2:11.

13:7 feeble . . . melt. The people will be utterly helpless (Jer. 6:24; Ezek. 7:17).

13:8 woman in labor. This comparison is used often in the Bible for intense pain and suffering (21:3; 49:24; 50:43; Ps. 48:6; Mic. 4:9; cf. Rom. 8:22).

13:10 stars . . . moon. These are figures for God's cosmic judgment (24:23; Joel 2:10, 31; Rev. 6:12–14).

light. See note 2:5. The ancients worshiped the heavenly bodies, but Scripture teaches that God is the Creator of them all (Deut. 4:19). Darkness symbolizes judgment. The imagery is also used for the final destruction of the world (34:3).

13:11 ruthless. See note 29:20.

13:13 make the heavens tremble . . . the earth will be shaken. These expressions depict the coming of God in judgment against His creation. The shaking of the world symbolizes the overthrow of all that unbelievers exalt as rivals to God (2:12–18). The king of Babylon is described as one "who made the earth tremble" (14:16).

13:14 turn . . . flee. The attractiveness of Babylon will become a phantom when people realize how short-lived human kingdoms are.

13:15, 16 thrust through . . . ravished. These are the terrors brought by war.

13:16 houses. See note 24:10.

13:17 Medes. These were inhabitants of the Zagros Mountains, east of Babylon and Assyria. They were never subjugated by Assyria and joined Babylon in the conquest of Assyria (612–609 B.C.). For the dating of this prophecy it is significant that Persia, which conquered Media in 549 B.C., is not mentioned.

13:19 kingdoms. See note on v. 4.

Sodom and Gomorrah. See note 1:9.

13:20 never be inhabited. This is the measure of God's judgment on human pride. Babylon was finally laid waste as described.

21 But [j]wild animals will lie down there,
and their houses will be full of
howling creatures;
there [k]ostriches[1] will dwell,
and there wild goats will dance.
22 Hyenas[2] will cry in its towers,
and [l]jackals in [m]the pleasant
palaces;
its time is close at hand
and its days will not be
prolonged.

The Restoration of Jacob

14 [n]For the LORD will have compassion
on Jacob and will again choose
Israel, and [o]will set them in their own land,
and [p]sojourners will join them and will
attach themselves to the house of Jacob.
2 And [q]the peoples will take them and bring
them to their place, and the house of Israel
will possess them in the LORD's land [r]as
male and female slaves. [s]They will take captive those who were their captors, [t]and rule
over those who oppressed them.

Israel's Remnant Taunts Babylon

3 When the LORD has given you rest from
your pain and turmoil and the hard service
with which you were made to serve, 4 you
will take up this [u]taunt against the king of
Babylon:

"How the oppressor has ceased,
[v]the insolent fury[3] ceased!
5 The LORD has broken the [w]staff of the
wicked,
the [w]scepter of rulers,
6 [x]that struck the peoples in wrath
with unceasing blows,
that ruled the nations in anger
with unrelenting persecution.
7 The whole earth is at rest and
quiet;
[y]they break forth into singing.
8 [z, a]The cypresses rejoice at you,
[b]the cedars of Lebanon, saying,
'Since you were laid low,
no woodcutter comes up
against us.'
9 Sheol beneath is stirred up
to meet you when you come;
it rouses the shades to greet you,
all who were leaders of the earth;
it raises from their thrones
all who were kings of the nations.
10 [c]All of them will answer
and say to you:
'You too have become as weak as we!
You have become like us!'
11 Your pomp is brought down to
Sheol,
the sound of your harps;
maggots are laid as a bed beneath
you,
and worms are your covers.
12 "How [d]you are fallen from heaven,
O Day Star, [e]son of Dawn!
How you are cut down to the
ground,
you who laid the nations low!

21 [j][ch. 34:13, 14] [k]ch. 34:13; Jer. 50:39
22 [l]ch. 35:7; Jer. 51:37 [m][ch. 25:2; Amos 3:15]
Chapter 14
1 [n]Ps. 102:13; Zech. 1:17 [o]2 Chr. 36:22, 23 [p]Zech. 8:22, 23; See Eph. 2:12-14
2 [q]ch. 49:22; 60:9; 66:20 [r]ch. 61:5 [s][Joel 3:8] [t]ch. 60:14
4 [u]Mic. 2:4; Hab. 2:6 [v][Jer. 51:13; Rev. 18:16]
5 [w][ch. 9:4]
6 [x][Jer. 50:23]
7 [y]ch. 44:23; 49:13; 54:1; 55:12
8 [z][Ezek. 31:16] [a][ch. 37:24] [b]See ch. 2:13
10 [c][Jer. 51:48]
12 [d][ch. 24:21; 34:3] [e][Job 38:7]

[1] Or *owls* [2] Or *foxes* [3] Dead Sea Scroll (compare Septuagint, Syriac, Vulgate); the meaning of the word in the Masoretic Text is uncertain

13:21, 22 wild animals . . . jackals. Babylon becomes unfit for human habitation; only wild animals haunt the site (34:11–15; Jer. 50:39; 51:37; Zeph. 2:14, 15).

14:1 choose. Election is God's choice, and He is free to set Israel aside, or to choose Israel again for a new future (41:8, 9; 44:1, 2; 45:4; 65:9; Ex. 19:6; Deut. 7:6; cf. Rom. 9–11).

14:2 peoples These are instruments of God's plan of redemption (55:5; 60:1–18; 61:5–7; 66:19, 20; cf. Ezra 1:1–8).

14:3–21 A taunt against the king of Babylon. Victors frequently sang taunt songs against their victims (v. 7; 12:1; Ex. 15:1).

14:3 rest. As in the first Exodus, God will liberate the people from oppression.

14:4 taunt. The Hebrew term has a range of meanings including brief sayings like those in the Book of Proverbs, and a figurative poem like the one here.

king of Babylon. This king is a chief representative of oppressive human power.

14:7 singing. Instead of "the song of the ruthless" (25:5), a new song will be heard in response to God's judgment and deliverance (24:14, 16; 26:1, 19; 44:23; 49:13). See note 12:1–6.

14:8 cypresses . . . cedars. Nature responds to God's acts of judgment and restoration (55:13; 60:13; contrast 37:24).

no woodcutter. Assyrian kings boast in their annals of the magnificent trees they carted off from pillaged lands to build their splendid palaces.

14:9–11 Sheol. Isaiah uses the popular conception of the realm of the dead with its shadowy figures welcoming newcomers in an ironic description of Babylon's fall and her descent into the lower regions. The use of these conventional ideas is poetic, and is not intended as a theology of the afterlife. See 5:14 and note; Prov. 1:12; 9:18 and notes.

14:9 thrones. The defeated kings had thrones in their royal graves. By contrast the king of Babylon is given a bed of maggots (v. 11).

14:12 fallen from heaven. This figure represents in an exaggerated way the fall of Babylon, with all its imperial ambitions, into destruction (cf. Lam. 2:1; Luke 4:6; 10:15).

O Day Star, son of Dawn. Lit. "shining one, son of dawn." Probably this refers to the planet Venus, rising in the morning and climbing toward the top of the sky, only to be overtaken by the sun. In the ancient world observations of this astronomical cycle gave rise to several myths. Babylon seems to have thought of itself as fulfilling such a heavenly destiny, and becoming an eternal and universal empire. But with the appearance of God (v. 22), Babylon's light would be extinguished.

13 You said in your heart,
[f]'I will ascend to heaven;
above the stars of God
[g]I will set my throne on high;
I will sit on the mount of assembly
in the far reaches of the north;[1]
14 I will ascend above the heights of the clouds;
I will make myself like the Most High.'
15 [h]But you are brought down to Sheol,
to the far reaches of the pit.
16 Those who see you will stare at you
and ponder over you:
'Is this [i]the man who made the earth tremble,
who shook kingdoms,
17 who made the world like a desert
and overthrew its cities,
[j]who did not let his prisoners go home?'
18 All the kings of the nations lie in glory,
each in his own tomb;[2]
19 but you are cast out, away from your grave,
like a loathed branch,
[k]clothed with the slain, those pierced by the sword,
who go down to the stones of the pit,
like a dead body trampled underfoot.
20 You will not be joined with them in burial,
because you have destroyed your land,
you have slain your people.

"May [l]the offspring of evildoers
nevermore be named!
21 Prepare slaughter for his sons
[m]because of the guilt of their fathers,
lest they rise and possess the earth,
and fill the face of the world with cities."

22 "I will rise up against them," declares
the LORD of hosts, "and will cut off from
Babylon name and [n]remnant, [o]descendants
and posterity," says the LORD. 23 "And I will
make it a possession of the [p]hedgehog,[3]
and pools of water, and I will sweep it with
the broom of destruction," declares the
LORD of hosts.

An Oracle Concerning Assyria

24 The LORD of hosts has sworn:
[q]"As I have planned,
so shall it be,
and as I have purposed,
so shall it stand,
25 that [r]I will break the Assyrian in my land,
and on my mountains trample him underfoot;
and [s]his yoke shall depart from them,
and [s]his burden from their shoulder."
26 This is the purpose that is purposed
concerning the whole earth,
and this is [t]the hand that is stretched out
over all the nations.
27 [u]For the LORD of hosts has purposed,
and who will annul it?
[t]His hand is stretched out,
and who will turn it back?

13 [f]Jer. 51:53; Amos 9:2; [Matt. 11:23; Luke 10:15] [g]Dan. 5:22, 23; [2 Thess. 2:4]
15 [h]Ezek. 32:23; Matt. 11:23; Luke 10:15
16 [i][Jer. 50:23]
17 [j][Jer. 50:33]
19 [k][Ezek. 32:20]
20 [l]Job 18:19; Ps. 21:10; 109:13
21 [m][Ex. 20:5; Matt. 23:35]
22 [n][Jer. 51:50, 62] [o]Job 18:19; [Gen. 21:23]
23 [p]ch. 34:11; Zeph. 2:14
24 [q][Prov. 19:21]
25 [r]ch. 37:36 [s]ch. 9:4; 10:27
26 [t][Deut. 4:34]
27 [u]2 Chr. 20:6; Job 9:12; Ps. 33:11; Prov. 21:30; Dan. 4:31, 33, 35 [t][See ver. 26 above]

1 Or *in the remote parts of Zaphon* 2 Hebrew *house* 3 Possibly *porcupine*, or *owl*

14:13 on the mount of assembly. According to Canaanite myths, the god El presided over an assembly of gods on a mountain in Syria. Babylon was ready to claim this honor for itself.

far reaches of the north. A traditional rendering of Hebrew *zaphon*. Psalm 48:1, 2 mentions "the far north" as belonging to the Lord alone.

14:14 Most High. See Gen. 14:19, 20. This is a restatement of v. 13. People may claim rule over every realm of God's kingdom, but God is still sovereign.

14:15 Sheol . . . pit. See vv. 9–11 and notes.

14:16 kingdoms. See note 13:4.

14:17 desert . . . prisoners. Babylon used the power of which it was so proud for destruction and cruelty.

14:18 the kings . . . lie in glory. The satirical contrast introduced in v. 9 is taken up again. The conquered kings are pictured in honored rest, while proud Babylon is thrown out like unhealthy refuse. To be deprived of a proper burial was regarded as a great misfortune.

14:22 remnant. Unlike Israel, Assyria has no remnant (v. 30; cf. 15:9; 17:3 and 1:9 note).

14:23 hedgehog. See note 13:21, 22. It is possible that a certain type of bird is meant, rather than a hedgehog.

14:25 yoke. See note 9:3, 4.

14:26, 27 the purpose . . . who will annul. These verses concluding the section that began at 13:1 are an eloquent statement of God's irresistible judgment over the whole earth (43:13).

An Oracle Concerning Philistia

28 In the year that [v]King Ahaz died came this [w]oracle:

29 Rejoice not, [x]O Philistia, all of you,
that [y]the rod that struck you is broken,
for from the serpent's root will come forth an adder,
and its fruit will be a [z]flying fiery serpent.
30 And the firstborn of [a]the poor will graze,
and [a]the needy lie down in safety;
but I will kill your root with famine,
and your remnant it will slay.
31 [b]Wail, O [c]gate; cry out, O city;
melt in fear, [x]O Philistia, all of you!
[d]For smoke comes out of the north,
and there is no straggler in his ranks.

32 What will one answer the messengers of the nation?
[e]"The LORD has founded Zion,
and in her the afflicted of his people find refuge."

An Oracle Concerning Moab

15 An [w]oracle concerning [f]Moab.

Because [g]Ar of Moab is laid waste in a night,
Moab is undone;
because [h]Kir of Moab is laid waste in a night,
Moab is undone.
2 He has gone up to the temple,[1] and to [i]Dibon,
to the high places[2] to weep;
over [j]Nebo and over [i]Medeba
Moab [k]wails.
On every head is [l]baldness;
every beard is shorn;
3 in the streets they wear sackcloth;
on the housetops and in the squares
everyone wails and melts in tears.
4 [m]Heshbon and [m]Elealeh cry out;
their voice is heard as far as [n]Jahaz;
therefore the armed men of Moab cry aloud;
his soul trembles.
5 My heart cries out for Moab;
her fugitives flee to Zoar,
to [n]Eglath-shelishiyah.
For at the [o]ascent of Luhith
they go up weeping;
on the road to [o]Horonaim
they raise a cry of destruction;
6 the waters of [p]Nimrim
are a desolation;
the grass is withered, the vegetation fails,
the greenery is no more.

28 [v]2 Kin. 16:20 [w]See ch. 13:1
29 [x]Ex. 15:14; [Ps. 60:8; 87:4; 108:9] [y][ch. 10:24] [z]ch. 30:6; Num. 21:6; [Jer. 46:22]
30 [a][ch. 29:19; Zeph. 3:12]
31 [b]ch. 13:6 [c]ch. 24:12 [x][See ver. 29 above] [d][ch. 29:1]
32 [e]Ps. 87:1, 5; 102:16; 132:13; [ch. 28:16]
Chapter 15
1 [w][See ver. 28 above] [f]See Jer. ch. 48; Ezek. 25:8-11; Amos 2:1-3; Zeph. 2:8, 9 [g]Num. 21:15, 28 [h][ch. 16:7, 11]
2 [i]Num. 21:30 [j]ch. 13:6 [k]Deut. 34:1 [l]See ch. 3:24
4 [m]Num. 32:37 [n]Jer. 48:34
5 [n][See ver. 4 above] [o]Jer. 48:5
6 [p][Num. 32:36]

1 Hebrew *the house* 2 Or *temple, even Dibon to the high places*

14:28 oracle. See note 13:1. This oracle could date from as early as 727 B.C., four years before Shalmaneser's attack on Samaria, or as late as 715 B.C., fourteen years before the fall of Samaria (2 Kin. 18:13). The later date is preferable since it corresponds to a time of Philistine revolt against Assyria.

14:29 rod. See note 10:5. This is an Assyrian king—either Tiglath-pileser III (d. 727 B.C.) or Sargon (d. 705 B.C.).

broken. This weakness in Assyria's hegemony is temporary.

adder . . . flying fiery serpent. There is no need to identify the snakes with particular kings, like Sennacherib, Esarhaddon, or Ashurbanipal. The idea is that Assyrian strength will go on for more than one generation despite successions of kings.

14:30 poor . . . needy. See 11:4; Ps. 19:8 and notes.

remnant. See note on v. 22.

14:31 smoke . . . out of the north. This reference is to the Assyrian invasion.

14:32 messengers. The Philistines sought to create a coalition with Judah and other nations, but God's response through Isaiah is clear. God will protect His own, in spite of the political and military turmoil.

15:1–16:14 This oracle of judgment against Moab was probably delivered around the time of Sargon's defeat of Moab in 715 B.C. See also 11:14; 25:10; Jer. 48; Ezek. 25:8–11; Amos 2:1–3; Zeph. 2:8–11. The oracle concerns Moab's distress (ch. 15) and the response to Moab's distress (ch. 16).

15:1 oracle. See note 13:1.

Moab. Moab was a nation east of the Dead Sea, between the Ammonites and the Edomites. Her relations with Judah were often tense.

Ar . . . Kir. The city of Ar was on the Arnon River, and Kir was the capital of Moab.

15:2 Dibon . . . high places. Dibon was a site north of the Arnon River devoted to the worship of the Moabite god Chemosh.

Nebo . . . Medeba. Nebo was a village north of the Arnon River, not far from the mountain where Moses went to look at the Promised Land (Deut. 34:1). Medeba was five miles to the southeast.

baldness. The customs of mourning included cutting the hair and shaving.

15:3 streets. See note 24:11.

sackcloth . . . tears. These were customs of mourning (v. 2; 22:12; Jer. 4:8; 41:5; 48:20, 34; Lam. 2:10).

15:4 Heshbon and Elealeh. These two towns were close together, about six miles north of Medeba (v. 2). Heshbon was captured by Israel under Moses (Num. 21:23–26).

Jahaz. Located on the Arnon River, about twenty miles south of Heshbon (Num. 21:23; Jer. 48:34).

15:5 My heart cries. Isaiah has noticeably more sympathy for Moab, Ruth's homeland (16:11), than for the other nations.

Zoar. The Moabites flee to Zoar, as their forefather Lot had done (Gen. 19:23–30).

Luhith . . . Horonaim. Unidentified cities probably close to Zoar (Jer. 48:3, 5, 34).

15:6 waters of Nimrim. Possibly a seasonal stream southeast of the Dead Sea (Jer. 48:34).

7 [q] Therefore the abundance they have
gained
and what they have laid up
they carry away
over the Brook of the Willows.
8 For a cry has gone
around the land of Moab;
her wailing reaches to Eglaim;
her wailing reaches to Beer-elim.
9 For the waters of [r] Dibon[1] are full of
blood;
for I will bring upon Dibon even
more,
[s] a lion for those of Moab who
escape,
for the remnant of the land.

16 [t] Send the lamb to the ruler of the
land,
from [u] Sela, by way of the desert,
to the mount of the daughter of
Zion.
2 Like fleeing birds,
like a scattered nest,
so are the daughters of Moab
at [v] the fords of the Arnon.
3 "Give counsel;
grant justice;
[w] make your shade like night
at the height of noon;
shelter the outcasts;
do not reveal the fugitive;
4 let [x] the outcasts of Moab
sojourn among you;
be a shelter to them[2]
from the destroyer.
When the oppressor is no more
and destruction has ceased,
and he who tramples underfoot has
vanished from the land,
5 [y] then a throne will be established in
steadfast love,
and on it will sit in faithfulness
in the tent of David
one who judges and seeks justice
and is swift to do
righteousness."
6 [z] We have heard of the pride of
Moab—
how proud he is!—
[a] of his arrogance, his pride, and his
insolence;
in his idle boasting he is not
right.
7 Therefore let Moab wail for Moab,
[b] let everyone wail.
Mourn, utterly stricken,
for the [c] raisin cakes of
[d] Kir-hareseth.
8 For the fields of Heshbon languish,
and [e] the vine of Sibmah;
the lords of the nations
have struck down its branches,
which reached to Jazer
and strayed to the desert;
its shoots spread abroad
and passed over the sea.
9 Therefore [f] I weep with [e] the weeping
of Jazer
for the vine of Sibmah;
I drench you with my tears,
O Heshbon and Elealeh;
for over [g] your summer fruit and your
harvest
the shout has ceased.

7 [q] Jer. 48:36
9 [r] [ver. 2]
[s] [2 Kin. 17:25; Jer. 50:17]
Chapter 16
1 [t] 2 Kin. 3:4
[u] ch. 42:11; 2 Kin. 14:7
2 [v] Judg. 11:18
3 [w] [1 Kin. 18:4]
4 [x] 1 Sam. 22:3
5 [y] ch. 32:1, 2; Dan. 7:14, 27; Mic. 4:7; Luke 1:33
6 [z] Jer. 48:29; Zeph. 2:10
[a] Judg. 3:14; 2 Kin. 13:20; [2 Chr. 20:1]
7 [b] ch. 15:3
[c] 2 Sam. 6:19; [ver. 9]
[d] 2 Kin. 3:25; [ch. 15:1]
8 [e] Jer. 48:32
9 [f] [ch. 15:5]
[g] [ver. 7]

1 Dead Sea Scroll, Vulgate (compare Syriac); Masoretic Text *Dimon* (twice in this verse) 2 Some Hebrew manuscripts, Septuagint, Syriac; Masoretic Text *let my outcasts sojourn among you; as for Moab, be a shelter to them*

15:7 Brook of the Willows. This may be the Zered River on the border between Moab and Edom (v. 8).

15:9 Dibon . . . blood. A city on the Arnon River.

a lion. The fugitives go from trouble to trouble (cf. Amos 5:19) in their flight southward. They finally turn to Judah in the west for asylum (16:1–5).

16:1 Send the lamb. The Moabites were shepherds (Num. 32:3, 4), and could send lambs as tokens of their submission (cf. 2 Kin. 3:4).

from Sela. The fugitives were either at Sela, a naturally fortified site in Edom or at a mountain stronghold (Hebrew *sela'* means "rock," or "cliff"). The tribute is sent from their outpost to Judah.

Zion. See note 1:8.

16:2 birds . . . at the fords. The fugitives became refugees fleeing to the south (15:8, 9).

16:3 shade. The verse requests protection from the heat of the day.

16:4 oppressor . . . he who tramples underfoot. Assyria.

16:5 in steadfast love. God had made a covenant with David (55:3; 2 Sam. 22:51; Ps. 89:28; see note 54:8). In Jesus, the Son of David, the nations find shelter (Acts 15:16, 17).

throne . . . tent of David. Hope lies in Yahweh and in His promises to David (9:2–7; 11:1–9; Amos 9:11, 12).

16:7 See "God Sees and Knows: Divine Omniscience" at Prov. 15:3.

16:8 Heshbon . . . Sibmah. These places were not far apart (15:4; Jer. 48:32).

vine. The imagery of the vineyard (5:1–7) is applied here to Moab.

Jazer . . . the sea. Jazer was the extreme north of Moabite territory.

16:9 I weep . . . I drench. Isaiah is moved by the desolation of the fine vineyards.

Elealeh. See 15:4.

10 [h]And joy and gladness are taken away
from [i]the fruitful field,
and in the vineyards no [j]songs are
sung,
no cheers are raised;
no [k]treader treads out wine [l]in the
presses;
I have put an end to the
shouting.
11 Therefore [m]my inner parts moan like
a lyre for Moab,
and my inmost self for
Kir-hareseth.

12 And when Moab presents himself,
when [n]he wearies himself on [o]the high
place, when he comes to his sanctuary to
pray, he will not prevail.
13 This is the word that the LORD spoke
concerning Moab [p]in the past. 14 But now
the LORD has spoken, saying, "In three
years, [q]like the years of a hired worker, the
glory of Moab will be brought into contempt, in spite of all his great multitude,
and those who remain will be [r]very few and
feeble."

An Oracle Concerning Damascus

17 An [s]oracle concerning [t]Damascus.

Behold, Damascus will cease to be a
city
and will become a heap of
ruins.
2 The cities of [u]Aroer are
deserted;
they will be for flocks,
which will lie down, and [v]none
will make them afraid.
3 The fortress will disappear from
[w]Ephraim,
and the kingdom from
[w]Damascus;
and the remnant of Syria will be
like [x]the glory of the children of
Israel,
declares the LORD of hosts.

4 And in that day [x]the glory of Jacob
will be brought low,
and [y]the fat of his flesh will grow
lean.
5 And it shall be [z]as when the reaper
gathers standing grain
and his arm harvests the ears,
and as when one gleans the ears of
grain
in [a]the Valley of Rephaim.
6 [b]Gleanings will be left in it,
as when an olive tree is
beaten—
two or three berries
in the top of the highest bough,
four or five
on the branches of a fruit tree,
declares the LORD God of Israel.

7 [c]In that day man will look to his Maker,
and his eyes will look on the Holy One of
Israel. 8 [d]He will not look to the altars, the
work of his hands, and he will not look on
what his own fingers have made, either the
[e]Asherim or the altars of incense.
9 [f]In that day their strong cities will be
like the deserted places of the wooded
heights and the hilltops, which they deserted because of the children of Israel, and
there will be desolation.

10 [h]Jer. 48:33 [i][ch. 9:3] [j][Judg. 9:27] [k]ch. 63:3; Jer. 25:30 [l]ch. 5:2
11 [m]ch. 15:5; Jer. 48:36
12 [n][1 Kin. 18:29] [o]ch. 15:2; [Num. 22:41; 23:14, 28]
13 [p]See Amos 2:1-3
14 [q]ch. 21:16 [r][ch. 10:22]
Chapter 17
1 [s]See ch. 13:1 [t]ch. 7:8; Zech. 9:1; See Jer. 49:23-27; Amos 1:3-5
2 [u]Deut. 2:36; Josh. 13:25 [v]Mic. 4:4

3 [w]ch. 7:16; 8:4 [x][1 Sam. 4:21]
4 [x][See ver. 3 above] [y]ch. 10:16
5 [z][ch. 24:1] [a]See 2 Sam. 5:18
6 [b]ch. 24:13
7 [c][Hos. 8:14]
8 [d]ch. 27:9; Mic. 5:13, 14 [e]Ex. 34:13; See Deut. 16:21
9 [f][ch. 27:10]

16:11 my inner parts moan . . . my inmost self. This describes deeply felt sorrow (v. 9; 21:3, 4; cf. Jer. 48:36). See note 15:5.

16:12 high place . . . sanctuary. See note 15:2.

16:13 the LORD spoke. This summary regarding Moab's distress is in prose form. Either it is a revelation in the past or a reference to the oracles in 15:1–9 or 15:1–16:12.

16:14 In three years. The desolation of Moab is at hand. Perhaps this is a reference to the quelling of the rebellion against Sargon, king of Assyria, in 715 B.C.

glory. The prophetic word applies to all who exalt themselves and trouble the people of God. Salvation is in the Messiah (v. 5), but those who seek refuge for political or economic reasons will not find shelter in Zion.

17:1–14 This oracle of judgment concerning Damascus may be dated to the Syro-Ephraimite crisis of 734–732 B.C.

17:1 oracle. See 13:1.

Damascus. Besides being the capital of Syria, it was also the commercial hub along the trade routes between Mesopotamia, Egypt and Arabia. Damascus was captured by Tiglath-pileser III in 732 B.C.

17:2 Aroer. This city was located on the Arnon River (2 Kin. 10:32, 33). Syria's political control extended at times to the Arnon.

17:3 fortress . . . Ephraim. The "strong cities" (v. 9) of Israel were already weakened by 732 B.C. (9:1 note) and ceased to exist in 722 B.C.

remnant. Unlike Israel, Syria has no remnant.

17:5 Valley of Rephaim. A lush valley southwest of Jerusalem, it was the gateway to the western plains (Josh. 15:8; 18:16; 2 Sam. 5:18, 22; 1 Chr. 14:9).

17:7 man. The faithful remnant look to their Creator.

Maker. The prophet contrasts the works of God with those of His creatures. See note 2:8.

17:8 Asherim. The Canaanite goddess Asherah was a fertility goddess, symbolized by sacred groves and poles (27:9; Ex. 34:13; Deut. 16:21; Judg. 2:13).

10 For [g]you have forgotten the God of
your salvation
and have not remembered the
[h]Rock of your refuge;
therefore, though you plant pleasant
plants
and sow the vine-branch of a
stranger,
11 though you make them grow[1] on the
day that you plant them,
and make them blossom in the
morning that you sow,
yet the harvest will flee away[2]
in a day of grief and incurable pain.
12 Ah, [i]the thunder of many peoples;
they thunder like the thundering
of the sea!
Ah, the roar of nations;
they roar like the roaring of mighty
waters!
13 [j]The nations roar like the roaring of
many waters,
[k]but he will rebuke them, and they
will flee far away,
chased [l]like chaff on the mountains
before the wind
and [m]whirling dust before the storm.
14 [n]At evening time, behold, terror!
Before morning, they are no more!
This is the portion of those who
loot us,
and the lot of those who plunder us.

An Oracle Concerning Cush

18 Ah, land of [o]whirring wings
that is beyond the rivers of [p]Cush,[3]
2 which [q]sends ambassadors by the sea,
in vessels of papyrus on the
waters!
Go, you swift messengers,
to a nation, [r]tall and smooth,
to a people feared near and far,
a nation [s]mighty and conquering,
whose land the rivers divide.
3 All you inhabitants of the world,
you who dwell on the earth,
when [t]a signal is raised on the
mountains, look!
When a trumpet is blown, hear!
4 For thus the LORD said to me:
"I will quietly look [u]from my
dwelling
like clear heat in sunshine,
like a cloud of dew in the heat of
harvest."
5 [v]For before the harvest, when the
blossom is over,
and the flower becomes a ripening
grape,
he cuts off the shoots with pruning
hooks,
and the spreading branches he
lops off and clears away.

10 [g]Ps. 106:21 [h]ch. 26:4; [Deut. 32:4, 18, 31]
12 [i]See ch. 22:5-7
13 [j][ch. 33:3] [k]Ps. 9:5; [Joel 3:2] [l]See Ps. 1:4 [m]Ps. 83:13
14 [n][Ps. 30:5]

Chapter 18
1 [o][ch. 8:8; 17:12] [p]2 Kin. 19:9
2 [q]ch. 30:4 [r]ver. 7 [s][2 Sam. 8:2]
3 [t]See ch. 5:26
4 [u]Ps. 11:4
5 [v][Ezek. 31:3, 12, 13]

[1] Or *though you carefully fence them* [2] Or *will be a heap* [3] Probably *Nubia*

17:10 forgotten . . . have not remembered. This expression describes apostasy (Deut. 4:9, 23; 8:11, 14, 19; 32:18).

Rock. See note 8:14, 15.

refuge. The Lord alone is the strength of His people (25:4; 27:5), in contrast to military and political solutions (v. 9; 23:11, 14; 30:2).

pleasant plants . . . stranger. This reference probably points to Canaanite fertility rituals. Israel had cultivated relations with her neighbors and had adapted their ways.

17:11 make them grow. Perhaps this alludes to a pagan practice in which potted plants were forced to sprout in order to secure fertile crops.

harvest. The end will bring nothing but disaster.

17:12 thundering of the sea . . . mighty waters. The destructive power of the nations appears to be like that of the "seas" and "mighty waters" (8:7 note). In ancient Near Eastern myths the sea represents chaos and death (Ezek. 28:2; 32:2 and notes).

17:13 chaff . . . whirling dust. To be driven away as chaff (cf. 29:5; 41:15, 16; Ps. 83:13) reveals a lack of life, value, and stability.

mountains. Grain is winnowed on windy hilltops.

17:14 terror. An unforeseen series of troubles (24:17, 18), appear on the day of the Lord's wrath (22:5). The Lord still protects His people. He is Immanuel (7:14 note; 8:8 note; 8:10 note), who repays the nations for the evil done to His people.

18:1 Ah. See note 1:4.

land of whirring wings. This may mean either a land of "many insects" or "many ships" (so ancient translations).

Cush. The biblical Ethiopia is the remote region of southern Egypt and beyond, including Nubia, south of the fourth cataract of the Nile. The Nubian Shabako ruled over lower Egypt from 715 B.C. (twenty-fifth Dynasty). His administration tried to extend his influence northward into the delta region.

18:2 vessels of papyrus. These are papyrus boats that the Nubians could use to send messengers to incite the nations to rebel against Assyria.

tall and smooth. The phrase possibly refers to the impressive appearance of the nation or nations that the remote Nubians were trying to stir up.

18:3 inhabitants of the world. Those addressed in this oracle will observe what the Lord is doing.

signal. See note 5:26. Trumpets were also commonly used as signals in war.

18:4 I will quietly look . . . dwelling. Yahweh patiently observes the rebellion of the nations (Ps. 2:1–4).

clear heat . . . cloud of dew. Expressive of the stillness as God waits to act (see 25:5).

18:5, 6 These verses contain two images of God's judgment. First, there is the pruning of the vines before harvest to encourage the development of the grapes, "shoots" and "branches." Second, there is the carcass on which the "birds of prey" and the wild animals feed. Contrast 31:5.

6 [v]They shall all of them be left
to the birds of prey of the
mountains
and to the beasts of the earth.
And the birds of prey will summer
on them,
and all the beasts of the earth will
winter on them.

7 [w]At that time tribute will be brought to
the LORD of hosts

from a people [x]tall and smooth,
from a people feared near and far,
a nation mighty and conquering,
whose land the rivers divide,

to [y]Mount Zion, the place of the [z]name of
the LORD of hosts.

An Oracle Concerning Egypt

19 An [a]oracle concerning [b]Egypt.

Behold, the LORD [c]is riding on a swift
cloud
and comes to Egypt;
and [d]the idols of Egypt will tremble
at his presence,
and the heart of the Egyptians will
[e]melt within them.

2 And I will stir up Egyptians against
Egyptians,
[f]and they will fight, each against
another
and each against his neighbor,
city against city, kingdom against
kingdom;

3 and the spirit of the Egyptians within
them will be emptied out,
and I will confound[1] their
[g]counsel;
and they will inquire of the idols and
the sorcerers,
and [h]the mediums and the
necromancers;

4 and I will give over the Egyptians
into the hand of [i]a hard master,
and a fierce king will rule over them,
declares the Lord GOD of hosts.

5 And the waters of the sea will be
dried up,
and the river will be dry and
parched,

6 and its canals will become foul,
and the branches of Egypt's Nile
will diminish and dry up,
reeds and rushes will rot away.

7 There will be bare places by the Nile,
on the brink of the Nile,
and all that is sown by the Nile will
be parched,
will be driven away, and will be no
more.

8 The [j]fishermen will mourn and lament,
all who cast a hook in the Nile;
and they will languish
who spread nets on the water.

9 The workers in [k]combed flax will be
in despair,
and the weavers of white cotton.

10 Those who are the [l]pillars of the land
will be crushed,
and all who [m]work for pay will be
grieved.

11 The princes of [n]Zoan are utterly
foolish;
the wisest counselors of Pharaoh
give stupid counsel.

6 [v][See ver. 5 above] 7 [w]Ps. 68:31 [x]ver. 2 [y][ch. 25:10] [z]2 Sam. 7:13
Chapter 19
1 [a]See ch. 13:1 [b][Joel 3:19]; See Jer. 46:13-26; Ezek. 29:1–31:2; 31:18–32:32 [c]Ps. 18:10, 11; 104:3; [Matt. 26:64; Rev. 1:7] [d]Ex. 12:12; [1 Sam. 5:3; Jer. 43:12; 50:2] [e]ch. 13:7; See Josh. 2:11
2 [f][Judg. 7:22]
3 [g]ver. 11
[h]ch. 8:19
4 [i]ch. 20:4; Jer. 46:26; Ezek. 29:19
8 [j][Num. 11:5]
9 [k][Ezek. 27:7]
10 [l][Gal. 2:9] [m]Jer. 46:21
11 [n]ch. 30:4; Num. 13:22; Ps. 78:43

[1] Or *I will swallow up*

18:6 summer . . . winter. The length of time implied emphasizes how extensive the carnage will be.

18:7 tribute. The nations offer tokens of submission (13:4 note; 16:1 note).

tall and smooth. See v. 2.

the place. The temple was the Old Testament token of God's kingdom (Deut. 12:5, 11).

19:1–20:6 An oracle of judgment concerning Egypt. In contrast to ch. 20, the language of ch. 19 is symbolic, not historically specific.

19:1 oracle. Prophetic message (13:1 note).

19:3 the idols and the sorcerers. On idolatry and divination, see 2:6, 8; 8:19.

19:4 hard master . . . fierce king. Egypt, too, will be subjugated; perhaps this is an allusion to Pharaoh's cruelty before the Exodus (Ex. 6:9).

Lord GOD of hosts. See note 1:9.

19:5 river . . . dry. This spells economic disaster for a country whose life depends on the Nile. God can easily dry up Egypt's many waters.

19:6 reeds and rushes. Contrast 35:6, 7.

19:7 sown by the Nile. Egypt was the bread-basket of many countries because of the regular flooding of the Nile (Gen. 41:57).

19:9 flax . . . white cotton. God's judgment against Egypt fell on the important industries of fishing (v. 8) and flax products, for which Egypt was famous.

19:10 pillars. The meaning of this Hebrew word is uncertain. Some believe it is a metaphor for the nobles as the "foundation" of the society in contrast to those "who work for pay." Others suggest "weavers" of cloth. The point is that all aspects of the society will suffer greatly.

19:11 Zoan. Also known as Tanis, this was a city in the Nile Delta (Num. 13:22; Ps. 78:12, 43) and Egypt's capital at the time.

foolish. God turns the wisdom of the wise into folly.

counselors . . . stupid counsel. See note 11:2.

son of the wise, a son of ancient kings. This sarcastic remark taunts Egypt's claim to wisdom (cf. 1 Kin. 4:29–31).

How can you say to Pharaoh,
"I am a son of the wise,
a son of ancient kings"?
12 Where then are your [o]wise men?
Let them tell you
that they might know what the
LORD of hosts has purposed
against Egypt.
13 The princes of [n]Zoan have become
fools,
and the princes of [p]Memphis are
deluded;
those who are the [q]cornerstones of
her tribes
have made Egypt stagger.
14 The LORD has mingled within her [r]a
spirit of confusion,
and they will make Egypt stagger in
all its deeds,
[s]as a drunken man staggers in his
vomit.
15 And there will be nothing for
Egypt
that [t]head or tail, palm branch or
reed, may do.

Egypt, Assyria, Israel Blessed

16 In that day the Egyptians will be [u]like
women, and [v]tremble with fear before the
hand that the LORD of hosts shakes over
them. 17 And the land of Judah will become
a terror to the Egyptians. Everyone to
whom it is mentioned will fear because of
the purpose that the LORD of hosts has purposed against them.
18 [w]In that day there will be [x]five cities in
the land of Egypt that [y]speak the language
of Canaan and swear allegiance to the LORD
of hosts. One of these will be called the
City of Destruction.[1]
19 In that day there will be an [z]altar to the
LORD in the midst of the land of Egypt, and
a [a]pillar to the LORD at its border. 20 [a]It will
be a sign and a witness to the LORD of hosts
in the land of Egypt. When they cry to the
LORD because of oppressors, [b]he will send
them a savior and defender, and deliver
them. 21 [c]And the LORD will make himself
known to the Egyptians, and the Egyptians
will know the LORD in that day [d]and worship with sacrifice and offering, and they
will make vows to the LORD and perform
them. 22 [e]And the LORD will strike Egypt,
striking and healing, and they will return to
the LORD, and he will listen to their pleas
for mercy and heal them.
23 [f]In that day there will be a highway
from Egypt to Assyria, and Assyria will
come into Egypt, and Egypt into Assyria,
[g]and the Egyptians will worship with the
Assyrians.
24 In that day Israel will be the third with
Egypt and Assyria, [h]a blessing in the midst
of the earth, 25 whom the LORD of hosts has
blessed, saying, "Blessed be Egypt [i]my people, and Assyria [j]the work of my hands,
and [k]Israel my inheritance."

A Sign Against Egypt and Cush

20 In the year that [l]the commander in
chief, who was sent by Sargon the
king of Assyria, came to [m]Ashdod and

1 Dead Sea Scroll and some other manuscripts *City of the Sun*

12 [o]1 Kin. 4:30; Acts 7:22
13 [n][See ver. 11 above] [p]Jer. 2:16; 44:1; 46:14, 19; Ezek. 30:13, 16 [q][Zech. 10:4]
14 [r][1 Kin. 22:22] [s][ch. 24:20; 29:9]
15 [t]ch. 9:14
16 [u]Jer. 50:37; 51:30; Nah. 3:13 [v]ch. 10:32
18 [w]ver. 21 [x][ch. 30:17; 2 Kin. 7:13] [y][Zeph. 3:9]
19 [z][2 Kin. 5:17] [a][Gen. 28:18]
20 [a][See ver. 19 above] [b][Obad. 21]
21 [c][ver. 25] [d]Zech. 14:16-18; [ch. 2:2]
22 [e]Jer. 46:25, 26
23 [f]ch. 11:16 [g][ver. 18, 21; Zeph. 3:9]
24 [h][Gen. 12:2, 3]
25 [i][Hos. 2:23] [j]ch. 29:23 [k]Deut. 32:9
Chapter 20
1 [l]2 Kin. 18:17 [m]1 Sam. 5:1

19:12 Where then are your wise men. These words addressed to Pharaoh continue to stand as a polemic against human pride (1 Cor. 1:20).

19:13 princes . . . cornerstones. These include political, economic, and religious leaders.

Memphis. This city in Lower Egypt was its ancient capital.

19:16 the hand. See note 14:26, 27.

19:18 five cities. Not just one but five cities will turn to the Lord.

language of Canaan. This shows how great a change is in view, because anything Canaanite was an abomination to the Egyptians (Gen. 43:32; 46:34).

swear allegiance to the LORD. That is, submit completely to God.

City of Destruction. This probably refers to Heliopolis ("City of the Sun," see text note). Jewish scribes parodied the name by changing the Hebrew word for "sun" to the almost identical Hebrew word for "destruction."

19:20 sign . . . witness. The altar (v. 19) signifies their commitment to the Lord (cf. Gen. 12:8; 28:22; Josh. 22:26–29).

savior and defender. God will fill these roles to deliver them from oppressors, as He did for Israel in the days of the judges (Judg. 2:18; 3:9, 15).

19:22 strike . . . heal. Divine discipline will draw the Egyptians to the Lord (30:26; Hos. 6:1; 14:1, 2, 4).

19:23 highway. Building this link between Egypt and Assyria symbolizes the removal of the alienation between them (cf. 11:16 note).

Egypt to Assyria. These two great cultures find unity in a common commitment to the Lord.

19:24 blessing in the midst of the earth. Israel, Egypt, and Assyria will join in the patriarchal promises (Gen. 12:2, 3).

19:25 people . . . work of my hands . . . inheritance. Each will share in full covenant membership, signified by three designations: "people" (cf. 10:24; 40:1 note; Ps. 100:3; Jer. 11:4; Hos. 2:23); "work of my hands" (60:21; Ps. 119:73; 138:8); "inheritance" (cf. Deut. 32:9).

20:1 Sargon. This is Sargon II, king of Assyria from 721 to 705 B.C.

Ashdod. This Philistine city rebelled against Assyria at the encouragement of Shabako, the Nubian king (18:1 note) in 713 B.C. It fell in 711. An inscription mentioning Sargon by name has been unearthed at Ashdod.

fought against it and captured it— 2 at that
time the LORD spoke by Isaiah the son of
Amoz, saying, "Go, and loose the sackcloth
from your waist and take off your sandals
from your feet," and he did so, walking
[n]naked and barefoot.
3 Then the LORD said, "As my servant
Isaiah has walked naked and barefoot for
three years [o]as a sign and a portent against
Egypt and Cush,[1] 4 so shall the [p]king of
Assyria lead away the Egyptian captives
and the Cushite exiles, both the young and
the old, naked and barefoot, with buttocks
uncovered, the nakedness of Egypt. 5 [q]Then
they shall be dismayed and ashamed
because of Cush their hope and of Egypt
their boast. 6 And the inhabitants of [r]this
coastland will say in that day, 'Behold, this
is what has happened to those in whom we
hoped and [s]to whom we fled for help to be
delivered from the king of Assyria! And we,
how shall we escape?'"

Fallen, Fallen Is Babylon

21 The [t]oracle concerning the wilderness of [u]the sea.

[v]As whirlwinds in the Negeb sweep on,
it comes from the wilderness,
from a terrible land.
2 A stern vision is told to me;
[w]the traitor betrays,
and the destroyer destroys.
Go up, O [x]Elam;
lay siege, O [y]Media;
all the [z]sighing she has caused
I bring to an end.
3 Therefore my loins are filled with
anguish;
[a]pangs have seized me,
like the pangs of a woman in labor;
I am bowed down so that I cannot
hear;
I am dismayed so that I cannot see.
4 My heart staggers; horror has
appalled me;
[b]the twilight I longed for
has been turned for me into
trembling.
5 [c]They prepare the table,
they spread the rugs,[2]
they eat, they drink.
Arise, O princes;
[d]oil the shield!
6 For thus the Lord said to me:
"Go, set a watchman;
let him announce what he sees.
7 When he sees riders, horsemen in
pairs,
riders on donkeys, riders on
camels,
let him listen diligently,
very diligently."
8 Then he who saw cried out:[3]
[e]"Upon a watchtower I stand, O Lord,
continually by day,
and at my post I am stationed
whole nights.

2 [n]Mic. 1:8, 11; [1 Sam. 19:24]
3 [o][ch. 8:18]
4 [p]ch. 19:4
5 [q]ch. 30:3, 5; [ch. 37:9]
6 [r]Jer. 47:7; [ch. 14:29, 31] [s][ch. 37:6]
Chapter 21
1 [t]See ch. 13:1 [u]Jer. 51:36, 42 [v]Jer. 51:1
2 [w]ch. 24:16; 33:1 [x]See ch. 11:11 [y]See ch. 13:17
[z]Ezek. 9:4
3 [a]See ch. 13:8
4 [b][Deut. 28:67]
5 [c]Jer. 51:39, 57 [d]2 Sam. 1:21
8 [e]Hab. 2:1

1 Probably *Nubia* 2 Or *they set the watchman* 3 Dead Sea Scroll, Syriac; Masoretic Text *Then a lion cried out*, or *Then he cried out like a lion*

20:2 sackcloth . . . barefoot. The Lord ordered Isaiah to be partially clad like a captive going into exile. Sackcloth was a garment for times of mourning (15:3; 22:12; 37:1, 2; 58:5), or else the distinctive prophetic garment (2 Kin. 1:8; Zech. 13:4).

20:3 my servant. The phrase refers to a position of trust and honor before God. Moses was God's friend and servant (Ex. 14:31; Num. 12:7, 8; Deut. 34:5). Also included among God's servants were Abraham (Ps. 105:42); Jacob (Ezek. 28:25); Joshua (Josh. 24:29); David (37:35; 2 Sam. 3:18; Ps. 132:10); the Suffering Servant (52:13–53:12); and groups of people, such as the prophets (44:26) and restored Israel (41:8, 9; 43:10; 44:1, 2, 21; 45:4; 48:20). God's servants may suffer, but they are promised a great heritage as "servants of the LORD" (54:17; 65:8, 9, 13–15; 66:14).

three years. It could designate the time that Isaiah walked about as a sign or the duration before the sign would be realized.

sign and a portent. The prophetic style of life (8:18; cf. Deut. 13:1, 2; Jer. 32:20) pointed out the folly of relying on Egypt, because Egypt, like any nation, was vulnerable.

20:4 king of Assyria. Esarhaddon fulfilled this prophecy in 671 B.C.

20:6 in that day. See note 2:11.

in whom we hoped. Egypt's fate will persuade the people that no ally can help them escape.

21:1 oracle. See note 13:1.

wilderness of the sea. This is probably a sarcastic parody. Babylon's southern region on the Persian Gulf, known as "Land of the Sea," will become a wilderness or as good as a wilderness to anyone looking for salvation from there.

21:2 stern vision. The prophet is overwhelmed by what he sees.

betrays . . . destroys. In the course of waging war.

Elam . . . Media. Elam was a major region of Persia. It was allied with Media in 700 B.C. Perhaps as a part of Assyria's army (5:26 note) Elam helped to conquer Babylon in 689 B.C., as they certainly did in 539 B.C. (11:11; 13:17 and notes).

the sighing. The indefinite subject could refer to the groan of Babylon under Assyrian domination or to the groan of the nations under Babylonian control. The former is more likely, because Babylon rose to power in 605 B.C.

21:3, 4 The expressions in these verses convey great psychological suffering on the prophet's part (16:9–11; 22:4; cf. Dan. 8:27; 10:16–17). The report of Babylon's fall may have distressed Isaiah because now no one could rescue Judah from Assyria.

21:5 oil the shield. Prepare for battle.

21:6 watchman. Isaiah is God's watchman in Judah.

21:7 riders . . . camels. Probably signs of an approaching army.

9 And behold, here come riders,
horsemen in pairs!"
[f] And he answered,
[g] "Fallen, fallen is Babylon;
[h] and all the carved images of her gods
he has shattered to the ground."
10 O [i] my threshed and winnowed one,
what I have heard from the LORD
of hosts,
the God of Israel, I announce to you.

11 The [j] oracle concerning [k] Dumah.

One is calling to me from [l] Seir,
"Watchman, what time of the
night?
Watchman, what time of the night?"
12 The watchman says:
"Morning comes, and also [m] the night.
If you will inquire, [n] inquire;
come back again."

13 The [o] oracle concerning [p] Arabia.

In the thickets in [p] Arabia you will
lodge,
O [q] caravans of [p] Dedanites.
14 To the thirsty bring water;
meet the fugitive with bread,
O inhabitants of the land of
[r] Tema.
15 For they have fled from the swords,
from the drawn sword,
from the bent bow,
and from the press of battle.

16 For thus the Lord said to me, "Within
a year, [s] according to the years of a hired
worker, all the glory of [t] Kedar will come to
an end. 17 And the remainder of the archers
of the mighty men of the sons of [t] Kedar
will be few, [u] for the LORD, the God of
Israel, has spoken."

An Oracle Concerning Jerusalem

22 The [v] oracle concerning [w] the valley
of vision.

What do you mean that you have
gone up,
all of you, to the housetops,
2 you who are full of shoutings,
tumultuous city, [x] exultant
town?
Your slain are [y] not slain with the
sword
or dead in battle.
3 [z] All your leaders have fled
together;
without the bow they were
captured.
All of you who were found were
captured,
though they had fled far away.
4 Therefore I said:
"Look away from me;
[a] let me weep bitter tears;
do not labor to comfort me
concerning the destruction of the
daughter of my people."

9 [f] [Hab. 2:2] [g] Jer. 51:8; Cited Rev. 14:8; 18:2 [h] ch. 46:1
10 [i] Jer. 51:33; Amos 1:3; [Mic. 4:13]
11 [j] See ch. 13:1 [k] Gen. 25:14; 1 Chr. 1:30 [l] Deut. 2:8; Ezek. 35:2
12 [m] [Job 36:20; Amos 5:8] [n] [Ps. 37:36]
13 [o] See ch. 13:1 [p] Gen. 25:3; Jer. 25:23, 24 [q] [Gen. 37:25]
14 [r] Job 6:19
16 [s] See ch. 16:14 [t] ch. 60:7; Gen. 25:13; Ps. 120:5, 6; S. of S. 1:5; Jer. 2:10; 49:28; Ezek. 27:21
17 [t] [See ver. 16 above] [u] ch. 1:20
Chapter 22
1 [v] See ch. 13:1 [w] ver. 5; Jer. 21:13; [Joel 3:12, 14]
2 [x] ch. 32:13 [y] Lam. 4:9
3 [z] [ch. 1:10]
4 [a] Jer. 9:1; Mic. 1:8

21:9 fallen is Babylon. Finally, the seductive power of Babylon, her religion (17:7–9; 27:9; 46:1–13), and her culture have come to an end (13:19).

21:10 my threshed and winnowed one. Judah is portrayed as an oppressed people, much like the grain under the threshing sledge (28:27, 28; 41:15, 16; Amos 1:3). See note 40:1.

21:11 oracle. See note 13:1.

Dumah. An oasis in Edom at the intersection of the roads from the Red Sea to Palmyra and from the Persian Gulf to Petra.

Seir. Edom. The Edomites ask the prophet what the future will hold.

21:12 Morning . . . night. The future holds both hope and judgment, specifically, relief from Assyrian domination followed by oppression from Babylon.

21:13 oracle. See note 13:1.

Dedanites. Dedan was an oasis 200 miles south of Dumah (Ezek. 27:20; 38:13).

21:14 Tema. This also was an oasis, located 90 miles north of Dedan (Jer. 25:23). The desert peoples provide food and water for the fugitives from the battle.

21:16 Within a year. Arabia's glory will be directly affected by what happens in Babylon.

Kedar. Arabia, including Syria; the area inhabited by Bedouin tribes (Jer. 49:28, 29).

22:1–25 An oracle of judgment concerning the Valley of Vision, Jerusalem. The placement of an oracle concerning Jerusalem in the midst of oracles against foreign nations may be explained by the historical association of Jerusalem with Babylon. Jerusalem had trusted in Babylon during the Assyrian hegemony, but ultimately was taken into captivity by her former ally. The occasion may be Ashdod's rebellion and the Assyrian campaign in 711 B.C., or the lifting of the siege on Jerusalem after the devastation of Judah in 701 B.C.

22:1 oracle. See note 13:1.

valley of vision. This may be intended as an insult, to the effect that the city built on a hill (2:1) is now a valley.

to the housetops. The Assyrians having left, the people gathered on the housetops for purposes of socializing and celebrating (v. 13).

22:2 full of shoutings . . . tumultuous . . . exultant. The noisy and excited citizenry has not seen what the prophet has seen. Rather they have become complacent (32:13; Zeph. 2:15; 3:11).

not slain with the sword. They had run away (v. 3).

22:3 your leaders have fled. The people were governed by unreliable and selfish leaders who abandoned them to save their own lives (2 Kin. 25:4–6). The prophet is critical of human leadership and of people who have no understanding of what is happening around them (1:23–26; 3:13–15; 9:14–17; 19:13–15; 28:7–13; 29:15).

22:4 do not labor to comfort me. His sorrow was too deep for consolation. See note 21:3–4.

5 [b]For the Lord GOD of hosts has [c]a day
of tumult and [d]trampling and
[e]confusion
in [w]the valley of vision,
a battering down of walls
and a shouting to the
mountains.
6 And [f]Elam bore the quiver
with chariots and horsemen,
and [g]Kir uncovered the shield.
7 Your choicest valleys were full of
chariots,
and the horsemen took their stand
at the gates.
8 He has taken away [h]the covering of
Judah.

In that day you looked to [i]the weapons
of the House of the Forest, 9 and you saw
that [j]the breaches of the city of David were
many. [k]You collected the waters of the
lower pool, 10 and you counted the houses
of Jerusalem, and you broke down the
houses to fortify the wall. 11 [k]You made a
reservoir between [l]the two walls for the
water of [m]the old pool. But [n]you did not
look to him who did it, or see him who
planned it long ago.

12 In that day [o]the Lord GOD of hosts
called for weeping and
mourning,
for [p]baldness and [q]wearing
sackloth;
13 and behold, joy and gladness,
killing oxen and slaughtering sheep,
eating flesh and drinking wine.
[r]"Let us eat and drink,
for tomorrow we die."
14 The LORD of hosts [s]has revealed
himself in my ears:
"Surely [t]this iniquity will not be
atoned for you [u]until you die,"
says the Lord GOD of hosts.

15 Thus says the Lord GOD of hosts,
"Come, go to this steward, to [v]Shebna,
who is over the household, and say to him:
16 What have you to do here, and whom
have you here, [w]that you have cut out here
a tomb for yourself, you [x]who cut out a
tomb on the height and carve a dwelling for
yourself in the rock? 17 Behold, the LORD
will hurl you away violently, O you strong
man. [y]He will seize firm hold on you 18 and
whirl you around and around, and throw
you like a ball into a wide land. There you
shall die, and there shall be [z]your glorious
chariots, you shame of your master's
house. 19 [a]I will thrust you from your office,
and you will be pulled down from your station. 20 In that day I will call my servant
[b]Eliakim the son of Hilkiah, 21 and [b]I will
clothe him with your robe, and will bind
your sash on him, and will commit your
authority to his hand. And he shall be [c]a
father to the inhabitants of Jerusalem and

5 [b][ch. 37:3] [c]ch. 10:6; 18:2 [d]Mic. 7:4 [e]ch. 2:12-17 [w][See ver. 1 above]
6 [f]See ch. 11:11 [g]2 Kin. 16:9
8 [h]ch. 30:1 [i]1 Kin. 10:17
9 [j]ver. 5, 10; [2 Chr. 32:5] [k][Neh. 3:16]
11 [k][See ver. 9 above] [l][2 Kin. 25:4] [m][ch. 7:3; 2 Kin. 20:20; 2 Chr. 32:3, 4] [n][ch. 5:12]
12 [o][Joel 2:17] [p]See ch. 3:24 [q]See 2 Sam. 3:31
13 [r]ch. 56:12; Cited 1 Cor. 15:32
14 [s]ch. 5:9 [t][ch. 27:9; 1 Sam. 3:14] [u][ver. 13]
15 [v]ch. 36:3, 11, 22; 37:2; 2 Kin. 18:18, 26, 37; 19:2
16 [w]2 Chr. 16:14 [x]Matt. 27:60
17 [y][Dan. 3:21]
18 [z][ch. 36:9]
19 [a][ver. 25]
20 [b]ch. 36:3; 37:2; 2 Kin. 18:18, 26, 37; 19:2
21 [b][See ver. 20 above] [c]Gen. 45:8

22:5 day. The day of the Lord. See note 2:11.

tumult and trampling and confusion. These images are a vivid description of desolation and destruction (18:2, 7; Deut. 28:20; Ezek. 7:7; Amos 3:9; Zech. 14:13).

battering down . . . shouting. There is frenzied anxiety and screams of anguish.

22:6 Elam . . . Kir. See notes 11:11; 21:2. These nations to the east of Babylon joined Assyria in the siege of Jerusalem (5:26 note).

22:8 the House of the Forest. This was apparently a storeroom for weapons next to the temple (1 Kin. 7:2–5).

22:9 city of David. Jerusalem.

lower pool. This may be the pool of Siloam. Hezekiah put buildings around it to ensure that people in Jerusalem could reach it, while denying it to enemies outside (Luke 13:4; John 9:7, 11).

22:11 old pool. Probably the Gihon Spring, also known as the "upper pool" (7:3; 36:2).

did not look . . . see him. While busying themselves with planning and fortifying Jerusalem, they forgot the Lord.

planned it long ago. God had planned the future of Jerusalem when He determined long before to create it (37:26). No one could change His plan or avert His judgment.

22:13 joy and gladness . . . drinking. This is the spirit of revelry (v. 2). It should be contrasted with the joy of God's people (35:10; 51:11).

wine. See 24:11.

Let us eat and drink, for tomorrow we die. This is a proverbial expression of contempt and disregard for God's purposes in history (1 Cor. 15:32; cf. Luke 12:19, 20).

22:14 this iniquity will not be atoned. God's judgment stands (Amos 7:1–9).

22:16 tomb . . . dwelling for yourself in the rock. Isaiah questions Shebna's preparation of a royal tomb in the hillside. Shebna should be providing leadership, not working on luxuries for himself. A tomb that may be Shebna's, cut in the rock, has been excavated in the Kidron Valley.

22:17 strong man. This ironic expression challenges Shebna's presumption.

22:18 throw you like a ball. Shebna is insignificant and is readily overthrown (cf. Jer. 22:26).

chariots. This emphasizes Shebna's luxurious way of life.

22:19 I will thrust you from your office. By 701 B.C. Shebna had been demoted to serve as secretary, and Eliakim had assumed Shebna's office (36:3, 22).

22:20 my servant. See note 20:3. God regarded Eliakim (36:3, 11, 22; 37:2) as His servant, a special designation for one close to God.

22:21 robe . . . sash. These were garments for a person in high office.

father. He would be a godly leader who serves the people well.

to the house of Judah. 22 And I will place
[d]on his shoulder [e]the key of the house of
David. [f]He shall open, and none shall shut;
and he shall shut, and none shall open.
23 And I will fasten him [g]like a peg in a
secure place, and he will become [h]a throne
of honor to his father's house. 24 And they
will hang on him the whole honor of his
father's house, the offspring and issue,
every small vessel, from the cups to all the
flagons. 25 In that day, declares the LORD of
hosts, [g]the peg that was fastened in a
secure place will give way, and it will be cut
down and fall, and the load that was on it
will be cut off, for the LORD has spoken."

An Oracle Concerning Tyre and Sidon

23 The [i]oracle concerning [j]Tyre.

Wail, O [k]ships of Tarshish,
for Tyre is laid waste, [l]without
house or harbor!
From [m]the land of Cyprus[1]
it is revealed to them.
2 Be still, O inhabitants of the coast;
the merchants of [n]Sidon, who
cross the sea, have filled you.
3 And on many waters
your revenue was the grain of Shihor,
the harvest of the Nile;
you were [o]the merchant of the
nations.
4 Be ashamed, O [n]Sidon, for the sea
has spoken,
the stronghold of the sea, saying:
"I have neither labored nor given
birth,
I have neither reared young men
nor brought up young women."
5 When the report comes to Egypt,
they will be in anguish[2] over the
report about Tyre.
6 [p]Cross over to Tarshish;
wail, O inhabitants of the coast!
7 Is this your exultant city
[q]whose origin is from days of old,
whose feet carried her
to settle far away?
8 Who has purposed this
against Tyre, the bestower of
crowns,
whose merchants were princes,
whose traders were the honored of
the earth?
9 The LORD of hosts has purposed it,
[r]to defile the pompous pride of all
glory,[3]
to dishonor all the honored of the
earth.
10 Cross over your land like the Nile,
O daughter of Tarshish;
there is no restraint anymore.
11 [s]He has stretched out his hand over
the sea;
he has shaken the kingdoms;
the LORD has given command
concerning Canaan
to destroy its strongholds.
12 And he said:
"You will no more exult,
O oppressed virgin daughter of
[t]Sidon;

22[d]Rev. 3:7 [e]ch. 9:6 [f][Job 12:14] 23[g][ch. 33:20; 54:2; Eccles. 12:11] [h][Rev. 3:21] 25[g][See ver. 23 above]
Chapter 23
1[i]See ch. 13:1 [j][Jer. 25:22; 27:2, 3]; See Ezek. 26:2–28:24; Joel 3:4-8; Amos 1:9, 10; Zech. 9:2-4 [k]ver. 14; 1 Kin. 10:22; 22:48 [l]ch. 24:10 [m]Jer. 2:10; See Gen. 10:4
2[n]ver. 4, 12; Gen. 10:15; Josh. 19:28; Jer. 25:22; 27:3; Ezek. 27:8; 32:30; Joel 3:4; Zech. 9:2
3[o]See Ezek. 27:3-23
4[n][See ver. 2 above]
6[p]ver. 12
7[q][Gen. 10:15]
9[r][Ezek. 28:7]
11[s][Ex. 14:21]
12[t]See ver. 2

[1] Hebrew *Kittim*; also verse 12 [2] Hebrew *they will have labor pains*
[3] The Hebrew words for *glory* and *hosts* sound alike

22:23 throne of honor. He will bring honor to his family and offspring, in contrast to Shebna the ("shame of your master's house," v. 18).

22:24 every small vessel. A metaphor for those who depended on God's servant.

22:25 In that day. Though Eliakim was faithful, he could not avert God's judgment on Judah.

23:1–18 An oracle of judgment concerning Tyre, concerning commercial systems that do not take God into consideration. The language is general and symbolic, not historically specific.

23:1 oracle. See note 13:1.

Tyre. A prominent Phoenician port on the Mediterranean, west of Mt. Hermon and Damascus. Judah had a longstanding relationship with Tyre, for Solomon had traded with Hiram of Tyre (1 Kin. 5:1, 8–11) and Phoenician sailors had manned Solomon's fleet (1 Kin. 9:27).

ships of Tarshish. These large vessels of the merchant fleet (1 Kin. 10:22; Ps. 48:7) traversed great distances to the Phoenician colonies along the Mediterranean coasts.

is laid waste. The fall of Tyre would require the ships to find another port.

Cyprus. This would be a port of call on the return voyage.

23:2 Sidon. Tyre and Sidon were the two most important Phoenician cities, both Mediterranean ports. The fall of one would affect the other.

23:3 Shihor. Egypt (cf. 19:7).

23:4 the sea has spoken. The sea laments the loss or destruction of its children. Hearing this, Sidon should not be overconfident.

23:6 Tarshish. Tartessus in Spain (Jon. 1:3). The nations join in the lament.

23:7, 8 exultant city . . . honored. Tyre was known for her revelry (22:2 note), "origin," far-flung influence, wealth, and fame (v. 8).

23:9–13 See "God Sees and Knows: Divine Omniscience" at Prov. 15:3.

23:9 LORD of hosts. See note 1:9.

purposed. Throughout his prophecy Isaiah seeks to bring to light something of God's counsel (11:2 note).

23:11 sea . . . kingdoms. God is Lord of land and sea.

Canaan. Canaan includes Tyre and Sidon.

23:12 virgin daughter. The inhabitants of Sidon (cf. 37:22; 47:1).

arise, [u]cross over to [v]Cyprus,
even there you will have no rest."

13 Behold the land of [w]the Chaldeans!
This is the people that was not;[1] Assyria
destined it for wild beasts. They erected
[x]their siege towers, they stripped her
palaces bare, they made her a ruin.

14 [y]Wail, O ships of Tarshish,
for your stronghold is laid waste.

15 In that day Tyre will be forgotten for [z]sev-
enty years, like the days[2] of one king. At
the end of [z]seventy years, it will happen to
Tyre as in the song of the prostitute:

16 "Take a harp;
go about the city,
O forgotten prostitute!
Make sweet melody;
sing many songs,
that you may be remembered."

17 At the end of [a]seventy years, the LORD
will visit Tyre, and she will return to her
wages and [b]will prostitute herself with all
the kingdoms of the world on the face of
the earth. 18 Her merchandise and her
wages will be holy to the LORD. It will not
be stored or hoarded, but her merchandise
will supply abundant food and fine clothing for those who dwell before the LORD.

Judgment on the Whole Earth

24 Behold, [c]the LORD will empty the
earth[3] and make it desolate,
and he will twist its surface and
scatter its inhabitants.
2 [d]And it shall be, as with the people,
so with the priest;
as with the slave, so with his master;
as with the maid, so with her
mistress;
[e]as with the buyer, so with the seller;
as with the lender, so with the
borrower;
[f]as with the creditor, so with the
debtor.
3 [g]The earth shall be utterly empty and
utterly plundered;
[h]for the LORD has spoken this word.

4 [i]The earth mourns and withers;
the world languishes and withers;
the highest people of the earth
languish.
5 The earth lies [j]defiled
under its inhabitants;
for [k]they have transgressed the laws,
violated the statutes,
broken the everlasting covenant.
6 Therefore [l]a curse devours the earth,
and its inhabitants [m]suffer for their
guilt;
therefore the inhabitants of the earth
are scorched,
and few men are left.
7 [n]The wine mourns,
the vine languishes,
all the merry-hearted sigh.

12 [u]ver. 6 [v]ver. 1
13 [w]ch. 47:1; 48:14 [x][2 Kin. 25:1; Jer. 6:27]
14 [y]See ver. 1
15 [z]Jer. 25:11, 22
17 [a]Jer. 25:11, 22 [b]Rev. 17:1, 2
Chapter 24
1 [c]ch. 13:9
2 [d]Hos. 4:9; [Lam. 4:16]; See ch. 3:1-3 [e][Ezek. 7:12, 13] [f][Jer. 15:10]
3 [g]ver. 1, 6 [h]See ch. 1:20
4 [i][ch. 16:8; Hos. 4:3]
5 [j]Num. 35:33 [k][ch. 2:6, 8]
6 [l]Zech. 5:3, 4 [m][Ps. 5:10]
7 [n][Joel 1:10, 12]

1 Or *that has become nothing* 2 Or *lifetime* 3 Or *land*; also throughout this chapter

23:13 Chaldeans . . . beasts. "Chaldeans" is another name for the Assyrians; they defeated Babylon in 689 B.C. Isaiah refers to the defeat as an example for Tyre.

23:15 seventy years. A period of time ordained by God; "seventy" signifies fullness. It is not possible to determine the specific time referred to.

song of the prostitute. A street song concerning a prostitute.

23:17 to her wages. Like a harlot, Tyre formed economic alliances with anyone who enriched her, regardless of ethics.

23:18 holy to the LORD. Tyre, too, will acknowledge the sovereignty of the Lord by paying tribute (Deut. 2:3–35; Josh. 6:17, 19).

abundant food and fine clothing. The wealth of the nations builds up the kingdom of God (45:14; 60:5, 11; 61:6; 66:12; Hag. 2:7, 8).

24:1–27:13 This section of Isaiah is often called an "apocalypse." The prophet holds before sinner and godly the clear teaching that the day of the Lord brings judgment on creation and the fullness of salvation for the saints. God's plan of redemption includes restoration from exile, the blessings of Christ in the church, and the establishment of God's kingdom in all nations. Ch. 24 focuses on God's overthrow of the corrupted earth; ch. 25, on the praise that comes to Him in response; and chs. 26 and 27 on God's interaction with His people. Brilliant assonances, incapable of translation, enhance the prophetic message.

24:1 the LORD will empty the earth. This is not annihilation, but a situation in which human structures can no longer operate (v. 3).

desolate. All human resources are removed (Nah. 2:10).

twist its surface. The world is filled with disturbances and distresses (Lam. 3:9).

scatter. God will judge the people more severely than He did at Babel, when He scattered them by confounding their languages (Gen. 11:8, 9).

24:2 people . . . priest. God will judge everyone, without making social distinctions.

24:3 spoken. See note 1:19, 20.

24:4 highest. People in their pride elevate themselves against God (2:11, 12, 17).

24:5 earth lies defiled . . . broken. The days of Noah will have returned to the earth (Gen. 6:5, 11–13). The earth itself is considered to be in danger of judgment due to the sins of those who live on it (Jer. 44:22; Rom. 8:20–22).

24:6 left. This Hebrew word is also translated "survivors" (1:9) and "remnant" (10:20, 21). As in the days of Noah (Gen. 6:8, 18), "few" will remain.

24:7–13 The prophet explains what the universal day of the Lord will be like. There will be sorrow instead of laughter (vv. 8–11; see notes 22:2, 13). The makers of music and song stop in the middle of their act (cf. 5:12).

8 [o]The mirth of the tambourines is stilled,
the noise of the jubilant has ceased,
the mirth of the lyre is stilled.
9 No more do they drink wine [p]with singing;
strong drink is bitter to those who drink it.
10 [q]The wasted city is broken down;
[r]every house is shut up so that none can enter.
11 [s]There is an outcry in the streets for lack of wine;
[t]all joy has grown dark;
the gladness of the earth is banished.
12 Desolation is left in the city;
the gates are battered into ruins.
13 For thus it shall be in the midst of the earth
among the nations,
[u]as when an olive tree is beaten,
as at the gleaning when the grape harvest is done.

14 They lift up their voices, they sing for joy;
over the majesty of the LORD they shout from the west.[1]
15 [v]Therefore in the east[2] give glory to the LORD;
in the coastlands of the sea, give glory to the name of the LORD, the God of Israel.
16 [w]From the ends of the earth we hear songs of praise,
of glory to [x]the Righteous One.
But I say, "I waste away,
I waste away. Woe is me!
For [y]the traitors have betrayed,
with betrayal the traitors have betrayed."
17 [z]Terror and the pit and the snare[3]
are upon you, O inhabitant of the earth!
18 [z]He who flees at the sound of the terror
shall fall into the pit,
and he who climbs out of the pit
shall be caught in the snare.
For [a]the windows of heaven are opened,
and [b]the foundations of the earth tremble.
19 The earth is utterly broken,
the earth is split apart,
the earth is violently shaken.
20 The earth [c]staggers like a drunken man;
it sways like a hut;
[d]its transgression lies heavy upon it,
and it falls, and will not rise again.

21 On that day the LORD will punish
the host of heaven, in heaven,
and [e]the kings of the earth, on the earth.
22 [f]They will be gathered together
as prisoners in a pit;
they will be shut up in a prison,
and after many days [g]they will be punished.
23 [h]Then the moon will be confounded
and the sun ashamed,
for [i]the LORD of hosts reigns
on Mount Zion and in Jerusalem,
and his glory will be before his elders.

8 [o]Jer. 7:34; Hos. 2:11; [Amos 8:10] 9 [p][Amos 6:5, 6] 10 [q][ch. 34:11] [r]ch. 23:1 11 [s][ver. 7; Ps. 144:14; Joel 1:5] [t][Joel 1:12] 13 [u]ch. 17:6; [Mic. 7:1] 15 [v][ch. 45:6] 16 [w][ver. 14] [x][ch. 26:2; 60:21]
[y]ch. 21:2; 33:1 17 [z]Jer. 48:43, 44; [Job 20:24; Amos 5:19] 18 [z][See ver. 17 above] [a]See Gen. 7:11 [b]Ps. 18:7 20 [c][ch. 19:14; 29:9] [d][ver. 5, 6] 21 [e]Ps. 76:12; [ch. 10:12; 31:8] 22 [f]Mic. 4:11, 12 [g]ch. 29:6 23 [h]See ch. 13:10 [i]Ps. 99:1, 2; Mic. 4:7

1 Hebrew *from the sea* 2 Hebrew *in the realm of light* 3 The Hebrew words for *terror, pit,* and *snare* sound alike

24:10 wasted city. That is, the city of desolation or desolate city; possibly Jerusalem, possibly meaning civilization in general.

house. What used to be a place of private security and enjoyment of life (5:9; 6:11; 13:16, 21; 32:13) is closed.

24:13 olive tree . . . gleaning. See note 17:4.

24:14 lift up their voices. The new song is in response to God's act of salvation (cf. ch. 12; 35:6; 42:10–13; 44:23; 49:13; 52:8, 9; 65:14). See v. 16; 14:7 note.

majesty. They sing of the greatness of Yahweh as over against human pride.

24:15 give glory to the LORD. This is a call to give God the recognition worthy of His name (25:3; 43:20; Ps. 22:23; Rev. 4:8–5:14). See note 37:16.

24:16 the ends of the earth. The nations will also join in.

But I. Isaiah, filled with tension as he looks forward to God's salvation, sees the corruption around him and is unable to join the hymn of praise.

traitors. The Hebrew evokes a sense of widespread corruption. Deception is everywhere.

24:18 windows . . . are opened. The judgment is like the Flood (cf. Gen. 7:11; 8:2).

foundations . . . tremble. The image of an earthquake is expanded in vv. 19, 20 and is an expression of a theophany (6:1 note; 13:13 note; Ps. 99:1 note).

24:21 host of heaven . . . kings. These include the gods of the nations, Satan's hosts, and human powers (cf. Eph. 6:11, 12). They are reserved for punishment and will be cast out from God's presence (2 Pet. 2:4; Rev. 17:8; 20:10).

24:23 moon . . . sun. See note 13:10.

Zion. See note 1:8. As those in Noah's ark found rest on Mount Ararat, so the remnant will find rest on Mount Zion.

God Will Swallow Up Death Forever

25 O LORD, [j]you are my God;
[k]I will exalt you; I will praise your name,
for you have done wonderful things,
[l]plans formed of old, faithful and sure.
2 For you have made the city [m]a heap,
the fortified city a ruin;
the foreigners' palace is a city no more;
it will never be rebuilt.
3 [n]Therefore strong peoples will glorify you;
cities of ruthless nations will fear you.
4 [o]For you have been a stronghold to the poor,
a stronghold to the needy in his distress,
[p]a shelter from the storm and a shade from the heat;
[q]for the breath of the ruthless is like a storm against a wall,
5 [r]like heat in a dry place.
You subdue the noise of the foreigners;
as heat by the shade of a cloud,
so the song of the ruthless is put down.
6 [s]On this mountain the LORD of hosts
will make for all peoples
a feast of rich food, a feast of well-aged wine,
[t]of rich food full of marrow, of aged wine well refined.
7 And he will swallow up [s]on this mountain
the covering that is cast over all peoples,
[u]the veil that is spread over all nations.
8 [v]He will swallow up death forever;
and [w]the Lord GOD will wipe away tears from all faces,
and [x]the reproach of his people he will take away from all the earth,
[y]for the LORD has spoken.
9 It will be said on that day,
"Behold, this is our God; [z]we have waited for him, that he might save us.
This is the LORD; we have waited for him;
[a]let us be glad and rejoice in his salvation."
10 For the hand of the LORD will rest
[s]on this mountain,
and [b]Moab shall be trampled down in his place,
as straw is trampled down in a dunghill.[1]
11 [c]And he will spread out his hands in the midst of it
as a swimmer spreads his hands out to swim,
but the LORD [d]will lay low his pompous pride together with the skill[2] of his hands.

Chapter 25
1 [j]Ex. 15:2 [k][Ps. 107:32] [l][2 Kin. 19:25]
2 [m][ch. 17:1; Jer. 51:37]
3 [n][ch. 18:7]
4 [o]Nah. 1:7 [p]ch. 4:6 [q][2 Chr. 32:18]
5 [r][ch. 32:2]
6 [s]ch. 2:2, 3; 11:9; 24:23 [t][Ps. 63:5]
7 [s][See ver. 6 above] [u][2 Cor. 3:15]
8 [v]Cited 1 Cor. 15:54; [Hos. 13:14] [w]Rev. 7:17; [ch. 30:19] [x][ch. 37:4] [y]See ch. 1:20
9 [z]ch. 26:8; [Gen. 49:18; Ps. 27:14] [a]Ps. 9:14
10 [s][See ver. 6 above] [b]See ch. 15:1
11 [c][ch. 16:12] [d][ch. 16:14]

1 The Hebrew words for *dunghill* and for the Moabite town *Madmen* (Jeremiah 48:2) sound alike 2 Or *in spite of the skill*

25:1 my God. A personal affirmation of confidence in God (7:13; 49:4, 5).

exalt . . . praise. See note 12:1.

faithful. See notes at 1:21; 11:5.

25:2 city. See 24:10 note.

25:3 glorify. The nations will acknowledge the Lord (24:14–16 and notes).

ruthless nations. Oppressive, tyrannical nations. See notes 19:24; 29:20.

25:4 stronghold. See note on "refuge" at 17:10.

poor . . . needy. See Ps. 9:18 note.

shelter . . . shade. See notes at 4:6; 30:2.

25:5 heat. Like "storm" in v. 4, this is a metaphor for oppression and persecution.

ruthless. The oppressors, troublers, and seducers of God's people.

25:6–8 Isaiah envisions the grand banquet that will celebrate God's victory.

25:6 mountain. Zion, the mountain of the Lord (vv. 7, 10). See note 2:2.

for all peoples. The guests come from all nations (24:14–16; Rev. 14:6).

rich food . . . aged wine. Ps. 23:5; Matt. 8:11; Luke 13:29; Rev. 19:9.

25:7 covering . . . veil. Perhaps these words refer to the grave as the covering for the dead.

25:8 swallow up death. Paradoxically, the devouring "mouth," from which no one can escape, will itself be swallowed up (5:14; Prov. 1:12 note).

Lord God. This title combines the Hebrew word for "lord, sovereign" with the covenant name of God (see 28:16; 40:10; 52:4; 65:13).

tears . . . reproach. All mourning (30:19; 35:10; 61:2–5; Rev. 7:17; 21:4), even death and the sting of death (1 Cor. 15:54), will be removed.

25:9 our God. The prophet identifies himself with the people of God (26:13; 40:3; 61:6).

waited. See 8:17 note.

be glad . . . salvation. See 12:1–3 and notes.

25:10 hand. This is the hand of judgment (9:12 and note; 9:17, 21; 10:4).

on this mountain. See note on v. 6.

Moab. Here Moab is representative of all the proud nations, as is Edom in 34:5–17; 63:1–6; Obad. 1.

25:11 pride . . . skill. See note 5:21.

12 And the high fortifications of his
walls he will bring down,
lay low, and cast to the ground, to
the dust.

You Keep Him in Perfect Peace

26 In that day [e]this song will be sung
in the land of Judah:

"We have a strong city;
he sets up [f]salvation
as walls and bulwarks.
2 [g]Open the gates,
that the righteous nation that
keeps faith may enter in.
3 [h]You keep him in perfect peace
whose mind is stayed on you,
because he trusts in you.
4 Trust in the LORD forever,
for the LORD GOD is an everlasting
rock.
5 [i]For he has humbled
the inhabitants of the height,
the lofty city.
He lays it low, lays it low to the
ground,
casts it to the dust.
6 The foot tramples it,
the feet of [j]the poor,
the steps of [j]the needy."
7 The path of the righteous is level;
[k]you make level the way of the
righteous.
8 In the path of your judgments,
O LORD, we wait for you;
[l]your name and [l]remembrance
are the desire of our soul.
9 My soul yearns for you in the
night;
my spirit within me earnestly seeks
you.
[m]For when your judgments are in the
earth,
the inhabitants of the world learn
righteousness.
10 [n]If favor is shown to the wicked,
he does not learn righteousness;
in the land of uprightness he deals
corruptly
and does not see the majesty of
the LORD.
11 O LORD, [o]your hand is lifted up,
but [p]they do not see it.
Let them see your zeal for your
people, and be ashamed.
Let [q]the fire for your adversaries
consume them.
12 O LORD, you will ordain [r]peace
for us;
you have done for us all our works.
13 O LORD our God,
[s]other lords besides you have ruled
over us,
[t]but your name alone we bring to
remembrance.
14 They are dead, they will not live;
they are shades, they will not arise;
to that end you have visited them
with destruction
and wiped out all remembrance of
them.
15 [u]But you have increased the nation,
O LORD,
you have increased the nation; you
are glorified;
[v]you have enlarged all the borders
of the land.
16 O LORD, [w]in distress they sought you;
they poured out a whispered prayer
when your discipline was upon
them.

Chapter 26
1 [e][ch. 27:2] [f][ch. 60:18]
2 [g]Ps. 118:19, 20
3 [h][ch. 30:15]
5 [i]ch. 25:12
6 [j][ch. 25:4]
7 [k]1 Sam. 2:9; Ps. 37:23
8 [l]Ex. 3:15
9 [m]ver. 16; [2 Chr. 33:12]
10 [n]See Ps. 73:3-11
11 [o][Mic. 5:9] [p][ch. 5:12] [q]Ps. 21:9; [ch. 33:14]
12 [r]ch. 9:7; Mic. 5:5
13 [s][ch. 2:8; 2 Kin. 16:3, 4] [t][ch. 2:20; Ps. 20:7]; See 2 Kin. 18:4-6
15 [u]ch. 9:3 [v][ch. 54:2, 3]
16 [w]Hos 5:15; See ch. 37:1-4

26:1 song. See note 14:7.

city. The city of God is the community of the redeemed (1:26; 2:2; 60:18 and notes; Ps. 46:4; 48:1–3, 12, 13; Rev. 21:2, 10).

salvation as walls and bulwarks. Since God is with His people, He provides salvation and security (12:2 note). God is like a wall protecting His people from disgrace (49:16).

26:2 Open the gates. The gates open for the entrance of the glorious King and His people (Ps. 15; 24:7, 9; 118:19, 20).

26:3 perfect peace. The "peace" of God that the righteous receive and promote (v. 12; 32:17, 18; 55:12; 66:12) will not be extended to the wicked (48:22; 59:8). This "peace" is found in Immanuel (9:6; 11:6–9; 14:7 and notes).

stayed . . . trusts. See notes 2:22; 8:12, 17.

26:4 everlasting rock. See 8:14, 15; cf. 1 Sam. 2:2.

26:5 humbled. As Nebuchadnezzar discovered (Dan. 4:37).

26:8 wait for you. This statement is a magnificent expression of what God desires: children who do His will, love Him, and wait trustingly for His full salvation.

26:10 favor. God's common grace (Matt. 5:45; Luke 6:35) is evidenced in His blessings in nature, procreation, health, and prosperity (Acts 14:17).

26:11 hand. The hand of judgment (9:12 and note; 9:17, 21; 10:4; 25:10).

fire. See note on "burning" at 4:4.

26:12 peace. See note on v. 3.

26:14 will not arise. Notice the contrast with v. 19 (cf. 14:22, 30).

remembrance. Their names, dynasty, and memorials are forgotten.

26:15 increased . . . enlarged. This verse describes the experience of restoration in earthly terms, fostering hope in the final restoration (9:3; 54:2).

17 [x]Like a pregnant woman
who writhes and cries out in her
pangs
when she is near to giving
birth,
so were we because of you,
O LORD;
18 [x]we were pregnant, we
writhed,
but we have given birth to
wind.
We have accomplished no
deliverance in the earth,
and the inhabitants of the world
have not fallen.
19 [y]Your dead shall live; their bodies
shall rise.
You who dwell in the dust, awake
and sing for joy!
For [z]your dew is a dew of light,
and the earth will give birth to the
dead.
20 Come, my people, enter your
chambers,
and shut your doors behind you;
hide yourselves [a]for a little while
until the fury has passed by.
21 [b]For behold, the LORD is coming out
from his place
to punish the inhabitants of [c]the
earth for their iniquity,
and the earth will disclose the blood
shed on it,
and will no more cover its
slain.

17 [x]See ch. 13:8
18 [x][See ver. 17 above]
19 [y][Ezek. 37:12; Dan. 12:2; Hos. 13:14] [z][Hos. 14:5]
20 [a]ch. 10:25
21 [b]Mic. 1:3 [c][ch. 24:5]

The Redemption of Israel

27 1 In that day the LORD with his hard and great and strong [d]sword will punish [e]Leviathan the fleeing serpent, [e]Leviathan the twisting serpent, and he will slay [f]the dragon that is in the sea.

2 In that day,
[g]"A pleasant vineyard,[1] [h]sing of it!
3 I, the LORD, am its keeper;
every moment I water it.
Lest anyone punish it,
I keep it night and day;
4 I have no wrath.
[i]Would that I had thorns and briers
to battle!
I would march against them,
I would burn them up
together.
5 Or let them lay hold of my
protection,
let them make peace with me,
let them make peace with me."
6 [j]In days to come[2] Jacob shall take
root,
Israel shall blossom and put forth
shoots
and fill the whole world with
fruit.
7 [k]Has he struck them [l]as he struck
those who struck them?
Or have they been slain [m]as their
slayers were slain?

Chapter 27
1 [d][Jer. 47:6] [e]Ps. 74:14 [f]ch. 51:9; Ezek. 29:3
2 [g]ch. 5:7 [h][ch. 26:1]
4 [i][ch. 10:17]
6 [j]ch. 37:31; Hos. 14:5, 6
7 [k]Hos. 6:1, 2 [l]See ch. 37:36-38 [m]ch. 37:18, 19

1 Many Hebrew manuscripts *a vineyard of wine* 2 Hebrew *In those to come*

26:18 given birth to wind. This expression of futility is due to the failure of the godly to establish God's kingdom (49:4). They suffered, but without apparent success.

deliverance in the earth. The hope of God's people both before and after the coming of Christ was the renewal of the earth and its transformation into a kingdom of peace and righteousness (cf. 42:4; 2 Pet. 3:13; cf. note on 12:2).

26:19 dead . . . bodies. This message of hope for the future is in contrast to v. 14 (cf. Ezek. 37:11, 12). The Old Testament expresses faith in the resurrection of the body since death is an invasion of God's created order (25:8 note; Job 19:26; Ps. 49:15; 73:24–26; Dan. 12:2; Hos. 13:14).

26:20 my people. That is, the remnant (vv. 7–9; 40:1 note).

enter . . . hide. As He protected Noah behind doors of safety (Gen. 7:16), so here God protects His own, as they await His salvation.

a little while. This "little while" is as long as God's judgment lasts. The present suffering is not worthy to be compared to the eternal glory that follows (v. 19; 54:7; Ps. 30:5; 2 Cor. 4:17; 2 Pet. 3:9).

fury. See 10:5 and note.

26:21 blood. See Gen. 4:10; 37:26; Ps. 9:12.

27:1 In that day. See note 2:11.

Leviathan . . . dragon. The Old Testament employs this image to denote evil, autocratic powers (30:7 note; 51:9; Ezek. 28:2; 32:2 and notes) and to assure the godly that the Lord will punish all such human expressions of power and resistance to His kingdom. Behind earth's tyrants is Satan, and behind the elect is Christ (Gen. 3:15; Rom. 16:20; Rev. 12:1–6).

27:2–13 The coming transformation is again portrayed.

27:2–6 This song of the vineyard is in sharp contrast to the parable of 5:1–7. For the vine and vineyard, see 3:14; 61:5; 65:21.

27:3 water . . . night and day. He provides for all the needs by His blessing and steadfast protection of His people (cf. Ps. 121:4, 5).

27:4 I have no wrath. The Lord is ready to forgive and to reconcile people to Himself.

burn. See note 4:4.

27:5 make peace. God welcomes all who are reconciled to Him (26:3).

27:6 take root . . . with fruit. These are indicators of a good and productive vine (John 15:1–8).

the whole world. The people of God (Jew and Gentile) make up the kingdom of God (1 Pet. 2:9–12).

27:7 struck . . . slain. The Lord has dealt more graciously with His people than with their oppressors. God fatally struck the nations, not Israel (10:5–23; 13:19–14:2; 47:4, 5).

8 [n] Measure by measure,[1] by exile you
contended with them;
[o] he removed them with his fierce
breath[2] in the day of the east
wind.
9 Therefore by this [p] the guilt of Jacob
will be atoned for,
and this will be the full fruit of the
removal of his sin:[3]
[q] when he makes all the stones of the
altars
like chalkstones crushed to pieces,
no [r] Asherim or incense altars will
remain standing.
10 [s] For the fortified city is solitary,
a habitation deserted and forsaken,
like the wilderness;
there the calf grazes;
there it lies down and strips its
branches.
11 When its boughs are dry, they are
broken;
women come and make a fire of
them.
[t] For this is a people without
discernment;
therefore he who made them will
not have compassion on
them;
he who formed them will show
them no favor.

12 In that day [u] from the river Euphrates
to the Brook of Egypt the LORD will thresh
out the grain, and you will be gleaned
one by one, O people of Israel.
13 And in
that day [v] a great trumpet will be blown,
[w] and those who were lost in the land of
Assyria and those who were driven out to
the land of Egypt [x] will come and worship
the LORD on the holy mountain at Jerusalem.

Judgment on Ephraim and Jerusalem

28 Ah, the proud crown of [y] the
drunkards of Ephraim,
and the fading flower of its
glorious beauty,
which is on the head of the rich
valley of those overcome with
wine!
2 Behold, the Lord has [z] one who is
mighty and strong;
like a storm of hail, a destroying
tempest,
like [a] a storm of mighty, overflowing
waters,
he casts down to the earth with his
hand.
3 [b] The proud crown of the drunkards of
Ephraim
will be trodden underfoot;

8 [n] [Jer. 10:24] [o] [Jer. 18:17] 9 [p] [ch. 22:14] [q] [2 Kin. 18:4] [r] See Deut. 16:21 10 [s] ch. 17:9; 32:14, 19; [Hos. 8:14; Mic. 5:11] 11 [t] Deut. 32:28; See ch. 30:16-18
12 [u] See Gen. 15:18 13 [v] Lev. 25:9; [Matt. 24:31; Rev. 11:15] [w] ch. 11:11, 16; Mic. 7:12 [x] [ch. 2:2]
Chapter 28
1 [y] [Hos. 7:5] 2 [z] [ch. 8:7] [a] ver. 15, 18 3 [b] ver. 1

1 Or *By driving her away*; the meaning of the Hebrew word is uncertain 2 Or *wind* 3 Septuagint *and this is the blessing when I take away his sin*

27:8 removed . . . east wind. The east wind brought dust and scorching heat from the desert, destroying vegetation. Here it is a figure for God's wrath.

27:9 guilt . . . sin. By undergoing God's discipline (v. 7), Jacob, that is to say Israel, will pay their debt to divine justice for their idolatry. The proof that the discipline has been effective will be the destruction of the places where they worshiped idols. This atonement and new obedience illustrates on a national level what Christ would accomplish in a perfect way on behalf of a greater number (John 11:52).

27:10 fortified city. That is, the city of man (26:1–6 note).

27:11 boughs. The mighty city will become brittle like dried out branches.

people without discernment. The city is inhabited by foolish idolaters (2:8 note; Rom. 1:20–23).

he who made. See 22:11 note.

he who formed. A frequent designation of God as Creator, Ruler, and Redeemer of His people. The verb denotes planning ("purposed," 46:11); authority, as of an artisan over his materials (41:25); creation and providence (45:18); and the formation of a new people (43:1, 21; 44:2, 21; 49:5; 64:8).

favor. This is the undeserved grace of God (26:10; 30:18, 19; 33:2).

27:12 thresh. This verb can refer to separating grain (by flailing the stalks, Ruth 2:17) or olives (by beating the branches, Deut. 24:20). It is frequently used as a metaphor for separating and gathering God's people from the world.

river . . . Brook. That is, the Euphrates River and the Wadi el-Arish, defining the boundaries of the territory of Canaan, given by promise to Abraham (Gen. 15:18). Assyria and Egypt will be connected by a highway (11:16; 35:8, 9) that leads from both to Jerusalem. People from different origins will be united in worship of the one God.

27:13 trumpet. Like the banner (11:10), the trumpet is used for summoning troops (Ex. 19:16, 19; 1 Sam. 13:3; 2 Sam. 6:15; Matt. 24:31; 1 Thess. 4:16).

lost. This could refer to the oppressed and scattered remnant (Jer. 50:6; Ezek. 34:4–6), to the dead (25:8; 26:14, 19), or to both.

mountain. That is, Zion (2:2 note). It is the place of both God's throne (14:13) and His blessed presence (25:6, 7). These promises are both already realized (e.g., Heb. 12:22) and still to come (e.g., Rev. 21:2, 3).

28:1–13 An oracle of woe on the occasion of Ephraim's fall (722 B.C.). This is the first section of woes (1:4 note) in chs. 28–33 (28:1; 29:1, 15; 30:1; 31:1; 33:1).

28:1 proud. Human arrogance stands in opposition to the "majesty" (same word in Hebrew) of the Lord (26:10).

crown. A symbol of royalty (Ezek. 21:31) or deity (2 Sam. 12:30), or if translated "wreath," a sign of social status or celebration (Song 3:11, of a garland worn at a wedding). The reference is to Samaria and its debauched leadership.

drunkards . . . wine. See 24:11.

28:2 mighty and strong. Assyria.

hail . . . waters. Assyria is likened to a powerful storm (7:2; 17:13; 28:17; 29:6; 30:30; 32:19). For God's protection, see 4:6.

4 [c]and the fading flower of its glorious
beauty,
which is on the head of the rich
valley,
will be like [d]a first-ripe fig before the
summer:
when someone sees it, he
swallows it
as soon as it is in his hand.

5 [e]In that day the LORD of hosts will be
a crown of glory,[1]
and a diadem of beauty, to the
remnant of his people,
6 and [f]a spirit of justice to him who
sits in judgment,
and [g]strength to those who turn
back the battle at the gate.

7 [h]These also reel with wine
and [i]stagger with strong
drink;
the priest and [j]the prophet reel with
strong drink,
they are swallowed by[2] wine,
they stagger with strong drink,
they reel in vision,
they stumble in giving
judgment.
8 For all tables are full of filthy vomit,
with no space left.

9 [k]"To whom will he teach
knowledge,
and to whom will he explain the
message?
Those who are weaned from the
milk,
those taken from the breast?
10 For it is precept upon precept,
precept upon precept,
line upon line, line upon line,
here a little, there a little."

11 [l]For by people of strange lips
and with a foreign tongue
the LORD will speak to this people,
12 to whom he has said,
[m]"This is rest;
give rest to the weary;
and this is repose";
yet they would not hear.
13 And the word of the LORD will be to
them
precept upon precept, precept upon
precept,
line upon line, line upon line,
here a little, there a little,
[n]that they may go, and fall backward,
and be broken, and snared, and
taken.

A Cornerstone in Zion

14 Therefore hear the word of the LORD,
you [o]scoffers,
who rule this people in Jerusalem!
15 Because you have said, "We have
made a covenant with death,
and with Sheol we have an
agreement,
when the [p]overwhelming whip passes
through
it will not come to us,
for we have made [q]lies our refuge,
and in falsehood we have taken
shelter";

4 [c][Amos 8:1, 2] [d]Hos. 9:10; Mic. 7:1
5 [e]ch. 2:11
6 [f][1 Kin. 3:28] [g][ch. 38:6]
7 [h][ch. 3:12] [i]Hos. 4:11 [j]ch. 9:15; 56:10, 12
9 [k]Jer. 6:10
11 [l]Cited 1 Cor. 14:21; See ch. 5:26-29
12 [m]ch. 30:15; [Matt. 11:28, 29]
13 [n]ch. 8:15
14 [o]ver. 22; ch. 29:20
15 [p]ver. 2, 18; [ch. 8:7, 8] [q][Rom. 1:25]

1 The Hebrew words for *glory* and *hosts* sound alike 2 Or *confused by*

28:4 first-ripe fig before the summer. The June figs were delightful because they foreshadowed the September harvest (Hos. 9:10; Mic. 7:1; Nah. 3:12). Ephraim with all her possibilities of achievement would be exiled, and the fruit of her labors would be enjoyed by the Assyrians.

28:5 In that day. See note 2:11.

remnant. See note 1:9; cf. 10:19–23.

28:6 spirit of justice. As such, He will be the Spirit of transformation (32:15; 44:3–5; 59:21; 61:1). See notes at 4:4; 11:2. Paul also contrasted being drunk with wine to the work of the Spirit (Eph. 5:18). The "spirit of justice" prevails in the messianic age (11:1–5; 42:1–4).

justice. See note 1:21.

28:7 wine . . . strong drink. See v. 1; 24:11.

priest and the prophet. The leaders of God's people had become sensual, hard of heart, and sarcastic (29:9–14; cf. Zeph. 3:4).

28:9 To whom will he teach. See note 27:7. The hardened, insulting leaders speak against Isaiah.

28:11 strange lips. That is, the foreign language of the oppressors (33:19; Jer. 5:15). The Assyrians will become Israel's teachers due to its own failed leadership. For Paul's application of this verse to "speaking in tongues," see 1 Cor. 14:21, 22.

28:12 rest. Israel could not enter the full rest in Canaan (Deut. 12:9) because of unbelief (Ps. 95:11). The hope for rest lay in the promises to Moses (1 Kin. 8:56) and to David (Ps. 132:8, 14, 17). Instead of enjoying the rest that comes by faith, Israel will be punished by her enemies.

28:13 word of the LORD. This revelation will come to Israel through the discipline of foreigners who teach Israel morals.

precept upon precept. Isaiah throws the taunts of the religious leaders (v. 10) back at them.

fall backward. God's word will have a hardening effect on its hearers.

28:14 scoffers . . . rule. These are foolish and wicked rulers (Prov. 1:22; 29:8).

28:15 covenant . . . agreement. They had chosen to ally themselves with Egypt for the purpose of remaining independent (30:2), but the choice was deadly.

lies . . . taken shelter. Their confidence was false (4:6 note).

16 therefore thus says the Lord God,
[r]"Behold, I am the one who has laid[1]
as a foundation [s]in Zion,
a stone, a tested stone,
a precious cornerstone, of a sure
foundation:
'Whoever believes will not be in
haste.'
17 And I will make justice [t]the line,
and righteousness [t]the plumb line;
and hail will sweep away the refuge
of lies,
and waters will overwhelm the
shelter."
18 Then [u]your covenant with death will
be annulled,
and your agreement with Sheol
will not stand;
when the overwhelming scourge
passes through,
you will be beaten down by it.
19 As often as it passes through it will
take you;
[v]for morning by morning it will
pass through,
by day and by night;
and it will be [w]sheer terror to
understand the message.
20 For the bed is too short to stretch
oneself on,
and the covering too narrow to
wrap oneself in.
21 For the LORD will rise up [x]as on
Mount Perazim;
[y]as in the Valley of [z]Gibeon he will
be roused;
to do his deed—strange is his deed!
and to work his work—alien is his
work!

16 [r]Cited Rom. 9:33; 1 Pet. 2:6; [Ps. 118:22; Matt. 21:42; Acts 4:11] [s]ch. 14:32
17 [t][2 Kin. 21:13]
18 [u]ver. 15
19 [v][ch. 50:4] [w][2 Chr. 32:18]
21 [x][2 Sam. 5:20; 1 Chr. 14:11] [y]See Josh. 10:10-14 [z]1 Chr. 14:16; See Josh. 9:3

22 Now therefore do not [a]scoff,
lest your bonds be made strong;
for I have heard [b]a decree of
destruction
from the Lord God of hosts against
the whole land.
23 Give ear, and hear my voice;
give attention, and hear my
speech.
24 Does he who plows for sowing plow
continually?
does he continually open and
harrow his ground?
25 [c]When he has leveled its surface,
does he not scatter dill, sow
cumin,
and put in wheat in rows
and barley in its proper place,
and emmer[2] as the border?
26 [d]For he is rightly instructed;
his God teaches him.
27 Dill is not threshed with a threshing
sledge,
nor is a cart wheel rolled over
cumin,
but dill is beaten out with a stick,
and cumin with a rod.
28 Does one crush grain for bread?
No, he does not thresh it forever;[3]
when he drives his cart wheel over it
with his horses, he does not
crush it.
29 This also comes from the LORD of
hosts;
he is [e]wonderful in counsel
and excellent in wisdom.

22 [a]ver. 14 [b]ch. 10:23
25 [c][ch. 55:10, 11]
26 [d][ch. 21:10]
29 [e]Jer. 32:19; [ch. 9:6]

1 Dead Sea Scroll *I am laying* 2 A type of wheat 3 Or *Grain is crushed for bread; he will surely thresh it, but not forever*

28:16 Lord God. See note 25:7.

stone . . . sure foundation. See note 8:14–15. The sure foundation is Jesus Christ (cf. Ps. 118:22; Rom. 9:33; 10:11; 1 Cor. 3:11; Eph. 2:20; 1 Pet. 2:4–8).

28:17 justice . . . righteousness. See note 1:21.

hail . . . waters. See note on v. 2.

refuge. See note 4:6.

28:19 As often as. The Assyrian army marched through Israel many times.

terror. Divine judgment in human history brings people face-to-face with God's power.

28:20 short . . . narrow. The things people depend on for safety are neither adequate nor comfortable.

28:21 Perazim . . . Gibeon. In the past the Lord struck the Philistines (2 Sam. 5:19, 20) and the Canaanites (Josh. 10:10) at these places.

work . . . alien. The Lord will turn against His own people.

28:22 scoff. They are responsible for any increased discipline.

decree. God ordains the events of history. See 10:22, 23.

28:23–29 As timing is important for success in farming, so God has times for grace and for judgment.

28:23 Give ear . . . hear. The prophet issues the call of divine wisdom (1:2; Prov. 1:8; 4:1; 5:1).

28:25 emmer. Probably rye (Ex. 9:32). The comparison follows the natural order of plowing, breaking up the clods, harrowing, and sowing (vv. 24, 25).

28:27 not . . . a threshing sledge. The different grains require different treatment; the Lord adjusts His judgment to circumstances and does not "plow continually" (v. 24).

28:29 counsel . . . wisdom. See note 11:2. The scoffing rulers foolishly mock the one who is wonderful in counsel (cf. 9:6).

The Siege of Jerusalem

29 Ah, Ariel, Ariel,
the city [f]where David encamped!
Add year to year;
let the feasts run their round.
2 Yet I will distress Ariel,
and there shall be moaning and lamentation,
and she shall be to me like an Ariel.[1]
3 [g]And I will encamp against you all around,
and will besiege you [h]with towers
and I will raise siegeworks against you.
4 [i]And you will be brought low; from the earth you shall speak,
and from the dust your speech will be bowed down;
your voice shall come from the ground like [j]the voice of a ghost,
and from the dust your speech shall whisper.

5 But the multitude of your foreign foes shall be like [k]small dust,
and the multitude of the ruthless like passing chaff.
[l]And in an instant, suddenly,
6 [m]you will be visited by the LORD of hosts
with thunder and with earthquake and great noise,
with whirlwind and tempest, and the flame of a devouring fire.
7 And [n]the multitude of all the nations that fight against Ariel,
all that fight against her and her stronghold and distress her,
shall be [o]like a dream, a vision of the night.
8 [p]As when a hungry man dreams he is eating
and awakes with his hunger not satisfied,
or as when a thirsty man dreams he is drinking
and awakes faint, with his thirst not quenched,
so shall the multitude of all the nations be
that fight against Mount Zion.

9 Astonish yourselves[2] and be astonished;
[q]blind yourselves and be blind!
Be drunk, but not with wine;
[r]stagger, but not with strong drink!
10 [s]For the LORD has poured out upon you
a spirit of deep sleep,
and has closed your eyes (the prophets),
and covered your heads (the seers).

11 And the vision of all this has become to you like the words of a book that is [t]sealed. When men give it to one who can read, saying, "Read this," he says, "I cannot, for it is sealed." 12 And when they give the book to one who cannot read, saying, "Read this," he says, "I cannot read."

13 And the Lord said:
"Because [u]this people [v]draw near with their mouth
and honor me with their lips,
while their hearts are far from me,
and their fear of me is a commandment taught by men,
14 therefore, behold, [w]I will again do wonderful things with this people,
with wonder upon wonder;
and [x]the wisdom of their wise men shall perish,
and the discernment of their discerning men shall be hidden."

Chapter 29
1 [f][2 Sam. 5:9] **3** [g][2 Kin. 25:1; Ezek. 4:2] [h][Ezek. 21:22; 26:8] **4** [i][ch. 2:11, 12] [j]See ch. 8:19 **5** [k]ch. 17:13; Ps. 18:42 [l][ch. 17:14; 37:36; 2 Kin. 19:35] **6** [m][1 Kin. 19:11, 12] **7** [n][Zech. 12:9]; See Mic. 4:11-13 [o]ch. 17:14; [Job 20:8] **8** [p][Ps. 73:20; 90:5]
9 [q][ch. 22:12, 13] [r][ch. 19:14; 24:20] **10** [s][ch. 6:10; Rom. 11:8] **11** [t]ch. 8:16; Dan. 12:4 **13** [u]Cited Matt. 15:8, 9; Mark 7:6, 7; [Ezek. 33:31] [v][ch. 1:12; 58:2] **14** [w]Hab. 1:5; See ch. 3:1-4 [x]Jer. 49:7; Cited 1 Cor. 1:19

[1] *Ariel* could mean *lion of God*, or *hero* (2 Samuel 23:20), or *altar hearth* (Ezekiel 43:15-16) [2] Or *Linger awhile*

29:1–14 An oracle of woe against Jerusalem.

29:1 Ah. See note 1:4.

David. Jerusalem's claim to be the city of God springs from David (cf. Ps. 132).

year . . . feasts. This points out the repetitious and tiring observance of empty rituals. See note 1:11–15.

29:3 besiege. God refers to Assyria's siege of Jerusalem in 701 B.C.

29:4 low . . . whisper. These images describe Jerusalem's experience of humiliation (2:10; 8:19).

29:5 ruthless. See note on v. 20.

29:6 thunder . . . fire. Nature rages when the Lord of the heavenly armies appears (6:4 note; Ex. 19:16–19; Judg. 5:4, 5; Ps. 18:7–15; Ezek. 32:6–8 note).

29:10 seers. See note 30:10.

29:13 draw near . . . far from me. God desires expressions of devotion from the heart and hates empty ritual (1 Cor. 1:19; Col. 2:20–23).

29:14 wisdom . . . hidden. God will shatter human wisdom and planning (30:1–5; 31:1–3).

15 Ah, [y]you who hide deep from the
LORD your counsel,
whose deeds are [z]in the dark,
and who say, "Who sees us? Who
knows us?"
16 [a]You turn things upside down!
Shall the potter be regarded as the clay,
that the thing made should say of its
maker,
"He did not make me";
or the thing formed say of him who
formed it,
"He has no understanding"?
17 Is it not yet a very little while
[b]until Lebanon shall be turned into
a fruitful field,
and the fruitful field shall be
regarded as a forest?
18 In that day [c]the deaf shall hear
[d]the words of a book,
and out of their gloom and darkness
[e]the eyes of the blind shall see.
19 [f]The meek shall obtain fresh joy in
the LORD,
and the poor among mankind shall
exult in the Holy One of Israel.
20 For the ruthless shall come to nothing
and [g]the scoffer cease,
and all who watch to do evil shall
be cut off,
21 who by a word make a man out to be
an offender,
and [h]lay a snare for him who
reproves in the gate,
and with an empty plea [i]turn aside
him who is in the right.

22 Therefore thus says the LORD, [j]who
redeemed Abraham, concerning the house
of Jacob:

"Jacob shall no more be ashamed,
no more shall his face grow pale.
23 For when he sees his children,
[k]the work of my hands, in his midst,
they will sanctify my name;
[l]they will sanctify the Holy One of
Jacob
and will stand in awe of the God
of Israel.
24 And those [m]who go astray in spirit
will come to understanding,
and those who murmur will accept
instruction."

Do Not Go Down to Egypt

30 "Ah, [n]stubborn children,"
declares the LORD,
[o]"who carry out a plan, but not mine,
and who make [p]an alliance,[1] but not
of my Spirit,
that they may add sin to sin;
2 [q]who set out to go down to Egypt,
without asking for my direction,
to take refuge in the protection of
Pharaoh
and to seek shelter in the shadow
of Egypt!

15[y][ch. 30:1] [z]Ezek. 8:12 16[a]See ch. 10:15 17[b][Ps. 107:33, 35] 18[c][ch. 32:3; 35:5; Matt. 11:5] [d]ver. 12 [e][ch. 35:5; Matt. 11:5] 19[f]ch. 61:1; [ch. 14:32; Zeph. 3:12; Matt. 5:3] 20[g]ch. 28:14, 22 21[h]Amos 5:10; [Ps. 127:5] [i]Amos 5:12 22[j][ch. 51:2] 23[k]ch. 19:25; 60:21; [Ps. 100:3] [l]ch. 8:13 24[m][ch. 28:7] Chapter 30 1[n][ch. 1:2, 4] [o][ch. 29:15] [p]ch. 25:7 2[q]ch. 31:1; 36:6

1 Hebrew *who weave a web*

29:15, 16 This oracle of woe against Jerusalem's sages begins the third section of woes in chs. 28–33 (28:1–13 note).

29:15 counsel . . . deeds. They oppose the plans and works of God (11:2 note; Ps. 10:11; 64:5, 6). They try to manipulate God rather than submit to Him.

29:16 potter . . . clay. They overturned God's order by their independent and haughty spirit (27:11 note; cf. Rom. 9:20).

29:17 Lebanon. The forests of Lebanon will become fields, and fields will become forests. Judgment brings about such reversals; "the last will be first, and the first last" (Matt. 20:16; Luke 1:52, 53).

29:18 In that day. See note 2:11.

deaf . . . blind. These words are used here as figures for the people's former spiritual conditions. The "deaf" are those formerly deaf to the message of God (42:18, 19; 43:8; cf. 6:10; 29:9). The "blind" formerly wandered from and did not discern the ways of God (42:7, 16; 56:10; 59:10; Lam. 4:14). The restoration of the spiritually "deaf" and "blind" is fulfilled today in Christ (61:1).

book. See notes on vv. 11, 12.

29:19 meek . . . poor. See Ps. 9:18 note.

the Holy One of Israel. See note 1:4.

29:20 ruthless. These people are the powerful and tyrannical oppressors of this world (13:11; 25:3–5; 29:5; 49:25; cf. Ps. 37:35; 86:14; Ezek. 28:7; 30:11; 32:12).

scoffer. This designation, common in wisdom literature, means a hardened and cynical person (28:14; Ps. 1:1; Prov. 1:22; 3:34; 9:7, 8; 21:24).

watch to do evil. Such a person is identified in v. 21.

29:22 redeemed Abraham. God accomplished redemption for Abraham by election and by covenant, promising him and his descendants the hope of the divine presence (cf. Josh. 24:14; Acts 7:2–4).

ashamed. Humiliated in defeat.

29:23 children. Jacob's hope lies in God's gracious dealing with his offspring from generation to generation (49:20–22; 54:1, 13; 65:23).

30:1 Ah. See note 1:4.

stubborn children. These are Hezekiah's counselors (cf. 1:2 note).

carry out a plan. The Hebrew could be translated "weaving a web" or "pouring out libations." Either refers to making political alliances.

not of my Spirit. Human plans (v. 2) are opposed to the plans of the Spirit of God.

add sin to sin. Here we see stubbornness increasing (1:2–4) from the plan to act independently of God to the sin of injustice (v. 12; 10:1–4 notes).

30:2 Egypt. In 701 B.C. Judah counted on Egyptian troops for help against Sennacherib (20:5, 6; 2 Kin. 8:21).

shadow. God alone provides His people with protection from danger (4:6; 16:3; 25:4, 5; 51:16; cf. Ps. 17:8; 36:7; 91:1; 121:5).

3 [r]Therefore shall the protection of
Pharaoh turn to your shame,
and the shelter in the shadow of
Egypt to your humiliation.
4 For though his officials are at [s]Zoan
and [t]his envoys reach [u]Hanes,
5 everyone comes to shame
through [v]a people that cannot
profit them,
that brings neither help nor profit,
but shame and disgrace."

6 An [w]oracle on [x]the beasts of [y]the Negeb.

Through a land of trouble and
anguish,
from where come the lioness and
the lion,
the adder and the [z]flying fiery
serpent,
they carry their riches on the backs
of donkeys,
and their treasures on the humps
of camels,
to a people that cannot profit
them.
7 Egypt's [a]help is worthless and empty;
therefore I have called her
[b]"Rahab who sits still."

A Rebellious People

8 And now, go, [c]write it before them
on a tablet
and inscribe it in a book,
that it may be for the time to come
as a witness forever.[1]
9 [d]For they are a rebellious people,
lying children,
children unwilling to hear
the instruction of the LORD;

3 [r][ver. 7; ch. 20:5] 4 [s]See ch. 19:11 [t][Ezek. 17:15] [u][Jer. 43:7] 5 [v][ver. 7; Jer. 2:36] 6 [w]See ch. 13:1 [x][ch. 51:9; Ps. 68:30] [y][Acts 8:26] [z][Deut. 8:15] 7 [a]ch. 36:6 [b]ch. 51:9 8 [c]Hab. 2:2 9 [d]ver. 1

10 [e]who say to [f]the seers, "Do not see,"
and to the prophets, "Do not
prophesy to us what is right;
speak to us [g]smooth things,
prophesy illusions,
11 leave the way, turn aside from the
path,
let us hear no more about the Holy
One of Israel."
12 Therefore thus says the Holy One of
Israel,
"Because you despise this word
and trust in [h]oppression and
perverseness
and rely on them,
13 therefore this iniquity shall be to you
[i]like a breach in a high wall,
bulging out, and about to
collapse,
whose breaking comes suddenly,
in an instant;
14 and its breaking is [j]like that of a
potter's vessel
that is smashed so ruthlessly
that among its fragments not a shard
is found
with which to take fire from the
hearth,
or to dip up water out of the
cistern."
15 For thus said the Lord GOD, the Holy
One of Israel,
"In [k]returning[2] and [l]rest you shall be
saved;
in quietness and in trust shall be
your strength."

10 [e]Amos 2:12; [Amos 7:12, 13] [f]See 1 Sam. 9:9 [g][1 Kin. 22:13]; See Jer. 28:1-11; Ezek. 13:8-16 12 [h][ch. 5:8, 20] 13 [i]Ps. 62:3 14 [j]Ps. 2:9 15 [k]Hos. 14:1 [l][Ex. 14:14]

1 Some Hebrew manuscripts, Syriac, Targum, Vulgate, and Greek versions; Masoretic Text *forever and ever* 2 Or *repentance*

30:3 shame. From this experience of utter failure, the Lord promises to deliver those who trust in Him (54:4; 61:7).

30:4 officials. Perhaps these were Judah's ambassadors who went to Zoan (19:11 note) and to Hanes (fifty miles south of Cairo).

30:6 oracle. See note 13:1.

30:7 Rahab who sits still. The name Rahab alludes to a chaos monster defeated by the gods in Canaanite creation mythology (Ezek. 28:2 and note). The prophet mocks both the mythical monster and Egypt with a title meaning roughly "Rahab, who does nothing."

30:8 tablet . . . book. The oracles concerning the folly of dependence on Egypt were to be written down as a witness to future generations.

30:9 children. See note 1:2.

instruction. The law that they are rejecting is the godly wisdom taught by Isaiah (cf. Prov. 2:1–5).

30:10 seers . . . prophets. The preaching of many prophets conformed to the expectations of the people (9:15; 28:7; 29:10; 44:25; 1 Kin. 22:8; Jer. 6:14; 14:13–16; 20:9, 10; 28:8, 9; Ezek. 13; Hos. 9:7–9; Amos 2:12; 7:12, 16; Mic. 2:6–11; 3:5, 11). Others, like Isaiah, spoke by inspiration of the Spirit and under compulsion of a divine vision.

30:11 the Holy One of Israel. See note 1:4.

30:12 Therefore. Since they would not listen to God's prophets, they will hear from Him in judgment.

word. That is, the word of God through Isaiah (vv. 8, 9).

oppression and perverseness. Jerusalem's leaders were unprincipled, and their diplomacy resulted in oppression.

30:13 iniquity. Their stubborn resistance to the Lord and dependence on Egypt will bring about their downfall.

30:15 Lord GOD. See note 25:7.

rest . . . quietness. The Lord can give His people what they searched for in Egypt.

be saved . . . strength. The Lord is the strength of His people and He will be victorious (12:2 note).

But you were unwilling, **16** and you
said,
"No! We will flee upon [m]horses";
therefore you shall flee away;
and, "We will ride upon swift steeds";
therefore your pursuers shall be
swift.
17 [n]A thousand shall flee at the threat of
one;
at the threat of five you shall flee,
till you are left
like a flagstaff on the top of a
mountain,
like a signal on a hill.

The LORD Will Be Gracious

18 Therefore the LORD [o]waits to be
gracious to you,
and therefore he [p]exalts himself to
show mercy to you.
For the LORD is a God of justice;
[q]blessed are all those who wait for
him.

19 For a people shall dwell [r]in Zion, in
Jerusalem; you shall weep no more. He
will surely be gracious to you at the sound
of your cry. As soon as he hears it, he
answers you. **20** And though the Lord give
you the [s]bread of adversity and the [s]water
of affliction, [t]yet your Teacher will not
hide himself anymore, but your eyes shall
see your Teacher. **21** [u]And your ears shall
hear a word behind you, saying, "This is
[v]the way, walk in it," when you turn to the
right or when you turn to the left. **22** Then
you will defile your carved idols overlaid
with silver and your gold-plated metal
images. [w]You will scatter them as unclean
things. You will say to them, "Be gone!"

23 [x]And he will give [y]rain for the seed with
which you sow the ground, and bread, the
produce of the ground, which will be rich
and plenteous. [z]In that day your livestock
will graze in large pastures, **24** and [a]the oxen
and the donkeys that work the ground will
eat seasoned fodder, which has been winnowed with shovel and fork. **25** And [b]on
every lofty mountain and every high hill
there will be brooks running with water,
in the day of the great slaughter, [c]when
the towers fall. **26** [d]Moreover, the light of the
moon will be as the light of the sun, and
the light of the sun will be sevenfold, as
the light of seven days, in the day when [e]the
LORD binds up [f]the brokenness of his people,
and heals the wounds inflicted by his blow.

27 Behold, the name of the LORD comes
from afar,
burning with his anger, and in
thick rising smoke;[1]
his lips are full of fury,
and his tongue is like a devouring
fire;
28 [g]his breath is [h]like an overflowing
stream
that reaches up to the neck;
to sift the nations with the sieve of
destruction,
and to place on the jaws of the
peoples [i]a bridle that leads
astray.

29 You shall have a song as in the night
when a holy feast is kept, and gladness of
heart, [j]as when one sets out to the sound
of the flute to go to [k]the mountain of the
LORD, to [l]the Rock of Israel. **30** And the LORD

16 [m]ch. 31:1, 3; [Hos. 14:3] **17** [n][Lev. 26:8; Deut. 32:30] **18** [o][Hab. 2:3] [p]ch. 5:16 [q]Ps. 2:12; 34:8; Prov. 16:20; Jer. 17:7 **19** [r][ch. 14:32] **20** [s]1 Kin. 22:27; Ps. 127:2; [Ezek. 4:10, 11] [t][ch. 3:1, 2] **21** [u][Jer. 31:33, 34] [v]ch. 35:8; [Acts 9:2] **22** [w]ch. 2:20; 31:7; [Hos. 14:8]

23 [x][ch. 32:20; Ps. 144:13, 14] [y][Jer. 5:24] [z][Ps. 65:13] **24** [a]See Gen. 45:6 **25** [b][ch. 33:21; Ps. 107:35; Joel 3:18] [c]ch. 32:19; [ch. 2:15] **26** [d]ch. 60:19, 20 [e][Hos. 6:1] [f][ch. 1:5, 6] **28** [g]ch. 11:4; 2 Thess. 2:8 [h][ch. 8:8; Nah. 1:8] [i]ch. 37:29 **29** [j]1 Sam. 10:5; 1 Kin. 1:40 [k]ch. 2:3 [l]ch. 26:4; 44:8; Deut. 32:18

[1] Hebrew *in weight of uplifted clouds*

30:16 horses. They depended on military strength and stratagems (2:7 note; 31:1, 3).

30:17 thousand . . . one. This is a reversal of God's promise to give His people victory (Lev. 26:7, 8; Deut. 32:30; Josh. 23:10).

30:18 justice. God upholds His kingdom in His patience (1:21 note).

30:19 weep. See note 25:7, 8; cf. Rev. 7:17; 21:4.

30:20 Teacher. For God's instruction, see 28:11–13; 29:11, 12. After His judgment they will see His salvation (29:24).

30:22 On Isaiah's polemic against idolatry, see 2:8.

defile. That is, desecrate (2 Kin. 23:4–8).

30:23 rain . . . bread. These blessings will come in response to the repentance apparent in the preceding verses (v. 20; cf. Deut. 28:11, 12).

In that day. See note 2:11.

30:25 brooks. Isaiah uses exaggeration to proclaim God's abundant blessings prepared for His children (cf. Joel 3:18; Amos 9:13).

day of the great slaughter. The day of the Lord (cf. 34:2, 6; Jer. 12:3; 19:6; 46:10; Zeph. 1:7, 8).

towers. Symbols of human pride (2:12–17).

30:26 sevenfold. Here the exaggerated figure indicates that God is with His people (2:5 note; 42:16; 60:19; Rev. 21:22, 23).

binds up . . . heals. God disciplines, but He remembers and heals the wounds of His people (19:22; 57:18; 61:1; Ps. 147:3; Jer. 3:22; 30:17; but cf. Is. 6:10).

30:27 name of the LORD. The covenant name represents God (12:2 note; cf. Ex. 3:14).

lips . . . tongue. Isaiah uses the resources of poetry to depict the angry power of God.

30:29 song . . . flute. This celebration is like that of a pilgrimage feast.

mountain. See note 2:2.

[m]will cause his majestic voice to be heard
and the descending blow of his arm to be
seen, in furious anger [n]and a flame of
devouring fire, with a cloudburst [o]and
storm and hailstones. 31 The Assyrians will
be terror-stricken at the voice of the LORD,
[p]when he strikes with his rod. 32 And every
stroke of the appointed staff that the LORD
lays on them [q]will be to the sound of tambourines and lyres. [r]Battling with brandished arm, he will fight with them. 33 For
[s]a burning place[1] has long been prepared;
indeed, for the king it is made ready, [t]its
pyre made deep and wide, with fire and
wood in abundance; [u]the breath of the
LORD, like a stream of sulfur, kindles it.

Woe to Those Who Go Down to Egypt

31 Woe to [v]those who go down to
Egypt for help
and rely on horses,
who [w]trust in chariots because they
are many
and in horsemen because they are
very strong,
but [x]do not look to the Holy One of
Israel
or consult the LORD!
2 And [y]yet he is wise and brings
disaster;
[z]he does not call back his words,
but [a]will arise against the house of
the evildoers
and against the helpers of [b]those
who work iniquity.
3 The Egyptians are man, and not God,
and their horses [c]are flesh, and not
spirit.
When the LORD stretches out hishand,
the helper will stumble, and he
who is helped will fall,
and they will all perish together.

4 For thus the LORD said to me,
[d]"As a lion or a young lion growls over
his prey,
and when a band of shepherds is
called out against him
is not terrified by their shouting
or daunted at their noise,
[e]so the LORD of hosts will come
down
to fight[2] on Mount Zion and on its
hill.
5 [f]Like birds hovering, so the LORD of
hosts
will protect Jerusalem;
he will protect and deliver it;
he will spare and
rescue it."

6 [g]Turn to him from whom people[3] have
[h]deeply revolted, O children of Israel.
7 For in that day [i]everyone shall cast away
his idols of silver and his idols of gold,
which your hands have sinfully made for
you.

8 [j]"And the Assyrian shall fall by a
sword, not of man;
and a sword, not of man, shall
devour him;
and he shall flee from the
sword,
and his young men shall be [k]put to
forced labor.
9 [l]His rock shall pass away in
terror,
and his officers desert the standard
in panic,"
declares the LORD, whose [m]fire is in
Zion,
and whose [n]furnace is in
Jerusalem.

30 [m]Ps. 18:13 [n]ch. 29:6 [o]ch. 28:2; [Josh. 10:11] **31** [p]ch. 9:4; [Mic. 6:9] **32** [q]Ex. 15:1 [r]ch. 11:15; 19:16; [ch. 2:19] **33** [s]2 Kin. 23:10; Jer. 7:31 [t]Ezek. 24:9, 10 [u]Ps. 18:8; Ezek. 20:48
Chapter 31
1 [v]ch. 30:2; 36:6 [w]Ps. 20:7; [ch. 30:16; 36:9] [x][ch. 22:11] **2** [y][Ps. 94:8-10] [z][Num. 23:19] [a][ch. 22:14] [b]Ps. 94:4 **3** [c]Jer. 17:5
4 [d]Hos. 11:10; Amos 1:2; 3:8 [e][ch. 42:13] **5** [f]Deut. 32:11; [Ps. 91:4] **6** [g][ch. 30:15] [h]ch. 1:5 **7** [i]ch. 2:20; 30:22 **8** [j]ch. 37:36 [k][Gen. 49:15; Prov. 12:24] **9** [l]Deut. 32:31; See ch. 30:29 [m]ch. 30:33 [n]Ps. 21:9; Mal. 4:1

1 Or *For Topheth* 2 The Hebrew words for *hosts* and *to fight* sound alike 3 Hebrew *they*

30:33 burning place. In Hebrew "Topheth." Topheth was a pit on the south side of Jerusalem where children had been sacrificed and a continual fire burned to consume the refuse that was thrown there (57:5; 2 Kin. 23:10; Jer. 7:31, 32; 19:6, 11–13).

31:1 Egypt . . . horsemen. Judah thought they could be delivered by Egyptian horses and chariots (30:2).

look to. One way of seeking the Lord is to consult His prophets (29:9, 10; 30:1).

the Holy One of Israel. See note 1:4.

31:2 he is wise. This prophetic sarcasm ridicules the royal counselors.

disaster. He is sovereign in judgment (45:7).

31:3 Egyptians . . . not spirit. This model of poetic parallelism contrasts flesh and spirit, creature and Creator (2:22; Ps. 56:4; John 4:24).

31:4 lion . . . not terrified. The Lord is as determined as a lion. Assyrian kings likened themselves to lions, proverbial for their strength and ferocity.

31:5 protect Jerusalem. The Lord cares for His people like a mother bird (Ex. 19:4; Deut. 32:11, 12).

31:7 in that day. See note 2:11.

idols . . . hands. On Isaiah's polemic against idolatry, see 2:8.

31:8 shall fall. Assyria will come to an end by God's hand and at His time, not by human stratagems (37:36).

31:9 rock. Assyria will be looking for a place to hide (Rev. 6:16).

fire . . . furnace. See 4:5 note; 10:17; 30:27, 30, 33.

A King Will Reign in Righteousness

32 Behold, [o]a king will reign in righteousness,
and princes will rule in justice.
2 [p]Each will be like a hiding place from the wind,
a shelter from the storm,
[q]like streams of water in a dry place,
like the shade of a great rock in a weary land.
3 [r]Then the eyes of those who see will not be closed,
and the ears of those who hear will give attention.
4 The heart of the hasty will understand and know,
[s]and the tongue of the stammerers will hasten to speak distinctly.
5 [t]The fool will no more be called noble,
nor the scoundrel said to be honorable.
6 For [u]the fool speaks folly,
and his heart is busy with iniquity,
to practice ungodliness,
to utter error concerning the LORD,
[v]to leave the craving of the hungry unsatisfied,
and to deprive the thirsty of drink.
7 As for the scoundrel—[w]his devices are evil;
he plans wicked schemes
to ruin the poor with lying words,
even when the plea of the needy is right.
8 But he who is noble plans noble things,
and on noble things he stands.

Chapter 32
1 [o]Ps. 72:1, 2, 4; Jer. 23:5; See ch. 11:1-4
2 [p]ch. 4:6; 25:4 [q]ch. 33:21
3 [r]See ch. 29:18
4 [s]ch. 35:6
5 [t][ch. 5:20]
6 [u]1 Sam. 24:13 [v][ch. 3:14, 15]
7 [w]Mic. 2:1, 2

Complacent Women Warned of Disaster

9 [x]Rise up, you women [y]who are at ease, hear my voice;
you complacent daughters, give ear to my speech.
10 In little more than a year
you will shudder, you complacent women;
for the grape harvest fails,
the fruit harvest will not come.
11 Tremble, you women [y]who are at ease,
shudder, you complacent ones;
[z]strip, and make yourselves bare,
[a]and tie sackcloth around your waist.
12 [b]Beat your breasts for the pleasant fields,
for the fruitful vine,
13 [c]for the soil of my people
growing up in thorns and briers,
[d]yes, for all the joyous houses
in the exultant city.
14 For the palace is forsaken,
the populous city deserted;
the hill and the watchtower
will become dens forever,
[e]a joy of wild donkeys,
a pasture of flocks;
15 until [f]the Spirit is poured upon us from on high,
and [g]the wilderness becomes a fruitful field,
and the fruitful field is deemed a forest.
16 Then justice will dwell in the wilderness,
and righteousness abide in the fruitful field.

9 [x]See ch. 3:16–4:1 [y]Amos 6:1
11 [y][See ver. 9 above] [z][ch. 47:2, 3] [a]See Gen. 37:34
12 [b][ch. 24:7]
13 [c]ch. 7:23; 34:13; Hos. 9:6 [d][ch. 24:11, 12]
14 [e]Jer. 2:24
15 [f][ch. 11:2; Joel 2:28] [g]ch. 35:1, 2; [ch. 29:17]

32:1–3 The peace and harmony of godly leadership.

32:1 king . . . princes. This means the Messiah (9:1–7; 11:1–9) and godly leaders (1:26; 1 Pet. 5:2).

32:2 shelter . . . great rock. The protective role of the king and his cohorts results from their dependence on the Lord (4:6 note); in contrast to any reliance on Egypt (30:1, 2, 12; 31:1, 3).

32:3 eyes . . . ears. This is in contrast to 6:9, 10; 29:9, 10; 30:1, 2; 31:1. See note 29:18.

32:4 heart . . . tongue. This is all in fulfillment of 29:24.

32:7 poor . . . needy. See Ps. 9:18 note.

32:8 he who is noble. He stands in contrast to the fool, who is willing to oppress the needy (vv. 5–7).

32:9 women . . . at ease. The people were confident of succeeding in their schemes (vv. 5–7; cf. 3:16–24; Amos 6:1; Zech. 1:15).

complacent. This is the same word rendered "trust" in v. 17 and "secure" in v. 18. The false security based on confidence in Egypt contrasts with the true security based on trust in God.

32:10 grape harvest . . . fruit harvest. Poor harvest is an indication of God's judgment.

32:13 soil . . . city. Everything will become a wasteland (cf. 5:5, 6; 16:8–10; 24:7–13; 34:13–15).

exultant city. See notes 22:2, 13.

32:15 Spirit. The Holy Spirit transforms everything according to God's order. He is the Spirit of restoration. See 11:2; 28:6; 42:1; 61:1; Ezek. 36:27; Joel 2:28, 29.

from on high. The Spirit is above all earthly powers (Ps. 93:4; Luke 24:49; Eph. 4:8).

wilderness . . . forest. See note 29:17.

17 [h] And the effect of righteousness will be peace,
and the result of righteousness, quietness and trust[1] forever.
18 My people will abide in a peaceful habitation,
in secure dwellings, and in quiet resting places.
19 [i] And it will hail when the forest falls down,
[j] and the city will be utterly laid low.
20 [k] Happy are you who sow beside all waters,
who let the feet of the ox and the donkey range free.

O Lord, Be Gracious to Us

33 [l] Ah, you destroyer,
who yourself have not been destroyed,
you traitor,
whom none has betrayed!
When you have ceased to destroy,
you will be destroyed;
and when you have finished betraying,
they will betray you.
2 O Lord, be gracious to us; [m] we wait for you.
Be our arm every morning,
our salvation in the time of trouble.
3 [n] At the tumultuous noise peoples flee;
when you lift yourself up, nations are scattered,
4 and your spoil is gathered as the caterpillar gathers;
[o] as locusts leap, it is leapt upon.

17 [h] James 3:18; [ch. 1:27; Ps. 72:3; 119:165]
19 [i] ch. 28:2, 17 [j] ch. 26:5
20 [k] Eccles. 11:1; [ch. 30:23]
Chapter 33
1 [l] ch. 21:2; [ch. 17:14]
2 [m] ch. 25:9; 26:8
3 [n] ch. 17:13; [2 Kin. 19:7]
4 [o] [Joel 2:4, 5]
5 [p] ch. 2:17; 5:15, 16
6 [q] [ch. 39:8]
7 [r] [ch. 36:22; 2 Kin. 18:37]
8 [s] [Judg. 5:6] [t] [ver. 1]; See 2 Kin. 18:14-17
9 [u] ch. 24:4; [Nah. 1:4]
10 [v] Ps. 12:5; 68:1; [ch. 10:26]
11 [w] [ch. 59:4; Ps. 7:14] [x] ch. 10:16, 17; [Ps. 80:16]
12 [x] [See ver. 11 above]

5 [p] The Lord is exalted, for he dwells on high;
he will fill Zion with justice and righteousness,
6 [q] and he will be the stability of your times,
abundance of salvation, wisdom, and knowledge;
the fear of the Lord is Zion's[2] treasure.

7 Behold, their heroes cry in the streets;
[r] the envoys of peace weep bitterly.
8 [s] The highways lie waste;
the traveler ceases.
[t] Covenants are broken;
cities[3] are despised;
there is no regard for man.
9 [u] The land mourns and languishes;
Lebanon is confounded and withers away;
Sharon is like a desert,
and Bashan and Carmel shake off their leaves.

10 [v] "Now I will arise," says the Lord,
"now I will lift myself up;
now I will be exalted.
11 [w] You conceive chaff; you give birth to stubble;
your breath is [x] a fire that will consume you.
12 And the peoples will be as if burned to lime,
[x] like thorns cut down, that are burned in the fire."

1 Or *security* 2 Hebrew *his* 3 Masoretic Text; Dead Sea Scroll *witnesses*

32:18 My people. See note 40:1.

32:19 hail. See note 28:2.

33:1–24 This sixth and final oracle of woe in chs. 28–33 is against Assyria. By focusing on Assyria's defeat and Judah's exaltation, the Lord, the King of Judah, is exalted.

33:1 destroyer . . . betrayed. Though Assyria is the reference in the historical context (cf. 10:5, 12, 24; 14:25; 30:31; 31:8; 2 Kin. 18:13–16; 19:32–37), it represents any power opposed to God.

33:2 This verse begins a prayer for mercy during the hour of judgment.

33:3 scattered. See Num. 10:35.

33:4 your spoil. The spoils go to the Lord, victor over the nations (23:18).

33:5 dwells on high. See note 32:15.

33:6 salvation. See note 12:2.

Zion's treasure. See text note. Probably the meaning is that the best gift a person can receive from God is the pure faith that is formed in response to the revelation of God's grace (Ps. 130:4; Prov. 9:10; Luke 5:10).

33:7–12 With all Judah's false hopes gone (vv. 7–9), the Lord acts to destroy Assyria.

33:7 heroes. Perhaps this sarcasm is directed at the three officials who conversed with Assyria (36:3, 22).

cry . . . weep. Human ploys have failed. International trade, diplomacy, and military expeditions have come to an end. The Assyrians accepted gifts and tribute from Judah but treacherously continued their siege.

33:9 land . . . Carmel. Areas famous for their fertility have become like deserts (2:13; 29:17; 32:13 and notes). For the transformation, see 35:1, 2.

33:10 Now. The time for divine intervention and the glorious establishment of His kingdom has arrived.

33:12 lime . . . thorns. These similes explain how completely Assyria will be destroyed (cf. 27:4; Amos 2:1).

13 Hear, you who are far off, what I
have done;
and you who are near,
acknowledge my might.
14 The sinners in Zion are afraid;
trembling has seized the godless:
[y]"Who among us can dwell [z]with the
consuming fire?
Who among us can dwell with
everlasting burnings?"
15 [a]He who walks righteously and speaks
uprightly,
who despises the gain of
oppressions,
who shakes his hands, lest they hold
a bribe,
who stops his ears from hearing of
bloodshed
[b]and shuts his eyes from looking on
evil,
16 he will dwell on the heights;
his place of defense will be the
fortresses of rocks;
[c]his bread will be given him; his
water will be sure.
17 [d]Your eyes will behold the king in his
beauty;
[e]they will see a land that stretches
afar.
18 [f]Your heart will muse on the terror:
"Where is he who counted, where
is [g]he who weighed the tribute?
Where is [h]he who counted the
towers?"
19 [i]You will see no more the insolent
people,
the people [j]of an obscure speech
that you cannot comprehend,
stammering in a tongue that you
cannot understand.

14 [y][Ps. 15:1; 24:3] [z]ch. 66:15; Heb. 12:29
15 [a][Ps. 15:2; 24:4] [b]Ps. 119:37
16 [c]ch. 30:23, 25
17 [d]ch. 6:5; [Zech. 9:9] [e][ch. 54:2, 3]
18 [f][Ps. 37:10] [g][2 Kin. 18:14] [h][Ps. 48:12]
19 [i][2 Kin. 19:32, 33] [j]ch. 28:11; Deut. 28:49, 50
20 [k]ch. 32:18 [l]ver. 6
21 [m]Ps. 46:4, 5 [n][ch. 2:16; Ps. 48:7]
22 [o][Judg. 2:16] [p]James 4:12 [q][1 Sam. 12:13]
23 [r][Gen. 49:27] [s][Ps. 68:12]
24 [t][ch. 1:5, 6] [u]ch. 1:25, 26; Jer. 50:20
Chapter 34
1 [v]Ps. 49:1; [Joel 3:1, 2]

20 Behold Zion, the city of our
appointed feasts!
[k]Your eyes will see Jerusalem,
an untroubled habitation, an
[l]immovable tent,
whose stakes will never be
plucked up,
nor will any of its cords be broken.
21 But there the LORD in majesty will be
for us
a place of [m]broad rivers and
streams,
[n]where no galley with oars can go,
nor majestic ship can pass.
22 For the LORD is our [o]judge; the LORD
is our [p]lawgiver;
the LORD is our [q]king; he will
save us.
23 Your cords hang loose;
they cannot hold the mast firm in
its place
or keep the sail spread out.
[r]Then prey and spoil in abundance
will be divided;
even [s]the lame will take the prey.
24 And no inhabitant will say, [t]"I am
sick";
[u]the people who dwell there will be
forgiven their iniquity.

Judgment on the Nations

34 Draw near, [v]O nations, to hear,
and give attention,
O peoples!
Let the earth hear, and all that fills it;
the world, and all that comes
from it.
2 For the LORD is enraged against all
the nations,
and furious against all their host;

33:13 Hear . . . acknowledge. People will confess that God's judgments in history are wise and powerful and submit to His sovereignty.

far off . . . near. See 57:19; these statements include every person, from whatever nation or tribe.

33:14 Who among us can dwell. This realization by sinners challenges them to repent and live in harmony with God's holy presence (Ps. 15:1; 24:3).

33:15 walks . . . shuts his eyes. These phrases describe conduct of the godly (Ps. 1:1, 2; 15:2–5; 24:4; Gal. 5:22–25; Eph. 5:1; James 3:13–18).

bribe. See note 1:23.

33:16 dwell on the heights. With God.

fortresses . . . water. He enjoys divine protection (cf. Ps. 18:1–3) and provision (49:10; 55:1, 2; 62:9; 65:13; contrast 30:20).

33:17 king. The arrival of God's kingdom and Messiah is of greater splendor than any previous manifestation (32:1 note).

33:18, 19 terror . . . stammering. Isaiah describes the misery of exile from home and oppression by foreigners.

33:20 tent . . . cords. The exile has ended. Jerusalem enjoys stability and prosperity (54:2; cf. Rev. 21:1–3).

33:21 broad rivers and streams. God provides all the needs of the citizens of His kingdom (41:18; 48:18).

galley . . . majestic ship. The kingdoms of this world can no longer intimidate and harass God's people.

33:22 See notes 2:4; 12:2; cf. 44:6; 51:4; Ps. 46; 48; 96–99; Zeph. 3:15, 17.

33:23 Your cords . . . sail. The people of the Lord are compared to a drifting ship.

33:24 inhabitant . . . people who dwell. See note on v. 14.

34:2 enraged . . . furious. See notes 5:25; 10:5.

he has [w]devoted them to
destruction,[1] has given them
over for slaughter.
3 Their slain shall be cast out,
and [x]the stench of their corpses
shall rise;
[y]the mountains shall flow with their
blood.
4 [z]All the host of heaven shall rot away,
and the skies roll up like a scroll.
All their host shall fall,
as leaves fall from the vine,
like leaves falling from the fig tree.

5 For my sword has drunk its fill in the
heavens;
behold, it descends for judgment
upon [a]Edom,
upon the people [b]I have devoted to
destruction.
6 The LORD has a sword; it is sated
with blood;
it is gorged with fat,
with the blood of lambs and goats,
with the fat of the kidneys of rams.
[c]For the LORD has a sacrifice in Bozrah,
a great slaughter in the land of
Edom.
7 [d]Wild oxen shall [e]fall with them,
and [f]young steers with [f]the mighty
bulls.
Their land shall drink its fill of blood,
and their soil shall be gorged
with fat.

8 [g]For the LORD has a day of vengeance,
a year of recompense for the cause
of Zion.
9 [h]And the streams of Edom[2] shall be
turned into pitch,
and her soil into sulfur;
her land shall become burning
pitch.

2 [w][Josh. 6:21] 3 [x]Joel 2:20 [y][Ezek. 39:4] 4 [z]Joel 2:31; 3:15; Matt. 24:29; Acts 2:20; Rev. 6:13, 14; [Ps. 102:26; Heb. 1:11] 5 [a]See ch. 63:1-6; Jer. 49:7-22; Obad. 1-21; Mal. 1:2-4 [b][ver. 2] 6 [c]ch. 63:1 7 [d]Num. 23:22 [e]ch. 47:1 [f]Ps. 22:12 8 [g]ch. 61:2; 63:4; Ps. 137:7 9 [h]Deut. 29:23

10 [i]ch. 66:24 [j][Rev. 14:11; 18:18; 19:3] [k]Mal. 1:4 11 [l]ch. 14:23; Zeph. 2:14; [Rev. 18:2] [m]2 Kin. 21:13; Lam. 2:8; See Amos 7:7-9 [n][ch. 24:10] 13 [o]See ch. 32:13 [p]ch. 13:22; Ps. 44:19; Mal. 1:3 14 [q]See ch. 13:21 15 [r]Deut. 14:13

10 Night and day [i]it shall not be
quenched;
[j]its smoke shall go up forever.
[k]From generation to generation it
shall lie waste;
none shall pass through it forever
and ever.
11 [l]But the hawk and the porcupine[3]
shall possess it,
the owl and the raven shall dwell
in it.
[m]He shall stretch the line of
[n]confusion[4] over it,
and the plumb line of emptiness.
12 Its nobles—there is no one there to
call it a kingdom,
and all its princes shall be nothing.

13 [o]Thorns shall grow over its
strongholds,
nettles and thistles in its fortresses.
It shall be the haunt of [p]jackals,
an abode for ostriches.[5]
14 [q]And wild animals shall meet with
hyenas;
the wild goat shall cry to his fellow;
indeed, there the night bird[6] settles
and finds for herself a resting
place.

15 There the owl nests and lays
and hatches and gathers her young
in her shadow;
indeed, there [r]the hawks are gathered,
each one with her mate.
16 Seek and read from the book of the
LORD:
Not one of these shall be missing;
none shall be without her mate.

1 That is, set apart (devoted) as an offering to the Lord (for destruction); also verse 5 2 Hebrew *her streams* 3 The identity of the animals rendered *hawk* and *porcupine* is uncertain 4 Hebrew *formlessness* 5 Or *owls* 6 Identity uncertain

devoted them to destruction . . . slaughter. They are consigned to destruction, as the Canaanites were (Josh. 6:17).

34:3 blood. The blood of the slain will be so great it will create mud slides (v. 7). This is imagery of the day of the Lord on earth.

34:4 roll up. See Heb. 1:10–12; 2 Pet. 3:12. As the Lord stretched out the heavens at creation (42:25), in the end He will roll them up (Mark 13:24, 25; Rev. 6:13).

34:5 descends. The Lord's avenging sword moves from demolishing the pantheon of heaven to Edom in particular.

Edom. Here representing the nations (63:1–6; Ezek. 35; Obad. 10–14; cf. Rev. 18:2).

34:6 sword. See Rev. 19:15.

Bozrah. An important city in Edom 30 miles southeast of the Dead Sea.

34:7 Wild oxen . . . mighty bulls. These terms refer to the Edomite leaders.

34:8 day of vengeance. The day of the Lord is the time when the Lord establishes His kingdom on earth by delivering and glorifying His saints and by punishing the wicked and the oppressors of His children (2:11 note; 35:4; 59:17, 18; 61:2; 63:4).

34:9 pitch . . . burning pitch. Alluding to the fall of Sodom and Gomorrah (Gen. 19:24–28; Ps. 11:6; Jer. 49:17, 18; Rev. 14:10, 11).

34:10 Night and day . . . generation to generation. God's judgment is everlasting (66:24; Matt. 18:8, 9; 25:41, 46; Mark 9:43, 48).

34:11 confusion . . . emptiness. The same Hebrew words are rendered "without form and void" in Gen. 1:2. God has decreed the desolation of powers that oppose His order. He brings disorder on those who have wreaked havoc with His order.

34:16 book of the LORD. Probably the prophecy of vv. 1–15. The Spirit will see to it that what the Word announces is fulfilled.

For the mouth of the LORD has commanded,
and his Spirit has gathered them.
17 [s]He has cast the lot for them;
his hand has portioned it out to them with the line;
they shall possess it forever;
from generation to generation they shall dwell in it.

The Ransomed Shall Return

35 [t]The wilderness and the dry land shall be glad;
[u]the desert shall rejoice and blossom like the crocus;
2 it shall blossom abundantly
and rejoice with joy and singing.
[v]The glory of Lebanon shall be given to it,
the majesty of [w]Carmel and [x]Sharon.
[y]They shall see the glory of the LORD,
the majesty of our God.

3 [z]Strengthen the weak hands,
and make firm the feeble knees.
4 Say to those who have an anxious heart,
"Be strong; fear not!
[a]Behold, your God
will come with vengeance,
with the recompense of God.
He will come and save you."

5 [b]Then the eyes of the blind shall be opened,
and the ears of the deaf unstopped;
6 [b]then shall the lame man leap like a deer,
and the tongue of the mute sing for joy.
[c]For waters break forth in the wilderness,
and streams in the desert;
7 [d]the burning sand shall become a pool,
and the thirsty ground springs of water;
in the haunt of [e]jackals, where they lie down,
the grass shall become reeds and rushes.

8 [f]And a highway shall be there,
and it shall be called the Way of Holiness;
[g]the unclean shall not pass over it.
It shall belong to those who walk on the way;
even if they are fools, they shall not go astray.[1]
9 No lion shall be there,
nor shall any ravenous beast come up on it;
they shall not be found there,
but the redeemed shall walk there.
10 [h]And the ransomed of the LORD shall return
and come to Zion with singing;
[i]everlasting joy shall be upon their heads;
they shall obtain gladness and joy,
and sorrow and sighing shall flee away.

17 [s][Ps. 78:55]
Chapter 35
1 [t]ch. 55:12, 13 [u][ch. 32:15]
2 [v]S. of S. 5:15 [w]S. of S. 7:5 [x]ch. 33:9; S. of S. 2:1 [y]ch. 40:5
3 [z]Cited Heb. 12:12; [ch. 40:1]
4 [a][ch. 40:10, 11]
5 [b]ch. 32:3, 4
6 [b][See ver. 5 above] [c][ver. 1; ch. 41:18; 43:19; 44:3, 4; John 7:38, 39]
7 [d]ch. 48:20, 21; 49:10 [e]See ch. 13:22
8 [f]ch. 40:3 [g]ch. 52:1
10 [h]ch. 51:11 [i]ch. 65:19; [ch. 25:8; Rev. 7:17; 21:4]

[1] Or *if they are fools, they shall not wander in it*

34:17 cast the lot. As God distributed the Promised Land by lot (Josh. 18:10), so He has divided Edom among the unclean animals (v. 11).

35:1 wilderness. See note 40:3. The presence of God's Spirit of restoration transforms nature and people, even when affected by this sinful world (32:15 note).

35:2 our God. For the revelation of God's kingdom, see notes 6:3; 33:17, 21.

35:4 fear not. This admonition often occurs as an assurance of deliverance from oppressors (7:4; 8:12 note; 10:24; 37:6; 41:10, 13; 43:5; 51:7).

vengeance . . . save. God will bring complete deliverance to the oppressed and establish justice on earth (34:8 note).

35:5, 6 blind . . . mute. These transformations are evidences of a supernatural restoration and are associated with the ministry of Jesus (Matt. 11:2–6; 12:22; Mark 7:37; Luke 7:21, 22).

waters. See note 1:30.

35:7 reeds and rushes. This is in contrast to 19:5, 6.

35:8 highway. See note 11:16; 40:3; contrast 33:8.

Way of Holiness. Only those who have been cleansed and consecrated are privileged to walk on the road of salvation that leads to Zion (4:3 note).

35:9 lion . . . ravenous beast. Contrast 13:21, 22; 34:11–15.

35:9, 10 redeemed . . . ransomed. These two Hebrew words often appear as parallels (Jer. 31:11; Hos. 13:14), and are almost synonymous. Both words are used to describe God's deliverance of Israel from Egypt (Ex. 6:6; 13:15, where the word "redeemed" translates the word for "ransomed" here). They play an important role in Isaiah's description of the future deliverance from the Exile as a new exodus (51:10, 11). The Lord is the "Redeemer" (41:14 and note; 49:26) who has forgiven Israel's sins (44:22; Ps. 103:3, 4).

35:10 sorrow and sighing. See note 25:8. Cf. 51:11.

Sennacherib Invades Judah

36 [j]In the fourteenth year of King
Hezekiah, [k]Sennacherib king of
Assyria came up against all the fortified
cities of Judah and took them. 2 [l]And the
king of Assyria sent the Rabshakeh[1] from
[m]Lachish to King Hezekiah at Jerusalem,
with a great army. And he stood [n]by the
conduit of the upper pool on the highway
to the Washer's Field. 3 And there came out
to him [o]Eliakim the son of Hilkiah, who
was over the household, and [o]Shebna the
secretary, and Joah the son of Asaph, the
recorder.

Chapter 36
1 [j]For ver. 1-22, see 2 Kin. 18:13, 17-37
[k][2 Chr. 32:1]
2 [l]2 Chr. 32:9
[m]Josh. 15:20, 39
[n]ch. 7:3
3 [o]ch. 22:15, 20, 21
4 [p][ch. 10:8]
6 [q]Ezek. 29:6, 7
7 [r]2 Kin. 18:4; See Deut. 12:2-5

4 And the Rabshakeh said to them, "Say
to Hezekiah, 'Thus says the [p]great king, the
king of Assyria: On what do you rest this
trust of yours? 5 Do you think that mere
words are strategy and power for war? In
whom do you now trust, that you have
rebelled against me? 6 [q]Behold, you are
trusting in Egypt, that broken reed of a
staff, which will pierce the hand of any man
who leans on it. Such is Pharaoh king of
Egypt to all who trust in him. 7 But if you
say to me, "We trust in the LORD our God,"
is it not he [r]whose high places and altars

1 *Rabshakeh* is the title of a high-ranking Assyrian military officer

36:1–39:8 This historical bridge between chs. 1–35 and 40–66 directly parallels 2 Kin. 18:13–20:19. It records the fulfillment of Isaiah's predictions that the Lord would judge Judah by bringing the Assyrian army to the gates of Jerusalem and would then judge that proud army by destroying it there, preserving a faithful remnant in the city. Hezekiah's faith contrasts with that of his father, Ahaz. Hezekiah by faith accepted a sign when confronted with illness (30:7, 8); Ahaz refused to ask for a sign (7:12).

36:1 fourteenth year. About 701 B.C. Hezekiah ruled with his father Ahaz as co-regent from 729–715 B.C. and was sole king from 715–686 B.C. Some explain the "fourteenth" year as a copyist's error for "twenty-fourth," while others suggest that Isaiah is referring to the beginning of Hezekiah's independent rule in 715 B.C.

Sennacherib. He was the king of Assyria from 705–681 B.C.

fortified cities. Sennacherib states in his annals that forty-six such cities were conquered during this campaign (2 Kin. 18:13 note).

36:2 the Rabshakeh. He was the royal counselor for military affairs. According to 2 Kin. 18:17 the king also sent his "Tartan" ("commander in chief"; cf. Is. 20:1) and his "Rab-saris" ("chief officer").

Lachish. This fortress town in the western hill country of Judah, guarded an important road that led into the highlands south of Jerusalem (Jer. 34:7).

great army. According to 37:36, 185,000 troops were killed in the siege of Jerusalem; the full army would have been much larger than that.

upper pool. Isaiah had met Ahaz there (7:3).

36:3 Eliakim . . . Shebna. See note 22:19.

Joah . . . recorder. He was an important office holder and the official spokesperson of the kings.

36:4 great king. An official title of Assyrian kings equivalent to "emperor." By contrast, Hezekiah is named without a title (vv. 13, 14).

36:5 In whom do you now trust. The challenge of loyalty to Assyria, other political powers, or to the Lord is the essential message of Isaiah (12:2 note).

36:6 Egypt. Hezekiah had depended on Egypt for support (30:2, 6, 7, 13; 31:1, 3 and notes). But as Isaiah had said Egypt could never deliver Judah because she too was under divine judgment (19:1–15; 20:3–6).

36:7 high places and altars. Hezekiah had removed many pagan and idolatrous sites in Judah (2 Kin. 18:4; 2 Chr. 31:1), no doubt to the dismay and anger of many Judeans.

this altar. This charge focuses on the requirement to worship exclusively at the temple of Solomon.

Assyrian Empire (650 B.C.). By 650 B.C. the Assyrian Empire, with its capital in Nineveh, stretched from the Persian Gulf in the east throughout the fertile crescent into Palestine and beyond, embracing for a short time all of Egypt in the southwest. Judah, while a free zone, still paid tribute to Assyria during the reign of Manasseh.

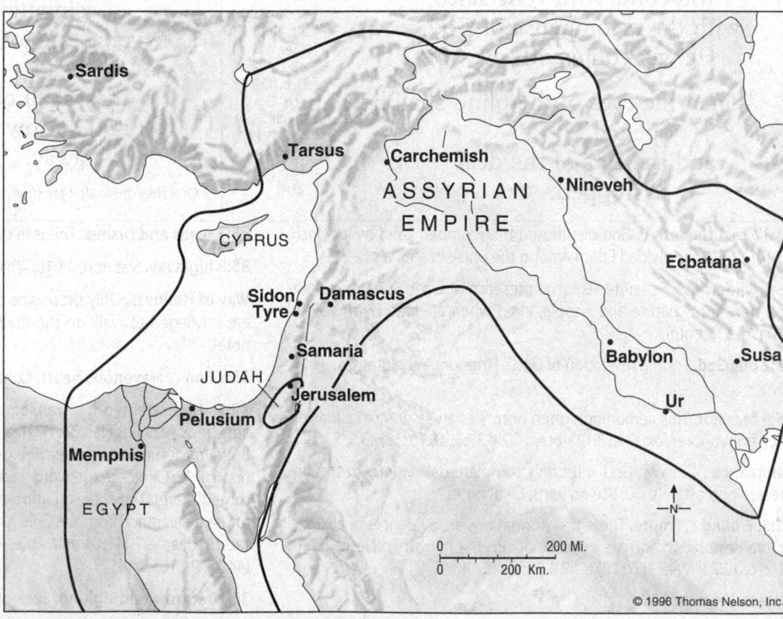

Hezekiah has removed, saying to Judah and
to Jerusalem, "You shall worship before this
altar"? 8 Come now, make a wager with my
master the king of Assyria: I will give you
two thousand horses, if you are able on
your part to set riders on them. 9 How then
can you repulse [s]a single captain among the
least of my master's servants, when [t]you
trust in Egypt for chariots and for horsemen? 10 Moreover, is it without the LORD
that I have come up against this land to
destroy it? [u]The LORD said to me, Go up
against this land and destroy it.'"
11 Then Eliakim, Shebna, and Joah said to
the Rabshakeh, "Please speak to your servants [v]in Aramaic, for we understand it. Do
not speak to us in the language of Judah
within the hearing of the people who are
on the wall." 12 But the Rabshakeh said,
"Has my master sent me to speak these
words to your master and to you, and not
to the men sitting on the wall, who are
doomed with you to eat their own dung
and drink their own urine?"
13 Then the Rabshakeh stood and called
out in a loud voice in the language of
Judah: "Hear the words of the great king,
the king of Assyria! 14 Thus says the king:
[w]'Do not let Hezekiah deceive you, for he
will not be able to deliver you. 15 Do not let
Hezekiah make you trust in the LORD by
saying, "The LORD will surely deliver us.
This city will not be given into the hand of
the king of Assyria." 16 Do not listen to
Hezekiah. For thus says the king of Assyria:
Make your peace with me[1] and come out to
me. Then each one of you will eat of his
own vine, and each one of his own fig tree,
and each one of you will drink the water of
his own cistern, 17 until [x]I come and take
you away to a land like your own land, a

9 [s][ch. 10:8] [t][ch. 20:5; 30:3, 7; 31:1]
10 [u]ch. 10:5, 6
11 [v]Ezra 4:7; Dan. 2:4
14 [w][ch. 37:10; 2 Chr. 32:6-8]
17 [x]2 Kin. 18:11

19 [y]ch. 37:13 [z]Jer. 49:23 [a][2 Kin. 17:6]
20 [b][2 Chr. 32:19]
22 [c]ver. 3; [ch. 33:7]
Chapter 37
1 [d]For ver. 1-38, see 2 Kin ch. 19
2 [e]See ch. 1:1
3 [f][ch. 22:5] [g][ch. 13:8; Hos. 13:13]
4 [h][ver. 28, 29] [i]ch. 1:9

land of grain and wine, a land of bread and
vineyards. 18 Beware lest Hezekiah mislead
you by saying, "The LORD will deliver us."
Has any of the gods of the nations delivered his land out of the hand of the king of
Assyria? 19 [y]Where are the gods of [z]Hamath
and [z]Arpad? Where are the gods of
Sepharvaim? [a]Have they delivered Samaria
out of my hand? 20 [b]Who among all the
gods of these lands have delivered their
lands out of my hand, that the LORD should
deliver Jerusalem out of my hand?'"
21 But they were silent and answered him
not a word, for the king's command was,
"Do not answer him." 22 [c]Then Eliakim the
son of Hilkiah, who was over the household, and Shebna the secretary, and Joah
the son of Asaph, the recorder, came to
Hezekiah with their clothes torn, and told
him the words of the Rabshakeh.

Hezekiah Seeks Isaiah's Help

37 [d]As soon as King Hezekiah heard it,
he tore his clothes and covered himself with sackcloth and went into the house
of the LORD. 2 And he sent Eliakim, who was
over the household, and Shebna the secretary, and the senior priests, covered with
sackcloth, to the prophet [e]Isaiah the son of
Amoz. 3 They said to him, "Thus says
Hezekiah, 'This day is a [f]day of distress, of
rebuke, and of disgrace; [g]children have
come to the point of birth, and there is no
strength to bring them forth. 4 [h]It may be
that the LORD your God will hear the words
of the Rabshakeh, whom his master the
king of Assyria has sent to mock the living
God, and will rebuke the words that the
LORD your God has heard; therefore lift up
your prayer for [i]the remnant that is left.'"

[1] Hebrew *Make a blessing with me*

36:8 horses . . . riders. Judah did not have cavalry; Assyria did.

36:10 The LORD said to me. He is trying to appeal to the religious people of Judah.

36:11 Aramaic. For many centuries Aramaic was the international language of diplomacy and commerce.

36:15 trust . . . deliver. These words testify to Hezekiah's public expression of faith in God.

trust in the LORD. This theme has been at the heart of Isaiah's preaching in chs. 7–35.

36:16 Make your peace. Lit. "make a blessing" (text note). The Rabshakeh appeals for renewal of a political covenant with Assyria. In contrast, see 27:5.

eat . . . drink. He tempts them with food and drink (37:30 note) in the midst of a harsh siege (v. 12). The Assyrians project an ideal and happy life, but the Lord alone can fulfill what they promise.

36:17 take you. The phrase reflects the Assyrian policy of exiling a rebellious population (cf. 2 Kin. 15:29).

37:1 tore his clothes . . . sackcloth. These expressions of mourning or repentance signify humility, dependence, and need for God.

37:2 Eliakim . . . Shebna. See 22:15–25.

senior priests. That is, representatives of the leading priestly families (Jer. 19:1).

37:3 distress . . . disgrace. This is a time of adversity when the loyalty of people is tested (cf. 25:4; 26:16; 33:2).

birth . . . no strength. Hezekiah admits the futility of human strategies in a time of acute crisis (26:17, 18).

37:4 the living God. These words express Hezekiah's renewed faith and zeal for the Lord's name.

remnant. The country had been decimated (1:9 note; 6:11).

5 When the servants of King Hezekiah
came to Isaiah, 6 Isaiah said to them, "Say
to your master, 'Thus says the LORD: Do
not be afraid because of the words that you
have heard, with which the young men of
the king of Assyria have reviled me.
7 Behold, [j] I will put a spirit in him, so that
[k] he shall hear a rumor and return to his
own land, and [l] I will make him fall by the
sword in his own land.'"
8 The Rabshakeh returned, and found the
king of Assyria fighting against [m] Libnah, for
he had heard that the king had left [m] Lachish.
9 Now the king heard concerning Tirhakah
king of [n] Cush,[1] "He has set out to fight
against you." And when he heard it, he sent
messengers to Hezekiah, saying, 10 "Thus
shall you speak to Hezekiah king of Judah:
[o] 'Do not let your God in whom you trust
deceive you by promising that Jerusalem will
not be given into the hand of the king of
Assyria. 11 Behold, you have heard what the
kings of Assyria have done to all lands,
devoting them to destruction.[2] And shall you
be delivered? 12 [p] Have the gods of the nations
delivered them, the nations that my fathers
destroyed, [q] Gozan, [r] Haran, Rezeph, and the
people of Eden who were in Telassar?
13 [p] Where is the king of Hamath, the king of
Arpad, the king of the city of Sepharvaim, the
king of Hena, or the king of Ivvah?'"

Hezekiah's Prayer for Deliverance

14 Hezekiah received the letter from the
hand of the messengers, and read it; and
Hezekiah went up to the house of the
LORD, and spread it before the LORD. 15 And
Hezekiah prayed to the LORD: 16 "O LORD
of hosts, God of Israel, [s] who is enthroned
above the cherubim, you are the God, you
alone, of all the kingdoms of the earth;
[t] you have made heaven and earth. 17 [u] Incline
your ear, O LORD, and hear; open
your eyes, O LORD, and see; and hear [v] all
the words of Sennacherib, which he has
sent to mock the living God. 18 Truly,
O LORD, [w] the kings of Assyria have laid
waste all the nations and their lands, 19 and
have cast their gods into the fire. For they
were no gods, but the work of men's
hands, wood and stone. Therefore they
were destroyed. 20 So now, O LORD our
God, save us from his hand, that all the
kingdoms of the earth may know that you
alone are the LORD."

Sennacherib's Fall

21 Then Isaiah the son of Amoz sent to
Hezekiah, saying, "Thus says the LORD, the
God of Israel: Because you have prayed to
me concerning Sennacherib king of
Assyria, 22 this is the word that the LORD
has spoken concerning him:

"'She despises you, she scorns you—
[x] the virgin daughter of Zion;
she wags her head behind you—
the daughter of Jerusalem.

7 [j] [ch. 19:14] [k] ver. 9 [l] ver. 38
8 [m] Josh. 10:31
9 [n] ch. 18:1, 2; 20:5
10 [o] [ch. 36:14]
12 [p] ch. 36:18, 19 [q] 2 Kin. 17:6 [r] Gen. 11:31, 32
13 [p] [See ver. 12 above]
16 [s] Ex. 25:22; Ezek. 10:1 [t] Acts 4:24; [Jer. 10:11]
17 [u] [2 Chr. 6:40] [v] 2 Chr. 32:19
18 [w] [ch. 10:13, 14]
22 [x] [Mic. 4:13]; See ch. 1:8

1 Probably *Nubia* 2 That is, setting apart (devoting) as an offering to the Lord (for destruction)

37:7 return . . . fall. See vv. 37, 38. Isaiah encouraged Hezekiah to trust the Lord, as he had encouraged Ahaz (7:4).

37:8–13 Sennacherib renewed his attempt at persuading Hezekiah to submit to and depend on Assyria. By making folly of the gods of the nations, he challenged Hezekiah to stop trusting in the Lord.

37:8 Libnah. A city in the western hill country of Judah a few miles north of Lachish (36:2 note).

37:9 king of Cush. Egypt was ruled by an Ethiopian dynasty at this time. Tirhakah commanded the Egyptian troops in 701 B.C. He became sole king about 689 B.C. For "Cush" see 18:1 note.

37:10, 11 Sennacherib assails the Lord's ability to deliver Judah (v. 4 note).

37:12 fathers. Sennacherib claims that his god is with him, because the Assyrian success went back several generations.

Gozan . . . Eden. Cities in Mesopotamia.

37:13 Hamath . . . Ivvah. Cities in Aram (Syria).

37:14–20 Hezekiah did not respond to Sennacherib's boast; instead, he turned to the Lord in prayer (38:2). Unlike Ahaz, Hezekiah confessed his complete trust in the Lord as King, Creator, and Redeemer. The theology of this prayer summarizes Isaiah's vision of God.

37:16 enthroned above the cherubim. God is with His people and rules over them (1 Sam. 4:4; 2 Sam. 6:2; Ps. 80:1; 99:1), truths represented by His presence in the Most Holy Place of the temple, which contained the ark of the covenant with the wings of two cherubim above it.

you are the God, you alone. Hezekiah attributes deity exclusively to the Lord (44:8; 45:5, 6, 14, 22; 46:9).

kingdoms. See note 13:4.

made heaven and earth. There is a distinct emphasis in Isaiah's prophecies on Yahweh as the sovereign and absolute Creator of all (27:10, 11; 42:5; 45:12, 18).

37:17 Incline Your ear . . . hear. Unlike the gods of Assyria, the Lord sees, hears, and acts.

37:19 On Isaiah's polemic against idolatry, see 2:8.

37:21 the LORD, the God of Israel. A formal title for the One whose covenant was with the twelve tribes of Israel.

37:22 the virgin daughter. Hebrew literary convention speaks of cities and people as young women (47:1; Lam. 2:10; Amos 5:2).

Zion. See note 1:8.

despises . . . wags her head. She expresses rejection and derision in this manner (Ps. 22:7; Jer. 18:16). This taunt song in vv. 22–29 is similar to the one in 14:4–21.

23 “ ‘Whom have you mocked and
reviled?
Against whom have you raised
your voice
and lifted your eyes to the heights?
Against [y]the Holy One of Israel!
24 By your servants you have mocked
the Lord,
and you have said, [z]With my many
chariots
I have gone up the heights of the
mountains,
to the far recesses of Lebanon,
[a]to cut down its tallest cedars,
its choicest cypresses,
to come to its remotest height,
its most fruitful forest.
25 I dug wells
and drank waters,
to dry up with the sole of my foot
all [b]the streams [c]of Egypt.

26 [d]“ ‘Have you not heard
that I determined it long ago?
I planned from days of old
what now I bring to pass,
that you should make fortified cities
crash into heaps of ruins,
27 while their inhabitants, shorn of
strength,
are dismayed and confounded,
and have become like plants of the
field
and like tender grass,
like grass on the housetops,
blighted[1] before it is grown.

28 “ ‘I know your sitting down
and your going out and coming in,
and your raging against me.
29 [e]Because you have raged
against me
and your complacency has come to
my ears,
I will put my hook in your nose
and my bit in your mouth,
and [f]I will turn you back on
the way
by which you came.’

30 “And this shall be the sign for you: this
year you shall eat what grows of itself, and
in the second year what springs from that.
Then in the third year sow and reap, and
plant vineyards, and eat their fruit. 31 And
the surviving remnant of the house of
Judah [g]shall again take root downward and
bear fruit upward. 32 [h]For out of Jerusalem
shall go a remnant, and out of Mount Zion
a band of survivors. [i]The zeal of the LORD
of hosts will do this.

33 “Therefore thus says the LORD concerning the king of Assyria: He shall not come
into this city or shoot an arrow there or
come before it with a shield or [j]cast up a
siege mound against it. 34 By the way that
he came, by the same he shall return, and
he shall not come into this city, declares
the LORD. 35 [k]For I will defend this city to
save it, for my own sake and for [l]the sake
of my servant David.”

36 [m]And the angel of the LORD went out
and struck down a hundred and eighty-five
thousand in the camp of the Assyrians.
And when people arose early in the morning, behold, these were all dead bodies.
37 Then Sennacherib king of Assyria departed and returned home and lived at

23 [y]ch. 10:17
24 [z][ch. 8:7, 8] [a][ch. 14:8]
25 [b][ch. 19:6] [c][ch. 20:4]
26 [d][ch. 10:5, 15; 25:1, 2]
29 [e][ch. 10:12] [f]ver. 34
31 [g]ch. 27:6
32 [h][ch. 14:32] [i]See ch. 9:7
33 [j][Hab. 1:10; Luke 19:43]
35 [k]ch. 31:5; 38:6 [l][ch. 29:1]
36 [m]ch. 17:14; 30:31; 31:8; [ch. 10:33; 14:25; 29:5]

1 Some Hebrew manuscripts and 2 Kings 19:26; most Hebrew manuscripts *like a field*

37:23 mocked . . . to the heights. Assyria had exalted herself against the Lord.

37:24 gone up the heights. This poetic expression, emphasizing superiority and pride (14:13, 14), is usually reserved for deity.

37:25 I dug . . . dry up. Absolute claims of authority over creation are an insult to God's prerogatives.

37:26 I bring to pass. Assyria is nothing but a tool to advance God's plans.

heaps of ruins. Assyria accomplished God's will among the kingdoms of this world (10:5–19; cf. Ps. 37:1, 2; Mic. 4:11–13). See note 27:10.

37:28 I know. God is sovereign over Assyria. They can never escape His scrutiny (cf. Ps. 139).

37:29 raged . . . complacency. God has seen what Assyria has done, holds her responsible, and decides her punishment.

hook. Assyrian monuments show their captives pierced with hooks or rings.

37:30 sign. The overthrow of Assyria and the restoration of a remnant was a witness to God's faithfulness in working out His plans (7:11 note).

eat their fruit. What Assyria had promised (36:16), the Lord alone can fulfill.

37:31 remnant. See note 1:9.

root . . . fruit. These events would fulfill God's promise to restore His vineyard (27:6 note). This restoration began in 701 B.C. and still continues, as all who are in Jesus Christ are grafted into the vine and become part of God's vineyard (John 15:1–8).

37:35 defend . . . save. See note 31:5. Sennacherib did not succeed in his siege of Jerusalem. God was faithful to the promise made to David (8:8, 10; 2 Sam. 7:16).

servant. See note 20:3.

37:36 angel of the LORD. Jerusalem's deliverance came by supernatural means, as did the death of the firstborn in Egypt (Ex. 12:12; cf. 2 Sam. 24:16).

[n]Nineveh. 38 And as he was worshiping in
the house of Nisroch his god, Adram-
melech and Sharezer, his sons, struck him
down with the sword. And after they
escaped into the land of [o]Ararat, [p]Esar-
haddon his son reigned in his place.

Hezekiah's Sickness and Recovery

38 [q]In those days Hezekiah became
[r]sick and was at the point of death.
And [s]Isaiah the prophet the son of Amoz
came to him, and said to him, "Thus says
the LORD: Set your house in order, for you
shall die, you shall not recover."[1] 2 Then
Hezekiah turned his face to the wall and
prayed to the LORD, 3 and said, "Please,
O LORD, remember how [t]I have walked
before you in faithfulness and with a whole
heart, and have done what is good in your
sight." And Hezekiah wept bitterly.

4 Then the word of the LORD came to
Isaiah: 5 "Go and say to Hezekiah, Thus
says the LORD, the God of David your
father: I have heard your prayer; I have
seen your tears. Behold, I will add [u]fifteen
years to your life.[2] 6 [v]I will deliver you and
this city out of the hand of the king of
Assyria, and will defend this city.

7 "This shall be the sign to you from the
LORD, that the LORD will do this thing that
he has promised: 8 [w]Behold, I will make the
shadow cast by the declining sun on
the dial of Ahaz turn back ten steps." So
the sun turned back on the dial the ten
steps by which it had declined.[3]

9 A writing of Hezekiah king of Judah,
after he had been sick and had recovered
from his sickness:

10 I said, [x]In the middle[4] of my days
I must depart;
I am consigned to the gates of Sheol
for the rest of my years.
11 I said, I shall not see the LORD,
the LORD [y]in the land of the living;
I shall look on man no more
among the inhabitants of the world.
12 My dwelling is plucked up and
removed from me
[z]like a shepherd's tent;
[a]like a weaver [b]I have rolled up my life;
[c]he cuts me off from the loom;
[d]from day to night you bring me to an
end;
13 [e]I calmed myself[5] until morning;
like a lion [f]he breaks all my bones;
from day to night you bring me to
an end.
14 Like [g]a swallow or a crane I chirp;
[h]I moan like a dove.
[i]My eyes are weary with looking
upward.
O Lord, I am oppressed; [j]be my
pledge of safety!
15 What shall I say? For he has spoken
to me,
and he himself has done it.
[k]I walk slowly all my years
because of the bitterness of my soul.
16 [l]O Lord, by these things men live,
and in all these is the life of my
spirit.
Oh restore me to health and make
me live!

37 [n]Gen. 10:11; Jonah 1:2; 3:3; 4:11
38 [o]Gen. 8:4 [p]Ezra 4:2
Chapter 38
1 [q]For ver. 1-8, see 2 Kin. 20:1-6, 9-11 [r]2 Chr. 32:24 [s]See ch. 1:1
3 [t]2 Kin. 18:5, 6
5 [u]2 Kin. 18:2, 13
6 [v]ch. 37:35
8 [w][2 Kin. 20:9, 10]
10 [x][Ps. 102:24]
11 [y]Ps. 27:13; [Ps. 88:5]
12 [z][2 Cor. 5:1] [a]Job 7:6 [b][Heb. 1:12] [c]Job 6:9 [d][Job 4:20; Ps. 73:14]
13 [e][Ps. 30:5] [f][Ps. 38:3]
14 [g][Jer. 8:7] [h]ch. 59:11 [i]Ps. 69:3 [j]Ps. 119:122; [Ps. 86:17; Heb. 7:22]
15 [k]1 Kin. 21:27
16 [l]Deut. 8:3

1 Or *live*; also verses 9, 21 2 Hebrew *to your days* 3 The meaning of the Hebrew verse is uncertain 4 Or *In the quiet* 5 Or (with Targum) *I cried for help*

37:38 the house of Nisroch. Sennacherib's death in the temple of Nisroch contrasts with the life Hezekiah found in the temple of the Lord (vv. 1, 14).

struck him down. Twenty years later he was murdered by his own sons (681 B.C.).

Ararat. This is a mountainous region in the extreme eastern part of modern Turkey.

Esarhaddon. He was king over Assyria from 681–669 B.C.

38:1 In those days. This expression refers to the general time of the siege of Jerusalem by the Assyrians (701 B.C.; 36:1 note).

38:2 prayed. In this second prayer (cf. 37:14–20) the king places his confidence in God's righteousness.

38:3 remember . . . good. This petition is a moving expression of loyalty to Yahweh (33:14–16).

in faithfulness . . . a whole heart. See 10:20 and note.

wept bitterly. Hezekiah was apparently without a male heir. He lived an additional fifteen years (v. 5). Manasseh, his successor to the throne, was twelve when Hezekiah died (2 Kin. 20:21–21:1).

38:5 fifteen years. This period ran from 701–686 B.C.

38:6 deliver . . . defend. See 37:33–35.

38:7 sign. See 7:11–14; 37:30.

38:9 A writing of Hezekiah. Verses 10–20 are a hymn combining elements of lament (vv. 10–15) and thanksgiving (vv. 16–20; 2 Chr. 29:30; Prov. 25:1).

38:10 my days . . . my years. Hezekiah expressed his anguish over the reality and sting of death (Ps. 55:4).

38:11 I shall not see the LORD. Hezekiah did not want to leave this life in which he served God. See 14:9–11 note; Phil. 1:24.

38:12 removed . . . bring me to an end. Hezekiah offered many metaphors for vexation with the brevity of life, as if God were his enemy (cf. Ps. 22; 32:3, 4).

38:14, 15 I am oppressed. He is determined to remain faithful and to abandon himself to the Lord's mysterious will, painful though it is.

17 [m] Behold, it was for my welfare
that I had great bitterness;
[n] but in love you have delivered
my life
from the pit of destruction,
[n] for you have cast all my sins
behind your back.
18 [o] For Sheol does not thank you;
death does not praise you;
those who go down to the pit do not
hope
for your faithfulness.
19 The living, the living, he
thanks you,
as I do this day;
[p] the father makes known to the
children
your faithfulness.
20 The LORD will save me,
and we will play my music on
stringed instruments
all the days of our lives,
[q] at the house of the LORD.

21 [r] Now Isaiah had said, "Let them take a
cake of figs and apply it to the boil, that he
may recover." 22 Hezekiah also had said,
"What is the sign that I shall go up to the
house of the LORD?"

Envoys from Babylon

39 [s] At that time Merodach-baladan the
son of Baladan, king of Babylon,
[t] sent envoys with letters and a present to
Hezekiah, for he heard that he had been
sick and had recovered. 2 And Hezekiah
welcomed them gladly. And he showed
them his treasure house, [u] the silver, the
gold, the spices, the precious oil, his whole
armory, all that was found in his storehouses. [v] There was nothing in his house or
in all his realm that Hezekiah did not show
them. 3 Then Isaiah the prophet came to
King Hezekiah, and said to him, "What did
these men say? And from where did they
come to you?" Hezekiah said, "They have
come to me from a far country, from
Babylon." 4 He said, "What have they seen
in your house?" Hezekiah answered, "They
have seen all that is in my house. There is
nothing in my storehouses that I did not
show them."

5 Then Isaiah said to Hezekiah, "Hear the
word of the LORD of hosts: 6 [w] Behold, the
days are coming, when all that is in your
house, and that which your fathers have
stored up till this day, shall be carried to
Babylon. Nothing shall be left, says the
LORD. 7 [x] And some of your own sons, who
will come from you, whom you will father,
shall be taken away, and they shall be
eunuchs in the palace of the king of
Babylon." 8 Then said Hezekiah to Isaiah,
"The word of the LORD that you have spoken is good." For he thought, [y] "There will
be peace and security in my days."

Comfort for God's People

40 [z] Comfort, comfort my people,
says your God.

17 [m] Ps. 119:67, 75 [n] [Ps. 103:12; Mic. 7:19]
18 [o] Ps. 88:10-12; 115:17; [Eccles. 9:10]
19 [p] Deut. 4:9; 6:7; Ps. 78:3, 4
20 [q] 2 Kin. 20:5
21 [r] 2 Kin. 20:7, 8
Chapter 39
1 [s] For ver. 1-8, see 2 Kin. 20:12-19 [t] [2 Chr. 32:31]
2 [u] [2 Kin. 18:15, 16] [v] [2 Chr. 32:25]
6 [w] 2 Kin. 24:13; See 2 Kin. 25:13-17
7 [x] Dan. 1:2, 3, 7
8 [y] [2 Chr. 32:26]
Chapter 40
1 [z] ch. 51:12; [Luke 2:25]

38:17 pit of destruction. Hebrew *sheol;* see 14:6–11 note.

38:18 thank . . . praise. Hezekiah's emphasis is on communal and personal praise in response to God's acts of salvation in this life. Praise is offered only in the land of the living.

38:19 father . . . to the children. The story of God's acts of redemption were to be told from generation to generation (cf. Ex. 12:25–27).

38:20 save me . . . all the days of our lives. Hope is alive (cf. Ps. 6:9; 22:22–24), as Hezekiah expects to join in the communal praise (vv. 18, 19).

stringed instruments. Musical accompaniment assisted the singing of psalms (cf. Ps. 33:1–3; 150).

house of the LORD. This was the place specially designed by God for worship from the time of Solomon until the time of the church.

38:21 apply it. All healing is of God. He may mediate it through medicine.

39:1 At that time. That is, some time after Hezekiah's illness (38:1 note).

39:2 silver . . . all that was found. These arms and wealth evidence Hezekiah's ability to support Babylon in its rebellion against Assyria.

39:3 Isaiah . . . Hezekiah. Isaiah came to speak for God and questioned Hezekiah.

39:4 all that is in my house. His action suggests he was trusting his might and political alliance with Babylon, not the Lord.

39:5 Hear the word. This phrase introduces the prophetic charge and judgment.

LORD of hosts. See note 1:9.

39:6 carried to Babylon. Isaiah predicts the Babylonian exile.

39:7 your own sons See 2 Kin. 24:15.

eunuchs. See Dan. 1:3–6.

39:8 word. See note on v. 5.

good . . . in my days. This response has a negative note, as the king shows little concern for his own descendants or for his people. Though an end did come to the Babylonian exile, the prophetic word is clear that there "is no peace . . . for the wicked" (48:22; 57:21). God's peace will extend to the children of Zion (66:12, 13).

40:1–55:13 Isaiah originally addressed these words to the future exiles in Babylon to encourage them to flee from there and return by faith to the Promised Land (e.g., 48:20, 21). The encouragement partially arises from their supernatural character (e.g., 41:21–27). These prophecies, delivered more than a century and a half beforehand (see Introduction: Interpretive Difficulties), astonish their audience by predicting Israel's (i.e., Judah's) immediate deliverance from Babylon by Cyrus (e.g.,

2 [a] Speak tenderly to Jerusalem,
and cry to her
that [b] her warfare[1] is ended,
that her iniquity is pardoned,
that she has received from the LORD's
hand
double for all her sins.

3 [c] A voice cries:[2]
[d] "In the wilderness prepare the way of
the LORD;
[e] make straight in the desert a
highway for our God.
4 [f] Every valley shall be lifted up,
and every mountain and hill be
made low;
the uneven ground shall become
level,
and the rough places a plain.
5 [g] And the glory of the LORD shall be
revealed,
and all flesh shall see it together,
[h] for the mouth of the LORD has
spoken."

The Word of God Stands Forever

6 A voice says, "Cry!"
And I said,[3] "What shall I cry?"
[i] All flesh is grass,
and all its beauty[4] is like the flower
of the field.
7 The grass withers, the flower fades
when the breath of the LORD blows
on it;
surely the people are grass.
8 [j] The grass withers, the flower fades,
but the word of our God will stand
forever.

The Greatness of God

9 Get you up to a high mountain,
O Zion, [k] herald of good news;[5]
lift up your voice with strength,
O Jerusalem, herald of good news;[6]
lift it up, fear not;
say to the cities of Judah,
"Behold your God!"
10 [l] Behold, the Lord GOD comes with
might,
and his arm rules for him;
[m] behold, his reward is with him,
and his recompense before him.

2 [a] Hos. 2:14 [b] [2 Chr. 36:22; Jer. 25:12]
3 [c] Cited Matt. 3:3; Mark 1:3; Luke 3:4; John 1:23 [d] Mal. 3:1; [ch. 57:14] [e] Ps. 68:4
4 [f] Cited Luke 3:5; [ch. 49:11]
5 [g] [Luke 3:6] [h] ch. 1:20
6 [i] Cited 1 Pet. 1:24, 25; [Job 14:2; Ps. 102:11; 103:15; James 1:10]
8 [j] Cited James 1:11
9 [k] ch. 52:7
10 [l] ch. 59:16, 17; [Luke 11:22] [m] ch. 62:11; [Rev. 22:12]

[1] Or *time of service* [2] Or *a voice of one crying* [3] Revocalization based on Dead Sea Scroll, Septuagint, Vulgate; Masoretic Text *And someone says* [4] Or *all its constancy* [5] Or *O herald of good news to Zion* [6] Or *O herald of good news to Jerusalem*

44:24–45:13), the coming of the suffering Christ to save them from their sins after they return to the land (42:1–7; 49:1–13; 50:4–11; 52:13–53:12), and Israel's final salvation in the last days (51:6). The near, more remote, and most remote prophecies merge together on the canvas. From Isaiah's perspective, the restoration after the Exile inaugurates the new age, and this first taste of salvation through God's servant, Cyrus, coalesces with the greater salvation that the Christ, God's servant, will bring His people. Today, the elect have even more confidence in words of prophecy because these have been fulfilled in Christ and are being fulfilled in His Church (2 Pet. 1:19).

40:1 Comfort, comfort. The verbs are plural in form. God is addressing His heavenly court and the prophetic messengers who participate in it (v. 6; 44:26). Other heralds will be encouraged to spread the good news (vv. 9–11; 52:7). The repetition is for emphasis and occurs in 51:9, 17; 52:1, 11; 57:14; 62:10.

my people. Though they have rebelled, they are still treated as the people of God. The phrase occurs frequently in Isaiah (1:3; 3:12, 15; 43:20; 51:4, 16; 53:8; 58:1; 65:10, 22). See 43:1 note.

40:2 warfare . . . iniquity. Isaiah refers to the exile of Israel and Judah of which he has spoken repeatedly. The suffering came on account of sin. See note 27:9.

double for all her sins. God has judged the punishment to be sufficient and is ready to forgive (43:25; 44:22; 48:9).

40:3 voice. Though the voice may have included earlier prophets, such as Isaiah, it finds fulfillment in the ministry of John the Baptist (Matt. 3:3; Mark 1:3, 4; Luke 1:76; 3:4, 5; John 1:23).

wilderness . . . desert. These are metaphors for alienation and anguish (14:17; 27:10; 64:10). God alone can transform the desert into a blooming and fruitful oasis, a figure for the fullness and joy of His salvation (32:15, 16; 35:1, 6; 41:18, 19; 43:19, 20; 48:21; 51:3).

prepare . . . make straight. "Prepare" means to "remove every obstruction" (57:14). God will remove all obstacles at His coming, but He expects His people to prepare for the kingdom (62:10) and requires the nations to assist the progress of His salvation.

way . . . a highway. See note 11:16. Here these are figures for human hearts that must be prepared through repentance (35:8–10; Luke 3:3–9). When that happens, God's glory appears on earth.

40:4 valley . . . rough places. At the Lord's appearance (6:4 note), nature submits to His will. He removes all obstacles and prepares a road by which the royal procession advances in the establishment of the kingdom.

40:5 revealed. God's kingdom is "revealed" in acts of salvation and judgment, especially in Jesus Christ (Luke 2:30, 31; John 1:14). The restoration from exile was a manifestation of God's glory.

all flesh . . . together. The revelation of His kingdom is public and visible in creation, in Christ, in the church, and in the new earth (Gen. 9:17; Matt. 2:1–11; 16:27; 24:30; Acts 28:28; 2 Cor. 3:18).

mouth. See note 1:20. This affirmation is expanded in vv. 6–8.

40:6 voice. An angelic voice addresses Isaiah (6:6–9).

40:7 breath. His wrath is likened to the destructive east wind (Ps. 103:16; Jer. 4:11; Ezek. 17:10).

40:9 Zion. See note 1:8.

good news. That is, the gospel. God has come to rescue His enslaved people.

40:10 comes. He arrives to inaugurate His kingdom on earth (35:4 note; 43:15; 44:6; 52:7–10).

arm. This metaphor describes the power of God as manifested in acts of deliverance and vengeance (v. 11; 48:14; 51:5, 9; 53:1; 59:16; 63:5, 12; Ex. 15:16; Ps. 44:3; 89:13; 98:1; 136:12).

reward. The spoils of victory here are the delivered people themselves. The rescued exiles both foreshadow and merge into the messianic community.

11 [n] He will tend his flock like a
shepherd;
[o] he will gather the lambs in his arms;
[p] he will carry them in his bosom,
and gently lead those that are with
young.
12 [q] Who has measured the waters in the
hollow of his hand
and marked off the heavens with a
span,
enclosed the dust of the earth in a
measure
and weighed the mountains in
scales
and the hills in a balance?
13 [r] Who has measured[1] the Spirit of the
LORD,
or what man shows him his
counsel?
14 Whom did he consult,
and who made him understand?
[s] Who taught him the path of justice,
and taught him knowledge,
and showed him the way of
understanding?
15 Behold, the nations are like a drop
from a bucket,
and are accounted [t] as the dust on
the scales;
behold, he takes up [u] the
coastlands like fine dust.
16 Lebanon would not suffice for fuel,
nor are [v] its beasts enough for a
burnt offering.
17 [w] All the nations are as nothing before
him,
they are accounted by him as less
than nothing and emptiness.
18 [x] To whom then will you liken God,
[y] or what likeness compare with
him?
19 [y] An idol! A craftsman casts it,
and a goldsmith overlays it with gold
and casts for it silver chains.
20 [z] He who is too impoverished for an
offering
chooses wood[2] that will not rot;
he seeks out a skillful craftsman
to set up an idol that will not move.
21 [a] Do you not know? Do you not hear?
Has it not been told you from the
beginning?
Have you not understood from the
foundations of the earth?
22 It is he who sits above the circle of
the earth,
and its inhabitants are [b] like
grasshoppers;
[c] who stretches out the heavens like a
curtain,
and spreads them like a tent to
dwell in;
23 [d] who brings princes to nothing,
and makes the rulers of the earth
as emptiness.
24 Scarcely are they planted, scarcely
sown,
scarcely has their stem taken root
in the earth,
when he blows on them, and they
wither,
[e] and the tempest carries them off
like stubble.
25 [f] To whom then will you compare me,
that I should be like him? says the
Holy One.
26 Lift up your eyes on high and see:
who created these?
[g] He who brings out their host by
number,
calling them all by name,

11 [n] Ezek. 34:23; Zech. 11:7; [John 10:11; 21:15; Acts 20:28] [o] [Matt. 18:12; Luke 15:5] [p] [Num. 11:12]
12 [q] [Prov. 30:4]
13 [r] Cited Rom. 11:34; [1 Cor. 2:16]
14 [s] Job 21:22
15 [t] ch. 29:5 [u] ch. 41:1
16 [v] [Ps. 50:10]
17 [w] Ps. 62:9; Dan. 4:35; [ch. 41:12]
18 [x] ver. 25; ch. 46:5; Acts 17:29 [y] [Hos. 13:2]
19 [y] [See ver. 18 above]
20 [z] ch. 46:6; Jer. 10:3-5; See ch. 44:9-15
21 [a] ver. 28; [Acts 14:17; Rom. 1:19, 20]
22 [b] [Num. 13:33] [c] Job 9:8; Ps. 104:2
23 [d] Job 12:21; Ps. 107:40
24 [e] ch. 41:2; [Ps. 83:13]
25 [f] ver. 18
26 [g] Ps. 147:4

[1] Or *has directed* [2] Or *He chooses valuable wood*

40:11 flock . . . lead. These are the expressions of the tender, shepherding care of the divine King (Ps. 23:1–4; 78:52; 80:1; Jer. 31:10; Ezek. 34:11–16; Mic. 2:12; John 10:11).

40:15 nations . . . coastlands. The Creator is sovereign over all human powers—which are as nothing (2:22).

40:16 Lebanon. Famous for its dense cedar forests (2:13 note).

40:18 compare. The Lord is incomparable (v. 25; 46:5). See "The Spiritual Nature of God" at 66:1.

40:19 silver chains. Possibly chains that kept the idol from toppling over. On Isaiah's polemic against idolatry, see 2:8.

40:21 not know . . . not understood. This charge is directed at rejection of God's revelation (52:6 note).

beginning . . . foundations. God's glory and power are revealed in nature (Rom. 1:20).

40:22 circle. This is either the horizon, or the hemisphere of the sky over the earth.

tent. God's creation is compared to a tent He has pitched (42:5; 44:24; 51:13; Ps. 18:11; 19:4).

40:24 planted . . . tempest. This verse develops the imagery introduced in vv. 6, 7.

stubble. See notes 17:13; 29:5.

40:26 Lift . . . see. God holds people responsible for discerning the revelation in creation (Rom. 1:18–32).

calling . . . might. The Lord knows and upholds His creation.

by the greatness of his might,
and because he is strong in power
not one is missing.

27 Why do you say, O Jacob,
and speak, O Israel,
[h]"My way is hidden from the LORD,
[i]and my right is disregarded by my God"?

28 Have you not known? Have you not heard?
The LORD is [j]the everlasting God,
the Creator of the ends of the earth.
He does not faint or grow weary;
[k]his understanding is unsearchable.

29 He gives power to the faint,
and to him who has no might he increases strength.

30 Even youths shall faint and be weary,
and young men shall fall exhausted;

31 but [l]they who wait for the LORD shall renew their strength;
they shall mount up with wings [m]like eagles;
they shall run and not be weary;
they shall walk and not faint.

27 [h][ch. 49:14] [i][ch. 49:4]
28 [j][Ps. 121:4] [k]Ps. 147:5
31 [l]Ps. 103:5 [m][Ex. 19:4]

Fear Not, For I Am with You

41 [n]Listen to me in silence,
[o]O coastlands;
let the peoples renew their strength;
let them approach, then let them speak;
let us together draw near for judgment.

2 [p]Who stirred up one from the east
whom victory meets at every [q]step?[1]
[r]He gives up nations before him,
so that he tramples kings underfoot;
he makes them like dust with his sword,
[s]like driven stubble with his bow.

3 He pursues them and passes on safely,
by paths his feet have not trod.

4 [t]Who has performed and done this,
calling the generations from the beginning?
[u]I, the LORD, the first,
and with the last; I am he.

5 [v]The coastlands have seen and are afraid;
the ends of the earth tremble;
they have drawn near and come.

6 Everyone helps his neighbor
and says to his brother, "Be strong!"

7 [w]The craftsman strengthens the goldsmith,
and he who smooths with the hammer him who strikes the anvil,
saying of the soldering, "It is good";
and they strengthen it with nails
[x]so that it cannot be moved.

Chapter 41
1 [n][Hab. 2:20; Zech. 2:13] [o]See ch. 11:11
2 [p]ch. 46:11; [ch. 45:1] [q][Judg. 4:10] [r]2 Chr. 36:23 [s]ch. 40:24
4 [t][ver. 26] [u]ch. 43:10, 11; 44:6; 48:12; Rev. 1:8, 17; 22:13
5 [v]See ch. 11:11
7 [w]ch. 40:19 [x][ch. 40:20]

[1] *Or whom righteousness calls to follow?*

40:27 Jacob . . . Israel. Isaiah has in mind the remnant in exile. See note 41:8.

hidden . . . disregarded. In His anger God hid His face from them (49:14; 54:8), but in His grace He is powerful to deliver (8:17 note).

40:28 known . . . heard. See note on v. 21; "The Self-existence of God" at Ps. 90:2.

everlasting God. The Creator is sovereign over time and space (9:6; 40:22).

40:31 wait. See notes 8:17; 26:8, 9.

mount up . . . run . . . walk. These verbs give a vivid picture of the spiritual transformation that comes through faith.

41:1 silence . . . together draw near. All nations are called upon to acknowledge the Lord's sovereignty and discern His hand in history.

coastlands . . . peoples. See notes 24:13, 16; 40:15.

their strength. The prophet exhorts the nations to accept the strength mediated by faith (40:31).

41:2 one from the east. Namely, Cyrus the Great of Persia (reigned 550–530 B.C.; v. 25; 44:28; 45:1 and notes).

victory. Cyrus was victorious in establishing a new order (1:21 note; 44:24–45:5, 13; 46:11).

gives . . . makes. The victories of Cyrus were the Lord's doing on behalf of Israel (43:3).

nations . . . kings. The nations are under the Lord's authority and they must acknowledge His name to participate in His plan of redemption (45:1; 49:22, 23; 60:3, 16).

41:3 pursues . . . passes. Cyrus's conquests were rapid (cf. 46:11).

41:4 beginning. God has ordered human history.

I, the LORD . . . I am he. This is a most significant formula of divine self-identification (41:13; 42:8; 43:3, 10, 13, 15; 44:24; 45:3, 5, 6; 46:4; 48:17; 49:23; 51:15; 60:22; note the use of "I am" in John 6:35; 8:12, 58; 9:5; 10:7, 9, 11, 14; 11:25; 14:6; 15:1, 5).

first . . . last. These words give assurance that everything is always under the Lord's control (44:6; 48:12; cf. Heb. 13:8; Rev. 1:8, 17; 2:8; 21:6; 22:13).

41:5, 6 afraid. Fear leads to rebellion in response to the Lord's challenge of v. 1.

41:7 On Isaiah's polemic against idolatry, see 2:8.

8 But you, Israel, [y]my servant,
Jacob, [z]whom I have chosen,
the offspring of Abraham, [a]my friend;
9 you whom I took from the ends of the earth,
and called [b]from its farthest corners,
saying to you, "You are [y]my servant,
[z]I have chosen you and not cast you off";
10 fear not, for I am with you;
be not dismayed, for I am your God;
I will strengthen you, I will help you,
I will uphold you with [c]my righteous right hand.

11 [d]Behold, all who are incensed against you
shall be put to shame and confounded;
those who strive against you
shall be as nothing and shall perish.
12 [e]You shall seek those who contend with you,
but you shall not find them;
[f]those who war against you
shall be as nothing at all.
13 For I, the LORD your God,
hold your right hand;
it is I who say to you, "Fear not,
I am the one who helps you."

14 Fear not, you [g]worm Jacob,
you men of Israel!
I am the one who helps you, declares the LORD;
your [h]Redeemer is the Holy One of Israel.
15 [i]Behold, I make of you a threshing sledge,
new, sharp, and having teeth;
you shall thresh [j]the mountains and crush them,
and you shall make the hills like chaff;
16 [k]you shall winnow them, and [l]the wind shall carry them away,
and the tempest shall scatter them.
[m]And you shall rejoice in the LORD;
in the Holy One of Israel you shall glory.

17 [n]When the poor and needy seek water,
and there is none,
and their tongue is parched with thirst,
I the LORD will answer them;
I the God of Israel will not forsake them.
18 [o]I will open rivers on the bare heights,
and fountains in the midst of the valleys.
[p]I will make the wilderness a pool of water,
and the dry land springs of water.
19 [q]I will put in the wilderness the cedar,
the acacia, the myrtle, and the olive.
I will set in the desert [r]the cypress,
the plane and the pine together,
20 that they may see and know,
may consider and understand together,
that [s]the hand of the LORD has done this,
the Holy One of Israel has created it.

8 [y]ch. 44:1, 2 [z]Deut. 7:6; 10:15; 14:2; Ps. 135:4; [1 Pet. 2:9] [a]2 Chr. 20:7; James 2:23
9 [b]ch. 43:5, 6 [y][See ver. 8 above] [z][See ver. 8 above]
10 [c]Ps. 48:10
11 [d][ch. 45:24]
12 [e]Ps. 37:10 [f]ch. 40:17
14 [g][Ps. 22:6] [h]ch. 54:5; [Ps. 78:35]; See ch. 43:14
15 [i]Mic. 4:13 [j][ch. 2:14]
16 [k][Jer. 51:2] [l][ver. 2] [m]ch. 45:25
17 [n][ch. 44:3]
18 [o]ch. 35:6, 7 [p]Ps. 107:35
19 [q]ch. 35:1, 2; 55:12, 13 [r]ch. 60:13
20 [s]Job 12:9

41:8 Israel . . . Jacob. These are parallel expressions for the godly children of Abraham (v. 14; 40:27; 42:24; 43:1, 22, 28; 44:1, 5, 21, 23; 45:4; 46:3; 48:1, 12; cf. Luke 1:54).

chosen. See note 14:1.

41:10 fear not. See notes 35:4; 10:24.

I am with you. The Lord is Immanuel (8:8, 10; 43:2, 5; cf. Acts 18:9, 10).

I am your God. The basic promise for the covenant (vv. 13, 14; 43:1, 5; 44:2, 8; 51:12; Gen. 17:7; 21:17; 26:24; Deut. 20:1; 31:6, 8; Lev. 26:12; Jer. 32:38; Ezek. 37:27; 2 Cor. 6:16).

strengthen . . . uphold. The Lord is present in graciously delivering, exalting, and vindicating His children (v. 13; 42:1; 44:2; 49:8; 50:7). See note 40:31.

righteous right hand. He establishes order on earth by His power, as He did at the Exodus (63:12; Ex. 15:6).

41:11 put to shame. See note 1:29.

41:14 worm. The same word occurs at Job 25:6 and Ps. 22:6.

Redeemer. The Hebrew term designates the family protector. For a distressed family member, among other things, he avenges a murder (Num. 35:19) and redeems family property and those who have become slaves (Lev. 25:23–49; Ruth 2:20 note). See also 35:9, 10 and note.

the Holy One of Israel. See note 1:4. The Lord, the Holy God, stoops to deliver His own people (43:14, 15; 45:11; 47:4; 48:17; 49:7; 54:5; 57:15).

41:15 mountains . . . hills. These represent the many enemies of Israel (vv. 11, 12; cf. 42:15).

41:17 poor and needy. These are the returning exiles and all who seek God's favor (11:4 note; Ps. 9:18 note).

41:18, 19 An abundance of water ("rivers . . . springs") and vegetation ("cedar . . . cypress") pictures a transformation of creation (12:3; 35:1 and note; 43:18–20; 49:9–11; 55:13).

41:20 created. See note 4:5.

The Futility of Idols

21 Set forth your case, says the LORD;
bring your proofs, says the King of Jacob.
22 Let them bring them, and [t]tell us
what is to happen.
Tell us the former things, what they are,
that we may consider them,
that we may know their outcome;
or declare to us the things to come.
23 [t]Tell us what is to come hereafter,
that we may know that you are gods;
[u]do good, or do harm,
that we may be dismayed and terrified.[1]
24 Behold, [v]you are nothing,
and your work is less than nothing;
an abomination is he who chooses you.
25 [w]I stirred up one from the north, and he has come,
[x]from the rising of the sun, [y]and he shall call upon my name;
he shall trample on rulers as on mortar,
as the potter treads clay.
26 [z]Who declared it from the beginning,
that we might know,
and beforehand, that we might say,
"He is right"?
There was none who declared it,
none who proclaimed,
none who heard your words.
27 [a]I was the first to say[2] to Zion,
"Behold, here they are!"
and [b]I give to Jerusalem a herald of good news.
28 [c]But when I look there is no one;
among these there is no counselor
who, when I ask, gives an answer.
29 [d]Behold, they are all a delusion;
their works are nothing;
their metal images are empty wind.

The LORD's Chosen Servant

42 [e]Behold [f]my servant, whom I uphold,
my chosen, [g]in whom my soul delights;
[h]I have put my Spirit upon him;
[i]he will bring forth justice to the nations.
2 He will not cry aloud or lift up his voice,
or make it heard in the street;
3 [j]a bruised reed he will not break,
and a faintly burning wick he will not quench;
[k]he will faithfully bring forth justice.

22 [t][ver. 26; ch. 44:7; 45:21; 46:10] 23 [t][See ver. 22 above] [u][ch. 45:7] 24 [v]ver. 29; [Ps. 115:8; 1 Cor. 8:4] 25 [w]Jer. 50:3 [x]ver. 2 [y][Ps. 44:5] 26 [z][ver. 22] 27 [a]ch. 51:12 [b]ch. 40:9; 52:7 28 [c]See ver. 21-24 29 [d][ver. 12]
Chapter 42
1 [e]Cited Matt. 12:18-20 [f]ch. 41:8; 43:10; 52:13; 53:11; [ver. 19; Ezek. 34:24; Zech. 3:8; Acts 3:26; 4:27; Phil. 2:7] [g]Matt. 3:17 [h]ch. 11:2; 61:1 [i][ch. 2:4] 3 [j][ch. 57:15] [k]Ps. 9:8

1 Or *that we may both be dismayed and see* 2 Or *Formerly I said*

41:21 case . . . proofs. God renews the challenge issued in v. 1.

41:22 what is to happen . . . outcome. The Lord alone plans, declares, and executes. See note at 11:2.

former things. See 42:9; 43:9; 46:9; 48:3. These include past prophecies of events, especially God's abandonment of Israel and Judah as recorded in chs. 1–35.

things to come. See 42:23; 44:7; 45:11; 46:10. These are prophecies of the Lord's favor and the full establishment of His kingdom, as in chs. 40–66.

41:23 do good, or do harm. God taunts the pagan gods for their inability to act in any direction.

41:24 nothing . . . abomination. God condemns those who turn away from Him.

41:25 stirred up . . . he has come. The Lord shows His sovereignty over the nations.

north . . . rising of the sun. Cyrus came from Persia in the east and conquered Media in 549 B.C., becoming master of territories north of Babylon. He executed the Lord's will (45:4, 5; 2 Chr. 36:23; Ezra 1:1–4).

potter. See note 27:11.

41:27 a herald. This probably refers to Isaiah (40:1 note).

good news. The gospel of God's grace (40:9 note).

41:28 no one . . . no counselor. The nations and their idols are impotent.

41:29 delusion . . . empty wind. The Lord's assessment of idols is that they are empty, worthless (40:18–20; 41:7, 21–24; 44:9).

42:1–9 This is the first of four "Servant Songs" in chs. 40–55 celebrating the Servant of the Lord (49:1–7; 50:4–11; 52:13–53:12; cf. ch. 61).

42:1 servant. See note 20:3. The servant imagery is fulfilled in Jesus (Matt. 12:15–21) and is also applicable to Israel (41:8 note) before His coming, and to the church later (1 Pet. 2:21–25). Israel as "Servant" includes only the faithful, not the unfaithful Israel (vv. 18–22).

uphold. See note 41:10.

chosen. See note 14:1.

delights. The Servant pleases God and is an object of His love and favor (60:10; 62:4; Matt. 3:17; Mark 1:11; Luke 9:35).

justice to the nations. God institutes His universal kingdom of justice and righteousness. "Justice" is emphatically repeated three times in vv. 1–4.

42:2 not cry aloud . . . lift up. The Servant does not clamor for attention, but speaks in a spirit of gentleness and patience.

42:3 bruised reed. This metaphor would be appropriate for the poor and needy (Ps. 9:18 note). Rather than break the weak, the Servant will heal them.

burning wick. This represents people who are close to losing faith and hope.

4 He will not grow faint or be
discouraged[1]
till he has established justice in the
earth;
and [l] the coastlands wait for his
law.
5 Thus says God, the LORD,
who created the heavens [m] and
stretched them out,
who spread out the earth and what
comes from it,
[n] who gives breath to the people on it
and spirit to those who walk in it:
6 "I am the LORD; [o] I have called you in
righteousness;
I will take you by the hand and
keep you;
I will give you [p] as a covenant for the
people,
[q] a light for the nations,
7 [r] to open the eyes that are blind,
to bring out the prisoners from the
dungeon,
[s] from the prison those who sit in
darkness.
8 I am the LORD; that is my name;
[t] my glory I give to no other,
nor my praise to carved idols.
9 Behold, the former things have come
to pass,
[u] and new things I now declare;
before they spring forth
I tell you of them."

4 [l] ch. 60:9; Gen. 10:5; [ch. 2:3; Matt. 12:21] **5** [m] ch. 44:24; 45:12 [n] Acts 17:25 **6** [o] ch. 41:9 [p] ch. 49:6, 8 [q] Luke 2:32 **7** [r] ch. 35:5; 49:9; 61:1; Heb. 2:14, 15 [s] Luke 1:79 **8** [t] ch. 48:11 **9** [u] [ch. 43:19]

Sing to the LORD a New Song

10 [v] Sing to the LORD a new song,
his praise from the end of the
earth,
[w] you who go down to the sea, and all
that fills it,
[l] the coastlands and their
inhabitants.
11 Let the desert and its cities lift up
their voice,
the villages that [x] Kedar inhabits;
let the habitants of [y] Sela sing
for joy,
let them shout from the top of the
mountains.
12 Let them give glory to the LORD,
and declare his praise in [l] the
coastlands.
13 [z] The LORD goes out like a mighty
man,
like a man of war [a] he stirs up his
zeal;
he cries out, [b] he shouts aloud,
he shows himself mighty against
his foes.
14 For a long time I have held my
peace;
I have kept still and restrained
myself;
now I will cry out [c] like a woman in
labor;
I will gasp and pant.

10 [v] See Ps. 36:3 [w] Ps. 107:23 [l] [See ver. 4 above] **11** [x] See ch. 21:16 [y] ch. 16:1 **12** [l] [See ver. 4 above] **13** [z] ch. 40:10 [a] [ch. 9:7; 50:17] [b] Ps. 78:65 **14** [c] See ch. 13:8

[1] Or *bruised*

42:4 justice . . . law. The Servant will practice godliness on earth (cf. 2:2–4). He will be greater than Moses (Deut. 18:15–18; Acts 3:22–26), mediating a new covenant that enables people to keep His law (v. 6; 2 Cor. 3:3; Heb. 8:7–13).

wait. See 8:17 note.

42:5 created the heavens . . . earth. God is above all creation as the Creator of everything (4:5 note).

breath . . . spirit. The Creator and Sustainer of life (Ps. 104:30; Acts 17:24, 25) will enable the Servant to transform the earth with new, spiritual life.

42:6 called . . . keep. These are expressions parallel to v. 1.

covenant for the people. Jesus Christ, as God's Servant, brought the new covenant to His people (see 53:4–6; Jer. 31:31–34; Heb. 8:6–13; 9:15). The covenant is also called the "covenant of peace" (54:10), the "everlasting covenant" (55:3; 61:8), and the "new covenant" (Jer. 31:31).

light for the nations. The recipients of God's light are a new community of light-bearers in a dark world (9:2; 49:6; 51:4; 60:1–3; Luke 2:30–32; Acts 26:17, 18, 23).

42:7 to open . . . darkness. The Babylonian exile is described as a kind of dark prison. Israel's salvation from exile prefigures a spiritual deliverance through Christ from the blindness, bondage, and darkness of sin (5:30; 29:18; 51:14 and notes).

42:8 glory. See "The Glory of God" at Ezek. 1:28.

42:9 former things. These "former things" include the judgments prophesied against Damascus, Samaria, Nineveh, and Judah (41:22 note).

new things. These "new things" include renewal of the covenant, restoration to the land, the messianic kingdom, inclusion of the Gentiles, and the new heaven and earth (41:22 note).

declare . . . tell. God plans, proclaims, and executes. His word will come to pass (11:2 note; 40:8).

42:10 new song. The redeemed will sing a new song as Moses and Miriam did when they had witnessed God's acts of salvation (Ex. 15:1, 21; cf. 12:1–6 and notes; Ps. 149:1; Rev. 5:9; 14:3).

end of the earth. Wherever God's children may be found (11:12).

42:11 Kedar. See note 21:16 (60:7; Ps. 120:5; Jer. 2:10; 49:28, 29).

Sela. See note 16:1.

42:12 glory. The Lord receives acclamation from His subjects (v. 8; 24:14–16 note; 1 Pet. 2:9).

42:13 zeal. Assurance comes from knowing that when the Lord's zeal is stirred, He will accomplish His plan (9:7 note).

mighty man . . . man of war. Isaiah describes the Lord as a Divine Warrior in whom hope lies (1:9; 5:26 and notes).

cries out. The Hebrew word here is different from the one in v. 2. This is a battle cry or call to arms, not a cry of distress.

15 [d] I will lay waste mountains and hills,
and dry up all their vegetation;
I will turn the rivers into islands,[1]
and dry up the pools.
16 [e] And I will lead the blind
in a way that they do not know,
in paths that they have not known
I will guide them.
I will turn the darkness before them
into light,
[f] the rough places into level
ground.
These are the things I do,
and I do not forsake them.
17 [g] They are turned back and utterly put
to shame,
who trust in carved idols,
who say to metal images,
"You are our gods."

Israel's Failure to Hear and See

18 Hear, you deaf,
and look, you blind, that you may
see!
19 Who is blind but my servant,
or deaf as my messenger whom I
send?
Who is blind as my dedicated one,[2]
or blind as the servant of the LORD?
20 [h] He sees many things, but does not
observe them;
[i] his ears are open, but he does not
hear.
21 The LORD was pleased, for his
righteousness' sake,
to magnify his law and make it
glorious.
22 But this is a people plundered and
looted;
they are all of them trapped in
holes
[j] and hidden in prisons;
they have become plunder with none
to rescue,
spoil with none to say,
"Restore!"
23 Who among you will give ear
to this,
will attend and listen for the time
to come?
24 Who gave up Jacob to the
looter,
and Israel to the plunderers?
Was it not the LORD, against whom
we have sinned,
in whose ways they would not
walk,
and whose law they would not
obey?
25 So he poured on him the heat of his
anger
and the might of battle;
it set him on fire all around, [k] but he
did not understand;
it burned him up, [l] but he did not
take it to heart.

Israel's Only Savior

43 But now thus says the LORD,
[m] he who created you, O Jacob,
he who formed you, O Israel:
[n] "Fear not, for I have redeemed
you;
[o] I have called you by name, you are
mine.
2 [p] When you pass through the waters,
I will be with you;
and through the rivers, they shall
not overwhelm you;
[p] when you walk through fire [q] you
shall not be burned,
and the flame shall not consume
you.

15 [d] ch. 50:2 16 [e] ch. 35:5, 8 [f] ch. 40:4 17 [g] ch. 1:29; 44:11; 45:16; Ps. 97:7 20 [h] See Rom. 2:21-23 [i] [Jer. 6:10] 22 [j] ch. 14:17 25 [k] [ch. 47:11; Hos. 7:9] [l] ch. 57:1, 11
Chapter 43
1 [m] ch. 44:2, 21, 24 [n] ch. 41:14 [o] ch. 45:3, 4; [Gen. 32:28] 2 [p] Ps. 66:12 [q] ch. 42:25; [Dan. 3:25, 27]

1 Or *into coastlands* 2 Or *as the one at peace with me*

42:16 lead . . . not forsake. God promises to be with His people and lead them, as He did Israel in the wilderness (Ex. 13:21, 22).

42:18 deaf . . . blind. They are "deaf" because they did not listen (v. 23), and "blind" because they refused to see the hand of God in their history (v. 20; 48:3–6).

42:19 my servant. The Lord exclaims at the blindness and deafness of Israel, who unaccountably were as weak spiritually as their neighbors.

42:21 magnify his law. High regard for God's law will extend His righteous kingdom on earth (v. 4 note).

42:22 plundered and looted . . . in prisons. These conditions came about because they rebelled against the Lord (v. 24).

42:24 Jacob . . . Israel. See note 41:8.

42:25 battle. God in effect fought against His own people through the Assyrian and Babylonian devastation of Samaria and Judah.

43:1–7 God will establish a new community.

43:1 created. See note 4:5.

formed. See note 27:10–11.

Fear not. See note at 10:24; 35:4.

redeemed. See note 35:8, 9.

called . . . name. The Lord called them to be His people and He knows them by name (v. 3 note; 45:3; 49:1; 62:2; John 10:3; Rev. 2:17). The basic blessing of God's covenant is expressed in Jer. 30:22, "You shall be my people, and I will be your God." See also Ex. 6:7; Lev. 11:45; Jer. 11:4.

43:2 waters . . . flame. These words describe the affliction through which God will bring His people to safety (Ps. 66:6, 12).

3 For [r]I am the LORD your God,
the Holy One of Israel, your Savior.
[s]I give Egypt as your ransom,
Cush and [t]Seba in exchange for you.
4 Because you are precious in my eyes,
and honored, and I love you,
I give men in return for you,
peoples in exchange for your life.
5 [u]Fear not, for I am with you;
[v]I will bring your offspring from the east,
and from the west I will gather you.
6 I will say to the north, Give up,
and to the south, Do not withhold;
bring [w]my sons from afar
and [w]my daughters from the end of the earth,
7 everyone who is called by my name,
whom I created for my glory,
whom I formed and made."

8 Bring out [x]the people who are blind,
yet have eyes,
who are deaf, yet have ears!
9 [y]All the nations gather together,
and the peoples assemble.
Who among them can declare this,
and show us the former things?
Let them bring their witnesses to prove them right,
and let them hear and say, It is true.
10 [z]"You are my witnesses," declares the LORD,
"and [a]my servant whom I have chosen,
that you may know and believe me
and understand that I am he.
[b]Before me no god was formed,
nor shall there be any after me.
11 [c]I, I am the LORD,
and besides me there is no savior.
12 I declared and saved and proclaimed,
when there was no strange god among you;
and [z]you are my witnesses," declares the LORD, "and I am God.
13 Also [d]henceforth I am he;
there is none who can deliver from my hand;
I work, and who can turn it back?"

14 Thus says the LORD,
your Redeemer, the Holy One of Israel:
[e]"For your sake I send to Babylon
and [f]bring them all down as fugitives,
[g]even the Chaldeans, in the ships in which they rejoice.
15 I am the LORD, your Holy One,
the Creator of Israel, your King."

16 Thus says the LORD,
[h]who makes a way in the sea,
a path in the mighty waters,
17 who [i]brings forth chariot and horse,
army and warrior;
they lie down, they cannot rise,
[j]they are extinguished, [k]quenched like a wick:
18 [l]"Remember not the former things,
nor consider the things of old.
19 [m]Behold, I am doing a new thing;
now it springs forth, do you not perceive it?
[n]I will make a way in the wilderness
[o]and rivers in the desert.
20 The wild beasts will honor me,
[p]the jackals and the ostriches,
[q]for I give water in the wilderness,
rivers in the desert,
to give drink to my chosen people,

3 [r]See Ex. 20:2 [s][ch. 45:14; 52:3, 4] [t]Ps. 72:10 **5** [u]ch. 41:10, 13, 14; 44:2; Jer. 30:10, 11 [v]ch. 49:12; [ch. 60:8, 9; Ps. 107:3] **6** [w][2 Cor. 6:18] **8** [x]ch. 42:19 **9** [y]ch. 41:1, 21, 22 **10** [z]ver. 12; ch. 44:8 [a]ch. 42:1 [b]See ch. 41:4 **11** [c]ch. 45:21; Hos. 13:4

12 [z][See ver. 10 above] **13** [d]ch. 41:4; Ps. 90:2; [John 8:58] **14** [e][ver. 4] [f][ch. 47:1] [g]ch. 23:13 **16** [h]ch. 51:10; Ex. 14:21, 22; Ps. 77:19 **17** [i]See Ex. 14:4-9 [j][Ps. 76:5, 6] [k]ch. 1:31; [Ps. 118:12] **18** [l][Jer. 16:14; 23:7] **19** [m][ch. 42:9; 2 Cor. 5:17; Rev. 21:9] [n]ch. 35:8 [o]ch. 11:18; 18:21 **20** [p]See ch. 13:22 [q][ch. 49:10]

43:3 Egypt . . . Cush . . . Seba. Seba is probably South Arabia, or Eritrea. For Cush, see Ps. 68:31 note. The Lord chose Israel above these nations (Ps. 147:20; Amos 3:1, 2) and transferred their land to His people (Deut. 4:20, 37, 38; Josh. 24:13; Ps. 78:55).

43:4 precious . . . honored. God's people are exalted by election (49:5; Ex. 19:5; Deut. 7:6–8).

43:8 blind . . . deaf. Here again is the community of rebels. See notes 29:18; 42:18, 19. Spiritually "blind" and "deaf" Israel fulfills the Lord's prophecies in spite of itself.

43:9 former things. See 41:22 note.

43:10 servant. See notes 20:3; 41:8; 42:1.

43:13 henceforth. The Lord alone from old willed the redemption of His people (40:21; 41:4).

deliver from my hand. See Deut. 32:39.

43:14 Redeemer. See 35:9; 41:14 and notes.

43:16 sea . . . mighty waters. Isaiah refers to the crossing of the Red Sea (Ex. 14; 15).

43:17 chariot and horse, army and warrior. The prophet recalls the chariots of Egypt that were destroyed before the face of the Lord (cf. 31:1).

43:19 new thing. The exodus from Egypt is less important than the new era of redemption (42:9 note).

wilderness . . . desert. See note 40:3.

rivers. See note 41:18.

43:20 beasts . . . ostriches. These creatures are associated with desolate areas (34:11–15). See note 13:20–22.

water. This recalls God's provision in the wilderness (Ex. 15:22–26). See note 1:30.

my chosen people. See notes on vv. 1, 3.

21 the people whom I formed for myself
[r] that they might declare my praise.

22 "Yet you did not call upon me, O Jacob;
but [s] you have been weary of me, O Israel!
23 [t] You have not brought me your sheep for burnt offerings,
or honored me with your sacrifices.
I have not burdened you with offerings,
[s] or wearied you with frankincense.
24 You have not bought me sweet cane with money,
or satisfied me with the fat of your sacrifices.
But you have burdened me with your sins;
you have wearied me with your iniquities.

25 "I, I am he
[u] who blots out [v] your transgressions for my own sake,
and I will not remember your sins.
26 Put me in remembrance; [w] let us argue together;
set forth your case, that you may be proved right.
27 [x] Your first father sinned,
and [y] your mediators transgressed against me.
28 Therefore [z] I will profane the princes of the sanctuary,
and [a] deliver Jacob to utter destruction
and Israel to reviling.

Israel the LORD's Chosen

44 "But now hear, [b] O Jacob my servant,
Israel whom I have chosen!
2 Thus says the LORD who made you,
[c] who formed you from the womb and will help you:
[d] Fear not, O Jacob my servant,
[e] Jeshurun whom I have chosen.
3 [f] For I will pour water on the thirsty land,
and streams on the dry ground;
I will pour my Spirit upon your offspring,
and my blessing on your descendants.
4 They shall spring up among the grass
[g] like willows by flowing streams.
5 [h] This one will say, 'I am the LORD's,'
another will call on the name of Jacob,
and another will write on his hand, 'The LORD's,'
and name himself by the name of Israel."

Besides Me There Is No God

6 Thus says the LORD, the King of Israel
and [i] his Redeemer, the LORD of hosts:

21 [r] Ps. 79:13; [Ps. 22:3; 105:1; Luke 1:74, 75; 1 Pet. 2:9]
22 [s] Mic. 6:3
23 [t] [Amos 5:25] [s] [See ver. 22 above]
25 [u] ch. 44:22; [Ezek. 36:25, 26] [v] [ch. 46:8]
26 [w] ch. 1:18
27 [x] [Ezek. 16:3] [y] [Jer. 5:31]
28 [z] Lam. 2:2 [a] [Jer. 24:9; 29:22]
Chapter 44
1 [b] See ch. 41:8
2 [c] ver. 24; ch. 49:15; [Ps. 71:6; Jer. 1:5; Gal. 1:15] [d] See ch. 43:5 [e] Deut. 32:15
3 [f] Joel 2:28; John 7:38; Acts 2:18; See ch. 35:6
4 [g] [Ps. 4:3]
5 [h] [ch. 14:1]
6 [i] See ch. 43:14

43:22 not call . . . been weary. Instead of presenting offerings and sacrifices, the people were hardened in their sins.

43:23 have not brought me your sheep. The people followed more than one religious practice, but these were not necessarily offered to God. On the emptiness of sacrifices which are mere external rituals, see Jer. 7:21–23 note.

43:24 sweet cane. An aromatic plant, possibly sugar cane.

43:25 I, I am he. A repetition for emphasis.

blots . . . remember. God forgives sin, as Israel had experienced after the incident of the golden calf (Ex. 34:6, 7; cf. Luke 5:21). The Lord graciously promises to forgive and to establish His word (37:35; 42:21; 48:9, 11).

43:26 set forth your case. They stood condemned, unable to refute God's charge.

43:27 first father. Jacob was the father of the twelve tribes (Hos. 12:2, 3).

mediators. These are the religious leaders, including prophets and priests.

43:28 princes . . . reviling. Judah was disgraced by the destruction of the temple and the exile of her people (63:18; cf. 2 Kin. 25:18–21).

44:1 servant. See notes 20:3; 41:8; 42:1.

chosen. See notes 14:1; 43:3.

44:2 formed. See note 27:11.

from the womb. God likens Himself to a mother who has conceived and will give birth (v. 24; 42:14; 66:9).

Fear not. See notes 10:24; 35:4.

Jeshurun. A poetic name for Israel (Deut. 32:15), meaning "upright one."

44:3 pour my Spirit . . . offspring. This passage develops the promises in 28:6; 32:15. The Spirit lives in the children of the covenant today (Joel 2:28, 29; Acts 2:38, 39).

blessing. The Spirit will also confirm God's promises. For the connection between water and the Spirit see Mark 1:8–10.

44:5 This one . . . another. Many will participate in the new age of restoration, as Gentiles and Jews together will confess the name of the Lord (cf. Ps. 87:4–6).

44:6–20 The Lord confronts the idols. On Isaiah's polemic against idolatry (vv. 9–20), see 2:8 note.

44:6 See theological note "One and Three: The Trinity."

Redeemer. See note 35:9, 10.

first . . . last. See note 41:4.

[j]"I am the first and I am the last;
besides me there is no god.
7 [k]Who is like me? Let him proclaim it.[1]
Let him declare and set it
before me,
since I appointed an ancient people.
Let them declare what is to come,
and what will happen.
8 Fear not, nor be afraid;
have I not told you from of old
and declared it?
[l]And you are my
witnesses!
[m]Is there a God besides me?
There is no [n]Rock; I know not
any."

6[j]ch. 48:12; Rev. 1:8; See ch. 41:4
7[k]ch. 41:26, 27
8[l]ch. 43:10 [m]ch. 45:5; Deut. 4:35, 39; 32:39; 1 Sam. 2:2; Joel 2:27 [n]See ch. 30:29
9[o]ch. 41:24, 29

The Folly of Idolatry

9 [o]All who fashion idols are nothing, and the things they delight in do not profit. Their witnesses neither see nor know, that

[1] Or *Who like me can proclaim it?*

One and Three: The Trinity

The Old Testament constantly insists that there is only one God, the self-revealed Creator, who must be worshiped and loved exclusively (Deut. 6:4–5; Is. 44:6–45:25). The New Testament agrees (Mark 12:29–30; 1 Cor. 8:4; Eph. 4:6; 1 Tim. 2:5), but speaks of three personal agents, Father, Son, and Holy Spirit, working together to bring about salvation (Rom. 8; Eph. 1:3–14; 2 Thess. 2:13–14; 1 Pet. 1:2). The historic formulation of the Trinity (from the Latin word *trinitas*, meaning "threeness") is not an attempt to explain it; that would be beyond us. It does provide a boundary and safeguard for our thoughts about this mystery, which confronts us with perhaps the most difficult thought that the human mind can know. It is not easy; but it is true.

The doctrine springs from the historical facts of redemption recorded and explained in the New Testament. Jesus prayed to His Father and taught His disciples to do the same. Yet He convinced them that He was personally divine. Belief in His divinity and in the rightness of offering Him worship and prayer is basic to New Testament faith (John 20:28–31, cf. 1:1–18; Acts 7:59; Rom. 9:5; 10:9–13; 2 Cor. 12:7–9; Phil. 2:5–6; Col. 1:15–17; 2:9; Heb. 1:1–12; 1 Pet. 3:15). Jesus promised to send "another Helper" or "Paraclete" (from the Greek; see text note at John 14:16) to carry on His work as the first Helper (John 14:16,17). A "Paraclete" is an advocate, helper, ally, and supporter (John 14:26; 15:26–27; 16:7–15). The promised Helper was the Holy Spirit, who came at Pentecost to fulfill His ministry. From the start He was recognized as the third divine Person: to lie to Him, said Peter not long after Pentecost, is to lie to God (Acts 5:3–4).

Christ prescribed baptism "in the name (singular: one God, one name) of the Father and of the Son and of the Holy Spirit"—three Persons who are the one God to whom Christians commit themselves (Matt. 28:19). So we meet the three Persons in the account of Jesus' own baptism: the Father acknowledged the Son, and the Spirit showed His presence in the Son's life and ministry (Mark 1:9–11). The blessing of 2 Cor. 13:14 is trinitarian, as is the prayer for grace and peace from the Father, the Spirit, and Jesus Christ in Rev. 1:4–5. John includes the Spirit between the Father and the Son only because he teaches that the Spirit is divine in the very same sense as are the Father and the Son. These are some of the more striking examples of trinitarian teaching in the New Testament. Though the technical language of later theology is not found there, trinitarian faith and thinking are present in all its pages. In this sense the Trinity is a biblical doctrine.

Basically the doctrine is that the unity of the one God is complex. The three personal "subsistences" (as they are called) are coequal and coeternal centers of self-awareness, each being "I" in relation to two who are "You," and each having the full divine essence of God, the specific existence that belongs to God alone. God is not one person who plays three separate roles; this is the error called "modalism." Nor are there three gods who only seem to be one because they always act together; this is "tritheism." The theologian B. B. Warfield put it simply: "when we have said these three things, then—that there is but one God, that the Father and the Son and the Spirit is each God, that the Father and the Son and the Spirit is each a distinct person—we have enunciated the doctrine of the Trinity in its completeness." This summarizes what was revealed through the words and works of Jesus, and is the reality underlying the salvation of the New Testament.

Practically speaking, the doctrine of the Trinity requires us to give equal honor to each of the three Persons in the unity of the one God. Moreover, knowing the doctrine establishes personal faith no less than it enriches a healthy sense of unity with other Christians.

44:8 Rock. See 8:14, 15 note; Deut. 32:4, 15, 31.

44:9 nothing . . . not profit. See 41:29 note.

they may be put to shame. **10** [p]Who fashions a god or casts an idol that is profitable
for nothing? **11** [q]Behold, all his companions
shall be put to shame, and the craftsmen
are only human. Let them all assemble, let
them stand forth. They shall be terrified;
they shall be put to shame together.
12 [p]The ironsmith takes a cutting tool and
works it over the coals. He fashions it with
hammers and works it with his strong arm.
He becomes hungry, and his strength fails;
he drinks no water and is faint. **13** The carpenter stretches a line; he marks it out with
a pencil. He shapes it with planes and
marks it with a compass. [r]He shapes it into
the figure of a man, with the beauty of a
man, to dwell in a house. **14** [s]He cuts down
cedars, or he chooses a cypress tree or an
oak and lets it grow strong among the trees
of the forest. He plants a cedar and the rain
nourishes it. **15** Then it becomes fuel for a
man. He takes a part of it and warms himself; he kindles a fire and bakes bread. Also
he makes a god and worships it; he makes
it an idol and falls down before it. **16** Half of
it he burns in the fire. Over the half he eats
meat; he roasts it and is satisfied. Also he
warms himself and says, "Aha, I am warm,
I have seen the fire!" **17** And the rest of it he
makes into a god, his idol, and falls down
to it and worships it. [t]He prays to it and
says, "Deliver me, for you are my god!"
18 They know not, nor do they discern,
for he has shut their eyes, so that they cannot see, and their hearts, so that they cannot understand. **19** No one considers, nor is
there knowledge or discernment to say,
"Half of it I burned in the fire; I also baked
bread on its coals; I roasted meat and have
eaten. And shall I make the rest of it an
[u]abomination? Shall I fall down before a
block of wood?" **20** [v]He feeds on [w]ashes; a
deluded heart has led him astray, and he
cannot deliver himself or say, "Is there not
[x]a lie in my right hand?"

The LORD Redeems Israel

21 Remember these things, O Jacob,
and Israel, for you are [y]my servant;
I formed you; you are my servant;
[z]O Israel, you will not be forgotten
by me.
22 [a]I have blotted out your
transgressions like a cloud
and your sins like mist;
return to me, for I have redeemed you.

23 [b]Sing, O heavens, for the LORD has
done it;
shout, O [c]depths of the earth;
break forth into singing, O mountains,
O forest, and every tree in it!
For the LORD has redeemed Jacob,
[d]and will be glorified[1] in Israel.
24 Thus says the LORD, [e]your Redeemer,
[f]who formed you from the womb:
[g]"I am the LORD, who made all things,
[h]who alone stretched out the
heavens,
who spread out the earth by
myself,
25 who frustrates the signs of liars
and makes fools of diviners,
[i]who turns wise men back
and makes their knowledge foolish,
26 [j]who confirms the word of his servant
and fulfills the counsel of his
messengers,
who says of Jerusalem, 'She shall be
inhabited,'
[k]and of the cities of Judah, 'They
shall be built,
and I will raise up their ruins';

[1] Or *will display his beauty*

10 [p][ch. 40:19, 20; 41:6, 7; 46:6, 7; Hab. 2:18]; See Jer. 10:3-5
11 [q]ch. 45:16; Ps. 115:8; See ch. 42:17
12 [p][See ver. 10 above]
13 [r]See Ps. 115:5-7
14 [s][ch. 40:20]
17 [t][ch. 45:20]
19 [u]Deut. 27:15
20 [v]Hos. 12:1 [w][Job 13:12]
[x]Ps. 144:8; [Rom. 1:25]
21 [y]ch. 42:19; See ch. 42:1 [z][ch. 49:15]
22 [a]ch. 43:25
23 [b]ch. 49:13; [ch. 55:12; Ps. 69:34; Jer. 51:48] [c]Ps. 63:9; [Hos. 2:21, 22] [d]ch. 49:3; [ch. 55:5; 60:9]
24 [e]See ch. 43:14 [f]See ver. 2 [g][ch. 42:5] [h]ch. 42:5; 45:12
25 [i][ch. 19:3, 14]
26 [j][2 Chr. 36:22] [k][Jer. 32:15, 44]

Their witnesses. The "witnesses" could be the idols or their makers. Neither has any power of sight or understanding (Ps. 115:8).

44:11 assemble . . . stand. The setting is a court of law (41:21).

44:12 An idol may be a work of art. But even the finest craftsman's mortality is revealed in his hunger and thirst. In contrast, see 40:28.

44:13 figure of a man. The carpenter makes his god in his own image (Deut. 4:16; Rom. 1:22, 23).

44:18 know . . . discern. They are utterly foolish (v. 9; 6:9, 10).

44:19 an abomination . . . block of wood. The prophet employs ridicule to expose the foolishness of idolatry. See "Mankind's Guilty Knowledge of God" at Rom. 1:19.

44:20 lie. The conclusion: idolatry is a deception, a hoax.

44:22 redeemed. The Lord alone is the Redeemer (35:9, 10; 41:14 and notes).

44:23 heavens . . . every tree. All creation will praise God for His salvation of Israel.

glorified. God will glorify the redeemed, who in turn will lead many to praise the Lord for His mighty acts (4:2 note; 49:3; 55:5; 60:21; 61:3).

44:25 diviners. Divination was strictly forbidden in Israel (2:6; 8:19 and notes).

44:26 word . . . counsel. These refer to the Lord's revelations of His plan (11:2 note).

servant. See notes 20:3; 41:8; 42:1.

ruins. These are the regions devastated by Babylon. The restoration of Judah was the beginning of a new stage in the history of redemption.

27 [l] who says to the deep, 'Be dry;
I will dry up your rivers';
28 who says of [m] Cyrus, 'He is [n] my shepherd,
and he shall fulfill all my purpose';
saying of Jerusalem, 'She shall be built,'
[o] and of the temple, 'Your foundation shall be laid.'"

Cyrus, God's Instrument

45 Thus says the LORD to [p] his anointed, to Cyrus,
[q] whose right hand I have grasped,
to subdue nations before him
and [r] to loose the belts of kings,
to open doors before him
that gates may not be closed:
2 "I will go before you
and [s] level the exalted places,[1]
[t] I will break in pieces the doors of bronze
and cut through the bars of iron,
3 [u] I will give you the treasures of darkness
and the hoards in secret places,
that you may know that it is I, the LORD,
the God of Israel, [v] who call you by your name.
4 For the sake of my servant Jacob,
and Israel my chosen,
[v] I call you by your name,
[w] I name you, though you do not know me.
5 [x] I am the LORD, and there is no other,
besides me there is no God;
[y] I equip you, though you do not know me,
6 [z] that people may know, from the rising of the sun
and from the west, that there is none besides me;
I am the LORD, and there is no other.
7 I form light and create darkness,
I make well-being and [a] create calamity,
I am the LORD, who does all these things.
8 [b] "Shower, O heavens, from above,
and [c] let the clouds rain down righteousness;
let the earth open, that salvation and righteousness may bear fruit;
let the earth cause them both to sprout;
I the LORD have created it.
9 [d] "Woe to him who strives with him who formed him,
a pot among earthen pots!
[e] Does the clay say to him who forms it, 'What are you making?'
or 'Your work has no handles'?
10 Woe to him who says to a father,
'What are you begetting?'
or to a woman, 'With what are you in labor?'"
11 Thus says [f] the LORD,
the Holy One of Israel, and the one who formed him:

27 [l] ch. 11:15; [ch. 51:10]
28 [m] ch. 45:1 [n] [2 Sam. 5:2; Ps. 78:72] [o] ch. 45:13; See 2 Chr. 36:22, 23; Ezra 1:1-3
Chapter 45
1 [p] [ch. 44:28] [q] [ch. 41:13] [r] Job 12:21; [ver. 5; ch. 22:21]
2 [s] ch. 40:4 [t] Ps. 107:16
3 [u] [Jer. 50:37; 51:13] [v] ch. 43:1
4 [v] [See ver. 3 above] [w] [ch. 62:2]
5 [x] See ch. 44:8 [y] Job 12:21; [ver. 5; ch. 22:21]
6 [z] [ch. 37:20; Mal. 1:11]
7 [a] [ch. 41:23; Amos 3:6]
8 [b] [Deut. 32:2] [c] Ps. 85:11; [Hos. 10:12]
9 [d] [Eccles. 6:10]; See ch. 10:15 [e] ch. 64:8; Cited Rom. 9:20
11 [f] Ezek. 39:7

1 Masoretic Text; Dead Sea Scroll, Septuagint *level the mountains*

44:27 deep . . . rivers. Possibly a reference to the crossing of the Red Sea (43:16, 19 and notes). The prophecy may have found a literal fulfillment when Cyrus diverted the water of the Euphrates River and marched his army through the gates that allowed it to flow through the city of Babylon (45:2 note).

44:28 my shepherd. Kings were often called shepherds (2 Sam. 5:2; Jer. 3:15; cf. Mic. 5:4). Cyrus ruled by God's decree.

Jerusalem . . . temple. These were rebuilt by Cyrus's royal decree (Ezra 1:2–4; 6:3–5).

45:1 his anointed. This title is not used elsewhere of anyone outside Israel, and its application to Cyrus would have shocked Isaiah's audience.

right hand I have grasped. He rules by Yahweh's authority (41:2; 48:14; cf. Ps. 2:8, 9; 110:1).

nations . . . kings. See note 41:2.

45:2 break . . . cut. Nothing can withstand the Lord's servant (cf. Ps. 107:16).

doors. The prophecy may have had a literal fulfillment when Cyrus used the gates that allowed the Euphrates to flow through Babylon (44:27 note).

45:3 darkness . . . secret places. Precious metals came from deep mines (Job 28:1–6). Cyrus plundered the fabulous wealth of Lydia in 546 B.C.

call you by your name. The Lord has raised up Cyrus and knows him (compare 43:1 note).

45:4 servant. See notes at 20:3; 41:8; 42:1.

chosen. See note 14:1.

name you. As God's "shepherd" (44:28) and "anointed" (v. 1), Cyrus has a title of honor.

you do not know me. Cyrus remained an unbeliever.

45:7 form. See note 27:11.

light . . . darkness. The Lord asserts His power over two fundamental poles of reality, as described in Gen. 1:3, 4. The parallel terms "well-being" and "calamity" include the political realities that Cyrus was going to disturb in fulfilling the counsel of God.

45:8 heavens . . . earth. Creation must prepare itself for the Lord's act of redemption, described by two synonyms: "righteousness" and "salvation" (12:2; 26:17, 18 and notes).

[g]"Ask me of things to come;
will you command me [h]concerning
my children and [i]the work of
my hands?[1]
12 [j]I made the earth
and created man on it;
it was my hands [k]that stretched out
the heavens,
and [l]I commanded all their host.
13 [m]I have stirred him up in
righteousness,
[n]and I will make all his ways level;
[o]he shall build my city
[p]and set my exiles free,
not for price or reward,"
says the LORD of hosts.

The LORD, the Only Savior

14 Thus says the LORD:
[q]"The wealth of Egypt and the
merchandise of Cush,
and the Sabeans, men of stature,
shall come over to you [r]and be yours;
they shall follow you;
they shall come over in chains and
bow down to you.
They will plead with you, saying:
'Surely God is in you, and there is
no other,
no god besides him.'"
15 [s]Truly, you are a God who hides
yourself,
O God of Israel, the Savior.
16 [t]All of them are put to shame and
confounded;
the makers of idols go in confusion
together.
17 But Israel is saved by the LORD
with everlasting salvation;
[u]you shall not be put to shame or
confounded
to all eternity.

11 [g][ch. 41:23] [h][Jer. 31:9] [i]ch. 29:23; 64:8
12 [j]Jer. 27:5 [k]ch. 42:5; 44:24 [l]Gen. 2:1
13 [m]ch. 41:2 [n][ver. 2] [o]See ch. 44:28 [p]ch. 49:25; 51:14; 52:3
14 [q][ch. 43:3] [r]ch. 14:2
15 [s]ch. 57:17
16 [t]See ch. 42:17
17 [u]ch. 54:4
18 [v]ch. 42:5 [w][Gen. 1:2] [x][Ps. 115:16]
19 [y]ch. 48:16; [Deut. 30:11] [z]Jer. 29:13, 14 [a]ver. 23
20 [b][ch. 41:1] [c][ch. 44:18, 19; 48:5-7] [d]ch. 46:1, 7; Jer. 10:5 [e][ch. 44:17]
21 [f][ch. 41:22, 26; 43:9] [g][ch. 43:11]
22 [h]ch. 11:12; 43:5, 6
23 [i]See Gen. 22:16 [j]ver. 19 [k]Cited Rom. 14:11; [Phil. 2:10]

18 [v]For thus says the LORD,
who created the heavens
(he is God!),
who formed the earth and made it
(he established it;
he [w]did not create it empty,
[x]he formed it to be inhabited!):
"I am the LORD, and there is no other.
19 [y]I did not speak in secret,
in a land of darkness;
I did not say to the offspring of Jacob,
[z]'Seek me in vain.'[2]
I the LORD speak [a]the truth;
I declare what is right.
20 [b]"Assemble yourselves and come;
draw near together,
you survivors of the nations!
[c]They have no knowledge
who [d]carry about their wooden idols,
[e]and keep on praying to a god
that cannot save.
21 [f]Declare and present your case;
let them take counsel together!
Who told this long ago?
Who declared it of old?
Was it not I, the LORD?
And there is no other god
besides me,
a righteous God [g]and a Savior;
there is none besides me.
22 "Turn to me and be saved,
[h]all the ends of the earth!
For I am God, and there is no other.
23 [i]By myself I have sworn;
from my mouth has gone out in
[j]righteousness
a word that shall not return:
[k]'To me every knee shall bow,
every tongue shall swear
allegiance.'[3]

1 A slight emendation yields *will you question me about my children, or command me concerning the work of my hands?* 2 Hebrew *in emptiness* 3 Septuagint *every tongue shall confess to God*

45:13 not for price. Although the Lord gave Cyrus a handsome reward (v. 3) for ransoming His people (43:3), this was not the reason Cyrus liberated them.

45:14 Egypt . . . Cush . . . Sabeans. See 43:3 note; Ps. 68:31. The nations will come to worship the one God (Zech. 8:23; Eph. 3:6).

45:15 a God who hides yourself. God is said to hide Himself when He seems not to be present to help His people (8:17; 54:8). He is also "hidden" in the sense that He is unaccountable to anyone, and His ways are often mysterious (55:8, 9; Ps. 77:19 note; Rom. 9:20; 11:33, 34).

45:17 everlasting salvation . . . to all eternity. God is unlike people and idols, who can never secure the future for themselves or for others (cf. Heb. 5:9).

45:18 empty. This word is translated "without form" in Gen. 1:2. This was the beginning, not the end of creation. In the same way God does not invite people to seek Him to no purpose. He will carry through with what He has begun (55:11; 66:9) and answer those who seek Him (55:3; Matt. 11:28; Heb. 11:6).

45:19 in secret, in a land of darkness. The Lord's revelation is unlike pagan oracles that were obscure and ambiguous. The Lord's revelation is clear and public, though the outworking of His promises may not conform to human expectations (48:16).

45:22 ends of the earth. See v. 14 and note.

45:23 By myself I have sworn. God's promises are guaranteed by His name (14:24; 62:8; Gen. 22:16; Ex. 32:13; Heb. 6:13–18).

every knee . . . every tongue. This is the goal of redemptive history (v. 14 and note; Rom. 14:11; 1 Cor. 15:25; Phil. 2:10, 11).

24 [l]"Only in the LORD, it shall be said
of me,
are righteousness and [m]strength;
to him shall come and be ashamed
[n]all who were incensed against him.
25 In the LORD all the offspring of Israel
shall be justified and shall glory."

The Idols of Babylon and the One True God

46 [o]Bel bows down; Nebo stoops;
their idols are on beasts and
livestock;
these things you carry are borne
as burdens on weary beasts.
2 They stoop; they bow down together;
they cannot save the burden,
but [p]themselves go into captivity.

3 "Listen to me, O house of Jacob,
all the remnant of the house of Israel,
[q]who have been borne by me from
before your birth,
carried from the womb;
4 [r]even to your old age I am he,
and to gray hairs I will carry you.
I have made, and I will bear;
I will carry and will save.

5 [s]"To whom will you liken me and
make me equal,
and compare me, that we may be
alike?
6 [t]Those who lavish gold from the purse,
and weigh out silver in the scales,
hire a goldsmith, and he makes it
into a god;
[u]then they fall down and worship!
7 [v]They lift it to their shoulders, they
carry it,
they set it in its place, and it
stands there;
[w]it cannot move from its place.
If one cries to it, it does not answer
or save him from his trouble.

8 "Remember this and stand firm,
recall it to mind, [x]you
transgressors,
9 remember the former things of old;
for I am God, and there is no other;
I am God, and there is none
like me,
10 [y]declaring the end from the
beginning
and from ancient times things not
yet done,
saying, [z]'My counsel shall stand,
and I will accomplish all my
purpose,'
11 [a]calling a bird of prey from the east,
the man of my counsel from a far
country.
[b]I have spoken, and I will bring it to
pass;
I have purposed, and I will do it.

12 "Listen to me, you stubborn of heart,
you who are far from
righteousness:
13 [c]I bring near my righteousness; it is
not far off,
and my salvation will not delay;
[d]I will put salvation in Zion,
for Israel my glory."

The Humiliation of Babylon

47 [e]Come down and sit in the dust,
O virgin [f]daughter of Babylon;
[g]sit on the ground without a throne,
O daughter of [h]the Chaldeans!
[i]For you shall no more be called
tender and delicate.
2 Take the millstones and [j]grind flour,
[k]put off your veil,
strip off your robe, uncover your
legs,
pass through the rivers.

24 [l][ch. 26:4; 44:8] [m][ch. 26:4; 44:8] [n][ch. 41:11]
Chapter 46
1 [o]Jer. 50:2; 51:44; [ch. 21:9]
2 [p][Jer. 48:7; Hos. 10:5, 6]
3 [q][Deut. 1:31; 32:11]
4 [r][Ps. 71:18]
5 [s]See ch. 40:18
6 [t]See ch. 44:10 [u]ch. 44:15
7 [v]See ch. 45:20 [w]Ps. 115:7
8 [x][ch. 43:25]
10 [y]ch. 41:26 [z]ch. 44:26, 28; Ps. 33:11; Prov. 19:21; [Heb. 6:17]
11 [a]See ch. 41:2 [b]Num. 23:19
13 [c]ch. 51:5; [ch. 56:1; Ps. 85:9] [d]ch. 62:11; [Joel 2:32]
Chapter 47
1 [e][ch. 43:14] [f]Ps. 137:8 [g]ch. 3:26 [h]ch. 23:13; 48:14 [i][ver. 5; ch. 13:19]
2 [j]Judg. 16:21; [Matt. 24:41] [k][ch. 20:4]

46:1, 2 Bel . . . Nebo. Babylonian gods.

bows . . . stoops. The idols were dead weight, a lifeless burden on the animals that had to carry them. On Isaiah's polemic against idolatry, see 2:8.

46:3 remnant. See note 1:9.

birth . . . womb. The Lord's care is like that of a mother for her children (44:2 note; 49:5; cf. Deut. 1:31; Hos. 11:3, 4).

46:4 old age . . . gray hairs. The Lord is constant in His care (Ps. 71:9, 18).

I am he. See note 41:4.

46:9 former . . . of old. See notes 41:22; 42:9.

46:11 east . . . man. This is Cyrus; see 41:2.

46:12 stubborn of heart. These are the transgressors of v. 8. As some in the first exodus looked back to Egypt (Num. 14:3), so also some in the second exodus longed for Babylon.

46:13 Zion. See note 1:8.

47:1–15 An oracle regarding the fall of Babylon, never to rise again.

47:1–3 Babylon, the queen of nations, is commanded to descend from her throne and become a menial slave girl. By contrast, Zion, a captive slave girl, will be commanded to ascend her throne (52:1, 2).

47:1 virgin daughter of Babylon. The city of Babylon and its inhabitants.

47:2 put off . . . pass through. All Babylon's privileges and status will be removed. She will be humiliated.

3 Your nakedness shall be uncovered,
and your disgrace shall be seen.
I will take vengeance,
and I will spare no one.
4 [l] Our Redeemer—the LORD of hosts is
his name—
is the Holy One of Israel.

5 [m] Sit in silence, and go into darkness,
O daughter of [h] the Chaldeans;
for you shall no more be called
[n] the mistress of kingdoms.
6 [o] I was angry with my people;
I profaned my heritage;
I gave them into your hand;
[p] you showed them no mercy;
on the aged you made your yoke
exceedingly heavy.
7 You said, "I shall be [q] mistress forever,"
so that you did not lay these
things to heart
or remember their end.

8 Now therefore hear this, [q] you lover
of pleasures,
[r] who sit securely,
who say in your heart,
[s] "I am, and there is no one
besides me;
[t] I shall not sit as a widow
or know the loss of children":
9 [u] These two things shall come to you
in a moment, [v] in one day;
the loss of children and widowhood
shall come upon you in full measure,
[w] in spite of your many sorceries
and the great power of your
enchantments.

10 You felt secure in your wickedness,
you said, "No one sees me";
your wisdom and your knowledge
led you astray,
and you said in your heart,
[x] "I am, and there is no one
besides me."

11 But evil shall come upon you,
which you will not know how to
charm away;
disaster shall fall upon you,
for which you will not be able to
atone;
[y] and ruin shall come upon you
suddenly,
of which you know nothing.

12 [z] Stand fast in your enchantments
and your many sorceries,
with which you have labored from
your youth;
perhaps you may be able to succeed;
perhaps you may inspire terror.
13 You are wearied with your many
counsels;
let them stand forth and save you,
[a] those who divide the heavens,
who gaze at the stars,
who at the new moons make known
what shall come upon you.

14 Behold, [b] they are like stubble;
[c] the fire consumes them;
they cannot deliver themselves
from the power of the flame.
No coal for warming oneself is this,
no fire to sit before!
15 Such to you are those with whom
you have labored,
who have done business with you
from your youth;
they wander about each in his own
direction;
there is no one to save you.

Israel Refined for God's Glory

48 Hear this, O house of Jacob,
[d] who are called by the name of Israel,
and [e] who came from the waters of
Judah,
[f] who swear by the name of the LORD
and confess the God of Israel,
but not in truth or right.

4 [l] See ch. 43:14
5 [m] [Jer. 8:14] [h] [See ver. 1 above] [n] [ver. 1]
6 [o] [Zech. 1:15] [p] [ch. 14:17; 51:23]
7 [q] [ver. 1]
8 [q] [See ver. 7 above] [r] Zeph. 2:15 [s] [ch. 45:6, 18; Jer. 50:29] [t] Lam. 1:1; [Rev. 18:7]
9 [u] [ch. 51:19] [v] [Jer. 50:31] [w] [ver. 12, 13; Nah. 3:4]
10 [x] [ch. 45:6, 18; Jer. 50:29]
11 [y] [Jer. 51:41; Ps. 35:8]
12 [z] [ver. 9]
13 [a] [ch. 44:25; Dan. 2:2, 10]
14 [b] ch. 41:2; Nah. 1:10; Mal. 4:1 [c] See ch. 10:17
Chapter 48
1 [d] ch. 43:1 [e] Ps. 68:26 [f] Jer. 7:9

47:4 Redeemer. See notes 35:9; 41:14.

47:7 mistress forever. Her boast was based on her contempt for the truths that God ruled history and that He would judge her for her cruelties (v. 6; Rev. 18:7). Her society and politics had no regard for God.

47:9 moment, in one day. Babylon's losses will occur suddenly.

loss of children and widowhood. Bereft of husband and children, she has no hope for the future and is consigned to slavery and extinction. Contrast 49:21–23; 54:1–6.

47:10 wisdom . . . knowledge. These are Babylon's traditions of religion, magic, and divination. See note 44:25.

I am. In brazen self-deification, Babylon usurps the name of God (45:5, 6, 18, 21, 22; 46:9).

47:13 counsels . . . stars. Babylon depended on omens from the heavenly bodies for her decisions (Dan. 2:2).

47:14 stubble . . . flame. See Rev. 18:17–19. Babylon's astrologers (v. 13) practiced their craft to save Babylon from these prophecies, but they cannot even save themselves (Dan. 2:10–13).

48:1 Hear. This final and urgent appeal was designed to lead deaf and blind Israel (vv. 6, 8; cf. 42:18–20; 46:3–12; 51:1) to recognize God's ways in creation and in history (vv. 12, 16).

2 For they call themselves after the
holy city,
[g] and stay themselves on the God of
Israel;
the LORD of hosts is his name.
3 "The former things [h] I declared of old;
they went out from my mouth and
I announced them;
then suddenly I did them and they
came to pass.
4 Because I know that [i] you are obstinate,
and your neck is an iron sinew
and your forehead brass,
5 [h] I declared them to you from of old,
before they came to pass I
announced them to you,
lest you should say, [j] 'My idol did
them,
my carved image and my metal
image commanded them.'
6 "You have heard; now see all this;
and will you not declare it?
From this time forth [k] I announce to
you new things,
hidden things that you have not
known.
7 They are created now, not long ago;
before today you have never heard
of them,
lest you should say, 'Behold, I
knew them.'
8 You have never heard, you have
never known,
from of old your ear has not been
opened.
For I knew that you would surely
deal treacherously,
and that [l] from before birth you
were called a rebel.
9 [m] "For my name's sake I defer my anger,
for the sake of my praise I restrain
it for you,
that I may not cut you off.

2 [g] [Mic. 3:11] 3 [h] ch. 41:26 4 [i] [Ex. 32:9] 5 [h] [See ver. 3 above] [j] See Jer. 44:15-17 6 [k] See ch. 43:19 8 [l] ch. 46:8 9 [m] [Mal. 3:6]

10 Behold, I have refined you, [n] but not
as silver;
[o] I have tried[1] you in the furnace of
affliction.
11 [p] For my own sake, for my own sake,
I do it,
for how should my name[2] be
profaned?
[q] My glory I will not give to
another.

The LORD's Call to Israel

12 "Listen to me, O Jacob,
and Israel, whom I called!
I am he; [r] I am the first,
and I am the last.
13 My hand [s] laid the foundation of the
earth,
and my right hand [s] spread out the
heavens;
[t] when I call to them,
they stand forth together.
14 "Assemble, all of you, and
listen!
[u] who among them has declared
these things?
The LORD loves him;
[v] he shall perform his purpose on
Babylon,
and his arm shall be against [w] the
Chaldeans.
15 [x] I, even I, have spoken and called
him;
I have brought him, and he will
prosper in his way.
16 [y] Draw near to me, hear this:
from the beginning I have not
spoken in secret,
from the time it came to be I have
been there."
And now [z] the Lord GOD has sent me,
and his Spirit.

10 [n] [1 Pet. 1:7] [o] [Deut. 4:20; Ezek. 22:18, 20, 22] 11 [p] ch. 43:25; Ezek. 20:9 [q] ch. 42:8 12 [r] See ch. 41:4 13 [s] ch. 51:13; [Ps. 102:25; Heb. 1:10] [t] [ch. 40:26] 14 [u] [ch. 41:26] [v] ch. 46:10, 11 [w] ch. 23:13; 47:1 15 [x] See ch. 45:1-3 16 [y] ch. 45:19 [z] ch. 61:1

[1] Or *I have chosen* [2] Hebrew lacks *my name*

48:3 former things. See notes 41:22; 42:9.

48:5 from of old, before they came to pass. The Lord alone decrees and executes His will according to His word.

48:6 heard; now see. The evidence speaks for itself, if only they would believe God's word.

new things, hidden things. An era of salvation and kingdom righteousness began with the restoration from exile, but these prophecies look forward to Christ's coming and the growth of His kingdom in its fullness (45:15; Rev. 1:19).

48:10 refined . . . tried. The Exile was a period of refining (1:22, 25; compare Ezek. 22:18–22; 1 Pet. 1:7).

48:12 I am he. Contrast Babylon's boast in 47:8, 10.

48:14 The LORD loves him. That is, Cyrus (41:2, 25; 45:4; 46:11 and notes).

48:15 called . . . prosper. The status and special success of Cyrus is given by the Lord.

48:16 I have been there. Christ appears to be speaking in this verse. As commonly translated, He reveals that His Spirit inspired the prophets (Rev. 19:10), and that He came into the world sent by the Father and the Spirit. Salvation is the work of the triune God.

17 Thus says the LORD,
your Redeemer, the Holy One of Israel:
"I am the LORD your God,
who teaches you to profit,
who leads you in the way you should go.
18 [a]Oh that you had paid attention to my commandments!
[b]Then your peace would have been like a river,
and your righteousness like the waves of the sea;
19 [c]your offspring would have been like the sand,
and your descendants like its grains;
their name would never be cut off
or destroyed from before me."

20 [d]Go out from Babylon, flee from [e]Chaldea,
declare this [f]with a shout of joy, proclaim it,
send it out to the end of the earth;
say, [g]"The LORD has redeemed his servant Jacob!"
21 [h]They did not thirst when he led them through the deserts;
[i]he made water flow for them from the rock;
he split the rock and the water gushed out.

22 [j]"There is no peace," says the LORD, "for the wicked."

18 [a]Ps. 81:13; Luke 19:42; [Deut. 32:29] [b]ch. 66:12
19 [c]ch. 10:22; Gen. 22:17; Hos. 1:10
20 [d]ch. 52:11; Jer. 50:8; 51:6, 45; Zech. 2:6, 7 [e]ch. 23:13; 47:1 [f][ch. 35:10; 52:9] [g]ch. 44:23; [Ex. 19:4-6]
21 [h][ch. 35:6; 44:3; Deut. 8:15] [i]ch. 43:19; Ex. 17:6; Num. 20:11
22 [j]ch. 57:21

Chapter 49
1 [k]See ch. 11:11 [l]ch. 33:13 [m]See ch. 44:2
2 [n]ch. 11:4; Hos. 6:5; [Heb. 4:12; Rev. 1:16] [o]ch. 51:16
3 [p]ch. 44:23
4 [q][ch. 65:23]; See ch. 50:6-8; 53:10-12
5 [r][ch. 50:4] [s][ch. 52:13]

The Servant of the LORD

49 Listen to me, [k]O coastlands,
and give attention, you peoples [l]from afar.
[m]The LORD called me from the womb,
from the body of my mother he named my name.
2 [n]He made my mouth like a sharp sword;
[o]in the shadow of his hand he hid me;
he made me a polished arrow;
in his quiver he hid me away.
3 And he said to me, "You are my servant,
Israel, [p]in whom I will be glorified."[1]
4 [q]But I said, "I have labored in vain;
I have spent my strength for nothing and vanity;
yet surely my right is with the LORD,
and my recompense with my God."

5 [r]And now the LORD says,
he [m]who formed me from the womb to be his servant,
to bring Jacob back to him;
and that Israel might be gathered to him—
for [s]I am honored in the eyes of the LORD,
and my God has become my strength—
6 he says:
"It is too light a thing that you should be my servant
to raise up the tribes of Jacob
and to bring back the preserved of Israel;

1 Or *I will display my beauty*

48:17 Redeemer. See note 35:9; 41:14.

48:18 Oh that you had paid attention. God reveals a compassionate longing for His people to find their peace in living for Him. As Dante said, "In His will is our peace."

river . . . waves of the sea. These similes represent abundant life (66:12; Amos 5:24).

righteousness. See note 1:21. Peace and righteousness go together (v. 22; 26:3 note; 32:17; 54:13, 14; 60:17; Ps. 85:10; Heb. 7:2).

48:19 offspring . . . sand. This is the promise first made to Abraham (Gen. 12:2; 22:17).

48:21 thirst . . . gushed out. The prophet remembers the exodus from Egypt and how God provided for His people then (41:17–20; 43:19–21; 44:3; cf. Ex. 17:6; Ps. 105:41).

48:22 no peace. See v. 18 note.

49:1–7 This is the second of the four "Servant Songs" (42:1–9; 49:1–7; 50:4–11; 52:13–53:12).

49:1 called . . . name. The faithful servant is called "Israel" (v. 3; 43:1; 44:2, 24; 45:3 and notes). He is distinct from unfaithful Israel (vv. 5, 6; 42:18; 46:12; 48:1 and notes).

49:2 mouth. The servant conquers through preaching (11:4 note; 51:16 note; 61:1). God's words are effective (40:8; 45:19; 55:10, 11).

sharp sword . . . polished arrow. These metaphors portray the effectiveness of the word (Eph. 6:17; Heb. 4:12; Rev. 1:16; 2:12, 16; 19:15).

49:3 servant. See notes 20:3; 41:8; 42:1.

49:4 labored in vain. The servant's complaint is fulfilled in Christ's rejection and suffering (42:2 note).

right. See 40:10; Gen. 15:1. The servant will be vindicated (50:8) and rewarded after His death and resurrection (53:8–10).

49:5 formed. See note 27:11.

bring . . . gathered. One purpose of the Servant is to reconcile the Jews with God.

49:6 light for the nations. A second purpose of the Servant is to bring the gospel to the nations (Luke 2:32; Acts 13:47; 26:23). He fulfills the call of Abraham (Gen. 12:3; 22:18) and of Israel (Ex. 19:5, 6). Today the ascended Christ brings the gospel to the nations through His body, the church (Matt. 28:18–20; 1 Pet. 2:9, 10).

[t] I will make you [u] as a light for the
nations,
that [v] my salvation may reach to
the end of the earth."

7 Thus says the LORD,
[w] the Redeemer of Israel and his
Holy One,
[x] to one deeply despised, abhorred by
the nation,
the servant of rulers:
[y] "Kings shall see and arise;
princes, and they shall prostrate
themselves;
because of the LORD, who is
faithful,
the Holy One of Israel, who has
chosen you."

The Restoration of Israel

8 Thus says the LORD:
[z] "In a [a] time of favor I have answered
you;
in a day of salvation I have helped
you;
I will keep you [b] and give you
as a covenant to the people,
to establish the land,
[c] to apportion the desolate
heritages,
9 [d] saying to the prisoners,
'Come out,'
to those who are in darkness,
'Appear.'
[e] They shall feed along the ways;
on all bare heights shall be their
pasture;
10 [f] they shall not hunger or thirst,
neither scorching wind nor sun
shall strike them,
for he who has pity on them [g] will
lead them,
and by springs of water will guide
them.

11 [h] And I will make all my mountains a
road,
and my highways shall be
raised up.
12 [i] Behold, these shall come from afar,
and behold, [j] these from the north
and from the west,[1]
and these from the land of Syene."[2]

13 [k] Sing for joy, O heavens, and exult,
O earth;
break forth, O mountains, into
singing!
for the LORD [l] has comforted his
people
and will have compassion on his
afflicted.

14 But Zion said, [m] "The LORD has
forsaken me;
my Lord has forgotten me."

15 [n] "Can a woman forget her nursing child,
that she should have no
compassion on the son of her
womb?
Even these may forget,
yet I will not forget you.
16 Behold, [o] I have engraved you on the
palms of my hands;
your walls are continually
before me.
17 Your builders make haste;[3]
[p] your destroyers and those who laid
you waste go out from you.
18 [q] Lift up your eyes around and see;
they all gather, they come to you.
[r] As I live, declares the LORD,
[s] you shall put them all on as an
ornament;
you shall bind them on as a bride
does.

6 [t] Cited Acts 13:47 [u] ch. 42:6 [v] [Ps. 98:3]
7 [w] ch. 48:17 [x] ver. 1; ch. 53:3; [ch. 50:6, 7] [y] ver. 23
8 [z] Cited 2 Cor. 6:2 [a] Ps. 69:13 [b] ch. 42:6 [c] ch. 61:4
9 [d] ch. 42:7 [e] [ch. 41:18]
10 [f] Cited Rev. 7:16 [g] Rev. 7:17; See ch. 40:11
11 [h] [ch. 40:4]
12 [i] ch. 43:5, 6 [j] [Ps. 107:3]
13 [k] See ch. 44:23 [l] ch. 40:1
14 [m] [ch. 40:27; 54:6; 62:4]
15 [n] [ch. 43:1; Ps. 27:10]
16 [o] S. of S. 8:6; Rev. 13:16
17 [p] See Zech. 1:18-21
18 [q] ch. 60:4 [r] Num. 14:21; See Ezek. 5:11 [s] [Jer. 43:12]

[1] Hebrew *from the sea* [2] Dead Sea Scroll; Masoretic Text *Sinim* [3] Dead Sea Scroll; Masoretic Text *Your children make haste*

49:7 Redeemer. See note 41:14.

servant of rulers. Paradoxically, the king who humbles himself to become the Servant of rulers will Himself receive their homage (4:2; 45:24; 52:15).

49:8 a time of favor. This time stands in contrast to the day of vengeance (12:2; 34:8 and notes; cf. 35:4; 59:17, 18; 61:2; 63:4; 2 Cor. 6:2).

establish . . . apportion. This restoration began with the return from exile (44:26; 45:8 note).

49:9 prisoners. See notes 42:7; 51:14; 61:1.

darkness. See note 5:30.

feed . . . pasture. The servant is the Shepherd and King of Israel (40:11).

49:10 guide. Isaiah alludes to the exodus from Egypt (42:16; 48:21; Ex. 15:13).

49:11 road . . . highways. See note 11:16.

49:12 come from afar . . . west. The salvation of true Israel is in view here (11:11 note).

Syene. To the east, possibly China, but the exact location is uncertain.

49:13 Sing. See note 14:7.

49:14 forsaken . . . forgotten. God seems to have abandoned Judah during the Exile (40:27; 54:7).

49:16 walls. See note 26:1.

19 "Surely your waste and your desolate
places
and your devastated land—
[t] surely now you will be too narrow for
your inhabitants,
and those who swallowed you up
will be far away.
20 [u] The children of your bereavement
will yet say in your ears:
[t] 'The place is too narrow for me;
make room for me to dwell in.'
21 Then you will say in your heart:
'Who has borne me these?
[u] I was bereaved and barren,
exiled and put away,
but who has brought up these?
Behold, I was left alone;
from where have these come?'"

22 Thus says the Lord GOD:
"Behold, I will lift up my hand to the
nations,
[v] and raise my signal to the peoples;
[w] and they shall bring your sons in
their bosom,
and your daughters shall be carried
on their shoulders.
23 [x] Kings shall be your foster fathers,
and their queens your nursing
mothers.
[y] With their faces to the ground they
shall bow down to you,
and [z] lick the dust of your feet.
Then you will know that I am the
LORD;
[a] those who wait for me [b] shall not
be put to shame."

24 Can the prey be taken from the
mighty,
or the captives of a tyrant[1] be
rescued?

19 [t] [Zech. 10:10]
20 [u] ch. 54:1 [t] [See ver. 19 above]
21 [u] [See ver. 20 above]
22 [v] ch. 11:12 [w] ch. 14:2
23 [x] ch. 69:8, 16 [y] ch. 60:14 [z] Ps. 72:9; [Mic. 7:17] [a] [ch. 40:31] [b] Ps. 25:3; Joel 2:27

25 For thus says the LORD:
[c] "Even the captives of the mighty shall
be taken,
and the prey of the tyrant be
rescued,
for I will contend with those who
contend with you,
and I will save your children.
26 [d] I will make your oppressors eat their
own flesh,
and they shall be drunk [e] with their
own blood as with wine.
Then all flesh shall know
that [f] I am the LORD your Savior,
and your Redeemer, the Mighty
One of Jacob."

Israel's Sin and the Servant's Obedience

50 Thus says the LORD:
"Where is [g] your mother's
certificate of divorce,
with which [h] I sent her away?
Or [i] which of my creditors is it
to whom I have sold you?
[j] Behold, for your iniquities you were
sold,
and for your transgressions your
mother was sent away.
2 [k] Why, when I came, was there no
man;
why, when I called, was there no
one to answer?
[l] Is my hand shortened, that it cannot
redeem?
Or have I no power to deliver?
[m] Behold, by my rebuke [n] I dry up the
sea,
[o] I make the rivers a desert;
[p] their fish stink for lack of water
and die of thirst.

25 [c] [Matt. 12:29; Luke 11:21, 22]
26 [d] [ch. 9:20; Zech. 11:9] [e] [Rev. 14:20; 16:6] [f] ch. 43:3; See Ex. 20:2

Chapter 50
1 [g] Deut. 24:1 [h] Jer. 3:8; [Hos. 2:2] [i] [2 Kin. 4:1; Matt. 18:25] [j] ch. 59:2
2 [k] [ch. 42:18-23] [l] ch. 59:1; Num. 11:23 [m] Ps. 104:7; 106:9; Nah. 1:4; [ch. 19:5, 6] [n] [Ex. 14:21] [o] Josh. 3:16 [p] [Ex. 7:18, 21]

1 Dead Sea Scroll, Syriac, Vulgate (see also verse 25); Masoretic Text *of a righteous man*

49:19 too narrow. The prophecy of vv. 19–21 looks beyond the return at the time of Cyrus. Nehemiah built only a small city. The prophecy is fulfilled in the new Israel, the church (54:1–3; Zech. 2:4, 5).

49:22 nations. These "nations" are not just Babylon, as had been the case at the time of Cyrus (v. 19 note; cf. Rom. 11:26).

49:23 Kings. Nations that formerly oppressed Israel will serve Christ and His Church, the true Israel, and in doing so find salvation (Gen. 12:3).

lick the dust. On the "Black Obelisk" of Shalmaneser III, Jehu, King of Israel, is shown bowing to the ground before the Assyrian ruler.

wait. See 40:31 and note.

49:25 contend . . . save. The Lord takes up the case of the needy and is just in His retribution (v. 26; Rev. 16:6; 18:20).

49:26 know. See note 52:6.

Mighty One. Isaiah reveals the vindication of the people of God. God Himself will fight for His people and redeem them from all adversity.

50:1 mother's. The inhabitants of Jerusalem who were taken into the Babylonian exile are here figuratively described as God's wife.

certificate of divorce. Had the Lord issued such a divorce, He could not have taken Israel back (Deut. 24:1–4; Jer. 3:1, 8).

creditors. Had the Lord sold Israel to creditors, He would have lost authority over their destiny (cf. 2 Kin. 4:1; Neh. 5:5).

for your iniquities. Since Israel was sold in payment for the debt of her sins, the Redeemer had the responsibility to buy them back (41:14; 52:3).

50:4–11 This is the third of four "Servant Songs" (42:1–9; 49:1–7; 50:4–11; 52:13–53:12). The reproach against believing Israel in the Exile (51:7) anticipates the rejection of Jesus Christ.

3 [q]I clothe the heavens with blackness
and make sackcloth their
covering."

4 The Lord GOD has given [r]me
the tongue of those who are taught,
that [s]I may know how to sustain
with a word
[t]him who is weary.
Morning by morning he awakens;
he awakens my ear
to hear as those who are taught.

5 [u]The Lord GOD has opened my ear,
[v]and I was not rebellious;
I turned not backward.

6 [w]I gave my back to those who strike,
and my cheeks to those who pull
out the beard;
I hid not my face
from disgrace and spitting.

7 But the Lord GOD helps me;
therefore I have not been
disgraced;
[x]therefore I have set my face like a flint,
and I know that I shall not be put
to shame.

8 [y]He who vindicates me is near.
Who will contend with me?
Let us stand up together.
Who is my adversary?
Let him come near to me.

9 [z]Behold, the Lord GOD helps me;
who will declare me guilty?
Behold, all of them will wear out like
a garment;
the moth will eat them up.

10 Who among you fears the LORD
and obeys [a]the voice of his
servant?
[b]Let him who walks in darkness
and has no light
trust in the name of the LORD
and rely on his God.

11 Behold, all you who kindle
a fire,
who equip yourselves with burning
torches!
Walk by the light of your fire,
and by the torches that you have
kindled!
[c]This you have from my hand:
you shall lie down in
torment.

The LORD's Comfort for Zion

51 [d]"Listen to me, you who pursue
righteousness,
you who seek the LORD:
look to the rock from which you
were hewn,
and to the quarry from which you
were dug.

2 Look to Abraham your father
and to Sarah who bore you;
for [e]he was but one when I called
him,
that I might bless him and
multiply him.

3 For the LORD [f]comforts Zion;
he comforts all her waste places
and makes her wilderness like
[g]Eden,
her desert like [h]the garden of the
LORD;
[i]joy and gladness will be found in
her,
thanksgiving and the voice
of song.

4 [j]"Give attention to me, my
people,
and give ear to me, my
nation;
[k]for a law[1] will go out from me,
and I will set my justice for a light
to the peoples.

3 [q]Jer. 14:22; Rev. 6:12
4 [r][Ex. 4:11] [s][ch. 40:1, 2] [t][Matt. 11:28]
5 [u]Ps. 40:6 [v][John 14:31; Phil. 2:8; Heb. 5:8; 10:7]
6 [w][ch. 53:5; Matt. 26:67; 27:26; Mark 15:19; Luke 22:63]
7 [x]Ezek. 3:8, 9
8 [y]Rom. 8:33, 34
9 [z]ch. 41:10
10 [a]ver. 4; ch. 49:2, 3 [b]ch. 42:16; [Mic. 7:8]
11 [c][John 9:39]
Chapter 51
1 [d]ver. 7
2 [e]Ezek. 33:24
3 [f]ch. 40:1; 52:9 [g]Gen. 2:8; Ezek. 28:13; 31:9; Joel 2:3 [h]Gen. 13:10 [i]ch. 35:10
4 [j]Ps. 78:1 [k]ch. 2:3

1 Or *for teaching*; also verse 7

50:4 word. See notes 45:23; 49:2.

weary. See Jer. 31:25.

50:6 back. Jesus Christ suffered such injustice as part of His obedience to God (53:5, 11, 12; Matt. 27:26; John 19:1).

pull out the beard. This is an act of humiliation (2 Sam. 10:4, 5; Neh. 13:25).

50:7 my face like a flint. Resolved and determined in the face of opposition (cf. Ezek. 3:8, 9; Jer. 1:18; Luke 9:51).

not be put to shame. Not put to shame by defeat.

50:11 who kindle a fire. The general sense is that they undertake plans relying on their own strength, rather than God's, and bring themselves to ruin as a result.

51:1 rock . . . quarry. They are asked to remember their descent from Abraham and Sarah (Deut. 26:5; compare Ezek. 16:6). Their origin was modest.

51:3 Eden. For this "garden of the LORD," see Gen. 2:8; Ezek. 28:13; 31:8, 9. The promise here is a transformation from curse to blessing.

joy and gladness. In Zion joy will replace sorrow (v. 11). The people in effect will regain the lost paradise of God (9:3; 12:3 and notes).

51:4 law . . . a light. The servant establishes justice in the last days (2:2–4; 42:1–4, 6; 49:6). See "God Is Light: Divine Holiness and Justice" at Lev. 11:44.

5 [l]My righteousness draws near,
my salvation has gone out,
and my arms will judge the peoples;
[m]the coastlands hope for me,
and for my arm they wait.
6 [n]Lift up your eyes to the heavens,
and look at the earth beneath;
[o]for the heavens vanish like smoke,
the earth will wear out like a garment,
and they who dwell in it will die in like manner;[1]
[p]but my salvation will be forever,
and my righteousness will never be dismayed.

7 [q]"Listen to me, you who know righteousness,
the people [r]in whose heart is my law;
[s]fear not the reproach of man,
nor be dismayed at their revilings.
8 [t]For the moth will eat them up like a garment,
and the worm will eat them like wool;
[p]but my righteousness will be forever,
and my salvation to all generations."

9 [u]Awake, awake, [v]put on strength,
O [w]arm of the LORD;
awake, [x]as in days of old,
the generations of long ago.
Was it not you who cut [y]Rahab in pieces,
that pierced [z]the dragon?
10 [a]Was it not you who dried up the sea,
the waters of the great deep,
who made the depths of the sea a way
for the redeemed to pass over?
11 [b]And the ransomed of the LORD shall return
and come to Zion with singing;
everlasting joy shall be upon their heads;
they shall obtain gladness and joy,
and sorrow and sighing shall flee away.

12 "I, I am he [c]who comforts you;
who are you that you are afraid of [d]man who dies,
of the son of man who is made [e]like grass,
13 and have forgotten the LORD, your Maker,
[f]who stretched out the heavens
and [g]laid the foundations of the earth,
and you fear continually all the day
because of the wrath of [h]the oppressor,
when he sets himself to destroy?
And where is the wrath of [h]the oppressor?
14 [i]He who is bowed down shall speedily be released;
he shall not die and go down [j]to the pit,
neither shall his bread be lacking.
15 I am the LORD your God,
[k]who stirs up the sea so that its waves roar—
the LORD of hosts is his name.
16 [l]And I have put my words in your mouth
[m]and covered you in the shadow of my hand,
[n]establishing[2] the heavens
and [o]laying the foundations of the earth,
and saying to Zion, 'You are my people.'"

5 [l]ch. 46:13 [m]See ch. 11:11
6 [n]ch. 40:26 [o]Ps. 102:26; [Matt. 24:25; 2 Pet. 3:10; Rev. 21:1] [p][Ps. 102:27, 28]
7 [q]ver. 1 [r]Ps. 37:31 [s]ch. 41:14; Matt. 10:28
8 [t]ch. 50:9 [p][See ver. 6 above]
9 [u]ver. 17; ch. 52:1 [v][Ps. 93:1] [w]ch. 40:10; 52:10; 53:1; Luke 1:51 [x]Ps. 44:1 [y]ch. 30:7 [z]ch. 27:1; Ps. 74:13, 14; Ezek. 29:3
10 [a]ch. 43:16; Ex. 14:21; Ps. 106:9
11 [b]See ch. 35:10
12 [c]ch. 40:1; 66:13 [d]Ps. 118:6 [e]See ch. 40:6
13 [f]ch. 40:22 [g]See ch. 48:13 [h]ch. 14:4
14 [i]ch. 45:13 [j]Zech. 9:11
15 [k]Jer. 31:35
16 [l]ch. 59:21; [ch. 50:4] [m]ch. 49:2 [n]ch. 40:22 [o]See ch. 48:13

1 Or *will die like gnats* 2 Or *planting*

51:5 near. The day of the Lord is always imminent (46:13; Zeph. 1:14; 1 Thess. 5:4–11; James 5:8).

51:6 like smoke . . . like a garment. The present creation is destined to be replaced (50:9; Ps. 68:2; 102:3, 26; Hos. 13:3; see also Is. 24:4; 34:4; Heb. 1:10–12; 2 Pet. 3:10).

51:7 in whose heart is my law. Notice the spiritual reality of the covenant (Jer. 31:31–34; Ezek. 36:27) in contrast to the state of the people in 29:13.

51:9 Awake, awake. The command implies that the Lord has appeared to be asleep (40:27, 28; Ps. 44:23).

Rahab. See note 30:7. The spiritual enemies of God's salvation are portrayed as the forces of chaos and evil. Such forces are overcome by God, not Israel or any other human power.

51:12 I, I am he. This is emphatic as in v. 15. The double pronoun corresponds to the double command, "Awake, awake" (v. 9).

grass. See 37:27; Ps. 129:6 note.

51:15 stirs up the sea so that its waves roar. See 51:9, 10 note. This power over the sea is representative of His power over all creation (Job 26:12; Ps. 107:25; Jer. 31:35).

51:16 my words in your mouth. The remnant prefigures the Servant, Jesus Christ (49:2 note).

17 [p] Wake yourself, wake yourself,
stand up, O Jerusalem,
[q] you who have drunk from the hand
of the LORD
the cup of his wrath,
who have drunk to the dregs
the bowl, [r] the cup of staggering.
18 [s] There is none to guide her
among all the sons she has borne;
there is none to take her by the hand
among all the sons she has
brought up.
19 [t] These two things have happened to
you—
who will console you?—
devastation and destruction, famine
and sword;
who will comfort you?[1]
20 [u] Your sons have fainted;
they lie at the head of every street
like an [v] antelope [w] in a net;
they are full of the wrath of
the LORD,
the rebuke of your God.

21 [x] Therefore hear this, you who are
afflicted,
who are drunk, but not with wine:
22 Thus says your Lord, the LORD,
your God [y] who pleads the cause of
his people:
"Behold, I have taken from your hand
[r] the cup of staggering;
the bowl of my wrath you shall drink
no more;
23 [z] and I will put it into the hand of
your tormentors,
[a] who have said to you,
'Bow down, that we may pass
over';
and [b] you have made your back like
the ground
and like the street for them to pass
over."

17 [p]ver. 9; ch. 52:1 [q]Job 21:20; Jer. 25:15; [Matt. 20:22; 26:39, 42; Mark 10:38; 14:36; Luke 22:42; John 18:11] [r]Ps. 60:3; Zech. 12:2
18 [s][Ps. 74:9; Jer. 5:31]
19 [t]ch. 47:9
20 [u]Lam. 2:11, 12 [v]Deut. 14:5 [w][Ps. 141:10]
21 [x]ch. 54:11
22 [y]Jer. 50:34; [ch. 49:25] [r][See ver. 17 above]
23 [z]Jer. 25:17, 26, 28 [a][ch. 47:6] [b][ch. 52:2]

Chapter 52
1 [c]ch. 51:17 [d][Ex. 28:2, 40]; See Zech. 3:1-4 [e]ch. 48:2; Neh. 11:1 [f]ch. 60:21; Joel 3:17; [ch. 35:8; Rev. 21:27]
2 [g][ch. 51:23] [h]ch. 51:14
3 [i]ch. 45:13; 50:1 [j][1 Pet. 1:18]
4 [k]Gen. 46:6
5 [l]Cited Rom. 2:24; [Ezek. 36:20, 23]
6 [m][ch. 49:26]
7 [n]Nah. 1:15; Cited Rom. 10:15 [o]ch. 40:9
8 [p]See ch. 62:6 [q][ch. 33:17, 22; 1 Cor. 13:12; 1 John 3:2; Rev. 22:4]

The LORD's Coming Salvation

52 [c] Awake, awake,
put on your strength, O Zion;
[d] put on your beautiful garments,
O Jerusalem, [e] the holy city;
[f] for there shall no more come
into you
the uncircumcised and the unclean.
2 [g] Shake yourself from the dust and
arise;
be seated, O Jerusalem;
[h] loose the bonds from your neck,
O captive daughter of Zion.

3 For thus says the LORD: [i] "You were sold
for nothing, and [j] you shall be redeemed
without money." 4 For thus says the Lord
GOD: [k] "My people went down at the first
into Egypt to sojourn there, and the
Assyrian oppressed them for nothing.
5 Now therefore what have I here," declares
the LORD, "seeing that my people are taken
away for nothing? Their rulers wail,"
declares the LORD, "and [l] continually all the
day my name is despised. 6 Therefore my
people shall know my name. [m] Therefore in
that day they shall know that it is I who
speak; here am I."

7 [n] How beautiful upon the
mountains
are the feet of him who brings
good news,
who publishes peace, [o] who brings
good news of happiness,
who publishes salvation,
who says to Zion, "Your God
reigns."
8 The voice of [p] your watchmen—they
lift up their voice;
together they sing for joy;
[q] for eye to eye they see
the return of the LORD to Zion.

1 Dead Sea Scroll, Septuagint, Syriac, Vulgate; Masoretic Text *how shall I comfort you*

51:17 Wake yourself, wake yourself. Double imperatives are also found in vv. 1, 9; 52:1, 11 (cf. Eph. 5:14). See note on v. 9.

cup of his wrath. An image of God's judgment (63:6; Ps. 75:8; Jer. 25:15–31; Ezek. 23:31–34; John 18:11; Rev. 14:10; 16:19).

51:20 antelope in a net. The graceful animal depicts Jerusalem, surrounded by the enemy and in danger of dying.

51:23 your tormentors. Preeminently the Babylonians (Lam. 1:4, 5).

52:1 beautiful garments. Jerusalem is magnificently dressed as a royal wife (61:10; Rev. 3:4, 5, 18; 4:4; compare 47:1–3).

the uncircumcised and the unclean. The wicked will have no share in the city of God (48:22; Nah. 1:15; Rev. 21:27; 22:14, 15).

52:3 sold for nothing. The idols gave Israel nothing.

without money. Salvation is free (45:13; 55:1).

52:4 sojourn. Israel was dependent on Egypt's promised hospitality, but Egypt betrayed that trust.

52:6 know my name. The phrase alludes to Ex. 3:13, 14; 6:2. The Lord glorifies His name through inspiring Isaiah's prophecies and bringing them to pass.

52:7 feet. Messengers run from the scene of battle across the hills to Zion with the good news that God reigns. They prefigure the evangelists who will announce the gospel of Jesus Christ (Rom. 10:15; Eph. 6:15).

9 [r] Break forth together into singing,
[s] you waste places of Jerusalem,
for [t] the LORD has comforted his people;
he has redeemed Jerusalem.
10 [u] The LORD has bared his holy arm
before the eyes of all the nations,
[v] and all the ends of the earth shall see
the salvation of our God.

11 [w] Depart, depart, go out from there;
touch no unclean thing;
go out from the midst of her; purify
yourselves,
[x] you who bear the vessels of the
LORD.
12 For you shall not [y] go out in haste,
and you shall not go in flight,
[z] for the LORD will go before you,
[a] and the God of Israel will be your
rear guard.

He Was Wounded for Our Transgressions

13 Behold, [b] my servant shall act wisely;[1]
he shall be high and lifted up,
and shall be exalted.
14 As many were astonished at you—
[c] his appearance was so marred,
beyond human semblance,
and his form beyond that of the
children of mankind—
15 so [d] shall he sprinkle[2] many nations;
[e] kings shall shut their mouths
because of him;
[f] for that which has not been told
them they see,
and that which they have not
heard they understand.

9 [r] Ps. 98:4 [s] ch. 58:12 [t] ch. 40:1; 51:3, 12
10 [u] See ch. 51:9 [v] Ps. 98:3; [Luke 3:6]
11 [w] ch. 48:20; Jer. 50:8; 51:6, 45; Zech. 2:6, 7; Cited 2 Cor. 6:17; [Rev. 18:4] [x] See Ezra 1:7-11
12 [y] [Ex. 12:11, 33, 39] [z] Mic. 2:13; [Ex. 14:19] [a] [ch. 58:8]
13 [b] See ch. 42:1
14 [c] [ch. 53:2, 3]
15 [d] Lev. 4:6, 17 [e] ch. 49:7, 23 [f] Cited Rom. 15:21; [Rom. 16:25]

Chapter 53
1 [g] Cited John 12:38; Rom. 10:16 [h] See ch. 51:9
2 [i] ch. 11:1 [j] [ch. 52:14]
3 [k] ch. 49:7; [Ps. 22:6; Mark 9:12] [l] [John 1:10, 11]
4 [m] [Matt. 8:17] [n] Ps. 69:26
5 [o] [Rom. 4:25] [p] Cited 1 Pet. 2:24
6 [q] Cited 1 Pet. 2:25; [Jer. 50:6, 17] [r] 2 Cor. 5:21; [ver. 10; Col. 2:14]

53 [g] Who has believed what they heard
from us?[3]
And to whom has [h] the arm of the
LORD been revealed?
2 For he grew up before him like a
young plant,
[i] and like a root out of dry ground;
[j] he had no form or majesty that we
should look at him,
and no beauty that we should
desire him.
3 [k] He was despised and rejected[4] by men;
a man of sorrows,[5] and acquainted
with[6] grief;[7]
and as one from whom men hide
their faces[8]
he was despised, and [l] we esteemed
him not.

4 [m] Surely he has borne our griefs
and carried our sorrows;
yet we esteemed him stricken,
[n] smitten by God, and afflicted.
5 [o] But he was wounded for our
transgressions;
he was crushed for our iniquities;
upon him was the chastisement that
brought us peace,
[p] and with his stripes we are healed.
6 [q] All we like sheep have gone astray;
we have turned every one to his
own way;
[r] and the LORD has laid on him
the iniquity of us all.

[1] Or *shall prosper* [2] Or *startle* [3] Or *Who has believed what we have heard?* [4] Or *forsaken* [5] Or *pains*; also verse 4 [6] Or *and knowing* [7] Or *sickness*; also verse 4 [8] Or *as one who hides his face from us*

52:9 waste places of Jerusalem. Restoration, after the Babylonian exile of the sixth century B.C., began with the rebuilding of Jerusalem's ruins (Ezra 3:8–13; Neh. 6:15–7:3). In the same sense, Christ is rebuilding His people who were being destroyed by sin (1 Pet. 2:5).

52:11 who bear the vessels. These people represent all of Zion and serve God as priests. They must be consecrated for holy service and remain undefiled (2 Cor. 6:17; Heb. 12:14; 1 Pet. 2:1–12; Rev. 18:4).

52:12 not . . . haste. The contrast is with the exodus from Egypt. Ex. 12:11 and Deut. 16:3 are the only other passages where this phrase occurs.

before you . . . rear guard. An allusion to the pillar of cloud and fire that protected Israel in their flight from Egypt (42:16; 58:8; Ex. 13:21, 22; 14:19, 20). God's presence guides His people into the fullness and brilliance of His everlasting kingdom (4:5, 6; 49:10).

52:13–53:12 This is the last of the four "Servant Songs" (42:1–9; 49:1–7; 50:4–11; 52:13–53:12). The "Suffering Servant" is Jesus Christ. This passage is quoted or referred to many times in the New Testament. Christ's suffering in the place of His sheep gives them eternal life.

52:13–15 The Lord vindicates and glorifies His servant.

52:13 act wisely. The Servant will discern and perform God's will, and as a result achieve His glorious purpose (Luke 24:26; 1 Pet. 5:10).

52:14 astonished . . . marred. Christ was disfigured by the abuse He suffered from Roman soldiers.

52:15 sprinkle. Participation in the benefits of a sacrifice is indicated by the sprinkling of blood. See Ex. 24:8 and note; Lev. 4:1–5:13 note; and Heb. 9:19 note.

53:1 what they heard from us. The gospel proclaimed by the believing remnant.

53:2 root out of dry ground. His origins were not promising (Zech. 4:10; John 1:46).

53:3 despised and rejected. See 49:7; Ps. 22:6; Lam. 1:1–3; 2:15, 16.

53:4 smitten by God. They believed this about the Servant because the Law said, "a hanged man is cursed by God" (Deut. 21:23; cf. Gal. 3:13). The onlookers thought Christ was suffering only what He deserved, but His experience of pain and anguish was for His people (1 Pet. 2:24). The extremity of His suffering shows that His compassion is real and not theoretical (Heb. 2:17, 18).

53:5 we are healed. The sufferings of Christ remove the penalty that His people would otherwise owe, and as a result He will undo the effects of sin in them. Death itself will be undone at last (1 Cor. 15:26).

53:6 All we. Even as we all sinned, so He died for all of us (2 Cor. 5:14, 15). See "Definite Redemption" at John 10:15.

7 He was oppressed, and he was
afflicted,
[s]yet he opened not his mouth;
[t]like a [u]lamb that is led to the
slaughter,
and like a sheep that before its
shearers is silent,
so he opened not his mouth.
8 By oppression and judgment he was
taken away;
and as for his generation, [v]who
considered
that he was cut off out of the land of
the living,
stricken for the transgression of my
people?
9 And they made his grave with the
wicked
[w]and with a rich man in his death,
although [x]he had done no
violence,
and there was no deceit in his
mouth.
10 Yet [y]it was the will of the LORD to
crush him;
he has put him to grief;[1]
[z]when his soul makes[2] an offering for
sin,
he shall see his offspring; he shall
prolong his days;
[a]the will of the LORD shall prosper in
his hand.
11 Out of the anguish of his soul he
shall see[3] and be satisfied;
by his knowledge shall [b]the righteous
one, my servant,
[c]make many to be accounted
righteous,
[d]and he shall bear their iniquities.
12 [e]Therefore I will divide him a portion
with the many,[4]
[f]and he shall divide the spoil with
the strong,[5]
because he poured out his soul to
death
and was numbered with the
transgressors;
[g]yet he bore the sin of many,
and makes intercession for the
transgressors.

The Eternal Covenant of Peace

54 [h]"Sing, O barren one, who did not
bear;
break forth into singing and cry
aloud,
you who have not been in labor!
For the children of [i]the desolate one
[j]will be more
than the children of her who is
married," says the LORD.
2 [k]"Enlarge the place of your tent,
and let the curtains of your
habitations be stretched out;
do not hold back; lengthen your cords
and strengthen your stakes.

7 [s]Matt. 26:63; Mark 14:61; John 19:9; 1 Pet. 2:23 [t]Cited Acts 8:32 [u][Jer. 11:19]
8 [v]ch. 57:1
9 [w]Matt. 27:57, 60 [x]Cited 1 Pet. 2:22; [Heb. 4:15; 1 John 3:5]
10 [y][ver. 4] [z][ver. 6] [a][ch. 44:28]
11 [b][1 John 2:1] [c]Acts 13:39; Rom. 5:18, 19 [d][ver. 5]
12 [e]ch. 52:13; [Phil. 2:9] [f][Col. 2:15] [g]ver. 6, 8, 10
Chapter 54
1 [h]Cited Gal. 4:27 [i]ch. 62:4 [j][1 Sam. 2:5]
2 [k][ch. 49:19, 20]

[1] Or *he has made him sick* [2] Or *when you make his soul* [3] Masoretic Text; Dead Sea Scroll *he shall see light* [4] Or *with the great* [5] Or *with the numerous*

sheep . . . astray. See 1 Pet. 2:25. See "Original Sin and Total Depravity" at Ps. 51:5.

laid. The guilt of our sins was transferred to Jesus, and He offered Himself as a sacrifice in our place. As Paul wrote, God "made him to be sin who knew no sin" (2 Cor. 5:21).

53:7 lamb . . . sheep. Christ is the Lamb of God (John 1:29; 1 Cor. 5:7; Rev. 5:6) in obedience and submission to God (cf. Matt. 26:63; 27:12, 14; 1 Pet. 2:23).

53:8 By oppression and judgment. He was put to death as a result of injustice. See "The Atonement" at Rom. 3:25.

53:9 wicked . . . rich. Although people supposed that Jesus was dying as a common criminal, through the intervention of Joseph of Arimathea Jesus was buried in honor. His suffering for sinners had been successfully completed.

violence . . . deceit. He was wise and righteous (1 Pet. 2:22), but died a criminal's death (Luke 23:33).

53:10 it was the will of the LORD. This amazing statement is true because Christ was delivered up "according to the definite plan and foreknowledge of God" (Acts 2:23).

offspring. The offspring are those who come to life through His death (John 12:24; Gal. 3:29).

53:11 knowledge. This is a reference to His insight into the divine plan (52:13 note).

righteous. See Rom. 5:19.

accounted righteous. Christ's righteousness is imputed to His people (53:6 note), and in return He accepted their guilt so as to "bear their iniquities." See "Justification and Merit" at Gal. 3:11.

53:12 Therefore I. The Lord divides the spoils of victory with His triumphant Servant (52:13).

poured out his soul. He gave Himself for the sins of others (v. 4; Luke 22:37; Phil. 2:7, 8; Heb. 9:28; 1 Pet. 2:24).

intercession. He prayed for sinners (Luke 23:34; Heb. 7:25).

54:1 Sing. See note 14:7.

barren . . . desolate. In exile, Judah and Israel felt forsaken by God and did not experience His blessing.

more than the children. The New Testament applies this verse to "the Jerusalem above . . . our mother" (Gal. 4:26, 27; cf. Heb. 12:22). See 49:21; 53:10.

54:2 Enlarge . . . strengthen. The tent is enlarged in anticipation of a great increase in the number of occupants (cf. 26:15; 33:20; 49:19 note; contrast Jer. 10:20).

3 [l]For you will spread abroad to the right and to the left,
and your offspring will possess the nations
and will people the desolate cities.
4 "Fear not, [m]for you will not be ashamed;
be not confounded, for you will not be disgraced;
for you will forget the shame of your youth,
and the reproach of your widowhood you will remember no more.
5 [n]For your Maker is your husband,
the LORD of hosts is his name;
[o]and the Holy One of Israel is your Redeemer,
[p]the God of the whole earth he is called.
6 [q]For the LORD has called you
like a wife deserted and grieved in spirit,
like a wife of youth when she is cast off,
says your God.
7 [r]For a brief moment I deserted you,
but with great compassion I will gather you.
8 [r]In overflowing anger for a moment
I hid my face from you,
[s]but with everlasting love I will have compassion on you,"
says the LORD, your Redeemer.
9 "This is like [t]the days of Noah[1] to me:
as I swore that the waters of Noah should no more go over the earth,
so I have sworn that I will not be angry with you,
and will not rebuke you.
10 For the mountains may depart
and the hills be removed,
but my steadfast love shall not depart from you,
and [u]my covenant of peace shall not be removed,"
says the LORD, who has compassion on you.
11 [v]"O afflicted one, storm-tossed and not comforted,
behold, [w]I will set your stones in antimony,
[x]and lay your foundations with sapphires.[2]
12 I will make your pinnacles of agate,[3]
your gates of carbuncles,[4]
and all your wall of precious stones.
13 [y]All your children [z]shall be taught by the LORD,
[a]and great shall be the peace of your children.
14 In righteousness you shall be established;
you shall be far from oppression,
for you shall not fear;
and from terror, for it shall not come near you.
15 [b]If anyone stirs up strife,
it is not from me;
whoever stirs up strife with you
shall fall because of you.
16 Behold, I have created the smith
who blows the fire of coals
and produces a weapon for its purpose.
I have also created the ravager to destroy;
17 no weapon that is fashioned against you shall succeed,
and you shall confute every tongue that rises against you in judgment.

3 [l][ch. 11:14; Gen. 28:14] 4 [m]ch. 45:17 5 [n]ch. 62:4, 5; [Hos. 2:7] [o]See ch. 43:14 [p]Zech. 14:9 6 [q]ver. 1; [ch. 49:14; 60:15; 62:4] 7 [r][ch. 26:20] 8 [r][See ver. 7 above] [s]ch. 55:3 9 [t]Gen. 8:21; 9:11 10 [u]Num. 25:12; Ezek. 34:25; 37:26; [Mal. 2:5] 11 [v]ch. 51:21 [w][ch. 60:10] [x][Rev. 21:19] 13 [y]Cited John 6:45 [z]Jer. 31:33, 34 [a][ch. 9:7; Ps. 119:165] 15 [b][ch. 8:9, 10]

1 Some manuscripts *For this is as the waters of Noah* 2 Or *lapis lazuli* 3 Or *jasper, or ruby* 4 Or *crystal*

54:3 possess . . . people. The expansion will be so great that they will possess the cities of their enemies (11:14 note; Gen. 22:17; 28:14).

54:4 shame of your youth. Israel's infidelity led to its oppression by Egypt and Assyria (52:4; Jer. 31:19).

reproach of your widowhood. This figure represents the Babylonian exile (vv. 6–8).

54:5 the Holy One of Israel is your Redeemer. See 41:14 notes.

God of the whole earth. The titles in v. 5 show that God did not give up Zion out of weakness or necessity (50:1–3).

54:6 deserted. See note 49:14.

54:9 waters of Noah. At the time of the Flood the Lord made a covenant with creation, symbolized by the rainbow (Gen. 9:1–17).

54:10 mountains . . . hills. In our experience the mountains and hills seem permanent and unchanging, but the commitment of God to His people will remain when they are gone (51:6; Ps. 46:2, 3; Matt. 24:35; Heb. 1:10–12).

54:11 storm-tossed. This metaphor represents the day of the Lord's wrath.

lay . . . sapphires. These metaphors describe the beauty and glory of Zion, the city of God (Rev. 21:19).

54:17 heritage. This heritage is the covenant and its promises, especially the promise of God's protection and righteousness (1:21 note).

This is the heritage of the servants of
the LORD
[c] and their vindication[1] from me,
declares the LORD."

The Compassion of the LORD

55 [d]"Come, everyone who thirsts,
come to the waters;
and he who has no money,
[e] come, buy and eat!
Come, buy wine and milk
without money and without price.
2 [f]Why do you spend your money for
that which is not bread,
and your labor for that which does
not satisfy?
Listen diligently to me, and eat what
is good,
and delight yourselves in rich food.
3 Incline your ear, and come to me;
[g] hear, that your soul may live;
[h] and I will make with you an
everlasting covenant,
[i] my steadfast, sure love for [j]David.
4 [k] Behold, I made him a witness to the
peoples,
[l] a leader and commander for the
peoples.
5 [k] Behold, you shall call a nation that
you do not know,
and [m]a nation that did not know
you shall run to you,
because of the LORD your God, and
of the Holy One of Israel,
[n] for he has glorified you.
6 [o]"Seek the LORD while he may be
found;
call upon him while he is near;
7 let the wicked forsake his way,
and the unrighteous man his
thoughts;
let him return to the LORD, that he
may have compassion on him,
and to our God, for he will
abundantly pardon.
8 For my thoughts are not your
thoughts,
neither are your ways my ways,
declares the LORD.
9 [p]For as the heavens are higher than
the earth,
so are my ways higher than your
ways
and my thoughts than your
thoughts.
10 [q]"For as the rain and the snow come
down from heaven
and do not return there but water
the earth,
making it bring forth and sprout,
[r] giving seed to the sower and bread
to the eater,
11 so shall my word be that goes out
from my mouth;
it shall not return to me empty,
but [s]it shall accomplish that which I
purpose,
and shall succeed in the thing for
which I sent it.
12 [t]"For you shall go out in joy
and be led forth in peace;
[u] the mountains and the hills before you
shall break forth into singing,
and all the trees of the field shall
clap their hands.

17 [c]ch. 45:24, 25
Chapter 55
1 [d]ch. 44:3; John 7:37; [Matt. 5:6] [e]Prov. 9:5
2 [f][John 6:27]
3 [g]Prov. 4:4 [h]ch. 61:8; Jer. 32:40; Ezek. 37:26; [ch. 54:8; 59:21] [i]Ps. 89:33–35; [Acts 13:34] [j]Jer. 30:9
4 [k]Ps. 18:43 [l]Dan. 9:25; Mic. 5:2; Acts 5:31; Rev. 17:14; 19:16; [ch. 9:6, 7]
5 [k][See ver. 4 above] [m]Zech. 8:22, 23 [n][ch. 44:23; Acts 3:13]
6 [o]Ps. 32:6; Amos 5:4
9 [p]Ps. 103:11
10 [q][Ps. 148:8] [r][2 Cor. 9:10]
11 [s]ch. 40:8
12 [t]ch. 35:10; [ch. 48:20, 21; 52:12] [u]ch. 44:23; Ps. 98:8

1 Or *righteousness*

55:1 everyone. This address follows logically on the previous section (vv. 13, 17) and expresses the worldwide applicability of the gospel.

thirsts . . . no money. The thirst is for spiritual things that money cannot buy (52:3; Deut. 8:3; Ps. 42:2; 63:1; Prov. 9:5, 6; Matt. 5:6; John 7:37, 38; Rev. 21:6; 22:17).

waters. Isaiah frequently describes the new era of salvation, God's kingdom and its divine blessings in terms of an abundance of water (1:30, 31 note).

buy . . . without money. This paradox signifies that salvation is a free gift for anyone who desires it (Matt. 11:28; Rom. 10:13; Titus 3:5).

wine and milk. These are symbols of complete satisfaction.

55:3 you. The promises of the Davidic covenant are now extended to all who come to God.

everlasting covenant. In the covenant as given to David, God promised him a permanent throne and lasting dynasty (2 Sam. 7:12–16; 1 Kin. 8:23–26; Ps. 89:27–37). David's royal house will rule over the nations. These elements are fulfilled in Christ and His church (4:2; 7:14; 9:6; 11:1, 2 and notes).

55:4 made him a witness. This was accomplished especially by raising Jesus Christ of the house of David from the dead (Acts 13:34).

55:7 wicked . . . unrighteous. God requires living faith, as indicated in repentance and change of behavior (James 2:18; 1 John 1:3–5).

compassion . . . abundantly pardon. The prophet repeats the invitation of 1:18 with great boldness and directness.

55:8 my thoughts are not your thoughts. Specifically, God's thoughts concerning grace exceed human imagination (64:4; 1 Cor. 2:9; Eph. 3:20; Rom. 11:33). See "God Sees and Knows: Divine Omniscience" at Prov. 15:3.

55:10, 11 rain. The rain falls abundantly and of its own accord, and in a familiar but mysterious way produces plants and useful crops, evidently for the purpose of supplying people's needs—the divine purpose in this is applied figuratively to the Word of God, to distinguish it from fallible human thoughts and plans.

55:12 go out. The exodus from Babylon, like the exodus from Egypt, is a picture of how God delivers His people from their sins (48:20, 21; 52:11, 12; John 10:3; Col. 1:13).

singing . . . clap. Creation rejoices in God's acts of redemption (44:23; 49:13; Ps. 96:11–13).

13 [v]Instead of the thorn shall come up
the cypress;
instead of the brier shall come up
the myrtle;
and it shall make a name for the LORD,
an everlasting sign that shall not
be cut off."

Salvation for Foreigners

56 Thus says the LORD:
"Keep justice, and do
righteousness,
[w]for soon my salvation will come,
and my deliverance be revealed.
2 Blessed is the man who does this,
and the son of man who holds it
fast,
[x]who keeps the Sabbath, not
profaning it,
and keeps his hand from doing
any evil."
3 Let not [y]the foreigner who has joined
himself to the LORD say,
"The LORD will surely separate me
from his people";
and let not the eunuch say,
"Behold, I am [z]a dry tree."
4 For thus says the LORD:
"To the eunuchs [x]who keep my
Sabbaths,
who choose the things that please me
and hold fast my covenant,
5 [a]I will give in my house and within
my walls
a [b]monument and a name
better than sons and daughters;
[c]I will give them an everlasting name
that shall not be cut off.
6 "And [y]the foreigners who join
themselves to the LORD,
to minister to him, to love the
name of the LORD,
and to be his servants,
everyone [x]who keeps the Sabbath
and does not profane it,
and holds fast my covenant—
7 [d]these I will bring to [e]my holy mountain,
and make them joyful in my house
of prayer;
[f]their burnt offerings and their
sacrifices
will be accepted on my altar;
for [g]my house shall be called a house
of prayer
for all peoples."
8 The Lord GOD,
[h]who gathers the outcasts of Israel,
declares,
[i]"I will gather yet others to him
besides those already gathered."

Israel's Irresponsible Leaders

9 [j]All you beasts of the field, come to
devour—
all you beasts in the forest.
10 [k]His watchmen are blind;
they are all without knowledge;
they are all silent [l]dogs;
they cannot bark,
dreaming, lying down,
loving to slumber.
11 [m]The dogs have a mighty appetite;
they never have enough.
But [n]they are shepherds who have no
understanding;
they have all turned to their own
way,
[o]each to his own gain, one and all.

13[v]ch. 35:1, 2; 41:19
Chapter 56
1[w]ch. 46:12, 13; 51:5, 6
2[x]ch. 58:13
3[y]ch. 14:1; [Deut. 23:7, 8] [z][Ezek. 17:24; 20:47]
4[x][See ver. 2 above]
5[a][1 Tim. 3:15; Rev. 3:12] [b][2 Sam. 18:18; John 1:12] [c][2 Tim. 2:19]
6[y][See ver. 3 above] [x][See ver. 2 above]
7[d]ch. 65:1; [ch. 19:24, 25] [e]ch. 2:2 [f][Rom. 15:16] [g]Cited Matt. 21:13; Mark 11:17; Luke 19:46
8[h]ch. 11:12 [i]John 10:16; Eph. 1:10; See Eph. 2:11-16
9[j]Jer. 12:9; Ezek. 34:8
10[k]ch. 62:6; Jer. 6:17 [l][Phil. 3:2]
11[m]Ezek. 34:2, 3 [n][Jer. 23:1] [o]Jer. 6:13

55:13 Instead of the thorn . . . cypress. Judgment is replaced by salvation (5:6; 32:13; 41:19).

everlasting sign. Compare the rainbow in Gen. 9:8–17.

56:1–66:24 These prophecies are addressed to the exiles returned from Babylon before the rebuilding of the temple in 520 B.C. (64:8–12). They still suffer from idolatry, hypocrisy and indifference. Isaiah prophesies concerning their responsibilities toward the coming glorious kingdom and the certainty of its arrival.

56:1 will come. See 50:8; 51:5; Phil. 4:5.

56:2 Sabbath. Keeping this day holy (Ex. 31:13–17) signifies loyalty to the Lord and to His covenant (58:13; Ezek. 20:20).

56:3 eunuch. Eunuchs were normally excluded from the covenant community (Deut. 23:1). The Ethiopian eunuch of Acts 8:26–39 fulfilled this promise through faith in Jesus, the Servant of Is. 53.

56:5 everlasting name. That is, everlasting life in God's temple (v. 7; 2:2; Ps. 23:6; Acts 8:27, 36–38).

56:7 house of prayer. Being here means being included in the covenant and enjoying the life of communion with God (2:2–4; Ps. 15:1; cf. 1 Kin. 8:41–43; Mark 11:17).

56:8 gathers the outcasts . . . others. The Lord gathers Jews and non-Jews into one community (John 10:16).

56:9 beasts of the field. A metaphor for hostile nations (18:6; Ezek. 34:5, 8, 25).

56:10 watchmen. They warn the city of approaching danger. The prophets were called to be spiritual watchmen (21:6; Jer. 6:17; Ezek. 3:17; 33:2–7).

blind. See note 29:18.

dogs. In the Near East, dogs are considered to be unclean, undesirable scavengers. Here they are a figure for those with insatiable greed.

56:11 shepherds. That is, rulers (v. 10 note; Ezek. 34:1–6; contrast 40:11 note).

12 [p]"Come," they say, "let me get wine;
let us fill ourselves with strong drink;
[q]and tomorrow will be like this day,
great beyond measure."

Israel's Futile Idolatry

57 The righteous man perishes,
and no one lays it to heart;
[r]devout men are taken away,
while no one understands.
For the righteous man is taken away
from calamity;
2 [s]he enters into peace;
they rest [t]in their beds
who walk in their uprightness.
3 But you, draw near,
sons of the sorceress,
[u]offspring of the adulterer and the
loose woman.
4 Whom are you mocking?
Against whom [v]do you open your
mouth wide
and stick out your tongue?
Are you not children of
[w]transgression,
[x]the offspring of deceit,
5 you who burn with lust among [y]the
oaks,[1]
under every green tree,
[z]who slaughter your children in the
valleys,
under the clefts of the rocks?
6 Among the smooth stones of [a]the
valley is your portion;
they, they, are your lot;
to them you have poured out a drink
offering,
you have brought a grain offering.
Shall I relent for these things?
7 [b]On a high and lofty mountain
you have set your bed,
and there you went up to offer
sacrifice.
8 Behind the door and the doorpost
you have set up your memorial;
for, deserting me, [c]you have
uncovered your bed,
you have gone up to it,
[d]you have made it wide;
and you have made a covenant for
yourself with them,
you have loved their bed,
you have looked on nakedness.[2]
9 You journeyed to the king with oil
and multiplied your perfumes;
[e]you sent your envoys far off,
and sent down even to Sheol.
10 You were wearied with the length of
your way,
[f]but you did not say, "It is
hopeless";
you found new life for your strength,
and so you were not faint.[3]
11 [g]Whom did you dread and fear,
[h]so that you lied,
and did not remember me,
did not lay it to heart?
[i]Have I not held my peace, even for a
long time,
and you do not fear me?
12 I will declare your righteousness and
your deeds,
but they will not profit you.
13 [j]When you cry out, let your collection
of idols deliver you!
The wind will carry them off,
a breath will take them away.
[k]But he who takes refuge in me shall
possess the land
and shall inherit [l]my holy
mountain.

12 [p][ch. 28:7] [q][ch. 22:13; Prov. 23:35; Luke 12:19; 1 Cor. 15:32]
Chapter 57
1 [r]Ps. 12:1
2 [s][Luke 2:29] [t]2 Chr. 16:14; Ezek. 32:25
3 [u][John 8:41, 42]
4 [v][Ps. 35:21] [w]ch. 46:8, 9 [x][ch. 1:4]
5 [y]ch. 1:29; 2 Kin. 16:4 [z]Ezek. 16:20, 21
6 [a][2 Kin. 23:10]
7 [b]1 Kin. 14:23; Ezek. 16:16, 24
8 [c]Ezek. 16:25; [Hos. 1:2] [d][Ezek. 23:17]
9 [e]Ezek. 16:26, 28, 29
10 [f]Jer. 2:25; 18:12
11 [g][ch. 51:12, 13] [h]Ps. 78:10, 36 [i]Ps. 50:21
13 [j]Jer. 11:12 [k]Ps. 37:9 [l]ch. 11:9; 56:7; 65:11, 25

1 Or *among the terebinths* 2 Or *on a monument* (see 56:5); Hebrew *on a hand* 3 Hebrew *and so you were not sick*

56:12 Come . . . tomorrow. See 22:13 and note; Luke 12:19; James 4:13.

57:3 sorceress. See 2:6 note; Deut. 18:10.

57:4 mocking . . . tongue. The ungodly are filled with sarcasm and criticism (cf. 5:18, 19; 28:9, 10; 37:3).

57:5 children. Child sacrifice was practiced in the worship of the Ammonite god Molech (v. 9 note; cf. 2 Kin. 23:10; Ps. 106:37, 38; Jer. 7:31; Ezek. 20:28, 31).

valleys . . . clefts. These are secret, hiding places (2:21; 7:19 note). The implication is that their practices are shameful.

57:7, 8 high and lofty mountain . . . nakedness. The people were involved in immoral and idolatrous practices at the hilltop shrines (Hos. 4:13). Their relation with these false gods is compared to sexual union.

57:9 the king. The name of their god, "Molech," is similar to the Hebrew word for "king" and is probably what is meant here.

sent down. Isaiah describes the energy they spent in willing service of their idols.

Sheol. This charge of visiting the realm of the dead (5:14 note) is either a figure of speech to express the depths to which they sank, or a reference to necromancy (communicating with the dead).

57:10 new life for your strength. They found a deceptive liveliness in immorality and idolatry that lead to death.

57:12 righteousness. This is sarcasm; the threat is to declare their sins (cf. 58:2, 3; 64:6).

57:13 possess the land. This promise is the blessing Jesus proclaimed to the meek (v. 15; Matt. 5:5).

Comfort for the Contrite

14 And it shall be said,
[m]"Build up, build up, prepare the way,
remove every obstruction from my people's way."
15 For thus says [n]the One who is high and lifted up,
who inhabits eternity, whose name is [o]Holy:
[p]"I dwell in the high and holy place,
and also [q]with him who is of a contrite and lowly spirit,
[r]to revive the spirit of the lowly,
and to revive the heart of the contrite.
16 [s]For I will not contend forever,
nor will I always be angry;
for the spirit would grow faint before me,
and the breath of life that I made.
17 Because of the iniquity of his [t]unjust gain I was angry,
I struck him; I hid my face and was angry,
but he went on backsliding in the way of his own heart.
18 I have seen his ways, [u]but I will heal him;
I will lead him [v]and restore comfort to him and his mourners,
19 [w]creating [x]the fruit of the lips.
[y]Peace, peace, [z]to the far and to the near," says the LORD,
[u]"and I will heal him.
20 [a]But the wicked are like the tossing sea;
for it cannot be quiet,
and its waters toss up mire and dirt.
21 [b]There is no peace," says my God,
"for the wicked."

14[m]ch. 62:10; [ch. 40:3]
15[n][Mic. 6:6] [o]Luke 1:49 [p]Ps. 113:6 [q]Ps. 34:18; 138:6 [r][ch. 42:3]
16[s]Gen. 6:3; Ps. 103:9
17[t]ch. 56:11; Jer. 6:13
18[u]Jer. 3:22 [v]ch. 61:3
19[w]ch. 50:4 [x]Heb. 13:15 [y][Eph. 2:17] [z]Acts 2:39 [u][See ver. 18 above]
20[a]Jude 13
21[b]ch. 48:22

True and False Fasting

58 "Cry aloud; do not hold back;
[c]lift up your voice like a trumpet;
[d]declare to my people their transgression,
to the house of Jacob their sins.
2 [e]Yet they seek me daily
and delight to know my ways,
as if they were a nation that did righteousness
and did not forsake the judgment of their God;
they ask of me righteous judgments;
they delight to draw near to God.
3 [f]'Why have we fasted, and you see it not?
Why have we humbled ourselves, and you take no knowledge of it?'
Behold, in the day of your fast you seek your own pleasure,[1]
[g]and oppress all your workers.
4 Behold, you fast only to quarrel and to fight
and to hit with a wicked fist.
Fasting like yours this day
will not make your voice to be heard on high.
5 [h]Is such the fast that I choose,
[i]a day for a person to humble himself?
Is it to bow down his head like a reed,
and to spread sackcloth and ashes under him?
Will you call this a fast,
and a day acceptable to the LORD?

[1] Or *pursue your own business*

Chapter 58
1[c]Lev. 25:9; [Joel 2:1] [d]Mic. 3:8
2[e][ch. 1:11; 29:13; Zech. 7:5, 6]
3[f][Mal 3:14] [g][ch. 60:17]; See Neh. 5:1-8
5[h]Zech. 7:5 [i]Lev. 16:29

57:14 prepare the way. See notes 11:16; 40:3.

obstruction. Specifically, the idolatry and immorality described in vv. 3–13.

my people's way. See note 40:1.

57:15 high and lifted up. An epithet for the Lord (6:1).

high and holy place. The Lord is transcendent over creation.

contrite and lowly spirit. Those who submit to God's law and repent under His judgment (Ps. 34:17, 18; 51:17; 1 Pet. 5:6).

57:16 not contend forever. In God's grace, judgment will end and God will create salvation (54:9; 57:18, 19; Ps. 130:3, 4).

57:18 heal . . . restore comfort. The Lord is physician (30:26 note), guide (49:10 note), and evangelist (40:1 note).

mourners. Those who lament Jerusalem's destruction (64:10–12; 25:8 note).

57:20 tossing sea. The wicked are constantly in motion, restless, and causing problems (Jude 13).

58:3 fasted . . . oppress. Despite their religiosity they were not concerned with justice for others (cf. 1:15–17; 59:2; Hos. 6:4–6; Amos 5:23, 24; Zech. 7:8–12). Instead of setting the day aside so that all can fast and pray, they wanted to rest while others worked.

58:4 quarrel . . . hit. These actions are expressions of their pride and hatred.

heard on high. God does not hear prayer when it is not in the spirit of love.

58:5 fast that I choose. See 1:10–15; Amos 5:21–23; Mic. 6:7, 8.

bow down . . . sackcloth and ashes. Conventional acts of mourning ceremonies that accompany fasting (Joel 1:13, 14). God looks for expressions of inner humility and brokenness before Him, rather than devotion to rituals (Matt. 6:16).

6 "Is not this the fast that I choose:
[j] to loose the bonds of wickedness,
to undo the straps [k] of the yoke,
to let the oppressed[1] go free,
and to break every yoke?
7 Is it not [l] to share your bread with the
hungry
and bring the homeless poor into
your house;
when you see the naked, to cover him,
[m] and not to hide yourself from your
own flesh?
8 [n] Then shall your light break forth like
the dawn,
[o] and your healing shall spring up
speedily;
[p] your righteousness shall go before you;
[q] the glory of the LORD shall be your
rear guard.
9 Then you shall call, and the LORD
will answer;
you shall cry, and he will say,
'Here I am.'
If you take away [r] the yoke from your
midst,
[s] the pointing of the finger, and
speaking wickedness,
10 [t] if you pour yourself out for the
hungry
and satisfy the desire of the afflicted,
[n] then shall your light rise in the
darkness
and your gloom be as the noonday.
11 And the LORD will guide you
continually
and satisfy your desire in scorched
places
and make your bones strong;
and you shall be [u] like a watered garden,
like a spring of water,
whose waters do not fail.
12 [v] And your ancient ruins shall be
rebuilt;
you shall raise up the foundations
of many generations;
you shall be called the repairer of the
breach,
the restorer of streets to dwell in.
13 [w] "If you turn back your foot from the
Sabbath,
from doing your pleasure[2] on my
holy day,
and call the Sabbath a delight
and the holy day of the LORD
honorable;
if you honor it, not going your own
ways,
or seeking [x] your own pleasure,[3] or
talking idly;[4]
14 then you shall take delight in the
LORD,
[y] and I will make you ride on the
heights of the earth;[5]
[z] I will feed you with the heritage of
Jacob your father,
[a] for the mouth of the LORD has
spoken."

6 [j] See Neh. 5:10-12 [k] ver. 9
7 [l] ver. 10; Ezek. 18:7; [Matt. 25:35] [m] Neh. 5:5
8 [n] [Job 11:17] [o] Jer. 30:17 [p] Ps. 85:13 [q] [ch. 52:12]
9 [r] ver. 6 [s] Prov. 6:13
10 [t] ver. 7, 8
11 [u] Jer. 31:12
12 [v] ch. 61:4; 65:21; [Ezra 6:14; Neh. 4:6]
13 [w] ch. 56:2; See Neh. 13:15-21 [x] ver. 3
14 [y] Deut. 32:13 [z] Jer. 50:19 [a] ch. 1:20
Chapter 59
1 [b] ch. 50:2; Num. 11:23
2 [c] Jer. 5:25

Evil and Oppression

59 Behold, [b] the LORD's hand is not
shortened, that it cannot save,
or his ear dull, that it cannot
hear;
2 [c] but your iniquities have made a
separation
between you and your God,
and your sins have hidden his face
from you
so that he does not hear.

1 Or *bruised* 2 Or *business* 3 Or *pursuing your own business* 4 Hebrew *or speaking a word* 5 Or *of the land*

58:6 fast that I choose. This verse presents a different idea of fasting: to rescue the oppressed and provide for the needy (Matt. 25:34–40).

58:7 own flesh. Relatives, and secondarily people from the same tribe or area (1 Tim. 5:8).

58:8 Then. This word connects human responsibility and the coming of God's kingdom.

light . . . glory. The glorious kingdom of God (9:2; 60:1–3; Luke 1:78, 79) will dawn with God's blessing and protection (2:5 note), and with His healing (30:26 note). It is the establishment of a new order (1:21 note), with the presence of the God of glory (4:2 note).

rear guard. Like the pillar of cloud and fire in the wilderness (4:5, 6; Ex. 13:21; 14:20).

58:9 call . . . cry. Then God will answer prayer (30:19; 65:24); in contrast see v. 4 note.

Here I am. Typically this is a courteous answer given by a person who is ready to hear a message or follow instructions (e.g., Gen. 22:1, 7; Ex. 3:4; 1 Sam. 3:4).

yoke . . . speaking wickedness. These expressions represent oppression, contempt, and improper speech (Prov. 6:13).

58:10 then. See v. 8 note. The dawning of the new age brings ever greater brightness (2:5; 5:30 and notes).

58:11 watered garden . . . spring. They will be greatly blessed and productive (1:30, 31 note; cf. John 7:38).

58:12 ancient ruins shall be rebuilt. The restored exiles were in need of the spiritual and economic resources to rebuild Judah (44:26, 28; 61:4; Ezek. 36:10; Amos 9:14, 15; Hag. 1:2–9; Acts 15:15–17).

58:13 Sabbath . . . holy day. The Lord does not reject ritual as such. This day is the sign of the covenant (56:2 note).

own ways . . . own pleasure. Their goals were social prestige, financial gain, and political importance (contrast 33:15 and note).

3 [d] For your hands are defiled with blood
and your fingers with iniquity;
your lips have spoken lies;
your tongue mutters wickedness.
4 [e] No one enters suit justly;
no one goes to law honestly;
they rely on empty pleas, they speak lies,
[f] they conceive mischief and give birth to iniquity.
5 They hatch adders' eggs;
they weave the spider's web;
he who eats their eggs dies,
and from one that is crushed a viper is hatched.
6 [g] Their webs will not serve as clothing;
men will not cover themselves with what they make.
Their works are works of iniquity,
and deeds of violence are in their hands.
7 [h] Their feet run to evil,
and they are swift to shed innocent blood;
their thoughts are thoughts of iniquity;
desolation and destruction are in their highways.
8 The way of peace they do not know,
and there is no justice in their paths;
they have made their roads crooked;
[i] no one who treads on them knows peace.
9 Therefore justice is far from us,
and righteousness does not overtake us;
[j] we hope for light, and behold, darkness,
and for brightness, but we walk in gloom.
10 [k] We grope for the wall like the blind;
we grope like those who have no eyes;
we stumble at noon as in the twilight,
[l] among those in full vigor we are like dead men.
11 We all growl like bears;
[m] we moan and moan like doves;
[n] we hope for justice, but there is none;
for salvation, but it is far from us.
12 For our transgressions are multiplied before you,
and our sins testify against us;
for our transgressions are with us,
and we know our iniquities:
13 transgressing, and denying the LORD,
and turning back from following our God,
[o] speaking oppression and revolt,
conceiving and uttering from the heart lying words.
14 [p] Justice is turned back,
and righteousness stands afar off;
for truth has stumbled in the public squares,
and uprightness cannot enter.
15 Truth is lacking,
and he who departs from evil makes himself a prey.

Judgment and Redemption

The LORD saw it, and it displeased him [1]
that there was no justice.
16 [q] He saw that there was no man,
and wondered that there was no one to intercede;
then his own arm brought him salvation,
and his righteousness upheld him.
17 [r] He put on righteousness as a breastplate,
and a helmet of salvation on his head;
he put on garments of vengeance for clothing,
and wrapped himself in [s] zeal as a cloak.

3 [d] ch. 1:15
4 [e] [ver. 14] [f] Job 15:35; Ps. 7:14
6 [g] Job 8:14
7 [h] Prov. 1:16; Cited Rom. 3:15-17
8 [i] ch. 48:22; 57:21
9 [j] [ver. 11; ch. 60:2]
10 [k] Deut. 28:29; Job 5:14; 12:25; See ch. 42:18-20
[l] [1 Cor. 4:9, 10]
11 [m] ch. 38:14 [n] [ver. 9; ch. 46:13; 56:1]
13 [o] [ver. 3, 4]
14 [p] [ch. 51:4, 5]
16 [q] [ch. 51:18; 63:5]
17 [r] 1 Thess. 5:8; See Eph. 6:13-17 [s] [ch. 9:7]

1 Hebrew *and it was evil in his eyes*

59:5 adders' eggs . . . spider's web. The comparison indicates wickedness that wants to grow and to ensnare others.

59:7 run . . . swift. They no longer hesitate to break God's laws (Prov. 1:16); their actions result in discord and chaos (Rom. 3:15–17).

59:8 way of peace. Those who deny others peace will themselves be kept from it (48:22; 57:21).

59:10 grope . . . stumble. These words describe the experience of one cursed (Deut. 28:29; Job 5:14).

59:16 no one to intercede. No one was available to help, except the Messiah (53:12; Rom. 5:7).

righteousness. This "righteousness" is His victorious salvation (46:13; 51:6, 8; 56:1).

59:17 breastplate . . . helmet. Today, Christians put on this armor of God (Eph. 6:13–17).

put on . . . wrapped. The Lord of Hosts will accomplish what no one else could do (42:13; 49:25; 52:10; Ex. 15:3).

18 [t]According to their deeds, so will he
repay,
wrath to his adversaries,
repayment to his enemies;
[u]to the coastlands he will render
repayment.
19 [v]So they shall fear the name of the
LORD from the west,
and his glory from the rising of the
sun;
[w]for he will come like a rushing
stream,[1]
which the wind of the LORD
drives.

20 [x]"And [y]a Redeemer will come to Zion,
to those in Jacob who turn from
transgression," declares the
LORD.

21 "And as for me, [z]this is my covenant with
them," says the LORD: "My Spirit that is
upon you, [a]and my words that I have put
in your mouth, shall not depart out of your
mouth, or out of the mouth of your offspring, or out of the mouth of your children's offspring," says the LORD, "from this
time forth and forevermore."

The Future Glory of Israel

60 [b]Arise, shine, for your light has
come,
and [c]the glory of the LORD has
risen upon you.
2 For behold, darkness shall cover the
earth,
and thick darkness the peoples;
but the LORD will arise upon you,
and his glory will be seen upon
you.
3 [d]And nations shall come to your
light,
and kings to the brightness of your
rising.
4 [e]Lift up your eyes all around, and see;
they all gather together, they come
to you;
[f]your sons shall come from afar,
and your daughters shall be carried
on the hip.
5 Then you shall see and [g]be radiant;
your heart shall thrill and exult,[2]
because the abundance of the sea
shall be turned to you,
[h]the wealth of the nations shall
come to you.
6 A multitude of camels shall cover you,
the young camels of [i]Midian and
[j]Ephah;
all those from [k]Sheba shall come.
[l]They shall bring gold and
frankincense,
and shall bring good news, the
praises of the LORD.
7 All the flocks of [m]Kedar shall be
gathered to you;
the rams of [n]Nebaioth shall
minister to you;
[o]they shall come up with acceptance
on my altar,
[p]and I will beautify my beautiful
house.
8 Who are these that fly like a cloud,
and [q]like doves to their
windows?

18 [t]ch. 63:4, 6 [u][ch. 41:1, 5]
19 [v][Ps. 113:3] [w][ch. 30:27, 28]
20 [x]Cited Rom. 11:26, 27; [ch. 40:9; Joel 2:32] [y]ch. 43:14
21 [z]Jer. 31:31; Heb. 8:10; 10:16 [a]ch. 51:16; [Deut. 4:10]
Chapter 60
1 [b][Eph. 5:14] [c]ch. 40:5; 58:8; Mal. 4:2
3 [d]ch. 42:6; 49:6; Rev. 21:24
4 [e]ch. 49:18 [f]ver. 9; ch. 66:20
5 [g]Ps. 34:5 [h]ch. 61:6
6 [i]Judg. 6:5 [j]Gen. 25:4 [k]1 Kin. 10:1; Ps. 72:10 [l][Matt. 2:11]
7 [m]See ch. 21:16 [n]Gen. 25:13; 28:9; 36:3 [o]ch. 56:7 [p]Hag. 2:7
8 [q]Hos. 11:11; [Gen. 8:9]

1 Hebrew *a narrow river* 2 Hebrew *your heart shall tremble and grow wide*

59:20 Redeemer. He will come in the person of Jesus Christ. This promise is quoted by Paul (Rom. 11:26, 27). See note 35:9, 10.

59:21 covenant. The Lord's covenant of grace is renewed (42:6 note).

Spirit. The role of the Spirit of God is mentioned several times in the Old Testament (32:15; 44:3; Jer. 31:31–34; Ezek. 37:14; Zech. 12:10). The Spirit works "by and with the Word in our hearts" (*Westminster Confession* 1.5). His continuing presence with His people was secured with the revelation of the New Testament (John 16:7, 13; 2 Cor. 5:5; Gal. 3:14; 4:6).

60:1 Arise. The imperative (feminine singular) is addressed to Zion (v. 14).

shine. Zion receives and reflects God's light (Luke 1:78, 79; Eph. 5:14; Rev. 21:23, 24).

60:2 darkness shall cover . . . LORD will arise. Although the world is in darkness, God's light shines on His people (John 1:15; Col. 1:13; 1 Pet. 2:9).

his glory. See 4:5; 40:5; John 1:14; Rev. 21:11.

60:3 nations shall come. See 11:1; 42:16; 49:6. The prophecy has been fulfilled day by day since the coming of the gospel (Acts 9:15; 11:18).

kings to the brightness. They come to Christ (42:6; 49:6). The wise men who came to see Jesus were Gentiles if not "kings" in some sense.

60:5 wealth . . . shall come. The prophecy began to be fulfilled with Darius's contribution to the temple (Ezra 6:8, 9). It has a much greater fulfillment through the ascended Christ, who rules in the hearts of His people.

60:6 Midian. A desert tribe famous for caravans and trade (Gen. 37:28, 36; Judg. 6:5, 6).

Ephah. A tribe related to Midian (Gen. 25:4).

Sheba. This country was renowned for its wealth (1 Kin. 10:1, 2).

60:7 Kedar. See note 21:16.

Nebaioth. Related to the Ishmaelites (Gen. 25:13), and later known as Nabateans. Their capital was at Petra, 50 miles south of the Dead Sea.

9 For [r] the coastlands shall hope for me,
[s] the ships of Tarshish first,
[t] to bring your children from afar,
their silver and gold with them,
for the name of the LORD your God,
and for the Holy One of Israel,
because [u] he has made you
beautiful.
10 [v] Foreigners shall build up your walls,
and [v] their kings shall minister to
you;
for in my wrath I struck you,
but in my favor I have had mercy
on you.
11 [w] Your gates shall be open continually;
day and night they shall not be
shut,
[w] that people may bring to you the
wealth of the nations,
with their kings led in procession.
12 [x] For the nation and kingdom
that will not serve you shall perish;
those nations shall be utterly laid
waste.
13 [y] The glory of Lebanon shall come to
you,
the cypress, the plane, and [z] the
pine,
to beautify the place of my sanctuary,
and I will make the place of my
feet glorious.
14 [a] The sons of those who afflicted you
shall come bending low to you,
[b] and all who despised you
shall bow down at your feet;
[c] they shall call you the City of the
LORD,
the Zion of the Holy One of Israel.

9 [r] ch. 51:5; See ch. 11:11 [s] See ch. 2:16 [t] Gal. 4:26 [u] ch. 44:23; 55:5
10 [v] ch. 45:1, 13; Zech. 6:15
11 [w] [Rev. 21:25, 26]
12 [x] [Zech. 14:17-19]
13 [y] ch. 35:2 [z] ch. 41:19
14 [a] [ch. 14:1, 2; Zech. 8:23] [b] ch. 49:23; [Rev. 3:9] [c] [ch. 1:26; 62:2]

15 [d] Whereas you have been forsaken and
hated,
with no one passing through,
[e] I will make you majestic forever,
a joy from age to age.
16 [f] You shall suck the milk of nations;
you shall nurse at the breast of
kings;
and you shall know that [g] I, the LORD,
am your Savior
and your Redeemer, [h] the Mighty
One of Jacob.

17 Instead of bronze I will bring gold,
and instead of iron I will bring silver;
instead of wood, bronze,
instead of stones, iron.
I will make your overseers peace
[i] and your taskmasters righteousness.
18 [j] Violence shall no more be heard in
your land,
devastation or destruction within
your borders;
[k] you shall call your walls Salvation,
and your gates Praise.

19 [l] The sun shall be no more
your light by day,
nor for brightness shall the moon
give you light;[1]
but the LORD will be your everlasting
light,
and your God will be your glory.[2]
20 Your sun shall no more go down,
nor your moon withdraw itself;
for the LORD will be your everlasting
light,
and [m] your days of mourning shall
be ended.

15 [d] ch. 54:6; 62:4 [e] Ps. 47:4; [ch. 65:18]
16 [f] [ch. 49:23; 66:11, 12] [g] ch. 43:3; 49:26; [ch. 47:4] [h] Gen. 49:24; Ps. 132:2
17 [i] [ch. 58:3]
18 [j] ch. 11:9 [k] ch. 26:1
19 [l] Zech. 14:6, 7; Rev. 21:23; 22:5; [ch. 24:23; 30:26]
20 [m] ch. 35:10; 65:19; Rev. 21:4

1 Masoretic Text; Dead Sea Scroll, Septuagint, Targum add *by night*
2 Or *your beauty*

60:9 coastlands shall hope for me. So also in 43:5–7, 14; 49:18; 51:5.

ships of Tarshish. See note 23:5. The resumption of maritime trade is another way the glory of the new age is described in terms of Solomon's splendor (1 Kin. 10:22).

silver and gold. See Hag. 2:7–9.

60:10 Foreigners. As Hiram, king of Tyre, helped build the first temple (1 Kin. 5), and Cyrus and Darius, kings of Persia, the second (Ezra 6), so also today people of many nations are building up the church, the temple of the Lord (Eph. 2:11–22).

kings shall minister. The exiles were promised that foreign kings would depart (49:17); now it is asserted that foreign kings will serve Mount Zion and worship God. In His wrath against kings, God will remember mercy and save some of them.

60:11 gates . . . day and night. Instead of attacking, the nations will bring tribute (Rev. 21:25–26).

60:12 perish. See Gen. 12:3; Heb. 2:3.

60:13 sanctuary. Precious wood glorified Solomon's temple as well (1 Kin. 6:15–18). This provides another connection between the former and latter glory (vv. 6, 9 and notes).

place of my feet. At first this expression referred to the ark of the covenant (Ps. 132:7; 1 Chr. 28:2); later, to the temple (Ezek. 43:7); and, finally, to the whole world (66:1).

60:16 nurse at the breast of kings. This is figurative language for the wealth brought by kings to Zion.

60:17 gold . . . silver . . . bronze . . . iron. Bronze and iron were important alloys used for making tools and weapons. Each material is replaced by one stronger and more valuable. By analogy, the cultural and social life of the country will be raised beyond what Solomon knew. Whatever the interim fulfillments of this prophecy, it looks ultimately to the splendor of the New Jerusalem (Rev. 21:9–27; see also Ps. 48).

60:18 walls. God's salvation and Israel's praise constitute the defense of the spiritual temple, Christ and His church (26:1 note; cf. Zech. 2:4, 5).

60:19 everlasting light. This is God's presence with His people (v. 1 note; Rev. 21:11, 23; 22:5).

21 [n]Your people shall all be righteous;
[o]they shall possess the land forever,
[p]the branch of my planting, the work
of my hands,
that I might be glorified.[1]
22 [q]The least one shall become a clan,
and the smallest one a mighty
nation;
[r]I am the LORD;
in its time I will hasten it.

The Year of the LORD's Favor

61 [s]The Spirit of the Lord GOD is
upon me,
because the LORD has [t]anointed me
to bring good news to the poor;[2]
he has sent me to bind up the
brokenhearted,
to proclaim liberty to the captives,
and [u]the opening of the prison to
those who are bound;[3]
2 [v]to proclaim the year of the LORD's
favor,
[w]and the day of vengeance of our
God;
to comfort all who mourn;
3 to grant to those who mourn in Zion—
[x]to give them a beautiful headdress
instead of ashes,
[y]the oil of gladness instead of mourning,
the garment of praise instead of a
faint spirit;
[z]that they may be called oaks of
righteousness,
the planting of the LORD, [a]that he
may be glorified.[4]
4 [b]They shall build up the ancient ruins;
they shall raise up the former
devastations;
they shall repair the ruined cities,
the devastations of many
generations.

21 [n]ch. 52:1; Jer. 31:34 [o]Ps. 37:9; See Ezek. 37:25 [p]ch. 61:3
22 [q][Matt. 12:31] [r]Hab. 2:3
Chapter 61
1 [s]ch. 11:2; 42:1; 48:16; Cited Luke 4:18, 19 [t]Ps. 45:7 [u]ch. 45:13; Ps. 146:7
2 [v][Lev. 25:10] [w]ch. 34:8
3 [x]ver. 10; [ch. 28:5] [y]Ps. 45:7; Heb. 1:9 [z][ch. 60:21] [a]John 15:8
4 [b]Amos 9:14; See ch. 58:12
5 [c]ch. 14:2; [ch. 60:10]
6 [d]Ex. 19:6; 1 Pet. 2:9; [Joel 1:9] [e]ch. 60:5, 11, 16
7 [f]ch. 40:2; [ch. 54:7, 8; Zech. 9:12]
8 [g]Ps. 11:7; [ch. 59:15] [h]ch. 40:10; 49:4 [i]See ch. 55:3
10 [j]Hab. 3:18 [k][ch. 59:17; Zech. 3:4]

5 [c]Strangers shall stand and tend your
flocks;
foreigners shall be your plowmen
and vinedressers;
6 [d]but you shall be called the priests of
the LORD;
they shall speak of you as the
ministers of our God;
[e]you shall eat the wealth of the
nations,
and in their glory you shall boast.
7 [f]Instead of your shame there shall be
a double portion;
instead of dishonor they shall
rejoice in their lot;
therefore in their land they shall
possess a double portion;
they shall have everlasting joy.
8 [g]For I the LORD love justice;
I hate robbery and wrong;[5]
[h]I will faithfully give them their
recompense,
[i]and I will make an everlasting
covenant with them.
9 Their offspring shall be known
among the nations,
and their descendants in the midst
of the peoples;
all who see them shall acknowledge
them,
that they are an offspring the LORD
has blessed.
10 [j]I will greatly rejoice in the LORD;
my soul shall exult in my God,
[k]for he has clothed me with the
garments of salvation;
he has covered me with the robe of
righteousness,

[1] Or *that I might display my beauty* [2] Or *afflicted* [3] Or *the opening* [of the eyes] *to those who are blind*; Septuagint *and recovery of sight to the blind* [4] Or *that he may display his beauty* [5] Or *robbery with a burnt offering*

61:1 Spirit. See 11:2; 42:1; 48:16 and notes; Luke 3:22; 4:18, 19. The prophecy was fulfilled in the ministry of Christ. Isaiah is included (62:1) as a shadow or forerunner of Jesus.

poor. See Ps. 9:18 note; Luke 7:22.

proclaim liberty. This phrase may be an allusion to the liberation of slaves in the Year of Jubilee (Lev. 25:10).

61:2 the year of the LORD's favor. Through His death and resurrection, Jesus inaugurated the "day of salvation" (2 Cor. 6:2) in which the gospel is preached all over the world, and those who were estranged can find peace in Him (Eph. 2:12, 13; 3:5; 2 Tim. 1:10).

day of vengeance. Jesus closed the book before reading this portion of Isaiah's oracle (Luke 4:18–20). The time of healing belongs to His first coming; the time of judgment to the second (1 Thess. 1:10). See note 34:8.

61:6 wealth of the nations. See note 60:5.

61:7 shame . . . dishonor. These words describe the experience of the Babylonian exile of the sixth century B.C. (30:3; 50:4–6).

61:8 everlasting covenant. See notes 42:6; 55:3.

61:9 descendants. The blessings of the covenant are extended to the children (59:21).

all who see . . . blessed. This alludes to the promise to Abraham (41:8; 51:2; Gen. 12:2, 3).

61:10 I. Zion is represented here as having received the blessings described in v. 3, for example, joy and the garments of praise. To be "clothed" with something is a common figure for a change in status or condition (52:1; Zech. 3:3–5; Matt. 22:11).

as a bridegroom decks himself [l]like a priest with a beautiful headdress,
[m]and as a bride adorns herself with her jewels.
11 For as the earth brings forth its sprouts,
and as a garden causes what is sown in it to sprout up,
so the Lord GOD will cause [n]righteousness and praise
to sprout up before all the nations.

Zion's Coming Salvation

62 [o]For Zion's sake I will not keep silent,
and for Jerusalem's sake I will not be quiet,
[p]until her righteousness goes forth as brightness,
and her salvation as a burning torch.
2 [q]The nations shall see your righteousness,
and all the kings your glory,
[r]and you shall be called by a new name
that the mouth of the LORD will give.
3 You shall be [s]a crown of beauty in the hand of the LORD,
and a royal diadem in the hand of your God.
4 [t]You shall no more be termed [u]Forsaken,[1]
and your land shall no more be termed Desolate,[2]
[r]but you shall be called [v]My Delight Is in Her,[3]
and your land Married;[4]
for the LORD delights in you,
and your land shall be married.
5 For as a young man marries a young woman,
so [w]shall your sons marry you,
and as the bridegroom rejoices over the bride,
so [x]shall your God rejoice over you.

6 On your walls, O Jerusalem,
I have set [y]watchmen;
all the day and all the night
they shall never be silent.
You who put the LORD in remembrance,
take no rest,
7 and give him no rest
until he establishes Jerusalem
and makes it [z]a praise in the earth.
8 The LORD has sworn [a]by his right hand
and by his mighty arm:
"I will not again give [b]your grain
to be food for your enemies,
[c]and foreigners shall not drink your wine
for which you have labored;
9 but [d]those who garner it shall eat it
and praise the LORD,
and [d]those who gather it shall drink it
in the courts of my sanctuary."[5]

10 Go through, go through the gates;
[e]prepare the way for the people;
[f]build up, build up the highway;
clear it of stones;
[g]lift up a signal over the peoples.
11 Behold, the LORD has proclaimed
to the end of the earth:
[h]Say to the daughter of Zion,
[i]"Behold, your salvation comes;
behold, his reward is with him,
and his recompense before him."
12 [j]And they shall be called The Holy People,
The Redeemed of the LORD;
[k]and you shall be called Sought Out,
A City Not Forsaken.

10 [l]ver. 3 [m]ch. 49:18; Rev. 21:2
11 [n][ch. 60:18; 62:7]
Chapter 62
1 [o]ver. 6, 7 [p][Prov. 4:18]
2 [q]ch. 60:3; Ps. 98:2 [r]ch. 60:14; [Rev. 2:17; 3:12]
3 [s]Zech. 9:16; [ch. 54:11, 12]
4 [t]Hos. 1:10; 1 Pet. 2:10; See ch. 54:6 [u]ch. 49:14; 54:1, 7; 60:15 [r][See ver. 2 above] [v]Mal. 3:12
5 [w][ch. 51:18] [x]ch. 65:19
6 [y]ch. 52:8; 56:10
7 [z]ch. 60:18; [ch. 61:11; Zeph. 3:20]
8 [a][Heb. 6:13] [b]Deut. 28:33; Jer. 5:17 [c][ch. 65:21, 22]
9 [d][Deut. 12:12; 14:23, 26]
10 [e]ch. 40:3 [f]ch. 57:14 [g]ch. 11:10; 49:22
11 [h]Zech. 9:9; [Matt. 21:5; John 12:15] [i]ch. 40:10
12 [j]ch. 61:6 [k]ver. 4; [ch. 61:4]

1 Hebrew *Azubah* 2 Hebrew *Shemamah* 3 Hebrew *Hephzibah* 4 Hebrew *Beulah* 5 Or *in my holy courts*

62:1 burning torch. This picture of salvation as a welcoming light is developed in 58:8; 60:1–3.

62:2 nations . . . kings. They witness the confirmation of the promises (2:2–4; 41:2 note; 52:10; 60:3; 61:11).

a new name. Like new clothes (61:10 note), the new name signifies a renewed relationship and enhanced privilege (vv. 4, 12; cf. 1:26; 56:5; 60:14, 18; cf. Gen. 17:5, 15; Rev. 2:17; 3:12).

62:3 crown of beauty. The Lord shares His glory with His people.

62:6 watchmen. A figure for prophets (56:10 note).

62:8 has sworn. See note 14:24.

by his right hand and by his mighty arm. That is, by Himself (40:10 note; 41:10; 51:9; 52:10; 53:1).

food for your enemies. The curse (Lev. 26:16; Deut. 28:33) will be replaced by blessing.

62:10 Go through, go through . . . build up, build up. These imperatives emphatically encourage the people to worship.

gates. These lead into the court of the sanctuary (v. 9).

62:12 Holy People. See 4:3; Ex. 19:6; 1 Pet. 2:9, 10.

Redeemed. See note 35:9.

The LORD's Day of Vengeance

63 Who is this who comes from [l]Edom,
in crimsoned garments from [l]Bozrah,
he who is splendid in his apparel,
[m]marching in the greatness of his strength?
"It is I, speaking in righteousness,
mighty to save."
2 Why is your [n]apparel red,
and your garments like his [o]who treads in the winepress?
3 [p]"I have trodden the winepress alone,
[q]and from the peoples no one was with me;
I trod them in my anger
and trampled them in my wrath;
their lifeblood[1] spattered on my garments,
and stained all my apparel.
4 [r]For the day of vengeance was in my heart,
and my year of redemption[2] had come.
5 I looked, but [s]there was no one to help;
I was appalled, but there was no one to uphold;
so my own arm brought me salvation,
and my wrath upheld me.
6 I trampled down the peoples in my anger;
[t]I made them drunk in my wrath,
and I poured out their lifeblood on the earth."

The LORD's Mercy Remembered

7 I will recount the steadfast love of the LORD,
the praises of the LORD,
according to all that the LORD has granted us,
[u]and the great goodness to the house of Israel
that he has granted them according to his compassion,
according to the abundance of his steadfast love.
8 For he said, "Surely they are my people,
children who will not deal falsely."
And he became their Savior.
9 [v]In all their affliction he was afflicted,[3]
and the angel of his presence saved them;
[w]in his love and in his pity he redeemed them;
[x]he lifted them up and carried them all the days of old.
10 [y]But they rebelled
[z]and grieved his Holy Spirit;
therefore he turned to be their enemy,
and himself fought against them.
11 Then he remembered [a]the days of old,
of Moses and his people.[4]
[b]Where is he who brought them up out of the sea
with the shepherds of his flock?
Where is he who put in the midst of them
his Holy Spirit,

Chapter 63
1 [l]ch. 34:6
[m][Ps. 68:7]
2 [n]Rev. 19:13
[o][Lam. 1:15; Rev. 14:20; 19:15]
3 [p][Joel 3:13]
[q][ch. 59:16]
4 [r]ch. 34:8
5 [s][ch. 59:16]
6 [t]ch. 49:26
7 [u]Ps. 145:7
9 [v]Judg. 10:16
[w]Deut. 7:7, 8; [Ezek. 16:5, 6] [x]See Deut. 32:10-12
10 [y]Ex. 15:24; Num. 14:11; Ps. 78:17, 56; 95:9; Ezek. 20:8 [z]Ps. 78:40; Acts 7:51; [Eph. 4:30]
11 [a]See Ps. 77:11-20
[b]See Ex. 14:19-22

1 Or *their juice*; also verse 6 2 Or *the year of my redeemed* 3 Or *he did not afflict* 4 Or *Then his people remembered the days of old, of Moses*

63:1 Edom. This nation is representative of the ungodly and proud nations (34:1–17, especially v. 5; Obad. 14, 15; Lam. 4:21, 22; Joel 3:19; Mal. 1:2–5).

Bozrah. An important city in Edom 30 miles southeast of the Dead Sea.

63:3 winepress . . . stained. This verse presents an extended metaphor for the day of the Lord (Lam. 1:15; Joel 3:13; Rev. 14:17–20; 19:15). The winepress represents the battle, and the juice pressed out represents the casualties of war.

63:4 my year of redemption. This phrase alludes to the laws concerning slaves and property in the Jubilee year (Lev. 25). This idea of redemption is developed throughout Isaiah, but especially in 61:1–63:6 (34:8; 35:9 and notes).

had come. The future is already seen through faith.

63:7 I will recount. Isaiah will proclaim aloud (Ps. 51:13–15; 89:1; 145:7) the Lord's mighty acts of the past, described as His "steadfast love."

63:8 children who will not deal falsely. These are faithful children of God (Ex. 4:22; Deut. 14:1), unlike the rebellious children described in 1:2–4.

63:9 affliction. Israel's sufferings in Egypt (Ex. 2:23–25).

angel of his presence. See Ex. 14:19; 23:20–23.

carried. Cf. Ex. 19:4; Deut. 1:31; 32:10–12.

63:10 grieved his Holy Spirit. Rebellion against God's word brought the patience of God's Spirit to an end (cf. Ps. 106:33; Acts 7:51; Eph. 4:30). Divine patience is long suffering, but it will not restrain God's judgment forever.

63:11 days of old. That is, the period of the Exodus and wilderness wanderings.

shepherds of his flock. Moses was this shepherd. Jesus is our shepherd (Heb. 3:1–6; 13:20).

12 who caused his glorious arm
to go at the right hand of Moses,
[c] who divided the waters before them
[d] to make for himself an everlasting name,
13 who led them through the depths?
Like a horse in the desert,
they did not stumble.
14 Like livestock that go down into the valley,
[e] the Spirit of the LORD gave them rest.
So you led your people,
[d] to make for yourself a glorious name.

Prayer for Mercy

15 [f] Look down from heaven and see,
[g] from your holy and beautiful[1] habitation.
Where are [h] your zeal and your might?
The stirring of your inner parts and your compassion
are held back from me.
16 For [i] you are our Father,
though Abraham does not know us,
and Israel does not acknowledge us;
you, O LORD, are our Father,
[j] our Redeemer from of old is your name.
17 O LORD, why do you make us wander from your ways
and [k] harden our heart, so that we fear you not?
[l] Return for the sake of your servants,
the tribes of your heritage.
18 [m] Your holy people held possession for a little while;[2]
[n] our adversaries have trampled down your sanctuary.
19 [o] We have become like those over whom you have never ruled,
like those who are not called by your name.

12 [c] Ex. 14:21; Josh. 3:16 [d] 2 Sam. 7:23; Neh. 9:10
14 [e] [Num. 10:33] [d] [See ver. 12 above]
15 [f] Deut. 26:15 [g] Ps. 33:14 [h] ch. 59:17; [Zech. 1:14]
16 [i] ch. 64:8; Deut. 32:6 [j] ch. 43:14
17 [k] ch. 6:10; [John 12:40] [l] Ps. 90:13
18 [m] [Deut. 4:25, 26] [n] ch. 64:11
19 [o] [Jer. 14:8]

Chapter 64
1 [p] [2 Sam. 22:10; Ps. 18:9; 144:5] [q] Judg. 5:5; Mic. 1:4
2 [r] [Josh. 2:9, 10]
3 [s] [Ex. 14:13; 15:11]
4 [t] [Ps. 31:19] [u] [1 Cor. 2:9]
6 [v] See ch. 59:12-15 [w] Ps. 90:5, 6
7 [x] ch. 43:22; Hos. 7:7

64 [p] Oh that you would rend the heavens and come down,
[q] that the mountains might quake at your presence—
2[3] as when fire kindles brushwood
and the fire causes water to boil—
[r] to make your name known to your adversaries,
and that the nations might tremble at your presence!
3 [s] When you did awesome things that we did not look for,
you came down, the mountains quaked at your presence.
4 [t] From of old no one has heard
or perceived by the ear,
[u] no eye has seen a God besides you,
who acts for those who wait for him.
5 You meet him who joyfully works righteousness,
those who remember you in your ways.
Behold, you were angry, and we sinned;
in our sins we have been a long time, and shall we be saved?[4]
6 [v] We have all become like one who is unclean,
and all our righteous deeds are like a polluted garment.
[w] We all fade like a leaf,
and our iniquities, like the wind, take us away.
7 [x] There is no one who calls upon your name,
who rouses himself to take hold of you;
for you have hidden your face from us,
and have made us melt in[5] the hand of our iniquities.

[1] Or *holy and glorious* [2] Or *They have dispossessed your holy people for a little while* [3] Ch 64:1 in Hebrew [4] Or *in your ways is continuance, that we might be saved* [5] Masoretic Text; Septuagint, Syriac, Targum *have delivered us into*

63:16 our Father. God has always been the Father of His people (64:8; Ex. 4:22, 23; Jer. 3:4, 19); they are His children by adoption (Deut. 32:6; Rom. 8:15).

Abraham. See 51:2.

63:17 make us wander. God makes those who reject Him stray (Rom. 1:20–25; 2 Thess. 2:10–12), and may confirm them in their sin (6:10; Ex. 4:21; Ps. 95:8).

63:18 our adversaries. The Babylonians (Ps. 74:4–8).

63:19 called by your name. To signify ownership (Deut. 28:10; Jer. 14:9).

64:1 Oh that you would . . . come down. With eloquence Isaiah pleads with God to make His presence unmistakably clear, especially in the fires of judgment (4:4, 5 and notes; Ex. 19:18; Heb. 12:18).

64:3 awesome things. An allusion to God's appearance on Mount Sinai after the Exodus (Ex. 19:16–18; Deut. 10:21; Ps. 66:3–6; 106:22; see Ezek. 32:6–8 note).

64:6 unclean. Unfit to be in God's presence (Lev. 13:45, 46; Hag. 2:13, 14).

polluted garment. Garments stained by menstruation (Lev. 15:19; Ezek. 36:17; cf. Phil. 4:7, 8). No one is sinless in God's sight (6:5; Job 15:14–16).

8 [y] But now, O LORD, you are our Father;
[z] we are the clay, and you are our potter;
[a] we are all the work of your hand.
9 [b] Be not so terribly angry, O LORD,
[c] and remember not iniquity forever.
Behold, please look, we are all your people.
10 [d] Your holy cities have become a wilderness;
Zion has become a wilderness,
Jerusalem a desolation.
11 [e] Our holy and beautiful[1] house,
where our fathers praised you,
has been burned by fire,
and all our pleasant places have become ruins.
12 [f] Will you restrain yourself at these things, O LORD?
Will you keep silent, and afflict us so terribly?

Judgment and Salvation

65 [g] I was ready to be sought by
[h] those who did not ask for me;
I was ready to be found by those who did not seek me.
I said, "Here am I, here am I,"
to a nation that was not called by[2] my name.
2 [i] I spread out my hands all the day
to a rebellious people,
who walk in a way that is not good,
following their own devices;
3 a people who provoke me
to my face continually,
[j] sacrificing in gardens
and making offerings on bricks;
4 who sit in tombs,
and spend the night in secret places;
[k] who eat pig's flesh,
and broth of tainted meat is in their vessels;
5 who say, "Keep to yourself,
do not come near me, for I am too holy for you."
[l] These are a smoke in my nostrils,
a fire that burns all the day.
6 Behold, [m] it is written before me:
[n] "I will not keep silent, but I will repay;
[o] I will indeed repay into their bosom
7 both your iniquities [p] and your fathers' iniquities together,
says the LORD;
[q] because they made offerings on the mountains
[q] and insulted me on the hills,
I will measure into their bosom
payment for their former deeds."[3]

8 Thus says the LORD:
[r] "As the new wine is found in the cluster,
and they say, 'Do not destroy it,
for there is a blessing in it,'
so I will do for my servants' sake,
[s] and not destroy them all.
9 [t] I will bring forth offspring from Jacob,
and from Judah possessors of my mountains;
my chosen shall possess it,
and my servants shall dwell there.
10 [u] Sharon shall become a pasture for flocks,
and [v] the Valley of Achor a place for herds to lie down,
for my people [w] who have sought me.

8 [y] ch. 63:16 [z] ch. 45:9; Rom. 9:20, 21 [a] ch. 29:23; 45:11
9 [b] [ch. 57:16; Ps. 74:1, 2] [c] Ps. 79:8
10 [d] Neh. 1:3; 2:3
11 [e] Hag. 1:9; 2:3; [2 Kin. 25:9; 2 Chr. 36:19; Ps. 74:7]
12 [f] ch. 42:14; [Zech. 1:12]
Chapter 65
1 [g] Cited Rom. 10:20; [Eph. 2:12, 13] [h] [ch. 2:2, 3; 18:7; 19:19, 25; Zech. 14:16]
2 [i] Rom. 10:21
3 [j] ch. 1:29; 66:17; [ch. 57:3-6]
4 [k] ch. 66:17
5 [l] ch. 1:31; 9:18
6 [m] [Jer. 2:22; 17:1] [n] Ps. 50:3 [o] Ps. 79:12; [Jer. 16:18]
7 [p] Ex. 20:5; [Matt. 23:35] [q] [Ezek. 20:27, 28]
8 [r] [ch. 17:6] [s] [ch. 2:21]
9 [t] [ch. 27:6; 37:31]
10 [u] ch. 33:9; 35:2 [v] Hos. 2:15; [Josh. 7:26] [w] [ch. 51:1]

1 Or *holy and glorious* 2 Or *that did not call upon* 3 Or *I will first measure their payment into their bosom*

64:8 our Father. See note 63:16.

clay . . . work of your hand. See notes 22:11; 27:11; cf. Rom. 9:20, 21.

64:9 Compare the promises of 43:25; 54:7, 8.

64:10 holy cities. The cities of Judah.

64:11 our fathers. The speakers are at least a generation removed from the fall of the temple in 586 B.C.

65:1 Here am I. This is repeated for emphasis. God's presence is salvation.

a nation that was not called by my name. That is, Gentiles (42:1; 49:6). Paul quotes this prophecy in Rom. 10:20. God's salvation does not conform to human expectations; it originates in His free decision. See Rom. 9:11, 12, 25, 26; 10:30, 31; 11:6, 17 on this important principle.

65:2 spread out my hands. Unlike the people whose "hands are full of blood" (1:15), the Lord reached out with love.

65:3 to my face. They did not hide their offensive, idolatrous acts.

sacrificing in gardens. These sacrifices were associated with fertility religions (1:29 note).

65:4 sit in tombs. They go there to consult the spirits of the dead (8:19; 29:4).

pig's flesh. Eating pork was prohibited (66:3, 17; Lev. 11:7, 8; Deut. 14:8).

65:5 smoke . . . fire. They are a constant annoyance to God.

65:6 repay. The principle of retribution applies in God's judgment (Obad. 15; Gal. 6:7; 1 Pet. 1:17; Rev. 20:12, 13; 22:12).

65:8 new wine. The new wine in the cluster is the remnant for whose sake the whole is preserved (Matt. 13:29). The remnant is among both Israel (1:9 note) and the nations (56:6; cf. Gen. 18:22–33).

65:9 my chosen shall possess it. The kingdom will be theirs (14:1 note; 57:13; cf. Obad. 19–21).

65:10 Sharon. This fertile plain south of Mt. Carmel, on the Mediterranean coast. It is a picture of how the Lord will transform creation (33:9; 35:1, 2 and notes).

Valley of Achor. South of Jericho (Josh. 7:24; Hos. 2:15).

11 But [x]you who forsake the LORD,
who forget [y]my holy mountain,
who [z]set a table for Fortune
and [z]fill cups of mixed wine for Destiny,
12 I will destine you to the sword,
and all of you shall bow down to the slaughter,
[a]because, when I called, you did not answer;
when I spoke, you did not listen,
[b]but you did what was evil in my eyes
and chose what I did not delight in."
13 Therefore thus says the Lord GOD:
"Behold, [c]my servants shall eat,
but you shall be hungry;
behold, my servants shall drink,
but you shall be thirsty;
behold, my servants shall rejoice,
but you shall be put to shame;
14 behold, [d]my servants shall sing for gladness of heart,
but you shall cry out for pain of heart
and shall wail for breaking of spirit.
15 You shall leave your name to [e]my chosen [f]for a curse,
and the Lord GOD will put you to death,
but his servants [g]he will call by another name.
16 So that he who [h]blesses himself in the land
shall bless himself by [h]the God of truth,
and he who takes an oath in the land
shall swear by [i]the God of truth;
[j]because the former troubles are forgotten
and are hidden from my eyes.

11 [x][Josh. 24:20] [y]ver. 25; Joel 3:17 [z]Ezek. 23:41; [1 Cor. 10:21] 12 [a]ch. 66:4; Prov. 1:24; Jer. 7:13 [b]ch. 66:4 13 [c]ch. 55:1; Ps. 22:26 14 [d][Ps. 5:11] 15 [e]ver. 9 [f][Deut. 28:37; Jer. 29:22; Zech. 8:13] 15 [g]ch. 62:2 16 [h]Jer. 4:2 [i][Deut. 32:4] [j][ch. 43:18, 19]

New Heavens and a New Earth

17 "For behold, [k]I create new heavens
and a new earth,
and the former things shall not be remembered
or come into mind.
18 But be glad and rejoice forever
in that which I create;
for behold, [l]I create Jerusalem to be a joy,
and her people to be a gladness.
19 [m]I will rejoice in Jerusalem
and be glad in my people;
[n]no more shall be heard in it the sound of weeping
and the cry of distress.
20 No more shall there be in it
an infant who lives but a few days,
or an old man who does not fill out his days,
for [o]the young man shall die a hundred years old,
and [p]the sinner a hundred years old shall be accursed.
21 [q]They shall build houses and inhabit them;
they shall plant vineyards and eat their fruit.
22 [q]They shall not build and another inhabit;
they shall not plant and another eat;
[r]for like the days of a tree shall the days of my people be,
and my chosen shall long enjoy[1] the work of their hands.
23 [s]They shall not labor in vain
[t]or bear children for calamity,[2]
for [u]they shall be the offspring of the blessed of the LORD,
and their descendants with them.
24 [v]Before they call I will answer;
[w]while they are yet speaking I will hear.

17 [k]ch. 66:22; 2 Pet. 3:13; Rev. 21:1 18 [l][Jer. 31:7] 19 [m]ch. 62:5; 66:10 [n]ch. 35:10; Rev. 21:4 20 [o][Prov. 3:2] [p]Eccles. 8:12 21 [q]Ezek. 28:26; [Deut. 28:30] 22 [q][See ver. 21 above] [r]See Ps. 92:12-14 23 [s]ch. 49:4 [t][Deut. 28:41] [u]ch. 61:9; See Ps. 115:12-15 24 [v][Ps. 32:5] [w][Dan. 9:21]

[1] Hebrew *shall wear out* [2] Or *for sudden terror*

65:11 Fortune . . . Destiny. Syrian gods.

65:15 for a curse. This is an even worse fate than being forgotten.

another name. See note 62:2.

65:16 God of truth. the Hebrew word translated "truth" is "amen"; see 2 Cor. 1:20; Rev. 3:14; also John 14:6; 1 John 5:20.

65:17 new heavens and a new earth. This prophecy awaits the Second Coming of Christ (2 Pet. 3:13; Rev. 21:1). In the meantime through faith the saints experience in part the blessing of the age to come (42:9; 43:19 and notes). See "Heaven" at Rev. 21:1.

the former. The adversities and disgrace brought on by sin (41:22 note).

65:18 create Jerusalem. It will be altogether new with no remembrance of the old (Rev. 21:1, 2).

65:20 infant . . . old man. Premature death of infants or persons in mid-career can provoke the thought that life is meaningless. Such early death, as also the transfer of one person's reward to another person who did not earn it (v. 22), is part of God's judgment on sin. God promises to remove this curse from His people (Amos 5:11 note).

25 [x]The wolf and the lamb shall graze
together;
the lion shall eat straw like the ox,
and [y]dust shall be the serpent's food.
[z]They shall not hurt or destroy
in all my holy mountain,"
says the LORD.

The Humble and Contrite in Spirit

66 [a]Thus says the LORD:
[b]"Heaven is my throne,
and the earth is my footstool;
what is the house that you would
build for me,
and what is the place of my rest?
2 [c]All these things my hand has made,
and so all these things came to be,
declares the LORD.
[d]But this is the one to whom I will look:
he who is humble and contrite in
spirit
and trembles at my word.
3 [e]"He who slaughters an ox is like one
who kills a man;
he who sacrifices a lamb, like one
who breaks a dog's neck;
he who presents a grain offering, like
one who offers [f]pig's blood;
he who makes a memorial offering
of frankincense, like one who
blesses an idol.
[g]These have chosen their own ways,
and their soul delights in their
abominations;
4 [h]I also will choose harsh treatment for
them
and bring [i]their fears upon them,
[j]because when I called, no one
answered,
when I spoke they did not listen;
[k]but they did what was evil in my eyes
and chose that in which I did not
delight."

5 Hear the word of the LORD,
you who tremble at his word:
"Your brothers who hate you
and cast you out for my name's
sake
have said, [l]'Let the LORD be
glorified,
that we may see your joy';
but it is they who shall be put to
shame.

6 "The sound of an uproar from the
city!
A sound from the temple!
The sound of the LORD,
[m]rendering recompense to his
enemies!

Rejoice with Jerusalem

7 [n]"Before she was in labor
she gave birth;
before her pain came upon her
she delivered a son.
8 Who has heard such a thing?
Who has seen such things?
Shall a land be born in
one day?
Shall a nation be brought forth in
one moment?
For [n]as soon as Zion was in labor
she brought forth her
children.
9 Shall I bring to the point of birth and
not cause to bring forth?"
says the LORD;
"shall I, who cause to bring forth,
shut the womb?"
says your God.

10 [o]"Rejoice with Jerusalem, and be glad
for her,
all you who love her;
rejoice with her in joy,
all you who mourn over her;

25 [x]ch. 11:6, 7 [y]Gen. 3:14; Mic. 7:17 [z]ch. 11:9
Chapter 66
1 [a]Cited Acts 7:40, 50; [1 Kin. 8:27; Acts 17:24] [b][Matt. 5:34, 35]
2 [c][1 Chr. 29:14] [d]ch. 57:15; Ps. 34:18
3 [e]ch. 1:11 [f]See ch. 65:4 [g]Jer. 7:24
4 [h][ch. 30:16] [i][ch. 51:12] [j]See ch. 65:12 [k][Jer. 7:31]
5 [l]ch. 5:19
6 [m]ch. 50:18; 63:4; 65:6
7 [n]See ch. 13:8
8 [n][See ver. 7 above]
10 [o]ch. 65:19

65:25 dust shall be the serpent's food. This alludes to Gen. 3:14. The curse on Satan is carried out.

66:1 See theological note "The Spiritual Nature of God" on next page.

66:3–4 The Lord hates empty religious expressions as much as paganism (Jer. 7:21–23 note).

66:3 kills a man. This may be an allusion to child sacrifice (cf. Jer. 7:31; Ezek. 23:39).

breaks a dog's neck. Only certain animals were prescribed for sacrifice. The dog was not even permitted for food (56:10 note; Lev. 11:26).

pig's blood. See 65:4.

66:5 who hate you. The opposition reflected in ch. 65 between God's servants and nominal Israel has intensified.

Let . . . joy. Such an expression of praise by rebellious people is hypocritical righteousness.

shall be put to shame. Humiliation is the fate of the persecutors. See v. 10 for the fate of the persecuted.

66:7 Before . . . birth. The birth of the new community will be sudden, and no human effort will contribute to it. Christ laid the foundation of the church in His lifetime, especially in the week of His death and resurrection (John 2:19).

66:9 The purposes of God will not be frustrated, or begun only to be left unfinished.

11 that you may nurse and be satisfied
from her consoling breast;
that you may drink deeply with delight
from her glorious abundance."[1]

12 For thus says the LORD:
[p]"Behold, I will extend peace to her
like a river,
and the glory of the nations like an
overflowing stream;
and [q]you shall nurse, you shall be
carried upon her hip,
and bounced upon her knees.
13 As one whom his mother comforts,
so [r]I will comfort you;
you shall be comforted in Jerusalem.
14 You shall see, and your heart shall
rejoice;
[s]your bones shall flourish like the
grass;
and [t]the hand of the LORD shall be
known to his servants,
and he shall show his indignation
against his enemies.

Final Judgment and Glory of the LORD

15 "For behold, [u]the LORD will come in fire,
and [v]his chariots like the whirlwind,
to render his anger in fury,
and his rebuke with flames of fire.

12 [p][ch. 48:18] [q]ch. 60:16
13 [r]ch. 51:12; [ch. 35:10]
14 [s]ch. 58:11 [t][Ezra 8:22, 31]
15 [u]ch. 33:14; Mal. 3:1, 2; [2 Thess. 1:7, 8] [v]Ps. 68:17

[1] Or *breast*

The Spiritual Nature of God

"God is Spirit," said Jesus to the Samaritan woman at the well (John 4:24). Though fully personal, God does not live in and through a body as we do, and so is not subject to the limits of space and time. Although nothing created can be omnipresent, God is everywhere in His fullness continually. All created things are limited by time, but for God there is no "present moment" into which He is locked as we are.

Theologians refer to God's freedom from limits and bounds as His infinity and His immensity (1 Kin. 8:27; Is. 40:12–26; 66:1). God upholds everything in being, and He has everything everywhere always before His mind, in its own relation to His all-inclusive plan and purpose for every thing and every person in His world (Dan. 4:34–35; Eph. 1:11).

God is immutable, or unchangeable. Nothing can increase or diminish God's perfection, and He does not change for the better or the worse. Because He is not in time He is not subject to change as creatures are (2 Pet. 3:8). Yet He is active in His world all the time, constantly making new things spring forth (Is. 42:9; 2 Cor. 5:17; Rev. 21:5). In all His works He expresses His perfect character with perfect consistency. True to His unchangeable character, He will fulfill every word He has spoken and the plans He has made (Num. 23:19; Ps. 33:11; Mal. 3:6; James 1:16–18). His immutability explains why, when people change their attitude to Him, He changes His attitude to them (Gen. 6:5–7; Ex. 32:9–14; 1 Sam. 15:11; Jon. 3:10).

God's unchangeable perfection does not mean He is impassive and unfeeling, but what He feels is a matter of His own choice, and is included in the unity of His infinite being. God is not driven by His reaction to events or the presence of feelings that arise within Him. But many scriptures represent God as having emotions, such as joy, sorrow, anger, and delight. It is a great mistake to forget that God feels—though of necessity in a way that transcends a finite being's experience of emotion.

All God's thoughts and actions involve the whole of Him; He is undivided in Himself, not composed of parts. This attribute is called His simplicity. God is not distracted, divided by competing interests, or obliged to ration His attention. He simultaneously gives total and undivided attention, not just to one thing at a time, but to everything and everyone anywhere in space or time (cf. Matt. 10:29–30).

The God who is Spirit must be worshiped in spirit and in truth (John 4:24). Worship "in spirit" means worship from a heart renewed by the Holy Spirit. No rituals, ceremony, or devotional formality is true worship without a willing heart, which the Holy Spirit alone can prepare. "In truth" means on the basis of God's revelation culminating in the incarnate Word, Jesus Christ, who is the truth (John 14:6). In the Spirit, "the LORD is near to all who call on him, to all who call on him in truth," wherever they may be (Ps. 145:18; cf. Heb. 4:14–16). Through the revelation of Christ, God invites limited, sinful creatures to claim Him who is the eternal, unchangeable God, as their own God. God is committed to His people through a covenant of divine promises as sure as His own faithfulness (Heb. 6:17, 18).

66:11 nurse . . . satisfied. See note 60:16.

66:12 her. Mother Jerusalem (vv. 8, 10).

66:13 mother. The Lord likens His tender love to that of a mother.

66:15 fire . . . whirlwind. These depict lightning and storm clouds respectively (Deut. 33:26; Ps. 18:10; Jer. 4:13), common accompaniments of God's appearance (10:17, 18; 29:6; Ezek. 32:6–8 note). Isaiah prayed for God to come in this way to bring judgment (64:1–3).

16 For [w]by fire [x]will the LORD enter into
judgment,
and by his sword, with all flesh;
and those slain by the LORD shall
be many.

17 [y]"Those who sanctify and purify themselves to go into the gardens, following one
in the midst, [z]eating pig's flesh and the
abomination and mice, shall come to an
end together, declares the LORD.

18 "For I know[1] their works and their
thoughts, and the time is coming[2] [a]to gather all nations and tongues. And they shall
come and shall see my glory, 19 [a]and I will
set a sign among them. And from them [b]I
will send survivors to the nations, to
[c]Tarshish, [d]Pul, and [d]Lud, who draw the
bow, to [e]Tubal and [e]Javan, [f]to the coastlands afar off, [g]that have not heard my fame
or seen my glory. And they shall declare my
glory among the nations. 20 [h]And they shall
bring all your brothers from all the nations
[i]as an offering to the LORD, on horses and in
chariots and in litters and on mules and on

16 [w]Ps. 97:3 [x]Joel 3:2
17 [y]ch. 65:3, 5 [z]See ch. 65:4
18 [a]ch. 2:2; Zech. 14:16
19 [b]ch. 45:20 [c]1 Kin. 10:22 [d]Jer. 46:9; Ezek. 27:10 [e]Gen. 10:2; Ezek. 27:13 [f]Gen. 10:5 [g][Rom. 15:20, 21]
20 [h]See ch. 14:2; 49:22 [i][Rom. 15:16]
21 [j]ch. 61:6; Ex. 19:6; [1 Pet. 2:9; Rev. 1:6]
22 [k]See ch. 65:17 [l]ch. 53:10; [Ps. 89:29]
23 [m][Zech. 14:16; Ps. 86:9]
24 [n]Mark 9:18 [o][Rev. 21:8]

dromedaries, to my holy mountain Jerusalem, says the LORD, just as the Israelites
bring their grain offering in a clean vessel to
the house of the LORD. 21 [j]And some of them
also I will take for priests and for Levites,
says the LORD.

22 "For as [k]the new heavens and the
new earth
that I make
shall remain before me, says the
LORD,
so [l]shall your offspring and your
name remain.
23 [m]From new moon to new moon,
and from Sabbath to Sabbath,
all flesh shall come to worship
before me,
declares the LORD.

24 "And they shall go out and look on the
dead bodies of the men who have rebelled
against me. For [n]their worm shall not die,
[o]their fire shall not be quenched, and they
shall be an abhorrence to all flesh."

1 Septuagint, Syriac; Hebrew lacks *know* 2 Hebrew *and it is coming*

66:16 sword. The Lord appears as a warrior (27:1; 34:5; Rev. 19:11–18). See notes 9:6; 13:4; 40:10; 42:13.

66:17 gardens . . . pig's flesh . . . abomination. See v. 3; 65:2–5.

66:18 their works and their thoughts. Probably the works and thoughts of those to be gathered.

all nations and tongues. There will be universal acknowledgement of the Lord's kingdom (Zech. 8:23; Rev. 7:9, 10).

glory. This is God's glory in His temple (Ezek. 11:22, 23; 44:4).

66:19 sign. This "sign" is probably remarkable acts of judgment on the false worshipers as the remnant is delivered from among them.

survivors. The true worshipers who survive persecution (v. 5; Matt. 24:9–14) bring God's glory to the nations (v. 18).

Tarshish. See note 23:5.

Pul, and Lud. In North Africa.

Tubal. South of the Black Sea in modern Turkey (Ezek. 38:2, 3; 39:1).

Javan. The people of Asia Minor or Greece (Ezek. 27:13, 19; Joel 3:6).

declare . . . nations. The Gentiles will submit themselves to the Lord and rejoice in His mighty acts (24:16 note).

66:20 all your brothers. The Gentiles will bring dispersed Israel back to the temple (43:5; 60:4, 9; Rom. 11:11–14).

66:22 new heavens . . . new earth. See note 65:17 (cf. 2 Pet. 3:13; Rev. 21:1).

your offspring and your name. The people of God will never again suffer reproach, but will enjoy everlasting glory (43:1 note; 65:18, 19; cf. Jer. 31:35, 36).

66:23 new moon . . . Sabbath. There will be universal worship of God at His appointed time (cf. Zech. 14:16).

66:24 worm . . . fire. Jerusalem's garbage dump became symbolic of perpetual punishment and anguish (30:33 note; Mark 9:47, 48).

THE BOOK OF

Jeremiah

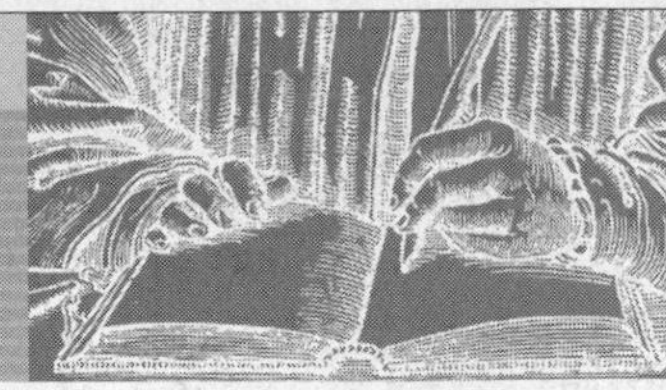

AUTHOR

Jeremiah prophesied during the reigns of the last kings of Judah: Josiah (640–609 B.C.), Jehoahaz (609), Jehoiakim (609–598), Jehoiachin (598–597) and Zedekiah (597–586). The kingdom of Judah ended in the exile of most of its people to Babylon, chiefly as a result of two invasions by King Nebuchadnezzar (597 and 586 B.C.), though the first deportations occurred as early as 605 (Dan. 1:1 note). The northern kingdom, Israel, had been conquered by the Assyrians a century before Jeremiah began his ministry. Assyria itself fell to Babylon in 612 B.C., and the northern kingdom was never restored. Jeremiah announced the coming judgment of God on His people and lived to see his prophecy fulfilled.

This prophet was also a priest, from the priestly town of Anathoth in the territory of Benjamin (1:1 note). A lonely figure because of his unpopular message (15:17), he was divinely forbidden to marry as a sign of the imminent cessation of normal life (16:2). He also found himself opposed to the authorities in the land and to all classes of people (26:8). As a result, his life was in serious danger more than once (11:18–23; 18:18; 26:8; 36:19; 38:6). His message placed him in the thick of political events. He was sought out especially by King Zedekiah for his comments on the likely outcome of the final onslaught of the approaching Babylonian armies (37:3, 17). Politically, it was a turbulent time as Egypt and Babylon contested the region. Jeremiah repeatedly prophesied a Babylonian victory, proclaiming that the Lord was using Nebuchadnezzar as His scourge. When Jerusalem fell, the Babylonian commander had a special commission from Nebuchadnezzar himself for the care of the prophet, whose fame had spread to the heart of the empire (39:11–14).

DATE AND OCCASION

The background to the prophecy is the long struggle in Judah between the idolatrous worship of foreign gods, deeply embedded since the reign of Manasseh (696–642 B.C.), and the worship of the Lord, which Josiah attempted to restore in his reform (see 2 Kin. 22; 23). The reform began in 628 B.C. (see 2 Chr. 34:3 note) and was given fresh impetus by the discovery of the Book of the Law in 621 B.C. (2 Kin. 22:8). Jeremiah's call came in 626 B.C. (1:2 note). His early ministry coincides with Josiah's reform. Jeremiah testifies, however, to the reform's failure to make significant impact on the people's lives, as the religious abuses of Manasseh reemerged under Josiah's successors.

CHARACTERISTICS AND THEMES

Jeremiah's message moved through phases that do not correspond exactly to the structure of the book: (a) He called Judah to repent and avoid judgment that would otherwise come (e.g., 7:1–15). (b) He announced that the time for repentance was past, since judgment was now determined against the people (19:10, 11 notes). Judgment is the dominant note in the book, and is understood as the invocation of the final curse of the covenant, namely, loss of the Promised Land (Lev. 26:31–33; Deut. 28:49–68). (c) The Lord would save His people, or a remnant of them, through the exile (24:4–7 notes). Though the Babylonians would prevail over Judah at the Lord's command, this would be for a limited time only—Babylon, in its turn, would also fall (25:9, 11, 12). This prophecy was fulfilled in 539 B.C., when Babylon was defeated by an alliance of Persians and Medes under Cyrus, paving the way for the exiles of Judah to return (50:3; 51:1, 27, 28; 2 Chr. 36:20–23). This promise of eventual deliverance was Jeremiah's answer to the false prophets who had constantly challenged his message of judgment (28:1–4).

Jeremiah also had a message of salvation, but only on the other side of judgment (29:11–14). That message is crystallized in the prophecy of the new covenant (central text: 31:31–34). The new covenant prophecy is built around the main ingredients of the Mosaic covenant at Sinai: it spoke of God's desire to have a relationship with His chosen people, and of the requirement upon them to return His love with obedience (Ex. 19:3–6; Deut. 7:6–11). The new covenant speaks of the empowerment of God's people to obey Him (31:33 note; 32:40 note). Although it is promised in national terms (31:31 and note), it is something new, which the New Testament shows to be fulfilled in the greater "Israel of God" (Gal. 6:16) through Christ (22:30 note; 23:5 note; 30:9; 31:33 note; 33:18 note).

Jeremiah reveals his personal involvement with his message more fully than the other prophets (but cf. Is. 22:4; Mic. 1:8, 9), and he feels the agony of the people at the approach of the Babylonian armies, even before they feel it themselves (4:19–21; 10:19–22; 14:19–22). He also feels the passion of the Lord concerning the sin he witnesses (8:21–9:3 notes). His role is mediatorial in nature. This role is most poignant in the series of passages often referred to as the prophet's "Confessions" (11:18–20; 12:1–4; 15:10–18; 17:14–18; 18:19–23; 20:7–18). In these he expresses his anguish at the great burden of his prophetic calling, prays for vengeance on his personal enemies, and even accuses the Lord of having forced or deceived him (15:18; 20:7). Some of these prayers elicit answers from the Lord containing rebuke and reassurance (11:21–23; 12:5, 6; 15:19–21). The reassurance to Jeremiah in 15:19–21 is later echoed in a prayer of Ephraim, which receives its own answer (31:18–20). The Lord's good intention toward Jeremiah, therefore, becomes an earnest of His intended faithfulness to the whole people, through and beyond the imminent judgment.

The book contains various materials that make reading it as a continually unfolding narrative difficult. Much of Jeremiah comprises poetic oracles spoken by the prophet (e.g., chs. 2–6). At other times an argument is developed in a style that is sermonic or prosaic (e.g., 7:1–15). There is also third-person narrative about the prophet himself, presumably penned by someone else (e.g., 37–45), and ch. 52 happens to be an editorial appendix (see the last sentence of 51:64). The composition is therefore complicated, as might be expected from the length of Jeremiah's ministry alone (25:3), and conveys the full breadth and force of Jeremiah's ministry from the perspective of the fulfillment of his repeated warnings of coming punishment.

If the work was completed during the Exile, the latest historical point reached in the book, the purpose would be to chasten the exiles by encouraging them to ponder the meaning of their exile. At the same time it seeks to engender hope, since the prophet who had pronounced judgment, and had been proven right, had also preached a message of Judah's eventual restoration to the land and the nation's privileged relationship with God. Jeremiah evidently was assisted by Baruch in compiling the book, and Baruch may also have recorded the third-person narratives.

A clue to the procedure by which the various prophecies and sermons might have become a book is found in 36:4–6, where Baruch writes down all the words from Jeremiah's mouth. When the scroll is destroyed by Jehoiakim, the Lord commands Jeremiah to rewrite the scroll, with more words added. Reference is also made in 51:60 to Jeremiah recording his prophecies in a book.

The contents of the book are not arranged in chronological order, but rather thematically. Chapters 21–24 are framed by prophecies concerning each of Josiah's successors up to (but excluding) Zedekiah. Similarly chs. 35; 36 refer back to the reign of Jehoiakim, after scenes which involved Zedekiah.

OUTLINE OF JEREMIAH

I. The Call of the Prophet (ch. 1)

II. Oracles Chiefly of Judgment on Judah (chs. 2–20)

- A. *Calls to Repent and Images of Judgment (chs. 2–6)*
- B. *The Lord's Freedom to Judge His People (chs. 7–10)*
- C. *The Covenant Broken: First Confessions (chs. 11–13)*
- D. *The Drought; Jeremiah as Intercessor (chs. 14; 15)*
- E. *Signs of Coming Judgment and a Confession (16:1–17:18)*
- F. *A Sermon About the Sabbath (17:19–27)*
- G. *The Potter, the Lord's Purposes, and the Trials of Jeremiah (chs. 18–20)*

OUTLINE OF JEREMIAH (Cont.)

III. The End of the Davidic Dynasty; Salvation Only Through Exile (chs. 21–24)
- A. *Judgment Against Kings (chs. 21; 22)*
- B. *Judgment Against Prophets (ch. 23)*
- C. *The Remaining Figs (ch. 24)*

IV. The Necessity of Babylonian Dominance over the Nations (chs. 25–29)
- A. *Seventy Years of Captivity (ch. 25)*
- B. *Arrest and Trial of Jeremiah (ch. 26)*
- C. *The False Prophets (chs. 27–29)*

V. Promises of Restoration (chs. 30–33)
- A. *Return to the Land (ch. 30)*
- B. *The New Covenant (ch. 31)*
- C. *Certainty of the Lord's Deliverance (chs. 32; 33)*

VI. Jerusalem's Last Days (chs. 34–39)
- A. *Rejection of the Word of the Lord (chs. 34–36)*
- B. *Imprisonments of Jeremiah (chs. 37; 38)*
- C. *The Fall of Jerusalem (ch. 39)*

VII. The Aftermath of the Fall of Jerusalem (chs. 40–45)
- A. *The Governorship and Assassination of Gedaliah (40:1–41:10)*
- B. *The Flight to Egypt; Prophecies There (41:11–44:30)*
- C. *The Promise to Baruch (ch. 45)*

VIII. Oracles of Judgment Against the Nations (chs. 46–51)
- A. *Against Egypt (ch. 46)*
- B. *Against Philistia (ch. 47)*
- C. *Against Moab (ch. 48)*
- D. *Against Ammon (49:1–6)*
- E. *Against Edom (49:7–22)*
- F. *Against Damascus (49:23–27)*
- G. *Against Arabian Tribes (49:28–33)*
- H. *Against Elam (49:34–39)*
- I. *Against Babylon (chs. 50; 51)*

IX. Appendix: the Fall of Jerusalem (ch. 52)

1 The words of Jeremiah, the son of
Hilkiah, one [a]of the priests who were
in [b]Anathoth in the land of Benjamin, **2** to
whom the word of the LORD came in the
days of [c]Josiah the son of Amon, king of
Judah, in [d]the thirteenth year of his reign.
3 It came also in the days of [e]Jehoiakim the
son of Josiah, king of Judah, and [f]until the
end of the eleventh year of [g]Zedekiah,
the son of Josiah, king of Judah, [h]until the
captivity of Jerusalem in the fifth month.

The Call of Jeremiah

4 Now the word of the LORD came to me,
saying,

5 [i]"Before I formed you in the womb I
knew you,
and before you were born [j]I
consecrated you;
I appointed you a prophet [k]to the
nations."

6 Then I said, "Ah, Lord GOD! Behold, [l]I do
not know how to speak, [m]for I am only a
youth." **7** But the LORD said to me,

"Do not say, 'I am only a youth';
for to all to whom I send you, you
shall go,
and [n]whatever I command you, you
shall speak.
8 [o]Do not be afraid of them,
[p]for I am with you to deliver you,
declares the LORD."

Chapter 1
1 [a]Ezek. 1:3 [b]ch. 29:27; 32:7; Josh. 21:18
2 [c]See 2 Kin. 22; 23:1-30 [d]ch. 25:3; 36:2
3 [e]ch. 25:1; 36:1; See 2 Kin. 23:34–24:6 [f]ch. 39:2 [g]See 2 Kin. 24:17–25:7 [h]See 2 Kin. 25:8-11
5 [i]See Isai. 44:2 [j][John 10:36] [k][Isai. 49:6]; See ch. 25:15-29; ch. 46–51
6 [l][Ex. 4:10] [m][1 Kin. 3:7]
7 [n]ver. 17; Ezek. 2:7 **8** [o]Ezek. 2:6; 3:9 [p]ch. 15:20; See Ex. 3:12

1:1–19 God calls Jeremiah to his prophetic ministry of announcing divine judgment on Judah for idolatry.

1:1–3 Jeremiah prophesied over a forty-year period up to the Babylonian exile of the people of Judah. During this time the word of the Lord came to him repeatedly (25:3).

1:1 priests who were in Anathoth. Anathoth was a priestly city from early times (Josh. 21:17, 18); cf. 11:21–23. Jeremiah was both a prophet and a priest.

1:2 to whom the word of the LORD came. This phrase often opens prophetic books (cf. Hos. 1:1; Joel 1:1; Mic. 1:1). Jeremiah's recorded words, therefore, are God's words.

Josiah. He was a godly king who undertook a major religious reform beginning in 628 B.C. (2 Kin. 22; 23; 2 Chr. 34; 35); Jeremiah approves of him (22:15, 16), though he makes few specific references to the reform.

thirteenth year. That is, 626 B.C.

1:5 I formed you . . . knew you. God's creation and election of Jeremiah belong together (for the verb "know" in the sense of "choose," see Gen. 18:19; Amos 3:2). This setting apart before birth is the ground of Jeremiah's prophetic standing. Compare also Moses, whose birth narrative (Ex. 2) has the same meaning, and Paul (Gal. 1:15).

to the nations. Jeremiah's message is chiefly for Judah, but he has words of judgment for other nations as well (25:8–37; 46–51).

1:6 I do not know how to speak. Moses made a similar protest (Ex. 4:10).

youth. This denotes a disqualifying immaturity (1 Kin. 3:7).

1:8 Do not be afraid. The reassurance necessarily recurs (10:5; 30:10; cf. Is. 43:1; Luke 12:32).

I am with you. These words are the Lord's essential promise to His people (Ex. 3:12; Is. 7:14; Matt. 1:23; 28:20).

9 [q]Then the LORD put out his hand and
[r]touched my mouth. And the LORD said to
me,

"Behold, I have put [s]my words in your
mouth.
10 See, I have set you this day [k]over
nations and over kingdoms,
[t]to pluck up and to break down,
to destroy and to overthrow,
to build and to plant."

11 And the word of the LORD came to me,
saying, [u]"Jeremiah, what do you see?" And
I said, "I see an almond[1] branch." 12 Then
the LORD said to me, "You have seen well,
for I am watching over my word to perform
it."

13 The word of the LORD came to me a
second time, saying, "What do you see?"
And I said, "I see [v]a boiling pot, facing
away [w]from the north." 14 Then the LORD
said to me, [w]"Out of the north disaster[2]
shall be let loose upon all the inhabitants
of the land. 15 For behold, [x]I am calling all
the tribes of the kingdoms of the north,
declares the LORD, [y]and they shall come,
and every one shall set his throne at the
entrance of the gates of Jerusalem, against
all its walls all around and against all the
cities of Judah. 16 And [z]I will declare my
judgments against them, for all their evil
[a]in forsaking me. [b]They have made offerings to other gods and [c]worshiped the
works of their own hands. 17 But you,
[d]dress yourself for work;[3] arise, and [e]say to
them everything that I command you. [f]Do
not be dismayed by them, lest I dismay you
before them. 18 And I, behold, I make you
this day [g]a fortified city, [h]an iron pillar, and
[i]bronze walls, against the whole land,
against the kings of Judah, its officials, its
priests, and the people of the land. 19 [i]They
will fight against you, but they shall not
prevail against you, for [j]I am with you,
declares the LORD, to deliver you."

Israel Forsakes the LORD

2 The word of the LORD came to me, saying, 2 "Go and proclaim in the hearing
of Jerusalem, Thus says the LORD,

"I remember the devotion of [k]your
youth,
your love [l]as a bride,
[m]how you followed me in the
wilderness,
[n]in a land not sown.
3 [o]Israel was holy to the LORD,
[p]the firstfruits of his harvest.
[q]All who ate of it incurred guilt;
disaster came upon them,
declares the LORD."

4 Hear the word of the LORD, O house of
Jacob, and all the clans of the house of
Israel. 5 Thus says the LORD:

[r]"What wrong did your fathers find
in me
that they went far from me,
[s]and went after [t]worthlessness, and
became worthless?

1 *Almond* sounds like the Hebrew for *watching* (compare verse 12)
2 The Hebrew word can mean *evil, harm,* or *disaster,* depending on context; so throughout Jeremiah 3 Hebrew *gird up your loins*

9 [q][Ezek. 2:9] [r][Isai. 6:7] [s]ch. 5:14
10 [k][See ver. 5 above] [t]ch. 18:7; 31:28; 45:4; [2 Cor. 10:4, 5]
11 [u][Amos 7:8]
13 [v]Ezek. 24:3; [Ezek. 22:21] [w]ch. 4:6; 6:1; 10:22
14 [w][See ver. 13 above]
15 [x][ch. 25:9] [y][ch. 39:3; 43:10]
16 [z]ch. 4:12 [a]ch. 19:4; 22:9 [b]ch. 7:9; 44:3 [c]ch. 25:6, 7; Isai. 2:8; Acts 7:41
17 [d][1 Kin. 18:46; 1 Pet. 1:13] [e]ver. 7 [f]ver. 8; Ezek. 3:9
18 [g][Isai. 50:7] [h]Rev. 3:12 [i]ch. 15:20; [ch. 6:27]
19 [i][See ver. 18 above] [j]ver. 8; [Acts 18:9, 10]
Chapter 2
2 [k]ch. 3:4 [l]Ezek. 16:8, 43, 60; [Rev. 2:4] [m]Deut. 2:7 [n]Deut. 8:2, 3
3 [o]Ex. 28:36; [Ex. 19:5, 6] [p]James 1:18; [Ex. 4:22] [q]ch. 12:14; Ezek. 25:12, 13; [Gen. 12:3]
5 [r]ver. 31; Isai. 5:4; Mic. 6:3 [s]2 Kin. 17:15 [t]ch. 10:15; 14:22; 16:19

1:9 touched my mouth. This indicates that Jeremiah was consecrated to speak the Lord's words (Is. 6:7).

words in your mouth. See Ex. 4:15; 2 Pet. 1:21.

1:10 pluck up . . . plant. The images stress Jeremiah's message of destruction, while also foreshadowing the Lord's reconstruction. The narrative of his call prepares for the prophet's ministry in all its variety. God's word accomplishes God's purposes (Is. 55:11).

1:11 word. The term can also designate revelatory visions (Amos 7:8).

1:13, 14 boiling . . . let loose. The second vision, like the first, affirms the inevitability of the imminent judgment on Judah. Jeremiah must himself believe the message in order to proclaim it.

1:14 north. Though Babylon lay to the east, their route of march would bring them from the north.

1:16 judgments. Judgment is a work of God, in relation to His covenant people (11:2), in which He implements the curses of the covenant (Deut. 28:15–68).

forsaking me . . . other gods. Judah's basic sin is apostasy; the central issue in the book is faithfulness to God.

made offerings. See note 11:13.

works of their own hands. Ironic polemic (Is. 46:6).

1:17 dress yourself. Lit. "gird up your loin," adjust the robe in preparation for battle or other activities (1 Kin. 18:46; 1 Pet. 1:13).

1:18 kings . . . land. Jeremiah's accusation will embrace the whole society of Judah, from greatest to least.

2:1–6:30 Jeremiah uses a number of vivid images (such as comparing Judah to a wild donkey and a prostitute) to indict Judah for unfaithfulness to God (2:1–3:5) and to warn of certain judgment if the nation will not repent and return to God (3:6–6:30).

2:2 Jerusalem. In Hebrew cities are personified as feminine (7:29 note).

devotion. On the Hebrew word (*ḥesed*), see Ps. 36:5 note.

youth . . . bride. Israel's early relationship with the Lord in the wilderness after the exodus from Egypt is remembered as pure and devoted, like a bride's with her groom. See Hos. 2:14–16 for a similar image.

2:3 holy . . . firstfruits. These terms are drawn from the life of worship. As holy, Israel was dedicated to the Lord (Ezek. 22:26); a "firstfruit" is something belonging specifically to the Lord (Deut. 26:2; Hos. 9:10).

incurred guilt. The offense resulted from unauthorized handling of holy things.

6 They did not say, [u]'Where is the
Lord
who brought us up from the land
of Egypt,
who led us [v]in the wilderness,
in a land of deserts and pits,
in a land of drought and deep
darkness,
in a land that none passes
through,
where no man dwells?'
7 [w]And I brought you into a plentiful
land
to enjoy its fruits and its good
things.
But when you came in, [x]you defiled
my land
and made my heritage an
abomination.
8 The priests did not say, 'Where is the
Lord?'
[y]Those who handle the law did not
know me;
[z]the shepherds[1] transgressed
against me;
[a]the prophets prophesied by Baal
and went after [b]things that do not
profit.
9 "Therefore [c]I still contend with you,
declares the Lord,
and [d]with your children's children
I will contend.
10 For cross to the coasts of [e]Cyprus
and see,
or send to [f]Kedar and examine
with care;
see if there has been such a thing.
11 [g]Has a nation changed its gods,
[h]even though they are no gods?
But my people [i]have changed their
glory
for [b]that which does not profit.
12 Be appalled, [j]O heavens, at this;
be shocked, be utterly desolate,
declares the Lord,
13 for my people have committed two
evils:
[k]they have forsaken [l]me,
the fountain of [m]living waters,
and hewed out cisterns for
themselves,
broken cisterns that can hold no
water.
14 [n]"Is Israel a slave? Is he a homeborn
servant?
Why then has he become a prey?
15 [o]The lions have roared against him;
they have roared loudly.
They have made his land a waste;
his cities are in ruins, [p]without
inhabitant.
16 Moreover, the men of [q]Memphis and
[r]Tahpanhes
[s]have shaved[2] the crown of your
head.
17 [t]Have you not brought this upon
yourself
by forsaking the Lord your God,
when [u]he led you in the way?
18 [v]And now what do you gain by going
to Egypt
to drink the waters of [w]the Nile?
[x]Or what do you gain by going to
Assyria
to drink the waters of [y]the
Euphrates?

6 [u][Isai. 63:11-13; Hos. 13:4, 5] [v]Deut. 8:15; 32:10 **7** [w]See Deut. 8:7-10 [x]Ps. 106:38; [Lev. 18:24, 25] **8** [y]ch. 18:18; [Mal. 2:7; Rom. 2:20] [z][ch. 5:5] [a]ch. 23:13; [ch. 5:31] [b][Hab. 2:18] **9** [c]ver. 35; Ezek. 17:20; 20:35, 36 [d]Ex. 20:5, 6 **10** [e]See Gen. 10:4 [f]See Isai. 21:16 **11** [g][Mic. 4:5]; See ch. 18:13-15 [h]ch. 16:20; Isai. 37:19; Gal. 4:8 [i]Ps. 106:20 [b][See ver. 8 above] **12** [j]Isai. 1:2 **13** [k]ch. 17:13 [l]Ps. 36:9 [m]John 4:10 **14** [n][Ex. 4:22] **15** [o]ch. 4:7; Isai. 5:29 [p]ch. 9:11; 46:19 **16** [q]ch. 44:1; 46:14; Ezek. 30:16 [r]ch. 43:7-9 [s][Deut. 33:20] **17** [t]ch. 4:18 [u]ver. 6 **18** [v]ver. 36; Isai. 30:1, 2; 31:1 [w]Isai. 23:3 [x][Hos. 7:11] [y]Gen. 31:21; Isai. 7:20; 8:7

[1] Or *rulers* [2] Hebrew *grazed*

2:7 defiled my land . . . my heritage. See Deut. 21:23. God's holy people (Deut. 7:6) dwell in the land He gave them for a heritage. The land can be defiled, or in religious terms be made "unclean," by sin, because it remains God's possession. See Lev. 25:23.

2:8 priests. These may also be "those who handle the law," (cf. 18:18; Deut. 31:9), or the latter may be a scribal group (8:8).

shepherds. A figure often used for rulers (23:1–4).

prophets. These prophets were an official group that Jeremiah frequently opposes for their apostasy (23:9–40; 28).

2:9 I still contend with you. The courtroom metaphor is resumed (v. 5; Hos. 4:1; Mic. 6:1, 2).

2:10 Cyprus . . . Kedar. These locations represent west and east respectively. The appeal takes its meaning from the special position of Israel, namely their covenant with the Lord, and Jeremiah's assertion that the nation's gods are impotent.

2:12 O heavens. See also Is. 1:2. Heaven and earth serve as witnesses of the covenant (Deut. 30:19; 31:28; 32:1).

2:13 two evils. Jeremiah stresses the seriousness of Judah's sin.

waters. God alone provides life-giving water (Is. 55:1; John 4:10, 7:37–39).

broken cisterns. The gods they took for themselves were useless, empty.

2:15 lions. These are Israel's enemies (4:7), announcing desolation.

2:16 Memphis . . . Tahpanhes. Egyptian cities. Egypt and Babylon fought over who would own Israel, 609 to 605 B.C.

crown. Possibly, a reference to Josiah, who was killed by Pharaoh Neco at the battle of Megiddo in 609 B.C. (2 Kin. 23:29).

2:18 Egypt . . . Assyria. One of Israel's and Judah's besetting sins was to seek help from political alliances, rather than the Lord (Hos. 12:1).

waters. Note the boasts of the Assyrian field commander to be a more reliable provider of basic needs than the Lord (2 Kin. 18:31).

19 [z]Your evil will chastise you,
and [a]your apostasy will reprove you.
Know and see that it is evil and [b]bitter
for [c]you to forsake the LORD your God;
the fear of me is not in you,
declares the Lord GOD of hosts.

20 "For long ago I [d]broke your yoke
and burst your bonds;
but you said, [e]'I will not serve.'
yes, [f]on every high hill
and under every green tree
you bowed down [g]like a whore.
21 [h]Yet I planted you a choice vine,
wholly of pure seed.
[i]How then have you turned degenerate
and become a wild vine?
22 Though you wash yourself with lye
and use much soap,
[j]the stain of your guilt is still before me,
declares the Lord GOD.
23 [k]How can you say, 'I am not unclean,
I have not gone after the Baals'?
Look at your way [l]in the valley;
know what you have done—
a restless young camel running here and there,
24 [m]a wild donkey used to the wilderness,
in her heat sniffing the wind!
Who can restrain her lust?
None who seek her need weary themselves;
in her month they will find her.
25 Keep [n]your feet from going unshod
and [o]your throat from thirst.
But you said, 'It is hopeless,
[p]for I have loved foreigners,
and after them I will go.'

26 "As a thief is shamed when caught,
so the house of Israel shall be shamed:
[q]they, their kings, their officials,
their priests, and their prophets,
27 who say to a tree, 'You are my father,'
and to a stone, 'You gave me birth.'
For they have turned their back to me,
and not their face.
But [r]in the time of their trouble they say,
'Arise and save us!'
28 But [s]where are your gods
that you made for yourself?
Let them arise, [t]if they can save you,
in your time of trouble;
for [u]as many as your cities
are your gods, O Judah.

29 "Why do you contend with me?
You have all transgressed against me,
declares the LORD.
30 In vain have I [v]struck your children;
they took no correction;
[w]your own sword devoured your prophets
like a ravening lion.
31 And you, O generation, behold the word of the LORD.
Have I been a wilderness to Israel,
or a land of thick darkness?
Why then do my people say, 'We are free,
we will come no more to you'?
32 [x]Can a virgin forget her ornaments,
or a bride her attire?
Yet [y]my people have forgotten me
days without number.

19 [z]Isai. 3:9; Hos. 5:5 [a]ch. 3:22; 5:6; 14:7 [b]ch. 4:18 [c]ver. 13, 17
20 [d]ch. 5:5; 30:8 [e]ver. 31 [f]ch. 3:2; 17:2 [g]ch. 3:1; Isai. 1:21
21 [h]Ex. 15:17; Ps. 44:2; 80:8; Isai. 5:2 [i]Isai. 5:4; [Deut. 32:32]
22 [j][ch. 17:1]
23 [k]ver. 35 [l]ch. 7:31, 32; 19:2, 6
24 [m]ch. 14:6
25 [n]Deut. 29:5 [o]Ex. 17:6 [p]ch. 3:13; Deut. 32:16
26 [q]ch. 13:13; 32:32; [ch. 8:1]
27 [r]Judg. 10:9, 10; Isai. 26:16
28 [s]Deut. 32:37, 38 [t]Isai. 45:20 [u]ch. 11:13
30 [v]ch. 5:3; Isai. 1:5; 9:13 [w]Neh. 9:26; 1 Thess. 2:15
32 [x]Isai. 3:20; 61:10 [y]ch. 3:21; 18:15; Deut. 32:18; Ps. 106:21; Isai. 17:10; Hos. 8:14

2:20 high hill . . . green tree. See Deut. 12:2; 1 Kin. 14:23. These were typical sites of shrines to the gods of Canaan.

whore. Judah is portrayed as a harlot, unfaithful to the Lord (Ezek. 23:1–8; Hos. 3:1–5; 4:10–14).

2:21 choice vine . . . wild vine. The "vine" metaphor is frequently used for Israel (12:10; Ps. 80:8–16; Is. 5:1–7; Ezek. 17:1–10). Jesus Christ is the true vine, and those who abide in Him are the branches (John 15:1–8).

wild. Lit. "foreign." Foreignness here connotes pagan religious practices.

2:22 wash. Sin is only effectively washed away when there is repentance toward the Lord Himself as the One who cleanses, through the blood of the everlasting covenant (Is. 53:4–6; Heb. 9:11–15; 13:20).

2:23 the valley. Probably this refers to the Hinnom Valley, immediately south of Jerusalem, where abominable worship practices occurred (7:31).

young camel. Characteristically irresolute, ready to follow any fresh impulse.

2:24 wild donkey . . . heat. This metaphor is a picture of lust.

2:28 your gods that . . . your cities. The association of gods with particular localities is a distinguishing feature of pagan religion.

2:32 virgin . . . bride. Such forgetfulness is so unlikely as to be virtually impossible.

my people have forgotten me. See Is. 1:2, 3.

33 "How well you direct your course
to seek love!
So that even to wicked women
you have taught your ways.
34 Also on your skirts is found
[z] the lifeblood of the guiltless poor;
you did not find them [a] breaking in.
Yet in spite of all these things
35 you say, 'I am innocent;
surely his anger has turned from me.'
[b] Behold, I will bring you to judgment
for [c] saying, 'I have not sinned.'
36 [d] How much you go about,
changing your way!
You shall be [e] put to shame by Egypt
as you were put to shame by
Assyria.
37 From it too you will come away
with [f] your hands on your head,
for the LORD has rejected those in
whom you trust,
and you will not prosper by them.

3 [g] "If[1] a man divorces his wife
and she goes from him
and becomes another man's wife,
will he return to her?
[h] Would not that land be greatly
polluted?
[i] You have played the whore with
many lovers;
and would you return to me?
declares the LORD.
2 Lift up your eyes to [j] the bare heights,
and see!
Where have you not been ravished?
[k] By the waysides you have sat
awaiting lovers
like an Arab in the wilderness.
[h] You have polluted the land
with your vile whoredom.
3 [l] Therefore the showers have been
withheld,
and the spring rain has not come;
yet you have [m] the forehead of a
whore;
you refuse to be ashamed.
4 Have you not just now [n] called to me,
'My father, you are the friend of my
youth—
5 [o] will he be angry forever,
will he be indignant to the end?'
Behold, you have spoken,
but you have done all the evil that
you could."

Faithless Israel Called to Repentance

6 The LORD said to me in the days of
[p] King Josiah: "Have you seen what she did,
that faithless one, Israel, [q] how she went up
on every high hill and under every green
tree, and there [i] played the whore? 7 And I
thought, 'After she has done all this she
will return to me,' but she did not return,
and her treacherous [r] sister Judah saw it.
8 She saw that for all the adulteries of that
faithless one, Israel, [s] I had sent her away
with [t] a decree of divorce. [u] Yet her treacherous sister Judah did not fear, but she too
went [i] and played the whore. 9 Because she
took her whoredom lightly, she polluted
the land, committing adultery with [v] stone
and tree. 10 Yet for all this her treacherous
sister Judah did not return to me [w] with her
whole heart, but in pretense, declares the
LORD."

11 And the LORD said to me, [x] "Faithless
Israel has shown herself more righteous
than treacherous Judah. 12 Go, and proclaim these words toward [y] the north, and
say,

[z] "'Return, faithless Israel,
declares the LORD.
I will not look on you in anger,
for [a] I am merciful,
declares the LORD;
[b] I will not be angry forever.

1 Septuagint, Syriac; Hebrew *Saying, "If*

34 [z] ch. 19:4; 2 Kin. 21:16; 24:4; Ps. 106:38 [a] Ex. 22:2
35 [b] Ps. 143:2 [c] Prov. 28:13; 1 John 1:8, 10
36 [d] [ch. 31:22] [e] Isai. 30:3
37 [f] 2 Sam. 13:19
Chapter 3
1 [g] See Deut. 24:1-4 [h] ver. 9; Ps. 106:38 [i] ch. 2:20
2 [j] ch. 3:21, 23; 4:11; 7:29; Num. 23:3 [k] Ezek. 16:25 [h] [See ver. 1 above]
3 [l] ch. 9:12; 14:22; Deut. 28:24 [m] [ch. 6:15]; See Ezek. 3:7, 8
4 [n] [Luke 15:18]
5 [o] Ps. 103:9
6 [p] ch. 1:2 [q] See ch. 2:20 [i] [See ver. 1 above]
7 [r] [Ezek. 16:46; 23:4]
8 [s] 2 Kin. 17:18; [Hos. 1:6, 9] [t] [Matt. 19:7; Mark 10:4]; See Deut. 24:1-4 [u] Ezek. 23:11 [i] [See ver. 1 above]
9 [v] ch. 2:27
10 [w] Hos. 7:14
11 [x] Ezek. 16:51, 52
12 [y] See ver. 18 [z] Prov. 28:13; See Deut. 30:1-10 [a] Ps. 86:5, 15 [b] Ps. 103:9

2:34 lifeblood . . . poor. This refers to the persecution of the weak by the strong (a great theme of Amos; Amos 2:6–8; 4:1).

2:37 hands on your head. A posture for captives of war.

3:1 divorces his wife. The bridal metaphor (2:2) now becomes one of divorce. The underlying law is Deut. 24:1–4; the finality of divorce is the background of the argument here.

3:6 King Josiah. See Introduction: Author; Date and Occasion and note on 1:2.

Israel. The northern kingdom was destroyed in 722 B.C.

played the whore. See "Syncretism and Idolatry" at Hos. 2:13.

3:8 decree of divorce. See note on v. 1. Israel was "divorced" by being deported by Assyria (722 B.C.), an exile from which she did not return.

3:9 stone and tree. This is a reference to idols. See "Syncretism and Idolatry" at Hos. 2:13.

3:12 toward the north. To those already deported by Assyria.

Return, faithless Israel. This call implies both repentance and a physical return to their territory; these two aspects go together in Jeremiah's message of salvation. See note 29:14.

I will not be angry forever. This statement answers the question of v. 5; cf. 31:20.

13 [c] Only acknowledge your guilt,
that you rebelled against the LORD your God
and scattered your favors among foreigners under [d] every green tree,
and that you have not obeyed my voice,
declares the LORD.
14 [e] Return, O faithless children,
declares the LORD;
[f] for I am your master;
I will take you, one from a city and two from a family,
and I will bring you to Zion.

15 "'And [g] I will give you shepherds after my
own heart, [h] who will feed you with knowledge and understanding. 16 And when you
have multiplied and increased in the land, in
those days, declares the LORD, they shall no
more say, "The ark of the covenant of the
LORD." It shall not come to mind or be
remembered or missed; it shall not be made
again. 17 At that time Jerusalem shall be
called the throne of the LORD, [i] and all
nations shall gather to it, [j] to the presence of
the LORD in Jerusalem, and they shall no
more stubbornly follow their own evil heart.
18 [k] In those days the house of Judah shall join
the house of Israel, and together they shall
come from the land [l] of the north to [m] the
land that I gave your fathers for a heritage.

19 "'I said
How I would set you among my sons,
and give you a pleasant land,
a heritage most beautiful of all nations.
And I thought you would [n] call me, My Father,
and would not turn from following me.
20 [o] Surely, as a treacherous wife leaves her husband,
so have you been treacherous to me, O house of Israel,
declares the LORD.'"
21 A voice on the [p] bare heights is heard,
[q] the weeping and pleading of Israel's sons
because they have perverted their way;
they have forgotten the LORD their God.
22 [r] "Return, O faithless sons;
[s] I will heal your faithlessness."
"Behold, we come to you,
for you are the LORD our God.
23 Truly [t] the hills are a delusion,
the orgies[1] on the mountains.
[u] Truly in the LORD our God
is the salvation of Israel.

24 "But from our youth the shameful
thing has devoured all for which our
fathers labored, their flocks and their
herds, their sons and their daughters.
25 [v] Let us lie down in our shame, and let
our dishonor cover us. For [w] we have
sinned against the LORD our God, we and
our fathers, from our youth even to this
day, and we have not obeyed the voice of
the LORD our God."

4

1 "If you return, O Israel,
declares the LORD,
[x] to me you should return.
If you remove your detestable things from my presence,
[y] and do not waver,
2 [z] and if you swear, 'As the LORD lives,'
in truth, in justice, and in righteousness,
then [a] nations shall bless themselves in him,
[b] and in him shall they glory."

1 Hebrew *commotion*

13 [c] Lev. 26:40 [d] ver. 6
14 [e] ver. 22; Hos. 14:1 [f] Isai. 54:5; 62:5; Hos. 2:19, 20; Mal. 2:11
15 [g] ch. 23:4; Ezek. 34:23; [John 10:11] [h] Acts 20:28
17 [i] Isai. 2:2, 3 [j] Isai. 60:9
18 [k] ch. 50:4; Isai. 11:13; Ezek. 37:21, 22; Hos. 1:11 [l] ver. 12; ch. 16:15; 23:8; 31:8 [m] Amos 9:15
19 [n] [Isai. 63:16]
20 [o] ver. 7, 8; ch. 5:11
21 [p] See ver. 2 [q] ch. 31:9
22 [r] ver. 14 [s] ch. 30:17; Isai. 57:18; Hos. 6:1
23 [t] ver. 21; [Ps. 121:1, 2] [u] Ps. 3:8
25 [v] Job 8:22; Ezra 9:6 [w] Ezra 9:7; Ezek. 2:3
Chapter 4
1 [x] Joel 2:12 [y] [1 Kin. 14:15]
2 [z] Deut. 6:13 [a] Isai. 65:16 [b] 1 Cor. 1:31; 2 Cor. 10:17

3:13 scattered your favors. Another use of the prostitution metaphor; see 2:20.

3:14 I am your master. Lit. "I am your husband." Although Israel was bound to be faithful to God as her true "husband," Jeremiah exposes her sin of spiritual adultery, her attachment to the gods of the nations. See Hos. 2:16, 17.

take . . . one . . . two. God will save a remnant from among the exiles (23:3 note; Is. 10:20–22 note).

3:16 multiplied and increased. These same words appear in reverse order in Gen. 1:28 ("Be fruitful and multiply"). God will make a new beginning with His people.

in those days. A future messianic age is now in view (cf. Is. 2:1–5).

The ark . . . shall not come to mind. The importance of the ark will be diminished because the Lord will be present in a new way.

3:17 throne. No longer is the ark the Lord's throne (Ex. 25:22; 1 Sam. 4:4), but Jerusalem itself: the Lord rules the whole earth from the midst of His people (Zech. 2:10–12).

3:20 a treacherous wife leaves. See 3:1; Hos. 1–3.

3:22 Return . . . faithless. This summons parallels Hos. 14:4. The call to repentance goes further: the Lord Himself will enable the people to return (Deut. 30:6).

3:24 devoured . . . daughters. This loss of possessions and family is the antithesis of blessing (Deut. 7:13). Children were often sacrificed to pagan gods (7:31).

3 For thus says the LORD to the men of
Judah and Jerusalem:

[c]"Break up your fallow ground,
and [d]sow not among thorns.
4 [e]Circumcise yourselves to the LORD;
remove the foreskin of your hearts,
O men of Judah and inhabitants of
Jerusalem;
[f]lest my wrath go forth like fire,
and burn with none to quench it,
[g]because of the evil of your deeds."

Disaster from the North

5 Declare in Judah, and proclaim in Jerusalem, and say,

[h]"Blow the trumpet through the land;
cry aloud and say,
[i]'Assemble, and let us go
into the fortified cities!'
6 [j]Raise a standard toward Zion,
flee for safety, stay not,
for I bring disaster from [k]the north,
[l]and great destruction.
7 [m]A lion has gone up from his thicket,
a destroyer of nations has set out;
he has gone out from his place
to make your land a waste;
your cities will be ruins
[n]without inhabitant.
8 For this [o]put on sackcloth,
lament, and wail,
for [p]the fierce anger of the LORD
has not turned back from us."

9 "In that day, declares the LORD, [q]courage
shall fail both king and officials. The priests
shall be appalled and the prophets
astounded." 10 Then I said, "Ah, Lord GOD,
[r]surely you have utterly deceived this people and Jerusalem, saying, 'It shall be well
with you,' whereas the sword has reached
their very life."

11 At that time it will be said to this people and to Jerusalem, "A hot wind from
[s]the bare heights in the desert toward the
daughter of my people, not to winnow or
cleanse, 12 a wind too full for this comes for
me. Now it is I who [t]speak in judgment
upon them."

13 Behold, he comes up like clouds;
[u]his chariots like the whirlwind;
his horses are [v]swifter than eagles—
woe to us, [w]for we are ruined!
14 O Jerusalem, [x]wash your heart from
evil,
that you may be saved.
How long shall your wicked thoughts
lodge within you?
15 For a voice [y]declares from Dan
and proclaims trouble from
[z]Mount Ephraim.
16 Warn the nations that he is coming;
announce to Jerusalem,
"Besiegers come [a]from a distant land;
they shout against the cities of
Judah.
17 Like keepers of a field [b]are they
against her all around,
because she has rebelled
against me,
declares the LORD.
18 Your ways and your deeds
have brought this upon you.
This is your doom, and [c]it is bitter;
it has reached your very heart."

Anguish over Judah's Desolation

19 [d]My anguish, my anguish! I writhe in
pain!
Oh the walls of my heart!
My heart is beating wildly;
I cannot keep silent,
for I hear the sound of the trumpet,
the alarm of war.
20 [e]Crash follows hard on crash;
the whole land is laid waste.
[f]Suddenly my tents are laid waste,
my curtains in a moment.
21 How long must I see the standard
and hear the sound of the
trumpet?

3 [c]Hos. 10:12 [d]Matt. 13:7, 22; Mark 4:7, 18; Luke 8:7, 14
4 [e]Deut. 10:16; [ch. 9:26; Rom. 2:28, 29] [f]ch. 21:12 [g]Deut. 28:20
5 [h][ch. 6:1; Hos. 5:8; Joel 2:1] [i]ch. 8:14
6 [j][ch. 50:2; 51:12, 27] [k]See ch. 1:13 [l][Isai. 1:28]
7 [m]ch. 2:15; 5:6; 49:19 [n]ch. 33:10; 34:22; 46:19; Isai. 5:9; 6:11
8 [o]ch. 4:8; 6:26; Isai. 22:12; 32:11 [p]Num. 25:4; Ps. 78:49; See Isai. 13:9-13
9 [q][Ps. 48:4, 5]
10 [r]Ezek. 14:9; [1 Kin. 22:22]
11 [s]See ch. 3:2
12 [t]ch. 1:16
13 [u]Isai. 5:28 [v]2 Sam. 1:23; Lam. 4:19 [w]ch. 9:19
14 [x]Ps. 51:2, 7; Isai. 1:16; James 4:8
15 [y]ch. 8:16 [z]See Josh. 24:33
16 [a]ch. 5:15
17 [b]ch. 6:3; See 2 Kin. 25:1-4
18 [c]ch. 2:19
19 [d]Isai. 16:11; Hab. 3:16; [ch. 9:1; Isai. 22:4]
20 [e]Ezek. 7:26 [f]ch. 10:20; 49:29

4:4 Circumcise . . . hearts. The outward signs of ownership by the Lord are nothing unless they correspond to an inner reality. Only God can circumcise the heart (31:31–34; Deut. 10:16; 30:6).

4:5 Blow the trumpet. A traditional method of warning (cf. Joel 2:1; Amos 3:6). Jeremiah begins to announce destruction at the hand of a foe from the north. Fear will drive country-dwellers to the cities for safety.

4:8 sackcloth . . . wail. Traditional actions of indicating grief; cf. Jon. 3:5.

4:9 In that day. A day of reckoning, when the things prophesied will come to pass (cf. Is. 2:11, 12).

4:11 hot wind. The sirocco winds blew from across the desert and caused tremendous damage to crops.

4:13 clouds . . . whirlwind . . . eagles. These comparisons drawn from nature indicate the strength and speed of the enemy.

4:17 Like keepers of a field. It is as if Judah's enemies already own the land.

4:21 How long. This cry is common in psalms of lament (e.g., Ps. 13:1).

22 "For [g]my people are foolish;
they know me not;
they are stupid children;
they have no understanding.
[h]They are 'wise'—in doing evil!
But how to do good they know not."

23 I looked on the earth, and behold, it
was [i]without form and void;
[j]and to the heavens, and they had
no light.
24 I looked on [k]the mountains, and
behold, they were quaking,
and all the hills moved to and fro.
25 [l]I looked, and behold, there was no
man,
and all the birds of the air had fled.
26 I looked, and behold, the [m]fruitful
land was a desert,
and all its cities were laid in ruins
before the LORD, before [n]his fierce
anger.

27 For thus says the LORD, "The whole
land shall be a desolation; [o]yet I will not
make a full end.

28 [p]"For this the earth shall mourn,
[q]and the heavens above be dark;
for I have spoken; I have purposed;
[r]I have not relented, nor will I turn
back."

29 At the noise of horseman and archer
every city takes to flight;
they enter thickets; they climb
among rocks;
all the cities are forsaken,
and [s]no man dwells in them.
30 And you, O desolate one,
what do you mean that you dress in
scarlet,
[t]that you adorn yourself with
ornaments of gold,
[u]that you enlarge your eyes with
paint?
In vain you beautify yourself.
[v]Your lovers despise you;
they seek your life.
31 For I heard [w]a cry as of a woman in
labor,
anguish as of one giving birth to
her first child,
the cry of the daughter of Zion
gasping for breath,
[x]stretching out her hands,
"Woe is me! I am fainting before
murderers."

Jerusalem Refused to Repent

5 [y]Run to and fro through the streets
of Jerusalem,
look and take note!
Search her squares to see
[z]if you can find a man,
one who does justice
and seeks truth,
[a]that I may pardon her.
2 [b]Though they say, "As the LORD lives,"
[c]yet they swear falsely.
3 O LORD, do not your eyes look for
truth?
[d]You have struck them down,
but they felt no anguish;
you have consumed them,
but they refused to take correction.
[e]They have made their faces harder
than rock;
they have refused to repent.
4 Then I said, "These are only the poor;
they have no sense;
[f]for they do not know the way of the
LORD,
the justice of their God.
5 I will go to the great
and will speak to them,
for they know the way of the LORD,
the justice of their God."
[g]But they all alike had broken the yoke;
they had burst the bonds.

22 [g]Ps. 82:5; Isai. 1:3 [h]Ps. 36:3; Isai. 1:16, 17; Rom. 16:19 **23** [i]Gen. 1:2 [j]Isai. 5:30 **24** [k]Nah. 1:5 **25** [l][Zeph. 1:3] **26** [m]Ps. 107:34 [n]See ver. 8 **27** [o]ch. 5:10, 18; 30:11; 46:28; Neh. 9:31; Ezek. 11:13 **28** [p]ch. 12:4; Hos. 4:3 [q]Isai. 50:3 [r][Num. 23:19] **29** [s]See ver. 7 **30** [t][Isai. 61:10] [u][2 Kin. 9:30] [v]Lam. 1:2, 19; Ezek. 23:22 **31** [w]ch. 6:24; See Isai. 13:8 [x]Isai. 1:15; Lam. 1:17
Chapter 5
1 [y][2 Chr. 16:9] [z]See Gen. 18:23-32 [a][ver. 7] **2** [b][Tit. 1:16] [c]ch. 7:9 **3** [d]See ch. 2:30 [e]Ezek. 3:8 **4** [f]ch. 8:7; Mic. 3:1 **5** [g]ch. 2:20; Ps. 2:3; 107:14

4:22 wise. Original wickedness is strengthened by habit and practice (9:5).

4:23 without form and void . . . heavens . . . had no light. Compare Gen. 1:2, 14, 15. Creation itself is undone by His judgment.

4:25 no man. The same phrase is used in Gen. 2:5. Again creation is returned to its original chaos.

4:26 fruitful land . . . a desert. Covenant blessings are now reversed (Deut. 8:7–16).

4:30 adorn yourself . . . paint. A vivid repetition of the harlot metaphor.

lovers . . . seek your life. These lines express the ironic truth of Judah's self-deception.

4:31 daughter of Zion. Jerusalem is personified (Lam. 1:6 note).

Woe . . . murderers. We hear her pathetic dying breath.

5:1 if you can find . . . pardon her. This search is an allusion to Abraham's prayer for Sodom (Gen. 18:22–32) and an implicit answer to Jeremiah's prayer for the city (later forbidden; 7:16). But the city is totally corrupt.

5:3 made their faces harder than rock. The people's determination not to repent is the chief frustration of the prophet (cf. Ezek. 3:7–9).

6 Therefore [h]a lion from the forest shall
strike them down;
a [i]wolf from the desert shall
devastate them.
[j]A leopard is watching their cities;
everyone who goes out of them
shall be torn in pieces,
because their transgressions are many,
their [k]apostasies are great.

7 [l]"How can I pardon you?
Your children have forsaken me
[m]and have sworn by those who are
no gods.
[n]When I fed them to the full,
[o]they committed adultery
[p]and trooped to the houses of
whores.
8 They were well-fed, lusty stallions,
[q]each neighing [r]for his neighbor's
wife.
9 [s]Shall I not punish them for these
things?
declares the LORD;
and shall I not avenge myself
on a nation such as this?

10 [t]"Go up through her vine rows and
destroy,
[u]but make not a full end;
strip away her branches,
for they are not the LORD's.
11 [v]For the house of Israel and the house
of Judah
have been utterly treacherous to me,
declares the LORD.
12 They have spoken falsely of the LORD
and have said, 'He will do nothing;
[w]no disaster will come upon us,
[x]nor shall we see sword or famine.
13 The prophets will become wind;
the word is not in them.
Thus shall it be done to them!'"

6 [h]See ch. 4:7 [i]Hab. 1:8; Zeph. 3:3 [j]Hos. 13:7 [k]ch. 2:19
7 [l][ver. 1] [m]Deut. 32:21; Josh. 23:7; 2 Chr. 13:9; Gal. 4:8 [n]Deut. 32:15 [o]ch. 9:2; 23:10 [p]Mic. 5:1
8 [q]ch. 13:27; 50:11 [r]Ezek. 22:11
9 [s]ver. 29; ch. 9:9; [Rom. 2:2]
10 [t][ch. 39:8] [u]See ch. 4:27
11 [v]ch. 3:20
12 [w][Gen. 3:4] [x][ch. 14:13; Isai. 28:15]
14 [y][ch. 1:9, 10] [z][Obad. 18; Zech. 12:6; Rev. 11:5]
15 [a]ch. 34:21, 22; Deut. 28:49; [ch. 1:15; Amos 6:14] [b]Isai. 33:19
16 [c]See Isai. 5:28 [d]Ps. 5:9
17 [e]Lev. 26:16; Deut. 28:31, 33, 51 [f][Hos. 8:14]
19 [g]ch. 13:22; 16:10, 11; 22:8, 9; Deut. 29:24, 25; 1 Kin. 9:8, 9 [h]Deut 4:27, 28; 28:47, 48, 68

The LORD Proclaims Judgment

14 Therefore thus says the LORD, the
God of hosts:
"Because you have spoken this
word,
behold, [y]I am making my words in
your mouth [z]a fire,
and this people wood, and the fire
shall consume them.
15 [a]Behold, I am bringing
against you
a nation from afar, O house of
Israel,
declares the LORD.
It is an enduring nation;
it is an ancient nation,
a nation whose language you do not
know,
[b]nor can you understand what
they say.
16 [c]Their quiver is like [d]an open tomb;
they are all mighty warriors.
17 [e]They shall eat up your harvest and
your food;
they shall eat up your sons and
your daughters;
they shall eat up your flocks and
your herds;
they shall eat up your vines and
your fig trees;
your [f]fortified cities in which you
trust
they shall beat down with the
sword."

18 "But even in those days, declares the
LORD, [u]I will not make a full end of you.
19 And when your people say, [g]'Why has
the LORD our God done all these things to
us?' you shall say to them, 'As you have forsaken me and served foreign gods in your
land, [h]so you shall serve foreigners in a
land that is not yours.'"

5:6 lion . . . wolf . . . leopard. Such breach of God's covenant brings the covenant curses on the people (Lev. 26:22).

5:7 I fed them . . . adultery. The motive for following false gods was the delusion that the gods of the land of Canaan had the power to make it fertile. The Lord claims the land's fertility as His own sphere (Hos. 2:8, 9 notes).

5:8 lusty stallions . . . neighing. Religious prostitution slips over into actual adultery. See a similar description in 2:23, 24.

5:9 Shall I not. Again the courtroom metaphor is used; an appeal to witnesses is implied. The Lord's justice must be accomplished.

5:10 not a full end. This hint that punishment will not be final is one of several such clues in the early part of the book (12:14–17; 16:14, 15; and 23:3 note).

are not the LORD's. In the same breath Judah's covenant status is annulled (Hos. 1:9 note). The apparently irreconcilable needs of judgment and salvation are both evident here.

5:12 They have spoken falsely. Wrong belief about God is related to every kind of untruth (9:3–6).

He will do nothing . . . famine. These words summarize the message of the false prophets. See 28:2–4.

5:13 wind. Jeremiah counters that those false prophets who claim to have the Spirit (Hebrew *ruaḥ*) are but wind (also *ruaḥ*).

5:17 eat . . . eat . . . eat . . . eat. That Judah's enemies will consume the bounty of the land is a reversal of covenant blessing. See Deut. 7:13 for the promise of the very things now to be lost.

20 Declare this in the house of Jacob;
proclaim it in Judah:
21 "Hear this, [i]O foolish and senseless
people,
[j] who have eyes, but see not,
who have ears, but hear not.
22 [k] Do you not fear me? declares the
LORD;
Do you not tremble before me?
I placed the sand [l]as the boundary
for the sea,
a perpetual barrier that it cannot
pass;
though the waves toss, they cannot
prevail;
though [m]they roar, they cannot
pass over it.
23 [n] But this people has a stubborn and
rebellious heart;
they have turned aside and gone
away.
24 They do not say in their hearts,
'Let us fear the LORD our God,
[o] who gives the rain in its season,
the autumn rain and the spring
rain,
and keeps for us
[p] the weeks appointed for the
harvest.'
25 [q] Your iniquities have turned these
away,
and your sins have kept good from
you.
26 For wicked men are found among my
people;
[r] they lurk like fowlers lying in
wait.[1]
[s] They set a trap;
they catch men.
27 Like a cage full of birds,
their houses are full of deceit;
therefore they have become great and
rich;
28 [t] they have grown fat and sleek.
They know no bounds in deeds of
evil;
[u] they judge not with justice
the cause of the fatherless, to make it
prosper,
and they do not defend the rights
of the needy.
29 [v] Shall I not punish them for these
things?
declares the LORD,
and shall I not avenge myself
on a nation such as this?"
30 An appalling and [w]horrible thing
has happened in the land:
31 [x] the prophets prophesy falsely,
and the priests rule at their
direction;
[y] my people love to have it so,
but what will you do when the end
comes?

Impending Disaster for Jerusalem

6 Flee for safety, [z]O people of
Benjamin,
from the midst of Jerusalem!
Blow the trumpet in [a]Tekoa,
and raise a signal on
[b]Beth-haccherem,
for disaster looms [c]out of the
north,
and great destruction.
2 The lovely and delicately bred I will
destroy,
[d] the daughter of Zion.[2]
3 [e] Shepherds with their flocks shall
come against her;
[f] they shall pitch their tents around
her;
they shall pasture, each in his
place.

21 [i]Deut. 32:6; Isai. 6:9 [j][Matt. 13:14]
22 [k]ch. 10:7 [l]Job 26:10; 38:10, 11; Ps. 104:9 [m]ch. 51:55; [Ps. 46:3]
23 [n]ch. 6:28
24 [o]ch. 14:22; Deut. 11:14; Job 5:10; Ps. 147:8; Matt. 5:45 [p]Gen. 8:22
25 [q]ch. 3:3
26 [r][Prov. 1:11] [s]Ps. 10:9; [Ps. 124:7]
28 [t]Deut. 32:15; Ps. 17:10 [u][ch. 7:6; Isai. 1:23; Zech. 7:10]
29 [v]See ver. 9
30 [w]ch. 23:14; Hos. 6:10
31 [x]ch. 6:13; 14:14, 18; 20:6; 23:21, 25; 27:10, 15; 29:9; Ezek. 13:6 [y][Mic. 2:11]
Chapter 6
1 [z][Judg. 1:21] [a]See 2 Sam. 14:2 [b]Neh. 3:14 [c]See ch. 1:14
2 [d]See 2 Kin. 19:21
3 [e][ch. 23:1] [f]ch. 4:17

1 The meaning of the Hebrew is uncertain 2 Or *I have likened the daughter of Zion to the loveliest pasture*

5:21 foolish. See Prov. 1:7.

who have eyes . . . hear not. See note Is. 6:10.

5:22 Do you not fear. Jeremiah argues from God's power in creation (Job 38–41; Rom. 1:18–20).

5:26 wicked men . . . catch men. The nature of wickedness is to entice even the innocent into it. Prov. 2:12–19 describes its blandishments.

5:27, 28 become great and rich. Jeremiah moves from specifically religious sins to social evils, for the two are closely related.

fat . . . sleek. This description symbolizes self-centered wealth, cf. Ps. 73:7.

fatherless . . . needy. Ps. 9:18 note.

6:1 Benjamin. This territory bordering Jerusalem to the north was part of the southern kingdom of Judah.

Tekoa. A city in Judah, the home of Amos (Amos 1:1).

Beth-haccherem. An unknown location in Judah.

north. See note 1:14.

6:2 lovely . . . daughter of Zion. See note 2:2. Though a personification of Jerusalem (4:31 note), the simile has in mind the city's refined women (Is. 3:16–26).

6:3 Shepherds with their flocks. These "shepherds" are enemy officers with their troops, taking possession of the land (cf. 4:15).

4 [g]"Prepare war against her;
arise, and let us attack [h]at noon!
Woe to us, for the day declines,
for the shadows of evening
lengthen!
5 Arise, and let us attack by night
and destroy her palaces!"

6 For thus says the LORD of hosts:
[i]"Cut down her trees;
[j]cast up a siege mound against
Jerusalem.
This is the city that must be
[k]punished;
there is nothing but oppression
within her.
7 [l]As a well keeps its water fresh,
so she keeps fresh her evil;
[m]violence and destruction are heard
within her;
sickness and wounds are ever
before me.
8 Be warned, O Jerusalem,
[n]lest I turn from you in disgust,
lest I make you [o]a desolation,
an uninhabited land."

9 Thus says the LORD of hosts:
[p]"They shall glean thoroughly as
a vine
the remnant of Israel;
like a grape-gatherer pass your hand
again
over its branches."
10 [q]To whom shall I speak and give
warning,
that they may hear?
[r]Behold, their ears are uncircumcised,
[s]they cannot listen;
behold, [t]the word of the LORD is to
them an object of scorn;
they take no pleasure in it.
11 Therefore I am full of the wrath of
the LORD;
[u]I am weary of holding it in.

[v]"Pour it out upon the children in the
street,
and upon the gatherings of young
men, also;
[w]both husband and wife [x]shall be
taken,
the elderly and the very aged.
12 [y]Their houses shall be turned over to
others,
their fields and wives together,
for I will stretch out my hand
against the inhabitants of the
land,"
declares the LORD.
13 [z]"For from the least to the greatest of
them,
everyone [a]is greedy for unjust
gain;
and from [b]prophet to priest,
everyone deals falsely.
14 They have healed the wound of my
people lightly,
saying, [c]'Peace, peace,'
[d]when there is no peace.
15 [e]Were they ashamed when they
committed abomination?
No, they were not at all
ashamed;
they did not know how to
blush.
Therefore they shall fall among those
who fall;
[f]at the time that I punish them,
they shall be overthrown,"
says the LORD.

16 Thus says the LORD:
"Stand by the roads, and look,
and ask for [g]the ancient paths,
where the good way is; and walk
in it,
[h]and find rest for your souls.
But they said, 'We will not walk
in it.'

4 [g]ch. 22:7; Joel 3:9; [ch. 51:27] [h]ch. 15:8
6 [i][Deut. 20:20] [j]2 Kin. 19:32; Isai. 37:33; Ezek. 26:8; Luke 19:43 [k]Luke 19:44
7 [l]Isai. 57:20 [m]Ps. 55:9; Ezek. 7:11, 23
8 [n]Ezek. 23:18; [Hos. 9:12] [o]See ch. 4:7
9 [p][Deut. 24:21]
10 [q]Isai. 28:9; 53:1 [r][Ex. 6:12; Acts 7:51] [s]ch. 7:26 [t]ch. 20:8
11 [u]ch. 20:9 [v]ch. 9:21 [w][Lam. 2:21] [x]ch. 8:9
12 [y]For ver. 12-15, see ch. 8:10-12
13 [z][ch. 31:34; 44:12; Jonah 3:5] [a]Isai. 56:11 [b]ch. 14:18; 23:11; Mic. 3:11; See ch. 5:31
14 [c]ch. 4:10; 14:13; 23:17; Ezek. 13:10; Mic. 3:5; [John 14:27] [d]Isai. 48:22; 57:21; Ezek. 7:25
15 [e][ch. 3:3; 8:12] [f][ver. 6]
16 [g]ch. 18:15; [Isai. 8:20; Mal. 4:4; Luke 16:29] [h]Matt. 11:29; [Ps. 116:7]

6:4, 5 at noon . . . by night. These are unusual times to attack: the enemy's strength is such that he is free to attack whenever he likes.

6:6 A new oracle is addressed to the Babylonians, the Lord's instrument of judgment.

oppression. The rich and powerful of Jerusalem have oppressed their own people.

6:7 a well . . . evil. Judah cannot help pouring out her wickedness, because that is her true nature (cf. Matt. 7:16).

6:9 glean thoroughly . . . the remnant. Farmers were not supposed to glean everything, but to leave something behind for the poor (Deut. 24:19–22); Babylon, however, may "glean" Judah completely (contrast 5:10). The Lord has deeper purposes behind the permission He gives (23:3 note). The curse was not absolute, for God did spare a remnant to fulfill His covenant of redemption (Introduction: Characteristics and Themes). See note 11:23.

6:14 Peace. More than absence of war, it is individual and social well-being that is the consequence of covenant-keeping.

Peace, peace. The easily welcomed message of false prophets cannot bring true peace (Mic. 2:6), whose counterpart is righteousness.

6:16 ancient paths. This figure describes the traditional religious life of the Israelites from the time of Moses.

17 [i]I set watchmen over you, saying,
'Pay attention to [j]the sound of the
trumpet!'
But they said, [k]'We will not pay
attention.'
18 Therefore hear, O nations,
and know, O congregation, what
will happen to them.
19 Hear, O earth; behold, I am bringing
disaster upon this people,
[l]the fruit of their devices,
because they have not paid attention
to my words;
and as for my law, they have
rejected it.
20 [m]What use to me is [n]frankincense that
comes from [o]Sheba,
or sweet cane from a distant land?
[p]Your burnt offerings are not
acceptable,
nor your sacrifices pleasing to me.
21 Therefore thus says the LORD:
[q]'Behold, I will lay before this people
stumbling blocks against which
they shall stumble;
fathers and sons together,
neighbor and friend shall perish.'"

22 Thus says the LORD:
[r]"Behold, a people is coming [s]from the
north country,
a great nation is stirring from [t]the
farthest parts of the earth.
23 They lay hold on bow and javelin;
they are [u]cruel and have no mercy;
[v]the sound of them is like the
roaring sea;
they ride on horses,
set in array as a man for battle,
against you, O daughter of Zion!"
24 We have heard the report of it;
[w]our hands fall helpless;

17 [i]Isai. 56:10; [Isai. 21:11] [j]Isai. 58:1; [ch. 4:19] [k]ch. 44:16
19 [l]Prov. 1:31
20 [m]Isai. 1:11 [n]Isai. 43:23; 60:6 [o]See 1 Kin. 10:1 [p]ch. 7:21, 22; 14:12; Ps. 40:6; Isai. 1:11; Amos 5:21
21 [q]Ezek. 3:20
22 [r]For ver. 22-24, see ch. 50:41-43 [s]See ch. 1:13 [t]ch. 25:32; 31:8
23 [u]Isai. 13:9, 18 [v]Isai. 17:12
24 [w]ch. 38:4; 49:24; Ezek. 21:7; See 2 Sam. 4:1; Ezek. 7:17 [x]See Isai. 13:8
25 [y]Ps. 31:13; Lam. 2:22; [Job 18:11]
26 [z]See ch. 4:8; Esth. 4:1 [a]ch. 25:34; Ezek. 27:30; [Lam. 3:16; Mic. 1:10] [b]Amos 8:10; Zech. 12:10
27 [c][ch. 1:18] [d]ch. 9:7
28 [e]ch. 5:23 [f]ch. 9:4; [Lev. 19:16] [g]Ezek. 22:18, 20
29 [g][See ver. 28 above] [h][Isai. 1:25]
30 [i]Isai. 1:22; Ezek. 22:19, 20
Chapter 7
2 [j]ch. 26:2
3 [k]ch. 18:11; 26:13
4 [l][ver. 8]

anguish has taken hold of us,
[x]pain as of a woman in labor.
25 Go not out into the field,
nor walk on the road,
for the enemy has a sword;
[y]terror is on every side.
26 O daughter of my people, [z]put on
sackcloth,
and [a]roll in ashes;
[b]make mourning as for an only son,
most bitter lamentation,
for suddenly the destroyer
will come upon us.

27 "I have made you [c]a tester of metals
among my people,
that you may know and [d]test their
ways.
28 [e]They are all stubbornly rebellious,
[f]going about with slanders;
they are [g]bronze and iron;
all of them act corruptly.
29 The [g]bellows blow fiercely;
the lead is consumed by the fire;
[h]in vain the refining goes on,
for the wicked are not removed.
30 [i]Rejected silver they are called,
for the LORD has rejected them."

Evil in the Land

7 The word that came to Jeremiah from
the LORD: 2 [j]"Stand in the gate of the
LORD's house, and proclaim there this
word, and say, Hear the word of the LORD,
all you men of Judah who enter these gates
to worship the LORD. 3 Thus says the LORD
of hosts, the God of Israel: [k]Amend your
ways and your deeds, and I will let you
dwell in this place. 4 [l]Do not trust in these
deceptive words: 'This is the temple of the
LORD, the temple of the LORD, the temple of
the LORD.'

6:17 watchmen. That is, the prophets (Is. 21:11; Ezek. 3:17; Hab. 2:1).

6:18 hear, O nations . . . O congregation. See 2:4; Mic. 1:2.

6:20 frankincense . . . sweet cane. These were expensive ingredients used in religious rituals (Ex. 30:23–38).

burnt offerings are not acceptable. This indictment is important in the Psalms and Prophets (Ps. 40:6–8; Is. 1:11–15; Mic. 6:6–8). See Matt. 23:23.

6:23 lay hold on bow and javelin . . . on horses. See the description of Babylon in Hab. 1:6–11. Though the Babylonians are God's instrument, He does not approve their cruelty.

6:27 a tester. Elsewhere in the book, the Lord Himself is the One who tests both the people (9:7; 17:10; 20:12) and Jeremiah (11:20; 12:3). The prophet acts as God's agent here.

6:29, 30 lead . . . silver. Lead was used in the process of refining silver. The process of refining Judah has yielded nothing of value.

7:2 gate. Probably this is the gate leading to the inner court of the temple. Jeremiah stands in the central place of Judah's worship to proclaim its falsehood. The power of this action is heightened by his being himself a priest.

all you men of Judah . . . to worship the LORD. Possibly this prophecy was delivered on one of the great annual feasts (Ex. 23:14–18), when all Israel was required to be present.

7:3 this place. The Promised Land. The force of Jeremiah's appeal here, perhaps a shock to complacent Judah, was that they could not take the land for granted.

7:4 deceptive words . . . the temple of the LORD. The repetition gives emphasis. The hypocrisy of their professed trust in the Lord and His temple is exposed at its lowest ebb.

5 "For if you truly [m]amend your ways and
your deeds, if you truly [n]execute justice
one with another, 6 if you [n]do not oppress
the sojourner, the fatherless, or the widow,
[n]or shed innocent blood in this place, [o]and
if you do not go after other gods to your
own harm, 7 [p]then I will let you dwell in
this place, [q]in the land that I gave of old to
your fathers forever.
8 "Behold, you trust in deceptive words
to no avail. 9 [r]Will you steal, murder, commit adultery, [s]swear falsely, [t]make offerings
to Baal, [o]and go after other gods that you
have not known, 10 and then come and
stand before me in this house, [u]which is
called by my name, and say, 'We are delivered!'—only to go on doing all these abominations? 11 [v]Has this house, [u]which is
called by my name, [w]become a den of robbers in your eyes? Behold, I myself have
seen it, declares the LORD. 12 Go now to [x]my
place that was in Shiloh, [y]where I made my
name dwell at first, and [z]see what I did to
it because of the evil of my people Israel.
13 And now, because you have done all
these things, declares the LORD, and [a]when
I spoke to you persistently you did not listen, and [b]when I called you, you did not
answer, 14 therefore I will do to [c]the house
[u]that is called by my name, and in which
you trust, and to the place that I gave to
you and to your fathers, [z]as I did to Shiloh.
15 [c]And I will cast you out of my sight, [d]as I
cast out all your kinsmen, all the offspring
of [e]Ephraim.
16 "As for you, [f]do not pray for this people, or lift up a cry or prayer for them, and
do not intercede with me, for I will not
hear you. 17 Do you not see what they are

5 [m]ch. 22:3 [n]Deut. 24:14
6 [n][See ver. 5 above] [o]ch. 13:10; 25:6; Deut. 6:14
7 [p]Deut. 4:40 [q]ch. 3:18
9 [r]Hos. 4:1, 2 [s]ch. 5:2 [t]ch. 1:16 [o][See ver. 6 above]
10 [u]ch. 32:34; 34:15
11 [v]Isai. 56:7 [u][See ver. 10 above] [w]Cited Matt. 21:13; Mark 11:17; Luke 19:46; [Ezek. 7:22]
12 [x]Judg. 18:31; 1 Sam. 1:3 [y]Deut. 12:11 [z]ch. 26:6; Ps. 78:60; See 1 Sam. 4:3-12
13 [a]ver. 25; 2 Chr. 36:15 [b]Prov. 1:24; [ver. 27; Isai. 50:2; 65:12]
14 [c]Deut. 12:5; 1 Kin. 9:7 [u][See ver. 10 above] [z][See ver. 12 above]
15 [c][See ver. 14 above] [d]2 Kin. 17:6, 23 [e]Ps. 78:67; Hos. 4:17; 5:3, 9; 6:4; 12:1
16 [f]ch. 11:14; 14:11; [Ex. 32:10; Deut. 9:14; 1 John 5:16]
18 [g]Hos. 7:4 [h]ch. 44:17, 19 [i][2 Kin. 23:13] [j]ch. 19:13 [k]ch. 11:17; Deut. 32:16, 21; 1 Kin. 14:9; 16:2; 2 Chr. 34:25
19 [l][Job 35:6] [m]ch. 51:51

doing in the cities of Judah and in the
streets of Jerusalem? 18 The children gather
wood, the fathers kindle fire, [g]and the
women knead dough, to [h]make cakes for
[i]the queen of heaven. And [j]they pour out
drink offerings to other gods, [k]to provoke
me to anger. 19 [l]Is it I whom they provoke?
declares the LORD. Is it not themselves, [m]to
their own shame? 20 Therefore thus says the
Lord GOD: behold, [n]my anger and my
wrath will be poured out on this place,
upon man and beast, upon the trees of the
field and the fruit of the ground; [o]it will
burn and not be quenched."
21 Thus says the LORD of hosts, the God
of Israel: [p]"Add your burnt offerings to
your sacrifices, and eat the flesh. 22 For in
the day that I brought them out of the land
of Egypt, I did not speak to your fathers or
command them [q]concerning burnt offerings and sacrifices. 23 But this command I
gave them: [r]'Obey my voice, and [s]I will be
your God, and you shall be my people.
[t]And walk in all the way that I command
you, [u]that it may be well with you.' 24 [v]But
they did not obey or incline their ear, [w]but
walked in their own counsels and [x]the
stubbornness of their evil hearts, and
[y]went backward and not forward. 25 From
the day that your fathers came out of the
land of Egypt to this day, [z]I have persistently sent all my servants the prophets to
them, day after day. 26 Yet they did not listen to me or incline their ear, [a]but stiffened their neck. [b]They did worse than
their fathers.

20 [n]ch. 42:18; 44:6; 2 Chr. 34:25; Lam. 4:11 [o]ch. 17:27 21 [p]See ch. 6:20
22 [q]Hos. 6:6 23 [r]ch. 11:4, 7; Ex. 15:26; Deut. 6:3 [s]Lev. 26:12 [t]Deut. 5:33 [u]ch. 42:6; Deut. 4:40 24 [v]Ps. 81:11 [w]Ps. 81:12 [x][ch. 3:17; Hos. 4:16] [y]ch. 2:19, 27; 8:5; 15:6; 32:33 25 [z]2 Chr. 36:15, 16 26 [a]2 Chr. 30:8 [b]ch. 16:12

7:5, 6 if you . . . to your own harm. The conditional language echoes the Mosaic covenant (Deut. 14:28, 29; Deut. 13:1–3).

shed innocent blood. This plea is not an exaggeration (19:4).

7:9 Will you steal. Notice the allusion to five of the Ten Commandments (compare Hos. 4:2), with a climactic stress on the first (Ex. 20:3).

7:10 this house, which is called by my name. See Deut. 12:5; 1 Kin. 8:43, where the "place" is identified as the Jerusalem temple.

delivered. False worship yields false security.

7:12 Shiloh . . . my name. Shiloh was a central place of worship for all Israel before David made Jerusalem the capital (Josh. 18:1; 1 Sam. 1:9). Now that Shiloh was no more (probably destroyed by the Philistines), it was a good proof of Jeremiah's point that even a place where the Lord had made His name to dwell was not immune to His judgment.

7:13 you did not listen. This is an important theme in the book (6:17; 11:7, 8; 25:3; cf. 2 Kin. 17:13, 14).

7:16 do not pray. Such prohibition is ominous because one of the prophetic roles was to intercede (Abraham served as an intercessor, Gen. 20:7; and Moses, Ex. 32:11–14). The prohibition is repeated at 11:14 (compare 15:1; 1 John 5:16).

7:18 children . . . fathers . . . women. A picture of the universal hold idolatry had on the people.

queen of heaven. A Babylonian name for the goddess Ishtar (44:19, 25).

7:20 man and beast . . . fruit of the ground. Breakdown in the relationship between God and His people affects all creation (see Hos. 2:18).

7:21–23 burnt offerings . . . sacrifices. Sacrifices without the inner worship of the heart were of no interest to God; the people might as well eat the sacrifices themselves if they offered them that way. This prophetic condemnation of empty ritual is all the more remarkable because the sacrificial system revealed to Moses was still in force. Jeremiah is not alone in speaking this way; see 1 Sam. 15:23; Is. 1:11–15; Hos. 6:6; Amos 5:21–25; Mic. 6:6–8.

7:24 walked . . . their evil hearts. This portrayal of Judah strongly suggests a native disposition towards evil in the human heart.

27 [c]"So you shall speak all these words to
them, but they will not listen to you. [d]You
shall call to them, but they will not answer
you. 28 And you shall say to them, 'This is
the nation that did not obey the voice of
the LORD their God, and did not accept discipline; [e]truth has perished; it is cut off
from their lips.

29 [f]" 'Cut off your hair and cast it away;
raise a lamentation on [g]the bare heights,
for the LORD has rejected and forsaken
the generation of his wrath.'

The Valley of Slaughter

30 "For the sons of Judah have done evil
in my sight, declares the LORD. They have
set [h]their detestable things in the house
[i]that is called by my name, to [h]defile it.
31 And they have built the high places of
[j]Topheth, which is in [k]the Valley of the Son
of Hinnom, [l]to burn their sons and their
daughters in the fire, [m]which I did not
command, nor did it come into my mind.
32 [n]Therefore, behold, the days are coming,
declares the LORD, when it will no more be
called [j]Topheth, or [k]the Valley of the Son of
Hinnom, but the Valley of Slaughter; [o]for
they will bury in Topheth, because there is
no room elsewhere. 33 [p]And the dead bodies of this people will be food for the birds
of the air, and for the beasts of the earth,
[q]and none will frighten them away. 34 [r]And
I will silence in the cities of Judah and in
the streets of Jerusalem the voice of mirth
and the voice of gladness, the voice of the
bridegroom and the voice of the bride, [s]for
the land shall become a waste.

8 "At that time, declares the LORD, the
bones of the kings of Judah, the bones
of its officials, the bones of the priests, the
bones of the prophets, and the bones of
the inhabitants of Jerusalem shall be
brought out of their tombs. 2 And they shall
be spread [t]before the sun and the moon
and all the host of heaven, which they have
loved and served, which they have gone
after, and which they have sought and worshiped. [u]And they shall not be gathered or
buried. [v]They shall be as dung on the surface of the ground. 3 [w]Death shall be preferred to life by all the remnant that
remains of this evil family [x]in all the places
where I have driven them, declares the
LORD of hosts.

Sin and Treachery

4 "You shall say to them, Thus says the LORD:
[y]When men fall, do they not rise again?
If one turns away, does he not return?
5 Why then has this people [z]turned away
in perpetual [a]backsliding?
[b]They hold fast to deceit;
they refuse to return.
6 [c]I have paid attention and listened,
but they have not spoken rightly;
no man relents of his evil,
saying, 'What have I done?'
Everyone turns to his own course,
[d]like a horse plunging headlong into battle.
7 Even the stork in the heavens
knows her times,
and [e]the turtledove, [f]swallow, and crane[1]
keep the time of their coming,
[g]but my people know not
the rules of the LORD.

27 [c]ch. 1:17 [d][ver. 13]
28 [e]ch. 9:3
29 [f][Job 1:20] [g]See ch. 3:2
30 [h]ch. 32:34; Ezek. 5:11; 7:20; [ch. 19:5; 2 Kin. 21:4, 7] [i]See ver. 10
31 [j]2 Kin. 23:10 [k][ch. 31:40; Josh. 18:16] [l]Ps. 106:38 [m]Deut. 17:3; [ver. 21, 22]
32 [n]ch. 19:6 [j][See ver. 31 above] [k][See ver. 31 above] [o]ch. 19:11; [Ezek. 6:5]
33 [p]ch. 12:9; 16:4; 19:7; 34:20; Deut. 28:26; Ps. 79:2 [q][Isai. 17:2]
34 [r]ch. 16:9; 25:10; Ps. 78:63; Isai. 24:7, 8; Rev. 18:22, 23; [Ezek. 26:13; Hos. 2:11] [s]ch. 27:17; 44:2, 6; Lev. 26:31, 33

Chapter 8
2 [t]Deut. 4:19; 2 Kin. 21:3; 23:5; [Job 31:26-28; Ezek. 8:16] [u][Job 27:19] [v]ch. 9:22; 16:4; 25:33
3 [w][Job 3:21, 22; 7:15, 16; Rev. 9:6] [x]ch. 23:3, 8; 29:14, 18; 32:37; Dan. 9:7
4 [y][Rom. 11:11]
5 [z]See ch. 7:24 [a]See ch. 2:19 [b]ch. 9:6
6 [c][2 Pet. 3:9] [d]See Job 39:19-25
7 [e]S. of S. 2:12 [f]Isai. 38:14 [g][ch. 5:4, 5; Isai. 1:3]

1 The meaning of the Hebrew word is uncertain

7:29 Cut off your hair. This command is in the grammatical feminine, and personifies Jerusalem as a woman (2:1); the shaving of her head is a sign of mourning or humility.

7:30 in the house. This verse is evidence of the presence of a foreign cult in the temple itself, as under Manasseh (2 Kin. 21:7). Josiah had removed the abomination, but it had returned, possibly in the time of Jehoiakim (Introduction: Author; Date and Occasion). Ezekiel also knows of such defilement (Ezek. 8:3–12). Such practices explain Jeremiah's reference to Judah's persistent rebelliousness.

7:31 high places. The usual name for pagan cult centers (2 Kin. 23:8, 9).

Topheth. Lit. "place of fire." This was in the Valley of the Son of Hinnom, where children were sacrificed to the foreign god Molech. Offering the firstborn child was practiced in the ancient world, but in Israel the firstborn child was to be "redeemed" by substituting an animal for sacrifice (Ex. 13:2; 34:19, 20). Child sacrifice was expressly forbidden (Lev. 18:21; 20:2–5). See also 2 Kin. 23:10 and note.

Valley of the Son of Hinnom. Southwest of Jerusalem; its equivalent name in Greek is *Gehenna*, or "hell" (Matt. 5:22 note).

7:33 dead bodies. See 1 Kin. 14:11 and note. Exhuming remains (8:1) inflicted an even greater dishonor (2 Kin. 23:16, 18) than leaving a corpse exposed to scavengers.

8:2 spread before the sun . . . moon . . . host of heaven. The irony in this curse is that they worshiped these heavenly bodies (2 Kin. 21:3–5). Is. 40:25, 26 declares the Creator to be greater than these created things.

8:6 turns. Instead of turning away from their sins, they turned toward them in a headlong rush.

8 [h]"How can you say, 'We are wise,
and the law of the LORD is with
us'?
But behold, the lying pen of the
scribes
has made it into a lie.
9 [i]The wise men shall be put to shame;
they shall be dismayed [j]and
taken;
behold, they have rejected the word
of the LORD,
so what wisdom is in them?
10 [k]Therefore I will give their wives to
others
and their fields to conquerors,
because from the least to the
greatest
everyone [l]is greedy for unjust gain;
from prophet to priest,
everyone deals falsely.
11 They have healed [m]the wound of my
people lightly,
saying, 'Peace, peace,'
when there is no peace.
12 Were they ashamed when they
committed abomination?
No, [n]they were not at all
ashamed;
they did not know how to blush.
[o]Therefore they shall fall among the
fallen;
when I punish them, they shall be
overthrown,
says the LORD.
13 When I would [p]gather them, declares
the LORD,
there are [q]no grapes on the vine,
[r]nor figs on the fig tree;
[s]even the leaves are withered,
and what I gave them has passed
away from them."[1]
14 Why do we sit still?
[t]Gather together; [t]let us go into the
fortified cities
and perish there,
for the LORD our God has doomed us
to perish
and has [u]given us [v]poisoned water
to drink,
because we have sinned against
the LORD.
15 [w]We looked for peace, but no good
came;
for a time of healing, but behold,
terror.
16 [x]"The snorting of their horses is heard
[y]from Dan;
at the sound of the neighing [z]of
their stallions
[a]the whole land quakes.
They come [b]and devour the land and
all that fills it,
the city and those who dwell in it.
17 For behold, I am sending among you
[c]serpents,
adders [d]that cannot be charmed,
[e]and they shall bite you,"
declares the LORD.

Jeremiah Grieves for His People

18 My joy is gone; grief is upon me;[2]
[f]my heart is sick within me.
19 Behold, the cry of the daughter of my
people
from [g]the length and breadth of
the land:
"Is the LORD not in Zion?
[h]Is her King not in her?"
[i]"Why have they provoked me to anger
with their carved images
and with their foreign idols?"
20 "The harvest is past, the summer is
ended,
and we are not saved."
21 For the wound of [j]the daughter of
my people is my heart
wounded;
[k]I mourn, and dismay has taken
hold on me.

8 [h][Rom. 2:17, 18]
9 [i][1 Cor. 1:19, 20] [j]Job 5:13
10 [k]For ver. 10-12, see ch. 6:12-15 [l][Isai. 56:11]
11 [m]ver. 21
12 [n]See ch. 3:3 [o][Hos. 4:5]
13 [p]Zeph. 1:2 [q]Isai. 5:1, 2; Joel 1:7 [r][Matt. 21:19; Luke 13:6] [s]Isai. 1:30
14 [t]ch. 4:5 [u]ch. 9:15; 23:15; Lam. 3:15, 19; Amos 6:12; [Rev. 8:11] [v]ch. 23:15; Deut. 29:18
15 [w]ch. 14:19; Job 30:26
16 [x]Job 39:20 [y]ch. 4:15 [z]Judg. 5:22 [a]ch. 49:21; 51:29; Ps. 60:2 [b]ch. 10:25; 47:2
17 [c][Lev. 26:22] [d]Ps. 58:4, 5; [Eccles. 10:11] [e]Num. 21:6
18 [f]Isai. 1:5; Lam. 1:13, 22; 5:17
19 [g]Isai. 39:3 [h]Isai. 33:17 [i]Deut. 32:21
21 [j]ver. 11; ch. 14:17 [k]Job 30:30; Lam. 4:8; Joel 2:6; Nah. 2:10

1 The meaning of the Hebrew is uncertain 2 Compare Septuagint; the meaning of the Hebrew is uncertain

8:8 wise . . . scribes. The wise are a group, perhaps the same group as the "scribes." See 2 Sam. 8:17; Ezra 7:6 and notes.

8:9 The wise . . . what wisdom. Unlike the wisdom expounded in Proverbs, the wisdom of these scribes is empty, having no real knowledge of the Lord's word. See Deut. 4:6.

8:13 no grapes on the vine. The vine symbolizes Judah (2:21). However, the language also suggests a loss of fertility, a blessing of God that the people had attributed to other gods (Hos. 2:8, 9).

8:14 Gather together. The word is the same as for "gathering" the harvest in v. 13. Ironically, what they intend as a gathering for safety will be a gathering for judgment.

8:17 serpents, adders. This may be taken literally, as a kind of plague (compare the "poisoned water," v. 14; Num. 21:6), or as a figure of speech for the enemy.

8:18 My joy is gone; grief is upon me. The Hebrew in this phrase is problematic (text note).

8:21 I mourn. Jeremiah participates in the suffering of the people (14:2).

22 Is there no [l]balm in Gilead?
Is there no physician there?
Why then has the health of the daughter of my people
not been restored?

9 [1] [m]Oh that my head were waters,
and my eyes a fountain of tears,
that I might weep day and night
for the slain of [j]the daughter of my people!
2 [2] Oh that I had in the desert
a travelers' lodging place,
that I might leave my people
and go away from them!
For they are all [n]adulterers,
a company of [o]treacherous men.
3 [p]They bend their tongue like a bow;
falsehood and not truth has grown strong[3] in the land;
for they proceed from evil to evil,
[q]and they do not know me, declares the LORD.

4 [r]Let everyone beware of his neighbor,
and put no trust in any brother,
for every [s]brother is a deceiver,
and every neighbor [t]goes about as a slanderer.
5 Everyone deceives his neighbor,
and no one speaks the truth;
they have taught their tongue to speak lies;
they weary themselves committing iniquity.
6 Heaping oppression upon oppression, and deceit upon deceit,
[u]they refuse to know me, declares the LORD.

7 Therefore thus says the LORD of hosts:
"Behold, [v]I will refine them and [w]test them,
for what else can I do, because of my people?
8 [x]Their tongue is a deadly arrow;
[y]it speaks deceitfully;
with his mouth [z]each speaks peace to his neighbor,
but in his heart [a]he plans an ambush for him.
9 [b]Shall I not punish them for these things? declares the LORD,
and shall I not avenge myself
on a nation such as this?

10 "I will take up weeping and wailing for the mountains,
and a lamentation for [c]the pastures of the wilderness,
[d]because they are laid waste so that no one passes through,
and the lowing of cattle is not heard;
[e]both the birds of the air and the beasts
have fled and are gone.
11 [f]I will make Jerusalem a heap of ruins,
[g]a lair of jackals,
[h]and I will make the cities of Judah a desolation,
without inhabitant."

12 [i]Who is the man so wise that he can
understand this? To whom has the mouth
of the LORD spoken, that he may declare
it? Why is the land ruined [j]and laid waste
like a wilderness, so that no one passes
through? 13 And the LORD says: [k]"Because
they have forsaken my law that I set before them, and have not obeyed my voice
or walked in accord with it, 14 but [l]have

22 [l]ch. 46:11; [Gen. 37:25]
Chapter 9
1 [m]See ch. 13:17 [j][See ver. 21 above]
2 [n]ch. 5:7, 8; 23:10; Hos. 7:4 [o]Isai. 21:2
3 [p][Ps. 64:3] [q][Judg. 2:10; Hos. 4:1]
4 [r]ch. 12:6; Ps. 41:9; Mic. 7:5 [s][Gen. 27:36] [t]ch. 6:28; [Lev. 19:16]
6 [u]ch. 8:5
7 [v]Isai. 1:25 [w]ch. 6:27
8 [x][Ps. 57:4] [y][Ps. 12:2; 120:3] [z]Ps. 28:3 [a]Hos. 7:6
9 [b]ch. 5:9, 29
10 [c]ch. 12:4; Ps. 65:12 [d]ver. 12 [e]ch. 4:25
11 [f]Isai. 25:2 [g]ch. 10:22; 49:33; 51:37 [h]ch. 34:22; 44:6
12 [i]ch. 23:18; Ps. 107:43; Hos. 14:9 [j]ver. 10
13 [k][Ps. 89:30-32]
14 [l]See ch. 3:17

[1] Ch 8:23 in Hebrew [2] Ch 9:1 in Hebrew [3] Septuagint; Hebrew *and not for truth they have grown strong*

8:22 no balm in Gilead. Gilead was known for its medicinal products (46:11).

no physician . . . restored. For the healing metaphor, and false healers, see 8:11. The desire for a physician is an appeal to God as such; He will come at the right time in the Person of Christ, the Great Physician (30:17; cf. Luke 4:18, 19).

9:1 that I might weep. Jeremiah's sympathy for the people will be shared later by Jesus (Luke 19:41).

9:3 like a bow. This is a military simile; their bow is falsehood, and they go out wielding it, as if to battle.

declares the LORD. God concurs in Jeremiah's estimation of the moral condition of the people (vv. 1, 2). The Lord's attitude is expressed through the prophet.

9:8 speaks peace. Such peace (Hebrew *shalom*) would be a true basis for society, and a product of covenant faithfulness; its opposite is falsehood, unfortunately the actual basis of the society.

9:10 I will take up weeping. Jeremiah weeps particularly for the desolation of the land God had given His people to be rich and populated, but which is desolate. See Mic. 1:8.

9:11 a lair of jackals. The lack of inhabitants marks the curse on the land in this common theme (Ps. 44:19; Is. 13:21, 22).

9:12 wise . . . understand. This language is reminiscent of the concept of wisdom as God-given knowledge (Prov. 1:2–5). The idea of wisdom as a recommendation of Israel among the nations (Deut. 4:6) has now been overturned.

9:13 that I set before them. See Deut. 4:8.

stubbornly followed their own hearts and
have gone after the Baals, as their fathers
taught them. 15 Therefore thus says the
LORD of hosts, the God of Israel: [m]Behold,
I will feed this people with bitter food, and
give them [n]poisonous water to drink. 16 [o]I
will scatter them among the nations
[p]whom neither they nor their fathers have
known, and I will [q]send the sword after
them, until I have consumed them."

17 Thus says the LORD of hosts:
[r]"Consider, and call for the mourning
women to come;
send for the skillful women to
come;
18 let them make haste [s]and raise a
wailing over us,
[t]that our eyes may run down with
tears
and our eyelids flow with water.
19 For a sound of wailing is heard from
Zion:
[u]'How we are ruined!
We are utterly shamed,
because we have left the land,
because they have cast down our
dwellings.'"
20 Hear, O women, the word of the
LORD,
and let your ear receive the word
of his mouth;
teach to your daughters a lament,
and each to her neighbor a dirge.
21 For death has come up into our
windows;
it has entered our palaces,
[v]cutting off the children from the
streets
and the young men from the
squares.

15 [m]Deut. 29:18; [Ps. 80:5] [n]See ch. 8:14
16 [o]Lev. 26:33; Deut. 28:64 [p]ch. 15:14 [q]ch. 14:12; [ch. 49:37; Ezek. 5:2, 12]
17 [r][2 Chr. 35:25]
18 [s]Amos 5:16; [Matt. 9:23; Mark 5:38] [t]ver. 1; ch. 14:17
19 [u]ch. 4:13
21 [v]ch. 6:11
22 [w]See ch. 8:2 [x][Lev. 23:22; Job 5:26]
23 [y]Prov. 3:5; 21:30; Eccles. 9:11
24 [z][Ps. 34:2; 1 Cor. 1:31; 2 Cor. 10:17] [a][Mic. 6:8; 7:18]
25 [b][Isai. 24:21]
26 [c][ch. 25:19-21] [d]ch. 25:23; 49:32; [Lev. 19:27] [e]Lev. 26:41; Deut. 10:16; Ezek. 44:7; Rom. 2:28, 29; [ch. 4:4]
Chapter 10
3 [f]Isai. 44:9 [g]Isai. 40:20; 45:20
4 [h]Isai. 40:19 [i]Isai. 41:7

22 Speak, "Thus declares the LORD:
[w]'The dead bodies of men shall fall
like dung upon the open field,
[x]like sheaves after the reaper,
and none shall gather them.'"

23 Thus says the LORD: [y]"Let not the wise
man boast in his wisdom, let not the
mighty man boast in his might, let not the
rich man boast in his riches, 24 but [z]let him
who boasts boast in this, that he understands and knows me, that I am the LORD
who practices steadfast love, justice, and
righteousness in the earth. [a]For in these
things I delight, declares the LORD."
25 "Behold, the days are coming, declares
the LORD, when [b]I will punish all those who
are circumcised merely in the flesh—
26 [c]Egypt, Judah, Edom, the sons of Ammon,
Moab, and [d]all who dwell in the desert who
cut the corners of their hair, for all these
nations are uncircumcised, and all the
house of Israel is [e]uncircumcised in heart."

Idols and the Living God

10 Hear the word that the LORD speaks
to you, O house of Israel. 2 Thus
says the LORD:

"Learn not the way of the nations,
nor be dismayed at the signs of the
heavens
because the nations are dismayed
at them,
3 [f]for the customs of the peoples are
vanity.[1]
[g]A tree from the forest is cut down
and worked with an axe by the
hands of a craftsman.
4 [h]They decorate it with silver and gold;
[i]they fasten it with hammer and nails
so that it cannot move.

[1] Or *vapor*, or *mist*

9:17 mourning women. The weeping theme is taken up again (vv. 1, 10), with the Old Testament's clearest allusion to professional wailing women, employed to lead in mourning for the dead (Amos 5:16).

9:21 death. The actions of death are poetically personified.

children . . . young men. See 6:11; Lam. 5:13–15 and notes.

9:24 See theological note "True Knowledge of God."

understands and knows me. See v. 12, which introduced the idea of wisdom into this chapter. In the end wisdom is knowing God, not abstractly, but personally.

steadfast love, justice, and righteousness. These three characteristic qualities of the Lord are revealed and exercised in the covenant.

9:25, 26 circumcised merely in the flesh. See 4:4. Israel is outwardly circumcised, but inwardly uncircumcised. The surrounding nations practiced circumcision, but not as a covenant sign of belonging to the Lord. Because Israel and Judah are uncircumcised in their hearts, they are effectively in the same condition as the nations. See Rom. 2:25–29; 4:9–12; 9:8; Gal. 5:6; 6:15.

10:2 dismayed. Terror characterizes the worship of false gods. Worship of heavenly bodies (8:2 and note) carries with it special fears because of unusual phenomena. A biblical understanding of creation takes away these fears, accepting such phenomena as God's created order (Gen. 1; Is. 40:26).

10:3 vanity. This word, used elsewhere by Jeremiah for idols (cf. v. 8), conveys their emptiness (2:5).

10:4 silver and gold. Although some idols were cast in precious metals (Ex. 32:4; Neh. 9:18), more often they were carved out of wood and decorated with gold or silver as described here (Is. 40:18–20). The most common household idols were molded from clay and fired like pottery (Judg. 18:17; Is. 30:22; 42:17).

5 Their idols[1] are like scarecrows in a
cucumber field,
and [j] they cannot speak;
[k] they have to be carried,
for they cannot walk.
Do not be afraid of them,
[l] for they cannot do evil,
neither is it in them to do good."

6 [m] There is none like you, O LORD;
you are great, and your name is
great in might.
7 [n] Who would not fear you, O King of
the nations?
For this is your due;
for among all the wise ones of the
nations
and in all their kingdoms
there is none like you.
8 [o] They are both [p] stupid and foolish;
the instruction of idols is but wood!
9 [q] Beaten silver is brought from
[r] Tarshish,
and gold from [s] Uphaz.
[q] They are the work of the craftsman
and of the hands of the
goldsmith;
their clothing is violet and purple;
[t] they are all the work of skilled
men.
10 [u] But the LORD is the true God;
[v] he is the living God and the
everlasting King.
At his wrath the earth quakes,
and the nations cannot endure his
indignation.

11 Thus shall you say to them: [w] "The gods
who did not make the heavens and the
earth [x] shall perish from the earth and from
under the heavens."[2]

5 [j] Ps. 115:5; 135:16; Hab. 2:18, 19; 1 Cor. 12:2 [k] Ps. 115:7; Isai. 46:7 [l] Isai. 41:23
6 [m] ch. 49:19; Ex. 15:11; Ps. 86:8, 10
7 [n] ch. 5:22; Rev. 15:4
8 [o] [Isai. 41:29; Hab. 2:18; Zech. 10:2] [p] ver. 21
9 [q] Isai. 40:19 [r] Gen. 10:4; See 1 Kin. 10:22 [s] Dan. 10:5 [t] Ps. 115:4
10 [u] Deut. 32:4; Ps. 31:5 [v] Ps. 42:2
11 [w] [Ps. 96:5] [x] ver. 15; Isai. 2:18; Zech. 13:2

[1] Hebrew *They* [2] This verse is in Aramaic

True Knowledge of God

In 1 Tim. 6:20–21 Paul warns Timothy against "what is falsely called 'knowledge,' for by professing it some have swerved from the faith." Paul's attack is against religious tendencies that developed into Gnosticism in the second century A.D. Teachers of such ideas told believers to see their Christian commitment as only a first step along the road to "knowledge" (*gnosis* in Greek), and urged them to take more steps along that road. These teachers viewed the material order as worthless and considered the body to be a prison for the soul. Their answer to human spiritual need was illumination, that is, to attain a certain "knowledge" reserved for the few. They denied that sin was part of the problem, and the "knowledge" they offered made use of celestial passwords and disciplines of mysticism and detachment. To them, Jesus was a supernatural teacher, but a human being only in appearance; they denied the Incarnation and the Atonement. They replaced Christ's call to a life of holy love with asceticism or licentiousness. Paul's letters to Timothy (1 Tim. 1:3–4; 4:1–7; 6:20–21; 2 Tim. 3:1–9); Jude 4, 8–19; 2 Pet. 2, and the first two letters of John (1 John 1:5–10; 2:9–11, 18–29; 3:7–10; 4:1–6; 5:1–12; 2 John 7–11) explicitly oppose beliefs and practices that would later be recognized as Gnosticism.

By contrast, Scripture speaks of "knowing" God as the spiritual person's ideal: namely, the fullness of a faith relationship that brings salvation and eternal life, generating love, hope, obedience, and joy (Ex. 33:13; Jer. 31:34; Dan. 11:32; John 17:3; Gal. 4:8, 9; Phil. 3:8–11; 2 Tim. 1:12; Heb. 8:8–12). The dimensions of this knowledge are intellectual (knowing the truth about God; Deut. 7:9; Ps. 100:3); volitional (trusting, obeying, and worshiping God); and moral (practicing justice and love; Jer. 22:16; 1 John 4:7–8). Faith's knowledge focuses on Jesus Christ, the incarnate God and the mediator between God and man. Faith seeks specifically to know Christ and His power (Phil. 3:8–14). The knowledge fostered by God's covenant agreement with us is reciprocal, with affection on both sides: we know God as ours because He knows us as His (John 10:14; Gal. 4:9; 2 Tim. 2:19).

10:7 fear. The biblical fear of God involves more than the dread of God's judgment. It includes awe, reverence, and adoration in response to God's majesty and holiness (Ps. 2:11, 12).

O King. This appellation counters claims to kingship by false deities, such as Bel Marduk in Babylon (cf. Is. 46:1; 43:15).

wise ones. Their wisdom is contrasted with the Lord's (v. 12).

10:8 stupid . . . foolish . . . instruction. The language is like that of wisdom literature.

10:9 Tarshish . . . Uphaz. The former is in Spain; Uphaz has not been identified.

10:10 true . . . living God. See Deut. 5:26.

everlasting King. See note on v. 7; also Ex. 15:18; 2 Sam. 7:13. The eternity of God's kingdom is affirmed, even though the house of David is about to come to its historical end.

wrath . . . indignation. Cf. Ps. 97:5.

12 [y]It is he who [z]made the earth by his power,
[z]who established the world by his wisdom,
and [a]by his understanding stretched out the heavens.
13 [b]When he utters his voice, there is a tumult of waters in the heavens,
[c]and he makes the mist rise from the ends of the earth.
[c]He makes lightning [d]for the rain,
[c]and he brings forth the wind [e]from his storehouses.
14 [f]Every man is stupid and without knowledge;
[g]every goldsmith is put to shame by his idols,
for his images are false,
[h]and there is no breath in them.
15 They are worthless, a work of delusion;
at the time of their punishment they shall perish.
16 Not like these is he who is [i]the portion of Jacob,
for he is the one who formed all things,
[j]and Israel is the tribe of his inheritance;
[k]the LORD of hosts is his name.
17 [l]Gather up your bundle from the ground,
O you who dwell under siege!
18 For thus says the LORD:
[m]"Behold, I am slinging out the inhabitants of the land
at this time,
[n]and I will bring distress on them,
that they may feel it."

19 Woe is me because of my hurt!
[o]My wound is grievous.
But I said, "Truly this is an affliction,
and I must bear it."
20 [p]My tent is destroyed,
and all my cords are broken;
my children have gone from me,
[q]and they are not;
there is no one to spread my tent again
and [p]to set up my curtains.
21 [r]For the shepherds [s]are stupid
and do not inquire of the LORD;
therefore they have not prospered,
[t]and all their flock is scattered.

22 A voice, a rumor! Behold, it comes!—
[u]a great commotion out of the north country
to make [v]the cities of Judah a desolation,
[v]a lair of jackals.

23 [w]I know, O LORD, that the way of man is not in himself,
that it is not in man who walks to direct his steps.
24 [x]Correct me, O LORD, but in justice;
not in your anger, lest you bring me to nothing.
25 [y]Pour out your wrath on the nations that know you not,
and on the peoples that call not on your name,
[z]for they have devoured Jacob;
they have devoured him and consumed him,
and have laid waste his habitation.

12 [y]For ver. 12-16, see ch. 51:15-19 [z]Gen. 1:1, 6, 9; Ps. 104:5; Prov. 3:19 [a]Job 9:8
13 [b][Job 38:34; Ps. 104:6, 7] [c]Ps. 135:7 [d]ch. 14:22; Job 5:10 [e]Job 38:22
14 [f]ver. 8; Prov. 30:2; [Rom. 1:22] [g]See Isai. 42:17 [h]Ps. 135:17; Hab. 2:19
16 [i]Ps. 16:5 [j]Deut. 32:9 [k]ch. 31:35; 32:18; 50:34
17 [l][ch. 6:1; Ezek. 12:3]
18 [m]1 Sam. 25:29 [n]Deut. 28:20
19 [o]ch. 14:17; 30:12
20 [p]ch. 4:20; [Isai. 54:2] [q]ch. 31:15
21 [r]ch. 23:1; Ezek. 34:2 [s]ver. 8 [t]Ezek. 34:5, 6
22 [u]See ch. 1:13 [v]See ch. 9:11
23 [w]Prov. 16:1; 20:24; Dan. 5:23
24 [x]ch. 30:11; 46:28; Ps. 6:1; 38:1
25 [y]Ps. 79:6, 7 [z]ch. 8:16; 30:16; Ps. 14:4

10:12 power . . . wisdom . . . understanding. The power of the true God in creation is appealed to again in the argument against foreign gods. For creation by God's wisdom, see Prov. 8:22–31, a passage that foreshadows Christ as the pre-existent wisdom of God (Col. 1:15; 2:3).

10:13 When he utters . . . from his storehouses. See Ps. 29:3, 4; 135:5–7. The Lord's control of the rain directly counters claims made for the Canaanite god Baal (see 1 Kin. 17:1).

10:16 portion of Jacob . . . his inheritance. For the Lord as one's portion or inheritance see Num. 18:20; Ps. 16:5. Originally this referred specifically to the Levites, but later it is used more broadly to describe what God promised Israel in His covenant with them.

10:19 Woe is me . . . grievous. See Jeremiah's cry in 4:19–21. The medical metaphor is a favorite in Jeremiah (6:7; 14:17; 30:12, 13, 15, 17).

10:20 my children have gone. The sorrows of losing children fill in the picture of the desolation of exile (16:3–5).

10:23 I know . . . his steps. This thought is found also in the wisdom literature (Prov. 16:9).

10:25 This verse closely resembles Ps. 79:6, 7 and may be a citation of it. Yet in its new context it may not be as well motivated as in the psalm. The chapter ends with a plea for the Lord to punish the Gentiles, even though its main burden has been to show that Judah deserves as severe a judgment.

The Broken Covenant

11 The word that came to Jeremiah
from the LORD: 2 [a]"Hear the words
of this covenant, and speak to the men of
Judah and the inhabitants of Jerusalem.
3 You shall say to them, Thus says the LORD,
the God of Israel: [b]Cursed be the man who
does not hear the words of this covenant
4 that I commanded your fathers when I
brought them out of the land of Egypt,
[c]from the iron furnace, saying, [d]Listen to
my voice, and do all that I command you.
[d]So shall you be my people, and I will be
your God, 5 [e]that I may confirm the oath
that I swore to your fathers, [f]to give them a
land flowing with milk and honey, as at
this day." Then I answered, "So be it,
LORD."

6 And the LORD said to me, [g]"Proclaim all
these words in the cities of Judah and in
the streets of Jerusalem: [h]Hear the words of
this covenant and do them. 7 For I solemnly warned your fathers when I brought
them up out of the land of Egypt, [i]warning
them persistently, even to this day, saying,
[d]Obey my voice. 8 [j]Yet they did not obey or
incline their ear, [k]but everyone walked in
the stubbornness of his evil heart.
Therefore I brought upon them all [g]the
words of this covenant, which I commanded them to do, but they did not."

9 Again the LORD said to me, [l]"A conspiracy exists among the men of Judah and the
inhabitants of Jerusalem. 10 They have
turned back to [m]the iniquities of their forefathers, who refused to hear my words.
[m]They have gone after other gods to serve
them. [n]The house of Israel and the house
of Judah have broken my covenant that I
made with their fathers. 11 Therefore, thus
says the LORD, behold, I am bringing disaster upon them that they cannot escape.
[o]Though they cry to me, I will not listen to
them. 12 Then the cities of Judah and the
inhabitants of Jerusalem [p]will go and cry to
the gods to whom they make offerings,
[p]but they cannot save them in the time of
their trouble. 13 [p]For your gods have
become as many as your cities, O Judah,
and as many as the streets of Jerusalem are
the altars you have set up to shame, [q]altars
to make offerings to Baal.

14 "Therefore [r]do not pray for this people,
or lift up a cry or prayer on their behalf,
[o]for I will not listen when they call to me in
the time of their trouble. 15 [s]What right has
my beloved in my house, [t]when she has
done many vile deeds? Can even sacrificial
flesh avert your doom? [u]Can you then
exult? 16 The LORD once called you [v]'a green
olive tree, beautiful with good fruit.' But
[w]with the roar of a great tempest he will set
fire to it, and [x]its branches will be consumed. 17 The LORD of hosts, [y]who planted
you, has decreed disaster against you,
because of the evil that the house of Israel
and the house of Judah have done, [z]pro-
voking me to anger by making offerings to
Baal."

18 The LORD made it known to me and
I knew;
then you showed me their
deeds.

Chapter 11
2 [a]ver. 6, 8; [2 Kin. 23:3]
3 [b]Deut. 27:26; Gal. 3:10
4 [c]Deut. 4:20 [d]ch. 7:22, 23; Lev. 26:3, 12
5 [e]Deut. 7:12, 13; Ps. 105:9, 10 [f]See Ex. 3:8
6 [g][ch. 19:2] [h]ver. 6, 8; [2 Kin. 23:3]
7 [i]ch. 7:25; See 2 Chr. 36:15 [d][See ver. 4 above]
8 [j]ch. 7:26; 32:23 [k]See ch. 3:17 [g][See ver. 6 above]
9 [l]Ezek. 22:25; [Isai. 8:12; Hos. 6:9]
10 [m][ch. 17:23; Ps. 78:8; 79:8; Ezek. 20:18] [n]Deut. 31:16, 20
11 [o]Prov. 1:28; Isai. 1:15; Ezek. 8:18; Mic. 3:4
12 [p]ch. 2:28; [Acts 17:16]
13 [p][See ver. 12 above] [q][Hos. 9:10]; See Judg. 6:25-32
14 [r]ch. 7:16; [Heb. 10:26; 1 John 5:16] [o][See ver. 11 above]
15 [s]Isai. 1:11, 12 [t][Ezek. 16:25] [u]Prov. 2:14
16 [v]Ps. 52:8; [Hos. 14:6] [w][Ps. 83:2] [x]Rom. 11:17, 20
17 [y]ch. 2:21; Isai. 5:2 [z]See ch. 7:18

11:1–13:27 Judah's idolatry is a violation of the covenant and will result in captivity as part of the curses of the covenant.

11:2 words. The commands of God in the Mosaic covenant (Deut. 1:1). The Mosaic covenant, unlike the covenant of Noah and the new covenant, depended on Israel's faithfulness rather than the Lord's (Heb. 8:6; Introduction: Characteristics and Themes).

covenant. A covenant is a solemn agreement between two or more parties. It is the kind of relationship into which God freely entered first with all mankind (Gen. 9:1–17), then with Abraham, as the father of Israel (Gen. 17:1–21), then with Israel at Sinai (Ex. 19–24), then with David (2 Sam. 7:12–16; Ps. 89:3), and finally with the whole people of God in the new covenant (31:31–34 notes).

11:3 Cursed be the man. See Deut. 27:15–26.

11:5 confirm the oath that I swore. The covenant with Abraham was in the form of a divine promise (Gen. 15:17–21; cf. Deut. 4:31). Under the terms of the Mosaic covenant, the temporal blessings of the Abrahamic covenant were administered on the basis of Israel's obedience (Ex. 19–24). Under the terms of the new covenant, the eternal blessings of the Abrahamic covenant are administered on the basis of Christ's obedience, while the believer's obedience proves the vitality of their professed faith (James 2:14–26).

a land flowing with milk and honey. See Ex. 3:8; Deut. 6:3.

So be it. The "So be it" (Hebrew *amen*) indicates acceptance of the terms laid down. See Deut. 27:15–26.

11:9 conspiracy. This could be resistance to Jeremiah's words, or to Josiah's reform.

11:10 house . . . with their fathers. Again, the covenant is traced back to the promise to the patriarchs (v. 5 and note). Judah's present breach of it is consistent with the pattern of Israel's history (see especially Judges).

11:13 make offerings. Incense was used in pagan worship and also in worship of the Lord (1:16; 7:9; 18:15; Ex. 30:7–9).

11:15 my beloved. Judah, also in 12:7. The term of endearment is in line with the courtship and bridal imagery of 2:2; 3:1.

in my house. See 7:10, 11; Ezek. 8:6–13.

sacrificial flesh . . . exult. The Hebrew is difficult; the criticism, however, is of unacceptable worship that produces a falsely based joy in God's salvation.

19 But I was [a]like a gentle lamb
led to the slaughter.
I did not know [b]it was against me
they devised schemes, saying,
"Let us destroy the tree with its fruit,
[c]let us cut him off from [d]the land of the living,
that his name be remembered no more."
20 But, O LORD of hosts, who judges righteously,
who [e]tests [f]the heart and the mind,
[g]let me see your vengeance upon them,
for to you have I committed my cause.

21 Therefore thus says the LORD concerning the men of [h]Anathoth, [i]who seek your
life, and say, [j]"Do not prophesy in the
name of the LORD, or you will die by our
hand"— 22 therefore thus says the LORD of
hosts: "Behold, I will punish them. The
young men shall die by the sword, their
sons and their daughters shall die by
famine, 23 and none of them shall be left.
For I will bring disaster upon the men of
[k]Anathoth, [l]the year of their punishment."

Jeremiah's Complaint

12 [m]Righteous are you, O LORD,
when I complain to you;
yet I would plead my case before you.
[n]Why does the way of the wicked prosper?
Why do all [o]who are treacherous thrive?
2 You plant them, and they take root;
they grow and produce fruit;
[p]you are near in their mouth
and far from their heart.
3 [q]But you, O LORD, know me;
[r]you see me, and test my heart toward you.
[s]Pull them out like sheep for the slaughter,
and set them apart for [t]the day of slaughter.
4 [u]How long will the land mourn
and the grass of every field wither?
[v]For the evil of those who dwell in it
[w]the beasts and the birds are swept away,
because they said, "He will not see our latter end."

The LORD Answers Jeremiah

5 "If you have raced with men on foot,
and they have wearied you,
how will you compete with horses?
And if in a safe land you are so trusting,
what will you do in [x]the thicket of the Jordan?
6 For [y]even your brothers and the house of your father,
[n]even they have dealt treacherously with you;
they are in full cry after you;
[z]do not believe them,
though they speak friendly words to you."
7 "I have forsaken my house;
I have abandoned [a]my heritage;
I have given [b]the beloved of my soul
into the hands of her enemies.
8 [a]My heritage has become to me
like a lion in the forest;
she has lifted up her voice against me;
therefore I hate her.
9 Is [a]my heritage to me like [c]a hyena's lair?
Are the [c]birds of prey against her all around?
Go, [d]assemble all the wild beasts;
bring them to devour.

19 [a]Isai. 53:7; [Rev. 5:6] [b]ch. 18:18; Lam. 3:60, 61 [c]Ps. 83:4; Isai. 53:8 [d]Ps. 27:13
20 [e]ch. 17:10; 20:12; Ps. 7:9; Rev. 2:23 [f]See 1 Sam. 16:7 [g]ch. 15:15; 17:18; 20:12; Lam. 3:64
21 [h]Josh. 21:18 [i][ch. 12:6; Matt. 13:57] [j]Isai. 30:10
23 [k]Josh. 21:18 [l]ch. 23:12
Chapter 12
1 [m]Ezra 9:15; Ps. 51:4; Lam. 1:18; Dan. 9:7 [n]Job 12:6; Ps. 37:1, 7; 92:7; Hab. 1:13; Mal. 3:15; See Job 21:7-15; Ps. 73:3-12 [o][Isai. 21:2]
2 [p]Isai. 29:13
3 [q]ch. 15:15; Ps. 130:1 [r]Ps. 17:3 [s][2 Pet. 2:12] [t]James 5:5
4 [u]ver. 11; ch. 9:10; 23:10 [v]Ps. 107:34 [w]ch. 4:25; 7:20; 9:10; Hos. 4:3; [Rom. 8:22]
5 [x]ch. 40:19; 50:44; Zech. 11:3; [Josh. 3:15]
6 [y]ch. 9:4; [ch. 11:19, 21] [n][See ver. 1 above] [z]Prov. 26:25
7 [a]Isai. 19:25 [b]ch. 11:15
8 [a][See ver. 7 above]
9 [a][See ver. 7 above] [c]Isai. 46:11 [d]ch. 7:33; Isai. 56:9; [Ezek. 39:17; Rev. 19:17]

11:19 like a gentle lamb led to the slaughter. A simile drawing on the practice of sacrifice (see Ps. 44:11). Jeremiah often uses the language of the "lament" psalms (see Introduction to Psalms). As a type of Christ, the sufferings of Christ are prefigured in Jeremiah's life (Is. 53:7).

tree with its fruit. Meaning Jeremiah and his message, or an emphatic reference to his life.

cut him off . . . remembered no more. Not to be remembered, by having no children, was the worst of fates. Those who tried to cut off Jeremiah's remembrance are themselves forgotten, while through his prophecy, Jeremiah is remembered today.

11:21 the men of Anathoth. They are from Jeremiah's own town (1:1). The details of the plot reveal that his worst opposition comes from those closest to him (Ps. 69:7–9; Matt. 10:36, citing Mic. 7:6). In this respect also Jeremiah resembles Christ (John 7:2–5; Acts 1:15–20).

11:23 none of them. This threat of total extinction contrasts the fate of Jeremiah's personal enemies with that of Judah in general (see 4:27; 5:10; 6:9, and notes).

12:6 your brothers and the house of your father. See 11:21–23.

12:7 heritage. God's "heritage" includes both the land given to Israel (Deut. 4:21), and the people themselves. See vv. 8, 9; 2:7.

beloved. See 11:15 and note.

12:8 like a lion. This first of a series of similes (cf. vv. 9, 10) shows how Judah's nature has been changed.

I hate her. As often in the Bible, "hate" is the only alternative to love (Mal. 1:2, 3).

10 Many shepherds have destroyed my
vineyard;
[e] they have trampled down my
portion;
they have made my pleasant portion
a desolate wilderness.
11 They have made it a desolation;
desolate, [u] it mourns to me.
The whole land is made desolate,
[f] but no man lays it to heart.
12 Upon all the bare heights in the desert
destroyers have come,
for the sword of the LORD devours
from one end of the land to the
other;
no flesh has peace.
13 [g] They have sown wheat and have
reaped thorns;
[h] they have tired themselves out but
profit nothing.
They shall be ashamed of their[1]
harvests
[i] because of the fierce anger of the
LORD."

14 Thus says the LORD concerning all [j] my evil neighbors [k] who touch the heritage that [l] I have given my people Israel to inherit: "Behold, I will pluck them up from their land, and I will pluck up the house of Judah from among them. 15 And after I have plucked them up, I will again have compassion on them, [m] and I will bring them again each to his heritage and each to his land. 16 And it shall come to pass, if they will diligently learn the ways of my people, [n] to swear by my name, 'As the LORD lives,' even as they taught my people to swear by Baal, [o] then they shall be built up in the midst of my people. 17 [p] But if any nation will not listen, then I will utterly pluck it up and destroy it, declares the LORD."

10 [e] Isai. 63:18 11 [u] [See ver. 4 above] [f] Isai. 42:25 13 [g] [Lev. 26:16; Deut. 28:38; Mic. 6:15; Hag. 1:6] [h] Isai. 55:2; Hab. 2:13 [i] ch. 4:8, 26; 25:37, 38; 30:24; 49:37; 51:45; Lam. 1:12; 4:11 14 [j] [Ps. 137:7]; See Ezek. ch. 25 [k] Zech. 2:8 [l] ch. 3:18 15 [m] ch. 48:47; 49:6 16 [n] ch. 4:2 [o] ch. 24:6; [1 Pet. 2:5] 17 [p] [Isai. 60:12]

Chapter 13
1 [q] Ex. 28:39; Lev. 16:4; [Acts 21:11] 4 [r] [ch. 51:59, 63] [s] Isai. 7:19 6 [q] [See ver. 1 above] 7 [q] [See ver. 1 above] [t] ch. 18:4 [u] [Ezek. 15:4, 5] 9 [v] [Ps. 137:1] [w] Lev. 26:19 10 [x] [ch. 3:17; 16:11, 12] [u] [See ver. 7 above] 11 [y] [Ex. 19:5] [z] ch. 33:9; Isai. 55:13; Zeph. 3:20

The Ruined Loincloth

13 Thus says the LORD to me, "Go and buy a linen loincloth and [q] put it around your waist, and do not dip it in water." 2 So I bought a loincloth according to the word of the LORD, and put it around my waist. 3 And the word of the LORD came to me a second time, 4 "Take the loincloth that you have bought, which is around your waist, and arise, [r] go to the Euphrates and hide it there in [s] a cleft of the rock." 5 So I went and hid it by the Euphrates, as the LORD commanded me. 6 And after many days the LORD said to me, "Arise, go to the Euphrates, and take from there [q] the loincloth that I commanded you to hide there." 7 Then I went to the Euphrates, and dug, and I took [q] the loincloth from the place where I had hidden it. And behold, the loincloth was [t] spoiled; it was [u] good for nothing.

8 Then the word of the LORD came to me: 9 "Thus says the LORD: [v] Even so will I spoil the pride of Judah and the great [w] pride of Jerusalem. 10 This evil people, who refuse to hear my words, [x] who stubbornly follow their own heart and have gone after other gods to serve them and worship them, shall be like this loincloth, which is [u] good for nothing. 11 For as the loincloth clings to the waist of a man, so I made the whole house of Israel and the whole house of Judah cling to me, declares the LORD, [y] that they might be for me a people, [z] a name, a praise, and a glory, but they would not listen.

The Jars Filled with Wine

12 "You shall speak to them this word: 'Thus says the LORD, the God of Israel, "Every jar shall be filled with wine."' And they will say to you, 'Do we not indeed

[1] Hebrew *your*

12:10 shepherds. That is, foreign rulers.

pleasant portion. See Is. 5:7.

12:12 no flesh has peace. The verse exposes the lie of false proclamations of peace (6:14).

12:14 evil neighbors. Though Judah's enemies are used by the Lord to punish her, they themselves will be judged.

pluck up. When God judges Judah's enemies by removing them from their own lands, He also will deliver and restore Judah, the theme to be developed in Jer. 30–33.

12:15 after I have plucked them up . . . his land. This prophecy is an astonishing turn in the thought, anticipating a restoration and salvation of all peoples. Jeremiah looks forward to the inclusion of the Gentiles in God's salvation (46:26; 48:47; 49:6) as do other prophets (e.g., Is. 42:6).

12:16 they shall be built up . . . my people. See Is. 19:25 for an equally surprising use of "my people"—for Egypt.

13:1 linen loincloth. The "loincloth" symbolizes the close relationship between God and His people.

13:4 Euphrates. A nearer location may actually be intended (possibly Parah, Josh. 18:23, close to Anathoth), whose similarity of name nevertheless suggested the Euphrates and therefore the Babylonian exile.

13:7 spoiled . . . good for nothing. Its ruin depicts the corruption of the people, no longer fit for a relationship with the Lord.

13:11 made the whole house . . . cling to me. The Lord spells out the meaning of the symbolic act as an illustration of His covenant with all Israel.

13:12 filled with wine. Wine is here used as a symbol of God's wrath (25:15–29).

know that [a]every jar will be filled with
wine?' 13 Then you shall say to them, 'Thus
says the LORD: [b]Behold, I will fill with
drunkenness all the inhabitants of this
land: [c]the kings who sit on David's throne,
[d]the priests, the prophets, and all the inhabitants of Jerusalem. 14 And I will [e]dash
them one against another, fathers and sons
together, declares the LORD. I will not pity
or spare or have compassion, that I should
not destroy them.'"

Exile Threatened

15 Hear and give ear; be not proud,
for the LORD has spoken.
16 [f]Give glory to the LORD your God
[g]before he brings darkness,
before your feet stumble
on the twilight mountains,
and [g]while you look for light
he turns it into gloom
and makes it [h]deep darkness.
17 But if you will not listen,
[i]my soul will weep in secret for
your pride;
my eyes will weep bitterly and run
down with tears,
because the LORD's flock has been
taken captive.

18 Say to [j]the king and [j]the queen
mother:
"Take a lowly seat,
for [k]your beautiful crown
has come down from your head."
19 [l]The cities of the Negeb are shut up,
with none to open them;
all Judah is taken into exile,
wholly taken into exile.

20 "Lift up your eyes [m]and see
those who come from the north.
Where is the flock that was given you,
your beautiful flock?
21 What will you say when they set as
head over you
those whom you yourself have
taught to be friends to you?
[n]Will not pangs take hold of you
like those of a woman in
labor?
22 And if you say in your heart,
[o]'Why have these things come
upon me?'
it is for the greatness of your
iniquity
that [p]your skirts are lifted up
and you suffer violence.
23 [q]Can the Ethiopian change his
skin
or [q]the leopard his spots?
Then also you can do good
who are accustomed to do evil.
24 I will scatter you[1] [r]like chaff
driven by the wind from the
desert.
25 [s]This is your lot,
the portion I have measured out
to you, declares the LORD,
because [t]you have forgotten me
and trusted in lies.
26 [p]I myself will lift up your skirts over
your face,
and your shame will be seen.
27 I have seen [u]your abominations,
your adulteries and [v]neighings,
your lewd whorings,
[w]on the hills in the field.
Woe to you, O Jerusalem!
How long will it be [x]before you
are made clean?"

Famine, Sword, and Pestilence

14 The word of the LORD that came to Jeremiah concerning [y]the drought:

[1] Hebrew *them*

12 [a]ch. 48:12
13 [b]Ezek. 23:33 [c]ch. 17:20; 19:3; 22:2 [d][ch. 18:18]
14 [e]Ps. 2:9; [ch. 19:10, 11]
16 [f][Josh. 7:19] [g]Isai. 5:30; 8:22; Amos 5:8; 8:9; [John 11:10] [h]Isai. 60:2
17 [i]ch. 9:1, 18; 14:17; Lam. 1:2, 16; 2:18; 3:49
18 [j]ch. 22:26; 2 Kin. 24:12 [k]Prov. 4:9; Isai. 28:5; 62:3; Lam. 5:16
19 [l][Josh. 6:1]
20 [m]ch. 1:13, 14; 6:22
21 [n]See Isai. 13:8
22 [o]See ch. 5:19 [p]ver. 26; Isai. 3:17; Lam. 1:8; Nah. 3:5; [Hos. 2:10]
23 [q][Matt. 19:26]
24 [r]Ps. 1:4; 83:13
25 [s]Job 20:29; Ps. 11:6 [t]ch. 2:32
26 [p][See ver. 22 above]
27 [u]ch. 6:15 [v]ch. 5:8 [w]See ch. 2:20 [x]Isai. 1:16; [Ezek. 24:13]
Chapter 14
1 [y]ch. 17:8

13:18 to the king and the queen mother. Probably Jehoiachin and his mother Nehushta (2 Kin. 24:8). This prophecy is thus close to the time of Nebuchadnezzar's attack on Jerusalem in 597 B.C. (Introduction: Author; Date and Occasion).

has come down. See 22:24–26. This judgment spells the end of the historical Davidic dynasty, and seems in conflict with the promise to David (2 Sam. 7). However, see 33:14–26 for the future fulfillment of the Davidic covenant.

13:19 The cities of the Negeb. These cities along the southern border were important defense against allies of Babylon (like Moab; 2 Kin. 24:2), but were unable to prevent the sack of Judah. They symbolize Judah's pride (v. 17), shown to be hollow.

13:20 the north. See 4:6. Judah is vulnerable from both north and south (v. 19).

13:22 your skirts. A picture of public shame, as of a prostitute.

13:23 Can the Ethiopian . . . his spots. A rhetorical question. It is typical of Jeremiah to assert Judah's inability to repent and obey the Lord—hence his new covenant theology (31:31–34 and notes). See "The Freedom and Bondage of the Will" at 17:9.

13:25 lot. The word "lot" recalls the lot cast for the division of the land (Josh. 14:2). Now it signifies expulsion from the same land.

14:1–15:21 The people are so hardened in their sin that God will not answer even Jeremiah's prayer for deliverance from the punishment of drought. In answer to Jeremiah's question whether God has rejected Judah completely (14:19), God replies that the coming judgment is inevitable because of Judah's sin, but He assures Jeremiah of personal deliverance from his enemies.

2 [z]"Judah mourns
and [a]her gates languish;
her people lament on the ground,
and [b]the cry of Jerusalem goes up.
3 Her nobles send their servants for water;
they come to the cisterns;
they find no water;
they return with their vessels empty;
they are [c]ashamed and confounded
and [d]cover their heads.
4 Because of the ground that is dismayed,
since there is [e]no rain on the land,
the farmers are ashamed;
they cover their heads.
5 Even [f]the doe in the field forsakes
her newborn fawn
because there is no grass.
6 [g]The wild donkeys stand on the bare heights;
they pant for air like jackals;
their eyes fail
because there is no vegetation.

7 "Though our iniquities testify against us,
act, O LORD, [h]for your name's sake;
[i]for our backslidings are many;
[j]we have sinned against you.
8 [k]O you hope of Israel,
its savior in time of trouble,
why should you be like a stranger in the land,
like a traveler who turns aside to tarry for a night?
9 Why should you be like a man confused,
[l]like a mighty warrior who cannot save?
Yet [m]you, O LORD, are in the midst of us,
and [n]we are called by your name;
[o]do not leave us."

10 Thus says the LORD concerning this people:
"They have loved to wander thus;
they have not restrained their feet;
[p]therefore the LORD does not accept them;
[q]now he will remember their iniquity
and punish their sins."

11 The LORD said to me: [r]"Do not pray for
the welfare of this people. 12 Though they
fast, I will not hear their cry, [s]and though
they offer burnt offering and grain offering,
I will not accept them. But I will consume
them [t]by the sword, by famine, and by
pestilence."

Lying Prophets

13 Then I said: "Ah, Lord GOD, behold,
the prophets [u]say to them, 'You shall not
see the sword, nor shall you have famine,
but I will give you assured peace in this
place.'" 14 And the LORD said to me: "The
[v]prophets are prophesying lies in my name.
[w]I did not send them, nor did I command
them or speak to them. They are prophesying to you a lying vision, [x]worthless divination, and [y]the deceit of their own minds.
15 Therefore thus says the LORD concerning
the prophets who prophesy in my name
although I did not send them, and who
say, 'Sword and famine shall not come
upon this land': [z]By sword and famine
those prophets shall be consumed. 16 And
the people to whom they prophesy shall be
cast out in the streets of Jerusalem, victims
of famine and sword, [a]with none to bury

2 [z]Lam. 1:4 [a]Isai. 3:26; [Lam. 2:8] [b][1 Sam. 5:12]
3 [c]Ps. 40:14 [d][2 Sam. 15:30]
4 [e]ch. 3:3
5 [f]Job 39:1; Ps. 29:9
6 [g]ch. 2:24
7 [h]ver. 21; Ps. 25:11 [i]ch. 2:19 [j]ver. 20
8 [k]ch. 17:13; 50:7; Ps. 71:5
9 [l][Isai. 59:1] [m][Ex. 29:45] [n]Dan. 9:18; [Eph. 3:15] [o]Ps. 119:121
10 [p]Hos. 8:13 [q]Hos. 9:9
11 [r]See ch. 7:16
12 [s]Prov. 1:28; Isai. 1:15; Ezek. 8:18; Mic. 3:4; See ch. 6:20 [t]ch. 16:4; 24:10; 32:24; Ezek. 14:21
13 [u][ch. 4:10; 6:14]
14 [v]See ch. 5:31 [w]ch. 23:21; 27:15; Deut. 18:20; [Matt. 7:15; Mark 13:22] [x]Ezek. 13:6; [ch. 27:9; 29:8] [y]ch. 23:26
15 [z][ch. 23:34]
16 [a]Ps. 79:3

14:3 cover their heads. A sign of mourning.

14:4 no rain. The Lord either gives or withholds the rain (Deut. 11:10–15; 28:12).

14:8 hope. The Hebrew word also means "pool," a striking word in time of drought.

savior. Or deliverer, as in battle.

14:9 called by your name. This calling explains the meaning of "for your name's sake" in v. 7. The Lord's honor is at stake in the fortunes of His people.

14:10 says the LORD. God responds directly to the prayer of vv. 7–9.

this people. Perhaps significantly, God does not use "my people."

14:11 Do not pray. See 7:16 and note. Here the prohibition follows the intercession in vv. 7–9.

14:12 fast . . . burnt offering and grain offering. Ritual for its own sake does not move God (7:21–23 note).

sword . . . famine . . . pestilence. The first of fifteen appearances of this combination in Jeremiah (e.g., 15:2). This is a typical summation of the horrors that judgment can bring (Deut. 32:24, 25).

14:13 the prophets. That is, those who falsely prophesy peace (6:1–4; 8:11). Jeremiah pleads on behalf of the people—that they have been misled.

14:16 And the people. The prophet's plea (v. 13) misses its mark: the people should have tested the prophets by their prophecies (Deut. 13:2, 3; 18:21, 22).

none to bury. See 7:33.

them—them, their wives, their sons, and their daughters. For I will pour out their evil upon them.

17 "You shall say to them this word:
[b]'Let my eyes run down with tears
night and day,
and let them not cease,
for the virgin [c]daughter of my people
is shattered with a great wound,
[d]with a very grievous blow.
18 [e]If I go out into the field,
behold, those pierced by the
sword!
[e]And if I enter the city,
behold, the diseases of famine!
[f]For both prophet and priest ply their
trade through the land
and have no knowledge.'"
19 [g]Have you utterly rejected Judah?
Does your soul loathe Zion?
Why have you struck us down
[h]so that there is no healing for us?
[i]We looked for peace, but no good
came;
for a time of healing, but behold,
terror.
20 [j]We acknowledge our wickedness,
O LORD,
and the iniquity of our fathers,
[j]for we have sinned against you.
21 Do not spurn us, [k]for your name's
sake;
do not dishonor your glorious
throne;
[l]remember and do not break your
covenant with us.
22 Are there any among [m]the false gods
of the nations [n]that can bring
rain?
Or can the heavens give showers?
Are you not he, O LORD our God?
We set our hope on you,
[o]for you do all these things.

17 [b]See ch. 13:17 [c]See ch. 8:21 [d]ch. 10:19; 30:12
18 [e]Ezek. 7:15 [f][ch. 5:31]
19 [g]Lam. 5:22 [h][ch. 15:18] [i]ch. 8:15
20 [j][Ps. 106:6; Dan. 9:5, 8]
21 [k]ver. 7 [l]Lev. 26:42; Ps. 106:45
22 [m]ch. 10:15; [Deut. 32:21] [n]Job 28:26; 38:26, 28; Zech. 10:1, 2 [o]Job 12:9; Isai. 66:2

Chapter 15
1 [p]Ps. 99:6; [Ezek. 14:14] [q][Ps. 106:23]; See Ex. 32:11-13 [r][1 Sam. 7:9; 8:6; 12:23; 15:11] [s]ch. 35:19; [ver. 19]
2 [t]ch. 14:12; 16:4; 21:9; 43:11; Ezek. 5:12; 6:11, 12; Zech. 11:9
3 [u]See Lev. 26:16-22 [v]Deut. 28:26 [w]Rev. 6:8
4 [x]ch. 24:9; 29:18; 34:17; Deut. 28:25 [y][2 Kin. 21:2, 11, 16, 17; 23:26; 24:3, 4]
5 [z]Isai. 51:19; [Nah. 3:7]
6 [a]Deut. 32:15 [b]See ch. 7:24 [c][Hos. 13:14]
7 [d][ch. 51:2; Isai. 41:16; Matt. 3:12; Luke 3:17] [e]Isai. 30:24 [f]ch. 5:3; Isai. 9:13; Amos 4:6, 8-11

The LORD Will Not Relent

15 Then the LORD said to me,
[p]"Though [q]Moses [r]and Samuel
[s]stood before me, yet my heart would not
turn toward this people. Send them out of
my sight, and let them go! 2 And when they
ask you, 'Where shall we go?' you shall say
to them, 'Thus says the LORD:

[t]"'Those who are for pestilence, to
pestilence,
and those who are for the sword,
to the sword;
those who are for famine, to famine,
and those who are for captivity, to
captivity.'

3 [u]I will appoint over them four kinds of
destroyers, declares the LORD: the sword to
kill, the dogs to tear, and [v]the birds of the
air [w]and the beasts of the earth to devour
and destroy. 4 [x]And I will make them a horror to all the kingdoms of the earth because
of what [y]Manasseh the son of Hezekiah,
king of Judah, did in Jerusalem.

5 [z]"Who will have pity on you,
O Jerusalem,
[z]or who will grieve for you?
Who will turn aside
to ask about your welfare?
6 [a]You have rejected me, declares the
LORD;
[b]you keep going backward,
so I have stretched out my hand
against you and destroyed
you—
[c]I am weary of relenting.
7 [d]I have winnowed them with [e]a
winnowing fork
in the gates of the land;
I have bereaved them; I have
destroyed my people;
[f]they did not turn from their
ways.

14:19 We looked for peace. Because of the false prophets' teaching (v. 13 and note).

14:21 your glorious throne. The temple is in view (see 2 Kin. 19:15; but cf. 1 Kin. 8:27).

your covenant. Jeremiah recalls the covenant with Abraham, Isaac, and Jacob (Gen. 15:12–21; 26:3–5; 28:13–15; Lev. 26:42–45).

15:1 Moses and Samuel. God calls to mind two great intercessors for Israel (Ex. 32:11–14; 1 Sam. 12:23). Note also Elijah in 1 Kin. 17:1. Prayer for the people is again prohibited (7:16; 11:14), and the prayer just offered (vv. 19–22) is specifically rejected.

15:3 sword . . . dogs . . . birds . . . beasts. See 7:33 note; 1 Kin. 21:23.

15:4 Manasseh. A son of the reformer King Hezekiah (2 Kin. 20:21) and one of the most wicked kings. Even after the reforms of his grandson Josiah, Judah's punishment and exile continues to be linked to him (2 Kin. 23:26). See Introduction: Author; Date and Occasion.

15:6 going backward. See 3:22.

I am weary of relenting. Such promises as in 31:20 are for the moment in the background.

15:7 winnowed. See 4:11, where the metaphor is used slightly differently. Here it means punishment (cf. Is. 41:16).

8 I have made their widows more in
number
than [g]the sand of the seas;
I have brought against the mothers of
young men
a destroyer at noonday;
I have made anguish and terror
fall upon them suddenly.
9 [h]She who bore seven has grown
feeble;
[i]she has fainted away;
[j]her sun went down while it was yet
day;
she has been shamed and
disgraced.
And the rest of them I will give to
the sword
before their enemies,
declares the LORD."

Jeremiah's Complaint

10 [k]Woe is me, my mother, that you bore
me, a man of strife and contention to the
whole land! [l]I have not lent, nor have I borrowed, yet all of them curse me. 11 The
LORD said, "Have I not[1] set you free for
their good? Have I not pleaded for you
before the enemy in the time of trouble and
in the time of distress? 12 Can one break
iron, iron [m]from the north, and bronze?
13 [n]"Your wealth and your treasures I will
give as [o]spoil, without price, for all your
sins, throughout all your territory. 14 I will
make you serve your enemies [p]in a land
that you do not know, [q]for in my anger a
fire is kindled that shall burn forever."

15 [r]O LORD, you know;
[s]remember me and visit me,
[s, t]and take vengeance for me on my
persecutors.
In your forbearance take me not
away;
[u]know that [v]for your sake I bear
reproach.

16 Your words were found, [w]and I ate
them,
and [x]your words became to me
a joy
and the delight of my
heart,
[y]for I am called by your name,
O LORD, God of hosts.
17 [z]I did not sit in the company of
revelers,
nor did I rejoice;
[a]I sat alone, because your hand was
upon me,
for you had filled me with
indignation.
18 Why is my pain unceasing,
[b]my wound incurable,
refusing to be healed?
Will you be to me [c]like a deceitful
brook,
like waters that fail?

19 Therefore thus says the LORD:
[d]"If you return, I will restore you,
and you shall [e]stand
before me.
If you utter what is precious, and
not what is worthless,
you shall be as my mouth.
They shall turn to you,
but you shall not turn to them.
20 [f]And I will make you to this
people
a fortified wall of bronze;
they will fight against you,
[g]but they shall not prevail over
you,
[h]for I am with you
to save you and deliver you,
declares the LORD.
21 [g]I will deliver you out of the hand of
the wicked,
and redeem you from the grasp of
[i]the ruthless."

1 The meaning of the Hebrew is uncertain

8 [g]Gen. 22:17; Ps. 139:18
9 [h]1 Sam. 2:5; [Lam. 1:1] [i]Job 11:20 [j]Amos 8:9
10 [k]ch. 20:14 [l]Ex. 22:25; Ps. 15:5; Isai. 24:2
12 [m]See ch. 1:13
13 [n]ch. 17:3 [o]Ps. 44:12
14 [p]ch. 9:16; 16:13; 17:4; 22:28 [q]Deut. 32:22
15 [r]ch. 12:3 [s][Judg. 16:28] [t]ch. 11:20; 20:12 [u]ch. 17:16 [v]Ps. 69:7
16 [w]Ezek. 3:1, 3; Rev. 10:9, 10 [x]Ps. 119:111, 162 [y]ch. 14:9
17 [z]Ps. 26:4 [a]Ps. 102:7; Lam. 3:28
18 [b]ch. 30:15; Job 34:6 [c]Job 6:15; Isai. 58:11
19 [d]ch. 3:14 [e][ver. 1]
20 [f][ch. 1:18; 6:27] [g]ch. 1:19; 20:11 [h]See ch. 1:8
21 [g][See ver. 20 above] [i]Isai. 13:11; 25:4, 5; 29:5

15:9 who bore seven. A picture of blessing (Ps. 127:5) is reversed.

rest of them . . . to the sword. Even the remnant left by the destruction is threatened with death. Compare Is. 6:13, where a similar thought is finally softened by the promise of the "seed."

15:12 Can one break iron. How could Jeremiah expect to change Judah's stubborn heart? See 13:23 and note.

15:14 serve your enemies. This prophecy is fulfilled for Jeremiah at 43:4–7.

15:16 Your words . . . I ate them. This verse recalls the sweet side of the bittersweet task of receiving God's words (Ezek. 3:1–3).

I am called by your name. This phrase is applied to the people in 14:9.

15:17 I sat alone. No doubt this is literally true, partly due to celibacy (16:2). But there can also be a profound sense of loneliness for the unwelcome prophet; note Elijah in 1 Kin. 19:10 and our Lord Jesus in Matt. 26:37, 38.

15:18 wound incurable. The wound is Judah's in 14:17. The whole phrase is applied to Judah in 30:12, together with a promise of healing (30:16, 17). See also 10:19, where it is used of Jeremiah.

a deceitful brook. Contrast 2:13; and cf. 20:7.

Famine, Sword, and Death

16 The word of the LORD came to me:
2 "You shall not take a wife, nor shall
you have sons or daughters in this place. 3 For
thus says the LORD concerning the sons and
daughters who are born in this place, and
concerning the mothers who bore them
and the fathers who fathered them in this
land: 4 [j]They shall die of deadly diseases.
[k]They shall not be lamented, nor shall they be
buried. [l]They shall be as dung on the surface
of the ground. [m]They shall perish by the
sword and by famine, [n]and their dead bodies
shall be food for the birds of the air and for
the beasts of the earth.

5 "For thus says the LORD: [o]Do not enter
the house of mourning, or go to lament or
grieve for them, for I have taken away my
peace from this people, my steadfast love
and mercy, declares the LORD. 6 Both great
and small shall die in this land. [k]They shall
not be buried, and no one shall lament for
them or [p]cut himself [q]or make himself bald
for them. 7 No one shall [r]break bread for
the mourner, to comfort him for the dead,
nor shall anyone give him the cup of consolation to drink for his father or his mother. 8 You shall not go into the house of
feasting to sit with them, to eat and drink.
9 For thus says the LORD of hosts, the God
of Israel: [s]Behold, I will silence in this
place, before your eyes and in your days,
the voice of mirth and the voice of gladness, the voice of the bridegroom and the
voice of the bride.

10 "And when you tell this people all these
words, and they say to you, [t]'Why has the
LORD pronounced all this great evil against
us? What is our iniquity? What is the sin
that we have committed against the LORD
our God?' 11 then you shall say to them:
[u]'Because your fathers have forsaken me,
declares the LORD, and [v]have gone after
other gods and have served and worshiped
them, and have forsaken me and have not
kept my law, 12 and because [w]you have done
worse than your fathers, for behold, [x]every
one of you follows his stubborn, evil will,
refusing to listen to me. 13 Therefore [y]I will
hurl you out of this land into [z]a land that
neither you nor your fathers have known,
[a]and there you shall serve other gods day
and night, for I will show you no favor.'

The LORD Will Restore Israel

14 [b]"Therefore, behold, the days are coming, declares the LORD, when it shall no
longer be said, [c]'As the LORD lives who
brought up the people of Israel out of the
land of Egypt,' 15 but 'As the LORD lives who
brought up the people of Israel [d]out of the
north country and out of all the countries
where he had driven them.' For [e]I will
bring them back to their own land that I
gave to their fathers.

16 "Behold, [f]I am sending for many fishers, declares the LORD, and they shall catch
them. And afterward I will send for many
hunters, and they shall hunt them from
every mountain and every hill, and out [g]of
the clefts of the rocks. 17 For [h]my eyes are on
all their ways. [i]They are not hidden from
me, nor is their iniquity concealed from my
eyes. 18 But first [j]I will doubly repay their
iniquity and their sin, because they have
polluted my land with the carcasses of their
detestable idols, and [k]have filled my inheritance with their abominations."

19 [l]O LORD, my strength and my
stronghold,
[m]my refuge in the day of trouble,
[n]to you shall the nations come
from the ends of the earth and say:

Chapter 16
4 [j]See ch. 15:2 [k]ch. 22:18, 19; 25:33 [l]See ch. 8:2 [m]See ch. 14:12 [n]See ch. 7:33
5 [o]See Ezek. 24:16-23
6 [k][See ver. 4 above] [p]Lev. 19:28; Deut. 14:1 [q]Job 1:20; [Isai. 3:24]
7 [r]Isai. 58:7; Ezek. 24:17; [Deut. 26:14; Hos. 9:4]
9 [s]See ch. 7:34
10 [t]See ch. 5:19
11 [u]ch. 5:19; 22:9; [Deut. 29:25, 26; 2 Kin. 22:17; 2 Chr. 34:25] [v]ch. 13:10
12 [w]ch. 7:26 [x]See ch. 3:17
13 [y]ch. 10:18; 22:26; Isai. 22:17, 18; See Deut. 4:26-28; 28:64, 65 [z]See ch. 15:14 [a]Deut. 28:36, 64
14 [b]For ver. 14, 15, see ch. 23:7, 8 [c]ch. 4:2
15 [d][Isai. 43:5, 6]; See ch. 3:18 [e]ch. 24:6; 30:3; 32:37
16 [f][Ezek. 12:13; Amos 4:2; Hab. 1:15] [g]ch. 13:4
17 [h]ch. 32:19; 2 Chr. 16:9; Job 34:21; Prov. 5:21 [i][Ps. 51:9; 90:8]
18 [j]ch. 17:18; Isai. 40:2 [k][Isai. 65:4]; See Ezek. 43:7-9
19 [l]2 Sam. 22:33; Ps. 28:7; 31:3, 4; Isai. 25:4 [m]ch. 17:17 [n][Isai. 9:2; 49:6, 22, 23]

16:1–17:18 Jeremiah is prohibited from marrying and taking part in other normal activities as a sign of coming judgment (ch. 16). A sharp contrast is drawn between the destinies of those who trust in man and in God (17:1–18).

16:2 You shall not take a wife. The prohibition is related exclusively to Jeremiah's role as a prophet of Judah's fate (1 Cor. 7:26). Jeremiah will be childless, a sign that there is no immediate future for Judah.

16:4 sword and by famine. See note 14:12.

16:8 shall not go into . . . feasting. After v. 2 and v. 5, there is yet a third symbolic prohibition.

16:9 silence . . . bridegroom and . . . bride. See also 7:34. Such sounds are typical of times of peace and hope (Matt. 24:38, 39; contrast 33:10, 11).

16:12 done worse than your fathers. Though the present generation shares guilt with its forefathers (14:20), it is responsible for its own sin (31:29, 30; Ezek. 18:2–4).

16:13 hurl you out of this land. That is, God will send them into exile (see Deut. 28:36, 64).

serve other gods. With a punishment to fit the crime, they would finally discover that these gods can provide no benefit.

16:16 fishers . . . hunters. Judah is pictured as the prey of the Lord.

every mountain and every hill . . . clefts of the rocks. There will be no escape (23:24; Is. 2:19).

16:17 my eyes are on all. See "God Sees and Knows: Divine Omniscience" at Prov. 15:3.

"Our fathers have inherited nothing
but lies,
[o]worthless things in which there is
no profit.
20 Can man make for himself [p]gods?
Such are not gods!"

21 "Therefore, behold, I will make them
know, this once I will make them know my
power and my might, and they shall know
that [q]my name is the LORD."

The Sin of Judah

17 "The sin of Judah is written with [r]a
pen of iron; with a point of diamond it is engraved on [s]the tablet of their
heart, and on [t]the horns of their altars,
2 while [u]their children remember their
altars and their [v]Asherim, [w]beside every
green tree and on the high hills, 3 [x]on the
mountains in the open country. [y]Your
wealth and all your treasures I will give for
spoil as the price of your high places for sin
throughout all your territory. 4 You shall
loosen your hand from your heritage that I
gave to you, [z]and I will make you serve
your enemies in a land that you do not
know, [a]for in my anger a fire is kindled that
shall burn forever."

5 Thus says the LORD:
"Cursed is the man [b]who trusts in man
and makes flesh his strength,[1]
whose heart turns away from the
LORD.
6 [c]He is like a shrub in the desert,
[d]and shall not see any good come.
He shall dwell in the parched places
of the wilderness,
in [e]an uninhabited salt land.

7 [f]"Blessed is the man who trusts in
the LORD,
[g]whose trust is the LORD.
8 [h]He is like a tree planted by
water,
that sends out its roots by the
stream,
and does not fear when heat
comes,
for its leaves remain green,
and is not anxious in the year of
drought,
for it does not cease to bear
fruit."

9 The heart is deceitful above all
things,
and desperately sick;
who can understand it?
10 [i]"I the LORD search the heart
[j]and test the mind,[2]
[k]to give every man according to his
ways,
according to the fruit of his
deeds."

11 Like the [l]partridge that gathers a
brood that she did not
hatch,
so is [m]he who gets riches but not
by justice;
[n]in the midst of his days they will
leave him,
[o]and at his end he will be a
fool.

12 A glorious throne set on high from
the beginning
is the place of our sanctuary.

1 Hebrew *arm* 2 Hebrew *kidneys*

19 [o]See ch. 18:15
20 [p][1 Cor. 8:4]; See ch. 2:11
21 [q]See ch. 33:2
Chapter 17
1 [r]Job 19:24 [s]Prov. 3:3; 7:3; [2 Cor. 3:3] [t]Ex. 27:2; Ps. 118:27
2 [u][ch. 19:5] [v]Judg. 3:7; See Deut. 16:21 [w][Isai. 1:29]; See ch. 2:20
3 [x]Ps. 48:1, 2; 87:1; Isai. 2:3 [y]ch. 15:13
4 [z]See ch. 15:14 [a]See Deut. 32:22
5 [b]2 Chr. 32:8; Ps. 146:3
6 [c]ch. 48:6 [d]ch. 29:32; Job 20:17; Ps. 34:12 [e]Deut. 29:23; Job 39:6
7 [f]Ps. 25:2; 34:8; 125:1; See Ps. 2:12 [g]Ps. 71:5
8 [h]Ps. 1:3; [Ezek. 47:12]
10 [i]1 Sam. 16:7; 1 Chr. 28:9; Ps. 139:23; Rom. 8:27 [j]See ch. 11:20 [k]ch. 32:19; Job 34:11; Ps. 62:12
11 [l][1 Sam. 26:20] [m]Ps. 39:6 [n][Ps. 55:23] [o][Luke 12:20]

16:21 know that my name is the LORD. Knowing the Lord's name here means recognizing His authority and power through His acts of judgment.

17:1 on the tablet of their heart. This metaphor recalls tablets for writing laws. See 31:33, where the law will be written on the heart, and Prov. 3:3; 7:3. In the new covenant, Christ writes the law on His people's hearts by His Spirit (2 Cor. 3:3).

on the horns of their altars. These altars should commemorate atonement for sin, but where the sin is unforgiven they continue to remind God of the sin itself.

17:2 their altars and their Asherim. See 2:20 note; Ex. 34:13; Deut. 7:5.

17:3 the mountains. Mount Zion, where the temple was, was plundered by Nebuchadnezzar (52:17–23).

17:4 heritage that I gave to you. The Promised Land (2:7).

17:7 trusts. The Lord repays trust because He is by nature trustworthy (Is. 7:9). The close similarity between vv. 7, 8 and Ps. 1:1–3 suggests that trust in the Lord entails obedience to His law.

17:8 a tree planted by water. This image is a potent symbol of strength in a dry country (Is. 44:4).

17:9 The heart. In the Old Testament, the "heart" is more than the seat of emotion. It represents the basis of character, including the mind and the will (4:19; Prov. 4:23; 16:23). See theological note "The Freedom and Bondage of the Will" on next page.

17:10 mind. Lit. "kidneys." In ancient Hebrew idiom, these organs represented the seat of the emotions.

17:11 Like the partridge . . . by justice. It was commonly believed that partridges would steal the eggs of other birds, but the hatchlings would return to their natural parent. In the same way a person will not be able to retain riches unjustly gained.

and at his end . . . fool. On the transience of riches, see Prov. 23:4, 5.

17:12 A glorious throne. See note 14:21; Ps. 99:1.

from the beginning. This implies that Zion was chosen as God's throne even before the temple was built (Ex. 15:17).

13 O LORD, [p]the hope of Israel,
[q]all who forsake you shall be put to shame;
those who turn away from you[1]
[r]shall be written in the earth,
for [s]they have forsaken [t]the LORD,
the fountain of living water.

Jeremiah Prays for Deliverance

14 [u]Heal me, O LORD, and I shall be healed;
save me, and I shall be saved,
for [v]you are my praise.
15 [w]Behold, they say to me,
"Where is the word of the LORD?
Let it come!"
16 I have not run away from being your shepherd,
nor have I desired the day of sickness.
[x]You know [x]what came out of my lips;
it was before your face.
17 Be not a terror to me;
[y]you are my refuge in the day of disaster.
18 [z]Let those be put to shame who persecute me,
but let me not be put to shame;
[z]let them be dismayed,
but let me not be dismayed;
[a]bring upon them the day of disaster;
destroy them with double destruction!

Keep the Sabbath Holy

19 Thus said the LORD to me: "Go and
stand in the People's Gate, by which [b]the
kings of Judah enter and by which they go
out, and in all the gates of Jerusalem, 20 and
say: 'Hear the word of the LORD, [b]you kings
of Judah, and all Judah, and all the inhabitants of Jerusalem, who enter by these
gates. 21 Thus says the LORD: Take care for
the sake of your lives, and [c]do not bear a
burden on the Sabbath day or bring it in by
the gates of Jerusalem. 22 And do not carry
a burden out of your houses on the Sabbath
[d]or do any work, but [e]keep the Sabbath day holy, as I commanded your fathers.
23 Yet [f]they did not listen or incline their ear,

1 Hebrew *me*

13 [p]See ch. 14:8 [q]Josh. 24:20; Ps. 73:27; Isai. 1:28 [r][Luke 10:20] [s]ch. 1:16 [t]ch. 2:13; [John 4:10, 14]
14 [u]Ps. 6:2 [v]Deut. 10:21
15 [w]Isai. 5:19; 2 Pet. 3:4
16 [x]ch. 15:15; Ps. 40:9; 139:4
17 [y]ch. 16:19
18 [z]Ps. 35:4; 40:14 [a]ch. 11:20; Ps. 35:8
19 [b]See ch. 13:13
20 [b][See ver. 19 above]
21 [c][John 5:10]; See Neh. 13:15-19
22 [d]See Num. 15:32-36 [e]Ex. 23:12; 31:13; Isai. 56:2; 58:13; Ezek. 20:12, 20; See Ex. 20:8-11; Deut. 5:12-15
23 [f]ch. 7:24, 26; [ch. 11:10]

The Freedom and Bondage of the Will

Proper understanding of the freedom of the will in the fallen human condition is assisted by distinguishing free agency from free will.

Free agency is a mark of humanity as such. All humans are free agents in the sense that they make their own decisions about what they will do, choosing as they please in the light of their conscience, inclinations, and thoughts. They are answerable to God and to the rest of humanity for their choices. Adam was a free agent before the Fall, and afterwards. He continued to have desires and thoughts and to put them into action through his will. Similarly, we are free agents now; we will continue to be so after the resurrection. The glorified saints exercise their wills, but they are confirmed in grace, so that they cannot sin. Their choices are the product of human free agency, made in accordance with their nature, but now these choices are good and right. The transformation of their hearts is complete and they desire to do what is right.

Free will has been defined by Christian teachers from the second century on as the ability to choose any at all of the moral options offered in a given situation. Augustine taught that this possibility was lost through the Fall. The loss is part of the burden of original sin. After the Fall, our natural hearts are not inclined toward God; they are in bondage to sin and cannot be freed from this slavery except by the grace of regeneration. Such an understanding of the fallen will is taught by Paul in Rom. 6:16–23.

Only a will that has been set free is able to choose righteousness freely and heartily. A permanent love of righteousness, that is, an inclination of the heart to the way of living that pleases God, is one aspect of the freedom that Christ gives (John 8:34–36; Gal. 5:1, 13).

17:13 written in the earth. They will soon be forgotten. Contrast the thought of Ex. 32:32.

17:15 Where is the word of the LORD. With this taunt Jeremiah is accused of being a false prophet (Deut. 18:21, 22). See Mic. 7:10; 2 Pet. 3:2–4.

17:18 dismayed . . . dismayed. Prayer for judgment upon his enemies is common in Jeremiah (11:20; 12:3; 15:15). The words are reminiscent of his call (1:17).

17:20 who enter by these gates. The message is given at the gates because of their role in commerce (see Neh. 13:15, 19).

17:22 keep the Sabbath day holy. Specific appeal is made to the Sabbath commandment (Ex. 20:8–11; Deut. 5:12–15; Neh. 10:31; Is. 56:2).

[g]but stiffened their neck, that they [h]might
not hear and receive instruction.
24 "'But if you listen to me, declares the
LORD, and [c]bring in no burden by the gates
of this city on the Sabbath day, but [e]keep
the Sabbath day holy and do no work on it,
25 then [i]there shall enter by the gates of this
city kings and princes who sit on the throne
of David, riding in chariots and on horses,
they and their officials, the men of Judah
and the inhabitants of Jerusalem. And this
city shall be inhabited forever. 26 And people
shall come from [j]the cities of Judah [k]and
the places around Jerusalem, [j]from the land
of Benjamin, [k]from the Shephelah, from the
hill country, [k]and from [l]the Negeb, bringing
[m]burnt offerings and sacrifices, grain offerings and frankincense, and [m]bringing thank
offerings to the house of the LORD. 27 But if
you do not listen to me, to [e]keep the
Sabbath day holy, [c]and not to bear a burden
and enter by the gates of Jerusalem on the
Sabbath day, then I will [n]kindle a fire in its
gates, and it shall [o]devour the palaces of
Jerusalem and [p]shall not be quenched.'"

The Potter and the Clay

18 The word that came to Jeremiah
from the LORD: 2 "Arise, and go down
to [q]the potter's house, and there I will let
you hear my words." 3 So I went down to
[r]the potter's house, and there he was working at his wheel. 4 And the vessel he was
making of clay was [s]spoiled in the potter's
hand, and [t]he reworked it into another vessel, as it seemed good to the potter to do.
5 Then the word of the LORD came to me:
6 "O house of Israel, [u]can I not do with you
as this potter has done? declares the LORD.
[v]Behold, like the clay in the potter's hand,
so are you in my hand, O house of Israel.
7 If at any time I declare concerning a
nation or a kingdom, that I will [w]pluck up
and break down and destroy it, 8 and if that
nation, concerning which I have spoken,
[x]turns from its evil, [y]I will relent of the disaster that I intended to do to it. 9 And if at
any time I declare concerning a nation or a
kingdom that I will [w]build and plant it,
10 and if it does evil in my sight, not listening to my voice, then I will relent of the
good that I had intended to do to it.
11 Now, therefore, say to the men of Judah
and the inhabitants of Jerusalem: 'Thus
says the LORD, behold, I am shaping disaster against you and devising a plan against
you. [z]Return, every one from his evil way,
and [a]amend your ways and your deeds.'
12 "But they say, [b]'That is in vain! We will
follow our own plans, and will every one
act according to [c]the stubbornness of his
evil heart.'

13 "Therefore thus says the LORD:
[d]Ask among the nations,
Who has heard the like of this?
The virgin Israel
has done [e]a very horrible thing.
14 Does the snow of Lebanon leave
the crags of Sirion?[1]
Do the mountain[2] waters run dry,[3]
the cold flowing streams?
15 [f]But my people have forgotten me;
they make offerings to [g]false gods;
they made them stumble in their ways,
[h]in the ancient roads,
and to walk into side roads,
[i]not the highway,
16 making their land [j]a horror,
a thing [j]to be hissed at forever.
[k]Everyone who passes by it is horrified
[l]and shakes his head.

23 [g][2 Chr. 30:8; Acts 7:51] [h]See ch. 5:3
24 [c][See ver. 21 above] [e][See ver. 22 above]
25 [i]ch. 22:4
26 [j]ch. 32:44; 33:13 [k]Zech. 7:7 [l]Gen. 13:1 [m]Lev. 7:12; 22:29; 2 Chr. 33:16; Ps. 107:22; 116:17
27 [e][See ver. 22 above] [c][See ver. 21 above] [n]ch. 21:14; 43:12; 49:27; 50:32; Lam. 4:11; Amos 1:14 [o]ch. 52:13; 2 Kin. 25:9 [p]ch. 7:20
Chapter 18
2 [q]ch. 19:1; 1 Chr. 4:23; [Zech. 11:13]
3 [r]ch. 19:1; 1 Chr. 4:23; [Zech. 11:13]
4 [s]ch. 13:7 [t][Rom. 9:21]
6 [u]Isai. 45:9; See Rom. 9:20-24 [v]Job 10:9; Isai. 64:8
7 [w]ch. 1:10; 42:10
8 [x]Ezek. 18:21 [y]ch. 26:3, 13, 19; Judg. 2:18; Jonah 3:10
9 [w][See ver. 7 above]
11 [z]ch. 35:15; 2 Kin. 17:13; Jonah 3:8 [a]ch. 7:3; 25:5; 35:15
12 [b]ch. 2:25 [c]See ch. 3:17
13 [d]ch. 2:10, 11 [e]ch. 5:30
15 [f]ch. 2:13, 32; 17:13 [g]ch. 2:5; 10:15; 16:19 [h]ch. 6:16 [i][Isai. 57:14]
16 [j]ch. 19:8; 25:9, 11, 18; 49:13, 17; 50:13; 51:37; 2 Chr. 29:8 [k]ch. 50:13; Lam. 2:15 [l]Job 16:4; Ps. 22:7; Matt. 27:39

1 Hebrew *the field* 2 Hebrew *foreign* 3 Hebrew *Are . . . plucked up?*

17:25, 26 This prophecy presents a picture (partly repeated in 22:4) of the restoration of the Davidic dynasty, the social structure, and the worship, that all centered on the temple. See also 23:5, 6; 30:9; 33:14–26. All that is threatened for Judah, therefore, can be reversed.

18:1–20:18 Just as a potter remolds a marred pot, God will remold His people by disciplining them in exile (18:1–17). Jeremiah portrays God's judgment by breaking a clay jar (ch. 19), and is mistreated because of his unpopular message (18:18–23; ch. 20).

18:2 the potter's house. Apparently in the Valley of the Son of Hinnom, near the Potsherd Gate (19:2); hence the command to "go down." See also 7:31.

18:4 reworked it into another vessel. The potter has freedom with respect to his plans. The spoiling of his first intention is not final.

18:6 O house of Israel. The analogy with Israel follows. The use of the term "Israel" recalls God's historic purposes of election for the whole people, to which Judah was now heir.

18:7, 8 The potter illustration (vv. 2–4) shows that the Lord's purposed judgment may be revoked by that nation's repentance.

18:13 very horrible thing. One of the strong terms used for idolatry (v. 15; cf. 5:30).

18:14 Do the mountain waters. As it would be against nature to turn from cold, running water to polluted, standing water, so it is hard to understand why anyone would turn from God to idolatry.

18:15 make offerings. See note 11:13.

ancient roads . . . side roads, not the highway. See note 6:16. The "side roads" are narrow, insufficient and dangerous.

17 [m]Like the east wind [n]I will scatter
them
before the enemy.
[o]I will show them my back, not my
face,
in the day of their calamity."

18 Then they said, [p]"Come, let us make
plots against Jeremiah, [q]for the law shall
not perish from the priest, nor counsel
from the wise, nor the word from the
prophet. [r]Come, let us strike him with the
tongue, and let us not pay attention to any
of his words."

19 Hear me, O LORD,
and [s]listen to the voice of my
adversaries.
20 [t]Should good be repaid with evil?
Yet [u]they have dug a pit for my life.
[v]Remember how I stood
before you
to speak good for them,
to turn away your wrath from them.
21 Therefore [w]deliver up their children
to famine;
give them over to the power of the
sword;
let their wives become childless [x]and
widowed.
May their men meet death by
pestilence,
their youths be struck down by the
sword in battle.
22 [y]May a cry be heard from their houses,
when you bring the plunderer
suddenly upon them!
For [u]they have dug a pit to take me
[z]and laid snares for my feet.
23 Yet [a]you, O LORD, know
all their plotting to kill me.
[b]Forgive not their iniquity,
nor blot out their sin from your
sight.
Let them be overthrown before you;
deal with them in the time of your
anger.

17 [m]ch. 13:24 [n]Gen. 41:6, 23, 27; Ex. 10:13; Job 27:21; Ps. 48:7; Ezek. 27:26; Hos. 13:15; Jonah 4:8 [o][ch. 2:27]
18 [p]ch. 11:19 [q][ch. 2:8; 5:13, 31; 6:13] [r]ch. 9:3, 8; Job 5:21; [Ps. 31:20]
19 [s]Ps. 35:1; Isai. 49:25
20 [t]Ps. 35:12 [u]Ps. 35:7; 57:6; 119:85 [v][Neh. 13:14]
21 [w]Ps. 109:10 [x]Ps. 109:9
22 [y][ch. 20:16] [u][See ver. 20 above] [z]Ps. 140:5
23 [a][Ps. 35:22] [b]Neh. 4:5

Chapter 19
1 [c]See ch. 18:2 [d]ver. 10 [e]2 Kin. 19:2; 23:1; Ezek. 8:1
2 [f]See Josh. 15:8
3 [g]ch. 17:20 [h]See ch. 13:13 [i]1 Sam. 3:11; 2 Kin. 21:12
4 [j]See ch. 1:16 [k]2 Kin. 21:16; See ch. 2:34
5 [l]ch. 7:31; 32:35; Lev. 18:21 [m]ch. 7:31; 32:35; Deut. 17:3
6 [n]ch. 7:32 [o]ver. 2
7 [p][Isai. 19:3] [q][Lev. 26:17] [r]See ch. 7:33
8 [s]See ch. 18:16
9 [t]Lev. 26:29; Deut. 28:53; Isai. 9:20; Lam. 2:20; 4:10; Ezek. 5:10 [u]Deut. 28:53, 55, 57

The Broken Flask

19 Thus says the LORD, "Go, buy [c]a
potter's earthenware [d]flask, and
take some of [e]the elders of the people and
some of [e]the elders of the priests, 2 and go
out [f]to the Valley of the Son of Hinnom at
the entry of the Potsherd Gate, and proclaim there the words that I tell you. 3 You
shall say, [g]'Hear the word of the LORD, [h]O
kings of Judah and inhabitants of
Jerusalem. Thus says the LORD of hosts,
the God of Israel: Behold, I am bringing
such disaster upon this place that [i]the
ears of everyone who hears of it will tingle. 4 [j]Because the people have forsaken
me and have profaned this place by making offerings in it to other gods whom neither they nor their fathers nor the kings of
Judah have known; [k]and because they
have filled this place with the blood of
innocents, 5 [l]and have built the high
places of Baal [l]to burn their sons in the
fire as burnt offerings to Baal, [m]which I
did not command or decree, nor did it
come into my mind— 6 therefore, [n]behold,
days are coming, declares the LORD, when
this place shall no more be called
Topheth, or [o]the Valley of the Son of
Hinnom, but the Valley of Slaughter.
7 And in this place [p]I will make void the
plans of Judah and Jerusalem, [q]and will
cause their people to fall by the sword
before their enemies, and by the hand of
those who seek their life. [r]I will give their
dead bodies for food to the birds of the air
and to the beasts of the earth. 8 And I will
make this city [s]a horror, [s]a thing to be
hissed at. Everyone who passes by it will
be horrified and will hiss because of all its
wounds. 9 [t]And I will make them eat the
flesh of their sons and their daughters,
and everyone shall eat the flesh of his
neighbor [u]in the siege and in the distress,
with which their enemies and those who
seek their life afflict them.'

18:17 east wind. Cf. 4:11.

my back, not my face. The meaning is withheld favor (2:27). He will turn His back on them.

18:20 Should good be repaid with evil. Cf. Ps. 35:12; 1 Pet. 2:19–24.

dug a pit. They had murderous intention (v. 22). See Jeremiah's actual experiences in 37:16; 38:6.

stood before you . . . for them. See note 15:1.

19:2 Valley of the Son of Hinnom. See note 18:2.

Potsherd Gate. A gate on the south of the city, possibly the Dung Gate (Neh. 2:13).

19:3 disaster . . . tingle. The words closely resemble 2 Kin. 21:12, which also concerns judgment on Judah and Jerusalem. The judgment is severe and shocking to anyone who hears of it.

19:9 eat the flesh . . . of his neighbor. Such a horror had occurred during the siege of 586 B.C. (Lam. 2:20 and note).

10 "Then [v]you shall break [w]the flask in the
sight of the men who go with you, 11 and
shall say to them, 'Thus says the LORD of
hosts: So will I break this people and this
city, [x]as one breaks a potter's vessel, [y]so
that it can never be mended. [z]Men shall
bury in Topheth because there will be no
place else to bury. 12 Thus will I do to this
place, declares the LORD, and to its inhabitants, making this city [a]like Topheth. 13 The
houses of Jerusalem and the houses of the
kings of Judah—[b]all the houses on whose
[c]roofs offerings have been offered [d]to all the
host of heaven, and [e]drink offerings have
been poured out to other gods—shall be
defiled [a]like the place of Topheth.'"

14 Then Jeremiah came from [f]Topheth,
where the LORD had sent him to prophesy,
[g]and he stood in the court of the LORD's
house and said to all the people: 15 "Thus
says the LORD of hosts, the God of Israel,
behold, I am bringing upon this city and
upon all its towns all the disaster that I
have pronounced against it, [h]because they
have stiffened their neck, [i]refusing to hear
my words."

Jeremiah Persecuted by Pashhur

20 Now [j]Pashhur the priest, the son of
[k]Immer, who was [l]chief officer in
the house of the LORD, heard Jeremiah
prophesying these things. 2 Then [j]Pashhur
beat Jeremiah the prophet, and put him
[m]in the stocks that were in the upper
[n]Benjamin Gate of the house of the LORD.
3 The next day, when [j]Pashhur released
Jeremiah from the stocks, Jeremiah said to
him, "The LORD does not call your name
[j]Pashhur, but Terror On Every Side. 4 For
thus says the LORD: Behold, I will make
you [o]a terror to yourself and to all your
friends. They shall fall by the sword of their
enemies while you look on. And I will give
all Judah into the hand of the king of
Babylon. He shall carry them captive to
Babylon, and shall strike them down with
the sword. 5 Moreover, [p]I will give all the
wealth of the city, all its gains, all its
[q]prized belongings, and all the treasures of
the kings of Judah into the hand of their
enemies, who shall plunder them and seize
them and carry them to Babylon. 6 And
you, [r]Pashhur, and all who dwell in your
house, shall go into captivity. To Babylon
you shall go, and there you shall die, and
there you shall be buried, you and all your
friends, [s]to whom you have prophesied
falsely."

7 O LORD, [t]you have deceived me,
and I was deceived;
[u]you are stronger than I,
and you have prevailed.
[v]I have become a laughingstock all
the day;
everyone mocks me.
8 For whenever I speak, I cry out,
I shout, [w]"Violence and
destruction!"
For [x]the word of the LORD has
become for me
[y]a reproach and [y]derision all day
long.
9 If I say, "I will not mention him,
or speak any more in his name,"
[z]there is in my heart as it were a
burning fire
shut up in my bones,
and [a]I am weary with holding it in,
and I cannot.

10 [v][ch. 51:63, 64] [w]ver. 1
11 [x]Ps. 2:9; Isai. 30:14; Lam. 4:2 [y][Prov. 6:15] [z]ch. 7:32
12 [a][2 Kin. 23:10]
13 [b]ch. 32:29; 44:18; 2 Kin. 23:12; Zeph. 1:5 [c]2 Sam. 11:2 [d]Deut. 4:19; Acts 7:42 [e]ch. 7:18; 44:18 [a][See ver. 12 above]
14 [f]ver. 2, 3 [g]ch. 26:2; [2 Chr. 20:5]
15 [h]ch. 7:26; 2 Chr. 30:8 [i]ch. 25:3
Chapter 20
1 [j]ch. 21:1; 38:1; 1 Chr. 9:12; [Ezra 2:38] [k]1 Chr. 24:14; Ezra 2:37 [l][ch. 29:26]
2 [j][See ver. 1 above] [m]ch. 29:26; Acts 16:24 [n]ch. 37:18
3 [j][See ver. 1 above]
4 [o]See ch. 6:25
5 [p][2 Kin. 20:17]; See 2 Kin. 24:12-16; 25:13-17 [q]Job 28:10; Ezek. 22:25
6 [r]ch. 21:1; 38:1; 1 Chr. 9:12; [Ezra 2:38] [s]See ch. 14:14
7 [t][Ezek. 14:9] [u][2 Pet. 1:21] [v]Ps. 119:51; Lam. 3:14
8 [w]ch. 6:7 [x]ch. 6:10 [y]Ps. 44:13; 79:4
9 [z]Job 32:18, 19; Ps. 39:3 [a]ch. 6:11

19:10 Then you shall break the flask. The climax of the scene is another symbolic prophetic action (see 13:1–11 and notes). The earthenware flask shatters on impact (Ps. 2:9). The metaphor was familiar in the ancient world.

19:11 can never be mended. Judah, hardened in sin, cannot be reshaped, but only destroyed.

Men shall bury . . . no place else to bury. See 7:32.

19:13 host of heaven. See 8:2 and note; also 2 Kin. 23:4, 5.

defiled like the place. Josiah had defiled Topheth (2 Kin. 23:10).

20:1 Pashhur. The name was apparently common (see 21:1; 38:1—each text possibly referring to a different man). Note that senior priests had been among Jeremiah's audience in the valley (19:1), and Pashhur was perhaps among them.

20:2 beat Jeremiah. Pashhur's duties as governor of the temple included restraining those whose actions disrupted temple worship (29:26; Deut. 25:2, 3). Jeremiah's prayer in 15:18 shows that faithful prophetic preaching was dangerous.

the prophet. This title affirms Jeremiah's status as a true prophet, despite the legal action against him.

20:3 Terror On Every Side. See 6:25. The people should be afraid to be associated with Pashhur, because he is a highly visible example of why the Lord's anger was falling on them. He had openly abused God's prophet.

20:7 deceived me . . . was deceived. Jeremiah had not foreseen the trials that his task would bring, and he receives his call (especially perhaps 1:7, 8) as an overpowering compulsion (4:10).

20:8 For whenever I speak . . . destruction. A compulsion he cannot control makes him utter his message of coming wrath.

20:9 a burning fire. Jeremiah's reluctance was profound, but God's word in him exerted a pressure he could not resist (see Amos 3:8; 1 Cor. 9:16; 2 Cor. 5:14).

10 [b] For I hear many whispering.
[c] Terror is on every side!
"Denounce him! [d] Let us denounce
him!"
say all my [e] close friends,
[f] watching for [g] my fall.
"Perhaps he will be deceived;
then [h] we can overcome him
and take our revenge on him."
11 But [i] the LORD is with me as a dread
warrior;
therefore my persecutors will
stumble;
[i] they will not overcome me.
[j] They will be greatly shamed,
for they will not succeed.
Their [k] eternal dishonor
will never be forgotten.
12 O LORD of hosts, who tests the
righteous,
[l] who sees the heart and the
mind,[1]
let me see your vengeance upon
them,
for to you have I committed my
cause.
13 [m] Sing to the LORD;
praise the LORD!
For he has delivered the life of the
needy
from the hand of evildoers.
14 [n] Cursed be the day
on which I was born!
The day when my mother bore me,
let it not be blessed!
15 Cursed be the man who brought the
news to my father,
"A son is born to you,"
[o] making him very glad.

10 [b] Ps. 31:13 [c] See ch. 6:25 [d] [ch. 36:16, 20] [e] Ps. 41:9; 55:13; [ch. 9:4; 38:22] [f] [Ps. 56:6] [g] Ps. 35:15 [h] ch. 1:19; 5:22
11 [i] See ch. 1:8 [j] ch. 17:18; 23:40 [k] ch. 23:40
12 [l] See ch. 11:20
13 [m] [Ps. 35:9, 10; 109:30, 31]
14 [n] ch. 15:10; Job 3:3
15 [o] [John 16:21]
16 [p] Gen. 19:25; Isai. 13:19 [q] ch. 18:22
17 [r] [Job 3:10, 11]
18 [s] [Job 3:20] [t] [Lam. 3:1, 2]
Chapter 21
1 [u] See ch. 20:1 [v] ch. 29:25; 37:3; 2 Kin. 25:18 [w] ch. 35:4; 2 Chr. 34:8
2 [x] [ch. 37:7] [y] [2 Kin. 25:1] [z] Ps. 105:2, 5
4 [a] [ch. 32:5; 37:10] [b] [Isai. 13:4]
5 [c] ch. 27:5; 32:17, 21; Ex. 6:6; Deut. 4:34; Ezek. 20:33 [d] ch. 32:37; Deut. 29:28

16 Let that man be like [p] the cities
that the LORD overthrew without
pity;
[q] let him hear a cry in the morning
and an alarm at noon,
17 [r] because he did not kill me in the
womb;
so my mother would have been my
grave,
and her womb forever great.
18 [s] Why did I come out from the womb
[t] to see toil and sorrow,
and spend my days in shame?

Jerusalem Will Fall to Nebuchadnezzar

21 This is the word that came to
Jeremiah from the LORD, when King
Zedekiah sent to him [u] Pashhur the son of
Malchiah and [v] Zephaniah the priest, the
son of [w] Maaseiah, saying, 2 [x] "Inquire of the
LORD for us, [y] for Nebuchadnezzar[2] king of
Babylon is making war against us. Perhaps
the LORD will deal with us according to [z] all
his wonderful deeds and will make him
withdraw from us."
3 Then Jeremiah said to them: 4 "Thus
you shall say to Zedekiah, 'Thus says the
LORD, the God of Israel: [a] Behold, I will turn
back the weapons of war that are in your
hands and with which you are fighting
against the king of Babylon and against the
Chaldeans who are besieging you outside
the walls. [b] And I will bring them together
into the midst of this city. 5 I myself will
fight against you [c] with outstretched hand
and strong arm, [d] in anger and in fury and
in great wrath. 6 And I will strike down the
inhabitants of this city, both man and

[1] Hebrew *kidneys* [2] Hebrew *Nebuchadrezzar*, another spelling for *Nebuchadnezzar* (king of Babylon) occurring frequently from Jeremiah 21–52; this latter spelling is used throughout Jeremiah for consistency

20:14 Cursed. The Spirit has permitted this record of Jeremiah's despair to be preserved. The prophet's words are like Job's (Job 3:1–26).

20:16 the cities . . . overthrew. Sodom and Gomorrah, whose fate was proverbial (Is. 1:9; Amos 4:11).

21:1–24:10 These chapters narrate the end of the Davidic dynasty, making it clear that disaster and exile are God's judgment on the sins of Judah's kings and people. Jeremiah denounces false prophets who lead the people astray (ch. 23), but also sounds a note of hope as God promises to gather a remnant of His people from captivity under the leadership of "a righteous Branch" from David's house (23:3–8). The twin messages of judgment and future restoration are repeated in Jeremiah's vision of two baskets of figs (ch. 24).

21:1 Zedekiah. The name means "the LORD is my righteousness."

sent to him. Zedekiah maintains a vacillating dependence on Jeremiah without the moral courage to obey his warnings (37:3, 21; 38:5, 14, 19, 24–26).

Pashhur. Not necessarily the same Pashhur as in 20:1 (see note) or 38:1.

Zephaniah. A priest and the son of Maaseiah (29:25, 29; 37:3; 52:24), not the same as the prophet Zephaniah (Zeph. 1:1).

21:2 Inquire. A request for guidance.

Nebuchadnezzar. King of Babylon, 605–562 B.C. His name is formed with "Nabu" (or "Nebo"), a Babylonian god (Is. 46:1; Dan. 1:1).

making war against us. Zedekiah was a vassal of Nebuchadnezzar (37:1), and rebelled against him in 589 B.C. Nebuchadnezzar laid siege to Jerusalem in 588.

21:5 I myself will fight against you . . . outstretched hand . . . strong arm. The language depicts the Lord's power in war, horrifyingly turned against His people (Deut. 4:34; 5:15; 7:19; Amos 5:18).

anger . . . fury . . . great wrath. See Deut. 29:23.

beast. They shall die of a great pestilence.
7 Afterward, declares the LORD, [e]I will give
Zedekiah king of Judah and his servants
and the people in this city who survive the
pestilence, sword, and famine into the
hand of Nebuchadnezzar king of Babylon
and into the hand of their enemies, into
the hand of those who seek their lives. He
shall strike them down with the edge of the
sword. [f]He shall not pity them or spare
them or have compassion.'
8 "And to this people you shall say:
[g]'Thus says the LORD: Behold, [h]I set before
you the way of life and the way of death.
9 He who stays in this city shall die [i]by the
sword, by famine, and by pestilence, but
he who goes out and [j]surrenders to the
Chaldeans who are besieging you shall live
[k]and shall have his life as a prize of war.
10 For [l]I have set my face against this city for
harm and [m]not for good, declares the LORD:
[n]it shall be given into the hand of the king
of Babylon, and he shall burn it with fire.'

Message to the House of David

11 "And to the house of the king of Judah
say, 'Hear the word of the LORD, 12 O house
of David! Thus says the LORD:

[o]"'Execute justice [p]in the morning,
and deliver from the hand of the
oppressor
him who has been robbed,
[q]lest my wrath go forth like fire,
and burn with none to quench it,
because of your evil deeds.'"

13 [r]"Behold, I am against you,
O inhabitant of the valley,
O rock of the plain,
declares the LORD;
you who say, [s]'Who shall come
down against us,
or who shall enter our habitations?'
14 [t]I will punish you according to [u]the
fruit of your deeds,
declares the LORD;
[v]I will kindle a fire in her forest,
[t]and it shall devour all that is
around her."

22 Thus says the LORD: "Go down to
the house of the king of Judah and
speak there this word, 2 and say, [w]'Hear the
word of the LORD, O King of Judah, who
sits on the throne of David, you, and your
servants, and your people who enter these
gates. 3 Thus says the LORD: [x]Do justice and
righteousness, and deliver from the hand
of the oppressor him who has been robbed.
And [y]do no wrong or violence [z]to the resident alien, [x]the fatherless, and the widow,
nor [a]shed innocent blood in this place.
4 For if you will indeed obey this word,
[b]then there shall enter the gates of this
house kings who sit on the throne of
David, riding in chariots and on horses,
they and their servants and their people.
5 But if you will not obey these words, I
[c]swear by myself, declares the LORD, that
[d]this house shall become a desolation. 6 For
thus says the LORD concerning the house of
the king of Judah:

"'You are like Gilead to me,
like the summit of [e]Lebanon,
yet surely I will make you a desert,
[f]an uninhabited city.[1]
7 [g]I will prepare destroyers against you,
each with his weapons,
[h]and they shall cut down your
choicest cedars
and cast them into the fire.

8 "'And many nations will pass by this
city, and every man will say to his neighbor, [i]"Why has the LORD dealt thus with
this great city?" 9 [j]And they will answer,
"Because they have forsaken the covenant
of the LORD their God and worshiped other
gods and served them."'"

10 [k]Weep not for him who is dead,
nor grieve for him,

[1] Hebrew *cities*

7 [e]ch. 37:17; 39:5; 52:9 [f]Deut. 28:50; 2 Chr. 36:17; Ezek. 5:11
8 [g]Deut. 30:15, 19 [h]ch. 38:2
9 [i]See ch. 15:2 [j]ch. 37:13, 14 [k]ch. 39:18; 45:5
10 [l]ch. 44:11; Lev. 20:3, 5; Ps. 34:16; Ezek. 14:8; [Amos 9:4] [m][ch. 14:11] [n]ver. 7; ch. 34:2; 37:8, 10; 38:17, 18, 23; 39:8; 52:13; 2 Chr. 36:19
12 [o]ch. 22:3; Zech. 7:9; [ch. 22:16] [p]Ps. 101:8 [q]ch. 4:4
13 [r][ver. 10]; See Ezek. 13:8 [s][ch. 49:4]
14 [t]ch. 9:25 [u]Prov. 1:31; Isai. 3:10
[v]Ezek. 20:47

Chapter 22
2 [w]ch. 21:12
3 [x]ch. 7:5, 6; 21:12 [y]Lev. 19:33 [z]Ps. 82:3; Isai. 1:17 [a]ver. 17; [ch. 26:15]
4 [b]ch. 17:25
5 [c]ch. 49:13; 51:14; Gen. 22:16; Amos 6:8; [Heb. 6:13] [d]ch. 7:34; 25:11, 18; 44:6, 22; Isai. 64:10; Ezek. 5:14
6 [e]ver. 20, 23 [f][ch. 6:8]
7 [g]ch. 6:4 [h]2 Kin. 19:23; Isai. 37:24
8 [i]See ch. 5:19
9 [j]Deut. 29:25, 26
10 [k][2 Chr. 35:24, 25]

21:12 Execute justice. See 9:24. This requirement of justice was expected both of the king and the messianic King (23:5; 2 Sam. 8:15; 1 Kin. 3:28; Ps. 72:1, 2).

22:2 O King of Judah. A word for any of the kings, serving as the prelude to a demonstration of their virtually unbroken failure.

22:5 I swear by myself. See Gen. 22:16; Is. 45:23 and notes.

22:6 Gilead . . . Lebanon. These were fertile regions (cf. 8:22 and note). Lebanon was well-watered and rich in forests, especially cedar, which was used for the Jerusalem temple (1 Kin. 5:6–10).

22:7 prepare. Lit. "consecrate." Language normally used of war undertaken by God for His people is used, shockingly, of a foreign army arrayed against God's people (6:4, 5; 21:4, 5).

22:10 dead . . . him who goes away. That is, Josiah and his son Shallum (v. 11). Shallum reigned briefly and was exiled to Egypt in 609 B.C. (2 Kin. 23:30–34). This saying probably dates from that year.

[l] but weep bitterly for him who goes away,
for he shall return no more
to see his native land.

Message to the Sons of Josiah

11 For thus says the LORD concerning
Shallum the son of Josiah, king of Judah,
who reigned instead of Josiah his father,
and [m] who went away from this place: "He
shall return here no more, 12 but [m] in the
place where they have carried him captive,
there shall he die, and he shall never see
this land again."

13 [n] "Woe to him who builds his house by [o] unrighteousness,
and his upper rooms by injustice,
[p] who makes his neighbor serve him for nothing
and does not give him his wages,
14 who says, 'I will build myself a great house
with spacious upper rooms,'
who cuts out windows for it,
paneling it with cedar
and [q] painting it with vermilion.
15 Do you think you are a king
because you compete in cedar?
Did not your father eat and drink
and [r] do justice and righteousness?
[s] Then it was well with him.
16 [t] He judged the cause of the poor and needy;
[s] then it was well.
Is not this [u] to know me?
declares the LORD.
17 But you have eyes and heart
only for your dishonest gain,
[v] for shedding innocent blood,
and for practicing oppression and violence."

18 Therefore thus says the LORD concerning Jehoiakim the son of Josiah, king of
Judah:

[w] "They shall not lament for him, saying,
[x] 'Ah, my brother!' or 'Ah, sister!'
They shall not lament for him, saying,
[y] 'Ah, lord!' or 'Ah, his majesty!'
19 With the burial of a donkey [z] he shall be buried,
dragged and dumped beyond the gates of Jerusalem."

20 "Go up to Lebanon, and cry out,
and lift up your voice in Bashan;
cry out from [a] Abarim,
for all [b] your lovers are destroyed.
21 I spoke to you in your prosperity,
but you said, 'I will not listen.'
[c] This has been your way from [d] your youth,
that you have not obeyed my voice.
22 [e] The wind shall shepherd all your shepherds,
and [b] your lovers shall go into captivity;
[f] then you will be ashamed and confounded
because of all your evil.
23 O inhabitant of [g] Lebanon,
nested among the cedars,
how you will be pitied when pangs come upon you,
[h] pain as of a woman in labor!"

24 [i] "As I live, declares the LORD, though
Coniah the son of Jehoiakim, king of
Judah, were [j] the signet ring on my right
hand, yet I would tear you off 25 and [k] give
you [l] into the hand of those who seek your
life, into the hand of those of whom you

10 [l] ver. 11
11 [m] [2 Kin. 23:34; 2 Chr. 36:4; Ezek. 19:4]
12 [m] [See ver. 11 above]
13 [n] Hab. 2:12; See Isai. 5:18-23 [o] [Mic. 3:10] [p] Lev. 19:13; 25:39, 40; Deut. 24:14, 15; James 5:4
14 [q] Ezek. 23:14
15 [r] [2 Kin. 23:25] [s] Ps. 128:2; Eccles. 8:12; Isai. 3:10
16 [t] Prov. 31:9; [Isai. 1:17] [s] [See ver. 15 above] [u] [Judg. 2:10]
17 [v] ver. 3; [ch. 26:15]
18 [w] Ps. 78:64; See ch. 16:4-6 [x] [1 Kin. 13:30] [y] [ch. 34:5]
19 [z] ch. 8:2; 36:30; [Isai. 14:19]
20 [a] Num. 27:12; Deut. 32:49 [b] [ch. 3:1]
21 [c] ch. 3:25 [d] Ps. 129:1, 2
22 [e] ch. 23:1; [Ezek. 34:10] [b] [See ver. 20 above] [f] ch. 3:25
23 [g] ver. 6 [h] ch. 6:24; See Isai. 13:8
24 [i] Isai. 49:18; See Ezek. 5:11 [j] 1 Kin. 21:8; S. of S. 8:6; Hag. 2:23
25 [k] ch. 34:20 [l] ch. 39:17; [Deut. 1:17]

22:15 Do you think . . . well with him. The contrast is between kingship seen as the exercise of justice (Josiah) and kingship as an opportunity for getting wealth (Jehoiakim).

22:16 Is not this to know me. See Ps. 9:18 note. Knowing the Lord requires being faithful to His commands (Mic. 6:6–8; John 14:15, 17).

22:17 your. That is, Jehoiakim.

dishonest gain . . . innocent blood . . . oppression. Jehoiakim was guilty of all the evils Jeremiah condemns (6:13; 7:6; 19:4; 21:12; and cf. 26:20–23).

22:19 burial of a donkey. The extreme shame of no burial. See 7:33; 8:1, 2 and notes; cf. 15:3.

22:20 Lebanon . . . Bashan . . . Abarim. These mountainous regions lie to the north, northeast, and southeast respectively. Jerusalem is pictured as wailing for help to former allies, themselves now powerless before Babylon, leaving Jerusalem to cry alone.

22:23 inhabitant of Lebanon. In the present context this phrase is a figure for Jerusalem, related to the close trade connections between Jerusalem and Lebanon. The temple and palace were built with cedar from Lebanon (v. 6 note). The name connotes the pride and false sense of security of Judah.

22:24–30 This oracle is against Jehoiachin (here called "Coniah"), in whose reign the first major deportations to Babylon occurred.

22:24 signet. This represents the identity of the owner, and to reject it is shocking. Later, the same language is used to promise a renewal of the Davidic kingdom (Hag. 2:23).

are afraid, even into the hand of
Nebuchadnezzar king of Babylon and into
the hand of the Chaldeans. 26 [m]I will hurl
you and [n]the mother who bore you into
another country, where you were not born,
and there you shall die. 27 But to the land to
which they will long to return, there they
shall not return."

28 Is this man [o]Coniah a despised,
broken pot,
a [p]vessel no one cares for?
Why are he and his children hurled
and cast
into a [q]land that they do not know?
29 [r]O land, land, land,
hear the word of the LORD!
30 Thus says the LORD:
"Write this man down as [s]childless,
a man who shall not succeed in his
days,
[t]for none of his offspring shall succeed
[t]in sitting on the throne of David
and ruling again in Judah."

The Righteous Branch

23 [u]"Woe to the shepherds who
destroy and scatter the sheep of my
pasture!" declares the LORD. 2 Therefore
thus says the LORD, the God of Israel, concerning [u]the shepherds who care for my
people: "You have scattered my flock and
have driven them away, and you have not
attended to them. [v]Behold, I will attend to
you for your evil deeds, declares the LORD.
3 [w]Then I will gather the remnant of my
flock [x]out of all the countries where I have
driven them, and I will bring them back to
their fold, [y]and they shall be fruitful and
multiply. 4 [z]I will set shepherds over them
who will care for them, and they shall fear
no more, nor be dismayed, neither shall
any be missing, declares the LORD.
5 [a]"Behold, the days are coming, declares
the LORD, when I will raise up for David a
righteous [b]Branch, and [c]he shall reign as
king and deal wisely, and shall execute justice and righteousness in the land. 6 In his
days Judah will be saved, and [d]Israel will
[e]dwell securely. And this is the name by
which he will be called: [f]'The LORD is our
righteousness.'
7 [g]"Therefore, behold, the days are coming, declares the LORD, when they shall no
longer say, 'As the LORD lives who brought
up the people of Israel out of the land of
Egypt,' 8 but 'As the LORD lives who brought
up and led the offspring of the house of
Israel out of the north country and out of all
the countries where he[1] had driven them.'
Then they shall dwell in their own land."

Lying Prophets

9 Concerning the prophets:

[h]My heart is broken within me;
[i]all my bones shake;
I am like a drunken man,
like a man overcome by wine,
because of the LORD
and because of his holy words.

26 [m]2 Kin. 24:15; 2 Chr. 36:10 [n][2 Kin. 24:8]
28 [o]ver. 24 [p][ch. 48:38; Ps. 31:12; Hos. 8:8] [q]See ch. 15:14
29 [r]Isai. 1:2
30 [s][1 Chr. 3:17; Matt. 1:12] [t]ch. 36:30
Chapter 23
1 [u]ch. 6:3; 10:21; 22:22; 25:34, 36; Isai. 56:11; Ezek. 34:2; Zech. 11:17; [John 10:12, 13]
2 [u][See ver. 1 above] [v]ver. 22; ch. 4:4
3 [w]ch. 29:14; 32:37; Deut. 30:3; Ezek. 20:34, 41; 37:21; [Ps. 107:3]; See Ezek. 34:11-16 [x][ch. 8:3] [y][Gen. 1:28]
4 [z]ch. 3:15
5 [a]For ver. 5, 6, see ch. 33:14-16 [b]Isai. 4:2; 11:1 [c]ch. 30:9; Isai. 32:1; Ezek. 37:24; Hos. 3:5; Zech. 9:9; Matt. 2:2; Luke 1:32; 19:38; John 1:49
6 [d]Deut. 33:28; [Zech. 14:11] [e]ch. 32:37 [f]Rom. 10:4; 1 Cor. 1:30
7 [g]For ver. 7, 8, see ch. 16:14, 15
9 [h]Ezek. 6:9 [i]Hab. 3:16

1 Septuagint; Hebrew *I*

22:26 you and the mother who bore you. See 13:18 and note.

into another country. This reference to exile in Babylon is fulfilled in 597 B.C. (29:2; 2 Kin. 24:15).

22:29 O land, land, land. In this address to the land we hear the Lord's grief over His inheritance, defiled by Judah's sin (2:7 and note; 12:4).

22:30 Write this man down as childless. Though Jehoiachin had children (1 Chr. 3:17, 18), none of them would reign as king over Judah. Promises of future Davidic kingship (e.g., 23:5, 6) were fulfilled beyond the scope of the historical Israelite and Judean kingdoms—in Christ the Son of Man (Dan. 7:13 and note), and the greater son of David (Matt. 22:41–46). Even the promise to Zerubbabel (Hag. 2:23), Jehoiachin's grandson (1 Chr. 3:19), finds fulfillment in Christ, since Zerubbabel never reigned as king. Israel was abandoned until Christ came (Mic. 5:3).

23:3 I will. The failure of the kings requires the Lord Himself to take control in a new way (24:7 note).

remnant. The gathering of the remnant shows the continuing care of the Lord for His people and His determination to fulfill His covenantal purposes. In the present context, the doctrine of the remnant suggests first of all the breaking off of certain of Judah's branches (vv. 1, 2; cf. Rom. 11:17–24) following the king's neglect and the due punishment (Introduction: Characteristics and Themes).

bring them back to their fold. The Lord Himself is now the Shepherd (Ps. 23).

23:4 I will set shepherds over them. Under the Shepherd there will be true shepherds, who will faithfully administer the kingdom in the new age (Mic. 5:5).

23:5, 6 raise up for David. This messianic promise is a fulfillment of the promise to David (2 Sam. 7:12; Matt. 1:1, 17).

23:5 a righteous Branch. A messianic term; see Is. 4:2; 11:1; and Zech. 6:12, where Zerubbabel is a type of Christ.

execute justice and righteousness. See note 21:12.

23:6 Judah . . . Israel. The reunification of Judah and Israel marks the messianic age (Ezek. 37:15–22).

securely. The blessings of the messianic kingdom will include deliverance from the political and military turmoil surrounding Judah.

name. Names were understood as designations of character, not arbitrary labels of identification. See "Immanuel" in Is. 7:14 and the names in Is. 9:6.

The LORD is our righteousness. Righteous rule is the hallmark of the Messiah's reign.

23:9 the prophets. See "Prophets" at Deut. 18:18.

10 [j] For the land is full of adulterers;
[k] because of the curse [l] the land mourns,
and [m] the pastures of the wilderness are dried up.
[n] Their course is evil,
and their might is not right.
11 [o] "Both prophet and priest are ungodly;
even [p] in my house I have found their evil,
declares the LORD.
12 [q] Therefore their way shall be to them
like slippery paths [r] in the darkness,
into which they shall be driven and fall,
for I will bring disaster upon them
[s] in the year of their punishment,
declares the LORD.
13 In the prophets of [t] Samaria
[u] I saw an unsavory thing:
[v] they prophesied by Baal
[w] and led my people Israel astray.
14 But in the prophets of Jerusalem
I have seen a horrible thing:
[x] they commit adultery and walk in lies;
[y] they strengthen the hands of evildoers,
so that no one turns from his evil;
[z] all of them have become like Sodom to me,
[z] and its inhabitants like Gomorrah."
15 Therefore thus says the LORD of hosts concerning the prophets:
[a] "Behold, I will feed them with bitter food
[a] and give them [b] poisoned water to drink,
for from the prophets of Jerusalem
ungodliness has gone out into all the land."

16 Thus says the LORD of hosts: "Do not listen to the words of the prophets who prophesy to you, [c] filling you with vain hopes. [d] They speak visions of their own minds, not from the mouth of the LORD.
17 They say continually to those who despise the word of the LORD, [e] 'It shall be well with you'; and to everyone who [f] stubbornly follows his own heart, they say, [g] 'No disaster shall come upon you.'"

10 [j] ch. 5:7, 8; 9:2 [k] Ps. 10:7; 59:12; Hos. 4:2, 3 [l] ch. 4:28 [m] ch. 9:10; 12:4; Ps. 107:34 [n] [ch. 22:17]
11 [o] [ver. 33, 34; Zeph. 3:4]; See ch. 6:13 [p] ch. 7:30; 32:34; Ezek. 8:16; 23:39
12 [q] Ps. 35:6; 73:18 [r] Prov. 4:19; [ch. 13:16] [s] ch. 11:23
13 [t] Lam. 2:14 [u] Isai. 7:9; Ezek. 16:46, 51, 53, 55; 23:4, 33 [v] ch. 2:8 [w] Isai. 9:16; Mic. 3:5
14 [x] ch. 29:23 [y] Ps. 64:5; Ezek. 13:22 [z] Isai. 1:9, 10; 13:19
15 [a] ch. 9:15; Prov. 5:4 [b] ch. 8:14
16 [c] [Ps. 12:2] [d] [ver. 21, 26; Num. 16:28]
17 [e] [Zech. 10:2]; See ch. 6:14 [f] See ch. 3:17 [g] ch. 5:12; Mic. 3:11

Omnipresence and Omnipotence

God is present in all places; however, we should not think of Him as filling space, for He has no physical dimensions. It is as spirit that He is everywhere. Although it surpasses the understanding of body-bound creatures like ourselves, God Himself is present everywhere in His majesty and power. Needy souls praying to Him anywhere in the world are in His sight and receive His personal attention. Belief in God's omnipresence is apparent in Ps. 139:7–10; Jer. 23:23, 24; Acts 17:24–28. When Paul speaks of the ascended Christ as filling all things (Eph. 4:8), Christ's availability everywhere in the fullness of His power is certainly part of the meaning. Father, Son, and Holy Spirit are omnipresent, though the personal presence of the glorified Son is not physical (in the body).

"I know that you can do all things, and that no purpose of yours can be thwarted" (Job 42:2). Job testifies that God is omnipotent. He is all-powerful, almighty. God has power to do everything that in His perfect wisdom and goodness He wills to do. Omnipotence does not mean that God can do literally everything: God cannot sin, lie, change His nature or deny the demands of His holy character (Num. 23:19; 1 Sam. 15:29; 2 Tim. 2:13; Heb. 6:18; James 1:13, 17). He cannot make a square circle, for the notion of a square circle is self-contradictory; He cannot cease to be God. But all that He wills and promises He can and will do.

Was it excessive for David to say, "I love you, O LORD, my strength. The LORD is my rock and my fortress and my deliverer; my God, my rock, in whom I take refuge; my shield, and the horn of my salvation, my stronghold" (Ps. 18:1, 2)? Was it excessive for another psalmist to declare, "God is our refuge and strength, a very present help in trouble" (Ps. 46:1)? It would have been a fault to say such things if God were less than omnipresent and omnipotent. But the knowledge of God's greatness, including His omnipresence and omnipotence, produces great faith and high praise.

23:14 they commit adultery . . . his evil. Right belief and right action are inseparable in the Old Testament; it is no accident that those who have not heard God's word actively encourage evil. See 29:21–23. **like Sodom . . . like Gomorrah.** See 20:16; Is. 1:9 and notes. The comparison of Jerusalem to Sodom and Gomorrah is shocking.

18 For [h]who among them has stood in
the council of the LORD
to see and to hear his word,
or who has paid attention to his
word and listened?
19 [i]Behold, the storm of the LORD!
Wrath has gone forth,
[j]a whirling tempest;
it will burst upon the head of the
wicked.
20 [k]The anger of the LORD will not turn
back
until he has executed and
[k]accomplished
the intents of his heart.
[l]In the latter days you will understand
it clearly.

21 [m]"I did not send the prophets,
yet they ran;
I did not speak to them,
yet they prophesied.
22 [n]But if they had stood in my council,
then they would have proclaimed
my words to my people,
[o]and they would have turned them
from their evil way,
and [p]from the evil of their deeds.

23 [q]"Am I a God at hand, declares the
LORD, and not a God afar off? 24 [q]Can a man
hide himself in secret places so that I cannot see him? declares the LORD. [r]Do I not
fill heaven and earth? declares the LORD. 25 I
have heard what the prophets have said
[s]who prophesy lies in my name, saying, [t]'I
have dreamed, I have dreamed!' 26 How
long shall there be lies in the heart of [u]the
prophets who prophesy lies, and who
prophesy the deceit of their own heart,
27 who think to make my people forget my
name by their dreams that they tell one
another, even as their [v]fathers forgot my
name for Baal? 28 [w]Let the prophet who has
a dream [x]tell the dream, but let him who
has my word speak my word faithfully.
[y]What has straw in common with wheat?
declares the LORD. 29 [y]Is not my word like
fire, declares the LORD, and [z]like a hammer
that breaks the rock in pieces? 30 [a]There-
fore, behold, I am against the prophets,
declares the LORD, who steal my words
from one another. 31 Behold, I am against
the prophets, declares the LORD, who use
their tongues and declare, 'declares the
LORD.' 32 Behold, I am against those who
prophesy lying dreams, declares the LORD,
and who tell them and [b]lead my people
astray by their lies and their recklessness,
when [c]I did not send them or charge them.
So they do not profit this people at all,
declares the LORD.

33 [d]"When one of this people, or a
prophet or a priest asks you, 'What is [e]the
burden of the LORD?' you shall say to them,
'You are the burden,[1] and [f]I will cast you
off, declares the LORD.' 34 And as for the
prophet, priest, or one of the people who
says, [e]'The burden of the LORD,' [d]I will
punish that man and his household.
35 Thus shall you say, every one to his
neighbor and every one to his brother,
'What has the LORD answered?' or 'What
has the LORD spoken?' 36 But [e]'the burden
of the LORD' you shall mention no more,
for the burden is every man's own word,
and [g]you pervert the words of [h]the living
God, the LORD of hosts, our God. 37 Thus
you shall say to the prophet, 'What has the
LORD answered you?' or 'What has the
LORD spoken?' 38 But if you say, [e]'The burden of the LORD,' thus says the LORD,
'Because you have said these words, "The
burden of the LORD," when I sent to you,
saying, "You shall not say, 'The burden
of the LORD,'" 39 therefore, behold, I will

[1] Septuagint, Vulgate; Hebrew *What burden?*

18 [h]ver. 22; Isai. 40:14
19 [i]ch. 30:23
[j]ch. 25:32
20 [k]ch. 30:24; [Isai. 55:11]
[l]ch. 30:24
21 [m]See ch. 14:14
22 [n]ver. 18
[o]ch. 25:5; [Luke 1:17]
[p]ver. 2
23 [q][Ps. 94:7, 9; Amos 9:2, 3]; See Ps. 139:7-12
24 [q][See ver. 23 above]
[r]Isai. 66:1; Acts 7:49
25 [s]See ch. 5:31 [t][Zech. 10:2]
26 [u][ver. 16, 21; Num. 16:28]
27 [v]Judg. 3:7; 8:33, 34
28 [w][Num. 12:6]
[x]ver. 25
[y][Luke 3:17]
29 [y][See ver. 28 above]
[z][Dan. 2:34, 45]
30 [a]Ezek. 13:8; [ch. 14:15; Deut. 18:20]
32 [b]ver. 13
[c]ver. 21; See ch. 14:14
33 [d]See Ezek. 14:1-11 [e]Mal. 1:1 [f][Hos. 4:6]
34 [e][See ver. 33 above]
[d][See ver. 33 above]
36 [e][See ver. 33 above]
[g][Matt. 15:6]
[h]Ps. 42:2
38 [e][See ver. 33 above]

23:18 stood in the council of the LORD. The Hebrew word translated "council" here and in v. 22 may also be translated "counsel," depending on whether the emphasis is on God's deliberations with the heavenly "council" (1 Kin. 22:19–22; Job 1:6) or on the "counsel" resulting from those deliberations. The word is translated "secret" in Amos 3:7.

23:21 I did not send. See 14:14.

yet they ran . . . prophesied. They are a picture of zeal in their self-serving propagation of falsehood. See "Prophets" at Deut. 18:18.

23:22 council. See note on v. 18.

23:23 at hand . . . afar. The point is that nothing, near or far, can escape God's knowledge (Ps. 139:2; Amos 9:2, 3).

23:24 See theological note "Omnipresence and Omnipotence."

23:25 dreamed . . . dreamed. The dream was one way in which a revelation might come to a prophet (Num. 12:6; cf. Joel 2:28); yet such claims should always be treated with due suspicion and tested against the rest of God's revelation (Deut. 13:1–3).

23:28 dream . . . word . . . straw . . . wheat. The false dream is to the true prophetic word as straw is to wheat; only the wheat has any value.

23:29 fire . . . hammer. There can be no mistaking the true word, because of its inevitable effects (Amos 3:8).

23:30 who steal my words. For a case of prophetic jealousy, see 1 Kin. 22:24.

23:31 declares the LORD . . . and declare, 'declares the LORD.' The false prophets disguise their own words as words from God by using the prophetic formula.

surely lift you up and [f]cast you away from
my presence, you and the city that I gave to
you and your fathers. **40**[i]And I will bring
upon you everlasting reproach and [i]perpet-
ual shame, which shall not be forgotten.'"

The Good Figs and the Bad Figs

24 [j]After Nebuchadnezzar king of
Babylon had taken into exile from
Jerusalem [k]Jeconiah the son of Jehoiakim,
king of Judah, together with [l]the officials
of Judah, the craftsmen, and the metal
workers, and had brought them to Babylon, the LORD showed me this vision: behold, [m]two baskets of figs placed before
the temple of the LORD. **2**One basket had
very good figs, [n]like first-ripe figs, but the
other basket had [o]very bad figs, so bad that
they could not be eaten. **3**And the LORD
said to me, "What do you see, Jeremiah?"
I said, "Figs, the good figs very good, and
the bad figs very bad, so bad that they cannot be eaten."
4Then the word of the LORD came to me:
5"Thus says the LORD, the God of Israel:
Like these good figs, so I will regard as
good the exiles from Judah, [p]whom I have
sent away from this place to the land of the
Chaldeans. **6**[q]I will set my eyes on them for
good, and I will bring them back to this
land. [r]I will build them up, and not tear
them down; [s]I will plant them, and not
uproot them. **7**[t]I will give them a heart to
know that I am the LORD, [u]and they shall
be my people [t]and I will be their God, [v]for
they shall return to me with their whole
heart.
8"But thus says the LORD: Like [w]the bad
figs that are so bad they cannot be eaten, so
will I treat [x]Zedekiah the king of Judah, his
officials, the remnant of Jerusalem who
remain in this land, and those who [y]dwell
in the land of Egypt. **9**I will make them [z]a
horror[1] to all the kingdoms of the earth, to
be [a]a reproach, [b]a byword, [a]a taunt, and [c]a
curse in all the places where I shall drive
them. **10**And I will send [d]sword, famine,
and pestilence upon them, until they shall
be utterly destroyed from the land that I
gave to them and their fathers."

Seventy Years of Captivity

25 [e]The word that came to Jeremiah
concerning all the people of Judah,
in the fourth year of Jehoiakim the son of
Josiah, king of Judah (that was the first
year of Nebuchadnezzar king of Babylon),
2which Jeremiah the prophet spoke to all
the people of Judah and all the inhabitants
of Jerusalem: **3**"For twenty-three years,
[f]from the thirteenth year of Josiah the son
of Amon, king of Judah, to this day, the
word of the LORD has come to me, and I
have spoken [g]persistently to you, [h]but you
have not listened. **4**[g]You have neither listened nor inclined your ears to hear, although the LORD [h]persistently sent to you
all his servants the prophets, **5**saying,
[i]'Turn now, every one of you, [j]from his evil
way and evil deeds, and [k]dwell upon the
land that the LORD has given to you and
your fathers from of old and forever. **6**[l]Do
not go after other gods to serve and worship them, [m]or provoke me to anger [m]with
the work of your hands. Then I will do you
no harm.' **7**[m]Yet you have not listened to
me, declares the LORD, [m]that you might
provoke me to anger [m]with the work of
your hands to your own harm.
8"Therefore thus says the LORD of hosts:
Because you have not obeyed my words,

[1] Compare Septuagint; Hebrew *horror for evil*

39[f][See ver. 33 above]
40[i]ch. 20:11
Chapter 24
1[j]Amos 8:1, 2 [k]2 Kin. 24:12; 2 Chr. 36:10 [l]Matt. 1:11; [ch. 22:18, 24, 28] [m]ch. 29:2; 2 Kin. 24:12, 14
2[n][Isai. 28:4] [o]ch. 29:17
5[p]ch. 29:20
6[q][Amos 9:4] [r]ch. 12:15; 29:10 [s]ch. 31:28; 42:10; [ch. 1:10; Amos 9:15]
7[t]ch. 32:39; Deut. 30:6; Ezek. 11:19; 36:26, 27 [u]See ch. 30:22; 31:33 [v]ch. 29:13; Joel 2:12, 13
8[w]ver. 2; ch. 29:17 [x]ch. 21:1 [y]See ch. 43; ch. 44
9[z]See ch. 15:4 [a]ch. 29:18; 49:13; Neh. 2:17; Isai. 43:28 [b]Deut. 28:37; 2 Chr. 7:20 [c]ch. 25:18; 26:6; 29:22; 2 Kin. 22:19
10[d]See ch. 14:12
Chapter 25
1[e]ch. 1:3; 36:1; [2 Kin. 24:1]
3[f]ch. 1:2 [g]ch. 7:13; 11:7, 8; 26:5; 29:19; 32:33; 35:14; 2 Chr. 36:15 [h]See ch. 7:13
4[g][See ver. 3 above] [h][See ver. 3 above]
5[i]See ch. 18:11 [j]ch. 23:22 [k]ch. 7:7
6[l]See ch. 7:6 [m][ch. 32:30]
7[m][See ver. 6 above]

24:1–10 A vision of two baskets of figs, one representing those exiled to Babylon, and the other those who would resist exile and with it the Lord's purpose of judgment and salvation. This prophecy reveals that it is too late to avert the exile by repentance (21:9).

24:1 Jeconiah . . . to Babylon. The first large deportation was in 597 B.C. (2 Kin. 24:14–16).

24:2 very good figs . . . very bad figs. There is in Judah a remnant who will be preserved for God's purposes ("good figs"), but their leaders are so corrupt that they are beyond redemption and can only be destroyed by judgment ("bad figs," vv. 8–10).

24:5–7 The "good figs" symbolize the exiles, those whom God preserves through the due punishment for Judah's sin, and in whom henceforth His purposes will be accomplished.

24:7 I will give them a heart to know. The Lord's answer to His people's inability to maintain the covenant relationship is for He Himself to intervene and create in them a new capacity for knowing Him.

they shall be my people and I will be their God. Use of the basic covenant formula (32:38; Lev. 26:12) shows that this answer is nothing less than a new covenant. The theology introduced here is developed at 31:31–34.

25:1–29:32 Jeremiah predicts seventy years of Babylonian captivity for Judah as judgment for persistent sin, and warns the neighboring nations as well of judgment at the hands of Babylon (ch. 25). His message meets opposition from false prophets, priests, and the people (chs. 26–29).

25:1 fourth year of Jehoiakim. Babylon began its attacks in Palestine and Judah became a Babylonian vassal state in 605 B.C.

25:3 thirteenth year of Josiah. See 1:2 and notes.

persistently. Jeremiah's persistence was part of a long prophetic mission to Israel. Like his predecessors, his ministry failed to obtain the desired response (7:13 and note).

9 [n]behold, I will send for all the tribes of the
north, declares the LORD, and for Nebuchadnezzar the king of Babylon, [o]my servant, and I will bring them against this land
and its inhabitants, and against all these
surrounding nations. I will devote them to
destruction, [p]and make them a horror, a
hissing, and an everlasting desolation.
10 Moreover, [q]I will banish from them the
voice of mirth and the voice of gladness,
the voice of the bridegroom and the voice
of the bride, [r]the grinding of the millstones
and [s]the light of the lamp. **11** [p]This whole
land shall become a ruin and a waste, and
[t]these nations shall serve the king of
Babylon [u]seventy years. **12** Then after seventy years are completed, [v]I will punish the
king of Babylon and that nation, [v]the land
of the Chaldeans, for their iniquity, declares
the LORD, [v]making the land an everlasting
waste. **13** I will bring upon that land all the
words that I have uttered against it, everything written [w]in this book, which Jeremiah
prophesied against all the nations. **14** [x]For
many nations [x]and great kings shall make
slaves even of them, [y]and I will recompense
them according to their deeds and the work
of their hands."

The Cup of the LORD's Wrath

15 Thus the LORD, the God of Israel, said
to me: [z]"Take from my hand this cup of the
wine of wrath, and make all the nations to
whom I send you drink it. **16** They shall
drink and stagger and be crazed because of
[a]the sword that I am sending among them."
17 So I took the cup from the LORD's
hand, [b]and made all the nations to whom
the LORD sent me drink it: **18** [c]Jerusalem and
the cities of Judah, its kings and officials,
[d]to make them a desolation and a waste,
a hissing and a curse, as at this day;
19 [e]Pharaoh king of Egypt, his servants, his
officials, all his people, **20** and [f]all the mixed
tribes among them; all the kings of [g]the
land of Uz and all the kings of [h]the land of
the Philistines ([h]Ashkelon, [h]Gaza, Ekron,
and the remnant of [i]Ashdod); **21** [j]Edom,
[k]Moab, and the sons of [l]Ammon; **22** all the
kings of [m]Tyre, all the kings of [m]Sidon, and
the kings of the coastland across [n]the sea;
23 [o]Dedan, [p]Tema, [q]Buz, and all who cut
[r]the corners of their hair; **24** all the [s]kings of
Arabia and all the kings of [f]the mixed tribes
who dwell in the desert; **25** all the kings of
Zimri, all the kings of [t]Elam, and all the
kings of [u]Media; **26** all the kings of [v]the
north, far and near, one after another, and
all the kingdoms of the world that are on
the face of the earth. And after them the
king of [w]Babylon[1] shall drink.

27 "Then you shall say to them, 'Thus
says the LORD of hosts, the God of Israel:
[x]Drink, be drunk and vomit, fall and rise
no more, because of [y]the sword that I am
sending among you.'

9 [n]ch. 1:15 [o]ch. 27:6; 43:10; [Isai. 44:28; 45:1]; See Ezek. 29:18-20 [p]See ch. 18:16
10 [q]See ch. 7:34 [r]Eccles. 12:4; Rev. 18:22 [s]Rev. 18:23
11 [p][See ver. 9 above] [t][ch. 28:14]; See ch. 27:3-6 [u]2 Chr. 36:21, 22; Ezra 1:1; Dan. 9:2; [Isai. 23:15]
12 [v]ch. 51:24, 26, 62; Isai. 13:19
13 [w]See ch. 46–51
14 [x]ch. 27:7; 50:9, 41; 51:27, 28 [y]ch. 50:29; 51:6, 24
15 [z]ch. 49:12; 51:7; Job 21:20; Ps. 60:3; 75:8; Isai. 51:17; Lam. 4:21; Rev. 14:10
16 [a][ch. 47:6]
17 [b][Isai. 51:22, 23]
18 [c][Zech. 12:2] [d]See ch. 18:16
19 [e]ch. 46:25
20 [f]ch. 50:37; [Ex. 12:38; Ezek. 30:5] [g]Job 1:1; Lam. 4:21 [h]ch. 47:1, 4, 5 [i][Isai. 20:1]
21 [j]ch. 9:26; See ch. 49:7-22 [k]See ch. 48 [l]See ch. 49:1-6 **22** [m]ch. 47:4; Isai. 23:1, 2 [n][ch. 49:23] **23** [o]ch. 49:8; Isai. 21:13 [p]Job 6:19 [q][Job 32:2, 6] [r]See ch. 9:26 **24** [s]2 Chr. 9:14 [f][See ver. 20 above] **25** [t]Isai. 11:11; See ch. 49:34-39 [u][2 Kin. 17:6] **26** [v]ch. 50:9 [w]ch. 51:41 **27** [x]Hab. 2:16 [y]Ezek. 38:21; [ver. 16]

1 Hebrew *Sheshach*, a code name for Babylon

25:9 tribes of the north. Babylon and her allies (1:15; 6:1).

Nebuchadnezzar . . . my servant. See also 27:6. He is God's "servant" in the sense of being appointed as an agent of His judgment. In the same way Cyrus is called God's "anointed" for the purpose of releasing the exiles to return to their land (Is. 45:1).

surrounding nations. See vv. 19–26. The judgment on Judah is only the beginning of a general judgment.

25:11, 12 seventy years. See 29:10. This period may be counted in round figures from 605 B.C. (v. 1; Dan. 1:1) to 538 B.C., when the exiles began to return home following Cyrus's decree (2 Chr. 36:20–23). The seventy years allow the Lord's word of judgment to have full effect before new salvation can be experienced.

punish the king of Babylon. This prophecy is developed further in chs. 50; 51. The agent of punishment is in turn punished for her own sins (50:18; cf. Is. 10:5–7, 12).

25:13 in this book. In the Septuagint (the ancient Greek translation of the Old Testament) the "oracles against the nations" from chs. 46–51 occur after this phrase. Those oracles appear in different orders in the Hebrew and Greek versions.

25:14 many nations and great kings. Possibly Persia and its allies, but more likely a general statement of the principle that agents of God's judgment are themselves subject to judgment (vv. 11, 12 note).

25:18 Jerusalem and . . . Judah. God's judgment is first visited upon His chosen people, as befits those who are most privileged (25:29; Amos 3:2).

25:20 Ashkelon . . . remnant of Ashdod. This list of Philistine cities omits Gath, apparently already destroyed (Amos 1:6–8). Ashdod had been partially destroyed by the Egyptians during the seventh century. See also 47:1–7.

25:21 Edom, Moab, and . . . Ammon. See 49:7–22; 48:1–49:6.

25:22 Tyre . . . Sidon. The principal cities of Phoenicia, both ports on the Mediterranean coast. See Ezek. 28:1–23.

25:23 Dedan, Tema. Tribes living in northern Arabia (Is. 21:13, 14). Buz was probably also an Arabian tribal group.

25:24 Arabia. See 49:28–33.

25:25 Zimri. Unknown.

Media. Having themselves been defeated by Cyrus, the Medes participated with the Persians in the conquest.

25:26 Babylon. In Hebrew "Sheshach." This word is an allusion to Babylon based on the word "Babel," using a familiar code that substitutes for each consonant the corresponding one from the alphabet written in reverse. In English, ABC would become ZYX.

28 "And if they refuse to accept the cup
from your hand to drink, then you shall say
to them, 'Thus says the LORD of hosts: [z]You
must drink! 29 For behold, [y]I begin to work
disaster at the city that is called by my
name, and shall you go unpunished? You
shall not go unpunished, [a]for I am summoning a sword against all the inhabitants
of the earth, declares the LORD of hosts.'

30 "You, therefore, shall prophesy against
them all these words, and say to them:

[b]" 'The LORD will roar from on high,
and from his holy habitation utter
his voice;
he will roar mightily against his fold,
[c]and shout, like those who tread
grapes,
against all the inhabitants of the
earth.
31 The clamor will resound to the ends
of the earth,
for [d]the LORD has an indictment
against the nations;
[e]he is entering into judgment with all
flesh,
and the wicked he will put to the
sword,
declares the LORD.'

32 "Thus says the LORD of hosts:
Behold, disaster is going forth
from nation to nation,
[f]and a great tempest is stirring
[g]from the farthest parts of the earth!

33 [h]"And those pierced by the LORD on
that day shall extend from one end of the
earth to the other. [i]They shall not be
lamented, [j]or gathered, or buried; [j]they
shall be dung on the surface of the ground.

34 [k]"Wail, [l]you shepherds, and cry out,
[m]and roll in ashes, you lords of the
flock,
for the days of your slaughter and
dispersion have come,
and you shall fall like a choice
vessel.
35 No refuge will remain [n]for the
shepherds,
nor escape for the lords of the
flock.
36 A voice—the cry of the
shepherds,
[o]and the wail of the lords of the
flock!
For the LORD is laying waste their
pasture,
37 [p]and the peaceful folds are
devastated
[q]because of the fierce anger of the
LORD.
38 Like a lion [r]he has left his
lair,
for their land has become a
waste
because of [s]the sword of the
oppressor,
[q]and because of his fierce
anger."

Jeremiah Threatened with Death

26 [t]In the beginning of the reign of
[u]Jehoiakim the son of Josiah, king
of Judah, this word came from the LORD:
2 "Thus says the LORD: [v]Stand in the court
of the LORD's house, and speak to all the
cities of Judah that come to worship in the
house of the LORD [w]all the words that I
command you to speak to them; [x]do not
hold back a word. 3 [y]It may be they will listen, and every one turn from his evil way,
[z]that I may relent of the disaster that I
intend to do to them [a]because of their evil
deeds. 4 You shall say to them, 'Thus says
the LORD: [b]If you will not listen to me, to
walk in my law that I have set before you,
5 [c]and to listen to the words of my servants
the prophets whom I send to you [c]urgent-
ly, [c]though you have not listened, 6 then I
will make this house [d]like Shiloh, and I will
make this city [e]a curse for all the nations of
the earth.'"

7 [f]The priests and the prophets and all the
people heard Jeremiah speaking these

28 [z]ch. 49:12
29 [y][See ver. 27 above] [a]Prov. 11:31; Isai. 10:12; Amos 3:2; Obad. 16; [1 Pet. 4:17]
30 [b]Joel 3:16; Amos 1:2 [c][Judg. 9:27; Isai. 16:9]
31 [d]Hos. 4:1 [e]Isai. 66:16; [Joel 3:2]
32 [f]ch. 23:19; 30:23 [g]ch. 6:22
33 [h]Isai. 66:16 [i]See ch. 16:4 [j]See ch. 8:2
34 [k]ch. 4:8 [l]See ch. 23:1 [m]ch. 6:26
35 [n]See ch. 23:1
36 [o]ch. 4:8
37 [p][Isai. 32:18] [q]See ch. 12:13
38 [r][Job 38:40] [s]ch. 46:16; 50:16 [q][See ver. 37 above]
Chapter 26
1 [t]ch. 27:1 [u]2 Kin. 23:36; 2 Chr. 36:5
2 [v]ch. 19:14 [w][Ezek. 3:10] [x]Deut. 4:2; 12:32; [Acts 20:27]
3 [y]ch. 36:3 [z]ver. 13, 19; See ch. 18:8 [a]ch. 4:4
4 [b]Lev. 26:14; Deut. 28:15
5 [c]See ch. 25:3, 4
6 [d]See ch. 7:12 [e]See ch. 24:9
7 [f]ch. 23:33

25:29 city that is called by my name. That is, Jerusalem; see notes 7:10–15. The Lord would not punish His own people while ignoring the wickedness of other nations. An important factor in the theology of judgment against the nations is that the honor of God's own name is at stake in the fate of His people.

25:31 indictment. A legal action in which the Lord claims His right to punish the guilty (2:9 note).

25:38 Like a lion. See note 2:15. Here Jeremiah refers to the Lord (Amos 3:8).

26:1 In the beginning of the reign of Jehoiakim. Possibly his first year (609–608 B.C.). The fuller account of the temple sermon (7:1–15) is not dated. This date formula brings Jehoiakim into the foreground as one who rejects Jeremiah's words (ch. 36).

26:2 the court. Probably the inner courtyard.

words in the house of the LORD. 8 And when
Jeremiah had finished speaking all that the
LORD had commanded him to speak to all
the people, then [f]the priests and the
prophets and all the people laid hold of
him, saying, "You shall die! 9 Why have you
prophesied in the name of the LORD, saying,
'This house shall be [d]like Shiloh, and this
city shall be desolate, [g]without inhabitant'?" And all the people gathered around
Jeremiah in the house of the LORD.
10 When [f]the officials of Judah heard
these things, they came up from the king's
house to the house of the LORD and took
their seat in the [h]entry of the New Gate of
the house of the LORD. 11 Then [i]the priests
and the prophets said to the officials and to
all the people, [j]"This man deserves the sentence of death, because he has prophesied
against this city, as you have heard with
your own ears."
12 Then Jeremiah spoke to all the officials
and all the people, saying, "The LORD sent
me to prophesy against this house and this
city all the words you have heard. 13 Now
therefore [k]mend your ways and your deeds,
[l]and obey the voice of the LORD your God,
[z]and the LORD will relent of the disaster
that he has pronounced against you.
14 [m]But as for me, behold, I am in your
hands. Do with me as seems good and
right to you. 15 Only know for certain that if
you put me to death, [n]you will bring innocent blood upon yourselves and upon this
city and its inhabitants, for in truth the
LORD sent me to you to speak all these
words in your ears."

Jeremiah Spared from Death

16 [o]Then the officials and all the people
said to the priests and the prophets, [p]"This
man does not deserve the sentence of death,
for he has spoken to us in the name of the
LORD our God." 17 [q]And certain of [r]the elders
of the land arose and spoke to all the assembled people, saying, 18 "Micah of Moresheth
prophesied in the days of Hezekiah king of
Judah, and said to all the people of Judah:
'Thus says the LORD of hosts,

[s]"'Zion shall be plowed as a field;
Jerusalem shall become a heap of ruins,
and the mountain of the house a wooded height.'

19 Did Hezekiah king of Judah and all Judah
put him to death? [t]Did he not fear the LORD
and entreat the favor of the LORD, [u]and did
not the LORD relent of the disaster that he
had pronounced against them? [v]But we are
about to bring great disaster upon ourselves."
20 There was another man who prophesied in the name of the LORD, Uriah the son
of Shemaiah from [w]Kiriath-jearim. He
prophesied against this city and against
this land in words like those of Jeremiah.
21 And when [x]King Jehoiakim, with all his
warriors and all the officials, heard his
words, the king sought to put him to
death. But when Uriah heard of it, he was
afraid and fled and escaped to Egypt.
22 Then [x]King Jehoiakim sent to Egypt certain men, [y]Elnathan the son of [z]Achbor
and others with him, 23 and they took Uriah
from Egypt and brought him to King
Jehoiakim, [a]who struck him down with the
sword and dumped his dead body into the
burial place of the common people.
24 But the hand of [b]Ahikam the son of
Shaphan was with Jeremiah so that he was
not given over to the people to be put to
death.

8 [f][See ver. 7 above]
9 [d][See ver. 6 above] [g]See ch. 4:7
10 [f][See ver. 7 above] [h]ch. 36:12
11 [i]ch. 36:10 [j]ch. 38:4; [ver. 16]
13 [k]See ch. 7:3 [l]Deut. 30:2 [z][See ver. 3 above]
14 [m]Josh. 9:25
15 [n][Matt. 27:24]
16 [o]ver. 8 [p][ver. 11]
17 [q][Acts 5:34] [r]See ch. 19:1
18 [s]Mic. 3:12
19 [t][2 Chr. 32:26] [u]Ex. 32:14; 2 Sam. 24:16; [1 Kin. 13:6] [v][Acts 5:39]
20 [w]Josh. 9:17; 1 Sam. 6:21; 7:1, 2; 1 Chr. 13:5, 6
21 [x]ver. 1; ch. 27:1
22 [x][See ver. 21 above] [y]ch. 36:12, 25 [z]2 Kin. 22:12, 14
23 [a][ch. 22:17; Neh. 9:26; Matt. 21:35; 23:37]
24 [b]2 Kin. 22:12

26:8 You shall die. This phrase was used in handing down the sentence for capital crimes (Ex. 21:15–17; Deut. 18:20). Jeremiah is evidently held to be a false prophet because of the people's belief that God's temple could never be destroyed.

26:10 the officials of Judah. These persons had legal duties in the royal administration; their arrival indicates that a formal proceeding against Jeremiah is about to begin.

New Gate. The gates were the normal place for court hearings (Ruth 4:1; Prov. 31:23).

26:16 This man does not deserve the sentence of death. Contrast v. 11. This verdict is a remarkable vindication of Jeremiah's authenticity as a prophet.

26:18, 19 Micah of Moresheth. His precedent is cited in support of the judgment just given, because as a result of his prophecy that Jerusalem would fall (Mic. 3:12), the people repented of their sin. King Hezekiah prayed for Jerusalem and avoided defeat by the Assyrians in 701 B.C. (cf. Is. 37:14–38).

26:20–23 The story of Uriah shows that Jeremiah was not alone in his preaching; it also stresses that Jeremiah's escape is not the most important point of this chapter, but rather the opposition in Judah to the word of God. Uriah died; Jeremiah lived, to complete his God-ordained ministry. Compare the various fates of the heroes of faith in Heb. 11:32–38.

26:22 Elnathan the son of Achbor. Contrast his action on Jeremiah's behalf in 36:12, 25—an evidence of shifting roles, which must have made Jeremiah's safety seem precarious.

26:23 burial place of the common people. The cemetery was located in the Kidron Valley, east of Jerusalem (2 Kin. 23:6).

26:24 Ahikam the son of Shaphan was with Jeremiah. An official under Josiah (2 Kin. 22:12, 14), his support may have been decisive in Jeremiah's deliverance.

The Yoke of Nebuchadnezzar

27 In the beginning of the reign of
Zedekiah[1] the son of Josiah, king of
Judah, this word came to Jeremiah from
the LORD. 2 Thus the LORD said to me:
[c]"Make yourself straps and [d]yoke-bars, and
put them on your neck. 3 Send word[2] to the
king of [e]Edom, the king of [e]Moab, the king
of the sons of [e]Ammon, the king of [e]Tyre,
and the king of Sidon by the hand of the
envoys who have come to Jerusalem to
Zedekiah king of Judah. 4 Give them this
charge for their masters: 'Thus says the
LORD of hosts, the God of Israel: This is
what you shall say to your masters: 5 "It is I
who [f]by my great power and my outstretched arm [g]have made the earth, with
the men and animals that are on the earth,
[h]and I give it to whomever it seems right to
me. 6 [i]Now I have given all these lands into
the hand of Nebuchadnezzar, the king of
Babylon, [j]my servant, [k]and I have given
him also the beasts of the field to serve
him. 7 [l]All the nations shall serve him and
[m]his son and [n]his grandson, [o]until the time
of his own land comes. [p]Then many
nations and great kings shall make him
their slave.
8 "'"But if any nation or kingdom will
not serve this Nebuchadnezzar king of
Babylon, [q]and put its neck under the yoke
of the king of Babylon, I will punish that
nation [r]with the sword, with famine, and
with pestilence, declares the LORD, until I
have consumed it by his hand. 9 So [s]do not
listen to your [t]prophets, your diviners,
your dreamers, your [u]fortune-tellers, or
your sorcerers, who are saying to you, 'You
shall not serve the king of Babylon.' 10 [v]For
it is a lie that they are prophesying to you,
with the result that you will be removed far
from your land, and I will drive you out,
and you will perish. 11 [w]But any nation that
will bring its neck under the yoke of the
king of Babylon and serve him, I will leave
on its own land, to work it and dwell there,
declares the LORD."'"
12 To [x]Zedekiah king of Judah I spoke in
like manner: [w]"Bring your necks under the
yoke of the king of Babylon, and [y]serve him
and his people and live. 13 [z]Why will you
and your people die [a]by the sword, by
famine, and by pestilence, [b]as the LORD has
spoken concerning any nation that will not
serve the king of Babylon? 14 [c]Do not listen
to the words of the prophets who are saying to you, 'You shall not serve the king of
Babylon,' [v]for it is a lie that they are prophesying to you. 15 I have not sent them,
declares the LORD, but [v]they are prophesying falsely in my name, with the result that
I will drive you out and you will perish, you
and the prophets who are prophesying to
you."
16 Then I spoke to the priests and to all
this people, saying, "Thus says the LORD:
[v]Do not listen to the words of your
prophets who are prophesying to you, saying, [d]'Behold, the vessels of the LORD's
house will now shortly be brought back
from Babylon,' [c]for it is a lie that they are
prophesying to you. 17 [c]Do not listen to
them; [w]serve the king of Babylon and live.
Why should this city [e]become a desolation? 18 If they are prophets, and if the word
of the LORD is with them, then [f]let them
intercede with the LORD of hosts, [g]that the
vessels that are left in the house of the
LORD, in the house of the king of Judah,
and in Jerusalem may not go to Babylon.
19 [h]For thus says the LORD of hosts concerning the pillars, the sea, the stands, and
the rest of the vessels that are left in this
city, 20 which Nebuchadnezzar king of

Chapter 27
2 [c][1 Kin. 22:11; Ezek. 7:23] [d]ch. 28:10, 12, 13; See Lev. 26:13
3 [e]ch. 25:21, 22
5 [f]Ps. 115:15; Isai. 45:12 [g]See ch. 21:5 [h]Ps. 115:16; Dan. 4:17, 25, 32
6 [i][Ezek. 30:21, 25] [j]See ch. 25:9 [k]ch. 28:14; Dan. 2:38
7 [l][Dan. 2:37, 38] [m]ch. 52:31 [n]Dan. 5:1, 30 [o]See ch. 25:12 [p]See ch. 25:14
8 [q]ver. 11, 12; [ch. 30:8] [r]See ch. 14:12
9 [s][ch. 14:14] [t][ch. 29:8] [u][Deut. 18:10; Isai. 2:6]
10 [v]See ch. 5:31
11 [w][ver. 2, 8]
12 [x]ch. 28:1; [ch. 27:1] [w][See ver. 11 above] [y]ver. 17; [ch. 38:17]
13 [z]Ezek. 18:31 [a]See ch. 14:12 [b]ver. 8
14 [c][ch. 14:14] [v][See ver. 10 above]
15 [v][See ver. 10 above]
16 [v][See ver. 10 above] [d]ch. 28:3; 2 Kin. 24:13; 2 Chr. 36:7, 10, 18 [c][See ver. 14 above]
17 [c][See ver. 14 above] [w][See ver. 11 above] [e]See ch. 7:34
18 [f][Isai. 59:16] [g]Dan. 1:2
19 [h][2 Kin. 25:13]

[1] Or *Jehoiakim* [2] Hebrew *send them*

27:3 Edom . . . Sidon. See 25:21, 22; these nations too are under the Lord's judgment.

envoys who have come . . . to Zedekiah. Probably they had come to discuss rebellion against Nebuchadnezzar, in league with Egypt.

27:5 great power and my outstretched arm. See 21:5.

have made the earth . . . give it to whomever it seems right. With an argument from creation, the Lord claims rights over all nations. See Dan. 2:38; 4:25 (also Nebuchadnezzar).

27:9 prophets . . . sorcerers. All these serve merely to bolster the political system, in this case with an exhortation not to submit to Babylon. These false prophets and other classes are forbidden in Israel (14:14; Lev. 19:26; Deut. 18:10, 11).

27:11 I will leave on its own land. Judah and its neighbors could still avoid total exile by accepting God's judgment of submission to Babylon.

27:12 serve him . . . and live. Jeremiah pleads with Judah to accept dominion by Babylon and the exile of some of its leaders (Jehoiachin and those taken in 597 B.C., 2 Kin. 24:15, 16) as part of God's plan for her ultimate salvation (24:5).

27:16 Behold. This false message was proclaimed by Hananiah (28:1–3).

vessels of the LORD's house. These vessels were carried off, some in 605 B.C. (Dan. 1:1, 2), some in 597 B.C. (2 Kin. 24:13).

Babylon did not take away, [i]when he took
into exile from Jerusalem to Babylon
Jeconiah the son of Jehoiakim, king of
Judah, and all the nobles of Judah and
Jerusalem— 21 thus says the LORD of hosts,
the God of Israel, [h]concerning the vessels
that are left in the house of the LORD, in the
house of the king of Judah, and in
Jerusalem: 22 [j]They shall be carried to
Babylon [k]and remain there [l]until the day
when I visit them, declares the LORD.
[m]Then I will bring them back [j]and restore
them to this place."

Hananiah the False Prophet

28 In that same year, at the beginning
of the reign of [n]Zedekiah king of
Judah, in the fifth month of the fourth
year, Hananiah the son of [o]Azzur, the
prophet from [p]Gibeon, spoke to me in
the house of the LORD, in the presence of
the priests and all the people, saying,
2 "Thus says the LORD of hosts, the God of
Israel: [q]I have broken the yoke of the king
of Babylon. 3 [r]Within [s]two years I will bring
back to this place all the vessels of the
LORD's house, which Nebuchadnezzar
king of Babylon took away from this place
and carried to Babylon. 4 I will also bring
back to this place [t]Jeconiah the son of
Jehoiakim, king of Judah, and all the exiles
from Judah who went to Babylon, declares
the LORD, [q]for I will break the yoke of the
king of Babylon."

5 Then the prophet Jeremiah spoke to
Hananiah the prophet in the presence of
the priests and all the people who were
standing in the house of the LORD, 6 and
the prophet Jeremiah said, [u]"Amen! May
the LORD do so; may the LORD make the
words that you have prophesied come
true, and bring back to this place from
Babylon the vessels of the house of the
LORD, and all the exiles. 7 Yet hear now this
word that I speak in your hearing and in
the hearing of all the people. 8 [v]The
prophets who preceded you and me from
ancient times prophesied war, famine, and
pestilence against many countries and
great kingdoms. 9 [w]As for the prophet who
prophesies peace, when the word of that
prophet comes to pass, then it will be
known that the LORD has truly sent the
prophet."

10 Then the prophet Hananiah took the
[x]yoke-bars from the neck of Jeremiah the
prophet and broke them. 11 And Hananiah
spoke in the presence of all the people, saying, [y]"Thus says the LORD: [z]Even so will I
break the yoke of Nebuchadnezzar king of
Babylon from the neck of [a]all the nations
within two years." But Jeremiah the
prophet went his way.

12 Sometime after the prophet [b]Hana-
niah had broken the yoke-bars from off
the neck of Jeremiah the prophet, the
word of the LORD came to Jeremiah:
13 "Go, tell Hananiah, 'Thus says the
LORD: You have broken wooden bars, but
you have made in their place bars of iron.
14 For thus says the LORD of hosts, the God
of Israel: I have put upon the neck of all
these nations [c]an iron yoke to serve
Nebuchadnezzar king of Babylon, [d]and
they shall serve him, [e]for I have given to
him even the beasts of the field.' " 15 And
Jeremiah the prophet said to the prophet
Hananiah, "Listen, Hananiah, [f]the LORD
has not sent you, [g]and you have made this
people trust in a lie. 16 Therefore thus says
the LORD: 'Behold, I will remove you from
the face of the earth. This year you shall
die, [h]because you have uttered rebellion
against the LORD.' "

17 In that same year, in the seventh
month, the prophet Hananiah died.

20 [i]2 Kin. 24:14, 15; Matt. 1:11, 12; See ch. 24:1
21 [h][See ver. 19 above]
22 [j]ch. 52:17, 20, 21; 2 Kin. 25:13; 2 Chr. 36:18 [k]ch. 32:5 [l]ch. 29:10; 2 Chr. 36:22; Ezra 1:1 [m]Ezra 1:7, 8; 5:14; 7:19
Chapter 28
1 [n]ch. 27:12 [o]Ezek. 11:1 [p]Josh. 9:3; 21:17
2 [q][ch. 27:2, 11, 12]
3 [r]ch. 27:16 [s]ver. 11
4 [t][ch. 22:10, 12, 26] [q][See ver. 2 above]
6 [u]1 Kin. 1:36
8 [v][ch. 26:18]
9 [w]Deut. 18:22; See ch. 6:14
10 [x]ch. 27:2
11 [y][1 Kin. 22:11] [z]ver. 2, 3 [a]ch. 27:7
12 [b]ver. 1, 10
14 [c]Deut. 28:48 [d][ch. 25:11] [e]See ch. 27:6
15 [f]ch. 29:31; Deut. 18:20; [Ezek. 13:22, 23] [g]See ch. 5:31
16 [h]ch. 29:32; Deut. 13:5

27:22 They shall be carried . . . day when I visit them. The fate of exile for a fixed time (25:11; 27:7) is now applied to the temple vessels.

28:1 In that same year . . . the fourth year. Since Zedekiah's reign began in 597 B.C., the events recounted here and in ch. 27 (27:1 note) occurred in 593 B.C.

28:2 yoke. Hananiah directly challenges Jeremiah's message (27:16–22).

28:3 Within two years. Since just over four years had already passed (v. 1), Hananiah predicts they will be gone no more than seven years. Contrast Jeremiah's seventy years (25:11, 12).

28:6 Amen. Jeremiah's first response reflects his love for the land and people. But the message God had revealed to him gave him no confidence in this hope.

28:8 preceded you and me. Jeremiah includes Hananiah with himself among the prophets and reminds him that the Lord's message has been principally judgment.

28:13 wooden bars . . . bars of iron. The Lord's will could not be frustrated by Hananiah's symbolic act. Hananiah dramatizes Judah's resistance, that can only make the inevitable servitude harsher.

28:16 remove. The same Hebrew word as "sent" (v. 15), an ironic play on words since this "sending" is to his death.

rebellion. The rebellion was ostensibly against Babylon, but really against God (Deut. 13:5).

Jeremiah's Letter to the Exiles

29 These are the words of the letter that Jeremiah the prophet sent from Jerusalem to [i]the surviving elders of the exiles, and to [j]the priests, [j]the prophets, and [j]all the people, whom Nebuchadnezzar had taken into exile from Jerusalem to Babylon. **2** This was after [k]King Jeconiah and the queen mother, the eunuchs, the officials of Judah and Jerusalem, the craftsmen, and the metal workers had departed from Jerusalem. **3** The letter was sent by the hand of Elasah the son of [l]Shaphan and Gemariah the son of [m]Hilkiah, whom Zedekiah king of Judah sent to Babylon to Nebuchadnezzar king of Babylon. It said: **4** "Thus says the LORD of hosts, the God of Israel, to all the exiles whom I have sent into exile from Jerusalem to Babylon: **5** [n]Build houses and live in them; plant gardens and eat their produce. **6** Take wives and have sons and daughters; take wives for your sons, and give your daughters in marriage, that they may bear sons and daughters; multiply there, and do not decrease. **7** But seek the welfare of the city where I have sent you into exile, and [o]pray to the LORD on its behalf, for in its welfare you will find your welfare. **8** For thus says the LORD of hosts, the God of Israel: [p]Do not let your prophets and [q]your diviners who are among you deceive you, and do not listen to the dreams that they dream,[1] **9** for [r]it is a lie that they are prophesying to you in my name; [s]I did not send them, declares the LORD.

10 "For thus says the LORD: [t]When seventy years are completed for Babylon, [u]I will visit you, [v]and I will fulfill to you my promise [v]and bring you back to this place. **11** [w]For I know the plans I have for you, declares the LORD, plans for wholeness and not for evil, [x]to give you a future and a hope. **12** [y]Then you will call upon me and come and pray to me, [y]and I will hear you. **13** [z]You will seek me and find me. When you seek me [a]with all your heart, **14** I will be found by you, declares the LORD, [b]and I will restore your fortunes and [c]gather you from all the nations and all the places [d]where I have driven you, declares the LORD, and I will bring you back to the place from which I sent you into exile.

15 "Because you have said, 'The LORD has raised up prophets for us in Babylon,' **16** thus says the LORD concerning [e]the king who sits on the throne of David, and concerning all the people who dwell in this city, your kinsmen who did not go out with you into exile: **17** 'Thus says the LORD of hosts, behold, I am sending on them [f]sword, famine, and pestilence, and I will make them like [g]vile figs that are so rotten they cannot be eaten. **18** I will pursue them with [f]sword, famine, and pestilence, [d]and will make them a horror to all the kingdoms of the earth, [h]to be a curse, [i]a terror, a hissing, and a reproach among all the nations [i]where I have driven them, **19** because they did not pay attention to my words, declares the LORD, [j]that I persistently sent to you by my servants the prophets, but you would not listen, declares the LORD.' **20** Hear the word of the LORD, all you exiles [k]whom I sent away from Jerusalem to Babylon: **21** 'Thus says the LORD of hosts, the God of Israel, concerning Ahab the son of Kolaiah and Zedekiah the son of Maaseiah, [l]who are prophesying a lie to you in my name: Behold, I will deliver them into the hand of Nebuchadnezzar king of Babylon, and he shall strike them down before your eyes. **22** [m]Because of them [n]this curse shall be used by all the exiles from Judah in Babylon: "The LORD make you like Zedekiah and Ahab, [o]whom the king of Babylon roasted in the fire," **23** because they have done an outrageous thing in Israel,

Chapter 29
1 [i]Ezek. 8:1 [j][ch. 23:33]
2 [k]ch. 24:1; 2 Kin. 24:12, 14
3 [l]2 Chr. 34:8 [m]1 Chr. 6:13
5 [n]ver. 28
7 [o][Ezra 6:10; 1 Tim. 2:1, 2]
8 [p][ch. 5:31; 6:14] [q]ch. 27:9, 15
9 [r]See ch. 5:31 [s]ver. 31
10 [t]See ch. 25:12 [u]ch. 27:22 [v]ch. 33:14; [ch. 24:6]
11 [w][Isai. 55:8, 9] [x]ch. 31:17
12 [y]ch. 33:3; Dan. 9:3
13 [z]2 Chr. 15:2; Ps. 32:6; 78:34; Prov. 8:17; Isai. 55:6; Hos. 3:5; See Lev. 26:39-42; Deut. 30:1-3 [a]ch. 24:7; Deut. 4:29
14 [b]ch. 30:3 [c]See ch. 23:3 [d]See ch. 8:3
16 [e]See ch. 22:2
17 [f]See ch. 24:10 [g]ch. 24:8
18 [f][See ver. 17 above] [d][See ver. 14 above] [h]See ch. 15:4 [i]ch. 18:16; 42:18; See ch. 24:9
19 [j]See ch. 25:4
20 [k]ch. 24:5
21 [l]ver. 9; See ch. 14:14
22 [m]See Isai. 65:15 [n]See ch. 24:9 [o][Dan. 3:6]

[1] Hebrew *your dreams, which you cause to dream*

29:3 Elasah the son of Shaphan. Possibly he was from the same family that had defended Jeremiah (26:24).

29:5 Build houses and live in them. An act of commitment to their new lives, showing acceptance of the Lord's judgment (cf. Ezek. 8:1).

29:7 welfare. Peace (6:14 and note) is the chief covenantal blessing. The peace lightly promised by the false prophets (8:11) gives way to a true peace (see also John 14:27).

pray. The Lord's blessing can come on any nation through the prayer and action of His people; compare Abraham (Gen. 20:17), Joseph (Gen. 37–50), and Daniel (Dan. 1–6).

29:14 This verse echoes Deut. 30:3–5 (similar in turn to Deut. 4:29, 30).

bring you back. The phrase implies a restoration of the relationship between the Lord and His people. See 30:3, 18; 31:23; 32:44; 33:7, 11, 26; 48:47; 49:6, 39.

29:16 the king. That is, Zedekiah. That Zedekiah still ruled in Jerusalem, albeit as a Babylonian vassal, may have been a focus of false hope for the exiles.

29:22 in the fire. A method of execution particularly associated in the Old Testament with the rule of Nebuchadnezzar (Dan. 3:6).

[p]they have committed adultery with their
neighbors' wives, and [p]they have spoken in
my name lying words that I did not command them. [q]I am the one who knows,
[q]and I am witness, declares the LORD.'"

Shemaiah's False Prophecy

24 To [r]Shemaiah of Nehelam you shall
say: 25 "Thus says the LORD of hosts, the
God of Israel: You have sent letters in your
name to all the people who are in
Jerusalem, and to [s]Zephaniah the son of
[t]Maaseiah the priest, and to all the priests,
saying, 26 'The LORD has made you priest
instead of Jehoiada the priest, to have
[u]charge in the house of the LORD [v]over
every madman who prophesies, to put him
in [w]the stocks and neck irons. 27 Now why
have you not rebuked Jeremiah [x]of
Anathoth who is prophesying to you? 28 For
he has sent to us in Babylon, saying, "Your
exile will be long; [y]build houses and live in
them, and plant gardens and eat their produce."'"

29 [s]Zephaniah the priest read this letter in
the hearing of Jeremiah the prophet.
30 [z]Then the word of the LORD came to
Jeremiah: 31 "Send to all the exiles, saying,
'Thus says the LORD concerning [a]Shemaiah
of Nehelam: Because [a]Shemaiah had
prophesied to you [b]when I did not send
him, and has made you trust in a lie,
32 therefore thus says the LORD: Behold, I
will punish [a]Shemaiah of Nehelam and his
descendants. He shall not have anyone living among this people, [c]and he shall not
see the good that I will do to my people,
declares the LORD, [d]for he has spoken
rebellion against the LORD.'"

Restoration for Israel and Judah

30 The word that came to Jeremiah
from the LORD: 2 "Thus says the
LORD, the God of Israel: [e]Write in a book
all the words that I have spoken to you.
3 [f]For behold, days are coming, declares the
LORD, [g]when I will restore [h]the fortunes of
my people, [i]Israel and Judah, says the
LORD, [j]and I will bring them back to the
land that I gave to their fathers, and they
shall take possession of it."

4 These are the words that the LORD
spoke concerning [i]Israel and Judah:

5 "Thus says the LORD:
We have heard a cry of panic,
of terror, and no peace.
6 Ask now, and see,
can a man bear a child?
[k]Why then do I see every man
with his hands on his stomach
[k]like a woman in labor?
[l]Why has every face turned pale?
7 Alas! [m]That day is so great
[n]there is none like it;
it is a time of distress for Jacob;
yet he shall be saved out of it.

8 "And it shall come to pass in that day,
declares the LORD of hosts, that I will
[o]break his [p]yoke from off your neck, and I
will [o]burst your bonds, [q]and foreigners
shall no more make a servant of him. [1] 9 But
they shall serve the LORD their God and
[r]David their king, whom I will raise up for
them.

10 [s]"Then fear not, [t]O Jacob my servant,
declares the LORD,
nor be dismayed, O Israel;
for behold, [s]I will save you from far
away,
[u]and your offspring from the land of
their captivity.
[s]Jacob shall return and have quiet and
ease,
and none shall make him afraid.
11 [v]For I am with you to save you,
declares the LORD;
[v]I will make a full end of all the nations
among whom I scattered you,
but of you I will not make a full
end.

1 Or *serve him*

23 [p]ch. 23:14 [q]Mal. 3:5
24 [r]ver. 31, 32
25 [s]ch. 21:1; 2 Kin. 25:18 [t]ch. 35:4
26 [u][ch. 20:1] [v][2 Kin. 9:11; Acts 26:24] [w]ch. 20:2
27 [x]ch. 1:1; 32:7
28 [y]ver. 5
29 [s][See ver. 25 above]
30 [z]ver. 1, 20
31 [a]ver. 24 [b]ver. 9; See ch. 5:31
32 [a][See ver. 31 above] [c]See ch. 17:6 [d]ch. 28:16
Chapter 30
2 [e]ch. 36:2; Hab. 2:2
3 [f]Hab. 2:3 [g]ver. 18; ch. 29:14; 31:23; 32:44; 33:7, 11, 26; Job 42:10; Lam. 2:14 [h]Ezra 2:1
[i]Isai. 11:12, 13; Hos. 1:11 [j]ch. 12:15; Ezek. 20:42; See ch. 16:15; 23:3
4 [i][See ver. 3 above]
6 [k]See Isai. 13:8 [l]Nah. 2:10; [Joel 2:6]
7 [m]Joel 2:11; Zeph. 1:14 [n]Dan. 12:1
8 [o]ch. 2:20; Nah. 1:13 [p]See ch. 27:2 [q]Ezek. 34:27
9 [r]Isai. 55:3, 4; Ezek. 34:23; 37:24; Hos. 3:5; [Luke 1:69, 70; Acts 13:22, 23]; See ch. 23:5
10 [s]ch. 42:11; 46:27, 28; See Isai. 43:5 [t]Isai. 41:8 [u]See ch. 3:18
11 [v]ch. 46:28

29:28 will be long. Jeremiah prophesied that the Exile would last seventy years (v. 10; 25:11, 12).

build houses . . . plant gardens. Shemaiah cites Jeremiah's letter (v. 5).

29:31, 32 The threat to Shemaiah parallels that made against Hananiah (28:15, 16).

30:1–33:26 These chapters contain promises of restoration and of the new covenant (31:31–34). The certainty of restoration is portrayed in Jeremiah's purchase of a field (ch. 32).

30:6 can a man . . . woman in labor. The anguish of childbirth is a picture of the suffering under the Babylonian armies (4:19, 31).

30:7 That day. The day of the Lord; see Amos 5:18; 8:9. Amos's generation expected it as a day of deliverance, but had to learn that it would bring judgment.

30:10 fear not, O Jacob my servant. See Is. 41:8, 10; 43:1; 44:1, 2.

none shall make him afraid. Contrast v. 5. This promise is a fulfillment of covenant blessing (Lev. 26:6).

[v] I will [w] discipline you in just measure,
and I will by no means leave you
unpunished.

12 "For thus says the LORD:
[x] Your hurt is incurable,
[y] and your wound is grievous.
13 There is none to uphold your cause,
no medicine for your wound,
[z] no healing for you.
14 [a] All your lovers have forgotten you;
they care nothing for you;
for I have dealt you the blow of [b] an
enemy,
the punishment [c] of a merciless foe,
because your guilt is great,
[d] because your sins are flagrant.
15 [x] Why do you cry out over your hurt?
[x] Your pain is incurable.
Because your guilt is great,
[d] because your sins are flagrant,
I have done these things to you.
16 [e] Therefore all who devour you shall
be devoured,
and [f] all your foes, every one of
them, shall go into captivity;
[g] those who plunder you shall be
plundered,
[h] and all who prey on you I will
make a prey.
17 [i] For I will restore [j] health to you,
and [k] your wounds I will heal,
declares the LORD,
because [l] they have called you an
outcast:
[l] 'It is Zion, for whom no one cares!'

18 "Thus says the LORD:
Behold, [m] I will restore the fortunes of
the tents of Jacob
and have compassion on his
dwellings;
the city shall be rebuilt on [n] its mound,
and the palace shall stand where it
used to be.
19 [o] Out of them shall come songs of
thanksgiving,
and the voices of those who
celebrate.
[p] I will multiply them, and they shall
not be few;
I will make them honored, and
they shall not be small.
20 [q] Their children shall be as they were
of old,
and their congregation shall be
established before me,
and I will punish all who oppress
them.
21 [r] Their prince shall be one of
themselves;
[r] their ruler shall come out from
their midst;
[s] I will make him draw near, and he
shall approach me,
[t] for who would dare of himself to
approach me?
declares the LORD.
22 [u] And you shall be my people,
and I will be your God."

23 [v] Behold [w] the storm of the LORD!
Wrath has gone forth,
a whirling tempest;
it will burst upon the head of the
wicked.
24 [x] The fierce anger of the LORD will not
turn back
until he has executed and
accomplished
the intentions of his mind.
[y] In the latter days you will
understand this.

The LORD Will Turn Mourning to Joy

31 [z] "At that time, declares the LORD, [a] I will be the God of all the clans of Israel, and they shall be my people."

2 Thus says the LORD:
"The people who survived the
sword
found grace in the
wilderness;
[b] when Israel sought for rest,

11 [v] ch. 46:28 [w] See ch. 10:24
12 [x] See ch. 15:18 [y] ch. 10:19; 14:17
13 [z] ch. 46:11
14 [a] Lam. 1:2; [ch. 4:30] [b] Job 13:24; 19:11; Isai. 63:10; Lam. 2:4 [c] Job 30:21; [ch. 6:23] [d] ch. 5:6
15 [x] [See ver. 12 above] [d] [See ver. 14 above]
16 [e] [ver. 11; ch. 10:25; Isai. 41:11] [f] [Ex. 23:22] [g] Isai. 33:1 [h] ch. 2:14
17 [i] ch. 33:6 [j] ch. 8:22 [k] Ps. 6:2; Hos. 6:1 [l] [Mic. 4:6, 7; Zeph. 3:19]
18 [m] [Amos 9:11]; See ver. 3 [n] Deut. 13:16
19 [o] ch. 31:12, 13; 33:11; Isai. 35:10; 51:11
[p] Ezek. 36:10, 37; Zech. 10:8
20 [q] Isai. 1:26
21 [r] [Gen. 49:10; Deut. 18:18] [s] Num. 16:5 [t] ch. 49:19; [Heb. 5:4]
22 [u] ch. 24:7; 31:1; 32:38; See ch. 31:33; Lev. 26:12
23 [v] ch. 23:19, 20 [w] ch. 25:32
24 [x] See ch. 12:13 [y] Hos. 3:5
Chapter 31
1 [z] ch. 30:24 [a] [2 Cor. 6:18]; See ch. 30:22
2 [b] [ch. 30:10; Ps. 95:11; Isai. 63:14]

30:20 as they were of old. This is probably an allusion to the time of David (v. 9).

congregation. A technical term denoting the political or religious assembly of the covenant people.

30:21 Their prince . . . ruler . . . from their midst. Whereas Judah is being ruled by a foreign power during its exile, Jeremiah looks forward to the restoration of its political independence and special relationship with the Lord (v. 22).

31:2 people who survived the sword. The remnant through whom God's purposes will continue (v. 7; 6:9 note; 23:3 note). Contrast 15:2.

wilderness. Judah's exile in Babylon and subsequent restoration are sometimes compared with Israel's wanderings in the wilderness prior to entering the Promised Land (see Is. 40:3, 4; 43:19, 20). Like the first exodus, this restoration will be a demonstration of the Lord's power to save.

3 the LORD appeared to him[1] from
far away.
[c]I have loved you with an everlasting
love;
therefore [d]I have continued [e]my
faithfulness to you.
4 [f]Again I will build you, and you shall
be built,
O virgin Israel!
[g]Again you shall adorn yourself with
tambourines
and shall go forth in [h]the dance of
the merrymakers.
5 [i]Again you shall plant vineyards
on the mountains of Samaria;
the planters shall plant
and shall enjoy the fruit.
6 For there shall be a day when
watchmen will call
in [j]the hill country of Ephraim:
[k]'Arise, and let us go up to Zion,
to the LORD our God.'"
7 For thus says the LORD:
[l]"Sing aloud with gladness for Jacob,
and raise shouts for [m]the chief of
the nations;
proclaim, give praise, and say,
[n]'O LORD, save your people,
the remnant of Israel.'
8 Behold, I will bring them [o]from the
north country
and [p]gather them from [q]the
farthest parts of the earth,
among them [r]the blind and the lame,
the pregnant woman and she who
is in labor, together;
a great company, they shall return
here.
9 [s]With weeping they shall come,
[t]and with pleas for mercy I will lead
them back,
I will make them [u]walk by brooks of
water,
[v]in a straight path in which they
shall not stumble,
for [w]I am a father to Israel,
and Ephraim is [x]my firstborn.
10 "Hear the word of the LORD,
O nations,
and declare it in the coastlands far
away;
say, 'He who scattered Israel will
[p]gather him,
and will keep him [y]as a shepherd
keeps his flock.'
11 [z]For the LORD has ransomed Jacob
and has redeemed him from
[a]hands too strong for him.
12 They shall come and sing aloud on
the height of Zion,
[b]and they shall be radiant [c]over the
goodness of the LORD,
[d]over the grain, the wine, and the oil,
and over the young of the flock
and the herd;
[e]their life shall be like a watered
garden,
[f]and they shall languish no more.
13 [g]Then shall the young women rejoice
in the dance,
and the young men and the old
shall be merry.
[h]I will turn their mourning into joy;
I will comfort them, and give them
gladness for sorrow.

3 [c]Deut. 7:8; 10:15; Mal. 1:2; Rom. 11:28 [d]Ps. 36:10 [e]Hos. 11:4
4 [f]ver. 28; ch. 33:7 [g]Isai. 61:10 [h]ver. 13; Ex. 15:20; Judg. 11:34; 21:21; See 2 Sam. 6:14
5 [i]Isai. 65:21; Amos 9:14
6 [j]See Josh. 24:33 [k]Isai. 2:3; 27:13
7 [l]Isai. 12:6; 65:18 [m]Amos 6:1 [n]Ps. 118:25
8 [o]See ch. 3:18 [p]See ch. 23:3 [q]See ch. 6:22 [r]Isai. 35:5, 6
9 [s]ch. 50:4; [Ezra 3:13; 10:1] [t]ch. 3:21; Zech. 12:10 [u]Isai. 35:6, 7; 49:10; [Ps. 23:2] [v]Isai. 35:8; 43:19; 49:11 [w]Rom. 8:15 [x][Ex. 4:22; Ps. 89:27]
10 [p][See ver. 8 above] [y]Isai. 40:11
11 [z]Isai. 43:1; 44:23; 48:20 [a][Isai. 49:24, 25]
12 [b]Isai. 2:2; Mic. 4:1 [c]Hos. 3:5 [d][Deut. 12:17] [e]Isai. 58:11 [f]Isai. 35:10
13 [g]See ver. 4 [h][John

[1] Septuagint; Hebrew *me*

31:3 from far away. This phrase probably carries forward the allusion to Sinai from the preceding verse (Ex. 19–24).

loved . . . everlasting love. The Lord's love for Israel was the ground of His election of them (Deut. 7:6, 7). The everlasting character of the covenant is affirmed in Gen. 17:7.

faithfulness. See note 9:24; contrast 16:5. This verse provides another sign of the reestablishment of the broken covenant.

31:4 virgin Israel. Contrast 18:13–15, where Israel's "virginity" has been squandered. See also 2:20, 22. In the new covenant the stain of defilement is finally cleansed.

dance. Such dances are acts of religious celebration (Judg. 21:19, 20).

31:5 plant vineyards . . . enjoy the fruit. This promise signifies the covenant blessing of fertility (Deut. 7:13; 28:4; contrast Deut. 28:30).

Samaria. The capital of the northern kingdom of Israel, or the northern kingdom as a whole. Its people were deported by Assyria in 722 B.C.

31:6 watchmen. Perhaps they were responsible for knowing the times of annual feasts, by observing the moon.

Ephraim . . . let us go up to Zion. Not as previously, to the apostate northern shrines of Jeroboam at Bethel and Dan (1 Kin. 12:26–33), but in renewed relationship with the Lord.

31:9 lead . . . brooks of water. See Ps. 23:2; Is. 48:21; 49:10.

straight path. See Is. 40:4.

father . . . firstborn. See 3:4; 31:20; Ex. 4:22; Hos. 11:1–4.

31:11 ransomed . . . redeemed. These verbs are closely related synonyms in Hebrew. The word translated "ransomed" means "to set free by paying a ransom," and it is used of the Lord's act of liberating Israel from Egypt (Deut. 7:8; 9:26). The second verb ("redeemed") is a technical term related to the responsibility of a "close relative" to purchase or "redeem" property which would otherwise be alienated from a family (32:8; Ruth 2:20 note). It is also used of God's deliverance of Israel from Egypt (Ex. 6:6, 7). The way that God has redeemed us to Himself through the ransom of Christ (cf. 1 Tim. 2:5, 6) is explained in the New Testament (see "The Atonement" at Rom. 3:25).

14 [i] I will feast the soul of the priests
with abundance,
and my people shall be satisfied
with my goodness,
declares the LORD."

15 Thus says the LORD:
[j] "A voice is heard in [k] Ramah,
lamentation and bitter weeping.
[l] Rachel is weeping for her children;
she refuses to be comforted for her
children,
[m] because they are no more."

16 Thus says the LORD:
"Keep your voice from weeping,
and your eyes from tears,
for there is a reward for your work,
declares the LORD,
and [n] they shall come back from
the land of the enemy.
17 [o] There is hope for your future,
declares the LORD,
and your children shall come back
to their own country.
18 I have heard [p] Ephraim grieving,
'You have disciplined me, and I was
disciplined,
like an untrained calf;
[q] bring me back that I may be restored,
for you are the LORD my God.
19 For after [r] I had turned away, I
relented,
and after I was instructed, [s] I
slapped my thigh;
[t] I was ashamed, and I was
confounded,
because I bore the disgrace of my
youth.'
20 [p] Is Ephraim my dear son?
[u] Is he my darling child?
For as often as I speak against him,
I do remember him still.
[v] Therefore my heart[1] yearns for him;
I will surely have mercy on him,
declares the LORD.

21 [w] "Set up road markers for yourself;
make yourself guideposts;
[x] consider well the highway,
[w] the road by which you went.
Return, O virgin Israel,
return to these your cities.
22 [y] How long will you waver,
[z] O faithless daughter?
For the LORD has created a new thing
on the earth:
a woman encircles a man."

23 Thus says the LORD of hosts, the God
of Israel: "Once more they shall use these
words in the land of Judah and in its cities,
[a] when I restore their fortunes:

[b] "'The LORD bless you, [c] O habitation of
righteousness,
[d] O holy hill!'

24 [e] And Judah and all its cities shall dwell
there together, and [e] the farmers and those
who wander with their flocks. 25 For I will
[f] satisfy the weary soul, and every languishing soul I will replenish."
26 At this I awoke and looked, and my
sleep was pleasant to me.
27 [g] "Behold, the days are coming, declares the LORD, when [h] I will sow the house
of Israel and the house of Judah with [i] the
seed of man and the seed of beast. 28 And it
shall come to pass that [j] as I have watched
over them [k] to pluck up and break down, to
overthrow, destroy, and bring harm, [k] so I
will watch over them [l] to build and to plant,
declares the LORD. 29 In those days they
shall no longer say:

[m] "'The fathers have eaten sour grapes,
and the children's teeth are set on
edge.'

30 [n] But everyone shall die for his own sin.
Each man who eats sour grapes, his teeth
shall be set on edge.

[1] Hebrew *bowels*

16:20]
14 [i] [ver. 25]
15 [j] Cited Matt. 2:18 [k] Josh. 18:25 [l] [Gen. 35:19, 20; 48:7; 1 Sam. 10:2] [m] ch. 10:20
16 [n] Ezra 1:5; Hos. 1:11
17 [o] ch. 29:11
18 [p] [ver. 9] [q] Ps. 80:3; Lam. 5:21
19 [r] Deut. 30:2 [s] Ezek. 21:12 [t] [ch. 3:25]
20 [p] [See ver. 18 above] [u] [Prov. 8:30] [v] S. of S. 5:4; Isai. 16:11
21 [w] [Isai. 57:14; 62:10] [x] ch. 50:4, 5
22 [y] ch. 2:18, 23, 36 [z] ch. 49:4
23 [a] See ch. 30:3 [b] Ps. 122:6, 7 [c] ch. 50:7; Isai. 1:26 [d] Zech. 8:3
24 [e] ch. 33:13
25 [f] Ps. 36:8; [ver. 14]
27 [g] ch. 9:25 [h] Ezek. 36:11; Hos. 2:23; Zech. 10:9 [i] [Ps. 22:30; Isai. 53:10]
28 [j] ch. 44:27; [ch. 32:42] [k] [ver. 40]; See ch. 1:10 [l] See ch. 24:6
29 [m] Ezek. 18:2, 3; [Lam. 5:7]
30 [n] Ezek. 18:4

31:15 A voice . . . in Ramah . . . Rachel is weeping. Ramah was in the region assigned to the tribe of Benjamin. Rachel weeps over the destruction of the north in 722 B.C. The words are quoted in Matt. 2:18 concerning Herod's slaughter of the innocents.

31:21 Set up road markers. Israel must remind itself to return not only to its land, but more importantly to God.

31:22 new thing. See Is. 42:9.

a woman . . . a man. The saying is obscure, but possibly the picture is of a mother protecting her son, that is, of security.

31:27 sow . . . seed. Both words are from the same Hebrew root. This makes an allusion to the promise of Gen. 15:18, where the Hebrew for "seed" is translated "offspring."

31:29 The fathers . . . set on edge. This proverb was used by the exiles to blame previous generations for the disaster of the Exile (Ezek. 18:2), possibly based on a misunderstanding of Ex. 20:5; Num. 14:18.

31:30 everyone shall die for his own sin. The principle that each person is judged individually is elaborated at length in Ezek. 18:4–32 (cf. Deut. 24:16). The point is that this generation fully deserves the punishment, even though the nation's guilt has been continuous (7:13; 11:7, 8).

The New Covenant

31 [o]"Behold, the days are coming, declares the LORD, when I will make [p]a new
covenant with the house of Israel and the
house of Judah, 32 not like the covenant
that I made with their fathers on the day
when [q]I took them by the hand to bring
them out of the land of Egypt, my covenant
that they broke, [r]though I was their husband, declares the LORD. 33 [s]But this is the
covenant that I will make with the house of
Israel after those days, declares the LORD: [s]I
will put my law within them, and I will
write it [t]on their hearts. [u]And I will be their
God, and they shall be my people. 34 And
no longer shall each one teach his neighbor
and each his brother, saying, 'Know the
LORD,' [v]for they shall all know me, [w]from
the least of them to the greatest, declares
the LORD. For [x]I will forgive their iniquity,
and [y]I will remember their sin no more."

35 Thus says the LORD,
who [z]gives the sun for light
by day
and [a]the fixed order of the moon
and the stars for light by
night,
who stirs up the sea so that its
waves roar—
[b]the LORD of hosts is his name:

31 [o]ver. 31-34, cited Heb. 8:8-12 [p]Luke 22:20; 2 Cor. 3:6
32 [q][Deut. 1:31] [r]See ch. 3:14
33 [s]ch. 32:40; Ezek. 37:26; Cited Heb. 10:16 [t]Ps. 37:31; 2 Cor. 3:3 [u]Hos. 2:23; Zech. 8:8; 13:9; Rev. 21:7; See ch. 30:22
34 [v]Isai. 54:13 [w]See ch. 6:13 [x]ch. 33:8; 36:3; 50:20; Mic. 7:18; Acts 10:43; Rom. 11:27; Cited Heb. 10:17 [y]Isai. 43:25
35 [z]Gen. 1:16 [a]See ver. 36 [b]See ch. 10:16
36 [c][Ps. 148:6; Isai. 54:9, 10]; For ver. 36, 37, see ch. 33:20-26
37 [d]Rom. 11:1
38 [e]ver. 27, 31 [f]Neh. 3:1; 12:39; Zech. 14:10 [g]2 Kin. 14:13
39 [h]Ezek. 40:3; Zech. 1:16; 2:1, 2; [Rev. 11:1]

36 [c]"If this fixed order departs
from before me, declares
the LORD,
then shall the offspring of Israel
cease
from being a nation before me
forever."

37 Thus says the LORD:
"If the heavens above can be
measured,
and the foundations of the earth
below can be explored,
[d]then I will cast off all the offspring of
Israel
for all that they have done,
declares the LORD."

38 [e]"Behold, the days are coming, declares the LORD, when the city shall be
rebuilt for the LORD [f]from the tower of
Hananel to [g]the Corner Gate. 39 [h]And the
measuring line shall go out farther, straight
to the hill Gareb, and shall then turn to
Goah. 40 [i]The whole valley of the dead bodies and the ashes, and all the fields as far
as the [j]brook Kidron, to the corner of [k]the
Horse Gate toward the east, [l]shall be sacred to the LORD. [m]It shall not be uprooted
or overthrown anymore forever."

40 [i][ch. 7:31, 32] [j]See 2 Sam. 15:23 [k]2 Chr. 23:15 [l]Isai. 52:1; Joel 3:17 [m][ver. 28]

31:31–34 Picking up themes first expounded by Moses in Deut. 30:1–10, Jeremiah prophesies that God will make a new covenant with His people. As the making of the old covenant (Ex. 19–24) followed the redemption from Egypt (Ex. 12–15), so the making of the new covenant will follow the redemption from sins (v. 34).

31:31, 32 The new covenant will stand in contrast to the old covenant, in that the new cannot be broken as the old was (v. 32; Heb. 8:7, 8). The guarantee that it will not be broken is the grace mediated by Christ through His death and resurrection (Heb. 9:12–15; 10:1–4, 10–18).

31:31 new covenant. See "God's Covenant of Grace" at Gen. 12:1. See also 1 Cor. 11:25; 2 Cor. 3:6; Heb. 9:15; 12:24.

with the house of Israel and the house of Judah. Using both names stresses the unity of God's covenant people.

31:32 not . . . my covenant that they broke. The new covenant will make good the deficiencies of the old, which lay in the people's inability to keep it (11:10; 2 Cor. 3:14; Heb. 8:7).

their husband. See 2:2; 3:14 note. Cf. Christ's relationship to the church (Eph. 5:25–27; Rev. 19:7; 21:2, 9).

31:33 Under the old covenant, the law of God was engraved on tablets of stone and placed in the Most Holy Place; under the new covenant God will write His law on the hearts of His people. The people then are like the temple in that the law of God is within them, but with the difference that they are a living temple, made of living stones (2 Cor. 3:3; 1 Pet. 2:5). See "God's Covenant of Grace" at Gen. 12:1.

after those days. The prophet speaks of a time after exile, without being specific. The New Testament shows that the time arrived with Christ, the Messiah.

I will. God will take the initiative to renew His people.

my law. The law of Moses required obedience from the heart (Deut. 6:6) but provided no enablement for that obedience (Deut. 5:29; 29:4). It did mediate forgiveness and hope, especially through the sacrifices. The law was a system of "types and shadows," that is, of significant elements foreshadowing Christ and inviting trust in God through Him.

I will be their God, and they . . . my people. This declaration is the summary of God's blessings promised in His covenant (Lev. 26:12; cf. 7:23).

31:34 Know the LORD. See "True Knowledge of God" at 9:24.

For I will forgive. The basis of the promises in vv. 32, 33 will be a new work of redemption that secures the forgiveness of sins (see Heb. 10:1–17).

remember their sin no more. The continuing cycle of sacrifices under the old covenant provided a constant reminder of sins (Heb. 10:3, 4, 11). The words "no more" underscore that the satisfaction made for sins in the redemption to come will be perfect, making any further sacrifices unnecessary.

31:35, 36 gives the sun . . . moon and the stars. The enduring order of the heavenly bodies is made the measure of God's commitment to His people (33:20, 21, 25, 26).

31:38 the city. Jerusalem.

Tower of Hananel . . . Corner Gate. Opposite ends of the city, signifying its entirety (see 2 Chr. 26:9; Zech. 14:10, 11). The restoration of Jerusalem will be the first sign of the fulfillment of the new covenant promise.

31:39 Gareb . . . Goah. Unidentified locations in Jerusalem.

31:40 valley. That is, the Valley of the Son of Hinnom (7:31 note).

Jeremiah Buys a Field During the Siege

32 The word that came to Jeremiah
from the LORD [n]in the tenth year of
Zedekiah king of Judah, [o]which was the
eighteenth year of Nebuchadnezzar. 2 At
that time the army of the king of Babylon
was besieging Jerusalem, and Jeremiah the
prophet [p]was shut up in [q]the court of the
guard that was in the palace of the king of
Judah. 3 For Zedekiah king of Judah had
imprisoned him, saying, "Why do you
prophesy and say, 'Thus says the LORD:
[r]Behold, I am giving this city into the hand
of the king of Babylon, and he shall capture
it; 4 [s]Zedekiah king of Judah shall not
escape out of the hand of the Chaldeans,
[r]but shall surely be given into the hand of
the king of Babylon, and shall speak with
him face to face and see him eye to eye.
5 And [t]he shall take Zedekiah to Babylon,
and there he shall remain until I visit him,
declares the LORD. [u]Though you fight
against the Chaldeans, you shall not succeed'?"
6 Jeremiah said, "The word of the LORD
came to me: 7 Behold, Hanamel the son of
Shallum your uncle will come to you and
say, [v]'Buy my field that is at [w]Anathoth,
[x]for the right of redemption by purchase is
yours.' 8 Then Hanamel my cousin came to
me in [q]the court of the guard, in accordance with the word of the LORD, and said
to me, 'Buy my field that is at [w]Anathoth in
the land of Benjamin, for the right of possession and redemption is yours; buy it for
yourself.' Then I knew that this was the
word of the LORD.
9 "And I bought the field at [w]Anathoth
from Hanamel my cousin, and [y]weighed
out the money to him, seventeen shekels
of silver. 10 [z]I signed the deed, [a]sealed it,
[b]got witnesses, and [y]weighed the money
on scales. 11 Then I took the sealed deed of
purchase, containing the terms and conditions and the open copy. 12 And I gave the
deed of purchase to [c]Baruch the son of
Neriah son of Mahseiah, in the presence
of Hanamel my cousin, in the presence of
[d]the witnesses who signed the deed of purchase, and in the presence of all the
Judeans who were sitting in [q]the court of
the guard. 13 I charged [c]Baruch in their
presence, saying, 14 'Thus says the LORD of
hosts, the God of Israel: Take these deeds,
both this sealed deed of purchase and this
open deed, and put them in an earthenware vessel, that they may last for a long
time. 15 For thus says the LORD of hosts,
the God of Israel: Houses and [e]fields and
vineyards shall again be bought in this
land.'

Jeremiah Prays for Understanding

16 "After I had given the deed of purchase
to [f]Baruch the son of Neriah, I prayed to
the LORD, saying: 17 'Ah, Lord GOD! It is
[g]you who has made the heavens and the
earth by your great power and by [h]your
outstretched arm! [i]Nothing is too hard for
you. 18 [j]You show steadfast love to thousands, [j]but you repay the guilt of fathers
[k]to their children after them, O great and
[l]mighty God, whose name is the [m]LORD of
hosts, 19 [n]great in counsel and [o]mighty in
deed, [p]whose eyes are open to all the ways
of the children of man, [q]rewarding each
one according to his ways and according
to the fruit of his deeds. 20 You have shown
[r]signs and wonders in the land of Egypt,
and to this day in Israel and among all
mankind, [s]and have made a name for
yourself, as at this day. 21 [t]You brought
your people Israel out of the land of Egypt
with signs and wonders, with a strong
hand and [u]outstretched arm, [t]and with
great terror. 22 And you gave them this land,
[v]which you swore to their fathers to give
them, [v]a land flowing with milk and honey.
23 And they entered and took possession of it.

Chapter 32
1 [n][ch. 37:5, 11; 39:1, 2; 52:4; 2 Kin. 25:2] [o][ch. 52:12; 2 Kin. 25:8]
2 [p]Ps. 88:8 [q]ver. 8, 12; ch. 33:1; 37:21; 38:6, 13; 39:14; [Neh. 3:25]
3 [r]ver. 25, 36, 43; ch. 21:10; 34:2; 37:17; 38:3
4 [s]ch. 34:3 [r][See ver. 3 above]
5 [t]ch. 39:7; 52:11 [u][ch. 21:4; 33:5]
7 [v]ver. 25 [w]ch. 1:1; 29:27; Josh. 21:18 [x]Lev. 25:25; [Ruth 4:4]
8 [q][See ver. 2 above] [w][See ver. 7 above]
9 [w][See ver. 7 above] [y]Gen. 23:16; Zech. 11:12; [Matt. 26:15]
10 [z]ver. 44 [a]Esth. 3:12 [b]ver. 25 [y][See ver. 9 above]
12 [c]ch. 36:4, 8, 10, 14, 26, 32; 43:3, 6; 45:1-3 [d][Isai. 8:2] [q][See ver. 2 above]
13 [c][See ver. 12 above]
15 [e]ver. 43
16 [f]See ver. 12
17 [g]Isai. 37:16 [h]See ch. 21:5 [i]ver. 27; See Gen. 18:14
18 [j]Ex. 20:6; 34:7; Deut. 5:9, 10 [k]Ps. 79:12; Isai. 65:6 [l]Isai. 9:6 [m]See ch. 10:16
19 [n]Isai. 28:29 [o][Ps. 66:3, 5] [p]See ch. 16:17 [q]See ch. 17:10
20 [r]Ps. 135:9 [s]2 Sam. 7:23; See Neh. 9:10
21 [t]Ex. 6:6; Deut. 4:34; 1 Chr. 17:21 [u]See ch. 21:5 **22** [v]Deut. 26:15; See Ex. 3:8

32:1 tenth year of Zedekiah. That is, 587 B.C. This chapter recounts the first of several exchanges between Jeremiah and Zedekiah in this period. See 21:3–7; 34:1–7; 37:3–8, 17–20; 38:14–28.

32:7 Anathoth. This village was Jeremiah's hometown; see 1:1.

right of redemption by purchase is yours. Hanamel may be selling because of debt, and asking Jeremiah to be the "close relative" who redeems (31:11 note). By normal standards, it is absurd to buy a field when the whole land is about to be lost.

32:9 seventeen shekels of silver. This amount is probably a normal price, though under the circumstances the field was worthless.

32:15 Houses and fields and vineyards . . . in this land. The significance of the purchase is that Judah will again possess its historic land and enjoy normal life in it. It therefore symbolizes that aspect of the new covenant promise (29:14 and note; 31:38–40).

32:20 signs and wonders. See Ex. 7:3.

and among all mankind. This confession stresses God's rule over the whole world.

32:21 This description is repeated from Deut. 26:8. See also v. 20; Ex. 15:14–16.

[w]But they did not obey your voice or walk in your law. They did nothing of all you commanded them to do. Therefore you have made all this disaster come upon them. **24** Behold, [x]the siege mounds have come up to the city to take it, and [y]because of sword and famine and pestilence [z]the city is given into the hands of the Chaldeans who are fighting against it. What you spoke has come to pass, and behold, you see it. **25** Yet you, O Lord GOD, have said to me, [a]“Buy the field for money [b]and get witnesses”—though [z]the city is given into the hands of the Chaldeans.’ ”

26 The word of the LORD came to Jeremiah: **27** “Behold, I am the LORD, [c]the God of all flesh. [d]Is anything too hard for me? **28** Therefore, thus says the LORD: [e]Behold, I am giving this city into the hands of the Chaldeans and into the hand of Nebuchadnezzar king of Babylon, and he shall capture it. **29** The Chaldeans who are fighting against this city [f]shall come and set this city on fire and burn it, [g]with the houses on whose roofs offerings have been made to Baal [g]and drink offerings have been poured out to other gods, [h]to provoke me to anger. **30** For the children of Israel and the children of Judah have done nothing but evil in my sight [i]from their youth. The children of Israel have done nothing but [h]provoke me to anger [j]by the work of their hands, declares the LORD. **31** This city has aroused my anger and wrath, from the day it was built to this day, [k]so that I will remove it from my sight **32** because of all the evil of the children of Israel and the children of Judah that they did to provoke me to anger—[l]their kings and their officials, their priests and their prophets, the men of Judah and the inhabitants of Jerusalem. **33** [m]They have turned to me their back and not their face. And though I have taught them [n]persistently, they have not listened [o]to receive instruction. **34** They set up [p]their abominations in the house that is called by my name, to defile it. **35** They built the high places of Baal [q]in the Valley of the Son of Hinnom, [r]to offer up their sons and daughters to Molech, [s]though I did not command them, nor did it enter into my mind, that they should do [p]this abomination, [t]to cause Judah to sin.

They Shall Be My People; I Will Be Their God

36 “Now therefore thus says the LORD, the God of Israel, concerning this city of which you say, [u]‘It is given into the hand of the king of Babylon by sword, by famine, and by pestilence’: **37** [v]Behold, I will gather them from all the countries [w]to which I drove them in [x]my anger and my wrath and in great indignation. I will bring them back to this place, [y]and I will make them dwell in safety. **38** [z]And they shall be my people, and I will be their God. **39** [a]I will give them one heart and one way, that they may fear me forever, [b]for their own good and the good of their children after them. **40** [c]I will make with them an everlasting covenant, that I will not turn away from doing good to them. [d]And I will put the fear of me in their hearts, that they may not turn from me. **41** [e]I will rejoice in doing them good, [f]and I will plant them in this land in faithfulness, with all my heart and all my soul.

42 “For thus says the LORD: [g]Just as I have brought all this great disaster upon this people, so I will bring upon them all the good that I promise them. **43** [h]Fields shall be bought in this land [i]of which you are saying, ‘It is a desolation, without man or beast; [j]it is given into the hand of the Chaldeans.’ **44** Fields shall be bought for money, and [k]deeds shall be signed and [k]sealed and [k]witnessed, [l]in the land of Benjamin, [l]in the places about Jerusalem, [l]and in the cities of Judah, [l]in the cities of the hill country, [l]in the cities of the Shephelah, and in the cities of the Negeb; for [m]I will restore their fortunes, declares the LORD.”

23 [w]Neh. 9:26, 27; See ch. 11:8; Dan. 9:10-14 **24** [x]ch. 33:4; See ch. 6:6 [y]See ver. 3 [z]ver. 36; See ch. 14:12 **25** [a]ver. 7 [b]ver. 10 [z][See ver. 24 above] **27** [c]Num. 16:22 [d]See Gen. 18:14 **28** [e]ver. 3 **29** [f]See ch. 21:10 [g]See ch. 19:13 [h]See ch. 7:18 **30** [i]ch. 3:25 [h][See ver. 29 above] [j]ch. 25:6, 7 **31** [k]2 Kin. 23:27; 24:3 **32** [l]ch. 2:26 **33** [m]ch. 2:27; [Ezek. 8:16]; See ch. 7:24 [n]See ch. 25:3 [o]See ch. 5:3 **34** [p]See ch. 7:30; 23:11 **35** [q]ch. 7:31; See Josh. 18:16 [r]Lev. 18:21 [s]ch. 7:31 [p][See ver. 34 above] [t][1 Kin. 16:19] **36** [u]See ver. 3 **37** [v]See ch. 23:3 [w]See ch. 8:3 [x]ch. 21:5; Deut. 29:28 [y]ch. 23:6; 33:16; Ezek. 34:25 **38** [z]See ch. 30:22; 31:33 **39** [a]Ezek. 11:19, 20 [b]Deut. 6:24 **40** [c]ch. 50:5; Ps. 89:34; Isai. 55:3; Ezek. 16:60 [d]See ch. 31:33 **41** [e][Deut. 28:63] [f]See ch. 24:6 **42** [g][ch. 31:28] **43** [h]ver. 15 [i]ch. 33:10 [j]See ver. 3 **44** [k]ver. 10 [l]See ch. 17:26 [m]See ch. 30:3

32:29 offerings have been made to Baal. Typical elements in Jeremiah’s accusation against Judah (1:16; 7:18; 19:13; cf. Deut. 31:29).

32:33 have not listened. See 2:30; 5:3; 7:24; 11:8.

32:35 Molech. “Molech” is probably the title of a god (rather than a proper name) who was worshiped by the Phoenicians, Moabites, Ammonites, and others in a ritual involving child sacrifice (Lev. 18:21; 20:2–5; 2 Kin. 23:10).

32:37 Jeremiah reaffirms Moses’ promise of restoration from exile (Deut. 30:3–5). The suddenness and improbability of this promise, following the tirade of vv. 26–35, is explained by the rhetorical question “Is anything too hard for me?” (v. 27; cf. v. 17).

32:40 everlasting covenant. See 31:31–36 and notes.

32:44 Benjamin . . . Negeb. These regions represent the territorial extent of Judah at the time of the Exile (17:26; 33:13).

The LORD Promises Peace

33 The word of the LORD came to
Jeremiah a second time, while he
was still [n]shut up in the court of the guard:
2 "Thus says [o]the LORD who made the
earth,[1] the LORD who formed it to establish
it—[p]the LORD is his name: 3 [q]Call to me and
I will answer you, [q]and will tell you great
and hidden things [r]that you have not
known. 4 For thus says the LORD, the God
of Israel, concerning the houses of this city
and the houses of the kings of Judah that
were torn down to make a defense against
[s]the siege mounds and against the sword:
5 They are coming in [t]to fight against the
Chaldeans and to fill them[2] with the dead
bodies of men whom I shall strike down
[u]in my anger and my wrath, [v]for I have hidden my face from this city because of all
their evil. 6 [w]Behold, I will bring to it health
and healing, and I will heal them and
reveal to them abundance of prosperity
and security. 7 [x]I will restore the fortunes of
Judah and the fortunes of Israel, [y]and
rebuild them as they were [z]at first. 8 [a]I will
cleanse them from all the guilt of their sin
against me, [b]and I will forgive all the guilt
of their sin and rebellion against me. 9 [c]And
this city[3] shall be to me a name of joy, a
praise and a glory before all the nations of
the earth who shall hear of all the good that
I do for them. They shall [d]fear and tremble
because of all the good and all the prosperity I provide for it.
10 "Thus says the LORD: In this place [e]of
which you say, 'It is a waste without man
or beast,' in the cities of Judah and the
streets of Jerusalem that are desolate, without man or inhabitant or beast, there shall
be heard again 11 [f]the voice of mirth and the
voice of gladness, the voice of the bridegroom and the voice of the bride, the voices of those who sing, as they bring [g]thank
offerings to the house of the LORD:

Chapter 33
1 [n]See ch. 32:2
2 [o][Isai. 37:26] [p][ch. 16:21; Ex. 6:3; Ps. 83:18; Amos 4:13]
3 [q]ch. 29:12; Ps. 91:15 [r]Isai. 48:6
4 [s]ch. 32:24
5 [t][ch. 32:5] [u]Ezek. 22:20 [v]Deut. 31:17, 18
6 [w]ch. 30:17
7 [x]See ch. 30:3 [y]See ch. 24:6 [z]Isai. 1:26
8 [a]Ezek. 36:25; [Ps. 51:2, 7; Heb. 9:13, 14] [b]See ch. 31:34
9 [c]See ch. 13:11 [d][Ps. 130:4; Isai. 60:5]
10 [e]ch. 32:43
11 [f]See ch. 7:34 [g]1 Chr. 16:34; Ps. 106:1; 107:1; Isai. 12:4 [h]ch. 30:19; Lev. 7:12; Ps. 107:22 [x][See ver. 7 above]
12 [i][Ezek. 36:11] [j][ch. 31:24; 50:19; Isai. 65:10; Ezek. 34:14, 15] [k]S. of S. 1:7
13 [l]See ch. 17:26 [m][Lev. 27:32] [n][John 10:3]
14 [o]For ver. 14-16, see ch. 23:5, 6 [p]ch. 29:10
15 [q]ch. 23:5; [Isai. 4:2; 11:1]
16 [r]ch. 23:6; 32:37 [s]ch. 23:6
17 [t]2 Sam. 7:16; 1 Kin. 2:4; Ps. 89:3, 4
18 [u][Isai. 66:21]
20 [v]For ver. 20-26, see ch. 31:36, 37 [w]ver. 25; [Isai. 54:9] [x]Gen. 8:22; Ps. 72:5

[h]"'Give thanks to the LORD of
hosts,
for the LORD is good,
for his steadfast love endures
forever!'

[x]For I will restore the fortunes of the land
as at first, says the LORD.
12 "Thus says the LORD of hosts: [i]In this
place that is waste, without man or beast,
and in all of its cities, there shall again be
[j]habitations of shepherds [k]resting their
flocks. 13 [l]In the cities of the hill country,
[l]in the cities of the Shephelah, [l]and in
the cities of the Negeb, in the land of
Benjamin, [l]the places about Jerusalem,
[l]and in the cities of Judah, [m]flocks shall
again pass under the hands [n]of the one
who counts them, says the LORD.

The LORD's Eternal Covenant with David

14 [o]"Behold, the days are coming, declares the LORD, when [p]I will fulfill the
promise I made to the house of Israel and
the house of Judah. 15 In those days and at
that time I will cause a righteous [q]Branch
to spring up for David, and he shall execute justice and righteousness in the land.
16 In those days Judah will be saved [r]and
Jerusalem will dwell securely. And this is
the name by which it will be called: [s]'The
LORD is our righteousness.'
17 "For thus says the LORD: [t]David shall
never lack a man to sit on the throne of the
house of Israel, 18 [u]and the Levitical priests
shall never lack a man in my presence to
offer burnt offerings, to burn grain offerings, and to make sacrifices forever."
19 The word of the LORD came to Jeremiah: 20 [v]"Thus says the LORD: [w]If you can
break my covenant with the day and my
covenant with the night, [x]so that day and
night will not come at their appointed time,

1 Septuagint; Hebrew *it* 2 That is, the torn-down houses 3 Hebrew *and it*

33:2 who made the earth. See note 10:12. God's creation is here the ground of His power both to judge and to save (32:17).

33:3 great and hidden things. A similar phrase in Is. 48:6 also speaks of salvation as new creation. See Dan. 2:47.

33:6 Behold. The change in the Lord's purpose is not motivated by any change in Judah, but by His decision. See 30:8, 16; 32:36, for similar transitions.

33:11 mirth . . . gladness . . . bridegroom . . . bride. Contrast 7:34; 16:9. These circumstances will be brought about by the new covenant.

33:17 This promise is not finally to restore the monarchy, but to inaugurate the messianic kingdom (23:5; 30:9; 2 Sam. 7:12–16; cf. 1 Kin. 2:4).

33:18 the Levitical priests. The priest's role was essential to the administration of the covenant (Ex. 28; 29; Deut. 10:8; 18:1). They also had a covenant of their own with the Lord (Num. 25:12, 13; 1 Sam. 2:30, 35). The promise of a perpetual priestly ministry is fulfilled by Christ Himself (Heb. 5:6–10; 7:11–25).

33:20, 21 covenant with the day and . . . night. The permanence of the institutions now envisaged is in stark contrast with 7:1–15. Such permanence is only comprehensible in the framework of the new covenant—though the need for faithfulness is never set aside (32:40 and note).

21[y]then also my covenant with David my
servant may be broken, so that he shall not
have a son to reign on his throne, and my
covenant with the Levitical priests my ministers. 22As [z]the host of heaven cannot be
numbered and [z]the sands of the sea cannot
be measured, so I will multiply the offspring of David my servant, and the
Levitical priests who minister to me."
23The word of the LORD came to
Jeremiah: 24"Have you not observed that
these people are saying, 'The LORD has
rejected the two clans that he chose'? Thus
they have despised my people so that they
are no longer a nation in their sight. 25Thus
says the LORD: [a]If I have not established my
covenant with day and night and the fixed
order of heaven and earth, 26then I will
reject the offspring of Jacob and David my
servant and will not choose one of his offspring to rule over the offspring of
Abraham, Isaac, and Jacob. [b]For I will
restore their fortunes and will have mercy
on them."

Zedekiah to Die in Babylon

34 The word that came to Jeremiah from
the LORD, when [c]Nebuchadnezzar
king of Babylon and all his army [d]and all the
kingdoms of the earth under his dominion
and all the peoples were fighting against
Jerusalem and all of its cities: 2"Thus says the
LORD, the God of Israel: Go and speak to
[e]Zedekiah king of Judah and say to him,
'Thus says the LORD: [f]Behold, I am giving
this city into the hand of the king of Babylon,
and he shall burn it with fire. 3[g]You shall not
escape from his hand but shall surely be captured and delivered into his hand. [g]You shall
see the king of Babylon eye to eye and speak
with him face to face. And you shall go to
Babylon.' 4Yet hear the word of the LORD, O
Zedekiah king of Judah! [h]Thus says the LORD
concerning you: [h]'You shall not die by the
sword. 5You shall die in peace. [i]And as
spices were burned for your fathers, the former kings who were before you, so people
shall [j]burn spices for you [k]and lament for
you, saying, "Alas, lord!"' For I have spoken
the word, declares the LORD."
6Then Jeremiah the prophet spoke all
these words to Zedekiah king of Judah, in
Jerusalem, 7when the army of the king of
Babylon was fighting against Jerusalem and
against all the cities of Judah that were left,
[l]Lachish and [m]Azekah, [n]for these were the
only [o]fortified cities of Judah that remained.
8The word that came to Jeremiah from
the LORD, after King Zedekiah [p]had made a
covenant with all the people in Jerusalem
[q]to make a proclamation of liberty to them,
9[r]that everyone should set free his Hebrew
slaves, male and female, [s]so that no one
should enslave a Jew, his brother. 10And
they obeyed, all the officials and all the people who had entered into the covenant that
everyone would set free his slave, male or
female, so that they would not be enslaved
again. They obeyed and set them free. 11But
afterward they turned around and took
back the male and female slaves [r]they had
set free, and brought them into subjection
as slaves. 12The word of the LORD came to
Jeremiah from the LORD: 13"Thus says the
LORD, the God of Israel: I myself made a
covenant with your fathers when [t]I brought
them out of the land of Egypt, out of the
house of bondage, saying, 14[u]'At the end of
seven years each of you must set free the fellow Hebrew who has been sold to you and
has served you six years; [r]you must set him

21 [y]Ps. 89:34
22 [z]Gen. 22:17
25 [a]Ps. 74:16, 17; 104:19
26 [b]ver. 7, 11; See ch. 30:3
Chapter 34
1 [c]ch. 39:1; 52:4; 2 Kin. 25:1 [d]ch. 1:15; [ch. 51:28]
2 [e]2 Kin. 25:2 [f]See ch. 21:10
3 [g]See ch. 32:4
4 [h][ch. 38:17, 20; 39:4, 7]
5 [i]1 Sam. 31:12; 2 Chr. 21:19 [j]2 Chr. 16:14 [k][ch. 22:18]
7 [l]Josh. 10:3 [m]Josh. 10:10; 15:35 [n]2 Kin. 18:13 [o]ch. 4:5
8 [p]ver. 15 [q]ver. 15, 17; Ex. 21:2; Lev. 25:10; [Isai. 61:1]
9 [r]See Lev. 25:39-46 [s][Neh. 5:8]
11 [r][See ver. 9 above]
13 [t]Ex. 20:2
14 [u]Ex. 21:2; Deut. 15:12 [r][See ver. 9 above]

33:22 cannot be numbered . . . sands of the sea. In these promises concerning the messianic kingdom, the promises to Abraham are also fulfilled (Gen. 22:17; contrast 15:8).

33:24 two clans. The reference to these "clans" is ambiguous. It could refer to the kingdoms of Israel and Judah (v. 14) or to the royal family of David and the priestly family of Levi (vv. 17, 18).

33:26 Abraham, Isaac, and Jacob. The new covenant is a fulfillment of the covenant with Abraham that embraced all peoples (Gen. 12:3). See note on v. 22.

34:1–36:32 These chapters narrate scenes of rejection of the word of the Lord that led to final judgment on Judah. King Zedekiah is condemned for going back on his promise to free slaves (ch. 34), and the people of Judah are reproved for failing to learn a lesson from the example of the faithful Rechabites (ch. 35). King Jehoiakim rejects Jeremiah's message and burns the prophet's scroll (ch. 36).

34:1 all the kingdoms . . . fighting against Jerusalem. It was required that vassal nations join in battle with their overlord.

34:4, 5 not die by the sword . . . die in peace. Zedekiah's precise fate was left obscure in 21:4–7; 32:3–5; but see 52:11. The point here is that he will not die in battle.

34:7 Lachish and Azekah. These were fortified cities of Judah (2 Chr. 11:5, 9). The verse gives a glimpse of the last days of Judah. Jerusalem knew the enemy was closing in as the outlying cities fell one by one. A pottery fragment dating from 588 B.C. carried this message to the commander at Lachish: "we are watching for the signals of Lachish . . . we cannot see Azekah."

34:8 proclamation of liberty to them. According to Ex. 21:2–11; Lev. 25:39–55; Deut. 15:12–18, slaves were to be released in the last year of a seven-year cycle. Zedekiah's "covenant" (or solemn undertaking) reflects his ambivalence between listening to Jeremiah and his own political advisers.

free from your service.' But [v]your fathers
did not listen to me or incline their ears to
me. 15 You recently repented and did what
was right in my eyes [p]by proclaiming liberty, each to his neighbor, and [w]you made a
covenant before me in the [x]house that is
called by my name, 16 but then you turned
around [y]and profaned my name when [y]each
of you took back his male and female
slaves, [z]whom you had set free according to
their desire, and you brought them into
subjection to be your slaves.
17 "Therefore, thus says the LORD: You
have not obeyed me [p]by proclaiming liberty, every one to his brother and to his
neighbor; [a]behold, I proclaim to you liberty
[b]to the sword, to pestilence, and to famine,
declares the LORD. [c]I will make you a horror
to all the kingdoms of the earth. 18 And the
men who transgressed my covenant and did
not keep the terms of [w]the covenant that
they made before me, I will make them
like[1] [d]the calf that they cut in two and
passed between its parts— 19 the officials of
Judah, the officials of Jerusalem, [e]the
eunuchs, the priests, and all the people of
the land who passed between the parts of
the calf. 20 And I will give them into the
hand of their enemies [f]and into the hand of
those who seek their lives. [g]Their dead bodies shall be food for the birds of the air and
the beasts of the earth. 21 And [h]Zedekiah
king of Judah and his officials I will give
into the hand of their enemies and into the
hand of those who seek their lives, into the
hand of the army of the king of Babylon
[i]which has withdrawn from you. 22 Behold,
[j]I will command, declares the LORD, and
will [k]bring them back to this city. [k]And they
will fight against it and take it and burn it
with fire. [l]I will make the cities of Judah a
desolation [m]without inhabitant."

The Obedience of the Rechabites

35 The word that came to Jeremiah
from the LORD in the days of [n]Jehoi-
akim the son of Josiah, king of Judah: 2 "Go
to the house of the [o]Rechabites and speak
with them and bring them to the house of
the LORD, into one of [p]the chambers; then
offer them wine to drink." 3 So I took
Jaazaniah the son of Jeremiah, son of
Habazziniah and his brothers and all his
sons and the whole house of the
Rechabites. 4 I brought them to the house
of the LORD into [p]the chamber of the sons
of Hanan the son of Igdaliah, [q]the man of
God, which was near [p]the chamber of the
officials, above [p]the chamber of [r]Maaseiah
the son of Shallum, [s]keeper of the threshold. 5 Then I set before the Rechabites
pitchers full of wine, and cups, and I said
to them, "Drink wine." 6 But they
answered, "We will drink no wine, for
[t]Jonadab the son of Rechab, our father,
commanded us, 'You shall not drink wine,
neither you nor your sons forever. 7 You
shall not build a house; you shall not sow
seed; you shall not plant or have a vineyard; but you shall live in tents all your
days, [u]that you may live many days in the
land where you sojourn.' 8 We have obeyed
the voice of Jonadab the son of Rechab, our
father, in all that he commanded us, to
drink no wine all our days, ourselves, our
wives, our sons, or our daughters, 9 and not
to build houses to dwell in. We have no
vineyard or field or seed, 10 but we have
lived in tents and have obeyed and done all
that Jonadab our father commanded us.
11 But [v]when Nebuchadnezzar king of
Babylon came up against the land, we said,
'Come, and let us go to Jerusalem for fear
of [w]the army of the Chaldeans and [w]the
army of the Syrians.' [x]So we are living in
Jerusalem."
12 Then the word of the LORD came to
Jeremiah: 13 "Thus says the LORD of hosts,
the God of Israel: Go and say to the people
of Judah and the inhabitants of Jerusalem,

[1] Hebrew lacks *them like*

14 [v]ch. 7:24, 26; 11:8; 17:23; 25:4; 35:15; 44:5
15 [p][See ver. 8 above] [w]ver. 8; [2 Kin. 23:3] [x]See ch. 7:10
16 [y]Lev. 18:21; 19:12 [z]ver. 11
17 [p][See ver. 8 above] [a][Matt. 7:2; Gal. 6:7; James 2:13] [b]See ch. 14:12 [c]See ch. 15:4
18 [w][See ver. 15 above] [d][Gen. 15:10]
19 [e]ch. 29:2
20 [f]See ch. 22:25 [g]See ch. 7:33
21 [h][ver. 2, 4, 8] [i]ch. 37:5, 11
22 [j]Isai. 10:6 [k]ch. 37:8; 38:3 [l]ch. 9:11 [m]See ch. 4:7
Chapter 35
1 [n]ch. 25:1
2 [o]1 Chr. 2:55 [p]1 Kin. 6:5, 6; 1 Chr. 9:26, 33
4 [p][See ver. 2 above] [q][Deut. 33:1] [r]ch. 21:1; 29:25; 37:3 [s]2 Kin. 12:9; 25:18
6 [t]2 Kin. 10:15, 23
7 [u][Ex. 20:12; Eph. 6:2, 3]
11 [v]ch. 46:2; 2 Kin. 24:1; [ver. 1] [w]2 Kin. 24:2 [x][ver. 7]

34:15, 16 repented . . . turned around. These two verbs effectively portray Judah's fickleness (3:6, 14 notes).

profaned my name. The blatant disregard for the law regarding the release of slaves is a repudiation of the Lord Himself (note the analogy between the "covenants" of vv. 8, 13).

34:18 the calf that they cut . . . between its parts. See Gen. 15:18 and note. This sort of action accompanied making a covenant. It illustrated the penalty that would fall on a person who broke the covenant.

35:2 house of the Rechabites. Most of what is known of this clan is in this chapter.

house of the LORD . . . chambers. These rooms were used for storage (1 Kin. 6:5; Neh. 13:4, 5).

35:3 Jeremiah. One of two persons other than the prophet himself named "Jeremiah," mentioned in the book (see 52:1).

35:4 man of God. Another name for a prophet (1 Kin. 12:22).

35:6, 7 The vow taken by Jonadab the son of Rechab commits his descendants to a nomadic life, with impermanent lodging and abstaining from wine. This life was a voluntary commitment not required by the Mosaic law (Deut. 6:10, 11; 7:13).

[y]Will you not receive instruction and listen to my words? declares the LORD. 14 The command that Jonadab the son of Rechab gave to his sons, to drink no wine, has been kept, and they drink none to this day, for they have obeyed their father's command. I have spoken to you [z]persistently, but you have not listened to me. 15 I have sent to you all my servants the prophets, sending them [z]persistently, saying, [a]'Turn now every one of you from his evil way, and amend your deeds, and [b]do not go after other gods to serve them, and then you shall dwell in the land that I gave to you and your fathers.' [c]But you did not incline your ear or listen to me. 16 The sons of Jonadab the son of Rechab have kept the command that their father gave them, but this people has not obeyed me. 17 Therefore, thus says the LORD, the God of hosts, the God of Israel: Behold, I am bringing upon Judah and all the inhabitants of Jerusalem all the disaster that I have pronounced against them, [d]because I have spoken to them and they have not listened, [d]I have called to them and they have not answered."

18 But to the house of the Rechabites Jeremiah said, "Thus says the LORD of hosts, the God of Israel: Because you have obeyed the command of Jonadab your father and kept all his precepts and done all that he commanded you, 19 therefore thus says the LORD of hosts, the God of Israel: Jonadab the son of Rechab shall never lack a man [e]to stand before me."

Jehoiakim Burns Jeremiah's Scroll

36 In the [f]fourth year of Jehoiakim the son of Josiah, king of Judah, this word came to Jeremiah from the LORD: 2 "Take [g]a scroll and [h]write on it all the words that I have spoken to you against Israel and [i]Judah [j]and all the nations, [k]from the day I spoke to you, from the days of Josiah until today. 3 [l]It may be that the house of Judah will hear all the disaster that I intend to do to them, [m]so that every one may turn from his evil way, and [n]that I may forgive their iniquity and their sin."

4 Then Jeremiah called [o]Baruch the son of Neriah, and [o]Baruch wrote on [g]a scroll at the dictation of Jeremiah all the words of the LORD that he had spoken to him. 5 And Jeremiah ordered [o]Baruch, saying, [p]"I am banned from going to the house of the LORD, 6 so you are to go, and [q]on a day of fasting in the hearing of all the people in the LORD's house you shall read the words of the LORD from the scroll that you have written at my dictation. You shall read them also in the hearing of all the men of Judah who come out of their cities. 7 [l]It may be that their plea for mercy will come before the LORD, [m]and that every one will turn from his evil way, for great is the anger and wrath that the LORD has pronounced against this people." 8 And Baruch the son of Neriah did all that Jeremiah the prophet ordered him about reading from the scroll the words of the LORD in the LORD's house.

9 [r]In the fifth year of Jehoiakim the son of Josiah, king of Judah, [s]in the ninth month, all the people in Jerusalem and all the people who came from the cities of Judah to Jerusalem [t]proclaimed a fast before the LORD. 10 Then, in the hearing of all the people, Baruch read the words of Jeremiah from the scroll, in the house of the LORD, in [u]the chamber of Gemariah the son of Shaphan the secretary, which was in the upper court, at the entry of the New Gate of the LORD's house.

11 When Micaiah the son of Gemariah, son of [v]Shaphan, heard all the words of the LORD from the scroll, 12 he went down to the king's house, into the secretary's chamber, and all the officials were sitting there: [w]Elishama the secretary, [x]Delaiah the son of Shemaiah, [x]Elnathan [y]the son of Achbor, [x]Gemariah the son of [z]Shaphan, Zedekiah the son of Hananiah, and all the officials. 13 And Micaiah told them all the words that

13 [y]See ch. 5:3
14 [z]See ch. 25:3
15 [z][See ver. 14 above] [a]2 Kin. 17:13; See ch. 18:11 [b]See ch. 7:6 [c]See ch. 34:14
17 [d][Isai. 50:2]
19 [e]See ch. 15:1
Chapter 36
1 [f]ch. 25:1; 45:1; [ver. 9]
2 [g]Ezra 6:2; Ps. 40:7; Ezek. 2:9; Zech. 5:1, 2 [h]ch. 30:2; [ch. 51:60] [i]ch. 25:2 [j]See ch. 25:15-26; ch. 46–51 [k]ch. 1:2; 25:3
3 [l]ch. 26:3; Ezek. 12:3; Zeph. 2:3; [Amos 5:15] [m][ch. 18:8] [n]See ch. 31:34
4 [o]See ch. 32:12
5 [o][See ver. 4 above] [p]ch. 32:2; 33:1; 39:15
6 [q][ver. 9]
7 [l][See ver. 3 above] [m][See ver. 3 above]
9 [r][ver. 1] [s]ver. 22 [t][2 Chr. 20:3]
10 [u][ch. 35:2]
11 [v]ch. 26:24; 40:5; 2 Chr. 34:8, 15, 18
12 [w]ch. 26:10 [x]ver. 20; ch. 41:1; 2 Kin. 25:25 [y]ver. 25 [z]ch. 26:22

35:19 shall never lack a man to stand before me. See 33:17, 18. Such a promise might be expected for a king, and even for priests, but not for the obscure Rechabites. It is used here to contrast ominously with what Jehoiakim and the Davidic dynasty can expect.

36:1 fourth year of Jehoiakim. That is, 605 B.C., the year of Nebuchadnezzar's first move against Jerusalem (25:1 note).

36:2 Take a scroll and write on it. The present account is an important guide to understanding how prophetic books were written. Jeremiah's oracles were spoken over a long period (25:3), and are here gathered into a collection (Is. 8:16 and note).

36:4 Baruch. This is the second mention of Jeremiah's scribe (32:12). His activity suggests that he had a role in compiling the Book of Jeremiah.

36:5 I am banned. This statement probably means he was banned from the temple area because of his unpopularity with the authorities (26:2–11).

36:9 In the fifth year . . . the ninth month. That is, December, 604 B.C.

he had heard, when Baruch read the scroll
in the hearing of the people. 14 Then all the
officials sent Jehudi the son of Nethaniah,
son of [a]Shelemiah, son of Cushi, to say to
Baruch, "Take in your hand the scroll that
you read in the hearing of the people, and
come." So Baruch the son of Neriah took
the scroll in his hand and came to them.
15 And they said to him, "Sit down and read
it." So Baruch read it to them. 16 When they
heard all the words, they turned one to
another in fear. And they said to Baruch,
[b]"We must report all these words to the
king." 17 Then they asked Baruch, "Tell us,
please, how did you write all these words?
Was it at his dictation?" 18 Baruch answered
them, "He dictated all these words to me,
[c]while I wrote them with ink on the scroll."
19 Then the officials said to Baruch, "Go
and hide, you and Jeremiah, and let no one
know where you are."
20 So they went into the court to the king,
having put the scroll in [d]the chamber of
Elishama the secretary, and they reported
all the words to the king. 21 Then the king
sent Jehudi to get the scroll, and he took it
from the chamber of Elishama the secretary. And Jehudi read it to the king and all
the officials who stood beside the king. 22 It
was [e]the ninth month, and the king was
sitting in [f]the winter house, and there was
a fire burning in the fire pot before him.
23 As Jehudi read three or four columns, the
king would cut them off with a knife and
throw them into the fire in the fire pot,
until the entire scroll was consumed in the
fire that was in the fire pot. 24 Yet [g]neither
the king nor any of his servants who heard
all these words was afraid, [h]nor did they
tear their garments. 25 Even when [i]Elnathan
and Delaiah and Gemariah [j]urged the king
not to burn the scroll, he would not listen
to them. 26 And the king commanded
Jerahmeel the [k]king's son and Seraiah the
son of Azriel and [l]Shelemiah the son of
Abdeel to seize [m]Baruch the secretary and
Jeremiah the prophet, but the LORD hid
them.
27 Now after the king had burned the
scroll with the words that Baruch wrote at
Jeremiah's dictation, the word of the LORD
came to Jeremiah: 28 "Take another scroll
and write on it all the former words that
were in the first scroll, which Jehoiakim the
king of Judah has burned. 29 And concerning Jehoiakim king of Judah you shall say,
'Thus says the LORD, You have burned this
scroll, saying, [n]"Why have you written in it
that the king of Babylon will certainly come
and destroy this land, and will cut off from
it man and beast?" 30 Therefore thus says
the LORD concerning Jehoiakim king of
Judah: [o]He shall have none [p]to sit on the
throne of David, [q]and his dead body shall
be cast out to the heat by day and the frost
by night. 31 [r]And I will punish him and his
offspring and his servants for their iniquity.
I will bring upon them and upon the
inhabitants of Jerusalem and upon the people of Judah all the disaster that I have pronounced against them, but they would not
hear.'"
32 Then Jeremiah took another scroll and
gave it to [s]Baruch the scribe, the son of
Neriah, who [t]wrote on it at the dictation of
Jeremiah all the words of the scroll that
Jehoiakim king of Judah had burned in the
fire. And many similar words were added
to them.

Jeremiah Warns Zedekiah

37 [u]Zedekiah the son of Josiah, [v]whom
Nebuchadnezzar king of Babylon
made king in the land of Judah, reigned
instead of [w]Coniah the son of Jehoiakim.
2 [x]But neither he nor his servants nor the
people of the land listened to the words of
the LORD that he spoke through Jeremiah
the prophet.
3 King Zedekiah sent [y]Jehucal the son of
[z]Shelemiah, and [a]Zephaniah the priest, the
son of [b]Maaseiah, to Jeremiah the prophet,
saying, "Please [c]pray for us to the LORD our

14 [a]ver. 26; ch. 37:3, 13; 38:1
16 [b]ver. 20
18 [c]ver. 32; [Rom. 16:22]
20 [d]ver. 12
22 [e]Amos 3:15 [f]ver. 9; [John 10:22]
24 [g][ver. 16] [h]See Josh. 7:6
25 [i]ver. 12 [j][Isai. 59:16]
26 [k][1 Kin. 22:26; Zeph. 1:8] [l]ver. 14 [m]See ch. 45:1-3
29 [n]See ch. 26:9
30 [o][ch. 22:30] [p][ch. 22:2, 4] [q][ch. 22:19]
31 [r][ch. 1:16]
32 [s]See ver. 4 [t]ver. 18
Chapter 37
1 [u]2 Kin. 24:17; 2 Chr. 36:10 [v]ch. 22:24 [w][Ezek. 17:13]
2 [x]See 2 Chr. 36:12-14
3 [y][ch. 38:1] [z]ver. 13; ch. 38:1 [a]See ch. 21:1 [b]See ch. 35:4 [c][ch. 21:2]

36:21 Jehudi. Baruch is no longer the reader, presumably being in hiding (v. 19). The absence of Jeremiah and Baruch focuses Jehoiakim's response on the words themselves.

36:23 the entire scroll was consumed in the fire. The contrast with Josiah could not be stronger (2 Kin. 22:11–13).

36:28 Take another scroll. God's word cannot be invalidated by the destruction of a scroll.

36:30 Jehoiakim . . . shall have none to sit on the throne of David. His son Jehoiachin's rule lasted only a few months (22:30 note; 2 Kin. 24:8).

37:1–39:18 These chapters recount Jeremiah's last warnings before the fall of Jerusalem and his imprisonment for his unpopular message. His repeated advice to surrender to the Babylonians is ignored, and he remains imprisoned until the fall of Jerusalem.

37:1 Zedekiah . . . reigned instead of Coniah. See 2 Kin. 24:17–18. The year was 597 B.C.

"God." 4 [d]Now Jeremiah was still going in and out among the people, [e]for he had not yet been put in prison. 5 [f]The army of Pharaoh had come out of Egypt. And when [g]the Chaldeans who were besieging Jerusalem heard news about them, [h]they withdrew from Jerusalem.

6 Then the word of the LORD came to Jeremiah the prophet: 7 "Thus says the LORD, God of Israel: Thus shall you say to the king of Judah who [i]sent you to me to inquire of me, 'Behold, [j]Pharaoh's army that came to help you is about to [k]return to Egypt, to its own land. 8 And [l]the Chaldeans shall come back and fight against this city. [l]They shall capture it and burn it with fire. 9 Thus says the LORD, Do not deceive yourselves, saying, "The Chaldeans will surely go away from us," for they will not go away. 10 [m]For even if you should defeat the whole army of Chaldeans who are fighting against you, and there remained of them only wounded men, every man in his tent, they would rise up and burn this city with fire.'"

Jeremiah Imprisoned

11 Now when [n]the Chaldean army had withdrawn from Jerusalem at the approach of Pharaoh's army, 12 Jeremiah set out from Jerusalem to go to [o]the land of Benjamin [p]to receive his portion there [q]among the people. 13 When he was at [r]the Benjamin Gate, a sentry there named Irijah the son of [s]Shelemiah, son of Hananiah, seized Jeremiah the prophet, saying, [t]"You are deserting to the Chaldeans." 14 And Jeremiah said, "It is a lie; I am not deserting to the Chaldeans." But Irijah would not listen to him, and seized Jeremiah and brought him to [u]the officials. 15 And the officials were enraged at Jeremiah, and they beat him [v]and imprisoned him in the house of Jonathan the secretary, for it had been made a prison.

16 [w]When Jeremiah had come to the dungeon cells and remained there many days, 17 King Zedekiah sent for him and received him. The king questioned him [x]secretly in his house and said, "Is there any word from the LORD?" Jeremiah said, "There is." Then he said, [y]"You shall be delivered into the hand of the king of Babylon." 18 Jeremiah also said to King Zedekiah, "What wrong have I done to you or your servants or this people, [v]that you have put me in prison? 19 [z]Where are your prophets who prophesied to you, saying, 'The king of Babylon will not come against you and against this land'? 20 Now hear, please, O my lord the king: [a]let my humble plea come before you and [b]do not send me back to the house of Jonathan the secretary, lest I die there." 21 So King Zedekiah gave orders, and they committed Jeremiah to [c]the court of the guard. And a loaf of bread was given him daily from the bakers' street, [d]until all the bread of the city was gone. So Jeremiah remained in [c]the court of the guard.

Jeremiah Cast into the Cistern

38 Now Shephatiah the son of Mattan, Gedaliah the son of Pashhur, [e]Jucal the son of Shelemiah, and [f]Pashhur the son of Malchiah heard the words that Jeremiah was saying to all the people, 2 "Thus says the LORD: [g]He who stays in this city shall die by the sword, by famine, and by pestilence, [g]but he who goes out to the Chaldeans shall live. He shall have his life as a prize of war, and live. 3 Thus says the LORD: [h]This city shall surely be given into the hand of the army of the king of Babylon and be taken." 4 Then the officials said to the king, [i]"Let this man be put to death, [j]for he is weakening the hands of the soldiers who are left in this city, and the hands of all the people, by speaking such words to them. For this man is not seeking [k]the welfare of this people, but their harm." 5 King Zedekiah said, "Behold, he is in your hands, [l]for the king can do nothing against you." 6 So they took Jeremiah [m]and cast him into the cistern of Malchiah, the king's son, which was in [n]the court of the guard, letting Jeremiah down [o]by ropes. [p]And there was no water in the cistern, but only mud, and [q]Jeremiah sank in the mud.

4 [d][Num. 27:17] [e][ch. 32:2; 33:1]
5 [f][Ezek. 17:15] [g]ch. 32:2 [h]ver. 11; ch. 34:21
7 [i][ch. 21:2] [j][Ezek. 29:2, 6] [k][ch. 46:17; 2 Kin. 24:7; Lam. 4:17]
8 [l]ch. 34:22
10 [m][ch. 21:4]
11 [n]ver. 5
12 [o]ch. 1:1; 32:8 [p][ch. 32:9] [q]ver. 4; ch. 39:14
13 [r]ch. 38:7; Zech. 14:10 [s]ver. 3; ch. 38:1 [t][ch. 21:9; 38:19; 39:9; 52:15]
14 [u]ch. 36:12
15 [v][Heb. 11:36]
16 [w]See ch. 38:6-14
17 [x]ch. 38:16 [y]See ch. 21:7
18 [v][See ver. 15 above]
19 [z][ch. 28:2, 11, 17]
20 [a][ch. 38:26] [b][ch. 38:28]
21 [c]See ch. 32:2 [d]ch. 38:9; 52:6; Ezek. 4:10, 16

Chapter 38
1 [e][ch. 37:3] [f]See ch. 20:1
2 [g]ch. 21:9; [ver. 17, 18]
3 [h]See ch. 32:3
4 [i]ch. 26:11 [j]See ch. 6:24 [k][ch. 33:9]
5 [l]See ver. 24-28
6 [m]ch. 37:16 [n]See ch. 32:2 [o]ver. 11, 13 [p][Gen. 37:24; Zech. 9:11] [q][Ps. 69:14]

37:5 Egypt . . . Chaldeans. See 34:10, 11. Egypt and Babylon were in contention for the region. Many in Judah were looking to Egypt for support (24:8); the Babylonians would have withdrawn to counter the Egyptian advance.

37:15 they beat him. This is the second mention of such punishment (20:2).

37:21 the court of the guard. The court was less severe than the "dungeon" (v. 16; see 32:2). Zedekiah here shows a measure of respect for God's prophet.

38:6 cistern. This was likely a deep pit with only a small opening in the top. Whether it was empty from water shortage or disuse is not clear. They may have hoped Jeremiah would die there.

Jeremiah Rescued from the Cistern

7 When [r]Ebed-melech [s]the Ethiopian, [t]a
eunuch who was in the king's house, heard
that they had put Jeremiah into the cistern—the king was sitting [u]in the Benjamin
Gate— 8 [r]Ebed-melech went from the king's
house and said to the king, 9 "My lord the
king, these men have done evil in all that
they did to Jeremiah the prophet by casting
him into the cistern, and he will die there
of [v]hunger, [w]for there is no bread left in the
city." 10 Then the king commanded [r]Ebed-
melech the Ethiopian, "Take three men
with you from here, and lift Jeremiah the
prophet out of the cistern before he dies."
11 So [r]Ebed-melech took the men with him
and went to the house of the king, to a
wardrobe in the storehouse, and took from
there old rags and worn-out clothes, which
he let down to Jeremiah in the cistern [x]by
ropes. 12 Then [r]Ebed-melech the Ethiopian
said to Jeremiah, "Put the rags and clothes
between your armpits and [x]the ropes."
Jeremiah did so. 13 Then they drew
Jeremiah up with [x]ropes and lifted him out
of the cistern. And Jeremiah remained in
the [n]court of the guard.

Jeremiah Warns Zedekiah Again

14 King Zedekiah sent for Jeremiah the
prophet and received him at the third
entrance of the temple of the LORD. The king
said to Jeremiah, "I will ask you a question;
hide nothing from me." 15 Jeremiah said to
Zedekiah, "If I tell you, will you not surely
put me to death? And if I give you counsel,
you will not listen to me." 16 Then King
Zedekiah swore [y]secretly to Jeremiah, [z]"As
the LORD lives, [a]who made our souls, I will
not put you to death or deliver you into the
hand of [b]these men who seek your life."

17 Then Jeremiah said to Zedekiah, "Thus
says the LORD, the God of hosts, the God of
Israel: [c]If you will surrender to [d]the officials
of the king of Babylon, [e]then your life shall
be spared, and this city shall not be burned
with fire, and you and your house shall live.
18 But if you do not surrender to [d]the officials of the king of Babylon, [f]then this city
shall be given into the hand of the
Chaldeans, [f]and they shall burn it with fire,
and you shall not escape from their hand."
19 King Zedekiah said to Jeremiah, "I am
afraid of the Judeans [g]who have deserted to
the Chaldeans, lest I be handed over to
them and they deal cruelly with me."
20 Jeremiah said, "You shall not be given to
them. Obey now the voice of the LORD in
what I say to you, [h]and it shall be well with
you, and your life shall be spared. 21 But if
you refuse to [c]surrender, this is the vision
which the LORD has shown to me: 22 Behold,
all the women left in the house of the king
of Judah were being led out to the officials
of the king of Babylon and were saying,

[i]"'Your trusted friends have deceived you
and prevailed against you;
now that your feet are sunk in the
mud,
they turn away from you.'

23 All your wives and [j]your sons shall be led
out to the Chaldeans, and you yourself
shall not escape from their hand, but shall
be seized by the king of Babylon, and this
city shall be burned with fire."
24 Then Zedekiah said to Jeremiah, "Let
no one know of these words, and you shall
not die. 25 If [k]the officials hear that I have
spoken with you and come to you and say
to you, 'Tell us what you said to the king
and what the king said to you; hide nothing from us and we will not put you to
death,' 26 then you shall say to them, [l]'I
made a humble plea to the king that he
would not send me back to the house of
Jonathan to die there.'" 27 Then all the officials came to Jeremiah and asked him, and
he answered them as the king had instructed him. So they stopped speaking with
him, for the conversation had not been
overheard. 28 And Jeremiah remained [m]in
the court of the guard until the day that
Jerusalem was taken.

7 [r]ch. 39:16 [s][Acts 8:27] [t]ch. 29:2; Isai. 56:3, 4 [u]See ch. 37:13
8 [r][See ver. 7 above]
9 [v]ch. 11:22; [ch. 14:16, 18; 19:9] [w][ch. 37:21]
10 [r][See ver. 7 above]
11 [r][See ver. 7 above] [x]ver. 6
12 [r][See ver. 7 above] [x][See ver. 11 above]
13 [x][See ver. 11 above] [n][See ver. 6 above]
16 [y]ch. 37:17 [z]See Ruth 3:13 [a][Isai. 57:16] [b]See ver. 1-9
17 [c]ver. 2, 21; [ch. 27:12, 13; 2 Kin. 24:12] [d]ch. 39:3 [e][ch. 34:4, 5]
18 [d][See ver. 17 above] [f]See ch. 21:10
19 [g]See ch. 37:13
20 [h]ch. 40:9
21 [c][See ver. 17 above]
22 [i]See ch. 20:10
23 [j]ch. 39:6; 41:10; 43:6
25 [k][ver. 5]
26 [l][ch. 37:20]
28 [m]See ch. 32:2

38:7 Ebed-melech. The name means "king's servant" and he would have held a position of responsibility in Zedekiah's household.

king was sitting in the Benjamin Gate. Probably he was hearing civil suits (2 Sam. 15:2–4).

38:12 rags . . . ropes. Here is a touching glimpse of Ebed-melech's kindness.

38:14 third entrance. This entrance is not mentioned elsewhere, but perhaps was for the private use of the king. The whole encounter breathes secrecy.

38:22 women . . . led out to the officials. The loss of a harem was a humiliating consequence for a king defeated in war.

Your trusted friends. Lit. "men of your peace." These "friends" included the officials who had counseled war (vv. 1, 4), and the false prophets (8:11). The expression ironically confirms Jeremiah's criticism of them.

The Fall of Jerusalem

39 [n]In the ninth year of Zedekiah king of Judah, in the tenth month, Nebuchadnezzar king of Babylon and all his army came against Jerusalem and besieged it. 2 In the eleventh year of Zedekiah, in the fourth month, on the ninth day of the month, a breach was made in the city. 3 Then all [o]the officials of the king of Babylon came [p]and sat in the middle gate: Nergal-sar-ezer, Samgar-nebu, Sar-sekim [q]the Rab-saris, Nergal-sar-ezer the Rab-mag, with all the rest of the officers of the king of Babylon. 4 When Zedekiah king of Judah and all the soldiers saw them, they fled, going out of the city at night by way of the king's garden through the gate between the two walls; and they went toward [r]the Arabah. 5 But the army of the Chaldeans pursued them and overtook Zedekiah in [s]the plains of Jericho. And when they had taken him, they brought him up to Nebuchadnezzar king of Babylon, at [t]Riblah, in the land of Hamath; [u]and he passed sentence on him. 6 The king of Babylon [v]slaughtered the sons of Zedekiah at [t]Riblah before his eyes, and the king of Babylon [v]slaughtered all the nobles of Judah. 7 [w]He put out the eyes of Zedekiah and bound him in chains to take him to Babylon. 8 [x]The Chaldeans burned the king's house and the house of the people, [y]and broke down the walls of Jerusalem. 9 Then [z]Nebuzaradan, the [a]captain of the guard, carried into exile to Babylon the rest of the people who were left in the city, [b]those who had deserted to him, and the people who remained. 10 Nebuzaradan, the captain of the guard, [c]left in the land of Judah some of the poor people who owned nothing, and gave them vineyards and fields at the same time.

The LORD Delivers Jeremiah

11 Nebuchadnezzar king of Babylon gave command concerning Jeremiah through Nebuzaradan, the captain of the guard, saying, 12 [d]"Take him, look after him well, and do him no harm, but deal with him as he tells you." 13 So [e]Nebuzaradan the captain of the guard, Nebushazban the Rab-saris, Nergal-sar-ezer the Rab-mag, [e]and all the chief officers of the king of Babylon 14 sent and took Jeremiah from [f]the court of the guard. They entrusted him to [g]Gedaliah the son of [h]Ahikam, son of [i]Shaphan, that he should take him home. So [j]he lived among the people.

15 The word of the LORD came to Jeremiah [k]while he was shut up in the court of the guard: 16 "Go, and say to [l]Ebed-melech the Ethiopian, 'Thus says the LORD of hosts, the God of Israel: [m]Behold, I will fulfill my words against this city for harm and [n]not for good, and they shall be accomplished before you on that day. 17 But I will deliver you on that day, declares the LORD, and you shall not be given into the hand of the men [o]of whom you are afraid. 18 For I will surely save you, and you shall not fall by the sword, but you shall have your [p]life as a prize of war, [q]because you have put your trust in me, declares the LORD.'"

Jeremiah Remains in Judah

40 The word that came to Jeremiah from the LORD [r]after Nebuzaradan the captain of the guard had let him go from [s]Ramah, when he took him [t]bound in chains along with all the captives of Jerusalem and Judah who were being exiled to Babylon. 2 The captain of the guard took Jeremiah and said to him, [u]"The LORD your God pronounced this disaster against this place. 3 The LORD has brought it about, and has done as he said. [v]Because you sinned against the LORD and did not obey his voice, this thing has come upon you. 4 Now, behold, I release you today from the chains on your hands. [w]If it seems good to you to come with me to Babylon, come, and I will look after you well, [w]but if it seems wrong to you to come with me to Babylon, do not come. [x]See, the whole land is before you; go wherever you think it good and right to go. 5 If you remain,[1] then return to [y]Gedaliah the son

Chapter 39
1 [n]For ver. 1-10, see ch. 52:4-16; 2 Kin. 25:1-12
3 [o]ch. 38:17, 18, 22 [p][ch. 1:15] [q]ver. 13; 2 Kin. 18:17
4 [r]See Deut. 1:1
5 [s]Josh. 5:10 [t]See 2 Kin. 23:33 [u][Ezek. 17:15]
6 [v]ch. 52:10
7 [w][ch. 32:4; Ezek. 12:13]
8 [x]See ch. 21:10 [y]Neh. 1:3; [Ps. 80:12; Isai. 5:5]
9 [z]ch. 40:1; 52:12; 2 Kin. 25:8 [a]Gen. 37:36 [b]See ch. 37:13
10 [c]ch. 40:7; 2 Kin. 25:12
12 [d]ch. 40:4
13 [e][ver. 3]
14 [f]ch. 38:28; See ch. 32:2 [g]ch. 43:6; See ch. 40:5-9, 11-16; 41:1-4, 6; 2 Kin. 25:22-25 [h]2 Kin. 22:12 [i]2 Kin. 22:3 [j]ch. 37:12
15 [k]ch. 36:5; 38:13
16 [l]See ch. 38:7 [m]Dan. 9:12 [n]ch. 21:10; [ch. 14:11]
17 [o]ch. 22:25
18 [p]ch. 21:9; 45:5 [q]Ps. 25:2; 37:40
Chapter 40
1 [r][ch. 39:14] [s]Josh. 18:25 [t][Ps. 149:8]
2 [u][Deut. 29:24, 28]
3 [v]ch. 44:3, 23; Deut. 29:25; See Dan. 9:10-12
4 [w][ch. 39:12] [x][Gen. 20:15]
5 [y]See ch. 39:14

[1] Syriac; the meaning of the Hebrew phrase is uncertain

39:1 tenth month. January, 588 B.C. (52:4; 2 Kin. 25:1).

39:2 ninth day . . . month. That is, July, 586 B.C. (52:5–7; 2 Kin. 25:2–4); the siege had lasted two and a half years.

39:3 sat in the middle gate. This fulfills 1:15. The officials' names are formed with those of Babylonian gods (Nebo, Nergal).

39:11, 12 Nebuchadnezzar . . . gave command concerning Jeremiah. How much of the prophet's message the king knew is not clear; he probably regarded him as a Babylonian sympathizer (though see 25:12).

40:5 Gedaliah. See 26:24. Gedaliah is receptive to Jeremiah's understanding of events.

of Ahikam, son of Shaphan, [z]whom the
king of Babylon appointed governor of the
cities of Judah, and dwell with him among
the people. Or go wherever you think it
right to go." So the captain of the guard
gave him an allowance of food and a present, and let him go. 6 Then Jeremiah went
to [y]Gedaliah the son of Ahikam, at
[a]Mizpah, and lived with him [b]among the
people [c]who were left in the land.
7 [d]When all the captains of the forces in
the open country and their men heard that
[e]the king of Babylon had appointed
Gedaliah the son of Ahikam governor in
the land and had committed to him men,
women, and children, those of [f]the poorest of the land who had not been taken
into exile to Babylon, 8 they went to
Gedaliah at [a]Mizpah—[g]Ishmael the son of
Nethaniah, [h]Johanan the son of Kareah,
Seraiah the son of Tanhumeth, the sons of
Ephai the Netophathite, [i]Jezaniah the son
of the Maacathite, they and their men.
9 Gedaliah the son of Ahikam, son of
Shaphan, swore to them and their men,
saying, "Do not be afraid to serve the
Chaldeans. Dwell in the land and serve the
king of Babylon, [j]and it shall be well with
you. 10 As for me, I will dwell at [a]Mizpah,
[k]to represent you before the Chaldeans
who will come to us. But as for you, [l]gath-
er wine and summer fruits and oil, and
store them in your vessels, and dwell in
your cities that you have taken." 11 Likewise, when all the Judeans who were in
[m]Moab and among [n]the Ammonites and in
[o]Edom and in other lands heard that the
king of Babylon had left a remnant in
Judah and had appointed Gedaliah the
son of Ahikam, son of Shaphan, as governor over them, 12 [p]then all the Judeans
returned from all the places to which they
had been driven and came to the land of
Judah, to Gedaliah at Mizpah. And they
[q]gathered wine and summer fruits in great
abundance.
13 Now [r]Johanan the son of Kareah and
[s]all the leaders of the forces in the open
country came to Gedaliah at Mizpah 14 and
said to him, "Do you know that Baalis the
king of [t]the Ammonites has sent Ishmael
the son of Nethaniah to take your life?" But
Gedaliah the son of Ahikam would not
believe them. 15 Then Johanan the son of
Kareah spoke secretly to Gedaliah at
Mizpah, "Please let me go and strike down
Ishmael the son of Nethaniah, and no one
will know it. Why should he take your life,
so that all the Judeans who are gathered
about you would be scattered, [u]and the
remnant of Judah would perish?" 16 But
Gedaliah the son of Ahikam said to
Johanan the son of Kareah, "You shall not
do this thing, for you are speaking falsely of
Ishmael."

Gedaliah Murdered

41 [v]In the seventh month, Ishmael the
son of Nethaniah, son of Elishama,
of the royal family, one of the chief officers
of the king, came with ten men to
Gedaliah the son of Ahikam, at [w]Mizpah.
As they [x]ate bread together there at
Mizpah, 2 [y]Ishmael the son of Nethaniah
and the ten men with him rose up and
struck down Gedaliah the son of Ahikam,
son of Shaphan, with the sword, and killed
him, [z]whom the king of Babylon had
appointed governor in the land. 3 Ishmael
also struck down all the Judeans who
were with Gedaliah at Mizpah, and the
Chaldean soldiers who happened to be
there.
4 On the day after the murder of
Gedaliah, before anyone knew of it, 5 eighty
men arrived from [a]Shechem and [b]Shiloh
and [c]Samaria, with [d]their beards shaved
and [e]their clothes torn, and [d]their bodies
gashed, [f]bringing grain offerings and
incense to present at the temple of the
LORD. 6 And Ishmael the son of Nethaniah
came out from [g]Mizpah to meet them,
weeping as he came. As he met them, he
said to them, "Come in to Gedaliah the son

5 [z]ch. 41:2
6 [y][See ver. 5 above] [a]ch. 41:6; Josh. 18:26 [b]ch. 37:12; 39:14 [c]ch. 39:10
7 [d]For ver. 7-9, see 2 Kin. 25:23, 24 [e]ver. 5 [f]ch. 39:10; 2 Kin. 25:12
8 [a][See ver. 6 above] [g]ver. 14, 15, 16; See ch. 41:1-3 [h]ver. 13, 15, 16; ch. 42:1, 8 [i]ch. 42:1
9 [j]ch. 38:20
10 [a][See ver. 6 above] [k]ch. 52:12; [Deut. 1:38] [l][ver. 12]
11 [m][Num. 22:1; 2 Sam. 8:2] [n]1 Sam. 11:1; 12:12 [o]Gen. 36:8
12 [p][ch. 43:5] [q][ver. 10]
13 [r]ver. 8, 15, 16; ch. 42:1, 8 [s]ch. 41:11; 42:1
14 [t][ch. 41:10]
15 [u][ch. 42:2]
Chapter 41
1 [v]2 Kin. 25:25 [w]See ch. 40:6, 8, 10 [x][Ps. 41:9]
2 [y][2 Sam. 13:28, 29] [z]ch. 40:5
5 [a]Josh. 17:7 [b]Josh. 18:1 [c]1 Kin. 16:24; See ch. 23:13 [d][ch. 48:37; Deut. 14:1; Isai. 15:2] [e]ch. 36:24 [f][2 Kin. 25:9]
6 [g]ch. 40:6, 8, 10

40:10 gather wine and summer fruits and oil. At the moment of judgment, we are given a glimpse of future blessing in the land. Contrast the drought conditions during parts of Jeremiah's earlier preaching (14:1–6 and notes).

41:1 As they ate bread together. This hospitality emphasizes the treachery of Ishmael the son of Nethaniah.

41:5 from Shechem . . . Shiloh . . . Samaria. These cities were important religious centers in the former northern kingdom that fell in 722 B.C. The men are a remnant of Israel's population who had made pilgrimages to Jerusalem for the great feasts (in accordance with Ex. 23:14–17). The time of year (the "seventh month," see v. 1) was the Feast of Booths.

with their beards shaved . . . bodies gashed. These actions are signs of mourning for the fall of Jerusalem.

the temple of the LORD. Although the temple had been destroyed, the temple mount was still regarded as holy.

of Ahikam." 7 When they came into the
city, Ishmael the son of Nethaniah and the
men with him slaughtered them and cast
them into a cistern. 8 But there were ten
men among them who said to Ishmael,
"Do not put us to death, for we have
[h]stores of wheat, barley, oil, and honey hidden in the fields." So he refrained and did
not put them to death with their companions.

9 Now the cistern into which Ishmael
had thrown all the bodies of the men
whom he had struck down along with[1]
Gedaliah was the large cistern that [i]King
Asa had made for defense against [i]Baasha
king of Israel; Ishmael the son of
Nethaniah filled it with the slain. 10 Then
Ishmael took captive all the rest of the
people who were in Mizpah, [j]the king's
daughters and all the people who were left
at Mizpah, whom [k]Nebuzaradan, the captain of the guard, had committed to
Gedaliah the son of Ahikam. Ishmael the
son of Nethaniah took them captive and
set out to cross over to [l]the Ammonites.

11 But when [m]Johanan the son of Kareah
and [n]all the leaders of the forces with him
heard of all the evil that Ishmael the son of
Nethaniah had done, 12 they took all their
men and went to fight against Ishmael the
son of Nethaniah. They came upon him at
[o]the great pool that is in [p]Gibeon. 13 And
when all the people who were with Ishmael
saw Johanan the son of Kareah and [q]all the
leaders of the forces with him, they
rejoiced. 14 [r]So all the people whom
Ishmael had carried away captive from
Mizpah turned around and came back, and
went to Johanan the son of Kareah. 15 But
Ishmael the son of Nethaniah escaped
from Johanan with eight men, and went to
[s]the Ammonites. 16 Then Johanan the son
of Kareah and [q]all the leaders of the forces
with him took from Mizpah all the rest of
the people whom he had recovered from
Ishmael the son of Nethaniah, after he
had struck down Gedaliah the son of
Ahikam—soldiers, [t]women, children, and
eunuchs, whom Johanan brought back
from [u]Gibeon. 17 And they went and stayed
at Geruth [v]Chimham near [w]Bethlehem,
intending to go to Egypt 18 because of the
Chaldeans. For they were afraid of them,
because Ishmael the son of Nethaniah had
struck down Gedaliah the son of Ahikam,
[x]whom the king of Babylon had made governor over the land.

Warning Against Going to Egypt

42 Then [y]all the commanders of the
forces, and [z]Johanan the son of
Kareah and Jezaniah the son of [a]Hoshaiah,
and all the people [b]from the least to the
greatest, came near 2 and said to Jeremiah
the prophet, "Let [c]our plea for mercy come
before you, and [d]pray to the LORD your
God for us, for all [e]this remnant—[f]because
we are left with but a few, as your eyes see
us—3 that [g]the LORD your God may show
us the way we should go, and the thing
that we should do." 4 Jeremiah the prophet
said to them, "I have heard you. Behold, I
will pray to the LORD your God according
to your request, and [h]whatever the LORD
answers you I will tell you. [h]I will keep
nothing back from you." 5 Then they said to
Jeremiah, [i]"May the LORD be a true and
[j]faithful witness against us [k]if we do not act
according to all the word [l]with which the
LORD your God sends you to us. 6 Whether
it is good or bad, we will obey the voice of
the LORD our God to whom we are sending
you, [m]that it may be well with us when we
obey the voice of the LORD our God."

7 [n]At the end of ten days the word of the
LORD came to Jeremiah. 8 Then he summoned [z]Johanan the son of Kareah and [y]all
the commanders of the forces who were
with him, and all the people [b]from the least
to the greatest, 9 and said to them, "Thus
says the LORD, the God of Israel, [o]to whom
you sent me to present your plea for mercy
before him: 10 If you will remain in this
land, [p]then I will build you up and not pull
you down; I will plant you, and not pluck

1 Hebrew *by the hand of*

8 [h][Judg. 6:11]
9 [i][1 Kin. 15:22; 2 Chr. 16:6]
10 [j]See ch. 38:23 [k][ch. 40:7] [l][ch. 40:14]
11 [m]See ch. 40:8 [n]ch. 40:13
12 [o][2 Sam. 2:13] [p]Josh. 9:3, 17
13 [q]ch. 40:13
14 [r]ver. 10, 16
15 [s][ch. 40:14]
16 [q][See ver. 13 above] [t]ch. 40:7
[u]Josh. 9:3, 17
17 [v][2 Sam. 19:37, 38] [w][Matt. 2:1, 14]; See Gen. 35:19
18 [x]ch. 40:5; 41:2
Chapter 42
1 [y]ch. 40:13; 41:11 [z]See ch. 40:8 [a]ch. 43:2 [b][ch. 6:13]
2 [c]See ch. 36:7 [d]ver. 20; [1 Sam. 7:8; 12:19] [e][ch. 40:15; Isai. 37:4] [f][Lev. 26:22]
3 [g][ch. 37:17; Ezra 8:21]
4 [h]1 Sam. 3:18; [Num. 22:18]
5 [i][Gen. 31:50] [j][Rev. 1:5; 3:14] [k]Judg. 11:10 [l]ver. 21
6 [m]ch. 7:23
7 [n][Ezek. 3:16]
8 [z][See ver. 1 above] [y][See ver. 1 above] [b][See ver. 1 above]
9 [o]ver. 2, 3
10 [p]See ch. 24:6

41:7 the city. That is, Mizpah (v. 6).

41:10 the king's daughters. Members of Zedekiah's court, not just the king's own daughters.

Ammonites. Part of the former alliance against Babylon (27:3), the Ammonite action is itself under God's judgment (27:8; 49:1–6).

41:11–44:30 Jeremiah is taken to Egypt by Jewish survivors fleeing from possible Babylonian reprisals.

41:15 escaped . . . with eight men. Two men were presumably lost in the skirmish (v. 2).

42:10 If you will remain in this land. This promise of blessing for the remnant left behind during the Exile was a new theme in Jeremiah's message (24:8; 40:6).

you up; [q]for I relent of the disaster that I
did to you. **11** [r]Do not fear the king of
Babylon, [r]of whom you are afraid. [s]Do not
fear him, declares the LORD, [s]for I am with
you, to save you and to deliver you from
his hand. **12** [t]I will grant you mercy, that he
may have mercy on you and let you remain
in your own land. **13** [u]But if you say, 'We
will not remain in this land,' disobeying
the voice of the LORD your God **14** and saying, 'No, [v]we will go to the land of Egypt,
where we shall not see war or [w]hear the
sound of the trumpet or [x]be hungry for
bread, and we will dwell there,' **15** then hear
the word of the LORD, O remnant of Judah.
Thus says the LORD of hosts, the God of
Israel: [y]If you set your faces to enter Egypt
[z]and go to live there, **16** then the sword [a]that
you fear shall overtake you there in the
land of Egypt, and the famine of which you
are afraid shall follow close after you to
Egypt, [b]and there you shall die. **17** All the
men who set their faces to go to Egypt to
live there shall die by the sword, by famine,
and by pestilence. They shall have [c]no remnant or survivor from the disaster that I will
bring upon them.

18 "For thus says the LORD of hosts, the
God of Israel: [d]As my anger and my wrath
were poured out on the inhabitants of
Jerusalem, so my wrath will be poured out
on you when you go to Egypt. [e]You shall
become an execration, a horror, a curse,
and a taunt. You shall see this place no
more. **19** The LORD has said to you, O remnant of Judah, [f]'Do not go to Egypt.' [g]Know
for a certainty that I have warned you this
day **20** that you have gone astray at the cost
of your lives. [h]For you sent me to the LORD
your God, saying, [h]'Pray for us to the LORD
our God, and [i]whatever the LORD our God
says declare to us and we will do it.' **21** And
I have this day declared it to you, but you
have not obeyed the voice of the LORD your
God in anything [j]that he sent me to tell
you. **22** [k]Now therefore know for a certainty
that you shall die by the sword, by famine,
and by pestilence in the place where you
desire to go to live."

10 [q]ch. 18:8; Gen. 6:6; [Deut. 32:36] **11** [r][ch. 22:25; 41:18] [s]ch. 30:10, 11; [Rom. 8:31] **12** [t][Neh. 1:11] **13** [u]ch. 43:4; [ch. 44:16, 17] **14** [v][ch. 41:17] [w]ch. 4:19 [x][ch. 37:21] **15** [y]ch. 44:12; [ver. 19; Deut. 17:16] [z]ch. 44:27; See ch. 44:1, 12-14 **16** [a]Ezek. 11:8 [b]ver. 22; ch. 44:12 **17** [c]Lam. 2:22 **18** [d]See ch. 7:20 [e]See ch. 18:16 **19** [f]ch. 43:2; [ver. 14-16] [g][Ezek. 2:5] **20** [h]ver. 2 [i]ver. 3 **21** [j]ver. 5 **22** [k]ver. 16, 17

Chapter 43
2 [l]ch. 42:1 [m]See ch. 40:8 [n]Ps. 86:14; Isai. 13:11; Mal. 4:1 **2** [o]ch. 42:19 **3** [p]See ch. 32:12 [q][ch. 38:22] [r][ch. 37:13] **4** [m][See ver. 2 above] [s]ch. 40:13 **5** [t][ch. 40:11, 12] **6** [u]ch. 44:20 [v]See ch. 38:23 [w]ch. 39:10; 40:7 [x]See ch. 39:14 **7** [y]ch. 2:16; 44:1; 46:14; [Isai. 30:4] **9** [y][See ver. 7 above] **10** [z]See ch. 25:9 [a]ch. 1:15 **11** [b]ch. 44:13; 46:13 [c]See ch. 15:2 **12** [d]See ch. 17:27 [e]ch. 46:25; Ezek. 30:13; [Ex. 12:12; Isai. 19:1]

Jeremiah Taken to Egypt

43 When Jeremiah finished speaking
to all the people all these words of
the LORD their God, with which the LORD
their God had sent him to them, **2** Azariah
the son of [l]Hoshaiah and [m]Johanan the son
of Kareah and [n]all the insolent men said to
Jeremiah, "You are telling a lie. The LORD
our God did not send you to say, [o]'Do not
go to Egypt to live there,' **3** but [p]Baruch the
son of Neriah [q]has set you against us, [r]to
deliver us into the hand of the Chaldeans,
that they may kill us or take us into exile in
Babylon." **4** So [m]Johanan the son of Kareah
and all [s]the commanders of the forces and
all the people did not obey the voice of the
LORD, to remain in the land of Judah. **5** But
Johanan the son of Kareah and all the commanders of the forces took [t]all the remnant
of Judah who had returned to live in the
land of Judah from all the nations to which
they had been driven— **6** [u]the men, the
women, the children, [v]the princesses, and
every person whom [w]Nebuzaradan the captain of the guard had left with [x]Gedaliah
the son of Ahikam, son of Shaphan; also
Jeremiah the prophet and Baruch the son
of Neriah. **7** And they came into the land of
Egypt, for they did not obey the voice of
the LORD. And they arrived at [y]Tahpanhes.

8 Then the word of the LORD came to
Jeremiah in Tahpanhes: **9** "Take in your
hands large stones and hide them in the
mortar in the pavement that is at the
entrance to Pharaoh's palace in [y]Tah-
panhes, in the sight of the men of Judah,
10 and say to them, 'Thus says the LORD of
hosts, the God of Israel: Behold, I will send
and take Nebuchadnezzar the king of
Babylon, [z]my servant, [a]and I will set his
throne above these stones that I have hidden, and he will spread his royal canopy
over them. **11** He shall come [b]and strike the
land of Egypt, [c]giving over to the pestilence
those who are doomed to the pestilence, to
captivity those who are doomed to captivity, and to the sword those who are doomed
to the sword. **12** [d]I shall kindle a fire [e]in the
temples of the gods of Egypt, and he shall

42:13–16 The Lord's word is still against seeking refuge in Egypt (Deut. 17:16). The issue, as ever, is false trust and the delusion of safety in human power and calculation (22:20, 22; 30:14).

43:7, 8 Egypt. Jeremiah's prophetic ministry continues even in Egypt. **Tahpanhes.** See 2:16. Tahpanhes was located in the eastern Nile delta.

43:9 Take in your hands large stones . . . hide them. A symbolic action whose interpretation follows. The action was designed to show that the word would surely come to pass.

43:10 Nebuchadnezzar . . . my servant. See note 25:9.

burn them [f]and carry them away captive.
[g]And he shall clean the land of Egypt [g]as a
shepherd cleans his cloak of vermin, and
he shall go away from there in peace. 13 He
shall break the [h]obelisks of Heliopolis,
which is in the land of Egypt, [e]and the temples of the gods of Egypt he shall burn with
fire.' "

Judgment for Idolatry

44 The word that came to Jeremiah
concerning all the Judeans who
lived in the land of Egypt, at [i]Migdol, at
[j]Tahpanhes, at Memphis, and in the land
of [k]Pathros, 2 "Thus says the LORD of hosts,
the God of Israel: You have seen all the disaster that I brought upon Jerusalem and
upon all the cities of Judah. Behold, this
day [l]they are a desolation, and no one
dwells in them, 3 because of the evil that
they committed, [m]provoking me to anger,
[n]in that they went to make offerings [o]and
serve other gods that they knew not, neither they, nor you, nor your fathers. 4 [p]Yet I
persistently sent to you all my servants the
prophets, saying, 'Oh, do not do this
abomination that I hate!' 5 [q]But they did
not listen [q]or incline their ear, to turn from
their evil and make no offerings to other
gods. 6 [r]Therefore my wrath and my anger
were poured out and kindled in the cities
of Judah and in the streets of Jerusalem,
[s]and they became a waste and a desolation,
as at this day. 7 And now thus says the LORD
God of hosts, the God of Israel: Why do
you commit this great evil [t]against yourselves, to cut off from you [u]man and
woman, [u]infant and child, from the midst
of Judah, leaving you no remnant? 8 [m]Why
do you provoke me to anger with the works
of your hands, [n]making offerings to other
gods in the land of Egypt where you have
come to live, so that you may be cut off and
become [v]a curse and a taunt among all the
nations of the earth? 9 Have you forgotten
the evil of your fathers, [w]the evil of the
kings of Judah, [x]the evil of their[1] wives,
your own evil, [y]and the evil of your wives,
which they committed in the land of Judah

12 [f][ch. 48:7] [g][Ps. 104:2; Isai. 49:18] 13 [h][Ex. 23:24] [e][See ver. 12 above]
Chapter 44
1 [i]ch. 46:14; Ex. 14:2 [j]See ch. 43:7-9 [k]ver. 15; See Isai. 11:11 2 [l]ver. 6 3 [m]ver. 8; See ch. 7:18, 19 [n]See ch. 1:16 [o]ch. 19:4; Deut. 6:14 4 [p]See 2 Chr. 36:15 5 [q]See ch. 34:14 6 [r]See ch. 7:20 [s]See ch. 7:34; 9:11 7 [t]Hab. 2:10; [Num. 16:38; Prov. 20:2] [u][ch. 38:23; Lam. 2:11] 8 [m][See ver. 3 above] [n][See ver. 3 above] [v]ch. 42:18; See ch. 18:16 9 [w][ch. 15:4] [x]1 Kin. 11:1, 8; 15:13; 2 Kin. 11:1 [y]ver. 15, 25
10 [z][Prov. 28:14] 11 [a]See ch. 21:10 12 [b]ch. 42:15 [c]ch. 42:16 [d]See ch. 6:13 [e]See ch. 18:16 [v][See ver. 8 above] 13 [f]ch. 43:11 14 [g]ch. 42:17 [h][ch. 22:27] [i][ver. 28] 15 [j]ver. 9, 25 [k]See ver. 1 16 [l]ch. 6:16; 42:13 17 [m][Judg. 11:36] [n]ch. 7:18 [o]ch. 19:13 [p][1 Kin. 11:33; 2 Kin. 21:3] 18 [n][See ver. 17 above] [q][Lam. 3:22] 19 [r]ch. 7:18 [s][Num. 30:6, 7]

and in the streets of Jerusalem? 10 They
have not humbled themselves even to this
day, [z]nor have they feared, nor walked in
my law and my statutes that I set before
you and before your fathers.
11 "Therefore thus says the LORD of hosts,
the God of Israel: [a]Behold, I will set my face
against you for harm, to cut off all Judah. 12 I
will take the remnant of Judah who have [b]set
their faces to come to the land of Egypt to
live, and they shall all be consumed. [c]In the
land of Egypt they shall fall; by the sword
and by famine [c]they shall be consumed.
[d]From the least to the greatest, they shall die
by the sword and by famine, [e]and they shall
become an oath, a horror, [v]a curse, and a
taunt. 13 [f]I will punish those who dwell in the
land of Egypt, as I have punished Jerusalem,
with the sword, with famine, and with pestilence, 14 [g]so that none of the remnant of
Judah who have come to live in the land of
Egypt shall escape or survive [h]or return to
the land of Judah, to which they desire to
return to dwell there. For they shall not
return, [i]except some fugitives."
15 Then all the men who knew that [j]their
wives had made offerings to other gods,
and all the women who stood by, a great
assembly, all the people who lived in
[k]Pathros in the land of Egypt, answered
Jeremiah: 16 "As for the word that you have
spoken to us in the name of the LORD, [l]we
will not listen to you. 17 [m]But we will do
everything that we have vowed, make offerings to [n]the queen of heaven [o]and pour out
drink offerings to her, [p]as we did, both we
and our fathers, our kings and our officials,
in the cities of Judah and in the streets of
Jerusalem. For then we had plenty of food,
and prospered, and saw no disaster. 18 But
since we left off making offerings to [n]the
queen of heaven and pouring out drink
offerings to her, we have lacked everything
[q]and have been consumed by the sword
and by famine." 19 And the women said,[2]
"When we made offerings to the queen of
heaven [r]and poured out drink offerings to
her, was it [s]without our husbands'

[1] Hebrew *his* [2] Compare Syriac; Hebrew lacks *And the women said*

43:13 obelisks. Characteristic examples of Egyptian architecture.

44:4 this abomination. Idolatrous worship of other gods.

44:7 no remnant. Possibly this oracle threatens that the restoration promised in 5:10 and 23:3 may not be carried out.

44:9 Have you forgotten the evil. And by implication the judgment that resulted. Similarly, 2 Kin. 17:18–20 uses the judgment of the northern kingdom as a warning to Judah before her fall.

44:19 without our husbands' approval. See Num. 30:6–15. The women evidently took the lead in worshiping the queen of heaven (7:18).

approval that we made cakes for her bearing her image and poured out drink offerings to her?"
20Then Jeremiah said to all the people,
[t]men and women, all the people who had
given him this answer: **21**[u]"As for the offerings that you offered in the cities of Judah
and in the streets of Jerusalem, you and
your fathers, your kings and your officials,
and the people of the land, [v]did not
the LORD remember them? Did it not
come into his mind? **22**[w]The LORD could
no longer bear your evil deeds and [x]the
abominations that you committed. [y]There-
fore your land has become [z]a desolation
and a waste and a curse, [a]without inhabitant, as it is this day. **23**It is because you
made offerings [b]and because you sinned
against the LORD and did not obey the
voice of the LORD or walk in his law and in
his statutes and in his testimonies [c]that
this disaster has happened to you, as at
this day."
24Jeremiah said to all the people and all
the women, "Hear the word of the LORD,
[d]all you of Judah who are in the land of
Egypt. **25**Thus says the LORD of hosts, the
God of Israel: [e]You and your wives have
declared with your mouths, and have fulfilled it with your hands, saying, 'We will
surely perform our vows that we have
made, [f]to make offerings to the queen of
heaven and to pour out drink offerings to
her.' Then confirm your vows and perform
your vows! **26**Therefore hear the word of
the LORD, [d]all you of Judah who dwell in
the land of Egypt: [g]Behold, I have sworn
by my great name, says the LORD, [h]that my
name shall no more be invoked by the
mouth of any man of Judah in all the land
of Egypt, [i]saying, 'As the Lord GOD lives.'
27[j]Behold, I am watching over them for
disaster and not for good. [k]All the men of
Judah who are in the land of Egypt shall be
consumed by the sword and by famine,
until there is an end of them. **28**[l]And those
who escape the sword shall return from
the land of Egypt to the land of Judah,
[m]few in number; and all the remnant of
Judah, who came to the land of Egypt to
live, [n]shall know whose word will stand,
mine or theirs. **29**This shall be the sign to
you, declares the LORD, that I will punish
you in this place, in order that you may
know that [o]my words will surely stand
against you for harm: **30**Thus says the
LORD, behold, I will give [p]Pharaoh Hophra
king of Egypt into the hand of his enemies
[q]and into the hand of those who seek his
life, as I gave [r]Zedekiah king of Judah into
the hand of Nebuchadnezzar king of
Babylon, who was his enemy and sought
his life."

Message to Baruch

45 The word that Jeremiah the prophet
spoke to [s]Baruch the son of Neriah,
[t]when he wrote these words in a book at
the dictation of Jeremiah, [u]in the fourth
year of Jehoiakim the son of Josiah, king of
Judah: **2**"Thus says the LORD, the God of
Israel, to you, O Baruch: **3**You said, [v]'Woe
is me! For the LORD has added sorrow to
my pain. [w]I am weary with my groaning,
[x]and I find no rest.' **4**Thus shall you say to
him, Thus says the LORD: [y]Behold, what I
have built I am breaking down, and what I
have planted I am plucking up—that is,
the whole land. **5**And [z]do you seek great
things for yourself? Seek them not, for
behold, [a]I am bringing disaster upon all
flesh, declares the LORD. But I will give you
[b]your life as a prize of war in all places to
which you may go."

Judgment on Egypt

46 The word of the LORD that came to
Jeremiah the prophet [c]concerning
the nations.
2About Egypt. [d]Concerning the army of
Pharaoh Neco, king of Egypt, which was by
the river Euphrates at Carchemish and
which Nebuchadnezzar king of Babylon

20 [t]ch. 43:6 **21** [u]ver. 17; [Ezek. 8:10, 11] [v][Ezek. 21:24] **22** [w]ch. 5:9, 29 [x]Ezek. 8:6 [y]See ch. 7:34 [z]See ch. 18:16 [a]See ch. 4:7 **23** [b]See ch. 40:3 [c][Deut. 31:29] **24** [d]ver. 15; See ch. 43:5-7 **25** [e]ver. 16 [f]ver. 17 **26** [d][See ver. 24 above] [g]See ch. 22:5 [h][Ezek. 20:39] [i][ch. 4:2] **27** [j]ch. 31:28 [k]ch. 42:16 **28** [l][ver. 14; Isai. 27:13] [m]Ezek. 6:8 [n]ver. 17, 25, 26 **29** [o]Prov. 19:21 **30** [p]ch. 46:17; See Ezek. 29:2-5; 30:21-24 [q]ch. 46:26 [r][ch. 39:5]
Chapter 45
1 [s]See ch. 32:12 [t]See ch. 36:4, 18 [u]ch. 36:1 **3** [v][ch. 36:26] [w]Ps. 6:6 [x]Lam. 1:3; 5:5 **4** [y]ch. 31:28; [Isai. 5:5] **5** [z][Ps. 131:1, 2; Rom. 12:16] [a][ch. 25:26, 29] [b]ch. 21:9; 39:18
Chapter 46
1 [c][ch. 1:5; 25:13]; See ch. 25:15-26 **2** [d]2 Kin. 23:29; 2 Chr. 35:20

44:23 law . . . statutes . . . testimonies. The requirements of the Mosaic covenant (Deut. 11:1, 32; 12:1).

44:29, 30 Pharaoh Hophra (reigned 589–570 B.C.) was killed by his enemies during a military revolt; his death is used as a sign that all the Lord's prophecies against the refugees in Egypt would come to pass.

45:1–5 This chapter contains God's promise to Baruch to spare his life, made many years earlier.

45:1 fourth year of Jehoiakim. The year in which Baruch prepared the first scroll of Jeremiah's words for public reading (36:1–3).

45:3 my pain. Baruch had evidently suffered along with Jeremiah as a result of Jeremiah's prophetic commission (cf. 11:18–23). See 36:19; 43:3.

rest. See Deut. 12:9; Ps. 95:11.

46:1–51:64 This section of Jeremiah comprises a series of judgment oracles against the surrounding nations.

46:2 Carchemish. Nebuchadnezzar defeated Pharaoh Neco at the battle of Carchemish on the upper Euphrates River in 605 B.C. and brought to a close Egypt's political and military influence over Palestine and Syria.

defeated in [e]the fourth year of Jehoiakim the son of Josiah, king of Judah:

3 [f]"Prepare buckler and shield,
and advance for battle!
4 [g]Harness the horses;
mount, O horsemen!
Take your stations with your helmets,
[f]polish your spears,
put on your armor!
5 Why have I seen it?
They are dismayed
and have turned backward.
Their [h]warriors are beaten down
and have fled in haste;
[i]they look not back—
[j]terror on every side!
declares the LORD.
6 The swift cannot flee away,
nor the warrior escape;
[d]in the north by the river Euphrates
[k]they have stumbled and fallen.

7 "Who is this, [l]rising like the Nile,
like rivers [m]whose waters surge?
8 Egypt rises like the Nile,
like rivers [m]whose waters surge.
He said, 'I will rise, I will cover the earth,
I will destroy cities and their inhabitants.'
9 [n]Advance, O horses,
and rage, O chariots!
Let the warriors go out:
men of Cush and [o]Put who handle the shield,
[p]men of Lud, skilled in handling the bow.
10 [q]That day is the day of the Lord GOD of hosts,
[r]a day of vengeance,
[s]to avenge himself on his foes.
[t]The sword shall devour and be sated
and drink its fill of their blood.
For the Lord GOD of hosts holds [u]a sacrifice
[v]in the north country [w]by the river Euphrates.
11 [x]Go up to Gilead, and take [x]balm,
O virgin daughter of Egypt!
In vain you have used many medicines;
[y]there is no healing for you.
12 The nations have heard of your shame,
and the earth is full of your cry;
[z]for warrior has stumbled against warrior;
they have both fallen together."

13 The word that the LORD spoke to
Jeremiah the prophet about the coming of
[a]Nebuchadnezzar king of Babylon to strike
the land of Egypt:

14 "Declare in Egypt, and proclaim in [b]Migdol;
proclaim in [b]Memphis and [b]Tahpanhes;
Say, [c]'Stand ready and be prepared,
for [d]the sword shall devour around you.'
15 Why are your [e]mighty ones face down?
They[1] do not stand
because the LORD thrust them down.
16 He made many stumble, [f]and they fell,
and they said one to another,
'Arise, and let us go back to our own people
and to the land of our birth,
[g]because of the sword of the oppressor.'
17 Call the name of [h]Pharaoh, king of Egypt,
'Noisy one who lets the hour go by.'

1 Hebrew *He*

2 [e]ch. 25:1; 36:1; 45:1
3 [f][ch. 51:11]
4 [g][Nah. 3:2] [f][See ver. 3 above]
5 [h][2 Sam. 1:19, 25] [i]ver. 21; ch. 47:3 [j]See ch. 6:25
6 [d][See ver. 2 above] [k][Dan. 11:19]
7 [l][ch. 47:2; Isai. 8:7, 8; Dan. 11:22] [m][Ezek. 32:2]
8 [m][See ver. 7 above]
9 [n]Nah. 3:2; [Judg. 5:22] [o]Ezek. 27:10 [p]Isai. 66:19
10 [q]Isai. 13:9; Joel 1:15 [r]ch. 50:15 [s]Isai. 1:24 [t][ver. 14; Isai. 34:5] [u][Isai. 34:6] [v]ver. 6 [w]ver. 2
11 [x][ch. 8:22] [y][Ezek. 30:21]
12 [z]ver. 6
13 [a]ch. 43:10, 11; 44:30; [Isai. 19:4; Ezek. 29:10]
14 [b]See ch. 44:1 [c][ver. 3, 4] [d][ver. 10]
15 [e]ch. 8:16; 47:3
16 [f]Lev. 26:37 [g]ch. 50:16
17 [h][Isai. 30:7]

fourth year of Jehoiakim. See 36:1; 45:1. The ascendancy of Babylon over Egypt was critical for Judah in her final years.

46:3, 4 Prepare buckler . . . put on your armor. These orders to the Egyptian army mock her military pretensions.

46:6 by the river Euphrates. That is, at Carchemish (v. 2 note).

46:9 men of Cush . . . Put . . . Lud. Mercenaries from Africa and Greece testify to Egypt's power.

46:11 Gilead. See note 8:22.

virgin daughter of Egypt. Suggesting vulnerability and innocence, though it could be meant ironically. See its use in connection with Israel in 14:17; 18:13.

46:14 Migdol . . . Memphis . . . Tahpanhes. See 2:16; 43:8; 44:1.

46:15 Why are your mighty ones face down. The Septuagint (Greek) reading is preferred by many interpreters: "Why has Apis run away?" Apis was the sacred bull of ancient Egypt, worshiped as an incarnation of the god Ptah, especially at Noph (Memphis, v. 14).

18 [i]"As I live, declares the King,
[j]whose name is the LORD of hosts,
like [k]Tabor among the mountains
and like [l]Carmel by the sea, shall
one come.
19 [m]Prepare yourselves baggage for exile,
O [n]inhabitants of Egypt!
For [o]Memphis shall become a waste,
a ruin, [p]without inhabitant.
20 "A beautiful [q]heifer is Egypt,
but a biting fly [r]from the north has
come upon her.
21 Even her hired soldiers in her midst
are like [s]fattened calves;
yes, they have turned and fled
together;
they did not stand,
for the day of their calamity has
come upon them,
[t]the time of their punishment.
22 "She makes [u]a sound like a serpent
gliding away;
for her enemies march in force
and come against her with axes
[v]like those who fell trees.
23 [v]They shall cut down her forest,
declares the LORD,
though it is impenetrable,
because [w]they are more numerous
than locusts;
they are without number.
24 The daughter of Egypt shall be put to
shame;
she shall be delivered into the hand
of [r]a people from the north."

25 The LORD of hosts, the God of Israel,
said: "Behold, I am bringing punishment
upon [x]Amon of [y]Thebes, and Pharaoh and
Egypt [z]and her gods and her kings, upon
Pharaoh and those who trust in him.
26 [a]I
will deliver them into the hand of those
who seek their life, into the hand of
Nebuchadnezzar king of Babylon and his
officers. [b]Afterward Egypt shall be inhabited
[c]as in the days of old, declares the LORD.

27 [d]"But fear not, O Jacob my servant,
nor be dismayed, O Israel,
for behold, I will save you from far
away,
and your offspring from the land of
their captivity.
Jacob shall return and have quiet and
ease,
and none shall make him afraid.
28 [d]Fear not, O Jacob my servant,
declares the LORD,
for I am with you.
I will make a full end of all the nations
to which I have driven you,
but of you I will not make a full end.
[e]I will discipline you in just measure,
and I will by no means leave you
unpunished."

Judgment on the Philistines

47 The word of the LORD that came to Jeremiah the prophet [f]concerning the Philistines, before Pharaoh struck down [g]Gaza.

2 "Thus says the LORD:
[h]Behold, waters are rising [i]out of the
north,
[h]and shall become an overflowing
torrent;
they shall overflow [j]the land and all
that fills it,
the city and those who dwell in it.
Men shall cry out,
and every inhabitant of the land
shall wail.
3 At the noise of the stamping of the
hoofs of [k]his stallions,
[l]at the rushing of his chariots, at
the rumbling of their wheels,
the fathers [m]look not back to their
children,
so feeble are their hands,
4 because of the day that is coming to
destroy
all [f]the Philistines,
to cut off from [n]Tyre and Sidon
every helper that remains.

18 [i]See ch. 4:2 [j]ch. 48:15; 51:57; Isai. 47:4; 48:2 [k]Judg. 4:6 [l]1 Kin. 18:42, 44
19 [m][ch. 48:18] [n][Ezek. 12:3] [o]See ch. 44:1 [p]See ch. 4:7
20 [q][Hos. 10:11] [r]ver. 6, 10, 24; See ch. 1:13
21 [s]Amos 6:4; Mal. 4:2 [t]ch. 50:27
22 [u][Isai. 29:4] [v][Isai. 10:34; 14:8]
23 [v][See ver. 22 above] [w][Judg. 6:5; 7:12]
24 [r][See ver. 20 above]
25 [x]Nah. 3:8 [y]Ezek. 30:14, 15, 16 [z]See ch. 43:12
26 [a]ch. 44:30; Ezek. 30:4; 32:11 [b]Ezek. 29:13, 14; See Isai. 19:22-25 [c]Isai. 51:9
27 [d]See ch. 30:10, 11; Isai. 43:5
28 [d][See ver. 27 above] [e]ch. 10:24
Chapter 47
1 [f]ch. 25:20; Ezek. 25:15, 16; Zeph. 2:5 [g]Amos 1:6, 7; Zeph. 2:4
2 [h][ch. 46:7, 8; Isai. 8:7] [i]See ch. 1:13 [j][ch. 8:16]
3 [k]ch. 46:15 [l]Nah. 3:2 [m]ch. 46:5
4 [f][See ver. 1 above] [n]Isai. 23:1, 2; Joel 3:4; See ch. 25:22

46:18 As I live. See Gen. 22:15.

the King. For God as King, see 8:19; 10:7, 10; 48:15; 51:57; Deut. 33:5. In the oracles against the nations, God's true kingship is contrasted with the vain pretensions of earthly kings.

Tabor . . . Carmel. These mountains in northern Israel stood at the eastern and western boundaries of the strategic Plain of Megiddo.

46:20 heifer. This may be an ironic allusion to Egyptian worship of the bull Apis (v. 15 note).

biting fly. That is, Nebuchadnezzar.

from the north. See 6:1.

46:25 Amon of Thebes. Amon was the chief Egyptian god. Thebes is in the south, suggesting even deeper penetration by Babylon.

47:4 Tyre and Sidon. These Phoenician cities afforded natural protection to the Philistines farther down the Mediterranean coast, though it is not known whether alliances ever existed between them.

Caphtor. The Philistines' place of origin, usually identified as Crete.

For the LORD is destroying the
Philistines,
[o] the remnant of the coastland of
[p] Caphtor.
5 [q] Baldness has come upon Gaza;
[r] Ashkelon has perished.
O remnant of their valley,
[s] how long will you gash yourselves?
6 [t] Ah, sword of the LORD!
How long till you are quiet?
Put yourself into your scabbard;
rest and be still!
7 How can it[1] be quiet
[u] when the LORD has given it a charge?
Against [v] Ashkelon and against the
seashore
[w] he has appointed it."

Judgment on Moab

48 [x] Concerning Moab.
Thus says the LORD of hosts, the God of Israel:

"Woe to [y] Nebo, for it is laid waste!
[z] Kiriathaim is put to shame, it is
taken;
the fortress is put to shame [a] and
broken down;
2 the renown of Moab is no more.
In [b] Heshbon they planned disaster
against her:
'Come, let us cut her off [c] from
being a nation!'
You also, O [d] Madmen, shall be
brought to silence;
the sword shall pursue you.
3 "Hark! A cry from [e] Horonaim,
'Desolation and great destruction!'
4 Moab is destroyed;
her little ones have made a cry.
5 [e] For at the ascent of Luhith
they go up weeping;[2]
for [e] at the descent of Horonaim
they have heard the distressed cry[3]
of destruction.
6 Flee! Save yourselves!
You will be like [f] a juniper in the
desert!
7 For, [g] because you trusted in your
works and your treasures,
you also shall be taken;
and [h] Chemosh [i] shall go into exile
with [j] his priests and his
officials.
8 [k] The destroyer shall come upon every
city,
and no city shall escape;
the valley shall perish,
and [l] the plain shall be destroyed,
as the LORD has spoken.

9 "Give wings to Moab,
for she would fly away;
her cities shall become a desolation,
with no inhabitant in them.

10 [m] "Cursed is he who does [n] the work of
the LORD with slackness, and cursed is he
who keeps back his sword from bloodshed.

11 "Moab has been at ease from his
youth
and has [o] settled on his dregs;
he has not been emptied from vessel
to vessel,
nor has he gone into exile;
so his taste remains in him,
and his scent is not changed.

12 "Therefore, behold, the days are coming, declares the LORD, when I shall send to
him pourers who will pour him, and empty
his vessels and break his[4] jars in pieces.
13 Then [p] Moab shall be ashamed of
Chemosh, as [q] the house of Israel was
ashamed of [r] Bethel, their confidence.

14 "How do you say, 'We are heroes
and mighty men of war'?

4 [o] Amos 1:8 [p] Gen. 10:14; Amos 9:7
5 [q] [ch. 48:37; Isai. 3:24] [r] ch. 25:20; [Judg. 1:18] [s] [ch. 48:37]
6 [t] Deut. 32:41; See Ezek. 21:3-5
7 [u] [Ezek. 14:17] [v] ch. 25:20; [Judg. 1:18] [w] Mic. 6:9
Chapter 48
1 [x] ch. 25:21; 2 Kin. 24:2; See Isai. ch. 15–16; Ezek. 25:8-11; Amos 2:1-3; Zeph. 2:8, 9 [y] ver. 22; Num. 32:3 [z] ver. 23; Num. 32:37; Josh. 13:19; Ezek. 25:9 [a] ver. 20, 39
2 [b] ver. 34, 45; ch. 49:3; Num. 32:37; Isai. 15:4 [c] [ch. 31:36] [d] [Isai. 10:31]
3 [e] Isai. 15:5; [ver. 34]
5 [e] [See ver. 3 above]
6 [f] ch. 17:6
7 [g] ch. 49:4 [h] Num. 21:29 [i] [Isai. 46:2] [j] ch. 49:3
8 [k] ch. 6:26 [l] ver. 21; Josh. 13:9, 17, 21; [Deut. 3:10]
10 [m] Judg. 5:23; [1 Sam. 15:3, 9; 1 Kin. 20:42] [n] [1 Cor. 15:58]
11 [o] Zeph. 1:12
13 [p] [Num. 21:29; Isai. 16:14] [q] [Hos. 10:6] [r] [1 Kin. 12:29]

1 Septuagint, Vulgate; Hebrew *you* 2 Hebrew *weeping goes up with weeping* 3 Septuagint (compare Isaiah 15:5) *cry* 4 Septuagint, Aquila; Hebrew *their*

48:1–47 This chapter records the oracle against Moab; cf. Is. 15; 16; Ezek. 25:8–11; Amos 2:1–3. Moab was an enemy of Israel (Judg. 3:12–14; 2 Kin. 3:4–27). It was an ally of Judah against Babylon (27:3), but supplied troops for Nebuchadnezzar against Jehoiakim (2 Kin. 24:2). Its defeat by Nebuchadnezzar may have come in 582 B.C. following a rebellion.

48:1 Nebo . . . Kiriathaim. Originally these towns were allocated to the tribe of Reuben (Num. 32:3, 37, 38; Josh. 13:15, 19).

48:2 Heshbon. This village was also assigned to Reuben (Num. 32:37; Josh. 13:17).

48:7 Chemosh. A god of Moab worshiped by Solomon (1 Kin. 11:7, 33; 2 Kin. 23:13). Images of defeated gods were often carried off into exile.

48:8 The destroyer. Probably Nebuchadnezzar.

48:11, 12 The wine left to age represents Moab's complacency. Their ease and security will vanish as quickly as a bottle empties when overturned.

48:13 Bethel. Possibly a reference to the name El Bethel used for the Lord in Jeroboam's apostate worship at Bethel (1 Kin. 12:28–30). That cult had not prevented the Assyrians from plundering the land in 722 B.C. (2 Kin. 18:9–12).

15 The destroyer of [s]Moab and his cities
has come up,
and the choicest of his young men
have [t]gone down to slaughter,
declares [u]the King, [u]whose name is
the LORD of hosts.
16 The calamity of Moab is near at hand,
and his affliction hastens swiftly.
17 [v]Grieve for him, all you who are
around him,
and all who know his name;
say, [w]'How the mighty scepter is
broken,
the glorious staff.'

18 [x]"Come down from your glory,
and sit on the parched ground,
O inhabitant of [y]Dibon!
For the destroyer of Moab has come
up against you;
he has destroyed your strongholds.
19 [z]Stand by the way [z]and watch,
O inhabitant of [a]Aroer!
Ask him who flees and her who
escapes;
say, 'What has happened?'
20 Moab is put to shame, for it is broken;
[v]wail and cry!
Tell it beside [b]the Arnon,
that [s]Moab is laid waste.

21 "Judgment has come upon [c]the tableland, upon Holon, and [d]Jahzah, and Mephaath, 22 and [y]Dibon, and [e]Nebo, and Beth-
diblathaim, 23 and [f]Kiriathaim, and Beth-
gamul, and [g]Beth-meon, 24 and [h]Kerioth, and
[i]Bozrah, and all the cities of the land of
Moab, far and near. 25 [j]The horn of Moab is
cut off, and [k]his arm is broken, declares the
LORD.
26 [l]"Make him drunk, [m]because he magnified himself against the LORD, so that
Moab shall [l]wallow in his vomit, [n]and he
too shall be held in derision. 27 [o]Was not
Israel a derision to you? [p]Was he found
among thieves, that whenever you spoke of
him [q]you wagged your head?

28 [r]"Leave the cities, and dwell in the
rock,
O inhabitants of Moab!
Be [s]like the dove that nests
in the sides of the mouth of a
gorge.
29 [t]We have heard of the pride of
Moab—
he is very proud—
of his loftiness, his pride, and his
arrogance,
and the haughtiness of his heart.
30 I know his insolence, declares the
LORD;
[u]his boasts are false,
his deeds are false.
31 [v]Therefore I wail for Moab;
I cry out for all Moab;
for the men of [w]Kir-hareseth I
mourn.
32 More than for [x]Jazer I weep for you,
[y]O vine of [z]Sibmah!
[a]Your branches passed over the sea,
reached to the Sea of [x]Jazer;
on your summer fruits and your
grapes
the destroyer has fallen.
33 [b]Gladness and joy have been taken
away
from the fruitful land of Moab;
I have made the wine cease from the
winepresses;
no one treads them with shouts
of joy;
the shouting is not the shout of joy.

34 [c]"From the outcry at Heshbon even to
Elealeh, as far as Jahaz they utter their
voice, from Zoar to [d]Horonaim and Eglath-
shelishiyah. For the waters of Nimrim also
have become desolate. 35 And I will bring to
an end in Moab, declares the LORD, him
who offers sacrifice in [e]the high place and
makes offerings to his god. 36 Therefore my
heart moans for Moab like a flute, and my
heart moans like a flute for the men of [f]Kir-
hareseth. [g]Therefore the riches they gained
have perished.
37 [h]"For every head is shaved and every
beard cut off. [i]On all the hands are gashes,
and [j]around the waist is sackcloth. 38 On all
the housetops of Moab and in the squares
there is nothing but lamentation, for I have

15 [s]ver. 8, 18, 20; Isai. 15:1 [t]ch. 50:27 [u]See ch. 46:18
17 [v][Isai. 15:4, 5; 16:7] [w][Isai. 9:4; 14:5]
18 [x]Num. 21:30; Isai. 15:2 [y][Isai. 47:1]
19 [z]Deut. 2:36; Josh. 13:9 [a][1 Sam. 4:13, 16; Nah. 2:1]
20 [v][See ver. 17 above] [b]Isai. 16:2 [s][See ver. 15 above]
21 [c]ver. 8; Num. 21:23 [d]Josh. 13:18
22 [y][See ver. 18 above] [e]Isai. 15:2; Num. 33:46
23 [f]See ver. 1 [g][Josh. 13:17; 1 Chr. 5:8]
24 [h]ver. 41; Amos 2:2 [i]ch. 49:13, 22; Isai. 63:1
25 [j][Ps. 75:10] [k][Ezek. 30:21]
26 [l]ch. 25:27; 51:39; Isai. 19:14 [m]ver. 42. Lam. 1:9 [n]ver. 39
27 [o]Zeph. 2:8; [Ezek. 25:8] [p][ch. 2:26] [q]Ps. 64:8; Lam. 2:15; Matt. 27:39
28 [r]ver. 9 [s]Ps. 55:6, 7; S. of S. 2:14
29 [t]Isai. 16:6
30 [u][ch. 50:36]
31 [v]Isai. 15:5; 16:7, 11 [w][2 Kin. 3:25]
32 [x]Num. 21:32 [y]Isai. 16:8, 9 [z]Josh. 13:19 [a][Ps. 80:11]
33 [b]Isai. 16:10
34 [c]See Isai. 15:4-6 [d]ver. 3
35 [e][Isai. 15:2; 16:12; Ezek. 20:29]
36 [f]See ver. 31 [g]Isai. 15:7
37 [h]Isai. 15:2, 3 [i][ch. 47:5] [j]ch. 49:3; Lam. 2:10; See ch. 4:8

48:19 Aroer. Southeast of Dibon, this border fortress on the Arnon River (v. 20) is here pictured anxiously watching the flight of the refugees.

48:20 Arnon. That is, in the region along the Arnon. It was the most important river in Moab.

48:28 dwell in the rock. See Is. 2:10.

48:32 Sibmah . . . Sea of Jazer. See Is. 16:8.

48:38 housetops of Moab. It was customary to offer incense upon rooftops as an act of worship (2 Kin. 23:12).

broken Moab like [k]a vessel for which no one cares, declares the LORD. 39 How it is broken! How they wail! [l]How Moab has turned his back in shame! So Moab [m]has become a derision and a horror to all that are around him."

40 For thus says the LORD:
"Behold, [n]one shall fly swiftly like an eagle
[o]and spread his wings against Moab;
41 [p]the cities shall be taken
and the strongholds seized.
[q]The heart of the warriors of Moab
shall be in that day
like the heart of [r]a woman in her birth pains;
42 Moab shall be [s]destroyed and be no longer a people,
because [t]he magnified himself against the LORD.
43 [u]Terror, pit, and snare
are before you, O inhabitant of Moab!
declares the LORD.
44 He who flees from the terror
shall fall into the pit,
and he who climbs out of the pit
shall be caught in the snare.
[v]For I will bring these things upon Moab,
the year of their punishment,
declares the LORD.
45 "In the shadow of Heshbon
fugitives stop without strength,
for fire came out from Heshbon,
flame from the house of Sihon;
it has destroyed [w]the forehead of Moab,
the crown of [w]the sons of tumult.
46 [x]Woe to you, O Moab!
The people of [y]Chemosh are undone,
for your sons have been taken captive,
and your daughters into captivity.

38 [k][ch. 22:28] 39 [l][ver. 6] [m]ver. 26 40 [n]ch. 49:22; [Deut. 28:49; Ezek. 17:3] [o][Isai. 8:8] 41 [p]ver. 24 [q][Isai. 13:7, 8] [r]See ch. 6:24 42 [s][Isai. 7:8] [t]ver. 26 43 [u]Isai. 24:17, 18; Lam. 3:47 44 [v][ch. 11:23] 45 [w]Num. 24:17 46 [x]See ver. 1 [y]ver. 13

47 [z]Yet I will restore the fortunes of Moab
in the latter days, declares the LORD."
Thus far is the judgment on Moab.

47 [z][ch. 46:27; 49:39]

Judgment on Ammon

49 [a]Concerning the Ammonites.
Thus says the LORD:
"Has Israel no sons?
Has he no heir?
Why then has [b]Milcom [c]dispossessed Gad,
and his people settled in its cities?
2 Therefore, behold, the days are coming,
declares the LORD,
when I will cause [d]the battle cry to be heard
against [e]Rabbah of the Ammonites;
it shall become a desolate [f]mound,
and its villages shall be burned with fire;
then Israel shall dispossess those
who dispossessed him,
says the LORD.
3 "Wail, O [g]Heshbon, for Ai is laid waste!
Cry out, O daughters of [e]Rabbah!
[h]put on sackcloth,
lament, and run to and fro among the hedges!
For [i]Milcom shall go into exile,
[j]with his priests and his officials.
4 Why do you boast of your valleys,[1]
[k]O faithless daughter,
[l]who trusted in her treasures, saying,
'Who will come against me?'
5 Behold, [m]I will bring terror upon you,
declares the Lord GOD of hosts,
from all who are around you,
and you shall be driven out, every
man straight before him,
with none to gather the fugitives.

Chapter 49
1 [a]ch. 25:21; [Ezek. 21:28; 25:2] [b][1 Kin. 11:5, 33; 2 Kin. 23:13] [c][Amos 1:13] 2 [d]ch. 4:19 [e]Ezek. 21:20; 25:5; Amos 1:14 [f]ch. 30:18 3 [g]ch. 48:2 [e][See ver. 2 above] [h]ch. 48:37; See ch. 4:8 [i][1 Kin. 11:5, 33; 2 Kin. 23:13] [j]ch. 48:7 4 [k]ch. 3:14 [l]ch. 48:7 5 [m][ch. 48:43]

1 Hebrew *valleys, your valley flows*

48:40 eagle. This would be Nebuchadnezzar (Ezek. 17:3).

48:45, 46 Derived from Num. 21:28, 29, but Jeremiah redirects Balaam's prophecy against the Amorites by applying it to Moab.

Sihon. He was an Amorite ruler in Moses' time, with his capital at Heshbon (Num. 21:21–30).

49:1–6 A prophecy against the Ammonites. See Ezek. 25:1–7; Amos 1:13–15. Ammon, an old enemy of Israel (Judg. 11:4–33; 1 Sam. 11:1–11; 2 Sam. 10; 1 Kin. 4:13–19), was located in Trans-Jordan just north of Moab. Like Moab, it was part of an alliance against Babylon (27:3), and like Moab it supplied troops to Nebuchadnezzar against Judah (2 Kin. 24:2). Its hostility to Gedaliah (40:13–41:3) suggests a rebellion against Babylon, probably leading to an attack that virtually ended its existence as an autonomous nation.

49:1 Milcom. The chief god of the Ammonites (32:35 note; 1 Kin. 11:5).

49:2 Rabbah. This city is identified with modern Amman in Jordan.

49:3 Heshbon. As a border town, it may have belonged to Ammon at some time also (Judg. 11:26).

Ai. Not the city of Ai familiar from the events of Josh. 8. Its location is not known.

[6]"But [n]afterward I will restore the fortunes of the Ammonites, declares the LORD."

Judgment on Edom

[7]Concerning [o]Edom.
Thus says the LORD of hosts:

[p]"Is wisdom no more in [p]Teman?
[q]Has counsel perished from the prudent?
[q]Has their wisdom vanished?
8 [r]Flee, turn back, dwell in the depths,
O inhabitants of [s]Dedan!
For I will bring the calamity of Esau upon him,
[t]the time when I punish him.
9 [u]If grape-gatherers came to you,
would they not leave [v]gleanings?
[u]If thieves came by night,
would they not destroy only enough for themselves?
10 [w]But I have stripped Esau bare;
[u]I have uncovered his hiding places,
and he is not able to conceal himself.
His children are destroyed, and his brothers,
and his neighbors; and [x]he is no more.
11 [y]Leave your fatherless children; I will keep them alive;
[y]and let your widows trust in me."

[12]For thus says the LORD: [z]"If those who
did not deserve to drink the cup must
drink it, [a]will you go unpunished? You
shall not go unpunished, but you must
drink. [13][b]For I have sworn by myself,
declares the LORD, that [c]Bozrah shall
become [d]a horror, a taunt, a waste, and a
curse, and all her cities shall be perpetual
wastes."

14 [e]I have heard a message from the LORD,
and an envoy has been sent among the nations:
[f]"Gather yourselves together and come against her,
and rise up for battle!
15 For behold, I will make you small among the nations,
despised among mankind.
16 The horror you inspire has deceived you,
and the pride of your heart,
you who live in the clefts of the rock,[1]
who hold the height of the hill.
Though you [g]make your nest as high as the eagle's,
I will bring you down from there,
declares the LORD.

[17][h]"Edom shall become a horror.
[i]Everyone who passes by it will be horrified
[i]and will hiss because of all its disasters.
[18][j]As when Sodom and Gomorrah and
their [k]neighboring cities were overthrown,
says the LORD, [l]no man shall dwell there,
[l]no man shall sojourn in her. [19][m]Behold,
[n]like a lion coming up from [o]the jungle of
the Jordan against a perennial pasture, I
will suddenly make him[2] run away from
her. And I will appoint over her whomever
I choose. [p]For who is like me? [q]Who will
summon me? [r]What shepherd can stand
before me? [20]Therefore hear the plan that
the LORD has made against [s]Edom and the
purposes that he has formed against the
inhabitants of [t]Teman: [u]Even the little ones
of the flock shall be dragged away. Surely
their fold shall be appalled at their fate.
[21]At the sound of their fall [v]the earth shall
tremble; the sound of their cry shall be
heard at the Red Sea. [22]Behold, [w]one shall
mount up and fly swiftly like an eagle and
spread his wings against [x]Bozrah, and the
heart of the warriors of Edom shall be in
that day like the heart [y]of a woman in her
birth pains."

[1] Or *of Sela* [2] Septuagint, Syriac *them*

6 [n][ver. 39; ch. 48:47] **7** [o]ch. 25:21; Isai. 34:5; Amos 1:11; Obad. 1; [Mal. 1:2]; See Ezek. 25: 12-14 [p]ver. 20; Obad. 9 [q][Isai. 19:11, 12] **8** [r]ver. 30 [s]ch. 25:23; Gen. 25:3 [t]ch. 50:27, 31; [ch. 46:21; 50:27] **9** [u]Obad. 5, 6 [v][Judg. 8:2] **10** [w]Mal. 1:3 [u][See ver. 9 above] [x]ch. 31:15; Isai. 17:14 **11** [y][Ps. 10:14, 18; 68:5] **12** [z]ch. 25:28; [Obad. 16] [a]ch. 25:29 **13** [b]See ch. 22:5 [c]ver. 22; See ch. 48:24 [d]See ch. 24:9 **14** [e]See Obad. 1-4

[f][Isai. 13:4] **16** [g][ch. 48:28] **17** [h]Ezek. 35:3, 7, 9 [i][ch. 50:13] **18** [j]See Isai. 13:19 [k][Deut. 29:23] [l]ver. 33 **19** [m]For ver. 19-21, see ch. 50:44-46 [n]See ch. 4:7 [o]See ch. 12:5 [p]See ch. 10:6 [q]Job 9:19 [r][ch. 30:21] **20** [s]Ezek. 35:3, 7, 9 [t]See ver. 7 [u]ch. 50:45 **21** [v]ch. 8:16; 50:46; [Ezek. 26:15] **22** [w]See ch. 48:40 [x]ver. 13 [y]ver. 24; See ch. 6:24

49:7–22 A prophecy against Edom. See also 27:3; Is. 21:11, 12; Ezek. 25:12–14; Amos 1:11, 12; Obad. 1–16. Edom was an old enemy of Israel (2 Sam. 8:13, 14) and had caused special bitterness by assisting Babylon against Judah.

49:7 Teman. A region of Edom representing the whole.

49:8 Esau. The brother of Jacob, whose name was another designation for Edom (Gen. 25:29, 30). See also Obad. 10.

49:13 Bozrah. The capital of Edom.

49:22 eagle. Probably Nebuchadnezzar (as 48:40), though the Edomites were also conquered decisively by Arabs during the sixth century B.C.

49:23–27 A prophecy against Syria, or Aram. Syria impinged chiefly on the northern kingdom of Israel in the Assyrian period (1 Kin. 20; Amos 1:3–5). The three states named here had fallen to Assyria in the eighth century B.C.

49:23 Damascus . . . Hamath . . . Arpad. These are major Aramean city-states.

Judgment on Damascus

23 Concerning [z]Damascus:

[a]"Hamath and [b]Arpad are confounded,
for they have heard bad news;
they melt in fear,
[c]they are troubled like the sea that
cannot be quiet.
24 [z]Damascus has become feeble, [d]she
turned to flee,
and panic seized her;
anguish and sorrows have taken hold
of her,
as [y]of a woman in labor.
25 How is [e]the famous city not
forsaken,
the city of my joy?
26 [f]Therefore her young men shall fall in
her squares,
and all her soldiers shall be
destroyed in that day,
declares the LORD of hosts.
27 And [g]I will kindle a fire in the wall of
[z]Damascus,
and it shall devour the strongholds
of [h]Ben-hadad."

Judgment on Kedar and Hazor

28 Concerning [i]Kedar and the kingdoms of
Hazor that Nebuchadnezzar king of Babylon struck down.

Thus says the LORD:
[j]"Rise up, advance against [i]Kedar!
Destroy [k]the people of the east!
29 [l]Their tents and their flocks shall be
taken,
their [l]curtains and all their goods;
their camels shall be led away from
them,
and men shall cry to them:
[m]'Terror on every side!'
30 [n]Flee, wander far away, dwell in the
depths,
O inhabitants of Hazor!
declares the LORD.
For Nebuchadnezzar king of Babylon
has made a plan against you
and formed a purpose against you.
31 [j]"Rise up, advance against a nation [o]at
ease,
[p]that dwells securely,
declares the LORD,
[p]that has no gates or bars,
that dwells alone.
32 [q]Their camels shall become plunder,
their herds of livestock a spoil.
[r]I will scatter to every wind
[s]those who cut the corners of their
hair,
and I will bring their calamity
from every side of them,
declares the LORD.
33 Hazor shall become [t]a haunt of
jackals,
an everlasting waste;
[u]no man shall dwell there;
[u]no man shall sojourn in her."

Judgment on Elam

34 The word of the LORD that came to
Jeremiah the prophet concerning [v]Elam, in
the beginning of the reign of [w]Zedekiah
king of Judah.
35 Thus says the LORD of hosts: "Behold, I
will break [x]the bow of [v]Elam, the mainstay
of their might. 36 And I will bring upon
[v]Elam the four winds from the four quarters of heaven. And I will scatter them to all
those winds, and there shall be no nation
to which those driven out of [v]Elam shall
not come. 37 I will [y]terrify [v]Elam before their
enemies and before those who seek their
life. I will bring disaster upon them, [z]my
fierce anger, declares the LORD. [a]I will send
the sword after them, until I have consumed them, 38 and I will set my throne in
[v]Elam and destroy their king and officials,
declares the LORD.
39 "But in the latter days [b]I will restore the
fortunes of [v]Elam, declares the LORD."

23 [z]Isai. 17:1; Amos 1:3 [a]1 Kin. 8:65; Zech. 9:2 [b]2 Kin. 18:34 [c]Zech. 9:4
24 [z][See ver. 23 above] [d][ch. 46:5] [y][See ver. 22 above]
25 [e][ch. 33:9]
26 [f]ch. 50:30
27 [g]See ch. 17:27 [z][See ver. 23 above] [h]1 Kin. 15:18; 20:1; 2 Kin. 6:24; 8:7; 13:3
28 [i]Isai. 21:16; 60:7 [j]ver. 14, 31 [k]Isai. 11:14; Ezek. 25:4, 10; See Judg. 6:3
29 [l]Ps. 120:5; S. of S. 1:5 [m]See ch. 6:25
30 [n]ver. 8
31 [j][See ver. 28 above] [o]Job 16:12 [p]Ezek. 38:8, 11
32 [q][Ezek. 38:12] [r]ver. 36 [s]See ch. 9:26
33 [t]See ch. 9:11 [u]ver. 18
34 [v]ch. 25:25; Gen. 14:1; Isai. 11:11; 21:2; Ezek. 32:24; Dan. 8:2 [w]2 Kin. 24:17, 18
35 [x]Isai. 22:6 [v][See ver. 34 above]
36 [v][See ver. 34 above]
37 [y][ch. 1:17] [v][See ver. 34 above] [z]See ch. 12:13 [a]See ch. 9:16
38 [v][See ver. 34 above]
39 [b][ch. 48:47] [v][See ver. 34 above]

49:28–33 A prophecy against Arabian kingdoms. Arab nomadic tribes posed a periodic threat to settled communities (Judg. 6:1–6). The present prophecy may have been occasioned by an Arab uprising against Nebuchadnezzar in 598 B.C.

49:28 Kedar. An Arab tribe well-known in the Old Testament period (Gen. 25:13; Is. 21:16, 17; 42:11).

Hazor. Also in the Arabian desert, and not the well-known Hazor in northern Israel; this name may have designated a number of Arab settlements including Teman, Buz, and Dedan (25:23, 24).

people of the east. Another designation for Arab tribal peoples (Judg. 6:3; 7:12; Job 1:3).

49:31 dwells securely . . . no gates or bars. These nomadic peoples typically lived in unwalled towns, not depending on fortified cities. See the description of Laish in Judg. 18:7. They were no match for a well-armed invader.

49:34–39 A prophecy against Elam, an important power to the east of Babylon, subjugated by Assyria, but resurgent in the Babylonian period. The prophecy possibly relates to a Babylonian containment campaign against Elam in 595 B.C.

Judgment on Babylon

50 The word that the LORD spoke concerning [c]Babylon, concerning the land
of the Chaldeans, [d]by Jeremiah the prophet:

2 "Declare among the nations and
proclaim,
set up a banner and proclaim,
conceal it not, and say:
[e]'Babylon is taken,
[f]Bel is put to shame,
Merodach is dismayed.
[e]Her images are put to shame,
her idols are dismayed.'

3 "For [g]out of the north a nation has come
up against her, [h]which shall make her land
a desolation, and none shall dwell in it;
[i]both man and beast shall flee away.

4 [j]"In those days and in that time,
declares the LORD, [j]the people of Israel and
the people of Judah shall come together,
[k]weeping as they come, and they [l]shall
seek the LORD their God. 5 [m]They shall ask
the way to Zion, with faces turned toward
it, [n]saying, 'Come, let us join ourselves to
the LORD in an [o]everlasting covenant that
will never be forgotten.'

6 [p]"My people have been lost sheep.
[q]Their shepherds have led them astray,
turning them away on the mountains.
From mountain to hill they have gone.
They have forgotten their fold. 7 All who
found them have devoured them, [r]and
their enemies have said, 'We are not guilty,
for [s]they have sinned against the LORD,
[t]their habitation of righteousness, the
LORD, [u]the hope of their fathers.'

8 [v]"Flee from the midst of Babylon, [v]and
go out of the land of the Chaldeans, and be
as male goats before the flock. 9 For behold,
I am stirring up and bringing against
Babylon [w]a gathering of great nations, from
the north country. And they shall array
themselves against her. From there she
shall be taken. Their arrows are like a
skilled warrior who does not return empty-
handed. 10 [x]Chaldea shall be plundered; all
who plunder her shall be sated, declares
the LORD.

11 [y]"Though you rejoice, though you exult,
O plunderers of my heritage,
though you frolic like a heifer in the
pasture,
and neigh like stallions,
12 your mother shall be utterly shamed,
and she who bore you shall be
disgraced.
Behold, she shall be the last of the
nations,
[z]a wilderness, a dry land, and a
desert.
13 [a]Because of the wrath of the LORD she
shall not be inhabited
but shall be an utter desolation;
[b]everyone who passes by Babylon
shall be appalled,
[b]and hiss because of all her wounds.
14 [c]Set yourselves in array against
Babylon all around,
[d]all you who bend the bow;
shoot at her, spare no arrows,
[e]for she has sinned against the LORD.
15 [f]Raise a shout against her all around;
she has surrendered;
her bulwarks have fallen;
[g]her walls are thrown down.
For [h]this is the vengeance of the LORD:
take vengeance on her;
[i]do to her as she has done.
16 Cut off from Babylon the sower,
and the one who handles the
sickle in time of harvest;
[j]because of the sword of the oppressor,
[k]every one shall turn to his own
people,
and every one shall flee to his own
land.

Chapter 50
1 [c]See Isai. 13:1–14:27; 21:1-10 [d][ch. 51:59, 60]
2 [e]Isai. 21:9 [f]See Isai. 46:1
3 [g]See ch. 1:14 [h]ver. 13, 23; ch. 51:29 [i]ch. 51:62; [Ps. 135:8]
4 [j]See ch. 3:18 [k]ch. 31:9, 18; Ezra 8:21; Ps. 126:6 [l]Hos. 3:5
5 [m][ch. 31:21] [n][Isai. 2:3] [o]See ch. 32:40
6 [p]ver. 17; Isai. 53:6; [Matt. 18:12; Luke 15:4] [q]Zech. 10:2; See Ezek. 34:1-6
7 [r][ch. 40:2, 3] [s][ver. 14] [t]ch. 31:23 [u]See ch. 14:8
8 [v]ch. 51:6, 45; See Isai. 48:20
9 [w]See ch. 25:14
10 [x][ch. 25:12]
11 [y][Lam. 4:21]
12 [z]ch. 51:43
13 [a]ver. 39 [b]See ch. 18:16
14 [c]ver. 9; ch. 51:11; Isai. 21:2 [d]ver. 29; [ch. 51:3] [e][ver. 7]
15 [f][Josh. 6:16] [g]ch. 51:58 [h]ch. 46:10; 51:6, 11 [i]ver. 29; ch. 51:56
16 [j]ch. 46:16 [k][ch. 51:9]; See Isai. 13:14

50:1–51:64 The prophecy against Babylon (cf. Is. 13:1–14:23; 21:1–9) is the climax of the book. The previous prophecies have served Jeremiah's purpose of showing that Babylon would prevail over "all the nations" (27:7) for a period. Babylon has appeared up to this point as the instrument of God's wrath. Finally, however (as in 25:17–26), "the word of the LORD" is uttered against Babylon itself, to show that its own time of judgment must come (25:11, 12). The Hebrew text of Jeremiah has placed the prophecy (actually delivered in 593 B.C.; see 51:59 note) at this point in the book so that the judgment on Babylon may occupy the climactic position. The relative length of the prophecy also shows how important Babylon is in the theology of the book.

50:2 Bel . . . Merodach. Merodach or "Marduk" was the creator and chief deity in Babylonian myth. He was also called Bel, an early form of the word "Baal" ("lord"). See also Is. 46:1.

50:3 out of the north a nation. See 1:14; 6:1. The tables are now turned on Babylon. The nation in question is not specified, but see 51:27, 28.

50:5 everlasting covenant. See 31:31–34; 32:40; 33:20, 21.

50:9 I am stirring up . . . against Babylon . . . from the north country. Cyrus is mentioned in Is. 41:25; 45:1. Members of the alliance are named in 51:27, 28.

50:12 your mother. The city of Babylon is personified.

last of the nations. She had seemed invincible (Is. 14:12–17).

17 [l]"Israel is a hunted sheep [m]driven away
by lions. [n]First the king of Assyria [o]devoured
him, and now at last [p]Nebuchadnezzar king
of Babylon [q]has gnawed his bones. **18** Therefore, thus says the LORD of hosts, the God of
Israel: Behold, [r]I am bringing punishment
on the king of Babylon and his land, [s]as I
punished the king of Assyria. **19** [t]I will
restore Israel to his pasture, and [t]he shall
feed on [u]Carmel and in [u]Bashan, and his
desire shall be satisfied on the hills of
Ephraim and in [u]Gilead. **20** In those days
and in that time, declares the LORD, [v]iniq-
uity shall be sought in Israel, and there
shall be none. And sin in Judah, and none
shall be found, for [w]I will pardon those
whom I leave as a remnant.

21 "Go up against the land of Merathaim,[1]
and against the inhabitants of
Pekod.[2]
Kill, [x]and devote them to destruction,[3]
declares the LORD,
and do all that I have commanded
you.
22 [y]The noise of battle is in the land,
and great destruction!
23 [z]How the hammer of the whole earth
is cut down and broken!
[a]How Babylon [b]has become
a horror among the nations!
24 [c]I set a snare for you and you were
taken, O Babylon,
and [d]you did not know it;
you were found and caught,
because you opposed the LORD.
25 The LORD has opened his armory
and brought out [e]the weapons of
his wrath,
for the Lord GOD of hosts has a work
to do
in the land of the Chaldeans.
26 Come against her from every quarter;
open her granaries;
[f]pile her up like heaps of grain, and
devote her to destruction;
let nothing be left of her.
27 Kill all [g]her bulls;
let them go down to the slaughter.
Woe to them, for their day has come,
[h]the time of their punishment.

28 "A voice! They [i]flee and escape from
the land of Babylon, [j]to declare in Zion the
vengeance of the LORD our God, vengeance
for [k]his temple.

29 [l]"Summon archers against Babylon, all
those who bend the bow. [l]Encamp around
her; let no one escape. [m]Repay her according to her deeds; do to her according to all
that she has done. For she has [n]proudly
defied the LORD, the Holy One of Israel.
30 [o]Therefore her young men shall fall in her
squares, and all her soldiers shall be destroyed on that day, declares the LORD.

31 "Behold, I am against you, O [n]proud
one,
declares the Lord GOD of hosts,
[p]for your day has come,
the time when I will punish you.
32 [n]The proud one shall stumble and fall,
with none to raise him up,
[q]and I will kindle a fire in his cities,
and it will devour all that is
around him.

33 "Thus says the LORD of hosts: [r]The
people of Israel are oppressed, and the people of Judah with them. All who took them
captive have held them fast; [s]they refuse to
let them go. **34** [t]Their Redeemer is strong;
[u]the LORD of hosts is his name. [v]He will
surely plead their cause, that he may give
rest to the earth, but unrest to the inhabitants of Babylon.

35 "A sword against the Chaldeans,
declares the LORD,
and against the inhabitants of
Babylon,
and against [w]her officials and her
[x]wise men!

1 *Merathaim* means *double rebellion* 2 *Pekod* means *punishment*
3 That is, set apart (devote) as an offering to the Lord (for destruction)

17 [l]See ver. 6 [m]ch. 2:15; 4:7; Isai. 5:29 [n]2 Kin. 17:6; 18:13 [o]ch. 51:34 [p]2 Kin. 24:10, 14; See 2 Kin. 25:1-11 [q][ch. 51:34]
18 [r]Isai. 10:12; 24:21; [Ps. 76:12] [s]Isai. 14:24, 25
19 [t]Ezek. 34:13, 14 [u]Mic. 7:14
20 [v][Isai. 40:2] [w]Isai. 33:24; See ch. 31:34
21 [x]ver. 26; [ch. 51:3]
22 [y]ch. 51:54
23 [z]Isai. 14:6 [a][Rev. 18:19, 21] [b]ver. 3, 13
24 [c][Ps. 141:9] [d][ch. 51:31; Dan. 5:30]
25 [e]Isai. 13:5
26 [f][Neh. 4:2]
27 [g][Ps. 22:12; Isai. 34:7, 8] [h]ch. 46:21
28 [i][ver. 8] [j]ch. 51:10; Ps. 64:9 [k][ch. 51:11; 52:13; Dan. 5:3, 23]
29 [l][ver. 14; Job 16:13] [m]ch. 25:14 [n]Isai. 47:10
30 [o]ch. 49:26
31 [n][See ver. 29 above] [p]ver. 27; ch. 49:8
32 [n][See ver. 29 above] [q]See ch. 17:27
33 [r][ver. 17] [s][Isai. 14:17]
34 [t]See Isai. 43:14 [u]See ch. 10:16 [v]ch. 51:36; Isai. 51:22
35 [w]ch. 51:57; Dan. 5:30 [x]Dan. 4:6

50:19 Carmel . . . Bashan . . . hills of Ephraim and in Gilead. These are the most fertile parts of Israel.

50:21 Merathaim . . . Pekod. These words are puns on Babylonian place-names (Marratu, Puqudu). The Hebrew words mean "double rebellion" and "punishment."

50:24 taken . . . you did not know it. The Persian defeat of Babylon was unexpected.

50:27 bulls. That is, Babylon's army (46:15 note).

50:28 They flee. Jewish escapees from Babylon returned to Jerusalem.

vengeance for his temple. The burning of the temple (52:13) was the definitive destruction of Jerusalem. The Lord ties His vengeance on Babylon specifically to that.

50:29 the Holy One of Israel. This name for God is frequent in Isaiah.

50:34 Redeemer. See note 31:11.

36 A sword against the diviners,
that they may become fools!
A sword against her [y]warriors,
that they may be destroyed!
37 A sword against her horses and
against her chariots,
and against all [z]the foreign troops
in her midst,
that [a]they may become women!
[b]A sword against all her treasures,
that they may be plundered!
38 [c]A drought against her waters,
that they may be dried up!
[d]For it is a land of images,
and they are mad over idols.

39 [e]"Therefore wild beasts shall dwell
with hyenas in Babylon, and ostriches shall
dwell in her. She shall never again have
people, nor be inhabited for all generations. 40 [f]As when God overthrew Sodom
and Gomorrah and their neighboring
cities, declares the LORD, [g]so no man shall
dwell there, and no son of man shall
sojourn in her.

41 [h]"Behold, a people comes from the
north;
a mighty nation and many kings
are stirring from the farthest parts
of the earth.
42 They lay hold of bow and spear;
they are cruel and have no mercy.
The sound of them is like the roaring
of the sea;
they ride on horses,
arrayed as a man for battle
against you, O daughter of
Babylon!

43 "The king of Babylon heard the report
of them,
and his hands fell helpless;
anguish seized him,
pain as of a woman in labor.

44 [i]"Behold, like a lion coming up from the
thicket of the Jordan against a perennial pasture, I will suddenly make them run away
from her, and I will appoint over her
whomever I choose. For who is like me?
Who will summon me? What shepherd [j]can
stand before me? 45 Therefore hear [k]the plan
that the LORD has made against Babylon,
[k]and the purposes that he has formed
against the land of the Chaldeans: [l]Surely
the little ones of their flock shall be dragged
away; surely their fold shall be appalled at
their fate. 46 [m]At the sound of the capture of
Babylon the earth shall tremble, and her cry
shall be heard among the nations."

The Utter Destruction of Babylon

51 Thus says the LORD:
"Behold, I will stir up [n]the
spirit of a destroyer
against Babylon,
against the inhabitants of
Leb-kamai,[1]
2 and I will send to Babylon winnowers,
and [o]they shall winnow her,
and they shall empty her land,
when they come against her from
every side
[p]on the day of trouble.
3 [q]Let not the archer bend his bow,
and let him not stand up in his
armor.
Spare not her young men;
[r]devote to destruction[2] all her
army.
4 They shall fall down slain in the land
of the Chaldeans,
[s]and wounded in her streets.
5 [t]For Israel and Judah have not been
forsaken
by their God, the LORD of hosts,
but the land of the Chaldeans[3] is full
of guilt
against the Holy One of Israel.

6 [u]"Flee from the midst of Babylon;
let every one save his life!
[v]Be not cut off in her punishment,
[w]for this is the time of the LORD's
vengeance,
the repayment he is rendering her.
7 Babylon was [x]a golden cup in the
LORD's hand,
[y]making all the earth drunken;
[z]the nations drank of her wine;
therefore the nations went mad.
8 [a]Suddenly Babylon has fallen and
been broken;
[b]wail for her!
[c]Take balm for her pain;
perhaps she may be healed.

36 [y]ch. 51:57
37 [z]See ch. 25:20 [a]ch. 51:30 [b][Isai. 45:3]
38 [c]Isai. 44:27; [ch. 51:36] [d]ver. 2; ch. 51:47, 52
39 [e]Isai. 13:21, 22
40 [f]Gen. 19:25; See Isai. 13:19 [g]ch. 51:43
41 [h]For ver. 41-43, see ch. 6:22-24
44 [i]For ver. 44-46, see ch. 49:19-21 [j]Job 41:10
45 [k]ch. 51:11, 12, 29; Isai. 14:24
[l]ch. 49:20
46 [m]See ch. 49:21
Chapter 51
1 [n][ch. 4:11; Isai. 21:1]
2 [o][Matt. 3:12]; See ch. 15:7 [p][ch. 2:28]
3 [q][ch. 50:14, 29] [r][ch. 50:21]
4 [s]ch. 49:26
5 [t]See Isai. 54:5-7
6 [u]ver. 45; ch. 50:8 [v][Gen. 19:15] [w]ch. 50:15
7 [x][Ps. 75:8; Rev. 17:4] [y]Rev. 14:8 [z]See ch. 25:15, 16
8 [a]See Isai. 21:9 [b]Isai. 13:6; Rev. 18:9, 11, 19; [ch. 48:20] [c][ch. 46:11]

1 A code name for Chaldea 2 That is, set apart (devote) as an offering to the Lord (for destruction) 3 Hebrew *their land*

9 We would have healed Babylon,
but she was not healed.
[d] Forsake her, and [e] let us go
each to his own country,
for [f] her judgment has reached up to
heaven
and has been lifted up even to the
skies.
10 [g] The LORD has brought about our
vindication;
[h] come, let us declare in Zion
the work of the LORD our God.

11 [i] "Sharpen the arrows!
Take up the shields!

[j] The LORD has stirred up the spirit of the
kings of [k] the Medes, because [l] his purpose
concerning Babylon is to destroy it, [m] for
that is the vengeance of the LORD, the vengeance for [m] his temple.

12 [n] "Set up a standard against the walls of
Babylon;
[o] make the watch strong;
set up watchmen;
prepare the ambushes;
[l] for the LORD has both planned and
done
what he spoke concerning the
inhabitants of Babylon.
13 [p] O you who dwell by many waters,
rich in treasures,
your end has come;
the thread of your life is cut.
14 [q] The LORD of hosts has sworn by
himself:
Surely I will fill you with men, [r] as
many as locusts,
[s] and they shall raise the shout of
victory over you.

15 [t] "It is he who made the earth by his
power,
who established the world by his
wisdom,
and by his understanding stretched
out the heavens.
16 When he utters his voice there is a
tumult of waters in the heavens,
and he makes the mist rise from
the ends of the earth.
He makes lightning for the rain,
and he brings forth the wind from
his storehouses.
17 Every man is stupid and without
knowledge;
every goldsmith is put to shame by
his idols,
for his images are false,
and there is no breath in them.
18 They are worthless, a work of
delusion;
at the time of their punishment
they shall perish.
19 Not like these is he who is the
portion of Jacob,
for he is the one who formed all
things,
and Israel is the tribe of his
inheritance;
the LORD of hosts is his name.

20 "You are my hammer and weapon of
war:
with you I [u] break nations in pieces;
with you I destroy kingdoms;
21 with you I break in pieces the horse
and his rider;
with you I break in pieces the
chariot and the charioteer;
22 with you I break in pieces man and
woman;
with you I break in pieces [v] the old
man and the youth;
with you I break in pieces [v] the young
man and the young woman;
23 with you I break in pieces the
shepherd and his flock;
with you I break in pieces the farmer
and his team;
with you I break in pieces
[w] governors and commanders.

24 [x] "I will repay Babylon and all the
inhabitants of Chaldea before your very
eyes for all the evil that they have done in
Zion, declares the LORD.

25 "Behold, I am against you,
O destroying mountain,
declares the LORD,
which destroys the whole earth;

9 [d] ver. 6, 45; ch. 50:8 [e] [ch. 50:16]; See Isai. 13:14 [f] Rev. 18:5
10 [g] Ps. 37:6; [ch. 23:6] [h] ch. 50:28
11 [i] ch. 46:4 [j] See Isai. 13:17 [k] 2 Kin. 17:6; Dan. 5:31 [l] [ch. 50:45] [m] ch. 50:28
12 [n] ver. 27; ch. 50:2; [Isai. 13:2] [o] [Isai. 21:5; Nah. 2:1] [l] [See ver. 11 above]
13 [p] Rev. 17:1, 15; [ver. 36]
14 [q] See ch. 22:5 [r] [Ps. 105:34; Joel 1:4; 2:25] [s] Isai. 16:9
15 [t] For ver. 15-19, see ch. 10:12-16
20 [u] [Dan. 7:7, 19, 23]
22 [v] 2 Chr. 36:17; [Isai. 13:16, 18]
23 [w] ver. 28, 57
24 [x] ch. 50:15, 29; [Ps. 137:8]

51:11 Medes. Babylon was conquered by an alliance of Medes and Persians (Introduction: Characteristics and Themes). See also Is. 13:17; 21:2.

51:13 by many waters. Babylon was renowned for its irrigation channels, fed by the Euphrates River.

51:14 sworn by himself. See Gen. 22:16 and note.

51:20 You are my hammer. Apparently addressed to Babylon; vv. 20–23 should be taken together with vv. 24–26. Babylon was God's "hammer" (50:23) against the nations, but later Babylon's own sin would cause it to be judged.

I will stretch out my hand against you,
and roll you down from the crags,
[y] and make you a burnt mountain.
26 No [z] stone shall be taken from you
for a corner
and no stone for a foundation,
but you shall be [a] a perpetual waste,
declares the LORD.

27 [b] "Set up a standard on the earth;
[c] blow the trumpet among the
nations;
[d] prepare [e] the nations for war
against her;
summon against her [f] the kingdoms,
[g] Ararat, Minni, and [h] Ashkenaz;
appoint a [i] marshal against her;
[j] bring up horses like bristling
locusts.
28 [d] Prepare [e] the nations for war
against her,
the kings of [k] the Medes, [l] with their
governors [l] and deputies,
and every [m] land under their
dominion.
29 [n] The land trembles and writhes in pain,
[o] for the LORD's purposes against
Babylon stand,
to make the land of Babylon a
desolation,
without inhabitant.
30 The warriors of Babylon have ceased
fighting;
they remain in their strongholds;
their strength has failed;
[p] they have become women;
[q] her dwellings are on fire;
[r] her bars are broken.
31 One [s] runner runs to meet another,
and one messenger to meet another,
to tell the king of Babylon
that his city is taken on every side;
32 the fords have been [t] seized,
the marshes are burned with fire,
and the soldiers are in panic.
33 For thus says the LORD of hosts, the
God of Israel:
[u] The daughter of Babylon is like [u] a
threshing floor
at the time when it is trodden;
yet a little while
and [v] the time of her harvest will
come."

34 "Nebuchadnezzar the king of Babylon
[w] has devoured me;
he has crushed me;
he has made me an empty vessel;
[x] he has swallowed me like [y] a
monster;
he has filled his stomach with my
delicacies;
he has rinsed me out.[1]
35 The violence done to me and to my
kinsmen be upon Babylon,"
let the inhabitant of Zion say.
"My blood be upon the inhabitants of
Chaldea,"
let Jerusalem say.
36 Therefore thus says the LORD:
"Behold, [z] I will plead your cause
and take vengeance for you.
[a] I will dry up her sea
and [b] make her fountain dry,
37 and Babylon shall become [c] a heap of
ruins,
[d] the haunt of jackals,
[e] a horror [e] and a hissing,
without inhabitant.

38 [f] "They shall roar together [g] like lions;
they shall growl like lions' cubs.
39 [h] While they are inflamed [h] I will
prepare them a feast
and [i] make them drunk, that they
may become merry,
[i] then sleep a perpetual sleep
and not wake, declares the LORD.
40 I will bring them down like lambs to
the slaughter,
like rams and male goats.

41 "How [j] Babylon[2] is taken,
[k] the praise of the whole earth
[l] seized!
How Babylon has become
a horror among the nations!
42 [m] The sea has come up on Babylon;
she is covered with its tumultuous
waves.

25 [y] Rev. 8:8; [Rev. 18:8, 9] 26 [z] [Ps. 118:22; Isai. 28:16] [a] ver. 62; ch. 25:12 27 [b] See ver. 12 [c] See ch. 4:5 [d] See ch. 6:4 [e] See ch. 25:14 [f] [ch. 50:41] [g] Gen. 8:4; 2 Kin. 19:37 [h] Gen. 10:3; 1 Chr. 1:6 [i] Nah. 3:17 [j] See ver. 14 28 [d] [See ver. 27 above] [e] [See ver. 27 above] [k] See ver. 11 [l] ver. 23, 57 [m] [ch. 34:1] 29 [n] See ch. 8:16 [o] ch. 50:45 30 [p] ch. 50:37; [Isai. 19:16] [q] Isai. 47:14 [r] Lam. 2:9; Nah. 3:13 31 [s] [2 Chr. 30:6] 32 [t] ver. 41 33 [u] See Isai. 21:10 [v] [Isai. 17:5; Joel 3:13; Rev. 14:15] 34 [w] ch. 50:17 [x] ver. 44 [y] Ps. 74:13 36 [z] ch. 50:34 [a] Isai. 44:27; [ch. 50:38] [b] [ver. 13] 37 [c] Isai. 25:2 [d] Isai. 13:22 [e] See ch. 18:16 38 [f] [Amos 3:4] [g] Nah. 2:11, 12 39 [h] [Isai. 21:5] [i] ver. 57 41 [j] ch. 25:26 [k] [Isai. 13:19] [l] ver. 32 42 [m] [ver. 55; Isai. 8:7, 8]

[1] Or *he has expelled me* [2] Hebrew *Sheshach*, a code name for Babylon

51:27 Ararat, Minni, and Ashkenaz. Assyrian administrative districts in Armenia.

51:30 her dwellings are on fire. Babylon's sacking of Judah (cf. 21:10) is being revenged by her Median conquerors.

51:33 daughter of Babylon. This figure both personifies Babylon and alludes to its women, made vulnerable by defeat. See 50:42; Lam. 1:6 and note.

51:36 plead . . . vengeance. See 50:15. The metaphors of revenge and courtroom judgment are mixed here.

43 Her cities have become a horror,
[n] a land of drought and a desert,
[o] a land in which no one dwells,
and through which no son of man
passes.
44 And I will punish [p] Bel in Babylon,
and [q] take out of his mouth [r] what
he has swallowed.
[s] The nations shall no longer flow to
him;
[t] the wall of Babylon has fallen.

45 "Go out of the midst of her, [u] my
people!
Let every one save his life
from [v] the fierce anger of the LORD!
46 Let not your heart faint, and be not
fearful
[w] at the report heard in the land,
[x] when a report comes in one year
and afterward a report in another
year,
and violence is in the land,
[x] and ruler is against ruler.

47 "Therefore, behold, the days are
coming
when [y] I will punish the images of
Babylon;
[z] her whole land shall be put to shame,
and all her slain shall fall in the
midst of her.
48 [a] Then the heavens and the earth,
and all that is in them,
shall sing for joy over Babylon,
[b] for the destroyers shall come
against them out of the north,
declares the LORD.
49 Babylon must fall for the slain of
Israel,
[c] just as for Babylon have fallen the
slain of all the earth.

50 [d] "You who have escaped from the
sword,
go, do not stand still!
Remember the LORD from far away,
and let Jerusalem come into your
mind:
51 [e] 'We are put to shame, for we have
heard reproach;
[e] dishonor has covered our face,
[f] for foreigners have come
into the holy places of the LORD's
house.'

52 "Therefore, behold, the days are
coming, declares the LORD,
when [y] I will execute judgment
upon her images,
[g] and through all her land
the wounded shall groan.
53 Though Babylon should [h] mount up
to heaven,
and though she should [i] fortify her
strong height,
yet destroyers would come from me
against her,
declares the LORD.

54 [j] "A voice! A cry from Babylon!
The noise of great destruction from
the land of the Chaldeans!
55 For the LORD is laying Babylon waste
and stilling her mighty voice.
[k] Their waves roar like many waters;
the noise of their voice is raised,
56 for a destroyer has come upon her,
upon Babylon;
her warriors are taken;
their bows are broken in pieces,
[l] for the LORD is a God of
recompense;
he will surely repay.
57 [m] I will make drunk her officials and
her wise men,
[n] her governors, her commanders,
and her warriors;
they shall sleep a perpetual sleep and
not wake,
declares [o] the King, whose name is
the LORD of hosts.

58 "Thus says the LORD of hosts:
The broad [p] wall of Babylon
shall be leveled to the ground,
[q] and her high gates
shall be burned with fire.

43 [n] ch. 50:12 [o] ch. 50:40
44 [p] ch. 50:2; See Isai. 46:1 [q] ver. 34; [Ezra 1:7, 8] [r] ver. 34 [s] [ch. 31:12; Isai. 2:2] [t] ver. 58
45 [u] See ver. 6 [v] See ch. 12:13
46 [w] [Isai. 37:7] [x] Matt. 24:6, 7
47 [y] [ch. 50:2] [z] [ch. 50:12]
48 [a] [Rev. 18:20]; See Isai. 44:23 [b] ch. 50:3
49 [c] [ver. 24]
50 [d] [ch. 44:28]
51 [e] ch. 7:19; Ps. 44:15, 16 [f] Lam. 1:10
52 [y] [See ver. 47 above] [g] Job 24:12; Ezek. 26:15
53 [h] [ver. 25]; See Isai. 14:13 [i] [ch. 49:16]
54 [j] ch. 50:22
55 [k] [ver. 42]; See ch. 5:22
56 [l] ch. 50:15; Isai. 59:18
57 [m] ver. 39 [n] ver. 23, 28 [o] See ch. 46:18
58 [p] ver. 44; ch. 50:15 [q] [Isai. 45:2]

51:44 what he has swallowed. He "swallowed" the nations taken into exile and their treasures. Judah's treasures were restored by Cyrus's decree (Ezra 1:5–11).

wall of Babylon. An enormously wide double wall, further protected by an intervening moat.

51:51 The exiles express their grief over the occupation of the temple by Nebuchadnezzar in 586 B.C., perhaps feeling that this defilement can never be cleansed.

51:53 Though Babylon should mount up to heaven. Probably this is a reference to its lofty ziggurats, symbols of its religious pride (Gen. 11:4).

51:58 high gates. The Ishtar Gate was known for its great height.

labor . . . the nations. The labor of subject nations in building Babylon's fortifications will be of no use when God brings His judgment.

[r]The peoples labor for nothing,
and [s]the nations weary themselves
only for fire."

59 The word that Jeremiah the prophet
commanded Seraiah [t]the son of Neriah, son
of Mahseiah, when he went with Zedekiah
king of Judah to Babylon, [u]in the fourth year
of his reign. Seraiah was the quartermaster.
60 [v]Jeremiah wrote in a book all the disaster
that should come upon Babylon, [w]all these
words that are written concerning Babylon.
61 And Jeremiah said to Seraiah: "When you
come to Babylon, see that you read all these
words, 62 and say, 'O LORD, you have said
concerning this place that you will cut it off,
so [x]that nothing shall dwell in it, neither
man nor beast, and it shall be [y]desolate forever.' 63 When you finish reading this book,
[z, a]tie a stone to it [z]and cast it into the midst
of the Euphrates, 64 and say, [z]'Thus shall
Babylon sink, to rise no more, because of
the disaster that I am bringing upon her,
[b]and they shall become exhausted.'"
Thus far are the words of Jeremiah.

58 [r]Hab. 2:13 [s]ver. 64
59 [t][ch. 32:12] [u][ch. 28:1]
60 [v][ch. 36:2] [w]See ver. 1-58; ch. 50:1-46
62 [x]ch. 50:3 [y]ver. 26
63 [z][ch. 19:10, 11] [a][Rev. 18:21]
64 [z][See ver. 63 above] [b]ver. 58

Chapter 52
1 [c]For ver. 1-27, see 2 Kin. 24:18–25:21
2 [d]2 Kin. 23:37; See ch. 22:13-17
4 [e]For ver. 4-16, see ch. 39:1-10

The Fall of Jerusalem Recounted

52 [c]Zedekiah was twenty-one years old
when he became king; and he
reigned eleven years in Jerusalem. His
mother's name was Hamutal the daughter
of Jeremiah of Libnah. 2 And he did what
was evil in the sight of the LORD, [d]accord-
ing to all that Jehoiakim had done. 3 For
because of the anger of the LORD things
came to the point in Jerusalem and Judah
that he cast them out from his presence.

And Zedekiah rebelled against the king
of Babylon. 4 [e]And in the ninth year of his
reign, in the tenth month, on the tenth day
of the month, Nebuchadnezzar king of
Babylon came with all his army against
Jerusalem, and laid siege to it. And they
built siegeworks all around it. 5 So the city
was besieged till the eleventh year of King
Zedekiah. 6 On the ninth day of the fourth
month the famine was so severe in the city
that there was no food for the people of the
land. 7 Then a breach was made in the city,
and all the men of war fled and went out

51:59 Seraiah the son of Neriah. An official in Zedekiah's administration, he was responsible for this expedition's billeting en route. He is the brother of Baruch, Jeremiah's scribe (32:12).

went with Zedekiah . . . to Babylon, in the fourth year of his reign. That is, in 593 B.C. The expedition may have been in response to a summons to explain Zedekiah's part in the uprising against Nebuchadnezzar (27:3 note).

51:60 a book. It may have contained the prophecies in chs. 50 and 51. See 36:2.

51:63, 64 This final symbolic act (13:1–11 note) reinforced the last word of Jeremiah, that Babylon would fall.

52:1–34 The final chapter of Jeremiah is an appendix describing the fall of Jerusalem and reminding the reader that Jeremiah's prophecies were fulfilled. Despite its message of divine judgment for sin, the Book of Jeremiah ends (like 2 Kings) on a hopeful note by calling attention to the mercy shown to King Jehoiachin of Judah while in Babylonian exile (52:31–34; cf. 2 Kin. 25:27–30).

52:1 Jeremiah of Libnah. Not Jeremiah the prophet, who was from Anathoth (1:1).

(Medo-) Babylonian Empire (560 B.C.) In 605 B.C. Nebuchadnezzar's two-year siege of Carchemish proved successful, and most of the Assyrian Empire rapidly became the Babylonian Empire. In 587 B.C. Nebuchadnezzar conquered all of Judah, besieging and destroying Jerusalem and the Jewish temple in the process. At its Zenith in 560 B.C. Babylon ruled the entire fertile crescent and Arabia, although Egypt regained autonomy.

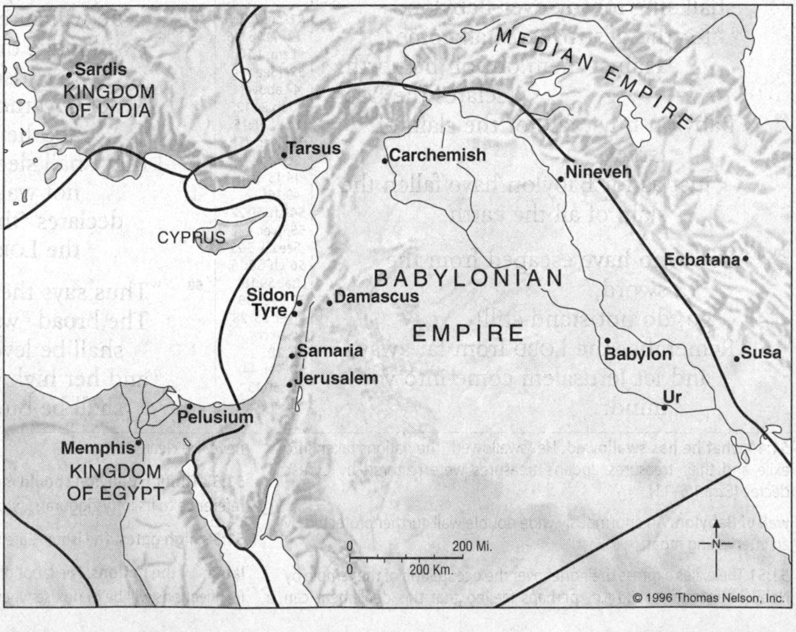

from the city by night by the way of a gate
between the two walls, by the king's garden, while the Chaldeans were around the
city. And they went in the direction of the
Arabah. 8 But the army of the Chaldeans
pursued the king and overtook Zedekiah in
the plains of Jericho. And all his army was
scattered from him. 9 Then they captured
the king and brought him up to the king of
Babylon at Riblah in the land of Hamath,
and he passed sentence on him. 10 The king
of Babylon slaughtered the sons of Zedekiah before his eyes, and also slaughtered
all the officials of Judah at [f]Riblah. 11 [g]He
put out the eyes of Zedekiah, and bound
him in chains, and the king of Babylon
took him to Babylon, and put him in
prison [g]till the day of his death.

The Temple Burned

12 [h]In the fifth month, on [i]the tenth day
of the month—that was [j]the nineteenth
year of King Nebuchadnezzar, king of
Babylon—Nebuzaradan the captain of the
bodyguard, who [k]served the king of
Babylon, entered Jerusalem. 13 And he
burned the house of the LORD, and the
king's house and all the houses of Jerusalem; every great house he burned
down. 14 And all the army of the Chaldeans,
who were with the captain of the guard,
broke down all the walls around Jerusalem.
15 And Nebuzaradan the captain of the guard
carried away captive some of the poorest of
the people and the rest of the people who
were left in the city and [l]the deserters who
had deserted to the king of Babylon, together with the rest of the artisans. 16 But
Nebuzaradan the captain of the guard left
some of the poorest of the land to be vinedressers and plowmen.

17 And the [m]pillars of bronze that were in
the house of the LORD, and the stands and
the [n]bronze sea that were in the house of
the LORD, the Chaldeans broke in pieces,
and [o]carried all the bronze to Babylon.
18 And they took away [p]the pots and the
shovels and the snuffers and the basins and
the dishes for incense and all the vessels of
bronze used in the temple service; 19 [q]also
the small bowls and the fire pans and the
basins and the pots and [r]the lampstands
and [s]the dishes for incense [s]and the bowls
for drink offerings. What was of gold the
captain of the guard took away as gold, and
what was of silver, as silver. 20 As for the
two pillars, the one sea, [t]the twelve bronze
bulls that were under the sea,[1] and the
stands, which Solomon the king had made
for the house of the LORD, the bronze of all
these things was beyond weight. 21 As for
the pillars, the height of the one pillar was
eighteen cubits,[2] [u]its circumference was
twelve cubits, and its thickness was four
fingers, and it was hollow. 22 On it was a
capital of bronze. The height of the one
capital was [v]five cubits. A network and
pomegranates, all of bronze, were around
the capital. And the second pillar had the
same, with pomegranates. 23 There were
ninety-six pomegranates on the sides; all
the pomegranates were a hundred upon
the network all around.

The People Exiled to Babylon

24 And the captain of the guard took
[w]Seraiah the chief priest, and [x]Zephaniah
the second priest, and the three keepers of
the threshold; 25 and from the city he took
an officer who had been in command of
the men of war, and [y]seven men of the
king's council, who were found in the city;
and the secretary of the commander of the
army who mustered the people of the land;
and sixty men of the people of the land,
who were found in the midst of the city.
26 And Nebuzaradan the captain of the
guard took them and brought them to the
king of Babylon at [z]Riblah. 27 And the king
of Babylon struck them down, and put
them to death at [z]Riblah in the land of
Hamath. So Judah was taken into exile out
of its land.

28 This is the number of the people whom
Nebuchadnezzar carried away captive: [a]in
the seventh year, 3,023 Judeans; 29 [b]in the
eighteenth year of Nebuchadnezzar he
carried away captive from Jerusalem 832
persons; 30 in the twenty-third year of

10 [f]ver. 26, 27 11 [g][Ezek. 12:13] 12 [h]ch. 1:3 [i][2 Kin. 25:8] [j][ver. 29] [k]ch. 40:10 15 [l]See ch. 37:13 17 [m]ch. 27:19; See 2 Chr. 4:12-15 [n]2 Chr. 4:2, 10 [o]See ch. 27:22 18 [p]2 Kin. 25:14 19 [q]1 Kin. 7:50; 2 Kin. 25:15 [r]1 Kin. 7:49 [s]Ex. 25:29; 37:16 20 [t]1 Kin. 7:25, 44 21 [u]1 Kin. 7:15 22 [v]1 Kin. 7:16; [2 Kin. 25:17] 24 [w][1 Chr. 6:14, 15] [x][ch. 29:25] 25 [y][Esth. 1:14] 26 [z]ver. 9, 10 27 [z][See ver. 26 above] 28 [a][2 Kin. 24:12, 14] 29 [b][ver. 12]

[1] Hebrew lacks *the sea* [2] A *cubit* was about 18 inches or 45 centimeters

52:12 the tenth day. 2 Kin. 25:8 has the "seventh day." One or the other text could be a copyist's error.

52:22 five. 2 Kin. 25:17 has "three." See note on v. 12.

52:25 seven. 2 Kin. 25:19 has "five." See note on v. 12.

52:28–30 These verses refer to the two main deportations of Jews to Babylon, in 597 B.C. ("the seventh year") and 586 B.C. (the "eighteenth year"; "nineteenth" in v. 12 is due to an alternate way of counting). A third, smaller deportation is also mentioned. The numbers here are smaller than those in 2 Kin. 24:14, 16, and may count only adult males.

Nebuchadnezzar, Nebuzaradan the captain of the guard carried away captive of the Judeans 745 persons; all the persons were 4,600.

Jehoiachin Released from Prison

31 [c]And in the thirty-seventh year of the exile of Jehoiachin king of Judah, in the twelfth month, on the twenty-fifth day of the month, Evil-merodach king of Babylon, in the year that he became king, lifted up the head of [d]Jehoiachin king of Judah and brought him out of prison.
32 And he spoke kindly to him, and gave him a seat above the seats of [e]the kings who were with him in Babylon.
33 So Jehoiachin put off his prison garments. And every day of his life he dined regularly at the king's table,
34 and for his allowance, a regular allowance was given him by the king according to his daily need, until the day of his death as long as he lived.

31 [c]For ver. 31-34, see 2 Kin. 25:27-30 [d]ch. 37:1; See ch. 22:24-30
32 [e][ch. 27:3]

52:31 twenty-fifth. 2 Kin. 25:27 has "twenty-seventh." See note on v. 12.

THE BOOK OF

Lamentations

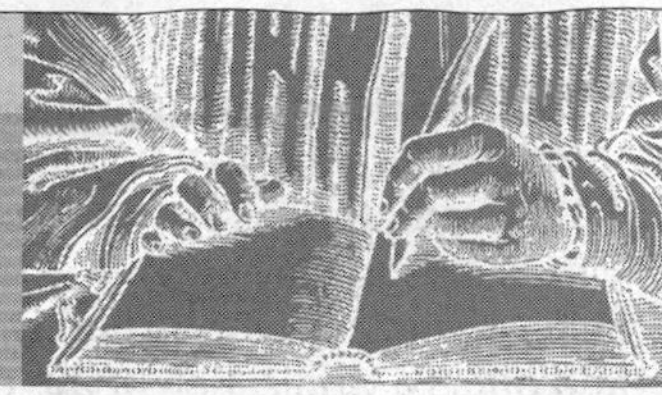

AUTHOR

The Book of Lamentations is traditionally attributed to the prophet Jeremiah. This has been true at least since the time of the Septuagint, the Greek translation of the Old Testament (c. 250 B.C.), where a note about the prophet's authorship of the book appears as a heading before the first verse. The idea of Jeremiah as the author may have been encouraged by 2 Chr. 35:25, where we are told that the prophet composed laments for King Josiah. There is no direct evidence in the book itself that Jeremiah was its author, although passages in the work distinctly recall his character and language, especially ch. 3 (Lam. 3:48–51; Jer. 14:17). However, since the book consists of five different poems that vary somewhat in style, sometimes seeming to be spoken by an individual (ch. 3) and sometimes by a community (ch. 5), it may be that the poems come from different pens.

DATE AND OCCASION

The link between Lamentations and Jeremiah remains plausible, however, not only because of similar expressions, but also because of the setting and theme of the poems. The setting is clearly Judah, particularly Jerusalem, and almost certainly the period after the fall of the kingdom of Judah to the Babylonians in 586 B.C. and before the restoration of exiles in 538 B.C. The lament concerning the loss of Judah's king (2:2, 9), in distinction from other devastations of Jerusalem, fixes this occasion for the laments.

A setting during the period of the Babylonian exile makes Lamentations a fitting sequel to the Book of Jeremiah. As Jeremiah had foretold the fall of Jerusalem, Lamentations expresses the pain of the event itself.

CHARACTERISTICS AND THEMES

The five chapters of the book are five poems. These poems take the form of laments, such as appear in other books of the Old Testament, principally the Psalms. Laments (both of the community and the individual) have certain typical characteristics, of which the most common are: (a) complaint about adversity, which the Lord either tolerated or even caused; (b) confession of trust; (c) appeal for deliverance, on the grounds of the Lord's character and His covenant; and (d) certainty of a hearing, often with an assurance that the enemies and persecutors will in turn experience the wrath of God (Ps. 74). The Book of Lamentations has these typical marks, though it represents a unique set of variations upon them. It is sometimes compared with a particular kind of lament, the funeral lament (Amos 5:1–3), but it does not quite fit this category, because Jerusalem is not uniformly portrayed as "dead."

The clearest evidence for meter in Hebrew poetry is the Book of Lamentations, which seems to use a line of five beats divided three-two. This meter is called *Qinah*, after the Hebrew name for Lamentations. It is most often found in poetry of this sorrowful kind.

A second poetic form found in Lamentations is the acrostic, in which lines or sets of lines are arranged according to the twenty-two letters of the Hebrew alphabet. Each line or group of lines begins with the succeeding letter. This method may indicate that the poet is giving a complete treatment of the subject matter. The acrostic also provides a form for the literary expression of grief, allowing the writer to deal with themes that are almost too deep for words.

The purpose of Lamentations cannot be stated in a single word. In a sense its production was itself a way of coming to terms with the destruction of Zion. The center of gravity is the wrath of God against His people. God's wrath is taken to be just. Judah had sinned, and the prophets had given God's warning. Amos had spoken long before of a day of the Lord against His people (Amos 5:18), a day that now had come (Lam. 1:12). Lamentations does not express total perplexity, as Job may at times appear to do. Instead, it justifies God's punishment of Judah and offers a vindication of the prophets who had predicted it.

Lamentations is anything but a work of passive resignation. God's wrath is accepted, but not without great emotional resistance. Could God behave like the enemy of His own people, and drive them to terrors that are painful even to describe (2:4, 5, 20–22)? Although the writer understands the justice of God, the agony and bewilderment of the event can be freely expressed. The book retains its power in times of anguish and sorrow.

Yet in his anguish this poet of the Exile is able to affirm that God is still merciful and faithful (3:22–36). This is the covenant God of Abraham, Isaac, and Jacob, whose faithfulness to the patriarchs was a continuing foundation for new appeals to Israel and Judah to put their trust in Him (Mic. 7:20). Lamentations may be counted, perhaps with Abraham himself, as one of the supreme examples in the Old Testament of faith in God. Jeremiah had prophesied that there would be a definite end to the Babylonian exile (Jer. 25:11). Lamentations looks for such an end, and even hopes that Judah's enemies will be judged for their crimes against her. In this hope there is an understanding of the sovereignty of God over all the nations, the sovereignty that embraces all mysteries (3:37–39). In the days before His own cry of abandonment (Matt. 27:46) and the mystery of His redemptive suffering, Jesus made His own lament over Jerusalem (Matt. 23:37–39; Luke 13:34, 35). The solemnity and compassion of His words expresses the goodness and severity of God that undergirds the gospel (Rom. 11:22, 23).

Lamentations points beyond the humiliation of Jerusalem to the humiliation and exaltation of Christ. With this anchor, the world can know that God is good, and He will do good in His time "... to those who wait for him" (3:25).

OUTLINE OF LAMENTATIONS

I. Jerusalem Once Great But Now Devastated (ch. 1)
II. The Lord's Anger with Judah (ch. 2)
III. The Grief of the Community (ch. 3)
IV. Zion's Degradation (ch. 4)
V. Disaster and Petition (ch. 5)

How Lonely Sits the City

1 [a]How lonely sits the city
that was full of people!
How like [b]a widow has she become,
she who was great among the
nations!
She who was [c]a princess among the
provinces
has become [d]a slave.

2 [e]She weeps bitterly in the night,
with tears on her cheeks;
[f]among all her lovers
she has [g]none to comfort her;
[h]all her friends have dealt
treacherously with her;
they have become her
enemies.

3 [i]Judah has gone into exile because
of affliction
and hard servitude;
[j]she dwells now among the
nations,
[k]but finds no resting place;
her pursuers have all overtaken her
in the midst of her distress.[1]

Chapter 1
1 [a][Jer. 7:34] [b][Jer. 15:8] [c][ch. 5:16; Ezra 4:20; Eccles. 2:8] [d]Isai. 31:8
2 [e]Ps. 6:6; Jer. 9:1; 13:17 [f]ver. 19; Jer. 22:22; 30:14 [g]ver. 9, 16, 17, 21; Eccles. 4:1 [h]See Ezek. 23:22-26
3 [i]Jer. 52:27 [j][ch. 2:9; Deut. 28:64, 65] [k]Jer. 45:3

1 Or *in the narrow passes*

1:1–22 The chosen city of Zion, once exalted, has been humbled.

1:1 How lonely. The first verse sets the theme of the lament: Jerusalem's loss of greatness. The city, once favored, is desolate from the Babylonians' plundering (Is. 1:21–26).

widow. Widowhood and solitude (Jer. 15:17) are typical pictures of abandonment.

slave. Slavery is contrary to God's ultimate design for Israel. They had become a nation when God delivered them from slavery in Egypt so that they could serve him (Deut. 6:20–25; Jer. 2:14; Deut. 15:12–18). The blessings of living in the Promised Land and serving according to the Law were replaced with the punishments of exile and forced labor (Deut. 28:47–50), because the people had often broken the covenant they accepted when they left Egypt (Ex. 24:7, 8).

1:2 lovers. This is a word often used in irony for Judah's idolatrous neighbors with whom she willingly consorted (Jer. 3:1).

none to comfort. See also vv. 7, 9, 16. This should be compared with the comfort promised in Is. 40:1. Here there is no limit to the effects of the Babylonian ravages.

1:3 For the fall of Judah, see 2 Kin. 24:20–25:30; Jer. 39–45, 52.

exile. This is the ultimate humiliation for the covenant people (Deut. 28:63–68).

no resting place. The covenant had promised rest from enemies (Deut. 12:9; 2 Sam. 7:1, cf. Deut. 28:65).

4 The roads to Zion mourn,
for none come to [l]the festival;
[m]all her gates are desolate;
her priests [n]groan;
her virgins have been afflicted,[1]
and she herself suffers bitterly.

5 [o]Her foes have become the head;
her [p]enemies prosper,
because [q]the LORD has afflicted her
[r]for the multitude of her
transgressions;
[s]her children have gone away,
captives before the foe.

6 From the daughter of Zion
all her majesty has departed.
Her princes have become like deer
[t]that find no pasture;
they fled without strength
before the pursuer.

7 Jerusalem remembers
in the days of her affliction and
wandering
[u]all the precious things
that were hers from [v]days of old.
When her people fell into the hand
of the foe,
and there was none to help her,
her foes gloated over her;
they [w]mocked at her downfall.

8 [x]Jerusalem sinned grievously;
therefore she became filthy;
all who honored her despise her,
[y]for they have seen her nakedness;
she herself [z]groans
and turns her face away.

4 [l]See ch. 2:6 [m]Jer. 14:2 [n]ver. 8, 11, 21, 22
5 [o][Deut. 28:13, 44; Jer. 13:21] [p]Jer. 12:1 [q]ver. 12; ch. 3:33 [r]Jer. 30:14, 15; Dan. 9:16 [s]2 Chr. 36:17, 20; See Jer. 52:28-30
6 [t][Jer. 14:6]
7 [u]ver. 10, 11 [v]ch. 2:17; Jer. 46:26 [w]Obad. 12, 13; [Ps. 119:51]
8 [x][Zech. 13:1] [y][Ezek. 16:37] [z]ver. 4, 21, 22

9 [a]Her uncleanness was [a]in her skirts;
[b]she took no thought of her future;[2]
therefore her fall is terrible;
[c]she has no comforter.
"O LORD, behold my affliction,
for the enemy has [d]triumphed!"

10 The enemy has stretched out
his hands
over all her [e]precious things;
for she has seen [f]the nations
enter her sanctuary,
those whom you [g]forbade
to enter your congregation.

11 All her people [z]groan
as [h]they search for bread;
they trade their [e]treasures for [i]food
to revive their strength.
"Look, O LORD, and see,
for I am despised."

12 "Is it nothing to you, all [j]you who
pass by?
[k]Look and see
if there is any sorrow like my sorrow,
which was brought upon me,
which [l]the LORD inflicted
on [m]the day of his fierce anger.

13 "From on high he [n]sent fire;
into my bones[3] he made it
descend;
[o]he spread a net for my feet;
he turned me back;
[p]he has left me stunned,
faint all the day long.

9 [a][Jer. 13:22] [b][Deut. 32:29; Isai. 47:7] [c]ver. 2 [d]Jer. 48:26
10 [e]ver. 7 [f]Ps. 79:1; Jer. 51:51 [g][Deut. 23:3; Neh. 13:1]
11 [z][See ver. 8 above] [h]ch. 2:12; 4:4; [Jer. 38:9; 52:6] [i]ver. 19
12 [j]Job 21:29; Ps. 80:12 [k][Dan. 9:12] [l]ver. 5 [m]See Jer. 12:13
13 [n]Ps. 102:3 [o]Ps. 9:15; Ezek. 12:13; 17:20 [p]ch. 3:11; See Jer. 8:18

[1] Septuagint, Old Latin *dragged away* [2] Or *end* [3] Septuagint; Hebrew *bones and*

1:4 The regular worship life of ancient Israel is pictured here.

roads to Zion. People who lived at a distance would travel these roads in pilgrimage to the temple (Ps. 84:5).

festival. The main yearly gatherings for worship were Unleavened Bread, Pentecost, and Booths (Ex. 23:14–17; Lev. 23:4–44). Jerusalem would be crowded, and priests presided over the vibrant celebrations.

virgins have been afflicted. This is a sign of defeat; contrast Jer. 31:13.

1:5 enemies prosper. See other complaints in Jer. 12:1; Ps. 73. Here the complaint comes with a confession of sin. As the prophets foretold, Judah's unfaithfulness brought her to grief.

1:6 daughter of Zion. This phrase personifies Jerusalem (Jer. 6:2); yet perhaps it also alludes to the women of the city, who feel its anguish most keenly.

1:7 Jerusalem remembers. Again the bitter present contrasts with an earlier, happier time, possibly that of David and Solomon.

1:8 Jerusalem sinned. The idea of sin as the cause of the Exile is developed, first with images of ritual impurity.

filthy. The word probably refers to menstruation (Lev. 15:19–33). The consequence of Judah's sin was similar, if not more severe: being cut off from God's worship, and perhaps also public humiliation (cf. Jer. 13:22, 26).

1:9 uncleanness. This intensifies the image of ritual uncleanness.

O LORD, behold. Zion is personified for the first time, introducing an element of appeal to the Lord, a normal part of the lament form (Introduction: Characteristics and Themes).

1:10 sanctuary. The temple was intended to attract the nations to worship the God of Israel (1 Kin. 8:41–43), but now it has brought invaders who desecrate it.

1:11 All . . . strength. The picture of desolation becomes vivid, with its intimation of food shortages.

1:12 all you who pass by . . . like my sorrow. The sufferer imagines that their suffering is unprecedented. Yet no one seems to sympathize.

the day of his fierce anger. The expression here is a grim confirmation of the prophecy of Amos that on the day of the Lord His anger would be against His own people (Amos 5:18).

1:13 he sent fire. Zion knows that the Lord Himself has afflicted them (Ps. 88:13–18).

14 "My transgressions were bound[1] into
[q]a yoke;
by his hand they were fastened
together;
they were set upon my neck;
he caused my strength to fail;
the Lord gave me into the hands
of those whom I cannot withstand.

15 "The Lord rejected
all my mighty men in my midst;
he summoned an assembly against me
to crush my young men;
[r]the Lord has trodden as in a
winepress
the virgin daughter of Judah.

16 "For these things [s]I weep;
my eyes flow with tears;
for [t]a comforter is far from me,
one to [u]revive my spirit;
my children are desolate,
for the enemy has prevailed."

17 [v]Zion stretches out her hands,
but [t]there is none to comfort her;
the LORD has commanded against
Jacob
that his neighbors should be his
foes;
Jerusalem has become
a filthy thing among them.

18 [w]"The LORD is in the right,
[x]for I have rebelled against his word;
but hear, all you peoples,
and see my suffering;
[y]my young women and my young men
have gone into captivity.

14[q]Deut. 28:48
15[r][Isai. 63:2, 3]
16[s]See Jer. 13:17 [t]ver. 2, 21 [u][ver. 11]
17[v]Isai. 1:15; Jer. 4:31 [t][See ver. 16 above]
18[w]See Jer. 12:1 [x]1 Sam. 12:14, 15 [y][Deut. 28:41]
19[z]See ver. 2 [a]ver. 11
20[b]ch. 2:11; Job 30:27; Isai. 16:11 [c]Deut. 32:25; Ezek. 7:15; See Jer. 15:2
21[d]ver. 4, 8, 11 [e]ver. 2, 16, 17 [f][ch. 4:21; Jer. 50:11] [f][ch. 4: 21; Jer. 50:11]
22[g]Ps. 109:14, 15 [h]ver. 12; ch. 2:20 [d][See ver. 21 above] [i]See Jer. 8:18
Chapter 2
1[j][ch. 3:44] [k][Matt. 11:23]; See Isai. 14:15 [l]1 Chr. 28:2

19 "I called to [z]my lovers,
but they deceived me;
my priests and elders
perished in the city,
while [a]they sought food
to revive their strength.

20 "Look, O LORD, for I am in distress;
[b]my stomach churns;
my heart is wrung within me,
because I have been very rebellious.
[c]In the street the sword bereaves;
in the house it is like death.

21 "They heard[2] [d]my groaning,
yet [e]there is no one to comfort me.
All my enemies have heard of my
trouble;
[f]they are glad that you have done it.
You have brought[3] the day you
announced;
[f]now let them be as I am.

22 [g]"Let all their evildoing come before you,
and deal with them
as [h]you have dealt with me
because of all my transgressions;
for [d]my groans are many,
and [i]my heart is faint."

The Lord Has Destroyed Without Pity

2 How the Lord in his anger
has set the daughter of Zion [j]under
a cloud!
[k]He has cast down from heaven to earth
the splendor of Israel;
he has not remembered [l]his footstool
in the day of his anger.

1 The meaning of the Hebrew is uncertain 2 Septuagint, Syriac *Hear*
3 Syriac *Bring*

1:15 the Lord has trodden. The Lord, formerly a warrior on Israel's behalf (Deut. 9:1–3), has turned His might against His own people.

1:16 a comforter is far from me. There is no one to help, no one to comfort—a dominant theme in these verses (2, 7, 9, 17).

1:17 Jacob. A historic name for Israel, derived from the name of their ancestor (Gen. 32:38).

his neighbors should be his foes. The presence of Judah as an unclean thing among the nations falsifies her intended role as a witness to the holiness of God (Ex. 19:5, 6).

1:18 The LORD is in the right. Zion justifies the Lord's punishment by an admission of sin. Yet the thought shifts quickly again to her slavery.

1:19 lovers. They fail in time of need.

1:21 my enemies. Zion appeals to the Lord because of the enemies' gloating. Their insults are deeply offensive to Judah's status as God's covenant people—and therefore to God Himself.

day. The day of the Lord now becomes a day of terror for Zion's enemies. Zion's lament follows the prophetic pattern, where the enemies who administer God's judgment finally come to suffer judgment themselves (Jer. 25:15–38).

1:22 Let . . . transgressions. Zion finally asserts that her enemies merit judgment as much as she does.

my groans. The petition to punish, however, does not diminish Zion's deep distress.

2:1–22 The second lament over Zion's loss of glory begins and the prophet portrays the Lord's anger with her.

2:1 How. Cf. 1:1 and note.

He has cast down . . . the splendor. Israel's fall into disfavor is compared to a falling star (Is. 14:12).

has not remembered. Judah is astonished that the promise to David is now apparently void (cf. Ps. 89, especially vv. 38–51). Isaiah had assured the people that God would protect Zion (e.g., Is. 37:35), and the people of Judah had absolutized these promises. They forgot their obligation to keep the terms of God's covenant with them (Ex. 24:1–3).

his footstool. Used normally for the ark of the covenant (1 Chr. 28:2; Ps. 132:7), or the earth (Is. 66:1), it is here applied to Zion (cf. Ps. 99:5).

2 The Lord [m]has swallowed up
[n]without mercy
all the habitations of Jacob;
in his wrath [o]he has broken down
the strongholds of the daughter of
Judah;
he has brought [p]down to the ground
[p]in dishonor
the kingdom [q]and its rulers.

3 He has cut down in [r]fierce anger
all [s]the might of Israel;
[t]he has withdrawn from them his
right hand
in the face of the enemy;
[u]he has burned like a flaming fire in
Jacob,
consuming all around.

4 [v]He has bent his bow like an enemy,
with his right hand set [w]like a foe;
and he has killed all who were
delightful in our eyes
in the tent of the daughter of Zion;
he has poured out his fury like fire.

5 [w]The Lord has become like an enemy;
[x]he has swallowed up Israel;
[y]he has swallowed up all its palaces;
he has laid in ruins its
strongholds,
and he has multiplied in the
daughter of Judah
[z]mourning and lamentation.

6 He has laid waste his booth like a
garden,
laid in ruins [a]his meeting place;
[a]the LORD has made Zion forget
festival and [b]Sabbath,
and in his fierce indignation has
spurned king and priest.

2 [m]ver. 16; [Ps. 35:25; 56:2; Ezek. 36:3] [n]ver. 17, 21; ch. 3:43; [Ezek. 9:5, 10] [o]Ps. 89:40 [p]Ps. 74:7 [q]Isai. 43:28
3 [r]See Jer. 12:13 [s]1 Sam. 2:1 [t]Ps. 74:11 [u]Ps. 79:5; 89:46
4 [v]ch. 3:12 [w]See Jer. 30:14
5 [w][See ver. 4 above] [x]ver. 16; [Ps. 35:25; 56:2; Ezek. 36:3] [y][2 Kin. 25:9] [z]Isai. 29:2
6 [a]ch. 1:4; Isai. 1:13; Zeph. 3:18 [b]Isai. 1:13
7 [c][Ps. 89:38] [d][Ezek. 24:21] [e]Deut. 32:30 [f]Ps. 74:4
8 [g][Jer. 5:10] [h]ver. 18 [i]See 2 Kin. 21:13 [j]Jer. 14:2
9 [k]Jer. 51:30; Nah. 3:13 [l][Hos. 3:4] [m]Ps. 74:9
10 [n]ch. 1:1; 3:28; Isai. 3:26 [o]Ezek. 3:15 [p]See Josh. 7:6 [q]Jer. 48:37; Ezek. 7:18; Amos 8:10; See Jer. 4:8
11 [r][ver. 18; ch. 5:17; Ps. 6:7] [s]See ch. 1:20 [t][Job 16:13] [u]ch. 3:48 [v][ch. 4:4; Jer. 44:7] [w]ver. 19; [Isai. 51:20]

7 [c]The Lord has scorned his altar,
[d]disowned his sanctuary;
[e]he has delivered into the hand of the
enemy
the walls of her palaces;
[f]they raised a clamor in the house of
the LORD
as on the day of festival.

8 [g]The LORD determined to lay in ruins
[h]the wall of the daughter of Zion;
[i]he stretched out the measuring line;
he did not restrain his hand from
destroying;
[j]he caused rampart and wall to lament;
[j]they languished together.

9 Her gates have sunk into the ground;
[h]he has ruined [k]and broken her
bars;
[l]her king and princes are among the
nations;
the law is no more,
and [m]her prophets find
no vision from the LORD.

10 The elders of the daughter of Zion
[n]sit on the ground [o]in silence;
[p]they have thrown dust on their heads
and [q]put on sackcloth;
the young women of Jerusalem
have bowed their heads to the
ground.

11 [r]My eyes are spent with weeping;
[s]my stomach churns;
[t]my bile is poured out to the ground
[u]because of the destruction of the
daughter of my people,
[v]because infants and babies [w]faint
in the streets of the city.

2:2 strongholds. The strength of the fortified cities of Judah had symbolized God's blessing in response to Judah's covenant faithfulness (2 Chr. 10:4–12).

2:3 might. The language used makes vivid the contrasts (a) between Judah and the enemies, as well as (b) between Judah's life as it should be and as it is.

2:4 bent his bow. Deut. 32:42. The harmful arrows that were meant for God's enemies (Deut. 32:42) are now aimed at His people (Hos. 5:10; Jer. 6:11; 7:20).

like an enemy. 1:15 note.

poured out his fury. This holy war imagery is classically used of God's judgment on the nations (Ps. 69:24).

2:5 daughter of Judah. See note 1:6.

2:6 his booth . . . his meeting place. These are references to the temple.

the LORD has made . . . forget festival and Sabbath. 1:4 note. This can be rendered "The LORD has made appointed feasts and Sabbaths forgotten things in Zion," an ironic justice since the people had first forgotten the Sabbaths themselves (Amos 8:5; Jer. 17:19–27).

2:7 his altar . . . his sanctuary. God's judgment destroys not only the place of His dwelling, but the means of Israel's approach to Him in worship. The shouts of triumphant enemies replace the cry of worshiping assemblies.

2:8 stretched out the measuring line. This was done as if to survey the city for destruction (Is. 34:11; Amos 7:7, 8).

2:9 law . . . prophets . . . vision. Not only are the religious institutions destroyed, but the Lord withholds revelation. The prophetic vision that accompanies preaching of the law has ceased (Jer. 8:8–10; 18:18; 1 Sam. 3:1).

2:10 The elders . . . dust . . . sackcloth . . . bowed their heads. These are the conventional gestures of mourning (Job 2:12, 13; and Lam. 1:4).

2:11 My eyes are spent with weeping. Compare the poet's natural suffering because of the agony of his people with the experiences of Jeremiah (Jer. 4:19), and note the pictures of desolation that accompany the prophet's expressions of anguish (Jer. 4:31).

12 They cry to their mothers,
[x]"Where is bread and wine?"
[w]as they faint like a wounded man
in the streets of the city,
as their life is poured out
on their mothers' bosom.

13 What can I say for you, [y]to what
compare you,
O daughter of Jerusalem?
[y]What can I liken to you, that I may
comfort you,
O virgin daughter of Zion?
[z]For your ruin is vast as the sea;
who can heal you?

14 [a]Your prophets have seen for you
false and deceptive visions;
[b]they have not exposed your iniquity
to [c]restore your fortunes,
[d]but have seen for you [e]oracles
that are false and misleading.

15 All who pass along the way
clap their hands at you;
[f]they hiss and wag their heads
at the daughter of Jerusalem;
"Is this the city that was called
[g]the perfection of beauty,
[g]the joy of all the earth?"

16 [h]All your enemies
rail against you;
they hiss, they gnash their teeth,
they cry: "We [i]have swallowed her!
Ah, this is the day we longed for;
now we have it; [j]we see it!"

17 The LORD has done what he
purposed;
he has carried out [k]his word,
which he commanded [l]long ago;
[m]he has thrown down [n]without pity;
[o]he has made the enemy rejoice over
you
and exalted the [p]might of your
foes.

18 Their heart cried to the Lord.
O [q]wall of the daughter of Zion,
[r]let tears stream down like a torrent
[s]day and night!
[t]Give yourself no rest,
[u]your eyes no respite!

19 "Arise, [v]cry out in the night,
at the beginning of the night
watches!
[w]Pour out your heart like water
before the presence of the Lord!
[x]Lift your hands to him
for the lives of your children,
[y]who faint for hunger
at the head of every street."

20 Look, O LORD, and see!
[z]With whom have you dealt thus?
[a]Should women eat the fruit of their
womb,
the children of [b]their tender care?
Should [c]priest and prophet be killed
in the sanctuary of the Lord?

21 In the dust of the streets
[d]lie the young and the old;
[d]my young women and my young
men
have fallen by the sword;
[e]you have killed them in the day of
your anger,
slaughtering [f]without pity.

12[x]See ch. 1:11 [w][See ver. 11 above] 13[y][ch. 1:12] [z]2 Sam. 5:20; [Ezek. 26:3] 14[a]See Jer. 5:31 [b][Isai. 58:1] [c]See Jer. 30:3 [d]See Jer. 5:31 [e][Jer. 23:33, 34] 15[f]See 2 Chr. 29:8 [g]Ps. 48:2; Ezek. 16:14 16[h]ch. 3:46; [Job 16:9, 10] [i]See ver. 2 [j][Ps. 35:21] 17[k]See Lev. 26:14-45; Deut. 28:15-68

[l]ch. 1:7; Jer. 46:26 [m]See ver. 2 [n]ver. 2, 21 [o][Ps. 38:16; 89:42] [p][ver. 3] 18[q]ver. 8 [r]See ver. 11 [s]Ps. 32:4; 42:3 [t]Ps. 77:2 [u]Ps. 17:8 19[v]Ps. 119:147, 148 [w]Ps. 62:8; [1 Sam. 7:6] [x][1 Tim. 2:8] [y]See ver. 11, 12 20[z]ch. 1:22 [a]ch. 4:10; See Jer. 19:9 [b]ver. 22 [c][ch. 4:13] 21[d][2 Chr. 36:17] [e]ch. 3:43 [f]ver. 2, 17

2:11, 12 infants and babies . . . their mothers. The prophet is especially moved by the sight of suffering children.

2:13 What can I say for you. The meaning seems to be, "What can I tell you about suffering, you who have suffered so much?" No ready answers occur to someone who witnesses sorrows like these.

comfort. See note 1:2.

2:14 deceptive visions. The thought advances from v. 9; prophets are now said to have prophesied falsely. The complex problem of false prophecy is a recurrent theme of the prophets (Jer. 5:12, 13; 23:9–40; 28). Deut. 18:21, 22 furnishes one criterion by which prophets may be judged true or false.

2:15 perfection of beauty . . . joy of all the earth. The beauty of the chosen place is extravagantly expressed (Ps. 50:2; 48:2), but by scoffers who mock the ruin and agony of Jerusalem.

2:16 We have swallowed her. In vv. 2 and 5, God Himself is said to have swallowed up the people. As this verse makes clear, He did this using Judah's enemies for His agents. The verse also shows how the nations proudly attribute their victory over Judah to their own strength.

2:17 carried out his word . . . commanded long ago. God's purposes of judgment were declared in the curses of the covenant (Lev. 26:23–39; Deut. 28:15–68); the present fate of Judah has happened in accordance with God's known purposes.

might. See note on v. 3.

2:18 O wall. There is irony in this futile cry to the city wall, a symbol of the nation's imagined strength.

day and night. Cf. Deut. 28:67.

2:19 children. See note on v. 12.

2:20 Should women . . . children. The theme of the suffering of innocent children reaches the height of pathos (Jer. 19:9). Its power as an appeal to God is enhanced by the knowledge that God knows motherly affection (Is. 66:13). As extreme in its own way is the outrage of sacrilege: the Lord's anointed ones are killed in His sanctuary.

priest and prophet. For the sins of priests and prophets, see 4:13.

2:21 the young and the old. The horror of death in youth is contrasted with the blessing of attaining a good age (Job 42:17).

22 You summoned as if to [g]a festival day
[h]my terrors on every side,
[i]and on the day of the anger of the
LORD
no one escaped or survived;
[j]those whom I held and raised
my enemy destroyed.

Great Is Your Faithfulness

3 [k]I am the man who has seen
affliction
under the [l]rod of his wrath;
2 he has driven and brought me
[m]into darkness without any light;
3 surely against me he turns his hand
again and again the whole day
long.

4 He has made my flesh and my skin
waste away;
[n]he has broken my bones;
5 [o]he has besieged and enveloped me
with [p]bitterness and tribulation;
6 [q]he has made me dwell in darkness
like the dead of long ago.

7 [r]He has walled me about so that [s]I
cannot escape;
he has made my chains heavy;
8 though [t]I call and cry for help,
he shuts out my prayer;
9 [r]he has blocked my ways with blocks
of stones;
he has made my paths crooked.

10 [u]He is a bear lying in wait for me,
a lion in hiding;
11 [v]he turned aside my steps and [u]tore
me to pieces;
[w]he has made me desolate;
12 [x]he bent his bow [y]and set me
as a target for his arrow.

13 He drove into my kidneys
[z]the arrows of his quiver;
14 [a]I have become the laughingstock of
all peoples,
[b]the object of their taunts all day
long.
15 [c]He has filled me with
bitterness;
he has sated me with
[d]wormwood.

16 [e]He has made my teeth grind
on gravel,
and [f]made me cower in ashes;
17 my soul is bereft of peace;
I have forgotten what
happiness[1] is;
18 [g]so I say, "My endurance has
perished;
so has my hope from the
LORD."

19 [h]Remember my affliction and my
wanderings,
[d]the wormwood and [i]the gall!
20 My soul continually
remembers it
[j]and is bowed down within me.
21 But this I call to mind,
and [k]therefore I have hope:

22[g][ver. 6] [h]See Jer. 6:25 [i][Jer. 42:17; 44:14] [j]ver. 20
Chapter 3
1[k]Jer. 20:18 [l]Ps. 2:9
2[m]Isai. 5:30
4[n]Ps. 51:8; Isai. 38:13; Jer. 50:17
5[o][Job 19:12] [p]ver. 19; Deut. 29:18
6[q]Ps. 143:3
7[r]Job 19:8 [s]Ps. 88:8
8[t]Job 19:7; 30:20; Ps. 22:2
9[r][See ver. 7 above]
10[u]See Hos. 13:8
11[v][Jer. 18:15] [u][See ver. 10 above] [w]ch. 1:13
12[x]ch. 2:4 [y][Job 16:12]
13[z]Job 6:4; Ps. 38:2
14[a]See Jer. 20:7 [b]ver. 63; Job 30:9; Ps. 69:12
15[c][Isai. 51:17, 21] [d]Jer. 9:15
16[e][Prov. 20:17] [f]See Jer. 6:26
18[g][Ps. 9:18]
19[h][ch. 1:9, 11, 20] [d][See ver. 15 above] [i]ver. 5
20[j]Ps. 42:6; 44:25
21[k][Ps. 42:5, 11]

1 Hebrew *good*

2:22 a festival day . . . terrors. This contrast between summoning to the joy of a feast and summoning to disaster is starkly powerful.

terrors. See Jer. 6:25; 20:10.

day of the anger of the LORD. The poem ends where it began, without alleviation of the dark picture.

3:1–66 As an individual expresses the grief of the community, hope and consolation are sustained by a knowledge of God's compassionate love.

3:1 I am the man. This chapter is an acrostic with three verses for each letter of the Hebrew alphabet. On the author's possible identity as Jeremiah, and the acrostic form in Hebrew poetry, see the Introduction, and further below. For portrayals of the Lord Himself as the One who has afflicted the speaker, see Job 19:21; Ps. 88:7, 15; Jer. 15:17, 18. In this poem an individual expresses the grief of his community (vv. 22, 40–47).

3:2 into darkness without any light. Contrast Is. 9:2. Darkness is a metaphor for the distress experienced as the absence of God; light stands for the opposite: salvation and blessing. The day of the Lord is described in these terms at Amos 5:18.

3:4 skin . . . bones. These are pictures of physical distress, perhaps due to age or illness (Job 13:28; Is. 38:13).

3:5 bitterness and tribulation. Emotional and physical effects of distress go hand in hand.

3:6 the dead of long ago. The distresses and diseases of life diminish its fullness, culminating in death. In his weakened condition, the prophet considers himself to have little more participation in life than if he were actually dead. From the perspective of the living, the dead exist not at all, or as shadows (Prov. 2:18; 9:18 and notes). For other pictures of death in the Old Testament, see Job 3:11–19; Ps. 6:5; 115:17; Is. 14:18, 19. Against this background the Old Testament is eloquent in its testimony to resurrection beyond the grave (Job 19:25–27; Ps. 16:9–11; 49:15; 73:24).

3:8 shuts out my prayer. For unheard prayer see Ps. 10:1; 13:1; 22:1, 2.

3:10–12 a bear . . . his arrow. Some of the hazards that could actually overtake the traveler are vivid ways of expressing terror and distress.

3:14 the laughingstock. See Jer. 20:7.

3:17 peace . . . happiness. These conditions, the sum of blessing, are totally absent.

3:18 My endurance . . . LORD. The expression of hopelessness in the poem reaches its climax here.

3:20 remembers. The poet's experience is a symbol of the people's; see the language in 1:7.

3:21 this I call to mind. Memory that once discouraged now encourages (Ps. 77:3–9, 10–15). The memory of God's devotion to His people brings hope out of hopelessness.

22 [l] The steadfast love of the LORD never
ceases;[1]
[l] his mercies never come to an end;
23 they are new [m] every morning;
[n] great is your faithfulness.
24 [o] "The LORD is my portion," says my soul,
[k] "therefore I will hope in him."

25 The LORD is good to those who [p] wait
for him,
to the soul who seeks him.
26 [q] It is good that one should wait quietly
for the salvation of the LORD.
27 [r] It is good for a man that he bear
the yoke [s] in his youth.

28 Let him [t] sit alone in silence
when it is laid on him;
29 [u] let him put his mouth in the dust—
there may yet be hope;
30 [v] let him give his cheek to the one
who strikes,
and let him be filled with insults.

31 [w] For the Lord will not
cast off forever,
32 but, though he [x] cause grief, [y] he will
have compassion
[z] according to the abundance of his
steadfast love;

22 [l] [Jer. 44:12, 18; Mal. 3:6] 23 [m] Job 7:18 [n] Ps. 36:5 24 [o] Ps. 16:5; 73:26 [k] [See ver. 21 above] 25 [p] Ps. 130:6; [Isai. 30:18] 26 [q] Ps. 130:5, 7; Mic. 7:7 27 [r] [Matt. 11:29] [s] [Eccles. 12:1] 28 [t] ch. 1:1; 2:10; Isai. 3:26 29 [u] Job 42:6 30 [v] Isai. 50:6; Matt. 5:39 31 [w] Ps. 103:9 32 [x] ch. 1:5 [y] Ps. 103:8 [z] Ps. 106:45

33 [a] [Heb. 12:6, 10] [b] [Heb. 12:11] 34 [c] [Ps. 107:10] 35 [d] [Hab. 1:13] 36 [d] [See ver. 35 above] 37 [e] [Ps. 33:9] 38 [f] Isai. 45:7; Amos 3:6 39 [g] Prov. 19:3 40 [h] Joel 2:12, 13 41 [i] Ps. 25:1; 119:48 42 [j] See Dan. 9:5 [k] Ps. 78:17

33 [a] for he does not willingly afflict
or [b] grieve the children of men.

34 To crush underfoot
all [c] the prisoners of the earth,
35 [d] to deny a man justice
in the presence of the Most High,
36 to subvert a man in his lawsuit,
[d] the Lord does not approve.

37 [e] Who has spoken and it came to
pass,
unless the Lord has
commanded it?
38 [f] Is it not from the mouth of the Most
High
that good and bad come?
39 [g] Why should a living man complain,
a man, about the punishment of
his sins?

40 Let us test and examine our ways,
[h] and return to the LORD!
41 [i] Let us lift up our hearts and hands
to God in heaven:
42 [j] "We have transgressed and
[k] rebelled,
and you have not forgiven.

1 Syriac, Targum; Hebrew *Because of the steadfast love of the LORD, we are not cut off*

3:22–24 The climactic point of the poem and the book is reached here. The lament form often has turning points where the experience of rejection by God turns unexpectedly to confidence, based on a knowledge of His character and of His past mercies. See the confessions of trust and hope in Ps. 22.

3:22, 23 See "God Is Love: Divine Goodness and Faithfulness" at Ps. 136:1.

3:22 steadfast love. On the Hebrew word (*ḥesed*) see Ps. 36:5 note. The plural form, used here, recalls many acts or perhaps the riches of divine love.

mercies. God's covenant devotion is always joined with His compassion, a term of profound emotion. We are not consumed because God's compassion is not consumed. God's wrath toward His people will end because His compassion cannot end (4:22; Hos. 11:8).

3:23 every morning. God's love will bring the morning of salvation (Ps. 90:14; Mal. 4:2; Luke 1:78).

faithfulness. The unqualified reliability of God makes Him worthy of faith (Hab. 2:4).

3:24 my portion. This phrase recalls the territorial allocations to the Israelite tribes. The priests and Levites, who were landless, had the Lord as their portion (Num. 18:20; cf. Ps. 73:26).

3:25 The LORD . . . seeks him. God is always good to those who seek, hope, and wait for Him (cf. 1 Chr. 28:9). The threefold "good" in this context (cf. vv. 26, 27) focuses on God's goodness.

3:27 in his youth. The reference is apparently to Jeremiah's suffering in early and middle life, possibly signifying a relief from it in old age. Perhaps the community, like an individual, should hope for the yoke to be lifted with the passage of time.

3:28–30 Let him . . . insults. The prophet exhorts the afflicted to bear present suffering, in the light of the affirmation in the next verses.

sit alone. Cf. 1:1.

3:30 let him give his cheek. The humiliation of Israel foreshadows Christ's humiliation (Is. 50:6; Matt. 26:67).

3:31–33 Since God is compassionate, the present experience of His wrath must be short-lived (Ps. 30:5; Is. 54:7; Hos. 6:1). Again, compassion is joined to God's unfailing love (Hebrew *ḥesed,* 3:22). God does not afflict men "willingly," that is, "cheerfully," or "from His heart" even in judgment.

3:34–36 The implication of these verses is that God cannot approve such things (Job 8:3). Of course, God has approved these very things, since He has brought them to pass. This is the problem of judgment and affliction that the poet faces.

3:37, 38 All that happens is by God's word (Gen. 1:3), calamity as well as good (Amos 3:6).

3:39 Since all things take place by the word of the Lord, no living man can complain when God brings calamity as punishment for sin.

the punishment of his sins. The sin of the people is an important part of the prophet's answer to the problem of judgment and affliction (dreadful though God's judgment is, 2:20–22). The phrase in Hebrew implies that sin and consequent punishment belong inescapably together.

3:40–47 Notice that the speaker is plural throughout this section.

3:40–42 Let us test . . . transgressed. This is a call to repentance, acknowledging sin. The impulse to confess sins seems to give way soon to renewed lamentation, following the statement, "you have not forgiven" (v. 42). The confession could have been superficial or hypocritical. In any case the penalties were not lifted.

43 "You have wrapped yourself with
anger and pursued us,
[l] killing without pity;
44 [m] you have wrapped yourself with a
cloud
so that no prayer can pass through.
45 [n] You have made us scum and garbage
among the peoples.

46 [o] "All our enemies
open their mouths against us;
47 [p] panic and pitfall have come upon us,
devastation and [q] destruction;
48 [r] my eyes flow with rivers of tears
because of the destruction of the
daughter of my people.

49 [r] "My eyes will flow without ceasing,
without respite,
50 [s] until the LORD from heaven
looks down and sees;
51 my eyes cause me grief
at the fate of all the daughters of
my city.

52 [t] "I have been hunted [u] like a bird
by those who were my enemies
[v] without cause;
53 [w] they flung me alive into the pit
[x] and cast stones on me;
54 [y] water closed over my head;
I said, [z] 'I am lost.'

55 [a] "I called on your name, O LORD,
from the depths of the pit;
56 [b] you heard my plea, 'Do not close
your ear to my cry for help!'
57 [c] You came near when I called on you;
you said, [d] 'Do not fear!'

58 "You have [e] taken up my cause,
[f] O Lord;
you have [e] redeemed my life.
59 You have seen the wrong done to
me, [g] O LORD;
judge my cause.
60 You have seen all their vengeance,
all [h] their plots against me.

61 [i] "You have heard their taunts, O LORD,
all [h] their plots against me.
62 The lips and thoughts [j] of my assailants
are against me all the day long.
63 [k] Behold their sitting and their rising;
[l] I am the object of their taunts.

64 [m] "You will repay them,[1] O LORD,
[n] according to the work of their
hands.
65 You will give them[2] dullness of heart;
your curse will be[3] on them.
66 You will pursue them[4] in anger and
[o] destroy them
from under [p] your heavens,
O LORD."[5]

The Holy Stones Lie Scattered

4 [q] How the gold has grown dim,
how the pure gold is changed!
The holy stones lie scattered
[r] at the head of every street.

2 The precious sons of Zion,
worth their weight in [s] fine gold,
how they are regarded as [t] earthen pots,
the work of a potter's hands!

43 [l] ch. 2:2, 17, 21 44 [m] ver. 8; [ch. 2:1] 45 [n] [1 Cor. 4:13] 46 [o] ch. 2:16, 17 47 [p] Isai. 24:17; Jer. 48:43 [q] Isai. 51:19 48 [r] ch. 1:16; See Jer. 13:17 49 [r] [See ver. 48 above] 50 [s] Ps. 14:2; Isai. 63:15 52 [t] ch. 4:18 [u] Ps. 11:1 [v] See Ps. 35:19 53 [w] Jer. 37:16; 38:6, 9, 10 [x] [Dan. 6:17] 54 [y] Ps. 69:2 [z] Ps. 88:5; [Ezek. 37:11] 55 [a] Ps. 130:1 56 [b] [Ps. 130:2] 57 [c] [James 4:8] [d] See Josh. 1:9

58 [e] Ps. 119:154 [f] [1 Sam. 24:15] 59 [g] Ps. 35:22, 23 60 [h] See Jer. 11:19 61 [i] ch. 5:1 [h] [See ver. 60 above] 62 [j] Ps. 18:39, 48 63 [k] [Ps. 139:2] [l] See ver. 14 64 [m] See Jer. 11:20 [n] Ps. 28:4; [2 Tim. 4:14] 66 [o] [Deut. 25:19; Jer. 10:11] [p] Ps. 8:3

Chapter 4 1 [q] [Isai. 1:22; Jer. 6:30] [r] ch. 2:19 2 [s] Ps. 19:10 [t] See Jer. 19:11

[1] Or *Repay them* [2] Or *Give them* [3] Or *Place your curse* [4] Or *Pursue them*
[5] Syriac (compare Septuagint, Vulgate); Hebrew *the heavens of the LORD*

3:43–45 You have wrapped . . . among the peoples. Here the prophet parodies the actions of God at the Exodus. Then God's anger helped Israel; it was their enemies who were slain without pity; and the cloud was a sign of favor. Israel was precious among the nations, not "scum and garbage."

3:48–66 The speech now reverts to the singular again.

3:48 rivers of tears. There are strong echoes of Jeremiah in this close association between the people's grief and the poet's grief. A link is suggested between the suffering of the people and of the poet.

3:49 My eyes will flow. These words reflect familiar lament language (Ps. 6:6; 42:3; Jer. 9:1; 18).

3:52 enemies without cause. Ps. 35:19; John 15:25.

3:53 into the pit. Ps. 28:1; 88:6. The life of Jeremiah may be in view again in these verses (Jer. 38:6).

3:55 I called . . . pit. See Ps. 16:10, 11; 30:1; and the experience of Jonah (Jon. 2:2–7). Christ's suffering as the righteous Servant of the Lord brings this recurring theme of the suffering prophets and their rescue by the Lord to its highest fulfillment.

3:56 you heard my plea. The turning point of the lament arrives when the poet is reassured that the Lord has heard his prayer (Ps. 6:8–10).

3:57 Do not fear. This is a common exhortation in Isaiah (e.g., Is. 41:10; cf. Mark 6:50).

3:58–66 This section takes up the biblical theme of innocent, vicarious suffering that reaches its consummation in Christ's death for those who brought it upon Him.

3:58–60 my cause . . . redeemed my life . . . my cause. In Jer. 50:34 the Lord is the Redeemer of Judah and pleads their case. Here the Lord pleads against them, because they have turned against His prophet.

3:64–66 repay them. The note of revenge is present in Jer. 12:1, as in Ps. 77:6, 7.

4:1–22 This chapter, containing the most vivid portrayal of Judah's agonies, laments Zion's punishment, but gives assurances that the punishment will cease.

4:1 the gold . . . The holy stones. The gold and the rich furnishings of Solomon's temple were laid waste by Nebuchadnezzar (2 Kin. 25:9).

4:2 The precious sons . . . fine gold. The idea of gold is quickly transferred to the people themselves, more valuable than the temple's riches. As God's "treasured possession" (Ex. 19:5) they had been exceedingly precious; now they are the most common clay.

3 Even jackals offer the breast;
they nurse their young,
but the daughter of my people has
become cruel,
like the ostriches in the wilderness.

4 The tongue of the nursing infant
[u]sticks
to the roof of its mouth for thirst;
[v]the children beg for food,
but no one gives to them.

5 Those who once feasted on delicacies
perish in the streets;
[w]those who were brought up in purple
embrace ash heaps.

6 [x]For the chastisement[1] of the daughter
of my people has been greater
than the punishment[2] of Sodom,
[y]which was overthrown in a moment,
and no hands were wrung for her.[3]

7 Her princes were purer than snow,
whiter than milk;
their bodies were more ruddy than
coral,
the beauty of their form[4] was like
sapphire.[5]

8 [z]Now their face is blacker than soot;
they are not recognized in the
streets;
their skin has shriveled on their bones;
it has become as dry as wood.

9 Happier were the victims of the sword
than the victims of hunger,
who wasted away, pierced
by lack of the fruits of the field.

10 [a]The hands of [b]compassionate women
[c]have boiled their own children;
[d]they became their food
during the destruction of the
daughter of my people.

11 [e]The LORD gave full vent to his wrath;
he poured out his hot anger,
and [f]he kindled a fire in Zion
that consumed its foundations.

12 [g]The kings of the earth did not
believe,
nor any of the inhabitants of the
world,
that foe or enemy could enter
the gates of Jerusalem.

13 This was for [h]the sins of her prophets
and [h]the iniquities of her priests,
who shed in the midst of her
the blood of the righteous.

14 [i]They wandered, blind, through the
streets;
they were so defiled with blood
[j]that no one was able to touch
their garments.

15 "Away! [k]Unclean!" people cried at
them.
"Away! Away! Do not touch!"
So they became fugitives and
wanderers;
people said among the nations,
"They shall stay with us no
longer."

4 [u]Ps. 22:15 [v][ch. 2:11]
5 [w][2 Sam. 1:24]
6 [x]Matt. 10:15; Luke 10:12 [y]Gen. 19:25; 2 Pet. 2:6; Jude 7
8 [z]ch. 5:10; Job 30:30; [Ps. 119:83]
10 [a]See Jer. 19:9 [b][1 Kin. 3:26; Isai. 49:15] [c][2 Kin. 6:29] [d]Deut. 28:57
11 [e]Ezek. 5:13 [f]See Jer. 17:27
12 [g][Isai. 52:15; 53:1]
13 [h][ch. 2:20]; See Jer. 5:31; 23:21
14 [i][Isai. 59:10] [j][Num. 19:16]
15 [k][Lev. 13:45]

1 Or *iniquity* 2 Or *sin* 3 The meaning of the Hebrew is uncertain 4 The meaning of the Hebrew is uncertain 5 Hebrew *lapis lazuli*

4:3 Even jackals. Is. 1:2, 3.

ostriches. These birds were a proverbial figure for the callousness of parents towards their children (Job 39:16). This indifference is a theme of the chapter (v. 10), developed from 2:20.

4:5 delicacies. The picture of someone rich and delicately bred falling suddenly into dire want and danger is echoed often in the prophets (Amos 4:1–3; 6:1; Jer. 6:2).

4:6 chastisement. The Hebrew word can be translated "punishment" or "iniquity" according to the context, because the two ideas are so intimately linked. The connection is strong in this chapter, where the intense suffering of Judah is linked repeatedly to her unnatural sin.

Sodom. The prophets often use Sodom as an archetype of divine judgment on sin (Deut. 29:23; Is. 1:10; Jer. 23:14; Ezek. 16:46; Hos. 11:8; Amos 4:11; Luke 17:28–30). The comparison with Sodom holds good both for the sins of the city and the dreadful judgment that fell upon it.

4:7 princes. Num. 6:1–21, note.

whiter . . . ruddy. These are colors often associated with the human body.

4:8 Now. Ironically, in the prevailing difficulties, no one is marked out as special; all distinctions have been obliterated.

4:9 Happier . . . sword. The misery of the people is desperate and wretched. Death by famine is not a summary, instant judgment; in its lingering it exposes the horrors of God's judgment to a dreadful degree (Deut. 28:54–57).

4:10 women . . . children. See v. 3.

4:11 wrath. The focus returns to God's wrath; there is an explanation even for these ills in Judah's sin.

4:12 The kings of the earth. Possibly this phrase refers to the assumed impregnability of Zion, reinforced by the dramatic failure of the Assyrians to take the city following Sennacherib's conquest of the rest of Judah in 701 B.C. (2 Kin. 18:13–19:37).

4:13 prophets . . . priests. See note 2:20 and Jer. 5:30, 31; Mic. 3:9–12.

4:14 wandered, blind, through the streets. Deut. 28:28, 29.

defiled with blood. God, in His wrath, had made Zion's priests and prophets ritually unclean. Elsewhere (Is. 59:3) the phrase refers to blood spilled by the guilty. Ironically, the blood that defiles these blind wanderers is their own.

4:15 Unclean. Lev. 13:45.

fugitives. The curse of Deut. 28:65–66 is fulfilled.

16 [l]The LORD himself[1] has scattered them;
he will regard them no more;
[m]no honor was shown to the priests,
[n]no favor to the elders.

17 [o]Our eyes failed, ever watching
[o]vainly for help;
in our watching we watched
for [p]a nation which could not save.

18 [q]They dogged our steps
so that we could not walk in our streets;
[r]our end drew near; our days were numbered,
for our end had come.

19 Our pursuers were [s]swifter
than the eagles in the heavens;
they chased us on the mountains;
they lay in wait for us in the wilderness.

20 [t]The breath of our nostrils, [u]the LORD's anointed,
was captured [v]in their pits,
of whom we said, [w]"Under his shadow
we shall live among the nations."

21 [x]Rejoice and be glad, O daughter of Edom,
you who dwell in [y]the land of Uz;
but to you also [z]the cup shall pass;
you shall become drunk and strip yourself bare.

16[l]ch. 2:17 [m][Isai. 24:2] [n]ch. 5:12
17[o]Ps. 119:82, 123; [Jer. 3:23] [p]Jer. 37:7, 8
18[q]ch. 3:52 [r]Ezek. 7:2, 3, 6; Amos 8:2
19[s]Jer. 4:13; [2 Sam. 1:23; Hab. 1:8]
20[t][Gen. 2:7] [u][ch. 2:9; 2 Kin. 25:5, 6] [v][Ezek. 12:13; 17:20; 19:4, 8] [w][Judg. 9:15; Ezek. 31:6, 17]
21[x][ch. 1:21] [y]Job 1:1; Jer. 25:20 [z]See Jer. 25:15, 16
22[a][Isai. 40:2] [b]Obad. 10
Chapter 5
1[c]Ps. 89:50 [d]ch. 3:61
2[e]Ps. 79:1
5[f][Josh. 10:24]
6[g][Hos. 12:1]
7[h]Jer. 31:29; Ezek. 18:2
8[i][Prov. 30:21, 22]

22 [a]The punishment of your iniquity,
O daughter of Zion, is accomplished;
he will keep you in exile no longer;[2]
but [b]your iniquity, O daughter of Edom, he will punish;
he will uncover your sins.

Restore Us to Yourself, O LORD

5 [c]Remember, O LORD, what has befallen us;
look, and see [d]our disgrace!

2 [e]Our inheritance has been turned over to strangers,
our homes to foreigners.

3 We have become orphans, fatherless;
our mothers are like widows.

4 We must pay for the water we drink;
the wood we get must be bought.

5 [f]Our pursuers are at our necks;[3]
we are weary; we are given no rest.

6 We have given the hand to [g]Egypt,
and to [g]Assyria,
to get bread enough.

7 Our fathers sinned, and are no more;
[h]and we bear their iniquities.

8 [i]Slaves rule over us;
there is none to deliver us from their hand.

1 Hebrew *The face of the LORD* 2 Or *he will not exile you again*
3 Symmachus *With a yoke on our necks*

4:17 a nation. Israel and Judah characteristically sought help in political alliances rather than in the Lord (Is. 7; 30:1–5; Jer. 24).

4:19 eagles. Jer. 4:13.

4:20 the LORD's anointed. This is a reference to hope in the Davidic king, especially following Josiah's reform (2 Kin. 22; 23). This reform, though religious, had also asserted Judah's independence and seemed to confirm the ancient promise to David (2 Sam. 7). The last king of Judah, deported by Nebuchadnezzar, was Zedekiah (2 Kin. 25:7). Yet Jeremiah promised final salvation through the righteous Branch of David, the Messiah (Jer. 23:5–8).

4:21, 22 O daughter of Edom. This is one of Israel's historic enemies. Her enmity was the more scandalous because of an ancient affinity of blood; Edom was another name for Jacob's brother, Esau (Gen. 25:30). But the nation of Edom will also fall in its turn (Obad. and Jer. 49:7–22).

The punishment of your iniquity . . . is accomplished. That is, "Your guilt will end." Because of God's mercy and compassion the guilt of His people will be ended, and they, in contrast to Edom, will be delivered. See Is. 40:2 and Jer. 49:7–22.

5:1–22 Rehearsing the continuing effects of Zion's degradation, the poet makes a final plea for restoration.

5:1 Remember . . . us. This is a typical opening for a communal lament. Zion no longer appears in the immediate throes of siege and plunder (as in ch. 4), but at a later stage of affliction, when the sudden violation of the land has given way to harsh and humiliating oppression.

5:2 Our inheritance. The land as a whole is Israel's inheritance from God (Deut. 4:21; 12:9), while the territory of Judah is given specifically to the tribe of that name (Josh. 15:20–63).

strangers . . . foreigners. God had given the land to Israel, and had even directed them to expel the foreigners. Now this was turned upside down.

5:3 orphans . . . widows. Their position was precarious and dependent. Israel was commanded to show care for them, because their condition denied them normal access to the land's goods (Deut. 14:28, 29).

5:4 We must pay for the water. This necessity is an ironic reversal of Deut. 6:10, 11, and especially Josh. 9:21–23.

5:5 no rest. This condition is another reversal of a blessing promised in Deuteronomy (Deut. 12:9; Lam. 1:3).

5:6 Egypt . . . Assyria. This kind of submission was not only humiliating but dangerous (2 Kin. 18:14).

5:7 Our fathers sinned . . . we bear their iniquities. A similar description of solidarity between generations is found in Ex. 20:5 and in the books of 1 and 2 Kings, with their records of guilt accumulated over the generations. Passages such as Ezek. 18 (notes; Jer. 31:29, 30) address those who questioned the justice of being judged for sins they did not commit. Ezekiel answers that those who share in their father's judgment have shared in their father's sins: each generation bears the guilt of its own sins, not of those of previous generations only.

5:8 Slaves. When Babylonian servants command Israel there has been an ironic distortion of the true relationships between God, Israel, and the nations. Israel is in truth a nation freed from slavery (Deut. 15:12–18); but those who do not serve the true God must be in bondage. See 1:1 and note.

9 [j] We get our bread at the peril of our lives,
because of the sword in the wilderness.
10 [k] Our skin is hot as an oven
with [l] the burning heat of famine.
11 Women are raped in Zion,
young women in the towns of Judah.
12 [m] Princes are hung up by their hands;
[n] no respect is shown to the elders.
13 Young men are compelled to [o] grind at the mill,
and boys stagger [p] under loads of wood.
14 [n] The old men have left the city gate,
the young men [q] their music.
15 [q] The joy of our hearts has ceased;
[r] our dancing has been turned to mourning.
16 [s] The crown has fallen from our head;
woe to us, for we have sinned!
17 For this [t] our heart has become sick,
for these things [u] our eyes have grown dim,
18 for Mount Zion which lies desolate;
[v] jackals prowl over it.
19 [w] But you, O LORD, reign forever;
your throne endures to all generations.
20 [x] Why do you forget us forever,
why do you forsake us for so many days?
21 [y] Restore us to yourself, O LORD, that we may be restored!
Renew our days as of old—
22 [z] unless you have utterly rejected us,
and you remain exceedingly angry with us.

9 [j] [Jer. 6:25] 10 [k] See ch. 4:8 [l] [Deut. 32:24] 12 [m] See 2 Kin. 25:19-21 [n] ch. 4:16 13 [o] [Judg. 16:21] [p] [Josh. 9:27] 14 [n] [See ver. 12 above] [q] [Isai. 24:8] 15 [q] [See ver. 14 above] [r] [Amos 8:10] 16 [s] Ps. 89:39; Jer. 13:18; [ch. 1:1] 17 [t] Isai. 1:5 [u] See ch. 2:11 18 [v] [Isai. 34:13] 19 [w] Ps. 9:7; 102:12; 145:13 20 [x] Ps. 13:1 21 [y] Jer. 31:18; [Ps. 80:3, 7, 19] 22 [z] Jer. 14:19

5:9 sword in the wilderness. This possibly speaks of wilderness robbers who took advantage of the weakened community.

5:11–13 Here are pictures of shame.

5:11 young women. The loss of virginity outside marriage brought shame on a woman and her family, and possibly additional serious consequences (Deut. 22:13–21).

5:12 hung up. This was a form of torture or of execution by exposure.

5:13 grind at the mill. This was degrading toil for a young man (Judg. 16:21).

5:14 This verse conveys something of the state of normal life in Judah by describing what has ceased. The "gate," which had legal and social functions, is now deserted. The light-hearted pleasures of the "young men" have been replaced by the harsh life depicted in the preceding verses.

5:16 The crown. Some take this to refer to Jerusalem in particular (Lam. 1:1; 2:15; 5:18). Probably it represents the glory of Israel and Judah among the nations (Ex. 19:6).

woe . . . sinned. See note on v. 7.

5:18 Mount Zion . . . desolate. The poet comes full circle from 1:1, resuming the theme of the scandal of the chosen city of God lying destroyed and abandoned.

5:19 you, O LORD, reign forever. Though the "royalty" of the people (v. 16) is no more, that of the Lord remains forever.

5:20 Why. The note of lament is struck again. There is no easy exit from the pain that has been expressed; but the affirmation of God's sovereignty is made in the midst of that pain (v. 19). The logic of vv. 19, 20 is paralleled in Ps. 89, vv. 1–37 praising God's sovereignty and vv. 38–51 asking "How long" (Ps. 89:46).

5:21 Restore us . . . restored. These two words are from the same Hebrew verb. Its use is ambiguous, since the restoration could be either a physical return of exiles to the land or a return that is moral and religious (repentance). The ambiguity is necessary, because the prophets never envisage a restoration to the land that is separate from repentance towards God. For an exact parallel of this thought, see Jer. 31:18.

5:22 unless. The poet declines to finish the lament on a high note. Nevertheless, the final note is not one of despair but of petition. The five poems in the book come to us out of the acute grief of the judgment experienced, but they also point to the compassion of God as grounds for future deliverance.

THE BOOK OF Ezekiel

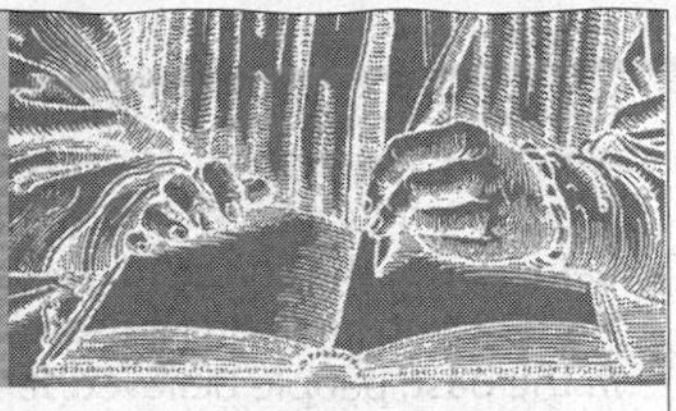

AUTHOR

We have no information about the prophet Ezekiel beyond what is known from the book bearing his name. Nebuchadnezzar had captured Jerusalem in 597 B.C. and carried away King Jehoiachin, the royal family, and the leading citizens and craftsmen (2 Kin. 24:14). Ezekiel was among this first group of deportees. His wife died during the captivity shortly before Jerusalem was destroyed by the Babylonians in 586 B.C. (24:15–18). If the prophet was thirty years old when he began his prophetic ministry (1:1), and this date corresponds to the fifth year of the exile of Jehoiachin (1:2, 3), Ezekiel was about twenty-six when he was carried into exile. The last date recorded in the book (April 26, 571 B.C., 29:17) shows that Ezekiel's ministry spanned at least twenty-three years, until he was about fifty. The circumstances of his death are not known.

Ezekiel was a priest (1:3). Priests ordinarily began their temple service at age thirty. However, in the year he would have begun his temple service Ezekiel was living in Babylon, seven hundred miles from Jerusalem. It was at this significant age in his life that God called Ezekiel to be a prophet. His prophetic endowment was recognized by the leaders among the exiles (8:1; 20:1).

"Ezekiel" means "God makes strong, hardens" (see note 3:8). God addresses Ezekiel many times by the phrase "Son of man," meaning "person, human being." The phrase in this book emphasizes human frailty and insignificance as compared with the transcendence of God (contrast its use as a messianic title in Dan. 7:13; Matt. 26:64; Mark 14:62; Rev. 14:14).

DATE AND OCCASION

Ezekiel witnessed much of the decline and fall of the Assyrian Empire. In place of the Assyrians the armies of Babylon under King Nebuchadnezzar were emerging as the dominant power in the ancient Near East. The city of Babylon was located in the region of Chaldea, and so the names "Chaldeans" and "Babylonians" are used interchangeably by biblical writers. The Babylonians and the armies of Pharaoh Neco of Egypt periodically fought over the territory formerly subject to the Assyrians along the coast of Syria and Israel; the kings of Judah in Jerusalem were caught in the middle.

Jehoiakim was placed on the throne of Jerusalem by Pharaoh Neco (2 Kin. 23:34) in 609 B.C. After the Egyptians were defeated by the Babylonians at Carchemish in 605 B.C., Jehoiakim switched his allegiance and became a vassal of Nebuchadnezzar. He remained a Babylonian vassal for three years, and then switched his allegiance back to Egypt (2 Kin. 24:1). Jehoiakim died in the same month Nebuchadnezzar set out on an expedition to punish him. He was succeeded by his son Jehoiachin, who was left to face Nebuchadnezzar's wrath. After a brief siege, Jehoiachin was taken into captivity with much of the population of Jerusalem, including Ezekiel, in 597 B.C. (2 Kin. 24:8–12). Ezekiel settled with a colony of Jewish captives, possibly near Tel-abib, on "the Chebar canal" (1:1), a canal flowing into the Euphrates southeast of Babylon.

Nebuchadnezzar installed Zedekiah, Jehoiachin's uncle, as ruler of Judah. He ruled until the destruction of Jerusalem in 586 B.C. Though in this way Zedekiah became the last king of Judah, Jehoiachin was considered the last legitimate ruler from the Davidic line. Dates in the Book of Ezekiel are all in terms of the years of Jehoiachin's exile. The reign of Zedekiah was characterized by a similar vacillation between Egypt and Babylon (17:15–19).

The exiles and many of those remaining in Jerusalem hoped that the Exile would be short, that those who had been deported would soon be returned to the city, and that Jerusalem would be spared further disaster. There were false prophets who wrongly encouraged this belief. Since the Lord had chosen Jerusalem as His dwelling and had Himself defended the city in the past, people believed Jerusalem was inviolable. Ezekiel had to warn the exiles that a worse fate was yet in store for Jerusalem.

No other prophetic book contains as many chronological notices. Ezekiel was conscious of the relevance of his message to the immediate historical situation. The chronology for the latter half of the first millennium B.C. (including the time of Ezekiel) is known from chronological records in the Bible and other documents in a variety of languages from the ancient Near East. Astronomical observations recorded by ancient scribes enable us to correlate the ancient and modern calendars with a high degree of confidence. The Book of Ezekiel contains indications of the date at more than a dozen places (1:1, 2; 8:1; 20:1; 24:1, etc.). These dates fall between 593 and 573 B.C.

CHARACTERISTICS AND THEMES

The Book of Ezekiel may be divided into three parts. In the first two, Ezekiel announces judgment on Jerusalem (1–24) and foreign nations (25–32). The first years of Ezekiel's ministry were concerned with the immediate prospects of Jerusalem. It is only after a messenger arrived reporting the destruction of Jerusalem (33:21, 22) that Ezekiel's preaching became dominated by the promises of restoration and mercy for the future (33–48). This three-part structure (judgment against Israel, judgment against foreign nations, grace and mercy for Israel) can be found also in Isaiah and Zephaniah.

Ezekiel is the only prophetic book that is entirely autobiographical, written in the first person from the vantage point of the prophet himself. The work also contains a larger number of symbolic actions than any other prophetic book (3:22–26; 4:1–14; 5:1–4; 12:10–20; 21:6, 7, 18–24; 24:15–24; 37:15–28). See note 4:1–3. Ezekiel identified closely with his own message: he suffered in his body the consequences of representing God before the nation and of representing the nation under God's judgment. Ezekiel also uses many parables (chs. 15; 16; 17; 19; 23) and proverbs (12:21, 22; 16:44; 18:2, 3). The prophecy of Ezekiel had a profound effect on the Book of Revelation; many themes from this prophet recur in that book.

Several themes in Ezekiel's teaching are used with some frequency.

1. The Holiness and Transcendence of God. Revelation to Ezekiel is often mediated by an angelic guide (chs. 8; 40–48). When Ezekiel does see a vision of God, it is "the appearance of the likeness of the glory of the LORD," God Himself remaining transcendent and hidden (1:28 note). God is Judge, all-knowing and all-powerful, surrounded in splendor and ruling over the affairs of nations.

God is holy. Sin is an affront to His holiness and must be judged. Israel is a rebellious nation, but the Exile is designed to produce a purged nation, a remnant ready to live in obedience before God (6:8; 9:8; 11:12, 13; 12:16; 14:22, 23).

2. The Grace and Mercy of God. God's judgment of Judah and Jerusalem does not frustrate His purpose in electing Israel. God will show mercy to a remnant; these will inherit His promises afresh and enjoy restoration to their land. God will again be in their midst (48:35; cf. 11:20; 14:11; 36:23, 27, 28). The nation will again live under a Davidic prince (37:24, 25; 45:7) who will rule righteously (34:23). God will give to His people a new heart and a new spirit (36:24–28).

3. The Sovereignty of God. God rules over the affairs and destiny not only of Israel, but also of all other nations (chs. 25–32). The words God spoke through the prophet will be performed.

4. Individual Responsibility. The Exile had come about in part as a result of the cumulative guilt of generations of Israelites who had lived in rebellion against God and His law. While guilt always has a corporate dimension, Ezekiel, more than any prophet before him, emphasized the individual consequences of disobedience and transgression. See notes 18:1–32; 33:1–20.

OUTLINE OF EZEKIEL

I. Judgment on Judah and Jerusalem (chs. 1–24)

- A. *The Prophet's Call (chs. 1–3)*
- B. *Symbolic Actions About the Destruction of Jerusalem (chs. 4; 5)*
- C. *Oracle Against the Mountains of Israel (ch. 6)*
- D. *The End (ch. 7)*
- E. *A Vision of Judgment in Jerusalem (chs. 8–11)*
- F. *Oracles About the Sins of Israel and Jerusalem (chs. 12–24)*
    1. Two Symbolic Actions (12:1–20)
    2. Popular Proverbs (12:21–28)
    3. False Prophets and Prophetesses (ch. 13)
    4. Consequences of Idolatry (ch. 14)
    5. Parable of the Vine (ch. 15)
    6. Jerusalem as Child and Harlot (ch. 16)
    7. Parable of Two Eagles (ch. 17)
    8. Individual Responsibility (ch. 18)
    9. Dirge Allegory for Israel's Kings (ch. 19)
    10. A Review of the Nation's History and Her Future (ch. 20)
    11. Babylon, God's Sword (ch. 21)
    12. The Sins of Jerusalem (ch. 22)
    13. A Parable of Two Sisters (ch. 23)
    14. A Cooking Pot (24:1–14)
    15. The Death of Ezekiel's Wife (24:15–27)

II. Oracles Against Foreign Nations (chs. 25–32)

- A. *Ammon (25:1–7)*
- B. *Moab (25:8–11)*
- C. *Edom (25:12–14)*
- D. *Philistia (25:15–17)*
- E. *Tyre (26:1–28:19)*
- F. *Sidon (28:20–26)*
- G. *Egypt (chs. 29–32)*

III. Blessing for Judah and Jerusalem (chs. 33–48)

- A. *Ezekiel the Watchman (ch. 33)*
- B. *The Shepherds of Israel (ch. 34)*
- C. *Against Edom (ch. 35)*
- D. *A Prophecy to the Mountains of Israel (ch. 36)*
- E. *The Valley of Dry Bones (37:1–14)*
- F. *Two Sticks Becoming One (37:15–28)*
- G. *Gog and Magog (chs. 38; 39)*
- H. *A Vision of a Restored Jerusalem (chs. 40–48)*
    1. The Plan of the New Temple (chs. 40–42)
    2. Regulations for the New Temple (chs. 43; 44)
    3. The Holy District in the Land (45:1–8)
    4. Regulations for Offerings (45:9–46:24)
    5. A Life-giving River (47:1–12)
    6. Boundaries and Allotment of the Land (47:13–48:29)
    7. The City Gates (48:30–35)

Ezekiel in Babylon

1 [a]In the thirtieth year, in the fourth
month, on the fifth day of the month,
as I was among the exiles by [b]the Chebar
canal, [c]the heavens were opened, and I saw
[d]visions of God.[1] **2** On the fifth day of the
month (it was [e]the fifth year of [f]the exile of
King Jehoiachin), **3** the word of the LORD
came to Ezekiel [g]the priest, the son of Buzi,
in the land of the Chaldeans by [b]the
Chebar canal, and [h]the hand of the LORD
was upon him there.

The Glory of the LORD

4 As I looked, behold, [i]a stormy wind
came [j]out of the north, and a great cloud,
with [k]brightness around it, and fire flashing
forth continually, and in the midst of the
fire, [l]as it were gleaming metal.[2] **5** And from
the midst of it came the likeness of [m]four
living creatures. [n]And this was their

Chapter 1
1 [a][ver. 3; Num. 4:3] [b]ch. 3:15, 23; 10:15, 20, 22; 43:3 [c][Matt. 3:16; Mark 1:10; Luke 3:21; John 1:51; Acts 7:56; 10:11; Rev. 10:11] [d]ch. 8:3; 40:2; [ch. 11:24; Num. 12:6]
2 [e][ch. 8:1]; See ch. 20:1 [f]2 Kin. 24:12, 15; [ch. 17:12; 19:8; 33:21; 40:1]
3 [g][ver. 1] [b][See ver. 1 above] [h]ch. 3:22; 8:1; 33:22; 37:1; 40:1; [1 Kin. 18:46; 2 Kin. 3:15]
4 [i]Jer. 23:19; 25:32; 30:23; [ch. 3:12] [j]See Jer. 1:14 [k]ver. 27 [l]ver. 27; ch. 8:2
5 [m]See Rev. 4:6-8 [n]ch. 10:14, 21

[1] Or *from God* [2] Or *amber*; also verse 27

1:1 thirtieth year. July, 593 B.C. The book appears to have a double superscription, one in the first person (v. 1) and the other in the third (vv. 2–3). The dates in the Book of Ezekiel are normally calculated from the year of the captivity of Jehoiachin (cf. 40:1). But the first date in the book specifies a "thirtieth" year (v. 1) and immediately refers to the "fifth year" (v. 2) of Jehoiachin. Probably the "thirtieth" year is Ezekiel's age at the time of his prophetic call, coinciding with the "fifth" year of Jehoiachin. A candidate for the priesthood ordinarily assumed the full responsibilities of the office at age thirty (Num. 4:3). Instead of achieving this important goal, Ezekiel was living in exile far from the temple in Jerusalem, unable to fulfill his calling as a priest.

Chebar canal. The Jews living outside their homeland commonly established places of worship along streams of water (Ps. 137:1; Acts 16:13). Two cuneiform texts from Nippur mention a *naru kabari* (meaning "Great River") that is probably the Chebar; it was a large irrigation canal that brought water from the Euphrates below Babylon.

1:4–3:15 Ezekiel's inaugural vision should be compared with the call narratives of Moses (Ex. 3), Isaiah (Is. 6), and Jeremiah (Jer. 1). Like Moses, the model prophet (Deut. 18:15, 18), those who followed him would ordinarily begin their prophetic careers by being admitted to the divine presence. In the heavenly council they hear the words of God. The prophets report such experiences not so much as autobiography but because their admission to the divine council was the basis for their claim to prophetic authority. It was a qualification that distinguished the true prophet from the false (1 Kin. 22:19–28; Jer. 23:16–18).

1:4 stormy wind. For the whirlwind or storm as a mode of theophany, see 2 Kin. 2:1, 11; Job 38:1; 40:6; Ps. 77:18; 83:15; 148:8; Is. 29:6; 66:15; Jer. 4:13; 23:19; 30:23; Nah. 1:3; Zech. 9:14.

1:5 When these "living creatures" appear again they are identified as "cherubim" (10:1, 15, 16, 20). There are points of similarity with the seraphim that attend God in Isaiah's call (Is. 6:2, 3), and with John's vision of the divine throne (Rev. 4:6–9). Their wings "touched one another" (v. 9) like the wings of the cherubim over the ark in the Most Holy Place of the temple (1 Kin. 6:27; 2 Chr. 3:11–12). Chronicles describes the ark as the divine chariot (1 Chr. 28:18).

appearance: they had a human likeness,
6 [o]but each had four faces, and each of
them had four wings. **7** Their legs were
straight, and the soles of their feet were like
the sole of a calf's foot. And they sparkled
[p]like burnished bronze. **8** Under their wings
[q]on their four sides [r]they had human
hands. And the four had their faces and
their wings thus: **9** their wings touched one
another. [s]Each one of them went straight
forward, [q]without turning as they went.
10 As for the likeness of their faces, [t]each
had a human face. The four had the face of
a lion on the right side, the four had the
face of an ox on the left side, and the four
had the face of an eagle. **11** Such were their
faces. And their wings were spread out
above. Each creature had two wings, each
of which touched the wing of another,
while [u]two covered their bodies. **12** [s]And
each went straight forward. [v]Wherever the
spirit would go, they went, without turning
as they went. **13** As for the likeness of the
living creatures, their appearance was [w]like
burning coals of fire, [w]like the appearance
of torches moving to and fro among the living creatures. [x]And the fire was bright, and
out of the fire went forth lightning. **14** And
the living creatures [y]darted to and fro, [z]like
the appearance of a flash of lightning.
15 [a]Now as I looked at the living creatures, I
saw a wheel on the earth beside the living
creatures, one for each of the four of them.[1]
16 [a]As for the appearance of the wheels and
their construction: their appearance was like
[b]the gleaming of beryl. [c]And the four had the
same likeness, their appearance and construction being as it were a wheel within a wheel.
17 [d]When they went, they went [e]in any of their
four directions[2] [f]without turning as they went.
18 And their rims were tall and awesome, [g]and
the rims of all four were full of eyes all around.
19 [h]And when the living creatures went, the
wheels went beside them; [i]and when the living creatures rose from the earth, the wheels
rose. **20** [j]Wherever the spirit wanted to go, they
went, and the wheels rose along with them,
[j]for the spirit of the living creatures[3] was in the
wheels. **21** [h]When those went, these went; and
when those stood, these stood; [i]and when
those rose from the earth, the wheels rose
along with them, [j]for the spirit of the living
creatures was in the wheels.
22 Over the heads of the living creatures
there was [k]the likeness of an expanse, shining like awe-inspiring [l]crystal, spread out
above their heads. **23** And under the
expanse their wings were [m]stretched out
straight, one toward another. [n]And each
creature had two wings covering its body.
24 And when they went, I heard the sound
of their wings [o]like the sound of many
waters, like [p]the sound of the [q]Almighty, a
sound of tumult [r]like the sound of an
army. When they stood still, they let down
their wings. **25** And there came a voice from
above [s]the expanse over their heads. When
they stood still, they let down their wings.
26 And above the expanse over their heads
there was [t]the likeness of a throne, [t]in appearance [u]like sapphire;[4] and seated above the
likeness of a throne was [v]a likeness with a
human appearance. **27** And [w]upward from
what had the appearance of his waist I saw as
it were [x]gleaming metal, like the appearance
of fire enclosed all around. And downward
from what had the appearance of his waist I
saw as it were the appearance of fire, and
[y]there was brightness around him.[5] **28** Like the
appearance of [z]the bow that is in the cloud
on the day of rain, so was the appearance of
the brightness all around.

Such was the appearance of the likeness
of [a]the glory of the LORD. And when I saw
it, [b]I fell on my face, and I heard the voice
of one speaking.

6 [o]ch. 10:21
7 [p]ch. 40:3; Rev. 1:15; 2:18
8 [q]ver. 17; ch. 10:11 [r]ch. 10:8, 21
9 [s]ch. 10:22 [q][See ver. 8 above]
10 [t]ch. 10:14, 21
11 [u]ver. 23; [Isai. 6:2]
12 [s][See ver. 9 above] [v]ch. 10:17
13 [w][Ps. 104:4] [x][Ps. 97:3, 4]
14 [y][Zech. 4:10] [z][Matt. 24:27; Luke 17:24]
15 [a]ch. 10:9; [Dan. 7:9]
16 [a][See ver. 15 above] [b][Dan. 10:6] [c]ch. 10:10
17 [d]ch. 10:11 [e]ver. 8 [f]ver. 9
18 [g]ch. 10:12; [Rev. 4:8]
19 [h]ch. 10:16 [i][ch. 10:19; 11:22]
20 [j]ch. 10:17
21 [h][See ver. 19 above] [i][See ver. 19 above] [j][See ver. 20 above]
22 [k][ver. 25, 26; ch. 10:1] [l][Rev. 4:6]
23 [m]ver. 7 [n]ver. 11
24 [o]ch. 43:2; [Rev. 1:15] [p]Ps. 29:3, 4; 68:33 [q]See Gen. 17:1 [r]Dan. 10:6; [Rev. 19:6]
25 [s][ver. 22]
26 [t]ch. 10:1; [1 Kin. 22:19] [u]Ex. 24:10 [v]Dan. 8:15; [Rev. 1:13]
27 [w]ch. 8:2; [ver. 4] [x]See ver. 4 [y]ver. 4
28 [z]Gen. 9:13; [Rev. 4:3; 10:1] [a]ch. 3:23; 8:4; 9:3; 10:4, 18, 19; 11:22, 23; 43:4, 5; 44:4; [Ex. 24:16] [b]ch. 3:23; 43:3; 44:4; [Gen. 17:3, 17; Josh. 5:14; Dan. 8:17; Acts 9:4; Rev. 1:17]

1 Hebrew *of their faces* 2 Hebrew *on their four sides* 3 Or *the spirit of life*; also verse 21 4 Or *lapis lazuli* 5 Or *it*

1:10 faces. The four faces probably represent the heads of four realms of creation. Man is supreme and faces outward. The ox is the head of domestic animals; the lion of wild animals; and the eagle of birds. The creatures apparently were in a square with the human faces looking outward to the four cardinal directions, making the other faces visible from the sides.

1:13, 14 coals of fire . . . torches . . . lightning. Fire is a regular component of the theophanies (manifestations or appearances of God) in the Old Testament (Gen. 15:17; Ex. 3:2; 13:21, 22; 14:24; 19:18; 24:17; Num. 11:1; Deut. 1:33; 4:11, 12, 24, 33, 36; 5:22–26; 9:3; Ps. 18:8; 78:14, 21).

1:24 sound. A distinctive loud sound accompanies theophanies involving the divine army (2 Sam. 5:24; 2 Kin. 7:6; Is. 13:4; 66:6; Joel 2:5; cf. Gen. 3:8; Ex. 19:19; Is. 6:4). See particularly 3:12, 13; 10:5.

1:27 brightness. The light radiating from the divine presence is overwhelming (Dan. 7:9), for God dwells "in unapproachable light" (1 Tim. 6:16). No one has seen God, and Ezekiel does not dare to describe Him. He can speak only of "the appearance of the likeness of the glory" of the Lord (1:28), a way of speaking essentially three steps removed from a direct description of God.

1:28 bow. The rainbow not only reflects the splendor around God but testifies to His dominion over the sea and His promise to Noah (Gen. 9:16, 17). See theological note "The Glory of God" on page 1148.

Ezekiel's Call

2 And he said to me, [c]"Son of man,[1] [d]stand
on your feet, and I will speak with you."
2 And as he spoke to me, [e]the Spirit entered
into me and [f]set me on my feet, and I heard
him speaking to me. 3 And he said to me,
"Son of man, I send you to the people of
Israel, to [g]nations of rebels, who have
rebelled against me. [h]They and their fathers
have transgressed against me to this very
day. 4 The descendants also are [i]impudent
and stubborn: I send you to them, and you
shall say to them, 'Thus says the Lord GOD.'
5 And [j]whether they hear or refuse to hear
(for they are [g]a rebellious house) [k]they will
know that a prophet has been among them.
6 And you, son of man, [l]be not afraid of
them, nor be afraid of their words, [m]though
briers and thorns are with you and you sit
on [n]scorpions.[2] Be not afraid of their words,
nor be dismayed at their looks, for they are
a rebellious house. 7 And you shall speak my
words to them, [j]whether they hear or refuse
to hear, for they are a rebellious house.
8 "But you, son of man, hear what I say to
you. [o]Be not rebellious like that rebellious
house; open your mouth and [p]eat what I
give you." 9 And when I looked, behold, [q]a
hand was stretched out to me, and behold,
[r]a scroll of a book was in it. 10 And he spread
it before me. And it had writing [s]on the
front and on the back, and there were written on it words of lamentation and mourning and woe.

3 And he said to me, [c]"Son of man, eat
whatever you find here. [t]Eat this scroll,
and go, speak to the house of Israel." 2 So I
opened my mouth, and he gave me this
scroll to eat. 3 And he said to me, "Son of
man, feed your belly with this scroll that I
give you and fill your stomach with it."
[u]Then I ate it, and it was in my mouth [v]as
sweet as honey.
4 And he said to me, [w]"Son of man, go to
the house of Israel and speak with my words
to them. 5 For you are not sent to a people of
foreign speech and a hard language, but to
the house of Israel— 6 not to many peoples
of foreign speech and a hard language,
whose words you cannot understand.
[x]Surely, if I sent you to such, they would listen to you. 7 [y]But the house of Israel will not
be willing to listen to you, for they are not
willing to listen to me. Because all the house
of Israel [z]have a hard forehead and a stubborn heart. 8 [a]Behold, I have made your face
as hard as their faces, and your forehead as
hard as their foreheads. 9 Like [b]emery harder
than flint have I made your forehead. [c]Fear
them not, nor be dismayed at their looks, for
they are a rebellious house." 10 Moreover, he
said to me, "Son of man, [d]all my words that
I shall speak to you receive [e]in your heart,
and hear with your ears. 11 And go to the
exiles, [f]to your people, and speak to them
and say to them, [g]'Thus says the Lord GOD,'
[h]whether they hear or refuse to hear."
12 [i]Then the Spirit[3] lifted me up, and I
heard behind me the voice[4] of [j]a great
earthquake: "Blessed be the glory of the
LORD from its place!" 13 It was the sound of
the wings of [k]the living creatures as they
touched one another, and the sound of the
wheels beside them, and the sound of [l]a
great earthquake. 14 [m]The Spirit lifted me up
and took me away, and I went in bitterness
in the heat of my spirit, the [n]hand of the

Chapter 2
1 [c]ch. 3:1, 3, 4, 17, 25; 4:1, 16; 5:1 [d]Dan. 10:11
2 [e]ch. 3:24 [f]ch. 3:24; Dan. 8:18
3 [g][ver. 5, 6, 8; ch. 3:26; 24:3; 44:6] [h]ch. 20:16, 18, 21
4 [i][ch. 3:7]
5 [j]ch. 3:11; [ch. 3:27; 17:12] [g][See ver. 3 above] [k]ch. 33:33
6 [l]ch. 3:9; Jer. 1:8 [m][ch. 28:24; 2 Sam. 23:6; Mic. 7:4] [n][Deut. 8:15]
7 [j][See ver. 5 above]
8 [o][Isai. 50:5] [p]Rev. 10:9; [ch. 3:1, 3]
9 [q]ch. 8:3; Dan. 10:10; Rev. 10:2 [r]Jer. 36:2
10 [s]Rev. 5:1
Chapter 3
1 [c][See ch. 2:1 above] [t][ch. 2:8]
3 [u]Jer. 15:16; Rev. 10:9, 10 [v][Ps. 19:10; 119:103]
4 [w]See ch. 2:1
6 [x][Matt. 11:21, 23]
7 [y][John 15:20] [z][ch. 2:4]
8 [a]See Jer. 1:18
9 [b][Isai. 50:7] [c]ch. 2:6
10 [d]Jer. 26:2 [e][ver. 3]
11 [f]ch. 33:2, 12, 17, 30 [g]ver. 27 [h]ch. 2:7
12 [i]ch. 8:3; 11:1, 24; 43:5; [ch. 37:1] [j][ch. 1:24]
13 [k]ch. 1:5, 15 [l][ch. 1:24] 14 [m]ch. 8:3; 11:1, 24; 43:5; [ch. 37:1] [n]See ch. 1:3

[1] Or *Son of Adam*; so throughout Ezekiel [2] Or *on scorpion plants* [3] Or *the wind*; also verse 14 [4] Or *sound*

2:1–8 In other call narratives, after the person comes into the divine presence, God announces the commission, normally with a statement that God is sending that person (2:3; Ex. 3:10; Judg. 6:14; Is. 6:8; Jer. 1:7).

2:1 Son of man. God addresses Ezekiel this way more than ninety times in this book. The phrase means "person, human being" and emphasizes the humanity and frailty of the prophet, all the more when it stands in such proximity to a vision of God's glory. This use of the phrase in Ezekiel should be distinguished from its use in the Gospels as the favorite self-designation of Jesus. Jesus uses the phrase to designate Himself as the "Son of Man" known from Dan. 7:13, 14.

2:2 Spirit. In the Old Testament the Spirit of God is preeminently the Spirit of prophecy, the Spirit who makes the prophet a channel of revelation (Num. 11:25, 26, 29; 1 Sam. 10:6; 19:20; Joel 2:28; Zech. 7:12).

2:6 briers . . . thorns . . . scorpions. These metaphors refer to those who are going to persecute Ezekiel for bringing an unpopular message from God (1 Kin. 18:4; Jer. 20:7–18; Matt. 23:29–31, 34, 37).

2:9–3:3 In other accounts of the prophetic call, once the commission is given God often provides a sign to confirm it (Ex. 3:12; Jer. 1:11–14). Moses had said that God would put His word into the mouths of the prophets (Deut. 18:18), and here that is seen in a graphic way. What food is to the body, so the word of God would be for Ezekiel's ministry.

2:10 front . . . back. Scrolls were ordinarily written only on one side, but see also Zech. 5:3; Rev. 5:1.

lamentation and mourning and woe. Most of the first half of the Book of Ezekiel is oracles of judgment against Judah (chs. 1–24) and foreign nations (chs. 25–32).

3:7 to you . . . to me. The Lord identifies His messengers with Himself (cf. Luke 10:16; John 13:20).

3:8 made your face as hard. Ezekiel's name in Hebrew means "God makes strong, hardens."

3:12 Spirit lifted me up. Ezekiel more than once describes his visionary experiences in terms of transport by the Spirit (3:12, 14; 8:3; 11:1, 24; 40:1–3; 43:5). See 2 Kin. 2:11, 16; 2 Cor. 12:1, 2.

LORD being strong upon me. 15 [o]And I came
to the exiles at Tel-abib, who were dwelling
[o]by the Chebar canal, and I sat where they
were dwelling.[1] And [p]I sat there [q]over-
whelmed among them [r]seven days.

A Watchman for Israel

16 [s]And at the end of seven days, the word
of the LORD came to me: 17 [t]"Son of man, [u]I
have made you a watchman for the house of
Israel. Whenever you hear a word from my
mouth, you shall [v]give them warning from
me. 18 [w]If I say to the wicked, [x]'You shall
surely die,' [v]and you give him no warning,
nor speak to warn the wicked from his
wicked way, in order to save his life, that
wicked person [y]shall die for[2] his iniquity,
[z]but his blood I will require at your hand.
19 [a]But if you warn the wicked, and he does
not turn from his wickedness, or from his
wicked way, he shall die for his iniquity,
[b]but you [c]will have delivered your soul.
20 [d]Again, if a righteous person turns from
his righteousness and commits injustice,
[e]and I lay a stumbling block before him, he
shall die. [v]Because you have not warned
him, he shall die for his sin, [d]and his righteous deeds that he has done shall not be
remembered, [z]but his blood I will require at
your hand. 21 But if you warn the righteous
person not to sin, and he does not sin, he
shall surely live, because he took warning,
and you will have delivered your soul."
22 [f]And the hand of the LORD was upon me
there. And he said to me, "Arise, go out into
[g]the valley,[3] and [h]there I will speak with you."

15 [o]See ch. 1:1 [p]Job 2:13; Ps. 137:1; Lam. 2:10 [q]ch. 4:17; Isai. 52:14; Jer. 14:9 [r][Gen. 50:10; 1 Sam. 31:13]
16 [s][Jer. 42:7]
17 [t]See ch. 2:1 [u]ch. 33:7; Isai. 52:8; 56:10; Jer. 6:17; [Heb. 13:17] [v]2 Chr. 19:10; [2 Kin. 6:10]; See ver. 18-21; ch. 33:4-6
18 [w]ch. 33:8 [x]Gen. 2:17 [v][See ver. 17 above] [y]ch. 18:18; Jer. 31:30; [John 8:21, 24] [z]ver. 20; ch. 33:6, 8; 34:10; [ch. 18:13; Acts 18:6; 20:26]
19 [a]ch. 33:9 [b][1 Tim. 4:16] [c]ch. 14:14, 20 **20** [d]See ch. 18:24 [e]Jer. 6:21 [v][See ver. 17 above] [z][See ver. 18 above] **22** [f]See ch. 1:3 [g]ch. 8:4; 37:1; Gen. 11:2 [h][Acts 9:6; 22:10]

[1] Or *Chebar, and to where they dwelt* [2] Or *in*; also verses 19, 20 [3] Or *plain*; also verse 23

The Glory of God

God's goal is His glory, but this needs careful explanation, for it is easily misunderstood. It points to a purpose, not of divine egoism, but of divine love. Certainly, God asks to be praised for His praiseworthiness and exalted for His greatness and goodness; He asks to be appreciated for what He is. But the glory that is His goal is a two-sided, two-stage relationship: on the one side He reveals His glory in acts of free generosity, and on the other, His people respond with adoration, giving Him glory with thanksgiving for what they have seen and received. Human beings were made for this reciprocal fellowship of love, and Christ's redemption makes it possible for those who had fallen. Human nature is fulfilled through seeing God's glory and returning praise to Him, just as God has pleasure in revealing His goodness to those who receive it (Zeph. 3:14–17).

"Glory" in the Old Testament is associated with value, riches, splendor, and dignity. When Moses asked to see God's glory, God proclaimed to Moses His name; that is, He revealed to Moses something of His nature, character, and power (Ex. 33:18–34:7; theological note " 'This Is My Name': God's Self-disclosure" at Ex. 3:15). Accompanying the proclamation was an awe-inspiring physical manifestation, a bright cloud like a burning fire (Ex. 24:17). This glory of God's presence is often called the "Shekinah" or the "Shekinah glory." It appeared at significant moments as a sign of God's active presence (Ex. 33:22; 34:5; cf. 16:10; 24:17; 40:34; Lev. 9:23–24; 1 Kin. 8:10–11; Ezek. 1:28; 8:4; 9:3; 10:4; 11:22–23; Matt. 17:5; Luke 2:9; cf. Acts 1:9; 1 Thess. 4:17; Rev. 1:7). New Testament writers proclaim that the glory of God is now revealed in Jesus Christ (John 1:14–18; 2 Cor. 4:3–6; Heb. 1:1–3).

God is glorified in the acts of salvation, because they exhibit His incomparable condescension, His inexhaustible love, and His limitless power. "Salvation belongs to the LORD" (Jon. 2:9), and those He saves have contributed nothing to their salvation except their need (Is. 42:8; 48:11). The praise for salvation belongs to no one except God. This is why Reformation theology was so insistent on the principle, "Glory to God *alone*" (*soli Deo gloria*), and why we need to maintain that principle with equal zeal today.

3:15 Tel-abib. Precise location not known.

overwhelmed. The Bible records similar periods of silence or incapacity on the part of others (Ezra 9:4; Job 2:13; Jer. 23:9; Dan. 8:27; Acts 9:9).

3:16 word of the LORD. This phrase occurs over fifty times in Ezekiel, more than in any other prophetic book.

3:17 watchman. Ezekiel will elaborate on his role as a watchman in 33:1–9. Being a watchman meant he was responsible for those he ministered to and had to warn them of any impending threat. Failure to issue the warning would make him accountable for any misfortune that resulted. People in a city would not ignore the cry of an ordinary watchman, yet they would not listen to Ezekiel (vv. 6, 7; cf. Is. 22:1–14).

3:22 hand of the LORD. Ezekiel uses this phrase to describe how revelation came to him (v. 14; 8:1; 33:22; 37:1; 40:1).

valley. The word means an open area between mountains and can be translated either "valley" or "plain." The term also occurs in Ezekiel's vision of the "valley" of dry bones (37:1).

23 So I arose and went out into the valley,
and behold, [i]the glory of the LORD stood
there, like the glory that I had seen [j]by the
Chebar canal, [i]and I fell on my face. 24 [k]But
the Spirit entered into me and set me on my
feet, and he spoke with me and said to me,
"Go, shut yourself within your house. 25 And
you, O son of man, behold, [l]cords will be
placed upon you, and you shall be bound
with them, so that you cannot go out among
the people. 26 And I will make your tongue
cling to the roof of your mouth, so that [m]you
shall be mute and unable to reprove them,
[n]for they are a rebellious house. 27 [o]But when
I speak with you, I will open your mouth,
and you shall say to them, [p]'Thus says the
Lord GOD.' [q]He who will hear, let him hear;
and he who will refuse to hear, let him
refuse, for they are a rebellious house.

The Siege of Jerusalem Symbolized

4 "And you, [r]son of man, [s]take a brick
and lay it before you, and engrave on it
a city, even Jerusalem. 2 [t]And put siegeworks against it, [u]and build a siege wall
against it, [v]and cast up a mound against it.
Set camps also against it, [w]and plant battering rams against it all around. 3 And you,
take an iron griddle, and place it as an iron
wall between you and the city; [x]and set
your face toward it, [y]and let it be in a state
of siege, and press the siege against it. This
is [z]a sign for the house of Israel.
4 "Then lie on your left side, and place the
punishment[1] of the house of Israel upon it.
For the number of the days that you lie on
it, [a]you shall bear their punishment. 5 For I
assign to you a number of days, [b]390 days,
[c]equal to the number of the years of their
punishment. [a]So long shall you bear [d]the
punishment of the house of Israel. 6 And
when you have completed these, you shall
lie down a second time, but on your right
side, and [e]bear [f]the punishment of the
house of Judah. [g]Forty days I assign you, a
day for each year. 7 [h]And you shall set your
face toward the siege of Jerusalem, [i]with
your arm bared, and you shall prophesy
against the city. 8 And behold, [j]I will place
cords upon you, so that you cannot turn
from one side to the other, till you have
completed [k]the days of your siege.
9 "And you, take wheat and barley, beans
and lentils, millet and emmer,[2] and put
them into a single vessel and make your
[l]bread from them. [m]During the number of
days that you lie on your side, [n]390 days,
you shall eat it. 10 And your food that you eat
shall be [o]by weight, [p]twenty shekels[3] a day;
from day to day[4] you shall eat it. 11 And
water you shall drink [o]by measure, the sixth
part of a hin;[5] from day to day you shall
drink. 12 And you shall eat it as a barley cake,
baking it [q]in their sight on human dung."
13 And the LORD said, "Thus shall the people
of Israel eat [r]their bread unclean, among the
nations where I will drive them." 14 Then I

23 [i]See ch. 1:28 [j]See ch. 1:1
24 [k]See ch. 2:2
25 [l]ch. 4:8
26 [m][Isai. 8:16] [n][ch. 2:3]
27 [o][ch. 24:27; 29:21] [p]ver. 11 [q][Rev. 22:11]
Chapter 4
1 [r]See ch. 2:1 [s][ver. 3; Jer. 13:1, 2]
2 [t][2 Kin. 25:1] [u]ch. 17:17; 21:22; 26:8 [v]Luke 19:43 [w]ch. 21:22; 26:9
3 [x]See ch. 21:2 [y][Isai. 29:3] [z]ch. 12:6, 11; 24:24, 27; [Isai. 8:18; 20:3]
4 [a]ch. 44:10, 12; [Lev. 16:22; Isai. 53:11, 12]
5 [b]ver. 9 [c][Num. 14:34] [a][See ver. 4 above] [d][ch. 23:4, 9, 10]
6 [e]ch. 44:10, 12; [Lev. 16:22; Isai. 53:11, 12] [f][ch. 23:11, 12] [g][Num. 14:34]
7 [h]See ch. 21:2 [i]Isai. 52:10
8 [j]ch. 3:25 [k][ver. 9; ch. 5:2]; See 2 Kin. 25:1-3; Jer. 39:1, 2; 52:4-6
9 [l][1 Kin. 22:27] [m]See ver. 8 [n]ver. 5
10 [o]ch. 12:19; [Jer. 37:21] [p]ch. 45:12 11 [o][See ver. 10 above] 12 [q]See ch. 12:3
13 [r]Hos. 9:3; [Dan. 1:8]

1 Or *iniquity*; also verses 5, 6, 17 2 A type of wheat 3 A *shekel* was about 2/5 ounce or 11 grams 4 Or *at a set time daily*; also verse 11
5 A *hin* was about 4 quarts or 3.5 liters

3:26 you shall be mute. The length and nature of Ezekiel's speechlessness is one of the most debated issues in the book. Whatever its beginning, it lasted until word reached the exiles that the city of Jerusalem had been destroyed (24:27; 33:22; cf. 29:21). The prophet was not completely mute, but spoke only when he received revelation from God. Ezekiel delivered many oracles to the exiles in the six years between his call and the destruction of Jerusalem.

4:1–3 The prophets of Israel used props like the brick as illustrations for their points; these object lessons are usually called "symbolic actions" (1 Kin. 11:30; 22:11; 2 Kin. 13:17; Is. 20:2–4; Jer. 13:1–14; 19:1–10). In several places in Mesopotamia bricks or clay tablets have been found with maps or architectural drawings inscribed on them. The prophet depicts the siege that was laid against Jerusalem in 586 B.C. and ended with its destruction.

4:3 iron griddle. The large flat griddle on which bread was baked in an oven. Since the prophet represented God in this miniature drama, the iron griddle standing on edge represented the wall between God and Jerusalem. Their prayers would not reach Him, and He would not intervene on their behalf.

4:4 place the punishment. The dual nature of the prophetic office—representing God to the people and the people to God—is seen in the second half of the symbolic action. Now the prophet represents the people and bears their sin (cf. Ex. 32:30–32; Rom. 9:3).

4:5, 6 390. The time period to which the figures 390 and 40 refer are hard to interpret. Each day represented one year (v. 6; cf. Num. 14:34; Dan. 9:24–27). It may be that the 40 days do not follow the 390 days (for a total of 430), but are concurrent with them. Some regard the total of 430 years as a symbolic reference to the length of Israel's sojourn in Egypt (Ex. 12:40–41).

4:8 place cords upon you. Lying on his side while bound probably means that Ezekiel was immobile a part of each day. For example, he still had to prepare his meals (vv. 8–13).

4:9–11 Ezekiel must exist on siege rations while he enacts the siege of Jerusalem. These rations reflect the privations during a siege (Deut. 28:52–57; 2 Kin. 6:25; 7:12; Jer. 15:2; 19:9).

4:10 twenty shekels. About eight ounces (see text note).

4:11 the sixth part of a hin. This water ration is 0.6 liter or just over a pint.

4:12–15 Ceremonial cleanness was all but impossible to observe during a siege, even for a priest like Ezekiel. Human excrement was considered impure (Deut. 23:13), and the prophet is repulsed by God's command to him, protesting that he had never violated the dietary laws restricting the kinds of food Israel was permitted to eat (44:31; Ex. 22:31; Lev. 7:19–24; 11:8, 39, 40; 22:8; Deut. 14:3, 8). God permitted him to substitute cattle manure, still a widely used fuel in parts of the Near East.

said, [s]"Ah, Lord GOD! Behold, I have never
defiled myself.[1] [t]From my youth up till now
I have never eaten [u]what died of itself or was
torn by beasts, nor has [v]tainted meat come
into my mouth." **15** Then he said to me, "See,
I assign to you cow's dung instead of human
dung, on which you may prepare your
bread." **16** Moreover, he said to me, [w]"Son of
man, behold, [x]I will break the supply[2] of
bread in Jerusalem. They shall eat bread [o]by
weight and with anxiety, and they shall
drink water [o]by measure and in dismay. **17** I
will do this that they may lack bread and
water, and [y]look at one another in dismay,
and [z]rot away because of their punishment.

Jerusalem Will Be Destroyed

5 "And you, [a]O son of man, take a [b]sharp
sword. Use it as [c]a barber's razor and
[d]pass it over your head and your beard.
Then take balances for weighing and divide
the hair. **2** [e]A third part you shall burn in the
fire [f]in the midst of the city, [g]when the days
of the siege are completed. And a third part
you shall take and strike with the sword all
around the city. [h]And a third part you shall
scatter to the wind, and [i]I will unsheathe
the sword after them. **3** [j]And you shall take
from these a small number and bind them
in the skirts of your robe. **4** [k]And of these
again you shall take some and cast them
into the midst of the fire and burn them in
the fire. From there a fire will come out into
all the house of Israel.
5 "Thus says the Lord GOD: [l]This is
Jerusalem. I have set her [m]in the center of
the nations, with countries all around her.
6 And she has rebelled against my rules by
doing wickedness [n]more than the nations,
and against my statutes more than [m]the
countries all around her; for they have
rejected my rules and have not walked in
my statutes. **7** Therefore thus says the Lord
GOD: Because you are [o]more turbulent
than the nations that are all around you,
[p]and have not walked in my statutes or
obeyed my rules, [q]and have not[3] even
acted according to the rules of the nations
that are all around you, **8** therefore thus
says the Lord GOD: Behold, I, even I, [r]am
against you. [s]And I will execute judgments[4] in your midst [t]in the sight of the
nations. **9** And because of all your abominations I will do with you [u]what I have
never yet done, and the like of which I will
never do again. **10** Therefore [v]fathers shall
eat their sons in your midst, and sons shall
eat their fathers. [s]And I will execute judgments on you, [w]and any of you who survive I will scatter to all the winds.
11 Therefore, [x]as I live, declares the Lord
GOD, surely, [y]because you have defiled my
sanctuary [z]with all your detestable things
and with all your [a]abominations, [b]there-
fore I will withdraw.[5] [c]My eye will not
spare, and I will have no pity. **12** [d]A third
part of you shall die of pestilence and be
consumed with famine in your midst; [d]a
third part shall fall by the sword all around
you; [d]and a third part I will scatter to all
the winds and will unsheathe the sword
after them.
13 [e]"Thus shall my anger spend itself,
and I will vent my fury upon them and satisfy myself. And they shall know that [f]I am
the LORD—that I have spoken in my jealousy—[e]when I spend my fury upon them.
14 Moreover, I will make you [g]a desolation
and [h]an object of reproach among [i]the
nations all around you and in the sight of
all who pass by. **15** You shall be[6] a reproach
and a taunt, a warning [j]and a horror, to
[i]the nations all around you, [k]when I execute judgments on you in anger and fury,
and [l]with furious rebukes—I am the LORD,
I have spoken—**16** when I send against
you[7] [m]the deadly arrows of famine, arrows

14 [s]ch. 9:8; 11:13; 20:49 [t][Acts 10:14] [u]ch. 44:31; [Lev. 7:24] [v]Isai. 65:4; [Lev. 7:18] **16** [w]See ch. 2:1 [x]ch. 5:16; 14:13; Lev. 26:26 [o][See ver. 10 above] **17** [y]See ch. 3:15 [z]ch. 24:23; 33:10; Lev. 26:39
Chapter 5
1 [a]See ch. 2:1 [b]Ps. 57:4; Isai. 49:2 [c][Isai. 7:20] [d][ch. 1:3; 44:20; Lev. 21:5] **2** [e]See ver. 12 [f][ver. 5; ch. 4:1] [g]See ch. 4:8 [h][ver. 10] [i]ver. 12; ch. 12:14; [Jer. 9:16] **3** [j][Jer. 40:6; 52:16] **4** [k][Jer. 42:18; 44:14] **5** [l][ver. 2; ch. 4:1] [m][ch. 38:12] **6** [n]See ch. 16:47, 48 [m][See ver. 5 above] **7** [o]Ps. 2:1; 46:6 [p]ch. 16:47 [q][ch. 11:12] **8** [r]See ch. 13:8 [s]ch. 11:9; 16:41; 23:10 [t]ch. 22:16 **9** [u][2 Kin. 21:12, 13; Lam. 1:12; Dan. 9:12] **10** [v]See Jer. 19:9 [s][See ver. 8 above] [w]ch. 12:14; 17:21; 22:15; 36:19; Deut. 28:64; Jer. 9:16; 15:4; Zech. 2:6; [ver. 2; ch. 36:19] **11** [x]See ch. 16:48; [y]ch. 8:3, 5, 6; 23:39; 2 Chr. 36:14; Jer. 7:30 [z]ch. 11:18 [a]ch. 7:20; 11:18, 21; [b]ch. 16:27 [c]ch. 7:4, 9; 8:18; 9:5, 10; [Jer. 21:7]

12 [d][ver. 2; ch. 6:11, 12; Jer. 15:2] **13** [e]ch. 6:12; 7:8; 20:8, 21; Lam. 4:11; [ch. 39:25] [f]ch. 36:5, 6; 38:19 **14** [g]ch. 6:6; See Jer. 22:5 [h]ch. 22:4; Neh. 2:17; Ps. 79:4; Jer. 24:9 [i]ver. 5, 6 **15** [j]ch. 14:8; Deut. 28:37 [i][See ver. 14 above] [k][ch. 14:21] [l]ch. 25:17 **16** [m]Deut. 32:23, 24

1 Hebrew *my soul* (or *throat*) *has never been made unclean* 2 Hebrew *staff* 3 Some Hebrew manuscripts and Syriac lack *not* 4 The same Hebrew expression can mean *obey rules*, or *execute judgments*, depending on context 5 Some Hebrew manuscripts *I will cut you down* 6 Dead Sea Scroll, Septuagint, Syriac, Vulgate, Targum; Masoretic Text *And it shall be* 7 Hebrew *them*

5:1 razor. God had prohibited Israelite men from shaving or cutting parts of their beard (Lev. 19:27). This law was reiterated for priests (Lev. 21:5), and Ezekiel was a priest (1:1). Cutting facial hair could be a matter of great personal shame (2 Sam. 10:4–5; Is. 7:20; 50:6) or a sign of mourning (Ezra 9:3; Is. 15:2; Jer. 7:29; 41:5; 48:37).

5:10–13 Ezekiel interprets the symbolism of vv. 1–4: the hairs burned in fire represent those who will die of plague or disease during the siege; the hairs struck with the sword represent those who will die in battle and the aftermath of the siege; the hairs dispersed by the wind represent those who will be carried into exile. It is striking that Ezekiel does not elaborate on the significance of the few hairs retained in the folds of his garment; they symbolize the survivors who will remain in Jerusalem (Jer. 40:7–12).

5:10 eat their sons. Cannibalism could be a consequence of a protracted siege (2 Kin. 6:26–29; Lam. 2:20). Moses had warned that this would happen if the nation did not obey (Deut. 28:53–57).

for destruction, which I will send to
destroy you, and when I bring more and
more famine upon [n]you and break your
supply[1] of bread. 17 I will send famine and
[o]wild beasts against you, [p]and they will
rob you of your children. Pestilence and
[q]blood shall pass through you, and I will
bring the sword upon you. I am the LORD;
I have spoken."

Judgment Against Idolatry

6 The word of the LORD came to me:
2 [r]"Son of man, [s]set your face toward
[t]the mountains of Israel, and [u]prophesy
against them, 3 and say, [v]You mountains of
Israel, hear the word of the Lord GOD!
Thus says the Lord GOD to [w]the mountains
and [x]the hills, to [y]the ravines and the valleys: Behold, I, even I, will bring a sword
upon you, [z]and I will destroy your high
places. 4 [z]Your altars shall become desolate, and your [a]incense altars shall be broken, and I will cast down your slain before
your idols. 5 [z]And I will lay the dead bodies of the people of Israel before their
idols, [b]and I will scatter your bones
around your altars. 6 Wherever you dwell,
[c]the cities shall be waste and [d]the high
places ruined, so that your altars will be
waste and ruined,[2] your idols broken and
destroyed, your [a]incense altars cut down,
and your works wiped out. 7 And the slain
shall fall in your midst, and you shall
know that I am the LORD.
8 [e]"Yet I will leave some of you alive.
When you have among the nations [f]some
who escape the sword, and when you are
scattered through the countries, 9 then
those of you who escape [g]will remember
me among the nations where they are
carried captive, how [h]I have been broken
over their whoring heart that has departed
from me and over their eyes [i]that go whoring after their idols. [g]And they will be
loathsome in their own sight for the evils
that they have committed, for all their
abominations. 10 And they shall know that I
am the LORD. [j]I have not said in vain that I
would do this evil to them."
11 Thus says the Lord GOD: [k]"Clap your
hands [l]and stamp your foot and say, Alas,
because of all the evil abominations of the
house of Israel, [m]for they shall fall by the
sword, by famine, and by pestilence. 12 [n]He
who is far off shall die of pestilence, and he
who is near shall fall by the sword, and
he who is left and is preserved shall die of
famine. [o]Thus I will spend my fury upon
them. 13 And you shall know that I am the
LORD, [p]when their slain lie among their
idols around their altars, [q]on every high
hill, [r]on all the mountaintops, [s]under every
green tree, and under [t]every leafy oak,
wherever [u]they offered pleasing aroma to
all their idols. 14 And [v]I will stretch out my
hand against them and [w]make the land
desolate and waste, [x]in all their dwelling
places, from the wilderness to [y]Riblah.[3]
Then [z]they will know that I am the LORD."

The Day of the Wrath of the LORD

7 The word of the LORD came to me:
2 "And you, [a]O son of man, thus says
the Lord GOD to the land of Israel: [b]An
end! The end has come upon the four cor-

16 [n]See ch. 4:16
17 [o]ch. 14:15; 33:27; 34:25; Deut. 32:24; [2 Kin. 17:25] [p][ch. 36:12] [q]ch. 38:22
Chapter 6
2 [r]See ch. 2:1 [s]ch. 13:17; 20:46; 21:2; 25:2; 28:21; 29:2; 35:2; 38:2; [Luke 9:51] [t]ch. 19:9; 33:28; 34:13, 14; 35:12; 36:1, 4, 8; 37:22; 38:8; 39:2, 4, 17 [u]ch. 37:4, 9; 38:2
3 [v]ch. 36:1, 4 [w]ch. 36:4, 6 [x][ver. 13] [y][ch. 31:12; Isai. 57:5, 6] [z]Lev. 26:30
4 [z][See ver. 3 above] [a]See 2 Chr. 14:5
5 [z][See ver. 3 above] [b][2 Kin. 23:14, 16]
6 [c]ch. 12:20; [Isai. 27:10] [d][ver. 3, 4] [a][See ver. 4 above]
8 [e]ch. 12:16; 14:22 [f]ch. 7:16
9 [g]ch. 16:61; 20:43; 36:31; Lev. 26:39, 40 [h][Jer. 23:9] [i]See Ex. 34:15
10 [j][Num. 23:19]
11 [k][ch. 21:14, 17] [l][ch. 25:6] [m]See ch. 5:12
12 [n][ch. 7:15] [o]See ch. 5:13
13 [p][ver. 4, 5] [q][ch. 20:28] [r]Hos. 4:13 [s]Jer. 2:20 [t]Isai. 1:29 [u]ch. 16:19; 20:28; Gen. 8:21
14 [v]ch. 25:7, 13, 16; 35:3; Isai. 5:25 [w]ch. 33:28 [x][Num. 33:46, 47; Jer. 48:22] [y][ver. 6] [z]See ver. 7
Chapter 7 2 [a]See ch. 2:1 [b]Lam. 4:18; [Isai. 10:23]

1 Hebrew *staff* 2 Or *and punished* 3 Some Hebrew manuscripts; most Hebrew manuscripts *Diblah*

6:1–3 Ezekiel's address to the mountains and hills of Jerusalem as if they were in sight has prompted some to suggest that for part of his ministry Ezekiel was in Israel instead of with the exiles in Babylon. However, though the hills and mountains of Israel were his metaphorical audience, the real audience was the exiles themselves. Compare Ezekiel's prophecy regarding the people of Edom addressed to Mount Seir (ch. 35).

6:3 high places. The Canaanites normally worshiped their gods on hilltops. God commanded the Israelites to eradicate the high places when they came into the land (Num. 33:52; Deut. 12:1–3; 33:29). However, the high places continued to flourish long after the temple was built (16:16; Jer. 7:31; 19:5; 32:35; 48:35). The people worshiped Canaanite gods there or converted the pagan shrines for use in a combination of Canaanite practices and their own. The continued existence of the high places was a particular offense to the writer of the Book of Kings (1 Kin. 11:7; 12:31, 32; 13:2, 32; 14:23; 2 Kin. 12:3; 14:4; 15:4, 35; 17:29; 23:5, 8, 13, 15, 19, 20).

6:5 dead bodies. The shrines would be desecrated by the presence of dead bodies (9:7; Num. 19:16, 18; 1 Kin. 13:2; 2 Kin. 23:14–16; 2 Chr. 23:14, 15; 34:5).

6:7 you shall know that I am the LORD. Ezekiel makes frequent use of this "recognition formula" (cf. 7:4, 9; 11:10, 12; 12:20). The Lord reveals Himself as the Ruler of history by announcing events beforehand.

6:8 escape. Ezekiel introduces the remnant theme (9:8; 11:12, 13; 12:16; 14:22, 23; 20:39–44). The remnant is a group or individual who has experienced some calamity, ordinarily in judgment for sin, and has survived. This group of survivors becomes the nucleus for the continuation of the group: they embody the future hopes of the people, and they inherit the promises of God afresh. The Exile was to be a period of purging and refining so that a pure people would emerge from it.

6:14 Riblah. See text note. The exact location is uncertain, although the context seems to require a well-known place. The Hebrew letters for "d" and "r" look similar and were occasionally confused by scribes. Riblah is in northern Lebanon where Pharaoh Neco and Nebuchadnezzar based some of their operations (2 Kin. 23:33; 25:6) in the last years of Judah. Ezekiel's audience would have understood the reference. From the wilderness to Riblah would mean from the southern to the northern boundaries of Judah and Israel.

ners of the land.[1] **3** Now [b]the end is upon
you, and [c]I will send my anger upon you;
[d]I will judge you according to your ways,
and I will punish you for all your abominations. **4** [e]And my eye will not spare you, nor
will I have pity, but [f]I will punish you for
your ways, while your abominations are in
your midst. [g]Then you will know that I am
the LORD.

5 "Thus says the Lord GOD: Disaster
[h]after disaster![2] Behold, it comes. **6** [b]An end
has come; the end has come; it has awak-
ened against you. Behold, it comes. **7** [i]Your
doom[3] has come to you, O inhabitant of
the land. [j]The time has come; the day is
near, a day of tumult, and not [k]of joyful
shouting on the mountains. **8** Now I will
soon [l]pour out my wrath upon you, and
[m]spend my anger against you, [d]and judge
you according to your ways, and I will punish you for all your abominations. **9** [e]And
my eye will not spare, nor will I have pity.
I will punish you according to your ways,
while your abominations are in your midst.
[n]Then you will know that I am the LORD,
who strikes.

10 [o]"Behold, the day! Behold, it comes!
[p]Your doom has come; [q]the rod has blossomed; pride has budded. **11** [r]Violence has
grown up into [q]a rod of wickedness. [s]None
of them shall remain, nor their abundance,
nor their wealth; neither shall there be preeminence among them.[4] **12** [j]The time has
come; the day has arrived. Let not [t]the
buyer rejoice, nor [t]the seller mourn, [u]for
wrath is upon all their multitude.[5] **13** For
[v]the seller shall not return to what he has
sold, while they live. [w]For the vision concerns all their multitude; it shall not turn
back; and because of his iniquity, none can
maintain his life.[6]

14 "They have blown the trumpet and
made everything ready, but none goes to
battle, [x]for my wrath is upon all their multitude. **15** [y]The sword is without; pestilence
and famine are within. [z]He who is in the
field dies by the sword, [z]and him who is in
the city famine and pestilence devour.
16 [a]And if any survivors escape, they will be
on the mountains, like [b]doves of the valleys, all of them moaning, each one over
his iniquity. **17** [c]All hands are feeble, and all
knees turn to water. **18** [d]They put on sackcloth, and [e]horror covers them. Shame is
on all faces, and [f]baldness on all their
heads. **19** They cast their silver into the
streets, and their gold is like an unclean
thing. [g]Their silver and gold are not able to
deliver them in the day of the wrath of the
LORD. They cannot satisfy their hunger or
fill their stomachs with it. [h]For it was [i]the
stumbling block of their iniquity. **20** [j]His
beautiful ornament they used for pride,
and [k]they made their abominable images
and their detestable things of it. Therefore
[l]I make it an unclean thing to them. **21** And
I will give it into the hands of [m]foreigners
for prey, [n]and to the wicked of the earth for
spoil, and [l]they shall profane it. **22** I will
turn my face from them, and [l]they shall
profane my treasured[7] place. Robbers shall
enter [l]and profane it.

23 [o]"Forge a chain![8] [p]For the land is full
of bloody crimes [q]and the city is full of violence. **24** I will bring [r]the worst of the
nations to take possession of their houses.
[s]I will put an end to the pride of the
strong, [t]and their holy places[9] shall be
profaned. **25** [u]When anguish comes, [v]they
will seek peace, but there shall be none.
26 [w]Disaster comes upon disaster; [x]rumor
follows rumor. [y]They seek a vision from
the prophet, while [z]the law[10] perishes
from the priest and [a]counsel from the elders. **27** The king mourns, the prince is
wrapped in despair, and the hands of the
people of the land are paralyzed by terror.

3 [b][See ver. 2 above] [c]See ver. 8 [d]See ch. 18:30 **4** [e]See ch. 5:11 [f]ch. 9:10; 11:21; 16:43; 22:31 [g]See ch. 6:7 **5** [h][ch. 5:9] **6** [b][See ver. 2 above] **7** [i]ver. 10 [j]Zeph. 1:14, 15; [ch. 12:23] [k][Jer. 25:30] **8** [l]ch. 9:8; 14:19; 20:8, 13, 21, 33, 34; 22:22; 36:18 [m]See ch. 5:13 [d][See ver. 3 above] **9** [e][See ver. 4 above] [n][ch. 6:7] **10** [o][ver. 2] [p]ver. 7 [q][Isai. 10:5; 14:5] **11** [r][ver. 23] [q][See ver. 10 above] [s][ch. 17:13] **12** [j][See ver. 7 above] [t][Isai. 24:2; 1 Cor. 7:29, 30] [u]ver. 14 **13** [v]Lev. 25:13, 14 [w]See ch. 9:8-10 **14** [x]ver. 12 **15** [y][ch. 6:12; Lam. 1:20] [z]Jer. 14:18

16 [a]ch. 6:8 [b][Isai. 38:14] **17** [c]ch. 21:7; Isai. 13:7; Jer. 6:24 **18** [d]Isai. 15:2, 3; Lam. 2:10; [e]Ps. 55:5 [f]See Isai. 3:24 **19** [g]Prov. 11:4; Zeph. 1:18; [h][1 Tim. 6:10] [i]ch. 14:3, 4, 7; 44:12 **20** [j][Isai. 64:11] [k][ch. 16:17]; See ch. 8:5-16 [l][ch. 9:7; 24:21; 25:3] **21** [m]See ch. 28:7 [n][ver. 24; ch. 23:46] [l][See ver. 20 above] **22** [l][See ver. 20 above]

23 [o][Jer. 27:2] [p]ch. 8:17; 9:9; 11:6; 22:3, 4; Jer. 6:7 [q][ver. 11] **24** [r][ver. 21; Hab. 1:6, 13] [s][ver. 11] [t]See ver. 20 **25** [u][ver. 2] [v][Jer. 6:14; 8:15; 1 Thess. 5:3] **26** [w][Jer. 4:20] [x]See Job 1:16-19 [y][ch. 20:1, 3; Ps. 74:9] [z][Mal. 2:7] [a][1 Kin. 12:6]

1 Or *earth* 2 Some Hebrew manuscripts (compare Syriac, Targum); most Hebrew manuscripts *Disaster! A unique disaster!* 3 The meaning of the Hebrew word is uncertain; also verse 10 4 The meaning of this last Hebrew sentence is uncertain 5 Or *abundance*; also verses 13, 14 6 The meaning of this last Hebrew sentence is uncertain 7 Or *secret* 8 Probably refers to an instrument of captivity 9 By revocalization (compare Septuagint); Hebrew *and those who sanctify them* 10 Or *instruction*

7:7 a day. The prophets of the Old Testament often speak of "the day" or "the day of the LORD" (30:3–9; Is. 2:12–17; 13:6–10; 34:8–12; 61:1–3; 63:3–6; Joel 2; 3; Amos 5:18–20; Obad. 8, 15; Zeph. 1:1–2:3; Zech. 14; Mal. 4:1–3). This was the day when the Lord would come to judge His enemies and to vindicate His name. Depending on the context in which it was spoken by the prophet, the day of the Lord could mean joy or sorrow for Israel. In the New Testament, see Rom. 2:16; 1 Cor. 1:8; 5:5; 2 Cor. 1:14; Phil. 1:6, 10; 2:16; 2 Tim. 1:12, 18; 4:8; Heb. 10:25; 2 Pet. 2:9; 3:12; Rev. 16:14.

7:22–27 Because the Lord had chosen Jerusalem as His dwelling and had miraculously fought on behalf of the city in the past (2 Kin. 18; 19; 2 Chr. 32; Is. 36:37), Judah had come to accept the notion that the city was inviolable as a theological truth. Ezekiel's contemporary, Jeremiah, was also warning the inhabitants of the city not to trust in the existence of the temple as a guarantee of their own security (Jer. 7:1–15; 26:1–19).

According to their way [b]I will do to them,
and according to their judgments I will
judge them, [c]and they shall know that I
am the LORD."

Abominations in the Temple

8 [d]In the sixth year, in the sixth month,
on the fifth day of the month, [e]as I sat
in my house, with [f]the elders of Judah sitting before me, [g]the hand of the Lord GOD
fell upon me there. **2** Then I looked, and
behold, [h]a form that had the appearance of
a man.[1] [h]Below what appeared to be his
waist was fire, and above his waist was
something like the appearance of brightness, like [i]gleaming metal.[2] **3** He [j]put out
the form of a hand and took me by a lock
of my head, and the Spirit lifted me up
[k]between earth and heaven and [l]brought
me in [m]visions of God to Jerusalem, [n]to
the entrance of the gateway of the inner
court that faces north, [o]where was the seat
of the [p]image of jealousy, [q]which provokes
to jealousy. **4** And behold, [r]the glory of the
God of Israel was there, like the vision that
I saw [s]in the valley.

5 Then he said to me, [t]"Son of man, lift
up your eyes now toward the north." So I
lifted up my eyes toward the north, and
behold, north of [u]the altar gate, in the
entrance, was this [p]image of jealousy.
6 And he said to me, "Son of man, [v]do you
see what they are doing, [w]the great abominations that the house of Israel are committing here, [x]to drive me far from my
sanctuary? But you will see still greater
abominations."

7 And he brought me to the entrance of
the court, and when I looked, behold,
there was a hole in the wall. **8** Then he said
to me, "Son of man, [y]dig in the wall." So
I dug in the wall, and behold, there was
an entrance. **9** And he said to me, "Go in,
and see [z]the vile abominations that they
are committing here." **10** So I went in and
saw. And there, [a]engraved on the wall all
around, was [b]every form of [c]creeping
things and loathsome beasts, and all the
idols of the house of Israel. **11** And before
them stood [d]seventy men of [e]the elders of
the house of Israel, with Jaazaniah the son
of [f]Shaphan standing among them. Each
had his censer in his hand, and [g]the
smoke of the cloud of incense went up.
12 Then he said to me, "Son of man, have
you seen what the elders of the house of
Israel are doing [h]in the dark, each [i]in his
room of pictures? For they say, [j]'The LORD
does not see us, the LORD has forsaken the
land.'" **13** He said also to me, [k]"You will
see still greater abominations that they
commit."

14 Then he brought me to [l]the entrance of
the north gate of the house of the LORD,
and behold, there sat women weeping for
Tammuz. **15** Then he said to me, "Have you
seen this, O [t]son of man? [k]You will see still
greater abominations than these."

16 And he brought me into [m]the inner
court of the house of the LORD. And
behold, at the entrance of the temple of the
LORD, [n]between the [o]porch and [p]the altar,
were about twenty-five men, [q]with their
backs to the temple of the LORD, and their
faces toward the east, worshiping [r]the sun

27 [b][ver. 4] [c]See ch. 6:7
Chapter 8
1 [d][ch. 1:2]; See ch. 20:1 [e][2 Kin. 6:32] [f]ver. 11, 12; ch. 14:1; 20:1, 3; [g]See ch. 1:3
2 [h]ch. 1:27 [i]ch. 1:4, 27
3 [j][Dan. 5:5]; See ch. 2:9 [k][2 Cor. 12:2, 4] [l]ch. 11:1, 24; 40:2 [m]See ch. 1:1 [n]ver. 14 [o][ch. 5:11] [p][Deut. 4:16] [q]Deut. 32:16, 21
4 [r]See ch. 1:28 [s]See ch. 3:22
5 [t]See ch. 2:1 [u]See ver. 16 [p][See ver. 3 above]
6 [v][ch. 47:6] [w]See ch. 5:11 [x][ch. 10:18, 19]
8 [y][ch. 12:5]
9 [z]See ch. 5:11
10 [a]ch. 23:14 [b]See Ex. 20:4 [c]Lev. 11:20; Rom. 1:23
11 [d][Ex. 24:1; Num. 11:16] [e]See ver. 1 [f]2 Chr. 34:8 [g][ch. 6:13]
12 [h][ver. 7] [i][ver. 10] [j]ch. 9:9; Ps. 10:11; Isai. 29:15
13 [k]ver. 6
14 [l]ver. 3
15 [t][See ver. 5 above] [k][See ver. 13 above]
16 [m]ch. 10:3; 40:28; 43:5; 45:19; 46:1; 1 Kin. 6:36 [n]Joel 2:17 [o]1 Kin. 6:3 [p]ver. 5; ch. 40:47; Ex. 40:6, 29; [ch. 9:2] [q][Jer. 2:27; 32:33] [r]See Jer. 8:2

1 By revocalization (compare Septuagint); Hebrew *of fire* 2 Or *amber*

8:1–18 The prophet sees four different types of idolatry flourishing in the city: (a) worship of the "image of jealousy" (vv. 5, 6); (b) worship of "beasts" (vv. 7–13); (c) the "Tammuz" cult (vv. 14, 15); and (d) worship of the "sun" (v. 16). All segments of society were involved: the elders (vv. 11, 12), the women (v. 14), and the priests (v. 16).

8:3 to Jerusalem. It is not necessary to conclude that Ezekiel went physically to Jerusalem. His visionary experience of transport is not unlike other visionary experiences in the Bible (3:12, 14; 37:1; 40:1; 2 Cor. 12:2).

north. This led from the outer to the inner court of the temple.

8:5 image of jealousy. The image is defined in v. 3 as something that "provokes to jealousy," that is, provokes the anger of the God who is jealous for His own honor (Ex. 20:5). God's glory belonged there (v. 4); the idol did not. This idol was probably an Asherah, an image of a Canaanite goddess who was possibly viewed as Yahweh's consort. Manasseh put an image of this kind in the temple (2 Kin. 21:7).

8:10 beasts. Worshiping beasts was worshiping the creature rather than the Creator (Rom. 1:25). Animals over which man was to rule and have dominion had become the object of veneration (Gen. 1:28).

8:11 Jaazaniah the son of Shaphan. Shaphan had been instrumental in Josiah's reform (2 Kin. 22:3–14; 2 Chr. 34:8, 15–20). Burning incense in the temple precincts was a rite reserved for the priests (Ex. 30:1–10; Num. 16:40; 18:1–7; 2 Chr. 26:16–21).

8:14 Tammuz. At the time of Ezekiel, Tammuz was worshiped both as a fertility god and the lord of the underworld. Rites used in worship of Tammuz were tied to the annual cycles of death and rebirth of vegetation. When plants withered under the heat of the summer sun, Tammuz was thought to have died and descended to the underworld; mourning rites marked his passing. The reappearance of vegetation was viewed as the return of Tammuz; fertility rites sought to ensure the productivity of the land.

8:16 twenty-five men. These were probably priests since access to the area between the altar and the portico of the temple was ordinarily restricted to priests. The temple faced east. Rather than face the temple to lament and mourn their sins and to intercede for the nation as they should have done (9:4; Joel 2:17), these men literally turned their backs on the house of God and worshiped the rising sun instead (2 Kin. 21:5; 23:11). Astral cults were common in the ancient Near East.

toward the east. 17 Then he said to me,
"Have you seen this, O [s]son of man? Is it
too light a thing for the house of Judah to
commit [t]the abominations that they commit here, that [u]they should fill the land
with violence and [v]provoke me still further
to anger? Behold, they put the branch to
their[1] nose. 18 Therefore [w]I will act in wrath.
[x]My eye will not spare, nor will I have pity.
[y]And though they cry in my ears with a
loud voice, I will not hear them."

Idolaters Killed

9 Then he cried in my ears with a loud
voice, saying, "Bring near the execu-
tioners of the city, [z]each with his destroying weapon in his hand." 2 And behold, six
men came from the direction of [a]the upper
gate, which faces north, each with his
weapon for slaughter in his hand, and with
them was [b]a man clothed in linen, with a
writing case at his waist. And they went in
and stood beside [c]the bronze altar.
3 Now [d]the glory of the God of Israel had
gone up from the cherub on which it rested
to [e]the threshold of the house. And he called
to [b]the man clothed in linen, who had the
writing case at his waist. 4 And the LORD said
to him, "Pass through the city, through
Jerusalem, and [f]put a mark on the foreheads
of the men who [g]sigh and groan over all the
abominations that are committed in it."
5 And to [h]the others he said in my hearing,
"Pass through the city after him, and strike.
[i]Your eye shall not spare, and you shall
show no pity. 6 [j]Kill old men outright, young
men and maidens, little children and
women, but [k]touch no one on whom is the
mark. And [l]begin at my sanctuary." So they
began with the elders who were before the
house. 7 Then he said to them, [m]"Defile the
house, and fill the courts with the slain. Go
out." So they went out and struck in the
city. 8 And while they were striking, and I
was left alone, [n]I fell upon my face, and
cried, [o]"Ah, Lord GOD! [p]Will you destroy all
the remnant of Israel [q]in the outpouring of
your wrath on Jerusalem?"
9 Then he said to me, [r]"The guilt of the
house of Israel and Judah is exceedingly
great. [s]The land is full of blood, and the
city full of injustice. For [t]they say, 'The
LORD has forsaken the land, and the LORD
does not see.' 10 As for me, [u]my eye will not
spare, nor will I have pity; [v]I will bring their
deeds upon their heads."
11 And behold, [w]the man clothed in linen,
with the writing case at his waist, brought
back word, saying, "I have done as you
commanded me."

The Glory of the LORD Leaves the Temple

10 Then I looked, and behold, [x]on the
expanse that was over the heads of
the cherubim there appeared above them
something [y]like a sapphire,[2] in appearance
like a throne. 2 And he said to [z]the man
clothed in linen, "Go in among [a]the
whirling wheels underneath the cherubim.
Fill your hands with [b]burning coals from
between the cherubim, and [c]scatter them
over the city."
And he went in [d]before my eyes. 3 Now
the cherubim were standing [e]on the south
side of the house, when the man went in,
and [f]a cloud filled [g]the inner court. 4 And

17 [s]See ch. 2:1 [t]See ch. 5:11 [u][ch. 7:11, 23] [v]Jer. 7:18, 19; [ch. 20:28]
18 [w]ch. 5:13 [x]See ch. 5:11 [y]Prov. 1:28; Isai. 1:15; Mic. 3:4
Chapter 9
1 [z][ch. 43:3]
2 [a]2 Kin. 15:35; Jer. 20:2 [b]ch. 10:2, 6, 7; Dan. 10:5; 12:6, 7 [c][ch. 8:16]
3 [d]See ch. 1:28 [e]ch. 10:4, 18; 46:2; 47:1 [b][See ver. 2 above]
4 [f]Rev. 3:12; 7:3; 9:4; 14:1; 22:4; [Ex. 12:7; Rev. 13:16, 17; 14:9; 20:4] [g][Ps. 119:53, 136, 158]
5 [h][ver. 2] [i]See ch. 5:11
6 [j][2 Chr. 36:17] [k][Rev. 9:4] [l]See Jer. 25:29
7 [m]ch. 7:21, 22
8 [n]ch. 11:13; [Num. 14:5] [o]See ch. 4:14 [p]ch. 11:13 [q]See ch. 7:8
9 [r]See 2 Chr. 36:14-16 [s]See ch. 7:23 [t]See ch. 8:12
10 [u]See ch. 5:11 [v]See ch. 7:4
11 [w]ch. 10:2, 6, 7; Dan. 10:5; 12:6, 7
Chapter 10
1 [x][ch. 1:22] [y]See ch. 1:26
2 [z]See ch. 9:2 [a]ver. 6, 13 [b]ch. 1:13 [c][Rev. 8:5] [d]ver. 19 3 [e][Luke 1:11] [f]See 1 Kin. 8:10 [g]See ch. 8:16

[1] Or *my* [2] Or *lapis lazuli*

8:17 violence. The sins denounced in this chapter are primarily in reference to corrupt religious practice, but not exclusively. Corrupt religion is inevitably accompanied by corrupt relations between people, so that the entire land is described as full of violence or lawlessness. This theme is further developed in 9:9 and 11:6.

branch to their nose. Some Assyrian reliefs show people holding branches before their faces in a gesture of reverence and worship; this may be a reference to that ritual gesture.

9:1 each with his destroying weapon. The idolatry of the nation would not go unpunished (cf. 2 Chr. 15:12, 13). Though the slayers are described as men (vv. 1, 2), they are probably angelic warriors (Ex. 12:23–30; 1 Chr. 21:15–20) assigned to the execution of the idolaters.

9:2 clothed in linen. Linen garments were worn by priests (Ex. 28:31–42), but angels and those in the presence of God were also so described (Dan. 10:5; 12:6, 7; Rev. 15:6; 19:8, 14).

a writing case. This man is a scribe, apparently charged with keeping the heavenly record (Ex. 32:32, 33; Ps. 69:28; 139:16; Dan. 12:1; Phil. 4:3; Rev. 3:5; 13:8; 17:8; 20:12, 15; 21:27). Ezekiel's vision is a reminder that idolaters have no place in the city of God (1 Cor. 5:11; 6:9; Eph. 5:5; Rev. 21:8; 22:15).

9:3 the glory. The glory cloud that revealed the divine presence was understood to dwell above the Most Holy Place in the temple; now the cloud has begun a journey visually portraying the way in which God will forsake Jerusalem (10:18, 19; 11:22, 23).

9:4 mark. The mark on the foreheads in this vision may have influenced John in Rev. 7:3; 14:9. The mark placed on the foreheads was the last letter of the Hebrew alphabet, *tau*. At the time of Ezekiel, *tau* was written like the English "X." Early Christian interpreters saw in this slanted cross an anticipation of the cross of Christ. Compare also the marking of the doorposts and lintels in the Passover narrative (Ex. 12:21–23).

9:9 blood. The indictments in ch. 8 had concentrated on idolatry and cultic offenses; here the issue is not the relationship between God and people, but relations among people. The prophet is elaborating on the violence and lawlessness mentioned in 8:17.

10:1 cherubim. See 1:5 note.

[h]the glory of the LORD [i]went up from the
cherub to the threshold of the house, and
the house [f]was filled with the cloud, and
the court was filled with [j]the brightness
of the glory of the LORD. 5 And [k]the sound
of the wings of the cherubim was heard as
far as the outer court, [k]like the voice of God
Almighty when he speaks.
6 And when he commanded [l]the man
clothed in linen, [m]"Take fire from between
[n]the whirling wheels, from between the
cherubim," he went in and stood beside a
wheel. 7 And a cherub stretched out his
hand from between the cherubim to the
fire that was between the cherubim, and
took some of it and put it into the hands of
the man clothed in linen, who took it and
went out. 8 The cherubim appeared to have
[o]the form of a human hand under their
wings.
9 [p]And I looked, and behold, there were
four wheels beside the cherubim, one
beside each cherub, and [q]the appearance of
the wheels was [r]like sparkling [s]beryl. 10 And
as for their appearance, the four had the
same likeness, as if a wheel were within a
wheel. 11 [t]When they went, they went in
any of their four directions[1] [u]without turning as they went, [v]but in whatever direction
the front wheel[2] faced, the others followed
without turning as they went. 12 [w]And their
whole body, their rims, and their spokes,
their wings,[3] and the wheels were full of
eyes all around—the wheels that the four
of them had. 13 As for the wheels, they were
called in my hearing "the whirling wheels."
14 [x]And every one had four faces: [y]the first
face was the face of the cherub, and the
second face was [z]a human face, and the
third the face of a lion, and the fourth
the face of an eagle.
15 [a]And the cherubim mounted up. These
were [b]the living creatures that I saw by [c]the
Chebar canal. 16 [d]And when the cherubim
went, the wheels went beside them. And
[d]when the cherubim lifted up their wings
to mount up from the earth, the wheels did
not turn from beside them. 17 [e]When they
stood still, these stood still, and when they
mounted up, these mounted up with
them, for the spirit of the living creatures[4]
was in them.
18 [f]Then [g]the glory of the LORD went out
from the threshold of the house, and stood
over the cherubim. 19 [h]And the cherubim
lifted up their wings and mounted up from
the earth [i]before my eyes as they went out,
with the wheels beside them. And they
stood at the entrance of the [j]east gate of the
house of the LORD, and [k]the glory of the
God of Israel was over them.
20 [l]These were the living creatures that I
saw [m]underneath the God of Israel by [n]the
Chebar canal; and I knew that they were
cherubim. 21 [o]Each had four faces, and each
four wings, and underneath their wings
[p]the likeness of human hands. 22 [q]And as
for the likeness of their faces, they were the
same faces whose appearance I had seen by
the Chebar canal. [r]Each one of them went
straight forward.

Judgment on Wicked Counselors

11 [s]The Spirit lifted me up and
brought me to [t]the east gate of the
house of the LORD, which faces east. And
behold, at the entrance of the gateway
there were [u]twenty-five men. And I saw
among them Jaazaniah [v]the son of Azzur,
and [w]Pelatiah the son of Benaiah, princes
of the people. 2 And he said to me, [x]"Son of
man, these are the men who devise iniquity and who give wicked counsel in this city;
3 [y]who say, [z]'The time is not near[5] to build
houses. [a]This city is the cauldron, and we
are the meat.' 4 Therefore prophesy against
them, prophesy, O son of man."
5 And [b]the Spirit of the LORD fell upon
me, and he said to me, "Say, Thus says the
LORD: So you think, O house of Israel. [c]For

4 [h]See ch. 1:28 [i]ver. 18, 19 [f][See ver. 3 above] [j][ch. 43:2]
5 [k]ch. 1:24
6 [l]See ch. 9:2 [m][ver. 2] [n]ver. 2
8 [o][ver. 21; ch. 1:8; 8:3]
9 [p][ch. 1:15] [q]ch. 1:16 [r][ch. 1:4] [s][ch. 1:16; Dan. 10:6]
11 [t]ch. 1:17 [u]ch. 1:9 [v][ver. 22]
12 [w][ch. 1:18]
14 [x][ch. 1:6] [y][ch. 1:10] [z][ch. 1:5, 10; 41:19]
15 [a]ver. 17, 19 [b]ch. 1:5; [c]See ch. 1:1
16 [d]ch.1:19
17 [e]ch. 1:20
18 [f][ver. 4] [g]ch. 43:2; See ch. 1:28
19 [h]ch. 11:22 [i]ver. 2 [j]ch. 11:1 [k]ch. 43:2; See ch. 1:28
20 [l]ch.1:5 [m]ch. 1:22, 26 [n]See ch. 1:1
21 [o][ch. 1:6] [p][ver. 8]
22 [q]ch. 1:10 [r][ver. 11]
Chapter 11
1 [s]ver. 24; See ch. 3:12 [t]ch. 10:19 [u]ch. 8:16 [v]Jer. 28:1 [w]ver. 13
2 [x]See ch. 2:1
3 [y][Jer. 29:28] [z][ch. 12:22, 27] [a]ch. 24:3, 6
5 [b]See ch. 2:2 [c]ch. 20:32; 38:10; [Isai. 29:15]

[1] Hebrew *to their four sides* [2] Hebrew *the head* [3] Or *their whole body, their backs, their hands, and their wings* [4] Or *spirit of life* [5] Or *Is not the time near . . . ?*

10:7 stretched out his hand. The cherub reaches inside the pillar of fire to retrieve the flames that will devour the city (v. 2).

10:12 eyes. See Deut. 11:12; 2 Chr. 16:9; Prov. 15:3; Zech. 3:9; 4:10; Rev. 4:8.

10:14 cherub. This face was an ox or bull in the earlier vision (1:10).

11:1 twenty-five men. These men appear to be political leaders, not priests, and so would not be the same as the twenty-five sun worshipers in 8:16.

Jaazaniah the son of Azzur. Not the same person as Jaazaniah the son of Shaphan (8:11).

11:3 cauldron . . . meat. The leadership of Jerusalem had already been deported by Nebuchadnezzar in 597 B.C.; this deportation included much of the royal family, the leaders of the military, and the craftsmen, leaving only "the poorest people of the land" (2 Kin. 24:13–16). Those who rose to prominence in the absence of the earlier ruling class appear to have had delusions of grandeur. The analogy they used of a cauldron and meat seems to mean that they considered those who had been deported from the city as the waste parts of a butchered animal, while they were the best parts.

I know the things that come into your
mind. 6 [d]You have multiplied your slain in
this city and have filled its streets with the
slain. 7 Therefore thus says the Lord GOD:
[e]Your slain whom you have laid in the
midst of it, [a]they are the meat, and [a]this
city is the cauldron, but you shall be
brought out of the midst of it. 8 [f]You have
feared the sword, and I will bring the
sword upon you, declares the Lord GOD.
9 And I will bring you out of the midst of
it, and [g]give you into the hands of foreigners, and [h]execute judgments upon you.
10 [i]You shall fall by the sword. I will judge
you at the border of Israel, [j]and you shall
know that I am the LORD. 11 [k]This city shall
not be your cauldron, nor shall you be the
meat in the midst of it. I will judge you at
the border of Israel, 12 and you shall know
that I am the LORD. For you have not
walked in my statutes, nor obeyed my
rules, [l]but have acted according to the
rules of the nations that are around you."
13 And it came to pass, while I was prophesying, [m]that [n]Pelatiah the son of Benaiah
died. [o]Then I fell down on my face and
cried out with a loud voice and said, [o]"Ah,
Lord GOD! [p]Will you make a full end of the
remnant of Israel?"

Israel's New Heart and Spirit

14 And the word of the LORD came to me:
15 [q]"Son of man, your brothers, even your
brothers, your kinsmen,[1] the whole house
of Israel, all of them, are those of whom the
inhabitants of Jerusalem have said, [r]'Go far
from the LORD; to us this land is given for
a possession.' 16 Therefore say, 'Thus says
the Lord GOD: Though I removed them far
off among the nations, and though I scattered them among the countries, yet [s]I
have been a sanctuary to them for a while[2]
in the countries where they have gone.'
17 Therefore say, 'Thus says the Lord GOD:
[t]I will gather you from the peoples and
assemble you out of the countries where
you have been scattered, [t]and I will give
you the land of Israel.' 18 And when they
come there, [u]they will remove from it all its
[v]detestable things and all its abominations.
19 [w]And I will give them one heart, and [x]a
new spirit I will put within them. [y]I will
remove the heart of stone from their flesh
[z]and give them a heart of flesh, 20 [a]that they
may walk in my statutes and keep my rules
and obey them. [b]And they shall be my
people, and I will be their God. 21 [c]But as
for those whose heart goes after their
detestable things and their abominations,[3]
[d]I will bring their deeds upon their own
heads, declares the Lord GOD."
22 [e]Then the cherubim lifted up their
wings, with the wheels beside them, [e]and
the glory of the God of Israel was over
them. 23 And the glory of the LORD went up
from the midst of the city and [f]stood on the
mountain that is on the east side of the
city. 24 [g]And the Spirit lifted me up and
brought me [h]in the vision by the Spirit of
God [i]into Chaldea, to the exiles. Then the
vision that I had seen went up from me.
25 And I told the exiles all the things that
the LORD had shown me.

Judah's Captivity Symbolized

12 The word of the LORD came to me:
2 [j]"Son of man, you dwell in the
midst of [k]a rebellious house, [l]who have
eyes to see, but see not, who have ears to
hear, but hear not, for they are [k]a rebellious
house. 3 As for you, son of man, prepare for
yourself [m]an exile's baggage, and go into

6 [d][ch. 7:23] **7** [e]ch. 24:7 [a][See ver. 3 above] **8** [f]Jer. 42:16 **9** [g]ch. 7:21 [h]See ch. 5:8 **10** [i]Jer. 39:6; See 2 Kin. 25:18-21; [j]See ch. 6:7 **11** [k][ver. 3, 7] **12** [l][ch. 8:10, 14, 16] **13** [m][Acts 5:5] [n]ver. 1 [o]ch. 9:8 [p][ch. 20:17] **15** [q]See ch. 2:1 [r][1 Sam. 26:19] **16** [s][ch. 37:26, 28; Isai. 8:14; Rev. 21:22] **17** [t]ch. 20:41; 28:25; 34:13; 36:24; 37:21; [ch. 38:8; 39:27; Isai. 11:12] **18** [u]ch. 37:23 [v]ch. 5:11 **19** [w]Jer. 32:39; [Acts. 4:32] [x]ch. 36:26; [ch. 18:31; Ps. 51:10; Jer. 31:33] [y][Zech. 7:12] [z][2 Cor. 3:3] **20** [a]Ps. 105:45 [b]ch. 14:11; 36:28; Lev. 26:12; See Jer. 30:22; 31:33 **21** [c]See ch. 9:4-6 [d]See ch. 7:4 **22** [e]ch. 10:19 **23** [f]Zech. 14:4; [ch. 43:2] **24** [g]ver. 1; See ch. 3:12 [h]See ch. 1:1 [i][ch. 8:3]
Chapter 12 **2** [j]See ch. 2:1 [k]See ch. 2:3, 5 [l]Isai. 42:18; Matt. 13:13 **3** [m]ver. 4, 7

1 Hebrew *the men of your redemption* 2 Or *in small measure* 3 Hebrew *To the heart of their detestable things and their abominations their heart goes*

11:7 meat. The prophet makes clear that the best part, the "meat" of the city, was the ones who had been killed. The new leaders had considered themselves to be this best part (v. 3 note).

11:13 Pelatiah. This name means "Yahweh provides escape." When this man dies suddenly and unexpectedly during Ezekiel's vision, Ezekiel fears that all hope of escape died with him. The prophet intercedes with the Lord once again on behalf of the remnant. See note 6:8; cf. 9:8.

11:15 brothers. In case of emergency, such as bankruptcy, a person's close relatives had an obligation to preserve the family and property (Ruth 2:20 note). If these relatives were far away, the property would not be safe.

11:16 sanctuary. Since the exiles were far from the temple in Jerusalem, God Himself would substitute as their sanctuary. Jesus later would take the place of the temple (Matt. 26:61; 27:40; John 2:19), and through the Spirit His followers would become His temple (1 Cor. 3:16, 17; 2 Cor. 6:16; 1 Pet. 2:5).

11:22–24 At the close of his vision Ezekiel sees the glory cloud depart from the city of Jerusalem and move east across the Kidron Valley to the Mount of Olives as it departs from the city. But God had not forsaken the city forever. Ezekiel later describes the glory of God returning to Jerusalem (ch. 43).

12:1–16 This is another symbolic action (4:1–3 note); the prophet enacts the exile of his countrymen in Jerusalem.

12:2 rebellious. See 2:3–8; 3:9, 26, 27.

eyes . . . ears. Compare Deut. 29:4; Prov. 20:12; Is. 6:9–10; 32:3; Jer. 5:21; Matt. 13:15, 16; Mark 8:18; Acts 28:26, 27; Rom. 11:8. The entire section makes frequent allusion to seeing (vv. 4–7, 12, 13).

exile by day [n]in their sight. You shall go
like an exile from your place to another
place [n]in their sight. [o]Perhaps they will
understand, though[1] they are a rebellious
house. 4 You shall bring out your baggage
by day in their sight, as baggage for exile,
and you shall go out yourself [p]at evening in
their sight, as those do who must go into
exile. 5 In their sight [q]dig through the wall,
and bring your baggage out through it. 6 In
their sight you shall lift the baggage upon
your shoulder and carry it out at dusk. You
shall cover your face that you may not see
the land, for I have made you [r]a sign for the
house of Israel."

7 [s]And I did as I was commanded. [t]I
brought out my baggage by day, as baggage
for exile, and in the evening I dug through
the wall with my own hands. I brought out
my baggage at dusk, carrying it on my
shoulder in their sight.

8 In the morning the word of the LORD
came to me: 9 [u]"Son of man, has not the
house of Israel, [v]the rebellious house, said
to you, [w]'What are you doing?' 10 Say to
them, 'Thus says the Lord GOD: This oracle
concerns[2] [x]the prince in Jerusalem and all
the house of Israel who are in it.'[3] 11 Say, [y]'I
am a sign for you: [z]as I have done, so shall
it be done to them. They shall go into exile,
into captivity.' 12 [a]And the prince who is
among them shall lift his baggage upon his
shoulder at dusk, and shall go out. [b]They
shall dig through the wall to bring him out
through it. [c]He shall cover his face, that he
may not see the land with his eyes. 13 [d]And I
will spread my net over him, and he shall be
taken in my snare. And [e]I will bring him to
Babylon, the land of the Chaldeans, [e]yet he
shall not see it, and he shall die there.
14 [f]And I will scatter toward every wind all
who are around him, his helpers and all his
troops, [g]and I will unsheathe the sword after
them. 15 [h]And they shall know that I am the
LORD, when I disperse them among the
nations and scatter them among the countries. 16 [i]But I will let a few of them escape
from the sword, from famine and pestilence,
that they may declare all their abominations
among the nations where they go, [j]and may
know that I am the LORD."

17 And the word of the LORD came to me:
18 [k]"Son of man, [l]eat your bread with quaking, and drink water with trembling and
with anxiety. 19 And say to the people of the
land, Thus says the Lord GOD concerning
the inhabitants of Jerusalem in the land of
Israel: [m]They shall eat their bread with anxiety, [m]and drink water in dismay. In this
way [n]her land will be stripped of all it contains, [o]on account of the violence of all
those who dwell in it. 20 [p]And the inhabited
cities shall be laid waste, and the land shall
become a desolation; and you shall know
that I am the LORD."

21 And the word of the LORD came to me:
22 "Son of man, [q]what is this proverb that
you[4] have about the land of Israel, saying,
[r]'The days grow long, and every vision
comes to nothing'? 23 Tell them therefore,
'Thus says the Lord GOD: I will put an end
to this proverb, and they shall no more use
it as a proverb in Israel.' But say to them,
[s]The days are near, and the fulfillment[5] of
every vision. 24 [t]For there shall be no more
any [u]false vision or flattering divination
within the house of Israel. 25 For I am the
LORD; I will speak [v]the word that I will
speak, and it will be performed. [w]It will no
longer be delayed, but in your days, [x]O
rebellious house, I will speak the word and
perform it, declares the Lord GOD."

3 [n]ch. 4:12; 21:6; 37:20; 43:11 [o]See Jer. 36:3
4 [p][2 Kin. 25:4; Jer. 39:4; 52:7]
5 [q][ch. 8:8]
6 [r]See ch. 4:3
7 [s]ch. 24:18; 37:7 [t][ver. 3]
9 [u]See ch. 2:1 [v]See ch. 2:3, 5 [w][ch. 17:12; 24:19; 37:18]
10 [x][ch. 21:25]; See 2 Chr. 36:11-13
11 [y][ver. 6] [z][ch. 24:24]
12 [a][2 Kin. 25:4] [b][ver. 5] [c][ver. 6]
13 [d]ch. 17:20; 19:8; 32:3; [Hos. 7:12] [e][2 Kin. 25:7; Jer. 32:4, 5; 52:11]
14 [f][2 Kin. 25:5]; See ch. 5:10
[g]See ch. 5:2
15 [h]See ch. 6:7
16 [i]ch. 6:8, 9; 14:22 [j]See ch. 6:7
18 [k]See ch. 2:1 [l][ch. 4:10, 11]
19 [m]ch. 4:16 [n][ch. 32:15; Zech. 7:14] [o]ch. 7:11, 23
20 [p]ch. 6:6
22 [q][ch. 16:44; 18:2, 3] [r][ver. 27; ch. 11:3; 2 Pet. 3:4]
23 [s][ch. 7:7, 12]
24 [t]ch. 13:23 [u]ch. 13:6, 7
25 [v]Isai. 55:11 [w]Isai. 13:22 [x]See ch. 2:3, 5

[1] Or *will see that* [2] Or *This burden is* [3] Hebrew *in the midst of them*
[4] The Hebrew for *you* is plural [5] Hebrew *word*

12:4 evening. Taking place under cover of darkness, this would be a furtive escape, like digging through the wall of a house (v. 5). Ezekiel portrays Zedekiah's abortive effort to escape from Nebuchadnezzar (vv. 10, 11; 2 Kin. 25:3–7).

12:6 cover. Covering the face was a gesture of shame or grief (24:17, 22; Lev. 13:45; 2 Sam. 19:4; Esth. 6:12; 7:8; Ps. 44:15; 69:7). In this context it suggests that the exiles will never see Jerusalem again, and more particularly, that Zedekiah will lose his sight (vv. 12, 13; 2 Kin. 25:7).

12:13 my net. God is described as a hunter or fowler (17:20; 32:3; Job 19:6; Is. 8:14; 24:18; 51:20; Jer. 50:24; Lam. 1:13; Hos. 7:12).

12:17–20 This is another symbolic action (see Introduction). The food and water of Ezekiel are presumably the siege rations he was allotted in 4:9–11. The prophet's physical weakness and trembling represented the lot of those in Jerusalem.

12:21–14:11 These passages are united by a concern with false prophecy. The Old Testament uses a number of criteria for distinguishing true from false prophecy. These criteria focus on what the message was, how it was received, and who received it. (a) The preeminent criterion for true or false prophecy is the fulfillment of the prophet's words (Deut. 18:21, 22). His message must not contradict earlier revelation (Deut. 13:1–5). The message of a true prophet often ran against popular sentiment, and the prophets were persecuted because of their unpopular pronouncements (Jer. 20:7–10; 38:1–13; cf. Matt. 23:34, 35). (b) Certain means of discerning God's will were forbidden (Deut. 18:9–14), such as divination, spiritism, and sorcery. However, prophets could receive revelation through dreams and visions (Num. 12:6–8). (c) The true prophet was admitted to God's confidence (Jer. 23:18). The experience of admission to God's counsel as if to a divine assembly was often reported in a call narrative (1:4–3:15 note). Finally, the prophet's character had to be consistent with the glory of the God he served.

26 And the word of the LORD came to me:
27 "Son of man, behold, they of the house of
Israel say, [y]'The vision that he sees is [z]for
many days from now, and he prophesies of
times far off.' **28** Therefore say to them,
Thus says the Lord GOD: [w]None of my
words will be delayed any longer, [v]but the
word that I speak will be performed,
declares the Lord GOD."

False Prophets Condemned

13 The word of the LORD came to me:
2 [a]"Son of man, prophesy against
the prophets of Israel, who are prophesying, and say to those [b]who prophesy from
their own hearts: 'Hear the word of the
LORD!' **3** Thus says the Lord GOD, Woe to
the foolish prophets who follow their own
spirit, and have seen nothing! **4** Your
prophets have been like jackals among
ruins, O Israel. **5** [c]You have not gone up
into the breaches, or built up a wall for the
house of Israel, that it might stand in battle in the day of the LORD. **6** [d]They have seen
false visions and lying divinations. They
say, 'Declares the LORD,' [e]when the LORD
has not sent them, and yet they expect him
to fulfill their word. **7** Have you not seen a
false vision and uttered a lying divination,
[f]whenever you have said, 'Declares the
LORD,' although I have not spoken?"
8 Therefore thus says the Lord GOD:
"Because you have uttered falsehood and
seen lying visions, therefore behold, [g]I am
against you, declares the Lord GOD. **9** My
hand will be against the prophets who see
false visions and who give lying divinations. They shall not be in the council of
my people, [h]nor be enrolled in the register
of the house of Israel, [i]nor shall they enter
the land of Israel. [j]And you shall know that
I am the Lord GOD. **10** Precisely because
they have misled my people, [k]saying,
'Peace,' when there is no peace, and
because, when the people build a wall,
[l]these prophets smear it with whitewash,[1]
11 say to those who smear it with whitewash
that it shall fall! [m]There will be a deluge of
rain, and you, O great hailstones, will fall,
and a stormy wind break out. **12** And when
the wall falls, will it not be said to you,
'Where is the coating with which you
smeared it?' **13** Therefore thus says the Lord
GOD: [m]I will make a stormy wind break out
in my wrath, [m]and there shall be a deluge
of rain in my anger, and great hailstones in
wrath to make a full end. **14** And I will break
down the wall that you have smeared with
whitewash, and bring it down to the
ground, so that its foundation will be laid
bare. When it falls, you shall perish in the
midst of it, [n]and you shall know that I am
the LORD. **15** Thus will I spend my wrath
upon the wall and upon those who have
smeared it with whitewash, and I will say
to you, The wall is no more, nor those who
smeared it, **16** the prophets of Israel who
prophesied concerning Jerusalem [k]and saw
visions of peace for her, when there was no
peace, declares the Lord GOD.
17 "And you, son of man, [o]set your face
against [p]the daughters of your people,
[q]who prophesy out of their own minds.
Prophesy against them **18** and say, Thus
says the Lord GOD: Woe to the women
[r]who sew magic bands upon all wrists, and
[s]make veils for the heads of persons of
every stature, in [t]the hunt for souls! Will
you hunt down souls belonging to my people and keep your own souls alive? **19** You
have profaned me among my people [u]for

27 [y][ver. 22; Amos 6:3] [z]ch. 38:8; Dan. 8:26; 10:14; [2 Pet. 3:4]
28 [w][See ver. 25 above] [v][See ver. 25 above]
Chapter 13
2 [a]See ch. 2:1 [b]ver. 17; Jer. 23:16, 26
5 [c]ch. 22:30; Ps. 106:23; [Ps. 80:12; Isai. 5:5; 58:12]
6 [d]ver. 23; ch. 12:24; 21:29; 22:28; Jer. 5:31 [e]See Jer. 14:14
7 [f]Jer. 23:21
8 [g]ch. 5:8; 21:3; 26:3; 28:22; 29:3; 30:22; 34:10; 35:3; 38:3; Jer. 21:13
9 [h][Ezra 2:59, 62; Neh. 7:5; Ps. 69:28; 87:6] [i]ch. 20:38; [j]See ch. 6:7
10 [k]ver. 16; Jer. 6:14; Mic. 3:5 [l]ch. 22:28
11 [m]ch. 38:22; Isai 28:2, 17; [Isai. 30:13]
13 [m][See ver. 11 above]
14 [n]See ch. 6:7
16 [k][See ver. 10 above]
17 [o]See ch. 6:2 [p][Ex. 15:20; Judg. 4:4; 2 Kin. 22:14] [q]ver. 2
18 [r]ver. 20 [s]ver. 21 [t]ver. 20
19 [u][Mic. 3:5]

1 Or *plaster*; also verses 11, 14, 15

12:27 times far off. The people scoff that the prophecy will not be fulfilled in their lifetimes. In the New Testament, a similar attitude of disbelief does not change the certainty of the return of Christ (2 Pet. 3:3, 4, 10; Rev. 10:6).

13:4 jackals. The prophet uses two images to describe the false prophets. They are like jackals among ruins (v. 4), separate from society and useless to it. In vv. 10, 11, they are compared to flimsy walls covered with whitewash (see v. 10 text note), untrustworthy and impermanent.

13:5 not gone up into the breaches. The focus is on the conduct of the false prophets: the true prophet so identified with God's people as to expose himself to risk on their behalf. When a wall was breached by an attacking army, the assignment of greatest danger was the task of repairing the gap. At such points, the false prophets were nowhere to be found. The Hebrew term for a gap is used to describe Moses, who "stood in the breach" (Ps. 106:23) on behalf of Israel. Ultimately only Jesus Christ can stand in the breach between God and humanity (1 Tim. 2:5).

13:9 register. Probably the census list and civil register of Israel, the earthly counterpart of the heavenly records. See 9:2 note.

13:10–12 The image of the gap in the wall (v. 5) may have prompted this further description of the actions of the false prophets. Their false visions and lying divinations were a wall of shoddy workmanship—when plastered over or whitewashed (v. 10 text note), it may have looked substantial, but it could not withstand the weather, much less the day of the Lord when God Himself would bring judgment on the city.

13:17–23 The Bible mentions several true prophetesses, like Miriam, Deborah, Huldah, and Anna (Ex. 15:20; Judg. 4:4; 2 Kin. 22:14; 2 Chr. 34:22; Luke 2:36), and some false ones (Neh. 6:14; Rev. 2:20). The women mentioned in these verses are practitioners of magic and sorcery, activities specifically forbidden for Israel (12:21–14:11 note). They made their living by selling amulets and charms.

handfuls of barley [v]and for pieces of bread,
putting to death souls who should not die
and keeping alive souls who should not
live, by your lying to my people, who listen
to lies.
20 "Therefore thus says the Lord GOD:
Behold, [w]I am against [x]your magic bands
with which you hunt the souls like birds,
and I will tear them from your arms, and I
will let the souls whom you hunt go free,
the souls like birds. 21 Your veils also I will
tear off and [y]deliver my people out of your
hand, and they shall be no more in your
hand as prey, [z]and you shall know that I
am the LORD. 22 [a]Because you have disheartened the righteous falsely, although I
have not grieved him, and [b]you have
encouraged the wicked, that [c]he should
not turn from his evil way to save his life,
23 [d]therefore you shall no more see false
visions nor practice divination. I will deliver my people out of your hand. And you
shall know that I am the LORD."

Idolatrous Elders Condemned

14 Then certain of the [e]elders of Israel
came to me [e]and sat before me.
2 And the word of the LORD came to me:
3 [f]"Son of man, these men have taken their
idols into their hearts, and set [g]the stumbling block of their iniquity before their
faces. [h]Should I indeed let myself be consulted by them? 4 Therefore speak to them
and say to them, Thus says the Lord GOD:
Any one of the house of Israel who takes
his idols into his heart and sets the stumbling block of his iniquity before his face,
and yet comes to the prophet, [i]I the LORD
will answer him as he comes with the multitude of his idols, 5 [j]that I may lay hold of
the hearts of the house of Israel, [k]who are
all estranged from me through their idols.
6 "Therefore say to the house of Israel,
Thus says the Lord GOD: [l]Repent and turn
away from your idols, and turn away your
faces from all your abominations. 7 For any
one of the house of Israel, or of the
strangers who sojourn in Israel, [k]who separates himself from me, taking his idols into
his heart and putting the stumbling block
of his iniquity before his face, and yet
comes to a prophet to consult me through
him, [m]I the LORD will answer him myself.
8 And [n]I will set my face against that man; I
[o]will make him a sign and a byword [n]and
cut him off from the midst of my people,
[p]and you shall know that I am the LORD.
9 And if the prophet is deceived and speaks
a word, [q]I, the LORD, have deceived that
prophet, and I will stretch out my hand
against him and will destroy him from the
midst of my people Israel. 10 And they shall
bear their punishment[1]—the punishment
of the prophet and the punishment of the
inquirer shall be alike— 11 that the house of
Israel may no more go astray from me, nor
[r]defile themselves anymore with all their
transgressions, [s]but that they may be my
people and I may be their God, declares
the Lord GOD."

Jerusalem Will Not Be Spared

12 And the word of the LORD came to me:
13 [t]"Son of man, when a land sins against
me [u]by acting faithlessly, and I stretch out
my hand against it and [v]break its supply[2]
of bread and send famine upon it, and [w]cut
off from it man and beast, 14 [x]even if these
three men, [y]Noah, [z]Daniel, and [a]Job, were
in it, [b]they would deliver but their own
lives by their righteousness, declares the
Lord GOD.
15 [c]"If I cause wild beasts to pass through
the land, and they ravage it, [d]and it be
made desolate, so that no one may pass

19 [v][Prov. 28:21]
20 [w]See ver. 8 [x]ver. 18
21 [y][ch. 34:10] [z]See ch. 6:7
22 [a][Jer. 14:14]; See Jer. 28:15 [b]Jer. 23:14 [c]See ch. 18:21
23 [d]See ver. 6, 7, 9
Chapter 14
1 [e]See ch. 8:1
3 [f]See ch. 2:1 [g]ch. 7:19; 44:12 [h]ch. 20:3, 31; 2 Kin. 3:13; [ch. 36:37]
4 [i][ver. 7]
5 [j][2 Thess. 2:11, 12] [k]Isai. 1:4
6 [l][ch. 18:30, 32]
7 [k][See ver. 5 above] [m][ver.4]
8 [n]ch. 15:7; Lev. 17:10; Jer. 44:11 [o]ch. 5:15; Deut. 28:37 [p]See ch. 6:7
9 [q][1 Kin. 22:23]
11 [r]ch. 37:23 [s]See ch. 11:20
13 [t]See ch. 2:1 [u]ch. 15:8; 17:20; 18:24; 20:27; 2 Chr. 36:14 [v]See ch. 4:16 [w]ver. 17, 19, 21
14 [x][Jer. 15:1] [y]See Gen. 6:9 [z]ch. 28:3; Dan. 9:23 [a]Job 1:1 [b]ch. 3:19
15 [c]See ch. 5:17 [d]ch. 6:6; 12:20

[1] Or *iniquity;* three times in this verse [2] Hebrew *staff*

14:3 set the stumbling block. This is one of the prophet's favorite phrases (vv. 4, 7; 7:19; 44:12). It may refer to secret idolatry.

14:9 I . . . have deceived . . . I will stretch out my hand. Numerous biblical passages integrate the sovereignty of God and the moral responsibility of human beings without allowing the predeterminate will of God to be used as an excuse for moral evil (Esth. 4:13, 14; Joel 2:32; Matt. 26:24, 25; Acts 2:23). In this section, idolaters without any intention of giving up their idolatry come to seek a prophetic word. By God's arrangement they find a prophet as false as they are, and both will come under God's judgment. The prophet who serves them, though induced by God, must bear the responsibility for his wrongdoing. See 1 Kin. 22:19–25.

14:14 even if. The prophet is apparently addressing the view held by some that the presence of a certain number of righteous people in Jerusalem would serve to protect the city (cf. Gen. 18:22–32).

Noah, Daniel, and Job. Though Noah was a righteous man and blameless among those of his generation (Gen. 6:9), the world was not spared because of his presence. Job too was blameless and upright (Job 1:1), but this did not spare his family. The identity of the "Daniel" mentioned is much debated. He is probably not Ezekiel's contemporary known from the Book of Daniel; the Hebrew spelling used here *(Dani'el)* is different from that used for the name of the prophet *(Daniyye'l)*. More probably this Daniel is a heroic figure mentioned in a text from ancient Ugarit. This story concerns a king named Dan'el known to some extent for his righteousness, wisdom (cf. 28:3), and pity. "Noah, Daniel, and Job" would then designate non-Israelite figures from remote times known for their uprightness. They could not save the world in their own day and even together could not save the city of Jerusalem (cf. v. 20).

through because of the beasts, **16** even if
these three men were in it, [e]as I live,
declares the Lord GOD, they would deliver
neither sons nor daughters. They alone
would be delivered, but [f]the land would be
desolate.
17 "Or [g]if I bring a sword upon that land
and say, Let a sword pass through the land,
[h]and I cut off from it man and beast,
18 [x]though these three men were in it, as I
live, declares the Lord GOD, they would
deliver neither sons nor daughters, but
they alone would be delivered.
19 "Or [i]if I send a pestilence into that land
and pour out my wrath upon it with blood,
to cut off from it man and beast, **20** even if
Noah, Daniel, and Job were in it, as I live,
declares the Lord GOD, they would deliver
neither son nor daughter. They would
deliver but their own lives by their righteousness.
21 "For thus says the Lord GOD: How
much more [j]when I send upon Jerusalem
my four disastrous acts of judgment,
[k]sword, [l]famine, [m]wild beasts, and [n]pesti-
lence, to cut off from it man and beast!
22 But behold, [o]some survivors will be left in
it, sons and daughters who will be brought
out; behold, when they come out to you,
and [p]you see their ways and their deeds,
you will be consoled for the disaster that I
have brought upon Jerusalem, for all that I
have brought upon it. **23** They will console
you, when you see their ways and their
deeds, and you shall know that I have not
done without cause all that I have done in
it, declares the Lord GOD."

Jerusalem, a Useless Vine

15 And the word of the LORD came to
me: **2** [q]"Son of man, how does [r]the
wood of the vine surpass any wood, the
vine branch that is among the trees of
the forest? **3** Is wood taken from it to make
anything? Do people take [s]a peg from it to
hang any vessel on it? **4** [t]Behold, it is given
to the fire for fuel. When the fire has consumed both ends of it, and the middle of it
is charred, is it useful for anything?
5 [u]Behold, when it was whole, it was used
for nothing. How much less, when the fire
has consumed it and it is charred, can it
ever be used for anything! **6** Therefore thus
says the Lord GOD: [v]Like the wood of the
vine among the trees of the forest, [t]which I
have given to the fire for fuel, so have I
given up the inhabitants of Jerusalem.
7 [w]And I will set my face against them.
Though [x]they escape from the fire, the fire
shall yet consume them, [y]and you will
know that I am the LORD, [w]when I set my
face against them. **8** [z]And I will make the
land desolate, because [a]they have acted
faithlessly, declares the Lord GOD."

The LORD's Faithless Bride

16 Again the word of the LORD came to
me: **2** [b]"Son of man, [c]make known
to Jerusalem her abominations, **3** and say,
Thus says the Lord GOD to Jerusalem: Your
origin and your birth are of the land of the
Canaanites; your father was an [d]Amorite
and your mother a [e]Hittite. **4** And as for
your birth, [f]on the day you were born your
cord was not cut, nor were you washed
with water to cleanse you, nor rubbed with
salt, nor wrapped in swaddling cloths. **5** No
eye pitied you, to do any of these things to
you out of compassion for you, [g]but you
were cast out on the open field, for you
were abhorred, [f]on the day that you were
born.
6 "And when I passed by you and saw
you wallowing [h]in your blood, I said to you
[h]in your blood, 'Live!' I said to you [h]in your
blood, 'Live!' **7** [i]I made you flourish like a
plant of the field. And you grew up and
became tall [j]and arrived at full adornment.
Your breasts were formed, and your hair
had grown; yet [k]you were naked and bare.
8 "When I passed by you again and saw
you, behold, you were at the age for love,
and [l]I spread the corner of my garment
over you and covered your nakedness; I
made my vow to you [m]and entered into a
covenant with you, declares the Lord GOD,
[n]and you became mine. **9** Then I bathed
you with water and washed off your blood
from you and [o]anointed you with oil. **10** [p]I
clothed you also with embroidered cloth

16 [e]See ch. 5:11 [f]ch. 6:14 **17** [g]ch. 21:3, 4, 9; Lev. 26:25; [Jer. 47:6, 7] [h]ver. 13 **18** [x][See ver. 14 above] **19** [i]ch. 38:22; [2 Sam. 24:15] **21** [j]ch. 5:17; Rev. 6:8; [ch. 33:27] [k]ver. 17 [l]ver. 13 [m]ver. 15 [n]ver. 19 **22** [o]ch. 6:8; 12:16 [p]ver. 23; ch. 20:43; [ch. 16:54]
Chapter 15
2 [q]See ch. 2:1 [r]See ver. 6 **3** [s][Isai. 22:23, 24] **4** [t][John 15:6] **5** [u][ver. 3]
6 [v][ch. 17:6; Ps. 80:8; Isai. 5:1]; See ch. 19:10-14 [t][See ver. 4 above] **7** [w]See ch. 14:8 [x][2 Kin. 25:9] [y]See ch. 6:7 **8** [z]ch. 6:14 [a]See ch. 14:13
Chapter 16
2 [b]See ch. 2:1 [c]ch. 22:2 **3** [d]ver. 45; Gen. 15:16; Deut. 7:1 [e]ver. 45; Deut. 7:1; Judg. 1:26 **4** [f][Hos. 2:3] **5** [g][Deut. 32:10] [f][See ver. 4 above] **6** [h]ver. 22 **7** [i][Ex. 1:7] [j][ver. 11, 13] [k]ver. 22, 39; ch. 23:29 **8** [l]Ruth 3:9; [Jer. 2:2] [m][Ex. 24:7, 8] [n]See Ex. 19:5 **9** [o]Ruth 3:3; [Ps. 23:5] **10** [p]ver 13, 18; [ch. 26:16; 27:7, 16; Ex. 26:36]

15:3 anything. The wood of the vine was not fit for any worthwhile object, not even a lowly peg. God reminds the exiles that His choice of Israel as His people was not because of any intrinsic worth in them, but solely a matter of His grace (Deut. 7:6–8).

15:4 charred. The partial burning of Israel is probably a reference to the partial exile that had already taken place in 597 B.C. with the deportation of Jehoiachin and a large portion of the city's upper class, including Ezekiel. After this partial damage, the city is worth even less. The prophet Zechariah likens the Babylonian exile to a fire when he describes the high priest as "a brand plucked from the fire" (Zech. 3:2).

and shod you with fine leather. I wrapped
you in fine linen and covered you with
silk.[1] **11** [q]And I adorned you with ornaments
and [r]put bracelets on your wrists and a
chain on your neck. **12** And I put a ring on
your nose and earrings in your ears and a
beautiful crown on your head. **13** Thus you
were adorned with gold and silver, and
your clothing was of fine linen and silk and
embroidered cloth. [s]You ate fine flour
and honey and oil. [t]You grew exceedingly
beautiful and advanced to royalty. **14** And
[u]your renown went forth among the
nations because of your beauty, for it was
perfect through the splendor that I had
bestowed on you, declares the Lord GOD.
15 [v]"But you trusted in your beauty [w]and
played the whore[2] because of your renown
[x]and lavished your whorings[3] on any
passerby; your beauty[4] became his. **16** You
took some of your garments and made for
yourself colorful shrines, and on them
played the whore. The like has never been,
nor ever shall be.[5] **17** You also took [y]your
beautiful jewels of my gold and of my silver, which I had given you, and [z]made for
yourself images of men, and with them
played the whore. **18** And you took your
embroidered garments to cover them, [a]and
set my oil and my incense before them.
19 [b]Also my bread that I gave you—[s]I fed
you with fine flour and oil and honey—you
set before them for [c]a pleasing aroma; and
so it was, declares the Lord GOD. **20** [d]And
you took your sons and your daughters,
whom you had borne to me, and [e]these
you sacrificed to them to be devoured.
Were your whorings so small a matter
21 that you slaughtered my children and
delivered them up as an offering by fire to
them? **22** And in all your abominations and
your whorings you did not remember [f]the
days of your youth, [g]when you were naked
and bare, wallowing in your blood.
23 "And after all your wickedness (woe,
woe to you! declares the Lord GOD), **24** you
built yourself [h]a vaulted chamber and
made yourself a lofty place in every square.
25 At the head of every street [i]you built your
lofty place and made [j]your beauty an
abomination, [k]offering yourself[6] to any
passerby and multiplying your whoring.
26 [w]You also played the whore [l]with the
Egyptians, your lustful neighbors, [m]multi-
plying your whoring, [n]to provoke me to
anger. **27** Behold, therefore, I stretched out
my hand against you [o]and diminished your
allotted portion [p]and delivered you to the
greed of your enemies, [q]the daughters of
the Philistines, who were ashamed of your
lewd behavior. **28** You played the whore also
[r]with the Assyrians, because you were not
satisfied; yes, you played the whore with
them, and still you were not satisfied.
29 You multiplied your whoring also [s]with
the trading land [t]of Chaldea, and even with
this you were not satisfied.
30 "How lovesick is your heart,[7] declares
the Lord GOD, because you did all these

11 [q][ch. 23:40] [r][ch. 23:42; Gen. 24:22, 30, 47]
13 [s]Deut. 32:13, 14 [t][ver. 15, 25; Ps. 48:2]
14 [u]Lam. 2:15; [ch. 23:10]
15 [v][ver. 13] [w]ch. 23:3, 8, 11, 12; Lev. 17:7; Isai. 1:21; 57:8; Jer. 2:20; 3:2, 6, 20; Hos 1:2 [x][ver. 25]
17 [y][ver. 11] [z][ch. 7:20; 23:14]
18 [a]ch. 23:41
19 [b][Hos. 2:8] [s][See ver. 13 above] [c]See ch. 6:13
20 [d][ver. 21, 36] [e]ch. 20:26, 31; 23:37
22 [f]ver. 43, 60 [g]ver. 6, 7
24 [h]ver. 39
25 [i]ver. 31; [Isai. 57:7; Jer. 2:20; 3:2] [j][ver. 14] [k][ver. 15]
26 [w][See ver. 15 above] [l]ch. 20:7, 8; 23:19-21 [m]ch. 23:14, 19 [n]Jer. 7:18, 19
27 [o][ch. 5:10, 11] [p][ver. 37] [q]ver. 57; [2 Sam. 1:20]
28 [r]ch. 23:12; Jer. 2:18, 36; See 2 Kin. 16:7-18; 2 Chr. 28:16-21
29 [s]See ver. 3 [t]See ch. 23:14-16

1 Or *with rich fabric* 2 Or *were unfaithful*; also verses 16, 17, 26, 28 3 Or *unfaithfulness*; also verses 20, 22, 25, 26, 29, 33, 34, 36 4 Hebrew *it* 5 The meaning of this Hebrew sentence is uncertain 6 Hebrew *spreading your legs* 7 Revocalization yields *How I am filled with anger against you*

16:1–63 Ezekiel tells the story of an unwanted child, her marriage, and infidelity. Hosea used marriage as an analogy of the covenant relationship between God and Israel (Hos. 1–3; see also Eph. 5:22–33; Rev. 19:7; 21:2, 9). Ezekiel's speech appears to have a judicial setting; he recounts God's charge against the nation from its earliest days to his own time.

16:3 origin. Jerusalem was originally a pagan city; the first inhabitants are variously described as Amorites, Canaanites, Jebusites, and Hittites (v. 45; Gen. 10:15, 16; Josh. 10:5; Judg. 1:21; 19:10; 2 Sam. 5:6). In this respect the city was not unlike the patriarchs, who were of pagan Syrian stock (Deut. 26:5; Josh. 24:14).

16:5 cast out. Undesired infants were often abandoned and left to die. The baby girl Ezekiel describes was abandoned before even being washed.

16:7 grew. The unwanted child grew to beautiful maturity. The onset of puberty appears with development of breasts (cf. 23:3) and the growth of hair; later the girl reaches the age of lovemaking (v. 8).

16:8 spread the corner of my garment over you. Covering a woman with one's garment is symbolic of entering into marital relations (Ruth 3:9). To "uncover" this relation is to violate it (Deut. 22:30).

I made my vow. The covenant relationship of God with Israel had been sealed with the oath, "you shall be my people, and I will be your God" (36:28; Lev. 26:12; Jer. 11:4; 30:22; contrast Hos. 1:9). For the divine oath, see Gen. 15:7–21; 26:3; Deut. 1:8.

16:9–14 The foundling has become a queen. She has received all the care she lacked when born and far more. Her life, status, wealth and beauty all derive from the gracious gift of the One who chose her.

16:17 All that the foundling-become-queen had received from her loving husband and king is now turned to wantonness and promiscuity (cf. Deut. 6:10–12). Her actions demonstrate the irrationality of sin: there could be no sound reason for such behavior.

16:20 sacrificed. For the practice of child sacrifice in Israel and among neighboring states, see v. 36; 20:31; Gen. 22:2, 13; Lev. 18:21; 20:2–5; Deut. 12:31; 18:10; 2 Kin. 16:3; 17:17; 21:6; 23:10; Ps. 106:37, 38; Jer. 32:35; Mic. 6:7. In Jerusalem these practices were associated with the Valley of the Son of Hinnom, south of the city.

16:26 played the whore. Israel's failure to obey God was not a matter of overt idolatry alone. Foreign alliances were also regarded as evidence of a failure to trust God in the face of political difficulty. Such alliances were a breach of Israel's exclusive allegiance to the Lord (cf. 23:7; 29:16; Is. 7; 8; 30; 31; Jer. 2:36, 37; 22:20–22; Hos. 7:11–13). The writer of Chronicles emphasizes this point particularly (2 Chr. 14:9–15; 16:1–9; 19:1, 2; 20; 25:6–8; 28).

things, the deeds of a brazen prostitute,
31 building your vaulted chamber at the
head of every street, and making your lofty
place in every square. Yet you were not like
a prostitute, [u]because you scorned payment. 32 Adulterous wife, who receives
strangers instead of her husband! 33 Men
give gifts to all prostitutes, [v]but you gave
your gifts to all your lovers, bribing them to
come to you from every side with your
whorings. 34 So you were different from
other women in your whorings. No one
solicited you to play the whore, and [v]you
gave payment, while no payment was given
to you; therefore you were different.
35 "Therefore, O prostitute, hear the word
of the LORD: 36 Thus says the Lord GOD,
Because your lust was poured out and your
nakedness uncovered in your whorings
with your lovers, and with all your abominable idols, [w]and because of the blood of
your children that you gave to them,
37 therefore, behold, [x]I will gather all your
lovers with whom you took pleasure, [y]all
those you loved and all those you hated. [z]I
will gather them against you from every
side [a]and will uncover your nakedness to
them, that [b]they may see all your nakedness. 38 [c]And I will judge you [d]as women
who commit adultery and [e]shed blood are
judged, and bring upon you the blood of
wrath and jealousy. 39 And I will give you
into their hands, and they shall throw
down your [f]vaulted chamber and break
down [g]your lofty places. [h]They shall strip
you of your clothes and take [i]your beautiful jewels and leave you [j]naked and bare.
40 [k]They shall bring up a crowd against you,
[l]and they shall stone you and cut you to
pieces with their swords. 41 [l]And they shall
[m]burn your houses and [n]execute judgments upon you in the sight of many
women. [o]I will make you stop playing the
whore, and [p]you shall also give payment no
more. 42 [q]So will I satisfy my wrath on you,
and my jealousy shall depart from you. I
will be calm and will no more be angry.
43 Because you have not remembered [r]the
days of your youth, but have enraged me
with all these things, therefore, behold, [s]I
have returned your deeds upon your head,
declares the Lord GOD. "Have you not
[t]committed lewdness in addition to all
your abominations?
44 "Behold, everyone [u]who uses proverbs
will use this proverb about you: 'Like
mother, like daughter.' 45 You are the
daughter of your mother, who loathed her
husband and her children; and you are the
sister of [v]your sisters, who loathed their
husbands and their children. [w]Your mother was a Hittite and [w]your father an Amorite. 46 And [x]your elder sister is Samaria,
who lived with her daughters to the north
of you; and [y]your younger sister, who lived
to the south of you, is Sodom with her
daughters. 47 [z]Not only did you walk in
their ways and do according to their abominations; within a very little time [a]you were
more corrupt than they in all your ways.
48 [b]As I live, declares the Lord GOD, your
sister [c]Sodom and her daughters have not
done as you and your daughters have
done. 49 Behold, this was the guilt of your
sister Sodom: she and her daughters had
pride, [d]excess of food, and prosperous
ease, but did not aid the poor and needy.
50 They were haughty and [e]did an abomination before me. So [f]I removed them,
when I saw it. 51 [g]Samaria has not committed half your sins. You have committed
more abominations than they, and [h]have
made your sisters appear righteous by all
the abominations that you have committed.

31 [u][ver. 33, 34]
33 [v][ver. 41; Hos. 8:9]
34 [v][See ver. 33 above]
36 [w][ver. 20, 21, 38]
37 [x]Hos 8:10 [y][ver. 27; ch. 23:28] [z]ch. 23:22 [a]ch. 23:10, 29; Hos. 2:10; Rev. 17:16; [ver. 39] [b]Lam. 1:8
38 [c]ch. 21:30 [d]ch. 23:45; Lev. 20:10; Deut. 22:22 [e]Gen. 9:6; [ch. 18:10; 23:37, 45]
39 [f]ver. 24 [g]ver. 25 [h]ch. 23:26; [Hos. 2:3] [i]ver. 11, 12 [j]ver. 7
40 [k]ch. 23:46 [l]ch. 23:47; [Josh. 7:24, 25]
41 [l][See ver. 40 above] [m]2 Kin. 25:9; Jer. 39:8; 52:13 [n]See ch. 5:8 [o]ch. 23:27, 48 [p][ver. 33, 34]
42 [q]See ch. 5:13
43 [r]ver. 22, 60 [s]See ch. 7:4 [t]ch. 22:9
44 [u][ch. 12:22; 18:2, 3]
45 [v][ver. 46] [w]See ver. 3
46 [x]ver. 51, 53, 55; [ch. 23:4, 33] [y]ver. 48, 49, 53, 55; [Isai. 1:10]
47 [z]ch. 5:7 [a]ver. 48, 51, 52; ch. 5:6; [2 Kin. 21:9; 2 Chr. 33:9; Jer. 2:10, 11]
48 [b]ch. 5:11; 14:16, 18, 20; 17:16, 19; 18:3; 20:3, 33; Isai. 49:18; Zeph. 2:9 [c]ver. 47; [Matt. 10:15; 11:24]
49 [d][Gen. 13:10] 50 [e]See Gen. 13:13 [f]See Gen. 19:24 51 [g]ver. 46, 47 [h]ver. 52; Jer. 3:11

16:37 gather them against you. She sought the loyalty and affection of her lovers; but instead, they become the instruments of her humiliation and punishment. Though the nations were used by God to punish His people, they would bear the guilt of the sins they committed (ch. 25; Is. 10:5, 12; Zech. 1:14, 15); see note 14:9.

uncover your nakedness. Public degradation by exposing the nakedness of prostitutes or adulteresses is also mentioned in Jer. 13:22, 26; Hos. 2:10; Nah. 3:5.

16:38 bring upon you the blood. For the wrath of a jealous husband, see Prov. 6:34. The wealth and garments of the woman will be taken, and she will be left as naked as she was when the story began. She would be covered not with the blood of childbirth (v. 6) but the blood from her wounds. Adultery was a capital offense, punishable by stoning (Lev. 20:10; Deut. 22:21–24; cf. John 7:53–8:11).

16:41 burn. See 23:47; cf. Jer. 32:29; 34:22; 37:8; 38:18. A large part of Jerusalem was burned by the Babylonian army (Jer. 39:8).

16:44 proverbs. Ezekiel more than once refers to popular proverbs (12:21–28; 18).

16:45 Hittite . . . Amorite. The moral depravity of the Hittites and Amorites is assumed; cf. v. 3.

16:49 Sodom. Readers of the Bible often think of the sins of Sodom as mainly sexual (Gen. 19:5–9), but Ezekiel indicts the city for materialism and neglect of the poor and needy. Jesus made a similar comparison with Capernaum in Matt. 11:23, 24. The sins of Jerusalem exceeded those of her sisters, the nearby cities.

52 [i]Bear your disgrace, you also, for you
have intervened on behalf of your sisters.
Because of your sins in which you acted
more abominably than they, they are more
in the right than you. So be ashamed, you
also, and bear your disgrace, for you have
made your sisters appear righteous.
53 [j]"I will restore their fortunes, both the
fortunes of Sodom and her daughters, and
the fortunes of Samaria and her daughters,
and I will restore your own fortunes in
their midst, 54 that you may bear your disgrace [k]and be ashamed of all that you have
done, [l]becoming a consolation to them.
55 As for your sisters, Sodom and her
daughters shall return to their former state,
[j]and Samaria and her daughters shall
return [m]to their former state, [j]and you and
your daughters shall return [m]to your former state. 56 Was not your sister Sodom a
byword in your mouth [n]in the day of your
pride, 57 before your wickedness was uncovered? Now you have become [o]an object
of reproach for the daughters of Syria[1] and
all those around her, and for [p]the daughters of the Philistines, [q]those all around
who despise you. 58 [r]You bear the penalty of
your lewdness and your abominations,
declares the LORD.

The LORD's Everlasting Covenant

59 "For thus says the Lord GOD: I will deal
with you as you have done, you [s]who have
despised the oath in breaking the covenant, 60 yet [t]I will remember my covenant
with you [u]in the days of your youth, [v]and I
will establish for you an everlasting
covenant. 61 [w]Then you will remember your
ways [x]and be ashamed when you take
[y]your sisters, both your elder and your
younger, and I give them to you [z]as daughters, but not on account of[2] the covenant
with you. 62 I will establish my covenant
with you, [a]and you shall know that I am
the LORD, 63 that you may remember and be
confounded, and [b]never open your mouth
again because of your shame, when I atone
for you for all that you have done, declares
the Lord GOD."

52 [i]See ch. 32:24
53 [j][ch. 29:14; 39:25; Zeph. 2:7; 3:20]
54 [k]ver 61 [l][ch. 14:22, 23]
55 [j][See ver. 53 above] [m]ch. 36:11
56 [n]See Isai. 2:6-11
57 [o]See 2 Kin. 16:5-7; Isai. 7:1, 2 [p]ver. 27; [2 Chr. 28:18] [q]ch. 28:24, 26
58 [r][ch. 14:10; 23:35, 49]
59 [s][ch. 17:15, 16, 18, 19]
60 [t]See Lev. 26:42 [u]ver. 8, 22, 43 [v]Jer. 32:40; 50:5
61 [w]See ch. 6:9 [x]ver. 54 [y][ver. 45, 46] [z][Isai. 54:1]
62 [a]See ch. 6:7
63 [b][Rom. 3:19]
Chapter 17
2 [c]See ch. 2:1 [d][ch. 20:49; 24:3]
3 [e]Jer. 48:40 [f]ver. 7 [g][Jer. 22:23] [h]ver. 22; ch. 31:3, 4, 10
5 [i]See Deut. 8:7-10 [j][Isai. 44:4]
6 [k][ver. 14] [l]ch. 15:6
7 [m][ver. 15] [n][ch. 31:4]
8 [i][See ver. 5 above]
9 [m][See ver. 7 above]
10 [o]ch. 19:12; [Hos. 13:15]

Parable of Two Eagles and a Vine

17 The word of the LORD came to me:
2 [c]"Son of man, [d]propound a riddle,
and speak a parable to the house of Israel;
3 say, Thus says the Lord GOD: [e]A great eagle
[f]with great wings and long pinions, [f]rich in
plumage of many colors, came [g]to Lebanon
[h]and took the top of the cedar. 4 He broke off
the topmost of its young twigs and carried it
to a land of trade and set it in a city of merchants. 5 Then he took of the seed of the land
[i]and planted it in fertile soil.[3] He placed it
beside abundant waters. [j]He set it like a wil-
low twig, 6 and it sprouted and became a
[k]low [l]spreading vine, and its branches turned
toward him, and its roots remained where it
stood. So it became a vine and produced
branches and put out boughs.
7 [m]"And there was another great eagle
with great wings and much plumage, [m]and
behold, this vine bent its roots toward him
and shot forth its branches toward him
from [n]the bed where it was planted, that he
might water it. 8 [i]It had been planted on
good soil by abundant waters, that it might
produce branches and bear fruit and
become a noble vine.
9 "Say, Thus says the Lord GOD: [m]Will it
thrive? Will he not pull up its roots and cut
off its fruit, so that it withers, so that all its
fresh sprouting leaves wither? It will not
take a strong arm or many people to pull it
from its roots. 10 Behold, it is planted; will
it thrive? [o]Will it not utterly wither when

[1] Some manuscripts (compare Syriac) *of Edom* [2] Or *not apart from*
[3] Hebrew *in a field of seed*

16:60 everlasting covenant. Jerusalem would once again have primacy over her sisters, but not on the basis of the previous covenant relationship between God and the city. There will be a new covenant, a new relationship between God and the city in the future. God Himself would atone for her sins.

17:1–24 This oracle has no date, but probably came between the dates given in 8:1 and 20:1, the sixth and seventh years of the exile of Jehoiachin (592–590 B.C.). Nebuchadnezzar laid siege to Jerusalem in 588 B.C. and removed Zedekiah from the throne in 586 B.C. (v. 20).

17:3 eagle. Ezekiel propounds an allegory. The great eagle is the imperial might of Babylon, represented by Nebuchadnezzar.

cedar. The lofty cedar represents the kingdom of Judah and the dynasty of David, that had endured by this time over three hundred years.

17:4 topmost of its young twigs. The removal of the topmost twig refers to the exile and captivity of Jehoiachin in Babylon. The exiles continued to regard Jehoiachin as the legitimate king of Judah.

17:6 vine. Nebuchadnezzar replaced the cedar with the far more humble and lowly vine, a reference to his installation of Zedekiah on the throne in Jerusalem after deporting Jehoiachin (2 Kin. 24:15–17). Nebuchadnezzar had done much for Zedekiah, just as the vine had fertile soil, abundant water, and prospered.

17:7 another great eagle. The turning of the vine toward another great eagle represents Zedekiah's shift in allegiance from Nebuchadnezzar to Egypt (vv. 15–17), with the result that the vine itself would be uprooted and destroyed.

the east wind strikes it—wither away on
the bed where it sprouted?”
11 Then the word of the LORD came to me:
12 “Say now to [p]the rebellious house, [q]Do
you not know what these things mean? Tell
them, behold, [r]the king of Babylon came to
Jerusalem, and took her king and her
princes and brought them to him to
Babylon. 13 [s]And he took one of the royal
offspring[1] [t]and made a covenant with him,
[u]putting him under oath ([v]the chief men of
the land he had taken away), 14 that the
kingdom might be humble and not lift
itself up, and keep his covenant that it
might stand. 15 [w]But he rebelled against him
by sending his ambassadors [x]to Egypt, that
they might give him horses and a large
army. [y]Will he thrive? Can one escape who
does such things? Can he [z]break the
covenant and yet escape?
16 [a]“As I live, declares the Lord GOD,
surely [b]in the place where the king dwells
[c]who made him king, whose oath he
despised, and whose covenant with him
he broke, in Babylon he shall die.
17 [d]Pharaoh with his mighty army and great
company will not help him in war, [e]when
mounds are cast up and siege walls built
to cut off many lives. 18 He despised the
oath in breaking the covenant, and
behold, he gave his hand and did all these
things; he shall not escape. 19 Therefore
thus says the Lord GOD: As I live, surely it
is my oath that he despised, and my
covenant that he broke. I will return it
upon his head. 20 [f]I will spread my net over
him, and he shall be taken in my snare,
and I will bring him to Babylon [g]and enter
into judgment with him there [h]for the
treachery he has committed against me.
21 And all the pick[2] of his troops shall fall
by the sword, [i]and the survivors shall be
scattered to every wind, and you shall
know that [j]I am the LORD; I have spoken.”
22 Thus says the Lord GOD: [k]“I myself
will take a sprig from the lofty top of the
cedar and will set it out. [l]I will break off
from the topmost of its young twigs a tender one, and [m]I myself will plant it on a
high and lofty mountain. 23 [n]On the mountain height of Israel will I plant it, that it
may bear branches and produce fruit and
become a noble cedar. [o]And under it will
dwell every kind of bird; in the shade of its
branches birds of every sort will nest.
24 And all the trees of the field shall know
that I am the LORD; [p]I bring low the high
tree, and make high the low tree, dry up
[q]the green tree, and make [q]the dry tree
flourish. [r]I am the LORD; I have spoken,
and I will do it.”

The Soul Who Sins Shall Die

18 The word of the LORD came to me:
2 “What do you[3] mean [s]by repeating
this proverb concerning the land of Israel,
[t]‘The fathers have eaten sour grapes, and
the children’s teeth are set on edge’? 3 [u]As I
live, declares the Lord GOD, [v]this proverb
shall no more be used by you in Israel.
4 Behold, all souls are mine; the soul of the
father as well as the soul of the son is mine:
[w]the soul who sins shall die.
5 “If a man is righteous and does [x]what is
just and right— 6 if he [y]does not eat upon
the mountains or [z]lift up his eyes to the
idols of the house of Israel, [a]does not defile
his neighbor’s wife [b]or approach [c]a woman

12 [p]See ch. 2:3-5 [q]See ch. 12:9-11 [r]2 Kin. 24:11, 12
13 [s]2 Kin. 24:17 [t]ver. 15, 16, 18; 2 Chr. 36:13 [u][ch. 21:23] [v]2 Kin. 24:14, 15
15 [w][ver. 7; ch. 23:27; 2 Kin. 24:20; 2 Chr. 36:13; Jer. 37:5-7] [x]Deut. 17:16; [Isai. 31:1, 3]; 36:6, 9 [y][ver. 9, 10] [z]ch. 16:59; [ver. 13]
16 [a]See ch. 16:48 [b][ch. 12:13] [c]ver. 13
17 [d]ver. 15; See Jer. 37:5-8 [e]See ch. 4:2
20 [f]See ch. 12:13 [g][ch. 20:35; 38:22] [h]See ch. 14:13
21 [i]See ch. 5:10 [j]ch. 21:17, 32; 26:5, 14; 28:10; 30:12; 34:24; 39:5; [ver. 24]
22 [k]ver. 3 [l]ver. 4 [m][Ps. 2:6]
23 [n]ch. 20:40; 34:14 [o]ch. 31:6; Dan. 4:12; Matt. 13:32
24 [p][ch. 21:26, 27] [q]ch. 20:47; [Luke 23:31] [r]ch. 22:14; 24:14; 36:36; 37:14
Chapter 18
2 [s][ch. 12:22; 16:44] [t]Jer. 31:29
3 [u]See ch. 16:48 [v]Jer. 31:29, 30
4 [w]ver. 20
5 [x]ver. 19, 21, 27 **6** [y]ver. 11, 15; ch. 22:9 [z]ch. 33:25 [a]ver. 11, 15; [ch. 22:11] [b]Lev. 18:19 [c]ch. 22:10

1 Hebrew *seed* 2 Some Hebrew manuscripts, Syriac, Targum; most Hebrew manuscripts *all the fugitives* 3 The Hebrew for *you* is plural

17:10 east wind. See note 19:12.

17:15 Egypt. Although the Old Testament histories do not mention Zedekiah’s appeal to Egypt for help, Jeremiah does mention it (Jer. 37:5–11; 44:30). One of the Lachish letters, written on broken pottery in the last days of the kingdom of Judah, reports that a commander of the army went down to Egypt, perhaps to ask for help. See 16:26; 29:6, 7; 30:20–26.

17:20, 21 See 2 Kin. 25:4–7.

17:22 twigs. The Bible often uses a branch or tree as a symbol of royalty (Dan. 4:9–12, 19–22), particularly as a figure of the Messiah. The messianic Branch belongs to the house of David (Is. 4:2; 11:1; 53:2; 60:21; Jer. 23:5; 33:15; Zech. 6:12). Ezekiel announces that someday God would take a descendant of Jehoiachin (cf. vv. 3, 4 and 12, 13) and restore him to kingship in Judah.

17:23 bird. Rather than be threatened by other kingdoms (birds like the eagles), this splendid cedar would become a haven for birds of all kinds (cf. Dan. 4:12, 21). The tree would be fruitful (2 Kin. 19:30; Is. 11:1; 37:31; Jer. 17:8; cf. John 15:4, 5, 8, 16).

18:1–32 The Exile was not the result of the sins of a single generation. Rather, the continued disobedience of Israel through many generations, “since the day their fathers came out of Egypt, even to this day” (2 Kin. 21:15), finally brought judgment on Judah. The cumulative guilt of the nation was being judged by God in the events that led up to the destruction of Jerusalem. The response of the exiles was to question the justice of God. The popular proverb (v. 2; cf. Jer. 31:29) in effect said, “It’s not our fault—we are being punished for what we did not do. Our fathers sinned, and we are the ones who are paying the price.” Ezekiel replies by emphasizing that God responds according to the acts of each individual and generation. The exiles cannot evade their guilt; they were suffering for their own sins as well.

18:6 not eat. Eating at the mountain shrines would refer to sacrificial meals at the high places (6:13; 20:28; 22:9; cf. Ex. 32:5, 6).

impurity. The law prohibited sexual intercourse during a woman’s period (22:10; Lev. 15:16–33; 18:19).

in her time of menstrual impurity, 7 [d]does
not oppress anyone, but [e]restores to the
debtor his pledge, [f]commits no robbery,
[g]gives his bread to the hungry [g]and covers
the naked with a garment, 8 [h]does not lend
at interest [h]or take any profit, withholds his
hand from injustice, [i]executes true justice
between man and man, 9 [j]walks in my
statutes, and keeps my rules by acting
faithfully—he is righteous; [k]he shall surely
live, declares the Lord GOD.
10 "If he fathers a son who is violent, [l]a
shedder of blood, who does any of these
things 11 (though he himself did none of
these things), [m]who even eats upon the
mountains, [n]defiles his neighbor's wife,
12 oppresses the poor and needy, [o]commits
robbery, [o]does not restore the pledge, [p]lifts
up his eyes to the idols, [q]commits abomination, 13 [r]lends at interest, and takes profit;
shall he then live? He shall not live. He has
done all these abominations; he shall surely die; [s]his blood shall be upon himself.
14 "Now suppose this man fathers a son
who sees all the sins that his father has
done; he sees, and does not do likewise:
15 he does not eat upon the mountains or
lift up his eyes to the idols of the house of
Israel, does not defile his neighbor's wife,
16 does not oppress anyone, [t]exacts no
pledge, [u]commits no robbery, [v]but gives
his bread to the hungry [v]and covers the
naked with a garment, 17 withholds his
hand from iniquity,[1] takes no interest or
profit, obeys my rules, [w]and walks in my
statutes; he shall not die for his father's
iniquity; [x]he shall surely live. 18 As for his
father, because he practiced extortion,
robbed his brother, and did what is not
good among his people, [y]behold, he shall
die for his iniquity.
19 "Yet you say, [z]'Why should not the son
suffer for the iniquity of the father?' When
the son has done [a]what is just and right,
and has been careful to observe all my
statutes, [b]he shall surely live. 20 [c]The soul
who sins shall die. [d]The son shall not suffer for the iniquity of the father, nor the
father suffer for the iniquity of the son.
[e]The righteousness of the righteous shall
be upon himself, [f]and the wickedness of
the wicked shall be upon himself.
21 [g]"But if a wicked person turns away
from all his sins that he has committed and
keeps all my statutes and does [h]what is just
and right, [i]he shall surely live; he shall not
die. 22 [j]None of the transgressions that he
has committed shall be remembered against
him; for the righteousness that he has done
he shall live. 23 [k]Have I any pleasure in the
death of the wicked, declares the Lord GOD,
and not rather that he should turn from his
way and live? 24 [l]But when a righteous person turns away from his righteousness and
does injustice and does the same abominations that the wicked person does, shall he
live? [m]None of the righteous deeds that he
has done shall be remembered; for [n]the
treachery of which he is guilty and the sin he
has committed, for them he shall die.
25 [o]"Yet you say, 'The way of the Lord is
not just.' Hear now, O house of Israel: Is
my way not just? Is it not your ways that
are not just? 26 When a righteous person
turns away from his righteousness and
does injustice, he shall die for it; for the
injustice that he has done he shall die.
27 Again, [p]when a wicked person turns away
from the wickedness he has committed
and does what is just and right, he shall
save his life. 28 Because he considered and
turned away from all the transgressions
that he had committed, he shall surely live;
he shall not die. 29 Yet the house of Israel
says, 'The way of the Lord is not just.' O
house of Israel, are my ways not just? Is it
not your ways that are not just?
30 "Therefore [q]I will judge you, O house
of Israel, every one according to his ways,
declares the Lord GOD. [r]Repent and turn
from all your transgressions, [s]lest iniquity

7 [d]ver. 12, 16; Ex. 22:21 [e]ver. 12; ch. 33:15; Ex. 22:26 [f]ver. 12, 16, 18 [g]ver. 16; Isai. 58:7; [Matt 25:35, 36] **8** [h]ver. 13, 17; ch. 22:12; Ex. 22:25; Ps. 15:5; [i]Deut. 1:16; Zech. 8:16 **9** [j]ver. 17 [k]ver. 17, 19, 21; ch. 20:11; Amos 5:4 **10** [l]See ch. 16:38 **11** [m]See ver. 6 [n]ver. 6; [Lev. 18:20] **12** [o]ver. 7 [p]ver. 6 [q]ch. 8:6, 17 **13** [r]See ver. 8 [s]ch. 33:4; Lev. 20:9, 11; See ch. 3:18 **16** [t][ver. 7, 12] [u]ver. 7 [v]See ver. 7 **17** [w]ver. 9 [x]See ver. 9 **18** [y]See ch. 3:18 **19** [z]Ex. 20:5; [ver. 2] [a]ver. 5, 21, 27 [b]See ver. 9 **20** [c]ver. 4 [d]See 2 Kin. 14:6 [e]Isai. 3:10, 11 [f][Rom. 2:9] **21** [g]See ver. 27 [h]ver. 5, 19 [i]ver. 9 **22** [j]ch. 33:16 **23** [k]ver. 32; ch. 33:11; 1 Tim. 2:4, 6; 2 Pet. 3:9; [Tit. 2:11] **24** [l]ch. 3:20; 33:12, 13, 18 [m][2 Pet. 2:20, 21] [n]See ch. 14:13 **25** [o]ch. 33:17, 20 **27** [p]ver. 21; ch. 33:19; [ch. 13:22; 33:11, 12] **30** [q]ch. 7:3, 8; 33:20; 36:19; [ch. 39:24] [r][ch. 14:6; Hos. 14:1] [s][Isai. 3:8]

[1] Septuagint; Hebrew *from the poor*

18:7 pledge. See vv. 12, 16; Ex. 22:26; Deut. 24:10–13, 17; Prov. 20:16; Amos 2:8. An ostracon (a piece of broken pottery with writing on it) of the late seventh century B.C. records the complaint of a field worker to a village official that his employer had taken his garment and kept it.

18:10 a son who is violent. Having a righteous father did not mean the unrighteous son would escape punishment for his sin.

18:14 his father. Conversely, having an unrighteous father would not bring judgment on a righteous son (v. 10 note; Deut. 24:16; 2 Kin. 14:6).

18:24 does injustice. God will not allow Himself to be merely an escape hatch in times of trouble; He cannot be looked to as Savior without also being received as Lord.

18:30–32 This is a summary statement. Sin can never be taken lightly in one's relationship with God. Yet within the solemn warnings about the gravity of sin and the threat it represents, there remains the assurance that God does not desire or delight in the death of the wicked (2 Pet. 3:9). Repentance is the way to life (2 Chr. 6:37–39; Is. 30:15; 59:20; Jer. 18:8; Matt. 4:17; Mark 1:4, 15; Luke 13:3, 5; 15:7, 10; 24:47; Acts 3:19; 17:30; 2 Cor. 7:10).

be your ruin.[1] 31 [t]Cast away from you all the
transgressions that you have committed,
and [u]make yourselves a new heart and a
new spirit! [v]Why will you die, O house of
Israel? 32 [w]For I have no pleasure in the
death of anyone, declares the Lord GOD;
[r]so turn, and live."

A Lament for the Princes of Israel

19 And you, [x]take up a lamentation for
the princes of Israel, 2 and say:

What was your mother? [y]A lioness!
Among lions she crouched;
in the midst of young lions
she reared her cubs.
3 And she brought up one of her cubs;
[z]he became a young lion,
[a]and he learned to catch prey;
he devoured men.
4 The nations heard about him;
[b]he was caught in their pit,
[c]and they brought him with hooks
to the land of Egypt.
5 When she saw that she waited in vain,
that her hope was lost,
[d]she took another of her cubs
and made him a young lion.
6 He prowled among the lions;
he became a young lion,
and he learned to catch prey;
he devoured men,
7 and seized[2] their widows.
He laid waste their cities,
and the land was appalled and all
who were in it
at the sound of his roaring.
8 [e]Then the nations set against him
from provinces on every side;
[f]they spread their net over him;
[b]he was taken in their pit.
9 With hooks [e]they put him in a
cage[3]
and [g]brought him to the king of
Babylon;
they brought him into custody,
that his voice should no more be
heard
on [h]the mountains of Israel.
10 Your mother was [i]like a vine in a
vineyard[4]
planted by the water,
[j]fruitful and full of branches
[k]by reason of abundant water.
11 Its strong stems became
rulers' scepters;
it towered aloft
among the thick boughs;[5]
it was seen in its height
with the mass of its branches.
12 But the vine was plucked up in fury,
cast down to the ground;
[l]the east wind dried up its fruit;
they were stripped off and
withered.
As for its strong stem,
fire consumed it.
13 [m]Now it is planted in the wilderness,
in a dry and thirsty land.
14 [n]And fire has gone out from the stem
of its shoots,
has consumed its fruit,
[o]so that there remains in it no strong
stem,
no scepter for ruling.

This is [p]a lamentation and has become a
lamentation.

31 [t][ch. 20:7] [u]See ch. 11:19 [v]ch. 33:11
32 [w]See ver. 23 [r][See ver. 30 above]
Chapter 19
1 [x]ch. 26:17; 27:2, 32; 28:12; 32:2; Amos 5:1; [Jer. 7:29]
2 [y][Gen. 49:9]
3 [z][ch. 22:25; 32:2; 2 Kin. 23:30, 31] [a]ch. 22:25, 27
4 [b]Lam. 4:20 [c][2 Kin. 23:33, 34; Jer. 22:11, 12]
5 [d]2 Kin. 23:34, 36
8 [e][2 Chr. 36:6] [f]See ch. 12:13 [b][See ver. 4 above]
9 [e][See ver. 8 above] [g][Jer. 22:26, 27] [h]See ch. 6:2
10 [i]See ch. 15:6 [j][Ps. 80:9] [k][Deut. 8:7]
12 [l]ch. 17:10; [Hos. 13:15]
13 [m][ch. 1:1; Hos. 2:3; See 2 Kin. 24:12-16]
14 [n][2 Kin. 24:20]; See ch. 17:15-19 [o][ver. 11, 12] [p]See ver. 1

[1] Or *lest iniquity be your stumbling block* [2] Hebrew *knew* [3] Or *in a wooden collar* [4] Some Hebrew manuscripts; most Hebrew manuscripts *in your blood* [5] Or *the clouds*

18:31 make yourselves a new heart and a new spirit. As Ezekiel himself recognized, the new heart and spirit were the gift of God (36:26) and not the product of human effort (cf. Eph. 2:8, 9). Ezekiel exhorts his audience to seek these not through their own merit but by repentance (v. 32).

19:1–14 Ezekiel presents another allegory in the kind of Hebrew poetry ordinarily used for funeral dirges and laments. This kind of poetry in Hebrew has a particular meter that Ezekiel's audience would recognize. The same rhythm is used in 26:17, 18; 27:12–19; 28:12–19; 32:2–8.

19:2 lioness. The lioness represents the nation of Israel or the city of Jerusalem, which produced these cubs, or kings; for the image of Jerusalem as a mother, see Ps. 87:5; Is. 50:1; 54:1; Gal. 4:26, 27. The lion as an image is frequently associated with Davidic kingship (Gen. 49:9; Mic. 5:8). The New Testament looks for "the Lion of the tribe of Judah" to reestablish the kingdom of God (Rev. 5:5).

19:4 Egypt. Jehoahaz reigned for only three months before he was taken to Egypt as a captive of Pharaoh Neco in 609 B.C. (2 Kin. 23:31–34; 2 Chr. 36:2–4).

19:5 another. Ezekiel omits any description of the reign of Jehoiakim and proceeds to his son Jehoiachin. Second Kings does not mention any exile for Jehoiakim (2 Kin. 23:36–24:7; cf. 2 Chr. 36:5–8); he apparently died in Jerusalem.

19:9 Babylon. Jehoiakim had rebelled against Nebuchadnezzar, and the wrath of the Babylonian king was directed against his son Jehoiachin. Ezekiel describes his deportation to Babylon in 597 B.C. (2 Kin. 24:8–16; 2 Chr. 36:9, 10). Jehoiachin was imprisoned until the reign of Evil-merodach (562–560 B.C.; 2 Kin. 25:27–30).

19:12 east wind. This is just as in 17:9, 10. The east wind is an instrument of Yahweh's will (Ex. 10:13; 14:21; Ps. 78:26; Hos. 13:15; Jon. 4:8). The east wind brought the desert heat and would wither the vine.

19:14 no strong stem. The end of the kingdom of Judah is described as a time when the vine was uprooted and no branch was left to make a ruler's scepter. For the use of a branch as a symbol of the messianic king, see note 17:22.

Israel's Continuing Rebellion

20 [q]In the seventh year, in the fifth
month, on the tenth day of the
month, certain of [r]the elders of Israel came
to inquire of the LORD, [s]and sat before me.
2 And the word of the LORD came to me:
3 [t]"Son of man, speak to the elders of Israel,
and say to them, Thus says the Lord GOD,
Is it to inquire of me that you come? [u]As I
live, declares the Lord GOD, [v]I will not be
inquired of by you. 4 [w]Will you judge them,
son of man, will you judge them? [x]Let
them know the abominations of their
fathers, 5 and say to them, Thus says the
Lord GOD: [y]On the day when I chose Israel,
[z]I swore[1] to the offspring of the house of
Jacob, [a]making myself known to them in
the land of Egypt; [z]I swore to them, saying,
I am the LORD your God. 6 On that day I
swore to them that [b]I would bring them
out of the land of Egypt into a land that I
had searched out for them, a land [b]flowing
with milk and honey, [c]the most glorious of
all lands. 7 And I said to them, [d]Cast away
the detestable things [e]your eyes feast on,
every one of you, and do not defile yourselves with [f]the idols of Egypt; [g]I am the
LORD your God. 8 [h]But they rebelled against
me and were not willing to listen to me.
[i]None of them cast away the detestable
things their eyes feasted on, nor did they
forsake the idols of Egypt.
"Then I said I would pour out my wrath
upon them [j]and spend my anger against
them in the midst of the land of Egypt. 9 [k]But
I acted [l]for the sake of my name, [m]that it
should not be profaned in the sight of the
nations among whom they lived, [n]in whose
sight I made myself known to them in bringing them out of the land of Egypt. 10 [o]So I led
them out of the land of Egypt and brought
them into the wilderness. 11 [p]I gave them my
statutes and made known to them my rules,
[q]by which, if a person does them, he shall
live. 12 Moreover, I gave them [r]my Sabbaths,
as a sign between me and them, [s]that they
might know that I am the LORD who sanctifies them. 13 [t]But the house of Israel rebelled
against me in the wilderness. [u]They did not
walk in my statutes but rejected my rules, by
which, if a person does them, he shall live;
[v]and my Sabbaths they greatly profaned.
[t]"Then I said I would pour out my wrath
upon them in the wilderness, to make a
full end of them. 14 But I acted for the sake
of my name, that it should not be profaned
in the sight of the nations, [w]in whose sight
I had brought them out. 15 Moreover, [x]I
swore to them in the wilderness [y]that I
would not bring them into the land that
I had given them, a land [z]flowing with milk
and honey, [z]the most glorious of all lands,
16 because they rejected my rules and did
not walk in my statutes, and profaned my
Sabbaths; [a]for their heart went after their
idols. 17 Nevertheless, [b]my eye spared them,
and I did not destroy them or [c]make a full
end of them in the wilderness.
18 "And I said to [d]their children in the
wilderness, Do not walk [e]in the statutes of
your fathers, nor keep their rules, [f]nor
defile yourselves with their idols. 19 [g]I am
the LORD your God; [h]walk in my statutes,
and be careful to obey my rules, 20 and
[i]keep my Sabbaths holy that [j]they may be a
sign between me and you, that you may
know that I am the LORD your God. 21 [k]But
the children [l]rebelled against me. [m]They
did not walk in my statutes and were not
careful to obey my rules, by which, if a person does them, he shall live; they profaned
my Sabbaths.
[n]"Then I said I would pour out my wrath
upon them and spend my anger against

Chapter 20
1 [q][ch. 1:2; 8:1; 24:1; 26:1; 29:1, 17; 30:20; 31:1; 32:1, 17; 33:21; 40:1] [r]See ch. 8:1 [s]ch. 14:1
3 [t]See ch. 2:1 [u]See ch. 16:48 [v]See ch. 14:3
4 [w]ch. 22:2; 23:36 [x]ch. 16:2; 22:2
5 [y]See Ex. 6:7 [z]ver. 15:23, 28, 42; ch. 36:7; 47:14; [Gen. 14:22] [a][Ex. 3:8; 4:31; 6:2]
6 [b]ver. 15; See Ex. 3:8 [c]ver. 15; [Jer. 3:19; Zech. 7:14]
7 [d][ver. 8; ch. 18:31] [e][ver. 24] [f][ver. 18; Lev. 18:3] [g]ver. 19; See Ex. 20:2
8 [h]ver. 21 [i][ver. 7] [j]See ch. 5:13
9 [k]ver. 22, 44 [l]Ps. 106:8 [m][Isai. 48:11] [n]ver. 14
10 [o]Ex. 13:18, 20
11 [p]Deut. 4:8; [Neh. 9:13, 14; Ps. 147:19, 20] [q]Lev. 18:5; Rom. 10:5; Gal. 3:12; See ch. 18:9
12 [r][ver. 13, 16, 21, 24]; See Ex. 20:8-11; Deut. 5:12-15 [s]ch. 37:28; [Lev. 21:23]
13 [t]ver. 21 [u]ver. 21, 24 [v]ver. 21, 24; ch. 22:8; 23:38
14 [w]ver. 9
15 [x]See ver. 5 [y]Ps. 95:11; See Num. 14:28-30 [z]ver. 6; See Ex. 3:8
16 [a][ver. 24; Num. 15:39; Ps. 78:37]
17 [b]See ch. 5:11 [c][ch. 11:13] **18** [d]ver. 21; [ch. 2:3] [e]Josh. 24:14; 1 Pet. 1:18 [f][ver. 7] **19** [g]ver. 5; See Ex. 20:2 [h]Deut. 5:32, 33 **20** [i]Jer. 17:22 [j]ver. 12; [Gen. 9:12; 17:11] **21** [k]Deut. 31:27 [l]ver. 8, 13 [m]ver. 13, 16 [n]ver. 8

[1] Hebrew *I lifted my hand*; twice in this verse; also verses 6, 15, 23, 28, 42

20:1 year. Once again the elders gather to seek instruction from the prophet, about a year later than the date last mentioned (8:1; cf. 14:1). The date would be the tenth of Ab (August, 591 B.C.), five years to the day before Jerusalem was put to the torch (Jer. 52:12).

20:5 I swore. This phrase is repeated several times in the chapter (vv. 5, 6, 15, 23, 28, 42). God had pledged Himself to Israel and would perform His promises. See Ex. 3:6–10; 6:2–8.

20:8 idols of Egypt. The Pentateuch does not record details about the religious life of the Israelites during their slavery in Egypt, but it is safe to infer that they had assimilated the religion of the culture there as they did later in Canaan. The incident with the golden calf (Ex. 32) should be understood against the background of idolatry in Egypt. See 23:3; Josh. 24:14.

20:11 statutes. The law was God's gracious gift to Israel; it was a way of life (Deut. 4:40; 32:46, 47; Josh. 1:7, 8).

20:12 Sabbaths. The Sabbath (vv. 13, 16, 21, 24) is singled out as a law unique to Israel, one that most clearly distinguished it from the nations. The Sabbath is often cited as an important example that stands for the whole law (22:8, 26; 23:38; 44:24; cf. Neh. 13:18; Is. 56:2, 4, 6; Jer. 17:19–27).

20:13 rebelled. The first generation in the wilderness rebelled against God (Ex. 17:2; Num. 14:18; 16; 17; 20:10, 24; 25; 26:9; 27:14; Deut. 1:26, 43; 9:7; 31:27).

my Sabbaths. See Num. 15:32–36.

them in the wilderness. 22 [o]But I withheld
my hand [p]and acted for the sake of my
name, [q]that it should not be profaned in
the sight of the nations, in whose sight I
had brought them out. 23 [r]Moreover,
[s]I swore to them in the wilderness [t]that I
would scatter them among the nations and
disperse them through the countries, 24 because they had not obeyed my rules, but
had rejected my statutes and profaned my
Sabbaths, [u]and their eyes were set on their
fathers' idols. 25 [v]Moreover, I gave them
statutes that were not good and rules by
which they could not have life, 26 and I
defiled them through [w]their very gifts [w]in
their offering up all their firstborn, that I
might devastate them. I did it [x]that they
might know that I am the LORD.
27 "Therefore, [y]son of man, speak to the
house of Israel and say to them, Thus says
the Lord GOD: In this also your fathers
blasphemed me, by [z]dealing treacherously
with me. 28 For when I had brought them
into the land that [a]I swore to give them,
then wherever they saw [b]any high hill or
any leafy tree, there they offered their sacrifices and there they presented [c]the provocation of their offering; there they sent up
their pleasing aromas, and there they
poured out their drink offerings. 29 (I said
to them, [d]What is the high place to which
you go? So its name is called Bamah[1] to
this day.)
30 "Therefore say to the house of Israel,
Thus says the Lord GOD: [e]Will you defile
yourselves after the manner of your fathers
and go [f]whoring after their detestable
things? 31 When you present your gifts and
[g]offer up your children in fire,[2] you defile
yourselves with all your idols to this day.
And [h]shall I be inquired of by you, O house
of Israel? [i]As I live, declares the Lord GOD,
I will not be inquired of by you.
32 [j]"What is in your mind shall never happen—the thought, [k]'Let us be like the
nations, like the tribes of the countries,
[l]and worship wood and stone.'

The LORD Will Restore Israel

33 [i]"As I live, declares the Lord GOD,
[m]surely with a mighty hand and an outstretched arm and [n]with wrath poured out
I will be king over you. 34 [o]I will bring you
out from the peoples and gather you out of
the countries where you are scattered, with
a mighty hand and an outstretched arm,
and with wrath poured out. 35 [p]And I will
bring you into the wilderness of the peoples, [q]and there I will enter into judgment
with you [r]face to face. 36 [s]As I entered into
judgment with your fathers in the wilderness of the land of Egypt, so I will enter
into judgment with you, declares the Lord
GOD. 37 I will make you [t]pass under the rod,
and I will bring you into the bond of the
covenant. 38 [u]I will purge out the rebels
from among you, and those who transgress
against me. [v]I will bring them out of the
land where they sojourn, [w]but they shall
not enter the land of Israel. [x]Then you will
know that I am the LORD.
39 "As for you, O house of Israel, thus says
the Lord GOD: [y]Go serve every one of you
his idols, now and hereafter, if you will not
listen to me; [z]but my holy name you shall
no more profane with your gifts and your
idols.
40 [a]"For on my holy mountain, the mountain height of Israel, declares the Lord GOD,

22 [o]ver. 14 [p]ver. 9, 14, 44 [q]ver. 9 **23** [r]ver. 15 [s]See ver. 5 [t]Deut. 28:64 **24** [u][ver. 16] **25** [v]Ps. 81:12; Acts 7:42; Rom. 1:24, 28; 2 Thess. 2:11, 12; [ver. 39] **26** [w][ver. 31; ch. 16:20, 21] [x]See ch. 6:7 **27** [y]See ch. 2:1 [z]See ch. 14:13 **28** [a]See ver. 5 [b][ch. 6:13] [c][ch. 8:17] **29** [d][ver. 40] **30** [e][ver. 7] [f]Ps. 106:39 **31** [g][ver. 26] [h]See ch. 14:3 [i]See ch. 16:48 **32** [j]See ch. 11:5 [k][Jer. 44:17] [l]Deut. 4:28; 2 Kin. 19:18; Dan. 5:4, 23; Rev. 9:20 **33** [i][See ver. 31 above] [m]See Jer. 21:5 [n][ver. 8] **34** [o][Jer. 31:8] **35** [p][ver. 10; Hos. 2:14] [q][ch. 17:20] [r][Deut. 5:4] **36** [s]See Num. 14:20-23, 28-30 **37** [t]Lev. 27:32 **38** [u]ch. 34:17, 20, 22; [Matt. 25:32, 33] [v][ver. 35] [w]ch. 13:9 [x]See ch. 6:7 **39** [y][ver. 25, 26; Judg. 10:14] [z]ch. 39:7; 43:7; [Jer. 44:25, 26] **40** [a]ch. 17:23; [ch. 28:14; Isai. 56:7]

1 *Bamah* means *high place* 2 Hebrew *and make your children pass through the fire*

20:23 scatter. The threat of exile existed even before the people entered the land (Lev. 26:32–35; Deut. 28:64–67; Ps. 106:26). Moses predicted that they would rebel against the Lord once in the land (Deut. 31:27, 29).

20:26 their firstborn. The law was God's gracious gift (v. 11 note), but when perverted it brought death. Ezekiel appears to regard the practice of child sacrifice in ancient Israel as a perversion of their laws regarding the firstborn (Ex. 13:1, 11–16; 22:29; 34:19, 20; Num. 18:15, 16). Every first-born belonged to the Lord, but children were not to be sacrificed.

20:29 high place. Second Kings measures almost every ruler of Judah in terms of what he or she did about the high places around Jerusalem.

20:32–38 The desire to be like the surrounding nations (v. 32) reflects 1 Sam. 8:20; the people had rejected God (1 Sam. 8:7, 8). But just as God would not abandon earlier generations of His chosen people, so now He promises a new exodus and a return to the wilderness experience (vv. 33–35). Just as only the faithful and obedient from those in the wilder-ness generation crossed into the land (Num. 14:30, 38), so too God would again purge the nation to bring a faithful people into the land (vv. 36–38).

20:35 wilderness of the peoples. Possibly this refers to the desolation of exile, which Israel was about to experience. Israel was going to be judged in a "wilderness" just as the wilderness generation had been.

20:37 pass under the rod. The phrase alludes to the practice of count-ing off animals for the tithe (Lev. 27:32, 33); it suggests that a tenth would be left (cf. Is. 6:13).

20:38 purge. The goal of the periodic catastrophes that befell Israel was commonly to produce a purified, purged, and faithful remnant (6:8 note).

20:40 holy mountain. Zion. The faithful remnant would worship at God's holy mountain. The glory of the grace of God is that He deals with us in mercy and not as our sins deserve (20:44; Ezra 9:13; Job 33:27; Ps. 103:10; Lam. 3:22, 23, 31–33).

there [b]all the house of Israel, all of them,
shall serve me in the land. [c]There I will
accept them, and there I will require your
contributions and the choicest of your
gifts, with all your sacred offerings. **41** As a
pleasing aroma I will accept you, when [d]I
bring you out from the peoples and gather
you out of the countries where you have
been scattered. And [e]I will manifest my
holiness among you in the sight of the
nations. **42** [f]And you shall know that I am
the LORD, when I bring you into the land of
Israel, the country that [g]I swore to give to
your fathers. **43** [h]And there you shall
remember your ways and all your deeds
with which you have defiled yourselves,
[h]and you shall loathe yourselves for all the
evils that you have committed. **44** And you
shall know that I am the LORD, [i]when I deal
with you for my name's sake, [j]not according to your evil ways, nor according to your
corrupt deeds, O house of Israel, declares
the Lord GOD."

45 [1] And the word of the LORD came to me:
46 [k]"Son of man, [l]set your face toward the
southland;[2] [m]preach against the south, and
prophesy against the forest land in the
Negeb. **47** Say to the forest of the Negeb,
Hear the word of the LORD: Thus says the
Lord GOD, Behold, [n]I will kindle a fire in
you, and it shall devour every [o]green tree in
you and every [o]dry tree. The blazing flame
shall not be quenched, and [p]all faces from
south to north shall be scorched by it. **48** [q]All
flesh shall see that I the LORD have kindled
it; it shall not be quenched." **49** Then I said,
[r]"Ah, Lord GOD! They are saying of me, [s]'Is
he not a maker of parables?'"

The LORD Has Drawn His Sword

21 [3] The word of the LORD came to me:
2 [t]"Son of man, [u]set your face toward
Jerusalem and [v]preach against the sanctuaries.[4] Prophesy against the land of Israel
3 and say to the land of Israel, Thus says the
LORD: [w]Behold, I am against you and will
draw [x]my sword from its sheath and [y]will
cut off from you both righteous and
wicked. **4** Because I will cut off from you
both righteous and wicked, therefore my
sword shall be drawn from its sheath
against all flesh from south to north. **5** [z]And
all flesh shall know that I am the LORD. I
have drawn [x]my sword from its sheath; [a]it
shall not be sheathed again.

6 "As for you, son of man, [b]groan; with
breaking heart and bitter grief, [c]groan
before their eyes. **7** [d]And when they say to
you, 'Why do you groan?' you shall say,
'Because of the news [e]that it is coming.
[f]Every heart will melt, and [g]all hands will
be feeble; every spirit will faint, and [g]all
knees will be weak as water. [h]Behold, it is
[e]coming, and it will be fulfilled,'" declares
the Lord GOD.

8 And the word of the LORD came to me:
9 [r]"Son of man, prophesy and say, Thus
says the Lord; Say:

> [i]"A sword, a sword is sharpened
> and also polished,
> **10** [j]sharpened for slaughter,
> [j]polished to flash like lightning!

(Or [k]shall we rejoice? You have despised
the rod, my son, [l]with everything of
wood.)[5] **11** So the sword is given to be polished, that it may be grasped in the hand.
It is sharpened and polished [m]to be given
into the hand of the slayer. **12** [n]Cry out and
wail, son of man, for it is against my people. It is against all the princes of Israel.
They are delivered over to the sword with
my people. [o]Strike therefore upon your
thigh. **13** For it will not be a testing—what
could it do if you despise [p]the rod?"[6]
declares the Lord GOD.

[1] Ch 21:1 in Hebrew [2] Or *toward Teman* [3] Ch 21:6 in Hebrew [4] Some Hebrew manuscripts, compare Septuagint, Syriac *against their sanctuary* [5] Probable reading; Hebrew *The rod of my son despises everything of wood* [6] Or *For it is a testing; and what if even the rod despises? It shall not be!*

40 [b]ch. 39:25 [c]ch. 43:27; Isai. 60:7; [Mal. 3:4; Rom. 12:1]
41 [d]ver. 34 [e]ch. 36:23; 39:27; [ch. 28:22; 38:16, 23; Num. 20:12; Isai. 8:13]
42 [f]See ch. 6:7 [g]See ver. 5
43 [h]See ch. 6:9
44 [i]ver. 9, 14, 22 [j][Ps. 103:10]
46 [k]See ch. 2:1 [l][ch. 21:2] [m]Amos 7:16; [Isai. 55:10, 11]
47 [n]Jer. 21:14 [o]ch. 17:24; [Luke 23:31] [p]ch. 21:4
48 [q]Isai. 40:5; [Isai. 30:33]
49 [r]See ch. 4:14 [s][ch. 17:2; 24:3]
Chapter 21
2 [t]See ch. 2:1 [u][ch. 20:46] [v]See ch. 20:46
3 [w]See ch. 13:8 [x]ver. 19, 30; [Deut. 32:41; Jer. 47:6] [y][ch. 20:47; Job 9:22]
5 [z][ch. 20:48] [x][See ver. 3 above] [a][ver. 30]
6 [b][ch. 6:11; 12:18] [c]See ch. 12:3
7 [d][ch. 12:9] [e][ch. 7:5, 6] [f]See Josh. 2:11 [g]See ch. 7:17 [h]ch. 39:8
9 [r][See ch. 20:49 above] [i]See ver. 3
10 [j][ver. 15, 28] [k][James 5:5] [l][ch. 20:47]
11 [m][ver. 19]
12 [n][ver. 6] [o]Jer. 31:19
13 [p][ver. 10]

20:45–48 This short prophecy against the South is explained in 21:1–5. Here and in 21:4 disaster comes "from south to north," and the disaster cannot be stopped (v. 48; 21:5). The threat was issued in Babylon, and Israel is described as lying to the south. Disaster is usually portrayed as coming from the north (Is. 14:31; 41:25; Jer. 1:13–15; 4:6; 6:1; 10:22; 25:9; 47:2; 50:9; 51:48; Joel 2:20).

20:49 They are saying of me. Ridicule and mocking were often a prophet's lot (2 Chr. 36:16; Matt. 20:19; 27:29).

21:1–32 The oracles of this chapter all use the figure of a sword (21:1–7, 8–27, 28–32). The Old Testament frequently describes God as a warrior. His sword was ordinarily wielded against Israel's enemies (Deut. 32:41; Is. 31:8; 34:5–8; 66:16; Jer. 25:31; 50:35–37; Zeph. 2:12). But now the sword was given to the Babylonians and would be wielded against Judah and Jerusalem (vv. 2, 12).

21:9 A sword. Probably Ezekiel is once again using some form of symbolic action (4:1–3 note). The prophet may have been whirling, cutting, and slashing with a sword in a dramatic dance as part of the oracle.

21:10, 13 rod. These verses along with v. 27 are united in part by their allusions to Judah's scepter (Gen. 49:10). A wooden rod was nothing against an iron sword, and Judah was no contest for Nebuchadnezzar.

14 "As for you, [q]son of man, prophesy.
[r]Clap your hands and let the sword come
down twice, [s]yes, three times,[1] the sword
for those to be slain. It is the sword for the
great slaughter, which surrounds them,
15 that their hearts may melt, and many
stumble.[2] At all their gates I have given the
glittering sword. Ah, it is made like lightning; [t]it is taken up[3] for slaughter. **16** Cut
sharply to the right; set yourself to the left,
wherever your face is directed. **17** I also will
[r]clap my hands, [u]and I will satisfy my fury;
[v]I the LORD have spoken."

18 The word of the LORD came to me
again: **19** "As for you, son of man, mark two
ways for [w]the sword of the king of Babylon
to come. Both of them shall come from the
same land. And make [x]a signpost; make it
[x]at the head of the way to a city. **20** Mark a
way [y]for the sword to come to Rabbah of
the Ammonites and to Judah, into
Jerusalem the fortified. **21** For the king of
Babylon stands [z]at the parting of the way,
at the head of the two ways, to use divination. He shakes the arrows; he consults
[a]the teraphim;[4] he looks at the liver. **22** Into
his right hand comes the divination for
Jerusalem, [b]to set battering rams, to open
the mouth with murder, to lift up the voice
with shouting, to set battering rams against
the gates, [c]to cast up mounds, to build
siege towers. **23** But to them it will seem like
a false divination. [d]They have sworn
solemn oaths, but he brings their guilt to
remembrance, [e]that they may be taken.

24 "Therefore thus says the Lord GOD:
Because you have made your guilt to be
remembered, in that your transgressions
are uncovered, so that in all your deeds
your sins appear—because you have come
to remembrance, [f]you shall be taken in
hand. **25** And you, O profane[5] [g]wicked one,
prince of Israel, [h]whose day has come, [i]the
time of your final punishment, **26** thus says
the Lord GOD: Remove the turban and take
off the crown. Things shall not remain as
they are. [j]Exalt that which is low, and bring
low that which is exalted. **27** A ruin, ruin,
ruin I will make it. [k]This also shall not be,
[l]until he comes, the one to whom judgment belongs, and I will give it to him.

28 "And you, [m]son of man, prophesy, and
say, Thus says the Lord GOD [n]concerning
the Ammonites and concerning their
reproach; say, [o]A sword, a sword [p]is drawn
for the slaughter. [o]It is polished to consume and to flash like lightning— **29** while
[q]they see for you false visions, while they
divine lies for you—to place you on the
necks of the profane wicked, [r]whose day
has come, the time of their final punishment. **30** [p]Return it to its sheath. In the
place where you were created, in the land
of your origin, [s]I will judge you. **31** And [t]I
will pour out my indignation upon you; [u]I
will blow upon you with the fire of my
wrath, and I will deliver you into the hands
of [v]brutish men, skillful to destroy. **32** You
shall be fuel for the fire. Your blood shall
be in the midst of the land. [w]You shall be
no more remembered, [x]for I the LORD have
spoken."

Israel's Shedding of Blood

22 And the word of the LORD came to
me, saying, **2** "And you, [y]son of
man, [z]will you judge, will you judge [a]the
bloody city? [b]Then declare to her all her
abominations. **3** You shall say, Thus says
the Lord GOD: A city that sheds blood in
her midst, so that [c]her time may come, and
that makes idols to defile herself! **4** You

14 [q]See ch. 2:1 [r]ch. 22:13; Num. 24:10 [s][2 Kin. 24:1, 10; 25:1]
15 [t]ver. 10
17 [r][See ver. 14 above] [u]See ch. 5:13 [v]See ch. 17:24
19 [w]ver. 11 [x][ver. 21]
20 [y]See ch. 25:1-5; Jer. 49:1-6; Amos 1:13-15
21 [z][ver. 19] [a]See Gen. 31:19
22 [b]ch. 4:2; 26:9 [c]See ch. 4:2
23 [d][ch. 17:13] [e][ch. 17:20]
24 [f][ch. 17:20]
25 [g][ch. 17:19; 2 Chr. 36:13; Jer. 52:2] [h]ver. 29; ch. 22:3, 4 [i]ch. 35:5
26 [j][ch. 17:24; Luke 1:52]
27 [k][ver. 13] [l]Gen. 49:10; Zech. 6:12, 13; John 1:49; [Rev. 17:14]
28 [m]See ch. 2:1 [n]See ver. 20 [o][ver. 9, 10] [p][ver. 5]
29 [q]See ch. 13:6 [r]ver. 25
30 [p][See ver. 28 above] [s]ch. 16:38
31 [t]See ch. 7:8 [u]ch. 22:20, 21 [v]See Ps. 49:10
32 [w]ch. 25:10 [x]See ch. 17:24
Chapter 22
2 [y]See ch. 2:1 [z]See ch. 20:4 [a][ch. 16:38; 23:37; 24:6; 2 Kin. 21:16]; See ch. 7:23 [b]ch. 16:2; 20:4
3 [c]ch. 21:25, 29

[1] Hebrew *its third* [2] Hebrew *many stumbling blocks* [3] The meaning of the Hebrew word rendered *taken up* is uncertain [4] Or *household idols* [5] Or *slain*; also verse 29

21:18–23 Nebuchadnezzar would be coming from the north, approaching a fork in the road. Ezekiel probably drew a map something like an inverted "Y" scratched in the dirt or on a brick (4:1–3 note). Coming from the north, the left fork in the road would take the Babylonian armies down the "King's Highway," a major highway passing through Jordan. The right fork would take the Babylonians down the "Via Maris," an important international highway on the coastal plain west of Jerusalem. These highways met near Damascus.

21:21 divination. The Babylonian king used several ways to obtain guidance from the gods. (a) The images (Hebrew *teraphim*) were religious objects used in worship. (b) Divination by examining the contours and markings on the livers of sacrificed birds or sheep (hepatoscopy) was a common practice in ancient times. (c) Arrows were used as a means of casting lots.

21:23 sworn solemn oaths. Nebuchadnezzar laid siege to Jerusalem by January, 588 B.C.

21:25 prince. The profane and wicked prince is Zedekiah, the last king of Judah (17:1–10 note).

21:28 Ammonites. From vv. 18–23 it might seem that the Babylonians would attack Jerusalem but spare Ammon. This third and last sword song explains that Ammon too would taste God's wrath in the fury of the Babylonians (Jer. 49:1–6). Ammon was allied with Jerusalem and Egypt against the Babylonians in 589 B.C. However, when Jerusalem came under attack, Ammon took advantage of her former ally (Jer. 27:3; 40:11, 14; 41:10, 15; cf. 2 Kin. 24:2).

22:2 bloody city. This first of three oracles in ch. 22 revolves around repeated references to blood (vv. 2, 3, 4, 6, 9, 12, 13; cf. v. 27). The city is indicted for both moral and ritual crimes.

have become guilty [a]by the blood that you
have shed, and defiled by the idols that
you have made, and you have brought
[c]your days near, the appointed time of[1] your
years has come. [d]Therefore I have made you
a reproach to the nations, and a mockery to
all the countries. 5 Those who are near and
those who are far from you will mock you;
[e]your name is defiled; [f]you are full of
tumult.
6 "Behold, [g]the princes of Israel in you,
every one according to his power, have
been bent on shedding blood. 7 Father and
mother [h]are treated with contempt in you;
the sojourner [i]suffers extortion in your
midst; the fatherless and the widow [i]are
wronged in you. 8 [j]You have despised my
holy things and [k]profaned my Sabbaths.
9 [l]There are men in you who slander to
shed blood, and people in you [m]who eat on
the mountains; [n]they commit lewdness in
your midst. 10 In you [o]men uncover their
fathers' nakedness; in you they violate
women who are unclean in their menstrual impurity. 11 [p]One commits abomination
with his neighbor's wife; [q]another lewdly
defiles his daughter-in-law; [r]another in you
violates his sister, his father's daughter.
12 In you [s]they take bribes to shed blood;
[t]you take interest and profit and make gain
of your neighbors by extortion; but [u]me
you have forgotten, declares the Lord GOD.
13 "Behold, [v]I strike my hand at [w]the dishonest gain that you have made, and at
[x]the blood that has been in your midst.
14 [y]Can your courage endure, or can your
hands be strong, in the days that I shall
deal with you? [z]I the LORD have spoken,
and I will do it. 15 [a]I will scatter you among
the nations and disperse you through the
countries, and [b]I will consume your
uncleanness out of you. 16 And [c]you shall
be profaned by your own doing [d]in the
sight of the nations, [e]and you shall know
that I am the LORD."
17 And the word of the LORD came to me:
18 [f]"Son of man, the house of Israel has
become [g]dross to me; all of them are
[h]bronze and tin and iron and lead in the
furnace; they are [i]dross of silver. 19 Therefore thus says the Lord GOD: Because you
have all become dross, therefore, behold,
I will gather you into the midst of
Jerusalem. 20 As one gathers silver and
bronze and iron and lead and tin into a
furnace, [j]to blow the fire on it in order to
melt it, so I will gather you [k]in my anger
and in my wrath, and I will put you in and
melt you. 21 I will gather you and blow on
you with the fire of my wrath, and you
shall be melted in the midst of it. 22 As silver is melted in a furnace, so you shall be
melted in the midst of it, and you shall
know that I am the LORD; [l]I have poured
out my wrath upon you."
23 And the word of the LORD came to
me: 24 "Son of man, say to her, You are a
land that is [m]not cleansed [n]or rained
upon in the day of indignation. 25 [o]The
conspiracy of her prophets in her midst is
[p]like a roaring lion [q]tearing the prey; they
have devoured human lives; they have
taken treasure and precious things; they
have made many widows in her midst.
26 [r]Her priests [s]have done violence to my
law and [t]have profaned my holy things.
[u]They have made no distinction between
the holy and the common, neither have
they taught the difference between the
unclean and the clean, and [v]they have disregarded my Sabbaths, [w]so that I am profaned among them. 27 [x]Her princes in her
midst are like wolves [y]tearing the prey,
[z]shedding blood, destroying lives to get
dishonest gain. 28 And [a]her prophets have
smeared whitewash for them, [b]seeing
false visions and divining lies for them,
saying, 'Thus says the Lord GOD,' when

4 [a][See ver. 2 above] [c][See ver. 2 above] [d]See ch. 5:14
5 [e][Isai. 1:21] [f]Isai. 22:2
6 [g]ver. 27
7 [h]Deut. 27:16; [Eph. 6:2]; See Ex. 20:12 [i]Ex. 22:21, 22
8 [j][ver. 26] [k]See ch. 20:13
9 [l]Lev. 19:16; [1 Sam. 22:9] [m]See ch. 18:6 [n]ch. 16:43
10 [o]Lev. 18:7, 8; 20:11
11 [p]Lev. 18:20; Jer. 5:8; [ch. 18:6] [q]Lev. 18:15; 20:12; [Amos 2:7] [r]Lev. 18:9; 20:17
12 [s]Deut. 27:25 [t]See ch. 18:8 [u]ch. 23:35; See Jer. 2:32
13 [v]ch. 21:14, 17; [w]ver. 27 [x]See ver. 2
14 [y][ch. 21:7] [z]See ch. 17:24
15 [a]See ch. 5:10 [b]ch. 24:11; [ver. 21, 22]
16 [c][ver. 26; ch. 7:24] [d]ch. 5:8 [e]See ch. 6:7
18 [f]See ch. 2:1 [g]Ps. 119:119; Isai. 1:22, 25 [h]Jer. 6:28 [i]Isai. 1:25
20 [j]ch. 21:31; [Mal. 3:3] [k]Jer. 33:5
22 [l]See ch. 7:8
24 [m]See ver. 2-4 [n][ch. 34:26]; See 1 Kin. 8:35, 36
25 [o]See Jer. 11:9 [p]See ch. 19:3 [q]ver. 27
26 [r][Mal. 2:8] [s]Zeph. 3:4 [t][ver. 8] [u]See Lev. 10:10 [v][Jer. 17:22, 24, 27] [w]See ch. 36:20
27 [x]ver. 6; Mic. 3:1, 2; Zeph. 3:3; [Matt. 7:15] [y]ver. 25 [z][ver. 13] 28 [a]ch. 13:10 [b]See ch. 13:6

1 Some Hebrew manuscripts, Septuagint, Syriac, Vulgate, Targum; most Hebrew manuscripts *until*

22:7 Father and mother. They abused their own parents (Deut. 5:16; Mic. 7:6; Rom. 1:30; Eph. 6:1; Col. 3:20; 2 Tim. 3:2).

the sojourner . . . the fatherless and the widow. See Ps. 9:18 note. Other references: Deut. 10:18; 14:29; 24:17; 26:12, 13; 27:19; Ps. 68:5; 72:4; 146:9; Is. 1:17; 10:1, 2; Jer. 7:6, 7; 22:3; Zech. 7:10; Mal. 3:5).

22:11 abomination. For the range of forbidden sexual relations, see Lev. 18:6–23; 20:10–21.

22:18 furnace. The periodic outpouring of divine judgment on Israel was designed to purge her of sin and to produce a pure people (6:8 note). Israel's experience in Egypt was likened to time in a furnace (Deut. 4:20; 1 Kin. 8:51; Jer. 11:4), and the Exile would be a refiner's furnace for Israel. Refining is a common image in the Bible (Ps. 66:10; 119:119; Prov. 17:3; 25:4; Is. 1:25; 48:10; Jer. 9:7; Zech. 13:9; Mal. 3:2, 3; 1 Cor. 3:12–15; 1 Pet. 1:7).

22:21 blow. God blows on the flame, the divine breath serving as a bellows to heat the fire hotter. The fear is that no silver will emerge from the furnace—only dross.

the LORD has not spoken. 29 The people of the land [c]have practiced extortion and committed robbery. They have oppressed the poor and needy, and [c]have extorted from the sojourner without justice. 30 [d]And I sought for a man among them [e]who should build up the wall [e]and stand in the breach before me for the land, that I should not destroy it, but I found none. 31 Therefore [f]I have poured out my indignation upon them. I have consumed them with the fire of my wrath. I have returned [g]their way upon their heads, declares the Lord GOD."

Oholah and Oholibah

23 The word of the LORD came to me: 2 [h]"Son of man, there were [i]two women, the daughters of one mother. 3 [j]They played the whore in Egypt; [j]they played the whore [k]in their youth; there their breasts were pressed and their virgin bosoms[1] handled. 4 Oholah was the name of the elder and Oholibah the name of her sister. [l]They became mine, and they [m]bore sons and daughters. As for their names, Oholah is [n]Samaria, and Oholibah is Jerusalem.

5 "Oholah played the whore [o]while she was mine, and [p]she lusted after her lovers [q]the Assyrians, warriors 6 clothed in purple, [r]governors and commanders, [s]all of them desirable young men, [t]horsemen riding on horses. 7 She bestowed her whoring upon them, the choicest men of Assyria all of them, and she defiled herself with all the idols of everyone after whom she lusted. 8 She did not give up her whoring [u]that she had begun in Egypt; for in her youth men had lain with her and handled her virgin bosom and poured out their whoring lust upon her. 9 Therefore [v]I delivered her into the hands of her lovers, into the hands of the Assyrians, after whom she lusted. 10 [w]These uncovered her nakedness; [x]they seized her sons and her daughters; and as for her, they killed her with the sword; and she became [y]a byword among women, [z]when judgment had been executed on her.

11 [a]"Her sister Oholibah saw this, and she became [b]more corrupt than her sister[2] in her lust and in her whoring, which was worse than that of her sister. 12 She lusted after the Assyrians, governors and commanders, warriors clothed in full armor, horsemen riding on horses, [s]all of them desirable young men. 13 And I saw that she was defiled; they both took the same way. 14 But she carried her whoring further. She saw men [c]portrayed on the wall, the [d]images of [e]the Chaldeans portrayed in vermilion, 15 wearing belts on their waists, with flowing turbans on their heads, all of them having the appearance of officers, a likeness of Babylonians whose native land was Chaldea. 16 When she saw them, she lusted after them and [f]sent messengers to them [e]in Chaldea. 17 And the Babylonians came to her [g]into the bed of love, and they defiled her with their whoring lust. And after she was defiled by them, [h]she turned from them in disgust. 18 When she carried on her whoring so openly and flaunted her nakedness, I turned in disgust from her, as I had turned in disgust from her sister. 19 Yet she increased her whoring, [i]remembering the days of her youth, when she played the whore in the land of Egypt 20 and lusted after her paramours there, whose members were like those of donkeys, and whose issue was like that of horses. 21 Thus you longed for the lewdness of your youth, when the Egyptians handled your bosom and pressed[3] your young breasts."

22 Therefore, O Oholibah, thus says the Lord GOD: "Behold, I will stir up against you your lovers [h]from whom you turned in disgust, [j]and I will bring them against you

1 Hebrew *nipples*; also verses 8, 21 2 Hebrew *than she* 3 Vulgate, Syriac; Hebrew *for the sake of*

29 [c][ver. 7]
30 [d]Isai. 59:16; Jer. 5:1 [e]See ch. 13:5
31 [f][ver. 21] [g]See ch. 7:4
Chapter 23
2 [h]See ch. 2:1 [i][ch. 16:45, 46]
3 [j]See ch. 16:15 [k][ch. 16:22]
4 [l]ch. 16:8 [m][ver. 37] [n][ch. 16:46]
5 [o]Num. 5:19, 20 [p][Hos. 2:5] [q]2 Kin. 15:19; 17:3; Hos. 8:9
6 [r]ver. 23 [s]ver. 23 [t]ch. 38:15; [Isai. 5:28]
8 [u][ver. 3, 19]
9 [v][2 Kin. 15:29]; See 2 Kin. 17:4-6, 23; 18:9-11
10 [w]ver. 29; See ch. 16:37 [x]ver. 25
[y][ch. 16:14] [z]See ch. 5:8
11 [a]Jer. 3:8, 9 [b]Jer. 3:11; See ch. 16:47
12 [s][See ver. 5 above]
14 [c]ch. 8:10 [d][ch. 16:17] [e]ch. 16:29; [2 Kin. 20:12, 13; 24:1]
16 [f][ver. 40; Isai. 57:9 [e][See ver. 14 above]
17 [g][ver. 41; Isai. 57:7, 8] [h]ver. 22, 28; [ch. 17:15]
19 [i][ver. 3]; See ch. 16:15
22 [h][See ver. 17 above] [j]ch. 16:37

22:30 breach. See 13:5 note.

23:1–49 Ezekiel propounds another allegory. The two sisters are a tale of two cities: "Oholah" is Samaria, the capital of the northern kingdom, and "Oholibah" is Jerusalem, capital of the southern kingdom.

23:3 played the whore. Though Ezekiel emphasized that each individual and generation would bear responsibility for its own sin (18:1–32 note), he also describes a cumulative guilt and a deferred punishment. The indictment of the two kingdoms begins with their prostitution in Egypt (16:26; 20:5–9).

23:4 mine. The sisters had a covenant relationship with the Lord.

23:5 lovers. Israel's oath of exclusive allegiance to the Lord would be broken by foreign alliances as well as by idolatry (vv. 5–10; 16:26 note; cf. Hos. 8:9). Prostitution did not secure the admiration or affection of the Assyrian lovers—quite the contrary (vv. 9, 10). Ultimately Assyria destroyed the northern kingdom (2 Kin. 17:5, 6).

23:14 further. Judah entered alliances of her own with the Babylonians (2 Kin. 20:12–18; 23:29; Is. 39:1). There were also overtures to Egypt (23:19–21).

from every side: 23 the Babylonians and all
the Chaldeans, [k]Pekod and Shoa and Koa,
and all the Assyrians with them, [l]desirable
young men, [l]governors and commanders
all of them, officers and men of renown, all
of them riding on horses. 24 And they shall
come against you from the north[1] with
chariots and wagons and a host of peoples.
[m]They shall set themselves against you on
every side with buckler, shield, and helmet; and [n]I will commit the judgment to
them, and [o]they shall judge you according
to their judgments. 25 And I will direct my
jealousy against you, [p]that they may deal
with you in fury. They shall cut off your
nose and your ears, and your survivors
shall fall by the sword. [q]They shall seize
your sons and your daughters, and your
survivors shall be devoured by fire. 26 [r]They
shall also strip you of your clothes and take
away your beautiful jewels. 27 [s]Thus I will
put an end to your lewdness and [t]your
whoring begun in the land of Egypt, so that
you shall not lift up your eyes to them or
remember Egypt anymore.
28 "For thus says the Lord GOD: [u]Behold,
I will deliver you into the hands of those
whom you hate, [v]into the hands of those
from whom you turned in disgust, 29 and
[w]they shall deal with you in hatred and take
away all the fruit of your labor [x]and leave
you naked and bare, and [y]the nakedness of
your whoring shall be uncovered. Your
lewdness and your whoring 30 have brought
this upon you, because [z]you played the
whore with the nations and defiled yourself with their idols. 31 You have gone the
way of your sister; [a]therefore I will give
[b]her cup into your hand. 32 Thus says the
Lord GOD:

"You shall drink your sister's cup
that is deep and large;
you shall be laughed at and held in
derision,
for it contains much;
33 you will be filled with [c]drunkenness
and sorrow.
[c]A cup of horror and desolation,
the cup of [d]your sister Samaria;

23 [k]Jer. 50:21 [l]ver. 6, 12
24 [m][2 Kin. 19:32] [n][ch. 9:5, 6] [o]2 Kin. 25:6
25 [p]ver. 29 [q]ver. 10
26 [r]ch. 16:39
27 [s]ver. 48; ch. 16:41 [t]ver. 3, 19
28 [u]ch. 16:37 [v]ver. 17, 22
29 [w]ver. 25 [x]ch. 16:7, 22, 39 [y]ver. 10; See ch. 16:37
30 [z]ch. 6:9; See Ex. 34:15
31 [a][ver. 9, 10] [b][Jer. 25:15]
33 [c]Isai. 51:17; Jer. 13:13; [Rev. 14:10] [d][ver. 4]
34 [e]Ps. 75:8
35 [f]ch. 22:12; See Jer. 2:32 [g]1 Kin. 14:9 [h][ver. 49; ch. 14:10; 16:58]
36 [i]See ch. 2:1 [j][ch. 20:4; 22:2]
37 [k]See ch. 16:38 [l][ch. 22:2] [m]ch. 16:20, 21; [ch. 7:23]
38 [n]See ch. 5:11 [o]See ch. 20:13
39 [p]ver. 37; ch. 16:20, 21, 36 [q]ch. 44:7 [r][2 Kin. 21:4]; See Jer. 23:11
40 [s][ver. 16] [t][2 Kin. 9:30; Jer. 4:30] [u][ch. 16:11, 12]
41 [v][Esth. 1:6] [w]ch. 16:18; [Prov. 7:17] [x][Hos. 2:8]
42 [y][Isai. 22:2] [z][ch. 16:11] [a][ch. 16:12]
45 [b][ver. 24]; See ch. 16:38

34 [e]you shall drink it and drain it out,
and gnaw its shards,
and tear your breasts;

for I have spoken, declares the Lord GOD.
35 Therefore thus says the Lord GOD:
Because [f]you have forgotten me and [g]cast
me behind your back, you yourself [h]must
bear the consequences of your lewdness
and whoring."
36 The LORD said to me: [i]"Son of man,
[j]will you judge Oholah and Oholibah?
Declare to them their abominations. 37 For
[k]they have committed adultery, [l]and blood
is on their hands. With their idols they
have committed adultery, and they have
even [m]offered up[2] to them for food the children whom they had borne to me.
38 Moreover, this they have done to me:
[n]they have defiled my sanctuary on the
same day and [o]profaned my Sabbaths.
39 For when [p]they had slaughtered their
children in sacrifice to their idols, on the
same day [q]they came into my sanctuary to
profane it. And behold, [r]this is what they
did in my house. 40 They even sent for men
to come from afar, [s]to whom a messenger
was sent; and behold, they came. For them
you bathed yourself, [t]painted your eyes,
[u]and adorned yourself with ornaments.
41 You sat on [v]a stately couch, with a table
spread before it [w]on which you had placed
my incense and [x]my oil. 42 The [y]sound of a
carefree multitude was with her; and with
men of the common sort drunkards[3] were
brought from the wilderness; and they put
[z]bracelets on the hands of the women, and
[a]beautiful crowns on their heads.
43 "Then I said of her who was worn out
by adultery, Now they will continue to use
her for a whore, even her![4] 44 For they have
gone in to her, as men go in to a prostitute.
Thus they went in to Oholah and to
Oholibah, lewd women! 45 But righteous
men [b]shall pass judgment on them with
the sentence of adulteresses, and with the
sentence of women who shed blood,

1 Septuagint; the meaning of the Hebrew word is unknown 2 Or *have even made pass through the fire* 3 Or *Sabeans* 4 The meaning of the Hebrew verse is uncertain

23:23 Pekod and Shoa and Koa. Probably Aramean tribes east of the Tigris River.

23:29 naked and bare. See 16:35–41.

23:31–34 The cup is a common metaphor in the Bible. In many cases it is symbolic of God's blessings (Ps. 16:5; 23:5; 116:13; 1 Cor. 10:16). It can also represent the anger of God (Ps. 75:7, 8; Is. 51:17–20; Jer. 25:15–29; 49:12; 51:7; Lam. 4:21; Hab. 2:16; Zech. 12:2; Rev. 14:9–11). This cup of wrath is mentioned by Jesus in the Garden of Gethsemane (Matt. 26:39, 42) and appears in John's account of Jesus' death (John 18:11; 19:28–30).

because they are adulteresses, and blood is
on their hands."
46 For thus says the Lord GOD: [c]"Bring up
a vast host against them, and make them
[d]an object of terror and [e]a plunder. 47 [f]And
the host shall stone them and cut them
down with their swords. [g]They shall kill
their sons and their daughters, and [h]burn
up their houses. 48 [i]Thus will I put an end
to lewdness in the land, that all women
may take warning and not commit lewdness as you have done. 49 And they shall
return your lewdness upon you, and [j]you
shall bear the penalty for your sinful idolatry, and [k]you shall know that I am the Lord
GOD."

The Siege of Jerusalem

24 [l]In the ninth year, in the tenth
month, on the tenth day of the
month, the word of the LORD came to me:
2 [m]"Son of man, write down the name of
this day, this very day. The king of Babylon
has laid siege to Jerusalem this very day.
3 And [n]utter a parable to [o]the rebellious
house and say to them, Thus says the Lord
GOD:

"Set on [p]the pot, set it on;
pour in water also;
4 put in it the pieces of meat,
all the good pieces, [q]the thigh and
the shoulder;
fill it with choice bones.
5 Take the choicest one of the flock;
pile the logs[1] under it;
boil it well;
seethe also its bones in it.

6 "Therefore thus says the Lord GOD:
[r]Woe to the bloody city, to [p]the pot whose
corrosion is in it, and whose corrosion has
not gone out of it! Take out of it piece after
piece, without making any choice.[2] 7 For
the blood she has shed is in her midst; she
put it on [s]the bare rock; [t]she did not pour
it out on the ground to cover it with dust.
8 To rouse my wrath, to take vengeance, I
have set on the bare rock the blood she
has shed, that it may not be covered.
9 Therefore thus says the Lord GOD: Woe
to the bloody city! [u]I also will make the
pile great. 10 Heap on the logs, kindle the
fire, boil the meat well, mix in the spices,[3]
and let the bones be burned up. 11 Then set
it empty upon the coals, that it may
become hot, and its copper may burn,
[v]that its uncleanness may be melted in it,
its corrosion consumed. 12 [w]She has wearied herself with toil;[4] its abundant corrosion does not go out of it. Into the fire with
its corrosion! 13 On account of your
unclean lewdness, because I would have
cleansed you and you were not cleansed
from your uncleanness, [x]you shall not be
cleansed anymore till [y]I have satisfied my
fury upon you. 14 [z]I am the LORD. I have
spoken; it shall come to pass; I will do it.
I will not go back; [a]I will not spare; [b]I will
not relent; [c]according to your ways and
your deeds you will be judged, declares
the Lord GOD."

Ezekiel's Wife Dies

15 The word of the LORD came to me:
16 [d]"Son of man, behold, I am about to take
the delight of your eyes away from you at a
stroke; yet you shall not mourn or weep,
nor shall your tears run down. 17 Sigh, but
not aloud; make no mourning for the dead.
[e]Bind on your turban, and [f]put your shoes
on your feet; do not cover your lips, [g]nor
eat the bread of men." 18 So I spoke to the

1 Compare verse 10; Hebrew *the bones* 2 Hebrew *no lot has fallen upon it* 3 Or *empty out the broth* 4 The meaning of the Hebrew is uncertain

46 [c]ch. 16:40 [d]Deut. 28:25 [e]ch. 7:21
47 [f]ch. 16:40, 41; [Josh. 7:24, 25] [g]ch. 24:21; See 2 Chr. 36:17 [h]2 Chr. 36:19
48 [i]ver. 27; [ch. 16:41]
49 [j][ver. 35] [k][See ch. 6:7]
Chapter 24
1 [l]See ch. 20:1
2 [m]See ch. 2:1
3 [n][ch. 17:2; 20:49] [o]See ch. 2:5 [p]ch. 11:3, 7, 11; 2 Kin. 4:38
4 [q]See 1 Sam. 9:24
6 [r]ch. 22:2; [Nah. 3:1] [p][See ver. 3 above]
7 [s]ch. 26:4, 14 [t][Lev. 17:13; Deut. 12:16, 24]
9 [u]Isai. 30:33
11 [v]ch. 22:15
12 [w][Jer. 2:22]
13 [x]Isai. 22:14 [y]See ch. 5:13
14 [z]See ch. 17:24 [a]See ch. 5:11 [b][Num. 23:19; 1 Sam 15:29] [c][ch. 20:43; 23:45]
16 [d]See ch. 2:1
17 [e]See Lev. 10:6 [f][2 Sam. 15:30; Isai. 20:2] [g]Hos. 9:4; See Jer. 16:5-7

24:1–14 Ezekiel provides another allegory. The image is a cooking pot, and two oracles applying it are introduced by the same phrase, "Woe to the bloody city" (vv. 6, 9).

24:1 year. The date is ordinarily identified as January 15, 588 B.C. (see also 2 Kin. 25:1; Jer. 52:4). The beginning of the siege of the city was commemorated with a fast among the exiles (Zech. 8:19). God revealed to the prophet information about events taking place hundreds of miles away in Jerusalem.

24:3 pot. Ezekiel has already used the image of a cooking pot in 11:2–12 (cf. Jer. 1:13, 14; Mic. 3:3). From this initial description it appears that preparations are being made for a festive meal; the best of meats are to be cooked.

24:6 corrosion. The prophet looks at the corrosion (lit. "rust") in the pot and likens it to the bloodshed and guilt in the city. Though its occupants were removed piece by piece and dispersed to the far corners of the world, the guilt of the city remained like scum in the bottom of the pot. Compare the denunciation of the bloodshed in the city in 22:1–16; 36:18; 2 Kin. 21:16; 24:4; Is. 26:21; 59:7; Lam. 4:13; Hos. 4:2; Joel 3:21; Mic. 3:10.

24:7 cover. Blood, shed and uncovered, cried out to be avenged; note the same concept in Gen. 4:10; Job 16:18.

24:11 hot. The cauldron is emptied in an effort to cleanse it, but the scum is so resistant that even heating the cauldron white-hot will not purify it. God will destroy the city.

24:16, 17 Customary mourning included lamenting and crying, removing headgear and covering the head with dust and ashes (Josh. 7:6; 1 Sam. 4:12; Job 2:12), removing sandals (2 Sam. 15:30; Is. 20:2), and covering the head or face (Esth. 6:12; Jer. 14:3, 4). Ezekiel would do none of these things; the ordinary practices associated with mourning were not sufficient to represent the depth of his sorrow.

people in the morning, and [h]at evening my
wife died. And on the next morning I did
[i]as I was commanded.
19 And [j]the people said to me, "Will you
not tell us what these things mean for us,
that you are acting thus?" 20 Then I said to
them, "The word of the LORD came to me:
21 'Say to the house of Israel, Thus says the
Lord GOD: [k]Behold, I will profane my
sanctuary, the pride of your power, the
delight of your eyes, and the yearning of
your soul, and [l]your sons and your daughters whom you left behind shall fall by the
sword. 22 And [m]you shall do as I have
done; [m]you shall not cover your lips, [g]nor
eat the bread of men. 23 [m]Your turbans
shall be on your heads and your shoes on
your feet; you shall not mourn or weep,
but [n]you shall rot away in your iniquities
and groan to one another. 24 Thus shall
Ezekiel be to you [o]a sign; [m]according to all
that he has done you shall do. When this
comes, then [p]you will know that I am the
Lord GOD.'
25 "As for you, [q]son of man, surely on the
day when I take from them [r]their stronghold, their joy and glory, the delight of
their eyes and their soul's desire, and also
their sons and daughters, 26 [s]on that day a
fugitive will come to you to report to you
the news. 27 On that day your mouth [t]will
be opened to the fugitive, and you shall
speak and be no longer mute. [u]So you will
be a sign to them, and [v]they will know that
I am the LORD."

Prophecy Against Ammon

25 The word of the LORD came to me:
2 [w]"Son of man, [x]set your face
toward [y]the Ammonites and prophesy
against them. 3 Say to the Ammonites, Hear
the word of the Lord GOD: [z]Thus says the
Lord GOD, Because you said, [a]'Aha!' over
my [b]sanctuary when it was profaned, and
over the land of Israel when it was made
desolate, and over the house of Judah
when they went into exile, 4 therefore
behold, I am handing you over to [c]the people of the East for a possession, and they
shall set their encampments among you
and make their dwellings in your midst.
They shall eat your fruit, and they shall
drink your milk. 5 I will make [d]Rabbah a
[e]pasture for camels and Ammon[1] [e]a fold
for flocks. [v]Then you will know that I am
the LORD. 6 For thus says the Lord GOD:
Because [f]you have clapped your hands
[g]and stamped your feet and [h]rejoiced with
all the [i]malice within your soul against the
land of Israel, 7 therefore, behold, [j]I have
stretched out my hand against you, and
[k]will hand you over as plunder to the
nations. And I will cut you off from the
peoples and will make you perish out of
the countries; I will destroy you. Then you
will know that I am the LORD.

Prophecy Against Moab and Seir

8 "Thus says the Lord GOD: Because
[l]Moab and [m]Seir[2] said, 'Behold, the [n]house
of Judah is like all the other nations,'
9 therefore [l]I will lay open the flank of
Moab from the cities, from its cities on its
frontier, the glory of the country, [o]Beth-
jeshimoth, [p]Baal-meon, and [q]Kiriathaim.
10 I will give it [r]along with the Ammonites
[s]to the people of the East as a possession,
[t]that the Ammonites may be remembered
no more among the nations, 11 [l]and I will
execute judgments upon Moab. [u]Then
they will know that I am the LORD.

18 [h][ver. 16] [i]ch. 12:7; 37:7
19 [j]See ch. 12:9
21 [k][Jer. 7:14]; See ch. 7:21 [l]ch. 23:47; See 2 Chr. 36:17
22 [m][ver. 17; ch. 12:11] [g][See ver. 17 above]
23 [m][See ver. 22 above] [n]See ch. 4:17
24 [o]ver. 27; See ch. 4:3 [m][See ver. 22 above] [p]See ch. 6:7
25 [q]See ch. 2:1 [r][ver. 21]
26 [s]See ch. 33:21, 22
27 [t]ch. 29:21; [ch. 3:26, 27] [u]ver. 24; See ch. 4:3 [v]See ch. 6:7
Chapter 25
2 [w]See ch. 2:1 [x]See ch. 6:2 [y]ch. 21:20, 28; See Jer. 49:1-6
3 [z]ch. 2:4; 3:11, 27
[a]ch. 26:2; 36:2 [b]See ch. 7:22
4 [c]Judg. 6:3
5 [d]2 Sam. 11:1; 12:26; See ch. 21:20 [e][Zeph. 2:15] [v][See ver. 27 above]
6 [f]Ps. 98:8; Isai. 55:12 [g][ch. 6:11] [h][Zeph. 2:8, 10] [i]ver. 15; ch. 36:5
7 [j]See ch. 6:14 [k][ver. 4; ch. 7:21]
8 [l]See Isai. 15:1-9; Jer. 48:1-47 [m]See ver. 12 [n]See Jer. 25:17-26
9 [l][See ver. 8 above] [o]Josh. 12:3 [p]1 Chr. 5:8; [q]See Jer. 48:1
10 [r]ver. 2 [s]ver. 4 [t]ch. 21:32
11 [l][See ver. 8 above] [u]See ch. 6:7

[1] Hebrew *and the Ammonites* [2] Septuagint lacks *and Seir*

24:27 be no longer mute. See 3:26 and note. Ezekiel's message would be vindicated when word reached the exiles that Jerusalem has been destroyed, and he would be released from the silence God had imposed on him.

25:1–32:32 Between warnings of the destruction of Jerusalem (chs. 1–24) and prophecies of hope and restoration (chs. 33–48), Ezekiel includes a section of oracles against foreign nations. Israel's prophets played an important role in the nation's warfare, often providing oracles concerning particular battles (1 Sam. 22:5; 1 Kin. 20:13, 14, 22; 22:5–23; 2 Kin. 3:11; 9:6, 7; 20:14; 2 Chr. 16:7; 20:14–20; 28:9; Jer. 28:8; 38:14). Archaeological evidence from the cultures surrounding Israel shows that they conducted ritual denunciations or rites of symbolic destruction. The nations denounced here by Ezekiel include most of the states of the ancient Near East, with Babylon as a notable exception (38:2 note).

25:1–7 Ezekiel had already spoken against Ammon (21:28–32). Israel's relationship with the Ammonites was long and varied, primarily a record of conflict. Oracles against Ammon are also found in Jer. 49:1–6; Amos 1:13–15; Zeph. 2:8, 9.

25:5 you will know. See note 6:7.

25:6, 7 Because . . . therefore. The punishment fits the crime: rejoicing at the harm done to Jerusalem, the Ammonites themselves become prey to a foreign power. Though many of the small states in the area escaped the destruction during the Babylonian invasion of 587–586 B.C., sources outside the Bible indicate that Nebuchadnezzar decimated Ammon and Moab in 582 B.C. The prophet makes the same point in 21:28–32.

25:8 Moab. Israel's relationships with Moab were largely a history of conflict; other prophets include oracles against this nation (Is. 15; 16; Jer. 48; Amos 2:1–3; Zeph. 2:8, 9). Moab would share Ammon's fate.

Prophecy Against Edom

12 "Thus says the Lord GOD: Because
[v]Edom acted revengefully against the house
of Judah and has grievously offended [w]in
taking vengeance on them, 13 therefore thus
says the Lord GOD, [x]I will stretch out my
hand against Edom and cut off from it man
and beast. And I will make it desolate; from
[y]Teman even to [z]Dedan they shall fall by
the sword. 14 And I will lay my vengeance
upon Edom [a]by the hand of my people
Israel, and they shall do in Edom according
to my anger and according to my wrath,
and [b]they shall know my vengeance,
declares the Lord GOD.

Prophecy Against Philistia

15 "Thus says the Lord GOD: Because [c]the
Philistines [d]acted revengefully and took
vengeance [e]with malice of soul to destroy
in never-ending enmity, 16 therefore thus
says the Lord GOD, [x]Behold, I will stretch
out my hand against the Philistines, and I
will cut off [f]the Cherethites and destroy the
rest of the seacoast. 17 I will execute great
vengeance on them [g]with wrathful rebukes.
[h]Then they will know that I am the LORD,
when I lay my vengeance upon them."

Prophecy Against Tyre

26 [i]In the eleventh year, on the first
day of the month, the word of the
LORD came to me: 2 [j]"Son of man, because
[k]Tyre said concerning Jerusalem, [l]'Aha, the
gate of the peoples is broken; it has swung
open to me. I shall be replenished, now
that she is laid waste,' 3 therefore thus says
the Lord GOD: [m]Behold, I am against you,
O Tyre, and will bring up [n]many nations
against you, [o]as the sea brings up its waves.
4 They shall destroy the walls of Tyre and
break down her towers, and I will scrape
her soil from her and [p]make her a bare
rock. 5 She [q]shall be in the midst of the sea
a place for the spreading of nets, [r]for I have
spoken, declares the Lord GOD. And she
shall become plunder for the nations, 6 and
her daughters on the mainland shall be
killed by the sword. [s]Then they will know
that I am the LORD.
7 "For thus says the Lord GOD: [t]Behold, I
will bring against Tyre [u]from the north
Nebuchadnezzar[1] king of Babylon, [v]king of
kings, with horses and chariots, and with
horsemen and a host of many soldiers. 8 He
will kill with the sword [w]your daughters on
the mainland. [x]He will set up a siege wall
against you and throw up a mound against
you, and raise [y]a roof of shields against you.
9 [z]He will direct the shock of his battering
rams against your walls, and with his axes
he will break down your towers. 10 His horses will be so many that their dust will cover
you. Your walls will shake at the noise of
the horsemen and wagons and chariots,
when he enters your gates as men enter a
city that has been breached. 11 With the
hoofs of his horses he will trample all your
streets. He will kill your people with the
sword, and your mighty pillars will fall to
the ground. 12 They will plunder [a]your riches and loot [a]your merchandise. They will
break down your walls and destroy your

12 [v]ver. 8; ch. 32:29; 35:2, 5; 2 Chr. 28:17; Ps. 137:7; Isai. 21:11; 34:5; Amos. 1:11, 12; See Jer. 49:7- 22; Obad. 1-21 [w]ver. 15
13 [x]See ch. 6:14 [y]1 Chr. 1:45; Amos 1:12 [z]ch. 27:15, 20; 38:13; Isai. 21:13
14 [a]Amos 9:12; Obad. 18 [b][ver. 17]
15 [c]Jer. 25:20; 47:1; Joel 3:4; Amos 1:6; Zeph. 2:4; See Isai. 14:29-31 [d]ver. 12 [e]ver. 6; ch. 36:5
16 [x][See ver. 13 above] [f]See 1 Sam. 30:14
17 [g]ch. 5:15 [h][ver. 14]
Chapter 26
1 [i]See ch. 20:1
2 [j]See ch. 2:1 [k]See Isai. 23:1-18 [l]ch. 25:3; 36:2
3 [m]See ch. 13:8 [n][ch. 32:3; Jer. 34:1] [o][Lam. 2:13]
4 [p]ch. 24:7
5 [q]ch. 47:10 [r]See ch. 17:24
6 [s]See ch. 6:7
7 [t][ch. 29:18] [u]See Jer. 1:14 [v]Ezra 7:12; Dan. 2:37; [Hos. 8:10]
8 [w]ver. 6 [x]See ch. 4:2 [y][2 Kin. 19:32] 9 [z]ch. 4:2; 21:22 12 [a]See ch. 27:12- 24

1 Hebrew *Nebuchadrezzar*; so throughout Ezekiel

25:12 Edom. Edom made incursions into Judah at the time of Jerusalem's fall (35:15; 36:5; Ps. 137:7–9; Lam. 4:21, 22). The enmity between Israel and Edom is traced in the Bible to the relationship between Jacob and Esau (Gen. 25:23, 30). Ezekiel includes a second oracle against Edom in ch. 35; other prophets make pronouncements against this state in Is. 34:5–11; Jer. 49:7–22; Amos 1:11, 12; Obad.; Mal. 1:3–5.

25:15 Philistines. The nations mentioned thus far were east of the Jordan River and the Dead Sea. The Philistines occupied the coastal plain west of Judah, controlling a long segment of the vital international coastal highway. Conflicting territorial claims and competing strategic interests made for a history of unfriendly relations with Israel. Ezekiel had already spoken of this enmity (16:27, 57). Other prophets also include oracles against the Philistines (Is. 14:29–31; Jer. 47; Joel 3:4–6; Amos 1:6–8; Zeph. 2:4–7; Zech. 9:5–7). The Philistines were Israel's most prominent enemy in the time of the judges and of Saul, David, and Solomon.

25:16 Cherethites. The Philistines appear to have entered Canaan in the latter half of the second millennium B.C. as part of the large migration of peoples known from Egyptian records as the "sea peoples." One group of Philistines was identified as "Cherethites," probably associating them with Crete. See 1 Sam. 30:14 note.

26:1–28:26 Ezek. 26–28 is devoted to oracles against Israel's Phoenician neighbors, primarily Tyre (26:1–28:19), but also Sidon (28:20–26). The chapters are divided into subsections, each introduced with the phrase "the word of the LORD came to me" (26:1; 27:1; 28:1, 11, 20). There was occasional military conflict between Israel and the Phoenicians, but the Bible mentions Tyre and Sidon primarily as the source of pagan cults, especially the Baal worship of Jezebel, a Phoenician princess (Judg. 10:6; 1 Kin. 11:1, 5, 33; 16:31; 2 Kin. 23:13). The Phoenicians provided Israel with trade and expert labor (2 Sam. 5:11; 1 Kin. 5:1, 6; 7:13, 14; 9:11; 2 Chr. 2:3, 13, 14; Ezra 3:7; Neh. 13:16; Acts 12:20). Other prophetic books also include oracles against Tyre and Sidon (Is. 23; Joel 3:4–6; Amos 1:9, 10; Zech. 9:2–4).

26:2 be replenished. The kingdom of Judah at times controlled trade routes leading through the coastal plains to Egypt, as well as Arabia and Africa via the port of Ezion Geber. Tyre would profit if Jerusalem lost control of these trade routes.

26:7 Tyre. Shortly after the fall of Jerusalem, Nebuchadnezzar laid siege to Tyre. The part of the city on the mainland fell quickly in 585 B.C., but the island fortress defied the armies of Babylon for thirteen years, until 572 B.C. (29:17, 18).

pleasant houses. Your stones and timber
and [b]soil they will cast into the midst of the
waters. 13 [c]And I will stop the music of your
songs, and [d]the sound of your lyres shall be
heard no more. 14 [p]I will make you a bare
rock. [q]You shall be a place for the spreading
of nets. You shall never be rebuilt, [r]for I am
the LORD; I have spoken, declares the Lord
GOD.

15 "Thus says the Lord GOD to Tyre: Will
not [e]the coastlands shake at the sound of
your fall, [f]when the wounded groan, when
slaughter is made in your midst? 16 Then all
[g]the princes of the sea will step down from
their thrones and [h]remove their robes and
strip off their embroidered garments. They
will clothe themselves with trembling;
[i]they will sit on the ground and [j]tremble
every moment and [k]be appalled at you.
17 And they will [l]raise a lamentation over
you and say to you,

"'How you have perished,
you who were inhabited from the seas,
O city renowned,
[m]who was mighty on the sea;
she and her inhabitants [n]imposed their terror
on all her inhabitants!

18 Now the coastlands tremble
on the day of your fall,
and the coastlands that are on the sea
are dismayed at your passing.'

19 "For thus says the Lord GOD: When I
make you a city laid waste, like the cities
that are not inhabited, [o]when I bring up
the deep over you, and the great waters
cover you, 20 then [p]I will make you go down
with those who go down to the pit, to the
people of old, and I will make you to dwell
in the world below, among ruins from of
old, [p]with those who go down to the pit, so
that you will not be inhabited; but I will set
beauty [q]in the land of the living. 21 I will
bring you [r]to a dreadful end, and you shall
be no more. [s]Though you be sought for,
you will never be found again, declares the
Lord GOD."

12 [b]ver. 4
13 [c][Isai. 24:8; Jer. 7:34; 16:9] [d][Isai. 5:12; 23:16]
14 [p][See ver. 4 above] [q][See ver. 5 above] [r][See ver. 5 above]
15 [e]ch. 27:35 [f]Jer. 51:52
16 [g][Isai. 23:8] [h][Jonah 3:6] [i]Isai. 3:26 [j]ch. 32:10 [k]ch. 27:35
17 [l]ch. 19:1; 27:2, 32; [Rev. 18:9] [m][Isai. 23:4] [n]See ch. 32:23
19 [o][ver. 3; ch. 27:34]
20 [p][ch. 31:14, 16; 32:18, 24] [q]ch. 32:23, 27, 32; Ps. 27:13
21 [r]ch. 27:36; 28:19 [s][Ps. 37:36]
Chapter 27
2 [t]See ch. 2:1 [u]See ch. 19:1
3 [v][Isai. 23:1] [w][Isai. 23:3] [x]ch. 28:12
4 [y]ver. 25, 27
5 [z]Deut. 3:9 [a]Judg. 9:15
6 [b]See Isai. 2:13 [c]See Gen. 10:4
7 [d]See ch. 16:10 [c][See ver. 6 above]
8 [e]Gen. 10:18 [f]ver. 27, 29
9 [g]1 Kin. 5:18; Ps. 83:7 [h]ver. 27
10 [i]ch. 38:5 [j]ch. 30:5; [Isai. 66:19; Jer. 46:9] [k][2 Sam. 8:7; S. of S. 4:4]

A Lament for Tyre

27 The word of the LORD came to me:
2 "Now you, [t]son of man, [u]raise a
lamentation over Tyre, 3 and say to Tyre,
who dwells at [v]the entrances to the sea,
[w]merchant of the peoples to many coastlands, thus says the Lord GOD:

"O Tyre, you have said,
'I am [x]perfect in beauty.'

4 Your borders are [y]in the heart of the seas;
your builders made perfect your beauty.

5 They made all your planks
of fir trees from [z]Senir;
they took [a]a cedar from Lebanon
to make a mast for you.

6 Of [b]oaks of Bashan
they made your oars;
they made your deck of pines
from [c]the coasts of Cyprus,
inlaid with ivory.

7 [d]Of fine embroidered linen from Egypt
was your sail,
serving as your banner;
blue and purple from [c]the coasts of Elishah
was your awning.

8 The inhabitants of Sidon and [e]Arvad
were your rowers;
your skilled men, O Tyre, were in you;
they were [f]your pilots.

9 The elders of [g]Gebal and her skilled men were in you,
[h]caulking your seams;
all the ships of the sea with their mariners were in you
to barter for your wares.

10 [i]"Persia and [j]Lud and [i]Put were in your
army as your men of war. [k]They hung the

26:19, 20 waters . . . pit. Waters and a pit are common biblical metaphors for death or the realm of the dead (waters: Ex. 15:5, 8, 10; Job 26:5; Ps. 32:6; 69:2, 14; Lam. 3:54. Pit: 31:14, 16; 32:18, 23, 24, 30; Job 33:18–30; Ps. 30:3, 9; 55:23; 88:4–6; 103:4; 143:7; Prov. 1:12; Is. 14:15; 38:18). These two images are combined in 28:8; Ps. 69:15; Jon. 2:5, 6. The prophet describes the mythological waters of chaos engulfing the island and its inhabitants (28:2 note).

27:3–6 The island city of Tyre is compared to a luxurious ship made of the finest materials and manned by an experienced crew.

27:5 Senir. The Amorite name for Mount Hermon (Deut. 3:9).

27:7 Elishah. Probably in Cyprus.

27:8 Arvad. An island city about two miles off the Mediterranean coast north of Byblos.

27:9 Gebal. Another name for Byblos on the Mediterranean coast north of Tyre.

shield and helmet in you; they gave you
splendor. 11 Men of [e]Arvad and Helech were
on your walls all around, and men of
Gamad were in your towers. They hung
their shields on your walls all around; they
made [x]perfect your beauty.
12 [l]"Tarshish did [m]business with you
because of your great wealth of every kind;
silver, iron, tin, and lead they exchanged
for your [n]wares. 13 [o]Javan, [p]Tubal, and
[p]Meshech traded with you; they exchanged
human beings and vessels of bronze for
your merchandise. 14 From [q]Beth-togarmah
they exchanged horses, war horses, and
mules [r]for your wares. 15 The men of
[s]Dedan[1] traded with you. Many coastlands
were your own special markets; they
brought you in payment ivory tusks and
ebony. 16 Syria [t]did business with you
because of your abundant goods; they
exchanged for your wares [u]emeralds, [u]pur-
ple, [v]embroidered work, [w]fine linen, coral,
and [x]ruby. 17 Judah and the land of Israel
traded with you; they exchanged for your
merchandise [y]wheat of [z]Minnith, meal,[2]
honey, oil, and [a]balm. 18 [b]Damascus did
business with you for your abundant
goods, because of your great wealth of
every kind; wine of Helbon and [c]wool of
Sahar 19 and casks of wine[3] from Uzal they
exchanged for your wares; wrought iron,
[d]cassia, and [e]calamus were bartered for
your merchandise. 20 Dedan traded with
you in saddlecloths for riding. 21 Arabia and
all the princes of [f]Kedar were your favored
dealers [f]in lambs, rams, and goats; in these
they did business with you. 22 The traders
of [g]Sheba and [g]Raamah traded with you;
they exchanged [h]for your wares [i]the best of
all kinds of spices and all precious stones
and gold. 23 [j]Haran, Canneh, [j]Eden, traders
of Sheba, [k]Asshur, and Chilmad traded
with you. 24 In your market these traded
with you in choice garments, in clothes of
[l]blue and [l]embroidered work, and in carpets of colored material, bound with cords
and made secure. 25 [m]The ships of [n]Tar-
shish traveled for you with your merchandise. So you were filled and heavily laden
[o]in the heart of the seas.

26 "Your rowers have brought you out
into the high seas.
[p]The east wind has wrecked you
in the heart of the seas.
27 Your riches, your wares, your
merchandise,
your mariners and [q]your pilots,
[r]your caulkers, your dealers in
merchandise,
and all your men of war who are in
you,
with all your crew
that is in your midst,
sink into the heart of the seas
[s]on the day of your fall.
28 At the sound of the cry of your pilots
[t]the countryside shakes,
29 and down from their ships
[u]come all who handle the oar.
The mariners and all the pilots of the
sea
stand on the land
30 [u]and shout aloud over you
and cry out bitterly.
[v]They cast dust on their heads
[w]and wallow in ashes;
31 they [x]make themselves bald for you
and put sackcloth on their waist,
and they weep over you in bitterness
of soul,
with bitter mourning.

11 [e][See ver. 8 above] [x][See ver. 3 above]
12 [l]ver. 25; ch. 38:13; See 1 Kin. 10:22 [m]ver. 16, 18, 21 [n]ver. 14, 16, 19, 22
13 [o]Gen. 10:2 [p]ch. 32:26; 38:2; 39:1
14 [q]ch. 38:6; Gen. 10:3 [r]ver. 12
15 [s]Gen. 10:7; See ch. 25:13
16 [t]ver. 12 [u]ch. 28:13 [v]ver. 7 [w]1 Chr. 15:27; Job 28:18 [x]Isai. 54:12
17 [y]See 1 Kin. 5:9, 11 [z]Judg. 11:33 [a]See Gen. 37:25
18 [b]Isai. 7:8; [ver. 16] [c]Rev. 1:14
19 [d]Ex. 30:24 [e][Ex. 30:23]
21 [f]Isai. 60:7
22 [g]ch. 38:13; Gen. 10:7 [h]ver. 12 [i]Ex. 30:23
23 [j]2 Kin. 19:12 [k]Gen. 10:22
24 [l]ver. 7
25 [m]Ps. 48:7; Isai. 2:16; 23:14 [n]See ver. 12 [o]ver. 4
26 [p]See Jer. 18:17
27 [q]ver. 8 [r]ver. 9 [s][ch. 26:18; 32:10]
28 [t][ch. 45:2; 48:15, 17]
29 [u][Rev. 18:17, 18]
30 [u][See ver. 29 above] [v]Lam. 2:10; Rev. 18:19 [w]See Jer. 6:26
31 [x]See Isai. 3:24

1 Hebrew; Septuagint *Rhodes* 2 The meaning of the Hebrew word is unknown 3 Probable reading; Hebrew *Vedan and Javan*

27:11 Gamad. Probably in northern Syria.

27:13 Tubal, and Meshech. These peoples (32:26; 38:2, 3; 39:1; Gen. 10:2; 1 Chr. 1:5) were in Asia Minor, in the northeast corner of the Mediterranean. They are also known from Assyrian inscriptions.

human beings. For Tyre's involvement in the slave trade, see Joel 3:4–6.

27:14 Beth-togarmah. A region of northeast Asia Minor (modern Turkey).

27:17 traded with you. Tyre was a maritime power and probably not self-sufficient in agriculture. The Bible several times mentions her trade with Israel for foodstuffs (1 Kin. 5:9–11; 2 Chr. 2:10; Ezra 3:7; Acts 12:20).

Minnith. A town east of the Jordan near Rabbah in Ammon (modern Amman), though the site has not been identified precisely (Judg. 11:33).

27:18 Helbon. A town northwest of Damascus. Akkadian texts and Greek historians mention the wine from this region.

27:22 Raamah. A region in southern Arabia (Gen. 10:7; 1 Chr. 1:9).

27:23 Canneh. Probably a city in northern Syria otherwise spelled "Calneh" (Amos 6:2) or "Calno" (Is. 10:9).

Eden. Beth Eden, a city located between the Euphrates and Balikh rivers (2 Kin. 19:12; Is. 37:12; Amos 1:5).

Chilmad. This name is otherwise unknown and may be a copyist's error for the words "all of Media."

27:25–36 No one thought Tyre could be defeated. But her strength, her wealth, and her skill were no match for seas that obeyed the command of God. Tyre's fate would be a warning to all other nations that watched from the shore.

32 In their wailing they [y] raise a
lamentation for you
and lament over you:
[z] ‘Who is like Tyre,
like one destroyed in the midst of
the sea?
33 When your wares came from the seas,
[a] you satisfied many peoples;
with your abundant wealth and
merchandise
[a] you enriched the kings of the earth.
34 Now [b] you are wrecked by the seas,
in the depths of the waters;
your merchandise and all your crew
in your midst
have sunk with you.
35 [c] All the inhabitants of the coastlands
are appalled at you,
and [d] the hair of their kings bristles
with horror;
their faces are convulsed.
36 [e] The merchants among the peoples
[f] hiss at you;
[g] you have come to a dreadful end
and shall be no more forever.’ ”

Prophecy Against the Prince of Tyre

28 The word of the LORD came to me:
2 [h] “Son of man, say to [i] the prince of
Tyre, Thus says the Lord GOD:

[j] “Because your heart is proud,
and [k] you have said, ‘I am a god,
I sit in the seat of the gods,
in the heart of the seas,’
yet [l] you are but a man, and no god,
[m] though you make your heart like
the heart of a god—
3 [n] you are indeed wiser [o] than [p] Daniel;
no secret is hidden from you;
4 by your wisdom and your
understanding
[q] you have made wealth for yourself,
and have gathered gold and silver
into your treasuries;
5 by your great wisdom in your trade
you have increased your wealth,
and [j] your heart has become proud
in your wealth—
6 therefore thus says the Lord GOD:
[r] Because you make your heart
like the heart of a god,
7 therefore, behold, I will bring
[s] foreigners upon you,
the most ruthless of the nations;
and they shall draw their swords
against [t] the beauty of your
wisdom
and defile [t] your splendor.
8 [u] They shall thrust you down into
the pit,
[v] and you shall die the death of
the slain
in the heart of the seas.
9 [w] Will you still say, ‘I am a god,’
in the presence of those who
kill you,
though [l] you are but a man, and
no god,
in the hands of those who slay you?
10 [x] You shall die the death of the
uncircumcised
by the hand of foreigners;
[y] for I have spoken, declares the
Lord GOD.”

A Lament over the King of Tyre

11 Moreover, the word of the LORD came
to me: 12 [z] “Son of man, [a] raise a lamentation
over [b] the king of Tyre, and say to him,
Thus says the Lord GOD:

“You were the signet of perfection,[1]
[c] full of wisdom and [d] perfect in
beauty.
13 You were in [e] Eden, the garden of God;
[f] every precious stone was your
covering,

1 The meaning of the Hebrew phrase is uncertain

32 [y] See ch. 19:1 [z] [Rev. 18:18]
33 [a] [Rev. 18:15, 19]
34 [b] [ch. 26:19]
35 [c] ch. 26:15, 16 [d] [ch. 32:10]
36 [e] Rev. 18:11 [f] See Jer. 18:16 [g] ch. 26:21; 28:19
Chapter 28
2 [h] See ch. 2:1 [i] [ver. 12] [j] [Rev. 18:7] [k] [ver. 9] [l] Isai. 31:3 [m] ver. 6
3 [n] [ver. 12; Zech. 9:2] [o] Dan. 1:17 [p] ch. 14:14
4 [q] [Zech. 9:3]
5 [j] [See ver. 2 above]
6 [r] ver. 2
7 [s] ver. 10; ch. 7:21; 30:12; 31:12 [t] [ver. 17]
8 [u] [ch. 32:18, 19] [v] [ch. 32:20]
9 [w] [ver. 2] [l] [See ver. 2 above]
10 [x] ch. 31:18; 32:19, 21, 24, 25 [y] See ch. 17:24
12 [z] See ch. 2:1 [a] See ch. 19:1 [b] [ver. 2] [c] [ver. 3] [d] ch. 27:3
13 [e] ch. 31:8, 9; See Isai. 51:3 [f] [ch. 27:16]

28:2 a god . . . in the heart of the seas. In the ancient Near East, the watery depths of the primeval ocean are a standard symbol for the powers of chaos and death. Archaeologists have discovered more than one mythical creation account in which “the Sea” appears as a dragon or sea monster to be killed by the gods. The threat of chaos to the created order is subdued and the gods rule the waves. In the Bible the sea is no threat to God; it obeys His commands. Ezekiel describes how the king of Tyre had become proud of the city’s wealth and power, and had begun to flatter himself as a god ruling over the sea (cf. Ps. 29:10; Rev. 17:1, 15). But the sea would swallow him (v. 8; 29:3 note).

28:3 Daniel. See 14:14 note.

28:12 a lamentation. See note 19:1–14.

king of Tyre. Ethbaal ruled Tyre at this time. The prophet describes the way God had favored Ethbaal by portraying the king as a primeval being, a figure like Adam, the crown and epitome of creation, living in the garden paradise that God had made. He remained there until wickedness was found in him (v. 15). Some take the prophet to be comparing the king of Tyre to Satan, a glorious being who fell from grace (1 Tim. 3:6).

28:13, 14 garden . . . mountain. The prophet joins two images for the dwelling place of God, a garden (Gen. 2; 3) and a mountain (20:40; Ex. 19:23; Deut. 33:2; Ps. 43:3; 48:1; 87:1; 99:9; Is. 27:13; 56:7; 57:13; 66:20). The temple was built on a mountain and was decorated with floral motifs (40:16–37; 41:18–20, 25–27; 1 Kin. 6:29, 32, 35; 7:18, 20, 22, 36, 42; 2 Chr. 3:5).

[g] sardius, topaz, and diamond,
beryl, onyx, and jasper,
sapphire,[1] [f] emerald, and
carbuncle;
and [h] crafted in gold were your
settings
and your engravings.[2]
[i] On the day that you were created
they were prepared.
14 You were an anointed [j] guardian
cherub.
I placed you;[3] you were on [k] the
holy mountain of God;
in the midst of the stones of fire
you walked.
15 You were blameless in your ways
[l] from the day you were created,
till unrighteousness was found in
you.
16 In the abundance of [m] your trade
you were filled with violence in
your midst, and you sinned;
so I cast you as a profane thing from
[k] the mountain of God,
and I destroyed you,[4] [j] O guardian
cherub,
from the midst of the stones of
fire.
17 [n] Your heart was proud because of
[o] your beauty;
you corrupted your wisdom for the
sake of your splendor.
I cast you to the ground;
I exposed you before kings,
to feast their eyes on you.
18 By the multitude of your iniquities,
in the unrighteousness of your
trade
you profaned your sanctuaries;
so [p] I brought fire out from your
midst;
it consumed you,
and I turned you to ashes on the
earth
[q] in the sight of all who saw you.
19 All who know you among the
peoples
are appalled at you;
[r] you have come to a dreadful end
and shall be no more forever."

13 [g] Rev. 4:3; 21:19, 20 [f] [ch. 27:16] [h] [ch. 26:13] [i] ver. 15
14 [j] Ex. 25:20; 1 Kin. 8:7 [k] [ch. 20:40]
15 [l] ver. 13
16 [m] [ver. 5] [k] [See ver. 14 above] [j] [See ver. 14 above]
17 [n] ver. 2, 5 [o] [ver. 7]
18 [p] [ch. 30:8, 14, 16; Rev. 18:8] [q] [ver. 17]
19 [r] ch. 26:21; 27:36

21 [s] See ch. 2:1 [t] See ch. 6:2 [u] See Isai. 23:2
22 [v] See ch. 13:8 [w] ch. 39:13; [Ex. 14:4, 17, 18] [x] See ch. 6:7 [y] ver. 26 [z] See ch. 20:41
23 [a] ch. 38:22
24 [b] Num. 33:55; Josh. 23:13 [c] [2 Cor. 12:7] [d] ch. 16:57
25 [e] See ch. 11:17 [z] [See ver. 22 above] [f] ch. 36:28; 37:25
26 [g] Jer. 23:6; 32:37 [h] ver. 22 [d] [See ver. 24 above] [x] [See ver. 22 above]
Chapter 29
1 [i] See ch. 20:1
2 [j] See ch. 2:1 [k] See ch. 6:2 [l] ch. 32:2 [m] See ch. 6:2 [n] See Isai.

Prophecy Against Sidon

20 The word of the LORD came to me:
21 [s] "Son of man, [t] set your face toward
[u] Sidon, and [t] prophesy against her 22 and
say, Thus says the Lord GOD:

"Behold, [v] I am against you, O Sidon,
and [w] I will manifest my glory in
your midst.
And [x] they shall know that I am the
LORD
[y] when I execute judgments in her
and [z] manifest my holiness in her;
23 for I will send [a] pestilence into her,
and blood into her streets;
and the slain shall fall in her midst,
by the sword that is against her on
every side.
Then they will know that I am the
LORD.

24 "And for the house of Israel [b] there shall
be no more a brier to prick or [c] a thorn to
hurt them among all their neighbors [d] who
have treated them with contempt. Then
they will know that I am the Lord GOD.

Israel Gathered in Security

25 "Thus says the Lord GOD: [e] When I
gather the house of Israel from the peoples
among whom they are scattered, and [z] manifest my holiness in them in the sight of the
nations, [f] then they shall dwell in their own
land that I gave to my servant Jacob. 26 [g] And
they shall dwell securely in it, and they
shall build houses and plant vineyards.
They shall dwell securely, [h] when I execute
judgments upon all their neighbors [d] who
have treated them with contempt. [x] Then
they will know that I am the LORD their
God."

Prophecy Against Egypt

29 [i] In the tenth year, in the tenth
month, on the twelfth day of the
month, the word of the LORD came to me:
2 [j] "Son of man, [k] set your face against
[l] Pharaoh king of Egypt, [m] and prophesy
against him and [n] against all Egypt; 3 speak,
and say, Thus says the Lord GOD:

1 Or *lapis lazuli* 2 The meaning of the Hebrew phrase is uncertain
3 The meaning of the Hebrew phrase is uncertain 4 Or *banished you*

28:21–23 Sidon was commonly paired with her trading partner Tyre, twenty-five miles south on the Mediterranean coast.

28:25 gather. God would bring His people back to their land. Israel would flourish since the nations that had been her adversaries had been eliminated.

28:26 vineyards. The prophets often describe God's future blessing of Israel in terms of agricultural prosperity (36:29, 30; 1 Kin. 4:25; Is. 65:21, 22; Jer. 32:15; Joel 3:18; Amos 9:13–15; Mic. 4:4; Zech. 3:10).

[o]"Behold, I am against you,
Pharaoh king of Egypt,
[p]the great dragon that lies
in the midst of his streams,
[q]that says, 'My Nile is my own;
I made it for myself.'
4 I will [r]put hooks in your jaws,
and make the fish of your streams
stick to your scales;
and I will draw you up out of the
midst of your streams,
with all the fish of your streams
that stick to your scales.
5 [s]And I will cast you out into the
wilderness,
you and all the fish of your
streams;
you shall fall [t]on the open field,
and [u]not be brought together or
gathered.
To the beasts of the earth and to the
birds of the heavens
[s]I give you as food.

6 Then all the inhabitants of Egypt [v]shall
know that I am the LORD.
"Because you[1] have been [w]a staff of reed to
the house of Israel; 7 [x]when they grasped you
with the hand, you broke and tore all their
shoulders; and when they leaned on you,
you broke and made all their loins to shake.[2]
8 Therefore thus says the Lord GOD: [y]Behold,
I will bring a sword upon you, and will cut
off from you man and beast, 9 and the land of
Egypt shall be a desolation and a waste.
[v]Then they will know that I am the LORD.
[z]"Because you[3] said, 'The Nile is mine,
and I made it,' 10 therefore, [z]behold, I am
against you and [a]against your streams, and
[a]I will make the land of Egypt an utter
waste and desolation, [b]from Migdol to
Syene, as far as the border of Cush. 11 [c]No
foot of man shall pass through it, and no
foot of beast shall pass through it; it shall
be uninhabited forty years. 12 [d]And I will
make the land of Egypt a desolation in the
midst of desolated countries, and her cities
shall be a desolation forty years among
cities that are laid waste. [e]I will scatter the
Egyptians among the nations, and disperse
them through the countries.
13 "For thus says the Lord GOD: At the end
of forty years [f]I will gather the Egyptians
from the peoples among whom they were
scattered, 14 and [g]I will restore the fortunes
of Egypt and bring them back to [h]the land of
Pathros, the land of their origin, and there
they shall be a lowly kingdom. 15 It shall be
the most lowly of the kingdoms, [i]and never
again exalt itself above the nations. And I
will make them so small that they will never
again rule over the nations. 16 And it shall
never again be [j]the reliance of the house of
Israel, recalling their iniquity, when they
turn to them for aid. [k]Then they will know
that I am the Lord GOD."
17 [l]In the twenty-seventh year, in the first
month, on the first day of the month, the
word of the LORD came to me: 18 [m]"Son of
man, [n]Nebuchadnezzar king of Babylon
made his army labor hard against Tyre.
Every head was made bald, and every
shoulder was rubbed bare, yet neither he
nor his army got anything from Tyre to pay

19:1
3 [o]See ch. 13:8 [p]ch. 32:2; Ps. 74:13, 14; Isai. 27:1; 51:9 [q]ver. 9
4 [r]ch. 19:9; 38:4; 2 Kin. 19:28
5 [s][ch. 32:4, 5] [t]Jer. 9:22 [u]See Jer. 8:2
6 [v]See ch. 6:7 [w]2 Kin. 18:21; Isai. 36:6
7 [x][ch. 17:17; Isai. 20:5; 30:3, 5; Jer. 2:36; 37:5, 7]
8 [y]See ch. 14:17
9 [v][See ver. 6 above] [z]ver. 3; See ch. 13:8
10 [z][See ver. 9 above]
[a][ch. 30:12] [b]ch. 30:6
11 [c]ch. 32:13; [ch. 35:7]
12 [d]ch. 30:7 [e]ch. 30:23, 26; [Jer. 46:19]
13 [f][Isai. 19:22, 23; Jer. 46:26]
14 [g][ch. 39:25] [h]ch. 30:14; See Isai. 11:11
15 [i][ch. 30:13]
16 [j][Isai. 30:2, 3; 36:4, 6; Lam. 4:17] [k]ver. 6; See ch. 6:7
17 [l]See ch. 20:1
18 [m]See ch. 2:1 [n][ch.

1 Hebrew *they* 2 Syriac (compare Psalm 69:23); Hebrew *to stand*
3 Hebrew *he*

29:1–32:32 The proclamations against foreign nations in chs. 25–28 were directed largely against lesser states and immediate neighbors of Israel. However, these four chapters are directed against Egypt, one of the great empires of the ancient world. The chapters contain seven prophecies against Egypt; all are dated (29:1, 17; 30:20; 31:1; 32:1, 17) except the oracle beginning in 30:1.

29:1 year. This was in 587 B.C., about a year after Nebuchadnezzar had laid siege to Jerusalem. See note 24:1.

29:3 dragon. Egypt is likened to a sea monster (vv. 3–5). The term used can designate both the abundant crocodiles of the Nile and the sea monster that represented chaos in the mythology of the ancient Near East. The Bible calls this mythological creature "dragon," "Leviathan," or "Rahab" (32:2; Job 3:8; 7:12; 9:13 note; 41:1; Ps. 74:13, 14; 89:10; Is. 27:1; 30:7; 51:9; cf. Rev. 12:15; 20:2). "Rahab" is also used as a poetic designation of Egypt (Ps. 87:4; Is. 30:7). In the mythology of the cultures surrounding Israel this sea monster was a god who rivaled other gods, but in the Bible it was simply another creature living in submission to the command of Yahweh.

29:4 hooks. God would pluck this dragon from the sea as easily as anglers haul in fish; He would leave it rotting on the shore. See note 28:2.

29:5 give you as food. The birds and animals had been given to mankind as food (Gen. 1:30; 9:2, 3); the reversal of this relationship is a proverbial curse (32:4; Deut. 28:26; Ps. 79:2; Jer. 7:33; 15:3; 16:4; 19:7; 34:20).

29:6 reed. Ezekiel's description of Egypt as a splintered reed recalls the Assyrian field commander's similar comments to Hezekiah (2 Kin. 18:21).

29:10 Migdol to Syene. That is, from north to south (see also 30:6). Migdol was in northern Egypt, a site on the route of the Exodus (Ex. 14:2; Num. 33:7; Jer. 44:1; 46:14). Syene was in southern Egypt at the first cataract on the Nile. It was the terminal point for deep water navigation of the Nile and represented Egypt's southern frontier.

29:11 forty years. It is difficult to fix a definite historical period of forty years for an Egyptian exile; the number may have been symbolic rather than intended as a definite period.

29:17 year. This oracle was delivered in April, 571 B.C., sixteen years after the preceding oracle (29:1). It is the latest date mentioned in the book.

29:18 got anything from Tyre. Nebuchadnezzar's siege of Tyre had lasted for thirteen years (26:7 note). The siege was long and expensive, and the rewards did not repay the effort.

for the labor that he had performed against
her. 19 Therefore thus says the Lord GOD:
[o]Behold, I will give the land of Egypt to
Nebuchadnezzar king of Babylon; [p]and he
shall carry off its wealth[1] [q]and despoil it
and plunder it; and it shall be the wages for
his army. 20 [r]I have given him the land of
Egypt as his payment for which he labored,
because they worked for me, declares the
Lord GOD.

21 "On that day [s]I will cause a horn to
spring up for the house of Israel, and [t]I will
open your lips among them. [u]Then they
will know that I am the LORD."

A Lament for Egypt

30 The word of the LORD came to me:
2 [v]"Son of man, prophesy, and say,
Thus says the Lord GOD:

[w]"Wail, 'Alas for the day!'
3 [w]For the day is near,
[x]the day of the LORD is near;
it will be [y]a day of clouds,
a time of doom for[2] the nations.
4 [z]A sword shall come upon Egypt,
[a]and anguish shall be in [b]Cush,
when the slain fall in Egypt,
and [c]her wealth[3] is carried away,
and [d]her foundations are torn down.

5 [b]Cush, and [e]Put, and Lud, and [f]all Arabia,
and Libya,[4] and the people of the land that
is in league,[5] shall fall with them by the
sword.

6 "Thus says the LORD:
[g]Those who support Egypt shall fall,
and [h]her proud might shall come down;
[i]from Migdol to Syene
they shall fall within her by the sword,
declares the Lord GOD.
7 [j]And they shall be desolated in the midst of desolated countries,
and their cities shall be in the midst of cities that are laid waste.
8 [k]Then they will know that I am the LORD,
when [l]I have set fire to Egypt,
and [w]all her helpers are broken.

9 "On that day [m]messengers shall go out
from me in ships to terrify the unsuspecting [b]people of Cush, and [a]anguish shall
come upon them on the day of Egypt's
doom;[6] for, behold, it comes!

10 "Thus says the Lord GOD:

[n]"I will put an end to the wealth of Egypt,
by the hand of Nebuchadnezzar king of Babylon.
11 He and his people with him, [o]the most ruthless of nations,
shall be brought in to destroy the land,
[z]and they shall draw their swords against Egypt
and fill the land with the slain.
12 And [p]I will [q]dry up the Nile
and will sell the land into the hand of [r]evildoers;
[s]I will bring desolation upon the land and everything in it,
by the hand of [t]foreigners;
[u]I am the LORD; I have spoken.

13 "Thus says the Lord GOD:

[v]"I will destroy the idols
and put an end to the images in [w]Memphis;
[x]there shall no longer be a prince from the land of Egypt;
so [y]I will put fear in the land of Egypt.
14 I will make [z]Pathros a desolation
and will set fire to [a]Zoan
[b]and will execute judgments on [c]Thebes.
15 And I will pour out my wrath on Pelusium,
the stronghold of Egypt,
and cut off the multitude[7] of Thebes.

1 Or *multitude* 2 Hebrew lacks *doom for* 3 Or *multitude*; also verse 10 4 With Septuagint; Hebrew *Cub* 5 Hebrew *and the sons of the land of the covenant* 6 Hebrew *the day of Egypt* 7 Or *wealth*

26:7] **19** [o]ch. 30:10, 24, 25; 32:11; Jer. 46:13 [p]ch. 30:4 [q]ch. 32:12 **20** [r][Isai. 43:3] **21** [s]Ps. 132:17; [Luke 1:69] [t]ch. 24:27; 33:22; [ch. 16:63] [u]See ch. 6:7
Chapter 30
2 [v]See ch. 2:1 [w]See Isai. 13:6 **3** [w][See ver. 2 above] [x]ch. 7:7, 12; Joel 1:15; 2:1; Zeph. 1:7 [y]ch. 34:12 **4** [z]ch. 29:8 [a][Isai. 21:3] [b][Isai. 43:3] [c]ch. 29:19 [d][ver. 6] **5** [b][See ver. 4 above] [e]See ch. 27:10 [f]See Jer. 25:20 **6** [g][ch. 32:21] [h]ver. 18; [ch. 33:28] [i]ch. 29:10 **7** [j]ch. 29:12
8 [k]ch. 29:6; See ch. 6:7 [l][ch. 28:18] [w][See ver. 2 above] **9** [m][Isai. 18:1, 2] [b][See ver. 4 above] [a][See ver. 4 above] **10** [n]See ch. 29:19 **11** [o]See ch. 28:7 [z][See ver. 4 above] **12** [p]Isai. 19:5, 6; [ch. 29:10] [q][ch. 29:3] [r][Isai. 19:4] [s][ch. 29:10] [t]See ch. 28:7 [u]See ch. 17:24 **13** [v]See Jer. 43:12 [w]Isai. 19:13 [x][ch. 29:15; Zech. 10:11] [y][Isai. 19:16] **14** [z]ch. 29:14; See Isai. 11:11 [a]See Num. 13:22 [b]ver. 19 [c]Jer.

29:21 horn. A horn is a common symbol for political power in the Bible (Deut. 33:17; 1 Sam. 2:10; 2 Sam. 22:3; Ps. 18:2; 75:4, 5, 10; 89:24; 92:10; 112:9; 132:17; 148:14; Jer. 48:25; Lam. 2:3, 17; Dan. 7:7, 8, 20, 21; Zech. 1:18–21; Rev. 17:12). This oracle against Egypt ends by finding hope for Israel; compare 28:24–26.

open your lips. See notes 24:27 and 33:22.

30:1–19 This is the only one of Ezekiel's oracles against Egypt that is not dated. It may have been given between January and April, 587 B.C. (29:1; 30:20).

30:14 Zoan. In the eastern Nile delta; also known as Tanis.

30:15 Pelusium. A fortress on the Mediterranean coast, it was Egypt's northeastern frontier.

16 And I will set fire to Egypt;
Pelusium shall be in great agony;
Thebes shall be breached,
and [w]Memphis shall face enemies[1]
by day.
17 The young men of On and of
Pi-beseth shall fall by the sword,
and the women[2] shall go into
captivity.
18 At [d]Tehaphnehes [e]the day shall be
dark,
when I break there the yoke bars
of Egypt,
and [f]her proud might shall come to
an end in her;
she shall be covered by a cloud,
and her daughters shall go into
captivity.
19 Thus [g]I will execute judgments on
Egypt.
[h]Then they will know that I am the
LORD."

Egypt Shall Fall to Babylon

20 [i]In the eleventh year, in the first
month, on the seventh day of the month,
the word of the LORD came to me: 21 [j]"Son
of man, [k]I have broken the arm of Pharaoh
king of Egypt, and behold, [l]it has not been
bound up, to heal it by binding it with a
bandage, so that it may become strong to
wield the sword. 22 Therefore thus says the
Lord GOD: Behold, I am against Pharaoh
king of Egypt and [m]will break his arms,
both the strong arm and the one that was
broken, and I will make the sword fall from
his hand. 23 [n]I will scatter the Egyptians
among the nations and disperse them
through the countries. 24 And [o]I will
strengthen the arms of the king of Babylon
and put [p]my sword in his hand, but I will
break the arms of Pharaoh, and he will
groan before him [q]like a man mortally
wounded. 25 I will strengthen the arms of
the king of Babylon, but the arms of
Pharaoh shall fall. [r]Then they shall know
that I am the LORD, [s]when I put my sword
into the hand of the king of Babylon and he
stretches it out against the land of Egypt.
26 And I will scatter the Egyptians among
the nations and disperse them throughout
the countries. Then they will know that I
am the LORD."

Pharaoh to Be Slain

31 [t]In the eleventh year, in the third
month, on the first day of the
month, the word of the LORD came to me:
2 [u]"Son of man, say to Pharaoh king of
Egypt and to [v]his multitude:

[w]"Whom are you like in your
greatness?
3 Behold, [x]Assyria was a [y]cedar in
[z]Lebanon,
with beautiful branches and [a]forest
shade,
[b]and of towering height,
its top among the clouds.[3]
4 The waters nourished it;
the deep made it grow tall,
making [c]its rivers flow
around the place of its planting,
sending forth its streams
to all the trees of the field.
5 So [d]it towered high
above all the trees of the field;
its boughs grew large
and its branches long
from [e]abundant water in its shoots.
6 [f]All the birds of the heavens
made their nests in its boughs;

46:25
16 [w][See ver. 13 above]
18 [d]See Jer. 2:16 [e][Jer. 15:9; Amos 8:9] [f]ver. 6
19 [g]ver. 14 [h]See ch. 6:7
20 [i]See ch. 20:1
21 [j]See ch. 2:1 [k][Jer. 48:25] [l][Jer. 30:13; 46:11]
22 [m]See ch. 13:8
23 [n]ch. 29:12
24 [o]ver. 10 [p]See ch. 21:3 [q]Job 24:12
25 [r]See ch. 6:7 [s][ver. 8]
Chapter 31
1 [t]See ch. 20:1
2 [u]See ch. 2:1 [v][ch. 29:19; 30:4; 32:12, 16, 20, 31, 32] [w][ver. 18; ch. 32:19]
3 [x][Isai. 10:34]; See Dan. 4:10, 20-22 [y]See Judg. 9:15 [z][ver. 15, 16] [a][ch. 17:23] [b][Isai. 10:33]
4 [c][ch. 17:7]
5 [d][Dan. 4:11] [e]ch. 17:5; [Ps. 1:3]
6 [f]ch. 17:23; Dan. 4:12, 21

[1] Or *distress* [2] Or *the cities*; Hebrew *they* [3] Or *its top went through the thick boughs*; also verses 10, 14

30:17 On. Near the southern vertex of the Nile delta, On was an important religious center for Egypt.

Pi-beseth. Mentioned only here in the Bible; it was in the eastern delta and was a capital city during the twenty-third and twenty-second dynasties (950–725 B.C.).

30:20 year. April, 587 B.C.

30:21 arm. Pharaoh Hophra had sent an army to the assistance of Zedekiah, but it was repulsed (Jer. 37:1–10; cf. Ezek. 17:15–17; 29:6, 7). The "arm" is a figure for military power. The exiles living in Babylon and the people in Jerusalem had hoped that Pharaoh would defeat Babylon, but this prophecy denies them. Instead, Babylon will break the arm of Pharaoh, leaving him unable to handle a sword, and useless as an ally for Israel.

31:1 year. June, 587 B.C., a few months after the preceding oracle (30:20). Jerusalem was besieged and within weeks of being destroyed by Nebuchadnezzar.

31:3 Assyria. The prophet uses the fate of Assyria as a warning to Egypt, for the once powerful Assyrian Empire had collapsed between 640 and 609 B.C. Some scholars think it unlikely that in an oracle against Egypt the primary focus should fall on Assyria (vv. 3–17). They suggest that a copyist's error has altered one of the consonants in the text, and translate "Assyria" as "cypress" or "to what can I compare you," a better parallel with the last clause in v. 2. With this correction, the whole passage is about Egypt.

cedar. Ezekiel has already used a similar symbol (ch. 17). Great trees can tower hundreds of feet and live for thousands of years; they provide an apt metaphor for kingdoms and dynasties (17:22–24). Much of the description of this tree resembles Nebuchadnezzar's dream in Dan. 4:1–12, 19–27. The lavishness of Ezekiel's description of this tree compares with the extravagance of his description of Tyre as a richly appointed merchant ship (27:3–11).

under its branches all the beasts of
the field
gave birth to their young,
and under its shadow
lived all great nations.
7 It was [g]beautiful in its greatness,
in the length of its branches;
[e]for its roots went down
to abundant waters.
8 [h]The cedars [i]in the garden of God
could not rival it,
nor the fir trees equal its
boughs;
neither were the plane trees
like its branches;
no tree [i]in the garden of God
was its equal in beauty.
9 I made it beautiful
in the mass of its branches,
and all the trees of [j]Eden envied it,
that were in the garden of God.

10 "Therefore thus says the Lord GOD:
Because [k]it[1] towered high and set its top
among the clouds, and [l]its heart was proud
of its height, 11 I will give it into the hand of
a mighty one of the nations. He shall surely deal with it as its wickedness deserves. I
have cast it out. 12 [m]Foreigners, [m]the most
ruthless of nations, have cut it down and
left it. [n]On the mountains and in all the
valleys its branches have fallen, and its
boughs have been broken in all [o]the
ravines of the land, and [p]all the peoples of
the earth have gone away from its shadow
and left it. 13 [q]On its fallen trunk dwell all
the birds of the heavens, and on its branches are all the beasts of the field. 14 [r]All this
is in order that no trees by the waters may
grow to towering height or set their tops
among the clouds, and that no trees that
drink water may reach up to them in
height. For they are all given over to death,
[s]to the world [t]below, among the children of
man,[2] with those who go down to the pit.
15 "Thus says the Lord GOD: On the day
[u]the cedar[3] went down to Sheol I caused
mourning; I closed the deep over it, and
restrained its rivers, and many waters were
stopped. I clothed Lebanon in gloom for it,
and all the trees of the field fainted because
of it. 16 [v]I made the nations quake at the
sound of its fall, [u]when I cast it down to
Sheol with those who go down to the pit.
[w]And all the trees of Eden, the choice and
best of Lebanon, all that drink water, [x]were
comforted in the world below. 17 They also
went down to Sheol with it, [y]to those who
are slain by the sword; yes, [z]those who
were its arm, [a]who lived under its shadow
among the nations.
18 [b]"Whom are you thus like in glory and
in greatness [w]among the trees of Eden?
[c]You shall be brought down with [w]the trees
of Eden to the world below. [d]You shall lie
among the uncircumcised, [y]with those
who are slain by the sword.
[b]"This is Pharaoh and all his multitude,
declares the Lord GOD."

A Lament over Pharaoh and Egypt

32 [e]In the twelfth year, in the twelfth
month, on the first day of the
month, the word of the LORD came to me:
2 [f]"Son of man, [g]raise a lamentation over
[h]Pharaoh king of Egypt and say to him:

"You consider yourself [i]a lion of the
nations,
but you are like [j]a dragon [k]in the
seas;
[l]you burst forth in your rivers,
trouble the waters with your feet,
and foul their rivers.
3 Thus says the Lord GOD:
[m]I will throw my net over you
with a host of [n]many peoples,
and [o]they will haul you up in my
dragnet.
4 And [p]I will cast you on the
ground;
on the open field I will fling you,
and will cause all the birds of the
heavens to settle on you,
and I will gorge the beasts of the
whole earth with you.
5 I will strew your flesh [q]upon the
mountains
and fill the valleys with your
carcass.[4]

7 [g][ver. 2] [e][See ver. 5 above]
8 [h][Amos 2:9] [i]ch. 28:13; [ver. 16, 18]
9 [j]See Isai. 51:3
10 [k][ver. 3] [l]Dan. 5:20; [Isai. 10:12]
12 [m]See ch. 28:7 [n][ch. 32:5] [o][ch. 6:3] [p][Dan. 4:14]
13 [q]ch. 32:4
14 [r][ver. 5] [s][ver. 16, 18; ch. 26:20; 32:18, 24] [t]Ps. 63:9
15 [u][ch. 32:18, 21; Isai. 14:9, 10]
16 [v][ch. 26:15] [u][See ver. 15 above] [w]ver. 9; [Isai. 14:8] [x][ch. 32:31]
17 [y]ch. 32:20, 21; 35:8 [z][ch. 30:5, 6, 8] [a][ver. 6]
18 [b][ver. 2] [w][See ver. 16 above] [c][Matt. 11:23; Luke 10:15] [d]ch. 28:10; 32:19, 21, 24, 25, 28 [y][See ver. 17 above]
Chapter 32
1 [e]See ch. 20:1
2 [f]See ch. 2:1 [g]See ch. 19:1 [h]ch. 29:2 [i]ch. 19:3, 5, 6; 38:13 [j]ch. 29:3 [k][Isai. 18:2] [l][ver. 14; Jer. 46:8]
3 [m]See ch. 12:13 [n][ch. 26:3] [o][ch. 29:4]
4 [p][ch. 29:5]
5 [q][ch. 31:12]

1 Syriac, Vulgate; Hebrew *you* 2 Or *of Adam* 3 Hebrew *it* 4 Hebrew *your height*

32:1 year. March, 585 B.C., two months after the exiles would have received news of the destruction of Jerusalem (33:21).

32:2 dragon. In the pagan mythology of the ancient Near East, the orderly universe emerges from chaos after a titanic battle between a god and a great sea monster or dragon called "Sea." After the battle, parts of the universe are created from the carcass of the dead monster. Ezekiel refers to this myth in several places (28:2 note; 29:3–5). Here Ezekiel compares Egypt to the great sea dragon, terrible but destined to be defeated by the Lord.

6 I will drench the land even to the
mountains
with your flowing blood,
and the ravines will be full of you.
7 [r]When I blot you out, [s]I will cover the
heavens
and make their stars dark;
I will cover the sun with a cloud,
and the moon shall not give its light.
8 All the bright lights of heaven
will I make dark over you,
and [t]put darkness on your land,
declares the Lord GOD.

9 "I will trouble the hearts of many peoples, when I bring your destruction among
the nations, into the countries that you
have not known. 10 [u]I will make many peoples appalled at you, and the hair of their
kings shall bristle with horror because of
you, when [v]I brandish my sword before
them. [w]They shall tremble every moment,
every one for his own life, on the day of
your downfall.
11 "For thus says the Lord GOD: [x]The
sword of the king of Babylon shall come
upon you. 12 I will cause [y]your multitude to
fall by the swords of mighty ones, all of
them [z]most ruthless of nations.

[a]"They shall bring to ruin the pride of
Egypt,
and all its multitude[1] shall perish.
13 I will destroy all its beasts
from beside many waters;
[b]and no foot of man shall trouble
them anymore,
nor shall the hoofs of beasts
trouble them.
14 Then [c]I will make their waters clear,
and cause their rivers to run like oil,
declares the Lord GOD.
15 When I make the land of Egypt
desolate,
and when the land [d]is desolate of
all that fills it,

7 [r][Isai. 14:12] [s][Isai. 13:10; Joel 2:31; Matt. 24:29; Mark 13:24, 25] 8 [t][Ex. 10:21; Isai. 5:30] 10 [u][ch. 27:35] [v][1 Chr. 21:16] [w]ch. 26:16; [Deut. 28:66] 11 [x][ch. 29:8, 19]; See Jer. 46:26 12 [y]See ch. 31:2 [z]See ch. 28:7 [a]ch. 29:19 13 [b]ch. 29:11 14 [c][ver. 2] 15 [d][ch. 12:19]

[e][Ex. 7:5]; See ch. 6:7 16 [f][ver. 2] [g]See ch. 31:2 17 [h]See ch. 20:1 18 [i]See ch. 2:1 [j][ver. 2] [g][See ver. 16 above] [k][ch. 26:20; 31:16] [l]See ch. 31:14 19 [m][ch. 31:2, 18] [n]ver. 32; See ver. 28-30 20 [o]ch. 31:17, 18 [p]See ch. 31:2 21 [q]Isai. 14:9, 10 [r][ch. 30:6, 8] [s]ch. 28:10; 31:18 [o][See ver. 20 above] 22 [t][ver. 24, 26, 29, 30] [u]ver. 25, 26 23 [v]Isai. 14:15 [w]ver. 24, 25, 26, 27; [ch. 26:17] [x]Ps. 27:13 24 [y][ver. 22] [z]Isai. 11:11; See Jer. 49:34-39 [a]ver. 20 [b]ver. 18; See ch. 31:14 [c]ver. 25, 30; ch. 16:52, 54; 36:7; 44:13; [ch. 34:29; 36:6; 39:26] 25 [d][Isai. 30:33] [e][ver. 22]

when I strike down all who dwell in it,
then [e]they will know that I am the
LORD.

16 [f]This is a lamentation that shall be chanted; the daughters of the nations shall chant
it; over Egypt, and over [g]all her multitude,
shall they chant it, declares the Lord GOD."
17 [h]In the twelfth year, in the twelfth
month,[2] on the fifteenth day of the month,
the word of the LORD came to me: 18 [i]"Son
of man, [j]wail over [g]the multitude of Egypt,
and [k]send them down, her and the daughters of majestic nations, [l]to the world
below, to those who have gone down to the
pit:
19 [m]'Whom do you surpass in beauty?
Go down and [n]be laid to rest with
the uncircumcised.'
20 They shall fall amid those [o]who are slain
by the sword. Egypt[3] is delivered to the
sword; drag her away, and [p]all her multitudes. 21 The mighty chiefs [q]shall speak of
them, [r]with their helpers, out of the midst
of Sheol: 'They have come down, they lie
still, [s]the uncircumcised, [o]slain by the
sword.'
22 [t]"Assyria is there, and all her company,
[u]its graves all around it, all of them slain,
fallen by the sword, 23 whose graves are set
in [v]the uttermost parts of the pit; and her
company is all around her grave, all of
them slain, fallen by the sword, [w]who
spread terror [x]in the land of the living.
24 [y]"Elam is [z]there, and all her multitude
around her grave; all of them [a]slain, fallen
by the sword, who went down uncircumcised into [b]the world below, who spread
their terror in the land of the living; and
[c]they bear their shame [b]with those who go
down to the pit. 25 [d]They have made her a
bed among the slain with all her multitude,
[e]her graves all around it, all of them uncircumcised, slain by the sword; for terror of

[1] Or *wealth* [2] Hebrew lacks *in the twelfth month* [3] Hebrew *She*

32:6–8 The language of this section is similar to that used to describe the day of the Lord in Is. 13:10; Joel 2:30, 31; 3:15; Amos 8:9. See note 7:7. The appearance of God as a divine warrior is accompanied by convulsions in the created order. The universe dissolves into the chaos that existed before creation, when the heavens were dark (38:18–23 note). Here the extravagant imagery is not meant literally but is used in connection with the death of a Pharaoh.

32:11 sword. God threatens to subdue the sea dragon Egypt by bringing the armies of Babylon against her. The "sword of the king of Babylon" was in effect the sword of the Lord (ch. 21; 30:25).

32:17 year. Probably the spring of 585 B.C.

32:18 to the world below. The prophet describes the descent of Egypt into the underworld. The proud empire becomes just one more among the many states that preceded her (Assyria, v. 22; Elam, v. 24; Meshech and Tubal, v. 26; Edom, v. 29; Sidon and "the princes of the north," v. 30). The underworld ("Sheol" or "the grave") was commonly portrayed as a vast burial chamber where the dead had a shadowy and joyless existence. See note Is. 14:9–11; also Gen. 37:35; Job 3:17–19; 7:9; 10:20–22; 17:13–16; Ps. 88:5, 11; 115:17; Prov. 1:12; 9:18; Eccl. 9:10; Is. 5:14; 38:18; Hab. 2:5.

them was spread in the land of the living,
and they bear their shame with those who
go down to the pit; they are placed among
the slain.
26 [f]"Meshech-Tubal is [e]there, and all her
multitude, [e]her graves all around it, all of
them uncircumcised, slain by the sword;
for they spread their terror in the land of
the living. **27** And [g]they do not lie with the
mighty, the fallen from among the uncircumcised, who went down to Sheol with
their weapons of war, whose swords were
laid under their heads, and whose iniquities are upon their bones; for the terror of
the mighty men was in the land of the living. **28** But as for you, you shall be broken
[h]and lie among the uncircumcised, with
those who are slain by the sword.
29 [i]"Edom is [j]there, her kings and all her
princes, who for all their might are laid
with those who are killed by the sword;
they lie with the uncircumcised, with those
who go down to the pit.
30 "The princes [k]of the north are there, all
of them, and all the [l]Sidonians, who have
gone down in shame with the slain, [m]for all
the terror that they caused by their might;
they lie uncircumcised with those who are
slain by the sword, and [n]bear their shame
with those who go down to the pit.
31 "When Pharaoh sees them, he [o]will be
comforted for [p]all his multitude, Pharaoh
and all his army, slain by the sword,
declares the Lord GOD. **32** [q]For I spread terror [r]in the land of the living; and he shall
be laid to rest among [s]the uncircumcised,
with those who are slain by the sword,
Pharaoh and all his multitude, declares the
Lord GOD."

Ezekiel Is Israel's Watchman

33 The word of the LORD came to me:
2 [t]"Son of man, speak to [u]your people and say to them, If [v]I bring the sword
upon a land, and the people of the land
take a man from among them, and make
him their [w]watchman, **3** and if he sees the
sword coming upon the land and [x]blows
the trumpet and warns the people, **4** then if
anyone who hears the sound of the trumpet does not take warning, and the sword
comes and takes him away, [y]his blood shall
be upon his own head. **5** [z]He heard the
sound of the trumpet and did not take
warning; his blood shall be upon himself.
But if he had taken warning, he would have
saved his life. **6** [a]But if the watchman sees
the sword coming and does not blow the
trumpet, so that the people are not
warned, and the sword comes and takes
any one of them, [a]that person is taken
away in his iniquity, but his blood I will
require at the watchman's hand.
7 [b]"So you, [t]son of man, I have made a
watchman for the house of Israel.
[b]Whenever you hear a word from my
mouth, you shall give them warning from
me. **8** If I say to the wicked, O wicked one,
you shall surely die, [c]and you do not speak
to warn the wicked to turn from his way,
[c]that wicked person shall die in his iniquity, but his blood I will require at your
hand. **9** [d]But if you warn the wicked to turn
from his way, and he does not turn from
his way, [d]that person shall die in his iniquity, [e]but you will have delivered your soul.

Why Will You Die, Israel?

10 "And you, [f]son of man, say to the
house of Israel, Thus have you said: 'Surely
our transgressions and our sins are upon
us, and [g]we rot away because of them.
[h]How then can we live?' **11** Say to them, [i]As
I live, declares the Lord GOD, [j]I have no
pleasure in the death of the wicked, but
that the wicked turn from his way and live;
[k]turn back, turn back from your evil ways,
[k]for why will you die, O house of Israel?
12 [t]"And you, son of man, say to [l]your
people, [m]The righteousness of the righteous shall not deliver him when he transgresses, [n]and as for the wickedness of the
wicked, he shall not fall by it when he
turns from his wickedness, [m]and the righteous shall not be able to live by his righteousness[1] when he sins. **13** Though I say to
the righteous that he shall surely live, yet
[m]if he trusts in his righteousness and does

26 [f]See ch. 27:13 [e][See ver. 25 above]
27 [g][Isai. 14:18, 19]
28 [h]ch. 28:10; 31:18
29 [i][ver. 22] [j]See ch. 25:12-14
30 [k][ch. 38:6; 39:2] [l]ch. 28:21; See Isai. 23:2 [m]ver. 23 [n]See ver. 24
31 [o][ch. 31:16] [p]See ch. 31:2
32 [q][ver. 10] [r]ver. 23 [s]ver. 21, 27
Chapter 33
2 [t]See ch. 2:1 [u]ver. 12, 17, 30; ch. 3:11; 37:18 [v]See ch. 14:17 [w][Mic. 7:4]
3 [x][Amos 3:6]
4 [y]ch. 18:13; See ch. 3:18
5 [z][ch. 3:19]
6 [a][ch. 3:18]
7 [b]See ch. 3:17 [t][See ver. 2 above]
8 [c]ver. 6
9 [d][ver. 4] [e]ch. 3:19; [1 Tim. 4:16]
10 [f]See ch. 2:1 [g]See ch. 4:17 [h][ch. 37:11; Isai. 49:14]
11 [i]See ch. 16:48 [j]See ch. 18:23 [k]ch. 18:31
12 [t][See ver. 2 above] [l]See ver. 2 [m][ver. 18]; See ch. 18:24 [n][2 Chr. 7:14]
13 [m][See ver. 12 above]

[1] Hebrew *by it*

32:26 Meshech-Tubal. See 27:13 note.

33:1–20 This chapter marks the beginning of the second part of Ezekiel. The first part of the book is primarily about Jerusalem in the past and present; the second part focuses on the future of the City of God. This part of the book begins by repeating two important themes: first, a reiteration of Ezekiel's call as watchman (vv. 1–9; cf. 3:16–21); and second, the doctrine of individual moral responsibility (vv. 10–20; ch. 18). The exiles hear the news of the destruction of Jerusalem in v. 21; the remainder of Ezekiel's utterances about Jerusalem do not anticipate judgment and destruction, but rather restoration.

injustice, none of his righteous deeds shall
be remembered, but in his injustice that he
has done he shall die. 14 Again, [o]though I
say to the wicked, [p]'You shall surely die,'
yet [q]if he turns from his sin and does what
is just and right, 15 if the wicked [r]restores
the pledge, [s]gives back what he has taken
by robbery, and walks [t]in the statutes of
life, not doing injustice, he shall surely live;
he shall not die. 16 [u]None of the sins that
he has committed shall be remembered
against him. He has done what is just and
right; he shall surely live.

17 "Yet [l]your people say, [v]'The way of the
Lord is not just,' when it is their own way
that is not just. 18 [w]When the righteous
turns from his righteousness and does
injustice, he shall die for it. 19 And [x]when
the wicked turns from his wickedness and
does what is just and right, he shall live by
them. 20 Yet you say, 'The way of the Lord
is not just.' O house of Israel, [y]I will judge
each of you according to his ways."

Jerusalem Struck Down

21 In the [z]twelfth year [a]of our exile, in the
tenth month, on the fifth day of the month,
[b]a fugitive from Jerusalem came to me and
said, [c]"The city has been struck down."
22 [d]Now [e]the hand of the LORD had been
upon me the evening before the fugitive
came; and he had opened my mouth by
the time the man came to me in the morning, so my mouth was opened, and I was
no longer mute.

23 The word of the LORD came to me:
24 [f]"Son of man, the inhabitants of these
[g]waste places in the land of Israel keep saying, [h]'Abraham was only one man, yet he
got possession of the land; but [i]we are
many; the land is surely given us to possess.'
25 Therefore say to them, Thus says the Lord
GOD: [j]You eat flesh with the blood and [k]lift
up your eyes to your idols and [l]shed blood;
shall you then possess the land? 26 [m]You rely
on the sword, [n]you commit abominations,
and [n]each of you defiles his neighbor's wife;
shall you then possess the land? 27 Say this to
them, Thus says the Lord GOD: [o]As I live,
surely those who are in [p]the waste places
shall fall by [q]the sword, and whoever is in
the open field I will give to [q]the beasts to be
devoured, and those who are in [r]strong-
holds and in caves shall die by [q]pestilence.
28 [s]And I will make the land a desolation and
a waste, and [t]her proud might shall come to
an end, and [u]the mountains of Israel shall
be so desolate that none will pass through.
29 [v]Then they will know that I am the LORD,
when I have made the land a desolation and
a waste because of all their abominations
that they have committed.

30 "As for you, [f]son of man, [w]your people
who talk together about you by the walls
and at the doors of the houses, say to one
another, each to his brother, 'Come, and
hear what the word is that comes from the
LORD.' 31 [x]And they come to you as people
come, and they sit before you as my people, and they hear what you say but they
will not do it; for [y]with lustful talk in their
mouths they act; their heart is set on their
gain. 32 And behold, you are to them like
one who sings lustful songs[1] with a beautiful voice and [z]plays well on an instrument,
for [a]they hear what you say, but they will
not do it. 33 [b]When this comes—and come
it will!—[c]then they will know that a
prophet has been among them."

Prophecy Against the Shepherds of Israel

34 The word of the LORD came to me:
2 [d]"Son of man, prophesy against
the shepherds of Israel; prophesy, and say

14 [o]ch. 3:18 [p][Gen. 2:17] [q]See ch. 18:27
15 [r]ch. 18:7 [s]Lev. 6:2, 4, 5; [Luke 19:8] [t]See ch. 20:11
16 [u]ch. 18:22
17 [l][See ver. 12 above] [v]ch. 18:25, 29
18 [w][ver.12, 13; See ch. 18:26]
19 [x]ch. 18:27; [ver. 11, 12]
20 [y]See ch. 18:30
21 [z]See ch. 20:1 [a]ch. 40:1; See ch. 1:2 [b]ch. 24:26 [c]ch. 40:1; [ch. 26:2]; See 2 Kin. 25:2-11
22 [d]ch. 24:26, 27 [e]See ch. 1:3
24 [f]See ch. 2:1 [g][ch. 36:4] [h]Isai. 51:2; [Acts 7:5] [i][Matt 3:9; Luke 3:8]
25 [j][Gen. 9:4; Lev. 3:17] [k]ch. 18:6 [l]See ch. 22:3
26 [m][Gen. 27:40] [n]ch. 22:11
27 [o]See ch. 16:48 [p][ch. 36:4] [q][ch. 14:21] [r][1 Sam. 23:29]
28 [s][ch. 35:3, 9; Jer. 44:2, 6, 22] [t][ch. 7:24; 30:6] [u]See ch. 6:2
29 [v]See ch. 6:7
30 [f][See ver. 24 above] [w]See ver. 2
31 [x]See ch. 8:1 [y]Ps. 78:36, 37; Isai. 29:13; Jer. 12:2; 1 John 3:18
32 [z][1 Sam. 16:17] [a][Matt. 7:26; Luke 6:49]
33 [b][ver. 29] [c]ch. 2:5
Chapter 34 2 [d]See ch. 2:1

[1] Hebrew *like the singing of lustful songs*

33:21 year. Jerusalem was destroyed by fire in the fifth month of the eleventh year of Jehoiachin's rule (2 Kin. 25:8–10; Jer. 52:12–14). If news did not reach the exiles until the twelfth year, tenth month, it took over a year and a half for the news to travel a distance covered by Ezra in four months (Ezra 7:9). A few Hebrew texts and one ancient translation of the Bible read "eleventh" year instead of "twelfth"; the difference is only one letter in Hebrew, and "twelfth" could be the mistake of a copyist.

33:22 opened my mouth. The prophet had been silent for a sustained period; see notes 3:26 and 24:27. Now that the news of Jerusalem's destruction has reached the exiles, his mouth is opened, and Ezekiel addresses (a) those who remained in Judah after the destruction of the city (vv. 23–29) and (b) his fellow exiles (vv. 30–33).

33:25 eat flesh with the blood. This practice was forbidden in Gen. 9:4; Lev. 7:26, 27; 17:10; Deut. 12:16, 23.

33:26 wife. See 18:6, 11, 15.

33:30 talk together about you. Ezekiel had been ignored and even ridiculed, but now that events had confirmed the truth of his words, he had become popular with the people. But they still were not hearing, still not listening so as to repent and obey (v. 11).

33:32 lustful songs. Now the exiles had begun to see Ezekiel as a source of entertainment. Hearing him seemed to be a way of passing an idle evening or afternoon (cf. 20:49 note).

34:2–10 Sheep that are weak, injured, or ill are the special care of a good shepherd, but Israel's kings often ignored this basic rule. See Ps. 9:18 note.

to them, even to the shepherds, Thus says
the Lord GOD: [e]Ah, shepherds of Israel
[f]who have been feeding yourselves!
[g]Should not shepherds feed the sheep?
3 [h]You eat the fat, you clothe yourselves
with the wool, [i]you slaughter the fat ones,
but you do not feed the sheep. 4 [j]The weak
you have not strengthened, the sick you
have not healed, [h]the injured you have
not bound up, [h]the strayed you have not
brought back, [k]the lost you have not
sought, and with force and [l]harshness you
have ruled them. 5 [m]So they were scattered,
because there was no shepherd, and [n]they
became food for all the wild beasts. 6 My
sheep were scattered; they wandered over
all the mountains and on every high hill.
My sheep were scattered over all the face of
the earth, [o]with none to search or seek for
them.

7 "Therefore, you shepherds, hear the
word of the LORD: 8 [p]As I live, declares the
Lord GOD, surely because [q]my sheep have
become a prey, and my sheep have
become food for all the wild beasts, since
there was no shepherd, and because my
shepherds have not searched for my
sheep, but the shepherds have fed themselves, and have not fed my sheep, 9 therefore, you shepherds, hear the word of the
LORD: 10 Thus says the Lord GOD, [r]Behold,
I am against the shepherds, and [s]I will
require my sheep at their hand and [t]put a
stop to their feeding the sheep. [u]No
longer shall the shepherds feed themselves. [v]I will rescue my sheep from their
mouths, that they may not be food for
them.

The Lord GOD Will Seek Them Out

11 "For thus says the Lord GOD: [w]Behold,
I, I [x]myself will search for my sheep and
will seek them out. 12 As a shepherd seeks
out his flock when he is among his sheep
that have been scattered, so will I seek out
my sheep, and I will rescue them from all
places where they have been scattered on
[y]a day of clouds and [z]thick darkness.
13 And I will bring them out from the peoples [a]and gather them from the countries,
and will bring them into their own land.
And I will feed them on [b]the mountains of
Israel, by the ravines, and in all the inhabited places of the country. 14 [c]I will feed
them with good pasture, and on the
mountain heights of Israel shall be their
grazing land. [d]There they shall lie down in
good grazing land, and on rich pasture
they shall feed on the mountains of Israel.
15 [e]I myself will be the shepherd of my
sheep, and I myself will make them lie
down, declares the Lord GOD. 16 [f]I will seek
the lost, [g]and I will bring back the strayed,
and I will bind up the injured, and I will
strengthen the weak, and [h]the fat and the
strong I will destroy.[1] I will feed them in
justice.

17 "As for you, my flock, thus says the
Lord GOD: [i]Behold, I judge between sheep
and sheep, between rams and [j]male goats.
18 Is it not enough for you to feed on the
good pasture, that you must tread down
with your feet the rest of your pasture; and
to drink of [k]clear water, that you must
muddy the rest of the water with your feet?
19 And must my sheep eat what you have
trodden with your feet, and drink what you
have muddied with your feet?

20 "Therefore, thus says the Lord GOD to
them: Behold, I, I myself will judge
between the fat sheep and the lean sheep.
21 Because you push with side and shoulder, and [l]thrust at all the [m]weak with your
horns, till you have scattered them abroad,
22 I will rescue[2] my flock; [n]they shall no
longer be a prey. And I will judge between
sheep and sheep. 23 And [o]I will set up over
them one shepherd, [p]my servant David,
and he shall feed them: he shall feed them
and be their shepherd. 24 And [q]I, the LORD,
will be their God, and my servant David
shall be prince among them. [r]I am the
LORD; I have spoken.

2 [e]See Jer. 23:1 [f][ver. 8, 10; Jude 12] [g][2 Cor. 12:14]
3 [h]Zech. 11:16 [i]Zech. 11:4, 5; [Mic. 3:2, 3]
4 [j][ver. 16, 21] [h][See ver. 3 above] [k][Matt. 18:12; Luke 15:4] [l]Ex. 1:13, 14; [1 Pet. 5:3]
5 [m]1 Kin. 22:17; Matt. 9:36 [n][Jer. 50:7, 17]
6 [o][ver. 11]
8 [p]See ch. 16:48 [q][ver. 22]
10 [r]See ch. 13:8 [s][Heb. 13:17]; See ch. 3:18 [t][Zech. 11:8] [u][ver. 2, 8] [v][ch. 13:21]
11 [w][Luke 19:10; John 10:11] [x][Mic. 4:6, 7]
12 [y]ch. 30:3 [z]Joel 2:2; Zeph. 1:15
13 [a]See ch. 11:17 [b]See ch. 6:2
14 [c]Ps. 23:2; [John 10:9] [d][Isai. 32:18; Jer. 33:12]
15 [e][ver. 23; Isai. 40:11]
16 [f][ver. 4] [g]Mic. 4:6 [h][ver. 20; Isai. 10:16; Amos 4:1]
17 [i]ver. 20, 22; [ch. 20:38; Matt. 25:32, 33] [j]Zech. 10:3
18 [k][ch. 32:14]
21 [l]Deut. 33:17; Dan. 8:4 [m][ver. 4]
22 [n][ver. 8]
23 [o]ch. 37:22, 24; Jer. 23:4, 5; Mic. 5:4; 7:14; [ver. 15; John 10:11, 16] [p]ch. 37:24, 25; [2 Sam. 5:2; Ps. 78:71, 72]
24 [q]See ch. 37:27; Ex. 29:45; Lev. 26:12 [r]See ch. 17:24

1 Septuagint, Syriac, Vulgate *I will watch over* 2 Or *save*

34:11 I myself. Having set aside the unfaithful undershepherds, God Himself takes the role of shepherd (Luke 15:3–7).

34:12 a day of clouds and thick darkness. This language is ordinarily associated with the day of the Lord (7:7 note; Joel 2:1, 2; Zeph. 1:15; Is. 60:2; Jer. 13:16; 23:12; Amos 5:18–20).

34:17 rams and male goats. God's judgment is not confined to the shepherds, but will include the livestock. Some of the animals in the herd had been bullying others; these probably represent members of the upper classes of Jerusalem society who had oppressed the poor. There was a similar situation in the restoration community (Neh. 5).

34:23 David. This promise of restoration (vv. 6, 10–16) looks forward to a messianic kingdom. God's Servant, One like David, would rule in peace, righteousness, and prosperity exceeding that known during the rule of the historical David. No descendant of David in the restoration period fulfilled Ezekiel's prophetic description of Israel's future. The New Testament identifies Jesus as the Good Shepherd (vv. 2–10 note).

The LORD's Covenant of Peace

25 [s]“I will make with them a covenant of
peace and [t]banish wild beasts from the
land, [u]so that they may dwell securely in
the wilderness and sleep in the woods.
26 And I will make them and the places all
around my hill [v]a blessing, and [w]I will send
down the showers in their season; they
shall be [x]showers of blessing. 27 [y]And the
trees of the field shall yield their fruit, and
the earth shall yield its increase, and they
shall be secure in their land. And [z]they
shall know that I am the LORD, when [a]I
break the bars of their yoke, and [a]deliver
them from the hand of those who enslaved
them. 28 [n]They shall no more be a prey to
the nations, [t]nor shall the beasts of the
land devour them. They shall dwell securely, and none shall make them afraid. 29 And
I will provide for them [b]renowned planta-
tions so that [c]they shall no more be consumed with hunger in the land, and no
longer [d]suffer the reproach of the nations.
30 And they shall know that [q]I am the LORD
their God with them, and that they, the
house of Israel, are my people, declares the
Lord GOD. 31 And you are my sheep, [e]hu-
man sheep of my pasture, and I am your
God, declares the Lord GOD.”

Prophecy Against Mount Seir

35 The word of the LORD came to me:
2 [f]“Son of man, [g]set your face [h]against
[i]Mount Seir, and prophesy against it, 3 and
say to it, Thus says the Lord GOD: [j]Behold,
I am against you, Mount Seir, and [k]I will
stretch out my hand against you, [l]and I
will make you a desolation and a waste. 4 [m]I
will lay your cities waste, and you shall
become a desolation, and you shall know
that I am the LORD. 5 Because [n]you cherished perpetual enmity and gave over the
people of Israel to the power of the sword
[o]at the time of their calamity, [p]at the time
of their final punishment, 6 therefore, [q]as I
live, declares the Lord GOD, I will prepare
you for blood, and blood shall pursue you;
[r]because you did not hate bloodshed,
therefore blood shall pursue you. 7 [l]I will
make Mount Seir a waste [m]and a desolation, and I will cut off from it [s]all who come
and go. 8 And I will fill [t]its mountains with
the slain. On your hills and in your valleys
and in all [t]your ravines [u]those slain with
the sword shall fall. 9 [l]I will make you a perpetual desolation, and [m]your cities shall
not be inhabited. Then [v]you will know that
I am the LORD.

10 “Because you said, [w]‘These two nations and these two countries shall be
mine, and [x]we will take possession of
them’—although the [y]LORD was there—
11 therefore, [q]as I live, declares the Lord
GOD, I will deal with you [z]according to the
anger and [z]envy that you showed because
of your hatred against them. And [a]I will
make myself known among them, when I
judge you. 12 And you shall know that I am
the LORD.

[b]“I have heard all the revilings that you
uttered against the mountains of Israel,
saying, ‘They are laid desolate; [c]they are
given us to devour.’ 13 And [b]you magnified
yourselves against me [d]with your mouth,
and multiplied your words against me; I
heard it. 14 Thus says the Lord GOD: [e]While
the whole earth rejoices, I will make you
desolate. 15 As you [f]rejoiced over the inheritance of the house of Israel, because it was
desolate, so I will deal with you; you shall
be desolate, [g]Mount Seir, and all Edom, all
of it. Then [h]they will know that I am the
LORD.

25 [s]ch. 37:26; See Isai. 54:10 [t]Lev. 26:6; Hos. 2:18; [Isai. 35:9]; See Isai. 11:6-9 [u]ch. 38:8, 14; 39:26
26 [v]Gen. 12:2; Isai. 19:24; Zech. 8:13; [w]Lev. 26:4; [ch. 22:24] [x]Mal. 3:10
27 [y]ch. 36:30; Lev. 26:4 [z]See ch. 6:7 [a]Jer. 30:8
28 [n][See ver. 22 above] [t][See ver. 25 above]
29 [b]Isai. 60:21; 61:3 [c]ch. 36:29 [d]See ch. 32:24
30 [q][See ver. 24 above]
31 [e]Ps. 74:1; 100:3; John 10:16
Chapter 35
2 [f]See ch. 2:1 [g]See ch. 6:2 [h]ch. 25:12; Isai. 21:11, 12; Amos 1:11; Mal. 1:4 [i]ch. 25:8; Gen. 32:3
3 [j]See ch. 13:8 [k]See ch. 6:14 [l][ch. 33:28]
4 [m][Isai. 17:9; 27:10]
5 [n][Ps. 137:7; Amos 1:11] [o]Obad. 13 [p]ch. 21:25
6 [q]See ch. 16:48 [r]See Gen. 9:6
7 [l][See ver. 3 above] [s]ch. 29:11 [m][See ver. 4 above]
8 [t][ch. 31:12] [u]ch. 31:17, 18; 32:20, 21
9 [l][See ver. 3 above] [m][See ver. 4 above] [v]See ch. 6:7
10 [w][ch. 37:22] [x][ch. 36:2, 3, 5; Ps. 83:6, 12] [y]See ch. 48:35 11 [q][See ver. 6 above] [z][ver. 15; Matt. 7:2] [a][ver. 9] 12 [b][2 Kin. 19:4, 28] [c][ver. 10] 13 [b][See ver. 12 above] [d][1 Sam. 2:3] 14 [e][Isai. 65:13, 14] 15 [f]ch. 36:5; Ps. 137:7 [g]ver. 2 [h]See ch. 6:7

34:24 prince. See note 37:24.

34:25 covenant of peace. The verses that follow spell out what this covenant entails. It includes safety and agricultural bounty in the land. The imagery is of paradise restored.

securely. Wild animals were a constant danger (Lev. 26:6; Deut. 33:20; Judg. 14:5, 6; 1 Sam. 17:34–37; 1 Kin. 13:24–28; 20:36; 2 Kin. 2:24; 17:25, 26; Ps. 7:2; 10:9; 17:12; Prov. 28:15; Is. 31:4; Jer. 5:6; Lam. 3:10; Hos. 13:8; Amos 3:4, 8, 12; 5:19; Mic. 5:8; cf. Is. 11:6–9; 65:25).

34:26 a blessing. Agricultural prosperity is a common theme in Old Testament portrayals of the blessed future of God's people (vv. 25–29); see note 28:26.

34:30 And they shall know. See note 6:7.

with them . . . my people. The essence of God's covenant with Israel was that the Lord would be their God, and they would be His people (11:20; 36:28; Ex. 6:7; Lev. 26:12; Deut. 7:6; 14:2; 27:9; 29:13; Ps. 50:7; Is. 51:22; Jer. 7:23; 11:4; 30:22; Joel 2:27).

35:2 Mount Seir. Edom was located along the margin of arable land southeast of the Dead Sea; Seir was the chief mountain range in the country. Mount Seir was used as a synonym for Edom (v. 15; Gen. 32:3; 36:8, 9; Deut. 2:8; Judg. 5:4; 2 Chr. 25:14).

35:10 two nations. Israel and Judah.

we will take possession of them. Contrast Deut. 2:2–6, a passage forbidding Israel to take the territory of Edom because God had given it to the descendants of Esau.

Prophecy to the Mountains of Israel

36 "And you, [i]son of man, prophesy to
[j]the mountains of Israel, and say, O
mountains of Israel, hear the word of the
LORD. 2 Thus says the Lord GOD: Because
[k]the enemy said of you, [l]'Aha!' and, 'The
ancient [m]heights have become our possession,' 3 therefore prophesy, and say, Thus
says the Lord GOD: Precisely because [n]they
made you desolate and crushed you from
all sides, so that you became the possession of the rest of the nations, and [o]you
became the talk and evil gossip of the people, 4 therefore, O mountains of Israel, hear
the word of the Lord GOD: Thus says the
Lord GOD to [p]the mountains and the hills,
the ravines and the valleys, [q]the desolate
wastes and the deserted cities, which have
become [r]a prey and derision to the rest of
the nations all around, 5 therefore thus says
the Lord GOD: Surely I have spoken in [s]my
hot jealousy against the rest of the nations
and [t]against all Edom, who [u]gave my land
to themselves as a possession [v]with wholehearted joy and [w]utter contempt, that they
might make its pasturelands a prey.
6 Therefore prophesy concerning the land
of Israel, and say to [j]the mountains and
hills, to the ravines and valleys, Thus says
the Lord GOD: [x]Behold, I have spoken in
my jealous wrath, because you have suffered [y]the reproach of the nations.
7 Therefore thus says the Lord GOD: [z]I
swear that the nations that are all around
you [y]shall themselves suffer reproach.

8 "But you, O mountains of Israel, [a]shall
shoot forth your branches and yield your
fruit to my people Israel, for [b]they will soon
come home. 9 For [c]behold, I am for you,
and I will turn to you, and [d]you shall be
tilled and sown. 10 And [e]I will multiply people on you, the whole house of Israel, all of
it. [f]The cities shall be inhabited and the
waste places rebuilt. 11 And I will multiply
on you [g]man and beast, and [h]they shall
multiply and be fruitful. And I will cause
you to be inhabited as in [i]your former
times, and [j]will do more good to you than
ever before. [k]Then you will know that I am
the LORD. 12 I will let people walk on you,
even my people Israel. [l]And they shall possess you, and you shall be their inheritance, and you shall no longer [m]bereave
them of children. 13 Thus says the Lord
GOD: Because they say to you, [n]'You
devour people, and you bereave your
nation of children,' 14 therefore you shall no
longer devour people and no longer
bereave your nation of children, declares
the Lord GOD. 15 And I will not let you hear
anymore [y]the reproach of the nations, and
you shall no longer bear the disgrace of the
peoples and no longer cause your nation to
stumble, declares the Lord GOD."

The LORD's Concern for His Holy Name

16 The word of the LORD came to me:
17 [o]"Son of man, when the house of Israel
lived in their own land, [p]they defiled it by
their ways and their deeds. Their ways
before me were [q]like the uncleanness of a
woman in her menstrual impurity. 18 So [r]I
poured out my wrath upon them [s]for the
blood that they had shed in the land, for
the idols [t]with which they had defiled it.
19 [u]I scattered them among the nations, and
they were dispersed through the countries.
[v]In accordance with their ways and their
deeds I judged them. 20 But when they
came to the nations, wherever they came,
[w]they profaned my holy name, in that people said of them, 'These are the people of
the LORD, and yet they had to go out of his
land.' 21 But I had concern [x]for my holy
name, which the house of Israel had profaned among the nations to which they
came.

I Will Put My Spirit Within You

22 "Therefore say to the house of Israel,
Thus says the Lord GOD: [y]It is not for your
sake, O house of Israel, that I am about to
act, but for the sake of my holy name,
[w]which you have profaned among the
nations to which you came. 23 [z]And I will
vindicate the holiness of my great name,
which has been profaned among the
nations, and which you have profaned
among them. [a]And the nations will know

Chapter 36
1 [i]See ch. 2:1 [j]See ch. 6:2
2 [k]ver. 5; ch. 35:10, 12 [l]ch. 25:3; 26:2 [m]Deut. 32:13
3 [n][ch. 6:3, 4] [o][Lam. 2:15, 16]
4 [p]ch. 6:3 [q][ch. 33:24, 27] [r][ch. 7:21]
5 [s]Deut. 4:24 [t]ch. 35:15 [u][ver. 3; ch. 35:10] [v]ch. 35:15 [w]ch. 25:6
6 [j][See ver. 1 above] [x][ver. 5] [y]See ch. 32:24
7 [z]See ch. 20:5 [y][See ver. 6 above]
8 [a]See ch. 17:23 [b]ch. 12:23; [Isai. 56:1]
9 [c][ch. 5:8] [d][ver. 34]
10 [e]ver. 37; ch. 37:26; Jer. 30:19 [f][ver. 33, 35]
11 [g]Jer. 31:27; [Jer. 33:12] [h][Gen. 1:28] [i][ch. 16:55] [j][Job 42:12] [k]See ch. 6:7
12 [l]Obad. 17 [m][ch. 5:17]
13 [n][Num. 13:32]
15 [y][See ver. 6 above]
17 [o]See ch. 2:1 [p]See Lev. 18:25 [q]See Lev. 18:19
18 [r]See ch. 7:8 [s]ch. 16:36; 22:3 [t]See ch. 5:11
19 [u]See ch. 5:10 [v]See ch. 18:30
20 [w]Isai. 52:5; [ch. 22:26; Rom. 2:24]
21 [x][ch. 20:9; Isai. 43:25; 48:11]
22 [y]ver. 32; [Deut. 9:5] [w][See ver. 20 above]
23 [z]See ch. 20:41 [a][ch. 30:19, 26; 38:23; 39:7, 21]; See ch. 6:7

36:1–38 The prophecy of judgment directed against Mount Seir (ch. 35) is followed by a prophecy of restoration directed to the mountains of Israel.

36:2 ancient heights. This phrase refers to the land God promised Israel, or if taken strictly, to the heights of Zion (17:23; 34:14; Deut. 32:13; Ps. 48:2; 78:69; Is. 58:14; Jer. 31:12).

36:12 children. Israel will prosper and be more populous than she had been before the recent disaster (vv. 11, 12; cf. Zech. 2:4). The prophets often describe God's future blessing on the land in terms of a multitude of children (37:25; Is. 49:20; 54:1; 59:21; Jer. 30:20; 31:17; Zech. 8:5).

36:17 impurity. See 18:6 note.

that I am the LORD, declares the Lord GOD,
when through you I vindicate my holiness
before their eyes. **24** [b]I will take you [c]from
the nations and gather you from all the
countries and [d]bring you into your own
land. **25** [e]I will sprinkle clean water on you,
and you shall be clean from [f]all your
uncleannesses, and [g]from all your idols [h]I
will cleanse you. **26** And I will give you [i]a
new heart, and [i]a new spirit I will put within you. [i]And I will remove the heart of
stone from your flesh and give you a heart
of flesh. **27** [j]And I will put my Spirit within
you, [i]and cause you to walk in my statutes
and [k]be careful to obey my rules. **28** [l]You
shall dwell in the land that I gave to your
fathers, and [m]you shall be my people, and
I will be your God. **29** And [n]I will deliver you
from all your uncleannesses. And [o]I will
summon the grain and make it abundant
and [p]lay no famine upon you. **30** [q]I will
make the fruit of the tree and the increase
of the field abundant, [o]that you may never
again suffer the disgrace of famine among
the nations. **31** Then [r]you will remember
your evil ways, and your deeds that were
not good, and you will loathe yourselves
for your iniquities and your abominations.
32 [y]It is not for your sake that I will act,
declares the Lord GOD; let that be known
to you. Be ashamed and confounded for
your ways, O house of Israel.
33 "Thus says the Lord GOD: On the day
that [s]I cleanse you from all your iniquities,
[t]I will cause the cities to be inhabited, and
the waste places shall be rebuilt. **34** And the
land that was desolate shall be tilled,
instead of being the desolation that it was
in the sight of all who passed by. **35** And
they will say, 'This land that was desolate
has become like [u]the garden of Eden, and
the waste and desolate and ruined cities
are now fortified and inhabited.' **36** Then
[v]the nations that are left all around you
shall know that I am the LORD; I have
rebuilt the ruined places and [w]replanted
that which was desolate. [x]I am the LORD; I
have spoken, and I will do it.
37 "Thus says the Lord GOD: This also [y]I
will let the house of Israel ask me to do for
them: [z]to increase their people like [a]a
flock. **38** Like the flock for sacrifices,[1] [b]like
the flock at Jerusalem during her appoint-
ed feasts, so [t]shall the waste cities be filled
with flocks of people. [c]Then they will know
that I am the LORD."

The Valley of Dry Bones

37 [d]The hand of the LORD was upon
me, and [e]he brought me out in the
Spirit of the LORD and set me down in the
middle of the valley;[2] it was full of bones.
2 And he led me around among them, and
behold, there were very many on the surface of the valley, and behold, they were
very dry. **3** And he said to me, [f]"Son of man,
[g]can these bones live?" And [h]I answered,
"O Lord GOD, you know." **4** Then he said to
me, [i]"Prophesy over these bones, and say
to them, [j]O dry bones, hear the word of the
LORD. **5** Thus says the Lord GOD to these
bones: Behold, I will cause [k]breath[3] to
enter you, and you shall live. **6** [l]And I will
lay sinews upon you, and will cause flesh

1 Hebrew *flock of holy things* 2 Or *plain*; also verse 2 3 Or *spirit*; also verses 6, 9, 10

24 [b]See ch. 11:17 [c]See Ps. 44:11 [d]ch. 37:12, 21
25 [e][Isai. 52:15; Heb. 10:22] [f]Isai. 4:4; [ver. 17] [g]ch. 37:23 [h]Jer. 33:8
26 [i]See ch. 11:19:20
27 [j]ch. 37:14 [i][See ver. 26 above] [k]ch. 37:24
28 [l]ch. 28:25 [m]See ch. 11:20
29 [n]ch. 37:23; [Matt. 1:21] [o]Joel 2:19; [Zech. 9:17] [p]ch. 34:29
30 [q]ch. 34:27 [o][See ver. 29 above]
31 [r]See ch. 6:9
32 [y][See ver. 22 above]
33 [s][ver. 25] [t][ver. 9, 10]
35 [u]See Isai. 51:3
36 [v][Ps. 126:2] [w][ch. 34:29] [x]See ch. 17:24
37 [y][ch. 14:3] [z]See ver. 10 [a][ch. 34:31]
38 [b][2 Chr. 35:7] [t][See ver. 33 above] [c]See ch. 6:7
Chapter 37
1 [d]See ch. 1:3 [e]See ch. 3:12
3 [f]See ch. 2:1 [g][1 Cor. 15:35] [h][Deut. 32:39; John 5:21]
4 [i][ch. 6:2] [j][John 5:28]
5 [k][Gen. 2:7]
6 [l][ver. 8]

36:25 sprinkle. The sprinkling or pouring of water refers to the ritual purifications for removing religious defilement (Ex. 30:17–21; Lev. 14:52; Num. 19:17–19). It is also used as a symbol for the gift of God's Spirit, in the anointing of kings and priests and in the prophetic call (Joel 2:28, 29). The outpouring of God's Spirit is a sign of the messianic age (37:14; 39:29; Is. 42:1; 44:3; 59:21). This rich symbolism attaches to baptism in the New Testament. The language of vv. 25–27 is closely paralleled in Ps. 51:7–11.

36:26 new heart . . . new spirit. See 11:19 and note on 18:31. Instead of a heart of stone, unable to respond to God with love and obedience, God will provide a new heart and a new spirit. Note that these come as the result of divine initiative and not human attainment. Jeremiah describes the new covenant in the same way (Jer. 31:33; and Prov. 3:3; 7:3; Rom. 2:15, 29; 2 Cor. 3:3).

36:27 my Spirit. The new spirit would be the Spirit of God transforming those in whom He dwells and enabling them to obey the law of God. Cf. Rom. 7:6; 8:2–17; Gal. 5:16–18, 22; 1 John 3:24.

36:33 waste places shall be rebuilt. See Is. 44:26; 58:12; 61:4.

36:35 Eden. Israel as a nation was God's garden; see notes 28:13, 14; 40:16; 47:1, 2.

37:1–14 Interpreters have long discussed the relationship between Ezekiel's vision and the general resurrection at the end of time. The Old Testament does not present a complete doctrine of resurrection; this awaited the coming of Christ (Job 14:14; 19:25, 26; Dan. 12:2; see also 1 Kin. 17:17–24; 2 Kin. 4:8–37; 13:21). Ezekiel's vision gave an immediate hope to the exiles longing to be restored to their own country (37:14), and it has a more permanent application to the general resurrection.

37:1 Spirit. The words "breath," "Spirit," and "wind" in this passage represent the same Hebrew word, adjusted by translations to the requirements of context (vv. 1, 5, 6, 8, 9, 10, 14).

valley. This is the same term used in 3:22; see note there. Since this word is only used in Ezekiel in these two passages, the locale of this vision may have been the same as that for the prophet's call. Some have suggested that the vision was in the environs of Jerusalem, possibly the Kidron Valley east of the city (47:1–6; Joel 3:12; Zech. 14:4).

37:4 Prophesy. The prophetic word was like God's word at creation. God spoke, and new life was created (Gen. 1). Ezekiel's words are similarly efficacious in this vision, for they are also God's words.

to come upon you, and [l]cover you with
skin, and put breath in you, and you shall
live, [m]and you shall know that I am the
LORD."
7 So I prophesied [n]as I was commanded.
And as I prophesied, there was a sound,
and behold, [o]a rattling,[1] and the bones
came together, bone to its bone. 8 And I
looked, and behold, there were sinews on
them, and flesh had come upon them, and
skin had covered them. But [p]there was no
breath in them. 9 Then he said to me,
[i]"Prophesy to the breath; prophesy, [f]son of
man, and say to the breath, Thus says the
Lord GOD: Come from [q]the four winds, O
breath, and breathe on these slain, that
they may live." 10 So I prophesied [n]as he
commanded me, and [r]the breath came into
them, and they lived and stood on their
feet, an exceedingly great army.
11 Then he said to me, [f]"Son of man,
these bones are the whole house of Israel.
Behold, they say, 'Our bones are dried up,
and [s]our hope is lost; [t]we are clean cut off.'
12 Therefore [i]prophesy, and say to them,
Thus says the Lord GOD: Behold, [u]I will
open your graves and raise you from your
graves, O my people. And [v]I will bring you
into the land of Israel. 13 And [w]you shall
know that I am the LORD, when I open your
graves, and raise you from your graves, O
my people. 14 And [x]I will put my Spirit
within you, and you shall live, and I will
place you in your own land. Then you shall
know that I am the LORD; [y]I have spoken,
and I will do it, declares the LORD."

I Will Be Their God, They Shall Be My People

15 The word of the LORD came to me:
16 [z]"Son of man, [a]take a stick[2] and write on
it, 'For [b]Judah, and [c]the people of Israel
associated with him'; then take another
stick and write on it, 'For [b]Joseph (the stick
of [d]Ephraim) and all the house of Israel
associated with him.' 17 And [e]join them one
to another into one stick, that [f]they may
become [g]one in your hand. 18 And when
[h]your people say to you, [i]'Will you not tell
us what you mean by these?' 19 say to them,
Thus says the Lord GOD: Behold, I am about
to take [j]the stick of Joseph (that is in the
hand of Ephraim) and the tribes of Israel
associated with him. And I will join with it
the [j]stick of Judah,[3] and [k]make them one
stick, [g]that they may be one in my hand.
20 When the sticks on which you write are in
your hand [l]before their eyes, 21 then say to
them, Thus says the Lord GOD: Behold, [m]I
will take the people of Israel from the
nations among which they have gone, and
will gather them from all around, and [m]bring
them to their own land. 22 And [n]I will make
them one nation in the land, on [o]the mountains of Israel. And [p]one king shall be king
over them all, and they shall be no longer
[q]two nations, and no longer divided into
two kingdoms. 23 [r]They shall not [s]defile
themselves anymore [t]with their idols and
their detestable things, or with any of their
transgressions. But [u]I will save them from all
the backslidings[4] in which they have sinned,
and will cleanse them; and [v]they shall be my
people, and I will be their God.
24 "My servant [w]David [x]shall be king over
them, and they shall all have [y]one shepherd. [z]They shall walk in my rules and be
careful to obey my statutes. 25 [a]They shall

6 [l][ver. 8] [m]See ch. 6:7 **7** [n]ch. 12:7; 24:18 [o][1 Kin. 19:11] **8** [p][ver. 5] **9** [i][See ver. 4 above] [f][See ver. 3 above] [q]Dan. 7:2; 11:4; Rev. 7:1 **10** [n][See ver. 7 above] [r]Rev. 11:11 **11** [f][See ver. 3 above] [s][ch. 33:10; Isai. 49:14] [t]Lam. 3:54 **12** [i][See ver. 4 above] [u][Isai. 26:19; Hos. 13:14] [v]ver. 21, 25; ch. 36:24 **13** [w]See ch. 6:7 **14** [x]ch. 36:27 [y]See ch. 17:24 **16** [z]See ch. 2:1 [a][Num. 17:2] [b][Zech. 10:6] [c]2 Chr. 11:12, 13, 16; 15:9; 30:11, 18; [d]Gen. 48:13, 14, 19; [Hos. 5:3, 5] **17** [e][ver. 22, 24] [f][Isai. 11:13] [g][ch. 35:10] **18** [h]See ch. 33:2 [i]See ch. 12:9 **19** [j][ver. 16] [k][ver. 17] [g][See ver. 17 above] **20** [l]See ch. 12:3 **21** [m]ver. 25; ch. 36:24; See ch. 11:17 **22** [n][ver. 17; Jer. 50:4] [o]See ch. 6:2 [p][ver. 24, 25; ch. 34:24] [q][ch. 35:10]

23 [r][ch. 36:25] [s]ch. 14:11 [t]ch. 36:25 [u]ch. 36:29 [v]ch. 34:24, 30; 2 Cor. 6:16; Rev. 21:3; See Ex. 29:45; Lev. 26:12 **24** [w]See ch. 34:23 [x]See Jer. 23:5 [y][ver. 22] [z]ch. 36:27 **25** [a]ch. 28:25

[1] Or *an earthquake* (compare 3:12, 13) [2] Or *one piece of wood*; also verses 17, 19, 20 [3] Hebrew *And I will place them on it, the stick of Judah* [4] Many Hebrew manuscripts; other Hebrew manuscripts *dwellings*

37:9 breath. The infusion of the breath of life recalls Gen. 2:7.

37:12 graves. The vision began with exposed and unburied bones (v. 2), but now broadens to include the opening of graves.

37:14 you shall know. Israel's restoration would be God's own testimony to His power and rule.

37:16 a stick. The prophet performs another symbolic action (4:1–3 note). Two sticks, one bearing the name of the southern kingdom Judah and the other bearing the name of the northern kingdom Ephraim, are held end to end in one of the prophet's hands so that they appeared to be joined.

37:18–23 The prophet interprets his symbolic actions (vv. 16, 17). Joseph's two sons were Ephraim and Manasseh; these two tribes were the central part of the northern kingdom, so much so that the northern kingdom (Israel) was sometimes designated simply as "Ephraim" (2 Chr. 25:7, 10; Is. 7:2, 9, 17; 11:13; 17:3; Jer. 31:20; Hos. 4:17; 6:4; 8:9; 9:8; 10:6; Zech. 9:13). It fell to the Assyrians almost a century and a half before the exile of Judah, and was dispersed among other nations and assimilated to them. This passage looks back to the united monarchy under David and Solomon, and forward to a future ideal restoration (33:24; Jer. 3:18; 23:5, 6; Hos. 1:11; Amos 9:11).

37:24 king. Ezekiel is reluctant to use the word "king" in reference to any of the historical rulers of Jerusalem, preferring instead to call them "prince" (v. 25; 12:10, 12; 19:1; 21:12, 25; 22:6; 34:24). Here, however, he describes the future Davidic ruler as "king" (v. 22, 24), possibly a subtle way of distinguishing this future ruler from the others. The New Testament reveals that this shepherd-king is Jesus (34:2–10, 23 and notes), who reigns over the renewed people of God forever (v. 25; 34:31; John 10:11, 14; Matt. 2:2; Acts 5:31).

37:25–28 forever . . . forevermore. The repetition of "forever" (vv. 25, 26, 28) indicates that the reunification in view is eschatological, that is, an event to occur in the last days.

dwell in the land that I gave to my servant
Jacob, where your fathers lived. They and
their children and their children's children
shall dwell there [b]forever, and David my
servant shall be their prince [c]forever. **26**[d]I
will make a covenant of peace with them. It
shall be [e]an everlasting covenant with them.
And I will set them in their land[1] and [f]mul-
tiply them, and will [g]set my sanctuary in
their midst forevermore. **27**[h]My dwelling
place shall be with them, [v]and I will be their
God, and they shall be my people. **28**Then
[i]the nations will know that [j]I am the LORD
who sanctifies Israel, when [g]my sanctuary is
in their midst forevermore."

Prophecy Against Gog

38 The word of the LORD came to me:
2[k]"Son of man, [l]set your face toward
[m]Gog, of the land of [n]Magog, the [o]chief
prince of [p]Meshech[2] and [p]Tubal, and
[q]prophesy against him **3**and say, Thus says
the Lord GOD: Behold, [r]I am against you, O
Gog, chief prince of Meshech[3] and Tubal.
4[s]And I will turn you about and [t]put hooks
into your jaws, and I will bring you out,
and [u]all your army, horses and horsemen,
all of them clothed in full armor, a great
host, all of them with buckler and shield,
wielding swords. **5**[v]Persia, [w]Cush, and [v]Put
are with them, all of them with shield and
helmet; **6**[x]Gomer and all his [y]hordes;
[z]Beth-togarmah from [a]the uttermost parts
of the north with all his hordes—[u]many
peoples are with you.
7[b]"Be ready and keep ready, you and all
your hosts that are assembled about you,
and be a guard for them. **8**[c]After many days
you will be mustered. [d]In the latter years
you will go against [d]the land that is
restored from war, the land whose people
[e]were gathered from many peoples upon
[f]the mountains of Israel, which had been a
continual waste. Its people were brought
out from the peoples and [g]now dwell
securely, all of them. **9**You will advance,
coming on [h]like a storm. You will be [i]like a
cloud covering the land, you and all your
[y]hordes, and many peoples with you.

25[b]Isai. 60:21; Joel 3:20; Amos 9:15 [c][John 12:34] **26**[d]ch. 34:25 [e]See Isai. 55:3 [f]See ch. 36:10 [g]ver. 28; ch. 43:7; See ch. 11:16 **27**[h]Lev. 26:11; Rev. 21:3 [v][See ver. 23 above] **28**[i]See ch. 36:23 [j]See ch. 20:12 [g][See ver. 26 above]
Chapter 38
2[k]See ch. 2:1 [l]See ch. 6:2 [m]ch. 39:1, 11; Rev. 20:8 [n]ch. 39:6; Gen. 10:2; Rev. 20:8 [o]ch. 39:1 [p]See ch. 27:13 [q][ver. 4, 9] **3**[r]See ch. 13:8 **4**[s]ch. 39:2 [t]See ch. 29:4 [u][ver. 15] **5**[v]ch. 27:10 [w]Gen. 10:8 **6**[x]Gen. 10:2 [y]ver. 22 [z]Gen. 10:3; See ch. 27:14 [a]ch. 39:2; [ch. 32:30] [u][See ver. 4 above] **7**[b][Isai. 8:9, 10] **8**[c]Isai. 24:22 [d][ver. 16] [e]See ch. 11:17 [f]See ch. 6:2 [g]ch. 34:25, 27, 28 **9**[h][Isai. 28:2] [i][Jer. 4:13] [y][See ver. 6 above]

1 Hebrew lacks *in their land* 2 Or *Magog, the prince of Rosh, Meshech* 3 Or *Gog, prince of Rosh, Meshech*

37:26 covenant of peace. See 34:25 and note.

everlasting covenant. This eternal covenant took effect through the offering of Christ's blood (Heb. 13:20).

37:27 their God . . . my people. See note 34:30.

37:28 sanctuary is in their midst forevermore. Ezekiel looks for a renewed city of God (chs. 40–48). More than six hundred years later John had a similar vision (Rev. 21), but of a city that needed no temple building (Rev. 21:22).

38:1–39:29 Before his description of the future city of God, the prophet first describes the defeat and removal of its foes. Gog, the prince of Magog (see note on v. 2), sums up the final opposition to the kingdom and people of God. God comes as a divine warrior, fighting for His people and visiting an apocalyptic defeat on His foes, preparing the way for the vision of the renewed city (chs. 40–48).

38:2 Gog. The identity of Gog is uncertain. He is often identified with Gyges, the king of Lydia, a land in Anatolia (modern Turkey). In Akkadian texts from the seventh century Gyges is known as an Assyrian vassal; later legend credited him with the invention of coinage. The name "Gog" is phonetically similar to the Akkadian word for "Gyges," but an identification of the two is by no means certain.

Magog. This land ruled by Gog is also otherwise unknown from extant geographical lists or citations in ancient literature; it may mean no more than "land of Gog."

Meshech and Tubal. Though the identification of Gog and Magog remain uncertain, the identification of Meshech and Tubal is not in doubt (27:13 note). From the ancient historians Herodotus and Josephus, as well as Assyrian documents from the twelfth to the eighth centuries B.C., they are known to be tribes from central and eastern Anatolia (modern Turkey). Considerable misunderstanding has resulted from misguided speculation regarding these geographical terms. Some have identified these locations with other sites known from contemporary geography and have made them part of conjectures about later political events. Meshech and Tubal are said to be Moscow and Tobolsk, two Russian cities far distant from the region Ezekiel mentions. The Hebrew word translated "prince" (v. 2) is *ro'sh,* and some have said that this means "Russia." Even if this word is a geographical name and not to be translated "prince," it is not "Russia." The name "Russia" was brought into the region north of Kiev by the Vikings in the Middle Ages, and was not in use in Ezekiel's time.

In describing the threats to Israel's existence, the Bible commonly refers to foes coming from the north (Is. 41:25; Jer. 1:13–15; 4:6; 6:22; 10:22; 13:20; 15:12; 25:9, 26; 46:10, 20, 24; 50:3, 9, 41, 49; Ezek. 26:7; 38:6, 15; 39:2; Dan. 11; Zech. 2:6; 6:6–8; cf. Is. 5:26–29; 13:1–13; Heb. 1:5–11; Nah. 2:2–10; 3:1–3). References to these northern foes before the Babylonian exile in the sixth century B.C. usually point to Assyria, Babylon, and Persia, Israel's traditional enemies. During and after the Babylonian exile, the foes from the north take on a more symbolic and apocalyptic coloring. In his description of conflict at the end of time, Ezekiel mentions tribes on the fringes of kingdoms to the north as an embodiment of the foes from the north that already figured in Israel's eschatology (their understanding of the last days). Rather than add to speculation about future history, modern readers should understand that Ezekiel himself uses these nations as symbolic references to all powers arrayed against God's people. Ezekiel contains many oracles against foreign nations (Ezek. 29–32), but there is none specifically against Babylon, where he and the exiles were held in captivity. Some have suggested that Magog, Meshech, and Tubal are veiled references to Babylon, the immediate enemy. Gog and Magog recur in John's apocalyptic description of future conflict between good and evil (Rev. 20:8).

38:5 Cush. See Is. 68:31 note.

38:6 Gomer. This is probably a group from the area north of the Black Sea, known to the Assyrians as the Gimirrai and to the Greeks as the Cimmerians. Gog leads a coalition of nations from the south and the north. The picture is of a total mobilization against the people of God. Compare the divine summons to war in Joel 3:9–11.

Beth-togarmah. See 27:14 note.

38:9 like a cloud. An innumerable foe assembles (Jer. 4:13; Joel 2:2).

10 "Thus says the Lord GOD: On that day,
[j]thoughts will come into your mind, and
you will devise an evil scheme 11 and say, 'I
will go up against [k]the land of unwalled villages. I will fall upon [l]the quiet people who
dwell securely, all of them dwelling without walls, and having no bars or gates,' 12 to
seize spoil and carry off plunder, to turn
your hand against [m]the waste places that
are now inhabited, and [m]the people who
were gathered from the nations, who have
acquired livestock and goods, [n]who dwell
at the center of the earth. 13 [o]Sheba and
[p]Dedan and the merchants of Tarshish and
all [q]its leaders[1] will say to you, 'Have you
come to seize spoil? Have you assembled
your hosts to carry off plunder, to carry
away silver and gold, to take away livestock
and goods, to seize great spoil?'
14 "Therefore, [r]son of man, prophesy, and
say to [s]Gog, Thus says the Lord GOD: On
that day when my people Israel are
[g]dwelling securely, [t]will you not know it?
15 You will come from your place out of [u]the
uttermost parts of the north, you and
[v]many peoples with you, [w]all of them riding on horses, a great host, a mighty army.
16 You will come up against my people
Israel, [i]like a cloud covering the land. [x]In
the latter days I will bring you against my
land, that the nations may know me, when
through you, O Gog, [y]I vindicate my holiness before their eyes.
17 "Thus says the Lord GOD: Are you [z]he
of whom I spoke in former days by my servants the prophets of Israel, who in those
days prophesied for years that I would
bring you against them? 18 But on that day,
the day that Gog shall come against the
land of Israel, declares the Lord GOD, [a]my
wrath will be roused in my anger. 19 For [b]in
my jealousy and in my blazing wrath I
declare, On that day [c]there shall be a great
earthquake in the land of Israel. 20 [d]The fish
of the sea and the birds of the heavens and
the beasts of the field and all creeping
things that creep on the ground, and all the
people who are on the face of the earth,
[e]shall quake at my presence. And [f]the
mountains shall be thrown down, and the
cliffs shall fall, and every wall shall tumble
to the ground. 21 [g]I will summon a sword
against Gog[2] on all my mountains, declares
the Lord GOD. [h]Every man's sword will be
against his brother. 22 With pestilence and
bloodshed [i]I will enter into judgment with
him, and [j]I will rain upon him and [k]his
hordes and the many peoples who are with
him [l]torrential rains and hailstones, [m]fire
and sulfur. 23 So I will show my greatness
and my [n]holiness and [o]make myself known
in the eyes of many nations. Then [p]they
will know that I am the LORD.

39 "And you, [q]son of man, [r]prophesy
against [s]Gog and say, Thus says the
Lord GOD: Behold, [t]I am against you, O
Gog, [u]chief prince of [v]Meshech[3] and
[v]Tubal. 2 [w]And I will turn you about and
drive you forward, and bring you up from
[x]the uttermost parts of the north, and lead
you against the [y]mountains of Israel. 3 Then
[z]I will strike your bow from your left hand,
and [z]will make your arrows drop out of
your right hand. 4 [a]You shall fall on [y]the
mountains of Israel, you and all your
[b]hordes and the peoples who are with you.
[c]I will give you to birds of prey of every sort
and to the beasts of the field to be
devoured. 5 You shall fall in the open field,
for [d]I have spoken, declares the Lord GOD.
6 [e]I will send fire on [f]Magog and on those
[g]who dwell securely in [h]the coastlands, and
[i]they shall know that I am the LORD.
7 "And [j]my holy name I will make known
in the midst of my people Israel, and [k]I will
not let my holy name be profaned anymore. And [l]the nations shall know that I
am [m]the LORD, the Holy One in Israel.
8 [n]Behold, it is coming and it will be
brought about, declares the Lord GOD.
That is the day [o]of which I have spoken.

10 [j]See ch. 11:5
11 [k][Zech. 2:4, 5] [l][Jer. 49:31]
12 [m][ver. 8] [n][ch. 5:5, 7, 14, 15]
13 [o]ch. 27:22 [p]ch. 25:13; 27:15 [q][ch. 32:2; Ps. 17:12]
14 [r]See ch. 2:1 [s]ver. 2, 3 [g][See ver. 8 above] [t][ver. 11]
15 [u]ver. 6; ch. 39:2 [v][ver. 6, 9, 22] [w]ch. 23:6
16 [i][See ver. 9 above] [x][ver. 8] [y]ver. 23; [ch. 39:13]; See ch. 20:41
17 [z][Jer. 6:22, 23]
18 [a][Ps. 18:8]
19 [b]See ch. 5:13 [c][Hag. 2:6, 7; Rev. 16:18]
20 [d][Hos. 4:3] [e][Ps. 114:7] [f]Jer. 4:24
21 [g]Jer. 25:29 [h][Judg. 7:22]
22 [i][ch. 17:20] [j]Ps. 11:6 [k]ver. 6:9 [l]ch. 13:11, 13 [m]Ps. 11:6; [ch. 39:6; Rev. 20:9]
23 [n]See ver. 16 [o]ch. 36:23; 37:28 [p]See ch. 6:7
Chapter 39
1 [q]See ch. 2:1 [r]ch. 38:2, 3 [s]ch. 38:2 [t]ch. 38:3; See ch. 13:8 [u]ch. 38:2, 3 [v]ch. 38:2
2 [w]ch. 38:4 [x]ch. 38:6, 15; [ch. 32:30] [y]See ch. 6:2
3 [z][Ps. 76:3]
4 [a][ch. 38:21] [b]ch. 38:6, 9, 22 [c][ver. 17]
5 [d]See ch. 17:21
6 [e][ch. 28:18; 30:8, 14, 16; 38:22] [f]ch. 38:2 [g]ch. 38:8, 14 [h]ch. 27:3, 6, 7, 15 [i]See ch. 6:7
7 [j][ver. 22] [k]See ch. 20:39 [l]See ch. 36:23 [m]Isai. 45:11 8 [n]ch. 21:7 [o]ch. 38:17

1 Hebrew *young lions* 2 Hebrew *against him* 3 Or *Gog, prince of Rosh, Meshech*

38:11 quiet people. Compare the strategy in Judg. 18:7, 8. Though Gog plotted against Israel, in reality God was bringing them to their own destruction (vv. 4, 16).

38:13 Sheba. The southwestern corner of the Arabian peninsula (modern Yemen). The Sabeans were famous for trading (23:42; 27:22; 1 Kin. 10:1, 2; Job 6:19; Joel 3:8).

Dedan. A territory in southern Edom (25:13; 27:20; Jer. 25:23; 49:8).

38:17 he of whom I spoke. Gog is not specifically mentioned in any other Old Testament prophecy. Ezekiel refers to earlier prophecies describing a foe from the north (v. 2 note).

38:18–23 God Himself will be Israel's defender. In passages describing the appearance of God as a divine warrior, the prophets commonly speak of a corresponding convulsion in the created order; creation dissolves into primeval chaos (32:6–8 note; Is. 13:13; 24:18–20; Jer. 4:23–26; Joel 2:10, 30, 31; Hag. 2:6, 7, 21; 3:16; cf. Judg. 5:4; Ps. 18:8; 46:3; 77:16–19).

9 "Then those who dwell in the cities of
Israel will go out and [p]make fires of the
weapons and burn them, shields and buck-
lers, bow and arrows, [q]clubs[1] and spears;
and they will make fires of them for seven
years, 10 so that they will not need to take
wood out of the field or cut down any out
of the forests, for [p]they will make their fires
of the weapons. [r]They will seize the spoil of
those who despoiled them, and plunder
those who plundered them, declares the
Lord GOD.

11 "On that day I will give to [s]Gog a place
for burial in Israel, the Valley of the
Travelers, east of the sea. It will block the
travelers, for there Gog and all his multitude will be buried. It will be called
the Valley of [t]Hamon-gog.[2] 12 For [u]seven
months the house of Israel will be burying
them, in order [v]to cleanse the land. 13 All
the people of the land will bury them, and
it will bring them renown on the day that
[w]I show my glory, declares the Lord GOD.
14 They will set apart men to travel through
the land regularly and bury those travelers
remaining on the face of the land, so as [v]to
cleanse it. At[3] the end of [x]seven months
they will make their search. 15 And when
these travel through the land and anyone
sees a human bone, then he shall set up a
sign by it, till the buriers have buried it in
the Valley of [y]Hamon-gog. 16 (Hamonah[4] is
also the name of the city.) Thus shall they
cleanse the land.

17 "As for you, [z]son of man, thus says the
Lord GOD: [a]Speak to [b]the birds of every
sort and to [b]all beasts of the field, 'Assemble and come, gather from all around
to [c]the sacrificial feast that I am preparing
for you, a great sacrificial feast on the
mountains of Israel, and you shall eat flesh
and drink blood. 18 [d]You shall eat the flesh
of the mighty, and drink the blood of the
princes of the earth—of rams, of lambs,
and of he-goats, of bulls, all of them [e]fat
beasts of Bashan. 19 And you shall eat fat till
you are filled, and drink blood till you are
drunk, at the sacrificial feast that I am
preparing for you. 20 And you shall be filled
at my table with horses and charioteers,
with mighty men and all kinds of warriors,'
declares the Lord GOD.

21 "And [f]I will set my glory among the
nations, and all the nations shall see [g]my
judgment that I have executed, and [g]my
hand that I have laid on them. 22 [h]The
house of Israel shall know that I am the
LORD their God, from that day forward.
23 And [i]the nations shall know that the
house of Israel went into captivity for their
iniquity, because they dealt so treacherously with me that [j]I hid my face from them
and [k]gave them into the hand of their
adversaries, and they all fell by the sword.
24 I dealt with them [l]according to their
uncleanness and their transgressions, and
hid my face from them.

The LORD Will Restore Israel

25 "Therefore thus says the Lord GOD: Now
[m]I will restore the fortunes of Jacob and have
mercy on [n]the whole house of Israel, and [o]I
will be jealous for my holy name. 26 They
shall [p]forget their shame and all the treachery
they have practiced against me, when [q]they
dwell securely in their land with [r]none to
make them afraid, 27 [s]when I have brought
them back from the peoples and gathered
them from their enemies' lands, [t]and
through them have vindicated my holiness

9 [p][Ps. 46:9; Isai. 9:5] [q][1 Sam. 17:40]
10 [p][See ver. 9 above] [r][Isai. 33:1]
11 [s]ch. 38:2 [t]ver. 15
12 [u][ver. 14] [v][Deut. 21:23]
13 [w]ch. 28:22
14 [v][See ver. 12 above] [x][ver. 12]
15 [y]ver. 11
17 [z]See ch. 2:1 [a][Rev. 19:17] [b]ver. 4; [Jer. 12:9] [c][Isai. 34:6; Zeph. 1:7]
18 [d][Rev. 19:18] [e][Ps. 22:12]
21 [f]ver. 7, 13; [ch. 28:22; 37:28; 38:23]; See ch. 36:23 [g][Ex. 7:4]
22 [h]ver. 28; Joel 2:27; See ch. 6:7
23 [i]See Deut. 29:24-28 [j]Deut. 31:17 [k][Lev. 26:25]
24 [l]See ch. 18:30]
25 [m]See Jer. 30:3 [n]ch. 20:40 [o][ch. 20:9]; See ch. 5:13
26 [p]See ch. 32:24 [q]ch. 34:25, 27, 28; 38:8 [r]ch. 34:28
27 [s]ch. 28:25; See ch. 11:17 [t]See ch. 20:41

1 Or *javelins* 2 *Hamon-gog* means *the multitude of Gog* 3 Or *Until*
4 *Hamonah* means *multitude*

39:9 make fires of the weapons. The prophet uses a vivid image to describe how large the enemy army will be and how total its defeat: the Israelites will gather the weapons of the vanquished and have sufficient firewood to last for seven years (Ps. 46:9).

39:11 place for burial. Gog's hordes will be buried on the borders of Israel, near the Dead Sea. After seven months of work, burial details will still be searching for bodies (vv. 14, 15).

39:14 cleanse. Contact with a corpse rendered one ceremonially unclean (Lev. 11:24–28, 39; 22:4), so the land would require cleansing.

39:15 Hamon-gog. The valley will be named "Valley of the Hordes of Gog."

39:17 sacrificial feast. See note 29:5. Usually sacrifice meant that animals became food. Here the image is reversed: the human enemies are sacrificed, and the animals eat. By such a reversal of the created order (Gen. 1:30; 9:2, 3) the prophet shows the universe dissolving into chaos under God's judgment (38:18–23 note). The same image is used in Rev. 19:17, 18 (Is. 34:6, 7; Jer. 46:10; Zeph. 1:7–9).

39:18 Bashan. A region east of the Sea of Galilee known for its fine cattle (Deut. 32:14; Ps. 22:12; Amos 4:1).

39:19 eat fat . . . drink blood. These parts of a sacrificial animal were ordinarily offered to God (44:15; Lev. 3:17).

39:23 went into captivity. The Babylonian exile did not show that God had failed in His promises—to the contrary, it demonstrated to Israel and to the nations alike that His sovereignty was universal. Though God afflicted His people, He had not abandoned them (vv. 25–29). After describing how God would crush His enemies (chs. 38; 39), the prophet turns to a description of the glorious restoration of the people of God (chs. 40–48).

39:25 restore . . . Jacob. With the enemy destroyed, the prophet turns to God's purposes for His people, their restoration and blessedness.

in the sight of many nations. 28 [h]Then they
shall know that I am the LORD their God,
because I sent them into exile among the
nations and then assembled them into their
own land. I will leave none of them remaining among the nations anymore. 29 [u]And I
will not hide my face anymore from them,
when [v]I pour out my Spirit upon the house
of Israel, declares the Lord GOD."

Vision of the New Temple

40 [w]In the twenty-fifth year [x]of our
exile, at the beginning of the year,
on the tenth day of the month, [y]in the fourteenth year after the city was struck down,
on that very day, [z]the hand of the LORD was
upon me, and he brought me to the city.[1]
2 In [a]visions of God he brought me to the
land of Israel, and set me down on [b]a very
high mountain, on which was a structure
like a city to the south. 3 When he brought
me there, behold, there was [c]a man whose
appearance was [d]like bronze, with [e]a linen
cord and [f]a measuring reed in his hand.
And he was standing in the gateway. 4 And
the man said to me, [g]"Son of man, [h]look
with your eyes, and [h]hear with your ears,
and set your heart upon all that I shall
show you, for you were brought here in
order that I might show it to you. [i]Declare
all that you see to the house of Israel."

The East Gate to the Outer Court

5 And behold, there was [j]a wall all around
the outside of the temple area, and the
length of the measuring reed in the man's
hand was six long cubits, [k]each being a
cubit and a handbreadth[2] in length. So he
measured the thickness of the wall, one
reed; and the height, one reed. 6 Then he
went into [l]the gateway facing east, [m]going
up its steps, and measured the threshold of
the gate, one reed deep.[3] 7 And [n]the side
rooms, one reed long and one reed broad;
and the space between the side rooms, five
cubits; and the threshold of the gate by the
vestibule of the gate at the inner end, one
reed. 8 Then he measured the vestibule of
the gateway, on the inside, one reed. 9 Then
he measured the vestibule of the gateway,
eight cubits; [o]and its jambs, two cubits;
and the vestibule of the gate was at the
inner end. 10 And there were three side
rooms on either side of the east gate. [p]The
three were of the same size, and the jambs
on either side were of the same size. 11 Then
he measured the width of the opening of
the gateway, ten cubits; and the length of
the gateway, thirteen cubits. 12 There was a
barrier before the side rooms, one cubit on
either side. And the side rooms were six
cubits on either side. 13 Then he measured
the gate from the ceiling of the one side
room to the ceiling of the other, a breadth
of twenty-five cubits; the openings faced
each other. 14 He measured also [q]the
vestibule, twenty cubits. And around the
vestibule of the gateway was the court.[4]
15 From the front of the gate at the entrance
to the front of the inner vestibule of the
gate was fifty cubits. 16 And the gateway had
[r]windows all around, narrowing inwards

28 [h][See ver. 22 above]
29 [u][ver. 23] [v][Joel 2:28]
Chapter 40
1 [w]See ch. 20:1 [x]ch. 33:21; See ch. 1:2 [y][ch. 26:1, 2] [z]See ch. 1:3
2 [a]See ch. 1:1 [b][ch. 43:12; Rev. 21:10]
3 [c]ch. 43:6; 47:3; See ch. 9:2 [d]See ch. 1:7 [e][ch. 47:3] [f][Rev. 11:1]; See ch. 42:16-19
4 [g]See ch. 2:1 [h]ch. 44:5 [i]ch. 43:10
5 [j]ch. 42:20 [k][ch. 41:8; 43:13]
6 [l]See ch. 43:1 [m][ver. 22]
7 [n]ver. 29, 33, 36
9 [o]ch. 41:1
10 [p][ver. 7]
14 [q]ver. 9, 16
16 [r]ch. 41:16, 26; [1 Kin. 6:4]

1 Hebrew *brought me there* 2 A *cubit* was about 18 inches or 45 centimeters; a *handbreadth* was about 3 inches or 7.5 centimeters
3 Hebrew *deep, and one threshold, one reed deep* 4 Text uncertain; Hebrew *And he made the jambs sixty cubits, and to the jamb of the court was the gateway all around*

39:29 pour out my Spirit. See 36:25 note; 11:19; 18:31; 37:14; Joel 2:28.

40:1–48:35 Ezekiel's vision of the restored city combines many strands of biblical tradition. Ezekiel weaves together the familiar understanding of Jerusalem as the city where God had chosen to dwell with references to Mount Sinai and the Garden of Eden.

An angel leads the prophet on a tour of the city, beginning at the gates to the outer court of the temple (40:6–27) and ending after several chapters with a division of land among the twelve tribes (47:13–48:35). Interpretations of these chapters vary widely. Many have seen in these passages a blueprint and building specifications for a normal city that was to be built (43:10, 11). However, elements of the prophetic vision seem to go beyond a literal understanding (e.g., 47:1–12). Other interpreters understand Ezekiel's temple vision as a largely symbolic description of the way God would bless His people, with the temple preeminently standing for the presence of God in the midst of His people. Through the use of vision and symbol (40:2; Num. 12:6), the prophet describes a point in the future when the presence of God among His people would transcend anything Israel had experienced in history.

40:2 high mountain. Presumably Mount Zion, site of the temple in Jerusalem (17:22–24; 20:40; cf. Ps. 48:1, 2; Is. 2:2; Mic. 4:1). The prophet would tour the holy mountain just as the psalmist had (Ps. 48:12, 13).

40:3 a man. The prophet is conducted on his tour of the city by an angelic guide (cf. Zech. 1:14).

measuring reed. See 2 Kin. 21:13; Amos 7:7, 8; Zech. 2:1, 2; Rev. 21:10, 15.

40:4 Declare all that you see. John received similar instructions (Rev. 1:11).

40:5 cubits. There were at least two standard cubits, the short cubit of about 17.4 inches, and the long cubit used here, of about 20.4 inches (43:13; 2 Chr. 3:3). The rod was about ten feet long.

40:6 going up its steps. The temple was approached by steps to a raised platform that was the outer court. More steps led to a higher platform that was the inner court (vv. 34, 37). A flight of stairs led from there to the temple building (v. 49; 41:8). The higher the elevation and the closer to the inner sanctuary, the greater the degree of sanctity.

40:9 vestibule. These gateways resemble gates of the Solomonic period unearthed in excavations at Hazor, Megiddo, and Gezer (1 Kin. 9:15). The way through the center of the gate was flanked by three guardrooms on each side.

40:16 palm trees. See also vv. 22, 31, 34, 37. The decoration in Israel's ancient sanctuaries was mainly botanical; varieties of trees and plants

toward the side rooms and toward their
[s]jambs, and likewise the vestibule had windows all around inside, and on the jambs
were [t]palm trees.

The Outer Court

17 Then he brought me into [u]the outer
court. And behold, there were [v]chambers
and a [w]pavement, all around the court.
[x]Thirty chambers faced the pavement.
18 And the pavement ran along the side of
the gates, corresponding to the length of
the gates. This was the lower pavement.
19 Then he measured the distance from the
inner front of the lower gate to the outer
front of the inner court,[1] a hundred cubits
on the east side and on the north side.[2]

The North Gate

20 As for [y]the gate that faced toward the
north, belonging to [u]the outer court, he
measured its length and its breadth. 21 Its
[n]side rooms, three on either side, and its
jambs and its vestibule were of the same
size as those of [z]the first gate. Its length
was [a]fifty cubits, and its breadth [b]twenty-
five cubits. 22 And [c]its windows, its
vestibule, and [c]its palm trees were of the
same size as those of the gate that faced
toward the east. And by seven steps [d]peo-
ple would go up to it, and find its vestibule
before them. 23 And opposite the gate on
the north, as on the east, was a gate to [e]the
inner court. And [f]he measured from gate to
gate, a hundred cubits.

The South Gate

24 And he led me toward the south, and
behold, there was a gate on the south. And
[g]he measured its jambs and its vestibule;
they had the same size as the others.
25 Both it and its vestibule [h]had windows all
around, like the windows of the others. Its
length was fifty cubits, and its breadth
twenty-five cubits. 26 And there were seven
steps leading up to it, and its vestibule was
before them, and it had [i]palm trees on its
jambs, one on either side. 27 And there was
a gate on the south of [j]the inner court. And
he measured from gate to gate toward the
south, a hundred cubits.

The Inner Court

28 Then he brought me to [j]the inner court
through the south gate, and [k]he measured
the south gate. It was of the same size as
the others. 29 Its [l]side rooms, its jambs, and
its vestibule were of the same size as the
others, and both it and its vestibule [m]had
windows all around. [m]Its length was fifty
cubits, and its breadth twenty-five cubits.
30 And there were vestibules all around,
twenty-five cubits long and five cubits
broad. 31 Its vestibule faced the outer court,
and [i]palm trees were on its jambs, and [n]its
stairway had eight steps.

32 Then he brought me to the inner court
on the east side, and [o]he measured the
gate. It was of the same size as the others.
33 Its side rooms, its jambs, and its vestibule
were of the same size as the others, and
both it and its vestibule had windows all
around. Its length was fifty cubits, and its
breadth twenty-five cubits. 34 [p]Its vestibule
faced the outer court, and it had palm trees
on its jambs, on either side, and its stairway had eight steps.

35 Then he brought me to [q]the north gate,
and [r]he measured it. It had the same size as
the others. 36 Its side rooms, its jambs, and
its vestibule were of the same size as the others,[3] and it had windows all around. Its
length was fifty cubits, and its breadth twenty-five cubits. 37 Its vestibule[4] faced the outer
court, and it had palm trees on its jambs, on
either side, and its stairway had eight steps.

38 There was [s]a chamber with its door in
the vestibule of the gate,[5] [t]where the burnt
offering was to be washed. 39 And in the
vestibule of the gate were two [u]tables on
either side, on which the [v]burnt offering

16 [s]ver. 9, 14 [t]ch. 41:18
17 [u]ch. 42:1; [Rev. 11:2] [v]ver. 38, 44, 45, 46; ch. 41:10; See 2 Kin. 23:11 [w][2 Chr. 7:3] [x]ch. 41:6; [ch. 45:5]
20 [y][ver. 6] [u][See ver. 17 above]
21 [n][See ver. 7 above] [z][ver. 6] [a][ver. 15] [b][ver. 13]
22 [c][ver. 16] [d][ver. 6]
23 [e]ver. 28; [ch. 8:3] [f]ver. 27
24 [g][ver. 21]
25 [h]ver. 22
26 [i][ver. 16]
27 [j]ver. 23; ch. 8:16
28 [j][See ver. 27 above] [k][ver. 24]
29 [l]See ver. 7 [m][ver. 25]
31 [i][See ver. 26 above] [n][ver. 22]
32 [o][ver. 21]
34 [p]ver. 31
35 [q]ch. 47:2 [r]ver. 32, 33
38 [s][ver. 17] [t][ch. 46:2; 2 Chr. 4:6]
39 [u][ver. 42] [v][ch. 46:2]; See Lev. 1:3, 4

1 Hebrew *distance from before the low gate before the inner court to the outside* 2 Or *cubits. So far the eastern gate; now to the northern gate.* 3 One manuscript (compare verses 29 and 33); most manuscripts lack *were of the same size as the others* 4 Septuagint, Vulgate (compare verses 26, 31, 34); Hebrew *jambs* 5 Hebrew *at the jambs, the gates*

decorated the sacred area (Ex. 25:34; 37:19; 1 Kin. 6:18, 29, 32, 35). In this respect the sanctuaries of Israel suggested the beauty of the Garden of Eden and set before Israel the goal of again dwelling in God's garden (28:13, 14 note).

40:17 outer court. Worshipers were admitted to the outer court, but only priests and Levites could enter the inner court. The text does not specify the use of the thirty rooms on the perimeter of the outer court (cf. Jer. 35:2).

40:20–27 The northern and southern gates were the same as the eastern gate (vv. 5–16).

40:28 inner court. The inner court was separated from the outer court by a wall; it too had three gateways (vv. 28–37).

40:38 washed. Animals offered for sacrifice were slaughtered in the gateways to the inner court (43:13–27). When the animals had been slaughtered, the parts were washed (Lev. 1:9, 13; 2 Chr. 4:6) and hung on hooks (v. 43).

and the [w]sin offering and the [x]guilt offering were to be slaughtered. **40** And off to the side, on the outside as one goes up to the entrance of the north gate, were two tables; and off to the other side of the vestibule of the gate were two tables. **41** [y]Four tables were on either side of the gate, eight tables, [z]on which to slaughter. **42** And there were four tables [a]of hewn stone for the burnt offering, a cubit and a half long, and a cubit and a half broad, and one cubit high, on which the instruments were to be laid with which the [v]burnt offerings and the sacrifices were slaughtered. **43** And hooks,[1] a handbreadth long, were fastened all around within. And on the tables the flesh of the offering was to be laid.

Chambers for the Priests

44 On the outside of the inner gateway there were two [b]chambers[2] in the [c]inner court, one[3] at the side of the north gate facing south, the other at the side of the south[4] gate facing north. **45** And he said to me, This chamber that faces south is for the priests [d]who have charge of the temple, **46** and the chamber that faces north is for the priests [e]who have charge of the altar. These are [f]the sons of Zadok, who alone[5] among the sons of Levi may come [g]near to the LORD to minister to him. **47** And he measured the court, [h]a hundred cubits long and [h]a hundred cubits broad, a square. And [i]the altar was in front of the temple.

The Vestibule of the Temple

48 Then he brought me to [j]the vestibule of the temple and measured the [k]jambs of the vestibule, five cubits on either side. And the breadth of the gate was fourteen cubits, and the sidewalls of the gate[6] were three cubits on either side. **49** [l]The length of the vestibule was twenty cubits, and the breadth twelve[7] cubits, and people would go up to it by ten steps.[8] And there were pillars beside the jambs, one on either side.

39 [w]ch. 42:13; See Lev. 4:2, 3 [x]ch. 42:13; 46:20; See Lev. 5:1-6
41 [y][ver. 39:40] [z][ver. 38]
42 [a][Ex. 20:25] [v][See ver. 39 above]
44 [b][ver. 17, 38] [c]1 Chr. 6:31, 32
45 [d]1 Chr. 9:23; [ch. 44:8, 14, 15, 16; 48:11]; See Lev. 8:35; Num. 1:53
46 [e][Num. 3:31]; See Num. 18:5 [f]ch. 43:19; 44:15; [1 Kin. 2:35; 1 Chr. 24:3, 6] [g]ch. 42:13; 45:4
47 [h]See ch. 41:13-15 [i][ch. 43:13; Ex. 40:29; Matt. 23:35]
48 [j]ch. 41:25, 26 [k][ver. 9]
49 [l]1 Kin. 6:3

Chapter 41
1 [m]ver. 21, 23; ch. 42:8 [n]ver. 3; ch. 40:9
2 [o]1 Kin. 6:17 [p]1 Kin. 6:2
3 [q]ch. 40:16
4 [r]1 Kin. 6:20; 2 Chr. 3:8 [s]1 Kin. 6:5 [t]ver. 21, 23; ch. 45:3; See 1 Kin. 6:16
5 [u]1 Kin. 6:5, 8; See ver. 6-9
6 [v]ch. 40:17 [w]1 Kin. 6:6
7 [x]1 Kin. 6:8
8 [y][ch. 40:5; 43:13]
9 [z][ver. 11]

The Inner Temple

41 Then he brought me to [m]the nave and measured the [n]jambs. On each side six cubits[9] was the breadth of the jambs.[10] **2** And the breadth of the entrance was ten cubits, and the sidewalls of the entrance were five cubits on either side. And he measured the length of the nave,[11] [o]forty cubits, and its breadth, [p]twenty cubits. **3** Then he went [q]into the inner room and measured the jambs of the entrance, two cubits; and the entrance, six cubits; and the sidewalls on either side[12] of the entrance, seven cubits. **4** And he measured [r]the length of the room, twenty cubits, and its breadth, twenty cubits, across [s]the nave. And he said to me, "This is [t]the Most Holy Place."

5 Then he measured the wall of the temple, six cubits thick, and the breadth of [u]the side chambers, four cubits, [u]all around the temple. **6** And the side chambers were in three stories, one over another, [v]thirty in each story. There were offsets[13] all around the wall of the temple to serve as supports for the side chambers, [w]so that they should not be supported by the wall of the temple. **7** And it became broader as it wound upward to the side chambers, because the temple was enclosed upward all around the temple. Thus the temple had a broad area upward, and [x]so one went up from the lowest story to the top story through the middle story. **8** I saw also that the temple had a raised platform all around; the foundations of the side chambers measured a full reed of [y]six long cubits. **9** The thickness of the outer wall of the side chambers was five cubits. [z]The free space between the side chambers

[1] Or *shelves* [2] Septuagint; Hebrew *were chambers for singers* [3] Hebrew lacks *one* [4] Septuagint; Hebrew *east* [5] Hebrew lacks *alone* [6] Septuagint; Hebrew lacks *was fourteen cubits, and the sidewalls of the gate* [7] Septuagint; Hebrew *eleven* [8] Septuagint; Hebrew *and by steps that would go up to it* [9] A *cubit* was about 18 inches or 45 centimeters [10] Compare Septuagint; Hebrew *tent* [11] Hebrew *its length* [12] Septuagint; Hebrew *and the breadth* [13] Septuagint, compare 1 Kings 6:6; the meaning of the Hebrew word is uncertain

40:46 Zadok. See 44:15 note.

40:48–41:4 Like Solomon's temple before it, the temple of Ezekiel's vision had three rooms: a vestibule or portico (40:48, 49); an outer sanctuary (41:1, 2); and the inner sanctuary or Most Holy Place (41:3, 4). The temple building was higher than the surrounding courtyard and reached by stairways leading to the portico (40:6 note). The increase in height represented increasing sanctity as one approached the inner room.

40:49 pillars. The pillars presumably resembled Jachin and Boaz, the pillars that stood outside Solomon's temple (1 Kin. 7:15–22).

41:3 he went into. Access to the Most Holy Place was restricted to the high priest on the Day of Atonement (Lev. 16; cf. Heb. 9:11–14); the angel could enter this room, but Ezekiel could not.

41:4 twenty cubits. The Most Holy Place in the tabernacle and in Solomon's temple as well was a cube, equal in length, width, and height (cf. Rev. 21:16).

41:5–12 Rooms were built around the north, west, and south sides of the temple building. Probably they were used to store equipment and the wealth of the temple (cf. 42:13; 1 Kin. 6:5–10). The second and third stories were offset so that each was a cubit wider than the level below.

of the temple and the 10 [a]other chambers
was a breadth of [b]twenty cubits all around
the temple on every side. 11 And the doors
of the [c]side chambers opened on [d]the free
space, one door toward the north, and
another door toward the south. And the
breadth of the free space was five cubits all
around.
12 The building that was facing [e]the separate yard on the west side was seventy
cubits broad, and the wall of the building
was five cubits thick all around, and its
length ninety cubits.
13 Then he measured the temple, [f]a hundred cubits long; and the yard and the
building with its walls, a hundred cubits
long; 14 also the breadth of the east front of
the temple and the yard, a hundred cubits.
15 Then he measured the length of [g]the
building facing the yard that was at the
back and [h]its galleries[1] on either side, a
hundred cubits.
The inside of the nave and the vestibules
of the court, 16 [i]the thresholds and [j]the narrow windows and the galleries all around
the three of them, opposite the threshold,
were paneled with wood all around, from
the floor up to the windows (now the windows were covered), 17 to the space above
the door, even to the inner room, and on
the outside. And on all the walls all
around, inside and outside, was a measured pattern.[2] 18 It was carved of [k]cheru-
bim and [l]palm trees, a palm tree between
cherub and cherub. Every cherub had two
faces: 19 [m]a human face toward the palm
tree on the one side, and the face of a
young lion toward the palm tree on the
other side. They were carved on the whole
temple all around. 20 From the floor to
above the door, cherubim and palm trees
were carved; similarly the wall of the nave.
21 The doorposts of [n]the nave were
squared, and in front of [o]the Holy Place
was something resembling 22 [p]an altar of
wood, three cubits high, two cubits long,
and two cubits broad.[3] Its corners, its
base,[4] and its walls were of wood. He said
to me, "This is [q]the table that is before the
LORD." 23 The nave and the Holy Place had
each [r]a double door. 24 The double doors
had two leaves apiece, [s]two swinging leaves
for each door. 25 And on the doors of the
nave were carved cherubim and palm trees,
[t]such as were carved on the walls. And
there was [u]a canopy[5] of wood in front of
[v]the vestibule outside. 26 And there were
[i]narrow windows and palm trees on either
side, on the sidewalls of the vestibule, [w]the
side chambers of the temple, and the
canopies.

The Temple's Chambers

42 Then he led me out into [x]the outer
court, [y]toward the north, and he
brought me to [x]the chambers that were
opposite [z]the separate yard and opposite
[a]the building on the north. 2 The length of
the building whose door faced north was [b]a
hundred cubits,[6] and [c]the breadth fifty
cubits. 3 Facing [d]the twenty cubits that
belonged to the inner court, and facing
[e]the pavement that belonged to the outer
court, was [f]gallery[7] against gallery in three
stories. 4 And [g]before the chambers was a
passage inward, ten cubits wide and [h]a
hundred cubits long,[8] and [g]their doors
were on the north. 5 Now the upper chambers were narrower, for the galleries took
more away from them than from the lower
and middle chambers of the building. 6 For
they were in three stories, and they had no
pillars like the pillars of the courts. Thus
the upper chambers were set back from the
ground more than the lower and the middle ones. 7 And [i]there was a wall outside
parallel to the chambers, toward the outer
court, opposite the chambers, [j]fifty cubits
long. 8 For the chambers on the outer court
were fifty cubits long, while those opposite
[k]the nave[9] were [l]a hundred cubits long.
9 Below these chambers was [m]an entrance
on the east side, as one enters them from
the outer court.
10 In the thickness of [n]the wall of the
court, on the south[10] also, opposite [o]the

10 [a]See ch. 40:17 [b]ch. 42:3
11 [c][ver. 5] [d][ver. 9]
12 [e]ch. 42:1, 10, 13; See ver. 13-15
13 [f]ch. 40:47
15 [g]ver. 12; ch. 42:1 [h]ch. 42:3, 5
16 [i]Isai. 6:4 [j]ver. 26; ch. 40:16, 25; [1 Kin. 6:4]
18 [k]ver. 20, 25; 1 Kin. 6:29, 32, 35; 7:36 [l]ch. 40:16, 22, 26, 31, 34, 37; 2 Chr. 3:5
19 [m][ch. 1:10; 10:14]
21 [n]ver. 1 [o]See ver. 4
22 [p]Rev. 11:1; See Ex. 30:1 [q]ch. 44:16; [ch. 23:41; Mal. 1:7, 12]
23 [r]See 1 Kin. 6:31-33
24 [s][1 Kin. 6:34]
25 [t]ver. 18, 20 [u]1 Kin. 7:6 [v]ch. 40:48
26 [i][See ver. 16 above] [w]See ver. 5-9

Chapter 42
1 [x]ch. 40:17 [y]ch. 40:20 [z]ver. 10, 13; ch. 41:12, 13 [a]ch. 41:12, 15
2 [b][ch. 41:13] [c][ver. 8]
3 [d]ch. 41:10 [e]ch. 40:17 [f][ver. 5; ch. 41:15, 16]
4 [g][ch. 46:19] [h][ver. 11]
7 [i][ver. 10, 12] [j][ver. 2]
8 [k]ch. 41:1, 21, 23 [l][ch. 41:13, 14]
9 [m]ch. 44:5; 46:19
10 [n][ver. 7] [o][ver. 1]

1 The meaning of the Hebrew term is unknown; also verse 16
2 Hebrew *were measurements* 3 Septuagint; Hebrew lacks *two cubits broad* 4 Septuagint; Hebrew *length* 5 The meaning of the Hebrew word is unknown; also verse 26 6 A *cubit* was about 18 inches or 45 centimeters 7 The meaning of the Hebrew word is unknown; also verse 5 8 Septuagint, Syriac; Hebrew *and a way of one cubit* 9 Or *temple* 10 Septuagint; Hebrew *east*

41:22 altar. The table of the bread of the Presence is described as an altar only here. Ezekiel probably does so because the bread was consumed by priests like part of a sacrificial meal, and because the incense set out with the bread was viewed as a memorial offering (Lev. 24:5–9; 1 Sam. 21:3–6).

42:1–14 These rooms should not be confused with those built on the perimeter of the temple building itself (41:5–12 note). These were along the north and south sides of the wall separating the inner and outer courts.

yard and opposite [o]the building, there were
[p]chambers **11**with [q]a passage in front of
them. They were similar to the chambers
on the north, of the same length and
breadth, with the same exits[1] and arrangements and [q]doors, **12**as were the entrances
of the chambers on the south. There was
an entrance at the beginning of the passage, the passage before [n]the corresponding wall on the east as one enters them.[2]

13Then he said to me, "The north chambers and the south chambers opposite [o]the
yard are the holy chambers, [r]where the
priests who approach the LORD [s]shall eat
the [t]most holy offerings. There they shall
put the most holy offerings—[t]the grain
offering, [u]the sin offering, and [u]the guilt
offering, for the place is holy. **14**When the
priests enter the Holy Place, they shall not
go out of it into the outer court [v]without
laying there the garments in which they
minister, for these are holy. [v]They shall put
on other garments before they go near to
that which is for the people."

15Now when he had finished measuring
the interior of the temple area, he led me
out by [w]the gate that faced east, and
measured the temple area all around.
16He measured the east side with [x]the
measuring reed, 500 cubits by the measuring reed all around. **17**He measured the
north side, 500 cubits by the measuring
reed all around. **18**He measured the south
side, 500 cubits by the measuring reed.
19Then he turned to the west side and
measured, 500 cubits by the measuring
reed. **20**He measured it on the four sides.
It had [y]a wall around it, [z]500 cubits long
and [z]500 cubits broad, [a]to make a separation between the holy and the common.

The Glory of the LORD Fills the Temple

43 Then he led me to [b]the gate, the
gate facing east. **2**And behold, [c]the
glory of the God of Israel was coming from
the east. And [d]the sound of his coming was
like the sound of many waters, and [e]the
earth shone with his glory. **3**And [f]the vision
I saw was just like the vision that I had
seen [g]when he[3] came to destroy the city,
and just like [h]the vision that I had seen [i]by
the Chebar canal. And [j]I fell on my face.
4As [c]the glory of the LORD [k]entered the
temple by the gate facing east, **5**[l]the Spirit
lifted me up and brought me into [m]the
inner court; and behold, [n]the glory of the
LORD filled the temple.

6[o]While the man was standing beside
me, [p]I heard one speaking to me out of the
temple, **7**and he said to me, [q]"Son of man,
this is [r]the place of my throne and [s]the
place of the soles of my feet, [t]where I will
dwell in the midst of the people of Israel
forever. And the house of Israel shall no
more [u]defile my holy name, neither they,
nor their kings, by their whoring and by
the dead bodies[4] of their kings at their high
places,[5] **8**by setting their threshold by my
threshold and their doorposts beside my
doorposts, with [v]only a wall between me
and them. They have [w]defiled my holy
name by their abominations that they have
committed, so I have consumed them in
my anger. **9**Now let them put away their
whoring and the dead bodies of their kings
far from me, [t]and I will dwell in their midst
forever.

10"As for you, [q]son of man, [x]describe to
the house of Israel the temple, that they
may be ashamed of their iniquities; and
they shall measure the plan. **11**And if they
are ashamed of all that they have done,
[x]make known to them the design of the
temple, its arrangement, [y]its exits and its

10[o][ver. 1] [p]See ch. 40:17
11[q][ver. 4]
12[n][See ver. 10 above]
13[o][See ver. 10 above] [r]ch. 40:43 [s]Lev. 6:16, 26; 10:13; 24:9 [t]Num. 18:9 [u]ch. 40:39
14[v]ch. 44:19; Lev. 6:11
15[w]See ch. 43:1
16[x][ch. 40:3]
20[y]ch. 40:5 [z][ch. 45:2; Rev. 21:16] [a][ch. 22:26; 43:12; 44:23; 48:15]
Chapter 43
1[b]ver. 4; ch. 10:19; 11:1; 40:6; 42:15; 44:1
2[c]ch. 10:18, 19; 11:23; [Rev. 21:11] [d]ch. 1:24; [Rev. 1:15] [e][ch. 10:4; Rev. 18:1]
3[f]See ch. 1:28 [g][ch. 9:1, 2, 5] [h]See ch. 1:4-28 [i]See ch. 1:1 [j]See ch. 1:28
4[c][See ver. 2 above] [k][ch. 44:2]
5[l]See ch. 3:12 [m]See ch. 8:16 [n]ch. 10:4; 44:4; 1 Kin. 8:10, 11; [Isai. 6:1]
6[o]See ch. 40:3 [p][Ex. 25:22]
7[q]See ch. 2:1 [r][Ps. 99:1] [s][1 Chr. 28:2; Isai. 60:13] [t]See ch. 37:26, 28 [u][ver. 8]; See ch. 20:39
8[v][ch. 42:20] [w][ver. 7]
9[t][See ver. 7 above]
10[q][See ver. 7 above] [x]ch. 40:4
11[x][See ver. 10 above] [y][ch. 44:5]

[1] Hebrew *and all their exits* [2] The meaning of the Hebrew verse is uncertain [3] Some Hebrew manuscripts and Vulgate; most Hebrew manuscripts *when I* [4] Or *the monuments*; also verse 9 [5] Or *at their deaths*

42:20 wall. The outer wall separated the sacred precincts from the secular; see note 40:7.

500. The 500 cubits is the sum of the lengths of the north outer gateway (50), part of the outer court (100), the north inner gateway (50), the inner court (100), the south inner gateway (50), part of the outer court (100), and the south outer gateway (50).

43:1–5 The prophet had an earlier vision of the glory of the Lord departing from the city (10:18–22; 11:22–24); now in his vision he witnesses its return. The glory comes from the east, the direction to which it had departed (11:23). The glory of the Lord had filled the tabernacle and Solomon's temple when they were dedicated (Ex. 40:34, 35; 1 Kin. 8:10, 11; 2 Chr. 5:13, 14; 7:1, 2; cf. Is. 60:1–3). See note 11:22–24. The temple of the restoration period, built by Zerubbabel, was not built according to Ezekiel's vision; it was smaller than Solomon's temple (Ezra 3:12, 13; Hag. 2:3). Yet Haggai prophesied that the glory of Zerubbabel's temple would exceed that of Solomon's (Hag. 2:7–9), because God's presence would be there.

43:7 throne. The Jerusalem temple was understood as the place where God had His throne; He was enthroned above the ark in the Most Holy Place (1 Sam. 4:4; 2 Sam. 6:2; 2 Kin. 19:15; 1 Chr. 13:6; Ps. 80:1; 99:1; 132:13, 14; Is. 6:1; 37:16).

43:10 plan. The patterns for Israel's past sanctuaries had come from God; so too the plans for the temple in Ezekiel's vision were of divine origin. See note 40:1–48:35. Like Moses who gave Israel the laws for the tabernacle, Ezekiel saw the promise only from a distance, in a vision (Num. 27:12, 13; Deut. 32:52; 34:4).

entrances, that is, its whole design; and make known to them as well all its statutes and its whole design and all its laws, and write it down [z]in their sight, so that they may observe all its laws and all its statutes and carry them out. **12** This is the law of the temple: the whole territory on the top of [a]the mountain [b]all around shall be most holy. Behold, this is the law of the temple.

The Altar

13 "These are the measurements of [c]the altar by cubits (the cubit being [d]a cubit and a handbreadth):[1] its base shall be one cubit high[2] and one cubit broad, with a rim of one span[3] around its edge. And this shall be the height of the altar: **14** from the base on the ground to the lower ledge, two cubits, with a breadth of one cubit; and from the smaller ledge to the larger ledge, four cubits, with a breadth of one cubit; **15** and the altar hearth, four cubits; and from the altar hearth projecting upward, [e]four horns. **16** The altar hearth shall be [f]square, twelve cubits long by twelve broad. **17** The ledge also shall be square, fourteen cubits long by fourteen broad, with a rim around it half a cubit broad, and its base one cubit all around. [g]The steps of the altar shall face east."

18 And he said to me, [h]"Son of man, thus says the Lord GOD: These are the ordinances for the altar: On the day when it is erected for offering burnt offerings upon it and [i]for throwing blood against it, **19** you shall give to [j]the Levitical priests [k]of the family of Zadok, who draw near to me to minister to me, declares the Lord GOD, [l]a bull from the herd for a sin offering. **20** And [m]you shall take some of its blood and put it on [e]the four horns of the altar and on the four corners of the ledge and upon [n]the rim all around. [o]Thus you shall purify the altar and make atonement for it. **21** You shall also take the bull of the sin offering, and [p]it shall be burned in the appointed place belonging to the temple, outside the sacred area. **22** And on the second day you shall offer a male goat without blemish for a sin offering; and the altar shall be purified, as it was purified with the bull. **23** When you have finished purifying it, you shall offer a bull from the herd without blemish and [q]a ram from the flock without blemish. **24** You shall present them before the LORD, and the priests [r]shall sprinkle salt on them and offer them up as a burnt offering to the LORD. **25** [s]For seven days you shall provide daily a male goat for a sin offering; also, a bull from the herd and a ram from the flock, without blemish, shall be provided. **26** Seven days shall they make atonement for the altar and cleanse it, and so consecrate it.[4] **27** And when they have completed these days, then [t]from the eighth day onward the priests shall offer on the altar your burnt offerings and your [u]peace offerings, and [v]I will accept you, declares the Lord GOD."

The Gate for the Prince

44 Then he brought me [w]back to the outer gate of the sanctuary, [x]which faces east. And it was shut. **2** And the LORD said to me, "This gate shall remain shut; it shall not be opened, and no one shall enter by it, for [y]the LORD, the God of Israel, has entered by it. Therefore it shall remain shut. **3** Only [z]the prince may sit in it [a]to eat bread before the LORD. He [b]shall enter by

11 [z]See ch. 12:3
12 [a][ch. 40:2] [b]See ch. 42:15-20
13 [c][ch. 40:47; 47:1]; See Ex. 27:1-8 [d]ch. 40:5; [ch. 41:8]
15 [e]See Ex. 27:2
16 [f][ch. 40:47; Ex. 27:1]
17 [g][Ex. 20:26]
18 [h]See ch. 2:1 [i]See Lev. 1:5
19 [j]ch. 44:15; Deut. 17:9; 18:1; 24:8; 27:9 [k]See ch. 40:46 [l]ch. 45:18; Ex. 29:1, 10
20 [m]ch. 45:19; Ex. 29:12; Lev. 8:15 [e][See ver. 15 above] [n][ver. 13, 17] [o]Ex. 29:36; [ch. 45:18]
21 [p]Ex. 29:14
23 [q][Ex. 29:1]
24 [r]Lev. 2:13
25 [s]Ex. 29:35, 36; Lev. 8:33, 35
27 [t]Lev. 9:1 [u]See Lev. 3:1 [v]See ch. 20:40
Chapter 44
1 [w][ch. 43:5] [x]See ch. 43:1
2 [y][ch. 43:4]
3 [z]ch. 34:24; 37:25; 45:7; 46:2 [a][Gen. 31:54] [b]ch. 46:2, 12

1 A *cubit* was about 18 inches or 45 centimeters; a *handbreadth* was about 3 inches or 7.5 centimeters 2 Or *its gutter shall be one cubit deep* 3 A *span* was about 9 inches or 22 centimeters 4 Hebrew *fill its hand*

43:12 law of the temple. Ezekiel's temple vision is the only body of ritual law in the Bible not from the mouth of Moses. Like Moses, Ezekiel had received this law on a high mountain (40:2; Ex. 25:9, 40).

43:13 cubits. See note 40:5.

altar. The altar was built as a series of platforms, each smaller than the one below, similar to a step-pyramid or ziggurat. The ancient rabbis had many discussions about this altar since its construction contradicted the command that the altar should not have steps (Ex. 20:24–26).

43:18 throwing blood. See Ex. 29:16; Lev. 4:6; 5:9.

43:19 family of Zadok. See note 44:15.

43:21 outside. See Ex. 29:14; Lev. 4:12, 21; 8:17; 9:11; 16:27. The writer of Hebrews interprets these instructions as an aspect of Christ's offering of Himself (Heb. 13:11–13).

44:1 shut. The prophet had been in the inner court (43:5), but is now taken to the eastern gate. That gate will remain closed because the glory of the Lord had entered the temple through it (v. 2; 43:4; cf. Ps. 24:7–10). That the gate is closed may also imply that the Lord will never leave the temple again (43:7, 9). The so-called Golden Gate in the eastern wall of the Old City of Jerusalem is walled shut. This gate from the Byzantine period (A.D. 300–650) was restored in the Crusader period (A.D. 1000–1100). It is no doubt positioned above the remains of gates from earlier periods. The gate was walled shut during the Muslim rule of Suleiman the Magnificent in the sixteenth century. Since this part of Ezekiel plays a role in Muslim eschatology, it may have provided a reason for walling up the gate. However, all the gates to the south and east of the temple platform were closed at this time in order to control access to the mosques on the platform above.

44:3 prince. Since the gate is closed, the gateway becomes a room; in this room the prince will be allowed to eat his portion of sacrificial meals. This provision has never been put into effect for any king of Israel. In Ezekiel's vision it represents the special relationship the promised king would maintain with the temple. See note 37:24.

way of the vestibule of the gate, and shall
go out by the same way."
4 Then he brought me by way of [c]the
north gate to the front of the temple, and I
looked, and behold, [d]the glory of the LORD
filled the temple of the LORD. And [e]I fell on
my face. 5 And the LORD said to me, [f]"Son
of man, mark well, [g]see with your eyes,
[g]and hear with your ears all that I shall tell
you concerning [h]all the statutes of the temple of the LORD and all its laws. And mark
well [h]the entrance to the temple and all the
exits from the sanctuary. 6 And say to [i]the
rebellious house,[1] to the [j]house of Israel,
Thus says the Lord GOD: O house of Israel,
[k]enough of all your abominations, 7 in [l]ad-
mitting foreigners, [m]uncircumcised in heart
and flesh, to be in my sanctuary, [n]profan-
ing my temple, when you offer to me my
food, the fat and the blood. You[2] have broken my covenant, in addition to all your
abominations. 8 And [o]you have not kept
charge of my holy things, but you have set
others to keep my charge for you in my
sanctuary.
9 "Thus says the Lord GOD: [p]No foreigner, uncircumcised in heart and flesh, of all
the foreigners who are among the people of
Israel, shall enter my sanctuary. 10 But [q]the
Levites who went far from me, going astray
from me after their idols [r]when Israel went
astray, [s]shall bear their punishment.[3]
11 They shall be [t]ministers in my sanctuary,
having oversight [u]at the gates of the temple
and ministering in the temple. They shall
slaughter the burnt offering and the sacrifice for the people, and [v]they shall stand
before the people, to minister to them.
12 Because they ministered to them before
their idols and became [w]a stumbling block
of iniquity to the house of Israel, therefore
I have [x]sworn concerning them, declares
the Lord GOD, and they shall bear their
punishment. 13 They [y]shall not come near
to me, to serve me as priest, nor come near
any of my holy things and the things that
are most holy, but [z]they shall bear their
shame and the abominations that they
have committed. 14 Yet I will appoint them
to keep [a]charge of the temple, [b]to do all its
service and all that is to be done in it.

Rules for Levitical Priests

15 "But [c]the Levitical priests, [c]the sons of
Zadok, who kept [a]the charge of my sanctuary [r]when the people of Israel went astray
from me, shall come near to me [d]to minister to me. And they shall stand before me
to offer me [e]the fat and the blood, declares
the Lord GOD. 16 They shall enter my sanctuary, and they shall approach [f]my table, to
minister to me, and they shall keep my
charge. 17 When they enter the gates of the
inner court, they shall wear [g]linen garments. They shall have nothing of wool on
them, while they minister at the gates of
the inner court, and within. 18 They shall
have linen turbans on their heads, and
linen undergarments around their waists.
They shall not bind themselves with anything that causes sweat. 19 And when they
go out into the outer court to the people,
they shall put off the garments in which
they have been ministering [h]and lay them
in the holy chambers. And [i]they shall put
on other garments, [j]lest they communicate
holiness to the people with their garments.
20 [k]They shall not shave their heads or [l]let
their locks grow long; they shall surely trim
the hair of their heads. 21 [m]No priest shall
drink wine when he enters the inner court.
22 [n]They shall not marry a widow or a
divorced woman, but only virgins of the
offspring of the house of Israel, or a widow

[1] Septuagint; Hebrew lacks *house* [2] Septuagint, Syriac, Vulgate; Hebrew *they* [3] Or *iniquity*; also verse 12

4 [c]ch. 40:20 [d]See ch. 43:5 [e]See ch. 1:28 **5** [f]See ch. 2:1 [g]ch. 40:4 [h][ch. 43:11] **6** [i]See ch. 2:3 [j]ch. 40:4 [k]ch. 45:9; [1 Pet. 4:3] **7** [l][ver. 9; Neh. 7:64, 65; Acts 21:28] [m][Jer. 9:26; Acts 7:51] [n]ch. 23:39 **8** [o][ch. 22:26] **9** [p][ver. 7] **10** [q][ver. 15; ch. 48:11] [r]ch. 48:11 [s]See ch. 4:4 **11** [t]ch. 46:24 [u][1 Chr. 26:1] [v]Num. 16:9 **12** [w]ch. 7:19; 14:3, 4, 7; [Mal. 2:8] [x]Ps. 106:26 **13** [y]Num. 18:3; 2 Kin. 23:9 [z]See ch. 32:24 **14** [a]See ch. 40:45; [b]1 Chr. 23:28, 32 **15** [c]See ch. 43:19 [a][See ver. 14 above] [r][See ver. 10 above] [d][ver. 11; Deut. 10:8] [e][ver. 7] **16** [f]See ch. 41:22 **17** [g]Ex. 28:39; 39:27 **19** [h]ch. 42:14 [i]Lev. 6:11 [j][ch. 46:20; Ex. 29:37; 30:29; Lev. 6:27] **20** [k]Lev. 21:5; [ch. 5:1] [l][Num. 6:5] **21** [m]Lev. 10:9 **22** [n]Lev. 21:7, 13, 14

44:4–9 While some portions of the Old Testament emphasize restrictions on the participation of foreigners in Israel's worship (Ex. 12:43; Lev. 22:25; Neh. 9:2; Jer. 51:51), other passages anticipate the participation of foreigners (47:22, 23; 1 Kin. 8:41, 43; 2 Chr. 6:32, 33; Is. 56:3, 6; cf. Zech. 14:21; Eph. 2:12, 19). Similar restrictions on foreigners characterize other writings from the period after the Babylonian exile (Ezra 4:1–3; 10:10–44; Neh. 13:1–9; Hag. 2:14). In the New Testament period there was a written warning at the entrance to the temple prohibiting Gentiles from entering the temple on pain of death (cf. Acts 21:26–30). In the New Israel of the new covenant, the church, all such distinctions between Jew and Gentile have been removed. Part of Christ's purpose was to destroy these barriers (Matt. 10:18; Luke 2:32; Acts 9:15; 10:28, 45; 11:1, 18; 13:46–48; Rom. 1:5, 16; 2:10; 3:29; 10:12; 15:16; Gal. 3:8, 28; Eph. 2:11–18; 3:6).

44:10–14 Though foreigners had served in the temple in the past (Josh. 9:3, 6, 21), they will no longer be allowed to enter. The tasks they had performed belonged to the Levites (Num. 1:50–53; 3:6, 8, 28–32; 1 Chr. 23:24–32; 2 Chr. 8:14, 15). Priestly families that had engaged in idolatry before the Babylonian exile (8:6) will now join their fellow Levites in the more menial tasks of the temple and as assistants to the priests. The priesthood itself will be restricted to the line of Zadok (v. 15; 40:45, 46).

44:15 Zadok. Zadok had served as high priest alongside Abiathar during the reign of David (2 Sam. 15:24–29; 20:25). Abiathar was dismissed because he had supported Adonijah against Solomon (1 Kin. 1:7; 2:26), but Zadok had supported Solomon and became the only high priest. The priesthood had earlier been restricted among the Levites to the descendants of Aaron (Ex. 28:1; Lev. 8:2–7; 9:1–24; Num. 20:25–28; 1 Chr. 6:48–53), and Ezekiel foresees a further restriction to one family from Aaron.

who is the widow of a priest. 23 [o]They shall teach my people the difference between the holy and the common, and [o]show them how to distinguish between the unclean and the clean. 24 [p]In a dispute, they shall act as judges, and they shall judge it according to my judgments. They shall keep my laws and my statutes in all my appointed feasts, and [q]they shall keep my Sabbaths holy. 25 [r]They shall not defile themselves by going near to a dead person. However, for father or mother, for son or daughter, for brother or unmarried sister they may defile themselves. 26 [s]After he has become clean, they shall count seven days for him. 27 And on the day that he goes into the Holy Place, [t]into the inner court, to minister in the Holy Place, [u]he shall offer his sin offering, declares the Lord GOD.

28 [v]"This shall be their inheritance: I am their inheritance: and [w]you shall give them no possession in Israel; I am their possession. 29 [x]They shall eat the grain offering, the sin offering, and the guilt offering, and [y]every devoted thing in Israel shall be theirs. 30 [z]And the first of all the firstfruits of all kinds, and every offering of all kinds from all your offerings, shall belong to the priests. [a]You shall also give to the priests the first of your dough, [b]that a blessing may rest on your house. 31 [c]The priests shall not eat of [d]anything, whether bird or beast, that has died of itself or is torn by wild animals.

The Holy District

45 "When [e]you allot the land as an inheritance, [f]you shall set apart for the LORD a portion of the land as a holy district, 25,000 cubits[1] long and 20,000[2] cubits broad. It shall be holy throughout its whole extent. 2 [g]Of this a square plot of 500 by 500 cubits shall be for the sanctuary, with fifty cubits for [h]an open space around it. 3 And [i]from this measured district you shall measure off a section 25,000 cubits long and 10,000 broad, [j]in which shall be the sanctuary, [k]the Most Holy Place. 4 [l]It shall be the holy portion of the land. It shall be for the priests, who minister in the sanctuary and approach the LORD to minister to him, and it shall be a place for their houses and a holy place for the sanctuary. 5 [m]Another section, 25,000 cubits long and 10,000 cubits broad, shall be for the Levites who minister at the temple, as their possession for cities to live in.[3]

6 "Alongside the portion set apart as the holy district [n]you shall assign for the property of the city an area 5,000 cubits broad and 25,000 cubits long. [o]It shall belong to the whole house of Israel.

The Portion for the Prince

7 [p]"And to [q]the prince shall belong the land on both sides of the holy district and the property of the city, alongside the holy district and the property of the city, on the west and on the east, corresponding in length to one of the tribal portions, and extending from the western to the eastern boundary 8 of the land. It is to be his property in Israel. And [r]my princes shall no more oppress my people, but [s]they shall let the house of Israel have the land according to their tribes.

9 "Thus says the Lord GOD: [t]Enough, O princes of Israel! Put away violence and oppression, and execute justice and righteousness. Cease [u]your evictions of my people, declares the Lord GOD.

10 [v]"You shall have just balances, a just ephah, and a just bath.[4] 11 The ephah and the bath shall be [w]of the same measure, [x]the bath containing one tenth of a homer,[5] and the ephah one tenth of a

23 [o][ch. 22:26]; See Lev. 10:10, 11
24 [p]Deut. 17:8, 9; [2 Chr. 19:8] [q][ch. 22:26]
25 [r]See Lev. 21:1-3
26 [s]Num. 19:11, 12
27 [t]ver. 17, 21 [u]ch. 40:39; 42:13; Lev. 4:2, 3
28 [v]See Num. 18:20 [w][ch. 45:4, 5]
29 [x]See Lev. 6:14-18, 25-29; 7:1-6 [y]Lev. 27:21, 28; Num. 18:14
30 [z]See Ex. 23:19 [a]See Num. 15:20 [b]Mal. 3:10
31 [c]Lev. 22:8; [Ex. 22:31]; See Lev. 7:24 [d]ch. 4:14
Chapter 45
1 [e][ch. 48:29]; See ch. 47:21, 22 [f]See ch. 48:8-10
2 [g]See ch. 42:16-20 [h][ch. 27:28; 48:15, 17]; See Lev. 25:34
3 [i][ver. 1] [j]ch. 48:10 [k]See ch. 41:4
4 [l][ch. 48:11, 12]
5 [m]ch. 48:13
6 [n]ch. 48:15 [o][ch. 48:18, 19]
7 [p]ch. 48:21 [q]See ch. 44:3
8 [r][ch. 22:27; 46:18] [s]ch. 47:13, 21; See ch. 48:1-7, 23-28
9 [t]ch. 44:6 [u][ch. 46:18]
10 [v]See Lev. 19:35, 36
11 [w][Deut. 25:14, 15] [x][Isai. 5:10]

1 A *cubit* was about 18 inches or 45 centimeters 2 Septuagint; Hebrew *ten* 3 Septuagint; Hebrew *as their possession, twenty chambers* 4 An *ephah* was about 3/5 of a bushel or 22 liters; a *bath* was about 6 gallons or 22 liters 5 A *homer* was about 6 bushels or 220 liters

44:24 judges. For the judicial role of the priests, see 1 Chr. 26:29; 2 Chr. 19:8–11.

44:25 dead person. Contact with death made a person unclean; priests, and especially the high priest, had to avoid such contact (Lev. 21:1–12).

44:31 eat. The prohibition against eating meat of an animal found dead applied to all Israel (Lev. 11:39, 40; Deut. 14:21).

45:1–8 The allocation of the land will be taken up in greater detail in ch. 47. The concern here is the sacred precincts. Ezekiel describes a sacred area in the middle of the land, a square about 8 miles (25,000 cubits) on a side, further subdivided into three strips of land (cf. Rev. 21:16). The northern zone (about 25 square miles) was set aside for the use of the Levites. The center zone contained the sanctuary and was set apart for the priests. The southern zone, about half the size of the other two, was given to the city itself. The area east and west of the 8-mile square was given to the prince, while the area north and south will be divided among the other tribes. Interestingly, in Ezekiel's vision the temple itself was outside the city proper.

45:10 just. Apparently the use of false weights and balances was common (Lev. 19:35, 36; Deut. 25:13–16; Prov. 11:1; Amos 8:5; Mic. 6:10–12).

ephah . . . bath. The ephah was a dry measure of about five gallons. The bath was a liquid measure of about six gallons.

45:11 homer. Ten baths or ephahs made a homer, or about fifty gallons.

homer; the homer shall be the standard
measure. **12**[y]The shekel shall be twenty
gerahs;[1] twenty shekels plus twenty-five
shekels plus fifteen shekels shall be your
mina.[2]
13[z]"This is the offering that you shall
make: one sixth of an ephah from each
homer of wheat, and one sixth of an ephah
from each homer of barley, **14**and as the
fixed portion of oil, measured in baths, one
tenth of a bath from each cor[3] (the cor, like
the homer, contains [a]ten baths).[4] **15**And
one sheep from every flock of two hundred,
from the watering places of Israel for grain
offering, burnt offering, and peace offerings, [b]to make atonement for them, declares the Lord GOD. **16**All the people of the
land shall be obliged to give this offering to
the prince in Israel. **17**[c]It shall be the
prince's duty to furnish the burnt offerings,
grain offerings, and drink offerings, at the
feasts, the new moons, and the Sabbaths,
all the appointed feasts of the house of
Israel: he shall provide the sin offerings,
grain offerings, burnt offerings, and peace
offerings, to make atonement on behalf of
the house of Israel.
18"Thus says the Lord GOD: In the first
month, [d]on the first day of the month, you
shall take a bull from the herd without
blemish, and [e]purify the sanctuary. **19**[f]The
priest shall take some of the blood of the
sin offering and put it [g]on the doorposts of
the temple, the four corners of the ledge of
the altar, and the posts of the gate of the
inner court. **20**You shall do the same on the
seventh day of the month for anyone who
has sinned through error or ignorance; so
you shall make atonement for the temple.
21[h]"In the first month, on the fourteenth
day of the month, you shall celebrate the
Feast of the Passover, and for seven days
unleavened bread shall be eaten. **22**On that
day the prince [i]shall provide for himself
and all the people of the land a young bull
for a sin offering. **23**And on [j]the seven days
of the festival he shall provide as a burnt
offering to the LORD seven young bulls and
seven rams without blemish, on each of the
seven days; and [k]a male goat daily for a sin
offering. **24**And [l]he shall provide as [m]a grain
offering an ephah for each bull, an ephah
for each ram, and a hin[5] of oil to each
ephah. **25**[n]In the seventh month, on the fifteenth day of the month and for the seven
days of the feast, [o]he shall make the same
provision for sin offerings, burnt offerings,
and grain offerings, and for the oil.

The Prince and the Feasts

46 "Thus says the Lord GOD: [p]The gate
of [q]the inner court that faces east
shall be shut on the six working days, but
on the Sabbath day it shall be opened, and
[r]on the day of the new moon it shall be
opened. **2**[s]The prince shall enter by the
vestibule of the gate from outside, and
shall take his stand by [t]the post of the gate.
[u]The priests shall offer his burnt offering
and his peace offerings, and he shall worship at [v]the threshold of the gate. Then he
shall go out, but the gate shall not be shut
until evening. **3**[w]The people of the land
shall bow down at the entrance of that gate
before the LORD on the Sabbaths and on
the new moons. **4**[x]The burnt offering that
the prince offers to the LORD [y]on the
Sabbath day shall be six lambs without
blemish and a ram without blemish. **5**And
[z]the grain offering with the ram shall be an
ephah,[6] and the grain offering with the
lambs shall be [a]as much as he is able,

[1] A *shekel* was about 2/5 ounce or 11 grams; a *gerah* was about 1/50 ounce or 0.6 gram [2] A *mina* was about 1 1/4 pounds or 0.6 kilogram [3] A *cor* was about 6 bushels or 220 liters [4] See Vulgate; Hebrew *(ten baths are a homer, for ten baths are a homer)* [5] A *hin* was about 4 quarts or 3.5 liters [6] An *ephah* was about 3/5 bushel or 22 liters

12[y]See Ex. 30:13 **13**[z]ch. 44:30 **14**[a]ver. 11 **15**[b]See Lev. 1:4 **17**[c][2 Chr. 30:24; 35:7]; See ch. 46:4-7 **18**[d][ch. 46:1, 3, 6] [e]Lev. 16:16; [ch. 43:20, 22, 23] **19**[f]See ch. 43:20 [g][Ex. 12:7] **21**[h]See Lev. 23:5 **22**[i][ver. 17] **23**[j]Lev. 23:8 [k]Num. 28:15 **24**[l]ch. 46:5, 7 [m]See Lev. 2:1 **25**[n]See Lev. 23:34 [o]See ver. 22-24

Chapter 46
1[p]ch. 45:19 [q]See ch. 8:16 [r][ch. 45:18] **2**[s]See ch. 44:3 [t][ch. 45:19] [u][ch. 40:38, 39] [v][ch. 9:3] **3**[w]ver. 9 **4**[x]ch. 45:17 [y][Num. 28:9, 10] **5**[z]ver. 14; ch. 45:24 [a][Deut. 16:17]

45:12 shekel . . . mina. A shekel was about two-fifths of an ounce; a mina of sixty shekels would be about a pound and a half. The mina was normally fifty shekels.

45:17 prince's duty. Israel's princes were also responsible to make offerings on behalf of the people (vv. 13–17). The people would give offerings in kind to the prince, who in turn provided them to the sanctuary (cf. 2 Chr. 30:24). See notes 37:24; 44:3.

45:18–25 These regulations cover aspects of the ceremonial observances in the first month (New Year's Day, vv. 18–20, and Passover, vv. 21–24) and seventh month (Tabernacles, v. 25). This legislation may have represented modifications of earlier liturgical practice. Once again, like Moses, Ezekiel provides religious and ceremonial law to Israel (see notes 43:10, 12).

45:19 altar. Compare the consecration of the altar in Ex. 29:35–37.

45:24 hin. A liquid measure of about one gallon.

46:2 prince. The prince will be allowed to enter as far as the inner threshold of the eastern gate into the inner courtyard on festival days; on other days he will enter and leave with the ordinary people (vv. 9, 10) unless he is making a freewill offering (v. 12). The prince has special privileges with reference to the eastern gate in the outer courtyard (44:1 note; 44:3 note). From his vantage point at the threshold of the inner gate, the prince will have a full view of the inner courtyard and the great altar; but entry to the inner court is restricted to priests and Levites.

46:4 burnt offering. The specifications for this offering differ from the Sabbath offerings in Num. 28:9, where two lambs and no ram are required.

together with a hin[1] of oil to each ephah.
6 On the day of the new moon he shall offer
a bull from the herd without blemish, and
six lambs and a ram, which shall be without blemish. 7 As a grain offering he shall
provide an ephah with the bull and an
ephah with the ram, and with the lambs
[b]as much as he is able, together with a hin
of oil to each ephah. 8 [c]When the prince
enters, he shall enter by the vestibule of the
gate, and he shall go out by the same way.
9 [d]"When the people of the land [e]come
before the LORD at the appointed feasts, he
who enters by the north gate to worship
shall go out by the south gate, and he who
enters by the south gate shall go out by the
north gate: no one shall return by way of
the gate by which he entered, but each
shall go out straight ahead. 10 When they
enter, [f]the prince shall enter with them,
and when they go out, he shall go out.
11 "At the feasts and the appointed festivals, [z]the grain offering with a young bull
shall be an ephah, and with a ram an
ephah, and with the lambs [b]as much as
one is able to give, together with a hin of
oil to an ephah. 12 When the prince provides [g]a freewill offering, either a burnt
offering or peace offerings as a freewill
offering to the LORD, [h]the gate facing east
shall be opened for him. And he shall offer
his burnt offering or his peace offerings [i]as
he does on the Sabbath day. Then he shall
go out, and after he has gone out the gate
shall be shut.
13 [j]"You shall provide a lamb a year old
without blemish for a burnt offering to the
LORD daily; morning by morning you shall
provide it. 14 And [k]you shall provide a
grain offering with it morning by morning,
one sixth of an ephah, and one third of a
hin of oil to moisten the flour, as a grain
offering to the LORD. This is a perpetual
statute. 15 Thus the lamb and the meal
offering and the oil shall be provided,
morning by morning, for [l]a regular burnt
offering.
16 "Thus says the Lord GOD: If the prince
makes a gift to any of his sons as his inheritance, it shall belong to his sons. It is their
property by inheritance. 17 But if he makes
a gift [m]out of his inheritance to one of his
servants, it shall be his to [n]the year of liberty. Then it shall revert to the prince; surely it is his inheritance—it shall belong to
his sons. 18 [o]The prince shall not take any of
the inheritance of the people, [p]thrusting
them out of their property. He shall give
his sons their inheritance out of his own
property, so that none of my people shall
be [q]scattered from his property."

Boiling Places for Offerings

19 Then he brought me through the
entrance, which was [r]at the side of the gate,
to the north row of [s]the holy chambers for
the priests, and behold, a place was there at
the extreme western end of them. 20 And he
said to me, "This is the place where the
priests [t]shall boil the guilt offering and
the sin offering, and where [u]they shall bake
the grain offering, in order not to bring
them out into the outer court and so [v]com-
municate holiness to the people."
21 Then he brought me out to the outer
court and led me around to the four corners
of the court. And behold, in each corner of
the court there was another court— 22 in the
four corners of the court were small[2] courts,
forty cubits[3] long and thirty broad; the four
were of the same size. 23 On the inside,
around each of the four courts was a row of
masonry, with hearths made at the bottom
of the rows all around. 24 Then he said to
me, "These are the kitchens where those
who [w]minister at the temple [t]shall boil the
sacrifices of the people."

7 [b]ver. 5
8 [c][ver. 2]
9 [d]ver. 3 [e][Deut. 16:16]; See Ex. 23:14-17
10 [f][Ps. 42:4]
11 [z][See ver. 5 above] [b][See ver. 7 above]
12 [g]Lev. 7:16; 22:23; Deut. 23:23 [h][ver. 1] [i][ver. 2]
13 [j]Ex. 29:38; Num. 28:3, 4
14 [k]ver. 5
15 [l]Num. 23:10, 15
17 [m][ch. 45:7] [n]See Lev. 25:10
18 [o][1 Sam. 8:14; 1 Kin. 21:3, 7] [p][ch. 45:8] [q][ch. 34:4, 5]
19 [r][ver. 1] [s][ch. 42:4]
20 [t]2 Chr. 35:13 [u][Lev. 2:4] [v]See ch. 44:19
24 [w]ch. 44:11 [t][See ver. 20 above]

1 A *hin* was about 4 quarts or 3.5 liters 2 Septuagint, Syriac, Vulgate; the meaning of the Hebrew word is uncertain 3 A *cubit* was about 18 inches or 45 centimeters

46:6 day of the new moon. The first day of the month. The specifications again differ from earlier legislation (Num. 28:11).

46:13 daily. Whereas most of the preceding regulations concerned offerings on particular days of the Old Testament liturgical calendar, God was to be worshiped in Israel every day (vv. 13–15). The provisions for these daily offerings differ from earlier practice (Num. 28:3–8; 2 Kin. 16:15; 1 Chr. 16:40; 2 Chr. 13:11; 31:3).

46:16–18 In redeeming Israel from Egypt and later Babylon, God removed them from the place of bondage, but also secured for them an inheritance in their own land. The land was supposed to be inalienable (Lev. 25:14–17, 23, 24; 1 Kin. 21), representing the permanence of the redemption and inheritance that God had provided (1 Pet. 1:4).

46:16 sons. Ezekiel envisaged the restoration of Davidic rule. See notes 37:24; 44:3.

46:17 year of liberty. This is most likely a reference to the Year of Jubilee (Lev. 25:8–17; 27:24; Is. 61:1, 2).

46:20 bake. Old Testament worship combined sacrifice and prayer with eating and social activity. These regulations specify the places where the Levites would prepare offerings for the sacrificial meals that are eaten by worshipers.

Water Flowing from the Temple

47 Then he brought me back to [x]the
door of the temple, and behold,
[y]water was issuing from below [z]the threshold of the temple toward the east (for the
temple faced east). The water was flowing
down from below the south end of the
threshold of the temple, south of [a]the altar.
2Then he brought me out by way of [b]the
north gate and led me around on the outside to [c]the outer gate that faces toward the
east; and behold, the water was trickling
out on the south side.
3Going on eastward with a measuring line
in his hand, [d]the man measured a thousand
cubits,[1] and then led me through the water,
and it was ankle-deep. **4**Again he measured
a thousand, and led me through the water,
and it was knee-deep. Again he measured a
thousand, and led me through the water,
and it was waist-deep. **5**Again he measured
a thousand, and it was a river that I could
not pass through, for the water had risen. It
was deep enough to swim in, a river that
could not be passed through. **6**And he said
to me, [e]"Son of man, [f]have you seen this?"
Then he led me back to the bank of the
river. **7**As I went back, I saw on the bank of
the river [g]very many trees on the one side
and on the other. **8**And he said to me,
"This water flows toward the eastern region
and goes down into [h]the Arabah, and
enters the sea;[2] when the water flows into
[i]the sea, the water will become fresh.[3] **9**And
wherever the river[4] goes, every living creature that swarms will live, and there will be
very many fish. For this water goes there,
that the waters of the sea[5] may become
fresh; so everything will live where the river
goes. **10**Fishermen will stand beside the
sea. From [j]Engedi to [k]Eneglaim it will be a
place for the spreading of nets. Its fish will
be of very many kinds, like the fish of [l]the
Great Sea.[6] **11**But its swamps and marshes
will not become fresh; they are to be left for
salt. **12**And on the banks, [m]on both sides of
the river, there will grow [n]all kinds of trees
for food. [o]Their leaves will not wither, nor
their fruit fail, [p]but they will bear fresh fruit
every month, because the water for them
flows from the sanctuary. Their fruit will be
for food, and [p]their leaves for healing."

Division of the Land

13Thus says the Lord GOD: "This is the
boundary[7] by which [q]you shall divide the
land for inheritance among the twelve
tribes of Israel. [r]Joseph shall have two portions. **14**And you shall divide equally what
[s]I swore [t]to give to your fathers. [u]This land
shall fall to you as your inheritance.
15"This shall be the boundary of the
land: On the north side, from [l]the Great

1 A *cubit* was about 18 inches or 45 centimeters 2 That is, the Dead Sea 3 Hebrew *will be healed*; also verses 9, 11 4 Septuagint, Syriac, Vulgate, Targum; Hebrew *two rivers* 5 Hebrew lacks *the waters of the sea* 6 That is, the Mediterranean Sea; also verses 15, 19, 20 7 Probable reading; Hebrew *The valley of the boundary*

Chapter 47
1 [x][ch. 43:1, 2] [y]Ps. 46:4; Joel 3:18; [Zech. 14:8; Rev. 22:1] [z]See ch. 9:3 [a]See ch. 43:13
2 [b]ch. 40:35 [c][ch. 40:6]
3 [d][ch. 40:3]
6 [e]See ch. 2:1 [f][ch. 8:6]
7 [g]ver. 12; [Rev. 22:2]
8 [h]See Deut. 1:1
[i]Deut. 3:17; 4:49; Josh. 3:16
10 [j]See 1 Sam. 23:29 [k]Isai. 15:8 [l]See Josh. 15:12
12 [m][ver. 7] [n][Gen. 2:9] [o]Ps. 1:3; [Jer. 17:8] [p][Rev. 22:2]
13 [q]ch. 45:8; See ch. 48:1-7, 23-28 [r][ch. 48:4, 5]; See Josh. 17:14-18
14 [s]See ch. 20:5 [t]See Gen. 12:7 [u][ch. 48:29]
15 [l][See ver. 10 above]

47:1, 2 The courtyard of the tabernacle had a large basin or laver where the priests washed (Ex. 30:17–21). In Solomon's temple there was a much larger Sea (1 Kin. 7:23–26). This Sea too was used for ritual washing (2 Chr. 4:6), but in addition it symbolized the primeval ocean, no longer as a menacing symbol of chaos (28:2 note), but subjected by God to the service of His temple. In Ezekiel's temple vision, these earlier basins are replaced by a life-giving river (Rev. 21:1; 22:1, 2). The tabernacle laver and the temple Sea stood south of the altar in the sanctuary courtyard; the river too originates from south of the altar. This passage should be compared with others that speak of a river in the city of God (Ps. 46:4), or describe the eruption of a stream in the city (Joel 3:18; Zech. 14:3–8). Since the temple in part symbolized paradise, Ezekiel's river recalls the rivers issuing from the Garden of Eden (Gen. 2:10–14).

47:3–12 The river brings life everywhere it goes, transforming Israel into a paradisal garden. Jerusalem is built on a geological watershed on top of a ridge of hills. Rain falling there flows into the Kidron Valley and makes its way into the Dead Sea. Jesus appealed to the images used in this passage to describe Himself. He told the Samaritan woman that He was the source of life-giving water (John 4:10–14). When the disciples were surprised that Jesus was talking with a Samaritan woman, He spoke to them of an unending harvest that had already begun (John 4:27–38), in effect drawing on Ezekiel's picture of trees bearing twelve crops a year. John also records Jesus' saying that He is the source of streams of living water, adding the comment that Jesus was speaking of God's Spirit (John 7:37–39).

47:10 Engedi. On the western shore of the Dead Sea (Josh. 15:62; 1 Sam. 23:29; 2 Chr. 20:2). **Eneglaim.** Near the northwest corner of the Dead Sea.

47:11 swamps and marshes. That the swamps and marshes would be left for salt may show familiarity with the tradition that the shallow southern reaches of the Dead Sea were the sites of the ancient cities of Sodom and Gomorrah (Gen. 19:27–29).

47:13 Joseph shall have two portions. In Ezekiel's vision the land would be divided equally among the twelve tribes. Since the tribe of Levi received its territorial inheritance inside the sacred precincts of Jerusalem (45:1–8 note), the number twelve was maintained by substituting for Joseph the two sons of Joseph, Ephraim and Manasseh (Gen. 48:1–6).

47:14 your inheritance. This is the land God promised to the patriarchs (Gen. 12:7; 15:18–21; 22:17; 28:4), and that was possessed during the reigns of David and Solomon (1 Kin. 8:65; 1 Chr. 13:5; 2 Chr. 9:26).

47:15 boundary. The boundaries detailed here (vv. 15–20) mention a number of sites that are not known, but they roughly correspond to other such lists (Num. 34:1–12; 1 Kin. 8:65). However, the allocation of the land (ch. 48) is quite different from the historical boundaries of the tribes. The eastern and western boundaries are easy to identify: on the east, the boundary began in the headwaters of the Jordan south of Damascus, down the Jordan River, and along the western shore of the Dead Sea; on the west, the border was the Mediterranean Sea. The northern and southern borders are more difficult to establish: in the north, the line began near Tyre and proceeded east to a point north of the Sea of Galilee; in the south, it ran from a point below the Dead Sea to the Brook of Egypt (the Wadi el-Arish) on the Mediterranean coast.

Sea [v]by way of Hethlon to Lebo-hamath,
and on to [w]Zedad,[1] 16 [x]Berothah, Sibraim
(which lies on the border between
[y]Damascus and [v]Hamath), as far as Hazer-
hatticon, which is on the border of Hauran.
17 So the boundary shall run from the sea to
[z]Hazar-enan, which is on the northern border of Damascus, with the border of
Hamath to the north.[2] This shall be the
north side.[3]
18 "On the east side, the boundary shall
run between Hauran and Damascus; along
the Jordan between [a]Gilead and the land of
Israel; to [b]the eastern sea and as far as
Tamar.[4] This shall be the east side.
19 "On the south side, it shall run from
[c]Tamar as far as [d]the waters of Meribah-
kadesh, from there along [e]the Brook of
Egypt[5] to [f]the Great Sea. This shall be the
south side.
20 "On the west side, the Great Sea shall
be the boundary to a point [v]opposite Lebo-
hamath. This shall be the west side.
21 [g]"So you shall divide this land among
you according to the tribes of Israel. 22 [h]You
shall allot it as an inheritance for yourselves and [i]for the sojourners who reside
among you and have had children among
you. [j]They shall be to you as native-born
children of Israel. With you they shall be
allotted an inheritance among the tribes of
Israel. 23 In whatever tribe the sojourner
resides, there you shall assign him his
inheritance, declares the Lord GOD.

48 "These are the names of the tribes:
Beginning at the northern extreme,
beside [k]the way of Hethlon [l]to Lebo-
hamath, as far as [m]Hazar-enan (which is on
the northern border of [n]Damascus over
against Hamath), and[6] extending from the
east side to the west,[7] [o]Dan, one portion.
2 Adjoining the territory of Dan, from the
east side to the west, [o]Asher, one portion.
3 Adjoining the territory of Asher, from the
east side to the west, [o]Naphtali, one portion. 4 Adjoining the territory of Naphtali,
from the east side to the west, Manasseh,
one portion. 5 Adjoining the territory of
Manasseh, from the east side to the west,
Ephraim, one portion. 6 Adjoining the territory of Ephraim, from the east side to the
west, Reuben, one portion. 7 Adjoining the
territory of Reuben, from the east side to
the west, Judah, one portion.
8 "Adjoining the territory of Judah, from
the east side to the west, shall be [p]the portion which you shall set apart, 25,000
cubits[8] in breadth, and in length equal to
one of the tribal portions, from the east
side to the west, with [q]the sanctuary in the
midst of it. 9 The portion that you shall set
apart for the LORD shall be 25,000 cubits in
length, and 20,000[9] in breadth. 10 [r]These
shall be the allotments of the holy portion:
the priests shall have an allotment measuring 25,000 cubits on the northern side,
10,000 cubits in breadth on the western
side, 10,000 in breadth on the eastern side,
and 25,000 in length on the southern side,
with the sanctuary of the LORD in the midst
of it. 11 This shall be for [s]the consecrated
priests, [t]the sons of Zadok, who kept my
charge, who did not go astray when the
people of Israel went astray, [u]as the Levites
did. 12 And it shall belong to them as a special portion from the holy portion of the
land, a most holy place, adjoining the territory of the Levites. 13 [v]And alongside the
territory of the priests, the Levites shall
have an allotment 25,000 cubits in length
and 10,000 in breadth. The whole length

1 Septuagint; Hebrew *the entrance of Zedad, Hamath* 2 The meaning of the Hebrew is uncertain 3 Probable reading; Hebrew *and as for the north side* 4 Compare Syriac; Hebrew *you shall measure* 5 Hebrew lacks *of Egypt* 6 Probable reading; Hebrew *and they shall be his* 7 Septuagint (compare verses 2-8); Hebrew *the east side the west* 8 A *cubit* was about 18 inches or 45 centimeters 9 Compare 45:1; Hebrew *ten*

15 [v]ch. 48:1 [w]Num. 34:8
16 [x]2 Sam. 8:8 [y]ch. 48:1; Isai. 7:8 [v][See ver. 15 above]
17 [z][ch. 48:1]
18 [a]Josh. 13:11 [b]Joel 2:20
19 [c]Gen. 14:7; 2 Chr. 20:2 [d]Num. 20:13 [e]Num. 34:5 [f]See Josh. 15:12
20 [v][See ver. 15 above]
21 [g]ver. 13
22 [h]ch. 45:1; 48:29 [i]Isai. 14:1; [Eph. 3:6] [j]Ex. 12:19, 48, 49; [Rom. 10:12; Gal. 3:28; Col. 3:11]
Chapter 48
1 [k]ch. 47:15 [l]ch. 47:20; See 1 Kin. 8:65 [m][ch. 47:17] [n]ch. 47:16, 17, 18 [o]Num. 2:25-31
2 [o][See ver. 1 above]
3 [o][See ver. 1 above]
8 [p]See ch. 45:1-6 [q]ver. 21
10 [r]ch. 45:4
11 [s]ch. 44:15 [t]See ch. 40:46 [u]ch. 44:10
13 [v]ch. 45:5

48:1–29 In Ezekiel's vision the allotment of the land among the tribes is different from what it was historically. Each tribe is allotted a horizontal strip of land connecting with the eastern and western borders. The status of Jacob's wives and of the individual tribes seem to be the determining factors in the arrangement of the tribes; cf. Num. 2; 3. The northernmost tribes (Dan, Asher, and Naphtali) were traditionally located in the north; the southernmost tribe (Gad, v. 27) was historically a northern tribe. These four tribes are the sons of Leah's servant Zilpah and Rachel's servant Bilhah (Gen. 30:3–8, 10–13); as such they are located at the outer extremities of the tribal allotments in Ezekiel's vision.

Judah is the closest tribe north of the sacred area in the center of the land (vv. 8–22; 45:1–8). Judah was historically a southern tribe; by presenting the tribe of David as part of the northern tribes, Ezekiel may be saying in effect that the North will have a portion in David (cf. 2 Sam. 20:1; 1 Kin. 12:16; 2 Chr. 10:16). Judah is in the place of honor that would have belonged to the firstborn Reuben; Reuben is immediately north of Judah. Next are the two tribes of Joseph, Ephraim and Manasseh, descendants of Jacob through the favored wife Rachel.

The nearest tribe south of the sacred area is Benjamin. Its favored place reflects the favored status of Rachel and balances the favored position of the Joseph tribes in the north. The remaining three southern tribes (Simeon, Issachar, and Zebulun) are the descendants of Leah; Issachar, Zebulun, and Benjamin historically held allotments in the north.

48:8–22 This description is an elaboration of 45:1–8.

48:11 sons of Zadok. See note 44:15.

shall be 25,000 cubits and the breadth
20,000.[1] 14 They [w]shall not sell or exchange
any of it. They shall not alienate [x]this
choice portion of the land, for it is holy to
the LORD.
15 [y]"The remainder, 5,000 cubits in
breadth and 25,000 in length, shall be [z]for
common use for the city, for dwellings and
for [a]open country. In the midst of it shall
be the city, 16 and these shall be its measurements: [b]the north side 4,500 cubits,
the south side 4,500, the east side 4,500,
and the west side 4,500. 17 And the city
shall have open land: on the north 250
cubits, on the south 250, on the east 250,
and on the west 250. 18 The remainder of
the length alongside the holy portion shall
be 10,000 cubits to the east, and 10,000 to
the west, and it shall be alongside the holy
portion. [c]Its produce shall be food for the
workers of the city. 19 And the workers of
the city, from all the tribes of Israel, shall
till it. 20 The whole portion that [d]you shall
set apart shall be 25,000 cubits square,
that is, the holy portion together with the
property of the city.
21 [e]"What remains on both sides of the
holy portion and of the property of the city
shall belong to the prince. Extending from
the 25,000 cubits of the holy portion to the
east border, and westward from the 25,000
cubits to the west border, parallel to the
tribal portions, it shall belong to the
prince. [f]The holy portion with the sanctuary of the temple shall be in its midst. 22 It
shall be separate from the property of the
Levites and the property of the city, which
are in the midst of that which belongs to
the prince. The portion of the prince shall
lie between the territory of Judah and the
territory of Benjamin.

14 [w][Lev. 27:10, 28, 33] [x][ch. 44:30]
15 [y]ch. 45:6 [z]See ch. 42:20 [a][ch. 27:28; 45:2]
16 [b][ver. 20; Rev. 21:16]
18 [c][ch. 45:6]
20 [d][ch. 40:47]
21 [e]ch. 45:7 [f]ver. 8, 10

28 [g]ch. 47:19 [h]ch. 47:10; See Josh. 15:12
29 [i]ch. 47:22
30 [j]Num. 34:4, 5, 8, 9, 12; Josh. 15:4, 7, 11 [k][ver. 16]
31 [l][Rev. 21:12, 13] [m]See Deut. 33:6-8
35 [n]Isai. 60:14; [Jer. 23:6; 33:16] [o]ch. 35:10; Jer. 3:17; Joel 3:21; [Zech. 2:10; Rev. 21:3]

23 "As for the rest of the tribes: from the
east side to the west, Benjamin, one portion. 24 Adjoining the territory of Benjamin,
from the east side to the west, Simeon,
one portion. 25 Adjoining the territory of
Simeon, from the east side to the west, Issachar, one portion. 26 Adjoining the territory of Issachar, from the east side to the
west, Zebulun, one portion. 27 Adjoining
the territory of Zebulun, from the east side
to the west, Gad, one portion. 28 And adjoining the territory of Gad to the south,
the boundary shall run [g]from Tamar to the
waters of [g]Meribah-kadesh, from there
along the Brook of Egypt[2] to [h]the Great
Sea.[3] 29 This is the land that [i]you shall allot
as an inheritance among the tribes of Israel,
and these are their portions, declares the
Lord GOD.

The Gates of the City

30 "These shall be [j]the exits of the city: On
the north side, which is to be [k]4,500 cubits
by measure, 31 [l]three gates, the gate of
[m]Reuben, the gate of [m]Judah, and the gate
of [m]Levi, the gates of the city being named
after the tribes of Israel. 32 On the east side,
which is to be 4,500 cubits, three gates, the
gate of Joseph, the gate of Benjamin, and
the gate of Dan. 33 On the south side, which
is to be 4,500 cubits by measure, three
gates, the gate of Simeon, the gate of Issachar, and the gate of Zebulun. 34 On the
west side, which is to be 4,500 cubits, three
gates,[4] the gate of Gad, the gate of Asher,
and the gate of Naphtali. 35 The circumference of the city shall be 18,000 cubits. And
[n]the name of the city from that time on
shall be, [o]The LORD is there."

1 Septuagint; Hebrew *10,000* 2 Hebrew lacks *of Egypt* 3 That is, the Mediterranean Sea 4 One Hebrew manuscript, Syriac (compare Septuagint); most Hebrew manuscripts *their gates three*

48:30–35 The city has twelve gates named for the twelve tribes (cf. Rev. 21:12–14). Since one gate is named after Levi, Ephraim and Manasseh are replaced by their father Joseph.

48:35 The LORD is there. From the beginning of the Old Testament God had revealed His intention to be with His people. He walked and spoke with them in the Garden of Eden and dwelled in sanctuaries built in their midst. The promise of a child named Immanuel pointed to a day when God would be "with us" (Is. 7:14 text note). The New Testament ends in much the same way as the Book of Ezekiel ends. John too describes the city of God, and a time when God will live with human beings (Rev. 21:3); he ends with the prayer, "Amen. Come, Lord Jesus" (Rev. 22:20).

THE BOOK OF

Daniel

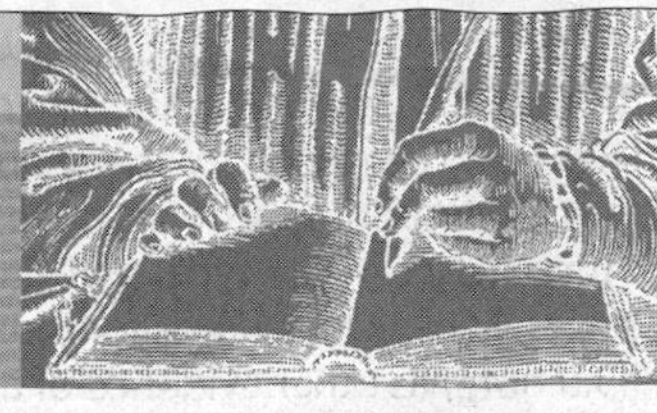

AUTHOR

The authorship and date of the Book of Daniel have been matters of considerable debate among biblical scholars. The dispute centers on the way Daniel's prophecies and visions look forward to a succession of four ancient empires, beginning with the Babylonian (chs. 2; 7; 11). Daniel describes in great detail the historical relations between the Seleucid and Ptolemaic kingdoms just prior to and during the time of Antiochus IV Epiphanes (ch. 11). To account for this detailed knowledge, many scholars conclude that the book must have been written by an unknown author about 170 B.C., during the lifetime of Antiochus IV Epiphanes and not during the time of Daniel, who was taken to Babylon in 605 B.C. However, representations in the book itself indicate that Daniel was its author (9:2; 10:2) and that it was written shortly after the capture of Babylon by Cyrus in 539 B.C. Also, Jesus quotes the prediction of "the abomination of desolation" found in this book as having been "spoken of by the prophet Daniel" (Matt. 24:15).

DATE AND OCCASION

The arguments that have been offered for dating the Book of Daniel during the time of Antiochus IV Epiphanes involve three basic issues: (a) the nature of Old Testament prophecy; (b) historical problems; and (c) the Hebrew and Aramaic language in the book. Each of these topics needs to be considered in turn.

Generally speaking, the prophets of Israel were primarily concerned with the religious and social circumstances confronting their contemporaries, rather than with predicting events in the distant future. When the prophets did predict future events, it was normally of incidents in the near term, such as Jeremiah's prophecies about the imminent fall of Jerusalem to the Babylonians. Daniel's vision concerning the "king of the north" and the "king of the south" parallels exactly the history of relations between the Seleucid and Ptolemaic empires existing at the time of Antiochus IV Epiphanes (11:2–39 and notes), while the description of the circumstances surrounding the death of the king (11:40–12:3) does not correspond to what is otherwise known about Antiochus's death. On this basis some scholars argue that the Book of Daniel was written in Antiochus's time, shortly before his death. However, the idea that Israelite prophets did not predict events in the more distant future depends on the assumption that the prophecies in Daniel are late, as also those of Isaiah concerning Cyrus (Is. 44:28; 45:1). It may also be the result of a rejection of prophecy in general.

Interpreters of the Book of Daniel who favor a late date of writing also propose that there are serious historical problems in the narratives about Daniel's experiences in Babylon, particularly concerning Belshazzar's relationship to Nebuchadnezzar (5:2 note) and the identity of "Darius the Mede" (6:1 note). They identify the four kingdoms foreseen by Daniel (chs. 2; 7) as the Babylonians, the Medes, the Persians, and finally the Greeks (including the Seleucids and Ptolemies). This identification is difficult because there is no evidence for a Median kingdom in an interval between the Babylonian and Persian kingdoms. Cyrus, the Persian king (550–530 B.C.), conquered the Medes in 549 B.C. and the Babylonians in 539 B.C. (5:1, 31 notes).

On the other hand, scholars who date the book in the time of Daniel interpret the sequence of kingdoms as the Babylonian, Medo-Persian, Greek, and finally Roman empires. They point to the reference to "the Medes and Persians" in 5:28 as evidence that Daniel considered them as together constituting one kingdom.

Concerning the date of the language used in Daniel, it first must be noted that a large segment

(2:4–7:28) is written in Aramaic rather than Hebrew. The reason for the change of language is not known. Some scholars have argued that the Aramaic is of a late type, pointing to the use of several Greek loanwords for musical instruments (3:5 note) as other evidence of a late date. Neither argument is convincing. There is abundant evidence of contacts between the Greeks and the Near East prior to the time of Alexander the Great. Such contacts are sufficient to explain the appearance of the Greek loanwords. The Aramaic and Hebrew of Daniel can be dated anywhere between the late sixth and early second centuries B.C. In other words, the language does not lend much weight to either the early or the late date proposal.

INTERPRETIVE DIFFICULTIES

The authorship and date of Daniel are not the only interpretive difficulties posed by the book. There are significant variations in overall approach to the book. These variations fall into three main categories. The first approach is taken by those who conclude that the book was written in the time of Antiochus Epiphanes. According to this view all references to events before the time of Antiochus are ordinary history, written after the events described. The only genuine prediction in the book would be of the anticipated death of Antiochus and the expected intervention of God to establish His kingdom. However, Antiochus did not die in the manner depicted (11:36–12:3 note) and the kingdom did not materialize as apparently anticipated. See notes 2:44; 7:14, 18.

A second, more traditional view finds the primary stress of the predictions of the book to be on the First Advent of Christ. This approach is usually associated with an amillennial or postmillennial eschatological position.

A third view finds one focus of the book to be primarily on Antiochus Epiphanes and the persecution of God's people during his reign. The other focus is on the divine intervention in human affairs at the end of time when God's kingdom is established. Stress does not fall on the First Advent of Christ (chs. 2; 9 notes), but rather on Antiochus and the Second Coming of Christ. This approach is usually associated with a premillennial eschatological position. Within this approach there are many differences in the interpretation of details by various commentators.

CHARACTERISTICS AND THEMES

Daniel contains two different types of material. Six historical narratives are found in chs. 1–6, while four visions are found in chs. 7–12. The visions are almost exclusively predictive. Among the six narratives, ch. 2 contains a vision given to Nebuchadnezzar and Daniel's interpretation of it.

Reflection on the content of the historical narratives reveals that they are not a connected historical discourse, but are independent units placed together for a specific purpose. The narratives do not give a history of Israel under Babylonian or Persian rule, nor do they give a biographical history of Daniel or his friends. The common thread is an emphasis on the way the absolute sovereignty of God operates in the affairs of all nations (2:47; 3:17, 18; 4:28–37; 5:18–31; 6:25–28). Jerusalem may be destroyed with its temple in ruins, God's people may be in exile, and wicked rulers may seem triumphant, but God remains supreme. God is greater than all circumstances, and His people should be true to Him in whatever situation they find themselves. Depiction of this truth is the controlling principle of Dan. 1–6.

Nebuchadnezzar's vision in ch. 2 shows that history is not under the control of other gods, nor can its mystery be discovered by human manipulation. History is under the control of the God who is utterly free to direct it and to reveal it as He pleases (Rev. 5:9). According to His sovereign pleasure He will intervene among the kingdoms of this world and establish a universal kingdom that will endure forever.

The visions (chs. 7–12) contain predictions of times in the future when this truth will be of particular importance for God's people. Although the Jews were persecuted during the time of their subjection to Babylonian and Persian rulers, there was no widespread and systematic attempt to abolish their faith. This did not happen until the time of Antiochus IV, who named himself "Epiphanes," meaning "God manifest," and ruled in the Seleucid Empire from 175–164 B.C. Antiochus tried to force the Jews to accept the culture of Hellenism and to abandon their religious practices. Many Jews submitted, but others refused and suffered severe persecution. One of the major reasons for writing the Book of Daniel was to prepare God's people for the time of Antiochus Epiphanes and to give them encouragement for this period of persecution. At the same time the book looks beyond the time of Antiochus Epiphanes to the coming of Christ. It is Christ who will destroy all human kingdoms and establish His eternal kingdom of righteousness and peace.

In addition to these overarching themes of Daniel, certain key concepts are relevant to discussion of the book. One of these is the "time of trouble" (12:1), commonly taken to be the "great tribulation" that is to precede the Second Advent of Christ (Matt. 24:21; Luke 21:23; Rev. 2:22; 7:14). Matthew links this trouble with "the abomination of desolation" (Matt. 24:15) predicted by Daniel (cf. Dan. 9:27; 12:11) and fulfilled by the Antichrist (the "man of lawlessness" in 2 Thess. 2:3, 4).

The "Antichrist" may also be included in Daniel's theology (Dan. 7:8, 20–22, 24–27; 11:36–45). The word does not occur outside the letters of John (1 John 2:18, 22; 4:3; 2 John 7), but references to a person of satanic hatred who appears in the final days of human history before Christ's Second Advent are found in both testaments. The Antichrist sets up the "abomination that makes desolate" (Dan. 11:31; cf. Matt. 24:15), exalts himself as a god (Dan. 11:36–39; 2 Thess. 2:3, 4) and is ultimately destroyed by Christ upon His return (Dan. 11:45; 2 Thess. 2:8 [cf. Is. 11:4]; Rev. 19:20).

The idea of the millennium also occurs in discussions of Daniel. The term "millennium" is derived from the Latin word for "one thousand" and designates the thousand-year period described in Rev. 20. The nature of the thousand years is understood differently by three general schools of interpretation, classified as follows: (a) Premillennialists believe that the thousand years is a worldwide kingdom of peace and righteousness on earth to be established on earth after the Second Coming of Christ (Is. 2:1–5; 11:1–10). (b) Postmillennialists believe that the thousand years is a period of peace and righteousness to be established through the worldwide preaching of the gospel, resulting in the conditions described in passages such as Is. 2:1–5; 11:1–10. (c) Amillennialists consider the thousand years as a figurative reference to the present age of the gospel. Accordingly, the millennium is not viewed as a future political order, but the spiritual kingdom of Christ's rule in the church.

In the postmillennial and amillennial views, the number "one thousand" is usually taken figuratively to mean a large unit of time rather than precisely 1,000 years.

OUTLINE OF DANIEL

I. The Narratives (chs. 1–6)

- A. *God's Vindication of Daniel and His Friends for Their Faithfulness (ch. 1)*
- B. *Daniel's Interpretation of Nebuchadnezzar's Dream (ch. 2)*
- C. *God's Deliverance of Daniel's Friends from the Fiery Furnace (ch. 3)*
- D. *God's Judgment on Nebuchadnezzar (ch. 4)*
- E. *God's Judgment on Belshazzar (ch. 5)*
- F. *God's Deliverance of Daniel from the Lions' Den (ch. 6)*

II. Daniel's Visions (chs. 7–12)

- A. *Vision of the Four Beasts and the Establishment of God's Kingdom (ch. 7)*
- B. *Vision of the Ram and the Goat (ch. 8)*
- C. *Vision of the Seventy Weeks (ch. 9)*
- D. *Vision of the Angel and the Future History of God's People (chs. 10–12)*
    1. The Angel's Message to Daniel (10:1–11:1)
    2. Near Eastern History from the Time of Daniel to Antiochus IV Epiphanes (11:2–20)
    3. The Rule of Antiochus IV Epiphanes (11:21–35)
        - a. *His Accession and Character (11:21–24)*
        - b. *His Career (11:25–31)*
        - c. *The Destiny of God's People During His Rule (11:32–35)*
    4. The Rule of the Antichrist (11:36–12:3)
        - a. *His Character (11:36–39)*
        - b. *His Activities (11:40–45)*
        - c. *The Destiny of God's People During His Rule (12:1–3)*
    5. A Final Message to Daniel (12:4–13)

Daniel Taken to Babylon

1 In the third year of [a]the reign of
Jehoiakim king of Judah, Nebuchadnezzar king of Babylon came to
Jerusalem and besieged it. 2 And the Lord
gave Jehoiakim king of Judah into his
hand, with some of [b]the vessels of the
house of God. And he brought them to
[c]the land of Shinar, to the house of his
god, [d]and placed the vessels in the treasury of his god. 3 Then the king commanded Ashpenaz, [e]his chief eunuch, to bring
some of the people of Israel, both of the
royal family[1] and of [f]the nobility, 4 youths
without [g]blemish, of good appearance and
[h]skillful in all wisdom, endowed with
knowledge, understanding learning, and
competent to stand in the king's palace,
and to [i]teach them the literature and language of the [j]Chaldeans. 5 The king
assigned them a daily portion of [k]the food
that the king ate, and of [l]the wine that he
drank. They were to be educated for
[m]three years, and at the end of that time
they were to [n]stand before the king.
6 Among these were [o]Daniel, [p]Hananiah,
[p]Mishael, and [p]Azariah of the tribe of
Judah. 7 And [e]the chief of the eunuchs [q]gave
them names: [r]Daniel he called Belteshazzar, Hananiah he called Shadrach,
Mishael he called Meshach, and Azariah he
called Abednego.

Chapter 1
1 [a]2 Kin. 24:1, 2; 2 Chr. 36:6
2 [b]ch. 5:2; 2 Kin. 24:13; 2 Chr. 36:7, 10; [Jer. 27:18] [c]Gen. 11:2; Zech. 5:11 [d]2 Chr. 36:7; Ezra 5:14
3 [e][2 Kin. 20:18; Isai. 39:7] [f]Esth. 1:3
4 [g][Lev. 24:19, 20; 2 Sam. 14:25] [h][ver. 17; ch. 9:22] [i][Isai. 47:10] [j]ch. 2:2, 4, 5, 10; 3:8; 4:7; 5:7, 11
5 [k]ch. 11:26 [l]ver. 8:16 [m][ver. 18] [n][ch. 2:2; 1 Kin. 10:8]; See Gen. 41:46
6 [o]Ezek. 14:14, 20; Matt. 24:15 [p]ch. 2:17
7 [e][See ver. 3 above] [q][2 Kin. 23:34; 24:17] [r]ch. 2:26; 4:8, 9, 18, 19; 5:12; 10:1
8 [s]2 Cor. 9:7 [t][Lev. 3:17; Ezek. 4:13; Hos. 9:3] [k][See ver. 5 above] [l][See ver. 5 above]

Daniel's Faithfulness

8 But Daniel [s]resolved that he would not
[t]defile himself with [k]the king's food, or with
[l]the wine that he drank. Therefore he asked
the chief of the eunuchs to allow him not to
[t]defile himself. 9 [u]And God gave Daniel favor
and compassion in the sight of the chief of
the eunuchs, 10 and the chief of the eunuchs
said to Daniel, "I fear my lord the king, who
assigned your food and your drink; for why
should he see that you were in worse condition than the youths who are of your own
age? So you would endanger my head with
the king." 11 Then Daniel said to the steward
whom the chief of the eunuchs had assigned
over Daniel, Hananiah, Mishael, and
Azariah, 12 "Test your servants for [v]ten days;
let us be given vegetables to eat and water to
drink. 13 Then let our appearance and the
appearance of the youths who eat [k]the king's
food be observed by you, and deal with your
servants according to what you see." 14 So he
listened to them in this matter, and tested
them for ten days. 15 At the end of ten days it
was seen that they were better in appearance
and fatter in flesh than all the youths who ate
the king's food. 16 [w]So the steward took away
their food and the wine they were to drink,
and gave them [x]vegetables.

9 [u][Gen. 39:21; Ps. 106:46; Prov. 16:7] 12 [v][Rev. 2:10] 13 [k][See ver. 7 above] 16 [w]ver. 11 [x]ver. 12

1 Hebrew *of the seed of the kingdom*

1:1 the third year. Jehoiakim's third year was 605 B.C. In that year Nebuchadnezzar defeated a coalition of Assyria and Egypt at Carchemish and initiated Babylon's rise to international power. After the battle of Carchemish, Nebuchadnezzar advanced against Jehoiakim (2 Kin. 24:1, 2; 2 Chr. 36:5–7) and took some Judeans captive, including Daniel. This was the first of three invasions of Judah by Nebuchadnezzar. The second was in 597 B.C. (2 Kin. 24:10–14), and the third in 587 B.C. (2 Kin. 25:1–24). In the Book of Jeremiah, Nebuchadnezzar's attack is dated to Jehoiakim's fourth year instead of the third (Jer 25:1; 46:2). The difference of one year occurs because in the Babylonian chronology, which Daniel apparently used, the king's reign was officially counted from the first day of the succeeding new year, rather than from the actual date of his accession to the throne.

Nebuchadnezzar king of Babylon. Nebuchadnezzar led the Babylonians to victory at Carchemish as crown prince and commander of the army. Shortly after this victory, he assumed the Babylonian throne when his father Nabopolassar died (626–605 B.C.). Nebuchadnezzar's reign (605–562 B.C.) is the historical context for much of Jeremiah, Ezekiel, and Daniel.

1:2 the Lord gave . . . into his hand. Israel's defeat by the Babylonians is not to be explained simply by analysis of military and political factors. God was at work in the affairs of the nations, and He used the Babylonians to judge His own people for their transgressions (2 Kin. 17:15, 18–20; 21:12–15; 24:3, 4).

the treasury of his god. Marduk (or Bel) was the chief god of the Babylonian pantheon (cf. Jer. 50:2).

1:4 literature and language of the Chaldeans. Babylonian literature was written in wedge-shaped characters impressed with a stylus on soft clay tablets that were later fired to make them permanent. Thousands of these tablets have been discovered by archaeologists. The Babylonians worshiped many gods, and their culture was filled with magic, sorcery, and astrology. The common language of Babylon was Aramaic (2:4 and note).

1:5 the food that the king ate. Jehoiachin later received such a provision under the rule of the Babylonian king, Evil-merodach (2 Kin. 25:27–30).

1:6 Daniel, Hananiah, Mishael, and Azariah. In these Hebrew names, the component *el* means "God," and *yah* is a form of God's name "Yahweh" (Ps. 50:1 note). Hence: Daniel means "my judge is God"; Hananiah, "Yahweh is gracious"; Mishael, "Who is what God is?" and Azariah, "Yahweh has helped."

1:7 Belteshazzar . . . Shadrach . . . Meshach . . . Abednego. Suggestions for the meanings of these names include: Belteshazzar, "May Bel protect his life"; Shadrach, "the command of Aku," (the Sumerian moon god); Meshach, "Who is what Aku is?" and Abednego, "servant of Nebo" (a Babylonian god). Bel is another name for Marduk, the chief Babylonian god (cf. 4:8).

1:8 he would not defile himself. The reason for Daniel's conclusion that he and his friends would be defiled by the king's food is not given. Perhaps it involved violation of the dietary laws of Moses (Lev. 11; 17).

1:15 they were better in appearance. The obedience of Daniel and his friends to God, and their refusal to compromise their faith in a heathen environment, were rewarded with God's blessing (cf. Deut. 8:3; Matt. 4:4).

17 As for these four youths, [y]God gave
them learning and [z]skill in all literature and
wisdom, and Daniel had [a]understanding in
all visions and dreams. 18 At the end of [b]the
time, when the king had commanded that
they should be brought in, the chief of the
eunuchs brought them in before Nebuchadnezzar. 19 And the king spoke with
them, and among all of them none was
found like Daniel, Hananiah, Mishael, and
Azariah. Therefore [c]they stood before the
king. 20 And in every matter of wisdom and
understanding about which the king
inquired of them, he found them ten times
better than all [d]the magicians and [e]en-
chanters that were in all his kingdom.
21 And Daniel [f]was there until the first year
of [g]King Cyrus.

Nebuchadnezzar's Dream

2 In the second year of the reign of
Nebuchadnezzar, Nebuchadnezzar
had dreams; [h]his spirit was troubled, and
[i]his sleep left him. 2 Then the king commanded that [d]the magicians, [e]the
enchanters, the [j]sorcerers, and [k]the Chaldeans be summoned to tell the king his
dreams. So they came in and [l]stood before
the king. 3 And the king said to them, "I
had a dream, and [h]my spirit is troubled to
know the dream." 4 Then [k]the Chaldeans
said to the king in Aramaic,[1] [m]"O king, live
forever! Tell your servants the dream, and
we will show the interpretation." 5 The king
answered and said to [k]the Chaldeans, "The
word from me is firm: if you do not make
known to me the dream and its interpretation, you shall be [n]torn limb from limb,
[n]and your [o]houses shall be laid in ruins.
6 But if you show the dream and its interpretation, [p]you shall receive from me gifts
and rewards and great honor. [q]Therefore
show me the dream and its interpretation."
7 They answered a second time and said,
"Let the king tell his servants the dream,
and we will show its interpretation." 8 The
king answered and said, "I know with certainty that you are trying to [r]gain time,
because you see that the word from me is
firm— 9 if you do not make the dream
known to me, [s]there is but one sentence
for you. You have agreed to speak lying and
corrupt words before me till [t]the times
change. [u]Therefore tell me the dream, and
I shall know that you can show me its interpretation." 10 [v]The Chaldeans answered the
king and said, "There is not a man on earth
who can meet the king's demand, for no
great and powerful king has asked such a
thing of any magician or enchanter or
[v]Chaldean. 11 The thing that the king asks is
difficult, and no one can show it to the king
except [w]the gods, whose dwelling is not
with flesh."

12 Because of this the king was angry and
[x]very furious, and [y]commanded that all
[z]the wise men of Babylon be destroyed.

17 [y][ch. 2:20, 23; Job 32:8; James 1:5] [z]ver. 4 [a]ch. 5:12; [ch. 9:23; 10:1, 11, 12]
18 [b][ver. 5]
19 [c]ch. 2:2
20 [d][ch. 2:27; Gen. 41:8, 24; Ex. 7:11, 22; 8:7, 18, 19; 9:11] [e]ch. 2:2, 10, 27; 4:7; 5:7, 11, 15
21 [f][ch. 6:28; 10:1] [g]See ch. 6:28
Chapter 2
1 [h][ch. 4:5; 5:9; Gen. 41:8] [i][ch. 6:18; Esth. 6:1]
2 [d][See ch. 1:20 above] [e][See ch. 1:20 above] [j]Deut. 18:10, 11; 2 Chr. 33:6; Isai. 47:9, 12 [k]See ch. 1:4 [l]See ch. 1:5
3 [h][See ver. 1 above]
4 [k][See ver. 2 above] [m]ch. 3:9; 5:10; 6:6, 21; See 1 Kin. 1:31
5 [k][See ver. 2 above] [n]ch. 3:29 [o]Ezra 6:11; [2 Kin. 10:27]
6 [p][ch. 5:7, 16] [q][ver. 7, 9]
8 [r]Eph. 5:16; Col. 4:5
9 [s]Esth. 4:11 [t][ver. 21; ch. 7:25] [u]ver. 6; [ver. 7]
10 [v]See ch. 1:4 **11** [w][ch. 5:11, 14] **12** [x][ch. 3:19] [y][ver. 24] [z]ch. 4:6

[1] The text from this point to the end of chapter 7 is in Aramaic

1:17 God gave them learning. God's blessing was not limited to physical well-being, but also included outstanding intellectual development during their three years of Babylonian education.

visions and dreams. With a view to what follows in the book (chs. 2; 4; 5), Daniel is distinguished from his companions in his ability to interpret dreams and visions, much as Joseph was in the court of Pharaoh (Gen. 40:8; 41:16).

1:18 At the end of the time. That is, after the three years mentioned in v. 5.

1:20 the magicians and enchanters. The term translated "magicians" is also used in Gen. 41:8, 24 and Ex. 7:11. The word translated "enchanters" occurs only here and in 2:2 and can be rendered "conjurer" or "soothsayer." Whatever means these royal advisers used to gain knowledge, Daniel and his friends were able to demonstrate superior insight on the matters they were questioned about.

1:21 until the first year of King Cyrus. Babylon fell to Cyrus in 539 B.C., or sixty-six years after Daniel had been taken captive to Babylon. Daniel lived through the entire period of the Babylonian captivity. Cyrus issued a decree in the first year of his reign permitting the Israelites to return from captivity, and to take with them the vessels from the temple that had been seized by Nebuchadnezzar (Ezra 1:7–11). The statement does not mean that Daniel died in the first year of Cyrus (10:1).

2:1 In the second year. Since the Babylonian system started counting Nebuchadnezzar's reign officially from the beginning of the year succeeding his actual succession, his "second year" could mean the end of Daniel's three years of training (1:5). Otherwise the events took place during his training.

his sleep left him. It was widely believed in the ancient Near East that the gods spoke to human beings in dreams.

2:2 magicians . . . enchanters. See note 1:20.

sorcerers . . . Chaldeans. "Sorcerers" practiced divination or witchcraft (Ex. 22:18; Deut. 18:10; Is. 47:9, 12; Jer. 27:9). Here "Chaldeans" probably means a class of soothsayers and astrologers, rather than the name of an ethnic group (as in 1:4; 3:8; 5:30; 9:1).

2:4 Aramaic. From here until the end of ch. 7 the text is written in Aramaic rather than Hebrew. Ezra 4:8–6:18; 7:12–26 are also written in Aramaic. There has been much speculation about why these verses are in Aramaic, but no generally accepted conclusion has been reached.

2:5 make known to me the dream. Nebuchadnezzar formulated a test to see whether the advisers to the court had access to hidden knowledge, as they claimed. If they could not tell him the dream, then he would have no confidence in their interpretation (cf. v. 9).

2:11 difficult. The wise men confess that they cannot do what the king asks. Only the gods have such power, but the gods, they protest, do not reveal such things to anyone (cf. Ex. 8:18, 19).

13 So the decree went out, and the wise men
were about to be killed; and they sought
[a]Daniel and his companions, to kill them.
14 Then Daniel replied with prudence and
discretion to [b]Arioch, the [c]captain of the
king's guard, who had gone out to kill the
wise men of Babylon. 15 He declared[1] to
Arioch, the king's captain, "Why is the
decree of the king [d]so urgent?" Then
Arioch made the matter known to Daniel.
16 And Daniel went in and requested the
king to appoint him a time, that he might
show the interpretation to the king.

God Reveals Nebuchadnezzar's Dream

17 Then Daniel went to his house and
made the matter known to [e]Hananiah,
[e]Mishael, and [e]Azariah, his companions,
18 [f]and told them to seek mercy from the
[g]God of heaven concerning this mystery, so
that Daniel and his companions might not
[h]be destroyed with the rest of the wise men
of Babylon. 19 Then the mystery was revealed to Daniel in [i]a vision of the night.
Then Daniel [j]blessed the [g]God of heaven.
20 Daniel answered and said:

> [k]"Blessed be the name of God forever
> and ever,
> [l]to whom belong wisdom and
> might.
> 21 [m]He changes times and seasons;
> [n]he removes kings and sets up
> kings;
> [o]he gives wisdom to the wise
> [o]and knowledge to those who have
> understanding;

13 [a]See ch. 1:4-7
14 [b]ver. 24, 25 [c][Gen. 37:36]
15 [d]ch. 3:22
17 [e]ch. 1:6
18 [f][Matt. 18:19] [g]ver. 19, 28, 37, 44; Rev. 11:13 [h][ver. 12, 24]
19 [i][Num. 12:6; Job 33:15, 16] [j]See Josh. 22:32
20 [k]1 Chr. 29:10; Ps. 72:18; 113:2; 115:18; Luke 1:68 [l][Isai. 28:29]
21 [m][ver. 9; ch. 7:25] [n][ch. 4:17; 5:20; Job 12:18; Ps. 75:7; Rom. 13:1] [o]See ch. 1:17

1 Aramaic *answered and said*; also verse 26

The Wisdom and Will of God

Wisdom in Scripture means choosing the best and noblest end at which to aim, along with the most appropriate and effective means of achieving that end. Old Testament wisdom literature, including Job, Proverbs, Ecclesiastes, and certain of the Psalms (Ps. 19; 37; 104; 107; 147; 148), dealt not only with the life of worship or religious exercise in the restricted sense, but also with everyday moral behavior in family, social, and business concerns. In the New Testament the letter of James might also be considered "wisdom literature" in its plain-spoken description of practical Christian living. In light of the wisdom literature of Scripture, Christian wisdom means making the "fear of the LORD"—reverent worship and service of Him—the goal of life (Prov. 1:7; 9:10; cf. Eccl. 12:13).

God's wisdom is seen in His works of creation, preservation, and redemption: it is His choice of His own glory as His goal (Ps. 46:10; Is. 42:8; 48:11), and His decision to achieve it first by creating a marvelous variety of things and people (Ps. 104:24; Prov. 3:19, 20), second by kindly providences of all sorts (Ps. 145:13–16; Acts 14:17), and third by the redemptive "wisdom" of "Christ crucified" (1 Cor. 1:18–2:16) and the resulting Christian church in the world (Eph. 3:10).

The outworking of God's wisdom involves the expression of His will in two different senses. In the first sense, God's will is "His eternal purpose, according to the counsel of His will, whereby, for His own glory, He hath foreordained whatsoever comes to pass" (*Westminster Shorter Catechism*, Q. 7). This "eternal purpose" is God's decreed will, referred to in Eph. 1:11. In the second sense, the will of God is His command, that is, His instruction given in Scripture, concerning how people should believe and behave. This is sometimes called His "preceptive will," and is spoken of in Rom. 12:2; Eph. 5:17; Col. 1:9; 1 Thess. 4:3–6. Some of its requirements are rooted in His holy character, which we are to imitate: such are the principles of the Decalogue, and the two great commandments (Ex. 20:1–17; Matt. 22:37–40; cf. Eph. 4:32–5:2). Some of its requirements spring simply from the divine institution. Such were circumcision and the sacrificial and purity laws of the Old Testament, and such are baptism and the Lord's Supper today. But all, in their respective times, bind the conscience, and God's plan of events (His "eternal purpose") already includes the "good works" of obedience that those who believe will perform (Eph. 2:10).

It is sometimes difficult, even impossible, for mortal humans to understand how obedience, putting us at a disadvantage in the world, is part of a predestined plan of furthering both God's glory and our good (Rom. 8:28). But we glorify God by believing that it is so, because He who cannot lie has said it. One day we will see it to be so, because His wisdom is perfect and never fails.

2:18 seek mercy from the God of heaven. Daniel also realized that human wisdom was insufficient to meet the king's demand (v. 11 note). Only divine revelation could provide the answer.

2:20 See theological note "The Wisdom and Will of God."

2:21 he removes kings and sets up kings. Daniel alludes to the content of the dream.

22 [p]he reveals deep and hidden things;
[p]he knows what is in the darkness,
[q]and the light dwells with him.
23 To you, O [r]God of my fathers,
[s]I give thanks and praise,
for [t]you have given me wisdom and might,
and have now made known to me what [u]we asked of you,
for you have made known to us the king's matter."

24 Therefore Daniel went in to [v]Arioch,
whom the king had appointed to destroy
the wise men of Babylon. He went and said
thus to him, "Do not destroy the wise men
of Babylon; bring me in before the king,
and I will show the king the interpretation."
25 Then [v]Arioch brought in Daniel before
the king [w]in haste and said thus to him: "I
have found [x]among the exiles from Judah a
man who will make known to the king the
interpretation." 26 The king said to Daniel,
[y]whose name was Belteshazzar, [z]"Are you
able to make known to me the dream that
I have seen and its interpretation?"
27 Daniel answered the king and said, "No
wise men, [a]enchanters, [a]magicians, or [b]as-
trologers can show to the king the mystery
that the king has asked, 28 but [c]there is a
God in heaven who reveals mysteries, and
he has made known to King Nebuchadnezzar [d]what will be in the latter days.
Your dream and [e]the visions of your head
as you lay in bed are these: 29 To you, O
king, as you lay in bed came thoughts of
what would be after this, [f]and he who
reveals mysteries made known to you what
is to be. 30 But [g]as for me, this mystery has
been revealed to me, not because of any
wisdom that I have more than all the living,
but in order that the interpretation may be
made known to the king, and that [h]you
may know the thoughts of your mind.

Daniel Interprets the Dream

31 "You saw, O king, and behold, a great
image. This image, mighty and of exceeding brightness, stood before you, and its
appearance was frightening. 32 [i]The head of
this image was of fine gold, [j]its chest and
arms of silver, its middle and [j]thighs of
bronze, 33 [k]its legs of iron, its feet partly of
iron and partly of clay. 34 As you looked, a
stone was cut out [l]by no human hand, and
it struck the image on its feet of iron and
clay, and [m]broke them in pieces. 35 Then
the iron, the clay, the bronze, the silver,
and the gold, [m]all together were broken in
pieces, and became [n]like the chaff of the
summer threshing floors; and the wind carried them away, so that [o]not a trace of
them could be found. But the stone that
struck the image became [p]a great mountain
[q]and filled the whole earth.
36 "This was the dream. Now we will tell
the king its interpretation. 37 You, O king,
[r]the king of kings, to whom [s]the God of
heaven [t]has given the kingdom, the power,
and the might, and the glory, 38 and into
whose hand he has given, wherever they
dwell, the children of man, [u]the beasts of
the field, and the birds of the heavens, making you rule over them all—you are [v]the
head of gold. 39 [w]Another kingdom inferior
to you shall arise after you, and yet a third
kingdom [v]of bronze, [x]which shall rule over
all the earth. 40 And [y]there shall be a fourth
kingdom, strong as iron, because iron
[z]breaks to pieces and shatters all things.
And like iron that crushes, it shall [z]break

22 [p]Job 12:22; [Ps. 25:14; 139:12; Amos 4:13; Heb. 4:13] [q]1 Tim. 6:16; James 1:17; 1 John 1:5; [John 1:4, 5] **23** [r][ch. 6:10] [s]Deut. 26:7; 1 Chr. 12:17; 29:18 [t][ver. 20]; See ch. 1:17 [u][ver. 18] **24** [v]ver. 14, 15 **25** [v][See ver. 24 above] [w]ch. 3:24 [x]ch. 5:13; Ezra 4:1; 6:16, 19, 20; 10:7, 16 **26** [y]See ch. 1:7 [z][ch. 5:16] **27** [a]See ch. 1:20 [b]ch. 4:7; 5:7 **28** [c]See ver. 22 [d]ch. 10:14; Hos. 3:5 [e]ch. 4:5; 7:15 **29** [f]ver. 45 **30** [g][Gen. 41:16; Acts 3:12] [h][Eccles. 3:18] **32** [i][ver. 38] [j][ver. 39] **33** [k][ver. 40] **34** [l][ch. 8:25; Job 34:20; Lam. 4:6; 2 Cor. 5:1] [m]ver. 40, 44, 45; Isai. 8:9; [Matt. 21:44; Luke 20:18] **35** [m][See ver. 24 above] [n]Ps. 1:4 [o][Rev. 20:11] [p][Isai. 2:2] [q][Ps. 80:9] **37** [r]Ezra 7:12; Ezek. 26:7 [s]ver. 19 [t]ch. 5:18; [Ezra 1:2]; See ver. 21 **38** [u]ch. 4:21; Jer. 27:6 [v][ver. 32] **39** [w][ver. 32; ch. 5:28, 31] [v][See ver. 38 above] [x][ch. 7:6] **40** [y][ch. 7:7, 23] [z]See ver. 34

2:22 he reveals deep and hidden things. Job 28 is a carefully drawn picture of wisdom as "hidden from the eyes of all" (Job 28:21) and inaccessible without God.

2:24 Do not destroy the wise men. Daniel urges the king to be merciful to the wise men even though their inability to know the dream has been exposed.

2:28 a God in heaven who reveals mysteries. Just as Joseph had done in Egypt (Gen. 40:8; 41:16), so also Daniel attributes his knowledge of the dream to God. Daniel's God revealed to this young man what astrology, magic, and the occult could not discover.

in the latter days. This expression seems to range in meaning from the "end time," technically called the "eschaton" (Ezek. 38:16), to simply the future in general (Gen. 49:1; Deut. 4:30; 31:29).

2:32, 33 gold . . . iron . . . clay. There is a progressive decrease in the value of the materials in the image from the head to the feet.

2:34 its feet of iron and clay. Some interpreters view the mixture of iron and clay in the feet of the image as representing a second phase of the fourth kingdom different from the legs of solid iron (cf. vv. 41–43).

2:37–40 king of kings . . . fourth kingdom. The four kingdoms have been widely understood since Josephus (1st century A.D.) to be the empires of Babylon, Medo-Persia, Greece, and Rome. Others understand them to be Babylon, Media, Persia, and Greece, a sequence in agreement with the critical view that the book was written, after the facts, by a living witness during the period of Greek ascendency in the Middle East. However, the animal symbols in 7:4–7 historically fit the former structure of a combined Medo-Persian Empire, leaving Greece as the third and Rome as the fourth kingdom. Darius's appeal to the single "law of the Medes and Persians" (6:12; cf. 5:28) agrees with the first order of empires.

and crush all these. **41** And as you saw [a]the
feet and toes, partly of potter's clay and
partly of iron, it shall be a divided kingdom,
but some of the [y]firmness of iron shall be in
it, just as you saw iron mixed with the soft
clay. **42** And as the toes of the feet were partly iron and partly clay, so the kingdom shall
be partly strong and partly brittle. **43** As you
saw the iron mixed with soft clay, so they
will mix with one another in marriage,[1] but
they will not hold together, just as iron does
not mix with clay. **44** And in the days of
those kings [b]the God of heaven will set up
[c]a kingdom that shall never be destroyed,
nor shall the kingdom be left to another
people. [d]It shall break in pieces all these
kingdoms and bring them to an end, and [c]it
shall stand forever, **45** just as [e]you saw that [f]a
stone was cut from a mountain by no
human hand, and that [d]it broke in pieces
the iron, the bronze, the clay, the silver,
and the gold. A [g]great God has made known
to the king what shall be after this. The
dream is certain, and its interpretation sure."

Daniel Is Promoted

46 Then King Nebuchadnezzar [h]fell upon
his face and [i]paid homage to Daniel, and
commanded that [j]an offering and [k]incense
be offered up to him. **47** The king answered
and said to Daniel, "Truly, your [l]God is
God of gods and [m]Lord of kings, and [n]a revealer of mysteries, for you have been able
to reveal this mystery." **48** Then the king
gave Daniel high honors and many great
[o]gifts, and made him ruler over the whole
[p]province of Babylon and [q]chief prefect
over all the wise men of Babylon. **49** Daniel
made a request of the king, and he [r]ap-
pointed [s]Shadrach, Meshach, and Abednego over the affairs of [p]the province of
Babylon. But Daniel [t]remained at the
king's court.

Nebuchadnezzar's Golden Image

3 King Nebuchadnezzar made an image
of gold, whose height was sixty cubits[2]
and its breadth six cubits. He set it up on
[u]the plain of Dura, in [v]the province of
Babylon. **2** Then King Nebuchadnezzar sent
to gather [w]the satraps, the prefects, and [x]the
governors, the counselors, the treasurers,
the justices, the magistrates, and all the officials of the provinces to come to the dedication of the image that King Nebuchadnezzar
had set up. **3** Then [w]the satraps, the prefects,
and the governors, the counselors, the treasurers, the justices, the magistrates, and all
the officials of the provinces gathered for the
dedication of the image that King Nebuchadnezzar had set up. And they stood
before the image that Nebuchadnezzar had
set up. **4** And the herald [y]proclaimed aloud,
"You are commanded, O [z]peoples, nations,
and languages, **5** that when you hear the
[a]sound of the horn, pipe, lyre, trigon, harp,
bagpipe, and every kind of music, you [b]are
to fall down and worship the golden image

1 Aramaic *by the seed of men* 2 A *cubit* was about 18 inches or 45 centimeters

41 [a][ver. 33] [y][See ver. 40 above]
44 [b]ver. 19 [c]ch. 4:3, 34; 6:26; 7:14, 27; Mic. 4:7; [Matt. 3:2; Luke 1:33; John 18:36] [d][Isai. 60:12]; See ver. 34
45 [e][ver. 34] [f][Isai. 28:16] [d][See ver. 44 above] [g]ver. 28
46 [h][2 Sam. 14:22] [i][Matt. 8:2; Acts 10:25] [j][Acts 14:13] [k][Ezra 6:10]
47 [l]Deut. 10:17 [m][1 Tim. 6:15; Rev. 17:14; 19:16] [n]See ver. 22
48 [o][ver. 6] [p]ch. 3:1, 12, 30; [Esth. 1:1] [q]ch. 5:11; [ch. 4:9]
49 [r]ch. 3:12 [s][ch. 1:7] [p][See ver. 48 above] [t]Esth. 2:19
Chapter 3
1 [u][Gen. 11:2] [v]ver. 12, 30; ch. 2:48, 49
2 [w]ver. 27; ch. 6:1, 2, 3, 4, 6, 7; [Ezra 8:36] [x]ch. 2:48
3 [w][See ver. 2 above]
4 [y]ch. 4:14; 5:7; [Rev. 18:2] [z]ver. 29; ch. 4:1; 5:19; 6:25; 7:14; [Rev. 5:9]
5 [a]ver. 7, 10, 15 [b][ch. 2:46]

2:43 they will mix . . . but . . . not hold together. The elements of the fourth kingdom cannot preserve their union. One possible interpretation of the image is that the iron represents the culture and laws of imperial Rome, while the clay represents the divergent political and social traditions of its many parts. The fourth kingdom, though strong, is temporary.

2:44 those kings. The most natural interpretation is that the kings are the rulers of the four powers making up the image just described. The other possibility is that they are a sequence of several rulers of the fourth kingdom only.

a kingdom that shall never be destroyed. The eternal kingdom is the kingdom of our Lord Jesus Christ (Is. 9:7; Luke 1:33; Heb. 1:8; Rev. 11:15). This kingdom was inaugurated and preached at the First Coming of Christ (Mark 1:15; Matt. 12:28; 24:14), but does not come in its fullness until His Second Advent. See "The Kingdom of God" at Luke 17:20.

2:46 King Nebuchadnezzar fell . . . paid homage to Daniel. In a reversal of roles, Daniel is exalted to a position of honor by the Lord's intervention on his behalf. For the king's reaction, compare Acts 14:11; Rev. 22:8.

2:47 God of gods. Nebuchadnezzar's statement does not necessarily mean that he recognized Israel's God as the only God. His exclamation is that Israel's God is superior to other gods.

Lord of kings. Nebuchadnezzar confesses that Israel's God is supreme over human rulers and kingdoms. This is the unifying theme of Dan. 1–6 (Introduction: Characteristics and Themes).

2:48 province of Babylon. The Babylonian Empire was divided into provinces. Daniel was appointed ruler (cf. 3:2) of the province where the capital city was. Joseph and Mordecai also rose as Jews to political power in a foreign land. See Gen. 41:37–44 (Joseph) and Esth. 8:1, 2 (Mordecai).

3:1 an image of gold. Although the narrow proportions could suggest an obelisk rather than a statue, the monument is called an "image." It was probably a figure standing on a pedestal. The gold was probably plating, the fabrication of the image being much like that described in Is. 40:19; 41:7; Jer. 10:3–9.

the plain of Dura. Probably about six miles south of Babylon.

3:2 satraps . . . officials. The precise responsibilities of these different officials are not known. Five of the seven terms are of Persian origin, perhaps indicating that Daniel did not finish writing the account until after the beginning of Persian rule in 539 B.C.

3:5 horn . . . harp. Of the six terms for musical instruments, the three translated "lyre," "harp," and "bagpipe" are borrowed from Greek. This is not surprising since the international exchange of musicians and musical instruments at royal courts had a long history. The presence of these three Greek terms in Daniel does not establish that the account was written after the time of Alexander the Great, as is sometimes argued.

that King Nebuchadnezzar has set up.
6 And whoever does not fall down and worship shall immediately [c]be cast into a burning fiery furnace." 7 Therefore, as soon as all
the peoples heard the sound of the horn,
pipe, lyre, trigon, harp, bagpipe, and every
kind of music, all [z]the peoples, nations,
and languages fell down and worshiped the
golden image that King Nebuchadnezzar
had set up.

The Fiery Furnace

8 Therefore at that time certain
[d]Chaldeans [e]came forward and maliciously
accused the Jews. 9 They declared[1] to King
Nebuchadnezzar, "O king, live forever!
10 You, O king, [f]have made a decree, that
every man who [g]hears the sound of the
horn, pipe, lyre, trigon, harp, bagpipe, and
every kind of music, [g]shall fall down and
worship the golden image. 11 And whoever
does not fall down and worship [c]shall be
cast into a burning fiery furnace. 12 There are
certain Jews whom you have [h]appointed
over the affairs of [v]the province of Babylon:
[i]Shadrach, Meshach, and Abednego. These
men, O king, [j]pay no attention to you; they
do not serve your gods or worship the gold-
en image that you have set up."
13 Then Nebuchadnezzar [k]in furious rage
commanded that [i]Shadrach, Meshach, and
Abednego be brought. So they brought
these men before the king. 14 Nebuchadnezzar answered and said to them, "Is it
true, O Shadrach, Meshach, and Abednego, that you do not serve my gods or
worship the golden image that I have set
up? 15 Now if you are ready when [l]you hear
the sound of the horn, pipe, lyre, trigon,
harp, bagpipe, and every kind of music, to
fall down and worship the image that I
have made, well and good.[2] But if you do
not worship, [d]you shall immediately be
cast into a burning fiery furnace. And [m]who
is the god who will deliver you out of my
hands?"
16 [i]Shadrach, Meshach, and Abednego
answered and said to the king, "O
Nebuchadnezzar, we have no need to
answer you in this matter. 17 If this be so,
[n]our God whom we serve is able to deliver
us from the burning fiery furnace, and he
will deliver us out of your hand, O king.[3]
18 But if not, be it known to you, O king,
that we will not serve your gods or worship
the golden image that you have set up."
19 Then Nebuchadnezzar was [o]filled with
fury, and the expression of his face [p]was
changed against [i]Shadrach, Meshach, and
Abednego. He ordered the furnace heated
seven times more than it was usually heated. 20 And he ordered some of the mighty
men of his army [q]to bind [i]Shadrach,
Meshach, and Abednego, and to cast them
into the burning fiery furnace. 21 Then these
men were [q]bound in their cloaks, their
tunics,[4] their hats, and their other garments, and they were thrown into the
burning fiery furnace. 22 Because the king's
order was [r]urgent and the furnace over-
heated, the flame of the fire killed those
men who took up [s]Shadrach, Meshach,
and Abednego. 23 And these three men,
Shadrach, Meshach, and Abednego, fell
[q]bound into the burning fiery furnace.
24 Then King Nebuchadnezzar was [t]aston-
ished and rose up [u]in haste. He declared to
his [v]counselors, "Did we not cast three men
[w]bound into the fire?" They answered and
said to the king, "True, O king." 25 He
answered and said, "But I see four men
unbound, [x]walking in the midst of the fire,
and they [y]are not hurt; and the appearance
of the fourth is like [z]a son of the gods."

6 [c][Jer. 29:22; Ezek. 23:25]
7 [z][See ver. 4 above]
8 [d]See ch. 1:4 [e]ch. 6:12
10 [f]ver. 29; ch. 4:6; 6:26 [g]ver. 5, 7, 15
11 [c][See ver. 6 above]
12 [h]ch. 2:49 [v][See ver. 1 above] [i][ch. 1:7] [j]ch. 6:13
13 [k]ch. 2:12 [i][See ver. 12 above]
15 [l]ver. 5, 7, 10 [d][See ver. 8 above] [m][ch. 6:20; Ex. 5:2; 2 Kin. 18:35]
16 [i][See ver. 12 above]
17 [n][ver. 15]
19 [o][ver. 13; Esth. 7:7] [p][ch. 2:49] [i][See ver. 12 above]
20 [q][ver. 24, 25] [i][See ver. 12 above]
21 [q][See ver. 20 above]
22 [r]ch. 2:15 [s][ch. 1:7]
23 [q][See ver. 20 above]
24 [t]ch. 4:19 [u]ch. 2:25 [v]ch. 4:36; 6:7 [w]ver. 20, 21, 23
25 [x][Isai. 43:2] [y][ch. 6:23] [z][ver. 28; Job 1:6]

1 Aramaic *answered and said*; also verses 24, 26 2 Aramaic lacks *well and good* 3 Or *If our God whom we serve is able to deliver us, he will deliver us from the burning fiery furnace and out of your hand, O king.* 4 The meaning of the Aramaic words rendered *cloaks* and *tunics* is uncertain; also verse 27

3:6 a burning fiery furnace. Furnaces or kilns were used in Babylon for firing bricks (Gen. 11:3). Execution by burning was not unknown (Jer. 29:22; cf. Herodotus 1:86; 4:69; 2 Macc. 7).

3:8 Chaldeans. See 2:2 note; here "Chaldeans" probably indicates nationality. The informers were prejudiced against the Jews (v. 12; cf. Esth. 3:5, 6), possibly because they were jealous of the Jews' privileged position.

3:12 Shadrach, Meshach, and Abednego. See note 1:7. Daniel was either not present or was exempted by his high position from having to demonstrate his loyalty (2:48, 49).

3:15 who is the god. From Nebuchadnezzar's polytheistic perspective there was no god capable of such deliverance. Unwittingly, Nebuchadnezzar challenged the power of the God of Israel.

3:17, 18 he will deliver . . . But if not. These verses express the central theme of the chapter. The idea is not that God will always protect His people from physical harm (Is. 43:1, 2). He may do that and certainly is able to. The central idea is that God's people should be obedient to Him whatever the consequences.

3:25 a son of the gods. How Nebuchadnezzar recognized the fourth person in the furnace as a divine being is not explained (v. 28 note). Perhaps the miraculous appearance was itself sufficient reason for the conclusion.

26 Then Nebuchadnezzar came near to
the door of the burning fiery furnace; he
declared, [s]"Shadrach, Meshach, and Abednego, servants of the [a]Most High God,
come out, and come here!" Then [s]Sha-
drach, Meshach, and Abednego came out
from the fire. 27 And the [b]satraps, the prefects, the governors, and [v]the king's counselors gathered together and saw that [c]the
fire had not had any power over the bodies of those men. The hair of their heads
was not singed, their [d]cloaks were not
harmed, and no smell of fire had come
upon them. 28 Nebuchadnezzar answered
and said, "Blessed be the God of [s]Sha-
drach, Meshach, and Abednego, who [e]has
sent his angel and [f]delivered his servants,
who [g]trusted in him, and set aside[1] the
king's command, and yielded up their
bodies rather than [h]serve and worship any
god except their own God. 29 Therefore [i]I
make a decree: Any [j]people, nation, or language that speaks anything against the
God of [s]Shadrach, Meshach, and Abednego [k]shall be torn limb from limb, and
their houses laid in ruins, for there is no
other god who is able to rescue in this
way." 30 Then the king promoted [s]Sha-
drach, Meshach, and Abednego in [l]the
province of Babylon.

Nebuchadnezzar Praises God

4 [2] King Nebuchadnezzar to all [m]peoples,
nations, and languages, [n]that dwell in
all the earth: [o]Peace be multiplied to you! 2 It
has seemed good to me to show the [p]signs
and wonders that the [q]Most High God has
done for me.

3 How great are [p]his
signs,
how mighty his
[p]wonders!
[r]His kingdom is an everlasting
kingdom,
[r]and his dominion endures from
generation to generation.

Nebuchadnezzar's Second Dream

4 [3]I, Nebuchadnezzar, was at ease in my
house and prospering in my palace. 5 I saw
a dream that made me afraid. As I lay in
bed the fancies and [s]the visions of my head
alarmed me. 6 So [t]I made a decree that [u]all
the wise men of Babylon should be
brought before me, that they might make
known to me the interpretation of the
dream. 7 Then [v]the magicians, the enchanters, the Chaldeans, and the astrologers came in, and I told them the dream,
but [w]they could not make known to me its
interpretation. 8 At last Daniel came in
before me—he who was named [x]Belte-
shazzar after the name of my god, and in
whom is [y]the spirit of the holy gods[4]—and
I told him the dream, saying, 9 "O Belteshazzar, [z]chief of the magicians, because I
know that [y]the spirit of the holy gods is in
you and that no [a]mystery is too difficult
for you, tell me [s]the visions of my dream
that I saw and their interpretation. 10 [s]The
visions of my head as I lay in bed were
these: I saw, and [b]behold, a tree in the
midst of the earth, and its height was great.

1 Aramaic *and changed* 2 Ch 3:31 in Aramaic 3 Ch 4:1 in Aramaic
4 Or *Spirit of the holy God*; also verses 9, 18

26 [s][See ver. 22 above] [a]ch. 4:2; 5:18, 21
27 [b]ver. 2 [v][See ver. 24 above] [c][Heb. 11:34] [d]ver. 21
28 [s][See ver. 22 above] [e]ch. 6:22 [f][ver. 15, 17; Ps. 34:7] [g][Ps. 25:2] [h][Ex. 20:3]
29 [i]See ver. 10 [j]See ver. 4 [s][See ver. 22 above] [k]ch. 2:5
30 [s][See ver. 22 above] [l]ver. 1, 12; ch. 2:48, 49
Chapter 4
1 [m]See ch. 3:4 [n]ch. 6:25 [o]1 Pet. 1:2; 2 Pet. 1:2
2 [p]ch. 6:27; [John 4:48] [q]ch. 3:26
3 [p][See ver. 2 above] [r]See ch. 2:44
5 [s]ch. 2:28; 7:15
6 [t]See ch. 3:10 [u]ch. 2:12
7 [v]See ch. 2:2 [w][ver. 18; ch. 2:27; 5:8, 15]
8 [x]See ch. 1:7 [y]ver. 18; ch. 2:11; 5:11; Gen. 41:38; [Isai. 63:14]
9 [z]ch. 5:11; [ch. 2:48] [y][See ver. 8 above] [a]ch. 2:18 [s][See ver. 5 above]
10 [s][See ver. 5 above] [b][Ezek. 31:3]

3:26 the Most High God. This is a title expressing God's universal authority. As in v. 29 and 2:47, such a confession on the lips of a pagan is not an acknowledgment that Daniel's Lord is the only God, but only that He is supreme over other gods (4:2, 17, 34). To a Jew it means there is only one God (4:24–32; 5:18, 21; 7:18–27).

3:28 angel. The "angel" may be identified with the Angel of the Lord (Gen. 16:7); if so, it is a visible manifestation of God Himself (Ex. 3:2). God promised His presence when Israel walked through fire (Is. 43:1–3).

4:1 King Nebuchadnezzar. This final incident in the Book of Daniel associated with Nebuchadnezzar must be placed late in the king's 43-year reign when his building projects were completed and his power was at its height (cf. vv. 4, 30). He represents the most powerful kingdom on earth (vv. 10–12 note) as opposed to the rule of the Most High God. Babylonian records of long periods of absence and blasphemous acts by King Nabonidus (ruled 556 to 539 B.C.; 5:1 note) resemble in some ways Daniel's account of Nebuchadnezzar. Another composition called the "Prayer of Nabonidus" was discovered among the Dead Sea Scrolls, documents hidden before A.D. 70 by a Jewish community at Qumran and found in 1947. This "Prayer" is also similar to what Daniel says about Nebuchadnezzar. Nabonidus is separated from society for seven years and restored with the help of a Jewish exile following confession of his sins. However, his affliction is described as a form of skin disease rather than mental illness.

4:2 the Most High God. See notes 2:47; 3:26.

4:3 How great. Nebuchadnezzar's confession in this verse and in vv. 34, 35 communicates the central theme of the Book of Daniel, namely, the absolute sovereignty of the God of Israel.

4:6, 7 See notes 1:20; 2:2.

4:8 Belteshazzar. See note 1:7.

the spirit of the holy gods. The Holy Spirit was the immediate author of the extraordinary power of Daniel to know and to interpret secrets (2:19 note). Nebuchadnezzar's words agree with this, although he may have been thinking of another god known to him rather than the God of Daniel.

4:10–12 a tree. See Ezek. 31 for an extensive description of Assyria using the imagery of a tree. Similar imagery is used both of righteous and wicked individuals and nations Ps. 1:3; 37:35; 52:8; 92:12; Jer. 11:16, 17; 17:8.

11 [c]The tree grew and became strong, and its top reached to heaven, and it was visible to the end of the whole earth. **12** [d]Its leaves were beautiful and its fruit abundant, and in it was food for all. [e]The beasts of the field found shade under it, and [e]the birds of the heavens lived in its branches, and all flesh was fed from it.

13 "I saw in [s]the visions of my head as I lay in bed, and behold, [f]a watcher, [g]a holy one, came down from heaven. **14** He [h]proclaimed aloud and said thus: [i]'Chop down the tree and [j]lop off its branches, [j]strip off its leaves and scatter its fruit. [j]Let the beasts flee from under it and the birds from its branches. **15** But leave the stump of its roots in the earth, bound with a band of iron and bronze, amid the tender grass of the field. Let him be wet with the dew of heaven. Let his portion be with the beasts in the grass of the earth. **16** Let his mind be changed from a man's, and let a beast's mind be given to him; [k]and let seven periods of time [l]pass over him. **17** The sentence is by the decree of [f]the watchers, the decision by the word of [g]the holy ones, to the end that the living may know that the Most High [m]rules the kingdom of men [n]and gives it to whom he will and [o]sets over it the lowliest of men.' **18** This dream I, King Nebuchadnezzar, saw. And you, O [p]Belteshazzar, tell me the interpretation, because [q]all the wise men of my kingdom are not able to make known to me the interpretation, but you are able, for [r]the spirit of the holy gods is in you."

Daniel Interprets the Second Dream

19 Then Daniel, whose name was [p]Belteshazzar, was [s]dismayed for a while, and [t]his thoughts alarmed him. The king answered and said, "Belteshazzar, let not the dream or the interpretation alarm you." Belteshazzar answered and said, "My lord, [u]may the dream be for those who hate you [u]and its interpretation for your enemies! **20** [v]The tree you saw, which grew and became strong, so that its top reached to heaven, and it was visible to the end of the whole earth, **21** [w]whose leaves were beautiful and its fruit abundant, and in which was food for all, under which beasts of the field found shade, and in whose branches the birds of the heavens lived— **22** [x]it is you, O king, who have grown and become strong. [y]Your greatness has grown and reaches to heaven, [y]and your dominion to the ends of the earth. **23** And because the king saw [z]a watcher, a holy one, coming down from heaven and saying, [a]'Chop down the tree and destroy it, but leave the stump of its roots in the earth, bound with a band of iron and bronze, in the tender grass of the field, and let him be wet with the dew of heaven, and let his portion be with the beasts of the field, till [b]seven periods of time pass over him,' **24** this is the interpretation, O king: It is a decree of the Most High, which has come upon my lord the king, **25** [c]that you shall be driven from among men, and your dwelling shall be with the beasts of the field. You shall be made [d]to eat grass like an ox, and you shall be wet with the dew of heaven, and [b]seven periods of time shall pass over you, till [e]you know that the Most High rules the kingdom of men and gives it to whom he will. **26** And as it was commanded [f]to leave the stump of the roots of the tree, your kingdom shall be confirmed for you from the time that you know that Heaven rules. **27** Therefore, O king, let my counsel be acceptable to you: break off your sins by [g]practicing righteousness, [h]and your iniquities by showing mercy to the oppressed, [i]that there may perhaps be a lengthening of your prosperity."

11 [c][Ps. 37:35]
12 [d]Ezek. 31:7 [e]Ezek. 31:6
13 [s][See ver. 5 above] [f]ver. 23 [g][Deut. 33:2; Zech. 14:5; Jude 14]
14 [h]See ch. 3:4 [i]ver. 23; [Matt. 3:10; Luke 3:9] [j][Ezek. 31:12]
16 [k][ver. 23, 25] [l][1 Chr. 29:30]
17 [f][See ver. 13 above] [g][See ver. 13 above] [m]ver. 25, 32; ch. 5:21 [n]Jer. 27:5 [o]See 1 Sam. 2:8
18 [p]See ch. 1:7 [q][ver. 7; ch. 5:8, 15; Gen. 41:8] [r]See ver. 8
19 [p][See ver. 18 above] [s]ch. 3:24 [t]ch. 5:6 [u][1 Sam. 25:26; 2 Sam. 18:32]
20 [v][ver. 10, 11]
21 [w][ver. 12]
22 [x][Ezek. 31:3] [y]See Jer. 27:6-8
23 [z]ver. 13 [a]ver. 14, 15 [b]ver. 16
25 [c]ver. 32, 33; [ch. 5:21] [d][Ps. 106:20] [b][See ver. 23 above] [e]ver. 17, 32
26 [f]ver. 15, 23
27 [g]Matt. 6:1 [h]Prov. 16:6; [Matt. 25:35, 36; Luke 11:41] [i][Jer. 18:8; Jonah 3:10; Acts 8:22; 2 Tim. 2:25]

4:11 its top reached to heaven. The term "heaven" is a key term in this chapter. Although Nebuchadnezzar's kingdom reaches from earth to heaven, heaven condemns his pride and reminds him that his power and even his sanity are gifts from God.

4:13 watcher. A name used of an angel only here in the Old Testament.

4:16 a beast's mind. The mental illness in which a person imagines himself to be an animal is called "zoanthropy" (a compound of the Greek words for "animal" and "man").

let seven periods of time pass over him. This means seven periods of unspecified duration (cf. vv. 23, 25), such as seasons, years, or months.

4:22 it is you, O king. With this statement, much like Nathan's to David (2 Sam. 12:7), Daniel applies the dream to Nebuchadnezzar.

4:25 your dwelling shall be with the beasts. With graphic detail Daniel explains how Nebuchadnezzar's mind will fail. He will be deprived of his throne, and he will lose his dignity as a human being created to rule animals and not to imitate them.

the Most High rules. The purpose of Nebuchadnezzar's humiliation was to compel him to recognize God's sovereignty.

4:26 your kingdom shall be confirmed for you. Nebuchadnezzar was promised that in spite of the severity and length of his illness, he would regain his throne when he acknowledged God's sovereignty.

Heaven rules. This is the first time in the Bible where "Heaven" is used as a substitute for "God" (4:37). Compare Matt. 5:3 with Luke 6:20.

Nebuchadnezzar's Humiliation

28 All this came upon King Nebuchadnezzar. 29 At the end of twelve months he
was walking on the roof of the royal palace
of Babylon, 30 and the king answered and
said, [j]"Is not this great Babylon, which I
have built by [k]my mighty power as a royal
residence and for [k]the glory of my
majesty?" 31 [l]While the words were still in
the king's mouth, there fell a voice from
heaven, "O King Nebuchadnezzar, to you it
is spoken: The kingdom has departed from
you, 32 [m]and you shall be driven from
among men, and your dwelling shall be
with the beasts of the field. And you shall
be made to eat grass like an ox, and seven
periods of time shall pass over you, [m]until
you know that the Most High rules the
kingdom of men and gives it to whom he
will." 33 Immediately the word was fulfilled
against Nebuchadnezzar. [m]He was driven
from among men and ate grass like an ox,
and his body was wet with the dew of heav-
en till his hair grew as long as eagles' feathers, and his nails were like birds' claws.

Nebuchadnezzar Restored

34 [n]At the end of the days I, Nebuchadnezzar, lifted my eyes to heaven, and [o]my
reason returned to me, and I blessed the
Most High, and praised and honored [p]him
who lives forever,

> [q]for his dominion is an everlasting
> dominion,
> and [q]his kingdom endures from
> generation to generation;

35
> [r]all the inhabitants of the earth are
> accounted as nothing,
> and [s]he does according to his will
> among the host of heaven
> and among the inhabitants of the
> earth;
> [t]and none can stay his hand
> or [u]say to him, "What have you
> done?"

36 At the same time [v]my reason returned to
me, and for [w]the glory of my kingdom, [w]my
majesty and splendor returned to me. [x]My
counselors and [y]my lords sought me, and I
was established in my kingdom, and still
more greatness was [z]added to me. 37 Now I,
Nebuchadnezzar, [a]praise and extol and
honor the [b]King of heaven, [c]for all his works
are right and his ways are just; and [d]those
who walk in pride he is able to humble.

The Handwriting on the Wall

5 [e]King Belshazzar [f]made a great feast for
a thousand of his [g]lords and drank
wine in front of the thousand.
2 [e]Belshazzar, when he tasted the wine,
commanded that [h]the vessels of gold and
of silver that Nebuchadnezzar his father[1]
had taken out of the temple in Jerusalem
be brought, that the king and his lords, his
wives, and his concubines might drink
from them. 3 Then they brought in [h]the
golden vessels that had been taken out of
the temple, the house of God in Jerusalem,
and the king and his lords, his wives, and
his concubines drank from them. 4 They
drank wine and [i]praised the [j]gods of gold
and silver, bronze, iron, wood, and stone.
5 [k]Immediately [l]the fingers of a human
hand appeared and wrote on the plaster
of the wall of the king's palace, opposite
the lampstand. And the king saw [m]the hand
as it wrote. 6 [n]Then the king's color
changed, [o]and his thoughts alarmed him;
[p]his limbs gave way, and [q]his knees
knocked together. 7 [r]The king called loudly
to bring in [r]the enchanters, the [s]Chaldeans,

[1] Or *predecessor*; also verses 11, 13, 18

30 [j][ch. 5:20] [k][ver. 36; ch. 2:37] **31** [l][ch. 5:5; Luke 12:20] **32** [m]ver. 17, 25; ch. 5:21 **33** [m][See ver. 32 above] **34** [n][ver. 26] [o]ver. 36 [p]ch. 6:26; 12:7; Rev. 4:10 [q][Ps. 10:16]; See ch. 2:44 **35** [r]Isai. 40:17 [s][Ps. 115:3; Heb. 1:13, 14] [t][Isai. 14:27] [u]Job 9:12 **36** [v][Isai. 45:9; Rom. 9:20] [w]ver. 34 [x][ver. 30; ch. 5:18] [y]ch. 3:24; 6:7 [z]ch. 5:1; 6:17 **37** [a][Job 42:12; Matt. 6:33] [b]ver. 34; [ch. 5:23] [c][Deut. 32:4; Ps. 33:4; Rev. 15:3] [d][ch. 5:20; Prov. 20:23]
Chapter 5
1 [e]ver. 22, 29, 30; ch. 7:1; 8:1 [f]See Esth. 1:3 [g]ch. 4:36; 6:17 **2** [e][See ver. 1 above] [h]ver. 23; See ch. 1:2 **3** [h][See ver. 2 above] **4** [i]ver. 23; [Judg. 16:24] [j]ver. 23; [Rev. 9:20]; See Ps. 115:4-7 **5** [k][ch. 4:31] [l][Ezek. 8:3] [m]ver. 24 **6** [n][ver. 10; ch. 7:28] [o][ch. 4:5, 19; 7:28] [p][Ps. 60:23; Isai. 45:1] [q]Nah. 2:10 **7** [r][ch. 2:2; 4:6] [s]See ch. 1:4

4:34, 35, 37 Although Nebuchadnezzar confesses God's sovereignty, he does not confess a belief that the God of Israel is the only God. See theological note "God Reigns: Divine Sovereignty."

4:37 King of heaven. This unique title brings together the theme of the chapter: the rule of God from heaven (vv. 3, 26 and notes).

5:1 King Belshazzar. The name "Belshazzar" means "Bel, protect the king" (not to be confused with "Belteshazzar," the Babylonian name given to Daniel, 1:7 note). From Babylonian sources we know that Belshazzar was placed in charge of affairs in Babylon while his father, Nabonidus, the last king of Babylon, spent extensive periods of time at Tema in Arabia. The events of this chapter took place in 539 B.C., the year of Babylon's fall to the Persians, forty-two years after the death of Nebuchadnezzar in 563 B.C.

5:2 when he tasted the wine. Under the influence of wine Belshazzar committed a sacrilegious act.

his father. The immediate father of Belshazzar was Nabonidus, not Nebuchadnezzar. It is not unusual for the terms "father" (vv. 11, 13, 18) and "son" (v. 22) to be used as equivalents for "predecessor" and "successor" (text notes).

5:4 praised the gods. The temple vessels were defiled, not only by being put to profane use, but also by being used to honor the false gods of Babylon.

5:7 the enchanters, the Chaldeans, and the astrologers. See notes 1:20; 2:2; cf. 2:27; 4:7.

shows me its interpretation. Once again a king requires Daniel's assistance to understand a message from God meant for him (2:5 note).

third ruler. That is, close in power to Nabonidus and Belshazzar (5:1 note). "Third ruler" is an official designation of a high office, but not necessarily the literal third in line to the throne.

and [t]the astrologers. The king declared[1] to
the wise men of Babylon, [u]"Whoever reads
this writing, and shows me its interpretation,
shall be clothed with purple and have a
chain of gold around his neck and [v]shall be
the third ruler in the kingdom." **8** Then all
the king's wise men came in, but [w]they could
not read the writing or make known to the
king the interpretation. **9** Then King Belshazzar was greatly [x]alarmed, and his [n]col-
or changed, and his [y]lords were perplexed.
10 The queen,[2] because of the words of
the king and his lords, came into the banqueting hall, and the queen declared,
[z]"O king, live forever! Let not your
thoughts alarm you [a]or your color change.
11 There is a man in your kingdom [b]in whom
is the spirit of the holy gods.[3] In the days of
your father, [c]light and understanding and
wisdom like the wisdom of the gods were
found in him, and King Nebuchadnezzar,
your father—your father the king—[d]made
him chief of the magicians, [r]enchanters,
Chaldeans, and astrologers, **12** [e]because an
excellent spirit, knowledge, and [f]under-
standing [f]to interpret dreams, explain riddles, and [g]solve problems were found in this
Daniel, [h]whom the king named Belteshazzar. Now let Daniel be called, and he
will show the interpretation."

Daniel Interprets the Handwriting

13 Then Daniel was brought in before the
king. The king answered and said to
Daniel, "You are that Daniel, one of [i]the
exiles of Judah, whom the king my father
brought from Judah. **14** I have heard of you
that [b]the spirit of the gods[4] is in you, and
that [c]light and understanding and excellent wisdom are found in you. **15** Now [j]the
wise men, the [k]enchanters, have been
brought in before me to read this writing
and make known to me its interpretation,
but [l]they could not show the interpretation of the matter. **16** [m]But I have heard
that you can give interpretations and

7 [t]ch. 2:27 [u]ver. 16, 29; [ch. 2:6] [v]ver. 16, 29
8 [w]ver. 15; ch. 4:7, 18; [ch. 2:27; Gen. 41:8]
9 [x][ch. 2:1] [n][See ver. 6 above] [y]ver. 1
10 [z]See ch. 2:4 [a][ver. 6, 9]
11 [b]See ch. 4:8 [c][ch. 1:20] [d]ch. 4:9; [ch. 2:48] [r][See ver. 7 above]
12 [e]ch. 6:3 [f]See ch. 1:17 [g]ver. 16 [h]See ch. 1:7
13 [i]See ch. 2:25
14 [b][See ver. 11 above] [c][See ver. 11 above]
15 [j]ver. 7 [k][ch. 2:2; 4:6] [l]See ver. 8
16 [m][ch. 2:26]

1 Aramaic *answered and said*; also verse 10 2 Or *queen mother;* twice in this verse 3 Or *Spirit of the holy God* 4 Or *Spirit of God*

God Reigns: Divine Sovereignty

The assertion of God's absolute sovereignty in creation, providence, and salvation is basic to biblical belief and biblical praise. The vision of God reigning from His throne is recurrent (1 Kin. 22:19; Is. 6:1; Ezek. 1:26; Dan. 7:9; Rev. 4:2; cf. Ps. 11:4; 45:6; 47:8, 9; Heb. 12:2; Rev. 3:21). We are constantly told in explicit terms that the Lord (Yahweh) reigns as king, exercising dominion over great and small alike (Ex. 15:18; Ps. 47; 93; 96:10; 97; 99:1–5; 146:10; Prov. 16:33; 21:1; Is. 24:23; 52:7; Dan. 4:34, 35; 5:21–28; 6:26; Matt. 10:29–31). God's dominion is total: He wills as He chooses, and carries out all that He wills, and none can stay His hand, or thwart His plans. He exercises His rule in the normal course of life, as well as in more remarkable interventions or miracles.

God's rational creatures, angelic and human, have free agency, that is, the power of personal decision as to what they will do. We would not be moral beings, answerable to God the Judge, if it were not so. Nor would it be possible to distinguish, as Scripture does, between the bad purposes of human agents and the good purposes of God, who sovereignly overrules human action as a planned means to His own goals (Gen. 50:20; Acts 2:23; 13:26–39). Yet the fact of free agency confronts us with mystery. God's control over our free actions, actions chosen by ourselves, is as complete as it is over anything else; but how this can be we do not know. Despite this control, God is not, and cannot be, the author of sin. God has conferred responsibility on moral agents for their thoughts, words, and deeds, according to His justice.

Ps. 93 teaches that God's sovereign rule (a) guarantees the stability of the world against all the forces of chaos (vv. 1–4), (b) confirms the trustworthiness of all God's utterances and directives (v. 5), and (c) calls for the worship of His people (v. 5). The whole psalm expresses joy, hope, and confidence in the Almighty.

5:10 The queen. It is unlikely that this was a wife of Belshazzar, since she was already present at the banquet (vv. 2, 3). Probably she is to be identified as the "queen mother," one of very few women to have significant power in ancient royal courts (cf. 1 Kin. 15:3; 2 Kin. 11:1–3; 24:12; Jer. 13:18).

5:11 the spirit of the holy gods. See note 4:8. It is not surprising that the queen mother was more familiar with Daniel's life and prominence than was Belshazzar. Daniel would be in his eighties by 539 B.C. He had been brought to Babylon as a young man sixty-six years before (605 B.C., 1:1 note).

5:12 found in this Daniel. This divine endowment can be understood as the presence of God's Spirit in an individual, or simply as the possession of a remarkable spirit characteristic of that individual.

Belteshazzar. See note 1:7.

[n]solve problems. [o]Now if you can read the
writing and make known to me its interpretation, [o]you shall be clothed with purple and have a chain of gold around your
neck and [p]shall be the third ruler in the
kingdom."
17 Then Daniel answered and said before
the king, [q]"Let your gifts be for yourself,
and give your rewards to another.
Nevertheless, I will read the writing to the
king and make known to him the interpretation. 18 O king, the [r]Most High God [s]gave
[t]Nebuchadnezzar your father [u]kingship
and greatness and glory and majesty. 19 And
because of the greatness that he gave him,
[v]all peoples, nations, and languages [w]trem-
bled and feared before him. Whom he
would, he killed, and whom he would, he
kept alive; whom he would, he raised up,
and whom he would, he humbled. 20 But
[x]when his heart was lifted up and his spirit was hardened so that he dealt proudly,
[y]he was brought down from his kingly
throne, and his glory was taken from him.
21 [z]He was driven from among the children
of mankind, and his mind was made like
that of a beast, and his dwelling was with
the wild donkeys. He was fed grass like an
ox, and his body was wet with the dew of
heaven, [z]until he knew that the [r]Most High
God rules the kingdom of mankind and
sets over it whom he will. 22 And you his
son,[1] [a]Belshazzar, [b]have not humbled your
heart, though you knew all this, 23 but you
have lifted up yourself against [c]the Lord of
heaven. And [d]the vessels of his house have
been brought in before you, and you and
your lords, your wives, and your concubines have drunk wine from them. [e]And
you have praised the gods of silver and
gold, of bronze, iron, wood, and stone,
which do not see or hear or know, [f]but the
God in whose hand is your breath, and
[g]whose are all your ways, [h]you have not
honored.
24 "Then from his presence [i]the hand was
sent, and this writing was inscribed. 25 And
this is the writing that was inscribed:
MENE, MENE, TEKEL, and PARSIN. 26 This is
the interpretation of the matter: MENE,
God has numbered[2] the days of your kingdom and brought it to an end; 27 TEKEL,
[j]you have been weighed[3] in the balances
and found wanting; 28 PERES, your kingdom
is divided and given to [k]the Medes and
[l]Persians."[4]
29 Then [a]Belshazzar gave the command,
and Daniel [m]was clothed with purple, a
chain of gold was put around his neck, and
a proclamation was made about him, that
he should be the third ruler in the kingdom.
30 [n]That very night [a]Belshazzar the [o]Chal-
dean king was killed. 31[5] And [p]Darius [k]the
Mede received the kingdom, being about
sixty-two years old.

1 Or *successor* 2 MENE sounds like the Aramaic for *numbered* 3 TEKEL sounds like the Aramaic for *weighed* 4 PERES (the singular of *Parsin*) sounds like the Aramaic for *divided* and for *Persia* 5 Ch 6:1 in Aramaic

16 [n]ver. 12 [o]ver. 7, 29 [p]ver. 7, 29
17 [q][2 Kin. 5:16]
18 [r]ch. 3:26; 4:2 [s][ch. 2:37; 4:22] [t]ver. 2 [u][ch. 4:36]
19 [v]See ch. 3:4 [w][ch. 6:26]
20 [x][ch. 4:30, 31; Ezek. 31:10, 11] [y]See ch. 2:21
21 [z][ch. 4:25, 32] [r][See ver. 18 above]
22 [a]See ver. 1 [b][2 Chr. 33:23]
23 [c][ch. 4:37] [d]ver. 3; See ch. 1:2 [e]ver. 4 [f]Job 12:10 [g]Jer. 10:23 [h][Acts 12:23; Rev. 16:9]
24 [i]ver. 5
27 [j]Job 31:6; Ps. 62:9
28 [k]ver. 31; [ch. 9:1; Isai. 13:17; 21:2; Jer. 51:28] [l]See ch. 6:28
29 [a][See ver. 22 above] [m][ver. 7, 16]
30 [n]ver. 7, 16; 51:31, 39, 57 [a][See ver. 22 above] [o]Jer. 50:24
31 [p]ch. 9:1 [k][See ver. 28 above]

5:16 third ruler in the kingdom. See note on v. 7.

5:17 Let your gifts be for yourself. Daniel may reject Belshazzar's offer of reward because he is conscious that it is only by God's mercy that he is able to respond to the king's request, and he does not want to use his God-given role as a means of personal profit (cf. Gen. 14:23; 1 Sam. 9:7 note). But why then did he accept them earlier (2:48) and later (v. 29)? Some interpreters believe he is here avoiding royal pressure to modify the ominous message (Num. 22:18; Mic. 3:5, 11).

5:18 Nebuchadnezzar your father. See note on v. 2.

5:21–28 See "God Reigns: Divine Sovereignty" at 4:34.

5:21 Most High God rules. This statement summarizes the book's theology (Introduction: Characteristics and Themes).

5:22 And you his son. See note on v. 2.

though you knew all this. Because the king is without excuse, even more than his father, the time of mercy is past (contrast a different case at 1 Tim. 1:13).

5:24 Then. The writing on the wall is God's answer to the arrogant challenge presented by Belshazzar's pride and his defiance of the God who had shown His existence and sovereignty in the time of Nebuchadnezzar.

5:25 MENE, MENE, TEKEL, and PARSIN. Aramaic, like Hebrew, is usually written without vowels, and this very short inscription would have been ambiguous.

5:26 MENE. The Aramaic word could be a verb meaning "numbered" or a noun meaning "mina," a unit of money. Daniel read it as the verb to signify that the length of Belshazzar's reign had been determined by God and was about to end (Jer. 50:18).

5:27 TEKEL. This word is also either a verb or a noun. Daniel read it as a verb meaning "weighed," signifying that Belshazzar failed to measure up to God's standards of righteousness.

5:28 PERES. If those present at the banquet understood the three terms as nouns indicating various units of money (*mina*, or sixty shekels; *tekel*, one shekel; *peres*, a half-shekel), it is not surprising that they could not understand the inscription.

Medes and Persians. See Introduction: Date and Occasion.

5:29 Belshazzar gave the command. Like Nebuchadnezzar, Belshazzar honors Daniel (2:48), but unlike his predecessor, he does not honor Daniel's God (2:46, 47).

5:30 Belshazzar . . . was killed. It is not known just how Belshazzar died. However, the Greek historians Herodotus and Xenophon report that Babylon was taken in a surprise attack by the Persians while the Babylonians were engaged in revelling and dancing.

5:31 Darius the Mede. It has long been alleged that this and other references to Darius the Mede in the Book of Daniel (6:1, 6, 9, 25, 28; 9:1; 11:1) are historical errors. For this discussion see note 6:1.

sixty-two. The mina probably weighed sixty shekels. This, with the shekel and two half-shekels (v. 25 note) came to sixty-two; since this is Darius's age, he may have been referred to in the prophecy.

Daniel and the Lions' Den

6 It pleased Darius to set over the kingdom [q]120 [r]satraps, to be throughout
the whole kingdom; 2 and over them [s]three
presidents, of whom Daniel was one, to
whom these [r]satraps should give account,
so that the king might suffer no loss. 3 Then
this Daniel became [t]distinguished above all
[s]the other presidents and [r]satraps, because
[u]an excellent spirit was in him. And the
king planned [v]to set him over the whole
kingdom. 4 Then [s]the presidents and [r]the
satraps [w]sought to find a ground for complaint against Daniel with regard to the
kingdom, [x]but they could find no ground
for complaint or any fault, because he was
faithful, [x]and no error or fault was found in
him. 5 Then these men said, "We shall not
find any ground for complaint against this
Daniel unless we find it in connection with
the law of his God."
6 Then these [s]presidents and [r]satraps
came by agreement[1] to the king and said to
him, "O [y]King Darius, live forever! 7 All the
[s]presidents of the kingdom, the prefects
and the satraps, the [z]counselors and the
governors are agreed that the king should
establish an ordinance and enforce an [a]in-
junction, that whoever makes petition to
any god or man for thirty days, except to
you, O king, shall be cast into the den of
lions. 8 Now, O king, establish [a]the injunction and sign the document, so that it cannot be changed, according to [b]the law of
[c]the Medes and the Persians, [d]which cannot be revoked." 9 Therefore King Darius
signed the document and [a]injunction.
10 When Daniel knew that the document
had been signed, he went to his house
where [e]he had windows in his upper chamber open [f]toward Jerusalem. He got down
on his knees [g]three times a day and prayed
and [h]gave thanks before his God, as he had
done previously. 11 Then these men came
by agreement and found Daniel making
petition and plea before his God. 12 Then
they [i]came near and said before the king,
concerning the injunction, "O king! Did
you not sign [j]an injunction, that anyone
who makes petition to any god or man
within thirty days except to you, O king,
shall be cast into the den of lions?" The
king answered and said, "The thing stands
fast, according to the law of [c]the Medes
and Persians, [d]which cannot be revoked."
13 Then they answered and said before the
king, [k]"Daniel, who is one [l]of the exiles
[k]from Judah, [m]pays no attention to you,
O king, or [j]the injunction you have signed,
but makes his petition [g]three times a day."
14 Then [n]the king, when he heard these
words, [n]was much distressed and set his
mind to deliver Daniel. And he labored till
the sun went down to rescue him. 15 Then
these men came by agreement to the king
and said to the king, "Know, O king, that
it is a law of the Medes and Persians that
no [j]injunction or ordinance that the king
establishes can be changed."
16 Then the king commanded, and Daniel
was brought and cast into the den of lions.
The king declared[2] to Daniel, "May [o]your

Chapter 6
1 [q][Esth. 1:1] [r]See ch. 3:2
2 [s][ch. 5:7, 16, 29] [r][See ver. 1 above]
3 [t][Esth. 3:1] [s][See ver. 2 above] [r][See ver. 1 above] [u]ch. 5:12 [v][Gen. 41:40; Esth. 10:3]
4 [s][See ver. 2 above] [r][See ver. 1 above] [w][Eccles. 4:4] [x][Ezek. 14:14, 20]
6 [s][See ver. 2 above] [r][See ver. 1 above] [y]ver. 21; See ch. 2:4
7 [s][See ver. 2 above] [z]ch. 3:24; 4:36 [a]ver. 12, 13, 15
8 [a][See ver. 7 above] [b]ver. 12, 15; Esth. 1:19 [c][ch. 8:20] [d][ver. 15; Esth. 8:8]
9 [a][See ver. 7 above]
10 [e][Ps. 137:5] [f][Ps. 28:2; 138:2] See 1 Kin. 8:48 [g]Ps. 55:17 [h][ch. 2:23]
12 [i]ch. 3:8 [j]ver. 7, 8, 9 [c][See ver. 8 above] [d][See ver. 8 above]
13 [k]ch. 1:6 [l]See ch. 2:25 [m]ch. 3:12 [j][See ver. 12 above] [g][See ver. 10 above]
14 [n][Matt. 14:9; Mark 6:26]
15 [j][See ver. 12 above]
16 [o][Acts 27:23]

1 Or *came thronging*; also verses 11, 15 2 Aramaic *answered and said*; also verse 20

6:1 Darius. See note 5:31. Darius the Mede is not referred to in surviving historical sources outside the Scripture, and there is no interval between Belshazzar and Nabonidus (5:1 note) and the accession of Cyrus of Persia. Commentators have suggested that "Darius the Mede" could be: a throne name for Cyrus, the founder of the Persian Empire (v. 28 note); a title; or a designation for Gobryas, a general who had defected from Nebuchadnezzar to Cyrus and later captured Babylon. Cyrus made Gobryas governor over the territories the Persians took from the Babylonians.

6:3 an excellent spirit was in him. See 1:17; 4:8; 5:12.

6:5 the law of his God. Unintentionally, Daniel's adversaries affirm not only his moral integrity but also the visible nature of his piety and commitment to the God of Israel.

6:7 are agreed. The false implication is that Daniel concurred with the proposal. These officials are hypocritical in their seeming devotion to Darius. Their scheme is an attempt to manipulate him for their own designs.

any god or man . . . except to you. The proposal would appear to Darius to be more political than religious, and would serve to consolidate his authority over newly conquered territories.

6:8 the law of the Medes and the Persians. The unchangeableness of their law is also attested in extrabiblical writings. The effect of the decree was to create a conflict for Daniel between allegiance to God and obedience to human government.

6:10 down on his knees. Standing may have been a regular posture in prayer (1 Chr. 23:30; Neh. 9:2–5), while kneeling, a mark of humility, occurred in circumstances of particular solemnity (1 Kin. 8:54; Ezra 9:5; Ps. 95:6; Luke 22:41; Acts 7:60; 9:40).

as he had done previously. Evidently Daniel's prayer habits were public knowledge.

6:13 one of the exiles from Judah. This ethnic identification of Daniel is perhaps indicative of prejudice towards the Jews on the part of the other officials (3:8).

6:14 set his mind to deliver Daniel. Darius immediately perceived that he had been victimized by the intrigue of his own officials in order to trap Daniel. His loyalty to Daniel remained unshaken.

6:16 May your God . . . deliver you. Against his own will Darius was forced to comply with the decree. Nevertheless, he is confident that Daniel's God will intervene on behalf of His faithful servant.

God, whom you serve continually, deliver
you!" 17 [p]And a stone was brought and laid
on the mouth of the den, [q]and the king
sealed it [r]with his own signet and with the
signet of his [s]lords, that nothing might be
changed concerning Daniel. 18 Then the
king went to his palace and spent the night
fasting; [t]no diversions were brought to
him, and [u]sleep fled from him.

19 Then, at break of day, the king arose
and went in haste to the den of lions. 20 As
he came near to the den where Daniel was,
he cried out in a tone of anguish. The king
declared to Daniel, "O Daniel, servant of
[v]the living God, [o]has your God, whom you
serve continually, [w]been able to deliver you
from the lions?" 21 Then Daniel said to the
king, [x]"O king, live forever! 22 My God [y]sent
his angel [z]and shut the lions' mouths, and
they have not harmed me, because I was
found blameless [a]before him; [a]and also
before you, O king, I have done no harm."
23 Then the king was exceedingly glad, and
commanded that Daniel be taken up out of
the den. So Daniel was taken up out of the
den, and [b]no kind of harm was found on
him, because he had trusted in his God.
24 And the king commanded, and [c]those
men who had maliciously accused Daniel
were brought and cast into the den of
lions—they, their children, and their
wives. And before they reached the bottom
of the den, the lions overpowered them
and broke all their bones in pieces.

25 Then King Darius wrote to all [d]the peoples, nations, and languages [e]that dwell in
all the earth: [f]"Peace be multiplied to you.
26 [g]I make a decree, that in all my royal
dominion [h]people are to tremble and fear
before the God of Daniel,

> for [i]he is [j]the living God,
> enduring forever;
> his kingdom shall never be
> destroyed,
> [j]and his dominion shall be [k]to the
> end.
>
> 27 He delivers and rescues;
> he works [l]signs and wonders
> in heaven and on earth,
> he who has [m]saved Daniel
> from the power of the lions."

28 So this Daniel prospered during the
reign of Darius and [n]the reign of [o]Cyrus the
Persian.

Daniel's Vision of the Four Beasts

7 In the first year of [p]Belshazzar king of
Babylon, [q]Daniel saw a dream and [r]visions of his head as he lay in his bed. Then
he wrote down the dream and told the sum
of the matter. 2 Daniel declared,[1] "I saw in
my vision by night, and behold, [s]the four
winds of heaven were stirring up the great
sea. 3 And four great beasts [t]came up out of
the sea, different from one another. 4 The
first was like a lion and had eagles' wings.
Then as I looked its wings were plucked
off, and it was lifted up from the ground
and made to stand on two feet like a man,
and the mind of a man was given to it.
5 And behold, [u]another beast, a second one,
like a bear. It was raised up on one side. It
had three ribs in its mouth between its
teeth; and it was told, 'Arise, devour much

17 [p][Lam. 3:53] [q]Matt. 27:66; Rev. 20:3 [r][Esth. 3:12] [s]ch. 4:36; 5:1
18 [t][Prov. 25:20] [u]Esth. 6:1; [ch. 2:1]
20 [v]ver. 26 [o][See ver. 16 above] [w][ch. 3:15]
21 [x]See ch. 2:4
22 [y]ch. 3:28 [z]Heb. 11:33; [Ps. 22:21; 2 Tim. 4:17] [a][ver. 4]
23 [b][ch. 3:25]
24 [c][Deut. 19:19]
25 [d]See ch. 3:4 [e]ch. 4:1 [f]See ch. 4:1
26 [g]See ch. 3:10
[h][ch. 5:19; Ps. 99:1; Eccles. 12:13] [i]ver. 20 [j]See ch. 4:34 [k]ch. 7:26
27 [l]ch. 4:2 [m][ch. 3:28, 29]
28 [n][ch. 1:21] [o]2 Chr. 36:22, 23; Ezra 1:2, 2; 4:3, 5; 6:3, 14; Isai. 44:28; 45:1; [ch. 1:21; 10:1]
Chapter 7
1 [p]See ch. 5:1 [q][ch. 1:17] [r]ver. 15; ch. 2:28; 4:5
2 [s]ch. 8:8; 11:4; [Ezek. 37:9; Zech. 2:6; Rev. 7:1]
3 [t][Rev. 13:1]
5 [u][ch. 2:39]

1 Aramaic *answered and said*

6:17 sealed it with his own signet. Signet rings and cylinder seals were used by the Assyrians, Babylonians, and Persians. The ring or cylinder was pressed into soft clay to leave the mark of the owner of the seal. Breaking seals was a violation of the law.

6:22 My God sent his angel. Possibly, although not necessarily in the context, this was the Angel of the Lord. See note 3:28.

6:23 the king . . . commanded. Darius could rescue Daniel without violating the decree since its demands had been fulfilled.

6:26 a decree. Compare 2:47; 3:28, 29; 4:2, 3, 34–37; 5:18–29. As in the previous narratives, God displays His sovereign control of nature and history, kingdoms and kings. The decree is an eloquent testimony to "the living God" and His indestructible kingdom. It is an official acknowledgment of Daniel's God, although it does not necessarily reflect personal faith on the part of Darius.

6:28 Daniel prospered. Although the government changed hands, God's favor sustained Daniel and continued his authority.

7:1 the first year of Belshazzar. See note 5:1. Belshazzar's administration under Nabonidus may have begun at the same time as the accession of his father (556 B.C.) or a few years later. In either case the visions of chs. 7 and 8 are chronologically between the events of chs. 4 and 5.

7:2 great sea. The sea is a common figure for the restlessness and dangerous turmoil of sinful men and nations (see v. 17; cf. Is. 17:12, 13; 57:20).

7:3 four great beasts. These four "beasts" represent four kingdoms (vv. 17, 23), corresponding closely to the four kingdoms of Nebuchadnezzar's dream in ch. 2. For identification of the four kingdoms, see note 2:37–40 and Introduction: Date and Occasion.

7:4 like a lion. The "lion" with "eagle's wings" is an appropriate symbol for the Babylonian Empire (cf. Jer. 50:44; Ezek. 17:3, 12). Winged lions with human faces were common in Babylonian art and were placed at the entrances of important public buildings.

wings were plucked off. Perhaps this is a reference to Nebuchadnezzar's humiliation and later restoration after a seven-year period of insanity (ch. 4).

7:5 another beast . . . like a bear. The Medo-Persian kingdom is symbolized as a "beast" with a voracious appetite. The raised side may represent the superior status of Persia, and the "three ribs" likely represent Persia's conquests over Lydia, (546 B.C.), Babylon (539 B.C.), and Egypt (525 B.C.). See note 8:3.

flesh.' 6 After this I looked, and behold,
another, like a [v]leopard, with four wings of
a bird on its back. And the beast had four
heads, and [w]dominion was given to it.
7 After this I saw in the night visions, and
behold, a fourth beast, [x]terrifying and
dreadful and exceedingly strong. It had
great iron teeth; [x]it devoured and broke in
pieces [x]and stamped what was left with its
feet. It was different from all the beasts that
were before it, and [y]it had ten horns. 8 I
considered the horns, and behold, [z]there
came up among them another horn, a little
one, [z]before which three of the first horns
were plucked up by the roots. And behold,
in this horn were eyes like the eyes of a
man, and [a]a mouth speaking great things.

The Ancient of Days Reigns

9 As I looked,

[b]thrones were placed,
and the [c]Ancient of Days took his seat;
[d]his clothing was white as snow,
and [e]the hair of his head like pure wool;
his throne was fiery flames;
[f]its wheels were burning fire.
10 [g]A stream of fire issued
and came out from before him;
[h]a thousand thousands [i]served him,
[h]and ten thousand times ten thousand [j]stood before him;
the [k]court sat in judgment,
and [l]the books were opened.

11 I looked then because of the sound of
[a]the great words that the horn was speaking. And as I looked, [m]the beast was killed,
and its body destroyed [m]and given over to
be burned with fire. 12 As for the rest of the
beasts, [n]their dominion was taken away,
but their lives were prolonged for a season
and a time.

The Son of Man Is Given Dominion

13 I saw in the night visions,

and [o]behold, with the clouds of heaven
there came one like a son of man,
and he came to the [y]Ancient of Days
and was presented before him.
14 [p]And to him was given dominion
and glory and a kingdom,
that all [q]peoples, nations, and languages
should serve him;
[r]his dominion is an everlasting dominion,
which shall not pass away,
and his kingdom one
that shall not be destroyed.

Daniel's Vision Interpreted

15 "As for me, Daniel, my spirit within
me[1] was anxious, and [s]the visions of my
head alarmed me. 16 I approached one of
those who stood there and asked him the
truth concerning all this. So he told me and

6 [v][Hab. 1:8; Rev. 13:2] [w][ch. 11:5]
7 [x]ver. 19, 23 [y]ver. 20; [Rev. 12:3; 13:1; 17:12]
8 [z][ver. 20, 21, 24; ch. 8:9] [a]ver. 20; [Rev. 13:5, 6]
9 [b]Rev. 20:4; [Matt. 19:28]; See 1 Kin. 22:19 [c]ver. 22; [Ps. 90:2] [d]Matt. 28:3 [e]Rev. 1:14 [f][Ezek. 1:16; 10:2]
10 [g][Ps. 21:9] [h]Ps. 68:17; Heb. 12:22; Rev. 5:11 [i]Ps. 103:21 [j][Zech. 3:4] [k]ver. 22, 26; Rev. 11:18; 20:4 [l]Rev. 20:12
11 [a][See ver. 8 above] [m]Rev. 19:20; [Rev. 20:10]
12 [n][ver. 14, 26]
13 [o]Matt. 26:64; Mark 14:62; Rev. 1:7; 14:14 [y][See ver. 7 above]
14 [p]Ps. 110:1, 2; Isai. 9:6, 7; Rev. 11:15 [q]See ch. 3:4 [r]See ch. 2:44
15 [s]See ver. 1

1 Aramaic *within its sheath*

7:6 another, like a leopard. The Greek Empire is symbolized by the "leopard," known for its quickness. Alexander the Great (356–323 B.C.) conquered the Persian Empire with great speed. Alexander died suddenly at age thirty-three, and the empire he established was divided into four parts (Macedonia under Cassander, Thrace and Asia Minor under Lysimachus, Syria under Seleucus, and Egypt under Ptolemy).

7:7 a fourth beast. This unidentified "beast" symbolizes Rome, the kingdom that ultimately assimilated the various parts of the divided Greek kingdom.

it had ten horns. The "ten horns" symbolize ten kings or kingdoms associated with the Roman Empire (v. 24). Some interpreters suggest that a second phase of the fourth kingdom, a revived Roman Empire is to be expected, from which the ten horns will come, at once or one after the other (2:44 note; cf. Rev. 13:1–10; 17:3, 12).

7:8 another horn, a little one. The ten horns are prior in time to the "little horn" which uproots three of them, symbolizing another phase of the fourth kingdom. Many interpreters suggest that the little horn represents the Antichrist (2 Thess. 2:3, 4, 8). This would be the first reference in Scripture to the Antichrist.

7:9 the Ancient of Days took his seat. The title "Ancient of Days" occurs in the Bible only in this chapter (vv. 13, 22). It is a designation for God on the throne and judgment.

his throne . . . its wheels. The depiction of God's throne resembles Ezekiel's vision of the throne chariot of God (Ezek. 1:15–28).

7:11, 12 A contrast is drawn between the complete destruction of the fourth kingdom and the measure of continuance granted the preceding kingdoms as their people and customs were absorbed into the succeeding kingdoms.

7:13 with the clouds of heaven. Elsewhere in the Old Testament it is only God who comes on the clouds (Ps. 104:3; Is. 19:1). Accordingly, the "son of man" originates in heaven and comes by divine initiative.

one like a son of man. The Aramaic for "son of man" would otherwise mean "a human being" as opposed to the preceding "beasts." The equivalent is used for Daniel in 8:17 and many times for Daniel's contemporary, Ezekiel (e.g., Ezek. 2:1, 3, 6). But, in contrast to the "beasts" who misruled the earth, this One will rule as God intended before humanity's fall (Gen. 1:26–28; Ps. 8:4–6). The expression "son of man" is used sixty-nine times in the synoptic Gospels and twelve times in the Gospel of John to refer to Christ. It is the title Jesus most often used of Himself.

7:14 all peoples . . . should serve him. The "son of man" is Christ, the Messiah. Jesus referred this passage to Himself, and doing so caused the religious leaders of His day to accuse Him of blasphemy (Matt. 26:64, 65; Mark 14:62–64).

an everlasting dominion. He is given God's sovereignty and exercises the rule symbolized by the stone that fell in Nebuchadnezzar's dream (2:34, 35, 44, 45).

made known to me the interpretation of
the things. 17 [t]'These four great beasts are
four kings who shall arise out of the earth.
18 But [u]the saints of the Most High shall
receive the kingdom and possess the kingdom forever, forever and ever.'
19 "Then I desired to know the truth
about [v]the fourth beast, which was different from all the rest, exceedingly terrifying,
with its teeth of iron and claws of bronze,
and which devoured and broke in pieces
and stamped what was left with its feet,
20 [w]and about the ten horns that were on its
head, and the other horn that came up and
before which three of them fell, the horn
that had eyes and a mouth that spoke great
things, and that seemed greater than its
companions. 21 As I looked, this horn
[x]made war with the saints and prevailed
over them, 22 until the [y]Ancient of Days
came, and [u]judgment was given for the
saints of the Most High, and the time came
when [u]the saints possessed the kingdom.
23 "Thus he said: 'As for [v]the fourth beast,

there shall be a fourth kingdom on
earth,
which shall be different from all
the kingdoms,
and it shall devour the whole earth,
and trample it down, and break it
to pieces.
24 As for the ten horns,
out of this kingdom ten kings shall
arise,
and another shall arise after them;
he shall be different from the former
ones,
and shall put down three kings.
25 [z]He shall speak words against the
Most High,
and shall wear out the saints of the
Most High,
and shall think to [a]change the
times and the law;
and they shall be given into his hand
for [b]a time, times, and half a time.
26 [c]But the court shall sit in judgment,
and [d]his dominion shall be taken
away,
to be consumed and destroyed [e]to
the end.
27 [f]And the kingdom and the dominion
and the greatness of the kingdoms
under the whole heaven
shall be given to the people of [f]the
saints of the Most High;
[g]their kingdom shall be an everlasting
kingdom,
and all dominions shall serve and
obey them.'

28 "Here is the end of the matter. [h]As for
me, Daniel, my [i]thoughts greatly alarmed
me, [j]and my color changed, but [k]I kept the
matter in my heart."

Daniel's Vision of the Ram and the Goat

8 In the third year of the reign of [l]King
Belshazzar a vision appeared to me,
Daniel, [m]after that which appeared to me
[m]at the first. 2 And I saw in the vision; and
when I saw, I was in [n]Susa the capital,[1]
which is in the province of [o]Elam. And [p]I
saw in the vision, [p]and I was at the [q]Ulai
canal. 3 I raised my eyes and saw, and

17 [t][ver. 3]
18 [u]ver. 22, 27; Matt. 25:34; [1 Cor. 6:2; Rev. 2:26; 20:4]
19 [v]ver. 7
20 [w]ver. 8
21 [x][ch. 8:24]
22 [y]ver. 9, 13 [u][See ver. 18 above]
23 [v][See ver. 19 above]
25 [z][ch. 11:36] [a]ch. 2:9, 21 [b]ch. 12:7; Rev. 12:14
26 [c]See ver. 10 [d][ver. 12, 14] [e]ch. 6:26
27 [f]See ver. 18 [g]See ch. 2:44
28 [h]ver. 15; [ch. 8:27; 10:8, 16; Jer. 23:9] [i]ch. 4:5, 19; 5:6 [j][ch. 5:6, 10] [k][Luke 2:19, 51]
Chapter 8
1 [l]See ch. 5:1 [m][ch. 7:1]
2 [n]See Neh 1:1 [o]See Isai. 11:11 [p]See Ezek. 1:1 [q]ver. 16

1 Or *the fortified city*

7:18 the saints of the Most High. See vv. 21, 22, 25, 27. The "saints" are not angels, but believers in God, who will share in Christ's kingdom (Matt. 19:28; 1 Cor. 6:1–3; 2 Tim. 2:12; Rev. 22:5).

7:21 made war with the saints. Daniel gives additional information about the hostility of the little horn, possibly the Antichrist (v. 8), toward the people of God (cf. Rev. 13:7).

7:22 until the Ancient of Days came. Although the Antichrist will prevail for a time against God's people, in the end he will fall under the judgment of God (Zech. 14:1–4; Rev. 13:7–17; 19:20).

7:25 for a time, times, and half a time. The word "time" is the same word used in 4:16 and 4:23, and as there may mean one year. Some interpreters take this verse to refer to the last half of the seventieth week of ch. 9 (see 9:27). Others do not assign a specific duration to the expression, but take it to be a period of time that is shortened because God intervenes.

7:27 the saints of the Most High. See note on v. 18.

8:1–12:13 Daniel resumes writing in Hebrew for the last five chapters. He used Aramaic in 2:4 to 7:28 (2:4 note).

8:1 In the third year of the reign of King Belshazzar. That is, two years after Daniel's dream in ch. 7 (7:1 note).

8:2 I saw . . . I was. Daniel had a visionary journey like that of Ezekiel (Ezek. 3:10–15).

in Susa the capital. In Daniel's time Susa was the capital of Elam, about 230 miles east of Babylon. It is not clear whether Elam was independent, or aligned with Babylon or Media. Later, however, as one of three royal cities, Susa was the diplomatic and administrative center of the Persian Empire (cf. Neh. 1:1; Esth. 1:2).

the Ulai canal. This canal near Susa connected two rivers that flowed into the Persian Gulf.

8:3 a ram . . . two horns. According to v. 20, the ram and its horns represent the kings of the Medo-Persian Empire.

one was higher than the other, and . . . came up last. Medo-Persian history clarifies the symbolism. The Medes became independent of Assyria after 612 B.C. The Persians were under the control of the Medes, but eventually rose to prominence when Cyrus of Anshan defeated his Median overlord in 550 B.C. Cyrus (reigned 559–530 B.C.) called himself "King of the World."

behold, [r]a ram standing on the bank of the
canal. It had two horns, and both horns
were high, but one was higher than the
other, and the higher one came up last. 4 I
saw [s]the ram charging westward and northward and southward. No [t]beast [u]could
stand before him, [v]and there was no one
who could rescue from his power. [w]He did
as he pleased and [x]became great.

5 As I was considering, behold, a [y]male
goat came from the west across the face of
the whole earth, without touching the
ground. And the goat had [y]a conspicuous
horn between his eyes. 6 He came to [z]the
ram with the two horns, which I had seen
standing on the bank of the canal, [a]and he
ran at him in his powerful wrath. 7 I saw
him come close to the ram, [b]and he was
enraged against him and struck the ram
and broke his two horns. [c]And the ram had
no power to stand before him, but he [d]cast
him down to the ground and trampled on
him. And there was no one who could rescue the ram from his power. 8 Then [y]the
goat [e]became exceedingly great, but when
he was strong, the great horn was broken,
and instead of it there came up four [f]con-
spicuous horns toward [f]the four winds of
heaven.

9 Out of one of them came [g]a little horn,
which grew exceedingly great toward [h]the
south, toward the east, and toward [i]the
glorious land. 10 [j]It grew great, [k]even to
the host of heaven. And some of the host
[k]and some[1] of [l]the stars it threw down to

3 [r][ver. 20]
4 [s][Deut. 33:17; Ezek. 34:21] [t][ch. 7:17] [u][ver. 7] [v][ch. 3:15] [w][ch. 11:3, 16, 36] [x]ver. 8
5 [y][ver. 21]
6 [z][ver. 20] [a][Job 15:26]
7 [b]ch. 11:11 [c][ver. 4] [d][Ps. 7:5]
8 [y][See ver. 5 above] [e]ver. 4 [f][ver. 5]; See ch. 7:2, 3
9 [g]ch. 7:8 [h][ch. 11:25] [i]ch. 11:16, 41; [Ps. 48:2; Ezek. 20:6, 15]
10 [j][ch. 11:28] [k]Isai. 14:13 [l][Rev. 12:4]

1 Or *host, that is, some*

8:4 charging westward and northward and southward. That is, his back was toward the east from where he had come (Is. 41:2). Cyrus first took Asia Minor, then northern and southern Mesopotamia. Subsequent rulers extended Medo-Persian control far to the East.

became great. The Persian Empire became larger than any previous empire in ancient Near Eastern history.

8:5 from the west . . . the goat had a conspicuous horn. According to v. 21, the goat represents Greece and the large horn between his eyes is the first king. The symbolism clearly depicts the rise of the Greek Empire under Alexander the Great (356–323 B.C.).

across . . . the whole earth, without touching the ground. These words describe the amazing speed and extent of Alexander's conquests (7:6 note). In only three years he defeated the powerful Persian Empire.

8:8 the goat became exceedingly great. Alexander's empire quickly exceeded the Persian Empire in size. By 327 B.C. Alexander had moved east into what is today Afghanistan and then on to the Indus River.

the great horn was broken. Alexander died in Babylon at the age of thirty-three.

instead of it there came up four conspicuous horns. According to v. 22, these horns are four kingdoms that emerged from Alexander's empire but were inferior to it in strength. After a time of internal struggle, four of Alexander's generals took portions of the Greek Empire as their own kingdoms. See note 7:6.

8:9 a little horn. According to v. 23, this "little horn" symbolizes a wicked ruler who will arise in one of the four Greek kingdoms after a long interval of time ("at the latter end of their kingdom"). The descriptions of the actions of this ruler (vv. 9–14; 23–25) indicate that he is Antiochus IV Epiphanes, ruler of the Seleucid kingdom from 175–164 B.C. This horn must be distinguished from the "little one" of 7:8 if that chapter refers to the Roman period and not the Greek.

toward the glorious land. That is, toward Palestine.

8:10 the host of heaven. The "host of heaven" or the "stars" (cf. Jer. 33:22) symbolize the people of God (cf. 12:3; Gen. 15:5) or a heavenly

Alexander's Greek Empire (323 B.C.). In 334 B.C. Alexander, son of Philip II of Macedon, began a military quest to destroy the Persian Empire. Moving from west to east, he was victorious in battle at Issus in 332 B.C. against the Persian Darius III. Moving south, Alexander defeated the Phoenicians at Tyre in 332 B.C., swept through Palestine, and conquered Egypt in 331 B.C. Reengaging Darius III near Nineveh, Alexander's campaign continued east into India, securing vast territory for the Greek Empire. He died in Babylon in 323 B.C.

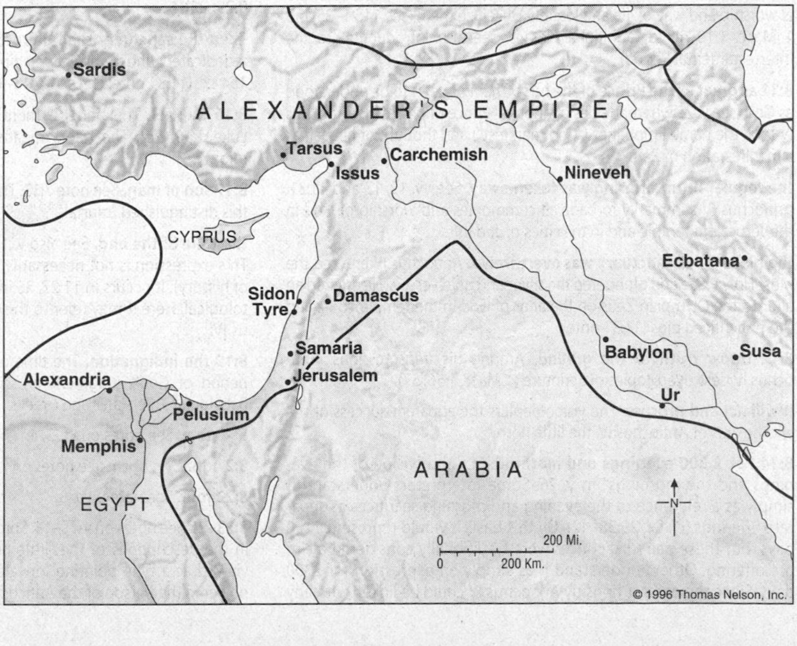

the ground and [m]trampled on them. **11** [n]It became great, even as great as [o]the Prince of the host. [p]And the regular burnt offering was taken away from him, and the place of his sanctuary was overthrown. **12** And a host will be given over to it together with the regular burnt offering because of transgression,[1] and it will throw truth to the ground, and [q]it will act and prosper. **13** Then I heard [r]a holy one speaking, and another holy one said to the one who spoke, [s]"For how long is the vision concerning the regular burnt offering, [t]the transgression that makes desolate, and the giving over of the sanctuary and host to be trampled underfoot?" **14** And he said to me,[2] "For 2,300 [u]evenings and mornings. Then the sanctuary shall be restored to its rightful state."

The Interpretation of the Vision

15 When I, Daniel, had seen the vision, I [v]sought to understand it. And behold, there stood before me one having [w]the appearance of a man. **16** [x]And I heard a man's voice [x]between the banks of the [y]Ulai, and it called, [z]"Gabriel, make this man understand the vision." **17** So he came near where I stood. And when he came, [a]I was frightened [b]and fell on my face. But he said to me, "Understand, [c]O son of man, that the vision is for [d]the time of the end."

18 And when he had spoken to me, [e]I fell into a deep sleep with my face to the ground. But [f]he touched me and made me stand up. **19** He said, "Behold, I will make known to you what shall be at the latter end of [g]the indignation, for it refers to [h]the appointed time of the end. **20** As for [i]the ram that you saw with the two horns, these are the kings of [j]Media and Persia. **21** And [k]the goat[3] is the king of Greece. And [k]the great horn between his eyes is [l]the first king. **22** [m]As for the horn that was broken, in place of which four others arose, four kingdoms shall arise from his[4] nation, [n]but not with his power. **23** And at the latter end of their kingdom, when the transgressors have reached their limit, a king of bold face, one who understands riddles, shall arise. **24** His power shall be great—[o]but not by his own power; and he shall cause fearful destruction [p]and shall succeed in what he does, [q]and destroy mighty men and the people who are the saints.

10 [m]ver. 7 **11** [n]ver. 25; See ch. 11:36 [o]Josh. 5:14 [p]ch. 11:31; 12:11 **12** [q]ver. 24; ch. 11:28, 30 **13** [r]See ch. 4:13 [s]ch. 12:6; [Rev. 6:10]; See ch. 9:21-27 [t]See ch. 11:31 **14** [u][ver. 26] **15** [v][1 Pet. 1:10, 11] [w]ch. 7:13; 10:16, 18; Ezek. 1:26; Rev. 1:13 **16** [x]See ch. 12:5-7 [y]ver. 2 [z]ch. 9:21; Luke 1:19, 26 **17** [a][Luke 1:12] [b]Ezek. 1:28 [c]See Ezek. 2:1 [d][ver. 19; ch. 11:27, 35, 40; 12:4, 9] **18** [e]ch. 10:9; [Luke 9:32] [f]ch. 9:21; 10:10, 18 **19** [g]ch. 11:36 [h][Ps. 102:13]; See ver. 17 **20** [i][ver. 3] [j][ch. 6:8] **21** [k][ver. 5] [l]ch. 10:20; ch. 11:3 **22** [m]ver. 8 [n]ver. 24 **24** [o]Rev. 17:17 [p]ver. 12; ch. 11:28, 30 [q][ch. 7:21]

1 Or *in an act of rebellion* 2 Hebrew; Septuagint, Theodotion, Vulgate *to him* 3 Or *the shaggy goat* 4 Theodotion, Septuagint, Vulgate; Hebrew *the*

army (Is. 14:13; also see 2 Macc. 9:10). The attack against the people of God amounts to an attack against heaven itself.

some of the host and some of the stars it threw down to the ground. This is a symbolic depiction of the severe persecution of God's people under Antiochus IV Epiphanes, who attempted to abolish their traditional worship and way of life and forcibly Hellenize them (see 11:21–35 and 1 Macc. 1:10–64 for additional details; see also Introduction to the Intertestamental Period).

8:11 as great as the Prince of the host. The "Prince" is to be understood as God (see v. 25 where the designation is "Prince of princes"). Antiochus IV took the name Epiphanes ("God manifest") and thought of himself as a manifestation of Zeus.

the regular burnt offering was taken away. See vv. 12, 13 and 11:31. Antiochus IV summarily forbade all ceremonies and worship of God in the Jerusalem temple and in the cities of Judah.

the place of his sanctuary was overthrown. Antiochus IV entered the Most Holy Place and plundered the silver and gold vessels. He erected an altar to the Olympian Zeus on the altar of God in the temple court and there sacrificed pigs (11:31 note).

8:12 throw truth to the ground. Among his transgressions, Antiochus IV destroyed copies of Scripture (1 Macc. 1:56, 57).

it will act and prosper. The vision depicts the apparent success of the wicked acts of Antiochus IV, the little horn.

8:14 For 2,300 evenings and mornings. Cf. the "vision of the evenings and the mornings" in v. 26. Some interpreters understand it simply as a reference to the evening and morning sacrifices as separate offerings (cf. Ex. 29:38–42). On this basis it would represent 1150 days, but these paired sacrifices were traditionally considered a single offering. Others understand it as simply an expression for 2300 days. Since the persecutions by Antiochus IV could be linked with any one of a number of incidents beginning as early as 171 B.C. and ending with the rededication of the temple in 164 B.C., it is difficult to say which understanding of the phrase is to be preferred. The multiple of the number twenty-three may simply be symbolic for a fixed period as in extrabiblical apocalypses (cf. the sixty-nine [23 x 3] weeks in 9:25, 26).

Then the sanctuary shall be restored. The temple was cleansed and rededicated under the leadership of Judas Maccabeus in December, 164 B.C. (11:34 note; cf. Zech. 9:13–17).

8:16 Gabriel. This angel is mentioned four times in Scripture (9:21; Luke 1:19, 26). The name means "mighty one of God" or "God is mighty."

8:17 son of man. See note 7:13. The "strong man of God" is speaking to this distinguished "mortal."

the time of the end. See also v. 19 ("the appointed time of the end"). This expression is not necessarily eschatological (referring to the end of history). It occurs in 11:27, 35 in contexts that are clearly not eschatological. Here it may refer to the end of the persecutions of Antiochus IV.

8:19 the indignation. The time of "the indignation" may refer to the period of God's judgment on Israel during their subjection to the Babylonians, Persians, and Greeks.

8:20 ram. See notes on vv. 3, 4.

8:21 goat . . . horn. See notes on vv. 5, 8.

8:22 four. See note on v. 8.

8:23–25 See notes on vv. 9–14. Some interpreters perceive the Antichrist in the descriptions of the "little horn" of this chapter. Antiochus IV is viewed as a type pointing forward to a later manifestation of satanic power in the person of the Antichrist.

25 [r]By his cunning he shall make deceit
prosper under his hand, and in his own
mind [s]he shall become great. [t]Without
warning he shall destroy many. And he
[s]shall even rise up against the Prince of
princes, and he shall be broken—but [u]by
no human hand. 26 The vision of [v]the
evenings and the mornings that has been
told [w]is true, but [x]seal up the vision, [y]for it
refers to many days from now."
27 And [z]I, Daniel, was overcome and lay
sick for some days. Then I rose and went
about the king's business, but I was
appalled by the vision [a]and did not understand it.

Daniel's Prayer for His People

9 [b]In the first year of [c]Darius the son of
Ahasuerus, by descent a [d]Mede, who
was made king over the realm of the
[e]Chaldeans— 2 in the first year of his
reign, I, Daniel, perceived in the books
the number of years that, according to
[f]the word of the LORD to Jeremiah the
prophet, must pass before the end of the
desolations of Jerusalem, namely, seventy
years.
3 Then I turned my face to the Lord God,
seeking him by [g]prayer and pleas for mercy
with fasting and sackcloth and ashes. 4 I
prayed to the LORD my God and [h]made
confession, saying, [i]"O Lord, the [i]great and
awesome God, who [j]keeps covenant and
steadfast love with those who love him
and keep his commandments, 5 [k]we have
sinned and done wrong and acted wickedly [l]and rebelled, turning aside from your
commandments and rules. 6 [m]We have not
listened to [n]your servants the prophets,
who spoke in your name to [o]our kings, our
princes, and our fathers, and to all the people of the land. 7 To you, [p]O Lord, belongs
righteousness, but to us open shame, as at
this day, to the men of Judah, to the inhabitants of Jerusalem, and to all Israel, [q]those
who are near and [q]those who are far away,
in [r]all the lands to which you have driven
them, because of [s]the treachery that they
have committed against you. 8 To us,
O Lord, belongs open shame, to our kings,
to our princes, and to our fathers, because
[k]we have sinned against you. 9 [t]To the Lord
our God belong mercy and forgiveness, for
we have rebelled against him 10 [m]and have
not obeyed the voice of the LORD our God
by walking in his laws, which he set before
us by [n]his servants the prophets. 11 [u]All
Israel has transgressed your law and turned
aside, [v]refusing to obey your voice. [w]And
the curse and oath [x]that are written in the
Law of [y]Moses the servant of God have
been poured out upon us, because [k]we
have sinned against him. 12 He has confirmed his words, which he spoke against
us and against [z]our rulers who ruled us,[1]
by [a]bringing upon us a great calamity. [b]For
under the whole heaven there has not been
done anything like what has been done
against Jerusalem. 13 [x]As it is written in the
Law of Moses, all this calamity has come
upon us; yet we have not entreated the
favor of the LORD our God, [c]turning from
our iniquities and gaining insight by your

25 [r][ch. 11:23] [s]ver. 11 [t][ch. 11:21, 24] [u]See ch. 2:34
26 [v][ver. 14] [w][ch. 10:1] [x][ch. 12:4, 9] [y]ch. 10:14
27 [z][ch. 7:28] [a][ver. 16]
Chapter 9
1 [b]ch. 11:1 [c]See ch. 5:31 [d][ch. 8:20] [e]ch. 5:30
2 [f][Ezra 1:1; Jer. 25:12]
3 [g]ver. 17, 18, 23; [Neh. 1:4]
4 [h]ver. 20; [Ezra 10:1; Neh. 1:6] [i]Neh. 1:5; 9:32 [j]Deut. 7:9
5 [k]ver. 15 [l]Lam. 3:42
6 [m]2 Chr. 36:15, 16 [n]Ezra 9:11; Zech. 1:6 [o]Ezra 9:7; Neh. 9:34
7 [p][ver. 14; Lam. 1:18] [q][Esth. 9:20] [r]See Jer. 8:3 [s]Lev. 26:40
8 [k][See ver. 5 above]
9 [t]Neh. 9:17; Ps. 86:15
10 [m][See ver. 6 above] [n][See ver. 6 above]
11 [u]See Isai. 1:4-6 [v][Jer. 40:3; 44:23] [w]Jer. 44:22 [x]See Lev. 26:14-45; Deut. 28:15-68 [y]1 Chr. 6:49; 2 Chr. 24:9; Neh. 10:29 [k][See ver. 5 above]
12 [z][Ps. 82:2, 3] [a]Jer. 39:16 [b]Ezek. 5:9; [Lam. 1:12] 13 [x][See ver. 11 above] [c]Hos. 7:10

1 Or *our judges who judged us*

8:25 Prince of princes. This is a reference to God (v. 11 note).

by no human hand. Antiochus IV died of a physical or nervous disorder in 164 B.C. For accounts of his death, see 1 Macc. 6:1–16 and 2 Macc. 9.

8:26 seal up the vision. The term "seal" can mean to authenticate or certify something, or to close up for confidentiality and safekeeping. The second sense seems best in this context (6:17 note).

it refers to many days from now. The words "from now" have been supplied by the translators. The conquests of Alexander (333–323 B.C.) occurred more than two centuries after Daniel's vision (c. 550 B.C.). The activities of Antiochus IV were about a century and a half after Alexander (171–164 B.C.).

9:1–27 Daniel recounts the revelation he received concerning the prophecy of Jeremiah about the seventy years of Jerusalem's desolation (Jer. 25:11, 12; 29:10). Significantly, the revelation follows Daniel's prayer confessing the sinfulness of God's people and the justice of Jerusalem's desolation, and seeking the favor of God for the restoration of the city and the temple.

9:1 the first year of Darius the son of Ahasuerus. See note 6:1. The word "Ahasuerus" (not the same person mentioned in Esth. 1:1) may be a royal title rather than a personal name. The first year of Darius was 539 B.C.

9:2 the desolations of Jerusalem . . . seventy years. Interpreters differ on the dates of the beginning and ending of the seventy-year period, and on whether it is to be understood as a round number for a human lifetime or exactly seventy years. Some date the period from 586 B.C. (the destruction of Jerusalem by Nebuchadnezzar) to 516 B.C., when the restoration of the temple was completed under Zerubbabel (Ezra 6:13–18). Others date the beginning of the period to the year of Daniel's own captivity (605 B.C., 1:1 note), which would suggest that Daniel recognized the end of the seventy years was imminent.

9:4–19 Daniel's prayer is rooted in a covenantal understanding of the Lord's relation to His people (blessing for obedience, cursing for disobedience, especially vv. 5, 7, 11, 12, 14; cf. Lev. 26:14–45; Deut. 28:15–68; 30:1–5). For a similar prayer, see Neh. 9. The prayer has four parts: (a) worship (v. 4); (b) a confession of sin (vv. 5–11); (c) recognition of the justice of God in His judgment on sin (vv. 11–14); and (d) a plea for God's mercy based on concern for His name, kingdom, and will (vv. 15–19). The prayer is grounded on God's promises (v. 2) and offered in a spirit of contrition and humility (v. 3). It is a model for the appropriate elements of effective prayer.

truth. 14 [d]Therefore the LORD has kept ready
the calamity and has brought it upon us,
[e]for the LORD our God is righteous in all the
works that he has done, and [f]we have not
obeyed his voice. 15 And now, O Lord our
God, who brought your people out of the
land of Egypt [g]with a mighty hand, and
[h]have made a name for yourself, as at this
day, [i]we have sinned, we have done
wickedly.
16 "O Lord, [j]according to all your righteous acts, let your anger and your wrath
turn away from your city Jerusalem, [k]your
holy hill, [l]because for our sins, and for
[m]the iniquities of our fathers, [n]Jerusalem
and your people have become [o]a byword
among all who are around us. 17 Now
therefore, O our God, listen to the prayer
of your servant and to his pleas for mercy,
and for your own sake, O Lord,[1] [p]make
your face to shine upon [q]your sanctuary,
which is desolate. 18 [r]O my God, incline
your ear and hear. Open your eyes and see
[s]our desolations, and [t]the city that is
called by your name. For we do not present our pleas before you because of our
righteousness, but because of your great
mercy. 19 O Lord, hear; O Lord, forgive.
O Lord, pay attention and act. [u]Delay not,
[v]for your own sake, O my God, because
[t]your city and [w]your people are called by
your name."

14 [d][Jer. 1:12] [e]Neh. 9:33; See ver. 7 [f]ver. 10
15 [g]Ex. 32:11; [Ex. 6:1; Neh. 1:10] [h]Ex. 14:18; Neh. 9:10 [i]See ver. 5
16 [j]Ps. 31:1; 71:2 [k]ver. 20; ch. 11:45; Jer. 31:23; Zech. 8:3 [l]Lam. 1:5 [m][Ex. 20:5] [n]Lam. 2:15, 16 [o]Ps. 44:13; 79:4; Ezek. 36:4; Mic. 6:16
17 [p]Num. 6:25 [q]Lam. 5:18
18 [r]2 Kin. 19:16; Isai. 37:17 [s]ver. 26 See ver. 27 [t]Jer. 25:29
19 [u]Ps. 40:17; 70:5 [v]Ps. 25:11; 79:9 [t][See ver. 18 above] [w]Jer. 14:9
20 [x]Isai. 65:24 [y]See ver. 16
21 [z]See ch. 8:16 [a]See ch. 8:18 [b]Ex. 29:39; [1 Kin. 18:36; Ezra 9:4, 5]
22 [c][ch. 8:16] [d][ch. 1:4, 17]
23 [e][ver. 20] [f][ch. 10:12, 14] [g]ch. 10:11, 19 [h][Matt. 24:15; Mark 13:14]

Gabriel Brings an Answer

20 [x]While I was speaking and praying,
confessing my sin and the sin of my people
Israel, and presenting my plea before the
LORD my God for [y]the holy hill of my God,
21 while I was speaking in prayer, the man
[z]Gabriel, whom I had seen in the vision at
the first, [a]came to me in swift flight at [b]the
time of the evening sacrifice. 22 [c]He made
me understand, speaking with me and saying, "O Daniel, I have now come out to give
you [d]insight and understanding. 23 [e]At the
beginning of your pleas for mercy a word
went out, [f]and I have come to tell it to you,
for [g]you are greatly loved. Therefore consider the word [h]and understand the vision.

The Seventy Weeks

24 [i]"Seventy weeks are decreed about
your people and [j]your holy city, to finish
[k]the transgression, to put an end to sin,
[l]and to atone for iniquity, [m]to bring in everlasting righteousness, to seal both vision
and prophet, and [n]to anoint a most holy
place.[2] 25 [o]Know therefore and understand
that [p]from the going out of the word to
restore and [q]build Jerusalem to the coming
of an [r]anointed one, a [s]prince, there shall
be seven weeks. Then for sixty-two weeks it

24 [i][Ezek. 4:6] [j]Neh. 11:1 [k]ch. 8:13 [l][Ps. 78:38; Heb. 2:17]; See Jer. 31:34 [m]Rom. 3:25, 26; See Jer. 23:5, 6 [n][Ps. 45:7; Isai. 61:1; Acts 4:26, 27] 25 [o][ver. 23] [p][2 Chr. 36:23; Ezra 1:3; 4:24; 6:15; Neh. 6:15] [q][Ps. 51:18] [r]John 1:41 [s]Isai. 55:4

1 Hebrew *for the Lord's sake* 2 Or *thing*, or *one*

9:21 Gabriel. See note 8:16.

9:24–27 The interpretation of these verses is disputed at many points. There are two fundamental approaches to the interpretation of the "weeks" (lit. "sevens"): symbolic periods of time or literal periods of time. In the symbolic view the seventy years of punishment (v. 2) are multiplied seven times in accordance with the covenantal curses (Lev. 26:18, 21, 24, 28). *Jubilees,* a Jewish book from the period between the Testaments, also structures the whole of history into periods of 490 years. Adherents of the literal view fall into three categories. As with other prophecies in Daniel, some commentators interpret the verses with reference to the time of Antiochus IV. Other interpreters may be divided into two groups: (a) those who interpret the passage as having its primary focus on events associated with the First Advent of Christ and shortly thereafter (first-advent view); (b) those who interpret the passage as having reference to events associated with both the first and second advents of Christ with an unstated time interval between the two (second-advent view). Within each of these categories individual interpreters differ on details.

9:24 Seventy weeks. Most interpreters view the units of "seventy weeks" as representing 490 years (9:24–27 note). These so-called seventy weeks of years are then divided into three subunits of 49 years ("seven weeks," v. 25); 434 years ("sixty-two weeks," v. 26); and 7 years ("one week," v. 27). Interpreters differ over whether these subunits are to be viewed as a continuous sequence or as having time intervals between them.

9:25 the going out of the word. The Hebrew term translated "word" may mean either word or command. This ambiguity has given rise to two primary interpretations for the beginning of the "seventy weeks": (a) some interpreters understand it to be the decree issued by Artaxerxes I in the seventh year of his reign, or 457 B.C. (Ezra 7:12–26). Forty-nine years later (408 B.C.) the streets and wall around Jerusalem had been completed (v. 25). (b) Other commentators understand the "seventy weeks" to begin in 587 B.C., the time of Jeremiah's prediction (his "word") that Jerusalem would be rebuilt (Jer. 31:38; 32:15, 37, 44). Forty-nine years later would be 538 B.C., the year that Cyrus permitted the Jews to fulfill Jeremiah's prophecy by returning to Palestine (Ezra 1:1–4).

to the coming of an anointed one. Advocates of interpretation (a) above understand "anointed one" to be a reference to Jesus. Linking the "seven weeks" (49 years) and the "sixty-two weeks" (434 years) as a continuous sequence yields 483 years, to run from 457 B.C. to A.D. 27, or approximately the beginning of Christ's three-year public ministry. Others take the 483 years to begin with the "command" of Artaxerxes I in the twentieth year of his reign (Neh. 2:1), 444 B.C., instead of the seventh year of his reign (Ezra 7:12–26) in 457 B.C. Using a 360-day lunar year (as in the Jewish calendar), this approach reaches a date for the crucifixion in A.D. 33. This date for the crucifixion is possible but not certain. Advocates of interpretation (b) above understand "anointed one" to refer to Cyrus (also called the Lord's "anointed," Is. 45:1). This view separates the "seven weeks" and the "sixty-two weeks." The "seven weeks" elapse between the destruction of Jerusalem in 586 B.C. and the decree of Cyrus in 538 B.C. The "sixty-two weeks" (434 years) is the time when the city is to be rebuilt, somewhere between 538 B.C. and A.D. 70 (when Jerusalem was destroyed). With this view, a time interval is required between the two periods of "weeks."

shall be built again with squares and moat,
[t]but in a troubled time. 26 And after the
sixty-two weeks, an anointed one shall [u]be
cut off and shall have nothing. And the
people of the prince who is to come [v]shall
destroy the city and the sanctuary. [w]Its[1]
end shall come with a flood, [x]and to the
end there shall be war. [y]Desolations are
decreed. 27 And he shall make a strong
covenant with many for one week, and for
half of the week he shall put an end to sacrifice and offering. [z]And on the wing of
abominations shall come one who makes
desolate, until [a]the decreed end is poured
out on the desolator."

Daniel's Terrifying Vision of a Man

10 [b]In the third year of Cyrus king of
Persia a word was revealed to
Daniel, [c]who was named Belteshazzar. And
[d]the word was true, and it was a great conflict.[2] And [e]he understood the word and
[e]had understanding of the vision.
2 In those days I, Daniel, was mourning
for [f]three weeks. 3 I ate no delicacies, no
meat or wine entered my mouth, nor did I
[g]anoint myself at all, for [f]the full three
weeks. 4 On the twenty-fourth day of the
first month, as I was standing [h]on the bank
of the great river ([i]that is, the Tigris) 5 [j]I lifted up my eyes and looked, and behold, [k]a
man clothed in linen, [l]with a belt of fine
[m]gold from Uphaz around his waist. 6 His
body was like [n]beryl, his face [o]like the
appearance of lightning, [p]his eyes like flaming torches, his arms and [q]legs like the
gleam of burnished bronze, and [q]the sound
of his words like the sound of a multitude.
7 [r]And I, Daniel, alone saw the vision, for
the men who were with me did not see the
vision, but a great trembling fell upon
them, and they fled to hide themselves. 8 So
I was left alone and saw this great vision,
and [s]no strength was left in me. My radiant
appearance was fearfully changed,[3] [t]and I
retained no strength. 9 Then I heard the
sound of his words, [u]and as I heard the
sound of his words, I fell on my face in
deep sleep [u]with my face to the ground.
10 And behold, [v]a hand touched me and
set me trembling on my hands and knees.
11 And he said to me, "O Daniel, [w]man
greatly loved, [x]understand the words that I
speak to you, and [y]stand upright, for [z]now
I have been sent to you." And when he had
spoken this word to me, I stood up trembling. 12 Then he said to me, [a]"Fear not,
Daniel, for from the first day that you [b]set
your heart to understand and [b]humbled
yourself before your God, [c]your words have
been heard, [d]and I have come because of

25 [t]See Neh. 4:7, 8, 16-18
26 [u]Isai. 53:8; [Mark 9:12; Luke 24:26] [v][Matt. 24:2; Mark 13:2; Luke 19:43, 44] [w]Nah. 1:8; [ch. 11:10, 22, 26, 40] [x]Matt. 24:6, 14 [y]ver. 18; See ver. 27
27 [z]Matt. 24:15; Mark 13:14; [Luke 21:20] [a]Isai. 10:23

Chapter 10
1 [b][ch. 1:21]; See ch. 6:28 [c]See ch. 1:7 [d][ch. 8:26] [e]See ch. 1:17
2 [f][ver. 13]
3 [g][Amos 6:6; Matt. 6:17] [f][See ver. 2 above]
4 [h][ch. 12:5] [i]Gen. 2:14
5 [j][Josh. 5:13] [k]Ezek. 9:2 [l][Rev. 1:13; 15:6] [m]Jer. 10:9
6 [n][Ezek. 1:16; 10:9] [o]Ezek. 1:14; Matt. 28:3 [p]Rev. 1:14 [q]Rev. 1:15
7 [r][Acts 9:7]
8 [s][ch. 7:28] [t]ver. 16
9 [u]ch. 8:18
10 [v]See Ezek. 2:9
11 [w]ver. 19; ch. 9:23 [x]See ch. 1:17 [y]Ezek. 2:1 [z][Heb. 1:14]
12 [a]ver. 19; [Judg. 6:23; Rev. 1:17] [b][ch. 9:3] [c][Acts 10:4] [d][ch. 9:23]

[1] Or *His* [2] Or *and it was about a great conflict* [3] Hebrew *My splendor was changed to ruin*

9:26 after the sixty-two weeks, an anointed one shall be cut off. Many interpreters understand this to refer to the crucifixion of Christ. According to view (b) above, the "anointed one" of v. 26 is Christ, and the "anointed one" of v. 25 is Cyrus.

the people of the prince. Many interpreters agree that the assailants are the armies of Titus who destroyed Jerusalem in A.D. 70. Some adherents of the second-advent view (9:24–27 note), however, argue that while the assailants are the armies of Titus, the "prince" himself is the Antichrist. This identification provides a transition to the second-advent interpretation of v. 27.

9:27 he shall make a strong covenant with many for one week. Advocates of the first-advent view (9:24–27 note) understand that "anointed one" will "make a strong covenant," that is, live out His public ministry. Advocates of the second-advent view posit a time interval between vv. 26 and 27 and understand that the "prince" will "make a strong covenant." The "prince" is identified as Antichrist, who will establish a covenant with Jewish people regathered in the land of Israel during a "tribulation" period (12:1; Matt. 24:21; Rev. 7:14) of seven years (the seventieth "week").

an end to sacrifice. According to advocates of the first-advent view (9:24–27 note) this refers to the termination of the Old Testament sacrificial system brought about by the death of Christ. According to advocates of the second-advent view this is a reference to the Antichrist's prohibition of "sacrifice and offering" (perhaps standing for religious practice in general) by the regathered Jewish people after three-and-a-half years (Rev. 11:2; 12:6, 14) of the tribulation period.

one who makes desolate. According to the first-advent view (9:24–27 note) this describes the destruction of Jerusalem that occurred in A.D. 70. According to the second-advent view it describes a catastrophe that will come upon Jerusalem in connection with the activities of the Antichrist. Phrases similar to "an abomination that makes desolate" occur in Dan. 8:13; 11:31; 12:11 (notes) as well as 1 Macc. 1:54. Dan. 8:13 and 1 Macc. 1:54 are clearly references to the activities of Antiochus IV. Jesus refers to this "abomination" in His prophecy of events yet future (Matt. 24:15; Mark 13:14).

10:1–12:13 The prophet reveals a final vision concerning the future reign of Antiochus IV Epiphanes, but looking beyond his reign to another that culminates at the end of the age.

10:1 the third year of Cyrus. That is, 537 B.C. See note 1:21. The repatriated exiles returned to the land to rebuild the temple (Ezra 1:1–4; 3:8), but would soon have to cease their efforts temporarily (Ezra 4:24).

10:2 mourning. Daniel probably mourns because of the state of Jerusalem (Neh. 1:4; Is. 61:3–4; 64:8–12; 66:10).

10:5 a man clothed in linen. Vv. 5, 6 give a detailed description of an angel, perhaps the one who spoke to Gabriel (8:16), or Gabriel himself (9:21). His appearance is much like that of the glory of the Lord (Ezek. 1:26–28; Rev. 1:12–16). For other references to angels, see Judg. 13:6; Ezek. 9:2, 3; 10:2; Luke 24:4.

10:7 great trembling. See Is. 6:5; Luke 5:8.

10:12 I have come because of your words. The vision and revelation that Daniel received came as a direct response to his prayers.

your words. 13 [e]The prince of the kingdom of Persia withstood me [f]twenty-one days, but [g]Michael, one of the chief princes, came to help me, for I was left there with the kings of Persia, 14 [d]and came to make you understand what is to happen to your people [h]in the latter days. For [i]the vision is for days yet to come."

15 When he had spoken to me according to these words, [j]I turned my face toward the ground [k]and was mute. 16 And behold, [l]one in the likeness of the children of man [m]touched my lips. Then I opened my mouth and spoke. I said to him who stood before me, "O my lord, by reason of the vision pains have come upon me, and [n]I retain no strength. 17 How can my lord's servant talk with my lord? For now no strength remains in me, and no breath is left in me."

18 Again [l]one having the appearance of a man [m]touched me and strengthened me. 19 And he said, [o]"O man greatly loved, [p]fear not, peace be with you; be strong and of good courage." And as he spoke to me, I was strengthened and said, "Let my lord speak, for you have strengthened me." 20 Then he said, "Do you know why I have come to you? But now I will return to fight against the [q]prince of Persia; and when I go out, behold, the prince of [r]Greece will come. 21 But I will tell you [s]what is inscribed in the book of truth: there is none who contends by my side against these except [t]Michael, your prince.

The Kings of the South and the North

11 And as for me, [u]in the first year of [u]Darius the Mede, I stood up to confirm and strengthen him.

2 "And now I will show you [v]the truth. Behold, three more kings shall arise in Persia, and a fourth shall be far richer than all of them. And when he has become strong through his riches, he shall stir up all against the kingdom of Greece. 3 Then [w]a mighty king shall arise, who shall rule with great dominion and [x]do as he wills. 4 And as soon as he has arisen, [y]his kingdom shall be broken and divided [y]toward the [z]four winds of heaven, but [a]not to his posterity, nor according to the authority with which he ruled, for his kingdom shall be plucked up and go to others besides these.

5 "Then the king of the south shall be strong, but one of his princes shall be stronger than he [b]and shall rule, and his authority shall be a great authority. 6 After some years [c]they shall make an alliance, and the daughter of the king of the south shall come to the king of the north to make an agreement. But she shall not retain the strength of her arm, and he and his arm

13 [e]ver. 20 [f][ver. 2, 3] [g]ver. 21; ch. 12:1; Jude 9; Rev. 12:7
14 [d][See ver. 12 above] [h]ch. 2:28 [i]ch. 8:26; [Hab. 2:3]
15 [j]ver. 9; ch. 8:18 [k]Ps. 39:2, 9
16 [l]See ch. 8:15 [m]Isai. 6:7 [n]ver. 8
18 [l][See ver. 16 above] [m][See ver. 16 above]
19 [o]ver. 11; ch. 9:23 [p]See ver. 12
20 [q]ver. 13 [r]ch. 8:21
21 [s]ch. 12:1, 4; [Ex. 32:32]
[t]See ver. 13

Chapter 11
1 [u]ch. 9:1
2 [v]ch. 10:21
3 [w][ch. 7:6; 8:5, 21] [x]ver. 16, 36; [ch. 8:4]
4 [y][ch. 8:8, 22] [z]See ch. 7:2 [a]Ps. 109:13
5 [b][ch. 7:6]
6 [c][ver. 23]

10:13 the prince of the kingdom of Persia withstood me. This "prince" is an evil but powerful spiritual being (cf. Is. 24:21; Luke 11:14–26) affecting Persian rule.

Michael. "Michael" is elsewhere in Scripture depicted as a commander of the holy angels (Jude 9; Rev. 12:7; cf. 2 Kin. 6:15–17). Here is a glimpse of spiritual battles waged in heavenly places and affecting events on earth (cf. Eph. 6:12; Rev. 12:7–9). The power of fallen angels is limited by God, as is made clear here and elsewhere in Scripture (Job 1:12; 2:6).

10:20 the prince of Persia. See note on v. 13.

the prince of Greece. This angel affects the affairs of the Greek kingdom (v. 13 note). Although both Persia and Greece would rule over God's people, Daniel must understand that their power is limited by the power of God.

10:21 the book of truth. This is a metaphor standing for God's knowledge and control of all history.

none . . . except Michael. Michael's interest to protect Israel (v. 13 note; cf. 12:1) corresponds with the interest of the messenger, who is directly concerned with God's purposes.

11:1 in the first year of Darius the Mede. Two years earlier (10:1 note) the angel who was speaking to Daniel had given assistance to Michael (10:13 note), perhaps in connection with the Persian decree to permit the Jews to return to their homeland.

11:2–12:4 The revelation given to Daniel in 11:2–12:4 is in three parts: 11:2–20 depicts Near Eastern history from the time of Daniel until the time of Antiochus IV Epiphanes; 11:21–35 describes the rule of Antiochus IV; and 11:36–12:4 apparently describes the time of the Antichrist.

11:2 three more kings. They are Cambyses, 529–523 B.C.; Pseudo-Smerdis (Gaumata), 523–522 B.C.; and Darius I, 522–486 B.C.

a fourth. Xerxes I, 485–464 B.C., known in the Old Testament as Ahasuerus.

his riches. See Esth. 1:4.

against the kingdom of Greece. Xerxes waged a number of campaigns against Greece beginning in 480 B.C.

11:3 a mighty king shall arise. Alexander the Great, 336–323 B.C. See notes 7:6; 8:5, 8.

11:4 his kingdom shall be broken. See notes 7:6; 8:8.

11:5 the king of the south. Ptolemy I Soter, 322–285 B.C.

one of his princes. Seleucus I Nicator, 312–280 B.C. Seleucus broke with Ptolemy, became king of Babylon, and controlled territories from the Indus River in the east to Syria in the west.

11:6–20 These verses contain detailed predictions of relations between the king of the North (the Seleucid kingdom) and the king of the South (the Ptolemaic kingdom). The section concerns events involving Laodice and Berenice (vv. 6–9), the career of Antiochus III (vv. 10–19), and the reign of Seleucus IV (v. 20).

11:6 the daughter of the king. Berenice, the daughter of Ptolemy II Philadelphus, 285–246 B.C.

to make an agreement. This is a marriage alliance (about 250 B.C.) between Antiochus II Theos (261–246 B.C.) of Syria and Ptolemy II of Egypt.

he and his arm shall not endure. Laodice, the former wife of Antiochus II, led a conspiracy that resulted in the death by poisoning of Berenice, Antiochus II, and their infant son.

shall not endure, but she shall be given up,
and her attendants, he who fathered her,
and he who supported[1] her in those times.
7 “And from a branch from her roots one
shall arise in his place. He shall come
against the army and enter the [d]fortress of
the king of the north, and he shall deal
with them and shall prevail. 8 He shall also
carry off to Egypt their gods with their
metal images and their precious [e]vessels of
silver and gold, and for some years he shall
refrain from attacking the king of the north.
9 Then the latter shall come into the realm
of the king of the south but shall return to
his own land.
10 “His sons shall wage war and assemble a multitude of great forces, which
shall keep coming [f]and overflow and pass
through, and again shall carry the war as
far as his [d]fortress. 11 Then the king of the
south, [g]moved with rage, shall come out
and fight with the king of the north. [h]And
he shall raise a great multitude, but it
shall be given into his hand. 12 And when
the multitude is taken away, his heart
shall be exalted, and he shall cast down
tens of thousands, but he shall not prevail. 13 For the king of the north shall again
[i]raise a multitude, greater than the first.
And [j]after some years[2] he shall come on
with a great army and abundant supplies.
14 “In those times many shall rise against
the king of the south, and the violent
among your own people shall lift themselves up in order to fulfill the vision, but
[k]they shall fail. 15 Then the king of the north
shall come and [l]throw up siegeworks and
take a well-fortified city. And the forces of
the south shall not stand, or even his best
troops, for there shall be no strength to
stand. 16 But he who comes against him
shall [m]do as he wills, and [n]none shall stand
before him. And he shall stand in [o]the glorious land, with destruction in his hand.
17 He shall [p]set his face to come with the
strength of his whole kingdom, and he
shall bring terms of an agreement and perform them. He shall give him the daughter
of women to destroy the kingdom,[3] but it
shall not stand or be to his advantage.
18 Afterward he shall turn his face to the
coastlands and shall capture many of them,
but a commander shall put an end to his
insolence. Indeed,[4] he [q]shall turn his insolence back upon him. 19 Then he shall turn
his face back toward the [r]fortresses of his
own land, but he shall [s]stumble and fall,
[t]and shall not be found.
20 “Then shall arise in his place one who
shall send an [u]exactor of tribute for the
glory of the kingdom. But within a few days
he shall be broken, neither in anger nor in
battle. 21 In his place shall arise a contemptible person to whom royal majesty
has not been given. [v]He shall come in without warning and obtain the kingdom [w]by
flatteries. 22 Armies shall be [x]utterly swept
away before him and broken, even the

7 [d][ver. 10, 19, 38, 39] 8 [e][ver. 43] 10 [f]ver. 26, 40; Isai. 8:8 [d][See ver. 7 above] 11 [g]ch. 8:7 [h]ver. 13 13 [i]ver. 11 [j][ch. 4:16]

14 [k]ver. 19, 33, 34 15 [l]See Ezek. 4:2 16 [m]ver. 3, 36 [n][Josh. 10:8] [o]ver. 41; See ch. 8:9 17 [p]See Jer. 42:15 18 [q][Hos. 12:14] 19 [r][ver. 7, 10, 38, 39] [s]Jer. 46:6 [t]Job 20:8; Ps. 37:36; Ezek. 26:21 20 [u][Isai. 60:17; Zech. 9:8] 21 [v]ver. 24 [w][ver. 34] 22 [x][ver. 10; Jer. 46:7]

1 Or *obtained* 2 Hebrew *at the end of the times* 3 Hebrew *her*, or *it*
4 The meaning of the Hebrew is uncertain

11:7 a branch from her roots. Ptolemy III Euergetes, 246–221 B.C., the brother of Berenice (v. 6 note).

enter the fortress. Ptolemy III attacked the Seleucid kingdom, executed Laodice (v. 6 note), and returned to Egypt with considerable booty.

11:9 the latter. Seleucus II Callinicus (246–226 B.C.), the son of Laodice, led an unsuccessful campaign against the Ptolemaic kingdom in 240 B.C.

11:10 His sons. Seleucus III Ceraunus, 226–223 B.C.; Antiochus III the Great, 223–187 B.C.

shall wage war. Antiochus III began to fight against the Ptolemies in 219 B.C. and for a time gained control of Palestine and western Syria.

his fortress. This probably refers to Raphia, a Ptolemaic fortress in southern Palestine, where a major battle was fought in 217 B.C.

11:11 the king of the south. Ptolemy IV Philopator, 221–203 B.C.

with the king of the north. Antiochus III. Antiochus suffered great losses, over 14,000 men, at the battle of Raphia in 217 B.C.

11:13 the king of the north. In alliance with Philip V of Macedon, Antiochus III raised an even larger army to invade the Ptolemaic kingdom. Ptolemy IV died under mysterious circumstances and was succeeded by Ptolemy V Epiphanes, 203–181 B.C., his four-year-old son.

11:15 take a well-fortified city. The victory of Antiochus III over the Egyptian general Scopas at Sidon in 198 B.C. marked the end of Ptolemaic rule in Palestine.

11:16 the glorious land. Palestine. See vv. 41, 45; 8:9.

11:17 it shall not stand or be to his advantage. After Cleopatra was given in marriage to Ptolemy V by her father Antiochus III, she aligned herself with the Egyptian cause, seeking Roman help against her father's attempt to take coastal cities in Asia Minor that were controlled by Egypt.

11:18 a commander. The Roman general Lucius Cornelius Scipio, who defeated Antiochus III in several battles and forced him to cede Asia Minor to Roman control (the Peace of Apamea, 188 B.C.). At this time the second son of Antiochus III, who became Antiochus IV Epiphanes, was taken hostage to Rome.

11:20 in his place one. Seleucus IV Philopator, 187–175 B.C. (the older son of Antiochus III).

tribute for the glory of the kingdom. For an account of Heliodorus's attempt to collect these taxes for Seleucus, see 2 Macc. 3:7–40.

11:21 a contemptible person. Antiochus IV Epiphanes (175–164 B.C.), who was not the legitimate successor of his brother Seleucus IV, since Seleucus IV had a son. See notes 8:9–14.

11:22 even the prince of the covenant. Perhaps this is a reference to the assassination in 171 B.C. of the high priest Onias III by supporters of Antiochus IV based in Jerusalem (see 2 Macc. 4:32–43).

prince of the covenant. **23** And from the
time that an alliance is made with him he
shall act deceitfully, and he shall become
strong with a small people. **24** [y]Without
warning he shall come into [z]the richest
parts[1] of the province, and he shall do
what neither his fathers nor his fathers'
fathers have done, scattering among them
plunder, spoil, and goods. He shall devise
plans against strongholds, but only for a
time. **25** And he shall stir up his power and
his heart against [a]the king of the south
with a great army. And the king of the
south shall wage war with an exceedingly
great and mighty army, but he shall not
stand, for plots shall be devised against
him. **26** Even those who eat his food shall
break him. His army shall be [b]swept away,
and many shall fall down slain. **27** And as
for the two kings, their hearts shall be bent
on doing evil. They shall speak lies at the
same table, but to no avail, for [c]the end is
yet to be at the time appointed. **28** And he
shall return to his land with great wealth,
but his heart shall be set against the holy
covenant. And he shall work his will and
return to his own land.
29 "At the time appointed he shall return
and come into the south, but it shall not be
this time as it was before. **30** For ships of
[d]Kittim shall come against him, and he
shall be afraid and withdraw, and shall
turn back and [e]be enraged and [e]take action
against the holy covenant. He shall turn
back and pay attention to those who forsake the holy covenant. **31** Forces from him
shall appear and [f]profane the temple and
fortress, and shall take away the regular
burnt offering. And [g]they shall set up the
abomination that makes desolate. **32** He
shall seduce with flattery those who violate
the covenant, but the people who know
their God shall stand firm and take action.
33 [h]And the wise among the people shall
make many understand, though for some
days they shall stumble by sword and
flame, by captivity and plunder. **34** When
they stumble, they shall receive a little
help. And many shall join themselves to
them with flattery, **35** and some of the wise
shall stumble, so that they may be refined,
[i]purified, and [j]made white, until [k]the time
of the end, [k]for it still awaits the appointed
time.
36 "And the king shall [l]do as he wills. [m]He
shall exalt himself and magnify himself
above every god, [n]and shall speak astonishing things against [o]the God of gods. [p]He
shall prosper [q]till the indignation is accomplished; for what is decreed shall be done.
37 He shall pay no attention to the gods of
his fathers, or to the one beloved by
women. He shall not pay attention to any
other god, for [m]he shall magnify himself
above all. **38** He shall honor the god of

24 [y]ver. 21 [z][Gen. 27:28, 39]
25 [a][ch. 8:9]
26 [b]ver. 10, 40
27 [c][ver. 35]
30 [d]Gen. 10:4; Num. 24:24 [e]See ver. 28
31 [f][ch. 12:11] [g]Matt. 24:15; Mark 13:14; [ch. 8:13; 12:11]
33 [h]ch. 12:3, 10
35 [i][Mal. 3:3, 4] [j][Rev. 7:14] [k][ver. 27, 40]
36 [l]ver. 3, 16 [m][ch. 7:25; 2 Thess. 2:4] [n][ch. 7:25; Rev. 13:5, 6] [o]Deut. 10:17 [p][ch. 8:12] [q][Isai. 10:25]; ch. 9:27
37 [m][See ver. 36 above]

1 Or *among the richest men*

11:25 the king of the south. Ptolemy VI Philometor, 181–146 B.C., son of Ptolemy V and Cleopatra, and the nephew of Antiochus (v. 17 note).

he shall not stand. Antiochus IV defeated Ptolemy VI at Pelusium, on the border of Egypt (cf. 1 Macc. 1:16–19).

11:28 he shall return . . . his heart shall be set against the holy covenant. In response to intrigues in Jerusalem against his supporters, Antiochus IV plundered the temple when he returned from Egypt to Syrian Antioch (cf. 1 Macc. 1:20–28).

11:29 into the south. Antiochus IV invaded Egypt again in 168 B.C.

11:30 ships of Kittim shall come. Roman armies under Gaius Popilius Laenas forced Antiochus IV to retreat from Egypt.

take action against the holy covenant. Antiochus IV determined to exterminate Jewish religion. See note 8:11.

11:31 the abomination that makes desolate. The desecration of the temple in December, 168 B.C. by Antiochus IV (cf. 1 Macc. 1:54, 59; 2 Macc. 6:2). See notes 8:11; 9:27; 12:11.

11:32 the people who know their God. Daniel speaks of those who opposed the Hellenizers and were ready to die for their faith (1 Macc. 1:60–63).

11:34 they shall receive a little help. Possibly this is a reference to Mattathias, an elderly priest, and his five sons (John, Simon, Judas, Eleazar, and Jonathan) who waged a guerrilla war against the forced hellenization of the Jews. Mattathias died in 166 B.C. His sons, known as the Maccabees, carried on the struggle. Victory was achieved under Judas Maccabeus in December, 164 B.C., when the temple was cleansed and daily sacrifices were restored (1 Macc. 4:36–39).

11:35 the end . . . the appointed time. See note 8:17.

11:36–12:3 Certain details in 11:36–12:3 cannot be harmonized with the events surrounding the death of Antiochus IV. For this reason some interpreters understand these verses to describe the Antichrist, who like Antiochus IV will persecute God's people just prior to the Second Advent of Christ (cf. 12:1–3). These verses describe the character of the Antichrist, his activities, and the destiny of God's people. This understanding requires a time interval between the events depicted in 11:21–35 and those in 11:36–12:3. Consequently, other interpreters have understood vv. 36–39 as a summary of Antiochus's religious policies; vv. 40–45 as a description of how his ambition leads to his defeat; and 12:1–3 as an anticipation of his defeat. The anticipated invasion of the Holy Land may be presented as a parallel to Nebuchadnezzar's earlier invasion, using the names of the nations of that time, sparing Israel's old enemies (v. 41), and climaxing in the anticipated defeat of Egypt itself (vv. 42, 43; cf. Ezek. 29). At his proudest moment Antiochus is destroyed at Mount Zion in the heart of the Holy Land (vv. 44, 45). Antiochus's defeat in 12:1–3 is described in terms of the absolute end of history. Because the prophecies in 11:40–12:3 have not been fulfilled historically, it is difficult to discern how literal or metaphorical they are, and their interpretation must be speculative. The interpretation that the future Antichrist is in view will be followed in the remaining notes.

11:36 till the indignation is accomplished. Just as with Antiochus IV (8:17 note; 11:35), the time of persecution is subject to God's control.

fortresses instead of these. A god whom his
fathers did not know he shall honor [r]with
gold and silver, with precious stones and
costly gifts. 39 He shall deal with the
strongest fortresses with the help of a foreign god. Those who acknowledge him he
shall load with honor. He shall make them
rulers over many and [s]shall divide the land
for a price.[1]
40 [t]"At the time of the end, the king of the
south shall attack[2] him, but the king of the
north shall rush upon him [u]like a whirlwind, with chariots and horsemen, and
with many ships. And he shall come into
countries and [v]shall overflow and pass
through. 41 He shall come into [w]the glorious
land. And tens of thousands shall fall, but
these shall be delivered out of his hand:
[x]Edom and [x]Moab and the main part of the
[x]Ammonites. 42 He shall stretch out his
hand against the countries, and the land of
Egypt shall not escape. 43 He shall become
ruler of the treasures of gold and of silver,
and all the precious things of Egypt, and
the [y]Libyans and the [z]Cushites shall follow
in his train. 44 But news from the east and
the north shall alarm him, and he shall go
out with great fury to destroy and devote
many to destruction.[3] 45 And he shall pitch
his palatial tents between the sea and the
glorious holy mountain. Yet he shall come
to his end, with none to help him.

The Time of the End

12 "At that time shall arise [a]Michael,
the great prince who has charge of
your people. And [b]there shall be a time of
trouble, such as never has been since there
was a nation till that time. But at that time
your people shall be delivered, [c]everyone
whose name shall be found written in the
book. 2 And many of those who [d]sleep in
[e]the dust of the earth shall [e]awake, [f]some
to everlasting life, and [f]some to shame and
everlasting contempt. 3 [g]And those who are
wise [h]shall shine like the brightness of the
sky above;[4] and [i]those who turn many to
righteousness, like the stars forever and
ever. 4 But you, Daniel, [j]shut up the words
and [k]seal the book, until [l]the time of the
end. [m]Many shall run to and fro, and
knowledge shall increase."
5 Then I, Daniel, looked, and behold,
two others stood, one on [n]this bank of the
stream and one on that bank of the
stream. 6 And someone said to [o]the man
clothed in linen, who was above the waters
of the stream,[5] [p]"How long shall it be till
the end of these wonders?" 7 And I heard
[o]the man clothed in linen, who was above
the waters of the stream; [q]he raised his
right hand and his left hand toward heav-
en and [r]swore by him who lives forever
that it would be for a [s]time, times, and half
a time, and that when the shattering of
[t]the power of [t]the holy people comes to an
end all these things would be finished. 8 I
heard, [u]but I did not understand. Then I
said, "O my lord, what shall be the outcome of these things?" 9 He said, [v]"Go your
way, Daniel, [w]for the words are shut up
and sealed until the time of the end.
10 [x]Many shall purify themselves and make
themselves white and be refined, but [y]the
wicked shall act wickedly. And none of the
wicked shall understand, [i]but those who
are wise shall understand. 11 And from the
time that [z]the regular burnt offering is
taken away and [a]the abomination that
makes desolate is set up, there shall be
1,290 days. 12 [b]Blessed is he who waits and
arrives at the 1,335 days. 13 [c]But go your
way till the end. [d]And you shall rest and
shall stand in your allotted place at [e]the
end of the days."

38 [r][Joel 3:5] 39 [s][Lam. 5:2, 6] 40 [t][ver. 27, 35] [u]Zech. 9:14 [v]ver. 10, 26 41 [w]ver. 16; See ch. 8:9 [x][Isai. 11:14] 43 [y][2 Chr. 12:3] [z]2 Chr. 12:3; Ezek. 30:4, 5; Nah. 3:9
Chapter 12
1 [a]See ch. 10:13 [b]Jer. 30:7; Matt. 24:21; Mark 13:19; [Rev. 16:18] [c]Ex. 32:32, 33; [Ezek. 13:9; Luke 10:20; Rev. 20:12] 2 [d][Ps. 17:15; John 11:11] [e][Isai. 26:19]; See Ezek. 37:1-10 [f]Matt. 25:46; John 5:28, 29; Acts 24:15; Rev. 20:12, 13 3 [g]ch. 11:33 [h]Matt. 13:43 [i][Mal. 2:6] 4 [j][ver. 9; ch. 8:26] [k]Isai. 8:16; 29:11; Rev. 5:1; 10:4; 22:10 [l][ver. 13]; See ch. 8:17 [m]Amos 8:12 5 [n][ch. 10:4] 6 [o]ch. 10:5; Ezek. 9:2 [p]ch. 8:13 7 [o][See ver. 6 above] [q]See Gen. 14:22 [r][Rev. 10:6] [s]ch. 7:25 [t][ch. 8:24] 8 [u][ch. 8:15] 9 [v]ver. 13 [w][ver. 4] 10 [x][ch. 11:35] [y][Rev. 9:20; 22:11] [i][See ver. 3 above] 11 [z]ch. 11:31 [a]See ch. 11:31 12 [b][Matt. 10:22] 13 [c]ver. 9 [d]Isai. 57:2; [Rev. 6:11] [e][Matt. 13:39]

[1] Or *land as payment* [2] Hebrew *thrust at* [3] That is, set apart (devote) as an offering to the Lord (for destruction) [4] Hebrew *the expanse*; compare Genesis 1:6-8 [5] Or *who was upstream*; also verse 7

11:40 At the time of the end. Here "end" carries an eschatological sense and refers to the end of this present age (8:17 note).

11:41 glorious land. Palestine (cf. vv. 16, 45; 8:9).

11:45 his end. See Joel 3; Zech. 14:1–4; 2 Thess. 2:8; Rev. 16:13–16; 19:11–21.

12:1 Michael. See note 10:13.

a time of trouble. This unparalleled time of trouble is sometimes identified with the "great tribulation" predicted by Jesus (Matt. 24:21; Mark 13:19).

your people shall be delivered. This deliverance is not necessarily from martyrdom (v. 2), but from the power of Satan, understood as his attempts to destroy people's faith during the time of distress.

12:2 everlasting life . . . and everlasting contempt. This verse is a clear prediction of the bodily resurrection of the godly and ungodly for the final judgment (Matt. 25:46; John 5:28, 29).

12:4 seal the book. Sealing the book preserves it unaltered as it awaits fulfillment (8:26 note).

12:7 a time, times, and half a time. See note 7:25.

12:11 the abomination that makes desolate is set up. See third note on 9:27. The similar activity of Antiochus IV prefigured this activity of the Antichrist (8:13).

1,290. The significance of these time frames is obscure. Three and one-half years is 1260 days of a 360-day year, or 1278 days of a 365-day year.

THE BOOK OF

Hosea

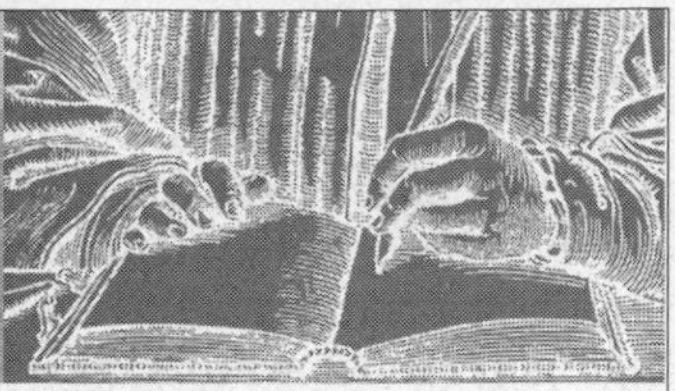

AUTHOR

Little is known about the background and training of the author of this book, the prophet Hosea, son of Beeri (1:1). Though it is not clearly stated in the book, Hosea's familiarity with the geography (4:15; 5:1, 8; 6:8, 9; 9:15; 10:5; 12:11) and history of the northern kingdom of Israel (5:13; 7:7, 11; 8:4, 9–14) suggests that he was a native of the northern kingdom.

DATE AND OCCASION

The Book of Hosea came from his prophetic ministry, which embraced the critical years of religious decline and decay in the northern kingdom, from about 750 B.C. until a few years before the fall of Samaria in 722 B.C. Hosea's preaching focused on Israel's breach of her covenantal relationship with God, mixing the pure worship of the Lord with the idolatry of the surrounding peoples (religious syncretism), and on the impending judgment. However, Hosea's proclamation of the nature of God's love sounds a more positive note in the book. For a discussion of Hosea's marriage and family life, see "Interpretive Difficulties" below.

During her final years, the northern kingdom of Israel was in a state of political and social decline. The economic prosperity and political security that the nation experienced during the reign of Jeroboam II (c. 793–753 B.C.) was followed by a period of political and social chaos and religious decline under the next six kings, who reigned for a combined period of twenty-five years (2 Kin. 15:8–17:41). Four of these kings were assassinated by those who usurped their thrones (Zechariah, Shallum, Pekahiah, and Pekah); one became a political prisoner (Hoshea, 2 Kin. 17:3, 4); and only one was succeeded by his son (Menahem, 2 Kin. 15:23).

Hosea's preaching reflects both the relative calm the kingdom experienced under Jeroboam II (2:5, 8, 13) and the later turmoil in domestic (7:3–7; 13:10, 11) and foreign affairs (7:8–12; 12:1). The Syro-Ephraimite war in particular (735–732 B.C.; 2 Kin. 15:27–30; 16:5–9; Is. 7:1–9) seems to stand behind Hosea's message in 5:8–10. Pekah of Israel had formed an alliance with Rezin of Syria in order to resist the expanding Assyrian Empire ruled by Tiglath-pileser III. Pekah then attacked Judah, which had refused to join the alliance with Syria. Assyria responded to Judah's request for assistance by attacking Syria's capital, Damascus, and systematically subjugating extensive territory in the northern kingdom of Israel.

The northern kingdom's political vacillation between Egypt and Assyria is also reflected in the text (5:13; 7:11; 8:9, 10; 9:3; 11:5; 12:1). This vacillation brought a further attack by the Assyrians, the arrest of King Hoshea, the siege of Samaria, and finally the end of the northern kingdom. Although this end is expected by Hosea, the fall of Samaria in 722 B.C. had not yet occurred at the time of his prophecy (13:16).

The northern kingdom was in a state of spiritual decline during the final phase of its history. The ancient faith of Israel, which Hosea describes so beautifully using analogies of marital and parental love (2:14–23; 11:1–4), had become polluted by elements of the Canaanite fertility religion. Such fertility cults focused especially on the worship of Baal, a god thought to be the giver of rain and fertility. The Israelites incorporated elements of the Canaanite fertility religion into the orthodox faith, notably sexual rites that included ritual prostitution and drunken orgies (4:10–13). The worship of the Lord and the worship of Baal (whose name lit. means "lord" or "master") became intermingled and even identified (2:5–13). Religious corruption evidenced itself not only in this popular, syncretistic form of religion, sometimes called a "baalized" form of Yahweh worship, but also in the lives of the religious leaders. Through corruption, greed, and hardness of heart they not only neglected to instruct the people in the true faith, but also tolerated, and in some cases even sponsored, syncretistic religion (4:4–13; 5:1; 6:9).

INTERPRETIVE DIFFICULTIES

The question of how to interpret the personal events of Hosea's life that symbolically parallel his prophetic message has long perplexed readers of the Book of Hosea. Are the details given in chs. 1 and 3 about Hosea's family life to be understood literally or allegorically? Because of the moral perplexity posed by the holy God's command that Hosea marry a prostitute, throughout the ages there always have been interpreters who have understood the details of Hosea's married life allegorically. Others, arguing that 1:2 refers to the future, reason that Gomer became a prostitute only after the birth of their first child. Still others, advocating a modified literal reading, argue that Gomer was not a common prostitute but rather a woman involved in cultic prostitution related to the fertility religion of Baal. However, the prophet's actual marriage to an unfaithful wife would make the analogy with the Lord's relationship to Israel most vivid, and this seems to be what the text intends.

Similarly, questions have been asked about Hosea's children. Their names, like that of the child born to Isaiah and the prophetess in Is. 8:1–4, are intended to have symbolic significance (cf. Is. 7:3; Ezek. 23). The names given to Hosea's children (Jezreel, Lo-ruhama, and Lo-ammi; 1:4, 6, 9 and notes) purposely illustrate Hosea's message about God's increasing displeasure with wayward Israel, but also convey the message of hope, renewal, love, and restoration (2:21–23 notes).

A related problem centers on the relationship between ch. 1, which presents a third-person account of Hosea's marriage to Gomer and the birth of their children, and ch. 3, which is an account in the first person of God's instructions to Hosea about loving an unfaithful woman. Although these chapters have most often been regarded as a chronologically sequential account of a single marriage, some argue that two different women and marriages are described in these chapters. Still others have suggested that the chapters are not sequential, but rather describe the same episode. Textual and translation difficulties in the Hebrew text stand behind these different views. For example, the word "again" in 3:1 stands between "said" and "go" in the Hebrew, and it could mean either "The LORD said again" or "The LORD said, 'Go again.'" Although these debates continue, the profound meaning of the prophet's marriage(s) as a picture of the Lord's relationship with Israel is clear.

CHARACTERISTICS AND THEMES

Hosea's book is not about Hosea, but about God and His relationship to His covenant people, Israel. God emphasizes His uniqueness and sovereignty (12:9; 13:4). Because of His unique holiness (11:9), adoration of Him is the only proper response (3:5), and He tolerates no rival claim. As Sovereign, all is under His rule, whether fertility (2:8), Israel's history (5:14, 15), or the nations (10:10).

A number of themes recur throughout the book, themes that continue to carry religious significance for the community of faith today (14:9 note). The theme of covenantal unfaithfulness, movingly symbolized by Hosea's relationship with his promiscuous wife, permeates the book. Closely related to this theme is that of repentance. Hosea calls wayward Israel to return to the Lord in order to reestablish the intimate relationship she earlier had experienced with Him in the wilderness period (2:7, 14, 19, 20). Promises of restoration, such as those in 1:11 and 2:23, will be fulfilled under the new covenant through Jesus Christ (Rom. 5:8; Eph. 2:4–10). The themes of unfaithfulness and repentance summon those within the covenant community to repent and to renew their love relationship with the Lord.

Another important theme in the book centers around what it means to "know" or "acknowledge" God (2:20; 4:1; 5:4; 6:3, 6; 13:4). This seems to be a technical term for covenant intimacy, loyalty, and obedience. The book teaches that true knowledge of God is not merely the possession of correct information about Him, but includes the intimacy typical of marriage and family life, an intimacy evidenced in worship, lifestyle, and loyalty to the covenant LORD. Hosea also warns that sin can delude people into thinking that they know and understand God, when in fact they are far from Him (8:2).

A polemic against religious syncretism (the mixture of true and false religion) also pervades the book (2:2–13; 4:10–19; 5:4; 9:1, 10). Over and over again Hosea points to the sin of the northern kingdom, which tried to wed the worship of the covenant LORD to Canaanite religion with its deification of sex and nature. The impossibility of such a marriage warns the church to remain loyal in a culture that encourages compromise and acceptance of principles and beliefs incompatible with biblical doctrine. Moreover, Hosea's vivid depictions of sin remind believers about the nature and consequences of human sin: it incurs divine judgment (9:9; 13:12); it causes severe crises in nature and society (4:3); and it corrupts the human personality. People become like the objects of their love (9:10).

Hosea's message is enhanced through his effective use of imagery. The strongest and most extended metaphors derive from the human experience of intimacy. Using the image of human marriage (chs. 1–3) and family life (11:1–4, 10), Hosea depicts God and His relationship with His people. In other figurative images God is compared to moth and rot (5:12), winter and spring rains (6:3), a lion (5:14; 11:10; 13:7–8), a leopard (13:7), a bear (13:8), and a cypress tree (14:8).

OUTLINE OF HOSEA

I. Superscription (1:1)

II. The Lesson from Hosea's Family Life (1:2–3:5)

- A. *Hosea's Wife and Children: A Parable of Judgment (1:2–2:1)*
- B. *Unfaithfulness and Punishment (2:2–13)*
- C. *Reconciliation and Restoration (2:14–23)*
- D. *Redeeming Wife and Nation (ch. 3)*

III. Hosea's Prophetic Message (chs. 4–14)

- A. *The Charge of Failure to Acknowledge God (4:1–6:3)*
  1. The Lord's Case Against Israel (ch. 4)
  2. Charges Against the Priests and People (ch. 5)
  3. Call to Repentance (6:1–3)
- B. *The Charge of Breaking God's Covenant (6:4–11:11)*
  1. Unfaithfulness and Decadence (6:4–7:16)
  2. Announcement of Judgment (ch. 8)
  3. Guilt and Punishment (chs. 9; 10)
  4. God's Unfailing Love (ch. 11)
- C. *The Charge of Faithlessness Toward the Lord (11:12–14:9)*
  1. Israel the Deceiver (11:12–12:14)
  2. The End of Compassion (ch. 13)
  3. Return and the Promise of Renewal (ch. 14)

1 The word of the LORD that came to
Hosea, the son of Beeri, [a]in the days of
Uzziah, Jotham, Ahaz, and Hezekiah, kings
of Judah, and in the days of [b]Jeroboam the
son of Joash, king of Israel.

Hosea's Wife and Children

2 When the LORD first spoke through
Hosea, the LORD said to Hosea, [c]"Go, take to
yourself a wife of whoredom and have [d]children of whoredom, for [e]the land commits
great whoredom by forsaking the LORD." 3 So
he went and took Gomer, the daughter of
Diblaim, and she conceived and bore him
a son.
4 And the LORD said to him, "Call his name
Jezreel, for in just a little while [f]I will punish
the house of Jehu for the blood of Jezreel,
and [g]I will put an end to the kingdom of the
house of Israel. 5 And on that day [h]I will break
the bow of Israel [i]in the Valley of Jezreel."
6 She conceived again and bore a daughter. And the LORD said to him, [j]"Call her
name No Mercy, [1] for [k]I will no more have

Chapter 1
1 [a]Isai. 1:1; Amos 1:1; Mic. 1:1 [b]2 Kin. 14:23; 15:1
2 [c][ch. 3:1] [d]ch. 2:4 [e][ch. 2:5]; See Ezek. 16:15
4 [f][2 Kin. 10:11] [g][Amos 7:9]
5 [h][2 Kin. 15:29] [i]Josh. 17:16; Judg. 6:33
6 [j][ver. 9; ch. 2:1, 23; Rom. 9:25; 1 Pet. 2:10] [k]ch. 2:4; 2 Kin. 17:6, 23

1 Hebrew *Lo-ruhama*, which means *she has not received mercy*

1:1 Hosea introduces his prophecy, naming himself as God's messenger. His name probably means "He [God] has saved."

Uzziah . . . Jeroboam. Whereas four kings of Judah are named, Uzziah (also called Azariah, 792–740 B.C.), Jotham (750–735 B.C.), Ahaz (735–715 B.C.), and Hezekiah (715–686 B.C.), the only northern king recorded is Jeroboam II (c. 793–753 B.C.). Perhaps the writer thought that the northern kings who reigned between Jeroboam II and the fall of the north in 722 (four were assassins) were not worthy of mention.

1:2 a wife of whoredom. See Introduction: Interpretive Difficulties. On the theme of marital and covenantal unfaithfulness, see Introduction: Characteristics and Themes.

the land commits great whoredom. Hosea's wife and children, together with all the inhabitants of the land, are deemed unfaithful.

1:3 Gomer. Her name has no symbolic significance, unlike the names of her children.

him. This pronoun is omitted in vv. 6, 8, but its absence does not necessarily imply that Hosea was not the father there also, since the indirect object may be implied.

1:4 Jezreel. Lit. "God sows" or "plants." This is the name of a beautiful and fertile valley between the mountain ranges of Samaria and Galilee (the site of Gideon's victory over the Midianites, Judg. 6:33), and of a town at the valley's southern end, where Jehu came to power through violence (1 Kin. 21:1; 2 Kin. 9; 10). This valley became the place of judgment in 733 B.C. (2 Kin. 15:29). This punishment through military defeat suggests the theme of covenant breaking since it reflects the curses recorded in Lev. 26:17; Deut. 28:25, 49–57. Yet Jezreel is also a sign of blessing and fertility in Hos. 2:22.

the house of Jehu. Jeroboam II was from the house of Jehu, a dynasty established through the bloodbath at Jezreel (2 Kin. 9:14–37; cf. 1 Kin. 19:16, 17) and ending with the murder of Zechariah (2 Kin. 15:8–10).

1:5 bow of Israel. Israel's military strength, symbolized by the bow (Gen. 49:24; 1 Sam. 2:4; Ezek. 39:3), was broken by the Assyrian army under Tiglath-pileser III, who conquered the northern territories of Israel.

1:6 No Mercy. Hebrew "Lo-ruhama." Lit. "she has not received mercy." The child's name signifies the imminent withdrawal of the compassion God had shown to Israel in spite of her covenant unfaithfulness.

mercy on the house of Israel, to forgive
them at all. 7 But [l]I will have mercy on the
house of Judah, and I will save them by the
LORD their God. I [m]will not save them by
bow or by sword or by war or by horses or
by horsemen."
8 When she had weaned No Mercy, she
conceived and bore a son. 9 And the LORD
said, [n]"Call his name Not My People,[1] for
[o]you are not my people, and I am not your
God."[2]
10 [3] Yet [p]the number of the children of
Israel shall be [q]like the sand of the sea,
which cannot be measured or numbered.
[r]And [s]in the place where it was said to
them, [o]"You are not my people," it shall be
said to them, [t]"Children[4] of [u]the living
God." 11 And [v]the children of Judah and the
children of Israel shall be gathered together, and [w]they shall appoint for themselves
one head. And they shall go up from the
land, for great shall be the day of Jezreel.

Israel's Unfaithfulness Punished

2 [5] Say to your brothers, [x]"You are my
people,"[6] and to your sisters, [y]"You
have received mercy."[7]

2 "Plead with your mother, plead—
for [z]she is not my wife,
and I am not her husband—
that she put away [a]her whoring from
her face,
and her adultery from between her
breasts;
3 lest [b]I strip her naked
and make her as [c]in the day she
was born,
and [d]make her like a wilderness,
and make her like a parched
land,
and kill her with thirst.
4 [e]Upon her children also I will have no
mercy,
[f]because they are children of
whoredom.
5 For [g]their mother has played the
whore;
she who conceived them has acted
shamefully.
For [h]she said, 'I will go after my
lovers,
who [i]give me my bread and my
water,
my wool and my flax, my oil and
my drink.'
6 Therefore [j]I will hedge up her[8] way
with thorns,
and [k]I will build a wall
against her,
so that she cannot find her
paths.

7 [l][ch. 11:12; 2 Kin. 19:35] [m][ch. 2:18; Zech. 4:6; 9:10]
9 [n]ver. 4, 6 [o]ch. 2:23; [Lev. 26:12]
10 [p][Ezek. 36:10, 37] [q]Gen. 22:17; See Gen. 13:16 [r]Cited Rom. 9:26 [s]Isai. 62:4 [o][See ver. 9 above] [t]Deut. 14:1; [2 Cor. 6:18] [u]Ps. 42:2; See Josh. 3:10
11 [v]Isai. 11:12, 13; Jer. 3:18; 50:4; Ezek. 34:23; Zech. 10:6; See Ezek. 37:16-24 [w][ch. 3:5]
Chapter 2
1 [x][ch. 1:9] [y][ch. 1:6]
2 [z][Isai. 50:1] [a][ch. 4:12; Ezek. 16:25]
3 [b][Ezek. 16:39] [c][Ezek. 16:4] [d][ver. 9; Ezek. 19:13]
4 [e]ch. 1:6 [f]ch. 1:2
5 [g][ch. 1:2] [h][ver. 12, 13] [i][ver. 8, 9; Jer. 44:17]
6 [j]Job 3:23 [k][Job 19:8; Lam. 3:7, 9]

1 Hebrew *Lo-ammi*, which means *not my people* 2 Hebrew *I am not yours* 3 Ch 2:1 in Hebrew 4 Or *Sons* 5 Ch 2:3 in Hebrew 6 Hebrew *ammi*, which means *my people* 7 Hebrew *ruhama*, which means *she has received mercy* 8 Hebrew *your*

1:7 I will have mercy. A reference to Jerusalem's miraculous deliverance from the Assyrians in 701 B.C. (Is. 37:14, 33–38; 2 Kin. 19:32–37).

1:9 Not My People. Hebrew "Lo-ammi." The name of the third child marks the high point of God's judgment, as God cancels the ancient covenantal formula (Ex. 6:7; Lev. 26:12; Deut. 26:17–19) and declares that the covenant is not in effect (v. 10 notes).

I am not your God. Lit. "I am not 'I AM' to you," a reference to the divine name for God used in Ex. 3:14.

1:10–2:1 The increasingly severe prophecies of judgment symbolized in the names of the three children are now dramatically reversed.

1:10 sand of the sea. A clear reference to the ancient patriarchal promise of innumerable descendants (Gen. 22:17; 32:12; cf. Gen. 13:16; 15:5; 26:24; 28:14).

You are not my people. The promise of restoration to these people was fulfilled at least in part when remnants of the north were joined with the south during the reign of Hezekiah (2 Chr. 30:11, 18) and after the Exile (1 Chr. 9:3; Ezra 8:35). The New Testament applies this promise to the church, the true Israel, composed of both Jews and Gentiles (Rom. 9:24–26; 1 Pet. 2:9, 10). For the apostles, the remnant of ethnic Israel was evidently a model for the remnant of the nations: what applied to the former applied to the latter.

Children of the living God. This unique expression suggests the kind of intimate relationship God desires with Israel, in which God gives life (as opposed to the lifeless relationship Israel had with Baal). In Is. 40:18–20; 44:9–20; 46:5–11, dead idols are contrasted with the living God. The living relationship is now provided in Jesus Christ (Matt. 16:16; Rom. 9:26).

1:11 one head. This reveals the completeness of reconciliation between both kingdoms and the Lord. Ultimately, this reunion takes place under Christ, the son of David (Matt. 1:23; 2:6, 15).

they shall go up from the land. Israel's restoration began in the return from exile. The phrase may also refer to resurrection from death (Ps. 71:20; Is. 43:6).

the day of Jezreel. See note 1:4.

2:1 brothers . . . sisters. The hostile siblings, Israel and Judah, will be fully reconciled, and the horrible indictments contained in the names Lo-ammi and Lo-ruhama will be reversed.

2:2 Plead. God brings a case against Israel in which the children are to accuse their mother.

she put away. Repentance and reconciliation are the final goals of God's judgment (vv. 9–23).

2:3 strip her naked. If repentance does not take place, the unfaithful wife (Gomer/Israel) will be publicly exposed (v. 10) and left destitute, punishments traditional for an adulteress (Ezek. 16:37–39; Nah. 3:5–7), though less severe than the death penalty (Deut. 22:22).

2:4 children of whoredom. God's love and mercy (1:6) will also be withdrawn from the children who, like their mother, are charged with promiscuity.

2:5 their mother has played the whore. The unfaithful mother (Israel) looked to Canaanite fertility religion and not to the Lord (v. 8) to provide the staples of life.

7 She shall pursue her lovers
but not overtake them,
and she shall seek them
but shall not find them.
[l]Then she shall say,
'I will go and return to [m]my first
husband,
[l]for it was better for me then than
now.'
8 And [n]she did not know
that it was [o]I who gave her
[p]the grain, the wine, and the oil,
and who lavished on [q]her silver and
gold,
[r]which they used for Baal.
9 Therefore [s]I will take back
my grain in its time,
and my wine in its season,
and [s]I will take away my wool and
my flax,
which were to cover her
nakedness.
10 Now [t]I will uncover her lewdness
in the sight of her lovers,
and no one shall rescue her out of
my hand.
11 [u]And I will put an end to all her
mirth,
her feasts, her [v]new moons, her
[v]Sabbaths,
and all her [w]appointed feasts.
12 And [x]I will lay waste her vines and
her fig trees,
[y]of which she said,
'These are [z]my wages,
which my lovers have given me.'

7 [l][Luke 15:17, 18] [m][Isai. 54:5, 6]
8 [n][ver. 20; Isai. 1:3] [o][Ezek. 16:19] [p]Deut. 7:13 [q]ch. 13:2 [r][Ezek. 16:17, 18]
9 [s][ver. 3; Joel 1:10]
10 [t]Lam. 1:8; Ezek. 16:37; 23:29
11 [u][Jer. 7:34; Amos 8:10] [v][Amos 8:5] [w][ch. 9:5; Isai. 1:13, 14]
12 [x][Isai. 5:5] [y][ver. 5] [z][Mic. 1:7]

Syncretism and Idolatry

Though there is only one God and only one true faith, that taught in the Bible, the apostate world (Rom. 1:18–25) has always been full of religions. The age-old urge toward syncretism (the assimilation of one religion's beliefs and practices into another) is still with us. Indeed, it has been revived in our time through renewed attempts to unify all religions and through persistent amalgams of Eastern and Western ideas that rise and fall in popularity.

The pressure to compromise is not new. After entering Canaan, Israel was constantly tempted to absorb into the worship of Yahweh the Canaanite worship of fertility gods and goddesses, if not to make images of Yahweh Himself—both practices being forbidden in the law (Ex. 20:3–6). The spiritual issue was whether Israel would remember that the covenant God was all-sufficient for them and that He claimed their exclusive allegiance, making the worship of other gods a spiritual adultery (Jer. 3; Ezek. 16; Hos. 2). This was a test the nation often failed.

Syncretism was widespread in the Roman Empire during the first centuries of Christianity. Polytheism was rife and all manner of mystery cults flourished. Early Christian teachers fought diligently to keep the faith from being assimilated to Gnosticism, a kind of theosophy that had no use for Christ's Incarnation and Atonement, since it saw the root problem of man as ignorance rather than sin. Neoplatonism and Manichaeism also saw the way of salvation mainly as a matter of ascetical detachment and escape from the physical world. Christian resistance to these movements was successful, and the classic formulations of the Trinity and the Incarnation in the creeds are a permanent legacy of these struggles.

Scripture condemns all idolatry as evil. Idols are mocked as delusive non-entities (Ps. 115:4–7; Is. 44:9–20), but they nevertheless enslave their worshipers in blind superstition (Is. 44:20). Paul adds that demons operate through idols, making them a spiritual menace (1 Cor. 8:4–6; 10:19–21). Biblical warnings against idolatry (e.g., 1 Cor. 10:14; 1 John 5:19–21) need to be taken to heart in the post-Christian Western culture, which is prepared to fill the spiritual vacuum that people feel by embracing religious syncretism, witchcraft, and experiments with the occult.

2:7 She shall pursue . . . seek. The woman's active initiative, representing all Israel, is stressed.

my first husband. The early period of intimacy is remembered fondly (cf. 11:1–4).

2:8 grain, the wine . . . silver and gold. The Lord's agricultural and commercial gifts (Deut. 7:13; 11:14; 28:1–12) were credited to Baal. In texts discovered at the ancient north Syrian city of Ugarit, Baal is seen as the god of the storm and worshiped as the provider of rain and fertility.

2:9–13 Therefore. Though not punished with death (v. 3 note; cf. Ezek. 16:37–40), the unfaithful and forgetful lover is severely chastised through a series of dramatic reversals in which God's gifts are withdrawn: failed harvests, exposure, and the end of festivals.

2:9 take back. The Hebrew indicates a forceful, snatching action.

2:11 Sabbaths. The Hebrew *shabbat* is derived from the verb meaning "stop" or "cease," making a sarcastic pun.

appointed feasts. The festivals had become occasions for religious syncretism, in which the worship of the Lord and Baal were intermingled. See Introduction: Date and Occasion.

2:12 wages . . . lovers have given. The prostitute's wages, which were in fact gifts from the Lord (v. 8), were to be destroyed.

I will make them a forest,
[a] and the beasts of the field shall
devour them.
13 And [b]I will punish her for [c]the feast
days of the Baals
when she burned offerings to them
and [d]adorned herself with her ring
and jewelry,
and went after her lovers
and forgot me, declares the LORD.

The LORD's Mercy on Israel

14 "Therefore, behold, I will allure her,
and [e]bring her into the wilderness,
and [f]speak tenderly to her.
15 And there I will give her her vineyards
and make the Valley of Achor[1] a
door of hope.
And there she shall answer [g]as in the
days of her youth,
as at the time when she came out
of the land of Egypt.

16 "And [h]in that day, declares the LORD,
you will call me 'My Husband,' and no
longer will you call me 'My Baal.' 17 For [i]I
will remove the names of the Baals from her
mouth, and they shall be remembered by
name no more. 18 And [j]I will make for them
a covenant on that day with the beasts of
the field, the birds of the heavens, and the
creeping things of the ground. And [k]I will
abolish[2] the bow, the sword, and war from
the land, and I will make you lie down in
[l]safety. 19 And I will betroth you to me [m]for-
ever. [n]I will betroth you to me in righteousness and in justice, in steadfast love and in
mercy. 20 [n]I will betroth you to me in faithfulness. And [o]you shall know the LORD.

21 "And [p]in that day [q]I will answer,
declares the LORD,
I will answer the heavens,
and they shall answer the earth,
22 and the earth shall answer the
grain, the wine, and the oil,
and they shall answer [r]Jezreel,[3]
23 and [s]I will sow her for myself in
the land.
And [t]I [u]will have mercy on No Mercy,[4]
and [v]I will say to Not My People,[5]
[w]'You are my people';
and he shall say, 'You are my
God.'"

12 [a][ch. 13:8] 13 [b][ch. 4:9] [c][ch. 11:2; 13:1, 2] [d]Ezek. 23:40; [Isai. 61:10] 14 [e][Ezek. 20:35] [f]Isai. 40:2 15 [g][ch. 9:10; 11:1; Jer. 2:2; Ezek. 16:22, 60] 16 [h]ver. 18, 21 17 [i]Zeph. 1:4; Zech. 13:2; [Ex. 23:13] 18 [j]Ezek. 34:25; [Job 5:23] [k]Ps. 46:9; Isai. 2:4; 9:5; Ezek. 39:9, 10 [l]Lev. 26:5; Jer. 23:6 19 [m][Ezek. 43:7] [n][ver. 7, 16; Jer. 3:14, 15; 2 Cor. 11:2] 20 [n][See ver. 19 above] [o]Jer. 31:34; John 17:3 21 [p]ver. 16 [q][Zech. 8:12] 22 [r][ch. 1:4, 11] 23 [s][ch. 1:10]; See Ezek. 36:9-11 [t]Cited Rom. 9:25, 26 [u]ch. 1:6 [v]ch. 1:9; 1 Pet. 2:10 [w]ver. 1; Zech. 13:9; See Lev. 26:12; Jer. 31:33

1 *Achor* means *trouble*; compare Joshua 7:26 2 Hebrew *break* 3 *Jezreel* means *God will sow* 4 Hebrew *Lo-ruhama* 5 Hebrew *Lo-ammi*

2:13 jewelry. On pagan goddesses, jewelry emphasized erotic areas of the anatomy.

her lovers. In vv. 7, 10, 12 these are probably synonymous with the Baals. The essence of the charge against Israel was that she had forgotten the Lord, whom she should have loved (cf. 4:6; 13:4–6). See theological note "Syncretism and Idolatry."

2:14 into the wilderness. There Israel is to love God alone (v. 16; cf. Jer. 2:2).

speak tenderly to her. Lit. "speak to the heart," an idiom used elsewhere for wooing, speaking kindly, and coaxing (Gen. 34:3; Judg. 19:3; Ruth 2:13).

2:15 Valley of Achor. Lit. "Valley of Trouble," this area was located near Jericho and was the site of the stoning of Achan (Josh. 7:24–26). Though associated with sin and death, this valley was to be transformed into a "door of hope."

2:16 My Baal. The Hebrew word *ba'al* can mean "master" or "husband," as well as refer to the pagan god Baal. In the future, Israel will be so zealous to stamp out anything associated with Baal worship that the word *ba'al* itself, in all its senses, will be avoided (v. 17).

2:18 I will make for them a covenant. Taking up the same theme in a later time, Jeremiah explains the covenant as entailing a new heart (Jer. 31:31–34).

with the beasts. The future kingdom is secure and peaceful, free from the threat of wild animals (Is. 11:6–9) and invasions (Ps. 46:9; Is. 2:4; Mic. 4:3). Wild animals were a threat, particularly after invading armies ravaged the land. The language may be figurative for a transformed humanity, with the resulting peace and security attending the renewal inaugurated by Christ at His First Advent and completed at His return.

2:19 betroth. Betrothal was the final step in the courtship process and involved paying a bride-price to the bride's father. Here the qualities of righteousness, justice, love, mercy, and faithfulness are a sort of bride-price that guarantees the permanence of the relationship.

righteousness. God's righteousness is expressed both in His fairness and in the salvation He bestows on His people (10:12; Amos 5:7).

justice. This term can denote the legal decisions and relationships by which justice and fairness are established and restored (5:11; 6:5; 10:4; Amos 5:15, 24; Mic. 6:8).

steadfast love. See note Ex. 15:13.

mercy. The term can refer to compassion, heartfelt sensitivity, and love (1:6; Gen. 43:14; Deut. 13:17; 2 Sam. 24:14).

2:20 faithfulness. This quality includes dependability, truthfulness, and steadfastness in relationships (Ps. 88:11; 89:1, 2, 5, 8, 24; 92:2; 98:3). Christ, by His active obedience, provided these covenant virtues for His people. By the Holy Spirit He inscribes His own nature on their hearts (2 Cor. 3:3).

know. The essence of the new covenant relationship involves knowing the Lord intimately (Jer. 31:34). Today Christ mediates this new covenant and renders the old covenant relationship obsolete (Heb. 8:7–13).

2:21 answer. The Lord will graciously answer Israel's cry, as she learns again to answer His appeals (v. 15 note).

the heavens. The Lord will show that He, not the storm-god Baal, commands the cycles of nature whereby the land becomes fertile and produces the crops that were earlier withheld (v. 9). See Introduction: Date and Occasion.

2:22 Jezreel. See note 1:4.

2:23 The promises of restoration come to a climax as Jezreel is redeemed (v. 22; cf. 1:4, 5), Lo-ruhama is shown God's love (1:6), and Lo-ammi becomes God's people (1:9).

You are my God. See Rom. 9:23–26 and 1 Pet. 2:9, 10 regarding the fulfillment of these promises.

Hosea Redeems His Wife

3 And the LORD said to me, [x]"Go again,
love a woman who is loved by another
man and is an adulteress, even as the LORD
loves the children of Israel, though they
turn to other gods and love cakes of
raisins." **2** So I bought her for fifteen shekels
of silver and a [y]homer and a lethech[1] of
barley. **3** And I said to her, "You must
[z]dwell as mine for many days. You shall
not play the whore, or belong to another
man; so will I also be to you." **4** For the children of Israel [z]shall dwell many days [a]with-
out king or prince, [b]without sacrifice or
[c]pillar, without [d]ephod or [e]household
gods. **5** Afterward [f]the children of Israel
shall return and [g]seek the LORD their God,
and [h]David their king, [i]and they shall come
in fear to the LORD and to his goodness in
the [j]latter days.

The LORD Accuses Israel

4 [k]Hear the word of the LORD,
O children of Israel,
for [l]the LORD has a controversy
with the inhabitants of the
land.
There is no faithfulness or
steadfast love,
and [m]no knowledge of God in
the land;
2 [n]there is swearing, lying, murder,
stealing, and committing
adultery;
they break all bounds, and
[o]bloodshed follows bloodshed.
3 Therefore [p]the land mourns,
and all who dwell in it languish,
[q]and also the beasts of the field
and the birds of the heavens,
[r]and even the fish of the sea are
taken away.

4 [s]Yet let no one contend,
and let none accuse,
for with you is [t]my contention,
O priest.[2]
5 You shall stumble by day;
the prophet also shall stumble
with you by night;
and I will destroy [u]your mother.
6 My people are destroyed [v]for lack of
knowledge;
[w]because you have rejected
knowledge,
I reject you [x]from being a priest
to me.
And since you have forgotten the law
of your God,
[y]I also will forget your children.

Chapter 3
1 [x][ch. 1:2, 3]
2 [y]Lev. 27:16; [Ezek. 45:11]
3 [z]Deut. 21:13
4 [z][See ver. 3 above] [a]ch. 10:3, 7 [b][ch. 9:4] [c][ch. 10:1, 2] [d]See Judg. 8:27 [e]See Gen. 31:19
5 [f][ch. 14:1] [g]Jer. 29:13; 50:4 [h]Ezek. 34:23; [ch. 1:11]; See Jer. 23:5 [i][Mic. 7:17] [j]Isai. 2:2; See Mic. 4:1-3

Chapter 4
1 [k]See ch. 5:1 [l]Isai. 3:13, 14; Jer. 25:31; Mic. 6:2 [m][ver. 6, 14; Jer. 4:22; 5:4]
2 [n][ch. 7:1] [o][ch. 6:9; 12:14; Mic. 3:10; 7:2]
3 [p]Isai. 24:4; Jer. 4:28; Joel 1:10 [q][Joel 1:18; Zeph. 1:3] [r][Ezek. 38:20]
4 [s][ver. 17] [t][Deut. 17:12]
5 [u]ch. 2:2
6 [v][ver. 1; Isai. 5:13] [w][Prov. 1:29] [x][Ex. 19:6] [y][Jer. 23:39]

1 A *shekel* was about 2/5 ounce or 11 grams; a *homer* was about 6 bushels or 220 liters; a *lethech* was about 3 bushels or 110 liters 2 Or *for your people are like those who contend with the priest*

3:1–5 Hosea recounts his reconciliation with his wife Gomer as an anticipation of God's reconciliation with Israel.

3:1 love . . . even as the LORD loves. God's apparently unreasonable request is patterned after His own loyal, protective, and bountiful love for undeserving Israel.

cakes of raisins. These delicacies, made from raisins pressed together, were associated with special occasions (2 Sam. 6:19), and may have been used in Baal worship as an aphrodisiac (cf. Song 2:5).

3:2 bought. Christ similarly fulfilled this picture of love in action when He redeemed His saints from the slave market of sin.

shekels. The payment, roughly half in silver and half in produce, amounted to about thirty shekels and approximated the price of a slave in Ex. 21:32. The New Testament teaches that the actual cost of redemption was Christ's blood (1 Pet. 1:18).

3:4 many days. The waiting period until the coming of Christ, the great and final King of the Davidic dynasty (v. 5).

without king . . . household gods. Israel's basic political and religious institutions, both legitimate (sacrifice and ephod, Ex. 28:31) and illegitimate (sacred stones or pillars, Deut. 16:21–22; idols or teraphim, Zech. 10:2), were going to be removed as punishment.

3:5 return and seek. Many Israelites repented with a full desire for intimacy with God at Pentecost (Acts 2:38–41).

David. This reference points to Jesus Christ, Son of David (1:11 note; 2 Sam. 7:12–16; Matt. 1:1; Rom. 1:3).

the latter days. See note Mic. 4:1.

4:1–19 In this striking example of a prophetic lawsuit against Israel for violating the terms of the covenant, Hosea gives an overview of the Lord's case against Israel and then focuses on the consequences of their rejection of the knowledge of God.

4:1 faithfulness . . . knowledge. See notes 2:19, 20.

4:2 swearing . . . bloodshed. These sins constituted violations of the foundational covenant document—the Decalogue (Ex. 20:2–17; Deut. 5:6–21).

4:3 the land mourns. Human sin results in crises within the natural order that endanger all of life (Lev. 18:28; Is. 24:4, 5).

4:4–10 Attention shifts to the sins of the priests, whose failure to instruct the nation in God's law has corrupted Israel (v. 6; Deut. 31:9–13; 33:10).

4:4 let no one contend. Or, "let no man bring a charge." According to the Mosaic law, the priests were entrusted with the task of rendering legal judgments (Deut. 17:9–13). But because of the general lack of knowledge and respect for God's law in Israel of Hosea's time, there was no point in bringing charges against another, because the verdicts would not be honored (the people were "like those who contend with the priest" [text note]; i.e., did not respect his decisions and teaching).

4:5 your mother. The nation of Israel (2:2, 5; Is. 50:1).

4:6 My people. The nation will lose her covenant relationship with God through lack of covenant knowledge (vv. 8, 12).

knowledge. Knowledge of God is inseparable from the law of God (Introduction: Characteristics and Themes). The priests, who were responsible for teaching the law—and their descendants—were to be punished for ignoring or forgetting the law (vv. 4–10 note).

7 [z] The more they increased,
the more they sinned against me;
[a] I will change their glory into
shame.
8 [b] They feed on the sin[1] of my people;
they are greedy for their iniquity.
9 [c] And it shall be like people, like
priest;
I will punish them for their ways
and repay them for their deeds.
10 [d] They shall eat, but not be satisfied;
they shall play the whore, but not
multiply,
because they have forsaken the LORD
to cherish 11 whoredom, wine, and
new wine,
which [e] take away the
understanding.
12 My people [f] inquire of a piece of
wood,
and their walking staff gives them
oracles.
For [g] a spirit of whoredom has led
them astray,
and they have left their God to
play the whore.
13 [h] They sacrifice on the tops of the
mountains
and burn offerings on the hills,
[i] under oak, poplar, and terebinth,
because their shade is good.
Therefore your daughters play the
whore,
and your brides commit adultery.
14 I will not punish your daughters
when they play the whore,
nor your brides when they commit
adultery;
for [j] the men themselves go aside
with prostitutes
and sacrifice with [k] cult prostitutes,
and a people [l] without understanding
shall come to ruin.
15 Though you play the whore, O [m] Israel,
let not [m] Judah become guilty.
[n] Enter not into [o] Gilgal,
nor go up to [p] Beth-aven,
and swear not, "As the LORD lives."
16 Like a stubborn heifer,
Israel is stubborn;
can the LORD now feed them
like a lamb in a broad pasture?
17 [q] Ephraim is joined to idols;
[r] leave him alone.
18 When their drink is gone, they give
themselves to whoring;
[s] their rulers[2] dearly love shame.
19 [t] A wind has wrapped them[3] in its
wings,
and they shall [u] be ashamed
because of their sacrifices.

7 [z] [ch. 13:6] [a] 1 Sam. 2:30; Mal. 2:9 8 [b] [Lev. 6:25, 26; 10:17] 9 [c] Isai. 24:2 10 [d] Lev. 26:26; Mic. 6:14; Hag. 1:6 11 [e] [1 Kin. 11:4; Prov. 20:1] 12 [f] [Judg. 18:5] [g] ch. 5:4; [ch. 2:2] 13 [h] Ezek. 6:13 [i] [Isai. 1:29]

14 [j] [ch. 9:10] [k] Deut. 23:17 [l] [ver. 1, 6] 15 [m] See ch. 6:4 [n] Amos 4:4, 5; 5:5 [o] ch. 9:15; 12:11 [p] ch. 5:8; 10:5; [ch. 10:8; 1 Kin. 12:29; Amos 1:5] 17 [q] [ver. 12; ch. 5:3] [r] [Matt. 15:14] 18 [s] [ch. 9:10] 19 [t] ch. 13:15; Jer. 4:11; 51:1; [Zech. 5:9] [u] [Isai. 1:29]

1 Or *sin offering* 2 Hebrew *shields* 3 Hebrew *her*

4:7 I will change their glory. Or, "they will change their glory." Ultimately, the Lord is Israel's glory (Is. 60:19; Jer. 2:11). In Rom. 1:23, Paul condemns the sin of exchanging God's glory for something corruptible.

shame. Idols or false gods (Deut. 32:16, 17).

4:8 They feed on the sin of my people. Taken literally, the priests, who ate portions of the animals sacrificed for sin, encouraged the people to sin. Then the priests would have more to eat (Lev. 6:26). Taken figuratively, the priests were gratified by the people's sin.

4:9 like people, like priest. No one is spared from judgment (cf. Is. 24:1–3).

4:10 eat . . . play the whore. Food will not satisfy (v. 8), and illicit sex will not produce increase. They have left the Lord, the source of life, to practice harlotry (vv. 12, 18; 2:4; 6:10; 9:1).

4:11 take away the understanding. Lit. "take away the [people's] heart," i.e., their ability to judge and think clearly (cf. Prov. 31:4, 5).

4:12 a piece of wood. Lit. "their wood." This may refer to the Asherah pole beside a Canaanite shrine (Deut. 16:21; Judg. 6:25–32), to some other deity (Hab. 2:18, 19), or to a sacred tree thought to give oracles (Judg. 9:37).

staff. Probably a divining rod, or perhaps a small figurine of Asherah.

spirit of whoredom. Their spiritual adultery is caused by an intoxicating and seductive power that draws them continuously into sin ("spirit of confusion," Is. 19:14; "spirit of deep sleep," Is. 29:10).

4:14 I will not punish. Not that God refused to punish the harlots and adulteresses at all (since the people as a whole will be judged), but that He would not allow them to be punished while the men who patronized them went free (cf. Gen. 38:24–26).

4:15–19 The theme of prophetic lawsuit against Israel continues as further charges of covenant disobedience are leveled (4:1–19 note).

4:15 Gilgal. This important Israelite sanctuary near Jericho was situated across the Jordan from Baal-peor. From the time of the conquest, Gilgal was an important place of worship (Josh. 4:19–5:12; 1 Sam. 10:8; 11:12–15). Later in Israel's history, Gilgal became associated with wicked and syncretistic religious practices (9:15; 12:11; Amos 4:4).

Beth-aven. This was a contemptuous nickname for Bethel ("House of God"), the important royal sanctuary (Amos 4:4; 5:5; 7:13; 1 Kin. 12:28–33).

As the LORD lives. This orthodox oath (Judg. 8:19; Ruth 3:13; 1 Sam. 14:39) was forbidden here because they were lying (v. 2), or because it was being misused by associating the Lord with Baal worship.

4:16 stubborn heifer. Israel was kicking against all of the Lord's efforts to care for them (cf. Jer. 31:18).

4:17 Ephraim. Because Ephraim was by far the largest of the ten northern tribes, the northern kingdom of Israel was sometimes called Ephraim (Deut. 33:17 note).

leave him alone. The plural verb here may indicate an address to other prophets.

4:19 wind . . . wings. A wordplay on the Hebrew word meaning "wind" or "spirit" is probably intended. Not only was a destructive storm wind of divine judgment about to sweep away the people (Job 1:19), but "the spirit of whoredom" (v. 12; 5:4) was leading them to ruin.

Punishment Coming for Israel and Judah

5 [v]Hear this, O priests!
Pay attention, O house of Israel!
Give ear, O house of the king!
For the judgment is for you;
for [w]you have been a snare at Mizpah
and a net spread upon [x]Tabor.
2 And [y]the revolters [z]have gone deep
into slaughter,
but [a]I will discipline all of them.
3 [b]I know Ephraim,
and Israel is not hidden from me;
for now, O Ephraim, you have played
the whore;
Israel is defiled.
4 [c]Their deeds do not permit them
to return to their God.
For [d]the spirit of whoredom is within
them,
and they know not the LORD.
5 [e]The pride of Israel testifies to his face;[1]
Israel and [f]Ephraim shall stumble
in his guilt;
[f]Judah also shall stumble with them.
6 [g]With their flocks and herds they
shall go
to seek the LORD,
[g]but they will not find him;
[h]he has withdrawn from them.
7 [i]They have dealt faithlessly with the
LORD;
for they have borne alien children.
Now the new moon shall devour
them with their fields.

8 [j]Blow the horn in [k]Gibeah,
the trumpet in [l]Ramah.
Sound the alarm at [m]Beth-aven;
we follow you,[2] O Benjamin!
9 Ephraim shall become a desolation
in the day of punishment;
among the tribes of Israel
I make known what is sure.
10 The princes of Judah have become
like [n]those who move the
landmark;
upon them I will pour out
my wrath like water.
11 Ephraim is [o]oppressed, crushed in
judgment,
because he was determined to go
after filth.[3]
12 But I am [p]like a moth to Ephraim,
and [p]like dry rot to the house of
Judah.
13 When Ephraim saw his sickness,
and Judah [q]his wound,
then Ephraim went [r]to Assyria,
and sent to the great king.[4]
[s]But he is not able to cure you
or heal [q]your wound.
14 For I will be [t]like a lion to [u]Ephraim,
and like a young lion to the house
of [u]Judah.
[v]I, even I, will tear and go away;
I will carry off, and no one shall
rescue.

Chapter 5
1 [v]ch. 4:1; Joel 1:2; Amos 3:1; Mic. 1:2 [w][ch. 6:9; 9:8] [x]Judg. 4:6
2 [y][ch. 9:15] [z][ch. 9:9; Isai. 29:15] [a][Ps. 50:21]
3 [b][Amos 3:2; 5:12]
4 [c][Isai. 59:2] [d]ch. 4:12
5 [e]ch. 7:10 [f]See ch. 6:4
6 [g]ch. 6:6; Isai. 1:11 [h]ch. 9:12
7 [i]ch. 6:7
8 [j]ch. 8:1; Jer. 4:5 [k]ch. 9:9; 10:9 [l]Josh. 18:25 [m]See ch. 4:15
10 [n]Deut. 19:14
11 [o]Deut. 28:33; Amos 4:1
12 [p][Job 13:28]
13 [q][Isai. 1:5, 6] [r]ch. 7:11; 8:9; 12:1; 2 Kin. 15:19 [s]ch. 14:3
14 [t]ch. 13:7 [u]See ch. 6:4 [v][Mic. 5:8]

[1] Or *in his presence* [2] Or *after you* [3] Or *to follow human precepts* [4] Or *to King Jareb*

5:1 priests . . . house of Israel . . . house of the king. The fate of the northern kingdom was bound up with that of its leaders. The priests were responsible to teach the law (4:6), and the royal house was responsible for administering justice.

snare. The leaders trapped their foolish subjects.

Mizpah. Probably this is the Mizpah in Benjamin, where Samuel judged (1 Sam. 7:5, 6; 10:17–24), not Mizpah in Gilead (Gen. 31:48, 49).

Tabor. A famous mountain site located on the northeastern edge of the Jezreel Valley (Judg. 4:6). These and other northern sites had become high places of the pagan cult of Baal.

5:3 Ephraim. See note 4:17.

5:4 spirit of whoredom. See note 4:12. They "know not the LORD" truly (4:1, 6), nor can they return or repent (cf. Jer. 13:23).

5:5 testifies. The sins of the people testify against them in the Lord's covenant lawsuit against His people (ch. 4 note).

5:6 With their flocks . . . to seek. The Lord will not be found through the offering of their ritual sacrifices (4:13; 1 Sam. 15:21–23; Is. 1:11–17; Mic. 6:6–8).

5:7 alien children. Like an unfaithful wife and mother, Israel gives birth to children that were literally and religiously illegitimate (4:6, 13, 14).

new moon. The festivals brought judgment, instead of the Lord's blessing on their wombs and crops as they had imagined would happen (cf. Is. 1:13, 14).

5:8 Blow . . . Sound the alarm. These commands sound the watchman's cry to warn of an approaching enemy (Judah) from the south (cf. 8:1). The Syro-Ephraimite war described in 2 Kin. 16:5–9 and 2 Chr. 28:5–21 seems to stand behind this warning. See Introduction: Date and Occasion.

Gibeah . . . Ramah . . . Beth-aven. These Benjaminite towns lie in a straight line running north from Jerusalem: Gibeah, three miles; Ramah, five miles; Beth-aven (Bethel), eleven miles. At various times in their history they were claimed by one or the other kingdom (1 Kin. 15:16–22).

5:10 move the landmark. The boundary lines dividing the Promised Land were considered sacred to the Lord (Deut. 19:14; 27:17; Job 24:2; Prov. 22:28; 23:10). See note Num. 27:1–11.

5:12 moth . . . dry rot. Like a moth, or possibly like an infection (some suggest that the Hebrew word translated "moth" means "pus"), God will bring inexorable and unpleasant decay upon sinful Ephraim.

5:13 sickness . . . wound. Instead of turning to the Lord for healing their miseries inflicted by an enemy (cf. Is. 1:5–9; Jer. 30:12, 13), Israel turned to Assyria. Assyrian records speak of the tribute paid by Israel's kings, Menahem and Hoshea (cf. 2 Kin. 15:17–20; 17:3).

5:14 I will be like a lion. Even with Assyrian help, Israel is helpless prey before the powerful lion, the Lord (13:7; Amos 1:2; 3:8).

15 [w] I will return again to my place,
until they acknowledge their guilt
and seek my face,
and [x] in their distress earnestly
seek me.

Israel and Judah Are Unrepentant

6 "Come, let us [y] return to the LORD;
for [z] he has torn us, that he
may heal us;
he has struck us down, and [a] he
will bind us up.
2 After two days [b] he will revive us;
on the third day he will raise
us up,
that we may live before him.
3 [c] Let us know; [c] let us press on to
know the LORD;
[d] his going out is sure as the dawn;
he will come to us [e] as the showers,
[f] as the spring rains that water the
earth."
4 What shall I do with you,
[g] O [h] Ephraim?
What shall I do with you,
O [h] Judah?
Your love is [i] like a morning cloud,
[i] like the dew that goes early away.
5 Therefore I have hewn them by the
prophets;
I have slain them [j] by the words of
my mouth,
and my judgment goes forth as the
light.
6 For [k] I desire steadfast love[1] and not
sacrifice,
[l] the knowledge of God rather than
burnt offerings.
7 But [m] like Adam they [n] transgressed
the covenant;
[o] there they dealt faithlessly
with me.
8 [p] Gilead is a city of evildoers,
[q] tracked with blood.
9 As robbers [r] lie in wait for a man,
so the priests band together;
they murder on the way to
[s] Shechem;
they commit villainy.
10 In the house of Israel I have seen a
horrible thing;
[t] Ephraim's whoredom is there;
[u] Israel is defiled.
11 For you also, O [u] Judah, [v] a harvest is
appointed,
when [w] I restore the fortunes of my
people.

15 [w] [Jer. 29:10-12; Ezek. 6:9]; See Lev. 26:40-42 [x] Isai. 26:16
Chapter 6
1 [y] ch. 14:1; [ch. 3:5] [z] ch. 5:14; [ch. 13:7, 8] [a] [Isai. 30:26]
2 [b] Ps. 71:20; [Luke 24:27, 44; John 2:22; 20:9; 1 Cor. 15:4]
3 [c] [ch. 4:6] [d] Mic. 5:2 [e] [ch. 14:5] [f] Joel 2:23
4 [g] [ch. 11:8] [h] ver. 10, 11; ch. 4:15; 5:5; 8:14; 10:11; 11:12; 12:1, 2; See ch. 5:9-14 [i] ch. 13:3
5 [j] Jer. 23:29; [Heb. 4:12]
6 [k] Cited Matt. 9:13; 12:7; [1 Sam. 15:22] [l] [ch. 2:20]
7 [m] [Gen. 3:11; Job 31:33; Rom. 5:14] [n] ch. 8:1; Deut. 17:2 [o] ch. 5:7
8 [p] [ch. 12:11] [q] See ch. 4:2
9 [r] [ch. 5:1; 7:6] [s] Josh. 24:1
10 [t] ch. 5:3; 7:4; [ch. 4:2, 12, 14; 9:10] [u] See ver. 4
11 [u] [See ver. 10 above] [v] See Joel 3:13 [w] Ps. 126:1; [Job 42:10]

[1] Septuagint *mercy*

5:15 I will return . . . my place. In His anger, God removes His saving presence from the people until they truly repent (3:5).

6:1–3 This song of repentance responds with the imagery of 5:11–14, but seems superficial in tone (v. 4).

6:1 let us. The priests may be quoted here, much as Israel was quoted in 2:7.

return. The call to return to the Lord is one of the central messages of the book (2:7; 3:5; 5:4, 15). True repentance and conversion bring reconciliation that includes healing of wounds (cf. Deut. 32:39).

6:2 two days . . . the third. This may simply denote a short period of time. Some, who view this as a prediction of Christ's resurrection, understand Paul to allude to this verse in 1 Cor. 15:4.

live before him. See Ps. 16:11.

6:3 press on to know the LORD. Like the call to return (v. 1), the call to true knowledge of the Lord is central to Hosea's message (2:8, 20; 4:1, 6; 5:4; 6:6). See Introduction: Characteristics and Themes.

as the dawn . . . as the showers. These similes compare God's reliability to the recurrent events of nature.

6:4 morning cloud . . . dew. Continuing the use of images from nature, God laments the temporary, transitory quality of Israel and Judah's covenant love, in contrast with His own faithfulness (v. 3).

6:5 light. Like the light of the sun whose rising dispels the darkness, God's justice consistently and inevitably goes forth (cf. Ps. 37:6), exposing the sins of those who have broken the covenant.

6:6 rather than burnt offerings. Covenant faithfulness or loyalty, not mere ritual, were required of the covenant people (Mic. 6:6–8 and notes).

6:7–10 These verses catalogue a number of crimes associated with specific places that were infamous in Hosea's day. Though the details are now lost, the record serves to indict the whole nation (v. 10).

6:7 like Adam. Several possible interpretations of this reference have been proposed: (a) the first man, Adam (Gen. 3); (b) a place identified with the ancient site Tell ed-Damiyeh on the Jordan River (Josh. 3:16), parallel to Gilead and Shechem (vv. 8, 9) and suggested by "there" in the second half of the verse; and (c) mankind. Because the elements of a covenant were present in God's relationship with Adam, the doctrine of God's covenant with Adam does not depend upon the interpretation of this text. See note Gen. 3.

6:8 Gilead. This was a mountainous region in the northern Transjordan, but the word may refer to the city of Ramoth-gilead.

evildoers. The term is used frequently in the Psalms to indicate the enemies of the righteous and of the Lord.

tracked with blood. This may allude to the fifty men of Gilead involved in the assassination of Pekahiah (2 Kin. 15:25).

6:9 Shechem. An important religious and political center, Shechem was located between Mount Gerizim and Mount Ebal (Deut. 27:4, 12–14; Josh. 8:30; 20:7; 24:1; Judg. 9:6; 1 Kin. 12:1).

6:10 horrible thing. The phrase suggests a religious sin, or the involvement of priests or prophets in gross wrongdoing (Jer. 5:30, 31; 18:13–15; 23:14).

whoredom. A common figure here for religious infidelity (7:4 and note).

6:11 harvest. A metaphor for God's judgment (Jer. 51:33; Joel 3:13; Matt. 13:39–43).

7 [x]When I would heal Israel,
the iniquity of Ephraim is revealed,
and the evil deeds of [y]Samaria;
for [z]they deal falsely;
the thief breaks in,
and the bandits raid outside.
2 But they do not consider
that [a]I remember all their evil.
Now [b]their deeds surround them;
[c]they are before my face.
3 By their evil [d]they make [d]the king
glad,
and the princes by their treachery.
4 [e]They are all adulterers;
they are like a heated oven
whose baker ceases to stir the fire,
from the kneading of the dough
until it is leavened.
5 On the day of [f]our king, the princes
became sick with the heat of wine;
he stretched out his hand with
mockers.
6 For with hearts like an oven [g]they
approach their intrigue;
all night their anger smolders;
in the morning it blazes like a
flaming fire.
7 All of them are hot as an oven,
and they devour their rulers.
All [h]their kings [i]have fallen,
and none of them calls upon me.

Chapter 7
1 [x][ch. 6:4] [y][Jer. 23:13] [z][ch. 4:2]
2 [a][ch. 5:3] [b]Ps. 9:16; Prov. 5:22 [c]Ps. 90:8
3 [d]ver. 5; [Rom. 1:32]
4 [e]See ch. 6:10
5 [f]ver. 3
6 [g]ch. 6:9
7 [h]ch. 8:4 [i]2 Kin. 15:10, 14, 25, 30
8 [j]Ps. 106:35
9 [k][ch. 8:7] [l]Isai. 42:25
9 [l]Isai. 42:25
10 [m]ch. 5:5 [n]Isai. 9:13
11 [o]ch. 4:11 [p][ch. 12:1; 2 Kin. 17:4] [q]See ch. 5:13
12 [r]See Ezek. 12:13 [s]ch. 10:10 [t]See Lev. 26:14-39; Deut. 28:15-68
13 [u]ch. 9:12 [v]ch. 13:14 [w][ch. 11:12; 12:1; Mic. 6:12]

8 Ephraim [j]mixes himself with the
peoples;
Ephraim is a cake not turned.
9 [k]Strangers devour his strength,
and [l]he knows it not;
gray hairs are sprinkled upon him,
and [l]he knows it not.
10 [m]The pride of Israel testifies to his
face;[1]
[n]yet they do not return to the LORD
their God,
nor seek him, for all this.
11 Ephraim is like a dove,
[o]silly and without sense,
calling to [p]Egypt, going to
[q]Assyria.
12 As they go, [r]I will spread over them
my net;
I will bring them down like birds
of the heavens;
[s]I will discipline them [t]according to
the report made to their
congregation.
13 [u]Woe to them, for they have strayed
from me!
Destruction to them, for they have
rebelled against me!
[v]I would redeem them,
but [w]they speak lies against me.

[1] Or *in his presence*

7:1 Ephraim . . . Samaria. Both terms refer to the northern kingdom, of which Samaria was the capital (4:17 note).

7:2 they do not consider. They have deceived even themselves (cf. Gal. 6:7).

7:3 king . . . princes. The royal leaders should have provided moral leadership, but savored instead the evil and treachery of those around them (2 Kin. 15:8–30).

7:4 adulterers. They left the Lord, to whom they were allied in the covenant, and joined themselves with other gods and other foreign allies (2:4; 4:12–14; Jer. 9:2; 23:10–14). See Introduction: Characteristics and Themes.

like a heated oven. The figures of an oven, a baker, and fire present a graphic word picture of the self-propagating passion, treachery, and wickedness that infested the political life of Israel during its last days and led to the series of violent assassinations of its kings (2 Kin. 15:8–30). The assassination of Pekah by Hoshea (2 Kin. 15:30) may be the occasion of the remarks in vv. 4–7.

7:5 day of our king. A royal celebration became an occasion for drunkenness, which in turn fueled wickedness (1 Kin. 16:9, 10; Prov. 31:4, 5; Amos 6:6).

7:6 they approach. Those plotting against the king, perhaps the priests (6:9).

7:7 rulers . . . kings. Even amid unrest that saw four kings assassinated within twenty years (2 Kin. 15:8–30), none of the leaders called upon God.

7:8 mixes himself with the peoples. A reference to Israel's shifting alliances with Egypt, Philistia, Aram, and Assyria.

a cake not turned. In this sarcastic figure for foolish national policy, Israel is compared to a useless half-baked cake because she refused to turn to the Lord.

7:9 devour his strength. They made Ephraim poor by exacting tribute.

he knows it not. This repeated phrase stresses Israel's ignorance of how politically weak and drained she had become. Lack of knowledge of God is here followed by lack of self-knowledge.

7:10 pride. Israel's blindness is attributed to stubborn arrogance that testifies against her (5:5). Turning back to the Lord was Israel's only hope (2:7; 3:5; 5:4; 6:1; Amos 4:6–12).

7:11 dove. The dove was reputed to be witless and easy to trap.

Egypt . . . Assyria. Like a dove, Israel fluttered from one nation to another seeking security and protection: Menahem submitted to Assyria and paid a vast tribute (2 Kin. 15:17–20); Pekah formed a coalition with Syria-Damascus against Assyria (2 Kin. 15:29, 37; 16:5); and Hoshea shifted his allegiance from Assyria to Egypt (2 Kin. 17:3, 4).

7:12 my net. The Lord's net of judgment will come down upon flitting Israel.

7:13 redeem. This term from commercial law meaning "buy back" (Lev. 27:27–31) is used also of Israel's deliverance from bondage (13:14; Ex. 15:13; Deut. 7:8; 9:26; Mic. 6:4).

lies. This may refer to the false ideas about the Lord that had been imported into Israel's religion, to insincere words of repentance (6:1–3), or more generally to the broken promises of the covenant.

14 [x]They do not cry to me from the heart,
but [y]they wail upon their beds;
for grain and wine they gash
themselves;
they rebel against me.
15 Although [z]I trained and strengthened
their arms,
yet they devise evil against me.
16 They [a]return, but not upward;[1]
they are [b]like a treacherous bow;
their princes shall fall by the sword
because of [c]the insolence of their
tongue.
This shall be their derision [d]in the
land of Egypt.

Israel Will Reap the Whirlwind

8 Set [e]the trumpet to your lips!
One [f]like a vulture is over the house
of the LORD,
because [g]they have transgressed my
covenant
and rebelled against my law.
2 To me they cry,
[h]My God, we—Israel—know you.
3 Israel has spurned the good;
the enemy shall pursue him.
4 [i]They made kings, [j]but not through me.
They set up princes, but I knew
it not.
With their silver and gold they made
idols
for their own destruction.

14 [x]Ps. 78:36, 37 [y][Amos 6:4, 5]
15 [z][ch. 11:3]
16 [a][ch. 6:1] [b]Ps. 78:57 [c]Ps. 73:9 [d]ch. 9:3
Chapter 8
1 [e]ch. 5:8 [f]See Deut. 28:49 [g]ch. 6:7
2 [h]See Matt. 7:21-23
4 [i]ch. 7:7; 1 Kin. 12:20 [j][2 Chr. 13:5]

5 [k]ch. 10:5, 6; [1 Kin. 12:28] [l][Jer. 13:27]
6 [k][See ver. 5 above] [m][Mic. 1:6, 7]
7 [n][ch. 10:12, 13] [o][ch. 7:9]
8 [p]2 Kin. 17:6 [q]Jer. 22:28
9 [r]See ch. 5:13 [s][Jer. 2:24]
10 [t][ch. 4:7, 10] [u]See Ezek. 26:7

5 [k]I have[2] spurned your calf,
O Samaria.
My anger burns against them.
[l]How long will they be incapable of
innocence?
6 For it is from Israel;
a craftsman made it;
it is not God.
[k]The calf of Samaria
[m]shall be broken to pieces.[3]
7 For [n]they sow the wind,
and they shall reap the
whirlwind.
The standing grain has no heads;
it shall yield no flour;
if it were to yield,
[o]strangers would devour it.
8 [p]Israel is swallowed up;
already they are among the
nations
as [q]a useless vessel.
9 For [r]they have gone up to
Assyria,
[s]a wild donkey wandering alone;
Ephraim has hired lovers.
10 Though they hire allies among the
nations,
I will soon gather them up.
And [t]the king and princes shall soon
writhe
because [u]of the tribute.

[1] Or *to the Most High* [2] Hebrew *He has* [3] Or *shall go up in flames*

7:14 from the heart. A responsible and loyal response, as suggested by a similar expression used in a contemporary Assyrian treaty.

wail upon their beds. This phrase could mean that they cried out to their gods on the beds of fertility-cult prostitution. If "gash themselves" is the best translation, this self-mutilation was yet another appeal to pagan gods (Deut. 14:1; 1 Kin. 18:26–29).

7:16 treacherous bow. See Ps. 78:57.

insolence of their tongue. These were directed against God and His prophets (6:5).

Egypt. The Egyptians would soon mock at the fall of those who only intermittently solicited their help.

8:1 trumpet. The urgent call for alarm (5:8) reports that Assyria, like an eagle (Deut. 28:49, 50; Is. 10:5, 6; Jer. 4:13; 48:40; Lam. 4:19; Hab. 1:8), is rapidly approaching to administer God's judgment.

the house of the LORD. This expression can refer to the land as well as the temple (9:15).

my covenant . . . my law. Rebellion against the terms of the covenant was tantamount to rebellion against God Himself (4:6; 6:6, 7; 7:13; 8:12).

8:2 we—Israel—know you. As they cry for help, the Israelites claim to know God, but their actions belie their words (6:1). See Introduction: Characteristics and Themes.

8:3 the good. This comprehensive term describes all the blessings under God's covenant; it may even refer to the "Good One," God Himself (Amos 5:14, 15; Mic. 6:8).

8:4 kings . . . princes. Israel's independence from God in the political sphere was apparent in their refusal to consult God in their choice of leaders. This led to a series of conspiracies and violent assassinations (7:3–7; 2 Kin. 15:8–30). See Introduction: Date and Occasion.

idols. In making gods of silver and gold, Israel expressed her defiant rejection of the good (v. 5; Ex. 20:3–6; 34:17; Lev. 19:4).

8:5 calf. A symbol of fertility and strength, the bull was frequently worshiped in the ancient Near East. Yet the golden calf of Samaria was established as an idol representing the Lord by Jeroboam I (1 Kin. 12:26–30; cf. Ex. 32) and is itself here described as the object of worship (10:5 note).

8:7 sow the wind . . . reap the whirlwind. This proverbial saying emphasizes the dire cause-and-effect relationship between sin and punishment (10:13; Job 4:8; Prov. 11:18; 22:8; Gal. 6:7–9).

8:9 gone up to Assyria. Probably a reference to Hoshea's submission to Assyria in his attempt to keep the power that he had seized following his murder of Pekah (7:11; 2 Kin. 15:30; 17:3). See Introduction: Date and Occasion.

wild donkey. Using a wordplay between the Hebrew for "wild donkey" and "Ephraim," Hosea condemns Ephraim (Israel) for stubbornly rejecting the Lord's company.

8:10 I will soon gather them. This gathering is for judgment, not restoration (Joel 3:2; Zeph. 3:8).

the king and princes. The king of Assyria (Is. 10:8).

11 Because Ephraim [v]has multiplied
altars for sinning,
they have become to him altars for
sinning.
12 [w]Were I to write for him my laws by
the ten thousands,
they would be regarded as a
strange thing.
13 As for my sacrificial offerings,
[x]they sacrifice meat and eat it,
but the LORD does not accept
them.
[y]Now he will remember their iniquity
and punish their sins;
[z]they shall return to Egypt.
14 For [a]Israel has forgotten [b]his Maker
and [c]built palaces,
and [a]Judah has multiplied fortified
cities;
so [d]I will send a fire upon his
cities,
and it shall devour her
strongholds.

The LORD Will Punish Israel

9 Rejoice not, O Israel!
Exult not like the peoples;
[e]for you have played the whore,
forsaking your God.
[f]You have loved a prostitute's
wages
on all threshing floors.
2 [g]Threshing floor and wine vat shall
not feed them,
and [g]the new wine shall fail them.
3 They shall not remain in [h]the land of
the LORD,
but [i]Ephraim shall return to Egypt,
and [j]they shall eat unclean food in
Assyria.
4 [k]They shall not pour drink offerings of
wine to the LORD,
[l]and their sacrifices shall not please
him.
It shall be like [m]mourners' bread to
them;
all who eat of it shall be defiled;
for their bread shall be for their
hunger only;
[n]it shall not come to the house of
the LORD.
5 [o]What will you do on the day of the
appointed festival,
and on the day of the feast of the
LORD?
6 For behold, they are going away from
destruction;
but [p]Egypt shall gather them;
Memphis shall bury them.
Nettles shall possess [q]their precious
things of silver;
[r]thorns shall be in their tents.
7 [s]The days of punishment have come;
the days of recompense have come;
Israel shall know it.
[t]The prophet is a fool;
the man of the spirit is mad,
because of your great iniquity
and great hatred.

11 [v]ch. 10:1; 12:11
12 [w][Deut. 4:6, 8]
13 [x]Jer. 7:21; [Amos 4:4] [y]ch. 9:9; Amos 8:7 [z]ch. 9:3; Deut. 28:68; [ch. 11:5]
14 [a]See ch. 6:4 [b]Isai. 17:7 [c][Amos 5:11] [d]Amos 2:5

Chapter 9
1 [e]ch. 1:2 [f]ch. 2:5; Jer. 44:17
2 [g][ch. 2:9]
3 [h]Jer. 2:7; 16:18; See Lev. 25:23 [i]See ch. 8:13 [j]Ezek. 4:13; Dan. 1:8
4 [k][ch. 3:4] [l][ch. 8:13] [m]Deut. 26:14; Ezek. 24:17 [n][Hag. 2:13]
5 [o][Isai. 10:3]
6 [p]See ch. 8:13 [q][ch. 10:8; Isai. 2:20] [r][ch. 10:8]
7 [s]See Isai. 10:3 [t]Ezek. 13:3

8:11 altars for sinning. Although built to atone for sin, northern altars instead became places to sin.

8:13 return to Egypt. God threatens them with captivity, here symbolized by the land where Israel earlier had been enslaved (9:3; Ex. 1:8–14; Deut. 28:68).

8:14 palaces . . . strongholds. Israel's confidence that buildings and fortifications bring spiritual, political, or military security was misguided.

fire. See Amos 1:4, 7, 10, 12, 14.

9:1–9 Because of divine judgment on her covenant disobedience, Israel would not enjoy the fruit of the land (Deut. 28:18), nor celebrate the annual agricultural feasts (Deut. 16:1–17 and notes).

9:1 threshing floors. The flat, open area used for threshing wheat and barley was also a place where Israel prostituted itself by indulging in sensual activities related to the fertility worship of Baal. See Introduction: Date and Occasion.

9:2 wine vat. This device was used for both wine and oil.

9:3 the land of the LORD. Also called the Lord's "house" (8:1; 9:15), the Promised Land is owned by the Lord and not by Baal—or even by Israel (Lev. 25:23 and note).

return to Egypt. See note 8:13.

unclean food. Other nations and the food they produced were considered unclean (Ezek. 4:13; Amos 7:17).

9:4 mourners' bread. Food in the house of mourners was unclean because of contact with a dead body (Num. 19:11–22; Deut. 26:14).

house of the LORD. They would not be able to sanctify their food through sacrifice while in exile.

9:5 the appointed festival. A probable reference to the annual fall harvest Feast of Booths or Tabernacles (Lev. 23:33–43; Deut. 16:13–15).

9:6 destruction. The Assyrian invasions.

Memphis shall bury them. Here poetically paired with Egypt, this Egyptian city was known for its great cemeteries, tombs, and pyramids.

precious things of silver . . . tents. The abandoned tents and valuables may have been religious shrines and idols, or their personal property in general.

9:7 prophet is a fool. In their sin, the Israelites consider the Lord's prophets to be foolish and idle talkers.

man of the spirit. Used in parallel with "prophet," this is probably another expression for "man of God" (1 Sam. 10:6; 1 Kin. 18:12; 22:21–28; 2 Kin. 2:9, 16).

mad. The Hebrew word indicates a nonsensical babbler or madman (1 Sam. 21:13–15; 2 Kin. 9:11; Jer. 29:26).

8 The prophet is [u]the watchman of
Ephraim with my God;
yet [v]a fowler's snare is on all his
ways,
and hatred in the house of his
God.
9 [w]They have deeply corrupted
themselves
as [x]in the days of Gibeah:
[w]he will remember their iniquity;
he will punish their sins.

10 Like grapes in the wilderness,
[y]I found Israel.
Like the first fruit on the fig tree
in its first season,
I saw your fathers.
But [z]they came to Baal-peor
and [a]consecrated themselves to the
thing of shame,
and [b]became detestable like the
thing they loved.
11 Ephraim's [c]glory shall fly away like a
bird—
[d]no birth, no pregnancy, no
conception!
12 [e]Even if they bring up children,
I will bereave them till none is left.
[f]Woe to them
when [g]I depart from them!
13 Ephraim, [h]as I have seen, was like a
young palm[1] planted in a
meadow;
but [e]Ephraim must lead his
children out to slaughter.[2]

14 Give them, O LORD—
what will you give?
Give them [i]a miscarrying womb
and dry breasts.

15 Every evil of theirs is in [j]Gilgal;
there I began to hate them.
Because of the wickedness of their
deeds
I will drive them out of my house.
I will love them no more;
all [k]their princes are [l]rebels.

16 Ephraim is stricken;
[m]their root is dried up;
they shall bear no fruit.
Even [n]though they give birth,
[e]I will put their beloved children to
death.
17 [o]My God will reject them
because they have not listened to
him;
[p]they shall be wanderers among the
nations.

10 [q]Israel is a luxuriant vine
that yields its fruit.
The more his fruit increased,
[r]the more altars he built;
as his country improved,
he improved his pillars.
2 Their heart is false;
now they must bear their guilt.
The LORD[3] will break down their altars
and destroy their pillars.

8 [u]Ezek. 3:17 [v]Ps. 91:3; [ch. 5:1]
9 [w][ch. 5:2] [x]ch. 10:9; Judg. 19:22
10 [y][Ps. 80:8; Isai. 5:1] [z]Num. 25:3; Ps. 106:28 [a][ch. 4:14] [b][Rom. 1:28, 29]
11 [c]ch. 10:5; [ch. 4:7] [d][Isai. 26:18]
12 [e]ch. 13:16 [f]ch. 7:13 [g]ch. 5:6; 1 Sam. 28:15, 16; Ezek. 10:18
13 [h][Ezek. 27:3] [e][See ver. 12 above]
14 [i][Luke 23:29]
15 [j]ch. 4:15; 12:11 [k]ch. 8:4 [l][ch. 5:2]
16 [m][ver. 11] [n][ver. 12, 13] [e][See ver. 12 above]
17 [o][ch. 8:5] [p]Deut. 28:64, 65
Chapter 10
1 [q]See Ps. 80:8-11 [r]ch. 8:11

1 Or *like Tyre* 2 Hebrew *to him who slaughters* 3 Hebrew *He*

9:8 watchman . . . fowler's snare. The prophets kept watch over Israel (5:8; Jer. 6:1; Ezek. 3:17; 33:1–7). But the one who sounded the alarm now found himself hunted like an animal and an object of hostility.

the house of his God. The land (8:1 note).

9:9 Gibeah. This town was infamous for the gang rape of the Levite's concubine and the war that followed (Judg. 19–21). The gravity of Israel's former sins also shows how deeply they require a complete renewal of their nature.

9:10 grapes in the wilderness. An unusual and delicious find.

first fruit on the fig tree. The early fig that ripens on the previous year's sprouts is not only very tender but quite uncommon (cf. Is. 28:4). These images stress how exceptional and pleasing was the Lord's initial covenant relationship with Israel.

Baal-peor. A reference to Israel's sexual and spiritual adultery in the wilderness (Num. 25 and notes)—behavior that was paralleled by Hosea's contemporaries.

became detestable. By joining themselves to Baal, the god of shame, the Israelites themselves became detestable.

9:11 glory. This could be her political and military power. But the context suggests that it is her large population. The blessing on Joseph and Ephraim had made them fruitful (Gen. 48:16; 49:22–26).

no birth. The practice of fertility religion generated a fertility curse, not a blessing (Deut. 28:18).

9:14 Give them. Hosea responds in prayer asking that God's fertility blessings be withdrawn (Gen. 49:25; Ex. 23:26; Deut. 28:4, 11). The prophet can only agree with God's righteous judgment.

9:15 Gilgal. See note 4:15; cf. 12:11.

drive them out of my house. Notice how this parallels God's banishment of the Canaanites (Ex. 23:29, 30; 33:2; Josh. 24:18; Judg. 6:9). See note 8:1.

9:16 Ephraim . . . fruit. "Ephraim" sounds like "fruit" in Hebrew, and the wordplay ironically underscores the tragedy of Ephraim's fruitlessness (Gen. 41:52). The name of this leading northern tribe is often used for the entire northern kingdom of Israel.

9:17 My God. Unlike the people who have turned away from God, the prophet remains faithful to the covenant.

wanderers. Having wandered from God (7:13), the Israelites, like Cain, are destined to be restless wanderers (Gen. 4:12).

10:1–8 In this section, unlike the preceding and following sections, the Lord does not speak but is spoken about.

10:1 more his fruit increased . . . more altars he built. Israel gives the credit for prosperity to their idols, and they devote more resources to the pagan cult whenever their prosperity increases.

10:2 heart is false. The covenant required single-minded devotion to the Lord (Deut. 6:5); Israel's divided loyalties called forth the judgment predicted in the covenant curses pronounced by Moses (Deut. 29:14–29).

3 For now they will say:
[s]"We have no king,
for we do not fear the LORD;
and a king—what could he do
for us?"
4 They utter [t]mere words;
with empty oaths they make
covenants;
so [u]judgment springs up like
poisonous weeds
[v]in the furrows of the field.
5 The inhabitants of Samaria tremble
for [w]the calf[1] of [x]Beth-aven.
Its people mourn for it, and so do its
idolatrous priests—
those who rejoiced over it and
[y]over its glory—
for it has departed[2] from them.
6 [z]The thing itself shall be carried to
Assyria
as tribute to [a]the great king.[3]
Ephraim shall be put to shame,
and Israel shall be ashamed [b]of his
idol.[4]

7 [c]Samaria's king shall perish
like a twig on the face of the waters.
8 The high places of [x]Aven, [d]the sin of
Israel,
shall be destroyed.
[e]Thorn and thistle shall grow up
on their altars,
and [f]they shall say to the mountains,
Cover us,
and to the hills, Fall on us.

9 From [g]the days of Gibeah, you have
sinned, O Israel;
there they have continued.
Shall not the war against the
unjust[5] overtake them in
Gibeah?
10 [h]When I please, [i]I will discipline
them,
and nations shall be gathered
against them
when they are bound up for [j]their
double iniquity.

11 Ephraim was a trained calf
that [k]loved to thresh,
and I spared her fair neck;
but I will put [l]Ephraim to the yoke;
[l]Judah must plow;
Jacob must harrow for himself.
12 [m]Sow for yourselves righteousness;
reap steadfast love;
[n]break up your fallow ground,
for it is the time to seek the LORD,
that he may come and [o]rain
righteousness upon you.

13 [p]You have plowed iniquity;
you have reaped injustice;
you have eaten the fruit of lies.
Because you have trusted in your
own way
and in the multitude of your
warriors,

3 [s][ver. 7, 15; 1 Sam. 12:12]
4 [t][ch. 4:2] [u]Amos 5:7; 6:12 [v]ch. 12:11
5 [w]See 1 Kin. 12:28 [x]See ch. 4:15 [y]ch. 9:11; [1 Sam. 4:21, 22]
6 [z][Isai. 46:2] [a]ch. 5:13 [b]ch. 11:6
7 [c][ver. 3]
8 [x][See ver. 5 above] [d]1 Kin. 12:30; Amos 8:14 [e][ch. 9:6] [f]Luke 23:30; Rev.6:16; [Isai. 2:19]
9 [g]ch. 9:9
10 [h][Ex. 32:34] [i]ch. 7:12 [j][1 Kin. 12:28]
11 [k][Deut. 25:4; 1 Cor. 9:9; 1 Tim. 5:18] [l]See ch. 6:4
12 [m][ch. 8:7; Gal. 6:8] [n]Jer. 4:3 [o]Isai. 45:8
13 [p][ch. 8:7]

1 Or *calves* 2 Or *has gone into exile* 3 Or *to King Jareb* 4 Or *counsel*
5 Hebrew *the children of injustice*

10:3 no king. Whether the king is still on the throne and is about to be deposed, or has already been deposed, without God's blessing he is useless.

10:4 empty oaths. The king's commitments could be covenants as a vassal to Assyria, which are deemed false because they were ratified by invoking Assyrian deities (cf. v. 6). More likely, the broken obligations in view are those of the king to his people (2 Sam. 3:21; 5:3), chief of which is to maintain justice.

poisonous weeds. Or "wormwood," as the Hebrew term is translated in Amos 6:12.

10:5 Samaria. The capital city of the northern kingdom.

calf of Beth-aven. The calf and its priests (2 Kin. 23:5; Zeph. 1:4) were probably not representative of a foreign deity. Rather, they exemplified a highly perverse form of worshiping the Lord in Israel (8:5 note; 13:2 note; 1 Kin. 12:31–33).

mourn. Hosea mocks the pious emotions that the people manifest for an idol.

10:8 high places of Aven. See 4:13, 14.

Cover us . . . Fall on us. The words speak of overwhelming devastation from the Lord. The people would rather die than face further judgments from Him. The passage is quoted by Jesus in Luke 23:30 and alluded to in Rev. 6:16.

10:9 Gibeah. See note 9:9.

10:10 double iniquity. This may refer to the past sin at Gibeah and the present sin of Israel, to Israel's religious sin and political faithlessness, or simply to Israel's repeated and unyielding transgressions.

10:11 Ephraim . . . Judah. Both kingdoms are in view.

trained calf . . . loved to thresh. A positive image of Israel's original calling as a teachable, unmuzzled animal threshing the harvested grain and free to eat as it worked (cf. 11:4; Deut. 25:4; Prov. 12:10; Jer. 50:11). Jesus also offers an easy yoke to His disciples (Matt. 11:28–30).

fair neck. That is, a strong neck capable of arduous work. Israel had not fulfilled the Lord's expectations. The easy yoke of covenant blessings would be replaced by the hard yoke of covenant curses in order to teach them obedience.

10:12 steadfast love. See note Ex. 15:13. Sowing that which is right and good brings a harvest of blessing from the Lord.

break up your fallow ground. When virgin and fallow ground is plowed, it produces a particularly abundant harvest.

rain righteousness. God must give the harvest (1 Cor. 3:6, 7).

10:13 plowed iniquity. Instead of cultivating a fruitful relationship with God, Israel has planted, reaped, and eaten wickedness and dishonesty (8:7; Gal. 6:7–9).

Because you have trusted in . . . your warriors. The punishment God will bring (a military defeat) is directly related to Israel's sin of depending on its own military power and not on the Lord (Jer. 9:23, 24).

14 therefore [q]the tumult of war shall
arise among your people,
and all your fortresses shall be
destroyed,
as [r]Shalman destroyed Beth-arbel on
the day of battle;
[s]mothers were dashed in pieces
with their children.
15 Thus it shall be done to you, O [t]Bethel,
because of your great evil.
At dawn [a]the king of Israel
shall be utterly cut off.

The LORD's Love for Israel

11 [u]When Israel was a child, [v]I loved
him,
and out of Egypt I [w]called [x]my son.
2 [y]The more they were called,
the more they went away;
[z]they kept sacrificing to the Baals
and burning offerings to idols.

3 Yet it was [a]I who taught Ephraim to
walk;
I took them up by their arms,
but they did not know that [b]I
healed them.
4 [c]I led them with cords of kindness,[1]
with the bands of love,
and [d]I became to them as one who
eases the yoke on their jaws,
and [e]I bent down to them and fed
them.

5 [f]They shall not[2] return to the land of
Egypt,
but [g]Assyria shall be their king,
[h]because [i]they have refused to
return to me.
6 [j]The sword shall rage against their
cities,
consume the bars of their gates,
and devour them [k]because of their
own counsels.
7 My people are bent [l]on turning away
from me,
and though [m]they call out to the
Most High,
he shall not raise them up at all.

8 How can I give you up, O Ephraim?
How can I hand you over, O Israel?
[n]How can I make you [o]like Admah?
How can I treat you [o]like Zeboiim?
[p]My heart recoils within me;
my compassion grows warm and
tender.
9 I will not execute my burning anger;
I will not again destroy Ephraim;
[q]for I am God and not a man,
[r]the Holy One in your midst,
and I will not come in wrath.[3]

14 [q][ch. 1:5] [r]2 Kin. 17:3 [s][ch. 13:16] 15 [t][ver. 5] [a][See ver. 6 above] **Chapter 11** 1 [u][ch. 2:15] [v]Deut. 7:8; [ch. 14:4] [w]Ex. 4:22; [Mal 1:6] [x]Cited Matt. 2:15 2 [y][ver. 7] [z][ch. 2:13; 13:1, 2] 3 [a][ch. 7:15; Deut. 1:31] [b]Ex. 15:26 4 [c]Jer. 31:3; [John 6:44; 12:32] [d]Lev. 26:13 [e]See Ps. 78:24-29 5 [f][ch. 8:13] [g][ch. 10:3] [h][2 Kin. 17:13, 14] [i][ch. 4:16; 7:16] 6 [j][ch. 10:14] [k]ch. 10:6 7 [l]ch. 14:4 [m][ver. 2] 8 [n][Gen. 19:24, 25; Jer. 49:18; 50:40; Amos 4:11; Jude 7] [o]Gen. 14:8; Deut. 29:23 [p][Deut. 32:36] 9 [q]See Num. 23:19 [r]See Isai. 12:6

1 Or *humaneness*; Hebrew *man* 2 Or *surely* 3 Or *into the city*

10:14 Shalman destroyed Beth-arbel. Hosea's audience must have remembered this now unknown event as particularly brutal. Shalman has been identified variously as Shalmaneser III of Assyria (859–824 B.C.), Shalmaneser V (727–722 B.C.), and Salamanu, a contemporary Moabite king. Beth-arbel is usually identified with the site of Irbid in Gilead.

10:15 Bethel. Often ironically called "Beth-aven" by Hosea (4:15 note; 5:8; 10:5).

At dawn. The time for battle to begin.

11:1–11 In language even more tender than the story of the prodigal son (Luke 15:11–32), God, the loving parent, proclaims His compassion for Israel. In spite of rebellion, God's election cannot be defeated. Beyond judgment there is hope.

11:1 loved. The language of love is used to describe both the father-son relationship and the covenantal relationship between a suzerain and vassal in ancient Near-Eastern treaties (Deut. 6:5; 7:8, 13; 10:15; 23:5).

out of Egypt I called my son. Here and in v. 4 reference is made to God's deliverance of Israel from slavery in Egypt (Ex. 4:22). Jesus, as the true Israel, was also brought out of Egypt in accordance with this prophecy (Matt. 2:15).

11:2 they were called . . . they went away. The Hebrew of this verse is difficult to translate. The meaning may be that the pagans or their gods, the Baals, tempted Israel, causing the nation to depart from the Lord. Alternatively, those who called may be the prophets, whose messages were ignored as Israel went after other gods.

11:3 I . . . taught Ephraim to walk. Probably a reference to God's tender leading of Israel through the wilderness to the Promised Land.

I healed them. God spared Israel from harm during the formative wilderness period (Ex. 15:26).

11:4 cords . . . bands . . . yoke . . . fed. The imagery apparently returns to Israel as a work animal (10:11), but here God pampers the creature.

11:5 They shall not . . . Egypt. The Hebrew word for "not" here seems to indicate that Israel will not return to Egypt (symbolic for bondage, 8:13 note), but such a reading appears to conflict with 8:13; 9:3; and 11:11. Some render this phrase as a rhetorical question ("shall he not return?"), while others emend the Hebrew word for "not" to mean "to it." Another reading, however, is indicated by the context of divine mercy in this passage (vv. 4, 8). Israel shall not return to Egypt (i.e., to her status before God called her as His covenant people, Deut. 4:34), but she will be punished for her sins by Assyria.

Egypt . . . Assyria. See notes 8:13; 9:3. Though deserved, the effect of this judgment is tempered in v. 11.

11:6 their cities. With fortified cities they were self-reliant (8:14).

gates. Some suggest that this difficult Hebrew word refers to people, specifically to false prophets who supplied the military counsel mentioned later in the verse.

11:8 How can I give you up. God now speaks directly to Israel. The contrast with vv. 5–7 heightens the impact of this deeply personal declaration of relentless compassion.

Admah . . . Zeboiim. These two cities on the plain near the southern end of the Dead Sea (Gen. 10:19; 14:2, 8) were destroyed along with Sodom and Gomorrah (Gen. 19:23–25), thus becoming examples of God's wrath (Deut. 29:23; Jer. 49:18).

11:9 Holy One. Holiness denotes God's difference from humans. Men seek revenge, but God works salvation.

10 [s]They shall go after the LORD;
[t]he will roar like a lion;
when he roars,
his children shall come trembling
[u]from the west;
11 they shall come trembling like birds
[v]from Egypt,
and [w]like doves [x]from the land of
Assyria,
and I will return them to their
homes, declares the LORD.
12[1] Ephraim [y]has surrounded me with
lies,
and the house of Israel with
deceit,
but Judah still walks with God
and is faithful to the Holy One.

12 Ephraim feeds on the wind
and pursues [z]the east wind all day
long;
they multiply [y]falsehood and violence;
[a]they make a covenant with Assyria,
and [b]oil is carried to Egypt.

The LORD's Indictment of Israel and Judah

2 [c]The LORD has an indictment against
Judah
and will punish Jacob according to
his ways;
he will repay him according to his
deeds.
3 [d]In the womb he took his brother by
the heel,
and in his manhood he strove with
God.
4 He strove with the angel and
prevailed;
he wept and sought his favor.
[e]He met God[2] at Bethel,
and there God spoke with us—
5 the LORD, the God of hosts,
[f]the LORD is his memorial name:
6 "So you, [g]by the help of your God,
return,
[h]hold fast to love and justice,
and wait continually for your
God."

7 A merchant, in whose hands are
[i]false balances,
he loves [j]to oppress.
8 Ephraim has said, "Ah, but [k]I am
rich;
I have found wealth for myself;
in all my labors [l]they cannot find in
me iniquity or sin."
9 [m]I am the LORD your God
from the land of Egypt;
I will again make you [n]dwell in tents,
as in the days of the appointed
feast.

10[s][ch. 3:5] [t]Isai. 31:4; Jer. 25:30; Joel 3:16; Amos 1:2 [u]Isai. 11:11; Zech. 8:7
11[v]See ch. 8:13 [w]Isai. 60:8 [x]Zech. 10:6, 10; [ch. 9:3]
12[y][ch. 7:13]
Chapter 12
1[z][ch. 13:15; Jer. 18:17] [y][See ch. 11:12 above] [a]See ch. 5:13 [b][ch. 7:11; 2 Kin. 17:4]
2[c]See ch. 4:1
3[d]Gen. 25:26; [Gen. 27:36]
4[e]Gen. 28:12, 19; 35:9, 10, 15
5[f]Ex. 3:15
6[g]ch. 14:1, 2; Joel 2:12, 13 [h][Mic. 6:8]
7[i]Amos 8:5; Mic. 6:11; [Prov. 11:1; 20:23] [j]Mic. 2:2
8[k]Zech. 11:5; Rev. 3:17 [l][Deut. 29:19]
9[m]ch. 13:4 [n]See Lev. 23:39-43; Neh. 8:14-18

[1] Ch 12:1 in Hebrew [2] Hebrew *him*

11:10 They shall go after the LORD. Restoration, not destruction, is the goal of God's judgment of His covenant people.

11:11 God compassionately tempers the effect of the judgment pronounced in v. 5.

from Egypt . . . Assyria. Again Egypt and Assyria are paired to symbolize the judgment of God's people through exile (8:13 note; 9:3; 11:5).

11:12–12:14 This section accuses Israel of betrayal and pronounces judgment. Recurrent themes are the past treachery of Israel (artistically linked with episodes from the life of Jacob) and the rejection of the word of the Lord as spoken by the prophets.

11:12 surrounded. The northern kingdom has God under siege.

Judah still walks with God. The Hebrew is difficult to translate. As rendered here, Judah is viewed positively and contrasted with Ephraim (i.e., Israel). But some translate the phrase to speak of Judah as "unruly against God," and thus like Ephraim.

12:1 feeds on. See Prov. 15:14; Is. 44:20.

wind . . . east wind. These images of futility (Job 15:2; Eccl. 1:14) and destruction (13:15; Jer. 18:17) are applied to Israel's alliances with Assyria (5:13; 7:11; 8:9; 14:3; 2 Kin. 17:3) and Egypt (7:16 note; 2 Kin. 17:4). Such alliances were not merely poor foreign policy, but expressions of faithlessness against the Lord.

falsehood. Examples of deception included Israel's vacillation between Assyria and Egypt (7:11), and playing off the latter against the former (2 Kin. 17:3, 4).

oil. Gifts were often given when making covenants.

12:2 indictment.. As in 4:1, the Lord acts as plaintiff, judge, and prosecutor in a court scene, bringing a covenant lawsuit against His people. He calls for punishment (v. 2) but also reconciliation (v. 6).

Jacob. That is, Israel (10:11; cf. Gen. 32:28).

12:3 took. The Hebrew here is the root for "Jacob" (Gen. 25:26) and is translated "cheated" in Gen. 27:36.

12:4 strove with the angel. The Hebrew root for "strove" is given as the source of the name "Israel" in Gen. 32:28. In tenaciously seeking God's blessing, Jacob set a positive example for the nation (v. 6).

Bethel. The place where God made Himself known to Jacob (Gen. 28:12–19; 35:1–15). See note 4:15.

12:5 the LORD, the God of hosts. A doxology, similar to those in Amos (Amos 4:13; 5:8, 9; 9:5, 6), here reminds Israel that the covenant God of the patriarchs (the LORD) is the God of hosts, the commander of Israel's armies, and sovereign over all creation (Zech. 1:3 note).

12:6 return. Like Jacob, who returned to Bethel to fulfill his vow (Gen. 35:1–15), Israel must return to the Lord.

12:7 merchant. The merchant Ephraim was not merely dishonest, but pagan.

12:9 I am the LORD your God . . . Egypt. The statement is one of self-presentation; it introduces an expression of the divine will to the covenant people (Ex. 20:2; Deut. 5:6).

tents . . . appointed feast. A reference to the Feast of Booths, when the people lived in booths in memory of Israel's time in the wilderness after leaving Egypt (Lev. 23:43). Just as Israel was judged with forty years of wilderness wandering (Num. 14:33), so here Israel is threatened with the "wilderness" of exile from the land.

10 [o] I spoke to the prophets;
it was I who multiplied [p] visions,
and through the prophets gave
parables.
11 [q] If there is iniquity in Gilead,
they shall surely come to nothing:
[r] in Gilgal they sacrifice bulls;
[s] their altars also are like stone heaps
[t] on the furrows of the field.
12 [u] Jacob fled to the land of Aram;
there Israel [v] served for a wife,
and for a wife he guarded sheep.
13 By [w] a prophet [x] the LORD brought
Israel up from Egypt,
and by a prophet he was guarded.
14 [y] Ephraim has given bitter
provocation;
so his Lord [z] will leave his
bloodguilt on him
[a] and will repay him for his
disgraceful deeds.

The LORD's Relentless Judgment on Israel

13 When Ephraim spoke, there was
trembling;
[b] he was exalted in Israel,
but he incurred guilt [c] through Baal
and died.
2 And now they sin more and
more,
and [d] make for themselves
metal images,
idols skillfully made of their
silver,
[e] all of them the work of
craftsmen.
It is said of them,
"Those who offer human sacrifice
[f] kiss calves!"
3 Therefore they shall be [g] like the
morning mist
or [g] like the dew that goes early
away,
[h] like the chaff that swirls from the
threshing floor
or [i] like smoke from a
window.
4 But [j] I am the LORD your God
from the land of Egypt;
[k] you know no God but me,
and [l] besides me there is no
savior.
5 [m] It was I who knew you in the
wilderness,
in the land of drought;

10 [o] [2 Kin. 17:13] [p] [Joel 2:28] 11 [q] ch. 6:8 [r] ch. 4:15; 9:15 [s] ch. 8:11 [t] ch. 10:4 12 [u] Gen. 28:5 [v] Gen. 29:20, 28 13 [w] [Deut. 18:15] [x] Ex. 12:50, 51; Ps. 77:20; See Isai. 63:11-14 14 [y] 2 Kin. 17:17 [z] See ch. 4:2 [a] ver. 2
Chapter 13
1 [b] [Amos 6:13] [c] See ch. 11:2
2 [d] ch. 2:8 [e] [Ps. 115:4; Isai. 40:19, 20] [f] [1 Kin. 19:18; Job 31:26, 27] 3 [g] ch. 6:4 [h] See Ps. 1:4 [i] See Ps. 68:2 4 [j] ch. 12:9 [k] See Ex. 20:3 [l] Isai. 43:11; 45:21 5 [m] Deut. 2:7; Amos 3:2

12:10 spoke to the prophets. No one could plead ignorance as an excuse (6:5; 12:13).

visions. A mode of revelation to the prophets (Num. 12:6; Job 33:14–16).

parables. These "parables" were figures of speech bearing divine messages (2 Sam. 12:1–4; Ps. 78:2; Is. 5:1–7; Ezek. 17:2–10).

12:11 Gilead. This region east of the Jordan, bordered by Moab on the south and Bashan on the north, was a place of illegal sacrifices, bloodshed, and idolatry. It was conquered by Assyria in 734–732 B.C. (2 Kin. 15:29; Hos. 6:8).

Gilgal. See note 4:15.

heaps on the furrows. Large stones struck by the farmer's plow were piled in heaps.

12:12 land of Aram. Paddan-aram (Gen. 28:2, 5).

served . . . guarded. Hosea compares Jacob's service to secure a wife from a foreign country with God's rescue of His people from Egypt.

12:13 prophet . . . prophet. The first prophet is clearly Moses (Deut. 18:15; 34:10–12) and the second probably is as well. The preserving prophet could, however, be a later prophet such as Samuel (Jer. 15:1) or Elijah (1 Kin. 19:9–18).

12:14 Ephraim has given bitter provocation. Again God's covenant faithfulness (v. 13) is contrasted with Israel's faithlessness. The Lord had been provoked by the worship of pagan gods (Deut. 32:21), but here even more offenses seem involved.

bloodguilt. This is a reference either to murder itself (4:2; 5:2; 6:8) or, as in ancient legal texts, to any capital crime. The verse concludes the lawsuit, and is parallel in structure to v. 2, which introduces the section. Covenant election entails covenant responsibility.

13:1 This begins an announcement of judgment for sins past (v. 1) and present (v. 2).

Ephraim. See note 4:17.

Baal. See 2:7, 8, 17; 9:10; 11:2.

died. Because of its idolatry, the northern kingdom (Ephraim) could be regarded as dead in trespasses and sins (cf. Eph. 2:1).

13:2 metal images . . . idols . . . calves. The collective picture is of small statues of calves molded of bronze and overlaid with silver (Ex. 32:4, 8; 34:17; Lev. 19:4; Deut. 19:16). The calf idol was Canaanite and linked with Baal worship, but the idolaters probably also associated it in their own minds with the Lord (8:5, 6; 10:5 and notes).

kiss. This was an act of devotion, adoration, or appeasement (1 Kin. 19:18).

13:3 mist . . . dew. See 6:4.

13:4 See note 12:9.

you know no God but me. This stands in contrast with the idolatry of v. 2. The statement, reminding Israel that the covenant relationship is exclusive, is cast in the language of the first commandment (Ex. 20:2, 3; Deut. 5:6, 7), but with the added idea of "knowing" God. Other so-called gods were worshiped, but only the one true God could be "known." See Introduction: Characteristics and Themes. Further linkage to the covenant requirements of the Decalogue is evident in the description of Israel's idolatry (vv. 1, 2), a clear violation of the second commandment (Ex. 20:4–6; Deut. 5:8–10).

13:5 I who knew you. Israel is represented in corporate solidarity by the Hebrew singular word for "you." This form of the pronoun emphasizes the personal nature of God's covenant relationship with His people. See Introduction: Characteristics and Themes; Gen. 17:7 note.

wilderness. During the difficult wilderness wanderings God knew and was preparing His people. Similarly, God will use the "wilderness" of exile to reclaim Israel (2:14–16).

6 [n]but when they had grazed,[1] they
became full,
[o]they were filled, and their heart
was lifted up;
[o]therefore they forgot me.
7 So [p]I am to them like a lion;
[q]like a leopard I will lurk beside the
way.
8 I will fall upon them [r]like a bear
robbed of her cubs;
I will tear open their breast,
and there I will devour them like a
lion,
[s]as a wild beast would rip them
open.

9 He destroys[2] you, O Israel,
for you are against me, against
[t]your helper.
10 [u]Where now is your king, to save you
in all your cities?
Where are all your rulers—
those of whom [v]you said,
"Give me a king and princes"?
11 [w]I gave you a king in my anger,
and [x]I took him away in my wrath.

12 The iniquity of Ephraim is
[y]bound up;
his sin is [y]kept in store.
13 [z]The pangs of childbirth come for
him,
but he is an unwise son,
for at the right time he does not
present himself
[a]at the opening of the
womb.

14 [b]Shall I ransom them from the power
of Sheol?
[b]Shall I redeem them from Death?
[c]O [d]Death, where are your
plagues?
[c]O [d]Sheol, where is your sting?
[e]Compassion is hidden from my
eyes.

15 Though [f]he may flourish among his
brothers,
[g]the east wind, the wind of the
LORD, shall come,
rising from the wilderness,
[h]and his fountain shall
dry up;
his spring shall be parched;
it shall strip [i]his treasury
of every precious thing.
16 [3] Samaria [j]shall bear her guilt,
because [k]she has rebelled against
her God;
they shall fall by the sword;
[l]their little ones shall be dashed in
pieces,
and their [m]pregnant women ripped
open.

6 [n][ch. 4:7] [o]Deut. 8:12, 14; [Deut. 32:15] 7 [p]ch. 5:14 [q]Jer. 5:6 8 [r]2 Sam. 17:8; Prov. 17:12 [s][ch. 2:12] 9 [t][Deut. 33:26] 10 [u][ch. 8:4; 10:3] [v]1 Sam. 8:5, 19 11 [w][1 Sam. 8:22] [x][1 Sam. 15:23] 12 [y]Job 14:17 13 [z]Isai. 13:8; 1 Thess. 5:3 [a][2 Kin. 19:3] 14 [b]Isai. 25:8; 26:19; Ezek. 37:12 [b]Isai. 25:8; 26:19; Ezek. 37:12 [c][1 Cor. 15:55] [d][Ezek. 14:21] [e][Ezek. 9:10] 15 [f][Gen. 41:52] [g][Ezek. 19:12; Jonah 4:8; Hab. 1:9] [h][Ezek. 17:10] [i][ch. 12:8] 16 [j][Hab. 1:11] [k]2 Kin. 18:12 [l][ch. 9:12; 10:14] [m][2 Kin. 8:12; 15:16; Amos 1:13]

1 Hebrew *according to their pasture* 2 Or *I will destroy* 3 Ch 14:1 in Hebrew

13:6 The verse describes a step-by-step process of descent in morals and worship (Deut. 32:10–18; Jer. 2).

forgot. This pitiful climax stands in sharp contrast to the former days of knowledge (vv. 4, 5 and notes; cf. Deut. 8:11–20).

13:7–9 This startling comparison of God to ferocious wild beasts that devour the flock echoes the covenant curses for disobedience (Lev. 26:21, 22; Deut. 32:24; Ezek. 14:21). These images depict the severity of divine judgment (5:14; Prov. 17:12; Jer. 5:6).

13:9 your helper. Israel's destruction is explained here in terms of the nation's rebellion against its Helper. There is no help like God (Ex. 18:4; Deut. 33:26–29; Ps. 10:14; 54:4; 115:9–11; 121:2–8; 146:5). To oppose Him is to invite destruction.

13:10 Give me a king. On Israel's request for a monarchy, see 1 Sam. 8. Asking for a king meant that they had rejected God as King (1 Sam. 13:9, 10). Their sense of security in having a king was a delusion.

13:11 gave . . . took. Though describing past action, the Hebrew verb tense suggests an ongoing process of giving and taking. The king is not specified. Perhaps this is a reference to the royal assassinations of Hosea's time (3:4; 7:7; 8:4; 10:3; cf. 2 Kin. 15:8–31; 17:1–6), to an early king such as Saul (who was alive when kingship was first requested), or even to all of the kings of the north (all twenty of whom "did what was evil in the sight of the LORD").

13:12 Lest they be diminished or forgotten, transgressions are figuratively tied up and then stored in a safe place for future retribution (7:2; 9:9; Deut. 32:34, 35; Job 14:17).

Ephraim. See note 4:17.

13:13 The predicament of Israel facing certain judgment is vividly compared to that of a mother and child during an unsuccessful birth (cf. 2 Kin. 19:3). This complex word picture compares Israel both to the mother (who faces sorrow and certain death) and to the child (who stubbornly refuses to be safely delivered).

an unwise son. Israel is depicted as a fetus that fails to position itself properly in the womb for delivery. This surprising figure relates to the theme of failure to acknowledge God (Introduction: Characteristics and Themes).

13:14 Compassion is hidden from my eyes. The Hebrew for "pity" can have the sense of "repentance" or "regret." God will not "repent" (i.e., change His mind) of His intention to vanquish death for His people.

13:15 Though he may flourish. This is Ephraim, whose name is from the same Hebrew root as "fruitful" (9:16 note).

east . . . wind of the LORD. See 12:1 and note. Here this destructive force is a symbol for Assyria as God's weapon of judgment against Israel (Introduction: Date and Occasion; Is. 10:5, 6).

13:16 Samaria. The capital city and driving force behind the northern kingdom's rebellion.

fall . . . dashed . . . ripped. Figurative language for destruction (vv. 3, 8, 15) here gives way to chilling expressions of hard reality.

A Plea to Return to the LORD

14 [n] Return, O Israel, to the LORD your God,
for [o] you have stumbled because of your iniquity.
2 Take with you words
and return to the LORD;
say to him,
"Take away all iniquity;
accept [p] what is good,
and we will pay with bulls
[q] the vows[1] of our lips.
3 [r] Assyria shall not save us;
[s] we will not ride on horses;
and [t] we will say no more, 'Our God,'
to the work of our hands.
[u] In you the orphan finds mercy."
4 I [v] will heal their apostasy;
[w] I will love them freely,
for my anger has turned from them.
5 [x] I will be like the dew to Israel;
[y] he shall blossom like the lily;
he shall take root like the trees [z] of Lebanon;
6 his shoots shall spread out;
his beauty shall be [a] like the olive,
and his fragrance like Lebanon.
7 They shall return and [b] dwell beneath my[2] shadow;
they shall flourish like the grain;
they shall blossom like the vine;
their fame shall be like the wine of Lebanon.

8 O [c] Ephraim, what have I to do with idols?
It is I who answer and look after you.[3]
I am like an evergreen cypress;
[d] from me comes your fruit.

9 [e] Whoever is wise, let him understand these things;
whoever is discerning, let him know them;
for the ways of the LORD are right,
and [f] the upright walk in them,
[f] but transgressors stumble in them.

Chapter 14
1 [n] ch. 6:1; 12:6; [ch. 3:5] [o] [ch. 13:9]
2 [p] [ch. 5:15] [q] Heb. 13:15; [Ps. 50:13, 14; 69:30, 31]
3 [r] ch. 5:13 [s] [Isai. 30:16; 31:1] [t] [ver. 8] [u] See Ps. 10:14
4 [v] Jer. 3:22; [ch. 6:1] [w] [ch. 11:1]
5 [x] [ch. 6:3] [y] Isai. 27:6 [z] [Ps. 92:12; Isai. 35:2]
6 [a] Ps. 52:8
7 [b] Ps. 91:1
8 [c] [ver. 3; Isai. 30:22] [d] [ch. 2:8, 23; John 15:4, 5]
9 [e] Ps. 107:43; Jer. 9:12; Dan. 12:10; John 8:47; 18:37 [f] [Prov. 10:29; Luke 2:34; 2 Cor. 2:16]

1 Septuagint, Syriac *pay the fruit* 2 Hebrew *his* 3 Hebrew *him*

14:1–3 The prophet speaks to the people, urging repentance before conveying God's promise of blessing (vv. 4–8).

14:1 Return. This thematic exhortation to return (2:7; 3:5; 6:1; 7:10; 12:6) is now addressed to those who have already fallen because of their sins.

14:2 Take with you words. Words of confession accompanied by obedience please God, not half-hearted sacrifices (5:6; 6:6; 8:11–13). A precise wording for confession is suggested in vv. 2, 3.

the vows of our lips. Or, "fruit of our lips" (text note). The Hebrew words for "bull calves" (here rendered "vows") and "fruit" are similar. See Prov. 12:14; 13:2; Heb. 13:15.

14:3 Assyria . . . horses. Israel was to give up trusting in foreign political powers (5:13; 7:11; 12:1), in her own military strength (10:13; cf. Ps. 33:16, 17), and in idolatrous and syncretistic religion (2:8, 13; 3:1; 4:12; 8:5, 6; 10:5, 6; 13:2).

orphan finds mercy. This alludes to the earlier theme of loss and restoration of love illustrated by Hosea's marriage and his daughter, Lo-ruhama (1:6; 2:2–4, 14–23). See Introduction: Characteristics and Themes.

14:4 I will heal. The promise of healing began to be realized when Israel returned from its sixth-century exile in Babylon. It finds much greater fulfillment in Jesus Christ and His church, and is consummated at His Second Coming.

apostasy. Israel's characteristic unfaithfulness (4:10–12; 5:4; 7:4; 11:7) will be healed by the great Healer, whose anger is now turned away.

love them freely. In this love song, we hear again the deep affection of God for His elect. This undeserved love is what the New Testament calls grace (Rom. 5:15; Eph. 2:5, 8).

14:5–7 In this section, resplendent with the language of love, colorful metaphors drawn from plant life—a blossoming lily (Song 2:1, 16), a deeply rooted, sprouting and fragrant cedar of Lebanon (Ps. 92:12; 104:16), a splendid olive tree (Ps. 52:8; Jer. 11:16), a shade tree (Song 2:3; Ezek. 17:22, 23), flourishing grain (2:8, 22), a flowering vine (10:1; Is. 5:1–7) and the fruit of the vine—depict a vigorous, renowned, stable, and prosperous Israel flourishing under God, who is likened to the life-giving dew (Deut. 33:13).

14:8 evergreen cypress. Like a tree renowned as a symbol of life (cf. Gen. 3:22; Rev. 22:2), God will give fruit to fruitless Ephraim (9:16 note).

14:9 Whoever is wise. This epilogue challenges every generation to consider carefully the ways of the Lord that are presented in the book (cf. Ps. 1; 18:21; Prov. 10:29). The choices that Israel faced are also set before the reader: wisdom or folly; discipleship or rebellion; life or death. The wise will "choose life" (Deut. 30:19, 20).

THE BOOK OF

Joel

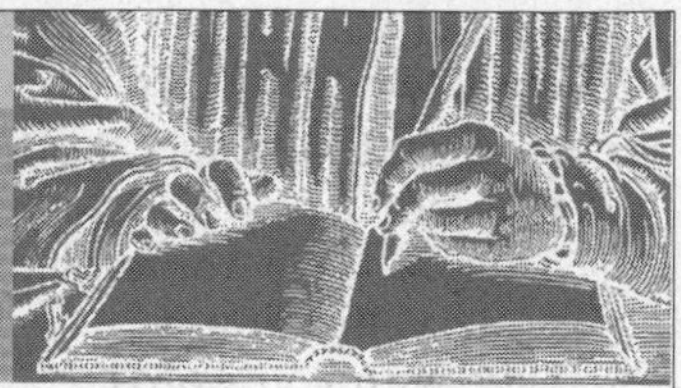

AUTHOR

The prophet Joel is identified only as "Joel, the son of Pethuel" (1:1). Joel's keen interest in Jerusalem, particularly in the temple and its functionaries (e.g., 1:9, 13, 14; 2:14–17, 32; 3:1, 6, 16, 17), suggests that he lived in Jerusalem and ministered as a temple prophet. Although he does not appear to have been a priest (1:9, 13; 2:17), Joel prayed on the people's behalf (1:19, 20).

DATE AND OCCASION

Since the Book of Joel contains no clear indications of when it was written, it is difficult to date the work. The book's vocabulary, linguistic parallels to other prophetic books, historical allusions, location in the canon, and other clues have been used in an effort to date the work. Some scholars date the book in the ninth century B.C., and others to the period just prior to the Jewish exile in Babylon during the sixth century B.C. But most scholars now prefer a date following this exile, some suggesting the early postexilic period (c. 520–500 B.C.), and others proposing a later date in the fifth or even the fourth century B.C. A date after the exile seems most convincing, although there is good reason to conclude with Calvin that the date of the book simply cannot be known with certainty.

CHARACTERISTICS AND THEMES

The unity of Joel was challenged by biblical critics of the late nineteenth and early twentieth centuries. These critics thought that the section describing events of the author's time (1:1–2:17) and the section dealing with future occurrences (2:18–3:21) were written by different authors. Today, however, most scholars accept the book's essential unity. Such features as the repeated theme of the "day of the LORD" (1:15; 2:1, 2, 11, 31; 3:14) and other identical or closely similar phrases shared by both sections (2:2 and 2:31; 2:10–11 and 3:16; 2:10 and 3:15; 2:11 and 31; 2:17 and 3:2; 2:27 and 3:17) point to the book's unity.

Interpreters throughout the ages have been faced with the question of whether to interpret the locusts in the Book of Joel literally or figuratively. Historically, the majority of interpreters have understood the locusts as symbols of future enemies (e.g., one manuscript of the Septuagint [Greek Old Testament] understood the four kinds of locusts to symbolize the Egyptians, Assyrians, Greeks, and Romans). But present-day interpreters see these creatures, at least in ch. 1, as actual locusts. Joel indeed moves quickly from an accurate description of a real devastation by locusts in ch. 1 to a description of the dreadful locust-like army of the Lord that blends the literal and figurative in ch. 2. It seems then that the destruction by locusts that Joel had seen became the vehicle for his prophecy proclaiming the need to repent in view of the coming day of the Lord.

The central message of the Book of Joel concerns the coming day of the Lord. Joel introduces that day in the context of the then-present destruction of the land's vegetation, a destruction that was a sign of judgment against the covenant community. Only their return to God would avert the imminent day of the Lord that would come "as destruction from the Almighty" (1:15). In this first instance then, Joel, like Amos (Amos 5:18–20; cf. Zeph. 1:7–13), declares that the day of the Lord is a day of judgment against God's own people. Similarly, in ch. 2 the day of the Lord is described as a "great and very awesome" day (2:11), "a day of darkness and gloom, a day of clouds and thick darkness" (2:2) in which the Lord leads His army against Israel. However, in the second part of the book, Joel introduces a second prophetic tradition about the day of the Lord, namely, that the day of the Lord is a day of judgment against the enemies of His people, whom He will protect and bless (Ezek. 25–32; Jer. 46–51; Is. 13). On the day of the Lord, the nations will be accountable for their crimes against the Lord's people and will be judged accordingly (3:2–16, 19). But the people of the Lord's inheritance will enjoy His protection and be spiritually and physically blessed (2:28–32; 3:16–18, 20, 21).

Repentance is a key theme in Joel's prophetic message. The call to repentance is given not merely to a select number of the covenant community, but rather to all the Lord's people who are called to return to Him: young and old, men and women, leaders and followers, and even those who might otherwise be exempted from community responsibilities (nursing mothers and newlyweds, 1:13, 14; 2:15–17). The return to God that Joel calls for involves the whole person. Such repentance is to be manifested externally through such actions as mourning, weeping, crying out to the Lord, and fasting (1:13, 14; 2:15–17). But merely external or ritual manifestations of repentance are not adequate, and the Lord calls the people to show the sincerity of their repentance by returning to the Lord their God "with all your heart" (2:12, 13). Joel also reminds God's people that motivation for repentance lies firmly in the nature of God: "he is gracious and merciful, slow to anger, and abounding in steadfast love" (2:13). Joel stresses that the hope of restoration lies ultimately in God, who exercises His sovereign freedom and grace in granting repentance and forgiveness to the people.

The Book of Joel has had an important place in the life of the church. The New Testament indicates that Jesus and His followers were familiar with the writings of Joel. The book's influence is most evident in the New Testament passages that speak of the end times. They use Joel's vivid images to describe the day of the Lord and the plague of locusts (e.g., Mark 13:24; Luke 21:25; Rev. 6:9; 9:2). Also important are the promises in Joel 2:28–32, which Peter quotes at Pentecost, claiming they have reached their fulfillment in the event of Pentecost (Acts 2:16–21). Paul in Rom. 10:13 also refers to the prophecy; he uses Joel 2:32 to show that "there is no distinction between Jew and Greek." Salvation is offered to all peoples. As Joel had said: "everyone who calls on the name of the LORD shall be saved" (2:32).

The church has continued to find the teaching in the Book of Joel on the day of the Lord to be an important source of hope and comfort on the one hand, and a word of warning on the other. In times of distress and trouble, Christians have found the promises about the ultimate blessing, protection, and vindication of the Lord's covenant community to be consoling and inspiring. At the same time, Joel's graphic depiction of the dreadful aspects of the day of the Lord has served as a reminder of God's holiness and judgment and as a continuing call to wholehearted repentance and holiness of life.

OUTLINE OF JOEL

I. Superscription (1:1)

II. Crises Demanding Repentance (1:2–2:17)

- A. *Recent Devastation by Locust and Drought (1:2–20)*
- B. *Future Assault by the Lord's Army (2:1–17)*

III. Responses of the Covenant God (2:18–3:21)

- A. *Physical Renewal of the Land (2:18–27)*
- B. *Spiritual Renewal of the Lord's People (2:28–32)*
- C. *Final Judgment (ch. 3)*
  1. Judgment of the Nations (3:1–15)
  2. Blessing on God's People (3:16–21)

1 The word of the LORD that came to Joel, the son of Pethuel:

An Invasion of Locusts

2 [a] Hear this, [b]you elders;
give ear, [b]all inhabitants of the land!
[c] Has such a thing happened in your days,
or in the days of your fathers?
3 [d] Tell your children of it,
and let your children tell their children,

Chapter 1
2 [a][Hos. 5:1] [b]ver. 14
[c][ch. 2:2]
3 [d][Ps. 78:4]

1:1 The word of the LORD. This short and simple title announces that what follows is the Lord's word, and compares most closely with Jon. 1:1. Compare with the more extended titles in Jer. 1:2; Ezek. 1:3; Hos. 1:1; Mic. 1:1; Zeph. 1:1; Hag. 1:1; Zech. 1:1; Mal. 1:1.

Joel. His name means "the LORD is God."

Pethuel. The only occurrence of this name in the Bible.

1:2–2:17 Two crises confront Judah with the consequences of their sins: (a) the recent devastation of the land by locusts (1:4–8) and drought (1:10–12, 16–20); and (b) the imminent assault on the land by the army of the Lord (2:1–17). If the people would be delivered from these calamities, they must repent of their sins and return to the Lord.

1:2–20 Joel appeals to elders (v. 2), drunkards (v. 5), farmers (v. 11), and priests (v. 13) to ponder the meaning of the recent locust plague and drought, and to repent.

1:2 Hear . . . give ear. This series of commands calls the people to recognize the personal and spiritual significance of the locust invasion. The repetition of thought in the first and second lines and in the third and fourth lines illustrates the parallelism typical of Hebrew poetry.

elders. This term designates the community and religious leaders. The same term used in 2:28 seems to refer to age, hence the translation "old men."

all inhabitants of the land. The entire population of Judah and Jerusalem is called to listen.

1:3 Tell . . . children . . . another generation. God's judgments, as well as His mercies, are to be passed on to future generations (cf. Deut. 4:9; 6:7; 32:7; Ps. 78:1–8).

The Prophets of Israel and Judah. During the early monarchy Elijah and Elisha had homes in the northern kingdom. Samuel's hometown of Ramah was the base of his yearly circuit as prophet and judge.

Among the writing prophets, only Hosea and Jonah were from the North. Hosea's home location is unknown. Jonah was from Gath-hepher, but his ministry extended beyond his home to the foreign city Nineveh.

Some prophets had homes in the South but prophesied to the North. Amos from Tekoa preached against the northern kingdom's worship at Bethel. Micah's message addressed Israel as well as Judah.

The messages of Isaiah, Jeremiah, Zephaniah, Ezekiel, Haggai, Zechariah, and Malachi span a long time period, but all concern either Jerusalem's destruction, fall, or later rebuilding.

Geographical information is lacking for Joel, Obadiah, and Habakkuk. All that is known about Nahum is the location of his home in Elkosh.

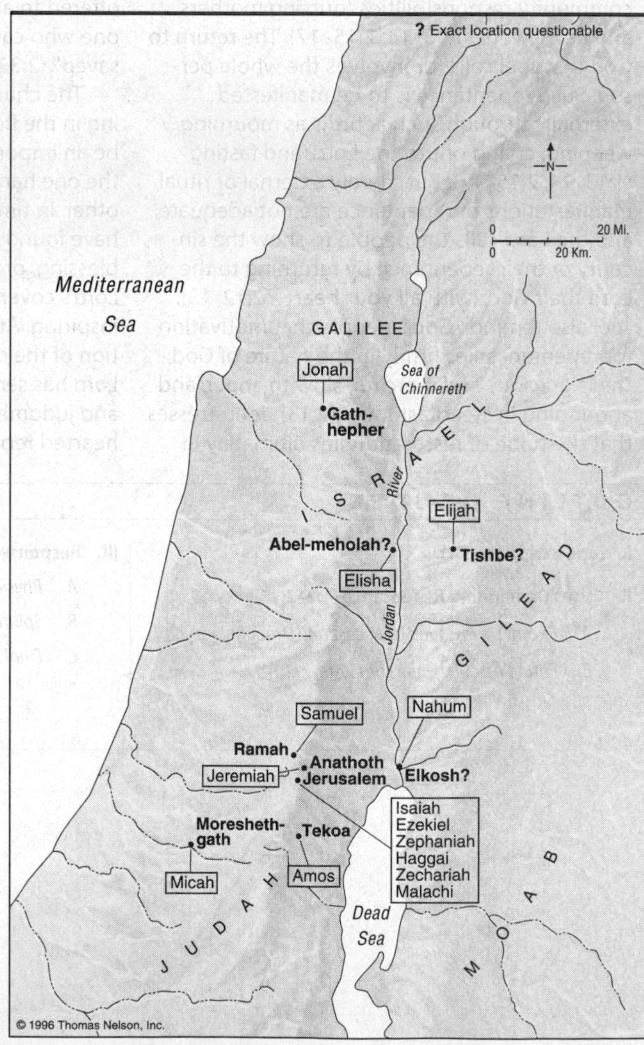

and their children to another
generation.

4 What [e] the cutting locust left,
[f] the swarming locust has eaten.
What the swarming locust left,
[g] the hopping locust has eaten,
and what the hopping locust left,
[h] the destroying locust has eaten.

5 Awake, you drunkards, and weep,
and [i] wail, all you drinkers of
wine,
because of [j] the sweet wine,
for it is cut off from your mouth.
6 For [k] a nation has come up against
my land,
[k] powerful and beyond number;
[l] its teeth are lions' teeth,
and it has the fangs of a lioness.
7 It has laid waste my vine
and splintered my [m] fig tree;
it has stripped off their bark and
thrown it down;
their branches are made white.

8 Lament like a virgin[1] [n] wearing
sackcloth
for the bridegroom of her youth.
9 [o] The grain offering and the drink
offering are cut off
from the house of the LORD.
[p] The priests mourn,
[p] the ministers of the LORD.
10 The fields are destroyed,
[q] the ground mourns,
because [r] the grain is destroyed,
[r] the wine dries up,
the oil languishes.

11 [s] Be ashamed,[2] O tillers of the soil;
wail, O vinedressers,
for the wheat and the barley,
[t] because the harvest of the field has
perished.
12 The vine dries up;
[u] the fig tree languishes.
Pomegranate, palm, and apple,
all the trees of the field are dried up,
and [v] gladness dries up
from the children of man.

A Call to Repentance

13 [w] Put on sackcloth and lament,
[p] O priests;
[x] wail, O ministers of the altar.
Go in, [w] pass the night in sackcloth,
[p] O ministers of my God!
[y] Because grain offering and drink
offering
are withheld from the house of
your God.

14 [z] Consecrate a fast;
[z] call a solemn assembly.
Gather [a] the elders
and [a] all the inhabitants of the land
to the house of the LORD your God,
and cry out to the LORD.

4 [e] ch. 2:25; Amos 4:9 [f] [Amos 7:1]; See Ex. 10:4 [g] ch. 2:25; Ps. 105:34; Nah. 3:15 [h] ch. 2:25; Ps. 78:46
5 [i] [Isai. 24:11] [j] ch. 3:18; Isai. 49:26; Amos 9:13
6 [k] ch. 2:2 [l] [Rev. 9:7, 8]
7 [m] [ver. 12]
8 [n] [ver. 13]; See 2 Sam. 3:31
9 [o] ver. 13; ch. 2:14 [p] ch. 2:17; [Isai. 61:6; Ezek. 45:4]
10 [q] See Hos. 4:3 [r] [Hos. 2:9]
11 [s] [Jer. 14:4] [t] ver. 17
12 [u] [ver. 7] [v] Isai. 24:11; Jer. 48:33
13 [w] [ver. 8; Jer. 4:8] [p] [See ver. 9 above] [x] [ver. 8; Mic. 1:8] [y] ver. 9; ch. 2:14
14 [z] ch. 2:15, 16; See 2 Chr. 20:3 [a] ver. 2

1 Or *young woman* 2 The Hebrew words for *dry up* and *be ashamed* in verses 10-12, 17 sound alike

1:4 locust. The poetic repetitions in every line emphasize the thoroughness of the locusts' destruction. The variety in the names of the locusts may refer to their different stages of development, although color differences or differences in type and regional origin may be reflected here and in 2:25. When locusts were understood as an instrument of divine punishment, repentance was the appropriate response (Deut. 28:38; Amos 7:1; Is. 33:4).

1:5 Awake . . . weep. The first call to respond is given to the drunkards. These represent the attitude of many who are oblivious to things that have spiritual significance. Only the alert are able to respond rightly to God's judgment.

1:6 my land. Personal pronouns are used throughout the book and point to the covenant relationship that binds the Lord, not only to the land and its vines and fig trees, but also to His people (1:7; 2:13, 14, 17, 18, 23, 26, 27; 3:2, 3, 17).

powerful . . . lioness. The locusts are compared to an invading nation that has the consuming passion of a lion (cf. 2:4–9; Rev. 9:7–9). Locusts and armies were often compared in ancient times. Mythical literature from the ancient city of Ugarit likens a large army to locusts (cf. Judg. 6:5; Prov. 30:27; Jer. 51:14, 27; Nah. 3:15–17).

1:7 vine . . . fig tree. The locusts' teeth effectively stripped the most valuable trees of the Lord's land.

1:8 Lament. The mourning is to be like that of a young woman who has lost her beloved before marriage.

sackcloth. This coarsely woven material was often made of goat's hair and worn during times of mourning. See v. 13; Gen. 37:34; 2 Sam. 3:31; 1 Kin. 21:27; Is. 32:11, 12.

1:9 grain offering . . . drink offering. These offerings, which were to be offered twice daily (Ex. 29:38–42; Lev. 2:1, 2; 23:13), were lacking because the crops were destroyed.

1:10 grain . . . wine . . . oil. The ingredients needed for the daily offerings traditionally appear in this order (2:19; Hos. 2:8).

dries up. Drought accompanied the locust invasion.

1:12 vine . . . fig . . . Pomegranate, palm . . . apple. Five kinds of trees are noted, leading up to the climactic statement that all the trees of the field are dried up.

gladness dries up. In an agricultural economy, human joy withers along with the vegetation.

1:13 sackcloth . . . lament. The priests are given precise instructions about how to respond personally to God's judgment.

1:14 Consecrate a fast. The priests are also to provide leadership in the community by proclaiming a public fast so that the entire nation could stop all regular activities for a time (probably for a day, Judg. 20:26; 1 Sam. 14:24; Jer. 36:6–9) to acknowledge God's judgment and to repent.

15 Alas for the day!
[b] For the day of the LORD is near,
and as destruction from the
Almighty[1] it comes.
16 Is not the food cut off
before our eyes,
[c] joy and gladness
from the house of our God?
17 [d] The seed shrivels under the clods;[2]
the storehouses are desolate;
the granaries are torn down
because [e] the grain has dried up.
18 How [f] the beasts groan!
The herds of cattle are perplexed
because there is no pasture for them;
even the flocks of sheep suffer.[3]

19 To you, [g] O LORD, I call.
[h] For fire has devoured
the pastures of the wilderness,
[h] and flame has burned
all the trees of the field.
20 Even the beasts of the field [i] pant for
you
because the water brooks are
dried up,
[h] and fire has devoured
the pastures of the wilderness.

The Day of the LORD

2 [j] Blow a trumpet in [k] Zion;
sound an alarm on [k] my holy mountain!
Let all the inhabitants of the land
tremble,
for [l] the day of the LORD is coming;
it is near,
2 [m] a day of darkness and gloom,
[m] a day of clouds and thick darkness!
Like blackness there is spread upon
the mountains
[n] a great and powerful people;
[o] their like has never been before,
nor will be again after them
through the years of all
generations.

3 [p] Fire devours before them,
and behind them a flame burns.
The land is like [q] the garden of Eden
before them,
but [r] behind them a desolate
wilderness,
and nothing escapes them.

4 [s] Their appearance is like the
appearance of horses,
and like war horses they run.
5 [t] As with the rumbling of chariots,
they leap on the tops of the
mountains,
like the crackling of [u] a flame of fire
devouring the stubble,
[n] like a powerful army
drawn up for battle.

6 Before them peoples are in anguish;
[v] all faces grow pale.
7 Like warriors they charge;
like soldiers they scale the wall.
They march each on his way;
they do not swerve from their paths.

15 [b] ch. 2:1, 11, 31; 3:14; Isai. 13:6, 9; Jer. 46:10; Ezek. 30:2, 3; Amos 5:18; Obad. 15; Zeph. 1:14, 15; Zech. 14:1; 2 Pet. 3:10
16 [c] [Deut. 12:6, 7; 16:14, 15]
17 [d] [Mal. 2:3] [e] ver. 11
18 [f] ch. 2:22; [Jer. 12:4; Hos. 4:3]
19 [g] Ps. 50:15 [h] Jer. 9:10
20 [i] [Job 38:41; Ps. 104:21; 145:15] [h] [See ver. 19 above]
Chapter 2
1 [j] ver. 15; Isai. 58:1; Hos. 5:8; Amos 3:6 [k] See ch. 3:17 [l] See ch. 1:15
2 [m] Amos 5:18, 20; Zeph. 1:15 [n] ch. 1:6; [ver. 11, 25] [o] [ch. 1:2]
3 [p] ch. 1:19, 20 [q] Gen. 2:8, 9; See Isai. 51:3 [r] Zech. 7:14
4 [s] Rev. 9:7
5 [t] Rev. 9:9; [Nah. 3:2] [u] Isai. 5:24; 47:14; Obad. 18; Nah. 1:10 [n] [See ver. 2 above]
6 [v] Nah. 2:10

1 *Destruction* sounds like the Hebrew for *Almighty* 2 The meaning of the Hebrew line is uncertain 3 Or *are made desolate*

1:15 the day of the LORD. A thematic phrase in Joel (1:15; 2:1, 11, 31; 3:14) and in other Old Testament prophetic books (Is. 13:6, 9; Ezek. 13:5; Amos 5:18, 20; Obad. 15; Zeph. 1:7, 14; Mal. 4:5). Here (and in 2:1, 11) it refers to a day of the Lord's wrath against Israel, though later in the book it refers to the Lord's wrath against the nations and blessing of the Lord's people (2:31; 3:14). The magnitude of the devastation points to an even more ominous day of judgment.

destruction from the Almighty. This phrase could be translated "might from the Almighty," capturing the sense of the Hebrew wordplay *shod* ("destruction") from *shaddai* ("the Almighty"; Is. 13:6).

1:16–18 Joel reinforces his point about the nearness of the day of the Lord by reminding his audience again of God's judgment, the signs of which could be seen in the drought conditions all around them.

1:19 To you, O LORD, I call. The prophet himself begins the lamentation. The devastation is from the Lord, and He is the source of restoration.

1:20 beasts of the field. Even the animals join Joel in his cry (Job 38:41; Ps. 104:21; 147:9).

fire has devoured. Divine judgment is often depicted as fire (Deut. 32:22; Ps. 50:3; 97:3). The metaphor describes the effects of drought (cf. 2:3, where the "fire" of locust devastation is depicted).

2:1–17 Joel urges "all the inhabitants of the land" (v. 1) to prepare for an imminent assault by the army of the Lord. A contrite heart among the people may bring God's compassion and blessing (v. 14).

2:1 a trumpet. The ram's horn (Hebrew *shophar*) was used in warfare and to signal danger. All trembled at the trumpet blast signaling the coming of the day of the Lord (Amos 3:6; Zeph. 1:14–16).

Zion . . . my holy mountain. Jerusalem.

2:2 day of darkness and gloom. This vivid word picture of the coming day of the Lord (cf. Zeph. 1:15; Amos 5:18, 20) corresponds to descriptions of the Lord's appearances in the past (Deut. 4:11; 5:22, 23; Ps. 97:2).

great and powerful people. Complex metaphors of an army and locust invasion combine to depict the judgment and devastation to occur (1:6 note).

2:3 desolate wilderness. The invaders raze the land. The bold contrast between "the garden of Eden" and this wilderness (Gen. 13:10; Is. 51:3; Ezek. 28:13–19; 31:8, 9, 16–18; 36:35) highlights the horror of the inescapable invasion.

2:5 Again the army of judgment is figuratively depicted as a locust invasion (1:6 note; cf. Rev. 9:1–11).

2:7–9 The army is disciplined, ruthless, and successful. The "city" (v. 9) is finally overrun (cf. the Egyptian plague of locusts in Ex. 10:6).

8 They do not jostle one another;
[w] each marches in his path;
they burst through the weapons
and are not halted.
9 [x] They leap upon the city,
they run upon the walls,
[y] they climb up into the houses,
[y] they enter through the windows
[z] like a thief.

10 [a] The earth quakes before them;
the heavens tremble.
[b] The sun and the moon are
darkened,
and the stars withdraw their
shining.
11 [c] The LORD utters his voice
before [d] his army,
for his camp is exceedingly great;
[e] he who executes his word is
powerful.
[f] For the day of the LORD is [g] great and
very awesome;
[h] who can endure it?

Return to the LORD

12 "Yet even now," declares the LORD,
[i] "return to me with all your heart,
[j] with fasting, with weeping, and with
mourning;
13 and [k] rend your hearts and not
[l] your garments."
Return to the LORD, your God,
[m] for he is gracious and merciful,
slow to anger, and abounding in
steadfast love;
[n] and he relents over disaster.
14 [o] Who knows whether he will not turn
and relent,
and [p] leave a blessing behind him,
[q] a grain offering and a drink offering
for the LORD your God?

15 [r] Blow the trumpet in Zion;
[s] consecrate a fast;
call a solemn assembly;
16 gather the people.
[t] Consecrate the congregation;
assemble the elders;
[u] gather the children,
even nursing infants.
[v] Let the bridegroom leave his room,
and the bride her chamber.

17 [w] Between the [x] vestibule and the [y] altar
[z] let the priests, the ministers of the
LORD, weep
and say, "Spare your people, O LORD,
and make not your heritage a
reproach,
a byword among the nations.[1]
[a] Why should they say among the
peoples,
'Where is their God?'"

The LORD Had Pity

18 [b] Then the LORD became jealous for his
land
[c] and had pity on his people.
19 The LORD answered and said to his
people,
"Behold, [d] I am sending to you
grain, wine, and oil,
[d] and you will be satisfied;

8 [w] Prov. 30:27 **9** [x] Isai. 33:4 [y] [Jer. 9:21] [z] [John 10:1] **10** [a] ch. 3:16; [Ps. 18:7; Amos 8:8] [b] ch. 3:15; Isai. 13:10; Ezek. 32:7; Matt. 24:29; [Rev. 9:2] **11** [c] ch. 3:16; [1 Thess. 4:16] [d] ver. 25 [e] Rev. 18:8 [f] See ch. 1:15 [g] ver. 31 [h] Mal. 3:2; [Num. 24:23] **12** [i] Deut. 4:30; 1 Sam. 7:3; Jer. 4:1; Hos. 12:6 [j] [1 Sam. 7:6] **13** [k] [Ps. 34:18] [l] See Gen. 37:29 [m] Ex. 34:6; Ps. 86:5, 15; Jonah 4:2 [n] [Num. 23:19; Ezek. 24:14]

14 [o] Jonah 3:9 [p] Hag. 2:19; Mal. 3:10 [q] ch. 1:9, 13 **15** [r] See ver. 1 [s] See ch. 1:14 **16** [t] See Josh. 3:5 [u] [2 Chr. 20:13] [v] [Deut. 24:5; Eccles. 3:5; Zech. 12:12-14; 1 Cor. 7:5] **17** [w] See ch. 1:9 [x] Ezek. 8:16 [y] 1 Kin. 6:3; 2 Chr. 3:4 [z] 2 Chr. 4:1 [a] Ps. 42:3; 79:10; 115:2 **18** [b] Zech. 1:14; 8:2 [c] [Ps. 103:13] **19** [d] [ch. 1:10; Ps. 4:7]; See Mal. 3:10-12

1 Or *reproach, that the nations should rule over them*

2:10 earth . . . stars. Such divine judgments are accompanied by a shaking and breakdown of the natural order. All creation is disturbed (v. 31; Jer. 4:23–26; Ezek. 32:7, 8; Nah. 1:5; Hab. 3:6, 10).

2:11 his army. The relentless army is the Lord's. He commands and His forces obey. The day of the Lord is great (2:31; Zeph. 1:14), dreadful (Mal. 4:5), and unbearable (Nah. 1:6; Mal. 3:2).

2:12 return to me. The Lord invites His people to escape by returning to Him with the whole heart.

fasting . . . weeping . . . mourning. The visible signs of repentance (Ezra 10:1–6; Esth. 4:3; Jon. 3:5–9).

2:13 not your garments. See "Legalism" at Matt. 23:4.

gracious . . . steadfast love. The call to return to the Lord is based on the Lord's dramatic self-revelation of His character to Moses in Ex. 34:6, 7, a description frequently repeated throughout the Old Testament (e.g., Num. 14:18; Ps. 86:15; 103:8; 145:8; Neh. 9:17; Jon. 4:2).

2:14 Who knows whether he will not turn and relent. God's sovereignty and freedom in forgiveness are seen in vv. 13, 14 (cf. Ex. 33:19; 2 Sam. 12:22; Lam. 3:29; Jon. 3:9; Zeph. 2:3). See note Gen. 6:6.

2:15, 16 Further instructions for returning to the Lord include a fast and an assembly (v. 15), a gathering and consecration of all the people, including the elders, children, nursing infants, and even those about to marry (v. 16). The staccato quality of the Hebrew poetry in these verses emphasizes the urgency of the situation.

2:17 Specific instructions are also given to the priests who are to weep and offer prayers of intercession.

Between the vestibule and the altar. This site in the temple was the usual place for priestly intercession (1 Kin. 8:22; Ezek. 8:16).

your heritage. The priestly lament appeals to the Lord's sense of ownership and pride in His covenant people (Deut. 9:26, 29; Ps. 44:11–14; 74:2; 79:10; 115:2; Mic. 7:10).

2:18–3:21 The Lord, the God of the covenant, promises to renew the land and His people, as they respond in repentance to the crises of 1:2–2:17. The redemptive renewal of God's people will someday lead to the final devastation of Zion's enemies and the final exaltation of Zion itself.

2:18–27 Repentance will bring renewed fruitfulness to the land.

2:18 Then. A change in subject, mood, and tense takes place at this point as the Lord promises restoration.

2:19 The prayers of God's people will be answered.

and I will no more make you
a reproach among the nations.

20 "I will remove the northerner far from you,
and drive him into a parched and desolate land,
his vanguard[1] into [e]the eastern sea,
and his rear guard[2] into [f]the western sea;
[g]the stench and foul smell of him will rise,
for he has done great things.

21 "Fear not, O land;
be glad and rejoice,
for [h]the LORD has done great things!
22 Fear not, [i]you beasts of the field,
for [j]the pastures of the wilderness are green;
[k]the tree bears its fruit;
the fig tree and [k]vine give their full yield.

23 [l]"Be glad, O children of Zion,
and [l]rejoice in the LORD your God,
for he has given [m]the early rain for your vindication;
he has poured down for you abundant rain,
[m]the early and [n]the latter rain, as before.

24 "The threshing floors shall be full of grain;
the vats shall overflow with wine and oil.

20[e]Ezek. 47:18; Zech. 14:8 [f]Zech. 14:8 [g]Isai. 34:3; [Amos 4:10]
21[h]Ps. 126:2, 3
22[i]See ch. 1:18 [j][ch. 1:19] [k][Zech. 8:12]
23[l]Ps. 100:1, 2; Hab. 3:18; Zech. 10:7 [m]Deut. 11:14; Jer. 5:24 [n]Hos. 6:3
25[o]ch. 1:4 [p]ver. 11
26[q]Lev. 25:19
27[r][Isai. 49:23] [s]ch. 3:17 [t]Hos. 11:9; See Ezek. 37:26 [u]See Ex. 20:2 [v][Isai. 44:8]
28[w]ver. 28-32, cited Acts 2:17-21 [x]Isai. 32:15; Ezek. 39:29; Zech. 12:10; John 7:39 [y][Acts 2:39] [z][Acts 21:9]
29[a][1 Cor. 12:13]

25 I will restore to you the years
that [o]the swarming locust has eaten,
[o]the hopper, [o]the destroyer, and [o]the cutter,
[p]my great army, which I sent among you.

26 [q]"You shall eat in plenty and be satisfied,
and praise the name of the LORD your God,
who has dealt wondrously with you.
And my people [q]shall never again be put to shame.
27 [r]You shall know that I am [s]in the midst of Israel,
and that [t]I am the LORD your God
[u]and there is none else.
And my people [v]shall never again be put to shame.

The LORD Will Pour Out His Spirit

28[3] [w]"And it shall come to pass afterward,
that [x]I will pour out my Spirit on all flesh;
[y]your sons and [z]your daughters shall prophesy,
your old men shall dream dreams,
and your young men shall see visions.
29 [a]Even on the male and female servants
in those days I will pour out my Spirit.

1 Hebrew *face* 2 Hebrew *his end* 3 Ch 3:1 in Hebrew

2:20 the northerner. Some interpreters have understood this to be a reference to the locusts of ch.1. More likely it refers to a large and mighty army that becomes the Lord's instrument of judgment. Unlike most locust invasions (which came from the east or south), foreign military invasions often came from the north. Cf. the references to the enemy from the north in Jer. 1:14, 15; 4:6; 6:1, 22; Ezek. 38:6, 15; 39:2.

2:21–24 Even the land and the wild animals are urged not to be afraid, and they are exhorted to be glad and rejoice with the people of Zion in the agricultural abundance from the Lord.

2:25 See note 1:4.

2:26 Abundance should lead to praise (cf. Deut. 8:10; Hos. 13:5, 6).

2:27 Restoration leads to a new realization that the Lord is in Israel, that He is the covenant God and there is no other.

2:28–32 Joel prophesies concerning the unprecedented outpouring of God's Spirit that will occur before the coming of the day of the Lord.

2:28, 29 Moses had earlier prayed that Israel as a whole would be a nation of prophets (Num. 11:29), and Joel also predicted this as part of Israel's glorious future. Peter proclaimed that the vision began to find fulfillment at Pentecost with the coming of the Holy Spirit (Acts 2:16–21), who empowers believers to bear witness to Jesus Christ (Acts 1:8). By introducing this prophecy with "the last days" (Acts 2:17), Peter links it with other prophecies regarding Israel's messianic future and so teaches that Pentecost inaugurates the promised new age (cf. 1 Pet. 1:10–12).

2:28 afterward. Joel gives notice of more distant promises.

pour out. Though the word here refers primarily to the pouring out of liquids (Gen. 9:6; Ex. 4:9), it is also used of the Holy Spirit (Ezek. 39:29; Zech. 12:10) who is given to all who believe without distinction as to sex, age, or social position (1 Cor. 12:13).

prophesy . . . dream dreams . . . see visions. See Num. 12:6; Jer. 31:31–34; Ezek. 36:26–29.

2:30, 31 The universal scope of events heralding "the great and awesome day of the LORD" is emphasized. See also Is. 13:10; Ezek. 32:7, 8; Amos 8:9; Zeph. 1:14–17.

2:32 calls on the name of the LORD. A reference to the worship of the Lord (Gen. 12:8; Ps. 105:1). Salvation is only found in returning to the true and exclusive worship of God.

survivors. These are those called by the Lord who have responded in faith.

30 "And I will show [b]wonders in the heavens and [b]on the earth, blood and fire and
columns of smoke. 31 [c]The sun shall be
turned to darkness, [d]and the moon to
blood, [e]before the great and awesome day
of the LORD comes. 32 And it shall come to
pass that [f]everyone who calls on the name
of the LORD shall be saved. [g]For in Mount
Zion and in Jerusalem there shall be those
who escape, as the LORD has said, and
among [h]the survivors shall be those whom
the LORD calls.

The LORD Judges the Nations

3 [1] "For behold, [i]in those days and at that
time, when I restore the fortunes of
Judah and Jerusalem, 2 [j]I will gather all the
nations and bring them down to the Valley
of Jehoshaphat. And [k]I will enter into judgment with them there, on behalf of my
people and my heritage Israel, because they
have scattered them among the nations
and have divided up my land, 3 and [l]have
cast lots for my people, and have traded a
boy for a prostitute, and have sold a girl for
wine and have drunk it.
4 "What are you to me, [m]O Tyre and
Sidon, and all [n]the regions of Philistia? Are
you paying me back for something? If you
are paying me back, [o]I will return your payment on your own head swiftly and speedily. 5 For [p]you have taken my silver and my
gold, and have carried my rich treasures
into your temples.[2] 6 You have sold [q]the
people of Judah and Jerusalem to the
Greeks in order to remove them far from
their own border. 7 Behold, I will stir them
up from the place to which you have sold
them, and [o]I will return your payment on
your own head. 8 I will sell your sons and
your daughters into the hand of the people
of Judah, and they will sell them to the
[r]Sabeans, to a nation far away, for the LORD
has spoken."

9 Proclaim this among the nations:
[s]Consecrate for war;[3]
stir up the mighty men.
Let all the men of war draw near;
let them come up.
10 [t]Beat your plowshares into swords,
and [t]your pruning hooks into
spears;
let the weak say, "I am a
warrior."
11 [u]Hasten and come,
all you surrounding nations,
and gather yourselves there.
[v]Bring down your warriors, O LORD.
12 Let the nations stir themselves up
and come up to [w]the Valley of
Jehoshaphat;
[x]for there I will sit to judge
all the surrounding nations.
13 [y]Put in the sickle,
[z]for the harvest is ripe.
[a]Go in, tread,
[a]for the winepress is full.
The vats overflow,
for their evil is great.

30 [b][Matt. 24:30; Luke 21:11]
31 [c]See ver. 10 [d]Rev. 6:12 [e]Mal. 4:5
32 [f]Cited Rom. 10:13 [g]Isai. 46:13; 59:20; Obad. 17 [h]Jer. 31:7; Mic. 4:7; Zech. 8:12
Chapter 3
1 [i]Jer. 30:3
2 [j][Zeph. 3:8]; See Zech. 14:2-4 [k]Isai. 66:16; Jer. 25:31
3 [l]Obad. 11; Nah. 3:10
4 [m]Isai. 23:1, 2; Jer. 47:4; Amos 1:9 [n][Ezek. 25:15, 16] [o][Obad. 15]
5 [p][2 Chr. 21:16, 17]
6 [q][ver. 3]
7 [o][See ver. 4 above]
8 [r]See 1 Kin. 10:1
9 [s][Mic. 3:5]
10 [t][Isai. 2:4]
11 [u][Isai. 54:15] [v][Zech. 14:5]
12 [w]ver. 2 [x]Ps. 96:13; 98:9; 110:6; Isai. 2:4; 3:13; Mic. 4:3
13 [y]Rev. 14:15 [z][Jer. 51:33; Hos. 6:11; Matt. 13:30, 39; Mark 4:29; John 4:35; Rev. 14:15, 18 [a]Rev. 14:20; [Isai. 63:2, 3]

1 Ch 4:1 in Hebrew 2 Or *palaces* 3 Or *Consecrate a war*

3:1–21 Joel prophesies the coming of that day of the Lord in which God will with finality judge Zion's enemies and make Zion a source of everlasting blessing.

3:1 in those days. In parallel with "at that time," this announcement marks the beginning of a further series of promises for God's people (Jer. 33:15; 50:4, 20).

3:2 Restoration will include the judgment of Israel's enemies ("all the nations") for their injustices against God's people and land.

Valley of Jehoshaphat. This place is identified as the "valley of decision" in v. 14. Its name is symbolic, the location unknown.

scattered . . . divided. Following deportation of the people, the land was redistributed to others. The particular historical event referred to here is not clear. The deportations of 722, 701, 598, and 586 B.C., or even smaller deportations involving border wars (e.g., Amos 1:9, 10) are possibilities.

3:3 Following the casting of lots for prisoners (Obad. 11; Nah. 3:10), defenseless children were traded and sold for purposes of debauchery (Amos 2:6).

3:4 paying me back. The legal charge against Tyre and Sidon (coastal Phoenicia) and the regions of Philistia (coastal Palestine, Josh. 13:2, 3) concerns their involvement in capturing and trading Israelites as prisoners of war. Both regions had sold Israelites as slaves to the Greeks (v. 6) and to Edom (Amos 1:6, 9).

3:5 my silver and my gold. The land's silver and gold, as well as its inhabitants, belonged to the Lord (Hag. 2:8).

3:7 them. God's restored people will inflict His punishment on Tyre, Sidon, and Philistia.

3:8 Sabeans. These were merchants from the distant land of Sheba (1 Kin. 10:1–13; Jer. 6:20).

3:9–12 Joel issues a bitterly ironic invitation to battle to those nations who will be defeated by the Lord.

3:10 plowshares . . . pruning hooks. Cf. Is. 2:4; Mic. 4:3.

3:11 there. The Valley of Jehoshaphat (v. 2 note) is the place of the great battle (v. 14 note).

3:13 Like grain ready to be cut down with the sickle (Is. 17:5) and like grapes waiting to be pressed (Is. 63:3), the wicked nations are ripe for a harvest of judgment (cf. Rev. 14:15, 18, 20).

winepress is full . . . vats overflow. The full winepress and overflowing vats emphasize the enormous wickedness of the nations massed in the valley for judgment.

14 Multitudes, multitudes,
in the valley of decision!
For [b]the day of the LORD is near
in the valley of decision.
15 [c]The sun and the moon are darkened,
and the stars withdraw their
shining.

16 [d]The LORD roars from Zion,
and [d]utters his voice from
Jerusalem,
[e]and the heavens and the earth
quake.
But the LORD is [f]a refuge to his
people,
a stronghold to the people of
Israel.

The Glorious Future of Judah

17 [g]"So you shall know that I am the
LORD your God,
[h]who dwells in Zion, [i]my holy
mountain.
And Jerusalem shall be holy,
and [j]strangers shall never again
pass through it.

18 "And in that day
[k]the mountains shall drip sweet wine,
and the hills shall flow with milk,
and [l]all the streambeds of Judah
shall flow with water;
[m]and a fountain shall come forth from
the house of the LORD
and water the Valley of [n]Shittim.

19 [o]"Egypt shall become a desolation
and [p]Edom a desolate wilderness,
[q]for the violence done to the people of
Judah,
because they have shed innocent
blood in their land.
20 [r]But Judah shall be inhabited forever,
and Jerusalem to all generations.
21 [s]I will avenge their blood,
blood I have not avenged,[1]
[h]for the LORD dwells in Zion."

[1] Or *I will acquit their bloodguilt that I have not acquitted*

14 [b]See ch. 1:15
15 [c]See ch. 2:10
16 [d]ch. 2:11; Amos 1:2; [Jer. 25:30] [e]ch. 2:10 [f]Isai. 4:6; 25:4
17 [g]ch. 2:27; [Ezek. 6:7] [h]ver. 21; [Ezek. 43:7] [i]ch. 2:1; Ps. 48:1; Isai. 65:11; Jer. 31:23 [j]Isai. 52:1; Nah. 1:15; Zech. 14:21; [Rev. 21:27; 22:15]
18 [k]Jer. 31:12; Amos 9:13 [l]Isai. 30:25 [m]Ezek. 47:1 [n]See Num. 25:1
19 [o]See Isai. 19:1-17 [p]See Isai. 34:5 [q]Obad. 10
20 [r]Ps. 125:1, 2; Ezek. 37:25
21 [s]Isai. 4:4; Ezek. 36:25, 29 [h][See ver. 17 above]

3:14 valley of decision. The Valley of Jehoshaphat is now identified as the "valley of decision" where the Lord's judgment will be passed upon multitudes.

near. The imminence of the day of the Lord as a day of judgment is again underlined (1:15; 2:1, 31).

3:15 sun . . . moon . . . stars. Nature responds to the appearance of the Lord on the day of judgment (2:10, 31; Amos 5:18).

3:16 The LORD roars. The Lord's voice is so powerful that even the earth and the sky tremble (Ps. 29:3–9; Jer. 25:30; Amos 1:2).

refuge . . . stronghold. Yet in the midst of the extraordinary manifestations of the Lord's anger against the nations, the Lord protects His covenant people (Is. 25:4; Ps. 46:1).

3:17 dwells in Zion. Judah's experience of the Lord's protection in the midst of His wrath deepened her knowledge of the reality of God's presence in her midst (in Zion, the Lord's holy and inviolable hill, Ps. 46:4; Is. 8:18; 52:1, 2; Zech. 2:10; 8:3; Rev. 21:3). Cf. 2:27.

3:18 The final scene of the drama is one of paradisal prosperity and blessing (cf. 2:19–26).

fountain shall come forth. The temple itself will be the source of a life-giving stream (Ezek. 47:1–12; Ps. 46:4; Rev. 22:1, 2), which will water even the dry and barren valley where acacia trees grow.

3:19 Egypt . . . Edom. Egypt (1 Kin. 14:25, 26; 2 Kin. 23:29) and Edom (Obad. 9–14), here representing all of Israel's enemies, are in ruins after this judgment.

3:20 inhabited forever. In contrast to her enemies, Judah and Jerusalem are blessed and promised perpetual habitation of the land (Jer. 17:25; Zech. 12:6) because "the LORD dwells in Zion" (v. 21).

THE BOOK OF

Amos

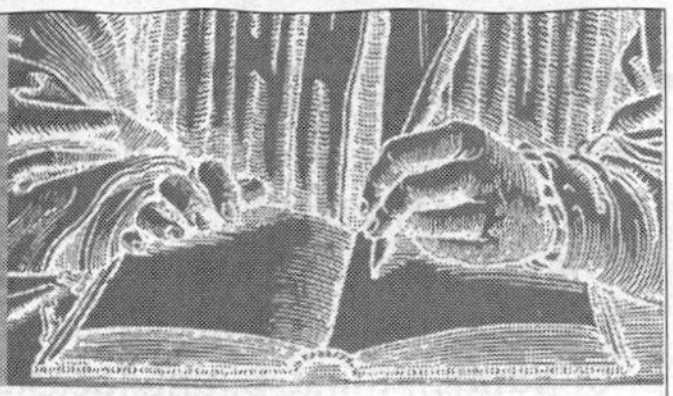

AUTHOR

Tekoa in Judah, a village some five miles south of Bethlehem, was the home of the prophet Amos (1:1). He was a man of several trades: shepherd (1:1), livestock breeder, and dresser of sycamore-fig trees (7:14). Although his background was rural and apparently isolated from centers of learning, Amos clearly knew the surrounding nations and was acquainted with international history (1:3–2:3). He was also familiar with both the history of God's covenant people and the covenant itself, as his numerous references to the Law make clear. Amos had not studied to be a prophet (7:14), but the Lord sovereignly called him to this office. He ministered primarily to the northern kingdom of Israel (7:15), although his prophecies also addressed the sins of Judah (2:4, 5; cf. 9:11).

DATE AND OCCASION

Amos's prophetic ministry took place during the reigns of Uzziah (sometimes called Azariah) of Judah (792–740 B.C.) and Jeroboam II of Israel (793–753 B.C.). During Jeroboam's reign there was peace between Judah and Israel. He had restored the boundaries of Israel in accordance with the prophecy of Jonah son of Amittai (2 Kin. 14:25). The northern kingdom had become wealthy and was enjoying a false sense of security, encouraged by the weakness of Egypt, Babylon, and especially Assyria, which had entered a temporary decline after the death of Adad-nirari III (810–783 B.C.). Israel faced no serious threat from Assyrian arms for about forty years.

Under Tiglath-pileser III (745–727 B.C.), Assyria gained strength and expanded to the north and west. Judah soon became an Assyrian vassal, and the state of Damascus, which had stood between Israel and Assyria, became part of the Assyrian empire (2 Kin. 16:7–9).

Tiglath-pileser III was succeeded by his son, Shalmaneser V (727–722 B.C.), who continued his father's policy of westward expansion, and forced Hoshea, king of Israel, to become his vassal. Hoshea rebelled, however, and mistakenly relied on Egypt for help that never came. Then Shalmaneser besieged Samaria; after three years the Israelite capital fell (722 B.C.) and the northern kingdom of Israel came to an end (2 Kin. 17:3–6).

CHARACTERISTICS AND THEMES

Amos may have delivered the prophecies of this book at different places in the northern kingdom, such as Samaria and Bethel. It is certain only that he fulfilled some of his prophetic ministry at Bethel (7:12, 13). Unlike the messages of earlier prophets (with the possible exception of Joel), the words of Amos were preserved in writing, like those of his contemporaries Isaiah and Hosea. It was essential that these great covenant lawsuit messages be preserved, both as reminders of Israel's history, and for the promises of restoration and redemption they contained.

Amos attacks two major areas of sin commonly indicted by the prophets: idolatry and social injustice. Israel's root problem was its false religion—"having the appearance of godliness, but denying its power" (2 Tim. 3:5). Although Israel maintained the ritual formalities of the law, and even exceeded them (4:4, 5), idolatry was commonplace (2 Kin. 17:9–17; Amos 5:26), as were violence and injustice (2:6–8; 4:1).

The God we encounter in Amos is the same Creator who made man in His image. He is God, and there is no other. He does not tolerate idolatry, which in reality is the worship of demons (Deut. 32:16, 17; 1 Cor. 10:20). The Lord is sovereign and is able to raise up one nation against another in judgment (1:3–2:3), a process that will continue until His return. God is also the Judge of His covenant people Israel, willing to raise up another nation against them (6:14). But for all this, He is a loving God who desires the life, not the death, of His people. Above all, He desires that they should "seek me and live" (5:4; 1 Tim. 2:3, 4).

The Lord sent warnings to Israel in the form of hunger, thirst, blight, locusts, plagues, and military defeat, but the people had refused to see His hand in these (4:6–11). Judgment must follow (4:12–5:20), and this punishment is portrayed in a series of verbal and visionary prophecies predicting wholesale destruction and exile. But the Lord chastises those He loves, and His judgment is really a sign of faithfulness to His covenant people. He promises to restore "the booth of David that is fallen" (9:11), and the ultimate future of His people is portrayed in a concluding description that resembles Eden in its fruitfulness and blessedness (9:13–15).

OUTLINE OF AMOS

I. Superscription and Introduction (1:1, 2)

II. Judgments Pronounced on the Nations (1:3–2:16)

- A. *Oracles Against Israel's Enemies (1:3–2:3)*
- B. *Oracles Against Judah and Israel (2:4–16)*

III. Prophecies Against Israel (chs. 3–6)

- A. *Divine Judgment Is Imminent (ch. 3)*
  1. Historical Background and Affirmation of Prophecy (3:1–8)
  2. Summons to Pagan Witnesses (3:9, 10)
  3. Judgment Announced (3:11–15)
- B. *Israel Is Unrepentant (ch. 4)*
  1. Indictment of Social and Religious Sin (4:1–5)
  2. Historical Review of Past Judgments (4:6–11)
  3. Further Judgment Announced (4:12, 13)
- C. *Lament and Call to Repentance (5:1–17)*
  1. Lament for Fallen Israel (5:1–3)
  2. Warnings and Indictments (5:4–17)
- D. *No Escape from God's Judgment (5:18–6:14)*
  1. Woe Oracles Against Israel's Syncretism and Complacency (5:18–6:7)
  2. Judgment Against Pride and Unrighteousness (6:8–14)

IV. Visions of Divine Retribution (7:1–9:10)

- A. *Judgment Averted by Intercession (7:1–6)*
  1. Vision of Locusts (7:1–3)
  2. Vision of Fire (7:4–6)
- B. *Judgment No Longer Averted (7:7–9:10)*
  1. Vision of a Wall and Plumb Line (7:7–9)
  2. Confrontation with Amaziah the Priest (7:10–17)
  3. Vision of Summer Fruit (ch. 8)
  4. Vision of the Lord by the Altar (9:1–10)

V. Restoration and Blessing (9:11–15)

- A. *Restoration of David's Dynasty (9:11, 12)*
- B. *Blessing of Abundance (9:13–15)*

1 The words of Amos, who was among
the [a]shepherds[1] of [b]Tekoa, which he
saw concerning Israel [c]in the days of
[d]Uzziah king of Judah and in the days of
[e]Jeroboam the son of Joash, king of Israel,
two years[2] before [f]the earthquake.

Judgment on Israel's Neighbors

2 And he said:

[g]"The LORD roars from Zion
and utters his voice from Jerusalem;
[h]the pastures of the shepherds mourn,
and the [i]top of [j]Carmel withers."

3 Thus says the LORD:

[k]"For three transgressions of
[l]Damascus,
and for four, [l]I will not revoke the
punishment,[3]

Chapter 1
1 [a]ch 7:14, 15 [b]2 Sam. 14:2 [c]See Hos. 1:1 [d]2 Kin. 15:1, 13, 30; 2 Chr. 26:1 [e]ch. 7:10; 2 Kin. 14:23 [f]Zech. 14:5; [Isai. 29:6]
2 [g]See Joel 3:16 [h][Ps. 65:12] [i]ch. 9:3 [j]See Josh. 19:26
3 [k]ver. 9, 11, 13; ch. 2:1, 4, 6; Prov. 30:15, 18, 21, 29 [l][Isai. 8:4]

[1] Or *sheep breeders* [2] Or *during two years* [3] Hebrew *I will not turn it back*; also verses 6, 9, 11, 13

1:1 Amos introduces himself and his prophecy, specifying the time when God's word came to him.

The words of Amos. The prophet's messages are introduced with this formula (cf. Jer. 1:1). The phrase has a covenant background (Deut. 1:1, "These are the words that Moses spoke."). Specifically, Amos the prophet is God's covenant lawsuit messenger, bringing God's suit against disobedient Israel.

shepherds. The Hebrew term probably refers to keepers of a particular kind of sheep known for its unusually fine wool. The king of Moab is identified as one owning such sheep (2 Kin. 3:4).

Tekoa. This village was five miles south of Bethlehem. Because of its good pastureland it supported many shepherds with their flocks.

the earthquake. Since this was a memorable event in an earthquake-prone region, it would have been remembered as an act of divine judgment, as in Zech. 14:5.

1:2 The LORD. See notes Ex. 3:15.

roars. Or, "will roar," since the action is future. As a shepherd, Amos could have known well the terrifying roar of a lion on the attack (1 Sam. 17:34–37). The Lord Himself roars from Zion to announce His judgment (Jer. 25:30; Joel 3:16). These opening words of judgment set the tone for what follows.

pastures . . . withers. The Lord's judgment will affect the whole land, from the pastures to the forested top of Carmel, rich in orchards and vineyards (Lev. 26:19; Deut. 28:23, 24).

1:3–2:16 This series of prophecies begins with six Gentile nations: Syria, Philistia, Phoenicia, Edom, Ammon, and Moab. Then the oracles dramatically turn against Judah (2:4–5) and Israel (2:6–16).

because they have threshed [m]Gilead
with threshing sledges of iron.
4 [n]So I will send a fire upon the house
of [o]Hazael,
and it shall devour the strongholds
of [o]Ben-hadad.
5 I will [p]break the gate-bar of
[l]Damascus,
and cut off the inhabitants from
the Valley of [q]Aven,[1]
and him who holds the scepter from
[r]Beth-eden;
and the people of [s]Syria shall go
into exile to [t]Kir,"
says the LORD.

6 Thus says the LORD:
[k]"For three transgressions of [u]Gaza,
and for four, I will not revoke the
punishment,
because [v]they carried into exile a
whole people
to deliver them up to Edom.
7 So I will send a fire upon the wall of
[u]Gaza,
and it shall devour her
strongholds.
8 I will cut off the inhabitants from
[w]Ashdod,
and him who holds the scepter
from Ashkelon;
I will turn my hand against
Ekron,
and the remnant of the
Philistines shall perish,"
says the Lord GOD.

9 Thus says the LORD:
[k]"For three transgressions of
[x]Tyre,
and for four, I will not revoke the
punishment,
because they delivered up a whole
people to Edom,

3 [m]ver. 13; [2 Kin. 10:33; Isai. 21:10] 4 [n]Jer. 49:27 [o]2 Kin. 13:24, 25 5 [p]Jer. 51:30 [l][See ver. 3 above] [q]See Hos. 4:15 [r]2 Kin. 19:12 [s]ch. 9:7; [2 Kin. 16:9] [t]ch. 9:7; 2 Kin. 16:9 6 [k][See ver. 3 above] [u]Jer. 47:1, 5; Zeph. 2:4; Zech. 9:5 [v]2 Chr. 28:18; See Joel 3:4-6
7 [u][See ver. 6 above] 8 [w]ch. 3:9; 1 Sam. 5:1 9 [k][See ver. 3 above] [x]See Joel 3:4

[1] Or *On*

1:3 For three transgressions . . . for four. This refrain, repeated with each prophecy, is an example of parallelism using ascending numbers for emphasis (cf. Ps. 62:11; Mic. 5:5). This standard device in ancient Near Eastern poetry is not intended literally, but means "for many transgressions."

Damascus. David defeated and garrisoned this royal city of Syria (2 Sam. 8:6). During Solomon's reign Damascus broke free, with Rezon as king (1 Kin. 11:23–25).

sledges of iron. The threshing sledge was a wooden board with teeth of iron or basalt fixed on the underside. An ox would pull the sledge over the grain while the driver stood on it. The Syrians are accused of having treated Gilead with extreme cruelty (2 Kin. 13:7).

1:4 I will send a fire. This refrain in each of the messages is also found in Hosea (8:14) and Jeremiah (17:27; 21:14; 29:27; 50:32). Fire was widely understood in the ancient Near East to be an instrument of divine judgment. It was often used in warfare, and was considered one way that a god purged a rebellious people. This pagan understanding also reflects a truth revealed in Scripture: the true God will in fact judge by fire (2 Pet. 3:7 note).

Hazael. The king of Syria (c. 841–801 B.C.), whose reign was predicted by the prophet Elisha (2 Kin. 8:13).

strongholds. These seem to have been fortified citadel-palaces of the nobility.

Ben-hadad. This is a throne name, like "Pharaoh" in Egypt. Probably the third king with this name is meant. The first assisted Judah's king Asa against Israel's Baasha (1 Kin. 15:18–20). The second, Ben-hadad II, was assassinated by the usurper Hazael (2 Kin. 8:14, 15). Hazael's son, Ben-hadad III, was contemporary with Jehoahaz of Israel (2 Kin. 13:25). It was he who made Israel's army "like the dust at threshing" (2 Kin. 13:7).

1:5 cut off. The verb is often used to indicate annihilation by war (Josh. 23:4; Is. 10:7).

the inhabitants. Lit. "the one who sits," probably the king. The Hebrew word is used of God sitting or enthroned as King in Ps. 2:4; 22:3 ("enthroned"); 29:10.

Valley of Aven. Lit. "Valley of Wickedness." Possibly it refers to ancient Syrian Heliopolis, now called Baalbek, in the Beqaa Valley of Lebanon. It was apparently a center for sun worship.

Beth-eden. This was probably a district about 200 miles northeast of Damascus (not to be confused with the Garden of Eden, Gen. 2:8 note), and ruled by a Syrian vassal king. The point of the parallelism between the Valley of Aven and Beth-eden is to indicate that not only Damascus, but its territories as well, will be undone.

Syria . . . to Kir. The original home of the Syrians (9:7), Kir will become their place of exile.

1:6 Gaza. The southernmost of the five Philistine royal cities, Ashkelon, Ashdod, Ekron, Gath, and Gaza. Located between Egypt and Canaan, Gaza was a natural center for trade.

whole people. That is, an entire group of exiles (also v. 9). The Philistine trade included slaves. Prisoners of war usually became slaves, but here a whole population was sold into slavery. The apparent reference is to the capture and sale of Israelites during the reign of Jehoram (2 Chr. 21:16, 17; Joel 3:3, 6).

to Edom. This ancient brother of Israel (Gen. 25:30) received Israelites as slaves from the Philistines. For its role in this unbrotherly sin, Gaza, which stands for Philistia as a whole, is now sentenced.

1:8 Ashdod. A strong and prosperous Philistine city, located eighteen miles northeast of Gaza.

Ashkelon. This third royal city lay halfway between Gaza and Ashdod on the Mediterranean coast.

Ekron. The precise location of this Philistine royal city is uncertain; a number of sites northeast of Ashdod have been suggested. Gath, the fifth royal city, is not mentioned because it had already been defeated by Hazael (2 Kin. 12:17), and again by Sargon II (722–705 B.C.). Assyria was the primary instrument of judgment against all these cities, and all four are subsequently mentioned in Assyrian annals as vassals of Esarhaddon (681–669) and Ashurbanipal (668–627).

1:9 Tyre. One of two major Phoenician cities (the other is Sidon) mentioned in the Canaanite Amarna letters (14th century B.C.). The name itself means "flint." Tyre was built on a large rock in the sea and was considered virtually impregnable until the fourth century B.C., when Alexander the Great conquered the city by building a causeway out to the city.

delivered up a whole people. See notes on v. 6.

and did not remember the
covenant of brotherhood.
10 So I will send a fire upon the wall of
[x]Tyre,
and it shall devour her
strongholds."

11 Thus says the LORD:

[k]"For three transgressions of [y]Edom,
and for four, I will not revoke the
punishment,
[y]because he pursued his brother with
the sword
[z]and cast off all pity,
[a]and his anger tore perpetually,
[a]and he kept his wrath forever.
12 So I will send a fire upon
[b]Teman,
and it shall devour the strongholds
of [c]Bozrah."

13 Thus says the LORD:

[k]"For three transgressions of the
[d]Ammonites,
and for four, I will not revoke the
punishment,
because [e]they have ripped open
pregnant women in [f]Gilead,
that they might enlarge their
border.
14 So I will kindle a fire in the wall of
[g]Rabbah,
[h]and it shall devour her
strongholds,
with shouting on the day of battle,
[h]with a tempest in the day of the
whirlwind;
15 and [i]their king shall go into exile,
he and his princes[1] together,"
says the LORD.

2

Thus says the LORD:

[k]"For three transgressions of [j]Moab,
and for four, I will not revoke the
punishment,[2]
because [k]he burned to lime
the bones of the king of Edom.
2 So I will send a fire upon Moab,
and it shall devour the strongholds
of [l]Kerioth,
and Moab shall die amid uproar,
amid shouting and the sound of
the trumpet;
3 [m]I will cut off the ruler from its
midst,
and will kill [m]all its princes[3]
with him,"
says the LORD.

[1] Or *officials* [2] Hebrew *I will not turn it back*; also verses 4, 6 [3] Or *officials*

10 [x][See ver. 9 above]
11 [k][See ver. 3 above] [y][2 Chr. 28:17] [z]Ps. 137:7; [Joel 3:19; Mal. 1:4] [a]Ezek. 35:5
12 [b]Obad. 9; See 1 Chr. 1:45 [c]Isai. 63:1; See 1 Chr. 1:44
13 [k][See ver. 3 above] [d]Jer. 49:1, 2; Zeph. 2:8, 9 [e]See Hos. 13:16 [f]ver. 3
14 [g]2 Sam. 11:1; 12:26; See Ezek. 21:20 [h][Ezek. 21:28, 29]
15 [i]Jer. 49:3
Chapter 2
1 [k][See ch. 1:3 above] [j]Zeph. 2:8, 9; See Isai. ch. 15 [k][2 Kin. 3:27]
2 [l]Jer. 48:24, 41
3 [m][Jer. 48:7]

did not remember the covenant. This phrase denotes the keeping of covenant obligations and is a standard phrase in ancient international covenants or treaties (cf. Gen. 9:15; Ex. 2:24; Lev. 26:42). Tyre did not keep its treaties with Israel.

of brotherhood. In the ancient Near East, kings entering into treaties styled themselves "brothers." So Hiram of Tyre called Solomon "my brother" (1 Kin. 9:13; cf. 1 Kin. 5:12), against a background of treaty relations with David (2 Sam. 5:11). Later, Ahab continued the close relation with Phoenicia by marrying Jezebel, daughter of Ethbaal, the king of Sidon (1 Kin. 16:31).

1:11 pursued his brother with the sword. See note on v. 6. These events of the reign of Jehoram include Edom's revolt and collusion with the Philistines and Arabs, who attacked Judah and entered Jerusalem, plundering the palace and deporting the royal household (2 Chr. 21:16, 17; Obad. 10–14).

1:12 Teman. Teman was a grandson of Esau (Gen. 36:11, 15). His descendant clan apparently gave its name to a region in the south of Edom, and to a village some fifteen miles from Petra. Here, the region is meant. Teman was famous for wisdom (Job 2:11; Jer. 49:7).

Bozrah. The northernmost Edomite city, some 35 miles north of Petra. By mentioning its northernmost and southernmost regions, Amos consigns all of Edom to destruction.

1:13 the Ammonites. The Ammonites descended from Ben-ammi, who was the offspring of the trickery and incest of Lot's younger daughter (Gen. 19:34–38). They lived between Aram and Moab.

ripped open pregnant women. This particular atrocity was practiced by others, including Hazael of Syria (2 Kin. 8:12), Menahem of Israel (2 Kin. 15:16), and Assyria (Hos. 13:16). The apparent purpose was to eliminate descendants who might try to reclaim the land.

enlarge their border. Ancient Near Eastern kings typically boasted that they extended the borders of their land. By doing so they fancied that they carried out the desire of their gods.

1:14 Rabbah. A short form of the fuller reference, "Rabbah of the Ammonites" (Deut. 3:11; 2 Sam. 12:26). This location is the modern Amman, in Jordan.

tempest . . . whirlwind. In Scripture, the figure of a violent and destructive storm is often used for the tumult of battle, as well as for the anger of God, or indeed for both at once (Ps. 83:15; Is. 5:28; 17:13; 29:6; 66:15; Jer. 4:13; 23:19; 25:32).

1:15 he and his princes together. According to regular Assyrian practice, a conquered king, his household, and his officials would be taken together into exile. Under Shalmaneser III (858–824 B.C.), Assyria conquered Ammon, making it an Assyrian vassal.

2:1 burned to lime the bones of the king of Edom. According to Hebrew tradition, these are the bones of the Moabite king Mesha. Such burning indicated special contempt, and was thought to deprive the dead of peace in the afterlife. Josiah burned the bones of false priests on the altar at Bethel (2 Kin. 23:15, 16).

2:2 Kerioth. Probably the name of a major Moabite city and religious center (Jer. 48:41). The exact site is uncertain. Alternatively, the Hebrew word could be taken to mean "cities," as the Septuagint (Greek Old Testament) translators understood it.

trumpet. This is the ram's horn (Hebrew *shophar*), the signal horn of ancient warfare.

2:3 I will cut off. See note 1:5.

Judgment on Judah

4 Thus says the LORD:

[n]"For three transgressions of Judah,
and for four, I will not revoke the
punishment,
because [o]they have rejected the law
of the LORD,
and have not kept his statutes,
but [p]their lies have led them astray,
those after which their fathers
walked.
5 So [q]I will send a fire upon Judah,
and it shall devour the strongholds
of Jerusalem."

Judgment on Israel

6 Thus says the LORD:

[n]"For three transgressions of Israel,
and for four, I will not revoke the
punishment,
because [r]they sell the righteous for
[s]silver,
and the needy for a pair of
sandals—
7 those who trample the head of the
poor [t]into the dust of the earth
and [u]turn aside the way of the
afflicted;
[v]a man and his father go in to the
same girl,
so that my holy name is profaned;
8 they lay themselves down beside
every altar
on garments [w]taken in pledge,
and in the house of their God they
drink
the wine of those who have been
fined.
9 "Yet [x]it was I who destroyed the
Amorite before them,
[y]whose height was like the height of
the cedars
and who was as strong as the oaks;
[z]I destroyed his fruit above
and his roots beneath.
10 [a]Also it was I who brought you up out
of the land of Egypt
[b]and led you forty years in the
wilderness,
[x]to possess the land of the Amorite.
11 And I raised up some of your sons
for prophets,
and some of your young men for
[c]Nazirites.
Is it not indeed so, O people of
Israel?"
declares the LORD.

4 [n]See ch. 1:3 [o]Lev. 26:14, 15; Neh. 1:7; Ezek. 20:13, 16, 24; [Dan. 9:11] [p]Jer. 16:19, 20; Rom. 1:25
5 [q]Jer. 17:27; Hos. 8:14
6 [n][See ver. 4 above] [r][Lev. 25:39; 2 Kin. 4:1] [s]ch. 8:6
7 [t]Lam. 2:10 [u]ch. 5:12; Job 24:4; Isai. 10:2 [v][1 Cor. 5:1]; See Ezek. 22:11
8 [w]See Ex. 22:26
9 [x]Deut. 2:31; Josh. 24:8; See Num. 21:21-25 [y][Num. 13:32, 33; Isai. 10:33] [z][Job 18:16]
10 [a]ch. 3:1; Ex. 12:17, 51 [b]See Deut. 8:2 [x][See ver. 9 above]
11 [c]Num. 6:2

2:4 Judah. The five oracles against pagan nations are concluded, and the southern kingdom of Judah is now addressed. Divine judgment moves ever closer to the northern kingdom of Israel, where Amos himself prophesied (v. 6).

rejected the law . . . statutes. For rejecting God's revealed covenant law, and so God Himself, they were particularly worthy of judgment (Ex. 15:26; Deut. 4:39, 40). Judah's covenant privileges implied greater responsibility (cf. Luke 12:48).

after which their fathers walked. The ancient Near Eastern idiom "to walk after" meant to follow in obedience as a vassal or servant. Judah was following lies, and serving as the vassal of false gods or demons (Deut. 32:17; Rom. 6:16; 1 Cor. 10:20).

2:5 I will send a fire. See note 1:4.

Jerusalem. The name means "city of peace." The Hebrew word for "peace" (*shalom*) denotes not only the absence of war, but also prosperity and wholeness. Because Judah had not sought integrity in the Lord, they would see destruction, not peace. This prophecy was fulfilled over 150 years later, when Nebuchadnezzar II conquered Jerusalem and burned every notable building, including the king's house (2 Kin. 25:8–10).

2:6 Israel. The indictment of the northern kingdom begins—Israel is guilty of social injustice, sexual immorality, and religious abuses (vv. 6–8).

sell the righteous for silver. A reference to the corrupt judicial system. Judges were willing to convict the innocent upon payment of a bribe.

the needy. The Lord had a special concern that their rights be protected (Ex. 23:6; Jer. 5:28), but they were being sold into slavery even for insignificant debts (here symbolized by a pair of sandals). Indigent slavery in Israel was legal, but was carefully limited by the law of Moses (Ex. 21:2; Deut. 15:12; 1 Pet. 2:18 and notes).

2:7 go in to the same girl. Amos decries uncontrolled sexual passion. Such behavior was contrary to God's original intention (Gen. 2:21–24; Matt. 19:4–6), and it profaned God's holy name (Lev. 18:24). The Mosaic law prohibited sexual union among persons closely related by blood (Lev. 18:6–18); while the Mosaic law does not mention this specific situation (the sharing of a common prostitute), the basic principle would still apply.

2:8 lay themselves down . . . on garments. They engaged in fertility cult prostitution beside the altars, further profaning the Lord's name. There were many altars in Israel, including those at Bethel (3:14), Dan (8:14), and Gilgal (Hos. 12:11). Their sins of sexual license and idolatry were compounded in that they slept on clothing taken as pledges for loans to the poor. Such garments were not to be kept overnight (Ex. 22:26; Deut. 24:12, 13).

wine of those who have been fined. Wine taken from the poor as payment for unjustly imposed fines. Perhaps the drinking accompanied the sexual indulgence just mentioned.

2:9 I . . . destroyed the Amorite. Faithful to His covenant promises (Gen. 15:16–21), the Lord had driven out the Canaanites (simply called "the Amorite" here) from the Promised Land. See note Gen. 10:16.

like . . . the cedars. The description recalls the report of the twelve spies (Num. 13:32, 33), but also God's wrath against all that is lofty and proud (Is. 2:12–18).

fruit above . . . roots beneath. A poetic expression for complete destruction.

2:10 out of the land of Egypt. By reminding them of His covenant faithfulness (cf. Gen. 50:24; Ex. 3:8), the Lord presses His case against Israel's unfaithfulness.

2:11 I raised up . . . prophets. The Lord sovereignly raised up prophets (Deut. 18:15–22), judges (Judg. 2:18), priests (1 Sam. 2:35), and kings (2 Sam. 7:12). The prophets served as covenant lawsuit messengers, sent to recall the people to obedience.

Nazirites. See note Num. 6:1–21. The Old Testament mentions Samson by name as a Nazirite (Judg. 13:4, 5). Samuel was probably a Nazirite as well (1 Sam. 1:11 note).

12 “But you made the Nazirites [d] drink wine,
and commanded the prophets, saying, [e] ‘You shall not prophesy.’
13 “Behold, I will press you down in your place,
as a cart full of sheaves presses down.
14 [f] Flight shall perish from the swift,
[f] and the strong shall not retain his strength,
[g] nor shall the mighty save his life;
15 he who handles the bow shall not stand,
and he who is [h] swift of foot shall not save himself,
[i] nor shall he who rides the horse save his life;
16 and he who is stout of heart among the mighty
shall flee away naked in that day,”
declares the LORD.

Israel's Guilt and Punishment

3 [j] Hear this word that the LORD has spoken against you, O people of Israel, against the whole family that I brought up out of the land of Egypt:

2 [k] “You only have I known
of all the families of the earth;
[l] therefore I will punish you
for all your iniquities.
3 “Do two walk together,
unless they have agreed to meet?
4 Does a lion roar in the forest,
when he has no prey?
Does a young lion cry out from his den,
if he has taken nothing?
5 Does a bird fall in a snare on the earth,
when there is no trap for it?
Does a snare spring up from the ground,
when it has taken nothing?
6 [m] Is a trumpet blown in a city,
and the people are not afraid?
[n] Does disaster come to a city,
unless the LORD has done it?
7 “For the Lord GOD does nothing
[o] without revealing his secret
to his servants the prophets.
8 The lion has roared;
who will not fear?
[p] The Lord GOD has spoken;
who can but prophesy?”

12 [d][Num. 6:3] [e]ch. 7:13, 16; Isai. 30:10; Mic. 2:6 14 [f][ch. 9:1; Eccles. 9:1] [g][Ps. 33:16] 15 [h][2 Sam. 2:18] [i][Ps. 33:17]
Chapter 3
1 [j]ch. 7:16; [ch. 2:10]
2 [k]Deut. 7:6; 10:15; Ps. 147:19, 20; [Hos. 5:3; 13:5; Mic. 2:3] [l][Matt. 10:15; 11:21, 22; Luke 10:13, 14; 12:47; Rom. 2:9] 6 [m]Ezek. 33:4; See Joel 2:1 [n][Isai. 45:7; Lam. 3:38; Mic. 1:12] 7 [o]Gen. 18:17; [Jer. 15:1] 8 [p][Num. 22:38]

2:12 But you. In contrast with the Lord's faithfulness, Israel sought to defeat God's purposes by commanding His messengers not to prophesy, and by making the Nazirites drink wine (in violation of their vow). They showed contempt for both the Lord and His law.

2:13 I will press you down. Just as a cart bogs down from the pressure of its contents and so becomes immovable, so Israel will be unable to flee (v. 14).

2:14 the swift . . . the strong. A vivid picture of helplessness: the fleet of foot will not escape and the strong will not stand their ground.

2:15 bow . . . foot . . . horse. All units of the army will fail before God's anger.

2:16 shall flee away naked. Even the bravest warriors not only cast away armor and weapons but also every impediment, including clothing, in the panic of their useless flight. Such naked flight is an utter humiliation.

in that day. This phrase often indicates the Lord's day of judgment (Zeph. 1:7 note). Here it refers the approaching day of Assyrian conquest.

3:1–15 God prosecutes a lawsuit against Israel through His servant Amos.

3:1 Hear this word. This solemn command occurs again at 4:1 and 5:1, and echoes commands to hear and obey the Lord in the original covenantal documents (Deut. 4:1; 5:1; 6:3). It occurs regularly in covenant lawsuit material (Jer. 2:4; Hos. 4:1).

3:2 You only have I known. In addition to cognition (Gen. 4:9), the Hebrew word for “know” has a wide range of meaning, including sexual relations (Gen. 4:1). Here the term denotes God's sovereign choice, or election, of Israel as the object of His loving concern (Gen. 18:19; cf. Deut. 7:7, 8).

therefore. The Lord's covenant graces include punishment for sins precisely because He loves His people too much to allow them to sin without discipline (Prov. 3:11, 12).

3:3–6 Amos presents a series of questions, to which the answer in every case is quite clear. Their purpose is to emphasize that the message of Amos comes from the Lord.

3:3 walk. To “walk together” with someone here means to agree with their destination and route. Implicitly, the prophet “walks” with the Lord.

3:4 roar. A silent hunter, the lion roars only after its victim's fate is sealed. Just as there is reason for the lion's roar, so also there must be a cause behind the prophet's utterance.

3:5 trap. No bird would be caught in an unbaited trap.

3:6 trumpet. See note 2:2. Siege was a fearful prospect in the ancient world, for it often resulted in starvation of the populace, followed by all the horrors of conquest: rape, pillage, slaughter, and burning.

disaster. Lit. “evil.” The Old Testament teaches that the Lord is the Creator of peace and of calamity (Is. 45:7). This does not mean that God is the author of evil, but rather that He sovereignly brings disaster or adversity on individuals and nations as just punishment. The curses pronounced in Gen. 3:14–19 show that the Lord brings such punishment.

3:7 GOD does nothing without revealing. The God who acts also reveals Himself and interprets His actions to and through the prophets. God revealed His plans for Sodom and Gomorrah to Abraham, the first “prophet” so designated in Scripture (Gen. 18:17; 20:7).

his servants the prophets. Moses, the supreme Old Testament prophet, was called “the servant of the LORD” (Deut. 34:5). Subsequent prophets were characterized by the similar phrase, “my servants the prophets” (Jer. 7:25; Ezek. 38:17; cf. Dan. 9:10).

3:8 who can but prophesy. Just as a lion's voice evokes fear, so the voice of the Lord compels the prophets to proclaim His word (Deut. 18:18; cf. 1 Cor. 9:16).

9 Proclaim to the strongholds in
[q]Ashdod
and to the strongholds in the land
of Egypt,
and say, "Assemble yourselves on
[r]the mountains of Samaria,
and see the great tumults within
her,
and [s]the oppressed in her midst."
10 "They do not know how to do right,"
declares the LORD,
[t]"those who store up violence and
robbery in their strongholds."

11 Therefore thus says the Lord GOD:
[u]"An adversary shall surround[1] the land
and bring down your defenses
from you,
and [v]your strongholds shall be
plundered."

12 Thus says the LORD: [w]"As the shepherd
rescues from the mouth of the lion two
legs, or a piece of an ear, [x]so shall the people of Israel [y]who dwell in Samaria be rescued, with the corner of a couch and part[2]
of a bed.

13 "Hear, [z]and testify against the house
of Jacob,"
declares the Lord GOD, [a]the God of
hosts,

9[q]ch. 1:8 [r]ch. 4:1; 6:1; [1 Kin. 16:24] [s]Ps. 94:5, 6; 103:6; See 1 Kin. 21:1-6 10[t][ch. 6:3; Isai. 3:14, 15]; See Mic. 6:10-12 11[u][2 Kin. 17:5, 6]; See 2 Kin. 18:9-12 [v][Isai. 39:6] 12[w][Ex. 22:13] [x]See Jer. 31:8, 9 [y][ch. 6:4] 13[z][Ps. 50:7; 81:8] [a]ch. 4:13; Ps. 80:4, 7, 14

14[b][Hos. 10:15]; See 1 Kin. 13:1-3 [c][2 Kin. 23:15] 15[d][ch. 6:11] [e]Jer. 36:22 [f]Judg. 3:20 [g]1 Kin. 22:39; Ps. 45:8
Chapter 4
1[h]Ps. 22:12 [i]ch. 3:9; 6:1 [j]Hos. 5:11 2[k]Ps. 89:35 [l][Jer. 16:16; Hab. 1:15]; See 2 Kin. 19:28

14 "that on the day I punish Israel for his
transgressions,
[b]I will punish the altars of Bethel,
and [c]the horns of the altar shall be
cut off
and fall to the ground.
15 [d]I will strike [e]the winter house along
with [f]the summer house,
and [g]the houses of ivory shall
perish,
and the great houses[3] shall come to
an end,"
declares the LORD.

4 "Hear this word, [h]you cows of
Bashan,
who are [i]on the mountain of
Samaria,
[j]who oppress the poor, [j]who crush
the needy,
who say to your husbands, 'Bring,
that we may drink!'
2 [k]The Lord GOD has sworn by his
holiness
that, behold, the days are coming
upon you,
[l]when they shall take you away with
hooks,
[l]even the last of you with
fishhooks.

1 Hebrew *An adversary and one who surrounds* 2 The meaning of the Hebrew word is uncertain 3 Or *many houses*

3:9 Proclaim. The command is in the plural, and is apparently directed at the Lord's servants the prophets.

Ashdod . . . Egypt. Amos poetically summons the pagan nobility to look upon the injustice that reigns in Samaria. Israel (the northern kingdom) should have been more righteous, not less, than her pagan neighbors; it is ironic that these pagans should be called as witnesses to Israel's misbehavior.

mountains of Samaria. Samaria was surrounded by mountains, from which the spectators are asked to view her.

tumults. Or, "disturbances," as the word is translated in 2 Chr. 15:5. Such conditions result from sin and are the opposite of "peace" (Hebrew *shalom*).

3:10 violence and robbery. The ill-gotten gains from their violent and thieving behavior. The rich have plundered and looted the poor.

3:11 adversary. Assyria. The thought of this verse echoes the substance of the covenant curse for disobedience (Deut. 28:52).

3:12 the shepherd rescues . . . a piece. According to ancient laws, shepherds were to demonstrate their diligence by rescuing a portion of a sheep taken by wild beasts (cf. Gen. 31:39 and note). The sheep of Israel will only be saved in a mutilated condition—in fact, the nation would be destroyed.

with the corner of a couch. The rich reclined idly on couches (as the Romans later did at their banquets), enjoying the luxury they extorted from the poor (6:4).

3:13 Hear, and testify. The command here (in the plural) may be to the pagans who have been summoned as witnesses, or to the Lord's messengers, who were commanded to summon the pagan witnesses (v. 9 note).

3:14 on the day . . . for his transgressions. The phrasing here recalls the original covenant documents (Ex. 32:34).

altars of Bethel. Jeroboam I had made a golden calf for Israel to worship at Bethel in the north, as an alternative to worship at Jerusalem in the south, and had installed an altar there (1 Kin. 12:25–33). Both altar and sanctuary were later destroyed by Josiah (2 Kin. 23:15).

horns of the altar. A fugitive could gain asylum by grasping the horns of the altar (1 Kin. 1:49–51), though this privilege was not always observed (1 Kin. 2:28–35). Even this last resort for sinful Israel will be cut off.

3:15 winter house . . . summer house. The possession of both a summer and a winter house was a great luxury, affordable only by kings and the very wealthy. The Lord would destroy these multiple houses and decorated mansions. Assyria, God's instrument of judgment (Is. 10:5, 6), was expert at such destruction and plunder, as the vast wealth of Nineveh amply testified (Nah. 2:9).

4:1–13 Through His servant Amos, God prosecutes a second covenant lawsuit against Israel.

4:1 Hear this word. See 3:1 and note.

cows of Bashan. The wealthy women of Samaria, who had been raised and cared for like the prime cattle of Bashan, a fertile area east of the Jordan River (Deut. 3:1 note).

4:2 sworn by his holiness. The same phrase occurs once elsewhere, in Ps. 89:35. No oath can be greater or more final (Heb. 6:13, 14).

fishhooks. The Assyrians frequently led prisoners by ropes attached to rings or hooks in their noses or lips.

3 [m] And you shall go out through the breaches,
each one straight ahead;
and you shall be cast out into Harmon,"
declares the LORD.

4 [n] "Come to Bethel, and transgress;
to [o] Gilgal, and multiply transgression;
[n] bring your [p] sacrifices every morning,
your tithes every three days;
5 offer a sacrifice of thanksgiving of [q] that which is leavened,
and proclaim [r] freewill offerings, publish them;
[s] for so you love to do,
O people of Israel!"
declares the Lord GOD.

Israel Has Not Returned to the LORD

6 "I gave you cleanness of teeth in all your cities,
and [t] lack of bread in all your places,
[u] yet you did not return to me,"
declares the LORD.
7 "I also [v] withheld the rain from you
when there were yet three months to the harvest;
[w] I would send rain on one city,
and send no rain on another city;
one field would have rain,
and the field on which it did not rain would wither;
8 so two or three cities [x] would wander to another city
to drink water, and would not be satisfied;
[u] yet you did not return to me,"
declares the LORD.

9 [y] "I struck you with blight and mildew;
your many gardens and your vineyards,
your fig trees and your olive trees
[z] the locust devoured;
[u] yet you did not return to me,"
declares the LORD.

10 "I sent among you a pestilence [a] after the manner of Egypt;
I killed your young men with the sword,
and [b] carried away your horses,[1]
and [c] I made the stench of your camp go up into your nostrils;
[u] yet you did not return to me,"
declares the LORD.

11 "I overthrew some of you,
[d] as when God overthrew Sodom and Gomorrah,
and you were [e] as a brand[2] plucked out of the burning;

3 [m] [Ezek. 12:5, 12] **4** [n] [ch. 5:5; Ezek. 20:39; Matt. 23:32] [o] [ch. 5:5; Hos. 4:15; 9:15; 12:11] [p] Num. 28:3, 4; [Jer. 7:21] **5** [q] Lev. 7:13 [r] Ex. 35:29; Lev. 22:18, 21; Deut. 12:6 [s] [Ps. 81:11, 12] **6** [t] [Deut. 28:57; Lam. 2:12] [u] Jer. 15:7; Hag. 2:17 **7** [v] Jer. 3:3; [Joel 2:23] [w] [Ex. 9:26] **8** [x] [ch. 8:12] [u] [See ver. 6 above] **9** [y] Deut. 28:22; Hag. 2:17 [z] Joel 1:4 [u] [See ver. 6 above] **10** [a] Deut. 28:27, 60; [Ex. 12:29; Ps. 78:50; Isai. 10:24, 26] [b] 2 Kin. 13:7 [c] [Joel 2:20] [u] [See ver. 6 above] **11** [d] [Isai. 13:19] [e] Zech. 3:2; [Jude 23]

[1] Hebrew *along with the captivity of your horses* [2] That is, a burning stick

4:3 cast out into Harmon. This location is now unknown.

4:4 Bethel . . . Gilgal. These were important sites in the earlier history of Israel; Bethel was a sanctuary during the period of the judges, and Samuel judged both there and at Gilgal (1 Sam. 7:16). They were also centers of syncretistic worship during the period of the divided kingdom (5:5).

every three days. Although the Hebrew word for "day" can stand for a year or for an unspecified longer period (Gen. 1:5 note), three literal days seem to be meant here. Israel's religious observances go even beyond what the law required. Though enthusiastic about ritual, they had no living relationship with God.

4:5 sacrifice . . . leavened. The covenant law made it clear that they were not to burn leavened bread as a sacrifice (Lev. 2:11; 6:17; 7:12). Amos sarcastically urges them to continue in their disobedience.

for so you love. In the ancient Near East, the term *to love* had special significance in covenants: the vassal's "love" for the sovereign entailed obedience (Deut. 6:5; cf. John 14:15). The nation's disobedience made it apparent that Israel loved rituals and idolatry rather than the Lord.

4:6–11 This section reviews what the Lord did in punishment to warn His people and draw their attention back to Him. The emphatic phrase "I also" indicates the change of subject. All the disasters mentioned were threatened in the covenant (Deut. 28). Israel should have understood this and repented. But as the refrain repeats, "you did not return to me" (4:6, 8, 9, 10, 11).

4:6 cleanness of teeth. Their teeth were clean because they had nothing to eat. The covenant had threatened hunger and want as a penalty for disobedience (Deut. 28:47, 48).

4:7, 8 rain. The winter rains from October through February were essential for the crops to begin their growth. The spring or "latter" rains of March and April would provide for mature growth (Jer. 5:24). The Lord had promised these rains, if Israel would obey His commands (Lev. 26:3, 4), but also warned that He would withhold them if they disobeyed (Lev. 26:18, 19; Deut. 28:23, 24).

4:9 blight and mildew. The Lord had threatened these in the covenant law (Deut. 28:22; cf. Hag. 2:17).

locust. The Hebrew word for this destructive insect probably derives from the verb meaning "to cut" (cf. Joel 1:4; 2:25). Ironically, the punishment described here is just what the Lord had inflicted on Egypt (Ps. 105:34–35), whose Pharaoh rebelled against God. Rebellious Israel has received the same punishment, and like Pharaoh has not repented.

4:10 pestilence . . . Egypt. The Lord had threatened a plague in His covenant with Israel (Deut. 28:21), along with all the diseases of Egypt (Deut. 28:21, 60, 61).

killed. Yet another covenant curse fulfilled (Ex. 22:24).

4:11 overthrew Sodom and Gomorrah. Similar or identical phrases are used in prophecies against Babylon (Is. 13:19; Jer. 50:40) and Edom (Jer. 49:18). The devastation of Sodom and Gomorrah provided a symbol of God's judgment against sin (Gen. 19:24, 25; Deut. 29:23 note); here God promises to overthrow Israel with equal thoroughness.

a brand plucked out of the burning. Despite God's repeated mercy to His people (e.g., 2 Kin. 13:3–5; cf. Zech. 3:2), they remained ungrateful and unrepentant.

[u] "yet you did not return to me,"
declares the LORD.

12 "Therefore thus I will do to you,
O Israel;
because I will do this to you,
prepare to meet your God, O Israel!"

13 For behold, [f] he who forms the
mountains and creates the wind,
and [g] declares to man what is his
thought,
[h] who makes the morning darkness,
and [i] treads on the heights of the
earth—
[j] the LORD, the God of hosts, is his
name!

Seek the LORD and Live

5 Hear this word that I [k] take up over you in lamentation, O house of Israel:

2 "Fallen, no more to rise,
is [l] the virgin Israel;
forsaken on her land,
with none to raise her up."

3 For thus says the Lord GOD:

"The city that went out a thousand
shall have a hundred left,
and that which went out a hundred
shall have ten left
to the house of Israel."

4 For thus says the LORD to the house of Israel:

[m] "Seek me and live;
5 but do not seek [n] Bethel,
and do not enter into [n] Gilgal
or cross over to [o] Beersheba;
for [n] Gilgal shall surely go into
exile,
and [n] Bethel shall come to
nothing."

6 [m] Seek the LORD and live,
[p] lest he break out like fire in the
house of Joseph,
and it devour, with none to
quench it for [n] Bethel,
7 O [q] you who turn justice to
wormwood[1]
and cast down righteousness to
the earth!

8 He who made the [r] Pleiades and
Orion,
and turns deep darkness into the
morning
and [s] darkens the day into night,
who [t] calls for the waters of the sea
[t] and pours them out on the surface
of the earth,
[u] the LORD is his name;

11 [u] [See ver. 6 above] 13 [f] [Ps. 102:25] [g] [Ps. 139:2] [h] [ch. 5:8; 8:9] [i] Isai. 58:14; Mic. 1:3 [j] ch. 3:13; 5:8; 9:6; See Jer. 10:16
Chapter 5
1 [k] Ezek. 19:1
2 [l] Lam. 2:1; [Isai. 47:1]
4 [m] 2 Chr. 15:2; Isai. 55:6; Zeph. 2:3
5 [n] See ch. 4:4 [o] ch. 8:14
6 [m] [See ver. 4 above] [p] [Isai. 9:18, 19] [n] [See ver. 5 above]
7 [q] [ch. 6:12]
8 [r] Job 9:9; 38:31 [s] Ps. 104:20; [ch. 4:13; 8:9] [t] ch. 9:6; [Gen. 6:17; Ps. 104:6, 7] [u] See ch. 4:13

1 Or *to bitter fruit*

4:12 thus I will do to you. Or, "because this is what I have done to you." The Hebrew is ambiguous. It either warns about the future, or cites the past as a reason to fear.

prepare . . . God. The phrase comes from Ex. 19:15–17, where, after three days of sanctification, the people met the Lord at Sinai. Then they met a God who was graciously forging a covenant with them. Now they would meet a God who was coming to judge their covenant disobedience.

4:13 who forms . . . declares . . . makes . . . treads. This verse is in the form of an ancient Near Eastern divine or royal title: a series of titles or epithets used to describe the deeds or powers of a god or king. Here they describe the great King, who is abundantly able to carry out the curses He originally threatened in the covenant (cf. Is. 44:24–28).

the LORD, the God of hosts. See note Zech. 1:3.

5:1 Hear this word. See 3:1 and note.

lamentation. As though in mourning for the dead, Amos pours out a lament for Israel. This literary device is frequently used in Old Testament prophecy (e.g., Jer. 7:29; Ezek. 19:1; 26:17; 27:2; 32:2).

5:2 Fallen. This term is used in other laments (e.g., 2 Sam. 1:19, 25, 27; 3:34; Lam. 2:21).

virgin Israel. This kind of personification is used of Israel (cf. Jer. 18:13; 2 Kin. 19:21) and of other nations such as Babylon (Is. 47:1) and Egypt (Jer. 46:11).

5:3 a thousand . . . ten. The drastic military reversals described here perhaps echo the prophecy of such disasters in the covenant, which the Lord warned would come because of idolatry (Deut. 32:15–18, 28–30).

5:4 Seek me and live. The Lord had promised to meet those who would seek Him, even in exile (Deut. 4:29; cf. Lam. 3:25). Tragically, the Lord's people often did not seek Him (Is. 9:13; Jer. 10:21).

5:5 Bethel . . . Gilgal. See note 4:4.

Beersheba. This ancient holy place (Gen. 21:31–33; 26:23–25; 46:1–5) was located 50 miles south-southwest of Jerusalem. People from the north evidently went there on pilgrimage (8:14). In the seventh century B.C., Josiah destroyed the high places "from Geba to Beersheba" during his reform (2 Kin. 23:8).

Gilgal . . . exile. The words form an alliterative wordplay in Hebrew.

5:6 fire. See note 1:4.

house of Joseph. Ephraim and Manasseh, the tribes descending from Joseph (Gen. 48:15 note), whose tribal areas contained Bethel (Ephraim) and Gilgal (Manasseh). These northern sanctuaries would be destroyed. Beersheba, in the south, would escape the fire of judgment that swept through the northern kingdom.

none to quench it. The Lord's judgment fire cannot be extinguished (Is. 1:31; Jer. 4:4; Matt. 3:12).

5:7 justice . . . righteousness. These often occur together in the Old Testament as qualities of life the Lord desires (v. 24; Is. 5:7).

5:8 made . . . turns . . . pours. See note 4:13. This majestic description of the Lord contrasts starkly with the previous verse.

Pleiades. A star cluster in the constellation Taurus, with six or seven prominent stars visible to the unaided eye.

Orion. In classical mythology, the constellation Orion is "the Hunter." In Job also, the Pleiades and Orion are named together as evidences of God's incomparable power and wisdom (Job 9:9; 38:31).

9 [y]who makes destruction flash forth
against the strong,
so that destruction comes upon
the fortress.
10 [w]They hate him who reproves [x]in the
gate,
and they [y]abhor him who speaks
the truth.
11 Therefore because you [z]trample on[1]
the poor
and you exact taxes of grain from
him,
[a]you have built houses of hewn stone,
but you shall not dwell in them;
[a]you have planted pleasant
vineyards,
but you shall not drink their wine.
12 For I know how many are your
transgressions
and how great are your sins—
you who afflict the righteous, who
[b]take a bribe,
and [c]turn aside the needy [x]in the
gate.
13 Therefore he who is prudent will
[d]keep silent in such a time,
[e]for it is an evil time.
14 [f]Seek good, and not evil,
that you may live;
and so the LORD, [g]the God of hosts,
will be with you,
as you have said.
15 [h]Hate evil, and love good,
and establish justice in the gate;
[i]it may be that the LORD, the God of
hosts,
will be gracious to the remnant of
Joseph.

16 Therefore thus says the LORD, [g]the God of
hosts, the Lord:
"In all the squares [j]there shall be
wailing,
and in all the streets they shall say,
'Alas! Alas!'
They shall call the farmers to
mourning
and [j]to wailing those who are
skilled in lamentation,
17 and in all vineyards there shall be
wailing,
for [k]I will pass through your
midst,"
says the LORD.

Let Justice Roll Down

18 Woe to you who desire [l]the day of
the LORD!

9 [y][Jer. 50:32]
10 [w]Isai. 29:21; [Prov. 15:5, 10] [x]See Ruth 4:1 [y][1 Kin. 22:8]
11 [z][James 2:6] [a]Deut. 28:30, 39; Mic. 6:15; Zeph. 1:13
12 [b]1 Sam. 8:3; 12:3; [Ps. 26:10] [c]ch. 2:7; Isai. 29:21 [x][See ver. 10 above]
13 [d][Eccles. 3:7] [e]Mic. 2:3
14 [f][Deut. 30:15, 19; Zeph. 2:3]
[g]ch. 3:13
15 [h]Ps. 97:10; Rom. 12:9 [i]Joel 2:14; [Ex. 32:30]
16 [g][See ver. 14 above] [j][Jer. 9:17, 18]
17 [k]Ex. 12:12
18 [l]See Joel 1:15

[1] Or *you tax*

5:10 They hate . . . they abhor. This verse contrasts with vv. 11, 12, which are in the second person. Such shifts of person are common in ancient Near Eastern writings of all kinds, and no significant difference of tone seems intended here.

who reproves . . . who speaks the truth. A reference to those who reprove falsehood in court and bear true witness there. Israel had come to hate such men, presumably because they threatened practices of corruption and dishonest gain (2:6 and note).

in the gate. Much of a city's legal business was transacted in its gate, a large passageway with adjoining rooms.

5:11 houses of hewn stone. These were costly to build, in contrast to the mud brick houses in which most people lived (cf. Is. 9:10).

you shall not dwell . . . you shall not drink. The curse of futility (failure to enjoy the fruit of one's labor) had fallen on the Canaanites as Israel dispossessed them from their cities (Deut. 6:10, 11). Now Israel will suffer the same fate, according to the words of Deut. 25:30 (cf. Is. 65:21–23; 1 Cor. 15:58).

5:12 For I know. Israel must realize that the Lord knows what they perhaps imagine He does not know (cf. Ps. 73:11; Job 22:13, 14).

bribe. The Hebrew term can refer to a common bribe (1 Sam. 12:3) or to a ransom for loss of life (Ex. 21:30). In view here may be the taking of a ransom for the life of a murderer, which was against the law (Num. 35:31).

5:13 an evil time. This phrase explains why the prudent will be silent: the times will be so bad that the truth will not be tolerated.

5:14 Seek good, and not evil. For this thought of effective repentance, see Is. 1:16–17. In 5:4 they were commanded to "Seek me"; only God is good (Matt. 19:17).

that you may live. Obedience to the Lord would bring them security and prosperity (Deut. 28:1–14); but the verse points to a deeper truth, that to know God is life itself (John 17:3).

God . . . with you. This is the deepest need of God's people, expressed prophetically in the name *Immanuel* ("God is with us," Is. 7:14; cf. Matt. 1:23).

as you have said. Israel complacently claimed that the Lord was with them, despite their rebelliousness, simply because He had made a covenant with them (cf. Matt. 3:9).

5:15 justice in the gate. See note on v. 10.

remnant of Joseph. The northern kingdom of Israel was dominated by the tribe of Ephraim, descendants of one of Joseph's sons (Deut. 33:17 note). Though Israel was relatively prosperous and strong, the phrase anticipates the future, after God's judgment, when He would graciously restore a remnant of the people.

5:17 all vineyards. The laments over Israel will be taken up in every part of the land, since every part will be punished.

I will pass through. The same verb appears at Ex. 12:12, where the Lord speaks of His impending judgment on Egypt. Ironically, because Israel has become as pagan as Egypt, He must now "pass through" Israel in judgment as well (7:2 note).

5:18–27 This second portion of ch. 5 treats the day of the Lord and His rejection of Israel.

5:18 the day of the LORD. Ultimately, this is the great and terrible "day of the LORD" when He comes in judgment (cf. Is. 2:12; 13:6–13; Obad. 15; Zeph. 1:7, 14). Every Old Testament judgment was also a "day of the LORD," and anticipated that final day. Joel described it as a day of terrible judgment and destruction (Joel 1:15–20; 2:11), although it would also be accompanied by a redemptive outpouring of God's Spirit (Joel 2:28–32).

Why would you have the day of
the LORD?
[m] It is darkness, and not light,
19 [n] as if a man fled from a lion,
and a bear met him,
or went into the house and leaned
his hand against the wall,
and a serpent bit him.
20 [m] Is not the day of the LORD darkness,
and not light,
and gloom with no brightness in it?
21 [o] "I hate, I despise your feasts,
and I take no delight in your
solemn assemblies.
22 [p] Even though you offer me your burnt
offerings and grain offerings,
I will not accept them;
and the peace offerings of your
fattened animals,
I will not look upon them.
23 Take away from me the noise of your
songs;
to [q] the melody of your harps I will
not listen.
24 But let justice roll down like waters,
and righteousness like an ever-
flowing stream.

18 [m] See Joel 2:1, 2
19 [n] [Isai. 24:18; Jer. 48:44]
20 [m] [See ver. 18 above]
21 [o] Isai. 1:14; [Jer. 6:20]
22 [p] Ps. 51:16, 17; Isai. 1:11
23 [q] [ch. 6:5; 8:3; Isai. 5:12]
25 [r] Cited Acts 7:42, 43
26 [s] [Deut. 32:17; Ezek. 20:16, 24] [t] [Isai. 46:7]
27 [u] 2 Kin. 17:6 [v] ch. 3:12 [g] [See ver. 14 above]
Chapter 6
1 [w] Isai. 32:9; Zeph. 1:12; Luke 6:24; James 5:1 [x] ch. 3:9; 4:1 [y] [Ezek. 22:6] [z] See Ex. 19:5
2 [a] Gen. 10:10; Isai. 10:9 [b] 1 Kin. 8:65; 2 Kin. 18:34; Isai. 10:9 [c] See 1 Sam. 17:4 [d] [Nah. 3:8]

25 [r] "Did you bring to me sacrifices and
offerings during the forty years in the
wilderness, O house of Israel? 26 [s] You [t] shall
take up Sikkuth your king, and Kiyyun
your star-god—your images that you made
for yourselves, 27 [u] and I will send you into
exile beyond [v] Damascus," says the LORD,
whose name is [g] the God of hosts.

Woe to Those at Ease in Zion

6 [w] "Woe to those who are at ease in
Zion,
and to those who feel secure on
[x] the mountain of
Samaria,
[y] the notable men of [z] the first of the
nations,
to whom the house of Israel
comes!
2 Pass over to [a] Calneh, and see,
and from there go to [b] Hamath the
great;
then go down to [c] Gath of the
Philistines.
[d] Are you better than these
kingdoms?
Or is their territory greater than
your territory,

darkness, and not light. The Lord alone has power to make day as dark as night, both literally and figuratively, in judgment (v. 8).

5:19 lion . . . bear. Amos vividly portrays the futility of trying to escape the Lord's judgment (Is. 24:17, 18).

5:20 brightness. In addition to denoting physical light, the Hebrew word for "brightness" is associated with the Lord (Ps. 18:12; Is. 4:5) and with the righteous (Prov. 4:18, 19; Is. 60:3; 62:1). There will be no light of righteousness in the land, and no brightness from the Lord's favorable countenance. Judgment will be black and total, engulfing the whole land.

5:21–24 For a similar condemnation of empty ritual and sacrifice without repentance, see Mic. 6:6–8 (cf. Matt. 5:23, 24; 1 Cor. 13:3).

5:21 I hate, I despise. Two Hebrew words here combine to express the attitude more forcefully than either could by itself. The result can be translated, "I reject with utter hatred."

I take no delight. The language refers to burnt offerings. In the Mosaic covenant, the Lord declares that if His people were disobedient, He would "not smell" the fragrance of their offerings (Lev. 26:31).

5:24 justice . . . righteousness. See note on v. 7.

ever-flowing stream. The streams, or wadis, of the Middle East are rocky watercourses through which torrents rush in the rainy season, but which are dry at other times. The Lord desires righteousness that is like His own, dependable and strong.

5:25 Did you bring. Offerings had been brought to the Lord during the wilderness wanderings (Ex. 18:12; Lev. 9:8–24). The question emphasizes that such offerings were not of primary importance to the Lord. Rather, He wants worship in spirit and in truth accompanied by true repentance.

5:26 take up Sikkuth . . . Kiyyun. Sikkuth (or Sakkuth) was an Assyrian deity associated with the planet Saturn. Kiyyun (or Kaiwan) was a Babylonian term for Saturn. Amos here refers to idols associated with astral deities that were carried in cultic processions. The Septuagint (Greek Old Testament) translated the Hebrew for "Sikkuth your king" as "tabernacle of Moloch" (the Hebrew letters are similar), a reading quoted by Stephen in Acts 7:43.

that you made for yourselves. Old Testament attacks against idolatry often focus on the merely man-made nature of the idols (Is. 44:9–20; Jer. 10:1–5; Mic. 5:13).

5:27 beyond Damascus. Banishment beyond Damascus in Syria implied exile to Assyria, as the prophet's audience well understood. Exile far from home was one of the original covenant curses (Deut. 28:36, 64).

6:1 Zion . . . mountain of Samaria. Zion (Jerusalem) and Samaria were the capitals of Judah and Israel respectively. Like his contemporaries Hosea, Isaiah, and Micah, Amos was given prophecies that addressed both the southern and northern kingdoms (Hos. 6:4–11; Mic. 1:5).

first of the nations. The same ironic Hebrew phrase occurs also at Num. 24:20 (referring to Amalek). Israel had become powerful and prosperous under Jeroboam II, and might fancy herself the first among the nations.

6:2 Calneh. The identity of this city is uncertain, but it may be the Calno mentioned in Is. 10:9, which was conquered by Sargon II of Assyria in 710 B.C.

Hamath the great. Located north of Dan on the Orontes River in Syria, it was restored to Israelite control by Jeroboam II (2 Kin. 14:23–25).

Gath. One of the five major Philistine cities (1:6 note), Judah's Uzziah had recaptured Gath from Syrian control (2 Kin. 12:17; 2 Chr. 26:6).

Are you better . . . is their territory greater. The precise historical context and meaning of this verse is debated. Some suggest that Calneh, Hamath, and Gath had been conquered, and that Israel should therefore not expect to escape conquest either. Others contend that Amos mentions other flourishing capitals of the region to show that Israel was as great as they, perhaps implying that Israel's territory is not so small that aggressors will ignore it and attack these other cities instead.

3 [e]O you who put far away the day of
disaster
[f]and bring near the seat of
violence?

4 "Woe to those [g]who lie on [h]beds of
ivory
[g]and stretch themselves out on
their couches,
and eat lambs from the
flock
[i]and calves from the midst of the
stall,

5 [j]who sing idle songs to the sound of
the harp
and like David [j]invent for
themselves instruments of
music,

6 [k]who drink wine in bowls
and [l]anoint themselves with the
finest oils,
but are not grieved over the ruin of
Joseph!

7 [m]Therefore they shall now be the first
of those who go into exile,
and the revelry of those who
stretch themselves out shall
pass away."

8 [n]The Lord GOD has sworn by himself,
declares the LORD, the God of hosts:

"I abhor [o]the pride of Jacob
and hate his strongholds,
[p]and I will deliver up the city and
all that is in it."

9 And [q]if ten men remain in one house,
they shall die. 10 And when one's relative,
[r]the one who anoints him for burial, shall
take him up to bring the bones out of the
house, and shall say to him who is in the
innermost parts of the house, "Is there still
anyone with you?" he shall say, "No"; and
he shall say, [s]"Silence! We must not mention the name of the LORD."

11 For behold, the LORD commands,
and [t]the great house shall be
struck down into fragments,
and the little house into bits.

12 Do horses run on rocks?
Does one plow there[1] with oxen?
[u]But you have turned justice into
[v]poison
[u]and the fruit of righteousness into
wormwood[2]—

13 you who rejoice in Lo-debar,[3]
who say, [w]"Have we not by our
own strength
captured Karnaim[4] for ourselves?"

3 [e][ch. 9:10; Ezek. 12:27] [f]See ch. 3:10
4 [g][ch. 3:12] [h][Esth. 1:6] [i][James 5:5]
5 [j]See ch. 5:23
6 [k][Isai. 5:12] [l][Dan. 10:3]
7 [m]ch. 7:11, 17
8 [n]Jer. 22:5; 51:14 [o]ch. 8:7; [Ps. 47:4] [p][Jer. 17:3]
9 [q][ch. 3:3]
10 [r]See 1 Sam. 31:12 [s][ch. 5:13; 8:3]
11 [t][ch. 3:15]
12 [u][ch. 5:7] [v]Deut. 29:18
13 [w][Mic. 4:13; 1 Kin. 22:11]

[1] Or *the sea* [2] Or *into bitter fruit* [3] *Lo-debar* means *nothing* [4] *Karnaim* means *horns* (a symbol of strength)

6:3 seat of violence. Israel has enthroned violence, such as extortion and abuse of the poor, as a way of life, while also denying that the day of judgment is coming.

6:4 ivory. A symbol of wealth and luxury (3:15; 1 Kin. 10:22).

calves . . . stall. Choice calves were kept in stalls and fattened for special occasions. Such was the normal fare for the wealthy of Samaria.

6:5 like David. An ironic comparison with David's musical interests. Unlike their frivolous endeavors, David composed many psalms to the glory of the Lord (2 Sam. 23:1).

6:6 in bowls. That is, from large bowls or basins. The same Hebrew word is used for the large bowls before the altar at the temple (Num. 7:13; Zech. 14:20). The prophet's hyperbole vividly portrays the excesses of the city.

Joseph. See note 5:6.

6:7 first of those who go into exile. This phrase is a Hebrew wordplay on the earlier phrase, "first of the nations" (v. 1). Israel fancied herself the first among the nations, but would find herself leading the exiles.

6:8–14 A series of judgment pronouncements follows the indictments of vv. 1–7.

6:8 sworn by himself. Similar to oaths in Gen. 22:16; Ex. 32:13; Is. 45:23, here indicating that the judicial sentence is unalterable (Heb. 6:13 note).

pride of Jacob. This refers both to Israel's pride and to that in which they took pride—their military strength. The word translated "strongholds" has the sense of "fortified palace" or "citadel."

6:9 ten men . . . one house. The meaning seems to be that small remnants hoping to escape will be found and killed.

6:10 relative . . . one who anoints. Lit. "a man's kinsman and his burner," probably one and the same individual. Fear of epidemics may have required cremation instead of burial. Or the burning could be a fire in honor of the dead (Jer. 34:5).

must not mention the name of the LORD. Previously, one might mention or invoke the Lord's name for help, since He was the God of Israel's covenant. But on the day of judgment one may not do this, because the God of the covenant is coming in judgment (cf. Is. 48:1).

6:11 commands. The Lord is rousing Assyria, His instrument of judgment, to come against Israel (cf. Is. 10:5, 6).

great house . . . little house. Both the great houses of the wealthy and the small houses of the poor will be shattered by the coming judgment. Here, as often in Hebrew, the word for "house" can also mean "household" or "family."

6:12 Do horses run on rocks? Obviously not; no one runs a horse in such treacherous footing. Neither would one plow on rocks. But Israel's injustice is just as absurd. A suggested reading of the second question, "Does one plow there with oxen," requires a different word division in the Hebrew and is attested by no ancient version. It is better to take "rocks" as understood, although not explicitly stated, in the second query.

6:13 Lo-debar . . . Karnaim. Lo-debar was a border town in Gilead, Karnaim a city on the plain of Bashan on the way to Damascus. Both were apparently retaken from Hazael by Jehoash (2 Kin. 10:32, 33; 13:25), but later conquered by Assyria (2 Kin. 15:29). The names respectively mean "nothing" and "horns." A wordplay is intended, by which Amos says that Israel rejoices in the conquest of nothing (the conquest of Lo-debar, soon to be taken by Assyria, was short-lived), and boasts of having taken "horns" (symbolic of military strength in the ancient Near East) by their own strength. Their conquests amount to nothing, and their strength will melt away before the Lord's judgment.

14 "For behold, [x]I will raise up against
you a nation,
O house of Israel," declares the
LORD, the God of hosts;
"and they shall oppress you from
[y]Lebo-hamath
to the Brook of [z]the Arabah."

Warning Visions

7 [a]This is what the Lord GOD showed me:
behold, [b]he was forming locusts when
the latter growth was just beginning to
sprout, and behold, it was the latter growth
after the king's mowings. 2 When they had
finished eating the grass of the land, I said,

"O Lord GOD, please forgive!
[c]How can Jacob stand?
He is so small!"
3 [d]The LORD relented concerning this;
"It shall not be," said the LORD.

4 [a]This is what the Lord GOD showed me:
behold, the Lord GOD was calling [e]for a judgment by fire, and it devoured the great deep
and was eating up the land. 5 Then I said,

"O Lord GOD, please cease!
[c]How can Jacob stand?
He is so small!"
6 [d]The LORD relented concerning this;
"This also shall not be," said the
Lord GOD.

7 [a]This is what he showed me: behold,
the Lord was standing beside a wall built
with [f]a plumb line, with a plumb line in his
hand. 8 And the LORD said to me, [g]"Amos,
what do you see?" And I said, "A plumb
line." Then the Lord said,

"Behold, I am setting [f]a plumb line
in the midst of my people Israel;
[g]I will never again pass by them;
9 [h]the high places of Isaac shall be
made desolate,
and the sanctuaries of Israel shall
be laid waste,
and I will rise against [i]the house of
Jeroboam with the sword."

Amos Accused

10 Then Amaziah [j]the priest of Bethel sent
to [k]Jeroboam king of Israel, saying, "Amos
has [l]conspired against you in the midst of
the house of Israel. The land is not able to

14 [x][Jer. 5:15] [y]2 Kin. 14:25 [z]See Deut. 1:1
Chapter 7
1 [a]ch. 8:1 [b][Joel 1:4]; See Ex. 10:4
2 [c][Ps. 130:3]
3 [d][Deut. 32:36; Joel 2:13]
4 [a][See ver. 1 above] [e][Rev. 8:7, 8]
5 [c][See ver. 2 above]
6 [d][See ver. 3 above]
7 [a][See ver. 1 above] [f][ver. 17]; See 2 Kin. 21:13
8 [g]ch. 8:2 [f][See ver. 7 above]
9 [h]Gen. 26:23, 25 [i]See 2 Kin. 15:8-12
10 [j]1 Kin. 12:32 [k]ch. 1:1 [l][Jer. 38:4]

6:14 a nation. Assyria.

Lebo-hamath . . . Brook of the Arabah. The northern and southern boundaries of the kingdom as restored by Jeroboam II (2 Kin. 14:25).

7:1–8:3 This long section contains four visions (7:1–3; 7:4–6; 7:7–9; 8:1–3) and an autobiographical section related to the third vision (7:10–17). The first two visions have the structure: (a) the Lord gives the vision; (b) Amos intercedes; (c) the Lord relents. Conversation between the Lord and His prophet is an integral part of the visionary experience.

7:1 locusts. This Hebrew word, occurring only here and in Nah. 3:17, denotes swarming locusts just hatched.

latter growth . . . king's mowings. This verse seems to indicate that the first crop (the "king's mowings") represented the king's share (cf. 5:11; 1 Kin. 12:4), while the farmer and his family depended on the second harvest for survival. Destruction of this second crop by locusts placed the population at risk of starvation.

7:2 eating the grass of the land. The Hebrew word for "grass" is general; all vegetation was destroyed, not just crops. In Hebrew, the whole phrase echoes the description of the locust plague in Ex. 10:12, 15 ("every plant in the land"). The Lord would punish Israel just as He punished Egypt before the Exodus.

7:3 relented. Moved by intercessory appeal, the Lord is willing to change His mind, or relent, concerning an intended punishment (cf. Ex. 32:12, 14; Joel 2:13; Jon. 3:10; Jer. 18:8). See note Gen. 6:6.

7:4 judgment by fire. See note 1:4; Is. 66:15–16.

great deep . . . land. The "great deep" could be the Mediterranean Sea, although the same phrase is also used of the chaotic subterranean waters (Gen. 7:11 note), and of the Red Sea at Israel's crossing (Is. 51:10). The prospect of a fire that will devour sea and land echoes the covenant judgment warning in Deut. 32:22. The language exceeds what happened in the Old Testament, but foreshadows the Last Judgment (cf. 2 Pet. 3:10; Rev. 21:1), of which all previous judgments are but types.

7:7 he showed me. This and the fourth vision (8:1–3) have the same structure: (a) the Lord gives the vision; (b) the Lord questions Amos; (c) Amos replies; (d) the Lord explains and judges. Similarly structured visionary experiences are recorded at Jer. 1:11, 12, 13–16.

a wall built with a plumb line. Most interpret this image to portray Israel being judged to see if they measured up to God's standard. Others, following another analysis of the words (the word translated "plumb" resembles the Accadian word for "tin"), render this "a wall of tin." The same "wall" symbolism in Egyptian literature stands for military capability (cf. "wall of bronze," Jer. 15:20; and "iron wall," Ezek. 4:3). The use of an Accadian (Assyrian) word for the metal indicates the source of the military power that the Lord will use to judge Israel.

with a plumb line in his hand. See note above. Many interpret this phrase as a reference to God's covenant law, His standard of judgment. Others render this phrase "with tin in his hand," a probable reference to Assyrian power, anticipating that He will put "tin" (i.e., Assyrian power) in the midst of His people (v. 8).

7:8 never again pass by them. No longer will the Lord pass over their transgressions (Mic. 7:18).

7:9 high places . . . sanctuaries. These high places were traditional sites of Canaanite idolatrous worship (Deut. 12:2; 2 Kin. 17:10–12). The sanctuaries were for idolatrous or syncretistic worship.

house of Jeroboam . . . sword. Jeroboam himself might not die by the sword, but his household or family would be affected. Although Jeroboam apparently died a natural death (2 Kin. 14:29), his son Zechariah was murdered (2 Kin. 15:10).

7:10–17 This autobiographical section apparently relates to the third vision, telling the reaction of Amaziah to the prophecies of Amos.

7:10 the priest of Bethel. Amaziah was probably the chief priest at the shrine of Bethel.

Amos has conspired. The political implications of the prophet's preaching are apparent. Jeremiah too was wrongly considered a traitor because of his prophecies against Judah (Jer. 26:11; 37:11–13; 38:1–6).

bear all his words. 11 For thus Amos has said,

"'Jeroboam shall die by the sword,
and [m] Israel must go into exile
away from his land.'"

12 And Amaziah said to Amos, [n] "O seer, go, flee away [o] to the land of Judah, and [p] eat bread there, and prophesy there, 13 but [q] never again prophesy at Bethel, for [r] it is the king's sanctuary, and it is a temple of the kingdom."

14 Then Amos answered and said to Amaziah, [s] "I was[1] no prophet, nor a prophet's son, but [t] I was a herdsman and a dresser of sycamore figs. 15 [u] But the LORD took me from following the flock, and the LORD said to me, 'Go, prophesy to my people Israel.' 16 [v] Now therefore hear the word of the LORD.

"You say, [n] 'Do not prophesy against
Israel,
and [w] do not preach against the
house of [x] Isaac.'

17 [y] Therefore thus says the LORD:

"'Your wife shall be a prostitute in the
city,
and your sons and your daughters
shall fall by the sword,
and your land [z] shall be divided up
with a measuring line;
you yourself shall die in an unclean
land,
and [m] Israel shall surely go into
exile away from its land.'"

The Coming Day of Bitter Mourning

8 [a] This is what the Lord GOD showed me: behold, a basket of summer fruit. 2 And he said, [b] "Amos, what do you see?" And I said, [c] "A basket of summer fruit." Then the LORD said to me,

[d] "The end[2] has come upon my people
Israel;
[b] I will never again pass by them.
3 [e] The songs of the temple[3] [f] shall
become wailings[4] in that day,"
declares the Lord GOD.
[g] "So many dead bodies!"
"They are thrown everywhere!"
[h] "Silence!"

4 Hear this, [i] you who trample on the
needy

11 [m] ch. 6:7
12 [n] See 1 Sam. 9:9
[o] [ch. 1:1]
[p] [Mic. 3:5, 11]
13 [q] See ch. 2:12 [r] See 1 Kin. 12:29–13:1
14 [s] ch. 1:1; [Zech. 13:5]
[t] ch. 1:1
15 [u] [Ps. 78:71]
16 [v] ch. 3:1
[n] [See ver. 12 above]
[w] Ezek. 20:46; 21:2; Mic. 2:6
[x] [ver. 9]
17 [y] [Jer. 28:16; 29:21, 31, 32]
[z] [ver. 7, 8]
[m] [See ver. 11 above]
Chapter 8
1 [a] ch. 7:1
2 [b] ch. 7:8
[c] [Jer. 24:1; Mic. 7:1]
[d] Lam. 4:18
[b] [See ver. 2 above]
3 [e] [ch. 5:23]
[f] [Jer. 47:2]
[g] [ch. 6:9]
[h] [ch. 6:10; Jer. 16:4, 6]
4 [i] [Ps. 14:4]

1 Or *am*; twice in this verse 2 The Hebrew words for *end* and *summer fruit* sound alike 3 Or *palace* 4 Or *The singing women of the palace shall wail*

7:11 Jeroboam shall die by the sword. Probably an allusion to the prophecy in v. 9. Amaziah misquotes Amos so as to make Jeroboam feel more personally threatened.

7:12 eat bread there . . . prophesy. Probably this means "earn your living by prophesying there in Judah." Although it was appropriate for a prophet to be paid for his work (1 Sam. 9:6–8; but cf. Mic. 3:5, 11), Amaziah accuses Amos of being merely a prophet for hire. Amaziah's commands here are an example of the sin of commanding the prophets not to prophesy (2:12).

7:13 king's sanctuary . . . temple of the kingdom. From the time when Jeroboam I established idolatry at Bethel (3:14 note) the kings of Israel had a major influence on the cult. Amaziah is concerned for the sanctuary of his earthly king, rather than for the sanctuary of the great King, the Lord. Ironically, Amaziah is the religious official concerned to protect earthly interests—the very charge which he brought against Amos (v. 12). A future generation of priests would likewise put to death Jesus, the greatest of the prophets, out of a wrong concern to protect their own kingdom and temple (John 11:48).

7:14 no prophet . . . prophet's son. Amos was not originally a prophet, nor one of the so-called "sons of the prophets" (i.e., disciples of the prophets; 1 Kin. 20:35; 2 Kin. 2:3, 5, 7, 15). He was not a paid professional prophet.

herdsman. See note 1:1.

dresser of sycamore figs. One who treated the fruit by appropriate cutting to ensure superior sweetness once the fruit was ripe. Amos was skilled in more than one trade (1:1 note).

7:15 the LORD took me . . . my people Israel. Amos flatly rejects Amaziah's accusation (7:12) and stresses his divine call to prophesy. The same phrasing is used for the Lord's choice of David as king (2 Sam. 7:8). The prophet's allusion to David's call indicates that the Lord has the sovereign right to choose both kings and prophets—and that His prophets have every right to prophesy at the "temple of the kingdom" (v. 13).

7:16 Do not prophesy. See 2:12 and note; 7:12, 13.

7:17 wife shall be a prostitute. Either by being ravished at the fall of the city, or out of desperation after the loss of family and wealth (cf. Deut. 28:30).

your sons and your daughters. Sons and daughters were often punished along with parents for covenant transgressions (Deut. 28:32, 53; Jer. 5:17; Ezek. 24:21); violent death was a typical covenant punishment (Is. 3:25; Jer. 39:18).

die in a unclean land. Exile would be especially distasteful for the priest Amaziah: by living in a pagan land he would become ritually unclean. See note Lev. 11–16.

Israel . . . land. Amos sarcastically quotes Amaziah's own words from v. 11 back at him.

8:2 summer fruit. The Hebrew words for "summer fruit" and "end" are similar, and are skillfully brought together here for effect. The vision of summer fruit indicates that the "end has come" for Israel.

never again pass by them. See note 7:8.

8:3 songs . . . wailings. The Lord would no longer tolerate the noise of the temple songs (5:23), which would turn to the wailing of bereavement when the Lord came in judgment.

that day. See note 5:18.

many dead bodies. An abundance of corpses was typical in defeated cities in the ancient Near East, especially when conquered by the Assyrians (Nah. 3:3).

8:4–14 God charges Israel with social injustice, commercial dishonesty, and indifference to holy days.

and bring the poor of the land to
an end,
5 saying, "When will [j] the new moon
be over,
that we may sell grain?
And [k] the Sabbath,
that we may offer wheat for sale,
that we may make [l] the ephah small
and the shekel[1] great
and deal deceitfully with false
balances,
6 that we may buy the poor for [m] silver
and the needy for a pair of sandals
and sell the chaff of the wheat?"
7 The LORD has sworn by [n] the pride of
Jacob:
"Surely [o] I will never forget any of their
deeds.
8 [p] Shall not the land tremble on this
account,
and everyone mourn who dwells
in it,
[q] and all of it rise like the Nile,
and be tossed about [r] and sink
again, like the Nile of Egypt?"
9 "And on that day," declares the Lord
GOD,
[s] "I will make the sun go down at
noon
and darken the earth in broad
daylight.
10 [t] I will turn your feasts into mourning
and all your songs into
lamentation;
[u] I will bring sackcloth on every waist
[u] and baldness on every head;
[v] I will make it like the mourning for
an only son
and the end of it like a bitter day.
11 "Behold, the days are coming,"
declares the Lord GOD,
"when [w] I will send a famine on the
land—
not a famine of bread, nor a thirst for
water,
[x] but of hearing the words of the
LORD.
12 [x] They shall wander from sea to sea,
and from north to east;
they shall run to and fro, to seek the
word of the LORD,
[y] but they shall not find it.
13 [z] "In that day the lovely virgins and the
young men
shall [a] faint for thirst.
14 Those who swear by [b] the Guilt of
Samaria,
and say, 'As your god lives, O Dan,'
and, 'As [c] the Way of [d] Beersheba lives,'
they shall fall, and never rise
again."

5 [j] See Num. 28:11 [k] [Neh. 13:15, 16] [l] Ezek. 45:10; Mic. 6:10, 11; See Hos. 12:7
6 [m] ch. 2:6
7 [n] ch. 6:8 [o] Hos. 8:13; 9:9
8 [p] [Hos. 4:3] [q] ch. 9:5 [r] [Zech. 10:11]
9 [s] Jer. 15:9; Mic. 3:6; Matt. 24:29; [ch. 4:13; 5:8]
10 [t] [Jer. 7:34; 16:9; Hos. 2:11] [u] Isai. 3:24 [v] Jer. 6:26; Zech. 12:10
11 [w] [Isai. 8:20, 21] [x] [Ps. 74:9; Prov. 29:18; Mic. 3:7]
12 [x] [See ver. 11 above] [y] [ch. 4:8]
13 [z] Isai. 51:20 [a] [Jonah 4:8]
14 [b] Deut. 9:21; 1 Kin. 12:29, 30; Hos. 10:8 [c] [Acts 9:2] [d] ch. 5:5

1 An *ephah* was about 3/5 bushel or 22 liters; a *shekel* was about 2/5 ounce or 11 grams

8:5 new moon . . . Sabbath. The New Moon festival was celebrated every fourth week, with various offerings (Num. 28:11–15). The Sabbath, observed every week, was founded on God's acts of creation (Ex. 20:8–11) and redemption (Deut. 5:12 note). Work was forbidden on these days.

ephah small . . . balances. Such dishonest business practices were against the Lord's law, and would result in His judgment (Lev. 19:36; Deut. 25:14).

8:6 silver . . . sandals. See notes 2:6.

chaff of the wheat. Lit. "the refuse of the wheat." The estate owners sold even the chaff, which fell to the floor when the wheat was threshed, mixing it with the wheat and cheating the buyer.

8:7 the pride of Jacob. See note 6:8. Here the phrase may refer to the Lord Himself, or to the land of Israel, which is elsewhere called "our heritage . . . the pride of Jacob" (Ps. 47:4).

8:8 tossed about and sink. Each year the Nile rose and overflowed its banks, flooding the countryside and leaving rich deposits of silt. The imagery is used here to depict a coming flood of judgment—the upheaval of the Assyrian invasion (cf. Is. 8:7, 8).

8:9 that day. See note 5:18.

I will make . . . darken. Though such idolatry was strictly prohibited by the covenant (Deut. 4:19), Judah and Israel engaged in star and sun worship (5:26 note; 2 Kin. 23:5, 11). The assertions here affirm that He alone is God, and the sun merely one of His creations (Gen. 1:16 and notes).

the earth. Or, "the land," since the land of Israel was to be punished. The phrase directly recalls the plague of darkness that the Lord brought upon the land of Egypt (cf. Ex. 10:21, 22; Ps. 105:28). Here again, the Lord is about to judge Israel with a judgment similar to that of Egypt.

8:10 sackcloth. This coarse material was worn as a sign of mourning to indicate that the pleasures of life no longer mattered to the mourner (Gen. 37:34; 2 Sam. 3:31).

baldness on every head. Shaving the head was a sign of mourning. It was prohibited in the covenant (Lev. 21:5; Deut. 14:1), perhaps because it was a pagan practice of bodily disfigurement that disgraced God's image (Is. 15:2, 3; Ezek. 27:30, 31). Ironically, it was prophesied for Israel and Judah (cf. Is. 3:24; Mic. 1:16).

bitter. A term describing the ultimate consequences of sin (2 Sam. 2:26; Prov. 5:4).

8:11 a famine . . . of hearing the words. This curse stems from the covenant law (Deut. 32:20; Hos. 3:4). So also in the period of the judges, when sin abounded (Judg. 21:25), "the word of the LORD was rare" (1 Sam. 3:1).

8:12 from sea to sea. A standard phrase in the ancient Near East denoting "the ends of the earth," this literally meant "from the Mediterranean to the Persian Gulf."

8:13 lovely virgins . . . young men. Even the young and robust will be at the end of their strength (cf. Is. 51:20).

thirst. The focus is on physical extremity (cf. 4:7, 8), though spiritual thirst may be in view as well (v. 11).

8:14 swear by the Guilt. To swear by a god in the ancient Near East implied the recognition and worship of that god. Israelites were commanded to swear only by the Lord (Deut. 6:13; 10:20; cf. Jer. 5:7; Zeph. 1:5).

The Destruction of Israel

9 I saw the LORD standing beside[1] the altar, and he said:

[e]"Strike the capitals until [e]the thresholds [f]shake,
[g]and shatter them on the heads of all the people;[2]
and those who are left of them I will kill with the sword;
[h]not one of them shall flee away;
not one of them shall escape.

2 [i]"If they dig into Sheol,
from there shall my hand take them;
[i]if they climb up to heaven,
from there I will bring them down.
3 If they hide themselves on [j]the top of Carmel,
from there I will search them out and take them;
[k]and if they hide from my sight at the bottom of the sea,
there I will command the serpent, and it shall bite them.
4 [l]And if they go into captivity before their enemies,
there I will command the sword, and it shall kill them;
[m]and I will fix my eyes upon them
for evil and not for good."

5 The Lord GOD of hosts,
he who touches the earth and [n]it melts,
and all who dwell in it mourn,
[o]and all of it rises like the Nile,
[o]and sinks again, like the Nile of Egypt;
6 [p]who builds his upper chambers in the heavens
and founds his vault upon the earth;
[q]who calls for the waters of the sea
and pours them out upon the surface of the earth—
[r]the LORD is his name.

7 "Are you not like [s]the Cushites to me,
O people of Israel?" declares the LORD.
[t]"Did I not bring up Israel from the land of Egypt,
and [u]the Philistines from [v]Caphtor
and the Syrians from [w]Kir?
8 Behold, [x]the eyes of the Lord GOD
are upon the sinful kingdom,
and I will destroy it from the surface of the ground,
[y]except that I will not utterly destroy the house of Jacob,"
declares the LORD.

9 "For behold, I will command,
[z]and shake the house of Israel
among all the nations
as one shakes with a sieve,
but no pebble shall fall to the earth.

Chapter 9
1 [e]Zeph. 2:14 [f][Isai. 6:4] [g]See Judg. 16:26-30 [h][ch. 2:14]
2 [i][Ps. 139:8-10]
3 [j]ch. 1:2 [k][Job 26:5]
4 [l][Deut. 28:65] [m]See Jer. 21:10
5 [n]Ps. 46:6 [o]ch. 8:8
6 [p][Ps. 104:3, 5] [q]See ch. 5:8 [r]See ch. 14:13
7 [s][Zeph. 3:10] [t]Ex. 20:2 [u]Jer. 47:4 [v]Gen. 10:14 [w]ch. 1:5
8 [x][ver. 4] [y]Jer. 30:11; [Obad. 17]
9 [z][Jer. 15:7; Matt. 3:12; Luke 3:17]

1 Or *on* 2 Hebrew *all of them*

9:1–6 In the other four visions, Amos was an intercessor or respondent to the Lord's questions (7:1–8:3 note; 7:7 note). In this vision, however, Amos has no active role, but simply records what he sees.

9:1 Strike the capitals. That is, of the pillars. The command seems to be for an angel (cf. 2 Sam. 24:16; 2 Kin. 19:35) to destroy the temple, bringing it down on the heads of those within (cf. Judg. 16:29, 30).

9:2 Sheol . . . heaven. This pair poetically expresses the comprehensiveness of God's dominion (Ps. 139:7–12; Is. 7:11).

9:3 Carmel. See 1:2 and note.

bottom of the sea. In contrast with the height of Mount Carmel. Since Carmel was on the coast of Israel, further flight would lead one into the sea.

serpent. This sea monster is perhaps the Leviathan of Is. 27:1. The Lord's sovereignty over all creation is poetically asserted; none can escape His justice.

9:4 captivity. One of the covenant curses for disobedience (Deut. 28:41).

9:5, 6 This section constitutes a short divine title (4:13 note), identifying the Lord as Judge.

9:5 touches . . . melts. For similar expressions of the Lord's awesome power, see Ps. 46:6; 104:32; Nah. 1:5.

rises . . . sinks. See note 8:8.

9:6 upper chambers. This can be rendered "palace" or "temple" (cf. Rev. 11:19). The Hebrew word means "steps" or "stairs," such as those used to enter the temple, particularly the temple of the end time (Ezek. 40:6, 22, 26, 31, 34).

vault. Here it perhaps means the arch or vault of heaven (Ex. 24:10 note).

the LORD is his name. An exact repetition of the phrase in 5:8.

9:7 like the Cushites. Lit. "like the sons of the Ethiopians," the dark-skinned tribes south of Egypt (Gen. 10:6). Sinful Israel has rejected the covenant and is no more privileged than the Ethiopians.

Egypt . . . Caphtor . . . Kir. By making Israel's Exodus from Egypt poetically parallel (and hence implicitly equal) to His dealings with other nations, God tells Israel that she has become no better than the pagans.

Caphtor. Crete.

Syrians from Kir. See note 1:5.

9:8 sinful kingdom. Israel.

not utterly destroy. A graciously chosen remnant will survive.

9:9 shake . . . among all the nations. The Lord would scatter His people among the nations, first by means of Assyria, which often resettled conquered peoples in different parts of its empire.

as one shakes. Figuratively separating the wheat (the faithful) from the chaff (the sinners), the experience of exile will serve to purify the nation of Israel (v. 10).

10 All the sinners of my people shall die
by the sword,
who say, [a]'Disaster shall not
overtake or meet us.'

The Restoration of Israel

11 "In that day [b]I will raise up
the booth of David that is fallen
and repair its breaches,
and raise up its ruins
and rebuild it as in the days of old,
12 [c]that they may possess the remnant of
Edom
and all the nations who are called
by my name,"[1]
declares the LORD who does this.

13 "Behold, the days are coming,"
declares the LORD,
[d]"when the plowman shall overtake
the reaper
and the treader of grapes him who
sows the seed;
[e]the mountains shall drip sweet
wine,
and all the hills shall flow with it.
14 [f]I will restore the fortunes of my
people Israel,
and [g]they shall rebuild the ruined
cities and inhabit them;
[h]they shall plant vineyards and drink
their wine,
[i]and they shall make gardens and
eat their fruit.
15 [j]I will plant them on their land,
[k]and they shall never again be
uprooted
out of the land [l]that I have given
them,"
says the LORD your God.

10 [a][ch. 6:3] 11 [b]Cited Acts 15:16 12 [c][Obad. 19] 13 [d]Cited Acts 15:17, 18 [e]Lev. 26:5 14 [f]Joel 3:18 [g]Jer. 30:3 [h]Isai. 61:4 [i]Jer. 31:5 15 [j]Jer. 24:6; Ezek. 34:29 [k][Joel 3:20] [l][Jer. 3:18]

1 Hebrew; Septuagint (compare Acts 15:17) *that the remnant of mankind and all the nations who are called by my name may seek the Lord*

9:10 Disaster shall not overtake. Denial of judgment, like denial of guilt, is characteristic of sin.

9:11–15 Amos concludes with an oracle of promised restoration ordered as follows: (a) reconstruction (v. 11); (b) conquest (v. 12); (c) fruitful abundance (v. 13); (d) rebuilding and replanting (v. 14); (e) enduring security (9:15). Amos assures his readers that once the judgment of exile is past, restoration is as certain as was dispersion.

9:11 In that day. The day of the Lord is here depicted as the time of Israel's deliverance (Zeph. 1:7 note).

booth. The "booth" represents the dynasty of David which, to the eyes of the prophet, was as good as fallen. But the tabernacle of David will be rebuilt. In Jesus, the greater Son of David, the dynasty of David has been reestablished (Acts 15:16, 17).

9:12 Edom. Though subject to divine judgment (1:11, 12), a remnant of Edom will be brought under the redemptive kingship of David's Son. Edom, indeed all the nations, will benefit from coming under the dominion of this future King (Ps. 2:8). In Acts 15:16, 17, James applies this passage to God's taking a people for Himself from among the Gentiles and including them in the church.

and all the nations. The addition of this phrase suggests that "the remnant of Edom" represents the redeemed from all nations.

who are called by my name. This phrase tells us that some, not all, from every Gentile group will come under the dominion of David's Son. Only those who bear God's name among all the nations will be included. The phrase (lit. "upon whom My name is called") indicates subordination to the Name and sometimes is used of Israel's subordination to God's covenant lordship (Deut. 28:10; Jer. 14:9). Amos foresees that the Lord will take possession of the remnant of all nations and will reign over them in a covenantal relationship through His messianic King (Acts 15:13–17).

9:13 A prediction of abundance, indeed more than abundance, follows the prophecies of disaster and desolation. The culmination of the Lord's redemptive work through David's Son is portrayed in terms of endless cycles of fruitfulness, reminiscent of Eden but surpassing it (cf. Joel 3:18).

9:14 restore the fortunes. Lit. "turn the captivity of my people," a recurring phrase in the prophetic covenant lawsuits (Jer. 29:14; Ezek. 16:53; Hos. 6:11).

rebuild . . . inhabit . . . plant . . . drink. These blessings reverse the earlier futility curses (5:11 and note).

9:15 I will plant them. The Lord promises lasting safety for His people. God's covenant with David had promised an eternal kingship (v. 11; 2 Sam. 7:10). David's greater Son, Jesus Christ, will guarantee redeemed Israel's permanent blessedness.

the land that I have given them. See note Gen. 13:15. The phrasing harks back to God's covenant with Abraham and his descendants (Gen. 12:1, 7; 13:14–17; 15:18; 17:8). The physical Promised Land is but a type of the New Israel's life in Christ; it points forward to the heavenly Jerusalem (Heb. 11:13–16; 12:22–24). The covenant land promise finds final fulfillment in the new heavens and the new earth (Rev. 21:1–22:6).

THE BOOK OF

Obadiah

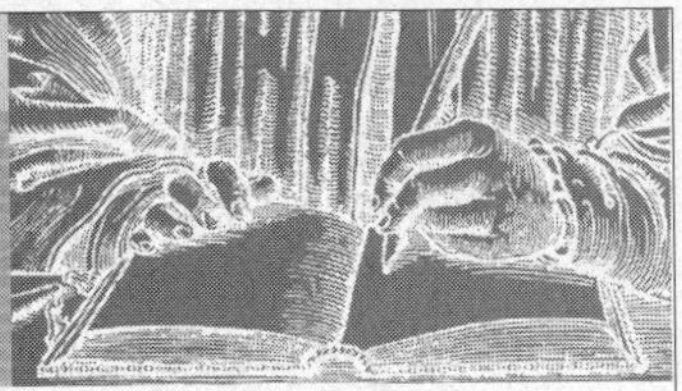

AUTHOR

We know little of the prophet other than his name, which means "servant of the LORD." The name itself is not unusual in the Old Testament. The value and authority of the message rests on the foundation that "the LORD has spoken" (v. 18), and not on the fame or prominence of the messenger.

DATE AND OCCASION

Students of this prophecy have long debated the date of its composition. The prophet has in view a military assault on Jerusalem in which the Edomites gleefully took part (vv. 11–14), but he does not provide information that clearly dates the catastrophe. Some date the book in relation to an invasion of Judah by Philistines and Arabs during King Jehoram's reign (848–841 B.C.), in which it is presumed that the Edomites participated (2 Kin. 8:20–22; 2 Chr. 21:8–10, 16, 17).

Others relate the events prompting this prophecy to the invasions of Judah by the Babylonians, which resulted eventually in her collapse in 586 B.C. Both Scripture (Ps. 137; Ezek. 35:1–15) and Jewish tradition explicitly mention the Edomites' involvement in this final catastrophe, and the text of Obadiah seems to refer more naturally to this event.

Although the striking similarities between vv. 1–9 of this prophecy and Jer. 49:7–22 must be more than an impressive coincidence, they do not resolve the problem of dating Obadiah. We know that Jeremiah prophesied from about 626 B.C. until after 586; but whether one prophet quotes the other, or whether both prophets used an earlier source, is uncertain.

CHARACTERISTICS AND THEMES

The prophecy is "concerning Edom" (v. 1) and is repeatedly addressed to that nation, but it was given to the covenant community as holy Scripture. The purpose, therefore, more than to warn Edom of imminent judgment, is to reassure God's people of His triumphant justice at work for them. Edom prospered, Judah lay defeated, and the moral order of the world appeared to have been overthrown by lawless forces. But the prophet Obadiah was raised up with a message of God's sovereign justice in order to strengthen His people's weakened faith. It is the righteous purpose of God, not the evil will of men, that determines history.

When the church suffers at the hands of God's enemies, she needs to return to the prophecy of Obadiah and renew her faith in the just God revealed there. He cares for His persecuted people, and behind their present circumstances He is always at work for them.

OUTLINE OF OBADIAH

I. God's Declaration of War on Edom (vv. 1–14)

A. *Superscription; Call to the Nations (v. 1)*

B. *God's Resolve to Humiliate Proud Edom (vv. 2–4)*

C. *God's Resolve to Loot Prosperous Edom (vv. 5–7)*

D. *Edom's Vulnerability to God's Judgment (vv. 8, 9)*

E. *Edom's Cruel Indifference to Judah's Trouble (vv. 10–14)*

II. God's Promise of a New Moral Order (vv. 15–21)

A. *Vengeance Against the Nations and Edom (vv. 15, 16)*

B. *Deliverance for Jerusalem (vv. 17, 18)*

C. *Land Possessed by the Lord's People (vv. 19–21)*

1 The vision of Obadiah.

Edom Will Be Humbled

Thus says the Lord GOD [a]concerning Edom:
[b]We have heard a report from the LORD,
and a messenger has been sent among the nations:
"Rise up! Let us rise against her for battle!"
2 Behold, I will make you small among the nations;
you shall be utterly despised.[1]
3 [c]The pride of your heart has deceived you,
you who live in the clefts of the rock,[2]
in your lofty dwelling,
[d]who say in your heart,
"Who will bring me down to the ground?"
4 Though you soar aloft like the eagle,
though your nest is set among the stars,
from there I will bring you down,
declares the LORD.
5 If [e]thieves came to you,
if plunderers came by night—
how you have been destroyed!—
would they not steal only enough for themselves?
If [e]grape gatherers came to you,
would they not leave gleanings?
6 [f]How Esau has been pillaged,
his treasures sought out!
7 All your allies have driven you to your border;
those at peace with you have deceived you;
they have prevailed against you;
[g]those who eat your bread[3] have set a trap beneath you—
[h]you have[4] no understanding.
8 [i]Will I not on that day, declares the LORD,
destroy the wise men out of Edom,
and understanding out of [j]Mount Esau?
9 And your mighty men shall be dismayed, [k]O Teman,
so that every man from [j]Mount Esau
will be cut off by slaughter.

Edom's Violence Against Jacob

10 [l]Because of the violence done to your brother Jacob,
shame shall cover you,
[m]and you shall be cut off forever.
11 [n]On the day that you stood aloof,
[o]on the day that strangers carried off his wealth

1 [a]See Jer. 49:7-22; Ezek. 25:12-14 [b]For ver. 1-4, see Jer. 49:14-16
3 [c][Num. 24:21, 22] [d][Isai. 14:13-15]
5 [e]Jer. 49:9
6 [f][Jer. 49:10]
7 [g][Ps. 41:9] [h][Jer. 49:7]
8 [i][Isai. 29:14] [j][Ezek. 35:2]
9 [k]Amos 1:12; See 1 Chr. 1:45 [j][See ver. 8 above]
10 [l]Num. 20:20, 21 [m][Ezek. 35:9]
11 [n]Ps. 137:7; [Jer. 12:14] [o]See 2 Kin. 25:10-20

[1] Or *Behold, I have made you small among the nations; you are utterly despised* [2] Or *Sela* [3] Hebrew lacks *those who eat* [4] Hebrew *he has*

1 vision. A supernatural revelation to the prophet's inner sight or hearing. Obadiah introduces the message he received from the Lord about Edom.

Thus says the Lord GOD. God revealed the content of the prophecy (cf. 2 Pet. 1:21). This raises the moral quality of its severity above human vengefulness to the purity of divine justice.

Edom. The bitterness between Edom and Israel began in the patriarchal period. God blessed Isaac and Rebekah with twin sons, Esau and Jacob (Gen. 25:21–26; cf. Mal. 1:2, 3; Rom. 9:10–13). The personal rivalry between Jacob and Esau (Gen. 27), from whom the nations of Israel and Edom descended, developed into longstanding national conflict (Ex. 15:13–15; Num. 20:14–21; 1 Sam. 14:47; 2 Sam. 8:13, 14; 1 Kin. 11:14, 15; 2 Kin. 8:20–22; 14:7). Edom also symbolically represents the enemies of God's people (Is. 63:1–6).

Let us rise against her. Speaking for his people, the prophet sees divine significance in the news of a conspiracy against Edom. Behind the human plot the Sovereign Lord is at work. That such news reached Obadiah's ears in connection with this vision was no coincidence; it was a token of the prophecy's fulfillment.

2–14 God declares war on Edom, resolving to humiliate (vv. 2–4) and loot (vv. 5–7) that nation. No wise statesman or brave warrior in Edom will withstand the divine assault (vv. 8–10). Edom, which had been cruelly indifferent to Judah's woes (vv. 11–14), will fall.

3 clefts of the rock. The Hebrew word for "rock" (*sela'*) was also the name of a fortress city in the rocky heights of Edom. The rugged mountain terrain of Edom deterred invasion from without and encouraged complacency within.

3, 4 Edom's arrogant question ("Who will bring me down?") is answered with God's solemn resolve ("I will bring you down").

4 like the eagle . . . among the stars. A hyperbolic depiction of the Edomites' false sense of security. Despite Edom's apparent safety, no one can rise above God. Though Edom seemed invincible, God called Israel to realize that no earthly power can evade His sovereign justice.

7 The conspiring nations of v. 1 turn out to be Edom's own allies. It is a matter of justice that Edom should be betrayed by friends, having stabbed his "brother Jacob" (v. 10) in the back.

8–10 Though wise and mighty, Edom will be no match for the Lord.

9 Teman. The personal name of a descendant of Esau (Gen. 36:11), which was also used for the Edomite nation.

11, 12 Edom is doomed because they broke the law of brotherly compassion by joining, in malicious merriment, with God's enemies as they destroyed Judah. The interplay between "your brother" in v. 10 and the invading "strangers" and "foreigners" here is powerful. The exploitation of a brother's adversity showed that Edom's true loyalty was toward getting ahead in the world, in disregard of moral and spiritual absolutes. The seeds of Edom's moral character were sown by their ancestor Esau, who showed that he cared more for earthly enjoyment than for God's kingdom by despising his birthright of covenant blessings and marrying Hittite wives (Gen. 25:29–34; 26:34, 35; cf. 27:46–28:1). Translated into New Testament terms, Edom embodies the spirit of "the world" (1 John 2:15–17).

and foreigners entered his gates
[p] and cast lots for Jerusalem,
you were like one of them.
12 [q] But do not gloat over the day of your brother
in the day of his misfortune;
[r] do not rejoice over the people of Judah
in the day of their ruin;
[s] do not boast[1]
in the day of distress.
13 [t] Do not enter the gate of my people
in the day of their calamity;
[t] do not gloat over his disaster
in the day of his calamity;
[u] do not loot his wealth
in the day of his calamity.
14 [v] Do not stand at the crossroads
to cut off his fugitives;
do not hand over his survivors
in the day of distress.

The Day of the LORD Is Near

15 For [w] the day of the LORD is near
upon all the nations.
[x] As you have done, it shall be done to you;
your deeds shall return on your own head.
16 [y] For as you have drunk on [z] my holy mountain,
so all the nations shall drink continually;
they shall drink and swallow,
and shall be as though they had never been.
17 [a] But in Mount Zion there shall be those who escape,
and it shall be holy,
[b] and the house of Jacob shall possess
their own possessions.
18 [c] The house of Jacob shall be a fire,
and the house of Joseph a flame,
and the house of Esau [d] stubble;
they shall burn them and consume them,
[e] and there shall be no survivor for the house of Esau,
for the LORD has spoken.

The Kingdom of the LORD

19 Those of [f] the Negeb [b] shall possess [g] Mount Esau,
and those of the Shephelah shall possess [h] the land of the Philistines;
they shall possess the land of Ephraim and the land of Samaria,
and Benjamin shall possess Gilead.
20 The exiles of this host of the people of Israel
shall possess the land of the Canaanites as far as [j] Zarephath,
and the exiles of Jerusalem who are in Sepharad
shall possess the cities of the Negeb.
21 [k] Saviors shall go up to Mount Zion
to rule [g] Mount Esau,
and [l] the kingdom shall be the LORD's.

11 [p] Joel 3:3 12 [q] [Ps. 22:17] [r] [Mic. 4:11; 7:8] [s] [1 Sam. 2:3] 13 [t] [Prov. 17:5] [u] [Ezek. 35:10] 14 [v] [Ezek. 21:21] 15 [w] See Joel 1:15 [x] Jer. 50:29; Ezek. 35:15; Hab. 2:8 16 [y] See Jer. 25:27, 28 [z] See Joel 3:17 17 [a] [Amos 9:8]; See Joel 2:32 [b] [Amos 9:12] 18 [c] Zech. 12:6; [Isai. 10:17; Jer. 5:14] [d] See Joel 2:5 [e] Ezek. 25:14 19 [f] [Josh. 10:40; Judg. 1:9] [b] [See ver. 17 above] [g] ver. 8 [h] Jer. 17:26 [i] See Jer. 23:13 20 [j] 1 Kin. 17:9; [Luke 4:26] 21 [k] [2 Kin. 13:5; Isai. 19:20; 1 Tim. 4:16; James 5:20] [g] [See ver. 19 above] [l] Ps. 22:28; Dan. 2:44; 7:14, 27; Zech. 14:9; Luke 1:33; 1 Cor. 15:24; Rev. 11:15; 19:6

1 Hebrew *do not enlarge your mouth*

15–18 The day of divine retribution will destroy all God's enemies and vindicate His people, through whom He will execute judgment.

15 day of the LORD is near upon all the nations. For the day of the Lord, see Is. 2:11, 12. Now the prophet sets the judgment of Edom against the larger backdrop of God's moral reckoning with all nations. This episode with Edom is only a small preview of God's judgment; He will not stop until He has cleansed His world of all His enemies. The connection between Edom and the rest of the nations is their shared rebellion against God.

16 The Edomites' drunken revelry on the sacred temple mount in Jerusalem is answered in kind with the cup of God's wrath forced to the lips of Edom and all the nations that have desecrated the things of God.

17 it shall be holy. No longer the victim of pillaging armies, Mount Zion will again be holy, pure, cleansed for God.

18 no survivor. Those survivors (v. 14) of Judah will rise up like a blazing fire of divine wrath to consume Edom, leaving her not a single survivor. Although powerful in Obadiah's day, from God's perspective Edom is as good as dead.

the LORD has spoken. Like a signature, this clause emphasizes the finality of God's intentions. He has committed Himself.

19, 20 God's exiled people will return to occupy the land of their inheritance, the boundaries of which will be restored and expanded.

19 God promises His people that the boundaries of the Davidic kingdom will be restored in the south (Mount Esau), the west ("the land of the Philistines"), the north ("the land of Ephraim and . . . of Samaria"), and the east ("Gilead").

20 The boundaries of the Davidic kingdom will not only be restored (v. 19), but also extend to reach northward to Zarephath, between Tyre and Sidon.

Sepharad. The location is uncertain. Proposals include Sardis in Asia Minor, Spain, and Media. God prompts His exiled people to believe that no earthly deportation can remove them beyond the reach of His love.

21 Saviors. God's people, transformed from fugitives (v. 14) into deliverers (text note), will reign over what was once enemy-held territory.

the kingdom shall be the LORD's. While all created reality is the Lord's right now (Ps. 47:2; 145:13), Obadiah is making a different point here—that the kingdom will be the Lord's in that He will judge His enemies and deliver His people with finality. God will be all in all, and His glorious, triumphant people will reign forever with Him. In this promise, Judah found hope for a future without Edomite persecution; here too the church finds hope for the future, when "the kingdom of the world has become the kingdom of our Lord and of his Christ" (Rev. 11:15).

THE BOOK OF

Jonah

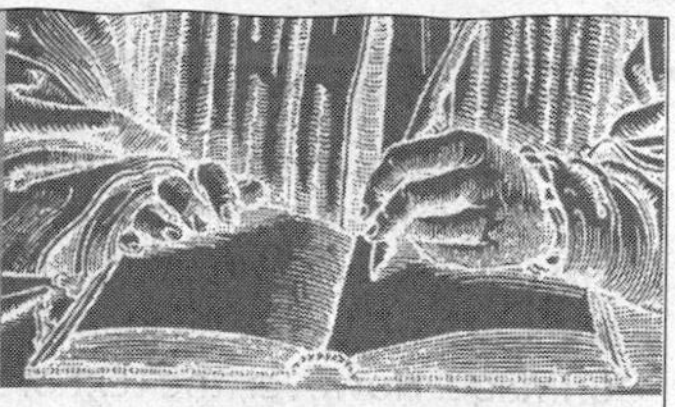

AUTHOR

This fifth book of the twelve Minor Prophets takes its name from its principal character, "Jonah the son of Amittai" (1:1). Of Amittai, nothing is known. Outside of this composition Jonah is mentioned only in 2 Kin. 14:25, as "Jonah the son of Amittai, the prophet, who was from Gath-hepher," the proclaimer of God's blessing to the northern kingdom of Israel during the reign of Jeroboam II (793–753 B.C.). In accordance with that prophecy, Jeroboam extended the borders of his kingdom beyond the frontier of Syria. The divine message to Nineveh found in this book was spoken through this same Jonah, although the author of the written narrative is unknown.

DATE AND OCCASION

Based on 2 Kin. 14:25, the events recorded in the Book of Jonah should be assigned to the eighth century B.C. Determining the chronology of the book's composition is a difficult task, however, and the book has been dated between the eighth and late third centuries B.C. It should be noted that there is no compelling evidence precluding an eighth-century date for the composition of the narrative (3:3 note).

The reign of Jeroboam II provides the setting for the Jonah story. This monarch was one of the strong military leaders of Israel's history. According to 2 Kin. 14:25–28, he imposed his authority on the territories of Damascus and Hamath, thereby restoring Israel's northern frontier to where it had been in the days of Solomon (1 Kin. 8:65). It is clear that Jeroboam's reign, together with that of his Judean contemporary Azariah (also called Uzziah, 792–740 B.C.), ushered in a period of remarkable peace and prosperity. As both Elisha and Jonah had prophesied (2 Kin. 13:19–25; 14:25), the northern kingdom enjoyed territorial expansion at the expense of Syria. By the outward appearances of population growth, territorial expansion, and commercial activity, Israel was indeed blessed by God.

However, this was not the picture that was painted a few years later by the prophets Hosea and Amos, when the kingdom fell into a state of social, moral, and religious decay. Their messages consisted, in part, of indictment and judgment of the nation for mixing the prescribed worship of the Lord with the idolatry of the surrounding peoples (religious syncretism) and for social injustice (Hos. 2:1–13; 4:1–5:14; Amos 2:6–16; 3:9–15).

Despite the narrative's focus on the prophet, the Book of Jonah is a story about the mercy and love of God. The Lord was the God of Israel, and that nation had been the special recipient of His covenant mercy and salvation. But Jonah, along with many of his countrymen, had responded with a national pride and ethnic particularism that blinded him to the grand scope of God's grace. Jonah was to learn, along with the nation, that Israel did not have a monopoly on the redemptive love of God (Acts 10:34, 35; Rom. 3:29). The story affirms the words of Ps. 145:8: "The LORD is gracious and merciful, slow to anger and abounding in steadfast love."

INTERPRETIVE DIFFICULTIES

Some scholars have challenged the literary unity of the book, suggesting theories of composite authorship or of substantial changes by a later editor. More recently, questions have been raised with regard to the authenticity of Jonah's thanksgiving psalm in 2:2–9. Such arguments for the literary disunity in the composition are not convincing.

As for the interpretation of the Jonah story proper, four distinct approaches have been suggested: allegory, midrash, parable, and historical narrative.

Allegory is a method of teaching truths or principles by means of symbolic fictional narrative. A good example is John Bunyan's *Pilgrim's Progress*, an exciting fictional story that conveys the truth that the Christian life is a spiritual pilgrimage. However, the text of Jonah lacks any compelling indication that would call for such an allegorical understanding.

Midrash is a type of commentary on Scripture classically carried on by Jewish scholars during the first thousand years of the Christian era. Jonah is treated by some as a type of early midrash, or commentary, on passages like Ex. 34:6, 7 (cf. Jon. 4:2), a commentary in which the events depicted are not necessarily historical. Such an approach fails to reckon with credible defenses of the book's historicity, and appears to conflict with Christ's witness regarding Jonah's experiences (Matt. 12:39–42; Luke 11:29–32).

The interpretation of the Book of Jonah as a parable is perhaps the most common. A parable is a brief and usually fictitious story that conveys moral, religious, or spiritual truths. Parables are best illustrated by the teachings of Jesus (e.g., Matt. 13:45, 46; Luke 10:29–37; 15:11–32). Nathan's parable in 2 Sam. 12:1–4 is a good Old Testament example. This view understands the Jonah narrative as a moral story with a teaching aim. There are a number of objections, however, to understanding the Book of Jonah as a parable, such as the unusual complexity and length of the story. This interpretation also deprives the book of its historical foundation.

In spite of its shocking surprises and sensational elements, Jonah should be understood as historical and prophetic narrative. The story centers on a specific figure and was written as a historical composition. Jewish tradition regarded the narrative as history, and Christ's allusions to the story (Matt. 12:38–41; Luke 11:29–32) lend further support to the historicity of the work. Jesus did not understand the Jonah story as a mere parable, but a narrative firmly rooted in historical reality.

Nevertheless, some scholars challenge the historical interpretation on several grounds, including the impossibility of the prophet's healthy survival inside the fish, the unlikelihood of the Ninevites' dramatic repentance, the size of Nineveh at the time, and the plant's fast rate of growth. Although some of these objections raise legitimate questions, most of the criticisms spring from assumptions that deny God's sovereignty in nature and history, including His ability to intervene supernaturally in the created order.

CHARACTERISTICS AND THEMES

In addition to teaching the ethnic universality of God's mercy and love, the theme of God's universal sovereignty over man and creation is maintained throughout the book. God is presented as Creator, the Maker of land and sea (1:9). Creation responds obediently to His every command (1:4, 15, 17; 2:10; 4:6–8). Like the Assyrians of Isaiah's day (Is. 10:5–7), creation serves the will of the Creator.

In the New Testament, Jonah's theme of God's mercy on the nations is used by Jesus as a rebuke to unrepentant Israel (Matt. 12:38–41; Luke 11:29–32). If the Ninevites repented at the preaching of the prophet Jonah, who was rescued from confinement in the huge fish, how much more should Israel repent at the preaching of Jesus, the Son of Man, who will be resurrected from the tomb. In a sense, then, Jesus magnifies God's mercy on the Gentiles in order to rouse Israel to envy and repentance; the apostle Paul would do the same by his preaching to the Gentiles (Rom. 11:11–14).

OUTLINE OF JONAH

I. Jonah Disobedient and Delivered (chs. 1; 2)

- *A. The Lord Commissions Jonah (1:1, 2)*
- *B. The Prophet Flees from the Lord (1:3)*
- *C. The Lord Pursues Jonah: The Great Storm (1:4–16)*
- *D. The Lord Preserves Jonah (1:17)*
- *E. Jonah's Thanksgiving and Deliverance (ch. 2)*

II. Jonah Obedient and Delivered (chs. 3; 4)

- *A. The Lord Commissions Jonah a Second Time (3:1, 2)*
- *B. The Prophet Responds in Obedience (3:3)*
- *C. Jonah Preaches; Nineveh Repents and Is Delivered (3:4–10)*
- *D. Jonah's Anger at God's Compassion (4:1–4)*
- *E. A Lesson in Divine Love (4:5–11)*

Jonah Flees the Presence of the Lord

1 Now the word of the LORD came to
[a]Jonah the son of Amittai, saying,
2 "Arise, go to [b]Nineveh, that [c]great city, and
call out against it, [d]for their evil[1] has come
up before me." 3 But Jonah [e]rose to flee to
[f]Tarshish from the presence of the LORD. He
went down to [g]Joppa and found a ship going
to [f]Tarshish. So he paid the fare and went on
board, to go with them to [f]Tarshish, [h]away
from the presence of the LORD.
4 But [i]the LORD hurled a great wind upon
the sea, and there was a mighty tempest on
the sea, so that the ship threatened[j] to break
up. 5 Then the mariners were afraid, and
[k]each cried out to his god. And [l]they hurled
the cargo that was in the ship into the sea to
lighten it for them. But Jonah had gone
down into the inner part of the ship and had
lain down and was fast asleep. 6 So the captain came and said to him, "What do you
mean, you sleeper? Arise, [k]call out to your
god! [m]Perhaps the god will give a thought to
us, that we may not perish."

Jonah Is Thrown into the Sea

7 And they said to one another, "Come,
let us [n]cast lots, that we may know on
whose account this evil has come upon
us." So they cast lots, and the lot fell on
Jonah. 8 Then they said to him, "Tell us on
whose account this evil has come upon us.
What is your occupation? And where do
you come from? What is your country? And
of what people are you?" 9 And he said to
them, "I am a Hebrew, and I fear [o]the
LORD, the God of heaven, [p]who made the
sea and the dry land." 10 Then the men
were exceedingly afraid and said to him,
"What is this that you have done!" For the
men knew that [h]he was fleeing from the
presence of the LORD, because he had told
them.
11 Then they said to him, "What shall we
do to you, that the sea may quiet down for
us?" For the sea grew more and more tempestuous. 12 He said to them, "Pick me up
and hurl me into the sea; then the sea
will quiet down for you, [q]for I know it
is because of me that this great tempest
has come upon you." 13 Nevertheless, the
men rowed hard[2] to get back to dry land,
but they could not, for the sea grew more
and more tempestuous against them.
14 Therefore they called out to the LORD,

Chapter 1
1 [a]2 Kin. 14:25
2 [b]Gen. 10:11, 12; 2 Kin. 19:36; Nah. 1:1; Zeph. 2:13; Matt. 12:41; Luke 11:30, 32 [c]ch. 3:3; 4:11 [d]Rev. 18:5
3 [e]ch. 4:2 [f]See 1 Kin. 10:22 [g]See Josh. 19:46 [h]Gen. 4:16; [Ps. 139:9, 10]
4 [i][Ps. 107:25] [j]1 Kin. 22:48; Ps. 48:7
5 [k][Ps. 107:28] [l][Acts 27:18, 19, 38]
6 [k][See ver. 5 above] [m][ch. 3:9]
7 [n][Judg. 20:9]
9 [o]Rev. 11:13 [p]Ps. 146:6
10 [h][See ver. 3 above]
12 [q][Josh. 7:20]

[1] The same Hebrew word can mean *evil* or *disaster*, depending on the context; so throughout Jonah [2] Hebrew *the men dug in* [their oars]

1:1–2:10 The book of the prophet Jonah falls into two main divisions, each introduced by the sentence, "Now the word of the LORD came to Jonah." The first division comprises two sections: the call, flight, and judgment of Jonah (ch. 1), and the thanksgiving psalm (ch. 2).

1:1–17 This passage depicts Jonah's disobedient response to the commission as a prophet to go to Nineveh, but does not tell us Jonah's reason for fleeing from God (which is not revealed until 4:2). Here we witness Jonah's interaction with the Gentile sailors, which involves a theme prominent in the book's second division—the Lord's mercy to Gentiles. Despite Jonah's disobedience and hypocrisy, the sailors do not despise Jonah's God, but see the clear hand of the God of Israel and respond in worship. In contrast with Jonah, the Gentile sailors are careful to avoid personal sin before God (v. 14). The prophet of God is judged, but the Gentiles are spared, an event that foreshadows the response and sparing of the Ninevites in the book's second division.

1:1 Now the word of the LORD came to Jonah. With some variations, wording like this is used some 112 times in the Old Testament to describe the giving of a divine message to a prophet.

Jonah the son of Amittai. The recipient of the Lord's revelation is Jonah ("dove"), the son of Amittai ("loyal" or "faithful"). This designation identifies the prophet as the historical character of 2 Kin. 14:25, who proclaimed that Jeroboam II (793–753 B.C.) would recover territory from the Syrians to the north. Contrast Jonah's message to Jeroboam's kingdom with the words of Amos and Hosea, who prophesied during the period of Israel's spiritual decline in the latter part of the same century (Introduction: Date and Occasion).

1:2 go to Nineveh. The Lord's sovereignty over all the nations is implicit in the command to Jonah. He is the Judge of all the earth (Gen. 18:25). The last capital of the Assyrian Empire, Nineveh was located on the east side of the Tigris River directly opposite the modern city of Mosul in northern Iraq. The site has been extensively excavated and boasts a long and rich history.

call out against it. Jonah understood that his pronouncement of the Lord's judgment on the feared and hated Assyrian Empire was reversible (4:2 note). He knew that his message offered the opportunity for repentance.

their evil has come up before me. In the later prophecy of Nahum (seventh century B.C.), the Assyrian capital of Nineveh is the focus of divine wrath and is depicted as the embodiment of evil and cruelty (Nah. 3:1–7). The Assyrian war machine was guilty of horrendous atrocities; in 612 B.C. that empire would itself fall victim to a cruel destroyer.

1:3 Tarshish. Precise identification of this Tarshish is difficult, though it is often identified with the mining port of Tartessus in southern Spain. Sometimes, however, the term designates distant Mediterranean coastlands in general.

from the presence of the LORD. Because God is present even "in the uttermost parts of the sea" (Ps. 139:9), escape was impossible.

1:4 the LORD hurled a great wind upon the sea. Jonah's God is the Creator and Lord of the sea (Gen. 1:10, 21; Ex. 14:21; Mark 4:41).

1:7 let us cast lots. The casting of lots was a common form of divination in the ancient world, a device used to discover the will of the gods. This method of discerning the will of the true God was not forbidden in ancient Israel, for the Lord ruled even over lots (Num. 26:55; Josh. 18:6–10; Neh. 10:34; Prov. 16:33; Acts 1:24–26).

1:9 I am a Hebrew. See note Gen. 14:13. Jonah identifies himself in ethnic terms. The term "Hebrew" was used by Israelites to identify themselves to foreigners (Gen. 40:15; Ex. 1:19; 3:18; 10:3).

I fear the LORD. Jonah also identifies himself in religious terms. The Lord his God is not just a personal, family, or national deity. He is the supreme and sovereign God, the Creator of land and sea.

the God of heaven. An old title (Gen. 24:3, 7) also commonly used in the Persian period after the Exile (2 Chr. 36:23; Ezra 1:2; Neh. 1:4, 5; 2:4).

"O LORD, let us not perish for this man's
life, and [r]lay not on us innocent blood, [s]for
you, O LORD, have done as it pleased you."
15 So they picked up Jonah and hurled him
into the sea, [t]and the sea ceased from its
raging. 16 Then the men feared the LORD
exceedingly, [u]and they offered a sacrifice to
the LORD [v]and made vows.

A Great Fish Swallows Jonah

17 [1] And the LORD appointed[2] a great fish to
swallow up Jonah. [w]And Jonah was in the
belly of the fish three days and three nights.

Jonah's Prayer

2 Then Jonah prayed to the LORD his
God from the belly of the fish, 2 saying,

[x]"I called out to the LORD, out of my
distress,
and he answered me;
[y]out of the belly of Sheol I cried,
[z]and you heard my voice.
3 [a]For you cast me into the deep,
into the heart of the seas,
and the flood surrounded me;
[b]all your waves and your billows
passed over me.
4 [c]Then I said, 'I am driven away
from your sight;
[d]Yet I shall again look
upon your holy temple.'
5 [e]The waters closed in over me [f]to take
my life;
the deep surrounded me;
weeds were wrapped about my head
6 at the roots of the mountains.
I went down to the land
whose bars closed upon me
forever;
yet you brought up my life from the
pit,
O LORD my God.
7 When my life was fainting away,
I remembered the LORD,
[g]and my prayer came to you,
into your holy temple.
8 [h]Those who pay regard to vain idols
[i]forsake their hope of steadfast
love.
9 [j]But I with the voice of thanksgiving
will sacrifice to you;
what I have vowed I will pay.
[k]Salvation belongs to the LORD!"

1 Ch 2:1 in Hebrew 2 Or *had appointed*

14 [r]Deut. 21:8 [s][Ps. 115:3]
15 [t]Ps. 65:7; Luke 8:24
16 [u][Gen. 8:20; 31:54] [v]See ch. 2:9
17 [w]Matt. 12:40; 16:4; [Luke 11:30]
Chapter 2
2 [x]Ps. 3:4; 120:1; Lam. 3:55 [y]Ps. 118:5 [z]Lam. 3:56
3 [a]Ps. 88:6, 7 [b]Ps. 42:7
4 [c]Ps. 31:22 [d][1 Kin. 8:35, 38]
5 [e][Lam. 3:54] [f]Ps. 69:1
7 [g][2 Chr. 30:27]
8 [h]Ps. 31:6; [2 Kin. 17:15; Jer. 2:5] [i][Jer. 2:13]
9 [j]Ps. 50:14; [Hos. 14:2; Heb. 13:15] [k]Ps. 3:8

1:17 the LORD appointed. The same Hebrew word also occurs in 4:6–8; each instance indicates a startling example of God's sovereignty over the natural world.

a great fish. The species of whale or fish that swallowed Jonah cannot be identified with certainty. Suggestions have included the sperm whale or a large shark. The fish was God's instrument to rescue Jonah from the depths of the sea ("the belly of Sheol," 2:2).

three days and three nights. Jesus referred to the Book of Jonah in order to communicate truths regarding His own message and mission (Matt. 12:38–41; 16:4; Luke 11:29–32). He speaks of the "sign of the prophet Jonah" not only with reference to the three days and three nights that Jonah was in the fish (Matt. 12:39, 40), but also with regard to the efficacy of Jonah's preaching. Without benefit of a miraculous sign, the Ninevites recognized Jonah's message as one with divine authority, and they responded in repentance.

2:1–10 Jonah's response to God's judgment is framed in the form of a thanksgiving psalm (v. 9). The cry of the prophet focuses on the desperate character of his situation by using terms typical in poetic descriptions of death or nearness to death. In his plight he looks to the Lord's holy temple, the physical token of the Lord's saving presence with His people. The psalm is a moving testimony to the heart of Israel's faith and to the heart of the prophet, but he still had much to learn. His vision of God's mercy was still narrow.

2:1 Jonah prayed. Consistent with Old Testament narrative style, the Jonah story is interrupted with a poem (vv. 2–9), a psalm of thanksgiving and celebration for the Lord's deliverance and mercy. The literary structure is typical of a thanksgiving psalm: (a) petition for deliverance (2:2); (b) review of crisis (2:3–6); (c) review of deliverance (2:6, 7); and (d) praise for deliverance (2:8, 9).

2:2 I called out . . . and he answered me. Using the poetic device of parallelism, Jonah's psalm is introduced in two couplets that tell of the prophet's prayer and the Lord's answer. Jonah acknowledges that he was rescued "out of the belly of Sheol" (a watery grave in the depths of the sea).

2:3–6 These verses contain a vivid recollection of the near-death crisis, its causes, and results. Jonah's plight was the Lord's judgment on his disobedience. The brush with a watery grave is presented with graphic imagery: entanglement in seaweed, the silence of deep water, and waves swelling high above the victim.

2:4 I am driven away from your sight. For the prophet, the ultimate horror of death was separation from the presence of the Lord (Ps. 88:4, 5, 10–12).

Yet I shall again look upon your holy temple. The Jerusalem temple was the earthly location of the divine presence. Jonah longed for the communion with God that the temple afforded. The prophet now laments losing the same divine presence that he earlier had sought to escape (1:3, 10).

2:6 I went down. Jonah was at death's door. His slow, silent descent through the depths, like a journey to the underworld, had brought him to "the gates of death" (Ps. 9:13).

you brought up my life from the pit. Here "pit" is used to describe the realm of death (Job 33:22, 24; Ps. 49:9; Is. 51:14). Despite the hopelessness of the circumstances, the repentant prophet is rescued from the realm of the dead and restored to communion with God.

2:7 I remembered the LORD. The context indicates that this prayer was answered; the importance and effectiveness of prayer are again emphasized, as in v. 2 (cf. Heb. 4:16).

2:8 Those who pay regard to vain idols. Recalling the ineffectiveness of the sailors' prayers and of their gods (1:5), Jonah condemns those who put their faith in idols.

2:9 Salvation belongs to the LORD. Like Joshua before him (Josh. 24:14, 15), Jonah declares his loyalty to the Lord and extols Him as the only source of salvation and deliverance. In imparting salvation to Jonah, the Lord moved the prophet from disobedience to repentance; in imparting salvation to the Ninevites, He will move them from idolatry to faith (3:5–10); in imparting salvation to the Gentiles now He sovereignly moves them to faith and repentance (Acts 11:17, 18).

10 And the LORD spoke to the fish, and it vomited Jonah out upon the dry land.

Jonah Goes to Nineveh

3 Then the word of the LORD came to
Jonah the second time, saying, 2 "Arise,
go to [l]Nineveh, that great city, and call out
against it the message that I tell you." 3 So
Jonah arose and went to Nineveh, according to the word of the LORD. Now [l]Nineveh
was an exceedingly great city,[1] three days'
journey in breadth.[2] 4 Jonah began to go
into the city, going a day's journey. And he
called out, "Yet forty days, and Nineveh
shall be overthrown!" 5 [m]And the people of
Nineveh believed God. [n]They called for a
fast and [o]put on sackcloth, from the greatest of them to the least of them.

The People of Nineveh Repent

6 The word reached[3] the king of Nineveh,
and [p]he arose from his throne, removed his
robe, covered himself with sackcloth, [q]and
sat in ashes. 7 And he issued a proclamation
and published through Nineveh, [r]"By the
decree of the king and his nobles: Let neither man nor [s]beast, herd nor flock, taste
anything. Let them not feed or drink water,
8 but let man and [s]beast be covered with
sackcloth, and let them call out mightily to
God. [t]Let everyone turn from his evil way
and from [u]the violence that is in his hands.
9 [v]Who knows? God may turn and relent
[w]and turn from his fierce anger, so that we
may not perish."
10 When God saw what they did, [x]how
they turned from their evil way, [x]God
relented of the disaster that he had said he
would do to them, and he did not do it.

Jonah's Anger and the LORD's Compassion

4 But it displeased Jonah exceedingly,[4]
and [y]he was angry. 2 And he prayed to
the LORD and said, "O LORD, is not this
what I said when I was yet in my country?
[z]That is why I made haste to flee to

Chapter 3
2 [l]See ch. 1:2
3 [l][See ver. 2 above]
5 [m][Matt. 12:41; Luke 11:32] [n]See 2 Chr. 20:3 [o]See 2 Sam. 3:31
6 [p][Job 1:20; Ezek. 26:16] [q]Job 2:8
7 [r][Dan. 6:26] [s][ch. 4:11; Ps. 36:6; Joel 1:18, 20]
8 [s][See ver. 7 above] [t]Jer. 18:11; 36:3 [u]Isai. 59:6
9 [v]2 Sam. 12:22; Joel 2:14 [w]Ps. 85:3
10 [x][Jer. 18:8]
Chapter 4
1 [y][ver. 4, 9]
2 [z]ch. 1:3

1 Hebrew *a great city to God* 2 Or *a visit was a three days' journey* 3 Or *had reached* 4 Hebrew *it was exceedingly evil to Jonah*

2:10 the LORD spoke . . . it vomited Jonah. Again creation responds obediently to the sovereign commands of the Creator (1:4, 15, 17). The fish, which might have been God's weapon of death, by grace became God's tool of deliverance.

3:1–4:11 In this second division of the book Jonah preaches the message God commanded, and the people of Nineveh respond with genuine repentance (ch. 3). When the Lord turns from threatened judgment, we learn the real reason why Jonah had fled the first time: he feared that God would show mercy to the hated Assyrians (4:2). In the object lessons that follow, the wideness of the Lord's mercy and compassion is revealed (4:5–11).

3:3 Jonah arose and went. Having learned that the call of God is irrevocable (cf. Rom. 11:29), Jonah responded to the Lord's renewed commission. Though he obeyed God this time, Jonah was "displeased" with the prospect of Ninevite repentance (4:1, 2).

Nineveh was. Some have suggested that the use of the past tense ("was") indicates that the city was no longer in existence at the time of writing. Given the city's destruction in 612 B.C. by the Medes and Babylonians, this interpretation would date the narrative sometime after the late seventh century B.C. The past tense does not preclude an eighth-century date, however, for it may simply indicate the status of the city when the prophet arrived.

an exceedingly great city, three days' journey. The Hebrew is difficult to translate. Many commentators interpret these phrases as a reference to the physical size of Nineveh. Archaeological exploration has shown that the city was between seven and eight miles in circumference with an estimated population of 120,000 people. Others suggest that the first formula should be translated "a very important city," or more lit. as "a great city to God" (emphasizing its significance rather than size). This latter reading fits the context better. The second expression (lit. "journey of three days") could indicate the duration of visit appropriate (in terms of ancient Near Eastern diplomatic protocol) for an emissary to such an important city.

3:5 the people of Nineveh believed. Jonah's worst fears were realized when the people believed, repented, proclaimed a fast, and adorned themselves in sackcloth (the traditional mourning garb of the ancient Near East). The repentance was swift and city-wide.

3:6 the king of Nineveh. Apparently a reference to the mighty king of Assyria. Although it is highly unlikely that Assyrian records would note this unusual occurrence, some scholars have associated this event with the religious reforms of Adad-nirari III (810–783 B.C.). The reign of Assur-dan III (772–755 B.C.) has also been suggested.

he arose . . . and sat in ashes. The king's response was as immediate and spontaneous as that of his subjects. Royal authority gave way to penitent humility. He exchanged his robes for sackcloth, his throne for a bed of ashes (cf. Job 42:6; Is. 58:5).

3:7 decree of the king. With the royal edict mandating prayer, mourning rites, and a fast for man and beast, Nineveh's repentance was complete. The inclusion of animals points to the thorough and genuine nature of their repentance. Later, it was customary among the Persians to include domestic animals in the rites of mourning.

3:8 Let everyone turn from . . . violence. This royal admonition addressed the most prominent of Nineveh's sins. Physical violence and social injustice were hallmarks of the Assyrian Empire (Nah. 3:1).

3:9 The king gives personal and corporate expression to the hope that genuine repentance will avert the divine judgment. The structure of 3:5–9 conforms to the typical Old Testament pattern of reporting corporate repentance (Jer. 36:3; Joel 2): (a) threat of judgment, (b) penitent response, and (c) divine decision to withhold punishment.

3:10 God saw what they did. The prophetic warning (v. 4) had an implied condition, namely, that judgment was imminent—if the city did not repent. In turning "from their evil way" the Ninevites met that condition. The Lord's change of mind (i.e., His sovereign choice to make His own action depend upon human response) is fully compatible with God's sovereignty and immutability, since He ordains the means as well as the ends of His sovereign will (Jer. 18:7–10). See note Gen. 6:6.

4:1–11 The book concludes with angry Jonah receiving a lesson in divine mercy and compassion from God Himself. Strikingly, we are not told how Jonah responded to this instruction. Instead, we are left with the contrast between Jonah's resentful attitude and God's great mercy to the Ninevites.

4:1 it displeased Jonah exceedingly. The Hebrew is particularly vivid (lit. "it was evil to Jonah as a great wrong"). Jonah's emotion is expressed in the strongest language possible: his greatest fear was that the Lord would bestow forgiveness on Israel's most hated enemy.

Tarshish; for I knew that you are a [a]gra-
cious God and merciful, slow to anger and
abounding in steadfast love, and [a]relenting
from disaster. 3 [b]Therefore now, O LORD,
please take my life from me, [c]for it is better
for me to die than to live." 4 And the LORD
said, [d]"Do you do well to be angry?"
5 Jonah went out of the city and sat to the
east of the city and [e]made a booth for himself there. He sat under it in the shade, till
he should see what would become of the
city. 6 Now the LORD God appointed a plant[1]
and made it come up over Jonah, that it
might be a shade over his head, to save him
from his discomfort.[2] So Jonah was exceedingly glad because of the plant. 7 But when
dawn came up the next day, God appointed
a worm that attacked the plant, so that it
withered. 8 When the sun rose, God
appointed a scorching [f]east wind, [g]and the
sun beat down on the head of Jonah so that
he [h]was faint. And he asked that he might
die and said, [c]"It is better for me to die than
to live." 9 But God said to Jonah, [i]"Do you
do well to be angry for the plant?" And he
said, "Yes, I do well to be angry, angry
enough to die." 10 And the LORD said, "You
pity the plant, for which you did not labor,
nor did you make it grow, which came into
being in a night and perished in a night.
11 And should not I pity [j]Nineveh, that great
city, in which there are more than 120,000
persons who do not know their right hand
from their left, and also much [k]cattle?"

2 [a]See Joel 2:13
3 [b][1 Kin. 19:4] [c][Eccles. 7:1]
4 [d][ver. 1, 9]
5 [e][Neh. 8:15]
8 [f]Jer. 18:17 [g][Ps. 121:6] [h][Amos 8:13] [c][See ver. 3 above]
9 [i][ver. 1, 4]
11 [j]See ch. 1:2 [k][ch. 3:7]

1 Hebrew *qiqayon*, probably the castor oil plant; also verses 7, 9, 10
2 Or *his evil*

4:2 you are a gracious . . . relenting from disaster. The reason for Jonah's initial flight to Tarshish is revealed. Despite his blatant disobedience and narrow-mindedness, Jonah understood the character of God. Here he echoes a liturgical formula describing God's mercy to an undeserving Israel (e.g., Ex. 34:6; Num. 14:18; Neh. 9:17; Ps. 103:8; Joel 2:13). Only here and in Joel 2:13 does the reference to divine repentance ("he relents over disaster") conclude the formula (3:10 note), an inclusion appropriate to the context of Nineveh's repentance and deliverance.

4:5 Jonah went out . . . made a booth. Grateful for his own deliverance, Jonah still refuses to accept that of the Ninevites. Hoping that the Lord will execute judgment, Jonah leaves the city for a vantage point from which to view the destruction of the city.

4:6 the LORD God appointed a plant. See note 1:17. Probably because of the shortage of timber in this dry region, Jonah's shelter was not adequate to provide protection from the hot Near Eastern sun. The type of vegetation provided is uncertain; some suggest the castor oil plant, which grows quickly to a height of 15 feet.

4:7, 8 The same divine hand that in mercy had provided the great fish and the shade now brings a worm to kill the plant, and a hot east wind (likely the feared scirocco of the Mediterranean world) to torment the bitter prophet.

4:9–11 The divine intention of the object lessons is now revealed. God's magnificent compassion for the people and animals He created and sustained (v. 11) is contrasted with Jonah's petty concern for the plant (v. 10). The reader recalls the compassion of Jesus as He looked upon the multitudes (Matt. 9:36; Mark 6:34; 8:2), and His statement in Matt. 10:29 that not a sparrow will fall to the ground apart from the will of the Father. In its infancy, the largely Jewish New Testament church would again wrestle with this issue of the wideness of God's mercy, as the Lord opened the hearts of the Gentiles to obey the gospel (Acts 11:18; 15:14; 28:28).

THE BOOK OF

Micah

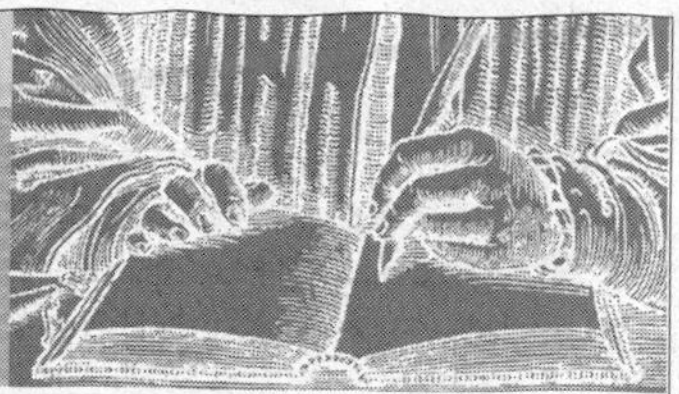

AUTHOR

Micah is identified by his hometown of Moresheth (1:1, 14), implying that he was an outsider to Jerusalem. Prophesying in the same period with Isaiah, he helped shape Israel's character and policies. Micah's inspired preaching (3:8) against injustice eventually brought Hezekiah to repentance and so saved Jerusalem (Jer. 26:17–19).

DATE AND OCCASION

Micah preached during the reigns of Jotham (750–735 B.C.), Ahaz (735–715 B.C.), and Hezekiah (715–686 B.C.), a time of Assyrian expansion and dominance in the ancient Near East. The northern kingdom of Israel was gradually overrun by the Assyrians, with the capital of Samaria finally falling in 722 B.C. to the Assyrian king Shalmaneser V (727–722 B.C.). Ahaz of Judah allied himself with Assyria and modeled the worship at Jerusalem after Assyrian practices (2 Kin. 16:7–18). Ahaz's son Hezekiah later revolted, and much of Judah was overrun by the Assyrian king Sennacherib, though Jerusalem itself was miraculously spared (2 Kin. 18:17–19:37).

Within Israel and Judah during this time, a shocking contrast between the extremely rich and the oppressed poor developed due to the exploitation of Israel's middle class (2:8, 9) by greedy landholders (2:1–5). The oppressors were supported by Israel's corrupt political and religious leaders (ch. 3). Because of this failed leadership, the whole nation became morally corrupt and ripe for judgment (6:9–16; 7:1–7).

God raised up Assyria as His wrathful rod against His sinful people (Is. 10:5–11). As Micah predicted (1:2–7), Samaria did fall to the invading Assyrians. Judah felt the force of divine judgment when Sennacherib marched through the Shephelah (Judah's western foothills) and up to the gate of Jerusalem, as Micah had also foretold (1:8–16).

CHARACTERISTICS AND THEMES

Micah arranges his nineteen prophecies into three cycles (Outline), each of which begins with prophecies of judgment and ends with a prophecy or prophecies of salvation, and each of which begins with the same Hebrew word rendered "hear" (1:2; 3:1; 6:1). The middle cycle has three prophecies of judgment (ch. 3) and seven of salvation (chs. 4; 5). The prophet uses word plays to predict judgment (see notes) and achieves vividness and immediacy by quoting his subjects (e.g., the false prophets trying to silence him, 2:6, 7; and the converted Gentiles going up to Jerusalem to worship, 4:2).

Micah primarily is a book of judgment proclaimed. The prophet declares that the holy and righteous God will no longer tolerate the persistent evil of His people (1:3). Many of Israel's sins are mentioned, ranging from idolatry and sorcery (5:12–14) to deceit and fraudulent dealings (6:10, 11). But Micah heaps special condemnation on those who oppressed the poor by seizing lands that God had intended as an inheritance for all His people (2:1–5; Num. 27:1–11 note). Judah's leaders, both political and spiritual, are also condemned for their oppression of the people and for their disregard of justice and truth (ch. 3).

Fundamental to Micah's proclamation of both judgment and restoration are the terms of the covenant relationship between God and His people. While God faithfully fulfilled His responsibilities under the covenant (6:1–5), the people wallowed in disobedience, and now the covenant curses were to be applied (6:13–16).

Despite his prevailing tone of impending punishment, Micah also looks beyond the judgment to future restoration and blessing. This too is rooted in God's covenant relationship with His people (Gen. 17:2 note). Faithful to His covenant promises to the patriarchs (7:20), the Lord will preserve a remnant of His people (2:12; 4:7; 5:3, 7, 8), and will raise up a Ruler out of Bethlehem in Judah—the Messiah Himself (5:1–5). Throughout the prophecies of salvation, Micah recognizes that Israel's restoration depends solely on the Lord's merciful forgiveness and sovereign initiative, not on the works of their hands (7:18, 19).

OUTLINE OF MICAH

I. Superscription (1:1)

II. First Cycle: Judgment and Deliverance (1:2–2:13)

- A. *Judgment on Samaria (1:2–7)*
- B. *Judgment on Judah (1:8–16)*
- C. *Sentencing of Greedy Landholders (2:1–5)*
- D. *Judgment Against False Prophets (2:6–11)*
- E. *A Remnant Restored (2:12, 13)*

III. Second Cycle: Degradation and Exaltation (chs. 3–5)

- A. *Evil Rulers Condemned (3:1–4)*
- B. *False Prophets Denounced (3:5–8)*
- C. *Zion to Be Leveled (3:9–12)*
- D. *Zion to Be Restored and Exalted (4:1–8)*
- E. *From Present Distress to Future Salvation (4:9–13)*
- F. *The Messianic Ruler (5:1–6)*
- G. *The Remnant of Jacob Among the Gentiles (5:7–9)*
- H. *The Lord Judges His People and the Nations (5:10–15)*

IV. Third Cycle: Hope in Darkness (chs. 6; 7)

- A. *The Lord's Allegation (6:1–8)*
- B. *Covenant Curses Fulfilled (6:9–16)*
- C. *Lament for a Broken and Corrupt Nation (7:1–7)*
- D. *Hymn of Victory (7:8–20)*

1 The word of the LORD that came to
Micah [a] of Moresheth [b] in the days of
Jotham, Ahaz, and Hezekiah, kings of
Judah, which he saw [c] concerning [d] Samaria
and Jerusalem.

The Coming Destruction

2 [e] Hear, you peoples, all of you;[1]
[f] pay attention, O earth, and all that is in it,
and [g] let the Lord GOD be a witness against you,
[h] the Lord from his holy temple.
3 For behold, [i] the LORD is coming out of [j] his place,
and will come down and [k] tread upon the high places of the earth.
4 And [l] the mountains will melt under him,
and the valleys will split open,
like wax before the fire,
like waters poured down a steep place.
5 All this is for [m] the transgression of Jacob
and for the sins of the house of Israel.
[n] What is the transgression of Jacob?
Is it not [d] Samaria?
And what is [o] the high place of Judah?
Is it not Jerusalem?
6 Therefore I will make [d] Samaria [p] a heap in the open country,
a place for planting vineyards,
and I will pour down her stones [q] into the valley
and [r] uncover her foundations.

Chapter 1
1 [a] [ver. 14] [b] Isai. 1:1; [c] Amos 1:1 [d] Isai. 7:9; Jer. 23:13
2 [e] ch. 3:1, 9; 6:1, 2; See Hos. 5:1 [f] See Isai. 1:2 [g] Mal. 3:5 [h] Ps. 11:4; Jonah 2:7; Hab. 2:20
3 [i] Isai. 26:21 [j] Ps. 115:3 [k] Amos 4:13; [Deut. 32:13]
4 [l] Ps. 97:5; [Judg. 5:5; Amos 9:5, 13; Nah. 1:5]
5 [m] See ch. 3:8 [n] [ver. 13] [d] [See ver. 1 above] [o] [2 Chr. 28:4]
6 [d] [See ver. 1 above] [p] [ch. 3:12] [q] [1 Kin. 16:24] [r] Ezek. 13:14

[1] Hebrew *all of them*

1:1 Micah of Moresheth. The name Micah is an abbreviated form of *Micayahu* ("Who is like Yahweh?"). The town of Moresheth was located near Gath in the Shephelah, or foothills, of Judah.

which he saw. The divine message to Micah took the form of a supernatural revelation to the prophet's inner sight or hearing.

1:2–7 This prophecy has four parts: summons of the nations to trial (v. 2); a symbolic vision of God overthrowing creation (vv. 3, 4); an accusation against Israel's capitals (v. 5); and the divine sentence for Samaria to be destroyed (vv. 6, 7).

1:2 all of you . . . against you. God's judgment of Samaria (vv. 6, 7) exemplifies and prefigures His judgment against all people who commit idolatry and social crimes.

1:3–5 Behind the march of the Assyrian army the prophet saw the hand of God (cf. Is. 10:5, 6). The depth of divine judgment against Jerusalem and Samaria is vividly portrayed in terms of a destruction of the created order itself.

1:3 high places. Whoever controlled Israel's heights controlled the land.

1:4 fire . . . down a steep place. These words link the symbolic vision with the historical overthrow of Samaria (vv. 6, 7), which was located on a hill (1 Kin. 16:24).

1:5 Jacob . . . Israel. "Jacob" and "Israel" often occur together in Micah, referring to the entire covenant people; sometimes "Jacob" represents the people as a whole (2:12; 3:1, 8, 9). The second occurrence of "Jacob" in this verse points to the northern kingdom (Israel) as distinct from Judah. In this book "Israel" designates Judah as representing the whole nation.

7 All [s] her carved images shall be
beaten to pieces,
[t] all her wages shall be burned with
fire,
and all her idols I will lay waste,
for from [t] the fee of a prostitute she
gathered them,
and to the fee of a prostitute they
shall return.

8 [u] For this I will lament and wail;
I will go [v] stripped and naked;
I will make lamentation [w] like the
jackals,
and mourning [x] like the
ostriches.
9 [y] For her wound is incurable,
and it has come to Judah;
it has reached to the gate of my
people,
to Jerusalem.
10 [z] Tell it not in [a] Gath;
weep not at all;
in Beth-le-aphrah
[b] roll yourselves in the dust.
11 Pass on your way,
inhabitants of Shaphir,
[c] in nakedness and shame;
the inhabitants of Zaanan
do not come out;
the lamentation of Beth-ezel
shall take away from you its
standing place.
12 For the inhabitants of Maroth
wait anxiously for good,
because disaster has come down
[d] from the LORD
to the gate of Jerusalem.
13 Harness the steeds to the chariots,
inhabitants of [e] Lachish;
it was the beginning of sin
to the daughter of Zion,
for in you were found
[f] the transgressions of Israel.
14 Therefore you shall give parting gifts[1]
to [g] Moresheth-gath;
the houses of [h] Achzib shall be a
deceitful thing
to the kings of Israel.
15 I will again bring [i] a conqueror
to you,
inhabitants of [h] Mareshah;
the glory of Israel
shall come to [j] Adullam.
16 [k] Make yourselves bald and cut off
your hair,
for the children of your delight;
[k] make yourselves as bald as the eagle,
for they shall go from you into
exile.

Woe to the Oppressors

2 [l] Woe to those who devise
wickedness
and work evil [m] on their beds!

7 s[Hos. 8:6] t[Hos. 2:12; 9:1] 8 u[Isai. 22:4] v See Isai. 20:2-4 w Job 30:29; Ps. 44:19 x Isai. 13:21 9 y[Hos. 5:13] 10 z 2 Sam. 1:20 a See 1 Sam. 17:4 b[Jer. 6:26] 11 c[Isai. 20:1,4; 47:3]
12 d See Amos 3:6 13 e Josh. 10:3; 2 Kin. 18:14, 17; 2 Chr. 32:9 f[ver. 5; Hos. 13:1] 14 g[ver. 1] h Josh. 15:44 15 i[ch. 2:4; Jer. 6:12] h[See ver. 14 above] j See 1 Sam. 22:1, 2 16 k See Isai. 22:12 Chapter 2 1 l[Isai. 10:1, 2] m[Ps. 36:4]

1 Or *give dowry*

1:7 her wages. Ancient Near Eastern fertility religions involved ritual prostitution, an activity strictly forbidden to Israel (Deut. 23:17). The wealth paid to them and used to make idols will be taken by the Assyrians and used in the same way.

1:8–16 This lament has three parts: an introduction, stating Micah's resolve to mourn Judah's exile (vv. 8, 9); a main body, with a series of wordplays on the names of Judah's stronghold predicting Judah's fall and exile (vv. 10–15); and a conclusion, calling the house of David to join in mourning rites because it will go into exile (v. 16).

1:8 stripped and naked. A symbolic act referring to the threat of captivity (Is. 20:2–4).

1:9 gate. Assyria's King Sennacherib reached Jerusalem's gate but did not take the city (v. 12; Introduction: Date and Occasion).

1:10 Tell it not in Gath. Micah's lament over the fall of David's house recalls David's lament over the fall of Saul's house under similar circumstances (2 Sam. 1:20).

roll yourselves in the dust. A vivid expression of grief over a humiliating defeat (Jer. 6:26).

1:11 Zaanan . . . out. Despite its name, this town will cower behind its wall and not "come out" into battle.

Beth-ezel. Lit. "adjoining house," the Hebrew word *'Ezel* resembles a verb meaning "withdraw" or "withhold." This town will withhold its protection from Judah because it has been annexed by the conqueror.

1:12 Maroth. Though it longed for good, this town would experience the bitterness of defeat.

1:13 steeds . . . chariots . . . Lachish. A major fortress town of Judah located southwest of Jerusalem, Lachish would have housed a contingent of chariots. Here the reference to "steeds" (the Hebrew term resembles "Lachish") perhaps implies that the chariots were to be used for flight rather than for fighting.

the beginning of sin. The precise nature of this sin is not explained. Many suggest that it involved the import of Egyptian horses for use in war (5:10; Deut. 17:16; 1 Kin. 10:28, 29), inducing Israel to rely on her military strength rather than on the Lord.

daughter of Zion. A personification of Jerusalem.

1:14 parting gifts. The dowry given by a father to his daughter as she departed for her husband's house (1 Kin. 9:16). The inhabitants of Moresheth-gath would depart into exile.

Achzib shall be a deceitful thing. The town's name closely resembles the Hebrew term for "deceitful," a word used for the "deceitful brook" in Jer. 15:18. The town of Achzib will disappoint the king of Judah.

1:15 glory of Israel . . . Adullam. As David had fled to the cave at Adullam (2 Sam. 23:13), so also the leaders ("glory") of Israel will flee. The body of the lament (vv. 10–15) begins and ends with literary references to David's career (v. 10 note).

2:1–5 This prophecy has three parts: (a) the accusation—evil and violent men unethically seize sacred property and destroy its owners (vv. 1, 2);

When the morning dawns, they perform it,
because it is in the power of their hand.
2 They covet fields and [n]seize them,
and houses, and take them away;
they oppress a man and his house,
a man and his inheritance.
3 Therefore thus says the LORD:
behold, against [o]this family I am devising disaster,[1]
from which you cannot remove your necks,
and you [p]shall not walk haughtily,
[q]for it will be a time of disaster.
4 In that day [r]they shall take up a taunt song against you
and moan bitterly,
and say, "We are utterly ruined;
[s]he changes the portion of my people;
[s]how he removes it from me!
[t]To an apostate he allots our fields."
5 Therefore you will have none [u]to cast the line by lot
in the assembly of the LORD.

6 [v]"Do not preach"—thus they preach—
[w]"one should not preach of such things;
[x]disgrace will not overtake us."
7 Should this be said, O house of Jacob?
[v]Has the LORD grown impatient?[2]
Are these his deeds?
Do not my words do good
to him who walks uprightly?
8 But lately [y]my people have risen up as an enemy;
you strip the rich robe from those who pass by trustingly
with no thought of war.[3]
9 The women of my people you drive out
from their delightful houses;
from their young children you take away
my splendor forever.
10 [z]Arise and go,
for this is no [a]place to rest,
because of [b]uncleanness that destroys
with a grievous destruction.
11 If a man should go about and [c]utter wind and lies,
saying, "I will preach to you [d]of wine and strong drink,"
he would be the preacher for this people!

12 I will surely assemble all of you, O Jacob;
[e]I will gather [f]the remnant of Israel;
I will set them together
like [g]sheep in a fold,
[h]like a flock in its pasture,
a noisy multitude of men.
13 [i]He who opens the breach goes up before them;
they break through and pass the gate,
[j]going out by it.
Their king passes on before them,
[k]the LORD at their head.

2 [n][Isai. 5:8] 3 [o][Amos 3:1, 2; Jer. 8:3] [p][Isai. 2:11, 17] [q]Amos 5:13 4 [r]Hab. 2:6; See Num. 23:7 [s][ch. 1:15] [t][Ps. 68:6] 5 [u]Deut. 32:8, 9; [Josh. 14:1, 2] 6 [v]See Amos 2:12 [w][Amos 8:11, 12] [x][Amos 8:10] 7 [v][See ver. 6 above]

8 [y][2 Chr. 28:8] 10 [z][ch. 1:11, 16] [a]Deut. 12:9; [Heb. 13:14] [b]Lev. 18:25 11 [c]Jer. 5:13 [d][Amos 2:12] 12 [e][2 Kin. 25:11] [f]See ch. 4:7 [g]See 1 Chr. 1:44 [h][Jer. 31:10] 13 [i][2 Kin. 25:10] [j][ch. 4:10] [k][Isai. 52:12]

1 The same Hebrew word can mean *evil* or *disaster*, according to context 2 Hebrew *Has the spirit of the LORD grown short?* 3 Or *returning from war*

(b) the sentence—the Lord sentences them to exile (v. 3) and loss of their lands to invaders (v. 4); (c) the conclusion—the robbers are cut off from the covenant people (v. 5). The accusation and sentence are linked by a play on words involving "who devise wickedness" (v. 1) and "I am devising disaster" (v. 3), which are virtually identical expressions in Hebrew. As the powerful took fields away from Israel's men (vv. 1, 2), so the Lord will send an enemy army to wrest the Promised Land from them (vv. 4, 5).

2:2 inheritance. A family's property was a permanent, sacred trust from God (Lev. 25:10, 13). See note Num. 27:1–11.

2:5 assembly. After the Babylonian exile the land would be redistributed (cf. Num. 26:55; Josh. 18:8–10), but neither the oppressors nor their descendants would then be present to claim an inheritance.

2:6–11 In this prophecy Micah defends his message against those who seek to silence him. Micah rebuffs their command to cease (v. 6). Then the Lord accuses the powerful of exploiting the defenseless (vv. 8, 9), and sentences them to exile because they have defiled the land (v. 10). Finally, the people are condemned for desiring false prophets who would tell them what they wish to hear (v. 11).

2:6 The Hebrew of v. 6 is difficult to translate. Some suggest that Micah confronts false prophets who support the land robbers and who have sought to silence him. In support of this interpretation, the Hebrew phrase rendered "thus they preach" could be translated "they prophesy." Others argue that the greedy and corrupt leaders themselves have tried to silence the prophet.

2:8, 9 robe . . . delightful houses . . . children. The oppressed belong to Israel's middle class (Introduction: Date and Occasion).

2:8 with no thought of war. Expecting peace in their homeland where they felt most secure, Israel's people were plundered instead.

2:12, 13 This prophecy of a remnant preserved like sheep in a pen recalls the remnant of Judah sheltered within Jerusalem while Sennacherib overran much of the land. The Lord then delivered them by decimating the Assyrian army (2 Kin. 18:17–19:37). Such provisional deliverances of God's chosen remnant anticipate the greater triumph of the Shepherd-King (5:2–5).

2:12 Jacob . . . Israel. A reference to Judah as representing the whole nation (1:5 note).

Rulers and Prophets Denounced

3 And I said:
[l]Hear, you heads of Jacob
and rulers of the house of Israel!
[m]Is it not for you to know justice?—
2 you [n]who hate the good and love the evil,
[o]who tear the skin from off my people[1]
and their flesh from off their bones,
3 [p]who eat the flesh of my people,
and flay their skin from off them,
and break their bones in pieces
and chop them up like meat in a pot,
like flesh in a cauldron.
4 [q]Then they will cry to the LORD,
but he will not answer them;
[r]he will hide his face from them at that time,
because they have made their deeds evil.

5 Thus says the LORD concerning [s]the prophets
who lead my people astray,
[t]who cry "Peace"
when they have something to eat,
but declare war against him
who puts nothing into their mouths.
6 Therefore [u]it shall be night to you, without vision,
and darkness to you, without divination.
[v]The sun shall go down on the prophets,
and the day shall be black over them;
7 [w]the seers shall be disgraced,
and the diviners put to shame;
[x]they shall all cover their lips,
for [y]there is no answer from God.
8 But as for me, [z]I am filled with power,
with the Spirit of the LORD,
and with justice and might,
to declare to Jacob [a]his transgression
and to Israel his sin.

9 [b]Hear this, you heads of the house of Jacob
and rulers of the house of Israel,
[c]who detest justice
and make crooked all that is straight,
10 [d]who build Zion with blood
and Jerusalem with iniquity.
11 [e]Its heads give judgment for a bribe;
[f]its priests teach for a price;
[g]its prophets practice divination for money;
[h]yet they lean on the LORD and [i]say,
"Is not the LORD in the midst of us?
[j]No disaster shall come upon us."
12 Therefore because of you
[k]Zion shall be plowed as a field;
Jerusalem [l]shall become a heap of ruins,
and [m]the mountain of the house [n]a wooded height.

The Mountain of the LORD

4 It shall come to pass [o]in the latter days
that the mountain of the house of the LORD
shall be established as the highest of the mountains,

Chapter 3
1 [l]See ch. 1:2 [m]Jer. 5:5; [Ezek. 22:6, 27]
2 [n][ver. 9] [o][Ezek. 34:3]
3 [p][Ps. 14:4; Isai. 3:15]
4 [q]See Prov. 1:28 [r]Isai. 1:15; See Deut. 31:17
5 [s]Jer. 23:13, 32; Ezek. 13:10 [t][Jer. 6:14]
6 [u]Ezek. 12:24; 13:23 [v]See Amos 8:9
7 [w]Zech. 13:4; [Jer. 37:19] [x][Lev. 13:45] [y]See Amos 8:11
8 [z][Jer. 6:11] [a]ch. 1:5; Isai. 58:1; [Ezek. 23:36]
9 [b]See ch. 1:2 [c][ver. 2]
10 [d]Jer. 22:13; Ezek. 22:27; Hab. 2:12
11 [e]ch. 7:3; Isai. 1:23 [f]See Jer. 6:13 [g][ver. 5; Ezek. 22:25] [h]Isai. 48:2 [i]Jer. 7:4; [Amos 5:14] [j][Jer. 23:17; Amos 9:10]
12 [k]Cited Jer. 26:18 [l][ch. 1:6] [m]ch. 4:2 [n][Luke 13:35]
Chapter 4
1 [o]For ver. 1-3, see Isai. 2:2-4

1 Hebrew *from off them*

3:1–12 The three prophecies of this chapter announce the rejection and punishment of Israel's incompetent, corrupt leadership. First, the leaders' treatment of the oppressed people is likened to cannibalism (vv. 1–4). Second, the false prophets who led the people astray are condemned (vv. 5–7) and contrasted with Micah, who prophesies true revelations from God (v. 8). Finally, the corrupt political and religious leaders are condemned and their complacency castigated (vv. 9–12).

3:1 And I said. An editorial addition, indicating that Micah edited his own book (Introduction: Characteristics and Themes).

Jacob . . . Israel. See note 1:5.

3:4 not answer. Just as the magistrates refused to hear the cries of the oppressed, so God will refuse to hear their cry in the time of judgment.

3:5 Peace . . . something to eat. These false prophets were opportunists, tailoring their pronouncements of peace and security to the desires of those who fed them. See Jer. 28.

3:6, 7 Those who had prophesied falsely will be judged and shamed by God's silence.

3:12 Zion . . . wooded height. This prophecy was given in the days of Hezekiah (Jer. 26:17–19). Because Hezekiah repented in 701 B.C., the judgment was delayed until 586 B.C.

4:1 the latter days. Micah's prophetic vision shifts from impending judgment in the short term to the "latter days," when the messianic reign of God is established in Zion. The expression points to a new epoch, which, though in the hidden future, decisively alters the course of history. Here it refers to the messianic age, begun at Christ's First Advent (Acts 2:7; Heb. 1:2) and consummated in the new heaven and earth (Rev. 21; 22).

mountain of the house of the LORD. Earthly Mount Zion prefigured the heavenly reality to which the church indeed has now come (Heb. 12:22–24). As part of the old covenant, the earthly religious center has been eclipsed by the coming new order (Heb. 8:13).

as the highest of the mountains. Pagan gods also had sacred mountains with temples. By being raised above them, God's eternal house (here symbolized by the temple on Mount Zion) will be established among the nations as the center of true worship.

and it shall be lifted up above the
hills;
and peoples shall flow to it,
2 and many nations shall come, and
say:
"Come, let us go up to the mountain
of the LORD,
to the house of the God of Jacob,
that he may teach us his ways
and that we may walk in his
paths."
For out of Zion shall go forth the
law,[1]
and the word of the LORD from
Jerusalem.
3 He shall judge between many
peoples,
and shall decide for strong nations
afar off;
and they shall [p]beat their swords into
plowshares,
and their spears into pruning
hooks;
nation shall not lift up sword against
nation,
neither shall they learn war
anymore;
4 [q]but they shall sit every man under
his vine and under his fig tree,
[r]and no one shall make them
afraid,
[s]for the mouth of the LORD of hosts
has spoken.
5 For [t]all the peoples walk
each in the name of its god,
but [u]we will walk in the name of the
LORD our God
forever and ever.

The LORD Shall Rescue Zion

6 [v]In that day, declares the LORD,
[w]I will assemble the [x]lame
and gather those who have been
driven away
and those whom I have afflicted;
7 and the lame I will make [y]the
remnant,
and those who were cast off,
a strong nation;
and [z]the LORD will reign over them
[a]in Mount Zion
from this time forth and
forevermore.
8 And you, O tower of the flock,
hill of the daughter of Zion,
to you shall it come,
the former dominion shall come,
kingship for the daughter of
Jerusalem.
9 Now why do you cry aloud?
[b]Is there no king in you?
[c]Has your counselor perished,
that [d]pain seized you like a
woman in labor?
10 [e]Writhe and groan,[2] O daughter
of Zion,
like a woman in labor,
for [f]now you shall go out from
the city
and dwell in the open country;
you [g]shall go to Babylon.
There you shall be rescued;
[h]there the LORD will redeem you
from the hand of your enemies.
11 Now [i]many nations
are assembled against you,
saying, "Let her be defiled,
and [j]let our eyes gaze upon Zion."
12 But [k]they do not know
the thoughts of the LORD;
they do not understand his plan,
that [l]he has gathered them as
sheaves to the threshing floor.
13 Arise and thresh,
O daughter of Zion,
for I will make your horn iron,
and I will make your hoofs bronze;

3 [p][Joel 3:10] 4 [q]See 1 Kin. 4:25 [r]Isai. 17:2 [s]See Isai. 1:20 5 [t][Jer. 2:11] [u][Zech. 10:12] 6 [v][ver. 1] [w]See Ezek. 11:17 [x]Ezek. 34:16; Zeph. 3:19 7 [y]ch. 2:12; 5:7, 8; Joel 2:32; Zeph. 2:7 [z]Isai. 24:23; [Dan. 7:14; Luke 1:33] [a]Ps. 2:6; Heb. 12:22 9 [b]Jer. 8:19 [c][Isai. 3:3] [d]Jer. 6:24 10 [e][John 16:20, 21] [f][ch. 2:13] [g]Isai. 39:6, 7 [h]See Isai. 44:22, 23 11 [i]Zech. 12:3 [j]ch. 7:10; Obad. 12 12 [k][Isai. 10:7] [l][Joel 3:13; Hab. 3:12; Matt. 3:12; Luke 3:17]

[1] Or *teaching* [2] Or *push*

4:6 In that day. See note on v. 1.

and. Perhaps better translated "even."

4:7 remnant. Just as God preserved a remnant that survived Sennacherib's invasion (2:12, 13 note), so also a remnant would survive the later Babylonian exile.

strong nation. A prophecy that finds final fulfillment in the church (1 Pet. 2:9, 10).

4:8 tower. Jerusalem (i.e., the heavenly Jerusalem, Heb. 12:22) will become a fortified tower around which the inhabitants will gather for protection.

4:9–13 This prophecy explains that Israel's present distress (the "now" of vv. 9, 11) will bring glorious salvation—liberation from the later Babylonian exile (vv. 9, 10) and release from Sennacherib's siege (vv. 11, 12).

4:10 like a woman in labor. The pain of judgment (exile, loss of king and land) for the remnant must precede the birth of the messianic age that will follow.

4:11 many nations. The Assyrian imperial army consisted of mercenaries from many nations.

you shall beat in pieces many peoples;
and [m] shall devote [1] [n] their gain to
the LORD,
their wealth to [o] the Lord of the
whole earth.

The Ruler to Be Born in Bethlehem

5 [2] Now muster your troops,
O daughter[3] of troops;
siege is laid against us;
with a rod [p] they strike the judge of
Israel
on the cheek.
2 [4] [q] But you, O Bethlehem Ephrathah,
who are too little to be among the
clans of [r] Judah,
from you shall come forth for me
one who is to be [s] ruler in Israel,
[t] whose origin is [u] from of old,
from ancient days.
3 Therefore he shall give them up
[v] until the time
when she who is in labor has given
birth;
then [w] the rest of his brothers shall
return
to the people of Israel.
4 And he shall stand [x] and shepherd his
flock [y] in the strength of the
LORD,
in the majesty of the name of the
LORD his God.
And they shall dwell secure, for now
[z] he shall be great
to the ends of the earth.
5 And he shall be [a] their peace.

[b] When the Assyrian comes into our
land
and treads in our palaces,
then we will raise against him seven
[c] shepherds
and eight princes of men;
6 they shall shepherd the land of
Assyria with the sword,
and the land of [d] Nimrod at its
entrances;
and he shall deliver us from the
Assyrian
[b] when he comes into our land
and treads within our border.

A Remnant Shall Be Delivered

7 Then [w] the remnant of Jacob shall be
in the midst of many peoples
like dew from the LORD,
like showers on the grass,
which delay not for a man
nor wait for the children of man.
8 And [w] the remnant of Jacob shall be
among the nations,
in the midst of many peoples,
like a lion among the beasts of the
forest,
like a young lion among the flocks
of sheep,
[e] which, when it goes through, treads
down
and tears in pieces, and there is
none to deliver.
9 Your hand shall [f] be lifted up over
your adversaries,
and all your enemies shall be cut off.
10 And [g] in that day, declares the LORD,
[h] I will cut off your horses from
among you
and will destroy your chariots;

13 [m] Lev. 27:28 [n] Isai. 23:18 [o] Ps. 97:5
Chapter 5
1 [p] See 1 Kin. 22:24
2 [q] Cited Matt. 2:6; [John 7:42] [r] [Heb. 7:14] [s] [Gen. 49:10; Isai. 9:6, 7; Jer. 30:21; Zech. 9:9] [t] Hos. 6:3 [u] Ps. 90:2; [Prov. 8:22, 23; John 1:1]
3 [v] [ch. 4:9, 10] [w] [ch. 4:7]
4 [x] Isai. 40:11; [ch. 7:14] [y] See Isai. 11:3-5 [z] Ps. 72:8; Isai. 52:13; Luke 1:32
5 [a] [Isai. 9:6; Zech. 9:10; Eph. 2:14] [b] [2 Kin. 18:13] [c] [Isai. 3:2, 3]
6 [d] Gen. 10:8, 10, 11 [b] [See ver. 5 above]
7 [w] [See ver. 3 above]
8 [w] [See ver. 3 above] [e] [Hos. 5:14]
9 [f] Isai. 26:11
10 [g] [ch. 4:1, 6] [h] Zech. 9:10; [Isai. 2:7; Hag. 2:22]

[1] Hebrew *devote to destruction* [2] Ch 4:14 in Hebrew [3] That is, city [4] Ch 5:1 in Hebrew

5:1–6 This prophecy also moves from present distress (v. 1) to the Messiah's advent and victory (vv. 2–6).

5:1 cheek. This insult to Israel's leader signifies that Jerusalem will fall to its Babylonian attackers, and all power to resist will be gone (cf. 2 Kin. 25:4–7).

5:2 Bethlehem Ephrathah. The town of David's birth (1 Sam. 16:1–13). Though the Davidic line of kings would temporarily cease (v. 3), God would yet raise up a ruler from David's family who would reign forever—Jesus Christ Himself (2 Sam. 7:12–17).

5:3 he shall give them up. Israel was without a Davidic king from the fall of Jerusalem in 586 B.C. until the Advent of Christ.

she who is in labor. A reference either to Mary, the mother of Jesus, or to the faithful remnant (see 4:10).

rest of his brothers. Thousands of Israelites were converted after Pentecost (Acts 2:41, 47).

5:5 the Assyrian. Assyria, the besieging nation of v. 1, here represents all enemies opposed to God's kingdom.

seven . . . eight. Seven is the number of perfection. There will be a more than sufficient supply of leaders to expand Christ's kingdom.

5:6 Nimrod. A reference to Babylon (Gen. 10:8 note).

5:7–9 This oracle has two parts: a prophecy that the remnant will become God's instrument of life and death (vv. 7, 8), and a petition for God to defeat all His foes (v. 9 and note). These statements find fulfillment in the church (2 Cor. 2:14–16).

5:7 delay . . . wait for. As rain proceeds from the divine initiative, so the remnant depends on God to refresh the earth.

5:9 Your hand shall. This verse is perhaps better translated as a petition for divine victory ("Let your hand be lifted against").

5:10–15 God will cleanse His nation (vv. 10–14) and cut off the pagan nations (v. 15). God's salvation cannot come otherwise than by stripping His nation of all vain and false military confidence (vv. 10, 11), sorceries (v. 12), and idolatry (v. 13).

11 [i] and I will cut off the cities of your land
and throw down all your strongholds;
12 and I will cut off [j] sorceries from your hand,
and [k] you shall have no more tellers of fortunes;
13 and [l] I will cut off your carved images
and [m] your pillars from among you,
[n] and you shall bow down no more to the work of your hands;
14 and I will root out your [o] Asherah images from among you
[i] and destroy your cities.
15 And in anger and wrath [p] I will execute vengeance
on the nations that did not obey.

The Indictment of the Lord

6 [q] Hear what the LORD says:
Arise, plead your case before the mountains,
and let the hills hear your voice.
2 [r] Hear, you mountains, [s] the indictment of the LORD,
and you enduring foundations of the earth,
for the LORD has an indictment against his people,
and he will contend with Israel.

3 "O my people, [t] what have I done to you?
[u] How have I wearied you?
Answer me!
4 For [v] I brought you up from the land of Egypt
and [w] redeemed you from the house of slavery,
and I sent before you Moses,
Aaron, and [x] Miriam.
5 O my people, remember [y] what Balak king of Moab devised,
and what Balaam the son of Beor answered him,
and what happened from [z] Shittim to Gilgal,
that you may know [a] the saving acts of the LORD."

What Does the Lord Require?

6 [b] "With what shall I come before the LORD,
and bow myself before [c] God on high?
Shall I come before him with burnt offerings,
with calves a year old?
7 [d] Will the LORD be pleased with[1] thousands of rams,
with ten thousands of rivers of oil?
[e] Shall I give my firstborn for my transgression,
the fruit of my body for the sin of my soul?"
8 He has told you, O man, what is good;
and [f] what does the LORD require of you
but to do justice, and to love kindness,[2]
and to [g] walk humbly with your God?

1 Or *Will the LORD accept* 2 Or *steadfast love*

11 [i] ver. 14; Isai. 17:9; 27:10; [Hos. 8:14; Zech. 2:4] **12** [j] [2 Kin. 9:22] [k] Deut. 18:10; [Isai. 2:6] **13** [l] Zech. 13:2 [m] Hos. 3:4 [n] [Isai. 17:8] **14** [o] Ex. 34:13; See Deut. 16:21 [i] [See ver. 11 above] **15** [p] [ver. 8; Ps. 149:7; 2 Thess. 1:8]
Chapter 6
1 [q] See ch. 1:2 **2** [r] Ps. 50:1, 4; Ezek. 36:4 [s] Isai. 1:18; See Hos. 4:1 **3** [t] Isai. 5:4; [Jer. 2:5, 31] [u] Isai. 43:22, 23; [Mal. 1:13]
4 [v] Ex. 12:51; Hos. 12:13; Amos 2:10 [w] 2 Sam. 7:23 [x] Ex. 15:20; Num. 12:1, 2 **5** [y] See Num. 22:5 [z] Num. 25:1; [a] [Judg. 5:11] **6** [b] [Hos. 5:6; Heb. 10:4] [c] Isai. 57:15 **7** [d] See 1 Sam. 15:22 [e] 2 Kin. 3:27; 16:3; 21:6; 23:10; [Lev. 18:21] **8** [f] [Deut. 10:12] [g] [Gen. 5:22]

5:15 vengeance. God's vengeance takes place when He secures His sovereignty by delivering His people and punishing their guilty oppressors. Only the sovereign Lord Himself has the ultimate right to use force to protect His kingdom, and the exercise of force by an individual or community without divine authorization springs from unbelief (Deut. 32:35; Rom. 12:19–21).

6:1–8 A classic example of the prophetic covenant lawsuit, in which the Lord pleads the terms of the covenant against His disobedient people. The message opens with a judgment scene in which the Lord is plaintiff, Micah is His envoy, the mountains are witnesses, and Israel is the accused (vv. 1, 2). God's own covenant faithfulness is then attested as He first gives Israel opportunity to voice any complaints (v. 3) and then recounts His mighty acts of deliverance (vv. 4, 5). The demand for covenant righteousness is then proclaimed—a righteousness consisting not merely in empty ritual but in heartfelt obedience (vv. 6–8).

6:1 Arise, plead your case. The Lord commands Micah, as His representative, to prosecute God's case against the people. Micah obeys the command in v. 2.

mountains. The Lord used the enduring mountains as witnesses to the covenant mediated by Moses (Deut. 4:26; 30:19 and note; 31:28; 32:1).

6:4, 5 These verses are framed by references to Egypt (from which Israel was delivered) and Gilgal (where Israel entered the Promised Land, Josh. 4:19). All God's saving acts during Israel's formative period are included: the Passover and Exodus, guidance by the pillar of fire and cloud, miraculous provision of food and water, the provision of able leaders ("Moses, Aaron, and Miriam"), and victory over enemies. God's wonderful provision for His people during this period foreshadowed the church's experience with Christ (John 6:33; 1 Cor. 5:7; 10:1–4).

6:5 remember. This command means not merely mental recall of past events, but that those events are to be means of actualizing them in the present. By faith such knowledge of the past is applied to present situations.

6:6, 7 Through the rhetorical escalation of sacrifices ("calves . . . thousands of rams . . . rivers of oil . . . my firstborn") Micah displays the absurdity of Israel's dependence on empty ritual and sacrifice to earn divine favor. Such reliance showed a profound misunderstanding of God's grace, for Israel's salvation was free and not earned (vv. 4, 5). Moreover, Israel's covenant obligations entailed social justice and mercy, not mere liturgy (v. 8). See also Amos 5:21–24.

6:8 humbly. Or, "prudently."

Destruction of the Wicked

9 The voice of the LORD cries to the
city—
and it is sound wisdom to fear
[h]your name:
"Hear of [i]the rod and of him who
appointed it![1]
10 Can I forget any longer the
treasures[2] of wickedness in the
house of the wicked,
and the scant measure that is
accursed?
11 Shall I acquit the man [j]with wicked
scales
and with a bag of deceitful weights?
12 Your[3] rich men are [k]full of violence;
your inhabitants [l]speak lies,
and [m]their tongue is deceitful in
their mouth.
13 Therefore I strike you with a grievous
blow,
[n]making you desolate because of
your sins.
14 [o]You shall eat, but not be satisfied,
and there shall be hunger within
you;
you shall put away, but not preserve,
and what you preserve I will give
to the sword.
15 [p]You shall sow, but not reap;
you shall tread olives, but not
anoint yourselves with oil;
you shall tread grapes, but not
drink wine.
16 For you have kept the statutes of
[q]Omri,[4]
and all the works of the house of
[r]Ahab;
and you have walked in their
counsels,
that I may make you [s]a desolation,
and your[5] inhabitants [s]a
hissing;
so you shall bear [t]the scorn of my
people."

9 [h]Isai. 30:27 [i]Isai. 10:5; 30:32 11 [j]See Hos. 12:7 12 [k]Amos 3:10; Hab. 1:2, 3 [l]Hos. 7:13 [m]Jer. 9:8 13 [n]ch. 7:13 14 [o]Hos. 4:10 15 [p][Zeph. 1:13; Hag. 1:6] 16 [q]1 Kin. 16:25, 26; [ch. 1:13] [r]See 1 Kin. 16:30-33; 21:25, 26 [s]See 2 Chr. 29:8 [t]Isai. 25:8

Chapter 7
1 [u]Isai. 24:13; [Isai. 17:6] [v]Hos. 9:10 2 [w][Ps. 12:1; Isai. 57:1] [x]Ps. 14:1, 3 [y][Ps. 10:9; Hos. 6:8, 9] [z]Isai. 9:19 3 [a][Zeph. 3:7] [b][Ps. 82:1, 2] [c]ch. 3:11 4 [d][2 Sam. 23:6, 7; Nah. 1:10]; See Ezek. 2:6 [e]See Ezek. 33:2 [f][ch. 3:6, 7; Isai. 22:5] 5 [g]Jer. 9:4 [h][Ps. 141:3] 6 [i]Ezek. 22:7; [Matt. 10:21, 35; Luke 12:53] [j]Cited Matt. 10:36 7 [k][Lam. 3:26]

Wait for the God of Salvation

7 Woe is me! For I have become
[u]as when the summer fruit has
been gathered,
as when the grapes have been
gleaned:
there is no cluster to eat,
no [v]first-ripe fig that my soul desires.
2 [w]The godly has perished from the earth,
and [x]there is no one upright
among mankind;
[y]they all lie in wait for blood,
and [z]each hunts the other with a
net.
3 [a]Their hands are on what is evil, to do
it well;
[b]the prince and [c]the judge ask for a
bribe,
and the great man utters the evil
desire of his soul;
thus they weave it together.
4 The best of them is [d]like a brier,
the most upright of them a thorn
hedge.
The day of [e]your watchmen, of your
punishment, has come;
[f]now their confusion is at hand.
5 [g]Put no trust in a neighbor;
have no confidence in a friend;
guard [h]the doors of your mouth
from her who lies in your arms;[6]
6 for [i]the son treats the father with
contempt,
the daughter rises up against her
mother,
the daughter-in-law against her
mother-in-law;
[j]a man's enemies are the men of
his own house.
7 But as for me, I will look to the LORD;
[k]I will wait for the God of my
salvation;
my God will hear me.

1 The meaning of the Hebrew is uncertain 2 Or *Are there still treasures* 3 Hebrew *whose* 4 Hebrew *For the statutes of Omri are kept* 5 Hebrew *its* 6 Hebrew *bosom*

6:9–16 This prophecy consists of an address to Jerusalem (v. 9), an accusation of falsity in business dealings and speech (vv. 10–12), and a judicial sentence of disease and ruin (v. 13–15). The covenantal context is apparent as the punishment reflects the covenant curses specified in the Mosaic law (v. 15; Lev. 26:20; Deut. 28:40, 51).

7:1–7 Micah laments that no righteous are found (vv. 1–4) and bemoans the resulting social and national confusion that is both the result and punishment of their sin (vv. 4–6). Particularly striking is the description of the breakdown of family order. Micah concludes, however, with the confidence that beyond God's judgment lies salvation (v. 7).

7:1 I have become . . . summer fruit. In his search for the righteous, Micah compares himself to a vinedresser searching for choice fruit after the best of the season is past.

7:2 no one upright. This verse explains the allegory of v. 1.

7:4 watchmen. A metaphor for the prophets who announced the coming judgment (Ezek. 3:17; 33:7).

7:5, 6 This passage was later used in Jewish extrabiblical apocalyptic literature to describe the conflict that will accompany the final day of the Lord, and Jesus quoted v. 6 in describing the conflict that results from His coming (Matt. 10:35–39; Luke 12:51–53).

8 [l] Rejoice not over me, O [m] my enemy;
[n] when I fall, I shall rise;
[o] when I sit in darkness,
the LORD will be a light to me.
9 [p] I will bear the indignation of the LORD
because I have sinned against him,
until [q] he pleads my cause
and executes judgment for me.
[r] He will bring me out to the light;
I shall look upon his vindication.
10 Then [s] my enemy will see,
and shame will cover her who [t] said to me,
"Where is the LORD your God?"
[u] My eyes will look upon her;
now she will be trampled down
[v] like the mire of the streets.
11 [w] A day for the building of your walls!
In that day [x] the boundary shall be far extended.
12 In that day they[1] will come to you,
[y] from Assyria and the cities of Egypt,
and from Egypt to [z] the River,
[a] from sea to sea and from mountain to mountain.
13 But [b] the earth will be desolate
because of its inhabitants,
for the fruit of their deeds.
14 [c] Shepherd your people [d] with your staff,
the flock of your inheritance,
who dwell alone in a forest
[e] in the midst of [f] a garden land;[2]
let them graze in Bashan and Gilead
as in the days of old.
15 [g] As in the days when you came out of the land of Egypt,
I will show them[3] marvelous things.
16 [h] The nations shall see and be ashamed of all their might;
[i] they shall lay their hands on their mouths;
their ears shall be deaf;
17 [j] they shall lick the dust like a serpent,
like the crawling things of the earth;
[k] they shall come trembling out of their strongholds;
[l] they shall turn in dread to the LORD our God,
and they shall be in fear of you.

God's Steadfast Love and Compassion

18 [m] Who is a God like you, [n] pardoning iniquity
and passing over transgression
[n] for the remnant of his inheritance?
[o] He does not retain his anger forever,
because he delights in steadfast love.
19 He will [p] again have compassion on us;
[q] he will tread our iniquities under foot.
[r] You will cast all our[4] sins
into the depths of the sea.
20 [s] You will show faithfulness to Jacob
and steadfast love to Abraham,
[t] as you have sworn to our fathers
from the days of old.

1 Hebrew *he* 2 Hebrew *of Carmel* 3 Hebrew *him* 4 Hebrew *their*

8 [l] [Jer. 50:11; Lam. 4:21] [m] ver. 10 [n] Ps. 37:24 [o] Ps. 112:4
9 [p] [Jer. 10:16,19] [q] See 1 Sam. 24:15 [r] Ps. 37:6
10 [s] ver. 8 [t] See Joel 2:17 [u] ch. 4:11 [v] Ps. 18:42; See 2 Sam. 22:43
11 [w] [Ps. 102:13] [x] Zeph. 2:2
12 [y] [Isai. 11:11, 16; 19:23, 24; 27:13; Hos. 11:11; Zech. 10:10] [z] See Gen. 31:21 [a] Zech. 9:10
13 [b] ch. 6:13
14 [c] Ps. 28:9; [ch. 5:4] [d] Ps. 23:4 [e] Jer. 50:19; [Zech. 10:10] [f] See Josh. 19:26
15 [g] Ps. 78:12; See Isai. 11:16
16 [h] [Isai. 26:11; 52:15] [i] See Judg. 18:19
17 [j] Ps. 72:9; Isai. 49:23 [k] Ps. 18:45 [l] [ch. 4:1]
18 [m] See Ex. 15:11 [n] Jer. 50:20; See Ex. 34:7 [o] Ps. 103:9
19 [p] Ps. 80:14 [q] [Rom. 6:14] [r] [Isai. 38:17]
20 [s] [Luke 1:72, 73] [t] Ps. 105:9, 10

7:8–20 This concluding hymn consists of four stanzas: (a) Lady Jerusalem in her fallen status confesses her sin and her faith in the Lord (vv. 8–10); (b) the prophet promises that she will become a sheepfold offering salvation to the world under judgment (vv. 11–13); (c) Micah prays that the Lord will again miraculously shepherd His people (v. 14), which the Lord promises to do (v. 15), and Micah then prophesies that the unbelieving enemy will be conquered (vv. 16, 17); and (d) the people celebrate God's forgiveness and faithfulness with a hymn of praise (vv. 18–20).

7:8 darkness. A dungeon without light is an apt figure for a city under divine judgment.

7:9 I shall look upon his vindication. The Lord's righteousness will be manifested in faithful Israel's salvation (vv. 8, 9) and her unbelieving enemy's destruction (v. 10).

7:11 day. See 4:1, 6; 5:10–15. The last day is symbolically depicted by the restoration of Jerusalem's city walls (v. 11) and the extension of the boundaries of the land to limits prophesied by Moses and enjoyed under David and Solomon (v. 12; Gen. 15:18; Ex. 23:31; Deut. 11:24; 1 Kin. 4:21, 25).

7:13 earth will be desolate. Outside the elect's secure borders is universal judgment. The Last Judgment is ultimately in view.

7:16 hands on their mouths . . . be deaf. These are signs of humiliation in the face of overwhelming divine power. They will no longer taunt Israel or listen to the vain boasts of others.

7:18 Who is a God like you. Micah, whose name means "Who is like the LORD" (1:1 note), perhaps employs a wordplay on his own name to emphasize God's pardoning grace.

7:19 cast . . . sea. As God began Israel's journey by casting the Egyptians into the Red Sea (v. 15; cf. Ex. 15:1–5), He will conclude her history by casting His people's iniquities into the depths.

7:20 show faithfulness. God's loving fidelity to the fathers is the basis of the church's hope (Rom. 4:17; Gal. 3:7–9, 29).

THE BOOK OF

Nahum

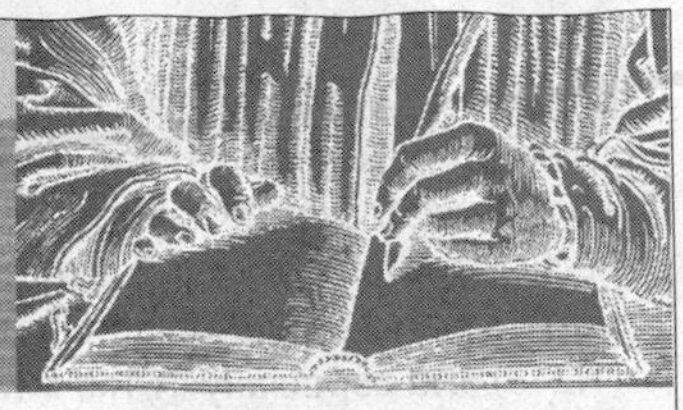

AUTHOR

Nahum means "comfort." His name is followed by the designation "of Elkosh," probably a reference to the location of his birth or where he prophesied. Attempts to provide a closer identification of Elkosh have been unsuccessful. Proposals have included locations near ancient Nineveh, in Galilee (the name "Capernaum" perhaps derives from the Hebrew for "village of Nahum"), and in Judah. The internal witness of the book supports Judah as the general vicinity of Nahum's prophetic activity (1:15).

As is the case in most prophetic books, the person of the prophet recedes behind his message. Nahum has been incorrectly regarded as a narrow nationalist who, inspired by feelings of hatred and vengeance, proclaimed a message of judgment against Nineveh, and at the same time extended the promise of unconditional salvation to his own people, Judah. But this view overlooks that this book reflects the usual literary form of prophecies against foreign nations, and is to be compared with similar proclamations in Is. 13–23; Jer. 46–51; Amos 1; 2; and Obadiah.

As a true prophet of Yahweh, Nahum was profoundly aware that the Lord, the incomparable and all-powerful God, held universal dominion over the kingdoms of this world. Like his predecessor Isaiah, Nahum was also a gifted poet. Using a wealth of imagery and pictorial language, the prophet portrays the total destruction of Nineveh by an anonymous enemy, and so voices the universal relief and joy of all who suffered under the oppressive regime of a merciless tyrant.

DATE AND OCCASION

Nahum's prophecy can be dated between the capture of Thebes by the Assyrian ruler Ashurbanipal in 663 B.C., which Nahum reports as a past event (3:8), and the fall of Nineveh in 612 B.C., which Nahum prophetically foretells (3:5–7).

During this period of the seventh century B.C., two major crises arose in the Assyrian empire. One came from the threat of the Medes and the advancing Scythians (642–638 B.C.). The other, larger crisis was the Babylonian revolt (652–648 B.C.) under the leadership of Ashurbanipal's elder brother who was supported by the Elamites and peoples from the Iranian highlands. Ripple effects of this revolt were experienced as far away as Palestine and Syria. Eventually the revolt was suppressed by bitter warfare that shook the whole empire. A date for Nahum's prophetic activities before or during this period of upheaval is attractive. Because the destruction of Thebes was apparently still fresh in the memory of his audience, a plausible date for Nahum's prophecy therefore falls between 660–650 B.C., in the days of King Manasseh of Judah, a loyal vassal of Assyria.

CHARACTERISTICS AND THEMES

The Book of Nahum has a double title (1:1). It is called an "oracle concerning Nineveh" and the "book of the vision of Nahum." "Oracle" often indicates a divine message of judgment against a foreign nation (Is. 13:1; Mal. 1:1 note). "Vision" refers to a supernatural revelation to the prophet's inner sight or hearing. At times a prophet was instructed to write down a specific message (Is. 8:1, 2; 30:8) or even "all the words" that the Lord required him to speak (Jer. 36). The written form then provided a strong additional witness to the certainty of the fulfillment of those divine pronouncements. The prophecy's double title is solid confirmation of the authenticity of this oracle of doom against Nineveh and the inescapability of God's imminent judgment on the Assyrian kingdom.

This often neglected and disparaged book

provides us with an important key for understanding past, present, and future history. Events do not occur as mere happenstance, but every particular of history is determined by the will, purpose, and power of God. In the opening hymn (1:2–8) and especially in 1:2, 3 (the "text" of Nahum's sermon), we learn that the Lord's government of history is in accordance with His character as the covenant God. He demands undivided submission everywhere and from everyone. Rejection of Him and of His law leads not only to the necessary consequences of chaos in society and in nature, but inevitably evokes His personal displeasure, resulting in just retribution.

God's patience must never be misunderstood as weakness. Corporate or individual sin will not be left unpunished. God ultimately ordains all the events of history. Nahum proclaimed the impending destruction of Nineveh as God's righteous judgment, and he invited his people to a joyful celebration of this event long before it took place.

Nineveh was a wicked, imperialistic, and deceitful metropolis with an arrogant and unscrupulous lust for power and domination manifested in merciless warmongering (3:1–4). In addition to its military exploits, Nineveh was condemned for its ruthless trade practices and insatiable materialism (3:16). Against this evil city Nahum delivered his message of divine vengeance and retribution (1:14; 3:5–7). No earthly power that defied God's law would finally escape His judgment.

Judgment, however, is not the Lord's final word. God's retributive judgment is also redemptive in that it furthers His loving purposes for His people and His covenant promises to them (1:15; 2:2). He destroys the forces of evil with the purpose of creating a new world of freedom (1:13), peace, and lasting comfort. "He knows those who take refuge in him" and cares for them (1:7). Those familiar with the message in the "book of the vision of Nahum" will better understand the necessity of the Cross of Jesus Christ, the Son of the jealous and avenging God. They will be able to proclaim from this book the glorified Christ, to whom all authority in heaven and on earth has been given (Matt. 28:18) and who is now guiding history toward that Great Day when He will hand over the kingdom to His Father, after He has destroyed all opposing powers, so "that God may be all in all" (1 Cor. 15:24–28).

OUTLINE OF NAHUM

I. Superscription (1:1)

II. Nineveh's Just and Merciful Judge (1:2–14)

- A. *The Lord's Jealousy and Power (1:2–8)*
- B. *Woe for the Wicked (1:9–14)*

III. Nineveh Powerless Before the Lord's Army (1:15–2:13)

- A. *Good News for Judah (1:15–2:2)*
- B. *Nineveh Captured and Plundered (2:3–10)*
- C. *Nineveh's Power Broken by the Lord (2:11–13)*

IV. Nineveh's Irreversible Destruction (ch. 3)

- A. *Judgment of the Wicked City Prophesied (3:1–7)*
- B. *Nineveh's Fate like That of Thebes (3:8–11)*
- C. *The Finality of Divine Judgment (3:12–19)*

1

[a]An oracle concerning [b]Nineveh. The book of the vision of Nahum of Elkosh.

God's Wrath Against Nineveh

2 [c]The LORD is a jealous and avenging
God;
the LORD is avenging and wrathful;
[d]the LORD takes vengeance on his
adversaries
and [e]keeps wrath for his enemies.
3 [f]The LORD is slow to anger and [g]great
in power,
and [h]the LORD will by no means
clear the guilty.
[i]His way is in whirlwind and storm,
and the clouds are the dust of his
feet.
4 [j]He rebukes the sea and makes it dry;
he dries up all the rivers;
[k]Bashan and [l]Carmel wither;
the bloom of [k]Lebanon withers.
5 [m]The mountains quake before him;
[n]the hills melt;
the earth heaves before him,
[o]the world and all who dwell in it.
6 [p]Who can stand before his
indignation?
Who can endure the heat of his
anger?
His wrath [q]is poured out like fire,
and [r]the rocks are broken into
pieces by him.
7 [s]The LORD is good,
[t]a stronghold in the day of trouble;
[u]he knows those who take refuge in
him.
8 But [v]with an overflowing flood
he will make a complete end of the
adversaries,[1]
and [w]will pursue his enemies into
darkness.
9 What [x]do you plot against the LORD?
[y]He will make a complete end;
trouble will not rise up a second
time.
10 For they are [z]like entangled thorns,
like drunkards as they drink;
[a]they are consumed like stubble
fully dried.
11 From you came one
[b]who plotted evil against the LORD,
a worthless counselor.
12 Thus says the LORD,
"Though they are at full strength and
many,
[c]they will be cut down and pass
away.

Chapter 1
1 [a]See Isai. 13:1 [b]ch. 2:8; 3:7; See Jonah 1:2
2 [c]See Ex. 20:5 [d][Ps. 92:9] [e][Ps. 103:9]
3 [f]See Ex. 34:6 [g]Job 9:4; Ps. 147:5 [h]See Ex. 34:7 [i][Ps. 97:2]; See Ps. 18:9-13
4 [j]Ps. 106:9; [Isai. 50:2] [k]Isai. 33:9 [l]See Josh. 19:26
5 [m][Jer. 4:24; Hab. 3:6] [n]Amos 9:13 [o]Ps. 98:7
6 [p][Mal 3:2] [q]2 Chr. 34:21; [Ps. 79:6] [r]Ezek. 38:20
7 [s]Jer. 33:11; See Ps. 100:5 [t]Ps. 46:1; Isai. 25:4 [u]Ps. 1:6; John 10:14, 27; 1 Cor. 8:3; 2 Tim. 2:19
8 [v][Isai. 30:28] [w]Isai. 8:22
9 [x][Isai. 10:7] [y][Jer. 4:27]
10 [z]See Mic. 7:4 [a]See Joel 2:5
11 [b][ver. 9; 2 Kin. 19:22, 23]
12 [c]Isai. 10:33, 34; [Isai.37:36]

[1] Hebrew *of her place*

1:1 Title of the book. See Introduction: Author; Date and Occasion.

1:2–14 The introductory hymn (vv. 2–8), which in the Hebrew forms an incomplete acrostic poem, movingly describes the Lord as the universal Judge with power to accomplish His will.

1:2, 3 The Lord's character forms the key to what follows.

1:2 jealous. This attribute refers to God's passionate reaction against any infringement on His holiness or any attempt to share His glory. His jealousy demands undivided loyalty and reveals itself as wrath against rejection of Him or His lordship.

avenging . . . avenging . . . takes vengeance. True to His nature, the universal Judge leaves no sin unpunished and metes out the just deserts of the wicked. The threefold repetition of the Hebrew word for "avenge" strongly emphasizes an inescapable and appropriate retribution.

adversaries . . . enemies. This terminology is typical of the Psalms and of holy-war imagery.

1:3 slow to anger. A well-known confession of God's patience with sinners (Ex. 34:6; Jon. 4:2).

great in power . . . by no means clear. God's patience never implies that He is weak or that He condones evil (Gen. 18:25).

1:3–6 The prophet offers a poetic portrayal of the power of the Lord as manifested in His control of nature at Creation and on other occasions of intervention on behalf of His people (Ex. 14:21, 22; Ps. 18:7–15; Matt. 8:26). The godly Israelite recognized the Lord's work in nature. But nature is not confused with God or worshiped as God; it is the theater of His revelation.

1:4 He rebukes. These words vividly portray the power of God in subjecting the forces of nature, as during creation or at the crossing of the Red Sea (Ex. 14).

sea . . . rivers. Used here as poetic parallels (Is. 50:2; Ps. 74:12–15). The abundant vegetation of the fertile "Bashan," "Carmel," and "Lebanon" withers when the hot desert wind, sent by the Lord, blows over it.

1:5 The displeasure of the approaching Lord fills the earth and its creatures with terror. All creation seems threatened by chaos when even the seemingly permanent things ("the mountains . . . the earth") tremble and disappear.

1:6 The rhetorical questions emphasize the irresistibility of God's anger. Divine wrath is compared to fire (Deut. 4:24; Heb. 12:29).

1:7 good. The term denotes the Lord's benevolence as the source of all true human well-being and prosperity, and is particularly a confession of His abundant covenant blessings and kindness (Ps. 73:1). The Lord's people experience His awesome power as holy love. When help is needed He is an impregnable fortress (Ps. 46).

1:8 flood . . . darkness. Striking images of severe judgment.

1:9–14 The downfall of the wicked, represented by Nineveh, culminates in the comfort of God's people, Judah.

1:9 plot. All Assyrian strategies will be futile. Their struggle and their plans are now against the Lord, who has decided on their destruction, and will bring it about once and for all.

1:11 who plotted evil. Perhaps a reference to Ashurbanipal (Introduction: Date and Occasion).

worthless. The word suggests something demonic.

1:12–14 A comforting divine message assures God's people that the downfall of Assyria implies the end of their humiliation.

1:12 Thus says the LORD. A well-known prophetic-messenger formula.

[d]Though I have afflicted you,
I will afflict you no more.
13 And now [e]I will break his yoke from off you
and will burst your bonds apart."
14 The LORD has given commandment about you:
[f]"No more shall your name be perpetuated;
from [g]the house of your gods I will cut off
the carved image and the metal image.
[h]I will make your grave, [i]for you are vile."

15[1] [j]Behold, upon the mountains, [k]the feet of him
who brings good news,
who publishes peace!
[l]Keep your feasts, O Judah;
[m]fulfill your vows,
[n]for never again shall the worthless pass through you;
he is utterly cut off.

The Destruction of Nineveh

2 [o]The scatterer has come up against you.
[p]Man the ramparts;
watch the road;
dress for battle;[2]
collect all your strength.
2 For [q]the LORD is restoring the majesty of Jacob
as the majesty of Israel,
for plunderers have plundered them
and [r]ruined their branches.

3 The shield of his mighty men is red;
[s]his soldiers are clothed in scarlet.
The chariots come with flashing metal
on the day he musters them;
the cypress spears are brandished.
4 [t]The chariots race madly through the streets;
they rush to and fro through the squares;
they gleam like torches;
they dart like lightning.
5 He remembers [u]his officers;
[v]they stumble as they go,
they hasten to the wall;
the siege tower[3] is set up.
6 [w]The river gates are opened;
the palace [x]melts away;

12 [d]ver. 9; [Isai. 9:1]
13 [e][Isai. 9:4; 10:27; 14:25]
14 [f][Ps. 109:13] [g][2 Kin. 19:37] [h][Isai. 30:33]; See Ezek. 32:21-23 [i][ch. 3:6]
15 [j]See Isai. 52:7 [k][Rom. 10:15] [l][Isai. 30:29] [m]See Num. 30:2 [n][ver. 12]; See Joel 3:17
Chapter 2
1 [o][Jer. 51:20] [p][Jer. 51:12]
2 [q][Isai. 37:31] [r]See Ps. 80:8-13; Isai. 5:1-7
3 [s][Ezek. 23:14, 15]
4 [t][ch. 3:2]
5 [u]ch. 3:18 [v]Jer. 46:12
6 [w][Isai. 45:1] [x][Isai. 14:31]

1 Ch 2:1 in Hebrew 2 Hebrew *gird your loins* 3 Or *the mantelet*

1:13 break his yoke . . . burst your bonds. Vivid poetic images of emancipation (Jer. 2:20; Ps. 2:3).

1:14 commandment. The word emphasizes authority and certainty.

your name. Complete extinction and loss of power and prestige await the Assyrians.

house of your gods. The temple and other objects of Assyria's trust and pride will also be destroyed.

grave. The term represents the final undoing of Nineveh, its king, and its people in 612 B.C.

1:15–2:13 This section is written in the prophetic present tense. Events still future are pictured as if already present, and events even more distantly future are portrayed as occurring at the same time with those happening much earlier. This vivid prophecy of judgment is a poetic "vision" (1:1; cf. Num. 12:6–8), and is not a precise and detailed historical account of events that took place later, in 612 B.C.

1:15 See Is. 52:7. The approach of a herald of "good news," whose feet tread "the mountains" of Judah, initiates a new period of grateful service to the Lord. The good news is summarized in the meaningful word "peace" (Hebrew *shalom*), signifying not only the end of hostilities but also the return to normal, abundant living conditions and general well-being.

Keep . . . vows. Periods of national crisis or foreign oppression often made celebration of the important temple feasts difficult, if not impossible. The "vows" made in the previous period of distress should now be fulfilled (Ps. 116:14, 17–19).

2:1 In sharp contrast to the call for Judah to celebrate is the ironic exhortation of Nineveh to prepare for an attack.

scatterer. The Assyrians, who destroyed many nations, including Israel, by scattering them over the face of the earth, will now experience a similar fate. In August, 612 B.C., the combined forces of the Medes and Babylonians destroyed Nineveh, and shortly afterward the Assyrian Empire collapsed.

2:2 majesty of Israel. God will restore the oppressed people to the happiness implied by the name "Israel." Jacob received this new name as a sign of his spiritual maturity and his willing acceptance of the destiny God intended for him from the beginning (Gen. 32:27, 28).

2:3 his mighty men. Probably a reference to the Lord's army (v. 2.). The warriors and chariots of the attackers fulfill His purposes. The armies of Assyria herself had earlier been God's instruments to accomplish His purposes of judgment (Is. 10:5–7).

red . . . scarlet. These terms emphasize the awe-inspiring appearance of the approaching army, whether the color refers to their actual robes or to the blood stains on them.

spears are brandished. The Hebrew is difficult but conveys the general impression of ready eagerness for war.

2:4 Nineveh is a beehive of frantic soldiers.

streets. Possibly open fields or plains outside the city; if so, the verse speaks of the approaching army and its chariots of war.

2:5 This may refer to the Assyrian king and his nobles, especially the military commanders. Alternatively, this verse may describe the attackers and their frenzied siege of Nineveh (the Hebrew word here rendered "siege tower" usually refers to a movable structure shielding the besiegers of a city).

2:6 river gates. The city of Nineveh was located on the bank of the Tigris River, and a smaller river flowed through the city. Conflicting ancient accounts ascribe the fall of Nineveh to flooding when the enemy redirected the dams and sluices of the water system. The description in Nahum is manifestly poetic, however. The term "gates" could simply refer to the five gates opening (cf. 3:13) in the direction of the Tigris River with its tributaries and canals. The location of the palace precluded the possibility of collapse by flooding.

palace. The seat of political and military organization.

7 its mistress[1] is [y]stripped;[2] she is
carried off,
her slave girls [z]lamenting,
moaning like doves
and [a]beating their breasts.
8 [b]Nineveh is like a pool
whose waters run away.[3]
"Halt! Halt!" they cry,
but [c]none turns back.
9 Plunder the silver,
plunder the gold!
There is no end of the treasure
or of the wealth of all precious
things.
10 [d]Desolate! Desolation and ruin!
[e]Hearts melt and [f]knees tremble;
[g]anguish is in all loins;
[h]all faces grow pale!
11 Where is the lions' den,
the feeding place of [i]the young
lions,
where the lion and lioness went,
where his cubs were, with [j]none to
disturb?
12 [k]The lion tore enough for his cubs
and [l]strangled prey for his lionesses;
he filled his caves with prey
and his dens with torn flesh.
13 [m]Behold, I am against you, declares the
LORD of hosts, and [n]I will burn your[4] chariots in smoke, and the sword shall devour
your young lions. I will cut off your prey
from the earth, and [o]the voice of your messengers shall no longer be heard.

7 [y][Isai. 22:8] [z]Isai. 38:14 [a][Ps. 68:25] 8 [b]See ch. 1:1 [c]Jer. 46:5 10 [d]See Zeph. 2:13-15 [e]Ps. 22:14; Isai. 13:7 [f]Dan. 5:6 [g]Isai. 21:3 [h]Joel 2:6 11 [i]Isai. 5:29; Jer. 2:15 [j]See Isai. 17:2 12 [k][Ezek. 19:4] [l][ver. 9; ch. 3:1] 13 [m]ch. 3:5; [Zeph. 2:5]; See Ezek. 13:8 [n][Ps. 46:9] [o][2 Kin. 19:9, 23]
Chapter 3
1 [p]Ezek. 24:9; [Hab. 2:12] [q][ch. 2:12] 2 [r][ch. 2:4] [s][Judg. 5:22] [t][Joel 2:5] 3 [u]Hab. 3:11 [v][2 Kin. 19:35] 4 [w][Rev. 17:2; 18:3] [x][Isai. 47:9, 12] 5 [m][See ch. 2:13 above] [y]Jer. 13:22, 26; [Isai. 3:17; 47:3]

Woe to Nineveh

3 Woe to [p]the bloody city,
all full of lies and plunder—
[q]no end to the prey!
2 The crack of the whip, and [r]rumble
of the wheel,
[s]galloping horse and [t]bounding
chariot!
3 Horsemen charging,
flashing sword and [u]glittering spear,
[v]hosts of slain,
heaps of corpses,
dead bodies without end—
they stumble over the bodies!
4 And all for the countless whorings of
the [w]prostitute,
[x]graceful and of deadly charms,
who betrays nations with her
whorings,
and peoples with her charms.
5 [m]Behold, I am against you,
declares the LORD of hosts,
and [y]will lift up your skirts over
your face;

[1] The meaning of the Hebrew word rendered *its mistress* is uncertain [2] Or *exiled* [3] Compare Septuagint; the meaning of the Hebrew is uncertain [4] Hebrew *her*

2:7 she. Nineveh is personified as a woman, a queen, going into exile. Her "slave girls," the inhabitants of the city, mourn the fate of their mistress.

2:8 pool. This striking image is often taken to portray Nineveh's full population and prosperity. Now it drains away.

2:10 Hearts melt . . . faces grow pale. The merciless devastation creates terror and paralysis among the once-mighty Ninevites.

2:11–13 This closing section is a taunt song in which the striking image of a pride of lions that met with destruction is employed to describe the imminent reversal of Nineveh's fortunes. God is the author of Nineveh's humiliation and disappearance.

2:11 Where. This rhetorical question emphasizes how the famous city will be reduced to oblivion.

the lions' den. An apt image for Nineveh as the home of the aggressive and ruthless Assyrians.

2:13 The real secret of Nineveh's full and final downfall is revealed. Confrontation with Israel's almighty covenant God is fatal to the Assyrian Empire.

I am against you. The opposite of the good tidings of salvation, "I will be with you" (Ex. 3:12; Josh. 1:5; Is. 43:2, 5).

messengers. The voices of the Assyrian envoys dictating terms and exacting tribute will be permanently silenced from the face of the earth.

3:1–19 The expression of woe that opens this chapter controls its mood until the last verse. The various parts all contribute to its literary unity, and together they emphasize the irreversible doom of Nineveh. The prophet no longer focuses on Israel and Judah alone, but places the fate of Nineveh in a universal perspective.

3:1–7 These vivid scenes of violence, death, and destruction confirm the city's expected doom. The charges against Nineveh (vv. 1–4) and her penalties (vv. 5–7) are set forth in stark detail.

3:1 bloody city. The phrase emphasizes the merciless cruelty openly boasted by the Assyrians in their official records.

lies. Deceitful diplomacy characterized their international dealings (Is. 36:16, 17).

plunder. See 2:12, 13. Friendly negotiations serve as a cover for rapacious behavior. In their insatiable lust for more they constantly move from one victim to another.

3:2, 3 These poetic verses provide one of the most vivid portrayals of a battle scene in the Old Testament. The staccato beat, economy of words, and gruesome detail all contribute to create an image of the Assyrian armies in action, reducing whole populations to "heaps of corpses" (v. 3).

3:4 With a change of imagery, Nineveh is likened to a beautiful and seductive "prostitute" for whose favor "nations" and "peoples" are sacrificed. Service of the gods, warfare, and commerce were closely intertwined. Seduction by Nineveh's power and pomp implied apostasy from true religion and subjection to her "charms," a term probably indicating the totality of pagan religion (Is. 47:12, 13).

3:5 Retribution by the universal Judge is inevitable. See 2:13.

lift up your skirts. The public humiliation by which harlots were punished.

and I will make nations look at [z]your
nakedness
and kingdoms at your shame.
6 I will throw filth at you
and [a]treat you with contempt
and make you [b]a spectacle.
7 And all who look at you [c]will shrink
from you and say,
Wasted is [d]Nineveh; [e]who will grieve
for her?
[f]Where shall I seek comforters for
you?
8 [g]Are you better than [h]Thebes[1]
that sat [i]by the Nile,
with water around her,
her rampart a sea,
and water her wall?
9 [j]Cush was her strength;
Egypt too, and that without
limit;
[k]Put and the [l]Libyans were her[2]
helpers.
10 [m]Yet she became an exile;
she went into captivity;
[n]her infants were dashed in
pieces
at the head of every street;
for her honored men [o]lots were
cast,
[p]and all her great men were bound
in chains.
11 [q]You also will be drunken;
you will go into hiding;
[r]you will seek a refuge from the
enemy.

5 [z]Hab. 2:16
6 [a]Mal. 2:9; [ch. 1:14] [b]Heb. 10:33; [1 Cor. 4:9]
7 [c]Jer. 51:9; Rev. 18:10 [d][Zeph. 2:13]; See ch. 1:1 [e]Isai. 51:19; Jer. 15:5 [f]Lam. 1:2, 9, 16, 17, 21
8 [g][Amos 6:2] [h]Jer. 46:25 [i][Ezek. 29:3]
9 [j]See Dan. 11:43 [k]Gen. 10:6 [l]See 2 Chr. 12:3
10 [m]Isai. 20:4 [n]Isai. 13:16 [o]Joel 3:3; Obad. 11 [p][Ps. 149:8]
11 [q]Jer. 25:17, 27; [Ps. 75:8; Isai. 51:17; Obad. 16] [r][Jer. 4:5, 6]

12 All your fortresses are [s]like fig
trees
with first-ripe figs—
if shaken they fall
into the mouth of the eater.
13 Behold, your troops
[t]are women in your midst.
The gates of your land
are wide open to your enemies;
fire has devoured your bars.
14 [u]Draw water for the siege;
[q]strengthen your forts;
go into the clay;
tread the mortar;
take hold of the brick mold!
15 There will the fire devour you;
the sword will cut you off.
It will [v]devour you [w]like the
locust.
Multiply yourselves [w]like the
locust;
multiply [w]like the grasshopper!
16 You increased [x]your merchants
more than the stars of the
heavens.
[w]The locust [y]spreads its wings and
flies away.
17 Your [z]princes are [w]like
grasshoppers,
[a]your scribes[3] like clouds of locusts
settling on the fences
in a day of cold—
when the sun rises, they fly away;
no one knows where they are.

12 [s][Rev. 6:13]
13 [t]Isai. 19:16; Jer. 51:30
14 [u][Isai. 22:11] [q][See ver. 11 above]
15 [v][Joel 2:3] [w][Joel 1:4, 6]
16 [x][Ezek. 27:23, 24] [w][See ver. 15 above] [y][ch. 2:9]
17 [z][Isai. 10:8] [w][See ver. 15 above] [a]Jer. 51:27

1 Hebrew *No-amon* 2 Hebrew *your* 3 Or *marshals*

3:6 The image of the harlot is continued. She will be made an object of scorn and an example to deter others from doing the same.

3:7 Wasted is Nineveh. The sight is so terrible that people will retreat from it in horror. So dreadful and truly deserved will be the disaster that no one will be found to mourn or comfort the nation in its downfall.

3:8 Thebes. See text note. The city of the god Amon. This ancient and magnificent metropolis of Upper Egypt fell to the Assyrians in 663 B.C. Located on the Nile some 400 miles upstream from Memphis, it may have had moats and canals as defenses. There is probably a figurative element in Nahum's emphasis on the sea. In Scripture, a river or sea is often an emblem for strength that only God can overcome (Ex. 15; Ps. 114:3–5; Is. 23:3, 4; Matt. 8:27).

3:9 Put. Traditionally identified with Libya.

3:11 drunken. Apparently a figurative reference to the cup of the Lord's anger, from which all who defy Him are forced to drink (Is. 51:17–23). Nineveh in her distress tries to hide and find refuge, but only the Lord provides refuge in times of trouble (1:7). Compared to Him even the most powerful are weak and vulnerable (vv. 12–17).

3:12 fig trees. This telling image emphasizes that the normally impregnable fortresses are now not only desirable but easy to take.

3:13 In the face of the approaching army all the Assyrian troops are like women (i.e., not trained for warfare). All barriers to slow the enemy's advance, such as gates and bars, have been removed.

3:14 Frantic efforts must be made to "strengthen . . . forts" and to prepare for a lengthy period of siege. The imperatives are ironic; vv. 14–17 reflect the mood of a derisive taunt song.

3:15 Even the most strenuous efforts to avoid invasion are useless. The city and its people succumb to fire and sword.

3:16 merchants. Assyria's international trade and commerce brought people and wealth to Nineveh. Under pressure from outside, the self-interest of these traders becomes clear. Having gathered like locusts, they seize what they can and disappear.

3:17 princes . . . scribes. See text note. These two terms are rare in Hebrew and may be Assyrian loan-words. They probably represent important officials in the government of the vast empire. When things become dangerous they run away. Riches, power, and organization fail miserably as the nation collapses.

sun rises. The appearance of the Lord's judgment will scatter His enemies as dramatically as the heat of day rouses and disperses sleeping locusts (cf. Ps. 84:11; Mal. 4:1–3).

18 Your shepherds [b]are asleep,
O king of Assyria;
[c]your nobles slumber.
Your people [d]are scattered on the mountains
with none to gather them.

19 There is no easing your hurt;
[e]your wound is grievous.
All who hear the news about you
[f]clap their hands over you.
For [g]upon whom has not come
your unceasing evil?

18[b][Ps. 76:5] [c]ch. 2:5 [d][1 Kin. 22:17] 19[e]Jer. 10:19; Mic. 1:9 [f]Lam. 2:15; [Zeph. 2:15] [g][Isai. 37:18]

3:18, 19 The finality of divine judgment on the cruel oppressor leads to universal rejoicing. These verses are reminiscent of funeral dirges and taunt songs of the period.

3:18 shepherds. A well-known metaphor for leaders indicates the subordinate rulers of the Assyrian king.

asleep . . . slumber. Striking euphemisms for death.

Your people . . . gather them. The pastoral image is extended to the people (or perhaps the army) as a flock of sheep. In the absence of shepherds, the people are scattered (cf. 1 Kin. 22:17).

3:19 The "news" of Nineveh's incurable "wound" and fatal "hurt" is received with general applause. The God of Israel, to whom alone vengeance belongs (Deut. 32:35; Rom. 12:19), has finally put an end to the continual wickedness that had caused such injustice and suffering. The vision of Nahum had its initial fulfillment in 612 B.C. but still awaits its final realization at the Second Coming of our Lord Jesus Christ.

THE BOOK OF

Habakkuk

AUTHOR

Our only reliable information about Habakkuk and his prophetic activity comes from this book. The meaning of his name is uncertain. It may be connected with a Hebrew word meaning "to embrace," or with the name of an Assyrian plant, the *hambakuku*. The former may refer to his closeness to the Lord; the latter may suggest the penetration of Assyrian culture into Judean society. The reference in 1:1 to Habakkuk as "the prophet" may imply that he was well known. His use of the cultic and wisdom traditions of Israel in his preaching have given rise to the doubtful notion that he was a prophet attached to the temple in Jerusalem, though the suggestion that he worked in Jerusalem is attractive. We can be sure, however, that in this book we meet a true prophet with a burning zeal for the glory of the Lord. His "oracle" (1:1 and note) is remarkable in that it is not, in the first place, a word directed to the people, but an answer to his own painful questions.

DATE AND OCCASION

Objective evidence for dating Habakkuk's prophetic activity is provided by 1:6. The reference to the Chaldeans, or Neo-Babylonians, as the threatening new world power indicates a period after the collapse of the Assyrian Empire (612–605 B.C.) but before the Chaldean armies of Nebuchadnezzar II captured Jerusalem and deported the young king Jehoiachin to Babylon in 597 B.C. (2 Kin. 24:8–17). Habakkuk apparently ministered during Jehoiakim's reign (609–598 B.C.) and was a younger contemporary of Jeremiah.

An important event during this period was the battle of Carchemish in 605 B.C., when Pharaoh Neco II and his Egyptian army, who had come to assist the Assyrians against Babylon, were soundly defeated by Nebuchadnezzar II. Soon afterward, Judah also, like the other previously independent kingdoms of Syro-Palestine, became subject to the powerful Neo-Babylonians. Habakkuk's inspired vision therefore may be dated to the period between 605 and 600 B.C. when the Babylonians became the dominant force on the international scene, mercilessly sweeping aside all opposition (1:5–17).

This time of international threat coincided with a period of increasing moral and spiritual deterioration in Judah. The evil reign of Jehoiakim formed a sad contrast to that of his father, the good king Josiah (Jer. 22:13–19; 26:20–23). As they insolently flouted the covenant laws, the people of Judah increasingly lost their unique character (1:2–4).

CHARACTERISTICS AND THEMES

Prophets were not only inspired preachers of divine messages to the people of God; they also shared the Lord's burden for His broken world and His deep concern for His wayward people. In this respect, Habakkuk closely resembles Jeremiah. But even more than with Jeremiah, Habakkuk's dialogue with God and his persistent prayers (2:1, 2; 3:2, 16) take the place of prophetic preaching as the heart of the message.

Habakkuk, a man with a burning passion for the honor of God (1:12; 3:3), experienced a profound spiritual crisis because of the Lord's seeming indifference to appalling spiritual conditions among His people (1:2–4). The absence of covenant life and obedience was dangerous to the people of God, but even more it was a rejection of the covenant Lord and an insult to Him. Because only divine intervention could change this deadly situation, Habakkuk was persistent in his appeal to the heavenly Judge, even when it seemed to be in vain (1:2). In response, the Lord revealed that the Chaldeans now appearing on the scene of history (1:6) would be His instruments of judgment. This cure seemed even worse than the disease and only added to the prophet's distress (1:12–17). How could the holy God, who cannot tolerate wrong (1:13), use such wicked people to fulfill His purposes? Does God really distinguish between good and evil in His sovereignty over history?

Convinced that the events of history were not determined by blind fate but by the righteous and holy God of Israel, Habakkuk expectantly waited on the Lord until he received an answer to his painful questions (2:1). The Lord's reply came in the vision introduced in 2:2, 3, which provides a true perspective on history and gives the divine promise about its outcome. This answer does not resolve all the painful questions, but it does teach God's people the way of covenant life in the here and now (2:3, 4). That way is to persevere in hope, waiting with confidence for the fulfillment of the Lord's unfailing promise. Although God's ways may be inscrutable, His purposes are consistent. They culminate in real life for the faithful, but woe and death for the self-sufficient and arrogant (2:4). The Lord's presence in His temple affirms His Lordship over history and assures us that in the end, His legitimate claim to the whole world will be universally acknowledged (2:14, 20; Is. 45:21–25; 1 Cor. 15:24–28).

The revelation of the Lord's sovereignty over history transforms Habakkuk's complaint into a hymn of joy (3:2–20). Instead of passively waiting for divine intervention, he now prayed positively that the Lord would act in accord with the deeds and qualities He displayed in the Exodus and at Sinai. Anticipating the future, Habakkuk in his prayer celebrates the Lord's coming (3:3–7), his judgment against nature and the nations (3:8–12), and His triumph over all opposition (3:13–15). From this perspective of faith, even the threat of severe calamity could not dampen Habakkuk's overwhelming joy in expectation of the coming salvation, a salvation guaranteed by the Lord's faithfulness to Himself and to His revelation (3:17–19).

Paul uses Hab. 2:4 as a foundational text for his proclamation of the gospel (Rom. 1:17; Gal. 3:11; cf. Heb. 10:35–39). Like Habakkuk (ch. 1), Paul knew that sin is incompatible with God's holiness and that the fatal tension between these opposites could only be resolved by divine intervention. The prophetic word to Habakkuk (ch. 2) reveals in principle the way God would deal with the incompatibility of sin and holiness. The Cross of Christ and the final Judgment are fulfillments of this revelation. Like Habakkuk, Paul also affirmed that true life was only possible in a relationship of total dependence on the Lord. Such dependence, based on the faithfulness of our God, transforms our existence in this world, filling our lives with joy in the certainty of God's faithfulness to His promises (2:3; 3:17–19).

For this reason, Habakkuk can be called a forefather of the Reformation. The key concepts of his preaching, as taken over by Paul, deeply influenced Luther and Calvin, and eventually became watchwords of the Reformation. Only the perspective of faith, or persevering and obedient trust in God, provides for meaningful existence in the world during the present period, between the "already" of initial fulfillment of God's promises and the "not yet" of their final realization.

OUTLINE OF HABAKKUK

I. Superscription (1:1)

II. First Complaint: Departure from Covenant Life by God's People (1:2–4)

III. First Response: The Lord Sends the Babylonians (1:5–11)

IV. Second Complaint: Why the Wicked Babylonians? (1:12–17)

V. Second Response: Life for the Faithful but Woe for the Wicked (ch. 2)

A. *The Crucial Distinction Revealed (2:1–5)*

B. *From Woe to Worship (2:6–20)*

VI. The Prayer of the Prophet (ch. 3)

A. *Superscription; Invocation (3:1, 2)*

B. *Divine Self-Revelation (3:3–15)*

C. *Faith's Expectation and Jubilation (3:16–19)*

1 [a]The oracle that Habakkuk the prophet saw.

Habakkuk's Complaint

2 O LORD, [b]how long shall I cry for
help,
and you will not hear?
Or cry to you [c]"Violence!"
and you will not save?
3 [d]Why do you make me see
iniquity,
and why do you idly look at
wrong?
Destruction [c]and violence are
before me;
strife and contention arise.
4 [e]So the law is paralyzed,
and justice never goes forth.
[f]For the wicked surround the
righteous;
so justice goes forth perverted.

The LORD's Answer

5 [g]"Look among the nations, and see;
wonder and be astounded.
[h]For I am doing a work in your
days
that you would not believe if
told.
6 For behold, [i]I am raising up the
Chaldeans,
that bitter and hasty nation,
[j]who march through the breadth of
the earth,
[k]to seize dwellings not their own.
7 They are dreaded and fearsome;
[l]their justice and dignity go forth
from themselves.
8 [m]Their horses are swifter than
leopards,
more fierce than [n]the evening
wolves;
their horsemen press proudly on.
Their horsemen come from afar;
[o]they fly like an eagle swift to
devour.
9 They all come [p]for violence,
all their faces [q]forward.
They gather captives [r]like sand.
10 At kings they scoff,
and at rulers they laugh.
[s]They laugh at every fortress,
for [t]they pile up earth and take it.
11 Then they sweep by like the wind
and go on,
[u]guilty men, [v]whose own might is
their god!"

Chapter 1
1 [a]See Nah. 1:1
2 [b]Ps. 13:1; 89:46 [c]Mic. 6:12
3 [d]See Jer. 9:2-6 [e][See ver. 2 above]
4 [e][Mic. 7:3] [f][Job 21:7; Jer. 12:1]
5 [g]Cited Acts 13:41 [h][Isai. 28:21; 29:14]
6 [i]See Jer. 5:15 [j][ch. 2:5] [k][ch. 2:6]
7 [l][ver. 10, 11]
8 [m]Jer. 4:13 [n]Jer. 5:6; Zeph. 3:3 [o]See Deut. 28:49
9 [p][ch. 2:17] [q][Hos. 13:15, 16] [r]See Josh. 11:4
10 [s][Nah. 3:12] [t][Ezek. 4:2]
11 [u][Hos. 13:16] [v][ver. 7]

1:1 oracle. Often a technical term for a prophecy of judgment against a foreign nation (Is. 13:1; 15:1; Nah. 1:1; Mal. 1:1 note).

Habakkuk the prophet. See Introduction: Author.

saw. The divine message took the form of a supernatural revelation to the prophet's inner sight or hearing (Mic. 1:1).

1:2–4 Habakkuk's first complaint: The prophet was grieved and shocked by how God's people continually departed from covenant life. They no longer lived like a chosen and saved people (Ex. 19:4–6). But Habakkuk is even more concerned about the Lord's apparent inactivity. Breach of the covenant was to bring curses and judgment (Deut. 28:15–68). He therefore appealed to the Lord in language reminiscent of the psalms of individual complaint to redress a seemingly hopeless situation. Habakkuk's passionate dialogue and anguished wrestling with the Lord dominate the first part of the book (1:2–2:20).

1:2 how long. The impatient question, characteristic of the psalms of lament (Ps. 13:2; 62:3; Jer. 47:6), indicates both importunity and perseverance in the prophet's appeal to the Lord, the final Judge in matters of covenant disobedience.

shall I cry. This indicates the loud cry of someone in deep distress (Ps. 22:24; 30:2).

Violence. This term summarizes the deliberate, brutal, and insensitive infringement of the rights and privileges of members of the covenant community.

you will not save. Habakkuk painfully observes the Lord's seeming indifference and inactivity in the face of undeserved suffering.

1:3 Why. The question continues the complaint (cf. Lam. 5:20).

iniquity. Lit. "labor" or "toil" that leads to distress, exhaustion, and despondency.

strife and contention. Unchecked wickedness results in a divided community riddled with suspicions, accusations, and personal attacks.

1:4 the law is paralyzed. Lit. "the law is numb." The word for "law" (Hebrew *torah*) denotes the divinely revealed standard for covenant life. The power and influence of the wicked had rendered the law ineffectual.

the wicked. Those in Israel who spurned the Lord's will and law.

1:5–11 God's first response: The Lord will send the Babylonians to judge His people. He uses strange instruments against His unfaithful people—the terrifying Babylonians (cf. Is. 10:5, 6).

1:5 astounded . . . not believe. God's method—the victory of the wicked over those "more righteous" (v. 13)—would pose a stumbling block to faith among Habakkuk's audience.

1:6 I am raising up. The sovereign God of Israel controls every power in history, including the aggressive Chaldeans.

Chaldeans. Also called Babylonians, or Neo-Babylonians, the Chaldeans rose to power as the Assyrian Empire fell. Nineveh, capital of Assyria, was destroyed in 612 B.C. The Chaldeans ruled until their capital, Babylon, was destroyed by the Persians in 539.

1:7 justice . . . from themselves. This describes the arrogance of the coming enemy whose standards of action and honor were entirely selfish.

1:8, 9 Vivid images portray the speed and resolution of these fierce and overpowering warriors.

1:10 At kings they scoff. The intimidating Babylonian armies look at obstacles as challenges and treat their opposition with contempt.

pile up earth. Siege ramps built by attackers to gain access to a fortified city's walls.

1:11 whose own might is their god. Or, "this his power is his god." Pride, especially the deification of one's own power, is offensive to God, the only One who deserves our worship.

Habakkuk's Second Complaint

12 Are you not [w]from everlasting,
O LORD my God, my Holy One?
[x]We shall not die.
O LORD, [y]you have ordained them as
a judgment,
and you, O [z]Rock, have
established them for reproof.
13 You who are [a]of purer eyes than to
see evil
and cannot look at wrong,
[b]why do you idly look at traitors
and [c]are silent when the wicked
swallows up
the man more righteous than he?
14 You make mankind like the fish
of the sea,
like crawling things that have
no ruler.
15 [d]He brings all of them up [e]with
a hook;
he drags them out with his net;
he gathers them in his dragnet;
so he rejoices and is glad.
16 [f]Therefore he sacrifices to his net
and makes offerings to his dragnet;
for by them he lives in luxury,[1]
and his food is rich.
17 Is he then to keep on emptying his
net
[g]and mercilessly killing nations
forever?

2 I will [h]take my stand at my
watchpost
and station myself on the tower,
and [i]look out to see [j]what he will say
to me,
and what I will answer concerning
my complaint.

The Righteous Shall Live by His Faith

2 And the LORD answered me:
[k]"Write the vision;
make it plain on tablets,
so he may run who reads it.
3 For still [l]the vision awaits its
appointed time;
it hastens to the end—it will not
lie.
If it seems slow, [m]wait for it;
[n]it will surely come; it will not
delay.
4 "Behold, his soul is puffed up; it is
not upright within him,

12 [w]Deut. 33:27; Ps. 90:2; 93:2 [x][Mal. 3:6] [y]See Isai. 10:5-7 [z]See Deut. 32:4
13 [a][Ps. 5:5] [b]Jer. 12:1 [c]Ps. 35:22
15 [d]Jer. 16:16; Amos 4:2 [e][Isai. 19:8]
16 [f][ver. 11]
17 [g][ch. 2:10]
Chapter 2
1 [h]Isai. 21:8 [i]Jer. 6:17; Ezek. 33:2 [j]Ps. 85:8
2 [k]Isai. 8:1; 30:8; [Rev. 1:19]
3 [l][Dan. 10:14]; See Ezek. 7:5-7 [m]Zeph. 3:8; See Isai. 8:17 [n]Cited Heb. 10:37; [2 Pet. 3:9]

1 Hebrew *his portion is fat*

1:12–17 Habakkuk's second complaint: The Lord's plan to use the wicked Babylonians to punish Israel seems to be in flagrant opposition to God's own revealed character.

1:12 from everlasting. As the eternal God of history and Lord of His people, He is free to choose the agents of chastisement.

my God, my Holy One. A personal relationship to the incomparable God, the Holy One, turns confusion into conviction that the present anguish will not be the end.

O Rock. This ancient Mosaic name for God emphasizes divine dependability and protection (Deut. 32:4 note).

1:14 You make mankind. A bold accusation by Habakkuk. If the Lord tolerates the evil actions of the Babylonians, He becomes responsible for the fate of their victims.

like the fish. Imagery of Babylon as a fisherman catching helpless fish is developed in vv. 14–17. Fishing was an important activity in Babylonia, which was located in the region of the Tigris and Euphrates rivers and was bordered on the south by the Persian Gulf. Some ancient Near Eastern wall reliefs portray victorious rulers carrying captives in fishnets.

no ruler. There was no one to protect them. Kings in the ancient Near East were seen as the protectors of their people (1 Sam. 8:20). An implicit accusation may also be present here, since the Lord was the ultimate King and protector of His people (Deut. 33:5; Is. 63:18, 19).

1:16 sacrifices. The instruments of their success are idolized and worshiped (v. 11 note).

2:1–20 Habakkuk receives an answer to his painful questions of 1:12–17. God will show that He is just and the justifier of those who have faith in Him. The final outcome of history will be worship of the one holy and just King (v. 20). The destiny of nations and individuals alike will be determined by their attitude toward God as it has found expression in persevering and faithful dependence or haughty rejection (Ps. 1; 2:2, 3).

2:1 Habakkuk's anguished questioning drove him to the fount of all wisdom to wait for an answer. His words express his determination to wait for an answer. God is sovereign in word as well as in deed—His revelation cannot be forced.

watchpost . . . tower. Military terms figuratively depict the prophet as a watchman on the lookout for a word from God.

2:2 Write . . . make it plain. In order that it might be preserved and transmitted (cf. Jer. 30:2; Nah. 1:1).

vision. See note 1:1.

so he may run who reads it. Perhaps a figure (though some suggest that Habakkuk actually wrote an oracle on large tablets) indicating that Habakkuk's prophecy was to be publicized. Either the writing was to be so clear that a courier could run with the tablets to read them, or that its clarity should enable passersby to read without difficulty (i.e., "that one may read it swiftly").

2:3 appointed time . . . not delay. A fixed period must elapse before the prophecy will be fulfilled, but this should not be regarded as failure or deception. Rather, this time can be endured with the Lord's guarantee of approaching fulfillment. Judgment on the Babylonians came (long after Habakkuk's vision) through Cyrus on October 29, 539 B.C.

2:4 The Lord now discloses the essential distinction He makes between the wicked, the Babylonians, and the righteous, the remnant of Judah. The wicked take paths that lead to death and defeat; the righteous by faith take a path that leads to life and victory. In brief, this distinction and the promise it contains for the righteous constitute the word of comfort to Habakkuk. It also marks the turning point in his personal struggle over the Lord's use of the wicked Babylonians as a rod of judgment against His people.

puffed up. The Babylonian king and kingdom, the embodiment of wickedness in the world. Habakkuk has earlier described their arrogance (1:7, 10, 11).

but [o]the righteous shall live by his
faith.[1]

5 "Moreover, wine[2] is [p]a traitor,
an arrogant man who is never
at rest.[3]
His greed is as wide as Sheol;
like death [q]he has never enough.
[r]He gathers for himself all nations
and collects as his own all
peoples."

Woe to the Chaldeans

6 Shall not all these [s]take up their taunt against him, with scoffing and riddles for him, and say,

[t]"Woe to him [u]who heaps up what is
not his own—
for [v]how long?—
and [w]loads himself with pledges!"
7 [x]Will not your debtors suddenly
arise,
and those awake who will make
you tremble?
Then you will be spoil for them.
8 [y]Because you have plundered many
nations,
all the remnant of the peoples
shall plunder you,
[z]for the blood of man and [y]violence to
the earth,
to cities and all who dwell in
them.

9 [t]"Woe to him who gets evil gain for his
house,
[a]to [b]set his nest on high,
to be safe from the reach of harm!
10 You have devised shame for your
house
[c]by cutting off many peoples;
you have forfeited your life.
11 For [d]the stone will cry out from the
wall,
and the beam from the woodwork
respond.

12 [t]"Woe to him [e]who builds a town with
blood
and founds a city on iniquity!
13 Behold, is it not from the LORD of
hosts
that [f]peoples labor merely for fire,
and nations weary themselves for
nothing?
14 [g]For the earth will be filled
with the knowledge of [h]the glory of
the LORD
as the waters cover the sea.

15 [t]"Woe to him [i]who makes his
neighbors drink—
you pour out your wrath and make
them drunk,
in order to gaze [j]at their nakedness!

4 [o]Cited Rom. 1:17; Gal. 3:11; Heb. 10:38; [John 3:36]
5 [p]ch. 1:13; Isai. 21:2 [q][Prov. 27:20] [r]Jer. 27:7; [ch. 1:6; Dan. 2:37, 38]
6 [s]Mic. 2:4; See Num. 23:7 [t]ver. 19; Isai. 5:8 [u][ch. 1:6] [v]See Zech. 1:12 [w][Ezek. 18:7]
7 [x]See Isai. 21:5-9
8 [y][Isai. 33:1] [z]ver. 17
9 [t][See ver. 6 above] [a][Isai. 14:13] [b]Jer. 49:16; [Num. 24:21]
10 [c][ch. 1:17]
11 [d][Luke 19:40]
12 [t][See ver. 6 above] [e]See Mic. 3:10
13 [f]Jer. 51:58
14 [g]Isai. 11:9 [h]Ps. 72:19
15 [t][See ver. 6 above] [i][ver. 5; Jer. 51:7] [j]Lam. 4:21; [Gen. 9:22]

1 Or *faithfulness* 2 Masoretic Text; Dead Sea Scroll *wealth* 3 The meaning of the Hebrew of these two lines is uncertain

by his faith. Or, "by his faithfulness." In context here, the Hebrew word denotes steadfast reliance on the Lord, a trust that perseveres. In the midst of a land filled with wickedness (1:2–4) and subject to the wrath of God, the Lord promises that a righteous remnant in Judah will trust in the God who remembers mercy in His wrath (3:2). The Hebrew recalls the words of Gen. 15:6 and applies them to Habakkuk's situation. By faith Abraham waited patiently for the fulfillment of God's promises (Heb. 6:15), and now Habakkuk and the remnant must wait patiently too (v. 3; 3:16). Here Paul found scriptural proof for the doctrine of justification by faith (Rom. 1:17; Gal. 3:11), and Habakkuk's word of comfort has been a key text for Protestant Reformation faith since the sixteenth century.

2:5 wine is a traitor . . . arrogant man. The arrogance and insatiability of the Babylonians is compared to a drunkard besotted with wine.

Sheol . . . death. It was proverbial that death was like a devouring mouth always ready for more to die (Prov. 1:12; 27:20; 30:15, 16).

2:6–20 This section of woes forms a distinct literary unit. Prophetic judgments are presented here in a taunt song, a poetic form that mocks the defeated.

2:6–8 The first woe. Those who plunder others will themselves be plundered.

2:6 all these. Judah and all those that suffered under the Babylonian oppressor. The prophecies of woe in vv. 6–20 are depicted in such general and proverbial terms that they acquire a universal applicability to the struggle of the persecuted righteous against the wicked.

Woe. The Hebrew word is apparently an interjection derived from the funeral lament (sometimes rendered "Alas," 1 Kin. 13:30), but is often used in prophecies of judgment.

pledges. The heavy tribute exacted by the Babylonians is figuratively depicted as articles taken in security for debts.

2:8 blood. The violence and bloodshed through which the Babylonians gained their plunder cries out to be avenged (v. 11; cf. Gen. 4:10).

2:9–11 The second woe condemns those who sought security and economic gain at the expense of others.

2:9 nest on high. Birds of prey often make their nests in high and inaccessible places. Likewise the Babylonians considered their position in world history to be secure (Is. 14:13, 14; 47:7).

2:11 stone will . . . respond. A striking personification. This cry against injustice emerges from building materials stolen from others or purchased with unjust gain.

2:12–14 The third woe pronounces judgment on the ruthless but futile efforts of the tyrant to perpetuate his fame.

2:12 builds a town with blood. Babylonian inscriptions confirm the high premium placed on building activities. Nebuchadnezzar, who used subjugated peoples as forced laborers, took special pride in his building of Babylon (Dan. 4:30). Such projects involved loss of life and were paid for with the spoils of war.

2:13 from the LORD . . . nothing. God sovereignly ensures that the efforts of the proud to perpetuate their own glory amount to nothing. Instead, the "earth will be filled with the knowledge of the glory of the LORD" (v. 14).

2:15–17 The fourth woe pronounces judgment on Babylon's sadistic and humiliating treatment of others.

16 You will have your fill [k]of shame
instead of glory.
[l]Drink, yourself, and show your
uncircumcision!
[l]The cup in the LORD's right hand
will come around to you,
and [m]utter shame will come upon
your glory!
17 [n]The violence [o]done to Lebanon will
overwhelm you,
as will the destruction of the
beasts that terrified them,
[n]for the blood of man and violence to
the earth,
to cities and all who dwell in
them.
18 [p]"What profit is an idol
when its maker has shaped it,
a metal image, [q]a teacher of
lies?
For its maker trusts in his own
creation
when he makes [r]speechless
idols!
19 [s]Woe to him [t]who says to a wooden
thing, Awake;
to a silent stone, Arise!
Can this teach?
Behold, it is overlaid with gold and
silver,
and [u]there is no breath at all in it.
20 But [v]the LORD is in his holy temple;
[w]let all the earth keep silence before
him."

16 [k]Nah. 3:5 [l]Jer. 25:15, 26 [m][Nah. 3:6] 17 [n]ver. 8 [o][Isai. 14:8; Jer. 22-23] 18 [p]Isai. 44:10 [q]Jer. 10:8, 14; Zech. 10:2 [r]Ps. 115:5; 1 Cor. 12:2 19 [s]ver. 6, 9, 12, 15 [t]See 1 Kin. 18:26, 27 [u]Ps. 135:17; Jer. 10:14 20 [v]Ps. 11:4; Mic. 1:2 [w][Zeph. 1:7; Zech. 2:13]

Chapter 3
2 [x]ver. 16; [Ps. 44:1] [y]Ps. 85:6 [z]Ps. 90:16 [a][Ps. 77:9] 3 [b]See 1 Chr. 1:45 [c]See Deut. 33:2 4 [d]See Ezek. 1:27 5 [e][2 Kin. 19:35]; See Ex. 12:29, 30; 1 Chr. 21:11-15 [f][Job 18:11] 6 [g][Ps. 60:6] [h]Gen. 49:26; Deut. 33:15 [i]Mic. 1:4; Nah. 1:5 [j][Isai. 51:9] 7 [k]Judg. 3:8 [l]See Judg. 8:19-21

Habakkuk's Prayer

3 A prayer of Habakkuk the prophet,
according to Shigionoth.

2 O LORD, [x]I have heard the report of
you,
and [y]your work, O LORD, do I fear.
In the midst of the years [z]revive it;
in the midst of the years make it
known;
[a]in wrath remember mercy.
3 God came from [b]Teman,
[c]and the Holy One from Mount
Paran.
His splendor covered the heavens,
and the earth was full of his praise.
Selah
4 [d]His brightness was like the light;
rays flashed from his hand;
and there he veiled his power.
5 [e]Before him went pestilence,
and plague followed [f]at his
heels.[1]
6 He stood [g]and measured the earth;
he looked and shook the nations;
then the [h]eternal mountains [i]were
scattered;
the everlasting hills sank low.
His were [j]the everlasting ways.
7 I saw the tents of [k]Cushan in
affliction;
[l]the curtains of the land of Midian
did tremble.

[1] Hebrew *feet*

2:16 cup in the LORD's right hand. This biblical metaphor indicates divine retribution (Is. 51:17–23). What the Babylonians did to others will be done to them (vv. 7, 8).

2:17 violence done to Lebanon. Military campaigns usually caused extensive damage to plants and animals. Trees supplied building material and firewood (Deut. 20:19, 20); wild and domestic animals were killed for food. Many cedar trees were lost during the Babylonian campaign against Lebanon (Is. 14:8). God's concern for His creation should be noted.

2:18–20 The fifth woe denounces idolatry, the worship of false gods, as futile and foolish (Is. 44:9–17; 57:12, 13).

2:20 temple. Lit. "palace," the heavenly sanctuary from which the Lord, the Great King, rules His world (Ps. 11:4).

let all the earth keep silence. A sharp contrast is drawn between the silent idols (v. 19) and the living God, before whom all others must keep silence. The woes of judgment on the proud and wicked culminate in the universal silence of worship in the glorious presence of the incomparable God (v. 14; Ps. 46:10).

3:1–19 This chapter records the persevering prayer of Habakkuk. In moving hymnic style, Habakkuk responds (vv. 16–19) to the Lord's revelation (2:2–5) of His imminent intervention in history on behalf of His people (vv. 3–15). As the Babylonians represented the proud and wicked on their way to ruin, Habakkuk now exemplifies the righteous faithful persevering and already rejoicing in hope of the Lord's promise of life.

3:1 prayer. Here perhaps a synonym for hymn (Ps. 72:20). The musical and liturgical notations in the heading, text, and conclusion of this prayer are like those commonly found in the psalms. See Introduction to Psalms: Characteristics and Themes.

3:2 The invocation or prologue to the hymn.

heard the report. Habakkuk's patience in standing before the Lord (2:1 note) was rewarded by a vision based on God's mighty deeds in the past.

revive it. Be present and active as You were in the time of Moses.

3:3–15 Habakkuk's prayer portrays a theophany, or visible self-manifestation of God, using imagery that is found in the traditional descriptions of God's appearances at the Exodus from Egypt, at the giving of the covenant law at Sinai, and during the conquest of Canaan (Ex. 15:1–18; Deut. 33:2, 3; Judg. 5:4, 5; Ps. 18:10; 68:7, 8, 24; 77:16–20).

3:3 Teman. The name of Esau's grandson represents the land of Edom (Amos 1:12 note).

Mount Paran. A mountain in the wilderness of the Sinai peninsula (Deut. 33:2).

3:5 pestilence, and plague. Habakkuk pictures ominous dimensions of God's coming in judgment (Deut. 28:21, 22).

3:7 Cushan . . . Midian. These are possibly alternative names for one people or area, perhaps for nomads from the Sinai peninsula.

8 [m] Was your wrath against the rivers,
O LORD?
Was your anger against the rivers,
[m] or your indignation against the sea,
[n] when you rode on your horses,
[n] on your chariot of salvation?
9 You stripped the sheath from your
bow,
[o] calling for many arrows.[1]
Selah
[p] You split the earth with rivers.
10 [q] The mountains saw you and writhed;
the raging waters swept on;
[r] the deep gave forth its voice;
[s] it lifted its hands on high.
11 [t] The sun and moon stood still in their
place
[u] at the light of your arrows as they
sped,
at the flash of your glittering spear.
12 [v] You marched through the earth in
fury;
[w] you threshed the nations in anger.
13 [v] You went out for the salvation of
your people,
for the salvation of [x] your anointed.
[y] You crushed the head of the house of
the wicked,
laying him bare from thigh to neck.[2]
Selah
14 You pierced with his own arrows the
heads of his warriors,
who came like a whirlwind to
scatter me,
rejoicing as if to devour the poor
in secret.
15 [z] You trampled the sea with your
horses,
the surging of mighty waters.
16 [a] I hear, and [b] my body trembles;
my lips quiver at the sound;
[c] rottenness enters into my bones;
my legs tremble beneath me.
Yet [d] I will quietly wait for the day of
trouble
to come upon people who
invade us.

Habakkuk Rejoices in the LORD

17 Though the fig tree should not
blossom,
nor fruit be on the vines,
the produce of the olive fail
and the fields yield no food,
the flock be cut off from the fold
and there be no herd in the stalls,
18 [e] yet I will rejoice in the LORD;
[f] I will take joy in the God of my
salvation.
19 GOD, the Lord, is my strength;
[g] he makes my feet like the deer's;
he makes me [h] tread on my [i] high
places.

[j] To the choirmaster: with [k] stringed[3]
instruments.

8 [m] [Ps. 114:5] [n] Deut. 33:26, 27; Ps. 18:10; 68:4, 17; 104:3; Isai. 19:1; 66:15
9 [o] See Ps. 105:8-11 [p] Ps. 78:15, 16
10 [q] Ex. 19:18; See Judg. 5:5 [r] Ps. 93:3 [s] [Ex. 14:22; 15:8]
11 [t] See Josh. 10:12, 13 [u] [ver. 5]; See 2 Sam. 22:15
12 [v] [Josh. 10:42] [w] [Mic. 4:12, 13]
13 [v] [See ver. 12 above] [x] 1 Chr. 16:22; Ps. 105:15
13 [y] Ps. 68:21; 110:6
15 [z] [Ps. 77:19]
16 [a] ver. 2 [b] Jer. 4:19 [c] [Prov. 12:4] [d] [Ps. 94:13; Isai. 14:3, 4]
18 [e] [Job 13:15] [f] Ps. 9:14; 13:5; 21:1; 35:9; Luke 1:47; See Joel 2:23
19 [g] See 2 Sam. 2:18 [h] Amos 4:13; Mic. 1:3 [i] Deut. 32:13; 33:29 [j] See Ps. 4 [k] Isai. 38:20

1 The meaning of the Hebrew line is uncertain 2 The meaning of the Hebrew line is uncertain 3 Hebrew *my stringed*

3:8–11 The prophet now directly addresses God. The approaching Lord is the invincible Divine Warrior who demonstrates His lordship over the cosmos. Similar poetic imagery is known from Canaanite and other mythologies.

3:11 stood still. See Josh. 10:12, 13.

3:12–15 The Lord of nature also has absolute power over the forces of history. He comes to deliver His people and judge the wicked.

3:12 threshed. An agricultural image derived from the way grain was threshed by violent beating or trampling (Amos 1:3 note).

3:13 You went out. In the past the Lord came out of His sanctuary for the salvation of His people in distress. This is what Habakkuk expects Him to do again.

for the salvation . . . anointed. Or, "to save Your Anointed." Possibly a synonym for the chosen people of Israel (cf. Ps. 105:15), but more probably a reference to the Davidic kingship as it came to final expression in the Messiah (Ps. 132:10).

3:15 the sea. Habakkuk refers again to the Exodus history in which God displayed His undisputed dominion over natural and historical forces.

3:16 Together with v. 2, this verse encloses the hymn of vv. 3–15 with autobiographical references at beginning and end.

my body trembles. Habakkuk describes in physical terms the profound effect that the divine self-revelation had on him (cf. Jer. 4:19). The Lord answered his painful questions and will hear his prayer.

I will quietly wait . . . of trouble. Awed by the divine majesty, Habakkuk may rest in the assurance that the Lord will judge the wicked.

3:17, 18 Even when crops and herds fail (a horrifying thought in the context of an agricultural economy), and society lives with hunger and poverty, Habakkuk's trusting expectation will not be crushed. Hope and trust transform his fear of the future into the desire to rejoice always in God his Savior (Rom. 8:35–39).

3:19 GOD, the Lord, is my strength. Total dependence on the sovereign covenant Lord is Habakkuk's key to life.

feet like the deer's . . . tread on my high places. This striking figure portrays the strength and confidence the Lord imparts to the righteous (Is. 40:29–31).

choirmaster. See note on v. 1.

THE BOOK OF

Zephaniah

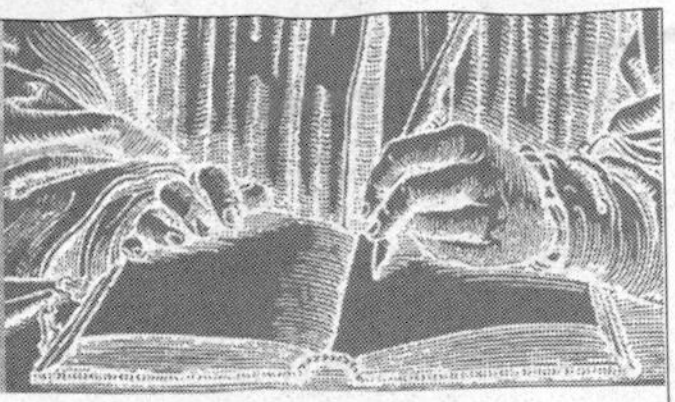

AUTHOR

Zephaniah's lineage is traced back to the fourth generation, which is unique in the prophetic literature. This may indicate that the Hezekiah (715–686 B.C.) mentioned in the fourth generation is the well-known king of Judah by that name. The name Zephaniah, which means "Yahweh [the LORD] hides," is used of a priest who was a contemporary of Jeremiah (21:1; 29:25) and of other persons in the Old Testament (Zech. 6:10, 14). Though the prophet employs priestly vocabulary at several points (1:4–5, 7–9; 3:4, 18), there is no conclusive evidence to indicate he was officially associated with the temple.

DATE AND OCCASION

Zephaniah prophesied in the southern kingdom of Judah when Josiah (640–609 B.C.) was king. However, there is some question as to whether the prophet's ministry preceded or followed Josiah's great reform of the nation's worship in 621 B.C. Zephaniah's denunciation of continuing syncretistic worship (mixing the idolatry of the surrounding peoples with the worship of the LORD) and of Baal worship points to a date prior to Josiah's reforms. All that can be said with certainty is that Nineveh had not yet been destroyed (2:13–15); therefore the prophet's message was spoken prior to its destruction in 612 B.C. Zephaniah would have been a contemporary of Jeremiah, whose call came in Josiah's thirteenth year (627 B.C.). If his ministry is dated in the earlier part of Josiah's reign, then he was instrumental in bringing about Josiah's reforms since the sins he attacked (1:4–6) are those abolished by Josiah's reforms (2 Kin. 23:4; 2 Chr. 34:1–7).

CHARACTERISTICS AND THEMES

The focal point of the prophet's message is the day of the Lord, in which a foreign enemy, the Lord's sword of judgment (2:12; Is. 10:5), would inflict severe destruction upon Jerusalem (1:4, 10, 11; 2:1). This enemy has been variously identified as the Scythians, the Assyrians, or the Babylonians, depending on when the book is dated. Zephaniah's treatment of this subject is extensive. The day is near (1:7) and will be a day in which the wrath and anger of Israel's sovereign Lord will be directed against the wicked (1:15, 18; 2:2, 3). It is a day of darkness and gloom (1:15). So determined is the Lord to root out evil that He conducts a thorough search to ensure that the wicked will be found and destroyed (1:12). In that day pride will be vanquished (3:11), and the humble of the land (the remnant) saved (3:12, 17). The Gentiles also will come to faith in the true and living God and will "call upon the name of the LORD" (3:9; cf. Joel 2:32).

A less obvious point, but one that is alluded to throughout Zephaniah, is the prophet's recognition of the importance of the Lord's covenant with His people. Although Zephaniah never uses the word "covenant," some passages echo details of previous covenantal encounters and provisions. Certainly the complaints against Judah reflect the Lord's anger at their neglect of the covenant obligations.

Like many of the other prophets, the book begins with a message of universal judgment (1:2, 3) and ends with an oracle of salvation in which both the nations (3:9) and the revitalized remnant of Israel (3:12, 13) are brought into a saving relationship with the Lord (3:19, 20). Zephaniah sees the judgment as transforming the world by bringing all people's works, both good and evil, under divine scrutiny. The restorative nature of God's wrath is indicated by the change of tone from the warnings of 1:2, 3 ("I will utterly sweep away everything") to the hope expressed in 3:14–17. Also, the prophet's terminology indicates his awareness of the messages of his predecessors (cf. 1:7 and Hab. 2:20; Zeph. 1:14 and Joel 1:15; Zeph. 1:7 and Is. 34:6).

OUTLINE OF ZEPHANIAH

I. Superscription (1:1)

II. Prophecies of Judgment (1:2–6)

- A. *Against All Nations (1:2, 3)*
- B. *Against Judah (1:4–6)*

III. The Day of the Lord: Accusation and Judgment (1:7–18)

IV. The Call to Repentance (2:1–3)

V. Prophecies Against the Nations (2:4–15)

- A. *Philistia (2:4–7)*
- B. *Moab and Ammon (2:8–11)*
- C. *Ethiopia (2:12)*
- D. *Assyria (2:13–15)*

VI. Accusation Against Jerusalem (3:1–5)

VII. Judgment Against All Nations (3:6–8)

VIII. The Purification and Restoration of Judah's Remnant (3:9–20)

1 The word of the LORD that came to Zephaniah the son of Cushi, son of Gedaliah, son of Amariah, son of Hezekiah, [a]in the days of [b]Josiah the son of Amon, king of Judah.

The Coming Judgment on Judah

2 [c]"I will utterly sweep away everything
from the face of the earth,"
declares the LORD.
3 "I will sweep away [d]man and beast;
I will sweep away the birds of the heavens
and [d]the fish of the sea,
and [e]the rubble[1] with the wicked.
I will [f]cut off mankind
from the face of the earth,"
declares the LORD.
4 "I will stretch out my hand against Judah
and against all the inhabitants of Jerusalem;
[g]and I will cut off from this place the remnant of Baal
and the name of the idolatrous priests along with the priests,
5 [h]those who bow down on the roofs
to the host of the heavens,
[i]those who bow down and swear to the LORD
and yet swear by [j]Milcom,
6 [k]those who have turned back from following the LORD,
[l]who do not seek the LORD or inquire of him."

The Day of the LORD Is Near

7 [m]Be silent before the Lord GOD!
For [n]the day of the LORD is near;

Chapter 1
1 [a]Jer. 1:2 [b]2 Kin. 22:1
2 [c]Jer. 8:13; [ver. 18; 2 Kin. 22:16, 17]
3 [d]Hos 4:3 [e]See Ezek. 7:19 [f]Ezek. 14:17
4 [g]See 2 Kin. 23:4
5 [h]Jer. 19:13 [i][1 Kin. 18:21; 2 Kin. 17:33, 41] [j]1 Kin. 11:5, 33
6 [k]Jer. 2:13, 17; 15:6 [l][Jer. 5:24; Heb. 11:6]
7 [m][Hab. 2:20] [n][ver. 14]; See Joel 1:15

1 Or *stumbling blocks* (that is, idols)

1:1 Superscription. See Introduction: Author; Date and Occasion.

word of the LORD. The phrase refers to revelation received from the Lord and communicated through a prophet.

1:2–6 The prophet begins with an announcement of universal judgment (vv. 2, 3), and quickly particularizes it against Judah and Jerusalem (v. 4). Three specific sins are denounced: idolatry (v. 4), syncretism (v. 5), and religious indifference (v. 6).

1:3 sweep away man. See Matt. 13:41, 42. The coming judgment is compared to that of the Genesis flood by use of the phrases "man and beast" and "birds of the heavens" (cf. Gen. 6:7; 7:23). This prophecy will be consummated at the end of history (2 Pet. 3:3–7).

1:4 stretch out my hand. This phrase refers to the power of God unleashed against His antagonists (2:13; Ex. 3:20; Deut. 4:34; Is. 5:25).

remnant of Baal. All that remains of Baal worship will be destroyed. This statement may mean that a religious renewal was already underway and that Baal worship was in decline.

1:5 those who bow down . . . to the host of the heavens. Baal worship and the worship of the stars were sins that had contributed to the demise of the northern kingdom in the eighth century B.C. (2 Kin. 17:16). Altars were apparently erected upon the roofs of the houses (2 Kin. 23:12; Jer. 19:13).

Milcom. Or, "Molech." Worship of this Ammonite god, which involved the hideous practice of child sacrifice, was strictly forbidden (Lev. 18:21 note; 20:2–5; cf. 1 Kin. 11:5; 2 Kin. 23:10; Jer. 32:35).

1:6 seek the LORD. See 2:3.

1:7 Be silent. See Hab. 2:20; Zech. 2:13; Ps. 46:10. The prophet calls for trustful submission to the sovereign, covenant God. The command to "be silent" is often linked to being in the presence of the holy God (Hab. 2:20; Zech. 2:13).

the day of the LORD. This term occurs frequently in the Old Testament prophets. It can refer to any specific time when the Divine Warrior, the Lord of Hosts, is glorious in victory: against Babylon through the Medes (Is. 13:1–14:27), against Egypt through Babylon (Ezek. 30:2–4), or against Israel through Assyria (Is. 10:5, 6, 20, 24). This day of the Lord's vengeance against the wicked is also depicted as the time of Israel's deliverance (Is. 34:2–35:10), when the Lord decisively defeats all of Israel's opposition (2:2, 9; 3:8–20; Joel 3:14–16). It is also the day of final judgment (Amos 5:18–20). See notes Ezek. 7:7 and Amos 5:18.

[o] the LORD has prepared a sacrifice
and [p] consecrated his guests.
8 And on the day of the LORD's
sacrifice—
[q] "I will punish the officials and the
king's sons
and [r] all who array themselves in
foreign attire.
9 On that day I will punish
everyone [s] who leaps over the
threshold,
and those who fill their master's[1]
house
with violence and fraud.

10 "On that day," declares the
LORD,
"a cry will be heard from [t] the Fish
Gate,
[u] a wail from [v] the Second Quarter,
a loud crash from the hills.
11 [w] Wail, O inhabitants of the Mortar!
For all the traders[2] are no more;
all who weigh out silver are
cut off.
12 At that time [x] I will search Jerusalem
with lamps,
and I will punish the men
[y] who are complacent,[3]
[z] those who say in their hearts,
'The LORD will not do good,
nor will he do ill.'
13 Their goods shall be [a] plundered,
and their houses laid waste.
[b] Though they build houses,
they shall not inhabit them;

7 [o] Isai. 34:6; Jer. 46:10; Ezek. 39:17, 19 [p] 1 Sam. 16:5
8 [q] 2 Kin. 24:12, 14; 25:7 [r] [Matt. 22:11]
9 [s] [1 Sam. 5:5]
10 [t] See 2 Chr. 33:14 [u] Zech. 11:3 [v] 2 Kin. 22:14
11 [w] Zech. 11:2; James 5:1
12 [x] Amos 9:3 [y] Jer. 48:11; [Amos 6:1] [z] Ps. 94:7; Ezek. 8:12; Mal. 2:17; 3:14, 15
13 [a] Isai. 42:22 [b] See Amos 5:11
[c] See Mic. 6:15
14 [d] [ver. 7; Ezek. 7:7, 12] [e] [Isai. 33:7]
15 [f] See Joel 1:15 [g] Job 30:3 [h] See Joel 2:2
16 [i] [Jer. 4:19] [j] [Isai. 2:15]
17 [k] Jer. 10:18 [l] Deut. 28:29; Isai. 59:10 [m] Ps. 79:3 [n] [Ps. 83:10]
18 [o] Ezek. 7:19; [Prov. 11:4] [p] [ch. 3:8] [q] Ezek. 36:5 [r] [ver. 2, 3]

[c] though they plant vineyards,
they shall not drink wine from
them."

14 [d] The great day of the LORD is near,
near and hastening fast;
the sound of the day of the LORD is
bitter;
[e] the mighty man cries aloud there.
15 [f] A day of wrath is that day,
a day of distress and anguish,
a day of [g] ruin and devastation,
[f] a day of darkness and gloom,
[h] a day of clouds and thick darkness,
16 [i] a day of trumpet blast and battle cry
[j] against the fortified cities
and against the lofty battlements.

17 [k] I will bring distress on mankind,
so that they shall walk [l] like the
blind,
because they have sinned against
the LORD;
[m] their blood shall be poured out like
dust,
and their flesh [n] like dung.
18 [o] Neither their silver nor their gold
shall be able to deliver them
on the day of the wrath of the
LORD.
[p] In the fire of his jealousy,
[q] all the earth shall be consumed;
[r] for a full and sudden end
he will make of all the inhabitants
of the earth.

1 Or *their Lord's* 2 Or *all the people of Canaan* 3 Hebrew *are thickening on the dregs* [of their wine]

the LORD has prepared a sacrifice. The imminent judgment coming upon Judah is compared to sacrifices. The nation is a sacrificial lamb (Is. 34:6; Jer. 46:10; Ezek. 39:17–19).

consecrated his guests. The invited guests may be the nations who serve as the divine instrument of judgment (Is. 10:5–10; Hab. 1:6). Alternatively, the invited guests (the covenant people) are themselves the sacrificial offerings. The consecration of guests is necessary to maintain the holiness of the Lord (Ex. 19:10; 24:9–11), and recalls elements of the covenant ritual at Mount Sinai (vv. 15, 16 note).

1:8 the officials. The sons of the king and other royal officials. Their lack of commitment to the covenant is evidenced by their adoption of foreign customs and attire, a sign of religious disloyalty.

1:9 threshold. The threshold of a pagan sanctuary. Probably a Philistine religious practice was being imitated (1 Sam. 5:5).

1:11 traders. Cries of anguish come from all parts of the city, depicting the extent of the evil and the judgment. The wealthier merchant class is singled out for their greed and corrupt business practices (Amos 8:4–6).

1:12 I will search. There is no escape from the divine scrutiny (Ps. 139; Amos 9:1–4).

who are complacent. See text note. The prophet draws a word picture from the wine-making process. Like the sediment of wine, which settles and thickens if left undisturbed, the citizens of Jerusalem have become settled (confirmed) in their indifference toward God. Because they are thoroughly complacent toward God, they regard Him as morally indifferent toward good or evil.

1:14–18 Zephaniah elaborates further on the day of the Lord, setting the stage for his strong plea for repentance in 2:1–3.

1:15, 16 The day of the Lord is presented in frightful images recalling the theophany that accompanied the establishment of the Mosaic covenant at Mount Sinai (Ex. 19:16), the terms of which Judah has broken. Some suggest that "day of the LORD" here can be regarded as the day of His covenant, when the Lord establishes His covenant or enforces its provisions.

1:17 they shall walk like the blind. One of the covenant curses found in Deut. 28:28, 29.

they have sinned. The reason for the Lord's judgment of Judah is stated in general terms. See note 3:1–5.

1:18 Neither their silver nor their gold. See Ps. 49:6–9; Prov. 11:4; Matt. 16:26; Luke 12:13–21.

jealousy. See Ex. 20:5; 34:14; Deut. 4:24. God's jealousy presupposes His covenant love. He has redeemed a people to make them His "treasured possession" (Ex. 19:5). God's covenant love demands the absolute loyalty of His people.

Judgment on Judah's Enemies

2 Gather together, yes, gather,
O [s]shameless nation,
2 [t]before the decree takes effect[1]
—before the day passes away [u]like chaff—
[v]before there comes upon you
the burning anger of the LORD,
before there comes upon you
the day of the anger of the LORD.
3 [w]Seek the LORD, [x]all you humble of the land,
who do his just commands;[2]
[y]seek righteousness; seek humility;
[y]perhaps [z]you may be hidden
on the day of the anger of the LORD.
4 [a]For Gaza shall be deserted,
and Ashkelon shall become a desolation;
Ashdod's people shall be driven out at noon,
and Ekron shall be uprooted.

5 Woe to [b]you inhabitants of the seacoast,
you nation of [c]the Cherethites!
[d]The word of the LORD is against you,
[e]O Canaan, land of the Philistines;
and I will destroy you [f]until no inhabitant is left.
6 [g]And you, O seacoast, [h]shall be pastures,
with meadows[3] for shepherds
and folds for flocks.
7 [i]The seacoast shall become the possession
of [j]the remnant of the house of Judah,
[k]on which they shall graze,
and in the houses of Ashkelon
they shall lie down at evening.
For the LORD their God [h]will be mindful of them
and [l]restore their fortunes.

8 "I have heard [m]the taunts of Moab
and [n]the revilings of the Ammonites,
how they have taunted my people
and made boasts [o]against their territory.
9 Therefore, [p]as I live," declares the LORD of hosts,
the God of Israel,
"Moab shall become [q]like Sodom,
and the Ammonites [q]like Gomorrah,
a land possessed by nettles and salt pits,
and a waste forever.
The remnant of my people shall plunder them,
and the survivors of my nation shall possess them."
10 This shall be their lot in return [r]for their pride,
because they taunted and boasted
against the people of the LORD of hosts.
11 The LORD will be awesome against them;
[s]for he will famish all the gods of the earth,
and [t]to him shall bow down,
each in its place,
all [u]the lands of the nations.

Chapter 2
1 [s]Jer. 6:15
2 [t][ch. 3:8] [u]Ps. 1:4 [v][2 Kin. 23:26]
3 [w]See Amos 5:6 [x]Ps. 76:9; Isai. 11:4 [y][Amos 5:14, 15] [z][Isai. 2:10; 26:20, 21]
4 [a]Zech. 9:5, 6; [Jer. 47:5]; See Amos 1:6-8
5 [b]Jer. 47:7; Ezek. 25:16 [c]See 1 Sam. 30:14 [d][Nah. 2:13] [e][Josh. 13:3] [f]ch. 3:6
6 [g]ver. 7 [h]Isai. 65:10
7 [i][Josh. 19:29] [j][ch. 3:13; Obad. 19] [k]Zech. 10:3; Luke 1:68 [h][See ver. 6 above] [l]ch. 3:20
8 [m][Jer. 48:27] [n]Ezek. 25:3, 6 [o][Jer. 49:1]
9 [p]Isai. 49:18; See Ezek. 16:48 [q]Deut. 29:23; See Isai. 13:19
10 [r]Isai. 16:6
11 [s][Isai. 17:4] [t]Ps. 22:27 [u]See Gen. 10:5

[1] Hebrew *gives birth* [2] Or *who carry out his judgment* [3] Or *caves*

2:1–3 As the Lord's representatives to enforce the covenant, the prophets often warned God's people (Is. 1:16–20; 55:1–6; Hos. 2:4, 5; 4:15; Amos 4:12; 5:5, 6; Mic. 6:8).

2:1 Gather together. They are called to assemble in order to hear (cf. Is. 34:1; Jer. 4:5; Joel 2:15, 16; 3:11). The call to hear these severe warnings is itself an act of divine grace, for the warnings are designed to elicit repentance.

2:3 Seek the LORD. See 1:6 and Is. 55:6, 7. Here this seeking of the Lord is further defined as "seek righteousness; seek humility." A similar pattern is evident in Amos, where the prophet commands, "Seek the LORD" and later "Seek good, and not evil" (Amos 5:6, 14).

perhaps you may be hidden. The prophet's tentative words here express both his hope that the "humble" remnant (v. 3) will find refuge from the Lord's wrath (cf. Is. 55:7), and his pessimism that the "shameless nation" (v. 1) will repent. Cf. Amos 5:15.

2:4–15 This section consists of four prophecies of judgment directed against the foreign nations. Such messages were to assure God's own people that His sovereign purposes extended over their enemies (1:5, 6) and that these nations were also morally accountable for their actions (Amos 1:3–2:3; Mic. 1:2).

2:5 Woe. The same word of doom later pronounced upon Jerusalem (3:1). It often introduces a prophecy of judgment.

2:7 The judgment of the nations will be accompanied by God's preservation of a remnant from His people (Deut. 32:27 note). Other references in Zephaniah to the remnant occur in v. 9 and 3:9–12.

restore their fortunes. This widely employed phrase refers to Israel's future salvation beyond the judgment (Deut. 30:3; Ps. 14:7; Jer. 30:3, 18; 32:44; Amos 9:14). Sometimes it refers to the physical return of exiles; in other instances a more general restoration of fortunes is indicated (e.g., Job 42:10).

2:9 Sodom . . . Gomorrah. These ancient cities symbolize sin and serve as types of God's final judgment on sinners (Gen. 18:20 note; Is. 1:9; Amos 4:11; Matt. 10:5; 2 Pet. 2:6).

2:11 bow down . . . all the lands of the nations. See 3:9, 10; Ps. 72:8–11; Is. 56:67.

12 [v]You also, O Cushites,
shall be slain by my sword.
13 And he will stretch out his hand
against the north
[w]and destroy Assyria,
and he [x]will make Nineveh a
desolation,
a dry waste like the desert.
14 [y]Herds shall lie down in her midst,
all kinds of beasts;[1]
[z]even the owl and the hedgehog[2]
shall lodge in her capitals;
a voice shall hoot in the window;
devastation will be on the
threshold;
for [a]her cedar work will be laid
bare.
15 This is the exultant city
[b]that lived securely,
that said in her heart,
"I am, and there is no one else."
What a desolation she has become,
[c]a lair for wild beasts!
[d]Everyone who passes by her
hisses and [e]shakes his fist.

Judgment on Jerusalem and the Nations

3 Woe to her who is rebellious and
defiled,
[f]the oppressing city!
2 She listens to no voice;
[g]she accepts no correction.
[h]She does not trust in the LORD;
she does not draw near to her
God.

3 [i]Her officials within her
are roaring lions;
her judges are [j]evening wolves
that leave nothing till the morning.
4 [k]Her prophets are fickle, treacherous
men;
[k]her priests [l]profane what is holy;
they do violence to the law.
5 The LORD within her [m]is righteous;
he does no injustice;
every morning he shows forth his
justice;
each dawn he does not fail;
but [n]the unjust knows no shame.

6 [o]"I have cut off nations;
their battlements are in ruins;
I have laid waste their streets
[p]so that no one walks in them;
their cities have been made desolate,
without a man, without an
inhabitant.
7 [q]I said, 'Surely you will fear me;
[r]you will accept correction.
Then your[3] dwelling would not be
cut off
according to all that I have
appointed against you.'[4]
But [s]all the more they were eager
to make all their deeds corrupt.
8 "Therefore [t]wait for me," declares the
LORD,
"for the day when I rise up to seize
the prey.

12 [v][ch. 3:10] 13 [w][Isai. 10:12] [x]Nah. 3:7 14 [y]Isai. 13:21, 22; 34:14 [z]Isai. 34:11 [a][Jer. 22:14, 15] 15 [b]Isai. 47:8 [c][Ezek. 25:5] [d]Jer. 19:8 [e][Nah. 3:19]
Chapter 3 1 [f]Jer. 6:6 2 [g]Jer. 5:3 [h][ver. 12]
3 [i]Ezek. 22:27; [Mic. 3:9, 10] [j]Hab. 1:8 4 [k]Jer. 23:11; Hos. 9:7 [l]Ezek. 22:26 5 [m][Jer. 12:1] [n][ch. 2:1] 6 [o]See ch. 2:4-15 [p][Zech. 7:14; 9:8] 7 [q][Jer. 36:3] [r][ver. 2] [s][Mic. 7:3] 8 [t]Hab. 2:3; See Isai. 8:17

[1] Hebrew *beasts of every nation* [2] The identity of the animals rendered *owl* and *hedgehog* is uncertain [3] Hebrew *her* [4] Hebrew *her*

2:12 my sword. See Is. 10:5.

2:13 destroy Assyria. Nineveh, the capital of Assyria, fell to the Babylonians and Medes in 612 B.C. This verse suggests that Zephaniah prophesied prior to that date (Introduction: Date and Occasion).

2:15 I am . . . no one else. This boast is phrased in language similar to what the sovereign Lord alone rightly may use (Deut. 4:39; Is. 45:5, 6; 47:10). Such self-deification meets with ruin, and those who boasted become objects of scorn.

3:1–5 The references here to prophets, priests, the sanctuary, and the law indicate that the prophet is addressing Jerusalem. The general accusation of 1:17 now becomes specific. Jerusalem's sins were particularly heinous because they were committed against the righteous covenant God who had graciously revealed Himself to His people (v. 5; Amos 2:4, 10–12; 3:2).

3:2 She listens to no voice. The people ignored God's voice revealed in the law (Deut. 31:9–13), through the prophets (Jer. 7:23–28; Hag. 1:12), and through the sages (Prov. 1:8).

she accepts no correction. See v. 7. Failure to receive correction leads to death (Prov. 5:23), but openness to it leads to life (Prov. 6:23; Jer. 2:30; 5:3; 7:28; 32:33; 35:13; Ps. 50:17).

draw near. The Hebrew verb here means "to approach God properly in worship" (cf. Lev. 10:3). Worship must come from the heart, not just the mouth (cf. Is. 29:13; John 4:24).

3:3, 4 See Mic. 3:9, 10.

3:3 officials within her. See note on v. 5.

roaring lions. The images of the unclean lion and wolf here describe the predatory and fierce nature of those corrupt government officials, whose proper office was to protect and give stability to society.

3:4 Her prophets . . . her priests. For similar condemnations of Israel's spiritual leaders, see Hos. 4:5, 6; Is. 28:7; Jer. 5:31; 6:13; Mic. 3:5–8, 11.

3:5 within her. Zephaniah contrasts the presence of the righteous Lord within Jerusalem and the presence of corrupt and unrighteous leadership within her (v. 3). The essence of God's covenant commitment is the promise of His presence with His people (Ex. 29:42–46 note; Num. 14:14; Is. 43:2). Here, God's presence threatens judgment (Hos. 11:9), but the same phrase in 3:17 signifies salvation.

3:6–8 Attention shifts from Jerusalem to the nations. The prophet notes God's previous judgment of the nations (v. 6), which should have been a lesson to Jerusalem (v. 7), before turning to the future judgment that awaits (v. 8).

3:7 you will accept correction. See v. 2.

For my decision is [u]to gather nations,
to assemble kingdoms,
to pour out upon them my
indignation,
all my burning anger;
for in the fire of my jealousy
[v]all the earth shall be consumed.

The Conversion of the Nations

9 "For at that time I will change the
speech of the peoples
to [w]a pure speech,
that all of them may call upon the
name of the LORD
and serve him with one accord.
10 [x]From beyond the rivers [y]of Cush
my worshipers, the daughter of my
dispersed ones,
shall bring my offering.
11 [z]"On that day [a]you shall not be put to
shame
because of the deeds by which you
have rebelled against me;
for then [b]I will remove from your
midst
your proudly exultant ones,
and [c]you shall no longer be haughty
in my holy mountain.
12 But I will leave in your midst
a people [d]humble and lowly.
[e]They shall seek refuge in the name of
the LORD,
13 [f]those who are left in Israel;
they [g]shall do no injustice
and speak no lies,
[h]nor shall there be found in their
mouth
a deceitful tongue.
[i]For they shall graze and lie down,
and none shall make them
afraid."

Israel's Joy and Restoration

14 [j]Sing aloud, O daughter of Zion;
shout, O Israel!
Rejoice and exult with all your heart,
O daughter of Jerusalem!
15 The LORD has taken away the
judgments against you;
he has cleared away your enemies.
[k]The King of Israel, [l]the LORD, is in
your midst;
you shall never again fear evil.
16 [z]On that day it shall be said to
Jerusalem:
"Fear not, O Zion;
[m]let not your hands grow weak.
17 [l]The LORD your God is in your
midst,
[n]a mighty one who will save;
[o]he will rejoice over you with
gladness;
he will quiet you by his love;
he will exult over you with loud
singing.

8 [u]Joel 3:2 [v][ch. 1:18] 9 [w]Isai. 19:18 10 [x]Ps. 68:31; Isai. 11:11; 60:4 [y][ch. 2:12] 11 [z]Isai. 2:11 [a][Isai. 54:4] [b][Mal. 4:1] [c]Jer. 7:4; [Matt. 3:9] 12 [d]Isai. 14:32; Zech. 11:7, 11; [Matt. 5:3] [e][ver. 2]

13 [f][ch. 2:7] [g]Isai. 60:21 [h][Rev. 14:5] [i]See Mic. 5:4 14 [j]Isai. 12:6; 54:1; Zech. 2:10; 9:9 15 [k]Matt. 27:42; John 1:49 [l]Ps. 46:5; Zech. 2:10; [Rev. 21:3] 16 [z][See ver. 11 above] [m][Isai. 35:3; Heb. 12:12] 17 [l][See ver. 15 above] [n][Isai. 63:1] [o]Isai. 62:5; Jer. 32:41

3:9–20 The dramatic reversal: Judgment is the prelude to restoration and purification both in Israel and among the nations (vv. 9, 12, 13). In a closing hymn of praise (3:14–20) the prophet sings of the future reign of the Lord, His victory over His enemies, and His love for and presence with His people. The church may sing this song now in celebration of Christ's victory on the Cross (Col. 2:15) and in anticipation of His triumph when He returns (2 Thess. 1:5–10).

3:9 change . . . a pure speech. To purify the lips is either to cleanse from sin in general (Is. 6:5) or to remove the names of foreign gods from the lips of a worshiper (Hos. 2:17).

of the peoples. The Gentiles will also call on His name (Is. 52:15; 65:1; 66:18).

all of them may call upon the name of the LORD. In contrast with the idolaters of 1:5, 6. See Gen. 4:26; 1 Kin. 18:24; Jer. 10:25; Joel 2:32; Acts 2:21; Rom. 10:12, 13.

3:11 proudly exultant ones. See Is. 2:12–18.

3:12 humble and lowly. These are contrasted with the proud and haughty of v. 11.

3:13 those who are left. See note 2:7.

shall do no injustice. The remnant will be like God. Identical words are used of the Lord in v. 5. A primary goal of salvation is ever-increasing conformity to the image of God (Matt. 5:48; 1 Pet. 1:15, 16).

and speak no lies. In contrast with the deceitful idolaters of 1:9.

graze and lie down. A common prophetic phrase (Is. 49:9; Mic. 7:14; Jer. 50:19; Ezek. 34:14) portraying the security that comes from trusting God and acknowledging His kingship (v. 15).

none shall make them afraid. See Mic. 4:4.

3:14 daughter of Zion. This personification of Jerusalem is based on the practice among poets of personifying places and objects in terms of grammatical gender. The word for "city" in Hebrew is feminine, and the prophet speaks of Zion as "daughter."

3:15 judgments . . . your enemies. The basis for the rejoicing in v. 14 is explained: both the judgments against God's people and the enemies that threaten them are overcome. This prophecy finds final fulfillment in Jesus Christ, who satisfied God's judgment against sin and overcame the enemies of God through His death on the Cross (Rom. 3:23–25; Col. 2:15 note).

The King of Israel . . . in your midst. See John 1:49. The promise of God's dwelling in the midst of His people points forward to Christ, the King of Israel (John 1:49) and incarnate glory of God (Ex. 26 note; John 1:14 note).

3:17 he will rejoice over you with gladness. This delight is grounded in the character of God, who "delights in steadfast love" (Mic. 7:18).

he will quiet you by his love. The phrase translated "quiet you" may also be rendered "is quiet" or "rests." In the larger context God has been revealed as the Warrior "mighty to save." The former war cry (1:14) is now quieted by victory and the loving relationship between God and His people. The Lord's purging and transforming work of grace creates a renewed people who acknowledge His rule and trust in His name (v. 12).

18 I will gather those of you who mourn
[p]for the festival,
so that you will no longer suffer
reproach.[1]
19 Behold, at that time [q]I will deal
with all your oppressors.
And [r]I will save the lame
and gather the outcast,
and I will change [s]their shame into
praise
and renown in all the earth.
20 [t]At that time I will bring you in,
at the time when I gather you
together;
for I will make you renowned and
praised
among all the peoples of the
earth,
[u]when I restore your fortunes
before your eyes," says the
LORD.

18 [p]Lam. 1:4; 2:6
19 [q][Isai. 60:14] [r]Mic. 4:6, 7; [Jer. 13:11; 33:9] [s]Isai. 61:7
20 [t]Isai. 11:12; Jer. 32:37; Ezek. 11:17 [u]ch. 2:7

[1] The meaning of the Hebrew is uncertain

3:19 praise and renown. See v. 20. The phrase goes back to Deut. 26:18, 19, where Israel as the Lord's special people is privileged to represent Him and be the tangible means whereby praise, honor, and glory are given to the Lord (cf. Is. 43:7; Jer. 13:11; 33:9). Paul sees the church in this role (Titus 2:14), as does Peter (1 Pet. 2:9–12).

THE BOOK OF

Haggai

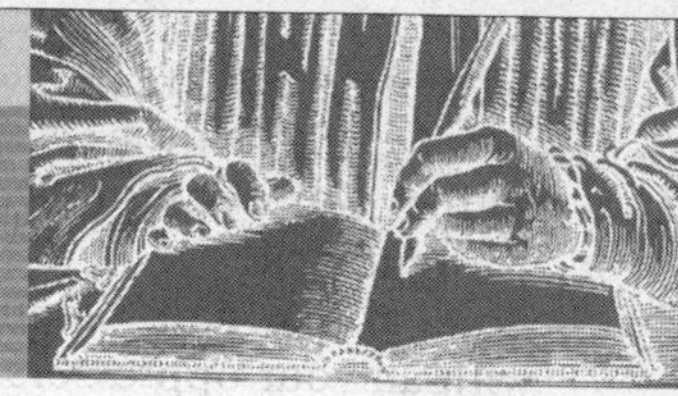

AUTHOR

The name "Haggai" means "festal," perhaps indicating that the prophet was born during a feast, but our knowledge of this prophet comes only from the Book of Haggai itself and from what the Book of Ezra mentions. The prophets Haggai and Zechariah cooperated to encourage the Jews who had returned from their sixth-century B.C. exile in Babylon to rebuild the temple at Jerusalem (Ezra 5:1; 6:14).

DATE AND OCCASION

Haggai and Zechariah share a common historical background, both having begun their ministries in "the second year of Darius the king" (520 B.C.). The Jews had returned to Palestine under the edict of the Persian king Cyrus in 538 B.C. and had begun to rebuild the temple. Opposition from the outside and discouragement from within caused them to abandon the project for about sixteen or seventeen years (Ezra 4:1–4). When Haggai and Zechariah began their work in 520 B.C., further opposition came from Tattenai, the Persian governor of Trans-Euphrates, which included Palestine (Ezra 5). But Darius I (Hystaspes), who ruled Persia from 522 to 486 B.C., reissued Cyrus's edict so that the temple was rebuilt within four years (Ezra 6:13–15). The second temple was dedicated on March 12, 516 B.C.

As for Haggai's messages themselves, we learn from his book that they were delivered between August and December of 520 B.C.

CHARACTERISTICS AND THEMES

Haggai consists of four messages headed by the phrase "the word of the LORD came by the hand of Haggai the prophet" (1:1; 2:1; 2:10; 2:20) or a similar phrase. These four alternate between calls to repentance in light of God's curses on their land (1:1–11; 2:10–19) and promises of greater blessings on the temple and of the Messiah through the Davidic line (2:1–9; 2:20–23).

Haggai, Zechariah, and Malachi use the title "Lord of hosts" more than ninety times (fourteen times in Haggai). This title has military connotations (God as the leader of Israel's armies, 1 Sam. 17:45), but also highlights God's glory (Ps. 24:10) and sovereign kingship over all creation (Amos 4:13).

Although Haggai is the second shortest book in the Old Testament, it is rich with profitable teaching for the church. Through Haggai His messenger (1:13), the Lord calls upon the unfaithful remnant of His covenant people to repent and rebuild His temple. God's concern is based upon His own sovereign pleasure and His desire to be honored (1:8). The people's lack of concern to build the temple showed their deeper lack of desire for God's special presence. They were under the curses of the covenant (1:6, 9, 11 and notes) but did not realize it. In response to Haggai's ministry, the Lord stirred up the spirit of the people (1:14), and they obeyed (1:12).

Haggai reaffirms that the Lord is with His people, just as when He brought them out of Egypt (1:13; 2:4, 5). Haggai's ministry was based on the expectation that God would renew His covenant promises to Israel when He brought them back into the land from captivity in Babylon. Haggai's words draw on those of earlier prophets at a number of points (2:7, 8 and notes). The rebuilding of the temple was an important part of that renewal, and Haggai developed that hope by associating the temple with the coming times of the Messiah (2:9, 23 and notes). The Messiah as God's anointed representative on earth would bring His glory, peace, and prosperity to God's people (2:9). Zerubbabel prefigures that Messiah in Haggai's day, but ultimately only Jesus the Messiah would fulfill the promise made to Zerubbabel to be God's royal ruler ("signet ring") on earth (2:23). Today we are the recipients of these promises and look forward to the final visible enthronement of Christ as Ruler, when once again the Lord will shake heaven and earth (Heb. 12:26).

OUTLINE OF HAGGAI

I. The First Message: A Call to Rebuild the Temple (ch. 1)
- A. *The People's Indifference and Poverty (1:1–11)*
- B. *The People's Response: Repentance (1:12–15)*

II. The Second Message: God's Greater Temple and Blessings (2:1–9)
- A. *Encouragement from God's Presence (2:1–5)*
- B. *Encouragement from God's Promise of Blessing (2:6–9)*

III. The Third Message: God's Blessing for a Defiled People (2:10–19)
- A. *The Cause of Their Defilement (2:10–14)*
- B. *The Results of Their Defilement: Covenant Curses (2:15–17)*
- C. *God's Determination to Bless Them (2:18, 19)*

IV. The Fourth Message: God's Victory for His People (2:20–23)
- A. *God's Overthrow of the Nations (2:20–22)*
- B. *The Enthronement of God's Ruler (2:23)*

The Command to Rebuild the Temple

1 [a]In the second year of Darius the king,
in the sixth month, on the first day of
the month, the word of the LORD came by
the hand of Haggai the prophet to
[b]Zerubbabel the son of [c]Shealtiel, governor
of Judah, and to [d]Joshua the son of
[e]Jehozadak, the high priest: **2** "Thus says the
LORD of hosts: These people say the time
has not yet come to rebuild the house of the
LORD." **3** Then the word of the LORD came [f]by
the hand of Haggai the prophet, **4** [g]"Is it a
time for you yourselves to dwell in your paneled houses, while [h]this house lies in ruins?
5 Now, therefore, thus says the LORD of
hosts: [i]Consider your ways. **6** [j]You have
sown much, and harvested little. [k]You eat,
but you never have enough; you drink, but
you never have your fill. You clothe yourselves, but no one is warm. And he who
[l]earns wages does so to put them into a bag
with holes.
7 "Thus says the LORD of hosts: [i]Consider
your ways. **8** Go up to the hills and bring
wood and build the house, that [m]I may
take pleasure in it and that [n]I may be glorified, says the LORD. **9** [j]You looked for much,
and behold, it came to little. And when you
brought it home, [o]I blew it away. Why?
declares the LORD of hosts. Because of my
house [h]that lies in ruins, while each of you
busies himself with his own house.
10 Therefore [p]the heavens above you have
withheld the dew, and the earth has

Chapter 1
1 [a]ver. 15; ch. 2:10; Ezra 4:24; 5:1; Zech. 1:1, 7 [b]See 1 Chr. 3:19 [c]See 1 Chr. 3:17 [d]See Ezra 3:2 [e]1 Chr. 6:15
3 [f]Ezra 5:1
4 [g][2 Sam. 7:2]; See Ps. 132:3-5 [h]Neh. 2:3, 17; Isai. 64:11; Jer. 33:10, 12
5 [i][ch. 2:15, 18]
6 [j]See Mic. 6:15 [k]Hos. 4:10
[l][Zech. 8:10]
7 [i][See ver. 5 above]
8 [m][Ps. 132:13, 14] [n][ch. 2:9] **9** [j][See ver. 6 above] [o][ch. 2:17] [h][See ver. 4 above] **10** [p][Jer. 5:24, 25; Zech. 8:12]; See 1 Kin. 8:35

1:1 sixth month . . . first day. Each of Haggai's sermons is carefully dated. This one occurred probably on August 29, 520 B.C. Haggai's message is addressed publicly to the leaders so that the people could respond as well (1:12).

Zerubbabel. He is likely the same person as Sheshbazzar (cf. Ezra 1:8), since both are said to have rebuilt the temple. Sheshbazzar could be an official Persian name. Zerubbabel was the grandson of King Jehoiachin (1 Chr. 3:19) and a descendant of David (2:23 note).

Joshua the son of Jehozadak. See 1 Chr. 6:15. A descendant of Zadok the priest. Under Persian rule, Zerubbabel had responsibility over the daily civil affairs of the region. As high priest, Joshua dealt with religious matters.

1:2 These people. An expression of implied displeasure (2:14). Verses 2–11 indict the spiritual indifference and misplaced priorities of God's people.

the time has not yet come. Their objection was not to the rebuilding itself, but to the timing of it. The objections may have been economic, because their land was in trouble (cf. vv. 10, 11), or religious, because according to Ezek. 37:24–27 the Messiah would rebuild the temple, or because according to Jer. 25:11–14, the nation must serve a foreign king seventy years. The original temple was destroyed in 586 B.C., and they may have falsely reasoned that they should not start building the new temple until 516 B.C. Such excuses showed that they were not pursuing God's kingdom and righteousness (cf. Matt. 6:33).

the house of the LORD. The temple was the dwelling place of God's special presence with His people (1 Kin. 8:27–30). Today God is graciously present in His temple, the church (1 Cor. 3:16, 17).

1:4 paneled houses. Haggai reveals the hypocrisy of their objections by a rhetorical question. The houses probably had elaborate wooden walls and ceilings (1 Kin. 7:3; Jer. 22:14). They were living in comparative luxury while God's house lay in ruins.

1:6 sown much, and harvested little. Their economic and social hardship was the effect of God's covenant curse on their disobedience (Deut. 11:8–15; 28:29, 38–40; Lev. 26:20). God frustrated their efforts because of their lack of concern for His glory.

1:8 take pleasure in it and that I may be glorified. God's purpose in the enterprise was the special joy He would take in this edifice and the appropriate honor He would thereby receive from His people. Their lack of concern for rebuilding indicated their lack of spiritual health.

1:9 his own house. The focus of their lives was on building personal fortunes rather than building God's kingdom.

withheld its produce. **11** And [q]I have called
for a drought on the land and the hills, on
[r]the grain, the new wine, the oil, on what
the ground brings forth, on man and beast,
and [s]on all their labors."

The People Obey the LORD

12 [t]Then [u]Zerubbabel the son of Shealtiel,
and [u]Joshua the son of Jehozadak, the high
priest, with all [v]the remnant of the people,
obeyed the voice of the LORD their God, and
the words of Haggai the prophet, as the
LORD their God had sent him. And the people feared the LORD. **13** Then Haggai, the
messenger of the LORD, spoke to the people
with the LORD's message, [w]"I am with you,
declares the LORD." **14** And [x]the LORD stirred
up the spirit of [u]Zerubbabel the son of
Shealtiel, governor of Judah, and the spirit of
[y]Joshua the son of Jehozadak, the high
priest, and the spirit of all [z]the remnant of
the people. And they came and [a]worked on
the house of the LORD of hosts, their God,
15 [b]on the twenty-fourth day of the month, in
the sixth month, in the second year of
Darius the king.

11 [q]2 Kin. 8:1; [Ps. 105:16] [r]Hos. 2:9 [s]ch. 2:17; Ps. 128:2
12 [t]Ezra 5:2; [u]ver. 1 [v]ch. 2:2
13 [w]ch. 2:4; [Isai. 43:5]
14 [x][2 Chr. 36:22; Ezra 1:1] [u][See ver. 12 above] [y]ver. 1 [z]ch. 2:2 [a][ch. 2:4; Ezra 5:8]
15 [b][ver. 1]

Chapter 2
1 [c][Lev. 23:34, 36]
2 [d]ch. 1:1
3 [e][Ezra 3:12] [f][ver. 9] [g][Zech. 4:10]
4 [h]Zech. 8:9; [Zech. 4:6, 7] [d][See ver. 2 above] [i][ch. 1:14] [j]ch. 1:13
5 [k]See Ex. 29:45 [l]Neh. 9:20 [m]Zech. 8:13, 15
6 [n]Cited Heb. 12:26 [o]ver. 21
7 [p][Isai. 60:1]
8 [q][1 Chr. 29:14, 16]

The Coming Glory of the Temple

2 [c]In the seventh month, on the twenty-
first day of the month, the word of
the LORD came by the hand of Haggai the
prophet, **2** "Speak now to [d]Zerubbabel the
son of Shealtiel, governor of Judah, and to
[d]Joshua the son of Jehozadak, the high
priest, and to all the remnant of the people,
and say, **3** [e]'Who is left among you who saw
this house [f]in its former glory? How do you
see it now? [g]Is it not as nothing in your eyes?
4 Yet now [h]be strong, O [d]Zerubbabel, declares the LORD. [h]Be strong, O [d]Joshua, son
of Jehozadak, the high priest. [h]Be strong, all
you people of the land, declares the LORD.
[i]Work, for [j]I am with you, declares the LORD
of hosts, **5** [k]according to the covenant that I
made with you when you came out of Egypt.
[l]My Spirit remains in your midst. [m]Fear not.
6 For thus says the LORD of hosts: [n]Yet once
more, in a little while, [o]I will shake the heavens and the earth and the sea and the dry
land. **7** And I will shake all nations, so that
the treasures of all nations shall come in, and
[p]I will fill this house with glory, says the
LORD of hosts. **8** [q]The silver is mine, and the

1:11 a drought. The drought on Judah's crops was God's curse on their agriculture, in keeping with His covenant (1:6 note; Deut. 7:13). The Hebrew word translated "ruins" in v. 9 sounds like the Hebrew word for "drought" here. Haggai's play on words reinforces the point that the drought was God's response to their neglect of His house.

1:12 remnant. A common term used by the prophets for those of God's people who remain faithful to Him in the midst of unbelief (Is. 10:22; cf. Zech. 13:9). Paul later points to a faithful remnant in Israel—the Jews who embraced Christ (Rom. 11:5).

voice of the LORD . . . words of Haggai. They recognized God's word through the voice of the prophet. God's word accomplishes its intended purpose (Is. 55:1; Heb. 4:12).

1:13 I am with you. As the people repented of their sin they received the greatest assurance possible, the presence of God. God's gracious presence with His people is the heart of the covenant relationship (Zech. 8:8 note).

1:14 stirred up the spirit. God Himself brought about the response of His people by His presence with them. Haggai emphasizes the internal response by the threefold repetition of "spirit." God's Spirit worked efficaciously through His word, in order to achieve His sovereign purpose (cf. Is. 55:11).

1:15 twenty-fourth day of the month. Probably September 21, 520 B.C.

2:1–9 The Lord again spoke to the people, this time encouraging them to continue building. Reports about the magnificence of the now-destroyed temple of Solomon were apparently a source of discouragement (v. 3). The Lord first assured them of His continued presence with them—a promise for the present (vv. 4, 5). Second, He assured them about the future goal of their project (vv. 6–9). Though it appeared humble in comparison, the glory of this temple would finally far outstrip Solomon's temple because it would be graced by the presence of the Messiah Himself (v. 9 note).

2:1 seventh month . . . twenty-first. October 17, 520 B.C. According to Lev. 23:33–43, this was the last day of the Feast of Tabernacles, during which God's people were to rejoice in God's provision for them in the wilderness and the blessings of the harvest. There was not much to rejoice in, however, since their harvest was meager (1:11).

2:2 the remnant of the people. Haggai's first sermon was addressed to the leaders because they had to initiate the work. The people are included here because this message is intended to encourage them about the task at hand.

2:3 this house in its former glory. Verses 1–3 suggest that the people were discouraged by the new temple's relative lack of splendor (cf. 2 Chr. 3; 4) and by the difficulty of the task ahead of them.

2:4 be strong. Threefold repetition adds emphasis to the command. Similar commands accompanied the building of Solomon's temple (1 Chr. 22:13; 28:20; cf. Gal. 6:9).

I am with you. The Lord's presence and His sustaining strength guarantee the ultimate success of their labors.

2:5 covenant that I made with you. God's covenant promises, made with His people in the Exodus from Egypt, now assure them of His presence (cf. Ex. 33:12–17; Num. 11:16–17). His mighty Spirit is present, just as in the days of the great deliverance from Egypt.

2:6 once more . . . I will shake. As is common in the prophets, the near and distant future are telescoped, or compressed together. Here references to the glory of the second temple are juxtaposed with a picture of the final universal judgment on the cosmos. While this shaking may be prefigured by political events occurring shortly after the time of Haggai (e.g., the defeat of Persia by the Greeks), the ultimate shaking of the created order is still to come (Heb. 12:26–28).

2:7 treasures of all nations. Though the Hebrew term translated "treasures" could refer to a person (i.e., the Messiah), the immediate context here favors a reference to the things desired by all nations (i.e., the things precious to them). Verse 8 speaks of such precious things, and the decree of King Darius, during whose reign Haggai ministered, alludes to precious things being contributed to the temple building project (Ezra 6:3–5, 8–9). Here Haggai probably echoes Isaiah's promise of an Israel made rich by the wealth of the nations (Is. 60:5). In other words, he speaks of the Messianic age.

fill this house with glory. God's intention is to honor Himself by manifesting His glorious presence before "all nations." As God's presence fills the temple, the nations come to the light (Is. 2:3–5; 60:3).

2:8 The silver . . . the gold. As the sovereign possessor of all things (cf. Ps. 24:1; 50:9–12), God will bring about both His own glorification and His people's inheritance of the nations' wealth (Is. 60:5). See note on v. 7.

gold is mine, declares the LORD of hosts.
9 [r]The latter glory of this house shall be
greater than the former, says the LORD of
hosts. And [s]in this place I will give peace,
declares the LORD of hosts.' "

Blessings for a Defiled People

10 [t]On the twenty-fourth day of the ninth
month, [u]in the second year of Darius, the
word of the LORD came by Haggai the prophet, 11 "Thus says the LORD of hosts: [v]Ask the
priests about the law: 12 'If someone carries
[w]holy meat in the fold of his garment and
touches with his fold bread or stew or wine
or oil or any kind of food, does it become
holy?' " The priests answered and said,
[x]"No." 13 Then Haggai said, [y]"If someone
who is unclean by contact with a dead body
[z]touches any of these, does it become
unclean?" The priests answered and said, "It
does become unclean." 14 Then Haggai
answered and said, [a]"So is it with this people, and with this nation before me, declares
the LORD, and so with every work of their
hands. And what they offer there is unclean.
15 Now then, [b]consider from this day onward.[1] Before stone was placed upon stone
in the temple of the LORD, 16 how did you
fare?[2] [c]When one came to a heap of twenty
measures, there were but ten. When one
came to the wine vat to draw fifty measures,
there were but twenty. 17 [d]I struck you and all
the products of your toil with blight and with
mildew and with hail, [e]yet you did not turn
to me, declares the LORD. 18 [b]Consider from
this day onward, [f]from the twenty-fourth day
of the ninth month. Since [g]the day that the
foundation of the LORD's temple was laid,
[b]consider: 19 [h]Is the seed yet in the barn?
Indeed, the vine, the fig tree, the pomegranate, and the olive tree have yielded nothing.
But from this day on [i]I will bless you."

Zerubbabel Chosen as a Signet

20 The word of the LORD came a second
time to Haggai [f]on the twenty-fourth day of
the month, 21 "Speak to [j]Zerubbabel, governor of Judah, saying, [k]I am about to shake
the heavens and the earth, 22 and [l]to overthrow the throne of kingdoms. I am about
to destroy the strength of the kingdoms of
the nations, and [m]overthrow the chariots
and their riders. And the horses and their
riders shall go down, [n]every one by the
sword of his brother. 23 On that day,
declares the LORD of hosts, I will take you,
O [j]Zerubbabel [o]my servant, the son of
[p]Shealtiel, declares the LORD, and make
you [q]like a[3] signet ring, [o]for I have chosen
you, declares the LORD of hosts."

[1] Or *backward*; also verse 18 [2] Probable reading (compare Septuagint); Hebrew *since they were* [3] Hebrew *the*

9 [r][ch. 1:8] [s][Zech. 6:13; Eph. 2:14]
10 [t]ver. 18, 20 [u]ch. 1:1
11 [v]See Lev. 10:10, 11
12 [w]Jer. 11:15 [x][ver. 14]
13 [y]Lev. 22:4, 6 [z][Num. 19:22]
14 [a][Isai. 64:6]
15 [b][ch. 1:5]
16 [c][ch. 1:6]
17 [d]Amos 4:9; [ch. 1:9; Deut. 28:22] [e]Jer. 5:3; Amos 4:6
18 [b][See ver. 15 above] [f]ver. 10 [g]Ezra 3:10; Zech. 8:9
19 [h][Zech. 8:12] [i]Joel 2:14
20 [f][See ver. 18 above]
21 [j]ch. 1:1; [Zech. 4:6] [k]ver. 6
22 [l]Dan. 2:44; Zech. 12:9; [Matt. 24:7] [m][Mic. 5:10] [n][Zech. 14:13]
23 [j][See ver. 21 above] [o][Isai. 43:10] [p]ch. 1:1 [q]Jer. 22:24

2:9 glory. This promise of greater glory is realized in Christ, the greatest manifestation of God's presence and glory (Mal. 3:1; John 1:14). Christ gives His glory to His church, the new temple of God (Eph. 2:21; 3:20, 21).

in this place I will give peace. This peace (Hebrew *shalom*) means more than the absence of conflict. It implies prosperity and a sense of total well-being. Christ gives peace to believers now (John 14:27), but ultimate fulfillment awaits the time when the Lord God Almighty and the Lamb are the temple of the New Jerusalem (Rev. 21:22).

2:10 twenty-fourth day of the ninth month. The sequence of time is important for interpreting the third message, which begins on a note of judgment (vv. 10–14). The people had repented and begun the work on Sept. 21, 520 B.C. (1:15), and Haggai brought a message of encouragement on Oct. 17 of the same year (2:1–9). Here, on Dec. 18, he brings another message of condemnation. The people had not yet seen the deeper issue—their defilement before the holy God. This is consistent with Zechariah's call to return to the Lord, issued *after* they began working on the temple (Zech. 1:3–6).

2:11–14 This portion of Haggai's third sermon, emphasizing the extensive defilement of the people and their efforts, builds on an object lesson taken from the Mosaic ceremonial law. The questions directed to the priests show that while ceremonial holiness is not transferable (v. 12), ceremonial defilement is (v. 13). Haggai then applies the lesson of the preceding questions to his hearers (v. 14). They defiled the work of the temple and their offerings because their estrangement from God was deeper than they realized. The mere presence of a rebuilt temple would not render them holy as a people (cf. Jer. 7:3–7); God demands genuine change of heart and life, not mere outward conformity.

2:15 Now. This word signals a transition from indictment to blessing. In spite of their past defilement, the holy God was determined to bless them (v. 19).

2:17 I struck . . . hail. This verse draws on Amos 4:9. Such natural disasters and lack of agricultural productivity, the bitter fruit of disobedience to the Lord's covenant (1:6 note; Deut. 28:22), were God's way of getting His people's attention.

2:19 I will bless you. God's grace overcomes the sin and defilement of His people. Though He chastises them, in the end mercy triumphs over judgment.

2:20–23 This last of Haggai's sermons, given the same day as the previous address (v. 10), returns to the theme of the latter-day glory of the temple (v. 6 note). Again future events are telescoped as Haggai interweaves mention of the coming Messiah (v. 23) with references to the shaking of the cosmos and the final victory of God over the nations (vv. 21, 22).

2:22 overthrow. The military and political powers of the nations finally submit to God's lordship (Dan. 2:44; 7:27).

2:23 On that day. See note Zech. 12:3.

my servant. Zerubbabel was God's chosen representative to accomplish His work. Isaiah spoke of a greater Servant who would come, whom Zerubbabel foreshadows (Is. 42:10). Jesus is both the descendant of Zerubbabel (Matt. 1:12) and the Servant of God (Acts 4:27, 30).

signet ring. This was a symbol of authority and power. Jeremiah uses the term to refer to one who is precious to God (Jer. 22:24).

THE BOOK OF

Zechariah

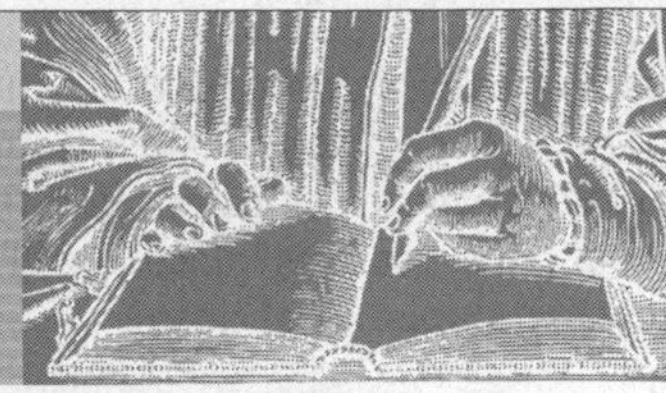

AUTHOR

Scholars differ widely on the authorship of Zechariah. The author is identified in 1:1 as "Zechariah, the son of Berechiah, son of Iddo." It has traditionally been held that this man was a sixth-century contemporary of Haggai and that the entire book was written by him. However, critical scholars have for some time argued that there were essentially two books (chs. 1–8 and 9–14). The first part is considered to be from the sixth century prophet himself, while the second part is assigned to a later time, usually the Maccabean era of the second century B.C. Various literary and historical arguments have been used to arrive at these conclusions, but all are tentative at best. There are no compelling reasons to conclude that Zechariah was not indeed the sole author of the book.

DATE AND OCCASION

The historical background of Zechariah is the same as that of Haggai (Introduction to Haggai), but their ministries differed in emphasis. Haggai's work centered on the rebuilding of the temple, while Zechariah's was largely designed to encourage God's people about the welfare of Jerusalem and its long-term future.

CHARACTERISTICS AND THEMES

Zechariah contains a variety of literary forms. The visions of the first part are similar to the visions of Ezekiel and Daniel, in part because later prophecy in Israel employed more visions. The book is often taken to be an example of early apocalyptic literature ("Introduction to Daniel: Characteristics and Themes"), and certainly methods and themes characteristic of such literature are present in Zechariah. In ch. 14 a description of a final war against Jerusalem is given in which God comes as a victorious warrior to save His people from their enemies. Similarly, the visions of the horsemen (1:7–11), the four chariots (6:1–8), and the woman in the basket (5:5–11) might also be viewed as apocalyptic.

Our understanding of the teaching of Zechariah is greatly helped when we recognize that the prophet gives pictures of the future in snapshot fashion, in which the pictures are not placed in any particular sequence. When we read a passage, we see only what is happening in that snapshot, not how it relates to other snapshots. Further, the prophet portrays even the present blessings that Christians enjoy in terms of the imagery and customs of Old Testament life.

Zechariah's visions combine the present and future in an interwoven fabric that is impossible to tear apart. That is why it is often difficult to ascertain what time period the prophet has in mind. The promises (e.g., 2:5, 11) relate to both the immediate audience in Zechariah's day and also to the distant future. This "telescoping," or compression of the near and distant future, is a common feature of the prophetic writings.

The welfare and future of Jerusalem as the holy city is a pervasive theme in Zechariah. Several of the visions develop this theme (1:7–17; 2:1–13; 5:1–4 and notes). Chapter 8 presents a picture of Jerusalem, with God in her midst, dwelling in beautiful tranquility. The book ends with a chapter developing this theme (ch. 14). Zechariah's focus on Jerusalem reflects the theme of the ideal Zion longed for in the Old Testament (Ps. 46; 48; 132).

Zechariah gives many explicit pictures of the Messiah, the Lord Jesus Christ. A pattern established between the Old Testament and the New Testament is that of Jesus as Messiah fulfilling promises the Lord spoke about Himself in the Old Testament. God's promises of what He will accomplish are realized through His Anointed

One. This explains the frequent citations in the New Testament from this book. The Messiah is portrayed as the King who comes riding into Jerusalem in 9:9, 10, a passage quoted by Matthew at Jesus' triumphal entry (Matt. 21:1–11). Christ's betrayal and death are spoken of in 13:7. Zechariah also develops the messianic figure of "the Branch," who combines the offices of priest and king (3:8 note; 6:12 note).

The era of the Messiah is touched on in other passages, even where the Messiah is not explicitly mentioned. The promise in 2:5, 10 of God's dwelling in the midst of His people is realized in Christ (John 1:14 and note). Similarly, the Feast of Tabernacles celebrated in 14:16–20 will find its fullest expression in the kingdom of the Messiah when the new Jerusalem comes down from heaven (Rev. 21:1–3).

OUTLINE OF ZECHARIAH

I. Encouragement for the Present (chs. 1–8)

- A. *Call to Repentance (1:1–6)*
- B. *The Eight Night Visions (1:7–6:8)*
  1. The Man Among the Myrtle Trees (1:7–17)
  2. Four Horns and Four Craftsmen (1:18–21)
  3. A Man with a Measuring Line (ch. 2)
  4. Clean Garments for the High Priest (ch. 3)
  5. The Gold Lampstand and the Two Olive Trees (ch. 4)
  6. The Flying Scroll (5:1–4)
  7. The Woman in a Basket (5:5–11)
  8. Four Chariots (6:1–8)
- C. *Appendix: The Crowning of Joshua as a Prophecy of the Coming Branch (6:9–15)*
- D. *Social Problems and the Transformation of Jerusalem (chs. 7; 8)*
  1. The Question Concerning Fasting (7:1–7)
  2. The Failure to Do Justice and Show Mercy (7:8–14)
  3. God's Blessings on Future Jerusalem (8:1–15)
  4. The Question of Fasting Answered (8:16–19)
  5. Extension of God's Blessings to Mankind (8:20–23)

II. The Future of God's Kingdom (chs. 9–14)

- A. *The First Prophetic Oracle (chs. 9–11)*
  1. The Coming of God the King from the North (9:1–8)
  2. The King's Arrival in Jerusalem (9:9, 10)
  3. The Coming of God the King from the South (9:11–17)
  4. The Shepherd-King's Destruction of Idols (ch. 10)
  5. A Poem on the Destruction of Proud Nations (11:1–3)
  6. A Picture of God's Shepherd (11:4–17)
- B. *The Second Prophetic Oracle (chs. 12–14)*
  1. God's Judgment on the Nations and the Salvation of Jerusalem (12:1–9)
  2. The Mourning of God's People in Jerusalem (12:10–14)
  3. The Cleansing of the Land of Judah (13:1–6)
  4. The Stricken Shepherd (13:7–9)
  5. The War Against Jerusalem (14:1–15)
  6. The Final Celebration of the Feast of Tabernacles (14:16–20)

A Call to Return to the LORD

1 In the eighth month, [a]in the second year
of Darius, the word of the LORD came
to the prophet [b]Zechariah, the son of
[c]Berechiah, son of [d]Iddo, saying, 2 [e]"The
LORD was very angry with your fathers.
3 Therefore say to them, Thus declares the
LORD of hosts: [f]Return to me, says the LORD
of hosts, and [g]I will return to you, says the
LORD of hosts. 4 [h]Do not be like your fathers,
[i]to whom the former prophets cried out,
'Thus says the LORD of hosts, [f]Return from
your evil ways and from your evil deeds.' But
[j]they did not hear or pay attention to me,
declares the LORD. 5 Your fathers, where are
they? And [k]the prophets, do they live forever?

Chapter 1
1 [a]See Hag. 1:1 [b]Ezra 6:14; Matt. 23:35 [c]1 Chr. 6:39 [d]Neh. 12:4, 16
2 [e][Jer. 2:5]
3 [f]Isai. 31:6; Jer. 3:1, 22; Ezek. 18:30; Mal. 3:7 [g]Jer. 12:15; Mic. 7:19
4 [h][Ps. 78:8] [i]See 2 Chr. 36:15 [f][See ver. 3 above] [j]ch. 7:11; 2 Chr. 36:16; See Jer. 35:15 5 [k][John 8:52]

1:1–6 Zechariah sets the stage for the record of night visions that follows in 1:7–6:8.

1:1 the eighth month, in the second year of Darius. October-November of 520 B.C. Compare the dates in Hag. 1:1, 15 to see how the two prophets ministered during the same time. Zechariah began his ministry two months *after* the returnees from Babylon began to rebuild the temple.

Zechariah, the son of Berechiah. See Introduction: Author; Date and Occasion. His name means "the LORD remembers."

1:2 The LORD was very angry. Verses 2–6 are a preface to the eight night visions of 1:7–6:8. This section shows that although the people had responded to Haggai's call to rebuild the temple, their hearts were still far from God. The Lord is still very angry with them.

1:3 the LORD of hosts. A divine title used extensively by the postexilic prophets Zechariah, Haggai, and Malachi. It has military connotations (God as leader of Israel's armies, 1 Sam. 17:45), but it also highlights God's sovereign kingship over all creation.

Return to me . . . I will return. Repentance involves a total turning away *from* sin and a turning *to* God. God's return would then bless His people with His presence (1:16; 2:11).

1:4 the former prophets. The preexilic prophets (e.g., Isaiah, Jeremiah).

they did not hear or pay attention to me. Their fathers showed obstinacy and rebellion (2 Kin. 17:13–15). As a consequence, the curses of the covenant (Deut. 28:15–68) came upon them for their disobedience.

declares the LORD. The Hebrew expression means an utterance that gives the prophets insight into the plan and will of God (Ps. 110:1).

6 [l]But my words and my statutes, which I
commanded [m]my servants the prophets, did
they not [n]overtake your fathers? So they
repented and said, [o]As the LORD of hosts purposed to deal with us for [p]our ways and
[p]deeds, so has he dealt with us."

A Vision of a Horseman

7 On the twenty-fourth day of the
eleventh month, which is the month of
Shebat, in the second year of Darius, the
word of the LORD came to the prophet
[b]Zechariah, the son of [c]Berechiah, son of
[d]Iddo, saying, 8 "I saw in the night, and
behold, [q]a man riding on a red horse! He

6 [l][Isai. 40:8; Matt. 24:35] [m]See Dan. 9:6 [n]Deut. 28:2, 15 [o]Lam. 2:17 [p][Ezek. 36:31]
7 [b][See ver. 1 above] [c][See ver. 1 above] [d][See ver. 1 above]
8 [q][Rev. 6:4]
[r][Rev. 6:4, 5, 8]; See ch. 6:2-7
9 [s][Rev. 22:6]
10 [q][See ver. 8 above] [t][Heb. 1:14]

was standing among the myrtle trees in the
glen, and behind him were [r]red, sorrel, and
white horses. 9 Then I said, 'What are
these, my lord?' [s]The angel who talked
with me said to me, 'I will show you what
they are.' 10 So [q]the man who was standing
among the myrtle trees answered, [t]'These
are they whom the LORD has sent to [u]patrol
the earth.' 11 And they answered [s]the angel
of the LORD who was standing among the
myrtle trees, and said, [u]'We have patrolled
the earth, and behold, all the earth [v]re-
mains at rest.' 12 Then [s]the angel of the

[u]ch. 6:7; [Job 1:7] 11 [s][See ver. 9 above] [u][See ver. 10 above] [v][ver. 15]
12 [s][Rev. 22:6]

Angels

Angels (the Greek *angelos* means "messenger") are one of two sorts of personal beings created by God, humanity being the other. Multitudinous in number (Matt. 26:53; Rev. 5:11), angels are intelligent moral agents. They are not embodied nor ordinarily visible, although they are able to manifest themselves in what appears as a physical form (Gen. 18:2–19:22; John 20:12, 13; Acts 12:7–10). They do not marry, and are not subject to death (Matt. 22:30; Luke 20:35, 36). They can move from one point in space to another, and many can be focussed in a tiny area (Luke 8:30, where the reference is to fallen angels).

Like human beings, the angels were originally under probation, and some of them fell into sin. The many who passed the test are now evidently confirmed in a state of holiness and immortal glory. Heaven is their dwelling place (Matt. 18:10; 22:30; Rev. 5:11), where they constantly worship God (Ps. 103:20, 21; 148:2) and from where they go out at God's command to render service to Christians (Heb. 1:14). These are the "holy" and "elect" angels (Matt. 25:31; Mark 8:38; Luke 9:26; Acts 10:22; 1 Tim. 5:21; Rev. 14:10), to whom God's work of grace in Christ continues to display an increasing measure of the divine wisdom and glory (Eph. 3:10; 1 Pet. 1:12).

Holy angels protect believers (Ps. 34:7; 91:11, 12), little ones in particular (Matt. 18:10), and they constantly observe what goes on in the church (1 Cor. 11:10). It is implied that they have a special ministry to believers at the time of their death (Luke 16:22), but we know no details about this. The world may watch Christians in the hopes of seeing them fall, but the angels watch to see the triumph of grace in their lives.

The mysterious "Angel of the LORD" or "Angel of God," who appears often in the early parts of the Old Testament, is sometimes identified with God, and other times distinguished from God (Gen. 16:7–13; 18:1–33; 22:11–18; 24:7, 40; 31:11–13; 32:24–30; 48:15–16; Ex. 3:2–6; 14:19; 23:20–23; 32:34–33:5; Num. 22:22–35; Josh. 5:13–15; Judg. 2:1–5; 6:11–23; 9:13–23). In certain instances at least, this Angel is in some sense God acting as His own messenger, and is commonly seen as a preincarnate appearance of God the Son.

Angelic activity was prominent at the great turning points in the divine plan of salvation (the days of the patriarchs, the time of the Exodus and giving of the law, the period of the Exile and restoration, and the birth, resurrection, and ascension of Jesus Christ). Angels will be prominent again when Christ returns (Matt. 25:31; Mark 8:38).

1:6 my servants the prophets. See note Is. 20:3.

they repented. See Neh. 9:1–10:27.

purposed to deal with us. The Hebrew word suggests that God's punishment of the preexilic fathers was in accord with a plan.

1:7–17 These verses record the first of eight night visions that Zechariah saw in the course of one night (v. 8). The visions are organized so that the first and last (6:1–8) correspond to one another in the imagery of horses and chariots. This first one emphasizes God's commitment to His covenant people; He is the rebuilder of Jerusalem and its protector against pagan forces in the outside world. The vision calls God's people to look beyond their present circumstances and place their trust in the promises of God.

1:8 red horse . . . red, sorrel, and white. The significance of these colors is uncertain.

1:9 angel who talked with me. This interpreting angel (1:19; 2:3; 3:1; 4:1) should be distinguished from the "Angel of the LORD" (v. 12 note; 3:1). See theological note "Angels."

1:11 all the earth remains at rest. The self-assured nations stand in contrast to the Jewish state struggling under Persian rule. Yet God assures His people that these proud nations will experience judgment (cf. Obadiah's words about Edom's false security, Obad. 3, 4, 8).

1:12 the angel of the LORD. See note Gen. 16:7. Many, though not all, scholars identify this Angel with the "man riding on a red horse" (v. 8).

LORD said, [w]'O LORD of hosts, [w]how long
will you [x]have no mercy on Jerusalem and
the cities of Judah, against which you have
been angry these [y]seventy years?' **13** And the
LORD answered [z]gracious and comforting
words to [s]the angel who talked with me.
14 So [s]the angel who talked with me said to
me, 'Cry out, Thus says the LORD of hosts:
[a]I am exceedingly jealous for Jerusalem and
for Zion. **15** [b]And I am exceedingly angry
with the nations that are [c]at ease; [d]for while
I was angry but a little, [e]they furthered the
disaster. **16** Therefore, thus says the LORD, [f]I
have returned to Jerusalem with mercy;
[g]my house shall be built in it, declares the
LORD of hosts, and [h]the measuring line
shall be stretched out over Jerusalem. **17** Cry
out again, Thus says the LORD of hosts: [i]My
cities shall again overflow with prosperity,
[j]and the LORD will again comfort Zion and
again [k]choose Jerusalem.'"

A Vision of Horns and Craftsmen

18 [l]And I lifted my eyes and saw, and
behold, [l]four horns! **19** And I said to [s]the
angel who talked with me, "What are these?"
And he said to me, [l]"These are the horns that
have scattered Judah, Israel, and Jerusalem."
20 Then the LORD showed me four craftsmen.
21 And I said, "What are these coming to do?"
He said, [l]"These are the horns that scattered
Judah, so that no one raised his head. And
these have come [m]to terrify them, to cast
down the horns of the nations [n]who lifted
up their horns against the land of Judah to
scatter it."

A Vision of a Man with a Measuring Line

2 [2] And I lifted my eyes and saw, and
behold, [o]a man with a measuring line
in his hand! **2** Then I said, "Where are you
going?" And he said to me, [p]"To measure
Jerusalem, to see what is its width and what
is its length." **3** And behold, [q]the angel who
talked with me came forward, and another
angel came forward to meet him **4** and said
to him, "Run, say to that young man,
[r]'Jerusalem shall be inhabited [s]as villages
without walls, because of [t]the multitude of
people and livestock in it. **5** And I will be to
her [u]a wall of fire all around, declares the
LORD, and I will be the glory in her midst.'"
6 Up! Up! [v]Flee from the land of the
north, declares the LORD. For I have
[w]spread you abroad as the four winds of
the heavens, declares the LORD. **7** [x]Up!
Escape to Zion, you who dwell with the
daughter of Babylon. **8** For thus said the
LORD of hosts, after his glory sent me[3] to
the nations who plundered you, [y]for he

12 [w]Ps. 80:4; 89:46; Hab. 2:6; Rev. 6:10 [x]Ps. 102:13 [y]ch. 7:5; Jer. 25:11; 29:10
13 [z]See Jer. 29:10, 11 [s][See ver. 9 above]
14 [s][See ver. 9 above] [a]ch. 8:2; Joel 2:18
15 [b][Joel 3:2] [c][ver. 11] [d][Isai. 54:7, 8] [e][Isai. 47:6]
16 [f]ch. 8:3 [g][ch. 4:9; Ezra 6:14] [h]Jer. 31:39; Ezra 40:3; 47:3
17 [i]ch. 2:4 [j]Isai. 40:1; 51:3 [k]ch. 2:12
18 [l][1 Kin. 22:1]
19 [s][See ver. 9 above] [l][See ver. 18 above]
21 [l][See ver. 18 above] [m]Deut. 28:26; Jer. 7:33 [n][Ps. 75:4, 5]
Chapter 2
1 [o]Ezek. 40:3; Rev. 11:1
2 [p][ch. 1:16]
3 [q]ch. 1:9, 19
4 [r][ch. 12:6; 14:10, 11] [s]See Esth. 9:19 [t]Isai. 49:19; Jer. 31:27
5 [u]Isai. 4:5; [ch. 9:8; Ps. 125:2]
6 [v]Isai. 48:20 [w][ch. 7:14; Ezek. 5:10; 17:21] **7** [x][Isai. 52:11] **8** [y]Jer. 12:14

[1] Ch 2:1 in Hebrew [2] Ch 2:5 in Hebrew [3] Or *he sent me after glory*

seventy years. A reference to the prophecy of Jer. 25:11, 12 where the Babylonian exile was announced.

1:13 gracious and comforting words. Words that reflect God's love for His people and reaffirm God's commitment not to forsake His people (Heb. 13:5).

1:14 I am exceedingly jealous for Jerusalem. The first expression of the theme of God's jealousy in the book (8:2). God's zealous love for His chosen people moves Him to act in their behalf. A similar theme is expressed in Zeph. 3:9–20.

1:15 I am exceedingly angry with the nations. Notice the contrast with v. 2 where God's past anger with His own people is expressed. Here God's love for His own (v. 14 above) moves Him to protect them by bringing judgment on the nations who have persecuted His people beyond measure.

1:17 The LORD will again . . . choose Jerusalem. A common theme in the visions (2:12; 3:2). God's choice of His people distinguishes them from the pagan nations. The result of His choice is to bring them prosperity ("My cities shall again overflow with prosperity").

1:18–21 The second vision focuses on the four horns. The "horn" was a symbol of power and pride in the ancient Near East (Ps. 75:4, 5). This vision is the counterpart of the first: Zion will be rebuilt and the nations destroyed. The identification of the four horns could be the same as those of Daniel's prophecies (Dan. 2:36–45; 7:17–28), and so correspond either to Babylonia, Medo-Persia, Greece, and Rome, or to Assyria, Babylon, Egypt, and Persia (10:10, 11). The horns could also have a greater significance and refer to "the four corners of the earth" (Rev. 20:8).

1:21 cast down the horns of the nations. The four craftsmen come to overthrow the power of the nations. This is symbolic of God's judgment coming on the nations that have persecuted His people, a fulfillment of God's promise to Abraham that He would curse those who cursed Abraham's descendants (Gen. 12:3).

2:1–5 Zechariah's third vision describes a man with a measuring line. This vision stresses God's protection of His people with His own personal presence (v. 5 notes). Jerusalem's walls were probably not rebuilt yet, and the city was subject to attack from roving bands.

2:1 a measuring line. An implement that became a symbol of rebuilding in Jeremiah's portrayal of a restored Jerusalem (Jer. 31:39).

2:4 without walls. The Old Testament prophets envision a time when Jerusalem will be the center of worship for the nations (v. 11; 8:20–23; Is. 2:1–4), and the city will overflow with people.

multitude of people and livestock. See note on v. 11.

2:5 a wall of fire all around. The day of full restoration is portrayed by the prophets as a second Exodus with the imagery of the pillar of fire (Is. 4:5, 6). As Israel was once protected from her enemies by God Himself, so He will again guard her from oppressors.

the glory. God's presence is far more than protection; it is the source of all blessing for His people. The essence of the renewed covenant is, "I will be their God, and they shall be my people" (Jer. 31:33).

2:6–13 In this section the prophet speaks to the Jews in Babylon (vv. 6–9) and in Jerusalem (vv. 10–13).

2:6 I have spread you abroad. A reference to God's judgment of Judah in the Exile as punishment for covenant disobedience (Deut. 28:36, 49, 50). The time of judgment is over; the time of restoration has come (v. 7).

who touches you touches [z]the apple of his
eye: **9** "Behold, [a]I will shake my hand over
them, [b]and they shall become plunder for
those who served them. Then [c]you will
know that the LORD of hosts has sent me.
10 [d]Sing and rejoice, O daughter of Zion, for
[e]behold, I come [f]and I will dwell in your
midst, declares the LORD. **11** [g]And many
nations shall join themselves to the LORD
in that day, and shall be my people. [f]And I
will dwell in your midst, and [c]you shall
know that the LORD of hosts has sent me to
you. **12** [h]And the LORD will inherit Judah as
his portion in the holy land, and will again
[i]choose Jerusalem."
13 Be silent, all flesh, before the LORD, for
he has roused himself from his holy
dwelling.

A Vision of Joshua the High Priest

3 Then he showed me [j]Joshua the high
priest standing before the angel of the
LORD, and [k]Satan[1] standing at his right
hand to accuse him. **2** And the LORD said to
Satan, [l]"The LORD rebuke you, O Satan! The
LORD who has [m]chosen Jerusalem rebuke
you! Is not this [n]a brand[2] plucked from the
fire?" **3** Now [j]Joshua was standing before the
angel, [o]clothed with filthy garments. **4** And
the angel said to [p]those who were standing
before him, [q]"Remove the filthy garments
from him." And to him he said, "Behold, [r]I
have taken your iniquity away from you,
and [s]I will clothe you with pure vestments."
5 And I said, [t]"Let them put a clean turban
on his head." So they put a clean turban on
his head and clothed him with garments.
And the angel of the LORD was standing by.
6 And the angel of the LORD solemnly
assured [j]Joshua, **7** "Thus says the LORD of
hosts: If you will walk in my ways and
[u]keep my charge, then you shall [v]rule my
house and have charge of my courts, and I
will give you the right of access among
[w]those who are standing here. **8** Hear now,
O Joshua the high priest, you and your
friends who sit before you, for [x]they are
men who are a sign: behold, I will bring
[y]my servant [z]the Branch. **9** For behold, on
[a]the stone that I have set before Joshua,

8 [z]See Deut. 32:10
9 [a]Isai. 11:15; 19:16 [b]Ezek. 39:10 [c]ch. 4:9; 6:15; Ezek. 33:33
10 [d]See Zeph. 3:14 [e]Ps. 40:7 [f]ch. 8:3; Isai. 12:6; Ezek. 37:27; Zeph. 3:15; 2 Cor. 6:16; See Lev. 26:12
11 [g]ch. 8:22; See Isai. 2:2 [f][See ver. 10 above] [c][See ver. 9 above]
12 [h]See Deut. 32:9 [i]ch. 1:17; [Hab. 2:20]

Chapter 3
1 [j]ch. 6:11; See Ezra 3:2 [k][1Chr. 21:1; Ps. 109:6]
2 [l]Jude 9 [m]ch. 1:17; [Rom. 8:33] [n]Amos 4:11
3 [j][See ver. 1 above] [o][Isai. 64:6; Jude 23]
4 [p][ver. 7; Luke 1:19] [q]Rev. 7:14 [r][ver. 9; Isai. 6:7] [s]Isai. 61:10 Luke 15:22; Rev. 19:8
5 [t]Job 29:14; [ch. 6:11] 6 [j][See ver. 1 above] 7 [u]Gen. 26:5; Mal. 3:14; See Lev. 8:35 [v][Deut. 17:9; Mal. 2:7] [w][ver. 4] 8 [x][Ezek. 12:11] [y]See Isai. 42:1 [z]ch. 6:12; Isai. 11:1; See Jer. 23:5 9 [a]Ps. 118:22; Isai. 28:16; [ch. 4:7]; See Ezra 3:9-11

[1] *Satan* means *the accuser* [2] That is, a burning stick

2:8 the apple of his eye. See note Deut. 32:10.

2:10 I will dwell in your midst. This promise assumes the sanctification of the people and land through the blood of the everlasting covenant (3:9 notes; 8:8 note; Heb. 13:20).

2:11 many nations. The extent of the vision transcends anything the Jews could accomplish in their day. The vision captures a time when salvation will not be limited to the Jewish nation but will extend God's grace to the world. That day has come in Christ's inauguration of the kingdom of God.

2:12 in the holy land. An expression used only here in the Scriptures. Judah will be holy because God will dwell there. Zechariah is envisioning the fullest realization of God's promise to Abraham (Gen. 12:3; 15:5).

2:13 Be silent. All mankind should revere God because of the great salvation declared in this chapter (Hab. 2:20).

he has roused himself. For the purpose of judgment. God will both judge the nations that oppressed His people and provide a safe home for His people.

3:1–10 The fourth vision concerns Joshua, the high priest (Ezra 3:2), and deals particularly with the problem of an impure priesthood. It begins by showing God's solution to the problem (vv. 4, 5) and ends by showing how God wipes away the sin of all His people (vv. 8, 9).

3:1 A courtroom scene similar to that in Job (Job 1:6–12). Satan has come to accuse Joshua of his unworthiness for the priesthood. The Hebrew term *Satan* means "adversary" or "accuser" (text note); here it may be descriptive (i.e., not a proper name).

standing. Joshua assumes the position of the priest who ministers in the presence of God. Accusation is a favorite ploy of Satan against believers. It differs from the conviction of the Holy Spirit. The Spirit convicts of sin in order to move us to repentance and forgiveness. Satan's goal is destruction, not redemption.

3:2 brand plucked from the fire. The fire is a metaphor for the Exile from which the people of God have been snatched. Amos 4:11 also uses the same expression to speak of the danger from which God redeems His people.

3:3 filthy garments. Here we see the basis of Satan's accusations that Joshua is unworthy. If the high priest is unclean, who can make atonement for sin? If he cannot make the atonement, how can the people be forgiven? The answer is given in a twofold manner below.

3:4 Remove the filthy garments. God makes Joshua fit for the priesthood by giving new garments. In this way Joshua is a type of the coming Branch (v. 8), who will fulfill a priestly function and provide clothing of righteousness for us from His own merit.

3:5 a clean turban. The turban was part of the high priest's dress. A new clean turban completes the restored garments, indicating that God has taken away the reproach on the priesthood (Ex. 28:36–38).

3:8 they are men who are a sign. These men foreshadow the coming Servant because they are priests, and He will act as a priest by making atonement for sin (v. 9 note).

my servant. A title of honor initially used for Moses (Num. 12:6–8). The term also was used as a title in Isaiah, sometimes for Israel (Is. 41:8; 44:1, 2) and sometimes (as here) for the Messiah, the Servant who would redeem His people (Is. 42:1–7; 52:13).

the Branch. A Messianic title combining the offices of priest and king (6:12 note: Is. 4:2 and note).

3:9 the stone. Possibly a reference to the Messiah. Several Old Testament passages about the stone were interpreted as messianic in the New Testament (Ps. 118:22; Is. 8:14; 28:16; Matt. 21:42; 1 Pet. 2:6–8).

seven eyes. The mixture of images is difficult to interpret but these eyes are symbols of God's omniscient and watchful care (also used in 4:10).

remove the iniquity of this land. God will take away His people's sin through the Branch. The priestly system in the Old Testament was not intended actually to cover sin but only to prefigure the One who would truly deal with man's sin (Heb. 10:1–18).

in a single day. The Day of Atonement (Lev. 16:30; 23:28) was an annual reminder of sin (Heb. 9:7–10), but Christ on a single day (Good Friday) once for all made atonement for the sins of God's people (Heb. 9:11–14).

on a single stone with [b]seven eyes,[1] I will
[c]engrave its inscription, declares the LORD
of hosts, and [d]I will remove the iniquity of
this land in a single day. **10** In that day,
declares the LORD of hosts, every one of
you will invite his neighbor to come [e]under
his vine and under his fig tree."

A Vision of a Golden Lampstand

4 And [f]the angel who talked with me
came again [g]and woke me, like a man
who is awakened out of his sleep. **2** And he
said to me, "What do you see?" I said, "I
see, and behold, [h]a lampstand all of gold,
with a bowl on the top of it, and [i]seven
lamps on it, with seven lips on each of the
lamps that are on the top of it. **3** And there
are [j]two olive trees by it, one on the right of
the bowl and the other on its left." **4** And I
said to [f]the angel who talked with me,
"What are these, my lord?" **5** Then the angel
who talked with me answered and said to
me, [k]"Do you not know what these are?" I
said, "No, my lord." **6** Then he said to me,
"This is the word of the LORD to
[l]Zerubbabel: [m]Not by might, nor by power,
but by my Spirit, says the LORD of hosts.
7 Who are you, [n]O great mountain? Before
[l]Zerubbabel [o]you shall become a plain.
And he shall bring forward [p]the top stone
amid shouts of 'Grace, grace to it!'"
8 Then the word of the LORD came to me,
saying, **9** [q]"The hands of [l]Zerubbabel have
laid the foundation of this house; his
hands shall also [r]complete it. [s]Then you
will know that the LORD of hosts has sent
me to you. **10** [t]For whoever has despised the
day of small things shall rejoice, and shall
see [u]the plumb line in the hand of
Zerubbabel.
[v]"These seven [v]are the eyes of the LORD,
[w]which range through the whole earth."
11 Then I said to him, "What are these [j]two
olive trees on the right and the left of the
lampstand?" **12** And a second time I answered and said to him, "What are these
[j]two branches of the olive trees, which are
beside the two golden pipes from which
the golden oil[2] is poured out?" **13** He said to
me, [x]"Do you not know what these are?" I
said, "No, my lord." **14** Then he said, [y]"These
are the two anointed ones[3] who stand by
[z]the Lord of the whole earth."

A Vision of a Flying Scroll

5 Again I lifted my eyes and saw, and
behold, a flying [a]scroll! **2** And he said to

9 [b]ch. 4:10; Rev. 5:6 [c][2 Tim. 2:19] [d][ver. 4]
10 [e]See 1 Kin. 4:25
Chapter 4
1 [f]ch. 1:9, 19 [g]Dan. 8:18; 10:9, 10
2 [h]See Ex. 25:31 [i]Ex. 25:37; [Rev. 1:12; 4:5]
3 [j][ver. 11; Rev. 11:4]
4 [f][See ver. 1 above]
5 [k]ver. 12
6 [l]See 1 Chr. 3:19 [m][Hos. 1:7]
7 [n][Jer. 51:25] [l][See ver. 6 above] [o]Isai. 40:4
[p]See ch. 3:9
9 [q][Ezra 3:10] [l][See ver. 6 above] [r][ch. 1:16] [s]See ch. 2:9
10 [t][Hag. 2:3] [u][ch. 1:16] [v]ch. 3:9 [w]2 Chr. 16:9; [Prov. 15:3]
11 [j][See ver. 3 above]
12 [j][See ver. 3 above]
13 [x]ver. 5
14 [y]Rev. 11:4 [z]ch. 6:5
Chapter 5
1 [a]Jer. 36:2, 28

[1] Or *facets* [2] Hebrew lacks *oil* [3] Hebrew *two sons of new oil*

3:10 under his vine . . . fig tree. An expression for peace and prosperity (1 Kin. 4:25; Mic. 4:4). The ultimate state of God's kingdom is in view.

4:1–14 The fifth vision describes a golden lampstand and two olive trees. The main problem addressed in the visions is how the work of rebuilding the temple will be completed. God's answer is that Joshua and Zerubbabel are only finite and limited human beings. The power for completing the task will come from God Himself.

4:2 lampstand all of gold. The lampstand was probably used to remind the people of the lampstand in the tabernacle and the temple (Ex. 25:31), although its shape was different. The lampstand may also have symbolized the responsibility of the postexilic Jewish community to be a "light for the nations" (Is. 42:6; 49:6).

seven lamps . . . seven lips. The numbers in this verse are somewhat confusing but they probably mean that there were seven lamps on the stand with one bowl to hold the lamp oil. Seven tubes from the bowl fed the lamps, while the bowl itself was filled from the olive trees (v. 12).

4:3 two olive trees. See v. 14 and note.

4:4 What are these. Zechariah's focus is on the olive trees, not on the lampstand. Here his question does not receive an immediate reply. It is answered in v. 14.

4:6 The key verse for understanding the vision.

Zerubbabel. Even though the vision includes Joshua as one of the olive trees, the focus is on Zerubbabel, as is evident from the repetition of his name in vv. 6, 7, 9, 10.

Not by might . . . power. That is, military strength or any other form of power (apart from God). God's people were repeatedly told not to depend on military power and foreign alliances to accomplish their calling (Is. 31:1–3; Ps. 20:7–9).

by my Spirit. The Spirit of God is often portrayed in the prophets as the One who enables God's servants to do God's work and overcome obstacles. Even the coming Servant of the Lord, the Messiah, is described in such terms (Is. 11:2; 42:1; 61:1).

4:7 the top stone. The last and most important stone, which presumably would ceremonially be put in place in the completed temple.

Grace, grace to it. The temple is completed amid shouts that ask for God's favor to rest on it. The phrase is repeated for emphasis (Is. 40:1 note).

4:10 the day of small things. It would have been easy to be discouraged with the meager results and progress. We find the people of Judah discouraged at the laying of the foundation of the second temple (Ezra 3:10–12) and also at the rebuilding in Haggai's day (520 B.C.; Hag. 2:3). The question in this verse reminds us not to judge God's work by human standards.

eyes of the LORD. See note 3:9.

4:14 These . . . anointed ones. See text note. "These" refers to Zerubbabel and Joshua. As God's chosen leaders they would be supplied by the Holy Spirit with the necessary strength to finish the temple. Together they foreshadow the Messiah, in whom the offices of priest and king (as well as prophet) will be joined in one Person (6:12 note). The total vision teaches both that God is the source of strength for doing His work and that He bestows His Spirit upon His chosen people for the work He has called them to do.

Lord of the whole earth. God is sovereign over all the affairs of men (Is. 40:15, 23, 24). Similarly, the title "Lord Almighty" shows that all the powers of the cosmos are at His disposal (1:3 note).

5:1–4 The sixth vision concerns a flying scroll. It teaches that the Lord who loves and restores His people is also righteous and will punish wickedness. This vision and the one to follow are warnings, but also encouragements that God will deal with the problem of sin in the land.

me, "What do you see?" I answered, "I see
a flying [a]scroll. Its length is twenty cubits,
and its width ten cubits."[1] 3 Then he said to
me, "This is [b]the curse that goes out over
the face of the whole land. For everyone
who [c]steals shall be cleaned out according
to what is on one side, and everyone who
[d]swears falsely[2] shall be cleaned out according to what is on the other side. 4 I will send
it out, declares the LORD of hosts, and it
shall enter the house of the thief, and the
house of [e]him who swears falsely by my
name. And [f]it shall remain in his house and
[g]consume it, both timber and stones."

A Vision of a Woman in a Basket

5 [h]Then the angel who talked with me
came forward and said to me, [i]"Lift your
eyes and see what this is that is going out."
6 And I said, "What is it?" He said, "This is
[j]the basket[3] that is going out." And he said,
"This is their iniquity[4] in all the land." 7 And
behold, the leaden cover was lifted, and
there was a woman sitting in the basket!
8 And he said, "This is Wickedness." And he
thrust her back into the basket, and thrust
down [j]the leaden weight on its opening.
9 Then I lifted my eyes and saw, and behold, two women coming forward! [k]The
wind was in their wings. They had wings like
the wings of a stork, and they lifted up the
basket between earth and heaven. 10 Then I
said to the angel who talked with me, "Where
are they taking the basket?" 11 He said to me,
"To the [l]land of Shinar, to build a house for
it. And when this is prepared, they will set
the basket down there on its base."

A Vision of Four Chariots

6 Again I lifted my eyes and saw, and
behold, four chariots came out from
between two mountains. And the mountains were mountains of [m]bronze. 2 The first
chariot had [n]red horses, the second [o]black
horses, 3 the third [p]white horses, and the
fourth chariot dappled horses—all of them
strong.[5] 4 Then I answered and said to [q]the
angel who talked with me, "What are these,
my lord?" 5 And the angel answered and
said to me, [r]"These are going out to the four
winds of heaven, after [s]presenting themselves before [t]the LORD of all the earth. 6 The
chariot with the black horses goes toward
[u]the north country, the white ones go after
them, and the dappled ones go toward [v]the
south country." 7 When the strong horses
came out, they were impatient to go and

2 [a][See ver. 1 above] 3 [b][Jer. 29:18; Ezek. 2:9, 10]; See Deut. 29:27 [c]See Ex. 20:15 [d]Ex. 20:7; [Eccles. 5:2] 4 [e]ch. 8:17; Lev. 19:12; Mal. 3:5 [f]Prov. 3:33 [g][Lev. 14:15] 5 [h]ch. 1:9 [i][ver. 1, 9; ch. 6:1] 6 [j][Ezek. 45:11] 8 [j][See ver. 3 above] 9 [k][Hos. 4:19] 11 [l]See Gen. 11:2
Chapter 6
1 [m]Dan. 2:39 2 [n]ch. 1:8; Rev. 6:4 [o]Rev. 6:5 3 [p]ch. 1:8; Rev. 6:2 4 [q]ch. 1:9 5 [r]Ps. 104:4; Heb. 1:7 [s]ch. 3:4 [t]ch. 4:14 6 [u]ver. 8; ch. 2:6; Jer. 1:13 [v][ch. 9:14]

1 A *cubit* was about 18 inches or 45 centimeters 2 Hebrew lacks *falsely* (supplied from verse 4) 3 Hebrew *ephah*; also verses 7-11. An *ephah* was about 3/5 bushel or 22 liters 4 One Hebrew manuscript, Septuagint, Syriac; most Hebrew manuscripts *eye* 5 Or *and the fourth chariot strong dappled horses*

5:2 twenty cubits . . . ten cubits. A large open scroll for all to read its words. As the context implies, the words on it are words of the law. Its large size was appropriate for its task of going out over the whole land to deal with every sin (v. 3).

5:3 curse. The curse contained in the Law (Deut. 28:15–68). As in Hag. 1:1–11, the prophet emphasizes that the obedience of God's people brings blessings, while disobedience brings God's curses.

everyone who steals . . . swears falsely. The curse was probably not directed at just two sins, but these are representative of the iniquity of the whole land. False swearing violates the third commandment and the first table of the law (one's duty to God). Theft violates the eighth commandment, found in the second table of the law (one's duty to neighbor). The Ten Commandments summarize the whole moral law and are a revelation of God's own character.

5:4 consume it. God's word will accomplish its intended purpose (Is. 55:11). Those who break God's law will surely suffer the consequences of their sin that this curse brings. Scripture many times emphasizes the certainty of judgment (Rom. 2:3; 1 Thess. 5:1–3; Heb. 2:3).

5:5–11 The seventh vision, of the woman in the measuring basket, stresses God's sovereign removal of wickedness from the land (v. 11 note). God's holy nature cannot tolerate sin in His people.

5:6 basket. See text note. The *ephah* was a unit of dry measure equivalent to about 21 quarts (Judg. 6:19; Ruth 2:17). Clearly, such a basket would not contain an adult, but precise realism is not necessarily characteristic of prophetic visions (Num. 12:6–8 and notes).

going out. The wickedness of the people was not limited to specific acts of sin (as one might conclude from the previous vision) but had infected the lives of all God's people.

5:7 a woman. Wickedness is personified by a woman, perhaps because the Hebrew word used for "wickedness" is grammatically feminine, or because Israel's idolatry was often characterized by the prophets as prostitution (Ezek. 16:25; Hos. 2:2).

5:9 two women . . . wind was in their wings. These are God's agents for removing wickedness out of the land. God's covenant faithfulness removes the sin of His people far from them (Ps. 103:11, 12; Mic. 7:19).

5:11 Shinar. This older word for Babylon is used possibly to evoke the Tower of Babel as a symbol of opposition to God (Gen. 11:2). Shinar, not Jerusalem, is the appropriate place for iniquity, since Jerusalem is the dwelling place of the Holy One of Israel (2:10–13; 8:3).

6:1–8 The last vision, the four chariots, recalls the four horses of the first vision (v. 1 note; cf. 1:7–17). The four chariots are symbolic of the "four winds of heaven" (v. 5), but beyond that the order and color of the horses may not have any special significance. The author of Revelation uses similar imagery in his portrayal of the four horsemen (Rev. 6:1–6).

6:1 mountains of bronze. The mountains probably symbolize the gate to heaven, though some suggest that the bronze reflects the bronze pillars of the temple (1 Kin. 7:13–22). In the first vision the riders went from the presence of God (1:10). Here the chariots are God's emissaries of judgment who emerge from between the bronze mountains.

6:5 four winds of heaven. The Hebrew word for "wind" can mean "spirit." Zechariah may be intentionally drawing on that ambiguity to say that as the winds cover the earth, so the angels of God cover the earth with God's presence (cf. v. 8 note).

the LORD of all the earth. The sovereign God commands His heavenly hosts to do His will (4:14 note).

6:7 impatient to go . . . the earth. The eager horses portray the immediacy of God's judgment.

[w]patrol the earth. And he said, "Go, [w]patrol
the earth." [w]So they patrolled the earth.
8 Then he cried to me, "Behold, those who
go toward [u]the north country have set my
Spirit at rest in [u]the north country."

The Crown and the Temple

9 And the word of the LORD came to me:
10 "Take from the exiles [x]Heldai, Tobijah,
and [y]Jedaiah, who have arrived from
Babylon, and go the same day to the house
of Josiah, the son of [z]Zephaniah. **11** Take
from them silver and gold, and make a
crown, [a]and set it on the head of [b]Joshua,
the son of Jehozadak, the high priest.
12 And say to him, 'Thus says the LORD of
hosts, "Behold, the man whose name is
[c]the Branch: for he shall branch out from
his place, and [d]he shall build the temple of
the LORD. **13** [e]It is he who shall build the
temple of the LORD [f]and shall bear royal
honor, and shall sit and rule on his throne.
And there shall be a priest on his throne,
[g]and the counsel of peace shall be between
them both."' **14** And the crown shall be in
the temple of the LORD as [h]a reminder to
[i]Helem,[1] [j]Tobijah, [j]Jedaiah, and Hen [j]the
son of Zephaniah.

15 [k]"And those who are far off shall come
and [l]help to build the temple of the LORD.
[m]And you shall know that the LORD of
hosts has sent me to you. [n]And this shall
come to pass, if you will diligently obey the
voice of the LORD your God."

A Call for Justice and Mercy

7 [o]In the fourth year of King Darius, the
word of the LORD came to Zechariah on
the fourth day of the ninth month, which is
[p]Chislev. **2** Now the people of Bethel had
sent Sharezer and Regem-melech and their
men [q]to entreat the favor of the LORD,
3 [r]saying to the priests of the house of the
LORD of hosts and [s]the prophets, "Should I
weep and [t]abstain in [u]the fifth month, as I
have done for so many years?"

4 Then the word of the LORD of hosts
came to me: **5** "Say to all the people of the
land and the priests, When you fasted and
mourned in [u]the fifth month and in [v]the
seventh, for these [w]seventy years, [x]was it
[x]for me that you fasted? **6** [y]And when you
eat and when you drink, do you not eat for
yourselves and drink for yourselves?
7 [z]Were not these the words that the LORD
proclaimed [a]by the former prophets, when
Jerusalem was inhabited and prosperous,
[b]with her cities around her, and the [b]South
and the [b]lowland were inhabited?"

8 And the word of the LORD came to
Zechariah, saying, **9** "Thus says the LORD
of hosts, [c]Render true judgments, show

7 [w][ch. 1:10]
8 [u][See ver. 6 above]
10 [x][ver. 14] [y]Neh. 7:39 [z]2 Kin. 25:18
11 [a][ch. 3:5] [b]ch. 3:1
12 [c]See ch. 3:8 [d][Matt. 16:18; Heb. 3:3]; See Eph. 2:20-22
13 [e]Ps. 21:5; Ezek. 21:27 [f]Ps. 110:4; Heb. 3:1 [g][Hag. 2:9]
14 [h][ver. 10] [i]ver. 10 [j]Ex. 12:14; [Matt. 26:13; Mark 14:9]
15 [k]Isai. 57:19; [Eph. 2:13, 19] [l]Isai. 60:10 [m]See ch. 2:9 [n]See Deut. 30:1-3
Chapter 7
1 [o][ch. 1:1, 7] [p]Neh. 1:1
2 [q]ch. 8:21, 22; 1 Sam. 13:12; Mal. 1:9
3 [r]Mal. 2:7 [s]ch. 8:9; [Ezra 5:1; 6:14] [t]ch. 8:19; [2 Kin.25:8] [u][ch. 12:12]
5 [u][See ver. 3 above] [v][2 Kin. 25:25] [w]See ch. 1:12 [x][Isai. 58:4, 5]
6 [y][1 Cor. 11:20, 21]
7 [z][ch. 1:5, 6] [a]ver. 12 [b]Jer. 17:26 **9** [c]Isai. 1:17; Jer. 21:12; Mic. 6:8; [Matt. 23:23]

1 An alternate spelling of *Heldai* (verse 10)

6:8 north country. The north is here representative of Israel's enemies because the geography of Palestine demanded that anyone attacking from the east, including the Persians, had to come by way of the north.

rest. If the north country were judged by God, then all other lands were securely under His judgment, and His protection of His people was complete. His Spirit could therefore rest.

6:9–15 This section is an appendix to the visions, offering additional comments on the fourth and fifth visions. It especially brings together the usually separate offices of priest and ruler in one Person—the Messiah (v. 13).

6:12 the Branch. A messianic title, the importance of which explains its occurrence here and in 3:8. Isaiah first used the term to denote the Messiah (Is. 4:2). Jeremiah then developed it as a title for the Davidic descendant who would rule on David's throne (Jer. 23:5, 6; 33:15, 16). Zechariah joins the royal and priestly offices in this title. Early Jewish interpreters saw it as a messianic title. All this shows the preparation in the Old Testament for the truth that Christ is our High Priest (Heb. 4:14; 7:24; 9:11) and our King (Heb. 1:8; Matt. 22:41–46). He is our Savior and our Lord.

6:13 he who shall build the temple of the LORD. The Messiah in His kingly function will build the temple. This was to encourage the Jews of Zechariah's day, but its fulfillment can be found in Jesus, who promised to build His church as a temple (John 2:19–21; 1 Cor. 3:16, 17; Eph. 2:19–21).

6:15 those who are far off. These are the nations who join in the Messiah's task of rebuilding the temple. This reflects Haggai's teaching that the nations will bring their wealth to the temple (Hag. 2:7 note). Since the church of Christ is the temple in this age, Gentiles build the temple by building the church, the living body of Christ on earth (1 Pet. 2:5).

7:1–14 This chapter deals with a question from the residents of the land about continuing to fast. The question shows their lack of understanding of the real issue of obedience. Zechariah answers that obedience is better than sacrifice (cf. 1 Sam. 15:22).

7:1 fourth year . . . fourth day . . . ninth month. December 7, 518 B.C., a little more than two years after the visions in chs. 1–6.

7:2 sent . . . to entreat the favor of the LORD. A delegation came from Bethel to inquire whether they should continue to fast in mourning for the destruction of the temple. The temple was destroyed in the fifth month (586 B.C.), according to 2 Kin. 25:8–15. The question is answered by the prophet in 8:18, 19. Chapter 7 shows that the restored community in Jerusalem was outwardly religious but was missing the fruits of true religion. True religion should result in good deeds (James 1:26, 27). See notes on vv. 9, 10.

7:5 seventh. The fast that mourned the assassination of Gedaliah, the governor of Judah appointed by the Babylonians (2 Kin. 25:25 note).

seventy years. It had been sixty-eight years since the destruction of the temple; Zechariah here speaks in round numbers.

was it for me. Zechariah's emphatic question points out the hypocrisy of their fasting: their fasts were motivated by self-interest rather than a desire to please God.

7:7 the South. See note Gen. 12:9.

7:9 Render true judgments. Zechariah calls on the people to do what their fathers did not. True justice meant applying God's word to the problems, both personal and social, confronting the restoration community. They must deliver the oppressed and punish the oppressor.

kindness and mercy to one another, 10 [d]do
not oppress the widow, the fatherless, the
sojourner, [e]or the poor, and [f]let none of
you devise evil against another in your
heart." 11 But [g]they refused to pay attention
[h]and turned a stubborn shoulder and
stopped their ears that they might not
hear.[1] 12 [i]They made their hearts diamond-
hard [i]lest they should hear the law and the
words that the LORD of hosts had sent [j]by
his Spirit through [k]the former prophets.
[l]Therefore great anger came from the LORD
of hosts. 13 [m]"As I[2] called, and they would
not hear, [m]so they called, and I would not
hear," says the LORD of hosts, 14 [n]"and I
scattered them with a whirlwind among all
[o]the nations that they had not known.
[p]Thus the land they left was desolate, [q]so
that no one went to and fro, [r]and the pleasant land was made desolate."

The Coming Peace and Prosperity of Zion

8 And the word of the LORD of hosts
came, saying, 2 "Thus says the LORD of
hosts: [s]I am jealous for Zion with great jealousy, and I am jealous for her with great
wrath. 3 Thus says the LORD: [t]I have
returned to Zion and [u]will dwell in the
midst of Jerusalem, [v]and Jerusalem shall be
called the faithful city, [w]and the mountain
of the LORD of hosts, the holy mountain.
4 Thus says the LORD of hosts: [x]Old men
and old women shall again sit in the streets
of Jerusalem, each with staff in hand
because of great age. 5 And the streets of the
city shall be full of boys and girls playing in
its streets. 6 Thus says the LORD of hosts: [y]If
it is marvelous in the sight of the remnant
of this people in those days, [z]should it also
be marvelous in my sight, declares the
LORD of hosts? 7 Thus says the LORD of
hosts: behold, [a]I will save my people [b]from
the east country and from the west country, 8 and I will bring them to dwell in the
midst of Jerusalem. [c]And they shall be my
people, and I will be their God, [d]in faithfulness and in righteousness."
9 Thus says the LORD of hosts: [e]"Let your
hands be strong, you who in these days have
been hearing these words from the mouth of
[f]the prophets who were present on [g]the day
that the foundation of the house of the LORD
of hosts was laid, that the temple might be
built. 10 For before those days [h]there was no
wage for man or any wage for beast, neither
was there any safety from the foe for him
who went out or came in, for I set every man
against his neighbor. 11 But now I will not
deal with the remnant of this people as in
the former days, declares the LORD of hosts.
12 [i]For there shall be a sowing of peace. The
vine shall give its fruit, and the ground shall
give its produce, [j]and the heavens shall give

10 [d]Isai. 1:23; Jer. 5:28; See Ex. 22:21, 22 [e]Prov. 22:22 [f]ch. 8:17
11 [g]ch. 1:4 [h]Neh. 9:29
12 [i][Ezek. 11:19; 36:26] [j][Neh. 9:30] [k]ver. 7 [l][2 Chr. 36:16; 1 Thess. 2:16]
13 [m][Isai. 1:15; Jer. 11:11]; See Prov. 1:24-28
14 [n][ch. 2:6] [o]See Deut. 28:33 [p]Ezek. 12:19 [q]ch. 9:8; [Zeph. 3:6] [r][Jer. 7:34]
Chapter 8
2 [s]ch. 1:14
3 [t]ch. 1:16 [u]See ch. 2:10 [v][Isai. 1:26] [w]See Isai. 2:3
4 [x][Ps. 128:6; Prov. 10:27]
6 [y][Ps. 118:23] [z]See Gen. 18:14
7 [a]ch. 10:6 [b]Ps. 107:3; Isai. 43:5; [Isai. 49:12; Ezek. 37:21]
8 [c]ch. 13:9; See Jer. 31:33 [d]Jer. 4:2
9 [e]2 Sam. 16:21; [Hag. 2:4] [f]ch. 7:3; Ezra 5:1, 2 [g]Hag. 2:18
10 [h][Hag. 1:6]
12 [i]Hos. 2:21, 22; Hag. 2:19 [j][Hag. 1:10]

1 Hebrew *and made their ears too heavy to hear* 2 Hebrew *he*

7:10 the widow, the fatherless, the sojourner, or the poor. These groups were easily exploited. God loves them (Ex. 22:21; Deut. 10:18) and ordered provision for their care (Deut. 24:17–22). God also pronounces curses on those who exploit them (Deut. 27:19). Injustices done to these groups are mentioned in Ps. 94:6 and Is. 10:1, 2.

devise evil . . . in your heart. The outward problem of mistreating others springs from inward hatred and disregard for others (Matt. 5:21, 22).

7:13 I would not hear. God's judgment, the Babylonian exile, was in proportion to their disobedience. The prophets repeatedly emphasize that formal acts of worship are nullified by disobedience. See especially 1 Sam. 15:22 and Is. 1:13–15.

7:14 the pleasant land was made desolate. The disobedience of their forefathers brought about God's judgment. Zechariah wants the people to understand that continued disobedience will be rewarded with judgment.

8:1–23 This chapter is a picture of the ultimate state of the kingdom of God, when God brings His final and fullest blessings on His people. Similar to Isaiah's portrayal of the future (Is. 65:17; 66:5–24), it gave the postexilic Jews hope that the Lord was still determined to bless them. Since the coming of Christ into the world, the beginning of these blessings is seen, but their full realization awaits the new heavens and new earth (Rev. 21:1).

8:2 I am jealous for her. God's zeal, or jealousy, for His people (not *of* them) is born of His covenant love and commitment to them (1:14), which in turn demands their wholehearted loyalty to Him.

8:3 faithful city. Faithful observance of God's law was rarely true of Israel, even in Zechariah's day. The prophet foresees a time when God's people will reflect His character in their dealings with one another (vv. 16, 17). See also Ex. 34:6, 7.

holy mountain. Mount Zion will be holy because God's presence will dwell there in a special way. The prophets repeatedly emphasize the day of salvation as a day of renewal of God's presence (2:5, 11).

8:4, 5 A picture of God's covenant blessings, in which God's blessing of long life (Ex. 20:12) and the joy of children playing reflect a state of *shalom*, total well-being.

8:6 marvelous. The Hebrew word denotes something beyond human strength and understanding, typically with reference to a divine action. For other examples of this emphasis see Gen. 18:14 ("hard") and Judg. 13:18.

remnant. Those faithful to God in the midst of disobedience. Paul speaks of "a remnant, chosen by grace" in Rom. 11:5. The elect of God are preserved to serve Him faithfully. See notes Is. 1:9 and Mic. 2:12.

8:7 save my people . . . the west. The covenant renewal of God's people involved restoration from foreign lands. See Deut. 30:1–5; Jer. 30:8–11.

8:8 they shall be my people . . . their God. This personal relationship is the essence of God's covenant with Abraham and his descendants (Gen. 17:7 and note), and of the new covenant (Jer. 31:33). It is the source of all other covenant blessings.

8:12 sowing . . . heavens. The blessings of God's final renewal are expressed in agricultural terms appropriate to the covenant promise of land. Because old Israel's life in the land is a type of New Israel's life in Christ (Gen. 13:15 note), today Christians experience the blessings of

their dew. [k]And I will cause the remnant of
this people to possess all these things. 13 And
as [l]you have been a byword of cursing
among the nations, O house of Judah and
house of Israel, [m]so will I save you, and [n]you
shall be a blessing. [o]Fear not, but [e]let your
hands be strong."

14 For thus says the LORD of hosts: [p]"As I
purposed to bring disaster to you when
your fathers provoked me to wrath, and I
did not relent, says the LORD of hosts, 15 so
again have I purposed in these days to
bring good to Jerusalem and to the house
of Judah; [o]fear not. 16 These are the things
that you shall do: [q]Speak the truth to one
another; [r]render in your gates judgments
[s]that are true and make for peace; 17 [t]do not
devise evil in your hearts against one
another, and [u]love no false oath, for all
these things I hate, declares the LORD."

18 And the word of the LORD of hosts came
to me, saying, 19 "Thus says the LORD of
hosts: The fast of the [v]fourth month and the
fast of the [w]fifth and the fast of the [x]seventh
and the fast of the [y]tenth shall be to the
house of Judah [z]seasons of joy and gladness
and cheerful feasts. Therefore love [a]truth
and peace.

20 "Thus says the LORD of hosts: Peoples
shall yet come, even the inhabitants of many
cities. 21 The inhabitants of one city shall go
to another, saying, [b]'Let us go at once [c]to
entreat the favor of the LORD and to seek the
LORD of hosts; I myself am going.' 22 [b]Many
peoples and strong nations shall come to
seek the LORD of hosts in Jerusalem and [c]to
entreat the favor of the LORD. 23 Thus says the
LORD of hosts: In those days [d]ten men [e]from
the nations of every tongue shall take hold of
the robe of a Jew, saying, 'Let us go with you,
for [f]we have heard that God is with you.'"

12 [k]See Jer. 3:18
13 [l][Isai. 43:28; 65:15] [m]ch. 10:6 [n]See Gen. 12:2, 3 [o]Hag. 2:5 [e][See ver. 9 above]
14 [p][Jer. 31:28; 32:42]
15 [o][See ver. 13 above]
16 [q]Cited Eph. 4:25; See Ps. 15:2 [r]See ch. 7:9 [s]ver. 19
17 [t]ch. 7:10 [u]See ch. 5:4
19 [v][Jer. 39:2] [w]ch. 7:3 [x]ch. 7:5 [y]2 Kin. 25:1 [z]Isai. 35:10 [a]ver. 16
21 [b][ch. 2:11; 14:16; Isai. 2:3] [c]See ch. 7:2
22 [b][See ver. 21 above] [c][See ver. 21 above]
23 [d]See Gen. 31:7 [e][Isai. 66:18; Rev. 5:9] [f][1 Cor. 14:25]
Chapter 9
1 [g]See Isai. 17:1
2 [h]Jer. 49:23; See 1 Kin. 8:65 [i]Josh. 19:28, 29; Isai. 23:1, 2 [j]See Ezek. 28:3-5
3 [k][Josh. 19:29] [l]Ezek. 28:4, 5
4 [m]Ezek. 26:17 [n]Ezek. 28:18

Judgment on Israel's Enemies

9 The burden of the word of the LORD
is against the land of Hadrach
and [g]Damascus is its resting place.
For the LORD has an eye on mankind
and on all the tribes of Israel,[1]
2 [h]and on Hamath also, which borders
on it,
[i]Tyre and [i]Sidon, though [j]they are
very wise.
3 Tyre has built herself [k]a rampart
and [l]heaped up silver like dust,
and fine gold like the mud of the
streets.
4 But behold, the Lord will strip her of
her possessions
and strike down [m]her power on
the sea,
and [n]she shall be devoured by fire.

1 Slight emendation yields *For to the LORD belongs the capital of Syria and all the tribes of Israel*

God's covenant renewal through Jesus (Matt. 26:28; 1 Cor. 11:25) and look forward to the total renewal of God's covenant blessings in the new heavens and earth (Rev. 21:1–22:5).

8:15 purposed. See note 1:6.

8:16, 17 The people are called on to order their lives in keeping with God's ethical standards. The godly behavior described here contrasts with the ungodliness that characterized much of Israel's history; truth and righteousness will reign in this final era of blessing (Amos 5:24).

8:19 This verse relates to the question in 7:3 and its reply. The fasts mentioned commemorated various aspects of Jerusalem's destruction.

fourth. The fast commemorating the fall of the walls of Jerusalem, the beginning of the end for the city (2 Kin. 25:3, 4). See notes 7:2, 5.

tenth. Nebuchadnezzar began his siege of Jerusalem in the tenth month (2 Kin. 25:1; Jer. 39:1–10).

8:20–23 These verses depict a great pilgrimage by the Gentile nations to Jerusalem, implying the extension of God's salvation beyond the borders of Israel (14:16–20; Is. 2:1–4; Mic. 4:1–3; Mal. 1:5).

8:22 strong nations. See Is. 2:2–4; Mic. 4:3.

8:23 ten men from the nations of every tongue. Emphasis is laid on the great numbers (v. 22, "many peoples") of Gentiles that will come to worship the true God. Revelation 5:9 speaks of the redeemed from "every tribe and language and people and nation." Salvation then is worldwide, not in the sense that every human being is redeemed, but that the children of God are chosen from every language and ethnic group of the world.

God is with you. The attraction of worship is the presence of God in the midst of His people (1 Cor. 14:24, 25).

9:1–11:17 The prophet turns his attention to the future of God's kingdom, developing his theme in two lengthy oracles (chs. 9–11; 12–14). The first prophecy of the book's latter half focuses on the coming of God the King in judgment. The opening verses (9:1–8) portray God as an avenging warrior who comes to take possession of His land by destroying all the pagan enemies who lie in His path (cf. Is. 9:6 note). He comes from the north to Jerusalem (cf. 9:14–17, where God is pictured as coming from the south to Jerusalem), an event that leads to the proclamation of 9:9. Some interpret the picture of a northern invasion as describing Alexander the Great's conquest of Palestine in 333 B.C. That may be, but its greater meaning concerns God Himself coming to avenge His people. See Introduction: Characteristics and Themes.

9:1 burden of the word of the LORD. This precise phrase is used twice in the Old Testament (here; 12:1). "Burden" implies that the prophet was under strong compulsion to deliver the message from God.

land of Hadrach. Known as Hatarikka in Assyrian cuneiform inscriptions, this is the northernmost city listed in vv. 1–8. The description here is rather general and a specific fulfillment ought not to be sought.

Damascus. The capital of Syria, Israel's neighbor to the north.

9:2 Hamath. Located on the Orontes River north of Damascus.

Tyre and Sidon. Phoenician cities on the Mediterranean coast. Both were commercial centers throughout the biblical period. Their description as "very wise" may relate to shrewdness in business. Judgment of these cities is a common prophetic theme (Jer. 47:1–7; Ezek. 28:11–23).

5 [o] Ashkelon shall see it, and be afraid;
Gaza too, and shall writhe in anguish;
Ekron also, because its hopes are confounded.
The king shall perish from Gaza;
Ashkelon shall be uninhabited;
6 [p] a mixed people[1] shall dwell in Ashdod,
and I will cut off the pride of Philistia.
7 I will take away [q] its blood from its mouth,
and [r] its abominations from between its teeth;
[s] it too shall be a remnant for our God;
it shall be like [t] a clan in Judah,
and Ekron shall be like the Jebusites.
8 Then [u] I will encamp at my house as a guard,
[v] so that none shall march to and fro;
[w] no oppressor shall again march over them,
[x] for now I see with my own eyes.

The Coming King of Zion

9 [y] Rejoice greatly, O daughter of Zion!
Shout aloud, O daughter of Jerusalem!
[z] behold, [a] your king is coming to you;
righteous and having salvation is he,
[b] humble and mounted on a donkey,
on a colt, the foal of a donkey.
10 [c] I will cut off the chariot from Ephraim
and [d] the war horse from Jerusalem;
and the battle bow shall be cut off,
and [e] he shall speak peace to the nations;
[f] his rule shall be from sea to sea,
and from [g] the River to the ends of the earth.
11 As for you also, because of [h] the blood of my covenant with you,
[i] I will set your prisoners free from [j] the waterless pit.
12 Return to your stronghold,
O [k] prisoners of hope;
today I declare that [l] I will restore to you double.
13 For [m] I have bent Judah as my bow;
I have made Ephraim its arrow.
I will stir up your sons, O Zion,
against your sons, [n] O Greece,
and wield you like a warrior's sword.

The LORD Will Save His People

14 Then the LORD will appear over them,
and [o] his arrow will go forth like lightning;
[p] the Lord GOD will sound the trumpet
and will march forth in [q] the whirlwinds [r] of the south.
15 The LORD of hosts [s] will protect them,
and [t] they shall devour, [u] and tread down the sling stones,
and [v] they shall drink and roar as if drunk with wine,
and be full like a bowl,
drenched [w] like the corners of the altar.

1 Or *a foreign people*; Hebrew *a bastard*

5 [o] See Zeph. 2:4
6 [p] [Deut. 23:2]
7 [q] See Lev. 3:17 [r] [Isai. 66:17] [s] [Isai. 14:1] [t] ch. 12:5, 6
8 [u] [ch. 2:5] [v] ch. 7:14 [w] ch. 10:4; [Isai. 60:17] [x] [ch. 12:4]
9 [y] See Zeph. 3:14 [z] Cited Matt. 21:5; [John 12:15] [a] See Jer. 23:5 [b] [Matt. 11:29]
10 [c] See Hos. 1:7 [d] See Mic. 5:10 [e] See Mic. 5:5 [f] Ps. 72:8 [g] See Ex. 23:31
11 [h] Ex. 24:8 [i] Isai. 42:7; 51:14; 61:1 [j] [Gen. 37:24; Jer. 38:6]
12 [k] [Jer. 31:17] [l] Isai. 61:7
13 [m] [ch. 10:3, 4] [n] Gen. 10:2; Ezek. 27:13
14 [o] See 2 Sam. 22:15 [p] [Isai. 27:13] [q] Isai. 21:1 [r] [ch. 6:6]
15 [s] ch. 12:8; [ch. 10:5] [t] ch. 12:6 [u] [ch. 10:5] [v] ch. 10:7 [w] [Lev. 4:18, 25]

9:5 Ashkelon . . . Gaza . . . Ekron. Strong cities of Philistia will not be able to withstand the power of the approaching warrior God. These cities are marked out for judgment many times in the Old Testament (Is. 14:28–32; Ezek. 25:15–17; Amos 1:6–8).

9:9, 10 This important Old Testament prophecy finds fulfillment both in Jesus' triumphal entry into Jerusalem (Matt. 21:1–11; John 12:12–16) and in His messianic reign (v. 10 note).

9:9 O daughter of Zion. A common title for God's holy city and people (Is. 1:8 note; 62:11; Zeph. 3:14).

your king. The royal descendant of David promised repeatedly (2 Sam. 7:12–14; Ps. 132:11; Is. 9:7; 11:1–5; Jer. 23:5, 6; 33:15–22; Ezek. 34:23, 24; 37:24, 25).

on a donkey. A sign of His humility. See note Matt. 21:1–11.

9:10 the chariot . . . the war horse. Implements of war will be abolished in the peaceful reign of the righteous King (Is. 2:1–4; 11:6–9). The Old Testament often predicts universal peace in the time of the messianic King (Is. 57:19; Mic. 4:1–5; cf. Eph. 2:12–18).

rule . . . to the ends of the earth. The universal, sovereign rule of God is foundational to Old Testament religion (Ps. 72:8; 96:3–5; Dan. 2:44–47; 7:13, 14, 27). Christ is the One who brings the Father's universal dominion to earth (Matt. 12:28; Phil. 2:9–11; Rev. 19:11–16).

9:11 blood of my covenant. A reference to the provision in God's covenant for covering sin (Ex. 24:8; Matt. 26:28).

9:13 O Greece. Lit. "O, Javan" (Gen. 10:2). This reference does not necessarily refer to the Maccabean wars (second century B.C.) of the intertestamental period, or indicate that the author lived in that period. Greece may be used as a symbol of the pagan nations that war against God's people.

9:14 whirlwinds of the south. The God of Israel is now portrayed as coming from the southern region of the desert riding on the storm clouds (2 Sam. 22:8–16; Ps. 29). Since Mount Sinai was the place He appeared when He brought the people out of Egypt, the Old Testament sometimes depicts God as coming from that region.

9:15 drink and roar as if drunk with wine. God's people will be exuberant with a holy joy because of God's victory and presence (Acts 2:13–21; Eph. 5:18).

16 On that day the LORD their God will
save them,
as [x]the flock of his people;
for [y]like the jewels of a crown
they shall shine on his land.
17 [z]For how great is his goodness, and
how great his beauty!
[a]Grain shall make the young men
flourish,
and new wine the young women.

The Restoration for Judah and Israel

10 Ask rain [b]from the LORD
in the season of [c]the spring rain,
from the LORD [d]who makes the storm
clouds,
and [e]he will give them showers of
rain,
to everyone the vegetation in the
field.
2 For [f]the household gods [g]utter
nonsense,
and the diviners see lies;
[h]they tell false dreams
and give empty consolation.
Therefore [i]the people wander like
sheep;
they are afflicted for lack of a
shepherd.

3 [j]"My anger is hot against the shepherds,
and [k]I will punish the leaders;[1]
for [l]the LORD of hosts cares for his
flock, the house of Judah,
and will make them like his
majestic steed in battle.
4 From him shall come [m]the
cornerstone,
from him [n]the tent peg,
from him the battle bow,
from him every ruler—[o]all of them
together.
5 They shall be like mighty men in
battle,
[p]trampling the foe in the mud of
the streets;
they shall fight because the LORD is
with them,
and they shall put to shame [q]the
riders on horses.

6 [r]"I will strengthen the house of Judah,
and [s]I will save the house of Joseph.
[t]I will bring them back [u]because I
have compassion on them,
and they shall be as though I had
not rejected them,
for [v]I am the LORD their God and
I will answer them.
7 Then Ephraim shall become like a
mighty warrior,
and [w]their hearts shall be glad as
with wine.
Their children shall see it and be glad;
their hearts shall rejoice in the LORD.

8 [x]"I will whistle for them and [y]gather
them in,
for I have redeemed them,
and [z]they shall be as many as they
were before.
9 [a]Though I scattered them among the
nations,
yet in far countries [b]they shall
remember me,
and with their children they shall
live and return.
10 [c]I will bring them home from the land
of Egypt,
and gather them from Assyria,
and [d]I will bring them to the land of
Gilead and to Lebanon,
[e]till there is no room for them.

16 [x]Ps. 100:3 [y]Isai. 62:3; [Mal. 3:17]
17 [z][Isai. 62:3, 4] [a][Isai. 62:8, 9; Jer. 31:12]
Chapter 10
1 [b]Jer. 14:22 [c]See Deut. 11:14 [d]Ps. 135:7 [e]Ezek. 34:26 [f]See Gen. 31:19 [g]Hab. 2:18
2 [h]Jer. 23:25 [i]Ezek. 34:5, 6
3 [j][Ezek. 34:10] [k][Ezek. 34:17] [l]Zeph. 2:7
4 [m][Ps. 118:22] [n]Isai. 22:23 [o][ch. 9:8]
5 [p][ch. 9:15] [q][Ps. 20:7]
6 [r][ver. 12] [s]ch. 8:7, 13 [t][Jer. 3:18] [u]Isai. 14:1 [v]ch. 13:9
7 [w]ch. 9:15
8 [x]Isai. 5:26 [y]Jer. 31:10, 11; See Hos. 1:11 [z]Ezek. 36:10, 11, 37
9 [a][Hos. 2:23] [b]Ezek. 6:9; See Deut. 30:1-3
10 [c]Isai. 11:11; 27:13; Hos. 11:11 [d][Mic. 7:14] [e]Isai. 49:20

1 Hebrew *the male goats*

9:16 the flock . . . jewels of a crown. God's people rest secure as sheep under His care (13:7; Ezek. 34:11–24; 37:24), and will become glorious as a result of God's presence (2 Cor. 3:18).

10:1–12 This chapter is a rebuke to the people, and especially the leaders, of Judah for seeking wisdom and advice from idols (v. 2). God's answer to their waywardness is that He Himself will be their shepherd. The Messiah is often portrayed (like David) as a Shepherd-King (Ezek. 34; Jer. 23:1–8).

10:1 Ask rain from the LORD. See note 8:12.

10:2 household gods . . . diviners. Occult attempts to tell the future are forbidden for God's people (Deut. 18:9–14), who are to derive their wisdom from the word of God (Prov. 1:7).

lack of a shepherd. Israel's and Judah's leaders were often rebuked for their godless leadership of God's people (Ezek. 34:1–10).

10:3 majestic steed. Judah will be strong like a horse arrayed for battle because of God's help (v. 6).

10:4 cornerstone . . . tent peg . . . battle bow. Symbolic references to the Messiah. Jesus was from the tribe of Judah (Heb. 7:14) and came in fulfillment of the promise of a ruler who would conquer every other ruler. See notes Gen. 49:10 and Mic. 5:2.

10:6 I am the LORD their God. Another strong reaffirmation of the covenant bond between God and His people. God saves His people because of His eternal commitment to them (8:8 note; Jer. 31:33).

10:8 whistle for them. As the shepherd whistles for his flock (cf. Is. 7:18), so God will recall the exiles from foreign lands (Deut. 30:1–10).

as they were before. As the Israelites had earlier multiplied (Ex. 1:7), in fulfillment of God's covenant promise to Abraham (Gen. 15:5; 17:6).

10:10–12 God's mighty act in summoning the exiles is depicted in language recalling Israel's Exodus from Egypt (Is. 43:16, 17).

11 [f]He shall pass through the sea of troubles
and strike down the waves of the sea,
[g]and all the depths of the Nile shall be dried up.
The pride of Assyria shall be laid low,
and [h]the scepter of Egypt shall depart.
12 [i]I will make them strong in the LORD,
and [j]they shall walk in his name,"
declares the LORD.

The Flock Doomed to Slaughter

11 Open your doors,
[k]O Lebanon,
that the fire may devour your cedars!
2 Wail, O cypress, for the cedar has fallen,
for the glorious trees are ruined!
Wail, [k]oaks of Bashan,
for the thick forest has been felled!
3 The sound of [l]the wail of [l]the shepherds,
for their glory is ruined!
The sound of the roar of [m]the lions,
[n]for the thicket of the Jordan is ruined!

4 Thus said the LORD my God: [o]"Become
shepherd of the flock doomed to slaughter.
5 [p]Those who buy them slaughter them and
go unpunished, and those who sell them
say, 'Blessed be the LORD, [q]I have become
rich,' and their own shepherds have no
pity on them. 6 For [r]I will no longer have
pity on the inhabitants of this land,
declares the LORD. Behold, I will cause
each of them to fall into the hand of his
neighbor, and each into the hand of his
king, and they shall crush the land, and I
will deliver none from their hand."

7 [s]So I became the shepherd of the flock
[t]doomed to be slaughtered by the sheep
traders. And I took two staffs, one I named
[u]Favor, the other I named [v]Union. [s]And
I tended the sheep. 8 In one month [w]I
destroyed the three shepherds. But I became impatient with them, and they also
detested me. 9 So I said, "I will not be your
shepherd. [x]What is to die, let it die. What
is to be destroyed, let it be destroyed. And
let those who are left devour the flesh of
one another." 10 And I took [y]my staff Favor,
and I broke it, annulling the covenant that
I had made with all the peoples. 11 So it was
annulled on that day, and [t]the sheep
traders, who were watching me, knew that
it was the word of the LORD. 12 Then I said
to them, "If it seems good to you, give me
my wages; but if not, keep them." And they
weighed out as my wages [z]thirty pieces of
silver. 13 Then the LORD said to me, "Throw
it to the potter"—[a]the lordly price at which
I was priced by them. So I took the [z]thirty
pieces of silver and threw them into the

11 [f]Isai. 11:15 [g][Amos 8:8] [h]Ezek. 30:13 **12** [i][ver. 6] [j]Mic. 4:5 **Chapter 11** **1** [k][Isai. 2:12, 13] **2** [k][See ver. 1 above] **3** [l]Jer. 25:34 [m]See Ezek. 19:1-3 [n][Jer. 12:5] **4** [o][ver. 7] **5** [p]Ezek. 34:3 [q]Hos. 12:8 **6** [r]Jer. 13:14 **7** [s][ver. 4] [t][Zeph. 3:12] [u]ver. 10 [v]ver. 14 **8** [w][ver. 3, 16; ch. 10:3; Jer. 22:11, 18, 24] **9** [x]Jer. 15:2 **10** [y]ver. 7 **11** [t][See ver. 7 above] **12** [z][Ex. 21:32; Matt. 26:15] **13** [a][Matt. 27:9, 10] [z][See ver. 12 above]

10:12 walk in his name. Following His guidance and wisdom in all that they do (Deut. 6:4–9; Mic. 4:5).

11:1–3 Scholars debate whether this small poetic section belongs with what precedes (chs. 9–10, God's judgment against the nations) or with what follows (11:4–17, God's judgment against Israel for their rejection of the Shepherd). The metaphors of large oaks, dense forests, and ravaging lions are drawn from the plants and animals of the Jordan Valley. The language is consistent with a number of judgments in Israel's history, but the preeminent judgment comes to those nations and individuals who reject the Good Shepherd, Jesus Christ (Acts 4:24–28).

11:2 cedar. Often used as a symbol of Lebanon (1 Kin. 5:6; Ps. 104:16).

Bashan. The fertile area northeast of the Dead Sea (Deut. 3:1 note).

11:4–17 The actors are difficult to identify with certainty in this section, although the general teaching is clear. The prophet is appointed to be a good shepherd, but because he is rejected he forsakes the flock (v. 9). As a good shepherd, the prophet is a type of the coming messianic Shepherd, Jesus Christ, who came as *the* Good Shepherd and laid down His life for the sheep (John 10:11–18).

11:4 Become shepherd. A command given to Zechariah.

the flock. The people of Israel.

11:6 I will no longer have pity. These words were appropriate before the Babylonian exile (Jer. 13:14; 15:5; 21:7); they occur here because of the continued rebellion of the people (Matt. 21:33–46).

11:7 Favor. Or, "grace." This word is also used of God Himself (Ps. 27:4; 90:17). The staff is symbolic of the grace that God has shown His people in His covenant (v. 10).

Union. Or, "unity." The unity of the divided nation (v. 14) was promised in the new covenant (Jer. 30:3; 31:27, 31; 33:7).

11:8 the three shepherds. These shepherds are difficult to identify. They could be symbolic of all leaders who fail to meet God's standards. In time the Good Shepherd of God's choice will depose all other rulers (Rev. 2:27).

11:9 The prophet as shepherd expresses his disgust with the rebellion and disobedience of the flock.

11:10 covenant . . . with all the peoples. The divinely imposed obligation on the nations not to injure God's people Israel (cf. Ezek. 34:25; Hos. 2:18). With the removal of God's favor toward Israel, the nations could afflict the flock of God.

11:12 thirty pieces of silver. Apparently the price of a slave (Ex. 21:32). Jewish officials paid Judas thirty shekels of silver to betray Jesus (Matt. 26:14–16).

11:13 threw them into the house of the LORD. A prophecy fulfilled when Judas threw down the thirty pieces of silver on the floor of the temple (Matt. 27:1–10; cf. Jer. 19:1–13).

house of the LORD, to the potter. 14 Then I
broke [b]my second staff Union, annulling
the brotherhood between Judah and Israel.
15 Then the LORD said to me, "Take once
more the equipment of [c]a foolish shepherd.
16 For behold, I am raising up in the land a
shepherd [d]who does not care for those
being destroyed, or seek the young or heal
the maimed or nourish the healthy, but
[e]devours the flesh of the fat ones, tearing
off even their hoofs.

17 [f]"Woe to my worthless shepherd,
[g]who deserts the flock!
May the sword strike his arm
and [h]his right eye!
Let his arm be wholly withered,
his right eye utterly blinded!"

The LORD Will Give Salvation

12 [i]The burden of the word of the
LORD concerning Israel: Thus
declares the LORD, [j]who stretched out the
heavens and [k]founded the earth and
[j]formed the spirit of man within him:
2 "Behold, I am about to make Jerusalem [l]a
cup of staggering to [m]all the surrounding
peoples. The siege of Jerusalem [n]will also
be against Judah. 3 [o]On that day I will make
Jerusalem a heavy stone for all the peoples.
[p]All who lift it will surely hurt themselves.
And [m]all the nations of the earth will gather against it. 4 [o]On that day, declares the
LORD, [q]I will strike every horse [r]with panic,
and its rider [r]with madness. But for the
sake of the house of Judah I will keep my
eyes open, when I strike every horse of the
peoples [r]with blindness. 5 Then the clans of
Judah shall say to themselves, 'The inhabitants of Jerusalem have strength through
the LORD of hosts, their God.'
6 [o]"On that day I will make the clans of
Judah [s]like a blazing pot in the midst of
wood, like a flaming torch among sheaves.
And [t]they shall devour to the right and to
the left all the surrounding peoples, while
[u]Jerusalem shall again be inhabited in its
place, in Jerusalem.
7 "And the LORD will give salvation to the
tents of Judah first, that the glory of the
house of David and the glory of the inhabitants of Jerusalem may not surpass that of
Judah. 8 [o]On that day [v]the LORD will protect
the inhabitants of Jerusalem, so that [w]the
feeblest among them on that day shall be
like David, and the house of David shall be
like God, [x]like the angel of the LORD, going
before them. 9 [o]And on that day [y]I will seek
to destroy all the nations that come against
Jerusalem.

Him Whom They Have Pierced

10 "And [z]I will pour out on the house of
David and the inhabitants of Jerusalem a
spirit of grace and [z]pleas for mercy, so that,
[a]when they look on me, on him whom they
have pierced, [b]they shall mourn for him,
[c]as one mourns for an only child, and weep
bitterly over him, as one weeps over a firstborn. 11 [l]On that day [d]the mourning in
Jerusalem will be as great [e]as the mourning
for Hadad-rimmon in the plain of Megiddo. 12 The land shall mourn, [f]each family[1] by itself: the family of the house of
David by itself, and their wives by themselves; the family of the house of [g]Nathan
by itself, and their wives by themselves;

14 [b]ver. 7
15 [c]See 2 Kin. 24:18-20
16 [d][Ezek. 34:4; John 10:13] [e]Ezek. 34:3
17 [f]Jer. 23:1 [g]John 10:12 [h][2 Kin. 25:7]
Chapter 12
1 [i]See Nah. 1:1 [j]See Isai. 42:5 [k]Isai. 48:13
2 [l]Isai. 51:17, 22, 23 [m][ch. 14:2] [n][ch. 14:14]
3 [o]ch. 13:1, 2, 4; 14:4, 6, 8; Isai. 2:11 [p][Matt. 21:44; Luke 20:18] [m][See ver. 2 above]
4 [o][See ver. 3 above] [q][Ps. 76:6] [r][Deut. 28:28]
6 [o][See ver. 3 above] [s][Jer. 5:14; Obad. 18] [t]ch. 9:15 [u]ch. 2:4; 14:10, 11
8 [o][See ver. 3 above] [v]ch. 9:15 [w][Isai. 60:22] [x][1 Sam. 29:9; 2 Sam. 14:17, 20; 19:27]
9 [o][See ver. 3 above] [y][ch. 14:3]
10 [z][Jer. 31:9] [a]Cited John 19:37; [Rev. 1:7] [b]Jer. 50:4 [c]Jer. 6:26; Amos 8:10
11 [l][See ver. 2 above] [d][Acts 2:37] [e][2 Chr. 35:24]
12 [f][ch. 7:3] [g]2 Sam. 5:14; Luke 3:31

1 Or *clan*; also verses 13, 14

11:14 annulling the brotherhood between Judah and Israel. The dissolution of the covenant nation because they rejected the Good Shepherd.

11:15–17 With the rejection of the Good Shepherd, worthless leaders take His place (cf. Ezek. 34:1–10). The loss of "arm" and "right eye" indicates the loss of power and insight necessary for leadership (v. 17). Some suggest that this prophecy refers to the Jewish leaders who led the nation into disastrous rebellions against Rome after the death of Christ (A.D. 66–74, 132–35).

12:1–14:21 The second oracle of the book's latter half focuses on God's judgment of the nations, climaxing with the salvation of Jerusalem and the final celebration of the Feast of Tabernacles.

12:1 burden of the word of the LORD. See note 9:1.

12:2 a cup of staggering. A common Old Testament image of God's wrath as a cup from which the nations will drink (Is. 51:17; Jer. 25:15–17, 27–29; Ezek. 23:32–34).

12:3 On that day. The day of the Lord (14:1). This phrase occurs numerous times in chs. 12–14, and indicates the fullness of God's judgment of the world and the final salvation of His people.

Jerusalem a heavy stone. The earthly Jerusalem of Zechariah's day was a type of the church, the heavenly Jerusalem in which we now live by faith (Heb. 12:22–24).

12:6 blazing pot . . . flaming torch. More images of Judah's devouring power.

12:10 spirit of grace and pleas for mercy. This describes God's gracious Spirit who produces humility in God's people. The Old Testament prophets emphasize that God's renewal of the covenant (Jer. 31:31–33) entailed renewal through His Spirit (Is. 59:21; Ezek. 36:26, 27; 39:29; Joel 2:28, 29).

look on me . . . whom they have pierced. Probably this means "look to the Messiah as the source of salvation." Many passages in John's Gospel speak of faith in terms of "seeing" (cf. John 6:40). The one looked upon in faith is none other than God Himself, who is pierced in the Person of His incarnate Son, the Messiah (John 1:14 and note; 19:37).

13 the family of the house of Levi by itself,
and their wives by themselves; the family of
[h]the Shimeites by itself, and their wives by
themselves; 14 and all the families that are
left, each by itself, and their wives by themselves.

13 [i]"On that day there shall be [j]a fountain opened for the house of David
and the inhabitants of Jerusalem, to
cleanse them from sin and uncleanness.

Idolatry Cut Off

2 "And [i]on that day, declares the LORD of
hosts, [k]I will cut off the names of the idols
from the land, so that [l]they shall be remembered no more. And also [m]I will remove
from the land the prophets and the spirit of
uncleanness. 3 And if anyone again prophesies, his father and mother who bore him
will say to him, [n]'You shall not live, for you
speak lies in the name of the LORD.' And his
father and mother who bore him shall
pierce him through when he prophesies.
4 "On that day [o]every prophet will be
ashamed of his vision when he prophesies.
He will not put on a hairy cloak in order to
deceive, 5 but he will say, [p]'I am no
prophet, I am a worker of the soil, for a
man sold me in my youth.'[1] 6 And if one
asks him, 'What are these wounds on your
back?'[2] he will say, 'The wounds I received
in the house of my friends.'

The Shepherd Struck

7 "Awake, O sword, against [q]my
shepherd,
against the man who stands next
to me,"
declares the LORD of hosts.
[r]"Strike the shepherd, and the sheep
will be scattered;
I will turn my hand against the
little ones.
8 In the whole land, declares the LORD,
two thirds shall be cut off and
perish,
[s]and one third shall be left alive.
9 And [t]I will put this third into the
fire,
and refine them as one refines
silver,
and test them as gold is tested.
[u]They will call upon my name,
and [v]I will answer them.
[w]I will say, 'They are my people';
and they will say, 'The LORD is my
God.'"

The Coming Day of the LORD

14 Behold, [x]a day is coming for the
LORD, when the spoil taken from
you will be divided in your midst. 2 For [y]I
will gather all the nations against Jerusalem to battle, and [z]the city shall be
taken [a]and the houses plundered [b]and the
women raped. [c]Half of the city shall go out
into exile, but the rest of the people shall
not be cut off from the city. 3 [d]Then the
LORD will go out and fight against those
nations as when he fights on a day of battle. 4 [e]On that day his feet shall stand [f]on
[g]the Mount of Olives that lies before
Jerusalem on the east, and [g]the Mount of
Olives shall be split in two from east to
west by [h]a very wide valley, so that one

13 [h]Num. 3:18
Chapter 13
1 [i]See ch. 12:3 [j][Ezek. 36:25]
2 [i][See ver. 1 above] [k]Mic. 5:13; [Jer. 10:11; Ezek. 30:13] [l]Ex 23:13 [m][ch. 10:2]
3 [n]See Deut. 13:1-11
4 [o][Mic. 3:7]
5 [p]Amos 7:14
7 [q][Isai. 40:11; Heb. 13:20]
[r][Matt. 26:31; Mark 14:27]
8 [s][ch. 14:2]
9 [t]Ps. 66:10, 12; Isai. 48:10; Mal. 3:2, 3; 1 Pet. 1:7
[u][Ps. 50:15]
[v]ch. 10:6
[w]ch. 8:8; See Ezek. 11:20
Chapter 14
1 [x]See Joel 1:15
2 [y]Joel 3:2
[z][Luke 21:24]
[a]Isai. 13:16
[b]Lam. 5:11
[c]ch. 13:8; [Matt. 24:40, 41]
3 [d][ch. 12:9]
4 [e][ver. 1]; See ch. 12:3
[f][Ezek. 11:23]
[g]2 Sam. 15:30 [h][ver. 10]

1 Or *for the land has been my possession since my youth* 2 Or *on your chest*; Hebrew *wounds between your hands*

13:1 On that day. See note 12:3.

fountain . . . from sin and uncleanness. The picture of a cleansing fountain indicates the abundance of forgiveness (cf. Jer. 2:13). Ultimately we find that abundance of forgiveness in Jesus and the Spirit (John 7:37–39).

13:3 lies in the name of the LORD. False prophecy includes both prophecy in the name of a false god and presumptuous speech in the name of the Lord (Deut. 13; 18:20–22). False prophets were to die by the sword (Deut. 13:12–15).

13:4 a hairy cloak. False prophets will deny that they were prophets for fear of punishment, and will refuse to wear the traditional clothing symbolic of the prophet (2 Kin. 1:8; Matt. 3:4).

13:6 wounds on your back. Probably wounds that were self-inflicted during idolatrous worship. Several Old Testament texts suggest that such practices were customary in pagan worship (Lev. 19:28; 21:5; Deut. 14:1; 1 Kin. 18:28). The accused prophet contends that his wounds were inflicted by friends, and were not the result of idolatrous worship.

13:7–9 These verses envision God's chosen Shepherd who suffers at the hand of God (v. 7). Out of this judgment emerges the true people of God (v. 9). No clearer picture of Jesus and His suffering church is given in the Old Testament. See the notes below.

13:7 Strike the shepherd. Astonishingly, God strikes His own chosen Shepherd. Jesus is the Shepherd who is stricken and afflicted (Matt. 26:31–35; Mark 14:27–31; Luke 22:31–34).

the sheep. God's people suffer along with their Shepherd (2 Cor. 1:5 note).

against the little ones. Possibly an indication of God's judgment against His sheep. The Hebrew word rendered "against" could also be translated "upon," indicating God's protection of the "little ones" in the midst of suffering.

13:8 two thirds . . . one third. The judgment sifts the true believers from the untrue. A common prophetic theme is that God's judgment will distinguish between the proud and humble (Zeph. 3:11, 12), between the true and false sheep (Ezek. 34:17–22).

14:1 a day is coming for the LORD. The Old Testament prophets proclaimed a "day of the Lord" for judgment and deliverance, both of which are present in this passage (Introduction to Zephaniah: Characteristics and Themes).

half of the Mount shall move northward,
and the other half southward. **5** And you
shall flee to the valley of my mountains,
for the valley of the mountains shall reach
to Azal. And you shall flee as you fled from
[i]the earthquake in the days of Uzziah king
of Judah. Then the LORD my God will
come, and all the holy ones with him.
6 [e]On that day [j]there shall be [j]no light,
cold, or frost.[1] **7** [k]And there shall be a unique[2]
day, [l]which is known to the LORD, neither
day nor night, but [m]at evening time there
shall be light.
8 [e]On that day [n]living waters shall flow
out from Jerusalem, half of them to [o]the
eastern sea[3] and half of them to [o]the western sea.[4] [p]It shall continue in summer as in
winter.
9 And [q]the LORD will be king over all the
earth. [r]On that day the LORD will be [s]one
and [t]his name one.
10 [u]The whole land shall be turned into a
plain from [v]Geba to [w]Rimmon south of
Jerusalem. But [x]Jerusalem shall remain aloft
[y]on its site from [z]the Gate of Benjamin to
the place of the former gate, to [a]the Corner
Gate, and from [b]the Tower of Hananel to
the king's winepresses. **11** And it shall be
inhabited, for [c]there shall never again be a
decree of utter destruction.[5] [d]Jerusalem
shall dwell in security.
12 And this shall be [e]the plague with
which the LORD will strike all the peoples
that wage war against Jerusalem: their flesh
will rot while they are still standing on their
feet, their eyes will rot in their sockets, and
their tongues will rot in their mouths.
13 And [f]on that day a great panic from the
LORD shall fall on them, so that [g]each will
seize the hand of another, and the hand of
the one will be raised against the hand of the
other. **14** Even [h]Judah will fight against
Jerusalem. And [i]the wealth of all the surrounding nations shall be collected, gold, silver, and garments in great abundance. **15** And
[j]a plague like this plague shall fall on the
horses, the mules, the camels, the donkeys,
and whatever beasts may be in those camps.
16 Then everyone who survives of all the
nations that have come against Jerusalem
[k]shall go up year after year to worship [l]the
King, the LORD of hosts, and [m]to keep [n]the
Feast of Booths. **17** And if [o]any of the families of the earth do not go up to Jerusalem to worship [l]the King, the LORD of
hosts, [p]there will be no rain on them.
18 And if the family of Egypt does not go
up and present themselves, then on them
there shall be no rain;[6] there shall be
[j]the plague with which the LORD afflicts
the nations that do not go up [m]to keep the
Feast of Booths. **19** This shall be the punishment to Egypt and the punishment to
all the nations that do not go up [m]to keep
the Feast of Booths.

5 [i]Amos 1:1
6 [e][See ver. 4 above] [j][Isai. 60:19; Rev. 21:23]
7 [k]Rev. 21:25 [l]Matt. 24:36 [m][Isai. 30:26]
8 [e][See ver. 4 above] [n]John 4:10; Rev. 22:1; [Isai. 33:21; Ezek. 47:1; Joel 3:18] [o]Joel 2:20 [p][Isai. 33:16]
9 [q]Ps. 47:7; [ver. 16, 17; Mal. 1:14] [r][ver. 1]; See ch. 12:3 [s]Eph. 4:5, 6 [t][ch. 13:2]
10 [u][ver. 4; Isai. 40:4] [v]Josh. 18:24 [w]Josh. 15:32 [x]Isai. 2:2 [y]ch. 12:6; [ch. 2:4] [z]See Jer. 37:13 [a]Jer. 31:38 [b]Neh. 3:1; Jer. 31:38
11 [c]Rev. 22:3 [d][Jer. 23:6]
12 [e][ver. 15, 18]
13 [f]See ch. 12:3 [g]Hag. 2:22; [1 Sam. 14:20]
14 [h][ch. 12:2] [i][Ezek. 39:10]
15 [j][ver. 12]
16 [k]See ch. 8:21 [l][ver. 9] [m][Nah. 1:15]; See Lev. 23:34 [n]See Lev. 23:39-43
17 [o]Isai. 60:12 [l][See ver. 16 above] [p]See 1 Kin. 17:1
18 [j][See ver. 15 above] [m][See ver. 16 above] **19** [m][See ver. 16 above]

1 Compare Septuagint, Syriac, Vulgate, Targum; the meaning of the Hebrew is uncertain 2 Hebrew *one* 3 That is, the Dead Sea 4 That is, the Mediterranean Sea 5 The Hebrew term rendered *decree of utter destruction* refers to things devoted (or set apart) to the Lord (or by the Lord) for destruction 6 Hebrew lacks *rain*

14:5 Azal. Clearly a place close to Jerusalem; its precise location is unknown.

holy ones. An expression found also in the New Testament (Jude 14; cf. Matt. 25:31). These are God's chosen servants, the angelic host (perhaps humans as well), coming to Jerusalem to liberate it from pagan aggressors. This day of battle ushers in the eternal bliss of God's special presence among His people.

14:7 a unique day . . . there shall be light. God Himself will be the light of the city (Is. 60:19, 20; Rev. 21:25; 22:5). Natural light from the heavenly bodies will have ceased (v. 6).

14:8 living waters . . . from Jerusalem. As the result of the Lord's presence, a refreshing stream of running water brings healing to those who seek refuge in the Lord. Such water symbolizes the blessings of salvation (Is. 55:1–5; Ezek. 47:1–12; John 4:10–14). Believers in Jesus receive the living water only He can give (John 7:37–39; Rev. 22:1).

14:9 king over all the earth. With the final victory, God's sovereignty over all is manifested.

the LORD will be one and his name one. These words clearly draw on Deut. 6:4, Israel's foundational confession (Mark 12:29 note). Only on this day of victory will the full meaning of this confession be understood.

14:10 This extensive geographical description is designed to stress that the whole land of God's people will be claimed by God Himself.

14:12 plague. This fearful plague recalls the plagues on Egypt (Ex. 7–12), as well as the covenant curses proclaimed by God upon disobedience (Lev. 26:16; Deut. 28:22).

14:15 like this plague. The plague will extend even to the animals belonging to the heathen enemies of God. Zechariah is emphasizing that the destruction of God's enemies will be final and complete. Even now Christians enjoy victory in faith (1 John 5:4) and await the final subjugation of God's enemies by Christ (1 Cor. 15:24–28).

14:16–20 The last part of the book pictures the universal blessing that God will bestow in the final state.

14:16 everyone who survives. The people in the pagan nations are not all destroyed. Some are converted and come to worship the true and living God in Jerusalem (6:15; 8:23 and notes).

Feast of Booths. The worship of the Gentiles is expressed in terms of this feast because it was one of joy and thankfulness to God for His blessings (Lev. 23:33–36, 39–43; Num. 29:12–34; Deut. 16:13–15). The feast occurred during the fall harvest season and therefore could symbolize the ingathering of the Gentiles.

[20] And [q] on that day there shall be inscribed on the bells of the horses, [r] "Holy to the LORD." And the pots in the house of the LORD shall be as the bowls before the altar.
[21] And every pot in Jerusalem and Judah shall be [r] holy to the LORD of hosts, so that all who sacrifice may come and take of them and boil the meat of the sacrifice in them. And [s] there shall no longer be [t] a trader[1] in the house of the LORD of hosts [q] on that day.

20 [q] See ch. 12:3 [r] Ex. 28:36; Isai. 23:18; Mic. 4:13
21 [r] [See ver. 20 above]

[s] Ezek. 44:9; See Joel 3:17 [t] [Deut. 7:1, 2] [q] [See ver. 20 above]

[1] Or *Canaanite*

14:20 Holy to the LORD. Originally inscribed on the high priest's turban (Ex. 28:36–38) to express dedication, the phrase is now applied to everything in Jerusalem, horses' bells and cooking pots, because God's presence sanctifies all around Him.

THE BOOK OF

Malachi

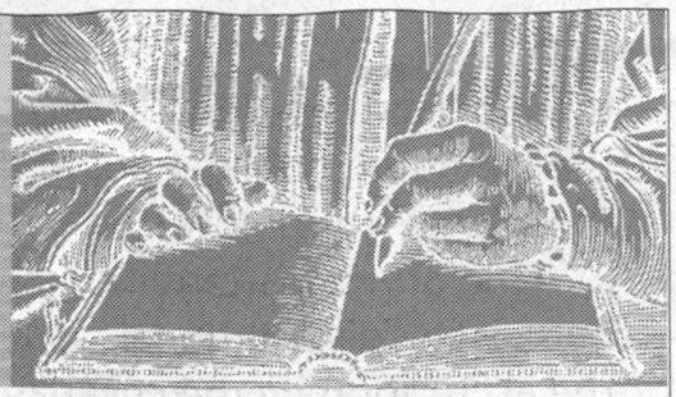

AUTHOR

The authorship of Malachi is a subject of debate. Scholars are divided as to whether the name "Malachi" is a personal name or a title. Both the Aramaic Targum and the Septuagint (Greek Old Testament translation) suggest something other than a personal name. The former identifies Malachi with Ezra. The latter translates the phrase "by Malachi" as "by the hand of his angel [or 'messenger']." The main arguments against viewing "Malachi" as the personal name of the prophet are the absence of specific data concerning his father and the lack of any mention of his place of birth. In addition, the phrase "oracle of the word," which occurs in 1:1, is alleged to be an anonymous addition to the text. Nevertheless, these are not compelling reasons for rejecting Malachi as a personal name. In the case of every other Old Testament prophetic book, a personal name is given. As with many of the prophets, we know little about the prophet's personal circumstances. But Malachi was "God's messenger," and the message he brought was from God (cf. Amos 3:7, 8).

DATE AND OCCASION

Malachi is to be dated about the time of Ezra and Nehemiah. The reference to the "governor" (1:8) locates the book in the Persian period, and Malachi's emphasis on the law (Mal. 4:4) would indicate the time of Ezra's ministry of restoring the prominence and authority of the law (Ezra 7:14, 25, 26; Neh. 8:18). Some date the book between the coming of Ezra (458 B.C.) and the coming of Nehemiah (445 B.C.). Others place Malachi in the period between Nehemiah's two visits to Jerusalem, about 433 B.C.

Also important is the recognition that the conditions and problems that confronted Ezra and Nehemiah are also found in the prophecy of Malachi. All three spoke out against marriage to foreign wives (e.g., 2:11–15; Neh. 13:23–27). They condemned neglect of the tithe (e.g., 3:8–10; Neh. 13:10–14). They castigated the evils of a degenerate priesthood (e.g., 1:6–2:9; Neh. 13:7, 8), and criticized social sins (e.g., 3:5; Neh. 5:1–13).

CHARACTERISTICS AND THEMES

The covenant theme is prominent in Malachi. Explicit references include: the covenant of Levi (2:5–9), the covenant of the fathers (2:10), the marriage covenant (2:14), and the messenger of the covenant (3:1). In addition to these direct references, the book begins with a rehearsal of God's covenant love (1:2–5). The seriousness of priestly incompetence and unfaithfulness is seen in the resulting erosion of covenant faithfulness among the common people, who broke faith in their marriages (2:10–16) and in their social and economic relationships (3:5), "profaning the covenant" (2:10). Unless they repent (3:7) they are under God's curse (3:9; Lev. 26:14–46; Deut. 28:15–68).

Malachi spoke to a disillusioned, discouraged, and doubting people whose experience did not harmonize with their understanding of the glorious promises found in the earlier prophets. Their vision of the coming messianic age did not materialize. Instead they experienced poverty, drought, and economic adversity, and they became disillusioned with God and their faith. Malachi's word confronts a people skeptical of the promises and therefore indifferent in their commitment to live in the light of those promises and to worship and serve the Lord with all their hearts. The book may serve as a catechism for times of doubt and disappointment, when the professing people of God are tempted to break faith with their covenant God. The prophet's ministry is to light the lamp of faith in a disheartened people by reminding them of God's electing love (1:2) and to set forth the continuing obligations of the covenant to those who truly know God (3:16–18).

One of the distinguishing features of this book is its "disputational" style. This is seen in the accusation by the covenant Lord against His people. The accusation is met by a cynical questioning of the charges. In response to the defiant response of the people, the prophet elaborates and defines the charges initially made. The book should be studied in the light of the structure, evident in the outline below, of six disputational dialogues. The structure reveals the role of this prophet as a covenant lawsuit advocate for God.

The uncommonly frequent use of the first person ("I") by the Lord in addressing the people lends an added sense of urgency and intimacy to the message of the book (1:2, 6, 14; 2:2; 3:5, 6, 10, 17; 4:5).

OUTLINE OF MALACHI

I. Israel Doubts God's Love for Them (1:1–5)

II. Degeneration of the Priesthood (1:6–2:9)

- A. *Contempt for God at the Altar (1:6–14)*
- B. *Neglect of God's Law (2:1–9)*

III. Israel's Failure in Marriage Practices (2:10–16)

- A. *Marriage to Idolatrous Wives (2:10–12)*
- B. *Divorce of Israelite Wives (2:13–16)*

IV. God's Response to Sin (2:17–3:5)

- A. *The Guilty Weary God with Excuses (2:17)*
- B. *The Purifying Work of the Messenger (3:1–5)*

V. God's Desire to Bless (3:6–12)

- A. *His Unchanging Promise to Forgive the Repentant (3:6, 7)*
- B. *Israel Robs God (3:8–12)*

VI. Distinction Between the Righteous and the Wicked (3:13–4:6)

- A. *The Harsh Words and Attitudes of the Cynical (3:13–15)*
- B. *The Godly Conduct of the Faithful (3:16–18)*
- C. *The Day of the Lord (4:1–6)*

1 The oracle of the word of the LORD to
Israel by Malachi.[1]

The LORD's Love for Israel

2 [a]"I have loved you," says the LORD. [b]But
you say, "How have you loved us?" "Is not
Esau [c]Jacob's brother?" declares the LORD.
"Yet [d]I have loved Jacob 3 but Esau I have
hated. [e]I have laid waste his hill country
and left his heritage to jackals of the
desert." 4 If Edom says, "We are shattered
but we will rebuild the ruins," the LORD of
hosts says, "They may build, but I will tear
down, and they will be called 'the wicked
country,' and 'the people with whom the
LORD is angry forever.'" 5 [f]Your own eyes
shall see this, and you shall say, "Great is
the LORD beyond the border of Israel!"

Chapter 1
2 [a]Deut. 7:8; Jer. 31:3 [b][ch. 2:14, 17; 3:7, 8, 13] [c][Amos 1:11; Obad. 10] [d]Cited Rom. 9:13
3 [e]Isai. 34:13; Jer. 49:10, 18; Ezek. 35:3, 4; Joel 3:19
5 [f]Ps. 91:8

1 *Malachi* means *my messenger*

1:1–5 Israel is not convinced that God loves them. This section is God's response to that cynical doubt. The Lord reminds Israel that Jacob, their ancestor, was chosen by God while Esau, Edom's forefather, was rejected. Therefore, although Israel has experienced the Lord's wrath for just a little while, Edom is a "people with whom the LORD is angry forever" (1:4). Furthermore, while Israel is heir of the everlasting promises of their covenant Lord, Edom will never rise again. The Lord's judgment on Edom will be cause for praise in Israel.

1:1 oracle of the word. Is. 13:1; Nah. 1:1; Hab. 1:1; Zech. 9:1; 12:1. Normally used in prophecies of judgment, "oracle" may point to the urgency felt by the prophet in issuing his proclamation. On this urgency, see also Jer. 20:9; Amos 3:8.

1:2 I have loved you. God's electing love is sovereign and unconditional. It is expounded principally in Deuteronomy where the verbs "to choose" and "to love" are parallel (Deut. 7:6–8). God's love is manifested in the covenant He initiates with His people. The nearness of God to Israel was to be the source of awe and amazement (Deut. 4:7, 8). God's love begins in eternity (Jer. 31:3) and is manifested in His covenantal dealings with Abraham, Moses, and David (Gen. 12:1–4; Ex. 19:5, 6; 2 Sam. 7). God's election of Jacob continued to have relevance for His dealings with Israel in the period of Malachi's ministry. Properly understood, God's love does not lead to moral complacency but to moral zeal. However, Israel's complacency and their cynicism about God's love led to the moral crises that Malachi addresses. See theological note "The Purpose of God: Predestination and Foreknowledge."

Jacob. One of the titles for God in the Psalms is "the God of Jacob" (Ps. 20:1; 46:7; 75:9; 76:6; 84:8). God's electing love is unique because He loves sinners, those who by nature were the objects of His displeasure and wrath (Luke 15:2; Rom. 5:6–8; Eph. 2:1–3). The history of Jacob and Esau in Genesis clearly points to God's choice of Jacob despite his lack of merit (Gen. 25:21–34; 27:1–40; Rom. 9:10–13).

1:3 hated. Although there is a usage of the verb "hate" which means "to love less" (Gen. 29:31; Luke 14:26), the context immediately following suggests that here "hate" means active rejection, displeasure, and disfavor manifested in retributive justice. It is not merely that Esau (Edom) suffers the absence or lessening of blessing, but that he receives judgment. For this usage of "hate," see Ps. 5:5; Is. 61:8; Hos. 9:15; Amos 5:21; Mal. 2:16. See "Election and Reprobation" at Rom. 9:18.

laid waste. The reference is most likely to the occupation of Edom by the Nabatean Arabs. In Amos 9:12 Edom is representative of all the nations who come under the saving influence of God's promise.

1:5 beyond the border of Israel. God is the sovereign Lord of history, whose redemptive purposes are accomplished both inside and outside ancient Israel (v. 11; Gen. 12:3).

The Priests' Polluted Offerings

6 [g]"A son honors his father, and a servant
his master. If then I am [h]a father, where is my
honor? And if I am [i]a master, where is my
fear? says the LORD of hosts to you, O priests,
who despise my name. [b]But you say, 'How
have we despised your name?' 7 [j]By offering
polluted food upon my altar. [b]But you say,
'How have we polluted you?' By saying that
[k]the LORD's table may be despised. 8 [l]When
you offer blind animals in sacrifice, is that
not evil? And when you offer those that are
lame or sick, is that not evil? Present that to
your governor; will he accept you or show
you favor? says the LORD of hosts. 9 And now
[m]entreat the favor of God, that he may be
gracious to us. With such a gift from your
hand, [n]will he show favor to any of you? says
the LORD of hosts. 10 [o]Oh that there were one
among you who would shut the doors, that
you might not kindle fire on my altar in vain!
I have no pleasure in you, says the LORD of
hosts, [p]and I will not accept an offering from
your hand. 11 For from the rising of the sun to
its setting my name [q]will be[1] great among the

6 [g]See Ex. 20:12 [h]Ex. 4:22; Hos. 11:1 [i][Luke 6:46] [b][See ver. 2 above]
7 [j][ver. 8; ch. 2:12; 3:3] [b][See ver. 2 above] [k][ver. 12]
8 [l][ver. 13]; See Lev. 22:22
9 [m]See Zech. 7:2 [n]See Deut. 10:17
10 [o][Isai. 1:13] [p][Isai. 1:11; Jer. 6:20; Amos 5:21]
11 [q][Isai. 2:2; 56:7; 60:3; 66:19]

[1] Or *is* (three times in verse 11; also verse 14)

The Purpose of God: Predestination and Foreknowledge

"Predestination" is a word often used to signify God's foreordaining of all the events of world history—past, present, and future. This usage is quite appropriate. In Scripture and historic Protestant theology, however, "predestination" refers specifically to God's decision, made in eternity before the world existed, regarding the final destinies of individual persons. In general, the New Testament speaks of the predestination, or election, of particular sinners for salvation and eternal life (Rom. 8:29; Eph. 1:4, 5, 11), although Scripture also on occasion ascribes to God an advance decision about those who are finally not saved (Rom. 9:6–29; 1 Pet. 2:8; Jude 4). For this reason it is usual in Protestant theology to define predestination as including both God's decision to save some from sin (election) and the corresponding decision not to save others (reprobation).

It is sometimes asserted that God's choice of individuals for salvation is based on His foreknowledge that they would choose Christ as their Savior. Foreknowledge in this case means passive foresight by God of what individuals will do apart from His foreordaining their action. But there are weighty objections to the view that election is based on passive foresight.

"Foreknow" in Rom. 8:29; 11:2 (cf. 1 Pet. 1:2, 20) indicates not only an advance recognition, but also an advance choice by God of His people. It does not express the idea of a spectator's passive anticipation of what will happen spontaneously. God's "knowledge" of His people in Scripture implies a special relationship of loving choice (Gen. 18:19).

Since all are naturally dead in sin (cut off from the life of God and unresponsive to Him), no one who hears the gospel will ever come to repentance and faith without the inner renewal that only God can impart (Eph. 2:4–10). Jesus said, "no one can come to me unless it is granted him by the Father" (John 6:65, cf. 6:44; 10:25–28). Sinners choose Christ because God chose them first, and moved them to their choice by graciously renewing their hearts.

Though all human acts are free in the sense of an immediate self-determination, such acts are also the outworking of God's eternal purpose and foreordination. We have difficulty understanding precisely how divine sovereignty and human freedom and responsibility are compatible, but Scripture everywhere assumes that they are so (Acts 2:23; 4:28 and notes).

Christians should thank God for their conversion, look to Him to keep them in His grace, and wait with confidence for His final triumph, according to His plan. See "Election and Reprobation" at Rom. 9:18 and "Effectual Calling and Conversion" at 2 Thess. 2:14.

1:6–2:9 A major reason for the Lord's anger with Israel is the priesthood's attitude toward God's name at the altar and toward God's law in teaching and judging. At the altar they offered diseased or imperfect animals in sacrifice, thereby reversing the intent of their labors and bringing curse and defilement where they should have brought blessing and cleansing. In their teaching and judging they violated the covenant with Levi (2:8), showing partiality and causing many to stumble.

1:6 honor. God is in Himself infinitely glorious, and He must receive the recognition of His people (Ps. 29:1, 2; 57:5, 11).

despise. The opposite of honoring and fearing the Lord (cf. 2 Sam. 12:9, 10). The word is used often in Proverbs (1:7; 15:20; 23:22).

1:7 polluted food. The reference is to animal sacrifices (v. 8). "Polluted" means ceremonially unclean and therefore unacceptable. God is not offended merely by ceremonial imperfections but by the attitude of contempt behind such imperfect sacrifices (Gen. 4:3–5 and notes; Heb. 11:4).

the LORD's table. This phrase, and the similar phrase in v. 12, occur only here in the Old Testament, both times referring to the altar.

1:8 lame or sick. The law expressly prohibited such offerings (Lev. 22:22; Deut. 15:21).

1:11 my name will be great among the nations. God promises the future triumph of His glorious kingdom. "From the rising of the sun to its setting," and similar phrases, often point to God's future judgment of the world and the restoration of His order (Ps. 50:1; Is. 45:6; 59:19).

nations, and in every place incense will be
offered to my name, and a pure offering. For
my name [q]will be great among the nations,
says the LORD of hosts. 12 But you profane it
when you say that [r]the Lord's table is polluted, and its fruit, that is, its food may be
despised. 13 But you say, [s]'What a weariness
this is,' and you snort at it, says the LORD of
hosts. [t]You bring what has been taken by
violence or is lame or sick, and this you bring
as your offering! Shall I accept that from your
hand? says the LORD. 14 Cursed be the cheat
who has [u]a male in his flock, and [v]vows it,
and yet sacrifices to the Lord what is blemished. For [w]I am a great King, says the LORD
of hosts, and my name [x]will be feared among
the nations.

The LORD Rebukes the Priests

2 "And now, [y]O priests, [z]this command is
for you. 2 [a]If you will not listen, if you
will not take it to heart to give honor to my
name, says the LORD of hosts, then I will
send [b]the curse upon you and I will curse
[c]your blessings. Indeed, I have already
cursed them, because you do not lay it to
heart. 3 Behold, [d]I will rebuke your offspring,[1] and [e]spread dung on your faces, the
[f]dung of your offerings, and you shall be
taken away with it.[2] 4 So shall you know that
I have sent [g]this command to you, that [h]my
covenant with Levi may stand, says the LORD
of hosts. 5 My covenant with him was one of
life and [i]peace, and I gave them to him. [j]It
was a covenant of fear, and he feared me. He
stood in awe of my name. 6 [k]True instruction[3] was in his mouth, and no wrong was
found on his lips. He walked with me in
peace and uprightness, and he [l]turned many
from iniquity. 7 For [m]the lips of a priest
should guard knowledge, and people[4]
should seek instruction from his mouth, for
he is the messenger of the LORD of hosts.
8 But you have turned aside from the way.
[n]You have caused many to stumble by your
instruction. You have corrupted [o]the
covenant of Levi, says the LORD of hosts,
9 and so [p]I make you despised and abased
before all the people, inasmuch as you do
not keep my ways but [q]show partiality in
your instruction."

Judah Profaned the Covenant

10 Have we not all [r]one Father? Has not
[s]one God created us? Why then are we
[t]faithless to one another, profaning the
covenant of our fathers? 11 Judah has been
[t]faithless, and abomination has been committed in Israel and in Jerusalem. For
[u]Judah has profaned the sanctuary of the
LORD, which he loves, and has married the

10 [r]1 Cor. 8:6; Eph. 4:6 [s]Acts 17:26 [t][Isai. 21:2; 24:16; 33:1] 11 [t][See ver. 10 above] [u]See Ezra 9:2

[1] Hebrew *seed* [2] Or *to it* [3] Or *law*; also verses 7, 8, 9 [4] Hebrew *they*

in every place. The imperfect sacrifices being offered during the prophet's time (vv. 7, 8) are contrasted with the pure offerings of worship in the future (Is. 2:2–4; 66:19–21; Zech. 14:16–21). The promise of this verse is being fulfilled even now as Christ gathers His kings and priests from among the nations (Rev. 5:9, 10), and it will be consummated in the future as the nations gather to worship God in purity (Rev. 21:27).

1:14 Cursed be the cheat. Laws regulating voluntary offerings required the giving of a perfect offering. This text implies an attempt to deceive the Lord (cf. Ps. 76:11).

I am a great King. God is not only their Father (1:6; Ex. 4:22) and their Master, but also their King. The idea of God as King arose early in Old Testament religion (Num. 23:21; 24:7; Deut. 33:5). See Ps. 93–100.

2:2 I will send the curse upon you. See Deut. 28:20.

I will curse your blessings. The blessings are either the physical and material blessings promised to the priests who received the peoples' tithes (Num. 18:21), or the pronouncements of blessing uttered by the priests at the time of the sacrifices (Num. 6:24–27), which then would become a curse.

2:5 one of life and peace. The central thrust of Deuteronomy is to show the connection between covenant obedience and life. Commitment to God leads to a full life. Some see in "covenant . . . of . . . peace" an allusion to the covenant with Phinehas mentioned in Num. 25:10–13.

2:7 lips of a priest should guard knowledge. See Ezra 7:10; Hos. 4:6. The connection between the true knowledge of the Lord and priestly instruction in the law is set forth vividly in 2 Chr. 15:3: "For a long time Israel was without the true God, and without a teaching priest and without law."

2:8 you have turned aside from the way. See Neh. 13:29. The priests' attitudes and actions set a bad example for the people. They abandoned their true calling, both to teach and practice the truth.

2:9 show partiality in your instruction. The basis for this censure is the character of God. God "is not partial and takes no bribe" (Deut. 10:17; cf. Lev. 19:15). Possibly the priests were favoring the rich and powerful of society.

2:10–16 Lack of faithfulness toward God leads to breakdowns in human relationships. Malachi addresses two problems. Marriage to idolatrous wives (vv. 10–12) and the divorcing of Israelite wives (vv. 13–16) are sternly rebuked.

2:10 one Father. Some interpret this as referring to Abraham (Is. 51:2). More likely it refers to God (1:6; Ex. 4:22, 23; Deut. 32:6; Is. 63:16; 64:8; Jer. 3:4, 19; 31:9).

2:11 has been faithless. This verb is used five times in vv. 10–16. It is used in Jer. 3:20 to refer to marital unfaithfulness.

abomination. The Hebrew word here, prominently employed in Deuteronomy, refers to idolatrous religious practices (Deut. 7:25, 26; 12:31; 13:14; 18:12). It can also refer to sexual transgression (Lev. 18:22, 26, 29, 30; Deut. 24:4).

profaned the sanctuary of the LORD. The Hebrew word translated "sanctuary" can also be understood as referring to the people themselves ("holy seed," Is. 6:13; cf. Ezra 9:2). It is the people who are loved by God and who defile themselves by disobedience in their marriage practices.

11 [q][Isai. 2:2; 56:7; 60:3; 66:19] 12 [r][ver. 7] 13 [s]Isai. 42:22; [ch. 3:14; Mic. 6:3] [t][ver. 8; Lev. 22:20] 14 [u]See Ex. 12:5 [v][Lev. 22:21] [w]See Zech. 14:9 [x]Ps. 47:2; 76:12
Chapter 2
1 [y]ch. 1:6 [z]ver. 4
2 [a]Lev. 26:14; See Deut. 28:15 [b][ch. 3:9] [c][Ps. 69:22]
3 [d][Joel 1:17; Hag. 2:17] [e]Nah. 3:6 [f][Ex. 29:14]
4 [g]ver. 1 [h]ver. 8; Num. 25:12, 13; Neh. 13:29; [Num. 3:45]
5 [i]See Isai. 54:10 [j][Lev. 16:2]
6 [k][Deut. 33:10] [l][Dan. 12:3; James 5:20]
7 [m]Deut. 17:9; See Lev. 10:11
8 [n][1 Sam. 2:17; Jer. 18:15; Ezek. 22:26] [o]See ver. 4
9 [p][1 Sam. 2:30] [q]Deut. 1:17; 16:19

daughter of a foreign god. 12 May the LORD cut off from the tents of Jacob, any descendant[1] of the man who does this, who [v]brings an offering to the LORD of hosts!
13 And this second thing you do. [w]You cover the LORD's altar with tears, with weeping and groaning because he no longer regards the offering or accepts it with favor from your hand. 14 [x]But you say, "Why does he not?" Because the LORD [y]was witness between you and the wife of your youth, [z]to whom [t]you have been faithless, though she is your companion and your wife by covenant.
15 [a]Did he not make them one, with a portion of the Spirit in their union?[2] And what was the one God[3] seeking?[4] [b]Godly offspring. So guard yourselves[5] in your spirit, and let none of you [t]be faithless to the wife of your youth.

12 [v][ch. 1:7]
13 [w][Zech. 7:3]
14 [x][ch. 1:2] [y]ch. 3:5
[z][ver. 11; Isai. 54:6]
[t][See ver. 10 above]
15 [a]Matt. 19:4, 5; See Gen. 2:24
[b][Ezra 9:2]
[t][See ver. 10 above]

1 Hebrew *any who wakes and answers* 2 Hebrew *in it* 3 Hebrew *the one* 4 Or *And not one has done this who has a portion of the Spirit. And what was that one seeking?* 5 Or *So take care*; also verse 16

Marriage and Divorce

Marriage is an exclusive relationship in which a man and a woman commit themselves to each other in covenant for life, and on the basis of this solemn vow become "one flesh" (Gen. 2:24; Mal. 2:14; Matt. 19:4–6).

The *Westminster Confession* (XXIV.2) states: "Marriage was ordained for the mutual help of husband and wife, for the increase of mankind with a legitimate issue, and of the church with an holy seed; and for preventing of uncleanness" (sexual license and immorality; Gen. 1:28; 2:18; 1 Cor. 7:2–9). God's ideal for marriage is that the man and the woman should complete each other (Gen. 2:23) and share in the creative work of making new people. Marriage is for Christians and non-Christians, but it is God's will that His people should marry only fellow believers (1 Cor. 7:39; cf. 2 Cor. 6:14; Ezra 9; 10; Neh. 13:23–27). Intimacy in its deepest dimension is impossible when the partners are not united in faith.

Paul uses Christ's relationship to His church to explain what Christian marriage is, so as to highlight the husband's special responsibility as the wife's leader and protector, and the wife's calling to accept her husband in that role (Eph. 5:21–33). The distinction of roles does not imply that the wife is an inferior person. As God's image-bearers, both man and wife have equal dignity and value, and they must fulfill their roles with a mutual respect grounded in recognition of this fact.

God hates divorce (Mal. 2:16), yet He provided a procedure for it that would protect the divorced wife (Deut. 24:1–4). This provision was made "because of your hardness of heart" (Matt. 19:8). The most natural understanding of Jesus' teaching (Matt. 5:31, 32; 19:8, 9) is that adultery, the sin of marital unfaithfulness, destroys the marriage covenant and warrants divorce (though reconciliation would be preferable), and that he who divorces his wife for any lesser reason becomes guilty of adultery when he remarries, and drives the woman into adultery if she remarries. The principle is that all cases of divorce and remarriage involve a disruption of God's ideal for the sexual relationship. When asked when divorce is lawful, Jesus replied that divorce is always deplorable (Matt. 19:3–6), but He did not deny that hearts continue to be hard, and that divorce, though an evil, may sometimes be permitted.

Paul says that a Christian who is deserted by an unbelieving partner is not "enslaved" (1 Cor. 7:15). This evidently means that the Christian may regard the relationship as finished. Whether this confers the right of remarriage has been disputed, and Reformed opinion has long been divided on the matter.

The *Westminster Confession* (XXIV.5, 6) states with cautious wisdom what Reformed Christians, reflecting on the Scriptures noted above, have down the centuries found themselves agreed on regarding divorce:

> In the case of adultery after marriage, it is lawful for the innocent party to sue out a divorce: and, after the divorce, to marry another, as if the offending party were dead.
>
> Although the corruption of man be such as is apt to study arguments unduly to put asunder those whom God hath joined together in marriage: yet, nothing but adultery, or such wilful desertion as can no way be remedied by the church, or civil magistrate, is cause sufficient of dissolving the bond of marriage: wherein, a public and orderly course of proceeding is to be observed; and the persons concerned in it not left to their own wills, and discretion, in their own case.

married the daughter of a foreign god. This phrase refers to marrying a woman still committed to a foreign god—an idolater outside the covenant (cf. Gen. 24:3, 4; Ex. 34:12–16; Deut. 7:3, 4; Josh. 23:12; 1 Kin. 11:1–10). The prohibition against marriage with unbelievers continues in the New Testament (1 Cor. 7:39; 2 Cor. 6:14).

2:14 wife of your youth. See v. 15; Prov. 5:18.

your wife by covenant. God's covenant faithfulness is to be mirrored in the marriage relationships of His people (Prov. 2:17; Eph. 5:22–33).

2:15 one. See Gen. 2:24.

16 "For [c] the man who hates and divorces, says
the LORD, the God of Israel, covers[1] his garment with violence, says the LORD of hosts.
So guard yourselves in your spirit, and [t] do
not be faithless."

The Messenger of the LORD

17 [d] You have wearied the LORD with your
words. [x] But you say, "How have we wearied him?" [e] By saying, "Everyone who does
evil is good in the sight of the LORD, and he
delights in them." Or by asking, [f] "Where is
the God of justice?"

3 1 [g] "Behold, I send [h] my messenger and
[i] he will prepare the way before me. And
the Lord [j] whom you seek will suddenly
come to his temple; and [k] the messenger of
the covenant in whom you delight, behold,
he is coming, says the LORD of hosts. 2 But
[l] who can endure the day of his coming, and
who can stand when he appears? For [m] he is
like a refiner's fire and like fullers' soap. 3 He
will sit [n] as a refiner and purifier of silver, and
he will purify the sons of Levi and refine
them like gold and silver, and they will bring
[o] offerings in righteousness to the LORD.[2]
4 [p] Then the offering of Judah and Jerusalem
will be pleasing to the LORD as in the days of
old and as in former years.
5 "Then I will draw near to you for judgment. I will be [q] a swift witness against the
sorcerers, against the adulterers, against
those who swear falsely, against those [r] who
oppress the hired worker in his wages, [s] the
widow and the fatherless, against those
who thrust aside the sojourner, and do not
fear me, says the LORD of hosts.

Robbing God

6 "For [t] I the LORD do not change; [u] therefore you, O children of Jacob, are not consumed. 7 [v] From the days of your fathers you
have turned aside from my statutes and have
not kept them. [w] Return to me, and I will
return to you, says the LORD of hosts. [x] But
you say, 'How shall we return?' 8 Will man
rob God? Yet you are robbing me. [x] But you
say, 'How have we robbed you?' [y] In your
tithes and contributions. 9 [z] You are cursed
with a curse, for you are robbing me, the
whole nation of you. 10 [a] Bring the full tithes

16 [c] Matt. 5:32; Mark 10:9, 11; Luke 16:18; 1 Cor. 7:10 [t] [See ver. 10 above]
17 [d] Isai. 43:24 [x] [See ver. 14 above] [e] [ch. 3:15; Isai. 5:20] [f] [ch. 3:1; 2 Pet. 3:4]
Chapter 3
1 [g] Cited Matt. 11:10; Mark 1:2; Luke 7:27; [ch. 4:5; Luke 1:76] [h] See ch. 2:7 [i] See Isai. 40:3 [j] [ch. 2:17] [k] [ch. 4:5]
2 [l] Joel 2:11 [m] Isai. 4:4
3 [n] Isai. 1:25; Zech. 13:9 [o] [ch. 1:7]
4 [p] Ezek. 20:40
5 [q] ch. 2:14; Jer. 29:23 [r] See Lev. 19:13 [s] See Deut. 24:17
6 [t] Ps. 102:27; See Num. 23:19 [u] Lam. 3:22
7 [v] Acts 7:51 [w] See Zech. 1:3 [x] [ch. 1:2]
8 [x] [See ver. 7 above] [y] [Neh. 13:10] 9 [z] [ch. 2:2] 10 [a] [Prov. 3:9, 10]

1 Probable meaning (compare Septuagint and Deuteronomy 24:1-4); or *For the LORD, the God of Israel, says that he hates divorce, and him who covers*
2 Or *and they will belong to the LORD, bringers of an offering in righteousness*

2:16 divorces. See Is. 50:1; Deut. 24:1–4; theological note "Marriage and Divorce."

garment. Entering into marriage and obtaining a wife is sometimes portrayed as covering with a garment (Ruth 3:9 text note; Ezek. 16:8).

2:17–3:5 Religious cynics charge the Lord with injustice. God responds with the promise that He will send a messenger to prepare the way before Him and then return to His temple. His presence among a wicked people requires judgment and gracious refinement (3:2, 3). He will change the Levites' hearts and they will then offer sacrifices in righteousness once again. The judgment will be exacting (3:5). The Lord Himself will be the chief witness for the prosecution of His people.

2:17 wearied the LORD. See Is. 43:24. In Malachi the offenses revolve around the cynical rejection of God's moral government and the attendant insolent spirit that constantly puts God on trial.

3:1–5 This section rebuts the two cynical statements of 2:17. The allegation that God does not differentiate between good and evil is answered in v. 2 by referring to the refining and purifying ministry of the messenger of the covenant. The second statement, "Where is the God of justice?" (2:17), is answered in v. 5. The Jews were looking for the Lord to judge the nations, but instead the Lord will come near to *them* for judgment (v. 5).

3:1 my messenger. See 4:5; also Is. 40:3 (where "prepare the way" also occurs). It was the practice in the Near East to send messengers in advance of a visiting king to announce his coming and to remove all hindrances or obstacles. This messenger (Matt. 11:10) will be the last of his kind to appear before the coming of the Lord, who is "the messenger of the covenant."

suddenly. This word is almost always associated in Scripture with an unhappy and calamitous circumstance (Num. 12:4; Is. 47:11; cf. 2 Pet. 3:10).

the messenger of the covenant. A person distinct from "my messenger," He will purify the sacrifices, the priests, and the nation (vv. 2–5). This "messenger of the covenant" is the Messiah, and this prophecy is fulfilled in Jesus who alone has performed the perfect sacrifice on behalf of His people.

3:3 he will purify the sons of Levi. The priests had been instrumental in leading the people astray. The work of purification will begin with them, and it will spread from them to the whole of the nation. The Levites were the pattern for the nation, which was to be "a kingdom of priests" (Ex. 19:6).

offerings in righteousness. See 1:11, "a pure offering." Because of the work of the messenger of the covenant, proper worship will again be offered, since the hearts and lives of the offerers will be purified (Ps. 4:5; Zeph. 3:9).

3:5 Then I will draw near to you for judgment. This section began with the religious cynics accusing the Lord of injustice. It ends with a covenant lawsuit in which the Lord brings charges against His people. The specific sins mentioned in v. 5 are clearly forbidden in the law of God. The root cause of these sins is that they "do not fear me."

3:6–12 The people were not only bringing defective offerings but also were withholding the tithe, apparently due to the field's meager returns. But withholding the tithe is stealing from the Lord. As a consequence the righteous Lord withheld blessing. Their sin also evidenced a lack of trust in the Lord to provide for their needs if they kept His commands. So the Lord urges them to put Him to the test. If they did so the consequent provision would be so great that the nations would see the difference and pronounce Israel blessed.

3:6 I . . . do not change. The immutability, or unchangeable character, of God is seen in His purpose to bless His elect people. Thus they are not destroyed (Ex. 34:6, 7; Jer. 30:11).

3:7 Return to me, and I will return to you. The command to repent is connected with a promise (cf. Zech. 1:3; James 4:8). Sin separates man from God and causes God to hide His face (Is. 59:2).

3:8 tithes. The word means a tenth. The practice of tithing is mentioned in the accounts of Abraham (Gen. 14:20) and Jacob (Gen. 28:22), and was codified in the law of Moses (Lev. 27:30; Num. 18:26; Deut. 14:22–29).

contributions. Portions of the animal sacrifices to which the priests were entitled (Ex. 29:27, 28; Lev. 9:22).

into the storehouse, that there may be food
in my house. And thereby [b]put me to the
test, says the LORD of hosts, if I will not open
[c]the windows of heaven for you and pour
down for you a blessing until there is no
more need. **11**I will rebuke [d]the devourer[1] for
you, so that it will not destroy the fruits of
your soil, and your vine in the field shall not
fail to bear, says the LORD of hosts. **12**Then
[e]all nations will call you blessed, for you will
be [f]a land of delight, says the LORD of hosts.
13[g]"Your words have been hard against
me, says the LORD. [h]But you say, 'How have
we spoken against you?' **14**You have said, [i]'It
is vain to serve God. [j]What is the profit of
our keeping his charge or of walking as in
mourning before the LORD of hosts? **15**And
now we call [k]the arrogant blessed. [k]Evildoers
not only prosper but [l]they put God to the
test and they escape.'"

The Book of Remembrance

16Then those who feared the LORD
[m]spoke with one another. The LORD paid
attention and heard them, and [n]a book of
remembrance was written before him of
those who feared the LORD and esteemed
his name. **17**"They shall be mine, says the
LORD of hosts, [o]in the day when I make up
[p]my treasured possession, and I will spare
them as a man spares his son who serves
him. **18**Then once more you shall [q]see the
distinction between the righteous and the
wicked, between one who serves God and
one who does not serve him.

The Great Day of the LORD

4 [2] "For behold, [r]the day is coming, [s]burn-
ing like an oven, when [t]all the arrogant
and [t]all evildoers [u]will be stubble. The day
that is coming [u]shall set them ablaze, says
the LORD of hosts, so that it will leave them
neither root nor branch. **2**But for you [v]who
fear my name, [w]the sun [x]of righteousness
shall rise [y]with healing in its wings. You
shall go out [z]leaping like calves from the
stall. **3**And you shall tread down the wicked,
for they will be ashes under the soles of your
feet, [a]on the day when I act, says the LORD
of hosts.
4[b]"Remember [c]the law of my servant
Moses, the statutes and rules that I commanded him at Horeb for all Israel.
5[d]"Behold, I will send you [e]Elijah the
prophet [f]before the great and awesome day
of the LORD comes. **6**And he will [g]turn the
hearts of fathers to their children and the
hearts of children to their fathers, lest I
come and [h]strike the land with a decree of
utter destruction."

10 [b]See 2 Cor. 9:6-8 [c]See Gen. 7:11
11 [d][Joel 1:4]
12 [e]Zeph. 3:19 [f][Isai. 62:4]
13 [g][ch. 2:17] [h][ch. 1:2]
14 [i][Zeph. 1:12] [j][Job 21:15]
15 [k][ch. 4:1] [l][Ps. 95:9]
16 [m][Deut. 6:6, 7] [n]See Ex. 32:32
17 [o][ch. 4:3; Acts 17:31] [p]Ex. 19:5; 1 Pet. 2:9
18 [q][ch. 4:1]
Chapter 4
1 [r][ver. 5; ch. 3:2] [s][2 Thess. 1:7, 8] [t]ch. 3:15 [u]Isai. 47:14; [Matt. 3:12; Luke 3:17]
2 [v]ch. 3:16 [w]Ps. 84:11; Luke 1:78; John 1:4; 8:12; 9:5; 12:46 [x][Jer. 23:6] [y]Isai. 53:5 [z][Jer. 50:11]
3 [a]See ch. 3:17
4 [b][Deut. 4:9, 10] [c]See Ex. 20:3-17; Deut. 4:10
5 [d][ch. 3:1] [e][Matt. 11:14; Mark 9:11; Luke 1:17] [f]Joel 2:31
6 [g][Luke 1:17] [h]Isai. 11:4; [Zech. 5:3]

1 Probably a name for some crop-destroying pest or pests 2 Ch 4:1-6 is ch 3:19-24 in the Hebrew

3:10 storehouse. This term refers to a room in the temple designated for the storage of gifts (2 Chr. 31:11; Neh. 10:38, 39; 12:44; 13:12).

put me to the test. This is a reversal of the ordinary biblical pattern, in which God typically tests human beings (Ps. 11:5; 26:2; 66:10; Prov. 17:3; Jer. 11:20; 12:3; 17:10). Only in a few instances are humans invited to test God (i.e., to prove His claims and justify His commands, Is. 7:11, 12; 1 Kin. 18:22–46).

windows of heaven. See Gen. 7:11.

3:13–4:6 The last section returns to the prophecy in 3:1–5 concerning the forerunner (Matt. 11:10) and the coming of God. In various ways the beginning of the section is reminiscent of a lament psalm. The complaints, however, are interpreted as hard words against the Lord. Yet there were those who sensed the same injustices without concluding that it was futile to serve the Lord. The first group spoke hard words and brought the Lord's response; the latter feared the Lord and caused Him to write words of remembrance concerning them. He promised that they would be His special possession in the great day of the Lord.

A reference to "the day" (v. 17) again introduces the last day of judgment, a day of destruction for the wicked but healing for the righteous. The final verses return to the promised forerunner and exhort the people to keep the law of Moses.

3:14 vain. The word means "empty" or "useless."

profit. The Hebrew term usually refers to unjust gain. Greed is inconsistent with a desire for God's truth (Ps. 119:36).

3:16 Then. The conversation and conduct of those who feared God is occasioned by the preceding words of murmuring and is placed in contrast to them.

book of remembrance. This exact phrase is found only here, but references to a special book are found elsewhere (Ex. 32:32; Ps. 69:28; Dan. 7:10).

3:17 They shall be mine. This phrase refers to the remnant described in v. 16.

my treasured possession. In the early stage of Old Testament revelation the nation of Israel is called God's "treasured possession" (Ex. 19:5; Deut. 7:6; 14:2).

4:1 shall set them ablaze. Two images of fire are used in Malachi to describe the Lord: a refining fire (3:2) and a destroying fire (4:1).

root nor branch. The wicked are compared to a tree (Amos 2:9) that will be consumed down to the roots, totally destroyed.

4:2 sun of righteousness. An expression unique to Malachi (cf. Ps. 84:12). The Davidic king will reign in righteousness (Is. 32:1) and will be called "a righteous Branch" (Jer. 23:5, 6).

healing. The Bible considers physical sickness and spiritual sickness or sin to be analogous. Salvation is often compared to bodily healing (Ex. 15:26; 2 Chr. 7:14; Ps. 103:3; Is. 53:5; Jer. 17:14).

4:5 Behold, I will send you Elijah the prophet. The literary connection of this verse with 3:1 indicates that "Elijah" is the same person as "my messenger." Both verses begin with the word "Behold," and use the same form of the verb "to send." In both cases the mission is to bring repentance in advance of the coming day of the Lord. The New Testament identifies this "Elijah" as John the Baptist (Matt. 11:14; 17:10; Mark 9:11–13; Luke 1:17).

4:6 turn the hearts of fathers to their children. Repentance and turning to God will be seen in the restoration of family relationships (Luke 1:17).

lest I come and strike the land with a decree. Malachi began with the announcement of God's electing love, yet the book ends with the threat of a curse. Malachi's dual thrust of mercy and judgment is echoed by Paul's pronouncement, "Note then the kindness and the severity of God" (Rom. 11:22).

into the storehouse, that there may be food
in my house. And thereby put me to the
test, says the LORD of hosts, if I will not open
the windows of heaven for you and pour
down for you a blessing until there is no
more need. 11 I will rebuke the devourer for
you, so that it will not destroy the fruits of
your soil, and your vine in the field shall not
fail to bear, says the LORD of hosts. 12 Then
all nations will call you blessed, for you will
be a land of delight, says the LORD of hosts.
13 "Your words have been hard against
me, says the LORD. But you say, 'How have
we spoken against you?' 14 You have said, 'It
is vain to serve God. What is the profit of
our keeping his charge or of walking as in
mourning before the LORD of hosts? 15 And
now we call the arrogant blessed. Evildoers
not only prosper but they put God to the
test and they escape.'"

The Book of Remembrance

16 Then those who feared the LORD
spoke with one another. The LORD paid
attention and heard them, and a book of
remembrance was written before him of
those who feared the LORD and esteemed
his name. 17 "They shall be mine, says the
LORD of hosts, in the day when I make up
my treasured possession, and I will spare
them as a man spares his son who serves
him. 18 Then once more you shall see the
distinction between the righteous and the
wicked, between one who serves God and
one who does not serve him.

The Great Day of the LORD

4 "For behold, the day is coming, burning like an oven, when all the arrogant
and all evildoers will be stubble. The day
that is coming shall set them ablaze, says
the LORD of hosts, so that it will leave them
neither root nor branch. 2 But for you who
fear my name, the sun of righteousness
shall rise with healing in its wings. You
shall go out leaping like calves from the
stall. 3 And you shall tread down the wicked,
for they will be ashes under the soles of your
feet, on the day when I act, says the LORD
of hosts.
4 "Remember the law of my servant
Moses, the statutes and rules that I commanded him at Horeb for all Israel.
5 "Behold, I will send you Elijah the
prophet before the great and awesome day
of the LORD comes. 6 And he will turn the
hearts of fathers to their children and the
hearts of children to their fathers, lest I
come and strike the land with a decree of
utter destruction."

[illegible]

3:17 They shall be mine. [illegible]

my treasured possession. [illegible]

4:1 shall set them ablaze. [illegible]

root nor branch. [illegible]

4:2 sun of righteousness. [illegible]

healing. [illegible]

4:5 Behold, I will send you Elijah the prophet. [illegible]

4:6 turn the hearts of fathers to their children. [illegible]

lest I come and strike the land with a decree. [illegible]

3:10 storehouse. [illegible]

put me to the test. [illegible]

windows of heaven. [illegible]

3:13 [illegible]

3:14 vain. [illegible]

3:15 [illegible]

3:16 [illegible]

book of remembrance. [illegible]

INTRODUCTION TO THE

Intertestamental Period

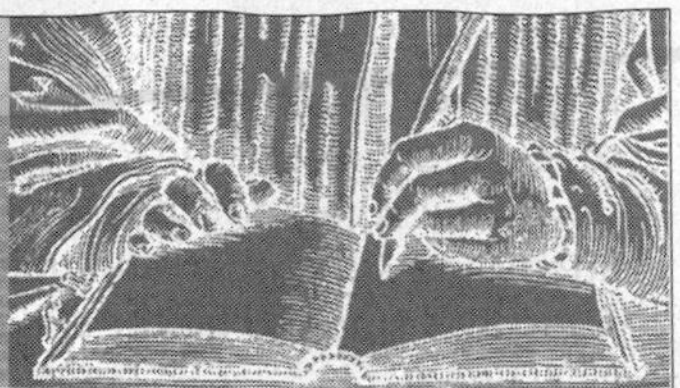

As the history of the Old Testament drew to a close, the Hebrew community was chastened, divided, and expectant. It was chastened because the people recognized the grievous sin that led the Lord to judge them. It was also divided. Many Jews had returned from exile and were worshiping God in Jerusalem, but many more had stayed in Persia, and still others had settled in Egypt and elsewhere. This scattering of the Jewish population is called the "Diaspora." But most of all, the people had not abandoned faith and hope. They knew the covenant promises of God to Abraham. They remembered the mighty arm of the Lord who redeemed His people from Egypt. And in them was developing an expectation for the Messiah who would accomplish God's saving purposes for His people and bring them the new Exodus they longed for.

Turning the page from the Book of Malachi to the first chapter of the New Testament is a leap of more than four hundred years. The Jews witnessed drastic changes in the surrounding cultures; inevitably, they too underwent serious internal transformation. The Persian Empire had given way to the whirlwind conquests of Alexander the Great. In the last third of the fourth century B.C., Alexander brought Greek culture, or "Hellenism," to the places he conquered, including much of the Middle East. After this, the affairs of the Jewish people were largely determined by confrontation with Greek culture.

THE PTOLEMIES

Alexander the Great died in 323 B.C., and Palestine came under the rule of one of his Greek generals, Ptolemy, who also ruled Egypt. Little is known about life in Judea under the Ptolemies. Apparently, the Jews retained considerable freedom to practice their religion as well as a measure of self-rule under their own high priest. His office originally had a strictly religious purpose, but in the absence of a Jewish king, the office became the Jews' major political symbol. At the same time the community felt increasing pressure to adopt Greek ways of life.

The Jewish colony in Alexandria, Egypt, seems to have flourished under the Ptolemies. Being in the capital city of a pagan culture, however, the colony had a direct need to reckon with the new environment. Some Jewish intellectuals wanted to teach Gentiles the history of the Hebrews. Others attempted to combine biblical religion with Greek philosophy, a process that culminated some time later in the allegorical interpretations of Philo of Alexandria. Among various literary productions, the translation of the Pentateuch from Hebrew into Greek was completed late in the third century B.C. This work, along with the later translations of the other Old Testament books, is called the Septuagint (commonly abbreviated with the Roman numeral "LXX"), named for the seventy scholars who according to tradition participated in the original translation. The New Testament authors wrote in Greek, and they often used the Septuagint when quoting the Old Testament.

THE SELEUCIDS

Another of Alexander's generals, Seleucus, became ruler of an empire that eventually extended from the western coast of Asia Minor (modern Turkey) to Babylon and beyond in the east. The Seleucid Empire established its capital in Antioch of Syria, north of Palestine, and presented a continual challenge to the Ptolemaic rulers. Finally, in 198 B.C., the Seleucid ruler Antiochus III was able to occupy Palestine.

No doubt the Jews were affected immediately by this change, but it was with the accession of Antiochus IV in 175 B.C. that Judea entered one of the most difficult periods ever faced by any Hebrew community. Also known as

Epiphanes ("God manifest"), Antiochus IV began to feel the threat of the Romans, who were slowly but surely advancing to the east. In an attempt to strengthen and unify his empire, Antiochus stepped up the process of Hellenizing Palestine.

Some Jews welcomed this development and embraced the new culture, in effect rejecting their religious identity. Such apostasy strengthened the resolve of other Jews to resist the policies of Antiochus. He did not understand the character of Judaism, and unleashed the terrors of religious persecution. Copies of the Hebrew Scriptures were burned, observance of the Sabbath was prohibited, circumcision was outlawed—and violators were put to death. In 167 B.C., Antiochus desecrated the Jewish temple by setting up a statue of Zeus and sacrificing pigs to it. Many Jews regarded this blasphemy as the fulfillment of the prophecy foretelling "the abomination that makes desolate" (Dan. 11:31; 12:11; cf. 9:27).

Shortly after this desecration, the Maccabean Revolt broke out. Under the leadership of Judas Maccabeus, or Judas the "Hammer," small bands of Jewish guerrilla fighters faced and repeatedly defeated large Seleucid armies. The Jews occupied Jerusalem and rededicated the Temple in 164 B.C. This event is still celebrated today in the Jewish feast of Hanukkah. The history of these and some subsequent events is related in 1 Maccabees, one of the group of books known as the Apocrypha (or in the Roman Catholic Church, the Deuterocanonicals).

THE HASMONEANS

Having tasted victory, the Jews were not happy with simply regaining the right to practice their religion. They fought to regain political freedom as well—something they had not enjoyed since their return from exile in Babylon in the sixth century B.C. After the death of Judas, his brothers Jonathan and Simon continued the war until 142, when Judea became independent and the Hasmonean dynasty was established. The name is derived from Hashmon, an ancestor of the Maccabees.

But the struggle with Hellenization was not over. Even before independence, Jonathan Maccabeus had taken over the office of high priest, despite his not belonging to the proper family (the line of Zadok). According to many scholars, it was this event that led a group of strict Jews to turn away from their nation and establish the Essene community of Qumran, near the Dead Sea. Considering themselves the true Israel, this community developed a monastic lifestyle. They interpreted the Old Testament prophecies as being fulfilled in their midst, and looked forward to a final and imminent war that would destroy God's enemies. An extensive collection of their literature—the Dead Sea Scrolls—was discovered in 1947.

The Hasmonean (Maccabean) rulers dominated the priesthood. They progressively adopted Greek ways of life. In general, they received the support of the Sadducees, an aristocratic group that sought to preserve political stability. This conservative "party" acknowledged only the Pentateuch as fully authoritative (while other books had a lesser authority) and on those grounds resisted the doctrine of the resurrection (cf. Matt. 22:23–33; Acts 23:6–8). The historical origin of the Sadducees, as well as that of the Pharisees, cannot be pinpointed. Both groups are first mentioned by the historian Josephus in connection with the rule of John Hyrcanus I (134–104 B.C.).

The Pharisees, though not primarily a political group, may be regarded as the party of the opposition for much of this period. They protested the inroads of Hellenization in Jewish life, developed an extensive oral tradition, and generally sought to preserve the purity regulations of Judaism. By means of their interpretations of the law, however, they altered many of the biblical requirements. This practice in effect lowered the standards of God's holiness and helped foster the illusion that people could please God by their own efforts (Mark 7:1–13; Luke 18:9–14).

THE ROMANS

In spite of some periods of prosperity, the Hasmonean dynasty, torn by internal strife, was unable to resist the advance of the Romans. In 63 B.C., the Roman general Pompey occupied Jerusalem. Continuing unrest led the Romans to make Herod the king of Judea. He was an Idumean by birth, but also a Jewish proselyte. He ruled from 37 B.C. until his death in 4 B.C.

Herod was obedient to Rome and ruled efficiently. His building projects, such as the construction of an artificial port in Caesarea—an astonishing engineering feat—made him famous in the ancient world. Of particular importance was his rebuilding of the temple in Jerusalem, an ambitious venture that began in 20 B.C. and continued until long after his death (John 2:20). These and other accomplishments earned him his name "Herod the Great." Unfortunately, Herod's vices overshadowed his strengths. Egotistical, jealous, and distrustful, Herod at times was a madman, going so far as to murder some of his own children.

As the New Testament story begins, the Jews are subjected to a foreign power, ruled by an able but despotic figure, and still waiting for a salvation yet unfulfilled.

THE NEW TESTAMENT

INTRODUCTION TO THE

Gospels and Acts

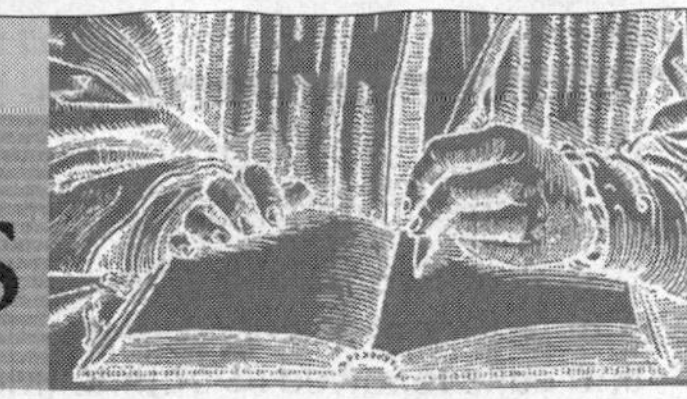

HISTORICAL BACKGROUND

When Jesus was born, Herod the Great was ruler of Judea and Samaria. Herod died in 4 B.C. and his kingdom passed to his son Archelaus (Matt. 2:19–22). Archelaus was guilty of misrule and was banished in A.D. 6. As a result, Judea and Samaria came directly under Roman administration through a series of governors or prefects, later known as procurators. Pontius Pilate was procurator of Judea during the ministry of Jesus.

The province of Galilee, where Jesus lived, had been given by Herod the Great to another of his sons, Herod Antipas (Matt. 14:1–12; Luke 23:6–15). In A.D. 39 Galilee passed to Herod Agrippa, a grandson of Herod the Great. A childhood friend of Agrippa was now the Roman emperor Claudius, and he made Agrippa king of Judea and Samaria as well. Agrippa was popular with the Jews, but his reign was short. He persecuted the apostles, and when he did not refuse to be praised as if he were a god, he was punished with sickness and died (A.D. 44; Acts 12:1–4, 19–23).

Agrippa's territory reverted to Roman governors, though a small portion was given to Agrippa II (Acts 25:13–26:32). Tensions between Judea and Rome increased during this period and led to a revolt in A.D. 66. The ensuing war was disastrous for the Jewish nation. In A.D. 70 Jerusalem was destroyed with terrible suffering.

CHARACTER OF NEW TESTAMENT NARRATIVE

Like the historical writings of the Old Testament, the Gospels and Acts do not provide us with every historical detail we might be interested in. The events included were carefully selected to present clearly and powerfully the message of the gospel.

It has long been noticed that the Gospels are not ordinary biographies. Two of them say nothing about Jesus' birth, and only one event from His youth has been recorded (Luke 2:41–52). Unlike what one would expect from a biography, a large proportion of each Gospel is devoted to the last week of Jesus' ministry. In the Book of Acts, only two apostles, Peter and Paul, are prominent. Moreover, the author gives about as much space to two "unproductive" years of imprisonment in Paul's life as he does to the apostle's three missionary journeys, which lasted at least seven years. Clearly, these books were not written to satisfy our curiosity but to proclaim a message.

When reading the New Testament narratives, therefore, we should make a special effort to determine why particular events were included. A detail that may seem insignificant at first sight (e.g., Paul's vow recorded in Acts 18:18) may subsequently prove quite important (Acts 21:20–24). Moreover, it is significant that God has given us four Gospels and not only one. Since many events in Jesus' life are recorded in more than one Gospel, we can discern their significance by reading about them in several books, each of which has its own theological points of emphasis.

THE SYNOPTIC PROBLEM

Even a quick reading of the four Gospels reveals that three of them (Matthew, Mark, and Luke) are alike, especially when contrasted with John. With a few important exceptions, the events and teachings included in John (e.g., chs. 3; 9; 11; 14) are not found in the first three Gospels, while these three have much material in common and share a similar perspective. For these reasons, the first three Gospels are called the "Synoptics."

A more detailed comparison, however, reveals a wide variety of differences as well as similarities. Sometimes the material recorded is exactly alike, while at other times there are minor verbal differences. In some cases the order of events is the same, but often it is not. From a literary point of view, these facts raise difficult questions. How did the Gospels originate? Did their authors use each other's work, and did they have other materials available to them?

The prevailing answer to these questions is that Mark was the first Gospel and that Matthew and Luke followed its outline (Mark 2:1–22; cf. Matt. 9:2–17; Luke 5:18–38). But Matthew and Luke have in common some important material not found in Mark (e.g., Matt. 7:24–27; Luke 6:47–49). This is explained by the suggestion that a second document, no longer extant, was used by these two writers. This solution is known as the "Two-Source Theory." In addition, clearly Matthew and Luke each had access to much unique information found only in their Gospels.

This proposal cannot account for all the facts, and alternate theories have been suggested. Some argue for the priority of Matthew rather than Mark; a few suggest that Luke was written first. Some have even argued that John was first. A number of scholars emphasize an oral tradition that must have preceded the writing of these documents, downplaying their literary interdependence. Most New Testament specialists continue to use the Two-Source approach as a working hypothesis but recognize that many questions remain unanswered.

Ultimately, God's guidance through inspiration was the controlling factor. God used historical developments as well as the personal research of the Gospel writers to accomplish His purposes (cf. Luke 1:1–4). Scholarly work on history and literature should therefore not be despised, since it often sheds light on the text. On the other hand, our confidence in the truth of Scripture does not rest on the ability of specialists to sort out literary problems, but on God's power to fulfill His promises (Is. 55:10, 11; 2 Tim. 3:16, 17).

THE GOSPEL ACCORDING TO

Matthew

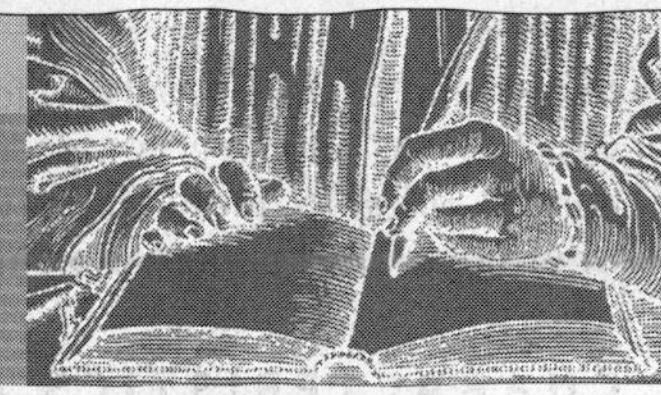

AUTHOR

Although this Gospel does not name its author, some early manuscripts have the inscription "according to Matthew," and Eusebius (c. A.D. 260–340) tells us that the early church father Papias (c. A.D. 60–130) spoke of Matthew as having arranged the "oracles" about Jesus. Subsequent tradition is unanimous that the disciple Matthew, also called Levi (9:9–13; Mark 2:13–17), was the author of this Gospel, and not until the eighteenth century was this tradition doubted.

There are some problems with the tradition. First, Papias apparently said that Matthew "arranged the oracles in the Hebrew dialect." This statement seems to indicate that Matthew wrote in Hebrew or Aramaic, and scholars point out that Matthew does not read like a translation from these languages. It is also quite similar to Mark (see "Introduction to the Gospels and Acts"), which was certainly written in Greek. It is possible that Matthew wrote in both Hebrew and Greek, much as Calvin wrote works in both Latin and French.

Secondly, since Papias did not say "gospel" but "oracles," some have identified these "oracles" as one of the sources lying behind our Gospels. But Eusebius appears to have understood "oracles" to mean "gospel," and Irenaeus (writing about A.D. 180) speaks of a "gospel" by Matthew written "for the Hebrews in their own dialect."

Other objections to Matthew's authorship are more speculative. Some suggest that the Gospel may have been the product of a group of writers ("school"). Its alleged dependence on Mark and supposedly late composition (see "Date and Occasion") are given as reasons to doubt Matthew's authorship. But these objections do not disprove the tradition that Matthew was the sole author.

Since the author did not identify himself, he probably thought that it was not essential for his readers to know his name. Working through the human author was the primary Author, the Holy Spirit.

DATE AND OCCASION

The earliest reference to the Gospel of Matthew is probably in the *Epistle to the Smyrnaeans* by Ignatius of Antioch (c. A.D. 110). Almost no one dates the book later than A.D. 100. Some scholars have dated it as early as A.D. 50, but many critics date it after the destruction of Jerusalem, usually between 80 and 100. Their reasons include the assumption that Jesus could not have predicted such future events as the destruction of Jerusalem, the view that the Gospel's trinitarian theology (28:19) and exalted christology (11:27) are late ideas that developed in a Hellenistic environment, and the assertion that the word "Rabbi" (mentioned in 23:5–10) was not used as a title before A.D. 70.

Some of these reasons, such as that Jesus could not have predicted the future or that a high christology is Hellenistic and therefore late, are highly dubious and reflect a rejection of supernatural revelation. Further, there is some evidence in the context of the book that Matthew was written before the destruction of Jerusalem in A.D. 70. The Gospel warns against the Sadducees, a group that rapidly declined from prominence after A.D. 70 and ultimately ceased to exist. The language used to describe the destruction of Jerusalem in ch. 24 reflects Old Testament prophecies of the divine judgment that Jesus foresaw as connected with the coming of His kingdom. There is no need to explain the content of ch. 24 as the author's memory of a historical event.

The writer of this Gospel probably used the Gospel of Mark. Assuming that Mark was composed with the help of the apostle Peter in Rome, an appropriate date for Matthew would be between A.D. 64 and 70.

Antioch in Syria is the most likely location for

the writing of the Gospel and for the church for which it was originally composed. Ignatius, the earliest writer to quote Matthew, was bishop of Antioch. The congregation in Antioch was of mixed Jewish and Gentile origin (Acts 15), and this would account for the problems of legalism and antinomianism that Matthew particularly addresses.

CHARACTERISTICS AND THEMES

Like all the Gospels, Matthew's purpose is to convey authoritative teaching by and about Jesus, whose coming marks the fulfillment of God's promises and the presence of God's kingdom. Matthew makes no division between history and theology. His history is the basis of the theology, and the theology gives its proper meaning to the history.

Matthew makes extensive use of "fulfillment" references to the Old Testament. His citations are not presented as isolated predictions and fulfillments, but as proof of the fulfillment of all the expectations of the Old Testament. This concern affects the way Matthew stresses certain elements in the history. Matthew shows us the illegality of the Sanhedrin's actions in the trial of Jesus (26:57–68), the distortion of the Old Testament by the scribes and Pharisees (15:1–9), and the covenantal nature of God's dealing with His people.

Also distinctive to Matthew is his presentation of the teaching of Jesus in five major discourses: ethics, discipleship and mission, the kingdom of heaven, the church, and the end time. These five divisions may have been patterned after the five books of Moses, to present Jesus as the Prophet like Moses of Deut. 18:18. Most scholars today recognize the five teaching discourses as the key to Matthew's basic design, especially since each discourse ends with an expression such as, "And when Jesus finished these sayings" (7:28). Further, there seems to be a relationship between each discourse and the narrative preceding it. Also note that the narrative portions deal primarily with the question of the King's identity, while the discourse material tends to focus on the King's people.

INTERPRETIVE DIFFICULTIES

Scholars today are in general agreement that both Matthew and Luke made use of the Gospel of Mark in writing their own Gospels (see "Introduction to the Gospels and Acts"). However, Matthew and Luke do not follow Mark at every point in the order of events of Jesus' life, or the order of His teachings. Matthew and Luke have some material in common not found in Mark, but here too they differ in its placement within Jesus' ministry.

To understand the chronology of the Gospels it is important to note that Mark's own account is not a complete diary. John reports that Jesus visited Jerusalem several times during a period of about three years, while in Mark the events are presented in what appears to be one year ending with a single, climactic visit to Jerusalem. In other words, the Holy Spirit had already led Mark in selecting and presenting the events of Jesus' ministry in a particular way. Matthew and Luke similarly were led by the Spirit in their own selection and presentation of events.

The Gospels do not simply present a schedule of Jesus' activities. Nor are they modern, technical biographies that follow methods unknown in their own day. The three Synoptic Gospels are individual and complementary works; they are not three incomplete attempts to do the same task. They are spiritual books; together with the Gospel of John they offer Jesus Christ, the incarnate Word, to all generations.

OUTLINE OF MATTHEW

I. Prologue (chs. 1; 2)

A. *The Genealogy of the King (1:1–17)*

B. *The Birth of the King (1:18–2:23)*

1. Announcement to Joseph and Child's Birth (1:18–25)
2. Adoration by the Wise Men (2:1–12)
3. "Out of Egypt I Called My Son" (2:13–23)

II. The Kingdom Comes (chs. 3–7)

A. *Initiating the Kingdom in Jesus (3:1–4:11)*

1. Jesus Baptized by John (ch. 3)
2. The Temptation in the Wilderness (4:1–11)

B. *Announcing the Kingdom (4:12–25)*

C. *First Discourse: Sermon on the Mount (chs. 5–7)*

1. The Beatitudes (5:1–12)
2. Interpreting the Law for the Kingdom (5:13–48)
3. Piety in the Kingdom: Charity, Prayer and Fasting (6:1–18)
4. A Heart for the Kingdom (6:19–34)
5. Standards of Judgment in the Kingdom (ch. 7)

III. The Works of the Kingdom (chs. 8–10)

A. *Healing the Sick and Calling Disciples (chs. 8; 9)*

B. *Second Discourse: Kingdom Mission (ch. 10)*

IV. The Nature of the Kingdom (chs. 11–13)

A. *The Identity of John and of Jesus (chs. 11; 12)*

1. Responding to the Works of Jesus and John (ch. 11)
2. Jesus, Lord of the Sabbath (12:1–13)
3. The Beginning of Opposition to Jesus (12:14–50)

B. *Third Discourse: Kingdom Parables (ch. 13)*

V. The Authority of the Kingdom (chs. 14–18)

A. *Jesus' Character and Authority (chs. 14–17)*

1. The Death of John the Baptist (14:1–12)
2. Feeding the Multitudes and the Leaven of the Pharisees (14:13–16:12)
3. Revealing the Son of God and His Mission (16:13–17:27)

B. *Fourth Discourse: Character and Authority of the Church (ch. 18)*

VI. Kingdom Blessings and Kingdom Judgments (chs. 19–25)

A. *From Galilee to Jerusalem (chs. 19; 20)*

1. Family Life Within the Kingdom (19:1–15)
2. Entering the Kingdom (19:16–20:16)
3. Opening the Eyes of the Spiritually and Physically Blind (20:17–34)

B. *The King Enters Jerusalem (chs. 21–23)*

1. Triumphal Entry and Cleansing the Temple (21:1–22)
2. Parables of Resistance to the King (21:23–22:14)
3. Conflict with the Pharisees and Sadducees (22:15–23:39)

C. *Fifth Discourse: Kingdom Judgment (chs. 24; 25)*

1. Signs of the End of the Age (24:1–31)
2. Parables Counseling Vigilance (24:32–25:46)

VII. Passion and Resurrection (chs. 26–28)

A. *Betrayal and Arrest (26:1–56)*

1. Preparing for Jesus' Death (26:1–16)
2. Last Supper and Gethsemane (26:17–56)

B. *The Trial and Execution of the King (26:57–27:56)*

1. Religious Trial Before the Sanhedrin (26:57–75)
2. Civil Trial Before Pilate (27:1–26)
3. The Crucifixion (27:27–56)

C. *Burial and Resurrection (27:57–28:20)*

1. Guarding the Tomb (27:57–66)
2. The Resurrection (28:1–15)
3. The Great Commission (28:16–20)

The Genealogy of Jesus Christ

1 [a]The book of the genealogy of Jesus
Christ, [b]the son of David, [c]the son of
Abraham.
2 [d]Abraham was the father of Isaac, and
[e]Isaac the father of Jacob, and [f]Jacob the
father of Judah and his brothers, 3 and
[g]Judah the father of Perez and Zerah by
Tamar, and Perez the father of Hezron, and
Hezron the father of Ram,[1] 4 and Ram the
father of Amminadab, and Amminadab the
father of Nahshon, and Nahshon the father
of Salmon, 5 and Salmon the father of Boaz
by [h]Rahab, and Boaz the father of Obed by
Ruth, and Obed the father of Jesse, 6 and
[i]Jesse the father of David the king.
And [j]David was the father of Solomon by
[k]the wife of Uriah, 7 and [l]Solomon the father
of Rehoboam, and Rehoboam the father of
Abijah, and Abijah the father of Asaph,[2]
8 and Asaph the father of Jehoshaphat, and
Jehoshaphat the father of Joram, [m]and
Joram the father of Uzziah, 9 and Uzziah
the father of Jotham, and Jotham the father
of Ahaz, and Ahaz the father of Hezekiah,
10 and Hezekiah the father of Manasseh,
and Manasseh the father of Amos,[3] and
Amos the father of Josiah, 11 and [n]Josiah
the father of [o]Jechoniah and his brothers,
at the time of the deportation to Babylon.
12 And after the deportation to Babylon:
[p]Jechoniah was the father of [q]Shealtiel,[4]
and [r]Shealtiel the father of Zerubbabel,
13 and Zerubbabel the father of Abiud, and
Abiud the father of Eliakim, and Eliakim
the father of Azor, 14 and Azor the father of
Zadok, and Zadok the father of Achim, and
Achim the father of Eliud, 15 and Eliud the
father of Eleazar, and Eleazar the father of
Matthan, and Matthan the father of Jacob,
16 and Jacob the father of [s]Joseph the husband of Mary, of whom Jesus was born,
who is called Christ.
17 So all the generations from Abraham to
David were fourteen generations, and from
David to the deportation to Babylon fourteen generations, and from the deportation
to Babylon to [t]the Christ fourteen generations.

The Birth of Jesus Christ

18 Now the birth of [u]Jesus Christ[5] took
place in this way. [v]When his mother Mary
had been betrothed[6] to Joseph, before they
came together she was found to be with
child [w]from the Holy Spirit. 19 And her husband Joseph, being a just man and unwilling [x]to put her to shame, resolved to
divorce her quietly. 20 But as he considered
these things, behold, [y]an angel of the Lord
appeared to him in a dream, saying,
"Joseph, son of David, do not fear to take
Mary as your wife, for that which is conceived in her is from the Holy Spirit. 21 She
will bear a son, and [z]you shall call his
name Jesus, [a]for he will save his people
from their sins." 22 [b]All this took place [c]to

Chapter 1
1 [a][Luke 3:23-38] [b]2 Sam. 7:12-16; Ps. 132:11; Isai. 11:1; Jer. 23:5; Luke 1:32, 69; John 7:42; Acts 2:30; 13:23; Rom. 1:3; 2 Tim. 2:8; Rev. 22:16 [c]Gen. 22:18; Gal. 3:16; [Rom. 9:5]
2 [d]Gen. 21:3 [e]Gen. 25:26 [f]Gen. 29:35
3 [g][Ruth 4:18-22; 1 Chr. 2:1-15]
5 [h]Josh. 6:25
6 [i]1 Sam. 16:1; 17:12 [j]2 Sam. 12:24 [k]2 Sam. 12:10
7 [l]For ver. 7-10, see 1 Chr. 3:10-14
8 [m][2 Kin. 15:1; 1 Chr. 3:11, 12]
11 [n]1 Chr. 3:15, 16 [o]Esth. 2:6; Jer. 24:1; 27:20
12 [p]1 Chr. 3:17-19 [q]Luke 3:27 [r]Ezra 3:2
16 [s]Luke 3:23
17 [t]ch. 2:4; 11:2; 16:16; 22:42; 23:10; Mark 8:29; Luke 3:15; [John 1:41; 4:25]
18 [u]ver. 1; Mark 1:1; John 1:17; 17:3; [ver. 16] [v]Luke 1:27 [w]Luke 1:35
19 [x][Deut. 24:1]
20 [y]ch. 2:13, 19; [ch. 2:12, 22] **21** [z]ver. 25; Luke 1:31; 2:21 [a]Luke 2:11; Acts 4:12; 5:31; 13:23, 38; [Acts 3:26] **22** [b]ch. 21:4; 26:56; John 19:36 [c]ch. 2:15, 23; 4:14; Mark 14:49

[1] Greek *Aram*; also verse 4 [2] *Asaph* is probably an alternate spelling for *Asa*; some manuscripts read *Asa*; also verse 8 [3] *Amos* is probably an alternate spelling for *Amon*; some manuscripts read *Amon*; twice in this verse [4] Greek *Salathiel*; twice in this verse [5] Some manuscripts *of the Christ* [6] That is, legally pledged to be married

1:1 book of the genealogy. The same phrase is used at Gen. 2:4; 5:1 in the Septuagint, the Greek translation of the Old Testament in common use following 150 B.C. Here it may refer not only to the genealogy immediately following, but to the account of Jesus' birth or the Gospel as a whole also.

Christ. This title comes from the Greek word *Christos,* meaning "anointed." "Messiah" represents the Hebrew word for "anointed"; see note 1 Sam. 2:10. In the Old Testament, anointing with oil could be performed for the office of prophet, priest, or king (Ex. 29:7; 1 Sam. 16:13; 1 Kin. 19:16). The Old Testament promises the coming of the righteous Servant of the Lord (Is. 42:1–9), who will be a prophet like Moses (Deut. 18:18, 19), a priest like Melchizedek (Ps. 110:4), and a king like David, the Lord's anointed (Is. 55:3–5; Jer. 30:9; Ezek. 34:24; Hos. 3:5; Zech. 12:8). Matthew reveals that Jesus is the Christ, the promised King and Deliverer.

1:2 The specifics of this genealogy differ from the one found in Luke; see note Luke 3:23–38.

1:3–16 Women are not usually named in Near Eastern genealogies, but they are intrinsic to God's purpose in sending Christ. The five women named in Jesus' genealogy all remind us that God often does the unexpected and chooses the unlikely. Tamar (v. 3) reminds us of Judah's failures (Gen. 38:6–30); Rahab (v. 5) was a harlot (Josh. 2); Ruth was a Moabite (Ruth 1:4) and thus subject to a special curse (Deut. 23:3–5); Uriah's wife Bathsheba (v. 6) was David's downfall (2 Sam. 11). Mary fulfills Is. 7:14 (v. 23), and the even more important promise of Gen. 3:15 (Gal. 4:4).

1:17 fourteen generations. Matthew organizes the genealogy into three groups of fourteen to show that God has a purpose in history. The early history leading to David, the monarchy leading to the Exile in Babylon, and the history of Israel after the Exile all lead up to, and point to Christ. Jechoniah (Jehoiachin) is included in both the second and third groups of fourteen; this enumeration is in keeping with Matthew's abbreviation of the genealogy (v. 5 cf. Josh. 2; v. 8 cf. 2 Chr. 21:4–26:13).

1:19 Joseph . . . resolved to divorce her quietly. Engagement was almost as binding as marriage, and infidelity during betrothal made divorce almost obligatory.

1:21 Jesus. The Greek equivalent of "Joshua," meaning "Yahweh is salvation," or "Yahweh saves." Often in names only the first syllable of God's name is used (e.g., *Eli*jah; *Isa*iah; *Jo*shua).

fulfill what the Lord had spoken by the
prophet:

23 [d]"Behold, the virgin shall conceive and
bear a son,
and they shall call his name
[e]Immanuel"

(which means, God [f]with us). 24 When
Joseph woke from sleep, he did as the
angel of the Lord commanded him: he
took his wife, 25 but knew her not until
she had given birth to a son. And [g]he called
his name Jesus.

The Visit of the Wise Men

2 Now [h]after Jesus was born in [i]Beth-
lehem of Judea [j]in the days of Herod
the king, behold, wise men[1] from [k]the east
came to Jerusalem, 2 saying, "Where is he
who has been born [l]king of the Jews? For
we saw [m]his star when it rose[2] and have
come to [n]worship him." 3 When Herod the
king heard this, he was troubled, and all
Jerusalem with him; 4 and assembling all
the chief priests and scribes of the people,
he inquired of them where [o]the Christ was
to be born. 5 They told him, "In Bethlehem
of Judea, for so it is written by the prophet:

6 [p]"'And you, O Bethlehem, in the land
of Judah,
are by no means least among the
rulers of Judah;
for from you shall come a ruler
who will [q]shepherd my people
Israel.'"

7 Then Herod summoned the wise men
secretly and ascertained from them what
time the star had appeared. 8 And he sent
them to Bethlehem, saying, "Go and search
diligently for the child, and when you have
found him, bring me word, that I too may
come and worship him." 9 After listening to
the king, they went on their way. And
behold, the star that they had seen when it
rose went before them until it came to rest
over the place where the child was. 10 When
they saw the star, they rejoiced exceedingly with great joy. 11 And going into the
house they saw the child with Mary his
mother, and they fell down and worshiped
him. Then, opening their treasures, [r]they
offered him gifts, [s]gold and [t]frankincense
and [u]myrrh. 12 And [v]being warned [w]in a
dream not to return to Herod, they departed to their own country by another way.

The Flight to Egypt

13 Now when they had departed, behold,
[x]an angel of the Lord appeared to Joseph in
a dream and said, "Rise, take the child and
his mother, and flee to Egypt, and remain
there until I tell you, for Herod is about to
search for the child, to destroy him." 14 And
he rose and took the child and his mother
by night and departed to Egypt 15 and
remained there until the death of Herod.
[y]This was to fulfill what the Lord had spoken by the prophet, [z]"Out of Egypt I called
my son."

Herod Kills the Children

16 Then Herod, when he saw that he had
been tricked by the wise men, became furious, and he sent and killed all the male
children in Bethlehem and in all that
region who were two years old or under,

[1] Greek *magi*; also verses 7, 16 [2] Or *in the east*; also verse 9

23 [d]Cited from Isai. 7:14 [e]Isai. 8:8, 10 [f]See ch. 28:20
25 [g]ver. 21
Chapter 2
1 [h]Luke 2:4-7 [i]Luke 2:15; John 7:42 [j]Luke 1:5 [k][Gen. 25:6; 1 Kin. 4:30]
2 [l]ch. 27:11, 37; Jer. 23:5; 30:9; Zech. 9:9 [m][Num. 24:17; Rev. 22:16] [n]See ch. 8:2
4 [o]See ch. 1:17
6 [p]Cited from Mic. 5:2 [q]Ezek. 34:23; John 21:15-17; [2 Sam. 5:2; Rev. 7:17]
11 [r][1 Sam. 9:7; Ps. 72:10] [s]Isai. 60:6 [t]Rev. 18:13 [u]Ex. 30:23; Ps. 45:8; John 19:39
12 [v]ver. 22; [ver. 13, 19] [w][ch. 27:19; Gen. 20:6; 31:11; Num. 12:6; Job 33:15]
13 [x]ver. 19; ch. 1:20; [ver. 12, 22]
15 [y]See ch. 1:22 [z]Cited from Hos. 11:1

1:23 virgin. See note Is. 7:14. Jesus' conception by a virgin is miraculous, announcing that God will soon redeem His people and is present with them. This quotation is the first of a number of Old Testament references Matthew uses to show that Jesus fulfills the Old Testament (2:6, 15, 18, 23 and notes). In the entire Gospel there are twelve such fulfillment formulas, and more than fifty Old Testament quotations. See "The Virgin Birth of Jesus" at Luke 1:27.

2:1 in the days of Herod the king. Herod the Great is known to have died in 4 B.C. Therefore Jesus was actually born in about 5 or 6 B.C. according to the standard dating of the Gregorian calendar.

wise men. The "Magi" were not kings, but priests or court advisers, such as Joseph or Daniel. They were probably from Mesopotamia, the region of ancient Babylon, although other locations east of Palestine have been suggested. There are numerous accounts of ancient astrologers interpreting astronomical phenomena as heralding the birth of kings.

2:2 star. This may have been a planetary conjunction, a supernova, or something purely supernatural. Whatever the case, it alludes to the star of Jacob (Num. 24:17), which was prophesied by another Gentile, Balaam.

2:6 The second line of the quotation in Matthew appears to say the opposite of the second line of Mic. 5:2 ("too little"), but the sense is that though Bethlehem appears to be insignificant, it is in truth important. The religious experts concluded from the prophets that the Messiah was to be born in Bethlehem, but not one of them bothered to make the short journey with the wise men to see Christ.

2:11 house. Jesus was no longer in a stable (Luke 2:7). This visit was some time after the birth (v. 1), perhaps a year or more (cf. v. 16). Although the wise men could scarcely have realized the full symbolic value of their gifts, Matthew records them to show the fulfillment of Old Testament passages where the Gentiles bring their wealth to Israel's king (Ps. 72:10; Is. 60:6).

2:15 fulfill. Hos. 11:1 refers to God's calling His son Israel out of Egypt in the Exodus. Matthew means that the history of God's redemption of Israel points forward to Jesus, the true Son of God.

according to the time that he had ascertained from the wise men. 17 [a]Then was fulfilled what was spoken by the prophet Jeremiah:

18 [b]"A voice was heard in Ramah,
weeping and loud lamentation,
Rachel weeping for her children;
she refused to be comforted,
because they [c]are no more."

The Return to Nazareth

19 But when Herod died, behold, an angel of the Lord appeared in a dream to Joseph in Egypt, 20 saying, "Rise, take the child and his mother and go to the land of Israel, for [d]those who sought the child's life are dead." 21 And he rose and took the child and his mother and went to the land of Israel. 22 But when he heard that Archelaus was reigning over Judea in place of his father Herod, he was afraid to go there, and [e]being warned in a dream he withdrew to the district of Galilee. 23 And he went and lived in a city called [f]Nazareth, [g]that what was spoken by the prophets might be fulfilled: "He shall be called a Nazarene."

John the Baptist Prepares the Way

3 [h]In those days [i]John the Baptist came preaching in [j]the wilderness of Judea, 2 [k]"Repent, for [l]the kingdom of heaven is at hand." 3 For this is he who was spoken of by the prophet Isaiah when he said,

[m]"The voice of one crying in the
wilderness:
[n]'Prepare[1] the way of the Lord;
make his paths straight.'"

4 Now John wore [o]a garment of camel's hair and a leather belt around his waist, and his food was [p]locusts and [q]wild honey. 5 Then Jerusalem and all Judea and all the region about the Jordan were going out to him, 6 and they were baptized by him in the river Jordan, [r]confessing their sins.

7 But when he saw many of [s]the Pharisees and [t]Sadducees coming for baptism, he said to them, [u]"You brood of [v]vipers! Who warned you to flee from [w]the wrath to come? 8 Bear fruit [x]in keeping with repentance. 9 And do not presume to say to yourselves, [y]'We have Abraham as our father,' for I tell you, God is able from [z]these stones to raise up children for Abraham. 10 Even now the axe is laid to the root of the trees. [a]Every tree therefore that does not bear good fruit is cut down and thrown into the fire.

17 [a]ch. 27:9; [ch. 1:22] **18** [b]Cited from Jer. 31:15 [c]Gen. 37:30; 42:13, 36; Lam. 5:7 **20** [d][Ex. 4:19] **22** [e]See ver. 12 **23** [f]ch. 4:13; Mark 1:9; Luke 1:26; 2:39; 4:16; John 1:45 [g]See ch. 1:22
Chapter 3
1 [h]For ver. 1-12, see Mark 1:2-8; Luke 3:2-17 [i]John 1:6, 7 [j]Josh. 15:61; [Judg. 1:16] **2** [k]ch. 4:17; Mark 1:15 [l]ch. 10:7; Dan. 2:44; [ch. 6:10]
3 [m]John 1:23; Cited from Isai. 40:3 [n]Luke 1:76 **4** [o]2 Kin. 1:8; Zech. 13:4; [Heb. 11:37] [p]Lev. 11:22 [q]1 Sam. 14:26 **6** [r]Acts 19:18 **7** [s]ch. 23:13, 15 [t]ch. 22:23 [u]ch. 12:34; 23:33 [v]Ps. 140:3 [w]Rom. 5:9; Eph. 5:6; Col. 3:6; 1 Thess. 1:10 **8** [x]Acts 26:20 **9** [y]John 8:39 [z][ch. 4:3]

10 [a]ch. 7:19; Luke 13:7, 9; John 15:2, 6

[1] Or *crying: Prepare in the wilderness*

2:18 Matthew is quoting from Jer. 31:15, from a prophecy about the return of Israel from exile. Rachel, the mother, represents all Israel in her weeping, and the departure of Christ to Egypt is like the departure of Rachel's sons, Joseph and Benjamin, to Egypt (Gen. 37:28; 43:15).

2:23 He shall be called a Nazarene. The Old Testament has no verse exactly corresponding to this, but note that Matthew introduces this reference to the prophets in more general terms than his other quotations. Nazareth was Christ's home, but Matthew's point is probably that Jesus would be despised, as people from Nazareth were (John 1:46; 7:42, 52). Is. 11:1 refers to the Messiah as a "branch" (Hebrew *netzer*) from the roots of Jesse; this verse may have been in mind.

3:2 Repent. The first command of both John the Baptist and Jesus (4:17). Repentance is not just sorrow for sin but a decisive change, a turning away from sin and to a life of obedience. "Repent" translates the Old Testament call to Israel to "return" to faithfulness to the covenant. It does not mean self-punishment, depression, or remorse. Judas was sorrowful and distressed (27:3) but he did not repent. See "Repentance" at Acts 26:20.

kingdom of heaven. The message of John the Baptist introduces the theme of Jesus' teaching. Mark and Luke call it the "kingdom of God" (4:17; cf. Mark 1:15). The kingdom or the reign of God is what the Old Testament prophets awaited: God's display of His sovereignty in the redemption of His people. John and Jesus proclaimed that the time of waiting was over and the King Himself had come. With the death and resurrection of Jesus and the spread of the good news to all nations, the Old Testament promises of God have been largely fulfilled for us, although we still await their complete realization when Christ returns in judgment (ch. 13 and notes).

is at hand. The beginning of God's work is the basis for the command to repent.

3:3 this is he. John the Baptist proclaims the coming of the Lord, using Is. 40:3. John's ministry pointed forward, like the Old Testament prophets, to a greater One who would follow (11:7–11; Acts 19:4, 5).

3:6 baptized. Christian baptism is not identical with the baptism of John for, although it retains the symbolism of repentance and purification (Acts 22:16; Eph. 5:26), it is performed in the name of the triune God (28:19) and symbolizes our union with Christ in His death and resurrection (Rom. 6:3–6; 1 Cor. 12:13; Gal. 3:27; Col. 2:12). See note Mark 1:4.

3:7 the wrath to come. The Old Testament promised the coming of the Lord in righteous judgment (Ps. 96:13; Zeph. 2:1, 2; Mal. 3:2). John will not allow the leaders to suppose that the cup of God's wrath is only for Israel's enemies, and that their own nation will escape. John was later puzzled that Jesus did not bring judgment (11:2, 3 and note).

3:8 fruit in keeping with repentance. Acts indicating an inner righteousness, not merely outward conformity. Since the Pharisees considered themselves to be the righteous of their day, the words of John must have cut deep.

3:9 Abraham as our father. Although being Jewish includes outward covenant privileges (Rom. 9:4, 5), the true children of God are so only by virtue of God's act. Only God can apply the water that changes hearts of stone (Ezek. 36:25, 26). Neither a Jew by birth nor a Christian by birth can expect to be spared judgment apart from the fruit that gives evidence of repentance and faith.

3:10 is cut down. Just as the kingdom is imminent, so is judgment; the coming of one implies the other. John did not yet know that Jesus'

11 [b]"I baptize you with water [c]for repentance, but [d]he who is coming after me is
mightier than I, whose sandals I am not
worthy to carry. He will baptize you [e]with
the Holy Spirit and with [f]fire. 12 His [g]win-
nowing fork is in his hand, and he will
clear his threshing floor and [h]gather his
wheat into the barn, [i]but the chaff he will
burn with [j]unquenchable fire."

The Baptism of Jesus

13 [k]Then Jesus came [l]from Galilee to the
Jordan to John, to be baptized by him.
14 [m]John would have prevented him, saying,
"I need to be baptized by you, and do you
come to me?" 15 But Jesus answered him,
"Let it be so now, for thus it is fitting for
[n]us to fulfill all righteousness." Then he
consented. 16 And when Jesus was baptized, immediately he went up from the
water, and behold, [o]the heavens were
opened to him,[1] and he [p]saw the Spirit
of God descending like a dove and coming
to rest on him; 17 and behold, [q]a voice from
heaven said, [r]"This is my beloved Son,[2]
with whom I am well pleased."

11 [b]John 1:26; Acts 1:5 [c]Acts 13:24; 19:4 [d]John 1:15, 27; 3:30, 31; Acts 13:25 [e]John 1:33; Acts 11:16 [f][Isai. 4:4; Mal. 3:2, 3; Acts 2:3] 12 [g]Isai. 30:24 [h]ch. 13:30 [i]Mal. 4:1 [j]Mark 9:43, 48 13 [k]For ver. 13-17, see Mark 1:9-11; Luke 3:21, 22; [John 1:32-34] [l]ch. 2:22 14 [m][John 13:6] 15 [n]John 9:4 16 [o]Acts 7:56 [p]John 1:32, 33; [Luke 4:18, 21; Acts 10:38] 17 [q]John 12:28 [r]ch. 17:5; 2 Pet. 1:17; [Ps. 2:7; Isai. 42:1; Eph. 1:6; Col. 1:13; 1 John 5:9]

Chapter 4
1 [s]For ver. 1-11, see Mark 1:12, 13; Luke 4:1-13 [t][Heb. 2:18; 4:15]

The Temptation of Jesus

4 [s]Then Jesus was led up by the Spirit
into the wilderness [t]to be tempted by
the devil. 2 And after fasting [u]forty days and
forty nights, he [v]was hungry. 3 And [w]the
tempter came and said to him, "If you are
[x]the Son of God, command [y]these stones
to become loaves of bread." 4 But he answered, [z]"It is written,

[a]"'Man shall not live by bread alone,
but by every word that comes from
the mouth of God.'"

5 [b]Then the devil took him to [c]the holy city
and set him on the pinnacle of the temple
6 and said to him, "If you are the Son of
God, throw yourself down, for it is written,

[d]"'He will command his angels
concerning you,'

and

2 [u][Deut. 9:9, 18; 1 Kin. 19:8] [v][John 4:6, 7] 3 [w]1 Thess. 3:5 [x]See ch. 14:33 [y][ch. 3:9] 4 [z]ver. 7, 10; Eph. 6:17 [a]Cited from Deut. 8:3; [John 4:34] 5 [b]Luke 4:9 [c]ch. 27:53; Neh. 11:18; Isai. 48:2; 52:1; Rev. 11:2; [Ps. 46:4; 48:1; Rev. 21:2; 22:19] 6 [d]Cited from Ps. 91:11, 12

1 Some manuscripts omit *to him* 2 Or *my Son, my* (or *the*) *Beloved*

immediate task was not to bring judgment, but to bear it Himself (11:2 note).

3:11 with the Holy Spirit and with fire. Cleansing with fire describes God's supernatural baptism, contrasted with the symbol of cleansing with water. The fire of the Spirit renews the people of God and consumes the wicked as chaff (Is. 4:4; Zech. 13:9; Mal. 3:2, 3; 4:1). John's witness to Jesus as the Lord who has come (v. 3) is extended. As Lord, Jesus baptizes with the Spirit and executes the Last Judgment. See "Baptism" at Rom. 6:3.

3:13–15 John was reluctant to baptize Jesus because he recognized that Jesus was the one person who had no need for repentance. But in order for "all righteousness" to be fulfilled, Jesus had to be identified with His people as the bearer of their sins (2 Cor. 5:21). Ultimately John's baptism pointed to Jesus, for only Jesus' death on a cross, which He called a "baptism" (Luke 12:50), could take away sins. Jesus' identification with His people included His baptism and death, His anointment with the Spirit, and His victory over temptation. See "The Baptism of Jesus" at Mark 1:9.

3:15 righteousness. God's kingdom (His sovereign rule in salvation and judgment) is defined by His righteousness. Jesus teaches the perfect righteousness that God requires (5:20, 48); He also secures God's righteousness for sinners. His baptism points to His death as "a ransom for many" (20:28) and shows the perfect obedience in which He fulfills all righteousness (Jer. 23:5, 6). Remission of sins and the gift of righteousness are received through faith in Jesus (8:10; 23:23; cf. 21:32). Those who lack God's righteousness, but hunger and thirst for it, will be filled (5:6; 6:33). Jesus calls those burdened with the load of self-righteousness to find their rest in Him (11:28–12:8).

3:16, 17 The testimony from heaven confirms Jesus' identification as the Servant of the Lord (Is. 42:1; cf. Ex. 4:22) and connects this with the messianic kingship (Ps. 2:7).

3:16 like a dove. The Spirit's appearance in the form of a dove reminds us of the Spirit's creative activity in Gen. 1:2 and may point to the beginning of the new creation through the ministry of Jesus (1:1 note).

4:1 tempted. Although God Himself tempts no one (James 1:13), our temptations are included in His sovereign plan for our good. If we overcome, we are strengthened; if we succumb, we recognize more clearly our need for further sanctification and grace.

The temptation of Jesus (vv. 1–11) parallels the testing of Israel in the wildernesss. The forty days correspond to the forty years of wandering (cf. Num. 14:34). This event recalls Deut. 8:1–5, used by Jesus in response to one of the temptations. The experience of Israel in the wilderness was the type or shadow of Jesus' temptation in the "wilderness" after His baptism.

The temptations appeal to common motivations: physical drives, pride, and the desire for possessions (1 John 2:16). But each is pointed specially at the Messiah. Satan appeals to Jesus in terms of His divine rights: "If You are the Son of God" (vv. 3, 6; cf. 27:40). The third temptation offers Jesus a path to kingship that avoids the Cross. Jesus was tempted in every way just as we are (Heb. 4:15), but He did not sin. He represents us before God as a "merciful and faithful high priest" (Heb. 2:17) because He knows through His human nature what it is to endure temptation. See "The Sinlessness of Jesus" at Heb. 4:15.

4:3 Son of God. See note 16:16.

4:4 by every word. In Deut. 8:3 this refers to God's word of direction in the wilderness and His provision of manna. Jesus will not abandon His trust in God to provide. Jesus replied to each of Satan's temptations with a reference to Scripture. The "sword of the Spirit" is God's Word (Eph. 6:17), and Jesus relied on Scripture for victory in His spiritual struggle. See "The Word of God: Scripture as Revelation" at Ex. 32:16.

4:5 pinnacle of the temple. Part of the temple wall was on the edge of the Kidron Valley with an enormous drop from the top to the bottom.

4:6 Satan quotes Scripture, but he uses Ps. 91:11, 12 in a way exactly opposite to the original meaning. Ps. 91 is an exhortation to trust in God; Satan attempts to replace trust with a test, casting doubt on God's faithfulness. Presumption is not too great a faith but no faith at all. See "Satan" at Job 1:6.

"'On their hands they will bear
you up,
lest you strike your foot against a
stone.'"

7 Jesus said to him, "Again [e]it is written,
[f]'You shall not [g]put the Lord your God to
the test.'" 8 [h]Again, the devil took him to a
very high mountain and showed him all
the kingdoms of the world and their glory.
9 And he said to him, "All these I will give
you, if you will fall down and worship me."
10 Then Jesus said to him, "Be gone, [i]Satan!
For [j]it is written,

[k]"'You shall worship the Lord your
God
and [l]him only shall you serve.'"

11 Then the devil left him, and behold, [m]an-
gels came and were ministering to him.

Jesus Begins His Ministry

12 Now when he heard that [n]John had
been arrested, [o]he withdrew into Galilee.
13 And leaving [p]Nazareth he went and lived
in [q]Capernaum by [r]the sea, in the territory
of [s]Zebulun and Naphtali, 14 [t]so that what
was spoken by the prophet Isaiah might be
fulfilled:

15 [u]"The land of Zebulun and the land of
Naphtali,
the way of the sea, beyond the
Jordan, Galilee of the
Gentiles—
16 [v]the people dwelling in darkness
have seen a great light,
and for those dwelling in the region
and [w]shadow of death,
on them a light has dawned."

7 [e]ver. 4, 10 [f]Cited from Deut. 6:16 [g][Isai. 7:12] 8 [h]Luke 4:5 10 [i]See 1 Chr. 21:1 [j]ver. 4, 7 [k]Cited from Deut. 6:13 [l]1 Sam. 7:3 11 [m]ch. 26:53; Luke 22:43 12 [n]ch. 14:3; Mark 1:14; Luke 3:19, 20; [John 3:24] [o]Luke 4:14 13 [p]See ch. 2:23 [q][ch. 9:1] [r]John 6:1 [s]Josh. 19:32-34 14 [t]See ch. 1:22 15 [u]Cited from Isai. 9:1, 2 16 [v]Isai. 42:7; Luke 1:79 [w]Job 3:5; Ps. 23:4; Amos 5:8 17 [x]Mark 1:14 [y]Acts 1:22; 10:37 [z]ch. 3:2 18 [a]For ver. 18-22, see Mark 1:16-20; [Luke 5:2-11; John 1:40-42] [b]ver. 13 19 [c]ch. 13:47 23 [d]Mark 1:39; Luke 4:15 [e]ch. 9:35; 13:54; Mark 1:21; John 18:20 [f]ch. 24:14; Luke 4:43; [ch. 13:19] [g]ch. 8:16; 14:35, 36; Mark 1:34; 6:55, 56 24 [h]Luke 2:2 [g][See ver. 23 above] [i]ch. 8:6 [j][John 10:21] [k]ch. 17:15 [l]ch. 9:2, 6

17 [x]From that time [y]Jesus began to preach,
saying, [z]"Repent, for the kingdom of heaven
is at hand."

Jesus Calls the First Disciples

18 [a]While walking by [b]the Sea of Galilee,
he saw two brothers, Simon (who is called
Peter) and Andrew his brother, casting a
net into the sea, for they were fishermen.
19 And he said to them, "Follow me, and
I will make you [c]fishers of men." 20 Immediately they left their nets and followed
him. 21 And going on from there he saw
two other brothers, James the son of
Zebedee and John his brother, in the boat
with Zebedee their father, mending their
nets, and he called them. 22 Immediately
they left the boat and their father and followed him.

Jesus Ministers to Great Crowds

23 [d]And he went throughout all Galilee,
[e]teaching in their synagogues and [f]pro-
claiming the gospel of the kingdom and
[g]healing every disease and every affliction
among the people. 24 So his fame spread
throughout all [h]Syria, and [g]they brought
him all the sick, those afflicted with various
diseases and [i]pains, [j]those oppressed by
demons, [k]epileptics, and [l]paralytics, and
he healed them. 25 [m]And great crowds followed him from Galilee and the [n]Deca-
polis, and from Jerusalem and Judea, and
from beyond the Jordan.

The Sermon on the Mount

5 Seeing the crowds, [o]he went up on the
mountain, and when he [p]sat down, his
disciples came to him.

25 [m]Mark 3:7, 8; Luke 6:17 [n]Mark 5:20
Chapter 5 1 [o]ch. 15:29 [p]Luke 4:20

4:10 Jesus rejects idolatry with all the zeal of true worship. He commands Satan to depart, for He has conquered the "strong man" (12:29).

4:15 Galilee of the Gentiles. Matthew stresses Jesus' focus on the nation of Israel during His earthly ministry (10:5, 6). However, his observation that Jesus' ministry fulfills Is. 9:2 shows that the commission to go to the Gentiles in Matt. 28:19 is not an afterthought; the ultimate goal always included the nations.

4:17 From that time. This phrase, which also occurs in 16:21, marks a turning point from the period of preparation to the period of Jesus' public ministry.

Repent. See "Repentance" at Acts 26:20.

4:23 teaching . . . proclaiming . . . healing. Teaching involved communicating the nature and purpose of God's kingdom, as seen in the Sermon on the Mount (chs. 5–7) and the parables of the kingdom (ch. 13). Preaching was proclaiming the good news that God's kingdom was near, that His sovereign purposes in history were finally being realized. Healing, as well as teaching and preaching, was a sign that this kingdom had come (11:5).

4:24 Syria. In Roman usage, "Syria" applied to virtually the whole of Palestine with the exception of Galilee (cf. Luke 2:2). A Galilean would probably have understood "Syria" to refer to the territory just north of Galilee, from the Mediterranean to Damascus.

epileptics. The only other use of this word in the New Testament is in 17:15, where it is applied to a demon-possessed boy who is exhibiting symptoms of epileptic seizures.

5:1–7:29 The Sermon on the Mount is the first of five great blocks of Jesus' teaching in Matthew (Introduction: Characteristics and Themes). It is the classic statement of the ethics of the kingdom of God. The early church favored a literal interpretation but fully applied the sermon only to special classes of Christians, especially monastics. Others, such as the Anabaptists, have attempted to apply it literally to every Christian. Still

The Beatitudes

2 And [q]he opened his mouth and taught
them, saying:
3 [r]"Blessed are [s]the poor [t]in spirit, for
[u]theirs is the kingdom of heaven.
4 "Blessed are [v]those who mourn, for they
shall be comforted.
5 "Blessed are [t]the [w]meek, for they [w]shall
inherit the earth.
6 "Blessed are those who hunger and
[x]thirst [y]for righteousness, for they shall be
satisfied.
7 "Blessed are [z]the merciful, for they shall
receive mercy.
8 "Blessed are [a]the pure in heart, for [b]they
shall see God.
9 "Blessed are [c]the peacemakers, for [d]they
shall be called [e]sons[1] of God.
10 [f]"Blessed are those who are persecuted
for righteousness' sake, for [u]theirs is the
kingdom of heaven.
11 [g]"Blessed are you when others revile
you and persecute you and utter all kinds
of evil against you falsely [h]on my account.
12 [i]Rejoice and be glad, for your reward is
great in heaven, for [j]so they persecuted the
prophets who were before you.

2 [q]Ps. 78:2
3 [r]For ver. 3-12, [Luke 6:20-23] [s][Isai. 61:1; 66:2] [t][ch. 11:29] [u][Luke 12:32]
4 [v]Isai. 61:2, 3; John 16:20; 2 Cor. 1:7; 7:10; Rev. 21:4; [James 4:9, 10]
5 [t][See ver. 3 above] [w]Ps. 37:11
6 [x]Ps. 42:2; Isai. 55:1, 2; John 7:37 [y]2 Tim. 2:22; [ch. 6:33]
7 [z]ch. 18:33; 25:34-36; Prov. 19:17; Luke 6:36; 2 Tim. 1:16; Heb. 6:10
8 [a]Ps. 24:4; 2 Tim. 2:22; [1 Pet. 1:22] [b]Heb. 12:14; 1 John 3:2, 3; Rev. 22:4; [1 Cor. 13:12]
9 [c]James 3:18 [d]1 John 3:1 [e]Rom. 8:14
10 [f]2 Tim. 2:12; James 5:11; 1 Pet. 3:14 [u][See ver. 3 above]

Salt and Light

13 "You are the salt of the earth, [k]but if
salt has lost its taste, how shall its saltiness
be restored? It is no longer good for anything except to be thrown out and trampled under people's feet.
14 [l]"You are the light of the world. A
city set on a hill cannot be hidden.
15 [m]Nor do people light a lamp and put
it under a basket, but on a stand, and it
gives light to all in the house. 16 In the
same way, let your light shine before
others, so [n]that they may see your good
works and [o]give glory to your Father who
is in heaven.

Christ Came to Fulfill the Law

17 [p]"Do not think that I have come to
abolish the [q]Law or the Prophets; I have
not come to abolish them [r]but to fulfill

11 [g]Heb. 11:26; 1 Pet. 4:14 [h]John 15:21 12 [i]Acts 5:41; Rom. 5:3; 2 Cor. 12:10; Col. 1:11, 24; Heb. 10:34; James 1:2; 1 Pet. 4:13 [j]See ch. 21:35 13 [k]Mark 9:50; Luke 14:34 14 [l]Eph. 5:8; Phil. 2:15; [John 8:12] 15 [m]Mark 4:21; Luke 8:16; 11:33 16 [n]Philem. 6; 1 Pet. 2:12 [o]John 15:8; 2 Cor. 9:13; Phil. 1:11; [ch. 9:8] 17 [p]Rom. 3:31 [q]ch. 7:12 [r][Rom. 10:4; 13:8; Gal. 3:24]

[1] Greek *huioi*; see preface

others have viewed it as legalistic, as a provisional, temporary code, or as a heightening of the law of Moses with the aim of inducing repentance (Luther). Finally, some have argued that the demands of the sermon are not to be understood literally, but that Jesus was concerned with inward disposition rather than outward conduct, or that the severity of the sermon is intended to compel a decision by the hearers either for or against God's demands on their lives.

We must recognize that the sermon is directed to the disciples and through them to the whole church today. The sermon addresses both inward motives and outward conduct (5:21, 22, 27, 28). These legitimate demands are so strict (5:48) that no one can completely obey them, and we are therefore driven to the grace and mercy of God. In some cases Jesus uses obviously intentional exaggeration to illustrate the absolute requirements of God's law (5:29, 30).

5:1 went up on the mountain. The content of this sermon is similar to the sermon on the plain recorded in Luke 6.

sat down. It was customary for teachers to sit while teaching (Luke 4:20).

5:3 Blessed. This means more than the emotional state represented by the word "happy." It includes spiritual well-being, having the approval of God, and thus a happier destiny (Ps. 1).

poor in spirit. Those with the greater spiritual need are more likely to perceive their need and depend on God alone and not their own goodness. Paul notes the same principle in Rom. 9:30, 31. The parallel in Luke 6:20 omits "in spirit." This has led many to suppose Jesus primarily spoke of the materially poor. Material poverty and recognition of spiritual need often go together (Ps. 9:18 note), but the two kinds of poverty are not identical.

5:4 those who mourn. The context indicates that these are mourning over sin and evil, especially their own, and over the failure of mankind to give proper glory to God.

5:5 the meek. This beatitude resembles and is perhaps based on Ps. 37:11. The meekness in view is spiritual meekness, an attitude of humility and submission to God. Our pattern for meekness is Jesus (the same Greek word is translated "gentle" in 11:29), who submits to the will of His Father.

inherit the earth. The ultimate fulfillment of the promise to Abraham, whom Paul calls "heir of the world" (Rom. 4:13; cf. Heb. 11:16).

5:6 hunger . . . for righteousness. Those who seek God's righteousness receive what they desire, not those who are confident of their own righteousness.

5:8 they shall see God. Because God is a spirit, His divine essence is invisible (Col. 1:15; 1 Tim. 1:17; 6:16). Nevertheless, believers will "see" God through the insight of faith, and Jesus assured His disciples that in seeing Him they had "seen the Father" (John 14:9). In the glorified state, God's children will "see him as he is" (1 John 3:2).

5:9 peacemakers. Spiritual peace, not the cessation of physical violence between nations, is in view. Although the term is usually understood to mean those who help others find peace with God, this peace can also be understood as those who have made their own peace with God and are called His children. The principle is extended in vv. 44, 45—the children of God make peace, even with their enemies.

5:13 salt. The primary value of salt was not as a flavoring but as a preservative. Disciples are to hinder the world's corruption. The salt deposits along the Dead Sea contain not just sodium chloride but a variety of other minerals as well. This salt can become good for nothing when the rain washes out its saltiness over the years. See "Christians in the World" at Col. 2:20.

5:14 See Is. 60:1–3.

5:16 See "The Mission of the Church in the World" at John 20:21.

5:17 Law or the Prophets. A way of referring to the whole Old Testament.

not come to abolish. The correctives of vv. 21–48 should be read in the light of this opening remark. In fulfilling the law, Jesus does not alter, replace, or nullify the former commands; rather, He establishes their true

them. **18** For truly, I say to you, [s]until heaven and earth pass away, not an iota, not a dot, will pass from the Law until all is accomplished. **19** [t]Therefore whoever relaxes [u]one of the least of these commandments and teaches others to do the same will be called least [v]in the kingdom of heaven, but whoever does them and teaches them will be called great [v]in the kingdom of heaven. **20** For I tell you, unless your righteousness exceeds [w]that of the scribes and Pharisees, you [x]will never enter the kingdom of heaven.

Anger

21 [y]"You have heard that it was said to those of old, [z]'You shall not murder; and whoever murders will be liable [a]to judgment.' **22** But I say to you that [b]everyone who is angry with his brother[1] will be liable to judgment; whoever insults[2] his brother will be liable to the council; and whoever says, 'You fool!' will be liable to [c]the hell[3] of fire. **23** [d]So if [e]you are offering your gift at the altar and there remember that your brother has something against you, **24** leave your gift there before the altar and go. First be reconciled to your brother, and then come and offer your gift. **25** [f]Come to terms quickly with your accuser while you are going with him to court, lest your accuser hand you over to the judge, and the judge to the guard, and you be put in prison. **26** Truly, I say to you, [g]you will never get out until you have paid the last penny.[4]

Lust

27 [h]"You have heard that it was said, [i]'You shall not commit adultery.' **28** But I say to you that [j]everyone who looks at a woman with lustful intent has already committed adultery with her in his heart. **29** [k]If your right eye [l]causes you to sin, tear it out and throw it away. For it is better that you lose one of your members than that your whole body be thrown into [m]hell. **30** [k]And if your right hand [l]causes you to sin, cut it off and throw it away. For it is better that you lose one of your members than that your whole body go into [m]hell.

Divorce

31 [h]"It was also said, [n]'Whoever divorces his wife, let him give her a certificate of divorce.' **32** [o]But I say to you that everyone who divorces his wife, except on the ground of sexual immorality, makes her commit adultery. And [p]whoever marries a divorced woman commits adultery.

Oaths

33 "Again [q]you have heard that it was said to those of old, [r]'You shall not swear falsely, but [s]shall perform to the Lord what you have sworn.' **34** But I say to you, [t]Do not

18 [s]Luke 16:17; [ch. 24:35] **19** [t][1 Cor. 3:12-15] [u][Gal. 3:10; James 2:10] [v]ch. 11:11; 18:1-4 **20** [w][Rom. 10:3; Phil. 3:9] [x]John 3:5 **21** [y]ver. 33; [ver. 27, 31, 38, 43] [z]Cited from Ex. 20:13; Deut. 5:17; [ch. 19:18; Mark 10:19; Luke 18:20; Rom. 13:9; James 2:11] [a][Deut. 16:18] **22** [b]1 John 3:15 [c]ch. 18:9; Mark 9:43; James 3:6; [ver. 29] **23** [d][ch. 6:15; Mark 11:25] [e]ch. 8:4; 23:18 **25** [f]Luke 12:58, 59 **26** [g][ch. 18:34, 35]

27 [h]See ver. 21 [i]Cited from Ex. 20:14; Deut. 5:18 **28** [j]Job 31:1; Prov. 6:25; [2 Sam. 11:2] **29** [k]ch. 18:8, 9; Mark 9:43-48 [l][ch. 13:41; Luke 17:1] [m]ch. 10:28; 23:15, 33; Luke 12:5; [ver. 22] **30** [k][See ver. 29 above]

[l][See ver. 29 above] [m][See ver. 29 above] **31** [h][See ver. 27 above] [n]ch. 19:7; Jer. 3:1; Cited from Deut. 24:1 **32** [o]ch. 19:9; Mark 10:11, 12; Luke 16:18; [1 Cor. 7:10, 11] [p]Rom. 7:3 **33** [q]Lev. 19:12; 1 Tim. 1:10 [r]Num. 30:2; Deut. 23:21; Eccles. 5:4 [s]James 5:12 **34** [t]ch. 23:22; Isai. 66:1; Acts 7:49; See Rev. 4:2

1 Some manuscripts insert *without cause* 2 Greek *says Raca to* (a term of abuse) 3 Greek *Gehenna*; also verses 29, 30 4 Greek *kodrantes*, Roman copper coin (Latin *quadrans*) worth about 1/64 of a *denarius* (which was a day's wage for a laborer)

intent and purpose in His teaching and accomplishes them in His obedient life. The Law, as well as the Prophets, points forward to Christ. See "The Law of God" at Ex. 20:1.

5:18 iota. A tiny extension on certain letters in the Hebrew alphabet.

until all is accomplished. The full manifestation of God's kingdom (chs. 24; 25) for which believers are to pray (6:10).

5:20 unless your righteousness exceeds. Jesus did not criticize the Pharisees for their strict observance of the law but for their emphasis on outward conformity to it without a proper inner attitude (ch. 23). By focusing on externals they avoided the real intent of the law and so obscured its real demands. The Qumran texts refer to the Pharisees as "seekers after smooth things" because they accommodated and compromised the law to fit the realities of life. Such accommodation removed awareness of the need for grace and dependence on God. In the following verses, Jesus restores the true nature of God's law as demanding total and radical holiness. Jesus demands a deeper obedience, not disregard of God's commands.

5:21 You have heard that it was said. Not the teaching of God's law itself, with its promises, but the teaching of the law by scribes and Pharisees (see note on v. 43).

5:22 You fool. Apparently Jewish law had sanctions against the specific insult *Raca,* but Jesus shows that any verbal abuse makes one liable to eternal damnation.

hell. This is *Gehenna,* the "valley of Hinnom," a trash dump outside Jerusalem where fires burned constantly. It was notorious as the location of human sacrifices by fire during the reigns of Ahaz and Manasseh (2 Chr. 28:3; 33:6). Jeremiah called it the "Valley of Slaughter" a symbol of God's fearful judgment (Jer. 7:32). See "Hell" at Mark 9:43.

5:25 Come to terms quickly. While vv. 23, 24 deal with the reconciliation of an offended brother, vv. 25, 26 appear to address the problem of conflict in larger society—in this case legal conflict. Christians are to work for reconciliation in all areas of life.

5:29 tear it out. The severity of the demand illustrates the radical nature of Jesus' ethic and our radical need. Jesus is not advocating self-mutilation; not the eyes or hands cause lust, but the heart and mind. Christians must not only avoid the act of adultery ("hand"), but also those things that would lead to a lustful attitude ("eye").

5:32 See 19:3–10 and notes; "Marriage and Divorce" at Mal. 2:16.

5:34 Do not take an oath. Some have understood Jesus' prohibition of oaths to be universal, but Jesus Himself submitted to oath (26:63), and Paul invoked God as his witness in Rom. 1:9. God Himself takes an oath so that we might be encouraged (Heb. 6:17). Jesus is addressing a narrow

take an oath at all, either by heaven, for [u]it
is the throne of God, 35 or by the earth, for
it is his footstool, or by Jerusalem, for it is
[v]the city of the great King. 36 And do not
take an oath by your head, for you cannot
make one hair white or black. 37 Let what
you say be simply 'Yes' or 'No'; [w]anything
more than this comes from [x]evil.[1]

Retaliation

38 [h]"You have heard that it was said, [y]'An
eye for an eye and a tooth for a tooth.'
39 But I say to you, [z]Do not resist the one
who is evil. But [a]if anyone [b]slaps you on
the right cheek, turn to him the other also.
40 And [z]if anyone would sue you and take
your tunic,[2] let him have your cloak as
well. 41 And if anyone [c]forces you to go one
mile, go with him two miles. 42 [d]Give to the
one who begs from you, and [e]do not refuse
the one who would borrow from you.

Love Your Enemies

43 [f]"You have heard that it was said, [g]'You
shall love your neighbor and [h]hate your
enemy.' 44 But I say to you, [i]Love your enemies and [j]pray for those who persecute
you, 45 [k]so that you may be sons of your
Father who is in heaven. For he makes his
sun rise on the evil and on the good, and
[l]sends rain on the just and on the unjust.
46 [m]For if you love those who love you, what
reward do you have? Do not even the tax
collectors do the same? 47 And if you greet
only your brothers,[3] what more are you
doing than others? Do not even [n]the Gentiles do the same? 48 [o]You therefore must be

34 [u]Ps. 48:2
35 [v][Prov. 10:19]
37 [w]See ch. 13:19 [x]See ver. 21
38 [h][See ver. 27] [y]Cited from Ex. 21:24; Lev. 24:20; Deut. 19:21
39 [z]1 Cor. 6:7; 1 Pet. 2:23 [a]For ver. 39-42, see Luke 6:29, 30; [Rom. 12:17] [b]ch. 26:67; Isai. 50:6; Lam. 3:30
40 [z][See ver. 39 above]
41 [c]ch. 27:32
42 [d]Ps. 37:21; Prov. 21:26 [e]Deut. 15:8; Ps. 37:26; 112:5; Luke 6:34, 35
43 [f]See ver. 21 [g]Cited from Lev. 19:18; See ch. 19:19 [h][Deut. 23:6]
44 [i]Luke 6:27, 28; Rom. 12:20; [Ex. 23:4; Job 31:29, 30; Ps. 7:4] [j]Luke 23:34; Acts 7:60; 2 Tim. 4:16; 1 Pet. 3:9
45 [k]Luke 6:35; [Eph. 5:1; Phil. 2:15] [l]Acts 14:17
46 [m]Luke 6:32
47 [n]ch. 6:7, 32
48 [o][Luke 6:36] [p]ch. 19:21; 1 Cor. 2:6; Phil. 3:15; Col. 1:28; 4:12; James 1:4; 3:2; See Gen. 17:1 [q][Lev. 19:2; 1 Pet. 1:15]

[p]perfect, [q]as your heavenly Father is perfect.

Giving to the Needy

6 "Beware of [r]practicing your righteousness before other people in order [s]to
be seen by them, for then you will have no
reward from your Father who is in heaven.
2 [t]"Thus, when you give to the needy,
sound no trumpet before you, as the hypocrites do in the synagogues and in the
streets, that they may [u]be praised by others. Truly, I say to you, they have [v]received
their reward. 3 But when you give to the
needy, do not let your left hand know what
your right hand is doing, 4 so that your giving may be in secret. [w]And your Father who
sees in secret will reward you.

The Lord's Prayer

5 "And when you pray, you must not be
like the hypocrites. For they love [x]to stand
and pray in the synagogues and at the street
corners, that they may be seen by others.
[y]Truly, I say to you, they have received their
reward. 6 But when you pray, [z]go into your
room and shut the door and pray to your
Father who is in secret. [a]And your Father
who sees in secret will reward you.
7 "And when you pray, do not heap up
empty phrases as [b]the Gentiles do, for

Chapter 6 **1** [r]1 John 2:29 [s]ver. 16; ch. 23:5 **2** [t][1 Cor. 13:3] [u]John 5:44 [v]Luke 6:24 **4** [w]ver. 6, 18 **5** [x]Mark 11:25; Luke 18:11 [y]ver. 2, 16 **6** [z]2 Kin. 4:33; Isai. 26:20 [a]ver. 4, 18 **7** [b]ver. 32; ch. 5:47

1 Or *the evil one* 2 Greek *chiton*, a long garment worn under the cloak next to the skin 3 Or *brothers and sisters*. The plural Greek word *adelphoi* (translated "brothers") refers to siblings in a family. In New Testament usage, depending on the context, *adelphoi* may refer either to *brothers* or to *brothers and sisters*

and misleading legalism that required a specific oath to make spoken words binding. The implication of such an approach to honesty is that we do not need to be truthful except under oath. Jesus demands an integrity of speech as though everything were under oath. He also prohibited the implicit idolatry of swearing by anything less than God. See "Honest Speech, Oaths, and Vows" at Neh. 5:12.

5:38 An eye for an eye. The original intent of Ex. 21:24, Lev. 24:20, and Deut. 19:21 is that punishment should be equitable and should fit the crime. These limitations prohibited exacting a greater vengeance (such as Lamech boasted in Gen. 4:23) or having different penalties for different social classes. Jesus contradicted those who saw in this principle grounds for personal vengeance.

5:39 Do not resist. In context this means "do not seek restitution in court." The slap on the right cheek is a backhanded one—an insult as well as injury. Jesus' remarks may refer back to the words of the Servant of the Lord in Is. 50:6.

5:41 if anyone forces you. The possibility of a Roman soldier coercing a person to serve as a guide or burden carrier was real. Even if compelled by force to do something for someone, one can demonstrate freedom by volunteering more than was demanded rather than begrudging the service.

5:43 hate your enemy. This is not in the Old Testament, but was a false conclusion in scribal teaching drawn from the narrow understanding of "neighbor" as simply one's fellow Jew. Jesus shows that the true intent of Lev. 19:18 extends even to one's enemies (Luke 10:29–37).

5:45 See "Providence" at Prov. 16:33.

5:48 be perfect. The standard that God demands of His people is His own perfect character. God's perfection includes the love of benevolent grace (v. 45). Although perfection is not attainable in this life, it is the goal of those who have become children of the Father (Phil. 3:12, 13).

6:1 your righteousness. Jesus affirms the positive value of such acts, but only when done in submission to God and love for Him, rather than in seeking *human* personal glory.

6:2 hypocrites. In the New Testament, the hypocrite is one who claims to have a relationship with God and to love righteousness, but is self-seeking and even self-deceived. The hypocrites denounced in ch. 23 were unaware of their hypocrisy.

6:5 pray. See "Prayer" at Luke 11:2.

6:7 do not heap up empty phrases. This prohibition does not contradict the principle that one should keep asking God for what is believed

[c]they think that they will be heard [d]for their
many words. **8** Do not be like them, [e]for
your Father knows what you need before
you ask him. **9** [f]Pray then like this:

[g]"Our Father in heaven,
[h]hallowed be [i]your name.[1]
10 [j]Your kingdom come,
[k]your will be done,[2]
[l]on earth as it is in heaven.
11 [m]Give us [n]this day our daily bread,[3]
12 and forgive us our debts,
as we also have forgiven our
debtors.
13 And [o]lead us not into temptation,
but [p]deliver us from [q]evil.[4]

14 [r]For if you forgive others their trespasses,
your heavenly Father will also forgive you,
15 [s]but if you do not forgive others their
trespasses, neither will your Father forgive
your trespasses.

Fasting

16 [t]"And [t]when you fast, do not look
gloomy like the hypocrites, for they disfig-
ure their faces that their fasting may be
seen by others. [u]Truly, I say to you, they
have received their reward. **17** But when you
fast, [v]anoint your head and wash your face,
18 that your fasting may not be seen by others but by your Father who is in secret.
[w]And your Father who sees in secret will
reward you.

Lay Up Treasures in Heaven

19 [x]"Do not lay up for yourselves treasures
on earth, where [y]moth and rust[5] destroy
and where [z]thieves break in and steal, **20** but
lay up for yourselves treasures in heaven,
where neither moth nor rust destroys and
where thieves do not break in and steal.
21 For where your treasure is, there your
heart will be also.

22 [a]"The eye is the lamp of the body. So,
if your eye is healthy, your whole body will
be full of light, **23** [a]but if [b]your eye is bad,
your whole body will be full of darkness. If
then the light in you is darkness, how great
is the darkness!

24 [c]"No one can serve two masters, for
either he will hate the one and love the
other, or he will be devoted to the one and
despise the other. You cannot serve God
and [d]money.[6]

Do Not Be Anxious

25 [e]"Therefore I tell you, [f]do not be anxious about your life, what you will eat or
what you will drink, nor about your body,
what you will put on. Is not life more than
food, and the body more than clothing?
26 [g]Look at the birds of the air: they neither
sow nor reap nor gather into barns, and yet
your heavenly Father feeds them. [h]Are you
not of more value than they? **27** And which
of you by being anxious can add a single
hour to his [i]span of life?[7] **28** And why are
you anxious about clothing? Consider the

7 [c]1 Kin. 18:26 [d]Prov. 10:19; Eccles. 5:2 **8** [e]ver. 32 **9** [f]For ver. 9-13, [Luke 11:2-4] [g]ver. 1 [h]Isai. 29:23; [Luke 1:49; 1 Pet. 3:15] [i]John 17:6 **10** [j][ch. 3:2; 4:17] [k]ch. 26:42; Luke 22:42; Acts 21:14; [ch. 12:50; Heb. 13:21] [l]Ps. 103:20, 21; Dan. 4:35 **11** [m]Prov. 30:8 [n][ver. 34] **13** [o]ch. 26:41; Mark 14:38; Luke 22:40, 46; [1 Cor. 10:13] [p]John 17:15; 2 Thess. 3:3; [2 Tim. 4:18] [q]See ch. 13:19 **14** [r]Mark 11:25; Luke 6:37; Eph. 4:32; Col. 3:13 **15** [s]ch. 18:35; See James 2:13 **16** [t]Isai. 58:5 [u]ver. 2, 5 **17** [v]Ruth 3:3; 2 Sam. 12:20 **18** [w]ver. 4, 6 **19** [x]ch. 19:21; Luke 12:21, 33, 34;18:22; 1 Tim. 6:9, 10, 17-19; Heb. 13:5 [y]James 5:2, 3 [z]ch. 24:43

22 [a]Luke 11:34, 35 **23** [a][See ver. 22 above] [b]ch. 20:15; Deut. 15:9; Prov. 28:22

24 [c]Luke 16:13; [Rom. 6:16; James 4:4] [d]Luke 16:9, 11, 13 **25** [e]For ver. 25-33, see Luke 12:22-31 [f]ver. 27, 28, 31, 34; ch. 10:19; 13:22 (Gk.); 1 Cor. 7:32 (Gk.); Phil. 4:6; 1 Pet. 5:7 **26** [g][Job 38:41; Ps. 147:9] [h]ch. 10:31 **27** [i]Luke 2:52

[1] Or *Let your name be kept holy*, or *Let your name be treated with reverence* [2] Or *Let your kingdom come, let your will be done* [3] Or *our bread for tomorrow* [4] Or *the evil one*; some manuscripts add *For yours is the kingdom and the power and the glory, forever. Amen* [5] Or *worm*; also verse 20 [6] Greek *mammon*, a Semitic word for money or possessions [7] Or *a single cubit to his stature*; a *cubit* was about 18 inches or 45 centimeters

to be His will (Luke 18), but corrects the idea that God is impressed with quantity of words.

6:9 This prayer is a model of brevity, asking first for God to be glorified and then for the needs of human life.

Our Father. See "Adoption" at Gal. 4:5.

hallowed be your name. Not just that God's creatures may keep it holy, but that God may Himself hallow it by being the holy Judge and Savior.

6:11 daily bread. The Greek word translated "daily" is known only from this prayer. It has been understood to mean "daily," "necessary," "future," or "tomorrow's" bread. There are three basic interpretations for it. The sacramental view is that it refers to the bread received in the Lord's Supper. Another view is that it symbolizes life in the coming kingdom, making the petition equivalent to "Your kingdom come" in v. 10. A third view takes it as a request for God's provision for our physical needs. This last view is perhaps the best, and this theme is developed in vv. 19–34 (Prov. 30:8).

6:12 debts. Spiritual debts are in view. Christians forgive others in response to God's forgiveness (18:32, 33); but if they do not forgive others, they cannot claim God's forgiveness for themselves (vv. 14, 15).

6:13 lead us not into temptation. The forgiven pray this petition because they trust God and they distrust themselves. The Father may test us (4:1; Deut. 8:2), but He will not allow us to be tempted beyond our capacity (1 Cor. 10:13).

6:17 anoint your head. This symbolized rejoicing (Ps. 23:5; 45:7; 104:15; Is. 61:3), but it was also part of daily routine except when fasting (Dan. 10:3). Not to anoint oneself could be an attempt to appear more pious than others.

6:19 "Rust" refers not only to ordinary corrosion but also to mildew, wood rot, and the like. Every material thing is subject to decay or loss.

6:23 light in you. The good eye looks to God as its "master" (v. 24) and fills the person with the "light" of God's will. The bad eye looks to "treasures on earth" (v. 19) and admits only the "darkness" of greed and self-interest. The person's whole life will be determined by the kind of "light" the "eye" lets in.

6:26 they neither sow nor reap. The point is not that birds are idle—an adult bird does not stay in its nest with open beak—but that birds do not worry about what the future holds. Anxious worry shows a lack of trust in God's knowledge and care (vv. 32, 33). See "Providence" at Prov. 16:33.

lilies of the field, how they grow: they neither toil nor spin, 29 yet I tell you, [j]even
Solomon in all his glory was not arrayed
like one of these. 30 But if God so clothes
the grass of the field, which today is alive
and tomorrow is thrown into the oven, will
he not much more clothe you, [k]O you of
little faith? 31 Therefore do not be anxious,
saying, 'What shall we eat?' or 'What shall
we drink?' or 'What shall we wear?' 32 For
[l]the Gentiles seek after all these things, and
[m]your heavenly Father knows that you
need them all. 33 But [n]seek first [o]the kingdom of God and his righteousness, [p]and all
these things will be added to you.
34 [q]"Therefore do not be anxious about
tomorrow, for tomorrow will be anxious
for itself. Sufficient for the day is its own
trouble.

Judging Others

7 [r]"Judge not, that you be not judged.
2 [s]For with the judgment you pronounce you will be judged, and [t]with the
measure you use it will be measured to
you. 3 Why do you see the speck that is in
your brother's eye, but [u]do not notice the
log that is in your own eye? 4 Or how can
you say to your brother, 'Let me take the
speck out of your eye,' when there is the
log in your own eye? 5 You hypocrite, first
take the log out of your own eye, and then
you will see clearly to take the speck out of
your brother's eye.
6 [v]"Do not give [w]dogs what is holy, and
do not throw your [x]pearls before pigs, lest
they trample them underfoot and turn to
attack you.

29 [j]1 Kin. 10:4-7 **30** [k]ch. 8:26; 14:31; 16:8; [ch. 17:20] **32** [l]ver. 7 [m]ver. 8 **33** [n][ch. 5:6, 20] [o]ver. 10 [p][1 Kin. 3:11-14; Mark 10:29, 30; 1 Tim. 4:8; 1 Pet. 3:9] **34** [q][James 4:13, 14]
Chapter 7
1 [r]For ver. 1-5, see Luke 6:37, 38, 41, 42; [Rom. 14:13; 1 Cor. 4:5; James 5:9] **2** [s]Rom. 2:1, 3; 14:10; James 2:13; 4:11, 12 [t]Mark 4:24; [Judg. 1:7] **3** [u][John 8:7-9] **6** [v]ch. 15:26; [Prov. 9:7, 8; 23:9] [w][Phil. 3:2; Rev. 22:15] [x]ch. 13:46
7 [y]For ver. 7-11, see Luke 11:9-13 [z]ch. 18:19; 21:22; Mark 11:24; John 14:13; 15:7, 16; 16:23, 24; James 1:5, 6, 17; 1 John 3:22; 5:14, 15 [a]1 Chr. 28:9; 2 Chr. 15:2; Prov. 8:17; Jer. 29:13; [Isai. 55:6] [b][Rev. 3:20] **9** [c]ch. 4:3 **11** [d]ch. 12:34; Gen. 6:5; 8:21 [z][See ver. 7 above] **12** [e]Luke 6:31 [f]See ch. 22:40

Ask, and It Will Be Given

7 [y]"Ask, [z]and it will be given to you;
[a]seek, and you will find; [b]knock, and it will
be opened to you. 8 For everyone who asks
receives, and the one who seeks finds, and
to the one who knocks it will be opened.
9 Or which one of you, if his son asks him
for [c]bread, will give him [c]a stone? 10 Or if he
asks for a fish, will give him a serpent? 11 If
you then, [d]who are evil, know how to give
good gifts to your children, how much
more will [z]your Father who is in heaven
give good things to those who ask him!

The Golden Rule

12 "So [e]whatever you wish that others
would do to you, do also to them, for this
is [f]the Law and the Prophets.
13 [g]"Enter by the narrow gate. For the
gate is wide and the way is easy[1] that leads
to destruction, and those who enter by it
are many. 14 For the gate is narrow and [h]the
way is hard that leads to life, and [i]those
who find it are few.

A Tree and Its Fruit

15 [j]"Beware of false prophets, who come
to you in sheep's clothing but inwardly are
[k]ravenous wolves. 16 You will recognize
them [l]by their fruits. Are grapes gathered
from thornbushes, or figs from thistles?
17 So, [m]every healthy tree bears good fruit,
but the diseased tree bears bad fruit. 18 A
healthy tree cannot bear bad fruit, nor can

13 [g]Luke 13:24 **14** [h]Ps. 16:11; [ch. 18:8; John 14:6] [i][Luke 13:23] **15** [j]ch. 24:11, 24; Deut. 13:1-3; Jer. 14:14; 23:16; Mark 13:22; Luke 6:26; Acts 13:6; 2 Pet. 2:1; 1 John 4:1 [k]Ezek. 22:27; Acts 20:29; [Mic. 3:5; John 10:12] **16** [l]Luke 6:43, 44; James 2:18 **17** [m]ch. 12:33-35

[1] Some manuscripts *for the way is wide and easy*

6:33 seek first the kingdom of God and his righteousness. We are to make God's sovereign rule, and a right relationship with Him, the highest priority in life (see 3:15 note on "righteousness"). Worry is inconsistent with this priority; it doubts the sovereignty or goodness of God and distracts from the true goals of life. God will meet all the needs of those who risk all for Him.

7:1 Judge not. Jesus prohibits one kind of judging, but approves a different kind. Condemning others for their faults is failure to exercise forgiveness (6:14, 15); only a gentle and humble criticism that first recognizes one's own greater faults can help. There is also a necessary, discerning kind of judgment that does not condemn but distinguishes unbelief from belief (v. 6). The method of discernment is given in v. 16.

7:6 what is holy. A reference to the evidences of the kingdom, such as the healings and the exorcisms, which may explain why Jesus did no miracles for unbelievers. But "what is holy" would also include the preaching of the kingdom; believers should not continue to preach to people who have rejected the gospel with contempt and scorn (10:14; 15:14). The Book of Acts illustrates the principle in practice (Acts 13:44–51; 18:5, 6; 28:17–28).

7:11 evil. The general sinfulness of humanity is assumed here, since even those who call God "Father" are said to be evil.

good things. These gifts from the Father are the things Jesus has been describing as necessary for disciples: righteousness, sincerity, purity, humility, and wisdom. Those who know their own need will ask God for them. The parallel in Luke 11:13 focuses on the one greatest gift—the Holy Spirit.

7:12 do also to them. Often called the "Golden Rule," this principle was stated by a number of ancient thinkers as, "Do not do to others what you do not want done to you." Jesus made it a positive obligation. Here it appears after the discussion of God's goodness and His willingness to give.

7:14 the way is hard. Presenting a rosy picture of the Christian life and minimizing that it is filled with trouble does not follow the lead of our Lord (Acts 14:22). It may be that the "false prophets" of v. 15 are especially those who deny that the way is narrow and hard.

7:15 sheep's clothing . . . ravenous wolves. The message of false prophets may be attractive and even seem orthodox. The only way to know for sure is to allow time to see "their fruits" (vv. 16–20). Some of the

a diseased tree bear good fruit. 19 [n]Every
tree that does not bear good fruit is cut
down and thrown into the fire. 20 Thus you
will recognize them [l]by their fruits.

I Never Knew You

21 [o]"Not everyone who [p]says to me, 'Lord,
Lord,' will [q]enter the kingdom of heaven, but
the one who [r]does the will of my Father
who is in heaven. 22 [s]On that day [t]many will
say to me, 'Lord, Lord, did we not [u]proph-
esy in your name, and cast out demons [v]in
your name, and do many mighty works in
your name?' 23 [t]And then will I declare to
them, 'I [w]never knew you; [x]depart from
me, [y]you workers of lawlessness.'

Build Your House on the Rock

24 [z]"Everyone then who hears these
words of mine and does them will be like
[a]a wise man who built his house on the
rock. 25 And the rain fell, and the floods
came, and the winds blew and beat on that
house, but it did not fall, because it had
been founded on the rock. 26 And everyone
who hears these words of mine and does
not do them will be like [a]a foolish man
who built his house on the sand. 27 And the
rain fell, and the floods came, and the
winds blew and beat against that house,
and it fell, and great was the fall of it."

The Authority of Jesus

28 And when Jesus finished these sayings,
[b]the crowds were astonished at his teaching, 29 [c]for he was teaching them as one
who had authority, and not as their scribes.

19 [n]See ch. 3:10
20 [l][See ver. 16]
21 [o]Luke 6:46; Rom. 2:13; James 1:22 [p][Hos. 8:2] [q][John 3:3, 5] [r]ch. 12:50
22 [s]ch. 25:11, 12; Luke 13:25-27 [t]Mal. 3:17, 18 [u][Num. 24:4; John 11:51; 1 Cor. 13:2] [v]See Mark 9:38
23 [t][See ver. 22 above] [w]ch. 10:33; [Ps. 101:4] [x]ch. 25:41; Ps. 6:8 [y]ch. 13:41; Ps. 5:5
24 [z]For ver. 24-27, see Luke 6:47-49 [a]ch. 25:2; [Ezek. 13:10-14]
26 [a][See ver. 24 above]
28 [b]ch. 13:54; 22:33; Mark 1:22; 6:2; 11:18; Luke 4:32; [Acts 13:12]
29 [c]John 7:46
Chapter 8
1 [d]ch. 4:25
2 [e]For ver. 2-4, see Mark 1:40-44; Luke 5:12-14 [f][ch. 18:26; Acts 10:25]
4 [g]ch. 9:30; 17:9; Mark 1:34; 5:43; 7:36; 8:26; See ch. 12:16 [h]Luke 17:14 [i]Lev. 14:2-32 [j]ch. 10:18; 24:14; Mark 6:11; Luke 9:5; James 5:3

Jesus Cleanses a Leper

8 When he came down from the mountain, [d]great crowds followed him.
2 [e]And behold, a leper[1] came to him and
[f]knelt before him, saying, "Lord, if you will,
you can make me clean." 3 And Jesus[2]
stretched out his hand and touched him,
saying, "I will; be clean." And immediately
his leprosy was cleansed. 4 And Jesus said
to him, [g]"See that you say nothing to anyone, but go, [h]show yourself to the priest
and [i]offer the gift that Moses commanded,
[j]for a proof to them."

The Faith of a Centurion

5 [k]When he entered Capernaum, a centurion came forward to him, appealing to him,
6 "Lord, my servant is lying paralyzed at
home, suffering terribly." 7 And he said to
him, "I will come and heal him." 8 But the
centurion replied, "Lord, I am not worthy to
have you come under my roof, but [l]only say
the word, and my servant will be healed.
9 For I too am a man under authority, with
soldiers under me. And I say to one, 'Go,'
and he goes, and to another, 'Come,' and he
comes, and to my servant,[3] 'Do this,' and he
does it." 10 When Jesus heard this, [m]he marveled and said to those who followed him,
"Truly, I tell you, with [n]no one in Israel[4]
have I found such faith. 11 I tell you, [o]many
will come from east and west and recline at
table with Abraham, Isaac, and Jacob in the

5 [k]For ver. 5-13, see Luke 7:1-10 **8** [l]Ps. 107:20; [ver. 16] **10** [m][Mark 6:6] [n]See ch. 9:2 **11** [o]Luke 13:29; Eph. 3:6; [Isai. 59:19; Mal. 1:11]

1 *Leprosy* was a term for several skin diseases; see Leviticus 13
2 Greek *he* 3 Greek *bondservant* 4 Some manuscripts *not even in Israel*

false prophets' fruits are mentioned in the New Testament: controversies (1 Tim. 1:3), divisions (1 Tim. 6:3, 4), destruction of faith (2 Tim. 2:18), and self-destruction by heresy (2 Pet. 2:1).

7:21 Lord, Lord. The doubling of a name was an address of intimacy (Gen. 22:11; 1 Sam. 3:10; 2 Sam. 18:33; Luke 22:31). It is not claims or feelings of intimacy with Jesus that matter, nor is it simply good works, even miraculous ones; only doing the will of the Father matters. Genuine intimacy with the Father means knowing God and being known by God (1 Cor. 8:2, 3).

7:25 the rain fell. Storms in Palestine are infrequent but can be violent. Although the houses of the foolish and the wise may for a long time appear equally secure, when the storm comes the destruction of the foolish one's house is total (Is. 28:14–18). So it is with the life of those who ignore the words of Jesus.

7:29 not as their scribes. The scribes, like the later rabbis, taught by referring to what previous teachers had said. Their authority was the tradition. Jesus taught directly from Scripture with His own authority. See theological note "The Teaching of Jesus."

8:1–9:38 The order of the miracles and events in these chapters differs from that found in Mark and Luke. Probably Matthew arranged them according to topic rather than chronology.

8:2 leper. A variety of skin diseases are referred to by the Greek word used here, probably not Hansen's disease (modern "leprosy"). Touching a leper made one ceremonially unclean (cf. Lev. 15:7), but in this case the leper is healed and becomes clean rather than Jesus becoming ritually defiled.

8:4 say nothing to anyone. The command to the leper to be silent was to prevent miracle seekers from hindering Jesus' main mission (Mark 1:45). By showing himself to the priest, the leper would fulfill the requirements of the Law and be able to rejoin Jewish society (Lev. 14:1–32).

8:5 centurion. A Roman military officer in charge of approximately one hundred men. This centurion had an appreciation for Jesus' authority that surpassed anything in Israel, an awareness of his own unworthiness, and faith that Jesus could overcome the difficulty of his unworthiness. Matthew, who often prefers a condensed style, does not mention the intermediaries that appear in the parallel account in Luke 7:1–10.

8:10–12 The faith of the Gentile centurion provides the occasion for the prediction that Israel will be hardened and the gospel will be extended to the Gentiles.

8:11 recline at the table with Abraham, Isaac, and Jacob. A reference to the messianic banquet theme of Is. 25:6–9. Gentiles now appear in place of the natural sons. This theme recurs in the parable of the wicked

kingdom of heaven, 12 [p]while the sons of the
kingdom [q]will be thrown into the outer
darkness. In that place [r]there will be weeping and gnashing of teeth." 13 And to the
centurion Jesus said, "Go; let it be done for
you [s]as you have believed." [t]And the servant
was healed at that very moment.

Jesus Heals Many

14 [u]And when Jesus entered Peter's house,
he saw [v]his mother-in-law lying sick with a
fever. 15 He [w]touched her hand, and the fever
left her, and she rose and began to serve him.
16 That evening they brought to him many
who were [x]oppressed by demons, and he
cast out the spirits [y]with a word and healed
all who were sick. 17 [z]This was to fulfill what
was spoken by the prophet Isaiah: [a]"He
took our illnesses and bore our diseases."

12 [p]Luke 13:28; [ch. 19:30; 21:41, 43] [q]ch. 22:13; 25:30 [r]ch. 13:42, 50; 22:13; 24:51; 25:30; Luke 13:28 13 [s]ch. 9:29 [t]John 4:53; [ch. 9:22] 14 [u]For ver. 14-16, see Mark 1:29-34; Luke 4:38-41

[v]1 Cor. 9:5 15 [w][ch. 9:25] 16 [x]ver. 28, 33; See ch. 4:24 [y][ver. 8] 17 [z]See ch. 1:22 [a]Cited from Isai. 53:4

The Teaching of Jesus

Jesus was the Son of God incarnate, and His teaching, given Him by His Father (John 7:16–18; 12:49, 50), will stand forever (Mark 13:31), finally to judge its hearers (Matt. 7:24–27; John 12:48). The importance of paying attention to it cannot be overstressed. Jesus taught as Jewish rabbis generally did, by short sayings rather than in flowing discourses, and many of His most vital utterances are in parables, proverbs, and isolated pronouncements responding to questions and reacting to situations. All His public teaching was marked by an authority that brought amazement (Matt. 7:28, 29; Mark 1:27; John 7:46), but some of the teaching was enigmatical, requiring thought and spiritual insight ("ears to hear," Matt. 11:15; 13:9, 43; Luke 14:35), and baffling the complacent and casual. Jesus' reason for teaching so cryptically about His messianic role, His atonement, resurrection, and future reign, was partly that only events could make these things clear, and partly that He was calling people to be His disciples through His personal impact on them, and then teaching them about Himself within that relationship, rather than offering detailed theological instruction to the uncommitted (Matt. 11:25–27; Mark 4:11, 12). But Jesus' statements often are clear, and many of the fuller presentations in the epistles of the New Testament are best read as expansions and explanations of what Jesus said.

Jesus' teaching had three regular points of reference. The first was His divine Father, who had sent and was directing Him, and to whom His disciples must learn to relate as their Father in heaven. The second was to people, both individuals and groups, the recipients of His constant and many-faceted calls to repentance and a new life. The third was Himself, the Son of Man, and the Messiah of Israel.

Out of Jesus' witness to His Father, to people in their need, and to His own messianic role, three theological themes emerge:

1. The kingdom of God. This "kingdom" is the reality that came with Jesus as the fulfillment of God's plan for history, of which Old Testament prophets had often spoken (Is. 2:1–4; 9:6, 7; 11:1–12:6; 42:1–9; 49:1–7; Jer. 23:5, 6). The kingdom is present with Jesus; His miracles are signs of it (Matt. 11:12; 12:28; Luke 16:16; 17:20, 21). The kingdom takes command of a person's life when he or she submits in faith to the lordship of Christ, a momentous commitment that brings salvation and eternal life (Mark 10:17–27; John 5:24). The kingdom will be preached and grow (Matt. 13:31–33; 24:14) until the Son of Man, now reigning in heaven, reappears to gather His elect from every corner of the world.

2. The saving work of Jesus. Having come down from heaven at the Father's will to bring chosen sinners to glory, Jesus died for them, calls and draws them to Himself, forgives their sins, and keeps them safe until the day of resurrection (Luke 5:20, 23; 7:48; John 6:37–40, 44, 45; 10:14–18, 27–29; 12:32; 17:1–26).

3. The ethics of God's family. The new life comes to sinners as a gift of God's free grace and must be expressed in a new lifestyle. Those who have received grace must be thankful; those who are greatly loved must show great love to others; those who live because they are forgiven must themselves forgive; those who know God as their loving heavenly Father must accept His providence without bitterness, honoring Him at all times by trusting in His protecting care. In a word, God's children must be like their Father and their Savior, and be utterly unlike the world (Matt. 5:43–48; 6:12–15; 18:21–35; 20:26–28; 22:35–40).

tenants (21:33–44, especially v. 43) and the banquet parable (22:1–14). Jesus' prediction is an early example of the principle developed by Paul in Rom. 9:30–32: Israel tries to pursue righteousness by works and does not obtain it, but Gentiles who know they deserve only condemnation seek God's mercy and obtain it.

8:12 darkness . . . weeping. These figures of speech represent the grief and despair of those who are excluded from the kingdom.

8:17 our illnesses. Is. 53:4 uses "griefs" to represent the sin for which they are the curse (Is. 53:5). Jesus came to bear the curse as well as the guilt of sin, and in His ministry He demonstrated His power over physical

The Cost of Following Jesus

18 Now [b]when Jesus saw a great crowd
around him, [c]he gave orders to go over to
the other side. **19** [d]And a scribe came up and
said to him, "Teacher, I will follow you
wherever you go." **20** And Jesus said to him,
"Foxes have holes, and birds of the air have
nests, but the Son of Man has nowhere to
lay his head." **21** Another of the disciples
said to him, "Lord, let me first go and bury
my father." **22** And Jesus said to him,
"Follow me, and leave [e]the dead to bury
their own dead."

Jesus Calms a Storm

23 [f]And when he got into the boat, his disciples followed him. **24** And behold, there
arose a great storm on the sea, so that the
boat was being swamped by the waves; but
[g]he was asleep. **25** And they went and woke
him, saying, [h]"Save us, Lord; we are perishing." **26** And he said to them, "Why are
you [i]afraid, [j]O you of little faith?" Then he
rose and [k]rebuked the winds and the sea,
and [l]there was a great calm. **27** And the men
[m]marveled, saying, "What sort of man is
this, that even [n]winds and sea obey him?"

Jesus Heals Two Demon-Possessed Men

28 [o]And when he came to the other side, to
the country of the Gadarenes,[1] two [p]demon-
possessed[2] men met him, coming out of the
tombs, so fierce that no one could pass that
way. **29** And behold, they [q]cried out, "What
have you to do with us, [r]O Son of God?
Have you come here to torment us [s]before
the time?" **30** Now a herd of many pigs was
feeding at some distance from them. **31** And
the demons begged him, saying, "If you cast
us out, send us away into the herd of pigs."
32 And he said to them, "Go." So they came
out and went into the pigs, and behold, the
whole herd rushed down the steep bank
into the sea and drowned in the waters.
33 The herdsmen fled, and going into the
city they told everything, especially what
had happened to the [t]demon-possessed
men. **34** And behold, all the city came out to
meet Jesus, and when they saw him, [u]they
begged him to leave their region.

Jesus Heals a Paralytic

9 And getting into a boat he crossed over
and came to [v]his own city. **2** [w]And
behold, some people brought to him a paralytic, lying on a bed. And when Jesus [x]saw
their faith, he said to the paralytic, [y]"Take
heart, my son; [z]your sins are forgiven."
3 And behold, some of the scribes said to
themselves, [a]"This man is blaspheming."
4 But Jesus, [b]knowing[3] their thoughts, said,
"Why do you think evil in your hearts?
5 For which is easier, to say, 'Your sins are

18 [b][ch. 14:22; John 6:15-17] [c]Mark 4:35; Luke 8:22 **19** [d]For ver. 19-22, see Luke 9:57-60 **22** [e][John 5:25] **23** [f]For ver. 23-27, see Mark 4:36-41; Luke 8:22-25; [John 6:16-21] **24** [g][John 4:6, 7] **25** [h][ch. 14:30] **26** [i]John 14:27 [j]See ch. 6:30 [k]Ps. 104:6, 7; [Luke 4:39] [l]Job 38:11; Ps. 65:7; [ch. 14:32] **27** [m][Mark 1:27] [n][Luke 5:9] **28** [o]For ver. 28-9:1, see Mark 5:1-21; Luke 8:26-40 [p]ver. 16; [Rev. 18:2] **29** [q]Mark 1:23, 24, 26; Luke 4:34; Acts 8:7 [r][ch. 4:3, 6]; See ch. 14:33 [s][Rev. 12:12] **33** [t]ver. 16 **34** [u][1 Kin. 17:18; Luke 5:8; Acts 16:39]
Chapter 9
1 [v]ch. 4:13; [Mark 2:1] **2** [w]For ver. 2-8, see Mark 2:3-12; Luke 5:18-26 [x]ver. 22, 29; ch. 8:10, 13; 15:28; Mark 10:52; Luke 7:9, 50; 17:19; 18:42; Acts 3:16; 14:9; James 5:15 [y]ver. 22 [z]Luke 7:48; [John 5:14] **3** [a]ch. 26:65; John 10:36 **4** [b]ch. 12:25; John 2:24, 25

[1] Some manuscripts *Gergesenes*; some *Gerasenes* [2] Greek *daimonizomai*; also verse 33; elsewhere rendered *oppressed by demons* [3] Some manuscripts *perceiving*

suffering. Yet He has not promised to remove sickness from the world or the church before the Second Coming (8:20–23; 1 Cor. 15:26; Rev. 21:4).

8:18–22 These two events show the radical commitment Jesus demands of disciples. Those who identify with Jesus will be "sojourners and exiles" in the world (1 Pet. 2:11). Honoring one's parents by providing a proper burial was a strict obligation in Jewish society, but Jesus demands a greater allegiance to Himself.

8:20 Son of Man. This title occurs only three times in the New Testament outside the Gospels (Acts 7:56; Rev. 1:13; 14:14). All of the many occurrences in the Gospels involve assertions made by Jesus about Himself and may be classified into three categories. "Son of Man" means "a human being," especially in statements about what is typical of humanity generally. This use is similar to God's calling Ezekiel "son of man" (Ezek. 2:1 note), or Paul's reference to the human race as "the sons of men" (Eph. 3:5). Jesus also refers to Himself by this title when He predicts the suffering, death, and resurrection He accomplished for humanity (17:22, 23 note). Finally, it can refer to the apocalyptic "Son of Man" who appears at the Judgment of the end time (24:30; 26:64 note). This usage stems from Dan. 7:13, 14 where "one like a son of man" appears before the Ancient of Days and receives world dominion and worship. Jesus may have used "Son of Man" and avoided using "Messiah" because of popular conceptions that the Messiah would be a political and military leader.

8:27 winds and sea obey him. Only God can still the seas and appear as Lord of the storm (Ps. 29:3, 4; 65:5–7; 89:9; 107:23–30).

8:28 two demon-possessed men. Probably only one of these two demoniacs was exceedingly violent, and so Mark and Luke mention only that one. Matthew is concerned about the double witness of the testimony.

8:29 Son of God. See note 16:16.

the time. The demons have an apparently legitimate complaint; it is not yet "the time," the Day of Judgment. But Jesus is present and is already breaking the powers of darkness (12:28).

8:31 demons. The Greek word translated "demons" is a broad term for "divinities" (Acts 17:18), and supernatural beings. "Unclean spirits" (10:1) caused havoc with men, sometimes by possession. They are in league with Satan, the prince of demons (9:34; 12:24–28). Jesus throws out Satan's servants as a sign of the arrival of God's kingdom (12:28).

8:32 Jesus permitted the demons to enter the pigs, perhaps because the Day of Judgment had not yet arrived. Subsequent events demonstrated the perverse values of the community, that preferred its pigs to the rescue of two human beings. Luke 8:31 reports the plea of the demons that they not be sent to the abyss.

9:2 your sins are forgiven. Forgiveness is the prerogative of the one who has been offended, and for Jesus to forgive sins was to claim divine authority (Is. 43:25).

9:5 which is easier. Ultimately, forgiving sins is more difficult than performing a miracle, as the scribes would know since they recognized that only God can forgive sins. But the forgiveness of sins cannot be seen by observers. Jesus performs the lesser deed to prove the greater.

forgiven,' or to say, 'Rise and walk'? 6 But
that you may know that the Son of Man
has authority on earth to forgive sins"—he
then said to the paralytic—"Rise, pick up
your bed and go home." 7 And he rose and
went home. 8 When the crowds saw it,
[c]they were afraid, and [c]they glorified God,
who had [d]given such authority to men.

Jesus Calls Matthew

9 [e]As Jesus passed on from there, he saw
a man called [f]Matthew sitting at the tax
booth, and he said to him, "Follow me."
And he rose and followed him.

10 And as Jesus[1] reclined at table in the
house, behold, many [g]tax collectors and
sinners came and were reclining with Jesus
and his disciples. 11 And when the Pharisees saw this, they said to his disciples,
[h]"Why does your teacher eat with [g]tax collectors and sinners?" 12 But when he heard
it, he said, "Those who are well have no
need of a physician, but those who are
sick. 13 Go and learn [i]what this means, [j]'I
desire mercy, and not sacrifice.' For [k]I
came not to call the righteous, [l]but sinners."

A Question About Fasting

14 Then [m]the disciples of John came to
him, saying, [n]"Why do we and [o]the
Pharisees fast,[2] but your disciples do not
fast?" 15 And Jesus said to them, [p]"Can the
wedding guests mourn as long as the bridegroom is with them? [q]The days will come
when the bridegroom is taken away from
them, and [r]then they will fast. 16 No one
puts a piece of unshrunk cloth on an
old garment, for the patch tears away from
the garment, and a worse tear is made.
17 Neither is new wine put into old [s]wine-
skins. If it is, the skins burst and the wine
is spilled and the skins are destroyed. But
new wine is put into fresh wineskins, and
so both are preserved."

A Girl Restored to Life and a Woman Healed

18 [t]While he was saying these things to
them, behold, a ruler came in and [u]knelt
before him, saying, "My daughter has just
died, but come and lay your hand on her,
and she will live." 19 And Jesus rose and followed him, with his disciples. 20 And
behold, a woman [v]who had suffered from a
discharge of blood for twelve years came
up behind him and touched [w]the fringe of
his garment, 21 for she said to herself, "If I
only touch his garment, I will be made
well." 22 Jesus turned, and seeing her he
said, [x]"Take heart, daughter; your faith
has made you well." [y]And instantly[3] the
woman was made well. 23 And when Jesus
came to the ruler's house and saw [z]the
flute players and the crowd making a commotion, 24 he said, "Go away, for [a]the girl is
not dead but [b]sleeping." And they laughed
at him. 25 But [c]when the crowd had been
put outside, he went in and [d]took her by
the hand, and the girl arose. 26 And the
report of this went through all that district.

Jesus Heals Two Blind Men

27 [e]And as Jesus passed on from there,
two blind men followed him, crying
aloud, "Have mercy on us, [f]Son of David."

8 [c]See Luke 7:16 [d]ch. 28:18
9 [e]For ver. 9-17, see Mark 2:14-22; Luke 5:27-38 [f]ch. 10:3; Mark 3:18; Luke 6:15; Acts 1:13
10 [g]ch. 11:19; See ch. 5:46
11 [h][Luke 15:2] [g][See ver. 10 above]
13 [i]ch. 12:7 [j]Cited from Hos. 6:6; [ch. 23:23; Mark 12:33] [k][Luke 15:7; John 9:39] [l]1 Tim. 1:15
14 [m]ch. 11:2; 14:12; Luke 11:1; John 1:35; 3:25; 4:1; [Acts 18:25; 19:3] [n][ch. 15:2] [o]Luke 18:12
15 [p]John 3:29 [q]See Luke 17:22 [r][John 16:20]
17 [s]Josh. 9:4
18 [t]For ver. 18-26, see Mark 5:22-43; Luke 8:41-56 [u]See ch. 8:2
20 [v]Lev. 15:25 [w]ch. 14:36; 23:5; [Num. 15:38, 39; Deut. 22:12]
22 [x]ver. 2; See Luke 7:50 [y]ch. 15:28; 17:18; [ch. 8:13]
23 [z]Rev. 18:22
24 [a][Acts 20:10] [b]John 11:4, 11
25 [c]Acts 9:40 [d]Mark 9:27; Acts 3:7; 9:41
27 [e][ch. 20:30-34] [f]ch. 12:23; 15:22; 20:30, 31; 22:42; See ch. 1:1

[1] Greek *he* [2] Some manuscripts add *much*, or *often* [3] Greek *from that hour*

9:11 Just as Jesus was not defiled by contact with lepers, so He was not defiled by contact with sinners. He is the Physician who heals spiritual as well as physical sickness. Those who thought they were well were puzzled by Jesus' activities and found Him offensive.

9:14 disciples of John. Although Luke notes that Pharisees asked about fasting, Mark includes both John's disciples and Pharisees among those who raised the question.

9:15 then they will fast. Jesus explained that because He was present as the Messiah, His disciples did not need to fast. Jesus recognizes a future time when the bridegroom will not be with them. This points out that, from the earliest stages of His ministry, Jesus anticipated a time between His initial coming in redemption and His final coming in the Judgment.

9:17 new wine put into old wineskins. New wine continues to ferment and builds up pressure that would burst a used wineskin. The old patterns of fasting are inappropriate for the fullness of the kingdom that has now arrived.

9:18–25 As usual, Matthew has a more condensed form of this story than Mark and Luke. Both the story of the ruler's daughter and the story of the woman with a hemorrhage illustrate the relation between the work of Jesus and the role of faith in the kingdom. The same point appears in the following accounts of the blind man and the mute demoniac. These works (raising the dead, healing the sick, etc.) are in response to faith, not because faith causes them, but because without faith in the King Himself they are not signs of the kingdom but only unaccountable events with no special meaning.

9:22 your faith has made you well. Her faith made her well because the blessings of the kingdom come to those who look to Jesus for the solution to their problems, not because of any power of faith in itself.

9:23 flute players and the crowd. Professional mourners and others who helped the bereaved express their grief.

9:24 not dead but sleeping. Jesus was prophesying that He would raise her up from death (John 11:11–14).

9:27–31 The healing of two blind men related here is similar to the account in 20:29–34, as well as to the healing of Bartimaeus narrated in Mark 10:46–52 (cf. Luke 18:35–43). Both Bartimaeus and the blind men in Matthew 9 and 20 express their faith by calling Jesus "Son of David," a

28 When he entered the house, the blind
men came to him, and Jesus said to them,
"Do you believe that I am able to do
this?" They said to him, "Yes, Lord."
29 [g]Then he touched their eyes, saying,
[h]"According to your faith be it done to
you." 30 And their eyes were opened. And
Jesus sternly warned them, [i]"See that no
one knows about it." 31 [j]But they went
away and spread his fame through all that
district.

Jesus Heals a Man Unable to Speak

32 As they were going away, behold, a
[k]demon-oppressed man who was mute
[l]was brought to him. 33 And when the
demon had been cast out, the mute man
spoke. And the crowds [m]marveled, saying,
"Never was anything like this seen in
Israel." 34 But the Pharisees said, "He casts
out demons by the prince of demons."

The Harvest Is Plentiful, the Laborers Few

35 [n]And Jesus went throughout all the
cities and villages, teaching in their synagogues and proclaiming the gospel of the
kingdom and healing every disease and
every affliction. 36 [o]When he saw the
crowds, [p]he had compassion for them,
because they were harassed and helpless,
[q]like sheep without a shepherd. 37 [r]Then he
said to his disciples, "The harvest is plentiful, but the laborers are few; 38 therefore
[s]pray earnestly to the Lord of the harvest to
[t]send out laborers into his harvest."

29 [g]Mark 8:25; John 9:6 [h]See ver. 2 **30** [i]See ch. 8:4 **31** [j]Mark 1:45; 7:36 **32** [k][ch. 12:22-24; Luke 11:14, 15] [l]See ch. 4:24 **33** [m][Mark 1:27] **35** [n]See ch. 4:23, 24 **36** [o][ch. 14:14] [p]Mark 6:34 [q]Num. 27:17; 1 Kin. 22:17; Ezek. 34:5 **37** [r]Luke 10:2; John 4:35 **38** [s][2 Thess. 3:1] [t]ch. 20:2; [Mark 1:12]
Chapter 10
1 [u]Mark 3:13-15; 6:7-13; Luke 6:13; 9:1, 2 **2** [v]For ver. 2-4, see Mark 3:16-19; Luke 6:14-16; Acts 1:13 [w]ch. 16:18; John 1:42 [x]ch. 4:18, 21 **3** [y]ch. 9:9 **5** [u][See ver. 1 above] [z]2 Kin. 17:24; Ezra 4:10; Luke 9:52; 10:33; 17:16; John 4:9, 39, 40; 8:48; Acts 8:25; [Acts 1:8]

The Twelve Apostles

10 [u]And he called to him his twelve
disciples and gave them authority
over unclean spirits, to cast them out, and
to heal every disease and every affliction.
2 [v]The names of the twelve apostles are
these: first, Simon, [w]who is called Peter,
and [x]Andrew his brother; [x]James the son of
Zebedee, and John his brother; 3 Philip and
Bartholomew; Thomas and [y]Matthew the
tax collector; James the son of Alphaeus,
and Thaddaeus;[1] 4 Simon the Cananaean,
and Judas Iscariot, who betrayed him.

Jesus Sends Out the Twelve Apostles

5 [u]These twelve Jesus sent out, instructing them, "Go nowhere among the
Gentiles and enter no town of [z]the Samaritans, 6 [a]but go rather to [b]the lost sheep
of [c]the house of Israel. 7 And proclaim as
you go, saying, [d]'The kingdom of heaven is
at hand.' 8 [e]Heal the sick, raise the dead,
cleanse lepers,[2] cast out demons. [f]You
received without paying; give without pay.
9 [g]Acquire no gold nor silver nor copper for

6 [a]ch. 15:24; [Acts 3:25, 26; 13:46] [b]Ps. 119:176; Isai. 53:6; Jer. 50:6; [ch. 9:36; 18:12] [c]Acts 2:36; 7:42; Heb. 8:8, 10 **7** [d]ch. 3:2; 4:17; Luke 10:9 **8** [e][ch. 11:5] [f][Isai. 55:1; Acts 3:6; 20:33, 35] **9** [g]For ver. 9-15, see Mark 6:8-11; Luke 9:3-5; [Luke 10:4-12; 22:35]

1 Some manuscripts *Lebbaeus*, or *Lebbaeus called Thaddaeus* 2 *Leprosy* was a term for several skin diseases; see Leviticus 13

messianic title. The similarities have suggested to some that both accounts in Matthew are based on the healing of Bartimaeus, but there are sufficient differences at least between the two accounts in Matthew as to indicate separate incidents.

9:35–38 This paragraph summarizes the activity of Jesus in chs. 5–9 (teaching, preaching, healing) and introduces the mission discourse of ch. 10. The background is Ezek. 34:5, 6. Jesus is the true Shepherd who is concerned for His sheep (John 10), and He is identified with the "Lord GOD" of Ezek. 34:11–16.

9:37 harvest. Often a metaphor for the end-time activity of God. That the harvest is "plentiful" indicates that the "harvest" is not the harvest time but the crop (as in Luke 10:2). The emphasis here is on the proclamation of the gospel, the eschatological announcement that precedes judgment and urges people to repent and have faith. The "laborers" are not the angels sent to gather for judgment (13:49) but disciples who imitate Jesus by proclaiming the coming of the kingdom (10:7). Jesus does not yet command His disciples to go into the harvest as laborers, but to pray to God to send workers. No one can do the work of harvest without being called to it and equipped for it by God.

10:2 apostles. The Greek word *apostolos* designates an authorized representative or emissary whose word has the authority of the sender (see 2 Cor. 8:23 where it is translated "messengers," and 2 Cor. 1:1 note). Here the Twelve receive authority to do exactly what Jesus was doing (vv. 7, 8).

10:4 Simon the Cananaean. A member of a revolutionary movement ("Simon . . . called the Zealot," Luke 6:15). According to Josephus, the Zealots were a political party whose religious enthusiasm led them to advocate armed rebellion against Rome. Simon may have been associated with this movement previously and continued to be called "the Cananaean" or "Zealot" to distinguish him from Simon Peter.

10:5–11:1 This section contains several lines of teaching regarding the Christian mission that are found in different places in the other Gospels. This does not mean Matthew invented the occasion. Matthew presents the teaching of Jesus in five major discourses, and he may have brought in relevant material delivered on other occasions. Particularly 10:17–22, which envisions a world mission and being "dragged before governors and kings" (v. 18), seems to go beyond v. 5, that restricts the mission to Israel. Nevertheless, the future mission of the disciples to the whole world (28:18–20) is linked to this early experience of preaching to Israel, and Matthew's grouping of the material is appropriate.

10:5 Go nowhere. Although Jesus has already responded to Gentile faith (8:10), the focus of this first mission of the disciples, like that of Jesus before His passion and resurrection (15:24), was to the natural heirs of the kingdom. Jesus does not prohibit preaching to Gentiles encountered during the mission to Israel, but He did not send the disciples at this point into Gentile areas.

10:7, 8 proclaim . . . Heal . . . raise. The same signs of the kingdom that Jesus performed in chs. 8 and 9 will be done by His disciples.

10:8 give without pay. The kingdom was given to the disciples freely; to peddle the message would insult God and obscure the nature of the gospel as a free gift. Nevertheless they will be sustained; they do not need extra travel money and provisions (vv. 9, 10). This is a model for Christian life in general.

your belts, 10 no bag for your journey, nor
two tunics[1] nor sandals nor a staff, for [h]the
laborer deserves his food. 11 And whatever
town or village you enter, find out who is
worthy in it and stay there until you
depart. 12 As you enter the house, [i]greet it.
13 And if the house is [j]worthy, let [i]your
peace come upon it, but if it is not worthy,
let [i]your peace [k]return to you. 14 And if anyone will not receive you or listen to your
words, [l]shake off the dust from your feet
when you leave that house or town.
15 Truly, I say to you, [m]it will be more bearable on the day of judgment for [n]the land
of Sodom and Gomorrah than for that
town.

Persecution Will Come

16 [o]"Behold, I am sending you out as
sheep in the midst of wolves, so be [p]wise as
serpents and [q]innocent as doves. 17 Beware
of men, for [r]they will deliver you over to
courts and flog you [s]in their synagogues,
18 [r]and you will be dragged before governors and kings for my sake, [t]to bear witness before them and the Gentiles.
19 [r]When [u]they deliver you over, [v]do not be
anxious how you are to speak or what you
are to say, for [w]what you are to say will be
given to you in that hour. 20 [x]For it is not
you who speak, but [y]the Spirit of your
Father speaking through you. 21 [z]Brother
will deliver brother over to death, and the
father his child, and children will rise
against parents and have them put to
death, 22 [a]and you will be hated by all for
my name's sake. [b]But the one who endures
to the end will be saved. 23 When they [c]per-
secute you in one town, [d]flee to the next,
for truly, I say to you, you will not have
gone through all the towns of Israel [e]before
the Son of Man comes.
24 [f]"A disciple is not above his teacher,
nor a servant[2] above his master. 25 It is
enough for the disciple to be like his
teacher, and the servant like his master. [g]If
they have called the master of the house
[h]Beelzebul, how much more will they
malign[3] those of his household.

Have No Fear

26 "So have no fear of them, [i]for nothing
is covered that will not be revealed, or hidden that will not be known. 27 What I tell
you in the dark, say in the light, and what
you hear whispered, proclaim on [j]the
housetops. 28 And [k]do not fear those who
kill the body but cannot kill the soul.
Rather fear him [l]who can destroy both soul
and body in hell.[4] 29 Are not two sparrows
sold for a penny?[5] And not one of them will

10 [h]1 Tim. 5:18; [1 Cor. 9:4, 7-14] **12** [i][1 Sam. 25:6; 1 Chr. 12:18] **13** [j][ch. 8:8; Acts 16:15] [i][See ver. 12 above] [k][Ps. 35:13] **14** [l]Acts 13:51 [Neh. 5:13; Acts 18:6] **15** [m]ch. 11:24 [n]Gen. 18:20; 19:28; 2 Pet. 2:6 **16** [o]Luke 10:3; [John 17:18] [p]Gen. 3:1 [q]Rom. 16:19 (Gk.); Phil. 2:15; [1 Cor. 14:20] **17** [r]See Mark 13:9, 11; Luke 12:11, 12 [s]See ch. 23:34 **18** [r][See ver. 17 above] [t]See ch. 8:4 **19** [r][See ver. 17 above] [u]For ver. 19-22, [Mark 13:11-13; Luke 21:12-19; 2 Tim. 4:16, 17] [v]See ch. 6:25 [w]Deut. 18:18; [Num. 23:5]; See Ex. 4:12 **20** [x]Luke 12:12; Acts 4:8; 6:10; 13:9; 1 Cor. 15:10; 2 Cor. 13:3; [ver. 40; 1 Thess. 2:13; Heb. 1:1] [y][John 15:26]

21 [z]ver. 35, 36 **22** [a]ch. 24:9; John 15:18-21 [b]ch. 24:13; Mark 13:13; [Dan. 12:12, 13; James 5:11; Rev. 2:10]; See Heb. 3:6 **23** [c]ch. 23:34 [d][ch. 12:15; Acts 8:1; 9:25, 30; 14:6; 17:10, 14] [e]ch. 16:28 **24** [f]Luke 6:40; John 13:16; 15:20; [Heb. 12:3] **25** [g]ch. 9:34; 12:24; Mark 3:22; Luke 11:15; See John 7:20 [h][2 Kin. 1:2] **26** [i]Mark 4:22; Luke 8:17; [1 Tim. 5:25]; For ver. 26-33, see Luke 12:2-9 **27** [j]See Luke 5:19 **28** [k]Isai. 8:12, 13; 51:12, 13; Jer. 1:8; 1 Pet. 3:14 [l]James 4:12

[1] Greek *chiton*, a long garment worn under the cloak next to the skin
[2] Greek *bondservant*; also verse 25 [3] Greek lacks *will they malign*
[4] Greek *Gehenna* [5] Greek *assarion*, Roman copper coin (Latin *quadrans*) worth about 1/16 of a *denarius* (which was a day's wage for a laborer)

10:14, 15 shake off the dust from your feet. That is, the dust on one's garment kicked up by the feet. Jews sometimes shook the dust off their clothing when returning from Gentile lands as a sign of contempt; Jesus uses it here as a sign of judgment. A town that did not receive the disciples did not receive Jesus, and became spiritually "pagan" and as subject to judgment as Sodom and Gomorrah (Acts 13:51).

10:17–20 These verses anticipate a later, more extensive mission than the immediate occasion of v. 5 (10:5–11:1 note). Persecution will occur at the hands of both Jewish (v. 17) and Gentile (v. 18) authorities. But disciples are not to respond to this as pagans do, by hiring professional orators to defend them in court. The Holy Spirit will provide their defense (Acts 4:8).

10:22 all. Every sort of people. The allusion is to Mic. 7:6, which Jesus later quotes (v. 35).

10:23 before the Son of Man comes. There are several interpretations of the coming of the Son of Man referred to in this verse.

(a) The "coming" is the Second Coming of Christ to judge the earth. This view fits most of the other occurrences of the phrase (24:30; 25:31; 26:64; but see 16:28). The chief difficulty is that the note of urgency in v. 23 seems incompatible with a delay until the Last Judgment.

(b) The "coming" is the resurrection and ascension of Jesus or the sending of the Spirit at Pentecost. However, there is no evidence that the disciples were persecuted with the intensity assumed in vv. 17–22 prior to Jesus' resurrection or Pentecost.

(c) The phrase "before the Son of Man comes" is a way of saying, "before I rejoin you." But again the persecution described in vv. 17–22 did not occur during this time, and the purpose for the coming of the Son of Man elsewhere (to bring judgment) makes this meaning unlikely.

(d) The "coming" refers to the destruction of Jerusalem in A.D. 70 as an act of judgment against the nation of Israel. This understanding retains the note of urgency and fits the experience of the church prior to A.D. 70. The other references to the coming of the Son of Man view it as a great and terrible display of God's judgment. Although these cannot be limited to the destruction of Jerusalem, that event was terrible in intensity and fell on what had been the central visible symbol of God's presence, the temple.

10:25 Beelzebul. Greek *beelzeboul*, a transliteration of a Hebrew or Aramaic name for the prince of demons (12:24–27). The name probably means "lord of heaven," and appears in the Old Testament in the intentionally distorted form Baal-zebub ("lord of the flies") as a name for the god of Ekron (2 Kin. 1:2).

10:26–31 This injunction to fear God and not people is perhaps a development of Is. 8:12, 13. It is supported by three arguments: first, the acts of the wicked will be shown for what they are; second, although people can kill the body, God can punish soul and body; and third, God orders everything, down to the fall of a sparrow and the number of hairs on the head. The Bible consistently teaches that fear and reverence are appropriate responses to God.

10:28 hell. See note 5:22.

fall to the ground apart from your Father. 30 But [m]even the hairs of your head are all numbered. 31 Fear not, therefore; [n]you are of more value than many sparrows. 32 [o]So everyone who acknowledges me before men, I also will acknowledge before my Father who is in heaven, 33 but [p]whoever denies me before men, [q]I also will deny before my Father who is in heaven.

Not Peace, but a Sword

34 [r]"Do not think that I have come to bring peace to the earth. [s]I have not come to bring peace, but a sword. 35 [r]For I have come [t]to set a man against his father, and a daughter against her mother, and a daughter-in-law against her mother-in-law. 36 [u]And a person's enemies will be those of his own household. 37 [v]Whoever loves father or mother more than me is not worthy of me, and whoever loves son or daughter more than me is not worthy of me. 38 And [w]whoever does not take his cross and [x]follow me is not worthy of me. 39 [y]Whoever finds his life will lose it, and whoever loses his life for my sake will find it.

Rewards

40 [z]"Whoever receives you receives me, and [a]whoever receives me receives him who sent me. 41 [b]The one who receives a prophet because he is a prophet will receive a prophet's reward, and the one who receives a righteous person because he is a righteous person will receive a righteous person's reward. 42 And [c]whoever gives one of [d]these little ones even a cup of cold water because he is a disciple, truly, I say to you, he will by no means lose his reward."

30 [m]See 1 Sam. 14:45
31 [n]ch. 6:26; 12:12
32 [o][Rom. 10:9, 10; Heb. 10:35; Rev. 3:5]
33 [p]2 Tim. 2:12; 2 Pet. 2:1; 1 John 2:23; [Mark 8:38] [q]ch. 7:23; 25:12; Luke 13:25
34 [r]See Luke 12:51-53 [s][Rev. 6:4]
35 [r][See ver. 34 above] [t]ver. 21; [Mic. 7:6]
36 [u]Cited from Mic. 7:6; [Ps. 41:9; 55:12, 13; John 13:18]
37 [v]Luke 14:26
38 [w]ch. 16:24; Mark 8:34; Luke 9:23; 14:27 [x]ch. 9:9; John 8:12; 12:26; 21:19
39 [y]ch. 16:25; Mark 8:35; Luke 9:24; 17:33; John 12:25
40 [z]Luke 10:16; John 13:20; Gal. 4:14; [ver. 20; ch. 18:5; 25:40] [a]Mark 9:37; Luke 9:48; [John 12:44, 45]
41 [b]1 Kin. 17:10-15; 18:4; 2 Kin. 4:8; [3 John 5-8]
42 [c]ch. 25:35, 40; Mark 9:41; Heb. 6:10 [d]ch. 18:10

Chapter 11
2 [e]For ver. 2-19, see Luke 7:18-35

Messengers from John the Baptist

11 When Jesus had finished instructing his twelve disciples, he went on from there to teach and preach in their cities. 2 [e]Now when John heard [f]in prison about the deeds of [g]the Christ, he sent word by [h]his disciples 3 and said to him, "Are you [i]the one who is to come, or shall we [j]look for another?" 4 And Jesus answered them, "Go and tell John what you hear and see: 5 [k]the blind receive their sight and the lame walk, lepers[1] are cleansed and the deaf hear, and the dead are raised up, and [l]the poor have good news preached to them. 6 And blessed is the one who [m]is not offended by me."

7 As they went away, Jesus began to speak to the crowds concerning John: "What did you go out [n]into the wilderness to see? [o]A reed shaken by the wind? 8 What then did you go out to see? A man[2] dressed in soft clothing? Behold, those who wear soft clothing are in kings' houses. 9 What then did you go out to see? [p]A prophet?[3] Yes, I tell you, and more than a prophet. 10 This is he of whom it is written,

> [q]" 'Behold, I send my messenger before
> your face,
> who will prepare your way before
> you.'

11 Truly, I say to you, among those born of women there has arisen no one greater than

[f]ch. 14:3; [ch. 4:12] [g]See ch. 1:17 [h]See ch. 9:14 3 [i]John 4:25; 6:14; 11:27 [j][Luke 3:15] 5 [k]See Luke 7:22 5 [l]Luke 4:18; [ch. 5:3; James 2:5] 6 [m]Isai. 8:14, 15; John 6:61; 16:1 7 [n]ch. 3:1; Luke 1:80 [o][Eph. 4:14; James 1:6] 9 [p]ch. 14:5; 21:26; Luke 1:76 10 [q]Mark 1:2; Cited from Mal. 3:1

[1] *Leprosy* was a term for several skin diseases; see Leviticus 13 [2] Or *Why then did you go out? To see a man . . .* [3] Some manuscripts *Why then did you go out? To see a prophet?*

10:35 a man against his father. Mic. 7:6 addresses the rebelliousness and strife characteristic of Israel during the time of Ahaz. Just as Israel's history foreshadows Jesus' history (2:15 note), its turmoil and strife foreshadow the strife that results from the coming of the Messiah, even to the division of families. Although coming to Christ brings peace to the heart (11:29), embracing the gospel also makes life more difficult in some respects, because Jesus demands allegiance that takes priority over the natural ties of life (vv. 37–39).

10:38 take his cross. This is to obey and identify with Jesus even unto death, not simply to bear some particular burden imposed by the Lord.

10:41 prophet . . . righteous person. This verse emphasizes the principle that receiving those who are emissaries of another is equivalent to receiving the person who sent them (v. 40).

10:42 little ones. While not excluding children, this phrase refers to all Jesus' disciples, who are to be like little children (18:1–6, 10, 14). Jesus' remark about reward underscores the importance of accepting and assisting even those believers who seem insignificant (25:40, 45).

11:2 the deeds of the Christ. Since Matthew seldom uses "Christ" as a name for Jesus, this phrase probably means "when John heard in prison about the messianic deeds." John the Baptist had predicted that the Coming One would bring judgment, chopping down the trees of wickedness (3:10, 12). But Jesus allowed His own forerunner to be imprisoned by the wicked Herod.

11:4–6 Jesus makes John's disciples witnesses of His miracles, miracles that directly fulfill Is. 35:5, 6.

11:9 more than a prophet. John the Baptist was the immediate forerunner of the One to whom all the prophets pointed, and hence he pointed to Christ more clearly than all of them. As such, he himself was the object of prophecy, the one predicted in Mal. 3:1, the fulfillment of the Elijah prophecy of Mal. 4:5, 6 (v. 14), the herald of the Servant of the Lord (3:3; Is. 40:3).

11:11 greater than he. The least in the kingdom are greater than John because, standing after the Cross and Resurrection and having received

John the Baptist. Yet the one who is least
in the kingdom of heaven is greater than
he. 12 [r]From the days of John the Baptist
until now the kingdom of heaven has suffered violence,[1] and the violent take it by
force. 13 [r]For all the Prophets and the Law
prophesied until John, 14 and if you are
willing to accept it, he is [s]Elijah who is to
come. 15 [t]He who has ears to hear,[2] let him
hear.

16 "But to what shall I compare this
generation? It is like children sitting in
the marketplaces and calling to their
playmates,

17 "'We played the flute for you, and you
did not dance;
we sang a dirge, and you did not
mourn.'

18 For John came [u]neither eating [v]nor drinking, and they say, 'He has a demon.' 19 The
Son of Man came [w]eating and drinking,
and they say, 'Look at him! A glutton and
a drunkard, [x]a friend of [y]tax collectors and
sinners!' Yet wisdom is justified by her
deeds."[3]

Woe to Unrepentant Cities

20 [z]Then he began to denounce the cities
where most of his mighty works had been
done, because they did not repent. 21 [a]"Woe
to you, Chorazin! Woe to you, Bethsaida!
For if the mighty works done in you had
been done in [a]Tyre and Sidon, they would
have repented long ago in sackcloth and
ashes. 22 [b]But I tell you, it will be more
bearable on [c]the day of judgment for [d]Tyre
and Sidon than for you. 23 And you,
[e]Capernaum, will you be exalted to heav-
en? You will be brought down to [f]Hades.
For if the mighty works done in you had
been done in Sodom, it would have
remained until this day. 24 [b]But I tell you
that [g]it will be more tolerable on [c]the day
of judgment for the land of Sodom than
for you."

Come to Me, and I Will Give You Rest

25 [h]At that time Jesus declared, "I thank
you, Father, [i]Lord of heaven and earth, that
[j]you have hidden these things from the
wise and understanding and [k]revealed
them to little children; 26 yes, Father, for
such was your [l]gracious will.[4] 27 [m]All things
have been handed over to me by my
Father, and no one knows the Son [n]except
the Father, and no one knows the Father
except the Son and anyone [o]to whom the
Son chooses to reveal him. 28 [p]Come to
[q]me, all who labor and are [r]heavy laden,
and I will give you rest. 29 Take my yoke
upon you, and [s]learn from me, for I am
[t]gentle and lowly in heart, and [u]you will
find rest for your souls. 30 For [v]my yoke is
easy, and my burden is light."

12 [r]Luke 16:16
13 [r][See ver. 12 above]
14 [s]ch. 17:10-13; Mal. 4:5; Mark 9:11-13; Luke 1:17; [John 1:21]
15 [t]ch. 13:9, 43; Luke 8:8; 14:35
18 [u]ch. 3:4; Mark 1:6 [v]Luke 1:15
19 [w]ch. 9:10; Luke 7:36; 14:1; John 2:1; 12:2 [x]ch. 9:11; Luke 15:2; 19:7 [y]ch. 18:17
20 [z][Ps. 81:11-13; Isai. 1:2-5]
21 [a]For ver. 21-24, see Luke 10:12-15
22 [b]ch. 15:21; Mark 3:8; [Isai. ch. 23; Ezek. 28:2-24; Amos 1:9, 10] [c][Luke 12:47, 48] [d]See Acts 17:31
23 [e]Cited from Isai. 14:13-15 [f]ch. 16:18; Luke 16:23; Acts 2:27
24 [b][See ver. 22 above] [g]ch. 10:15 [c][See ver. 22 above]
25 [h]For ver. 25-27, see Luke 10:21, 22 [i]See Acts 17:24 [j]Job 37:24; 1 Cor. 1:19-27; 2 Cor. 3:14
[k]ch. 21:16; Ps. 8:2; [ch. 13:11; 16:17] 26 [l]Luke 12:32; Gal. 1:15 27 [m]See ch. 28:18 [n][John 1:18; 6:46; 7:29; 8:19; 10:15; 17:25] [o][John 17:26] 28 [p]John 7:37; [John 6:37] [q][ver. 3] [r][ch. 23:4; Luke 11:46] 29 [s]John 13:15; Eph. 4:20; Phil. 2:5; 1 Pet. 2:21; 1 John 2:6 [t]Zech. 9:9; 2 Cor. 10:1; Phil. 2:7, 8; [ch. 5:5] [u]Jer. 6:16
30 [v]1 John 5:3

[1] Or *has been coming violently* [2] Some manuscripts omit *to hear*
[3] Some manuscripts *children* (compare Luke 7:35) [4] Or *for so it pleased you well*

the fullness of the Spirit, they participate in what the prophets saw from a distance (1 Pet. 1:10–12).

11:12 suffered violence. The kingdom is pressing ahead with force, although violent men, such as Herod who had imprisoned John the Baptist, are trying to overcome it by force. It is not the strong and forceful who obtain the kingdom but the weak and helpless (vv. 28–30), who know their own weakness and are ready to depend on God (cf. Luke 16:16 note).

11:14 he is Elijah. Jesus identifies John the Baptist as the Elijah prophesied by Malachi to come as the forerunner of the Messiah (Mal. 4:5). This identification required the eyes of faith ("if you are willing to accept it"). There may have been some misunderstanding that Elijah would be reincarnated, but John denied that he was Elijah (John 1:21). Gabriel's announcement was that John would come "in the spirit and power" of Elijah (Luke 1:17).

11:19 Son of Man. See note 8:20.

wisdom is justified by her deeds. Jesus uses a proverb to make a point about Himself. The "children" in view are His own messianic deeds (vv. 2–5). The things done by Christ as "wisdom" (1 Cor. 1:30) "justify" Him, or demonstrate that He is right (James 3:17, 18).

11:25 you have hidden . . . and revealed. God is sovereign in choosing those to whom He will reveal His truth. No one can know God by worldly wisdom and learning (1 Cor. 1:26–31).

11:27 handed over to me. Jesus here makes extraordinary claims. He claims that God's sovereign disposition of all things has been committed to Him. As in Dan. 7, the Son of Man has received all power and dominion. He claims that He alone knows the Father and the Father alone knows Him. Jesus' knowledge is equal to the Father's, and His sonship is unique. He claims that His sovereignty extends even to deciding who will know the Father. This idea parallels v. 25, but here it is Jesus who reveals the Father.

11:28 Come to Me. Jesus has the authority to invite people to Himself. He does not extend His invitation to the strong but to the weary and burdened. Jesus uses the language of the wisdom tradition, calling the burdened to Himself as the incarnate wisdom of God (v. 19 note).

11:29, 30 Though the law had been given by God as a help to His people, the oral traditions of the scribes and Pharisees went far beyond the demands of God and became a heavy burden (12:2 note; 15:2). When the law was understood as a way of salvation, it became a "yoke of slavery" (Gal. 5:1). By contrast, the yoke of Jesus, while demanding, is "easy" because it is from One who is "gentle and lowly in heart" and can provide true rest for the soul. See "The Humble Obedience of Christ" at John 5:19.

Jesus Is Lord of the Sabbath

12 At that time [w]Jesus went through
the grainfields on the Sabbath. His
disciples were hungry, and [x]they began to
pluck heads of grain and to eat. 2 But when
the Pharisees saw it, they said to him,
[y]"Look, your disciples are doing [z]what is
not lawful to do on the Sabbath." 3 He said
to them, [a]"Have you not read what David
did when he was hungry, and those who
were with him: 4 how he entered the house
of God and ate [b]the bread of the Presence,
which it was not lawful for him to eat nor
for those who were with him, but only for
the priests? 5 Or have you not read [c]in the
Law how on the Sabbath the priests in the
temple profane the Sabbath and are guiltless? 6 I tell you, [d]something greater than
the temple is here. 7 And if you had known
[e]what this means, [f]'I desire mercy, and not
sacrifice,' you would not have condemned
the guiltless. 8 For [g]the Son of Man is lord
of the Sabbath."

A Man with a Withered Hand

9 He went on from there and [h]entered
their synagogue. 10 And a man was there
with a withered hand. And they asked him,
[i]"Is it lawful to heal on the Sabbath?"—[j]so
that they might accuse him. 11 He said to
them, "Which one of you who has a sheep,
[k]if it falls into a pit on the Sabbath, will not
take hold of it and lift it out? 12 [l]Of how
much more value is a man than a sheep! So
[m]it is lawful to do good on the Sabbath."
13 Then he said to the man, "Stretch out
your hand." And [n]the man stretched it out,
and it was restored, healthy like the other.
14 But the Pharisees went out and conspired
against him, how to destroy him.

God's Chosen Servant

15 Jesus, aware of this, [o]withdrew from
there. And [p]many followed him, and he
healed them all 16 and [q]ordered them not to
make him known. 17 [r]This was to fulfill
what was spoken by the prophet Isaiah:

18 [s]"Behold, my [t]servant whom I have chosen,
my beloved with whom my soul is well pleased.
[u]I will put my Spirit upon him,
and he will proclaim justice to the Gentiles.
19 He will not quarrel or cry aloud,
nor will anyone hear his voice in the streets;
20 a bruised reed he will not break,
and a smoldering wick he will not quench,
until he brings justice to victory;
21 [v]and in his name the Gentiles will hope."

Blasphemy Against the Holy Spirit

22 [w]Then a demon-oppressed man who
was blind and mute was brought to him,

Chapter 12 1 [w]For ver. 1-8, see Mark 2:23-28; Luke 6:1-5 [x]Deut. 23:25 2 [y][ver. 10; Luke 13:14; 14:3; John 5:10; 7:23; 9:16] [z][Ex. 20:9-11] 3 [a]1 Sam. 21:1-6; See ch. 21:16 4 [b]Ex. 25:30; Lev. 24:5-9 5 [c]Num. 28:9, 10; [1 Chr. 9:32; John 7:22, 23] 6 [d]ver. 41, 42; [ver. 8; Hag. 2:9; Mal. 3:1] 7 [e]ch. 9:13 [f]Cited from Hos. 6:6; [Mic. 6:6-8] 8 [g][ch. 9:6] 9 [h]For ver. 9-14, see Mark 3:1-6; Luke 6:6-11 10 [i][Luke 14:3]; See ver. 2 [j][Luke 11:54; 20:20; John 8:6] 11 [k][Ex. 23:4, 5; Deut. 22:4] 12 [l]ch. 6:26; 10:31 [m][John 5:16, 17] 13 [n][1 Kin. 13:4] 15 [o]Mark 3:7; John 10:39; See ch. 10:23 [p]ch. 19:2 16 [q]Mark 1:25 (Gk.); 3:12; 8:30; Luke 4:41 (Gk.); 9:21; See ch. 8:4

17 [r]See ch. 1:22 18 [s]Cited from Isai. 42:1-3 [t]Acts 4:27, 30 [u][Isai. 61:1; Luke 4:18; John 3:34; Acts 10:38] 21 [v]Isai. 42:4 (Gk.); [Isai. 11:10; Rom. 15:12] 22 [w]For ver. 22-24, see Luke 11:14, 15; [ch. 9:32-34]

12:2 not lawful. The Old Testament does not prohibit plucking grain on the Sabbath in order to eat—the disciples were not farmers engaged in the work of harvest. The Pharisees' objections were based on an oral tradition that failed to understand the true purpose of the Law. See "Christian Liberty" at Gal. 5:1.

Sabbath. The Sabbath is a symbol of God's sovereignty over the whole created universe (Ex. 20:8). It is a reminder of His redemption of His people (Deut. 5:12), and it is a representation of the hope of eternal rest at the Consummation (Heb. 4:9). Jesus as Lord of the Sabbath fulfills all aspects of the meaning of the Sabbath (Col. 2:16, 17).

12:3–6 In His reply to the accusations of the Pharisees, Jesus uses two arguments from the lesser to the greater, both focusing on His own person and authority. David's transgression of the ceremonial law in an hour of need had been allowed, and now One with much greater authority was present. Similarly, the demands of temple worship excuse priests from certain requirements of the Law and now "something greater than the temple" is here (v. 6).

12:6 something greater than the temple. As the genuine needs of people are more important to God than ceremonial symbols, so the One in whom God dwells is greater than the symbolic dwelling place. Jesus, Immanuel ("God with us"), is the true temple, to whom the symbol pointed (John 1:14; 2:21). The disciples, being in the presence of Jesus, had a far greater service than the priests who served in the Jerusalem temple.

12:7 I desire mercy. Again quoting Hos. 6:6 (cf. 9:13), Jesus condemns the misuse of the law by the Pharisees. The Sabbath was given by God as a help to humanity, but the Pharisees were perverting this purpose by turning the Sabbath against those in need and making it a burden (Mark 2:27).

12:8 lord of the Sabbath. The Son of Man has received dominion over creation (8:20 note) and redemption (20:28). So too He has dominion over the Sabbath, the sign of God's sovereignty in creation and redemption (v. 2 note). The claims Jesus makes here doubtless shocked the Pharisees, furthering their resolve to kill Him (v. 14).

12:9–14 Another example of Christ's lordship over the Sabbath. Again, there is no Old Testament prohibition of healing on the Sabbath, and it is always lawful to do good. Jesus does not teach that the Sabbath is abolished by the coming of the kingdom. He came not to destroy the law, but to fulfill it (5:17 note). The problem was not that the Pharisees observed the Sabbath but that they misinterpreted it, and turned what should have been a delight into a burden.

12:16–21 ordered them not to make him known. Is. 42:1–4 is cited as an explanation of why Jesus commanded people not to tell who He was. He came to proclaim and establish justice, but not by a showy display of power, and not by leading a political or military movement. Since the role of the Messiah was so misunderstood among the people, Jesus had to dampen the misguided enthusiasm that was bound to spring up.

and he healed him, so that the man spoke
and saw. **23** [x]And all the people were
amazed, and said, [x]"Can this be the Son of
David?" **24** But when the Pharisees heard it,
they said, [y]"It is only by Beelzebul, the
prince of demons, that this man casts out
demons." **25** [z]Knowing their thoughts, [a]he
said to them, "Every kingdom divided
against itself is laid waste, and no city or
house divided against itself will stand.
26 And if Satan casts out Satan, he is divided against himself. How then will his kingdom stand? **27** And if I cast out demons by
Beelzebul, [b]by whom do [c]your sons cast
them out? Therefore they will be your
judges. **28** But if it is [d]by the Spirit of God
that I cast out demons, then [e]the kingdom
of God has come upon you. **29** Or [f]how can
someone enter a strong man's house and
plunder his goods, unless he first binds the
strong man? Then indeed [g]he may plunder
his house. **30** [h]Whoever is not with me is
against me, and whoever does not gather
with me scatters. **31** [i]Therefore I tell you,
every sin and blasphemy will be forgiven
people, but [j]the blasphemy against the
Spirit will not be forgiven. **32** And whoever
speaks a word [k]against the Son of Man [l]will
be forgiven, but [j]whoever speaks against
the Holy Spirit will not be forgiven, either
in [m]this age or in the age to come.

A Tree Is Known by Its Fruit

33 [n]"Either make the tree good and its
fruit good, or make the tree bad and its fruit
bad, [o]for the tree is known by its fruit.
34 [p]You brood of vipers! How can you speak
good, [q]when you are evil? [r]For out of the
abundance of the heart the mouth speaks.
35 [r]The good person out of his good treasure brings forth good, and the evil person
out of his evil treasure brings forth evil. **36** I
tell you, [s]on the day of judgment [t]people
will give account for [u]every careless word
they speak, **37** for [v]by your words you will be
justified, and by your words you will be
condemned."

The Sign of Jonah

38 Then some of the scribes and Pharisees
answered him, saying, "Teacher, [w]we wish
to see a sign from you." **39** But he answered
them, [x]"An evil and [y]adulterous generation
seeks for a sign, but no sign will be given to
it except the sign of the prophet Jonah.
40 For [z]just as Jonah was three days and
three nights in the belly of the great fish,
[a]so will the Son of Man be three days and
three nights in the heart of the earth.
41 [b]The men of Nineveh will rise up at the
judgment with this generation and [c]con-
demn it, for [d]they repented at the preaching of Jonah, and behold, [e]something
greater than Jonah is here. **42** [f]The queen of
the South will rise up at the judgment with
this generation and condemn it, for she
came from the ends of the earth to hear the
wisdom of Solomon, and behold, [e]some-
thing greater than Solomon is here.

Return of an Unclean Spirit

43 "When [g]the unclean spirit has gone
out of a person, it passes through [h]water-
less places seeking rest, but finds none.
44 Then it says, 'I will return to my house
from which I came.' And when it comes, it
finds the house empty, swept, and put in
order. **45** Then it goes and brings with it
seven other spirits more evil than itself,
and they enter and dwell there, and [i]the
last state of that person is worse than the

23 [x]John 4:29; 7:26, 31; See ch. 9:27
24 [y]Mark 3:22; See ch. 10:25
25 [z]See ch. 9:4 [a]For ver. 25-29, see Mark 3:23-27; Luke 11:17-22
27 [b][Acts 19:13] [c][2 Kin. 2:7]
28 [d][ver. 18] [e]ch. 19:24; 21:31, 43; Luke 17:21
29 [f]Isai. 49:24 [g][Isai. 53:12]
30 [h]Luke 11:23; [Mark 9:40; Luke 9:50]
31 [i]For ver. 31, 32, see Mark 3:28-30; [Luke 12:10; Heb. 6:4-6; 10:26; 1 John 5:16] [j][Acts 7:51; Heb. 10:29]
32 [k]ch. 11:19; John 7:12; 9:24 [l]1 Tim. 1:12, 13 [j][See ver. 31 above] [m][Eph. 1:21]
33 [n]ch. 7:16-20 [o]Luke 6:43, 44
34 [p]ch. 3:7; 23:33 [q]ch. 7:11 [r]ch. 15:18, 19; Luke 6:45; [ch. 13:52; Eph. 4:29]
35 [r][See ver. 34 above]
36 [s][Eph. 5:4, 11; 2 Pet. 1:8] [t]Eccles. 12:14; Rom. 14:12; 1 Pet. 4:5 [u]See Acts 17:31
37 [v][ch. 5:22; James 3:2-12]
38 [w]ch. 16:1; Mark 8:11, 12; Luke 11:16; 23:8; John 2:18; 4:48; 6:30; 1 Cor. 1:22

39 [x]ch. 16:4; For ver. 39-42, see Luke 11:29-32; [Mark 8:11, 12] [y]Isai. 57:3; Mark 8:38; James 4:4 **40** [z]Jonah 1:17 [a][ch. 17:22, 23] **41** [b]Jonah 1:2 [c]Heb. 11:7; [Jer. 3:11; Ezek. 16:51, 52; Rom. 2:27] [d]Jonah 3:5 [e]ver. 6 **42** [f]1 Kin. 10:1; 2 Chr. 9:1 [e][See ver. 41 above] **43** [g]For ver. 43-45, see Luke 11:24-26 [h][Ps. 63:1; Jer. 2:6] **45** [i]2 Pet. 2:20-22; [John 5:14]

12:24 Beelzebul. See note 10:25.

12:29 binds the strong man. By His victory over Satan in the wilderness (4:10 note) and exorcism of demons, Jesus demonstrated that He had bound the "strong man" and that Satan was powerless to prevent the coming of the kingdom. The binding of Satan was a symbol of the messianic age in Jewish apocalyptic literature (see also Rev. 20:2).

12:31, 32 Speaking against the Spirit, calling the work of the Spirit the work of Satan, involves an explicit, willful, and decisive rejection of the very Power that can bring about repentance. The notion of the "unforgivable sin" has caused needless anxiety. Anyone who has been convicted of sin by the Spirit (John 16:8) and now believes the truth cannot possibly have committed it. See "The Unpardonable Sin" at Mark 3:29.

12:36, 37 Jesus indicates that words, even carelessly spoken words, are eternally important. In the Bible verbal sins such as lies, gossip, or insults are condemned as severely as adultery and murder (5:22, 37; 2 Cor. 12:20; 1 Tim. 1:10; James 3:6; Rev. 21:8).

12:38 sign. That they should ask for a sign is incredible in the light of what they had already seen. Jesus does not do miracles on demand.

12:39 sign of . . . Jonah. Jonah was as good as dead and then restored to life again, and the Son of Man's rising from the dead (v. 40) is the greatest sign of all that the kingdom has come.

12:40 three days and three nights. An emphatic way of saying "three days."

12:43–45 Unless the Holy Spirit resides in the heart, unholy spirits may enter (Rom. 8:9). If people will not commit themselves to the King whose power they have experienced, their final state will be worse than if the kingdom had never come (Heb. 6:4–6).

first. So also will it be with this [j]evil generation."

Jesus' Mother and Brothers

46 While he was still speaking to the people, behold, [k]his mother and his [l]brothers stood outside, asking to speak to him.[1] 48 But he replied to the man who told him, "Who is my mother, and who are my brothers?" 49 And stretching out his hand toward his disciples, he said, "Here are my mother and my brothers! 50 For [m]whoever [n]does the will of my Father in heaven is my brother and sister and mother."

The Parable of the Sower

13 That same day Jesus went out of the house [o]and sat beside the sea. 2 And great crowds gathered about him, [p]so that he got into a boat and sat down. And the whole crowd stood on the beach. 3 And [q]he told them many things in parables, saying: [r]"A sower went out to sow. 4 And as he sowed, some seeds fell along the path, and the birds came and devoured them. 5 Other seeds fell on rocky ground, where they did not have much soil, and immediately they sprang up, since they had no depth of soil, 6 but [s]when the sun rose they were scorched. And since they had no root, [t]they withered away. 7 Other seeds fell among [u]thorns, and the thorns grew up and choked them. 8 Other seeds fell on good soil and produced grain, some [v]a hundredfold, some sixty, some thirty. 9 [w]He who has ears,[2] let him hear."

The Purpose of the Parables

10 Then the disciples came and said to him, "Why do you speak to them in parables?" 11 And he answered them, [x]"To you it has been given to know [y]the secrets of the kingdom of heaven, but to them it has not been given. 12 [z]For to the one who has, more will be given, and he will have an abundance, but from the one who has not, [a]even what he has will be taken away. 13 This is why I speak to them in parables, because [b]seeing they do not see, and hearing they do not hear, [c]nor do they understand. 14 Indeed, in their case the prophecy of Isaiah is fulfilled that says:

> [d]"'You will indeed hear but never understand,
> and you will indeed see but never perceive.
> 15 For this people's heart has grown dull,
> and with their ears [e]they can barely hear,
> and [f]their eyes they have closed,
> lest they should see with their eyes
> and hear with their ears
> and [g]understand with their heart
> and [h]turn, and I would heal them.'

16 But [i]blessed are your eyes, for they see, and your ears, for they hear. 17 [i]Truly, I say to you, [j]many prophets and righteous people longed to see what you see, and did not see it, and to hear what you hear, and did not hear it.

45 [j]ver. 39
46 [k]For ver. 46-50, see Mark 3:31-35; Luke 8:19-21 [l]ch. 13:55; Mark 6:3; John 2:12; 7:3, 5, 10; Acts 1:14; 1 Cor. 9:5; Gal. 1:19
50 [m][John 15:14; Heb. 2:11] [n]ch. 7:21; [Luke 11:28]
Chapter 13
1 [o]For ver. 1-15, see Mark 4:1-12; Luke 8:4-10
2 [p][Mark 3:9; Luke 5:1-3]
3 [q]ver. 34 [r][Isai. 55:10; Amos 9:13]
6 [s]James 1:11 [t]John 15:6
7 [u]Jer. 4:3
8 [v]ver. 23; Gen. 26:12
9 [w]See ch. 11:15
11 [x]ch. 19:11; Col. 1:27; [1 Cor. 2:6-10; 1 John 2:20, 27];See ch. 11:25 [y]See Rom. 16:25
12 [z]ch. 25:29; Mark 4:25; Luke 8:18; 19:26; [John 15:2; James 4:6] [a][Rev. 2:5]
13 [b]Deut. 29:4; Jer. 5:21; Ezek. 12:2; Rom. 11:8; 2 Cor. 3:14; 4:4; [Isai. 42:19, 20] [c]ver. 19, 51; ch. 15:10; 16:12; Mark 8:21
14 [d]John 12:40; Acts 28:26, 27; Cited from Isai. 6:9, 10 15 [e][Heb. 5:11] [f][John 9:39, 41] [g][Rom. 10:10] [h]See Luke 22:32 16 [i]Luke 10:23, 24; [ch. 16:17] 17 [i][See ver. 16 above] [j]Heb. 11:13; 1 Pet. 1:10-12; [John 8:56]

[1] Some manuscripts insert verse 47: *Someone told him, "Your mother and your brothers are standing outside, asking to speak to you"* [2] Some manuscripts add here and in verse 43 *to hear*

13:1–53 This collection of parables on the nature of the kingdom of heaven is the third great discourse in Matthew (Introduction: Characteristics and Themes).

13:3 parables. Although the term "parable" can have a broad range of meanings, Jesus' "parables" are His distinctive teaching through brief comparisons or narratives. They usually have one central point or idea. Most of Jesus' parables are clear, but they also contain a depth of meaning that only one with a right relationship to Jesus can comprehend. It is only to the disciples that Jesus gives the interpretation of the parable of the sower (vv. 18–23) and the parable of the weeds (vv. 36–43). The ungodly miss this deeper meaning because their lack of a proper relationship with God has darkened their thoughts and hearts (Rom. 1:21).

13:10 in parables. See "The Teaching of Jesus" at Matt. 7:28.

13:11–17 It is difficult to escape the note of election here. Even the ability to understand God's message, let alone respond to it, is the gift of God. The ears that hear are blessed by God.

13:11 To you . . . to them. The "secrets" of the kingdom are the things that were indicated in veiled manner in the Old Testament, but are now made clear to the disciples by the coming of the King. See "Illumination and Conviction" at 1 Cor. 2:10.

13:12 To those who have a relationship with Jesus, parables deepen understanding and foster that relationship, but to those who do not, parables increase the confusion and ignorance. Thus the function of parables is both to enlighten and to conceal.

13:13 because seeing. Mark 4:12 (cf. Luke 8:10) phrases this statement even more strongly, with "so that" rather than "because." For Mark Jesus' purpose in telling parables is to prevent understanding and to cause unbelief (Mark 4:11 note); in Matthew Jesus' parables are in response to people's unbelief and inability to understand. Though some argue that Matthew softens the note of divine sovereignty seen in Mark, the word "lest" in v. 15 indicates that God's sovereign choice lies behind the hardening of their hearts whether it precedes (Matthew) or follows (Mark) an encounter with Jesus' teaching. While in this passage Matthew highlights the moral responsibility of those who reject Christ, his inclusion of the reference to Is. 6:9, 10 illustrates the compatibility of God's sovereignty and human responsibility. The parables served as an instrument of judgment by hardening the impenitent.

The Parable of the Sower Explained

18 [k]“Hear then the parable of the sower: 19 When anyone hears the word of [l]the kingdom and [m]does not understand it, [n]the evil one comes and snatches away what has been sown in his heart. This is what was sown along the path. 20 As for what was sown on rocky ground, this is the one who hears the word and immediately [o]receives it with joy, 21 yet he has no root in himself, but [p]endures for a while, and when tribulation or persecution arises on account of the word, immediately [q]he falls away.[1] 22 As for what was sown among thorns, this is the one who hears the word, but [r]the cares of [s]the world and [t]the deceitfulness of riches choke the word, and it proves unfruitful. 23 As for what was sown on good soil, this is the one who hears the word and [m]understands it. He indeed [u]bears fruit and yields, in one case [v]a hundredfold, in another sixty, and in another thirty.”

The Parable of the Weeds

24 He put another parable before them, saying, [w]“The kingdom of heaven may be compared to a man who sowed good seed in his field, 25 but while his men were sleeping, his enemy came and sowed weeds[2] among the wheat and went away. 26 So when the plants came up and bore grain, then the weeds appeared also. 27 And the servants[3] of the master of the house came and said to him, ‘Master, did you not sow good seed in your field? How then does it have weeds?’ 28 He said to them, ‘An enemy has done this.’ So the servants said to him, ‘Then do you want us to go and gather them?’ 29 But he said, [x]‘No, lest in gathering the weeds you root up the wheat along with them. 30 Let both grow together until the harvest, and at harvest time I will tell the reapers, [y]Gather the weeds first and bind them in bundles to be burned, but gather the wheat into my barn.’”

The Mustard Seed and the Leaven

31 He put another parable before them, saying, [z]“The kingdom of heaven is like [a]a grain of mustard seed that a man took and sowed in his field. 32 It is the smallest of all seeds, but when it has grown it is larger than all the garden plants and becomes a tree, so that the birds of the air come and make nests in its branches.”

33 He told them another parable. [b]“The kingdom of heaven is like leaven that a woman took and hid in [c]three measures of flour, till it was [d]all leavened.”

Prophecy and Parables

34 [e]All these things Jesus said to the crowds in parables; indeed, he said nothing to them without a parable. 35 This was to fulfill what was spoken by the prophet:[4]

> [f]“I will open my mouth in parables;
> [g]I will utter what has been hidden
> [h]since the foundation of the world.”

The Parable of the Weeds Explained

36 Then he left the crowds and went into [i]the house. And his disciples came to him, saying, [j]“Explain to us the parable of the weeds of the field.” 37 He answered, “The one who sows the good seed is the Son of Man.

18 [k]For ver. 18-23, see Mark 4:13-20; Luke 8:11-15
19 [l]ver. 38; ch. 4:23; 8:12 [m]See ver. 13 [n]ch. 5:37; 6:13; John 17:15; Eph. 6:16; 2 Thess. 3:3; 1 John 2:13, 14; 3:12; 5:18, 19
20 [o][Isai. 58:2; Ezek. 33:31, 32; Mark 6:20; John 5:35]
21 [p]Gal. 1:6; [Hos. 6:4; Gal. 5:7] [q]See ch. 11:6
22 [r]See ch. 6:25 [s]2 Tim. 4:10 [t]1 Tim. 6:9, 10, 17; [ch. 19:23; Mark 10:23; Acts 5:1-11; Heb. 3:13]
23 [m][See ver. 19 above] [u]Hos. 14:8; John 15:5, 16; Phil. 1:11; Col. 1:6 [v]ver. 8
24 [w]ver. 37-42; [Mark 4:26-29]
29 [x][1 Cor. 4:5]
30 [y]ch. 3:12
31 [z]For ver. 31, 32, see Mark 4:30-32; Luke 13:18, 19 [a]ch. 17:20; Luke 17:6
33 [b]Luke 13:20, 21 [c]Gen. 18:6 [d]1 Cor. 5:6; Gal. 5:9
34 [e]ver. 3; Mark 4:33, 34; [John 16:25, 29]
35 [f]Cited from Ps. 78:2 [g][ver. 11; Rom. 16:25, 26; 1 Cor. 2:7] [h]ch. 25:34; Luke 11:50; [John 17:24; Eph. 1:4; 1 Pet. 1:20]
36 [i]ver. 1 [j]ver. 24-30; [ch. 15:15]

[1] Or *stumbles* [2] Probably *darnel*, a wheat-like weed [3] Greek *bondservants*; also verse 28 [4] Some manuscripts *Isaiah the prophet*

13:19 of the kingdom. See “The Kingdom of God” at Luke 17:20.

13:22 deceitfulness of riches. Wealth is a blessing from God, but it is a dangerous blessing if it captivates the heart.

13:23 who hears the word and understands it. Only hearing and understanding the word (obedience being implied) results in fruit. There are those who temporarily receive the word but who fall away to avoid earthly discomfort or lose their commitment in pursuit of earthly wealth (v. 22). Likewise there are differing levels of bearing fruit. There are ultimately only two kinds of ground, that which genuinely receives the word to bear fruit and that which does not.

13:24–30 Again, Jesus Himself provides the interpretation (vv. 36–43). The field is the whole world, not just Israel or the church, and God withholds immediate judgment for the sake of the elect who are in the world. The righteous have had to live in the midst of the unrighteous from the beginning.

13:31 mustard seed. The mustard scrub can grow to a height of ten feet. The things of God may appear small in the world, yet have great results. Certainly the kingdom of heaven at that point in history appeared to be nothing in comparison with Rome, yet it would prove to be much greater.

13:32 The picture of a tree with birds nesting in the branches recalls Ezek. 17:23, where the birds represent the Gentile nations taking refuge in the Messiah and enjoying the blessings of the covenant.

13:33 like leaven. Although leaven or yeast is often a symbol of evil (16:11), here the point is that the kingdom permeates the world. Jesus’ concerns extended beyond Israel to the whole world.

13:34, 35 Parables reveal as well as conceal. Jesus quotes from Ps. 78:2, where the “parables” or “dark sayings” are a recital of the history of God’s redemption of His people climaxing in the choice of David to shepherd Israel. The redemptive events themselves were not “hidden,” but their meaning was not obvious. The psalmist revealed their meaning.

13:37 Son of Man. See note 8:20.

38 The field is the world, and the good seed
is [k]the children of the kingdom. The weeds
are [l]the sons of the evil one, 39 and the enemy
who sowed them is the devil. [m]The harvest
is [n]the close of the age, and the reapers are
angels. 40 Just as the weeds [o]are gathered
and burned with fire, so will it be at [n]the
close of the age. 41 [p]The Son of Man will
send his angels, and they will gather out of
his kingdom all [q]causes of sin and [r]all lawbreakers, 42 [s]and throw them into the fiery
furnace. In that place [t]there will be weeping and gnashing of teeth. 43 Then [u]the
righteous will shine like the sun [v]in the
kingdom of their Father. [w]He who has ears,
let him hear.

The Parable of the Hidden Treasure

44 "The kingdom of heaven [x]is like treasure hidden in a field, which a man found
and covered up. Then in his joy [y]he goes
and sells all that he has and [z]buys that field.

The Parable of the Pearl of Great Value

45 "Again, the kingdom of heaven is like a
merchant in search of fine pearls, 46 who,
on finding [a]one pearl of great value, [y]went
and sold all that he had and [z]bought it.

The Parable of the Net

47 "Again, the kingdom of heaven is [b]like
a net that was thrown into the sea and
[c]gathered fish of every kind. 48 When it was
full, [d]men drew it ashore and sat down and
sorted the good into containers but threw
away the bad. 49 So it will be at [e]the close of
the age. The angels will come out and [f]sep-
arate the evil from the righteous 50 [g]and
throw them into the fiery furnace. In that
place [g]there will be weeping and gnashing
of teeth.

New and Old Treasures

51 [h]"Have you understood all these
things?" They said to him, "Yes." 52 And he
said to them, "Therefore every [i]scribe [j]who
has been trained for the kingdom of heaven
is like a master of a house, who [k]brings out
of his treasure what is new and what is
old."

Jesus Rejected at Nazareth

53 And when Jesus had finished these
parables, he went away from there, 54 [l]and
coming to [m]his hometown [n]he taught them
in their synagogue, so that [o]they were
astonished, and said, "Where did this man
get this wisdom and these mighty works?
55 [p]Is not this [q]the carpenter's son? Is not
his mother called Mary? And are not [r]his
brothers James and Joseph and Simon and
Judas? 56 And are not all his sisters with us?
Where then did this man get all these
things?" 57 And [s]they took offense at him.
But Jesus said to them, [t]"A prophet is not
without honor except in his hometown
and in his own household." 58 And he did
not do many mighty works there, [u]because
of their unbelief.

The Death of John the Baptist

14 [v]At that time [w]Herod the tetrarch
heard about the fame of Jesus, 2 and
he said to his servants, [x]"This is John the
Baptist. He has been raised from the dead;
that is why these miraculous powers are at
work in him." 3 For [y]Herod had seized John
and bound him and [z]put him in prison for
the sake of Herodias, his brother Philip's

38 [k]ch. 8:12; [ver. 43] [l]John 8:44; Acts 13:10; 1 John 3:10; [ch. 23:15]; See ver. 19
39 [m]Joel 3:13; Rev. 14:15 [n]ver. 49; ch. 24:3; 28:20; [Dan. 12:13; Heb. 9:26]
40 [o]John 15:6; [ch. 3:12] [n][See ver. 39 above]
41 [p]ch. 24:31 [q]ch. 16:23; 18:7; [Zeph. 1:3] [r]ch. 7:23
42 [s]ver. 50; Rev. 9:2; [Rev. 19:20; 20:10] [t]See ch. 8:12
43 [u]Prov. 4:18; Dan. 12:3; [1 Cor. 15:41, 42] [v][ver. 38; ch. 25:34; 26:29; Luke 12:32] [w]See ch. 11:15
44 [x]Prov. 2:4 [y][ch. 25:9; Prov. 23:23; Phil. 3:7, 8] [z][Isai. 55:1; Rev. 3:18]
46 [a]ch. 7:6 [y][See ver. 44 above] [z][See ver. 44 above]
47 [b]ch. 4:19 [c][ver. 38; ch. 22:10; 25:2]
48 [d]John 21:11
49 [e]See ver. 39 [f]ch. 25:32; [ver. 41]
50 [g]See ver. 42
51 [h]ver. 10-16; [John 10:6; 16:29]
52 [i]ch. 23:34 [j]ch. 28:19 [k][ch. 12:35]
54 [l]For ver. 54-58, see Mark 6:1-6; [Luke 4:16-30] [m]ch. 2:23; Luke 4:23 [n]See ch. 4:23 [o]See ch. 7:28
55 [p][Luke 4:22; John 6:42] [q][Mark 6:3] [r]See ch. 12:46
57 [s]See ch. 11:6 [t]Luke 4:24; John 4:44; [Jer. 11:21; 12:6; John 7:5]
58 [u][ch. 17:20]

Chapter 14 1 [v]For ver. 1-12, see Mark 6:14-29; Luke 9:7-9 [w]Luke 3:1; Acts 13:1
2 [x]ch. 16:14 3 [y]Luke 3:19, 20 [z]ch. 11:2; John 3:24

13:41 gather out. The final Judgment will not only be a separation of the ungodly from the godly, but of ungodliness from the godly. Note that the Son of Man will send *His* angels—Jesus clearly asserts divine authority.

13:42 fiery furnace. See "Hell" at Mark 9:43.

13:43 shine like the sun. An allusion to Dan. 12:3, a promise of the future resurrection.

13:44, 45 Jesus made known the hidden things of the kingdom by parables (v. 35), but they remain hidden for most people, who cannot see their value. But like the man who finds treasure or the trader in pearls, those who do perceive the value of the kingdom will sacrifice anything to obtain it (Phil. 3:8).

13:52 every scribe. These teachers were frequently castigated by Jesus (23:13–32), not because of their positions as teachers, but because of their hypocrisy.

trained for the kingdom. The Greek phrase may also be rendered "has become a disciple of the kingdom." Since this saying immediately follows Jesus' asking the disciples if they understand, the implication is that the disciples will become teachers, and will, like a hospitable host, share with others the "treasures" they have received—an understanding of both the old redemptive history that points to Christ and the new redemptive acts that mark the presence of the kingdom.

13:55 carpenter's son. The Greek word translated "carpenter" is also a general term for any craftsman of worker. Joseph could have worked with wood or stone.

13:58 Jesus' refusal to do many miracles in Nazareth was not because He needed the faith of people to empower Him, but because miracles are of little value to those without faith (cf. 1 Cor. 13:2).

14:3 Herod . . . his brother Philip's wife. See notes Mark 6:14, 17. The genealogy of the Herods is confusing, with multiple marriages, marriages of close relatives, and reuse of similar names.

wife,[1] 4 because John had been saying to
him, [a]"It is not lawful for you to have her."
5 And though he wanted to put him to
death, [b]he feared the people, because they
held him to be [c]a prophet. 6 But when
Herod's [d]birthday came, the daughter of
Herodias danced before the company and
pleased Herod, 7 so that he promised with
an oath to give her whatever she might ask.
8 Prompted by her mother, she said, "Give
me the head of John the Baptist here on a
platter." 9 And the king was sorry, but
because of his oaths and his guests he commanded it to be given. 10 He sent and had
John beheaded in the prison, 11 and his
head was brought on a platter and given to
the girl, and she brought it to her mother.
12 And [e]his disciples came and took the
body and buried it, and they went and told
Jesus.

Jesus Feeds the Five Thousand

13 Now when Jesus heard this, [f]he withdrew from there in a boat to a desolate
place by himself. But when the crowds
heard it, they followed him on foot from
the towns. 14 When he went ashore he [g]saw
a great crowd, and [g]he had compassion on
them and healed their sick. 15 Now when it
was evening, the disciples came to him and
said, "This is a desolate place, and the day
is now over; [h]send the crowds away to go
into the villages and buy food for themselves." 16 But Jesus said, "They need not
go away; [i]you give them something to
eat." 17 They said to him, "We have only five
loaves here and two fish." 18 And he said,
"Bring them here to me." 19 Then he
ordered the crowds to sit down on the
grass, and taking the five loaves and the
two fish, [j]he looked up to heaven and [k]said
a blessing. Then he broke the loaves and
gave them to the disciples, and the disciples gave them to the crowds. 20 And they
all ate and were satisfied. And they took
up twelve baskets full of the broken pieces
left over. 21 And those who ate were about
five thousand men, besides women and
children.

Jesus Walks on the Water

22 [l]Immediately he [m]made the disciples
get into the boat and go before him to the
other side, while he dismissed the crowds.
23 And after he had dismissed the crowds,
[n]he went up on the mountain by himself to
pray. When [o]evening came, he was there
alone, 24 but the boat by this time was a
long way[2] from the land,[3] beaten by the
waves, for the wind was against them.
25 And [l]in the fourth watch of the night he
came to them, walking on the sea. 26 But
when the disciples saw him walking on the
sea, [p]they were terrified, and said, "It is a
ghost!" and they cried out in fear. 27 But
immediately Jesus spoke to them, saying,
[q]"Take heart; it is I. [q]Do not be afraid."
28 And Peter answered him, "Lord, if it is
you, command me to come to you on the
water." 29 He said, "Come." So Peter got
out of the boat and [r]walked on the water
and came to Jesus. 30 But when he saw the
wind,[4] he was afraid, and beginning to sink
he cried out, [s]"Lord, save me." 31 Jesus
immediately reached out his hand and
took hold of him, saying to him, [t]"O you of
little faith, why did you [u]doubt?" 32 And
when they got into the boat, [s]the wind
ceased. 33 And [v]those in the boat [w]wor-
shiped him, saying, [x]"Truly you are [y]the
Son of God."

Jesus Heals the Sick in Gennesaret

34 [z]And when they had crossed over, they
came to land at [a]Gennesaret. 35 And when
the men of that place recognized him, they
sent around to all that region and [b]brought
to him all who were sick 36 and implored
him that they might only touch [c]the fringe
of his garment. And [d]as many as touched it
were made well.

4 [a]Lev. 18:16; 20:21
5 [b]ch. 21:26; [ch. 21:46] [c]See ch. 11:9
6 [d]Gen. 40:20
12 [e]See ch. 9:14
13 [f]For ver. 13-21, see Mark 6:32-44; Luke 9:10-17; John 6:1-13; [ch. 15:32-38; 16:9; Mark 8:2-9]
14 [g][ch. 9:36]
15 [h]ver. 22; [ch. 15:23]
16 [i][2 Kin. 4:42-44]
19 [j]Mark 7:34; John 11:41; 17:1 [k]ch. 26:26; 1 Sam. 9:13; Mark 8:7; 14:22; Luke 24:30; [1 Cor. 14:16]
22 [l]For ver. 22-33, see Mark 6:45-51; John 6:15-21 [m][ch. 8:18]
23 [n]Luke 6:12; 9:28; [Mark 1:35; Luke 5:16] [o][Mark 13:35]
25 [l][See ver. 22 above]
26 [p][Luke 24:37]
27 [q]ch. 17:7; [Deut. 31:6; Isai. 41:13; 43:1, 2; John 16:33]
29 [r][John 21:7]
30 [s][ch. 8:25, 26]
31 [t]See ch. 6:30 [u][James 1:6]
32 [s][See ver. 30 above]
33 [v]ver. 22 [w]See ch. 8:2 [x][John 6:14] [y]ch. 16:16; 26:63; Ps. 2:7; Mark 1:1; Luke 1:35; 4:41; John 1:49; 9:35; 10:36; 11:27; 20:31; [ch. 3:17]
34 [z]For ver. 34-36, see Mark 6:53-56; [John 6:24, 25]
[a]Luke 5:1 35 [b]ch. 4:24 36 [c]See ch. 9:20 [d]Mark 3:10; Luke 6:19; [Acts 5:15]

1 Some manuscripts *his brother's wife* 2 Greek *many stadia, a stadion* was about 607 feet or 185 meters 3 Some manuscripts *was out on the sea* 4 Some manuscripts *strong wind*

14:6 the daughter of Herodias. A daughter by an earlier marriage to Herod Philip. According to the Jewish historian Josephus, the daughter's name was Salome and she later married another son of Herod the Great, Philip the tetrarch of Ituraea and Trachonitis (Luke 3:1).

14:13 heard this. According to v. 2, enough time had elapsed following the death of John the Baptist for reports of Jesus' miracles to come back to Herod. Jesus heard about Herod's renewed inquiries.

14:15–21 As God provided manna for Israel in the wilderness, so Jesus provided bread for the people in a remote place. Jesus challenges the disciples to provide for the crowd, then makes them ministers of His provision (vv. 16, 19).

14:25 fourth watch. Between 3:00 and 6:00 A.M.

14:30 Cf. Ps. 69:1–3.

14:33 Son of God. This title recognizes the messiahship of Jesus and His display of divine power (16:16 note).

Traditions and Commandments

15 [e]Then Pharisees and [f]scribes came
to Jesus [f]from Jerusalem and said,
2 [g]"Why do your disciples break [h]the tradition of [i]the elders? [j]For they do not wash
their hands when they eat." **3** He answered
them, "And why do you break the commandment of God for the sake of your tradition? **4** For God commanded, [k]'Honor
your father and your mother,' and, [l]'Whoever reviles father or mother must surely
die.' **5** But you say, 'If anyone tells his father
or his mother, What you would have
gained from me is given to God,[1] **6** he need
not honor his father.' So for the sake of
your tradition you have [m]made void the
word[2] of God. **7** [n]You hypocrites! Well did
Isaiah prophesy of you, when he said:

8 [o]"'This people honors me with their
lips,
but their heart is far from me;
9 in vain do they worship me,
teaching as [p]doctrines the
commandments of men.'"

What Defiles a Person

10 And he called the people to him and
said to them, [q]"Hear and understand: **11** [r]it
is not what goes into the mouth that defiles
a person, but what comes out of the
mouth; this defiles a person." **12** Then the
disciples came and said to him, "Do you
know that the Pharisees were [s]offended
when they heard this saying?" **13** He
answered, [t]"Every plant that my heavenly
Father has not planted [u]will be rooted up.
14 Let them alone; [v]they are blind guides.[3]
And [w]if the blind lead the blind, both will
fall into a pit." **15** But Peter said to him,
[x]"Explain the parable to us." **16** And he said,
[y]"Are you also still without understanding?
17 Do you not see that [z]whatever goes into
the mouth passes into the stomach and is
expelled?[4] **18** But [a]what comes out of the
mouth proceeds from the heart, and this
defiles a person. **19** For out of the heart
come [b]evil thoughts, [c]murder, adultery,
sexual immorality, theft, false witness,
[d]slander. **20** [e]These are what defile a person.
But [f]to eat with unwashed hands does not
defile anyone."

The Faith of a Canaanite Woman

21 [g]And Jesus went away from there and
withdrew to the district of Tyre and Sidon.
22 And behold, [h]a Canaanite woman from
that region came out and was crying,
[i]"Have mercy on me, O Lord, Son of David;
my daughter is severely oppressed by a
demon." **23** But he did not answer her a
word. And his disciples came and begged
him, saying, [j]"Send her away, for she is crying out after us." **24** He answered, [k]"I was
sent only to the lost sheep of the house of
Israel." **25** But she came and [l]knelt before
him, saying, "Lord, help me." **26** And he
answered, "It is not right to take the children's bread and [m]throw it to the dogs."
27 She said, "Yes, Lord, yet even the dogs
eat [n]the crumbs that fall from their masters' table." **28** Then Jesus answered her,
"O woman, [o]great is your faith! [p]Be it done
for you as you desire." [q]And her daughter
was [p]healed instantly.[5]

Jesus Heals Many

29 [r]Jesus went on from there and walked
[s]beside the Sea of Galilee. And he [t]went up
on the mountain and sat down there.
30 And great crowds came to him, bringing
with them [u]the lame, the blind, the crippled, the mute, and many others, and they
put them at his feet, and he healed them,

Chapter 15
1 [e]For ver. 1-20, see Mark 7:1-23 [f]Mark 3:22
2 [g][ch. 9:11] [h]Gal. 1:14; Col. 2:8 [i]Heb. 11:2 [j]Luke 11:38
4 [k]Cited from Ex. 20:12 [l]Cited from Ex. 21:17
6 [m]Gal. 3:17 (Gk.); [Rom. 2:23]
7 [n]ch. 23:13
8 [o]Cited from Isai. 29:13; [Ezek. 33:31]
9 [p]Col. 2:22; Tit. 1:14
10 [q]ch. 13:51
11 [r]See Acts 10:14, 15
12 [s]See ch. 5:29
13 [t][Isai. 60:21; 61:3; John 15:1, 2; 1 Cor. 3:9] [u]Jude 12
14 [v]ch. 23:16, 24; [Isai. 56:10; Mal. 2:8] [w]Luke 6:39
15 [x][ch. 13:36]
16 [y]ch. 16:9
17 [z][1 Cor. 6:13]
18 [a]ch. 12:34; James 3:6
19 [b]James 2:4 [c]ch. 5:22, 28; See Ex. 20:13-16 [d]Eph. 4:31; Col. 3:8; 1 Tim. 6:4
20 [e]1 Cor. 6:9, 10 [f]Mark 7:2, 5
21 [g]For ver. 21-28, see Mark 7:24-30
22 [h]Gen. 10:15, 19; Judg. 1:30-33 [i]See ch. 9:27
23 [j][ch. 14:15]
24 [k]Rom. 15:8; See ch. 10:5, 6
25 [l]See ch. 8:2
26 [m]ch. 7:6
27 [n][Luke 16:21]
28 [o]See ch. 9:2 [p][ch. 8:13] [q]ch. 9:22; 17:18; [John 4:52, 53] **29** [r]For ver. 29-31, [Mark 7:31-37] [s]ch. 4:18; John 6:1 [t]ch. 5:1 **30** [u]See ch. 11:5

[1] Or *an offering* [2] Some manuscripts *law* [3] Some manuscripts add *of the blind* [4] Greek *is expelled into the latrine* [5] Greek *from that hour*

15:2 tradition of the elders. This oral law was regarded by the Pharisees as having equal authority with the written law. It was codified as the *Mishnah* in the second century. One of its treatises covers details of hand washing, such as how much water is to be used, how many rinsings are necessary, and so on.

15:3–6 Jesus makes a sharp distinction between human traditions and the divine commands of Scripture. Cherished traditional understandings must not supplant or obscure the Bible itself, nor should customs be elevated to the level of divine law. See "Legalism" at Matt. 23:4.

15:11 what comes out of the mouth. What one says is a reflection or product of what is inside (12:36, 37 note).

15:24 only to the lost sheep . . . of Israel. Prior to the resurrection, the "wall of hostility" (Eph. 2:14) still stood. Jesus came as the Messiah and heir to the throne of David. Jesus graciously responds only after it was clear that the woman had no presumption of deserving the blessing promised to Israel; rather, she hoped to benefit from the overflow of those blessings.

15:26 throw it to the dogs. The context indicates that house pets rather than strays are in view. The expression is not equivalent to the common insult "Gentile dog."

15:29–39 Mark indicates that these events took place in the Decapolis (Mark 7:31), a predominantly Gentile area. It follows the story of the Canaanite woman.

31 [v]so that the crowd wondered, when they
saw the mute speaking, [w]the crippled
healthy, the lame walking, and the blind
seeing. And [x]they glorified [y]the God of
Israel.

Jesus Feeds the Four Thousand

32 [z]Then Jesus called his disciples to him
and said, [a]"I have compassion on the
crowd because they have been with me
now three days and have nothing to eat.
And I am unwilling to send them away
hungry, lest they faint on the way." 33 And
the disciples said to him, "Where are we to
get enough bread in such a desolate place
to feed so great a crowd?" 34 And Jesus said
to them, "How many loaves do you have?"
They said, [b]"Seven, and a few small fish."
35 And directing the crowd to sit down on
the ground, 36 he took the seven loaves and
the fish, and [c]having given thanks he broke
them and gave them to the disciples, and
the disciples gave them to the crowds.
37 And [d]they all ate and were satisfied. And
they took up seven baskets full of the broken
pieces left over. 38 Those who ate were
four thousand men, besides women and
children. 39 And after sending away the
crowds, he got into the boat and went to
the region of [e]Magadan.

The Pharisees and Sadducees Demand Signs

16 [f]And the Pharisees and Sadducees
came, and [g]to test him [h]they asked
him to show them [i]a sign from heaven. 2 He
answered them, [1][j]"When it is evening, you
say, 'It will be fair weather, for the sky is
red.' 3 And in the morning, 'It will be
stormy today, for the sky is red and threatening.'
[k]You know how to interpret the
appearance of the sky, but you cannot
interpret [l]the signs of the times. 4 [m]An evil
and adulterous generation seeks for a
sign, but no sign will be given to it except
the sign of Jonah." So [n]he left them and
departed.

The Leaven of the Pharisees and Sadducees

5 When the disciples reached the other
side, they had forgotten to bring any bread.
6 Jesus said to them, "Watch and [o]beware
of [p]the leaven of the Pharisees and
Sadducees." 7 And they began discussing it
among themselves, saying, "We brought
no bread." 8 But [q]Jesus, aware of this, said,
[r]"O you of little faith, why are you discussing
among yourselves the fact that you
have no bread? 9 [s]Do you not yet perceive?
Do you not remember [t]the five loaves for
the five thousand, and how many baskets
you gathered? 10 Or [u]the seven loaves for
the four thousand, and how many baskets
you gathered? 11 How is it that you fail to
understand that I did not speak about
bread? [o]Beware of the leaven of the
Pharisees and Sadducees." 12 [v]Then they
understood that he did not tell them to
beware of the leaven of bread, but of [w]the
teaching of the Pharisees and Sadducees.

Peter Confesses Jesus As the Christ

13 [x]Now when Jesus came into the district
of Caesarea Philippi, he asked his disciples,
"Who do people say that the Son of Man
is?" 14 And they said, "Some say [y]John the
Baptist, others say [z]Elijah, and others
Jeremiah or one of the prophets." 15 He said
to them, "But who do you say that I am?"
16 Simon Peter replied, [a]"You are [b]the
Christ, [c]the Son of [d]the living God." 17 And
Jesus answered him, [e]"Blessed are you,

31 [v]See ch. 9:33 [w]ch. 18:8; Mark 9:43 [x]ch. 9:8 [y]Isai. 29:23; Luke 1:68; Acts 13:17
32 [z]For ver. 32-39, see Mark 8:1-10; [ch. 14:14-21] [a][ch. 9:36]
34 [b]ch. 16:10
36 [c]ch. 26:27; Mark 14:23; Luke 22:17, 19; John 6:11, 23; Acts 27:35; Rom. 14:6; 1 Cor.10:30; 11:24; 14:16; 1 Tim. 4:3, 4
37 [d][2 Kin. 4:42-44]
39 [e][Mark 8:10]
Chapter 16
1 [f]For ver. 1-12, see Mark 8:11-21 [g]See [John 8:6] [h]1 Cor. 1:22; See ch. 12:38 [i]Luke 11:16; 21:11
2 [j][Luke 12:54, 55]
3 [k]Luke 12:56 [l][ch. 12:28; Luke 19:44]
4 [m]See ch. 12:39 [n]ch. 4:13; 21:17
6 [o]Luke 12:1 [p]1 Cor. 5:6-8; Gal. 5:9
8 [q]ch. 26:10 [r]See ch. 6:30
9 [s]ch. 15:16 [t]ch. 14:17-21
10 [u]ch. 15:34-38
12 [v]ch. 17:13 [w][ch. 5:20; 23:3]
13 [x]For ver. 13-16, see Mark 8:27-29; Luke 9:18-20
14 [y]ch. 14:2; Mark 6:14; Luke 9:7 [z]Mark 6:15; Luke 9:8; [ch. 17:10; Mark 9:11; John 1:21]
16 [a]John 11:27 [b]See ch. 1:17 [c]See ch. 14:33 [d]Deut. 5:26; Josh. 3:10; Ps. 42:2; Jer. 10:10; Dan. 6:20; Hos. 1:10; Acts 14:15; 2 Cor. 3:3; 1 Tim. 4:10
17 [e][ch. 13:16]

[1] Some manuscripts omit the following words to the end of verse 3

16:1 a sign from heaven. Jesus referred the Pharisees to a literal sign from heaven, the sky itself. His analogy shows that the problem was not lack of evidence, but an unwillingness to accept its significance. Jesus had performed many signs already.

16:4 sign of Jonah. See note 12:39.

16:11 not . . . about bread. Jesus frequently spoke in parables, but was misunderstood here by His disciples who thought He was speaking literally (v. 7). They should have realized from His feeding miracles that Jesus could provide food if that was what was needed, and so recognized that He was speaking metaphorically about the "leaven" (the doctrine, v. 12) of the Pharisees and Sadducees (Mark 8:15 note).

16:12 False teaching, like leaven in dough, can quickly permeate the church and corrupt its holiness.

16:13 Caesarea Philippi. A small town at the foot of Mount Hermon, about twenty-five miles north of Galilee.

16:15 who do you say that I am. The "you" is plural; Peter answers on behalf of the Twelve.

16:16 Christ. Peter declares that Jesus is the Messiah and King prophesied in the Old Testament (1:1 note).

the Son of the living God. The meaning of the title "Son of God" is different from that of pagan literature. In the Old Testament, the anointed king was called a "son" of God (2 Sam. 7:14; Ps. 2:7). Israel as a whole is also God's "son" (Ex. 4:22), and Jesus fulfills this status of Israel (2:15 note). As applied to Jesus, the title reflects Jesus' unique relation to the Father (11:27; 21:38). He is acknowledged by the Father as "my beloved Son" (3:17; 17:5). Peter's understanding was given to him from above, going beyond what he could have discerned on his own.

[f]Simon Bar-Jonah! For [g]flesh and blood has
not revealed this to you, [h]but my Father
who is in heaven. **18** And I tell you, [i]you are
Peter, and [j]on this rock[1] I will build my
church, and [k]the gates of [l]hell[2] shall not
prevail against it. **19** I will give you [m]the keys
of the kingdom of heaven, and [n]whatever
you bind on earth shall be bound in heav-
en, and whatever you loose on earth shall
be loosed[3] in heaven." **20** [o]Then he strictly
charged the disciples to tell no one that he
was the Christ.

Jesus Foretells His Death and Resurrection

21 [p]From that time Jesus began to show
his disciples that [q]he must go to Jerusalem
and [r]suffer many things from the elders and
chief priests and scribes, and be killed, and
on [s]the third day be raised. **22** And Peter
took him aside and began to rebuke him,
saying, "Far be it from you, Lord![4] This
shall never happen to you." **23** But he
turned and said to Peter, [t]"Get behind me,
Satan! You are [u]a hindrance[5] to me. For
you [v]are not setting your mind on the
things of God, but on the things of man."

Take Up Your Cross and Follow Jesus

24 Then Jesus told his disciples, "If anyone would come after me, let him [w]deny
himself and [x]take up his cross and follow
me. **25** For [x]whoever would save his life will
lose it, but whoever loses his life for my
sake will find it. **26** For [y]what will it profit a
man if he gains the whole world and forfeits his life? Or [z]what shall a man give in
return for his life? **27** [a]For the Son of Man is
going to come with [b]his angels in the glory
of his Father, and [c]then he will repay each
person according to what he has done.
28 Truly, I say to you, there are some standing here who will not [d]taste death [e]until
they see the Son of Man [f]coming in his
kingdom."

The Transfiguration

17 [g]And after six days Jesus took with
him [h]Peter and James, and John his
brother, and led them up a high mountain
by themselves. **2** And he was [i]transfigured
before them, and [j]his face shone like the
sun, and [k]his clothes became white as

17 [f][John 1:42; 21:15-17] [g]1 Cor. 15:50; Gal. 1:16; Eph. 6:12; Heb. 2:14 [h]1 Cor. 2:10; 12:3; [ch. 11:25; John 6:45] **18** [i][ch. 10:2; John 1:42] [j]Eph. 2:20; Rev. 21:14; [ch. 7:24] [k]Job 38:17; Isai. 38:10 [l]See ch. 11:23 **19** [m][Isai. 22:22; Rev. 1:18; 3:7] [n][ch. 18:18; John 20:23] **20** [o]Mark 8:30; Luke 9:21; [ch. 17:9]; See ch. 12:16 **21** [p]For ver. 21-28, see Mark 8:31–9:1; Luke 9:22-27; [ch. 17:12, 22, 23; 20:17-19] [q]ch. 20:18; [Luke 13:33] [r]ch. 17:12, 22, 23; Luke 24:7 [s]See ch. 27:63; John 2:19 **23** [t][ch. 4:10] [u]See ch. 13:41 [v]Rom. 8:5; Phil. 3:19; Col. 3:2; [Phil. 2:5]

24 [w][2 Tim. 2:12, 13] [x]See ch. 10:38, 39 **25** [x][See ver. 24 above] **26** [y][Luke 12:20] [z][Ps. 49:7, 8] **27** [a]ch. 24:30; 25:31; 26:64; Dan. 7:10, 13; Zech. 14:5; John 1:51; Acts 1:11; 1 Thess. 1:10; 4:16; Jude 14; Rev. 1:7; [Deut. 33:2] [b]ch. 13:41 [c]Rom. 2:6; 14:12; 2 Cor. 5:10; Heb. 9:27; 1 Pet. 1:17; Rev. 2:23; 20:12; 22:12; See Acts 10:42; 1 Cor. 3:8 **28** [d]John 8:52; Heb. 2:9 [e][ch. 10:23; 23:36; 24:34] [f]Luke 23:42
Chapter 17 **1** [g]For ver. 1-8, see Mark 9:2-8; Luke 9:28-36 [h]ch. 26:37; Mark 5:37 **2** [i][2 Cor. 3:18 (Gk.)] [j]Rev. 1:16; 10:1 [k]Dan. 7:9; [ch. 28:3; Ps. 104:2]

[1] *Peter* sounds like the Greek word for *rock* [2] Greek *the gates of Hades* [3] Or *shall have been bound . . . shall have been loosed* [4] Or "[May God be] *merciful to you, Lord!*" [5] Greek *stumbling block*

16:17 flesh . . . has not revealed this. Recognition of who Jesus is must come from God.

16:18 Peter . . . rock. The name "Peter" is a play on the Greek word for "rock" (*petra*). There are four leading interpretations of this play on words: (a) Peter's confession that Jesus is "the Christ" (v. 16) is the rock upon which the church is built; (b) Jesus Himself is the rock, as Peter later testifies (1 Pet. 2:5–8); (c) Peter, as the representative apostle, is a foundation in the church (Eph. 2:20); (d) Peter represents by his confession the type of person on which the true church will be built.

The first and second possibilities are often defended by pointing out that Peter's name is petros and the rock is petra. But this linguistic difference is not significant for this context. The second possibility is unlikely because Jesus describes Himself in this passage as not the foundation but the builder of the church.

If it had not been for the abuse of this passage by the Roman Catholic Church, it is unlikely that any doubt would have arisen that the reference is to Peter. But the foundational rock is Peter as a representative apostle (v. 15 note) whose confession of Christ has been revealed to him by the Father. As Peter himself later declares (1 Pet. 2:4–8), all believers have become "living stones" by virtue of their association with Christ, with the apostles as the foundation (Eph. 2:20, 21; Rev. 21:14). When Peter says that Jesus must not go to the cross, he is not called a foundation rock, but a stumbling block (v. 23 and text note).

gates of hell. In the Old Testament and other literature the "gates of Sheol" or the "gates of death" are equivalent to "death." "The gates of hell" may also be a reference to "death."

16:19 keys of the kingdom. This metaphor specifies how the apostles are foundational to the church; they have been given binding and loosing powers, or "keys," which lock and unlock doors. The apostles open the kingdom to those who share Peter's confession and exclude those who will not receive their testimony to Christ (10:14, 15). Through them Jesus reveals His own word of kingdom authority. The apostolic foundation of the church is laid in the written Word of God, the Scriptures, which are now the keys of Christ's authority in the church (Eph. 2:20; 3:5) through the power of the Spirit (18:18). See "Church Discipline and Excommunication" at Matt. 18:15.

16:20 tell no one. See 8:4. Popular conceptions of the Messiah were far from recognizing His suffering ministry. To allow His disciples to proclaim His messiahship openly might have instigated a political movement that would have hampered His real mission (John 6:15).

16:21 From that time. This phrase marks a new phase of Jesus' ministry (4:17 note). Matthew turns from the public preaching of Jesus in Galilee to His careful instruction of the disciples about His death and resurrection, His role as Messiah and theirs as disciples.

16:24 See note 10:38. Here Jesus adds the command to deny oneself. The call to discipleship demands that one completely abandon the natural desire to seek comfort, fame, or power.

16:28 will not taste death until. Although this statement has been interpreted as referring to the Transfiguration (17:1, 2), the language implies a period longer than a week. Another possibility is the destruction of Jerusalem (10:23 note), but the context here is not specifically related to the judgment of Israel. The "coming" of the Son of Man more likely here relates to the entire process by which Jesus receives dominion, especially His resurrection, ascension, and sending of the Spirit. All these things happened during the lifetime of the disciples. The Transfiguration could also be the initial event in this process witnessed by the disciples.

17:1 after six days. Such an exact time reference is rare in the Gospels; it must have been included to make clear the connection between the confession at Caesarea Philippi and the Transfiguration. Now that the disciples have begun to recognize who Jesus is, He is ready to move

light. 3 And behold, there appeared to them
Moses and Elijah, talking with him. 4 And
Peter said to Jesus, "Lord, it is good that we
are here. If you wish, I will make three
[l]tents here, one for you and one for Moses
and one for Elijah." 5 He was still speaking
when, behold, [m]a bright cloud overshadowed them, and [m]a voice from the cloud
said, [n]"This is my beloved Son,[1] with whom
I am well pleased; [o]listen to him." 6 When
[p]the disciples heard this, [q]they fell on their
faces and were terrified. 7 But Jesus came
and [r]touched them, saying, "Rise, and
[s]have no fear." 8 And when they lifted up
their eyes, they saw no one but Jesus only.
9 [t]And as they were coming down the
mountain, Jesus commanded them, [u]"Tell
no one the vision, until the Son of Man is
raised from the dead." 10 And the disciples
asked him, "Then why do the scribes say
[v]that first Elijah must come?" 11 He
answered, "Elijah does come, and [w]he will
restore all things. 12 But I tell you that Elijah
has already come, and they did not recognize him, but [x]did to him whatever they
pleased. [y]So also the Son of Man will certainly suffer at their hands." 13 [z]Then the
disciples understood that he was speaking
to them of John the Baptist.

Jesus Heals a Demon-Possessed Boy

14 [a]And when they came to the crowd, a
man came up to him and, kneeling before
him, 15 said, "Lord, have mercy on my son,
for he is [b]an epileptic and he suffers terribly. For often he falls into the fire, and
often into the water. 16 And I brought him
to your disciples, and [c]they could not heal
him." 17 And Jesus answered, "O [d]faithless
and [d]twisted generation, how long am I to
be with you? [e]How long am I to bear with
you? Bring him here to me." 18 And Jesus
[f]rebuked him, and the demon came out of
him, and [g]the boy was healed instantly.[2]
19 Then the disciples came to Jesus privately and said, "Why could we not cast it
out?" 20 He said to them, [h]"Because of your
little faith. For [i]truly, I say to you, [j]if you
have faith like a grain of mustard seed,
[k]you will say to this mountain, 'Move from
here to there,' and it will move, and [l]noth-
ing will be impossible for you."[3]

Jesus Again Foretells Death, Resurrection

22 [m]As they were gathering[4] in Galilee,
Jesus said to them, "The Son of Man is
about to be delivered into the hands of
men, 23 and they will kill him, and he will
be raised on [n]the third day." And they were
greatly distressed.

The Temple Tax

24 [o]When they came to Capernaum, the
collectors of [p]the half-shekel tax went up to
Peter and said, "Does your teacher not pay
the tax?" 25 He said, "Yes." And when he
came into the house, Jesus spoke to him
first, saying, [q]"What do you think, Simon?
From whom do kings of the earth take [r]toll
or [r]tax? From their sons or from others?"

4 [l][Neh. 8:15] **5** [m]2 Pet. 1:17; [Ex. 24:15, 16] [n]See ch. 3:17 [o]Acts 3:22 **6** [p]2 Pet. 1:18 [q][Gen. 17:3; Ezek. 1:28; Rev. 1:17] **7** [r]Dan. 8:18; 9:21; 10:10, 18 [s]ch. 14:27 **9** [t]For ver. 9-13, see Mark 9:9-13 [u]See ch. 8:4; 12:16 **10** [v]See ch. 11:14 **11** [w]Mal. 4:6; Luke 1:16, 17; [Acts 1:6; 3:21] **12** [x]ch. 14:3, 10 [y]ch. 16:21 **13** [z]ch. 16:12 **14** [a]For ver. 14-19, see Mark 9:14-28; Luke 9:37-42 **15** [b]ch. 4:24 **16** [c][ch. 10:1; Mark 6:7; Luke 10:17] **17** [d]Phil. 2:15; [John 20:27] [e][John 14:9] **18** [f]ch. 8:26; Zech. 3:2; Mark 1:25; Luke 4:35, 39; Jude 9 [g]See ch. 9:22 **20** [h][John 11:40]; See ch. 6:30 [i]ch. 21:21, 22; Mark 11:23 [j]Luke 17:6; [ch. 13:31] [k]ver. 9; [1 Cor. 13:2] [l]Mark 9:23 **22** [m]For ver. 22, 23, see Mark 9:30-32; Luke 9:43-45; [ch. 16:21-28; 20:17-19]

23 [n]See Mark 8:31 **24** [o]Mark 9:33 [p]Ex. 30:13; 38:26 **25** [q]ch. 18:12; 21:28 [r]ch. 22:17, 19; Mark 12:14; Rom. 13:7

[1] Or *my Son, my* (or *the*) *Beloved* [2] Greek *from that hour* [3] Some manuscripts insert verse 21: *But this kind never comes out except by prayer and fasting* [4] Some manuscripts *remained*

toward the climax in Jerusalem. The Transfiguration is part of Jesus' preparation for that crisis. See "The Transfiguration of Jesus" at Mark 9:2.

17:3 Moses and Elijah. Since the Law and the Prophets testify to Jesus, Moses the lawgiver, and Elijah, one of the greatest prophets of Israel, are here privileged to appear with Jesus. According to Luke 9:31 they discussed Jesus' coming death.

17:5 This is my beloved Son, with whom I am well pleased. The words from heaven show the disciples how foolish Peter's suggestion was (v. 4), and they begin to realize who Jesus is. "My beloved Son," the designation also given at Jesus' baptism, is the term reserved by the Father for His "only Son" (John 3:16).

listen to him. The word of God spoken through Moses and the prophets pointed to Jesus. Now the final word is spoken by God's Son (Heb. 1:1–4).

17:9 Tell no one. See note 16:20.

17:11 Elijah does come. See note 11:14. The scribes were right but failed to recognize both Elijah and the Messiah when they came.

17:17 Jesus, like Moses, came down from the mount of glory to encounter unbelief (Ex. 32:15–21).

17:20 little faith. The disciples' shortage of faith was not that they lacked confidence or did not expect success—they were apparently surprised by their failure—but because their expectation was not properly grounded in relationship to God. A tiny grain of true faith, rooted in submissiveness to God, is effective. Mark 9:29 makes this point even clearer by speaking of prayer as the key.

17:22, 23 This statement is the second prediction of suffering and resurrection in Matthew (16:21–24). Jesus will undertake the suffering He describes as the Servant of the Lord (Is. 53). It appears that no one before Jesus had ever identified the Messiah, the Son of Man, and the Suffering Servant of the Old Testament as three aspects of the one Redeemer and King. The disciples are so overwhelmed by their difficulty in accepting the suffering of the Messiah that they apparently do not even hear the promise of the Resurrection. At least they did not initially believe it (Luke 24:25, 37, 38).

17:24–27 The temple tax was prescribed in Ex. 30:13. The passage is not about paying taxes to the civil authority (22:21). Jesus' point is that the Christ and His disciples enjoy a relationship with God that frees them from the obligations imposed upon "others." Yet Jesus is willing to conform to previous requirements in order to avoid giving offense. Paul advised (Rom. 14:13–21) and practiced (Acts 16:3; 21:26) similar continued observance of some ritual requirements of the Old Testament law.

26 And when he said, "From others," Jesus
said to him, "Then the sons are free. 27 However, not [s]to give offense to them, go to the
sea and cast a hook and take the first fish
that comes up, and when you open its
mouth you will find a shekel. Take that and
give it to them for me and for yourself."

Who Is the Greatest?

18 [t]At that time the disciples came to
Jesus, saying, "Who is the greatest
in the kingdom of heaven?" 2 And calling
to him a child, he put him in the midst of
them 3 and said, "Truly, I say to you,
unless you [u]turn and [v]become like children, you [w]will never enter the kingdom of
heaven. 4 [x]Whoever humbles himself like
this child is the [w]greatest in the kingdom
of heaven.
5 [y]"Whoever receives one such child in
my name receives me, 6 but [z]whoever causes
one of these [a]little ones who believe in me
to sin,[1] it would be better for him to have a
great millstone fastened around his neck
and to be drowned in the depth of the sea.

Temptations to Sin

7 "Woe to the world for [b]temptations to
sin![2] [c]For it is necessary that temptations
come, [d]but woe to the one by whom the
temptation comes! 8 [e]And if your hand or
your foot causes you to sin, cut it off and
throw it away. It is better for you to enter
life crippled or lame than with two hands
or two feet to be thrown into [f]the eternal
fire. 9 [e]And if your eye causes you to sin,
tear it out and throw it away. It is better for
you to enter life with one eye than with two
eyes to be thrown into the [e]hell[3] of fire.

The Parable of the Lost Sheep

10 "See that you do not despise [g]one of
these little ones. For I tell you that in
heaven [h]their angels always [i]see the face of
my Father who is in heaven.[4] 12 [j]What do
you think? [k]If a man has a hundred sheep
and one of them has gone astray, does he
not leave the ninety-nine on the mountains
and go in search of the one that went
astray? 13 And if he finds it, truly, I say to
you, he rejoices over it more than over the
ninety-nine that never went astray. 14 So [l]it
is not the will of my[5] Father who is in
heaven that one of these little ones should
perish.

If Your Brother Sins Against You

15 [m]"If your brother sins against you, [n]go
and tell him his fault, between you and
him alone. If he listens to you, you have
[o]gained your brother. 16 But if he does not
listen, take one or two others along with
you, that every charge may be established
[p]by the evidence of two or three witnesses.
17 If he refuses to listen to them, [q]tell it to
the church. And if he refuses to listen even
to the church, [r]let him be to you as [s]a
Gentile and [s]a tax collector. 18 Truly, I say
to you, [t]whatever you bind on earth shall

27 [s]See ch. 5:29
Chapter 18
1 [t]ch. 17:24; For ver. 1-5, see Mark 9:33-37; Luke 9:46-48; [ch. 20:20-28]
3 [u]See Luke 22:32 [v]ch. 19:14; Mark 10:15; Luke 18:17; [Ps. 131:2; 1 Cor. 14:20; 1 Pet. 2:2] [w][ch. 5:19, 20]
4 [x]ch. 20:27; 23:11, 12 [w][See ver. 3 above]
5 [y][ch. 10:40, 42]
6 [z]Mark 9:42 [a]Luke 17:2; [1 Cor. 8:12]
7 [b]See ch. 13:41 [c]Luke 17:1; See 1 Cor. 11:19 [d]ch. 26:24
8 [e]ch. 5:29, 30; Mark 9:43-48 [f]See ch. 25:41
9 [e][See ver. 8 above]
10 [g][ch. 6:29; 25:40, 45; Luke 15:7, 10] [h]Acts 12:15; [Ps. 34:7; 91:11; Heb. 1:14] [i]Luke 1:19; Rev. 8:2; [Esth. 1:14]
12 [j]ch. 17:25; 21:28 [k]For ver. 12-14, [Luke 15:4-7]
14 [l]John 6:39; 10:28; [John 17:12]
15 [m]Luke 17:3 [n]2 Thess. 3:15; [Tit. 3:10; James 5:19]; See Lev. 19:17 [o]1 Cor. 9:19-22; 1 Pet. 3:1 **16** [p]Deut. 19:15; 2 Cor. 13:1; [Num. 35:30; John 8:17; 1 Tim. 5:19; Heb. 10:28] **17** [q][1 Cor. 5:4, 5; 6:1-6] [r][Rom. 16:17; 1 Cor. 5:9-13; 2 Thess. 3:6, 14; 2 John 10] [s]ch. 5:46, 47 **18** [t][ch. 16:19; John 20:23]

[1] Greek *causes . . . to stumble*; also verses 8, 9 [2] Greek *stumbling blocks* [3] Greek *Gehenna* [4] Some manuscripts add verse 11: *For the Son of Man came to save the lost* [5] Some manuscripts *your*

18:1–35 This chapter is the fourth of the five great discourses in Matthew (Introduction: Characteristics and Themes).

18:3 like children. Jesus makes this comparison not because children are supposed to be innocent, but because they are dependent upon others and willingly accept from them what they cannot provide for themselves.

18:5 Whoever receives. Since Jesus' followers must become "like children," the "child" represents any disciple. Response to Jesus' disciples is a response to Jesus Himself, and causing a disciple to sin is a grave offense (v. 6).

18:7 Universal human depravity will result in inevitable offenses, but individual responsibility ("woe to the one by whom the temptation comes") is not diminished by the commonplace occurrence of sin.

18:8, 9 See notes 5:1–7:29 and 5:29.

18:10 their angels. Scripture teaches that angels guard and minister to God's people (Ps. 91:11; Heb. 1:14) and that these spiritual beings may be assigned specific areas of responsibility (Dan. 12:1). Though this verse is sometimes interpreted to mean that each believer has a personal angelic guardian (Acts 12:15 and note), this popular belief goes beyond the biblical evidence. Nevertheless, God's care of His people through angels should be an encouragement to Christians.

18:12–14 The concern for the one is not at the expense of the ninety-nine, but indicates God's commitment to each disciple, and His special concern for one straying or in danger. God elects, seeks out, and preserves not only His church as a whole, but each individual within the church. Ezek. 34:11–16 probably lies behind this parable.

18:15 If your brother sins. This three-stage procedure for dealing with a Christian in sin is at the heart of all church discipline. The goal is to bring about repentance while keeping general public awareness of the sin to a minimum. At no point is the matter to be broadcast to the world at large. See theological note "Church Discipline and Excommunication."

18:17 church. The use of the word "church" by Jesus may appear premature, but only if the "church" is divorced from its moorings in the Old Testament. In the Greek translation of the Old Testament (the Septuagint), the "assembly" of the people of God is called the *ekklesia*, or "church." Jesus' use of Deut. 19:15 in v. 16 implies that the church is equivalent to Old Testament Israel.

let him be to you as a Gentile and a tax collector. Such individuals are to be cut off from fellowship and suspended from full social relations with other Christians. Paul applies this discipline in 1 Cor. 5 and 1 Tim. 1:20.

18:18 See note 16:19.

be bound in heaven, and whatever you
loose on earth shall be loosed[1] in heaven.
19 Again I say to you, if two of you [u]agree on
earth about anything they ask, [v]it will be
done for them by my Father in heaven.
20 For where two or three are [w]gathered in
my name, [x]there am I among them."

The Parable of the Unforgiving Servant

21 Then Peter came up and said to him,
"Lord, how often [y]will my brother sin against
me, and I forgive him? [z]As many as seven
times?" 22 Jesus said to him, "I do not say to
you seven times, but seventy times seven.[2]

23 "Therefore the kingdom of heaven may
be compared to a king who wished [a]to settle accounts with his servants.[3] 24 When he
began to settle, one was brought to him
who owed him [b]ten thousand [c]talents.[4]
25 [d]And since he could not pay, his master
ordered him [e]to be sold, with his wife and
[f]children and all that he had, and payment
to be made. 26 So the servant[5] [g]fell on his
knees, imploring him, 'Have patience with
me, and I will pay you everything.' 27 And

19 [u][Acts 12:5, 12; Philem. 22] [v]See ch. 7:7 **20** [w][Acts 4:30, 31; 1 Cor. 5:4] [x][ch. 28:20; John 12:26; 20:20, 26] **21** [y]ver. 15 [z]Luke 17:3, 4; [Col. 3:13] **23** [a]ch. 25:19 **24** [b]Esth. 3:9 [c]ch. 25:15 **25** [d][Luke 7:42] [e]Ex. 21:2; Lev. 25:39 [f]2 Kin. 4:1; Neh. 5:5 **26** [g]Acts 10:25; See ch. 8:2

1 Or *shall have been bound . . . shall have been loosed* 2 Or *seventy-seven times* 3 Greek *bondservants*; also verses 28, 31 4 A *talent* was a monetary unit worth about twenty years' wages for a laborer 5 Greek *bondservant*; also verses 27, 28, 29, 32, 33

Church Discipline and Excommunication

Making Christian disciples involves a whole range of activities for nurture, instruction, and training. To produce mature disciples, Christian learning, devotion, worship, righteousness, and service, are all to be taught in a context of care and accountability (Matt. 28:20; John 21:15–17; 2 Tim. 2:14–26; Titus 2; Heb. 13:17) among the other believers. Not abstractly, but in this context Reformed theology has emphasized the importance of church discipline as the official procedures of the church permitting it to define its membership and maintain its standards of belief and practice, derived from the Bible.

Since believers are required to be holy, unspotted by the morals of the world, the church itself is separated from the world, and it is necessary to define the boundary between the world and the church. The New Testament clearly shows that in the whole context of church life judicial procedures have a significant place for the health of churches and individuals (1 Cor. 5:1–13; 2 Cor. 2:5–11; 2 Thess. 3:6, 14, 15; Titus 1:10–14; 3:9–11).

Jesus instituted church discipline by authorizing the apostles to prohibit or permit certain kinds of behavior; this is the power of "binding" and "loosing" sins (Matt. 18:18; John 20:23). The "keys of the kingdom," first given to Peter and defined as power to bind and loose (Matt. 16:19), have usually been understood as authority to oversee doctrine and impose discipline. This authority was given by Christ to the church in general and to its ordained leadership in particular.

The *Westminster Confession* (30.3) explains:

> Church censures are necessary, for the reclaiming and gaining of offending brethren, for deterring of others from the like offenses, for purging out of that leaven which might infect the whole lump, for vindicating the honor of Christ, and the holy profession of the gospel, and for preventing the wrath of God, which might justly fall upon the church, if they should suffer His covenant, and the seals thereof [the sacraments] to be profaned by notorious and obstinate offenders.

Church censures may have to escalate from admonition through exclusion from the Lord's Supper to expulsion from the congregation (excommunication), which is described as handing a person over to Satan, the prince of this world (Matt. 18:15–17; 1 Cor. 5:1–5, 11; 1 Tim. 1:20; Titus 3:10, 11). Public sins (that is, those that are open to the whole church's view) should be publicly corrected in the church's presence (1 Tim. 5:20; cf. Gal. 2:11–14). Jesus teaches a procedure for dealing privately with those who have given personal offence, in hope that it will not be necessary to ask for the church's public censure of them (Matt. 18:15–17).

The purpose of church censure in all its forms is not to punish for punishment's sake, but to call forth repentance and so recover the straying sheep. Ultimately, there is only one sin for which a church member is excommunicated—impenitence. When repentance is apparent, the church is to declare the sin remitted and receive the offender into fellowship once again.

18:19, 20 These verses should be taken in the larger context as still dealing with church discipline. V. 19 is a further application of v. 18, and v. 20 states that Jesus is present to validate the judicial activity of the church.

18:23–35 See 5:7 and 7:2. Those who know God's mercy must operate on the principle of mercy. If they do not show mercy but insist on justice, they will not receive mercy, but justice. An unforgiving heart is an unforgiven heart and is subject to torment "until he should pay all" (v. 34; 6:12 note). A truly forgiving heart is one result of spiritual rebirth (John 3:3).

18:24 talents. A talent was the highest monetary unit of currency, equivalent to six thousand denarii or drachmas (v. 28 note). Such a sum of money was practically uncountable and illustrates the enormous debt of sin that all have incurred before God.

out of pity for him, the master of that servant released him and [d]forgave him the
debt. 28 But when that same servant went
out, he found one of his fellow servants
who owed him a hundred [h]denarii,[1] and
seizing him, he began to choke him, saying, 'Pay what you owe.' 29 So his fellow servant fell down and pleaded with him,
'Have patience with me, and I will pay
you.' 30 He refused and went and put him
in prison until he should pay the debt.
31 When his fellow servants saw what had
taken place, they were greatly distressed,
and they went and reported to their master
all that had taken place. 32 Then his master
summoned him and said to him, 'You
wicked servant! I forgave you all that debt
because you pleaded with me. 33 [i]And
should not you have had mercy on your fellow servant, as I had mercy on you?' 34 [j]And
in anger his master delivered him to the
jailers,[2] [k]until he should pay all his debt.
35 [l]So also my heavenly Father will do to
every one of you, if you do not forgive your
brother [m]from your heart."

Teaching About Divorce

19 Now when Jesus had finished these
sayings, he went away from [n]Gal-
ilee and [o]entered [p]the region of Judea
beyond the Jordan. 2 And [q]large crowds followed him, and he healed them there.
3 And Pharisees came up to him and
[r]tested him by asking, [s]"Is it lawful to
divorce one's wife for any cause?" 4 He
answered, [t]"Have you not read that he who
created them from the beginning made
them male and female, 5 and said,
[u]'Therefore a man shall leave his father and
his mother and hold fast to his wife, and
[v]they shall become one flesh'? 6 So they are
no longer two but one flesh. [w]What therefore God has joined together, let not man
separate." 7 They said to him, [x]"Why then
did Moses command one to give a certificate of divorce and to send her away?" 8 He
said to them, "Because of your [y]hardness of
heart Moses allowed you to divorce your
wives, but from the beginning it was not
so. 9 [z]And I say to you: whoever divorces
his wife, except for sexual immorality, and
marries another, commits adultery."[3]
10 The disciples said to him, "If such is
the case of a man with his wife, it is better
not to marry." 11 But he said to them,
[a]"Not everyone can receive this saying, but
only [b]those to [c]whom it is given. 12 For
there are eunuchs who have been so from
birth, and there are eunuchs who have
been made eunuchs by men, and there are
eunuchs who have made themselves
eunuchs [d]for the sake of the kingdom of
heaven. Let the one who is able to receive
this receive it."

Let the Children Come to Me

13 [e]Then children were brought to him
that he might lay his hands on them and
pray. The disciples [f]rebuked the people,
14 but Jesus said, [g]"Let the little children
[h]come to me and do not hinder them, for
to such belongs the kingdom of heaven."
15 And he laid his hands on them and went
away.

27 [d][See ver. 25]
28 [h]ch. 20:2; 22:19; Mark 6:37; 14:5; Luke 7:41; 10:35; John 6:7
33 [i][ch. 6:12; Eph. 4:32; Col. 3:13; 1 John 4:11]
34 [j]See James 2:13 [k]ver. 30; [ch. 5:25, 26]
35 [l]ch. 6:15; [Prov. 21:13] [m]1 Pet. 1:22; [Rom. 6:17]
Chapter 19
1 [n]ch. 17:24 [o]For ver. 1-9, see Mark 10:1-12 [p]Luke 9:51; 17:11; John 10:40; [ch. 4:25]
2 [q]ch. 12:15
3 [r]See [John 8:6] [s]ch. 5:31
4 [t]Gen. 1:27; 2:18, 21-23; 5:2; [ch. 21:16]
5 [u]Eph. 5:31; Cited from Gen. 2:24
[v]1 Cor. 6:16; [Mal. 2:15]
6 [w]1 Cor. 7:10
7 [x]Deut. 24:1-4
8 [y]Mark 16:14; [Mark 3:5; 6:52; Heb. 3:8]
9 [z]See ch. 5:32
11 [a]1 Cor. 7:2, 7-9, 17 [b][ch. 20:23] [c]ch. 13:11
12 [d][1 Cor. 7:32]
13 [e]For ver. 13-15, see Mark 10:13-16; Luke 18:15-17 [f]Mark 10:48
14 [g]ch. 18:3 [h][Mark 9:39]

1 A *denarius* was a day's wage for a laborer 2 Greek *torturers*
3 Some manuscripts add *and whoever marries a divorced woman commits adultery*; other manuscripts *except for sexual immorality, makes her commit adultery, and whoever marries a divorced woman commits adultery*

18:28 a hundred denarii. The Roman denarius was a daily wage for workers (20:2) and was equivalent to the Greek drachma (Acts 19:19). The sum owed by the second servant to the first is nothing compared to the debt of the first servant to the king; it was less than one part in a hundred thousand.

19:3 Is it lawful. The Pharisees' question may reflect the opinion of Hillel, a rabbi who allowed divorce for the slightest reasons on the basis of Deut. 24:1–4. He was opposed by another teacher, Shammai, who regarded only gross indecency as proper grounds. Jesus' answer transcends this debate about Deuteronomy and returns to the order of creation by God. Jesus views divorce as a fundamental denial of God's created order and the nature of marriage.

19:7, 8 Hearing Jesus' view of marriage, the Pharisees thought they could set Him against Moses. But Jesus shows that Moses in Deut. 24:1–4 was not giving a justification for divorce, but making provisions in the event of divorce. Deut. 24:1–4 consists of a long introductory conditional statement ("if then"), ending with the prohibition for a man to remarry a woman he had earlier divorced. A hardness of heart with respect to marriage and divorce is specifically restrained by this case law.

19:9 except for sexual immorality. The Greek word for "sexual immorality" is fairly broad, including a number of sexual sins besides adultery. In this clause (present also in 5:32 but omitted in Mark 10:11), Jesus recognizes that marital infidelity potentially destroys the marital tie between spouses and is, therefore, ground for legal divorce. However, divorce is not mandatory and reconciliation (see 18:23–35 note) is preferable. See "Marriage and Divorce" at Mal. 2:16.

19:10 it is better not to marry. The disciples' reaction seems cynical. Jesus accepts their response and indicates that it may be better not to marry, but only for the sake of the kingdom, not because God has an unworkable view of marriage (cf. 1 Cor. 7:7–9).

19:14 Let the little children come. The disciples viewed children as a distraction from the work of Jesus, but He welcomes them as subjects of the kingdom and blesses them. Since entrance into the kingdom is by God's grace and not human achievement, dependent little ones have a special title to covenant blessing (18:1–9). See "Infant Baptism" at Gen. 17:11.

The Rich Young Man

16 [i]And behold, a man came up to him,
saying, "Teacher, what good deed must I
do to [j]have [k]eternal life?" **17** And he said to
him, "Why do you ask me about what is
good? There is only one who is good. [l]If
you would enter life, keep the commandments." **18** He said to him, "Which ones?"
And Jesus said, [m]"You shall not murder,
You shall not commit adultery, You shall
not steal, You shall not bear false witness,
19 Honor your father and mother, and, [n]You
shall love your neighbor as yourself." **20** The
young man said to him, [o]"All these I have
kept. What do I still lack?" **21** Jesus said to
him, "If you would be [p]perfect, go, [q]sell
what you possess and give to the poor, and
you will have [r]treasure in heaven; and
come, follow me." **22** [s]When the young man
heard this he went away sorrowful, for he
had great possessions.
23 And Jesus said to his disciples, "Truly,
I say to you, [t]only with difficulty will a rich
person enter the kingdom of heaven.
24 [u]Again I tell you, it is easier for a camel
to go through the eye of a needle than for
a rich person to enter [v]the kingdom of
God." **25** When the disciples heard this,
they were greatly astonished, saying,
"Who then can be saved?" **26** But Jesus
[w]looked at them and said, [x]"With man this
is impossible, but with God all things are
possible." **27** Then Peter said in reply, "See,
[y]we have left everything and followed you.
What then will we have?" **28** Jesus said to
them, "Truly, I say to you, in the new
world,[1] [z]when the Son of Man will sit on
his glorious throne, you who have followed me [a]will also sit on twelve thrones,
[b]judging the twelve tribes of Israel. **29** [c]And
everyone who has left houses or brothers
or sisters or father or mother or children or
lands, for my name's sake, will receive a
hundredfold[2] and will [d]inherit eternal life.
30 But [e]many who are [f]first will be last, and
the last first.

Laborers in the Vineyard

20 "For the kingdom of heaven is like
a master of a house who went out
early in the morning to hire laborers for his
vineyard. **2** After agreeing with the laborers
for a denarius[3] a day, he sent them into his
vineyard. **3** And going out about the third
hour he saw others standing idle in the
marketplace, **4** and to them he said, 'You go
into the vineyard too, and whatever is right
I will give you.' **5** So they went. Going out
again about the sixth hour and the ninth
hour, he did the same. **6** And [g]about the
eleventh hour he went out and found others standing. And he said to them, 'Why do
you stand here idle all day?' **7** They said to
him, 'Because no one has hired us.' He
said to them, 'You go into the vineyard
too.' **8** And [h]when evening came, the owner
of the vineyard said to his [i]foreman, 'Call
the laborers and pay them their wages,
beginning with the last, up to the first.'
9 And when those hired about the eleventh
hour came, each of them received a denarius. **10** Now when those hired first came,
they thought they would receive more, but
each of them also received a denarius.
11 And on receiving it they grumbled at the
master of the house, **12** saying, 'These last
worked only one hour, and you have made
them equal to us who have borne the burden of the day and [j]the scorching heat.'
13 But he replied to one of them, [k]'Friend, I
am doing you no wrong. Did you not agree
with me for a denarius? **14** Take [l]what
belongs to you and go. I choose to give to
this last worker as I give to you. **15** [m]Am I

16 [i]For ver. 16-29, see Mark 10:17-30; Luke 18:18-30; [Luke 10:25-28] [j][ver. 29] [k]ch. 25:46; [ch. 18:8] **17** [l]Lev. 18:5; Neh. 9:29; Ezek. 20:11, 13, 21; Rom. 10:5; Gal. 3:12 **18** [m]Rom. 13:9; Cited from Ex. 20:12-16; Deut. 5:16-20; [ch. 5:21, 27] **19** [n]ch. 5:43; 22:39; Mark 12:31; Luke 10:27; Gal. 5:14; James 2:8; Cited from Lev. 19:18 **20** [o][Phil. 3:6] **21** [p]See ch. 5:48 [q]Luke 12:33; [Luke 16:9; 19:8; Acts 2:45; 4:34, 35; 1 Tim. 6:18, 19] [r]ch. 6:19, 20 **22** [s][Ezek. 33:31] **23** [t][1 Cor. 1:26]; See ch. 13:22 **24** [u][Mark 10:24] [v]See ch. 12:28 **26** [w]Mark 10:21; Luke 22:61 [x]Gen. 18:14; Job 42:2; Jer. 32:17, 27; Zech. 8:6; Mark 14:36; Luke 1:37 **27** [y]ch. 4:20, 22; Mark 1:18, 20 **28** [z]See ch. 16:27 [a]Luke 22:30; Rev. 3:21 [b][1 Cor. 6:2] **29** [c][Luke 14:26] [d][ver. 16]; See ch. 25:34 **30** [e]ch. 20:16; Mark 10:31; Luke 13:30 [f][ch. 21:31, 32]

Chapter 20 **6** [g][1 Cor. 15:8] **8** [h]Lev. 19:13; Deut. 24:15 [i]Luke 8:3; [ch. 24:45] **12** [j]Luke 12:55; James 1:11 (Gk.); **13** [k]ch. 22:12; 26:50 **14** [l]ch. 25:25 **15** [m][Rom. 9:15-24]

[1] Greek *in the regeneration* [2] Some manuscripts *manifold* [3] A *denarius* was a day's wage for a laborer

19:16 have eternal life. This expression is equivalent to "enter the kingdom of God" (v. 24) and "be saved" (v. 25).

19:21 sell what you possess. Jesus' instruction to the young man to sell all he had demonstrated that what he lacked was the attitude that abandons everything (16:24) for the sake of God's unearned grace (Phil. 3:7–9).

19:23–26 Wealth was considered evidence of God's approval, and the rich would seem to be the likeliest candidates for the kingdom. Jesus turned this idea upside-down, and the result was not lost on the disciples: "Who then can be saved?" (v. 25).

19:28 judging. Governing, not sentencing to punishment.

19:29 will receive a hundredfold. The blessings of salvation far exceed anything which one must forsake to obtain them (1 Cor. 2:9).

19:30 first will be last. Positions of honor or prestige in this life by no means assure heavenly approval; indeed, often the reverse will be true. Similarly, as the following parable illustrates (20:1–16), length of earthly labor may not correspond to one's heavenly reward.

20:1–15 This parable is only a hard saying for those who fail to recognize their absolute dependence on grace for any good thing from God's hand. There is no room for a Christian to be jealous of the good gifts God has given to another.

20:2 a denarius. See note 18:28.

not allowed to do what I choose with what belongs to me? Or [n]do you begrudge my generosity?'[1] 16 So [o]the last will be first, and the first last."

Jesus Foretells His Death a Third Time

17 [p]And as Jesus was going up to Jerusalem, he took the twelve disciples aside, and on the way he said to them, 18 "See, [q]we are going up to Jerusalem. And the Son of Man will be delivered over to the chief priests and scribes, and they will [r]condemn him to death 19 and [s]deliver him over to the Gentiles [t]to be mocked and flogged and [u]crucified, and he will be raised on [v]the third day."

A Mother's Request

20 [w]Then [x]the mother of the sons of Zebedee came up to him with her sons, and [y]kneeling before him she asked him for something. 21 And he said to her, "What do you want?" She said to him, "Say that these two sons of mine [z]are to sit, one at your right hand and one at your left, [a]in your kingdom." 22 Jesus answered, [b]"You do not know what you are asking. Are you able [c]to drink the cup that I am to drink?" They said to him, "We are able." 23 He said to them, [d]"You will drink [e]my cup, but to sit at my right hand and at my left is not mine to grant, [f]but it is for those for whom it has been [g]prepared by my Father." 24 And when the ten heard it, they were indignant at the two brothers. 25 But Jesus called them to him and said, [h]"You know that the rulers of the Gentiles [i]lord it over them, and their great ones exercise authority over them. 26 [j]It shall not be so among you. But whoever would be great among you must be your servant,[2] 27 and whoever would be first among you must be your slave,[3] 28 even as the Son of Man came not to be served but [k]to serve, and [l]to give his life as a ransom for [m]many."

Jesus Heals Two Blind Men

29 [n]And as they went out of Jericho, a great crowd followed him. 30 And behold, there were two blind men sitting by the roadside, and when they heard that Jesus was passing by, they cried out, "Lord,[4] have mercy on us, [o]Son of David!" 31 The crowd [p]rebuked them, telling them to be silent, but they cried out all the more, "Lord, have mercy on us, Son of David!" 32 And stopping, Jesus called them and said, "What do you want me to do for you?" 33 They said to him, "Lord, let our eyes be opened." 34 And Jesus in pity touched their eyes, and immediately they recovered their sight and followed him.

The Triumphal Entry

21 [q]Now when they drew near to Jerusalem and came to Bethphage, to [r]the Mount of Olives, then Jesus [s]sent two disciples, 2 saying to them, "Go into the village in front of you, and immediately

15 [n]ch. 6:23; Deut. 15:9; Prov. 23:6 **16** [o]See ch. 19:30 **17** [p]For ver. 17-19, see Mark 10:32-34; Luke 18:31-33; [ch. 16:21-28; 17:12, 22, 23] **18** [q]See ch. 16:21 [r]ch. 26:66; John 19:7 **19** [s]ch. 27:2; John 18:30, 31; Acts 3:13; [Acts 2:23; 4:27; 21:11] [t]ch. 27:26-31 [u]ch. 26:2; Luke 24:7; John 12:32, 33; 18:32 [v]ch. 16:21; 27:63 **20** [w]For ver. 20-28, see Mark 10:35-45 [x]ch. 4:21; 27:56 [y]See ch. 8:2 **21** [z][ch. 19:28] [a]ch. 16:28; 25:31, 34; Luke 23:42 **22** [b][Luke 9:33; 23:34] [c]ch. 26:29, 42; Mark 14:36; Luke 22:42; John 18:11; [Isai. 51:22] **23** [d][Rom. 8:17; Phil. 3:10] [e]Acts 12:2; Rev. 1:9 [f][ch. 19:11] [g]ch. 25:34 **25** [h]For ver. 25-28, [ch. 18:1-4; Luke 22:25-27] [i]1 Pet. 5:3 **26** [j]ch. 23:11; [Luke 9:48]

28 [k]John 13:4, 13-15; Phil. 2:7; [2 Cor. 8:9] [l]Isai. 53:10; Dan. 9:26; John 10:15; 11:51, 52; Rom. 4:25; Gal. 1:4; 2:20; 1 Tim. 2:6; Tit. 2:14; 1 Pet. 1:18, 19 [m]ch. 26:28; Isai. 53:11, 12; Heb. 2:10; 9:28; [Rom. 5:15; Rev. 5:9] **29** [n]For ver. 29-34, see Mark 10:46-52; Luke 18:35-43; [ch. 9:27-31] **30** [o]ch. 21:9; 22:42; See ch. 1:1 **31** [p]ch. 19:13

Chapter 21 1 [q]For ver. 1-9, see Mark 11:1-10; Luke 19:29-38; John 12:12-15 [r]ch. 24:3; 26:30; Zech. 14:4; [John 8:1]; [Acts 1:12] [s][Mark 14:13]

[1] Or *is your eye bad because I am good?* [2] Greek *diakonos* [3] Greek *bondservant* (*doulos*) [4] Some manuscripts omit *Lord*

20:16 See note 19:30.

20:17–19 This is Jesus' third prediction of His passion and resurrection (16:21 note; 17:22, 23 note).

20:23 cup. In the Old Testament the "cup" normally signifies the outpouring of God's wrath (Ps. 75:8; Is. 51:17, 22; Jer. 25:15, 16). That the disciples would drink this cup means they would experience suffering, but note that Jesus calls it "my cup." Because Jesus drank the cup of God's wrath for His own, believers do not drink the wrath they deserve. In and through Christ's suffering they have already undergone judgment. They are now justified in Christ and heirs of His glory (Rom. 8:17). Yet their privilege is to be identified with Christ in His sufferings (1 Pet. 2:21).

20:28 ransom. This term refers to the price paid to deliver someone from slavery or imprisonment. The price of freedom from sin and condemnation is Jesus' life, given for us (1 Pet. 1:18, 19). Since the elect are ransomed from the wrath of God, the ransom was offered to God Himself. Jesus drinks the cup of God's wrath (v. 23), not for His own sins, but as the means of ransoming many.

for many. The Greek preposition translated "for" can also be translated "in the place of." It expresses the substitutionary nature of Jesus' suffering. That Jesus says "many" here (cf. Is. 53:11, 12) rather than "all people" indicates a specific or definite focus to His redemptive activity. Nevertheless, it is "many" and not a "few." See notes John 17:9; 1 Tim. 2:6.

20:29 went out. Luke says that they were entering Jericho rather than leaving. One possibility is that Matthew and Mark refer to the ruins of Old Testament Jericho, about a mile away from the newer town of Jericho built by Herod (Luke 18:35 note).

20:30 two blind men. Once again Matthew mentions two men where Mark and Luke mention only one (8:28 note).

21:1–11 Of the Synoptic Gospels, only Matthew mentions the colt's mother, probably to emphasize that it was a young colt, not yet weaned and therefore not yet ridden (cf. Mark 11:2), and because the quotation from Zech. 9:9 prophesies that the coming king would ride on "a colt, the foal of a donkey." Jesus chooses to make the fulfillment of prophecy unmistakable.

The Triumphal Entry is clearly a symbolic act. Zech. 9:9 was recognized as messianic by Jews, and the shout "Hosanna to the Son of David!" (v. 9) as well as the spreading of cloaks on the ground (cf. 2 Kin. 9:13) indicates that the crowd recognizes Jesus' claim to be the Messiah. Note David's proclamation of Solomon as his designated heir by having him ride into the city on a donkey (1 Kin. 1:33, 38, 44).

you will find a donkey tied, and a colt with
her. Untie them and bring them to me. **3**If
anyone says anything to you, you shall say,
'The Lord needs them,' and he will send
them at once." **4**This took place [t]to fulfill
what was spoken by the prophet, saying,

5 [u]"Say to the daughter of Zion,
'Behold, your king is coming to you,
[v]humble, and mounted on a
donkey,
and[1] on a colt, the foal of a beast
of burden.'"

6The disciples went and did as Jesus had
directed them. **7**They brought the donkey
and the colt and put on them their cloaks,
and he sat on them. **8**Most of the crowd
[w]spread their cloaks on the road, and others cut branches from the trees and spread
them on the road. **9**And the crowds that
went before him and that followed him
were shouting, [x]"Hosanna to [y]the Son of
David! [z]Blessed is he who comes in the
name of the Lord! Hosanna [a]in the highest!" **10**And [b]when he entered Jerusalem,
the whole city was stirred up, saying, "Who
is this?" **11**And the crowds said, "This is
[c]the prophet Jesus, [d]from Nazareth of
Galilee."

Jesus Cleanses the Temple

12[e]And Jesus entered the temple[2] and
drove out all who sold and bought in the
temple, and he overturned the tables of
[f]the money-changers and the seats of those
who sold [g]pigeons. **13**He said to them, "It
is written, [h]'My house shall be called a
house of prayer,' but [i]you make it a den of
robbers."
14[j]And the blind and the lame came to
him in the temple, and he healed them.
15[k]But when the chief priests and the
scribes saw the wonderful things that he
did, and the children crying out in the temple, [x]"Hosanna to the Son of David!" they
were indignant, **16**and they said to him,
"Do you hear what these are saying?" And
Jesus said to them, "Yes; [l]have you never
read,

[m]"'Out of the mouth of [n]infants and
nursing babies
you have prepared praise'?"

17And [o]leaving them, he [p]went out of the
city to [q]Bethany and lodged there.

Jesus Curses the Fig Tree

18[r]In the morning, as he was returning to
the city, [s]he became hungry. **19**[t]And seeing
a fig tree by the wayside, he went to it and
found nothing on it but only leaves. And
he said to it, "May no fruit ever come from
you again!" And the fig tree withered at
once.
20When the disciples saw it, they marveled, saying, "How did the fig tree wither
at once?" **21**And Jesus answered them,
[u]"Truly, I say to you, [v]if you have faith and
[w]do not doubt, you will not only do what
has been done to the fig tree, but even if
you say to this mountain, [x]'Be taken up
and thrown into the sea,' it will happen.
22And [v]whatever you ask in prayer, you will
receive, [y]if you have faith."

The Authority of Jesus Challenged

23[z]And when he entered the temple, the
chief priests and the elders of the people
came up to him [a]as he was teaching, and
said, [b]"By what authority are you doing
these things, and who gave you this
authority?" **24**Jesus answered them, "I also

4 [t]See ch. 1:22 **5** [u]Cited from Zech. 9:9; [Isai. 62:11] [v]ch. 11:29 **8** [w]2 Kin. 9:13 **9** [x][Rev. 7:10]; See Ps. 118:25 (Heb.) [y]ch. 20:30 [z]ch. 23:39; Cited from Ps. 118:26 [a]Luke 2:14; [Ps. 148:1] **10** [b]Mark 11:11 **11** [c]ver. 46; Luke 7:16; 13:33; 24:19; John 4:19; 6:14; 7:40; 9:17; [Mark 6:15; Luke 9:8, 19; John 1:21] [d]See ch. 2:23 **12** [e]For ver. 12-16, see Mark 11: 15-18; Luke 19:45-47; [John 2:14-16] [f][Ex. 30:13] [g]Lev. 1:14; 5:7; 12:8; Luke 2:24 **13** [h]Cited from Isai. 56:7 [i]Jer. 7:11 **14** [j]ch. 11:5; 15:31 **15** [k][Luke 19:39, 40] [x][See ver. 9 above] **16** [l]ver. 42; ch. 12:3, 5; 19:4; 22:31 [m]Cited from Ps. 8:2 (Gk.) [n]ch. 11:25 **17** [o]ch. 16:4 [p]Mark 11:19; [Luke 21:37] [q]Mark 11:1; Luke 19:29; 24:50; John 11:18 **18** [r]For ver. 18-22, see Mark 11:12-14, 20-24 [s]ch. 4:2 **19** [t][Luke 13:6-9] **21** [u]ch. 17:20 [v][John 14:12] [w]Acts 10:20; Rom. 4:20; 14:23; James 1:6 [x][Ps. 46:2; 1 Cor. 13:2; Rev. 8:8] **22** [v][See ver. 21 above] [y]See ch. 7:7 **23** [z]For ver. 23-27, see Mark 11:27-33; Luke 20:1-8 [a]See ch. 26:55 [b][Ex. 2:14; John 1:25; Acts 4:7]

1 Or *even* 2 Some manuscripts add *of God*

21:7 he sat on them. Jesus rode the colt (Mark 11:2). Perhaps "them" refers to the garments.

21:9 Hosanna. A Hebrew expression meaning, "Save, now."

21:12, 13 John 1:13–17 recounts a cleansing of the temple early in Jesus' ministry rather than during the final week. Many scholars, both liberal and conservative, propose that either John or the Synoptic Gospels changed the occasion for theological or other reasons. Others conclude that Jesus drove out money-changers on two separate occasions (Mark 11:15 note).

21:13 den of robbers. The phrase is from Jer. 7:11. Through the prophet the Lord denounced the idea that the physical temple guaranteed His blessing in spite of Judah's wickedness. This same superstitious notion prevailed in Jesus' time.

21:16 Jesus' quotation of Ps. 8:2 to justify the children's praises is astounding, for Ps. 8 says that God ordained worship for Himself from the lips of children. Jesus indirectly claims the prerogative of deity.

21:18–20 Matthew condenses an incident that took place on two separate days (cf. Mark 11:12–14, 20–26). The linking of this incident with the cleansing of the temple hints at God's imminent punishment of Israel by the destruction of the city and the temple (Jer. 24:1–8).

21:21, 22 This is similar to 17:20, but here the emphasis is on not doubting. Freedom from doubt arises from an awareness that something is truly God's will. True faith receives what it asks for; trust in God is not presumptive arrogance but submission to His will.

will ask you one question, and if you tell
me the answer, then I also will tell you by
what authority I do these things. 25 The
baptism of John, [c]from where did it come?
[d]From heaven or from man?" And they discussed it among themselves, saying, "If we
say, 'From heaven,' he will say to us, [e]'Why
then did you not believe him?' 26 But if we
say, 'From man,' [f]we are afraid of the
crowd, for they all hold that John was [g]a
prophet." 27 So they answered Jesus, "We
do not know." And he said to them,
"Neither will I tell you by what authority I
do these things.

The Parable of the Two Sons

28 [h]"What do you think? A man had two
sons. And he went to the first and said,
'Son, go and work in [i]the vineyard today.'
29 And he answered, 'I will not,' but afterward he [j]changed his mind and went.
30 And he went to the other son and said
the same. And he answered, 'I go, sir,' but
did not go. 31 Which of the two did the will
of his father?" They said, "The first." Jesus
said to them, "Truly, I say to you, [k]the tax
collectors and [l]the prostitutes go into [m]the
kingdom of God before you. 32 For John
came to you [n]in the way of righteousness,
and [o]you did not believe him, but [p]the tax
collectors and the prostitutes believed him.
And even when you saw it, you did not
afterward [j]change your minds and believe
him.

The Parable of the Tenants

33 [q]"Hear another parable. There was a
master of a house who planted [r]a vineyard
[s]and put a fence around it and dug a winepress in it and built a tower and [t]leased it
to tenants, and [u]went into another country.
34 When the season for fruit drew near, he
sent his servants[1] to the tenants [t]to get his
fruit. 35 [v]And the tenants took his servants
and beat one, killed another, and [w]stoned
another. 36 [x]Again he sent other servants,
more than the first. And they did the same
to them. 37 Finally he sent his son to them,
saying, 'They will respect my son.' 38 But
when the tenants saw the son, they said to
themselves, [y]'This is the heir. Come, [z]let us
kill him and have his inheritance.' 39 And
they took him and [a]threw him out of the
vineyard and killed him. 40 [b]When therefore
the owner of the vineyard comes, what will
he do to those tenants?" 41 They said to
him, [c]"He will put those wretches to a miserable death and [d]let out the vineyard to
other tenants who will give him the fruits
in their seasons."

42 Jesus said to them, [e]"Have you never
read in the Scriptures:

[f]"'The stone that the builders rejected
has become the cornerstone;[2]
this was the Lord's doing,
and it is marvelous in our eyes'?

43 Therefore I tell you, the kingdom of God
[g]will be taken away from you and given to
a people [h]producing its fruits. 44 And [i]the
one who falls on this stone will be broken
to pieces; and [j]when it falls on anyone, [k]it
will crush him."[3]

45 When the chief priests and the Pharisees heard his parables, they perceived
that he was speaking about them. 46 And
[l]although they were seeking to arrest him,
[m]they feared the crowds, because they held
him to be [n]a prophet.

The Parable of the Wedding Feast

22 And again Jesus [o]spoke to them in
parables, saying, 2 [p]"The kingdom
of heaven may be compared to a king who
gave [q]a wedding feast for his son, 3 and
[r]sent his servants[4] to call those who were
invited to the wedding feast, but they

25 [c][ch. 13:54] [d]Luke 15:18, 21; John 3:27 [e]ver. 32; Luke 7:30
26 [f]ver. 46; ch. 14:5 [g][John 5:35]; See ch. 11:9
28 [h]ch. 17:25; 18:12 [i]ver. 33; ch. 20:1
29 [j]ver. 32; ch. 27:3; Heb. 7:21
31 [k]Luke 7:29 [l]Luke 7:37-50 [m]See ch. 12:28
32 [n][ch. 3:8-12, 15; Prov. 8:20; 2 Pet. 2:21] [o]ver. 25; ch. 11:18 [p]Luke 3:12, 13 [j][See ver. 29 above]
33 [q]For ver. 33-46, see Mark 12:1-12; Luke 20:9-19 [r]ver. 28; Ps. 80:8; Isai. 5:1 [s]Isai. 5:2 [t]S. of S. 8:11, 12 [u]ch. 25:14, 15; [Mark 13:34]
34 [t][See ver. 33 above]
35 [v]ch. 5:12; 22:6; 23:34, 37; [2 Chr. 24:19; 36:15, 16; Neh. 9:26; Jer. 37:15; 38:6; Acts 7:52; 2 Cor. 11:24-26; 1 Thess. 2:15; Heb. 11:36, 37] [w][2 Chr. 24:21; John 10:31-33; Acts 7:59]
36 [x]ch. 22:4
38 [y]Heb. 1:2; [John 1:11; Rom. 8:17] [z][1 Kin. 21:19]
39 [a]Heb. 13:12
40 [b][ch. 24:50; 25:19]
41 [c]Luke 19:27 [d]ver. 43; Acts 13:46; 18:6; 28:28; [ch. 8:11, 12]

42 [e]ver. 16 [f]Acts 4:11; 1 Pet. 2:7; Cited from Ps. 118:22, 23 43 [g][Luke 14:24] [h][ch. 3:10; Isai. 5:4, 7] 44 [i]Isai. 8:14, 15; Rom. 9:32, 33; 1 Pet. 2:8 [j]Dan. 2:34, 35, 44, 45 [k]Amos 9:9 46 [l]Mark 11:18; Luke 19:47, 48; John 7:25, 30, 44; [ch. 26:4] [m]ver. 26 [n][ver. 11]
Chapter 22 1 [o]ch. 13:34 2 [p]For ver. 2-14, [Luke 14:16-24] [q]See Rev. 19:7 3 [r][Esth. 6:14; Prov. 9:3, 5]

1 Greek *bondservants*; also verses 35, 36 2 Greek *the head of the corner*
3 Some manuscripts omit verse 44 4 Greek *bondservants*; also verses 4, 6, 8, 10

21:33–46 This parable is based on Is. 5:1, 2 and possibly also Ps. 80:8–18. The meaning is clear: the landowner is God, the vineyard is the kingdom of God (v. 43), the servants are the prophets, the son is Jesus, the tenants are the Jews who oppose Jesus, the killing of the son is the Crucifixion, and the removal of the tenants is the transferral of the kingdom to a new people of God that includes Gentiles.

21:42 In response to the challenge to His authority (v. 23), Jesus quotes Ps. 118:22, 23 as evidence that His authority is given by God rather than derived from human institutions.

21:44 This saying combines the prophecies of Is. 8:14 and Dan. 2:34, 44. Jesus claims to be the destroyer of earthly kingdoms, the founder of God's kingdom on earth, and at the same time points out that the Jewish leaders are, as prophesied, opposed to this kingdom. Jesus' quotation of Ps. 118 and the allusion to Is. 8:14 and Dan. 2 provide the ground for the "stone" as a reference to Christ that appears frequently in the New Testament (Acts 4:11; Rom. 9:33; 1 Pet. 2:6–8).

22:1–14 Although there are similarities between this parable and Luke 14:16–24, there are few verbal parallels and some great differences.

would not come. 4 [s]Again he sent other servants, saying, 'Tell those who are invited, See, I have prepared my [t]dinner, [u]my oxen and my fat calves have been slaughtered, and everything is ready. Come to the wedding feast.' 5 But [v]they paid no attention and went off, one to his farm, another to his business, 6 while the rest seized his servants, [w]treated them shamefully, and [x]killed them. 7 The king was angry, and he sent his troops and [y]destroyed those murderers and burned their city. 8 Then he said to his servants, 'The wedding feast is ready, but those invited were not [z]worthy. 9 Go therefore to [a]the main roads and invite to the wedding feast as many as you find.' 10 And those servants went out into the roads and [b]gathered all whom they found, both bad and good. So the wedding hall was filled with guests.

11 "But when the king came in to look at the guests, he saw there [c]a man who had no wedding garment. 12 And he said to him, [d]'Friend, how did you get in here without a wedding garment?' And he was speechless. 13 Then the king said to the attendants, 'Bind him hand and foot and [e]cast him into the outer darkness. In that place [e]there will be weeping and gnashing of teeth.' 14 For many are [f]called, but few are [f]chosen."

Paying Taxes to Caesar

15 [g]Then the Pharisees went and plotted how [h]to entangle him in his talk. 16 And they sent [i]their disciples to him, along with [j]the Herodians, saying, "Teacher, [k]we know that you are true and teach [l]the way of God truthfully, and you do not care about anyone's opinion, for [m]you are not swayed by appearances.[1] 17 Tell us, then, what you think. Is it lawful to pay [n]taxes to [o]Caesar, or not?" 18 But Jesus, aware of their malice, said, "Why [p]put me to the test, you hypocrites? 19 Show me the coin for the tax." And they brought him a denarius.[2] 20 And Jesus said to them, "Whose likeness and inscription is this?" 21 They said, "Caesar's." Then he said to them, [q]"Therefore render to Caesar the things that are Caesar's, and to God the things that are God's." 22 When they heard it, they marveled. And they [r]left him and went away.

Sadducees Ask About the Resurrection

23 The same day [s]Sadducees came to him, [t]who say that there is no resurrection, and they asked him a question, 24 saying, "Teacher, Moses said, [u]'If a man dies having no children, his brother must marry the widow and raise up children for his brother.' 25 Now there were seven brothers among us. The first married and died, and having no children left his wife to his brother. 26 So too the second and third, down to the seventh. 27 After them all, the woman died. 28 In the resurrection, therefore, of the seven, whose wife will she be? For they all had her."

29 But Jesus answered them, "You are wrong, [v]because you know neither the Scriptures nor [w]the power of God. 30 For in the resurrection they neither [x]marry nor [x]are given in marriage, but are like angels in heaven. 31 And as for the resurrection of the dead, [y]have you not read what was said to you by God: 32 [z]'I am the God of Abraham, and the God of Isaac, and the God of Jacob'? He is not God of the dead,

4 [s]ch. 21:36 [t]Luke 11:38; John 21:12, 15 (Gk.) [u]Prov. 9:2
5 [v][Heb. 2:3]
6 [w]Luke 18:32; Acts 14:5; 1 Thess. 2:2 [x]See ch. 21:35
7 [y]ch. 21:41; Luke 19:27
8 [z]ch. 10:11; Acts 13:46; Rev. 3:4; [Luke 20:35]
9 [a]Ezek. 21:21; Obad. 14
10 [b]See ch. 13:47
11 [c][Rev. 19:8; 22:14]
12 [d]ch. 20:13; 26:50
13 [e]See ch. 8:12
14 [f]Rev. 17:14
15 [g]For ver. 15-32, see Mark 12:13-27; Luke 20:20-38 [h][Luke 11:54]
16 [i]Mark 2:18 [j]Mark 3:6; [Mark 8:15] [k][John 3:2] [l]Acts 18:26; [Acts 13:10] [m]See Acts 10:34
17 [n]ch. 17:25 [o]Luke 2:1; 3:1
18 [p]See John 8:6
21 [q]Rom. 13:7
22 [r]Mark 12:12
23 [s]ver. 34; ch. 3:7; 16:1; Acts 4:1; 5:17; 23:6 [t]Acts 23:8; [Acts 4:2]
24 [u][Deut. 25:5]
29 [v]John 20:9 [w]1 Cor. 6:14
30 [x]ch. 24:38; Luke 17:27
31 [y]See ch. 21:16
32 [z]Acts 7:32; Cited from Ex. 3:6

1 Greek *for you do not look at people's faces* 2 A *denarius* was a day's wage for a laborer

They should be understood as different parables given on different occasions. The first part of the parable (vv. 1–10) continues the theme begun in the previous chapter that the heirs of the kingdom have rejected it, and the kingdom has been offered to others. God's servants have the task of offering the gospel to all people (v. 9). The second part (vv. 11–14) affirms that receiving an invitation to God's kingdom does not guarantee inclusion; one must be properly clothed (cf. Zech. 3:3–5; Rev. 3:18; 19:8). Although everyone who hears the gospel has been invited, and although many may claim to be in the kingdom, only those clothed with Christ's righteousness are actually presentable to God. Only those who are chosen will be present at the marriage supper of the Lamb, and this election does not depend on any previous status (8:11, 12).

22:13 outer darkness. A description of eternal punishment. There will be no middle ground between heaven and hell.

22:14 called . . . chosen. See "Effectual Calling and Conversion" at 2 Thess. 2:14.

22:17 taxes. The hated poll tax symbolized submission to Rome. If Jesus simply advocated payment of the tax, He would alienate the people; if He encouraged nonpayment the Herodians would accuse Him of treason. Jesus' answer turns the question to a deeper issue, ultimate allegiance to God. The coin bearing the image of Caesar belongs to him; human beings made in the image of God belong to God.

22:21 to Caesar. See "Christians and Civil Government" at Rom. 13:1.

22:31, 32 have you not read. Jesus quotes from the Pentateuch (Ex. 3:6), a portion of Scripture particularly valued by the Sadducees. That God "is" (not "was") the God of the patriarchs proclaims the resurrection because "He is not God of the dead, but of the living." The eternal God calls His saints to an eternal relationship with Himself. All this implies that the patriarchs continue to live in the presence of God and will be resurrected in the future.

but of the living." 33 And when the crowd
heard it, [a]they were astonished at his
teaching.

The Great Commandment

34 [b]But when the Pharisees heard that he
had silenced [c]the Sadducees, they gathered
together. 35 [d]And one of them, [e]a lawyer,
asked him a question [f]to test him.
36 "Teacher, which is the great commandment in the Law?" 37 And he said to him,
[g]"You shall love the Lord your God with all
your heart and with all your soul and with
all your mind. 38 This is the great and first
commandment. 39 And [h]a second is like it:
[i]You shall love your neighbor as yourself.
40 [j]On these two commandments depend
[k]all the Law and the Prophets."

Whose Son Is the Christ?

41 [l]Now while the Pharisees [m]were gathered together, Jesus asked them a question,
42 saying, "What do you think about [n]the
Christ? Whose son is he?" They said to
him, [n]"The son of David." 43 He said to
them, "How is it then that David, [o]in the
Spirit, calls him Lord, saying,

44 [p]"'The Lord said to my Lord,
Sit at my right hand,
until I put your enemies under
your feet'?

45 If then David calls him Lord, [q]how is he
his son?" 46 [r]And no one was able to answer
him a word, [s]nor from that day did anyone
dare to ask him any more questions.

33 [a]See ch. 7:28 34 [b]For ver. 34-40, see Mark 12:28-33 [c]ver. 23 35 [d][Luke 10:25-28] [e]See Luke 7:30 [f]ver. 18 37 [g]Luke 10:27; Cited from Deut. 6:5 39 [h][1 John 4:21] [i]Cited from Lev. 19:18; See ch. 19:19 40 [j][Rom. 13:8, 10] [k]ch. 7:12; [Gal. 5:14] 41 [l]For ver. 41-45, see Mark 12:35-37; Luke 20:41-44 [m]ver. 34 42 [n]See ch. 1:1, 17 43 [o]Rev. 1:10; 4:2; [2 Sam. 23:2] 44 [p]Acts 2:34, 35; Heb. 1:13; Cited from Ps. 110:1; [1 Cor. 15:25; Heb. 10:13] 45 [q][Rom. 1:3, 4] 46 [r][Luke 14:6] [s]Mark 12:34; Luke 20:40

Chapter 23 [t]For ver. 1, 2, 5-7, see Mark 12:38, 39; Luke 20:45, 46; [Luke 11:43] 2 [u][Ezra 7:6, 10, 25; Neh. 8:4]

Seven Woes to the Scribes and Pharisees

23 Then Jesus [t]said to the crowds and
to his disciples, 2 [u]"The scribes and
the Pharisees [v]sit on Moses' seat, 3 so practice and observe whatever they tell you—
[w]but not what they do. [x]For they preach,
but do not practice. 4 [y]They tie up heavy
burdens, hard to bear,[1] and lay them on
people's shoulders, but they themselves
are not willing to move them with their finger. 5 [t]They do all their deeds [z]to be seen by
others. For they make [a]their phylacteries
broad and [b]their fringes long, 6 and they
[c]love the place of honor at feasts and [d]the
best seats in the synagogues 7 and [d]greet-
ings in [e]the marketplaces and being called
[f]rabbi[2] by others. 8 [g]But you are not to be
called rabbi, for you have one teacher, and
you are [h]all brothers.[3] 9 [i]And call no man
your father on earth, for [j]you have one
Father, who is in heaven. 10 Neither be
called instructors, for you have one instructor, [k]the Christ. 11 [l]The greatest among you
shall be your servant. 12 [m]Whoever exalts
himself will be humbled, and whoever
humbles himself will be exalted.
13 "But woe [n]to you, scribes and Pharisees, hypocrites! For you [o]shut the kingdom of heaven in people's faces. For you

[v][Deut. 17:10, 11; John 9:28, 29] 3 [w][ch. 5:20; 15:3-13] [x]Rom. 2:17-23 4 [y]Luke 11:46; [ch. 11:28-30; Acts 15:10] 5 [t][See ver. 1 above] [z]ch. 6:1, 16; [John 5:44] [a]Ex. 13:9; Deut. 6:8; 11:18 [b]See ch. 9:20 6 [c]Luke 14:7, 8 [d]Luke 11:43 7 [d][See ver. 6 above] [e]ch. 11:16; 20:3 [f]See John 1:38 8 [g]James 3:1 [h]Luke 22:32; John 21:23; See Philem. 16 9 [i][1 Cor. 1:12; 3:4] [j]ch. 6:9; Mal. 1:6; See ch. 7:11 10 [k]See ch. 1:17 11 [l]ch. 20:26 12 [m]Luke 14:11; 18:14; [ch. 18:4; Prov. 29:23; Ezek. 21:26; James 4:6, 10; 1 Pet. 5:5, 6] 13 [n]Luke 11:52 [o][ch. 16:19]

[1] Some manuscripts omit *hard to bear* [2] *Rabbi* means *my teacher*, or *my master*; also verse 8 [3] Or *brothers and sisters*

22:37 shall love. See "Love" at 1 Cor. 13:13.

22:40 all the Law and the Prophets. A way of referring to the entire Old Testament. Love fulfills the law because it sums up God's commandments and motivates obedience to them (Rom. 13:8–10; 1 Cor. 13). It does not dissolve God's norms for conduct, but illumines and deepens them (5:17; Rom. 8:4). See "The Law of God" at Ex. 20:1.

22:42 What do you think. The Pharisees had tested Jesus; now Jesus tests them. He focuses on the crucial issue—the identity of the Messiah (Christ)—and His quotation from Ps. 110 shows that the common view of the Messiah was too limited.

Christ. See note 1:1.

23:1–39 Some regard this chapter as another discourse (making six discourses rather than five; Introduction: Characteristics and Themes), or as part of the eschatological discourse in chs. 24; 25. However, it is not concluded by the phrase that closes the other discourses ("when Jesus had finished all these sayings"). It continues Jesus' prophetic activity of delivering oracles of woe to the unfaithful leaders of Israel (vv. 13–36 note). It is related to the following discourse in that it provides the reason for the doom of Jerusalem, announced in the language of Old Testament prophecy.

23:2 sit on Moses' seat. Though Jesus elsewhere condemns the scribes and Pharisees for adding human tradition to the law and for evading the spirit of the law (vv. 13–32; 15:1–9), here He recognizes the legitimate teaching office that they occupied (Deut. 17:8–13).

23:4 See theological note "Legalism."

23:5 phylacteries. See note Ex. 13:9.

23:8–10 In forbidding the use of the titles "Rabbi" (v. 8), "father" (v. 9), and "instructors" (lit. "leaders," v. 10), Jesus does not prohibit organization or the use of all titles in the church (cf. Acts 20:17; 1 Cor. 9:1; 1 Tim. 3:1, 2, 8, 12; Titus 1:5–7). His warning is against the temptation to accord human leaders the authority and prerogatives that belong to God alone—a temptation here exemplified by the use of pretentious forms of address.

23:13–36 Luke 11:37–54 records an earlier proclamation of six woes. This series of seven woes was a prophetic pronouncement; it brought God's lawsuit against His people and announced the imminent realization of the covenant curses (cf. Is. 5:8–23; Hab. 2:6–20). Such warnings express God's concern for His people and His desire that they repent (vv. 37–39).

23:13 hypocrites. See note at 6:2.

shut the kingdom. The teachers of the law and Pharisees did this by turning people away from Christ and His righteousness. The disciples are to do the opposite, freely proclaiming the gospel.

[p]neither enter yourselves nor allow those
who would enter to go in.[1] **15** Woe to you,
scribes and Pharisees, hypocrites! For you
travel across sea and land to make a single
[q]proselyte, and when he becomes a proselyte, you make him twice as much a [r]child
of [s]hell[2] as yourselves.
16 "Woe to [t]you, [u]blind guides, who say,
[v]'If anyone swears by the temple, it is nothing, but if anyone swears by the gold of the
temple, he is bound by his oath.' **17** You
blind fools! For which is greater, the gold
or [w]the temple that has made the gold
sacred? **18** And you say, 'If anyone swears by
the altar, it is nothing, but if anyone swears
by [x]the gift that is on the altar, he is bound
by his oath.' **19** You blind men! For which is
greater, the gift or [y]the altar that makes the
gift sacred? **20** So whoever swears by the
altar swears by it and by everything on it.
21 And whoever swears by the temple
swears by it and by [z]him who dwells in it.

13 [p][ch. 5:20; 21:31; Luke 7:30] **15** [q]Acts 2:10; 6:5; 13:43 [r][John 17:12; 2 Thess. 2:3] [s]See ch. 5:29 **16** [t]See ch. 15:14 [u]ver. 17, 19, 26; John 9:39-41; Rom. 2:19; 2 Pet. 1:9; Rev. 3:17 [v][ch. 5:33-35] **17** [w]Ex. 30:29 **18** [x]ch. 5:23 **19** [y]Ex. 29:37 **21** [z]1 Kin. 8:13; 2 Chr. 6:2; Ps. 26:8; 132:14

22 [a][ch. 21:25] [b]See ch. 5:34 [c]See Rev. 4:2 **23** [d]Luke 11:42 [e]Deut. 14:22; [Luke 18:12] [f]Isai. 28:25, 27

22 And whoever swears by [a]heaven swears
by [b]the throne of God and by [c]him who sits
upon it.
23 [d]"Woe to you, scribes and Pharisees,
hypocrites! For [e]you tithe mint and dill and
[f]cumin, and have neglected the weightier
matters of the law: [g]justice and mercy and
faithfulness. [h]These you ought to have
done, without neglecting the others. **24** You
blind guides, straining out a gnat and swallowing [i]a camel!
25 [j]"Woe to you, scribes and Pharisees,
hypocrites! For [k]you clean the outside of
[l]the cup and the plate, but inside they are
full of [m]greed and self-indulgence. **26** You
blind Pharisee! First clean the inside of [l]the

[g]Ps. 33:5; Jer. 5:1; Mic. 6:8; Zech. 7:9 [h][1 Sam. 15:22] **24** [i]ch. 19:24 **25** [j]For ver. 25-28, [ch. 15:11-20] [k]Luke 11:39, 40 [l]Mark 7:4 [m]Luke 16:14; 20:47 **26** [l][See ver. 25 above]

1 Some manuscripts add here (or after verse 12) verse 14: *Woe to you, scribes and Pharisees, hypocrites! For you devour widows' houses and for a pretense you make long prayers; therefore you will receive the greater condemnation* 2 Greek *Gehenna*; also verse 33

Legalism

The New Testament views Christian obedience as the practice of "good works." Christians are to be "rich in good works" (1 Tim. 6:18; cf. Matt. 5:16; Eph. 2:10; 2 Tim. 3:17; Titus 2:7, 14; 3:8, 14). A good deed is one done according to the right standard, God's revealed will; from a right motive, love for God and others; and with a right purpose, the glory of God.

Legalism is a distortion of obedience that can never produce good works in this sense. It skews motive and purpose, seeing good deeds as ways to earn God's favor. It can be arrogant and contemptuous of those who do not labor in the same way. Finally, legalism's self-advancing purpose squeezes humble kindness and compassion out of the heart.

In the New Testament we meet different kinds of legalism. Legalists among the Pharisees thought that because they were descended from Abraham they were guaranteed approval by God, while paradoxically they formalized daily observance of the law, down to minutest details, as the rule of life. In doing so they avoided what the law truly required. Judaizers were legalists who taught Christian believers that they must go on to become Jews by being circumcised and observing the religious calendar and ritual laws, and in this way gain favor with God. Jesus attacked the legalism of the Pharisees; Paul, the Judaizers.

The Pharisees that opposed Jesus thought of themselves as faithful keepers of the Mosaic law. Yet in emphasizing minor details they neglected what matters most (Matt. 23:23, 24). Their elaborate and misguided interpretations of the law denied its true spirit and aim (Matt. 15:3–9; 23:16–24). They substituted human tradition for God's authoritative law, binding consciences where God had left them free (Mark 2:16–3:6; 7:1–8). At heart they were hypocritical, seeking human approval for themselves and condemning others (Luke 20:45–47; Matt. 6:1–8; 23:2–7).

The Judaizers opposed by Paul added to the gospel requirements for salvation that obscured and denied the all-sufficiency of Christ (Gal. 3:1–3; 4:21; 5:2–6). The idea that there must be additional requirements to perfect the gospel was the root of their error. Paul opposed this idea no matter who advanced it (Col. 2:8–23), because it corrupted the way of salvation. Like Jesus, he would not tolerate those who brought new burdens to lay on the sheep.

23:15 hell. See note at 5:22. Those who were legalists made converts like themselves, prejudiced against receiving the righteousness that is by faith.

23:16 If anyone swears. See 5:33–37. This way of taking oaths is like children making promises with their fingers crossed behind their backs. God desires truth in all our words (5:37).

23:24 gnat . . . camel. The gnat was the smallest unclean animal and the camel was the largest. In Aramaic the two words sound similar.

cup and the plate, that the outside also
may be clean.
27 [n] "Woe to you, scribes and Pharisees,
hypocrites! For you are like [o] whitewashed
tombs, which outwardly appear beautiful,
but within are full of dead people's bones
and [p] all uncleanness. 28 So you also [q] outwardly appear righteous to others, but
within you are full of [r] hypocrisy and lawlessness.
29 [s] "Woe to you, scribes and Pharisees,
hypocrites! For you build the tombs of the
prophets and decorate the monuments of
the righteous, 30 saying, 'If we had lived in
the days of our fathers, we would not have
taken part with them in shedding the
blood of the prophets.' 31 Thus you witness against yourselves that you are [t] sons
of those who murdered the prophets.
32 [u] Fill up, then, the measure of your
fathers. 33 You serpents, [v] you brood of
vipers, how are you to escape being sentenced to [w] hell? 34 [x] Therefore [y] I send you
[z] prophets and wise men and [a] scribes,
[b] some of whom you will kill and crucify,
and [b] some you will [c] flog in your synagogues and [d] persecute from town to
town, 35 so that on you may come all [e] the
righteous blood shed on earth, from the
blood of innocent [f] Abel to the blood of
[g] Zechariah the son of Barachiah,[1] whom
you murdered between [h] the sanctuary
and [i] the altar. 36 Truly, I say to you, [j] all
these things will come upon this generation.

27 [n] Luke 11:44 [o] [Acts 23:3] [p] Eph. 5:3; [Num. 19:16; 2 Kin. 23:16]
28 [q] ver. 5 [r] Luke 12:1
29 [s] Luke 11:47, 48
31 [t] Acts 7:51, 52
32 [u] Gen. 15:16; Dan. 8:23; 1 Thess. 2:15, 16
33 [v] ch. 3:7; 12:34 [w] ver. 15
34 [x] For ver. 34-36, [Luke 11:49-51] [y] ch. 10:16 [z] See Acts 13:1; 1 Cor. 12:28 [a] ch. 13:52 [b] See ch. 21:35 [c] ch. 10:17; Mark 13:9; Luke 21:12; Acts 22:19; 26:11; [Luke 12:11] [d] ch. 10:23
35 [e] Rev. 18:24 [f] Gen. 4:4, 8. Heb. 11:4; 1 John 3:12 [g] [Zech. 1:1] [h] See Luke 1:9 [i] Ex. 40:6; 2 Kin. 16:14; Ezek. 40:47
36 [j] [ch. 10:23; 16:28; 24:34]

Lament over Jerusalem

37 [k] "O Jerusalem, Jerusalem, the city that
[l] kills the prophets and stones those who
are sent to it! How often would I have
[m] gathered [n] your children together [o] as a hen
gathers her brood [p] under her wings, and
[q] you would not! 38 See, [r] your house is left
to you desolate. 39 For I tell you, you will
not see me again, until you say, [s] 'Blessed is
he who comes in the name of the Lord.'"

Jesus Foretells Destruction of the Temple

24 [t] Jesus left the temple and was going
away, when his disciples came to
point out to him the buildings of the temple. 2 But he answered them, "You see all
these, do you not? Truly, I say to you,
[u] there will not be left here one stone upon
another that will not be thrown down."

Signs of the Close of the Age

3 As he sat on [v] the Mount of Olives, the
disciples came to him [w] privately, saying,
"Tell us, [x] when will these things be, and
what will be the sign of your [y] coming and
of [z] the close of the age?" 4 And Jesus
answered them, [a] "See that no one leads
you astray. 5 For [b] many will come in my
name, saying, 'I am [c] the Christ,' and they
will lead many astray. 6 And you will hear of

37 [k] For ver. 37-39, see Luke 13:34, 35; [Luke 19:41-44] [l] See ch. 21:35 [m] [Ps. 147:2; Prov. 1:24] [n] Luke 23:28 [o] [Deut. 32:11, 12] [p] Ruth 2:12 [q] John 5:40 38 [r] [Isai. 64:11; Jer. 12:7; 22:5]
39 [s] ch. 21:9; Cited from Ps. 118:26
Chapter 24 1 [t] [ch. 21:23]; For ver. 1-51, see Mark 13:1-37; Luke 21:5-36
2 [u] Luke 19:44 3 [v] See ch. 21:1 [w] [Mark 4:34] [x] [Acts 1:6, 7] [y] ver. 27, 37, 39; See 1 Thess. 2:19 [z] See ch. 13:39 4 [a] Jer. 29:8; Eph. 5:6; Col. 2:8; 2 Thess. 2:3; 1 John 3:7 5 [b] ver. 11, 24; Jer. 14:14; 1 John 2:18 [c] See ch. 1:17

[1] Some manuscripts omit *the son of Barachiah*

23:35 Abel . . . Zechariah. Abel was the first person to be killed for righteousness' sake (Gen. 4:8). The identity of Zechariah is problematic, and all suggested solutions have difficulties. Zechariah the prophet was the "son of Barachiah," but there is no evidence that he was martyred. There was a Zechariah, son of Baruch, who was killed by Zealots as mentioned by Josephus (*Jewish Wars* 4:334–44). He was killed in the temple area, but probably not between the sanctuary and the altar. Zechariah, son of Jehoiada, is the last martyr mentioned in the Old Testament in the Hebrew canonical order (2 Chr. 24:20–22). He was killed in the temple courtyard by command of Joash. If not for the words "son of Barachiah," the Zechariah of 2 Chr. 24 would be most likely, since Abel and Zechariah are the first and last martyrs in the Hebrew canon. It is remotely possible that "son of Barachiah" was an insertion by an early copyist (Luke 11:51 does not have it).

whom you murdered. By persecuting Christ, the Pharisees became identified with their murderous ancestors.

23:36 The punishment that "this generation" experienced was the destruction of Jerusalem and the temple in A.D. 70. See note 24:34.

23:39 you will not see me again, until. Some interpret this verse as a promise of an end-time conversion of the Jews (Rom. 11:25–32 and note), though the context seems to point more to the judgment of national Israel and the extension of the promises to spiritual Israel, made up of Gentiles as well as Jews (v. 38; cf. 21:43).

24:1–25:46 These two chapters are the last of Jesus' five great discourses in Matthew. Sometimes called the "Olivet discourse" because of its setting, most of the discourse is also recorded in Mark 13. The language is symbolic, and it deals with a number of events, not just a single incident.

There are three basic interpretive approaches to this discourse: first, all or most of ch. 24 (at least through v. 35) is concerned exclusively with the destruction of Jerusalem, and the "coming" of the Son of Man (24:30) is the exaltation of Jesus in heaven. Second, all of the sermon is about the Second Coming of Christ in judgment. Third, the sermon combines the destruction of Jerusalem and the judgment of the world in such a way that it is difficult to separate the references to the events surrounding the fall of Jerusalem and the Second Coming.

24:2 one stone. This was fulfilled during the Roman conquest of Jerusalem in A.D. 70 (Mark 13:2 note).

24:4–14 Wars, earthquakes, persecutions, and false prophets are all signs of Jesus' coming, but they indicate only the certainty of judgment, not its time (vv. 6, 8). Such signs characterize the entire period between His resurrection and His coming in judgment. Knowing when Jesus would return would lead His disciples to laziness and laxity in their watchfulness. The "when" (v. 3) that Jesus gives is task oriented: it is after the gospel has been preached to the nations (v. 14).

wars and rumors of wars. See that you [d]are
not alarmed, for this [e]must take place, but
the end is not yet. 7 For [f]nation will rise
against nation, and [g]kingdom against kingdom, and there will be [h]famines and earthquakes in various places. 8 All these are but
the beginning of [i]the birth pains.
9 "Then [j]they will deliver you up [k]to
tribulation and [l]put you to death, and [m]you
will be hated by all nations for my name's
sake. 10 And then many will fall away[1] and
[n]betray one another and hate one another.
11 And many [o]false prophets will arise [p]and
lead many astray. 12 And because lawlessness will be increased, [q]the love of many
will grow cold. 13 [r]But the one who endures
to the end will be saved. 14 And this gospel
of the kingdom [s]will be proclaimed
throughout the whole world [t]as a testimony
[u]to all nations, and [v]then the end will come.

The Abomination of Desolation

15 "So when you see the abomination of
desolation [w]spoken of by the prophet
Daniel, standing in [x]the holy place ([y]let the
reader understand), 16 then let those who
are in Judea flee to the mountains. 17 [z]Let
the one who is on [a]the housetop not go
down to take what is in his house, 18 and let
the one who is in the field not turn back to
take his cloak. 19 And [b]alas for women who
are pregnant and for those who are nursing
infants in those days! 20 Pray that your flight
may not be in winter or on a Sabbath. 21 For
then there will be [c]great tribulation, [d]such

6 [d]2 Thess. 2:2 [e]Rev. 1:1 **7** [f]2 Chr. 15:6; [Rev. 6:4] [g]Isai. 19:2 [h]Acts 11:28; Rev. 6:8, 12 **8** [i]John 16:21; Acts 2:24 (Gk.); Rom. 8:22 **9** [j]ch. 10:17, 21 [k]ver. 21, 29; Rev. 2:10 [l]ch. 23:34; John 16:2 [m]See ch. 10:22 **10** [n]ch. 10:21 **11** [o]See ch. 7:15 [p]ver. 5, 24 **12** [q][Luke 18:7; Rev. 2:4] **13** [r]See ch. 10:22 **14** [s]Rom. 10:18; Col. 1:6, 23; [Mark 14:9] [t]ch. 10:18 [u]ch. 28:19 [v][ver. 6] **15** [w]Dan. 9:27; 11:31; 12:11 [x][John 11:48; Acts 6:13; 21:28] [y][Dan. 9:22, 23, 25; Rev. 1:3] **17** [z]Luke 17:31 [a]See Luke 5:19 **19** [b]Luke 23:29 **21** [c]ver. 29; Dan. 12:1; [Rev. 7:14] [d]Rev. 16:18 **22** [e]ver. 24, 31; Isai. 65:8, 9; Luke 18:7; [ch. 22:14] **23** [f]Luke 17:23; [ver. 5, 26]

as has not been from the beginning of the
world until now, no, and never will be.
22 And if those days had not been cut short,
no human being would be saved. But for
[e]the sake of the elect those days will be cut
short. 23 [f]Then if anyone says to you, 'Look,
here is the Christ!' or 'There he is!' do not
believe it. 24 For [g]false christs and [h]false
prophets will arise and [i]perform great signs
and wonders, [j]so as to lead astray, if possible, even the elect. 25 See, [k]I have told you
beforehand. 26 So, if they say to you, 'Look,
[l]he is in the wilderness,' do not go out. If
they say, 'Look, he is in the inner rooms,'
do not believe it. 27 [m]For as the lightning
comes from the east and shines as far as
the west, so will be [n]the coming of the Son
of Man. 28 [o]Wherever the corpse is, there
the vultures will gather.

The Coming of the Son of Man

29 "Immediately after [p]the tribulation of
those days [q]the sun will be darkened, and
the moon will not give its light, and [r]the
stars will fall from heaven, and the powers
of the heavens will be shaken. 30 Then [s]will
appear in heaven [t]the sign of the Son of
Man, and then [u]all the tribes of the earth
will mourn, and [v]they will see the Son of

24 [g][1 John 2:18] [h]ver. 11 [i]Deut. 13:1-3; 2 Thess. 2:9-11; Rev. 13:13, 14; 16:14; 19:20; [Acts 8:9] [j]John 13:19; 14:29; [2 Pet. 3:17] **25** [k]Acts 21:38 **26** [l]Luke 17:24 **27** [m]ver. 3, 37, 39 [n]Luke 17:37; [Job 39:30] **28** [o]ver. 21 **29** [p]Isai. 13:10; 24:23; Ezek. 32:7; Joel 2:10, 31; 3:15; Acts 2:20; [Amos 5:20; 8:9; Zeph. 1:15; Rev. 6:12; 8:12] [q]Rev. 6:13; [Isai. 14:12; 34:4] [r]Dan. 7:13 **30** [s][ver. 3] [t]Rev. 1:7; [Zech. 12:12] [u]See ch. 16:27 [v]ch. 26:64; Mark 9:1; [ch. 25:31]

1 Or *stumble*

24:14 the whole world. See "The Mission of the Church in the World" at John 20:21.

24:15–21 Although some interpreters take this passage to refer exclusively to the Second Coming, there are unmistakable references to the destruction of Jerusalem in A.D. 70, as is clear from the parallel account in Luke 21:20–24. The destruction of Jerusalem was a foretaste of the Last Judgment and so is a sign of the coming wrath. It stands as a unique declaration of the end of the old age, and so is a specific and uniquely important sign.

24:15 abomination of desolation. The phrase is from Daniel; in Dan. 9:27; 11:31 it refers to the desecration of the temple by Antiochus Epiphanes. In 168 B.C. Antiochus erected a pagan altar in the temple. According to Josephus, he also sacrificed swine there. Shortly before A.D. 70 the Zealots were in the temple precincts during the war with Rome, and their presence could have been considered a desecration. In A.D. 70 the Romans entered the temple with military standards, ceremonial insignia that were elements of their religion. They took away the sacred vessels, including the lampstand, and burned the temple. Sculptures of their troops carrying the vessels are visible on the Arch of Titus in Rome.

let the reader understand. Possibly not a comment by the evangelist but by Jesus. In either case, the sense is not "whoever reads this Gospel," but "whoever reads Daniel."

24:16 flee to the mountains. According to the early church historian Eusebius, the Christians did flee Jerusalem during the Jewish war in obedience to a prophecy.

24:22 those days. Although this verse is usually taken with vv. 15–21, it is also possible to understand it as reverting to the general "beginning of the birth pains" of vv. 4–14.

24:24 if possible. Although the false prophets try to deceive the elect, there is no real possibility that they will succeed. God will keep the elect secure in His love (Rom. 8:31–39; cf. John 10:28, 29). See "Perseverance of the Saints" at Rom. 8:30.

24:27 as the lightning. The coming of Christ will be evident, unambiguous, and clear to all.

24:28 Wherever the corpse is. The sign of Jesus' coming will be as clear as where carrion is, eagles gather.

24:29–31 Some have understood these verses to represent the defeat of Satan's forces, the Son of Man's vindication, and the spread of the gospel to all the world, as having occurred symbolically at the destruction of Jerusalem. But the language of v. 31 is parallel to passages like 13:41; 16:27; and 25:31, as well as to passages such as 1 Cor. 15:52 and 1 Thess. 4:14–17. The passage most naturally refers to the Second Coming.

24:30 sign. Christ Himself, or the first moments of His appearing.

mourn. The mourning of the nations is an allusion to Zech. 12:10–12,

Man coming on the clouds of heaven [w]with power and great glory. 31 And [x]he will send out his angels with a loud [y]trumpet call, and they will [z]gather [a]his elect from the four winds, [b]from one end of heaven to the other.

The Lesson of the Fig Tree

32 "From the fig tree learn its lesson: as soon as its branch becomes tender and puts out its leaves, you know that summer is near. 33 So also, when you see all these things, you know that he is near, [c]at the very gates. 34 [d]Truly, I say to you, this generation will not pass away until all these things take place. 35 [e]Heaven and earth will pass away, but [f]my words will not pass away.

No One Knows That Day and Hour

36 "But concerning that day and hour [g]no one knows, not even the angels of heaven, [h]nor the Son,[1] [i]but the Father only. 37 [j]As were the days of Noah, [k]so will be the coming of the Son of Man. 38 [j]For as in those days before the flood they were eating and drinking, [l]marrying and giving in marriage, until [m]the day when Noah entered the ark, 39 and they were unaware until the flood came and swept them all away, [k]so will be the coming of the Son of Man. 40 Then two men will be in the field; one will be taken and one left. 41 [n]Two women will be grinding [o]at the mill; one will be taken and one left. 42 Therefore, [p]stay awake, for you do not know on what day [q]your Lord is coming. 43 [r]But know this, that if the master of the house had known in what part of the night [s]the thief was coming, he would have stayed awake and would not have let his house be broken into. 44 Therefore you also must be [t]ready, for [u]the Son of Man is coming at an hour you do not expect.

45 "Who then is [v]the faithful and [w]wise servant,[2] whom his master has set over his household, to give them their food at the proper time? 46 [x]Blessed is that servant whom his master will find so doing when he comes. 47 Truly, I say to you, [y]he will set him over all his possessions. 48 But if that wicked servant says to himself, 'My master [z]is delayed,' 49 and begins to beat his fellow servants[3] and eats and drinks with [a]drunkards, 50 the master of that servant will come [b]on a day when he does not expect him and at an hour he does not know 51 and will cut him in pieces and put him with the hypocrites. In that place [c]there will be weeping and gnashing of teeth.

The Parable of the Ten Virgins

25 "Then the kingdom of heaven will be like [d]ten virgins who took their lamps[4] and went to meet [e]the bridegroom.[5] 2 Five of them were foolish, and five were [w]wise. 3 For when the foolish took their lamps, they took no oil with them, 4 but the wise took flasks of oil with their lamps. 5 As the bridegroom [f]was delayed, they all became drowsy and slept. 6 But [g]at midnight there was a cry, 'Here is the bridegroom! Come out to meet him.' 7 Then all those virgins rose and [h]trimmed their lamps. 8 And the foolish said to the wise, 'Give us some of your oil, for our lamps are going out.' 9 But the wise answered, saying, 'Since there will not be enough for us and for you, go rather to the dealers and buy for yourselves.' 10 And while they were going to buy, the bridegroom came, and [i]those who were ready went in with him to [j]the marriage feast, and [k]the door was shut. 11 Afterward the other virgins came also, saying, [l]'Lord,

30 [w]ch. 13:41
31 [x]1 Cor. 15:52; 1 Thess. 4:16 [y][ch. 23:37; 2 Thess. 2:1] [z]ver. 22, 24 [a]Dan. 7:2; Zech. 2:6; Rev. 7:1 [b]Deut. 4:32; 30:4
33 [c]James 5:9; Rev. 3:20
34 [d]See ch. 16:28
35 [e]Ps. 102:26; Isai. 51:6; 2 Pet. 3:10; [ch. 5:18; Heb. 12:27] [f]Ps. 119:89; Isai. 40:8; 1 Pet. 1:23, 25
36 [g]ch. 25:13; 1 Thess. 5:1, 2 [h][Phil. 2:6, 7] [i][Zech. 14:7; Acts 1:7]
37 [j]Luke 17:26, 27 [k]ver. 27
38 [j][See ver. 37] [l]ch. 22:30 [m]Gen. 7:7-16
39 [k][See ver. 27 above]
41 [n]Luke 17:35 [o]Ex. 11:5; Isai. 47:2
42 [p]ch. 25:13; 26:41; Mark 14:34-38; Luke 12:37; 21:36; Acts 20:31; 1 Cor. 16:13; 1 Thess. 5:6; 1 Pet. 5:8 [q]John 13:13
43 [r]For ver. 43-51, [Luke 12:39-46] [s][1 Thess. 5:2; 2 Pet. 3:10; Rev. 3:3]
44 [t]ch. 25:10 [u]ver. 27
45 [v]ch. 25:21; 1 Cor. 4:2; Heb. 3:5 [w]ch. 7:24; 10:16; 25:2; Luke 16:8; 1 Cor. 10:15
46 [x]John 13:17; Rev. 16:15
47 [y]ch. 25:21, 23
48 [z]ch. 25:5
49 [a]1 Thess. 5:7 50 [b]2 Pet. 3:12; [ch. 25:13] 51 [c]See ch. 8:12
Chapter 25 1 [d]Luke 19:13 [e]ch. 9:15; John 3:29; Rev. 19:7; 21:2, 9 2 [w][See ch. 24:25 above] 5 [f]ch. 24:48; [ver. 19; Heb. 10:37; 2 Pet. 3:4, 9] 6 [g]Mark 13:35 7 [h][Luke 12:35] 10 [i]ch. 24:44 [j]ch. 22:2 [k]For ver. 10, 12, [Luke 13:25-27] 11 [l][ch. 7:22, 23]

[1] Some manuscripts omit *nor the Son* [2] Greek *bondservant*; also verses 46, 48, 50 [3] Greek *bondservants* [4] Or *torches* [5] Some manuscripts add *and the bride*

and the coming on the clouds refers to Christ's assumption of dominion prophesied in Dan. 7:13, 14.

24:34 this generation. The phrase naturally means the people living as Jesus spoke. Some suggest it means "this race," or somewhat better, "this sort of people," that is, evil and adulterous people, 12:39.

all these things. That is, "all these things" referred to in v. 33, which are distinguished from the consummation itself. They are the "beginning of the birth pains" (v. 8) and signs that point to the final coming of Christ, including the siege and fall of Jerusalem. All of the elements of this prophecy, except for the Second Coming itself, had occurred in some form before the disciples died (Luke 21:32 note).

24:36 no one knows. This remains true, and attempts to predict the time of the end are effectively stopped by it. See "The Humanity of Jesus" at 2 John 7.

24:42 stay awake. An active state, not passive waiting, according to vv. 45–51.

is coming. See "The Return of Jesus Christ" at 1 Thess. 4:16.

25:1–13 The delay of Christ's return distinguishes the wise from the foolish. Being ready means being prepared for a long delay; short-lived zeal is inadequate.

lord, open to us.' 12 [l]But he answered,
'Truly, I say to you, [m]I do not know you.'
13 [n]Watch therefore, for you [o]know neither
the day nor the hour.

The Parable of the Talents

14 [p]"For [q]it will be like a man [r]going on a
journey, who called his servants[1] and
entrusted to them his property. 15 To one
he gave five [s]talents,[2] to another two, to
another one, [t]to each according to his ability. Then he [r]went away. 16 He who had
received the five talents went at once and
traded with them, and he made five talents
more. 17 So also he who had the two talents
made two talents more. 18 But he who had
received the one talent went and [u]dug in
the ground and hid his master's money.
19 Now [v]after a long time the master of
those servants came and [w]settled accounts
with them. 20 And he who had received the
five talents came forward, bringing five talents more, saying, 'Master, you delivered to
me five talents; here I have made five talents more.' 21 His master said to him, 'Well
done, good and [x]faithful servant.[3] [y]You
have been faithful over a little; [z]I will set
you over much. Enter into [a]the joy of your
master.' 22 And he also who had the two talents came forward, saying, 'Master, you
delivered to me two talents; here I have
made two talents more.' 23 His master said
to him, 'Well done, good and faithful servant. You have been faithful over a little; I
will set you over much. Enter into the joy
of your master.' 24 He also who had
received the one talent came forward, saying, 'Master, I knew you to be [b]a hard man,
reaping [c]where you did not sow, and gathering where you scattered no seed, 25 so I
was afraid, and I went and hid your talent
in the ground. Here [d]you have what is
yours.' 26 But his master answered him,
'You [e]wicked and [e]slothful servant! You
knew that I reap where I have not sowed
and gather where I scattered no seed?
27 Then you ought to have invested my
money with the bankers, and at my coming
I should have received what was my own
with interest. 28 So take the talent from him
and give it to him who has the ten talents.
29 [f]For to everyone who has will more be
given, and he will have an abundance. But
from the one who has not, even what he
has will be taken away. 30 And [g]cast [h]the
worthless servant into the outer darkness.
In that place [g]there will be weeping and
gnashing of teeth.'

The Final Judgment

31 [i]"When the Son of Man comes in his
glory, and all the angels with him, [j]then he
will sit on his glorious throne. 32 Before him
[k]will be gathered [l]all the nations, and [m]he
will separate people one from another as a
shepherd separates [n]the sheep from the
goats. 33 And he will place the sheep on his
right, but the goats on the left. 34 Then [o]the
King will say to [p]those on his right, 'Come,
you [q]who are blessed by my Father, [r]inher-
it [s]the kingdom [t]prepared for you [u]from the
foundation of the world. 35 For [v]I was hungry and you gave me food, I was thirsty and
you [w]gave me drink, [x]I was a stranger and
you welcomed me, 36 [v]I was naked and you
clothed me, [y]I was sick and you [z]visited
me, [a]I was in prison and you came to me.'
37 Then the righteous will answer him, saying, 'Lord, when did we see you hungry
and feed you, or thirsty and give you drink?
38 And when did we see you a stranger and
welcome you, or naked and clothe you?
39 And when did we see you sick or in
prison and visit you?' 40 And [b]the King will
answer them, [c]'Truly, I say to you, as you
did it to one of the least of these [d]my brothers,[4] you did it to me.'
41 "Then he will say to those on his left,

12 [l][See ver. 11] [m]ch. 10:33; [2 Tim. 2:19] 13 [n]ch. 24:42 [o][ch. 24:50] 14 [p]For ver. 14-30, [Luke 19:12-27] [q][Mark 13:34] [r]ch. 21:33 15 [s]ch. 18:24 [t][Rom. 12:6; 1 Cor. 12:11; Eph. 4:7; 1 Pet. 4:10] [r][See ver. 14 above] 18 [u][ch. 13:44] 19 [v][ver. 5] [w]ch. 18:23; Rom. 14:12; [Luke 16:2] 21 [x]ver. 23; ch. 24:45 [y]Luke 16:10; 1 Cor. 4:2; [1 Tim. 3:13] [z]ch. 24:47 [a]Heb. 12:2; [Isai. 53:11; John 15:11] 24 [b]1 Sam. 25:3 [c][2 Cor. 8:12] 25 [d]ch. 20:14 26 [e]ch. 18:32; Prov. 20:4; Rom. 12:11

29 [f][Luke 12:48]; See ch. 13:12 30 [g]See ch. 8:12 [h][Luke 17:10] 31 [i]See ch. 16:27, 28 [j]ch. 19:28 32 [k][ch. 24:31] [l]Joel 3:12; [ch. 24:14; 28:19] [m]ch. 13:49 [n]Ezek. 34:17 34 [o]ver. 40; Luke 19:38; Rev. 17:14; 19:16; [Isai. 6:5] [p]1 Kin. 2:19; Ps. 45:9; 110:1 [q][Ps. 37:22; Isai. 65:23; Eph. 1:3] [r]ch. 19:29; 1 Pet. 3:9; Rev. 21:7 [s]Luke 12:32; 22:29 [t]ch. 20:23; [1 Cor. 2:9; Heb. 11:16] [u]See ch. 13:35

35 [v]Isai. 58:7; Ezek. 18:7, 16; [James 2:15, 16] [w]ch. 10:42 [x]Job 31:32; Rom. 12:13; Heb. 13:1, 2; 3 John 5 36 [v][See ver. 35 above] [y][Luke 10:33, 34] [z]James 1:27 [a]2 Tim. 1:16; [Heb. 10:34; 13:3] 40 [b]ver. 34 [c]See ch. 10:40, 42 [d]ch. 28:10; John 20:17; Rom. 8:29; Heb. 2:11; [ch. 12:50]

[1] Greek *bondservants*; also verse 19 [2] A *talent* was a monetary unit worth about twenty years' wages for a laborer [3] Greek *bondservant*; also verses 23, 26, 30 [4] Or *brothers and sisters*

25:15 talents. See notes 18:24, 28. The English word "talent" meaning a natural endowment or special ability is derived from this parable.

25:24 I knew you to be a hard man. The third servant was unwilling to do the work of investing the talent for the benefit of another.

25:31 Son of Man. See note 8:20.

25:32 sheep. The image of Christ's people as sheep is found in Ezek. 34 and is a part of Jesus' teaching (10:16; 18:12). The division concerns individuals, not nations.

25:40 the least of these my brothers. Christ's disciples (10:42; 12:48, 49; 18:14), not the poor and needy in general. The judgment of the nations depends on how they respond to Christians and to the gospel (10:40–42), not only because it is through the testimony of Christians that the Gentiles can hear and believe (Rom. 10:14), but also because Christ identifies with His people. Their suffering is His suffering, and compassion shown to them is compassion shown to Him.

25:41 See theological note "The Final Judgment" on next page.

[e]'Depart from me, you [f]cursed, into [g]the
eternal fire prepared for [h]the devil and his
angels. 42 For [i]I was hungry and you gave
me no food, I was thirsty and you gave
me no drink, 43 I was a stranger and you
did not welcome me, naked and you did
not clothe me, sick and in prison and you
did not visit me.' 44 Then they also will
answer, saying, 'Lord, when did we see you
hungry or thirsty or a stranger or naked or
sick or in prison, and did not minister to
you?' 45 Then he will answer them, saying,
'Truly, I say to you, as you did not do it to
one of the least of these, [j]you did not do it
to me.' 46 And these will go away [k]into eternal punishment, but the righteous [k]into
[l]eternal life."

41 [e]ch. 7:23 [f][Heb. 6:8] [g]ch. 13:40, 42; 18:8; Mark 9:43, 48; Jude 7; [Luke 16:24]; See 2 Thess. 1:8 [h]2 Pet. 2:4; Jude 6; Rev. 12:7
42 [i]Job 22:7
45 [j][Luke 10:16; Acts 9:5; 1 Cor. 8:12]
46 [k]Dan. 12:2; John 5:29; [Acts 24:15] [l]Rom. 2:7; 5:21; 6:23

The Plot to Kill Jesus

26 When Jesus had finished all these
sayings, he said to his disciples,
2 [m]"You know that after two days [n]the
Passover is coming, and [o]the Son of Man
[p]will be delivered up to be crucified."
3 [q]Then the chief priests and the elders of
the people gathered in [r]the palace of the
high priest, whose name was [s]Caiaphas,
4 [t]and plotted together in order to arrest
Jesus by stealth and kill him. 5 But they
said, "Not during the feast, [u]lest there be
an uproar among the people."

Chapter 26 **2** [m]For ver. 2-5, see Mark 14:1, 2; Luke 22:1, 2 [n]See John 6:4 [o]ver. 24 [p]See ch. 20:18, 19 **3** [q][Ps. 2:2; John 11:47; Acts 4:27] [r]ver. 58, 69; Luke 11:21; John 18:15; [Rev. 11:2] [s]ver. 57; Luke 3:2; John 11:49; 18:13; Acts 4:6 **4** [t]John 11:53; See ch. 21:46 **5** [u]ch. 27:24

The Final Judgment

The certainty of final judgment is the background against which the New Testament message of saving grace is set. Paul no less than Jesus stresses this certainty. According to Paul, Jesus Christ saves us from "the wrath to come" (1 Thess. 1:10) on "the day of wrath when God's righteous judgment will be revealed" (Rom. 2:5; cf. John 3:36; Rom. 5:9; Eph. 5:6; Col. 3:6; Rev. 6:17; 19:15). Throughout Scripture, God's "indignation," "anger," and "fury" are judicial; these words point to the holy Creator as the active Judge of sin. The message of coming judgment for all mankind, with Jesus Christ completing the work of His mediatorial kingdom by acting as Judge on His Father's behalf, runs throughout the New Testament (Matt. 13:40–43; 25:41–46; John 5:22–30; Acts 10:42; 2 Cor. 5:10; 2 Tim. 4:1; Heb. 9:27; 10:25–31; 12:23; 2 Pet. 3:7; Jude 6, 7; Rev. 20:11–15). When Christ comes again and history is completed, all people of all times will be raised for the judgment and take their place before Christ's throne. The event surpasses imagination, but the human imagination is not the measure of what God will do.

At the judgment every person will give an individual account to God, and God through Christ "will render to each one according to his works" (Rom. 2:6; cf. Ps. 62:12; Matt. 16:27; 2 Cor. 5:10; Rev. 22:12). The regenerate, who as servants of Christ have learned to love righteousness and desire the glory of heaven, will be acknowledged, and on the basis of Christ's merit on their behalf they will be awarded the righteousness they seek. The rest will go to a destiny commensurate with the godless way of life they have chosen, a place assigned to them on the basis of their own demerit (Rom. 2:6–11). How much they knew of the will of God will determine the severity of their condemnation (Matt. 11:20–24; Luke 11:42–48; Rom. 2:12).

The judgment will demonstrate the perfect justice of God. In a world of sinners, where God has "allowed all the nations to walk in their own ways" (Acts 14:16), evil is rampant, and doubts arise about how God, if He is sovereign, can be just, or, if He is just, can be sovereign. But God will be glorified in rendering just judgment, and the Last Judgment will answer every suspicion that He has ceased to care about righteousness (Ps. 50:16–21; Rev. 6:10; 16:5–7; 19:1–5).

For those who profess to belong to Christ, a review of their words and works (Matt. 12:36, 37) will show whether their profession is the fruit of an honest and good heart (Matt. 12:33–35), or a deceptive hypocrisy (Matt. 7:21–23). Everything will be exposed on Judgment Day (1 Cor. 4:5), and each person will receive from God what fairly belongs to them. Those whose professed faith did not express itself in a new life, marked by hatred of sin and love of righteousness, will be lost (Matt. 18:23–35; 25:34–46; James 2:14–26). Yet God has announced the day of judgment before the time, commanding everyone to repent and love life rather than death (Deut. 30:19; Luke 13:24).

25:46 eternal punishment. See "Hell" at Mark 9:43.

26:5 Not during the feast. Although the officials expected to postpone the murder of Jesus until after Passover (Mark 14:1 note), God's purpose (v. 2) was for it to take place on or just before the feast (v. 17 note).

Jesus Anointed at Bethany

6 [v]Now when Jesus was at [w]Bethany in
the house of Simon the leper,[1] **7** a woman
came up to him with an alabaster flask of
very expensive ointment, and she poured it
on his head as he reclined at table. **8** And
when the disciples saw it, they were indignant, saying, "Why this waste? **9** For this
could have been sold for a large sum and
[x]given to the poor." **10** But [y]Jesus, aware of
this, said to them, "Why do you trouble
the woman? For she has done a beautiful
thing to me. **11** For [z]you always have the
poor with you, but [a]you will not always
have me. **12** In pouring this ointment on my
body, she has done it [b]to prepare me for
burial. **13** Truly, I say to you, wherever [c]this
gospel is proclaimed in the whole world,
what she has done will also be told [d]in
memory of her."

Judas to Betray Jesus

14 [e]Then one of the twelve, whose name
was [f]Judas Iscariot, went to the chief
priests **15** and said, "What will you give me
if I deliver him over to you?" And they
[g]paid him [h]thirty pieces of silver. **16** And
from that moment he sought an opportunity [i]to betray him.

The Passover with the Disciples

17 [j]Now on [k]the first day of Unleavened
Bread the disciples came to Jesus, saying,
"Where will you have us prepare for you to
eat the Passover?" **18** He said, "Go into the
city to a certain man and say to him, [l]'The
Teacher says, [m]My time is at hand. I will
keep the Passover at your house with my
disciples.'" **19** And the disciples did as Jesus
had directed them, and they prepared the
Passover.

20 [n]When it was evening, he reclined at
table with the twelve.[2] **21** And as they were
eating, [o]he said, "Truly, I say to you, one of
you will betray me." **22** And they were very
sorrowful and began to say to him one after
another, "Is it I, Lord?" **23** He answered, [p]"He
who has dipped his hand in the dish with
me will betray me. **24** The Son of Man goes
[q]as it is written of him, but [r]woe to that
man by whom the Son of Man is betrayed!
[s]It would have been better for that man if
he had not been born." **25** Judas, who would
betray him, answered, "Is it I, [t]Rabbi?" He
said to him, [u]"You have said so."

Institution of the Lord's Supper

26 [v]Now as they were eating, Jesus took
bread, and [w]after blessing it broke it and
gave it to the disciples, and said, "Take,
eat; [x]this is my body." **27** And he took a cup,
and when he [y]had given thanks he gave it

6 [v]For ver. 6-13, see Mark 14:3-9; John 12:1-8; [Luke 7:37-39] [w]ch. 21:17; John 11:18
9 [x][John 13:29]
10 [y]ch. 16:8
11 [z]Deut. 15:11 [a]ch. 9:15; See John 7:33
12 [b]John 19:40
13 [c][ch. 24:14] [d]Acts 10:4
14 [e]For ver. 14-16, see Mark 14:10, 11; Luke 22:3-6; [John 13:2, 27, 30] [f]ch. 10:4; 27:3; Acts 1:16; [John 6:71; 12:4]
15 [g]Zech. 11:12; [Gen. 23:16; Jer. 32:9] [h]ch. 27:3, 9; Ex. 21:32
16 [i]See ch. 20:18, 19
17 [j]For ver. 17-19, see Mark 14:12-16; Luke 22:7-13 [k]Ex. 12:18
18 [l]See John 11:28 [m][ver. 45; John 7:6, 8, 30; 8:20; 13:1; 17:1]
20 [n]For ver. 20-24, see Mark 14:17-21; [Luke 22:14, 21-23; John 13:21-26]

21 [o][John 6:70, 71] **23** [p][John 13:18] **24** [q]ver. 54, 56; Mark 9:12; Luke 18:31; 24:25-27, 46; Acts 17:2, 3; 26:22, 23; 1 Cor. 15:3; 1 Pet. 1:10, 11 [r]ch. 18:7 [s]John 17:12; **25** [t]ver. 49; See John 1:38 [u]ver. 64; See Luke 22:70 **26** [v]For ver. 26-29, see Mark 14:22-25; Luke 22:18-20; 1 Cor. 11:23-25 [w]See ch. 14:19 [x]1 Cor. 10:16; [John 6:53] **27** [y]See ch. 15:36

1 *Leprosy* was a term for several skin diseases; see Leviticus 13
2 Some manuscripts add *disciples*

26:6–13 Mark 14:3–9 agrees with Matthew's account regarding the time (two days before Passover, v. 2) and the method of anointing (on Jesus' head). John 12:1–8 differs chronologically (six days before Passover), but although certain details are different (Mary anoints His feet), none conflict (John 12:3 note). These three accounts probably relate the same incident. Luke 7:36–38, however, bears only superficial similarity to this story.

26:8 they were indignant. John reports the hypocritical objection of Judas (John 12:4–6), and Matthew indicates that the others agreed with him.

26:11 the poor. Care for the poor is commanded by God, but the commandment cannot have a higher priority than Jesus, the One sent by the Author of the commandment. Similarly, God commands honor of father and mother, but not above honor to Jesus (10:37; 15:4–6; 19:29).

26:17 the first day of Unleavened Bread. The day of preparation for Passover, presumably 14 Nisan (the first month of the Jewish calendar). Jesus celebrated Passover that evening, 15 Nisan, and was crucified the next afternoon. The Gospel of John seems to present Jesus as crucified on the day before Passover (John 18:28; 19:14, 31), making the Lord's Supper not a Passover meal.

Calvin understood Preparation Day to be the day before Passover, and argued that the Jews according to some traditions combined the Passover with the weekly Sabbath (John 19:14 note). Then Matt. 27:62 would refer to the Preparation Day observed by the Jewish leadership. There is some difficulty, however, in seeing how Jesus' disciples could have had their lamb slaughtered in advance of the official schedule, and Mark 14:12 clearly indicates that Jesus arranged for Passover on the day when the lambs were customarily slaughtered. Whatever the solution, Matthew clearly identifies the meal that Jesus ate with His disciples on the eve of His crucifixion as the Passover meal.

26:18 My time. Again Jesus emphasizes that all the terrible events soon to take place were totally under God's control.

26:24 Son of Man. See 8:20 note.

as it is written of him. Jesus' atoning death was no mere contrivance of the misguided authorities. The event and its circumstances, including betrayal by His friend (Ps. 41:9; 55:12–14), had been appointed by God since before the world was formed. Nevertheless, those who brought about Jesus' death remain responsible for their actions ("woe to that man;" cf. Acts 2:23).

26:26–29 In the old covenant, the Passover meal was a memorial celebration of Israel's deliverance from Egypt. By transforming His last Passover meal to institute the Lord's Supper, Jesus shows the consistent focus on redemption throughout God's revelation. The Lord's Supper demonstrates the essential continuity between the old and the new covenants by revealing that the true meaning of the Passover lies in the deliverance effected by Jesus' death.

26:26 this is my body. In Roman Catholicism these words are quoted in support of the doctrine of transubstantiation, which teaches that the

to them, saying, "Drink of it, all of you,
28 for [x]this is my [z]blood of the[1] covenant,
which is poured out for [a]many [b]for the forgiveness of sins. 29 I tell you I will not drink
again of this fruit of the vine until that day
when I drink it new with you [c]in my
Father's kingdom."

Jesus Foretells Peter's Denial

30 [d]And when they had sung a hymn,
[e]they went out to [f]the Mount of Olives.
31 Then Jesus said to them, "You will all fall
away because of me this night. For it is
written, 'I will [g]strike the shepherd, and
the sheep of the flock will be scattered.'
32 But after I am raised up, [h]I will go before
you to Galilee." 33 [i]Peter answered him,
"Though they all fall away because of you,
I will never fall away." 34 [j]Jesus said to him,
"Truly, I tell you, this very night, [k]before
the rooster crows, you will deny me three
times." 35 [l]Peter said to him, "Even if I must
die with you, I will not deny you!" And all
the disciples said the same.

Jesus Prays in Gethsemane

36 [m]Then Jesus went with them [e]to a place
called Gethsemane, and he said to his disciples, "Sit here, while I go over there and
pray." 37 And taking with him [n]Peter and
[o]the two sons of Zebedee, he began to
be sorrowful and troubled. 38 Then he said
to them, [p]"My soul is very sorrowful, even
to death; remain here, and [q]watch[2] with
me." 39 And going a little farther he fell on
his face [r]and prayed, saying, "My Father, if
it be possible, let [s]this cup pass from me;
[t]nevertheless, not as I will, but as you will."
40 And he came to the disciples and found
them sleeping. And he said to Peter, "So,
could you not watch with me one hour?
41 [q]Watch and [u]pray that you [v]may not
enter into temptation. The spirit indeed is

28 [x][See ver. 26] [z]Ex. 24:8; [Zech. 9:11; Heb. 13:20] [a]See ch. 20:28 [b]Mark 1:4; [Luke 1:77]
29 [c][ch. 13:43]
30 [d]For ver. 30-35, see Mark 14:26-31 [e]Luke 22:39; John 18:1 [f]See ch. 21:1
31 [g]Cited from Zech. 13:7; [John 16:32]
32 [h]ch. 28:7, 10, 16; Mark 16:7
33 [i][Luke 22:31, 33]
34 [j]Luke 22:34; John 13:38 [k]ver. 75
35 [l]Luke 22:33; John 13:37
36 [m]For ver. 36-46, see Mark 14:32-42; Luke 22:40-46 [e][See ver. 30 above]
37 [n]ch. 17:1 [o]ch. 4:21
38 [p][Ps. 42:5, 6; John 12:27] [q]See ch. 24:42
39 [r]Heb. 5:7 [s]See ch. 20:22 [t]ver. 42; John 5:30; 6:38; Phil. 2:8
41 [q][See ver. 38 above] [u]1 Pet. 4:7 [v]ch. 6:13

willing, but the flesh is weak." 42 Again, for
the second time, he went away and prayed,
"My Father, if this cannot pass unless I
drink it, [w]your will be done." 43 And again
he came and found them sleeping, for
[x]their eyes were heavy. 44 So, leaving them
again, he went away and prayed for [y]the
third time, saying the same words again.
45 Then he came to the disciples and said to
them, "Sleep and take your rest later on.[3]
See, [z]the hour is at hand, and [a]the Son of
Man is betrayed into the hands of sinners.
46 Rise, let us be going; see, my betrayer is
at hand."

Betrayal and Arrest of Jesus

47 [b]While he was still speaking, [c]Judas
came, one of the twelve, and with him a
great crowd with swords and clubs, from
the chief priests and the elders of the people. 48 Now the betrayer had given them a
sign, saying, "The one I will kiss is the
man; seize him." 49 And he came up to Jesus
at once and said, "Greetings, [d]Rabbi!" And
he kissed him. 50 Jesus said to him,
[e]"Friend, [f]do what you came to do."[4] Then
they came up and laid hands on Jesus and
seized him. 51 And behold, one of those
who were with Jesus stretched out his
hand and drew his [g]sword and struck the
servant[5] of the high priest and cut off his
ear. 52 Then Jesus said to him, "Put your
sword back into its place. For [h]all who take
the sword will perish by the sword. 53 [i]Do
you think that I cannot appeal to my
Father, and he will at once send me [j]more
than twelve [k]legions of angels? 54 [l]But how

42 [w]ver. 39; See ch. 6:10
43 [x]Luke 9:32
44 [y][2 Cor. 12:8]
45 [z]John 12:23, 27; 13:1; 17:1; [ver. 18; Luke 22:53] [a]ch. 17:22; 20:18

47 [b]For ver. 47-56, see Mark 14:43-50; Luke 22:47-53; John 18:3-11 [c]ver. 14; Acts 1:16 49 [d]ver. 25 50 [e]ch. 20:13; 22:12 [f][John 13:27] 51 [g][Luke 22:38] 52 [h]Rev. 13:10; [Gen. 9:6; Ezek. 35:6] 53 [i][John 10:18] [j][ch. 4:11; 2 Kin. 6:17; Dan. 7:10; Luke 22:43; John 18:36] [k]Luke 8:30 54 [l]See ver. 24; ch. 1:22

[1] Some manuscripts insert *new* [2] Or *keep awake*; also verses 40, 41 [3] Or *Are you still sleeping and taking your rest?* [4] Or *Friend, why are you here?* [5] Greek *bondservant*

outward, physical attributes of the bread and wine remain unchanged, while the invisible essence is transformed into the body and blood of Christ. Calvin and the other Reformers recognized that the elements *represent* Christ's body and blood. Jesus uttered these words while physically present with His disciples, so a literal identification of the elements with His physical substance would not have occurred to them. The bread and wine are more than conventional symbols, however, for through the Holy Spirit they communicate *visibly* what is *read* and *heard* in the gospel (1 Cor. 10:16). See "The Lord's Supper" at 1 Cor. 11:23.

26:28 my blood of the covenant. The Mosaic covenant was inaugurated with a sacrifice (Ex. 24:28), and the new covenant prophesied by Jeremiah (Jer. 31:31–34; cf. Luke 22:17–20; 1 Cor. 11:23–25) is inaugurated by the sacrifice of Christ, to which the Lord's Supper points. See "The Sacraments" at 28:19.

26:31 I will strike the shepherd. In the context of Zech. 13:7, the Lord strikes the Shepherd, the "man who stands next to me," and God's "little ones" are scattered. Subsequently they are renewed and truly become God's people. The disciples' desertion of Jesus is representative of the nation's apostasy, as well as of the remnant that God will save.

26:39 cup. See 20:23 note. Jesus is horrified at the prospect of enduring His Father's wrath. Jesus had to face death knowing that His Father would not be with Him, but against Him in wrath of judgment.

26:52 Put your sword back into its place. Jesus did not bring His kingdom with force, like earthly kings.

then should the Scriptures be fulfilled, that
it must be so?" 55 At that hour Jesus said to
the crowds, "Have you come out as against
a robber, with swords and clubs to capture
me? Day after day [m]I sat in the temple
[n]teaching, and you did not seize me. 56 But
[l]all this has taken place that the Scriptures
of the prophets might be fulfilled." [o]Then
all the disciples left him and fled.

Jesus Before Caiaphas

57 [p]Then [q]those who had seized Jesus led
him to [r]Caiaphas the high priest, where the
scribes and the elders had gathered. 58 And
[s]Peter was following him at a distance, as
far as [r]the courtyard of the high priest, and
going inside he sat with [t]the guards to see
the end. 59 Now the chief priests and the
whole Council[1] [u]were seeking false testimony against Jesus that they might put
him to death, 60 but they found none,
[v]though many false witnesses came forward. At last [w]two came forward 61 and
said, "This man said, [x]'I am able to [y]de-
stroy the temple of God, and to rebuild it
in three days.'" 62 And the high priest stood
up and said, "Have you no answer to
make? What is it that these men testify
against you?"[2] 63 [z]But Jesus remained silent.
[a]And the high priest said to him, [b]"I adjure
you by [c]the living God, [d]tell us if you are
[e]the Christ, [f]the Son of God." 64 Jesus said
to him, [g]"You have said so. But I tell you,
from now on [h]you will see the Son of Man
[i]seated at the right hand of Power and
[h]coming on the clouds of heaven." 65 Then
the high priest [j]tore his robes and said,
[k]"He has uttered blasphemy. What further
witnesses do we need? You have now heard
his blasphemy. 66 What is your judgment?"
They answered, [l]"He deserves death."
67 Then [m]they spit in his face [n]and [o]struck
him. And some slapped him, 68 saying,
"Prophesy to us, you [p]Christ! Who is it that
struck you?"

Peter Denies Jesus

69 [q]Now Peter was sitting outside [r]in the
courtyard. And a servant girl came up to
him and said, "You also were with Jesus
the Galilean." 70 But he denied it before
them all, saying, "I do not know what you
mean." 71 And when he went out to the
entrance, another servant girl saw him, and
she said to the bystanders, "This man was
with Jesus [s]of Nazareth." 72 And again he
denied it with an oath: "I do not know the
man." 73 After a little while the bystanders
came up and said to Peter, "Certainly you
too are one of them, for [t]your accent
betrays you." 74 Then he began to invoke a
curse on himself and to swear, "I do not
know the man." And immediately the rooster crowed. 75 And Peter remembered the
saying of Jesus, [u]"Before the rooster crows,
you will [v]deny me three times." And he
went out and wept bitterly.

Jesus Delivered to Pilate

27 [w]When morning came, all the chief
priests and the elders of the people
[x]took counsel against Jesus to put him to
death. 2 And they bound him and [y]led him
away and [z]delivered him over to [a]Pilate the
governor.

55 [m][John 8:2]; [Luke 2:46; John 18:20] [n]ch. 21:23; [ch. 4:23]
56 [l][See ver. 54] [o]ver. 31; [Ps. 88:8, 18; John 16:32]
57 [p]Luke 22:54 [q]For ver. 57-68, see Mark 14:53-65; [John 18:12, 13, 19-24] [r]ver. 3
58 [s][John 18:15] [r][See ver. 57 above] [t]John 7:32; 18:3
59 [u]See Acts 6:11
60 [v]Ps. 27:12; 35:11 [w]Deut. 19:15
61 [x][Acts 6:14]; See John 2:19 [y]ch. 27:40
63 [z]ch. 27:12, 14; Isai. 53:7; John 19:9 [a]For ver. 63-66, [Luke 22:67-71] [b][Lev. 5:1; 1 Sam. 14:24, 26; Mark 5:7] [c]See ch. 16:16 [d]John 10:24 [e][ch. 22:42-45]; See ch. 1:17 [f]See ch. 14:33
64 [g]ver. 25 [h]See ch. 16:27; 24:30 [i]Ps. 110:1; Heb. 1:3; [Mark 16:19]
65 [j]Num. 14:6; Acts 14:14 [k]ch. 9:3; John 10:36
66 [l]See Lev. 24:16
67 [m]ch. 27:30; Isai. 50:6; Mark 10:34

[n][Luke 22:63-65; John 18:22] [o]ch. 5:39; Acts 23:2 **68** [p]ver. 63 **69** [q]For ver. 69-75, see Mark 14:66-72; Luke 22:55-62; John 18:16-18, 25-27 [r]ver. 3 **71** [s]ch. 2:23 **73** [t][Judg. 12:6] **75** [u]ver. 34 [v][Acts 3:13, 14]
Chapter 27 **1** [w]Mark 15:1; Luke 22:66 [x]See ch. 26:4 **2** [y]Luke 23:1; John 18:28 [z]See ch. 20:19 [a]Luke 3:1; 13:1; Acts 3:13; 4:27; 1 Tim. 6:13

1 Greek *Sanhedrin* 2 Or *Have you no answer to what these men testify against you?*

26:54, 56 be fulfilled. Jesus knows that the Scriptures prophesying salvation through His death must be fulfilled (Luke 22:37). Some commentators suggest that Zech. 13:7 is still in view (v. 31), but more probably that Jesus is referring broadly to His death and resurrection (see Luke 24:44–46).

26:59–61 Apparently the Sanhedrin had difficulty finding false witnesses. Finally they used a charge that was a distortion of something Jesus had said (John 2:19). The numerous irregularities in this trial have often been pointed out. This is not evidence of historical unreliability, but of the extreme actions the Jewish leaders took to rid themselves of Jesus.

26:63 I adjure you. Jesus did not answer, and Caiaphas comes to the point: does Jesus claim to be the Messiah sent from God?

26:64 You have said so. Jesus' answer is reluctantly affirmative, probably because the high priest's understanding of the Messiah's role was so different from the role Jesus actually fulfilled. Jesus responds in the same way to a similar question from Pilate in 27:11.

from now on you will see. Jesus probably speaks of the process of exaltation to the right hand of the Father that in a sense begins with His humiliation and death. The Jewish leaders would soon "see" in the resurrection reports of the soldiers (28:11–15) and Stephen's eyewitness testimony of the majesty of the exalted Christ (Acts 7:56) that the One whom they had killed was the Messiah He had claimed to be.

26:69–75 Peter's three denials are recorded in all four Gospels (Mark 14:66–72; Luke 22:54–62; John 18:15–18, 25–27), although the accounts differ in certain details. Peter's oaths (vv. 72, 74) mean that he appealed to God to witness to something that was not true (see 5:33–37; Ex. 20:7). All the Gospels record this incident, showing how deeply it impressed the mind of the early church. It is a testimony both to human weakness and the greatness of God's mercy.

Judas Hangs Himself

3 Then when [b]Judas, his betrayer, saw
that Jesus[1] was condemned, [c]he changed
his mind and brought back [d]the thirty
pieces of silver to the chief priests and the
elders, **4** saying, "I have sinned by betraying
innocent blood." They said, "What is that
to us? [e]See to it yourself." **5** And throwing
down the pieces of silver into the temple,
[f]he departed, and he went and hanged
himself. **6** But the chief priests, taking the
pieces of silver, said, "It is not lawful to put
them into [g]the treasury, since it is blood
money." **7** So they took counsel and bought
with them the potter's field as a burial
place for strangers. **8** Therefore [h]that field
has been called the Field of Blood [i]to this
day. **9** [j]Then was fulfilled what had been
spoken by the prophet Jeremiah, saying,
[k]"And they took the thirty pieces of silver,
the price of him on whom a price had been
set by some of the sons of Israel, **10** and they
gave them for the potter's field, as the Lord
directed me."

Jesus Before Pilate

11 [l]Now Jesus stood before the governor,
and the governor asked him, "Are you [m]the
King of the Jews?" Jesus said, [n]"You have
said so." **12** [o]But when he was accused by
the chief priests and elders, he gave no
answer. **13** Then Pilate said to him, [p]"Do
you not hear how many things they testify
against you?" **14** But he gave him no answer,
not even to a single charge, so that the governor was greatly amazed.

The Crowd Chooses Barabbas

15 [q]Now at the feast the governor was
accustomed to release for the crowd any
one prisoner whom they wanted. **16** And
they had then a notorious prisoner called
Barabbas. **17** So when they had gathered,
Pilate said to them, "Whom do you want
me to release for you: Barabbas, or [r]Jesus
who is called Christ?" **18** For he knew that it
was out [s]of envy that they had delivered
him up. **19** Besides, while he was sitting on
[t]the judgment seat, his wife sent word to
him, "Have nothing to do with [u]that righteous man, for I have suffered much
because of him today [v]in a dream." **20** Now
the chief priests and the elders persuaded
the crowd to [w]ask for Barabbas and destroy
Jesus. **21** The governor again said to them,
"Which of the two do you want me to
release for you?" And they said, "Barabbas." **22** Pilate said to them, "Then what
shall I do with Jesus who is called Christ?"
[x]They all said, "Let him be crucified!"
23 And he said, "Why, [y]what evil has he
done?" But they shouted all the more, "Let
him be crucified!"

Pilate Delivers Jesus to Be Crucified

24 So when Pilate saw that he was gaining
nothing, but rather that [z]a riot was beginning, he took water and [a]washed his hands
before the crowd, saying, "I am innocent of
[b]this man's blood;[2] [c]see to it yourselves."
25 And all the people answered, [d]"His blood
be on us and [e]on our children!" **26** Then he
released for them Barabbas, and having
[f]scourged[3] Jesus, delivered him to be crucified.

Jesus Is Mocked

27 [g]Then the soldiers of the governor took
Jesus into the [h]governor's headquarters,[4]
and they gathered the whole [i]battalion
before him. **28** And they stripped him and

3 [b]See ch. 26:14 [c]ch. 21:29 [d]ch. 26:15
4 [e]ver. 24
5 [f][2 Sam. 17:23; Acts 1:18]
6 [g]Mark 12:41, 43; Luke 21:1; John 8:20
8 [h]Acts 1:19 [i]ch. 28:15
9 [j]See ch. 1:22 [k]Cited from Zech. 11:13
11 [l]For ver. 11-14, see Mark 15:2-5; Luke 23:2, 3; John 18:29-38 [m]ver. 29, 37; ch. 2:2; John 18:39; 19:3; [ver. 42] [n][1 Tim. 6:13]; See Luke 22:70
12 [o]See ch. 26:63
13 [p]John 19:10
15 [q]For ver. 15-26, see Mark 15:6-15; Luke 23:18-25; John 18:39, 40; 19:16
17 [r]ver. 22
18 [s][John 12:19]
19 [t]John 19:13 [u]ver. 24; [Luke 23:47] [v]See ch. 2:12
20 [w]Acts 3:14
22 [x]Acts 13:28
23 [y][Luke 23:41; John 8:46]
24 [z]ch. 26:5 [a][Deut. 21:6-8; Ps. 26:6; 73:13] [b]ver. 19 [c]ver. 4
25 [d][ch. 23:35, 36; Josh. 2:19; Acts 5:28] [e][Ex. 20:5; Lam. 5:7]
26 [f]ch. 20:19; Isai. 50:6; 53:5; [Luke 23:16; John 19:1]
27 [g]For ver. 27-31, see Mark 15:16-20; John 19:2, 3 [h]John 18:28, 33; 19:9; Acts 23:35; Phil. 1:13 (Gk.) [i]See Acts 10:1

1 Greek *he* 2 Some manuscripts *this righteous blood*, or *this righteous man's blood* 3 A Roman judicial penalty, consisting of a severe beating with a multi-lashed whip containing imbedded pieces of bone and metal 4 Greek *praetorium*

27:3 changed his mind. Judas's remorse is not the same as repentance (3:2 note).

27:4 They cannot claim indifference to the question of "innocent blood" for which they paid the price (26:15). This attempt at passing responsibility is no more effective than Pilate's in v. 24.

27:5 hanged himself. See Acts 1:18 note.

27:9 spoken by . . . Jeremiah. Most of the words in the quotation are from Zech. 11:12, 13, but the content is also closely related to Jer. 19:1–13, which is a prophecy of judgment for the shedding of innocent blood (Jer. 19:4). Jeremiah twice speaks of a potter (Jer. 19:1, 11), and Matthew's "Field of Blood" recalls his designation of Tophet as the "Valley of Slaughter" (Jer. 19:6), which also was to become a burial ground (Jer. 19:11). Matthew finds in Judas's and the priests' actions a fulfillment of the judgment prophecies of Zechariah and Jeremiah.

27:14 Jesus' silence fulfills Is. 53:7.

27:25 His blood be on us. When Pilate seemed reluctant to act, the people were not afraid to say they would take the responsibility themselves. Their guilt, Pilate's guilt, and Judas's, is not determined by them but by God (cf. Acts 4:27). According to Ezekiel, descendants do not share the guilt of their parents unless they cooperate in their sins (Ezek. 18:20; cf. Acts 2:23, 39).

27:26 scourged. The Roman scourge was a multi-stranded whip to the ends of which bits of bone were tied. Prisoners often died from this punishment.

put [j]a scarlet robe on him, **29** and twisting
together a crown of thorns, they put it on
his head and put a reed in his right hand.
And kneeling before him, they [k]mocked
him, saying, "Hail, [l]King of the Jews!"
30 And [m]they spit on him and took the reed
and struck him on the head. **31** And when
they had mocked him, they stripped him of
the robe and put his own clothes on him
and [n]led him away to crucify him.

The Crucifixion

32 [o,p]As they went out, they found a man
of Cyrene, Simon by name. They compelled this man to carry his cross. **33** [q]And
when they came to a place called Golgotha
(which means Place of a Skull), **34** [r]they
offered him wine to drink, mixed with
[s]gall, but when he tasted it, he would not
drink it. **35** And when they had crucified
him, [t]they divided his garments among
them by casting lots. **36** Then they sat down
and [u]kept watch over him there. **37** And
over his head they put the charge against
him, which read, "This is Jesus, [v]the King
of the Jews." **38** Then two [w]robbers were
crucified with him, [x]one on the right and
one on the left. **39** And [y]those who passed
by [z]derided him, [a]wagging their heads
40 and saying, [b]"You who would destroy the
temple and rebuild it in three days, save
yourself! [c]If you are [d]the Son of God, come
down from the cross." **41** So also the chief
priests, with the scribes and elders, mocked
him, saying, **42** [e]"He saved others; [f]he cannot save himself. [g]He is the King of Israel;
let him come down now from the cross,
and we will believe in him. **43** [h]He trusts in
God; let God deliver him now, if he desires
him. For he said, 'I am the Son of God.'"
44 [i]And the robbers who were crucified with
him also reviled him in the same way.

The Death of Jesus

45 Now from the sixth hour[1] there was
darkness over all the land[2] until the ninth
hour.[3] **46** And about the ninth hour Jesus
[j]cried out with a loud voice, saying, [k]"Eli,
Eli, lema sabachthani?" that is, "My God,
my God, why have you forsaken me?"
47 And some of the bystanders, hearing it,
said, "This man is calling Elijah." **48** And
one of them at once ran and took a sponge,
filled it with [l]sour wine, and put it on a
reed and [m]gave it to him to drink. **49** But the
others said, "Wait, let us see whether
Elijah will come to save him." **50** And Jesus
[n]cried out again with a loud voice and
[o]yielded up his spirit.
51 And behold, [p]the curtain of the temple
was torn in two, from top to bottom. And
[q]the earth shook, and the rocks were split.
52 The tombs also were opened. And many
bodies of [r]the saints [s]who had fallen asleep
were raised, **53** and coming out of the tombs

28 [j]Rev. 18:12, 16; [Luke 23:11] **29** [k]ch. 20:19 [l]See ver. 11 **30** [m]See ch. 26:67 **31** [n]Isai. 53:7 **32** [o]Mark 15:21; Luke 23:26; [John 19:17] [p]Heb. 13:12; [ch. 21:39; Num. 15:35] **33** [q]For ver. 33-51, see Mark 15:22-38; Luke 23:32-38, 44-46; John 19:17-19, 23, 24, 28-30 **34** [r][Ps. 69:21] [s]Acts 8:23 **35** [t]Ps. 22:18 **36** [u]ver. 54; [Ps. 22:17] **37** [v]ver. 11, 29 **38** [w][John 18:40] [x][ch. 20:21] **39** [y]Ps. 22:7; 109:25; [Lam. 1:12] [z]Luke 22:65; 23:39; [James 2:7] [a]Job 16:4; Isai. 37:22; Jer. 18:16; Lam. 2:15 **40** [b]ch. 26:61 [c]ch. 4:3, 6 [d]ver. 43; ch. 26:63; See ch. 14:33

42 [e][Luke 4:23] [f][ch. 26:53, 54; John 10:18] [g]John 1:49; 12:13; [ver. 37] **43** [h]Cited from Ps. 22:8

44 [i][Luke 23:39-43] **46** [j][Heb. 5:7] [k]Cited from Ps. 22:1 **48** [l]Ruth 2:14 [m]Ps. 69:21 **50** [n]ver. 46 [o][John 10:18] **51** [p]Ex. 26:31-33; 2 Chr. 3:14 [q]ver. 54 **52** [r][Dan. 7:18, 22] [s]John 11:11-13; Acts 7:60; 13:36; 1 Cor. 15:6, 18, 20; 1 Thess. 4:13-15; 2 Pet. 3:4

[1] That is, noon [2] Or *earth* [3] That is, 3 P.M.

27:28 robe. Lit. "cloak," of a Roman soldier. Matthew calls the robe "scarlet," although Mark and John call it "purple." Matthew's detail emphasizes the indignity and may hint at the popular conception of the Messiah as a military and political deliverer.

27:32–37 Crucifixion was a slow and agonizing death. Nails were probably driven through the wrists rather than the palms. The weight of the suspended body made breathing difficult and painful. Involuntary efforts by the legs to ease the pressure greatly increased pain in the feet. This ordeal continued until the exhausted victim could no longer breathe; this might take several days.

27:34 gall. Any of several bitter herbs; Mark mentions myrrh. Commentators often note that myrrh mixed with wine is a painkiller. But the offer of galled wine was probably not a gesture of compassion but of mockery, as in Ps. 69:21. Jesus' thirst would have been great, but the gall made the wine undrinkable.

27:35 divided His garments. This action fulfilled Ps. 22:18, as is made explicit in John 19:23, 24. The events surrounding the crucifixion of Jesus include numerous fulfillments of Ps. 22.

27:37 the King of the Jews. The placard at the head of the cross specified the crime. Pilate was insulting the Jewish leaders, but the irony of its truth was apparent to the early church.

27:38 The term translated "robbers" is the word Josephus uses for rebels. Robbers were not ordinarily crucified. Perhaps these two were cohorts of Barabbas (Mark 15:7).

27:40 Again note the irony. Jesus *was* going to return after three days, and "rebuild" the temple of His body. Precisely because He was the Son of God, He would not come down from the cross.

27:45 from the sixth hour . . . until the ninth hour. From noon to 3:00 P.M.

27:46 why have you forsaken me. Jesus' desolate cry is a fulfillment of Ps. 22:1 showing the depth of His distress as He suffers separation from His Father. Later the apostles realized that Jesus was enduring the dreadful wrath of God's judgment on sin. This was all the more agonizing to One whose relationship with the Father was perfect in love. The cry is Aramaic, except the Hebrew "Eli." Mark gives the Aramaic "Eloi."

27:48, 49 The fulfillment of Ps. 69:21 (v. 34 note).

27:51 curtain . . . was torn. The veil of the temple was the curtain separating the Most Holy Place from the rest of the sanctuary. It symbolized the unapproachability of God (Heb. 9:8). Jesus' death was His sacrifice at the heavenly altar (Heb. 9:12, 24, 25), which opened the way to God (Heb. 10:19, 20), removing the veil. Heaven had been opened through the royal priesthood of Christ (1 Pet. 2:9).

from top to bottom. Implying a divine action.

27:52 were raised. The resurrection of the "many . . . saints," although mentioned here to show the connection with the rending of the veil, occurred after Jesus' resurrection. This resurrection was a partial, symbolic fulfillment of Dan. 12:2. There is no way of knowing who these

after his resurrection they went into [t]the
holy city and appeared to many. 54 [u]When
the centurion and those who were with
him, [v]keeping watch over Jesus, saw the
earthquake and what took place, they were
filled with awe and said, [w]"Truly this was
the Son[1] of God!"

55 There were also [x]many women there,
looking on [y]from a distance, who had followed Jesus from Galilee, [z]ministering to
him, 56 among whom were [z]Mary Magdalene and Mary the mother of James and
Joseph and [a]the mother of the sons of
Zebedee.

Jesus Is Buried

57 [b]When it was evening, there came a
rich man from Arimathea, named Joseph,
who also was a disciple of Jesus. 58 He
went to Pilate and asked for the body of
Jesus. Then Pilate ordered it to be given to
him. 59 And Joseph took the body and
wrapped it in a clean linen shroud 60 and
[c]laid it in his own new tomb, [d]which he
had cut in the rock. And he rolled [e]a great
stone to the entrance of the tomb and
went away. 61 Mary Magdalene and [f]the
other Mary were there, sitting opposite
the tomb.

The Guard at the Tomb

62 Next day, that is, after the day of
[g]Preparation, the chief priests and the
Pharisees gathered before Pilate 63 and said,
"Sir, we remember how [h]that impostor
said, while he was still alive, [i]'After three
days I will rise.' 64 Therefore order the tomb
to be made secure until the third day, [j]lest
his disciples go and steal him away and tell
the people, 'He has risen from the dead,'
and the last fraud will be worse than the
first." 65 Pilate said to them, "You have [k]a
guard[2] of soldiers. Go, make it as secure as
you can." 66 So they went and made the
tomb secure by [l]sealing the stone and setting a guard.

53 [t]See ch. 4:5
54 [u]For ver. 54-56, see Mark 15:39-41; Luke 23:47, 49 [v]ver. 36 [w]ver. 43
55 [x]John 19:25 [y]Ps. 38:11 [z]See Luke 8:2, 3
56 [z][See ver. 55 above] [a]ch. 20:20; [Mark 15:40]
57 [b]For ver. 57-61, see Mark 15:42-47; Luke 23:50-56; John 19:38-42
60 [c][Isai. 53:9] [d]Isai. 22:16 [e]Mark 16:4; [John 11:38]
61 [f]ver. 56; ch. 28:1
62 [g]Mark 15:42; Luke 23:54; John 19:14, 31, 42
63 [h][ver. 64; John 7:12] [i]ch. 16:21; 17:23; 20:19; 28:6; Mark 8:31; 10:34; Luke 9:22; 18:33; 24:6, 7; [ch. 26:61; John 2:19]
64 [j][ch. 28:13]
65 [k]ch. 28:11
66 [l]Dan. 6:17

Chapter 28
1 [m]For ver. 1-8, see Mark 16:1-8; Luke 24:1-10; John 20:1 [n]ch. 27:56, 61
2 [o][John 20:12]
3 [p]Dan. 10:6 [q][Dan. 7:9; Mark 9:3; John 20:12; Acts 1:10]
4 [r][Rev. 1:17]
6 [s]ch. 27:63
7 [t]ver. 10, 16; ch. 26:32
8 [u][Ps. 2:11]
9 [v][Mark 16:9; John 20:14] [w]2 Kin. 4:27 [x]ver. 17; Luke 24:52; See ch. 8:2

The Resurrection

28 [m]Now after the Sabbath, toward the
dawn of the first day of the week,
Mary Magdalene and [n]the other Mary went
to see the tomb. 2 And behold, there was a
great earthquake, for [o]an angel of the Lord
descended from heaven and came and
rolled back the stone and sat on it. 3 [p]His
appearance was like lightning, and [q]his
clothing white as snow. 4 And for fear of
him the guards trembled and [r]became like
dead men. 5 But the angel said to the
women, "Do not be afraid, for I know that
you seek Jesus who was crucified. 6 He is
not here, for he has risen, [s]as he said.
Come, see the place where he[3] lay. 7 Then
go quickly and tell his disciples that he has
risen from the dead, and behold, [t]he is
going before you to Galilee; there you will
see him. See, I have told you." 8 So they
departed quickly from the tomb [u]with fear
and great joy, and ran to tell his disciples.
9 And behold, Jesus [v]met them and said,
"Greetings!" And they came up and [w]took
hold of his feet and [x]worshiped him.
10 Then Jesus said to them, "Do not be
afraid; [y]go and tell [z]my brothers to go to
Galilee, and there they will see me."

The Report of the Guard

11 While they were going, behold, some
of [a]the guard went into the city and told
the chief priests all that had taken place.
12 And when they had assembled with the
elders and taken counsel, they gave a sufficient sum of money to the soldiers 13 and
said, "Tell people, [b]'His disciples came by
night and stole him away while we were
asleep.' 14 And if this comes to [c]the governor's ears, we will [d]satisfy him and keep
you out of trouble." 15 So they took the
money and did as they were directed. And

10 [y]See John 20:18 [z]John 20:17; [Ps. 22:22; Rom. 8:29; Heb. 2:11, 12, 17]
11 [a]ch. 27:65, 66 13 [b][ch. 27:64] 14 [c]ch. 27:2 [d]See Acts 12:20 (Gk.)

[1] Or *a son* [2] Or *Take a guard* [3] Some manuscripts *the Lord*

people were, or whether they died again or were translated directly to heaven.

27:54 Truly this was the Son of God. Although they may not have understood fully the phrase they used (16:16; Mark 15:39 and notes), the soldiers made an appropriate confession while the natural heirs of the covenant were deriding their Messiah.

27:57 a rich man. Joseph's gift of a tomb completes Jesus' fulfillment of Is. 53:9. See note Luke 23:50, 51.

27:62–66 Matthew includes this as background for 28:11–15.

27:62 Next day. The Sabbath. See note John 19:14.

28:6 has risen. See "The Resurrection of Jesus" at Luke 24:2.

28:10 my brothers. All Jesus' disciples (12:49, 50; 25:40).

28:11–15 This incident shows that clear evidence may have no effect on those who are committed to unbelief. That the story of the disciples stealing Jesus' body was still circulated in the days of Justin Martyr (c. 160) indicates something of the desperation felt by Jewish leaders in explaining the empty tomb.

this story has been spread among the Jews
[e]to this day.

The Great Commission

16 Now the eleven disciples [f]went to
Galilee, to the mountain to which Jesus
had directed them. 17 And when they saw
him they [g]worshiped him, but some
doubted. 18 And Jesus came and said to
them, [h]"All authority [i]in heaven and on
earth has been given to me. 19 [j]Go therefore
and [k]make disciples of [l]all nations, [j]baptizing them [m]in[1] [n]the name of the Father
and of the Son and of the Holy Spirit,
20 teaching them [o]to observe all that [p]I have
commanded you. And behold, [q]I am with
you always, to [r]the end of the age."

15 [e]ch. 27:8 16 [f]ver. 7 17 [g]ver. 9 18 [h]ch. 11:27; Dan. 7:13, 14; John 3:35; 13:3; 17:2; Acts 2:36; Rom. 14:9; 1 Cor. 15:27; Eph. 1:10, 20-22; Phil. 2:9, 10; Col. 2:10; Heb. 1:2; 2:8; 1 Pet. 3:22; [ch. 9:6; John 5:27] [i][ch. 6:10; Luke 2:14] 19 [j]Mark 16:15, 16 [k]ch. 13:52 [l]Luke 24:47; [ch. 24:14; Mark 11:17; Rom. 1:5] [m]See Acts 8:16 [n][2 Cor. 13:14] 20 [o]John 14:15 [p][Acts 1:2] [q][ch. 1:23; 18:20; John 12:26; 14:3; 17:24; Acts 18:10] [r]See ch. 13:39

1 Or *into*

The Sacraments

Christ instituted two rites for His followers to observe: baptism, a once-for-all rite of initiation (Matt. 28:19; Gal. 3:27), and the Lord's Supper, a regular rite of remembrance (1 Cor. 11:23–26). These are called "sacraments" in the Western church, "mysteries" in the Eastern Orthodox church, or "ordinances." Scripture has no technical term for the two rites or the corresponding Old Testament observances, that is, circumcision of males as a rite of initiation (Gen. 17:9–14, 23–27) and the annual passover as a rite of remembrance (Ex. 12:1–27). Biblical teaching, however, warrants classifying them all together as signs and seals of a covenant relationship with God.

"Sacrament" is from a Latin word meaning sacred. Study of the Christian rites themselves leads to a definition of sacrament as a ritual action instituted by Christ in which signs perceived by the senses present to us the grace of God in Christ and the blessings of His covenant. They communicate and confirm these blessings to believers, who in receiving the sacraments respond to God's grace and declare their faith and allegiance to Him. The sacraments "put a visible difference between those that belong unto the Church and the rest of the world." They solemnly "engage [Christians] to the service of God in Christ, according to His Word" (*Westminster Confession*, XXVII.1).

It was a mistake of the medieval church to classify as sacraments five more rites (confirmation, penance, marriage, ordination, and extreme unction). These five are not seals of a covenant relationship with God. They were not instituted by Christ, and they do not have "any visible sign or ceremony ordained of God" (*Thirty-Nine Articles*, XXV).

The sacraments are means of grace, for God uses them to strengthen faith's confidence in His promises and to call forth acts of faith for receiving the good gifts signified. The efficacy of the sacraments is not from the faith or virtue of the minister, but from the faithfulness of God, who, having given the signs, is now pleased to use them. Christ and the apostles speak of the sign as if it were the thing signified, and as if receiving the former is the same as receiving the latter (Matt. 26:26–28; 1 Cor. 10:15–21; 1 Pet. 3:21, 22). As the preaching of the Word makes the gospel audible, so the sacraments make it visible.

Sacraments strengthen faith by correlating Christian beliefs with the testimony of our senses. The *Heidelberg Catechism* illustrates this in its answer to Question 75. The key words are "as sure as."

> Christ has commanded me . . . to eat of this broken bread and to drink of this cup in memory of Him, and therewith has given assurance: first, that His body was . . . broken on the cross for me, and His blood shed for me, as sure as I see with my eyes the bread . . . broken for me and the cup communicated to me; and, further, that with His crucified body and shed blood He Himself feeds and nourishes my soul to eternal life, as sure as I take and taste the bread and cup . . . which are given me as sure tokens of the body and blood of Christ.

28:18 Jesus now has "all authority." The Son of Man has come before the Ancient of Days and received the promised dominion (Dan. 7:13, 14). The last stage of history has begun, but it will not be completed until Christ comes to earth in glory (26:64). See "Jesus' Heavenly Reign" at Acts 7:55.

28:19 Go therefore. The Great Commission is given on Christ's authority. Since Christ's dominion is universal, the gospel must go to the whole world. This commandment is the primary reason for evangelism and missions.

nations. The same Greek word often translated "Gentiles." The great promise that in Abraham all the nations would be blessed (Gen. 12:3) is ready to be fulfilled.

baptizing them. See note 3:6. Those who become disciples are baptized in (lit. "into") the triune name. There is one name (not "names"), and one baptism; Father, Son, and Spirit are one God. Disciples are baptized "in" this name because they belong to God, having been brought into the new covenant that expresses the will of the triune God. See theological note "The Sacraments."

28:20 teaching them to observe. Disciples are not just taught what to believe, but how to obey. Jesus taught practical holiness.

I am with you always. Jesus was named Immanuel ("God with us") at His birth (1:23), and now He promises to be with His disciples to the end of the age. He is with them specifically in the responsibility of teaching His will to the world. See "The Mission of the Church in the World" at John 20:21.

THE GOSPEL ACCORDING TO

Mark

AUTHOR

All four Gospels are anonymous, and together they provide the church an authorized, collective witness of Jesus' person and work through the apostles—a theme often emphasized in Mark (3:14; 4:10; 5:37; 8:32 and notes). There is nothing inconsistent about the apostles' using fellow workers such as John Mark, whose name appears above this Gospel, to put this collective and individual witness into writing. For John Mark's relations with the apostles, see Acts 12:12, 25; 13:5, 13; Col. 4:10; 2 Tim. 4:11; Philem. 24.

Mark's authorship is established by certain external considerations. Although the title, "According to Mark," is not original, it appears in all the ancient canonical lists and many ancient manuscripts and is thought to have been added very early in the history of the text. Second, early church fathers such as Papias (A.D. 140), Justin Martyr (A.D. 150), Irenaeus (A.D. 185), and Clement of Alexandria (A.D. 195) all affirm that Mark wrote the second Gospel. Papias refers to Mark as Peter's "interpreter." Another reason to accept the authenticity of Marcan authorship is that in the second and third centuries of the church, books falsely claiming apostolic authorship usually claimed well-known apostles as their authors rather than secondary figures such as John Mark.

Within the text itself a veiled indication of Mark's connection with this Gospel may be seen in an otherwise apparently irrelevant notice of a "young man" who fled when Jesus was arrested. Some interpreters have suggested that this is Mark's way of referring to himself on that occasion (14:51 note). Possible evidence of Mark's position as Peter's "interpreter" (above) is the simplified chronological order of events in Mark that mirrors Peter's rehearsal of those events in the Book of Acts (Acts 3:13, 14; 10:36–43).

DATE AND OCCASION

If Mark was used by Matthew and Luke, it is the earliest of the Gospels and cannot be dated later than about A.D. 70. It is generally thought that Matthew and Luke were written about A.D. 80–90. However, if Luke and Acts were finished around A.D. 62, when the narrative of Acts ends, Mark would be even earlier. Beyond these considerations, an argument can be made that all the books of the New Testament were written before A.D. 70, the date of the destruction of the temple in Jerusalem, and so come from the first, apostolic generation.

The church fathers held that Mark was addressed to the church in Rome or in Italy generally. This is supported by Mark's association with Peter, who in 1 Pet. 5:13 addresses Christians in "Babylon" (a probable reference to Rome), by the influence of Latin in the Greek text, and by the probable reference to members of the Roman church (15:21; cf. Rom. 16:13). The translation of Semitic terms (3:17; 5:41; 15:22) and careful explanation of Jewish customs (7:2–4; 15:42) suggests that a Gentile readership is anticipated, though not excluding Gentile converts to Judaism.

CHARACTERISTICS AND THEMES

1. The Purpose of the Gospel. Mark's prime purpose is to present in writing the witness of the apostles to the facts of the life, death, and resurrection of Jesus. Mark does not intend to write a full biography or even a complete account of Jesus' public ministry. The historical record is simplified, conforming to the basic structure of gospel proclamation: the beginning of Jesus' ministry with John the Baptist; Jesus' public ministry in Galilee and the surrounding regions; and His final journey to Jerusalem for the sacrifice of the cross. According to the Gospel of John, Jesus made at least five visits to Jerusalem (Mark 1:14 note). Matthew and Luke record more of Jesus' teaching than Mark, but Mark's goal is different. Using historical details, he presents an enlarged account of what the apostles preached about the cross of Christ (Acts 1:21, 22; 2:22–24; 1 Cor. 2:2).

2. Jesus as the True Israelite. Mark depicts Jesus as the true Israelite whose whole life demonstrates the necessity of submitting to the written Word of God (1:13 note; 12:35–37). In this, as more generally in service and in suffering (8:34–9:1), Jesus is presented and presents Himself as the model for His disciples.

3. Jesus as the Son of God. Mark presents the divinity of Jesus as Son of God and Son of Man (1:11; 2:10, 28; 3:11; 5:7; 9:7; 14:62; 15:39) shining through the ambiguous state of humiliation necessary for His earthly messianic calling. Mark also calls attention to the desire of Jesus to hide His true identity as Messiah and Son of God (the so-called "messianic secret") from those who would inevitably misinterpret it (1:34, 44; 3:12; 5:43; 7:36, 37; 8:26, 30; 9:9).

4. The Gospel as the Power of God. Mark emphasizes the importance of the preaching and teaching of the gospel message, not just as theological truth but as the "power of God" (12:24; cf. Rom. 1:16) over evil and sickness (1:27; cf. 16:15–18).

5. The Mission to the Gentiles. Mark shows Jesus' interest in the Gentiles and the validity of the church's mission to the Gentiles. This emphasis appears in the basic outline of the book, the care taken to explain Jewish terms and customs, the declaration that the temple was a "house of prayer for all the nations" (11:17), and the final confession of Christ from the mouth of a Gentile (15:39).

INTERPRETIVE DIFFICULTIES

The question of the literary type of the Gospel of Mark has occupied scholars continuously, especially in the last two hundred years. The question is important because it determines the context for interpreting individual elements of the Gospel. Some believe that the Gospels are a unique type of literature corresponding to the unique Christian message. Others think the Gospels should be compared to Greek and Roman biographies that combine in one literary work extraordinary deeds and memorable teachings. The Gospels differ from such biographies, most notably in the emphasis they place on the last days and death of Jesus, and their silence about most of His adult life. It has been well said that the Gospels are Passion narratives with long introductions.

Mark himself situates the beginning of his Gospel in the Old Testament (1:1–4 and notes), and its basic point of reference is to be found there, especially in the Book of Exodus. Exodus is a covenant document whose focal point is the account of how the covenant was inaugurated under the leadership of Moses. This focus corresponds in the Gospels to the significance of the death of Jesus, in which He shed the blood of the new covenant (14:24 and note). The rest of Exodus concerns the career of Moses, the covenant mediator; a record of the signs that God performed through him to establish the faith of God's people in the midst of unbelieving Egypt; and a record of the covenant legislation. Jesus likewise has called forth a new people, demonstrating His authority through miracles and signs, and has given His teaching as the "new commandment" (John 13:34) of the new covenant. As a record of Jesus' life and teachings, Mark takes its place in the history of redemption as a canonical document of the New Testament.

OUTLINE OF MARK

I. Prologue: The Inauguration of Jesus' Ministry (1:1–13)

- A. *John's Witness to Jesus (1:1–8)*
- B. *Jesus' Baptism and the Father's Witness (1:9–11)*
- C. *Jesus' Temptation (1:12, 13)*

II. The Public Ministry of Jesus in Galilee (1:14–6:44)

- A. *The Early Ministry (1:14–3:12)*
  1. Arrival in Galilee (1:14, 15)
  2. Call of the First Disciples (1:16–20)
  3. Exorcisms and Healings in Capernaum (1:21–34)
  4. Ministry in the Whole of Galilee (1:35–45)
  5. A Healing in Capernaum (2:1–12)
  6. Calling of Levi (2:13–17)
  7. Controversies with the Authorities (2:18–3:12)
- B. *The Later Ministry (3:13–6:44)*
  1. Calling of the Twelve (3:13–19)
  2. Controversies in Capernaum (3:20–35)
  3. Parables of the Kingdom (4:1–34)

OUTLINE OF MARK (Cont.)

4. Incursion into the Decapolis (4:35–5:20)
5. Return to Galilee (5:21–6:6)
6. Mission of the Twelve in Galilee (6:7–30)
7. Feeding of the Five Thousand in Galilee (6:31–44)

III. Ministry to Gentile Regions (6:45–9:32)

A. Visit to Gennesaret (6:45–7:23)

B. Ministry in Tyre, Sidon, and the Decapolis (7:24–8:9)

C. Ministry to the Region of Caesarea Philippi (8:10–9:32)

IV. Return to Capernaum; Conclusion of the Galilean Ministry (9:33–50)

V. Final Journey to Judea and Jerusalem (ch. 10)

A. Teaching on the Way to Jerusalem (10:1–45)

B. A Healing in Jericho (10:46–52)

VI. The Passion (chs. 11–15)

A. Triumphal Entry into Jerusalem (11:1–11)

B. Cleansing of the Temple (11:12–26)

C. Controversies in the Temple Courts (11:27–12:44)

D. Prophecies on the Mount of Olives (ch. 13)

E. Anointing at Bethany (14:1–11)

F. Passover Meal in Jerusalem (14:12–31)

G. Arrest and Trial of Jesus (14:32–15:20)

H. Death and Burial of Jesus (15:21–47)

VII. Resurrection Appearances in Jerusalem (ch. 16)

John the Baptist Prepares the Way

1 The beginning of the gospel of Jesus
Christ, [a]the Son of God.[1]
2 [b]As it is written in Isaiah the prophet,[2]
[c]"Behold, I send my messenger before
your face,
who will prepare your way,
3 [d]the voice of one crying in the
wilderness:
[e]'Prepare[3] the way of the Lord,
make his paths straight,'"
4 [f]John appeared, baptizing in [g]the wilderness and proclaiming [h]a baptism of [i]repen-
tance [j]for the forgiveness of sins. 5 And all
the country of Judea and all Jerusalem were
going out to him and were being baptized
by him in the river Jordan, [k]confessing
their sins. 6 Now John was [l]clothed with
camel's hair and [l]wore a leather belt
around his waist and ate [m]locusts and
[n]wild honey. 7 And he preached, saying,
[o]"After me comes he who is mightier than
I, the strap of whose sandals I am not worthy to stoop down and untie. 8 [p]I have baptized you with water, but [q]he will baptize
you with the Holy Spirit."

Chapter 1
1 [a]See Matt. 14:33
2 [b]For ver. 2-8, see Matt. 3:1-11; Luke 3:2-16 [c]Matt. 11:10; Luke 1:17, 76; 7:27; Cited from Mal. 3:1
3 [d]John 1:23; Cited from Isai. 40:3 [e]Luke 1:76
4 [f]John 1:6, 7 [g]Josh. 15:61; [Judg. 1:16] [h]Acts 2:38 [i]ver. 15 [j]Matt. 26:28; [Luke 1:77]
5 [k]Acts 19:18
6 [l][2 Kin. 1:8; Zech. 13:4; Heb. 11:37] [m]Lev. 11:22 [n]1 Sam. 14:26 7 [o]John 1:15, 27; 3:30, 31; Acts 13:25 8 [p]John 1:26; Acts 1:5; 11:16 [q]See John 1:33

1 Some manuscripts omit *the Son of God* 2 Some manuscripts *in the prophets* 3 Or *crying: Prepare in the wilderness*

1:1 The beginning. Unlike Matthew and Luke, Mark does not contain an account of Jesus' birth. The "beginning" (cf. Gen. 1:1; John 1:1) is identified with the ministry of John the Baptist (cf. Acts 1:22) and with the Old Testament prophecies announcing John's coming.

gospel. A term from political or personal reporting and correspondence, meaning "good news." The Greeks used this word for events such as the birth of an emperor or a major military victory.

of Jesus Christ. This phrase can be understood as either "about Jesus Christ" or "from Jesus Christ." The gospel is "about" Jesus, but it is also "from" Him (Rom. 1:9; 1 Cor. 9:12; 2 Cor. 10:14). The Gospel of Mark claims divine authority and offers itself as the word of Christ through His apostles to the church (cf. Rev. 1:1).

Son of God. Mark presents Jesus at the beginning of the Gospel as the divine, eternal Son. See notes 13:32; 14:36; 15:39; cf. Rom. 1:3.

1:2 it is written. By placing this citation of the Old Testament here, Mark intends to show the organic progress of revelation under the divine Lord of history. If the Old Testament is the Gospel's beginning and source, the Gospel revealed through Jesus Christ is the final and inspired interpretation of the Old Testament message.

the prophet. See text note. The citation is a chain of texts (Ex. 23:20; Mal. 3:1; Is. 40:3) concerning messengers that God had sent by way of preparation.

1:4 John. The Old Testament citations locate John the Baptist in the preplanned history of God's covenantal dealings with His people.

in the wilderness. John's preaching in the wilderness symbolically reminds Israel of her covenantal origins in the Exodus (cf. Jer. 2:2). The wilderness is the traditional meeting place between God and His people.

baptism of repentance. The Qumran community, with which John may have had contact in his youth, practiced ritual cleansings and baptisms. Also, converts to Judaism were baptized. John's innovation was to require a one-time baptism of Israelites already within the covenant community. For him to require such a gesture of radical repentance is a sign of the approach of the new covenant. See note Matt. 3:6.

for the forgiveness of sins. John does not actually bestow forgiveness of sins. Definitive forgiveness of sins belongs to the new covenant (Jer. 31:34), which the Messiah will bring.

1:5 all. This is literary exaggeration, indicating that the covenant people went out to John in a great crowd, no doubt as entire families (4:1; 6:44 and notes).

1:6 camel's hair. John's clothing and food identify him as a classic type of Old Testament prophet (2 Kin. 1:8; Zech. 13:4).

1:7 he preached. The identity of the One whom John announces and before whom he feels unworthy to kneel is evident from the Old Testament prophecies already cited. It is the "Lord" who "will suddenly come to his temple; and the messenger of the covenant," having been preceded by "my messenger" (Mal. 3:1).

1:8 Holy Spirit. The new covenant brings renewal to the people of God (Jer. 31:33, 34; Ezek. 37:14) through the Son and the Spirit, whom the Son possesses in full measure (Is. 42:1; 61:1).

The Baptism of Jesus

9 [r]In those days Jesus [s]came from Nazareth of Galilee and was baptized by John
in the Jordan. 10 And when he came up out
of the water, immediately he [t]saw [u]the
heavens opening [v]and the Spirit descending on him like a dove. 11 And [w]a voice
came from heaven, [x]"You are my beloved
Son;[1] with you I am well pleased."

The Temptation of Jesus

12 [y]The Spirit immediately drove him out
into the wilderness. 13 [y]And he was in the
wilderness forty days, being [z]tempted by
[a]Satan. And he was with the wild animals, and [b]the angels were ministering to
him.

Jesus Begins His Ministry

14 [c]Now after John was arrested, Jesus
[d]came into Galilee, proclaiming the gospel

9 [r]For ver. 9-11, see Matt. 3:13-17; Luke 3:21, 22; [John 1:32-34] [s]Matt. 2:23 10 [t]Acts 7:56 [u]Isai. 64:1 [v]John 1:32, 33; [Luke 4:18, 21; Acts 10:38] 11 [w]John 12:28 [x][ch. 9:7; Ps. 2:7; Isai. 42:1; Eph. 1:6; Col. 1:13; 2 Pet. 1:17; 1 John 5:9]

12 [y]See Matt. 4:1-11; Luke 4:1-13 13 [y][See ver. 12 above] [z][Heb. 2:18; 4:15] [a]See 1 Chr. 21:1 [b]Matt. 26:53; Luke 22:43 14 [c]Matt. 4:12; 14:3; Luke 3:20; [John 3:24] [d]Matt. 4:17, 23

1 Or *my Son, my* (or *the*) *Beloved*

The Baptism of Jesus

There is continuity between John's baptism of repentance (Mark 1:4) and the trinitarian baptism instituted by Jesus (Matt. 28:19). Both were symbols of cleansing, and had remission of sins in view (Mark 1:4; Acts 2:38). But they were not identical. Those baptized by John needed Christian baptism as well (Acts 19:5). Christian baptism is a sign of initiation pointing to a relationship with the Christ who has come; John's baptism was a preparatory rite, signifying readiness for the coming of the Christ and for His judgment (Matt. 3:7–12; Luke 3:7–18; Acts 19:4).

Jesus insisted that John, His cousin, must baptize Him, overriding John's protests (Matt. 3:13–15). In His role as Messiah, "born under the law" (Gal. 4:4), Jesus had to submit to all God's requirements for Israel, and to identify with those whose sins He had come to bear. His baptism proclaimed that He had come to take the sinner's place under God's judgment. It is in this sense that He was baptized to "fulfill all righteousness" (Matt. 3:15; cf. Is. 53:11).

At Christ's baptism there was a manifestation of the Trinity: the Father spoke from heaven, and a dove descended, as a sign of the Spirit's anointing. The significance of the dove descending and abiding was not that Jesus was being filled with the Spirit for the first time but that He was being marked as the bearer of the Spirit who would baptize with the Spirit (John 1:32, 33), and so bring in the age of the Spirit that was to fulfill Israel's hopes (Luke 4:1, 14, 18–21).

1:9 In those days. According to John 2:20, one of Jesus' earliest acts following His baptism took place when the rebuilding of the temple was in its forty-sixth year. Since Herod began reconstruction in 19 B.C., Jesus was baptized in about A.D. 27.

baptized by John. Jesus knows this to be part of the divine plan "to fulfill all righteousness" (Matt. 3:15), by which, in His humanity, He identifies fully with the human condition, and begins the process of bearing the sins of humanity. See theological note "The Baptism of Jesus."

1:10 immediately. This important word (sometimes translated "straightway") is characteristic of Mark (twelve times in the rest of the New Testament, forty-two times in Mark). It perhaps suggests not speed but rather the sureness and inevitability of God's sovereign plan, recalling the "straight" (same root as "straightway") paths divinely prepared for Jesus' coming and ministry.

Spirit descending. This descent of the Spirit is a sign of Jesus' messiahship (v. 8 note). In Jesus' baptism, as later in Christian baptism (Matt. 28:19), all three Persons of the Trinity are involved. The initiative of the Father, the vicarious work of the Son, and the glorifying, enabling power of the Spirit are all present.

1:11 You are my beloved Son. The mystery of the person of Jesus finds expression in the divine declaration. He, the Second Person of the Godhead, is at the same time the representative believer and the one true and faithful "son" of Israel (Ex. 4:23), who pleases the Father, and whom the Father acknowledges as Son in both a personal and an official sense (Ps. 2:7; Is. 42:1). See note on v. 1.

1:12 drove him. The verb "drove" is strong, giving the idea of divine and scriptural necessity. The Spirit is driving Jesus out into the "wilderness," just as Israel, called "son" (Ex. 4:23) and "baptized into Moses . . . in the sea" (1 Cor. 10:2; cf. Ex. 14:13–31), was led by the Spirit in the pillars of cloud and fire (Ex. 14:19, 20) along the path of wilderness testing.

1:13 forty days. Possibly a symbolic reference to the forty years of Israel's wilderness experience (Deut. 1:3; cf. v. 12 note).

wild animals. This detail emphasizes that the wilderness is a place of curse where the devil is master (Matt. 12:43; cf. Eph. 2:2). Jesus enters this domain and binds the strong man (see note 3:23–27). This is a kind of reenactment of the testing of Adam. Although Adam was in a garden and was not threatened by wild beasts, he fell to Satan's tempting. In the wilderness, Jesus, the second Adam, begins His defeat of the devil and His work of redemption by passing the test of filial obedience.

angels were ministering. Angels accompanied Israel in the Exodus (Ex. 14:19; 23:20; 32:34; 33:2). Jesus' experience in the wilderness is a type of that of the Christian in the world, which is experienced as Satan's domain (Eph. 6:12). See note 10:30.

1:14 after John . . . into Galilee. It is often claimed that the chronology of the first three (Synoptic) Gospels is irreconcilable with that of John for three main reasons: (a) the cleansing of the temple is placed in different periods of Jesus' ministry (11:15 note); (b) in the Synoptic Gospels Jesus is in Jerusalem only once, for the last week of His ministry, while in John He is there five times (c) in John Jesus has an early Judean ministry concurrent with that of John the Baptist (John 3:22–24), while in the Synoptic Gospels Jesus begins His ministry in Galilee. However, in saying that a Galilean ministry begins only after John the Baptist's arrest, Mark is not denying that there was an earlier Judean ministry; it is simply not part of his story.

of God, 15 and saying, [e]"The time is fulfilled, and [f]the kingdom of God is at hand;
[g]repent and believe in the gospel."

Jesus Calls the First Disciples

16 [h]Passing alongside the Sea of Galilee,
he saw Simon and Andrew the brother of
Simon casting a net into the sea, for they
were fishermen. 17 And Jesus said to them,
"Follow me, and I will make you become
[i]fishers of men." 18 And immediately they
left their nets and followed him. 19 And
going on a little farther, he saw James the
son of Zebedee and John his brother, who
were in their boat mending the nets. 20 And
immediately he called them, and they left
their father Zebedee in the boat with the
hired servants and followed him.

Jesus Heals a Man with an Unclean Spirit

21 [j]And they went into Capernaum, and
immediately [k]on the Sabbath [l]he entered
the synagogue and was teaching. 22 And
[m]they were astonished at his teaching, [m]for
he taught them as one who had authority,
and not as the scribes. 23 And immediately
there was in their synagogue a man with an
unclean spirit. And he cried out, 24 [n]"What
have you to do with us, Jesus of Nazareth?
Have you come to destroy us? [o]I know who
you are—[p]the Holy One of God." 25 But
Jesus [q]rebuked him, saying, "Be silent, and
come out of him!" 26 And the unclean
spirit, [r]convulsing him and [s]crying out with
a loud voice, came out of him. 27 And they
were all [t]amazed, so that they questioned
among themselves, saying, "What is this?
[u]A new teaching with authority! He commands even the unclean spirits, and they
obey him." 28 And at once his fame spread
everywhere throughout all the surrounding
region of Galilee.

Jesus Heals Many

29 [v]And immediately he[1] [w]left the synagogue and entered the house of Simon and
Andrew, with James and John. 30 Now
[x]Simon's mother-in-law lay ill with a fever,
and immediately they told him about her.
31 And he came and [y]took her by the hand
and lifted her up, and the fever left her, and
she began to serve them.

32 That evening at sundown they brought
to him all who were sick or [z]oppressed by
demons. 33 And the whole city was gathered
together at the door. 34 [a]And he healed
many who were sick with various diseases,
and cast out many demons. And [b]he would
not permit the demons to speak, because
they knew him.

15 [e]Dan. 9:25; Gal. 4:4; Eph. 1:10; [Luke 21:8; John 7:8] [f]See Matt. 3:2 [g]Acts 19:4; 20:21; Heb. 6:1 **16** [h]For ver. 16-20, see Matt. 4:18-22; [Luke 5:2-11; John 1:40-42] **17** [i]Matt. 13:47 **21** [j]Matt. 4:13; For ver. 21-28, see Luke 4:31-37 [k]See ch. 6:2 [l]ver. 39; See Matt. 4:23 **22** [m]See Matt. 7:28, 29 **24** [n]See Matt. 8:29 [o][ver. 34; Acts 19:15; James 2:19] [p]John 6:69; Acts 3:14; Rev. 3:7; [Luke 1:35; Heb. 7:26; 1 John 2:20] **25** [q]See Matt. 12:16 **26** [r]ch. 9:26 [s]ch. 5:7; Acts 8:7 **27** [t][Matt. 8:27] [u]Acts 17:19 **29** [v]For ver. 29-34, see Matt. 8:14-16; Luke 4:38-41 [w]ver. 21, 23 **30** [x]1 Cor. 9:5 **31** [y]ch. 9:27; Acts 3:7; 9:41 **32** [z]See Matt. 4:24 **34** [a]See Matt. 4:23 [b]ch. 3:11, 12; [Acts 16:17, 18]

[1] Some manuscripts *they*

1:15 The time is fulfilled. The past times, especially of God's acts of salvation for His people Israel, reach their climax in this present time of salvation through Jesus.

the kingdom of God is at hand. The kingdom of God is that final state of affairs where God's supreme reign is fully realized over the transformed universe and in the hearts of all His redeemed and glorified people. This kingdom is "at hand" in the sense that the coming of Jesus sets in motion all that will bring about its actualization. God requires repentance and belief in response to this news. See note on v. 4.

1:16 Sea of Galilee. An inland lake thirteen miles long and eight miles wide, otherwise known in the New Testament as the Lake of Gennesaret (Luke 5:1) or the Sea of Tiberias (John 6:1).

1:17 Follow Me . . . fishers of men. Mark immediately shows Jesus calling disciples to follow Him and to call others to Him. This first appointed ministry of the emerging church has as its primary goal seeking the lost. This emphasis on evangelism was not lost on the apostle Paul, who said, "Woe to me if I do not preach the gospel" (1 Cor. 9:16).

1:19 James . . . John. Note that Jesus does not recruit His apostles and "fishers of men" from the religious intelligentsia but from ordinary walks of life.

1:20 hired servants. This detail suggests a small prosperous business.

1:22 as one who had authority. Jesus' teaching is unlike that of the scribes because it is tied to His person (2:10) and to His interpretation of Scripture (12:35–40). Its content is new, announcing the coming of the kingdom (v. 15) and the defeat of Satan (v. 27).

1:24 What have you to do with us. This idiom distances the speaker from the person addressed. It occurs one other place in the New Testament (John 2:4).

Nazareth. Lit. "Nazarene." Nazareth, west of the Sea of Galilee, was Jesus' hometown.

Holy One of God. Jesus is described this way only in this incident (Luke 4:34). The demons quake in the presence of divine holiness.

1:25 Be silent. This strong term emphasizes Jesus' power to establish His kingdom in the face of evil.

1:29 James and John. See v. 19.

1:30 Simon's mother-in-law. Peter was married (see also 1 Cor. 9:5), showing that marriage is normal for Christian leaders. At the same time celibacy remains a legitimate possibility (Matt. 19:12; 1 Cor. 7:7, 8, 32).

1:32 at sundown. Jesus had already healed on the Sabbath day (v. 25). On this occasion the people waited till sunset, when the Sabbath ended, to carry their sick to Jesus.

1:34 many demons. The extent of demon possession in Galilee's Jewish population (v. 32 note) is startling, though the Gentile or pagan influence in Galilee must not be forgotten.

he would not permit the demons to speak. This is the first instance of what has been called the "messianic secret" (v. 43; 3:12; 4:10, 11; 5:19; 8:30; 9:9). The revelation of Jesus as the Messiah had to begin discreetly and proceed by stages so that the plan of God for the death of His Servant would not be jeopardized by any excesses of popular enthusiasm.

Jesus Preaches in Galilee

35 [c]And rising very early in the morning,
while it was still dark, he departed and
went out to a desolate place, and [d]there he
prayed. 36 And Simon and those who were
with him searched for him, 37 and they
found him and said to him, [e]"Everyone is
looking for you." 38 And he said to them,
"Let us go on to the next towns, that I may
preach there also, for [f]that is why I came
out." 39 [g]And [h]he went throughout all Galilee, preaching in their synagogues and casting out demons.

Jesus Cleanses a Leper

40 [i]And a leper[1] came to him, imploring
him, and [j]kneeling said to him, [k]"If you
will, you can make me clean." 41 Moved
with pity, he stretched out his hand and
touched him and said to him, "I will; be
clean." 42 And immediately the leprosy left
him, and he was made clean. 43 And [l]Jesus[2]
sternly charged him and sent him away at
once, 44 and said to him, [m]"See that you say
nothing to anyone, but go, [n]show yourself
to the priest and [o]offer for your cleansing
what Moses commanded, [p]for a proof to
them." 45 [q]But he went out and began to
talk freely about it, and to spread the news,
so that Jesus could no longer openly enter
[r]a town, but was out in [r]desolate places,
and [s]people were coming to him from
every quarter.

Jesus Heals a Paralytic

2 And when he returned to [t]Capernaum
after some days, it was reported that he
was at home. 2 And many were gathered
together, so that there was no more room,
not even at the door. And he was preaching
the word to them. 3 [u]And they came, bringing to him a paralytic carried by four men.
4 And when they could not get near him
because of the crowd, [v]they removed the
roof above him, and when they had made
an opening, they let down the bed on
which the paralytic lay. 5 And when Jesus
[w]saw their faith, he said to the paralytic,
"My son, [x]your sins are forgiven." 6 Now
some of the scribes were sitting there,
questioning in their hearts, 7 "Why does
this man speak like that? [y]He is blaspheming! [z]Who can forgive sins but God alone?"
8 And immediately Jesus, [a]perceiving in his
spirit that they thus questioned within
themselves, said to them, "Why do you
question these things in your hearts?
9 Which is easier, to say to the paralytic,
'Your sins are forgiven,' or to say, 'Rise,
take up your bed and walk'? 10 But that you
may know that [b]the Son of Man has
authority on earth to forgive sins"—he said
to the paralytic—11 "I say to you, rise, pick
up your bed, and go home." 12 And he rose
and immediately picked up his bed and
went out before them all, so that they were
all amazed and [c]glorified God, saying, "We
never saw anything like this!"

Jesus Calls Levi

13 He went out again beside the sea, and
[d]all the crowd was coming to him, and he

35 [c]For ver. 35-38, see Luke 4:42, 43 [d]Luke 5:16; See Matt. 14:23
37 [e][John 12:19]
38 [f]Isai. 61:1
39 [g][Luke 4:44] [h]ver. 21
40 [i]For ver. 40-44, see Matt. 8:2-4; Luke 5:12-14 [j]ch. 10:17; Matt. 17:14; 27:29 [k][ch. 9:22, 23; Matt. 9:28]
43 [l]Matt. 9:30
44 [m]ch. 1:34; 5:43; 7:36; 8:26; Matt.9:30; 17:9; See Matt. 12:16 [n]Luke 17:14 [o]Lev. 14:2-32 [p]ch. 6:11; Matt. 10:18; 24:14; Luke 9:5; James 5:3
45 [q]ch. 7:36; Matt. 9:31; [Luke 5:15, 16] [r]2 Cor. 11:26 [s]ch. 2:2, 13; 3:7; [John 6:2]
Chapter 2
1 [t][Matt. 9:1]
3 [u]For ver. 3-12, see Matt. 9:2-8; Luke 5:18-26
4 [v][Luke 5:19]
5 [w]ch. 10:52; Matt. 8:10, 13; 9:22, 29; 15:28; Luke 7:9, 50; 17:19; 18:42; Acts 3:16; 14:9; James 5:15 [x]Luke 7:48; [John 5:14]
7 [y]ch. 14:64; John 10:36 [z]Ps. 32:5; Isai. 43:25 **8** [a]See John 2:25 **10** [b][ver. 28]
12 [c]See Luke 7:16 **13** [d]See ch. 1:45

1 *Leprosy* was a term for several skin diseases; see Leviticus 13 2 Greek *he*; also verse 45

1:35 desolate place. Lit. "deserted place," the place where Jesus fights His spiritual battle (v. 12; cf. v. 3), and which is also, as with ancient Israel, a type of the present Christian walk (1 Cor. 10:1–11; Heb. 13:12, 13).

1:38 for that is why I came out. Jesus states His program of evangelistic preaching with compelling clarity. He says in Luke 19:10, "For the Son of Man came to seek and to save the lost." And so He is on the move, touring Galilee several times (v. 39; 6:6; Luke 8:1).

1:40 a leper. Under the Mosaic law, certain skin diseases made a person ceremonially unclean, excluding him from communal life (Lev. 13:46).

1:43 sternly charged. See note on v. 34. The Greek verb expresses deep emotion, as in the case of Jesus before the tomb of Lazarus (John 11:33, 38).

1:44 for a proof. Jesus respects the Mosaic law as the great high priest of another line (Heb. 7:11–8:13), but He is not bound or limited by it. Although touching the leper was a violation of the laws of ritual purity (Lev. 5:3), Jesus did so as He healed him.

1:45 talk freely. This was not the time for unbridled proclamation (v. 34 note), though there would come a time in the history of redemption (after the Resurrection) when open preaching would be proper (Matt. 10:27; Luke 12:2, 3).

2:1 at home. Jesus was from Nazareth, about twenty miles away, and Simon Peter's house (1:29) may have served as His home in Capernaum, a village more centrally located and with direct access to the Sea of Galilee.

2:4 removed the roof. Houses had flat roofs made of branches and dried clay supported by wooden beams.

2:5 your sins are forgiven. Jesus' response is extraordinary for two reasons. First, the man had come for physical healing, but Jesus speaks about the more profound illness of sin, of which physical illness generally is a consequence; and about the radical healing of forgiveness, of which this particular physical healing was a sign. Second, Jesus claims for Himself the power to forgive sins, which in all the Bible can be attributed only to God (Ex. 34:7; Is. 1:18). The teachers of the law immediately accuse Jesus of "blaspheming" (v. 7; 3:29 note), a proper conclusion if He were a mere man.

2:9 Which is easier. Jesus asks the scribes to reconsider their judgment in the light of His power to heal (cf. John 5:36; 10:25, 38), which is ultimately a divine power (Ps. 41:1; Jer. 3:22; Hos. 14:4).

2:10 Son of Man. Jesus used this phrase regularly to designate Himself,

was teaching them. 14 [e]And as he passed by, he saw [f]Levi the son of Alphaeus sitting at the tax booth, and he said to him, "Follow me." And he rose and followed him.

15 And as he reclined at table in his house, many [g]tax collectors and sinners were reclining with Jesus and his disciples, for there were many who followed him. 16 And [h]the scribes of[1] the Pharisees, when they saw that he was eating with sinners and tax collectors, said to his disciples, [g]"Why does he eat[2] with tax collectors and sinners?" 17 And when Jesus heard it, he said to them, "Those who are well have no need of a physician, but those who are sick. [i]I came not to call the righteous, [j]but sinners."

A Question About Fasting

18 Now [k]John's disciples and the Pharisees were fasting. And people came and said to him, [l]"Why do John's disciples and [m]the disciples of the Pharisees fast, but your disciples do not fast?" 19 And Jesus said to them, [n]"Can the wedding guests fast while the bridegroom is with them? As long as they have the bridegroom with them, they cannot fast. 20 [o]The days will come when the bridegroom is taken away from them, and [p]then they will fast in that day. 21 No one sews a piece of unshrunk cloth on an old garment. If he does, the patch tears away from it, the new from the old, and a worse tear is made. 22 And no one puts new wine into old [q]wineskins. If he does, the wine will burst the skins—and the wine is destroyed, and so are the skins. But new wine is for fresh wineskins."[3]

Jesus Is Lord of the Sabbath

23 [r]One Sabbath he was going through the grainfields, and as they made their way, his disciples [s]began to pluck heads of grain. 24 And the Pharisees were saying to him, "Look, [t]why are they doing [u]what is not lawful on the Sabbath?" 25 And he said to them, [v]"Have you never read [w]what David did, when he was in

14 [e]For ver. 14-22, see Matt. 9:9-17; Luke 5:27-38 [f][Matt. 9:9]
15 [g]Matt. 11:19; Luke 15:2
16 [h]Acts 4:5; 23:9 [g][See ver. 15 above]
17 [i][Luke 15:7; John 9:39] [j]1 Tim. 1:15
18 [k]Matt. 11:2; 14:12; Luke 11:1; John 1:35; 3:25; 4:1; [Acts 18:25; 19:3] [l][ch. 7:5] [m]Luke 18:12
19 [n]John 3:29
20 [o]See Luke 17:22 [p][John 16:20]
22 [q]Josh. 9:4
23 [r]For ver. 23-28, see Matt. 12:1-8; Luke 6:1-5 [s]Deut. 23:25
24 [t][Matt. 9:11] [u][Ex. 20:9-11]
25 [v]See Matt. 21:16 [w]1 Sam. 21:1-6

[1] Some manuscripts *and* [2] Some manuscripts add *and drink* [3] Some manuscripts omit *but new wine is for fresh skins*

associating Himself in His ministry with the heavenly "Son of Man" of Dan. 7:13, 14 (v. 28; 8:31; 9:31; 10:33, 45; 13:26). See note Matt. 8:20.

2:14 Levi the son of Alphaeus. In the parallel account in Matt. 9:9–13 this person is named "Matthew." Since Matthew appears in Mark's list of apostles (3:18) and there is no mention of Levi, it appears that Levi was surnamed "Matthew," and it was by that name that he was best known in the early church.

tax booth. Tax booths were set up on highways, bridges, and canals for tolls, and at the lakeside to tax fishing. See note Luke 3:12.

he rose. The radical demand of Jesus' call and the unconditional obedience of the one who hears are thrown into sharp relief for the reader.

2:15 sinners. A term of disdain used by the Pharisees for all Jews who did not follow their traditions of legal purity.

reclining with. Contact with sinners would make Jesus a sinner, since rabbinic regulations specifically prohibited such table fellowship. On the other hand, the "sinners" would see in this a gesture of friendship and acceptance (14:20 note).

2:16 Pharisees. Theological descendants of the Hasidim, a second-century B.C. movement of piety, learning, and faithfulness to the Mosaic law against Greek pagan influence. At the time of Jesus, strict observance of the law, and especially ritual purity, was regulated by a body of ethical teachings known as "the tradition of the elders" (7:3), developed by the rabbis as an application of the law to specific situations. The difficulty of knowing this tradition and all its many subtle interpretations created a social and religious gap between a sanctimonious elite, "the righteous," and the general population, "the sinners."

2:17 he said . . . I came not. Note the clear declaration of the priority of His mission (cf. 1:38). There is both truth and biting irony in Jesus' words. Tax collectors, prostitutes, and the like are indeed spiritually "sick," but Jesus does not really intend the Pharisees to think of themselves as "healthy" (cf. Luke 18:9–14). Jesus is breaking down the artificial categories of all legalistic, works-righteousness religion. Like the Old Testament (Ps. 14:1–3), Jesus teaches that all are sinners (7:1–8), and that righteousness is first and foremost a gift of God to repentant sinners (Ps. 51:1–18; Luke 19:9; Rom. 3:22).

2:18 fasting. The Mosaic law required only one fast annually, on the Day of Atonement (Lev. 16:29–31; cf. Acts 27:9, which calls this day "the Fast"). Nevertheless, as a sign of contrition and penitence associated with prayer, fasting was a part of Old Testament piety from the time of the judges (Judg. 20:26; 1 Kin. 21:27), sometimes becoming an empty ritual (Is. 58:3). The Pharisees and their adherents apparently fasted twice a week (Luke 18:12). Since the message of John the Baptist centered on repentance (Matt. 3:11), fasting was appropriate for his disciples. Jesus, whose own message included repentance, did not insist upon fasting.

2:19 Jesus said to them. The reason Jesus gives sets Him off from all that was before, for the "bridegroom" has now come, the "new" (vv. 21, 22) is present. By comparing Himself to the bridegroom, Jesus affirms the presence of the kingdom as a time for celebration, like a wedding. Jesus eats and drinks with publicans and sinners, bringing joy and salvation to them (Luke 19:6, 9).

2:20 will fast. The present celebration (v. 19) is provisional, for Jesus has yet to suffer and die, and "the bridegroom [will be] taken away from them." See Acts 13:2; 14:23.

2:21, 22 The images of new cloth and new wineskins again emphasize the new situation brought about by the coming of the kingdom and of its King, and seek to show through the symbols of unwise action the inappropriateness of fasting in this new situation.

2:23 One Sabbath. The problem with the legalistic reasoning by certain Pharisees is illustrated in this incident. In reality the disciples were not stealing or doing farm work (Deut. 23:25). Their accusers counted even plucking the "heads of grain" as reaping, which was prohibited on the Sabbath (Ex. 34:21).

2:25 he said to them, "Have you never read . . . ?" Jesus' question suggests an ironic criticism of their knowledge of Scripture (John 3:10; 5:39, 47). Jesus does not justify Himself by laying Scripture aside. He rather shows His understanding of its depth and its proper application to human need.

need and was hungry, he and those who
were with him: 26 how he entered the
house of God, in the time of [x]Abiathar
the high priest, and ate [y]the bread of the
Presence, which it is not lawful for any
but the priests to eat, and also gave it
to those who were with him?" 27 And he
said to them, [z]"The Sabbath was made
for man, [a]not man for the Sabbath. 28 So
[b]the Son of Man is lord even of the
Sabbath."

A Man with a Withered Hand

3 [c]Again [d]he entered the synagogue, and
a man was there with a withered
hand. 2 And [e]they watched Jesus,[1] to see
whether he would heal him on the
Sabbath, so that they might accuse him.
3 And he said to the man with the withered
hand, "Come here." 4 And he said to them,
[f]"Is it lawful on the Sabbath to do good or
to do harm, to save life or to kill?" But they
were silent. 5 And he [g]looked around at
them with anger, grieved at [h]their hardness of heart, and said to the man,
"Stretch out your hand." [i]He stretched it
out, and his hand was restored. 6 [j]The
Pharisees went out and immediately [j]held
counsel with [k]the Herodians against him,
how to destroy him.

A Great Crowd Follows Jesus

7 [l]Jesus withdrew with his disciples to the
sea, and [m]a great crowd followed, from
Galilee and Judea 8 and Jerusalem and
[n]Idumea and from beyond the Jordan and
from around [o]Tyre and Sidon. When the
great crowd heard all that he was doing,
they came to him. 9 And he told his disciples to [p]have a boat ready for him because
of the crowd, lest they [q]crush him, 10 for [r]he
had healed many, so that all who had [s]dis-
eases pressed around him [t]to touch him.
11 [u]And whenever the unclean spirits saw
him, they [v]fell down before him and cried
out, "You are [w]the Son of God." 12 And [x]he
strictly ordered them not to make him
known.

The Twelve Apostles

13 [y]And he went up on the mountain and
called to him those [z]whom he desired, and
they came to him. 14 [y]And he appointed
twelve (whom he also named apostles) so
that they might be with him and he might
send them out to preach 15 [y]and have authority

26 [x]1 Chr. 24:6; [1 Sam. 21:1; 2 Sam. 8:17] [y]Ex. 25:30; Lev. 24:5-9 **27** [z]Ex. 23:12; Deut. 5:14 [a]Col. 2:16 **28** [b][ver. 10] **Chapter 3** **1** [c]For ver. 1-6, see Matt. 12:9-14; Luke 6:6-11 [d]ch. 1:29 **2** [e]Luke 14:1; 20:20; [Luke 11:54; John 8:6] **4** [f][Luke 14:3] **5** [g]ver. 34; ch. 5:32; 10:23; [ch. 10:21] [h]ch. 6:52; Rom. 11:25; Eph. 4:18 [i][1 Kin. 13:4] **6** [j]See Matt. 12:14 [k]ch. 12:13; Matt. 22:16; [ch. 8:15] **7** [l]Matt. 12:15 [m]Matt. 4:25; Luke 6:17 **8** [n]Isai. 34:5; Ezek. 35:15 [o]See Matt. 11:21 **9** [p]ch. 6:32, 45 (Gk.); 8:10 (Gk.) [q]ch. 5:24, 31 **10** [r]See Matt. 4:23 [s]ch. 5:29, 34 [t]ch. 6:56; Matt. 9:20, 21; 14:36; Luke 6:19 **11** [u]ch. 1:26, 34; Luke 4:41 [v]Luke 8:28 [w]See Matt. 14:33 **12** [x]See Matt. 12:16 **13** [y]Matt. 10:1; Luke 6:12, 13; [ch. 6:7-13; Luke 9:1, 2] [z]John 13:18; 15:16, 19 **14** [y][See ver. 13 above] **15** [y][See ver. 13 above]

1 Greek *him*

David. Executing a divine mission (1 Sam. 21:5) as the Lord's anointed, David ate the consecrated bread normally reserved for the priests. Christ, as the Son of David allows His disciples to fulfill their physical needs so they might continue their mission of redemption, a work that is always lawful to be done.

2:26 Abiathar. According to 1 Sam. 21:1–6, it was Abiathar's father, Ahimelech, who gave David the consecrated bread. However, Abiathar was certainly alive, and perhaps even present, when the incident referred to occurred. So the phrase "in the time of Abiathar" is strictly correct. Probably Jesus referred to Abiathar because he was so well known as one of David's chief supporters.

2:28 lord even of the Sabbath. Again (cf. v. 10) Jesus declares His authority as the Son of Man who brings blessings, this time as the Mediator of the Old Testament Law concerning the Sabbath. This claim is made against traditions that had turned the life-promoting fourth commandment (Ex. 20:8–11) into a burden. Since the Sabbath was instituted at creation and not only under Moses, the Lord of the Sabbath is also Lord of creation.

3:1 withered hand. This was not a life and death illness, whose healing on the Sabbath would be permitted by the rules of the Pharisees (v. 4 note). Jesus' action would appear to be a deliberate provocation as well as an act of mercy.

3:2 they watched Jesus. The Pharisees (v. 6) make Jesus' action a test case, as Jesus evidently wanted them to do.

3:4 Is it lawful. Jesus anticipates their criticism by reiterating the Sabbath teaching He began in 2:25–28. The Pharisees held that only essential aid to the sick was lawful on the Sabbath. Jesus shows that their interpretation was against the spirit of the commandment, which existed for the promotion of good (2:27). The good that Jesus does in bringing redemption is required, not forbidden, by the divine law.

3:6 Herodians. A non-religious, political group supporting the dynasty of the Herods. They supported and depended upon the alliance with Rome. In collaborating with the Herodians, the Pharisees had moved far from the Old Testament ideal for the people of God (cf. Deut. 17:15). For more on this conspiracy, see 8:15; 12:13.

3:8 great crowd. The phrase is repeated twice (vv. 8, 9). Jesus' public ministry, in spite of the opposition of the ruling elite (v. 6), is becoming a mass movement. Jesus is so crowded that He must take refuge in a small boat (v. 9). People are coming to Galilee from everywhere to hear Him.

3:11 whenever the unclean spirits saw him. Although the crowds are Jewish (cf. 7:26–29), Jesus is constantly meeting people possessed with evil spirits. In the presence of Jesus the true nature of the combat (Eph. 6:12) becomes evident. The demons are exposed, and they expose the true identity of Jesus, the Son of God (1:1; 15:39 and notes).

3:12 strictly ordered. See 1:34, 43.

3:13 those whom he desired. Mark emphasizes that the choice of the apostles has its origin in Jesus' determined purpose.

3:14 he appointed twelve. In such a context, the significance of the number "twelve" could hardly be missed. Jesus was setting up the constitution of the renewed Israel (Matt. 19:28). See "The Apostles" at Acts 1:26.

that they might be with him. A signal point of the uniqueness of the Twelve is the time they spend with the earthly Jesus, a time of preparation.

preach. Again (1:14, 17) the priority is a preaching mission coupled with exorcism. The time of preparation has a markedly practical emphasis.

to cast out demons. 16 He appointed the
twelve: [a]Simon (to whom [b]he gave the
name Peter); 17 [c]James the son of Zebedee
and John the brother of James (to whom
he gave the name Boanerges, that is, Sons
of Thunder); 18 Andrew, and Philip, and
Bartholomew, and [d]Matthew, and Thomas,
and James the son of Alphaeus, and Thaddaeus, and Simon the Cananaean, 19 and
Judas Iscariot, who betrayed him.
20 Then he went [e]home, and the crowd
gathered again, [f]so that they could not
even eat. 21 [g]And when [h]his family heard it,
they went out to seize him, for they were
saying, "He [i]is out of his mind."

Blasphemy Against the Holy Spirit

22 And [j]the scribes who came down from
Jerusalem were saying, [k]"He is possessed
by Beelzebul," and "by the prince of
demons he casts out the demons." 23 [l]And
he called them to him and said to them in
parables, "How can Satan cast out Satan?
24 If a kingdom is divided against itself, that
kingdom cannot stand. 25 And if a house is
divided against itself, that house will not be
able to stand. 26 And if Satan has risen up
against himself and is divided, he cannot
stand, but is coming to an end. 27 But [m]no
one can enter a strong man's house and
plunder his goods, unless he first binds the
strong man. [n]Then indeed he may plunder
his house.
28 [o]"Truly, I say to you, all sins will be forgiven the children of man, and whatever
blasphemies they utter, 29 but whoever
[p]blasphemes against the Holy Spirit never
has forgiveness, but is guilty of an eternal
sin"— 30 for they had said, "He has an
unclean spirit."

Jesus' Mother and Brothers

31 [q]And his mother and his [r]brothers
came, and standing outside they sent to
him and called him. 32 And a crowd was sitting around him, and they said to him,
"Your mother and your brothers[1] are outside, seeking you." 33 And he answered
them, "Who are my mother and my brothers?" 34 And [s]looking about at those who sat
around him, he said, "Here are my mother
and my brothers! 35 [t]Whoever [u]does the will
of God, he is my brother and sister and
mother."

The Parable of the Sower

4 Again [v]he began to teach beside the
sea. And a very large crowd gathered
about him, [w]so that he got into a boat and
sat in it on the sea, and the whole crowd
was beside the sea on the land. 2 And [x]he
was teaching them many things in parables, and in his teaching he said to them:
3 "Listen! [y]A sower went out to sow. 4 And as
he sowed, some seed fell along the path,
and the birds came and devoured it. 5 Other
seed fell on rocky ground, where it did not

16 [a]For ver. 16-19, see Matt. 10:2-4; Luke 6:14-16; Acts 1:13 [b]Matt. 16:18; John 1:42
17 [c]Matt. 4:21
18 [d]Matt. 9:9
20 [e]ch. 7:17; 9:28 [f]ch. 6:31
21 [g][John 7:5] [h][ver. 31] [i]2 Cor. 5:13; [John 10:20; Acts 26:24]
22 [j]ch. 7:1; Matt. 15:1 [k]Matt. 9:34; 12:24; Luke 11:15; [Matt. 10:25]; See John 7:20
23 [l]For ver. 23-27, see Matt. 12:25-29; Luke 11:17-22
27 [m]Isai. 49:24 [n][Isai. 53:12]
28 [o]For ver. 28-30, see Matt. 12:31, 32; [Luke 12:10; Heb. 6:4-6; 10:26; 1 John 5:16]
29 [p][Acts 7:51; Heb. 10:29]
31 [q]For ver. 31-35, see Matt. 12:46-50; Luke 8:19-21 [r]ch. 6:3; Matt. 13:55; John 2:12; 7:3, 5, 10; Acts 1:14; 1 Cor. 9:5; Gal. 1:19
34 [s]ver. 5
35 [t][John 15:14; Heb. 2:11] [u]Matt. 7:21; [Luke 11:28]
Chapter 4 1 [v]For ver. 1-12, see Matt. 13:1-15; Luke 8:4-10 [w][ch. 3:9; Luke 5:1-3] 2 [x]ver. 33 3 [y][Isai. 55:10; Amos 9:13]

1 Other early manuscripts add *and your sisters*

3:18 Thaddaeus. Mark and Matt. 10:2–4 list identical names for the Twelve. The parallel list in Luke 6:12–16 (cf. Acts 1:13) had "Judas" instead of "Thaddaeus." A possible explanation of this difference is that Thaddaeus had a second name, Judas.

Cananaean. See note Matt. 10:4.

3:19 Iscariot. Some believe that Judas was a political revolutionary because "Iscariot" may have been derived from the Latin *itsicarius,* "assassin." More likely the word has a semitic origin—*ish* meaning "man (of)," *Kerioth,* a town in Israel close to Hebron (Josh. 15:25).

3:21 his family. Some interpreters identify these as Jesus' family, others propose associates, or friends. However, the group is possibly identified in v. 31 as "his mother and his brothers."

out of his mind. The phrase expresses an attitude of unbelief toward Jesus by those who humanly were closest to Him.

3:22 Beelzebul. Greek *beelzeboul,* the god of Ekron (2 Kin. 1:2; Matt. 10:25 note). The Pharisees use it as a name for Satan and accuse Jesus of casting out demons by the power of Satan.

3:23–27 parables. See note 4:2. This parable illustrates Jesus' claim that the kingdom of God has come (Matt. 12:28), for one stronger than the "strong man" is here, able to bind Satan and to free people from his kingdom.

3:29 blasphemes against the Holy Spirit. For various forms of blasphemy, see 2:7; Ex. 22:28; Lev. 24:10–16; Ezek. 35:12, 13; John 10:33–36; Acts 6:11. The unforgivable blasphemy specified here is the act of deliberately associating the power and the work of Jesus, who is full of the Holy Spirit, with the work of Satan. This is to equate supreme spiritual good with supreme spiritual evil, hardening one's heart in a way that makes repentance, and therefore forgiveness, impossible. See theological note "The Unpardonable Sin."

3:31 mother . . . brothers. See v. 21 and note. Roman Catholic commentators, for whom the eternal virginity of Mary is a dogma, stress that "brother" can refer to wider family relations, pointing to Gen. 13:8; 14:16; Lev. 10:4; 1 Chr. 23:22. However, in Mark the term always seems to mean siblings from the same parents. Matt. 1:25 indicates that Mary and Joseph began normal marital relations after the birth of Jesus, giving added meaning to Luke's designation of Jesus as Mary's "firstborn" (Luke 2:7).

3:35 Whoever does the will of God. The arrival of the kingdom of God changes human relationships. Those who oppose its progress, whether mothers or brothers, must be left; those in the kingdom become a person's closest associates, nearer and dearer than any others.

4:2 parables. See Matt. 13:3 note.

4:3–8 a sower . . . to sow. In first-century Palestine, sowing preceded plowing. Paths made by villagers and thorny areas had the seed plowed into them. Rocky places, covered by a thin layer of soil, only became visible after plowing.

have much soil, and immediately it sprang
up, since it had no depth of soil. 6 And [z]when
the sun rose it was scorched, and since it
had no root, [a]it withered away. 7 Other seed
fell among [b]thorns, and the thorns grew up
and choked it, and it yielded no grain.
8 And other seeds fell into good soil and
produced grain, growing up and increasing
and yielding thirtyfold and sixtyfold and [c]a
hundredfold." 9 And he said, [d]"He who has
ears to hear, let him hear."

The Purpose of the Parables

10 And [e]when he was alone, those around
him with the twelve asked him about the
parables. 11 And he said to them, [f]"To you
has been given [g]the secret of the kingdom
of God, but for [h]those outside everything is
in parables, 12 [i]so that

> "they [j]may indeed see but not
> perceive,
> and may indeed hear but not
> understand,
> lest they [k]should turn and be
> forgiven."

13 [l]And he said to them, "Do you not understand this parable? How then will you
understand all the parables? 14 [m]The sower

6 [z]James 1:11 [a]John 15:6 7 [b]Jer. 4:3 8 [c]ver. 20; Gen. 26:12 9 [d]See Matt. 11:15 10 [e]ver. 34 11 [f]Matt. 19:11; Col. 1:27; [1 Cor. 2:6-10; 1 John 2:20, 27]; See Matt. 11:25 [g]See Rom. 16:25 [h]1 Cor. 5:12, 13; Col. 4:5; 1 Thess. 4:12; 1 Tim. 3:7 12 [i]Isai. 6:9, 10 [j]Deut. 29:4; Jer. 5:21; Ezek. 12:2; Rom. 11:8; 2 Cor. 3:14; 4:4; [Isai. 42:19, 20] [k]See Luke 22:32 13 [l]For ver. 13-20, see Matt. 13:18- 23; Luke 8:11-15 14 [m][Matt. 13:37; John 4:36, 37]

The Unpardonable Sin

Jesus' solemn warning about a kind of sin that will not be forgiven, either in this world or the next, is found in three Gospels: Matt. 12:31, 32; Mark 3:28–30; Luke 12:10. It is specifically "blasphemy against the Spirit." This blasphemy is an act performed by speaking, understood as an expression of the thoughts of the heart (Matt. 12:33–37; cf. Rom. 10:9, 10). In the particular context the opponents of Jesus were saying that the Power doing good works among them was not God but the devil. Jesus distinguishes between this blasphemy and other sins, both other sins of speech and other sins in general. As the Bible teaches, God forgave sins of incest, murder, lying, and even Paul's persecution of the church, which Paul did while "breathing threats and murder" against God's people (Acts 9:1).

What makes the unpardonable sin different from others is its relation to the Holy Spirit. It is the Holy Spirit's work to enlighten the mind of sinners (Eph. 1:17, 18), to reveal and teach the gospel (John 14:26), persuading souls to repent and believe the truth (cf. Acts 7:51). The Spirit not only explains the Word of God, but He opens the mind so that it is perceived (2 Cor. 3:16, 17). When His influence is deliberately and knowingly refused, in opposition to the light, then the irreversible sin can be committed as a voluntary, informed act of malice. In response there is a hardening of the heart from God that rules out repentance and faith (Heb. 3:12, 13). God permits the decision of the human will to be permanent in this case. God does not do this lightly or without cause, but in response to an offense against His love.

A person who wants to repent, that is, to reverse the sins they may be guilty of, has not suffered this hardening and has not committed the profound act of hatred that God has determined He will not forgive. Anyone who has been born again will not commit this sin, because the Spirit lives in that person, and God is not divided against Himself (1 John 3:9).

The other verses dealing with the unpardonable sin are Heb. 6:4–6; 10:26–29; and 1 John 5:16, 17. These show that the possibility of this sin depends on there being particular enlightenment and understanding from God and that it is not a common, everyday matter. Jesus said "all sins" and "whatever blasphemies" will be forgiven, excepting only this one sin.

4:9 He who has ears. See also v. 23; Matt. 11:15; 13:9, 43; Luke 8:8; 14:35; Rev. 2:7; cf. Ps. 115:6. This phrase is a call for close attention.

4:10 when he was alone. Jesus was alone with His disciples, in particular with the Twelve (3:14 note) giving them special instruction. This aspect of Jesus' earthly ministry is in all the Gospels.

4:11 secret . . . parables. The "secret" refers to special divine revelation (Rom. 16:25; Eph. 1:9; 3:3, 9), the Old Testament notion of the prophet who by the Spirit is present in God's deliberative council. What he hears becomes his authoritative, divinely inspired message for the people (Ex. 24:15–18; Deut. 33:2; 1 Kin. 22:19; Is. 6:1–13; Jer. 23:18; Amos 3:7). Such revelation reaches its fulfillment in the gospel, which Paul will later call "the mystery of Christ" (Eph. 3:4; Col. 4:3) or "the mystery of the gospel" (Eph. 6:19). Here, the mystery of the kingdom is that the kingdom comes with Jesus, because He is the King. This "mystery," revealed to the disciples, is contrasted with "parables" told to "those who are outside." To those "outside," the parable is a riddle (contrast John 16:29), veiling their understanding as the Scripture had prophesied (v. 12, citing Is. 6:9, 10). To them Jesus remains a provocative enigma, as He will throughout His ministry.

4:13 all the parables. This explanation of the function of parables applies to all parables. See note Matt. 13:13.

4:14–20 The "mystery" of the parable is not its moral teaching about the hardness of human hearts. The "mystery" is to be found in the paradox that the coming of God's reign is to be identified with a fragile seed. The

sows [n]the word. 15 And these are the ones along the path, where the word is sown: when they hear, Satan immediately comes and takes away the word that is sown in them. 16 And these are the ones sown on rocky ground: the ones who, when they hear the word, immediately receive it [o]with joy. 17 And they have no root in themselves, but [p]endure for a while; then, when tribulation or persecution arises on account of the word, immediately [q]they fall away.[1] 18 And others are the ones sown among thorns. They are those who hear the word, 19 but [r]the cares of [s]the world and [t]the deceitfulness of riches and the desires for other things enter in and choke the word, and it proves unfruitful. 20 But those that were sown on the good soil are the ones who hear the word and accept it and [u]bear fruit, [v]thirtyfold and sixtyfold and a hundredfold."

A Lamp Under a Basket

21 [w]And he said to them, [x]"Is a lamp brought in to be put under a basket, or under a bed, and not on a stand? 22 [y]For nothing is hidden except to be made manifest; nor is anything secret except to come to light. 23 [z]If anyone has ears to hear, let him hear." 24 And he said to them, "Pay attention to what you hear: [a]with the measure you use, it will be measured to you, and still more will be added to you. 25 [b]For to the one who has, more will be given, and from the one who has not, even what he has will be taken away."

The Parable of the Growing Seed

26 And he said, [c]"The kingdom of God is as if a man should scatter seed on the ground. 27 He sleeps and rises night and day, and the seed sprouts and grows; [d]he knows not how. 28 The earth produces by itself, first the blade, then the ear, then the full grain in the ear. 29 But when the grain is ripe, at once [e]he puts in the sickle, because the harvest has come."

The Parable of the Mustard Seed

30 [f]And he said, "With what can we compare the kingdom of God, or what parable shall we use for it? 31 It is like [g]a grain of mustard seed, which, when sown on the ground, is the smallest of all the seeds on earth, 32 yet when it is sown it grows up and becomes larger than all the garden plants and puts out large branches, so that the birds of the air can make nests in its shade."

33 [h]With many such parables he spoke [i]the word to them, [j]as they were able to hear it. 34 He did not speak to them [k]without a parable, but [l]privately to his own disciples he [m]explained everything.

Jesus Calms a Storm

35 [n]On that day, when evening had come, he said to them, "Let us go across to the other side." 36 And leaving the crowd, they took him with them in the boat, just as he was. And other boats were with him. 37 And a great windstorm arose, and the waves [o]were breaking into the boat, so that the boat was already filling. 38 But he was in the stern, asleep on the cushion. And they woke him and said to him, "Teacher, do you not care that we are perishing?" 39 And he awoke and [p]rebuked the wind

14 [n]ver. 33; ch. 2:2; 16:20; Luke 1:2; Acts 8:4; James 1:21
16 [o][ch. 6:20; Isai. 58:2; Ezek. 33:31, 32; John 5:35]
17 [p]Gal. 1:6; [Hos. 6:4; Gal. 5:7] [q]See Matt. 11:6
19 [r]See Matt. 6:25 [s]2 Tim. 4:10 [t]1 Tim. 6:9, 10, 17; [ch. 10:23; Matt. 19:23; Acts 5:1-11; Heb. 3:13]
20 [u]Hos. 14:8; John 15:5, 16; Phil. 1:11; Col. 1:6 [v]ver. 8
21 [w]For ver. 21-25, see Luke 8:16-18 [x]Matt. 5:15; Luke 11:33
22 [y]Matt. 10:26; Luke 12:2; [1 Tim. 5:25]
23 [z]ver. 9
24 [a]Matt. 7:2; Luke 6:38
25 [b]See Matt. 13:12
26 [c][Matt. 13:24-30]
27 [d][Eccles. 11:5, 6]
29 [e]Joel 3:13; Rev. 14:15
30 [f]For ver. 30-32, see Matt. 13:31, 32; Luke 13:18, 19
31 [g]Matt. 17:20; Luke 17:6
33 [h]Matt. 13:34 [i]See ver. 14 [j]John 16:12; 1 Cor. 3:2; Heb. 5:12
34 [k][John 16:25] [l]ver. 10; [ch. 13:3] [m][2 Pet. 1:20] 35 [n]For ver. 35-41, see Matt. 8:18, 23-27; Luke 8:22-25; [John 6:16-21] 37 [o][Acts 27:14] 39 [p]Ps. 104:7; [Luke 4:39]

[1] Or *stumble*

Son of Man who exercises all authority on earth (2:11, 27) appears as Jesus of Nazareth. The coming of the kingdom is not equally visible to everyone, although it is a kingdom of power. Those on the outside have unreceptive hearts. For those with ears to hear, the parable unveils the "mystery" of redemption, hidden in the person and work of Christ Himself (1:34 note).

4:19 deceitfulness of riches. Cf. Eph. 4:22.

4:22 nothing is hidden . . . made manifest. During Christ's earthly ministry things are hidden, but the day will come, from the Resurrection on, when all will begin to be revealed (Matt. 10:26, 27; Luke 12:2, 3).

4:24 with the measure you use. The future spread of the mystery of the kingdom will be rewarded in direct measure to one's faithfulness to that task.

4:25 more will be given. This principle is illustrated in the parables of the talents (Matt. 25:14–30) and of the minas (Luke 19:11–27).

4:30–32 The parable of the mustard seed is again concerned with the kingdom's present manifestation in the person of Jesus.

4:32 birds of the air. In Dan. 4:21 the same metaphor refers to the world-wide dominion of Nebuchadnezzar.

4:33, 34 See vv. 10–12.

4:35 the other side. According to 3:7, Jesus is in Galilee. The "other side" of the lake is the region of the Gadarenes in the Decapolis (5:1 note).

4:37 great windstorm. The Sea of Galilee is about 700 feet below sea level, thirteen miles long and eight miles wide. At its southern end is a deep, cliff-lined valley. The wind funnelling through the surrounding hills and through this valley can whip the lake into sudden violent storms.

4:38 he was . . . asleep. Jesus had been teaching all day, and was no doubt exhausted. Mark, like John (John 4:6; 11:35, 38), emphasizes the full humanity of Jesus.

and said to the sea, "Peace! Be still!" And
the wind ceased, and [q]there was a great
calm. 40 He said to them, "Why are you [r]so
afraid? Have you still no faith?" 41 And they
were filled with great fear and said to one
another, [s]"Who then is this, that even
[t]wind and sea obey him?"

Jesus Heals a Demon-Possessed Man

5 [u]They came to the other side of the
sea, to the country of the Gerasenes.[1]
2 And when Jesus[2] had stepped out of the
boat, immediately there met him out of the
tombs a man with an unclean spirit. 3 [v]He
lived among the tombs. And no one could
bind him anymore, not even with a chain,
4 for he had often been bound with shackles and chains, but he wrenched the chains
apart, and he broke the shackles in pieces.
No one had the strength to subdue him.
5 Night and day among the tombs and on
the mountains he was always crying out
and bruising himself with stones. 6 And
when he saw Jesus from afar, he ran and
[w]fell down before him. 7 And [x]crying out
with a loud voice, he said, "What have you
to do with me, Jesus, [y]Son of [z]the Most
High God? [a]I adjure you by God, do not
torment me." 8 For he was saying to him,
"Come out of the man, you unclean spirit!"
9 And Jesus asked him, "What is your
name?" He replied, "My name is [b]Legion,
for we are many." 10 And he begged him
earnestly not to send them out of the country. 11 Now a great herd of pigs was feeding
there on the hillside, 12 and they begged
him, saying, "Send us to the pigs; let us
enter them." 13 So he gave them permission. And the unclean spirits came out,
and entered the pigs, and the herd, numbering about two thousand, rushed down
the steep bank into the sea and were
drowned in the sea.

14 The herdsmen fled and told it in the
city and in the country. And people came
to see what it was that had happened.
15 And they came to Jesus and saw the
demon-possessed[3] man, the one who had
had [c]the legion, sitting there, [d]clothed and
in his right mind, and they were afraid.
16 And those who had seen it described to
them what had happened to the demon-
possessed man and to the pigs. 17 And [e]they
began to beg Jesus[4] to depart from their
region. 18 As he was getting into the boat,
the man who had been possessed with
demons begged him that he might be with
him. 19 And he did not permit him but said
to him, "Go home to your friends and [f]tell
them how much the Lord has done for
you, and how he has had mercy on you."
20 And he went away and began to proclaim
in [g]the Decapolis how much Jesus had
done for him, and everyone marveled.

Jesus Heals a Woman and Jairus's Daughter

21 And when Jesus had crossed again in
the boat to the other side, a great crowd
gathered about him, and he was beside the

39 [q]Job 38:11; Ps. 65:7; [ch. 6:51; Matt. 14:32]
40 [r]John 14:27
41 [s][ch. 1:27] [t][Luke 5:9]
Chapter 5
1 [u]For ver. 1-21, see Matt. 8:28–9:1; Luke 8:26-40
3 [v][Rev. 18:2]
6 [w]See Matt. 8:2
7 [x]ch. 1:26; Acts 8:7 [y][Matt. 4:3, 6]; See Matt. 14:33 [z]Gen. 14:18; Num. 24:16; Ps. 57:2; Dan. 3:26; Luke 1:32; 6:35; Acts 16:17 [a]Matt. 26:63; Acts 19:13; [James 2:19]
9 [b]Matt. 26:53
15 [c][Luke 8:27] [d]ver. 9
17 [e][1 Kin. 17:18; Luke 5:8; Acts 16:39]
19 [f]Ps. 66:16; [ch. 1:44]
20 [g]ch. 7:31; Matt. 4:25

1 Some manuscripts *Gergesenes*; some *Gadarenes* 2 Greek *he*; also verse 9 3 Greek *daimonizomai*; also verses 16, 18; elsewhere rendered *oppressed by demons* 4 Greek *him*

4:39 Peace! Be still! Lit. "be muzzled." Jesus has authority on earth to forgive sins (2:10), He is Lord of the Sabbath (2:28), He has authority in His teaching (1:22) and over the demons (1:27), and now He demonstrates His authority over nature. This calming of the storm resembles His exorcisms; there is the demonic expression of violence (1:26; 5:4, 13), the command to be "silent" (1:25 note), and the resultant calm (5:15). Jesus binds "the strong man" (3:23–27) and reclaims from his power the physical creation.

5:1 the country of the Gerasenes. Gerasa was thirty miles southeast of the lake. There is also a village named Khersa on the eastern shore with the kind of cliffs and tombs described in the story. Jesus enters the Decapolis, a political association of ten independent Greek city-states, anticipating the future Gentile mission of the church. The Gentile character of the population is apparent since the Jews did not raise pigs, which were unclean under Mosaic law.

5:2 out of the tombs. This demon-possessed man was exiled from normal human contacts, separated from his village and family (v. 19).

5:3 no one could bind him. Violence and unusual physical strength leading to slow self-destruction (v. 5; 9:22) often seem to characterize the demon-possessed (v. 13; 1:26; 9:18, 20, 22, 26), but before the spiritual strength of Jesus the demons cower and flee.

5:7 What have you to do with me. See 1:24.

5:9 What is your name. Naming someone was believed to be a way of gaining power over them. The demons had already identified Jesus (v. 7; cf. 1:24, 34), but by this question Jesus reveals His superior power.

Legion. Jesus forces the demon to unmask himself. He is not one but many. A Roman legion was six thousand men.

5:10 he begged. The demon cowers before Jesus, even invoking God's name as a form of protection (v. 7), recognizing that Jesus has absolute power over him.

5:13 he gave them permission. Jesus permits the demons to enter the pigs, who then hurl themselves over the cliff. This exorcism is a dramatic demonstration of Jesus' power over evil (vv. 14, 16) and of the presence of the kingdom in His ministry (Luke 11:20). See "Demons" at Deut. 32:17.

5:15 sitting. In comparison with his previous violent behavior and the recent destruction of the pigs, the man "sitting there, clothed and in his right mind" gives eloquent expression to the peace and life-giving restoration that comes from Jesus' power (4:39; 9:26, 27).

5:19 Go home. This man becomes the first Gentile missionary. Jesus usually demands silence (1:34 note), but in this instance He allows the preparation for the future mission of the church to begin. Jesus will later command silence regarding a healing performed in the Decapolis, but to no avail (7:31–37).

sea. 22 [h]Then came one of [i]the rulers of the synagogue, Jairus by name, and seeing him, he fell at his feet 23 and implored him earnestly, saying, "My little daughter is at the point of death. Come and [j]lay your hands on her, so that she may be made well and live." 24 And he went with him.

And a great crowd followed him and [k]thronged about him. 25 And there was a woman [l]who had had a discharge of blood for twelve years, 26 and who had suffered much under many physicians, and had spent all that she had, and was no better but rather grew worse. 27 She had heard the reports about Jesus and came up behind him in the crowd and touched his garment. 28 For she said, "If I touch even his garments, I will be made well." 29 [m]And immediately the flow of blood dried up, and she felt in her body that she was healed of her [n]disease. 30 And Jesus, perceiving in himself that [o]power had gone out from him, immediately turned about in the crowd and said, "Who touched my garments?" 31 And his disciples said to him, "You see the crowd pressing around you, and yet you say, 'Who touched me?'" 32 And he looked around to see who had done it. 33 But the woman, knowing what had happened to her, came in fear and trembling and fell down before him and told him the whole truth. 34 And he said to her, "Daughter, [p]your faith has made you well; [p]go in peace, and be healed of your [n]disease."

35 While he was still speaking, there came from [q]the ruler's house some who said, "Your daughter is dead. Why [r]trouble [s]the Teacher any further?" 36 But overhearing[1] what they said, Jesus said to [q]the ruler of the synagogue, "Do not fear, only believe." 37 And he allowed no one to follow him except [t]Peter and James and [u]John the brother of James. 38 They came to the house of the ruler of the synagogue, and Jesus[2] saw a commotion, people weeping and wailing loudly. 39 And when he had entered, he said to them, [v]"Why are you making a commotion and weeping? The child is not dead but [w]sleeping." 40 And they laughed at him. But he [x]put them all outside and took the child's father and mother and those who were with him and went in where the child was. 41 [y]Taking her by the hand he said to her, "Talitha cumi," which means, "Little girl, I say to you, [z]arise." 42 And immediately the girl got up and began walking (for she was twelve years of age), and they were immediately overcome with amazement. 43 And [a]he strictly charged them that no one should know this, and told them to give her something to eat.

Jesus Rejected at Nazareth

6 [b]He went away from there and came to [c]his hometown, and his disciples followed him. 2 And [d]on the Sabbath he began to teach in the synagogue, and [e]many who heard him were astonished, saying, "Where did this man get these things? What is the wisdom given to him? How are such mighty works done by his hands? 3 [f]Is

22 [h]For ver. 22-43, see Matt. 9:18-26; Luke 8:41-56 [i]Luke 13:14; Acts 13:15; 18:8, 17
23 [j]ch. 6:5; 7:32; 8:23, 25; 16:18; Matt. 9:18; Luke 4:40; 13:13; Acts 9:12, 17; 28:8
24 [k]ver. 31; ch. 3:9
25 [l]Lev. 15:25
29 [m]Matt. 15:28; 17:18 [n]See ch. 3:10
30 [o]Luke 5:17; 6:19; 8:46; [Acts 10:38]
34 [p]See Luke 7:50 [n][See ver. 29 above]
35 [q]ver. 22
35 [r]Luke 7:6 [s]See John 11:28
36 [q][See ver. 35 above]
37 [t]ch. 9:2; 14:33 [u]ch. 3:17
39 [v][Acts 20:10] [w]John 11:4, 11
40 [x]Acts 9:40
41 [y]See ch. 1:31 [z]Luke 7:14, 22; [Matt. 11:5; John 11:43]
43 [a]ch. 9:9; See Matt. 8:4
Chapter 6
1 [b]For ver. 1-6, see Matt. 13:54-58; [Luke 4:16-30] [c]Matt. 2:23; Luke 4:23
2 [d]ch. 1:21; Luke 4:31; 6:6; 13:10; [Acts 13:14]; See Matt. 4:23
[e]See Matt. 7:28 3 [f][Luke 4:22; John 6:42]

1 Or *ignoring*; some manuscripts *hearing* 2 Greek *he*

5:22 rulers of the synagogue. Though he was a layman, a ruler's responsibilities were socially and religiously important, including not only the upkeep of the building but also the proper conduct of the service and the choice of Torah readings.

5:25 discharge of blood. The woman's condition was not only physically debilitating, but it disqualified her from marriage (Lev. 20:18) as well as religious life in general (Lev. 15:25–33).

5:29 immediately. See 1:10 note.

5:30 Who touched my garments. The touch of faith is felt by Jesus, even though in such a dense crowd many people were touching Him. The phrase "power had gone out from him" occurs only here.

5:32 he looked around. For a woman who has been a social outcast for many years, the healing is only complete when Jesus has publicly identified her, commends her faith, and declares to all that she is healed (v. 34) and cleansed.

5:37 Peter and James and John. Jesus built around Himself a hierarchy of closeness. There are numerous disciples (4:10) from whom twelve are appointed apostles (3:13–19), and within the Twelve some (Peter, James, John, and sometimes Andrew) enjoy Jesus' fullest intimacy, most notably at the Transfiguration (9:2–13) and in Gethsemane (14:32, 33).

5:38 wailing. In the Middle Eastern cultures, wailing is a customary expression of grief, sometimes calling for professional mourners.

5:40 put them all outside. Jesus is not interested in a grand spectacle of healing. Rather, He is concerned for the suffering of the girl, the faith of her parents, and the ultimate goal of His mission (v. 43).

5:41 Talitha cumi. Aramaic was the popular language spoken in Palestine. Mark gives the translation for other Aramaic terms (3:17; 7:11, 34; 10:46; 14:36) in order to clarify his narrative for those unfamiliar with that language.

5:43 strictly charged them. See notes on v. 19 and 1:34.

6:1 his hometown. Nazareth, some twenty miles southwest from Capernaum and the Sea of Galilee.

his disciples. The Twelve (v. 7).

6:2 Sabbath. Although He is Lord of the Sabbath (2:28), Jesus observes weekly Sabbath worship (1:21; 3:1; Luke 4:16–30).

astonished. See 1:22; 7:37; 10:26; 11:18.

not this [g]the carpenter, the son of Mary
and [h]brother of James and Joses and Judas
and Simon? And are not his sisters here
with us?" And [i]they took offense at him.
4And Jesus said to them, [j]"A prophet is not
without honor, except in his hometown
and among his relatives and in his own
household." **5**And [k]he could do no mighty
work there, except that [l]he laid his hands
on a few sick people and healed them.
6And [m]he marveled because of their unbelief.
[n]And he went about among the villages
teaching.

Jesus Sends Out the Apostles

7[o]And he called the twelve and began to
send them out two by two, and gave them
authority over the unclean spirits. **8**He
charged them to take nothing for their
journey except a staff—no bread, no bag,
no money in their belts— **9**but to [p]wear
sandals and not put on two tunics.[1] **10**And
he said to them, "Whenever you enter a
house, stay there until you depart from
there. **11**And if any place will not receive
you and they will not listen to you, when
you leave, [q]shake off the dust that is on
your feet [r]as a testimony against them."
12[s]So they went out and [t]proclaimed [u]that
people should repent. **13**[t]And they cast out
many demons and [v]anointed with oil many
who were sick and healed them.

The Death of John the Baptist

14[w]King Herod heard of it, for Jesus'[2]
name had become known. Some[3] said,

3[g][Matt. 13:55] [h]See ch. 3:31 [i]See Matt. 11:6
4[j]Luke 4:24; John 4:44; [Jer. 11:21; 12:6; John 7:5]
5[k][ch. 9:23; Gen. 19:22] [l]See ch. 5:23
6[m]Isai. 59:16; [Matt. 8:10] [n]Matt. 9:35; 11:1; Luke 8:1; 13:22
7[o]ch. 3:13-15; For ver. 7-11, see Matt. 10:1, 5, 9-14; Luke 9:1, 3-5; [Luke 10:4-11; 22:35]
9[p]Acts 12:8
11[q]Acts 13:51; [Neh. 5:13; Acts 18:6] [r]See ch. 1:44
12[s]Luke 9:6 [t]Matt. 10:7, 8 [u]Matt. 3:2; 4:17
13[t][See ver. 12 above] [v]James 5:14
14[w]For ver. 14-29, see Matt. 14:1-12; Luke 9:7-9
[x]ch. 8:28; Matt. 16:14
15[x][See ver. 14 above] [y]See Matt. 21:11
17[z]Luke 3:19, 20 [a]Matt. 11:2; John 3:24
18[z][See ver. 17 above] [b]Lev. 18:16; 20:21
20[c][Matt. 14:5; 21:26] [d]ch. 12:37; [ch. 4:16]

[x]"John the Baptist[4] has been raised from
the dead. That is why these miraculous
powers are at work in him." **15**[x]But others
said, "He is Elijah." And others said, "He is
[y]a prophet, like one of the prophets of
old." **16**But when Herod heard of it, he
said, "John, whom I beheaded, has been
raised." **17**[z]For it was Herod who had sent
and seized John and [a]bound him in prison
for the sake of Herodias, his brother
Philip's wife, because he had married her.
18[z]For John had been saying to Herod, [b]"It
is not lawful for you to have your brother's
wife." **19**And Herodias had a grudge against
him and wanted to put him to death. But
she could not, **20**for Herod [c]feared John,
knowing that he was a righteous and holy
man, and he kept him safe. When he heard
him, he was greatly perplexed, and yet he
[d]heard him gladly.
21But an opportunity came when Herod
[e]on his birthday [f]gave a banquet for his
nobles and military commanders and the
leading men of Galilee. **22**For when Herodias's daughter came in and danced, she
pleased Herod and his guests. And the king
said to the girl, "Ask me for whatever you
wish, and I will give it to you." **23**And he
vowed to her, "Whatever you ask me, I will
give you, [g]up to half of my kingdom."
24And she went out and said to her mother,
"For what should I ask?" And she said,
"The head of John the Baptist." **25**And she

21[e]Gen. 40:20 [f]1 Kin. 3:15; Esth. 1:3; 2:18 **23**[g]Esth. 5:3; 7:2

[1] Greek *chiton*, a long garment worn under the cloak next to the skin
[2] Greek *his* [3] Some manuscripts *He* [4] Greek *baptizer*; also verse 24

6:3 carpenter. Could also mean "builder." Jesus' work in this occupation prior to His ministry might explain His use of building metaphors, especially when describing His own essential ministry (14:58; 15:29; Matt. 7:24; 16:18; 21:33; Luke 12:18; 17:28). The remark concerning manual labor is probably not derogatory as such, for all rabbis were expected to have a trade. Paul had been trained as a rabbi and was a maker of tents or awnings (Acts 18:3; 22:3; 26:5; Phil. 3:5, 6). The accusation is that Jesus (who teaches "wisdom" in v. 2) is a common worker without religious or academic credentials.

son of Mary. See 3:31.

6:4 own household. Not only is Jesus rejected by the people of the town and the wider circle of relatives there, but also by His own family (3:31).

6:7 the twelve. Having already been appointed to be with Jesus (3:14 note) and receive special instruction concerning the mystery of His person and role (4:10, 11 notes), the Twelve are now permitted to share His ministry and authority.

send them out. The verb has the same root as the noun *apostle,* and underlines their link with Jesus as His personal representatives (3:14 note).

two by two. The biblical principle that testimony should be established by at least two witnesses (Num. 35:30; Deut. 17:6; 19:15; Matt. 18:16; John 8:17; 2 Cor. 13:1; 1 Tim. 5:19; Heb. 10:28) was also applied in the missionary activity of the early church in the ministries of Peter and John (Acts 3:1; 4:1), Paul and Barnabas (Acts 13:2), and Paul and Silas (Acts 15:40).

6:8 no bread. Matt. 10:10 gives the reason, "the laborer deserves his food."

6:11 shake off the dust. Strict Jews shook the foreign dust from their feet after travel in pagan territories. Refusal of the gospel invites the same reaction.

6:14 King Herod heard. Herod Antipas, son of Herod the Great, was "tetrarch" (ruler of a dependent state) of Galilee and Perea.

6:15 one of the prophets. Speculation about the identity of Jesus will lead to the accounts of the miraculous feedings (vv. 30–44; 8:1–9) and walking on water (vv. 47–52), all of which point to Jesus' personal divinity. But first Mark will relate the circumstances of the death of John the Baptist, with whom Herod and others had identified Jesus.

6:17 his brother Philip's wife. Herodias was a daughter of Aristobulus, one of the sons of Herod the Great. Other sons of Herod the Great included Herod Antipas and Herod Philip (by different wives). After marrying her half-uncle Herod Philip, Herodias left him for an adulterous relationship with his brother, Herod Antipas. Such were the loose morals, typical of the Herodian dynasty, against which John the Baptist preached (cf. Lev. 18:16, 20).

came in immediately with haste to the king and asked, saying, "I want you to give me at once the head of John the Baptist on a platter." **26** And the king was exceedingly sorry, but because of his oaths and his guests he did not want to break his word to her. **27** And immediately the king sent an executioner with orders to bring John's[1] head. He went and beheaded him in the prison **28** and brought his head on a platter and gave it to the girl, and the girl gave it to her mother. **29** When his [h]disciples heard of it, they came and took his body and laid it in a tomb.

Jesus Feeds the Five Thousand

30 [i,j]The apostles returned to Jesus and told him all that they had done and taught. **31** And he said to them, "Come away by yourselves to a desolate place and rest a while." For many were coming and going, and [k]they had no leisure even to eat. **32** [l]And they went away in [m]the boat to a desolate place by themselves. **33** Now many saw them going and [n]recognized them, and they ran there on foot from all the towns and got there ahead of them. **34** When he went ashore he [o]saw a great crowd, and [o]he had compassion on them, because they were like sheep without a shepherd. And he began to teach them many things. **35** And when it grew late, his disciples came to him and said, "This is a desolate place, and the hour is now late. **36** [p]Send them away to go into the surrounding countryside and villages and buy themselves something to eat." **37** But he answered them, [q]"You give them something to eat." And [r]they said to him, [s]"Shall we go and buy two hundred denarii[2] worth of bread and give it to them to eat?" **38** And he said to them, "How many loaves do you have? Go and see." And when they had found out, they said, [t]"Five, and two fish." **39** Then he commanded them all to sit down in groups on the green grass. **40** So they sat down in groups, by hundreds and by fifties. **41** And taking the five loaves and the two fish he [u]looked up to heaven and [v]said a blessing and broke the loaves and gave them to the disciples to set before the people. And he divided the two fish among them all. **42** And they all ate and were satisfied. **43** And they took up twelve baskets full of broken pieces and of the fish. **44** And those who ate the loaves were five thousand men.

Jesus Walks on the Water

45 [w]Immediately he [x]made his disciples get into [y]the boat and go before him to the other side, [z]to Bethsaida, while he dismissed the crowd. **46** And after he had taken leave of them, [a]he went up on the mountain to pray. **47** And when [b]evening came, the boat was out on the sea, and he was alone on the land. **48** And he saw that they were making headway painfully, for the wind was against them. And about [b]the fourth watch of the night[3] he came to them, walking on the sea. [c]He meant to pass by them, **49** but when they saw him walking on the sea they thought it was a ghost, and cried out, **50** for they all saw him and [d]were terrified. But immediately he spoke to them and said, [e]"Take heart; it is I. [e]Do not be afraid." **51** And he got into the

29 [h]See Matt. 9:14
30 [i]Luke 9:10 [j]Matt. 10:2; Luke 6:13; 17:5; 22:14; 24:10
31 [k]ch. 3:20
32 [l]For ver. 32-44, see Matt. 14:13-21; Luke 9:10-17; John 6:1-13; [ch. 8:2-9] [m]See ch. 3:9
33 [n]ver. 54
34 [o][Matt. 9:36]
36 [p]ver. 45; [Matt. 15:23]
37 [q][2 Kin. 4:42-44] [r][John 6:7] [s][Num. 11:13, 21, 22]
38 [t]ch. 8:19
41 [u]ch. 7:34; John 11:41; 17:1 [v]ch. 8:7; 14:22; 1 Sam. 9:13; Matt. 26:26; Luke 24:30; [1 Cor. 14:16]
45 [w]For ver. 45-51, see Matt. 14:22-32; John 6:15-21 [x][Matt. 8:18] [y]ver. 32 [z]ch. 8:22; [Luke 9:10; John 6:17]
46 [a]Luke 6:12; 9:28; [ch. 1:35; Luke 5:16]
47 [b][ch. 13:35]
48 [b][See ver. 47 above] [c][Gen. 32:26; Luke 24:28]
50 [d][Luke 24:37] [e]Matt. 17:7; [Deut. 31:6; Isai. 41:13; 43:1, 2; John 16:33]

1 Greek *his* 2 A *denarius* was a day's wage for a laborer 3 That is, between 3 A.M. and 6 A.M.

6:31 by yourselves. Being alone with Jesus, who then instructs them in the mystery of the kingdom (4:10, 11), is part of their preparation for future ministry (4:34; 9:2, 28; 13:3; cf. John 13:1; 16:29).

6:34 he had compassion. Jesus does what God promised to do in Ezek. 34:11, 14: "I myself will search for my sheep and will seek them out. . . . I will feed them with good pasture." Jesus acts as the Shepherd of God's people, like Moses (Num. 27:15–17; Ps. 77:20), David (Ps. 78:70–72), and God Himself (Ps. 23:1; 74:1; 78:52, 53; 80:1; Ezek. 34:15).

sheep without a shepherd. Ancient Israel, abandoned by unfaithful leaders, was also described in this way (Jer. 50:6; Ezek. 34:1–10).

6:40 by hundreds and by fifties. This detail recalls the ordering of ancient Israel in the wilderness under Moses (Ex. 18:21).

6:42 all ate and were satisfied. This feeding story recalls the miraculous provision of manna in the wilderness under Moses (Ex. 16:1–36, especially v. 16). Jesus is the new Moses bringing the new covenant.

6:43 they took up. A further reference to the provision of manna where nothing was to be left till the morning (Ex. 16:19).

twelve baskets full. The number recalls the twelve tribes of ancient Israel and suggests the important role that the Twelve would play in the constitution of the New Israel (3:14 note).

6:44 five thousand men. Mark does not use the Greek word that means "human being," but a term distinguishing men from women, with perhaps the idea of "head of family" (Matt. 14:21 adds "besides women and children"). The crowd may have numbered between fifteen and twenty thousand.

6:48 fourth watch. Since the Romans divided the night into four periods, the fourth watch would be the three hours ending at dawn.

6:49 a ghost. Lit. "phantasm," used in the New Testament only here and in Matt. 14:26. It has the connotation of superstitious imagination.

6:50 it is I. The Greek phrase (lit. "I am") is also the Septuagint (the Greek translation of the Old Testament) rendering of the divine name "I AM" revealed to Moses (Ex. 3:14; Deut. 32:39; Is. 41:4; 43:10, 13, 25; 45:18; 52:6; Hos. 13:4; Joel 2:27). This account has all the usual marks of biblical theophany narratives (various modes of visible, divine self-revelation), including human dread, divine identification, and words of assurance.

boat with them, and the wind ceased. And
they were utterly astounded, 52 for [f]they did
not understand about the loaves, but their
hearts [g]were hardened.

Jesus Heals the Sick in Gennesaret

53 [h]When they had crossed over, they
came to land at [i]Gennesaret and moored to
the shore. 54 And when they got out of the
boat, the people immediately [j]recognized
him 55 and ran about the whole region and
began to bring [k]the sick people [l]on their
beds to wherever they heard he was. 56 And
wherever he came, in villages, cities, or
countryside, [m]they laid the sick in the marketplaces and implored him that they
might touch even [n]the fringe of his garment. And [o]as many as touched it were
made well.

Traditions and Commandments

7 [p]Now when the Pharisees gathered to
him, with some of the scribes [q]who
had come from Jerusalem, 2 they saw that
some of his disciples ate with hands that
were [r]defiled, that is, unwashed. 3 (For the
Pharisees and all the Jews do not eat unless
they wash[1] their hands, holding to [s]the tradition of [t]the elders, 4 and when they come
from the marketplace, they do not eat
unless they wash.[2] And there are many
other traditions that they observe, such as
[u]the washing of [v]cups and pots and copper
vessels and dining couches.[3]) 5 And the
Pharisees and the scribes asked him, "Why
do your disciples not walk according to
[s]the tradition of [t]the elders, [w]but eat with
[r]defiled hands?" 6 And he said to them,
"Well did Isaiah prophesy of you [x]hyp-
ocrites, as it is written,

[y]"'This people honors me with their
lips,
but their heart is far from me;
7 in vain do they worship me,
teaching as [z]doctrines the
commandments of men.'

8 You leave the commandment of God and
hold to the tradition of men."

9 And he said to them, "You have a fine
way of [a]rejecting the commandment of
God in order to establish your tradition!
10 For Moses said, [b]'Honor your father and
your mother'; and, [c]'Whoever reviles father
or mother must surely die.' 11 But you say,
'If a man tells his father or his mother,
Whatever you would have gained from
me is Corban' (that is, given to God)[4]—
12 then you no longer permit him to do anything for his father or mother, 13 thus [d]mak-
ing void the word of God by your tradition
that you have handed down. And many
such things you do."

What Defiles a Person

14 And he called the people to him again
and said to them, [e]"Hear me, all of you,
and understand: 15 [f]There is nothing outside a person that by going into him can

52 [f]ch. 8:17-21 [g]John 12:40; Rom. 11:7; 2 Cor. 3:14; See ch. 3:5
53 [h]For ver. 53-56, see Matt. 14:34-36; [John 6:24, 25] [i]Luke 5:1
54 [j]ver. 33
55 [k]Luke 5:18 [l]Matt. 4:24
56 [m]Acts 5:15 [n]See Matt. 9:20 [o]ch. 3:10; Luke 6:19
Chapter 7
1 [p]For ver. 1-30, see Matt. 15:1-28 [q]ch. 3:22
2 [r][Acts 10:14; Rom. 14:14 (Gk.)]
3 [s]Gal. 1:14; Col. 2:8 [t]Heb. 11:2
4 [u]Heb. 9:10; [John 2:6] [v]Matt. 23:25; Luke 11:39
5 [s][See ver. 3 above] [t][See ver. 3 above] [w]Luke 11:38
[r][See ver. 2 above]
6 [x]Matt. 23:13 [y]Cited from Isai. 29:13; [Ezek. 33:31]
7 [z]Col. 2:22; Tit. 1:14
9 [a]Luke 7:30; Gal. 2:21 (Gk.); Heb. 10:28 (Gk.)
10 [b]Cited from Ex. 20:12 [c]Cited from Ex. 21:17
13 [d]Gal. 3:17 (Gk.); [Rom. 2:23]
14 [e]Matt. 13:51 15 [f]See Acts 10:14, 15

[1] Greek *unless they wash with a fist*, probably indicating a kind of ceremonial washing [2] Greek *unless they baptize*; some manuscripts *unless they purify themselves* [3] Some manuscripts omit *and dining couches* [4] Or *an offering*

6:52 they did not understand about the loaves. This remark suggests that the miracle of the feeding contains the same mystery concerning Jesus as does His walking on water. Jesus, as to His humanity, is indeed the new Moses. But He is also, and at the same time, the God who provided bread from heaven (Ex. 16:4).

6:53 Gennesaret. A village on the western shore of the Sea of Galilee (Luke 5:1).

6:56 his garment. See note 5:30.

7:1 Pharisees. See note 2:16.

scribes. Scribes were teachers of the law, mostly Pharisees.

7:2 defiled. The disciples had not washed in the manner prescribed by "the tradition of the elders" (vv. 3, 4), and so were considered ceremonially unclean. Jesus is critical of these traditional expansions of the ceremonial law by the scribes and Pharisees because they had so extended their traditions as to permit actual transgression of the moral law (vv. 9–13). His cross will finally bring the ceremonial law to an end.

7:3 wash. By their tradition, the Pharisees extended the biblical injunctions for priestly washing at the moment of temple sacrifice (Ex. 30:19; 40:12) to the eating of bread by all Jews.

tradition of the elders. The Pharisees believed that in addition to the written words of the law, Moses received instructions for its interpretation and application. This oral law was passed on by word of mouth from teacher to teacher. In His arguments with them, Jesus consistently appeals to Scripture and always seeks to get back to its true meaning (vv. 6–8).

7:5 Why do your disciples not. The Pharisees and scribes are not genuinely interested in the meal practice of the disciples, but in why Jesus, as their teacher, does not require them to observe "the tradition" generally.

7:6 Isaiah. Jesus' motivation is to bring people back into conformity with Scripture.

7:8 leave the commandment of God. The verb "leave" can mean "cancel," "abandon," or "neglect." Jesus is not an antinomian. Like the psalmist, He is consumed with longing for the law of God (Ps. 119:20), which He fulfills, protects (Matt. 5:17–20), and defends. He is not even against tradition, but only against that which annuls Scripture.

7:11 Corban. A Hebrew and Aramaic word (which Mark translates for his Gentile readers), designating something as dedicated to a religious purpose. By a simple vow to reserve their possessions as a gift to God, a person could avoid responsibility to support their parents.

defile him, but the things that come out of a person are what defile him."[1] 17 And when he had entered [g]the house and left the people, [h]his disciples asked him about the parable. 18 And he said to them, "Then [i]are you also without understanding? Do you not see that whatever goes into a person from outside cannot defile him, 19 since it enters not his heart [j]but his stomach, and is expelled?"[2] ([k]Thus he declared all foods clean.) 20 And he said, [l]"What comes out of a person is what defiles him. 21 For from within, out of the heart of man, come evil thoughts, sexual immorality, theft, [m]murder, adultery, 22 coveting, wickedness, deceit, [n]sensuality, [o]envy, [p]slander, [q]pride, [r]foolishness. 23 [s]All these evil things come from within, and they defile a person."

The Syrophoenician Woman's Faith

24 And from there he arose and went away to the region of Tyre and Sidon.[3] And he entered a house and did not want anyone to know, yet he could not be hidden. 25 But immediately a woman whose little daughter was possessed by an unclean spirit heard of him and came and fell down at his feet. 26 [t]Now the woman was a [u]Gentile, [v]a Syrophoenician by birth. And she begged him to cast the demon out of her daughter. 27 And he said to her, "Let the children be [w]fed first, for it is not right to take the children's bread and [x]throw it to the dogs." 28 But she answered him, "Yes, Lord; yet even the dogs under the table eat the children's [y]crumbs." 29 And he said to her, "For this statement you may [z]go your way; the demon has left your daughter."

17 [g]ch. 3:19; 9:28 [h][Matt. 13:36; 15:15]
18 [i]ch. 8:17, 18
19 [j][1 Cor. 6:13] [k][Luke 11:41; Acts 10:15; 11:9]
20 [l]Matt. 12:34; James 3:6
21 [m]Matt. 5:22, 28; See Ex. 20:13, 14, 17
22 [n]2 Cor. 12:21; Gal. 5:19; Eph. 4:19; 2 Pet. 2:7; Jude 4 [o]See Matt. 6:23 [p]Eph. 4:31; Col. 3:8; 1 Tim. 6:4 [q]See Luke 1:51 [r][Eph. 5:17]
23 [s]1 Cor. 6:9, 10
26 [t][John 12:20, 21] [u][1 Cor. 12:13] [v][Acts 21:2, 3]
27 [w][Acts 3:26; Rom. 1:16] [x]Matt. 7:6
28 [y][Luke 16:21]
29 [z]John 4:50
31 [a]For ver. 31-37, [Matt. 15:29-31] [b]Matt. 4:18; John 6:1 [c]ch. 5:20; Matt. 4:25
32 [d]Isai. 35:5, 6
32 [e]See ch. 5:23
33 [f]ch. 8:23
34 [g]See ch. 6:41 [h]ch. 8:12; [John 11:33]
35 [d][See ver. 32 above]
36 [i]ch. 9:9; See Matt. 8:4

30 And she went home and found the child lying in bed and the demon gone.

Jesus Heals a Deaf Man

31 [a]Then he returned from the region of Tyre and went through Sidon to [b]the Sea of Galilee, in the region of the [c]Decapolis. 32 And they brought to him [d]a man who was deaf and [d]had a speech impediment, and they begged him to [e]lay his hand on him. 33 And [f]taking him aside from the crowd privately, he put his fingers into his ears, and [f]after spitting touched his tongue. 34 And [g]looking up to heaven, [h]he sighed and said to him, "Ephphatha," that is, "Be opened." 35 [d]And his ears were opened, his tongue was released, and he spoke plainly. 36 And [i]Jesus[4] charged them to tell no one. But [j]the more he charged them, the more zealously they proclaimed it. 37 And they were [k]astonished beyond measure, saying, "He has done all things well. He even makes the deaf hear and the mute speak."

Jesus Feeds the Four Thousand

8 [l]In those days, when again a great crowd had gathered, and they had nothing to eat, he called his disciples to him and said to them, 2 [m]"I have compassion on the crowd, because they have been with me now three days and have nothing to eat. 3 And if I send them away hungry to their homes, they will faint on the way. And some of them have come from far away."

[j]ch. 1:45; Matt. 9:31 37 [k]ch. 10:26
Chapter 8 1 [l]For ver. 1-10, see Matt. 15:32-39; [ch. 6:32-44] 2 [m][Matt. 9:36]

[1] Some manuscripts add verse 16: *If anyone has ears to hear, let him hear* [2] Greek *goes out into the latrine* [3] Some manuscripts omit *and Sidon* [4] Greek *he*

7:20 What comes out of a person. Jesus is generalizing about the natural and constant way in which fallen human nature expresses itself, and His list of vices (vv. 21, 22) is meant to bring horrifying self-knowledge (cf. Rom. 1:24–32; 2:17–24).

defiles. Jesus goes to the essence of the matter—uncleanness of the heart, of which ceremonial uncleanness is really a symbol.

7:24 Tyre. Jesus moves north into a markedly Gentile region (cf. Matt. 11:21, 22), to the vicinity of the ancient Phoenician port city of Tyre (in modern Lebanon).

7:26 Gentile. She was of Syrian descent but spoke Greek.

7:27 first. Though in Gentile territory, Jesus maintains the temporal priority of Israel ("the children") in the divine plan of salvation, as Paul does later (Rom. 1:16; 2:10; cf. Acts 1:8; 13:46, 47).

dogs. The term is certainly derogatory (Matt. 7:6; Phil. 3:2; Rev. 22:15), though the Greek word includes the nuance "little dogs" or "pets." It should be seen as an example of Jesus' colorful imagery of table fellowship to explain the plan of salvation, namely, that "salvation is from the Jews" (John 4:22). The woman takes it in this sense, as her reply indicates.

7:31 Decapolis. See note 5:1. Jesus remains in Gentile territory, first going north to Sidon and then southeast to the Decapolis.

7:33 put his fingers into his ears. These physical actions accompany the miracle of healing, but are not its cause.

7:34 Ephphatha. An Aramaic word which Mark again translates for his Greek-speaking readers (5:41 note).

7:35 spoke plainly. For a deaf person, clearly expressed spoken language must usually be learned over a period of time.

7:36 tell no one. Regarding Jesus' command of secrecy, see notes 1:34 and 5:19.

8:1–10 A second miraculous feeding. Jesus later points to deep theological significance in the two feedings (8:18–21).

8:2 I have compassion. Since this feeding probably took place in the Decapolis (7:31), it is evident that Jesus extends His compassion from the lost sheep of the house of Israel (6:34) to the Gentiles, as His healing of the Syrophoenician woman's daughter (7:24–30) and His ministry in Gentile territory (7:31–37) would suggest. By His actions Jesus announces the world-wide mission of the future church.

4 And his disciples answered him, "How
can one feed these people with bread here
in this desolate place?" 5 And he asked
them, "How many loaves do you have?"
They said, [n]"Seven." 6 And he directed the
crowd to sit down on the ground. And he
took the seven loaves, and [o]having given
thanks, he broke them and gave them to
his disciples to set before the people; and
they set them before the crowd. 7 And they
had a few small fish. And [p]having blessed
them, he said that these also should be set
before them. 8 And [q]they ate and were satisfied. And they took up the broken pieces
left over, [n]seven baskets full. 9 And there
were about four thousand people. And he
sent them away. 10 And immediately he got
into [r]the boat with his disciples and went
to the district of [s]Dalmanutha.[1]

The Pharisees Demand a Sign

11 [t]The Pharisees came and began to
argue with him, [u]seeking from him [v]a sign
from heaven [w]to test him. 12 And [x]he sighed
deeply [y]in his spirit and said, "Why does
this generation seek a sign? Truly, I say to
you, no sign will be given to this generation." 13 And [z]he left them, got into the boat
again, and went to the other side.

The Leaven of the Pharisees

14 Now they had forgotten to bring bread,
and they had only one loaf with them in
the boat. 15 And he cautioned them, saying,
"Watch out; [a]beware of [b]the leaven of the
Pharisees and the leaven of [c]Herod."[2] 16 And
they began discussing with one another the
fact that they had no bread. 17 And [d]Jesus,
aware of this, said to them, "Why are you
discussing the fact that you have no bread?
[e]Do you not yet perceive [f]or understand?
[f]Are your hearts hardened? 18 [g]Having eyes
do you not see, and having ears do you not
hear? And do you not remember? 19 When I
broke [h]the five loaves for the five thousand,
how many baskets full of broken pieces did
you take up?" They said to him, "Twelve."
20 "And [i]the seven for the four thousand,
how many baskets full of broken pieces did
you take up?" And they said to him,
"Seven." 21 And he said to them, "Do you
not yet understand?"

Jesus Heals a Blind Man at Bethsaida

22 And they came [j]to Bethsaida. And
some people brought to him a blind man
and begged him to touch him. 23 And [k]he
took the blind man by the hand and led
him out of the village, and when [k]he had
[l]spit on his eyes and [m]laid his hands on
him, he asked him, "Do you see anything?"
24 And he looked up and said, "I see men,
but they look like trees, walking." 25 Then
Jesus[3] laid his hands on his eyes again; and
he opened his eyes, his sight was restored,
and he saw everything clearly. 26 And he
sent him to his home, saying, [n]"Do not
even enter the village."

Peter Confesses Jesus As the Christ

27 [o]And Jesus went on with his disciples
to the villages of Caesarea Philippi. And on

[1] Some manuscripts *Magadan*, or *Magdala* [2] Some manuscripts *the Herodians* [3] Greek *he*

5 [n]Matt. 16:10 **6** [o]ch. 14:23; Matt. 26:27; Luke 22:17, 19; John 6:11, 23; Acts 27:35; Rom. 14:6; 1 Cor. 10:30; 11:24; 14:16; 1 Tim. 4:3, 4 **7** [p]See Matt. 14:19 **8** [q][2 Kin. 4:42-44] [e][See ver. 5 above] **10** [r]See ch. 3:9 [s][Matt. 15:39] **11** [t]For ver. 11-21, see Matt. 16:1-12 [u]1 Cor. 1:22; See Matt. 12:38 [v]Luke 11:16; 21:11 [w]See [John 8:6] **12** [x]ch. 7:34 [y]John 11:33 **13** [z]Matt. 4:13; 21:17 **15** [a]Luke 12:1 [b]1 Cor. 5:6-8; Gal. 5:9 [c][ch. 3:6; 12:13 **17** [d]Matt. 26:10 [e]ch. 7:18 [f]ch. 6:52 **18** [g]Jer. 5:21; Ezek. 12:2; [Isai. 42:18, 19; 43:8; Matt. 13:13] **19** [h]ch. 6:41, 44 **20** [i]ver. 6, 9 **22** [j]See ch. 6:45 **23** [k]ch. 7:33 [l]John 9:6 [m]See ch. 5:23 **26** [n]ver. 23; [Matt. 8:4] **27** [o]For ver. 27-29, see Matt. 16:13-16; Luke 9:18-20

8:4 this desolate place. See note 1:4. The disciples' question, in view of what Jesus had previously done in similar circumstances, justifies Jesus' reproach in vv. 17, 18.

8:10 Dalmanutha. Presumably on the western shore of the Sea of Galilee, though its exact location is not known (see text note).

8:11 Pharisees. See note 2:16.

sign from heaven. Jesus does not perform signs on demand, especially not for those "testing" Him (cf. 1:13; Matt. 4:1–11, where the same Greek verb is translated "tempting"). The Pharisees wanted a sign to confirm that Jesus was the political messiah they were expecting (v. 15 note).

8:14 one loaf. This narrative detail ties this passage and the two feeding miracles together.

8:15 leaven of the Pharisees and . . . Herod. Jesus uses an everyday ingredient of bread as a metaphor (Luke 12:1 note). What seems like an innocent, indeed legitimate request for a sign (on Herod's desire for miracles, see Luke 23:8) is actually a rejection of His ministry and all His previous signs. Jesus is warning His disciples against superficial conceptions of His role and preparing them for His teaching concerning the true meaning of His coming and of His cross (vv. 27, 31). Such teaching remained incomprehensible to many Jews (1 Cor. 1:22, 23).

8:17 no bread. The disciples' thoughts are still dominated by material concerns, leaving them blind to the true vocation of their master and open to being tempted by the "leaven" of the Pharisees.

8:21 Do you not yet understand. Here Jesus' role in teaching and training the Twelve comes into the foreground of the narrative (3:14 note). His question to them is a reproach for failing to realize that the Lord who miraculously provided for five thousand and four thousand men with their families is capable of taking care of twelve men's physical needs. Indeed, they should know that Jesus is worthy of their total faith in all that He will reveal to them in the days to come.

8:22 Bethsaida. A fishing town on the northern shore of the Sea of Galilee and home of Philip, Andrew, and Peter.

8:23 spit on his eyes. See note 7:33.

8:24 trees, walking. The restoration of sight in this case is gradual.

8:26 Do not even enter the village. Jesus had led him out of the town (v. 23), so it is likely that the message of this miracle was intended for His disciples. They must realize that Jesus is gradually healing their spiritual sight. While in v. 21 they still do not understand who Jesus is, they too, like the blind man (v. 25), are about to see "clearly" the mystery of His person (vv. 27–30).

8:27 Caesarea Philippi. A town at the foot of Mount Hermon and close

the way he asked his disciples, "Who do people say that I am?" 28 And they told him, [p]"John the Baptist; and others say, [q]Elijah; and others, one of the prophets." 29 And he asked them, "But who do you say that I am?" Peter answered him, [r]"You are [s]the Christ." 30 [t]And he strictly charged them to tell no one about him.

Jesus Foretells His Death and Resurrection

31 [u]And he began to teach them that [v]the Son of Man must [w]suffer many things and [x]be rejected by the elders and the chief priests and the scribes and be killed, and [y]after three days rise again. 32 And he said this [z]plainly. And Peter took him aside and began to rebuke him. 33 But turning and seeing his disciples, he rebuked Peter and said, [a]"Get behind me, Satan! For you [b]are not setting your mind on the things of God, but on the things of man."

34 And he called to him the crowd with his disciples and said to them, "If anyone would come after me, let him [c]deny himself and [d]take up his cross and follow me. 35 For [d]whoever would save his life will lose it, but whoever loses his life for my sake [e]and the gospel's will save it. 36 [f]For what does it profit a man to gain the whole world and forfeit his life? 37 For [g]what can a man give in return for his life? 38 For [h]whoever is ashamed of me and of my words in this [i]adulterous and sinful generation, of him will the Son of Man also be ashamed [j]when he comes in the glory of his Father with [k]the holy angels."

9 And he said to them, "Truly, I say to you, there are some standing here who will not [l]taste death [m]until they see the kingdom of God after it has come [n]with power."

The Transfiguration

2 [o]And after six days Jesus took with him [p]Peter and James and John, and led them

28 [p]ch. 6:14; Matt. 14:2; Luke 9:7
28 [q]ch. 9:15; Luke 9:8; [ch. 9:11; Matt. 17:10; John 1:21]
29 [r]John 11:27 [s]ch. 14:61, 62; See Matt. 1:17
30 [t]Matt. 16:20; Luke 9:21; See Matt. 12:16
31 [u]For ver. 31–ch. 9:1, see Matt. 16:21-28; Luke 9:22-27 [v]ch. 10:33; [Luke 13:33] [w]ch. 9:30, 31; Matt. 17:12, 22, 23; Luke 24:7 [x]Luke 17:25; 1 Pet. 2:4; [ch. 12:10] [y]ch. 10:34; Matt. 27:63; [Matt. 12:40]; See John 2:19
32 [z]John 16:25
33 [a][Matt. 4:10] [b]Rom. 8:5; Phil. 3:19; Col. 3:2; [Phil. 2:5]
34 [c][2 Tim. 2:12, 13]

[d]See Matt. 10:38, 39 **35** [d][See ver. 34 above] [e]ch. 10:29; [1 Cor. 9:23; 2 Tim. 1:8; Philem. 13] **36** [f][Luke 12:20] **37** [g][Ps. 49:7, 8] **38** [h]Rom. 1:16; 2 Tim. 1:8, 12, 16; Heb. 11:16; 1 John 2:28; [Matt. 10:33] [i]Isai. 57:3; Matt. 12:39; James 4:4 [j]Dan. 7:10, 13; Zech. 14:5; Matt. 24:30; 25:31; 26:64; John 1:51; Acts 1:11; 1 Thess. 1:10; 4:16; Jude14; Rev. 1:7; [Deut. 33:2] [k]Acts 10:22; Rev. 14:10; [Matt. 13:41; 16:27]
Chapter 9 **1** [l]John 8:52; Heb. 2:9 [m][ch. 13:30; Matt. 10:23; 23:36; 24:34] [n]ch. 13:26; 14:62; [Matt. 25:31] **2** [o]For ver. 2-8, see Matt. 17:1-8; Luke 9:28-36 [p]ch. 5:37; 14:33

to the source of the Jordan river. Herod the Great built a marble temple to Caesar Augustus there, and his son Philip changed the town's name from Paneas to Caesarea. To distinguish it from the other Caesarea, the well-known Mediterranean port, it was known as Philip's Caesarea.

8:29 But who do you say that I am. Again the preeminence of the Twelve in the revelation of the person of Jesus is emphasized (v. 21; 3:14). Jesus dismisses what people say (v. 27), but retains as divinely revealed truth the confession of the Twelve (Matt. 16:16, 17 and notes).

the Christ. Lit. "the anointed One" (1 Sam. 2:10; Matt. 1:1 and notes). This is the first time in Mark's narrative that the name "Christ" appears (it does appear in the title at 1:1). Peter's confession (as spokesperson for the Twelve), along with the Transfiguration that follows (9:2–13), are a high point in the revelation of Jesus' person and a turning point in His earthly ministry. From now on His teaching will concentrate on His impending death, and He will soon begin to travel to Jerusalem.

8:30 tell no one. See notes 1:34; 5:19; cf. 9:9. Strangely, at this high point of revelation comes the order to keep it secret. But with hindsight the reason is clear. Jesus will not allow political notions of messiahship to compromise His true calling to be the suffering Messiah whose essentially moral and spiritual work of redemption will be total.

8:31–10:52 This section recounts the turning point of Jesus' earthly ministry (8:29 note). It contains three predictions of Jesus' death and resurrection (8:31; 9:31; 10:33, 34); relates the beginning of His journey to Jerusalem, and gives sustained teaching on true messiahship and discipleship.

8:31 Son of Man. See note 2:10.

must. Behind this small word is all the weight of scriptural prophecy and divinely ordained necessity (9:31; Luke 22:37; 24:7, 26, 44). Jesus' predictions concerning His death and resurrection come out of His understanding of the Old Testament Scriptures.

suffer many things. The prediction of the suffering Messiah comes particularly from Is. 52:13–53:12. See also Zech. 9:9; 12:10; 13:7; and the Old Testament generally for the theme of the righteous sufferer.

elders. Lay members of the Sanhedrin, the court that governed Jewish affairs. The court was composed of elders, chief priests, and teachers of the law (the scribes).

chief priests. Jesus predicts that the wealthy high-priestly families who were affiliated with the Sadducees will be involved in His death.

after three days. See Hos. 6:2. This is also a conventional expression for a short period.

rise again. See Is. 52:13; 53:10; cf. Ps. 110:1; Dan. 7:13, 14.

8:32 he said this plainly. In contrast to His public teaching in parables (4:10, 11), the Twelve privately receive plain instruction (cf. John 16:25, 29). Jesus' clear, private teaching will become the basis of His disciples' public preaching after Easter (Acts 2:29; 4:13, 29, 31; 28:31).

Peter . . . began to rebuke him. When even Peter, leader among the Twelve, fails to accept that the Messiah must suffer, one can appreciate the wisdom of Jesus' secrecy regarding His messianic office. Note Paul's remark that for many "the word of the cross is folly" (1 Cor. 1:18; cf. Gal. 3:13).

8:33 Get behind me, Satan. Satan is now at work even among Jesus' own disciples, not only in Judas but even in Peter, whose intervention would have annulled the plan of redemption and accomplished Satan's goal.

8:34 take up his cross. Condemned prisoners were generally made to carry the crossbar of their cross to the site of execution (cf. 15:21).

8:37 in return for his life. No monetary or material value can be placed on this (Ps. 49:7–9, to which Jesus is perhaps alluding).

8:38 in the glory of his Father. Though in the present time of humiliation "the Son of Man has nowhere to lay his head" (Matt. 8:20), one day He will be revealed with divine splendor as the Son of God (12:6–11; 14:62; cf. Dan. 7:13).

9:1 kingdom of God after it has come with power. The coming of the kingdom "with power" would seem to be associated with Jesus' resurrection since it will be witnessed by "some standing here," and it is also described as a coming "in power" (Rom. 1:4). The Transfiguration, which follows this utterance, is an intermediate and immediate fulfillment of Jesus' words, since it anticipates the manifestation of resurrection power and divine glory. See note Matt. 16:28.

9:2 after six days. In Ex. 24:16, "six days" is also the period of preparation for receiving revelation and witnessing a vision of divine glory (a theophany; 6:50 note).

up a high mountain by themselves. And he
was [q]transfigured before them, **3** and [r]his
clothes became radiant, intensely white, as
no one[1] on earth could bleach them. **4** And
there appeared to them Elijah with Moses,
and they were talking with Jesus. **5** And
Peter said to Jesus, [s]"Rabbi,[2] it is good that
we are here. Let us make three [t]tents, one
for you and one for Moses and one for
Elijah." **6** For [u]he did not know what to say,
for they were terrified. **7** And [v]a cloud overshadowed them, and [v]a voice came out of
the cloud, [w]"This is my beloved Son;[3] [x]lis-
ten to him." **8** And suddenly, looking
around, they no longer saw anyone with
them but Jesus only.
9 [y]And as they were coming down the
mountain, [z]he charged them to tell no one
what they had seen, [a]until the Son of Man
had risen from the dead. **10** [b]So they kept
the matter to themselves, [c]questioning
what this rising from the dead might mean.
11 And they asked him, "Why do the scribes
say [d]that first Elijah must come?" **12** And he
said to them, "Elijah does come first [e]to
restore all things. And [f]how is it written of
the Son of Man that he should [g]suffer many
things and [h]be treated with contempt?
13 But I tell you that Elijah has come, and
[i]they did to him whatever they pleased, as
it is written of him."

Healing of a Boy with an Unclean Spirit

14 [j]And when they came to the disciples,
they saw a great crowd around them, and

2 [q][2 Cor. 3:18 (Gk.) **3** [r]Dan. 7:9; [Ps. 104:2; Matt. 28:3] **5** [s]See John 1:38 [t][Neh. 8:15] **6** [u][ch. 14:40; Luke 9:33] **7** [v]2 Pet. 1:17; [Ex. 24:15, 16] [w]ch. 12:6; See Matt. 3:17 [x]Acts 3:22 **9** [y]For ver. 9-13, see Matt. 17:9-13 [z]ch. 5:43; See Matt. 8:4 [a]ch. 8:31 **10** [b]Luke 9:36 [c][John 16:17] **11** [d]See Matt. 11:14 **12** [e]Mal. 4:6; Luke 1:16, 17; [Acts 1:6; 3:21] [f]Ps. 22:6, 7; Isai. 53:2, 3; Dan. 9:26; Zech. 13:7; [Phil. 2:7]; See Matt. 26:24 [g]See ch. 8:31 [h]Luke 23:11; Acts 4:11 **13** [i]ch. 6:17, 27 **14** [j]For ver. 14-28, see Matt. 17:14-19; Luke 9:37-42

1 Greek *no cloth refiner* 2 *Rabbi* means *my teacher*, or *my master* 3 Or *my Son, my* (or *the*) *Beloved*

The Transfiguration of Jesus

Recorded in three of the Gospels (Matt. 17:1–8; Mark 9:2–8; Luke 9:28–36), and testified to by Peter and John (cf. 2 Pet. 1:16–18; John 1:14), the Transfiguration was a revelation of Jesus' deity. The transformation in Jesus' appearance as He prayed (Luke 9:29) was a momentary transition from the concealment of His divine glory that marked His days on earth to the manifestation of glory that will be revealed when He returns.

The bright light that shone from Jesus as His face changed (Luke 9:29) was the glory intrinsic to Him as the divine Son, "the radiance of the glory" (Heb. 1:3). The voice from the cloud confirmed the identification that the vision had already given.

The Transfiguration was also a significant event in the revelation of God's kingdom. Moses and Elijah represented the law and the prophets witnessing to Jesus and being superseded by Him. The "departure" (Greek exodus) of which they and Jesus talked (Luke 9:31 and text note) was Jesus' death, resurrection, and ascension. These events were not just a way of leaving this world, but of redeeming His people, just as the Exodus from Egypt led by Moses was Israel's liberation from slavery.

Peter and James and John. These three can represent the Twelve just as Peter alone can (8:29; Matt. 16:18; Acts 2:14).

a high mountain. Both Moses (on Sinai; Ex. 24) and Elijah (on Horeb; 1 Kin. 19) were given a vision of God's theophanic presence on high mountains.

transfigured. Lit. "changed in form." This Greek verb is used by Paul to describe the present work of the Spirit in the inner life of the believer (Rom. 12:2; 2 Cor. 3:18). That work will be completed when this same Spirit gives "life to your mortal bodies" as when He raised Jesus from the dead (Rom. 8:11), and as here in Jesus' momentary glorification. See theological note "The Transfiguration of Jesus."

9:4 Elijah with Moses. The Transfiguration ties the old covenant to the new, directly linking Moses and Elijah, representatives of the law and the prophets, with Jesus and His apostles, messengers of redemption's completion.

9:5 Let us make three tents. Peter perhaps wishes to capture and prolong the glory so as to avoid the suffering of which Jesus had already spoken (8:31–33).

9:7 This is my beloved Son. The heavenly declaration is a high point of divine revelation concerning the identity of Jesus. Just as God had revealed Himself in the theophany on Sinai as "the LORD, a God merciful and gracious" (Ex. 34:6), so now He reveals Himself as the one who speaks through His beloved Son (John 1:17; 3:16; Heb. 1:2).

listen to him. This phrase represents a rebuke to Peter as well as a declaration concerning the authority of the Son as revealer and prophet of the new covenant. These words echo Deut. 18:15, and identify Jesus as the great prophet like Moses.

9:9 charged them to tell no one. See notes 1:34; 8:30.

until the Son of Man had risen from the dead. Open, public testimony to Jesus' glory is to be withheld until after the full accomplishment of redemption.

9:10 questioning what this rising from the dead might mean. The disciples' confusion arises from Jewish expectation of a general resurrection in the last days, but not an individual resurrection in the midst of history.

9:12 Elijah does come first. Though John the Baptist is not personally Elijah risen from the dead (6:14–16; cf. John 1:21), Jesus teaches that Elijah was indeed the Old Testament type who prefigured the Baptist's ministry (cf. Luke 1:17).

9:13 they did to him. Just as Elijah suffered at the hands of Ahab and Jezebel (1 Kin. 19:1–10), so John suffered at the hands of Herod and Herodias (6:18 note). If John, who restored all things by calling the people of God to repentance and godliness, was put to death, should it be surprising (v. 12) that the Son of Man faces the same lot?

scribes arguing with them. 15 And immediately all the crowd, when they saw him,
[k]were greatly amazed and ran up to him
and greeted him. 16 And he asked them,
"What are you arguing about with them?"
17 And someone from the crowd answered
him, "Teacher, I brought my son to you,
for he has [l]a spirit that makes him mute.
18 And whenever it seizes him, it throws
him down, and he foams and grinds his
teeth and becomes rigid. So I asked your
disciples to cast it out, and [m]they were not
able." 19 And he answered them, "O [n]faith-
less generation, [n]how long am I to be with
you? How long am I to bear with you?
Bring him to me." 20 And they brought the
boy to him. And when the spirit saw him,
immediately it [o]convulsed the boy, and he
fell on the ground and rolled about, foaming at the mouth. 21 And Jesus asked his
father, "How long has this been happening
to him?" And he said, "From childhood.
22 And it has often cast him into fire and
into water, to destroy him. But [p]if you can
do anything, have compassion on us and
help us." 23 And Jesus said to him, [p]"If you
can! [q]All things are possible for one who
believes." 24 Immediately the father of the
child cried out[1] and said, "I believe; [r]help
my unbelief!" 25 And when Jesus saw that
[s]a crowd came running together, he
rebuked the unclean spirit, saying to it,
[t]"You mute and deaf spirit, I command
you, come out of him and never enter him
again." 26 And after crying out and [o]con-
vulsing him terribly, it came out, and the
boy was like a corpse, so that most of them
said, "He is dead." 27 But Jesus [u]took him by
the hand and lifted him up, and he arose.

15 [k][ch. 10:32]
17 [l]ver. 25; Luke 11:14
18 [m][ch. 6:7; Matt. 10:1; Luke 10:17]
19 [n][John 14:9; 20:27]
20 [o]ch. 1:26
22 [p][ch. 1:40; Matt. 9:28]
23 [p][See ver. 22 above]
[q][ch. 6:5, 6; Matt. 17:20]
24 [r][Luke 17:5]
25 [s]ver. 15
[t]ver. 17
26 [o][See ver. 20 above]
27 [u]See ch. 1:31

1 Some manuscripts add *with tears*

Hell

The New Testament views hell as the final abode of those condemned to eternal punishment at the Last Judgment (Matt. 25:41–46; Rev. 20:11–15). It is described as a place of fire and darkness (Jude 7, 13), of "weeping and gnashing of teeth" (Matt. 8:12; 13:42, 50; 22:13; 24:51; 25:30), of destruction (2 Thess. 1:7–9; 2 Pet. 3:7; 1 Thess. 5:3) and torment (Rev. 20:10; Luke 16:23). These terms are probably symbolic rather than literal, but, if anything, the reality will be more terrible than the symbol. New Testament teaching about hell is meant to appall us and fill us with horror, persuading us that though heaven will be better than we could dream, so hell will be worse than we can imagine. These are the issues of eternity that must be realistically faced.

Hell is not so much the absence of God, as the consequence of His wrath and displeasure. God is like a consuming fire (Heb. 12:29), and His righteous condemnation for defying Him and clinging to the sins He loathes will be experienced in hell (Rom. 2:6, 8, 9, 12). According to Scripture, hell is unending (Jude 13; Rev. 20:10). There is no biblical warrant for speculations about a "second chance" after death, or an annihilation of the ungodly at some stage.

Those in hell will realize that they have sentenced themselves to be there because they have loved darkness rather than light, refusing to have their Creator as their Lord. They preferred the self-indulgence of sin to self-denying righteousness, rejecting the God that made them (John 3:18–21; Rom. 1:18, 24, 26, 28, 32; 2:8; 2 Thess. 2:9–11). General revelation confronts everyone with a certain evidence of God, and from this standpoint hell has a basis in God's respect for human choice. All receive what they chose, either to be with God forever, or to be without Him. Those who are in hell will know, not only that for their doings they deserve it, but that in their hearts they chose it.

The purpose of the Bible's teaching about hell is to make us turn with gratitude to the grace of Christ that saves us from it (Matt. 5:29, 30; 13:48–50). For this reason God's warning to us is merciful; He has "no pleasure in the death of the wicked, but that the wicked turn from his way and live" (Ezek. 33:11).

9:17 has a spirit. Demon possession is clearly distinguished from normal illness (7:31–37), though in both cases the person cannot speak. Compare 1:24, 25; 5:2–15.

9:19 O faithless generation. Jesus' impatience with the disciples' lack of faith, and frustration with the general scene of unbelief and impotence as He returns from the mount of Transfiguration, is reminiscent of Moses coming down from Mount Sinai to find unbelief and unfaithfulness in the Israelite camp (Ex. 32).

9:25 a crowd came running. The situation is still volatile. The blind enthusiasm of the crowd constantly places Jesus in the dilemma of compassionately wanting to minister to people's suffering, while not jeopardizing the overarching plan of redemption.

I command you. The spiritual power of Jesus causes the demon to cry out (v. 26). See "Demons" at Deut. 32:17.

28 And when he had [v]entered the house, his
disciples asked him privately, "Why could
we not cast it out?" 29 And he said to them,
"This kind cannot be driven out by anything but prayer."[1]

Jesus Again Foretells Death, Resurrection

30 [w]They went on from there and passed
through Galilee. And he did not want anyone to know, 31 for he was teaching his disciples, saying to them, "The Son of Man is
going to be delivered into the hands of
men, and they will kill him. And when he
is killed, [x]after three days he will rise."
32 [y]But they did not understand the saying,
and were afraid to ask him.

Who Is the Greatest?

33 And [z]they came to Capernaum. And
when he was in the house [a]he asked them,
"What were you discussing on the way?"
34 But they kept silent, for on the way [b]they
had argued with one another about who
was the greatest. 35 And he sat down and
called the twelve. And he said to them, [c]"If
anyone would be first, he must be last of all
and servant of all." 36 And he took a child
and put him in the midst of them, and
[d]taking him in his arms, he said to them,
37 [e]"Whoever receives one such child in my
name receives me, and [e]whoever receives
me, receives not me but him who sent me."

Anyone Not Against Us Is for Us

38 [f]John said to him, "Teacher, we saw
someone [g]casting out demons in your
name,[2] and [h]we tried to stop him, because
he was not following us." 39 But Jesus said,
"Do not stop him, for no one who does a
mighty work in my name will be able soon
afterward to speak evil of me. 40 [i]For the
one who is not against us is for us. 41 For
truly, I say to you, [j]whoever gives you a cup
of water to drink because you belong to
Christ will by no means lose his reward.

Temptations to Sin

42 [k]"Whoever causes one of [l]these little
ones who believe in me to sin,[3] [m]it would
be better for him if a great millstone were
hung around his neck and he were thrown
into the sea. 43 [n]And if your hand causes
you to sin, cut it off. It is better for you to
enter life crippled than with two hands
to go to [o]hell,[4] to [p]the unquenchable fire.[5]
45 [q]And if your foot causes you to sin, cut it
off. It is better for you to enter life lame
than with two feet to be thrown into [o]hell.
47 [r]And if your eye causes you to sin, tear it
out. It is better for you to enter the kingdom of God with one eye than with two
eyes to be thrown into [s]hell, 48 'where [t]their
worm does not die and [u]the fire is not
quenched.' 49 For everyone will be salted
with fire.[6] 50 [v]Salt is good, [w]but if the salt

28 [v]ch. 3:19; 7:17 30 [w]For ver. 30-32, see Matt. 17:22, 23; Luke 9:43-45; [ch. 8:31; 10:32-34] 31 [x]See ch. 8:31 32 [y]ch. 6:52; Luke 2:50; 18:34; 24:25; John 10:6; 12:16; 16:17-19; [ver. 10] 33 [z]Matt. 17:24 [a]For ver. 33-37, see Matt. 18:1-5; Luke 9:46-48; [ch. 10:35-45] 34 [b]Luke 22:24; [ver. 50] 35 [c]ch. 10:43, 44; Matt. 20:26, 27; 23:11, 12; Luke 22:26 36 [d]ch. 10:16 37 [e][Matt. 10:40, 42] 38 [f]For ver. 38-40, see Luke 9:49, 50 [g]ch. 16:17; Matt. 7:22; Luke 10:17; Acts 19:13; [Matt. 12:27] [h][Num. 11:28] 40 [i][Matt. 12:30; Luke 11:23] 41 [j]See Matt. 10:42 42 [k]Matt. 18:6; Luke 17:2; [1 Cor. 8:12] [l][Zech. 13:7] [m][ch. 14:21] 43 [n]Matt. 5:30; 18:8 [o]See Matt. 5:22, 29 [p]ver. 48; Matt. 3:12; See Matt. 25:41 45 [q]Matt. 18:8 [o][See ver. 43 above] 47 [r]Matt. 5:29; 18:9 [s]See Matt. 5:22, 29 48 [t]Isai. 66:24 [u]ver. 44 50 [v]Luke 14:34 [w]Matt. 5:13

[1] Some manuscripts add *and fasting* [2] Some manuscripts add *who does not follow us* [3] Greek *to stumble*; also verses 43, 45, 47 [4] Greek *Gehenna*; also verse 47 [5] Some manuscripts add verses 44 and 46 (which are identical with verse 48) [6] Some manuscripts add *and every sacrifice will be salted with salt*

9:28 privately. See note 8:32.

9:31 teaching his disciples. Again and again Jesus gives priority to the training of the Twelve. Jesus repeats, for emphasis and because the lesson was still unlearned, what He had previously taught in 8:31.

9:33 house. See note 2:1.

9:34 who was the greatest. Given the importance of honor in that society, such considerations played a significant role in people's minds (cf. 10:35–45). Jesus is bringing about a revolution in this way of thinking, though without destroying the notion of functional hierarchy. See note 5:37.

9:35 called the twelve. Again the Twelve are singled out (3:14), and their position of leadership is explicitly recognized.

If anyone would be first. Jesus is not attacking leadership positions, but showing the way in which such roles should be exercised (i.e., as the "last . . . and servant of all"). This principle is exemplified by Jesus Himself who "came not to be served but to serve, and to give his life as a ransom for many" (10:45). The self-giving manner in which Jesus fulfills His messianic role, which is the first and foremost role in the kingdom, provides the standard for His disciples in whatever secondary roles they might exercise in the kingdom of God.

9:36 a child. Lit. "infant." The God-given dignity of every human being is exemplified by the little child. This weakest of human beings must be served in the same way as the greatest (9:35 note).

9:38 he was not following us. This phrase does not deny that the man was not a follower of Jesus; he was casting out demons in Jesus' name. Probably what is meant is that he does not recognize the authority of the Twelve. Without taking away the prerogatives of the Twelve, but sensing their pride and exclusivism (9:35 note; 10:35–45), Jesus refuses to denounce the one they are talking about. Instead He teaches that the support and fellowship of all who support His cause should be gratefully acknowledged.

9:41 whoever gives. All acts of mercy, care, and healing, done in Jesus' name (that is, with understanding and work and the purpose of serving Him) are eternally acknowledged as evidence of true discipleship.

9:42 Whoever causes . . . to sin. "Little ones" can refer either to infants (v. 36), or to insignificant believers (v. 39). Derailing the faith of those of little worldly importance, for example, through an inconsiderate, egotistical use of power (v. 35 note), calls for the most severe punishment (v. 43).

9:43 cut it off. This admonition should be understood as a kind of exaggeration used in speech to make a point (cf. vv. 45–47). Jesus is talking about costly renunciations of sinful habits. See theological note "Hell."

9:44–46 See text notes. Verses 44 and 46 do not appear in some early manuscripts, but the phrase is also found in v. 48.

9:49 salted with fire. Salt is associated with sacrifice in Lev. 2:13; Ezek. 43:24. The saying may mean that by contrast to the fire of destruction just spoken of, believers will persevere through fire and be purified by it.

has lost its saltiness, how will you make it
salty again? [x]Have salt in yourselves, and
[y]be at peace with one another."

Teaching About Divorce

10 [z]And he left there and went [a]to the
region of Judea and beyond the
Jordan, and crowds gathered to him again.
And again, as was his custom, he taught
them.
2 And Pharisees came up and in order [b]to
test him asked, [c]"Is it lawful for a man to
divorce his wife?" 3 He answered them,
"What did Moses command you?" 4 They
said, [d]"Moses allowed a man to write a certificate of divorce and to send her away."
5 And Jesus said to them, "Because of your
[e]hardness of heart he wrote you this commandment. 6 But [f]from the beginning of
creation, 'God made them [g]male and
female.' 7 [h]'Therefore a man shall leave his
father and mother and hold fast to his
wife,[1] 8 and [i]they shall become one flesh.'
So they are no longer two but one flesh.
9 [j]What therefore God has joined together,
let not man separate."
10 And in the house the disciples asked
him again about this matter. 11 And he said
to them, [k]"Whoever divorces his wife and
marries another commits adultery against
her, 12 and [l]if she divorces her husband and
marries another, she commits adultery."

50 [x]Ezek. 43:24; Col. 4:6; [Eph. 4:29] [y]Rom. 12:18; 2 Cor. 13:11; 1 Thess. 5:13; [ver. 34]; See Rom. 14:19
Chapter 10
1 [z]For ver. 1-12, see Matt. 19:1-9 [a]Luke 9:51; 17:11; John 10:40; [Matt. 4:25]
2 [b]Matt. 5:31 [c]See John 8:6
4 [d]Deut. 24:1-4
5 [e]ch. 16:14; [ch. 3:5; 6:52; Heb. 3:8]
6 [f]ch. 13:19; 2 Pet. 3:4; [Rom. 1:20] [g]Cited from Gen. 1:27; 5:2
7 [h]Eph. 5:31; Cited from Gen. 2:24
8 [i]1 Cor. 6:16; [Mal. 2:15]
9 [j]1 Cor. 7:10
11 [k]See Matt. 5:32
12 [l]1 Cor. 7:11, 13
13 [m]For ver. 13-16, see Matt. 19:13-15; Luke 18:15-17 [n]ver. 48
14 [o]Matt. 18:3 [p][ch. 9:39]
15 [q][John 3:3, 5] [r][Luke 8:13; James 1:21]

Let the Children Come to Me

13 [m]And they were bringing children to
him that he might touch them, and the disciples [n]rebuked them. 14 But when Jesus
saw it, he was indignant and said to them,
[o]"Let the children come to me; [p]do not
hinder them, for to such belongs the kingdom of God. 15 [q]Truly, I say to you, whoever does not [r]receive the kingdom of God
like a child shall not enter it." 16 And [s]he
took them in his arms and blessed them,
[t]laying his hands on them.

The Rich Young Man

17 [u]And as he was setting out on his journey, a man ran up and [v]knelt before him
and asked him, "Good Teacher, what must
I do to [w]inherit eternal life?" 18 And Jesus
said to him, "Why do you call me good?
No one is good except God alone. 19 You
know the commandments: [x]'Do not murder, Do not commit adultery, Do not steal,
Do not bear false witness, Do not defraud,
Honor your father and mother.'" 20 And he
said to him, "Teacher, [y]all these I have kept
from my youth." 21 And Jesus, [z]looking at
him, [a]loved him, and said to him, "You lack

16 [s]ch. 9:36 [t]Rev. 1:17 17 [u]For ver. 17-30, see Matt. 19:16-29; Luke 18:18-30; [Luke 10:25-28] [v]See ch. 1:40 [w][Matt. 19:16]; See Matt. 25:34 19 [x]Rom. 13:9; Cited from Ex. 20:12-16; Deut. 5:16-20; [Matt. 5:21, 27] 20 [y][Phil. 3:6] 21 [z]ver. 27; Luke 22:61; John 1:42; [ch. 3:5] [a][John 11:5; 13:23]

[1] Some manuscripts omit *and hold fast to his wife*

9:50 Have salt in yourselves. The image of salt describes true discipleship. Salt is a preservative. Jesus is telling His disciples to use humility and service to preserve the peace of the church, rather than dividing it through a desire to be great (v. 34).

10:1 region of Judea. The Roman province of Judea included most of central Palestine, with Jerusalem at its center. This journey into Judea begins the process that will lead Jesus to His death (Luke 9:51).

10:2 Is it lawful . . . to divorce. The question is vague, because Deut. 24:1–4 already indicates that the answer depends on the circumstances. Perhaps the Pharisees wanted to draw Jesus into the debate about Herod Antipas and his unlawful wife (6:17 note).

10:6 from the beginning. As usual, Jesus does not argue from "tradition" (7:3–12 notes) but seeks the intention of Scripture and its real requirements (see Matt. 5:20–22, 27, 28, 31, 32). Regarding marriage, Jesus shows that in the time of the new covenant, despite the continuing presence of sin, the conditions of life prior to the Fall will again be realized in an appropriate way (see Eph. 5:22–33).

10:8 one flesh. The creation order is to be maintained. Monogamous marriage is to be received and cherished.

10:11 Whoever divorces. This is a basic commandment about the inviolability of marriage. However, Jesus specifies one valid ground for divorce—marital infidelity (Matt. 5:32; 19:9). Paul seems to add another (1 Cor. 7:12–16).

10:13 children. Lit. "infants" (9:36 note). They were young enough to be brought by their parents and taken by Jesus in His arms.

10:14 do not hinder them. Jesus is expressing the typical Old Testament notion of covenant solidarity. These small children belong in the kingdom, initially because of the faith of their parents, though they must exercise faith personally as soon as they can. Small children model true believers who know they have nothing to bring and everything to receive (v. 15).

10:16 blessed them. To receive God's blessing means to be called by God's name (Gen. 48:16; Num. 6:22–27) and to be included in the blessings of the covenant (Gen. 22:16–18; Deut. 7:13).

10:17 a man. This man had great wealth (v. 22), was a ruler (Luke 18:18), and was young (Matt. 19:22). He had everything and yet lacked the most important thing—eternal life.

what must I do to inherit. The two verbs "do" and "inherit" placed together, the list of moral achievements, and the young man's understanding of goodness (v. 18 note) indicate a religious outlook based on works righteousness.

10:18 Why do you call me good. Jesus' reply does not mean that He does not consider Himself good. He rather wants to show the man that "No one is good except God alone," so that the man may realize that all his works do not make him good, and that he is not capable of earning eternal life.

10:21 You lack one thing. The young man's love of riches (v. 22) and refusal to give them up to follow Jesus shows that he has broken the greatest commandment of all: "You shall love the LORD your God with all your heart and with all your soul and with all your might" (Deut. 6:5; cf. Matt. 22:37). Lacking the total righteousness that God requires, he stands condemned.

one thing: go, [b]sell all that you have and give to the poor, and you will have [c]treasure in heaven; and come, follow me." **22** [d]Disheartened by the saying, he went away sorrowful, for he had great possessions.

23 And Jesus [e]looked around and said to his disciples, [f]"How difficult it will be for those who have wealth to enter [g]the kingdom of God!" **24** And the disciples [h]were amazed at his words. But Jesus said to them again, [i]"Children, [j]how difficult it is[1] to enter [g]the kingdom of God! **25** It is easier for a camel to go through the eye of a needle than for a rich person to enter [g]the kingdom of God." **26** And they were exceedingly astonished, and said to him,[2] "Then who can be saved?" **27** Jesus [k]looked at them and said, [l]"With man it is impossible, but not with God. For all things are possible with God." **28** Peter began to say to him, "See, [m]we have left everything and followed you." **29** Jesus said, "Truly, I say to you, [n]there is no one who has left house or brothers or sisters or mother or father or children or lands, for my sake and [o]for the gospel, **30** who will not receive a hundredfold [p]now in this time, houses and brothers and sisters and mothers and children and lands, [q]with persecutions, and in [r]the age to come eternal life. **31** But [s]many who are first will be last, and the last first."

Jesus Foretells His Death a Third Time

32 [t]And they were on the road, going up to Jerusalem, and [u]Jesus was walking ahead of them. And [v]they were amazed, and those who followed were afraid. And taking the twelve again, he began to tell them what was to happen to him, **33** saying, "See, [w]we are going up to Jerusalem, and the Son of Man will be delivered over to the chief priests and the scribes, and they will [x]condemn him to death and [y]deliver him over to the Gentiles. **34** And they will [z]mock him and [a]spit on him, and flog him and kill him. And [b]after three days he will rise."

The Request of James and John

35 [c]And James and John, [d]the sons of Zebedee, came up to him and said to him, "Teacher, we want you to do for us [e]whatever we ask of you." **36** And he said to them, [f]"What do you want me to do for you?" **37** And they said to him, "Grant us [g]to sit, one at your right hand and one at your left, [h]in your glory." **38** Jesus said to them, [i]"You do not know what you are asking. Are you able [j]to drink the cup that I drink, or [k]to be baptized with the baptism with which I am baptized?" **39** And they said to him, "We are able." And Jesus said to them, [l]"The cup that I drink [m]you will drink, and with the baptism with which I am baptized, [n]you will be baptized, **40** but to sit at my right hand or at my left is not mine to grant, [o]but it is for those for whom it has been [p]prepared."

20 [b]Luke 12:33; [Luke 16:9; 19:8; Acts 2:45; 4:34, 35; 1 Tim. 6:18, 19] [c]Matt. 6:19, 20
22 [d][Ezek. 33:31]
23 [e]See ch. 3:5 [f][1 Cor. 1:26]; See Matt. 13:22 [g]See Matt. 12:28
24 [h]ver. 32 [i]ch. 2:5 (Gk.); [John13:33; 21:5] [j]Job 31:24; Ps. 49:6; 52:7; Prov. 11:28; 1 Tim. 6:17 [g][See ver. 23 above]
25 [g][See ver. 23 above]
27 [k]ver. 23 [l]ch. 14:36; Gen. 18:14; Job 42:2; Jer. 32:17, 27; Zech. 8:6; Luke 1:37
28 [m]ch. 1:18, 20; Matt. 4:20, 22
29 [n][Luke 14:26] [o]See ch. 8:35
30 [p][Matt. 6:33] [q]2 Cor. 12:10; 2 Thess. 1:4; 2 Tim. 3:11, 12; [John 15:20; Acts 14:22] [r]Matt. 12:32; Eph. 1:21; [Luke 20:35]
31 [s]See Matt. 19:30
32 [t]For ver. 32-34, see Matt. 20:17-19; Luke 18:31-33 [u]Luke 9:51; 19:28 [v]ver. 24
33 [w]See Matt. 16:21 [x]Matt. 26:66; John 19:7 [y]Matt. 27:2; John 18:30, 31; Acts 3:13; [Acts 2:23; 4:27; 21:11]
34 [z]Matt. 27:26-31 [a]ch. 14:65; 15:19; See Matt. 26:67 [b]See ch. 8:31
35 [c]For ver. 35-45, see Matt. 20:20-28 [d]ch. 1:19 [e][Matt. 18:19]
36 [f]ver. 51
37 [g][Matt. 19:28] [h][Luke 9:26]
38 [i][Luke 9:33; 23:34] [j]ch. 14:36; Matt. 26:29, 42; Luke 22:42; John 18:11; [Isai. 51:22] [k]Luke 12:50
39 [l][Rom. 8:17; Phil. 3:10] [m]Acts 12:2; Rev. 1:9 [n][Rom. 6:3]
40 [o][Matt. 19:11] [p]Matt. 25:34

[1] Some manuscripts add *for those who trust in riches* [2] Some manuscripts *to one another*

10:23 How difficult it will be for those who have wealth. The difficulty is not because riches in themselves are evil and disqualify those who possess them, but because the rich are tempted to depend upon their riches and may be unable to admit their need of God.

10:25 camel . . . eye of a needle. An excellent example of Jesus' colorful, proverbial language, here expressing the idea of impossibility (v. 27). The suggestion that there was a small gate, called "the needle's eye," through which camels could barely pass is unsupported and trivializes Jesus' image.

10:26 Then who can be saved. The disciples understood Jesus' meaning. No one can be saved by good works.

10:27 With man it is impossible. Salvation is from the Lord, through sovereign divine initiative (Ps. 3:8; 68:19, 20), not by human effort.

10:28 we have left everything. While salvation cannot be earned, it imposes this radical condition.

10:30 a hundredfold. The phrase "this time" with its counterpart "the age to come" reflects the teaching of the rabbis about the two-tiered present evil age and the future age of the Messiah. The resurrection of Jesus significantly altered that view. In the period between the resurrection of Jesus and that of all believers the "two ages" exist side by side. The old is passing away, and the new is present, but not in its fullness. Hence there can be both a "hundredfold" blessing and persecution.

10:33 Son of Man will be delivered. See note 8:31.

Gentiles. The new element in this third prediction of the Passion is the mention of the Gentiles (that is, the Romans). The scourging and mockery He predicted are details of His death prophesied in the Scriptures (Ps. 22), and were normal Roman practice.

10:35 James and John. See 1:19 and 3:17. In Matt. 20:20 it is their mother who makes the request, so apparently the whole family was involved.

10:37 sit . . . at your right. Jesus' teaching on greatness (9:34, 35 and notes) clearly had yet to change their attitudes.

10:38 drink the cup. An Old Testament symbol for suffering and wrath (Ps. 75:8; Is. 51:17–22; Jer. 25:15; Ezek. 23:31–34).

baptism. Here the word is a metaphor for the experience of death-threatening judgment, with the hope of ultimate deliverance (Rom. 6:3–7; 1 Cor. 10:2; Col. 2:11–13).

10:40 not mine to grant. Jesus recognizes areas where only the Father has authority (13:32). Such places are decided in accordance with the principle that Jesus gives concerning service (9:35).

41 And when the ten heard it, they began to
be indignant at James and John. 42 [q]And
Jesus called them to him and said to them,
"You know that those who are considered
rulers of the Gentiles [r]lord it over them,
and their great ones exercise authority over
them. 43 But [s]it shall not be so among you.
But whoever would be great among you
must be your servant,[1] 44 and whoever
would be first among you must be [t]slave[2]
of all. 45 For even the Son of Man came not
to be served but [u]to serve, and [v]to give his
life as a ransom for [w]many."

Jesus Heals Blind Bartimaeus

46 [x]And they came to Jericho. And [y]as he
was leaving Jericho with his disciples and a
great crowd, Bartimaeus, [z]a blind beggar,
the son of Timaeus, was sitting by the roadside. 47 And when he heard that it was
[a]Jesus of Nazareth, he began to cry out and
say, "Jesus, Son of David, have mercy on
me!" 48 And many [b]rebuked him, telling
him to be silent. But he cried out all the
more, "Son of David, have mercy on me!"
49 And Jesus stopped and said, "Call him."
And they called the blind man, saying to
him, [c]"Take heart. Get up; he is calling
you." 50 And throwing off his [d]cloak, he
sprang up and came to Jesus. 51 And Jesus
said to him, [e]"What do you want me to do
for you?" And the blind man said to him,
[f]"Rabbi, let me recover my sight." 52 And

42 [q]For ver. 42-45, [ch. 9:33-36; Luke 22:25-27] [r]1 Pet. 5:3
43 [s]Matt. 23:11; [Luke 9:48]
44 [t]2 Cor. 4:5
45 [u]John 13:4, 13-15; Phil. 2:7; [2 Cor. 8:9] [v]Isai. 53:10; Dan. 9:26; John 10:15; 11:51, 52; Rom. 4:25; Gal. 1:4; 2:20; 1 Tim. 2:6; Tit. 2:14; 1 Pet. 1:18, 19 [w]ch. 14:24; Isai. 53:11, 12; Heb. 2:10; 9:28; [Rom. 5:15; Rev. 5:9]
46 [x]For ver. 46-52, see Matt. 20:29-34; Luke 18:35-43 [y][Luke 18:35; 19:1] [z]John 9:1, 8
47 [a]ch. 1:24
48 [b]Matt. 19:13
49 [c]John 16:33
50 [d]ch. 13:16 (Gk.)
51 [e]ver. 36 [f]John 20:16
52 [g]ch. 5:34; Matt. 9:22; Luke 7:50; 8:48; 17:19 [h]ch. 5:23, 28; 6:56

Jesus said to him, "Go your way; [g]your
faith has [h]made you well." And immediately he recovered his sight and followed
him on the way.

The Triumphal Entry

11 [i]Now when they drew near to
Jerusalem, to [j]Bethphage and Bethany, at [k]the Mount of Olives, Jesus[3] sent
[l]two of his disciples 2 and said to them, "Go
into the village in front of you, and immediately as you enter it you will find a colt
tied, [m]on which no one has ever sat. Untie
it and bring it. 3 If anyone says to you, 'Why
are you doing this?' say, 'The Lord has need
of it and will send it back here immediately.'" 4 And they went away and found a colt
tied at a door outside in the street, and they
untied it. 5 And some of those standing
there said to them, "What are you doing,
untying the colt?" 6 And they told them
what Jesus had said, and they let them go.
7 And they brought the colt to Jesus and
threw their cloaks on it, and he sat on it.
8 And many [n]spread their cloaks on the
road, and others spread leafy branches that
they had cut from the fields. 9 And those
who went before and those who followed
were shouting, [o]"Hosanna! [p]Blessed is he

Chapter 11 1 [i]For ver. 1-10, see Matt. 21:1-9; Luke 19:29-38; John 12:12-15; [Zech. 9:9] [j]Matt. 21:17; Luke 24:50; John 11:18 [k]Zech. 14:4; Matt. 24:3; 26:30; John 8:1; [Acts 1:12] [l][ch. 14:13] 2 [m][Luke 23:53] 8 [n]2 Kin. 9:13 9 [o]See Ps. 118:25 (Heb.) [p]Matt. 23:39; Cited from Ps. 118:26

1 Greek *diakonos* 2 Greek *bondservant* (*doulos*) 3 Greek *he*

10:41 indignant. Perhaps the others were indignant, not because John and James failed to put Jesus' teaching into practice (9:35 note), but because they wanted the same high places. Jesus desires to eliminate in the Twelve, and by extension in all His disciples, such notions of power and authority.

10:45 the Son of Man came not to be served. What finally breaks the stony hearts of Jesus' disciples is the example that He Himself gives. Jesus, the Son of Man who will inherit "dominion and glory and a kingdom" (Dan. 7:14), has come as a servant, fulfilling the prophecy of Is. 52:13–53:12.

ransom. A price paid to free the guilty from a sentence (Ex. 21:30), or debtors from their debt (Ex. 30:12; cf. Is. 53:10).

many. See Is. 53:12. In the Qumran writings (the Dead Sea Scrolls) this is a term for all the members of the community.

10:46 Jericho. Fifteen miles northeast of Jerusalem and 800 feet below sea level. See note Luke 18:35.

son of Timaeus. The translation shows that Mark was writing for an audience unfamiliar with Semitic languages (5:31 note).

10:47 Son of David. A popular messianic title (11:10; 12:35) drawn from the Old Testament (Is. 11:1–3; Jer. 23:5, 6; Ezek. 34:23, 24).

10:49 Jesus stopped. One of the marks of Jesus' public ministry is the time He gives to suffering individuals in the midst of crowds (5:30–34).

11:1 when they drew near to Jerusalem. The journey (10:1 note) reaches its destination, and what is called Passion Week begins. Jesus' decision to come up to Jerusalem is clearly determined by His understanding of the Old Testament and His prophecies concerning His own death (8:31 note).

Bethphage. Hebrew for "house of unripe figs," a small village east of Jerusalem.

Bethany. Hebrew for "house of sadness," two or three miles east of Jerusalem.

Mount of Olives. East of Jerusalem and rising about two hundred feet higher than the temple mount, this high hill commands a spectacular view of Jerusalem and especially of the temple. In Jesus' time it was covered with olive trees, but was stripped of them by the Romans during the siege of Jerusalem in A.D. 70.

11:2 you will find. This text witnesses to the supernatural knowledge of Jesus (cf. John 1:48–50).

colt. A young donkey (Matt. 21:2; John 12:15). The Old Testament prophesied Jesus' actions (Zech. 9:9), which in this case identify Him clearly as the Messiah. Zechariah prophesied the coming of a righteous and gentle King to bring salvation.

11:8 cloaks on the road. A recognition of Jesus' royal dignity.

branches. See Ps. 118:27. This psalm celebrates the procession of the royal Messiah.

11:9 Hosanna. A Greek transliteration of the Aramaic words for "Save us . . . O LORD" (Ps. 118:25). The crowd is shouting phrases from that psalm.

who comes in the name of the Lord!
10 Blessed is [q]the coming [r]kingdom of [s]our
father [r]David! [o]Hosanna [t]in the highest!"
11 [u]And he entered Jerusalem and went
into the temple. And when he had looked
around at everything, as it was already late,
[v]he went out to Bethany with the twelve.

Jesus Curses the Fig Tree

12 [w]On the following day, when they
came from Bethany, [x]he was hungry.
13 [y]And seeing in the distance a fig tree in
leaf, he went to see if he could find anything on it. When he came to it, he found
nothing but leaves, for [z]it was not the season for figs. 14 And he said to it, "May no
one ever eat fruit from you again." And his
disciples heard it.

Jesus Cleanses the Temple

15 [a]And they came to Jerusalem. And he
entered the temple and began to drive out
those who sold and those who bought in
the temple, and he overturned the tables of
[b]the money-changers and the seats of those
who sold [c]pigeons. 16 And he would not
allow anyone to carry anything through the
temple. 17 And he was teaching them and
saying to them, "Is it not written, [d]'My
house shall be called a house of prayer for
all the nations'? But [e]you have made it a
den of robbers." 18 And the chief priests
and the scribes heard it and [f]were seeking
a way to destroy him, for they feared him,
because [g]all the crowd was astonished at
his teaching. 19 [h]And when evening came
they[1] went out of the city.

The Lesson from the Withered Fig Tree

20 [i]As they passed by in the morning, they
saw the fig tree withered away to its roots.
21 And Peter remembered and said to him,
[j]"Rabbi, look! The fig tree that you cursed
has withered." 22 And Jesus answered them,
"Have [k]faith in God. 23 [l]Truly, I say to you,
whoever says to this mountain, [m]'Be taken
up and thrown into the sea,' and does not
[n]doubt in his heart, but [o]believes that what
he says will come to pass, it will be done
for him. 24 Therefore I tell you, [p]whatever
you ask in prayer, [o]believe that you [q]have
received[2] it, and it will be yours. 25 And
whenever [r]you stand praying, [s]forgive, [t]if
you have anything against anyone, so that
[u]your Father also who is in heaven may forgive you your trespasses."[3]

The Authority of Jesus Challenged

27 [v]And they came again to Jerusalem.
And as he was walking in the temple, the
chief priests and the scribes and the elders
came to him, 28 and they said to him, [w]"By
what authority are you doing these things,

10 [q]See Luke 1:32 [r][Ezek. 37:24, 25] [s][Acts 2:29] [o][See ver. 9 above] [t]Luke 2:14; [Ps. 148:1] **11** [u]Matt. 21:10 [v]ver. 19; Matt. 21:17 **12** [w]For ver. 12-14, see Matt. 21:18, 19 [x]Matt. 4:2 **13** [y][Luke 13:6-9] [z]ch. 13:28 **15** [a]For ver. 15-18, see Matt. 21:12-16; Luke 19:45- 47; [John 2:14-16] [b][Ex. 30:13] [c]Lev. 1:14; 5:7; 12:8; Luke 2:24 **17** [d]Cited from Isai. 56:7 [e]Jer. 7:11 **18** [f]See Matt. 21:46 [g]See Matt. 7:28 **19** [h]Luke 21:37; [ver. 11] **20** [i]For ver. 20-24, see Matt. 21:19-22 **21** [j]See John 1:38 **22** [k]Eph. 3:12; Phil. 3:9 **23** [l]Matt. 17:20 [m][Ps. 46:2; 1 Cor. 13:2; Rev. 8:8] [n]Acts 10:20; Rom. 4:20; 14:23; James 1:6 [o][ch. 16:17; John 14:12] **24** [p]See Matt. 7:7 [o][See ver. 23 above] [q][Isai. 65:24; Matt. 6:8] **25** [r]Matt. 6:5; Luke 18:11 [s]See Matt. 6:14 [t]Col. 3:13; [Matt. 5:23; 6:15] [u]Matt. 7:11 **27** [v]For ver. 27-33, see Matt. 21:23- 27; Luke 20:1-8 **28** [w][Ex. 2:14; John 1:25; Acts 4:7]

[1] Some manuscripts *he* [2] Some manuscripts *are receiving* [3] Some manuscripts add verse 26: *But if you do not forgive, neither will your Father who is in heaven forgive your trespasses*

11:11 he went out to Bethany. In Matt. 21:12–22, Jesus proceeds to cleanse the temple upon His arrival and curses the fig tree the next day. In Mark, Jesus returns to Bethany for the night; in the morning He curses the fig tree and then cleanses the temple. Probably Matthew treats the material topically (no specific time reference for the cleansing is given in Matt. 21:12), while Mark, who places stories within stories (5:21–43; 6:7–30), treats it chronologically.

11:13 not the season for figs. See note Matt. 21:18–20.

11:14 May no one ever eat fruit from you again. Jesus curses this tree for making a display but having no fruit, just as He will judge the temple (vv. 15–17) and predict its destruction (13:2). This would indicate that the rebuilding of the temple in Jerusalem will no longer be a goal of redemptive history. Jeremiah used figs as a symbol of judgment on Jerusalem (Jer. 24).

11:15 temple. That is, the Gentile court, the outermost court in the complex of structures surrounding the temple proper. It was the only area where Gentiles were allowed (cf. v. 17).

began to drive out. John 2:12–22 describes the temple cleansing at the beginning of Jesus' ministry, while all three Synoptic Gospels report one occurring at the end. It is likely that Jesus cleansed the temple twice. John's account is carefully dated (John 2:20; Mark 1:9 note), and the accounts are by no means identical. In John, Jesus comes with His disciples, and His actions recall to their minds Ps. 69:9. In the Synoptic accounts, Jesus comes in triumphal messianic glory and justifies His actions by quoting Is. 56:7 and Jer. 7:11. Jesus was no doubt aware that the prophet Jeremiah twice cursed the temple (Jer. 7:1–14; 26:2–6).

money-changers. This service was necessary because the temple tax and offerings had to be paid in the local currency, but it had become so corrupt that Jesus described the scene as "a den of robbers" (v. 17; Luke 19:45, 46 note). Jesus is also judging the Sadducean high-priestly families who were not attuned to the character of the Father whose house it was (cf. 12:18–27).

11:16 not allow anyone to carry anything. Not only had the court become a market, but it was being used as a shortcut by merchants of all kinds. Mark sees in Jesus' gesture a defense of Gentile rights and perhaps an indication of the future mission to the Gentiles.

11:18 chief priests and the scribes. Jesus acted under the eyes of those He knew would kill Him (8:31).

astonished at His teaching. See note 1:22.

11:20 withered away to its roots. This phrase indicates complete destruction (v. 14 note).

11:25 anything against anyone. See Matt. 5:23, 24.

11:26 This verse is lacking in certain ancient manuscripts (see text note). A similar saying is found in Matt. 6:14, 15.

11:27 chief priests. See note 11:18.

11:28 By what authority. The Jerusalem "authorities" seek to expose Jesus as an upstart, with no official status to act within the temple.

or who gave you this authority to do
them?" 29 Jesus said to them, "I will ask you
one question; answer me, and I will tell
you by what authority I do these things.
30 Was the baptism of John [x]from heaven or
from man? Answer me." 31 And they discussed it with one another, saying, "If we
say, 'From heaven,' he will say, [y]'Why then
did you not believe him?' 32 But shall we
say, 'From man'?"—[z]they were afraid of
the people, for they all held that John really
was [a]a prophet. 33 So they answered Jesus,
"We do not know." And Jesus said to
them, "Neither will I tell you by what
authority I do these things."

The Parable of the Tenants

12 [b]And he began to speak to them in
parables. "A man planted [c]a vineyard [d]and put a fence around it and dug a
pit for the winepress and built a tower, and
[e]leased it to tenants and [f]went into another
country. 2 When the season came, he sent a
servant[1] to the tenants to get from them
some of the fruit of the vineyard. 3 [g]And
they took him and beat him and sent him
away empty-handed. 4 [g]Again [g]he sent to
them another servant, and [h]they struck
him on the head and [i]treated him shamefully. 5 [j]And he sent another, and him they
killed. And so with many others: some they
beat, and some they killed. 6 He had still
one other, [k]a beloved son. [l]Finally he sent
him to them, saying, 'They will respect my
son.' 7 But those tenants said to one another,
[m]'This is the heir. Come, [n]let us kill him,
and the inheritance will be ours.' 8 And
they took him and killed him and [o]threw
him out of the vineyard. 9 What will the
owner of the vineyard do? [p]He will [q]come
and destroy the tenants and [r]give the vineyard to others. 10 [s]Have you not read [t]this
Scripture:

> [u]"'The stone that the builders rejected
> has become the cornerstone;[2]
> 11 this was the Lord's doing,
> and it is marvelous in our eyes'?"

12 And [v]they were seeking to arrest him
[w]but feared the people, for they perceived
that he had told the parable against them.
So they [x]left him and went away.

Paying Taxes to Caesar

13 [y]And they sent to him some of [z]the
Pharisees and some of [z]the Herodians, to
[a]trap him in his talk. 14 And they came and
said to him, "Teacher, [b]we know that you
are true and do not care about anyone's
opinion. For [c]you are not swayed by appearances,[3] but truly teach [d]the way of
God. Is it lawful to pay [e]taxes to [f]Caesar, or
not? Should we pay them, or should we
not?" 15 But, knowing [g]their hypocrisy, he
said to them, "Why [h]put me to the test?

30 [x]Luke 15:18, 21; John 3:27 **31** [y]Matt. 21:32; Luke 7:30 **32** [z]Matt. 14:5; 21:46 [a][John 5:35]; See Matt. 11:9 **Chapter 12** **1** [b]For ver. 1-12, see Matt. 21:33-46; Luke 20:9-19 [c]Ps. 80:8; Isai. 5:1; Matt. 21:28 [d]Isai. 5:2 [e]S. of S. 8:11, 12 [f]ch. 13:34; Matt. 25:14, 15 **3** [g]Matt. 5:12; 22:6; 23:34, 37; [2 Chr. 24:19; 36:15, 16; Neh. 9:26; Jer. 37:15; 38:6 Acts 7:52; 2 Cor. 11:24-26; 1 Thess. 2:15; Heb. 11:36, 37] **4** [g][See ver. 3 above] [h]Matt. 22:4 [i][Acts 14:19] **5** [j]Acts 5:41 (Gk.) **6** [k]See Matt. 3:17 [l][Heb. 1:1] **7** [m]Heb. 1:2; [John 1:11; Rom. 8:17] [n][1 Kin. 21:19] **8** [o]Heb. 13:12 **9** [p][Luke 19:27] [q][Matt. 24:50; 25:19] [r]Matt. 21:43; Acts 13:46; 18:6; 28:28; [Matt. 8:11, 12] **10** [s]See Matt. 21:16 [t]Luke 4:21; Acts 8:35 [u]Acts 4:11; 1 Pet. 2:7; Cited from Ps. 118:22, 23 **12** [v]ch. 11:18; Luke 19:47, 48; John 7:25, 30, 44; [Matt. 26:4] [w]ch. 11:32 [x]Matt. 22:22 **13** [y]For ver. 13-27, see Matt. 22:15- 32; Luke 20:20-38 [z]ch. 3:6; [ch. 8:15] [a]Luke 11:54 **14** [b][John 3:2] [c]See Acts 10:34 [d]Acts 18:25, 26; [Acts 13:10] [e]Matt. 17:25 [f]Luke 2:1; 3:1 **15** [g]Matt. 23:28; Luke 12:1 [h]See John 8:6

[1] Greek *bondservant*; also verse 4 [2] Greek *the head of the corner*
[3] Greek *you do not look at people's faces*

11:30 from heaven. Jesus' answer silences the officeholders and professional theologians, for it undercuts the claims of such "official" authority to be absolute. Prophetic authority cannot, by definition, have a human source (Gal. 1:11, 12). It is attested by God and demands submission. With Jesus' answer is an *unspoken* and ultimate question: "Do you recognize and submit to My authority?"

12:1 them. This pronoun apparently refers to the chief priests and scribes since it agrees with "they" in v. 12 (those who look for a way to arrest Him). This parable was also a provocation (11:18 note).

parables. See notes 4:2, 11. Although it is incorrect to seek a special, symbolic meaning for every detail of the parable, the essential point is clear.

vineyard. The parable is based on the "Song of the Vineyard" (Is. 5:1–5), which pictures Israel and her unfaithfulness.

12:2 servant. Often a term for the prophets (Ex. 14:31; 2 Chr. 1:3; Is. 20:3; Amos 3:7), whom Jesus sees as those whom God had sent to call Israel to faithfulness and who often suffered death (Matt. 23:37).

tenants. Those with "official" authority over the people of God, in particular those for whom the parable is told.

12:6 a beloved son. In the three Synoptic Gospels, the theme of Jesus as God's beloved son is rare (Mark 1:11; 9:7; cf. Matt. 16:16), but it is unmistakably present.

12:9 give the vineyard to others. Matt. 21:43 reads, "will be . . . given to a people producing its fruits," suggesting both the community of disciples forming around Jesus (Luke 22:29, 30) and the mission to the Gentiles (Matt. 8:11, 12; Rom. 9:22–26).

12:10 The stone that the builders rejected. Jesus cites Ps. 118:22, 23; that psalm celebrates the victory that God gives to His Messiah, establishing Him on His throne. Such is the faith of Jesus in His Father and in the Scripture, that in face of the death He has just predicted for Himself ("they took him and killed him," v. 8), He can rejoice in the promised victory.

12:13 Pharisees and some of the Herodians. The alliance between the Pharisees and the Herodians re-emerges (3:6). This alliance was possible because both parties accepted the Roman occupation, the former as divine punishment, the latter for political advantage.

12:14 taxes to Caesar. In addition to numerous customs taxes, tolls, and other charges (2:14 note), each Roman province was obliged to pay the imperial tribute. The same sum was exacted from all, rich and poor alike. This tax was very unpopular with the people.

12:15 Why put me to the test. His opponents' question was apparently an attempt to brand Jesus as a political revolutionary.

Bring me [i]a denarius[1] and let me look at
it." **16** And they brought one. And he said to
them, "Whose likeness and inscription is
this?" They said to him, "Caesar's." **17** Jesus
said to them, [j]"Render to Caesar the things
that are Caesar's, and to God the things
that are God's." And they marveled at him.

The Sadducees Ask About the Resurrection

18 And [k]Sadducees came to him, [l]who say
that there is no resurrection. And they
asked him a question, saying, **19** "Teacher,
Moses wrote for us that [m]if a man's brother
dies and leaves a wife, but leaves no child,
the man[2] must take the widow and raise
up offspring for his brother. **20** There were
seven brothers; the first took a wife, and
when he died left no offspring. **21** And the
second took her, and died, leaving no offspring. And the third likewise. **22** And the
seven left no offspring. Last of all the
woman also died. **23** In the resurrection,
when they rise again, whose wife will she
be? For the seven had her as wife."
24 Jesus said to them, "Is this not the reason you are wrong, because [n]you know neither the Scriptures nor [o]the power of God?
25 For when they rise from the dead, they
neither [p]marry nor [p]are given in marriage,
but are like angels in heaven. **26** And as for
the dead being raised, [q]have you not read
in [r]the book of Moses, in [s]the passage
about the bush, how God spoke to him,
saying, [t]'I am the God of Abraham, and the
God of Isaac, and the God of Jacob'? **27** He
is not God of the dead, but of the living.
You are quite wrong."

The Great Commandment

28 [u]And one of the scribes came up and
heard them disputing with one another,
and seeing that he answered them well,
asked him, "Which commandment is the
most important of all?" **29** Jesus answered,
"The most important is, [v]'Hear, O Israel:
The Lord our God, [w]the Lord is one. **30** And
you shall love the Lord your God with all
your heart and with all your soul and with
all your mind and with all your strength.'
31 [x]The second is this: [y]'You shall love your
neighbor as yourself.' There is no other
commandment [z]greater than these." **32** And
the scribe said to him, "You are right,
Teacher. You have truly said that [w]he is
one, and [a]there is no other besides him.
33 And to love him with all the heart and
with all [b]the understanding and with all
the strength, and to love one's neighbor as
oneself, [c]is much more than all [d]whole
burnt offerings and sacrifices." **34** And when
Jesus saw that he answered wisely, he said
to him, "You are not far from the kingdom
of God." [e]And after that no one dared to
ask him any more questions.

15 [i]See Matt. 18:28 **17** [j]Rom. 13:7 **18** [k]Matt. 3:7; 16:1; 22:34; Acts 4:1; 5:17; 26:6 [l]Acts 23:8; [Acts 4:2] **19** [m][Deut. 25:5] **24** [n]John 20:9 [o]1 Cor. 6:14 **25** [p]Matt. 24:38; Luke 17:27 **26** [q]See Matt. 21:16 [r][Luke 3:4; 20:42; Acts 1:20; 7:42] [s]Ex. 3:1-4, 17 [t]Acts 7:32; Cited from Ex. 3:6

28 [u]For ver. 28-34, see Matt. 22:34-40, 46; [Luke 10:25-28] **29** [v]Luke 10:27; Cited from Deut. 6:4, 5 [w]Rom. 3:30; 1 Cor. 8:4, 6; Gal. 3:20; Eph. 4:6; 1 Tim. 1:17; 2:5; James 2:19; 4:12; Jude 25; [Matt. 19:17; 23:9] **31** [x][1 John 4:21] [y]Cited from Lev. 19:18; See Matt. 19:19 [z][Matt. 23:23] **32** [w][See ver. 29 above] [a]Cited from Deut. 4:35 (Gk.)

33 [b]Deut. 4:6; Luke 2:47; Col. 1:9; 2:2 [c]1 Sam. 15:22; Hos. 6:6; Mic. 6:6-8; Matt. 9:13; 12:7 [d]Ps. 40:6; Heb. 10:6, 8 **34** [e]Luke 20:40

1 A *denarius* was a day's wage for a laborer 2 Greek *his brother*

denarius. Numerous currencies were in circulation in Palestine. Jesus asks for the Roman denarius, about a day's wage, bearing on one side a picture of Caesar and on the other a scene glorifying his reign.

12:17 Render to Caesar. Jesus takes the occasion to affirm that Rome's political power is legitimate, as at His trial He declares that it is from God (John 19:11). The early church followed this teaching of Jesus (Rom. 13:1–7; Col. 1:16; 1 Tim. 2:1–6; Titus 3:1, 2; 1 Pet. 2:13–17).

12:18 Sadducees. The high-priestly families at the time of Jesus were members of this group. The Sadducees denied the resurrection, the existence of angels, and rejected the oral tradition of the Pharisees. Their name probably derives from Zadok, David's high priest (2 Sam. 8:17; 1 Chr. 15:11; 29:22) and appointed officer over the Aaronic priestly line (1 Chr. 27:17), who was given the exclusive right to be high priest (Ezek. 40:46; 43:19).

12:19 Moses wrote. The story they tell to Jesus (vv. 19–23) is based on the "kinsman-redeemer" law of Deut. 25:5–10, which provides for a family line to be perpetuated by the nearest of kin in the event of a premature death (Ruth 2:20 note).

12:24 the power of God. Probably refers to the ongoing work of God and His powerful manifestations in the future (including the resurrection) through His Messiah (Luke 22:69; Rom. 1:16; 1 Cor. 1:18, 24).

12:25 neither marry. The final resurrection is the transformation of the physical universe (Rom. 8:21; 1 Cor. 15:52, 53), and the creation mandate of marriage and reproduction (Gen. 1:27, 28; 2:24) will no longer be appropriate.

12:26 the passage about the bush. See Ex. 3:1–6. The God who appears with miraculous power in the theophany of the burning bush is the Lord not of "the dead," but of the "living," those united to Him in an eternal covenant of grace. The teaching about resurrection, Jesus implies, is not limited to certain Old Testament proof texts (e.g., Job 19:25–27; Ps. 16:9–11; 17:15; 73:24–26; Is. 26:19; 53:11; Ezek. 37:1–14; Dan. 12:2; Hos. 6:2; 13:14), but is grounded in the Person of the living and life-giving God.

12:27 You are quite wrong. This strong phrase recalls Jesus' damning indictment of those whose father is not God but the devil (John 8:42–47).

12:29 Hear, O Israel. Again the debate is about Scripture. Jesus cites Deut. 6:4, known as the "Shema" (from the Hebrew for "hear"), the central confession of Israel's monotheistic faith.

12:31 The second. Jesus joins Lev. 19:18 to Deut. 6:4, 5, a text that James calls "the royal law" (James 2:8).

12:33 burnt offerings. The scribe approves Jesus' answer and adds a scriptural proof of his own (1 Sam. 15:22; Hos. 6:6).

12:34 not far from the kingdom. Compare the rich young ruler of 10:21 ("You lack one thing") and Nicodemus (John 3:1–21). In each case there is a need for new birth into eternal life (which is entering into the kingdom of God), something made possible by the death and resurrection of the Son of Man (John 3:3, 14, 15).

Whose Son Is the Christ?

35 [f]And as [g]Jesus taught in the temple, he
said, "How can the scribes say that [h]the
Christ is the son of David? 36 David himself,
[i]in the Holy Spirit, declared,

[j]"'The Lord said to my Lord,
Sit at my right hand,
until I put your enemies [k]under
your feet.'

37 David himself calls him Lord. So [l]how is
he his son?" And the great throng [m]heard
him gladly.

Beware of the Scribes

38 [n]And in his teaching he said, "Beware
of the scribes, who like to walk around in
long robes and like greetings in the marketplaces 39 and have the best seats in the
synagogues and [o]the places of honor at
feasts, 40 [p]who devour widows' houses and
[q]for a pretense make long prayers. They
will receive the greater condemnation."

The Widow's Offering

41 [r]And he sat down opposite [s]the treasury and watched the people [t]putting
money into the offering box. Many rich
people put in large sums. 42 And a poor
widow came and put in two [u]small copper
coins, which make a penny.[1] 43 And he

35 [f]For ver. 35-37, see Matt. 22:41-45; Luke 20:41-44 [g]See Matt. 26:55 [h]See Matt. 1:1, 17
36 [i][Luke 10:21; 1 Cor. 12:3] [j]Acts 2:34, 35; Heb. 1:13; Cited from Ps. 110:1; [1 Cor. 15:25; Heb. 10:13] [k][Acts 7:49]
37 [l][Rom. 1:3, 4] [m]ch. 6:20
38 [n]For ver. 38, 39, see Matt. 23:1, 2, 5-7; Luke 20:45, 46; [Luke 11:43]
39 [o]Luke 14:7, 8
40 [p][Luke 11:39; 16:14] [q][Matt. 6:5, 7]
41 [r]For ver. 41-44, see Luke 21:1-4 [s]Matt. 27:6; John 8:20 [t]2 Kin. 12:9
42 [u]Luke 12:59
43 [v][2 Cor. 8:2, 12]
44 [w]Phil. 4:11 [x]Luke 8:43

called his disciples to him and said to them,
"Truly, I say to you, [v]this poor widow has
put in more than all those who are contributing to the offering box. 44 For they all
contributed out of their abundance, but she
out of her [w]poverty has put in everything
she had, all [x]she had to live on."

Jesus Foretells Destruction of the Temple

13 [y]And as he came out of the temple,
one of his disciples said to him,
"Look, Teacher, what wonderful stones
and what wonderful buildings!" 2 And Jesus
said to him, "Do you see these great buildings? [z]There will not be left here one stone
upon another that will not be thrown down."

Signs of the Close of the Age

3 And as he sat on [a]the Mount of Olives
opposite the temple, [b]Peter and James and
John and [c]Andrew asked him [d]privately,
4 "Tell us, [e]when will these things be, and
what will be the sign when all these things
are about to be accomplished?" 5 And Jesus
began to say to them, [f]"See that no one
leads you astray. 6 [g]Many will come in my

Chapter 13 **1** [y]For ver. 1-37, see Matt. 24:1-51; Luke 21:5-36 **2** [z]Luke 19:44 **3** [a]See Matt. 21:1 [b]Matt. 17:1 [c]ch. 1:16, 29 [d][ch. 4:34] **4** [e][Acts 1:6, 7] **5** [f]ver. 9, 23, 33; Jer. 29:8; Eph. 5:6; Col. 2:8; 1 Thess. 2:3; 1 John 3:7 **6** [g]ver. 22; Jer. 14:14; 1 John 2:18

[1] Greek *two lepta,* which make a *kodrantes*; a *kodrantes* (Latin *quadrans*) was a Roman copper coin worth about 1/64 of a *denarius* (which was a day's wage for a laborer)

12:35 temple. See note 11:15. In addition to the Gentile court, there was also the women's court, and the court of Israel that was reserved for Jewish men.

12:36 David himself. Jesus' interpretation hangs on the Davidic authorship of this psalm.

in the Holy Spirit, declared. Jesus ascribes to David's psalm full divine inspiration, as do His disciples later (Acts 1:16; 4:25).

12:37 David himself calls him Lord. Jesus argues that, while the Messiah is descended from David, His royal dignity and power far surpass those of David, for David addresses this King as "my Lord" (Ps. 110:1). This king is uniquely associated with the LORD (Ps. 110:2). Such clear and faithful interpretation of Scripture is heard "gladly" (cf. Luke 24:32).

12:38 Beware of the scribes. The superficiality of the scribes' messianic doctrine and exegesis brings Jesus to criticize their superficial lifestyle in general. A similar warning is found in 8:15.

12:40 devour widows' houses. It was considered improper for anyone to receive a salary for interpreting the Scriptures. Consequently, they relied upon and sometimes took advantage of the hospitality of the people, among whom widows were especially vulnerable.

long prayers. See Matt. 6:5, 6 for a similar judgment of ostentatious and hypocritical spirituality.

12:41 treasury. The offering boxes were situated in the women's court of the temple, which gave access to all.

12:42 two small copper coins. This coin, the lepton, was the lowest denomination in circulation.

a penny. A Roman coin worth one sixty-fourth of a denarius (the denarius was one day's wage). Mark translates into Greek for Gentile readers (5:41 note).

13:1–37 This chapter is known as the "Little Apocalypse" or the Olivet Discourse. It makes predictions in three areas: the coming destruction of the temple (vv. 1–4); future persecutions (vv. 5–25); and the coming of the Son of Man (vv. 26–37).

13:1 what wonderful stones and what wonderful buildings. Herod the Great began rebuilding the temple in 19 B.C., using marble and gold as decorative materials. The outer court measured five hundred by three hundred yards. It was bordered by walls of massive white stones, some of which were sixteen feet long and three to four feet high. On top of these were magnificent, covered cloisters or walkways with richly carved wooden ceilings.

13:2 one stone. Jerusalem was sacked and the temple burned and destroyed in A.D. 70 by Titus, the Roman general (later emperor). The Arch of Titus commemorating his victory still stands in Rome.

13:3 Peter and James and John and Andrew asked him privately. Mark informs us that this teaching is part of the special instruction given to the Twelve (4:10, 11; 8:29).

13:4 when will these things be. The disciples' question has in view the predicted destruction of the temple. Jesus' reply seems to include both this particular event and the time leading to the coming of the Son of Man (v. 26; cf. Matt. 24:3). The events surrounding the destruction of the temple seem to anticipate and typify those associated with the Second Coming.

13:6 Many will come. In A.D. 130, Bar Kochba, the leader of a Jewish rebellion against the Romans, claimed to be and was accepted by his followers as the messiah, and the list has gone on since then.

name, saying, [h]'I am he!' and they will lead
many astray. 7 And when you hear of wars
and rumors of wars, [i]do not be alarmed.
This [j]must take place, but the end is not
yet. 8 For [k]nation will rise against nation,
and [l]kingdom against kingdom. There will
be [m]earthquakes in various places; there
will be [n]famines. These are but the beginning of the birth pains.
9 [o]"But [p]be on your guard. For they will
deliver you over to councils, and you will
be beaten [q]in synagogues, and you will stand
before [r]governors and [s]kings for my sake,
[t]to bear witness before them. 10 And the
gospel must first be proclaimed [u]to all
nations. 11 And when they bring you to trial
and deliver you over, [v]do not be anxious
beforehand what you are to say, but say
[w]whatever is given you in that hour, [x]for it
is not you who speak, but the Holy Spirit.
12 [y]And brother will deliver brother over to
death, and the father his child, and children will rise against parents and have
them put to death. 13 [z]And you will be
hated by all for my name's sake. [a]But the
one who endures to the end will be saved.

The Abomination of Desolation

14 "But when you see [b]the abomination of
desolation standing where it ought not to
be ([c]let the reader understand), then let
those who are in Judea flee to the mountains. 15 [d]Let the one who is on [e]the housetop not go down, nor enter his house, to
take anything out, 16 and let the one who is
in the field not turn back to take his cloak.
17 And [f]alas for women who are pregnant
and for those who are nursing infants in
those days! 18 Pray that it may not happen
in winter. 19 For in those days there will be
[g]such [h]tribulation as has not been [i]from
the beginning of the creation that [j]God
created until now, and never will be. 20 And
if the Lord had not cut short the days, no
human being would be saved. But for [k]the
sake of the elect, whom [l]he chose, he
shortened the days. 21 And [m]then if anyone
says to you, 'Look, here is the Christ!' or
'Look, there he is!' do not believe it.
22 [n]False christs and false prophets will arise
and [o]perform signs and wonders, [p]to lead
astray, if possible, [q]the elect. 23 But [r]be on
guard; [s]I have told you all things beforehand.

6 [h]See John 8:24 **7** [i]2 Thess. 2:2 [j]Rev. 1:1 **8** [k]2 Chr. 15:6; [Rev. 6:4] [l]Isai. 19:2 [m]Rev. 6:12 [n]Acts 11:28; Rev. 6:8 **9** [o]For ver. 9, 11-13, [Matt. 10:17-22; Luke 12:11, 12] [p]ver. 5; 2 John 8 [q]See Matt. 23:34 [r]Acts 17:6; 18:12; 24:1; 25:6 [s][Acts 27:24; 2 Tim. 4:16] [t]See Matt. 8:4 **10** [u]Matt. 28:19; Rom. 10:18; Col. 1:6, 23; [ch. 14:9] **11** [v]See Matt. 6:25 [w]Deut. 18:18; [Num. 23:5]; See Ex. 4:12 [x]Acts 4:8; 6:10; 13:9; 1 Cor. 15:10; 2 Cor. 13:3; [1 Thess. 2:13; Heb. 1:1] **12** [y]Matt. 10:35, 36 **13** [z]John 15:18-21; [Luke 6:22]

[a][Dan. 12:12, 13; James 5:11; Rev. 2:10]; See Heb. 3:6 **14** [b]Dan. 9:27; 11:31; 12:11 [c][Dan. 9:23, 25; Rev. 1:3] **15** [d]Luke 17:31 [e]See Luke 5:19 **17** [f]Luke 23:29 **19** [g]ver. 24; Dan. 12:1; [Rev. 7:14] [h]Rev. 16:18 [i]See ch. 10:6; [Deut. 4:32] [j]Gen. 1:1 **20** [k]ver. 22, 27; Isai. 65:8, 9; Luke 18:7; [Matt. 22:14] [l]John 13:18; 15:19; Eph. 1:4 **21** [m]Luke 17:23; [ver. 6] **22** [n][1 John 2:18] [o]Deut. 13:1-3; 2 Thess. 2:9-11; Rev. 13:13, 14; 16:14; 19:20; [Acts 8:9] [p]ver. 6 [q]ver. 20, 27 **23** [r]ver. 5 [s]John 13:19; 14:29;

I am he. This phrase is also the name of God (Ex. 3:14) and the title chosen by Jesus (John 8:28, 58).

13:7 the end. According to the parallel text (Matt. 24:3), "the end" is "the close of the age."

13:8 birth pains. The Jews expected a time of suffering before the coming of the Messiah and described it in this way, as does Paul in Rom. 8:22.

13:9 councils. Synagogue councils had the right to order floggings, limited to forty strokes (Deut. 25:1–3). The apostles suffered imprisonments and floggings (Acts 4:21; 5:18, 40; 2 Cor. 6:9; 11:23, 24).

13:10 proclaimed to all nations. The time between the resurrection of Christ and His Second Coming is not simply a time of suffering and persecution, but a time of grace and of evangelism throughout the earth in fulfillment of the prophecy of Is. 49:6.

13:11 what you are to say. This is a promise of special assistance in time of need, rather than a reference to the ministry of the Spirit among the Twelve in establishing their proclamation of Jesus (John 14:25, 26; 15:26, 27; 16:12–15).

13:13 endures to the end. See note on v. 7. This statement may also mean the end of each person's life. Such perseverance is often associated with suffering (Rom. 8:18–25; 12:12; Heb. 10:32; 12:2; 1 Pet. 2:20).

will be saved. Such steadfastness does not merit salvation but is the proof that true salvation, in one sense, has already taken place (Rom. 8:24).

13:14 the abomination of desolation. Dan. 11:31 predicts the coming of the king of the North who will desecrate the temple. That prediction was first fulfilled in 168 B.C. when Antiochus Epiphanes set up a pagan altar and sacrificed a pig in the Most Holy Place. In A.D. 70 the Old Testament text was definitively fulfilled when Titus, the Roman general (later emperor), sacked the temple.

let the reader understand. This phrase could either be an aside by Mark (indicating that he knew the destruction of the temple had already occurred), or Jesus' own wish that His hearers, as readers of the Old Testament, would realize that He was citing Dan. 9:25–27 and 11:31 (cf. 2:25; 12:10, 26).

flee to the mountains. When the Romans on their way to Jerusalem in A.D. 69 sacked Qumran, the members of their community hid their manuscripts in caves high up in the mountains overlooking the Dead Sea. Eusebius, the fourth-century church historian, states that the Christians left Jerusalem at that time and founded the church at Pella, east of the Jordan and forty to fifty miles north of Jerusalem.

13:19 tribulation as has not been. The Roman historian Tacitus and the Jewish historian Josephus describe the destruction of the temple as a catastrophe of supernatural dimensions, with armies appearing in the sky and a supernatural voice. According to Josephus the suffering was unparalleled.

13:20 cut short. This may refer to the limited period surrounding the destruction of the temple, or to a similar period before the Second Coming, or to both (v. 4 note).

the sake of the elect. The people of God (vv. 22, 27).

13:21 Look, here is the Christ. See note on v. 6.

13:22 signs and wonders. Jesus associates these with messianic manifestations, even though He recognizes such manifestations to be fraudulent.

The Coming of the Son of Man

24 “But in those days, after [t]that tribulation, [u]the sun will be darkened, and the
moon will not give its light, 25 and [v]the stars
will be falling from heaven, and the powers
in the heavens will be shaken. 26 And then
they will see [w]the Son of Man coming in
clouds [x]with great power and glory. 27 And
then [y]he will send out the angels and
[z]gather [a]his elect from [b]the four winds,
from [c]the ends of the earth [d]to the ends of
heaven.

The Lesson of the Fig Tree

28 “From the fig tree learn its lesson: as
soon as its branch becomes tender and
puts out its leaves, you know that summer
is near. 29 So also, when you see these
things taking place, you know that he is
near, [e]at the very gates. 30 [f]Truly, I say to
you, this generation will not pass away
until all these things take place. 31 [g]Heaven
and earth will pass away, but [h]my words
will not pass away.

No One Knows That Day or Hour

32 “But concerning that day or that hour,
[i]no one knows, not even the angels in
heaven, [j]nor the Son, [k]but only the Father.

[2 Pet. 3:17] **24** [t]ver. 19 [u]Isai. 13:10; 24:23; Ezek. 32:7; Joel 2:10, 31; 3:15; Acts 2:20; [Amos 5:20; 8:9; Zeph. 1:15; Rev. 6:12; 8:12] **25** [v]Rev. 6:13; [Isai. 14:12; 34:4] **26** [w]See Dan. 7:13 [x]ch. 9:1; Matt. 26:64; [Matt. 25:31] **27** [y]Matt. 13:41 [z][Matt. 23:37; 2 Thess. 2:1] [a]ver. 20, 22 [b]Dan. 7:2; Zech. 2:6; Rev. 7:1 [c][Acts 1:8] [d]Deut. 4:32; 30:4 **29** [e]James 5:9; Rev. 3:20 **30** [f]See ch. 9:1 **31** [g]Ps. 102:26; Isai. 51:6; 2 Pet. 3:10; [Matt. 5:18; Heb. 12:27] [h]Ps. 119:89; Isai. 40:8; 1 Pet. 1:23, 25 **32** [i]Matt. 25:13; 1 Thess. 5:1, 2 [j][Phil. 2:6, 7]

33 [l]Be on guard, [m]keep awake.[1] For you do
not know when the time will come. 34 [n]It is
like a man [o]going on a journey, when he
leaves home and puts his servants[2] in
charge, [p]each with his work, and commands [q]the doorkeeper to stay awake.
35 [r]Therefore stay awake—for you do not
know when the master of the house will
come, [s]in the evening, or [s]at midnight, or
[t]when the cock crows,[3] or [u]in the morning— 36 lest [v]he come suddenly and [w]find
you asleep. 37 And what I say to you I say to
all: [r]Stay awake.”

The Plot to Kill Jesus

14 [x]It was now two days before [y]the
Passover and the Feast of Unleavened Bread. And the chief priests and
the scribes [z]were seeking how to arrest him
by stealth and kill him, 2 for they said, “Not
during the feast, [a]lest there be an uproar
from the people.”

[k][Zech. 14:7; Acts 1:7] **33** [l]ver. 5 [m]Eph. 6:18; Heb. 13:17; [ch. 14:38] **34** [n][Matt. 25:14] [o][ch. 12:1; Matt. 21:33] [p][Rom. 12:6-8] [q]Ezek. 44:11; John 10:3; [Luke 12:36] **35** [r]ch. 14:34-38; Matt. 25:13; 26:41; Luke 12:37; 21:36; Acts 20:31; 1 Cor. 16:13; 1 Thess. 5:6; 1 Pet. 5:8 [s]ch. 1:32; Luke 12:38 [t]ch. 14:30, 68, 72; [Judg. 7:19] [u][ch. 6:48; Ex. 14:24] **36** [v][1 Thess. 5:1-6] [w]ch. 14:40 **37** [r][See ver. 35 above]

Chapter 14 **1** [x]For ver. 1, 2, see Matt. 26:2-5; Luke 22:1, 2 [y]See John 6:4 [z]John 11:53; See Matt. 21:46 **2** [a]Matt. 27:24

1 Some manuscripts add *and pray* 2 Greek *bondservants* 3 That is, the third watch of the night, between midnight and 3 A.M.

13:24 in those days. Since this is a technical Old Testament term for the last days (Jer. 3:16; Joel 3:1; Zech. 8:23), Jesus may be starting to speak of the end (cf. v. 7). According to some interpreters, in v. 26 the Second Coming is in view.

the sun will be darkened. Although these phrases often refer to the time of God's cosmic and final judgment (Is. 13:10; 34:4; Joel 2:10, 31), here they may signify another event so momentous that after it the world will never be the same again. Peter interprets Joel 2:31 in Acts 2:16–21 as a prophecy of the outpouring of the Spirit at Pentecost.

13:26 coming in clouds. Clouds sometimes signify divine presence (Ex. 19:9; 24:15–18). If the first coming of the Son of Man is characterized by suffering and humiliation (8:31 note), His future coming at the end will be an open declaration of His divine glory. Such a coming recalls the visible manifestations of God (theophanies) in the Old Testament (Ex. 19:16; 34:5; Ezek. 1:4; 10:3, 4), with the difference that this one will be universal. But vv. 24–27 may point, not to Christ's appearance in universal judgment, but to human realization that Jesus is reigning in the kingdom of God (Dan. 7:13), a realization triggered by the fall of Jerusalem (God's final judgment on the city). Then v. 27 would refer to the worldwide spread of the gospel that followed that event. The "angels" there would be the messengers of the gospel (*angelos* is the Greek word for "messenger," either human or angelic). On this view, Jesus' first reference to the end (His Second Coming) is not until v. 32 ("that day").

13:27 from the four winds. A poetic way of affirming the universality of the new people of God.

13:28 fig tree. There does not seem to be any specific symbolic sense to this "fig tree" (such as the re-emergence of the nation of Israel), especially since the parallel passage (Luke 21:29) adds "and all the trees." Jesus is simply saying that just as there are signs of what is to come in the natural realm, so it is in the spiritual.

13:30 this generation. For the event of the destruction of the temple, the phrase refers to Jesus' own generation.

13:31 Heaven and earth will pass away. Jesus makes His words equal to the words of Scripture, with eternal value (cf. Matt. 5:18). See "The Teaching of Jesus" at Matt. 7:28.

13:32 nor the Son. Jesus was conscious of His unique relationship to the Father as the eternal Son, yet there was a limitation of His knowledge during His incarnation. What the Father had not revealed to Him about the future He did not know. In that sense the man Jesus (the Son with regard to His human nature) was not omniscient.

13:35 in the evening. See 6:48 note.

14:1 It was now two days. That is, "on the second (or 'next') day"; compare 8:31. Mark appears to place the plotting of the chief priests and scribes on Wednesday of Passion Week.

the Passover. The Passover was one of the most important of the Jewish feasts, since it celebrated the deliverance from Egypt when the angel of death "passed over" the homes of the people of Israel (Ex. 12:1–30). At the time of Jesus, the Passover was celebrated on the fifteenth day of the first month of the Jewish calendar (Nisan, which corresponds to the end of March and beginning of April). It was observed the last day before the first full moon after the spring equinox. From that day when the paschal lambs were killed and eaten, all leaven (symbolizing sin) was to be removed from the house, and only unleavened bread was to be eaten for seven days. This observance was known as the "Feast of Unleavened Bread" (14:12; Ex. 12:15–20), and was closely associated with Passover.

chief priests. See note 8:31.

scribes. See note 7:1.

14:2 Not during the feast. Being one of the Jewish pilgrimage feasts, the Passover drew enormous numbers of people to Jerusalem. Josephus

Jesus Anointed at Bethany

3 [b]And while he was at [c]Bethany in the
house of Simon the leper,[1] as he was reclining at table, a woman came with an
alabaster flask of ointment of pure nard,
very costly, and she broke the flask and
poured it over his head. 4 There were some
who said to themselves indignantly, "Why
was the ointment wasted like that? 5 For
this ointment could have been sold for
more than three hundred denarii[2] and [d]giv-
en to the poor." And they [e]scolded her.
6 But Jesus said, "Leave her alone. Why do
you trouble her? She has done a beautiful
thing to me. 7 For [f]you always have the
poor with you, and whenever [g]you want,
you can do good for them. But [h]you will
not always have me. 8 [i]She has done what
she could; she has anointed my body
beforehand [j]for burial. 9 And truly, I say to
you, wherever [k]the gospel is proclaimed in
the whole world, what she has done will be
told [l]in memory of her."

Judas to Betray Jesus

10 [m]Then [n]Judas Iscariot, who was one of
the twelve, [n]went to the chief priests in
order to betray him to them. 11 And when
they heard it, they were glad and promised
to give him money. And he sought an opportunity to [o]betray him.

The Passover with the Disciples

12 [p]And on [q]the first day of Unleavened
Bread, when they [r]sacrificed the Passover
lamb, his disciples said to him, "Where
will you have us go and prepare for you to
eat the Passover?" 13 And he sent [s]two of his
disciples and said to them, "Go into the
city, and a man carrying a jar of water will
meet you. Follow him, 14 and wherever he
enters, say to the master of the house,
[t]'The Teacher says, Where is [u]my guest
room, where I may eat the Passover with
my disciples?' 15 And he will show you [v]a
large upper room furnished and ready;
there prepare for us." 16 And the disciples
set out and went to the city and found it
just as he had told them, and they prepared the Passover.
17 [w]And when it was evening, he came
with the twelve. 18 And as they were reclining at table and eating, [x]Jesus said, "Truly,
I say to you, one of you will betray me,
[y]one who is eating with me." 19 They began

3 [b]For ver. 3-9, see Matt. 26:6-13; John 12:1-8; [Luke 7:37-39] [c]Matt. 21:17; John 11:18
5 [d][John 13:29] [e]John 11:33, 38 (Gk.)
7 [f]Deut. 15:11 [g][2 Cor. 9:7] [h]ch. 2:20; See John 7:33
8 [i][ch. 12:43; Luke 21:3; 2 Cor. 8:12] [j]John 19:40
9 [k][Matt. 24:14] [l]Acts 10:4
10 [m]For ver. 10, 11, see Matt. 26:14-16; Luke 22:3-6; [John 13:2, 27, 30] [n]ch. 3:19; Matt. 27:3; Acts 1:16; [John 6:71; 12:4]
11 [o]See Matt. 20:18, 19
12 [p]For ver. 12-16, see Matt. 26:17-19; Luke 22:7-13 [q]Ex. 12:18 [r]1 Cor. 5:7
13 [s][ch. 11:1]
14 [t]See John 11:28
[u]Luke 2:7 (Gk.) 15 [v][Acts 1:13] 17 [w]For ver. 17-21, see Matt. 26:20-24; [Luke 22:14, 21-23; John 13:21-26] 18 [x][John 6:70, 71] [y][Ps. 41:9; John 13:18]

1 *Leprosy* was a term for several skin diseases; see Leviticus 13
2 A *denarius* was a day's wage for a laborer

estimated that the population of 50,000 increased to 3,000,000. Though his figures are generally considered greatly exaggerated (250,000 is more likely), there was a reason for the authorities' fears.

14:3 Bethany. See note 11:1.

Simon the leper. No doubt no longer a leper, he may have been healed by Jesus. He was clearly an important member of the wider circle of disciples since Jesus chose to visit his house at this time.

reclining. People reclined rather than sat at the table (Luke 22:14 note).

a woman. According to John 12:3, this woman was Mary, the sister of Lazarus and Martha. John also indicates that the meal occurred "six days before the Passover" (John 12:1), before Jesus had entered Jerusalem. Mark may have placed the account here to more closely associate this pre-anointing for burial (v. 8 note) with the plot to kill Jesus (v. 1), and was subsequently followed by Matthew (Matt. 26:3–13).

alabaster flask. Alabaster is a type of gypsum, in its pure form white or translucent, found in limestone deposits in caves and at the exit of springs. It was often used for making ointment jars, and was considered a luxury item.

pure nard. A rare perfume made from the root of a plant grown in the Himalayas. Its value of "three hundred denarii" (v. 5) was roughly equivalent to a year's wages.

broke the flask. To prevent loss, amounts suitable for a single application were sealed into flasks that were then broken at the neck at the time of use. According to John 12:3, the flask contained twelve ounces of perfume.

14:6 a beautiful thing. Jesus approves of what others see as a waste, for by this gesture she shows the inestimable worth of Jesus, of His death (v. 8), and of the profound communion that His sacrifice on the cross will establish. This gesture recalls the precious ointment poured over Aaron the high priest, which the psalmist compares to the priceless blessing of the fellowship of believers (Ps. 133).

14:8 anointed my body beforehand for burial. Jesus alludes to the anointing of dead bodies with spices and perfume that was widely practiced in Palestine at that time.

14:10 Judas Iscariot. Judas was to receive thirty silver coins (not even half the value of the perfume) for his betrayal of Jesus (v. 11).

the twelve. See note 3:14.

14:12 Unleavened Bread. This feast symbolized the removal of sin in the life of Israelite believers (Ex. 12:14–20). The Passover meal fell on the first day of this feast (v. 1 note; Ex. 12:14, 15), the fourteenth day after the beginning of the Jewish year (Ex. 12:6).

sacrificed the Passover lamb. Jesus died at Passover, the feast that celebrates how the blood of a lamb protected the Israelites in Egypt from God's wrath. Jesus' death shows the profound continuity in the divine plan of redemption (cf. 1 Cor. 5:7). In the order of these feasts is affirmed the priority of God's act of salvation (Passover and redemption) over against all our works of righteousness (Feast of Unleavened Bread and the believer's putting away of sin).

14:13 man carrying a jar of water. Women usually carried water jars. For Jesus' knowledge of future and distant events, see 11:1, 2 and John 1:48. Jesus could and did exercise on earth divine powers of knowledge (13:32 note).

14:17 with the twelve. The Gospels record that those present at this high point in the ministry of Jesus were the twelve He had chosen at the beginning (cf. 3:14). According to Luke 22:30, at this time Jesus announced their future ministry as judges of the new people of God. They were witnesses at the inauguration of the new covenant.

to be sorrowful and to say to him one after
another, "Is it I?" **20** He said to them, "It is
[z]one of the twelve, [y]one who is dipping
bread into the dish with me. **21** For the Son
of Man goes [a]as it is written of him, but
[b]woe to that man by whom the Son of Man
is betrayed! [c]It would have been better for
that man if he had not been born."

Institution of the Lord's Supper

22 [d]And as they were eating, he took
bread, and after [e]blessing it broke it and
gave it to them, and said, "Take; [f]this is my
body." **23** And he took a cup, and when he
had [g]given thanks he gave it to them, and
they all drank of it. **24** And he said to them,
[f]"This is my [h]blood of the[1] covenant,
which is poured out for [i]many. **25** Truly, I
say to you, I will not drink again of the fruit
of the vine until that day when I drink it
new in the kingdom of God."

Jesus Foretells Peter's Denial

26 [j]And when they had sung a hymn,
[k]they went out to [l]the Mount of Olives.
27 And Jesus said to them, "You will all fall
away, for it is written, 'I will [m]strike the
shepherd, and the sheep will be scattered.'
28 But after I am raised up, [n]I will go before
you to Galilee." **29** [o]Peter said to him, "Even
though they all fall away, I will not." **30** And
[p]Jesus said to him, "Truly, I tell you, this
very night, before [q]the rooster crows twice,
you will deny me three times." **31** But [r]he
said emphatically, "If I must die with you,
I will not deny you." And they all said the
same.

Jesus Prays in Gethsemane

32 [s]And they went [k]to a place called
Gethsemane. And he said to his disciples,
"Sit here while I pray." **33** And he took with
him [t]Peter and James and John, and began
[u]to be greatly distressed and troubled.
34 And he said to them, [v]"My soul is very
sorrowful, even to death. Remain here and
[w]watch."[2] **35** And going a little farther, he
fell on the ground [x]and prayed that, if it
were possible, [y]the hour might pass from
him. **36** And he said, [z]"Abba, Father, [a]all
things are possible for you. Remove [b]this
cup from me. [c]Yet not what I will, but what
you will." **37** And he came and found them
sleeping, and he said to Peter, "Simon, are
you asleep? Could you not watch one
hour? **38** [w]Watch and [d]pray that you may
not [e]enter into temptation. The spirit
indeed is willing, but the flesh is weak."
39 And again he went away and prayed, [f]saying the same words. **40** And again he came
and found them sleeping, for [g]their eyes
were very heavy, and [h]they did not know

20 [z]ver. 10 [y][See ver. 18 above]
21 [a]ver. 49; ch. 9:12; Luke 18:31; 24:25–27:46; Acts 17:2, 3; 26:22, 23; 1Cor. 15:3; 1 Pet. 1:10, 11 [b]Matt. 18:7 [c]John 17:12
22 [d]For ver. 22-25, see Matt. 26:26-29; Luke 22:18-20; 1 Cor. 11:23-25 [e]See Matt. 14:19 [f]1 Cor. 10:16; [John 6:53]
23 [g]See Matt. 15:36
24 [f][See ver. 21 above] [h]Ex. 24:8; [Zech. 9:11; Heb. 13:20] [i]See Matt. 20:28
26 [j]For ver. 26-31, see Matt. 26:30-35 [k]Luke 22:39; John 18:1 [l]See Matt. 21:1
27 [m]Cited from Zech. 13:7; [John 16:32]
28 [n]ch. 16:7; Matt. 28:7, 10, 16
29 [o][Luke 22:31, 33]
30 [p]Luke 22:34; John 13:38 [q]ver. 68, 72
31 [r]Luke 22:36; John 13:37
32 [s]For ver. 32-42, see Matt. 26:36-46; Luke 22:40-46 [k][See ver. 26 above]
33 [t]ch. 5:37; 9:2 [u]ch. 9:15; 10:32 **34** [v][Ps. 42:5, 6; John 12:27] [w]See Matt. 24:42
35 [x]Heb. 5:7 [y]ver. 41; John 12:23, 27; 13:1; 17:1; [Luke 22:53; John 16:4]
36 [z]Rom. 8:15; Gal. 4:6 [a]See Matt. 19:26 [b]See ch. 10:38 [c]John 5:30; 6:38; Phil. 2:8 **38** [w][See ver. 34 above] [d]1 Pet. 4:7 [e]Matt. 6:13 **39** [f]ver. 36 **40** [g]Luke 9:32 [h][ch. 9:6; Luke 9:33]

[1] Some manuscripts insert *new* [2] Or *keep awake*; also verses 37, 38

14:20 one of the twelve. Jesus' prediction of the betrayal comes from His intimate knowledge of Judas, and also from His understanding of the Scriptures (v. 21; Ps. 41:9).

dipping bread into the dish with me. Bread or meat was dipped into a central bowl of sauce. The detail emphasizes the deep personal betrayal, since table fellowship was a token of genuine friendship (cf. 2:16).

14:21 as it is written. See 8:31 note.

14:22 as they were eating. The sacramental meal of the new covenant is intrinsically related to and grows out of that of the old (note the parallelism with Ex. 24:9–11). Jesus takes two elements of the Passover meal, unleavened bread and wine, to express His new work of redemption. See "The Lord's Supper" at 1 Cor. 11:23.

14:24 my blood. In the original Passover the blood of the lamb protected the Israelites from death (Ex. 12:23, 30). The phrase "blood of the covenant" comes from Ex. 24:8, and recalls that biblical covenants are sealed in blood (Gen. 15:9–21; 17:9–14; Ex. 24:4–8).

poured out for many. Jesus is alluding to Is. 53:12 where the Servant of the Lord "poured out His soul to death" and "bore the sin of many."

14:25 I will not drink. Jesus is hereby predicting the imminence of His death.

drink it new. Jesus expresses His faith in God who will not abandon Him in death.

14:26 sung a hymn. This mention of singing is a reference to the Passover liturgy. Jesus and His disciples sing Ps. 115–118, the traditional close of the meal.

14:28 to Galilee. The angel at the tomb remembers this promise and alludes to Peter's denial (16:7).

14:30 before the rooster crows twice. For other examples of Jesus' knowledge of future events, see note on v. 13. The seemingly specific reference could also be a poetic way of saying "before dawn."

14:33 Peter and James and John. See note 5:37.

troubled. This verb is unique to Mark, and each time expresses deep emotional distress (9:15; 16:5, 6).

14:36 Abba. A colloquial Aramaic word for "father," which expresses Jesus' close relation with God the Father. Mark records the Semitic word (5:41; 7:34; 11:9; 14:45; 15:22, 34).

cup. See note 10:38.

14:37 one hour. In spite of noble intentions (14:29, 31), Peter is incapable of one hour of true discipleship.

14:38 Watch. This exhortation recalls the warning of 13:32–37 to watch and not fall asleep before the coming of the Son of Man. "Temptation" is the trap of Satan to cause God's people (in this case the Twelve) to fall and, if possible, to bring to nothing the plan of redemption.

what to answer him. 41 And he came the
third time and said to them, "Are you still
sleeping and taking your rest? [i]It is enough;
[j]the hour has come. [k]The Son of Man is
betrayed into the hands of sinners. 42 Rise,
let us be going; see, my betrayer is at
hand."

Betrayal and Arrest of Jesus

43 [l]And immediately, while he was still
speaking, [m]Judas came, one of the twelve,
and with him a crowd with swords and
clubs, from the chief priests and the scribes
and the elders. 44 Now the betrayer had
given them a sign, saying, "The one I will
kiss is the man. Seize him and lead him
away under guard." 45 And when he came,
he went up to him at once and said,
[n]"Rabbi!" And he [o]kissed him. 46 And they
laid hands on him and seized him. 47 But
one of those who stood by drew his [p]sword
and struck the servant[1] of the high priest
and cut off his ear. 48 And Jesus said to
them, "Have you come out as against a robber, with swords and clubs to capture me?
49 [q]Day after day I was with you in the temple [r]teaching, and you did not seize me.
But [s]let the Scriptures be fulfilled." 50 [t]And
they all left him and fled.

A Young Man Flees

51 And a young man followed him, with
nothing but [u]a linen cloth about his body.
And they seized him, 52 but he left the linen
cloth and ran away naked.

Jesus Before the Council

53 [v]And [w]they led Jesus to the high priest.
And all the chief priests and the elders and
the scribes came together. 54 [w]And [x]Peter
had followed him at a distance, [y]right into
[z]the courtyard of the high priest. And he
was sitting with [a]the guards and [b]warming
himself at the fire. 55 Now the chief priests
and the whole Council[2] were seeking testimony against Jesus to put him to death,
but they found none. 56 [c]For many bore
false witness against him, but their testimony [d]did not agree. 57 And some stood up
and bore false witness against him, saying,
58 [e]"We heard him say, [f]'I will destroy this
temple [g]that is made with hands, and in
three days I will build another, [h]not made
with hands.'" 59 Yet even about this their
testimony did not agree. 60 And the high
priest stood up in the midst and asked
Jesus, "Have you no answer to make? What
is it that these men testify against you?"[3]
61 But [i]he remained silent and made no
answer. [j]Again the high priest asked him,
"Are you [k]the Christ, the Son of [l]the
Blessed?" 62 And Jesus said, "I am, and
[m]you will see the Son of Man [n]seated at the
right hand of Power, and [m]coming with the
clouds of heaven." 63 And the high priest

41 [i][Luke 22:38] [j]See ver. 35 [k]ch. 9:31; 10:33 **43** [l]For ver. 43-50, see Matt. 26:47-56; Luke 22:47-53; John 18:3-11 [m]ver. 10; Acts 1:16 **45** [n]See John 1:38 [o]Luke 7:38, 45; 15:20; Acts 20:37 (Gk.) **47** [p][Luke 22:38] **49** [q][John 8:2]; [Luke 2:46; John 18:20] [r]Matt. 21:23; [Matt. 4:23] [s]See ver. 21; Matt. 1:22 **50** [t]ver. 27; [Ps. 88:8, 18; John 16:32] **51** [u]ch. 15:46; Judg. 14:12; Prov. 31:24

53 [v]For ver. 53-65, see Matt. 26:57-68; [John 18:12, 13, 19-24] [w]Luke 22:54, 55 **54** [w][See ver. 53 above] [x][John 18:15] [y][ver. 68] [z]See Matt. 26:3 [a]John 7:32; 18:3 [b]ver. 67; John 18:18 **56** [c]Ps. 27:12; 35:11 [d][Deut. 17:6; 19:15] **58** [e][Acts 6:14]

[f]ch. 15:29; See John 2:19 [g]Acts 7:48; 17:24; Heb. 9:11, 24 [h]2 Cor. 5:1 **61** [i]ch. 15:4, 5; Isai. 53:7; John 19:9 [j]For ver. 61-63, [Luke 22:67-71] [k]ch. 8:29; See Matt. 1:17 [l][Rom. 1:25] **62** [m]See Matt. 16:27; 24:30 [n]Ps. 110:1; Heb. 1:3; [ch. 16:19]

1 Greek *bondservant* 2 Greek *Sanhedrin* 3 Or *Have you no answer to what these men testify against you?*

14:43 crowd. Probably a force sent by the Sanhedrin since the three categories of members of that body are mentioned (v. 53; 8:31 note).

14:44 kiss. A sign of respect that disciples showed to teachers. After eating from the same dish (v. 20 note) Judas now feigns submission and respect.

14:48 as against a robber. The Greek can mean either "robber" or "insurrectionist," but in view of the charges brought against Jesus at His trial (Luke 23:2), "insurrectionist" is better.

14:49 let the Scriptures be fulfilled. See note 8:31. In view of v. 50, the passage Jesus had in mind may be Zech. 13:7 (see v. 27).

14:51 young man. Some interpreters have suggested that in this cryptic detail, as in the mention of the linen garment (a sign of wealth), there might be a veiled reference to Mark himself, since he was from a well-to-do family in Jerusalem (Acts 12:12).

14:53–15:15 This section of the narrative concerns Jesus' trials before the Jews and the Romans. These trials were full of errors and irregularities, with the principles of justice subordinated to expediency and politics. The Jewish trial had three parts: a hearing before Annas (reported only in John 18:12-14, 19-23); a trial before the Sanhedrin, led by Caiaphas in his house (14:53-65); and an early morning session of the Sanhedrin (15:1). The Roman trial was likewise in three parts: before Pilate (15:2-5); before Herod Antipas, (reported only in Luke 23:6-12); and before Pilate again (15:6-15).

14:54 courtyard of the high priest. Normally the Sanhedrin held its sessions in the marketplace near the temple. This trial took place in the high priest's residence. The trial was irregular in time (at night) and place, and in its unusual haste.

14:57 false witness. Deut. 19:15-21 requires that for guilt to be established there must be two or three corroborating witnesses. False witnesses would receive the same punishment that the accused was threatened with. These regulations were not applied in the case of Jesus.

14:58 I will destroy this temple that is made with hands. The first three (Synoptic) Gospels do not record Jesus saying this. However, it is found in John's account of the temple cleansing (John 2:19). This would support the probability that Christ cleansed the temple twice, since the lapse of three years would help explain the false witnesses' garbled version.

14:61 Christ. From the Greek word meaning "anointed one." "Messiah" represents the Hebrew word of the same meaning (1 Sam. 2:10 note).

Son of the Blessed. "The Blessed" is an indirect substitute for "God," used by the Jews to avoid the risk of taking God's name in vain. The whole title means "Son of God," and in the context indicates royal messiahship rather than absolute divinity.

14:62 I am. See notes 6:50; 13:6.

Son of Man. See note 2:10. Jesus modifies the title "Messiah" in terms of the divine figure of Dan. 7.

clouds. See note 13:26.

[o]tore his garments and said, "What further
witnesses do we need? 64 You have heard
[p]his blasphemy. What is your decision?"
And they [q]all condemned him as [r]deserv-
ing death. 65 [s]And some began [t]to spit on
him and [u]to cover his face and to strike
him, saying to him, "Prophesy!" And the
guards received him [v]with blows.

Peter Denies Jesus

66 [w]And as Peter was below in the courtyard, one of the servant girls of the high
priest came, 67 and seeing Peter [x]warming
himself, she looked at him and said, "You
also were with the Nazarene, Jesus." 68 But
he denied it, saying, "I neither know nor
understand what you mean." And he went
out into the gateway[1] and [y]the rooster
crowed.[2] 69 And the servant girl saw him
and began again to say to the bystanders,
"This man is one of them." 70 But again he
denied it. And after a little while the
bystanders again said to Peter, "Certainly
you are one of them, for you are a
Galilean." 71 But he began to invoke a curse
on himself and to swear, "I do not know
this man of whom you speak." 72 And
immediately the rooster crowed [z]a second
time. And Peter remembered how Jesus
had said to him, [a]"Before the rooster crows
twice, you will [b]deny me three times." And
he broke down and wept.[3]

Jesus Delivered to Pilate

15 [c]And as soon as it was morning, the
chief priests [d]held a consultation
with the elders and scribes and the whole
Council. And [e]they bound Jesus and [f]led
him away and [g]delivered him over to
[h]Pilate. 2 [i]And Pilate asked him, [j]"Are you
the King of the Jews?" And he answered
him, [k]"You have said so." 3 And the chief
priests accused him of many things. 4 And
Pilate again asked him, [l]"Have you no
answer to make? See how many charges
they bring against you." 5 But Jesus [l]made
no further answer, so that Pilate was
amazed.

Pilate Delivers Jesus to Be Crucified

6 [m]Now at the feast he used to release for
them one prisoner for whom they asked.
7 And among the rebels in prison, who had
[n]committed murder [o]in the insurrection,
there was a man called Barabbas. 8 And the
crowd came up and began to ask Pilate to
do as he usually did for them. 9 And he
answered them, saying, "Do you want me
to release for you the King of the Jews?"
10 For he perceived that [p]it was out of envy
that the chief priests had delivered him up.
11 But the chief priests stirred up the crowd
to have him release for them Barabbas
instead. 12 And Pilate again said to them,
"Then what shall I do with [q]the man you
call the King of the Jews?" 13 And they cried
out again, "Crucify him." 14 And Pilate said
to them, "Why, [r]what evil has he done?"
But they shouted all the more, "Crucify

63 [o]Num. 14:6; Acts 14:14
64 [p]Matt. 9:3; John 10:36 [q][Luke 23:50, 51] [r]See Lev. 24:16
65 [s]Luke 22:63, 64 [t]ch. 10:34; 15:19; Isai. 50:6 [u][Esth. 7:8] [v]Matt. 5:39; [Acts 23:2]
66 [w]For ver. 66-72, see Matt. 26:69-75; Luke 22:55-62; John 18:16-18, 25-27
67 [x]ver. 54
68 [y]ver. 30, 72
72 [z]ver. 68 [a]ver. 30 [b][Acts 3:13, 14]
Chapter 15
1 [c]Matt. 27:1; Luke 22:66 [d]ch. 3:6 [e]Matt. 27:2 [f]Luke 23:1; John 18:28 [g]See ch. 10:33 [h]Luke 3:1; 13:1; Acts 3:13; 4:27; 1 Tim. 6:13
2 [i]For ver. 2-5, see Matt. 27:11-14; Luke 23:2, 3; John 18:29-38 [j]ver. 9, 12, 18, 26; Matt. 2:2; John 18:39; 19:3; [ver. 32] [k][1 Tim. 6:13]; See Luke 22:70
4 [l][John 19:10]; See Matt. 26:63

5 [l][See ver. 4 above] **6** [m]For ver. 6-15, see Matt. 27:15-26; Luke 23:18-25; John 18:39, 40; 19:16 **7** [n]Acts 3:14 [o][Acts 5:36, 37] **10** [p][John 12:19] **12** [q][John 19:15] **14** [r][Luke 23:41; John 8:46]

[1] Or *forecourt* [2] Some manuscripts omit *and the rooster crowed*
[3] Or *And when he had thought about it, he wept*

14:63 tore his garments. A symbolic gesture expressing great sorrow or horror (Gen. 37:29; 2 Kin. 18:37; 19:1; Ezra 9:3; Jer. 36:24; Joel 2:13).

What further witnesses. The high priest makes the whole Sanhedrin witness to Jesus' blasphemy.

14:64 blasphemy. Jesus is condemned, not for insurrection, but for His claim to deity, the essence of His message. The prescribed punishment for blasphemy (insulting the honor of God's name) was death by stoning (Lev. 24:16), but at this time only Roman courts could order capital punishment. Jesus would die by a Roman punishment (John 18:31, 32 and notes).

14:65 spit on him. In their agreement with the accusation of the high priest, all the members of the Sanhedrin "condemned Him" (v. 64), and some expressed their agreement with physical and personal violence. Spitting in the face indicated exclusion from the group (Num. 12:14, 15), as if by ritual defilement. At this point, the Sanhedrin broke decisively with the Messiah.

14:67 Nazarene. See note 1:24.

14:70 Galilean. The Jews of Judea held the Galilean Jews in contempt as culturally and religiously inferior. Peter's manner and accent gave him away, especially in the courtyard of a Sadducean aristocrat.

15:1 as soon as it was morning. Probably at dawn. The purpose of the new meeting was apparently to draw up a civil charge (cf. Luke 23:2).

Pilate. The Apostles' Creed mentions Pilate as the representative of Rome who faced Jesus in this trial. Pilate was Roman governor of Judea from A.D. 26 to 36. As magistrate, only he had the legal right to pronounce capital sentences (14:64 note).

15:2 King of the Jews. This title is ambiguous. In a political sense, the Herods were kings and Jesus was not. Nevertheless Jesus was King of the Jews, offered to them as the fulfillment of their messianic hopes.

15:4 Have you no answer. Pilate apparently wanted to make Jesus realize that, before the law, silence meant consent.

15:7 Barabbas. Apparently he was an insurrectionist seeking the military overthrow of Rome. Matt. 27:16 (in some manuscripts) gives his first name as "Jesus," a common name of the period. The choice Pilate proposes to the crowd (v. 9) is unwittingly ironic: Jesus Barabbas, the would-be political savior of Israel, or Jesus of Nazareth, the true Savior of the world.

15:13 Crucify. Of Persian origin and adopted by the Romans, this cruel and shameful form of capital punishment was used mainly against rebellious slaves and insurrectionists. Metal spikes were driven through the

him." 15 So Pilate, wishing to satisfy the crowd, released for them Barabbas, and having [s]scourged[1] Jesus, he delivered him to be crucified.

Jesus Is Mocked

16 [t]And the soldiers led him away inside [u]the palace (that is, [v]the governor's headquarters),[2] and they called together the whole [w]battalion. 17 And they clothed him in [x]a purple cloak, and twisting together a crown of thorns, they put it on him. 18 And they began to salute him, [y]"Hail, King of the Jews!" 19 And they were striking his head with a reed and [z]spitting on him and [a]kneeling down in homage to him. 20 And when they had [b]mocked him, they stripped him of [x]the purple cloak and put his own clothes on him. And they [c]led him out to crucify him.

The Crucifixion

21 [d]And they compelled a passerby, Simon of Cyrene, who was coming in from the country, the father of Alexander and Rufus, to carry his cross. 22 [e]And they brought him to the place called Golgotha (which means Place of a Skull). 23 And they offered him wine mixed with [f]myrrh, but he did not take it. 24 And they crucified him and [g]divided his garments among them, casting lots for them, to decide what each should take. 25 And [h]it was the third hour[3] when they crucified him. 26 And the inscription of the charge against him read, [i]"The King of the Jews." 27 And with him they crucified two [j]robbers, [k]one on his right and one on his left.[4] 29 And [l]those who passed by derided him, [m]wagging their heads and saying, [n]"Aha! [o]You who would destroy the temple and rebuild it in three days, 30 save yourself, and come down from the cross!" 31 So also the chief priests with the scribes mocked him to one another, saying, [p]"He saved others; [q]he cannot save himself. 32 Let [r]the Christ, [s]the King of Israel, come down now from the cross that we may [t]see and believe." [u]Those who were crucified with him also reviled him.

15 [s]ch. 10:34; Isai. 50:6; 53:5; [Luke 23:16; John 19:1] **16** [t]For ver. 16-20, see Matt. 27:27-31; John 19:2, 3 [u]See Matt. 26:3 [v]John 18:28, 33; 19:9; Acts 23:35; Phil. 1:13 (Gk.) [w]See Acts 10:1 **17** [x]Rev. 18:12, 16; [Luke 23:11] **18** [y]See ver. 2 **19** [z]See ch. 14:65 [a]See Matt. 8:2 **20** [b]ch. 10:34 [x][See ver. 17 above] [c]Isai. 53:7 **21** [d]Matt. 27:32; Luke 23:26; [John 19:17] **22** [e]For ver. 22-38, see Matt. 27:33-51; Luke 23:32-38, 44-46; John 19:17-19, 23, 24, 28-30 **23** [f]Matt. 2:11; See John 19:39 **24** [g]Ps. 22:18 **25** [h][John 19:14]

26 [i]ver. 2 **27** [j][John 18:40] [k][ch. 10:37] **29** [l]Ps. 22:7; 109:25; [Lam. 1:12] [m]Job 16:4; Jer. 18:16; Lam. 2:15 [n]Ps. 35:25; 40:15 [o]ch. 14:58 **31** [p][Luke 4:23] [q][Matt. 26:53, 54; John 10:18] **32** [r]See Matt. 1:17 [s]John 1:49; 12:13; [ver. 26] [t]John 20:29 [u][Luke 23:39-43]

[1] A Roman judicial penalty, consisting of a severe beating with a multi-lashed whip containing imbedded pieces of bone and metal [2] Greek *the praetorium* [3] That is, 9 A.M. [4] Some manuscripts insert verse 28: *And the Scripture was fulfilled that says, "He was numbered with the transgressors"*

wrists or hands (John 20:25) and heels of the victim who suffered terrible pain. Death usually resulted over the course of days from the effects of the injuries, hunger, dehydration, and exposure. Breaking the condemned's legs (John 19:33) caused rapid death by asphyxiation, since the legs could no longer lift the body to help the person breathe. As Paul notes, the crucifixion of Jesus brought Him publicly under the curse of God (Gal. 3:13; cf. Deut. 21:23).

15:15 scourged. In Roman custom flogging preceded crucifixion.

15:16 palace. Originally the word for a military headquarters or barracks generally. In the Gospels it refers to an official residence (cf. Acts 23:35).

whole battalion. Lit. "cohort" or tenth part of a Roman legion of nominally six hundred men.

15:17 clothed him in a purple cloak. Purple was expensive and hard to produce, and for this reason was a mark of high rank (Esth. 1:6; Prov. 31:22; Luke 16:19; Rev. 17:4), especially of royalty (2 Chr. 2:7, 14; 3:14; Song 3:10).

crown of thorns. Jesus bore the divine curse (v. 13 note) on the ground, which produced thorns after Adam sinned (Gen. 3:17, 18).The soldiers used the crown to ridicule the idea that Jesus was a king.

15:18 Hail. This salutation and the homage paid (v. 19) are mockeries of the respect due to royalty.

15:21 Cyrene. Cyrene was an important city in what is today Libya. There was a large Jewish settlement in Cyrene going back several hundred years (Acts 6:9).

Alexander and Rufus. Simon's sons may have been members of the Christian community to which Mark wrote, probably at Rome (cf. Rom. 16:13).

carry his cross. Usually the condemned man would carry the crossbeam, weighing thirty to forty pounds. Simon, in taking up the cross of Jesus, became a visual image of the true discipleship that Jesus demands (8:34).

15:22 Place of a Skull. An ominous name, possibly referring to the shape of the hill where executions were carried out.

15:23 wine mixed with myrrh. A primitive form of painkiller. Myrrh was an expensive spice used as a cosmetic. It was offered to Jesus at His birth as a gift for a king (Matt. 2:11), and used in His burial by Nicodemus (John 19:39, 40).

15:24 divided his garments. These were the spoils reserved for the execution squad. This seemingly unimportant detail is a fulfillment of Ps. 22:18, a psalm that describes the agony of a violent and undeserved death (Ps. 22:16).

15:25 third hour. About 9:00 A.M.

15:26 the charge. Called the *titulus,* in Latin, this was a sign carried before the prisoner on the way to execution, and affixed to the cross over his head.

15:27 two robbers. Though the Greek word often means "robber," it can also mean "insurrectionist" (14:48 note) or more generally "criminal." Since robbery was not punishable by crucifixion (v. 13 note), one of the latter two meanings is more probable here.

15:28 This verse is lacking in the most ancient manuscripts, although it is present in the vast majority of existing manuscripts. It is possible that early copyists inserted the citation of Is. 53:12, relying on the parallel passage of Luke 22:37.

15:29 See note 14:58.

15:30 come down. This is both an insult and a diabolical temptation similar to those proposed to Jesus at the beginning of His ministry (Matt. 4:2–6). The devil is still seeking to subvert the work of redemption at the very moment of its accomplishment, when Jesus is at His greatest physical weakness (14:38).

The Death of Jesus

33 And when the sixth hour[1] had come,
there was darkness over the whole land
until the ninth hour.[2] 34 And at the ninth
hour Jesus [v]cried with a loud voice, [w]"Eloi,
Eloi, lema sabachthani?" which means,
"My God, my God, why have you forsaken
me?" 35 And some of the bystanders hearing
it said, "Behold, he is calling Elijah." 36 And
someone ran and filled a sponge with [x]sour
wine, put it on a reed [y]and gave it to him
to drink, saying, "Wait, let us see whether
Elijah will come to take him down." 37 And
Jesus [z]uttered a loud cry and [a]breathed his
last. 38 And [b]the curtain of the temple was
torn in two, from top to bottom. 39 [c]And
when the centurion, who stood facing him,
saw that in this way he[3] breathed his last,
he said, [d]"Truly this man was the Son[4] of
God!"

40 There were also [e]women looking on
[f]from a distance, among whom were [g]Mary
Magdalene, and Mary the mother of James
[h]the younger and of Joses, and [i]Salome.
41 When he was in Galilee, they followed
him and [g]ministered to him, and there
were also many other women who [j]came
up with him to Jerusalem.

Jesus Is Buried

42 [k]And when evening had come, since it
was [l]the day of Preparation, that is, the day
before the Sabbath, 43 Joseph of Arimathea,
[m]a respected member of the Council, who
[n]was also himself looking for the kingdom
of God, took courage and went to Pilate
and asked for the body of Jesus. 44 Pilate
was surprised to hear that he should have
already died.[5] And summoning [o]the centurion, he asked him whether he was already
dead. 45 And when he learned from [o]the
centurion that he was dead, he granted the
corpse to Joseph. 46 And Joseph[6] bought [p]a
linen shroud, and taking him down,
wrapped him in the linen shroud and [q]laid
him in a tomb [r]that had been cut out of
the rock. And he rolled [s]a stone against the
entrance of the tomb. 47 [t]Mary Magdalene

34 [v][Heb. 5:7] [w]Cited from Ps. 22:1
36 [x]Ruth 2:14 [y]Ps. 69:21
37 [z]ver. 34 [a][John 10:18]
38 [b]Ex. 26:31-33; 2 Chr. 3:14
39 [c]For ver. 39-41, see Matt. 27:54-56; Luke 23:47, 49 [d]Matt. 27:43
40 [e]John 19:25 [f]Ps. 38:11 [g]See Luke 8:2, 3 [h]Luke 19:3 [i]ch. 16:1; [Matt. 27:56]
41 [g][See ver. 40 above]
[j]Luke 2:4
42 [k]For ver. 42-47, see Matt. 27:57-61; Luke 23:50-56; John 19:38-42 [l]See Matt. 27:62
43 [m]Acts 13:50; 17:12 [n]Luke 2:25, 38
44 [o]ver. 39
45 [o][See ver. 44 above]
46 [p]See ch. 14:51 [q][Isai. 53:9] [r]Isai. 22:16 [s]ch. 16:4; [John 11:38] 47 [t]ver. 40

1 That is, noon 2 That is, 3 P.M. 3 Some manuscripts insert *cried out and* 4 Or *a son* 5 Or *Pilate wondered whether he had already died* 6 Greek *he*

15:33 sixth hour. Noon.

darkness. This recalls the darkness in Egypt, which lasted three days before the death of the firstborn sons (Ex. 10:22). See also the prophecy of Amos 8:9, 10 where the Lord promises to "darken the earth in broad daylight," in a time "like the mourning for an only son."

ninth hour. About 3:00 P.M.

15:34 Eloi . . . sabachthani. This is the first verse of Ps. 22 in Aramaic. Even in the jaws of death, Jesus' life is determined by what is written in Scripture.

15:35 Elijah. Some mistook the word *Eloi* for "Elijah," perhaps because in some circles it was believed that Elijah would return (6:15; 8:28).

15:36 sour wine. A cheap wine that has almost become vinegar. Unlike the offer of wine and myrrh (v. 23), there is no humanitarian desire to relieve the suffering here, but rather a cruel intention to prolong it by reviving Jesus, in order to see if "Elijah" would come at His call.

15:37 uttered a loud cry. Jesus had been hanging on the cross for six hours (vv. 25, 34). Crucifixion could last two or three days (v. 13 note).

15:38 the curtain of the temple was torn in two. The death of Jesus is the final and definitive sacrifice for sin (Heb. 7:27). The old dispensation of the covenant of grace is brought to a decisive end. No longer would the high priest need to enter into the Most Holy Place behind the veil to atone for the sins of the people (Ex. 26:31–33; cf. Heb. 9:1–10). Jesus is the new and eternal High Priest (Heb. 8:1), and also the perfect sacrificial victim (Heb. 9:14) who obtains for His people "eternal redemption" (Heb. 9:12).

15:39 centurion. A Roman officer responsible for one hundred men. This centurion was apparently responsible for the detachment that put Jesus to death. He was well placed to observe the death of Jesus.

Son of God. The Greek could be translated "a son of God." A Roman would not see in this term the Old Testament Messiah nor the eternal Son of the Trinity, but rather the Hellenistic idea of a human being favored by the gods. Nevertheless, the confession stands as the goal and climax of Mark's Gospel, filled with the content of the Christian message (cf. 1:1).

15:40 Mary Magdalene. That is, from Magdala on the southwestern shore of the Sea of Galilee (cf. 16:9; Luke 8:2).

Mary the mother of James the younger and of Joses. Known only from this incident (cf. Matt. 27:56).

Salome. Mother of James and John (Matt. 27:56; cf. 20:20, 21).

15:41 many other women. All the men had fled, except the beloved disciple (John 19:26, 35).

15:42 day of Preparation. The day before the Sabbath (Friday; John 19:14 note). Food was prepared before sunset, when the Sabbath began. Joseph would have to buy the linen, make arrangements for Jesus' burial, and ready the tomb (vv. 43–46) in the three hours remaining between Jesus' death and sunset.

15:43 Joseph of Arimathea. Perhaps from Ramah in Judea, twenty miles northwest of Jerusalem, the city of the prophet Samuel (1 Sam. 1:1). See note Luke 23:50, 51.

Council. The Sanhedrin (8:31 note).

kingdom of God. See note 1:15. Joseph was no doubt a pious Pharisee, but also a secret follower of Jesus.

took courage. This is apparently Joseph's first act of faith, but it comes at a time when all Jesus' own disciples had fled. Joseph puts himself in conflict with the decision of the Sanhedrin, and jeopardizes his entire future.

15:44 Pilate was surprised. Pilate's surprise again confirms the unusual character of Jesus' death (v. 37 note).

15:46 tomb . . . cut out of the rock. According to Matt. 27:60, the tomb belonged to Joseph and his family. Such a family burial site would consist of an ornately painted vestibule from which a passageway would lead to individual benches or shelves cut into the rock where the bodies were laid. The tomb would be sealed by a heavy stone that was rolled along a groove cut into the rock at the entrance.

and Mary the mother of Joses saw where he
was laid.

The Resurrection

16 [u,v]When the Sabbath was past,
[w]Mary Magdalene and [w]Mary the
mother of James and [i]Salome [x]bought
spices, so that they might go and anoint
him. 2 And very early on the first day of the
week, when the sun had risen, they went
to the tomb. 3 And they were saying to one
another, "Who will roll away [y]the stone for
us from the entrance of the tomb?" 4 And
looking up, they saw that the stone had
been rolled back—[z]it was very large. 5 And
[a]entering the tomb, they saw a young man
sitting on the right side, [b]dressed in [c]a
white robe, and [d]they were alarmed. 6 And
he said to them, [d]"Do not be alarmed. You
seek Jesus of Nazareth, who was crucified.
He has risen; he is not here. See the place
where they laid him. 7 But go, tell his disciples and Peter that [e]he is going before
you to Galilee. There you will see him,
[e]just as he told you." 8 And they went out
and fled from the tomb, for trembling and
astonishment had seized them, and they
said nothing to anyone, for they were
afraid.

[SOME OF THE EARLIEST MANUSCRIPTS DO NOT INCLUDE 16:9-20.][1]

Jesus Appears to Mary Magdalene

9 [[Now when he rose early on the first
day of the week, [f]he appeared first to [g]Mary
Magdalene, [g]from whom he had cast out
seven demons. 10 [h]She went and told those
who had been with him, [i]as they [j]mourned
and wept. 11 But when they heard that he
was alive and had been seen by her, they
[k]would not believe it.

Jesus Appears to Two Disciples

12 [l]After these things [m]he appeared in
[n]another form to two of them, as they were
walking into the country. 13 [o]And they went
back and told the rest, but they did not
believe them.

The Great Commission

14 Afterward [m]he appeared [p]to the eleven
themselves as they were reclining at table,
and he rebuked them for their [q]unbelief
and [r]hardness of heart, because [s]they had
not believed those who saw him after he
had risen. 15 And he said to them, [t]"Go into
all the world and [u]proclaim the gospel to
[v]the whole creation. 16 [w]Whoever believes
and is [x]baptized [y]will be saved, but [z]who-
ever [w]does not believe will be condemned.

Chapter 16
1 [u]For ver. 1-8, see Matt. 28:1-8; Luke 24:1-10; John 20:1 [v][ch. 1:32] [w]ch. 15:40 [i][See 15:40] [x]Luke 23:56; [John 19:39, 40]
3 [y]ch. 15:46
4 [z]Matt. 27:60
5 [a][John 20:11, 12 [b][ch. 9:3; Dan. 7:9; John 20:12; Acts 1:10] [c]Rev. 6:11; 7:9 [d]ch. 9:15
6 [d][See ver. 5 above]
7 [e]ch. 14:28
9 [f]John 20:14; [Matt. 28:9] [g]Luke 8:2
10 [h]John 20:18; [Matt. 28:10; Luke 24:10] [i]John 16:20 [j]Luke 6:25
11 [k]Luke 24:11; [ver. 16]
12 [l]Luke 24:13-31 [m]ver. 14; [John 21:1, 14] [n]Luke 9:29 (Gk.)
13 [o]Luke 24:33-35
14 [m][See ver. 12 above] [p]Luke 24:36; 1 Cor. 15:5 [q][Luke 24:41] [r]See ch. 10:5 [s]ver. 11, 13
15 [t]Matt. 28:19 [u]Col. 1:23; [ch. 13:10; Acts 1:8; Rom. 10:18] [v]Rom. 8:22
16 [w][John 3:18] [x]John 3:5; [y]Acts 16:31; Rom. 10:9; 1 Pet. 3:21 [z]ver. 11; Luke 24:11, 41; Acts 28:24; 1 Pet. 2:7; [2 Thess. 2:12]

1 Some manuscripts end the book with 16:8; others include verses 9-20 immediately after verse 8. A few manuscripts insert additional material after verse 14; one Latin manuscript adds after verse 8 the following: *But they reported briefly to Peter and those with him all that they had been told. And after this, Jesus himself sent out by means of them, from east to west, the sacred and imperishable proclamation of eternal salvation.* Other manuscripts include this same wording after verse 8, then continue with verses 9-20

16:1 Sabbath was past. At sunset (6:00 P.M.) on Saturday evening, a time appropriate for buying spices but not for visiting tombs.

anoint. Anointing was a way of showing affection (14:8 note), as in the West today one sends flowers.

16:3 Who will roll away the stone. They had seen the "very large" (v. 4) stone put in its place (15:46 note).

16:5 entering the tomb. They entered the vestibule of the burial chamber, at the far end of which was the individual niche (a bench or shelf) where Jesus' body had been laid (15:46 note).

young man. Matt. 28:2 says the women met an angel at the tomb.

16:6 of Nazareth. See note 1:24.

He has risen. If the Gospel of Mark reaches its climax in the confession that Jesus is the Son of God (15:39 note), a second climax is reached with the declaration of His resurrection, which attests that His preaching concerning the coming of the kingdom in power is true. See notes 1:15 and 9:1; "The Resurrection of Jesus" at Luke 24:2.

16:7 and Peter. These two words make all the difference in the enormous role that Peter would play in the subsequent history of redemption. By them Mark indicates, as he brings his Gospel to an end (16:9–20 note), that Jesus' work of preparation of the Twelve will not be lost.

he is going before. See note 14:28.

16:8 afraid. If vv. 9–20 are not original (see below), then the Gospel of Mark ends with this sentence. This would be a surprising conclusion for a document that purports to be a "gospel," a proclamation of "good news." An opposing consideration is that the word translated "afraid" also means "reverential fear," and the same state of mind is produced in the disciples at the sight of Jesus' Transfiguration (9:6), a type of the future resurrection. But the women's initial silence was really disobedience (v. 7).

16:9–20 Scholars differ regarding whether these verses were originally part of this Gospel. Some important early Greek manuscripts lack these verses, other manuscripts have vv. 9–20 (known as the "Longer Ending"), and still others have a "Shorter Ending" (roughly one verse long). A few manuscripts have both the "Shorter Ending" and the "Longer Ending." Because of these differences, some scholars believe that vv. 9–20 were added later and not written by Mark. On the other hand, the verses are cited by writers from the late second century and are found in the overwhelming majority of existing Greek manuscripts of the Gospel of Mark. For other scholars, these facts establish the authenticity of the passage.

16:9 Mary Magdalene. See note 15:40.

16:12 two of them. Compare Luke 24:13–35.

16:15 Go into all the world. Compare Matt. 28:19.

16:16 baptized. See "Infant Baptism" at Gen. 17:11.

[17]And [a]these signs will accompany those
who believe: [b]in my name they will cast out
demons; [c]they will speak in new tongues;
[18][d]they will pick up serpents with their
hands; and if they drink any deadly poison,
it will not hurt them; [e]they will lay their
hands [f]on the sick, and they will recover."
[19]So then the Lord Jesus, [g]after he had
spoken to them, [h]was taken up into heaven
and [i]sat down at the right hand of God.
[20]And they went out and preached everywhere, while [j]the Lord worked with them
and confirmed [k]the message [l]by accompanying signs.]]

17 [a][ch. 11:23] [b]Acts 5:16; 8:7; 16:18; 19:12; See ch. 9:38 [c]Acts 2:4; 10:46; 19:6; 1 Cor. 12:10, 28, 30; 13:1; 14:2, 4 **18** [d]Luke 10:19; Acts 28:3-5 [e]See ch. 5:23 [f]Acts 5:15, 16; 8:7; 9:12, 17; 28:8; James 5:14, 15; [John 14:12] **19** [g]Acts 1:3 [h]Luke 9:51; 24:51; John 6:62; Acts 1:2; 1 Tim. 3:16; [John 20:17; Eph. 4:8-10; Heb. 4:14] [i]Acts 7:55, 56; Rom. 8:34; Eph. 1:20; Col. 3:1; Heb. 1:3; 8:1; 10:12; 12:2; 1 Pet. 3:22; Rev. 3:21; See Matt. 22:44; Acts 2:33 **20** [j]Heb. 2:3, 4; See 1 Cor. 3:9 [k]See ch. 4:14 [l]See Acts 5:12

16:17 signs. All of the things predicted here (except drinking deadly poison) are recorded in the New Testament, especially in Acts. See also Rom. 15:19; Heb. 2:3, 4. Stories about some of the apostles surviving being forced to drink poison are found in early Christian literature outside the Bible.

16:19 right hand of God. A position symbolizing the authority that Jesus shares with God the Father (14:62; Phil. 2:9; cf. Ps. 110:1).

16:20 confirmed the message by accompanying signs. See note on v. 17.

THE GOSPEL ACCORDING TO

Luke

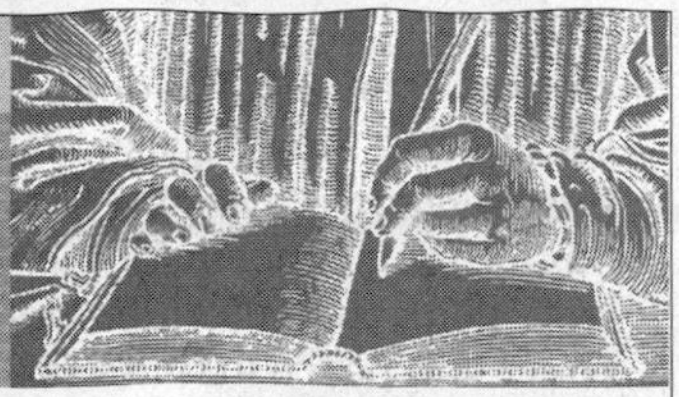

AUTHOR

It is commonly accepted that Luke and Acts have a single author; the style and vocabulary are similar and both books are addressed to Theophilus. Although the author never names himself, several passages using the pronoun "we" suggest that the author was a companion of Paul on some of his travels (Acts 16:10–17; 20:5–16; 21:1–18; 27:1–28:16). Among the persons named in the letters Paul wrote from Rome (where the "we" sections end), the most likely candidate is Luke. In agreement with this, tradition unanimously ascribes the book to Luke (see "Introduction to Acts").

The preface to Luke shows that the writer was not an eyewitness of the events recorded in the Gospel. All of Luke and Acts shows that Luke was a man of culture who had searched out the information he needed, but was not one of the original followers of Jesus. It is sometimes urged against Luke's authorship that his theology, especially in Acts, does not agree with Paul. But there is no reason why Luke should repeat what Paul said, and no evidence that he had read Paul's letters. Nor is it likely that Luke was one of Paul's converts. The writer does not contradict Paul, and we must allow for a certain independence. The objection reduces to the notion that Luke writes in his own way.

Nothing certain is known about Luke other than what we can glean from his two books. According to tradition he came from Antioch and was a physician (Col. 4:14). An argument has been made that Luke uses medical language. However, it seems that physicians in New Testament times did not have a technical language of their own, and Luke's vocabulary does not go beyond what was used by lay people. But there is nothing inconsistent with the tradition that he was a physician, and the author certainly shows an interest in the sick.

DATE AND OCCASION

Luke and Acts may have been written about A.D. 63. Acts ends with Paul still under house arrest in Rome, and it is reasonable to think that if Luke knew of Paul's release or death he would have mentioned it. Luke notes that the prophecy of Agabus was fulfilled (Acts 11:28); he would surely have done the same with Jesus' prophecy of the destruction of Jerusalem (Luke 21:20) if he was writing after A.D. 70. Acts mentions nothing that must be dated after A.D. 62 and shows no knowledge of Paul's letters. All these factors argue for an early date.

Some interpreters argue for a date of A.D. 75–85, saying that some of Luke's wording presupposes the destruction of Jerusalem, which occurred in A.D. 70 (e.g., 19:43; 21:20, 24). But these passages speak of what was customary in sieges of the time, and not much can be made of them if no more is said than that Jesus predicted that current policies meant disaster in due course. A few critics have argued for a date in the second century, but there seems to be no good reason for this. With the information at our disposal a date in the early 60s is reasonable.

Luke tells us in the preface that his purpose is to provide an accurate, well-ordered account of the basic Christian message, to enable his reader to "know the certainty" of the things he has learned (1:4). Both the Gospel and Acts are dedicated to the "most excellent Theophilus." Such a dedication is common in books intended for a wider audience.

CHARACTERISTICS AND THEMES

Luke was clearly a cultured person, able to write in a variety of styles. His opening paragraph is classical in style, while in other places his language resembles the Septuagint (the Greek translation of the Old Testament). Clearly he saw this as a suitable style for the religious writing in which he was engaged.

His main interest is salvation history, the

story of what God has done in Jesus to bring salvation to sinners. Luke makes it clear that this salvation is available for sinful people. He has a strong concern for the disreputable, who were neglected in contemporary religion but could find peace in God's salvation. Luke records a number of predictions of the suffering and death of Christ and devotes much space to it. He is sometimes said to have little interest in eschatology (the last things). This is scarcely fair to Luke, for the thought that the kingdom of God will come in power at the end time is certainly present (12:35–48; 17:22–37; 21:25–36).

Luke concerns himself with many people who would be neglected by most writers of his day—children, women, and the poor. Though these were commonly regarded as having no great significance, Luke demonstrates Jesus' special concern for them.

Prominent in the literary structure of the Gospel is Luke's description of Jesus' journey toward Jerusalem and the sacrifice of the Cross (9:51–19:44). The sovereignty of God in Jesus' ministry and death is highlighted as Jesus moves toward the city where He must die for sinners (9:22; 17:25; 18:31–33; cf. Acts 4:28).

The importance of prayer is stressed. Luke records that Jesus prayed before crucial occasions of His ministry. Nine of Jesus' prayers are included in the Gospel (seven of them found only in Luke), along with parables on prayer found only in Luke.

Expressions of joy often accompany the good news of the Messiah in Luke. Only this Gospel includes the magnificent songs of joy that accompanied the birth of the Messiah (1:46–55, 68–79; 2:14, 29–32).

OUTLINE OF LUKE

I. Preface (1:1–4)

II. The Infancy Stories (1:5–2:52)

III. The Ministry of John the Baptist (3:1–20)

IV. Introduction to Jesus' Ministry (3:21–4:13)

- A. *Baptism (3:21, 22)*
- B. *Genealogy (3:23–38)*
- C. *Temptation (4:1–13)*

V. Jesus in Galilee (4:14–9:50)

- A. *The Sermon at Nazareth (4:14–30)*
- B. *Teaching and Healing in Galilee (4:31–5:39)*
- C. *The Sabbath (6:1–11)*
- D. *Choosing the Twelve (6:12–16)*
- E. *The Sermon on the Plain (6:17–49)*
- F. *Healing Miracles (7:1–17)*
- G. *John the Baptist's Questions and His Greatness (7:18–35)*
- H. *Jesus and Women (7:36–8:3)*
- I. *Teaching in Parables (8:4–18)*
- J. *Jesus' Mighty Works (8:19–56)*
- K. *Training of the Twelve (9:1–50)*
    1. Mission of the Twelve (9:1–9)
    2. The Miraculous Feeding of the Multitude (9:10–17)
    3. Discipleship and the Transfiguration (9:18–50)

VI. Jesus' Journey from Galilee to Jerusalem (9:51–19:44)

- A. *More Teaching on Discipleship (9:51–10:42)*
- B. *Prayer (11:1–13)*
- C. *Evil Spirits (11:14–26)*
- D. *Blessedness and Judgment (11:27–13:9)*
- E. *Teaching About the Kingdom (13:10–14:35)*
    1. The Power of the Kingdom (13:10–21)
    2. Entering the Kingdom (13:22–35)
    3. Dinner with a Pharisee (14:1–24)
    4. Discipleship (14:25–35)
- F. *Three Parables About the Lost (ch. 15)*
- G. *Teaching About Money and Service (16:1–17:10)*
- H. *Ten Men with Leprosy (17:11–19)*
- I. *The Coming Kingdom (17:20–19:10)*
    1. The Coming Unannounced (17:20–37)
    2. Parables About Prayer (18:1–14)
    3. Jesus and the Children (18:15–17)
    4. The Rich Young Ruler (18:18–30)
    5. A Prophecy of Jesus' Death and Resurrection (18:31–34)
    6. Sight to the Blind (18:35–43)
    7. Zacchaeus (19:1–10)
- J. *Parable of the Minas (19:11–27)*
- K. *Jesus Enters Jerusalem (19:28–44)*

VII. Jesus in Jerusalem (19:45–21:38)

- A. *Cleansing the Temple (19:45, 46)*
- B. *Teaching in the Temple (19:47–20:18)*
- C. *Controversies (20:19–47)*
- D. *Olivet and the Temple (ch. 21)*

VIII. The Climax (22:1–24:53)

- A. *The Betrayal of Jesus (22:1–6)*
- B. *The Upper Room (22:7–38)*

OUTLINE OF LUKE (Cont.)

C. *Gethsemane (22:39–53)*
D. *Peter's Denial (22:54–62)*
E. *The Trial of Jesus (22:63–23:25)*
F. *The Crucifixion (23:26–56)*
G. *The Resurrection (24:1–49)*
H. *The Ascension (24:50–53)*

Dedication to Theophilus

1 Inasmuch as many have undertaken to
compile a narrative of the things that
[a]have been accomplished among us, **2** [b]just
as those who [c]from the beginning were [d]eye-
witnesses and [e]ministers of [f]the word [g]have
delivered them to us, **3** it seemed good to me
also, having followed all things closely for
some time past, to write [h]an orderly account
for you, [i]most excellent [j]Theophilus, **4** that
you may have [k]certainty concerning the
things [l]you have been taught.

Birth of John the Baptist Foretold

5 [m]In the days of Herod, king of Judea,
there was a priest named Zechariah,[1] [n]of
[o]the division of Abijah. And he had a wife
from the daughters of Aaron, and her name
was Elizabeth. **6** And they were both [p]righ-
teous before God, walking [q]blamelessly in
all the commandments and statutes of the
Lord. **7** But they had no child, because
[r]Elizabeth was barren, and [s]both were
advanced in years.
8 Now [t]while he was serving as priest
before God when [u]his division was on duty,
9 according to the custom of the priesthood,
he was chosen by lot [v]to enter [w]the temple
of the Lord and burn incense. **10** And the
whole multitude of the people [x]were praying [y]outside at the hour of incense. **11** And
there appeared to him an angel of the Lord
standing on the right side of [z]the altar of
incense. **12** And Zechariah was troubled
when he saw him, and [a]fear fell upon him.
13 But the angel said to him, "Do not be
afraid, Zechariah, for [b]your prayer has been
heard, and your wife Elizabeth will bear
you a son, and [c]you shall call his name
John. **14** And you will have joy and gladness,
and many will [d]rejoice at his birth, **15** for he
will be [e]great before the Lord. And [f]he
must not drink wine or strong [g]drink, and
[g]he will be [h]filled with the Holy Spirit,
[i]even from his mother's womb. **16** And he
will turn many of the children of Israel to
the Lord their God, **17** and [j]he will go before
him [k]in the spirit and power of Elijah, [l]to

Chapter 1
1 [a]2 Tim. 4:5, 17 (Gk.); [Acts 3:18]
2 [b][Heb. 2:3] [c]1 Cor. 11:2, 23 [d]John 15:27; 16:4; [Mark 1:1; Acts 11:15] [e]2 Pet. 1:16; 1 John 1:1, 3; [Acts 4:20; 1 Pet. 5:1] [f]Acts 26:16; 1 Cor. 4:1 [g]See Mark 4:14
3 [h]Acts 11:4 [i]Acts 23:26; 24:3; 26:25 [j]Acts 1:1
4 [k]Acts 2:36 (Gk.); [2 Pet. 1:16, 19] [l]Acts 18:25; Rom. 2:18; 1 Cor. 14:19; Gal. 6:6 (Gk.)
5 [m]Matt. 2:1 [n]1 Chr. 24:10 [o]ver. 8
6 [p]ch. 2:25 [q]Phil. 2:15; 3:6; 1 Thess. 2:10; 3:13; 5:23; [Acts 23:1; 24:16]
7 [r]ver. 36; [Judg. 13:2; 1 Sam. 1:2] [s][Gen. 18:11; Heb. 11:11, 12]

8 [t]1 Chr. 24:19; 2 Chr. 8:14; 31:2; [ver. 23] [u]ver. 5 **9** [v]Ex. 30:7, 8; 1 Sam. 2:28; 1 Chr. 23:13; 2 Chr. 29:11 [w]ver. 21, 22; Rev. 11:2, 19; [Heb. 9:2, 3] **10** [x]Ps. 141:2; [Rev. 5:8; 8:3, 4] [y][Lev. 16:17] **11** [z]Ex. 30:1-10; 40:26, 27 **12** [a]Acts 19:17 **13** [b][Acts 10:4, 31] [c]ver. 60, 63 **14** [d][ver. 58] **15** [e]ch. 7:28; Matt. 11:11 [f]ch. 7:33; Num. 6:3; Judg. 13:4, 7, 14; Matt. 11:18 [g][Acts 2:15, 17; Eph. 5:18] [h]ver. 41, 67; See Acts 2:4 [i]Isai. 49:1, 5; Jer. 1:5; Gal. 1:15 **17** [j]ver. 76; John 3:28 [k]See Matt. 11:14 [l]Cited from Mal. 4:6

[1] Greek *Zacharias*

1:1–4 The opening paragraph is written in Greek reminiscent of the classical style, the kind of opening expected in a literary book written for a wide circulation. Luke addresses Theophilus and explains why he has written.

1:1 many. Many writings of the early church have been lost.

accomplished. The purpose of God had been worked out in the things about which they wrote.

1:2 eyewitnesses. There was reliable evidence for what was written, although Luke distinguishes himself from those who were eyewitnesses.

1:3 for some time past. He had gone back to the start of the Christian movement, the events surrounding the birth of Jesus Himself.

most excellent. An address for a person of rank (Acts 23:26; 24:3).

1:4 certainty. The Christian faith is well grounded.

taught. The Greek word is the source of the English word "catechism."

1:5 Herod. Herod the Great, who reigned 37–4 B.C.

the division. There was only one temple, and priests served it on a rotating roster. The division of Abijah was the eighth of the twenty-four divisions (1 Chr. 24:10); each ministered for a week twice a year.

1:6 blamelessly. The expression does not mean that they never sinned but that they were godly and upright people. It must have been a serious disappointment to have no children, for children were regarded as God's reward for faithful service (Ps. 127:3–5).

1:7 advanced in years. Priests had no retirement age.

1:9 The large number of priests serving the one temple meant that a priest's opportunities for taking part in the ritual were few. He might not offer incense more than once in his life (some priests never had the privilege). This was the high point in Zechariah's career. He would go into the Holy Place with other priests, but they would withdraw leaving him alone to perform the offering.

1:11 the right side. Probably the south side; the angel would have been between the incense altar and the golden lampstand.

1:13 your prayer. This may have been a prayer for a son, but more probably at such a moment it was prayer for the redemption of Israel. Either way, the answer to the prayer would be seen in the birth of a son.

John. The name means "the Lord is gracious."

1:15 wine. That he would not drink alcoholic beverages leads many to think he would be a Nazirite, but Luke does not say this, and there is no reference to the hair being left uncut. More probably John had a unique position, neither priest nor Nazirite. He is the only person in the New Testament said to have been filled with the Holy Spirit from birth.

1:17 in the spirit and power of Elijah. See Mal. 3:1; 4:5.

turn the hearts of the fathers to the children, and [m] the disobedient to the wisdom
of the just, [n] to make ready for the Lord a
people prepared."
18 And Zechariah said to the angel, [o] "How
shall I know this? For I am an old man, and
my wife is advanced in years." **19** And the
angel answered him, "I am [p] Gabriel, [q] who
stands in the presence of God, and I was
sent to speak to you and to bring you this
good news. **20** And behold, [r] you will be
silent and unable to speak until the day
that these things take place, because you
did not believe my words, which will be
fulfilled in their time." **21** And the people
were waiting for Zechariah, and they were
wondering at his delay in [s] the temple.
22 And when he came out, he was unable to
speak to them, and they realized that he
had seen a vision in [s] the temple. And [t] he
kept making signs to them and remained
mute. **23** And [u] when his time of [v] service was
ended, he went to his home.
24 After these days his wife Elizabeth conceived, and for five months she kept herself
hidden, saying, **25** "Thus the Lord has done
for me in the days when he looked on me,
[w] to take away my reproach among people."

Birth of Jesus Foretold

26 In the sixth month the angel [x] Gabriel
was sent from God to a city of Galilee
named [y] Nazareth, **27** [z] to a virgin betrothed[1]
to a man whose name was Joseph, [a] of the
house of David. And the virgin's name was
Mary. **28** And he came to her and said,
"Greetings, [b] O favored one, [c] the Lord is
with you!"[2] **29** But [d] she was greatly troubled
at the saying, and tried to discern what sort
of greeting this might be. **30** And the angel
said to her, "Do not be afraid, Mary, for
[e] you have found favor with God. **31** And
behold, [f] you will conceive in your womb
and bear a son, and [g] you shall call his
name Jesus. **32** He will be great and will be
called the Son of [h] the Most High. And the
Lord God [i] will give to him the throne of
[j] his father David, **33** and he will reign over
the house of Jacob [k] forever, and of his
kingdom there will be no end."
34 And Mary said to the angel, "How will
this be, since I am a virgin?"[3]
35 And the angel answered her, [l] "The
Holy Spirit will come upon you, and the
power of [h] the Most High will overshadow
you; therefore the child to be born[4] will be
called [m] holy—[n] the Son of God. **36** And
behold, your relative Elizabeth in her old
age has also conceived a son, and this is
the sixth month with her [o] who was called
barren. **37** For [p] nothing will be impossible
with God." **38** And Mary said, "Behold, I am
the servant[5] of the Lord; let it be to me
according to your word." And [q] the angel
departed from her.

17 [m] Rom. 10:21 [n] ch. 7:27; Mal. 3:1; Matt. 11:10; Mark 1:2
18 [o] Gen. 15:8; [Gen. 17:17]
19 [p] ver. 26; Dan. 8:16; 9:21 [q] Rev. 8:2; [1 Kin. 17:1; Job 1:6; Isai. 63:9; Matt. 18:10]
20 [r] [Ezek. 3:26; 24:27]
21 [s] See ver. 9
22 [s] [See ver. 21 above] [t] ver. 62
23 [u] 2 Chr. 23:8; [ver. 8; 2 Kin. 11:5; 1 Chr. 9:25] [v] Heb. 10:11
25 [w] [Gen. 30:23; 1 Sam. 1:6; Ps. 113:9; Isai. 4:1]
26 [x] ver. 19 [y] See Matt. 2:23
27 [z] Matt. 1:16, 18 [a] ch. 2:4; Matt. 1:20
28 [b] [Ps. 45:2; Dan. 9:23] [c] Judg. 6:12
29 [d] See ver. 12
30 [e] Acts 7:46
31 [f] Isai. 7:14 [g] ch. 2:21; Matt. 1:21, 25
32 [h] ver. 76; ch. 6:35; Acts 7:48; See Mark 5:7 [i] ver. 69; 2 Sam. 7:11-13, 16; Ps. 89:4; 132:11; Isai. 9:6, 7; 16:5; Acts 2:30; [Rev. 3:7] [j] See Matt. 1:1 **33** [k] Dan. 2:44; 7:14, 18, 27; Heb. 1:8; Rev. 11:15; [John 12:34] **35** [l] Matt. 1:18, 20 [h] [See ver. 32 above] [m] John 6:69 [n] See Matt. 14:33 **36** [o] ver. 7 **37** [p] Cited from Gen. 18:14 (Gk.); See Matt. 19:26 **38** [q] [Judg. 6:21; Acts 12:10]

1 That is, legally pledged to be married 2 Some manuscripts add *Blessed are you among women!* 3 Greek *since I do not know a man* 4 Some manuscripts add *of you* 5 Greek *bondservant*; also verse 48

turn the hearts of the fathers to the children. He will restore unity to broken families, undoing the effects of sin (Ex. 34:7).

make ready. The climax is that John would prepare the way for the Lord. This is the reason he is especially remembered.

1:19 Gabriel. Gabriel and Michael are the only two angels named in the Bible. That Gabriel stands in God's presence shows his greatness—such a one should be believed. The Greek verb translated "bring you this good news" is the usual term for "preaching the gospel." Zechariah receives a sign: he will be silent until the boy is born.

1:21 temple. The holy place. The people were in the temple court, waiting for Zechariah to come out and pronounce the blessing. Offering incense did not take long, so the delay was puzzling. When Zechariah did not speak but made gestures (v. 22), the people concluded that he had seen a vision.

1:24 As the angel had promised, Elizabeth became pregnant. Childlessness was considered a divine punishment, but Elizabeth would bear this reproach no more (cf. Gen. 30:23).

1:27 betrothed. More binding than a modern engagement, this was virtually a form of marriage. The couple did not live together, but a divorce was needed to beak the relationship. See theological note "The Virgin Birth of Jesus."

1:28, 29 Mary was humbled and puzzled that the angel should say she was "favored" (a correct translation of the word sometimes rendered "full of grace"). The word indicates that Mary received grace, not that she was the source of grace to others.

1:31 Jesus. The name means "Yahweh is salvation."

1:32 great. There is a fuller meaning here than when the term was applied to John (v. 15). Jesus will be "the Son of the Most High."

the throne of his father. Luke points to the Messiah as a descendant of David (2 Sam. 7:12–16; Ps. 89:29).

1:33 The kingdom having no end is the kingdom of God.

1:34 Mary perceived that the angel was not talking about the children she would have in the course of her marriage to Joseph. She understood the angel to mean something miraculous—birth without a human father. The virgin conception is a distinctively Christian idea. Greek parallels sometimes cited relate stories of gods having sexual intercourse with women.

1:36 your relative. Elizabeth, and therefore Mary, was a descendant of Aaron (v. 5). The reference to "his father David" (v. 32) shows that Mary was also of Davidic descent. One of her parents was evidently descended from Aaron and the other from David.

Mary Visits Elizabeth

39 In those days Mary arose and went
with haste into [r]the hill country, to a town
in Judah, 40 and she entered the house of
Zechariah and greeted Elizabeth. 41 And
when Elizabeth heard the greeting of Mary,
the baby leaped in her womb. And
Elizabeth [s]was filled with the Holy Spirit,
42 and she exclaimed with a loud cry,
[t]"Blessed are you among women, and
[u]blessed is [v]the fruit of your womb! 43 And
why is this granted to me that the mother
of [w]my Lord should come to me? 44 For
behold, when the sound of your greeting
came to my ears, the baby in my womb
leaped for joy. 45 And [x]blessed is she who
believed that there would be[1] a fulfillment
of what was spoken to her from the Lord."

The Magnificat

46 And Mary said,

[y]"My [z]soul [a]magnifies the Lord,
47 [b]and my [z]spirit rejoices in [c]God
my Savior,
48 for [d]he has looked on the humble
estate of his servant.
For behold, from now on all
generations [e]will call me
blessed;
49 for [f]he who is mighty [g]has done great
things for me,
and [h]holy is his name.
50 And [i]his mercy is for those who fear
him
from generation to generation.
51 [j]He has shown strength with his arm;
[k]he has scattered the proud in the
thoughts of their hearts;
52 [j]he has brought down the mighty
from their thrones
[l]and exalted those of humble
estate;
53 he has filled [m]the hungry with good
things,

39 [r]ver. 65; Josh. 20:7; 21:11 41 [s]ver. 15, 67 42 [t][Judg. 5:24] [u][Deut. 28:4] [v]Ps. 127:3 43 [w]ch. 20:42; John 20:28; [ch. 2:11] 45 [x]John 20:29; [ver. 20] 46 [y]For ver. 46-53, [1 Sam. 2:1-10] [z]1 Thess. 5:23 [a]Ps. 34:2, 3; 69:30; Acts 10:46; 19:17 47 [b]Ps. 35:9; Isai. 61:10; Hab. 3:18; [Acts 16:34] [z][See ver. 46 above] [c]Ps. 106:21; 1 Tim. 1:1; 2:3; Tit. 1:3; 2:10; 3:4; Jude 25; [2 Tim. 1:9] 48 [d]1 Sam. 1:11; Ps. 138:6; [ch. 9:38]

[e]ch. 11:27; Ps. 72:17; [Mal. 3:12] 49 [f]Ps. 89:8; Zeph. 3:17 [g]Ps. 71:19; 126:2, 3 [h]Ps. 99:3; 111:9; Isai. 57:15 50 [i]Deut. 5:10; 7:9; Ps. 89:1, 2; 103:17 51 [j]Ps. 89:10; 98:1; 118:16; Isai. 51:9 [k]Dan. 4:37; See James 4:6 52 [j][See ver. 51 above] [l]Job 5:11; Ps. 75:7; 107:40, 41; 113:7, 8; 147:6; Ezek. 21:26; [James 4:10] 53 [m]Ps. 34:10; 107:9; [ch. 6:21, 24, 25]

[1] Or *believed, for there will be*

The Virgin Birth of Jesus

Matt. 1:18–25 and Luke 1:26–56; 2:4–7, two complementary but independent stories, agree in their record of Jesus' birth as the result of a miraculous conception. His mother Mary became pregnant by the Holy Spirit's creative action before she had any relationship with a man (Matt. 1:20; Luke 1:35).

Most Christians accepted the virgin birth without hesitation until the nineteenth century. Then it became a pivotal issue in the debate about Christian supernaturalism and the divinity of Jesus. Modernism, hoping to reinterpret Jesus as no more than a uniquely godly and insightful teacher, surrounded the virgin birth with a spirit of unnecessary skepticism.

In reality, the virgin birth belongs with the rest of the New Testament message about Jesus. The eternal dignity and glory that Jesus had before the world began (John 1:1–9) made it natural that He should enter into incarnate life in a way that proclaimed the glorious role He was coming to fulfill (Matt. 1:21–23; Luke 1:31–35).

Matthew and Luke are interested in how through this unique birth as a human being Jesus came to fulfill God's purposes of redemption, especially in tasting human sorrow and dying for sinners. They are less concerned with the virginal conception as a physical wonder or an apologetic weapon.

It is impossible to say whether the virgin birth was the only way Jesus could have come to earth and identified with His people. As it is, it testifies to Jesus' deity, setting Him apart from all others. It is appropriate that He should be born in this unusual way, since He was not implicated in sin, like all others since the Fall. Mary was not an exception in this respect, any more than David or Peter, though her sins are not recorded as theirs were. Through His death, Jesus became her Savior and the Savior of the rest of the church with her.

1:39 with haste. Mary must have left right away. Elizabeth was six months pregnant (v. 36); Mary stayed for three months and apparently went home before John's birth (vv. 56, 57).

1:41 filled with the Holy Spirit. The Holy Spirit enabled Elizabeth to pay tribute to the faith of Mary (v. 45).

1:46–55 This song of praise, called the *Magnificat* from its opening word in Latin, is revolutionary in its concern for the poor and despised of this world, and its rejection of the rich and proud.

1:48 servant. The word means "a slave" and expresses humility. Mary emphasizes God's mercy to the poor and His holiness and power.

1:51–53 The acts of God referred to are not necessarily in the past. Mary rejects accepted ideas of privilege for the rich as she speaks of what God will do for the poor (Ps. 9:18 note).

and the rich [n]he has sent empty
away.
54 He has [o]helped [p]his servant Israel,
[q]in remembrance of his mercy,
55 [r]as he spoke to our fathers,
[q]to Abraham and to his offspring
forever."

56 And Mary remained with her about three
months and returned to her home.

The Birth of John the Baptist

57 Now the time came for Elizabeth to
give birth, and she bore a son. 58 And her
neighbors and relatives heard that the Lord
[s]had shown great mercy to her, and they
rejoiced with her. 59 And [t]on the eighth day
they came to circumcise the child. And
they would have called him Zechariah after
his father, 60 but his mother answered, "No;
[u]he shall be called John." 61 And they said
to her, "None of your relatives is called by
this name." 62 And [v]they made signs to his
father, inquiring what he wanted him to be
called. 63 And he asked for [w]a writing tablet
and wrote, [u]"His name is John." And they
all wondered. 64 [x]And immediately his
mouth was opened and his tongue [y]loosed,
and he spoke, [z]blessing God. 65 And [a]fear
came on all their neighbors. And all these
things were talked about through all [b]the
hill country of Judea, 66 and all who heard
them [c]laid them up in their hearts, saying,
"What then will this child be?" For [d]the
hand of the Lord was with him.

Zechariah's Prophecy

67 And his father Zechariah [e]was filled
with the Holy Spirit and [f]prophesied, saying,

68 [g]"Blessed be the Lord [h]God of Israel,
for he has [i]visited and [j]redeemed
his people
69 and [k]has raised up [l]a horn of
salvation for us
[m]in the house of his servant David,
70 [n]as [o]he spoke by the mouth of his
holy prophets from of old,
71 [p]that we should be saved from our
enemies
and from the hand of all who
hate us;
72 [q]to show the mercy promised to our
fathers
and [r]to remember his holy
[s]covenant,
73 [t]the oath that he swore to our father
Abraham, to grant us
74 that we, being delivered from the
hand of our enemies,
might serve him [u]without fear,
75 [v]in holiness and righteousness
before him [w]all our days.
76 And you, child, will be called [x]the
prophet of [y]the Most High;
for [z]you will go before the Lord to
prepare his ways,
77 to give knowledge of salvation to his
people
[a]in the forgiveness of their sins,
78 because of the [b]tender mercy of
our God,
whereby [c]the sunrise shall [d]visit
us[1] [e]from on high
79 to [f]give light to [g]those who sit in
darkness and in the shadow
of death,
to guide our feet into [h]the way
of [i]peace."

53 [n]Job 22:9 54 [o]Isai. 41:8, 9; Heb. 2:16 [p]Isai. 44:21; 49:3 [q]Ps. 98:3; Mic. 7:20; [ver. 72, 73] 55 [r]Gen. 17:19; Ps. 132:11; Gal. 3:16 [q][See ver. 54 above] 58 [s]Gen. 19:19 59 [t]ch. 2:21; Gen. 17:12; Lev. 12:3; Phil. 3:5 60 [u]ver. 13 62 [v]ver. 22 63 [u][See ver. 60 above] [w]Isai. 8:1; 30:8 64 [x]ver. 20 [y]Mark 7:35 [z]ch. 2:28; 24:53 65 [a]ch. 5:26; 7:16 [b]See ver. 39 66 [c][ch. 2:19, 51] [d]Acts 11:21; 13:11 67 [e]ver. 15, 41 [f]Joel 2:28 68 [g]1 Kin. 1:48; 1 Chr. 29:10; Ezra 7:27; Ps. 41:13; 72:18; 106:48 [h]Isai. 29:23; Matt. 15:31; Acts 13:17 [i]ch. 7:16; Ex. 4:31; [ver. 78; Acts 15:14; Heb. 2:6] [j]ch. 2:38; Ps. 111:9; 130:7, 8; [ch. 24:21; Isai. 43:1; 59:20]

69 [k]1 Sam. 2:1, 10; Ps. 132:17; Ezek. 29:21 [l]2 Sam. 22:3; Ps. 18:2 [m]ver. 32 70 [n]Rom. 1:2; [Jer. 23:5, 6] [o]Acts 3:21 71 [p]Ps. 106:10 72 [q]Mic. 7:20 [r]Lev. 26:42; Ps. 105:8, 9; [ver. 54, 55] [s]See Rom. 9:4 73 [t]Gen. 22:16-18; 26:3; Heb. 6:13, 14 74 [u]Zeph. 3:15 75 [v]Eph. 4:24; [1 Thess. 2:10; Tit. 2:12] [w][Jer. 32:39; Matt. 28:20 (Gk.) 76 [x]ch. 7:26; 20:6; Matt. 11:9; 14:5 [y]See ver. 32 [z]ver. 17; ch. 3:4; 7:27; Mal. 3:1; Matt. 3:3; Mark 1:2, 3 77 [a][Matt. 26:28; Mark 1:4] 78 [b]Col. 3:12 (Gk.) [c]Mal. 4:2; Eph. 5:14; 2 Pet. 1:19 [d]See ver. 68 [e]ch. 24; 49 79 [f]Isai. 9:2; Matt. 4:16; [Acts 26:18]; See John 8:12 [g]Ps. 107:10; Isai. 42:7 [h]Rom. 3:17 [i]See ch. 2:14

1 Or *when the sunrise shall dawn upon us*; some manuscripts *since the sunrise has visited us*

1:54 helped. God's help through the Messiah is probably in mind.

1:55 Abraham. A reference to the covenant between God and Israel.

1:59 the eighth day. Jewish circumcision was on the eighth day (Gen. 17:12), but this is the earliest evidence for the custom of naming on that day.

1:63 writing tablet. A writing tablet was a board covered with wax that could be written on with a pointed instrument.

1:65 fear. The emotion of awe and reverence appropriate to the presence of God.

1:68 Blessed. A common way of beginning a thanksgiving (Ps. 72:18; 124:6).

redeemed. God's people are not rescued without cost.

1:69 horn. The horn was a symbol of strength.

his servant David. This phrase shows that Zechariah is talking about Jesus, not John.

1:72 his holy covenant. There are several covenants in the Old Testament, but that with Abraham was always seen as specially significant (Gen. 17).

1:76 you, child. Zechariah turns his attention to John and says he will be the forerunner of the Lord.

1:78 the sunrise. This refers to the Messiah (Mal. 4:2). The Greek means simply "rising," and some think of a shoot from Jesse (Is. 11:1). But the word is commonly used of the "rising" of the sun, and so a reference to the dawn is more likely.

80 [j]And the child grew and became strong in
spirit, and he was [k]in the wilderness until
the day of his public appearance to Israel.

The Birth of Jesus Christ

2 In those days [l]a decree went out from
[m]Caesar Augustus that all the world
should be [n]registered. 2 This was the first
[n]registration when[1] Quirinius [o]was governor of Syria. 3 And all went to be registered,
each to his own town. 4 And Joseph also
went up [p]from Galilee, from the town of
[q]Nazareth, to Judea, to [r]the city of David,
which is called [s]Bethlehem, [t]because he
was of the house and lineage of David, 5 to
be registered with Mary, his betrothed,[2]
who was with child. 6 And [t]while they were
there, the time came for her to give birth.
7 And she gave birth to her firstborn son
and [u]wrapped him in swaddling cloths and
[v]laid him in a manger, because there was
no place for them in [w]the inn.

The Shepherds and the Angels

8 And in the same region there were shepherds out in the field, keeping watch over
their flock by night. 9 And an angel of the
Lord [x]appeared to them, and [y]the glory of
the Lord shone around them, and they
were filled with fear. 10 And the angel said
to them, "Fear not, for behold, I bring you
good news of a great joy that will be for all
[z]the people. 11 For [a]unto you is born this
day in [b]the city of David [c]a Savior, who is
[d]Christ [e]the Lord. 12 And [f]this will be a sign
for you: you will find a baby [g]wrapped in
swaddling cloths and lying in a manger."
13 And suddenly there was with the angel [h]a
multitude of the heavenly host praising
God and saying,

14 "Glory to God in the highest,
and on earth peace among those
with whom he is pleased!"[3]

15 When the angels went away from them
into heaven, the shepherds said to one
another, "Let us go over to Bethlehem and
see this thing that has happened, which
the Lord has made known to us." 16 And
they went with haste and found Mary and
Joseph, and the baby [m]lying in a manger.
17 And when they saw it, they made known
the saying that had been told them concerning this child. 18 And all who heard it
wondered at what the shepherds told
them. 19 But [n]Mary treasured up all these
things, pondering them in her heart. 20 And
the shepherds returned, [o]glorifying and
praising God for all they had heard and
seen, as it had been told them.

80 [j]ch. 2:40 [k]Matt. 3:1; 11:7
Chapter 2
1 [l]Acts 17:7 [m][ch. 3:1] [n][Acts 5:37]
2 [n][See ver. 1 above] [o]ch. 3:1
4 [p]ch. 1:26 [q]See Matt. 2:23 [r]ver. 11; John 7:42; [1 Sam. 16:1] [s]Matt. 2:1 [t]ch. 1:27
6 [t][See ver. 4 above]
7 [u]ver. 12 [v]ver. 16 [w]ch. 22:11 (Gk.)
9 [x]ch. 24:4; Acts 12:7 [y]ch. 9:31; Acts 7:55; 2 Cor. 3:18
10 [z]ver. 32; John 11:50; [Zech. 9:9]
11 [a]Isai. 9:6 [b]ver. 4 [c]Matt. 1:21; John 4:42 [d]Acts 2:36; 10:36; [ch. 23:2]; See Matt. 1:17 [e][ch. 1:43]
12 [f]1 Sam. 2:34; 2 Kin. 19:29; 20:8, 9; Isai. 7:11, 14 [g]ver. 7
13 [h]Gen. 28:12; 32:1, 2; 1 Kin. 22:19; 2 Chr. 18:18; Ps. 103:21; 148:2; Dan. 7:10; Rev. 5:11
14 [i]ch. 19:38; [Ps. 148:1; Matt. 21:9] [j][ch. 10:21; Matt. 6:10; 28:18; John 17:4; Acts 7:49; Eph. 3:15; Col. 1:16, 20; Rev. 5:13] [k]ch. 1:79; Ps. 85:10; Isai. 9:6, 7; Hag. 2:9; Acts 10:36; Rom. 5:1; Eph. 2:14, 17; Col. 1:20 [l][ch. 3:22; 12:32; Eph. 1:5, 9; Phil. 2:13] **16** [m]ver. 7, 12 **19** [n]ver. 51; [ch. 1:66; Gen. 37:11]
20 [o]See ch. 7:16

1 Or *This was the registration before* 2 That is, one legally pledged to be married 3 Some manuscripts *peace, good will among men*

1:80 in the wilderness. John grew up in the wilderness and may have had contact with religious communities like that at Qumran, an ascetic community whose writings, the Dead Sea Scrolls, were discovered in 1946.

2:1–3 Luke dates the birth of Jesus by the common method of referring to the political rulers (3:1). There is no other record of a worldwide census under Augustus, but he did reorganize the administration of the empire and conducted censuses for taxation purposes. Quirinius was governor of Syria when a census was carried out in A.D. 6 and may have been there earlier (10–7 B.C.). It seems to have been the custom to conduct a census at intervals of fourteen years. Luke may be referring to a census preceding the well-known and unpopular census taken by Quirinius in A.D. 6.

2:3 to be registered. People went to their ancestral homes for registration. This would have made it easier to list families.

2:5 his betrothed. See note 1:27.

2:7 The birth of the baby is described simply. "Swaddling cloths" were strips of cloth used to wrap a baby. That the Child was put in a manger may mean that the birth was in a stable. There is a tradition that Jesus was born in a cave, which could have been used as a stable. Mangers were often outdoors, so it is possible that Jesus was born in the open air. Another possibility is that the place was the home of a poor family, where the animals would be under the same roof.

there was no place for them in the inn. This may mean that the innkeeper did not want to have them there.

2:8 shepherds out in the field. Animals to be used for the temple sacrifices were kept in the open, even in winter. The presence of shepherds outdoors does not prove that Jesus was born in a warm time of year. Shepherds were a despised class because their work prevented them from keeping the ceremonial law, and as they moved about the country it was common for them to be regarded as thieves. They were considered unreliable and were not allowed to give evidence in the courts.

2:9 angel. An angel is a messenger. In the New Testament, an "angel" is usually a supernatural messenger from God.

2:10 The angel began by reassuring the frightened men (cf. 1:13, 30), and went on to use strong terms for the great joy and the good news he was telling them.

all the people. The Greek phrase normally refers to the whole people of Israel.

2:11 Jesus is called "Savior" only twice in the four Gospels (cf. John 4:42). "Christ" means "Messiah," while "Lord" is regularly used in the Septuagint (the Greek translation of the Old Testament) for God's own name, conventionally translated with small capitals ("LORD"). The most outstanding terms are used for the new Baby.

2:12 The sign would enable them to find the Baby and it would prove to them the truth of what the angel said.

2:13 the heavenly host. "Host" is a military term, and it is remarkable that an army should announce peace (v. 14). The "peace" is peace with God, a peace that Christ would bring.

2:20 Luke often mentions praise to God (5:25, 26; 7:16; 13:13).

21 And [p] at the end of eight days, when he
was circumcised, [q] he was called Jesus, the
name given by the angel before he was conceived in the womb.

Jesus Presented at the Temple

22 And [r] when the time came for their
purification according to the Law of Moses,
they brought him up to Jerusalem [s] to present him to the Lord 23 (as it is written in
[t] the Law of the Lord, [u] "Every male who
first opens the womb shall be called holy to
the Lord") 24 and to offer a sacrifice according to what is said in [t] the Law of the Lord,
[v] "a pair of turtledoves, or two young
pigeons." 25 Now there was a man in Jerusalem, whose name was Simeon, and this
man was [w] righteous and [x] devout, [y] waiting
for [z] the consolation of Israel, and the Holy
Spirit was upon him. 26 And it had been
revealed to him by the Holy Spirit that he
would not [a] see death before he had seen
[b] the Lord's Christ. 27 And he came in the
Spirit into the temple, and when [c] the parents brought in the child Jesus, to do for
him according to the custom of the Law,
28 he took him up in his arms and [d] blessed
God and said,

29 "Lord, now you are letting your
servant[1] depart [e] in peace,
[f] according to your word;
30 for [g] my eyes have seen your
[h] salvation
31 [i] that you have prepared in the
presence of all peoples,
32 [j] a light for revelation to the
Gentiles,
and [k] for glory to [l] your people
Israel."

21 [p] See ch. 1:59 [q] ch. 1:31; Matt. 1:21, 25
22 [r] Lev. ch. 12; [ver. 21, 27; Gal. 4:4] [s] [1 Sam. 1:22, 24]
23 [t] ver. 39; Ex. 13:9; 2 Chr. 31:3 [u] [Ex. 13:2, 12]
24 [t] [See ver. 23 above] [v] Cited from Lev. 12:8
25 [w] ch. 1:6 [x] Acts 2:5; 8:2; 22:12 [y] ver. 38; ch. 23:51; Isai. 25:9; Mark 15:43; [Gen. 49:18] [z] Isai. 40:1; 57:18
26 [a] Ps. 89:48; John 8:51; Heb. 11:5; [Acts 2:27] [b] [ch. 9:20; 23:35; 1 Sam. 24:6]
27 [c] ver. 33, 41, 43, 48-51
28 [d] ch. 1:64
29 [e] Gen. 15:15 [f] ver. 26
30 [g] Isai. 52:10 [h] See ch. 3:6
31 [i] Ps. 98:2; See ch. 24:47
32 [j] Isai. 42:6; 49:6; 52:10; 60:3; John 8:12; Acts 13:47; 26:23 [k] [Isai. 45:25; 46:13] [l] ver. 10
33 [m] ver. 27
34 [n] [Isai. 8:14; Matt. 21:44; John 9:39; 1 Cor. 1:23, 24; 2 Cor. 2:16; 1 Pet. 2:8, 9] [o] Acts 28:22
36 [p] See Ex. 15:20
37 [q] 1 Tim. 5:5

33 And [m] his father and his mother marveled at what was said about him. 34 And
Simeon blessed them and said to Mary his
mother, "Behold, this child is appointed
[n] for the fall and rising of many in Israel,
and for a sign [o] that is opposed 35 (and a
sword will pierce through your own soul
also), so that thoughts from many hearts
may be revealed."
36 And there was [p] a prophetess, Anna, the
daughter of Phanuel, of the tribe of Asher.
She was advanced in years, having lived
with her husband seven years from when
she was a virgin, 37 and then as a widow
until she was eighty-four.[2] She did not
depart from the temple, [q] worshiping with
[r] fasting and prayer night and day. 38 And
coming up at that very hour she began to
give thanks to God and to speak of him to
all who were [s] waiting for the redemption of
Jerusalem.

The Return to Nazareth

39 And when they had performed everything according to [t] the Law of the Lord,
they returned into Galilee, to their own
town of [u] Nazareth. 40 [v] And the child grew
and became strong, filled with wisdom.
And the favor of God was upon him.

The Boy Jesus in the Temple

41 Now [w] his parents went [x] to Jerusalem
every year at [y] the Feast of the Passover.
42 And when he was twelve years old, [z] they
went up according to custom. 43 And when
the feast [a] was ended, as they were return-

[r] ch. 5:33; Matt. 6:16-18; Acts 13:2; 14:23; 2 Cor. 6:5; 11:27 38 [s] ver. 25; See ch. 1:68 39 [t] ver. 23 [u] ver. 4 40 [v] ch. 1:80 41 [w] ver. 27 [x] [1 Sam. 1:3] [y] Ex. 23:15; Deut. 16:1; John 2:13 42 [z] John 11:55 43 [a] Ex. 12:15; Lev. 23:8; Deut. 16:3

1 Greek *bondservant* 2 Or *as a widow for eighty-four years*

2:21–24 Jesus was circumcised on the eighth day as the law prescribed (Gen. 17:12; cf. Gal. 4:4, 5). The need for purification arose from the mother's being ceremonially unclean for seven days after the birth of a son. For another thirty-three days she was to keep away from holy things (these times were doubled for a daughter, Lev. 12:1–5). The mother was then to offer a lamb plus a dove or pigeon. If she was poor her offering was two doves or pigeons (Lev. 12:6–8). Mary gave the offering of the poor. The first male child of every mother was presented to the Lord (Ex. 13:2).

2:25 the consolation of Israel. This title for the Messiah refers to the comfort that He would bring.

2:28–32 blessed God. Simeon's blessing is often called the "Nunc Dimittis" from its opening words in Latin.

2:30 your salvation. This phrase signifies the Child who would bring God's salvation to humanity.

2:31 all peoples. This phrase is plural and refers to the Gentiles as well as Israel (v. 10 note).

2:34 fall and rising. If the "fall and rising" applies to one group, then it means they must be humbled in repentance before they can rise into salvation. If it describes two groups, then it indicates that those who reject Jesus will fall eternally, but those who accept Him will rise to be with God.

2:35 sword. The sword imagery means that all this will not be without cost to Mary as she sees her Son rejected and crucified.

2:36 Anna. Prophets were rare in Israel in those days, but the aged Anna was a prophetess.

2:41 The Passover was one of three feasts that had to be observed in Jerusalem (Ex. 23:14–17; 34:23).

2:42 twelve years old. Jesus may have gone up with His parents every year, but Jewish custom specified that a boy should be taken to the feast a year or two before he was thirteen, when he would be made a "son of the commandment" and become an adult member of the Jewish religious community.

2:43–45 Luke does not say why Jesus stayed behind or how Joseph and

ing, the boy Jesus stayed behind in Jerusalem. [w]His parents did not know it, 44 but
supposing him to be in the group they
went a day's journey, but then they began
to search for him among their relatives and
acquaintances, 45 and when they did not
find him, they returned to Jerusalem,
searching for him. 46 After three days they
found him in the temple, [b]sitting among
[c]the teachers, listening to them and asking
them questions. 47 And all who heard him
were amazed at his understanding and his
answers. 48 And when his parents[1] saw him,
they were astonished. And his mother said
to him, "Son, why have you treated us so?
Behold, [d]your father and I have been
searching for you in great distress." 49 And
he said to them, "Why were you looking
for me? Did you not know that [e]I must be
in [f]my Father's house?"[2] 50 And [g]they did
not understand the saying that he spoke to
them. 51 And he went down with them and
came to Nazareth and was submissive to
them. And [h]his mother treasured up all
these things in her heart.
52 And Jesus [i]increased in wisdom and in
stature[3] and in [i]favor with God and man.

John the Baptist Prepares the Way

3 In the fifteenth year of the reign of
[j]Tiberius Caesar, [k]Pontius Pilate [l]being
governor of Judea, and [m]Herod being
tetrarch of Galilee, and his brother Philip
tetrarch of the region of Ituraea and
Trachonitis, and Lysanias tetrarch of
Abilene, 2 during [n]the high priesthood of
Annas and [o]Caiaphas, [p]the word of God
came to [q]John the son of Zechariah in [r]the
wilderness. 3 And he went into all the
region around the Jordan, proclaiming [s]a
baptism of repentance [t]for the forgiveness
of sins. 4 As it is written in [u]the book of the
words of Isaiah the prophet,

[v]"The voice of one crying in the
wilderness:
[w]'Prepare the way of the Lord,[4]
make his paths straight.
5 [x]Every valley shall be filled,
[y]and every mountain and hill shall
be made low,
[z]and the crooked shall become
straight,
and the rough places shall become
level ways,
6 [a]and all flesh shall see [b]the salvation
of God.'"

7 He said therefore to the crowds that
came out to be baptized by him, [c]"You
brood of [d]vipers! Who warned you to flee
from [e]the wrath to come? 8 Bear fruits [f]in
keeping with repentance. And do not begin
to say to yourselves, [g]'We have Abraham as
our father.' For I tell you, God is able from
[h]these stones to raise up children for

43 [w][See ver. 41 above] 46 [b]See Matt. 26:55 [c]ch. 5:17 48 [d]ver. 27; [ver. 49] 49 [e]See ch. 13:33 [f]John 2:16; 14:2 50 [g][ch. 18:34]; See Mark 9:32 51 [h]See ver. 19 52 [i][1 Sam. 2:26]
Chapter 3
1 [j][ch. 2:1] [k]See Matt. 27:2 [l]ch. 2:2 [m]ver. 19; ch. 8:3; 9:7, 9; 13:31; 23:7; Matt. 14:1; Acts 4:27; 13:1; [Mark 6:14]
2 [n]John 18:13, 24; Acts 4:6 [o]See Matt. 26:3 [p]For ver. 2-17, see Matt. 3:1-12; Mark 1:2-8 [q]John 1:6, 7 [r]ch. 1:80; Josh. 15:61; [Judg. 1:16]
3 [s]Acts 2:38 [t]Matt. 26:28; [ch. 1:77]
4 [u]ch. 4:17; [Acts 8:28] [v]John 1:23; Cited from Isai. 40:3-5 [w]ch. 1:76
5 [x][Isai. 57:14] [y]Isai. 49:11; Zech. 4:7 [z]Isai. 42:16; 45:2
6 [a]Isai. 52:10; [Ps. 98:2, 3] [b]ch. 2:30; Acts 28:28; [ch. 1:69, 71, 77; Tit. 2:11] 7 [c]Matt. 12:34; 23:33 [d]Ps. 140:3 [e]Rom. 5:9; Eph. 5:6; Col. 3:6; 1 Thess. 1:10 8 [f]Acts 26:20 [g]John 8:39 [h][ch. 4:3]

[1] Greek *they* [2] Or *about my Father's business* [3] Or *years* [4] Or *crying, Prepare in the wilderness the way of the Lord*

Mary came to leave Him behind, but in a large caravan it would be easy to assume that a boy was with friends. If later custom was followed, the women and small children went ahead and the men followed. Each parent might think a twelve-year-old boy was with the other.

2:46–48 The temple courts were commonly used for teaching. Jesus both listened and asked questions, showing a determination to learn. In Jewish education there was an emphasis on discussion of problems, which is perhaps behind the reference to "his understanding and his answers" (v. 47). But Joseph and Mary did not understand (v. 50); there is reproach in Mary's words.

2:49 my Father's house. Already at twelve years of age, Jesus was conscious of a special relationship to the heavenly Father. The Jews did not speak in this way, but said "our Father" or added "in heaven" or the like.

2:51 submissive. Despite His understanding of His relationship to the heavenly Father, Jesus was a dutiful Son on earth and was obedient to Joseph and Mary as He grew. Mary did not understand it all, but she did not forget.

2:52 increased. Luke notes Jesus' well-rounded personal development: intellectual, social, and spiritual.

3:1 Luke's lengthy chronological reference comes at the beginning of John's ministry, probably about A.D. 27–29.

Pontius Pilate. In his will, Herod the Great left Judea to his son Archelaus, and other territories to his sons Philip and Antipas. But Archelaus ruled so badly that the Romans removed him in A.D. 6 and appointed their own governor. Pontius Pilate was the fifth governor of Judea, serving there from A.D. 26–36.

tetrarch. A tetrarch was a kind of petty prince. "Herod" here is Herod Antipas. Philip's region was northeast of the Sea of Galilee. Nothing more is known of Lysanias, but Abilene was north of the other regions.

3:2 The Jews had only one high priest at a time. Annas had been deposed by the Romans who appointed instead Caiaphas, his son-in-law. The Romans saw to it that Caiaphas exercised the official functions, but many Jews still considered Annas the true high priest.

the word of God came. John's message was not his own but the dynamic word of God Himself.

3:3 baptism of repentance. The Jews baptized Gentiles if they wished to become part of the people of God. The sting in John's practice was his call on Jews to undergo a rite they saw as fit only for Gentiles. John looked for a change of heart in Jews. See notes Matt. 3:6; Mark 1:4.

3:4–6 All four Gospels apply Is. 40:3 to John and agree that John saw himself as only a herald. But only Luke adds Is. 40:4, 5, emphasizing the thought of God's salvation.

3:7, 8 A strong warning is directed at those who claimed Abraham as father. Being a Jew would not deliver one from the coming wrath.

Abraham. 9 Even now the axe is laid to the
root of the trees. [i]Every tree therefore that
does not bear good fruit is cut down and
thrown into the fire."
10 And the crowds asked him, [j]"What
then shall we do?" 11 And he answered
them, [k]"Whoever has two tunics[1] is to
share with him who has none, and whoever has food is to do likewise." 12 [l]Tax collectors also came to be baptized and said to
him, "Teacher, [j]what shall we do?" 13 And
he said to them, [m]"Collect no more than
you are authorized to do." 14 Soldiers also
asked him, "And we, [j]what shall we do?"
And he said to them, [m]"Do not extort
money from anyone by threats or by false
accusation, and be content with your
[n]wages."
15 As the people were in expectation, and
all were questioning in their hearts concerning John, [o]whether he might be [p]the
Christ, 16 [q]John answered them all, saying,
"I baptize you with water, but [r]he who is
mightier than I is coming, [s]the strap of
whose sandals I am not worthy to untie.
He will baptize you [t]with the Holy Spirit
and with [u]fire. 17 His [v]winnowing fork is in
his hand, to clear his threshing floor and to
[w]gather the wheat into his barn, [x]but the
chaff he will burn with [y]unquenchable
fire."
18 So [z]with many other exhortations he
preached good news to the people. 19 But
[a]Herod the tetrarch, who had been reproved
by him for Herodias, his brother's wife,
and for all the evil things that Herod had
done, 20 added this to them all, that [b]he
locked up John in prison.
21 Now when all the people were baptized, and when [c]Jesus also had been
baptized and was praying, [d]the heavens
were opened, 22 and [e]the Holy Spirit
descended on him in bodily form, like a
dove; and [f]a voice came from heaven,
[g]"You are my beloved Son;[2] with you I am
well pleased."[3]

The Genealogy of Jesus Christ

23 Jesus, [h]when he began his ministry,
was about [i]thirty years of age, being [j]the
son (as was supposed) of Joseph, the son
of Heli, 24 the son of Matthat, the son of
Levi, the son of Melchi, the son of Jannai,
the son of Joseph, 25 the son of Mattathias,
the son of Amos, the son of Nahum, the
son of Esli, the son of Naggai, 26 the son of
Maath, the son of Mattathias, the son of
Semein, the son of Josech, the son of Joda,
27 the son of Joanan, the son of Rhesa, [k]the
son of Zerubbabel, the son [l]of Shealtiel,[4]
the son of Neri, 28 the son of Melchi, the
son of Addi, the son of Cosam, the son of

9 [i]ch. 13:7, 9; Matt. 7:19; John 15:2, 6 **10** [j]Acts 2:37; 16:30; 22:10 **11** [k]Isai. 58:7; Dan. 4:27; Eph. 4:28; James 2:15, 16; 1 John 3:17; [ch. 18:22] **12** [l]ch. 7:29; Matt. 21:32 [j][See ver. 10 above] **13** [m]ch. 19:8 **14** [j][See ver. 10 above] [m][See ver. 13 above] [n]1 Cor. 9:7 (Gk.) **15** [o]John 1:19, 20 [p]See Matt. 1:17 **16** [q]John 1:26; Acts 1:5 [r]John 1:15, 27; 3:30, 31; Acts 13:25 [s]Isai. 5:27 [t]John 1:33; Acts 11:16 [u][Isai. 4:4; Mal. 3:2, 3; Acts 2:3] **17** [v]Isai. 30:24 [w]Matt. 13:30 [x]Mal. 4:1 [y]Mark 9:43, 48 **18** [z][John 20:30; 21:25] **19** [a]Matt. 14:3; Mark 6:17, 18; See ver. 1 **20** [b][John 3:24] **21** [c]For ver. 21, 22, see Matt. 3:13-17; Mark 1:9-11; [John 1:32-34]

[d]Acts 7:56 **22** [e][ch. 4:18, 21; Acts 10:38] [f]John 12:28 [g][ch. 9:35; Ps. 2:7; Isai. 42:1; Eph. 1:6; Col. 1:13; 2 Pet. 1:17; 1 John 5:9] **23** [h]Matt. 4:17; Acts 1:1, 22 [i][Num. 4:3] [j]ch. 4:22; Matt. 13:55; John 1:45; 6:42; For ver. 23-38, [Matt. 1:1-16] **27** [k]Matt. 1:12 [l]Ezra 3:2

[1] Greek *chiton*, a long garment worn under the cloak next to the skin [2] Or *my Son, my* (or *the*) *Beloved* [3] Some manuscripts *beloved Son; today I have begotten you* [4] Greek *Salathiel*

3:9 axe is laid to the root. This phrase points to certain and speedy judgment.

fire. A symbol of judgment.

3:11 The tunic was an undergarment; normally only one was worn. John suggests that the man who owns two should give the spare to someone without one, and so also with food.

3:12 Tax collectors. Roman taxes were collected by agents who bid for the rights to collect taxes in a city. They would pay the Romans what they bid and collect more for their own salaries. There was a strong temptation for them to enrich themselves by collecting much more than what was reasonable. Jewish tax collectors were despised as collaborators with the occupying Roman forces. They were excluded from the religious life of the synagogue and the temple.

3:14 Like tax collectors, soldiers were tempted to use their position to enrich themselves. John enjoins honesty on all. All four Gospels have an account of the ministry of John the Baptist as he called people to repent in preparation for the coming of Jesus. Luke alone tells us what John said to questioners who were unclear about what it would mean for them.

3:15 Messianic speculations were in the air, but John said clearly he was no messiah. A greater One was coming.

3:16 not worthy to untie. In the rabbinic schools a student did not pay his teacher. He was required to perform services, but not the loosing of the sandal, which was considered too menial. John took a lowly place.

fire. The baptism with fire points to judgment (v. 9 note). The winnowing fork (v. 17) is another symbol for judgment. Workers used the fork to throw harvested grain into the wind, letting the grains fall directly to the ground and the chaff blow away. When the threshing floor was cleared, the chaff would be burned.

3:19, 20 Herod Antipas divorced his wife and married his niece Herodias who was married to his own brother (Mark 6:17 note). John denounced this scandalous deed, and Herod imprisoned him in the fortress of Machaerus, east of the Dead Sea.

3:21 Jesus identified Himself with sinners by undergoing their baptism. See "The Baptism of Jesus" at Mark 1:9.

3:22 All four Gospels tell us that the Holy Spirit came upon Jesus at this time. Doves were important in the Old Testament sacrificial system. Within that culture, they were regarded as affectionate and gentle. In the Scripture the dove is used often in imagery and comparisons, not always with the same meaning. See also Gen. 1:2; 8:8–12.

3:23–38 Luke's genealogy differs from that in Matthew (Matt. 1:2–17) in going all the way back to Adam rather than just to Abraham. Some of the names differ and the order is different. Some suggest that Matthew has Joseph's line and Luke Mary's, but Luke specifically starts with "Joseph." It may be that Matthew is giving not direct ancestors but those who would have been legally in line for the throne of David. Both evangelists emphasize that Jesus was of Davidic descent.

Elmadam, the son of Er, 29 the son of
Joshua, the son of Eliezer, the son of Jorim,
the son of Matthat, the son of Levi, 30 the
son of Simeon, the son of Judah, the son
of Joseph, the son of Jonam, the son of Eliakim, 31 the son of Melea, the son of Menna,
the son of Mattatha, the son of [m]Nathan,
the son of David, 32 [n]the son of Jesse, the
son of Obed, the son of Boaz, the son of
Sala, the son of Nahshon, 33 the son of Amminadab, the son of Admin, the son of
Arni, the son of Hezron, the son of Perez,
the son of Judah, 34 [o]the son of Jacob, [p]the
son of Isaac, [q]the son of Abraham, [r]the son
of Terah, the son of Nahor, 35 the son of
Serug, the son of Reu, the son of Peleg, the
son of Eber, the son of Shelah, 36 the son of
Cainan, the son of Arphaxad, the son of
Shem, the son of Noah, the son of Lamech,
37 the son of Methuselah, the son of Enoch,
the son of Jared, the son of Mahalaleel,
the son of Cainan, 38 the son of Enos, the
son of Seth, the son of Adam, the son of
God.

The Temptation of Jesus

4 [s]And Jesus, [t]full of the Holy Spirit, [u]re-
turned from the Jordan and was led
[v]by the Spirit in the wilderness 2 for [w]forty
days, [x]being tempted by the devil. [w]And he
ate nothing during those days. And when
they were ended, [y]he was hungry. 3 The
devil said to him, "If you are [z]the Son of
God, command [a]this stone to become
bread." 4 And Jesus answered him, [b]"It is
written, [c]'Man shall not live by bread
alone.'" 5 [d]And the devil took him up and
showed him all the kingdoms of the world
in a moment of time, 6 and said to him, "To
you [e]I will give all this authority and their
glory, [e]for it has been delivered to me, and
I give it to whom I will. 7 If you, then, will
worship me, it will all be yours." 8 And
Jesus answered him, [f]"It is written,

> [g]" 'You shall worship the Lord your
> God,
> and [h]him only shall you serve.' "

9 [i]And he took him to Jerusalem and set
him on the pinnacle of the temple and said
to him, "If you are [j]the Son of God, throw
yourself down from here, 10 for it is written,

> [k]" 'He will command his angels
> concerning you,
> to guard you,'

11 and

> [k]" 'On their hands they will bear
> you up,
> lest you strike your foot against a
> stone.' "

12 And Jesus answered him, "It is said, [l]'You
shall not [m]put the Lord your God to the
test.'" 13 And when the devil had ended
every temptation, he departed from him
[n]until an opportune time.

Jesus Begins His Ministry

14 [o]And Jesus returned [p]in the power of
the Spirit to Galilee, and [q]a report about
him went out through all the surrounding
country. 15 And [r]he taught in their synagogues, being glorified by all.

Jesus Rejected at Nazareth

16 [s]And he came to [t]Nazareth, where he
had been brought up. And [u]as was his custom, [v]he went to the synagogue on the
Sabbath day, and he stood up [w]to read.
17 And [x]the scroll of the prophet Isaiah was

31 [m]2 Sam. 5:14; 1 Chr. 3:5; 14:4; Zech. 12:12
32 [n]1 Sam. 16:1; 17:12; [Ruth 4:18-22; 1 Chr. 2:1-15]
34 [o]Gen. 29:35 [p]Gen. 25:26 [q]Gen. 21:3 [r]For ver. 34-38, see Gen. 5:3-32; 11:10-26; 1 Chr. 1:1-4, 24-27
Chapter 4
1 [s]For ver. 1-13, see Matt. 4:1-11; Mark 1:12, 13 [t]ver. 18; ch. 3:22; John 1:33; 3:34; Acts 10:38; [ch. 1:15; Acts 6:5] [u]ch. 3:3, 21 [v]ver. 14
2 [w][Deut. 9:9, 18; 1 Kin. 19:8] [x][Heb. 2:18; 4:15] [y][John 4:6, 7]
3 [z]See Matt. 14:33 [a][ch. 3:8]
4 [b]ver. 8, 10; Eph. 6:17 [c]Cited from Deut. 8:3; [John 4:34]
5 [d]Matt. 4:8
6 [e]Rev. 13:2
8 [f]ver. 4; [ver. 12] [g]Cited from Deut. 6:13 [h]1 Sam. 7:3
9 [i]Matt. 4:5 [j]ver. 3
10 [k]Cited from Ps. 91:11, 12
11 [k][See ver. 10 above]
12 [l]Cited from Deut. 6:16 [m][Isai. 7:12]
13 [n][ch. 22:53; John 14:30]
14 [o]Matt. 4:12 [p]ver. 1; [Acts 1:8] [q]ver. 37
15 [r]See Matt. 4:23 16 [s]For ver. 16-30, [Matt. 13:54-58; Mark 6:1-6] [t]ch. 2:39, 51 [u][Acts 17:2] [v]ver. 31; See Mark 6:2 [w]Acts 13:15, 27; 15:21 17 [x]ch. 3:4; [Acts 8:28]

4:1 Jesus was "full of the Holy Spirit . . . and was led by the Spirit," showing that the temptation was in the plan of God. Right at the beginning, Jesus faced the question of what sort of Messiah He was to be.

4:3–13 The devil seeks to deflect Jesus from His divinely appointed mission. In His victory over Satan, Jesus binds the strong man and proceeds to plunder his possessions (11:21, 22). Luke's account highlights the parallel between Jesus' temptation and the trials of Israel in the wilderness. Jesus was tempted for forty days in the wilderness, and Israel wandered for forty years in the wilderness (Num. 14:34). Israel failed the test of obedience, while Jesus was fully obedient to the Father.

4:5–8 This temptation comes third in Matthew. The reason for the different order is not known. The temptation is for Jesus to set up a mighty world empire, but at the cost of worshiping Satan. Again Jesus rejects the temptation by citing Scripture (Deut. 6:13).

4:9 the pinnacle. This may have been the top of the temple wall overlooking the Kidron Valley or perhaps the highest point of the temple itself. Jesus was tempted to make a public display of miraculous power, but He responds by quoting Scripture (v. 12). The passage quoted (Deut. 6:16) again recalls Israel's experience in the wilderness.

4:14 Jesus carried out an extensive ministry before going back to Nazareth.

4:16–20 This account is the oldest known report of the order of worship in a synagogue service. The service included a reading from the Law and one from the Prophets. Jesus or the ruler of the synagogue may have chosen Is. 61:1, 2 and 58:6. It was customary to stand for the reading as a mark of respect for God's Word, and to sit for the sermon. The reading chosen shows a strong concern for the poor (1:51–53 note; Ps. 9:18 note).

given to him. He unrolled the scroll and
found the place where it was written,

18 [y]"The Spirit of the Lord [z]is upon me,
because he has anointed me
to [a]proclaim good news to the
poor.
[b]He has sent me to proclaim liberty to
the captives
and [c]recovering of sight to the
blind,
[d]to set at liberty those who are
oppressed,
19 [e]to proclaim the year of the Lord's
favor."

20 And he rolled up the scroll and gave it
back to the attendant and [f]sat down. And
the eyes of all in the synagogue were [g]fixed
on him. 21 And he began to say to them,
"Today [h]this Scripture [i]has been fulfilled in
your hearing." 22 And all spoke well of him
and marveled at [j]the gracious words that
were coming from his mouth. And they
said, [k]"Is not this [l]Joseph's son?" 23 And he
said to them, "Doubtless you will quote to
me this proverb, [m]'Physician, heal yourself.' What we have heard you did [n]at
Capernaum, do here in your hometown as
well." 24 And he said, "Truly, I say to you,
[o]no prophet is acceptable in his hometown. 25 But in truth, I tell you, there were
many widows in Israel in the days of Elijah,
when [p]the heavens were shut up three
years and six months, and a great famine
came over all the land, 26 and Elijah was
sent to none of them [q]but only to
Zarephath, in the land of Sidon, to a
woman who was a widow. 27 And [r]there
were many lepers[1] in Israel in the time of
the prophet Elisha, and none of them was
cleansed, [s]but only Naaman the Syrian."
28 When they heard these things, all in the
synagogue were filled with wrath. 29 And
they rose up and [t]drove him out of the
town and brought him to the brow of the
hill on which their town was built, so that
they could throw him down the cliff. 30 But
[u]passing through their midst, he went
away.

Jesus Heals a Man with an Unclean Demon

31 [v]And he [w]went down to Capernaum, a
city of Galilee. And [x]he was teaching them
[y]on the Sabbath, 32 and [z]they were astonished at his teaching, [z]for his word possessed authority. 33 And [x]in the synagogue
there was a man who had the spirit of an
unclean demon, and he cried out with a
loud voice, 34 "Ha![2] [a]What have you to do
with us, Jesus of Nazareth? Have you come
to destroy us? [b]I know who you are—[c]the
Holy One of God." 35 But Jesus [d]rebuked
him, saying, "Be silent and come out
of him!" And when the demon had thrown
him down in their midst, he came out
of him, having done him no harm. 36 And
[e]they were all amazed and said to one
another, "What is this word? [e]For with
authority and power he commands the
unclean spirits, and they come out!" 37 And
[f]reports about him went out into every
place in the surrounding region.

Jesus Heals Many

38 [g]And he arose and left the synagogue
and entered Simon's house. Now [h]Simon's
mother-in-law was ill with a high fever, and
they appealed to him on her behalf. 39 And
he stood over her and [i]rebuked the fever,
and it left her, and immediately she rose
and began to serve them.
40 Now when the sun was setting, all

18 [y]Cited from Isai. 61:1, 2 [z]ver. 1; [Acts 1:2] [a]Matt. 11:5; [ch. 6:20] [b]Ps. 146:7, 8 [c][Isai. 42:7; John 9:39; Acts 26:18] [d]Isai. 58:6 **19** [e]Lev. 25:10; [Isai. 49:8; 2 Cor. 6:2] **20** [f]Matt. 26:55; [John 8:2]; [Matt. 5:1; 13:2] [g]Acts 3:4; [ch. 19:48] **21** [h]Mark 12:10; Acts 8:35 [i]See Matt. 1:22 **22** [j]Ps. 45:2 [k][Matt. 13:55; John 6:42] [l]ch. 2:27; 3:23 **23** [m][ch. 23:39; Matt. 27:42] [n]Matt. 11:23; Mark 2:1-12; John 4:46-53 **24** [o]See Matt. 13:57 **25** [p]1 Kin. 17:1; 18:1; James 5:17; [Rev. 11:6] **26** [q]1 Kin. 17:9 **27** [r][2 Kin. 7:3] [s]2 Kin. 5:1-14 **29** [t][Num. 15:35; Acts 7:58] **30** [u]John 8:59; 10:39 **31** [v]For ver. 31-37, see Mark 1:21-28 [w]Matt. 4:13 [x]ver. 15, 16; See Matt. 4:23 [y]See Mark 6:2 **32** [z]ver. 36; See Matt. 7:28, 29 **33** [x][See ver. 31 above] **34** [a]See Matt. 8:29 [b][Acts 19:15; James 2:19] [c]John 6:69; Acts 3:14; Rev. 3:7; [ch. 1:35; Heb. 7:26; 1 John 2:20] **35** [d]ver. 41; See Matt. 12:16 **36** [e]ver. 32; [Matt. 8:27] **37** [f]ver. 14 **38** [g]For ver. 38-41, see Matt. 8:14-16; Mark 1:29-34 [h]1 Cor. 9:5 **39** [i]ch. 8:24; 9:42; Matt. 8:26; 17:18; Mark 4:39; 9:25

[1] *Leprosy* was a term for several skin diseases; see Leviticus 13 [2] Or *Leave us alone*

4:21–27 By presenting the rejection at Nazareth at the beginning of Jesus' ministry, Luke highlights certain main characteristics of that ministry: (a) the response of wonder at His teachings coupled with persistent unbelief and rejection (vv. 22, 28); (b) His ministry as the fulfillment of Scripture (v. 21); (c) His concern for the poor and oppressed (vv. 18, 19); and (d) His ultimate aim of including Gentiles among the people of God (vv. 26, 27).

4:32 astonished. In contrast to the Pharisees and teachers of the law, who appealed to tradition and previous teachers, Jesus astonished people because He did not cite authorities.

4:33 There are few examples of demon possession in the Old Testament or in the New Testament outside the Gospels. In Scripture such possession is primarily part of the opposition of evil to the coming of God's Son.

4:33–35 This demon was cast out on the Sabbath. Luke tells of four other cures Jesus did on the Sabbath (v. 38; 6:6; 13:14; 14:1), and there are two in John (John 5:8, 9; 9:14).

4:34 The demon recognized Jesus as the "Holy One of God"—a term that denotes Jesus' special relationship to God and His empowerment by the Spirit (John 6:69). Luke makes it clear that part of the mission of Jesus was to defeat the powers of evil.

4:38, 39 Matthew and Mark both report this miracle, but only Luke mentions a high fever, which may indicate his medical interest. That Jesus "rebuked the fever" may mean that He saw Satan behind it in some way.

those who had any who were sick with various diseases brought them to him, and [j]he
laid his hands on every one of them and
healed them. **41** [k]And demons also came out
of many, [l]crying, "You are [m]the Son of
God!" But he rebuked them and [k]would
not allow them to speak, because they
knew that he was [n]the Christ.

Jesus Preaches in Synagogues

42 [o]And when it was day, he departed and
went [p]into a desolate place. And [q]the people sought him and came to him, and
would have kept him from leaving them,
43 but he said to them, [r]"I must [s]preach the
good news of the kingdom of God to the
other towns as well; for I was sent for this
purpose." **44** And he was preaching [t]in the
synagogues of Judea.[1]

Jesus Calls the First Disciples

5 On one occasion, while the crowd was
pressing in on him to hear the word of
God, he was standing by [u]the lake of
Gennesaret, **2** [v]and he saw two boats by the
lake, but the fishermen had gone out of
them and were [w]washing their nets.
3 Getting into one of the boats, which was
Simon's, he asked him to put out a little
from the land. And [x]he sat down and
taught the people from the boat. **4** And
when he had finished speaking, he said to
Simon, [y]"Put out into the deep and let
down your nets for a catch." **5** And Simon
answered, "Master, [z]we toiled all night and
took nothing! But at your word I will let
down the nets." **6** And when they had done
this, [a]they enclosed a large number of fish,
and [a]their nets were breaking. **7** They signaled to [b]their partners in the other boat to
come and help them. And they came and
filled both the boats, so that they began to
sink. **8** But when Simon Peter saw it, he fell
down at Jesus' knees, saying, [c]"Depart
from me, for [d]I am a sinful man, O Lord."
9 For he and all who were with him were
astonished at the catch of fish that they
had taken, **10** and so also were James and
John, sons of Zebedee, who were partners
with Simon. And Jesus said to Simon, "Do
not be afraid; from now on you will be
catching men." **11** And when they had
brought their boats to land, [e]they left everything and followed him.

Jesus Cleanses a Leper

12 While he was in one of the cities, [f]there
came a man full of leprosy.[2] And when he
saw Jesus, he [g]fell on his face and begged
him, "Lord, [h]if you will, you can make me
clean." **13** And Jesus[3] stretched out his hand
and touched him, saying, "I will; be clean."
And immediately the leprosy left him.
14 And he charged him [i]to tell no one, but
"go and show [j]yourself to the priest, and
[k]make an offering for your cleansing, as
Moses commanded, [l]for a proof to them."
15 [m]But now even more the report about
him went abroad, and great crowds gathered to hear him and to be healed of their
infirmities. **16** But [n]he would withdraw to
desolate places and [n]pray.

Jesus Heals a Paralytic

17 On one of those days, as he was teaching, Pharisees and [o]teachers of the law were

40 [j]See Mark 5:23
41 [k]Mark 3:11, 12; [Acts 16:17, 18] [l]ver. 33 [m]See Matt. 14:33 [n]See Matt. 1:17
42 [o]For ver. 42, 43, see Mark 1:35-38 [p]ch. 5:16 [q][Mark 1:36]
43 [r]See ch. 13:33 [s]ch. 8:1; 16:16; Matt. 4:23; 24:14; Acts 8:12
44 [t][Mark 1:39]
Chapter 5
1 [u]Num. 34:11; Deut. 3:17; Josh. 12:3; John 6:1; [Matt. 14:34]
2 [v]For ver. 2-11, [Matt. 4:18-22; Mark 1:16-20; John 1:40-42] [w][Mark 1:19]
3 [x][Matt. 5:1]
4 [y][John 21:6]
5 [z][John 21:3]
6 [a][John 21:11]
7 [b]Job 41:6
8 [c]See Matt. 8:34 [d]Isai. 6:5
11 [e]ch. 18:28; Matt. 19:27; [ver. 28]
12 [f]For ver. 12-14, see Matt. 8:2-4; Mark 1:40-44 [g]See ch. 17:16 [h][Matt. 9:28; Mark 9:22, 23]
14 [i]Matt. 9:30; 17:9; Mark 1:34; 5:43; 7:36; 8:26; See Matt. 12:16 [j]ch. 17:14 [k]Lev. 14:2-32 [l]ch. 9:5; Matt. 10:18; 24:14; Mark 6:11; James 5:3 **15** [m][Mark 1:45] **16** [n]Mark 1:35; See Matt. 14:23 **17** [o]ch. 2:46; Acts 5:34; 1 Tim. 1:7 (Gk.); [Matt. 22:35]

1 Some manuscripts *Galilee* 2 *Leprosy* was a term for several skin diseases; see Leviticus 13 3 Greek *he*

4:41 You are the Son of God. Again it is the demons who discern that Jesus is the Son of God. People might see in Him no more than another man, but the forces of evil recognized Him. "The Christ" means "the anointed One," the Messiah (see 1 Sam. 2:10 note).

4:43 I must. This phrase points to the divine compulsion in the mission of Jesus. The kingdom was central.

kingdom of God. This is Luke's first mention of the kingdom of God, Jesus' most frequent topic for preaching.

5:1 lake of Gennesaret. The Sea of Galilee; see Mark 1:16 note.

5:2 washing their nets. After each fishing trip the nets were checked, mended, and cleaned for the next trip. The boats were not in use, so Jesus could sit in Simon's boat and escape the crowd.

5:3 he sat. The normal posture for teaching (4:16–20 note).

5:5 all night. Night was the preferred time for fishing.

5:6 large number. This catch was the reward of obedience, not the result of skill or technique.

5:8 sinful man. Suddenly aware that he was in the presence of One who exercised the power of God, Peter was conscious of his sinfulness (cf. Gen. 18:27; Job 42:6; Is. 6:5).

5:12 Several skin diseases were called leprosy. They made a person ceremonially unclean, and could be disfiguring or fatal. Quarantine was the only defense against spread of the disease.

5:14 The priest was a kind of health inspector who could certify that the leper was cured. The priest would also offer the appropriate sacrifices to end the ritual defilement (Lev. 14).

5:17 Pharisees. Josephus indicates that there were more than six thousand Pharisees. They saw themselves as God's "separated ones" and sought to serve Him well. Many were godly, but their emphasis on outward acts and ritual taboos made others hard and formal. Such men opposed Jesus vigorously.

teachers of the law. Scribes whose work centered on interpreting the law of God. Many were Pharisees.

sitting there, who had come from every village of Galilee and Judea and from
Jerusalem. And [p]the power of the Lord was
with him to heal.[1] 18 [q]And behold, some
men were bringing [r]on a bed a man who
was paralyzed, and they were seeking to
bring him in and lay him before Jesus,
19 but finding no way to bring him in,
because of the crowd, they went up on [s]the
roof and let him down with his bed
[t]through the tiles into the midst before
Jesus. 20 And [u]when he saw their faith, he
said, "Man, [v]your sins are forgiven you."
21 And the scribes and the Pharisees began
to question, saying, "Who is this who
speaks [w]blasphemies? [x]Who can forgive
sins but God alone?" 22 When Jesus [y]per-
ceived their thoughts, he answered them,
"Why do you question in your hearts?
23 Which is easier, to say, 'Your sins are forgiven you,' or to say, 'Rise and walk'? 24 But
that you may know that [z]the Son of Man
has authority on earth to forgive sins"—he
said to the man who was paralyzed—"I say
to you, rise, pick up your bed and go
home." 25 And immediately he rose up
before them and picked up what he had
been lying on and went home, [a]glorifying
God. 26 And amazement seized them all,
and they [a]glorified God and were filled
[a]with awe, saying, "We have seen extraordinary things today."

Jesus Calls Levi

27 [b]After this he went out and saw [c]a tax
collector named [d]Levi, sitting at the tax
booth. And he said to him, "Follow me."
28 And [e]leaving everything, he rose and followed him.
29 And Levi made him a great feast in his
house, and there was a large company [f]of
tax collectors and others reclining at table
with them. 30 And the Pharisees and [g]their
scribes grumbled at his disciples, saying,
[h]"Why do you eat and drink with tax collectors and sinners?" 31 And Jesus answered
them, "Those who are well have no need of
a physician, but those who are sick. 32 [i]I
have not come to call the righteous [j]but
sinners [k]to repentance."

A Question About Fasting

33 And they said to him, [l]"The disciples of
John [m]fast often and [m]offer prayers, [n]and so
do the disciples of the Pharisees, but yours
eat and drink." 34 And Jesus said to them,
[o]"Can you make wedding guests fast while
the bridegroom is with them? 35 [p]The days
will come when the bridegroom is taken
away from them, and [q]then they will fast in
those days." 36 He also told them a parable:
"No one tears a piece from a new garment
and puts it on an old garment. If he does,
he will tear the new, and the piece from the
new will not match the old. 37 And no one
puts new wine into old [r]wineskins. If he
does, the new wine will burst the skins and
it will be spilled, and the skins will be
destroyed. 38 But new wine must be put
into fresh wineskins. 39 And no one after
drinking old wine desires new, for he says,
'The old is good.'"[2]

Jesus Is Lord of the Sabbath

6 [s]On a Sabbath,[3] while he was going
through the grainfields, his disciples
[t]plucked and ate some heads of grain, rubbing them in their hands. 2 But some of the

17 [p]See ch. 8:46 18 [q]For ver. 18-26, see Matt. 9:2-8; Mark 2:3-12 [r]Mark 6:55 19 [s]Deut. 22:8; 1 Sam. 9:25; Neh. 8:16; Matt. 10:27; 24:17; Acts 10:9 [t][Mark 2:4] 20 [u]ch. 7:9, 50; 17:19; 18:42; Matt. 8:10, 13; 9:22, 29; 15:28; Mark 10:52; Acts 3:16; 14:9; James 5:15 [v]ch. 7:48; [John 5:14] 21 [w]Matt. 26:65; John 10:36 [x]Ps. 32:5; Isai. 43:25 22 [y]See John 2:25 24 [z][ch. 6:5] 25 [a]See ch. 7:16 26 [a][See ver. 25 above] 27 [b]For ver. 27-38, see Matt. 9:9-17; Mark 2:14-22 [c]Matt. 11:19; See Matt. 5:46 [d][Matt. 9:9] 28 [e][ver. 11] 29 [f][ch. 15:1, 2] 30 [g]Acts 4:5; 23:9 [h]ch. 15:2; Matt. 11:19 32 [i][ch. 15:7; John 9:39] [j]1 Tim. 1:15 [k]ch. 13:3, 5; 15:10; 24:47; Matt. 4:17; 11:20; Mark 1:15; Acts 5:31 33 [l]ch. 11:1; Matt. 11:2; 14:12; John 1:35; 3:25; 4:1; [Acts 18:25; 19:3] [m]ch. 2:37 [n]ch. 18:12 34 [o]John 3:29 35 [p]See ch. 17:22 [q][John 16:20] 37 [r]Josh. 9:4

Chapter 6 1 [s]For ver. 1-5, see Matt. 12:1-8; Mark 2:23-28 [t]Deut. 23:25

1 Some manuscripts *was present to heal them* 2 Some manuscripts *better* 3 Some manuscripts *On the second first Sabbath* (that is, on the second Sabbath after the first)

5:19 up on the roof. Houses often had flat roofs and outside stairs.

5:20 their faith. This includes the friends as well as the paralyzed man. Jesus begins with forgiveness, not healing.

5:21 Who is this. See note Mark 2:5.

5:24 that you may know. Jesus links the power to forgive with the power to heal (Mark 2:9 note).

the Son of Man. Jesus' favorite self-designation, used many times in the Gospels and in them only by Jesus Himself. It refers to His heavenly origin and vocation (Dan. 7:13, 14). See note Matt. 8:20.

5:27 tax collector. See note 3:12.

5:28 leaving everything. Levi would never be able to go back to tax collecting; his action was final.

5:30 The Pharisees would have been outside. They regarded table fellowship with sinners as especially defiling.

5:33 The only fast prescribed in the law was on the Day of Atonement (Lev. 23:27), but religious people fasted on other days (e.g., Zech. 7:3, 5). Jesus did not command fasts, though He Himself fasted (4:2) and permitted it among His followers (Matt. 6:16–18).

5:36–38 Making a patch from a new garment for an old one spoils both—the new by having the patch torn from it, the old because the patch does not match. New wine in old wineskins ferments and bursts the skins; both wine and skins are lost.

6:1 Sabbath. A principal source of controversy between Jesus and the Pharisees was the right use of the Sabbath. They hedged it with repressive regulations so as to avoid the possibility of breaking the Sabbath. Jesus did not so much argue that the regulations should be relaxed as that they had misunderstood the Sabbath—it was a day on which good deeds should be done.

plucked and ate some heads of grain. This was permitted in the law

Pharisees said, [u]"Why are you doing [v]what
is not lawful to do on the Sabbath?" 3 And
Jesus answered them, [w]"Have you not read
[x]what David did when he was hungry, he
and those who were with him: 4 how he
entered the house of God and took and ate
[y]the bread of the Presence, [y]which is not
lawful for any but the priests to eat, and
also gave it to those with him?" 5 And he
said to them, [z]"The Son of Man is lord of
the Sabbath."

A Man with a Withered Hand

6 On another Sabbath, [a]he entered the
synagogue [b]and was teaching, and a man
was there whose right hand was withered.
7 And the scribes and the Pharisees
[c]watched him, to see whether he would
heal on the Sabbath, [d]so that they might
find a reason to accuse him. 8 But [e]he knew
their thoughts, and he said to the man with
the withered hand, "Come and stand
here." And he rose and stood there. 9 And
Jesus said to them, "I ask you, [f]is it lawful
on the Sabbath to do good or to do harm,
to save life or to destroy it?" 10 And [g]after
looking around at them all he said to him,
"Stretch out your hand." And [h]he did so,
and his hand was restored. 11 But they were
filled with [i]fury and discussed with one
another what they might do to Jesus.

The Twelve Apostles

12 In these days [j]he went out to the
mountain to pray, and all night he continued in prayer to God. 13 And when day
came, [k]he called his disciples [l]and [m]chose
from them twelve, whom he named [n]apos-
tles: 14 Simon, [o]whom he named Peter,
and [p]Andrew his brother, and [p]James and
John, and Philip, and Bartholomew, 15 and
[q]Matthew, and Thomas, and James the
son of Alphaeus, and Simon who was
called [r]the Zealot, 16 and [s]Judas the son of
James, and Judas Iscariot, who became a
traitor.

Jesus Ministers to a Great Multitude

17 And [t]he came down with them and
stood on a level place, with [u]a great crowd
of his disciples and a great multitude of
people from all Judea and Jerusalem and
the seacoast of [v]Tyre and Sidon, 18 who
came to hear him and to be healed of their
diseases. [w]And those who were troubled
with unclean spirits were cured. 19 And all
the crowd [x]sought to touch him, for [y]power
came out from him and healed them all.

The Beatitudes

20 And [z]he lifted up his eyes on his disciples, [a]and said:

"Blessed are you who are poor, for [b]yours
is the kingdom of God.

21 [c]"Blessed are you who are hungry now,
for you shall be satisfied.

[d]"Blessed are you who weep now, for
you shall laugh.

22 "Blessed are you when [e]people hate
you and when they [f]exclude you and revile
you and [g]spurn your name as evil, [h]on
account of the Son of Man! 23 [i]Rejoice in
that day, and leap for joy, for behold, your

2 [u][Matt. 9:11] [v][Ex. 20:9-11] 3 [w]See Matt. 21:16 [x]1 Sam. 21:1-6 4 [y]Ex. 25:30; Lev. 24:5-9 5 [z][ch. 5:24] 6 [a]For ver. 6-11, see Matt. 12:9-14; Mark 3:1-6 [b]See Mark 6:2 7 [c]ch. 14:1; 20:20; [ch. 11:54] [d][John 8:6] 8 [e]See Matt. 9:4 9 [f]ch. 14:3 10 [g]Mark 3:34; 5:32; 10:23; [Mark 10:21] [h][1 Kin. 13:4] 11 [i]2 Tim. 3:9 (Gk.) 12 [j]See Matt. 14:23 13 [k]ch. 9:1; Matt. 10:1; Mark 3:13; 6:7 [l]For ver. 13-16, see Matt. 10:2-4; Mark 3:16-19; Acts 1:13 [m]See John 13:18 [n]See Mark 6:30
14 [o]Matt. 16:18; John 1:42 [p]Matt. 4:18, 21 15 [q]Matt. 9:9 [r][Acts 21:20] 16 [s]John 14:22 17 [t][ver. 12; Matt. 5:1] [u]Matt. 4:25; Mark 3:7, 8 [v]See Matt. 11:21 18 [w]Matt. 4:24 19 [x]Matt. 14:36; Mark 3:10; [Acts 5:15]

[y]See ch. 8:46 20 [z]John 6:5 [a]For ver. 20-23, [Matt. 5:3-12] [b][ch. 12:32] 21 [c][ch. 1:53] [d]Isai. 25:8; 57:18; See Matt. 5:4 22 [e]See Matt. 10:22 [f][John 9:22; 12:42; 16:2] [g]Heb. 11:26; 1 Pet. 4:14 [h]John 15:21 23 [i]See Matt. 5:12

(Deut. 23:25); that it was done on the Sabbath was seen by the Pharisees as unlawful.

6:4 the bread of the Presence. Prepared in a special way for use in temple service, this bread was to be eaten only by priests (Lev. 24:5–9). In a time of need David used it for his companions (1 Sam. 21:3–6).

6:5 lord of the Sabbath. The Sabbath was instituted by God (Gen. 2:3; Ex. 20:8–11), but Jesus is Lord over it. Jesus claims divine authority to interpret the law.

6:9 is it lawful. Jesus presents a choice between doing good and doing evil on the Sabbath, not between doing good and doing nothing. He saw the failure to do good as in itself evil.

6:12 all night he continued in prayer. Prolonged prayer preceded the important choice of the Twelve.

6:13 apostles. The word means a "messenger," someone sent (see 2 Cor. 1:1 note). It is not often used in the Gospels ("the twelve" is more common) but is frequent in Acts and the Epistles. Until now Luke has spoken of "Simon," but from this point on he usually calls him "Peter."

6:17 a level place. This phrase accounts for the sermon being called "The Sermon on the Plain." Luke describes a ministry of teaching and healing that had wide appeal.

6:20–49 There are many similarities to the Sermon on the Mount (Matt. 5–7), and some see this as a variant account of the same sermon. But this sermon is much shorter, and Luke has parallels to other parts of Matt. 5–7 elsewhere. It is more likely that Jesus used much the same material on a number of occasions, a practice common among preachers.

6:20 Blessed. This term implies more than "fortunate" or "happy;" it is a religious term and means those who enjoy the favor of God.

you who are poor. Luke is especially concerned with the blessings that the gospel brings to the poor (see notes 1:46–55, 51–53; Ps. 9:18 note). Poverty can be a curse (Prov. 30:8, 9), and disciples know that they must rely on God for all things. They have no resources of their own and are "poor," but God blesses them with "the kingdom."

6:21 The hungry realize their need and look to God for satisfaction.

6:22, 23 A blessing for the persecuted is most unexpected. It is not suffering in general that is pronounced blessed, but suffering "on account of the Son of Man."

reward is great in heaven; for [j]so their
fathers did to the prophets.

Jesus Pronounces Woes

24 [k]"But woe to you who are rich, [l]for you
[m]have received your consolation.
25 "Woe to you who are full now, for [n]you
shall be hungry.
"Woe to [o]you who laugh now, [o]for you
shall mourn and weep.
26 "Woe to you, [p]when all people speak
well of you, for [q]so their fathers did to [r]the
false prophets.

Love Your Enemies

27 "But I say to you who hear, [s]Love your
enemies, [t]do good to those who hate you,
28 [u]bless those who curse you, [s]pray for those
who abuse you. 29 [v]To one who [w]strikes you
on the cheek, offer the other also, and from
one who takes away your cloak do not
withhold your tunic[1] either. 30 [x]Give to
everyone who begs from you, and from one
who takes away your goods do not demand
them back. 31 And [y]as you wish that others
would do to you, do so to them.
32 [z]"If you love those who love you, what
benefit is that to you? For even sinners love
those who love them. 33 And if you do good
to those who do good to you, what benefit
is that to you? For even sinners do the
same. 34 And [a]if you [b]lend to those from
whom you expect to receive, what credit is
that to you? Even sinners lend to sinners,
to get back the same amount. 35 But [c]love
your enemies, and do good, and lend,
expecting nothing in return, and your
reward will be great, and [d]you will be sons
of [e]the Most High, for [f]he is kind to the
ungrateful and the evil. 36 [g]Be merciful,
even as [h]your Father is merciful.

Judging Others

37 [i,j]"Judge not, and you will not be
judged; condemn not, and you will not be
condemned; [j]forgive, and you will be forgiven; 38 [k]give, and it will be given to you.
Good measure, pressed down, shaken
together, running over, will be put [l]into
your lap. For [m]with the measure you use it
will be measured back to you."
39 He also told them a parable: [n]"Can a
blind man lead a blind man? Will they not
both fall into a pit? 40 [o]A disciple is not
above his teacher, but everyone when he is
[p]fully trained will be like his teacher.
41 [i]Why do you see the speck that is in your
brother's eye, but [q]do not notice the log
that is in your own eye? 42 How can you say
to your brother, 'Brother, let me take out
the speck that is in your eye,' when you
yourself do not see the log that is in your
own eye? You hypocrite, first take the log
out of your own eye, and then you will see
clearly to take out the speck that is in your
brother's eye.

A Tree and Its Fruit

43 "For [r]no good tree bears bad fruit, nor
again does a bad tree bear good fruit, 44 for
[s]each tree is known by its own fruit. For
figs are not gathered from thornbushes,
nor are grapes picked from a bramble bush.
45 [t]The good person out of the good treasure of his heart produces good, and the
evil person out of his evil treasure produces
[u]evil, [v]for out of the abundance of the heart
his mouth speaks.

Build Your House on the Rock

46 [w]"Why [x]do you call me 'Lord, Lord,'
and not do what I tell you? 47 [y]Everyone
who comes to me and hears my words and
does them, I will show you what he is like:
48 he is like a man building a house, who

23 [j]See Matt. 21:35 **24** [k]Amos 6:1; James 5:1; [ch. 12:21] [l][ch. 16:25] [m]Matt. 6:2 **25** [n]Isai. 65:13 [o]Isai. 65:14; [Prov. 14:13; James 4:9] **26** [p][John 15:19; 17:14; James 4:4; 1 John 4:5] [q]Jer. 5:31; [Isai. 30:10; Mic. 2:11] [r]See Matt. 7:15 **27** [s]See Matt. 5:44 [t]Prov. 25:21, 22; Rom. 12:20, 21 **28** [u]1 Pet. 3:9 [s][See ver. 27 above] **29** [v]For ver. 29, 30, see Matt. 5:39-42; [Rom. 12:17] [w]Isai. 50:6; Lam. 3:30; Matt. 26:67 **30** [x]Ps. 37:21; Prov. 21:26 **31** [y]Matt. 7:12 **32** [z]Matt. 5:46 **34** [a][ch. 14:12-14; Prov. 19:17; Matt. 5:42] [b]Ps. 37:26 **35** [c]ver. 27 [d]Matt. 5:45 [e]ch. 1:32; See Mark 5:7 [f][James 1:5] **36** [g][Matt. 5:7, 48; Eph. 5:1, 2; James 3:17] [h]James 5:11 **37** [i]For ver. 37, 38, 41, 42, see Matt. 7:1-5; [Rom. 14:13; 1 Cor. 4:5; James 5:9] [j][Matt. 6:14; 18:23-35] **38** [k]2 Cor. 9:6-8 [l]Ps. 79:12; Isai. 65:6, 7; Jer. 32:18 [m]Mark 4:24; [Judg. 1:7] **39** [n]Matt. 15:14

40 [o]See Matt. 10:24 [p]2 Cor. 13:11; Heb. 13:21; 1 Pet. 5:10; [1 Cor. 1:10; 2 Tim. 3:17] **41** [i][See ver. 37 above] [q][John 8:7-9] **43** [r]For ver. 43, 44, see Matt. 7:16, 20 **44** [s]Matt. 12:33 **45** [t][Matt. 12:35; 15:18, 19; [Matt. 13:52; Eph. 4:29] [u][Matt. 5:37] [v]Matt. 12:34 **46** [w][Mal. 1:6]; See Matt. 7:21 [x]John 13:13 **47** [y]For ver. 47-49, see Matt. 7:24-27

[1] Greek *chiton*, a long garment worn under the cloak next to the skin

6:24–26 The "woes" correspond to the blessings of the previous verses. Those who do not realize their spiritual poverty but rely on their own achievement will reap disaster in the end. The term "woe" often introduces a prophetic oracle of doom.

6:30 A disciple must be free from the love of possessions.

6:31 Jesus is the first to give the "Golden Rule" in this positive form; see note Matt. 7:12.

6:32–34 The world's standards are not to guide the followers of Jesus.

6:35 sons of the Most High. God's people are to be like God, as merciful as He is.

6:37 Judge not, and you will not be judged. Jesus elsewhere teaches that His disciples must sometimes judge what others do (Matt. 18:15–17), and that the character of a person's heart can be recognized from the actions that flow from it (vv. 43–45; Matt. 7:15, 16). What He warns against here is the hypocrisy of those who condemn others for what they themselves are guilty of (vv. 41, 42), and the failure to show mercy (v. 36).

you will be forgiven. Such forgiveness is not a reward, but unless we forgive others we do not have genuine repentance and faith, and so exclude ourselves from forgiveness.

6:46–49 To call Jesus "Lord" is to say that He should be obeyed.

dug deep and laid the foundation on the
rock. And when a flood arose, the stream
broke against that house and could not
shake it, because it had been well built.[1]
49 [z]But the one who hears and does not do
them is like a man who built a house on
the ground without a foundation. When
the stream broke against it, immediately it
fell, and [a]the ruin of that house was great."

Jesus Heals a Centurion's Servant

7 After he had finished all his sayings in
the hearing of the people, [b]he entered
Capernaum. 2 Now a centurion had a servant[2] who was sick and at the point of
death, who was highly valued by him.
3 When the centurion[3] heard about Jesus,
[c]he sent to him elders of the Jews, asking
him to come and heal his servant. 4 And
when they came to Jesus, they pleaded
with him earnestly, saying, [d]"He is worthy
to have you do this for him, 5 for he loves
our nation, and he is the one who built us
[e]our synagogue." 6 And Jesus went with
them. When he was not far from the house,
the centurion sent friends, saying to him,
"Lord, [f]do not trouble yourself, for I am
not worthy to have you come under my
roof. 7 Therefore I did not presume to come
to you. But [g]say the word, and let my servant be healed. 8 For I too am a man set
under authority, with soldiers under me:
and I say to one, 'Go,' and he goes; and to
another, 'Come,' and he comes; and to my
servant, 'Do this,' and he does it." 9 When
Jesus heard these things, [h]he marveled at
him, and turning to the crowd that followed him, said, "I tell you, not even in
Israel have I found such [i]faith." 10 And
when those who had been sent returned to
the house, they found the servant well.

Jesus Raises a Widow's Son

11 Soon afterward[4] he went to a town
called Nain, and his disciples and a great
crowd went with him. 12 As he drew near to
the gate of the town, behold, a man who
had died was being carried out, [j]the only
son of his mother, and she was a widow,
and a considerable crowd from the town
was with her. 13 And when the Lord saw
her, [k]he had compassion on her and [l]said
to her, "Do not weep." 14 Then he came up
and touched [m]the bier, and the bearers
stood still. And he said, "Young man, I say
to you, [n]arise." 15 And the dead man sat up
and began to speak, and Jesus[5] [o]gave him
to his mother. 16 Fear seized them all, and
[p]they glorified God, saying, [q]"A great
prophet has arisen among us!" and [r]"God
has visited his people!" 17 And this report
about him spread through the whole of
Judea and all the surrounding country.

Messengers from John the Baptist

18 [s, t]The disciples of John reported all
these things to him. And John, 19 calling
two of his disciples to him, sent them to
the Lord, saying, "Are you the one [u]who is
to come, or [v]shall we look for another?"
20 And when the men had come to him,
they said, "John the Baptist has sent us to

49 [z][Ezek. 13:10-16] [a]Amos 6:11
Chapter 7
1 [b]For ver. 1-10, see Matt. 8:5-13
3 [c][Matt. 8:5]
4 [d][Acts 10:22]
5 [e]ch. 4:31, 33
6 [f]ch. 8:49; Mark 5:35; [Matt. 9:36 (Gk.)]
7 [g]Ps. 107:20; [Matt. 8:16]
9 [h][Mark 6:6] [i]See Matt. 9:2
12 [j][ch. 8:42; 9:38; Judg. 11:34; Heb. 11:17]
13 [k]Matt. 20:34 [l]ch. 8:52
14 [m]2 Sam. 3:31 [n]ch. 8:54; Mark 5:41; [ver. 22; Matt. 11:5; John 11:43; Acts 9:40]
15 [o][1 Kin. 17:23; 2 Kin. 4:36; Heb. 11:35]
16 [p]ch. 2:20; 23:47; Matt. 9:8; 15:31; Acts 4:21; 11:18; 21:20; [Matt. 5:16]; See ch. 13:13 [q]ver. 39; See Deut. 18:15; Matt. 21:11 [r]See ch. 1:68
18 [s]For ver. 18-35, see Matt. 11:2-19 [t]See Matt. 9:14
19 [u]John 4:25; 6:14; 11:27 [v][ch. 3:15]

1 Some manuscripts *founded upon the rock* 2 Greek *bondservant*; also verses 3, 8, 10 3 Greek *he* 4 Some manuscripts *The next day* 5 Greek *he*

7:2 centurion. Nominally in command of a hundred men, though the actual number varied. The centurions in the New Testament are all men of good character (7:4; 23:47; Acts 10:2; 27:43).

servant. The Greek word means "slave." This centurion was a humane person, concerned for his slaves.

7:3 elders of the Jews. That leading men among the Jews would plead for him shows the regard in which the centurion was held.

7:5 loves our nation. This attitude was unusual in a conqueror.

built us our synagogue. The centurion was interested in Jewish worship. He may even have been a "God-fearer," a Gentile who attached himself to the synagogue and worshiped God, but without being circumcised and becoming a Jewish proselyte.

7:6–8 In Matt. 6:8, the man comes in person. Matthew appears to mean that what a man does through agents he does himself. For Luke, the messengers were important in that they show the man's humility (vv. 6, 7).

7:8 under authority. The centurion was familiar with authority exercised at a distance.

7:9 marveled. Only twice is Jesus said to have marveled: here at the faith of a foreigner (cf. Matt. 8:10), and in Mark 6:6 at unbelief in Nazareth.

7:13 saw her. The mother would have been walking in front of the bier, so Jesus would have met her first. Nobody asked Him to help, but out of compassion He took action.

7:15 The first of Jesus' three miracles of raising the dead (8:40–56; John 11:1–44). Such miracles were powerful messianic signs (v. 22). These "resurrections" differ from the resurrection of Christ, however, for these three were reunited with their mortal bodies only to die once more. As the first to be clothed with an imperishable, spiritual body (1 Cor. 15:42–44), Jesus is indeed the "firstborn from the dead" (Col. 1:18; cf. 1 Cor. 15:20).

7:16 A great prophet. Inadequate, but probably the highest title they knew. They recognized the presence of God's power among them.

7:18, 19 John had borne witness to Jesus (3:16–17), so questions like these are unexpected. Some think his faith had failed in the harsh conditions of Herod's prison, others that his patience had given out and he was suggesting that Jesus should actively bring in the kingdom. More probably he looked for Jesus to bring judgment, a note that John had stressed in his own ministry. He could not understand why Jesus did not punish sinners, but constantly performed deeds of mercy. Would somebody else come to carry out the threats of judgment?

you, saying, 'Are you the one [u]who is to
come, or [v]shall we look for another?'" **21** In
that hour [w]he healed many people of diseases and plagues and evil spirits, and [x]on
many who were blind he bestowed sight.
22 And he answered them, "Go and tell
John what you have seen and heard: [y]the
blind receive their sight, the lame walk,
[z]lepers[1] are cleansed, and [a]the deaf hear,
[b]the dead are raised up, [c]the poor have
good news preached to them. **23** And
blessed is the one who is [d]not offended by
me."
24 When John's messengers had gone,
Jesus[2] began to speak to the crowds concerning John: "What did you go out [e]into
the wilderness to see? [f]A reed shaken by
the wind? **25** What then did you go out to
see? A man dressed in soft clothing?
Behold, those who are dressed in splendid
clothing and live in luxury are in kings'
courts. **26** What then did you go out to
see? [g]A prophet? Yes, I tell you, and more
than a prophet. **27** This is he of whom it is
written,

[h]"'Behold, I send my messenger before
your face,
who will prepare your way
before you.'

28 I tell you, among those born of women
none is greater than John. Yet the one who
is least in the kingdom of God is greater
than he." **29** (When all the people heard
this, and [i]the tax collectors too, they
declared God just,[3] [j]having been baptized
with [k]the baptism of John, **30** [l]but the
Pharisees and [m]the lawyers [n]rejected [o]the
purpose of God for themselves, not having
been baptized by him.)
31 "To what then shall I compare the people of this generation, and what are they
like? **32** They are like children sitting in the
marketplace and calling to one another,

"'We played the flute for you, and you
did not dance;
we sang a dirge, and you did not
weep.'

33 For John the Baptist has come [p]eating no
bread and [q]drinking no wine, and you say,
'He has a demon.' **34** The Son of Man has
come [r]eating and drinking, and you say,
'Look at him! A glutton and a drunkard, [s]a
friend of tax collectors and sinners!' **35** Yet
[t]wisdom is justified by all her children."

A Sinful Woman Forgiven

36 [u]One of the Pharisees asked him to eat
with him, and he went into the Pharisee's
house and took his place at the table.
37 [v]And behold, a woman of the city, who
was a sinner, when she learned that he was
reclining at table in the Pharisee's house,
brought an alabaster flask of ointment,
38 and standing behind him at his feet,
weeping, she began to wet his feet with her
tears and [w]wiped them with the hair of her
head and kissed his feet and anointed them
with the ointment. **39** Now when the
Pharisee who had invited him saw this, he
said to himself, "If [x]this man were [y]a
prophet, he [z]would have known who and
what sort of woman this is who is touching
him, for she is a sinner." **40** And Jesus answering said to him, "Simon, I have something to say to you." And he answered,
"Say it, Teacher."
41 "A certain moneylender had two
debtors. One owed five hundred [a]denarii,
and the other fifty. **42** [b]When they could not
pay, he [c]cancelled the debt of both. Now
which of them will love him more?"
43 Simon answered, "The one, I suppose, for
whom he cancelled the larger debt." And

20 [u][See ver. 19 above] [v][See ver. 19 above]
21 [w]Mark 1:34 [x]ch. 18:42; Matt. 9:30; 12:22; 15:31; 20:34; 21:14; Mark 8:25; John 9:7
22 [y]Isai. 29:18; 35:5, 6; Matt. 15:30 [z]ch. 17:14 [a]Mark 7:35 [b]See ver. 14 [c]ch. 4:18; [Matt. 5:3; James 2:5]
23 [d]Isai. 8:14, 15; John 6:61
24 [e]ch. 1:80; 3:2 [f][Eph. 4:14; James 1:6]
26 [g]ch. 1:76; 20:6; Matt. 14:5
27 [h]Mark 1:2; Cited from Mal. 3:1; [ch. 1:17, 76]
29 [i][ch. 20:6] [j]ch. 3:12; Matt. 21:32 [k]Acts 18:25; 19:3
30 [l][Matt. 21:25, 32; 23:13] [m]ch. 10:25; 11:45, 46, 52; 14:3; Matt. 22:35 [n]See Mark 7:9 [o]Acts 2:23; 13:36; 20:27
33 [p]Matt. 3:4; Mark 1:6 [q]ch. 1:15
34 [r]ver. 36; ch. 14:1; Matt. 9:10; John 2:1; 12:2 [s]ch. 15:2; 19:7; Matt. 9:11
35 [t][ch. 11:49; Prov. 8:1-36]
36 [u]ch. 11:37; 14:1
37 [v]For ver. 37-39, [Matt. 26:6-13; Mark 14:3-9; John 12:1-8]
38 [w]ver. 44; John 11:2
39 [x][ch. 15:2] [y]ver. 16; John 4:19 [z][ch. 22:64] **41** [a]See Matt. 18:28 **42** [b]Matt. 18:25 [c]Eph. 4:32; Col. 2:13; 3:13; [Rom. 8:32 (Gk.)]

1 *Leprosy* was a term for several skin diseases; see Leviticus 13
2 Greek *he* 3 Greek *they justified God*

7:21–23 See Is. 35:5, 6; 61:1.

7:24–28 Jesus praises John as the greatest of men, cast in the mold of the prophets of Israel and unmoved by expediency or luxury. Yet as a prophet he belonged to an era that was being withdrawn as the kingdom of God was introduced. In this sense he was less than those who were in the kingdom.

7:32 like children. Jesus compares that generation with children at play, who sometimes reject whatever games anyone might suggest.

7:37, 38 At a dinner like this the house would be open and people could come in and watch. A sinful woman (perhaps a prostitute) would not have been welcome; it took courage for her to come. Guests at dinner reclined on couches. Leaning on the left side, they took the food with their right hands.

7:37 alabaster. A translucent stone used to make containers for costly perfumes.

7:38 weeping. The woman's tears and her anointing of Jesus' feet demonstrated penitence and humility.

7:39 this man . . . would have known. A Pharisee would have no contact with sinful people, and was sure that no prophet would have such contact either. As Jesus did not dismiss the woman, Simon thought that He either did not know that she was sinful or did not care. In either case, in Simon's view Jesus could not be a prophet.

he said to him, "You have judged rightly."
44Then turning toward the woman he said
to Simon, "Do you see this woman? I
entered your house; [d]you gave me no water
for my feet, but [e]she has wet my feet with
her tears and wiped them with her hair.
45[f]You gave me no kiss, but from the time I
came in she has not ceased to [g]kiss my feet.
46[h]You did not anoint my head with oil,
but she has anointed my feet with ointment. **47**Therefore I tell you, her sins,
[i]which are many, are forgiven—for she
loved much. But he who is forgiven little,
loves little." **48**And he said to her, [j]"Your
sins are forgiven." **49**Then those who were
at table with him began to say among[1]
themselves, [k]"Who is this, who even forgives sins?" **50**And he said to the woman,
[l]"Your faith has saved you; [m]go in peace."

Women Accompanying Jesus

8 Soon afterward he went on [n]through
cities and villages, proclaiming and
[o]bringing the good news of the kingdom of
God. And the twelve were with him, **2**and
also [p]some women who had been healed of
evil spirits and infirmities: [q]Mary, called
Magdalene, [r]from whom seven demons
had gone out, **3**and [s]Joanna, the wife of
Chuza, Herod's household manager, and
Susanna, and many others, who provided
for them[2] out of their means.

The Parable of the Sower

4[t]And when a great crowd was gathering
and people from town after town came to
him, he said in a parable: **5**[u]"A sower went
out to sow his seed. And as he sowed,
some fell along the path and was trampled
underfoot, and the birds of the air devoured it. **6**And some fell on the rock, and
as it grew up, [v]it withered away, because it
had no moisture. **7**And some fell among
[w]thorns, and the thorns grew up with it
and choked it. **8**And some fell into good
soil and grew and yielded [x]a hundredfold."
As he said these things, he called out, [y]"He
who has ears to hear, let him hear."

The Purpose of the Parables

9And when his disciples asked him what
this parable meant, **10**he said, [z]"To you it
has been given to know [a]the secrets of the
kingdom of God, but for others they are in
parables, so [b]that 'seeing they may not see,
and hearing they may not understand.'
11[c]Now the parable is this: The seed is [d]the
word of God. **12**The ones along the path are
those who have heard. Then the devil
comes and takes away the word from their
hearts, so that they may not [e]believe and be
saved. **13**And the ones on the rock are those
who, when they hear the word, receive it
[f]with joy. But these have no root; they [g]be-
lieve for a while, and in time of testing [h]fall
away. **14**And as for what fell among the
thorns, they are those who hear, but [i]as
they go on their way they are choked by the
[j]cares and riches and pleasures of life, and
their fruit does not mature. **15**As for that in
the good soil, they are those who, hearing
the word, hold it fast in an honest and
good heart, and [k]bear fruit [l]with patience.

44 [d]1 Tim. 5:10; See Gen. 18:4 [e]ver. 38 **45** [f]2 Sam. 15:5; 19:39; 20:9 [g]ver. 38 **46** [h]Ps. 23:5; 141:5; Eccles. 9:8; Matt. 6:17 **47** [i][ver. 39] **48** [j]ch. 5:20; Matt. 9:2; Mark 2:5; James 5:15; 1 John 2:12; [John 20:23] **49** [k]ch. 5:21 **50** [l]ver. 9; [ver. 47; 1 Tim. 1:14]; See Mark 10:52; Eph. 2:8 [m]ch. 8:48; 1 Sam. 1:17; Mark 5:34
Chapter 8
1 [n]See Mark 6:6 [o]See ch. 4:43 **2** [p]ch. 23:49, 55; Matt. 27:55; Mark 15:40, 41; Acts 1:14 [q]ch. 24:10; Matt. 27:56, 61; 28:1; John 19:25; 20:1, 18 [r]Mark 16:9 **3** [s]ch. 24:10 **4** [t]For ver. 4-10, see Matt. 13:1-15; Mark 4:1-12 **5** [u][Isai. 55:10; Amos 9:13]
6 [v]John 15:6 **7** [w]Jer. 4:3 **8** [x]Gen. 26:12 [y]See Matt. 11:15 **10** [z]Matt. 19:11; Col. 1:27; [1 Cor. 2:6-10; 1 John 2:20, 27]; See Matt. 11:25 [a]See Rom. 16:25
[b]Isai. 6:9, 10; See Matt. 13:13 **11** [c]For ver. 11-15, see Matt. 13:18-23; Mark 4:13-20 [d]ch. 1:2; Mark 2:2; 4:33; 16:20; Acts 8:4; James 1:21 **12** [e]See Mark 16:16 **13** [f][Isai. 58:2; Ezek. 33:31, 32; Mark 6:20; John 5:35] [g]Gal. 1:6; [Hos. 6:4; Gal. 5:7] [h]1 Tim. 4:1; Heb. 3:12; [2 Thess. 2:3] **14** [i][James 1:11] [j]See Matt. 6:25 **15** [k]Hos. 14:8; John 15:5, 6; Phil. 1:11; Col. 1:6 [l]James 5:7; See Heb. 10:36

1 Or *to* 2 Some manuscripts *him*

7:44–46 Simon had omitted the courtesies normally given to guests. But the woman made up for this.

7:47 for. The woman was forgiven because of faith (v. 50). Her love showed that she understood what God's forgiveness meant for her.

7:48–50 Again Jesus authoritatively declares sins to be forgiven, an act that arouses comment (cf. 5:20, 21). But His concern is for the woman.

8:2 Rabbis refused to teach women, so Jesus' acceptance of them into His group of followers was unusual.

Magdalene. From the town of Magdala.

8:3 out of their means. This provides a glimpse of the way Jesus and His band were supported throughout His ministry.

8:4 parable. From this point, parables feature more prominently. Crowds were coming to Jesus but He looked for more than casual contact. Parables required people to think carefully about what He was saying.

8:5 Seed was sown first, then plowed into the soil. Pathways through the fields would not be plowed, and seed that fell there was wasted; it could not sink into the ground.

8:6 on the rock. That is, rock covered with a layer of soil too shallow to hold sufficient moisture.

8:7 thorns. That is, hardy, fast-growing weeds.

8:8 a hundredfold. Matthew and Mark speak of thirtyfold and sixtyfold, but Luke emphasizes abundance far beyond what any crop could be expected to produce.

8:10 secrets. The kingdom of God involves truths that are beyond human insights and wisdom, but that God has now made known.

others. These are the people to whom Isaiah's prophecy refers—they do not respond to Jesus' teaching. They hear the story but do not understand the meaning.

that. Jesus' teaching in parables has a twofold purpose—to reveal the mysteries of the kingdom to those who have "ears to hear" (v. 8) and to conceal the truth of the kingdom from those who do not. See notes Matt. 13:13; Mark 4:11.

8:13 they believe for a while. One test of a true and living faith is perseverance. Those who finally depart from the way of truth reveal that they were never actually part of God's family (1 John 2:19).

A Lamp Under a Jar

16[m,n] "No one after lighting a lamp covers
it with a jar or puts it under a bed, but puts
it on a stand, so that those who enter may
see the light. 17[o] For nothing is hidden that
will not be made manifest, nor is anything
secret that will not be known and come to
light. 18[p] Take care then how you hear, [q] for
to the one who has, more will be given, and
from the one who has not, even what he
thinks that he has will be taken away."

Jesus' Mother and Brothers

19[r] Then his mother and [s] his brothers
came to him, but they could not reach him
because of the crowd. 20 And he was told,
"Your mother and your brothers are standing outside, desiring to see you." 21 But he
answered them, "My mother and my
brothers are those [t] who hear the word of
God and do it."

Jesus Calms a Storm

22[u] One day he got into a boat with his
disciples, and he said to them, "Let us go
across to the other side of [v] the lake." So
they set out, 23 and as they sailed he fell
asleep. And a windstorm came down on
[v] the lake, and they were filling with water
and were in danger. 24 And they went and
woke him, saying, "Master, Master, we are
perishing!" And he awoke and [w] rebuked
the wind and the raging waves, and they
ceased, [x] and there was a calm. 25 He said to
them, "Where is your faith?" And they
[y] were afraid, and they [z] marveled, saying to
one another, "Who then is this, that [a] he
commands even winds and water, and they
obey him?"

Jesus Heals a Demon-Possessed Man

26[b] Then they sailed to the country of the
Gerasenes,[1] which is opposite Galilee. 27 When
Jesus[2] had stepped out on land, there met
him a man from the city who had demons.
For a long time he had worn no clothes,
and he had not lived in a house [c] but
among the tombs. 28 When he saw Jesus, he
[d] cried out and fell down before him and
said [d] with a loud voice, "What have you to
do with me, Jesus, [e] Son of [f] the Most High
God? I beg you, do not torment me." 29 For
he had commanded the unclean spirit to
come out of the man. (For many a time it
had seized him. He was kept under guard
and bound with chains and shackles, but
he would break the bonds and be driven by
the demon [g] into the desert.) 30 Jesus then
asked him, "What is your name?" And he
said, [h] "Legion," for many demons had
entered him. 31 And they begged him not to
command them to depart into [i] the abyss.
32 Now a large herd of pigs was feeding
there on the hillside, and they begged him
to let them enter these. So he gave them
permission. 33 Then the demons came out
of the man and entered the pigs, and the
herd rushed down the steep bank into [j] the
lake and were drowned.
34 When the herdsmen saw what had
happened, they fled and told it in the city
and in the country. 35 Then people went out
to see what had happened, and they came
to Jesus and found the man from whom
the demons had gone, sitting [k] at the feet of
Jesus, [l] clothed and in his right mind, and
they were afraid. 36 And those who had seen
it told them how the demon-possessed[3]
man had been healed. 37 Then all the
people of the surrounding country of the

16 [m] For ver. 16-18, see Mark 4:21-25 [n] ch. 11:33; Matt. 5:15
17 [o] ch. 12:2; Matt. 10:26; [1 Tim. 5:25]
18 [p] [ver. 11-15] [q] See Matt. 13:12
19 [r] For ver. 19-21, see Matt. 12:46-50; Mark 3:31-35 [s] Matt. 13:55; Mark 6:3; John 2:12; 7:3, 5, 10; Acts 1:14; 1 Cor. 9:5; Gal. 1:19
21 [t] ch. 11:28; See James 1:22
22 [u] For ver. 22-25, see Matt. 8:23-27; Mark 4:36-41; [John 6:16-21] [v] ver. 33; See ch. 5:1
23 [v] [See ver. 22 above]
24 [w] ch. 4:39; Ps. 104:7 [x] Job 38:14; Ps. 65:7; [Matt. 14:32; Mark 6:51]
25 [y] John 14:27 [z] [Mark 1:27] [a] [ch. 5:9]
26 [b] For ver. 26-40, see Matt. 8:28–9:1; Mark 5:1-21
27 [c] [Rev. 18:2]
28 [d] ch. 4:33, 34; Mark 1:23, 24, 26; Acts 8:7 [e] [ch. 4:3, 9]; See Matt. 14:33 [f] ch. 1:32; 6:35; Gen. 14:18; Num. 24:16; Ps. 57:2; Isai. 14:14; Dan. 3:26; Acts 16:17
29 [g] [ch. 11:24; Matt. 12:43] 30 [h] Matt. 26:53 31 [i] See Rev. 9:1 33 [j] ver. 22, 23
35 [k] [ver. 27] [l] ch. 10:39

[1] Some manuscripts *Gadarenes*; others *Gergesenes*; also verse 37
[2] Greek *he*; also verses 38, 42 [3] Greek *daimonizomai*; elsewhere rendered *oppressed by demons*

8:16–18 The whole purpose of lighting a lamp is that it may give light. The teaching Jesus gives is to be made known and in the end, on Judgment Day, nothing can be kept hidden. Therefore it is important to hear the teaching in the right way. All those who do this will find that their stock of truth keeps growing. To neglect what we have is to lose it.

8:19 brothers. Those who believe that Mary remained a virgin all her life regard these as cousins, or as children of Joseph by an earlier marriage. But there is little evidence for this view.

8:21 Jesus' words are not a repudiation of His earthly family; He took care of Mary even as He hung on the cross (John 19:26, 27). His point is that the service of God, and His work as Messiah, is more important than any natural relation.

8:22, 23 The Sea of Galilee is seven hundred feet below sea level and bounded by mountains. Cool air can sweep down and whip up sudden storms. Jesus' sleep followed the labors of a busy day.

8:26 Gerasenes. It is not clear what place name should be read here (see text note; Matt. 8:28; Mark 5:1 note). Both Gadara and Gerasa were towns situated some miles from the lake.

8:27 Demon possession took many forms. This man was deranged.

8:28 Like the demoniac of 4:34, this one knew who Jesus was (contrast the disciples in v. 25).

8:30 Legion. There may have been a great number of demons in the man (a Roman legion had about six thousand soldiers).

8:31 the abyss. The place of confinement for evil spirits (Rev. 20:1–3).

8:32, 33 Jesus permitted but did not order the demons to enter the swine.

Gerasenes [m]asked him to depart from
them, for they were seized with great fear.
So he got into the boat and returned. 38 The
man from whom the demons had gone
begged that he might be with him, but
Jesus sent him away, saying, 39 "Return to
your home, and [n]declare how much God
has done for you." And he went away, proclaiming throughout the whole city how
much Jesus had done for him.

Jesus Heals a Woman and Jairus's Daughter

40 Now when Jesus returned, the crowd
[o]welcomed him, for they were all waiting
for him. 41 [p]And there came a man named
Jairus, who was [q]a ruler of the synagogue.
And falling at Jesus' feet, he implored him
to come to his house, 42 for he had [r]an only
daughter, about twelve years of age, and
she was dying.

As Jesus went, the people [s]pressed
around him. 43 And there was a woman
[t]who had had a discharge of blood for
twelve years, and though she had spent all
her [u]living on physicians,[1] she could not be
healed by anyone. 44 She came up behind
him and touched [v]the fringe of his garment, and [w]immediately her discharge of
blood ceased. 45 And Jesus said, "Who was
it that touched me?" When all denied it,
Peter[2] said, "Master, the crowds surround
you and are pressing in on you!" 46 But
Jesus said, "Someone touched me, for I
perceive that [x]power has gone out from
me." 47 And when the woman saw that she
was not hidden, she came trembling, and
falling down before him declared in the
presence of all the people why she had
touched him, and how she had been
immediately healed. 48 And he said to her,
"Daughter, [y]your faith has made you well;
[y]go in peace."

49 While he was still speaking, someone
from [z]the ruler's house came and said,
"Your daughter is dead; [a]do not trouble
[b]the Teacher any more." 50 But Jesus on
hearing this answered him, "Do not fear;
only believe, and she will be well." 51 And
when he came to the house, he allowed no
one to enter with him, except [c]Peter and
[d]John and James, and the father and
mother of the child. 52 And all were weeping and [e]mourning for her, but he [f]said,
"Do not weep, for [g]she is not dead but
[h]sleeping." 53 And they laughed at him,
knowing that she was dead. 54 But [i]taking
her by the hand he called, saying, "Child,
[j]arise." 55 And [k]her spirit returned, and she
got up at once. And he directed that something should be given her to eat. 56 And her
parents were amazed, but [l]he charged
them to tell no one what had happened.

Jesus Sends Out the Apostles

9 [m]And he called the twelve together and
gave them power and authority over all
demons and to cure diseases, 2 [n]and he sent
them out to [o]proclaim the kingdom of God
and to heal. 3 [p]And he said to them, "Take
nothing for your journey, [q]no staff, nor

37 [m][ch. 5:8; 1 Kin. 17:18; Acts 16:39] **39** [n]Ps. 66:16; [ch. 5:14] **40** [o]ch. 9:11 **41** [p]For ver. 41-56, see Matt. 9:18-26; Mark 5:22-43 [q]ch. 13:14; Acts 13:15; 18:8, 17 **42** [r]See ch. 7:12 [s]ver. 45; Mark 3:9 **43** [t]Lev. 15:25 [u]ch. 21:4; Mark 12:44 **44** [v]Matt. 14:36; 23:5; [Num. 15:38, 39; Deut. 22:12] [w]Matt. 15:28; 17:18 **46** [x]ch. 5:17; 6:19; [Acts 10:38] **48** [y]See ch. 7:50 **49** [z]ver. 41 [a]ch. 7:6 [b]See John 11:28 **51** [c]ch. 9:28; Mark 14:33 [d]Mark 3:17 **52** [e]ch. 23:27; Matt. 11:17 [f]ch. 7:13 [g][Acts 20:10] [h]John 11:4, 11 **54** [i]See Mark 1:31 **54** [j]ch. 7:14, 22; [Matt. 11:5; John 11:43] **55** [k][Judg. 15:19; 1 Sam. 30:12] **56** [l]See Matt. 8:4
Chapter 9
1 [m]Matt. 10:1; Mark 3:13-15; 6:7 **2** [n]Matt. 10:5, 7, 8; [ver. 11; ch. 10:1, 9] [o]ver. 11, 60; See ch. 4:43 **3** [p]For ver. 3-5, see Matt. 10:9-14; Mark 6:8-11; [ch. 10:4-11; 22:35] [q][Mark 6:8]

[1] Some manuscripts omit *and though she had spent all her living on physicians,* [2] Some manuscripts add *and those who were with him*

8:37 Fear caused these people to reject the most wonderful opportunity of their lives. They may have been afraid of the power they saw in the healing or upset by the loss of a herd of swine.

8:38, 39 With Jesus gone it was important that the man work for God in that region. Notice that what "God has done" is identified with what Jesus had done.

8:41 a ruler of the synagogue. The man who would arrange the service, choosing those who would read Scripture or lead in prayer.

8:43 a discharge of blood. The woman's condition would make her ceremonially unclean (Lev. 15:25), cutting her off from many social relationships.

8:44 the fringe of his garment. Perhaps the tassel prescribed in Num. 15:37–40.

8:45 The woman's cure needed to be known publicly in order for her to be taken back into normal social life. Jesus was careful to arrange this.

8:48 Daughter. She is the only woman Jesus calls "Daughter," a tender statement.

8:52 Luke does not explain who "all" these people were. They would certainly include relatives and friends, probably people from the neighborhood and professional mourners (including flute players, Matt. 9:23). Mourning was normally demonstrative, and there would have been much wailing. Jesus forbade it all and said that the girl was "sleeping." This does not mean that she had not died, but that Jesus was prepared to waken her from death.

8:54 arise. Luke describes the miracle simply (Mark 5:41 retains the Aramaic words Jesus used, but Luke translates them).

8:56 The effect of the miracle was astonishment. This time Jesus forbade publicity; He often did not want news of His miracles to spread (Mark 1:34 note).

9:1, 2 The Twelve were evidently not together all the time (some had homes and families). But for this important mission Jesus gathered them all. He equipped them with power over demons (see "Demons" at Deut. 32:17) and sickness, and commissioned them to continue His work of preaching and healing.

9:3 They were to take the barest minimum, relying on God's provision.

no staff. No complete explanation has been given as to why Mark 6:8 allows a staff; perhaps both are ways of saying "Go as you are; make no special preparation."

bag, nor bread, nor money; and do not
have two tunics.[1] 4 And whatever house
you enter, stay there, and from there
depart. 5 And wherever they do not receive
you, when you leave that town [r]shake off
the dust from your feet [s]as a testimony
[t]against them." 6 [u]And they departed and
went through the villages, preaching the
gospel and healing everywhere.

Herod Is Perplexed by Jesus

7 [v]Now [w]Herod the tetrarch heard about
all that was happening, and he was perplexed, because it was said by some that
[x]John had been raised from the dead, 8 [x]by
some that Elijah had appeared, and [x]by
others that one of the prophets of old had
risen. 9 Herod said, "John I beheaded, but
who is this about whom I hear such
things?" And [y]he sought to see him.

Jesus Feeds the Five Thousand

10 On their return [z]the apostles told him
all that they had done. [a]And he took them
and withdrew apart to a town called
Bethsaida. 11 When the crowds learned it,
they followed him, and he [b]welcomed
them and [c]spoke to them of the kingdom
of God and [c]cured those who had need of
healing. 12 Now [d]the day began to wear
away, and the twelve came and said to him,
[e]"Send the crowd away to go into the surrounding villages and countryside to find
lodging and get provisions, for we are here
in a desolate place." 13 But he said to them,
[f]"You give them something to eat." They
said, "We have no more than [g]five loaves
and two fish—unless we are to go and buy
food for all these people." 14 For there were
about five thousand men. And he said to
his disciples, "Have them sit down in
groups of about fifty each." 15 And they did
so, and had them all sit down. 16 And taking the five loaves and the two fish, [h]he
looked up to heaven and [i]said a blessing
over them. Then he broke the loaves and
gave them to the disciples to set before the
crowd. 17 And they all ate and were satisfied. And what was left over was picked up,
twelve baskets of broken pieces.

Peter Confesses Jesus As the Christ

18 [j]Now it happened that as he was praying alone, the disciples were with him. And
he asked them, "Who do the crowds say
that I am?" 19 And they answered, [k]"John
the Baptist. But others say, [l]Elijah, and
others, that one of the prophets of old has
risen." 20 Then he said to them, "But who
do you say that I am?" And Peter answered,
[m]"The Christ of God."

Jesus Foretells His Death

21 [n]And he strictly charged and commanded them to tell this to no one, 22 [o]say-
ing, [p]"The Son of Man must [q]suffer many
things and [r]be rejected by the elders and
chief priests and scribes, and be killed, and
on [s]the third day be raised."

Take Up Your Cross and Follow Jesus

23 And he said to all, "If anyone would
come after me, let him [t]deny himself and
[u]take up his cross [v]daily and follow me.

5 [r]Acts 13:51; [Neh. 5:13; Acts 18:6] [s]See Mark 1:44 [t]James 5:3
6 [u]Mark 6:12
7 [v]For ver. 7-9, see Matt. 14:1-12; Mark 6:14-29 [w]ch. 3:1, 19; Acts 13:1 [x]ver. 19
8 [x][See ver. 7 above]
9 [y]ch. 23:8
10 [z]Mark 6:30 [a]For ver. 10-17, see Matt. 14:13-21; Mark 6:32-44; John 6:1-13; [Matt. 15:32-38; Mark 8:2-9]
11 [b]ch. 8:40 [c]ver. 2
12 [d]ch. 24:29 (Gk.); Jer. 6:4 [e][Matt. 15:23]
13 [f][2 Kin. 4:42-44] [g]Matt. 16:9; Mark 8:19
16 [h]Mark 7:34; John 11:41; 17:1 [i]ch. 24:30; 1 Sam. 9:13; Matt. 26:26; Mark 8:7; 14:22; [1 Cor. 14:16]
18 [j]For ver. 18-20, see Matt. 16:13-16; Mark 8:27-29
19 [k]ver. 7; Matt. 14:2; Mark 6:14 [l]ver. 8; Mark 6:15; [Matt. 17:10; Mark 9:11; John 1:21]
20 [m]ch. 23:35; Acts 3:18; Rev. 12:10; See Matt. 1:17

21 [n]Matt. 16:20; Mark 8:30; See Matt. 12:16 **22** [o]For ver. 22-27, see Matt. 16:21-28; Mark 8:31–9:1 [p]ch. 18:31; [ch. 13:33] [q]ch. 24:7; Matt. 17:12, 22, 23; Mark 9:30, 31 [r]ch. 17:25; 1 Pet. 2:4; [ch. 20:17] [s]ch. 18:33; 24:7, 46; See Matt. 27:63; John 2:19 **23** [t][2 Tim. 2:12, 13] [u]See Matt. 10:38, 39 [v]1 Cor. 15:31

[1] Greek *chiton*, a long garment worn under the cloak next to the skin

bag. The bag a traveler would take to carry belongings and provisions for his journey.

9:4 They would rely on hospitality, but staying in one house limited the time they spent in any one place.

9:5 shake off the dust from your feet. Strict Jews removed defiling dust from their feet when they returned from Gentile lands. The disciples' action symbolically said that those who rejected the preachers did not belong to God's people.

9:7 Herod. Herod Antipas, who ruled Galilee.

John had been raised from the dead. This became Herod's view (Mark 6:16), but at this time he simply believed that John was dead; Herod himself had ordered him beheaded.

9:8 Elijah. See the prophecy of Mal. 4:5.

9:10–17 The one miracle, apart from the Resurrection, found in all four Gospels.

9:10 took them . . . apart. They retired to a private place, evidently to report to Jesus and relax after the preaching tour.

Bethsaida. This must mean in the vicinity of Bethsaida, for it was "a desolate place" (v. 12).

9:11 welcomed them. This was a gracious act when Jesus was looking for time to rest.

9:20 who do you say. This question distinguishes the disciples from the crowds; the word "you" is emphatic.

Christ. This word means "anointed" (1 Sam. 2:10; Matt. 1:1 and notes); Christ is the One God has chosen above all others, the One who will bring salvation. Peter's answer is more than a penetrating assessment; it is not a human discovery but a revelation from God (Matt. 16:17).

9:21 strictly charged. The disciples would almost certainly have been misunderstood if they had told anyone; people would have thought they were proclaiming a political deliverer. Jesus went on to explain the Messiah must suffer, be rejected, die, and be raised on the third day (v. 22).

9:23–25 To take up the cross means to renounce selfish ambition; it is a death to a whole way of life.

24 For [u]whoever would save his life will lose it, but whoever loses his life for my sake will save it. 25 [w]For what does it profit a man if he gains the whole world and loses or forfeits himself? 26 For [x]whoever is ashamed of me and of my words, of him will the Son of Man be ashamed [y]when he comes in [z]his glory and the glory of the Father and of [a]the holy angels. 27 But I tell you truly, there are some standing here who will not [b]taste death [c]until they see the kingdom of God."

The Transfiguration

28 [d]Now about eight days after these sayings he took with him [e]Peter and John and James and [f]went up on the mountain to pray. 29 And as he was praying, the appearance of his face was [g]altered, and [h]his clothing became dazzling white. 30 And behold, two men were talking with him, Moses and Elijah, 31 who appeared in glory and spoke of his departure,[1] which he was about to accomplish at Jerusalem. 32 Now Peter and those who were with him [i]were heavy with sleep, but when they became fully awake [j]they saw his glory and the two men who stood with him. 33 And as the men were parting from him, Peter said to Jesus, "Master, it is good that we are here. Let us make three [k]tents, one for you and one for Moses and one for Elijah"—[l]not knowing what he said. 34 As he was saying these things, [m]a cloud came and overshadowed them, and they were afraid as they entered the cloud. 35 And [m]a voice came out of the cloud, saying, "This is my Son, [n]my Chosen One;[2] [o]listen to him!" 36 And when the voice had spoken, Jesus was found alone. [p]And they kept silent and told no one in those days anything of what they had seen.

Healing of a Boy with an Unclean Spirit

37 [q]On the next day, when they had come down from the mountain, a great crowd met him. 38 And behold, a man from the crowd cried out, "Teacher, I beg you to look at my son, for [r]he is my only child. 39 And behold, a spirit seizes him, and he suddenly cries out. It convulses him so that he foams at the mouth; and shatters him, and will hardly leave him. 40 And I begged your disciples to cast it out, but [s]they could not." 41 Jesus answered, "O [t]faithless and twisted generation, [u]how long am I to be with you and bear with you? Bring your son here." 42 While he was coming, the demon threw him to the ground and convulsed him. But Jesus [v]rebuked the unclean spirit and healed the boy, and [w]gave him back to his father. 43 And all were astonished at the majesty of God.

Jesus Again Foretells His Death

But while they were all marveling at everything he was doing, Jesus[3] said to his disciples, 44 "Let these words sink into your ears: [z]The Son of Man is about to be delivered into the hands of men." 45 [a]But they did not understand this saying, and [b]it was concealed from them, so that they might

24 [u][See ver. 23 above] **25** [w][ch. 12:20] **26** [x]Rom. 1:16; 2 Tim. 1:8, 12, 16; Heb. 11:16; 1 John 2:28; [Matt. 10:33] [y]Dan. 7:10, 13; Zech. 14:5; Matt. 24:30; 25:31; 26:64; John 1:51; Acts 1:11; 1 Thess. 1:10; 4:16; Jude 14; Rev. 1:7; [Deut. 33:2] [z]Matt. 19:28; 25:31; Mark 10:37; John 17:24 [a]Acts 10:22; Rev. 14:10; [Matt. 13:41; 16:27 **27** [b]John 8:52; Heb. 2:9 [c][ch. 21:31, 32; Matt. 10:23; 23:36; 24:34; Mark 13:30] **28** [d]For ver. 28-36, see Matt. 17:1-8; Mark 9:2-8 [e]ch. 8:51; Mark 14:33 [f]See Matt. 14:23 **29** [g]Mark 16:12 (Gk.) [h]Dan. 7:9; [Ps. 104:2; Matt. 28:3] **32** [i]Dan. 8:18; Matt. 26:43 [j]See John 1:14 **33** [k][Neh. 8:15] [l][Mark 9:6; 14:40] **34** [m]2 Pet. 1:17; [Ex. 24:15, 16] **35** [m][See ver. 34 above] [n]ch. 23:35; Isai. 42:1; [Ps. 89:3; Isai. 49:7] [o]Acts 3:22

36 [p]Matt. 17:9; Mark 9:9, 10 **37** [q]For ver. 37-42, see Matt. 17:14-19; Mark 9:14-28 **38** [r]See ch. 7:12 **40** [s][ch. 9:1; 10:17; Matt. 10:1; Mark 6:7] **41** [t]Phil. 2:15; [John 20:27] [u][John 14:9] **42** [v]ch. 4:35, 39; Zech. 3:2; Matt. 8:26; Mark 1:25; Jude 9 [w]See ch. 7:15 **43** [x]2 Pet. 1:16 [y]For ver. 43-45, see Matt. 17:22, 23; Mark 9:30-32 [z]ver. 22**44** [z][See ver. 43 above] **45** [a]ch. 2:50; 18:34; 24:25; Mark 6:52; John 10:6; 12:16; 16:17-19; [Matt. 17:13; Mark 9:10] [b]ch. 18:34; [ch. 24:16]

1 Greek *exodus* 2 Some manuscripts *my Beloved* 3 Greek *he*

9:27 see the kingdom of God. Suggestions as to the meaning of this phrase include the Transfiguration, Jesus' resurrection and ascension, Pentecost, the spread of the gospel, the destruction of Jerusalem, and the Second Advent. See note Matt. 16:28.

9:28 the mountain. The location of the Transfiguration is not known. Mount Tabor is the traditional site, but it is a long way from Caesarea Philippi and a military post was located there at that time. Mount Hermon is a more likely suggestion. See "The Transfiguration of Jesus" at Mark 9:2.

9:30 two men. Moses was the giver of the law, and Elijah represents the prophets.

9:31 his departure. Lit. His "exodus" (2 Pet. 1:15 has the same Greek word). Only Luke reports the subject of this conversation. That Jesus' death was discussed during this revelation of glory shows its centrality for His mission. It was by His death that glory would come to sinners.

9:32 heavy with sleep. The Transfiguration may have taken place at night, since v. 37 refers to "the next day" and Jesus sometimes prayed all night (6:12).

9:33 three tents. Peter suggests building structures of some kind, perhaps to enable the experience to be prolonged.

9:34 a cloud. As in the Old Testament, the cloud is associated with the presence of God.

9:35 my Son. This designation emphasizes the divine relationship, and the command "listen to him" His divine authority. Both set Jesus apart as different from and superior to Moses and Elijah.

9:37–40 The contrast between the glory on the mountaintop and the disciples' inability to defeat the forces of evil on the plain is striking. They had cast out demons previously (vv. 1–6; cf. Mark 9:29).

9:41 faithless and twisted generation. These words are apparently addressed to the crowds that had come without faith, evidently expecting Jesus to be able to do nothing. In contrast, the boy's father had faith even though it was imperfect (Mark 9:24).

9:44 The word "your" is emphatic. Over against the general unbelief, the disciples are to be different. Jesus then predicts His betrayal and death in general terms, but they did not understand.

9:45 it was concealed. This may mean that they were actively prevented

not perceive it. And they were afraid to ask
him about this saying.

Who Is the Greatest?

46 [c]An argument arose among them as to
which of them was the greatest. 47 But
Jesus, knowing the reasoning of their
hearts, took a child and put him by his side
48 and said to them, [d]"Whoever receives
this child in my name receives me, and
[d]whoever receives me receives him who
sent me. For [e]he who is least among you all
is the one who is great."

Anyone Not Against Us Is For Us

49 [f]John answered, "Master, we saw
someone [g]casting out demons in your
name, and [h]we tried to stop him, because
he does not follow with us." 50 But Jesus
said to him, "Do not stop him, [i]for the one
who is not against you is for you."

A Samaritan Village Rejects Jesus

51 When the days drew near for [j]him to
be taken up, [k]he set his face [l]to go to
Jerusalem. 52 And [m]he sent messengers
ahead of him, who went and entered a village of [n]the Samaritans, to make preparations for him. 53 But [o]the people did not
receive him, because [p]his face was set
toward Jerusalem. 54 And when his disciples James and John saw it, they said,
"Lord, do you want us to tell [q]fire to come
down from heaven and consume them?"[1]
55 But he turned and rebuked them.[2] 56 And
they went on to another village.

46 [c]For ver. 46-48, see Matt. 18:1-5; Mark 9:33-37; [Matt. 20:20-28; Mark 10:35-45]
48 [d][Matt. 10:40, 42] [e]ch. 22:26
49 [f]For ver. 49, 50, see Mark 9:38-40 [g]ch. 10:17; Matt. 7:22; Mark 16:17; Acts 19:13; [Matt. 12:27] [h][Num. 11:28]
50 [i][ch. 11:23; Matt. 12:30]
51 [j]See Mark 16:19 [k]2 Kin. 12:17; Isai. 50:7; Jer. 42:15 [l]ch. 13:22; 17:11; 18:31; 19:11, 28
52 [m][ch. 10:1] [n]See Matt. 10:5
53 [o]John 4:9; [ch. 10:33] [p]John 4:20
54 [q]See Rev. 13:13
57 [r]ver. 51 [s]For ver. 57-60, see Matt. 8:19-22
60 [t][John 5:25] [u]ver. 2
61 [v][1 Kin. 19:20]
62 [w][Phil. 3:13]
Chapter 10
1 [x]Ex. 24:1, 9; Num. 11:16 [y][ch. 9:2, 52]
2 [z]Matt. 9:37, 38; John 4:35

The Cost of Following Jesus

57 As they were going [r]along the road,
[s]someone said to him, "I will follow you
wherever you go." 58 And Jesus said to him,
"Foxes have holes, and birds of the air have
nests, but the Son of Man has nowhere to
lay his head." 59 To another he said,
"Follow me." But he said, "Lord, let me
first go and bury my father." 60 And Jesus[3]
said to him, "Leave [t]the dead to bury their
own dead. But as for you, go and [u]proclaim
the kingdom of God." 61 Yet another said,
"I will follow you, Lord, [v]but let me first
say farewell to those at my home." 62 Jesus
said to him, [w]"No one who puts his hand
to the plow and looks back is fit for the
kingdom of God."

Jesus Sends Out the Seventy-Two

10 After this the Lord appointed [x]seventy-
two[4] others and [y]sent them on
ahead of him, two by two, into every town
and place where he himself was about to
go. 2 [z]And he said to them, "The harvest is
plentiful, but the laborers are few. [a]There-
fore pray earnestly to the Lord of the harvest to send out laborers into his harvest.
3 Go your way; [b]behold, I am sending you
out as lambs in the midst of wolves. 4 [c]Carry
no moneybag, no knapsack, no sandals,

[a][2 Thess. 3:1] 3 [b]Matt. 10:16; [John 17:18] 4 [c]For ver. 4-12, [ch. 9:1-5; 22:35; Matt. 10:9-15; Mark 6:8-11]

1 Some manuscripts add *as Elijah did* 2 Some manuscripts add *and he said, "You do not know what manner of spirit you are of; for the Son of Man came not to destroy people's lives but to save them"* 3 Greek *he*
4 Some manuscripts *seventy;* also verse 17

from understanding, or simply that before the Resurrection it seemed contradictory to the disciples that salvation could come by way of Jesus' death.

9:46 greatest. Luke contrasts the disciples' wish to have the best place for themselves with Jesus' concern for others.

9:47 child. Children were typically considered unimportant. To be concerned with them and to take the lowest place is to be truly great.

9:49, 50 For John, it was not enough to do miracles in Jesus' name; it was necessary to "follow with us." Jesus is saying that there is no neutrality in the struggle against evil. Those not against us are for us, a test we should apply to others. In 11:23 we find a test we should apply to ourselves.

9:51 From this point to 19:44, Luke gives an account of Jesus' journey to Jerusalem. There is no parallel to this unit as a whole in the other Gospels, though there are parallels to some of the individual sections. Luke presents the solemn progress to the capital city where Jesus would die for sinners in accordance with the will of God. On the way He gives the disciples teaching that would be important for them when they were left to carry on as Christian leaders without His physical presence.

9:52, 53 Jesus and His disciples would be enough to strain the resources of a small village if they dropped in unexpectedly. Jesus gave due notice but was met with the traditional hostility of the Samaritans for the Jews.

9:54 The disciples had zeal for their task but did not understand the mercy of God.

9:59 bury my father. The father may have been alive. The words would then indicate that the potential disciple wanted to continue to care for his father until his death. If the father was dead, Jesus' words are all the more shocking, since filial piety demanded that a son should look after the burial arrangements for his father. Either way, Jesus is saying that the demands of the kingdom override all earthly loyalties.

10:1 seventy-two others. This mission is found only in Luke, but the instructions are similar to some of those given earlier to the Twelve (9:1–6; Matt. 10:5–15; Mark 6:7–13). The Greek manuscripts are divided between 70 and 72 as the number sent out (see text note), and there is no way of being sure which is original. Both represent the number of the nations of the world in Gen. 10 (the Hebrew text has 70 names, the Greek has 72).

two by two. Jesus had sent out the Twelve in pairs (Mark 6:7). This gave mutual support and also the testimony of two witnesses (cf. Deut. 17:6).

10:3 lambs in the midst of wolves. See "Christians in the World" at Col. 2:20.

10:4 sandals. This is probably not a command to go barefoot, but a prohibition against carrying an extra pair of sandals.

and [d]greet no one on the road. 5 Whatever
house you enter, first say, [e]'Peace be to this
house!' 6 And if a son of peace is there, your
peace will rest upon him. But if not, [f]it will
return to you. 7 And remain in the same
house, eating and drinking what they provide, for [g]the laborer deserves his wages.
Do not go from house to house. 8 Whenever you enter a town and they receive you,
eat what is set before you. 9 Heal the sick in
it and say to them, [h]'The kingdom of God
has come near to you.' 10 But whenever you
enter a town and they do not receive you,
go into its streets and say, 11 [i]'Even the dust
of your town that clings to our feet we wipe
off against you. Nevertheless know this,
that [j]the kingdom of God has come near.'
12 [k]I tell you, [l]it will be more bearable on
[m]that day for Sodom than for that town.

Woe to Unrepentant Cities

13 "Woe to you, Chorazin! Woe to you,
Bethsaida! For if the mighty works done in
you had been done in [n]Tyre and Sidon,
they would have repented long ago, sitting
in sackcloth and ashes. 14 [o]But it will be
more bearable in the judgment for [n]Tyre
and Sidon than for you. 15 And you, Capernaum, [p]will you be exalted to heaven? You
shall be brought down to [q]Hades.
16 [r]"The one who hears you hears me,
and [s]the one who rejects you rejects me,
and [t]the one who rejects me rejects him
who sent me."

The Return of the Seventy-Two

17 [u]The seventy-two returned with joy,
saying, "Lord, [v]even the demons are subject to us in your name!" 18 And he said to
them, [w]"I saw Satan [x]fall like lightning
from heaven. 19 Behold, I have given you
authority [y]to tread on serpents and scorpions, and over all the power of [z]the enemy,
and [a]nothing shall hurt you. 20 [b]Never-
theless, do not rejoice in this, that the spirits are subject to you, but rejoice that [c]your
names are written in heaven."

Jesus Rejoices in the Holy Spirit

21 [d]In that same hour [e]he rejoiced [f]in the
Holy Spirit and said, "I thank you, Father,
[g]Lord of heaven and earth, that [h]you have
hidden these things from the wise and
understanding and [i]revealed them to little
children; yes, Father, for [j]such was your
gracious will.[1] 22 [k]All things have been
handed over to me by my Father, and no
one knows who the Son is [k]except the
Father, or who the Father is [k]except the
Son and anyone [l]to whom the Son chooses
to reveal him."

23 Then turning to the disciples he said
privately, [m]"Blessed are the eyes that see
what you see! 24 For I tell you [n]that many
prophets and kings desired to see what you
see, and did not see it, and to hear what
you hear, and did not hear it."

The Parable of the Good Samaritan

25 [o]And behold, a [p]lawyer stood up to
[q]put him to the test, saying, "Teacher, what
shall I do to [r]inherit eternal life?" 26 He said
to him, "What is written in the Law? How
do you read it?" 27 And he answered, [s]"You

4 [d]2 Kin. 4:29 **5** [e]1 Sam. 25:6 **6** [f][Ps. 35:13] **7** [g]See 1 Tim. 5:18 **9** [h]ver. 11; See Matt. 3:2 **11** [i]Acts 13:51; [Neh. 5:13; Acts 18:6] [j]ver. 9 **12** [k]For ver. 13-15, see Matt. 11:21-23 [l]See Matt. 10:15 [m]Matt. 7:22 **13** [n][Isai. 23; Ezek. 28:2-24; Amos 1:9, 10] **14** [o][ch. 12:47, 48] [n][See ver. 13 above] **15** [p]Cited from Isai. 14:13-15 [q]ch. 16:23; Matt. 16:18; Acts 2:27 **16** [r]See Matt. 10:40 [s]John 12:48; 1 Thess. 4:8; [Matt. 25:45] [t]John 5:23 **17** [u]ver. 1 [v]See Mark 16:17 **18** [w][John 12:31; 16:11; Col. 2:15; Rev. 12:8, 9] [x][Isai. 14:12; Rev. 9:1] **19** [y]Ps. 91:13; Mark 16:18; Acts 28:5 [z]Matt. 13:39 [a]ch. 21:18; [Rom. 8:28, 39] **20** [b][Matt. 7:22, 23] [c]Ex. 32:32, 33; Ps. 69:28; Isai. 4:3; Ezek. 13:9; Dan. 12:1; Phil. 4:3; Heb. 12:23 **21** [d]For ver. 21, 22, see Matt. 11:25-27

[e][Isai. 53:11 [f][Mark 12:36] [g]See Acts 17:24 [h]Job 37:24; 1 Cor. 1:19-27; 2 Cor. 3:14 [i]Ps. 8:2; Matt. 21:16; [ch. 8:10; Matt. 16:17] [j][ch. 12:32] **22** [k]John 1:18; 6:46; 7:29; 8:19; 10:15; 17:25; See Matt. 28:18 [l][John 17:26] **23** [m]Matt. 13:16, 17; [Matt. 16:17] **24** [n]Heb. 11:13; 1 Pet. 1:10-12; [John 8:56] **25** [o]For ver. 25-28, [ch. 18:18-20; Matt. 19:16-19; 22:34-39; Mark 10:17-19] [p]See ch. 7:30 [q]See John 8:6 **25** [r]Matt. 19:29; 25:34, 46 **27** [s]Matt. 22:37; Mark 12:30; Cited from Deut. 6:5

[1] Or *for so it pleased you well*

greet no one. The customary greetings were elaborate, and to avoid them would be highly unusual.

10:6 it will return to you. God's peace comes only to those who respond.

10:11 the dust of your town. See note 9:5.

10:12 Sodom's wickedness was proverbial, but rejecting the preachers of God's kingdom is worse even than Sodom's deeds.

that day. Judgment Day.

10:13 Chorazin . . . Bethsaida. Having heard and rejected Jesus, these towns were more guilty than Tyre and Sidon, which were infamous for their evil.

10:15 Capernaum. Capernaum was a town where Jesus did much of His work.

10:16 To reject God's messengers is to reject God also.

10:18 In its context the saying seems to mean that the ministry of the preachers had inflicted a defeat upon Satan.

10:19 authority. When they are sent by God, they are safe from snakes and scorpions (cf. Acts 28:3–5). God's messengers are protected as they do what God calls them to do.

10:21 revealed them to little children. See "Illumination and Conviction" at 1 Cor. 2:10.

10:22 The relationship of Jesus and the Father is unique. Knowledge of it does not come to the world by natural means.

10:23, 24 The greatest of prophets and kings in earlier days had not seen the Messiah, as these disciples had (cf. 7:24–28 note).

10:25 lawyer. An expert in the law of God, and so a religious man. Yet he was not genuinely looking for information but for something that would enable him to accuse Jesus.

10:27 The lawyer showed insight; Jesus summed up the law in much the same way (Matt. 22:37–40).

shall love the Lord your God with all your heart and with all your soul and with all your strength and with all your mind, and [t]your neighbor as yourself." 28 And he said to him, "You have answered correctly; [u]do this, and you will live."

29 But he, [v]desiring to justify himself, said to Jesus, "And who is my neighbor?" 30 Jesus replied, "A man [w]was going down from Jerusalem to Jericho, and he fell among robbers, who stripped him and beat him and departed, leaving him half dead. 31 Now by chance a [x]priest was going down that road, and when he saw him he passed by on the other side. 32 So likewise [x]a Levite, when he came to the place and saw him, passed by on the other side. 33 But a [y]Samaritan, as he journeyed, came to where he was, and when he saw him, he had compassion. 34 He went to him and [z]bound up his wounds, pouring on [z]oil and wine. Then he set him on his own animal and brought him to an inn and took care of him. 35 And the next day he took out two [a]denarii[1] and gave them to the innkeeper, saying, 'Take care of him, and whatever more you spend, I will repay you when I come back.' 36 Which of these three, do you think, proved to be a neighbor to the man who fell among the robbers?" 37 He said, "The one who showed him mercy." And Jesus said to him, "You go, and do likewise."

Martha and Mary

38 Now as they went on their way, Jesus[2] entered a village. And a woman named [b]Martha [c]welcomed him into her house. 39 And she had a sister called [b]Mary, who [d]sat at the Lord's feet and listened to his teaching. 40 But Martha was distracted with much serving. And she went up to him and said, "Lord, do you not care that my sister has left me to serve alone? Tell her then to help me." 41 But the Lord answered her, "Martha, Martha, you are [e]anxious and troubled about many things, 42 but one thing is necessary.[3] Mary has chosen [f]the good portion, which will not be taken away from her."

The Lord's Prayer

11 Now Jesus[4] was praying in a certain place, and when he finished, one of his disciples said to him, "Lord, teach us to pray, [g]as John taught his disciples." 2 And he said to them, [h]"When you pray, say:

[i]"Father, [j]hallowed be [k]your name.
[l]Your kingdom come.
3 [m]Give us [n]each day our daily bread,[5]
4 and [o]forgive us our sins,
for we ourselves forgive everyone
who is indebted to us.
And [p]lead us not into temptation."

5 And he said to them, "Which of you who has a friend will go to him at midnight and say to him, 'Friend, lend me three loaves, 6 for a friend of mine has arrived on a journey, and I have nothing to set before him'; 7 and he will answer from within, 'Do not bother me; the door is now shut, and my children are with me in bed. I cannot get up and give you anything'? 8 I tell you, though he will not get up and give him any-

1 A *denarius* was a day's wage for a laborer 2 Greek *he* 3 Some manuscripts *few things are necessary, or only one* 4 Greek *he* 5 Or *our bread for tomorrow*

27 [t]Cited from Lev. 19:18; See Matt. 19:19
28 [u]Lev. 18:5; Neh. 9:29; Ezek. 20:11; Rom. 10:5; Gal. 3:12
29 [v]ch. 16:15
30 [w][ch. 18:31; 19:28]
31 [x]John 1:19; [Num. 8:19]
32 [x][See ver. 31 above]
33 [y]See Matt. 10:5
34 [z]Isai. 1:6
35 [a]See Matt. 18:28
38 [b]John 11:1, 19, 20; 12:2, 3 [c]ch. 19:6
39 [b][See ver. 38 above] [d]ch. 8:35; [Acts 22:3]
41 [e][1 Cor. 7:32-34]; See ch. 12:22
42 [f]Ps. 16:5
Chapter 11
1 [g]See ch. 5:33
2 [h]For ver. 2-4, [Matt. 6:9-13] [i]John 20:17; 1 Pet. 1:17 [j]Isai. 29:23; [ch. 1:49; 1 Pet. 3:15] [k]John 17:6 [l][Matt. 3:2; 4:17]
3 [m]Prov. 30:8 [n][Matt. 6:34]
4 [o]See ch. 7:48 [p]ch. 22:40, 46; Matt. 26:41; Mark 14:38; [1 Cor. 10:13]

10:28 do this. God's will is the way of life.

10:29–37 The parable answers the question "Who is my neighbor," not the question concerning what one must do to be saved. The Jews had various ideas about the "neighbor," but they confined it to Israel.

10:33, 34 Listeners would expect a priest and a Levite to be followed by a lay Israelite in an anti-clerical story. The Samaritan is totally unexpected, as is his kindness. Oil and wine were common remedies of that time and expressed the Samaritan's compassion.

10:35 two denarii. See Matt. 18:28 note. The coins would have paid for the man's board for several days.

10:38 a village. Bethany, about two miles from Jerusalem (John 11:1).

10:40, 41 Martha's preparations may have been unnecessarily elaborate. Mary knew that listening to Jesus was an extraordinary opportunity, to be given preference over other concerns (see Mark 19:7).

11:1 Lord, teach us to pray. Religious teachers were expected to teach their disciples how to pray.

11:2–4 This form of the "Lord's Prayer" differs slightly from that in Matt. 6:9–13. In Matthew, the prayer is given in a sermon; here it is given in answer to a question.

11:2 Father. This corresponds to the Aramaic *Abba,* the usual word for addressing a father in the family.

name. Names are representative of the person. The petition is that people will reverence God.

kingdom come. Jesus taught often about God's kingdom, and the prayer asks for it to be established. See theological note "Prayer."

11:4 forgive us . . . for we ourselves forgive. Sinners need the forgiveness of sins each day. If people do not forgive others they are not in a condition to receive forgiveness themselves.

11:7 In a one-room house the whole family would sleep on a raised platform, and for one person to get up would disturb them all.

11:8 Friendship is not enough to make him get up, but persistence is.

thing [q]because he is his friend, yet because
of his impudence[1] he will rise and give him
whatever he needs. 9 And I tell you, [r]ask, and
[s]it will be given to you; [t]seek, and you will
find; [u]knock, and it will be opened to you.
10 For everyone who asks receives, and the
one who seeks finds, and to the one who
knocks it will be opened. 11 What father
among you, if his son asks for[2] [v]a fish, will
instead of a fish give him [v]a serpent; 12 or if
he asks for an egg, will give him a scorpion?
13 If you then, [w]who are evil, know how to
give good gifts to your children, how much
more will the heavenly Father [x]give the
Holy Spirit to those who ask him!"

Jesus and Beelzebul

14 [y]Now he was casting out a demon that
was mute. When the demon had gone out,
the mute man spoke, and the people marveled. 15 But some of them said, "He casts
out demons [z]by Beelzebul, the prince of
demons," 16 while others, [a]to test him, kept
seeking from him a sign from heaven.
17 [b]But he, [c]knowing their thoughts, said to
them, "Every kingdom divided against
itself is laid waste, and a divided household
falls. 18 And if Satan also is divided against
himself, how will his kingdom stand? For
you say that I cast out demons by Beelzebul. 19 And if I cast out demons by Beelzebul, [d]by whom do [e]your sons cast them
out? Therefore they will be your judges.
20 But if it is by [f]the finger of God that I cast

8 [q][ch. 18:1-6] 9 [r]For ver. 9-13, see Matt. 7:7-11 [s]Matt. 18:19; 21:22; Mark 11:24; John 14:13; 15:7, 16; 16:23, 24; James 1:5, 6, 17; 1 John 3:22; 5:14, 15 [t]1 Chr. 28:9; 2 Chr. 15:2; Prov. 8:17; Jer. 29:13; [Isai. 55:6] [u][Rev. 3:20] 11 [v]ch. 4:3 13 [w]Gen. 6:5; 8:21; Matt. 12:34 [x][John 4:10; Acts 2:38] 14 [y]For ver. 14, 15, see Matt. 12:22-24; [Matt. 9:32-34] 15 [z]See Matt. 10:25

16 [a]See John 8:6 17 [b]For ver. 17-22, see Matt. 12:25-29; Mark 3:23-27 [c]See Matt. 9:4 19 [d][Acts 19:13] [e][2 Kin. 2:7] 20 [f]Ex. 8:19; 31:18; Deut. 9:10; Ps. 8:3]

1 Or *persistence* 2 Some manuscripts insert *bread, will give him a stone; or if he asks for*

Prayer

God made us and redeemed us for fellowship with Himself, and prayer is an important part of that relationship. God speaks to us in and through the contents of the Bible, which the Holy Spirit opens up and applies to us and enables us to understand. We then speak to God about Himself, ourselves, and people in His world, shaping what we say as response to what He has said. This unique form of two-way conversation continues as long as life lasts.

The Bible teaches us how to pray both privately (Matt. 6:5–8) and in company with each other (Acts 1:14; 4:24). In prayer, God's people express adoration and praise; confess their sins and ask for forgiveness; give thanks for God's goodness; and make petitions for themselves and others. The Lord's Prayer (Matt. 6:9–13; Luke 11:2–4) includes adoration, petition, and confession; the Psalter provides models of these three and of petition and intercession as well.

In petition the persons praying make their requests known to God, expressing their faith and dependence on Him for all things. Petition is the dimension of prayer most often highlighted through the Bible. As with the other aspects of prayer, petitions should ordinarily be directed to the Father, as the Lord's Prayer shows; but prayer may be directed to Christ, as in the days of His incarnation (Rom. 10:8–13; 2 Cor. 12:7–9), and to the Holy Spirit (Rev. 1:4).

Jesus teaches that petition to the Father is to be made in His name (John 14:13, 14; 15:16; 16:23, 24). This means invoking His mediation, as the One who secures our access to the Father, and looking to Him for support, as our intercessor in the Father's presence.

We may pray to God with fervent persistence when we bring our needs to Him (Luke 11:5–13; 18:1–8), and know that He will answer our prayers. But God knows what is best in a way that we do not, and He may deny our specific requests. If He denies us, it is because He has something better for us, as when Christ refused to heal Paul's thorn in the flesh (2 Cor. 12:7–9). To say, "your will be done," surrendering our own preference to the Father's wisdom, as Jesus did in Gethsemane (Matt. 26:39–44), is an explicit way of expressing faith in the goodness of what God has planned.

In intercession, we represent to God the needs and concerns of others. In doing this we exercise God-given love for them. Moses is a model for such a prayer in the Old Testament. In the New Testament it is at the center of what Jesus came to do, as John 17 reveals. The same prayer shows that the glory of God gives the ultimate purpose of intercession. In the same way, the Lord's Prayer puts God's glory first, making God's name the guide for our petitions and confessions as well.

11:13 you . . . evil. Universal sinfulness is presupposed.

11:14, 15 Jesus' enemies did not deny that He expelled demons, but ascribed His power to Beelzebul, the name of a heathen god (2 Kin. 1:2; Matt. 10:25 note).

11:17, 18 Unity is strength; Satan is not casting out his own workers.

11:20 the finger of God. As in Ex. 8:19, this figure describes the work of God Himself; Matt. 12:28 reads "the Spirit of God." Both statements bring out the truth that Jesus did not cast out demons by Beelzebul. The power

out demons, then [g] the kingdom of God has come upon you. 21 When a strong man, fully armed, guards his own palace, his goods are safe; 22 [h] but when one stronger than he attacks him and [i] overcomes him, he takes away his [j] armor in which he trusted and [k] divides his spoil. 23 [l] Whoever is not with me is against me, and whoever does not gather with me scatters.

Return of an Unclean Spirit

24 [m] "When the unclean spirit has gone out of a person, it passes through [n] waterless places seeking rest, and finding none it says, 'I will return to my house from which I came.' 25 And when it comes, it finds the house swept and put in order. 26 Then it goes and brings seven other spirits more evil than itself, and they enter and dwell there. And [o] the last state of that person is worse than the first."

True Blessedness

27 As he said these things, [p] a woman in the crowd raised her voice and said to him, [q] "Blessed is the womb that bore you, and the breasts at which you nursed!" 28 But he said, [r] "Blessed rather are those [s] who hear the word of God and [t] keep it!"

The Sign of Jonah

29 [u] When the crowds were increasing, he began to say, [v] "This generation is an evil generation. [w] It seeks for a sign, but no sign will be given to it except the sign of Jonah. 30 For as [x] Jonah became a sign to the people of Nineveh, so will the Son of Man be to this generation. 31 [y] The queen of the South will rise up at the judgment with the men of this generation and [z] condemn them, for she came from the ends of the earth to hear the wisdom of Solomon, and behold, [a] something greater than Solomon is here. 32 [b] The men of Nineveh will rise up at the judgment with this generation and [z] condemn it, for [c] they repented at the preaching of Jonah, and behold, [a] something greater than Jonah is here.

The Lamp of the Body

33 [d] "No one after lighting a lamp puts it in a cellar or under a basket, but on a stand, so that those who enter may see the light. 34 Your eye is [e] the lamp of your body. When your eye is healthy, your whole body is full of light, but when it is [f] bad, your body is full of darkness. 35 [e] Therefore be careful lest the light in you be darkness. 36 If then your whole body is full of light, having no part dark, it will be wholly bright, [g] as when a lamp with its rays gives you light."

Woes to the Pharisees and Lawyers

37 While Jesus[1] was speaking, [h] a Pharisee asked him to dine with him, so he went in and reclined at table. 38 The Pharisee was astonished to see [i] that he did not first wash before dinner. 39 And the Lord said to him, [j] "Now you Pharisees cleanse the outside of

20 [g] ch. 17:21; Matt. 19:24; 21:31, 43
22 [h] Isai. 49:24-26 [i] [John 16:33] [j] Eph. 6:11 [k] [Isai. 53:12]
23 [l] Matt. 12:30; [ch. 9:50; Mark 9:40]
24 [m] For ver. 24-26, see Matt. 12:43-45 [n] [Ps. 63:1; Jer. 2:6]
26 [o] 2 Pet. 2:20-22; [John 5:14]
27 [p] ch. 12:13 [q] [2 Chr. 9:7]; See ch. 1:48
28 [r] [Rev. 1:3; 22:7] [s] ch. 8:21; See James 1:22 [t] Lev. 22:31
29 [u] ch. 12:1 [v] For ver. 29-32, see Matt. 12:39-42; [Mark 8:11, 12] [w] ver. 16; See Matt. 12:38
30 [x] Jonah 1:17
31 [y] 1 Kin. 10:1; 2 Chr. 9:1 [z] Heb. 11:7; [Jer. 3:11; Ezek. 16:51, 52; Rom. 2:27] [a] [Matt. 12:6]
32 [b] Jonah 1:2 [z] [See ver. 31 above] [c] Jonah 3:5 [a] [See ver. 31 above]
33 [d] ch. 8:16; Matt. 5:15; Mark 4:21
34 [e] Matt. 6:22, 23

[f] Deut. 15:9; Prov. 28:22; Matt. 20:15 **35** [e] [See ver. 34 above] **36** [g] [Matt. 5:16]
37 [h] ch. 7:36; 14:1 **38** [i] Matt. 15:2; Mark 7:3, 4 **39** [j] Matt. 23:25, 26; [ch. 20:47]

1 Greek *he*

of God was at work in Him. This points to a further truth: in the coming of Jesus the kingdom of God has come. The miracles He performs are evidence for those who have eyes to see that God is at work.

11:21, 22 Satan is like a strong man in complete control of his house, the people under his power. But Jesus is stronger than Satan and overthrows him. This parable teaches that the kingdom of God is not simply a matter of helpful teaching; it comes with power to overcome Satan.

11:23 There can be no neutrality. The message of the kingdom brings the possibility of overcoming evil, and anyone who rejects this message accepts the ways of evil. There is no middle course.

11:24 house from which I came. The demon talks about the place he left as if he still owned it.

11:25 swept and put in order. The man has cleaned up his life, but nothing more. His life is empty, and therefore open to any evil influence.

11:28 rather. Jesus does not deny that Mary was blessed; He is saying that hearing and obeying God's word is more important.

11:29 a sign. Here Jesus responds to the demand for a "sign from heaven" (v. 16). Such a request could only have been motivated by unbelief, especially in view of the many demonstrations of messianic power already performed by Jesus (7:20–23). For Luke, Jesus' own presence is a "sign" of God's redemptive activity (2:34; 11:30).

11:30 Just as Jonah's three days inside the fish was a sign to the people of Nineveh, so Jesus' resurrection after three days in the tomb would be a sign to the Jews of His day.

11:31 The queen of the South. That is, the queen of Sheba (in southern Arabia) who made a long and difficult journey to hear Solomon (1 Kin. 10).

11:32 men of Nineveh. The Ninevites who repented when Jonah preached (Jon. 3:6–10). In both cases the argument is from the lesser to the greater. People responded to Solomon and to Jonah; much more should they respond to the Son of God.

11:34 the lamp of your body. When the eye is functioning correctly the body receives the benefit of light ("is full of light"; cf. Ps. 18:28). The people seeking a sign did not need more light, but better receptiveness to the light they already had. What God was doing in Jesus was plain enough.

11:38 wash before dinner. Such washing was not for reasons of hygiene, but ceremonial purity. The hands made contact with all sorts of things, some of which may have been ritually defiling. Scrupulous Jews purified themselves by washing their hands before eating so that defiled hands would not contaminate their food.

11:39, 40 Pharisees were scrupulous about the rules for outward ceremonial cleanness. Yet people could keep them all and still be defiled inwardly.

the cup and of the dish, but inside you are
full of [k]greed and wickedness. 40 [l]You fools!
[j]Did not he who made the outside make
the inside also? 41 But [m]give as alms those
things that are within, and behold, [n]every-
thing is clean for you.
42 [o]"But woe to you Pharisees! For [p]you
tithe the mint and rue and every herb, and neglect [q]justice and [r]the love of God. [s]These
you ought to have done, without neglecting the others. 43 Woe to you Pharisees! For
[t]you love the best seat in the synagogues
and greetings in the marketplaces. 44 Woe
to you! [u]For you are like unmarked graves,
and people walk over them without knowing it."
45 One of [v]the lawyers answered him,
"Teacher, in saying these things you insult us
also." 46 And he said, "Woe to you [w]lawyers
also! For [x]you load people with burdens
hard to bear, and you yourselves do not
touch the burdens with one of your fingers.
47 [y]Woe to you! For you build the tombs of
the prophets whom your fathers killed. 48 [z]So
you are witnesses and you [a]consent to the
deeds of [b]your fathers, for they killed them,
and you build their tombs. 49 Therefore also
[c]the Wisdom of God said, [d]'I will send them
[e]prophets and apostles, [f]some of whom
they will [g]kill and persecute,' 50 so that [h]the
blood of all the prophets, shed [i]from the
foundation of the world, may be [j]charged
against this generation, 51 from the blood of
[k]Abel to the blood of [l]Zechariah, who perished between [m]the altar and the sanctuary.
Yes, I tell you, it will be [j]required of this
generation. 52 Woe to you [n]lawyers! [o]For
you have taken away the key of [p]knowl-
edge. You [q]did not enter yourselves, and
you hindered those who were entering."
53 As he went away from there, the
scribes and the Pharisees began to press
him hard and to provoke him to speak
about many things, 54 [r]lying in wait for him,
[s]to catch him in something he might say.

Beware of the Leaven of the Pharisees

12 In the meantime, [t]when so many
thousands of the people had gathered together that they were trampling one
another, he began to say to his disciples
first, [u]"Beware of [v]the leaven of the Pharisees, [w]which is hypocrisy. 2 [x]Nothing is
covered up that will not be revealed, or hidden that will not be known. 3 Therefore
whatever you have said in the dark shall be
heard in the light, and what you have whispered in [y]private rooms shall be proclaimed
on [z]the housetops.

Have No Fear

4 "I tell you, my friends, [a]do not fear
those who kill the body, and after that have

[k][ch. 16:14] **40** [l]ch. 12:20 [j][See ver. 39 above] **41** [m]ch. 12:33; [ch. 16:9; Dan. 4:27] [n][Tit. 1:15] **42** [o]Matt. 23:23 [p]ch. 18:12; Deut. 14:22 [q]Ps. 33:5; Jer. 5:1; Mic. 6:8; Zech. 7:9 [r][1 John 3:17] [s][1 Sam. 15:22] **43** [t]ch. 20:46; Matt. 23:6, 7; Mark 12:38, 39; [ch. 14:7] **44** [u]Matt. 23:27 **45** [v]ver. 46, 52; See ch. 7:30 **46** [w]ver. 45, 52 [x]Matt. 23:4; [Matt. 11:28-30; Acts 15:10] **47** [y]Matt. 23:29, 30 **48** [z]Matt. 23:31 [a]See Rom. 1:32 [b]Acts 7:51, 52 **49** [c][ch. 7:35; Prov. 8:12, 22, 23, 30; Matt. 11:19; 1 Cor. 1:24, 30; Col. 2:3] [d]For ver. 49-51, [Matt. 23:34-36] [e]See Acts 13:1; 1 Cor. 12:28 [f]See Matt. 21:35 [g]1 Thess. 2:15 (Gk.)

50 [h]Rev. 18:24 [i]See Matt. 13:35 [j]Gen. 42:22; 2 Chr. 24:22; Ezek. 3:18 **51** [k]Gen. 4:4, 8; Heb. 11:4; 1 John 3:12 [l]2 Chr. 24:20, 21 [m]Ex. 40:6; 2 Kin. 16:14; Ezek. 40:47 [j][See ver. 50 above] **52** [n]ver. 45, 46 [o]Matt. 23:13; [Mal. 2:7, 8] [p]Rom. 2:20 [q][ch. 7:30; Matt. 5:20; 21:31] **54** [r]ch. 20:20; Mark 3:2; John 8:6; [Isai. 29:21] [s]Matt. 22:15; Mark 12:13
Chapter 12 **1** [t]ch. 11:29 [u]Matt. 16:6, 11, 12; Mark 8:15 [v]1 Cor. 5:6-8; Gal. 5:9 [w]Matt. 23:28; Mark 12:15 **2** [x]ch. 8:17; Mark 4:22; [1 Tim. 5:25]; For ver. 2-9, see Matt. 10:26-33 **3** [y]Matt. 6:6 [z]See ch. 5:19 **4** [a]Isai. 8:12, 13; 51:12, 13; Jer. 1:8; 1 Pet. 3:14

11:41 give as alms . . . within. Lit. "Give the inner things as alms." Jesus is saying that there must be a right inner attitude when one gives to the poor and, when the inside is right, all is clean.

11:42 woe. See note 6:24–26.

tithe. Tithing was intended as a joyful and thankful offering expressing love for God, but the Pharisees, by counting up stalks of mint and the like, had turned it into a burdensome duty.

11:43 greetings. Elaborate salutations that showed the recipients to be important people.

11:44 unmarked graves. Touching a grave made a person ceremonially defiled (Num. 19:16), so graves were whitewashed to warn people. An unmarked grave was a hidden source of ritual impurity.

11:45 lawyers. See note 10:25.

11:46 burdens hard to bear. The legal experts added to the law many regulations meant to ensure that the law itself would not be broken, but which imposed a heavy burden.

11:47 tombs of the prophets. They saw themselves as honoring those great men of God, but building tombs could not hide their complicity with those who killed them (v. 48).

11:49 I will send . . . persecute. The source of the quotation has not been discovered. Jesus Himself may be saying that this is the way God's wisdom works out.

11:50, 51 Jesus' own generation was guilty, for in rejecting Jesus it rejected the prophets who had spoken of Him. Thus, these people shared in the guilt for the deaths of righteous men. Abel was the first person murdered (Gen. 4:8), and Zechariah's murder may be the last in the Old Testament (2 Chr. 24:21–22; cf. Matt. 23:35 note).

11:52 taken away the key of knowledge. Through their traditional interpretation of the law, the "lawyers" had made it impossible for ordinary people to understand the true meaning of the law. The Pharisees and lawyers themselves also used their traditions to evade the demands of the law (cf. Mark 7:5–13).

12:1 thousands. The word strictly means "ten thousands" but was used generally of any large number. Jesus' teaching was addressed primarily to His disciples, though the crowds would also have heard and profited.

leaven. People were familiar with the way a little leaven slowly permeates and transforms a large mass of dough. Jesus elsewhere uses the figure of leaven to illustrate the hidden working of God's kingdom (13:21), but here it describes the negative influence of the Pharisees (Mark 8:15 note).

12:2, 3 On Judgment Day everything will be brought into the open; all hypocrisy will be unmasked.

12:3 private rooms. Mud brick walls could be dug through, so storerooms where valuables could be kept were well away from outside walls (and therefore secret).

nothing more that they can do. 5 But I will
warn you whom to fear: fear him [b]who,
after he has killed, has authority to cast
into hell.[1] Yes, I tell you, fear him! 6 Are not
five sparrows sold for two pennies?[2] And
[c]not one of them is forgotten before God.
7 Why, [d]even the hairs of your head are all
numbered. Fear not; [e]you are of more value
than many sparrows.

Acknowledge Christ Before Men

8 "And I tell you, [f]everyone who acknowledges me before men, the Son of Man also
will acknowledge [g]before the angels of
God, 9 but [h]the one who denies me before
men [i]will be denied [g]before the angels of
God. 10 And [j]everyone who speaks a word
[k]against the Son of Man [l]will be forgiven,
but the one who [m]blasphemes against the
Holy Spirit will not be forgiven. 11 [n]And
when they [o]bring you before the synagogues and [p]the rulers and [p]the authorities,
[q]do not be anxious about how you should
defend yourself or what you should say,
12 [r]for the Holy Spirit will teach you in that
very hour what you ought to say."

The Parable of the Rich Fool

13 [s]Someone in the crowd said to him,
"Teacher, tell my brother to divide the
inheritance with me." 14 But he said to him,
[t]"Man, [u]who made me a judge or arbitrator
over you?" 15 And he said to them, [v]"Take
care, and be on your guard against all covetousness, for one's life does not consist in
the abundance of his possessions." 16 And
he told them a parable, saying, [w]"The land
of a rich man produced plentifully, 17 and
he thought to himself, [x]'What shall I do,
for I have nowhere to store my crops?'
18 And he said, 'I will do this: I will tear
down my [y]barns and build larger ones, and
there I will store all my grain and my
goods. 19 And I will say to my soul, Soul,
you have ample goods laid up [z]for many
years; relax, [a]eat, drink, be merry.' 20 But
God said to him, [b]'Fool! [z]This night [c]your
soul is required of you, and the things you
have prepared, [d]whose will they be?' 21 So is
the one [e]who lays up treasure for himself
and is not rich toward God."

Do Not Be Anxious

22 And he said to his disciples, [f]"Therefore I tell you, [g]do not be anxious about
your life, what you will eat, nor about your
body, what you will put on. 23 For life is
more than food, and the body more than
clothing. 24 [h]Consider the ravens: they neither sow nor reap, they have neither storehouse nor barn, and yet God feeds them.
[i]Of how much more value are you than the
birds! 25 And which of you by being anxious can add a single hour to his [j]span of
life?[3] 26 If then you are not able to do as
small a thing as that, why are you anxious
about the rest? 27 Consider the lilies, how
they grow: they neither toil nor spin,[4] yet
I tell you, [k]even Solomon in all his glory
was not arrayed like one of these. 28 But
if God so clothes the grass, which is alive
in the field today, and tomorrow is thrown
into the oven, how much more will he
clothe you, [l]O you of little faith! 29 And do
not seek what you are to eat and what
you are to drink, nor [m]be worried. 30 For

5 [b]James 4:12
6 [c][Ps. 50:11]
7 [d]See 1 Sam. 14:45 [e]Matt. 6:26; 12:12
8 [f][Rom. 10:9, 10; Heb. 10:35; Rev. 3:5] [g][ch. 15:10; Matt. 25:31; 1 Tim. 5:21; Rev. 3:5]
9 [h]2 Tim. 2:12; 2 Pet. 2:1; 1 John 2:23; [Mark 8:38] [i]ch. 13:25; Matt. 7:23; 25:12 [g][See ver. 8 above]
10 [j][Matt. 12:31, 32; Mark 3:28-30; Heb. 6:4-6; 10:26; 1 John 5:16] [k]Matt. 11:19; John 7:12; 9:24 [l]1 Tim. 1:12, 13 [m][Acts 7:51; Heb. 10:29]
11 [n]Matt. 10:17, 19; [ch. 21:12, 14; Mark 13:11] [o]See Matt. 23:34 [p]Tit. 3:1 [q]See ver. 22
12 [r]See Matt. 10:19, 20
13 [s]ch. 11:27
14 [t]Mic. 6:8; Rom. 2:1, 3; 9:20 [u][Ex. 2:14; Acts 7:27]
15 [v]1 Tim. 6:6-11; [Heb. 13:5]
16 [w][Ps. 49:16-20]
17 [x][Eccles. 5:10]
18 [y]ver. 24
19 [z][Prov. 27:1; James 4:13-15] [a]Eccles. 2:24; 11:9; 1 Cor. 15:32; [ch. 15:23]
20 [b]Jer. 17:11; [Matt. 16:26]
20 [z][See ver. 19 above] [c]Job 27:8 [d]Ps. 39:6; [Job 27:17-22; Eccles. 2:18, 21]
21 [e]Matt. 6:19, 20 22 [f]For ver. 22-31, see Matt. 6:25-33 [g]ver. 11; ch. 10:41; Matt. 10:19; 13:22 (Gk.); 1 Cor. 7:32 (Gk.); Phil. 4:6; 1 Pet. 5:7 24 [h][Job 38:41; Ps. 147:9] [i]See ver. 7 25 [j]ch. 2:52 27 [k]1 Kin. 10:4-7 28 [l]Matt. 8:26; 14:31; 16:8; [ch. 17:6] 29 [m][James 1:6]

[1] Greek *Gehenna* [2] Greek *two assaria*; an *assarion* was a Roman copper coin worth about 1/16 of a *denarius* (which was a day's wage for a laborer) [3] Or *a single cubit to his stature*; a *cubit* was about 18 inches or 45 centimeters [4] Some manuscripts *Consider the lilies; they neither spin nor weave*

12:5 authority to cast into hell. Only God has this power. The word translated "hell" here is *Gehenna,* the place of final punishment (not *Hades,* a general word for the place of all the dead). *Gehenna* derives from Hebrew words meaning "valley of Hinnom," located outside Jerusalem (Matt. 5:22 note).

12:6 five sparrows sold for two pennies. The "pennies" are the assarion, equal to one-sixteenth of a denarius (a typical day's wage). Five sparrows sold for roughly an hour's pay, but God remembers them all.

12:10 Blasphemy against the Holy Spirit attributes to Satan the work of the Holy Spirit through Christ in the face of overwhelming moral evidence to the contrary. Such deliberate rejection of the truth is a decisive rejection of the One (the Holy Spirit) who can bring a person to repentance and faith; such sin makes forgiveness impossible. See "The Unpardonable Sin" at Mark 3:29.

12:13 The rule for inheritance was given in Deut. 21:17, and cases in dispute were often settled by rabbis. This man clearly wanted only a decision in his favor; he was not seeking a just arbitration.

12:22–34 Jesus provides four weighty arguments against anxiety. First, concern for worldly goods is foolish because life itself is more important (v. 23). Second, God will take care of His own, just as He cares for the birds of the air (v. 24). Third, anxiety accomplishes nothing (vv. 25, 26). Finally, as heirs of the inexhaustible riches of the kingdom of God, believers should not worry about earthly details (vv. 32, 33). Jesus calls His followers to order their priorities correctly by focusing their hearts on the kingdom (v. 34).

12:25 a single hour to his span of life. Or, "make his life any longer."

12:27 lilies. It is not certain what precise flower is meant.

Solomon. Solomon was proverbial for his wealth and splendor.

[n]all the nations of the world seek after these
things, and [n]your Father knows that you
need them. 31 Instead, [o]seek [p]his[1] kingdom,
[q]and these things will be added to you.
32 [r]"Fear not, little [s]flock, for [t]it is your
Father's good pleasure to give you [u]the
kingdom. 33 [v]Sell your possessions, and
[w]give to the needy. [x]Provide yourselves
with moneybags that do not grow old, with
[y]a treasure in the heavens that does not
fail, where no thief approaches and no
moth destroys. 34 [z]For where your treasure
is, there will your heart be also.

You Must Be Ready

35 "Stay dressed for action[2] and keep your
lamps burning, 36 and be like men who are
[c]waiting for their master to come home
from the wedding feast, so that they may
open the door to him at once when he
comes and [d]knocks. 37 [e]Blessed are those
servants[3] whom the master finds [e]awake
when he comes. Truly, I say to you, [f]he will
dress himself for service and [g]have them
recline at table, and he will come and serve
them. 38 If he comes in the second watch,
or in the third, and finds them awake,
blessed are those servants! 39 [h]But know
this, that if the master of the house had
known at what hour [i]the thief was coming,
he[4] would not have left his house to be
broken into. 40 You also must be [j]ready, for
[k]the Son of Man is coming at an hour you
do not expect."

41 Peter said, "Lord, [l]are you telling this
parable for us or for all?" 42 And the Lord
said, "Who then is [m]the faithful and [m]wise
[n]manager, whom his master will set over
his household, to give them their portion
of food at the proper time? 43 [o]Blessed is
that servant[5] whom his master will find so
doing when he comes. 44 Truly, I say to you,
[p]he will set him over all his possessions.
45 But if that servant says to himself, 'My
master [q]is delayed in coming,' and begins
to beat the male and female servants, and
to eat and drink and [r]get drunk, 46 the master of that servant will come [s]on a day
when he does not expect him and [s]at an
hour he does not know, and will cut him in
pieces and put him with the unfaithful.
47 [t]And that servant who [u]knew his master's
will but [v]did not get ready [u]or act according to his will, will receive a [w]severe beating. 48 [x]But the one who did not know, and
did what deserved a beating, [y]will receive a
light beating. [z]Everyone to whom much
was given, of him much will be required,
and from him to whom they entrusted
much, they will demand the more.

Not Peace, but Division

49 [a]"I came to cast fire on the earth, and
would that it were already kindled! 50 [b]I
have a baptism to be baptized with, and
how [c]great is my distress until it is accomplished! 51 [d]Do you think that I have come

30 [n]Matt. 6:8
31 [o][Matt. 5:6, 20] [p]ch. 11:2 [q][1 Kin. 3:11-14; Mark 10:29, 30; 1 Tim. 4:8; 1 Pet. 3:9]
32 [r]Isai. 41:14; 44:2 [s]Isai. 40:11; Matt. 26:31; John 10:16; 21:15-17; Acts 20:28, 29; 1 Pet. 5:2, 3 [t][ch. 10:21; Matt. 11:26; Eph. 1:5, 9; Phil. 2:13] [u]ch. 22:29; See Matt. 13:19
33 [v]See Matt. 19:21 [w]ch. 11:41 [x][ch. 16:9] [y]Matt. 6:20; [ver. 21; 1 Pet. 1:4]
34 [z]Matt. 6:21
35 [a]Eph. 6:14; 1 Pet. 1:13 [b][Matt. 25:7]
36 [c]See 2 Pet. 3:12 [d]Rev. 3:20
37 [e]See Matt. 24:42, 46 [f]John 13:4; [ver. 35; ch. 17:8] [g][ch. 22:27]
39 [h]For ver. 39-46, [Matt. 24:43-51] [i][1 Thess. 5:2; 2 Pet. 3:10; Rev. 3:3]
40 [j]ver. 47; Matt. 25:10 [k]ch. 21:27
41 [l][Mark 13:37]
42 [m]See Matt. 24:45 [n]ch. 16:1; 1 Pet. 4:10

43 [o]John 13:17; Rev. 16:15 44 [p]Matt. 25:21, 23 45 [q]Matt. 25:5; [Heb. 10:37; 2 Pet. 3:4, 9] [r]1 Thess. 5:7 46 [s]2 Pet. 3:12; [ver. 40] 47 [t][Matt. 11:24; John 15:22, 24] [u][James 4:17; 2 Pet. 2:21] [v]ver. 40 [w][Deut. 25:2, 3] 48 [x]Lev. 5:17; [Num. 15:29, 30] [y]Rom. 1:19, 20; 2:14, 15; [1 Tim. 1:13] [z][Matt. 25:29]; See Matt. 13:12 49 [a][Matt. 3:11] 50 [b]Mark 10:38 [c]2 Cor. 5:14 (Gk.); Phil. 1:23
51 [d]For ver. 51-53, see Matt. 10:34, 35

[1] Some manuscripts *God's* [2] Greek *Let your loins stay girded*; compare Exodus 12:11 [3] Greek *bondservants* [4] Some manuscripts add *would have stayed awake and* [5] Greek *bondservant*; also verses 45, 46, 47

12:31 seek his kingdom. The disciples were already in the kingdom. Therefore they should concentrate their energies on the interests of that kingdom.

12:33 Sell your possessions, and give to the needy. Central to this verse is the contrast between earthly goods that are perishable and a source of anxiety, and the treasures of the kingdom of God that are a lasting source of peace. Some of Jesus' followers had at least moderate wealth (10:38; John 19:27), and He is not demanding that all His disciples be poor. But they must be generous and not set their hearts on earthly possessions (v. 34).

12:35 dressed for action. That is, to be ready for service. Long robes hindered free movement and were kept above the knees with a belt when necessary.

12:37 dress himself. This is a reversal of roles, the master taking the place of the servant (cf. 22:27).

12:38 second watch, or . . . third. The Jews divided the night into three watches (Judg. 7:19), and the Romans into four. Jesus uses the Jewish division here. These servants watch for their master throughout the night.

12:42 faithful and wise manager. The manager was a slave put in charge of the whole estate by the owner. The owner was free from the burden of administration and the manager had considerable authority.

12:44 all his possessions. The reward of faithful service is the opportunity to perform higher service.

12:45, 46 The punishment for failure to make proper use of opportunities for service is severe.

12:47, 48 People are punished for failing to do right as well as for doing wrong. Ignorance can be blameworthy when there is the opportunity to know what is required. God makes His people's duty plain (Rom. 1:20; 2:14, 15).

12:49 fire. The fire of judgment.

12:50 baptism. Jesus' death is also a "baptism," another image that points to death (to "baptize" a city was to subject it to near total destruction). Liturgically, baptism came to symbolize death to an old way of life and rising to a new way. Jesus accepted His own death as the divine plan for bringing salvation to sinners.

accomplished. On the cross, Jesus spoke of the completion of His work (John 19:30).

to give peace on earth? [e]No, I tell you, but
rather division. 52 For from now on in one
house there will be five divided, three
against two and two against three. 53 They
will be divided, [f]father against son and son
against father, mother against daughter and
daughter against mother, mother-in-law
against her daughter-in-law and daughter-
in-law against mother-in-law."

Interpreting the Time

54 He also said to the crowds, [g]"When
you see [h]a cloud rising in the west, you say
at once, 'A shower is coming.' And so it
happens. 55 And [g]when you see the south
wind blowing, you say, 'There will be [i]scorch-
ing heat,' and it happens. 56 You hypocrites!
[j]You know how to interpret the appearance
of earth and sky, but why do you not know
how to interpret the present time?

Settle with Your Accuser

57 "And why [k]do you not judge [l]for yourselves what is right? 58 [m]As you go with your
accuser before the magistrate, make an
effort to settle with him on the way, lest he
drag you to the judge, and the judge hand
you over to the officer, and the officer put
you in prison. 59 I tell you, [n]you will never
get out until you have paid the very last
[o]penny."[1]

Repent or Perish

13 There were some present at that
very time who told him about the
Galileans whose blood [p]Pilate had mingled
with their sacrifices. 2 And he answered
them, [q]"Do you think that these Galileans
were worse sinners than all the other
Galileans, because they suffered in this way?
3 No, I tell you; but unless you [r]repent, you
will all likewise perish. 4 Or those eighteen
on whom the tower in [s]Siloam fell and killed
them: do you think that they were worse
offenders than all the others who lived in
Jerusalem? 5 No, I tell you; but unless you
[r]repent, you will all likewise perish."

The Parable of the Barren Fig Tree

6 And he told this parable: "A man had [t]a
fig tree planted in his vineyard, and he
came seeking fruit on it and found none.
7 And he said to the vinedresser, 'Look, for
three years now I have come seeking fruit
on this fig tree, and I find none. [u]Cut it
down. Why should it use up the ground?'
8 And he answered him, 'Sir, let it alone this
year also, until I dig around it and put on
manure. 9 Then if it should bear fruit next
year, well and good; but if not, you can cut
it down.'"

A Woman with a Disabling Spirit

10 Now [v]he was teaching in one of the
synagogues on the Sabbath. 11 And there
was a woman who had had [w]a disabling
spirit for eighteen years. She was bent over
and could not fully straighten herself.
12 When Jesus saw her, he called her over
and said to her, "Woman, you are freed
from your disability." 13 And he [x]laid his
hands on her, and immediately she was
made straight, and she [y]glorified God.
14 But [z]the ruler of the synagogue, indignant because Jesus [a]had healed on the
Sabbath, said to the people, [b]"There are six
days in which work ought to be done.
Come on those days and be healed, and
not on the Sabbath day." 15 Then the Lord
answered him, "You hypocrites! [c]Does not

1 Greek *lepton*, a Jewish bronze or copper coin worth about 1/128 of a *denarius* (which was a day's wage for a laborer)

51 [e][Rev. 6:4]
53 [f]Matt. 10:21; [Mic. 7:6]
54 [g][Matt. 16:2, 3] [h]1 Kin. 18:43, 44
55 [i]See Matt. 20:12
56 [j]Matt. 16:3
57 [k]ch. 21:30 [l]John 7:24; 1 Cor. 11:13
58 [m]Matt. 5:25, 26; [Prov. 25:8]
59 [n][Matt. 18:34, 35] [o]ch. 21:2; Mark 12:42
Chapter 13
1 [p]ch. 3:1
2 [q][Job 4:7; John 9:2; Acts 28:4]
3 [r]See ch. 5:32
4 [s]Isai. 8:6; John 9:7, 11
5 [r][See ver. 3 above]
6 [t]Matt. 21:19; Mark 11:13; [Isai. 5:2]
7 [u]ch. 3:9; Matt. 7:19
10 [v]See Matt. 4:23; Mark 6:2
11 [w]Acts 16:16; [ver. 16]
13 [x]See Mark 5:23 [y]ch. 5:25; 17:15; 18:43; See ch. 7:16
14 [z]See ch. 8:41 [a]See Matt. 12:2 [b]Ex. 20:9; Ezek. 46:1
15 [c]ch. 14:5; [Matt. 12:11]

12:54–56 The people could discern that a west wind (from the Mediterranean) meant rain and a south wind (from the desert) meant heat. But they did not discern what God was doing in their midst.

12:57–59 In legal matters, anyone with a bad case does well to secure an out-of-court settlement before the case comes to trial. Sinners should be reconciled to God now; they will perish if they wait until Judgment Day.

13:1 Pilate. To kill people in the act of worship is a grave offense. This incident, not recorded elsewhere, no doubt contributed to Pilate's reputation for cruelty.

13:2 Disaster was commonly held to be the result of sin (John 9:1, 2), but Jesus denies that these Galileans were especially sinful.

13:3 all likewise perish. All are sinners, so Jesus calls on His hearers to repent—otherwise they will perish. The Galileans had had no time to repent at the time of their deaths, and Jesus' unrepentant hearers might also face deaths that would give them no time to prepare. See "Repentance" at Acts 26:20.

13:4 This incident is unknown to us apart from this passage.

13:6–9 A vineyard was fertile soil for a fig tree and "three years" points to an established tree. It was unlikely that it would ever bear fruit, but it was given one more chance. That God does not punish sinners immediately does not mean that He approves of their sin. Rather, His patience shows He is merciful and they should repent while there is time.

13:10 on the Sabbath. The right use of the Sabbath was a continuing dispute between Jesus and His enemies.

13:11–13 The woman did not ask for healing. Jesus took the initiative.

13:14 ruler of the synagogue. See note 8:41.

13:15 hypocrites. The Jews cared for their animals and looked after them on the Sabbath as on other days, but this ruler of the synagogue objects to Jesus' act of compassion for this woman.

each of you on the Sabbath untie his ox or
his donkey from the manger and lead it
away to water it? 16 And ought not this
woman, [d]a daughter of Abraham whom
[e]Satan bound for eighteen years, be loosed
from this bond on the Sabbath day?" 17 As
he said these things, [f]all his adversaries
were put to shame, and [g]all the people
rejoiced at all the glorious things that were
done by him.

The Mustard Seed and the Leaven

18 [h]He said therefore, "What is the kingdom of God like? And to what shall I compare it? 19 It is like [i]a grain of mustard seed
that a man took and sowed in his garden,
and it grew and became a tree, and the
birds of the air made nests in its branches."
20 And again he said, "To what shall I compare the kingdom of God? 21 [j]It is like leaven
that a woman took and hid in [k]three measures of flour, until it was [l]all leavened."

The Narrow Door

22 [m]He went on his way through towns
and villages, teaching and [n]journeying
toward Jerusalem. 23 And someone said to
him, "Lord, [o]will those who are saved be
few?" And he said to them, 24 [p]"Strive [q]to
enter through the narrow door. For many,
I tell you, will seek to enter and will not be
able. 25 [r]When once the master of the house
has risen and shut the door, and you begin
to stand outside and to knock at the door,
saying, [s]'Lord, open to us,' then he will
answer you, [t]'I do not know where you
come from.' 26 Then you will begin to say,
[u]'We ate and drank in your presence, and
you taught in our streets.' 27 But he will say,
'I tell you, [t]I do not know where you come
from. [v]Depart from me, all you workers of
evil!' 28 [w]In that place there will be weeping
and gnashing of teeth, when you see
[w]Abraham and Isaac and Jacob and all the
prophets in the kingdom of God but [w]you
yourselves cast out. 29 And [w]people will
come from east and west, and from north
and south, and [x]recline at table in the kingdom of God. 30 And behold, [y]some are last
who will be first, and some are first who
will be last."

Lament over Jerusalem

31 At that very hour some Pharisees came
and said to him, "Get away from [z]here, for
[a]Herod wants to kill you." 32 And he said to
them, "Go and tell that fox, 'Behold, I cast
out demons and perform cures today and
tomorrow, and the third day [b]I finish my
course. 33 Nevertheless, [c]I [d]must go on
my way today and tomorrow and the
day following, for it cannot be that [e]a
prophet should perish away from Jerusalem.' 34 [f]O Jerusalem, Jerusalem, the city
that [g]kills the prophets and stones those
who are sent to it! [h]How often would I have
[i]gathered [j]your children together [k]as a hen
gathers her brood [l]under her wings, and
[m]you would not! 35 Behold, [n]your house is

16 [d]ch. 19:9 [e][ver. 11; Acts 10:38; 1 Cor. 5:5; 2 Cor. 12:7]; See 1 Chr. 21:1 **17** [f]Ps. 132:18; 1 Pet. 3:16 [g]ch. 18:43 **18** [h]For ver. 18, 19, see Matt. 13:31, 32; Mark 4:30-32 **19** [i]ch. 17:6; Matt. 17:20 **21** [j]Matt. 13:33 [k]Gen. 18:6 [l]1 Cor. 5:6; Gal. 5:9 **22** [m]See Mark 6:6 [n][ver. 33]; See ch. 9:51 **23** [o]Acts 2:47; 1 Cor. 1:18; 2 Cor. 2:15 **24** [p]1 Tim. 4:10; Heb. 12:4; [1 Tim. 6:12 (Gk.)]; See 1 Cor. 9:25 [q]Matt. 7:13 **25** [r]For ver. 25-27, [Matt. 25:10-12] [s]Matt. 7:22, 23 [t]Matt. 10:33; 25:12; [2 Tim. 2:19]

26 [u][Ex. 24:11] **27** [t][See ver. 25 above] [v]See Ps. 6:8 **28** [w]See Matt. 8:11, 12 **29** [w][See ver. 28 above] [x][ch. 14:15; 22:30] **30** [y]See Matt. 19:30 **31** [z][Matt. 19:1; Mark 10:1] [a]See ch. 3:1

32 [b]Heb. 2:10; 5:9; 7:28 **33** [c][John 11:9] [d]Acts 3:21; 17:3 [e]See Matt. 21:11 **34** [f]For ver. 34, 35, see Matt. 23:37-39; [ch. 19:41-44] [g]See Matt. 21:35 [h][Matt. 26:55] [i][Ps. 147:2; Prov. 1:24] [j]ch. 23:28 [k][Deut. 32:11, 12] [l]Ruth 2:12 [m]John 5:40 **35** [n][Isai. 64:11; Jer. 12:7; 22:5]

13:21 three measures. A large amount; in Greek, three *sata* (Hebrew *seahs*) the amount used by Sarah (Gen. 18:6).

13:22 See note 9:51. Luke presents Jesus making unhurried progress toward Jerusalem where the climax would be reached. On the way He continued to serve the people.

13:23 few. The Jews generally agreed that all Israel (except for a few especially sinful people) would be in the number of the saved.

13:24 Strive. This does not mean that salvation is by works; it is a strong way of saying that people must be in earnest about salvation.

narrow door. Jesus does not say what the narrow gate is, but clearly He is speaking of the way into salvation.

13:25 shut the door. There is a limit to the offer of salvation; it must be accepted while the offer is present.

I do not know where you come from. See Matt. 7:23; 25:12.

13:26, 27 To have had social fellowship with Jesus and to have heard His teaching were not enough.

13:28 weeping and gnashing. There will be weeping in grief and gnashing of teeth in anger as they see the great ones with whom they had always classed themselves in bliss, while they themselves are thrown out.

13:29 east . . . south. The saved will be people from all over the world.

recline. This imagery of the messianic banquet describes the great joy there will be in the kingdom (14:15; Rev. 19:9). There will be a complete reversal of many ideas strongly held among humankind (v. 30).

13:31 Get away from here. Jesus may have been in Perea where Herod ruled. The Pharisees preferred to see Him in Judea where they had more influence.

13:32 that fox. The Jews used the metaphor of a "fox" to mean worthless and sly. Jesus is unmoved by Herod's threats and says He will continue with His ministry. There is a limit to His time as the reference to the third day shows.

13:33 must. There was a compelling divine necessity to what Jesus was doing. Notice also the further reference to the certainty that Jerusalem was the place where He would die (cf. 9:31).

13:34, 35 This lament over the city was probably uttered as Jesus reached the city (Matt. 23:37, 38), and is included here by Luke because of its relevance to what Jesus has just said.

13:34 How often. Jesus must have been in Jerusalem more often than the Synoptic Gospels explicitly report; the Gospel of John records several visits.

13:35 your house. This may mean the temple or the city as a whole.

forsaken. And I tell you, you will not see
me until you say, [o]'Blessed is he who
comes in the name of the Lord!' "

Healing of a Man on the Sabbath

14 One Sabbath, [p]when he went to
dine at the house of a ruler of the
Pharisees, they were [q]watching him carefully. **2** And behold, there was a man before
him who had dropsy. **3** And Jesus responded to [r]the lawyers and Pharisees, saying,
[s]"Is it lawful to heal on the Sabbath, or
not?" **4** But they remained silent. Then he
took him and healed him and sent him
away. **5** And he said to them, [t]"Which of
you, having a son[1] or an ox that has fallen
into a well on a Sabbath day, will not
immediately pull him out?" **6** [u]And they
could not reply to these things.

The Parable of the Wedding Feast

7 Now he told a parable to those who
were invited, when he noticed [v]how they
chose the places of honor, saying to them,
8 "When you are invited by someone to a
wedding feast, do not sit down in a place of
honor, lest someone more distinguished
than you be invited by him, **9** and he who
invited you both will come and say to you,
'Give your place to this person,' and then
you will begin with shame to take the lowest place. **10** But when you are invited, go
and sit in the lowest place, [w]so that when
your host comes he may say to you,
'Friend, move up higher.' Then you will be
honored in the presence of all who sit at
table with you. **11** For [x]everyone who exalts
himself will be humbled, and he who humbles himself will be exalted."

35 [o]ch. 19:38; Cited from Ps. 118:26
Chapter 14
1 [p]ch. 7:36; 11:37 [q]ch. 20:20; Mark 3:2
3 [r]See ch. 7:30 [s]ch. 13:14; Matt. 12:10
5 [t]ch. 13:15; [Deut. 22:4; Matt. 12:11]
6 [u][Matt. 22:46]
7 [v]See ch. 11:43
10 [w]Prov. 25:6, 7
11 [x]ch. 18:14; [Prov. 29:23; Ezek. 21:26; Matt. 18:4; James 4:6, 10; 1 Pet. 5:5, 6]
12 [y]John 21:12 (Gk.) [z][ch. 6:34]
13 [a][Neh. 8:10, 12; Esth. 9:22] [b]ver. 21
14 [c]1 Cor. 15:23; 1 Thess. 4:16; [John 11:24; Rev. 20:4, 5] [d]Acts 24:15
15 [e]Rev. 19:9 [f][ch. 13:29; 22:16, 30]
16 [g]For ver. 16-24, [Matt. 22:2-14] [h][Isai. 25:6]
17 [i][Esth. 6:14; Prov. 9:3, 5]
20 [j]Deut. 24:5
21 [k]ver. 13

The Parable of the Great Banquet

12 He said also to the man who had invited him, "When you give [y]a dinner or a
banquet, do not invite your friends or your
brothers[2] or your relatives or rich neighbors, [z]lest they also invite you in return
and you be repaid. **13** But when you give a
feast, [a]invite [b]the poor, the crippled, the
lame, the blind, **14** and you will be blessed,
because they cannot repay you. You will be
repaid [c]at [d]the resurrection of the just."

15 When one of those who reclined at
table with him heard these things, he said
to him, [e]"Blessed is everyone who will [f]eat
bread in the kingdom of God!" **16** But he
said to him, [g]"A man once [h]gave a great
banquet and invited many. **17** And at the
time for the banquet he [i]sent his servant[3]
to say to those who had been invited,
'Come, for everything is now ready.' **18** But
they all alike began to make excuses. The
first said to him, 'I have bought a field, and
I must go out and see it. Please have me
excused.' **19** And another said, 'I have
bought five yoke of oxen, and I go to examine them. Please have me excused.' **20** And
another said, [j]'I have married a wife, and
therefore I cannot come.' **21** So the servant
came and reported these things to his master. Then the master of the house became
angry and said to his servant, 'Go out
quickly to the streets and lanes of the city,
and bring in [k]the poor and crippled and
blind and lame.' **22** And the servant said,
'Sir, what you commanded has been done,

1 Some manuscripts *a donkey* 2 Or *your brothers and sisters*. The plural Greek word *adelphoi* (translated "brothers") refers to siblings in a family. In New Testament usage, depending on the context, *adelphoi* may refer either to *brothers* or to *brothers and sisters* 3 Greek *bondservant*; also verses 21, 22, 23

forsaken. The inevitable result of faithlessness.

until you say. See note Matt. 23:39.

14:1 watching him carefully. Evidently to detect any violation of Sabbath observance.

14:2 dropsy. A disease in which fluid collected in the cavities of the body (mentioned only here in the New Testament).

14:3 Is it lawful. The law of Moses did not forbid healing on the Sabbath, but the "traditions of the elders" (Mark 2:16 note) did prohibit medical treatment unless the condition was life threatening.

14:5 a son or an ox. The Jews would pull a child or an animal out of a well on the Sabbath, though technically this was work. Their acts in an emergency showed that deeds of mercy were lawful on the Sabbath, and Jesus had performed a deed of mercy.

14:10 Jesus is not giving worldly advice but advocating genuine humility, as v. 11 shows (cf. 18:14; Matt. 23:12).

14:15 Blessed is everyone who. A pious and conventional utterance, perhaps meant to change the subject.

14:16, 17 Evidently those invited accepted the invitation; none is said to have declined. A second invitation when all was ready was customary (cf. Esth. 5:8; 6:14).

14:18–20 The excuses are transparently dishonest. No one buys a field or oxen without prior inspection, and if anyone did there was no hurry—the field and the oxen would be there tomorrow. The man who had married might cite Deut. 24:5, but that freed a man from military service, not social contacts.

14:21–24 This parable is a prophecy of the extension of the gospel to those the Pharisees thought unworthy. The "poor and crippled and blind and lame" (v. 21) represent the despised Jews who were not able to observe the traditional laws of ritual purity (sometimes called "the people of the land"), while those outside the city along the "highways and hedges" (v. 23) represent the Gentiles. The parable concludes with a warning to the elite of Israel who reject the Messiah that they will not be given a second chance.

and still there is room.' **23** And the master
said to the servant, 'Go out to the highways
and hedges and [l]compel people to come in,
that my house may be filled. **24** For I tell
you,[1] [m]none of those men who were invited shall taste my banquet.' "

The Cost of Discipleship

25 Now great crowds accompanied him,
and he turned and said to them, **26** [n]"If anyone comes to me and [o]does not hate his
own father and mother and wife and children and brothers and sisters, [p]yes, and
even his own life, he cannot be my disciple.
27 [q]Whoever does not [r]bear his own cross
and come after me cannot be my disciple.
28 For which of you, desiring to build a
tower, does not [s]first sit down and count
the cost, whether he has enough to complete it? **29** Otherwise, when he has laid a
foundation and is not able to finish, all
who see it begin to mock him, **30** saying,
'This man began to build and was not able
to finish.' **31** Or what king, going out to
encounter another king in war, will not [t]sit
down first and deliberate whether he is
able with ten thousand to meet him who
comes against him with twenty thousand?
32 And if not, while the other is yet a great
way off, he sends a delegation and asks for
terms of peace. **33** [u]So therefore, any one of
you who [v]does not renounce all that he has
cannot be my disciple.

Salt Without Taste Is Worthless

34 [w]"Salt is good, [x]but if salt has lost its
taste, how shall its saltiness be restored?
35 It is of no use either for the soil or for the
manure pile. It is thrown away. [y]He who
has ears to hear, let him hear."

The Parable of the Lost Sheep

15 Now [z]the tax collectors and sinners
were all drawing near to hear him.
2 And the Pharisees and the scribes [a]grum-
bled, saying, [b]"This man receives sinners
and [c]eats with them."
3 So he told them this parable: **4** [d]"What
man of you, having a hundred sheep, [e]if he
has lost one of them, does not leave the
ninety-nine [f]in the open country, and [g]go
after the one that is lost, until he finds it?
5 And when he has found it, [h]he lays it on
his shoulders, rejoicing. **6** And when he
comes home, he calls together his friends
and his neighbors, saying to them, 'Rejoice
with me, for [i]I have found my sheep that
was lost.' **7** Just so, I tell you, there will be
more joy in heaven over one sinner who
[j]repents than over ninety-nine [k]righteous
persons who need no repentance.

The Parable of the Lost Coin

8 "Or what woman, having ten silver
coins,[2] if she loses one coin, does not light
a lamp and sweep the house and seek diligently until she finds it? **9** And when she
has found it, she calls together her friends
and neighbors, saying, 'Rejoice with me,
for I have found the coin that I had lost.'
10 Just so, I tell you, there is joy before [l]the
angels of God over one sinner who
repents."

The Parable of the Prodigal Son

11 And he said, "There was a man who
had two sons. **12** And the younger of them
said to his father, 'Father, give me [m]the

1 The Greek word for *you* here is plural 2 Greek *ten drachmas*; a *drachma* was a Greek coin approximately equal in value to a Roman *denarius*, worth about a day's wage for a laborer

23 [l]Matt. 14:22; Mark 6:45
24 [m]Matt. 21:43; Acts 13:46
26 [n]ver. 33; Matt. 10:37; [Deut. 33:9] [o]ch. 16:13 [p]John 12:25; Acts 20:24; Rev. 12:11
27 [q]ch. 9:23; Matt. 10:38; 16:24; Mark 8:34 [r]John 19:17
28 [s][Prov. 24:27]
31 [t]ver. 28
33 [u][Phil. 3:7] [v][ver. 26; ch. 18:28]
34 [w]Mark 9:50 [x]Matt. 5:13
35 [y]See Matt. 11:15

Chapter 15
1 [z]See Matt. 11:19
2 [a]ch. 19:7; [Ex. 16:2, 7, 8; Num. 14:2; Josh. 9:18] [b][ch. 7:39] [c]ch. 5:30; Matt. 9:11; 11:19; Mark 2:16; [Acts 11:3; 1 Cor. 5:11; Gal. 2:12]
4 [d]For ver 4-7, [Matt. 18:12-14] [e]Ezek. 34:6; [1 Pet. 2:25] [f]Ex. 3:1; 1 Sam. 17:28 [g]Ezek. 34:4, 11, 12, 16; [ch. 19:10]
5 [h][Isai. 40:11; 49:22; 60:4; 66:12]
6 [i]1 Pet. 2:25
7 [j]ver. 10; See ch. 5:32 [k][ch. 5:32; Matt. 9:13]
10 [l]See ch. 12:8
12 [m]Deut. 21:17

14:26 hate. This means to love less (cf. Gen. 29:31, 33; Deut. 21:15–17, where "unloved" translates a word meaning "hated"). Discipleship means loving the Master so much that all other loves are hatred by comparison.

14:27 bear his own cross. See note 9:23–25.

14:28 Calculating the cost is important before undertaking any serious project. The "tower" could be a watchtower or a farm building. That one must "sit down" points to a careful and unhurried process.

14:34 salt. Salt was a flavoring agent and a preservative. The salt in use at that time was far from pure and it was possible for the sodium chloride to leach out of it, leaving a residue that was useless.

15:1 tax collectors. See note 3:12.

sinners. People who were immoral or who followed occupations that the scribes held to be incompatible with keeping God's law. A rabbinic rule stated that "one must not associate with an ungodly man," and the rabbis would not even teach such a person. Notice that ch. 14 ends with "let him hear" and ch. 15 begins with these "sinners" gathering around to hear Jesus.

15:3 The rabbis taught that God would welcome a penitent sinner, but these parables teach that God seeks out the sinner.

15:8 silver coins. The drachma (occurs only here in the New Testament) was the Greek equivalent of the Roman denarius, about a day's wage for a laborer. The ten coins may have been the woman's life savings, or they may have been strung together as a headdress.

light a lamp. Houses had no windows or perhaps small ones, so a lamp was needed even in the daytime.

15:11–32 The parable of the prodigal son could be called the "parable of the waiting father." While the repentance of the son is important to the parable, the father's willingness to forgive and his unexpected actions (v. 20 note, 22–23) are a striking illustration of the fatherly love of God for wayward human beings.

15:11, 12 The firstborn son was entitled to two-thirds of his father's property (Deut. 21:17). Sometimes the father would give the rights to the

share of property that is coming to me.'
And he divided [n]his property between
them. 13 Not many days later, the younger
son gathered all he had and took a journey
into a far country, and there he squandered
his property in [o]reckless living. 14 And when
he had spent everything, a severe famine
arose in that country, and he began to be in
need. 15 So he went and hired himself out
to[1] one of the citizens of that country, who
sent him into his fields to feed pigs. 16 And
he [p]was longing to be fed with the pods
that the pigs ate, and no one gave him anything.
17 "But [q]when he [r]came to himself, he
said, 'How many of my father's hired servants have more than enough bread, but I
perish here with hunger! 18 I will arise and
go to my father, and I will say to him,
"Father, [s]I have sinned against [t]heaven and
before you. 19 [u]I am no longer worthy to be
called your son. Treat me as one of your
hired servants."' 20 And he arose and came
to his father. But while he was still a long
way off, his father saw him and felt compassion, and [v]ran and [w]embraced him and
[x]kissed him. 21 And the son said to him,
'Father, I have sinned against heaven and
before you. [u]I am no longer worthy to be
called your son.'[2] 22 But the father said to
his servants,[3] 'Bring quickly [y]the best robe,
and put it on him, and put [z]a ring on his
hand, and [a]shoes on his feet. 23 And bring
[b]the fattened calf and kill it, and let us eat
and [c]celebrate. 24 For this my son [d]was
dead, and is alive again; he was lost, and is
found.' And they began to celebrate.
25 "Now his older son was in the field,
and as he came and drew near to the
house, he heard music and dancing. 26 And
he called one of the servants and asked
what these things meant. 27 And he said to
him, 'Your brother has come, and your
father has killed the fattened calf, because
he has received him back safe and sound.'
28 But he was angry and refused to go in.
His father came out and entreated him,
29 but he answered his father, 'Look, these
many years I have served you, and I never
disobeyed your command, yet you never
gave me a young goat, that I might [e]cele-
brate with my friends. 30 But when this son
of yours came, [f]who has devoured [g]your
property with prostitutes, you killed the
fattened calf for him!' 31 And he said to
him, 'Son, [h]you are always with me, and all
that is mine is yours. 32 It was fitting [e]to celebrate and be glad, for this your brother
[i]was dead, and is alive; he was lost, and is
found.'"

The Parable of the Dishonest Manager

16 He also said to the disciples, "There
was a rich man who had [j]a manager, and charges were brought to him that
this man was wasting his possessions.
2 And he called him and said to him, 'What
is this that I hear about you? Turn in the
account of your [k]management, for you can
no longer be manager.' 3 And the manager
said to himself, 'What shall I do, since my
master is taking the management away
from me? I am not strong enough to dig,
and I am ashamed to beg. 4 I have decided
what to do, so that when I am removed
from management, people may receive me
into their houses.' 5 So, summoning his
master's debtors one by one, he said to the

12 [n]ver. 30; Mark 12:44
13 [o][Eph. 5:18; Tit. 1:6; 1 Pet. 4:4
16 [p][ch. 16:21]
17 [q][1 Kin. 8:47] [r][Acts 12:11]
18 [s][Ex. 10:16] [t]Matt. 21:25; John 3:27
19 [u][ch. 7:6, 7]
20 [v][James 4:8] [w]Gen. 33:4; 45:14; 46:29; Acts 20:37 [x]2 Sam. 14:33
22 [y]Zech. 3:3-5 [z]Gen. 41:42; Esth. 3:10; 8:2 [a]Ezek. 16:10
23 [b][1 Sam. 28:24] [c]ch. 12:19
24 [d]ver. 32; [Rom. 11:15; Eph. 2:1; Col. 2:13; Rev. 3:1]
29 [e]ver. 23
30 [f]Prov. 29:3 [g]ver. 12
31 [h]John 8:35
32 [e][See ver. 29 above] [i]ver. 24
Chapter 16
1 [j]ch. 12:42
2 [k]See 1 Cor. 9:17

1 Greek *joined himself to* 2 Some manuscripts add *treat me as one of your hired servants* 3 Greek *bondservants*

property (which meant that he could not dispose of it himself, though the son could sell it) and retain the income (if the son sold the property, the buyer could not take possession until the father's death). But to give the property to one of the sons as in this parable was unusual.

15:15 Swine were unclean (Lev. 11:7); no Jew would take this job willingly.

15:20 The father was apparently watching intently for his son's return. It was undignified for an older man to lift up his robes and run.

15:22, 23 The father's actions indicate complete forgiveness and restoration of relationship. The "best robe" is a mark of distinction and the ring signifies authority (Gen. 41:42; Esth. 3:10; 8:2). Because slaves did not wear shoes, the shoes point to the status of a free man. The fattened calf was reserved for special occasions.

15:25 The older son's attitude illustrates the judgmental spirit of the Pharisees who were annoyed at the presence of "sinners" (vv. 1–3).

15:28 As with the younger son (v. 20), the father takes the initiative in restoring the relationship. The parable as a whole points to the sovereign love of God who actively seeks out unworthy sinners, those who do not seek Him (19:10).

15:29 served you. This statement indicates that the older brother viewed his relationship with the father as the reward for meritorious behavior. Like the father's loving response to the undeserving younger son shows, salvation is not a reward for good works but entirely the gracious gift of God (Eph. 2:8, 9).

15:31 all that is mine is yours. The property settlement remains unchanged. The attitude of the older son (v. 29 note) has caused him to lose sight of the relationship he does have with his father.

16:1 manager. The man who ran the estate, freeing the owner from being involved in every detail. Because he was not closely supervised it was easy for him to be dishonest or lazy.

first, 'How much do you owe my master?'
6He said, 'A hundred measures[1] of oil.' He
said to him, 'Take your bill, and sit down
quickly and write fifty.' **7**Then he said to
another, 'And how much do you owe?' He
said, 'A hundred measures[2] of wheat.' He
said to him, 'Take your bill, and write
eighty.' **8**The master commended the dishonest manager for his [l]shrewdness. For
[m]the sons of this world[3] are [l]more shrewd
in dealing with their own generation than
[n]the sons of light. **9**And I tell you, [o]make
friends for yourselves by means of [p]un-
righteous wealth,[4] so that when it fails they
may receive you into the eternal dwellings.
10[q]"One who is [r]faithful in a very little is
also faithful in much, and one who is dishonest in a very little is also dishonest in
much. **11**If then you have not been faithful
in the unrighteous wealth, who will entrust
to you the true riches? **12**And if you have
not been faithful in [s]that which is another's, who will give you that which is your
own? **13**[p]No servant can serve two masters,
for either he will hate the one and love the
other, or he will be devoted to the one and
despise the other. You cannot serve God
and money."

The Law and the Kingdom of God

14[t]The Pharisees, who were [u]lovers of
money, heard all these things, and they
[v]ridiculed him. **15**And he said to them,
"You are those who [w]justify yourselves
before men, but [x]God knows your hearts.
For what is exalted among men [y]is an
abomination in the sight of God.
16[z]"The Law and the Prophets were until
John; since then [a]the good news of the
kingdom of God is preached, and [b]every-
one forces his way into it.[5] **17**But [c]it is easier for heaven and earth to pass away than
for one dot of the Law to become void.

Divorce and Remarriage

18[d]"Everyone who divorces his wife and
marries another commits adultery, and he
who marries a woman divorced from her
husband commits adultery.

The Rich Man and Lazarus

19"There was a rich man who was
clothed in [e]purple and fine linen and [f]who
feasted sumptuously every day. **20**And at
his gate [g]was laid a poor man named
Lazarus, covered with sores, **21**who desired
to be fed with [h]what fell from the rich
man's table. Moreover, even the dogs came
and licked his sores. **22**The poor man died
and was carried by [i]the angels [j]to
Abraham's side.[6] The rich man also died

8 [l]See Matt. 25:2 [m]ch. 20:34; See ch. 10:6 [n]John 12:36; 1 Thess. 5:5; [Eph. 5:8]
9 [o][ch. 12:33; Matt. 6:20; 19:21; 1 Tim. 6:10, 17-19] [p]ver. 11, 13; Matt. 6:24
10 [q]Matt. 25:21, 23 [r]ch. 19:17
12 [s][1 Chr. 29:14, 16]
13 [p][See ver. 9 above]
14 [t][ch. 11:39; 20:47] [u]2 Tim. 3:2; [1 Tim. 6:10]
[v]ch. 23:35
15 [w]ch. 10:29 [x]1 Sam. 16:7; 1 Chr. 28:9; Prov. 21:2 [y]Prov. 16:5
16 [z]Matt. 11:12, 13 [a]See ch. 4:43 [b][ch. 15:1]
17 [c]Matt. 5:18
18 [d]See Matt. 5:32
19 [e]Esth. 8:15; Rev. 18:16 [f][James 5:5]
20 [g][Acts 3:2]
21 [h][Matt. 15:27]
22 [i]ch. 15:10; Matt. 18:10; Acts 12:15; Heb. 1:13, 14; See ch. 12:8 [j][John 13:23]

[1] About 875 gallons [2] Between 1,000 and 1,200 bushels [3] Greek *age* [4] Greek *mammon*, a Semitic word for money or possessions; also verse 11; rendered *money* in verse 13 [5] Or *everyone is forcefully urged into it* [6] Greek *bosom*; also verse 23

16:6 The manager may simply have been dishonest, but Jews were forbidden to take usury and one way around the regulation was to overcharge. The man might have borrowed four hundred gallons of oil and had the bill made out for eight hundred, the extra being the equivalent of a high rate of interest. By significantly reducing the amount of interest the debtor owed, the manager would have obliged the debtor to assist him personally (v. 4), at least for a time, without diminishing the principal owed to his own master.

16:8 With the original bills destroyed, the owner was in an awkward position. It would be difficult to establish his claim to the full amount, which included the interest. His praise of the shrewdness of his manager was a recognition that he had been outwitted. Jesus uses the parable to illustrate that worldly people often use what they have to further their own worldly ends more wisely than the people of the light do to further the quite different aims of God's kingdom.

16:9 Jesus' disciples are to use what wealth they have, not for selfish purposes, but to "make friends" (alms for the poor are probably in view here).

receive you. The text does not explicitly specify who is doing the receiving. Possibilities include the poor who have been helped in this life, or perhaps God Himself. In either case, salvation by works is not being taught (15:29 note). The loving help given to others in this life is a sign of genuine discipleship and salvation already enjoyed rather than a meritorious ground of salvation.

16:11 true riches. Heavenly treasures.

16:12 If "that which is your own" is the "true riches" mentioned in v. 11, then Jesus is saying that faithfulness as a manager in this life determines one's reward in the heavenly kingdom (Matt. 25:34).

16:13 servant. A household slave.

16:16 The Law and the Prophets. A reference to the entire Old Testament.

were until John. Luke here indicates that the ministry of John the Baptist signaled the great turning point of redemptive history (Matt. 11:11 note).

everyone forces his way into it. A difficult statement to translate and interpret. Some suggest that Jesus is exhorting His followers by describing the zeal necessary for entering the kingdom (13:24). Others suggest that "forcing his way" is meant in a negative sense, depicting hostile powers fighting against the kingdom (Matt. 11:12 note).

16:17 dot. A tiny projection on some Hebrew letters; it was the smallest part of a letter. The entire law comes from God, and it is as sure as its Author.

16:18 Jewish men at that time could divorce their wives easily and for slight cause. Jesus had a higher view of marriage; the law's provision for divorce (Deut. 24:1–4) was because of hardness of heart (Mark 10:5). He sees such casual divorce as causing adultery (Matt. 5:31, 32; 19:9). See "Marriage and Divorce" at Mal. 2:16.

16:19 a rich man. This man is sometimes called "Dives," from the Latin word meaning "rich."

purple and fine linen. The expensive clothing of the rich. Purple would be used for the outer garment and linen for the undergarment.

16:20 Lazarus. The only character given a name in Jesus' parables.

16:22 Jesus says nothing about the religious condition of either, but it is implied that Lazarus was right with God whereas the rich man was not.

Abraham's side. The image of "side" relates to being the guest of honor at a banquet (see John 13:23).

and was buried, 23 and in [k]Hades, being in
torment, he lifted up his eyes and [l]saw
Abraham far off and Lazarus [j]at his side.
24 And he called out, [m]'Father Abraham,
have mercy on me, and send Lazarus to dip
the end of his finger in water and [n]cool my
tongue, for [o]I am in anguish in this flame.'
25 But Abraham said, 'Child, remember that
[p]you in your lifetime received your good
things, and Lazarus in like manner bad
things; but now he is comforted here, and
you are in anguish. 26 And besides all this,
between us and you a great chasm has
been fixed, in order that those who would
pass from here to you may not be able, and
none may cross from there to us.' 27 And he
said, 'Then I beg you, father, to send him
to my father's house— 28 for I have five
brothers[1]—so that he may warn them, lest
they also come into this place of torment.'
29 But Abraham said, 'They have [q]Moses
and the Prophets; [r]let them hear them.'
30 And he said, 'No, [s]father Abraham, but if
someone goes to them from the dead, they
will repent.' 31 He said to him, 'If they do
not hear [q]Moses and the Prophets, [t]neither
will they be convinced if someone should
rise from the dead.'"

Temptations to Sin

17 And he said to his disciples,
[u]"Temptations to sin[2] are [v]sure to
come, but [w]woe to the one through whom
they come! 2 [x]It would be better for him if a
millstone were hung around his neck and
he were cast into the sea than that he
should cause one of these little ones to
sin.[3] 3 Pay attention to yourselves! [y]If your
brother sins, [z]rebuke him, and if he repents,
[a]forgive him, 4 and if he sins against you
[b]seven times in the day, and turns to you
seven times, saying, 'I repent,' you must
forgive him."

Increase Our Faith

5 [c]The apostles said to the Lord, [d]"Increase our faith!" 6 And the Lord said, [e]"If
you had faith like [f]a grain of mustard seed,
you could say to this [g]mulberry tree, 'Be
uprooted and planted in the sea,' and it
would obey you.

Unworthy Servants

7 "Will any one of you who has a servant[4]
plowing or keeping sheep say to him when
he has come in from the field, 'Come at
once and recline at table'? 8 Will he not
rather say to him, 'Prepare supper for me,
and [h]dress properly,[5] and serve me while I
eat and drink, and afterward you will eat
and drink'? 9 Does he thank the servant
because he did what was commanded?
10 So you also, when you have done all that
you were commanded, say, 'We are [i]un-
worthy servants;[6] we have only done what
was our duty.'"

Jesus Cleanses Ten Lepers

11 [j]On the way to Jerusalem [k]he was passing along between Samaria and Galilee.
12 And as he entered a village, he was met
by ten lepers,[7] [l]who stood at a distance
13 and lifted up their voices, saying, "Jesus,
Master, have mercy on us." 14 When he saw
them he said to them, "Go and [m]show

23 [k]See Matt. 11:23 [l]Matt. 8:11, 12 [j][See ver. 22 above]
24 [m]ver. 30; John 8:33, 39, 53 [n][Zech. 14:12] [o][Isai. 66:24]; See Matt. 25:41
25 [p][ch. 6:24; Job 21:13; Ps. 17:14]
29 [q]ver. 31; ch. 24:27; Acts 26:22; 28:23 [r][John 5:45-47]
30 [s]ver. 24
31 [q][See ver. 29 above] [t][Matt. 28:11-15; John 12:10, 11]
Chapter 17
1 [u]Matt. 18:7; See 1 Cor. 11:19 [v]See Matt. 13:41 [w]ch. 22:22
2 [x]Matt. 18:6; Mark 9:42
3 [y]Matt. 18:15, 21, 22 [z]Lev. 19:17
[a]See Matt. 6:14
4 [b][Matt. 18:21]
5 [c]See Mark 6:30 [d][Mark 9:24]
6 [e]Matt. 17:20 [f]Matt. 13:31 [g][ch. 19:4]
8 [h]John 13:4; [ch. 12:35, 37]
10 [i]Matt. 25:30; [Job 22:2, 3; 35:7; Rom. 11:35]
11 [j]See ch. 9:51 [k][John 4:3, 4]; See Matt. 19:1
12 [l]See Lev. 13:45, 46
14 [m]ch. 5:14; Lev. 13:2–14:32; Matt. 8:4

1 Or *brothers and sisters* 2 Greek *Stumbling blocks* 3 Greek *stumble* 4 Greek *bondservant*; also verse 9 5 Greek *gird yourself* 6 Greek *bondservants* 7 *Leprosy* was a term for several skin diseases; see Leviticus 13

16:23 in Hades. The usual Greek name for the place of the dead. In the New Testament it is not used with reference to the righteous. Here it is clearly a place of torment. See "Hell" at Mark 9:43.

16:24 Even in Hades the rich man is arrogant, thinking that he can have Lazarus sent to do his bidding.

16:25 The address "Child" is tender, but it cannot alter the facts. A great chasm separates them, and there is a whole new order with a complete reversal of earthly values.

your good things. The rich man had received what he saw as good things. He could have chosen the things of God, but he preferred physical pleasures.

16:27, 28 For the first time the rich man thinks of someone else, though he still remains within his own family. And he still assumes that Lazarus may be sent to do his bidding.

16:29 Moses and the Prophets. A reference to the Old Testament as a whole. The rich man assumed that the appearance of Lazarus would be effective. Jesus is saying that they have the witness of the Word of God; having rejected it, they will not accept another.

17:1 Temptations to sin. The Greek word originally designated the bait stick of a trap; it came to mean anything that trips people up and traps them (see text note).

17:2 little ones. Children or humble believers (cf. 10:21), who are helpless apart from God's aid.

17:5, 6 Apparently the apostles thought great faith would be needed to be so forgiving. Jesus points to what even small faith can bring about. More important than the quantity of faith is the object of faith—a great and powerful God.

17:12 lepers. People with leprosy were required by law to keep away from healthy people (Lev. 13:46); these came as close as they dared and called out loudly.

17:14 See note 5:14.

yourselves to the priests." And as they went
they were cleansed. 15 Then one of them,
when he saw that he was healed, turned
back, [n]praising God with a loud voice;
16 and [o]he fell on his face at Jesus' feet, giving him thanks. Now he was [p]a Samaritan.
17 Then Jesus answered, "Were not [q]ten
cleansed? Where are the nine? 18 Was no
one found to return and [r]give praise to God
except this [s]foreigner?" 19 And he said to
him, "Rise and go your way; [t]your faith has
[t]made you well."[1]

The Coming of the Kingdom

20 Being asked by the Pharisees [u]when the
kingdom of God would come, he answered
them, "The kingdom of God [v]is not coming
with signs to be observed, 21 nor [w]will they
say, 'Look, here it is!' or 'There!' for behold,
the kingdom of God is in the midst of you."[2]
22 And he said to the disciples, [x]"The
days are coming when you will desire [y]to
see one of the days of the Son of Man, and
you will not see it. 23 [z]And they will say to
you, 'Look, there!' or 'Look, here!' Do not
go out or follow them. 24 [a]For as the lightning flashes and lights up the sky from
one side to the other, so will the Son of
Man be [b]in his day.[3] 25 But first [c]he must
suffer many things and [c]be rejected by

15 [n]See ch. 7:16; 13:13 16 [o]ch. 5:12; Num. 16:22; [Matt. 26:39] [p]See Matt. 10:5 17 [q]ver. 12 18 [r]See John 9:24 [s]Isai. 66:5 19 [t]See Mark 10:52 20 [u]ch. 19:11; Acts 1:6 [v][ch. 12:39] 21 [w][ver. 23] 22 [x]ch. 5:35; 21:6; Matt. 9:15; Mark 2:20; [ch. 19:43; 23:29; John 4:21] [y]John 8:56; [Amos 5:18] 23 [z]ch. 21:8; Matt. 24:23; Mark 13:21; [ver. 21] 24 [a]Matt. 24:27 [b]See 1 Cor. 1:8 25 [c]See ch. 13:33; Matt. 16:21; 17:22; Mark 8:31

[1] Or *has saved you* [2] Or *within you*, or *within your grasp* [3] Some manuscripts omit *in his day*

The Kingdom of God

The theme of the kingdom of God runs through both Testaments, focusing God's purpose for world history. In the Old Testament God declared that He would exercise His kingship (His sovereignty, Dan. 4:34, 35) by ruling over people's lives and circumstances through His chosen King, the Davidic Messiah (Is. 9:6, 7) in a golden age of blessing. This kingdom came with Jesus and is known wherever the lordship of Jesus is acknowledged. Jesus is enthroned in heaven as ruler over all things (Matt. 28:18; Col. 1:13), King of kings and Lord of lords (Rev. 17:14; 19:16). The golden age of blessing is an era of salvation from sin and fellowship with God leading to a future state of complete joy in a reconstructed universe. The kingdom is present in its beginnings but future in its fullness; in one sense it is here already, but in the richest sense still to come (Luke 11:20; 16:16; 17:21; 22:16, 18, 29, 30).

The kingdom came bringing mercy but also judgment, just as John the Baptist, its forerunner, had said (Matt. 3:1–12). Those who received Jesus' word and put their destiny in His hands found mercy, while those who would not were judged.

The task of the church is to make the invisible kingdom visible through faithful Christian living and witness. The gospel of Christ is still the gospel of the kingdom (Matt. 4:23; 24:14; Acts 20:25; 28:23, 31), the good news of righteousness, peace, and joy in the Holy Spirit. The church makes its message credible by manifesting the reality of kingdom life.

The coming of the kingdom meant a new stage in God's redemptive program. All that was typical, temporary, and imperfect in the arrangements God made for Israel's communion with Him became things of the past. God's Israel, the seed of Abraham, was revealed as the company of believers in Jesus (Gal. 3:16, 26–29). The Spirit was poured out, and a new way of life became a reality for this world. A new internationalism of global church fellowship and global evangelism was born (Matt. 28:19, 20; Eph. 2:11–18; 3:6, 14, 15; Col. 1:28, 29; Rev. 5:9, 10; 7:9).

as they went. Jesus' command, when nothing had yet happened to the men, was a test of faith. They were healed as they went in obedience to Jesus' word.

17:15, 16 Gratitude brought one man straight back, praising God for what had happened. That he was a Samaritan made this all the more interesting, for he would not be expected to show much gratitude to a Jewish healer.

17:20–37 Jesus' answer to questions regarding the coming of the kingdom of God points to the dynamic character of that kingdom. In this passage, Jesus presents the kingdom both as present reality (v. 21) and as yet to be fully revealed (vv. 22–37). Jesus often presented the kingdom as a hidden and growing reality (Matt. 13:31–33), which is both present and future. In the earthly ministry of Jesus, the kingdom is already present (11:20), but the full reality of the kingdom is yet to be manifested (cf. 19:11). Christians are to pray for the full realization of God's kingdom (11:2). See theological note "The Kingdom of God."

17:21 the kingdom of God is in the midst of you. Cf. text note. The translation "in the midst of you" points to the presence of the kingdom in the person of Jesus.

17:22 one of the days of the Son of Man. A probable reference to the full manifestation of the kingdom at the Second Coming of Christ (vv. 26, 30). Christians long for the coming of Christ and for the peace and justice that the Second Coming will bring.

17:23–25 Though some will seek after false messiahs (21:8, 9), the final coming of Christ will be so public that everybody will know.

17:25 must suffer many things. The word "must" is important; it indicates the sovereign purpose of God (Acts 4:27, 28).

this generation. 26 [d]Just as it was in the days
of [e]Noah, so will it be in the days of the
Son of Man. 27 [f]They were eating and drinking and marrying and being given in marriage, until the day when Noah entered the
ark, and the flood came and destroyed
them all. 28 Likewise, just as it was in the
days of [g]Lot—they were eating and drinking,
buying and selling, planting and building,
29 [h]but on the day when Lot went out from
Sodom, fire and sulfur rained from heaven
and destroyed them all— 30 so will it be [i]on
the day when the Son of Man is revealed.
31 On that day, [j]let the one who is on [k]the
housetop, with his goods in the house, not
come down to take them away, and likewise let the one who is in the field not turn
back. 32 [l]Remember Lot's wife. 33 [m]Whoever
seeks to preserve his life will lose it, but
whoever loses his life will [n]keep it. 34 I tell
you, in that night there will be two in one
bed. One will be taken and the other left.
35 [o]There will be two women [p]grinding
together. One will be taken and the other
left."[1] 37 And they said to him, "Where,
Lord?" He said to them, [q]"Where the
corpse[2] is, there the vultures[3] will gather."

The Parable of the Persistent Widow

18 And he told them a parable to the
effect that they ought [r]always to
pray and not [s]lose heart. 2 He said, "In a
certain city there was a judge who [t]neither
feared God nor respected man. 3 And there
was a widow in that city who kept coming
to him and saying, 'Give me justice against
my adversary.' 4 For a while he refused, but
afterward he said to himself, [u]'Though I
neither fear God nor respect man, 5 yet
because this widow keeps bothering me, I
will give her justice, so that she will not
beat me down by her continual coming.'"
6 And the Lord said, "Hear what the
unrighteous judge says. 7 And [v]will not God
give justice to [w]his elect, [x]who cry to him
day and night? [y]Will he delay long over
them? 8 I tell you, he will give justice to
them [a]speedily. Nevertheless, when the
Son of Man comes, [b]will he find faith on
earth?"

The Pharisee and the Tax Collector

9 He also told this parable to some [c]who
trusted [d]in themselves that they were righteous, [e]and treated others with contempt:
10 "Two men [f]went up into the temple to
pray, one a Pharisee and the other a tax collector. 11 The Pharisee, [g]standing by himself,
prayed[4] [h]thus: 'God, I thank you that I am
not like other men, extortioners, unjust,
adulterers, or even like this tax collector.
12 [i]I fast twice a week; [j]I give tithes of all
that I get.' 13 But the tax collector, [g]standing

26 [d]Gen. 6:5; 7:7; Matt. 24:37; [1 Thess. 5:3] [e]Heb. 11:7; 1 Pet. 3:20; 2 Pet. 2:5 27 [f]Matt. 24:38, 39 28 [g]2 Pet. 2:7 29 [h]Gen. 19:16, 24; 2 Pet. 2:6 30 [i]1 Cor. 1:7; 2 Thess. 1:7; 1 Pet. 1:7, 13; 4:13; [Matt. 16:27; 24:44] 31 [j]ch. 21:21; Matt. 24:17, 18; Mark 13:15, 16 [k]See ch. 5:19 32 [l]Gen. 19:26 33 [m]See Matt. 10:39 [n]Acts 7:19 (Gk.) 35 [o]Matt. 24:41 [p]Ex. 11:5; Isai. 47:2 37 [q]Matt. 24:28; [Job 39:30]

Chapter 18
1 [r]ch. 21:36; Rom. 12:12; Eph. 6:18; Col. 4:2; 1 Thess. 5:17; [ch. 11:5-9] [s]2 Cor. 4:1, 16; 2 Thess. 3:13 (Gk.) 2 [t][2 Cor. 8:21] 4 [u][ch. 11:8] 7 [v]Rev. 6:10; [Isai. 63:4] [w]Rom. 8:33; Col. 3:12; Tit. 1:1; See Mark 13:20 [x]Ps. 88:1 [y]James 5:7 (Gk.) [z]2 Pet. 3:9 8 [a]Heb. 10:37 [b]ch. 17:26-30; [Matt. 24:12] 9 [c]ch. 16:15; [Matt. 5:20] [d]2 Cor. 1:9 [e]Prov. 30:12; Isai. 65:5; John 7:48, 49 10 [f]1 Kin. 10:5; 2 Kin. 20:5, 8; Acts 3:1; [ver. 14] 11 [g]Matt. 6:5; Mark 11:25 [h][Rev. 3:17] 12 [i]Matt. 9:14 [j]ch. 11:42

1 Some manuscripts add verse 36: *Two men will be in the field; one will be taken and the other left* 2 Greek *body* 3 Or *eagles* 4 Or *standing, prayed to himself*

17:26–29 People in the times of Noah and Lot carried on with the normal life of this world (Jesus does not speak of their sins) and neglected their opportunity. Noah and Lot were sinners, but they heeded God's warning and were saved. They were not wholly taken up with the things of this life.

17:32 Lot's wife came close to deliverance, but her backward look doomed her (Gen. 19:26).

17:33 Jesus repeats the teaching of 9:24 that the selfish and self-affirming life means spiritual death.

17:34, 35 Close proximity to some saved person will not help in the day of Christ's coming.

17:37 Where the corpse is. Jesus apparently uses a popular proverb to teach that just as dead bodies attract vultures, so the spiritually dead invite judgment.

18:1–8 The preceding verses (17:22–37) and the reference to the Second Coming in v. 8 indicate that persistence in prayer for the coming of Christ and His final triumph over evil, even when that coming is seemingly delayed, is particularly in view (1 Cor. 16:22; Rev. 22:20). On the general principle concerning the importance of continued prayer in all matters, see 11:5–8 and notes.

18:3 The widow was a helpless person with nothing but right on her side. She wanted justice, not revenge.

18:5 beat me down. A picturesque expression, lit. "give me a black eye." The judge may be afraid that the woman will ruin his reputation by making him seem unable to help his clients, and compelling them to beg at his door.

18:7 If even an "unrighteous" judge (v. 6) will do what is right, how much more God?

delay long. God will not keep putting them off like the judge in this parable; any delay will have a reason.

18:8 speedily. This is in God's time (2 Pet. 3:8), not ours.

will he find faith. This does not mean that there will be no believers, but that faith will not be characteristic of all.

18:10 Private prayer could be offered in the temple at any time of day, not only in formal services.

18:11 standing. A common posture for prayer.

18:12 fast twice a week. The only fast prescribed in the law of Moses was on the Day of Atonement (Lev. 16:29–31; 23:27), though voluntary fasting could accompany prayer (Ps. 35:13), penitence (1 Kin. 21:27), and mourning (2 Sam. 1:12). By the time of Christ, Jewish oral tradition had increased the number of fasts expected of the pious. Fasting can be a useful religious exercise (5:33–35; Acts 13:2, 3), but Jesus roundly condemned the practice when it was seen as a way of meriting God's favor (vv. 11, 12) or when it became an ostentatious display (Matt. 6:16–18; cf. Is. 58:1–6).

far off, [k]would not even lift up his eyes to
heaven, but [l]beat his breast, saying, 'God,
[m]be merciful to me, a sinner!' 14 I tell you,
this man went down to his house justified,
rather than the other. For [n]everyone who
exalts himself will be humbled, but the
one who humbles himself will be exalted."

Let the Children Come to Me

15 [o]Now they were bringing even infants
to him that he might touch them. And
when the disciples saw it, they [p]rebuked
them. 16 But Jesus called them to him, saying, [q]"Let the children come to me, and [r]do
not hinder them, [q]for to such belongs the
kingdom of God. 17 [s]Truly, I say to you,
whoever does not [t]receive the kingdom of
God like a child shall not enter it."

The Rich Ruler

18 [u]And a ruler asked him, "Good Teacher,
what must I do to [v]inherit eternal life?"
19 And Jesus said to him, "Why do you call
me good? No one is good except God
alone. 20 You know the commandments:
[w]'Do not commit adultery, Do not murder,
Do not steal, Do not bear false witness,
Honor your father and mother.'" 21 And he
said, [x]"All these I have kept from my
youth." 22 When Jesus heard this, he said to
him, "One thing you still lack. [y]Sell all that
you have and distribute to the poor, and
you will have [z]treasure in heaven; and
come, follow me." 23 [a]But when he heard
these things, he became very sad, for he
was extremely rich. 24 Jesus, looking at him
with sadness, said, [b]"How difficult it is for
those who have wealth to enter [c]the kingdom of God! 25 For it is easier for a camel to
go through the eye of a needle than for a
rich person to enter [c]the kingdom of God."
26 Those who heard it said, "Then who can
be saved?" 27 But he said, [d]"What is impossible with men is possible with God."
28 And Peter said, "See, [e]we have left our
homes and followed you." 29 And he said to
them, "Truly, I say to you, [f]there is no one
who has left house or wife or brothers[1] or
parents or children, for the sake of the
kingdom of God, 30 who will not receive
[g]many times more [h]in this time, and in [i]the
age to come eternal life."

Jesus Foretells His Death a Third Time

31 [j]And taking the twelve, he said to
them, "See, [k]we are going up to Jerusalem,
and [l]everything that is written about the
Son of Man by the prophets will be accomplished. 32 For he will be [m]delivered over to
the Gentiles and will be [n]mocked and
shamefully treated and [o]spit upon. 33 And
after flogging him, they will kill him, and
on [p]the third day he will rise." 34 [q]But they
understood none of these things. [r]This saying was hidden from them, and they did
not grasp what was said.

Jesus Heals a Blind Beggar

35 [s]As he drew near to Jericho, [t]a blind
man was sitting by the roadside beg-
ging. 36 And hearing a crowd going by, he

13 [k]Ezra 9:6 [l]ch. 23:48 [m]Ps. 79:9; Ezek. 16:63; Dan. 9:19 **14** [n]See ch. 14:11 **15** [o]For ver. 15-17, see Matt. 19:13-15; Mark 10:13-16 [p]ver. 39 **16** [q]Matt. 18:3 [r][Mark 9:39] **17** [s][John 3:3, 5] [t][ch. 8:13; James 1:21] **18** [u]For ver. 18-30, see Matt. 19:16-29; Mark 10:17- 30; [ch. 10:25-28] [v][Matt. 19:16]; See Matt. 25:34 **20** [w]Rom. 13:9; Cited from Ex. 20:12-16; Deut. 5:16-20; [Matt. 5:21, 27] **21** [x][Phil. 3:6] **22** [y]ch. 12:33; [ch. 16:9; 19:8; Acts 2:45; 4:34, 35; 1 Tim. 6:18, 19] [z]Matt. 6:19, 20 **23** [a][Ezek. 33:31] **24** [b][1 Cor. 1:26]; See Matt. 13:22 [c]See Matt. 12:28 **25** [c][See ver. 24 above] **27** [d]ch. 1:37; Gen. 18:14; Job 42:2; Jer. 32:17, 27; Zech. 8:6; Matt. 14:36

28 [e]Matt. 4:20, 22; Mark 1:18, 20 **29** [f][ch. 14:26] **30** [g][Job 42:10] [h][Matt. 6:33] [i]Matt. 12:32; Eph. 1:21; [ch. 20:35] **31** [j]For ver. 31-33, see Matt. 20:17- 19; Mark 10:32-34 [k]See ch. 9:51 [l]Ps. 22; See Matt. 1:22; 26:24 **32** [m]Matt. 27:2; John 18:30, 31; Acts 3:13; [Acts 2:23; 4:27; 21:11] [n]Matt. 27:26-31 [o]Mark 14:65; 15:19; See Matt. 26:67 **33** [p]See ch. 9:22 **34** [q]See Mark 9:32 [r]ch. 9:45; [ch. 24:16] **35** [s]For ver. 35-43, see Matt. 20:29-34; Mark 10:46-52 [t]John 9:1, 8

[1] Or *wife or brothers and sisters*

18:13 lift up his eyes to heaven. Looking upward was usual while praying, but this man was too conscious of unworthiness to do this. He simply asked for mercy as he acknowledged his sin.

18:14 justified. The Pharisee relied on his own merits, not having discovered that no human righteousness is sufficient before a God who demands perfection (Matt. 5:48). The tax collector relied on God's mercy and found it.

18:18 ruler. A general term meaning someone from the upper classes.

Good Teacher. This was not a usual form of address in Judaism; it was mere flattery. The man assumed that his deeds would bring him to eternal life.

18:19 Why do you call me good. Jesus challenges the ruler's flattery by reminding him that true goodness is an attribute of God alone. That his flattery was indeed insincere is shown by his failure to do what the "Good Teacher" taught him (v. 23).

18:22 Sell all. This challenge revealed that the young man had not really understood the commandments. When he was faced with the choice, it became clear that his possessions came before God.

18:23–25 See note Mark 10:25. The wealthy are tempted to rely on earthly things, together with those whose wealth is achievement in intellectual, artistic, or other fields. Great achievers often find it difficult to rely wholly on the mercy of God.

18:26, 27 If the rich with all their advantages cannot easily be saved, who can be? The answer is that salvation, for rich or poor, is always the gift of God.

18:28–30 Jesus' answer to Peter means that God's gifts surpass anything we can give up for Him. It does not mean that we can make sacrifices as a means of getting a better reward.

18:31–34 In His predictions of the Passion (cf. 5:35; 9:22, 43–45; 12:50; 13:32, 33; 17:25), this is the first time Jesus speaks of being handed over to the Gentiles.

18:35 draw near to Jericho. Luke implies Jesus was entering Jericho, whereas Matthew and Mark say the incident occurred as they "went out" of Jericho (Matt. 20:30; Mark 10:46). There seem to have been two "Jerichos" about a mile apart: the ruins of the Old Testament city conquered by Joshua (Josh. 6), and a city built by Herod the Great. The encounter may have happened as Jesus was leaving the old city and entering the new.

a blind man. Matthew mentions two blind men (cf. Matt. 8:28 and note),

inquired what this meant. 37 They told him,
[u]"Jesus of Nazareth is passing by." 38 And
he cried out, "Jesus, [v]Son of David, have
mercy on me!" 39 And those who were in
front [w]rebuked him, telling him to be
silent. But he cried out all the more, "Son
of David, have mercy on me!" 40 And Jesus
stopped and commanded him to be
brought to him. And when he came near,
he asked him, 41 [x]"What do you want me to
do for you?" He said, "Lord, let me recover
my sight." 42 And Jesus said to him, "Recover your sight; [y]your faith has [z]made you
well." 43 And immediately he recovered his
sight and followed him, [a]glorifying God.
And [b]all the people, when they saw it, gave
praise to God.

Jesus and Zacchaeus

19 [c]He entered Jericho and was passing through. 2 And there was a man
named Zacchaeus. He was a chief tax collector and was rich. 3 And [d]he was seeking
to see who Jesus was, but on account of the
crowd he could not, because he was small
of stature. 4 So he ran on ahead and
climbed up into [e]a sycamore tree to see
him, for he was about to pass that way.
5 And when Jesus came to the place, he
looked up and said to him, "Zacchaeus,
hurry and come down, for [f]I must stay at
your house today." 6 So he hurried and
came down and [g]received him joyfully.
7 And when they saw it, they all [h]grumbled,
"He has gone in to be the guest of a man
who is a sinner." 8 And Zacchaeus stood
and said to the Lord, "Behold, Lord, the
half of my goods [i]I give to the poor. And if
I have [j]defrauded anyone of anything, I
restore it [k]fourfold." 9 And Jesus said to
him, "Today salvation has come to this
house, since [l]he also is a son of Abraham.
10 For [m]the Son of Man came to seek and to
save the lost."

The Parable of the Ten Minas

11 As they heard these things, he proceeded to tell a parable, because he was
near to Jerusalem, and because [n]they supposed that the kingdom of God was to
appear immediately. 12 He said therefore,
[o]"A nobleman went into a far country to
receive for himself a kingdom and then
return. 13 Calling [p]ten of his servants,[1] he
gave them ten minas,[2] and said to them,
'Engage in business [q]until I come.' 14 But
[r]his citizens hated him and sent a delegation after him, saying, 'We do not want this
man to reign over us.' 15 When he returned,
having received the kingdom, he ordered
these servants to whom he had given the
money to be called to him, that he might
know what they had gained by doing business. 16 The first came before him, saying,
'Lord, your mina has made ten minas
more.' 17 And he said to him, 'Well done,
good servant![3] Because you have been

37 [u]Matt. 2:23
38 [v]See Matt. 1:1; 9:27
39 [w]ver. 15
41 [x]Mark 10:36
42 [y]ch. 7:50; 8:48; 17:19; Matt. 9:22; Mark 5:34 [z]ch. 7:3; 8:36, 50
43 [a]See ch. 7:16; 13:13 [b][ch. 19:37]
Chapter 19
1 [c]ch. 18:35; [Matt. 20:29; Mark 10:46]
3 [d][John 12:21]
4 [e]1 Kin. 10:27; 1 Chr. 27:28; Ps. 78:47; Isai. 9:10; [ch. 17:6]
5 [f][ch. 13:33]
6 [g]ch. 10:38
7 [h]See ch. 15:2
8 [i][ch. 18:22] [j]ch. 3:14 [k]Ex. 22:1; 2 Sam. 12:6
9 [l]John 8:33; Rom. 4:11, 12, 16; Gal. 3:7
10 [m]Ezek. 34:11, 16; [ch. 15:4; Matt. 9:13; 10:6; 15:24; 18:12]
11 [n][ch. 17:20; Acts 1:6]
12 [o]For ver. 12-27, [Matt. 25:14-30; Mark 13:34]
13 [p]Matt. 25:1 [q][John 21:22, 23]
14 [r][John 1:14]

1 Greek *bondservants*; also verse 15 2 A *mina* was about three months' wages for a laborer 3 Greek *bondservant*; also verse 22

while Luke and Mark mention only one (named Bartimaeus, Mark 10:46); he may have been the spokesman for the two.

18:38 Son of David. A messianic title.

18:42 your faith. Faith was the means by which the gift was received.

has made you well. This might be translated "has saved you," which would fit in with his following Jesus and praising God.

19:2 chief tax collector. The term is found nowhere else, but clearly it means the head of the local taxing agents. Jericho was near a major trade route and famous balsam groves. There was much to tax, and Zacchaeus was accordingly quite rich.

19:4 sycamore tree. A tree frequently planted by the roadside; it was easy to climb.

19:8 I restore. The verb is in the present tense for vividness and emphasis.

fourfold. The law required the amount plus a fifth (Lev. 6:5; Num. 5:7); Zacchaeus was going far beyond what the law demanded.

19:9 salvation. Jesus has just said that it is hard for a rich person to be saved (18:24, 25); the salvation of Zacchaeus shows it is not impossible (18:27). See "Salvation" at Acts 4:12.

a son of Abraham. This phrase may point to Zacchaeus as one of the lost sheep of Israel, to whom Jesus felt a special mission (cf. 13:16; Matt. 10:6; 15:24).

19:10 the Son of Man. Jesus' favorite way of referring to Himself (5:24 note).

19:11 Jesus' journey to Jerusalem was nearing its end, and some thought He would set up a magnificent earthly kingdom there.

19:12 The parable of the talents (Matt. 25:14–29) resembles this one, but there the amounts are larger and vary in size, testing the servants for their fitness for larger tasks. Here the amounts are small and the same for all (v. 13). The parable teaches that everyone has one basic task—to serve God faithfully.

a far country. Herod's sons were examples of noblemen who went to Rome hoping to be made king.

19:13 ten minas. Each servant received one mina, the equivalent of one hundred drachmas (15:8 note), or several months' wages.

19:14 When Herod's son Archelaus went to Rome seeking his kingdom, his Jewish subjects sent a delegation to ask that he not be made king over them.

19:16–19 Two servants did well and were rewarded with further opportunities of service in proportion to their success. Notice their modesty ("your mina has made") and the much greater responsibility allotted to them.

[s]faithful in a very little, [t]you shall have
authority over ten cities.' 18 And the second
came, saying, 'Lord, your mina has made
five minas.' 19 And he said to him, 'And you
are to be over five cities.' 20 Then another
came, saying, 'Lord, here is your mina,
which I kept laid away in [u]a handkerchief;
21 for I was afraid of you, because you are [v]a
severe man. You take [w]what you did not
deposit, and reap what you did not sow.'
22 He said to him, [x]'I will condemn you
with your own words, [y]you wicked servant!
You knew that I was [v]a severe man, taking
what I did not deposit and reaping what I
did not sow? 23 Why then did you not put
my money in the bank, and at my coming
I might have collected it with interest?'
24 And he said to those who stood by, 'Take
the mina from him, and give it to the one
who has the ten minas.' 25 And they said to
him, 'Lord, he has ten minas!' 26 'I tell you
that [z]to everyone who has, more will be
given, but from the one who has not, even
what he has will be taken away. 27 But [r]as
for these enemies of mine, who did not
want me to reign over them, bring them
here and [a]slaughter them before me.' "

The Triumphal Entry

28 And when he had said these things,
[b]he went on ahead, [c]going up to Jerusalem.
29 [d]When he drew near to Bethphage and
[e]Bethany, at [f]the mount that is called
Olivet, he sent [g]two of the disciples, 30 saying, "Go into the village in front of you,
where on entering you will find a colt tied,
[h]on which no one has ever yet sat. Untie it
and bring it here. 31 If anyone asks you,
'Why are you untying it?' you shall say this:
'The Lord has need of it.' " 32 So those who
were sent went away and found it [i]just as
he had told them. 33 And as they were untying the colt, its owners said to them, "Why
are you untying the colt?" 34 And they said,
"The Lord has need of it." 35 And they
brought it to Jesus, and throwing their
cloaks on the colt, they set Jesus on it.
36 And as he rode along, they [j]spread their
cloaks on the road. 37 As he was drawing
near—already on the way down the Mount
of Olives—[k]the whole multitude of his disciples began to rejoice and praise God with
a loud voice [l]for all the mighty works that
they had seen, 38 saying, [m]"Blessed is [n]the
King who comes in the name of the Lord!
Peace in heaven and [o]glory in the highest!"
39 [p]And some of the Pharisees in the crowd
said to him, "Teacher, rebuke your disciples." 40 He answered, "I tell you, if these
were silent, [q]the very stones would cry out."

Jesus Weeps over Jerusalem

41 [r]And when he drew near and saw the
city, [s]he wept over it, 42 saying, [t]"Would
that you, even you, had known on this day
the things that make for peace! But now
[u]they are hidden from your eyes. 43 For [v]the
days will come upon you, when your enemies [w]will set up a barricade around you
and [x]surround you and hem you in on
every side 44 [y]and tear you down to the
ground, you and your children within you.
And [z]they will not leave one stone upon

17 [s]ch. 16:10; 1 Cor. 4:2; [1 Tim. 3:13] [t][Matt. 24:47] **20** [u]John 11:44; 20:7; Acts 19:12 (Gk.) **21** [v][1 Sam. 25:3] [w][2 Cor. 8:12] **22** [x]2 Sam. 1:16; Job 9:20; 15:6 [y]Matt. 18:32 [v][See ver. 21 above] **26** [z][ch. 12:48]; See Matt. 13:12 **27** [r][See ver. 14 above] [a]ch. 20:16; Matt. 22:7; [1 Sam. 15:33] **28** [b]Mark 10:32 [c]See ch. 9:51; 10:30 **29** [d]For ver. 29-38, see Matt. 21:1-9; Mark 11:1-10; John 12:12-15; [Zech. 9:9] [e]ch. 24:50; Matt. 21:17; John 11:18 [f]Zech. 14:4; Matt. 24:3; 26:30; [John 8:1]; [Acts 1:12] [g][Mark 14:13] **30** [h][ch. 23:53] **32** [i]ch. 22:13 **36** [j]2 Kin. 9:13 **37** [k][ch. 18:43] [l][John 12:17, 18] **38** [m]ch. 13:35; Cited from Ps. 118:26 [n]See Matt. 25:34; John 1:49 [o]ch. 2:14; [Ps. 148:1] **39** [p][Matt. 21:15, 16]

40 [q]Hab. 2:11 **41** [r]For ver. 41-44, [ch. 13:34, 35; 23:28-31] [s][John 11:35; Heb. 5:7] **42** [t][Deut. 32:29] [u][John 12:40] **43** [v]See ch. 17:22 [w]Isai. 29:3; 37:33; Jer. 6:6; Ezek. 4:2; 26:8 [x]ch. 21:20 **44** [y]Ps. 137:9; Hos. 13:16; Nah. 3:10 [z]ch. 21:6

19:20, 21 Fear kept the third man from doing anything, though he knew his master expected much. Nothing is said about the other seven. The parable is concerned with two classes: those who worked and those who did not.

19:22–26 The punishment for not using what one has is to lose it, a principle of wide application. Those who use their spiritual opportunities find more, while those who do nothing about them lose what ability they did have.

19:28 See note 9:51.

19:29 Bethany. A village about two miles from Jerusalem. Bethphage must have been nearby; it was regarded as the outer limit of Jerusalem.

19:30 colt. This could refer to a horse or a donkey; the other Gospels make it clear it was a donkey. It had never been used and was therefore fit for a sacred purpose (Num. 19:2; 1 Sam. 6:7).

19:35, 36 throwing their cloaks on the colt. The clothing evidently served as a saddle. The clothes on the road formed a triumphal carpet.

19:37 This entry into Jerusalem fulfilled prophecy (Zech. 9:9) and was a public claim to messiahship, but messiahship of a distinctive kind, since the donkey was the animal of a man of peace. A conquering king would ride a horse. The people seem to have recognized the kingship, but not to have seen the emphasis on peace.

19:38 A quotation from Ps. 118:26, but with an explicit reference to the King. Luke alone has the words "peace" and "glory." He does not have "Hosanna," which his Gentile readers might not have understood.

19:39 rebuke your disciples. The Pharisees would not have wanted anything that disturbed the peace and brought trouble from the Romans.

19:41, 42 Only Luke records Jesus' lament as He drew near the city. Jesus knew that the excitement of the crowds did not correspond to genuine spiritual perception and that the actions being pursued would inevitably bring war, not peace.

19:43 set up a barricade. A description of a typical siege of a city. The embankment was erected as a protection for the invaders and a base from which to launch attacks.

19:44 The city will be completely destroyed. The people must live with their rejection of God's Messiah.

another in you, because you did not know
[a]the time of your [b]visitation."

Jesus Cleanses the Temple

45 [c]And he entered the temple and began
to drive out those who sold, **46** saying to
them, "It is written, [d]'My house shall be a
house of prayer,' but [e]you have made it a
den of robbers."

47 [f]And he was teaching daily in the temple. [g]The chief priests and the scribes and
the principal men of the people were seeking to destroy him, **48** but they did not find
anything they could do, for all the people
were hanging on his words.

The Authority of Jesus Challenged

20 [h]One day, [i]as Jesus[1] was teaching the
people in the temple and preach-
ing the gospel, [j]the chief priests and the
scribes with the elders came up **2** and said
to him, "Tell us [k]by what authority you do
these things, or who it is that gave you this
authority." **3** He answered them, "I also will
ask you a question. Now tell me, **4** Was the
baptism of John [l]from heaven or from
man?" **5** And they discussed it with one
another, saying, "If we say, 'From heaven,'
he will say, [m]'Why did you not believe
him?' **6** But if we say, 'From man,' all the
people will stone us to death, for they are
convinced that John was [n]a prophet." **7** So
they answered that they did not know
where it came from. **8** And Jesus said to
them, "Neither will I tell you by what
authority I do these things."

[a][Dan. 9:24] [b]1 Pet. 2:12
45 [c]For ver. 45-47, see Matt. 21:12-16; Mark 11:15-18; [John 2:14-16]
46 [d]Cited from Isai. 56:7 [e]Jer. 7:11
47 [f]ch. 20:1; See Matt. 26:55 [g]See Matt. 21:46
Chapter 20
1 [h]For ver. 1-8, see Matt. 21:23-27; Mark 11:27-33 [i]ch. 19:47 [j]Acts 4:1; 6:12
2 [k][Ex. 2:14; John 1:25; Acts 4:7]
4 [l]ch. 15:18, 21; John 3:27
5 [m]ch. 7:30; Matt. 21:32
6 [n][John 5:35]; See Matt. 11:9
9 [o]For ver. 9-19, see Matt. 21:33-46; Mark 12:1-12 [p]Ps. 80:8; Isai. 5:1; Matt. 21:28 [q]S. of S. 8:11, 12 [r]Matt. 25:14, 15; [Mark 13:34]
10 [q][See ver. 9 above] [s]Matt. 5:12; 22:6; 23:34, 37; [2 Chr. 24:19; 36:15, 16; Neh. 9:26; Jer. 37:15; 38:6; Acts 7:52; 2 Cor. 11:24-26; 1 Thess. 2:15; Heb. 11:36, 37]

The Parable of the Wicked Tenants

9 [o]And he began to tell the people this
parable: "A man planted [p]a vineyard and
[q]let it out to tenants and [r]went into
another country for a long while. **10** When
the time came, he sent a servant[2] to the
tenants, so that [q]they would give him some
of the fruit of the vineyard. [s]But the tenants
beat him and sent him away empty-
handed. **11** [t]And [s]he sent another servant.
But they also beat and [u]treated him shamefully, and sent him away empty-handed.
12 [s]And he sent yet a third. This one also
they wounded and cast out. **13** Then the
owner of the vineyard said, 'What shall I do?
I will send my [v]beloved son; perhaps they
will respect him.' **14** But when the tenants
saw him, they said to themselves, [w]'This is
the heir. [x]Let us kill him, so that the inheritance may be ours.' **15** And they [y]threw him
out of the vineyard and killed him. What
then will the owner of the vineyard do to
them? **16** [z]He will [a]come and destroy those
tenants and [b]give the vineyard to others."
When they heard this, they said, "Surely
not!" **17** But he [c]looked directly at them and
said, "What then is this that is written:

> [d]"'The stone that the builders rejected
> has become the cornerstone'?[3]

11 [t]Matt. 22:4 [s][See ver. 10 above] [u]Acts 5:41 (Gk.) **12** [s][See ver. 10 above] **13** [v]See Matt. 3:17 **14** [w]Heb. 1:2; [John 1:11; Rom. 8:17] [x][1 Kin. 21:19] **15** [y]Heb.13:12 **16** [z][ch. 19:27] [a][Matt. 24:50; 25:19] [b]Matt. 21:43; Acts 13:46; 18:6; 28:28; [Matt. 8:11, 12] **17** [c]See Mark 10:21 [d]Acts 4:11; 1 Pet. 2:7; Cited from Ps. 118:22

1 Greek *he* 2 Greek *bondservant*; also verse 11 3 Greek *the head of the corner*

19:45, 46 All four Gospels speak of Jesus driving traders out of the temple precincts, but the first three place it at the end of Jesus' ministry and John at the beginning. There were probably two cleansings (Mark 11:15 note). The merchants in the temple courts were money-changers and sellers of sacrificial animals. Only coins from Tyre were accepted in the temple, and money had to be changed before an offering could be made. It was convenient to have them close to the temple, but their presence in the temple courts themselves made true worship difficult. The traders would have been in the court of the Gentiles, the only place Gentiles could go to pray.

19:47, 48 The temple was a normal place for teaching. Jesus' opposition now includes a new group—"the principal men of the people." Evidently prominent lay people had now joined the priests and the scribes.

20:1 preaching the gospel. Jesus was bringing God's good news at the very time His enemies were plotting against Him.

chief priests . . . scribes . . . elders. This appears to be a delegation from the Sanhedrin.

20:2 these things. Things such as driving the traders out of the temple.

20:3, 4 Jesus was not avoiding their question. John had testified that Jesus was the Messiah. If they answered Jesus' question, they would have the answer to their own.

20:5, 6 Notice that they were not concerned with the truth, but with the consequences of their possible answers.

20:7, 8 Jesus will not talk about authority to men who refuse to reply to an important religious question, the answer to which they already know.

20:9–12 The tenants are a vivid picture of the nation that persistently rejected the messengers of God who were sent to call them to repentance.

20:13 Normally a landowner confronted with persistent refusal to pay and with abuse of his messengers would have taken strong measures. But just as this landowner keeps giving the tenants the opportunity for repentance, so God continues to reach out to sinners.

20:14 This is the heir. The tenants had refused to acknowledge an owner by paying rent, and they apparently reasoned that with the heir out of the way, they could establish their own title to the land. Jesus is making the point that the nation had behaved outrageously toward God.

20:17 Jesus quotes Ps. 118:22, which points to a complete reversal of accepted values.

cornerstone. Lit. "the head of the corner." It may be a large stone in the foundation, laid at the corner and determining the position of two walls. Or it may be the stone at the top of the corner binding the building together.

18 [e]Everyone who falls on that stone will be
broken to pieces, and when it falls [f]on anyone, [g]it will crush him."

Paying Taxes to Caesar

19 [h]The scribes and the chief priests
sought to lay hands on him at that very
hour, for they perceived that he had told
this parable against them, but they feared
the people. 20 [i]So they [j]watched him and
sent spies, who [k]pretended to be sincere,
that they might [l]catch him in something he
said, so as to deliver him up to the authority and jurisdiction of [m]the governor. 21 So
they asked him, "Teacher, [n]we know that
you speak and teach rightly, and [o]show no
partiality,[1] but truly teach [p]the way of God.
22 Is it lawful for us to give [q]tribute to
[r]Caesar, or not?" 23 But he perceived their
[s]craftiness, and said to them, 24 "Show me
[t]a denarius.[2] Whose likeness and inscription does it have?" They said, "Caesar's."
25 He said to them, "Then [u]render to Caesar
the things that are Caesar's, and to God the
things that are God's." 26 And they were not
able in the presence of the people [v]to catch
him in what he said, but marveling at his
answer they became silent.

Sadducees Ask About the Resurrection

27 There came to him [w]some Sadducees,
[x]those who deny that there is a resurrection, 28 and they asked him a question, saying, "Teacher, Moses wrote for us [y]that if a
man's brother dies, having a wife but no
children, the man[3] must take the widow
and raise up offspring for his brother. 29 Now
there were seven brothers. The first took a
wife, and died without children. 30 And the
second 31 and the third took her, and likewise all seven left no children and died.
32 Afterward the woman also died. 33 In the
resurrection, therefore, whose wife will the
woman be? For the seven had her as wife."

34 And Jesus said to them, [z]"The sons of
this age [a]marry and [a]are given in marriage,
35 but those who are [b]considered worthy to
attain to [c]that age and to the resurrection
from the dead [d]neither marry [d]nor are
given in marriage, 36 for [e]they cannot die
anymore, because they are [f]equal to angels
and [g]are [h]sons of God, being [i]sons[4] of the
resurrection. 37 But that the dead are raised,
[j]even Moses showed, in [k]the passage about
the bush, where he calls [l]the Lord the God
of Abraham and the God of Isaac and the
God of Jacob. 38 Now he is not God of the
dead, but of the living, for all [m]live to him."
39 Then some of the scribes [n]answered,
"Teacher, you have spoken well." 40 For [o]they
no longer dared to ask him any question.

Whose Son Is the Christ?

41 [p]But he said to them, "How can they
say that [q]the Christ is [q]David's son? 42 For
David himself says in the Book of Psalms,

18 [e]Isai. 8:14, 15; Rom. 9:32, 33; 1 Pet. 2:8 [f]Dan. 2:34, 35, 44, 45 [g]Amos 9:9 19 [h]ch. 19:47, 48 20 [i]For ver. 20-38, see Matt. 22:15-32; Mark 12:13-27 [j]ch. 14:1; Mark 3:2 [k][1 Kin. 14:6] [l]ver. 26; ch. 11:54 [m]Matt. 27:2, 11; 28:14; See Acts 23:24 21 [n][John 2:2] [o]See Acts 10:34 [p]Acts 18:25, 26; [Acts 13:10] 22 [q]Matt. 17:25 [r]ch. 2:1; 3:1 23 [s]1 Cor. 3:19; 2 Cor. 4:2; 11:3; Eph. 4:14; [2 Cor. 12:16] 24 [t]See Matt. 18:28 25 [u]Rom. 13:7 26 [v]ver. 20 27 [w]Matt. 3:7; 16:1; 22:34; Acts 4:1; 5:17; 23:6 [x]Acts 23:8; [Acts 4:2] 28 [y][Deut. 25:5]

34 [z]ch. 16:8; See ch. 10:6 [a]ch. 17:27; Matt. 24:38; [ver. 35] 35 [b]Acts 5:41; 2 Thess. 1:5, 11; [ch. 21:36]; See Matt. 22:8 [c][ch. 18:30]; See Mark 10:30 [d][ver. 34] 36 [e]1 Cor. 15:54, 55; Rev. 21:4 [f][Heb. 2:7, 9] [g][Gen. 1:26; Ps. 82:6] [h][Rom. 8:19, 23; 1 Cor. 15:52] [i]See ch. 10:6 37 [j]ver. 28 [k]Ex. 3:1–4:17 [l]Acts 7:32; Cited from Ex. 3:15; [Ex. 3:6] 38 [m]Rom. 6:11; 14:7, 8; 2 Cor. 5:15; Gal. 2:19; 1 Thess. 5:10; 1 Pet. 4:2; [Heb. 9:14] 39 [n]Mark 12:28; [Matt. 22:34] 40 [o]Matt. 22:46; Mark 12:34 41 [p]For ver. 41-44, see Matt. 22:41-45; Mark 12:35-37 [q]See Matt. 1:1, 17

1 Greek *and do not receive a face* 2 A *denarius* was a day's wage for a laborer 3 Greek *his brother* 4 Greek *huioi*; see preface

20:19 The religious teachers were hostile to Jesus but could find no legal way of harming him.

20:20 the governor. Clearly the "spies" hoped Jesus would say something that would make the Romans arrest Him.

20:21 The flattering approach was doubtless meant to put Jesus off guard.

20:22 Is it lawful. This means "Is it in accordance with God's law?" (it was required by Roman law). From the point of view of the questioners the answer had to put Jesus at odds with either the Romans or the Jews, who resented the taxes.

20:24 a denarius. Jesus asked for the silver coin that was the proper coinage for paying the tax, roughly equivalent to a day's wage (15:8 note). It bore an image of the emperor with his titles of honor. There was only one answer to Jesus' question, and it opened the way for His unexpected reply. Jesus could not be accused of disloyalty to either the Jews or the Romans. He made it clear that there are duties owed to God, but also duties to the state.

20:27 Sadducees. Luke mentions the Sadducees only here. None of their writings survive, so we know them only as their opponents saw them. They were conservative and aristocratic, and counted the high priests among their ranks. They rejected the oral tradition of the Pharisees and found no basis for a doctrine of resurrection in the Old Testament.

20:28–33 When a Jew died childless his brother was required to marry the widow, and the first son would become the heir of the deceased (Deut. 25:5–10). The Sadducees clearly thought that their story made nonsense of the doctrine of resurrection.

20:34–36 The Sadducees assumed that if there were an afterlife it would be something like a repetition of this life. Jesus denies this. Marriage is an essential part of this life but not of the next; therefore, their question was invalid.

20:36 equal to angels. At the Resurrection there will be a change in nature, and believers will have resurrection bodies like that of Christ (1 Cor. 15:35–58 and notes). Jesus' point is not that human beings will be exactly like angels, but that the mode of existence of angels, and in particular their immortality, provides a clue to the post-resurrection existence of believers, who will also be immortal (1 Cor. 15:42, 52–55). Marriage and procreation will no longer be necessary or appropriate to immortal bodies. See "Resurrection and Glorification" at 1 Cor. 15:21.

20:37 the passage about the bush. Before the addition of chapter and verse divisions, passages in Scripture were referred to by their content. Jesus draws an interesting proof that people live after this life from a well-known part of Scripture (Mark 12:26 note).

20:41 How can they say. Earlier generations were regarded as greater and wiser than the present one, and this opened the way for Jesus to

[r]"'The Lord said to my Lord,
Sit at my right hand,
43 until I make your enemies [s]your
footstool.'

44 David thus calls him Lord, so [t]how is he
his son?"

Beware of the Scribes

45 [u]And in the hearing of all the people he
said to his disciples, 46 "Beware of the
scribes, who like to walk around in long
robes, and love greetings in the marketplaces and the best seats in the synagogues
and [v]the places of honor at feasts, 47 [w]who
devour widows' houses and [x]for a pretense
make long prayers. They will receive the
greater condemnation."

The Widow's Offering

21 [y]Jesus[1] looked up and saw the rich
[z]putting their gifts into [a]the offering
box, 2 and he saw a poor widow put in two
[b]small copper coins.[2] 3 And he said, "Truly,
I tell you, [c]this poor widow has put in more
than all of them. 4 For they all contributed
out of their abundance, but she out of her
[d]poverty put in all [e]she had to live on."

Jesus Foretells Destruction of the Temple

5 [f]And while some were speaking of the
temple, how it was adorned with noble
stones and offerings, he said, 6 "As for these
things that you see, [g]the days will come
when there will not be left here one stone
upon another that will not be thrown
down." 7 And they asked him, "Teacher,
[h]when will these things be, and what will
be the sign when these things are about to
take place?" 8 And he said, [i]"See that you
are not led astray. For [j]many will come in
my name, saying, [k]'I am he!' and, [l]'The
time is at hand!' Do not go after them.
9 And when you hear of wars and tumults,
do not be [m]terrified, for these things [n]must
first take place, but the end will not be at
once."

Nation Will Rise Against Nation

10 Then he said to them, [o]"Nation will
rise against nation, and [p]kingdom against
kingdom. 11 There will be great [q]earth-
quakes, and in various places [r]famines and
pestilences. And there will be [s]terrors and
great [t]signs from heaven. 12 But before all
this [u]they will lay their hands on you and
persecute you, delivering you up to [v]the
synagogues and [w]prisons, and you [x]will
be brought before [y]kings and [z]governors
for my name's sake. 13 [a]This will be your
opportunity to bear witness. 14 Settle it therefore in your minds [b]not to meditate beforehand how to answer, 15 for [c]I will give you a
mouth and [d]wisdom, which none of your
adversaries will be able to withstand or
[e]contradict. 16 You will be delivered up
[f]even by parents and brothers[3] and relatives and friends, and some of you they will
put to death. 17 [g]You will be hated by all for
my name's sake. 18 But [h]not a hair of your
head will perish. 19 By your [i]endurance you
will gain your lives.

Jesus Foretells Destruction of Jerusalem

20 "But [j]when you see Jerusalem surrounded by armies, then know that [k]its
desolation has come near. 21 Then let those

42 [r]Acts 2:34, 35; Heb. 1:13; Cited from Ps. 110:1; [1 Cor. 15:25; Heb. 10:13] **43** [s][Acts 7:49] **44** [t][Rom. 1:3, 4] **45** [u]For ver. 45, 46, see Matt. 23:1, 2, 5-7; Mark 12:38, 39; [ch. 11:43] **46** [v]ch. 14:7, 8 **47** [w][ch. 11:39; 16:14] [x][Matt. 6:5, 7]
Chapter 21
1 [y]For ver. 1-4, see Mark 12:41-44 [z]2 Kin. 12:9 [a]Matt. 27:6; John 8:20 **2** [b]ch. 12:59 **3** [c][2 Cor. 8:2, 12] **4** [d]Phil. 4:11 [e]ch. 8:43 **5** [f]For ver. 5-36, see Matt. 24:1-51; Mark 13:1-37 **6** [g]ch. 19:43, 44; See ch. 17:22 **7** [h][Acts 1:6, 7] **8** [i]Jer. 29:8; Eph. 5:6; Col. 2:8; 2 Thess. 2:3; 1 John 3:7 [j]Jer. 14:14; 1 John 2:18 [k]See John 8:24 [l][Matt. 3:2; 4:17; Mark 1:15]
9 [m]ch. 24:37 [n]Rev. 1:1 **10** [o]2 Chr. 15:6; [Rev. 6:4] [p]Isai. 19:2 **11** [q]Rev. 6:12 [r]Acts 11:28; Rev. 6:8 [s]Isai. 19:17 [t]ch. 11:16; Matt. 16:1; Mark 8:11; [ver. 25; Rev. 12:1, 3; 13:13; 15:1]

12 [u]For ver. 12-17, [Matt. 10:17-22] [v]Acts 22:19; 26:11 [w]Acts 4:3; 5:18; 8:3; 12:4; 16:24; 24:27; 2 Cor. 11:23 [x]See Acts 16:19 [y][Acts 27:24; 2 Tim. 4:16, 17] [z]Acts 17:6; 18:12; 24:1; 25:6 **13** [a][Phil. 1:13, 14, 19] **14** [b]ch. 12:11 **15** [c][Ex. 4:12; Jer. 1:9] [d]Acts 6:10 [e][Acts 4:14] **16** [f][ch. 12:53; Matt. 10:35] **17** [g]John 15:18-21; [ch. 6:22] **18** [h][ver. 16; John 10:28]; See 1 Sam. 14:45 **19** [i]Rom. 5:3; James 1:3; [Matt. 10:22; 24:13]; See Heb. 10:36 **20** [j]See ch. 19:43 [k]Dan. 9:27

1 Greek *He* 2 Greek *two lepta*; a *lepton* was a Jewish bronze or copper coin worth about 1/128 of a *denarius* (which was a day's wage for a laborer) 3 Or *parents and brothers and sisters*

pose a question of His own. By popular definition, David was more important than any of his descendants. How could David call the Messiah his "Lord" (Ps. 110:1)? Jesus is teaching that the Messiah is not simply the Son of David; He is the Son of God and so David's Lord. Jesus' messiahship may be understood in part from His title "Son of David," but there are other aspects as well. He could not be regarded simply as "David" all over again.

20:45–47 See note Mark 12:40.

21:1 the offering box. In the court of the women there were thirteen trumpet-shaped collection boxes with inscriptions showing the use to which donations would be put.

21:2 poor. An unusual word (only here in New Testament) meaning "very poor." Her total livelihood (v. 4) was two copper coins of the lowest value (see text note).

21:5 noble stones. See note Mark 13:2.

21:6 This was fulfilled during the destruction of Jerusalem in A.D. 70.

21:8 I am He. False teachers will claim to be the Christ.

21:9 the end. The end of all things. Some sections of this discourse refer to the destruction of Jerusalem in A.D. 70 and others to Jesus' coming at the end of the age (Mark 13:4 note).

21:12 synagogues. Synagogues were centers for discipline as well as places of worship.

21:13 Trouble for the church also means opportunity to bear witness.

21:16–19 This passage is a strong affirmation of God's overriding control. For some of His followers there will be a martyr's death, for others deliverance. Either way, God is bringing His purposes to pass.

21:20 Jerusalem. This section refers to the destruction of the city, not the end time (v. 9 note).

who are in Judea flee to the mountains,
and let those who are inside the city
depart, and let not those who are out in the
country enter it, 22 for these are [l]days of
[m]vengeance, to fulfill [n]all that is written.
23 [o]Alas for women who are pregnant and
for those who are nursing infants in those
days! For there will be great distress upon
the earth and [p]wrath against this people.
24 They will fall by the edge of the sword
and [q]be led captive among all nations, and
[r]Jerusalem will be trampled underfoot by
the Gentiles, [s]until the times of the
Gentiles are fulfilled.

The Coming of the Son of Man

25 "And [t]there will be signs in sun and
moon [u]and stars, and on the earth [v]distress
of nations in perplexity because of the roaring of the sea and the waves, 26 people fainting with fear and with foreboding of what
is coming on the world. For [w]the powers of
the heavens will be shaken. 27 And then
they will see [x]the Son of Man coming in a
cloud [y]with power and great glory. 28 Now
when these things begin to take place,
straighten up and [z]raise your heads, because [a]your redemption is drawing near."

The Lesson of the Fig Tree

29 And he told them a parable: "Look at
the fig tree, and all the trees. 30 As soon as
they come out in leaf, you see [b]for yourselves and know that the summer is
already near. 31 So also, when you see these
things taking place, you know that the
kingdom of God is near. 32 [c]Truly, I say to

22 [l]Isai. 34:8; 63:4; Hos. 9:7 [m][ch. 18:7, 8] [n]See Matt. 1:22
23 [o]ch. 23:29 [p]1 Thess. 2:16
24 [q][Deut. 28:64] [r]Rev. 11:2; [Ps. 79:1; Isai. 63:3, 18; Dan. 8:13; Zech. 12:3] [s][Dan. 12:7; Rom. 11:25]
25 [t]Isai. 13:10; 24:23; Ezek. 32:7; Joel 2:10, 31; 3:15; Acts 2:20; [Amos 5:20; 8:9; Zeph. 1:15; Rev. 6:12; 8:12] [u]Rev. 6:13; [Isai. 14:12; 34:4] [v][Ps. 65:7]
26 [w][Isai. 34:4]
27 [x]See Dan. 7:13 [y]Matt. 26:64; Mark 9:1; [Matt. 25:31]
28 [z]Job 10:15 [a]Rom. 8:23; Eph. 4:30; [Rom. 13:11]; See ch. 1:68
30 [b]ch. 12:57; [Matt. 16:3]
32 [c]See ch. 9:27
33 [d]Ps. 102:26; Isai. 51:6; 2 Pet. 3:10; [Matt. 5:18; Heb. 12:27] [e]Ps. 119:89; Isai. 40:8; 1 Pet. 1:23, 25
34 [f][Rom. 13:13; 1 Thess. 5:6, 7; 1 Pet. 4:7]

you, this generation will not pass away
until all has taken place. 33 [d]Heaven and
earth will pass away, but [e]my words will
not pass away.

Watch Yourselves

34 "But watch yourselves [f]lest [g]your
hearts be weighed down with dissipation
and drunkenness and [h]cares of this life,
and [i]that day come upon you suddenly
[j]like a trap. 35 For it will come [j]upon all who
dwell on the face of the whole earth. 36 But
[k]stay awake at all times, [l]praying that you
may [m]have strength to escape all these
things that are going to take place, and [n]to
stand before the Son of Man."
37 And [o]every day he was teaching in the
temple, but [p]at night he went out and
lodged on [q]the mount called Olivet. 38 And
early in the morning [o]all the people came
to him in the temple to hear him.

The Plot to Kill Jesus

22 [r]Now the Feast of Unleavened
Bread drew near, which is called
[s]the Passover. 2 And the chief priests and
the scribes [t]were seeking how to put him to
death, for they feared the people.

Judas to Betray Jesus

3 [u]Then [v]Satan entered into [w]Judas called
Iscariot, who was of the number of the

[g]James 5:5 [h][Matt. 13:22] [i]1 Thess. 5:3, 4; [ch. 12:40] [j]Eccles. 9:12; Isai. 24:17 **35** [j][See ver. 34 above] **36** [k]ch. 12:37; Matt. 25:13; 26:41; Mark 14:34-38; Acts 20:31; 1 Cor. 16:13; 1 Thess. 5:6; 1 Pet. 5:8 [l]See ch. 18:1 [m][Hos. 12:4; James 5:16] [n]See Rev. 6:17 **37** [o]See Matt. 26:55 [p]ch. 22:39; Matt. 21:17; Mark 11:19; [John 8:1; 18:2] [q]See Matt. 21:1 **38** [o][See ver. 37 above]
Chapter 22 **1** [r]For ver. 1, 2, see Matt. 26:2-5; Mark 14:1, 2 [s]See John 6:4 **2** [t]John 11:53; See Matt. 21:46 **3** [u]For ver. 3-6, see Matt. 26:14-16; Mark 14:10, 11; [John 13:2, 27, 30] [v][Acts 5:3] [w]ch. 6:16; Matt. 27:3; Acts 1:16; [John 6:71; 12:4]

21:21 flee to the mountains. People would normally flee to a walled city for shelter from an invading army, but Jerusalem is doomed. People must run away from it, not try to enter it.

21:22 vengeance. Not meaningless suffering, but the divine penalty.

21:23 Alas. The siege of Jerusalem in A.D. 70 in fact brought extreme suffering.

21:24 the times of the Gentiles. This may mean the time when the Gentiles will have their triumph over Israel, or the time when the gospel is preached to the Gentiles, or both.

fulfilled. A divine purpose will be worked out (cf. Rom. 11:1–32).

21:25, 26 Attention moves to the Second Coming of Christ (v. 9 note). It will be preceded by signs that will puzzle many.

21:27 coming. Jesus' return will be a coming in splendor to reign.

21:28 redemption. This word means deliverance on payment of a price. Jesus paid the price at Calvary, and He here looks forward to the final fulfillment of what that deliverance means.

21:30 The appearance of leaves on the trees announces that summer is at hand. So the signs tell us that the kingdom is near.

21:32 generation. The Greek word usually means all the people alive at a given time, but it can also mean all of a certain kind of people (e.g., wicked or righteous). The term can also mean "race"; if this is the meaning here it signifies that the Jews will continue to the end.

21:36 stay awake . . . praying. Watchfulness and prayer are Christian duties to the end of time.

to stand before the Son of Man. This signifies salvation at the last day.

21:37, 38 Jesus' last days were spent teaching in Jerusalem, while at night He stayed on the Mount of Olives nearby.

22:1 the Feast . . . Passover. Strictly speaking, Passover and the Feast of Unleavened Bread were different but immediately successive festivals (Num. 28:26, 27), but by New Testament times the names were used interchangeably. The feast commemorated the great deliverance of Israel from Egypt (Ex. 12:17; Mark 14:1 note).

22:2 chief priests. The chief priests had the political power among the Jews and they, not the Pharisees, led the final opposition to Jesus.

22:3–6 Satan took control of Judas (John 13:2), and it was Judas who sought the chief priests, not they who sought him. The "officers" of the temple guard were mostly Levites.

twelve. **4** He went away and conferred with
the chief priests and [x]officers how he might
betray him to them. **5** And they were glad,
and agreed to give him money. **6** So he consented and sought an opportunity to [y]be-
tray him to them in the absence of a crowd.

The Passover with the Disciples

7 [z]Then came [a]the day of Unleavened
Bread, on which the Passover lamb had to
be sacrificed. **8** So Jesus[1] sent Peter and
John, saying, "Go and prepare the Passover
for us, that we may eat it." **9** They said to
him, "Where will you have us prepare it?"
10 He said to them, "Behold, when you have
entered the city, a man carrying a jar of
water will meet you. Follow him into the
house that he enters **11** and tell the master
of the house, [b]'The Teacher says to you,
Where is [c]the guest room, where I may eat
the Passover with my disciples?' **12** And he
will show you [d]a large upper room furnished; prepare it there." **13** And they went
and found it [e]just as he had told them, and
they prepared the Passover.

Institution of the Lord's Supper

14 [f]And when the hour came, he reclined
at table, and the apostles with him. **15** And
he said to them, "I have earnestly desired to
eat this Passover with you before I suffer.
16 For I tell you I will not eat it[2] [g]until it is fulfilled in the kingdom of God." **17** And he
took a cup, and [h]when he had given thanks
he said, "Take this, and divide it among
yourselves. **18** [i]For I tell you that from now
on I will not drink of the fruit of the vine
[g]until the kingdom of God comes." **19** [j]And
he took bread, and [h]when he had given
thanks, he broke it and gave it to them, saying, [k]"This is my body, which is given for
you. Do this in remembrance of me." **20** And
likewise the cup after they had eaten, saying,
[k]"This cup that is poured out for you is [l]the
new [m]covenant in my blood.[3] **21** [n]But behold,
the hand of him who betrays me is [o]with
me on the table. **22** For the Son of Man goes
[p]as it has been determined, but woe to that
man by whom he is betrayed!" **23** And they
began to question one another, which of
them it could be who was going to do this.

Who Is the Greatest?

24 [q]A dispute also arose among them, as
to which of them was to be regarded as the
greatest. **25** [r]And he said to them, "The
kings of the Gentiles [s]exercise lordship
over them, and those in authority over
them are called benefactors. **26** [t]But not so
with you. Rather, let [s]the greatest among
you become as the youngest, and the
leader as one who serves. **27** For who is the
greater, [u]one who reclines at table or one
who serves? Is it not the one who reclines
at table? But [v]I am among you as the one
who serves.

28 "You are those who have stayed with

4 [x]Acts 4:1; 5:24, 26 **6** [y]See Matt. 20:18, 19 **7** [z]For ver. 7-14, see Matt. 26:17-19; Mark 14:12-16 [a]Ex. 12:18; 1 Cor. 5:7 **11** [b]See John 11:28 [c]ch. 2:7 (Gk.) **12** [d][Acts 1:13] **13** [e]ch. 19:32 **14** [f]Matt. 26:20; Mark 14:17 **16** [g][ver. 30; ch. 14:15; Rev. 19:9] **17** [h]See Matt. 15:36 **18** [i]Matt. 26:29; Mark 14:25

[g][See ver. 16 above] **19** [j]For ver. 19, 20, see Matt. 26:26-28; Mark 14:22-24; 1 Cor. 11:23-25 [h][See ver. 17 above] [k]1 Cor. 10:16; [John 6:53] **20** [k][See ver. 19 above] [l]See 2 Cor. 3:6 [m]Ex. 24:8; [Zech. 9:11; Heb. 13:20] **21** [n]For ver. 21-23, see Matt. 26:21-24; Mark 14:18-21; [John 13:21-26] [o][Ps. 41:9; John 13:18]

22 [p]Acts 2:23 **24** [q]ch. 9:46; Mark 9:34 **25** [r]For ver. 25-27, [Matt. 18:1-4; 20:25-28; Mark 10:42-45] [s]1 Pet. 5:3 **26** [t]ch. 9:48; [Matt. 23:11] [s][See ver. 25 above] **27** [u][ch. 12:37] [v]See Matt. 20:28

1 Greek *he* 2 Some manuscripts *never eat it again* 3 Some manuscripts omit, in whole or in part, verses 19b-20 (*which is given . . . in my blood*)

22:7 Passover. According to Ex. 12:5 the animal could be a lamb or a young goat. It would be killed at twilight (Ex. 12:6).

22:8–12 Jesus was ready to die, but at the time of His own choosing. This may be the reason for the way Jesus made arrangements for the feast. None of the disciples knew where they would eat it.

22:10 carrying a jar. A man carrying a pitcher of water would stand out, because pitchers were used by women, and men carried water in skins.

22:14 reclined. The normal posture at such a meal. The diners leaned on their left elbows, facing the table with their feet away from it, and ate with the right hand.

22:15, 16 Jesus had intense desire for fellowship with His disciples at the Passover.

22:17 And he took a cup. At the Passover meal, each person would drink four cups of red wine. The wine was diluted, usually three parts of water to one of wine.

22:18 until the kingdom of God comes. This is an important aspect of the Lord's Supper as a sacrament; it points forward to the Second Coming of Christ (1 Cor. 11:26).

22:19 This is my body. There has been much discussion of these words (Matt. 26:26 note). The verb "is" in this instance does not mean "is identical with," but something more like "represents," "signifies," or perhaps "conveys." One Reformed communion service instructs the worshiper to "feed on Him in thy heart" when the bread is received. See "The Lord's Supper" at 1 Cor. 11:23.

Do this. The one thing Jesus commanded His followers to do as a remembrance of Him referred to His death, underlining the centrality of the Cross for the Christian faith.

22:20 the new covenant. By His death, Jesus offers the sacrifice that ratifies the new covenant of Jer. 31:31.

22:22, 23 Jesus immediately speaks of betrayal by one of those at the table. That Judas was enjoying table fellowship with Jesus made his crime all the worse. Jesus would fulfill prophecy and go as it had been decreed, but this does not lessen the guilt of the one who betrayed Him.

22:24–27 Only Luke has the account of this dispute that showed how far even the Twelve were from understanding what Jesus had come to do.

22:25 benefactors. A number of kings in antiquity took the title "Benefactor," often with little justification. The disciples must serve, as Jesus did.

22:28–30 That the disciples should serve rather than seek greatness does not mean they will go unnoticed. Jesus makes it clear that He knows how they have stood with Him, and that there will be a place for them in the kingdom. They are promised a wonderful future that includes judging the tribes of Israel (v. 30).

me [w]in my trials, 29 and [x]I assign to you, as
my Father assigned to me, a kingdom,
30 [y]that you may eat and drink at my table
in my kingdom and [z]sit on thrones judging
[a]the twelve tribes of Israel.

Jesus Foretells Peter's Denial

31 "Simon, Simon, behold, [b]Satan demanded to have you,[1] [c]that he might sift
you like wheat, 32 but [d]I have prayed for you
that your faith may not fail. And when you
have turned again, [e]strengthen your brothers." 33 Peter[2] said to him, "Lord, I am
ready to go with you both [f]to prison and
[g]to death." 34 [h]Jesus[3] said, "I tell you, Peter,
the rooster will not crow this day, until you
deny three times that you know me."

Scripture Must Be Fulfilled in Jesus

35 And he said to them, [i]"When I sent
you out with no moneybag or knapsack or
sandals, did you lack anything?" They said,
"Nothing." 36 He said to them, "But now let
the one who has a moneybag take it, and
likewise a knapsack. And let the one who
has no sword sell his cloak and buy one.
37 For I tell you that [j]this Scripture must be
fulfilled in me: [k]'And he was numbered
with the transgressors.' For [l]what is written
about me has its fulfillment." 38 And they
said, "Look, Lord, here are two [m]swords."
And he said to them, [n]"It is enough."

Jesus Prays on the Mount of Olives

39 [o]And he came out and went, [p]as was
his custom, to [q]the Mount of Olives, and
the disciples followed him. 40 [r]And when he
came to [s]the place, he said to them, [t]"Pray
that you may not [u]enter into temptation."
41 And he withdrew from them about a
stone's throw, and [v]knelt down and
prayed, 42 saying, [w]"Father, if you are willing, remove [x]this cup from me. [y]Never-
theless, not my will, but yours, be done."
43 And there appeared to him [z]an angel
from heaven, strengthening him. 44 And
[w]being in an agony he prayed more earnestly; and his sweat became like great
drops of blood falling down to the
ground.[4] 45 And when he rose from prayer,
he came to the disciples and found them
sleeping for sorrow, 46 and he said to them,
"Why are you sleeping? Rise and [a]pray that
you may not enter into temptation."

Betrayal and Arrest of Jesus

47 [b]While he was still speaking, there
came a crowd, and the man called [c]Judas,
one of the twelve, was leading them. He
drew near to Jesus to kiss him, 48 but Jesus
said to him, "Judas, would you betray the
Son of Man with a kiss?" 49 And when those
who were around him saw what would follow, they said, "Lord, shall we strike [d]with
the sword?" 50 And one of them struck the
servant[5] of the high priest and cut off his
right ear. 51 But Jesus said, "No more of
this!" And he touched his ear and healed
him. 52 Then Jesus said to the chief priests
and [e]officers of the temple and elders, who
had come out against him, "Have you
come out as against a robber, with swords
and clubs? 53 When [f]I was with you day
after day in the temple, you did not lay

28 [w]Heb. 2:18; 4:15 **29** [x]2 Tim. 2:12; [John 17:18]; See Matt. 25:34; 28:18; Acts 14:22; Rev. 1:6 **30** [y][ver. 16; ch. 13:29; 14:15; Matt. 8:11] [z]See Matt. 19:28 [a]Acts 26:7; James 1:1; Rev. 21:12 **31** [b]Job 1:6-12; 2:1-6; [2 Cor. 2:11; 1 Pet. 5:8]; See 1 Cor. 5:5 [c]Amos 9:9; [John 16:32] **32** [d]John 17:9, 11, 15 [e][Ps. 51:13; John 21:15-17] **33** [f][Acts 12:4] [g][John 21:19] **34** [h][Matt. 26:33-35; Mark 14:29-31; John 13:37, 38] **35** [i]ch. 9:3; 10:4; Matt. 10:9, 10; Mark 6:8 **37** [j][Acts 1:16]; See ch. 13:33; Matt. 1:22 [k]Cited from Isai. 53:12 [l][John 17:4; 19:30] **38** [m][ver. 49] [n][Deut. 3:26; Mark 14:41] **39** [o]Matt. 26:30; Mark 14:26; [John 18:1] [p]ch. 21:37; John 18:2 [q]See Matt. 21:1 **40** [r]For ver. 40-46, see Matt. 26:36-46; Mark 14:32-42 [s]John 18:2

[t]1 Pet. 4:7 [u]Matt. 6:13 **41** [v]See Acts 7:60 **42** [w]Heb. 5:7 [x]See Matt. 20:22 [y]See Matt. 6:10 **43** [z]Matt. 4:11; [Heb. 1:14] **44** [w][See ver. 42 above] **46** [a]ver. 40 **47** [b]For ver. 47-53, see Matt. 26:47-56; Mark 14:43-50; John 18:3-11 [c]ver. 3 **49** [d]ver. 38 **52** [e]See ver. 4 **53** [f][John 8:2]; [ch. 2:46; John 18:20]

1 The Greek word for *you* (twice in this verse) is plural; in verse 32, all four instances are singular 2 Greek *He* 3 Greek *He* 4 Some manuscripts omit verses 43 and 44 5 Greek *bondservant*

22:31 Simon, Simon. The repetition gives solemnity and emphasis. It is a form of intimate, personal address.

demanded to have you. The word "you" is plural. Satan had asked permission to trouble all the disciples. Notice that Satan has no power to act outside the area God allows him.

22:32 you. Here the word "you" is singular. When Peter has come through the trial he is to strengthen others.

22:35, 36 The future will not be as easy for the disciples as the past.

22:36 sword. This is probably not meant literally (cf. vv. 49–51; Matt. 26:51, 52), but is a way of saying that they face a dangerous future. Jesus Himself faces the fulfillment of Is. 53:12 and His followers will surely experience resistance and persecution.

22:38 enough. The disciples take the words about the sword literally, and Jesus' reply means, "Enough of that sort of talk."

22:40 the place. Gethsemane (Mark 14:32), an olive grove (John 18:1).

22:41 Luke's account does not mention Peter, James, and John (who slept while Jesus prayed). Luke's emphasis is on Jesus' prayer, not the disciples' failings. People generally prayed standing (18:11, 13), but at this solemn time Jesus knelt.

22:42 this cup. A symbol of suffering and divine anger (Is. 51:17; Ezek. 23:33).

not my will. As One who had taken upon Himself a complete human nature, it was natural for Jesus to shrink from the horror of the Cross, a horror magnified by His knowledge that in dying He would be forsaken by God and experience the weight of divine anger on sin. Nevertheless, Jesus is determined to follow the will of His Father.

22:43, 44 Luke alone tells of the angel who strengthened Jesus and of the sweat "like great drops of blood."

22:47 kiss. The kiss was a common greeting (1 Thess. 5:26), and to use it in this way was a horrible form of betrayal.

hands on me. But this is [g]your hour, and [h]the power of darkness."

Peter Denies Jesus

54 [i]Then they seized him and led him away, bringing him into the high priest's house, [j]and Peter was following at a distance. 55 [k]And when they had kindled a fire in the middle of [l]the courtyard and sat down together, Peter sat down among them. 56 Then a servant girl, seeing him as he sat in the light and looking closely at him, said, "This man also was with him." 57 But he denied it, saying, "Woman, I do not know him." 58 And a little later someone else saw him and said, "You also are one of them." But Peter said, "Man, I am not." 59 And after an interval of about an hour still another [m]insisted, saying, "Certainly this man also was with him, for he too is a Galilean." 60 But Peter said, "Man, I do not know what you are talking about." And immediately, while he was still speaking, the rooster crowed. 61 And the Lord turned and [n]looked at Peter. And Peter remembered the saying of the Lord, how he had said to him, [o]"Before the rooster crows today, you will [p]deny me three times." 62 And he went out and wept bitterly.

Jesus Is Mocked

63 [q]Now the men who were holding Jesus in custody were mocking him as they beat him. 64 [q]They also blindfolded him and kept asking him, [r]"Prophesy! [r]Who is it that struck you?" 65 And they said many other things against him, [s]blaspheming him.

Jesus Before the Council

66 [t]When day came, [u]the assembly of the elders of the people gathered together, both chief priests and scribes. And they led him away to their [v]council, and they [w]said, 67 [x]"If you are [y]the Christ, tell us." But he said to them, "If I tell you, you will not believe, 68 and if I ask you, you will not answer. 69 But from now on the Son of Man shall be seated [z]at the right hand of the power of God." 70 So they all said, "Are you [a]the Son of God, then?" And he said to them, [b]"You say that I am." 71 Then they said, "What further testimony do we need? We have heard it ourselves from his own lips."

Jesus Before Pilate

23 [c]Then the whole company of them arose and brought him before Pilate. 2 And they began to accuse him, saying, "We found this man [d]misleading our nation and [e]forbidding us to give tribute to [f]Caesar, and saying that he himself is Christ, [g]a king." 3 [h]And Pilate asked him, [i]"Are you the King of the Jews?" And he answered him, [j]"You have said so." 4 Then Pilate said to the chief priests and the

53 [g][Mark 14:35, 41; John 12:27; 16:4] [h]Eph. 6:12; Col. 1:13; [Acts 26:18]
54 [i]Matt. 26:57; Mark 14:53 [j]Matt. 26:58; Mark 14:54; John 18:15
55 [k]For ver. 55-62, see Matt. 26:69-75; Mark 14:66- 72; John 18:16-18, 25-27 [l]See Matt. 26:3
59 [m]Acts 12:15
61 [n]See Mark 10:21 [o]ver. 34 [p][Acts 3:13, 14]
63 [q][Matt. 26:67, 68; Mark 14:65; John 18:22, 23]
64 [q][See ver. 63 above] [r][ch. 7:39]
65 [s]See Matt. 27:39
66 [t]Matt. 27:1; Mark 15:1; John 18:28 [u]Acts 22:5 (Gk.) [v]See Matt. 5:22 [w]For ver. 67-71, [Matt. 26:63-66; Mark 14:61-64; John 18:19-21]
67 [x]John 10:24, 25 [y]See Matt. 1:17
69 [z]Mark 16:19; Acts 7:56; Heb. 1:3 **70** [a]See Matt. 14:33 [b]ch. 23:3; Matt. 27:11; Mark 15:2; [Matt. 26:25]
Chapter 23 **1** [c]Matt. 27:2; Mark 15:1; John 18:28 **2** [d]ver. 14; [Acts 17:6, 7; 24:5] [e][ch. 20:25] [f]ch. 2:1; 3:1 [g]John 18:33, 36, 37; 19:12; [Acts 17:7] **3** [h]Matt. 27:11; Mark 15:2 [i]ver. 37, 38; Matt. 2:2; John 18:39; 19:3 [j]See ch. 22:70

22:53 your hour. A furtive arrest at night suits this effort of the forces of spiritual darkness (cf. Eph. 6:12; Col. 1:13).

22:54 the high priest's house. Jesus was taken first to the high priest who had ordered His arrest. All four Gospels give more space to the trial than to the Crucifixion. They are answering questions about why the Jews condemned Jesus and why the Romans executed Him, and bringing out His identity as the Son of God and King of the Jews.

22:55–62 All four Gospels say that the first challenge came from a servant girl, but the second variously from the same girl (Mark 14:69), a different girl (Matt. 26:71), or a man (Luke 22:58). Servants were around a fire in a courtyard; a challenge from any of them would be taken up by the others and there would have been several voices challenging Peter. The threefold denial fulfills the prediction of v. 34.

22:63–65 Jesus was evidently left to a guard of soldiers who made sport of Him.

22:66–71 No single Gospel gives a complete account of Jesus' trial. It is clear that there were two main stages: the Jews tried Him before the Sanhedrin and obtained a verdict that He was a blasphemer and deserved to die. However, only the Romans had the right to execute Him, and they would not execute a man for blasphemy. There had to be a further trial before the Romans for a violation of Roman law.

22:66 day. Jewish trials had to be held in the daytime. Luke's description of those present points to the Sanhedrin.

22:67–69 Luke does not speak of a formal accusation or of a trial according to proper procedure. The Sanhedrin simply required Jesus to incriminate Himself according to their understanding of the Messiah. This He declines to do, as they would not believe Him. But He does say that a change is coming ("from now on," v. 69) and that He will be in the place of highest honor in heaven.

22:71 Jesus had conceded to the Sanhedrin's charge that He claimed to be the Son of God, and as far as they were concerned He was guilty of blasphemy (cf. Matt. 26:65). Persuading the Romans would require a different charge, but for the Sanhedrin the matter was over. Jesus was guilty in their eyes, and it remained only to secure His execution.

23:1 the whole company. All the members of the Sanhedrin were not needed, but their united front would impress Pilate with their seriousness.

23:2 misleading our nation. A curiously imprecise charge.

forbidding us to give tribute to Caesar. Jesus did the opposite (20:25).

saying that he . . . is Christ, a King. Jesus specifically refused to use the title (22:67, 68). All the charges were false.

23:3 You have said so. In one sense Jesus was King of the Jews, but in the sense in which Pilate understood the title He was not. His answer means something like "So you say" (cf. John 18:33–38). From this reply Pilate concluded that Jesus was no revolutionary (v. 4).

crowds, [k]"I find no guilt in this man." 5 But
they were urgent, saying, "He stirs up the
people, teaching throughout all Judea,
[l]from Galilee even to this place."

Jesus Before Herod

6 When Pilate heard this, he asked
whether the man was a Galilean. 7 And
when he learned that he belonged to
[m]Herod's jurisdiction, he sent him over to
Herod, who was himself in Jerusalem at
that time. 8 When Herod saw Jesus, he was
very glad, [n]for he had long desired to see
him, [o]because he had heard about him,
and he was hoping [p]to see some sign done
by him. 9 So he questioned him at some
length, but he made no answer. 10 The chief
priests and the scribes stood by, vehemently accusing him. 11 And Herod with his soldiers [q]treated him with contempt and
[r]mocked him. Then, [s]arraying him in
splendid clothing, he sent him back to
Pilate. 12 And [t]Herod and Pilate became
friends with each other that very day, for
before this they had been at enmity with
each other.
13 Pilate then called together the chief
priests and [u]the rulers and the people,
14 and said to them, "You brought me this
man [v]as one who was misleading the people. And [w]after examining him before you,
behold, I [x]did not find this man guilty of
any of your charges against him. 15 Neither
did Herod, for [y]he sent him back to us.
Look, nothing deserving death has been
done by him. 16 [z]I will therefore punish and
release him." [1]

Pilate Delivers Jesus to Be Crucified

18 [a]But they all cried out together, [b]"Away
with this man, and release to us Barabbas"— 19 a man who had been thrown into
prison for an insurrection started in the
city and [c]for murder. 20 Pilate addressed
them once more, desiring to release Jesus,
21 but they kept shouting, "Crucify, crucify
him!" 22 A third time he said to them,
"Why, [d]what evil has he done? [e]I have
found in him no guilt deserving death. [f]I
will therefore punish and release him."
23 But they were urgent, demanding with
loud cries that he should be crucified. And
their voices prevailed. 24 So Pilate decided
that their demand should be granted. 25 He
released the man who had been thrown
into prison [g]for insurrection and murder,
for whom they asked, [h]but he delivered
Jesus over to their will.

The Crucifixion

26 [i]And as they led him away, they seized
one Simon of Cyrene, who was coming in
from the country, and laid on him the
cross, to carry it behind Jesus. 27 And there
followed him a great multitude of the people and of women who were [j]mourning
and lamenting for him. 28 But turning to
them Jesus said, "Daughters of Jerusalem,
do not weep for me, but weep for yourselves and for your children. 29 For behold,
[k]the days are coming when they will say,
[l]'Blessed are the barren and the wombs
that never bore and the breasts that never
nursed!' 30 [m]Then they will begin to say to
the mountains, 'Fall on us,' and to the
hills, 'Cover us.' 31 For [n]if they do these
things when [o]the wood is green, what will
happen [o]when it is dry?"

4 [k]ver. 14, 22; John 18:38; 19:4, 6; [Matt. 27:24; 1 Pet. 2:22]
5 [l]ch. 4:14; Matt. 4:12, 23; Mark 1:14; John 1:43; 2:11
7 [m]See ch. 3:1
8 [n]ch. 9:9 [o]Matt. 14:1; Mark 6:14 [p]See Matt. 12:38
11 [q]Mark 9:12; Acts 4:11 [r]ch. 18:32 [s][Matt. 27:28; Mark 15:17]
12 [t]Acts 4:27; [Ps. 2:2]
13 [u]See ch. 24:20
14 [v]ver. 2 [w]Acts 3:13 [x]ver. 4
15 [y]ver. 11
16 [z]ver. 22; John 19:1; [Acts 5:40]
18 [a]For ver. 18-25, see Matt. 27:15-26; Mark 15:6-15; John 18:39, 40; 19:16 [b][Acts 21:36; 22:22]
19 [c]Acts 3:14
22 [d][ver. 41; John 8:46] [e]ver. 14, 15 [f]ver. 16
25 [g]ver. 19 [h]John 19:16
26 [i]Matt. 27:32; Mark 15:21; [John 19:17]
27 [j]ch. 8:52; Matt. 11:17
29 [k]See ch. 17:22 [l]ch. 21:23; Matt. 24:19; Mark 13:17
30 [m]Hos. 10:8; Rev. 6:16; [Isai. 2:19]
31 [n][Prov. 11:31; 1 Pet. 4:17] [o]Ezek. 20:47

1 Here, or after verse 19, some manuscripts add verse 17: *Now he was obliged to release one man to them at the festival*

23:5–7 In the Roman Empire, a trial was usually held in the province where the offense was committed, but it could be transferred to the province from which the accused came. Pilate seized on this to send Jesus to Herod. Only Luke mentions this.

23:9 made no answer. Herod was the only person to whom Jesus refused to speak.

23:11 Herod mocked Jesus, not taking the charge seriously.

23:16 I will . . . release him. Under Roman law a person might be beaten and warned to be more careful in the future. Pilate was evidently hoping that this would placate the Jews and enable him to release One he knew was innocent.

23:17 The custom of releasing a prisoner at Passover is not attested outside the Gospels, but this sort of thing was widely done at this time and there is nothing improbable about it.

23:18 Barabbas. The crowds clamored for Barabbas, a man otherwise unknown. His name means "son of the father," and Luke reports that his crimes were insurrection and murder.

23:26 Simon of Cyrene. It was customary for the condemned to carry the horizontal crossbeam to the site of the crucifixion. Jesus started to carry His cross (John 19:17), but He would have been weakened by the heavy scourging that usually preceded crucifixion (Mark 15:15). The soldiers conscripted a passer-by named Simon from Cyrene in North Africa. His sons apparently were known in the church (Mark 15:21 note).

23:27–31 Only Luke records this incident. There must have been many supporters of Jesus in Jerusalem; only a comparatively small number could crowd around the judgment hall where the opposition was concentrated.

23:28 Daughters of Jerusalem. These were local people, not pilgrims from Galilee. Jesus is concerned for them, not Himself, and turns their attention to the terrible troubles that would come upon the land (21:20–24).

23:31 Evidently a proverbial saying, possibly meaning that if Jesus (who

32 [p]Two others, who were criminals, were
led away to be put to death with him.
33 [q]And when they came to the place that is
called The Skull, there they crucified him,
and the criminals, [p]one on his right and
one on his left. 34 And Jesus said, "Father,
[r]forgive them, [s]for they know not what they
do."[1] And they cast lots [t]to divide his garments. 35 And [u]the people stood by, watching, [v]but [w]the rulers [x]scoffed at him,
saying, [y]"He saved others; [z]let him save
himself, [a]if he is [b]the Christ of God, [c]his
Chosen One!" 36 The soldiers also mocked
him, coming up and [d]offering him sour
wine 37 and saying, [e]"If you are [f]the King of
the Jews, save yourself!" 38 [g]There was also
an inscription over him,[2] "This is [f]the King
of the Jews."

39 [h]One of the criminals who were
hanged [i]railed at him,[3] saying, "Are you
not [j]the Christ? Save yourself and us!"
40 But the other rebuked him, saying, "Do
you not fear God, since you are under the
same sentence of condemnation? 41 And we
indeed justly, for we are receiving the due
reward of our deeds; but this man has
done nothing wrong." 42 And he said,
"Jesus, remember me [k]when you come into
your kingdom." 43 And he said to him,
"Truly, I say to you, today you will be with
me in [l]Paradise."

The Death of Jesus

44 [m]It was now about the sixth hour,[4] and
there was darkness over the whole land
until the ninth hour,[5] 45 while the sun's
light failed. And [n]the curtain of the temple
was torn in two. 46 Then Jesus, [o]calling out
with a loud voice, said, "Father, [p]into your
hands I [q]commit my spirit!" And having
said this [r]he breathed his last. 47 Now
[s]when the centurion saw what had taken
place, [t]he praised God, saying, "Certainly
this man was innocent!" 48 And all the
crowds that had assembled for this spectacle, when they saw what had taken place,
returned home [u]beating their breasts.
49 And all [v]his acquaintances and [w]the
women who had followed him from Galilee
[x]stood at a distance watching these things.

Jesus Is Buried

50 [y]Now there was a man named Joseph,
from the Jewish town of Arimathea. He was
a member of the council, a good and righteous man, 51 who had not consented to
their decision and action; and he [z]was
looking for the kingdom of God. 52 This
man went to Pilate and asked for the body
of Jesus. 53 Then he took it down and
wrapped it in a linen shroud and [a]laid him
in a tomb cut in stone, [b]where no one
had ever yet been laid. 54 It was the day of

32 [p]Matt. 27:38; Mark 15:27; John 19:18; [Matt. 20:21] 33 [q]Matt. 27:33; Mark 15:22; John 19:17 [p][See ver. 32 above] 34 [r]Isai. 53:12; See Matt. 5:44 [s][Mark 10:38]; See Acts 3:17 [t]Ps. 22:18; Matt. 27:35; Mark 15:24; John 19:23 35 [u]Ps. 22:7, 17 [v]Matt. 27:41, 42; Mark 15:31, 32 [w]See ch. 24:20 [x]ch. 16:14 [y][ch. 4:23] [z][Matt. 26:53, 54; John 10:18] [a][ch. 4:3, 9] [b]See ch. 9:20; Matt. 1:17 [c]ch. 9:35; Isai. 42:1; [Matt. 12:18; 1 Pet. 2:4] 36 [d][Ps. 69:21; Matt. 27:48; Mark 15:36; John 19:29] 37 [e]ver. 35 [f]See ver. 3 38 [g]Matt. 27:37; Mark 15:26; John 19:19; [John 19:21, 22] [f][See ver. 37 above] 39 [h][Matt. 27:44; Mark 15:32] [i]See Matt. 27:39 [j]ver. 35, 37

42 [k][Matt. 16:28] 43 [l]2 Cor. 12:4; Rev. 2:7 44 [m]Matt. 27:45; Mark 15:33; [John 19:14] 45 [n]Ex. 26:31-33; 2 Chr. 3:14 46 [o][Matt. 27:50; Mark 15:37; John 19:30] [p]Cited from Ps. 31:5; [Acts 7:59] [q]1 Pet. 4:19 [r][John 10:18] 47 [s]Matt. 27:54; Mark 15:39 [t]See ch. 7:16 48 [u]ch. 18:13 49 [v]Ps. 88:8 [w]ver. 55; John 19:25; See ch. 8:2 [x]Ps. 38:11 50 [y]For ver. 50-56, see Matt. 27:57-61; Mark 15:42-47; John 19:38-42 51 [z]ch. 2:25, 38 53 [a][Isai. 53:9] [b][Mark 11:2]

1 Some manuscripts omit the sentence *And Jesus . . . what they do*
2 Some manuscripts add *in letters of Greek and Latin and Hebrew*
3 Or *blasphemed him* 4 That is, noon 5 That is, 3 P.M.

was innocent) was crucified, what would happen to the Jews (who were guilty)?

23:33 The Skull. From the Latin word *calvaria,* "a skull." All four Gospels say that Jesus was crucified between two criminals; in His death He "was numbered with the transgressors" (Is. 53:12).

23:34 them. Both Jews and Romans.

his garments. The clothing of a crucified person was given to those who carried out the execution. In this way they fulfilled Ps. 22:18.

23:35 The rulers, not the people, were sneering. They speak of "the Christ" and the "Chosen One," although Jesus seems not to have used either title much.

23:42 into your kingdom. This request indicates some measure of trust. The man was confident that Jesus was not about to be annihilated in death but was going to a heavenly kingdom.

23:43 Paradise. A Persian word for "garden," which came to mean the place of the righteous dead (2 Cor. 12:4; Rev. 2:7).

23:44 about the sixth hour. About noon.

darkness. This was a supernatural darkness.

23:45 the curtain. A curtain separating the Most Holy Place from the rest of the temple. Jesus' death opened the way into the presence of God.

23:46 Matthew and Mark stress how terrible Jesus' death was. Luke does not deny this, but records Jesus' words showing that His death was in accordance with the will of the Father.

breathed his last. This is not the usual way of referring to death. None of the Gospels employs standard terminology for Jesus' death.

23:47 innocent. The way He died showed Him to be "innocent." Matthew and Mark have "Son of God"; in this context, the two terms have much the same meaning (Mark 15:39 note).

23:48 beating their breasts. A sign of grief. The crowd had come to be entertained, but Jesus' death disturbed them. Luke does not say what effect the death had on the disciples who witnessed it.

23:50, 51 Joseph of Arimathea is mentioned in all four Gospels as taking the leading role in Jesus' burial. The location of Arimathea is uncertain (Mark 15:43 note). Joseph was a member of the Sanhedrin and must have been absent when the vote to execute Jesus was taken, for "all" agreed to this (Mark 14:64). That he was "looking for the kingdom of God" (v. 51) means that he was a follower of Jesus.

23:53 linen. The linen cloth was a shroud (placed over the linen strips mentioned in John 19:40).

a tomb cut in stone. A rock tomb generally held several bodies (Mark 15:46 note), but this one was empty.

[c]Preparation, and the Sabbath was beginning.[1] 55 [d]The women [e]who had come with
him from Galilee followed and saw the
tomb and how his body was laid. 56 Then
they returned and [f]prepared spices and
ointments.

On the Sabbath they rested [g]according to
the commandment.

The Resurrection

24 [h]But on the first day of the week, at
early dawn, they went to the tomb,
[i]taking the spices they had prepared. 2 And
they found [j]the stone rolled away from the
tomb, 3 but when they went in they did not
find the body of the Lord Jesus. 4 While
they were perplexed about this, behold,
[k]two [l]men stood by them in dazzling
apparel. 5 And as they were [m]frightened and
bowed their faces to the ground, the men
said to them, "Why do you seek the living
among the dead? 6 He is not here, but has
risen. Remember how he told you, [n]while
he was still in Galilee, 7 [n]that the Son of
Man [o]must be delivered into the hands of
sinful men and [p]be crucified and on [q]the
third day rise." 8 And [r]they remembered his
words, 9 and returning from the tomb they
[s]told all these things to the eleven and to
all the rest. 10 Now it was [t]Mary Magdalene
and [u]Joanna and Mary the mother of James
and the other women with them who told
these things to the apostles, 11 but these
words seemed to them an idle tale, and
[v]they did not believe them. 12 But [w]Peter
rose and ran to the tomb; stooping and

54 [c]See Matt. 27:62
55 [d]Matt. 28:1 [e]ver. 49
56 [f]ch. 24:1; Mark 16:1; [John 19:39] [g]Ex. 20:10; Deut. 5:14
Chapter 24
1 [h]For ver. 1-10, see Matt. 28:1-8; Mark 16:1-8; John 20:1 [i]ch. 23:56
2 [j]Matt. 27:60; Mark 15:46; [John ch. 11]
4 [k]John 20:12 [l][Acts 1:10; 10:30]
5 [m]ver. 37
6 [n]ch. 9:22, 44; Matt. 17:22, 23; Mark 9:30, 31; [ver. 44]

7 [n][See ver. 6 above] [o]See ch. 13:33 [p]See Matt. 20:19 [q]See ch. 9:22 **8** [r]John 2:22; 12:1 **9** [s][John 20:18] **10** [t]Matt. 27:56; Mark 15:40, 41 [u]ch. 8:3 **11** [v]Mark 16:11; See Mark 16:16 **12** [w]John 20:3-6

1 Greek *was dawning*

The Resurrection of Jesus

Jesus' resurrection was a divine act involving all three Persons of the Godhead (John 10:17, 18; Acts 13:30–35; Rom. 1:4). It was not just a revival of the broken physical body that was taken down from the cross and buried. It was a transformation of Jesus' humanity that enabled Him to appear, vanish, and move unseen from one location to another (Luke 24:31, 36). It was the creative renewing of His body, to become the body that is now fully glorified and deathless (Phil. 3:21; Heb. 7:16, 24). The Son of God in heaven lives in and through His body, and will do so forever. In 1 Cor. 15:50–54, Paul envisages that Christians who are alive on earth at the moment of Christ's return will undergo a similar transformation. Those who have died in Christ before His return will likewise be transformed never to die again.

Christianity rests on the certainty of Jesus' resurrection as an occurrence in history. The Gospels have it as their goal, with the empty tomb and resurrection appearances, and Acts insists on it (Acts 1:3; 2:24–35; 3:15; 4:10; 5:30–32; 13:33–37). Paul regarded the Resurrection as indisputable proof that the message about Jesus as Judge and Savior is true (Acts 17:31; 1 Cor. 15:1–11, 20).

Jesus' resurrection demonstrated His victory over death (Acts 2:24; 1 Cor. 15:54–57), vindicated Him as righteous (John 16:10) and indicated His divine identity (Rom. 1:4). It led on to His ascension, and His present heavenly reign. It guarantees the believer's present forgiveness and justification (Rom. 4:25; 1 Cor. 15:17), and it is the hope of eternal life in Christ for the believer (John 11:25, 26; Rom. 6; Eph. 1:18–2:10; Col. 2:9–15; 3:1–4).

23:54 Preparation. Friday, the day on which people prepared for the Sabbath (John 19:14 note).

23:55, 56 There was not time on Friday to do all that Jesus' followers would have liked for His burial. The women took note of where the body was laid, evidently to know where to come when the Sabbath was over to complete the burial. Joseph and Nicodemus placed a considerable quantity of myrrh and aloes with the body as they laid it in the tomb (John 19:38, 39), but the women wanted to make their own contribution.

24:1–53 Each Gospel deals with the Resurrection in its own way, though none describes how it happened. Some things are clear in all four: the empty tomb, the slowness of the disciples to believe that the Resurrection had happened, and the prominence of women in the first appearances. But each Gospel also has something that does not appear in the others. Luke includes the account of the walk to Emmaus and related events.

24:1 the first day of the week. This began at sunset on Saturday. The women would have had the hours of darkness to complete their preparations before setting out for the tomb at daybreak.

24:2 See theological note "The Resurrection of Jesus."

24:2, 3 A stone tomb would be closed by rolling a stone in front of the opening (Mark 15:46 note). Matthew notes that a seal was placed on the stone (Matt. 27:66).

24:9 all the rest. This indefinite expression shows that there was a large band of Jesus' followers in Jerusalem at this time. Many would have been Galileans in Jerusalem for the Passover.

24:10 Mary Magdalene was the first to see the risen Lord (Mark 16:9; John 20:10–18). She is mentioned in all four Gospels in connection with the Crucifixion and the Resurrection, but otherwise we hear of her only in 8:2.

24:11 they did not believe them. In general the testimony of women was not highly regarded by first-century Jews.

looking in, he saw [x]the linen cloths by
themselves; and he went home marveling
at what had happened.

On the Road to Emmaus

13 That very day [y]two of them were going
to a village named Emmaus, about seven
miles[1] from Jerusalem, 14 and they were
talking with each other about all these
things that had happened. 15 While they
were talking and discussing together, Jesus
himself drew near and went with them.
16 [z]But their eyes were kept from recognizing him. 17 And he said to them, "What is
this conversation that you are holding with
each other as you walk?" And they stood
still, looking sad. 18 Then one of them,
named Cleopas, answered him, "Are you
the only visitor to Jerusalem who does not
know the things that have happened there
in these days?" 19 And he said to them,
"What things?" And they said to him,
"Concerning Jesus of Nazareth, a man who
was [a]a prophet [b]mighty in deed and word
before God and all the people, 20 and [c]how
our chief priests and [d]rulers delivered him
up to be condemned to death, and crucified him. 21 But we had hoped that he was
[e]the one to redeem Israel. Yes, and besides
all this, it is now [f]the third day since these
things happened. 22 Moreover, some women
of our company amazed us. [g]They were at
the tomb early in the morning, 23 and
[h]when they did not find his body, they
came back saying that [i]they had even seen
a vision of angels, who said that he was
alive. 24 [j]Some of those who were with us
went to the tomb and found it just as the
women had said, but him they did not
see." 25 And he said to them, "O foolish
ones, and slow of heart to believe all that
the prophets have spoken! 26 [k]Was it not
necessary that [l]the Christ should suffer
these things and enter into [m]his glory?"
27 And [n]beginning with [o]Moses and [p]all the
Prophets, he interpreted to them in all the
Scriptures the things concerning himself.
28 So they drew near to the village to
which they were going. [q]He acted as if he
were going farther, 29 but they urged him
strongly, saying, "Stay with us, for it is
toward evening and [r]the day is now far
spent." So he went in to stay with them.
30 When he was at table with them, he took
the bread and [s]blessed and broke it and
gave it to them. 31 [t]And their eyes were
opened, and they recognized him. And [u]he
vanished from their sight. 32 They said to
each other, [v]"Did not our hearts burn within us while he talked to us on the road,
while he [w]opened to us the Scriptures?"
33 And they rose that same hour and
returned to Jerusalem. And they [x]found the
eleven and [y]those who were with them
gathered together, 34 saying, "The Lord has
risen indeed, and [z]has appeared to Simon!"
35 Then they told what had happened on
the road, and [a]how he was known to them
in [b]the breaking of the bread.

Jesus Appears to His Disciples

36 As they were talking about these things,
[c]Jesus himself stood among them, and said
to them, "Peace to you!" 37 But they were
[d]startled and [e]frightened and [f]thought they
saw a spirit. 38 And he said to them, "Why
are you troubled, and why do doubts arise
in your hearts? 39 See my hands and my feet,
that it is I myself. [g]Touch me, and see. For
a spirit does not have flesh and bones as
you see that I have." 40 And when he had
said this, [h]he showed them his hands and
his feet. 41 And while they still disbelieved
[i]for joy and were marveling, [j]he said to
them, "Have you anything here to eat?"

12 [x]John 19:40 13 [y]Mark 16:12 16 [z]John 20:14; 21:4; [ver. 31; ch. 9:45; 18:34] 19 [a]See Matt. 21:11 [b]Acts 2:22; [Acts 7:22] 20 [c]Acts 2:23; 5:30; 13:27, 28; 1 Thess. 2:15 [d]ch. 23:13, 35; John 3:1; 7:26, 48; 12:42; Acts 3:17; 4:5, 8; 13:27; [1 Cor. 2:8] 21 [e]See ch. 1:68; 1 Pet. 1:18 [f]ver. 7 22 [g]ver. 1 23 [h]ver. 3 [i]ver. 4, 5, 9 24 [j]ver. 12; John 20:3 26 [k]ver. 7, 44, 46; Heb. 2:10; 12:2; 1 Pet. 1:11; See Acts 3:18 [l]See Matt. 1:17 [m]See ch. 9:26

27 [n]Acts 8:35 [o]Gen. 3:15; 12:3; 22:18; Num. 21:9; 24:17; [John 1:45; 5:46] [p]2 Sam. 7:12-16; Isai. 7:14; 9:6; 50:6; 52:13–53:12; 61:1; Jer. 23:5, 6; Dan. 7:13, 14; 9:24-27; Mic. 5:2; Zech. 6:12; 9:9; 12:10; 13:7; [Acts 13:27] 28 [q][Mark 6:48] 29 [r]ch. 9:12 (Gk.) 30 [s]See Matt. 14:19 31 [t][ver. 16] [u][ch. 4:30] 32 [v]Ps. 39:3 [w]ver. 45 33 [x]Acts 17:3; Mark 16:13 [y][Acts 1:14]

34 [z]1 Cor. 15:5 35 [a]ver. 30, 31 [b]See Acts 2:42 36 [c]Mark 16:14; John 20:19 37 [d]ch. 21:9 [e]ver. 5 [f][Matt. 14:26; Mark 6:49] 39 [g]1 John 1:1; [John 20:27] 40 [h]John 20:20 41 [i]Acts 12:14; [Gen. 45:26] [j]John 21:5

1 Greek *sixty stadia*; a *stadion* was about 607 feet or 185 meters

24:13 Emmaus. The exact site is not known.

24:16 their eyes were kept. This appears to mean that God prevented them from recognizing Jesus at this time.

24:18 Cleopas is not mentioned elsewhere.

24:20 our chief priests and rulers. The disciples place the principal responsibility for Jesus' death on their own people, not the Romans.

24:21 redeem. The word means to set free by paying a price. Clearly, the two were thinking of the political deliverance of their nation.

24:26 suffer . . . enter . . . glory. See vv. 44–47. Peter gives a similar outline of the message of the Old Testament in 1 Pet. 1:10, 11.

24:27 See 24:44 note.

24:30 took the bread . . . gave it to them. These were actions a host would perform at a meal (cf. 22:19).

24:31 opened. This was apparently by divine action (cf. v. 16).

24:34 They had not believed the women (v. 11), but an appearance to Simon Peter was convincing.

24:36 The sudden appearance of Jesus among them, although the doors were locked (John 20:19), indicates that the risen Lord was not limited as ordinary human beings are.

24:39 my hands and my feet. That is, to see the nail marks.

42 They gave him a piece of broiled fish,[1]
43 and he took it and ate before them.
44 Then he said to them, [k]"These are my
words that I spoke to you while I was still
with you, [l]that everything written about
me in the Law of Moses and the Prophets
and the Psalms must be fulfilled." 45 Then
[m]he opened their minds to understand the
Scriptures, 46 and said to them, "Thus [n]it is
written, [o]that the Christ should suffer and
on the third day [p]rise from the dead, 47 and
that [q]repentance and forgiveness of sins
should be proclaimed [r]in his name [s]to all
nations, [t]beginning from Jerusalem. 48 [u]You
are witnesses of these things. 49 And behold,
I am sending [v]the promise of my Father
upon you. But stay in the city until you [w]are
clothed with [x]power [y]from on high."

The Ascension

50 Then [z]he led them out as far as [a]Beth-
any, and lifting up his hands he blessed
them. 51 While he blessed them, [b]he parted
from them and was carried up into heaven.
52 And they [c]worshiped him and [z]returned to
Jerusalem [d]with great joy, 53 and [e]were continually in the temple [f]blessing God.

44 [k]See ver. 6 [l]See ver. 27 45 [m]ver. 32; [Job 33:16; Ps. 119:18; Acts 16:14; 1 John 5:20] 46 [n]See Matt. 26:24 [o]See ver. 7, 26 [p]John 20:9 47 [q]Acts 5:31; See Acts 2:38 [r]See Acts 4:12 [s]ch. 2:32; Gen. 12:3; Ps. 22:27; Isai. 2:2; 49:6; Hos. 2:23; Mal. 1:11; Matt. 28:19 [t]Gal. 3:8; Acts 10:37

48 [u]Acts 1:8, 22; 2:32; 3:15; 4:33; 5:32; 10:39, 41; 13:31; 1 Pet. 5:1; [John 15:27; 1 Cor. 15:15] 49 [v]John 14:26; Acts 1:4; [Acts 2:33; Eph. 1:13]; See Acts 2:16, 17 [w]Job 29:14; Ps. 132:9 [x]Acts 1:8 [y]ch. 1:78; Isai. 32:15 50 [z]Acts 1:12 [a]Matt. 21:17; John 11:18 51 [b]See Mark 16:19 52 [c]Matt. 28:9 [z][See ver. 50 above] [d]See John 16:22 53 [e]Acts 2:46; 3:1; 5:21, 42 [f]ch. 1:64; 2:28

1 Some manuscripts add *and some honeycomb*

The Ascension of Jesus

Jesus' ascension was His Father's act of withdrawing Him from His disciples' gaze upward (a sign of exaltation) into a cloud (a sign of God's presence, Acts 1:9–11). This act was not a form of space travel, but the next step following the Resurrection of Jesus' return from death to the height of glory. Jesus foretold the Ascension (John 6:62; 14:2, 12; 16:5, 10, 17, 28; 17:5; 20:17), and Luke described it (Luke 24:50–53; Acts 1:6–11). Paul celebrates it and affirms Christ's consequent lordship (Eph. 1:20; 4:8–10; Phil. 2:9–11; 1 Tim. 3:16), and Hebrews applies this truth for encouragement of the fainthearted (Heb. 1:3; 4:14; 9:24). Jesus Christ is Lord of the universe, a source of enormous encouragement to all believers.

The Ascension was from one standpoint the restoration of the glory that the Son had before the Incarnation, from another the glorifying of human nature in a way that had never happened before, and from a third the start of a reign that had not existed in this form before. The Ascension establishes three facts:

1. Christ's personal ascendancy. Ascension means accession. To sit at the Father's right hand is to occupy the position of ruler on God's behalf (Matt. 28:18; 1 Cor. 15:27; Eph. 1:20–22; 1 Pet. 3:22).

2. Christ's spiritual omnipresence. In the heavenly sanctuary of the heavenly Zion (Heb. 9:24; 12:22–24), Jesus is accessible to all who invoke His name (Heb. 4:14), and powerful to help them, anywhere in the world (Heb. 4:16; 7:25; 13:6–8).

3. Christ's heavenly ministry. The reigning Lord intercedes for His people (Rom. 8:34; Heb. 7:25). Though requesting from the Father is part of what He does (John 14:16), the essence of Christ's intercession is intervention in our interest rather than supplication on our behalf (as if His position were one of sympathy without status or authority). In sovereignty He now lavishes upon us the benefits that His suffering won for us. From His throne He sends the Holy Spirit constantly to enrich His people (John 16:7–14; Acts 2:33) and equip them for service (Eph. 4:8–12).

24:42 broiled fish. The risen Christ ate and drank, proving that He was not merely a visionary appearance.

24:44 everything . . . must be fulfilled. Notice the word "must." It is no accident that Scripture is fulfilled, for it reveals the purposes of God.

the Law of Moses and the Prophets and the Psalms. The threefold division of the Hebrew Bible. Jesus is saying that every part of Scripture bears witness to Him.

24:45 opened their minds. Jesus showed them the way to understand the Bible. Christ's death and resurrection were foretold in Scripture (v. 26 note). In addition, the calling of people to repentance and remission of sin were foretold (v. 47). These are based on Christ's atoning work. See "The Mission of the Church in the World" at John 20:21.

24:48 witnesses. The preachers are not to produce some novel concepts of their own, but to bear witness to what God has done.

24:49 The risen Jesus will send what His Father has promised, the gift of the Holy Spirit (Joel 2:28–32; Acts 2:1–4).

24:50 Luke gives no time indication here, but later he states that the Ascension took place forty days after the Resurrection (Acts 1:3).

Bethany. A village on the Mount of Olives about two miles east of Jerusalem (John 11:18).

24:51 he parted from them. Luke's account of the Ascension is a brief but fitting conclusion to his Gospel, which is an account of "all that Jesus began to do and teach, until the day when he was taken up" (Acts 1:1, 2). Luke provides a more detailed ascension account at the beginning of his second book (Acts 1:9–11). The Ascension marks the end of the work Jesus came to do on earth and the beginning of what He continues to do in and through the church. See theological note "The Ascension of Jesus."

24:52 they worshiped him. Whatever their view of Jesus in earlier days, they now recognized His divinity and worshiped Him. The separation did not bring sadness, but "great joy."

24:53 The Gospel ends as it began, in Jerusalem with the worship of God.

THE GOSPEL ACCORDING TO
John

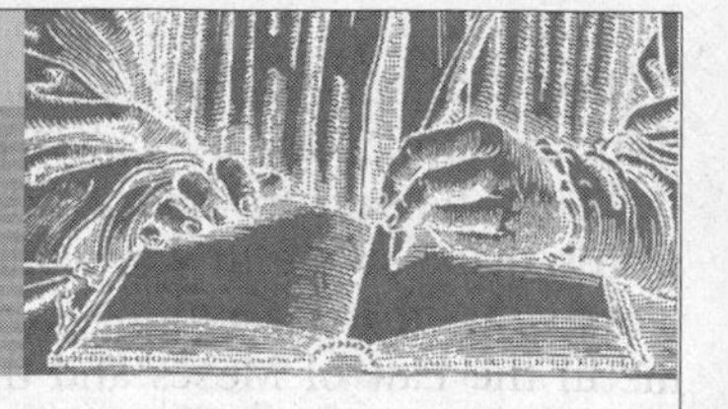

AUTHOR

The author of this Gospel was almost certainly a Jew. He displays an intimate knowledge of Jewish customs, festivals, and beliefs. His detailed geographical knowledge suggests that he was a native of Palestine, and it appears that he was an eyewitness of many of the events recorded in his Gospel (19:35).

Although the work is anonymous, it contains some hints about its authorship. This is the only Gospel that refers to one of the apostles with the expression the disciple "whom Jesus loved" (13:23) rather than by name. This disciple is the one identified as the eyewitness who "is bearing witness about these things, and who has written these things" (21:24). Moreover, any careful reader would notice that John, son of Zebedee, who was one of the most prominent disciples, is not mentioned by name in the Gospel. It is difficult to explain this omission unless one assumes that the Gospel was written by John and that he refrained from identifying himself.

Early church tradition, such as the writings of Irenaeus in the second century, consistently and explicitly attributes this Gospel to the apostle John. Modern doubts about the reliability of that tradition have led many scholars to reject John's authorship of the book, but no other view gives as satisfactory an account of the facts.

DATE AND OCCASION

Early church tradition suggests that John wrote the Gospel toward the end of his life, around A.D. 90. Some scholars of the late nineteenth and early twentieth centuries, having abandoned authorship by John, argued that the Gospel was as late as the middle of the second century. The discoveries of the Rylands papyrus (a manuscript fragment dated to about A.D. 125, containing a few lines from John 18) and of the Dead Sea Scrolls (which improved our understanding of Palestine in the first century) have led most scholars to return to the Gospel's traditional date. Some specialists have gone further and dated it before A.D. 70.

The author himself describes his purpose for writing: "that you may believe that Jesus is the Christ, the Son of God, and that by believing you may have life in his name" (20:31).

INTERPRETIVE DIFFICULTIES

A special challenge to interpreters of John's Gospel is the relation between seeing "signs" and belief. The author places great emphasis on the unique significance of Jesus' miracles because they reveal much about His Person and work (20:30, 31). But some passages seem to suggest that belief based solely upon having personally seen the signs is not a good thing. In 4:48, for instance, Jesus rebukes His hearers, "Unless you see signs and wonders you will not believe." This passage brings to mind the statement of Thomas in 20:25, "Unless I see . . . I will never believe." Therefore, many readers have concluded that an ideal faith has no interest in miracles. The problem with this conclusion is twofold. First, if faith resulting from miracles is not good, why does Jesus perform miracles? Second, why does John link these signs to faith in Christ (20:31)?

To believe in Jesus means not only to acknowledge His ability to perform miracles, but also to accept what those miracles as "signs" reveal about His Person and work. The evangelist indicates that the written record of Jesus' signs is sufficient testimony for those who are not eyewitnesses. This understanding is implied by what Jesus said to Thomas, "Blessed are those who have not seen and yet have believed" (20:29). Paul's formulation gives a similar relation between faith and sight: "we walk by faith, not by sight" (2 Cor. 5:7; cf. Rom. 8:24, 25).

Faith can be produced and encouraged by the signs Jesus performed. But the goal of this faith is to apprehend Jesus in His fullness, not merely as a miracle worker. Jesus is revealed by His "signs" as the eternal Word of God, one in glory with the Father and the Spirit. It is not necessary to be an eyewitness of the signs; the record of them is sufficient to convey their power for eliciting and strengthening faith in Jesus as the Messiah, the Son of God.

CHARACTERISTICS AND THEMES

The teachings of Jesus recorded in John tend to be lengthy discussions of a single topic, in contrast to the pithy, proverb-like sayings usually found in the other three Gospels. The teaching material is often embedded in conversations, as Jesus interacts with individual people or groups in discussion. There are almost no parables in this Gospel.

Jesus' interaction with those who did not receive Him although they were "his own" (1:11) is an important focus of the public ministry (chs. 1–12). Jesus appears often in Jerusalem at the time of the Jewish feasts. These feasts have special importance because of the way Jesus relates His own work to what the feasts signify (7:37–39). Despite this ministry, His nation did not receive Him, a fact that John explains as the result of human sin. Jesus is rejected, not because He is a stranger, but because people love darkness rather than light.

The Gospel of John makes use of sharp contrasts: light and darkness (1:4–9), love and hatred (15:17, 18), from above and from below (8:23), life and death (6:57, 58), truth and falsehood (8:32–47). Other distinctive features are the theme of misunderstanding (2:21; 6:51–58 and notes), the use of twofold or double meanings (3:14; 6:62 and notes), and the role of the "I am" sayings (6:35 note).

John highlights the reality of sin in various ways, but especially by emphasizing our total dependence on God for salvation. Just as our physical birth was not the result of our own effort or will, so our spiritual birth is not due to us, but to God's will and the power of His Spirit (1:12, 13; 3:5–8). Sinful men and women are unable to come to Jesus for salvation unless they are drawn by the Father (6:44). But when they come to Jesus, they have "eternal life," and do not "come into judgment" (5:24); they belong to the Father, and He will not let them die (10:27–29).

One of the most striking distinctives of this Gospel is the Prologue (1:1–18) that presents Jesus as the eternal Logos, or Word, the One who reveals the Father. Christ reveals the Father because He shares in the Father's deity. He is the One who made the universe (1:3). He met the needs of the Israelites in the wilderness, and now He provides spiritual water and bread (4:13, 14; 6:35). In short, He is one with the Father, the "I am" (5:18; 8:58; 10:30–33; cf. Ex. 3:14).

OUTLINE OF JOHN

I. Prologue (1:1–18)

II. Public Ministry (1:19–12:50)

- A. *John the Baptist's Witness (1:19–34)*
- B. *Calling of First Disciples (1:35–51)*
- C. *First Miracle: Changing Water to Wine at Cana (2:1–12)*
- D. *Cleansing the Temple at Jerusalem (2:13–25)*
- E. *Nicodemus (3:1–21)*
- F. *Testimony of John the Baptist (3:22–36)*
- G. *Jesus in Samaria (4:1–42)*
  1. Journey to Sychar (4:1–6)
  2. Samaritan Woman at the Well (4:7–30)
  3. Spiritual Food (4:31–38)
  4. Samaritan Belief (4:39–42)
- H. *Healing Official's Son in Cana of Galilee (4:43–54)*
- I. *Visit to Jerusalem (ch. 5)*
  1. Healing at Pool of Bethesda (5:1–15)
  2. Jesus and the Father (5:16–47)
- J. *The One Sent from the Father (ch. 6)*
  1. Feeding of the Five Thousand (6:1–15)
  2. Jesus Walks on Water (6:16–21)
  3. Discourse and Controversy: Jesus the Bread of Life (6:22–71)
- K. *Jesus Attends the Feast of Tabernacles in Jerusalem (chs. 7; 8)*
  1. Journey to Jerusalem (7:1–13)
  2. Is Jesus the Messiah? (7:14–52)
  3. The Woman Caught in Adultery (7:53–8:11)
  4. Jesus Testifies Concerning Himself (8:12–59)

OUTLINE OF JOHN (Cont.)

- L. *Healing of Man Born Blind (ch. 9)*
- M. *Good Shepherd Discourse (10:1–21)*
- N. *Jesus Attends the Feast of Dedication in Jerusalem (10:22–39)*
- O. *Ministry Across the Jordan (10:40–42)*
- P. *Lazarus Raised from the Dead (11:1–54)*
- Q. *Conclusion of the Public Ministry (11:55–12:50)*
  1. Anointing at Bethany (11:55–12:11)
  2. Triumphal Entry (12:12–19)
  3. Gentiles Come to Jesus (12:20–36)
  4. Unbelief of the Jews (12:37–50)

III. The Passion Week (chs. 13–19)

- A. *Jesus' Private Ministry to the Disciples (chs. 13–17)*
  1. Footwashing; Betrayal Foretold (ch. 13)
  2. Farewell Discourse (chs. 14–16)
  3. Intercessory Prayer (ch. 17)
- B. *Arrest and Trial (ch. 18)*
- C. *Crucifixion, Death, and Burial (ch. 19)*

IV. The Resurrection (ch. 20)

V. Epilogue (ch. 21)

- A. *The Miraculous Catch of Fish (21:1–14)*
- B. *Peter Reinstated (21:15–25)*

The Word Became Flesh

1 [a]In the beginning was [b]the Word, and
[c]the Word was with God, and [d]the
Word was God. **2** He was in the beginning
with God. **3** [e]All things were made through
him, and without him was not any thing
made that was made. **4** [f]In him was life,[1]
and [g]the life was the light of men. **5** [h]The
light shines in the darkness, and the darkness has not overcome it.

6 There was a man [i]sent from God, whose
name was [j]John. **7** He came as [k]a witness, to
bear witness about the light, [l]that all might
believe through him. **8** [m]He was not the
light, but came to bear witness about the
light.

9 [n]The true light, which enlightens everyone, was coming into the world. **10** He was
in the world, and the world was made
through him, yet [o]the world did not know
him. **11** He came to [p]his own,[2] and [q]his own
people[3] [r]did not receive him. **12** But to all
who did receive him, [s]who believed in his
name, [t]he gave the right [u]to become [v]chil-
dren of God, **13** who [w]were born, [x]not of
blood [y]nor of the will of the flesh nor of the
will of man, but of God.

Chapter 1
1 [a]Gen. 1:1; [Col. 1:17; 1 John 1:1; Rev. 1:4, 8, 17; 3:14; 21:6; 22:13] [b]Rev. 19:13; [Heb. 4:12; 1 John 1:1] [c]1 John 1:2; [ch. 17:5] [d]Phil. 2:6 **3** [e]ver. 10; Ps. 33:6; 1 Cor. 8:6; Col. 1:16; Heb. 1:2 **4** [f]ch. 5:26; 11:25; 1 John 1:2; 5:11 [g]ch. 8:12; 9:5; 12:46 **5** [h][ch. 3:19] **6** [i]ver. 33; ch. 3:28; Mal. 3:1 [j]Matt. 3:1; Mark 1:4; Luke 3:2 **7** [k]ch. 3:26; 5:33; 10:41 [l]Acts 19:4 **8** [m]ver. 20 **9** [n]Isai. 49:6; 1 John 2:8 **10** [o][ch. 16:3; 1 John 3:1] **11** [p]Matt. 21:38 [q]ch. 13:1 [r]ch. 5:43; [ch. 3:11, 32] **12** [s]See 1 John 5:13 [t]1 John 5:1 [u]1 John 3:1; [Matt. 5:45] [v][Gal. 3:26]; See ch. 11:52 **13** [w]James 1:18; [ch. 3:3; 1 Pet. 1:3] [x]1 Pet. 1:23 [y]ch. 3:6

[1] Or *was not any thing made. That which has been made was life in him*
[2] Greek *to his own things*; that is, to his own domain, or to his own people
[3] *People* is implied in Greek

1:1–18 This "Prologue" to the Gospel is a preface to the narrative beginning at v. 19.

1:1 the Word. The term "Word" (Greek *logos*) designates God the Son with respect to His deity; "Jesus" and "Christ" refer to His incarnation and saving work. During the first three centuries, doctrines of the Person of Christ focused intensely on His position as the Logos. In Greek philosophy, the Logos was "reason" or "logic" as an abstract force that brought order and harmony to the universe. But in John's writings such qualities of the Logos are gathered in the Person of Christ. In Neo-Platonic philosophy and the Gnostic heresy (second and third centuries A.D.), the Logos was seen as one of many intermediate powers between God and the world. Such notions are far removed from the simplicity of John's Gospel.

In this verse the Word is expressly affirmed to be God. The Word existed already "in the beginning" (a clear reference to the opening words of the Bible), which is a way of denoting the eternity that is unique to God. John states clearly, "the Word was God." Some have observed that the word translated "God" here has no definite article, and argued on this basis that it means "a god" rather than "God." This is a misunderstanding; the article is omitted because of the word order in the Greek sentence (the predicate "God" has been placed first for emphasis). The New Testament never endorses the idea of "a god," an expression that implies polytheism and is in sharp conflict with the consistent monotheism of the Bible. In the New Testament, the Greek word for "God" occurs often without the definite article, depending on the requirements of Greek grammar.

That "the Word was with God," indicates a distinction of Persons within the unity of the Godhead. Father, Son, and Holy Spirit are not successive forms of appearance of one Person, but are eternal Persons present from "the beginning" (v. 2). "With" suggests a relationship of close personal intimacy. See "One and Three: The Trinity" at Is. 44:6.

1:3 All things were made through him. This verse also emphasizes the deity of the Word, since creation belongs to God alone. See also v. 10; Col. 1:16–17; "God the Creator" at Ps. 148:5.

1:4 In him was life. Another affirmation of deity: the Son as well as the Father has "life in himself" (5:26).

1:5 has not overcome it. It is characteristic of the style of this Gospel to emphasize contrasting concepts (see Introduction). The plot of this Gospel could be seen in terms of a struggle between the forces of faith and unbelief.

1:7, 9 all . . . everyone. The universal relevance of the gospel is asserted (v. 7) as well as the enlightening activity of God's common grace (v. 9). God's saving activity is not restricted to any particular people.

1:9 The true light. In this Gospel, "truth" and "true" are often employed to signify what is everlasting or heavenly, as opposed to the merely temporal or earthly. See notes 4:24; 6:32; "Mankind's Guilty Knowledge of God" at Rom. 1:19.

1:11 did not receive him. Jesus' public ministry was one of rejection by "his own people" (see text notes).

1:12 Fallen human beings are not children of God by nature; this is the privilege only of those who have faith, a faith generated in them by the sovereign action of God (v. 13). See "Adoption" at Gal. 4:5.

1:13 who were born. Early Latin versions understood this to describe the virgin birth of Christ. However, the plural verb "were born" shows

[14]And [z]the Word [a]became flesh and
[b]dwelt among us, [c]and we have seen his
glory, glory as of the only Son from the
Father, full of [d]grace and [e]truth. [15]([f]John
bore witness about him, and cried out,
"This was he of whom I said, [g]'He who
comes after me ranks before me, because
he was before me.'") [16]And from [h]his fullness we have all received, [i]grace upon
grace. [17]For [j]the law was given through
Moses; [k]grace and truth came through
Jesus Christ. [18][l]No one has ever seen God;
[m]the only God,[1] who is at the Father's
side,[2] [n]he has made him known.

The Testimony of John the Baptist

[19]And this is the [o]testimony of John,
when the Jews sent priests and Levites
from Jerusalem to ask him, [p]"Who are
you?" [20][q]He confessed, and did not deny,
but confessed, "I am not the Christ." [21]And
they asked him, "What then? [r]Are you
Elijah?" He said, "I am not." "Are you [s]the
Prophet?" And he answered, "No." [22]So
they said to him, "Who are you? We need
to give an answer to those who sent us.
What do you say about yourself?" [23]He
said, "I am [t]the voice of one crying out in
the wilderness, 'Make straight[3] the way of
the Lord,' as the prophet Isaiah said."

[24](Now they had been sent from the
Pharisees.) [25]They asked him, [u]"Then why
are you baptizing, if you are neither the
Christ, nor Elijah, nor the Prophet?" [26]John
answered them, [v]"I baptize with water, but
among you stands one you do not know,
[27]even [w]he who comes after me, the strap
of whose sandal I am not worthy to untie."
[28]These things took place in Bethany across
the Jordan, where John was baptizing.

Behold, the Lamb of God

[29]The next day he saw Jesus coming
toward him, and said, "Behold, [x]the Lamb
of God, who [y]takes away the sin [z]of the
world! [30]This is he of whom I said, [a]'After

14 [z]ver. 1 [a]Rom. 1:3; 8:3; Gal. 4:4; Phil. 2:7, 8; Col. 1:22; 1 Tim. 3:16; Heb. 2:14; 1 John 4:2; 2 John 7; [ch. 6:51] [b]Rev. 7:15; 21:3 [c]See ver. 7 [d][ch. 14:6] [e]ch. 2:11; Luke 9:32; 2 Pet. 1:16, 17; 1 John 1:1; 4:14 **15** [f]See ver. 7 [g]ver. 27, 30; See Matt. 3:11 **16** [h]Eph. 1:23; 3:19; 4:13; Col. 1:19; 2:9 [i][Matt.25:29] **17** [j]ch. 7:19; Ex. 20:1 [k]ver. 14; [Rom. 5:21] **18** [l]ch. 5:37 6:46; Ex. 33:20; Col. 1:15; 1 Tim. 6:16; 1 John 4:12, 20; [ch. 12:45] [m]ver. 14; See ch. 3:16 [n][Matt. 11:27]; See ch. 3:32 **19** [o]ch. 3:26

[p][ch. 8:25] **20** [q]ver. 8; ch. 3:28; Acts 13:25; [Luke 3:15] **21** [r][Matt. 11:14; 16:14] [s]See Deut. 18:15, 18 **23** [t]Cited from Isai. 40:3; See Matt. 3:3 **25** [u]Matt. 3:6; Mark 1:4; Luke 3:3, 7 **26** [v]Matt. 3:11; Mark 1:7, 8; Luke 3:16; Acts 1:5; 13:25 **27** [w]ver. 15, 30 **29** [x]ver. 36; Ex. 12:3; Isai. 53:7; Acts 8:32; 1 Pet. 1:19; [Gen. 22:8; Rev. 5:6] [y]1 John 3:5; [Heb. 10:4, 11] [z][ch. 3:16, 17; 4:42; 12:47; 1 John 2:2; 4:14] **30** [a]ver. 15, 27

[1] Or *the only One, who is God*; some manuscripts *the only Son* [2] Greek *in the bosom of the Father* [3] Or *crying out, 'In the wilderness make straight*

that this verse is about the new birth of Christian believers (cf. 3:3, 5, 7, 8). This new birth takes place by the action of the Spirit giving life to those who were "dead in . . . trespasses and sins" (Eph. 2:1). The new birth, often called "regeneration," is explained more fully in 3:1–21. Paul uses the metaphor of a resurrection from death in sin rather than the image of rebirth (Rom. 6:4–6; Eph. 2:5, 6; Col. 2:13; 3:1; cf. John 5:24). God's work of salvation is wholly sovereign and gracious, but the reality of the human response in believing and receiving is never cancelled. See "Election and Reprobation" at Rom. 9:18.

1:14 the Word became flesh. This is the climactic assertion of the Prologue. To some of John's contemporaries, spirit and the divine were utterly opposed to matter and flesh. To others, the gods were thought to visit the earth disguised as human beings (Acts 14:11). But here a chasm is bridged: the eternal Word of God did not merely appear to be a human being, but actually became flesh. He took to Himself a full and genuine human nature. See theological note "Jesus Christ, God and Man" on next page.

dwelt among us. "Dwelt" means "pitched His tent." This not only indicates the temporary nature of Jesus' earthly existence, but does so in a way that recalls ancient Israel's tabernacle, where God could be found (Ex. 40:34, 35).

we have seen his glory. His "glory" is beheld, even as God's was in the wilderness (Ex. 16:1–10; 33:18–23), in the tabernacle (Ex. 40:34–35), and later in the temple (1 Kin. 8:1–11). There may also be a reference to the Transfiguration, since John witnessed it (Matt. 17:1–5). "Glory" applies supremely to God, who is the Creator and Ruler of the universe, and before whom all knees must bow. The Son has the divine glory by right (17:5). The Reformers declared their faith with the motto, *Soli Deo Gloria* ("To God alone the glory").

the only Son. This phrase translates a single Greek word and explicitly points to the eternal generation of the Son in the Trinity.

full of grace and truth. These words correspond to Old Testament terms describing God's covenant mercy that are often translated "steadfast love and faithfulness" (Gen. 24:27; Ps. 25:10; Prov. 16:6; cf. Ex. 34:6; Ps. 26:3). The Word made flesh fully manifests the gracious covenant-making and covenant-keeping character of God.

1:15 John the Baptist's ministry preceded the public ministry of Jesus (Matt. 3), yet the Word, being eternal, existed before John (cf. 8:58).

1:16 grace. This word, frequent in Paul's epistles, appears in John's writings only in this passage and as a customary greeting in Rev. 1:4; 22:21. It emphasizes that salvation is a gift. The Reformation expressed this with the motto *Sola Gratia* ("by grace alone").

1:17 Moses . . . Jesus Christ. There is both contrast and comparison. Grace and truth truly existed in Moses' day, but they were fully revealed in the coming of Christ.

1:18 No one has ever seen God. It is fundamental that God is invisible and without form (1 Tim. 6:16). Yet Christ reveals God. He brings the invisible and the visible together in a way that has no parallel or analogy.

1:19 testimony of John. John the Baptist's testimony to those who question him reveals that his role was to prepare the world for Christ.

1:21 Are you Elijah. In Matt. 11:14 Jesus, clearly referring to Mal. 4:5, tells the crowd that John is "Elijah who is to come." John comes in the "spirit and power of Elijah" (Luke 1:17), but the Baptist here affirms that he is not Elijah himself.

the Prophet. There were different expectations among first-century Jews concerning the "prophet like me" that Moses announced in Deut. 18:15. Here the priests and Levites want to know whether John considers himself to be this Prophet.

1:23 In quoting Is. 40:3, John applies to Christ what is said of Yahweh in that passage. The same truth appears even more clearly in Mark 1:1–3.

1:29 Behold, the Lamb of God. Compare v. 36. Whether "the Lamb" is the Passover lamb or the Servant lamb of Is. 53:7 cannot be easily determined. There is some evidence that the two figures were combined very early in Christian thought.

who takes away the sin of the world. The "world" designates humanity in its hostility to God, as elsewhere in this Gospel. Although not all persons without exception will be saved, the sacrifice is the only atonement for human sin, and its effectiveness is not limited by time or place (3:16 note).

Jesus Christ, God and Man

Trinity and Incarnation belong together. The doctrine of the Trinity declares that Christ is truly divine; the doctrine of the Incarnation declares that the same Christ is also fully human. Together they proclaim the full reality of the Savior revealed in the New Testament, the Son who came from the Father's side at the Father's will to become the sinner's substitute on the cross (Matt. 20:28; 26:36–46; John 1:29; 3:13–17; Rom. 5:8; 8:32; 2 Cor. 5:19–21; 8:9; Phil. 2:5–8).

The doctrine of the Trinity was defined at the Council of Nicaea (A.D. 325), when the church countered the Arian idea that Jesus was God's first and noblest creature by affirming that He was of the same "substance" or "essence" as the Father. The distinction between Father and Son is within the divine unity, so that the Son is God in the same sense as the Father is. In saying that Son and Father are "of one substance," and that the Son is "begotten, not made" (echoing "only Son," John 1:14, 18; 3:16, 18), the Nicene Creed unequivocally recognized the deity of Jesus Christ.

The church's confession of the doctrine of the Incarnation was expressed at the Council of Chalcedon (A.D. 451), where the church countered both the Nestorian idea that Jesus was two "persons," not one, and the Eutychian idea that Jesus' divinity had swallowed up His humanity. Rejecting both, the Council affirmed that Jesus is one person in two natures (that is, with two sets of capacities for experience, expression, and action). The two natures are united in Him without mixture, confusion, separation, or division, and each nature retains its own attributes. In other words, all that is in us, as well as all that is in God, is and always will be truly and distinguishably present in the one Christ. Thus the Chalcedonian formula strongly affirms the full humanity of the Lord.

The Incarnation, the mysterious miracle at the heart of historic Christianity, is central in the New Testament witness. Jesus came first to the Jews, whose central affirmation of faith is that there is only one God. The apostles were Israelites, yet they and the writers of the New Testament taught that Jesus the Messiah should be worshiped and trusted. This is to say that He is God no less than He is man. It is amazing that this testimony could prevail among them.

John's Gospel opens its eye-witness narratives (John 1:14; 19:35; 21:24) with the declaration that Jesus is the eternal divine Logos, agent of creation and source of life and light (vv. 1–5, 9). Through becoming "flesh," the Logos was revealed as the Son of God and the source of "grace and truth," "the only Son from the Father" (vv. 14, 18). The Gospel is punctuated with "I am" statements that have special significance because "I am" was used as a divine name on account of the Greek translation of Ex. 3:14; when John reveals Jesus as the "I am," the claim to deity is explicit. Examples of this are John 8:28, 58, and the seven declarations of Jesus as (a) the bread of life, giving spiritual food (6:35, 48, 51); (b) the light of the world, banishing darkness (8:12; 9:5); (c) the door for the sheep, giving access to God (10:7, 9); (d) the good shepherd, protecting from peril (10:11, 14); (e) the resurrection and life, overcoming death (11:25); (f) the way, truth, and life, guiding to the Father (14:6); (g) the true vine, nurturing for fruitfulness (15:1, 5). Climactically, Thomas worships Jesus as "My Lord and my God" (20:28). Jesus pronounces His blessing on all who share Thomas's faith (20:29–31).

Paul says about Jesus that "in him the whole fullness of deity dwells bodily" (Col. 2:9; cf. 1:19). Paul hails Jesus the Son as the Father's image and as His agent in creating and upholding everything (Col. 1:15–17). Paul declares Him to be "Lord," to whom one must pray for salvation just as one calls on Yahweh (Joel 2:32; Rom. 10:9–13). Jesus is "God over all" (Rom. 9:5), our "God and Savior" (Titus 2:13). Paul prays to Him personally (2 Cor. 12:8, 9), and looks to Him as a source of divine grace (2 Cor. 13:14). The testimony is explicit: faith in Jesus' deity is basic to Paul's theology and religion.

The writer to the Hebrews, revealing the perfection of Christ's high priesthood, declares the full deity and unique dignity of the Son of God (Heb. 1:3, 6, 8–12). He then celebrates Christ's full humanity (ch. 2). The high priesthood that he describes Christ as exercising depends on the conjunction of an endless, unfailing divine life with a full human experience of temptation and suffering (Heb. 2:14–17; 4:14–5:2; 7:13–28; 12:2, 3). The New Testament forbids worship of angels (Col. 2:18; Rev. 22:8, 9), but commands worship of Jesus. Outspokenly it presents the divine-human Savior as the proper object of faith, hope, and love. A religion without this emphasis cannot be Christian.

me comes a man who ranks before me, because he was before me.' 31 I myself did not know him, but [b]for this purpose I came baptizing with water, that he might be revealed to Israel." 32 And John [c]bore witness: [d]"I saw the Spirit descend from heaven like a dove, and [e]it remained on him. 33 I myself did not know him, but [f]he who sent me to baptize [g]with water said to me, 'He on whom you see the Spirit descend and remain, [h]this is he who baptizes [g]with the Holy Spirit.' 34 And I have seen and have borne witness that this is the Son of God."

Jesus Calls the First Disciples

35 The next day again John was standing with two of his disciples, 36 and he looked at Jesus as he walked by and said, "Behold, [i]the Lamb of God!" 37 The two disciples heard him say this, and they followed Jesus. 38 Jesus turned and saw them following and said to them, [j]"What are you seeking?" And they said to him, [k]"Rabbi" (which means Teacher), "where are you staying?" 39 He said to them, "Come and you will see." So they came and saw where he was staying, and they stayed with him that day, for it was about the tenth hour.[1] 40 [l]One of the two who heard John speak and followed Jesus[2] was Andrew, Simon Peter's brother. 41 He first found his own brother Simon and said to him, "We have found [m]the Messiah" (which means Christ). 42 He brought him to Jesus. Jesus looked at him and said, "So you are Simon the son of [n]John? You shall be called [o]Cephas" (which means [p]Peter[3]).

Jesus Calls Philip and Nathanael

43 [q]The next day Jesus decided [r]to go to Galilee. He found Philip and said to him, "Follow me." 44 Now [s]Philip was from Bethsaida, the city of Andrew and Peter. 45 Philip found [t]Nathanael and said to him, "We have found him of whom [u]Moses in the Law and also the prophets wrote, Jesus [v]of Nazareth, [w]the son of Joseph." 46 Nathanael said to him, [x]"Can anything good come out of Nazareth?" Philip said to him, "Come and see." 47 Jesus saw Nathanael coming toward him and said of him, "Behold, [y]an Israelite indeed, [z]in whom there is no deceit!" 48 Nathanael said to him, "How [a]do you know me?" Jesus answered him, "Before Philip called you, when you were under the fig tree, I saw you." 49 Nathanael answered him, [b]"Rabbi, [c]you are the Son of God! You are the [d]King of Israel!" 50 Jesus answered him, "Because I said to you, 'I saw you under the fig tree,'

31 [b]Luke 1:17, 76, 77 **32** [c]See ver. 7 [d]Matt. 3:16; Mark 1:10; Luke 3:22 [e][Isai. 11:2; Acts 10:38] **33** [f]ver. 6; Luke 3:2 [g][ch. 3:5] [h]Matt. 3:11; Mark 1:8; Luke 3:16; Acts 1:5 **36** [i]See ver. 29 **38** [j]ch. 18:4, 7; 20:15 [k]ver. 49; ch. 3:2, 26; 6:25; [ch. 20:16; Mark 10:51] **40** [l]For ver. 40-42, [Matt. 4:18-22; Mark 1:16-20; Luke 5:2-11] **41** [m]ch. 4:25 **42** [n]ch. 21:15-17 [o]1 Cor. 1:12; 3:22 [p]Matt. 16:18 **43** [q][ver. 35; ch. 2:1] [r][ver. 28] **44** [s]ch. 12:21 **45** [t]ch. 21:2 [u]See Luke 16:16; 24:27 [v]See Matt. 2:23 [w]ch. 6:42; Luke 3:23 **46** [x][ch. 7:41, 52] **47** [y]Ps. 73:1; Rom. 9:4, 6 [z]Ps. 32:2; Zeph. 3:15; [Rev. 14:5]

48 [a]ch. 2:24, 25 **49** [b]See ver. 38 [c][ch. 6:69; 11:27; 20:28] [d]ch. 12:13; Zeph. 3:15; Matt. 27:11, 42; [Zech. 9:9]

1 That is, about 4 P.M. 2 Greek *him* 3 *Cephas* and *Peter* are from the word for *rock* in Aramaic and Greek, respectively

1:31 I myself did not know him. Though John the Baptist may have had previous personal contact with Jesus (cf. Luke 1:39–45), he did not know who Jesus was (the Lamb and Son of God) until the Spirit identified Him (v. 32). See "The Baptism of Jesus" at Mark 1:9.

1:33 who baptizes with the Holy Spirit. The Old Testament anticipated the time of redemption as the time when the Spirit would be poured out on God's people. Paul refers to Jesus as the second Adam who became "a life-giving spirit," (1 Cor. 15:45 note). It is after Jesus returns to heaven that He sends this heavenly Helper to dwell with His people on earth (14:26; 16:7). The baptism of the Holy Spirit occurs with the new birth that constitutes helpless sinners as sons and daughters of God (vv. 12, 13; 1 Cor. 12:13). This baptism also empowers them for Christian service (Luke 24:49; Acts 1:8).

1:34 this is the Son of God. This is John's way of reporting the heavenly voice that accompanied the heaven-sent Spirit, as recorded in Matt. 3:17, "This is my beloved Son, with whom I am well pleased." While "son of God" was used variously by Jews (2 Sam. 7:14; Ps. 2:7) and Gentiles (Mark 15:39 note), the Baptist's witness, that of the last of the prophets of the old order (Matt. 11:11–14) is clear. Jesus is *the* Son of God, the "only Son from of the Father" (v. 14).

1:35–51 Jesus calls His first disciples. Since the apostles had unique authority from Christ to bear witness, the witness on which the church would be established (Eph. 2:20), it was necessary that they be particularly identified as having been selected by Christ Himself (cf. 15:16).

1:37 they followed. Traditionally, the students of a Jewish rabbi walked behind him. Jesus' disciples followed Him physically, but more is in view. Following Jesus takes on deeper levels of meaning throughout this Gospel (13:36–38; cf. 21:15–22).

1:45 of whom Moses . . . the prophets wrote. Philip recognizes that all the Old Testament, both Law and Prophets, anticipated a great redemptive work of God to be accomplished by a special anointed One. The Old Testament anticipation of Christ and His work was affirmed by Christ Himself (Luke 24:25–27, 44–47) and was central in the preaching of the apostles (Acts 2:29–32; 3:18, 21, 24; 7:52, 53; 8:30–35; 26:22, 23; 28:23).

the son of Joseph. This does not imply a denial of the virgin birth, of which Philip may not in any case have been aware; it is simply a reference identifying Jesus by His town and family (Matt. 1:24).

1:46 Can anything good come out of Nazareth. Nathanael apparently expresses contemporary skepticism that a prophet could arise from Galilee (7:52). Nazareth was an insignificant village, not mentioned in the Old Testament or other Jewish literature of the time.

1:47 an Israelite indeed. The phrase is probably meant to call to mind Israel as the people of God, to whom the Messiah was promised. This phrase also alludes to vv. 50, 51, where Nathanael is promised an experience similar to that of the first person named Israel (Gen. 28:12; 32:28), whose deceitful character was transformed by God.

1:49 Rabbi, you are the Son of God. Nathanael's confession may seem like an overreaction to Jesus' supernatural knowledge. But Philip had already indicated to Nathanael that Jesus was the One anticipated by the Law and the Prophets (v. 45). Nathanael comes to Jesus looking for reasons to believe or disbelieve, and he finds Jesus' knowledge convincing.

King of Israel. This is a title for the Messiah, used in shouts of praise at the Triumphal Entry (12:13), similar to the announcement of the wise men (Matt. 2:2) and to the inscription on the cross (19:19).

do you believe? You will see greater things
than these." 51 And he said to him, "Truly,
truly, I say to you, you will see [e]heaven
opened, and [f]the angels of God ascending
and descending on [g]the Son of Man."

The Wedding at Cana

2 On [h]the third day there was a wedding
at [i]Cana in Galilee, and the mother of
Jesus was there. 2 Jesus also was invited to
the wedding with [j]his disciples. 3 When the
wine ran out, the mother of Jesus said to
him, "They have no wine." 4 And Jesus said
to her, [k]"Woman, [l]what does this have to
do with me? [m]My hour has not yet come."
5 His mother said to the servants, "Do
whatever he tells you."
6 Now there were six stone water jars there
[n]for the Jewish rites of purification, each
holding twenty or thirty [o]gallons.[1] 7 Jesus
said to the servants, "Fill the jars with
water." And they filled them up to the brim.
8 And he said to them, "Now draw some out
and take it to the master of the feast." So
they took it. 9 When the master of the feast
tasted [p]the water now become wine, and did
not know where it came from (though the
servants who had drawn the water knew),
the master of the feast called the bridegroom
10 and said to him, "Everyone serves the
good wine first, and when people have
drunk freely, then the poor wine. But you
have kept the good wine until now." 11 This,
the first of his signs, Jesus did at Cana in
Galilee, and manifested [q]his glory. And [r]his
disciples believed in him.
12 After this he went down to Capernaum, with his mother and [s]his brothers[2]
and his disciples, and they stayed there for
a few days.

Jesus Cleanses the Temple

13 [t]The Passover of the Jews was at hand,
and Jesus [u]went up to Jerusalem. 14 [v]In the
temple he found those who were selling
oxen and sheep and pigeons, and the
money-changers sitting there. 15 And making a whip of cords, he drove them all out
of the temple, with the sheep and oxen.
And he poured out the coins of the money-
changers and overturned their tables.
16 And he told those who sold the pigeons,
"Take these things away; do not make [w]my
Father's house a house of trade." 17 His disciples remembered that it was written,
[x]"Zeal for your house will consume me."

51 [e]Ezek. 1:1; Matt. 3:16; Luke 3:21 [f][Gen. 28:12] [g]See Dan. 7:13
Chapter 2
1 [h][ch. 1:29, 35, 43] [i]ch. 4:46; 21:2
2 [j]ch. 1:40-49
4 [k]ch. 19:26 [l]See 2 Sam. 16:10 [m]ch. 7:30; 8:20; 13:1
6 [n]ch. 3:25; [Mark 7:3, 4] [o]2 Chr. 4:5 (Gk.)
9 [p]ch. 4:46
11 [q]See ch. 1:14 [r]ver. 2
12 [s]See Matt. 12:46
13 [t]ch. 11:55; See ch. 6:4 [u]ver. 23; Deut. 16:1-6; Luke 2:41
14 [v]For ver. 14-17, [Matt. 21:12, 13; Mark 11:15-17; Luke 19:45, 46, with Mal. 3:1-3]
16 [w][ch. 14:2; Luke 2:49]
17 [x]Cited from Ps. 69:9

1 Greek *two or three measures* (*metrētas*); a *metrētēs* was about 10 gallons or 35 liters 2 Or *brothers and sisters*. The plural Greek word *adelphoi* (translated "brothers") refers to siblings in a family. In New Testament usage, depending on the context, *adelphoi* may refer either to *brothers* or to *brothers and sisters*

1:50 greater things than these. Jesus' earthly miracles are signs of His redemptive power and work. The miracles are to be appreciated, not merely for themselves, but for the redemptive realities they promise. Greater than such works is the salvation Christ brings (v. 51).

1:51 heaven opened, and the angels of God ascending and descending. This verse alludes to Jacob's vision of a ladder or stairway stretching from earth to heaven (Gen. 28:12). Jesus presents Himself as the reality to which the stairway pointed. Jacob saw in a dream the reunion of heaven and earth; Christ brought it about in reality.

Son of Man. Jesus uses this name often for Himself. It emphasizes His human nature that enabled Him to die for His people. It also refers to the heavenly, messianic figure known from Daniel (Dan. 7:13; see Matt. 8:20 note).

2:1–11 Jesus' first sign: turning water into wine at Cana. This miracle signifies the transformation of the old order (symbolized by the stone water jars used for ceremonial washing, v. 6) into the new (the wine standing for eternal life in God's kingdom) through Jesus Christ (cf. 2 Cor. 5:17). See Is. 25:6–9 for the background image of salvation as a banquet.

2:3 wine. This is the normal term employed in the New Testament for the fermented drink. Paul uses it when he says, "do not get drunk with wine" (Eph. 5:18).

2:4 Woman. This is a respectful way of addressing a woman within that culture and is the way Jesus normally addresses women (4:21; 8:10).

what does this have to do with me. Jesus answers Mary's request, not because she is His mother, but as part of His work as the Messiah. This indicates that Mary's special role as Jesus' mother gives her no authority to intervene in Christ's messianic career—a strong argument against offering prayer to Mary.

My hour. Usually Jesus' "hour" refers to the time of His suffering and death (12:27). Here Jesus is asserting that He and not Mary must determine the timetable of His earthly ministry.

2:11 manifested his glory. The theme of Christ's glory had already been introduced (1:14 note). In the Old Testament, God manifested His glory in a variety of miraculous events, and John's comment indicates that he wants his readers to recognize Jesus' deity.

And his disciples believed in him. See also v. 23 and 20:31, where John's purpose for writing the book is disclosed.

2:12–23 Jesus is the final and full expression of what was only a shadow in the Old Testament (Heb. 10:1). Here He indicates that God is present in Him. The temple in Jerusalem could be destroyed, but not the temple that Jesus would rebuild in three days, His own body that was to be raised from the dead. John's record of the temple cleansing immediately after the miracle at Cana (vv. 1–11 note) offers an important key to the whole of Jesus' ministry. In these events are signaled replacement of the old order (water of ceremonial cleansing, Herod's temple) with the new (the wine of salvation, Is. 25:6–9; the risen Lamb as the new temple, Rev. 21:22).

Matthew, Mark, and Luke report a cleansing of the temple in the week of Jesus' crucifixion. In spite of some similarities, these are best viewed as different incidents (Mark 11:15 note). It is noteworthy that Jesus' statement about destroying the temple, which John alone records (v. 19), probably was the basis for the accusation by the false witnesses (Matt. 26:61; Mark 14:58), and again for the taunting comment of some spectators at the crucifixion (Matt. 27:40; Mark 15:29). The first three Gospels confirm the historical character of John's narrative. An echo of the same thought is found in the accusation against Stephen (Acts 6:14).

2:12 his brothers. See Matt. 12:46.

2:15 a whip of cords. Jesus fulfills the prophecy of Mal. 3:1–4. He comes suddenly to the temple and purifies the sons of Levi, as a demonstration of His zeal for God and for keeping God's ordinances holy.

18 So the Jews said to him, [y]"What sign
do you show us for doing these things?"
19 Jesus answered them, [z]"Destroy this temple, and in three days [a]I will raise it up."
20 The Jews then said, "It has taken forty-six
years to build this temple, and will you
raise it up in three days?" 21 But he was
speaking about [b]the temple of his body.
22 When therefore he was raised from the
dead, [c]his disciples remembered that he had
said this, and they believed [d]the Scripture
and the word that Jesus had spoken.

Jesus Knows What Is in Man

23 Now when he was in Jerusalem at the
Passover Feast, many believed in his name
[e]when they saw the signs that he was
doing. 24 But Jesus [f]on his part did not
entrust himself to them, because [g]he knew
all people 25 and needed no one to bear
witness about man, for [g]he himself knew
what was in man.

You Must Be Born Again

3 Now there was a man of the Pharisees
named [h]Nicodemus, [i]a ruler of the
Jews. 2 This man came to Jesus[1] [j]by night
and said to him, [k]"Rabbi, [l]we know that
you are a teacher come from God, for no
one can do these signs that you do [m]unless
God is with him." 3 Jesus answered him,
"Truly, truly, I say to you, unless one is
[n]born [o]again[2] he cannot [p]see the kingdom
of God." 4 Nicodemus said to him, "How
can a man be born when he is old? Can he
enter a second time into his mother's
womb and be born?" 5 Jesus answered,
"Truly, truly, I say to you, unless one is
born [q]of water and the Spirit, he cannot
enter the kingdom of God. 6 [r]That which is
born of the flesh is [s]flesh, and that which is
born of the Spirit is spirit.[3] 7 [t]Do not marvel
that I said to you, 'You must be born
[u]again.' 8 [v]The wind[4] blows [w]where it wishes, and you hear its sound, but you do not
know where it comes from or where it
goes. So it is with everyone who is born of
the Spirit."
9 Nicodemus said to him, [x]"How can
these things be?" 10 Jesus answered him,
"Are you the teacher of Israel [y]and yet you
do not understand these things? 11 Truly,

18 [y]ch. 4:48; 6:30; [Ex. 4:1, 8; 7:9]; See Matt. 12:38 **19** [z][Matt. 26:61; 27:40; Mark 14:58; 15:29] [a]ch. 10:18 **21** [b][ch. 1:14; 1 Cor. 6:19; Col. 2:9 **22** [c]ch. 12:16; Luke 24:8 [d]ch. 20:9; Ps. 16:10 **23** [e]ch. 11:45 **24** [f][ch. 6:14, 15] [g]ch. 1:48; 5:42; 16:30; [ch. 6:61, 64]; See Matt. 9:4 **25** [g][See ver. 24 above]
Chapter 3
1 [h]ch. 7:50; 19:39 [i]See Luke 24:20 **2** [j][ch. 12:42] [k]See ch. 1:38 [l][ch. 9:29; Matt. 22:16] [m]Acts 10:38; [ch. 5:36; 9:33; Acts 2:22] **3** [n]See ch. 1:13 [o][2 Cor. 5:17; Gal. 6:15; 1 Pet. 1:3, 23] [p]ver. 36
5 [q][Ezek. 36:25-27; Mark 16:16; Acts 2:38; Eph. 5:26; Tit. 3:5; Heb. 10:22] **6** [r]1 Cor. 15:50 [s]ch. 6:63 **7** [t]ch. 5:28 [u]See ver. 3 **8** [v][Eccles. 11:5; Ezek. 37:9] [w]1 Cor. 12:11 **9** [x]ch. 6:52, 60 **10** [y][ch. 9:30]

1 Greek *him* 2 Or *from above*; the Greek is purposely ambiguous and can mean both *again* and *from above*; also verse 7 3 The same Greek word means both *wind* and *spirit* 4 The same Greek word means both *wind* and *spirit*

2:20 forty-six years. The sentence itself does not indicate whether the temple was finished or was still under construction after these years of building. The first century Jewish historian Josephus (*Antiquities*, 15.380) says that the temple was begun in the eighteenth year of Herod the Great (around 19 B.C.) and was not completed until the reign of Herod Agrippa (A.D. 63), indicating that construction was still continuing in Jesus' time.

will you raise it up in three days. The Jews (and the disciples, v. 22) misunderstand Jesus' ambiguous statement. Such initial misunderstanding is common in John's Gospel (e.g., 3:4; 6:52). Those who "receive" Jesus (1:12) are led on to full understanding, but those who reject Him remain at the level of complete misunderstanding (1:5).

2:22 his disciples remembered. During His final instruction of the disciples before His arrest, Jesus promised that what He had taught them would be brought to their remembrance by the Holy Spirit (14:25, 26). The ability to predict events otherwise unknowable is evidence of divine authority. This applies to the prophecies of the Old Testament and to the predictions made by Jesus, especially about His resurrection.

2:23 believed in his name. In biblical times the "name" summed up a person's character, activity, and place in God's purpose. The faith of those mentioned here remained superficial, however, because they came to it only because "they saw the signs" (see Introduction: Interpretive Difficulties). For that reason, Jesus "did not entrust himself to them" (v. 24).

2:24, 25 Although Jesus did not exercise divine omniscience in the days of His flesh (11:34; Mark 13:32), He often displayed supernatural knowledge, important for His redemptive work, that indicated the divine endorsement of His claims and mission (1:48; Matt. 9:4; 17:27; Mark 11:2–4; 14:13–16).

3:1–21 This is the first of many teaching discourses recorded by John. Typically on being asked a question, Jesus answers in a way that steers the discussion into a deeper realm, often through misunderstandings that are corrected for those becoming true disciples. The new understanding reveals Jesus more fully.

3:2 by night. This might betray a fear of being seen, or it might be a sign of deference to Jesus, a rabbi who should not be distracted during the day. Understood symbolically, Nicodemus is a person living in the darkness of this world, who now encounters the light (8:12; cf. 9:4; 11:10; 13:30).

a teacher . . . from God. Nicodemus understands that God attests His messengers through giving them power to perform miracles, but this understanding falls far short of Jesus' true identity.

3:3 born again. See text note. The translation "born from above" accords well with the discussion of "earthly" and "heavenly" things in v. 12, and the discussion of ascending and descending in v. 13. This is the meaning of the Greek adverb in other places in this Gospel (19:11, 23). Nicodemus apparently understood it to mean "a second time." It is possible that both meanings are intended—a new birth that is a birth from above. See theological note "Regeneration: The New Birth" on the next page.

3:5 born of water and the Spirit. Some suggest that the "water" is the release of fluid that accompanies physical birth, but linguistic considerations point to understanding "water" and "Spirit" as referring to a single spiritual birth. Many interpreters understand "water" here as the water of baptism, but such a reference, before Christian baptism was instituted, would have been meaningless to Nicodemus. Others find a reference to John's baptism, but Jesus nowhere makes John's baptism a requirement for salvation. Probably the statement refers to Old Testament passages in which the terms "water" and "Spirit" are linked to express the pouring out of God's Spirit in the end times (Is. 32:15; 44:3; Ezek. 36:25–27). The presence of such rich Old Testament imagery accounts for Jesus' reproof of Nicodemus (v. 10): as a "teacher of Israel," he should have understood.

3:6–8 This passage emphasizes the priority and sovereignty of God in the work of salvation. It does not exclude the reality of human response in repentance and faith.

truly, I say to you, [z]we speak of what we
know, and bear witness to what we have
seen, but [z]you do not receive our testimony. 12 If I have told you earthly things
and you do not believe, how can you
believe if I tell you heavenly things? 13 [a]No
one has [b]ascended into heaven except [c]he
who descended from heaven, the Son of
Man.[1] 14 And [d]as Moses lifted up the serpent in the wilderness, so must the Son of
Man [e]be lifted up, 15 that whoever believes
[f]in him [g]may have eternal life.[2]

11 [z]See ver. 32
13 [a]Prov. 30:4; [Acts 2:34; Eph. 4:9] [b][ch. 7:34] [c]ver. 31; ch. 6:38, 42, 62; 1 Cor. 15:47; [Rom. 10:6]
14 [d]Num. 21:9 [e]ch. 8:28; 12:32, 34
15 [f][ch. 15:4; 16:33; 1 John 5:12, 20] [g]ver. 36

For God So Loved the World

16 "For [h]God so loved [i]the world,[3] [j]that
he gave his only Son, that whoever believes
in him should not [k]perish but have eternal
life. 17 For [l]God did not send his Son into
the world [m]to condemn the world, but
in order that the world might be saved

16 [h]Rom. 5:8; Eph. 2:4; 2 Thess. 2:16; 1 John 3:1; 4:9, 10 [i]See ch. 1:29 [j]Rom. 8:32 [k]ch. 10:28 17 [l]ch. 5:36, 38; 6:29, 57; 7:29; 8:42; 10:36; 11:42; 17:3; 20:21; Rom. 8:3; 1 John 4:9, 10, 14 [m]ch. 5:45; 8:15; 12:4

1 Some manuscripts add *who is in heaven* 2 Some interpreters hold that the quotation ends at verse 15 3 Or *For this is how God loved the world*

Regeneration: The New Birth

Regeneration is the act of God alone, in which He renews the human heart, making it alive when it was dead. In regeneration, God acts at the origin and deepest point of the human person. This means that there is no preparation, no preceding disposition in a sinner that requests or contributes to the new life given by God.

Regeneration is necessary because all descendants of Adam and Eve have inherited their sin and are morally unable to do what is good. Paul wrote to the Ephesians that people are by nature dead in trespasses and sins. In this state, they are without God and without hope in the world. Not in response to their merit, but freely and in love, God speaks the word that raises the dead.

The classic verses of John 3 that use the language of being "born again" or being "born from above" give the outlines of regeneration their sharpest edge. Jesus says that unless you are born again, you cannot see the kingdom of heaven. Without the grace of God, sinners cannot find the door, let alone force their way in. Elsewhere Jesus said, "Without me, you can do nothing"; and in speaking about salvation, "Without God, nothing is possible."

Jesus showed surprise that Nicodemus was puzzled by the demand to be born again. Nicodemus should have understood from the Old Testament that he was a sinner, and in need of new life; and he must have known the prophets, who promised that God would remove their hearts of flesh and replace them with hearts ready to do God's will. God would raise the dead, give sight to the blind, and preach the good news to those who could not save themselves.

Regeneration is the gift of God's grace. It is the immediate, supernatural work of the Holy Spirit wrought in us. Its effect is to quicken us to spiritual life from spiritual death. It changes the disposition of our souls, inclining our hearts to God. The fruit of regeneration is faith. Regeneration precedes faith.

Infants can be born again, although the faith that they exercise cannot be as visible as that of adults. For many Christians, the moment that they were born again is clearly known; but for others, it may not be, especially if they received new life in childhood. We are responsible to know whether we are spiritually alive, not the time and place we were born again.

3:11 I say to you . . . you do not receive our testimony. The first "you" is singular (Nicodemus) and the second "you" is plural (you and those whom you represent).

3:13 who descended from heaven. It could be said that in His divine nature Christ continued to dwell "in heaven" even during His life on earth. The point is that He has authority to speak of heavenly things. Later in the Gospel, Jesus' origin "from heaven" becomes a chief matter of dispute (6:41, 42).

the Son of Man. See note at Matt. 8:20.

3:14 Moses. Num. 21:4–9 records the story of the rebellious Israelites, who murmured and complained. God sent fiery serpents into their midst to punish them. Then God told Moses to put a bronze serpent on a pole, with the promise that whoever looked at it would live.

must . . . be lifted up. Here is a key term in this Gospel (8:28; 12:32, 34) which carries the double meaning of crucifixion and exaltation. Christ's death on the cross, His resurrection, and His glorification together reveal the glory of God. The word "must" points to God's sovereign purpose. The crucifixion was the keystone of God's eternal plan to save His people (Acts 4:27, 28).

3:16 God so loved the world. Some have insisted that God sent Jesus to die for the purpose of bringing salvation to everyone without exception, but only as a possibility. However, Jesus makes clear that the salvation of those whom the Father "gives me," and only those, is not a mere possibility but an absolute certainty; "will come to me" (6:37–40; 10:14–18; 17:9). The point made by "the world" is that Christ's saving work is not limited to one time or place but applies to the elect from all over the world. Those who do not receive the remedy God has provided in Christ will perish. It remains true that anyone who believes will not die (be separated from God) but live in God's presence forever. See "God Is Love: Divine Goodness and Faithfulness" at Ps. 136:1.

3:17 to condemn the world. Jesus elsewhere says that judgment does attend His coming into the world (9:39). His point is not that He will not judge, but that the time is not ready. The world was already under threat

through him. 18 [n]Whoever believes in him is
not condemned, but whoever does not
believe is condemned already, because he
has not [o]believed in the name of the only
Son of God. 19 [p]And this is the judgment:
[q]the light has come into the world, and
[r]people loved the darkness rather than the
light because [s]their deeds were evil. 20 [t]For
everyone who does wicked things hates the
light and does not come to the light, [u]lest
his deeds should be exposed. 21 But whoever [v]does what is true [w]comes to the light,
so that it may be clearly seen that his deeds
have been carried out in God."

John the Baptist Exalts Christ

22 After this Jesus and his disciples went
into the Judean countryside, and he
remained there with them and [x]was baptizing. 23 John also was baptizing at Aenon
near Salim, because water was plentiful
there, and people were coming and being
baptized 24 (for [y]John had not yet been put
in prison).
25 Now a discussion arose between some
of John's disciples and a Jew over [z]purifica-
tion. 26 And they came to John and said to
him, [a]"Rabbi, he who was with you across
the Jordan, [b]to whom you bore witness—
look, he is baptizing, and [c]all are going to
him." 27 John answered, [d]"A person cannot
receive even one thing [e]unless it is given
him [f]from heaven. 28 You yourselves bear
me witness, that I said, [g]'I am not the
Christ, but [h]I have been sent before him.'
29 [i]The one who has the bride is the bridegroom. [j]The friend of the bridegroom, who
stands and hears him, [k]rejoices greatly at
the bridegroom's voice. Therefore this joy
of mine is now complete. 30 [l]He must
increase, but I must decrease."[1]
31 [m]He who comes from above [n]is above
all. He who is of the earth belongs to the
earth and [o]speaks in an earthly way. [p]He
who comes from heaven [n]is above all.
32 [q]He bears witness to what he has seen
and heard, [r]yet no one receives his testimony. 33 Whoever receives his testimony
[s]sets his seal to this, [t]that God is true.
34 For he whom [u]God has sent utters the
words of God, for he gives the Spirit [v]with-
out measure. 35 [w]The Father loves the Son
and [x]has given all things into his hand.
36 [y]Whoever believes in the Son has eternal
life; [z]whoever does not obey the Son shall
not [a]see life, but the wrath of God remains
on him.

Jesus and the Woman of Samaria

4 Now when Jesus learned that the
Pharisees had heard that Jesus was
making and [b]baptizing more disciples than
John 2 (although Jesus himself did not baptize, but only his disciples), 3 he left Judea
and departed [c]again for Galilee. 4 [d]And he

18 [n]ch. 5:24; [Mark 16:16] [o]See 1 John 5:13
19 [p][ch. 9:39] [q]See ch. 1:4, 5, 9 [r][Isai. 30:10; Jer. 5:31] [s]ch. 7:7
20 [t][Job 24:13; Rom. 13:12; Eph. 5:13] [u]Eph. 5:11, 13
21 [v]1 John 1:6 [w]Ps. 139:23, 24
22 [x]ver. 26; ch. 4:1, 2
24 [y][ch. 5:35]; See Matt. 4:12
25 [z]ch. 2:6
26 [a]ver. 2 [b]See ch. 1:7 [c]ch. 12:19
27 [d]1 Cor. 4:7; Heb. 5:4 [e]ch. 6:65; [James 1:17] [f]See Matt. 21:25
28 [g]See ch. 1:20 [h]Mal. 3:1; Mark 1:2; Luke 1:17; Acts 19:4
29 [i]See Matt. 25:1 [j]Judg. 14:20; S. of S. 5:1 [k]Matt. 9:15
30 [l]Matt. 3:11
31 [m]ch. 8:23 [n]Rom. 9:5; Eph. 1:21 [o][1 John 4:5] [p]See ver. 13
32 [q]ver. 11 [r][ver. 19; ch. 1:11; 5:43; 12:37] **33** [s][ch. 6:27; Rom. 15:28; 2 Cor. 1:22; Eph. 1:13; Rev. 7:3-8]
[t][1 John 5:10] **34** [u]See ver. 17 [v][Ezek. 4:11, 16] **35** [w]See ch. 5:20 [x]See Matt. 28:18 **36** [y]ver. 15, 16; ch. 5:24; 6:40, 47, 54; 1 John 5:12, 13; [ch. 11:25, 26; 20:31]; See Matt. 19:16 [z][Rom. 2:8; Eph. 5:6; Col. 3:6] [a]ver. 3
Chapter 4 **1** [b]ch. 3:22, 26 **3** [c]ch. 2:11, 12 **4** [d][Luke 13:33]

[1] Some interpreters hold that the quotation continues through verse 36

of judgment before He came, but with His coming salvation became a reality offered to a hostile world (Matt. 23:37; Rom. 5:8).

3:18 Unbelief is not the only basis for condemnation, but it constitutes the climax of rebellion by resisting even God's gracious offer of salvation in Christ. Jesus comes into a world that is already condemned because of its rejection of God's self-revelation (Rom. 1:18–32).

3:19 people loved the darkness rather than the light. Jesus gives the reason for the world's rejection of Him: He is the light who exposes whether a person is righteous or not.

3:21 whoever does what is true comes to the light. Jesus speaks of "doing" the truth. This indicates that "truth" is a matter of both thought and practice. Living by the truth is contrasted with doing what is evil (v. 20).

3:22–36 There are three sections here. In vv. 22–24 we are told that Jesus and His disciples went into Judea, where John was. In vv. 25–30 the Baptist affirms once more that his entire role is to prepare for Christ. Verses 31–36 appear to be a continuation of the Baptist's words, or possibly a comment by the Gospel writer.

3:24 John . . . not yet . . . in prison. See Matt. 14:3–12; Mark 6:17–29.

3:26 baptizing. See "Baptism" at Rom. 6:3.

3:27 A person cannot receive. God is the Author of all that we receive (1 Cor. 4:7).

3:31 He who comes from above. Jesus is distinguished from all other humans who are "of the earth" (v. 13 note).

3:32 no one receives his testimony. John repeats the idea of 1:10, 11, that neither His own nation nor the world at large was ready to receive Christ. The barrier is the sin and blindness that God alone can penetrate (v. 3; 1:5).

3:33 Whoever receives. The world refused the light, but John immediately mentions those who are coming to the light, especially himself as the first exponent of the truth. John's preaching is the culmination of the Old Testament and the beginning of the New (1:15; Matt. 11:11).

3:34 for he gives the Spirit without measure. These words could certainly apply to the Spirit-empowered earthly ministry of Jesus (Luke 3:22; 4:1). But it is also possible that they refer to the fullness of the Spirit that Jesus gives to those who serve Him, and some ancient and modern commentators have understood the text this way. Later, Jesus is the agent who sends the Spirit (15:26).

3:35 The Father loves the Son. See 5:20.

4:1–42 The background of this incident is the profound contempt that the Jews and the Samaritans felt for each other (v. 9). Not surprisingly, the Samaritans responded with enmity toward the Jews. When traveling between Galilee and Judea, many Jews would cross the Jordan twice rather than pass through Samaria. Jesus did not follow this practice (Luke 9:52).

had to pass through Samaria. **5**So he came
to a town of Samaria called Sychar, near the
field [e]that Jacob had given to his son
Joseph. **6**Jacob's well was there; so Jesus,
[f]wearied as he was from his journey, was
sitting beside the well. It was about the
sixth hour.[1]
7There came a woman of Samaria to
draw water. Jesus said to her, [f]"Give me a
drink." **8**(For his disciples had gone away
into the city to buy food.) **9**The Samaritan
woman said to him, "How is it that you, a
Jew, ask for a drink from me, a woman of
Samaria?" ([g]For Jews have no dealings with
Samaritans.) **10**Jesus answered her, "If you
knew the gift of God, and who it is that is
saying to you, 'Give me a drink,' you would
have asked him, and he would have given
you [h]living water." **11**The woman said to
him, "Sir, you have nothing to draw water
with, and the well is deep. Where do you
get that living water? **12**[i]Are you greater
than our father Jacob? [j]He gave us the well
and drank from it himself, as did his sons
and his livestock." **13**Jesus said to her,
"Everyone who drinks of this water will be
thirsty again, **14**but [k]whoever drinks of the
water that I will give him [l]will never be
thirsty forever. The water that I will give
him will become [m]in him a spring of water
welling up to eternal life." **15**The woman
said to him, "Sir, [n]give me this water, so
that I will not be thirsty or have to come
here to draw water."

5 [e]ver. 12; Gen. 33:19; 48:22; Josh. 24:32
6 [f]ch. 19:28; [Matt. 4:2; 8:24; 21:18]
7 [f][See ver. 6 above]
9 [g]Luke 9:53; [ch. 8:48; Ezra 4:3, 10]; See Matt. 10:5
10 [h]ch. 7:38; Jer. 2:13; 17:13
12 [i][ch. 8:53] [j]ver. 5
14 [k][ch. 6:35, 51, 58; 7:37] [l][Isai. 49:10; Rev. 7:16] [m]ch. 7:38
15 [n][ch. 6:34]
16 [o]ch. 16:8
19 [p]ch. 9:17; [ch. 6:14] [q]Luke 7:16, 39; See Matt. 21:11
20 [r]Gen. 12:6, 7; 33:18, 20; Deut. 11:29; 27:12; Josh. 8:33 [s]Judg. 9:7 [t]See Deut. 12:5 [u][ch. 11:48]
21 [v]ch. 2:4 [w]ver. 23; ch. 5:25, 28; 16:2, 25, 32 [x]Zeph. 2:11; Mal. 1:11; 1 Tim. 2:8
22 [y][2 Kin. 17:28-34; Acts 17:23] [z]Ps. 147:19, 20; Isai. 2:3; Rom. 3:1, 2; 9:4, 5 [a]Matt. 2:4, 5; Acts 13:23; Rom. 11:26

16Jesus said to her, "Go, [o]call your husband, and come here." **17**The woman
answered him, "I have no husband." Jesus
said to her, "You are right in saying, 'I have
no husband'; **18**for you have had five husbands, and the one you now have is not
your husband. What you have said is true."
19The woman said to him, "Sir, I perceive
that [p]you are [q]a prophet. **20**[r]Our fathers
worshiped on [s]this mountain, but you say
that [t]in Jerusalem is [u]the place where people ought to worship." **21**Jesus said to her,
[v]"Woman, believe me, [w]the hour is coming
when [x]neither on this mountain nor in
Jerusalem will you worship the Father.
22[y]You worship what you do not know; [z]we
worship what we know, for [z]salvation is
[a]from the Jews. **23**But [b]the hour is coming,
and is now here, when the true worshipers
will worship the Father [c]in spirit and
[d]truth, for the Father [e]is seeking such people to worship him. **24**God is spirit, and
those who worship him must worship in
spirit and truth." **25**The woman said to
him, "I know that [f]Messiah is coming (he
who is called Christ). When he comes, [g]he
will tell us all things." **26**Jesus said to her,
[h]"I who speak to you am he."
27Just then [i]his disciples came back. They
marveled that he was talking with a woman,
but no one said, "What do you seek?" or,

23 [b]ver. 21 [c][Rom. 8:15; Eph. 2:18; 6:18; Phil. 3:3] [d]Ps. 145:18; [ch. 1:17] [e][ch. 6:44] **25** [f]See ch. 1:41 [g]Deut. 18:18; [ver. 29] **26** [h]ch. 9:35-37 **27** [i]ver. 8

1 That is, about noon

4:6 wearied. Jesus experienced fatigue and even exhaustion by virtue of His human nature (Matt. 8:24). See "The Humanity of Jesus" at 2 John 7.

the sixth hour. Noon.

4:9 Jews have no dealings with Samaritans. This phrase could also be translated, "Jews use nothing in common with Samaritans," referring to the legislation that forbade a Jew to eat or drink with Samaritans, who were more lax in their understanding of ritual cleanness. The surprise was not so much that Jesus would speak with a Samaritan, but that He would drink from a Samaritan vessel.

4:10 the gift of God. This expression emphasizes that salvation is not earned but given (Eph. 2:8). Jesus Himself is the gift of God (3:16; Gal. 2:20; Eph. 5:25).

living water. In the Old Testament, living or running water was employed figuratively as a reference to divine activity (Jer. 2:13; Zech. 14:8). See also v. 14 and 7:37–39.

4:11 Like the Jews and Nicodemus before her, the Samaritan woman misunderstands the key terms Jesus uses (v. 15; 2:19–21; 3:3–10).

4:13 will be thirsty again. Jesus contrasts temporary with eternal satisfaction, teaching that all earthly pleasures, even if legitimate, are fading.

4:14 "I will give" expresses the divine origin of the blessing: "welling up" is its great abundance; "eternal life" is its endless duration.

4:18 you have had five husbands. Jesus' knowledge of the Samaritan woman's previous life is like His knowledge of Nathanael (1:48).

4:20 Our fathers worshiped on this mountain. Some time after the northern kingdom fell to Assyria (721 B.C.), a split arose between the Jews in Jerusalem and the Israelites living in Samaria. These Samaritans later built a temple on Mount Gerizim, which was destroyed about 130 B.C. They continue to worship on Mount Gerizim even into modern times.

4:23 the hour is coming, and is now here. See 6:25. The time is soon coming when divisions between Jews and Samaritans will be removed (v. 21), and the temple worship will be superseded. The time "is now here" because Jesus is present and has begun the work leading to the presence of the Holy Spirit in the church (7:39; 20:22).

4:24 must worship in spirit and truth. "True" worship is contrasted with the worship regulated by the temporary provisions of the law, especially the separation of Jews and Gentiles and the requirement of temple worship at Jerusalem. The ceremonial and sacrificial aspects of the law were not false; they were temporary and provisional. Worship "in spirit" is worship in the Holy Spirit. He continues the work begun by Jesus (14:16–18; Acts 2:33). Prominent marks of the age of the Spirit are the removal of the barrier between Jews and Gentiles, and the ability of Christians to worship without the need for a temple of any kind.

4:26 I . . . am he. This is the one occasion before His trial when Jesus is recorded designating Himself as the Messiah. Perhaps the political overtones associated with this title made it unwise for Jesus to use it often (cf. 6:14, 15).

4:27 marveled. The disciples' attitude reflects both the contempt of the

"Why are you talking with her?" 28 So the
woman left her water jar and went away
into town and said to the people, 29 "Come,
see a man [j]who told me all that I ever did.
Can this be the Christ?" 30 They went out of
the town and were coming to him.
31 Meanwhile the disciples were urging
him, saying, [k]"Rabbi, eat." 32 But he said to
them, "I have food to eat that you do not
know about." 33 So the disciples said to one
another, [l]"Has anyone brought him something to eat?" 34 Jesus said to them, [m]"My
food is [n]to do the will of him who sent me
and [o]to accomplish his work. 35 Do you not
say, 'There are yet four months, then
comes the harvest'? Look, I tell you, lift up
your eyes, and see that [p]the fields are white
for harvest. 36 Already the one who reaps is
receiving wages and gathering fruit for
eternal life, so that [q]sower and [r]reaper [s]may
rejoice together. 37 For here the saying
holds true, [t]'One sows and another reaps.'
38 I sent you to reap [u]that for which you did
not labor. Others have labored, [v]and you
have entered into their labor."
39 Many Samaritans [w]from that town
believed in him [x]because of [y]the woman's
testimony, "He told me all that I ever did."
40 So when the Samaritans came to him,
they asked him to stay with them, and he
stayed there two days. 41 And many more
believed [z]because of his word. 42 They said
to the woman, "It is no longer because of
what you said that we believe, for we have
heard for ourselves, [a]and we know that this
is indeed [b]the Savior [c]of the world."
43 After [d]the two days he departed for
Galilee. 44 (For Jesus himself had testified
[e]that a prophet has no honor in his own
hometown.) 45 So when he came to Galilee,
the Galileans welcomed him, [f]having seen
all that he had done in Jerusalem at the
feast. For [g]they too had gone to the feast.

Jesus Heals an Official's Son

46 So he came again to [h]Cana in Galilee,
[i]where he had made the water wine. And at
Capernaum there was an official whose son
was ill. 47 When this man heard that Jesus
[j]had come from Judea to Galilee, he went
to him and asked him to come down and
heal his son, for he was at the point of
death. 48 So Jesus said to him, [k]"Unless you
see signs and wonders you will not
believe." 49 The official said to him, "Sir,
come down [l]before my child dies." 50 Jesus
said to him, "Go; your son will live." The
man believed the word that Jesus spoke to
him and went on his way. 51 As he was
going down, his servants[1] met him and
told him that his son was recovering. 52 So
he asked them the hour when he began to
get better, and they said to him, "Yesterday
at the seventh hour[2] the fever left him."
53 The father knew that was the hour when
Jesus had said to him, "Your son will live."
And he himself believed, [m]and all his
household. 54 [n]This was now the second
sign that Jesus did when he had come from
Judea to Galilee.

The Healing at the Pool on the Sabbath

5 After this there was a [o]feast of the Jews,
and Jesus went up to Jerusalem. 2 Now
there is in Jerusalem by [p]the Sheep Gate a
pool, in Aramaic[3] called Bethesda,[4] which
has five roofed colonnades. 3 In these lay a
multitude of invalids—blind, lame, and
[q]paralyzed.[5] 5 One man was there who had

29 [j]ver. 17, 18; [ver. 25]
31 [k]See ch. 1:38
33 [l][ver. 11, 15; ch. 2:20; 3:4; 6:34, 52]
34 [m][Job 23:12] [n]ch. 5:30; 6:38; 14:31 [o]ch. 5:36; 17:4
35 [p]Matt. 9:37; Luke 10:2; [ver. 25, 30]
36 [q][Matt. 13:37; Mark 4:14] [r]ver. 38 [s]Isai. 9:3; [Amos 9:13]
37 [t][Job 31:8]
38 [u]Josh. 24:13 [v][Acts 8:5-17, 25]
39 [w]ver. 5, 8 [x][ch. 17:20] [y]ver. 29
41 [z]ch. 8:30
42 [a][1 John 5:20] [b]1 John 4:14; [ch. 3:17; 12:47; 1 Tim. 4:10] [c]See ch. 1:29
43 [d]ver. 40
44 [e]See Matt. 13:57
45 [f]ch. 2:23; 3:2
[g]ver. 20
46 [h]ch. 2:1 [i]ch. 2:9
47 [j]ver. 3, 54
48 [k]ch. 2:18; 6:30; [ch. 20:29]
49 [l][ch. 11:21, 32; Mark 5:35; Luke 8:49]
53 [m]Acts 16:34; 18:8; See Acts 11:14
54 [n][ch. 2:11 with ver. 45, 46]
Chapter 5
1 [o]See ch. 6:4
2 [p]Neh. 3:1, 32; 12:39
3 [q]Matt. 12:10

1 Greek *bondservants* 2 That is, at 1 P.M. 3 Or *Hebrew* 4 Some manuscripts *Bethsaida* 5 Some manuscripts insert, wholly or in part, *waiting for the moving of the water; 4for an angel of the Lord went down at certain seasons into the pool, and stirred the water: whoever stepped in first after the stirring of the water was healed of whatever disease he had*

Jews for the Samaritans and the male chauvinism that regarded giving instruction to a woman as a waste of time.

4:30 They went out. The witness of the woman was more effective than the visit of the twelve apostles.

4:37 One sows and another reaps. Jesus makes it clear that His disciples have a responsibility distinct from His own. They will harvest what Jesus sowed. The saying may deliberately anticipate 12:23, 24.

4:42 the Savior of the world. They recognized that Jesus was more than a prophet (vv. 19, 29, 39); He is the Savior (1 John 4:14).

4:44 no honor in his own hometown. "His own hometown" is probably Galilee rather than Judea (cf. v. 3). Galilee is considered to be the place of Jesus' origin in this Gospel (1:46; 2:1; 7:42, 52). Though the Galileans "welcomed him" (v. 45), the text indicates that Jesus was displeased with their need to "see signs and wonders" in order to believe (v. 48; see Introduction: Interpretive Difficulties).

4:46 official. An officer in the service of Herod Antipas, tetrarch of Galilee (cf. Matt. 14:1–12; Luke 23:7).

4:50 your son will live. This was a word with power to heal, not merely a prophecy that he would recover.

4:52 the seventh hour. 1:00 P.M.

4:54 second sign. While Jesus had performed many other signs (2:23), this is the second that took place at Cana in Galilee (cf. 2:11). The repetition of "your son will live" (vv. 50, 53) shows the purpose of the sign is to reveal that Jesus has the power to give life. Corresponding to this repetition is the progression of the official's faith (vv. 48, 50, 53). This focus on life through the power of Jesus' word prepares the reader for the following discourse on life through the Son (5:19–30).

5:1 a feast of the Jews. Probably one of the pilgrimage feasts that were observed in Jerusalem, either Booths, Passover, or Pentecost.

been an invalid for thirty-eight years.
6 When Jesus saw him lying there and knew
that he had already been there a long time,
he said to him, "Do you want to be
healed?" 7 The sick man answered him, "Sir,
I have no one to put me into the pool when
the water is stirred up, and while I am going
another steps down before me." 8 Jesus said
to him, [r]"Get up, take up your bed, and
walk." 9 [r]And at once the man was healed,
and he took up his bed and walked.
[s]Now that day was the Sabbath. 10 So the
Jews said to the man who had been healed,
"It is the Sabbath, and [t]it is not lawful for
you to take up your bed." 11 But he answered them, "The man who healed me,
that man said to me, 'Take up your bed,
and walk.'" 12 They asked him, "Who is the
man who said to you, 'Take up your bed
and walk'?" 13 Now the man who had been
healed did not know who it was, for [u]Jesus
had withdrawn, as there was a crowd in the
place. 14 Afterward Jesus found him in the
temple and said to him, "See, you are well!
[v]Sin no more, [w]that nothing worse may
happen to you." 15 The man went away and
told the Jews that it was Jesus who had
healed him. 16 And this was why the Jews
[x]were persecuting Jesus, [y]because he was
doing these things on the Sabbath. 17 But
Jesus answered them, "My Father is working until now, and I am working."

Jesus Is Equal with God

18 This was why the Jews [z]were seeking
all the more to kill him, [a]because not only
was he [b]breaking the Sabbath, but he was
even calling God [c]his own Father, [d]making
himself equal with God.

The Authority of the Son

19 So Jesus said to them, "Truly, truly, I
say to you, [e]the Son [f]can do nothing of his
own accord, but only what he sees the
Father doing. For whatever the Father[1]
does, that the Son does likewise. 20 For [g]the
Father loves the Son and shows him all
that he himself is doing. And [h]greater
works than these will he show him, so that
[i]you may marvel. 21 For as the Father
[j]raises the dead and [k]gives them life, so [l]al-
so the Son gives life [m]to whom he will.
22 [n]The Father judges no one, but [o]has
given all judgment to the Son, 23 that all
may honor the Son, just as they [p]honor the
Father. [q]Whoever does not honor the Son
does not honor the Father who sent him.
24 Truly, truly, I say to you, [r]whoever hears
my word and [s]believes him who sent me
has eternal life. He [t]does not come into
judgment, but [u]has passed from death to
life.
25 "Truly, truly, I say to you, [v]an hour is
coming, and is now here, when [w]the dead
will hear [x]the voice of the Son of God, and
those who hear [w]will live. 26 [y]For as the
Father has life in himself, [z]so he has granted
the Son also to have life in himself. 27 And

8 [r]Matt. 9:6, 7; Mark 2:9, 11, 12; Luke 5:24, 25 **9** [r][See ver. 8 above] [s]ch. 9:14 **10** [t]Ex. 20:10; Neh. 13:19; Jer. 17:21, 22; [ch. 7:23; 9:16; Matt. 12:2; Mark 2:24; 3:4; Luke 6:2; 13:14 **13** [u][ch. 6:15] **14** [v][ch. 8:11] [w][Ezra 9:14] **16** [x]ch. 15:20; [Acts 9:4, 5] [y]ch. 7:23; 9:16 **18** [z]See ch. 7:1 [a]See ch. 10:33 [b]ver. 16 [c][Rom. 8:32] [d]Phil. 2:6 **19** [e]See ver. 30 [f][ch. 16:13] **20** [g]ch. 3:35; 10:17; 15:9, 10; 17:23-26; [Matt. 3:17] [h][ch. 14:12] [i]ch. 7:21 **21** [j][Deut. 32:39; 2 Cor. 1:9] [k]Rom. 4:17; 8:11 [l][ch. 6:33; 11:25]; See 1 Cor. 15:45 [m][Rom. 9:18] **22** [n][Acts 17:31] [o]ver. 27; ch. 9:39; Acts 10:42; [ch. 3:17]; See ch. 17:2 **23** [p]ch. 8:49 [q]Luke 10:16; [ch. 15:23; 1 John 2:23] **24** [r][ch. 8:51] [s]ch. 20:31; 1 John 5:9-13; [ch. 3:15, 36; 12:44] [t]ch. 3:18; [ver. 29] [u]1 John 3:14 **25** [v]See ch. 4:21, 23 [w]See Eph. 2:1, 5 [x][ch. 11:43] **26** [y][ch. 6:57] [z]See ch. 1:4; 17:2

1 Greek *he*

5:5 an invalid. The exact disease is not specified, but the event indicates that it hindered the man's movement and walking.

5:8 take up your bed. Jewish tradition had interpreted the Sabbath prohibition against work to forbid carrying burdens. Jeremiah protested against loading and unloading on the Sabbath (Jer. 17:21, 22).

5:9 the man was healed. It is not stated that faith in Jesus was required of the man, as was the case in many of Jesus' miracles (Matt. 9:22; 13:58; Mark 6:5, 6). The focus here is on Jesus' power.

5:14 nothing worse. The point of the admonition is not necessarily that the man had brought his illness on himself by some specific sin. Some sins can provoke God to physical and temporal judgment (1 Cor. 11:28–32), but illness is not necessarily related to particular sins (9:3).

5:17–47 Jesus debates the Jews regarding His relation to the Sabbath and to God. Jesus does not argue with His opponents about whether they understand the Sabbath legislation correctly. His interest is whether they understand who He is. Jesus claims to be God by indicating some of His divine prerogatives (vv. 17–30) and shows the basis for His claim (vv. 31–47).

5:17 My Father . . . and I am working. Jesus does not dispute with the Jews whether they are right to criticize the lame man. He denies that they can criticize Him, because He is only doing what His Father does. The Jews understood Him to be saying this, since they accused Him of making Himself equal with God (v. 18).

5:18 making himself equal with God. Jesus represented Himself as One who had the same authority over the Sabbath as the Author of the Sabbath (Luke 6:5), which was given not only at Sinai but in the creation order itself.

5:19 the Son can do nothing. This does not express personal inability, but emphasizes the complete unity of purpose and action in the Trinity. See theological note "The Humble Obedience of Christ."

5:20 greater works than these. There is a greater work than healing the sick. This work, according to v. 21, is raising the dead.

5:21 the Father raises the dead. A clear affirmation of what is expressed less clearly in the Old Testament. Jesus agrees with the Pharisees against the Sadducees, who denied the resurrection (Matt. 22:23). Raising the dead is possible only for God, yet Jesus claims the power for Himself (v. 25).

5:23 honor. Here "honor" is the holy fear of God awakened by the knowledge of coming judgment (v. 22). The Son, no less than the Father, is One to whom all will give an account.

5:24 eternal life. Salvation is not only an object of hope for the future, but a present reality for the believer; such a one "has passed from death to life" (cf. 6:47).

5:26 life in himself. See "The Self-existence of God" at Ps. 90:2.

he [a]has given him authority to execute
judgment, because he is the Son of Man.
28 Do not marvel at this, for [v]an hour is
coming when [b]all who are in the tombs will
hear his voice 29 and come out, [c]those who
have done good to the resurrection of life,
and those who have done evil to the resurrection of judgment.

Witnesses to Jesus

30 [d]"I can do nothing on my own. As I
hear, I judge, and my [e]judgment is just,
because [f]I seek not my own will [g]but the
will of him who sent me. 31 [h]If I alone bear
witness about myself, my testimony is not
deemed true. 32 There is [i]another who bears
witness about me, and [j]I know that the testimony that he bears about me is true.
33 [k]You sent to John, and he has borne witness to the truth. 34 Not that [l]the testimony
that I receive is from man, but I say these
things so that you may be saved. 35 He was
a burning and [m]shining lamp, and [n]you
were willing to rejoice for a while in his
light. 36 But [l]the testimony that I have is
greater than that of John. For [o]the works
that the Father has given me [p]to accomplish,
the very works that I am doing, [q]bear witness about me that [r]the Father has sent

27 [a]ver. 22 28 [v][See ver. 25 above] [b]ch. 11:24; 1 Cor. 15:52; [ch. 11:44, 45] 29 [c]See Dan. 12:2 30 [d]ver. 19; ch. 8:28; 14:10 [e]ch. 8:16 [f]ch. 4:34; 6:38; [ch. 7:18; Rom. 15:3] [g]See Matt. 26:39 31 [h][ch. 8:13, 14, 18, 54; 18:21] 32 [i]ver. 37 [j]ch. 7:28, 29 33 [k]See ch. 1:7, 19

34 [l]1 John 5:9 35 [m]2 Pet. 1:19 [n][Matt. 13:20; 21:26] 36 [l][See ver. 34 above] [o]ch. 10:25, 38; 14:11; 15:24; [ch. 2:23; Matt. 11:4] [p]See ch. 4:34 [q][ch. 3:2] [r]See ch. 3:17

The Humble Obedience of Christ

Humility in Scripture does not mean pretending to be worthless and refusing positions of responsibility, but knowing and keeping the place God has appointed for one. Being humble is a matter of accepting God's arrangement, whether it means the high exposure of leadership (Moses was humble as a leader, Num. 12:3), or the obscurity of being a servant. When Jesus said that He was "lowly in heart" (Matt. 11:29), He meant that He was following the Father's plan for His earthly life.

The three Persons of the Trinity are eternal and self-existent, having equally all aspects and attributes of deity, and always acting together. But the Persons are distinct in their mutual relationships. Something of what this means is revealed in the humble submission of Christ to the Father's will, and also in the way that the Holy Spirit is sent by the Father and the Son to confirm the work of salvation in human hearts.

The Father's will for Christ is sometimes called the covenant of redemption. It is called a "covenant" because it is an agreement between two parties. The Westminster Confession summarizes the agreement (the Father's purpose, accepted by the Son) as follows:

> It pleased God, in His eternal purpose, to choose and ordain the Lord Jesus, His only-begotten Son, to be the Mediator between God and man, the Prophet, Priest, and King; the Head and Saviour of His Church, the Heir of all things, and Judge of the world: unto whom He did, from all eternity, give a people to be His seed, and to be by Him in time redeemed, called, justified, sanctified, and glorified (*Westminster Confession,* VIII.1).

Christ fulfilled this covenant through two stages called His "humiliation" and His "exaltation." In His humiliation, He left behind the eternal glory that was His, taking on a perfect and complete human nature: body, soul, and spirit. Through His incarnation He lived a life of poverty and suffering. He was rejected by His nation, finally to die the shameful death of a common criminal (2 Cor. 8:9; Gal. 3:13; Phil 2:6–8).

In His exaltation, Christ rose from the dead, ascended to heaven, and reigns as King over the world and the church. Together with the Father, He has sent the Holy Spirit to complete the work of redemption that He won for us.

The redemptive obedience of Christ has two sides, called "active" and "passive." In His active obedience, Christ fulfilled the positive commandments of God on behalf of His people, serving God and doing good. This positive righteousness is granted as a gift through faith to believers, securing for them a righteous standing before God. In His passive obedience, Christ paid the penalty owed by sinners to God. He did this by suffering death on the cross. "Passive" means "permitting" or "allowing," not being inactive, detached, or unfeeling. Jesus came to do the Father's will, not to avoid it, and His heart was wholly conformed to it.

5:29 resurrection. See "Resurrection and Glorification" at 1 Cor. 15:21.

5:31–47 Jesus addresses four types of testimony that establish His claims: the testimony of John the Baptist; of Jesus' own works; of God the Father; and of Scripture, especially Moses.

5:31 my testimony is not deemed true. Jesus' testimony would not be false even if He alone spoke it. By "not true," He means not permitted in court according to the Mosaic law (Deut. 17:6; 19:15).

5:36 the very works that I am doing. This is the principle acknowl-

me. 37 And the Father who sent me [s]has
himself borne witness about me. His voice
you have never heard, [t]his form you have
never seen, 38 and [u]you do not have his
word abiding in you, for you do not believe
the one whom he has sent. 39 [v]You search
the Scriptures because you think that in
them you have eternal life; and [w]it is they
that bear witness about me, 40 yet [x]you
refuse to come to me that you may have
life. 41 [y]I do not receive glory from people.
42 But [z]I know that you do not have [a]the
love of God within you. 43 I have come [b]in
my Father's name, and [c]you do not receive
me. [d]If another comes in his own name,
you will receive him. 44 How can you
believe, when you receive glory from one
another and [e]do not seek the glory that
comes from [f]the only God? 45 Do not think
that I will accuse you to the Father. There
is one who accuses you: Moses, [g]on whom
you have set your hope. 46 If you believed
Moses, you would believe me; for [h]he
wrote of me. 47 But [i]if you do not believe his
writings, how will you believe my words?"

Jesus Feeds the Five Thousand

6 After this [j]Jesus went away to the other
side of [k]the Sea of Galilee, which is [l]the
Sea of Tiberias. 2 And a large crowd was following him, because they saw the signs
that he was doing on the sick. 3 Jesus went
up on [m]the mountain, and there he sat
down with his disciples. 4 Now [n]the Passover, the [o]feast of the Jews, was at hand.
5 [p]Lifting up his eyes, then, and seeing that
a large crowd was coming toward him,
Jesus said to [q]Philip, "Where are we to buy
bread, so that these people may eat?" 6 He
said this to test him, for he himself knew
what he would do. 7 [r]Philip answered him,
"Two hundred denarii[1] would not buy
enough bread for each of them to get a little." 8 One of his disciples, [s]Andrew, Simon
Peter's brother, said to him, 9 "There is a
boy here who has five [t]barley loaves and
two fish, but [t]what are they for so many?"
10 Jesus said, "Have the people sit down."
[u]Now there was much grass in the place.
So the men sat down, about five thousand
in number. 11 Jesus then took the loaves,
and [v]when he had given thanks, he distributed them to those who were seated. So
also the fish, as much as they wanted.
12 And when they had eaten their fill, he
told his disciples, "Gather up the leftover
fragments, that nothing may be lost." 13 So
they gathered them up and filled twelve
baskets with fragments from the five barley
loaves, left by those who had eaten.
14 When the people saw the sign that he
had done, they said, [w]"This is indeed [x]the
Prophet [y]who is to come into the world!"
15 [z]Perceiving then that they were about

37 [s]ch. 8:18; [Matt. 3:17] [t]See ch. 1:18
38 [u][1 John 2:14; 4:13, 14; 5:10]
39 [v][Acts 17:11; 2 Tim. 3:15]; [w]See Luke 24:27
40 [x]ver. 43. ch. 3:19; 7:17; [Matt. 23:37; Luke 13:34]
41 [y]ver. 34; [Matt. 6:1, 2; 1 Thess. 2:6]
42 [z]See ch. 2:24, 25 [a]Luke 11:42; See Jude 21
43 [b]ch. 10:25; 12:13; 17:12 [c]ch. 1:11; 3:11, 32 [d][Matt. 24:5]
44 [e]Rom. 2:29 [f]ch. 17:3
45 [g][ch. 9:28, 29; Rom. 2:17]
46 [h]ver. 47; Num. 21:9; Deut. 18:15; Luke 24:27; [ch. 12:41]
47 [i][Luke 16:31]
Chapter 6
1 [j]For ver. 1-13, see Matt. 14:13-21; Mark 6:32-44; Luke 9:10-17 [k]See Matt. 4:18 [l]ch. 21:1
3 [m]ver. 15
4 [n]ch. 2:13; 11:55; See Ex. ch. 12 [o]ch. 5:1; 7:2
5 [p]Luke 6:20 [q]ch. 1:44
7 [r][Mark 6:37]
8 [s]ch. 1:40, 44 9 [t]2 Kin. 4:42, 43 10 [u][Mark 6:39] 11 [v]ver. 23; See Matt. 15:36
14 [w]See ch. 4:19 [x]ch. 1:21; 7:40; See Matt. 21:11 [y]ch. 11:27; See Matt. 11:3
15 [z][ch. 12:12-15]

1 A *denarius* was a day's wage for a laborer

edged by Nicodemus (3:2). The power given by God to work miracles is a sign of His approval (10:25, 38), although not every wonderful work is a miracle in this sense (Ex. 7:11, 12; Matt. 7:22, 23; 24:24; Rev. 13:13).

5:37, 38 His voice . . . his word. These terms probably refer to Scripture, which is God's "voice" and "word," but which the unbelievers did not receive.

5:39 the Scriptures . . . bear witness about me. Jesus agrees that the Old Testament leads to eternal life (cf. 2 Tim. 3:15), while going on to reveal that this life is in Him, the Author of eternal life. The searching of those who refuse to find Christ in the Scriptures is futile, because it lacks the enlightenment of the Spirit (2 Cor. 3:6).

5:45 one who accuses you. Moses will accuse those who do not believe in Christ, because Moses wrote about Him. Jesus does not refer to any single text in Moses (such as Deut. 18:15), but to what "he wrote" (v. 46) in a general way. This is similar to what Jesus told His disciples after the resurrection on the road to Emmaus (Luke 24:27, 44–46), as well as to the preaching of the apostles (Acts 3:18; 17:2, 3; 18:28; 26:22, 23; 28:23).

6:1–71 This chapter is a major turning point in chs. 2–12. It reveals the identity of Jesus as One sent from the Father (vv. 38, 44, 46, 50, 51, 57); it graphically distinguishes belief and unbelief through the illustration of eating Jesus' flesh and blood (vv. 53–58); and it chronicles the growing rejection, motivated by unbelief, that confronted Jesus (vv. 41, 42, 60–66). The signs in this chapter call to mind corresponding saving events in the history of Israel. They indicate that Jesus fulfills the typology of the Passover, the Exodus, and the provision of food in the wilderness.

6:1–4 Jesus leaves Jerusalem and travels to the far side of the Sea of Galilee, around the time of the Passover. This feast was established in Ex. 12:43–51 to commemorate how God "passed over" the Israelites and killed the Egyptians. The Old Testament passages read during the Passover in Jesus' time probably included Gen. 1–8, Ex. 11–16, and Num. 6–14. There are strong similarities between these texts and Jesus' comments in this discourse.

6:1 Sea of Tiberias. Another name for the Sea of Galilee, in honor of the town of Tiberias, built by Herod between A.D. 20–30.

6:2 signs. John has reported only one healing in Galilee, of the official's son (4:46–54). Jesus must have done other such miracles as well (cf. 21:25).

6:3 Jesus went up on the mountain. This detail may be intended to suggest a comparison of Jesus and Moses, who went up on Mount Sinai (v. 14 note).

6:5–15 The feeding of the five thousand. Jesus brings food to a multitude, as Moses did in the wilderness (Num. 11).

6:5 that these people may eat. Reminiscent of Num. 11:13, where Moses asks God a similar question.

6:7 Two hundred denarii. A denarius was about one day's wage (Matt. 20:2).

6:10 five thousand. The figure does not include women and children (Matt. 14:21; cf. 2 Kin. 4:42–44).

6:14 the Prophet. That is, the Prophet like Moses (Deut. 18:15).

to come and take him by force to make him
king, Jesus [a]withdrew again to [b]the mountain by himself.

Jesus Walks on Water

16 When evening came, his disciples went
down to the sea, 17 got into a boat, and
started across the sea to Capernaum. It was
now dark, and Jesus had not yet come to
them. 18 The sea became rough because a
strong wind was blowing. 19 When they had
rowed about three or four miles,[1] they saw
Jesus walking on the sea and coming near
the boat, and they were frightened. 20 [c]But
he said to them, "It is I; do not be afraid."
21 Then they were glad to take him into the
boat, and immediately the boat was at the
land to which they were going.

I Am the Bread of Life

22 On the next day the crowd that
remained on the other side of the sea saw
that there had been only [d]one boat there,
and that Jesus had not entered the boat
with his disciples, but that his disciples
had gone away alone. 23 Other boats from
Tiberias came near the place where they
had eaten the bread after the Lord [e]had
given thanks. 24 [f]So when the crowd saw
that Jesus was not there, nor his disciples,
they themselves got into the boats and
[g]went to Capernaum, seeking Jesus.

25 When they found him on the other
side of the sea, they said to him, [h]"Rabbi,
when did you come here?" 26 Jesus answered them, "Truly, truly, I say to you,
[i]you are seeking me, not because you saw
[j]signs, but because you ate your fill of the
loaves. 27 [k]Do not labor for the food that
perishes, but for [l]the food that endures to
eternal life, which [m]the Son of Man will
give to you. For on [n]him God the Father
has [o]set his seal." 28 Then they said to him,
"What must we do, to be doing [p]the works
of God?" 29 Jesus answered them, "This is
the work of God, [q]that you believe in him
whom [r]he has sent." 30 So they said to him,
[s]"Then what sign do you do, that we may
see and believe you? What work do you
perform? 31 [t]Our fathers ate the manna in
the wilderness; as it is written, [u]'He gave
them bread from heaven to eat.'" 32 Jesus
then said to them, "Truly, truly, I say to
you, it was not Moses who gave you the
bread from heaven, but my Father gives
you the true bread from heaven. 33 For the
bread of God is [v]he who comes down
from heaven and gives life to the world."
34 They said to him, [w]"Sir, give us this bread
always."

35 Jesus said to them, [x]"I am the bread of
life; [y]whoever comes to me shall not
hunger, and whoever believes in me shall
never thirst. 36 But I said to you that you
have seen me and yet do not believe. 37 [z]All
that [a]the Father gives me will come to me,
and [b]whoever comes to me I will never cast
out. 38 For [c]I have come down from heaven,

15 [a]For ver. 15-21, see Matt. 14:22-33; Mark 6:45-51; [Matt. 8:18] [b]ver. 3
20 [c][Luke 24:38, 39]
22 [d]ch. 21:8
23 [e]ver. 11
24 [f]For ver. 24, 25, [Matt. 14:34-36; Mark 6:53-56] [g]ver. 17, 59
25 [h]See ch. 1:38
26 [i]ver. 24 [j]ver. 2
27 [k]Isai. 55:2 [l][ver. 35, 50, 51, 54, 58] [m]See Dan. 7:13 [n][ch. 5:36, 37; 10:36] [o][Ezek. 9:4; Rom. 4:11; 1 Cor. 9:2; 2 Tim. 2:19]; See ch. 3:33
28 [p]1 Cor. 15:58; Rev. 2:26
29 [q]1 John 3:23 [r]See ch. 3:17
30 [s]See Matt. 12:38
31 [t]ver. 49, 58; Ex. 16:15; Num. 11:7-9 [u]Cited from Neh. 9:15; [Ps. 78:24, 25; 105:40; 1 Cor. 10:3]
33 [v]ver. 50
34 [w]See ch. 4:15, 33
35 [x]ver. 41, 48, 51; [ver. 58] [y]ch. 4:14; 7:37; [ch. 5:40; Matt. 11:28; Rev. 7:16]
37 [z]ver. 39; ch. 17:2 [a]ch. 10:29; 17:6, 9, 24 [b]ch. 10:28; 17:12 **38** [c]See ch. 3:13

[1] Greek *twenty-five or thirty stadia*; a *stadion* was about 607 feet or 185 meters

6:15 to make him king. The kingship of the Messiah was to be spiritual, not political. While accepting the title "King of Israel" (1:49), Jesus refused the offer of Satan (Matt. 4:8, 9; Luke 4:5, 6) and the misguided efforts of the people.

6:16–21 This miracle is recorded in Matt. 14:22–33 and in Mark 6:47–51. It should not be confused with the calming of the storm found in Matt. 8:23–27; Mark 4:36–41; and Luke 8:22–25.

6:21 immediately. Some understand this to be an additional miracle; others take it to mean that after Jesus' entrance into the boat, no further difficulties were encountered.

6:26 not because you saw signs. Although they saw the miracle of the loaves and fishes, they did not recognize it as a sign identifying Jesus as the Messiah. It was merely as an opportunity for a meal to them.

6:27 Jesus points to the spiritual meaning of the miracle, which is to set God's seal of approval on His ministry and to identify Him as the Son of Man, the promised Messiah.

6:31 They expected that the coming of the Messiah would be marked by a miracle as great as or greater than the giving of the manna in the desert.

6:32 the true bread from heaven. The word "true" has a special meaning. Jesus refers to what is everlasting, as opposed to something merely representative. The bread God provided through Moses (Ex. 16; Num. 11) was only material and temporary, not spiritual and eternal. See note at 4:24.

6:33 he who comes down from heaven. This is Jesus Christ, whose incarnation is described as "coming down" (vv. 38, 41, 42, 50, 51, 58; 3:13, 31; Eph. 4:9–10).

gives life to the world. Christ provides eternal life to those who are dead in trespasses and sins (Eph. 2:1). They are chosen not only from the Jews but from the whole world. Jesus does not here teach universal salvation, but the universal relevance and appeal of His saving work (3:16 note).

6:34 give us this bread. They misinterpreted Jesus' statement by taking it on a purely physical level, as Nicodemus (3:4) and the Samaritan woman (4:15) had done.

6:35 I am the bread of life. This is the first of seven such "I am" sayings in this Gospel (8:12; 9:5; 10:7, 9, 11, 14; 11:25; 14:6; 15:1, 5). The expression looks back to Ex. 3:14 and is an implicit claim to deity (8:58, 59 and notes).

6:37 All that the Father gives me. God leads to faith all whom He plans to redeem. The redemption of the elect is certain. The Son promises acceptance to anyone who truly believes.

not to do [d]my own will but [d]the will of him
[e]who sent me. 39 And [f]this is the will of him
who sent me, [g]that I should lose nothing of
[h]all that he has given me, but [i]raise it up on
the last day. 40 For this is the will of my
Father, that everyone who [j]looks on the
Son and [k]believes in him [l]should have eternal life, and I will raise him up on the last
day."
41 So the Jews grumbled about him,
because he said, [m]"I am the bread that
came down from heaven." 42 They said, [n]"Is
not this Jesus, [o]the son of Joseph, whose
father and mother [p]we know? How does
he now say, 'I have come down from
heaven'?" 43 Jesus answered them, "Do not
grumble among yourselves. 44 No one can
come to me unless the Father who sent me
[q]draws him. And [r]I will raise him up on the
last day. 45 It is written in the Prophets,
[s]'And they will all be [t]taught by God.'
[u]Everyone who has heard and learned from
the Father comes to me— 46 [v]not that anyone has seen the Father except [w]he who is
from God; he [x]has seen the Father. 47 Truly,
truly, I say to you, [y]whoever believes has
eternal life. 48 [z]I am the bread of life.
49 [a]Your fathers ate the manna in the wilderness, and [b]they died. 50 [c]This is the
bread that comes down from heaven, so
that one may eat of it [d]and not die. 51 I am
the living bread [e]that came down from
heaven. If anyone eats of this bread, he will
live forever. And the bread that I will give
[f]for the life of the world is [g]my flesh."
52 The Jews then [h]disputed among themselves, saying, [i]"How can this man give us
his flesh to eat?" 53 So Jesus said to them,
"Truly, truly, I say to you, unless you eat
the flesh of [j]the Son of Man and drink his
blood, you [k]have no life in you. 54 Whoever
feeds on my flesh and drinks my blood [l]has
eternal life, and [m]I will raise him up on the
last day. 55 For my flesh is true food, and
my blood is true drink. 56 Whoever feeds on
my flesh and drinks my blood [n]abides in
me, and I in him. 57 As [o]the living Father
[p]sent me, and [q]I live because of the Father,
so whoever feeds on me, he also will live
because of me. 58 [r]This is the bread that
came down from heaven, not as the fathers
ate and died. Whoever feeds on this bread
will live forever." 59 Jesus[1] said these things
in the synagogue, as he taught [s]at Capernaum.

The Words of Eternal Life

60 [t]When many of his disciples heard it,
they said, "This is [u]a hard saying; who can
listen to it?" 61 But Jesus, [v]knowing in himself that his disciples were grumbling about
this, said to them, "Do you take offense at

38 [d]See ch. 5:30 [e]See ch. 4:34 **39** [f]ch. 10:28, 29; Matt. 18:14 [g]ch. 17:12; 18:9 [h]ver. 37 [i]ver. 40, 44, 54; [ch. 11:25; 1 Cor. 6:14] **40** [j]ch. 12:45; 14:17, 19 [k]ver. 47; ch. 3:15, 16 [l]ver. 27, 54; ch. 4:14 **41** [m]ver. 33, 35, 38 **42** [n]See Matt. 13:55 [o]See ch. 1:45 [p]ch. 7:27, 28 **44** [q]ch. 12:32; Jer. 31:3; Hos. 11:4; [ver. 65; ch. 4:23] [r]ver. 39 **45** [s]Cited from Isai. 54:13; [Jer. 31:33, 34; Heb. 8:10, 11] [t]1 Cor. 2:13; 1 Thess. 4:9; 1 John 2:20 [u][ver. 37] **46** [v]See ch. 1:18 [w]See ch. 7:29 [x][ch. 3:32; 8:38] **47** [y]See ch. 3:36 **48** [z]See ver. 35 **49** [a]See ver. 31 [b]ver. 58 **50** [c]ver. 33 [d]ver. 51, 58 **51** [e]ch. 3:13 [f]ver. 57; Luke 22:19 [g]ver. 53-56; [ch. 1:14]

52 [h]ch. 9:16; 10:19 [i]ver. 60; ch. 3:9 **53** [j]ver. 27 [k]See ch. 20:31 **54** [l]See ver. 40 [m]ver. 39 **56** [n]ch. 15:4, 5; 1 John 3:24; 4:13, 15, 16 **57** [o][ch. 5:26]; See Matt. 16:16 [p]See ch. 3:17 [q]ch. 11:25; Rev. 1:18 **58** [r]ver. 31, 33, 49-51 **59** [s]ver. 24 **60** [t]ver. 66; [ver. 64] [u]Jude 15 **61** [v][ch. 2:24, 25]

[1] Greek *He*

6:38 not to do my own will. The will of the Son and the will of the Father agree; there is no competition or disagreement. Jesus' submission to the Father shows this agreement.

6:39 lose nothing . . . but raise. The Father's will is more than that Jesus should make an offer to lost sinners. He will at last raise up all who are given Him by the Father and lose not one from that group. God graciously perseveres with true believers, ensuring their final salvation. See "Perseverance of the Saints" at Rom. 8:30.

6:41 the Jews grumbled about him. This response is similar to that of the Israelites in the wilderness, who complained against Moses and Aaron (Ex. 16:7; 17:3; Num. 11:1).

came down from heaven. Jesus' origin establishes His identity as Messiah and Son of God (vv. 29, 33, 38; 1:1, 2, 14, 18, 45, 46; 3:2, 13, 17, 31; 5:36–38). Those confronted with this revelation must respond either in belief or in rejection. There is no middle ground.

6:44 unless the Father who sent me draws him. Jesus teaches that no one can respond positively to His warning and invitation apart from the Father's work of drawing the individual to Jesus. The heart is naturally hard and will not accept God's invitation, unless a special work of God's grace takes place (v. 65). See "Effectual Calling and Conversion" at 2 Thess. 2:14.

6:45 they will all be taught by God. In its original context Is. 54:13 is a promise of final redemption. Jesus indicates in the next sentence that those who participate in this redemption are those who come to Him, thereby identifying Himself as the One in whom that final redemption comes.

Everyone who has heard . . . comes to me. Whoever wishes may come, and they come because they have "learned from the Father," who draws them (v. 44).

6:51–58 Jesus' hearers continue to misunderstand His statements, taking them on a purely physical level (cf. v. 34). Understood literally, what Jesus said would be highly objectionable since it would involve cannibalism and a use of blood that was strictly forbidden in the Law (Gen. 9:4; Lev. 7:26, 27; 17:10–14; Deut. 12:23, 24). Jesus uses the language of eating and drinking to illustrate the intimacy of the union between Christ and the believer. This spiritual union, by which Christ imparts new life to the believer, is portrayed later in the Gospel as the union of a vine and its branches (15:1–8). It is sometimes called the "mystical union," and is a recurrent topic in Paul's letters (Gal. 2:20; Eph. 1:3–14).

Though some see here a reference to the Lord's Supper, a mention of that sacrament at this point would have been incomprehensible to Jesus' listeners. This passage is best understood as pointing to the spiritual reality the Lord's Supper also signifies—union with Christ and all the benefits of salvation received through Him.

6:51 the living bread. See note on v. 32.

the world. See note 4:42.

6:53 unless you eat . . . and drink. Apart from personal union with the Savior there is no salvation. See "The Lord's Supper" at 1 Cor. 11:23.

6:60 many of his disciples. These disciples took offense at Jesus' words, refused to listen to Jesus' explanation, and were unwilling to accept the message of salvation by grace.

6:61, 64, 70. Three examples of supernatural knowledge (cf. 2:24, 25).

this? 62 Then what if you were to see [w]the
Son of Man [x]ascending to [y]where he was
before? 63 [z]It is the Spirit who gives life; [a]the
flesh is of no avail. [b]The words that I have
spoken to you are spirit and life. 64 But
[c]there are some of you who do not
believe." (For Jesus [v]knew from the beginning who those were who did not believe,
and [d]who it was who would betray him.)
65 And he said, "This is why I told you [e]that
no one can come to me unless it is granted
him by the Father."

66 [f]After this many of his disciples turned
back and no longer walked with him. 67 So
Jesus said to [g]the Twelve, "Do you want to
go away as well?" 68 Simon Peter answered
him, "Lord, to whom shall we go? You have
[h]the words of eternal life, 69 and [i]we have
believed, and have come to know, that [j]you
are [k]the Holy One of God." 70 Jesus
answered them, [l]"Did I not choose you,
[f]the Twelve? And yet one of you is [m]a
devil." 71 He spoke of Judas [n]the son of
Simon Iscariot, for [o]he, one of the Twelve,
was going to betray him.

Jesus at the Feast of Booths

7 After this Jesus went about in Galilee.
He would not go about in Judea,
because [p]the Jews[1] were seeking to kill
him. 2 Now [q]the Jews' Feast of [r]Booths was
at hand. 3 [s]So his brothers[2] said to him,
"Leave here and go to Judea, that your disciples also may see the works you are
doing. 4 For no one works in secret if he
seeks to be known openly. If you do these
things, [t]show yourself to the world." 5 [u]For
not even [v]his brothers believed in him.
6 Jesus said to them, [w]"My time has not yet
come, but your time is always here. 7 The
world cannot hate you, but [x]it hates me
because I testify about it that [y]its works are
evil. 8 You go up to the feast. I am not[3]
going up to this feast, for [z]my time has not
yet fully come." 9 After saying this, he remained in Galilee.

10 But after [a]his brothers had gone up to
the feast, then he also went up, not publicly but in private. 11 [b]The Jews [c]were looking for him at the feast, and saying, "Where
is he?" 12 And there was much [d]muttering
about him among the people. [e]While some
said, "He is a good man," others said, "No,
[f]he is leading the people astray." 13 Yet [g]for
fear of the Jews no one spoke openly of
him.

14 About the middle of the feast Jesus
went up [h]into the temple and began teaching. 15 The Jews therefore [i]marveled, saying,
"How is it that this man has learning,[4]
when he has never studied?" 16 So Jesus

62 [w]ver. 27 [x]See Mark 16:19 [y][ch. 17:5]; See ch. 3:13
63 [z][1 Cor. 15:45; 2 Cor. 3:6] [a]ch. 3:6 [b]ver. 68
64 [c]ver. 66 [v][See ver. 61 above] [d]ver. 71; ch. 13:11
65 [e]ver. 44, 45; ch.3:27
66 [f]ver. 60, 64
67 [g]ver. 70, 71
68 [h]Acts 5:20; [ch. 12:50; 17:8]
69 [i][ch. 11:27; 1 John 4:16] [j]See ch. 1:49 [k]See Mark 1:24
70 [l]See ch. 13:18 [f][See ver. 66 above] [m]ch. 13:2, 27; 17:12
71 [n]ch. 13:26 [o]ver. 64, 67

Chapter 7
1 [p]ch. 5:18; 8:37, 40; 11:53
2 [q]ch. 5:1; 6:4 [r]See Lev. 23:34
3 [s]ver. 5, 10; See Matt. 12:46
4 [t][ch. 14:22; 18:20]
5 [u][Matt. 13:57; Mark 3:21] [v]ver. 3, 10
6 [w][ver. 8, 30]; See ch. 2:4
7 [x]ch. 15:18, 24 [y]ch. 3:19; [Col. 1:21; 1 John 3:12] **8** [z]See ch. 2:4 **10** [a]ver. 3, 5 **11** [b]ver. 1 [c]ch. 11:56 **12** [d]ver. 32 [e][ver. 40-43] [f]ver. 47 **13** [g]ch. 19:38; 20:19; [ch. 9:22; 12:42] **14** [h]ver. 28 **15** [i][ver. 46; Luke 2:47; 4:22; Acts 4:13]

[1] Or *Judeans* [2] Or *brothers and sisters*; also verses 5, 10 [3] Some manuscripts add *yet* [4] Or *this man knows his letters*

6:62 see the Son of Man ascending. Like "lifted up" (3:14 note), "ascend" here probably refers to the events beginning with Christ's being "lifted up" on the cross and climaxing in His exaltation at the right hand of the Father. If many of His disciples grumbled at the hard sayings of vv. 53–58, what would their response be to the scandal of the crucifixion? See "The Ascension of Jesus" at Luke 24:51.

where he was before. A reference to the eternal preexistence of the living Word (1:1–3).

6:63 the Spirit who gives life; the flesh is of no avail. This makes it plain that a merely physical understanding of Jesus' words was utterly mistaken. Note the close cooperation of the Father (vv. 37–40, 44–46, 57, 65), the Son, and the Holy Spirit (v. 63) shown in this passage.

6:65 no one can come to me unless. It is impossible for anyone to come to Christ without the enabling call of God. The sinner's moral inability to choose Christ must be overcome by the gracious and sovereign power of the Spirit (3:5–21).

6:66–71 A crucial turning point in this Gospel. Many disciples, together with the crowds, reject Christ in unbelief, while His remaining disciples (as exemplified by Peter's confession) deepen their faith in Him.

6:67 Do you . . . go away. Jesus' question elicits the firm confession of Peter as the spokesman for the Twelve. A parallel situation is found in Matt. 16:13–20; Mark 8:27–29; Luke 9:18–20.

7:2 Feast of Booths. The longest festival of the Jewish year (lasting seven days), this feast followed the Jewish New Year and the Day of Atonement (*Yom Kippur,* Lev. 23; Deut. 16). It was a celebration of God's gracious provision for the Israelites in the wilderness and the completion of the year's harvest. There was a ceremonial water-drawing (commemorating the provision of water in the wilderness, Num. 20:2–13) and a lamp-lighting ritual. The first of these ceremonies provides the setting for Jesus' proclamation in vv. 37, 38, the second for His statement in 8:12.

7:3, 5, 10 his brothers. Cf. 2:12; Matt. 12:46. Some of the brothers later believed in Jesus (Acts 1:14).

7:6 My time. See vv. 8, 30; 2:4; 8:20; 12:23; 13:1; 17:1; Matt. 26:18; Mark 14:41. Such passages show the concern of Jesus to conform to God's schedule.

7:7 The world. Humanity in its opposition to God and His purpose.

evil. Evildoers resent being unmasked by the good (3:19, 20).

7:8 I am not going up to this feast. Jesus does indeed later go to the Feast. His brothers have asked Him to present Himself openly to the crowds. But Jesus asserts that He is "not" yet ready to appear in such a public way.

7:13 for fear of the Jews. This is not a reference to all those who were natural descendants of Abraham. Rather, the term refers to Jewish leaders and officials who were hostile toward Jesus.

7:15 has never studied. Jesus was not known to have been taught by any rabbi, yet His knowledge and wisdom astounded those who heard Him (cf. 3:2; Matt. 7:28; Luke 2:47).

answered them, [j]"My teaching is not mine,
but his [k]who sent me. 17 [l]If anyone's will is
to do God's[1] will, [m]he will know whether
the teaching is from God or whether I [n]am
speaking on my own authority. 18 The one
who speaks on his own authority [o]seeks his
own glory, but the one who seeks the glory
of him who sent him is true, and in him
there is no falsehood. 19 [p]Has not Moses
given you the law? Yet none of you keeps
the law. [q]Why do you seek to kill me?"
20 The crowd answered, [r]"You have a
demon! Who is seeking to kill you?"
21 Jesus answered them, "I did [s]one deed,
and you all marvel at it. 22 [t]Moses gave you
circumcision (not that it is from Moses, but
[u]from the fathers), and you circumcise a
man on the Sabbath. 23 If on the Sabbath a
man receives circumcision, so that the law
of Moses may not be broken, [v]are you
angry with me because on the Sabbath I
made a man's whole body well? 24 [w]Do not
judge by appearances, but judge with right
judgment."

Can This Be the Christ?

25 Some of the people of Jerusalem therefore said, "Is not this the man whom [x]they
seek to kill? 26 And here he is, [y]speaking
openly, and they say nothing to him! Can
it be that [z]the authorities really know that
this is the Christ? 27 But [a]we know [b]where
this man comes from, and when the Christ
appears, [c]no one will know where he
comes from." 28 So Jesus proclaimed, [d]as he
taught in the temple, [a]"You know me, and
you know where I come from? But [e]I have
not come of my own accord. [f]He who sent
me is true, [g]and him you do not know. 29 [h]I
know him, for I come [i]from him, and [j]he
sent me." 30 [k]So they were seeking to arrest
him, but [l]no one laid a hand on him, [m]be-
cause his hour had not yet come. 31 Yet
[n]many of the people believed in him. They
said, [o]"When the Christ appears, will he do
more signs than this man has done?"

Officers Sent to Arrest Jesus

32 The Pharisees heard the crowd [p]mut-
tering these things about him, and the
chief priests and Pharisees sent [q]officers to
arrest him. 33 Jesus then said, [r]"I will be
with you a little longer, and then [s]I am
going to him who sent me. 34 [t]You will seek
me and you will not find me. Where I am
you cannot come." 35 The Jews said to one
another, "Where does this man intend to
go that we will not find him? [u]Does he
intend to go to [v]the Dispersion among [w]the
Greeks and teach the Greeks? 36 What does
he mean by saying, [x]'You will seek me and

16 [j]ch. 8:28; 12:49; 14:10, 24; [ch. 3:34] [k]See ch. 3:17 17 [l][ch. 8:31, 32; 14:21, 23] [m][ch. 8:43; Ps. 25:9; Dan. 12:10; Phil. 3:15] [n]See ch. 5:30 18 [o]ch. 5:41; 8:50 19 [p]ver. 23; See ch. 1:17 [q]ver. 1 20 [r]ch. 8:48, 52; 10:20; [Matt. 11:18; Mark 3:22; Luke 7:33] 21 [s]ver. 23; ch. 5:2-9 22 [t]Lev. 12:3 [u]Gen. 17:10 23 [v]ch. 5:16; See Matt. 12:2 24 [w]ch. 8:15; [Isai. 11:3; 2 Cor. 10:7]; See Deut. 1:16, 17 25 [x]ver. 1 26 [y]ch. 18:20 [z]ver. 48 27 [a][ch. 6:42; 8:14, 19; 9:29] [b]ch. 19:9 [c][ver. 42] 28 [d]ver. 14 [a][See ver. 27 above] [e]ch. 8:42; [ch. 5:43] [f]See ch. 8:26 [g]ch. 8:19; 15:21; [ch. 4:22; 8:55]

29 [h]ch. 8:55; See Matt. 11:27 [i]ch. 6:46; 9:16, 33; [ch. 1:14] [j]See ch. 3:17 30 [k]ver. 44; ch. 10:39; [Matt. 21:46] [l]ch. 8:20 [m]ver. 6 31 [n]ch. 8:30; 10:42; 11:45; 12:11; [ch. 2:23; 12:42; Matt. 21:11] [o]Matt. 12:23 32 [p]ver. 12 [q]ver. 45, 46 33 [r]ch. 12:35; 13:33; 14:19; 16:16-19 [s]ch. 16:5 34 [t]ch. 8:21; 13:33 35 [u][ch. 8:22] [v]James 1:1; 1 Pet. 1:1; [Isai. 11:12 Zeph. 3:10 [w]ch. 12:20 36 [x]ver. 34

[1] Greek *his*

7:16 his who sent me. Jesus indicates the source of His teaching. His message is not original with Himself but comes from His Father.

7:17 will know. A true perception of the divine nature of Christ's teaching is granted to those who earnestly desire to do God's will (Ps. 25:14).

7:18 on his own authority. A contrast is established between self-seeking messengers and Jesus, whose guiding principle is to be true to His mission (12:49). See 1:14, 17; 14:6; 18:37; 2 Cor. 11:10; Rev. 3:7, 14; 19:11—passages where Christ and His message are identified with truth. This is also said of God the Father (7:28; 8:26; 17:3; Ps. 31:5; Is. 65:16; Rom. 3:4; 1 Thess. 1:9; 1 John 5:20; Rev. 6:10; 15:3; 16:7) and of the Holy Spirit (14:17; 15:26; 16:13; 1 John 4:6; 5:6). The same applies to the Scripture and apostolic preaching (17:17; Ps. 119:30, 43, 138, 142, 151, 160; Eph. 1:13; Col. 1:5; 2 Tim. 2:15; James 1:18). This is in sharp contrast with Satan who is "a liar" (8:44).

7:19 Moses . . . the law. The blessing of having received the law as the revelation of God's will (cf. Ps. 103:7; Rom. 3:2; 9:4) becomes a bane through disobedience (Rom. 7:7–12).

7:20 have a demon. Compare 8:48–52; 10:19–20; Matt. 12:24.

7:21 I did one deed. Jesus refers to the one deed He had done in their region, the healing of the lame man (5:1–15).

7:22 circumcision. Circumcision was prescribed in the law of Moses (Lev. 12:3), but it was previously instituted by God in the days of Abraham (Gen. 17:10–14). The regulation that it had to be performed on the eighth day was commonly regarded as taking precedence over the law of rest on the Sabbath.

7:23 whole body well. Jesus calls attention to the inconsistency of His accusers. There were a number of activities permitted on the Sabbath, including circumcision. He compares these activities with the work of healing.

7:27 we know where this man comes from. The people knew that Jesus was from Galilee (vv. 41, 52), and this seemed to conflict with the prevailing view that the Messiah would come from Bethlehem (v. 42; Matt. 2:5, 6) or that His origin would be unknown. Jesus in response points to His divine origin rather than an earthly location. In failing to acknowledge His divine mission they showed their ignorance of God's plan, in spite of the miracles, which were proof of God's endorsement (v. 31).

7:30 they were seeking to arrest him. The plots against Christ's life could not succeed until God's own time had come.

7:34 You will seek me and you will not find me. This is not in contradiction with Matt. 7:7. There Jesus is speaking about a thirst for God (cf. v. 37) that only the Holy Spirit creates in someone; but here He is referring to an effort to find Him geographically, which would be futile since He would be in heaven. Note the contrast between unbelievers (v. 34) and believers (14:3).

7:35 Where does this man intend to go. The Jews were puzzled as to Christ's origin and so could not understand His destination, which was heaven. They understood it merely in geographical terms and were not pleased at the thought that He would exercise His ministry among the Greeks, heathens that they despised.

you will not find me,' and, 'Where I am
you cannot come'?"

Rivers of Living Water

37 [y]On the last day of the feast, the great
day, Jesus stood up and cried out, [z]"If anyone thirsts, let him [a]come to me and drink.
38 Whoever believes in me, [b]as[1] the Scripture has said, [c]'Out of his heart will flow
rivers of [d]living water.'" **39** Now [e]this he
said about the Spirit, [f]whom those who
believed in him were to receive, [g]for as yet
the Spirit had not been [h]given, [i]because
Jesus was not yet glorified.

Division Among the People

40 When they heard these words, [j]some
of the people said, "This really is [k]the
Prophet." **41** Others said, "This is [l]the
Christ." But some said, [m]"Is the Christ to
come from Galilee? **42** Has not the Scripture
said that the Christ comes [n]from the offspring of David, and comes [o]from Bethlehem, the village [p]where David was?" **43** So
there was [q]a division among the people
over him. **44** [r]Some of them wanted to arrest
him, but no one laid hands on him.

45 [s]The officers then came to the chief
priests and Pharisees, who said to them,
"Why did you not bring him?" **46** The officers answered, [t]"No one ever spoke like
this man!" **47** The Pharisees answered them,
[u]"Have you also been deceived? **48** [v]Have
any of the authorities or the Pharisees be-

37 [y]Lev. 23:36; Num. 29:35; Neh. 8:18 [z]Isai. 55:1; See ch. 4:14 [a]See ch. 6:35
38 [b][Isai. 12:3; Ezek. 47:1] [c]ch. 4:14; [Prov. 18:4] [d]See ch. 4:10
39 [e]Isai. 44:3; [1 Cor. 12:13; Gal. 3:14] [f]Joel 2:28; Acts 2:16-18; [ch. 1:33; 20:22; Luke 24:49] [g]Acts 2:4, 33 [h]ch. 3:34; Luke 11:13 [i]ch. 14:16, 17; 16:7
40 [j]See ver. 31 [k]ch. 1:21; 6:14; See Matt. 21:11
41 [l]ver. 26 [m][ver. 52; ch. 1:46]
42 [n][Ps. 89:3, 4]; See Matt. 1:1 [o]Mic. 5:2; Matt. 2:1, 5; Luke 2:4 [p]1 Sam. 16:1
43 [q]ch. 9:16; 10:19; [ver. 12]
44 [r]ver. 30
45 [s]ver. 32
46 [t]See Matt. 7:29
47 [u]ver. 12
48 [v]1 Cor. 1:20, 26; 2:8; [ch. 12:42]
50 [w]ch. 3:1; 19:39
51 [x]Deut. 17:6; 19:15; [Acts 23:3]

lieved in him? **49** But this crowd that does
not know the law is accursed." **50** [w]Nico-
demus, who had gone to him before, and
who was one of them, said to them,
51 [x]"Does our law judge a man without
first [y]giving him a hearing and learning
what he does?" **52** They replied, [z]"Are you
from Galilee too? Search and see that [a]no
prophet arises from Galilee."

[THE EARLIEST MANUSCRIPTS DO NOT INCLUDE JOHN 7:53–8:11][2]

The Woman Caught in Adultery

8 **53** [[They went each to his own house,
1 but Jesus went to the Mount of
Olives. **2** [b]Early in the morning he came
again to the temple. All the people came to
him, and [c]he sat down and taught them.
3 The scribes and the Pharisees brought a
woman who had been caught in adultery,
and placing her in the midst **4** they said to
him, "Teacher, this woman has been
caught in the act of adultery. **5** Now [d]in the
Law Moses commanded us [e]to stone such
women. So what do you say?" **6** This they
said [f]to test him, [g]that they might have
some charge to bring against him. Jesus
bent down and wrote with his finger on the
ground. **7** And as they continued to ask

[y]Deut. 1:16; Prov. 18:13 **52** [z]ver. 41 [a][2 Kin. 14:25 with Josh. 19:13]
Chapter 8 **2** [b][Luke 21:38] [c]Matt. 5:1; Luke 4:20 **5** [d]Lev. 20:10; Deut. 22:22 [e]Deut. 22:24; Ezek. 16:38, 40 **6** [f]Matt. 16:1; 19:3; 22:18, 35; Mark 8:11; 10:2; 12:15; Luke 10:25; 11:16 [g]See Luke 11:54

1 Or *let him come to me, and let him who believes in me drink. As* 2 Some manuscripts do not include 7:53–8:11; others add the passage here or after 7:36 or after 21:25 or after Luke 21:38, with variations in the text

7:37, 38 At the climax of the feast, Jesus repeated dramatically the message He had given to the Samaritan woman (4:10–14) making clear that coming to Him meant believing in Him.

7:38 as the Scripture has said. What follows is not an exact quotation from the Old Testament, but there are several Old Testament passages that connect water with the end-time gift of the Spirit (e.g., Is. 44:3; Ezek. 36:25–27) and the blessings of the present (messianic) age (e.g., Is. 12:3; 58:11). Jesus fulfills the meaning of the Feast of Booths (v. 2 note).

rivers. This implies great abundance, benefiting not only believers, but also those around them.

7:39 the Spirit had not been given. Jesus is referring to the blessing of Pentecost. Of course, the Holy Spirit was present in the Old Testament period, but at Pentecost He entered into a more intimate relationship with believers (14:17; 1 Cor. 6:19). This is the Messiah's gift to His people: He baptizes with the Spirit (Matt. 3:11; Mark 1:8; Luke 3:16), but this blessing in its full measure and glory must await the ascension of Christ who will pour out the Spirit from heaven upon His people (16:7; cf. Eph. 4:8).

7:40 the Prophet. A reference to Deut. 18:15. It is interesting to observe the testimony of those outside the group of disciples who were not blinded by prejudice. They understood that Jesus could be "the Prophet" promised by Moses. They knew that His miracles were worthy of the Messiah they expected (v. 31). Some called him "the Christ" (v. 41), and they testified that no one ever spoke like Him (v. 46).

7:41–43 Dispute over the identity of Jesus continues to focus on His origin (cf. vv. 25–36 and notes). The people's questioning remains trapped within the limits of this world (3:1–15; 4:1–26).

7:45–52 The strong prejudice of the chief priests and Pharisees is apparent in their condemnation of the temple guards (vv. 47, 48), of the crowd (v. 49), and even of Nicodemus, one of their number (v. 52).

7:52 Galilee was held in contempt by the Sanhedrin as a mixed-race region where the law was not zealously observed.

7:53–8:11 These verses are not present in some Greek manuscripts, and in others they appear at different locations, such as after 7:36, or even in Luke.

8:5 the Law. The punishment prescribed by law for adultery was death (Lev. 20:10; Deut. 22:22). Stoning was not specified, except in one case (Deut. 22:24).

8:6 to test him. If Jesus told them to carry out the stoning, He would violate the Roman law by which the Romans reserved to themselves the execution of the death penalty in occupied lands (18:31). If Jesus told them to release the woman, He would appear to condone adultery and violate the law of Moses.

wrote. This is the only passage where Jesus is said to write. Nothing is said about what He wrote.

8:7 Jesus' challenge showed the accusers to be disqualified as judges. Their purpose was not to enforce Moses' law but to entrap Jesus, and they were using this woman as a pawn to achieve their wicked design.

him, he stood up and said to them, [h]“Let
him who is without sin among you [i]be the
first to throw a stone at her.” 8 And once
more he bent down and wrote on the
ground. 9 But when they heard it, they went
away one by one, beginning with the older
ones, and Jesus was left alone with the
woman standing before him. 10 Jesus stood
up and said to her, “Woman, where are
they? Has no one condemned you?” 11 She
said, “No one, Lord.” And Jesus said, [j]“Neither do I condemn you; go, and from now
on [k]sin no more.”]]

I Am the Light of the World

12 [l]Again Jesus spoke to them, saying, [m]“I
am the light of the world. Whoever [n]fol-
lows me will not [o]walk in darkness, but
will have the light of life.” 13 So the Pharisees said to him, [p]“You are bearing witness
about yourself; your testimony is not true.”
14 Jesus answered, “Even if I do bear witness about myself, [q]my testimony is true,
for I know [r]where I came from and [s]where
I am going, but [t]you do not know where I
come from or where I am going. 15 [u]You
judge according to the flesh; [v]I judge no
one. 16 Yet even if I do judge, [w]my judgment
is true, for [x]it is not I alone who judge, but
I and the Father[1] who sent me. 17 [y]In your
Law it is written that the testimony of two
men is true. 18 I am the one who bears witness about myself, and [z]the Father who
sent me bears witness about me.” 19 They
said to him therefore, “Where is your
Father?” Jesus answered, [a]“You know neither me nor my Father. [b]If you knew me,
you would know my Father also.” 20 These
words he spoke in [c]the treasury, as he
taught in the temple; but [d]no one arrested
him, because [e]his hour had not yet come.
21 So he said to them again, [f]“I am going
away, and [g]you will seek me, and [h]you will
die in your sin. Where I am going, you cannot come.” 22 So the Jews said, [i]“Will he kill
himself, since he says, ‘Where I am going,
you cannot come’?” 23 He said to them,
[j]“You are from below; I am from above.
[k]You are of this world; [l]I am not of this
world. 24 I told you that you [m]would die in
your sins, for [n]unless you believe that [o]I am
he you will die in your sins.” 25 So they said
to him, [p]“Who are you?” Jesus said to
them, “Just what I have been telling you
from the beginning. 26 I have much to say
about you and much to judge, but [q]he who
sent me is true, and I declare [r]to the world
[s]what I have heard from him.” 27 They did
not understand that [t]he had been speaking
to them about the Father. 28 So Jesus said to
them, “When you have [u]lifted up the Son
of Man, [v]then you will know that [w]I am he,
and that [x]I do nothing on my own authority, but [y]speak just as the Father taught
me. 29 And [z]he who sent me is with me.
[z]He has not left me alone, for [a]I always do
the things that are pleasing to him.” 30 As
he was saying these things, [b]many believed
in him.

7 [h]Rom. 2:1, 22 [i]Deut. 17:7 **11** [j]ver. 15; [ch. 3:17; Luke 12:14] [k]ch. 5:14 **12** [l]ch. 7:37, 38 [m][Ps. 36:9; Isai. 42:6; 49:6; Mal. 4:2]; See ch. 1:4, 9 [n]ch. 12:26; 21:19 [o]See ch. 12:35 **13** [p]ch. 5:31 **14** [q][Rev. 3:14] [r]ch. 13:3; 16:28 [s]ver. 21; ch. 7:33 [t][ch. 7:28; 9:29] **15** [u]ch. 7:24; 1 Sam. 16:7; [Job 10:4] [v]ch. 12:47; [ver. {11}] **16** [w]ch. 5:30 [x]ver. 29; ch. 16:32 **17** [y]See Num. 35:30 **18** [z]ch. 5:37 **19** [a]ver. 55; ch. 16:3 [b]ch. 14:7 **20** [c]See Matt. 27:6 [d]ch. 7:30 [e]ch. 7:8 **21** [f]ch. 14:28; [ch. 14:2, 3; 16:7] [g]See ch. 7:34 [h]ver. 24; Ezek. 3:18; 33:8 **22** [i][ch. 7:35] **23** [j][ver. 44; ch. 3:31] [k]1 John 4:5 [l]ch. 17:14, 16 **24** [m]ver. 21 [n]ch. 16:9 [o]Mark 13:6; Luke 21:8 **25** [p][ch. 1:19] **26** [q]ch. 3:33; 7:28; Rom. 3:4 [r][ch. 18:20] [s]ver. 40; ch. 15:15; [ch. 3:32; Rev. 1:1] **27** [t]ver. 18, 26 **28** [u]ch. 3:14; 12:32, 34 [v][ch. 16:8-11] [w]See ver. 24 [x]See ch. 5:30 [y]See ch. 7:16 **29** [z]ver. 16; ch. 16:32; Acts 10:38; See ch. 10:38 [a]ch. 4:34; 5:30; 6:38; [1 John 3:22] **30** [b]See ch. 7:31

[1] Some manuscripts *he*

8:11 condemn. This is a legal term referring to the sentence of a court. Jesus indicates that no such lawful procedures have been followed and therefore there is no basis for the capital punishment proposed. Jesus admonished the woman not to go on sinning.

8:12 I am the light of the world. In Jesus' time, candles were used as part of the celebration of the Feast of Booths. During this feast, the rock that provided water in the wilderness and the pillar of fire that provided light and guidance were remembered (Ex. 13:21). The rock pointed to Jesus (1 Cor. 10:4), and He also is the light to which the pillar of fire as a type pointed. Since God is light (1 John 1:5), Jesus' words amount to a claim of deity. Again, "I am" points back to Ex. 3:14 (6:35 note).

8:13 your testimony is not true. This discussion, which runs through v. 19, pivots on the question of valid testimony. The Pharisees say that Jesus' testimony is not legally acceptable because it lacks corroboration (Deut. 17:6; 19:15).

8:14 I know where I came from. Since Jesus knows where He "came from" (heaven), He knows that His testimony is valid and true. Jesus' origin is again the point of conflict (7:41–43, 52 and notes).

8:16 not I alone. Since the Father is His witness, Christ's testimony is legally acceptable. In any case, one who has the witness of God needs nothing more.

8:19 The Pharisees misunderstood Jesus' claim as a reference to His physical father, and they may have been eager to challenge Him as a child allegedly born out of wedlock. In speaking of His Father, however, Jesus was not talking about Joseph but about God. Knowledge of the Father comes through the Son (1:18; 14:9; 1 John 5:20). The Pharisees' blindness to Jesus shows that their technical knowledge of the law did not give them the knowledge of God.

8:21 I am going away. Jesus speaks of His death, resurrection, and ascension.

die in your sin. Jesus clearly states the two destinies of humanity. Not all will be saved; some cannot go where Jesus is going. The only way of salvation is to believe (v. 24; 3:16, 18).

8:24, 28 I am he. Here Jesus applies Old Testament language for Yahweh to Himself (Ex. 3:14; Is. 43:10), an identification that becomes unambiguous in v. 58.

8:28 lifted up. See note at 3:14.

8:30 believed in him. From what is said later (vv. 33, 37, 39), it is apparent that their profession was superficial. True believers are those who abide in His word (v. 31). Perseverance distinguishes those who are truly born of God (15:2, 6; 1 John 2:19).

The Truth Will Set You Free

31 So Jesus said to the Jews who had
believed in him, [c]"If you abide in my word,
you are truly my disciples, 32 and you will
[d]know the truth, and the truth [e]will set you
free." 33 They answered him, [f]"We are offspring of Abraham and have never been
enslaved to anyone. How is it that you say,
'You will become free'?"

34 Jesus answered them, "Truly, truly, I
say to you, [g]everyone who commits sin is a
slave[1] to sin. 35 [h]The slave does not remain
in the house forever; [i]the son remains forever. 36 So if the Son sets you free, you will
be free indeed. 37 I know that you are offspring of Abraham; yet [j]you seek to kill me
because my word finds no place in you. 38 [k]I
speak of what I have seen with my Father,
and you do what you have heard [l]from
your father."

You Are of Your Father the Devil

39 They answered him, [m]"Abraham is our
father." Jesus said to them, [n]"If you were
Abraham's children, you would be doing
what Abraham did, 40 but now [o]you seek to
kill me, a man who has told you the truth
[p]that I heard from God. This is not what
Abraham did. 41 You are doing what your
father did." They said to him, [q]"We were
not born of sexual immorality. We have
[r]one Father—even God." 42 Jesus said to
them, [s]"If God were your Father, you
would love me, for [t]I came from God and
[u]I am here. [v]I came not of my own accord,
but [w]he sent me. 43 [x]Why do you not understand what I say? It is because you cannot
[y]bear to hear my word. 44 [z]You are of your
father the devil, and your will is to do your
father's desires. [a]He was a murderer from
the beginning, and [b]has nothing to do with
the truth, because there is no truth in him.
[c]When he lies, he speaks out of his own
character, for he is a liar and the father of
lies. 45 But because I tell the truth, you do
not believe me. 46 Which one of you convicts me of sin? If I tell the truth, why do
you not believe me? 47 [d]Whoever is of God
hears the words of God. [e]The reason why

31 [c]ch. 15:7, 8; 2 John 9 **32** [d]2 John 1 [e]ver. 36; Rom. 6:18, 22; 8:2; 1 Cor. 7:22; 2 Cor. 3:17; Gal. 5:1, 13; James 1:25; 2:12; 1 Pet. 2:16 **33** [f]ver. 37, 39; Matt. 3:9; [Luke 19:9; Rom. 9:7] **34** [g]Rom. 6:16-20; Tit. 3:3; 2 Pet. 2:19 **35** [h]Gen. 21:10; Gal. 4:30 [i]Luke 15:31 **37** [j]ver. 40; See ch. 7:1 **38** [k]ch. 3:32; 5:19; 6:46 [l]ver. 41, 44 **39** [m]ver. 33, 56 [n][Gal. 3:7, 9] **40** [o]ver. 37

[p]ver. 26 **41** [q][Hos. 2:4] [r]Deut. 32:6; Isai. 63:16; 64:8; [ver. 47] **42** [s][1 John 5:1]

[t]1 John 5:20; [Heb. 10:9] [u]ch. 16:28; 17:8 [v]ch. 7:28 [w]See ch. 3:17 **43** [x]ch. 7:17 [y]Jer. 6:10; [1 Cor. 2:14] **44** [z]1 John 3:8, 12; [ver. 23]; See Matt. 13:38 [a]Gen. 4:8, 9; 1 John 3:12, 15; [Rom. 5:12] [b][1 John 2:4] [c]Gen. 3:4; 2 Cor. 11:3; Rev. 12:9 **47** [d][ch. 18:37; 1 John 4:6] [e][ch. 10:26]

[1] Greek *bondservant*; also verse 35

8:32 you will know the truth. Holding to the teaching of Christ who is the truth (14:6) leads one to the truth that sets a person free from slavery to sin. Salvation is not obtained by intellectual knowledge as the Gnostics imagined, but by a vital relationship with Jesus Christ and a commitment to the truth He revealed (18:37).

8:33 We . . . have never been enslaved. The Jews had been enslaved in Egypt and later were ruled by the Philistines, the Assyrians, and others. Since they could hardly deny this, they were probably saying that they had been a nation under God since the Exodus, no matter what else had happened to them. It is also possible that they were speaking about the time of the Romans, when they had certain liberties, including official recognition as a religion.

8:34 everyone who commits sin is a slave. Jesus describes the gravity of sin and the predicament of humanity under sin. His hearers did not understand the freedom He offered them as they did not understand the bondage they were in. See "The Freedom and Bondage of the Will" at Jer. 17:9.

8:36 if the Son sets you free. Regeneration (the new birth) is the work of the Holy Spirit (3:3–8), accomplished on the basis of Christ's death and resurrection on our behalf (3:14–16).

free indeed. Jesus was not speaking of political freedom, nor merely a freedom by which we are relieved from physical bondage. True freedom is to serve God, to fulfill the purposes of those specially created in God's image. Sin deprives us of this fulfillment because sin clouds our minds, degrades our feelings, and enslaves our wills. This is what the Reformers called "total depravity"; its only remedy is the grace of God in spiritual rebirth (3:3). See "Christian Liberty" at Gal. 5:1.

8:37 offspring of Abraham. God is interested in spiritual descent rather than physical ancestry. It does not matter how good a person's ancestors have been if he or she is walking in the path of disobedience (Ezek. 18). Likewise it does not matter how bad a person's ancestors have been if that person is renewed by God's Spirit and walks in the way of faith.

8:40 This is not what Abraham did. Abraham was obedient to God's direction even when it was painful for him. Jesus' audience claimed to be Abraham's descendants, but Jesus shows they are not like their ancestor in the essential matter of obedience. True sonship is not defined by biology but by obedience.

8:41 born of sexual immorality. This may well have been a sarcastic suggestion that Jesus was illegitimate.

Father . . . God. The Jews seldom addressed God as "Father." The fatherhood of God is a leading feature of Christ's teaching. God is the Father of those who are saved and received into God's household by adoption. God is the Father of the Son in a unique sense (1:14 note; 3:16; 20:17).

8:42 you would love me. The unity between Father and Son is so profound that no one can belong to the Father and reject the Son. Again Jesus' origin is a point of contention (7:41–43 note).

8:44 You are of your father the devil. The relation of truth and righteousness has been prominent in this Gospel. People love darkness (error) rather than light (truth), because their deeds are evil (3:10). A frightful contrast is apparent here; there are just two options: God or Satan. By God's grace, Abraham (vv. 39–41) had walked in the way of faith and obedience. Those who rejected Jesus were doing the opposite.

your will. Sinners desire to do what is evil. Only a supernatural act of grace can redirect a person's will to desire the good.

He was a murderer . . . a liar. Among all the sins that could be mentioned as characteristic of Satan, murder and lying are singled out: lying because it is the direct opposite of "truth," the central emphasis of this section (vv. 32–47); and murder because they desired to kill Jesus (v. 40). Satan contrasts sharply with Jesus who is "the truth, and the life" (14:6) and the giver of life (10:10, 28).

8:46 Which one of you convicts me of sin. No one can convict Jesus of sin, or prove any charge against Him. Jesus is free of all sin (2 Cor. 5:21), "holy, innocent, unstained, separated from sinners" (Heb. 7:26), doing always what pleases the Father (v. 29).

you do not hear them is that [f]you are not
of God."

Before Abraham Was, I Am

48 The Jews answered him, "Are we not
right in saying that you are a Samaritan and
[g]have a demon?" 49 Jesus answered, "I do
not have a demon, but [h]I honor my Father,
and you dishonor me. 50 Yet [i]I do not seek
my own glory; there is One who seeks it,
and he is the judge. 51 Truly, truly, [j]I say to
you, if anyone keeps my word, he will
never [k]see death." 52 The Jews said to him,
"Now we know that you have a demon!
[l]Abraham died, as did the prophets, yet
[m]you say, 'If anyone keeps my word, he
will never [n]taste death.' 53 [o]Are you greater
than our father Abraham, who died? And
the prophets died! Who do you make yourself out to be?" 54 Jesus answered, [p]"If I glorify myself, my glory is nothing. [q]It is my
Father who glorifies me, [r]of whom you say,
'He is our God.'[1] 55 But [s]you have not
known him. [t]I know him. If I were to say
that I do not know him, I would be [u]a liar
[v]like you, but I do know him and I keep his
word. 56 [w]Your father Abraham [x]rejoiced
[y]that he would see my day. [z]He saw it and
was glad." 57 So the Jews said to him, "You
are not yet fifty years old, and have you
seen Abraham?"[2] 58 Jesus said to them,
"Truly, truly, I say to you, before Abraham
was, [a]I am." 59 So [b]they picked up stones to
throw at him, but Jesus hid himself and
went out of the temple.

Jesus Heals a Man Born Blind

9 As he passed by, he saw a man blind
from birth. 2 And his disciples asked
him, [c]"Rabbi, [d]who sinned, [e]this man or
[f]his parents, that he was born blind?"
3 Jesus answered, "It was not that this man
sinned, or his parents, but [g]that the works
of God might be displayed in him. 4 We
must [h]work the works of him who sent me
[i]while it is day; night is coming, when no
one can work. 5 As long as I am in the
world, [j]I am the light of the world."
6 Having said these things, [k]he spat on the

47 [f][ver. 41]
48 [g]See ch. 7:20
49 [h]ch. 5:23; [ch. 7:18]
50 [i]ver. 54; ch. 5:41
51 [j]ch. 5:24; 11:26 [k]See Luke 2:26
52 [l][Zech. 1:5] [m]ver. 51 [n]Matt. 16:28; Heb. 2:9
53 [o][ch. 4:12]
54 [p]ver. 50 [q]ch. 13:32; 17:1; Acts 3:13; Heb. 5:5; 2 Pet. 1:17 [r]ver. 41
55 [s]ver. 19; ch. 7:28 [t]ch. 7:29; See Matt. 11:27 [u]1 John 1:6 [v]ver. 44
56 [w]ver. 39 [x]See Matt. 13:17 [y]Luke 17:22 [z][Heb. 11:13]
58 [a]See Ex. 3:14
59 [b]ch. 10:31
Chapter 9
2 [c]See ch. 1:38 [d][Luke 13:2, 4] [e][ver. 34] [f]Ex. 20:5
3 [g][ch. 11:4]
4 [h]See ch. 4:34 [i]ch. 11:9; 12:35; [Rom. 13:12; Gal. 6:10] 5 [j]See ch. 1:4, 5, 9; 8:12
6 [k]Mark 7:33; 8:23

[1] Some manuscripts *your God* [2] Some manuscripts *has Abraham seen you?*

8:47 you do not hear. Sin paralyzes our spiritual senses. Only an act of God's grace enables a sinner to hear His voice (cf. v. 43; 10:3, 4, 16, 27).

8:48 a Samaritan. A term of insult, possibly implying that Jesus was born out of wedlock (v. 41 note).

have a demon. When cornered by the truth, Jesus' enemies turn to blasphemy (Matt. 12:24, 31).

8:49 I do not have a demon. Jesus' conduct, in honoring the Father and not seeking self-glory, is the opposite of what a demon-possessed person would do. Jesus is not afraid to refer the matter to God's judgment (cf. 17:4).

8:51 if anyone keeps my word, he will never see death. Death, as eternal separation from fellowship with God, is the judicial punishment for sin (Rom. 6:23). Since Jesus died as the substitute for His people, those who belong to Him are freed from the penalty of sin because Christ endured it for them.

never. In extending the promise beyond this life, Jesus lays claim to a divine prerogative. The Jews understood the statement as promising avoidance of physical death (v. 52). Earlier statements made clear what Jesus meant (5:24–29).

8:53 Are you greater than our father Abraham. Abraham and the prophets, great as they were in the history of redemption, could not take away death. Only Christ has triumphed over the grave.

8:54 my glory. In the days of His earthly ministry, Jesus did not seek honor even though it belonged to Him as the Son of God. Christ's glory was visible to those who had eyes to see it (1:14). It was apparent in His resurrection and ascension (1 Tim. 3:16), and will be seen fully at His Second Coming.

8:56 Abraham . . . saw it and was glad. Abraham saw Christ's day as he embraced in faith many promises given to him by God, promises that demanded the coming of Christ to be fulfilled. Since the context of the discussion has been Satan as a murderer and Jesus as one whose death delivers from death, it may have special reference to God's providing the ram as a substitute when Abraham was prepared to sacrifice Isaac. This statement shows clearly that even in Old Testament times, believers were saved through faith in Christ presented to them in the foreshadowing given by God to reveal His redemptive plan (cf. Acts 4:12).

8:57 fifty years old. Jesus was closer to thirty (Luke 3:23).

8:58 before Abraham was, I am. This is a clear reference to Jesus' eternal preexistence. Since this is an attribute of God alone, this text is a forceful statement of Jesus' deity. The present tense of the verb suggests the eternal present of God's eternity. "I am" is also reminiscent of God's name in Ex. 3:14 (vv. 24, 28 note). See "Jesus Christ, God and Man" at 1:14.

8:59 they picked up stones. The Jews would not accept Christ's claim to be God, but treated it as blasphemy, for which stoning was required in the law (Lev. 24:16; cf. John 10:31; Matt. 26:65).

9:2 who sinned. Many Jews, like Job's friends, believed that every temporal misfortune was God's punishment for some specific sin. With a congenital affliction the explanation could be that the sin had been committed in the womb, or by the parents whose sinful act victimized their child. Jesus dismisses these as improper explanations (v. 3), but this is not to say that certain trials are not the God-ordained punishment for certain sins (e.g., the life of David after His adultery and murder, 2 Sam. 12–21). Neither does Jesus here dismiss the biblical doctrine of original sin (Rom. 5:12–21), which teaches that all suffering is the consequence of our corporate sin and rebellion in Adam. But it is unwise and uncharitable to judge that the sufferings of others are specifically punitive (Matt. 7:1). The question put to Jesus presents a false dilemma. Only two possibilities were given as reasons for the man's affliction, his own sin or the sin of his parents. Jesus offers a third option (v. 3).

9:3 that the works of God might be displayed. Some of our sufferings, like the trials of Job, are for God's glory, either through our resulting refinement or through a spectacular healing as in the present case. God's purpose is not always presently known to us, but we have God's assurance that His purpose is good (Rom. 8:28).

9:6 he spat on the ground. In Mark 8:23–25, Jesus also used saliva in the course of a healing. It was not a medical agent, but provided an opportunity for the man to show his faith by obeying Jesus' command (v. 7).

ground and made mud with the saliva.
[l]Then he anointed the man's eyes with the
mud **7** and said to him, "Go, wash in [m]the
pool of Siloam" (which means Sent). So he
went and washed and [n]came back seeing.
8 The neighbors and those who had seen
him before as a beggar were saying, [o]"Is
this not the man who used to sit and beg?"
9 Some said, "It is he." Others said, "No,
but he is like him." He kept saying, "I am
the man." **10** So they said to him, "Then
how were your eyes opened?" **11** He answered, [p]"The man called Jesus made mud
and anointed my eyes and said to me, 'Go
to Siloam and wash.' So I went and washed
and received my sight." **12** They said to him,
"Where is he?" He said, "I do not know."
13 They brought to the Pharisees the man
who had formerly been blind. **14** [q]Now it
was a Sabbath day when Jesus made the
mud and opened his eyes. **15** [r]So the Pharisees again asked him how he had received
his sight. And he said to them, "He put
mud on my eyes, and I washed, and I see."
16 Some of the Pharisees said, "This man is
not [s]from God, [t]for he does not keep the
Sabbath." But others said, [u]"How can a
man who is a sinner do such signs?" And
[v]there was a division among them. **17** So
they said again to the blind man, "What do
you say about him, since he has opened
your eyes?" He said, [w]"He is a prophet."
18 [x]The Jews did not believe that he had
been blind and had received his sight, until
they called the parents of the man who had
received his sight **19** and asked them, "Is
this your son, who you say was born blind?
How then does he now see?" **20** His parents
answered, "We know that this is our son
and that he was born blind. **21** But how he
now sees we do not know, nor do we know
who opened his eyes. Ask him; he is of age.
He will speak for himself." **22** (His parents
said these things [y]because they feared the
Jews, for [z]the Jews had already agreed that
if anyone should [a]confess Jesus[1] to be
Christ, [b]he was to be put out of the synagogue.) **23** Therefore his parents said, [c]"He
is of age; ask him."
24 So for the second time they called the
man who had been blind and said to him,
[d]"Give glory to God. We know that [e]this
man is a sinner." **25** He answered, "Whether
he is a sinner I do not know. One thing I
do know, that though I [f]was blind, now I
see." **26** They said to him, "What did he do
to you? How did he open your eyes?" **27** He
answered them, [g]"I have told you already,
and you would not listen. Why do you
want to hear it again? Do you also want to
become his disciples?" **28** And they reviled
him, saying, "You are his disciple, but [h]we
are disciples of Moses. **29** We know that
God has spoken to Moses, but as for this
man, [i]we do not know where he comes
from." **30** The man answered, "Why, this is
[j]an amazing thing! [k]You do not know
where he comes from, and yet he opened
my eyes. **31** We know that [l]God does not listen to sinners, but [m]if anyone is a worshiper of God and does his will, God
listens to him. **32** Never since the world
began has it been heard that anyone
opened the eyes of a man born blind. **33** [n]If
this man were not from God, he could do
nothing." **34** They answered him, [o]"You
were born in utter sin, and would you
teach us?" And they [p]cast him out.
35 Jesus heard that they had cast him out,
and having found him he said, "Do you
believe in [q]the Son of Man?"[2] **36** He answered, [r]"And who is he, sir, that I may
believe in him?" **37** Jesus said to him, "You

6 [l]See Matt. 9:29
7 [m]Isai. 8:6; Luke 13:4 [n]ch. 11:37
8 [o][Acts 3:2, 10]
11 [p]ver. 6, 7
14 [q]ch. 5:9
15 [r]ver. 10
16 [s]See ch. 7:29 [t]See Matt. 12:2 [u]ver. 33 [v]ch. 7:43; 10:19
17 [w]See ch. 4:19; 6:14
18 [x]ver. 22; [ver. 13]
22 [y]See ch. 7:13 [z][ch. 7:45-52] [a][Rom. 10:9] [b]ch. 12:42; 16:2
23 [c]ver. 21
24 [d]Josh. 7:19; Jer. 13:16; [1 Sam. 6:5; Isai. 42:12; Luke 17:18; Acts 12:23] [e]ver. 16
25 [f]ver. 18, 24
27 [g]ver. 15
28 [h][ch. 5:45]
29 [i]See ch. 8:14
30 [j][ch. 12:37; Mark 6:6] [k][ch. 3:10]
31 [l]Job 27:9; Ps. 66:18; Prov. 28:9 [m]Ps. 34:15, 16; 145:19; Prov. 15:20; [James 5:16]
33 [n]ver. 16; [ch. 3:2; 1:21]
34 [o][ver. 2] [p][ver. 22]
35 [q]ch. 10:36
36 [r][Rom. 10:14]

[1] Greek *him* [2] Some manuscripts *the Son of God*

9:9 he is like him. The miracle was so amazing that onlookers could not believe it was the same man.

9:12 I do not know. As the story develops, the healed man moves forward in the path of faith. Here, he does not know where Jesus is; later he asserts that Jesus is a prophet (v. 17); later still he raises doubts about the accusation that Jesus is a sinner (v. 25); and finally, after meeting Jesus again, he acknowledges that Jesus is the Son of God and worships Him (vv. 35–38). These steps of faith illustrate what the author of the Gospel wants for his readers (20:31).

9:16 Sabbath. Instead of being grateful for this supernatural work of God's grace, the Pharisees began to haggle about the observance of the Sabbath. Their concern was specifically about their traditional interpretation of what the fourth commandment required. Not one of the actions involved (spitting, applying mud, going as far as Siloam, washing one's face, healing a blind man) was forbidden by the law. Rather than question their own understanding of the law, they rejected Jesus and His ministry.

9:18–23 An inquiry with the blind man's parents establishes the reality of his blindness and the cure.

9:24–34 A second investigation with the healed man brings no new facts to light, but the investigators' position is hardened. The Pharisees call Jesus a "sinner" (v. 24) whose origin is unknown (v. 29), and they excommunicate the man whose replies only irritate them (vv. 27, 30). His replies are to the point: The man born blind had been healed, and "God does not listen to sinners" (v. 31).

9:35–38 In this second encounter with Jesus, the healed man's faith moves from a general confidence in Jesus' godly mission to a joyful acceptance of Him as the Messiah, worthy to be worshiped.

have seen him, and [s]it is he who is speaking to you." 38 He said, "Lord, I believe,"
and he worshiped him. 39 Jesus said, [t]"For
judgment I came into this world, [u]that
those who do not see may see, and [v]those
who see may become blind." 40 Some of the
Pharisees near him heard these things, and
said to him, [w]"Are we also blind?" 41 Jesus
said to them, "If you were blind, [x]you
would have no guilt;[1] but now that you
say, 'We see,' your guilt remains.

37 [s]ch. 4:26
39 [t]See ch. 5:22 [u][Matt. 11:25; Luke 4:18] [v][Matt. 9:13; 13:13; Mark 4:12; 2 Cor. 2:16]
40 [w]Rom. 2:19
41 [x]ch. 15:22, 24; [ch. 19:11; James 1:17; 1 John 1:8]

I Am the Good Shepherd

10 "Truly, truly, I say to you, he who
does not enter the sheepfold by the
door but climbs in by another way, that
man is a thief and a robber. 2 But he who

[1] Greek *you would not have sin*

Definite Redemption

Definite redemption, also called "particular redemption," or "limited atonement," is the historic Reformed doctrine about the intention of the triune God in the death of Jesus Christ. Without questioning the infinite worth of Christ's sacrifice or the genuineness of God's sincere invitation to all who hear the gospel (Rev. 22:17), the doctrine states that Christ in dying intended to accomplish what He did accomplish: to take away the sins of God's elect, and to ensure that they would all be brought to faith through regeneration and preserved through faith for glory. Christ did not intend to die in this efficacious sense for everyone. The proof of that, as Scripture and experience unite to teach us, is that not all are saved.

In discussing the atonement, some say that Christ died for all, and that all without exception will be saved. This is an actual universalism. A second doctrine is that Christ died for all, but that His death has no saving effect without an added faith and repentance not foreseen in His death. In other words, He died for the general purpose of making salvation possible, but the salvation of particular individuals was not included in His death. This is a hypothetical universalism. The third doctrine is that although Christ's death was infinite in value, it was offered to save only some, those who were known beforehand. This is the limited or definite atonement.

Scripture does not teach that all will be saved, ruling out actual universalism. The other two views do not differ about how many will be saved, but about the purpose for which Christ died. Scripture addresses this question. The New Testament teaches that God chose for salvation a great number of the fallen race and sent Christ into the world to save them (John 6:37–40; 10:27–29; 11:51, 52; Rom. 8:28–39; Eph. 1:3–14; 1 Pet. 1:20). Christ is said to have died for a particular people, with the clear implication that His death secured their salvation (John 10:15–18, 27–29; Rom. 5:8–10; 8:32; Gal. 2:20; 3:13, 14; 4:4, 5; 1 John 4:9, 10; Rev. 1:4–6; 5:9, 10). Before He died, Christ prayed for those the Father had given Him, and not for the world (John 17:9, 20). Jesus' prayer lifted up those for whom He was going to die, and He promised them that He would not fail to save them. Such passages present the idea of a definite atonement. The Old Testament, with its emphasis on the election of grace, provides strong support.

The free offer of the gospel, and the commandment to preach the good news everywhere, is not inconsistent with the teaching that Christ died for His elect people. All who come to Christ will find mercy (John 6:35, 47–51, 54–57; Rom. 1:16; 10:8–13). The gospel offers Christ, who knows His sheep. He died for them; He calls them by name, and they hear Him. This is the gospel that He commanded His disciples to preach in all the world, in order to save sinners.

9:39–41 In this epilogue Jesus brings to light the impact of His coming: those who falsely imagine they have special insight into the things of God become blind opponents of God's ways, and those who seem less informed are able to see when the Spirit of God opens their eyes and leads them to faith.

9:39 For judgment I came. The First Coming of Christ did not bring in the Last Judgment (3:17; 12:47), but He confronted people with the obligation to decide for or against Him (Matt. 12:30; Luke 11:23). Until the Second Coming of Christ, this is still the age of redemption during which the blind are made to see, and those dead in trespasses and sins are raised to newness of life (Eph. 2:4).

9:41 We see. The opponents lacked the elementary humility of acknowledging that they were sinners.

10:1–42 This chapter is divided into three sections: the good shepherd discourse (vv. 1–21), the discourse with the Jews at the Feast of Dedication (vv. 22–38), and a closing section (vv. 39–42). The chapter is unified by the teaching on the certain character of Christ's saving activity.

10:1 For God as the Shepherd of His people, see Gen. 48:15; 49:24; Ps. 23:1; 28:9; 78:52; 80:1; Is. 40:11; Jer. 31:10; Ezek. 34:11–16. A prophecy in Zech. 13:7 concerning "the shepherd" of Israel was applied by Jesus to Himself (Matt. 26:31). Jesus here presents His ministry as the work of a shepherd. In other parts of the New Testament, Jesus is referred to as the "great shepherd" (Heb. 13:20) and "the chief Shepherd" (1 Pet. 5:4); and Rev. 7:17 says that "the Lamb . . . will be their shepherd."

the sheepfold. A fenced enclosure with one entrance. Thieves and predators might climb over the fence to steal or even kill the sheep (vv. 8, 10).

enters by the door is the shepherd of the
sheep. 3 To him the gatekeeper opens.
The sheep hear his voice, and he calls his
own sheep by name and leads them out.
4 When he has brought out all his own, he
goes before them, and the sheep follow
him, for they know his voice. 5 [y]A stranger
they will not follow, but they will flee
from him, for they do not know the voice
of strangers." 6 This figure of speech Jesus
[z]used with them, but they [a]did not understand what he was saying to them.
7 So Jesus again said to them, "Truly,
truly, I say to you, [b]I am the door of the
sheep. 8 All who came before me are thieves
and robbers, but the sheep did not listen to
them. 9 I am the door. If anyone enters by
me, [c]he will be saved and will go in and out
and [d]find pasture. 10 The thief comes only
to steal and [e]kill and destroy. I came that
they may have life and have it abundantly.
11 [f]I am the good shepherd. The good shepherd [g]lays down his life for the sheep. 12 He
who is [h]a hired hand and not a shepherd,
who does not own the sheep, sees the wolf
coming and [i]leaves the sheep and flees,
and the wolf snatches them and [j]scatters
them. 13 He flees because [k]he is a hired
hand and [l]cares nothing for the sheep. 14 [m]I
am the good shepherd. [n]I know my own
and [o]my own know me, 15 [p]just as the
Father knows me and I know the Father;
and [q]I lay down my life for the sheep.
16 And [r]I have other sheep that are not of
this fold. [s]I must bring them also, and [t]they
will listen to my voice. So there will be [u]one
flock, [v]one shepherd. 17 [w]For this reason the
Father loves me, [x]because [y]I lay down my
life that I may take it up again. 18 [z]No one
takes it from me, but [y]I lay it down [a]of my
own accord. I have authority to lay it down,
and [b]I have authority to take it up again.
[c]This charge I have received from my
Father."

Chapter 10
5 [y][ver. 12, 13]
6 [z]ch. 9:40 [a]See Mark 9:32
7 [b]ver. 9; [ch. 14:6; Eph. 2:18]
9 [c][ch. 5:34] [d]Ps. 23:2; Ezek. 34:14
10 [e][Jer. 23:1; Ezek. 34:3]
11 [f]Isai. 40:11; Ezek. 34:12, 23; 37:24; Zech. 13:7; Heb. 13:20; 1 Pet. 2:25; 5:4; [ch. 21:15-17; Ps. 23; Rev. 7:17] [g]ver. 15, 17; ch. 15:13; 1 John 3:16; [Matt. 20:28; Mark 10:45]
12 [h][Ezek. 34:2-6] [i]Zech. 11:17; 13:7 [j][Jer. 23:1-3]
13 [k][1 Pet. 5:2] [l]Zech. 11:16
14 [m]See ver. 11 [n]ver. 27. Nah. 1:7; 2 Tim. 2:19 [o]ver. 4
15 [p]See Matt. 11:27 [q]See ver. 11
16 [r]Isai. 56:8 [s][Ezek. 34:11-13; Matt. 8:11, 12; Eph. 2:13-18; 1 Pet. 2:25] [t]ch. 5:25; 18:37; [Acts 28:28] [u][ch. 11:52; 12:32; 17:11, 21, 22] [v]Ezek. 34:23; 37:24
17 [w]Phil. 2:9; See ch. 5:20 [x]Isai. 53:7, 8, 12; Heb. 2:9 [y]ver. 11
18 [z][ch. 18:6; Matt. 26:53] [y][See ver. 17 above] [a][ch. 5:30] [b]ch. 2:19; [Phil. 2:7] [c]ch. 12:49; 14:31; 15:10

10:2 enters by the door. The shepherd does not need to climb over the fence, but is admitted by the watchman. The language here implies that several flocks are kept in one fold, and that a proper shepherd attended to his own sheep.

10:3 The sheep hear. The shepherd knows his sheep "by name" and the sheep recognize their shepherd's voice and come to him. This is a vivid image of how God has marked some people to be His in the midst of fallen humanity.

10:4 know his voice. Electing grace is also effective grace: Jesus, who knows the sheep, reveals Himself to them in such a way that they will respond. He does not force them to follow Him, but through the work of regeneration He makes them willing.

10:5 A stranger they will not follow. This comforting promise does not exclude the need to warn believers against deceitful teachers (Mark 13:22, 23; 2 Tim. 3:5; 4:2–5; 1 John 2:26).

10:6 they did not understand. In some cases the disciples themselves did not understand what Jesus was teaching (Matt. 13:10–17, 36; 15:15).

10:7 I am the door. Jesus changes the metaphor from "shepherd" to "door." As the "door of the sheep," Jesus is the One through whom eternal life is received (cf. 14:6; Matt. 7:13, 14). The "I am" phrase here continues the series of seven such expressions in this Gospel (6:35 note).

10:8 thieves and robbers. This does not refer to the Old Testament prophets sent by God (Matt. 21:34–36; 23:29–36), but to anyone who falsely claimed to be the Messiah.

10:9 If anyone enters by me, he will be saved. This guarantees that salvation is given to those who trust in Christ (Acts 16:31; Rom. 10:9, 10). In 14:6, it is made plain that these only are saved. Christ is necessary and sufficient for salvation (3:36).

go in and out. The sheep would come into the fold for safety and go out under their shepherd's guidance for pasture.

10:10 that they may have life . . . abundantly. The life that Jesus gives is unique because it is eternal, and He gives this life in ever-growing abundance to His redeemed.

10:11 good shepherd. Jesus now returns to the illustration with which the chapter started (vv. 2–5).

lays down his life. Jesus as Shepherd does more than risk His life (cf. 1 Sam. 17:34–36), He gives His life, enduring death on behalf of sinners. This is intimated in the name "Lamb of God" declared by John the Baptist (1:29) and in other statements by Jesus Himself (2:19; 3:14; 6:51).

for the sheep. This sacrifice is for "the sheep." It is for those whom the Father has given Him (17:2, 6, 24), the elect. It is they who through the death of Jesus Christ on their behalf will be justified and enjoy fellowship with God.

10:12 a hired hand. Jesus sharpens the picture by contrasting His sacrificial service with the cowardly abandonment of the sheep by those who are controlled by self-interest. Thieves rob the sheep; hired hands abandon the sheep; Christ lays down His life for the sheep.

10:14 I know my own and my own know me. This is placed in parallel with the intimacy between the Father and the Son (v. 15; cf. 17:21–23). It is clear that "know" here, as so often in Scripture, means more than a mental grasp; it includes personal understanding and a commitment of will. To say that God "knows" a person in this way refers to His gracious redemptive commitment to that individual.

10:15 See theological note "Definite Redemption."

10:16 other sheep. The gospel is not confined to Israel, but extends to the rest of the world.

10:17 the Father loves me. The self-sacrifice of the Son is an act of loving obedience to the Father that reveals the love among the three Persons of the Trinity.

10:17, 18 I . . . take it up again. The resurrection of Christ is described as the act of each of the three Persons of the Trinity: the Son, the Father (Acts 2:32; 3:15; 4:10; Gal. 1:1), and the Holy Spirit (Rom. 8:10–11).

10:18 No one takes it from me, but I lay it down of my own accord. This is a claim to deity, as even His enemies understood (v. 33), because God alone is the Author and Giver of life. The verse also underscores that Christ was not a victim but freely offered Himself for sinners. See "The Humble Obedience of Christ" at 5:19.

19 [d]There was again a division among the
Jews because of these words. 20 Many of
them said, [e]"He has a demon, and [f]is
insane; why listen to him?" 21 Others said,
"These are not the words of one who is
oppressed by a demon. [g]Can a demon
open the eyes of the blind?"

I and the Father Are One

22 At that time the Feast of Dedication
took place at Jerusalem. It was winter,
23 and Jesus was walking in the temple, [h]in
the colonnade of Solomon. 24 So the Jews
gathered around him and said to him,
"How long will you keep us in suspense? If
you are [i]the Christ, [j]tell us plainly." 25 Jesus
answered them, "I told you, and you do
not believe. [k]The works that I do [l]in my
Father's name bear witness about me,
26 but [m]you do not believe because you are
not part of my flock. 27 [n]My sheep hear my
voice, and I know them, and they follow
me. 28 [o]I give them eternal life, and [p]they
will never perish, and [q]no one will snatch
them out of my hand. 29 My Father, [r]who
has given them to me,[1] [s]is greater than all,
and no one is able to snatch them out of
[t]the Father's hand. 30 [u]I and the Father are
one."

31 [v]The Jews picked up stones again to
stone him. 32 Jesus answered them, "I have
shown you many good works from the
Father; for which of them are you going to
stone me?" 33 The Jews answered him, "It is
not for a good work that we are going to
stone you but [w]for blasphemy, because
you, being a man, [x]make yourself God."
34 Jesus answered them, "Is it not written in
[y]your Law, [z]'I said, you are gods'? 35 If he
called them gods to whom the word of God
came—and Scripture cannot be [a]broken—
36 do you say of him whom [b]the Father consecrated and [c]sent into the world, 'You are
blaspheming,' because [d]I said, 'I am the
Son of God'? 37 [e]If I am not doing the works
of my Father, then do not believe me; 38 but

19 [d]ch. 7:43; 9:16 **20** [e]See ch. 7:20 [f][Mark 3:21] **21** [g][Ex. 4:11; Ps. 146:8]; See ch. 9:33 **23** [h]Acts 3:11; 5:12 **24** [i]ch. 1:41 [j]Matt. 26:63; Luke 22:67 **25** [k]ver. 38. See ch. 5:36 [l]See ch. 5:43 **26** [m][ch. 8:47] **27** [n]ver. 14, 16 **28** [o][1 John 2:25; 5:11] [p]ch. 17:12; 18:9 [q]ch. 6:37 **29** [r]ch. 6:37; 17:2 [s][ch. 14:28] [t][Deut. 32:39; Isai. 49:2; 51:16] **30** [u]ch. 17:11, 22; [ch. 5:19; 14:9] **31** [v]ch. 8:59 **33** [w]See Lev. 24:16; Matt. 9:3 [x]ch. 5:18 **34** [y][ch. 12:34; 15:25; 1 Cor. 14:21]

[z]Cited from Ps. 82:6 **35** [a][Matt. 5:17, 19] **36** [b][ch. 6:27] [c]See ch. 3:17 [d]ch. 5:17, 18; [ver. 30] **37** [e]ch. 15:24

1 Some manuscripts *What my Father has given to me*

10:19 division. See 7:43; 9:16.

10:20 See 7:20.

10:22 Feast of Dedication. This festival, now called Hanukkah, is celebrated in December. It commemorates the restoration of the temple in the time of Judas Maccabeus and the Jewish revolt against Antiochus Epiphanes (164 B.C.).

10:23 colonnade of Solomon. A portico with roof and supporting columns on the east side of the court of the Gentiles in Herod's temple (Acts 3:11; 5:12).

10:24 If you are the Christ. This was the key question arising from Jesus' ministry. The disciples had reached that conclusion (6:69; Matt. 16:16; Mark 8:29; Luke 9:20). The question will be raised again at Jesus' trial, and the high priest will regard Jesus' answer as blasphemy (Matt. 26:63–65; Mark 14:61–64; Luke 22:67–71).

10:25 I told you. Jesus had affirmed this to the Samaritan woman (4:26) and to the man born blind (9:37), and He had accepted the confession of the disciples (v. 24 note; 1:49). In His discussions with the Jewish authorities, He had implied as much (8:28, 58). Here He again affirms His messianic identity absolutely.

The works. Jesus had referred to His works as evidence of the trustworthiness of His claims (5:36), and He pressed this point later before the disciples (14:11; 15:24). The man born blind had reasoned the same way (9:32, 33).

10:26 you do not believe. They closed their eyes to the clear evidence.

because you are not part of my flock. Only those who are Christ's, whom the Father has given Him, come to faith. Others are so blinded by their sinful prejudice that they refuse to believe. Only the regenerate, who have been "born again" (3:3, 7) believe.

10:27 My sheep. They listen to Jesus (vv. 3–5), and they follow Him (v. 4). These believers show renewal in the new direction and commitment of their lives.

10:28 The Lord gives His sheep the endless life of fellowship with God (17:2–3). He protects them from perishing, according to the infallibility of divine grace; and He allows no one to snatch them from His hand. The saints persevere because God preserves them. The sheep are not able to snatch themselves out of God's hand because the divine Shepherd will keep all of His true sheep from eternally straying (cf. 17:12). The solemn warnings of Scripture against apostasy are not intended to cause doubts about God's perseverance with those He has saved (cf. 1 John 2:19). See "Perseverance of the Saints" at Rom. 8:30.

10:29 the Father's hand. The hand of the Shepherd is also the Father's hand, and the supreme power of God is the ultimate guarantee of the sheep's safety.

10:30 one. Not identical Persons but one in essence (the Greek word for "one" is neuter). The Father and the Son and the Holy Spirit possess alike the fullness of the divine nature. This essential unity underlies their unity in the redemptive purpose. The verse indicates more than unity of purpose.

10:31–33 The Jews understood Jesus' claim to deity, and were preparing to stone Him for blasphemy (8:59).

10:34–38 In the Old Testament, human judges could be called "gods" because they were viewed as acting in God's place in dispensing justice. The Hebrew word *'elohim* is used not only to refer to the one true God but also to denote false gods, angels, and, very rarely, men exercising divine functions. Jesus' argument may be understood as follows: "Rather than taking offense because this word is used of Me, you should examine My credentials that prove My Father has sent Me into this world."

10:34 your Law. The quotation is found in Ps. 82:6. The term "law" was not restricted to the Pentateuch, or *Torah,* but referred to any part of the Old Testament as also having legal authority (15:25).

10:35 to whom the word of God came. This is not a reference to the writing of Scripture, but to the divine appointment of the judges.

Scripture cannot be broken. A strong statement of the authority of Scripture. In this serious confrontation that was to end in His death, Jesus did not hesitate to base His whole argument on one word of a minor psalm of Asaph. See "The Authority of Scripture" at 2 Tim. 3:16.

10:37 the works of my Father. The miracles and the whole course of His life attested to the correctness of Jesus' claim of a heavenly origin and mission. See "Miracles" at 1 Kin. 17:22.

if I do them, [f]even though you do not believe me, believe the works, that you may
know and understand that [g]the Father is in
me and I am in the Father." **39** [h]Again they
sought to arrest him, but he escaped from
their hands.
40 He went away again across the Jordan
to the place [i]where John had been baptizing at first, and there he remained. **41** And
many came to him. And they said, "John
did no sign, but [j]everything that John said
about this man was true." **42** And [k]many
believed in him there.

The Death of Lazarus

11 Now a certain man was ill, Lazarus
of Bethany, the village of [l]Mary and
her sister Martha. **2** [m]It was Mary who
anointed the Lord with ointment and
wiped his feet with her hair, whose brother
Lazarus was ill. **3** So the sisters sent to him,
saying, "Lord, [n]he whom you love is ill."
4 But when Jesus heard it he said, [o]"This illness does not lead to death. It is for [p]the
glory of God, so that the Son of God may
be glorified through it."
5 Now [q]Jesus loved Martha and her sister
and Lazarus. **6** So, when he heard that
Lazarus[1] was ill, [r]he stayed two days longer
in the place where he was. **7** Then after this
he said to the disciples, [s]"Let us go to
Judea again." **8** The disciples said to him,
[t]"Rabbi, [u]the Jews were just now seeking to
stone you, and are you going there again?"
9 Jesus answered, [v]"Are there not twelve
hours in the day? [w]If anyone walks in the
day, he does not stumble, because he sees
the light of this world. **10** But [x]if anyone
walks in the night, he stumbles, because
the light is not [x]in him." **11** After saying
these things, he said to them, "Our friend
Lazarus [y]has fallen asleep, but I go to
awaken him." **12** The disciples said to him,
"Lord, if he has fallen asleep, he will recover." **13** Now Jesus had spoken of his
death, but they thought that he meant taking rest in sleep. **14** Then Jesus told them
plainly, "Lazarus has died, **15** and for your
sake I am glad that I was not there, so that
you may believe. But let us go to him."
16 [z]So Thomas, called the Twin,[2] said to his
fellow disciples, "Let us also go, [a]that we
may die with him."

I Am the Resurrection and the Life

17 Now when Jesus came, he found that
Lazarus had already been in the tomb [b]four
days. **18** Bethany was near Jerusalem, about
two miles[3] off, **19** and many of the Jews had
come to Martha and Mary [c]to console them
concerning their brother. **20** [d]So when Martha
heard that Jesus was coming, she went and
met him, but Mary remained seated in the
house. **21** Martha said to [e]Jesus, "Lord, [f]if
you had been here, my brother would not
have died. **22** But even now I know that
whatever you ask from God, [g]God will give
you." **23** Jesus said to her, "Your brother will
rise again." **24** [h]Martha said to him, "I know
that he will rise again in [i]the resurrection

38 [f]ver. 25; [ch. 14:11] [g]ch. 14:10, 11, 20; 17:21, 23; [ch. 8:29]
39 [h]ch. 7:30, 44
40 [i]ch. 1:28
41 [j]ch. 1:7, 29-34; 3:27-30; 5:33
42 [k]See ch. 7:31
Chapter 11
1 [l]See Luke 10:38, 39
2 [m]ch. 12:3
3 [n]ver. 5, 11, 36
4 [o][ver. 11; Matt. 9:24] [p]ver. 40; [ch. 9:3; 13:31]
5 [q]ver. 3
6 [r][ch. 2:4; 7:6, 8]
7 [s]ch. 10:40
8 [t]See ch. 1:38 [u]ch. 8:59; 10:31
9 [v][Luke 13:33] [w]See ch. 9:4; 1 John 2:10
10 [x]Jer. 13:16
11 [y]See Matt. 27:52
16 [z]ch. 14:5; 20:24, 26-28; 21:2; Matt. 10:3; Mark 3:18; Luke 6:15; Acts 1:13 [a][ch. 13:37]
17 [b]ver. 39
19 [c]ver. 31; Job 2:11
20 [d][Luke 10:38, 39]
21 [e]ver. 32 [f][ver. 37]
22 [g][ver. 42; ch. 9:31]
24 [h][ver. 39] [i]ch. 5:29; Luke 14:14; See ch. 6:39

[1] Greek *he*; also verse 17 [2] Greek *Didymus* [3] Greek *fifteen stadia*; a *stadion* was about 607 feet or 185 meters

10:38 the Father is in me and I am in the Father. This mutual indwelling is characteristic of relationships within the Trinity.

10:39 he escaped. John does not give us details but makes it plain that nothing could happen to Jesus until God's appointed hour (7:44; 8:59).

11:1–54 The miracle of raising Lazarus from the dead is a climax to all the preceding signs that have revealed God's glory through Jesus. Here death itself, the final enemy of humanity, is successfully confronted by the One who is Himself the Resurrection and the Life. Yet even this glorious sign divides those who witness it. Those who reject the glory revealed commit themselves to pursuing Jesus' death (vv. 46–50).

11:1 Lazarus. Not the Lazarus of Luke 16:20. Lazarus is named only in John's Gospel.

11:2 Mary. Mary's anointing of Jesus is related in 12:1–8.

11:3 he whom you love is ill. This was a distress call, apparently sent shortly before Lazarus died.

11:4 This illness does not lead to death. In so speaking, Jesus is not denying that Lazarus will be dead for four days, but denying that death will finally triumph.

11:6 two days longer. A delay the sisters would have a hard time understanding.

11:8 the Jews were just now seeking to stone you. Jesus' death did not happen by accident or miscalculation; it was what He came to do. Jesus and His disciples knew that if He went to Jerusalem His life would be at risk.

11:11 fallen asleep. In the New Testament death is frequently represented as sleep (Acts 7:60; 1 Cor. 15:51; 1 Thess. 4:13). This is a common way of talking about death and says nothing in favor of the doctrine of "soul-sleep" for departed saints. Scripture is clear that conscious awareness continues after death.

11:16 that we may die with him. The hostility toward Jesus has now reached the point that the disciples are convinced that a trip to Jerusalem will result in Jesus' death. If they cannot talk Him out of the trip, they are at least willing to die with Him.

11:17 four days. This reference to the duration of time in the tomb, repeated in v. 39, is designed to show that Lazarus was really dead, and not merely sick.

11:21 if you had been here. The first statement of each sister (cf. v. 32).

11:22 even now. Martha still expected some miracle, although it seemed that her brother was beyond recovery. When Jesus speaks of resurrection, she relates it to the distant future, the "last day" (v. 24). Martha's faith was better informed than the Saddueces, who said there is no resurrection (Matt. 22:23).

on the last day." 25 Jesus said to her, [j]"I am
the resurrection and [k]the life.[1] Whoever
believes in me, [l]though he die, [m]yet shall
he live, 26 and everyone who lives and believes in me [n]shall never die. Do you
believe this?" 27 She said to him, "Yes, Lord;
[o]I believe that [p]you are the Christ, the Son
of God, [q]who is coming into the world."

Jesus Wept

28 When she had said this, she went and
called her sister Mary, saying in private,
[r]"The Teacher is here and is calling for
you." 29 And when she heard it, she rose
quickly and went to him. 30 Now Jesus had
not yet come into the village, but was still
in the place where Martha had met him.
31 When the Jews [s]who were with her in
the house, consoling her, saw Mary rise
quickly and go out, they followed her, supposing that she was going to the tomb to
weep there. 32 Now when Mary came to
where Jesus was and saw him, she fell at
his feet, saying to him, [t]"Lord, if you had
been here, my brother would not have
died." 33 When Jesus saw her weeping, and
the Jews who had come with her also
weeping, he [u]was deeply moved in his
spirit and [v]greatly troubled. 34 And he said,
"Where have you laid him?" They said to
him, "Lord, come and see." 35 [w]Jesus wept.
36 So the Jews said, "See [x]how he loved
him!" 37 But some of them said, "Could not
he [y]who opened the eyes of the blind man
[z]also have kept this man from dying?"

Jesus Raises Lazarus

38 Then Jesus, [a]deeply moved again, came
to the tomb. It was [b]a cave, and [c]a stone lay
against it. 39 Jesus said, "Take away the
stone." Martha, the sister of the dead man,
said to him, "Lord, by this time there will
be an odor, for [d]he has been dead four
days." 40 Jesus said to her, [e]"Did I not tell
you that if you believed you would see [f]the
glory of God?" 41 So they took away the
stone. And Jesus [g]lifted up his eyes and
said, "Father, I thank you that you have
heard me. 42 [h]I knew that you always hear
me, but I said this [i]on account of the people standing around, [j]that they may believe
that you sent me." 43 When he had said
these things, he cried out with a loud
voice, "Lazarus, come out." 44 [k]The man
who had died came out, [l]his hands and
feet bound with linen strips, and [m]his face
wrapped with a cloth. Jesus said to them,
"Unbind him, and let him go."

The Plot to Kill Jesus

45 [n]Many of the Jews therefore, [o]who had
come with Mary and [p]had seen what he
did, believed in him, 46 but some of them
went to the Pharisees and told them what
Jesus had done. 47 So the chief priests and
the Pharisees [q]gathered [r]the Council and
said, [s]"What are we to do? For this man
performs many signs. 48 If we let him go on
like this, everyone will believe in him, and
[t]the Romans will come and take away both
our [u]place and our nation." 49 But one of
them, [v]Caiaphas, [w]who was high priest
that year, said to them, "You know nothing at all. 50 Nor do you understand that [x]it

25 [j][ch. 5:21; 6:40, 44; 1 Cor. 15:21 [k]ch. 14:6; [ch. 6:57; Col. 3:4]; See ch. 1:4 [l][ch. 12:25] [m]See ch. 3:36
26 [n]ch. 6:50, 51; 8:51
27 [o]ch. 6:69; 20:31; 1 John 5:1, 5; [ch. 8:24; 13:19; 1 John 4:16] [p]Matt. 16:16 [q]ch. 6:14; See Matt. 11:3
28 [r]Matt. 26:18; Mark 14:14; Luke 22:11; See ch. 13:13
31 [s]ver. 19
32 [t]ver. 21
33 [u]ver. 38; Mark 14:5 (Gk.) [v]ch. 12:27; 13:21
35 [w][Luke 19:41]
36 [x]ver. 3
37 [y]ch. 9:6, 7 [z][ver. 21, 32]
38 [a]ver. 33 [b]Isai. 22:16 [c]ch. 20:1; Matt. 27:60; Mark 15:46; Luke 24:2
39 [d]ver. 17
40 [e]ver. 25, 26 [f]ver. 4; [Rom. 6:4]
41 [g]ch. 17:1
42 [h][ver. 22; Matt. 26:53] [i]ch. 12:29, 30 [j]ch. 17:8, 21; See ch. 3:17
44 [k]ch. 5:28, 29 [l]ch. 19:40 [m][ch. 20:7]
45 [n]ch. 12:11; [Acts 9:42] [o]ver. 19 [p]ch. 2:23
47 [q]See Matt. 26:3

[r]See Matt. 5:22 [s]ch. 12:19; [Acts 4:16] 48 [t][ch. 6:15; 18:36, 37] [u]Acts 21:28 49 [v]See Matt. 26:3 [w]ver. 51; ch. 18:13 50 [x]ch. 18:14

[1] Some manuscripts omit *and the life*

11:25 I am the resurrection and the life. This is repeated in part in 14:6 (Acts 3:15; Heb. 7:16). Life for the believer does not end at death, but continues eternally as an endless life of fellowship with God. This is true for those who, like Lazarus, were in the tomb as well as for those who are still alive. See note 6:35.

11:27 you are the Christ. The conversation elicits from Martha a confession of faith that parallels that of Peter (Matt. 16:16).

11:28 The Teacher. A characterization of Jesus' ministry. He did not disdain, as others often did, to teach a woman (Luke 10:39, 42).

11:33 he . . . troubled. The outward expression of sorrow did not leave Jesus unmoved. He shed tears (v. 35) in sympathy for the bereaved.

11:34 Where have you laid him. John's Gospel teaches both the deity of Christ (1:1, 18) and His full humanity. As the Mediator, Christ acted within the limits of His sinless humanity, without laying aside His deity. He experienced human emotions and could express ignorance of fact. See "The Humanity of Christ" at 2 John 7.

11:37 Could not he. The questions raised are what sort of power Jesus has and when He will choose to use it. Lazarus was allowed to die and the sisters to mourn, in order that God's glory might be manifested (v. 4; 9:3). The healing of the blind man is remembered as clearly supernatural.

11:41 Father, I thank you. Jesus offers thanks for the answer to His prayer. He is careful to relate this miracle to His mission as Messiah.

11:43 Lazarus, come out. The dead cannot hear, but Jesus wanted those present to see that God's voice can raise the dead (5:28, 29). This divine call that gives life to the dead vividly illustrates God's call to the spiritually dead that raises them to spiritual life (Eph. 2:5).

11:45–47 This work of God had a double result: faith in some, and resistance and unbelief in others (cf. 2 Cor. 3:15, 16).

11:48 The Sanhedrin, which had supreme religious authority in the land, feared that Jesus' ministry would provoke a popular uprising that the Romans would crush by force of arms.

11:49 Caiaphas. He was a Sadducee and the son-in-law of Annas, who had been deposed as high priest by the Romans but had considerable influence over the religious leaders (18:13).

is better for you that one man should die
for the people, not that the whole nation
should perish." 51 He did not say this of his
own accord, but [y]being high priest that
year [z]he prophesied that Jesus would die
for the nation, 52 and [a]not for the nation
only, but also [b]to gather into one the children of God who are scattered abroad. 53 So
from that day on they [c]made plans to put
him to death.

54 Jesus therefore [d]no longer walked
openly among the Jews, but went from
there to the region near the wilderness, to
a town called Ephraim, and there he stayed
with the disciples.

55 Now [e]the Passover of the Jews was at
hand, and [f]many went up from the country
to Jerusalem before the Passover [g]to purify
themselves. 56 [h]They were looking for[1] Jesus
and saying to one another as they stood in
the temple, "What do you think? That he
will not come to the feast at all?" 57 Now the
chief priests and the Pharisees had given
orders that if anyone knew where he was,
he should let them know, so that they
might arrest him.

Mary Anoints Jesus at Bethany

12 Six days before [i]the Passover, [j]Jesus
therefore came to Bethany, [k]where
Lazarus was, whom Jesus had raised from
the dead. 2 So they gave a dinner for him
there. [l]Martha served, and Lazarus was one
of those reclining with him at the table.
3 [m]Mary therefore took a pound[2] of expensive ointment made from pure nard, and
anointed the feet of Jesus and wiped his
feet with her hair. The house was filled
with the fragrance of the perfume. 4 But
Judas Iscariot, one of his disciples (he who
was about to betray him), said, 5 "Why was
this ointment not sold for three hundred
denarii[3] and [n]given to the poor?" 6 He said
this, not because he cared about the poor,
but because he was a thief, and [n]having
charge of the moneybag he used to help
himself to what was put into it. 7 Jesus said,
"Leave her alone, so that she may keep it[4]
for the day of my burial. 8 The poor you
always have with you, but you do not
always have me."

The Plot to Kill Lazarus

9 When the large crowd of the Jews
learned that Jesus[5] was there, they came,
not only on account of him but also to see
Lazarus, [o]whom he had raised from the
dead. 10 [p]So the chief priests made plans to
put Lazarus to death as well, 11 because [q]on
account of him many of the Jews were
going away and believing in Jesus.

The Triumphal Entry

12 The next day [r]the large crowd that had
come to the feast heard that Jesus was
coming to Jerusalem. 13 So they took
branches of [s]palm trees and went out to
meet him, crying out, [t]"Hosanna! Blessed
is [u]he who comes in the name of the Lord,

51 [y]ver. 49 [z][Ex 28:30; Num. 27:21; 1 Sam. 23:9; 30:7; Ezra 2:63; Neh. 7:65]
52 [a]Isai. 49:6; 1 John 2:2 [b]See ch. 10:16
53 [c]See ch. 7:1
54 [d]ch. 7:1, 4
55 [e]See ch. 6:4 [f]Luke 2:42 [g]2 Chr. 30:17, 18; [ch. 18:28; Acts 21:24]
56 [h]See ch. 7:11
Chapter 12
1 [i]ver. 12, 20; ch. 11:55 [j]For ver. 1-8, see Matt. 26:6-11; Mark 14:3-8 [k]ch. 11:1
2 [l]Luke 10:38, 40
3 [m][Luke 7:37, 38]
5 [n]ch. 13:29
6 [n][See ver. 5 above]
9 [o]ch. 11:44
10 [p][Luke 16:31]
11 [q]ver. 18; ch. 11:45
12 [r]For ver. 12-15, see Matt. 21:4-9; Mark 11:7-10; Luke 19:35-38
13 [s][Rev. 7:9] [t]Ps. 118:25, 26 [u][ch. 5:43]

1 Greek *were seeking for* 2 Greek *litra*; a *litra* (or Roman pound) was equal to about 11 1/2 ounces or 327 grams 3 A *denarius* was a day's wage for a laborer 4 Or *Leave her alone; she intended to keep it* 5 Greek *he*

11:50 Caiaphas callously suggests that executing an innocent person may be excused if it secures an advantage for the nation. He had forgotten the message of Prov. 17:15.

11:51 he prophesied. In the purposes of God, Caiaphas unknowingly uttered a prophecy. It was a blessing that Jesus died, because His death was necessary for the salvation, not only of Jews, but of the elect of the whole world.

11:54–57 The increasing hostility of the Jewish leaders led Jesus to withdraw for a time from Jerusalem.

12:1–11 The anointing of Jesus recounted in Luke 7:36–50 is a different incident from this anointing by Mary, which is related also in Matt. 26:6–12 and Mark 14:3–9.

12:3 expensive ointment. Judas evaluates this at a year's wages (v. 5), almost three times as much as Judas accepted to betray Jesus.

anointed the feet of Jesus. Matthew and Mark indicate that she poured some perfume on His head, which would be the common practice. To attend to His feet and wipe them with her hair was a tribute of humility and devotion.

12:4–6 Judas (and the other disciples, Matt. 26:8) objected strongly, calling the act a waste of money. His remarks were inconsiderate of Jesus and cruel toward Mary. The interest in the poor is unmasked as artificial.

12:7 Leave her alone. Jesus defends Mary while hinting at the nearness of His death. For this pivotal point of God's redemptive work, no expense is too great.

12:8 always . . . not always. There would always be poverty in a fallen world, together with the responsibilities of ministering to the poor as an expression of God's love. The opportunity of being present with Jesus and serving Him during His time on earth would not be repeated.

12:9, 10 Instead of recognizing God's hand in Lazarus's resurrection, the chief priests plotted to kill both Jesus and Lazarus.

12:11 many of the Jews. The religious leaders were losing popularity: Nicodemus seemed to have defected (7:50–52); some Jews had believed in Christ, however superficially (8:30 note); some were impressed by the healing of the man born blind (10:21); Jesus seemed to be gaining followers across the Jordan (10:41, 42); and now Lazarus's resurrection was leading still more to faith in Him (vv. 17, 18; 11:45). All this prepared for the acclaim that Jesus would receive at His triumphal entry, which led the Pharisees to say, "the world has gone after him" (v. 19).

12:13 Hosanna. The salutation was borrowed in part from Ps. 118:25, 26, to which was added the reference to "the King of Israel." This was particularly disquieting to the Jewish leaders, who feared a popular uprising under Jesus' leadership.

even [v]the King of Israel!" 14 And Jesus
found a young donkey and sat on it, just as
it is written,

15 [w]"Fear not, daughter of Zion;
behold, your king is coming,
sitting on a donkey's colt!"

16 [x]His disciples did not understand these
things at first, but [y]when Jesus was glorified, then [z]they remembered that these
things had been written about him and had
been done to him. 17 [a]The crowd that had
been with him when he called Lazarus out
of the tomb and raised him from the dead
continued to bear witness. 18 The reason
why the crowd went to meet him [b]was that
they heard he had done this sign. 19 So the
Pharisees said to one another, [c]"You see
that you are gaining nothing. Look, [d]the
world has gone after him."

Some Greeks Seek Jesus

20 Now [e]among those who went up to
worship at the feast were some [f]Greeks.
21 So these came to [g]Philip, who was from
Bethsaida in Galilee, and asked him, "Sir,
we wish to see Jesus." 22 Philip went and
told [h]Andrew; Andrew and Philip went and
told Jesus. 23 And Jesus answered them,
[i]"The hour has come [j]for the Son of Man to
be glorified. 24 Truly, truly, I say to you,
[k]unless a grain of wheat falls into the earth
and dies, it remains alone; but if it dies, it
bears much fruit. 25 [l]Whoever loves his life
loses it, and [m]whoever [n]hates his life in this
world will keep it for eternal life. 26 If anyone serves me, he must [o]follow me; and
[p]where I am, there will my servant be also.
[q]If anyone serves me, [r]the Father will
honor him.

The Son of Man Must Be Lifted Up

27 [s]"Now is my soul troubled. And what
shall I say? 'Father, [t]save me from [u]this
hour'? But [v]for this purpose I have come to
[u]this hour. 28 Father, glorify your name."
Then [w]a voice came from heaven: "I have
glorified it, and I will glorify it again." 29 The
crowd that stood there and heard it said
that it had thundered. Others said, [x]"An
angel has spoken to him." 30 Jesus answered, [y]"This voice has come for your
sake, not mine. 31 [z]Now is the judgment of
this world; now will [a]the ruler of this world
[b]be cast out. 32 And I, [c]when I am lifted up
from the earth, [d]will draw [e]all people to
myself." 33 He said this [f]to show by what
kind of death he was going to die. 34 So the
crowd answered him, "We have heard from
the Law that [g]the Christ remains forever.

13 [v]See ch. 1:49 **15** [w]Cited from Zech. 9:9 **16** [x][ch. 13:7]; See Mark 9:32 [y]ver. 23; See ch. 7:39 [z]ch. 2:22 **17** [a][Luke 19:37] **18** [b]ver. 9-11 **19** [c]ch. 11:47 [d][ch. 3:26] **20** [e][1 Kin. 8:41-43; Acts 8:27] [f]Acts 17:4; [Mark 7:26]; See ch. 7:35 **21** [g]ch. 1:44 **22** [h]See Mark 13:3 **23** [i]ch. 17:1; [ver. 27; ch. 13:31, 32; Mark 14:41]; See ch. 2:4 [j]ver. 16 **24** [k]1 Cor. 15:36 **25** [l]See Matt. 10:39 [m][ch. 11:25] [n]See Luke 14:26 **26** [o]ch. 8:12; 21:18 [p]ch. 14:3; 17:24; [2 Cor. 5:8; 1 Thess. 4:17] [q]ch. 14:21, 23; 16:27] [r]1 Sam. 2:30; Ps. 91:15 **27** [s]ch. 11:33; 13:21; [Luke 22:44] [t]Mark 14:35; [Heb. 5:7] [u]ver. 23 [v][ch. 18:37]

28 [w]Matt. 3:17; 17:5; Mark 1:11; 9:7; Luke 3:22; 9:35; 2 Pet. 1:17 **29** [x]Acts 23:9 **30** [y]ch. 11:42 **31** [z]ch. 16:11; [ch. 16:33] [a]ch. 14:30; 2 Cor. 4:4; Eph. 2:2; 6:12; [Matt. 13:19; Luke 4:6; 1 John 4:4; 5:19] [b][Luke 10:18; Col. 2:15; 1 John 3:8] **32** [c]ch. 3:14; 8:28 [d]See ch. 6:44 [e]Rom. 5:18; 8:32; 2 Cor. 5:15; 1 Tim. 2:6; Heb. 2:9; 1 John 2:2 **33** [f]ch. 18:32 **34** [g]Ps. 89:4; 110:4; Isai. 9:7; Ezek. 37:25; Luke 1:33

12:14, 15 The precise circumstances had been prophesied in Zech. 9:9. This prophecy is noted also in Matthew, and was understood in retrospect by the disciples.

12:20 some Greeks. An ironic footnote to the statement of the Pharisees in v. 19. These "Greeks" were probably not Jews of the dispersion (the Greek word is different from that translated "Hellenists" in Acts 6:1). Rather, they were perhaps proselytes or, more probably, Gentile "God-fearers" (as they were called) who participated in synagogue worship but did not undergo circumcision and full reception into the Jewish religion (Acts 8:27; 13:26; 17:4).

12:23 The hour has come. In contrast to earlier statements that His time had not yet come (2:4; 7:6, 8, 30; 8:20), this is the first of a number of statements that Christ's death and resurrection are at hand (v. 27; 13:1; 16:32; 17:1). The cross and burial themselves are described elsewhere as His humiliation (Phil. 2:8). This humiliation is the way by which Christ the Mediator, following the days of His resurrection on earth, must enter the glory of His ascension to the Father's right hand (13:31, 32; cf. Phil. 2:8, 9).

12:24 a grain of wheat. Jesus uses the growth of wheat from a seed as an explanation of His own work. His death in a certain time and place will open the doors of salvation for people of every age and nation.

12:25 Whoever loves his life. Those who are absorbed by the interests of life on earth encounter ruin, while those detached from worldly interests will through Christ's work attain to eternal life (Matt. 10:39; Luke 17:33). It is in the service of Christ and in union with Him that the truth of this statement is experienced (ch. 14).

12:27 Now is my soul troubled. Jesus is greatly troubled by the prospect of bearing the wrath of His holy Father in the place of sinners. Nevertheless He accepts His role and reasserts His commitment to it.

12:28 a voice came from heaven. In three places in the Gospels the Father speaks directly from heaven about Jesus: at His baptism (Matt. 3:17), at the Transfiguration (Matt. 17:5), and here. For the benefit of the disciples (v. 30), the Father places His seal of approval upon Jesus' saving work.

12:29 The crowd . . . heard it. A situation similar to the circumstances of Paul's conversion, where those who accompanied him heard a noise but could not distinguish the words (Acts 9:7; 22:9).

12:31 Now is the judgment of this world. By His coming death, Jesus will end the power of sin over Adam's race, judging and condemning it.

the ruler of this world. Satan (cf. 14:30; 16:11; 2 Cor. 4:4; Eph. 2:2; 1 John 4:4; 5:19). Satan has power in fact, not by right. When God destroys Satan's power, He is not violating his rights, or breaking any agreement made with him.

12:32 lifted up. This refers to the Crucifixion (v. 33), but also to the glorification of Christ. As Mediator, He will be "lifted up" to the right hand of God (3:14 note).

will draw all people. The Cross exerts a universal attraction, and people of all nationalities, Gentiles as well as Jews, will be saved through it. "All" means all kinds of people without distinction, not all members of the human race without exception.

12:34 the Law. One of the terms used for the whole Old Testament Scripture (10:34; 15:25). This is a possible reference to Ps. 89:36; 110:4; Is. 9:7; Ezek. 37:25; Dan. 7:14; Mic. 5:2.

How can you say that [h]the Son of Man
must be lifted up? Who is this Son of
Man?" **35** So Jesus said to them, [i]"The light
is among you [j]for a little while longer.
[k]Walk while you have the light, lest darkness [l]overtake you. [m]The one who walks in
the darkness does not know where he is
going. **36** While you have the light, believe
in the light, that you may become [n]sons of
light."

The Unbelief of the People

When Jesus had said these things, he
departed and hid himself from them.
37 Though he had done so many signs
before them, they still did not believe in
him, **38** [o]so that the word spoken by the
prophet Isaiah might be fulfilled:

> [p]"Lord, who has believed what he
> heard from us,
> and to whom has the arm of the
> Lord been revealed?"

39 Therefore they [q]could not believe. For
again Isaiah said,

40 [r]"He has blinded their eyes
> and [s]hardened their heart,
> lest they see with their eyes,
> and understand with their heart,
> and turn,
> and I would heal them."

41 Isaiah said these things because [t]he saw
his glory and [u]spoke of him. **42** Nevertheless, [v]many even of the authorities believed
in him, but [w]for fear of the Pharisees they
did not [x]confess it, so that they would not
be [x]put out of the synagogue; **43** [y]for they
loved the glory that comes from man more
than the glory that comes from God.

Jesus Came to Save the World

44 And Jesus cried out and said, [z]"Whoever believes in me, believes not in me but
[a]in him who sent me. **45** And [b]whoever [c]sees
me sees him who sent me. **46** [d]I have come
into the world as light, so that whoever
believes in me may not remain in darkness.
47 If anyone [e]hears my words and does not
keep them, [f]I do not judge him; for [g]I did
not come to judge the world but to save the
world. **48** [h]The one who rejects me and does
not receive my words has a judge; [i]the
word that I have spoken will judge him [j]on
the last day. **49** For [k]I have not spoken on
my own authority, but the Father [l]who
sent me has himself given me [m]a commandment—what to say and what to
speak. **50** And I know that his commandment is eternal life. What I say, therefore, I
say as the Father has told me."

Jesus Washes the Disciples' Feet

13 Now [n]before [o]the Feast of the
Passover, when Jesus knew that
[p]his hour had come [q]to depart out of this
world to the Father, [r]having loved [s]his own
who were in the world, he loved them to

34 [h]ver. 32 **35** [i]ver. 46; See ch. 1:4, 9; 8:12 [j]See ch. 7:33 [k]Jer. 13:16; Eph. 5:8 [l]1 Thess. 5:4 [m]Isai. 9:2; 1 John 1:6; 2:11; [ch. 11:10] **36** [n]See Luke 10:6 **38** [o][Matt. 1:22] [p]Rom. 10:16; Cited from Isai. 53:1 **39** [q][ch. 5:44] **40** [r][Isai. 6:10]; See Matt. 13:14, 15 [s]See Mark 6:52 **41** [t]Isai. 6:1 [u][ch. 5:46] **42** [v]ch. 3:1; [ch. 7:48] [w]See ch. 7:13 [x]See ch. 9:22 **43** [y]ch. 5:44 **44** [z][ch. 13:20]; See Matt. 10:40 [a]ch. 14:1; [ch. 5:24; 1 Pet. 1:21] **45** [b]ch. 14:9 [c]ch. 6:40 **46** [d]ver. 35, 36; See ch. 1:4, 5, 9; 8:12 **47** [e][ch. 3:36] [f]ch. 8:15 [g]See ch. 3:17; 4:42 **48** [h]Luke 10:16 [i]Deut. 18:18, 19 [j][Rom. 2:16] **49** [k]See ch. 5:19, 30

[l]See ch. 3:17 [m]ch. 10:18; 15:10
Chapter 13 1 [n]ch. 12:1 [o]See ch. 6:4 [p]See ch. 12:23 [q]ver. 3; ch. 16:28 [r]ver. 34 [s]ch. 1:11; 17:6, 9-11

the Son of Man. They understood this title to be a claim to be the promised Messiah.

lifted up. They understood this to be a reference to hanging or crucifixion, and on the basis of scriptures such as Ps. 89:36, 37 they could not reconcile Christ's death with their view of the Messiah.

12:35 the light. Jesus is the "light" (v. 46; 1:4–9; 8:12; 9:5). His impending death will bring a period of darkness.

12:38 Isaiah might be fulfilled. Jesus' earthly public ministry was a fulfillment of Isaiah's prophecy, which was largely one of judgment upon unbelieving Israel. Jesus pronounces the judgment, previously announced by Isaiah, that must precede the coming kingdom.

12:39 they could not believe. No one will truly believe unless God opens that person's understanding by a supernatural work of the Spirit (3:3–7).

12:41 saw his glory. Isaiah had received a vision of the glory of the enthroned God (Is. 6:1) and prophesied about the divine Suffering Servant (Is. 52:13–53:12).

12:42 many . . . believed in him. Isaiah's announced judgment came true, yet even some leaders (e.g., Joseph and Nicodemus, 19:38–40) were believers despite the threat of excommunication by their unbelieving peers.

12:44 believes in me . . . him who sent me. The close relationship of Jesus with the Father (cf. 17:21–23) is stressed in three respects: to believe in Christ is to believe in the Father; to see Christ is to see the Father (v. 45); to hear Christ is to hear the Father (v. 50). On the other hand, rejection of Christ and His words is also a rejection of the Father and His words. This rejection results in judgment, although the leading purpose of Christ's incarnation was the salvation of His own and not the condemnation of those who do not believe.

12:48 the word that I have spoken. See "The Teaching of Jesus" at Matt. 7:28.

13:1–17:26 These five chapters recount the ministry of Jesus to the disciples in the upper room, a ministry accompanied by a meal. The other Gospels indicate that the Lord's Supper was instituted on this occasion, but John does not say so, perhaps because he viewed the institution as sufficiently covered in the three Synoptic Gospels, Matthew, Mark, and Luke.

The relationship between the Synoptic accounts and John's Gospel has been extensively discussed by many commentators. The Synoptic Gospels all state that the meal alluded to in 13:2 was the Passover meal (Matt. 26:17–30; Mark 14:12–26; Luke 22:7–23). John, on the other hand, implies that the meal took place on the eve of the Passover, and that Jesus died at the precise time when the Passover lambs were being slaughtered (13:1, 29; 18:28; 19:14, 31, 42). Among scholars who accept the truthfulness of John and the Synoptic Gospels, several possible solutions have been proposed. See notes 19:14; Matt. 26:17.

13:1 he loved them to the end. Great emphasis is placed in chs. 13–17

the end. **2** During supper, when [t]the devil
had already put it into the heart of Judas
Iscariot, Simon's son, to betray him,
3 Jesus, knowing [u]that the Father had given
all things into his hands, and that [v]he had
come from God and [w]was going back to
God, **4** rose from supper. He laid aside his
outer garments, and taking a towel, [x]tied it
around his waist. **5** Then he [y]poured water
into a basin and began to wash the disciples' feet and to wipe them with the towel
that was wrapped around him. **6** He came
to Simon Peter, who said to him, "Lord, do
you wash my feet?" **7** [z]Jesus answered him,
"What I am doing [a]you do not understand
now, but afterward you will understand."
8 [b]Peter said to him, "You shall never wash
my feet." Jesus answered him, [c]"If I do not
wash you, you have no share with me."
9 Simon Peter said to him, "Lord, not my
feet only but also my hands and my head!"
10 Jesus said to him, "The one who has
bathed does not need to wash, [d]except for
his feet,[1] but is completely clean. And
[e]you[2] are clean, [f]but not every one of you."
11 [g]For he knew who was to betray him;
that was why he said, "Not all of you are
clean."

12 When he had washed their feet and
[h]put on his outer garments and resumed
his place, he said to them, [i]"Do you understand what I have done to you? **13** [j]You call
me [k]Teacher and Lord, and you are right,
for so I am. **14** If I then, your Lord and
Teacher, have washed your feet, [l]you also
ought to wash one another's feet. **15** For I
have given you an example, [m]that you also
should do just as I have done to you.
16 Truly, truly, I say to you, [n]a servant[3] is
not greater than his master, nor is a messenger greater than the one who sent him.
17 If you know these things, [o]blessed are
you if you do them. **18** [p]I am not speaking of
all of you; I know [q]whom I have chosen.
But [r]the Scripture will be fulfilled,[4] [s]'He
who ate my bread has lifted his heel against
me.' **19** [t]I am telling you this now, before it
takes place, that when it does take place
you may believe that I am he. **20** Truly, truly,
I say to you, [u]whoever receives the one I
send receives me, and whoever receives me
receives the one who sent me."

One of You Will Betray Me

21 After saying these things, [v]Jesus was
troubled in his spirit, and testified,
[w]"Truly, truly, I say to you, [x]one of you will
betray me." **22** [y]The disciples looked at
one another, uncertain of whom he spoke.

2 [t]ver. 11, 27; [Acts 5:3]; See ch. 6:70, 71
3 [u]See ch. 17:2; Matt. 11:27; Rev. 2:27 [v]ch. 8:42; 16:28 [w]See ch. 14:12
4 [x][ch. 21:7; Luke 22:27]
5 [y][2 Kin. 3:11]
7 [z][ver. 36] [a]ver. 12; [ch. 12:16; 15:15]
8 [b][Matt. 16:22] [c][1 Cor. 6:11; Eph. 5:26; Tit. 3:5; Heb. 10:22]
10 [d]See Gen. 18:4 [e]ch. 15:3 [f]ver. 18
11 [g]ver. 2; ch. 6:64; See ch. 2:24, 25
12 [h]ver. 4 [i]ver. 7
13 [j]Luke 6:46 [k]Matt. 23:8, 10; 1 Cor. 8:6; 12:3; Phil. 2:11; [Eph. 6:9]
14 [l]1 Tim. 5:10; [1 Pet. 5:5]
15 [m]See Matt. 11:29
16 [n]ch. 15:20; Matt. 10:24
17 [o]See Luke 11:28; James 1:22
18 [p]ver. 10, 11 [q]ch. 6:70; 15:16, 19; [Mark 3:13; Luke 6:13; Acts 1:2] [r][ch. 17:12]; See Matt. 1:22 [s]Cited from Ps. 41:9; [ver. 26; Matt. 26:23] **19** [t]ch. 14:29; 16:4 **20** [u]See Matt. 10:40 **21** [v]ch. 12:27 [w]Matt. 26:21; Mark 14:18; Luke 22:21 [x]Acts 1:17
22 [y]Luke 22:23

[1] Some manuscripts omit *except for his feet* [2] The Greek words for *you* in this verse are plural [3] Greek *bondservant* [4] Greek *But in order that the Scripture may be fulfilled*

on Christ's love. This love is illustrated in the moving scene of the footwashing in which the Son of God does not disdain performing the most menial tasks of a servant (Phil. 2:7, 8).

13:2 A vivid contrast between self-serving Judas and self-giving Jesus.

13:3 Jesus, knowing. Jesus' humble conduct was not because He forgot His rank as incarnate God the Son. His act demonstrates that rank and privilege are not occasions for arrogance, but are higher credentials for service.

13:5 wash the disciples' feet. Footwashing was a common element of hospitality in a dusty country where people wore sandals (cf. Luke 7:44). This task was usually performed by the lowliest member of the household.

13:6–10 Peter, with his usual impulsiveness (Luke 5:8; Matt. 16:22; Acts 10:14), objected to Jesus' action of washing his feet. He could not understand the humility of Christ. Jesus answers that whatever Peter's own expectations may have been, Peter must accept Jesus in the path that God has chosen for the Messiah to follow (Is. 55:7–9; Matt. 16:23).

13:11 he knew. John emphasizes that Judas's betrayal was not an unforeseen development, but that Jesus proceeded in full awareness of coming events and of Judas's role in them. Judas's action was his own free and responsible decision—yet carried out according to the plan of God.

13:13 Teacher and Lord. This double title gives special significance to the claim of Christ over the disciples' lives. Later, they would call Him "Lord" in acknowledgement of His deity (20:28).

13:15 I have given you an example. The humility of Christ is a pattern for His disciples. Instead of aspiring to dominate, they must be eager to serve (Matt. 20:26–28; Phil. 2:5–8; 1 Pet. 2:21).

13:17 if you do them. Intellectual perception is not enough, but must be backed up by commitment of life. This does not mean that our works are the basis of our acceptance by God, but that they are the evidence of a true faith. Trust and obedience are inseparable.

13:18 not . . . all of you. Jesus chose Judas to be one of the Twelve, but He did not bring him to salvation. Judas was not one of the elect (Matt. 26:24), yet he was in no way coerced into his betrayal.

fulfilled. Jesus remarks on the fulfillment of Scripture in many details of His life. The quotation from Ps. 41:9 is a possible reference to the treason of Ahithophel (2 Sam. 15:31).

13:19 before it takes place. The truth of a prior prediction was the mark of a true prophet, and false prediction was a sure way to discern a false prophet (Deut. 18:18–22).

I am he. The word "he" is supplied here for the English text. The original Greek reads "I am," a claim to deity derived from Ex. 3:14.

13:21 troubled in his spirit. Compare 11:33; 12:27. From the beginning Jesus knew what Judas would do, but His soul still felt it as the time approached.

13:22 uncertain. Judas had hidden his betrayal so carefully that the other disciples had no inkling of it. Each one began to fear that he might be the weak link (Matt. 26:22). Judas, too, mouthed the question (Matt. 26:25), but the disciples apparently did not hear Jesus' response.

23 [z]One of his disciples, whom Jesus loved,
was reclining at table [a]close to Jesus,[1] 24 so
Simon Peter motioned to him to ask Jesus[2]
of whom he was speaking. 25 [b]So that disciple, [c]leaning back against Jesus, said to
him, "Lord, who is it?" 26 Jesus answered,
[d]"It is he to whom I will give this morsel of
bread [e]when I have dipped it." So when he
had dipped the morsel, [f]he gave it to Judas,
[g]the son of Simon Iscariot. 27 Then after he
had taken the morsel, [h]Satan entered into
him. Jesus said to him, [i]"What you are
going to do, do quickly." 28 Now no one at
the table knew why he said this to him.
29 Some thought that, [j]because Judas had
the moneybag, Jesus was telling him, "Buy
what we need [k]for the feast," or that he
should [l]give something to the poor. 30 So,
after receiving the morsel of bread, he
immediately went out. [m]And it was night.

A New Commandment

31 When he had gone out, Jesus said,
[n]"Now is the Son of Man glorified, and
[o]God is glorified in him. 32 If God is glorified in him, [p]God will also glorify him in
himself, and [q]glorify him at once. 33 Little
children, [r]yet a little while I am with you.
You will seek me, and just [s]as I said to the
Jews, so now I also say to you, 'Where I am
going you cannot come.' 34 [t]A new commandment [u]I give to you, [v]that you love
one another: [w]just as I have loved you, you
also are to love one another. 35 [x]By this all
people will know that you are my disciples,
if you have love for one another."

Jesus Foretells Peter's Denial

36 Simon Peter said to him, "Lord, where
are you going?" [y]Jesus answered him,
"Where I am going [z]you cannot follow me
now, [a]but you will follow afterward."
37 [b]Peter said to him, "Lord, why can I not
follow you now? I will lay down my life for
you." 38 Jesus answered, "Will you lay
down your life for me? Truly, truly, I say to
you, [c]the rooster will not crow till you have
denied me three times.

I Am the Way, and the Truth, and the Life

14 [d]"Let not your hearts be troubled.
[e]Believe in God;[3] believe also in me.
2 In [f]my Father's house are many rooms. If
it were not so, would I have told you that
[g]I go to prepare a place for you? 3 And if I
go and prepare a place for you, I will come
again and will take you [h]to myself, that
[i]where I am you may be also. 4 And you

23 [z]ch. 19:26; 20:2; 21:7, 20 [a][Luke 16:22] 25 [b]Mark 4:36 [c]ch. 21:20 26 [d]Matt. 26:23; Mark 14:20 [e]Ruth 2:14 [f][Matt. 26:25] [g]ch. 6:71 27 [h]Luke 22:3; [ver. 2; 1 Cor. 11:27] [i][Luke 12:50] 29 [j]ch. 12:6 [k]ver. 1 [l]ch. 12:5 30 [m][1 Sam. 28:8] 31 [n]See ch. 7:39 [o]ch. 14:13; 15:8; 17:1, 4; 1 Pet. 4:11 32 [p]ch. 17:1, 5 [q]See ch. 12:23 33 [r]See ch. 7:33 [s]ch. 7:34; 8:21 34 [t]1 John 2:7, 8; 3:11; 2 John 5 [u]ch. 15:12, 17; 1 John 3:23; 4:21 [v]Lev. 19:18; Rom. 13:8; Col. 3:14; 1 Thess. 4:9; 1 Tim. 1:5; 1 Pet. 1:22 [w]ch. 15:12; Eph. 5:2; 1 John 4:10, 11

35 [x][1 John 3:14; 4:20] 36 [y][ver. 7] [z][ch. 7:34; 14:2] [a]ch. 21:18, 19; 2 Pet. 1:14 37 [b]Matt. 26:33-35; Mark 14:29-31; Luke 22:33, 34 38 [c]ch. 18:27
Chapter 14 1 [d]ver. 27; [ch. 16:22, 23; 1 Pet. 3:14] [e]See ch. 12:44 2 [f][ch. 2:16] [g]ch. 16:7; [ch. 8:21, 22; 13:33, 36] 3 [h]ver. 18, 28; [ch. 21:22, 23] [i]See ch. 12:26

1 Greek *in the bosom of Jesus* 2 Greek lacks *Jesus* 3 Or *You believe in God*

13:23 whom Jesus loved. This reference appears in 19:26; 20:2; 21:7, 20, and has generally been understood to be John, the author of the Gospel. The remark does not imply a lack of love for the other disciples, but indicates a special affinity for John (19:26, 27).

close to Jesus. In a formal banquet people were not seated but reclined at the table (Luke 22:14 note). John's position would not be unusual on such an occasion.

13:26 this morsel of bread. This was apparently a favor reserved for a guest of honor.

13:27 Satan entered into him. Judas's refusal to respond to Jesus' appeal opened up his heart to the control of Satan. He was still a responsible agent, but had surrendered to the dominion of evil (cf. 8:34).

do quickly. Jesus is still in control of the timetable and makes no further effort to check Judas on his fateful way.

13:31, 32 glorified. The verb is repeated five times. One could have expected the opposite word ("humiliated"), for in the language of Paul, Jesus was on the threshold of His deepest humiliation, hanging on the Cross under the divine curse (Gal. 3:13). But John focuses on the revelation of God's glory through Christ so as to bring out the glory of God revealed especially in the Cross.

13:33 You will seek me. This restriction is a temporary one. In time His disciples will go where Jesus is, when He has prepared a place for them (14:2).

13:34 A new commandment. There is nothing new about the command to love, since Lev. 19:18 teaches to "love your neighbor as yourself." The new element is the change from "neighbor" to "one another" and the change from "as yourself" to "as I have loved you." Christian love has Christ's sacrificial love as its model, and the community of believers as the primary (though by no means exclusive) place in which it is expressed (cf. Matt. 25:40; Gal. 6:10; Eph. 5:25). See "Love" at 1 Cor. 13:13.

13:36 you will follow afterward. This is a prophecy about the martyrdom of Peter (21:18, 19).

13:37 I will lay down my life for you. Peter was undoubtedly sincere, but he did not know himself.

13:38 the rooster will not crow. The expression "crows twice" (as reported in Mark 14:30) refers to the same confirmation of Peter's denials.

14:1 Let not your hearts be troubled. This passage of supreme comfort is offered by Jesus in an hour darkened by the shadow of Judas's treachery and Peter's failure, only a few hours away from the agony of Gethsemane and death on the cross (13:21). Yet the statement conveys a sense of sublime peace, and is intended to minister to the fears of the disciples rather than to Jesus' own needs.

14:2 many rooms. While the road is narrow and the gate small that lead to life (Matt. 7:14), it is also true that the number of Abraham's children is like the sand on the shore and the stars in the sky (Gen. 22:17), "a great multitude that no one could number" (Rev. 7:9).

prepare a place for you. Christ prepares the place in heaven for His own, and the Holy Spirit prepares the redeemed on earth for their place in heaven. See "Heaven" at Rev. 21:1.

14:3 take you to myself. In 1:51, Jesus has compared Himself to a ladder between heaven and earth. He is the One who takes His people to heaven.

know the way to where I am going."[1]
5 [j]Thomas said to him, "Lord, [k]we do not
know where you are going. How can we
know the way?" 6 Jesus said to him, "I am
[l]the way, and [m]the truth, and [n]the life. No
one comes to the Father except through
me. 7 [o]If you had known me, you would
have [p]known my Father also.[2] From now
on you do know him and [q]have seen him."
8 [r]Philip said to him, "Lord, [s]show us the
Father, and it is enough for us." 9 Jesus said
to him, "Have I been with you so long, and
you still do not know me, Philip? [t]Whoever
has seen me has seen the Father. How can
you say, 'Show us the Father'? 10 Do you
not believe that [u]I am in the Father and the
Father is in me? The words that I say to you
[v]I do not speak on my own authority, but
the Father who dwells in me does his
works. 11 Believe me that [u]I am in the
Father and the Father is in me, or else [w]be-
lieve on account of the works themselves.
12 "Truly, truly, I say to you, [x]whoever
believes in me will also do the works that I
do; and greater works than these will he
do, because I [y]am going to the Father.
13 [z]Whatever you ask in my name, this I will
do, that [a]the Father may be glorified in the
Son. 14 [z]If you ask me[3] anything in my
name, I will do it.

Jesus Promises the Holy Spirit

15 [b]"If you love me, you will [c]keep my
commandments. 16 And I will ask the
Father, and he will give you another
[d]Helper,[4] to be with you forever, 17 even
[e]the Spirit of truth, [f]whom the world cannot receive, because it neither sees him nor
knows him. You know him, for he dwells
with you and [g]will be in you.
18 "I will not leave you as orphans; [h]I will
come to you. 19 [i]Yet a little while and the
world will see me no more, but [j]you will
see me. [k]Because I live, you also will live.
20 [l]In that day you will know that [m]I am in
my Father, and [n]you in me, and [o]I in you.
21 [p]Whoever has my commandments and

5 [j]See ch. 11:16 [k]ch. 13:36 6 [l]Heb. 9:8; 10:20; [Eph. 2:18] [m]ch. 1:14, 17; [1 John 5:20] [n]See ch. 11:25 7 [o]ch. 8:19 [p]1 John 2:13, 14 [q][ch. 6:46] 8 [r]ch. 1:43, 44; 12:21 [s][Ex. 33:18] 9 [t]ch. 12:45; [ch. 10:30; 15:24; Col. 1:15; Heb. 1:3] 10 [u]See ch. 10:38 [v]See ch. 5:19, 20 11 [u][See ver. 10 above] [w]See ch. 5:36 12 [x][Matt. 17:20; 21:21; Mark 11:23; 16:17] [y]ver. 28; ch. 16:28; [ch. 7:33; 13:1, 3; 16:5, 10, 17; 17:11, 13; 20:17] 13 [z]ch. 15:16; 16:23, 24; See Matt. 7:7 [a]See ch. 13:31

14 [z][See ver. 13 above] 15 [b]ver. 21, 23; ch. 15:10; 1 John 5:3; 2 John 6 [c]See 1 John 2:3 16 [d]ver. 26; ch. 15:26; 16:7 17 [e]ch. 15:26; 16:13; [1 Cor. 2:12-14; 1 John 2:27; 4:6; 5:7] [f]1 Cor. 2:14 [g]Acts 2:4; [1 John 2:27; 2 John 2]; See Rom. 8:9 18 [h]ver. 3, 28 19 [i]See ch. 7:33 [j][ch. 12:45; 16:16] [k][Rom. 5:10; Eph. 2:5; Rev. 20:4] 20 [l]ch. 16:23, 26 [m]ver. 10 [n][ch. 15:4-7]; See 1 John 2:28 [o]ch. 17:21, 23, 26 21 [p][ch. 7:17; 8:31, 32]

1 Some manuscripts *Where I am going you know, and the way you know* 2 Or *If you know me, you will know my Father also*, or *If you have known me, you will know my Father also* 3 Some manuscripts omit *me* 4 Or *Advocate*, or *Counselor*; also 14:26; 15:26; 16:7

14:6 the life. Not existence as such, but existence in fulfillment of God's design that we should be His living temple (1:4).

except through me. This is a strong affirmation that Christ alone is the way of salvation. To imagine and proclaim other ways is to mislead people and forget the necessity of His coming and redemption (Acts 4:12; Rom. 10:14, 15; 1 John 5:12).

14:7 If you had known me. All the blessings previously named are summed up in the knowledge of God, which is more than a mere mental grasp, as it involves wholehearted commitment.

14:8 show us the Father. Philip's request shows misunderstanding, a theme throughout the Gospel (2:21 note), but it opens the way for the development that follows.

14:9 has seen the Father. Jesus is not denying the distinction of Persons in God. He is reminding Philip that He is the one who reveals God.

14:10 I am in the Father and the Father is in me. This is the reciprocal indwelling announced in 10:38 and developed here, also in v. 20, and again in 17:21. Three great unities are proclaimed in Scripture: the unity of the three Persons of the Trinity; the unity of the divine and human natures of Christ; and the unity of Christ and His people in redemption.

14:11 See "Miracles" at 1 Kin. 17:22.

14:12 greater works than these. History proves that Jesus is not affirming that each believer will do greater miracles than He did. The church's work in the power of the Holy Spirit will be "greater" than Jesus' works in number and territory.

14:13 Whatever you ask in my name. This does not guarantee that God will do whatever we ask if only we add to our prayer the words "in Christ's name." To pray in Christ's name is to identify with the purpose of Christ to the extent that our will has become identified with the will of God (1 John 5:14). Those who do not obtain what they specifically request are often surprised by a different but better answer—and "no" is sometimes the best answer. See "Prayer" at Luke 11:2.

that the Father may be glorified in the Son. The close relationship of the Persons of the Trinity is shown in Jesus' teaching on prayer.

14:15 keep. The proof of love to Christ is not an oral profession but living obedience.

14:16 I will ask the Father, and he will give. Both the Father and the Son are active in sending the Holy Spirit. He is the Spirit of God, the Spirit of the Father (Gen. 1:2; Is. 11:2; Matt. 10:20), and the Spirit of Christ, the Son (Rom. 8:9; Gal. 4:6; Phil. 1:19; 1 Pet. 1:11).

another Helper. See text note. The Greek word translated "Helper" was used in legal language for an advocate for the defense (1 John 2:1), and more generally for one called upon for help. Jesus was such a help for the disciples; and after His ascension the Holy Spirit would take over this work. The term emphasizes the personality of the Holy Spirit as distinct from the Father and the Son, and also His unity with them in the work of redemption.

14:17 the Spirit of truth. Here also the Spirit is in equality with the Father (Is. 65:16) and the Son (v. 6). The "Spirit of truth" is the authority behind the Bible: see "The Authentication of Scripture" at 2 Cor. 4:6.

the world. Sinful humanity as contrasted with God's redeemed people (15:18, 19; 17:9; 1 John 2:15–17; 4:5; 5:4, 5, 19).

with you and will be in you. The Spirit lives in believers (1 Cor. 3:16, 17; 6:19; 2 Cor. 6:16; Eph. 2:21).

14:18 I will come to you. Jesus refers primarily to the coming of the Holy Spirit at Pentecost, since the mutual indwelling, "you in me, and I in you" (v. 20), will not await the Second Coming of Christ. But these words are also appropriate for the hope of the church. Jesus will return to take the redeemed with Him (vv. 3, 19, 28; Acts 1:11).

14:19 Because I live, you also will live. This emphasizes again the truth of 11:25, 26. Life is to be found only in Jesus Christ (v. 6; 1:4).

14:20 I am in my Father. See notes on v. 10 and 10:38. The mutual indwelling in the Trinity is paralleled by the mutual indwelling of Christ and the believer.

[q]keeps them, he it is who loves me. And
[r]he who loves me [s]will be loved by my
Father, and I will love him and [t]manifest
myself to him." 22 [u]Judas (not Iscariot) said
to him, "Lord, how is it [v]that you will manifest yourself to us, and not to the world?"
23 Jesus answered him, [w]"If anyone loves
me, he will keep my word, and my Father
will love him, and [x]we will come to him
and [y]make our home with him. 24 Whoever
does not love me does not keep my words.
And [z]the word that you hear is not mine
but the Father's who sent me.

25 "These things I have spoken to you
while I am still with you. 26 But the [a]Helper,
the Holy Spirit, [b]whom the Father will send
in my name, [c]he will teach you all things
and [d]bring to your remembrance all that I
have said to you. 27 [e]Peace I leave with you;
[f]my peace I give to you. Not as the world
gives do I give to you. [g]Let not your hearts
be troubled, neither [h]let them be afraid.
28 [i]You heard me say to you, [j]'I am going
away, and I will come to you.' If you loved
me, you would have rejoiced, because I
[k]am going to the Father, for [l]the Father is
greater than I. 29 And [m]now I have told you
before it takes place, so that when it does
take place you may believe. 30 I will no
longer talk much with you, for [n]the ruler of
this world is coming. [o]He has no claim on
me, 31 but I do [p]as the Father has commanded me, [q]so that the world may know
that I love the Father. Rise, let us go from
here.

I Am the True Vine

15 "I am the [r]true vine, and my Father
is [s]the vinedresser. 2 [t]Every branch
of mine that does not bear fruit [u]he takes
away, and every branch that does bear fruit
he prunes, [v]that it may bear more fruit.
3 Already [w]you are clean [x]because of the
word that I have spoken to you. 4 [y]Abide [z]in
me, and I in you. As the branch cannot

21 [q]ver. 15; 1 John 2:5 [r]ch. 16:27 [s][ch. 12:26] [t]See ch. 7:4 **22** [u]Luke 6:16; Acts 1:13 [v][Acts 10:40, 41] **23** [w]See ver. 15, 21 [x]Rev. 3:20 [y][2 Cor. 6:16; 1 John 2:24] **24** [z][ver. 10]; See ch. 7:16 **26** [a]See ver. 16 [b][Luke 24:49; Acts 2:33, with ch. 15:26; 16:7] [c]ch. 16:13; 1 Cor. 2:10; 1 John 2:20, 27 [d]See ch. 2:22 **27** [e]ch. 20:19, 21, 26; Luke 24:36 [f]ch. 16:33; Col. 3:15; [Eph. 2:17; Phil. 4:7] [g]ver. 1 [h]2 Tim. 1:7 **28** [i]ver. 2-4 [j]See ch. 8:21 [k]See ver. 12 [l][ch. 10:29; Phil. 2:6]

29 [m]ch. 13:19; 16:4 **30** [n]See ch. 12:31 [o][ch. 17:14; 18:36; Heb. 4:15] **31** [p]ch. 12:49, 50; Phil. 2:8; Heb. 5:8 [q]ch. 17:21, 23

Chapter 15 **1** [r][Jer. 2:21] [s][1 Cor. 3:9] **2** [t]ver. 6. Matt. 3:10; 7:19; [Rom. 11:17; 2 Pet. 1:8] [u][Matt. 15:13; Rom. 11:22] [v][Matt. 13:12] **3** [w]ch. 13:10 [x]ch. 17:17; [ver. 7; Eph. 5:26] **4** [y]ver. 5-7; 1 John 2:6; [Phil 1:11; Col. 1:23]; See ch. 6:56 [z]See ch. 3:15

14:21 he who loves me will be loved. Just as there is reciprocal indwelling, there is also the deepest mutuality of love (v. 15 note).

14:22 to us, and not to the world. The disciple understood Jesus correctly, but he was probably hoping also for a political triumph that would be visible to all.

14:23 our home. As the Holy Spirit indwells the believer, so also the Father and the Son (Rom. 8:9–11; Rev. 3:20).

14:26 the Holy Spirit, whom the Father will send. In 15:26, it is the Son who sends the Spirit. The Father and Son concur in this sending. See theological note "The Holy Spirit" on the next page.

will teach you all things. All things that they needed to know for their mission (16:13).

bring to your remembrance all. This statement shows the divine intention in the teaching work of the Holy Spirit: the Spirit's teaching agrees with the teaching of Jesus Himself. He will ensure that the words of Jesus will be preserved for the instruction of the church (Matt. 24:35). These promises given to the apostles were fulfilled in the preaching of the apostles and in the completion of the New Testament Scriptures. They continue to be fulfilled as God's people learn from the inspired Scripture.

14:27 Peace. This was a common Hebrew salutation used in greeting or farewell. Jesus gives it a new and deeper sense that reappears in the salutations of the New Testament letters. Jesus' peace is true reconciliation with God, purchased with His death (Acts 10:36; Rom. 5:1; 14:17; Eph. 2:14–17; Phil. 4:7; Col. 3:15). It is the supreme remedy for all fears (v. 1), and the legacy Jesus left for His heirs.

14:28 you would have rejoiced. The Lord's departure and return are necessary to complete His mediatorial work (v. 3); they are the end of His humiliation and the revelation of His glory.

the Father is greater than I. This statement must be understood in light of the witness of this Gospel to the full deity of the Son, His equality and oneness with the Father (v. 9; 1:1; 10:30). The Son voluntarily veiled His divine glory to follow the way of humble obedience (Phil. 2:6–11).

14:29 I have told you. The fulfillment of Jesus' prophecies will be a convincing proof that He was sent by God.

14:30 the ruler of this world. Satan (cf. 12:31; 16:11). This statement points to the momentous spiritual conflict of Christ with Satan at the Cross.

He has no claim. This is a reaffirmation of Jesus' sinlessness (v. 31; 8:29, 46; 2 Cor. 5:21; Heb. 7:26, 27). He is the only member of the human race about whom this may be said.

14:31 Rise, let us go. This statement would appear to indicate that Jesus and the disciples left the upper room, but it seems that chs. 15–17 take place still in the room. Several options are possible. (a) Jesus gave the signal but some time elapsed before they left the room. (b) They left at once, but Jesus continued His discourse on the way to Gethsemane. This would bring the prayer of ch. 17 into sharp contrast with the agony in the garden. (c) John has arranged his material topically rather than chronologically. (d) The statement of Jesus was a challenge to meet Satan rather than a signal to leave the room (that is, "up then, let us go to meet the foe").

15:1–17 The union of Christ the Mediator and His redeemed people is portrayed in Scripture in a variety of ways. These portrayals work together in explaining the nature of this relationship. There is: (a) the foundation and the building (1 Cor. 3:11; Eph. 2:20–22); (b) the vine and the branches (15:1–17; Rom. 6:5); (c) the head and the body (1 Cor. 6:15, 19; 12:12; Eph. 1:22, 23; 4:15, 16); (d) the husband and the wife (Rom. 7:4; Eph. 5:31, 32; Rev. 19:7); (e) Adam and his descendants (Rom. 5:12, 18–21; 1 Cor. 15:22, 45, 49). The comparison with vine and branches indicates an organic union and a relation of complete dependence.

15:1 I am the true vine. As elsewhere in this Gospel, "true" means "genuine." Jesus is the final, real "vine," as compared to Israel, which was a type foreshadowing the reality. Israel is called God's "vine" or "vineyard" in the Old Testament (Ps. 80:8–16; Jer. 2:21). Israel is judged for not bearing fruit, while Jesus is and does what the type signified. This is the last of the "I am" sayings in the Gospel (6:35 note).

15:2 does not bear fruit. No branch that is Christ's can be wholly fruitless. But branches that belong to Christ will bear fruit, and undergo the pruning necessary to increase. The lack of fruit described in Ps. 80, Is. 5:1, and Jer. 2:21 is failure to be obedient to God. These Old Testament discussions of the vine and its fruit, combined with Christ's command to love in this chapter, indicate that "fruit" refers to a Christ-like life produced by the Holy Spirit (Gal. 5:22, 23), rather than to the number of people converted under a believer's ministry.

15:4 Abide. Jesus emphasizes permanence and steadfastness in His relationship with the disciples. "Abide" is repeated ten times in vv. 4–10.

bear fruit by itself, unless it abides in the
vine, neither can you, unless you abide in
me. **5** I am the vine; [a]you are the branches.
Whoever abides in me and I in him, he it is
that [b]bears much fruit, for apart from me
you can do nothing. **6** If anyone does not
abide in me [c]he is thrown away like a
branch and withers; [d]and the branches are
gathered, thrown into the fire, and burned.
7 If [e]you abide in me, and my words abide
in you, [f]ask whatever you wish, and it will
be done for you. **8** [g]By this my Father is glorified, that you [h]bear much fruit and so

5 [a]Rom. 6:5 [b]ver. 16; Col. 1:6, 10
6 [c]See ver. 2 [d]Matt. 13:40-42; [Ezek. 15:4]
7 [e]See ch. 8:31 [f]See ch. 14:13
8 [g]Isai. 61:3; Matt. 5:16; 2 Cor. 9:13; Phil. 1:11 [h]ver. 5
9 [i]See ch. 5:20 [j]See ch. 13:34
10 [k][ch. 14:15, 23]

prove to be my disciples. **9** [i]As the Father
has loved me, [j]so have I loved you. Abide
in my love. **10** [k]If you keep my commandments, you will abide in my love, just as [l]I
have kept [m]my Father's commandments
and abide in his love. **11** These things I have
spoken to you, [n]that my joy may be in you,
and that [o]your joy may be full.
12 [p]"This is my commandment, that you
love one another as I have loved you.
13 [q]Greater love has no one than this, [r]that

[l]ch. 8:55; 17:4; Phil. 2:8 [m]See ch. 10:18 **11** [n][2 Cor. 2:3] [o]ch. 3:29; 16:24; 17:13; 1 John 1:4; 2 John 12 **12** [p]See ch. 13:34 **13** [q]Rom. 5:7, 8; Eph. 5:2 [r]See ch. 10:11

The Holy Spirit

Before Jesus' death, He promised that He and the Father would send to His disciples "another Helper" (John 14:16, 26; 15:26; 16:7). The Greek word translated "Helper" is *parakletos*. It means a lawyer or assistant in a legal question. In a wider context it means a person who provides encouragement, counsel, and strength. Jesus will send "another" Helper, One like Himself who will carry on after Him the teaching and testimony that He began (John 16:7–15).

The work of such a Helper is work carried out by a personal Being. The Old Testament reveals much about the Spirit's activity in creation (Gen. 1:2; Ps. 33:6), revelation (Is. 61:1–3; Mic. 3:8), empowerment (Ex. 31:2–6; Judg. 15:14, 15; Is. 11:2), and inward renewal (Ps. 51:10–12; Ezek. 36:25–27). But it was for the New Testament to reveal clearly the Spirit as a distinct divine Person, coequal with the Father and the Son. The Spirit is said to speak (Acts 1:16; 8:29; 10:19; 13:2), teach (John 14:26), witness (John 15:26), search (1 Cor. 2:10), will (1 Cor. 12:11), and intercede (Rom. 8:26, 27). All these are the acts of an individual Person.

The divinity of the Spirit appears from the way the Father, Son, and Holy Spirit are named together in benedictions (2 Cor. 13:14; Rev. 1:4–6) and in the formula of baptism (Matt. 28:19). To lie to the Spirit is to lie to God (Acts 5:3, 4). The Spirit is called "seven spirits" in Rev. 1:4; 3:1; 4:5; 5:6 as an expression of His fullness and the diversity of His work in the church in many places, represented by the seven churches in Asia (Rev. 1:11–20). This divine perfection was foreshadowed in Zech. 3:9; 4:2, 10; the number "seven" expresses the perfection of the one Spirit. The Spirit is the third Person of the Trinity, equal to the Father and the Son in glory, and worthy with them of worship, love, and obedience.

The work of the Spirit is to glorify Jesus Christ by showing His disciples who He is (John 16:7–15) and what He means to them (Rom. 8:15–17; Gal. 4:6). The Spirit enlightens (Eph. 1:17, 18), regenerates (John 3:5–8), sanctifies (Gal. 5:16–18), and transforms (2 Cor. 3:18; Gal. 5:22, 23). He gives God's people what they need to serve Him (1 Cor. 12:4–11).

The Spirit's full ministry began on Pentecost, after Jesus ascended to heaven (Acts 2:1–4). John the Baptist foretold that Jesus would baptize in the Spirit (Mark 1:8; John 1:33) as the fulfillment of a promise made in the Old Testament and repeated by Jesus (Jer. 31:31–34; Joel 2:28–32; Acts 1:4, 5). Pentecost marked the opening of the last era of world history, that will end when Christ returns.

At the time they are born again, believers in Jesus receive the Spirit according to the fullness of the New Testament (Acts 2:38; Rom. 8:9; 1 Cor. 12:13). All the gifts for life service that appear subsequently in a Christian's life flow from this initial baptism in the Spirit, because in this baptism the sinner is united to the risen Christ.

The metaphor of the vine illustrates the point; it is only when nutrients flow freely to the branches that fruit can be borne.

15:5 apart from me you can do nothing. The total inability of the unregenerate sinner makes saving grace absolutely necessary for the beginning, the development, and the completion of salvation.

15:6 If anyone does not abide in me. Those that do not remain show that they never had a saving relationship with Christ. Their destiny is described with the language of damnation (cf. Matt. 3:12; 25:41; Jude 7; Rev. 20:14).

15:8 so prove to be my disciples. The works spoken of are not the ground of acceptance with God, but the result of a saving union with Christ received through grace, not merit.

15:11 my joy. Many imagine that obedience to Christ is burdensome because it requires sacrificial self-surrender and service (Rom. 12:1, 2). Jesus teaches the opposite, associating obedience with joy.

15:12 my commandment. See note 13:34.

someone lays down his life for his friends.
14You are [s]my friends [t]if you do what I
command you. **15**[u]No longer do I call you
servants,[1] for [v]the servant[2] [w]does not know
what his master is doing; but I have called
you friends, for [x]all that I have heard from
my Father [y]I have made known to you.
16You did not choose me, but [z]I chose you
and appointed you that you should go and
[a]bear fruit and that your fruit should abide,
so that [b]whatever you ask the Father in my
name, he may give it to you. **17**These things
I command you, [c]so that you will love one
another.

The Hatred of the World

18[d]"If the world hates you, know that it
has hated me before it hated you. **19**[e]If you
were of the world, the world would love
you as its own; but because [f]you are not of
the world, but I chose you out of the world,
therefore the world hates you. **20**Remember
the word that I said to you: [g]'A servant is
not greater than his master.' If they persecuted me, [h]they will also persecute you. [i]If
they kept my word, they will also keep
yours. **21**But [j]all these things they will do to
you [k]on account of my name, [l]because they
do not know him who sent me. **22**If I had
not come and spoken to them, [m]they
would not have been guilty of sin,[3] but
now they have no excuse for their sin.
23[n]Whoever hates me hates my Father also.

14[s]Luke 12:4 [t][ver. 10; Matt. 12:50] **15**[u][ver. 20] [v][Rom. 7:15] [w][ch. 13:7, 12] [x]ch. 3:32; 8:26, 40; [ch. 16:13] [y]ch. 17:26; [Gen. 18:17; 1 Cor. 2:16; 13:9, 10] **16**[z]See ch. 13:18 [a][2 John 8] [b][ver. 7]; See ch. 14:13 **17**[c]ver. 12 **18**[d]ch. 7:7; 1 John 3:13; [ver. 23, 24] **19**[e][1 John 4:5] [f]ch. 17:14, 16; [Luke 6:26; Gal. 1:4; James 4:4] **20**[g]ch. 13:16; Matt. 10:24; [ver. 15] [h]ch. 16:33; 1 Cor. 4:12; 2 Cor. 4:9; 1 Thess. 2:15; 2 Tim. 3:12 [i][Ezek. 3:7]; See ch. 8:51 **21**[j]ch. 16:3 [k]Matt. 10:22; 24:9; Rev. 2:3; [Acts 5:41; 1 Pet. 4:14, 16] [l]See Acts 3:17 **22**[m][Matt. 11:22, 24; Luke 12:47, 48]; See ch. 9:41 **23**[n]See ch. 5:23

24[o]If I had not done among them the works
that no one else did, [m]they would not be
guilty of sin, but now they have [p]seen and
hated both me and my Father. **25**But [q]the
word that is written in their Law must be
fulfilled: [r]'They hated me without a cause.'
26"But [s]when the Helper comes, whom I
will send to you from the Father, the
Spirit of truth, who proceeds from the
Father, [t]he will bear witness about me.
27And [u]you also will bear witness, [v]be-
cause you have been with me [w]from the
beginning.

16 "I have said all these things to you to
keep you from falling away. **2**[x]They
will put you out of the synagogues. Indeed,
[y]the hour is coming when [z]whoever kills
you will think he is offering service to God.
3And they will do these things [a]because
they have not known the Father, nor me.
4But [b]I have said these things to you, that
when [c]their hour comes you may remember that I told them to you.

The Work of the Holy Spirit

"I did not say these things to you from
the beginning, [d]because I was with you.

24[o]ch. 3:2; 7:31; 9:32; Matt. 9:33; [ch. 10:32, 37] [m][See ver. 22 above] [p]See ch. 14:9 **25**[q]See ch. 12:38; 10:34 [r]Cited from Ps. 35:19, or 69:4 **26**[s]See ch. 14:16, 17, 26 [t]1 Cor. 12:3; 1 John 5:7 **27**[u]ch. 19:35; 21:24; 1 John 1:2; 4:14; [3 John 12]; See Luke 24:48 [v]See Acts 4:20 [w][Luke 1:2; Acts 1:21, 22; 1 John 2:7]
Chapter 16 **2**[x]ch. 9:22; 12:42 [y]See ch. 4:21 [z]Acts 8:1; 9:1; 26:9-11 **3**[a]ch. 8:19, 55; 15:21; 17:25 **4**[b]ch. 13:19; 14:29 [c]See Luke 22:53 [d][Matt. 9:15]

[1] Greek *bondservants* [2] Greek *bondservant*; also verse 20 [3] Greek *they would not have sin*; also verse 24

15:13 lays down his life. Rom. 5:7, 8 describes Christ's amazing self-sacrifice, not for the righteous, but for sinners who are at enmity with God.

15:14 my friends. The test of friendship with Christ is obedience.

15:15 No longer do I call you servants. There is no previous record of Jesus Christ calling the disciples "servants," except possibly 12:26; yet Jesus had a right to do this, as He had the right to be called "Lord" (13:13). "Friend" suggests a close relation, and the language of brotherhood is closer still (Heb. 2:10, 11).

all . . . I have made known. Christ did not have a higher revelation reserved for an inner group; He revealed Himself to the disciples unstintingly.

15:16 You did not choose me, but I chose you. Jesus does not mean that His disciples exercised no will of their own; they did choose to follow Him. Rather, He is indicating that the first initiative, the original and saving choice, was His. Had He not chosen them, they would not have chosen Him. The immediate reference is to service as apostles, but the principle applies to many other matters including election to salvation (Eph. 1:4, 11).

appointed you. This too emphasizes the sovereign activity of God exercised without violation of the human act of decision.

go. This verb marks the direction of Christian service, like Matt. 28:19 and Acts 1:8.

fruit. The figure refers to individual sanctification (Gal. 5:22, 23) and to effectiveness in evangelism (Matt. 13:3–8; Rom. 1:13).

fruit should abide. A distinguishing characteristic of Christian service is that the results have eternal significance.

whatever you ask . . . give it to you. Effective prayer is accompanied by obedience and identification with the will of God (14:13 note; Ps. 66:18).

15:17 love one another. Repeated for the third time in this episode (v. 12; 13:34).

15:18 the world. The opposition between the world and God's elect is stated in the strongest terms (14:17). The world's hatred is not due to what the disciples do wrong, but to what they do right.

15:22 they would not have been guilty of sin. The sin here is the particular sin of hating Jesus and those who belong to Him; it is not sin in the general sense (v. 24).

15:25 in their Law. Those who received the law are condemned by it. This quotation is from the Psalms; "law" refers to the Old Testament in general rather than just to the Pentateuch (10:34 note).

15:26 the Helper. See note 14:16.

send to you. This refers to the work of the Holy Spirit in the plan of redemption, not His eternal relationships within the Godhead.

15:27 because you have been with me from the beginning. The apostles were eyewitnesses, and through the operation of the Holy Spirit, they were to provide the foundational and authoritative witness to Christ for the church (Luke 24:48; Acts 1:21, 22; Eph. 2:20). Following the conclusion of their unique work there can be no more apostles, and the church's present witness to Christ is dependent on the apostolic witness as it is written in the New Testament and illumined by the Holy Spirit.

5 But now [e]I am going to him who sent me,
and [f]none of you asks me, 'Where are you
going?' **6** But because I have said these
things to you, [g]sorrow has filled your heart.
7 Nevertheless, I tell you the truth: it is to
your advantage that I go away, for [h]if I do
not go away, [i]the Helper will not come to
you. But [j]if [k]I go, [l]I will send him to you.
8 [m]And when he comes, he will [n]convict the
world concerning sin and righteousness
and judgment: **9** concerning sin, [o]because
they do not believe in me; **10** [p]concerning
righteousness, [q]because I go to the Father,
and you will see me no longer; **11** [r]concern-
ing judgment, because the ruler of this
world [s]is judged.
12 "I still have many things to say to you,
but you cannot bear them now. **13** When
[t]the Spirit of truth comes, [u]he will [v]guide
you into all the truth, for he will not speak
on his own authority, but [w]whatever he
hears he will speak, and he will declare to
you the things that are to come. **14** He will
[x]glorify me, for he will take what is mine
and declare it to you. **15** [y]All that the Father
has is mine; [z]therefore I said that he will
take what is mine and declare it to you.

Your Sorrow Will Turn into Joy

16 [a]"A little while, and you will see me no
longer; and [b]again a little while, and you
will see me." **17** So [c]some of his disciples
said to one another, "What is this that he
says to us, [d]'A little while, and you will not
see me, and again a little while, and you
will see me'; and, [e]'because I am going to
the Father'?" **18** So they were saying, "What
does he mean by 'a little while'? [f]We do not
know what he is talking about." **19** [g]Jesus
knew that they wanted to ask him, so he
said to them, "Is this what you are asking
yourselves, what I meant by saying, 'A little
while and you will not see me, and again a
little while and you will see me'? **20** Truly,
truly, I say to you, [h]you will weep and
lament, but [i]the world will rejoice. You will
be sorrowful, but [j]your sorrow will turn
into joy. **21** [k]When a woman is giving birth,
she has sorrow because her hour has come,
but when she has delivered the baby, she
no longer remembers the anguish, for joy
that a human being has been born into the
world. **22** [l]So also you have sorrow now, but
[m]I will see you again and [n]your hearts will
rejoice, and no one will take your joy from
you. **23** [o]In that day you will [p]ask nothing of
me. Truly, truly, I say to you, [q]whatever you
ask of the Father in my name, [r]he will give
it to you. **24** Until now you have asked nothing in my name. [s]Ask, and you will receive,
[t]that your joy may be full.

I Have Overcome the World

25 "I have said these things to you in figures of speech. [u]The hour is coming when

5 [e]See ch. 14:12 [f][ch. 13:36; 14:5]
6 [g]ver. 22. ch. 14:1
7 [h]ch. 7:39 [i]ch. 15:26; [ch. 14:16] [j][Acts 2:33] [k]ch. 14:2 [l]See ch. 14:26
8 [m][ch. 8:28] [n][ch. 8:46]
9 [o]ch. 8:24; [Acts 2:36, 37; 1 Cor. 12:3]
10 [p][Acts 17:31] [q]ver. 16, 17, 19
11 [r]See ch. 12:31 [s][Col. 2:15; Heb. 2:14]
13 [t]See ch. 14:17 [u]See ch. 14:26 [v]Acts 8:31; [ch. 1:17; 14:6; Ps. 25:5] [w][ch. 15:15]
14 [x]See ch. 7:39
15 [y]ch. 17:10 [z]ver. 14
16 [a]See ch. 7:33 [b][ver. 22; 1 John 2:8]
17 [c][Mark 9:10, 32] [d]ver. 16 [e]ver. 10
18 [f][ch. 14:5]
19 [g][ver. 30]; See ch. 2:24, 25
20 [h]Matt. 9:15; Mark 16:10; Luke 23:27 [i][Rev. 11:10]
[j]Jer. 31:13; See Matt. 5:4 **21** [k]Isai. 26:17; [Ps. 48:6; Isai. 13:8; 1 Thess. 5:3; Rev. 12:2] **22** [l]ver. 6; [2 Cor. 6:10] [m][ver. 16] [n]Ps. 33:21; Isai. 66:14; Luke 24:52; Acts 2:46; 8:8, 39; 13:5 **23** [o]ver. 26. ch. 14:20 [p]ver. 19, 30 [q]See ch. 14:13 [r]ch. 15:16; [Eph. 1:3] **24** [s]See Matt. 7:7 [t]See ch. 15:11 **25** [u]ver. 2

16:5 none of you asks me. Although Peter had formally asked this and Thomas had practically done so (13:36; 14:5), their questions had been prompted by the prospect of Jesus' departure rather than the desire to know the nature and meaning of Jesus' destination (v. 6).

16:7 if I do not go away. Although news of Jesus' departure disturbed the disciples, it was necessary if they were to enjoy the permanent presence of the Spirit.

16:8 he will convict the world concerning sin. This is probably not a reference to the conviction that leads to repentance and salvation, but to the exposure of humanity's inexcusable guilt. See "Illumination and Conviction" at 1 Cor. 2:10.

16:9 concerning sin. Unbelief is an especially serious sin.

16:11 concerning judgment. Satan and those over whom he rules will ultimately be condemned by divine justice, whose verdict has already been rendered.

16:13 he will guide you into all the truth. This refers to the truth about God, not temporal knowledge of every kind. The Spirit guided the New Testament writers who prepared the new written revelation that would take its place beside the Old Testament Scriptures. The Spirit will remind the writers of the past (14:26; the Gospels), interpret the gospel for the present (14:26; 15:26; Acts and the Epistles), and reveal things to come (Rev. 1:19).

16:14 He will glorify me. Since the plan of redemption centers on Christ, this is the topic on which the Spirit will concentrate His teaching (15:26).

16:16 A little while . . . a little while. The first refers undoubtedly to the Crucifixion that will take Jesus away from them, the second may refer to the Resurrection, the coming of the Spirit, or to the Second Coming of Christ. The Resurrection fits best for the immediate time of the prophecy; the Second Coming fits best for the full scope of the joy in view.

16:17 I am going to the Father. The disciples connected what Jesus said in v. 10 with the statement of v. 16, and that made it more difficult to understand Christ's meaning, since one statement refers to the Ascension and the other to the Crucifixion.

16:22 I will see you again. See note on v. 16.

no one will take your joy. The blessings of God's redemption cannot be canceled by any power, human or satanic. The gracious purpose of God ensures the ongoing joy of salvation in the world (10:28; Phil. 1:6).

16:23 ask . . . ask. There are two different Greek verbs here, the first ordinarily relating to inquiry, and the second to petition. If we observe this distinction, we will note that after the Ascension the disciples will receive revealed truth through the Holy Spirit. Prayers will be directed mainly to the Father in Christ's name (in a spirit of complete agreement with the will and purposes of Christ). See "Prayer" at Luke 11:2.

16:24 Until now. Their prayers were too timid in the light of the salvation they were soon to know.

I will no longer speak to you in figures of
speech but will tell you plainly about the
Father. 26 In that day you will ask in my
name, and I do not say to you that I will
ask the Father on your behalf; 27 [v]for the
Father himself loves you, because [w]you
have loved me and [x]have believed that I
came from God.[1] 28 [y]I came from the Father
and have come into the world, and now [z]I
am leaving the world and going to the
Father."

29 His disciples said, "Ah, now you are
speaking plainly and not [a]using figurative
speech! 30 Now we know that [b]you know all
things and do not need anyone to question
you; this is why we believe that [c]you came
from God." 31 Jesus answered them, "Do
you now believe? 32 Behold, [d]the hour is
coming, indeed it has come, when [e]you
will be scattered, each to his own home,
and [f]will leave me alone. [g]Yet I am not
alone, for the Father is with me. 33 I have
said these things to you, that [h]in me you
may have peace. [i]In the world you will have
[j]tribulation. But [k]take heart; [l]I have overcome the world."

The High Priestly Prayer

17 When Jesus had spoken these
words, [m]he lifted up his eyes to
heaven, and said, "Father, [n]the hour has
come; [o]glorify your Son that the Son may
[p]glorify you, 2 since [q]you have given him
authority over all flesh, [r]to give eternal life
to all [s]whom you have given him. 3 [t]And
this is eternal life, [u]that they know you [v]the
only [w]true God, and [x]Jesus Christ whom
you have sent. 4 I [y]glorified you on earth,
[z]having accomplished the work that you
gave me to do. 5 And now, Father, [a]glorify
me in your own presence with the glory
[b]that I had with you [c]before the world
existed.

6 [d]"I have manifested your name to the
people [e]whom you gave me out of the
world. [f]Yours they were, and you gave
them to me, and they have kept your word.
7 Now they know that everything [f]that you
have given me is from you. 8 For I have
given them [g]the words that you gave me,
and they have received them and have
come to know in truth that [h]I came from
you; and [i]they have believed that you sent
me. 9 I am praying for them. [j]I am not praying for the world but for those [k]whom you
have given me, for [l]they are yours. 10 [m]All

27 [v][ch. 14:21, 23; 17:23] [w]ch. 21:15-17; [1 Cor. 16:22] [x]ver. 30. ch. 17:8 **28** [y]ch. 8:14; 13:3 [z]See ch. 14:12 **29** [a]ver. 25 **30** [b]ch. 21:17; See ch. 2:24, 25 [c][ver. 27, 28; ch. 3:2] **32** [d][ch. 4:21, 23] [e]Matt. 26:31; Mark 14:27 [f][Isai. 63:2] [g]See ch. 8:16, 29 **33** [h]See ch. 14:27; Col. 3:15 [i][ch. 15:18-21] [j]Rev. 1:9; See Acts 14:22 [k]ch. 14:1, 27 [l][Rom. 8:37; 1 John 4:4; 5:4, 5; Rev. 3:21; 12:11]
Chapter 17
1 [m]ch. 11:41 [n][ch. 7:30]; See ch. 12:23 [o]See ch. 7:39 [p]ver. 4 **2** [q]See Matt. 28:18; Rev. 2:26, 27 [r]ch. 10:28; 1 John 2:25 [s]ver. 6, 9, 24; ch. 6:37, 39; 10:29; 18:9; Heb. 2:13 **3** [t][1 John 5:20] [u]Hos. 2:20; 6:3; 2 Pet. 1:2, 3 [v]ch. 5:44 [w]1 Thess. 1:9; 1 John 5:20; [Jer. 10:10] [x]See ch. 3:17 **4** [y]ver. 1; See ch. 13:31 [z][ch. 19:30; Luke 22:37] **5** [a]ch. 13:32 [b]ch. 1:1, 2; [Rev. 3:21] [c]ver. 24; Prov. 8:23; See ch. 8:58 **6** [d]ver. 26; Ps. 22:22 [e]See ver. 2 [f]ver. 9 **7** [f][See ver. 6 above] **8** [g]ver. 14; ch. 15:15; [ch. 8:26; 12:49] [h]ch. 8:42; 16:27 [i]ver. 21, 25; ch. 6:69; 11:42; 16:30 **9** [j][ver. 20, 21] [k]See ver. 2 [l]ver. 6 **10** [m]ch. 16:15

[1] Some manuscripts *from the Father*

16:26 I do not say . . . that I will ask the Father on your behalf. Jesus is not saying that He will cease to pray for them (Rom. 8:34; Heb. 7:25; 1 John 2:1); it means that the disciples will have reached a certain maturity in prayer, so that He will not need to pray in their stead.

16:27 the Father himself loves you. The three Persons of the Trinity are united in their love for believers (3:16). Believers respond with faith and love toward all three Persons of the Godhead.

16:30 you know all things. Only God is omniscient; the disciples acknowledge the origin and the deity of Christ.

16:32 I am not alone. In most of His suffering, Christ was not alone. But His cry of distress, "My God, my God, why have you forsaken me?" (Matt. 27:46; Mark 15:34), makes it clear that Jesus endured a real separation from the Father. This was the climax of what He endured as our sin-bearer.

17:1 Father. This word occurs over one hundred times in John's Gospel. In the prayer of ch. 17 it is found six times.

the hour has come. Jesus was fully conscious of what was going to happen.

glorify your Son that the Son may glorify you. The perfect life of the Son in His incarnation gives glory to the Godhead. The Son is glorified in His crucifixion, resurrection, and enthronement at God's right hand—these events are viewed as a composite unity in this Gospel. See notes 12:23; 13:31.

17:2 given. This verb is used sixteen times in this prayer.

eternal life. See note 3:16.

to all whom you have given him. God's sovereign choice is emphasized in this expression (used again in vv. 6, 9, 24; cf. 6:44; 10:29).

17:3 that they know you . . . and Jesus Christ. Life consists in fellowship with God "who created us for Himself, so that our soul is restless unless it finds its rest in Him," as Augustine expressed it. Knowledge, here as so often in Scripture, means more than mere intellectual grasp; it involves affection and commitment as well. By placing Himself and the Father together as the source of eternal life, Christ affirms His own deity. See "True Knowledge of God" at Jer. 9:24.

17:4 accomplished the work. This anticipates the cry of victory from the cross, "It is finished" (19:30).

17:5 glorify me . . . with the glory. Jesus affirms as part of His petition that His glory existed "before the world existed," signifying that He was preexistent and uncreated. Second, He refers to the kind of "glory" He enjoyed there. Throughout the Bible, this is the glory always associated with the true, living, and only God.

17:6 manifested your name. Here, "name" denotes God in the beauty of His perfection as revealed to humanity.

Yours they were. Everything and everyone belongs to God by virtue of creation, but here possession by redemption is in view. God gave the elect to the Redeemer: "you gave me" (cf. Heb. 2:10–13).

17:9 I am not praying for the world. Jesus' work of redemption has particular reference to the elect—those whom the Father has given Him (10:14, 15, 27–29). This verse strongly supports a doctrine of definite redemption: the prayer of Jesus before His sacrificial death specifies His purpose in dying. In other contexts, where the specific purpose of Jesus' offering is not in precise focus, Jesus prays for His enemies, as we also are to do (Matt. 5:44; Luke 23:34). See "Definite Redemption" at 10:15.

mine are yours, and yours are mine, and [n]I
am glorified in them. **11** And I am no longer
in the world, but [o]they are in the world,
and [p]I am coming to you. [q]Holy Father,
[r]keep them in your name, [s]which you have
given me, [t]that they may be one, [u]even as
we are one. **12** [v]While I was with them, I
kept them in your name, which you have
given me. I have [w]guarded them, and [x]not
one of them has been lost except [y]the son
of destruction, [z]that the Scripture might be
fulfilled. **13** But now [a]I am coming to you,
and these things I speak in the world, that
they may have [b]my joy fulfilled in themselves. **14** [c]I have given them your word, and
[d]the world has hated them [e]because they
are not of the world, [f]just as I am not of the
world. **15** I [g]do not ask that you [h]take them
out of the world, but that you [i]keep them
from [j]the evil one.[1] **16** [k]They are not of the
world, just as I am not of the
world.
17 [l]Sanctify them[2] in the truth; [m]your word
is truth. **18** [n]As you sent me into the world,
so I have sent them into the world. **19** And
[o]for their sake [p]I consecrate myself,[3] that
they also [q]may be sanctified[4] in truth.
20 "I do not [r]ask for these only, but also
for those [s]who will believe in me through
their word, **21** [t]that they may all be one, just
as you, Father, are in me, and I in you, that
[u]they also may be in [v]us, so that the world
[w]may believe that you have sent me. **22** [x]The
glory that you have given me [y]I have given
to them, [t]that they may be one even as we
are one, **23** [z]I in them and you in me, [a]that
they may become perfectly one, [b]so that
the world may know that you sent me and
[c]loved them even as [d]you loved me.
24 Father, I desire that they also, whom you

10 [n]2 Thess. 1:10 **11** [o]ch. 13:1 [p]See ch. 14:12 [q][ver. 25] [r]ver. 12, 15; Jude 1 [s][Ex. 23:21; Phil. 2:9; Rev. 19:12] [t]ver. 21, 22; [ch. 10:16; Rom. 12:5; Gal. 3:28; Eph. 1:10; 4:4] [u]ch. 10:30 **12** [v]See ch. 14:25 [w]2 Thess. 3:3; Jude 24 [x]ch. 18:9; [ch. 6:39; 10:28] [y]2 Thess. 2:3 [z]Ps. 109:8; Acts 1:16-20; [ch. 13:18] **13** [a]See ch. 14:12 [b]See ch. 15:11 **14** [c]ver. 3 [d]See ch. 15:19 [e]ver. 16 [f]ch. 8:23 **15** [g]ver. 9 [h][1 Cor. 5:10] [i]ver. 11 [j]See Matt. 13:19

16 [k]ver. 14 **17** [l][1 Thess. 5:23; 2 Thess. 2:13; 1 Pet. 1:22]; See ch. 15:3 [m]2 Sam. 7:28; Ps. 119:160 **18** [n]ch. 20:21; [ch. 4:38; Matt. 10:5] **19** [o][Tit. 2:14] [p]ch. 10:36 [q][1 Cor. 1:2, 30; 6:11; Heb. 2:11; 10:10] **20** [r]ver. 9 [s][ch. 4:39; Rom. 10:14; 1 Cor. 3:5] **21** [t]See ver. 11; [1 Cor. 6:17] [u]1 John 1:3; 3:24; 5:20 [v]ch. 14:23 [w]See ver. 8 **22** [x]ver. 24; [ch. 1:14; Luke 9:26] [y]Rom. 8:30 [t][See ver. 21 above] **23** [z]ver. 26; ch. 14:20; Rom. 8:10; 2 Cor. 13:5 [a]1 John 2:5; [Col. 3:14; 1 John 4:12, 17] [b]ver. 21; ch. 14:31 [c]ch. 16:27 [d]ver. 24, 26; See ch. 5:20

[1] Or *from evil* [2] Greek *Set them apart* (for holy service to God) [3] Greek *I set myself apart* (for holy service to God); or *I sanctify myself* [4] Greek *may be set apart* (for holy service to God)

17:10 I am glorified in them. It is surprising that God's glory could be associated with the actions of human beings, who are so insignificant compared to the divine majesty. Yet people like Elihu in the Book of Job show that humans may give glory to God, and Paul affirms it of the most common activities of human beings, such as eating and drinking (1 Cor. 10:31).

17:11 Holy Father. This form of address is used only here in the New Testament.

that they may be one, even as we are one. The unity of Persons in the Trinity is the example for the unity of believers with one another through their union with Christ (14:10 note). There is a unity of purpose and essence in the invisible church, the body of Christ. This perfect unity (Eph. 4:12–16), to be manifested on the day of Christ, already forms and shapes God's people so "that the world may believe" (v. 21). Organized unity is no substitute for spiritual unity, although organizational divisions and separations among Christians undoubtedly bear a negative witness in the world (1 Cor. 1:10–13; 12:25; Gal. 5:20).

17:12 the son of destruction. The same term is used to denote the Antichrist in 2 Thess. 2:3. This fulfills Ps. 41:9. Judas's betrayal was necessary for the fulfillment of many other passages descriptive of our Lord's suffering. Jesus understood many Scriptures as containing prophetic announcements of various details of His messianic career. He stressed that all these would be fulfilled because they were the Word of God.

17:14 I have given them your word. This refers to Jesus' teaching.

they are not of the world. The new birth implies a radical division in humanity. Believers continue to live in the world, but they do not truly belong to it (v. 16).

17:15 keep them from the evil one. Jesus knows that the world will hate His disciples as it hated Him, but He does not ask for the disciples to be protected from suffering, but rather that they would be kept from the evil one. It is not the physical or social troubles of the world from which Jesus wishes His disciples to be "kept," but from its moral corruption. See "Christians in the World" at Col. 2:20.

17:17 Sanctify them. Jesus does not pray for the temporal well-being of the disciples, but for their sanctification. He wishes above all that they should be holy. "Truth" is the means by which holiness is attained. Error and deception are basic to evil, and truth is basic to godliness.

your word is truth. This testimony refers immediately to the Old Testament that the disciples possessed. It extends also to the teaching of Jesus, called God's "word" (v. 14), and it comes to include the books of the New Testament canon (v. 20; Luke 8:11–15, 21; 11:28; Acts 4:31; 6:7; 8:14, 25; 1 Thess. 2:13). This is a powerful attestation of the authority and divine origin of Scripture. See "The Authority of Scripture" at 2 Tim. 3:16.

17:18 As you sent me . . . so I have sent them. Compare 20:21. Jesus is the supreme pattern for Christian missions. Any true Christian is a "missionary," sent into the world to bear witness to Christ, to reach out to the lost where they may be found in order to lead them to the Savior.

into the world. Note the prepositions: not "of" the world (vv. 14, 16), nor "out of" the world (v. 15), but "into" the world and "in" the world (16:33).

17:19 I consecrate myself. Jesus, being supremely holy, does not need moral improvement (Heb. 7:26, 27). As the High Priest He consecrates Himself (Ex. 28:41) to His sacred task, especially His supreme sacrifice.

17:20 those who will believe. In a sublime turn of thought, the Lord now embraces in His prayer the whole body of believers, even those yet to come to faith in future ages. Every true Christian can be assured of being included in this prayer.

17:21 that the world may believe that you have sent me. This prayer for unity is not merely for a "spiritual" or invisible unity, but for a unity that is visible to the world, "that the world may believe." See note on v. 11.

17:23 perfectly one. There is a pattern of unity that characterizes the relationship of the Father and the Son, and the Son and the Christian. See note 14:10.

	Father to Son	**Son to Believer**
Unity	vv. 21, 23	vv. 21, 23, 26
Glory	vv. 22, 24	v. 22
Love	vv. 23, 24, 26	vv. 23, 26; 13:1
Mission	vv. 18, 23, 25	v. 18
Knowledge	v. 25	vv. 3, 8, 25, 26

loved them even as you loved me. This statement brings to light the love of God the Father for the redeemed (3:16), sometimes overlooked because of emphasis on the love of Christ for them.

have given me, may be [e]with me [f]where I
am, [g]to see my glory that you have given
me because you loved me [h]before the
foundation of the world. **25** [i]O righteous
Father, even though [j]the world does not
know you, I know you, and these know
that you have sent me. **26** [k]I made known to
them your name, and I will continue to
make it known, that the love [l]with which
you have loved me may be in them, and [m]I
in them."

Betrayal and Arrest of Jesus

18 When Jesus had spoken these
words, [n]he went out with his disciples across [o]the Kidron Valley, where there
was a garden, which he and his disciples
entered. **2** Now Judas, who betrayed him,
also knew [p]the place, for [q]Jesus often met
there with his disciples. **3** [r]So Judas, having
procured a band of soldiers and some officers from the chief priests and the
Pharisees, went there with lanterns and
torches and weapons. **4** Then Jesus, [s]know-
ing all that would happen to him, came forward and said to them, [t]"Whom do you
seek?" **5** They answered him, "Jesus of
Nazareth." Jesus said to them, "I am he."[1]
Judas, who betrayed him, was standing
with them. **6** [u]When Jesus[2] said to them, "I
am he," they drew back and fell to the
ground. **7** So he asked them again, [t]"Whom
do you seek?" And they said, "Jesus of
Nazareth." **8** Jesus answered, "I told you
that I am he. So, if you seek me, let these
men go." **9** [v]This was to fulfill the word that
he had spoken: "Of those whom you gave
me I have lost not one." **10** Then Simon
Peter, [w]having a sword, drew it and struck
the high priest's servant[3] and cut off his
right ear. (The servant's name was Malchus.) **11** So Jesus said to Peter, "Put your
sword into its sheath; [x]shall I not drink the
cup that the Father has given me?"

Jesus Before the High Priest

12 So the band of soldiers and their captain and the officers of the Jews arrested
Jesus and bound him. **13** First they [y]led him
to [z]Annas, for he was the father-in-law of
[a]Caiaphas, who was high priest that year.
14 It was Caiaphas who had advised the
Jews [b]that it would be expedient that one
man should die for the people.

24 [e]2 Tim. 2:11, 12 [f]See ch. 12:26 [g]ch. 1:14; 2 Cor. 3:18; [1 John 3:2] [h]Eph. 1:4; 1 Pet. 1:20; See ver. 5
25 [i]Jer. 12:1; Rev. 16:5; [ver. 11]; See 1 John 1:9 [j]See ch. 8:55; 10:15
26 [k]ver. 6; ch. 15:15 [l]ver. 23; ch. 15:9 [m]See ver. 23
Chapter 18
1 [n]Matt. 26:30, 36; Mark 14:26, 32; Luke 22:39 [o]See 2 Sam. 15:23
2 [p]Luke 22:40 [q][Luke 21:37; 22:39]
3 [r]For ver. 3-11, see Matt. 26:47-56; Mark 14:43-50; Luke 22:47-53
4 [s]ch. 13:1 [t]ver. 7; ch. 1:38; 20:15
6 [u][ch. 10:18; Matt. 26:53; Rev. 1:17]
7 [t][See ver. 4 above]
9 [v]ch. 17:12
10 [w][Luke 22:38]
11 [x]Matt. 20:22; 26:39, 42; [Isai. 51:22] **13** [y][Matt. 26:57] [z]ver. 24; Luke 3:2; Acts 4:6 [a]ver. 24, 28; See Matt. 26:3 **14** [b]ch. 11:50

[1] Greek *I am*; also verses 6, 8 [2] Greek *he* [3] Greek *bondservant*; twice in this verse

17:24 to see my glory. Jesus does not request temporal prosperity for either the disciples or the church; rather, He prays for holiness and unity on earth and for the gathering of His saints in heaven. To be with Christ is the supreme yearning of the Christian (Phil. 1:23; 1 Thess. 4:17).

17:26 The prayer ends by sounding again some of the notes heard throughout: unity, knowledge, mission, and love. This is a fitting climax to the teaching of Jesus in the whole Gospel.

18:1–40 This chapter has three sections. The arrest of Jesus is recorded in vv. 1–18, the trial before Annas in vv. 19–27, and the trial before Pilate in vv. 28–40.

The accounts of the four Gospels cover the major events of the arrest, trial, execution, and resurrection of Jesus. While some difficulties arise in the correlation of details, the main elements are in complete harmony. Jesus was arrested at night. His trial before the Jewish authorities had at least two phases, and during this part of the trial Peter denied Jesus three times. The trial before secular powers had three phases, and Jesus was executed by Pilate's soldiers. He was buried in Joseph of Arimathea's tomb, and on the first day of the week He arose from the dead and was seen alive in a variety of appearances to His disciples. None of the difficulties in the correlation of details is insuperable, but in a number of cases more than one explanation is possible, and in the absence of fuller data, it is difficult to choose among them.

18:3 officers from the chief priests. These were probably the same as the officers of 7:32, 45. They obviously expected resistance to the arrest, both from Jesus and His disciples.

18:4 knowing all . . . came forward and said to them. Note here, and at vv. 7 and 11, that Jesus was ready to be arrested and tried. He made no attempt to escape what He had come to do.

18:5–7 I am he. Here we may have a simple identification, but "he" is supplied in the English text, so Jesus' response coincides with a solemn name for God ("I AM") used in the Greek translation of the Old Testament in Ex. 3:14 (6:35 note).

18:8 let these men go. Even at this crucial time, Jesus was concerned for His disciples (17:12).

18:10 Peter . . . struck the high priest's servant. An ill-conceived act of resistance. John alone records that Peter carried the sword and that Malchus was the name of the servant; Luke alone records that Jesus healed him (Luke 22:51).

18:11 Put your sword into its sheath. Jesus' rebuke does not concern the propriety of self-defense or civil resistance; the point is that Jesus has come to give His life a ransom for many, and He must not be dissuaded from this task (cf. Matt. 16:21–23).

shall I not drink the cup. This "cup" is the cup of the wine of God's wrath (Ps. 75:8; Is. 51:17; Jer. 25:15–17, 27–38). The "cup" that Jesus chooses to drink is not merely death, but the wrath of God upon sin (cf. Matt. 20:22; Mark 10:38).

18:13 Annas. One of the most influential Jewish leaders of that age. Although deposed from the high priesthood by the Romans, he was still known by this title among the Jews. It is difficult to determine whether this verse and vv. 19–24 represent one or two phases of a trial before the Jewish authorities. Matthew, Mark, and Luke refer to an additional phase before the Sanhedrin. Judging from the description of rules for trials found in the *Mishnah* of some two hundred years later, the proceedings here were marked by serious irregularities and violations of Jewish law. The Sanhedrin was not supposed to meet at night; the death penalty could not be declared on the day of the trial; there was false evidence, and false witnesses were used (Matt. 26:59, 60); Jesus was exposed to blows from attendants during the trial (v. 22; Mark 14:65). In addition to all this, it was illegal for the Sanhedrin to meet for a capital case on the eve of a Sabbath or a feast day. These violations show that Jesus' condemnation by the Jewish authorities was a travesty of justice.

Peter Denies Jesus

15[c]Simon Peter followed Jesus, and so
did another disciple. Since that disciple
was known to the high priest, he entered
with Jesus into the court of the high priest,
16[d]but Peter stood outside at the door. So
the other disciple, who was known to the
high priest, went out and spoke to the servant girl who kept watch at the door, and
brought Peter in. 17[e]The servant girl at the
door said to Peter, "You also are not one of
this man's disciples, are you?" He said, "I
am not." 18Now the servants[1] and officers
had made a charcoal fire, because it was
cold, and they were standing and warming
themselves. [f]Peter also was with them,
standing and warming himself.

The High Priest Questions Jesus

19[g]The high priest then questioned Jesus
about his disciples and his teaching. 20Jesus
answered him, "I have spoken [h]openly [i]to
the world. I have always taught in synagogues and in the temple, where all Jews
come together. [j]I have said nothing in
secret. 21Why do you ask me? Ask those
who have heard me what I said to them;
they know what I said." 22When he had
said these things, one of the officers standing by struck Jesus with his hand, saying,
[k]"Is that how you answer the high priest?"
23Jesus answered him, "If what I said is
wrong, bear witness about the wrong; but if
what I said is right, why do you strike me?"
24[l]Annas then sent him bound to [l]Caiaphas
the high priest.

Peter Denies Jesus Again

25[m]Now Simon Peter was standing and
warming himself. So they said to him, "You
also are not one of his disciples, are you?"
He denied it and said, "I am not." 26One of
the servants of the high priest, a relative of
[n]the man whose ear Peter had cut off,
asked, "Did I not see you [o]in the garden
with him?" 27Peter again denied it, and [p]at
once a rooster crowed.

Jesus Before Pilate

28[q]Then they led Jesus [r]from the house of
Caiaphas to [s]the governor's headquarters.[2]
It was early morning. They themselves did
not enter the governor's headquarters, [t]so
that they would not be defiled, [u]but could
eat the Passover. 29[v]So Pilate went outside
to them and said, "What accusation do you
bring against this man?" 30They answered
him, "If this man were not doing evil, we
would not have delivered him over to you."
31Pilate said to them, [w]"Take him yourselves and judge him by your own law."
The Jews said to him, "It is not lawful for us
to put anyone to death." 32[x]This was to fulfill the word that Jesus had spoken [y]to show
by what kind of death he was going to die.

15 [c]Matt. 26:58; Mark 14:54; Luke 22:54 **16** [d]For ver. 16-18, see Matt. 26:69, 70; Mark 14:66-68; Luke 22:55-57 **17** [e]Acts 12:13 **18** [f]ver. 25; Mark 14:54 **19** [g]For ver. 19-24, [Matt. 26:59-68; Mark 14:55-65; Luke 22:63-71] **20** [h]ch. 7:26; [Matt. 26:55] [i][ch. 8:26] [j]Isai. 45:19; 48:16; [ch. 7:4] **22** [k][Acts 23:4] **24** [l]ver. 13 **25** [m]For ver. 25-27, see Matt. 26:71-75; Mark 14:69-72; Luke 22:58-62 **26** [n]ver. 10 [o]ver. 1 **27** [p]ch. 13:38 **28** [q]Matt. 27:2; Mark 15:1 Luke 23:1 [r]ver. 24 [s]ver. 33; ch. 19:9; See Matt. 27:27 [t]Acts 10:28; 11:3; [ch. 11:55] [u][ch. 19:14]

29 [v]For ver. 29-38, see Matt. 27: 11-14; Mark 15: 2-5; Luke 23:2, 3 **31** [w][ch. 19:6] **32** [x][ch. 13:18] [y]ch. 12:32, 33; Matt. 20:19; 26:2; Mark 10:33; Luke 18:32

1 Greek *bondservants*; also verse 26 2 Greek *the praetorium*

18:15 another disciple. Probably this was John since of the three closest to Jesus (Peter, James, and John), he is the only one not mentioned by name in the Gospel.

known to the high priest. He was admitted to the palace, even allowed to invite a guest (v. 16).

18:17 The account of Peter's denial is interrupted in John's Gospel by part of the trial proceedings (vv. 19–24). It would appear that there were three occasions of denial rather than three single sentences by Peter. This is what one would expect with a number of people coming and going and warming themselves by a fire. There may be different legitimate ways of distinguishing the occasions to yield the figure three predicted by Jesus (13:38). All four Gospels agree that the first denial was in response to a question of a "servant girl," in other words, a harmless person of no great importance in the household.

I am not. Peter's denial points out that when Jesus endures God's punishment against sin, He does so without comfort or consolation. Peter's denial is foretold in Zech. 13:6, 7. Jesus' solitude in His suffering is anticipated in Ps. 69:20.

18:19 The high priest then questioned. This may be Annas or Caiaphas in the house of Annas (v. 24). An accused person was not to be questioned until witnesses had first established a presumption of guilt. For this reason, some call this a hearing, not a trial.

18:22 one of the officers . . . struck Jesus. This obviously was highly irregular, particularly when the prisoner was bound (v. 24).

18:26 a relative. A question by this man endangered Peter more than the previous ones, since he might have wanted to avenge Malchus.

18:28 the governor's headquarters. The Roman trial of Jesus appears to have had three phases: an appearance before Pilate (vv. 28–38); an appearance before Herod (Luke 23:5–12); and a second appearance before Pilate (18:39–19:16). John describes only the first and third parts, but in more detail than the other Gospels.

so that they would not be defiled. The Roman Praetorium was a site of hostility between the Romans and the Jews, and an unclean place for Jews. Remarkably, it is the place where they collaborated to put Jesus to death. See note on chs. 13–17.

18:29 What accusation. The Jews had no charge that would be recognized in a Roman court, let alone be viewed as a capital offense.

18:31 Take him yourselves and judge him. A logical response. Pilate's point is that if they were not willing to specify charges, they should not expect Him to conduct a trial.

not lawful for us to put anyone to death. This was the usual provision in countries occupied by Rome, perhaps in order to protect those who supported Rome. The Jews were not always so obedient; note the death of Stephen (Acts 7:57–60).

18:32 what kind of death. See 3:14; 12:32–34. Stoning was the Jewish method of capital punishment. Hanging and crucifixion, as implied in the words "lifted up," were used by the Romans. This shows the divine control over the whole procedure, even though it was marked by flagrant injustice.

My Kingdom Is Not of This World

33 [z]So Pilate entered his headquarters
again and called Jesus and said to him,
[a]"Are you the King of the Jews?" 34 Jesus
answered, "Do you say this of your own
accord, or did others say it to you about
me?" 35 Pilate answered, "Am I a Jew? Your
own nation and the chief priests have delivered you over to me. What have you done?"
36 Jesus answered, [b]"My kingdom [c]is not of
this world. If my kingdom were of this
world, [d]my servants would have been fighting, that [e]I might not be delivered over to
the Jews. But my kingdom is not from the
world." 37 Then Pilate said to him, "So you
are a king?" Jesus answered, [f]"You say that I
am a king. [g]For this purpose I was born and
for this purpose [h]I have come into the
world— [i]to bear witness to the truth.
[j]Everyone who is [k]of the truth [l]listens to my
voice." 38 Pilate said to him, "What is truth?"

33 [z]ch. 19:9 [a][ch. 19:12] 36 [b][ch. 6:15; Dan. 2:44; 7:14, 27; Luke 17:21] [c]ch. 8:23; [ch. 15:19; 17:14, 16; 1 John 2:16; 4:5] [d][Matt. 26:53] [e]ch. 19:16 37 [f]See Luke 22:70 [g][ch. 12:27; Rom. 14:9] [h]ch. 16:28 [i]ch. 3:11, 32; 5:31; 8:13, 14, 18 [j]1 John 4:6; [ch. 8:47] [k]1 John 2:21; 3:19 [l]ch. 10:16, 27
38 [m]ch. 19:4 [n]ch. 19:4, 6; See Luke 23:4

After he had said this, [m]he went back
outside to the Jews and told them, [n]"I find
no guilt in him. 39 [o]But you have a custom
that I should release one man for you at the
Passover. So do you want me to release to
you the King of the Jews?" 40 They cried out
again, [p]"Not this man, but Barabbas!" Now
Barabbas was a robber.

Jesus Delivered to Be Crucified

19 Then Pilate took Jesus and [q]flogged
him. 2 [r]And the soldiers twisted together a crown of thorns and put it on his
head and arrayed him in a purple robe.
3 They came up to him, saying, "Hail, King
of the Jews!" and struck him with their
hands. 4 Pilate went out again and said to
them, "See, I am bringing him out to you

39 [o]For ver. 39, 40, see Matt. 27:15-18, 20-23; Mark 15:6-14; Luke 23:18-23
40 [p]Acts 3:14
Chapter 19 1 [q]Matt. 20:19; 27:26; Mark 15:15; Luke 23:16 2 [r]Matt. 27:27-30; Mark 15:16-19

18:33 King of the Jews. Jesus was not the "King of the Jews" in the sense that He promoted sedition against Rome, as charged by the Jewish leaders (Luke 23:2), but He was the King of the Jews in the messianic sense (12:13; Matt. 2:2; Luke 1:32, 33; 19:38).

18:36 My kingdom is not of this world. Jesus is a King, but He will not establish His kingdom by force. This greatly puzzles Pilate. See "Jesus' Heavenly Reign" at Acts 7:55.

18:37 You say. Pilate's question elicits the marvelous answer of Jesus, whose kingdom and mission are founded in the truth (1:8, 14, 17; 8:32; 14:6).

18:38 What is truth. Truth does not matter to those who, like Pilate, are motivated by expediency. Likewise, truth does not matter to skeptics who have despaired of knowing it.

I find no guilt in him. Pilate finds no crime in Jesus and is reluctant to put Jesus to death. Ironically, it is the pagan Roman governor who tries to release Jesus, while "his own" (1:11) want Him to die.

18:39 you have a custom. The custom of pardoning a criminal at the Passover is relevant to the festival itself, which commemorates God's sparing the Israelites from death.

18:40 Barabbas. This name means "son of the father." Instead of him, the true Son of the Father died.

19:1 flogged him. The Roman scourge was cruel and sometimes fatal. The whip had metal or bone fragments in it to tear the flesh.

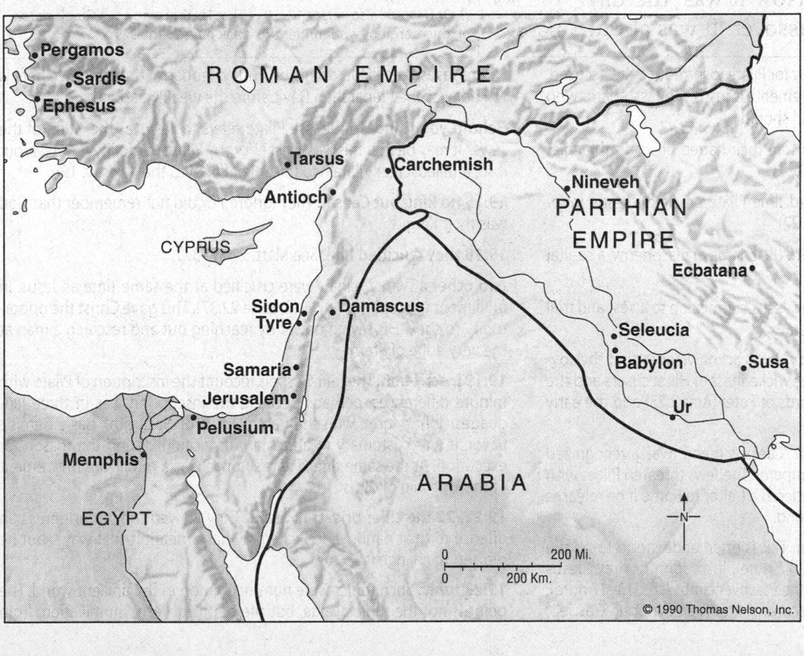

Roman Control of Palestine at the Time of Christ. Following a successful military campaign against the Seleucids in 64 B.C., Pompey turned the Roman armies southward and took control of Jerusalem in 63 B.C. Initially the Roman army had been invited by some of the Jews to protect them from the Nabateans. Once the Romans became established in Palestine, they never left, despite repeated Jewish revolts against Roman control.

that you may know that [s]I find no guilt in
him." 5 So Jesus came out, wearing [t]the
crown of thorns and the purple robe. Pilate
said to them, [u]"Behold the man!" 6 When
the chief priests and the officers saw him,
they cried out, "Crucify him, crucify him!"
Pilate said to them, [v]"Take him yourselves
and crucify him, for [w]I find no guilt in
him." 7 The Jews answered him, "We have
a law, and [x]according to that law he ought
to die because [y]he has made himself the
Son of God." 8 When Pilate heard this
statement, [z]he was even more afraid. 9 [a]He
entered his headquarters again and said to
Jesus, [b]"Where are you from?" But [c]Jesus
gave him no answer. 10 So Pilate said to
him, "You will not speak to me? Do you
not know that I have authority to release
you and authority to crucify you?" 11 Jesus
answered him, [d]"You would have no
authority over me at all unless it had
been given you from above. Therefore [e]he
who delivered me over to you [f]has the
greater sin."
12 From then on [g]Pilate sought to release
him, but the Jews cried out, "If you release
this man, you are not Caesar's friend.
[h]Everyone who makes himself a king
opposes Caesar." 13 So when Pilate heard
these words, he brought Jesus out and sat
down on [i]the judgment seat at a place
called The Stone Pavement, and in
Aramaic[1] Gabbatha. 14 Now it was [j]the day
of Preparation of the Passover. It was about

4 [s]ver. 6; ch. 18:38
5 [t]ver. 2 [u][ver. 14]
6 [v][ch. 18:31] [w]ver. 4
7 [x]Lev. 24:16; [ch. 10:33] [y]ch. 5:17, 18; 10:36; Matt. 26:63; Luke 22:70
8 [z][Matt. 27:19]
9 [a]ch. 18:33 [b]ch. 7:27 [c][ch. 18:37]; See Matt. 26:63
11 [d][Rom. 13:1] [e][ch. 18:14, 28-32; Matt. 27:2] [f]See ch. 9:41
12 [g]Acts 3:13 [h]See Luke 23:2
13 [i]Matt. 27:19
14 [j][ch. 18:28]; See Matt. 27:62
[k][ver. 5]
15 [l]Luke 23:18; [Acts 21:36]
16 [m]Matt. 27:26; Mark 15:15; Luke 23:25 [n]ch. 18:36-40
17 [o]Matt. 27:33; Mark 15:22; Luke 23:33 [p]Luke 14:27; [Matt. 27:32; Mark 15:21; Luke 23:26]
18 [q]Matt. 27:38; Mark 15:24, 27; Luke 23:32, 33

the sixth hour.[2] He said to the Jews,
[k]"Behold your King!" 15 They cried out,
[l]"Away with him, away with him, crucify
him!" Pilate said to them, "Shall I crucify
your King?" The chief priests answered,
"We have no king but Caesar." 16 [m]So he
[n]delivered him over to them to be crucified.

The Crucifixion

So they took Jesus, 17 and [o]he went out,
[p]bearing his own cross, to the place called
the place of a skull, which in Aramaic is
called Golgotha. 18 [q]There they crucified
him, and with him two others, one on
either side, and Jesus between them.
19 Pilate [r]also wrote an inscription and put
it on the cross. It read, "Jesus of Nazareth,
the King of the Jews." 20 Many of the Jews
read this inscription, for [s]the place where
Jesus was crucified was near the city, and it
was written in Aramaic, in Latin, and in
Greek. 21 So the chief priests of the Jews
said to Pilate, "Do not write, 'The King of
the Jews,' but rather, 'This man said, I am
King of the Jews.'" 22 Pilate answered,
[t]"What I have written I have written."
23 [u]When the soldiers had crucified Jesus,
they took his garments and divided them
into four parts, one part for each soldier;
also his tunic.[3] But the tunic was seamless,
woven in one piece from top to bottom,

19 [r][Matt. 27:37; Mark 15:26; Luke 23:38] 20 [s]ver. 17; [Num. 15:35, 36; Heb. 13:12] 22 [t][Gen. 43:14; Esth. 4:16] 23 [u]Matt. 27:35; Mark 15:24; Luke 23:34

[1] Or *Hebrew*; also verses 17, 20 [2] That is, about noon [3] Greek *chiton*, a long garment worn under the cloak next to the skin

19:5 Behold the man. A natural way for Pilate to introduce the accused, but providentially a significant statement. Jesus is the last Adam, who sums up all that humanity could and should be.

19:6 the chief priests . . . cried out. In their hatred of Jesus, the chief priests become the leaders of a mob.

I find no guilt in him. For the third time Pilate proclaims Jesus' innocence (18:38; 19:4; cf. Luke 23:4, 14, 22).

19:7 he ought to die. The appeal is to the charge of blasphemy, a capital offense in Jewish law (Lev. 24:16).

19:9 But Jesus gave him no answer. Jesus' submission to arrest and trial is part of His surrender as a self-offering.

19:11 You would have no authority. Jesus acknowledges that the sovereign plan of God includes even the wickedness of His accusers and the cowardice of Pilate. See also the words of Peter (Acts 2:23) and the early church (Acts 4:28).

19:12 you are not Caesar's friend. "Caesar's friend" was a recognized title for political supporters of the emperor. The Jews threaten Pilate with the suggestion that he will be considered a traitor to Rome if he releases someone who talks about being a king.

19:14 Preparation of the Passover. This is often understood to be the Thursday before Passover (Matt. 27:17 note). If so, John portrays Jesus being crucified at the same time as the Passover lambs (chs. 13–17 note). This appears to conflict with the record of the three Synoptic Gospels, where Jesus' crucifixion occurs on Friday. Probably, the reference here is to Friday as the Preparation Day before the weekly Sabbath.

Behold your King. To the last, Pilate refers to Jesus as the "King of the Jews." It may be that this was a last effort by Pilate to mollify the Jews, but if so, it failed. Later Pilate had this title affixed to the cross (v. 19).

19:15 no king but Caesar. They ignored or did not remember that God was their King.

19:18 they crucified him. See Matt. 27:32–37.

two others. Two criminals were crucified at the same time as Jesus, in fulfillment of prophecy (Is. 53:12; Luke 22:37). This gave Christ the opportunity to show His saving power by reaching out and rescuing a man at the very edge of eternity.

19:19 inscription. The four Gospels recount the inscription of Pilate with minute differences, perhaps because the inscription was in three languages. John's form, with the name "Jesus of Nazareth," has a Semitic flavor. It was customary to attach an inscription stating the reason for execution. At the same time, Pilate's notice was a public announcement of the kingship of Christ.

19:21, 22 the chief priests . . . said. They viewed the inscription as an offense to their nation, and Pilate may have meant it that way—but he refused to change it.

19:23 tunic. Such tunics were not uncommon in the ancient world. The point is not the tunic's value, but the depth of Jesus' humiliation, from

24 so they said to one another, "Let us not
tear it, but cast lots for it to see whose it
shall be." [v]This was to fulfill the Scripture
which says,

> [w]"They divided my garments among
> them,
> and for my clothing they cast lots."

So the soldiers did these things, 25 [x]but
standing by the cross of Jesus were his
mother and his mother's sister, Mary the
wife of Clopas, and Mary Magdalene.
26 When Jesus saw his mother and [y]the disciple whom he loved standing nearby, he
said to his mother, [z]"Woman, behold, your
son!" 27 Then he said to the disciple,
"Behold, your mother!" And from that
hour the disciple took her to [a]his own
home.

The Death of Jesus

28 After this, Jesus, knowing that all was
now [b]finished, said ([v]to fulfill the
Scripture), [c]"I thirst." 29 A jar full of sour
wine stood there, [d]so they put a sponge full
of the sour wine on a hyssop branch and
held it to his mouth. 30 When Jesus had
received the sour wine, he said, [e]"It is finished," and he bowed his head and [f]gave
up his spirit.

Jesus' Side Is Pierced

31 Since it was [g]the day of Preparation,
and [h]so that the bodies would not remain
on the cross on the Sabbath (for that
Sabbath was [i]a high day), the Jews asked
Pilate that their legs might be broken and
that they might be taken away. 32 So the soldiers came and broke the legs of the first,
and of the other [j]who had been crucified
with him. 33 But when they came to Jesus
and saw that he was already dead, they did
not break his legs. 34 But one of the soldiers
pierced his side with a spear, and at once
there came out [k]blood and water. 35 [l]He
who saw it has borne witness—[m]his testimony is true, and he knows that he is
telling the truth—[n]that you also may
believe. 36 [o]For these things took place that
the Scripture might be fulfilled: [p]"Not one
of his bones [q]will be broken." 37 And again
another Scripture says, [r]"They will look on
him whom they have pierced."

Jesus Is Buried

38 [s]After these things Joseph of Arimathea, who was a disciple of Jesus, but
secretly [t]for fear of the Jews, asked Pilate
that he might take away the body of Jesus,
and Pilate gave him permission. So he
came and took away his body. 39 [u]Nico-
demus also, who earlier had come to Jesus[1]
by night, came [v]bringing a mixture of
[w]myrrh and aloes, about seventy-five
pounds[2] in weight. 40 So they took the body
of Jesus and [x]bound it in [y]linen cloths with
the spices, as is the burial custom of the
Jews. 41 Now in the place where he was crucified there was a [z]garden, and [a]in the garden a new tomb [b]in which no one had yet
been laid. 42 So because of the Jewish [c]day

24 [v]See ch. 13:18 [w]Cited from Ps. 22:18
25 [x]Matt. 27:55, 56; Mark 15:40, 41; Luke 23:49
26 [y]See ch. 13:23 [z]ch. 2:4
27 [a][ch. 1:11; 16:32]
28 [b][ver. 30] [v][See ver. 24 above] [c]Ps. 69:21; See ch. 4:6, 7
29 [d]Matt. 27:48; Mark 15:36; [Luke 23:36]
30 [e][ver. 28; Acts 13:29]; See ch. 17:4 [f]Matt. 27:50; Mark 15:37; Luke 23:46
31 [g]ver. 14 [h]Deut. 21:23; Josh. 8:29; 10:26, 27 [i]Ex. 12:16
32 [j]ver. 18
34 [k]1 John 5:6, 8
35 [l]1 John 1:1-3; Rev. 1:2; See ch. 15:27 [m][ch. 21:24] [n][ch. 20:31]
36 [o]See Matt. 1:22 [p]Cited from Ex. 12:46; Num. 9:12; [1 Cor. 5:7] [q]Ps. 34:20
37 [r]Cited from Zech. 12:10; [Rev. 1:7]
38 [s]For ver. 38-42, see Matt. 27: 57-61; Mark 15: 42-47; Luke 23: 50-56
[t]See ch. 7:13 39 [u]ch. 3:1, 2; 7:50 [v][Mark 16:1; Luke 24:1] [w]Ps. 45:8; Prov. 7:17; S. of S. 4:14 40 [x]ch. 11:44; [2 Chr. 16:14; Acts 5:6] [y]ch. 20:5-7; Luke 24:12 41 [z][ch. 20:15] [a]2 Kin. 21:18, 26 [b]Luke 23:53; [Mark 11:2] 42 [c]ver. 14, 31

1 Greek *him* 2 Greek *one hundred litras*; a *litra* (or Roman pound) was equal to about 11 1/2 ounces or 327 grams

whom everything was taken as He offered Himself. It is also the fulfillment of Ps. 22:18.

19:25 by the cross. "Clopas" may be the same as "Cleopas," mentioned in Luke 24:18. The courage of the four women is noteworthy. Some are present again at Jesus' burial (Matt. 27:61; Mark 15:47) and at the Resurrection (20:1–18; Matt. 28:1; Mark 16:1).

19:26 Woman, behold your son. "Woman" is not a harsh form of address in Aramaic (2:4 note). Even in the midst of dying on the cross as the Mediator of the new covenant, Jesus fulfills his duty as the Son of Mary in a splendid example of obedience to the letter and spirit of the fifth commandment. In a time of intense physical pain and mental anguish, the Lord thought of others, as is shown in the first statements from the cross (Luke 23:34, 43).

19:28–30 all . . . finished. The worst ordeal, that of bearing in the place of His people the wrath of God against sin (Matt. 27:46; Mark 15:34), appears to be over.

19:31 day of Preparation. See note on v. 14.

bodies would not remain on the cross. This would ceremonially defile the land (Deut. 21:23). It is a starkly revealing example of their depraved insensitivity that they joined forces to commit murder and at the same time were so punctilious about enforcing the ceremonial law.

legs . . . broken. Breathing was so difficult in crucifixion that if the legs could not help by lifting the torso, a person would quickly die.

19:34 pierced his side with a spear. This act proves that Jesus was not in a coma but was dead, as shown by the burial preparations (vv. 39, 40) and the specification of a particular tomb (v. 41). Both the preserving of His bones (v. 33) and the piercing of His side fulfill Old Testament Scripture (vv. 36, 37; Ps. 34:20; Zech. 12:10).

blood and water. John emphasizes this physical evidence that Jesus was a real human being and that He was dead. It has been suggested that rupture of the heart caused by extreme agony is indicated, but more recent medical research has shown that such trauma occurs only when the heart is already damaged by disease. Others see a symbolic significance linked with 1 John 5:6–8.

19:38 Joseph of Arimathea. A secret supporter of Jesus mentioned in all four Gospels in connection with Jesus' burial, but nowhere else in the New Testament. See note Luke 23:50, 51.

of Preparation, [d]since the tomb was close
at hand, they laid Jesus there.

The Resurrection

20 [e]Now on the first day of the week
Mary Magdalene came to the tomb
early, while it was still dark, and saw that
[f]the stone had been taken away from the
tomb. 2 So she ran and went to Simon Peter
and the other disciple, [g]the one whom
Jesus loved, and said to them, "They have
taken the Lord out of the tomb, and [h]we
do not know where they have laid him."
3 [i]So Peter went out with the other disciple,
and they were going toward the tomb.
4 Both of them were running together, but
the other disciple outran Peter and reached
the tomb first. 5 And stooping to look in, he
saw [j]the linen cloths lying there, but he did
not go in. 6 Then Simon Peter came, following him, and went into the tomb. He saw
the linen cloths lying there, 7 and [k]the face
cloth, which had been on Jesus'[1] head, not
lying with the linen cloths but folded up in
a place by itself. 8 Then the other disciple,
[l]who had reached the tomb first, also went
in, and he saw and believed; 9 for as yet
[m]they did not understand the Scripture,
[n]that he must rise from the dead. 10 Then
the disciples went back to their homes.

Jesus Appears to Mary Magdalene

11 But Mary stood weeping outside the
tomb, and as she wept she stooped to look
into the tomb. 12 And [o]she saw [p]two angels
in white, sitting where the body of Jesus
had lain, one at the head and one at the
feet. 13 They said to her, [q]"Woman, why are
you weeping?" She said to them, [r]"They
have taken away my Lord, and I do not
know where they have laid him." 14 Having
said this, she turned around and [s]saw Jesus
standing, [t]but she did not know that it was
Jesus. 15 Jesus said to her, [u]"Woman, why
are you weeping? [v]Whom are you seeking?"
Supposing him to be [w]the gardener, she
said to him, "Sir, if you have carried him
away, tell me where you have laid him,
and I will take him away." 16 Jesus said to
her, "Mary." She turned and said to him
in Aramaic,[2] [x]"Rabboni!" (which means
Teacher). 17 Jesus said to her, "Do not cling
to me, for I have not yet ascended to the
Father; but go to [y]my brothers and say to
them, [z]'I am ascending to my Father and
your Father, to [a]my God and your God.'"
18 Mary Magdalene [b]went and announced

42 [d]ver. 41
Chapter 20
1 [e]Matt. 28:1; Mark 16:1, 2; Luke 24:1 [f]Matt. 27:60, 66; 28:2; Mark 15:46; 16:3, 4; Luke 24:2
2 [g]See ch. 13:23 [h]ver. 13
3 [i]Luke 24:12
5 [j]ch. 19:40
7 [k]ch. 11:44
8 [l]ver. 4
9 [m]Matt. 22:29 [n]Ps. 16:10; Luke 24:46; Acts 2:25-31; 13:34, 35; 17:3; 1 Cor. 15:4
12 [o][Mark 16:5] [p]Luke 24:4
13 [q]ver. 15; [ch. 2:4] [r]ver. 2
14 [s]Mark 16:9; [Matt. 28:9] [t]ch. 21:4; Luke 24:16, 31
15 [u]ver. 13 [v]ch. 1:38; 18:4, 7 [w][ch. 19:41]
16 [x]See ch. 1:38
17 [y]See Matt. 28:10 [z][Mark 16:19]; See ch. 14:12 [a]Matt. 27:46; Eph. 1:17; Rev. 3:2, 12; [1 Cor. 3:23]
18 [b]Mark 16:10; [Matt. 28:10; Luke 24:10, 22, 23]

1 Greek *his* 2 Or *Hebrew*

20:1–31 The four Gospels have accounts of several resurrection appearances; together with Acts 1:3–8 and 1 Cor. 15:5–8, there are twelve appearances, the first six in Jerusalem, four in Galilee, one on the Mount of Olives, and one on the road to Damascus.

20:2 Peter . . . the other disciple. Peter and John. See note 13:23.

we do not know. "We" indicates that several women were there, as recorded by the other Gospels. They were the same women who stood at the foot of the Cross, perhaps with the exception of Mary, Jesus' mother, who is not mentioned.

where they have laid him. Neither Mary nor the disciples were expecting the Resurrection, in spite of what Jesus had told them (cf. v. 9).

20:5–8 he saw the linen cloths. John took the first cursory look and saw that only the burial clothes were there. Peter and John then made a closer inspection. The graveclothes were in good order (v. 7). If someone had violated the tomb and removed the corpse, the linen cloths would not have been so well arranged, and the handkerchief would not likely have been folded.

20:9 they did not understand the Scripture. Later, as a result of Jesus' instruction, they understood His resurrection as a necessary fulfillment of prophecy (Luke 24:26, 27, 44–47; Acts 2:25–32; 13:35–37). Clearly the disciples did not expect a resurrection, or try to invent one in order to fit their own religious view. See "The Resurrection of Jesus" at Luke 24:2.

20:12 two angels in white. Matt. 28:2 records "an angel"; Mark 16:5 "a young man"; and Luke 24:4 "two men" (called "a vision of angels" in Luke 24:23). There is no necessary contradiction since the angels must have appeared in human form and one of them may be singled out, perhaps because he was the speaker. What Mary saw may also differ from what the other women saw since she remained alone at the tomb after Peter and John had left.

20:14 she . . . saw Jesus standing. Matthew reveals that Jesus had already appeared once to the group of women on their way to Jerusalem to tell the news about the empty tomb (Matt. 28:8–10).

did not know that it was Jesus. Jesus was often not immediately recognized after His resurrection (v. 20; 21:4). On some occasions this may have been due to skepticism or grief; in Luke it is sometimes due to supernatural hindrance (Luke 24:16, 31). In addition, the resurrection involves a change in appearance (1 Cor. 15:35–49).

20:16 Rabboni. The voice of Jesus calling "Mary" revealed clearly who He was. "Rabboni" is a lengthened form of "Rabbi," occurring one other time in the New Testament (Mark 10:51).

20:17 Do not cling to me. There is no impropriety in touching the resurrection body; in v. 27 Jesus tells Thomas to touch Him (see also Matt. 28:9). Jesus reminds Mary that He is not merely recovered but resurrected. She need not "cling to" Jesus as an earthly being who has been healed; rather, she should recognize Him as One whose resurrection marks Him as Lord and Christ. The kind of relationship that had been enjoyed by His friends up to now cannot continue unchanged. There is a continuing intimacy to be sure, but not of the former kind. There is no reason to suppose that Jesus ascended to the Father between His encounters with Mary and Thomas. See "The Ascension of Jesus" at Luke 24:51.

my brothers. Jesus' disciples; the same language is used in Matt. 28:10.

my Father and your Father, to my God and your God. Jesus distinguishes pointedly His unique Sonship from the sonship of the disciples. Jesus' relation to the Godhead is different from that of redeemed humans; He is the Lord from heaven (1:18; 3:13, 31).

to the disciples, "I have seen the Lord"—
and that he had said these things to her.

Jesus Appears to the Disciples

19 [c]On the evening [d]of that day, the first
day of the week, [e]the doors being locked
where the disciples were [f]for fear of the
Jews, Jesus came and stood among them
and said to them, [g]"Peace be with you."
20 When he had said this, [h]he showed them
his hands and his side. Then [i]the disciples
were glad when they saw the Lord. 21 Jesus
said to them again, "Peace be with you. As
[j]the Father has sent me, [k]even so I am
sending you." 22 And when he had said
this, he [l]breathed on them and said to
them, [m]"Receive the Holy Spirit. 23 [n]If you
forgive the sins of anyone, they are forgiven; if you withhold forgiveness from
anyone, it is withheld."

Jesus and Thomas

24 Now [o]Thomas, one of the Twelve,
called the Twin,[1] was not with them when
Jesus came. 25 So the other disciples told
him, "We have seen the Lord." But he said
to them, [p]"Unless I see in his hands the
mark of the nails, and place my finger into
the mark of the nails, and place my hand
into his side, I will never believe."
26 Eight days later, his disciples were
inside again, and Thomas was with them.
[q]Although the doors were locked, Jesus

[1] Greek *Didymus*

19 [c]1 Cor. 15:5; [ver. 26] [d]Luke 24:33, 36 [e]ver. 26 [f]See ch. 7:13 [g]See ch. 14:27
20 [h]Luke 24:40 [i]ch. 16:22
21 [j]ch. 17:18; [Heb. 3:1]; See ch. 3:17 [k]ch. 13:20; See Acts 1:2
22 [l]Gen. 2:7 [m][Acts 2:4]; See ch. 7:39
23 [n][Matt. 16:19; 18:18; 1 Cor. 5:4, 5]
24 [o]See ch. 11:16
25 [p]ver. 20; [Ps. 22:16]
26 [q]ver. 19

The Mission of the Church in the World

"Mission" comes from a Latin word meaning "to send." Jesus commanded His first disciples as representatives of those to follow, "As the Father has sent me, even so I am sending you" (John 20:21; cf. 17:18). This mission is still valid: the universal church, including every local congregation and every Christian in it, is sent into the world to fulfill a definite task.

The appointed task has two parts. First and fundamentally, it is the work of worldwide witness, making disciples and planting churches (Matt. 24:14; 28:19, 20; Mark 13:10; Luke 24:47, 48). The church proclaims Jesus Christ everywhere as God incarnate, Lord and Savior, and announces God's invitation to enter life through turning to Christ in repentance and faith (Matt. 22:1–10; Acts 17:30). Paul's ministry as a church-planter and evangelist to all the world, so far as was possible, is a model for carrying out this primary commitment (Rom. 1:14; 15:17–29; 1 Cor. 9:19–23; Col. 1:28, 29).

Second, all Christians are called to do works of mercy and compassion. Relying on God's commandment to love our neighbor, Christians should respond with generosity and compassion to all forms of human need (Matt. 25:34–40; Luke 10:25–37; Rom. 12:20, 21). Jesus healed the sick, fed the hungry, and taught the ignorant (Matt. 15:32; 20:34; Mark 1:41; 10:1), and those who are new creatures in Christ must practice the same compassion. In doing so they make credible the gospel they preach, about a Savior whose love transforms sinners into those who love God and other people (Matt. 5:16; cf. 1 Pet. 2:11, 12).

Though Jesus foresaw the mission to the Gentiles (Matt. 24:14; John 10:16; 12:32), His earthly ministry was directed to "the lost sheep of the house of Israel" (Matt. 15:24). Paul, the apostle to the Gentiles, always went to the Jews first as he preached (Acts 13:42–48; 14:1; 17:1–4, 10; 18:4–7, 19). Because the right of the Jews to hear the gospel first is a matter of divine appointment (Acts 3:26; 13:46; Rom. 1:16), it is important for Christians to continue bearing witness to the Jews. As Paul said, it was from Israel, according to the flesh, that Christ came to be the Savior of the world (Rom. 9:5).

20:19 the doors being locked. The impression is that the risen Jesus passed through the closed doors (also v. 26), not that they were opened in some way (compare Acts 12:10). This shows the transformation involved in the resurrection of the body (1 Cor. 15:35–49).

the disciples. Probably includes more than the ten apostles (twelve minus Judas and Thomas). In Acts 1:14, the women, Jesus' mother and brothers, and probably others (Acts 1:23) were together in the upper room after Jesus' ascension.

Peace be with you. Everyday words but a most welcome greeting, since they might have expected a rebuke for having abandoned Jesus at the time of His arrest.

20:20 his hands and his side. The marks of His wounds would identify Jesus, and also prove that He was not a ghost.

20:21 As the Father has sent me, even so I am sending you. This is a brief statement of the commission Jesus gave His disciples. A fuller statement is found in Matt. 28:18–20 and in Luke 24:44–53. Jesus is the supreme example for evangelism and missions. See theological note "The Mission of the Church in the World."

20:22 Receive the Holy Spirit. The gift is essential for the performance of the task given the disciples. This occasion is a foreshadowing of the fullness of the Spirit to be bestowed on the church at Pentecost.

20:23 If you forgive the sins of anyone. The apostles, as the founders of the church and acting for it, receive the authority to declare God's judgment on sins. Fundamentally, this declaration is made in the preaching of the gospel. See "Church Discipline and Excommunication" at Matt. 18:15.

came and stood among them and said,
[q]"Peace be with you." 27 Then he said to
Thomas, [r]"Put your finger here, and see my
hands; and put out your hand, and place it
in my side. Do not disbelieve, but believe."
28 Thomas answered him, [s]"My Lord and
my God!" 29 Jesus said to him, "Have you
believed because you have seen me?
[t]Blessed are those who have not seen and
yet have believed."

The Purpose of This Book

30 [u]Now Jesus did many other signs [v]in
the presence of the disciples, which are not
written in this book; 31 [w]but these are written so that you may [x]believe that Jesus is
the Christ, [y]the Son of God, and that by
believing [z]you may have life [a]in his name.

Jesus Appears to Seven Disciples

21 After this Jesus [b]revealed himself
[c]again to the disciples by [d]the Sea
of Tiberias, and he revealed himself in this
way. 2 Simon Peter, [e]Thomas (called the
Twin), Nathanael of [f]Cana in Galilee, [g]the
sons of Zebedee, and two others of his disciples were together. 3 Simon Peter said to
them, "I am going fishing." They said to
him, "We will go with you." They went out
and got into the boat, but [h]that night they
caught nothing.
4 Just as day was breaking, Jesus stood on
the shore; yet the disciples [i]did not know
that it was Jesus. 5 [j]Jesus said to them,
"Children, do you have any fish?" They
answered him, "No." 6 [k]He said to them,
"Cast the net on the right side of the boat,
and you will find some." So they cast it,
and now they were not able to haul it in,
because of the quantity of fish. 7 That disciple [l]whom Jesus loved therefore said to
Peter, "It is the Lord!" When Simon Peter
heard that it was the Lord, [m]he put on his
outer garment, for he was [n]stripped for
work, and [o]threw himself into the sea.
8 The other disciples came in the boat,
dragging the net full of fish, for they were
not far from the land, but about a hundred
yards[1] off.
9 When they got out on land, they saw a
charcoal fire in place, with fish laid out on
it, and bread. 10 Jesus said to them, "Bring
some of the fish that you have just caught."
11 So Simon Peter went aboard and hauled
the net ashore, full of large fish, 153 of
them. And although there were so many,
the net was not torn. 12 Jesus said to them,
[p]"Come and [q]have breakfast." Now [r]none
of the disciples dared ask him, "Who are
you?" They knew it was the Lord. 13 Jesus
came and [s]took the bread and gave it to
them, and so with the fish. 14 [t]This was now
the third time that Jesus was revealed to
the disciples after he was raised from the
dead.

Jesus and Peter

15 When they had [u]finished breakfast,
Jesus said to Simon Peter, [v]"Simon, [w]son of
John, [x]do you love me more than these?"
He said to him, "Yes, Lord; you know that
I love you." He said to him, "Feed [y]my

[1] Greek *two hundred cubits*; a *cubit* was about 18 inches or 45 centimeters

26 [q]ver. 19
27 [r]ver. 20; 1 John 1:1; [Luke 24:39]
28 [s][ch. 1:1, 49]
29 [t]1 Pet. 1:8; [2 Cor. 5:7]
30 [u]ch. 21:25 [v]Acts 10:41
31 [w]1 John 5:13 [x]See ch. 11:27 [y]See Matt. 14:33 [z]ch. 3:15, 16; 5:40; 6:53; 10:10 [a][Acts 10:43; 1 Cor. 6:11]; See Acts 3:6
Chapter 21
1 [b]ver. 14; [Mark 16:12, 14]; See ch. 7:4 [c]ch. 20:19, 26 [d]ch. 6:1
2 [e]See ch. 11:16 [f]ch. 2:1; 4:46 [g]Matt. 4:21; Luke 5:10
3 [h][Luke 5:5]
4 [i]ch. 20:14
5 [j]Luke 24:41
6 [k][Luke 5:4, 6, 7]
7 [l]See ch. 13:23 [m]ver. 18; [ch. 13:4] [n]1 Sam. 19:24; Isai. 20:2; Micah 1:8 [o][Matt. 14:29]
12 [p]Acts 10:41 [q]ver. 15 [r][ch. 4:27]
13 [s]ver. 9
14 [t]ver. 1; ch. 20:19, 26
15 [u]ver. 12 [v][Matt. 16:17; Luke 22:31] [w]ch. 1:42 [x][Matt. 26:33; Mark 14:29] [y]ch. 10:11-16; [Isai. 40:11]

20:28 My Lord and my God. This is probably the clearest and simplest confession of the deity of Christ to be found in the New Testament. The two highest words, "Lord" (used in the Greek translation of the Old Testament for the divine name "Yahweh"), and "God," are used together and addressed to Jesus in recognition of His glory. Jesus accepts this worship without hesitation. This is in sharp contrast to the angels who were mistakenly worshiped in Rev. 19:10; 22:9.

20:29 Blessed are those who have not seen. While commending Thomas's faith, Jesus blesses those who will come to believe through the witness of the disciples (17:20; cf. 1 Pet. 1:8, 9). This blessing introduces the reason for the writing of the Gospel (vv. 30, 31).

20:30 many other signs. None of the Gospels is an attempt to give a complete or a strictly chronological record, such as a modern biography (cf. 21:25). See Introduction to Matthew: Interpretive Difficulties.

20:31 these are written so that you may believe. This states the purpose of this Gospel. Through the signs narrated, the reader is to come to faith in Jesus as more than a miracle worker. He is Christ, the incarnate Word, with the Father and the Spirit as Triune God. Through believing, we find life in Him who is the source of life (6:32–58).

21:1–25 This chapter appears to be a kind of postscript, prepared by the same author as the rest of the Gospel, with the possible exception of vv. 24, 25.

21:3 I am going fishing. Perhaps Peter, having denied the Lord, thought he had forfeited the privilege of being a witness of Jesus' resurrection.

that night they caught nothing. Fishing at night was not unusual. The circumstances are reminiscent of the miraculous draught of fish recounted in Luke 5:4–11 and associated with the call of Peter and other disciples.

21:4 the disciples did not know. See note 20:14.

21:7 That disciple whom Jesus loved. See note 13:23. He was quick to recognize Jesus.

put on his outer garment. This is strange for someone about to jump into the water. It seems to be a gesture of reverence for Jesus, before whom Peter did not want to appear unclothed.

21:14 the third time. Not the third appearance absolutely, but the third to a group of the apostles (cf. 20:19–23, 24–28).

21:15 Simon, son of John. Jesus used this name at the beginning of His solemn declaration in response to Peter's confession (Matt. 16:17).

do you love me more than these. It is possible to construe this question in several ways. "Do you love Me more than these others love Me?"; "Do you love Me more than you love these others?"; "Do you love Me more

lambs." **16** He said to him a second time,
"Simon, son of John, do you love me?" He
said to him, "Yes, Lord; you know that I
love you." He said to him, [z]"Tend [y]my
sheep." **17** He said to him the third time,
"Simon, son of John, do you love me?"
Peter was grieved because he said to him
[a]the third time, "Do you love me?" and he
said to him, "Lord, [b]you know everything;
you know that I love you." Jesus said to
him, "Feed [c]my sheep. **18** [d]Truly, truly, I say
to you, when you were young, [e]you used
to dress yourself and walk wherever you
wanted, but when you are old, you will
stretch out your hands, and another will
dress you and carry you where you do not
want to go." **19** (This he said to show [f]by
what kind of death he was to glorify God.)
And after saying this he said to him,
[g]"Follow me."

Jesus and the Beloved Apostle

20 Peter turned and saw [h]the disciple
whom Jesus loved following them, [i]the one
who had been reclining at table close to
him and had said, "Lord, who is it that is
going to betray you?" **21** When Peter saw
him, he said to Jesus, "Lord, what about
this man?" **22** Jesus said to him, "If it is my
will that he remain [j]until [k]I come, what is
that to you? [l]You follow me!" **23** So the saying spread abroad among [m]the brothers[1]
that this disciple was not to die; yet Jesus
did not say to him that he was not to die,
but, "If it is my will that he remain until I
come, what is that to you?"

24 This is the disciple [n]who is bearing witness about these things, and who has written these things, and [o]we know [p]that his
testimony is true.

25 Now [q]there are also many other things
that Jesus did. Were every one of them to
be written, I suppose that [r]the world itself
could not contain the books that would be
written.

16 [z]Acts 20:28; 1Pet. 5:2; Rev. 7:17 (Gk.) [y][See ver. 15 above] **17** [a][ch. 13:38] [b]See ch. 2:25 [c]ver. 16 **18** [d][ch. 13:36] [e]ver. 7 **19** [f]2 Pet. 1:14 [g]ver. 22; Matt. 16:24; [ch. 13:36]; See ch. 8:12 **20** [h]ver. 7 [i]ch. 13:25 **22** [j]Matt. 10:23; 16:28; 1 Cor. 4:5; 11:26; James 5:7; Rev. 2:25 [k][ch. 14:3, 18, 28; Heb. 10:37; Rev. 2:5, 16; 3:3, 11; 16:15; 22:7, 12, 20]; See Matt. 16:27 [l]ver. 19

23 [m]Acts 1:15; 9:30; 11:1; 12:17; 15:1; 16:2, 40; 21:7, 17; 1 John 3:14, 16 **24** [n]See ch. 15:27 [o]1 John 3:2, 14; 5:15, 18-20; [ch. 19:35] [p]3 John 12 **25** [q]ch. 20:30 [r][Amos 7:10]

[1] Or *brothers and sisters*

than you love these nets and fish?" (cf. v. 3 note). The Greek verb translated "love" in Jesus' question changes when the question is raised the third time (v. 17), and Peter's answer has this second verb each time. Some have thought that there is a difference intended in the use of the two verbs. This is possible but not necessary, for two reasons. First, John interchanges these verbs elsewhere in His Gospel. Second, other differences of wording in this conversation do not seem to indicate a difference of purpose. For example, "Feed my lambs," "Tend my sheep," and "Feed my sheep" are equivalent.

Feed my lambs. "My lambs" and "my sheep" correspond to "my church" (10:14, 26, 27; Matt. 16:18). When Peter writes to his fellow elders (1 Pet. 5:1, 2), he urges them, "Shepherd the flock of God that is among you," apparently having taken to heart the words of Jesus.

21:17 the third time. Peter was grieved not because of the change of wording in this last question, but because Jesus repeated the question itself three times. Perhaps Peter was reminded of the three times he had denied Christ (13:38; 18:27). Whether Jesus intended such a reminder or not, He was giving Peter an opportunity to confess his love and to reaffirm his calling to follow Christ. With this knowledge Peter calls Jesus the "chief Shepherd" (1 Pet. 5:4).

21:19 by what kind of death. An ancient tradition says that Peter was martyred by being crucified upside down.

Follow me. This is like the original call given by Jesus to His apostles (Matt. 4:19; Luke 5:27; cf. John 21:22). The whole incident restores Peter to his place as an apostle, which his denial threatened to take from him.

21:20 the disciple whom Jesus loved. This further description, combined with 13:23–25, leaves little doubt that this was John, son of Zebedee.

21:24 the disciple who is bearing witness. See v. 20; 13:23 and notes.

we know. This is the certification of a contemporary who was in a position to know John personally. Therefore, the whole Gospel, including ch. 21, was accepted immediately by the early church.

21:25 the world itself could not contain. The writer uses exaggeration to make the point that the Gospel writers had to be selective of the facts and details included in their accounts.

THE ACTS OF THE APOSTLES

Acts

AUTHOR

According to tradition the Book of Acts is written by Luke the physician, a companion of Paul on his second and third missionary journeys and on the voyage to Rome. Evidence from the early church is that Luke was the author. Irenaeus (c. A.D. 130–200), Clement of Alexandria (A.D. 153–217), the anonymous Muratorian Canon (c. A.D. 170), and Eusebius (c. A.D. 325) all credit Luke as the author.

Evidence for Luke's authorship is found in the well-known "we" passages of the latter half of the book (16:10–17; 20:5–15; 21:1–18; 27:1–28:16). These passages show that the narrator of Acts accompanied Paul from Troas in Asia Minor to Philippi on the continent of Europe, returning with him to Troas. Later he and Paul traveled from Palestine to Rome.

The author was probably an educated Gentile, as attested by the style and the high level of Greek used in Luke and Acts. His Greek is sometimes fully classical (Luke 1:1–4). The author's methodical approach to writing and his interest in research reveal an educated, highly trained man.

It appears from Col. 4:14 that Paul was with "Luke the beloved physician." In the late nineteenth and early twentieth centuries, scholars drew attention to the medical terminology found in Luke and Acts and to the author's interest in diseases (Luke 4:38; 8:43–44; Acts 3:7; 12:23; 13:11; 20:7–11; 28:3, 8). More recently it has been argued that medical terms were in common use among ancient writers, so that the author need not have been a physician. Still, an interest in medical matters is apparent in Luke and Acts, and it is reasonable to think that Luke the physician was the author.

DATE AND OCCASION

Three dates suggested for Acts are: before A.D. 70; 80 to 85; and 105 to 130. The later dates are based in part on the theory that the author of Acts was probably not Luke, and obtained his information about the revolutionaries Theudas and Judas (5:36, 37) from the writings of the Jewish historian Josephus (*Antiquities* 18.4–10 and 20.97–98), who wrote during the latter half of the first century. But the Theudas mentioned in Acts may have been one of many revolutionaries who arose about the time Herod the Great died, and not the later Theudas mentioned by Josephus. Luke's knowledge of Judas was not necessarily derived from Josephus, any more than Josephus's knowledge was derived from Luke. Some argue that Luke made use of Josephus's account of the death of Herod Agrippa I in A.D. 44 (12:19–22), since both use similar words in describing the event. The two accounts, however, differ considerably.

The view that Luke and Acts were written before the destruction of Jerusalem in A.D. 70 is supported by the following considerations. First, ch. 28 ends with Paul under house arrest. While waiting to appear before Caesar, he is free to preach to all who come to him. This had to occur before A.D. 64, when a great fire swept through Rome and the Emperor Nero said that Christians were to blame. Second, Acts does not mention Paul's death, which appeared to be imminent in 2 Tim. 4 and which occurred about A.D. 68. Third, near the end of Acts, Luke portrays the Roman government as benevolent toward Christianity, an attitude that changed after A.D. 64. Fourth, certain vocabulary points to an early date. This vocabulary includes "disciple"; "the first day of the week" (later to become "the Lord's Day," Rev. 1:10); a reference to "the peoples of Israel" in 4:27 (a term later to include both Jews and Gentiles; Titus 2:14); the early title "Son of Man" (7:56); as well as language about geographical and political details.

Luke 1:3 and Acts 1:1 are both addressed to Theophilus. He may have been Luke's patron, or benefactor. Certainly he was a Gentile who received Christian instruction (Luke 1:4). As

Luke's patron, Theophilus would have provided a living for Luke to enable him to do research and write his two books. By way of comparison, the historian Josephus had the Roman generals Vespasian and Titus as patrons, as well as another benefactor, a certain Epaphroditus, to whom he dedicated his book *Against Apion*.

Luke collected material from his own experience and from Semitic sources inside and outside Palestine. He mentions the names of several people who may have helped him (16:11; 20:4). He could have talked to Mary, Jesus' mother, in addition to others who were "eyewitnesses and ministers of the word" (Luke 1:2).

CHARACTERISTICS AND THEMES

Acts is a careful history of the development of the early church. Luke's descriptions of geographical and provincial details, of governmental officials and their actions, of imperial procedure, of a sea voyage to Italy, replete with accurate nautical terms—all these come from a careful researcher who was himself an eyewitness of many of the events he records.

Luke had several purposes. In 1:1, 2 he says that in the Gospel he has explained the life of Jesus until the Ascension. He summarizes the general theme of Acts as follows: the Lord is going to expand his work "in Jerusalem and in all Judea and Samaria, and to the end of the earth." Acts is called the "Acts of the Apostles," yet Luke traces only the ministries of Peter (chs. 1–12) and Paul (chs. 13–28). Some have detected an interest in defending Christianity or showing that Christianity was not a threat to Rome. Acts is a map of the progress of the church into the ancient world, showing how the present age began.

OUTLINE OF ACTS

I. Peter and the Gospel to the Jews in Jerusalem, Judea and Samaria (1:1–12:24)

A. *Instructions from Jesus and the Wait for the Spirit (ch. 1)*

B. *Founding of the Church in Jerusalem (chs. 2–7)*
1. The Outpouring of the Holy Spirit and Peter's First Sermon (2:1–41)
2. The Fellowship of Believers (2:42–47)
3. The Beggar Healed and Peter's Second Sermon (ch. 3)
4. Persecution from the Sanhedrin (4:1–31)
5. The Church: Community and Discipline (4:32–5:11)
6. Further Persecution from the Sanhedrin (5:12–42)
7. Choosing of the Seven (6:1–7)
8. Persecution and Death of Stephen (6:8–7:60)

C. *Scattered by Persecution, the Gospel Spreads to Judea, Samaria, and Beyond (8:1–12:24)*
1. Philip Preaches in Samaria and to the Ethiopian Eunuch (ch. 8)
2. The Conversion of Saul (9:1–31)
3. Peter's Ministry in Lydda and Joppa (9:32–43)
4. Peter's Ministry in Caesarea: the Holy Spirit Poured Out on the Gentiles (10:1–11:18)
5. The Church in Syrian Antioch (11:19–30)
6. Herod Agrippa I's Persecution of the Church and Death (12:1–24)

II. Paul and the Gospel to the Gentiles (12:25–28:31)

A. *Paul Extends the Gospel into Asia Minor and Europe (12:25–21:16)*
1. Paul's First Missionary Journey—Cyprus and Asia Minor (12:25–14:28)
2. The Jerusalem Council (15:1–35)
3. Paul's Second Missionary Journey—Return to Asia Minor and on to Europe (15:36–18:22)
4. Paul's Third Missionary Journey—Strengthening the Churches of Asia Minor, Macedonia and Greece (18:23–21:16)

B. *Paul Takes the Gospel to Rome (21:17–28:31)*
1. Paul's Arrest, Trial, and Imprisonment in Palestine (21:17–26:32)
2. The Voyage to Rome (27:1–28:16)
3. Paul's Two Years of Ministry in Rome (28:17–31)

The Promise of the Holy Spirit

1 In the first book, O [a]Theophilus, I
have dealt with all that Jesus began [b]to
do and teach, **2** until the day when [c]he was
taken up, after he [d]had given commands
[e]through the Holy Spirit to the apostles
whom he had chosen. **3** [f]To them he presented himself alive after his suffering by
many proofs, appearing to them during
forty days and speaking about the kingdom
of God.

4 And while staying[1] with them [g]he
ordered them not to depart from Jerusalem, but to wait for the promise of the
Father, which, he said, "you heard from
me; **5** for [h]John baptized with water, [h]but
you will be baptized [i]with[2] the Holy Spirit
not many days from now."

The Ascension

6 So when they had come together, they
asked him, "Lord, [j]will you at this time
[k]restore the kingdom to Israel?" **7** He said
to them, [l]"It is not for you to know [m]times
or seasons that the Father has fixed by
his own authority. **8** But you will receive
[n]power [o]when the Holy Spirit has come
upon you, and [p]you will be [q]my witnesses
in Jerusalem and in all Judea and [r]Samaria,
and [s]to the end of the earth." **9** And when
he had said these things, as they were looking on, [t]he was lifted up, and [u]a cloud took
him out of their sight. **10** And while they
were gazing into heaven as he went,
behold, [v]two [w]men stood by them in
[x]white robes, **11** and said, [y]"Men of Galilee,
why do you stand looking into heaven?
This Jesus, who was taken up from you
into heaven, [z]will [a]come in the same way
as you saw him go into heaven."

Matthias Chosen to Replace Judas

12 Then [b]they returned to Jerusalem from
the mount called Olivet, which is near
Jerusalem, a Sabbath day's journey away.
13 And when they had entered, they went
up to [c]the upper room, where they were

Chapter 1
1 [a]Luke 1:3 [b]Luke 24:19
2 [c]See Mark 16:19 [d][ch. 10:42; Matt. 28:19, 20; Mark 16:15; Luke 24:47; John 20:21] [e][ch. 10:38; Luke 4:1, 18; John 20:22]
3 [f]ch. 10:40, 41; 13:31; Matt. 28:17; Mark 16:14; Luke 24:34, 36-51; John 20:19-29; 21; 1 Cor. 15:5-7
4 [g]Luke 24:49
5 [h]ch. 11:16; See Matt. 3:11 [i]ch. 2:1-4
6 [j]See Luke 17:20 [k][Mic. 4:8; Matt. 17:11; Mark 9:12; Luke 19:11]
7 [l][Matt. 24:36; Mark 13:32] [m]Dan. 2:21; 1 Thess. 5:1
8 [n]ch. 4:33; Luke 24:49; 1 Thess. 1:5; [ch. 10:38; Luke 4:14] [o]ver. 5 [p][ver. 22]; See Luke 24:48 [q][Isai. 43:12] [r]ch. 8:1, 14; [Matt. 10:5] [s]ch. 13:47; [Mark 16:15; Col. 1:23]
9 [t]ver. 2 [u]See 1 Thess. 4:17
10 [v][Luke 24:4] [w]Josh. 5:13; Dan. 9:21; 10:5; 12:6, 7; Zech. 1:8-11 [x]Matt. 28:3; Mark 16:5; John 20:12
11 [y]ch. 2:7; 13:31 [z][Phil. 3:20; 1 Thess. 1:10]; See Matt. 16:27 [a]2 Thess. 1:10
12 [b]Luke 24:50, 52
13 [c]ch. 9:37, 39; 20:8

[1] Or *eating* [2] Or *in*

1:1 In the first book. The Gospel of Luke as shown by the reference to Theophilus (Luke 1:3).

all that Jesus began to do and teach. A fitting summary of what Luke records in the Gospel.

1:2 taken up. Luke 24:50–52 locates the Ascension near Bethany, on the east side of the Mount of Olives, east of Jerusalem.

commands through the Holy Spirit. After the Resurrection Jesus communicated to His apostles the reality of His resurrection (John 20; 21), the truth of His calling as Messiah (Luke 24:44–49), the blessing of the Holy Spirit (John 20:22, 23), and the reality of His physical resurrection body (Luke 24:37–43).

he had chosen. A reference to Jesus' original choice of His apostles (Luke 6:12–16), one of whom (Judas) Jesus knew would become a traitor.

1:3 presented himself . . . many proofs. Christ's resurrection appearances (Matt. 28; Mark 16; Luke 24; John 20; 21; 1 Cor. 15:5–7) were important as an unshakable confirmation of Christ's supernatural person and work. It was important that Jesus' resurrection should be seen by the disciples (v. 22).

forty days. The time from the Resurrection to the Ascension. After Jesus ascended to heaven, the disciples stayed ten days in Jerusalem waiting for the promised outpouring of the Holy Spirit that occurred on Pentecost, the fiftieth day after Passover.

1:4 while staying with them. Jesus often communed with His friends and disciples over a meal: at the feeding of the five thousand (Luke 9:16), with tax collectors and sinners (Mark 2:15, 16; Luke 5:29), at the Pharisee's house (Luke 7:37), at the Last Supper (Matt. 26:21, 26), and after the Resurrection (Luke 24:42; John 21:9–15).

wait for the promise of the Father. The Holy Spirit was the gift of the Father and the gift of Jesus the Son (John 14:1, 26; 15:26).

1:5 John baptized with water. John the Baptist baptized large crowds of people (Matt. 3:5, 6, 13–15; Mark 1:5, 9; Luke 3:7–16, 21). John's water baptism of repentance (Mark 1:4) pointed forward to the messianic baptism with the Holy Spirit and fire (Luke 3:16). See "The Baptism of Jesus" at Mark 1:9.

not many days from now. A few days would pass before Pentecost.

1:6 at this time restore the kingdom to Israel. From what Jesus said in Matt. 19:28, the disciples thought that He might overthrow the Romans and restore the physical kingdom to Israel.

1:7 not for you to know times or seasons. The specific years or dates (which some in all ages try to predict) of the Second Coming of Christ (cf. 1 Thess. 5:2).

1:8 Holy Spirit has come upon you. Jesus means that the Holy Spirit will show His control of their lives with visible manifestations: the blowing of a violent wind, the appearance of tongues of fire, and speaking in foreign languages (ch. 2).

my witnesses in Jerusalem and in all Judea and Samaria, and to the end of the earth. The Book of Acts follows this strategy. The Jerusalem witness (ch. 2) gives in miniature form God's worldwide ministry: the "Jews . . . from every nation" (2:5) who heard and believed carried the message far and wide. In the rest of Acts the gospel spreads to Jerusalem (3:1–8:1), to Judea and Samaria, up to Antioch of Syria (8:1–12:25), and to the ends of the earth (13:1–28:31).

1:9 he was lifted up. See "The Ascension of Jesus" at Luke 24:51.

1:10 two men . . . in white robes. Persons described as dressed in white are commonly supernatural or glorified beings: Jesus Christ (Matt. 17:2; Mark 9:3; Rev. 1:14), angels (Matt. 28:3; Mark 16:5; Luke 24:4; John 20:12), and glorified saints (Luke 9:30, 31; Rev. 3:4, 5, 18; 4:4; 7:14).

1:11 Men of Galilee. The eleven were from Galilee; Judas Iscariot was from Kerioth in Judah.

in the same way. Jesus will return in His resurrection body, coming with the clouds of heaven (Matt. 24:30; 26:64; Mark 14:62; 1 Thess. 4:16, 17; Rev. 1:7). See "The Return of Christ" at 1 Thess. 4:16.

1:12 the mount called Olivet. A hill beyond the Kidron Valley just east of the walled city of Jerusalem. The disciples had been with Jesus on the Mount near Bethany (Luke 24:50).

a Sabbath day's journey. From the city, a distance calculated by the rabbis to be about 1,100 meters or three-fourths of a mile.

1:13 up to the upper room, where they were staying. Probably where

staying, [d]Peter and John and James and
Andrew, Philip and Thomas, Bartholomew
and Matthew, James the son of Alphaeus
and Simon [e]the Zealot and Judas the son of
James. 14 All these [f]with one accord [g]were
devoting themselves to prayer, together
with [h]the women and Mary the mother of
Jesus, and [i]his brothers.[1]
15 In those days Peter stood up among
[j]the brothers (the company of persons was
in all about 120) and said, 16 "Brothers,
[k]the Scripture had to be fulfilled, which the
Holy Spirit spoke beforehand by the mouth
of David concerning Judas, [l]who became a
guide to those who arrested Jesus. 17 For
[m]he was numbered among us and was allotted his share in [n]this ministry." 18 (Now
this man [o]bought a field with [p]the reward
of his wickedness, and falling headlong[2] he
burst open in the middle and all his bowels gushed out. 19 And it became known to
all the inhabitants of Jerusalem, so that the
field was called [q]in their own language
Akeldama, that is, Field of Blood.) 20 "For it
is written in the Book of Psalms,

> [r]"'May his camp become desolate,
> and let there be no one to dwell
> in it';

and

> [s]"'Let another take his office.'

21 So one of the men who have accompanied us during [t]all the time that the Lord
Jesus [u]went in and out among us, 22 [v]be-
ginning from the baptism of John until the
day when [w]he was taken up from us—one
of these men must become with us [x]a
witness to his resurrection." 23 And they
put forward two, Joseph called [y]Barsabbas,
who was also called [z]Justus, and [a]Mat-
thias. 24 And [b]they prayed and said, "You,
Lord, [c]who know the hearts of all, show
which one of these two you have chosen
25 to take the place in [d]this ministry and
[e]apostleship from which Judas turned
aside to go to his own place." 26 And they
cast lots for them, and the lot fell on
Matthias, and he was numbered with the
eleven apostles.

13 [d]See Matt. 10:2-4; Mark 3:16-19; Luke 6:14-16 [e][ch. 21:20] **14** [f]ch. 2:46; 4:24; 5:12;15:25; Rom. 15:6 [g]ch. 2:42; 6:4; Rom. 12:12; Col. 4:2; [Eph. 6:18] [h]Luke 8:2, 3 [i]See Matt. 12:46 **15** [j]See John 21:23 **16** [k]Luke 24:44; [Luke 22:37] [l]Matt. 26:47; Mark 14:43; Luke 22:47; John 18:3 **17** [m]John 6:71; 13:21 [n]ver. 25; ch. 20:24; 21:19; Rom. 11:13; 2 Cor. 4:1 **18** [o][Matt. 27:5-8] [p][Matt. 26:14-16] **19** [q][ch. 21:40] **20** [r]Cited from Ps. 69:25 [s]Cited from Ps. 109:8 **21** [t][John 15:27] [u]Num. 27:17; Deut. 31:2; 1 Sam. 18:13 **22** [v]ch. 13:24; Mark 1:1-4 [w]ver. 2, 9 [x]ch. 4:33; [ver. 8; 1 Pet. 1:3]; See Luke 24:48 **23** [y][ch. 15:22] [z][ch. 18:7; Col. 4:11] [a]ver. 26 **24** [b]ch. 6:6; 13:3 [c]See 1 Sam. 16:7; Rom. 8:27 **25** [d]See ver. 17 [e]Rom. 1:5; 1 Cor. 9:2; Gal. 2:8

[1] Or *brothers and sisters*. The plural Greek word *adelphoi* (translated "brothers") refers to siblings in a family. In New Testament usage, depending on the context, *adelphoi* may refer either to men or to both men and women who are siblings (brothers and sisters) in God's family, the church; also verse 15 [2] Or *swelling up*

the disciples had been hiding for fear of the Jews. This may have been the same room in which they had celebrated the Passover and Jesus had instituted the Lord's Supper (Mark 14:15), or a room in the house of Mary, the aunt of Barnabas (Col. 4:10), where the Christians later held meetings (12:12). It was probably located close to the temple courts where the visiting Jewish crowds were assembled (2:5–12).

Bartholomew. Also known as Nathanael (John 1:45; 21:2).

James the son of Alphaeus. Also known as James the younger (Mark 15:40).

Zealot. Possibly referring to Simon's former membership in the Zealot revolutionary group.

Judas the son of James. Also known as Thaddaeus (Matt. 10:3; Mark 3:18).

1:14 devoting themselves to prayer. Jesus established a pattern of prayer in the lives of His disciples. For examples of Jesus praying, see Luke 3:21; 5:16; 6:12; 9:18, 28, 29; 11:1; 22:32, 41; 23:34, 46.

with the women. Certain women who had followed Jesus, supported His work, and cared for Him in His death (Matt. 27:55, 56; 28:1; Mark 15:40, 41; Luke 8:2, 3; 23:49; 24:1, 22).

Mary the mother of Jesus. This is the last reference in the New Testament to Jesus' mother.

his brothers. Jesus' half brothers, the sons of Mary and Joseph (Matt. 13:55; Luke 14:26; John 7:3, 10).

1:15 In those days. The ten days between the Ascension and Pentecost (2:1).

1:16 Brothers. Males are particularly addressed here because Peter is talking about replacing Judas Iscariot, one of the Twelve whom Jesus had originally chosen as apostles (Matt. 10:2–4).

the Scripture had to be fulfilled. Ps. 69:25 and 109:8, quoted in v. 20, are applied by Peter to Judas Iscariot, who as an enemy of God had been deposed from his apostleship. Now "his office" (Ps. 109:8) had to be filled again.

the Holy Spirit spoke . . . by the mouth of David. The Holy Spirit inspired David to compose these words using his poetic skills.

1:17 allotted his share in this ministry. In His plan God allowed Judas, the enemy of the Savior, to serve for a time in the ministry of the disciples.

1:18 this man bought a field. Judas indirectly bought the field when he returned the money to the chief priests and elders who in turn purchased a burial place for foreigners called "Field of Blood."

with the reward. The thirty silver coins (Matt. 26:15), probably worth about 120 denarii, or 120 days' labor (Matt. 20:2).

falling headlong. Matthew writes that Judas "hanged himself" (Matt. 27:5). Apparently during or soon after the hanging his body fell to the ground and was broken or decomposed.

1:21 among us. This includes the whole time of Jesus' public ministry from His baptism to His ascension.

1:23 put forward two. Evidently Joseph and Matthias were chosen from a larger number of witnesses (according to v. 15, about 120 persons were present). Neither is mentioned elsewhere in Scripture.

1:24 you have chosen. Peter and the disciples recognized that their human responsibility and choice of a man to succeed Judas occurred within the bounds of God's sovereign will.

1:26 cast lots. Lots are mentioned in the Old Testament as a means of ascertaining God's will (Ex. 28:30 note).

apostles. See theological note "The Apostles" on the next page.

The Coming of the Holy Spirit

2 When [f]the day of Pentecost arrived,
they were all together in one place.
2 And suddenly there came from heaven a
sound like [g]a mighty rushing wind, and
[h]it filled the entire house where they were
sitting. 3 And divided tongues [i]as of fire
appeared to them and rested[1] on each one
of them. 4 And they were all [j]filled with the
Holy Spirit and began [k]to speak in other
tongues [l]as the Spirit gave them utterance.
5 Now there were dwelling in Jerusalem
Jews, devout men from every nation under
heaven. 6 And [m]at this sound the multitude
came together, and they were bewildered,
because each one was hearing them speak
in his own language. 7 And [n]they were
amazed and astonished, saying, "Are not
all these who are speaking [o]Galileans?
8 And how is it that we hear, each of us in
his own native language? 9 Parthians and

Chapter 2
1 [f]ch. 20:16; 1 Cor. 16:8; [Lev. 23:15]
2 [g][1 Kin. 19:11; Job 38:1; Ezek. 1:4] [h][ch. 4:31; 16:26]
3 [i]Matt. 3:11
4 [j]ch. 4:31; 13:52 [k]See Mark 16:17 [l][1 Cor. 12:10, 11]
6 [m]ver. 2
7 [n]ver. 12 [o]ch. 1:11; [Matt. 26:73]

1 Or *And tongues as of fire appeared to them, distributed among them, and rested*

The Apostles

Although the Gospels call the same people "disciples" and "apostles" (Matt. 10:1, 2; Luke 6:13), the terms are not synonyms. "Disciple" means "pupil, learner"; "apostle" means "emissary, representative," one sent with the authority of the sender. The twelve apostles (Rev. 21:14), as distinct from the apostles ("messengers") of the churches (2 Cor. 8:23 and text note), and from the rest of the disciples, were chosen and sent by Jesus (Mark 3:14) just as Jesus Himself, "the apostle . . . of our confession" (Heb. 3:1), was foreordained and sent by the Father (1 Pet. 1:20). As rejecting Jesus is rejecting the Father, so rejecting the apostles is rejecting Jesus (Luke 10:16).

Paul, the "apostle to the Gentiles" (Rom. 11:13; Gal. 2:8), announces himself as an apostle in the opening words of most of his letters. Because he had seen Christ on the Damascus road and been commissioned by Him (Acts 26:16–18) he was as truly a witness to Jesus' resurrection (which an apostle had to be, Acts 1:21, 22; 10:41, 42) as were the others. James, Peter, and John accepted Paul into apostolic partnership (Gal. 2:9), and God confirmed his status by the signs of an apostle (miracles and signs, 2 Cor. 12:12; Heb. 2:3, 4), and by the fruitfulness of his ministry (1 Cor. 9:2).

The apostles were agents of God's revelation of the truths that would become the Christian rule of faith and life. As such, and through Christ's appointment of them as His authorized representatives (2 Cor. 10:8; 13:10), the apostles exercised a unique authority in the church. There are no apostles today, though some Christians fulfill ministries that are in particular ways apostolic in style. No new canonical revelation is being given; apostolic teaching authority resides in the canonical Scriptures. The absence of new revelation does not put the contemporary church at a disadvantage compared with the church of apostolic days, for the Holy Spirit interprets and applies the Scriptures to God's people continually.

2:1 day of Pentecost. Lit. the "Fiftieth Day" after the Sabbath of the Passover week (Lev. 23:4–7, 15–16). Pentecost was celebrated on the first day of the week and was one of the three great annual feasts of Israel, preceded by Passover (Lev. 23:4–8; Num. 28:16–25) and followed four months later by the Feast of Booths (Lev. 23:33–43; Num. 29:12–38; cf. John 7:1–44). Pentecost is also called the "Feast of Weeks," because it was celebrated seven weeks after Passover (Deut. 16:10); the "Feast of Harvest," because the first fruits of the harvest were gathered then (Ex. 23:16); and the "day of the firstfruits" (Num. 28:26).

they were all together. All of the apostles (1:16) were there, and probably many of the 120 mentioned earlier (1:15).

2:2 a sound like a mighty rushing wind. Three signs (wind, fire, and inspired speech) of God's presence were witnessed (Ex. 3:2; 13:21; 24:17; 40:38; 1 Kin. 19:11–13). Wind is a symbol of the Holy Spirit's presence (Ezek. 37:9, 13; John 3:8), while fire is a symbol of His cleansing and judging power (Matt. 3:11, 12). The tongues were various languages spoken in all parts of the eastern Mediterranean region, from Rome to Persia.

2:4 all. All of the 120 (1:15). See Joel 2:28 which speaks of God's Spirit poured out "on all flesh."

filled with the Holy Spirit. They were under the special guidance and influence of the Spirit, particularly evidenced by their speaking in known languages ("tongues") which they had not previously learned (see 10:46; 19:6). Paul discusses the spiritual gift of tongues in 1 Cor. 12–14. The coming of the Spirit is the fulfillment of Jesus' promise reported in 1:5, 8 and Luke 24:49, but this does not mean that the Holy Spirit was not present and working with God's people in the Old Testament ("Holy Spirit" occurs in Ps. 51:11; Is. 63:10, 11; "Spirit of the LORD" in Judg. 3:10; 1 Sam. 10:6; Is. 11:2). See "The Holy Spirit" at John 14:26.

the Spirit gave them utterance. In all of the Christian life nothing is accomplished apart from God (Eph. 2:10; Phil. 2:12, 13).

2:5 Jews, devout men. See 8:2; 22:12; Luke 2:25. Probably most of these were visiting Jerusalem for Pentecost.

2:6, 7 The crowd was amazed that rural Galileans with their peculiar accents could have learned all these foreign languages.

2:8–11 The list of people from fifteen nations starts with the east ("Parthians and Medes and Elamites and residents of Mesopotamia," where Jews had been taken captive to Assyria and Babylon). The list proceeds west to Judea, and then north to Asia Minor (Cappadocia, Pontus, Asia, Phrygia, and Pamphylia), from there to North Africa (Egypt, parts of Libya near Cyrene), then to Rome. Finally the list includes two widely separated places, Crete and Arabia.

[p]Medes and [q]Elamites and residents of
Mesopotamia, Judea and Cappadocia,
Pontus and Asia, 10 Phrygia and Pamphylia,
Egypt and the parts of Libya belonging
to Cyrene, and visitors from Rome, 11 both
Jews and [r]proselytes, Cretans and Arabians—we hear them telling in our own
tongues the mighty works of God." 12 And
[s]all were amazed and perplexed, saying to
one another, "What does this mean?" 13 But
others [t]mocking said, "They are filled with
new wine."

Peter's Sermon at Pentecost

14 But Peter, standing with the eleven,
lifted up his voice and addressed them,
"Men of Judea and all who dwell in Jerusalem, let this be known to you, and give
ear to my words. 15 For these men are not
drunk, as you suppose, [u]since it is only the
third hour of the day.[1] 16 But this is what
was uttered through the prophet Joel:

17 [v]"'And in the last days it shall be, God
declares,
[w]that I will pour out my Spirit [x]on
all flesh,
and your sons and [y]your daughters
shall prophesy,
and your young men shall see
visions,
and your old men shall dream
dreams;
18 even on my male servants[2] and
female servants
in those days I will pour out my
Spirit, and [z]they shall
prophesy.
19 And I will show wonders in the
heavens above
and signs on the earth below,
blood, and fire, and vapor of
smoke;
20 [a]the sun shall be turned to darkness
and the moon to blood,
before [b]the day of the Lord
comes, the great and
magnificent day.
21 And it shall come to pass that
[c]everyone who calls upon
the name of the Lord shall
be saved.'

22 "Men of Israel, hear these words: Jesus
of Nazareth, [d]a man attested to you by God
[e]with [f]mighty works and wonders and
signs that [g]God did through him in your
midst, as you yourselves know— 23 this
Jesus, [h]delivered up according to [i]the definite plan and [j]foreknowledge of God, [k]you
crucified and killed by the hands of lawless
men. 24 [l]God raised him up, loosing the
pangs of death, because [m]it was not possible for him to be held by it. 25 For David
says concerning him,

[n]"'I saw the Lord always before me,
for he is at my right hand that I
may not be shaken;
26 therefore my heart was glad, and my
tongue rejoiced;
my flesh also will dwell [o]in hope.
27 For you will not abandon my soul to
[p]Hades,
[q]or let your [r]Holy One [s]see
corruption.

9 [p]2 Kin. 17:6 [q]Gen. 14:1, 9; Isai. 11:11; Dan. 8:2 11 [r]ch. 6:5; 13:43; Matt. 23:15 12 [s]ver. 7 13 [t][ch. 17:32; 1 Cor. 14:23] 15 [u][1 Thess. 5:7] 17 [v]Cited from Joel 2:28-32 [w]ver. 18, 33; Isai. 32:15; 44:3; Ezek. 36:27; See Rom. 5:5 [x][ch. 10:45; Tit. 3:6] [y]ch. 21:9 18 [z]ch. 11:28; 21:10; 1 Cor. 12:10 20 [a]See Matt. 24:29 [b][1 Thess. 5:2; Rev. 16:14] 21 [c]Rom. 10:13; [ch. 16:31] 22 [d]See John 3:2 [e]ch. 10:38; Luke 24:19 [f]2 Cor. 12:12; 2 Thess. 2:9; Heb. 2:4 [g][Matt. 12:28] 23 [h]Matt. 26:24; [ch. 3:13; Matt. 20:19]; See Luke 24:20 [i]Luke 22:22; [ch. 3:18; 4:28; 13:27] [j]1 Pet.1:2; [1 Pet. 1:20; Rev. 13:8] [k]See ch. 5:30

24 [l]ver. 32; ch. 3:15; 4:10; 10:40; 13:30, 33, 34, 37; 17:31; Rom. 4:24; 6:4; 8:11; 10:9; 1 Cor. 6:14; 15:15; 2 Cor. 4:14; Gal. 1:1; Eph. 1:20; Col. 2:12; 1 Thess. 1:10; Heb. 13:20; 1 Pet. 1:21; [Eph. 2:5] [m][Luke 24:5; John 10:18; 2 Tim. 1:10; Heb. 2:14; Rev. 1:17, 18] 25 [n]Cited from Ps. 16:8-11 26 [o]Rom. 4:18 27 [p]ver. 31; See Matt. 11:23 [q]ch. 13:35 [r]See Heb. 7:26 [s][Luke 2:26]

1 That is, 9 A.M. 2 Greek *bondservants*; twice in this verse

2:15 only the third hour. Counting 6:00 A.M. as the first hour makes this 9:00 A.M. It was customary to fast on feast days until at least the fourth hour. Thus the alleged drunkenness was most unlikely.

2:17–21 The quotation is from the Greek Old Testament text of Joel 2:28–32 (3:1–5). Peter's use of the words "in the last days" (cf. Is. 2:2; Hos. 3:5; Mic. 4:1; 1 Tim. 4:1; 2 Tim. 3:1; 1 Pet. 1:20; 1 John 2:18) makes explicit that Joel is referring to the last times promised by God. Peter interprets Joel's words as referring to the new covenant in contrast to the former days of the old covenant (Heb. 8:7; 9:1).

2:22 Jesus of Nazareth. This title is used elsewhere by Luke (6:14; 10:38; 22:8; 26:9; Luke 18:37; 24:19). In the sermon Peter emphasizes these important facts about Jesus: His death (v. 23), His bodily resurrection (vv. 24–32), His exaltation (v. 33), His coronation (vv. 34, 36), and the conquest at His Second Coming (v. 35).

attested to you by God with mighty works and wonders and signs. Although coming from Nazareth was a stumbling block (cf. John 1:46), God amply demonstrated that Jesus was the Messiah through the attestation of miracles.

2:23 according to the definite plan and foreknowledge of God. Although wicked men, both Jews and Gentiles (4:27, 28), had of their own will put Jesus to death, their actions were within the sovereign determination of God (cf. 17:26; 2 Chr. 25:16; Jer. 21:10; Dan. 11:36). God ordained the death of His Son, but the immediate perpetrators bear the guilt for crucifying Jesus (3:17, 18; 4:27, 28; 13:27). God ordains the means as well as the ends of human events without violating human freedom and responsibility. The Jews could not pass their guilt to the Romans; they had asked the Romans to crucify Jesus. Peter teaches that the Jews were accountable (3:15; 4:10; 5:30; 10:39).

crucified. Luke again emphasizes how Jesus died (Luke 24:39). Archaeologists have discovered in Palestine the pierced heel bones of a first-century A.D. victim of crucifixion.

2:25 David says. In Ps. 16 David is primarily speaking about his own human experience and suffering, but in the verses quoted here he is ultimately talking about Jesus (v. 25), God's Holy One whose body did not see decay (v. 27).

28 You have made known to me the
paths of life;
you will make me full of gladness
with your presence.'

29 "Brothers, I may say to you with confidence about [t]the patriarch David [u]that he
both died and [v]was buried, and [w]his tomb
is with us to this day. 30 [x]Being therefore a
prophet, and knowing that [y]God had
sworn with an oath to him that he would
set one of his descendants on his throne,
31 he foresaw and spoke about the resurrection of the Christ, that [z]he was not abandoned to Hades, nor did his flesh see
corruption. 32 This Jesus [a]God raised up,
[b]and of that we all are witnesses. 33 [c]Being
therefore [d]exalted at the right hand of God,
and having received from [e]the Father [f]the
promise of the Holy Spirit, [g]he has poured
out this that you yourselves are seeing and
hearing. 34 For [h]David did not ascend into
the heavens, but he himself says,

[i]"'The Lord said to my Lord,
Sit at my right hand,
35 until I make your enemies your
footstool.'

36 Let all the house of Israel therefore know
for certain that [j]God has made him [k]both
Lord and Christ, this Jesus [l]whom you crucified."

37 Now when [m]they heard this they were
cut to the heart, and said to Peter and the

29 [t]ch. 7:8, 9; Heb. 7:4 [u][ch. 13:36] [v]1 Kin. 2:10 [w]Neh. 3:16 30 [x][2 Sam. 23:2; Matt. 22:43; Heb. 11:32] [y]See Luke 1:32 31 [z]ver. 27 32 [a]ver. 24 [b]ch. 1:22; 4:33 33 [c]ch. 5:31; Eph. 1:20; Phil. 2:9; Heb. 2:9; 1 Pet. 3:22 [d]Ex. 15:6; Ps. 98:1 [e]ch. 1:4; [John 16:7] [f]Gal. 3:14 [g]ver. 17 34 [h][John 3:13] [i]Cited from Ps. 110:1 36 [j]See Matt. 28:18 [k]Rom. 14:9; 2 Cor. 4:5 [l]ver. 23 37 [m][ch. 5:33; 7:54]

2:33 exalted at the right hand of God. God's plan went beyond the resurrection of His Son, who must be exalted to the position He occupied with the Father from eternity (John 17:5).

and having received from the Father . . . Holy Spirit . . . poured out. The doctrine of the Trinity is implied: Peter showed how the Father (vv. 32, 33) worked in the life, death, resurrection, and exaltation of Jesus, His Son, and the Holy Spirit produced the miracle of causing His servants to speak in tongues.

2:36 In this climactic statement Peter not only stresses that Jesus is God's Messiah of the Old Testament (3:18, 20; 4:26; 5:42; Is. 11:1; Luke 4:18–21), but that He is the exalted Lord (Rom. 10:9; Phil. 2:9–11), and the conquering King (1 Cor. 15:24, 25; Rev. 19:16).

The Work of the Holy Spirit (2:4)

In the beginning

- Active and present at creation, hovering over the unordered conditions (Gen. 1:2)

In the Old Testament

- The origin of supernatural abilities (Gen. 41:38)
- The giver of artistic skill (Ex. 31:2–5)
- The source of power and strength (Judg. 3:9, 10)
- The inspiration of prophecy (1 Sam 19:20, 23)
- The equipper of God's messenger (Mic. 3:8)

In the Old Testament prophecy

- The cleansing of the heart for holy living (Ezek. 36:25–29)

In salvation

- Regenerates the believer (Titus 3:5)
- Indwells the believer (Rom. 8:9–11)
- Sanctifies the believer (2 Thess. 2:13)

In the New Testament

- Declares the truth about Christ (John 16:13, 14)
- Endows with power for gospel proclamation (Acts 1:8)
- Pours out God's love in the heart (Rom 5:5)
- Makes intercession (Rom. 8:26)
- Imparts gifts of ministry (1 Cor. 12:4–11)
- Enables the fruit of holy living (Gal. 5:22, 23)
- Strengthens the inner being (Eph. 3:16)

In the written Word

- Inspired the writing of Scripture (2 Tim. 3:16; 2 Pet. 1:21)

rest of the apostles, "Brothers, [n]what shall
we do?" 38 And Peter said to them, [o]"Repent
and [p]be baptized every one of you [q]in the
name of Jesus Christ [r]for the forgiveness of
your sins, and you will receive [s]the gift of
the Holy Spirit. 39 For [t]the promise is for
you and [u]for your children and for all [v]who
are far off, everyone [w]whom the Lord our
God calls to himself." 40 And with many
other words he bore witness and continued
to exhort them, saying, [x]"Save yourselves
from this [y]crooked generation." 41 So those
who received his word were baptized, and
[z]there were added that day about three
thousand souls.

The Fellowship of the Believers

42 And [a]they devoted themselves to the
apostles' [b]teaching and [c]fellowship, to [d]the
breaking of bread and the prayers. 43 And
awe[1] came upon every soul, and [e]many
wonders and signs were being done
through the apostles. 44 And all who
believed were together and [f]had all things
in common. 45 And [f]they were selling their
possessions and belongings and distributing the proceeds to all, as any had need.
46 And day by day, [g]attending the temple
[h]together and [i]breaking bread in their
homes, they received their food [j]with glad
and generous hearts, 47 praising God and
[k]having favor with all the people. And the
Lord [l]added to their number [m]day by day
those who [n]were being saved.

37 [n]ch. 16:30; Luke 3:10 **38** [o]ch. 3:19; 20:21; 26:18, 20; Luke 24:47 [p]ch. 22:16; [ch. 8:12]; See Mark 16:16 [q]ch. 10:48; See ch. 8:16 [r]See Mark 1:4 [s]ch. 10:45; [ch. 8:15, 20; 11:17]; See John 7:39 **39** [t]Rom. 9:4 [u]ch. 3:25; Isai. 54:13; [Isai. 44:3] [v]ch. 22:21; Isai. 57:19; Eph. 2:13, 17 [w]Joel 2:32; Rom. 8:30 **40** [x][ver. 21, 47] [y]Deut. 32:5; Matt. 17:17; Phil. 2:15 **41** [z]ver. 47 **42** [a][Heb. 10:25]; See ch. 1:14 [b]See 1 Cor. 14:6 [c]Gal. 2:9; Phil. 1:5; 1 John 1:3 [d]Luke 24:35; [ver. 46]; See ch. 20:7 **43** [e]See Mark 16:20 **44** [f]ch. 4:32, 34, 35; [Matt. 19:21] **45** [f][See ver. 44 above] **46** [g]ch. 3:1; 5:21, 42; Luke 24:53 [h]See ch. 1:14 [i][ver. 42] [j][ch. 16:34]; See John 16:22

The Lame Beggar Healed

3 Now Peter and John were [o]going up to
the temple at [p]the hour of prayer, [q]the
ninth hour.[2] 2 And a man [r]lame from birth
was being carried, [s]whom they laid daily at
the gate of the temple that is called the
Beautiful Gate [t]to ask alms of those entering the temple. 3 Seeing Peter and John
about to go into the temple, he asked to
receive alms. 4 And Peter directed his gaze
at him, as did John, and said, "Look at us."
5 And he fixed his attention on them,
expecting to receive something from them.
6 But Peter said, [u]"I have no silver and gold,
but what I do have I give to you. [v]In the
name of Jesus Christ of Nazareth, rise up
and walk!" 7 And he took him by the right
hand and raised him up, and immediately
his feet and ankles were made strong. 8 And
[w]leaping up he stood and began to walk,
and entered the temple with them, walking
and leaping and praising God. 9 And [x]all
the people saw him walking and praising
God, 10 and recognized him as the one who
sat at the Beautiful Gate of the temple, asking for alms. And they were filled with
wonder and amazement at what had happened to him.

47 [k]ch. 5:13 [l]ver. 41; ch. 5:14; 11:24 [m]ch. 16:5 [n]1 Cor. 1:18; [ver. 21, 40; ch. 16:31]
Chapter 3 **1** [o]See Luke 18:10 [p]Ps. 55:17 [q]ch. 10:3, 30; Matt. 27:46; [1 Kin. 18:29] **2** [r]ch. 14:8 [s][Luke 16:20] [t][John 9:8] **6** [u]2 Cor. 6:10 [v][ch. 9:34] **8** [w]ch. 14:10; Isai. 35:6 **9** [x]ch. 4:16, 21

[1] Or *fear* [2] That is, 3 P.M.

2:38 Repent and be baptized. Repentance (turning to God in sorrow for sin) and baptism were important parts of the message of John the Baptist (Matt. 3:1; Mark 1:4) and of Jesus (Matt. 4:17; 11:20; Luke 13:3, 5), and were central in the church's preaching and teaching (Matt. 28:18, 19). See "Baptism" at Rom. 6:3.

in the name of Jesus Christ. A summary of Matt. 28:18, 19 (baptism in the name of the Father, Son, and Holy Spirit), with only Jesus mentioned here, since Peter's sermon had to do with Jesus and His ministry.

for the forgiveness of your sins. Baptism is a sign and seal of spiritual cleansing the Spirit effects through the forgiveness of sins (Titus 3:5).

the gift of the Holy Spirit. The gift of the indwelling Person of the Holy Spirit, as well as the gift of forgiveness (Eph. 1:7), and of empowering for ministry. It is significant that Peter does not speak here of receiving the gift of tongues. The gifts of forgiveness and the indwelling Holy Spirit are essential for producing the fruit of the Spirit in the lives of believers (Gal. 5:22, 23) and for exercising the gifts the Spirit chooses to give at different times to different believers (1 Cor. 12:4–11).

2:39 Peter proclaims that salvation through God's Messiah is promised to the Jews, to their children, and to all those far off (i.e., the Gentiles, Eph. 2:11–13). Here again is the message of Acts—the gospel is for Jews and Gentiles. See "Infant Baptism" at Gen. 17:11.

everyone whom the Lord our God calls. Salvation is based on God's choice and calling (John 6:37; Eph. 1:4, 5).

2:42 the apostles' teaching and fellowship, to the breaking of bread and the prayers. This is a summary of the essential elements needed in Christian discipleship. They are elements the apostles had learned from their experience with Jesus: His teaching about His person and work (Matt. 16:18, 19; Luke 24:46) and their Christian responsibility as His followers (Matt. 5–7), the fellowship of Christ with His disciples (John 13), the Lord's Supper—the breaking of bread (Matt. 26:17–30), and His prayer life for and with the disciples (Matt. 6:5–13; Luke 11:1–13; John 17).

2:44 all who believed were together. This demonstrates the unity of the Spirit Paul later advocates (Eph. 4:3).

2:45 selling their possessions. Unified in the Spirit, the believers were attuned to the physical needs of others and voluntarily (4:34; 5:4) gave to meet those needs (4:32, "they had everything in common").

2:46 breaking bread in their homes. This refers to the common daily meals shared in the homes.

2:47 the Lord added. The church belongs to the Lord, and He is the one who sovereignly builds His church (Matt. 16:18; 1 Cor. 3:9).

3:1 the temple. The temple courts, and particularly the part near the gate called Beautiful (v. 2). This may have been the "Nicanor Gate" made of Corinthian bronze. Its exact location is uncertain.

3:3 into the temple. As Jews, Peter and John could walk through the Court of Women into the Court of Israel, but non-Jews would be restricted to the Court of the Gentiles.

Peter Speaks in Solomon's Portico

11 [y]While he clung to Peter and John, all
the people ran together to them in [z]the
portico called Solomon's, astounded.
12 And when Peter saw it he addressed the
people: "Men of Israel, why do you wonder
at this, or why do you stare at us, as though
by our own power or piety we have made
him walk? 13 [a]The God of Abraham, the
God of Isaac, and the God of Jacob, [b]the
God of our fathers, [c]glorified his servant[1]
Jesus, whom [d]you delivered over and [e]de-
nied in the presence of Pilate, [f]when he
had decided to release him. 14 But you
denied [g]the Holy and [h]Righteous One, and
[i]asked for a murderer to be granted to you,
15 and you killed [j]the Author of life, [k]whom
God raised from the dead. To this we are
witnesses. 16 And [l]his name—by [m]faith in
his name—has made this man strong
whom you see and know, and the faith that
is [n]through Jesus[2] has given the man this
perfect health in the presence of you all.
17 "And now, brothers, I know that [o]you
acted in ignorance, as did also your rulers.
18 But what God [p]foretold [q]by the mouth of
all the prophets, that [r]his Christ would
[s]suffer, he thus fulfilled. 19 [t]Repent therefore, and [u]turn again, that [v]your sins may
be blotted out, 20 that times of refreshing
may come from the presence of the Lord,
and that he may send the Christ [w]appoint-
ed for you, Jesus, 21 [x]whom heaven must
receive until the time for [y]restoring all the
things about which [z]God spoke by the
mouth of his holy prophets long ago.
22 Moses said, 'The Lord God will raise up
for you [a]a prophet like me from your brothers. You shall listen [b]to him in whatever he
tells you. 23 And it shall be that every soul
who does not listen to that prophet [c]shall
be destroyed from the people.' 24 And [d]all
the prophets who have spoken, from
Samuel and those who came after him, also
proclaimed these days. 25 [e]You are the sons
of the prophets and of [f]the covenant that
God made with your fathers, saying to
Abraham, [g]'And in your offspring shall all
the families of the earth be blessed.'
26 [h]God, [i]having raised up his servant, sent
him to you first, [j]to bless you [k]by turning
every one of you from your wickedness."

Peter and John Before the Council

4 And as they were speaking to the people, the priests and [l]the captain of the
temple and [m]the Sadducees came upon
them, 2 greatly annoyed because they were
teaching the people and proclaiming [n]in
Jesus the resurrection from the dead. 3 And
they arrested them and [o]put them in
custody until the next day, for it was
already evening. 4 But many of those who

11 [y]ch. 4:14 [z]ch. 5:12; John 10:23 **13** [a]Matt. 22:32 [b]ch. 5:30; 22:14; [ch. 7:32] [c]Isai. 55:5; [Isai. 52:13]; See John 8:54 [d]See Matt. 20:19 [e]ch. 13:28; John 19:7, 12, 15 [f]Luke 23:14, 16; John 19:12 **14** [g][ch. 4:27, 30]; See Mark 1:24 [h]ch. 7:52; 22:14; 1 Pet. 3:18; 1 John 2:1; 3:7; [James 5:6] [i]Luke 23:18, 19, 25 **15** [j]ch. 5:31 [k]See ch. 2:24 **16** [l][ver. 6] [m][John 1:12] [n][1 Pet. 1:21] **17** [o]ch. 13:27; [ch. 26:9; Luke 23:34; John 16:3; 1 Cor. 2:8; 1 Tim. 1:13] **18** [p]See ch. 2:23 [q]ch. 17:3; 26:22, 23; [Heb. 2:10]; See Luke 24:26, 27 [r]See Luke 9:20 [s]Matt. 17:12; Luke 22:15; 24:46; Heb. 13:12 **19** [t]See ch. 2:38 [u]See Luke 22:32 [v]Ps. 51:1, 9; Isai. 43:25; 44:22; Col. 2:14

20 [w]ch. 22:14; 26:16 **21** [x][ch. 1:11; Luke 24:26] [y][Matt. 17:11; Rom. 8:21] [z]Luke 1:70 **22** [a]ch. 7:37, cited from Deut. 18:15, 18, 19 [b]Matt. 17:5 **23** [c]Lev. 23:29 **24** [d]ch. 13:20; 1 Sam. 3:20; Heb. 11:32 **25** [e]See ch. 2:39 [f]See Rom. 9:4, 5 [g]Cited from Gen. 22:18; See Gen. 12:3 **26** [h]Rom. 1:16; 2:9; 15:8; [Mark 7:27] [i]ver. 22 [j]ver. 25 [k]Rom. 11:26; [Ezek. 3:19]; See Matt. 1:21
Chapter 4 **1** [l]ch. 5:24, 26; Luke 22:4, 52; [1 Chr. 9:11; Neh. 11:11] [m]See Matt. 22:23 **2** [n]ch. 17:18; [ch. 3:15] **3** [o]See Luke 21:12

[1] Or *child*; also verse 26 [2] Greek *him*

3:11 the portico called Solomon's. A porch built by Herod the Great along the east side of the temple platform. Jesus taught here on occasion (John 10:22).

3:13 The God of Abraham, the God of Isaac, and the God of Jacob. Appeal to the patriarchs was important in the sermons of Christ's servants (7:32; 13:17).

3:14 denied the Holy and Righteous One. The phrase "the Holy," referring to God, appears a number of times in the Old Testament. The phrase "the Holy One of Israel" occurs in Is. 1:4 and 5:24 (cf. Luke 1:35). Isaiah also speaks of God as "the Righteous One" (Is. 24:16; cf. Acts 7:52; 22:14). In applying this description to Jesus, Peter indicates the deity of Christ.

3:18 foretold by the mouth of all the prophets. See Luke 24:26, 27, 44–47. Peter could also have cited such passages as Deut. 18:15 (quoted in v. 22); Is. 53; Ps. 2; 16:8–11; 22 (cf. 1 Pet. 1:10, 11).

3:19 Repent . . . turn. Peter's sermon illustrates the two sides of repentance, that is, turning aside in sorrow from sin, and turning to God in faith. The call to repentance and faith is a necessary element of the apostolic preaching (2:38; 17:30; 20:21).

sins . . . blotted out. In the order of the gospel, repentance and faith receive from God forgiveness and removal of sins.

3:20 times of refreshing. This phrase, like "restoring all the things" (v. 21), seems to refer to the Second Coming of the Messiah.

3:25 saying to Abraham, 'And in your offspring . . .' As a climax, Peter refers to another patriarch and prophet, Abraham, through whom God sent Abraham's "offspring," the Messiah (Gal. 3:16), to bless all peoples on earth. As members of Abraham's spiritual posterity, all those who belong to Christ are also called "Abraham's offspring" (Gal. 3:29).

4:1 the priests. Several priests serving their allotted week's temple service (Luke 1:8, 23) were near Solomon's Colonnade and could hear Peter's declarations about Jesus the Messiah. Alarmed at what was considered dangerous teaching against Jewish authority, they probably alerted the captain of the temple guard. This captain was the commander of the temple police force and a member of one of the important priestly families. The priests also alerted the Sadducees, who held prominent positions in the Sanhedrin, the Jewish council.

4:2 proclaiming in Jesus the resurrection from the dead. The Sadducees were distressed because the apostles were teaching the people about the resurrection (1 Cor. 15:12–20). The Sadducees, unlike the Pharisees, did not believe in the bodily resurrection (23:6–8).

4:3 put them in custody . . . for it was already evening. This action was necessary because the temple sacrifices had been concluded and the temple gates were closed; official actions by the Sanhedrin would have to be taken the next day.

4:4 Despite the persecution, the church grew from three thousand on the day of Pentecost to five thousand. The emphasis here is on men, because in that time the men would have gathered together by them-

had heard the word believed, and [p]the number of the men came to about five thousand.
5 On the next day their rulers and elders
and scribes gathered together in Jerusalem,
6 with [q]Annas the high priest and [r]Caiaphas
and John and Alexander, and all who were
of the high-priestly family. 7 And when they
had set them in the midst, they inquired,
[s]"By what power or [t]by what name did you
do this?" 8 Then Peter, [u]filled with the Holy
Spirit, said to them, "Rulers of the people
and elders, 9 if we are being examined today
[v]concerning a good deed done to a crippled
man, by what means this man has been
healed, 10 let it be known to all of you and
to all the people of Israel that [w]by the name
of Jesus Christ of Nazareth, whom you crucified, [x]whom God raised from the dead—
by him this man is standing before you
well. 11 [y]This Jesus[1] is the stone that was
[z]rejected by you, the builders, which has
become the cornerstone.[2] 12 And there is
[a]salvation [b]in no one else, for [c]there is no
other [d]name under heaven given among
men by which we must be saved."
13 [e]Now when they saw the boldness of
Peter and John, and perceived that they
were uneducated, common men, they were
astonished. And they recognized that they
had been with Jesus. 14 But seeing the man
who was healed [f]standing beside them,
[g]they had nothing to say in opposition.
15 But when they had commanded them to
leave the council, they conferred with one
another, 16 saying, [h]"What shall we do with
these men? For that [i]a notable sign has
been performed through them is evident to
all the inhabitants of Jerusalem, and we
cannot deny it. 17 But in order that it may
spread no further among the people, let us
warn them [j]to speak no more to anyone
in this name." 18 So they called them and
charged them not to speak or teach at all in
the name of Jesus. 19 But Peter and John
answered them, [k]"Whether it is right in the
sight of God to listen to you rather than to
God, you must judge, 20 for [l]we cannot but
speak of what [m]we have seen and heard."
21 And when they had further threatened
them, they let them go, finding no way to
punish them, [n]because of the people, for
all were praising God [o]for what had happened. 22 For the man on whom this sign of
healing was performed was more than forty
years old.

The Believers Pray for Boldness

23 When they were released, they went to
their friends and reported what the chief
priests and the elders had said to them.
24 And when they heard it, they lifted their
voices [p]together to God and said, "Sovereign

4 [p][ch. 2:41]
6 [q]Luke 3:2; John 18:13, 24 [r]See Matt. 26:3
7 [s][Matt. 21:23] [t][ver. 10]
8 [u]See Matt. 10:20
9 [v]ch. 3:7, 8
10 [w]ch. 3:6 [x]See ch. 2:24
11 [y]See Ps. 118:22 [z]Mark 9:12; Luke 23:11
12 [a][1 Tim. 2:5] [b]ch. 13:26; 28:28; John 4:22; Heb. 2:3; Jude 3 [c][Gal. 1:7] [d]ch. 10:43; Luke 24:47; John 20:31
13 [e][John 7:15]
14 [f]ch. 3:11 [g][Luke 21:15]
16 [h][John 11:47; 12:19] [i]ver. 21; ch. 3:9, 10
17 [j]ch. 5:28, 40
19 [k]ch. 5:29
20 [l][Amos 3:8; John 15:27; 1 Cor. 9:16] [m]ch. 22:15; 1 John 1:1, 3
21 [n]ch. 5:13, 26; [Matt. 21:26, 46; Mark 11:32; Luke 20:6, 19; 22:2] [o]ch. 3:7, 8
24 [p]See ch. 1:14

[1] Greek *This one* [2] Greek *the head of the corner*

selves to hear the message, and the women would have been in the Court of Women (cf. John 6:10). In modern Israel men and women are separated in their worship at the Wailing Wall.

4:5 rulers and elders and scribes. These groups constituted the Jewish religious council, the Sanhedrin. Luke 22:66 describes the body of chief priests and scribes as "their council." This body would include the high priest, members of his family (v. 6), Sadducees, and Pharisees (Matt. 27:62) such as Nicodemus (who is called a "ruler of the Jews" and "teacher of Israel," John 3:1, 10) and Gamaliel (5:34; 22:3).

4:6 The men listed in this verse constituted what might be called the executive committee of the council. Annas, the father-in-law of Caiaphas who was the official high priest (John 18:13), is here called the high priest. He was the power behind the office and probably still regarded as high priest by many Jews since the office was held for life. The Romans had deposed Annas in A.D. 15. John is possibly Jonathan, son of Annas who was appointed high priest in A.D. 36, or Jonathan ben Zaccai, who became president of the Great Synagogue after the fall of Jerusalem. Nothing is known of Alexander.

4:7 by what name. The answer is given in v. 10: "the name of Jesus Christ of Nazareth." There is frequent emphasis on the name of Jesus or the name of the Lord (stressing the person and work of the Lord) in Acts (2:21, 38; 3:16; 4:10, 12; 8:16; 9:15, 28; 15:26; 16:18).

4:8 filled with the Holy Spirit. See 2:4; Eph. 5:18.

4:11 stone . . . rejected . . . the cornerstone. In Acts, defense of the gospel often includes reference to the fulfillment of Old Testament prophecy; here Ps. 118:22 is quoted (also cited in Matt. 21:42; 1 Pet. 2:7; cf. Rom. 9:33).

4:12 no other name. Just as the name of Jesus had been the only hope for physical healing of the man crippled from birth, so also the name of Jesus is the only hope for the spiritual healing of mankind. This exclusive and total reliance upon Christ for salvation is the clear teaching of both Jesus and the New Testament generally (John 14:6; 1 Tim. 2:5). See theological note "Salvation" at 2 Cor. 6:5.

4:13 uneducated. The courage and ready witness of Peter and John is a fulfillment of Christ's promise to the disciples in Matt. 10:19, 20. The courage and knowledge of the unschooled Galilean fishermen astonished the Sanhedrin. In taking note that these men "had been with Jesus," the council no doubt remembered how Jesus too, though without formal training, had surprised them with His teaching (Luke 2:46, 47; John 7:15).

4:19 to listen to you rather than to God. The duty of religious worship and speech is prior to the rights of the state, and the duty of a Christian conscience before God in proclaiming the gospel is above the rights of the Sanhedrin. The state is a servant ordained by God to maintain peace and order (Rom. 13:1–7). See "Christians and Civil Government" at Rom. 13:1.

4:24 lifted their voices together to God. This activity was a natural result of the apostles' training with Jesus and the habits they had formed (2:42).

Sovereign Lord. A term used to express the total creative power and control of the Lord over all His physical creation and over the affairs of humanity (cf. vv. 25, 26; Jer. 10:12).

Lord, [q]who made the heaven and the earth
and the sea and everything in them, 25 who
through the mouth of our father David,
your servant,[1] said by the Holy Spirit,

[r]"'Why did the Gentiles rage,
and the peoples plot in vain?
26 The kings of the earth set
themselves,
and [s]the rulers were gathered
together,
against the Lord and against his
[t]Anointed'[2] —

27 for truly in this city there were gathered
together against your [u]holy servant Jesus,
[v]whom you anointed, both [w]Herod and
[x]Pontius Pilate, along [y]with the Gentiles
and [z]the peoples of Israel, 28 [a]to do whatever your hand and [b]your plan had predestined to take place. 29 And now, Lord, [c]look
upon their threats and grant to your servants[3] to continue to speak your word with
all [d]boldness, 30 while [e]you stretch out your
hand to heal, and signs and wonders are
performed [f]through the name of your [g]holy
servant Jesus." 31 And when they had
prayed, [h]the place in which they were gathered together was shaken, and [i]they were
all filled with the Holy Spirit and [j]contin-
ued to speak the word of God with boldness.

They Had Everything in Common

32 Now the full number of those who
believed were of [k]one heart and [l]soul, and
no one said that any of the things that
belonged to him was his own, but [m]they
had everything in common. 33 And with
great [n]power the apostles were giving their
testimony to the resurrection of the Lord
Jesus, and [o]great grace was upon them all.
34 [p]There was not a needy person among
them, for [q]as many as were owners of lands
or houses sold them and brought the proceeds of what was sold 35 and [r]laid it at the
apostles' feet, and [s]it was distributed to
each as any had need. 36 Thus Joseph, who
was also called by the apostles Barnabas
(which means [t]son of encouragement), a
Levite, a native of Cyprus, 37 sold a field
that belonged to him and brought the
money and [u]laid it at the apostles' feet.

Ananias and Sapphira

5 But a man named Ananias, with his
wife Sapphira, sold a piece of property,
2 and with his wife's knowledge [v]he kept
back for himself some of the proceeds and
brought only a part of it and [w]laid it at the
apostles' feet. 3 But Peter said, "Ananias,

24 [q]Ex. 20:11; 2 Chr. 2:12; Neh. 9:6; Ps. 102:25; 124:8; 134:3; 146:6 **25** [r]Cited from Ps. 2:1, 2 **26** [s]ver. 5 [t]ch. 10:38; Luke 4:18; Heb. 1:9; [Dan. 9:24; Rev. 11:15] **27** [u]ver. 30 [v]ver. 26 [w]Luke 23:7-11 [x]Matt. 27:2 [y]See Matt. 20:19 [z]Matt. 26:3 **28** [a][Isai. 46:10] [b]See ch. 2:23 **29** [c][2 Kin. 19:16] [d]ver. 13, 31; ch. 9:27, 29; 13:46; 14:3; 18:26; 19:8; 28:31; Eph. 6:19 **30** [e][Ps. 138:7; Prov. 31:20; Isai. 1:25; Zeph. 1:4] [f]ch. 3:6; [Matt. 7:22; Mark 9:39; 16:17] [g]ver. 27 **31** [h][ch. 2:2; 16:26; Ps. 77:18] [i]See ch. 2:4 [j][Phil. 1:14]

32 [k]2 Chr. 30:12; Ezek. 11:19 [l]Phil. 1:27 [m]ch. 2:44 **33** [n]See ch. 1:8, 22 [o][ch. 11:23] **34** [p][2 Cor. 8:14, 15] [q]ch. 2:45 **35** [r]ver. 37; ch. 5:2 [s][ch. 6:1] **36** [t][Mark 3:17] **37** [u]ver. 35
Chapter 5 **2** [v]ver. 3 [w]ch. 4:35, 37

1 Or *child*; also verses 27, 30 2 Or *Christ* 3 Greek *bondservants*

4:25 through the mouth of our father David. A succinct summary of verbal inspiration. The Scripture writers spoke and wrote under the guidance of the Spirit (2 Pet. 1:21).

4:27 Herod and Pontius Pilate . . . Gentiles . . . peoples of Israel. The believers properly understood that both Jews and Gentiles were responsible for the crucifixion of Jesus. These were Herod Antipas, who was the son of Herod the Great and tetrarch (i.e., subordinate ruler under the Romans) of Galilee and Perea (Luke 3:1; 23:6, 7) and Pontius Pilate, who was the Roman procurator (governor) of Palestine from A.D. 26–36 (Luke 3:1; 23:1–24). The chief priests and elders persuaded the people to reject Jesus and ask for Barabbas (Matt. 27:20–26).

4:28 your hand and your plan. A clear affirmation that nothing, not even the wrongful death of God's Son, happens apart from God's sovereign will and control. The certainty of God's plan for the world is established by His sovereign "plan" and ensured by His almighty "hand." The early chapters of Acts teach the compatibility of divine sovereignty and human responsibility. While the murderers of Jesus acted in accord with what God had determined, they were morally responsible agents and were held accountable (3:15).

4:29 This prayer of the believing community illustrates the way in which the church should be empowered and encouraged by God's sovereignty. In the face of the threat of physical violence, the church affirmed God's control of the situation (v. 28) and, encouraged by this, they petitioned for greater boldness.

Lord. The Greek word for "Lord" is *kyrios,* used in the Septuagint (the Greek Old Testament) to translate the divine name *Yahweh.* It is used in the New Testament to refer both to God and also to Christ specifically (2:36; 7:31).

4:32–35 Because the believers were "of one heart" (v. 32), they were conscious of the needy in the church and consequently they helped by selling land and giving the proceeds to the apostles for those needs. This Christian giving was proportional to real need. It was voluntary, not compulsory (5:4).

4:33 the resurrection of the Lord Jesus. The crowning proof of the salvation accomplished in Jesus Christ was His resurrection from the dead. The apostles, as chief witnesses, had to testify about this redemptive event (1:22).

grace. Grace in witnessing and living.

4:36 Joseph . . . Barnabas . . . a Levite. In the Old Testament, the Levites did not have inherited land, as the other tribes had, although the Levites were allotted towns (Josh. 21). However, by New Testament times a Levite such as Joseph Barnabas may well have been able to own land. This probably was true of a country outside of Palestine, such as Cyprus. On the other hand, the land owned may have belonged to his wife. The introduction of Barnabas here lays the foundation for further reference to the significant influence of this outstanding believer in the life of the Jewish and Gentile churches and in the life of Paul.

4:37 sold a field that belonged to him. As "son of encouragement" (v. 36), Barnabas presented a good example of a Christian who gave to the needs of others (contrasted with the selfish example of Ananias and Sapphira, 5:1–11). Barnabas also interceded for Saul (9:27), encouraged the church at Antioch in Syria (11:22), led in missionary work abroad (13:2, 3), and continued in missionary work despite a disagreement with Paul (15:37–39).

5:2 he kept back . . . some of the proceeds. Ananias and his wife had the right to keep all of the proceeds from their land since the land and

why has [x]Satan filled your heart to lie [y]to
the Holy Spirit and [z]to keep back for yourself part of the proceeds of the land?
4 While it remained unsold, did it not
remain your own? And after it was sold,
was it not at your disposal? Why is it that
you have contrived this deed in your heart?
You have not lied to men but [a]to God."
5 When Ananias heard these words, he [b]fell
down and breathed his last. And [c]great fear
came upon all who heard of it. **6** The young
men rose and [d]wrapped him up and carried him out and buried him.

7 After an interval of about three hours
his wife came in, not knowing what had
happened. **8** And Peter said to her, "Tell me
whether you[1] sold the land for so much."
And she said, "Yes, for so much." **9** But
Peter said to her, "How is it that you have
agreed together [e]to test [f]the Spirit of the
Lord? Behold, the feet of those who have
buried your husband are at the door, and
they will carry you out." **10** Immediately she
fell down at his feet and breathed her last.
When the young men came in they found
her dead, and they carried her out and
buried her beside her husband. **11** And
[g]great fear came upon the whole church
and upon all who heard of these things.

Many Signs and Wonders Done

12 Now many signs and wonders were
regularly done among the people [h]by the
hands of the apostles. And they were all
[i]together in [j]Solomon's Portico. **13** None of
the rest dared join them, but [k]the people
held them in high esteem. **14** And [l]more
than ever believers were added to the Lord,
multitudes of both men and women, **15** [m]so
that they even [n]carried out the sick into the
streets and laid them on cots and mats,
that as Peter came by [o]at least his shadow
might fall on some of them. **16** The people
also gathered from the towns around Jerusalem, [p]bringing the sick and those afflicted with unclean spirits, and they were
all healed.

The Apostles Arrested and Freed

17 But the high priest rose up, and all who
were with him (that is, the party of [q]the
Sadducees), and filled with [r]jealousy **18** they
arrested the apostles and [s]put them in the
public prison. **19** But during the night [t]an
angel of the Lord [u]opened the prison doors
and brought them out, and said, **20** "Go and
stand in the temple and speak to the people all [v]the words of [w]this [x]Life." **21** And
when they heard this, [y]they entered the
temple [z]at daybreak and began to teach.

Now when the high priest came, and
those who were with him, they called
together the council and all the senate of
Israel and sent to the prison to have them
brought. **22** But when the officers came,
they did not find them in the prison, so
they returned and reported, **23** "We found
the prison securely locked and the guards
standing at the doors, but when we opened
them we found no one inside." **24** Now
when [a]the captain of the temple and the
chief priests heard these words, they were
greatly perplexed about them, wondering
what this would come to. **25** And someone
came and told them, "Look! The men
whom you put in prison [b]are standing in
the temple and teaching the people."
26 Then [c]the captain with the officers went
and brought them, but not by force, for

3 [x][Luke 22:3; John 13:2, 27] [y][ver. 4, 9] [z]ver. 2
4 [a][ver. 3, 9]
5 [b][Ezek. 11:13] [c]ver. 11
6 [d][ch. 8:2; Ezek. 29:5; John 19:40]
9 [e][ch. 15:10; 1 Cor. 10:9] [f][ver. 3, 4]
11 [g]ver. 5
12 [h]ch. 2:43; 4:30; 14:3; 19:11; Mark 16:20; Rom. 15:19; 2 Cor. 12:12; Heb. 2:4 [i]See ch. 1:14 [j]ch. 3:11; John 10:23
13 [k]ver. 26; ch. 2:47; 4:21
14 [l][ch. 6:1, 2]
15 [m][ch. 19:12] [n]Mark 6:55, 56
[o][2 Kin. 4:29; Matt. 14:36]
16 [p]Mark 16:17, 18
17 [q]See Matt. 22:23 [r]ch. 13:45; James 3:14, 16; [ch. 7:9; 17:5]
18 [s]See Luke 21:12
19 [t]See ch. 8:26 [u]ch. 12:10; 16:26
20 [v][John 6:63, 68; Phil. 2:16] [w][ch. 13:46; 22:4; 28:28] [x]ch. 3:15; 11:18
21 [y]ver. 25, 42 [z][John 8:2]
24 [a]ver. 26; See ch. 4:1
25 [b]ver. 21
26 [c]ver. 24

1 The Greek for *you* is plural here

the money was theirs (v. 4). The testimony of the whole church was at risk because of the sins of a few (cf. Lev. 10:1, 2; Num. 16:23–35; Josh. 7:19–25; 2 Sam. 6:1–7).

5:3 Satan filled your heart. Another example of Satan's influence is seen in the life of Peter (Mark 8:33). Later, Peter warned Christians against Satan's potential influence over them (1 Pet. 5:8).

lie to the Holy Spirit. In v. 4 Peter tells Ananias that he has lied to God. Peter's words indicate that the Holy Spirit is God (v. 9).

5:11 the whole church. This is the first of more than twenty occurrences in Acts of the Greek word *ekklesia,* usually translated "church." Stephen uses this word for the Old Testament "congregation" of the people (7:38). In the Septuagint (the Greek Old Testament), the worshiping assembly of God's people is often designated with this word. In ancient Greece, the *ekklesia* was the political "assembly" of citizens (19:32). The New Testament uses the word initially to refer to an organized body of believers (8:1; 11:22; 13:1).

5:13 None of the rest dared join them. No insincere, superficial followers dared to identify with the church. The standards of morality were high.

5:14 believers . . . both men and women. Believers came forward and joined the church. Luke mentions women often in the Gospel (Luke 7:28; 8:2, 3; 17:35; 23:27, 29, 49, 55) and in Acts (1:14; 8:3, 12; 9:2, 36; 13:50; 16:1, 13, 14; 17:4, 12, 34; 18:2; 21:5).

5:15 shadow. As when Jesus' healing power flowed from His garment at the touch of the woman who had been subject to bleeding (Mark 5:27, 28), here God allows the shadow of Peter to effect a cure, as He did also through cloths and aprons that Paul had used (19:11, 12).

5:21 the council. The great Jewish religious council at Jerusalem, the Sanhedrin, composed of about seventy men. It included Sadducees, Pharisees, and their associates. Under the Romans the Sanhedrin had broad authority in Palestine. According to ancient Jewish tradition, the members sat in a semicircle with two clerks and three rows of students at the front.

[d]they were afraid of being stoned by the
people.
27 And when they had brought them, they
set them before the council. And the high
priest questioned them, 28 saying, [e]"We
strictly charged you not to teach in this
name, yet here you have filled Jerusalem
with your teaching, and you [f]intend to bring
this man's blood upon us." 29 But Peter and
the apostles answered, [g]"We must obey
God rather than men. 30 [h]The God of our
fathers [i]raised Jesus, [j]whom you killed by
hanging him on [k]a tree. 31 God exalted [l]him
at his right hand as [m]Leader and [n]Savior, [o]to
give [p]repentance to Israel and [o]forgiveness
of sins. 32 And [q]we are witnesses to these
things, and [r]so is the Holy Spirit, [s]whom
God has given to those who obey him."
33 When they heard this, they [t]were
enraged and wanted to kill them. 34 But a
Pharisee in the council named [u]Gamaliel,
[v]a teacher of the law held in honor by all
the people, stood up and gave orders to
put the men outside for a little while.
35 And he said to them, "Men of Israel, take
care what you are about to do with these
men. 36 For [w]before these days Theudas
rose up, [x]claiming to be somebody, and a
number of men, about four hundred,
joined him. He was killed, and all who followed him were dispersed and came to
nothing. 37 After him Judas the Galilean
rose up in the days of [y]the census and drew
away some of the people after him. He too

26 [d]ver. 13; See ch. 4:21 **28** [e]ch. 4:18 [f]ch. 2:23, 36; 3:15; 4:10; 7:52; Matt. 27:25 **29** [g][ch. 4:19, 20] **30** [h]See ch. 3:13 [i]See ch. 2:24 [j]ch. 10:39; Gal. 3:13; See Luke 24:20 [k]ch. 13:29; 1 Pet. 2:24 **31** [l]See ch. 2:33 [m]See ch. 3:15 [n]See Luke 2:11 [o]Luke 24:47; See Luke 5:32 [p]ch. 11:18; 2 Tim. 2:25; [Rom. 2:4] **32** [q]See Luke 24:48 [r][ch. 15:28; John 15:26, 27; Heb. 2:4; 1 John 5:7] [s]See ch. 2:4 **33** [t]ch. 7:54; [ch. 2:37] **34** [u]ch. 22:3 [v]See Luke 5:17 **36** [w][ch. 21:38] [x]ch. 8:9; [Gal. 2:6; 6:3] **37** [y][Luke 2:2] **38** [z]Lam. 3:37 **39** [a]Prov. 21:30; Isai. 8:9, 10; Nah. 1:9 [b]2 Chr. 13:12; [ch. 11:17] **40** [c]ch. 4:18 [d][ch. 22:19; Mark 13:9; Luke 23:16]

perished, and all who followed him were
scattered. 38 So in the present case I tell
you, keep away from these men and let
them alone, for [z]if this plan or this undertaking is of man, it will fail; 39 but [a]if it is of
God, you will not be able to overthrow
them. You [b]might even be found opposing
God!" So they took his advice, 40 and [c]when
they had called in the apostles, [d]they beat
them and charged them not to speak in the
name of Jesus, and let them go. 41 Then
they left the presence of the council, [e]re-
joicing that they were counted worthy [f]to
suffer dishonor for [g]the name. 42 And every
day, [h]in the temple and from house to
house, they did not cease teaching and
[i]preaching [j]Jesus as the Christ.

Seven Chosen to Serve

6 Now in these days [k]when the disciples
were increasing in number, a complaint by the Hellenists[1] arose against the
Hebrews because their widows were being
neglected in [l]the daily distribution. 2 And
the twelve summoned the full number of
the disciples and said, "It is not right that
we should give up preaching the word of
God to serve tables. 3 [m]Therefore, brothers,[2]
pick out from among you seven men [n]of
good repute, [o]full of the Spirit and of wis-

41 [e]1 Pet. 4:13, 14, 16; See Matt. 5:12 [f]ch. 9:16; 21:13; [Rom. 1:5]; See John 15:21 [g]Lev. 24:11, 16; Phil. 2:9; 3 John 7 **42** [h]ch. 2:46 [i]ch. 8:35; 11:20; 17:18 [j]See ch. 18:5
Chapter 6 **1** [k]ch. 2:41, 47; 4:4; 5:14; [ver. 7] [l][ch. 4:35] **3** [m][Deut. 1:13] [n][1 Tim. 3:7] [o]ver. 5; ch. 7:55; 11:24; [Luke 1:15; 4:1]

1 That is, Greek-speaking Jews 2 Or *brothers and sisters*

5:28 bring this man's blood upon us. In 2:23; 3:15, 16; and 4:10, 11, Peter and his associates blamed the members of the Sanhedrin for the death of Jesus. The people had heard this accusation.

5:31 God exalted him at his right hand. This declaration would be understood by the Sanhedrin as a reference to the Resurrection. Such an exaltation by God would make this resurrected Jesus equal with God (cf. John 5:18; 10:33).

5:34 Gamaliel. One of the most famous rabbis of his time, Gamaliel was Paul's teacher (22:3) and probably a grandson of Rabbi Hillel, the leader of one of the two great schools of Jewish legal interpretation. In contrast to the school of Shammai, Gamaliel and the school of Hillel were known for their lenient interpretation of the law (Matt. 19:3 and note).

5:37 Judas the Galilean. The Jewish historian Josephus (*Jewish War* 20.118) speaks of a certain Galilean who stirred up a revolt because he resisted subservience and paying taxes to the Romans. The revolt failed, but it may have laid the groundwork for the party of the Zealots. The apostle Simon the Zealot (1:13; Matt. 10:4 and note) may have previously been a member of this group.

days of the census. Not the census of Luke 2:1, which was ordered by the Emperor Augustus about 8 B.C. (but was delayed until 5 or 6 B.C.), but the census fourteen years later in A.D. 6, in the time of the Procurator Coponius.

5:40 beat them. The apostles received the traditional "forty lashes less one" (2 Cor. 11:24).

6:1 widows were being neglected. The Old Testament required care of the poor and needy (Ps. 9:18 note). This concern is seen in the social action set forth in 2:44, 45; 4:34–37. Here the age-old problem of discrimination had emerged: the widows of Greek-speaking Jews (see text note) were considered outsiders by native-born Jews and so were not getting their share of the food distribution, probably deriving in part from the generous giving of 4:34–37.

6:2 the twelve. The twelve apostles including Matthias (1:26). This is a shift from "the eleven" (1:26; 2:14; Luke 24:9, 33).

disciples. The first of a number of times the believers are called "disciples" in Acts (e.g., v. 7; 9:1; 11:26; 13:52). Paul does not use this term to identify Christians.

the word of God. In this initial organization of the New Testament church, two important ministries are listed: the ministry of the word and prayer (v. 4); and the ministry of meeting people's physical needs, such as serving at table. The Greek verb is *diakoneo* ("serve"), from which English derives the word "deacon." In 6:1, the related noun is translated "distribution," and in v. 4 "the ministry." The office of deacon, which may have had its beginning here, is described in 1 Tim. 3:8–13.

6:3 brothers, pick out . . . seven men. The members of the church elected the seven, and the apostles set them apart (ordained) by prayer and the laying on of hands (v. 6).

full of the Spirit and of wisdom. The two requirements for the ministry of service in all ages are obedience to the Spirit and action guided by wisdom.

dom, whom we will appoint to this duty.
4 But [p]we will devote ourselves to prayer
and to the ministry of the word." **5** And
what they said pleased the whole gathering, and they chose Stephen, [q]a man full of
faith and [r]of the Holy Spirit, and [s]Philip,
and Prochorus, and Nicanor, and Timon,
and Parmenas, and Nicolaus, [t]a proselyte
of Antioch. **6** These they set before the apostles, and [u]they prayed and [v]laid their hands
on them.
7 And [w]the word of God continued to
increase, and the number of the disciples
multiplied greatly in Jerusalem, and a great
many of the priests [x]became obedient to
[y]the faith.

Stephen Is Seized

8 And Stephen, full of grace and [z]power,
was doing great wonders and signs among
the people. **9** Then some of those who
belonged to the synagogue of the Freedmen (as it was called), and of the Cy-
renians, and of the Alexandrians, and of
those from Cilicia and Asia, rose up and
disputed with Stephen. **10** But [a]they could
not withstand the wisdom and the Spirit
with which he was speaking. **11** Then [b]they
secretly instigated men who said, "We have
heard him speak blasphemous words
against Moses and God." **12** And they
stirred up the people and the elders and
the scribes, and they came upon him and
seized him and brought him before the
council, **13** and they [c]set up [d]false witnesses
who said, "This man never ceases to speak
words against [e]this holy place and the law,
14 for we have heard him say that this Jesus
of Nazareth [f]will destroy this place and will
[g]change [h]the customs that Moses delivered
to us." **15** And gazing at him, all who sat in
the council saw that his face [i]was like the
face of an angel.

Stephen's Speech

7 And the high priest said, "Are these
things so?" **2** And Stephen said:
[j]"Brothers and fathers, hear me. [k]The
God [l]of glory appeared to our father Abraham when he was in Mesopotamia, [m]before
he lived in Haran, **3** and said to him, [n]'Go
out from your land and from your kindred
and go into the land that I will show you.'
4 [m]Then he went out from the land of the
Chaldeans and lived in Haran. And [o]after
his father died, [p]God removed him from
there into this land in which you are now
living. **5** Yet he gave him no inheritance in
it, not even a foot's length, but promised
[q]to give it to him as a possession and to his
offspring after him, [r]though he had no
child. **6** And God spoke to this effect—that
[s]his offspring would [t]be sojourners in a
land belonging to others, who would enslave them and afflict them [u]four hundred
years. **7** 'But [v]I will judge the nation that
they serve,' said God, 'and after that they
shall come out [w]and worship me in this
place.' **8** And [x]he gave him the covenant of

4 [p]See ch. 1:14
5 [q]ch. 11:24 [r]ver. 3 [s]ch. 8:5; 21:8 [t]ch. 2:10; 13:43; Matt. 23:15
6 [u]ch. 1:24; 13:3 [v]1 Tim. 4:14; 5:22; 2 Tim. 1:6; [ch. 8:17; 9:17; 19:6; Heb. 6:2]
7 [w]ch. 12:24; 19:20; [Col. 1:5, 6] [x]See Rom. 1:5 [y]ch. 13:8; 14:22; 16:5
8 [z]See ch. 1:8
10 [a]See Luke 21:14, 15
11 [b][1 Kin. 21:10, 13; Matt. 26:59, 60]
13 [c]ver. 11 [d]ch. 7:58
[e][ch. 21:28; 25:8; Matt. 24:15]
14 [f][Dan. 9:26; Matt. 26:61] [g][Matt. 5:17] [h]ch. 15:1; 21:21
15 [i][Judg. 13:6; Eccles. 8:1]
Chapter 7
2 [j]ch. 22:1 [k][Gen. 15:7; Josh. 24:3; Neh. 9:7] [l]Ps. 29:3; [1 Cor. 2:8; James 2:1] [m]Gen. 11:31
3 [n]Cited from Gen. 12:1
4 [m][See ver. 2 above] [o]Gen. 11:32 [p]Gen. 12:4, 5

5 [q]Gen. 12:7; 13:15; 15:18; 17:8; 48:4; Heb. 11:8, 9 [r]Gen. 15:3; 18:10 6 [s]Cited from Gen. 15:13, 14 [t][Ex. 2:22; Heb. 11:9] [u]ver. 17; See Ex. 12:40 7 [v][Jer. 25:12; 30:20] [w][Ex. 3:12] 8 [x]Gen. 17:9-12

6:5 Stephen . . . Nicolaus. All seven men had Greek names, which may point to their being Jews from the Dispersion, although many Palestinian Jews also had Greek names. Attributes are listed for the first and last of the seven: for Stephen ("full of faith and of the Holy Spirit") who appears in 6:8–7:60, and for Nicolaus, "a proselyte of Antioch." Antioch soon became a center of missionary activity. Philip's later ministry to Samaria and to the Ethiopian eunuch is described in ch. 8.

6:8 Stephen . . . doing great wonders and signs. Philip, another of the seven, also did miracles later like the apostles who had ordained them (8:6).

6:9 synagogue of the Freedmen. Composed of Jews freed from slavery, who in this case were from Cyrene, a well-known town of North Africa.

Cilicia. A Roman province in the southeast part of Asia Minor, with Paul's hometown of Tarsus (9:11, 30; 11:25) as one of its chief cities.

Asia. The Roman province in the western part of modern-day Turkey.

6:11 blasphemous words against Moses and God. Although in the light of the gospel he may have begun to express concern about hollow observance of the technical details of the law, all that Stephen said, as is evident in ch. 7, was that Moses, like Jesus and like Stephen himself, was rejected by the people (7:35, 39). This could not be taken as blasphemy against Moses and God.

6:13 against this holy place and the law. Stephen did not speak against the temple, but only declared that God was not confined to an earthly temple since heaven was His home and throne (7:48–50). Stephen actually supported the Mosaic law and its teaching, especially as they pointed forward to Christ (7:37, 38).

6:14 Jesus of Nazareth will destroy this place. The Jewish leadership had heard the misinterpreted quotation of Jesus in John 2:19, but there is no evidence that Stephen had known or used it.

7:2 The God of glory. This title recalls the divine glory God showed His people in the time of Moses: the pillar of cloud (Ex. 14:19; 16:10; Ps. 105:39), the pillar of fire (Ex. 14:24), the glory of the Lord on the mountain (Ex. 24:15–18; 2 Cor. 3:7), and the glory on the tabernacle (Ex. 40:34, 35; cf. John 1:14).

7:4 land of the Chaldeans. Babylonia, in southern Mesopotamia (modern Iraq).

7:6 four hundred years. Ex. 12:40 has "430," but Stephen is speaking in round numbers, and may have been following the text of Gen. 15:13 which has "four hundred years."

7:8 covenant of circumcision. God established this covenant with Abraham. He was the father of all Israel but lived centuries before Moses came. Moses instituted the customs that Stephen's adversaries tried to protect (6:14).

circumcision. And [y]so Abraham became
the father of Isaac, and [z]circumcised him
on the eighth day, and [a]Isaac became the
father of Jacob, and [b]Jacob of the twelve
patriarchs.
9 "And the patriarchs, [c]jealous of Joseph,
[d]sold him into Egypt; but [e]God was with
him 10 and rescued him out of all his afflictions and [f]gave him favor and wisdom
before Pharaoh, king of Egypt, [g]who made
him ruler over Egypt and over all his household. 11 Now [h]there came a famine throughout all Egypt and Canaan, and great
affliction, and our fathers could find no
food. 12 [i]But when Jacob heard that there
was grain in Egypt, he sent out our fathers
on their first visit. 13 And [j]on the second
visit [k]Joseph made himself known to his
brothers, and [l]Joseph's family became
known to Pharaoh. 14 And [m]Joseph sent and
summoned Jacob his father and all his kindred, [n]seventy-five persons in all. 15 And
[o]Jacob went down into Egypt, and [p]he
died, he [q]and our fathers, 16 and [r]they were
carried back to Shechem and laid in the
tomb that [s]Abraham had bought for a sum
of silver from the sons of Hamor in
Shechem.
17 "But [t]as the time of the promise drew
near, which God had granted to Abraham,
[u]the people increased and multiplied in
Egypt 18 until there arose over Egypt another king [v]who did not know Joseph. 19 [w]He
dealt shrewdly with our race and forced
our fathers to expose their infants, [x]so that
they would not be kept alive. 20 [y]At this
time Moses was born; and he was beautiful
in God's sight. And he was brought up for
three months in his father's house, 21 and
[z]when he was exposed, Pharaoh's daughter
adopted him and brought him up as her
own son. 22 And Moses [a]was instructed in
[b]all the wisdom of the Egyptians, and he
was [c]mighty in his words and deeds.
23 "When he was forty years old, it came
into his heart [d]to visit his brothers, the children of Israel. 24 And seeing one of them
being wronged, he defended the oppressed
man and avenged him by striking down the
Egyptian. 25 He supposed that his brothers
would understand that God was giving
them salvation by his hand, but they did
not understand. 26 [e]And on the following
day he appeared to them as they were
quarreling and tried to reconcile them, saying, 'Men, you are brothers. Why do you
wrong each other?' 27 But the man who was
wronging his neighbor thrust him aside,
saying, [f]'Who made you a ruler and a judge
over us? 28 Do you want to kill me as you
killed the Egyptian yesterday?' 29 At this
retort [g]Moses fled and became an exile in
the land of Midian, [h]where he became the
father of two sons.
30 "Now when forty years had passed, [i]an
angel appeared to him [j]in the wilderness of
Mount Sinai, in a flame of fire in a bush.
31 When Moses saw it, he was amazed at
the sight, and as he drew near to look,
there came the voice of the Lord: 32 [k]'I am
the God of your fathers, the God of
Abraham and of Isaac and of Jacob.' And
Moses trembled and did not dare to look.
33 Then the Lord said to him, [l]'Take off the
sandals from your feet, for the place where
you are standing is holy ground. 34 [m]I have
surely seen the affliction of my people who
are in Egypt, and [n]have heard their groaning, and [o]I have come down to deliver
them. [p]And now come, I will send you to
Egypt.'
35 "This Moses, whom they rejected, [q]say-
ing, 'Who made you a ruler and a
judge?'—this man God sent as both ruler
and redeemer [r]by the hand of the angel
who appeared to him in the bush. 36 [s]This
man led them out, performing [t]wonders

8 [y]Gen. 21:2-4 [z]See Luke 1:59 [a]Gen. 25:26 [b]Gen. 29:31-35; 30:5-24; 35:18, 23-26 **9** [c]Gen. 37:11 [d]Gen. 37:28; 45:4; Ps. 105:17 [e]Gen. 39:2, 21, 23 **10** [f]Gen. 41:37-40 [g]Gen. 41:41, 43, 46; 42:6; Ps. 105:21 **11** [h]Gen. 41:54, 55; 42:5; Ps. 105:16 **12** [i]Gen. 42:1-3 **13** [j]Gen. 43:2-15 [k]Gen. 45:1-4 [l]Gen. 45:16 **14** [m]Gen. 45:9, 10, 27 [n][Gen. 46:26, 27; Ex. 1:5; Deut. 10:22] **15** [o]Gen. 46:5, 28; Ps. 105:23 [p]Gen. 49:33 [q]Ex. 1:6 **16** [r]Gen. 50:25; Ex. 13:19; Josh. 24:32 [s][Gen. 23:16 with Gen. 33:19; Josh. 24:32] **17** [t]ver. 5-7 [u]ch. 13:17; Ex. 1:7, 12; Ps. 105:24 **18** [v]Cited from Ex. 1:8 **19** [w]Ex. 1:9, 10; Ps. 105:25 [x]Ex. 1:16-18, 22 **20** [y]Ex. 2:2; Heb. 11:23 **21** [z]Ex. 2:3-10 **22** [a][Dan. 1:4, 17] [b]1 Kin. 4:30; [Isai. 19:11] [c][Luke 24:19]

23 [d]Ex. 2:11, 12 **26** [e]Ex. 2:13, 14 **27** [f]ver. 35; [Luke 12:14] **29** [g]Ex. 2:15 [h]Ex. 2:22; 18:3, 4 **30** [i]Ex. 3:2 [j][Ex. 3:1]

32 [k]Cited from Ex. 3:6 **33** [l]Ex. 3:5; Josh. 5:15 **34** [m]Ex. 3:7 [n]Ex. 2:24 [o]Ex. 3:8 [p]Ex. 3:10 **35** [q]ver. 27 [r][Ex. 3:2; 14:19; 23:20; Num. 20:16] **36** [s]Ex. 12:41; 33:1; Heb. 8:9 [t]Ex. 7:3

7:14 seventy-five persons. The Hebrew text of Ex. 1:5 has "seventy." But the Greek translation of the Old Testament text, which this sermon is basically following, and the fragments of Exodus found among the Dead Sea Scrolls read "seventy-five." The explanation of the "seventy-five" is to be found in the five additional descendants of Joseph included in the Greek translation of Gen. 46:20, where two sons of Manasseh, two sons of Ephraim, and one grandson of Ephraim are included.

7:16 the tomb that Abraham had bought . . . in Shechem. Stephen has condensed the events regarding the patriarchs' burial purchases. Jacob was buried in the cave of Machpelah at Hebron (Gen. 50:13), and according to Josephus (*Antiquities* 2.199) Joseph's brothers were buried in Hebron. Joseph's bones, however, were placed in the land Jacob had bought from the sons of Hamor (Gen. 33:19; 50:25; Ex. 13:19; Josh. 24:32). Stephen's audience knew that Jacob and his sons were buried in two different places (Hebron and Shechem). The narrative here is highly condensed.

7:22 Moses was instructed in all the wisdom of the Egyptians. Ex. 2:10 states that when the child Moses grew older the nurse (Moses' mother) took him to Pharaoh's daughter and "he became her son," with the assumption that in the royal household he would be given a full Egyptian education. Two first-century scholars, the historian Josephus and Philo the philosopher, tell of the extensive learning of Moses.

and signs [u]in Egypt and [v]at the Red Sea and
[w]in the wilderness for [x]forty years. 37 This is
the Moses who said to the Israelites, 'God
will raise up for you [y]a prophet like me
from your brothers.' 38 This is the one [z]who
was in the congregation in the wilderness
with [a]the angel who spoke to him at Mount
Sinai, and with our fathers. [b]He received
[c]living [d]oracles to give to us. 39 Our fathers
refused to obey him, but thrust him aside,
and [e]in their hearts they turned to Egypt,
40 saying to Aaron, [f]'Make for us gods who
will go before us. As for this Moses who led
us out from the land of Egypt, we do not
know what has become of him.' 41 And
[g]they made a calf in those days, and offered
a sacrifice to the idol and [h]were rejoicing in
[i]the works of their hands. 42 But [j]God
turned away and [k]gave them over to worship
[l]the host of heaven, as it is written in
the book of the prophets:

[m]"'Did you bring to me slain beasts and
    sacrifices,
  [n]during the forty years in the
    wilderness, O house of Israel?
43 You took up the tent of [o]Moloch
  and the star of your god Rephan,
    the images that you made to
      worship;
  and I will send you into exile beyond
    Babylon.'

44 "Our fathers had [p]the tent of witness in
the wilderness, just as he who spoke to
Moses [q]directed him to make it, according
to the pattern that he had seen. 45 Our
fathers in turn [r]brought it in with Joshua
when they [s]dispossessed the nations [t]that
God drove out before our fathers. So it was
[u]until the days of David, 46 [v]who found
favor in the sight of God and [w]asked to find
a dwelling place for [x]the God of Jacob.[1]
47 But it was [y]Solomon who built a house
for him. 48 [z]Yet the Most High does not
dwell [a]in houses made by hands, as the
prophet says,

49 [b]"'Heaven is my throne,
  [c]and the earth is my footstool.
What kind of house will you build
    for me, says the Lord,
  or what is the place of my rest?
50 Did not my hand make all these
    things?'

51 [d]"You stiff-necked people, [e]uncircumcised
in heart and ears, you always resist
the Holy Spirit. [f]As your fathers did, so do
you. 52 [g]Which of the prophets did not your
fathers persecute? And they killed those
who announced beforehand the coming of
[h]the Righteous One, [i]whom you have now
betrayed and murdered, 53 you who received
the law [j]as delivered by angels and [k]did not
keep it."

The Stoning of Stephen

54 Now when they heard these things
[l]they were enraged, and they [m]ground their
teeth at him. 55 But he, [n]full of the Holy
Spirit, gazed into heaven and saw [o]the glory
of God, and Jesus standing [p]at the right
hand of God. 56 And he said, "Behold, I see
[q]the heavens opened, and [r]the Son of Man

36 [u]Ex. 7-12; Ps. 78:43-51; 105:27-36 [v]Ex. 14:21, 27-31; Ps. 78:53; 106:9 [w]Ex. 16:1, 35; 17:1-6; Ps. 78:15 [x]ver. 42; ch. 13:18; Ex. 16:35; Num. 14:33, 34; Ps. 95:10; Heb. 3:9, 17 **37** [y]ch. 3:22; Cited from Deut. 18:15 **38** [z]Ex. 19:3, 17, 18 [a][ver. 53; Isai. 63:9] [b]Deut. 5:27, 31; 33:4; See John 1:17 [c][Deut. 32:47] [d]Rom. 3:2; Heb. 5:12; 1 Pet. 4:11 **39** [e]Ex. 16:3; Num. 11:4, 5; 14:3, 4; Ezek. 20:8, 24 **40** [f]Cited from Ex. 32:1, 23 **41** [g]Ex. 32:4-6, 35; Deut. 9:16; Ps. 106:19 [h]Amos 6:13 [i]Isai. 2:8; Jer. 1:16; 25:6, 7 **42** [j][Josh. 24:20; Isai. 63:10] [k]Ps. 81:12; Ezek. 20:39; Rom. 1:28 [l]Deut. 4:19; 2 Kin. 17:16; 21:3; 23:5; Jer. 19:13; Zeph. 1:5 [m]Cited from Amos 5:25-27 [n]See ver. 36 **43** [o]See 1 Kin. 11:7 **44** [p]Rev. 15:5; See Ex. 38:21 [q]See Ex. 25:40 **45** [r]Josh. 3:14-17 [s]Num. 32:5; Deut. 32:49 [t]ch. 13:19; Josh. 3:10; 23:9; 24:18; 2 Chr. 20:7 [u]2 Sam. 7:1 **46** [v]ch. 13:22; 1 Sam. 16:1; Ps. 89:19 [w]1 Kin. 8:17; 1 Chr. 22:7; Ps. 132:5 [x][Gen. 49:24; Isai. 49:26] **47** [y]2 Sam. 7:13; 1 Kin. 6:1, 2; 8:20; 2 Chr. 3:1 **48** [z][1 Kin. 8:27; 2 Chr. 2:6] [a]ch. 17:24 **49** [b][Ps. 11:4] [c]Matt. 5:34, 35; Cited from Isai. 66:1, 2 **51** [d]Deut. 10:16; See Ex. 32:9 [e]Lev. 26:41;Jer. 6:10; 9:26; Ezek. 44:7, 9 [f]Mal. 3:7 **52** [g]1 Kin. 19:10; 2 Chr. 36:16; Jer. 2:30; Matt. 23:31, 37; See Matt. 5:12; 21:35 [h]See ch. 3:14 [i]See ch. 5:28 **53** [j]Gal. 3:19; Heb. 2:2; [ver. 38; Deut. 33:2] [k]John 7:19 **54** [l]ch. 5:33; [ch. 2:37] [m]Job 16:9; Ps. 35:16; 37:12 **55** [n]ch. 6:5 [o]Ex. 24:16; Luke 2:9; John 12:41 [p]Ps. 110:1; See Mark 16:19 **56** [q]See John 1:51 [r]See Dan. 7:13

1 Some manuscripts *for the house of Jacob*

7:38 the congregation in the wilderness. "Congregation" translates the Greek word *ekklesia* ("church," see 5:11 note).

the angel who spoke to him at Mount Sinai. Although Moses received the law from God on Mount Sinai (Ex. 20:1, 21), angels had some part in its institution (v. 53; Deut. 33:2; Gal. 3:19; Heb. 2:2). On the Angel of the Lord, see notes Gen. 16:7 and Judg. 2:1.

7:44 tent of witness. The Old Testament tabernacle contained the ark of the covenant and the tablets of the Ten Commandments, which are called "the Testimony." Further symbolizing God's presence and life-giving power were the table of the consecrated bread (Ex. 37:10–16; Heb. 9:2), the seven-branched lampstand (Ex. 37:17–23; cf. John 8:12; Rev. 1:12–18), and the altar of incense (Ex. 37:25–29) pointing to the prayers of God's people rising up to the ever-present God (Ps. 141:2; Rev. 8:3, 4).

7:51 You stiff-necked people, uncircumcised in heart and ears. They would not listen from their hearts, nor obey the Lord and the Scriptures Stephen had cited. These metaphors are Old Testament figures meaning spiritually stubborn and unregenerate (Ex. 32:9; 33:3, 5; Deut. 9:6; 10:16; 30:6; Jer. 4:4).

7:52 the Righteous One. A title used for the Lord Almighty (Is. 24:16), and for Jesus Christ (22:14; 1 John 2:1).

7:55 the glory of God. The brilliance of God's presence (cf. Rev. 15:8; 21:11, 23).

standing at the right hand of God. Usually Jesus is said to be sitting at the right hand of God because His work was finished (Rom. 8:34; Col. 3:1; Heb. 10:12), but here He is standing to receive Stephen or to defend him. In this scene the Son of Man is both Judge and Advocate. See theological note "Jesus' Heavenly Reign" on the next page.

7:56 I see . . . the Son of Man. Stephen's vision of the Son of Man in heaven must have vividly reminded the Sanhedrin that when they asked Jesus, "Are you the Christ," He replied, "I am, and you will see the Son of Man seated at the right hand of Power, and coming with the clouds of

standing [p]at the right hand of God." [57]But
they cried out with a loud voice and
stopped their ears and rushed together[1] at
him. [58]Then [s]they cast him out of the city
and [t]stoned him. And [u]the witnesses laid
down their garments [v]at the feet of a young
man named Saul. [59]And as they were stoning Stephen, [w]he called out, "Lord Jesus,
[x]receive my spirit." [60]And [y]falling to his
knees he cried out with a loud voice,
[z]"Lord, do not hold this sin against them."
And when he had said this, [a]he fell asleep.

Saul Ravages the Church

8 And [b]Saul [c]approved of his execution.
And there arose on that day a great
persecution against the church in Jerusalem, and [d]they were all scattered
throughout the regions of Judea and
Samaria, except the apostles. [2]Devout men
buried Stephen and made great lamentation over him. [3]But [e]Saul was ravaging the
church, and entering house after house, he
[f]dragged off men and women and committed them to prison.

Philip Proclaims Christ in Samaria

[4]Now [g]those who were scattered went
about preaching the word. [5][h]Philip went
down to the city[2] of Samaria and proclaimed to them the Christ. [6][i]And the
crowds with one accord paid attention to
what was being said by Philip when they
heard him [j]and saw the signs that he did.
[7]For [k]unclean spirits came out of many
who were possessed, crying with a loud
voice, and many who were paralyzed or
lame were healed. [8]So [l]there was much joy
in that city.

Simon the Magician Believes

[9]But there was a man named Simon,
[m]who had previously practiced magic in

56[p][See ver. 55 above] **58**[s]Lev. 24:14-16; Num. 15:35; 1 Kin. 21:13; [Luke 4:29; Heb. 13:12] [t]Matt. 21:35; 23:37; Heb. 11:37 [u]ch. 6:13; [Deut. 13:9, 10; 17:7] [v]ch. 8:1; 22:20; [ch. 22:4] **59**[w]ch. 9:14 [x]Ps. 31:5; Luke 23:46 **60**[y]ch. 9:40; 20:36; 21:5; Luke 22:41; Eph. 3:14 [z]See Matt. 5:44 [a]See Matt. 27:52
Chapter 8
1[b]ch. 7:58; 22:20 [c]See Rom. 1:32 [d]ch. 11:19; See Matt. 10:23 **3**[e]ch. 9:1, 13, 21; 22:4, 19; 26:10, 11; 1 Cor. 15:9; Gal. 1:13; Phil. 3:6; 1 Tim. 1:13 [f][James 2:6] **4**[g]ver. 1 **5**[h]ch. 6:5 **6**[i][John 4:38] [j]John 2:23 **7**[k]See Mark 16:17, 18 **8**[l]ver. 39; See John 16:22 **9**[m]ver. 11; ch. 13:6

1 Or *rushed with one mind* 2 Some manuscripts *a city*

Jesus' Heavenly Reign

Christ's present role in glory is commonly referred to as His heavenly "session," His "sitting" at God's right hand. The New Testament pictures Jesus' heavenly activity as standing ready to act (Acts 7:56; Rev. 1:12–16; 14:1), walking among His people (Rev. 2:1), and riding to battle (Rev. 19:11–16), but it regularly expresses His present authority by saying that He sits at the Father's right hand—not to rest, but to rule. The picture is not of inactivity but of authority.

In Ps. 110 God sets the Messiah at His right hand as king and priest—as king to bring His enemies under His feet (v. 1), and as priest to serve God and direct God's grace forever (v. 4).

Christ rules over all spheres of authority whether angelic or human (Matt. 28:18; 1 Pet. 3:22). His kingdom in a direct sense is the church, the body over which He is the Head, governing it by His word and Spirit (Eph. 1:22, 23). As for the state: it is not related to the kingdom of God as it was in the Old Testament. The sword is not to be used to enforce Christ's kingdom (John 18:36), but Christ uses secular authority to maintain civil peace and order, and commands His disciples to submit to rulers (Matt. 22:21; Rom. 13:1–7). Christians seek in every sphere of life to do His will, reminding themselves and others that all are accountable to Christ as Judge, whatever their position in life may be (Matt. 25:31; Acts 17:31; Rom. 2:16; 2 Cor. 5:10).

Christ's session will continue until all His enemies and ours, including death, are brought to nothing. Death, the last enemy, will cease to exist when Christ at His appearing raises the dead for judgment (John 5:28, 29). Once judgment has been executed, the work of the mediatorial kingdom will be over, and Christ will triumphantly deliver the kingdom to the Father (1 Cor. 15:24–28).

heaven" (Mark 14:61, 62). Stephen saw the same Jesus standing in heaven at God's right hand, proving the truth of what he was saying and condemning the Sanhedrin.

7:58 a young man named Saul. Saul, later called Paul, was a Pharisee and associated with the Sanhedrin (Phil. 3:5). Possibly he was an instigator of Stephen's trial (8:3; 9:1, 2). At this point Luke introduces Saul, the second great figure of his book.

7:60 do not hold this sin against them. Compare the statement of Jesus in Luke 23:34.

8:3 Saul was ravaging the church. The Greek verb is strong; not just harassment, but an attempt to destroy the church is meant.

8:4 scattered . . . preaching the word. Through persecution the message was spread farther and more rapidly (11:19). As Tertullian said, "The blood of Christians is the seed of the church."

8:9 Simon. Simon Magus the sorcerer is frequently mentioned in ancient writings outside the Bible as the archenemy of the church and one of the leaders of the Gnostic heresy. Gnosticism (named from the Greek word *gnosis*, meaning "knowledge") taught that a person gained salvation not by the merit of Christ's death for sinners, but by special knowledge about

the city and amazed the people of Samaria,
[n]saying that he himself was somebody
great. 10 They all paid attention to him,
from the least to the greatest, saying, [o]"This
man is the power of God that is called
[p]Great." 11 And they paid attention to him
because for a long time he had [q]amazed
them with his magic. 12 But when [r]they
believed Philip as he preached good news
[s]about the kingdom of God and the name
of Jesus Christ, [r]they were baptized, both
men and women. 13 Even Simon himself
believed, and after being baptized he continued with Philip. And [t]seeing signs and
[u]great miracles[1] performed, [v]he was
amazed.
14 Now when [w]the apostles at Jerusalem
heard that [x]Samaria had received the word
of God, they sent to them Peter and John,
15 who came down and prayed for them
[y]that they might receive the Holy Spirit,
16 for [z]he had not yet [a]fallen on any of
them, but [b]they had only been baptized
in the name of the Lord Jesus. 17 Then [c]they
laid their hands on them and [d]they
received the Holy Spirit. 18 Now when
Simon saw that the Spirit was given
through the laying on of the apostles'
hands, he offered them money, 19 saying,
"Give me this power also, so that anyone
on whom I lay my hands may receive the
Holy Spirit." 20 But Peter said to him, [e]"May
your silver perish with you, because you
thought you could obtain the gift of God
[f]with money! 21 You have neither part nor
lot in this matter, for [g]your heart is not
right before God. 22 Repent, therefore, of
this wickedness of yours, and pray to the
Lord that, [h]if possible, the intent of your
heart may be forgiven you. 23 For I see that
you are in [i]the gall[2] of bitterness and in
[j]the bond of iniquity." 24 And Simon
answered, [k]"Pray for me to the Lord, that
nothing of what you have said may come
upon me."
25 Now when they had testified and spoken the word of the Lord, they returned to
Jerusalem, [l]preaching the gospel to many
villages of the Samaritans.

Philip and the Ethiopian Eunuch

26 Now [m]an angel of the Lord said to
Philip, "Rise and go toward the south[3] to the
road that goes down from Jerusalem to
Gaza." This is a desert place. 27 And he rose
and went. And [n]there was an [o]Ethiopian, a
eunuch, a court official of Candace, queen
of the Ethiopians, [p]who was in charge of all
her treasure. [q]He had come to Jerusalem to
worship 28 and was returning, seated in his
chariot, and he was reading the prophet
Isaiah. 29 And the Spirit said to Philip, "Go
over and join this chariot." 30 So Philip ran
to him and heard him reading Isaiah the
prophet and asked, "Do you understand
what you are reading?" 31 And he said,
[r]"How can I, unless someone [s]guides me?"
And [t]he invited Philip to come up and sit
with him. 32 Now the passage of the
Scripture that he was reading was this:

[u]"Like a sheep he was led to the
slaughter
and like a lamb before its shearer
is silent,
so he opens not his mouth.
33 In his [v]humiliation justice was
denied him.
Who can describe his generation?
For his life is taken away from
the earth."

34 And the eunuch said to Philip, "About
whom, I ask you, does the prophet say this,
about himself or about someone else?"

9 [n]See ch. 5:36
10 [o]ch. 14:11; 28:6 [p][ch. 19:27, 28]
11 [q]ver. 9; [ver. 13; Gal. 3:1]
12 [r]ch. 16:33, 34; 18:8; Mark 16:16 [s]ch. 1:3
13 [t]ver. 6, 7 [u]ch. 19:11 [v][ver. 9]
14 [w]ver. 1 [x]ch. 1:8
15 [y]ch. 2:38
16 [z][ch. 19:2] [a]ch. 10:44; 11:15 [b]ch. 19:5; [ch. 2:38; 10:47, 48; Matt. 28:19; 1 Cor. 1:13, 15; Gal. 3:27]
17 [c]ch. 9:17; 19:6; [ch. 6:6; Heb. 6:2] [d]See ch. 2:4
20 [e][2 Kin. 5:16; Dan. 5:17] [f]Isai. 55:1
21 [g]2 Kin. 10:15; Ps. 78:37
22 [h]Dan. 4:27; 2 Tim. 2:25
23 [i]Deut. 29:18; 32:32; Heb. 12:15 [j]Isai. 58:6; [Eph. 4:3; Col. 3:14]
24 [k][Ex. 8:8; 9:28; 10:17]
25 [l][ver. 6-8; John 4:38]
26 [m]ch. 5:19; 10:3; 11:13; 12:7, 23; 27:23; [Judg. 6:12; 13:3]
27 [n][Jer. 38:7] [o]Ps. 68:31; 87:4; Zeph. 3:10 [p]Ezra 7:21 [q][1 Kin. 8:41, 42; John 12:20]
31 [r]See Rom. 10:14 [s]John 16:13 [t][1 Kin. 20:33; 2 Kin. 10:15]
32 [u]Cited from Isai. 53:7, 8
33 [v][Phil. 2:8]

1 Greek *works of power* 2 That is, a bitter fluid secreted by the liver; bile 3 Or *go at about noon*

God. Justin Martyr (died c. A.D. 165), himself a Samaritan, says that almost all the Samaritans considered Simon the highest god (the "power of God," v. 10). Irenaeus (died c. A.D. 180), who wrote extensively against the Gnostics, regards Simon as one of the sources of their heresies. Although the Simon of v. 9 could be another Simon, the church fathers equate the two, and the context of 8:9–11 (his character and the Samaritans' attitude about him) certainly points to the two as the same person.

8:15 receive the Holy Spirit. The believing Samaritans to this point had not received evidence of the dynamic inward presence of the Holy Spirit, although as believers the Holy Spirit was living in them (Rom. 8:9). We are not told what evidence the Holy Spirit gave.

8:22, 23 By his words and actions Simon proved that he did not believe in Christ. He was still poisoned by "bitterness" (cf. Deut. 29:18; Heb. 12:15) and "in the bond of iniquity" (see Rom. 6:16; 8:8). A profession of faith without repentance is invalid.

8:27 eunuch. This word refers to either an emasculated official in the royal court or to a high official of government. The biblical Ethiopia (or Cush) is the remote area south of Egypt, including parts of modern Eritrea, Ethiopia, and Sudan.

Candace. The title of the queen mother who ruled in the place of her son. He was thought to be too sacred to be involved in secular affairs.

8:28 reading the prophet Isaiah. If the Ethiopian had been reading the passage about the Lord's mercy to eunuchs (Is. 56:3–5; cf. Deut. 23:1), it would have been natural for him also to read Is. 53 (v. 35 note).

8:30 heard him. In ancient times people normally read out loud.

35 Then Philip opened his mouth, and [w]be-
ginning with this Scripture [x]he told him
the good news about Jesus. 36 And as they
were going along the road they came to
some water, and the eunuch said, "See,
here is water! [y]What prevents me from
being baptized?"[1] 38 And he commanded
the chariot to stop, and they both went
down into the water, Philip and the
eunuch, and he baptized him. 39 And when
they came up out of the water, [z]the Spirit
of the Lord [a]carried Philip away, and the
eunuch saw him no more, and went on his
way rejoicing. 40 But Philip found himself at
Azotus, and as he passed through he
preached the gospel to all the towns until
he came to Caesarea.

The Conversion of Saul

9 But Saul, [b]still [c]breathing threats and
murder against the disciples of the
Lord, went to [d]the high priest 2 and asked
him for letters [e]to the synagogues at
Damascus, so that if he found any belonging to [f]the Way, men or women, he might
bring them bound to Jerusalem. 3 [g]Now as
he went on his way, he approached
Damascus, and suddenly a light from heav-
en flashed around him. 4 And falling to the
ground he heard a voice saying to him,
"Saul, Saul, why are you persecuting [h]me?"
5 And he said, "Who are you, Lord?" And
he said, "I am Jesus, [h]whom you are persecuting. 6 But [i]rise and enter the city, and
you will be told [j]what you are to do." 7 [k]The
men who were traveling with him stood
speechless, [l]hearing the voice but seeing no
one. 8 Saul rose from the ground, and
although his eyes were opened, [m]he saw
nothing. So they led him by the hand and
brought him into Damascus. 9 And for
three days he was without sight, and neither ate nor drank.

10 Now there was a disciple at Damascus
named [n]Ananias. The Lord said to him in a
vision, "Ananias." And he said, [o]"Here I
am, Lord." 11 And the Lord said to him,
"Rise and go to the street called Straight,
and at the house of Judas look for a man
[p]of Tarsus named Saul, for behold, he is
praying, 12 and he has seen in a vision a
man named Ananias come in and [q]lay his
hands on him so that he might regain his
sight." 13 But Ananias answered, "Lord, I
have heard from many about this man,
[r]how much evil he has done to [s]your
[t]saints at Jerusalem. 14 And here he has
authority from [u]the chief priests to bind all
who [v]call on your name." 15 But the Lord
said to him, "Go, for [w]he is a chosen instrument of mine to carry my name [x]before the
Gentiles and [y]kings and the children of
Israel. 16 For [z]I will show him how much
[a]he must suffer [b]for the sake of my name."
17 So [c]Ananias departed and entered the
house. And [d]laying his hands on him he
said, "Brother Saul, the Lord Jesus who
appeared to you on the road by which you

35 [w]Luke 24:27; [ch. 17:2; 18:28] [x]See ch. 5:42 **36** [y]ch. 10:47 **39** [z]1 Kin. 18:12; 2 Kin. 2:16; Ezek. 3:12, 14; 8:3; 11:1, 24; 43:5 [a]See 2 Cor. 12:2
Chapter 9
1 [b]ver. 13, 21; See ch. 8:3 [c][Ps. 27:12] [d]ch. 22:5; 26:10 **2** [e]ch. 22:19; [Luke 12:11; 21:12] [f]ch. 19:9, 23; 24:14, 22; [ch. 16:17; 18:25, 26; 22:4; Isai. 30:21; 35:8; Amos 8:14] **3** [g]For ver. 3-8, see ch. 22:6-11; 26:12-18; [1 Cor. 15:8] **4** [h][Isai. 63:9; Zech. 2:8] **5** [h][See ver. 4 above] **6** [i][Ezek. 3:22; Gal. 1:1] [j]ver. 16; [1 Cor. 9:16] **7** [k][Dan. 10:7] [l][ch. 22:9, with John 12:29]
8 [m][ch. 22:11] **10** [n]ch. 22:12 [o]Gen. 22:1; Isai. 6:8 **11** [p]ch. 21:39; 22:3 **12** [q]ver. 17; See Mark 5:23 **13** [r]ver. 1, 2 [s]1 Thess. 3:13; 2 Thess. 1:10 [t]Rom. 15:25, 26, 31
14 [u]ver. 21 [v]ch. 22:16; Rom. 10:13; 1 Cor. 1:2; [ch. 7:59; 2 Tim. 2:22] **15** [w][ch. 13:2; Rom. 1:1; Gal. 1:15; Eph. 3:7] [x]Rom. 1:5 (Gk.); 11:13; 15:16; Gal. 1:16; 2:2, 7-9; Eph. 3:7, 8; 1 Tim. 2:7; 2 Tim. 4:17 [y]ch. 25:22, 23; 26:1, 32; 2 Tim. 4:16 **16** [z]ch. 20:23; 21:4, 11; 1 Thess. 3:3 [a]ver. 6; [ch. 14:22; 2 Cor. 6:4, 5; 11:23-28] [b]See ch. 5:41 **17** [c]ch. 22:12-14 [d]ver. 12

[1] Some manuscripts add all or most of verse 37: *And Philip said, "If you believe with all your heart, you may." And he replied, "I believe that Jesus Christ is the Son of God."*

8:35 told him the good news about Jesus. Philip began from Is. 53, and identified the servant in the passage as the Suffering Servant, Jesus. Luke implies that he went on to other Old Testament passages to identify Jesus as the Messiah.

8:40 Azotus. Ancient Old Testament Ashdod (1 Sam. 5:1), one of the five Philistine cities, about twenty miles north of Gaza and sixty miles south of Caesarea on the coast. Philip preached the gospel in all the towns along the coast until he reached Caesarea, a large city Herod the Great had rebuilt (near Strato's Tower). It had an excellent harbor that Herod expanded for important sea traffic (21:8), and it served as headquarters for the Roman procurators such as Pilate, Felix (23:33–24:4), and Festus (25:6). Philip must have settled in Caesarea because years later he still resided there (21:8).

9:1 Saul. Saul was introduced in 7:58 and he is the main character in 9:1–31. A third brief glimpse of Saul is seen again in 11:25–30 before Saul, soon to be called Paul, becomes the main character in chs. 13–28.

still breathing threats. Even though he had helped to eliminate Stephen, Saul continued to persecute the Christian heresy.

9:2 the Way. Other names used in Acts for the early Christians are: "Christians" (used only in 11:26; 26:28; 1 Pet. 4:16), "disciples" (vv. 10, 19), "saints" (v. 13), "all who call on your name" (v. 14), and "brothers" (v. 30). "The Way" identifies the Christian cause as composed of followers of Jesus, who is "the way" (John 14:6). It is used a number of times in Acts (19:9, 23; 22:4; 24:14, 22).

9:3 a light from heaven. A supernatural light brighter than the sun (26:13) caught his attention.

9:4 Saul, Saul. The repetition signifies intimate personal address (cf. Gen. 22:11; 46:2; Ex. 3:4; 1 Sam. 3:10; Luke 10:41; 22:31).

persecuting me. To persecute Jesus' disciples was to persecute Jesus (Matt. 5:10–12; John 15:19, 20).

9:7 The men . . . hearing the voice. In 22:9 Paul says that "they did not understand the voice"; the Greek word can mean "sound" or "voice." Saul's companions heard a sound but could not understand what was being said.

9:15 chosen instrument . . . before the Gentiles and kings and the children of Israel. Paul considered himself to be an apostle to the Gentiles (Rom. 1:13, 14) as Peter was to the Jews (Gal. 2:8), but Paul also preached many times to the Jews, particularly in their synagogues (v. 20; Rom. 1:16; 1 Cor. 9:20).

9:17 Jesus who appeared to you. Saul had not had a dream or seen a

came has sent me so that you may regain
your sight and [e]be filled with the Holy
Spirit." 18 And immediately something like
scales fell from his eyes, and [f]he regained
his sight. Then [g]he rose and was baptized;
19 and [h]taking food, he was strengthened.

Saul Proclaims Jesus in Synagogues

For [i]some days he was with the disciples
at Damascus. 20 And immediately he proclaimed Jesus in the synagogues, saying,
[j]"He is the Son of God." 21 And all who
heard him were amazed and said, "Is not
this the man who [k]made havoc [l]in Jerusalem of those who called upon this name?
And has he not come here for this purpose,
to bring them bound before the chief
priests?" 22 But Saul [m]increased all the more
in strength, and [n]confounded the Jews who
lived in Damascus by proving [o]that Jesus
was the Christ.

Saul Escapes from Damascus

23 [p]When many days had passed, the
Jews plotted to kill him, 24 but their [q]plot
became known to Saul. [r]They were watching the gates day and night in order to kill
him, 25 but his disciples took him by night
and [s]let him down through an opening in
the wall,[1] lowering him in a basket.

Saul in Jerusalem

26 And [t]when he had come to Jerusalem,
he attempted to join the disciples. And
they were all afraid of him, for they did not
believe that he was a disciple. 27 But
[u]Barnabas took him and [v]brought him to
the apostles and declared to them [w]how on
the road he had seen the Lord, who spoke
to him, and [x]how at Damascus he had
[y]preached boldly in the name of Jesus. 28 So
he went [z]in and out among them at
Jerusalem, preaching boldly in the name of
the Lord. 29 And he spoke and disputed
against [a]the Hellenists.[2] But [b]they were
seeking to kill him. 30 And when [c]the brothers learned this, they brought him down to
Caesarea and sent him off [d]to Tarsus.
31 So [e]the church throughout all Judea
and Galilee and Samaria had peace and
was being built up. And [f]walking in the fear
of the Lord and in the comfort of the Holy
Spirit, [g]it multiplied.

The Healing of Aeneas

32 Now [h]as Peter went here and there
among them all, he came down also to the
saints who lived at Lydda. 33 There he
found a man named Aeneas, bedridden for
eight years, who was paralyzed. 34 And
Peter said to him, "Aeneas, [i]Jesus Christ
heals you; rise and make your bed." And
immediately he rose. 35 [j]And all the residents of Lydda and [k]Sharon saw him, and
[l]they turned to the Lord.

Dorcas Restored to Life

36 Now there was in [m]Joppa a disciple
named Tabitha, which, translated, means
Dorcas.[3] She was full of [n]good works and
acts of charity. 37 In those days she became
ill and died, and when they had washed
her, they laid her in [o]an upper room.
38 Since Lydda was near Joppa, the disciples, hearing that Peter was there, sent two
men to him, urging him, [p]"Please come to
us without delay." 39 So Peter rose and went
with them. And when he arrived, they took
him to [q]the upper room. All the widows
stood beside him weeping and showing
tunics[4] and other garments that Dorcas
made while she was with them. 40 But Peter
[r]put them all outside, and [s]knelt down and
prayed; and turning to the body [t]he said,
"Tabitha, arise." And she opened her eyes,
and when she saw Peter she sat up. 41 And
he gave her his hand and raised her up.
Then calling the saints and widows, he presented her alive. 42 And it became known

17 [e]See ch. 2:4
18 [f]ch. 22:13 [g]ch. 22:16
19 [h][ver. 9] [i]ch. 26:20
20 [j][ver. 22]
21 [k]ver. 13, 14 [l]Gal. 1:13, 23
22 [m]See 1 Tim. 1:12 [n]ch. 18:28 [o][ver. 20]
23 [p][Gal. 1:17, 18]
24 [q]ch. 20:3, 19; 23:30; [ch. 23:12; 25:3] [r]2 Cor. 11:32
25 [s]2 Cor. 11:33; [Josh. 2:15; 1 Sam. 19:12]
26 [t]ch. 22:17-20; 26:20
27 [u]ch. 4:36 [v][Gal. 1:18, 19] [w]ver. 3-6 [x]ver. 19, 20, 22 [y]See ch. 4:29
28 [z]ch. 1:21
29 [a]See ch. 6:1 [b][ch. 22:18]
30 [c]See John 21:23 [d][ch. 11:25; Gal. 1:21]
31 [e][ch. 8:1; 16:5] [f][Neh. 5:9] [g]ver. 35, 42
32 [h][ch. 8:25]
34 [i][ch. 3:6]
35 [j][ver. 31, 42] [k]1 Chr. 5:16; 27:29; S. of S. 2:1 [l]ch. 11:21; 2 Cor. 3:16
36 [m]See Josh. 19:46 [n]1 Tim. 2:10
37 [o]ver. 39; ch. 1:13; 20:8
38 [p]Num. 22:16 (Heb.; Gk.)
39 [q]ver. 37
40 [r]Matt. 9:25 [s]See ch. 7:60 [t][Mark 5:41; John 11:43]

[1] Greek *through the wall* [2] That is, Greek-speaking Jews [3] The Aramaic name *Tabitha* and the Greek name *Dorcas* both mean *gazelle* [4] Greek *chiton*, a long garment worn under the cloak next to the skin

vision, but had seen the Lord (cf. Is. 6:1, 5).

be filled with the Holy Spirit. Cf. 2:38. Nothing is said about any supernatural gifts, but emphasis is placed on his powerful preaching about Jesus as the Son of God (v. 20).

9:18 something like scales. Luke frequently calls attention to physical afflictions (13:11; 28:3–8). See Introduction: Author.

9:26 when he had come to Jerusalem. According to Gal. 1:18, 19, Paul saw only Peter and James the Lord's brother at Jerusalem. The others may have been afraid to meet with him or were preaching the gospel in other areas.

9:35 Sharon. The news concerning the healing of the paralytic had dramatic effects; it traveled to the Plain of Sharon, which extends north of Joppa up the coast forty to fifty miles.

9:36 Joppa. An ancient seaport (modern Jaffa, south of Tel Aviv), about thirty-eight miles northwest of Jerusalem, the port from which Jonah sailed (Jon. 1:3).

Tabitha. See text note on *Dorcas*.

9:37 washed her. Probably before the anointing with spices (cf. John 19:40). In Jerusalem, Jesus' body had been buried on the day of death, but outside the city a longer period was allowed (up to three days).

throughout all Joppa, and [u]many believed
in the Lord. 43 And he stayed in Joppa for
many days [v]with one Simon, a tanner.

Peter and Cornelius

10 At Caesarea there was a man
named Cornelius, a centurion of
[w]what was known as the Italian Cohort, 2 a
devout man [x]who feared God with all his
household, gave alms generously to the
people, and prayed continually to God.
3 [y]About the ninth hour of the day[1] [z]he saw
clearly in a vision [a]an angel of God come in
and say to him, "Cornelius." 4 And he
stared at him in terror and said, "What is
it, Lord?" And he said to him, "Your
prayers and your alms [b]have ascended [c]as a
memorial before God. 5 And now send men
to Joppa and bring one Simon who is called
Peter. 6 He is lodging [d]with one Simon, a
tanner, whose house is by the seaside."
7 When the angel who spoke to him had
departed, he called two of his servants and
a devout soldier from among those who
attended him, 8 and having related everything to them, he sent them to Joppa.

Peter's Vision

9 The next day, as they were on their journey and approaching the city, [e]Peter went
up [f]on the housetop about [g]the sixth hour[2]
to pray. 10 And he became hungry and
wanted something to eat, but while they
were preparing it, he fell into [h]a trance
11 and saw [i]the heavens opened and something like a great sheet descending, being
let down by its four corners upon the earth.
12 In it were all kinds of animals and reptiles
and birds of the air. 13 And there came a
voice to him: "Rise, Peter; kill and eat."
14 But Peter said, "By no means, Lord; [j]for I
have never eaten anything that is [k]common
or [l]unclean." 15 And the voice came to him
again a second time, [m]"What God has
made clean, do not call common." 16 This
happened three times, and the thing was
taken up at once to heaven.
17 Now while Peter was inwardly perplexed as to what [n]the vision that he had
seen might mean, behold, [o]the men who
were sent by Cornelius, having made
inquiry for Simon's house, stood at the
gate 18 and called out to ask whether Simon
who was called Peter was lodging there.
19 And while Peter was pondering [n]the
vision, [p]the Spirit said to him, "Behold,
three men are looking for you. 20 Rise and
go down and [q]accompany them without
hesitation, for I have sent them." 21 And
Peter went down to the men and said, "I
am the one you are looking for. What is the
reason for your coming?" 22 And they said,
"Cornelius, a centurion, an upright and
[r]God-fearing man, who is well spoken of by
the whole Jewish nation, was directed by [s]a
holy angel to send for you to come to his
house and [t]to hear what you have to say."
23 So he invited them in to be his guests.
The next day he rose and went away with
them, and [u]some of [v]the brothers from
Joppa accompanied him. 24 And on the following day they entered Caesarea. Cornelius was expecting them and had called
together his relatives and close friends.
25 When Peter entered, Cornelius met him
and [w]fell down at his feet and [x]worshiped
him. 26 But Peter lifted him up, saying,
[y]"Stand up; I too am a man." 27 And as he
talked with him, he went in and found

42 [u][John 11:45; 12:11] 43 [v]ch. 10:6
Chapter 10
1 [w]Matt. 27:27; Mark 15:16; John 18:3, 12
2 [x]ver. 22; ch. 13:16, 26
3 [y]ver. 17, 19 [z]See ch. 3:1 [a]See ch. 8:26
4 [b]Rev. 8:4; [Ps. 141:2; Dan. 10:12] [c]Matt. 26:13; Mark 14:9; [ver. 31; Heb. 6:10]
6 [d]ch. 9:43
9 [e]For ver. 9-32, see ch. 11:5-14 [f][2 Kin. 23:12; Jer. 19:13; 32:29; Zeph. 1:5]; See 1 Sam. 9:25 [g]Ps. 55:17
10 [h]ch. 22:17
11 [i]See John 1:51
14 [j]Ezek. 4:14; Dan. 1:8 [k]ver. 28 [l]Lev. 11:2-47; 20:25; Deut. 14:4-20
15 [m]Rom. 14:2, 14, 20; 1 Tim. 4:4; Tit. 1:15; [Matt. 15:11; Mark 7:15, 19; 1 Cor. 10:25]
17 [n]ver. 3 [o]ver. 7, 8
19 [n][See ver. 17 above] [p]See ch. 8:29
20 [q][ch. 15:7-9]
22 [r]See ver. 2 [s]See Mark 8:38 [t]ch. 11:14
23 [u]ver. 45; [ch. 11:12] [v]See John 21:23
25 [w]ch. 16:29; Dan. 2:46 [x]See Matt. 8:2
26 [y]Rev. 19:10; 22:8, 9; [ch. 14:15]

[1] That is, 3 P.M. [2] That is, noon

9:43 Simon, a tanner. Jews believed tanning to be an unclean profession because it involved contact with dead animals (Lev. 5:2). Peter was willing to stay with a tanner because the message of the gospel was beginning to break down barriers between people. This also anticipates Peter's vision in 10:9–23.

10:1 Caesarea. Caesarea Maritima (Caesarea by the Sea) was a seaport on the Mediterranean sixty-five miles northwest of Jerusalem. It was rebuilt and improved on an ambitious scale by Herod the Great.

10:2 feared God. A term that may indicate that Cornelius was partly converted to Judaism, a Gentile who worshiped God but who was not circumcised (13:16, 26).

10:9 on the housetop . . . to pray. Peter probably prayed three times a day (cf. 3:1; Dan. 6:10); this was his midday prayer. Houses typically had flat roofs reached by an outside stairway.

10:10 a trance. Peter's consciousness was withdrawn from external things in preparation for the vision (cf. 22:17).

10:12 all kinds of animals. Both clean and unclean animals (Lev. 11).

10:13 kill and eat. Peter was unwilling to violate the Old Testament laws that prohibited eating unclean animals (v. 14).

10:15 God has made clean. Through this vivid illustration, God told Peter that He had abrogated the laws of ritual cleanliness; see Mark 7:14–19.

10:16 three times. The vision was repeated to impress Peter.

10:24 the following day. It took the group two days to travel thirty miles from Joppa to Caesarea.

10:25 Peter entered. Peter was now willing to enter the house of a Gentile (v. 28).

fell down at his feet and worshiped him. Cornelius was overawed at Peter's presence; he had been instructed by God to send for the apostle.

many persons gathered. 28 And he said to
them, “You yourselves know how unlawful
it is for a Jew [z]to associate with or to visit
anyone of another nation, but [a]God has
shown me that I should not call any person
common or unclean. 29 So when I was sent
for, I came without objection. I ask then
why you sent for me.”
30 And Cornelius said, [b]“Four days ago,
about this hour, I was praying in my house
at [c]the ninth hour,[1] and behold, [d]a man
stood before me in bright clothing 31 and
said, ‘Cornelius, [e]your prayer has been
heard and your alms have been remembered before God. 32 Send therefore to
Joppa and ask for Simon who is called
Peter. He is lodging in the house of Simon,
a tanner, by the sea.’ 33 So I sent for you at
once, and you have been kind enough to
come. Now therefore we are all here in the
presence of God to hear all that you have
been commanded by the Lord.”

Gentiles Hear the Good News

34 So Peter opened his mouth and said:
“Truly I understand that [f]God [g]shows no
partiality, 35 but [f]in every nation anyone
who fears him and [h]does what is right is
acceptable to him. 36 As for [i]the word that
he sent to Israel, [j]preaching good news of
[k]peace through Jesus Christ ([l]he is Lord of
all), 37 you yourselves know what happened
throughout all Judea, [m]beginning [n]from
Galilee after the baptism that John proclaimed: 38 how [o]God anointed Jesus of
Nazareth [p]with the Holy Spirit and with
[q]power. He went about doing good and
healing all [r]who were oppressed by the
devil, [s]for God was with him. 39 And [t]we are
witnesses of all that he did both in the
country of the Jews and in Jerusalem.
[u]They put him to death by hanging him on
a tree, 40 but [v]God raised him on [w]the third
day and made him to [x]appear, 41 [y]not to all
the people but to us who had been chosen
by God as [z]witnesses, who ate and drank
with him after he rose from the dead.
42 And [a]he commanded us to preach to the
people and to testify [b]that he is the one
appointed by God to be judge [c]of the living
and the dead. 43 [d]To him [e]all the prophets
bear witness that [f]everyone who believes in
him receives [g]forgiveness of sins [h]through
his name.”

The Holy Spirit Falls on the Gentiles

44 While Peter was still saying these
things, [i]the Holy Spirit fell on all who
heard the word. 45 And the believers from
among [j]the circumcised who had come
with Peter were amazed, because [k]the gift
of the Holy Spirit [l]was poured out even on
the Gentiles. 46 For they were hearing them
[m]speaking in tongues and extolling God.
Then Peter declared, 47 [n]“Can anyone withhold water for baptizing these people, who
have received the Holy Spirit [o]just as we
have?” 48 And he [p]commanded them [q]to be
baptized in the name of Jesus Christ. Then
they asked him to remain for some days.

Peter Reports to the Church

11 Now the apostles and [r]the brothers[2] who were throughout Judea
heard that the Gentiles also had received
the word of God. 2 So when Peter went up
to Jerusalem, [s]the circumcision party criticized him, saying, 3 [t]“You went to uncircumcised men and [u]ate with them.” 4 But
Peter began and explained it to them in
order: 5 [v]“I was in the city of Joppa praying,
and in a trance I saw a vision, something
like a great sheet descending, being let

28 [z][ch. 11:3; John 4:9; 18:28; Gal. 2:12] [a][ver. 35]; See ver. 14, 15
30 [b]ver. 9, 23, 24 [c]See ch. 3:1 [d][ch. 1:10]
31 [e]See ver. 4
34 [f][ver. 28; ch. 15:19; Deut. 1:17; Rom. 3:29]; See Deut. 10:17 [g]Prov. 24:23; James 2:1, 9; [Jude 16]
35 [f][See ver. 34 above] [h]Isai. 64:5
36 [i]ch. 13:26; Ps. 107:20; 147:18, 19 [j]Isai. 52:7; Nah. 1:15; Eph. 2:17 [k]See Luke 2:14 [l]Rom. 10:12; [Rev. 17:14; 19:16]; See ch. 2:36; Matt. 28:18
37 [m]Luke 24:47 [n]Matt. 4:12; Mark 1:14
38 [o][Matt. 3:16; John 1:32, 33]; See ch. 4:26 [p][ch. 1:2; 2:22; Matt. 12:28; Luke 4:18; Rom. 1:4] [q][Luke 6:19] [r]See Matt. 4:24; Luke 13:16 [s]See John 8:29; 10:38
39 [t]ver. 41; See ch. 2:32; Luke 24:48 [u]ch. 5:30
40 [v]See ch. 2:24 [w]See Luke 9:22 [x]ch. 1:3
41 [y][John 14:21, 22]
[z]ver. 39
42 [a]See ch. 1:2 [b]ch. 17:31; 24:25; John 5:22, 27; 2 Cor. 5:10; See Matt. 16:27

[c]2 Tim. 4:1; 1 Pet. 4:5; [Rom. 14:9, 10; 1 Thess. 4:15, 17] 43 [d]ch. 26:22; Rom. 3:21; [Jer. 31:34] [e]ch. 3:18, 24; Luke 24:27 [f]ch. 2:38; 4:12; John 20:31; 1 John 2:12 [g]ch. 11:17; 13:39; 15:9; Rom. 9:33; 10:11; Gal. 3:22 [h]ch. 5:31
44 [i]11:15; 15:8; 1 Thess. 1:5; See ch. 2:4 45 [j]ver. 23; [ch. 11:2] [k]See ch. 2:17 [l]See ch. 2:38 46 [m]See Mark 16:17 47 [n]ch. 8:36 [o]ch. 2:4; 11:17; 15:8
48 [p][1 Cor. 1:14-17] [q]ch. 2:38; See ch. 8:12, 16
Chapter 11 1 [r]ver. 29; See John 21:23 2 [s]ch. 10:45; Gal. 2:12; Col. 4:11; Tit. 1:10; [Rom. 4:12] 3 [t]Gal. 2:12, 14; [ch. 10:28] [u][Luke 15:2] 5 [v]For ver. 5-14, see ch. 10:9-32

1 That is, 3 P.M. 2 Or *brothers and sisters*

10:28 God has shown me. He refers to the vision he had seen (v. 15).

10:34 God shows no partiality. The gospel is for both Jews and Gentiles (1:8; Rom. 1:16).

10:36 preaching good news of peace through Jesus Christ. The peace of reconciliation with God through the blood of Jesus, our peace (Eph. 2:13, 14).

Lord of all. Jesus is Lord of both Jews and Gentiles.

10:44 the Holy Spirit fell on all. They were anointed by the Spirit's power and were praising God and speaking in tongues (v. 46).

10:45 the circumcised . . . were amazed. It was difficult for strict Jews who had not seen Peter's vision to realize that God did not show favoritism in His offer.

10:48 in the name of Jesus Christ. Forgiveness of sins is through the name of Jesus (v. 43).

11:2 the circumcision party. Other Jewish believers criticized Peter for accepting Gentiles.

11:3 ate with them. Eating with non-Jews was a clear violation of the ceremonial law because Gentiles did not follow the Old Testament dietary laws (Lev. 11) or ceremonial washings (Mark 7:5).

down from heaven by its four corners, and it came down to me. 6 Looking at it closely, I observed animals and beasts of prey and reptiles and birds of the air. 7 And I heard a voice saying to me, 'Rise, Peter; kill and eat.' 8 But I said, 'By no means, Lord; for nothing common or unclean has ever entered my mouth.' 9 But the voice answered a second time from heaven, 'What God has made clean, do not call common.' 10 This happened three times, and all was drawn up again into heaven. 11 And behold, at that very moment three men arrived at the house in which we were, sent to me from Caesarea. 12 And the Spirit told me to go with them, [w]making no distinction. [x]These six brothers also accompanied me, and we entered the man's house. 13 And he told us how he had seen the angel stand in his house and say, 'Send to Joppa and bring Simon who is called Peter; 14 [y]he will declare to you a message by which [z]you will be saved, you and all your household.' 15 As I began to speak, [a]the Holy Spirit fell on them [b]just as on us at the beginning. 16 And I remembered the word of the Lord, how he said, [c]'John baptized with water, but you will be baptized with the Holy Spirit.' 17 If then [d]God gave [e]the same gift to them as he gave to us [f]when we believed in the Lord Jesus Christ, [g]who was I [h]that I could stand in God's way?" 18 When they heard these things they fell silent. And they [i]glorified God, saying, [j]"Then to the Gentiles also God has [k]granted [l]repentance that leads to life."

The Church in Antioch

19 [m]Now those who were scattered because of the persecution that arose over Stephen traveled as far as Phoenicia and Cyprus and Antioch, speaking the word to no one except Jews. 20 But there were some of them, men of Cyprus and Cyrene, who on coming to Antioch spoke to the Hellenists[1] also, [n]preaching the Lord Jesus. 21 And [o]the hand of the Lord was with them, and a great number who believed [p]turned to the Lord. 22 The report of this came to the ears of the church in Jerusalem, and they sent Barnabas to Antioch. 23 When he came and saw [q]the grace of God, he was glad, and he exhorted them all to remain faithful to the Lord [r]with steadfast purpose, 24 for he was a good man, [s]full of the Holy Spirit and of faith. And a great many people [t]were added to the Lord. 25 So Barnabas went to [u]Tarsus to look for Saul, 26 and when he had found him, he brought him to Antioch. For a whole year they met with the church and taught a great many people. And in Antioch the disciples were first called [v]Christians.

27 Now in these days [w]prophets came down from Jerusalem to Antioch. 28 And one of them named [x]Agabus stood up and foretold [y]by the Spirit that there would be a great [z]famine over all the world (this took place in the days of [a]Claudius). 29 So the disciples determined, everyone according to his ability, [b]to send relief to [c]the brothers[2] living in Judea. 30 [d]And they did so, sending it to [e]the elders by the hand of Barnabas and Saul.

James Killed and Peter Imprisoned

12 About that time Herod the king laid violent hands on some who belonged to the church. 2 He killed [f]James the brother of John [g]with the sword, 3 and when he saw [h]that it pleased the Jews, he proceeded to arrest Peter also. This was

12 [w]ch. 15:9 [x]ch. 10:23, 45 **14** [y]ch. 10:22 [z]ch. 10:2; 16:15, 31-34; 18:8; John 4:53 **15** [a]ch. 10:44 [b]ch. 2:4 **16** [c]ch. 1:5; [ch. 19:2]; See Matt. 3:11 **17** [d]See ch. 10:47 [e]See ch. 2:38 [f]Eph. 1:13; See ch. 10:43 [g][Rom. 9:20] [h]ch. 10:47; See ch. 5:39 **18** [i]ch. 21:20 [j][ch. 13:47; Matt. 8:11]; See ch. 10:34, 35 [k]See ch. 5:31 [l][2 Cor. 7:10] **19** [m]ch. 8:1, 4 **20** [n]See John 7:35; See ch. 5:42 **21** [o]ch. 13:11; Luke 1:66; [Ps. 80:17; 89:21] [p]ch. 9:35 **23** [q]ch. 13:43; 14:26; 20:24, 32; Rom. 5:15; 2 Cor. 6:1; Eph. 3:2, 7; Col. 1:6; Tit. 2:11; Heb. 12:15; 1 Pet. 5:12; [ch. 4:33; 15:40] [r]2 Tim. 3:10 **24** [s]ch. 6:5 [t]ch. 5:14; [ver. 26] **25** [u]ch. 9:30 **26** [v]ch. 26:28; 1 Pet. 4:16 **27** [w]See ch. 13:1 **28** [x]ch. 21:10 [y]See ch. 2:18; 8:29 [z]Matt. 24:7 [a]ch. 18:2 **29** [b][ch. 24:17; Rom. 15:26] [c]ver. 1

30 [d]ch. 12:25 [e]ch. 14:23; 15:2, 4, 6; 16:4; 20:17; 21:18; 1 Tim. 5:17, 19; Tit. 1:5; James 5:14; 2 John 1; 3 John 1
Chapter 12 **2** [f]Matt. 4:21; 20:23 [g]Heb. 11:37 **3** [h][ch. 24:27; 25:9]

[1] Or *Greeks* (that is, Greek-speaking non-Jews) [2] Or *brothers and sisters*

11:14 you and all your household. God's saving grace is often extended to whole families, as consistently appears in the Old Testament (e.g., Abraham, Isaac, and Jacob and their families) and the New (2:38, 39; 16:31; Luke 19:9).

11:17 the Lord Jesus Christ. This full title of Jesus is first used here.

I could stand in God's way. It was God's will to save both Jews and Gentiles; no doubt some of those present were reminded of God's promise to Abraham: "in you all the families of the earth shall be blessed" (Gen. 12:3; cf. Gal. 3:8).

11:18 repentance that leads to life. Biblical repentance means sorrow for sin and a change of heart that turns from sin toward God (20:21). The fruits of repentance are the good works to which God calls us (26:20; Luke 3:8; Eph. 2:10).

11:21 hand of the Lord. The men preached, but people were saved as God called them to believe in Him (1 Cor. 3:6).

11:26 called Christians. The word "Christian" occurs three times in the New Testament: here, 26:28, and 1 Pet. 4:16. It means a person belonging to or following Christ. The name may have originated in the church, or it may at first have been a derogatory term used by outsiders.

11:28 all the world. Widespread, not local.

12:3 it pleased the Jews . . . arrest Peter also. God's sovereign purpose was carried out in the lives of His equally dedicated servants: at this time James died by the sword, while Peter was delivered from prison.

during [i]the days of Unleavened Bread.
4 And when he had seized him, he put him
[j]in prison, delivering him over to four
[k]squads of soldiers to guard him, intending
after the Passover to bring him out to the
people. 5 So Peter was kept in prison, but
earnest prayer for him was made to God
[l]by the church.

Peter Is Rescued

6 Now when Herod was about to bring
him out, on that very night, Peter was
sleeping between two soldiers, [m]bound
with two chains, and sentries before the
door were guarding the prison. 7 And
behold, [n]an angel of the Lord [o]stood next
to him, and a light shone in the cell. [p]He
struck Peter on the side and woke him, saying, "Get up quickly." And [q]the chains fell
off his hands. 8 And the angel said to him,
"Dress yourself and [r]put on your sandals."
And he did so. And he said to him, "Wrap
your cloak around you and follow me."
9 And he went out and followed him. He
did not know that what was being done by
the angel was real, but [s]thought he was seeing a vision. 10 When they had passed the
first and the second guard, they came to
the iron gate leading into the city. [t]It
opened for them of its own accord, and
they went out and went along one street,
and immediately the angel left him.
11 When Peter [u]came to himself, he said,
"Now I am sure that [v]the Lord has sent his
angel and [w]rescued me from the hand of
Herod and from all that the Jewish people
were expecting."
12 When he realized this, he went to the
house of Mary, the mother of [x]John whose
other name was Mark, where many were
gathered together and [y]were praying. 13 And
when he knocked at the door of the gateway, [z]a servant girl named Rhoda came to
answer. 14 Recognizing Peter's voice, [a]in her
joy she did not open the gate but ran in
and reported that Peter was standing at the
gate. 15 They said to her, "You are out of
your mind." But she kept insisting that it
was so, and they kept saying, "It is [b]his
angel!" 16 But Peter continued knocking,
and when they opened, they saw him and
were amazed. 17 But [c]motioning to them
with his hand to be silent, he described to
them how the Lord had brought him out of
the prison. And he said, "Tell these things
to [d]James and to [e]the brothers."[1] Then he
departed and went to another place.
18 Now when day came, there was no little disturbance among the soldiers over
what had become of Peter. 19 And after
Herod searched for him and did not find
him, he examined the sentries and [f]ordered
that they should be put to death. Then he
went down from Judea to Caesarea and
spent time there.

The Death of Herod

20 Now Herod was angry with the people
of Tyre and Sidon, and they came to him
with one accord, and [g]having persuaded
Blastus, the king's chamberlain, they asked
for peace, because [h]their country depended
on the king's country for food. 21 On an
appointed day Herod put on his royal
robes, took his seat upon the throne, and
delivered an oration to them. 22 And the
people were shouting, "The voice of a god,
and not of a man!" 23 Immediately [i]an angel
of the Lord struck him down, because [j]he
did not give God the glory, and he was
eaten by worms and breathed his last.
24 But [k]the word of God increased and
multiplied.
25 [l]And Barnabas and Saul returned from[2]
Jerusalem when they had completed their

3 [i]ch. 20:6; Ex. 12:14, 15; 23:15
4 [j]See Luke 21:12 [k][John 19:23]
5 [l]2 Cor. 1:11; Eph. 6:18
6 [m]ch. 21:33
7 [n]See ch. 8:26 [o]Luke 2:9; 24:4 [p][1 Kin. 19:7] [q]ch. 16:26
8 [r]Mark 6:9
9 [s]Ps. 126:1
10 [t]ch. 5:19; 16:26
11 [u][Luke 15:17] [v]Ps. 34:7; 91:11; Dan. 3:28; 6:22 [w]Ps. 33:18, 19; 2 Cor. 1:10
12 [x]ver. 25; ch. 13:5, 13; 15:37, 39; Col. 4:10; 2 Tim. 4:11; Philem. 24; 1 Pet. 5:13 [y]ver. 5
13 [z]John 18:16, 17
14 [a]Luke 24:41; [Gen. 45:26]
15 [b]Matt. 18:10; See Heb. 1:14
17 [c]ch. 13:16; 19:33; 21:40 [d]ch. 15:13; 21:18; [Gal. 1:19; 2:9, 12] [e]See John 21:23
19 [f][ch. 16:27; 27:42]
20 [g]Matt. 28:14 (Gk.) [h][1 Kin. 5:9; Ezra 3:7; Ezek. 27:17]
23 [i][2 Sam. 24:16; 2 Kin. 19:35]; See ch. 8:26 [j]Ps. 115:1
24 [k]See ch. 6:7
25 [l]ch. 11:29, 30

[1] Or *brothers and sisters* [2] Some manuscripts *to*

during the days of Unleavened Bread. With so many zealous Jews visiting the city at the feast, it was an opportune time to make the arrest.

12:7 an angel of the Lord . . . a light shone. An angel was an assurance of God's presence, and the light would probably remind Peter of the Old Testament glory of the Lord (9:3; Ex. 3:2; 13:22; 40:34).

12:10 iron gate leading into the city. The Antonian Fortress had an entrance into the temple courts on the south as well as other entrances to the city.

12:15, 16 The disciples prayed fervently to God (cf. 4:23, 24) to protect and deliver Peter, but then failed to believe that the Lord had done what they requested.

12:15 his angel. They thought it was his personal angelic guardian (Matt. 18:10; Heb. 1:14). The popular conception was that such a guardian could assume the appearance of the human person protected.

12:19 put to death. According to Roman law, if a prisoner escaped, the guard was liable to be punished as the prisoner would have been (cf. 16:27, 28).

12:23 did not give God the glory. In his pride, he accepted for himself the praise that belongs to God.

eaten by worms. The Jewish historian Josephus (*Antiquities* 19.346–350) records that Herod Agrippa I experienced heart pains together with pain in his abdomen and died after five days. Herod died in A.D. 44, the fourth year of Claudius Caesar.

12:25 Barnabas and Saul . . . had completed their service. This was

service, bringing with them [m]John, whose
other name was Mark.

Barnabas and Saul Sent Off

13 Now there were in the church at
Antioch [n]prophets and [n]teachers,
[o]Barnabas, Simeon who was called Niger,[1]
Lucius of Cyrene, Manaen a member of the
court of [p]Herod the tetrarch, and Saul.
2 While they were worshiping the Lord and
fasting, [q]the Holy Spirit said, [r]"Set apart for
me Barnabas and Saul [s]for the work to
which I have called them." 3 Then after fasting and [t]praying they laid their hands on
them and [u]sent them off.

Barnabas and Saul on Cyprus

4 So, being sent out [v]by the Holy Spirit,
they went down to Seleucia, and from there
they sailed to Cyprus. 5 When they arrived
at Salamis, they proclaimed the word of
God [w]in the synagogues of the Jews. And
they had [x]John to [y]assist them. 6 When they
had gone through the whole island as far as
Paphos, they came upon a certain [z]magi-
cian, [a]a Jewish false prophet named Bar-
Jesus. 7 He was with [b]the proconsul, Sergius
Paulus, a man of intelligence, who summoned Barnabas and Saul and sought to
hear the word of God. 8 But Elymas the
magician (for that is the meaning of his
name) [c]opposed them, seeking to turn [d]the
proconsul away from the faith. 9 But Saul,
who was also called Paul, [e]filled with the
Holy Spirit, looked intently at him 10 and
said, "You [f]son of the devil, you enemy of
all righteousness, full of all deceit and [g]vil-
lainy, will you not stop [h]making crooked
[i]the straight paths of the Lord? 11 And now,
behold, [j]the hand of the Lord is upon you,
and you will be blind and unable to see the
sun for a time." Immediately mist and
darkness fell upon him, and he went about
seeking [k]people to lead him by the hand.
12 Then the proconsul believed, when he
saw what had occurred, for he was astonished at [l]the teaching of the Lord.

Paul and Barnabas in Antioch of Pisidia

13 Now Paul and his companions set sail
from Paphos and came to Perga in Pamphylia. And [m]John left them and returned
[n]to Jerusalem, 14 but they went on from
Perga and came to Antioch in Pisidia. And
[o]on the Sabbath day [p]they went into the
synagogue and sat down. 15 After [q]the reading from [r]the Law and the Prophets, [s]the
rulers of the synagogue sent a message to
them, saying, "Brothers, if you have any
[t]word of exhortation for the people, say it."
16 So Paul stood up, and [u]motioning with
his hand said:

25 [m]See ver. 12
Chapter 13
1 [n]ch. 11:27; 15:32; 19:6; 21:9, 10; Rom. 12:6, 7; See 1 Cor. 12:28, 29 [o]ch. 11:22-26 [p]See Luke 3:1
2 [q][ch. 20:28]; See ch. 8:29 [r]Rom. 1:1; Gal. 1:15 [s]See ch. 9:15
3 [t]See ch. 6:6 [u]ch. 14:26
4 [v]ver. 2; [ch. 16:6, 7]
5 [w]ver. 14; ch. 9:20; 14:1; 17:1, 2, 10, 17; 18:4, 19; 19:8; [ver. 46]; See Mark 6:2 [x]See ch.12:12 [y][ch. 19:22]
6 [z]ch. 8:9, 11 [a]See Matt. 7:15
7 [b]ver. 8, 12; ch. 18:12; 19:38
8 [c][Ex. 7:11; 2 Tim. 3:8] [d]ver. 7, 12
9 [e]ch. 4:8
10 [f][ch. 18:14] [g]See Matt. 13:38 [h]Mic. 3:9 [i]Hos. 14:9; 2 Pet. 2:15; [ch. 18:25, 26]
11 [j]ch. 11:21; Ex. 9:3; 1 Sam. 5:6, 7, 11; Ps. 32:4; [Heb. 10:31; 1 Pet. 5:6] [k][ch. 9:8; 22:11] **12** [l][ver. 49; ch. 15:35] **13** [m]ver. 5 [n]ch. 12:12 **14** [o]See ver. 5 [p]ver. 42, 44; ch. 16:13; 17:2; 18:4 **15** [q]ch. 15:21 [r]See Luke 16:16 [s]See Mark 5:22 [t]Heb. 13:22 **16** [u]See ch. 12:17

[1] *Niger* is a Latin word meaning *black*, or *dark*

the mission of bringing the Antioch famine relief gift to Jerusalem (11:27–30).

John . . . Mark. Possibly the young man who fled the night of Jesus' arrest (Mark 14:51, 52). Mark, the writer of the second Gospel (cf. 1 Pet. 5:13), accompanied Paul and Barnabas down to Antioch and went with them on the first missionary journey (13:4) as far as Perga in Pamphylia (13:13).

13:1 Barnabas. See note 4:36.

Simeon . . . called Niger. His second name means "black" in Latin and he may have come from Africa. He may be the same as Simon of Cyrene (Luke 23:26) whose sons, Alexander and Rufus, were among the Christians at Rome (Mark 15:21; cf. Rom. 16:13).

Lucius of Cyrene. Cyrene was the capital of the Roman province of Cyrenaica (in modern Libya).

13:3 laid their hands on them. They officially placed their hands on Barnabas and Saul in recognition of what the Holy Spirit had already done (v. 2) and what He was going to do in sending them out (v. 4; cf. 14:23; 1 Tim. 4:14).

13:4 Seleucia. The port of Antioch, sixteen miles west of Antioch.

Cyprus. An island in the Eastern Mediterranean, inhabited largely by Greeks but also by many Jews.

13:5 arrived at Salamis. They sailed directly west about 130 miles from Seleucia to the east coast of Cyprus. Salamis was the most important city on the island; the provincial capital was Paphos, ninety miles southwest.

13:6 a certain magician. The Greek *magos* means "wise man" (Matt. 2:1), "sorcerer," "magician." Sorcery was forbidden in Judaism, but was not unknown. Bar-Jesus ("son of Joshua") was indeed a false prophet.

13:7 Sergius Paulus. Possibly Lucius Sergius Paulus, who had been an official in the reign of Claudius and then became proconsul (the chief officer in a senatorial province) at Paphos in Cyprus (cf. 18:12; 2 Cor. 9:2). By contrast, Palestine was an imperial province and had a procurator responsible directly to the emperor.

13:8 Elymas. Another name for Bar-Jesus. This man was in the proconsul's court; he tried to keep Paulus from believing the Christian message.

13:9 Saul . . . called Paul. "Saul" was his Jewish name and "Paul" his Roman name, probably going back to his life in Tarsus. Luke uses the occasion of the conversion of a prominent Gentile official, Sergius Paulus, to introduce the familiar name of the apostle to the Gentiles.

13:13 came to Perga in Pamphylia. The city of Perga was in Pamphylia, an economically poor Roman province on the south coast of Asia Minor (modern Turkey). Perga was five miles inland. It was at this time that John Mark left Paul and Barnabas and returned home.

13:14 Antioch in Pisidia. This Antioch was about a hundred miles north of Perga and 3,600 feet above sea level. It was in Phrygia but near Pisidia, and to distinguish it from another Antioch in Phrygia it was popularly called "Antioch in Pisidia."

13:15 reading from the Law and the Prophets. A worship service in the synagogue would include the creed (Deut. 6:4), the prayer of "Eighteen Blessings," a reading from the Law and another from the Prophets, an exposition and application (Luke 4:16–30), and a concluding benediction.

"Men of Israel and [v]you who fear God,
listen. 17 [w]The God of this people Israel
[x]chose our fathers and [y]made the people
great [z]during their stay in the land of
Egypt, and [a]with uplifted arm he led them
out of it. 18 And for about [b]forty years [c]he
put up with[1] them in the wilderness. 19 And
[d]after destroying [e]seven nations in the land
of Canaan, [f]he gave them their land as an
inheritance. 20 All this took about 450
years. And after that [g]he gave them judges
until [h]Samuel the prophet. 21 Then [i]they
asked for a king, and God gave them Saul
[j]the son of Kish, a man of the tribe of
Benjamin, for forty years. 22 And [k]when he
had removed him, [l]he raised up David to
be their king, of whom he testified and
said, [m]'I have found in David the son of
Jesse [n]a man after my heart, [o]who will do
all my will.' 23 [p]Of this man's offspring God
has brought to Israel [q]a Savior, Jesus, [r]as he
promised. 24 Before his coming, [s]John had
proclaimed [t]a baptism of repentance to all
the people of Israel. 25 And as John was finishing his course, [u]he said, 'What do you
suppose that I am? I am not he. No, but
behold, after me one is coming, the sandals
of whose feet I am not worthy to untie.'
26 "Brothers, sons of the family of Abraham, and those among you [v]who fear God,
to us has been sent [w]the message of [x]this
salvation. 27 For those who live in
Jerusalem and their rulers, because [y]they
did not recognize him nor understand [z]the
utterances of the prophets, which are read
every Sabbath, [a]fulfilled them by condemning him. 28 And [b]though they found
in him no guilt worthy of death, [c]they
asked Pilate to have him executed. 29 And
when [d]they had carried out all that was
written of him, [e]they took him down from
[f]the tree and laid him in a tomb. 30 But
[g]God raised him from the dead, 31 and for
many days [h]he appeared to those [i]who had
come up with him [j]from Galilee to
Jerusalem, [k]who are now [l]his witnesses to
the people. 32 And we bring you the good
news [m]that what God promised to the
fathers, 33 [n]this he has fulfilled to us their
children by raising Jesus, as also it is written in the second Psalm,

16 [v]ver. 26; ch. 10:2, 22 **17** [w]See Matt. 15:31 [x]Deut. 7:6-8 [y]Num. 24:7 [z]ch. 7:17; Ex. 1:1, 7, 12; Ps. 105:23, 24 [a]Ex. 6:6; 13:14, 16 **18** [b]See ch. 7:36 [c][Deut. 9:5-24] **19** [d]See ch. 7:45 [e]Deut. 7:1 [f]Josh. 14:1, 2; 19:51; Ps. 78:55; 136:21, 22 **20** [g]Judg. 2:16; 3:9 [h]See ch. 3:24 **21** [i]1 Sam. 8:5; 1 Sam. 10:1 [j]1 Sam. 9:1, 2 **22** [k]1 Sam. 15:23, 26, 28; 16:1; [Hos. 13:11] [l]1 Sam. 16:13; 2 Sam. 2:4; 5:3 [m]Cited from Ps. 89:20 [n]ch. 7:46; Cited from 1 Sam. 13:14 [o]ver. 36 **23** [p]See Matt. 1:1 [q]Ps. 132:11; [ver. 32, 33] [r]See Luke 2:11 **24** [s]ch. 1:22; Matt. 3:1 [t]ch. 19:4; Mark 1:4; Luke 3:3; [ch. 2:38; Matt. 3:11] **25** [u]John 1:20, 27; [Matt. 3:11; Mark 1:7; Luke 3:16] **26** [v]ver. 16 [w]ch. 10:36; [Eph. 1:13] [x][ch. 5:20]; See ch. 4:12 **27** [y][2 Cor. 3:14, 15]; See ch. 3:17 [z]ver. 15; [ch. 15:21] [a]See Luke 24:20, 26, 27, 44 **28** [b][Mark 14:55; Luke 23:22] [c]ch. 2:23; 3:14, 15; Luke 23:23 **29** [d]Luke 18:31; 24:44; John 19:28, 30, 36, 37 [e]Matt. 27:59, 60; Mark 15:46; Luke 23:53; John 19:38, 41, 42 [f]See ch. 5:30 **30** [g]See ch. 2:24 **31** [h]See ch. 1:3 [i]Mark 15:41 [j]ch. 1:11; 2:7 [k]See Luke 24:48 [l]See ch. 1:8 **32** [m]ch. 26:6; Rom. 4:13; 15:8; Gal. 3:16; [Rom. 9:4] **33** [n][ver. 23; Luke 1:69-73]

1 Some manuscripts *he carried* (compare Deuteronomy 1:31)

13:20 about 450 years. About four hundred years plus the forty years in the wilderness and the period of Joshua's conquest (7:6 note).

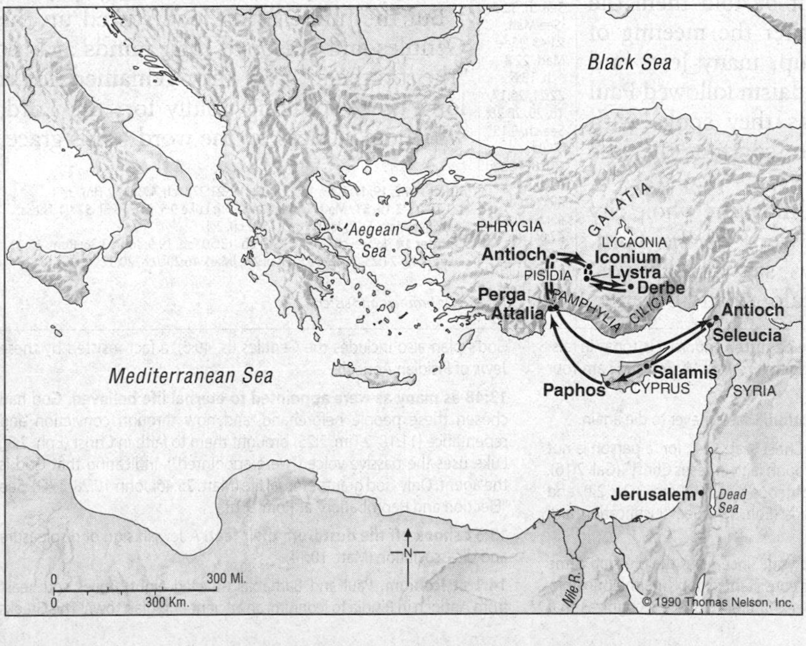

Paul Goes to Galatia (The First Missionary Journey). Sent out from the church at Antioch (Acts 13:1-3), Paul and Barnabas went to the cities of Galatia in Asia Minor. The Jewish synagogues in these cities provided Paul a platform for preaching the gospel. At times, however, he even encountered opposition from the synagogues.

[o]"'You are my Son,
today I have begotten you.'
34 And as for the fact that he raised him
from the dead, [p,q]no more to return to corruption, he has spoken in this way,

"'I will give you [r]the holy and sure
blessings of David.'

35 Therefore he says also in another psalm,

[s]"'You will not let your Holy One see
corruption.'

36 For David, after he had [t]served the purpose of God in his own generation, [u]fell
asleep and [v]was laid with his fathers and
saw corruption, 37 but he whom [w]God
raised up did not see corruption. 38 Let it be
known to you therefore, brothers, [x]that
through this man [y]forgiveness of sins is
proclaimed to you, and by him [z]everyone
who believes is freed from everything
39 [a]from which you could not be freed by
the law of Moses. 40 Beware, therefore, lest
what is said in the Prophets should come
about:

41 [b]"'Look, you scoffers,
be astounded and perish;
for I am doing a work in your days,
a work that you will not believe,
even if one tells it to you.'"

42 As they went out, the people begged
that these things might be told them the
next Sabbath. 43 And after the meeting of
the synagogue broke up, many Jews and
[c]devout [d]converts to Judaism followed Paul
and Barnabas, who, as they spoke with
them, urged them [e]to continue in [f]the
grace of God.

44 The next Sabbath almost the whole city
gathered to hear the word of the Lord.
45 [g]But [h]when the Jews saw the crowds,
they were filled with [i]jealousy and began to
contradict what was spoken by Paul, [j]revil-
ing him. 46 And Paul and Barnabas spoke
out boldly, saying, "It was necessary that
the word of God [k]be spoken first to you.
[l]Since you thrust it aside and judge yourselves [m]unworthy of eternal life, behold, we
[n]are turning to the Gentiles. 47 [o]For so the
Lord has commanded us, saying,

[p]"'I have made you [q]a light for the
Gentiles,
that you may [r]bring salvation to
the ends of the earth.'"

48 And when the Gentiles heard this, they
began rejoicing and [s]glorifying the word of
the Lord, and as many as were appointed
to eternal life believed. 49 And the word
of the Lord was spreading throughout the
whole region. 50 [t]But the Jews incited
the devout [u]women of high standing and
the leading men of the city, [v]stirred up persecution against Paul and Barnabas, and
[w]drove them out of their district. 51 But they
[x]shook off the dust from their feet against
them and went to Iconium. 52 And the disciples were filled [y]with joy and [z]with the
Holy Spirit.

Paul and Barnabas at Iconium

14 Now at Iconium [a]they entered
together into the Jewish synagogue
and spoke in such a way that a great number of both Jews and Greeks believed.
2 [b]But the [c]unbelieving Jews stirred up the
Gentiles and poisoned their minds against
[d]the brothers.[1] 3 So they remained for a
long time, speaking boldly for [e]the Lord,
who bore witness to [f]the word of his grace,

33 [o]Heb. 1:5; 5:5; Cited from Ps. 2:7 **34** [p]Rom. 6:9; [Heb. 9:25-28] [q]ver. 35-37 [r]Cited from Isai. 55:3 **35** [s]ch. 2:27; Cited from Ps. 16:10 **36** [t]ver. 22; ch. 20:27 [u]2 Sam. 7:12; 1 Kin. 2:10; [ch. 2:29] [v]Judg. 2:10 **37** [w]ver. 30 **38** [x]Luke 24:47; 1 John 2:12 [y]ch. 5:31 [z]Rom. 3:28; See ch. 10:43 **39** [a]Rom. 2:13; 3:20; 8:3; Gal. 2:16; 3:11; Eph. 2:9; 2 Tim. 1:9; Tit. 3:5; [Heb. 7:19] **41** [b]Cited from Hab. 1:5; [Isai. 29:14] **43** [c]ver. 50; ch. 17:4, 17; [ch. 16:14] [d]ch. 2:10; 6:5; Matt. 23:15 [e][Jude 21] [f]Jude 4; See ch. 11:23 **45** [g][ch. 19:9] [h][1 Thess. 2:16] [i]See ch. 5:17

[j]ch. 18:6; 26:11; 1 Tim. 1:20 **46** [k]ver. 5, 14; See ch. 3:26 [l]See Matt. 21:43 [m]See Matt. 22:8 [n]ch. 18:6; 22:21; 26:17, 18, 20; 28:28; See ch. 9:15 **47** [o][ch. 11:18] [p]Cited from Isai. 49:6; [Isai. 45:22] [q]Isai. 42:6; Luke 2:32 [r][ver. 26; ch. 1:8] **48** [s][2 Thess. 1:12]

50 [t][ch. 14:2, 19; 17:5, 13; 18:12; 20:3, 19; 21:27] [u]ch. 17:12 [v]2 Tim. 3:11 [w]1 Thess. 2:15 **51** [x]Matt. 10:14; Mark 6:11; Luke 9:5; [ch. 18:6] **52** [y][1 Thess. 1:6]; See Matt. 5:12; John 16:22 [z]See ch. 2:4
Chapter 14 **1** [a]See ch. 13:5 **2** [b]See ch. 13:50 [c]ch. 19:9; John 3:36; Rom. 15:31 [d]See John 21:23 **3** [e]ch. 15:8; Heb. 2:4; [Mark 16:20] [f]ch. 20:32

1 Or *brothers and sisters*

13:33 You are my Son, today I have begotten you. That is, today in raising You from the dead, I am declaring that You are My Son and I am Your Father (Heb. 1:5 note).

13:34 no more to return to corruption. That is, never to die again.

13:39 The law points the sinner to Christ (Gal. 3:24), for "a person is not justified by works of the law but through faith in Jesus Christ" (Gal. 2:16). To be justified is to be declared righteous by God (Rom. 3:21, 22), and therefore granted forgiveness of sins (Eph. 1:7). See "Justification and Merit" at Gal. 3:11.

13:46 the word of God . . . first to you. Since Jesus the Messiah came through the Jews (Gen. 12:3), Paul is consistent in applying the principle, "to the Jew first and also to the Greek" (Rom. 1:16). He recognizes that God's plan also includes the Gentiles (Is. 49:6), a fact resisted by these Jews of Pisidian Antioch.

13:48 as many as were appointed to eternal life believed. God had chosen these people beforehand, and now through conviction and repentance (11:18; 2 Tim. 2:25) brought them to faith in Christ (Eph. 2:8). Luke uses the passive voice ("were appointed"), indicating that God is the agent. Only God grants eternal life (Matt. 25:46; John 10:28; 17:2). See "Election and Reprobation" at Rom. 9:18.

13:51 shook off the dust from their feet. A Jewish sign of displeasure and disassociation (Matt. 10:14).

14:1 at Iconium. Paul and Barnabas traveled eighty miles southeast from Antioch in Pisidia to Iconium, an ancient Phrygian town. The Greeks

[g]granting signs and wonders to be done by
their hands. **4**But the people of the city
[h]were divided; [i]some sided with the Jews
and some with the apostles. **5**When an
attempt was made by both Gentiles and
Jews, with their rulers, [j]to mistreat them
and [k]to stone them, **6**they learned of it and
[l]fled to [m]Lystra and Derbe, cities of
Lycaonia, and to the surrounding country,
7and there they continued to preach the
gospel.

Paul and Barnabas at Lystra

8Now at Lystra there was a man sitting
who could not use his feet. He was [n]crip-
pled from birth and had never walked. **9**He
listened to Paul speaking. And Paul, looking intently at him and [o]seeing that he had
faith to be made well,[1] **10**said in a loud
voice, "Stand upright on your feet." And he
[p]sprang up and began walking. **11**And
when the crowds saw what Paul had done,
they lifted up their voices, saying in
Lycaonian, [q]"The gods have come down to
us in the likeness of men!" **12**Barnabas they
called [r]Zeus, and Paul, Hermes, because he
was the chief speaker. **13**And the priest of
[r]Zeus, whose temple was at the entrance to
the city, brought oxen and garlands to the
gates and [s]wanted to offer sacrifice with the
crowds. **14**But when the apostles Barnabas
and Paul heard of it, they [t]tore their garments and rushed out into the crowd, crying out, **15**"Men, [u]why are you doing these
things? We also are men, [v]of like nature
with you, and we bring you good news,
that [w]you should turn from these [x]vain
things to [y]a living God, [z]who made the
heaven and the earth and the sea and all
that is in them. **16**In past generations he
[a]allowed all the nations [b]to walk in their
own ways. **17**Yet [c]he did not leave himself
without witness, for he [d]did good by [e]giv-
ing you rains from heaven and [f]fruitful seasons, satisfying your hearts with [g]food and
[h]gladness." **18**Even with these words they
scarcely restrained the people from offering
sacrifice to them.

Paul Stoned at Lystra

19[i]But Jews came from Antioch and
Iconium, and having persuaded the
crowds, [j]they stoned Paul and dragged him
out of the city, supposing that he was dead.
20But when the disciples gathered about
him, he rose up and entered the city, and
on the next day he went on with Barnabas
to Derbe. **21**When they had preached the
gospel to that city and had [k]made many
disciples, they returned to Lystra and to
Iconium and to Antioch, **22**[l]strengthening
the souls of the disciples, encouraging
them [m]to continue in [n]the faith, and saying
that [o]through many tribulations we must
enter the kingdom of God. **23**And when
they had [p]appointed [q]elders for them in
every church, with prayer and fasting [r]they
committed them to the Lord in whom they
had believed.

Paul and Barnabas Return to Antioch in Syria

24Then they passed through Pisidia and
came to Pamphylia. **25**And when they had
spoken the word in Perga, they went down

3 [g]ch. 4:29, 30 **4** [h][ch. 23:7] [i][ch. 17:4, 5; 19:9; 28:24] **5** [j]1 Thess. 2:2; [2 Cor. 12:10] [k][ver. 19] **6** [l]See Matt. 10:23 [m]2 Tim. 3:11 **8** [n]ch. 3:2 **9** [o]See Matt. 9:2 **10** [p]ch. 3:8; Isai. 35:6 **11** [q]ch. 8:10; 28:6 **12** [r][ch. 19:35; 28:11 (Gk.)] **13** [r][See ver. 12 above] [s][Dan. 2:46] **14** [t]See Gen. 37:29 **15** [u]See ch. 10:26 [v]James 5:17 [w]ch. 15:19; 26:18, 20; Luke 1:16; 1 Thess. 1:9; [ch. 15:3; James 5:19, 20]; See ch. 9:35 [x]Deut. 32:21; 1 Sam. 12:21; Jer. 14:22; [1 Cor. 8:4] [y]See Matt. 16:16 [z]ch. 17:24; Gen. 1:1; Ex. 20:11; Ps. 146:6; Rev. 4:11; 10:6; 14:7 **16** [a][ch. 17:30; 1 Pet. 4:3] [b][Ps. 81:13; Mic. 4:5]

17 [c][ch. 17:27; Rom. 1:19, 20] [d]Num. 10:32 [e]Lev. 26:4; Deut. 11:14; 28:12; Job 5:10; Ps. 65:10; 147:8, 18; Ezek. 34:26; Joel 2:23 [f]Ps. 67:6; 85:12; Ezek. 34:27; Joel 2:24; Zech. 8:12 [g]Ps. 104:27 [h]Ps. 104:15 **19** [i]See ch. 13:45, 50 [j]2 Cor. 11:25; [ver. 5; 2 Tim. 3:11]; See ch. 7:58 **21** [k]Matt. 28:19 **22** [l]ch. 15:32, 41; [ch. 18:23; 1 Thess. 3:2, 13] [m]ch. 13:43; Col. 1:23 [n]See ch. 6:7 [o]John 15:20; 16:33; 1 Thess. 3:3; 2 Tim. 3:12; [ch. 9:16; Mark 10:30; Luke 22:28, 29; Rom. 8:17; Phil. 1:20; 2 Thess. 1:5; 2 Tim. 2:12; 1 Pet. 5:10; Rev. 1:9] **23** [p][Tit. 1:5] [q]See ch. 11:30 [r]ch. 20:32

[1] Or *be saved*

made it a city state, and under Augustus it became a city in the province of Galatia.

14:4 apostles. For the first time in Acts, the term has a broader meaning that includes men like Barnabas in addition to the apostles chosen by Jesus (1:24–26; Matt. 10:1–4; 2 Cor. 1:1 note).

14:5 stone them. Stoning was the way the Jews executed the death penalty for religious blasphemy (7:58, 59).

14:6 Lystra and Derbe. These two cities along with Iconium belonged strictly to the Roman province of Galatia, although they were part of the subdistrict called Lycaonia. From A.D. 37–72 Iconium was linguistically and politically on the Phrygian side of the border.

14:8 Lystra. In 6 B.C. Augustus fortified this settlement and made it into a Roman colony of the province of Galatia. He also settled the colony with Roman army veterans.

14:10 he sprang up and began walking. See "Miracles" at 1 Kin. 17:22.

14:12, 13 An ancient legend circulated in Lystra that the Greek gods Zeus and Hermes disguised themselves as men and came to the Phrygian hill country, seeking hospitality. Only one couple welcomed them, and in return their cottage was changed into a temple with a golden roof and marble columns. The houses of those who had refused the gods were destroyed. The Lystrans may have been thinking of this legend when they welcomed Barnabas and Paul and prepared to sacrifice oxen.

14:14 tore their garments. A conventional sign of grief or distress.

14:15–17 The content of Paul's sermon is similar to his later sermon at Athens (17:22–31). Both sermons were addressed to pagan crowds who would not understand quotations from and explanations of Old Testament Scriptures. Paul stressed that God's creative and providential power extended everywhere. See "General Revelation" at Ps. 19:1.

14:16 allowed all the nations. See "Mankind's Guilty Knowledge of God" at Rom. 1:19.

14:20 Derbe. A Lycaonian border town in southeastern Galatia, sixty-five miles southeast of Lystra.

to Attalia, 26 and from there they sailed to
Antioch, [s]where they had been [t]commend-
ed to the grace of God for the work that
they had fulfilled. 27 And when they arrived
and gathered the church together, [u]they
declared all that God had done with them,
and [v]how he had [w]opened [x]a door of faith
to the Gentiles. 28 And they remained no little time with the disciples.

The Jerusalem Council

15 [y]But some men came down from
Judea and were teaching [z]the
brothers, "Unless you are [a]circumcised
[b]according to the custom of Moses, you
cannot be saved." 2 And after Paul and
Barnabas had no small dissension and [c]de-
bate with them, Paul and Barnabas and
[d]some of the others were appointed to go
up to Jerusalem to [e]the apostles and the
elders about this question. 3 So, [f]being sent
on their way by the church, they passed
through both Phoenicia and Samaria, [g]de-
scribing in detail the conversion of the
Gentiles, and [h]brought great joy to all [i]the
brothers.[1] 4 [j]When they came to Jerusalem,
they were welcomed by the church and
[k]the apostles and the elders, and [g]they
declared all that God had done with them.
5 But some believers who belonged to [l]the
party of the Pharisees rose up and said,
[m]"It is necessary [n]to circumcise them and
to order them to keep the law of Moses."

6 [o]The [k]apostles and the elders were gathered together to consider this matter. 7 And
after there had been much [p]debate, Peter
stood up and said to them, "Brothers, you
know that in the early days God made a
choice among you, [q]that by my mouth the
Gentiles should hear [r]the word of [s]the
gospel and believe. 8 And God, [t]who knows
the heart, [u]bore witness to them, [v]by giving
them the Holy Spirit just as he did to us,
9 and [w]he made no distinction between us
and them, [x]having cleansed their hearts [y]by
faith. 10 Now, therefore, why [z]are you putting God to the test [a]by placing a yoke on
the neck of the disciples [b]that neither our
fathers nor we have been able to bear?
11 But we [c]believe that we will be [d]saved
through [e]the grace of the Lord Jesus, [w]just
as they will."

12 And all the assembly fell silent, and
they listened to Barnabas and Paul [f]as they
related what signs and wonders God had
done through them among the Gentiles.
13 After they finished speaking, [g]James
replied, "Brothers, listen to me. 14 [h]Simeon
has related how God first visited the
Gentiles, to take from them [i]a people for
his name. 15 And with this the words of the
prophets agree, just as it is written,

16 [j]"'After this I will return,
and I will rebuild the tent of David
that has fallen;
I will rebuild its ruins,
and I will restore it,
17 that the remnant[2] of mankind [k]may
seek the Lord,
and all the Gentiles [l]who are called
by my name,
says the Lord, who makes these
things 18 [m]known from of old.'

19 Therefore [n]my judgment is that we should
not trouble those of the Gentiles who [o]turn
to God, 20 but should write to them [p]to
abstain from [q]the things polluted by idols,

26 [s]ch. 13:3 [t]ch. 15:40 **27** [u]ch. 15:4; [ch. 15:3, 12; 21:19] [v][ch. 11:18] [w]1 Cor. 16:9; 2 Cor. 2:12; Col. 4:3; Rev. 3:8 [x][Hos. 2:15]
Chapter 15
1 [y]ver. 24 [z]ver. 3, 22, 23, 36, 40; See John 21:23 [a]ver. 5; Gal. 5:2; [1 Cor. 7:18; Gal. 2:11, 14] [b]ch. 6:14; Lev. 12:3 **2** [c]ver. 7 [d][Gal. 2:1, 2] [e]ver. 4, 6, 22, 23; ch. 16:4; See ch. 5:12; 11:30 **3** [f]ch. 21:5; Rom. 15:24; 1 Cor. 16:6, 11; 2 Cor. 1:16; Tit. 3:13; 3 John 6; [ch. 17:15] [g]See ch. 14:27 [h]ch. 11:18 [i]ver. 1 **4** [j][ch. 21:17] [k]ver. 2 [g][See ver. 3 above] **5** [l]See ch. 24:5 [m]ver. 1 [n]Gal. 5:3 **6** [o][ver. 12, 25] [k][See ver. 4 above] **7** [p]ver. 2 [q]ch. 10:20 [r][Eph. 1:13; Col. 1:5; 1 Thess. 1:5] [s]ch. 20:24 **8** [t]ch. 1:24 [u]ch. 14:3 [v]ch. 10:44, 47; 11:15, 17; [ver. 28; Gal. 3:2] **9** [w]ch. 11:12; Rom. 3:22-24; Eph. 3:6; [ch. 10:28, 34] [x]Ps. 51:10; [ch. 26:18; 2 Cor. 7:1; 1 Pet. 1:22] [y]See ch. 10:43

10 [z]Ps. 106:14; Isai. 7:12 [a]Gal. 5:1; [ver. 28] [b][Matt. 11:28; 23:4; Luke 11:46] **11** [c][ch. 16:31] [d]Eph. 2:5, 8; 2 Tim. 1:9; Tit. 2:11; 3:7; [Rom. 3:24; 1 Thess. 5:9] [e]Rom. 5:15 [w][See ver. 9 above] **12** [f]ver. 4; See ch. 14:27 **13** [g]See ch. 12:17 **14** [h][ver. 7] [i][ch. 18:10; Deut. 7:6; Isai. 43:21; Rom. 9:24-26] **16** [j]Cited from Amos 9:11, 12; [Jer. 12:15] **17** [k][ch. 17:27] [l]Isai. 43:7; Jer. 14:9; Dan. 9:19 **18** [m][Isai. 45:21] **19** [n][ver. 28] [o]See ch. 14:15 **20** [p]ch. 21:25 [q][ver. 29; Ezek. 4:13, 14; Dan. 1:8; Mal. 1:7, 12]

[1] Or *brothers and sisters*; also verse 22 [2] Or *rest*

15:1 The reports of Paul's and Barnabas's direct contact with the Gentiles on the first missionary journey may have reached Judea and Jerusalem through John Mark after he returned home (13:13). Also, others from Antioch may have brought the news during Paul's and Barnabas's extended stay there. This caused the Jewish Christians to fear that their Jewish heritage was threatened; they thought that the converted Gentiles must be brought into Judaism through circumcision. Paul recognized that forcing Gentiles to be circumcised might make them think that salvation must be earned (cf. Gal. 2:15, 16). He knew that the Judaizers had to be opposed lest they hinder the extension of the gospel to the Gentiles (1 Thess. 2:14–16).

15:6 apostles and the elders were gathered together. The church leaders took the lead in the discussion, but v. 12 indicates that the whole assembly was present.

15:13 James replied. James was the half brother of Jesus (Matt. 13:55; Introduction to James: Author). He seems by now to have become a prominent leader of the Jerusalem church (Gal. 2:9). James added a third testimony that Gentile believers should not be burdened with keeping the details of the Jewish ceremonial law; his speech concentrated on Old Testament Scriptures and their application to Gentile conversion.

15:19 my judgment. James finds support in the Scriptures and in the testimonies of Simon Peter, Barnabas, and Paul that God wants the Gentiles to be free from the ceremonial law and the demands of the Judaizers. He proposes that both Jews and Gentiles practice moderation. The Jewish Christians are to recognize that Gentiles are not to be bound by Jewish ceremonial law. The Gentile believers must consider the scruples of Jewish Christians and not offend them by eating food sacrificed to idols, or eating the meat of strangled animals, or blood (Lev. 17:10–14; 19:26).

and from [r]sexual immorality, and from
[s]what has been strangled, and from [s]blood.
21 For from ancient generations Moses has
had in every city those who proclaim him,
[t]for he is read every Sabbath in the synagogues."

The Council's Letter to Gentile Believers

22 Then it seemed good to [u]the apostles
and the elders, with the whole church, to
choose men from among them and send
them to Antioch with Paul and Barnabas.
They sent Judas called [v]Barsabbas, and
[w]Silas, leading men among [x]the brothers,
23 with the following letter: [x]"The brothers,
both [u]the apostles and the elders, to the
brothers[1] who are of the Gentiles in
Antioch and Syria and Cilicia, [y]greetings.
24 Since we have heard that [z]some persons
have gone out from us and [a]troubled you[2]
with words, unsettling your minds,
although we gave them no instructions, 25 it
has seemed good to us, having come [b]to
one accord, to choose men and send them
to you with our [c]beloved Barnabas and
Paul, 26 [d]men who have [e]risked their lives
for the sake of our Lord Jesus Christ. 27 We
have therefore sent [f]Judas and Silas, who
themselves will tell you the same things by
word of mouth. 28 For it has seemed good
[g]to the Holy Spirit and [h]to us [i]to lay on you
no greater burden than these requirements: 29 [j]that you abstain from [k]what has
been sacrificed to idols, and from blood,
and from what has been strangled, and
from sexual immorality. If you keep yourselves from these, you will do well.
Farewell."

30 So when they were sent off, they went
down to Antioch, and having gathered the
congregation together, they delivered the
letter. 31 And when they had read it, they
rejoiced because of its encouragement.
32 And Judas and Silas, who were themselves [l]prophets, encouraged and [m]strength-
ened [n]the brothers with many words. 33 And
after they had spent some time, they were
sent off [o]in peace by the brothers to those
who had sent them.[3] 35 But [p]Paul and Barnabas remained in Antioch, teaching and
preaching the word of the Lord, with many
others also.

Paul and Barnabas Separate

36 And after some days Paul said to
Barnabas, "Let us return and visit the
brothers [q]in every city where we proclaimed the word of the Lord, and see how
they are." 37 Now Barnabas wanted to take
with them [r]John called Mark. 38 But Paul
thought best not to take with them one
[s]who had withdrawn from them in
Pamphylia and had not gone with them to
the work. 39 And there arose [t]a sharp disagreement, so that they separated from
each other. [u]Barnabas took Mark with him
and sailed away to Cyprus, 40 but Paul
chose Silas and departed, [v]having been
commended by [w]the brothers to [x]the grace
of the Lord. 41 And he went through Syria
and Cilicia, [y]strengthening the churches.

Timothy Joins Paul and Silas

16 Paul[4] came also to Derbe and to
Lystra. A disciple was there, named
[z]Timothy, [a]the son of a Jewish woman who
was a believer, but his father was a Greek.
2 He was well spoken of by [b]the brothers[5] at
Lystra and Iconium. 3 Paul wanted Timothy
to accompany him, and he [c]took him and
circumcised him because of the Jews who
were in those places, for they all knew that
his father was a Greek. 4 As they went on

20 [r]1 Cor. 10:7, 8; Rev. 2:14, 20; See 1 Cor. 6:18 [s]See Lev. 3:17
21 [t]ch. 13:15; 2 Cor. 3:14, 15; [ch. 13:27]
22 [u]ver. 2 [v][ch. 1:23] [w]See 1 Pet. 5:12 [x]ch. 23:26; James 1:1; [2 John 10, 11]
23 [x][See ver. 22 above] [u][See ver. 22 above] [y]ver. 1
24 [z]ver. 1; [Gal. 2:4; 5:12; Tit. 1:10] [a]Gal. 1:7; 5:10
25 [b]See ch. 1:14 [c][2 Pet. 3:15]
26 [d]ch. 9:23-25; 14:19 [e][ch. 20:24; 21:13; 2 Cor. 4:11; 1 John 3:16]
27 [f]ver. 22, 32
28 [g][ver. 8; ch. 5:32; John 16:13; 1 Cor. 7:40] [h][ver. 19] [i][ver. 10; Rev. 2:24]
29 [j]See ver. 20 [k]ch. 21:25; 1 Cor. 8:1, 4, 7, 10; 10:19; Rev. 2:14, 20
32 [l]See ch. 13:1 [m]ver. 1 [n]See ch. 14:22
33 [o]Gen. 26:29; Heb. 11:31; [1 Cor. 16:11]
35 [p]ch. 13:1
36 [q]ch. 13:4, 13, 14, 51; 14:6, 24, 25
37 [r]See ch. 12:12
38 [s]ch. 13:13
39 [t][ch. 17:16 (Gk.)] [u][Col. 4:10]
40 [v]ch. 14:26 [w]ver. 1 [x]ver. 11; [ch. 11:23]; See Rom. 16:20
41 [y]ver. 32; ch. 16:5

Chapter 16 1 [z]ch. 17:14; 18:5; 19:22; 20:4; Rom. 16:21; 1 Cor. 4:17; Phil. 2:19; Col. 1:1; 1 Thess. 3:2; 2 Thess. 1:1; 1 Tim. 1:2, 18; 2 Tim. 1:2 [a]2 Tim. 1:5; 3:15
2 [b]See John 21:23 3 [c][Gal. 2:3]

[1] Or *brothers and sisters*; also verses 32, 33, 36 [2] Some manuscripts *some persons from us have troubled you* [3] Some manuscripts insert verse 34: *But it seemed good to Silas to remain there* [4] Greek *He* [5] Or *brothers and sisters*; also verse 40

15:23 The brothers. The Jewish Christians used this expression to set the Gentile Christians at ease.

15:28 to the Holy Spirit and to us. They were filled with the Spirit (2:1–41; 4:8; 6:5; 9:17; 13:4) and recognized the Spirit's role in their debate and decision.

15:32 Judas and Silas . . . prophets. Bringing encouragement and strength to believers was a primary function of the New Testament prophet (a spokesman for God).

15:39 disagreement . . . separated. The failure of Barnabas to support the Gentile Christians (Gal. 2:13) may have also contributed to the disagreement about Mark. Though the remainder of Acts contains no further record of Paul working with Barnabas, Paul mentions Barnabas in a positive light in 1 Cor. 9:6. Paul's later high regard for Mark is evident in Col. 4:10; Philem. 24; 2 Tim. 4:11.

Barnabas took Mark . . . Cyprus. Barnabas took his cousin Mark (Col. 4:10) on a missionary journey to the island of Cyprus, Barnabas's home. This would also provide an opportunity for Barnabas to encourage (4:36) the younger man.

16:1 A disciple . . . Timothy. In the small Jewish community of Lystra Paul found this young man, part Jew and part Greek. Like his father, Timothy had been reared as a Greek, and so had not been circumcised. His mother was Jewish. Paul did not think he was compromising the principles of Gentile freedom by circumcising Timothy (v. 3).

their way through the cities, they delivered
to them for observance [d]the decisions [e]that
had been reached by [f]the apostles and elders who were in Jerusalem. 5 [g]So the
churches were strengthened in [h]the faith,
and they increased in numbers [i]daily.

The Macedonian Call

6 And [j]they went through the region of
Phrygia and Galatia, having been forbidden
by the Holy Spirit to speak the word in
Asia. 7 And when they had come up to
Mysia, they attempted to go into Bithynia,
but [k]the Spirit of Jesus did not allow them.
8 So, passing by Mysia, they went down [l]to
Troas. 9 And a vision appeared to Paul in
the night: a man of Macedonia was standing there, urging him and saying, "Come
over to Macedonia and help us." 10 And
when Paul[1] had seen the vision, immediately [m]we sought to go on into Macedonia,
concluding that God had called us to
preach the gospel to them.

The Conversion of Lydia

11 So, setting sail from Troas, we [n]made a
direct voyage to Samothrace, and the following day to Neapolis, 12 and from there to
[o]Philippi, which is a leading city of the[2]
district of Macedonia and [p]a Roman
colony. We remained in this city some
days. 13 And [q]on the Sabbath day we went
outside the gate [r]to the riverside, where we
supposed there was a place of prayer, and
we [s]sat down and spoke to the women who
had come together. 14 One who heard us
was a woman named Lydia, from the city of
Thyatira, a seller of purple goods, [t]who was
a worshiper of God. The Lord [u]opened her
heart to pay attention to what was said by
Paul. 15 And after she was baptized, [v]and
her household as well, she urged us, saying, "If you have judged me to be faithful to
the Lord, come to my house and stay." And
she [w]prevailed upon us.

Paul and Silas in Prison

16 As we were going to [x]the place of
prayer, we were met by a slave girl who had
[y]a spirit of [z]divination and [a]brought her
owners much gain by fortune-telling. 17 She
followed Paul and us, [b]crying out, "These
men are [c]servants[3] of [d]the Most High God,
who proclaim to you [e]the way of salvation." 18 And this she kept doing for many
days. Paul, having become greatly annoyed,
turned and said to the spirit, [f]"I command
you [g]in the name of Jesus Christ to come
out of her." And [h]it came out that very
hour.

4 [d]ch. 17:7 [e]ch. 15:28, 29 [f]See ch. 15:2
5 [g][ch. 9:31] [h]See ch. 6:7 [i]ch. 2:47
6 [j]ch. 18:23; [Gal. 4:13]
7 [k]Rom. 8:9; Gal. 4:6; Phil. 1:19; 1 Pet. 1:11; [ver. 6; ch. 8:29]
8 [l]ch. 20:5, 6; 2 Cor. 2:12; 2 Tim. 4:13
10 [m]ver. 11-17; ch. 20:5-8, 13-15; 21:1-18; 27:1–28:16; [Col. 4:14]
11 [n]ch. 21:1
12 [o]Phil. 1:1; 1 Thess. 2:2 [p][ver. 21]
13 [q]See ch. 13:14 [r][Ezra 8:15, 21; Ps. 137:1] [s]Matt. 5:1
14 [t]ch. 18:7 [u]See Luke 24:45
15 [v]See ch. 11:14 [w]Gen. 19:3; Luke 24:29
16 [x]ver. 13 [y]Luke 13:11 [z]See Lev. 19:31 [a]ver. 19
17 [b]See James 2:19 [c]Dan. 3:26 [d]See Mark 5:7 [e][ch. 9:2; Matt. 7:14]
18 [f][Mark 1:25, 34] [g]See Mark 9:38 [h][Matt. 17:18]

[1] Greek *he* [2] Or *that* [3] Greek *bondservants*

16:6 Phrygia and Galatia. This is the southern part of the larger province of Galatia. It included the Phrygian district, Antioch of Pisidia, and the surrounding area.

Holy Spirit . . . Asia. The province of Asia, located in the western sector of Asia Minor, included the famous city of Ephesus where God wanted Paul to go at a later date (ch. 19). The Holy Spirit's identity coincides with both the Spirit of Jesus (v. 7) and God (v. 10; cf. 2 Cor. 3:17 note). These verses point to the Christian doctrine of the Trinity (cf. 2 Cor. 13:14).

16:7, 8 Mysia . . . Troas. Paul and Silas came from Derbe and Lystra northwest to Mysia, a region to the south of the Hellespont. They were unable to go north to Bithynia (toward the Black Sea), and instead went west to Troas on the Aegean coast. Troas was an established seaport; the site of ancient Troy was ten miles inland.

16:9 Macedonia. Macedonia was across the Aegean Sea from Troas. Mount Olympus is in the south of Macedonia.

16:10 we. The first of several passages using the plural pronoun "we" starts here, indicating that the author was with Paul and Silas.

16:11 Samothrace. A prominent island in the north Aegean where vessels regularly stopped. It was about halfway between Troas and Neapolis, the seaport serving Philippi.

16:12 Philippi. Philip II of Macedon, the father of Alexander the Great, had established a large Greek colony here and named it Philippi. The Romans conquered it in 167 B.C. and made it part of the province of Macedonia.

16:13 a place of prayer. According to Jewish law at least ten men were required to form a synagogue. Failing that, a place of prayer could be established outdoors, preferably near water.

women who had come together. They would meet to read and study the Scriptures, and they welcomed the assistance of any Jewish teacher who happened to visit there.

16:14 from the city of Thyatira. Southeast of Pergamum and about forty miles inland, Thyatira was in Asia Minor, across the Aegean Sea from Athens. Thyatira was known for wool and dying. Purple was an expensive dye.

The Lord opened her heart. Divine illumination and persuasion is necessary for the heart blinded by sin to respond to the gospel (Jer. 13:23; John 6:44, 65; Rom. 9:16; 1 Cor. 2:14). This effectual call of God ensures that all who have been chosen by God will believe (13:48; 2 Thess. 2:13, 14; 2 Tim. 1:9, 10).

16:15 she was baptized, and her household as well. Throughout redemptive history it has often been God's practice to save entire family units at the same time (2:38, 39; 11:14; 16:31; Gen. 17:7–14). The household baptisms of Acts are striking examples of this (10:47, 48; 16:31–33; cf. 1 Cor. 1:16). Such household baptisms were apparently standard practice.

16:16 a spirit of divination. Lit. "a python spirit." The term originally referred to a mythical serpent believed to guard the temple and oracle of the Greek god Apollo at Delphi. Later the phrase meant a demon-possessed person or even a ventriloquist. The people at Philippi must have thought of her as having a demon that could tell fortunes.

16:17 the Most High God. A Jew would understand this to be Yahweh; a Gentile would apply it to Zeus.

16:18 name of Jesus Christ to come out. Following the common understanding of the expression "the Most High God," everyone would realize that Paul meant to convey the thought that Jesus, as deity, expelled the demon.

19 But [i]when her owners saw that their hope of gain was gone, they seized Paul and Silas and [j]dragged them into the marketplace before the rulers. 20 And when they had brought them to the magistrates, they said, "These men are Jews, and they are disturbing our city. 21 They [k]advocate customs that are not lawful for us [l]as Romans to accept or practice." 22 The crowd joined in attacking them, and the magistrates tore the garments off them and gave orders [m]to beat them with rods. 23 And when they had inflicted many blows upon them, they threw them into prison, ordering the jailer to keep them safely. 24 Having received this order, he put them into the inner [n]prison and fastened their feet in [o]the stocks.

The Philippian Jailer Converted

25 [p]About midnight Paul and Silas were praying and singing hymns to God, and the prisoners were listening to them, 26 and suddenly [q]there was a great earthquake, so that the foundations of the prison were shaken. And immediately [r]all the doors were opened, and [s]everyone's bonds were unfastened. 27 When the jailer woke and saw that the prison doors were open, he drew his sword and [t]was about to kill himself, supposing that the prisoners had escaped. 28 But Paul cried with a loud voice, "Do not harm yourself, for we are all here." 29 And the jailer[1] called for lights and rushed in, and trembling with fear he [u]fell down before Paul and Silas. 30 Then he brought them out and said, "Sirs, [v]what must I do to be [w]saved?" 31 And they said, [x]"Believe in the Lord Jesus, and you will be saved, you [y]and your household." 32 And they spoke the word of the Lord to him and to all who were in his house. 33 And he took them [z]the same hour of the night and washed their wounds; and he [a]was baptized at once, he and all his family. 34 Then

19 [i]ver. 16; [ch. 19:25, 26] [j]ch. 17:6-8; 21:30; James 2:6; [ch. 8:3; 18:12; Matt. 10:18] **21** [k][Esth. 3:8] [l][ver. 12] **22** [m]2 Cor. 6:5; 11:23-25; 1 Thess. 2:2 **24** [n]See Luke 21:12 [o]Job 13:27; 33:11; Jer. 20:2, 3; 29:26 **25** [p]Job 35:10; Ps. 42:8; 77:6; 119:62 **26** [q]See ch. 4:31 [r]ch. 5:19; 12:10 [s]ch. 12:7 **27** [t][ch. 12:19; 27:42; 1 Kin. 20:39] **29** [u]ch. 10:25 **30** [v]ch. 2:37; 22:10; Luke 3:10, 12, 14; [John 6:28, 29] [w][ver. 17] **31** [x]See Mark 16:16 [y]See ch. 11:14 **33** [z]ver. 25 [a]See ch. 8:12

1 Greek *he*

16:19 seized Paul and Silas. Because both Paul and Silas were Jews and leaders of the missionary team, they were seized. Their companions were Gentiles (Luke, a Gentile from Syrian Antioch, and Timothy, a half-Gentile from Lystra) and were not charged.

16:21 advocate customs . . . not lawful for us . . . Romans. The charge was that Paul and Silas were propagating an illegal religion and disturbing the peace. The charge was inflamed by cultural and religious prejudice.

16:22 beat them. Paul and Silas were Roman citizens (v. 37) and should have been exempt from such treatment. But in the mob atmosphere this was ignored.

16:24 in the stocks. They were treated like criminals.

16:27 prison doors were open. See 5:19; 12:10.

about to kill himself. The jailer was liable to punishment if his prisoners escaped (12:19).

16:31 you and your household. For other instances of household salvation, see v. 15 note; 2:38, 39; 10:24, 48; 1 Cor. 1:16. When a person accepted a religion, the whole family was involved (v. 34). See "The Christian Family" at Eph. 5:22.

16:33 baptized. See "Baptism" at Rom. 6:3.

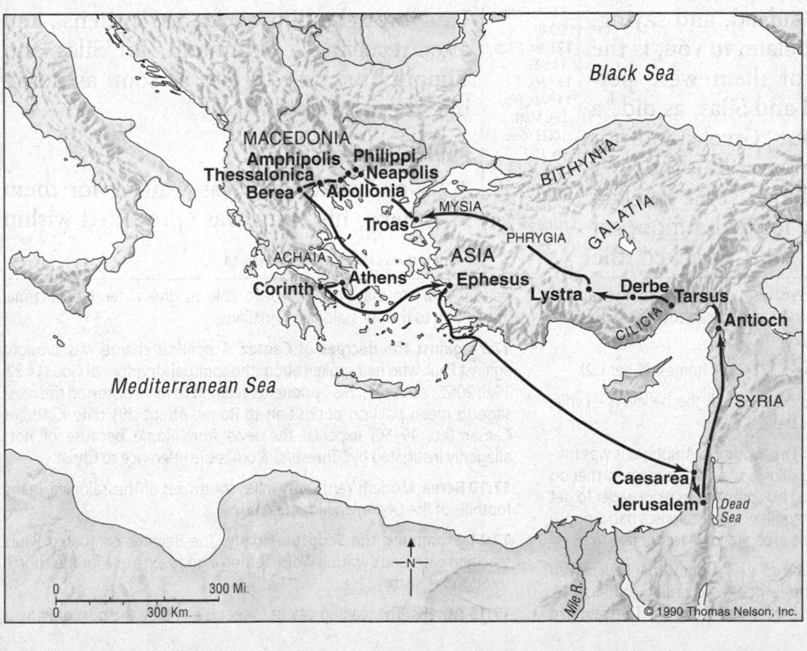

Paul Goes to Greece (The Second Missionary Journey). Starting from Jerusalem, Paul took Silas to visit again the churches of Galatia. Young Timothy joined them in Lystra. Together they went to Macedonia and Achaia, present-day Greece. On this journey the Philippian jailer was saved, the Bereans were "examining the Scriptures daily" (Acts 17:11), and Paul preached at the Areopagus.

he brought them up into his house and set
food before them. And he [b]rejoiced along
with his entire household that he had
believed in God.
35 But when it was day, the magistrates
sent the police, saying, "Let those men go."
36 And the jailer reported these words to
Paul, saying, "The magistrates have sent to
let you go. Therefore come out now and go
in peace." 37 But Paul said to them, "They
have beaten us publicly, [c]uncondemned,
men who are Roman citizens, and have
thrown us into prison; and do they now
throw us out secretly? No! Let them come
themselves and take us out." 38 The police
reported these words to the magistrates,
and [c]they were afraid when they heard that
they were Roman citizens. 39 So they came
and apologized to them. And they took
them out and [d]asked them to leave the city.
40 So they went out of the prison and visited
[e]Lydia. And when they had seen [f]the brothers, they encouraged them and departed.

Paul and Silas in Thessalonica

17 Now when they had passed
through Amphipolis and Apollonia,
they came to [g]Thessalonica, where there
was a synagogue of the Jews. 2 And Paul
went in, [h]as was his custom, and on three
Sabbath days he reasoned with them [i]from
the Scriptures, 3 [j]explaining and proving
that it was necessary for [k]the Christ to suffer and [l]to rise from the dead, and saying,
"This Jesus, whom I proclaim to you, is the
Christ." 4 And [m]some of them were persuaded and joined Paul and Silas, as did [n]a
great many of the devout [o]Greeks and not
a few of the leading women. 5 [p]But the Jews
[q]were jealous, and taking [r]some wicked
men of the rabble, they formed a mob, set
the city in an uproar, and attacked the
house of Jason, seeking to bring them out
to the crowd. 6 And when they could not
find them, [s]they dragged Jason and some of
the brothers before the city authorities,
shouting, "These men who have turned the
world upside down have come here also,
7 and Jason has received them, and they are
all acting against [t]the decrees of Caesar,
saying that there is [u]another king, Jesus."
8 And the people and the city authorities
were disturbed when they heard these
things. 9 And when they had taken money
as security from Jason and the rest, they let
them go.

Paul and Silas in Berea

10 [v]The brothers[1] immediately sent Paul
and Silas away by night to Berea, and when
they arrived they [w]went into the Jewish
synagogue. 11 Now these Jews were more
noble than those in Thessalonica; they received the word with all eagerness, [x]exam-
ining the Scriptures daily to see if these
things were so. 12 [y]Many of them therefore
believed, with not a few Greek [z]women of
high standing as well as men. 13 But when
the Jews from Thessalonica learned that
the word of God was proclaimed by Paul at
Berea also, they came there too, [a]agitating
and stirring up the crowds. 14 Then the
brothers [b]immediately sent Paul off on his
way to the sea, but Silas and [c]Timothy
remained there. 15 [d]Those who conducted
Paul brought him as far as [e]Athens, and
after receiving a command [f]for Silas and
Timothy to come to him as soon as possible, they departed.

Paul in Athens

16 Now while Paul was waiting for them
at Athens, his spirit was [g]provoked within

34 [b]Ps. 9:14; 13:5; Isai. 25:9; Luke 1:47; 1 Pet. 1:6, 8; [ch. 2:46]
37 [c]ch. 22:25, 29
38 [c][See ver. 37 above]
39 [d][Matt. 8:34]
40 [e]ver. 14 [f]See John 21:23
Chapter 17
1 [g]ch. 20:4; Phil. 4:16; 1 Thess. 1:1
2 [h]See ch. 13:5 [i]See ch. 8:35
3 [j]Luke 24:26, 32 [k]See ch. 3:18 [l]See John 20:9
4 [m][1 Thess. 2:1, 2]; See ch. 14:4 [n]See John 7:35 [o]ver. 12
5 [p]1 Thess. 2:14-16; See ch. 13:50 [q]See ch. 5:17 [r][Judg. 9:4; 11:3; 2 Chr. 13:7]
6 [s]ch. 16:19-21
7 [t]ch. 16:4; Luke 2:1 [u]See Luke 23:2
10 [v]ver. 14; See John 21:23 [w]ver. 2
11 [x][Isai. 34:16; John 5:39]
12 [y]ver. 4 [z]ch. 13:50
13 [a]ver. 8
14 [b]ver. 10; See Matt. 10:23 [c]See ch. 16:1
15 [d][ch. 15:3] [e]ch. 18:1; 1 Thess. 3:1 [f]ch. 18:5
16 [g][2 Pet. 2:8]

[1] Or *brothers and sisters*; also verse 14

16:37 Roman citizens. Roman citizens were exempted from scourging and torture. If Roman citizens were tried in a Roman court, they had the right to appeal their case to Caesar (25:11; 26:32).

16:40 Lydia. Early Christians often met in private homes (Philem. 2).

seen the brothers. "Brothers" would include all the believers—Lydia, her household, the jailer, Luke, and others.

17:1 Amphipolis and Apollonia . . . Thessalonica. Amphipolis was thirty miles southwest of Philippi and Apollonia twenty-five miles farther on the highway to Thessalonica. Paul and his companions were eager to get to Thessalonica, forty miles beyond Apollonia. Thessalonica had a population of 200,000 and was the provincial capital of Macedonia.

17:2 three Sabbath days. The Pauline epistles suggest that Paul stayed in Thessalonica much longer than three weeks. According to Phil. 4:16, the church at Philippi repeatedly sent him aid, and the Thessalonian epistles indicate that Paul had been able to give extensive doctrinal instruction to the Thessalonian Christians.

17:7 against the decrees of Caesar. A political charge was brought against Paul, who had spoken about the spiritual kingdom of God (14:22; 19:8; 20:25; 28:23, 31). His opponents seemed to have distorted the message to mean political opposition to Rome. About this time, Claudius Caesar (A.D. 49–50) expelled the Jews from Rome because of riots allegedly instigated by "Chrestus," a probable reference to Christ.

17:10 Berea. Modern Verria, fifty miles southwest of Thessalonica, in the foothills of the Olympian Mountains.

17:11 examining the Scriptures daily. The Bereans compared Paul's teaching with God's written Word, setting a good example for the church throughout history.

17:16 Athens. The leading city of Greece, served by the port of Piraeus

him as he saw that the city was [h]full of
idols. 17 So [i]he reasoned in the synagogue
with the Jews and the devout persons, and
in the marketplace every day with those
who happened to be there. 18 Some of the
Epicurean and Stoic philosophers also conversed with him. And some said, [j]"What
does this babbler wish to say?" Others said,
"He seems to be a preacher of foreign
divinities"—because [k]he was preaching
[l]Jesus and the resurrection. 19 And they
took hold of him and brought him to [m]the
Areopagus, saying, "May we know what
this [n]new teaching is that you are presenting? 20 For you bring some [o]strange things
to our ears. We wish to know therefore
what these things mean." 21 Now all the
Athenians and the foreigners who lived
there would spend their time in nothing
except telling or hearing something new.

Paul Addresses the Areopagus

22 So Paul, standing in the midst of the
Areopagus, said: "Men of Athens, I perceive that in every way you are very religious. 23 For as I passed along and observed
the objects of your worship, I found also an
altar with this inscription, [p]'To the
unknown god.' [p]What therefore you worship [q]as unknown, this I proclaim to you.
24 [r]The God who made the world and everything in it, being [s]Lord of heaven and
earth, [t]does not live in temples made by
man,[1] 25 nor is he served by human hands,
[u]as though he needed anything, since he
himself [v]gives to all mankind [w]life and
breath and everything. 26 And [x]he made
from one man every nation of mankind to
live [y]on all the face of the earth, [z]having
determined allotted periods and [a]the
boundaries of their dwelling place, 27 [b]that
they should seek God, in the hope that
[c]they might feel their way toward him and
find him. [d]Yet he is actually not far from
each one of us, 28 for

[e]"'In him we live and move and have
our being';[2]

as even some of [f]your own poets have said,

"'For we are indeed his offspring.'[3]

29 [g]Being then God's offspring, [h]we ought
not to think that the divine being is like
gold or silver or stone, an image formed by
the art and imagination of man. 30 [i]The
times of ignorance [j]God overlooked, but
[k]now he [l]commands all people everywhere
to repent, 31 because he has fixed [m]a day on
which [n]he will judge the world [o]in righteousness by a man whom he has appointed;

16 [h][Isai. 2:8] **17** [i]See ch. 13:5 **18** [j][1 Cor. 4:10] [k]See ch. 5:42 [l]ver. 31, 32; ch. 4:2; [1 Cor. 15:12] **19** [m]ver. 22; [ver. 34] [n]Mark 1:27; [John 7:16; Heb. 13:9] **20** [o]1 Pet. 4:4, 12; [Hos. 8:12] **23** [p][John 4:22; 1 Cor. 15:34] [q][ver. 30] **24** [r]Isai. 42:5; See ch. 14:15 [s]Matt. 11:25; [Deut. 10:14; Ps. 115:16] [t]See ch. 7:48 **25** [u]Ps. 50:8-12; [1 Chr. 29:14, 16; Job 22:2] [v]1 Tim. 6:17; James 1:5, 17 [w]Gen. 2:7; 7:22; Job 33:4; [Job 27:3; Eccles. 12:7; Zech. 12:1]; See ver. 28 **26** [x][Gen. 3:20; Mal. 2:10] [y]Gen. 11:8; Luke 21:35 [z][Job 12:23; 14:5] [a]Deut. 32:8; [Ps. 74:17]

27 [b][ch. 15:17] [c][Job 23:3, 8, 9] [d][Deut. 4:7; Ps. 145:18; Jer. 23:23, 24]; See ch. 14:17 **28** [e]Job 12:10; Dan. 5:23; [Heb. 2:11] [f][Tit. 1:12] **29** [g][Luke 3:38; Heb. 12:9] [h]Isai. 40:18, 19, 25; 46:5; [Rom. 1:23] **30** [i]Eph. 4:18; 1 Pet. 1:14; [ver. 23] [j][Rom. 3:25]; See ch. 14:16 [k][Mark 1:15; Tit. 2:11, 12; 1 Pet. 4:3] [l]Mark 6:12 **31** [m]Matt. 12:36; Rom. 2:16; 1 Cor. 3:13; 2 Pet. 2:9; 1 John 4:17; [Isai. 2:12] [n]2 Tim. 4:8; See ch. 10:42 [o]Ps. 9:8; 96:13; 98:9; 1 Pet. 2:23; [Rom. 3:6]

[1] Greek *made by hands* [2] Probably from Epimenides of Crete [3] From Aratus's poem "Phainomena"

on the Aegean Sea. Athens reached its zenith in the fifth century B.C. under Pericles (495–429 B.C.), when the Parthenon and other magnificent structures were built. The classical poets Aeschylus, Sophocles, Euripides, and Aristophanes flourished at this time. Although conquered by the Romans in 146 B.C., Athens continued to be a great intellectual and cultural center.

full of idols. There were statues of gods or goddesses in the Parthenon and other temples on the Acropolis, as well as in the public, commercial, and temple buildings below.

17:18 Epicurean and Stoic. Epicurus (342–270 B.C.) taught that the purpose of life was pleasure and freedom from pain, passions, and fears. On the other hand, the Cypriot Zeno (340–265 B.C.), founder of Stoicism, stressed living in harmony with nature and depending on reason and other self-sufficient powers. Both schools stressed the quest for peace of mind. Zeno viewed God pantheistically as the "world-soul."

babbler. A derogatory term meaning a scrap collector or peddler of assorted ideas.

17:19 the Areopagus. The name means "Mars' Hill." This is a hill near the Acropolis where in ancient times a council had met. The council became the city council of Athens, and in Roman times it was the court supervising morals, education, and religion. In Paul's time, the court met in the Royal Portico, in the marketplace below the Acropolis.

17:23 To the unknown god. Possibly a reference to the Altar of the Twelve Gods at Athens, erected to ensure that no god was left out of their worship. Paul used this point of contact to begin his discourse about the God who made the world, who is not carved out of stone or confined to any temple, and who controls the times and places where people live.

17:26 from one man See "The Fall" at Gen. 3:6.

17:28 In him we live and move and have our being. Paul says that God brought all people into being and they only exist by His providence. In the ancient world the three great mysteries of philosophy and science were the questions of life, motion, and being. See "General Revelation" at Ps. 19:1.

some of your own poets. Paul knew that the Athenians did not know the Old Testament, and he quoted from three of their own poets. Although their words originally referred to Zeus, the head of the Greek gods, Paul applied the quotations to the living God of heaven. The poets are Epimenides (c. 600 B.C.), Cleanthes (331–233 B.C.), and Aratus (c. 315–240 B.C.).

17:29 not . . . like gold or silver. See "The Self-Existence of God" at Ps. 90:2.

17:30 times of ignorance God overlooked. That is, God took into consideration the limitations of their knowledge about God, but now Paul has revealed the truth about the living God. With all people, they are called upon to repent of their sins.

17:31 a day on which he will judge . . . by a man whom he has appointed. The final Day of Judgment (Rev. 20:12–15). Rejection by the Athenians of the Man whom God appointed will result in Jesus finally and justly rejecting them on that Day of Judgment. Paul stresses that God's call to repentance and faith is not an invitation but a command.

and [p] of this he has given assurance to all
[q] by raising him from the dead."
32 Now when they heard of [r] the resurrection of the dead, [s] some mocked. But others
said, [t] "We will hear you again about this."
33 So Paul went out from their midst. 34 But
some men joined him and believed, among
whom also were Dionysius [u] the Areopagite
and a woman named Damaris and others
with them.

Paul in Corinth

18 After this Paul[1] left Athens and
went to Corinth. 2 And he found a
Jew named [v] Aquila, a native of Pontus,
recently come from Italy with his wife
[v] Priscilla, because [w] Claudius had commanded all the Jews to leave Rome. And he
went to see them, 3 and [x] because he was of
the same trade he stayed with them and
worked, for they were tentmakers by trade.
4 And [y] he reasoned in the synagogue [y] every
Sabbath, and tried to persuade Jews and
Greeks.
5 [z] When Silas and Timothy arrived from
Macedonia, Paul [a] was occupied with the
word, [b] testifying to the Jews that the Christ
was [c] Jesus. 6 And when they opposed and
reviled him, [d] he shook out his garments
and said to them, [e] "Your blood be on your
own heads! [f] I am innocent. [g] From now on
I will go to the Gentiles." 7 And he left there
and went to the house of a man named
Titius [h] Justus, [i] a worshiper of God. His
house was next door to the synagogue.
8 [j] Crispus, the ruler of the synagogue,
believed in the Lord, together [k] with his
entire household. And many of the
Corinthians hearing Paul believed and
were baptized. 9 And the Lord said to Paul
[l] one night in [m] a vision, [n] "Do not be afraid,
but go on speaking and do not be silent,
10 [n] for I am with you, and [o] no one will attack you to harm you, for [p] I have many in
this city who are my people." 11 And he
stayed a year and six months, teaching the
word of God among them.
12 But when Gallio was [q] proconsul of
Achaia, [r] the Jews made a united attack on
Paul and [s] brought him before the tribunal,
13 saying, "This man is persuading people
to worship God contrary to [t] the law." 14 But
when Paul was about to open his mouth,
Gallio said to the Jews, "If it were a matter
of wrongdoing or vicious [u] crime, O Jews, I
would have reason to accept your complaint. 15 But [v] since it is a matter of questions about words and names and [w] your
own law, see to it yourselves. I refuse to be
a judge of these things." 16 And he drove
them from the tribunal. 17 And they all
seized Sosthenes, the ruler of the synagogue, and beat him in front of the tribunal. But Gallio paid no attention to any of
this.

31 [p] [John 16:10, 11; Rom. 1:4] [q] See ch. 2:24 **32** [r] Heb. 6:2; See ver. 18 [s] [ch. 2:13; 26:8] [t] ch. 24:25 **34** [u] ver. 19, 22
Chapter 18
2 [v] ver. 18, 26; Rom. 16:3; 1 Cor. 16:19; 2 Tim. 4:19 [w] ch. 11:28 **3** [x] ch. 20:34; 1 Cor. 4:12; 9:15; 2 Cor. 11:7; 12:13; 1 Thess. 2:9; 2 Thess. 3:8 **4** [y] ch. 17:17; See ch. 13:5, 14 **5** [z] ch. 17:15; 1 Thess. 3:6 [a] 2 Cor. 5:14; [Job 32:18; Jer. 6:11; 20:9; Amos 3:8] [b] ch. 20:21 [c] ver. 28; ch. 2:36; 5:42; 17:3; [ch. 3:20; 8:5; 9:22] **6** [d] Neh. 5:13; [ch. 13:51] [e] Ezek. 18:13; 33:4; [2 Sam. 1:16; Matt. 27:25] [f] ch. 20:26 (Gk.); [Ezek. 3:18, 19] [g] See ch. 13:46 **7** [h] [ch. 1:23; Col. 4:11] [i] ch. 16:14 **8** [j] 1 Cor. 1:14 [k] See ch. 11:14

9 [l] ch. 23:11; 27:23 [m] [ch. 26:16; 2 Cor. 12:1-4] [n] ch. 27:24; Josh. 1:5, 6; Jer. 1:8; Matt. 28:20 **10** [n] [See ver. 9 above] [o] [Luke 21:18; 2 Thess. 3:2] [p] [John 10:16] **12** [q] See ch. 13:7 [r] See ch. 13:50 [s] See ch. 16:19 **13** [t] ver. 15 **14** [u] [ch. 13:10] **15** [v] ch. 23:29; 25:19; [1 Tim. 6:4; 2 Tim. 2:14] [w] ver. 13

[1] Greek *he*

raising him. See "The Resurrection of Jesus" at Luke 24:2.

18:1 Corinth. Since 27 B.C., this city had been the capital of the Roman province of Achaia. It was fifty miles southwest of Athens, near the isthmus that joins Attica and the Peloponnesus. Corinth was large and prosperous in the eighth to sixth centuries B.C., but it declined and was captured in 338 B.C. by Philip II of Macedon. In 196 B.C., it was taken by the Romans. They sacked it in 146 B.C. in punishment for a revolt, but it was restored by Julius Caesar as a Roman colony in 44 B.C. In New Testament times Corinth had over 200,000 inhabitants, including Greeks, freedmen from Italy, Roman army veterans, businessmen, government officials, people from the Near East, a large number of Jews, and many slaves. Corinth was thoroughly pagan and immoral. The city was filled with pagan temples and on the south there was a high acropolis with a temple of Aphrodite. From the fifth century B.C., the expression "to Corinthianize" meant to be sexually immoral.

18:2 Aquila, a native of Pontus . . . Priscilla. Pontus was on the north coast of Asia Minor (modern Turkey). Priscilla is frequently listed before her husband (vv. 18, 19, 26; Rom. 16:3; 2 Tim. 4:19). She may have had higher social status or have been more prominent in their tent-making business.

18:6 Your blood be on your own heads. They were responsible for their own sins.

18:7 house of . . . Justus. The first home of the Corinthian church. Titius Justus was a Gentile adherent to the faith at the synagogue, and a Roman citizen. He could have belonged to one of the families Julius Caesar sent to colonize Corinth. He may have been the Gaius of Rom. 16:23, who was baptized by Paul (1 Cor. 1:14); Gaius could have been a third name standing before Titius Justus.

18:8 Crispus, the ruler of the synagogue. As synagogue ruler, Crispus was in charge of the physical arrangements for the synagogue services. It is this Crispus (and presumably his household) whom Paul baptized (1 Cor. 1:14).

his entire household. See 16:15 and note; 16:31–33.

18:10 I have many in this city. Jesus promises that Paul's labors in Corinth will be fruitful because God's own people (those God has appointed to eternal life, 13:48) live in that city. Even though the elect Corinthians had not yet believed the gospel, and some had not even heard it, they nevertheless were known to God.

18:12 when Gallio was proconsul of Achaia. Luke's identification of the administrative head of this senatorial province as a proconsul is correct. An inscription found at Delphi, Greece, identifies Gallio as the proconsul in A.D. 52.

18:13 contrary to the law. That is, contrary to the Roman law forbidding the practice of religions not legally recognized by Rome. Judaism was legally recognized, and Christianity as an offshoot of Judaism was also a legal religion (*religio licita*).

Paul Returns to Antioch

18 After this, Paul stayed many days longer and then took leave of [x]the brothers[1] and set sail for Syria, and with him [y]Priscilla and Aquila. At [z]Cenchreae [z]he had cut his hair, [a]for he was under a vow. 19 And they came to [b]Ephesus, and he left them there, but [c]he himself went into the synagogue and reasoned with the Jews. 20 When they asked him to stay for a longer period, he declined. 21 But on taking leave of them he said, "I will return to you [d]if God wills," and he set sail from Ephesus.

22 When he had landed at Caesarea, he [e]went up and greeted the church, and then went down to Antioch. 23 After spending some time there, he departed and [f]went from one place to the next through the region of Galatia and Phrygia, [g]strengthening all the disciples.

Apollos Speaks Boldly in Ephesus

24 Now a Jew named [h]Apollos, a native of Alexandria, came to Ephesus. He was an eloquent man, [i]competent in the Scriptures. 25 He had been instructed in [j]the way of the Lord. And [k]being fervent in spirit,[2] he spoke and taught accurately the things concerning Jesus, though he knew only [l]the baptism of John. 26 He began to speak boldly in the synagogue, but when [m]Priscilla and Aquila heard him, they took him and explained to him [n]the way of God more accurately. 27 And when he wished to cross to [o]Achaia, [p]the brothers encouraged him and [q]wrote to the disciples to welcome him. When he arrived, [r]he greatly helped those who through grace had believed, 28 for he powerfully refuted the Jews in public, showing by the Scriptures [s]that the Christ was Jesus.

Paul in Ephesus

19 And it happened that while [t]Apollos was at Corinth, Paul passed [u]through the inland[3] country and came to Ephesus. There he found some disciples. 2 And he said to them, [v]"Did you receive the Holy Spirit when you believed?" And they said, "No, [w]we have not even heard that there is a Holy Spirit." 3 And he said, [x]"Into what then were you baptized?" They said, "Into [y]John's baptism." 4 And Paul said, [y]"John baptized with the baptism of repentance, telling the people [z]to believe in the one who was to come after him, that is, Jesus." 5 On hearing this, [a]they were baptized in[4] the name of the Lord Jesus. 6 And [b]when Paul had laid his hands on them, the Holy Spirit came on them, and [c]they began speaking in tongues and [d]prophesying. 7 There were about twelve men in all.

8 And [e]he entered the synagogue and for three months spoke boldly, reasoning and persuading them [f]about the kingdom of God. 9 [g]But when some became stubborn and [h]continued in unbelief, speaking evil of [i]the Way before the congregation, he withdrew from them and took the disciples with him, reasoning daily in the hall of

18 [x]See John 21:23 [y]ver. 2 [z][ch. 21:23, 24; Num. 6:2, 18] [a]Rom. 16:1 **19** [b]ch. 19:1; 20:16, 17; 1 Cor. 15:32; 16:8; Eph. 1:1; 1 Tim. 1:3; 2 Tim. 1:18 [c]ver. 4 **21** [d]1 Cor. 4:19; 16:7; Heb. 6:3; James 4:15; [Rom. 15:32; 1 Pet. 3:17] **22** [e]ch. 11:2; 21:15 **23** [f]ch. 16:6 [g]See ch. 14:22 **24** [h]ch. 19:1; 1 Cor. 1:12; 3:5, 6; 4:6; 16:12; Tit. 3:13 [i][Ezra 7:6] **25** [j]See ch. 9:2 [k]Rom. 12:11 [l]ch. 19:3; Luke 7:29 **26** [m]Matt. 22:16; [ver. 25] [n][ch. 19:1] **27** [o]ver. 18 [p][2 Cor. 3:1] [q]1 Cor. 3:6 [r][ch. 11:21, 23; 15:11; Eph. 2:8] **28** [s]See ver. 5

Chapter 19

1 [t]See ch. 18:24 [u][ch. 18:23] **2** [v][ch. 11:16, 17] [w][ch. 8:16; John 7:39] **3** [x]See ch. 8:16 [y]ch. 18:25; [Heb. 6:2]; See ch. 13:24, 25 **4** [y][See ver. 3 above] [z]John 1:7 **5** [a]See ch. 8:12, 16 **6** [b]See ch. 8:17 [c]ch. 10:46; See Mark 16:17 [d]See ch. 13:1 **8** [e]See ch. 13:5 [f]ch. 1:3; 28:23 **9** [g][ch. 13:45, 46; 1 Cor. 16:9] [h]See ch. 14:2 [i]ver. 23; See ch. 9:2

[1] Or *brothers and sisters;* also verse 27 [2] Or *in the Spirit* [3] Greek *upper* (that is, highland) [4] Or *into*

18:18 he was under a vow. Though this phrase could apply to Aquila, Paul is probably in view. The Nazirite vow required rigorous ceremonial purity that would have been impractical in Gentile lands (Num. 6:1–21), so this vow was more likely a private one undertaken by Paul as a religious exercise. The hair was allowed to grow during the period of the vow, and cutting it marked the conclusion of the vow and was perhaps an expression of gratitude to God.

18:23 some time there. Presumably Paul was in Antioch for several months, from about the fall of A.D. 52 to the spring of A.D. 53.

Galatia and Phrygia. Paul started his third missionary journey in the Phrygian part of Galatia in southern Asia Minor, the area nearest his former work.

19:1 the inland country. When he had finished his ministry in Phrygian Galatia (18:23), Paul continued westward by land through the region of Colosse, Laodicea, and Hierapolis (Col. 4:13) in the Lycus Valley, and finally arrived at Ephesus. Here he ministered for about three years (vv. 8, 10), from about A.D. 53 to 56.

Ephesus. The capital of the Roman province of Asia, Ephesus had been founded in about the twelfth century B.C. by Ionians from Athens. It became a great commercial power, but its economic prosperity declined, mainly because erosion into the river had silted and clogged the harbor. The city derived wealth and prestige from its temple of Artemis, built in honor of the goddess of fertility. The Ephesus of Paul's day had passed its zenith but was still an important commercial and religious center.

some disciples. According to v. 7, "about twelve."

19:2 receive the Holy Spirit. As followers of John the Baptist, these believers had not been instructed about the coming of the Spirit. Note that all categories of people received the baptism of the Holy Spirit: Jews, God-fearing Greeks, Samaritans, and Gentiles.

19:4 baptism of repentance . . . who was to come after him . . . Jesus. John's baptism of repentance (Mark 1:4; Luke 3:3) was directed toward repentance of sins and looked forward to the redeeming work of Jesus.

19:6 speaking in tongues and prophesying. The experience the Ephesian Gentiles had when receiving the Holy Spirit parallels that of the Jews (2:4, 11), Samaritans (8:14–17), and God-fearing Gentiles (10:44–46). This episode is an extension of the Pentecost experience to yet another group of people (v. 2 note). "Prophesying" in this passage may be equivalent to "telling . . . the mighty works of God" (2:11) or speaking so as to extol God (10:46).

19:9 hall of Tyrannus. Nothing further is known about Tyrannus. Some

Tyrannus.[1] **10** This continued for [j] two years,
so that [k] all the residents of Asia heard the
word of the Lord, both Jews and Greeks.

The Sons of Sceva

11 And [l] God was doing extraordinary miracles by the hands of Paul, **12** [l] so that even
handkerchiefs or aprons that had touched
his skin were carried away to the sick, and
their diseases left them and [m] the evil spirits came out of them. **13** Then some of the
itinerant Jewish [n] exorcists [o] undertook to
invoke the name of the Lord Jesus over
those who had evil spirits, saying, [p] "I
adjure you by the Jesus, whom Paul proclaims." **14** Seven sons of a Jewish high
priest named Sceva were doing this. **15** But
the evil spirit answered them, [q] "Jesus I
know, and Paul I recognize, but who are
you?" **16** And the man in whom was the evil
spirit leaped on them, mastered all[2] of
them and overpowered them, so that
they fled out of that house naked and
wounded. **17** And this became known to all
the residents of Ephesus, both Jews and
Greeks. And fear fell upon them all, and
[r] the name of the Lord Jesus was extolled.
18 Also many of those who were now believers came, [s] confessing and divulging their
practices. **19** And a number of those who
had practiced magic arts brought their
books together and burned them in the
sight of all. And they counted the value
of them and found it came to fifty thousand pieces of silver. **20** So the word of the
Lord [t] continued to increase and prevail
mightily.

A Riot at Ephesus

21 Now after these events Paul resolved in
the Spirit [u] to pass through [v] Macedonia and
Achaia and [w] go to Jerusalem, saying, "After
I have been there, [x] I must also see Rome."
22 And having sent into Macedonia two of
[y] his helpers, [z] Timothy and Erastus, he
himself stayed in Asia [a] for a while.
23 About that time [b] there arose no little

10 [j] [ver. 8; ch. 20:31] [k] [2 Tim. 1:15] **11** [l] [ch. 5:15]; See ch. 5:12 **12** [l] [See ver. 11 above] [m] See Mark 16:17 **13** [n] [Matt. 12:27; Luke 11:19] [o] See Mark 9:38 [p] Matt. 26:63; Mark 5:7 **15** [q] See James 2:19 **17** [r] [2 Thess. 1:12] **18** [s] Matt. 3:6; Mark 1:5; Rom. 14:11; James 5:16 **20** [t] ch. 6:7; 12:24 **21** [u] 1 Cor. 16:5; [ch. 20:1] [v] Rom. 15:26; 1 Thess. 1:7, 8 [w] ch. 20:16, 22; Rom. 15:25; 2 Cor. 1:16; [1 Cor. 16:3, 4] [x] Rom. 15:24, 28; [ch. 23:11; Rom. 1:13]

22 [y] Col. 4:7; 2 Tim. 1:18; 4:11; Philem. 13; [ver. 29; ch. 13:5] [z] See ch. 16:1 [a] [1 Cor. 16:8, 9] **23** [b] [2 Cor. 1:8]

1 Some manuscripts add *from the fifth hour to the tenth* (that is, from 11 A.M. to 4 P.M.) 2 Or *both*

manuscripts add, "from the fifth to the tenth hour" (11:00 A.M. to 4:00 P.M.). Tyrannus could have used the room in the cool morning hours, and given it to Paul for the rest of the day.

19:10 Asia. The Roman province in the western part of Asia Minor. As a result of this teaching, groups of believers were formed in numerous places (Col. 4:13, 16; Rev. 2; 3).

19:12 handkerchiefs or aprons . . . his skin. That is, sweat cloths or work aprons that Paul used as he worked at making tents or awnings (18:3). **to the sick.** This was not Paul's doing; because of their pagan religious background, the Ephesians were used to employing superstitious means (v. 19). God accommodated His gracious work to their ignorance.

19:13 evil spirits. In ancient times it was common practice to use magical names to drive out evil spirits. Jews in Ephesus presumed "to invoke the name of the Lord Jesus" over those possessed, trying to imitate what Paul did (v. 12; 16:18).

19:19 their books. These were scrolls with the names and incantations used in their magic.

Asia and Greece Revisited (Paul's Third Missionary Journey). Paul visited the churches of Galatia for a third time and then settled in Ephesus for more than two years. Upon leaving Ephesus, Paul traveled again to Macedonia and Achaia (Greece) for a three-month stay. He returned to Asia by way of Macedonia.

On this third journey Paul wrote 1 Corinthians from Ephesus, 2 Corinthians from Macedonia, and the letter to the Romans from Corinth.

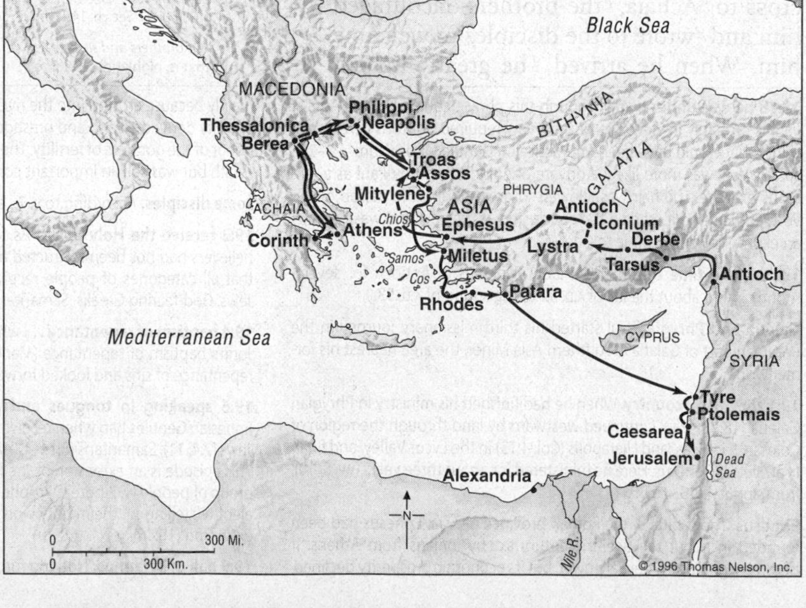

disturbance concerning [c]the Way. 24 For a
man named Demetrius, a silversmith, who
made silver shrines of Artemis, [d]brought no
little business to the craftsmen. 25 [d]These he
gathered together, with the workmen in
similar trades, and said, "Men, you know
that from this business we have our wealth.
26 And you see and hear that not only in
Ephesus but in almost all of Asia this Paul
has persuaded and turned away a great
many people, [e]saying that [f]gods made with
hands are not gods. 27 And there is danger
not only that this trade of ours may come
into disrepute but also that the temple of
the [g]great goddess Artemis may be counted
as nothing, and that she may even be
deposed from her magnificence, she whom
all Asia and the world worship."

28 When they heard this they were
enraged and were crying out, [g]"Great is
Artemis of the Ephesians!" 29 So the city
was filled with the confusion, and they
rushed together into the theater, dragging
with them Gaius and [h]Aristarchus, Mace-
donians who were Paul's [i]companions in
travel. 30 But when Paul wished to go in
among the crowd, the disciples would not
let him. 31 And even some of the Asiarchs,[1]
who were friends of his, sent to him and
were urging him not to venture into the
theater. 32 [j]Now some cried out one thing,
some another, for the assembly was in confusion, and most of them did not know
why they had come together. 33 Some of the
crowd prompted Alexander, whom the
Jews had put forward. And Alexander,
[k]motioning with his hand, wanted to make
a defense to the crowd. 34 But when they
recognized that he was a Jew, for about two
hours they all cried out with one voice,
[l]"Great is Artemis of the Ephesians!"

35 And when the town clerk had quieted
the crowd, he said, "Men of Ephesus, who
is there who does not know that the city of
the Ephesians is temple keeper of the great
Artemis, and of the sacred stone that fell
from [m]the sky?[2] 36 Seeing then that these
things cannot be denied, you ought to be
quiet and do nothing rash. 37 For you have
brought [n]these men here who are neither
[o]sacrilegious nor blasphemers of our goddess. 38 If therefore Demetrius and the
craftsmen with him have a complaint
against anyone, the courts are open, and
there are [p]proconsuls. Let them bring
charges against one another. 39 But if you
seek anything further,[3] it shall be settled in
the regular assembly. 40 For we really are in
danger of being charged with rioting today,
since there is no cause that we can give to
justify this commotion." 41 And when he
had said these things, he dismissed the
assembly.

Paul in Macedonia and Greece

20 After the uproar ceased, Paul sent
for the disciples, and after encouraging them, he said farewell and [q]departed
for Macedonia. 2 When he had gone
through those regions and had given them
much encouragement, he came to Greece.
3 There he spent three months, and when [r]a
plot was made against him by the Jews as
he was about to set sail for Syria, he decided to return through Macedonia. 4 Sopater
of Berea, the son of Pyrrhus from Berea,
accompanied him; and of the Thessalonians, [s]Aristarchus and Secundus; and
[s]Gaius of Derbe, and [t]Timothy; and the
Asians, [u]Tychicus and [v]Trophimus. 5 These

23 [c]ver. 9 **24** [d][ch. 16:16, 19] **25** [d][See ver. 24 above] **26** [e]ch. 14:15; 17:29; 1 Cor. 8:4 [f]Deut. 4:28; 2 Kin. 19:18; Ps. 115:4; Isai. 44:10-20; Jer. 10:3-6; Rev. 9:20 **27** [g][ch. 8:10] **28** [g][See ver. 27 above] **29** [h]ch. 20:4; 27:2; Col. 4:10; Philem. 24 [i]2 Cor. 8:19; [ver. 22; ch. 20:34] **32** [j]ch. 21:34 **33** [k]See ch. 12:17 **34** [l]ver. 28 **35** [m][ch. 14:12] **37** [n]ver. 29 [o]Rom. 2:22 **38** [p]See ch. 13:7
Chapter 20
1 [q]See ch. 19:21 **3** [r]ver. 19; [ch. 13:50]; See ch. 9:24 **4** [s]ch. 14:6, 21; See ch. 19:29 [t]See ch. 16:1 [u]Eph. 6:21; Col. 4:7; 2 Tim. 4:12; Tit. 3:12 [v]ch. 21:29; 2 Tim. 4:20

[1] That is, high-ranking officers of the province of Asia [2] The meaning of the Greek is uncertain [3] Some manuscripts *seek about other matters*

19:23 the Way. See note 9:2.

19:24 Demetrius, a silversmith. An important guild of silversmiths had developed at Ephesus on account of the large numbers of religious pilgrims. The pilgrims came to worship the goddess Diana (Artemis in Greek) who was portrayed by a famous statue at Ephesus as a fertility goddess with many breasts. Her "image" which had fallen "from the sky" (v. 35) was probably a meteorite that the people had begun to worship. The temple of Artemis was one of the seven wonders of the ancient world. Not only was it the object of religious pilgrimage, but it was a banking depository as well. Making silver shrines and images of the goddess was an important trade.

19:27 temple of the great goddess Artemis. The archaic Ionic temple of Artemis measured 220 by 425 feet, with 127 marble columns each 62 feet high. The lowest drums of the 36 western columns were carved with reliefs. The statue of the goddess was displayed in an inner room of the temple.

19:32 assembly. The Greek word *ekklesia* is used here and in vv. 39 and 41 to denote a secular assembly of people (5:11 note).

19:37 neither sacrilegious nor blasphemers of our goddess. These were common charges of Gentiles against Jews and Jewish Christians (Josephus, *Antiquities* 4.207; *Against Apion* 2.237).

20:1 departed for Macedonia. Paul went up the coast of Asia Minor from Ephesus, either by road or by ship, probably as far as Troas and then by ship to Macedonia (cf. 16:8–10) and Philippi (cf. 16:11–40), visiting groups of believers as he went. While in Macedonia, Paul may have extended his ministry as far as Illyricum (modern Albania; Rom. 15:19).

20:2 came to Greece. Paul arrived at Corinth, where he spent the winter of A.D. 56–57. During this time he wrote Romans (Rom. 15:26; 16:23, 24).

20:4 Paul's traveling companions are listed by name. They may have been official church representatives appointed to travel with Paul to

went on ahead and were waiting for [w]us at [x]Troas, **6** but we sailed away from Philippi after [y]the days of Unleavened Bread, and in five days we came to them at Troas, where we stayed for seven days.

Eutychus Raised from the Dead

7 [z]On the first day of the week, when we were gathered together [a]to break bread, Paul talked with them, intending to depart on the next day, and he prolonged his speech until midnight. **8** There were many lamps in [b]the upper room where we were gathered. **9** And a young man named Eutychus, sitting at the window, sank into a deep sleep as Paul talked still longer. And being overcome by sleep, he [c]fell down from the third story and was taken up dead. **10** But Paul went down and [d]bent over him, and taking him in his arms, said, [e]"Do not be alarmed, for his life is in him." **11** And when Paul had gone up and [f]had broken bread and eaten, he conversed with them a long while, until daybreak, and so departed. **12** And they took the youth away alive, and were not a little comforted.

13 But going ahead to the ship, we set sail for Assos, intending to take Paul aboard there, for so he had arranged, intending himself to go by land. **14** And when he met us at Assos, we took him on board and went to Mitylene. **15** And sailing from there we came the following day opposite Chios; the next day we touched at Samos; and[1] the day after that we went to Miletus. **16** For Paul had decided to sail past Ephesus, so that he might not have to spend time in Asia, for he was hastening [g]to be at Jerusalem, if possible, [h]on the day of Pentecost.

Paul Speaks to the Ephesian Elders

17 Now from Miletus he sent to Ephesus and called [i]the elders of the church to come to him. **18** And when they came to him, he said to them:

[j]"You yourselves know [k]how I lived among you the whole time [j]from the first day that I set foot in Asia, **19** [l]serving the Lord [m]with all humility and with [n]tears and with trials that happened to me through [o]the plots of the Jews; **20** how I [p]did not shrink from declaring to you anything that was profitable, and [q]teaching you in public and from house to house, **21** [r]testifying both to Jews and to Greeks of [s]repentance toward God and of [t]faith in our Lord Jesus Christ. **22** And now, behold, I am going to Jerusalem, constrained [u]by[2] the Spirit, not knowing what will happen to me there, **23** except that [v]the Holy Spirit testifies to me in every city that [w]imprisonment and [x]afflictions await me. **24** But [y]I do not account my life of any value nor as precious to myself, if only [z]I may finish my course and [a]the ministry [b]that I received from the Lord Jesus, [c]to testify to [d]the gospel of [e]the grace of God. **25** And now, behold, [f]I know that none of you among whom I have gone

5 [w]ver. 6-8, 13-15 [x]ch. 16:8-11
6 [y]ch. 12:3; Ex. 12:14, 15; 23:15
7 [z]1 Cor. 16:2; [Mark 16:9; John 20:19; Rev. 1:10] [a]ver. 11; 1 Cor. 10:16; 11:23, 24; See ch. 2:42
8 [b]ch. 1:13; 9:37, 39
9 [c]2 Kin. 1:2
10 [d][1 Kin. 17:21; 2 Kin. 4:34] [e][Matt. 9:23, 24; Mark 5:39]
11 [f]ver. 7
16 [g]ver. 22; ch. 24:11; [ver. 6; ch. 19:21; 1 Cor. 16:8] [h]ch. 2:1
17 [i]See ch. 11:30
18 [j]1 Thess. 1:5; [ver. 31, 34] [k]ch. 18:19; 19:1, 10
19 [l][Rom. 12:11; Col. 3:24] [m]1 Thess. 2:6, 7]; See Eph. 4:2 [n][ver. 31; 2 Cor. 2:4; Phil. 3:18] [o]See ver. 3
20 [p]ver. 27 [q][ver. 31]
21 [r]ver. 24; ch. 18:5 [s]Mark 1:15; Heb. 6:1; See ch. 2:38 [t][Eph. 1:15; Col. 1:4; 1 Tim. 3:13]
22 [u][ch. 17:16]
23 [v][ch. 21:4, 11]; See ch. 8:29; 9:16 [w]ch. 21:33 [x]ch. 14:22; 1 Thess. 3:3 **24** [y]See ch. 21:13 [z]2 Tim. 4:7 [a]ch. 1:17; 1 Tim. 1:12 [b]Gal. 1:1; 1 Thess. 2:4; [ch. 26:16; Tit. 1:3] [c]ver. 21 [d]ch. 15:7 [e][ver. 32; 1 Tim. 1:14]; See ch. 11:23 **25** [f][Phil. 1:25]

1 Some manuscripts add *after remaining at Trogyllium* 2 Or *bound in*

deliver money collected for relief of the Jerusalem church (1 Cor. 16:1–4; 2 Cor. 9:1–5). Sopater may be the "Sosipater" mentioned in Rom. 16:21. Aristarchus had faithfully accompanied Paul during the third missionary journey (19:29), and he accompanied the apostle to Rome (27:2) where he shared Paul's imprisonment (Col. 4:10). Secundus is not mentioned elsewhere in the New Testament. Gaius may be different from the Macedonian Gaius mentioned in 19:29. On Timothy, see Introduction to 1 Timothy: Date and Occasion. Tychicus was later Paul's representative to various churches during the apostle's imprisonments (Eph. 6:21; Col. 4:7–9; 2 Tim. 4:12). Trophimus accompanied Paul to Jerusalem where his presence in the city led to Paul's arrest (21:29). He apparently accompanied Paul after the apostle's release from the first Roman imprisonment (2 Tim. 4:20).

20:5 waiting for us. Luke again uses the first person plural pronoun, indicating that he traveled with Paul to Jerusalem.

20:7 first day of the week. Sunday.

to break bread. Since they were gathered together for worship on the first day of the week, the Lord's Day (Rev. 1:10), this celebration included communion (2:42) and was not just a fellowship meal (2:46).

Paul talked. This was a Sunday evening preaching-teaching service.

20:8–12 Luke records that Eutychus was "taken up dead," the likely result of such a fall. Paul's restoration of the young man to life is one of two such raisings of the dead by apostles recorded in Acts (9:40; cf. Luke 7:11–17; 8:49–56; John 11:1–44).

20:13 set sail for Assos. Paul went by road the twenty miles from Troas to Assos, while Luke went with the ship.

20:15 the following day . . . Chios . . . Samos . . . Miletus. They sailed down the coast to Miletus, about thirty miles south of Ephesus.

20:17 elders. These were the ordained representatives of the Ephesian congregation, called to be overseers and shepherds of the church of God (v. 28; cf. 1 Tim. 3:1–7; Titus 1:5–9).

20:20 teaching you in public and from house to house. Paul's teaching during his three-year stay (v. 31) in Ephesus was extensive, including public lectures at the synagogue and the lecture hall of Tyrannus, 19:8–10) as well as more private instruction in homes.

20:21 repentance . . . faith. See note 3:19. Both Jews and Gentiles must come to God in the same way—in repentance for sin (26:20; Luke 24:47) and faith in Jesus Christ.

20:22 constrained by the Spirit. Probably this refers to the urging of the Holy Spirit. Such explicit guidance by the Holy Spirit often occurred during Paul's ministry (16:6–10).

about [g]proclaiming the kingdom will see my face again. **26** Therefore [h]I testify to you this day that [i]I am innocent of the blood of all of you, **27** for [j]I did not shrink from declaring to you [k]the whole counsel of God. **28** [l]Pay careful attention to yourselves and to all [m]the flock, in which [n]the Holy Spirit has made you [o]overseers, [p]to care for [q]the church of God,[1] which he [r]obtained [s]with his own blood.[2] **29** I [r]know that after my departure [t]fierce wolves will come in among you, [u]not sparing the flock; **30** and [v]from among your own selves will arise men speaking twisted things, to draw away the disciples after them. **31** Therefore [w]be alert, remembering that [x]for three years I did not cease night or day [y]to admonish everyone [z]with tears. **32** And now [a]I commend you to God and to [b]the word of his grace, which is able to [c]build you up and to give you [d]the inheritance among all those who are sanctified. **33** [e]I coveted no one's silver or gold or apparel. **34** [f]You yourselves know that [g]these hands ministered to my necessities and [h]to those who were with me. **35** In all things [i]I have shown you that [j]by working hard in this way we must [k]help the weak and [l]remember the words of the Lord Jesus, how he himself said, 'It is more blessed [m]to give than to receive.'"

36 And when he had said these things, [n]he knelt down and prayed with them all. **37** And [o]there was much weeping on the part of all; [p]they embraced Paul and [p]kissed him, **38** being sorrowful most of all because of [q]the word he had spoken, that they would not see his face again. And [r]they accompanied him to the ship.

Paul Goes to Jerusalem

21 And when [s]we had parted from them and set sail, we [t]came by a straight course to Cos, and the next day to Rhodes, and from there to Patara.[3] **2** And having found a ship crossing to Phoenicia, we went aboard and set sail. **3** When we had come in sight of Cyprus, leaving it on the left we sailed to Syria and landed at Tyre, for there the ship was to unload its cargo. **4** And having sought out the disciples, we stayed there for seven days. And [u]through the Spirit they were telling Paul not to go on to Jerusalem. **5** When our days there were ended, we departed and went on our journey, and they all, with wives and children, [v]accompanied us until we were outside the city. And [w]kneeling down on the beach, we prayed **6** and said farewell to one another. Then we went on board the ship, and they returned home.

7 When we had finished the voyage from Tyre, we arrived at Ptolemais, and we greeted [x]the brothers[4] and stayed with them for

25 [g]See ch. 28:31
26 [h]Deut. 8:19 [i]See ch. 18:6
27 [j]ver. 20; [Jer. 26:2; Ezek. 33:8] [k]ch. 13:36; Luke 7:30; [ch. 2:23; Eph. 1:11; Heb. 6:17]
28 [l][1 Tim. 4:16] [m]ver. 29; [Eph. 4:11]; See Luke 12:32 [n][ch. 13:2; 1 Cor. 12:8-11] [o]Phil. 1:1; 1 Tim. 3:2; Tit. 1:7; [ver. 17] [p]See John 21:16 [q]1 Cor. 1:2; 10:32; 11:16; 15:9 [r][2 Pet. 2:1] [s]Heb. 9:12, 14; [Eph. 1:7; 1 John 1:7]
29 [r][See ver. 28 above] See 1 Pet. 1:18, 19; Rev. 5:9 [t]See Matt. 7:15 [u]John 10:12; [Col. 2:8]
30 [v][1 Cor. 11:19; 2 Cor. 11:13; 1 Tim. 1:19, 20; 1 John 2:18, 19]
31 [w][Heb. 13:17]; See Matt. 24:42 [x][ch. 19:8, 10; 24:17] [y]Col. 1:28 [z][Heb. 13:17]; See ver. 19
32 [a]ch. 14:23 [b]ch. 14:3; [ver. 24] [c]See Col. 2:7 [d]ch. 26:18; Eph. 1:14, 18; 5:5; Col. 1:12; 3:24; Heb. 9:15; [1 Pet. 1:4]; See Matt. 25:34; Rom. 8:17 **33** [e]1 Cor. 9:12; 2 Cor. 7:2; 11:9; 12:17; [1 Sam. 12:3; Matt. 10:8; 1 Thess. 2:5] **34** [f][ver. 18] [g]See ch. 18:3 [h]ch. 19:22, 29 **35** [i]2 Thess. 3:7 [j]Eph. 4:28 [k]1 Thess. 5:14; [1 Cor. 12:28] [l]ch. 11:16 [m]Matt. 10:8 **36** [n]See ch. 7:60 **37** [o][2 Tim. 1:4] [p]See Luke 15:20 **38** [q]ver. 25 [r]See ch. 15:3
Chapter 21 **1** [s]See ch. 16:10 [t]ch. 16:11 **4** [u]ver. 11; ch. 20:23 **5** [v]ch. 20:38 [w]ch. 20:36 **7** [x]See John 21:23

[1] Some manuscripts *of the Lord* [2] Or *with the blood of his Own* [3] Some manuscripts add *and Myra* [4] Or *brothers and sisters*; also verse 17

20:25 will see my face again. Paul's statement was based on his own judgment of the situation rather than on divine revelation. Because of continued plots against his life by the Jews (v. 3), the divine revelation that "imprisonment and afflictions" awaited him (v. 23), and his own intention to focus his future ministry on the western Mediterranean (Rom. 15:23–29), Paul considered it likely that he was seeing the Ephesian elders for the last time. However, it appears that Paul was later able to return to Ephesus after his release from prison in Rome (1 Tim. 1:3).

20:27 whole counsel of God. The revelation of God culminating in His Son Jesus Christ. Paul did not suppress any truths of the gospel but preached the full gospel to Jew and Gentile. He always used tact and discretion but never compromised the good news.

20:28 with his own blood. The phrasing is remarkable in the way it acknowledges that the blood of Christ is the blood of God. Many ancient manuscripts have a different word order, reading "the blood of His own," that is, of Christ.

20:29 not sparing the flock. See "Pastors and Pastoral Care" at 1 Pet. 5:2.

20:30 from among your own selves. Paul's prophetic warning in this verse was fulfilled as the Ephesian church was soon to be plagued by false teachers, some of whom apparently were leaders of the church (1 Tim. 1:3, 7, 19, 20; 6:3–5; Introduction to 2 Timothy: Interpretive Difficulties).

20:37 kissed him. The ancient practice of the Christian kiss of greeting (Luke 7:45; 1 Thess. 5:26; 1 Pet. 5:14), is still practiced in some cultures today.

21:1 Cos . . . Rhodes . . . Patara. They sailed on a direct course through the islands off the coast of Asia Minor to the port of Patara. The small island of Cos was a free state in the province of Asia. Rhodes, the capital on the north end of the island of Rhodes, was famous and prosperous in the earlier Greek period. Patara, a port on the southwest coast of Asia Minor, was an important harbor for ancient ships sailing the eastern Mediterranean, thus bringing Syria, Palestine, and Egypt into contact with Asia Minor, Macedonia, and Achaia.

21:2 Phoenicia. Syria controlled Phoenicia in the Roman period.

21:3 Tyre. This port, famous in Old Testament times and conquered by Alexander the Great, was about four hundred miles southeast of Patara, a sea journey of about five days.

21:4 through the Spirit. Paul was not disobedient to the Spirit; the Holy Spirit was compelling him to go to Jerusalem (20:22 note). It was "through the Spirit" that Paul's friends learned he was soon to suffer prison and hardship (20:23), and in response to this revelation they tried to persuade Paul "not to go on to Jerusalem" (cf. vv. 11, 12).

21:7 Ptolemais. A port twenty-five miles south of Tyre, where the ship unloaded cargo.

one day. 8 On the next day we departed and came to Caesarea, and we entered the house of [y]Philip [z]the evangelist, who was one of the seven, and stayed with him. 9 He had four unmarried daughters, [a]who prophesied. 10 While we were staying for many days, a prophet named [b]Agabus came down from Judea. 11 And coming to us, he [c]took Paul's belt and bound his own feet and hands and said, [d]"Thus says the Holy Spirit, [e]'This is how the Jews at Jerusalem will bind the man who owns this belt and [f]deliver him into the hands of the Gentiles.'" 12 When we heard this, we and the people there [g]urged him not to go up to Jerusalem. 13 Then Paul answered, [g]"What are you doing, weeping and breaking my heart? For [h]I am ready not only to be imprisoned but even to die in Jerusalem [i]for the name of the Lord Jesus." 14 And since he would not be persuaded, [j]we ceased and said, [k]"Let the will of the Lord be done."

15 After these days we got ready and went up to Jerusalem. 16 And some of the disciples from Caesarea went with us, bringing us to the house of Mnason of Cyprus, an early disciple, with whom we should lodge.

Paul Visits James

17 When we had come to Jerusalem, [l]the brothers received us gladly. 18 On the following day Paul went in with us to [m]James, and all [n]the elders were present. 19 After greeting them, [o]he related one by one [p]the things that God had done among the Gentiles through his [q]ministry. 20 And when they heard it, they [r]glorified God. And they said to him, "You see, brother, how many thousands there are among the Jews of those who have believed. They are all [s]zealous for the law, 21 and they have been told about you that you teach all [t]the Jews who are among the Gentiles to forsake Moses, [u]telling them [v]not to circumcise their children or [w]walk according to [x]our customs. 22 What then is to be done? They will certainly hear that you have come. 23 Do therefore what we tell you. We have four men [y]who are under a vow; 24 take these men and [z]purify yourself along with them and pay their expenses, [y]so that they may shave their heads. Thus all will know that there is nothing in what they have been told about you, but that you yourself also live in observance of the law. 25 But as for the Gentiles who have believed, [a]we have sent a letter with our judgment that they should abstain from what has been sacrificed to idols, and from blood, and from what has been strangled,[1] and from sexual immorality." 26 Then Paul took the men, and the next day [z]he purified himself along with them and [b]went into the temple, giving notice when the days of purification would be fulfilled and [c]the offering presented for each one of them.

Paul Arrested in the Temple

27 When [c]the seven days were almost completed, [d]the Jews from Asia, [e]seeing him in the temple, stirred up the whole crowd and laid hands on him, 28 crying out, "Men of Israel, help! This is the man who [f]is teaching everyone everywhere against the people and [g]the law and [g]this place.

8 [y]ch. 6:5; 8:5 [z]Eph. 4:11; 2 Tim. 4:5
9 [a]ch. 2:17, 18; Luke 2:36; 1 Cor. 11:5; See ch. 13:1
10 [b]ch. 11:28
11 [c][1 Sam. 15:27, 28; 1 Kin. 11:30; Isai. 20:3; Jer. 13:1-11; 27:2] [d]See ch. 20:23 [e][ver. 33]; See ch. 9:16 [f][ver. 31-33; Matt. 20:19]
12 [g][Matt. 16:21-23]
13 [g][See ver. 12 above] [h]ch. 20:24; Rom. 8:36; 2 Cor. 4:16; 12:10; Phil. 2:17; [ch. 15:26] [i]See ch. 5:41
14 [j][Ruth 1:18] [k]See Matt. 6:10
17 [l]ver. 7; [ch. 15:4]
18 [m]See ch. 12:17 [n]See ch. 11:30
19 [o]See ch. 14:27 [p][Rom. 15:18, 19] [q]See ch. 1:17
20 [r]ch. 11:18 [s]ch. 22:3; Rom. 10:2; Gal. 1:14
21 [t][James 1:1] [u]ver. 28 [v][Rom. 2:28, 29; 1 Cor. 7:19] [w][Mark 7:5; Gal. 2:14] [x]ch. 6:14; 15:1
23 [y][ch. 18:18]
24 [z]ver. 26; ch. 24:18; [John 11:55] [y][See ver. 23 above]
25 [a]See ch. 15:19, 20, 29
26 [z][See ver. 24 above] [b][Num. 6:13] [c][Num. 6:9-12] 27 [c][See ver. 26 above] [d]See ch. 13:50 [e]ch. 24:18; 26:21 28 [f]ver. 21 [g]See ch. 6:13

1 Some manuscripts omit *and from what has been strangled*

21:8 Caesarea. This seaport, built by Herod the Great, was the provincial capital of Judea; it was thirty-two miles south of Ptolemais (10:1 note).

Philip . . . one of the seven. One of the seven chosen to handle the food distribution (6:1–6). He had preached to the Samaritans, the Ethiopian eunuch, and the people along the Palestinian coast (ch. 8).

21:10 prophet named Agabus. The same Agabus who fifteen years earlier prophesied the severe famine in Judea and the surrounding area (11:27, 28).

21:11 says the Holy Spirit. In the first century context of the apostles, Agabus, as a prophet, was led directly by the Spirit to give God's inspired message.

21:15 went up to Jerusalem. Pentecost, the fiftieth day after Passover, was fast approaching (they had spent at least thirty-six days traveling from Philippi to Caesarea, and they had spent several days at Caesarea), and Paul wanted to be at Jerusalem for this feast.

21:20 zealous for the law. Thousands of Jewish Christians in Jerusalem strictly observed the Mosaic law. While many of these no doubt resented the fact that Gentile Christians were not required to observe the ceremonial law of Moses (v. 25; 15:1–31), the charge here was that Paul was encouraging Jews to forsake the law as well (v. 21). Such a charge may have been prompted by reports that Paul himself did not follow the Jewish ceremonial law when in Gentile company. Though Paul had no objection to Jews following their ancestral customs, he opposed any attempt to make such observance in some way necessary for salvation (Rom. 14:1–8; Gal. 5:2–6). Always careful to avoid giving unnecessary offense, Paul's flexibility in such matters shows that the interests of the gospel were always foremost in his mind (1 Cor. 9:19–23).

21:24 purify yourself . . . expenses. This was the Nazirite vow (Num. 6:1–21), during which the devotee let his hair grow. When the period of the vow was over, he shaved off his hair, dedicated it to the Lord, and burned it together with the sacrifice for the fellowship offering (Num. 6:18). Paul paid the expenses for four Nazirites, went to the priest with them for the sacrifices, and participated in the purification rites. In this way Paul publicly demonstrated that he was a law-abiding Jew.

Moreover, he even brought Greeks into the
temple and [h]has defiled [g]this holy place."
29 For they had previously seen [i]Trophimus
the Ephesian with him in the city, and they
supposed that Paul had brought him into
the temple. 30 Then all the city was stirred
up, and the people ran together. They
seized Paul and [j]dragged him out of the
temple, and at once the gates were shut.
31 [j]And as they were seeking to kill him,
word came to the tribune of [k]the cohort
that all Jerusalem was in confusion. 32 [l]He
at once took soldiers and centurions and
ran down to them. And when they saw the
tribune and the soldiers, they stopped
beating Paul. 33 Then the tribune came up
and arrested him and ordered him [m]to be
bound [n]with two chains. He inquired who
he was and what he had done. 34 [o]Some in
the crowd were shouting one thing, some
another. And as he could not learn the
facts because of the uproar, he ordered him
to be brought into [p]the barracks. 35 And
when he came to the steps, he was actually carried by the soldiers because of the violence of the crowd, 36 for the mob of the people
followed, crying out, [q]"Away with him!"

Paul Speaks to the People

37 As Paul was about to be brought into
the barracks, he said to the tribune, "May I
say something to you?" And he said, "Do
you know Greek? 38 Are you not [r]the
Egyptian, then, who recently stirred up a
revolt and led the four thousand men of
the Assassins out [s]into the wilderness?"
39 Paul replied, [t]"I am a Jew, from Tarsus in
Cilicia, a citizen of no obscure city. I beg
you, permit me to speak to the people."
40 And when he had given him permission,
Paul, standing on the steps, [u]motioned
with his hand to the people. And when
there was a great hush, he addressed them
in [v]the Hebrew language,[1] saying:

22 [w]"Brothers and fathers, hear the
defense that I now make before
you."

2 And when they heard that he was
addressing them in [x]the Hebrew language,
they became even more quiet. And he said:
3 [y]"I am a Jew, born in Tarsus in Cilicia,
but brought up in this city, educated [z]at
the feet of [a]Gamaliel[2] [b]according to the
strict manner of the law of our fathers, [c]being zealous for God [d]as all of you are this
day. 4 [e]I persecuted [f]this Way [g]to the death,
binding and delivering to prison both men
and women, 5 as [h]the high priest and [i]the
whole council of elders can bear me witness. From them I received letters to [j]the
brothers, and I journeyed toward Damascus to take those also who were there and
bring them in bonds to Jerusalem to be
punished.

6 [k]"As I was on my way and drew near to
Damascus, about noon a great light from
heaven suddenly shone around me. 7 And I
fell to the ground and heard a voice saying
to me, 'Saul, Saul, why are you persecuting
me?' 8 And I answered, 'Who are you,
Lord?' And he said to me, 'I am [l]Jesus of
Nazareth, whom you are persecuting.'
9 [m]Now those who were with me saw the
light but did not understand[3] the voice of
the one who was speaking to me. 10 And I
said, [n]'What shall I do, Lord?' And the
Lord said to me, 'Rise, and go into Damascus, and there you will be told all that
is appointed for you to do.' 11 And since I
could not see because of the brightness of
that light, I was led by the hand by those
who were with me, and came into Damascus.

12 "And [o]one Ananias, a devout man [p]according to the law, [q]well spoken of by all
the Jews who lived there, 13 [r]came to me,
and standing by me said to me, 'Brother
Saul, receive your sight.' And [s]at that very
hour I received my sight and saw him.
14 And he said, [t]'The God of our fathers
[u]appointed you to know his will, [v]to see

28 [h]ch. 24:6 [g]See ch. 6:13
29 [i]ch. 20:4
30 [j]ch. 26:21; [2 Kin. 11:15]
31 [j][See ver. 30 above] [k]See ch. 10:1
32 [l][ch. 23:27]
33 [m]ch. 20:23; [ver. 11] [n]ch. 12:6; [ch. 22:29; 26:29; 28:20; Eph. 6:20; 2 Tim. 1:16]
34 [o]ch. 19:32 [p]ch. 22:24; 23:10
36 [q]ch. 22:22; [Luke 23:18; John 19:15]
38 [r][ch. 5:36] [s]Matt. 24:26
39 [t]ch. 9:11; 22:3
40 [u]See ch. 12:17 [v]ch. 22:2; 26:14
Chapter 22
1 [w]ch. 7:2
2 [x]ch. 21:40
3 [y]ch. 9:11; 21:39; Rom. 11:1; 2 Cor. 11:22; Phil. 3:5 [z]Deut. 33:3; 2 Kin. 4:38; [Luke 10:39] [a]ch. 5:34 [b]ch. 26:5 [c][John 16:2; Phil. 3:6]; See ch. 21:20 [d]Rom. 10:2
4 [e]ver. 19; See ch. 8:3 [f][ch. 5:20]; See ch. 9:2 [g]ch. 26:10; [ver. 20; ch. 8:1]
5 [h]ch. 9:1 [i]Luke 22:66 (Gk.); 1 Tim. 4:14 (Gk.) [j]ch. 28:21
6 [k]For ver. 6-11, see ch. 9:3-8; 26:12-18
8 [l]ch. 26:9
9 [m][Dan. 10:7]; See ch. 9:7
10 [n]See ch. 16:30
12 [o]ch. 9:10 [p]ch. 24:14 [q]ch. 10:22
13 [r]ch. 9:17 [s]ch. 9:18
14 [t]See ch. 3:13 [u]ch. 9:15; 26:16 [v]ver. 18; ch. 9:17; 26:16; 1 Cor. 9:1; 15:8; [ver. 15]

1 Or *the Hebrew dialect* (that is, Aramaic); also 22:2 2 Or *city at the feet of Gamaliel, educated* 3 Or *hear with understanding*

21:37 Do you know Greek. The tribune was surprised to hear Paul speak Greek; he had thought him to be an insurrectionist Jew from Egypt, who three years before had appeared there claiming to be a prophet (Josephus, *Jewish War* 2.261–263).

21:38 Assassins. Lit. "dagger men," militant Jewish nationalists.

21:40 on the steps. Probably the stairs leading from the temple area to the Antonian Fortress (rebuilt by Herod the Great and named after Mark Antony) on the north edge of the temple platform.

Hebrew language. That is, Aramaic, as commonly spoken by Jews in Palestine, although the priests and Levites would also have known Hebrew. Greek was the common language of the Roman and Mediterranean world.

22:3 Tarsus. An important city, located in Cilicia on the eastern Mediterranean coast north of Cyprus. It was a noted intellectual center.

22:12 Ananias. An appropriate person to meet Saul, who was a zealous Pharisee, "a Hebrew of Hebrews" (Phil. 3:5, 6). Being known to Ananias

[w]the Righteous One and [x]to hear a voice
from his mouth; 15 for [y]you will be a witness for him to everyone of what [z]you have
seen and heard. 16 And now why do you
wait? [a]Rise and be baptized and [b]wash
away your sins, [c]calling on his name.'
17 [d]"When I had returned to Jerusalem
and [e]was praying in the temple, I fell into
[f]a trance 18 and saw him saying to me,
[g]'Make haste and get out of Jerusalem
quickly, because they will not accept your
testimony about me.' 19 And I said, 'Lord,
they themselves know that in one synagogue after another [h]I imprisoned and
[i]beat those who believed in you. 20 And
when the blood of Stephen [j]your witness
was being shed, [k]I myself was standing by
and [j]approving and [l]watching over the garments of those who killed him.' 21 And he
said to me, 'Go, for I will send you [m]far
away to the Gentiles.'"

Paul and the Roman Tribune

22 Up to this word they listened to him.
Then they raised their voices and said,
[n]"Away with such a fellow from the earth!
For [o]he should not be allowed to live."
23 And as they were shouting and throwing
off their cloaks and flinging dust into the
air, 24 the tribune ordered him to be
brought into [p]the barracks, saying that he
should be [q]examined by flogging, to find
out why they were shouting against him
like this. 25 But when they had stretched
him out for the whips,[1] Paul said to the
centurion who was standing by, "Is it lawful for you to flog [r]a man who is a Roman
citizen and uncondemned?" 26 When the
centurion heard this, he went to the tribune and said to him, "What are you about
to do? For this man is a Roman citizen."

14 [w]See ch. 3:14 [x][Gal. 1:12]
15 [y]ch. 23:11 [z]ver. 14; ch. 4:20
16 [a]ch. 9:18 [b]1 Cor. 6:11; Heb. 10:22; [Ps. 51:2]; See ch. 2:38 [c]See ch. 9:14
17 [d]ch. 9:26; 26:20 [e]ch. 3:1; Luke 18:10 [f]ch. 10:10; 11:5; [2 Cor. 12:1-4]
18 [g][ch. 9:29]
19 [h]ver. 4 [i]ch. 26:11; See Matt. 10:17
20 [j][Rev. 2:13] [k]ch. 7:58 [l]ch. 8:1; [ch. 26:10]; See Rom. 1:32
21 [m]See ch. 2:39; 9:15
22 [n]See ch. 21:36 [o]ch. 25:24
24 [p]ch. 21:34; 23:10 [q]ver. 29
25 [r]ch. 16:37
29 [s]ver. 24 [t]ch. 16:38 [u][ch. 23:27] [v]ch. 21:33
30 [w]ver. 24; ch. 23:28
Chapter 23
1 [x]2 Cor. 1:12; 2 Tim. 1:3; [ch. 24:16; Job 27:5, 6; 1 Cor. 4:4; 2 Cor. 4:2; 5:11; Heb. 13:18]
2 [y]ch. 24:1 [z]1 Kin. 22:24; Lam. 3:30; Mic. 5:1; 2 Cor. 11:20
3 [a][Matt. 23:27] [b][Isai. 30:13; Ezek. 13:10-14] [c]Deut. 25:1, 2; See John 7:51
4 [d][1 Sam. 2:28; Ps. 106:16]

27 So the tribune came and said to him,
"Tell me, are you a Roman citizen?" And he
said, "Yes." 28 The tribune answered, "I
bought this citizenship for a large sum."
Paul said, "But I am a citizen by birth."
29 So those who were about [s]to examine
him withdrew from him immediately, and
the tribune also [t]was afraid, [u]for he realized
that Paul was a Roman citizen and that [v]he
had bound him.

Paul Before the Council

30 But on the next day, [w]desiring to know
the real reason why he was being accused
by the Jews, he unbound him and commanded the chief priests and all the council to meet, and he brought Paul down and
set him before them.

23 And looking intently at the council,
Paul said, "Brothers, [x]I have lived
my life before God in all good conscience
up to this day." 2 And the high priest
[y]Ananias commanded those who stood by
him [z]to strike him on the mouth. 3 Then
Paul said to him, "God is going to strike
you, you [a]whitewashed [b]wall! Are you sitting to judge me according to the law, and
yet [c]contrary to the law you [c]order me to be
struck?" 4 Those who stood by said,
"Would you revile [d]God's high priest?"
5 And Paul said, [e]"I did not know, brothers,
that he was the high priest, for it is written,
[f]'You shall not speak evil of a ruler of your
people.'"
6 Now when Paul perceived that one part
were [g]Sadducees and the other Pharisees,
he cried out in the council, "Brothers, [h]I
am a Pharisee, a son of Pharisees. It is [i]with

5 [e][ch. 24:17] [f]Cited from Ex. 22:28 **6** [g]See Matt. 22:23 [h]ch. 26:5; Phil. 3:5 [i]ch. 24:15, 21; 26:6-8; 28:20

[1] Or *when they had tied him up with leather strips*

would recommend Paul to other Jews in the city who would otherwise be suspicious of him (9:10–19).

22:16 be baptized. Baptism in the New Testament is an outward sign of an inward cleansing. As such, it parallels circumcision in the Old Testament (Deut. 10:16; 30:6; Ezek. 44:7).

22:24 flogging. The Roman scourge was a whip of leather thongs loaded with bits of metal or bone; it could maim for life or kill. Jesus was scourged with such a whip (John 19:1). Paul had been beaten (2 Cor. 11:24, 25) but had never endured this particular punishment.

22:25 stretched him. The soldiers either stretched Paul's arms around a pole to expose his back or tied his hands and hoisted him from the ground to administer the whipping.

22:26 Roman citizen. Paul appealed again to his Roman citizenship, knowing that he was going to be punished without trial (16:37). Roman citizenship was highly prized, usually given only to those of high position or those who had performed some valuable service to the state. It was then passed on to one's family.

23:2 high priest Ananias. Son of Nebedaeus, a brutal and violent man who ruled as high priest from A.D. 48–59. This is not the earlier Annas of John 18:13. Ananias was assassinated early in the war with Rome (A.D. 66–70).

23:3 you whitewashed wall. Tombs were often whitewashed to make them more visible (Matt. 23:27, 28). Paul paid a fitting tribute to a corrupt official.

contrary to the law. According to Jewish law, Paul had to be tried and found guilty before being punished.

23:6 Sadducees . . . Pharisees. These two groups emerged during the period between the Old and New Testaments. They had different political and religious views. Paul seized the opportunity to emphasize their religious differences by identifying himself as a Pharisee and a believer in

respect to the [j]hope and the resurrection of the dead that I am on trial." 7 And when he had said this, a dissension arose between the Pharisees and the Sadducees, and the assembly was divided. 8 For the Sadducees [k]say that there is no resurrection, nor angel, nor spirit, but the Pharisees acknowledge them all. 9 Then a great clamor arose, and some of [l]the scribes of the Pharisees' party stood up and contended sharply, [m]"We find nothing wrong in this man. What [n]if a spirit or an angel spoke to him?" 10 And when the dissension became violent, the tribune, afraid that Paul would be torn to pieces by them, commanded the soldiers to go down and take him away from among them by force and bring him into [o]the barracks.

11 [p]The following night [q]the Lord stood by him and said, [r]"Take courage, for [s]as you have testified to the facts about me in Jerusalem, so you must [t]testify also in Rome."

A Plot to Kill Paul

12 When it was day, [u]the Jews made a plot and [v]bound themselves by an oath neither to eat nor drink till they had killed Paul. 13 There were more than forty who made this conspiracy. 14 They went to the chief priests and elders and said, "We have strictly bound ourselves by an oath to taste no food till we have killed Paul. 15 Now therefore you, along with the council, give notice to the tribune to bring him down to you, as though you were going to determine his case more exactly. And we are ready to kill him before he comes near."

16 Now the son of Paul's sister heard of their ambush, so he went and entered [w]the barracks and told Paul. 17 Paul called one of the centurions and said, "Take this young man to the tribune, for he has something to tell him." 18 So he took him and brought him to the tribune and said, "Paul [x]the prisoner called me and asked me to bring this young man to you, as he has something to say to you." 19 The tribune took him by the hand, and going aside asked him privately, "What is it that you have to tell me?" 20 And he said, [y]"The Jews have agreed to ask you to bring Paul down to the council tomorrow, as though they were going to inquire somewhat more closely about him. 21 But do not be persuaded by them, for more than forty of their men are lying in ambush for him, who [z]have bound themselves by an oath neither to eat nor drink till they have killed him. And now they are ready, waiting for your consent." 22 So the tribune dismissed the young man, charging him, "Tell no one that you have informed me of these things."

Paul Sent to Felix the Governor

23 Then he called two of the centurions and said, "Get ready two hundred soldiers, with seventy horsemen and two hundred spearmen to go as far as Caesarea at the third hour of the night.[1] 24 Also provide mounts for Paul to ride and bring him safely to [a]Felix [b]the governor." 25 And he wrote a letter to this effect:

26 "Claudius Lysias, to [c]his Excellency the governor Felix, [d]greetings. 27 [e]This man was seized by the Jews and [f]was about to be killed by them [f]when I came upon them with the soldiers and rescued him, [g]having learned that he was a Roman citizen. 28 And [h]desiring to know the charge for which they were accusing him, I brought him down to their council. 29 I found that he was being accused [i]about questions of their law, but [j]charged with nothing deserving death or imprisonment. 30 [k]And when it was disclosed to me [l]that there would be a plot against the man, I sent him to you at once, [m]ordering his accusers also to state before you what they have against him."

31 So the soldiers, according to their

6 [j][ch. 2:26, 27]; See Col. 1:5
8 [k]Luke 20:27; [1 Cor. 15:12]
9 [l]ch. 4:5; Mark 2:16; Luke 5:30 [m][ver. 29] [n][ch. 22:7, 17, 18; John 12:29]
10 [o]ver. 16, 32; ch. 21:34; 22:24
11 [p]ch. 18:9; 27:23 [q]1 Sam. 3:10 [r][2 Tim. 4:17] [s][ch. 19:21] [t]ch. 22:15
12 [u]ver. 30 [v]ver. 14, 21
16 [w]ver. 10, 32
18 [x]See Eph. 3:1
20 [y]ver. 14, 15
21 [z]ver. 12, 14
24 [a]ver. 26; ch. 24:3; 25:14 [b]ver. 33; ch. 24:1, 10; 26:30; See Luke 20:20
26 [c]ch. 24:3 [d]See ch. 15:23
27 [e]ch. 21:27 [f][ch. 21:32, 33] [g][ch. 22:25-29]
28 [h]ch. 22:30
29 [i]ch. 18:15; 25:19 [j]ch. 25:25; 26:31; 28:18; [ver. 9]
30 [k]ver. 20 [l]ver. 12; See ch. 9:24 [m]ver. 35; [ch. 24:19; 25:16]

[1] That is, 9 P.M.

the resurrection of the dead, against the Sadducees who denied the resurrection and the existence of angels and spirits (Matt. 22:23–32).

23:9 scribes of the Pharisees' party. These were teachers, expert interpreters of Jewish law.

23:16 the son of Paul's sister. Evidently some members of Paul's family were in Jerusalem.

told Paul. Prisoners received their necessary supplies from relatives and friends who regularly visited them.

23:23, 24 Heavily equipped infantry and cavalry delivered Paul safely to Felix, the procurator of the imperial province of Judea. The official provincial headquarters was at Caesarea.

23:26 governor Felix. Felix was a former slave, and as a freedman had ascended to an influential position in the Roman government. In A.D. 52, the emperor Claudius sent him as governor to Caesarea. Felix was addressed as "most excellent Felix" (24:2) during his eight-year administration. The Roman historian Tacitus said that Felix "occupied the office of a king while having the mind of a slave, saturated with cruelty and lust" (*History* 5.9).

instructions, took Paul and brought him by
night to Antipatris. **32** And on the next day
they returned to [n]the barracks, letting the
horsemen go on with him. **33** When they
had come to Caesarea and delivered the
letter to the governor, they presented Paul
also before him. **34** On reading the letter, he
asked what [o]province he was from. And
when he learned [p]that he was from Cilicia,
35 he said, "I will give you a hearing [q]when
your accusers arrive." And he commanded
him to be guarded in Herod's [r]praetorium.

Paul Before Felix at Caesarea

24 And [s]after five days the high priest
[t]Ananias came down with some
elders and a spokesman, one Tertullus.
They laid before [u]the governor their case
against Paul. **2** And when he had been summoned, Tertullus began to accuse him, saying:
"Since through you we enjoy much
peace, and since by your foresight, [v]most
excellent Felix, reforms are being made for
this nation, **3** in every way and everywhere
we accept this with all gratitude. **4** But, to
detain[1] you no further, I beg you in your
kindness to hear us briefly. **5** For we have
found this man a plague, [w]one who stirs up
riots among all the Jews throughout the
world and is a ringleader of [x]the sect of
the Nazarenes. **6** [y]He even tried to profane
the temple, but we seized him.[2] **8** By examining him yourself you will be able to find
out from him about everything of which we
accuse him."
9 The Jews also joined in the charge,
affirming that all these things were so.
10 And when the governor had nodded to
him to speak, Paul replied:
"Knowing that for many years you have
been a judge over this nation, I cheerfully
make my defense. **11** You can verify that [z]it
is not more than twelve days since I [a]went
up [b]to worship in Jerusalem, **12** and [c]they
did not find me disputing with anyone or
stirring up a crowd, either in the temple or
in the synagogues or in the city. **13** [d]Neither
can they prove to you what they now bring
up against me. **14** But this I confess to you,
that according to [e]the Way, which they call
[f]a sect, [g]I worship [h]the God of our fathers,
believing everything [i]laid down by the Law
and written in the Prophets, **15** [j]having [k]a
hope in God, which these men themselves
accept, that there will be [l]a resurrection [m]of
both the just and the unjust. **16** So I always
[n]take pains to have a [o]clear conscience
toward both God and man. **17** Now [p]after
several years [q]I came to bring alms to [r]my
nation and to present [s]offerings. **18** While I
was doing this, they found me [t]purified in
the temple, without any crowd or tumult.
But [u]some Jews from Asia— **19** [v]they ought
to be here before you and to make an accusation, should they have anything against
me. **20** Or else let these men themselves say
what wrongdoing they found when I stood
before the council, **21** other than this one
thing [w]that I cried out while standing
among them: 'It is with respect to the resurrection of the dead that I am on trial
before you this day.' "

Paul Kept in Custody

22 But Felix, having a rather accurate
knowledge of [x]the Way, put them off, saying, "When Lysias the tribune comes
down, I will decide your case." **23** Then he
gave orders to the centurion that he
[y]should be kept in custody but have some
liberty, and that [z]none of his friends
should be prevented from attending to his
needs.

32 [n]ver. 10, 16 **34** [o]ch. 25:1 [p]ch. 21:39 **35** [q]ver. 30 [r]See Matt. 27:27
Chapter 24
1 [s][ch. 21:18, 27 with ver. 11] [t]ch. 23:2 [u]ch. 23:24
2 [v]ch. 23:26; Luke 1:3
5 [w]See Luke 23:2 [x]ver. 14; ch. 5:17; 15:5; 26:5; 28:22
6 [y]ch. 21:27-29
11 [z]See ver. 1 [a]ch. 8:27; John 12:20 [b]ch. 20:16
12 [c][ch. 25:8]
13 [d]ch. 25:7
14 [e]ver. 22; See ch. 9:2 [f]ver. 5 [g]2 Tim. 1:3; [ch. 27:23; Luke 1:74; Rom. 1:9; Heb. 9:14; 12:28] [h]See ch. 3:13; 22:3 [i]ch. 26:22; 28:23; [Rom. 3:21]
15 [j]See ch. 23:6 [k]Tit. 2:13; [Gal. 5:5] [l]Luke 14:14 [m]See Dan. 12:2
16 [n][1 Tim. 4:7, 15] [o]1 Cor. 10:32; Phil. 1:10; [Jude 24]; See ch. 23:1
17 [p][ch. 20:31] [q]Rom. 15:25-28, 31; 1 Cor. 16:1-3; 2 Cor. 8:1-4; 9:1, 2, 12; [Gal. 2:10] [r]ch. 26:4; 28:19 [s][ver. 11; ch. 20:16]
18 [t]ch. 21:26; 26:21 [u]ch. 21:27
19 [v]See ch. 23:30
21 [w]See ch. 23:6
22 [x]ver. 14; See ch. 9:2
23 [y][ch. 28:16] [z][ch. 27:3]

[1] Or *weary* [2] Some manuscripts add *and we would have judged him according to our law. [7]But the chief captain Lysias came and with great violence took him out of our hands, [8]commanding his accusers to come before you.*

23:31 Antipatris. A town built by Herod the Great in honor of his father, Antipater, about thirty miles northwest of Jerusalem.

23:35 Herod's praetorium. The official residence built by Herod the Great. It became a Roman praetorium or official residence and included prisoners' cells (John 18:28; Phil. 1:13).

24:1 Tertullus. As an orator, Tertullus was a kind of lawyer, possibly a Jew (he refers to Jewish law as "our" law, v. 6, text note).

24:5–7 Tertullus charged that Paul was a chronic troublemaker, the leader of a disreputable religious sect, and a person who threatened to profane the temple. Paul replied to these accusations in his defense before Felix (vv. 10–21).

24:5 the Nazarenes. Christians were identified as followers of Jesus of Nazareth. "Nazareth" may have been a term of contempt (John 1:46).

24:14 I worship . . . God. Paul assured Felix that as a Jew he followed a religion protected by Rome. As a follower of "the Way," Paul worshiped the "God of our fathers" and believed in the resurrection of the dead (Dan. 12:1, 2; 1 Thess. 4:13–18; 2 Thess. 1:8).

24:21 the resurrection of the dead. Paul made one critical statement that pertained not to Roman political interests but to Jewish and Christian theology.

24:23 he should be kept . . . liberty. As a Roman citizen whose case was still pending, Paul was given some freedom (28:16).

24 After some days Felix came with his
wife Drusilla, who was Jewish, and he sent
for Paul and heard him speak about [a]faith
[b]in Christ Jesus. 25 And as he reasoned
[c]about righteousness and self-control and
the coming judgment, Felix was alarmed
and said, "Go away for the present. [d]When
I get an opportunity I will summon you."
26 At the same time he hoped [e]that money
would be given him by Paul. So he sent for
him often and conversed with him.
27 When two years had elapsed, Felix was
succeeded by Porcius [f]Festus. And [g]desir-
ing to do the Jews a favor, [h]Felix left Paul
in prison.

Paul Appeals to Caesar

25 Now three days after Festus had
arrived in [i]the province, he went up
to Jerusalem from Caesarea. 2 And the chief
priests and the principal men of the Jews
[j]laid out their case against Paul, and they
urged him, 3 asking as a favor against Paul[1]
that he summon him to Jerusalem—
because [k]they were planning an ambush to
kill him on the way. 4 Festus replied that
Paul was being kept at Caesarea and that
he himself intended to go there shortly.
5 "So," said he, "let the men of authority
among you go down with me, and if there
is anything wrong about the man, let them
bring charges against him."
6 After he stayed among them not more
than eight or ten days, he went down to
Caesarea. And the next day he took his seat
on [l]the tribunal and ordered Paul to be
brought. 7 When he had arrived, the Jews
who had come down from Jerusalem stood
around him, bringing many and serious
charges against him [m]that they could not
prove. 8 Paul argued in his defense,
"Neither [n]against [o]the law of the Jews, nor
against the temple, nor [p]against Caesar
have I committed any offense." 9 But
Festus, [q]wishing to do the Jews a favor,
said to Paul, "Do you wish to go up to
Jerusalem and there be tried on these
charges before me?" 10 But Paul said, "I am
standing before Caesar's [r]tribunal, where I
ought to be tried. To the Jews I have done
no wrong, as you yourselves know very
well. 11 If then I am a wrongdoer and have
committed anything for which I deserve to
die, I do not seek to escape death. But if
there is nothing to their charges against
me, no one can give me up to them. [s]I
appeal to Caesar." 12 Then Festus, when he
had conferred with his council, answered,
"To Caesar you have appealed; to Caesar
you shall go."

Paul Before Agrippa and Bernice

13 Now when some days had passed,
Agrippa the king and Bernice arrived at
Caesarea and greeted Festus. 14 And as they
stayed there many days, Festus laid Paul's
case before the king, saying, [t]"There is a
man left prisoner by Felix, 15 and when I
was at Jerusalem, the chief priests and the
elders of the Jews laid out their case
[u]against him, asking for a sentence of condemnation against him. 16 [v]I answered
them that it was not the custom of the
Romans to give up anyone [w]before the
accused met the accusers face to face and
had opportunity to make his defense concerning the charge laid against him. 17 [x]So
when they came together here, I made no
delay, but on the next day took my seat on
[y]the tribunal and ordered the man to be
brought. 18 When the accusers stood up,
they brought no charge in his case of such
evils as I supposed. 19 Rather they [z]had certain points of dispute with him about their
own religion and about [a]a certain Jesus,
who was dead, but whom Paul asserted to
be alive. 20 Being at a loss how to investigate
these questions, I [b]asked whether he wanted to go to Jerusalem and be tried there

24 [a]See ch. 20:21 [b]Gal. 2:16; [Rom. 3:24]
25 [c][Tit. 2:12, 13] [d]ch. 17:32; [2 Tim. 4:2]
26 [e][ver. 17]
27 [f]ch. 25:1; 26:24 [g]ch. 25:9; [ch. 12:3; Mark 15:15] [h]ch. 25:14; See Luke 21:12
Chapter 25
1 [i]ch. 23:34
2 [j]ver. 15
3 [k]See ch. 9:24
6 [l]ver. 10, 17; See Matt. 27:19
7 [m]ch. 24:13
8 [n][ch. 24:12; 28:17]; See ch. 6:13 [o]John 7:5; 19:7 [p]John 19:12
9 [q]ch. 24:27
10 [r]ver. 6, 17
11 [s]ch. 26:32; 28:19
14 [t]ch. 24:27
15 [u]ver. 2, 3
16 [v]ver. 4, 5 [w][John 7:51]; See ch. 23:30
17 [x]ver. 7, 24 [y]ver. 6, 10
19 [z]ch. 18:15; 23:29 [a][ch. 17:18]
20 [b]ver. 9

[1] Greek *him*

24:24 Drusilla. Daughter of Herod Agrippa I (12:1–23) and sister of Herod Agrippa II (25:13; 26:3 note) and Bernice (25:13 note), Drusilla left Azizus, king of Emesa in Syria, to marry Felix. She probably died along with her son Agrippa in the eruption of Mt. Vesuvius at Pompeii, A.D. 79.

24:27 Porcius Festus. Festus was from a noble family in Rome. Though Felix had been greedy and evil, Festus was wise and honorable.

25:4 Felix had to protect Paul while he was in Roman custody and he refused the request of the Jews, saving Paul from their plot.

25:11 I appeal to Caesar. Fearing that Festus was going to grant the Jews their request, Paul exercised his right as a Roman citizen to be tried before Caesar (Nero) in Rome. At this time Nero was under the benevolent influence of the Stoic philosopher Seneca, and had not yet shown his hostility to Christianity. Paul could hope to be acquitted by Nero.

25:13 Agrippa the king. This was Herod Agrippa II, son of Agrippa I and great-grandson of Herod the Great (26:3 note).

Bernice. The oldest daughter of Herod Agrippa I, Bernice was twice widowed before entering into an incestuous relationship with her brother, Herod Agrippa II. Despite the scandal of this relationship, she was frequently presented as Herod's queen on official occasions (e.g., vv. 13, 23).

regarding them. 21 But [c]when Paul had
appealed to be kept in custody for the decision of [d]the emperor, I ordered him to be
held until I could send him to Caesar."
22 Then [e]Agrippa said to Festus, "I would
like to hear the man myself." "Tomorrow,"
said he, "you will hear him."
23 So on the next day [f]Agrippa and
Bernice came with great pomp, and they
entered the audience hall with the military
tribunes and the prominent men of the
city. Then, at the command of Festus, Paul
was brought in. 24 And Festus said, "King
Agrippa and all who are present with us,
you see this man about whom [g]the whole
Jewish people petitioned me, both in
Jerusalem and here, [h]shouting that he
ought not to live any longer. 25 But I found
that [i]he had done nothing deserving death.
And [j]as he himself appealed to [k]the emper-
or, I decided to go ahead and send him.
26 But I have nothing definite to write to my
lord about him. Therefore I have brought
him before you all, and especially before
you, King Agrippa, so that, after we have
examined him, I may have something to
write. 27 For it seems to me unreasonable,
in sending a prisoner, not to indicate the
charges against him."

Paul's Defense Before Agrippa

26 So [l]Agrippa said to Paul, "You have
permission to speak for yourself."
Then Paul stretched out his hand and
made his defense:
2 "I consider myself fortunate that it is
before you, King Agrippa, I am going to
make my defense today [m]against all the
accusations of the Jews, 3 especially because you are familiar with all the [n]customs
and [o]controversies of the Jews. Therefore I
beg you to listen to me patiently.
4 [p]"My manner of life from my youth,
spent from the beginning among [q]my own
nation and in Jerusalem, is known by all
the Jews. 5 They have known for a long
time, if they are willing to testify, that [r]ac-
cording to the strictest [s]party of our [t]reli-
gion I have lived as [u]a Pharisee. 6 And now
I stand here on trial because of my hope in
[v]the promise made by God to our fathers,
7 [w]to which [x]our twelve tribes hope to [y]at-
tain, as they earnestly worship night and
day. And for this hope [z]I am accused by
Jews, O king! 8 Why is it thought [a]incredi-
ble by any of you that God raises the dead?
9 [b]"I myself was convinced that I ought to
do many things in opposing the name of
[c]Jesus of Nazareth. 10 [d]And I did so in
Jerusalem. I not only locked up many of
the saints in prison after receiving authority
[e]from the chief priests, but [f]when they
were put to death I cast my vote against
them. 11 And [g]I punished them often in all
the synagogues and tried to make them
[h]blaspheme, and [i]in raging fury against
them I [j]persecuted them even to foreign
cities.

Paul Tells of His Conversion

12 "In this connection [k]I journeyed to
Damascus with the authority and commission of the chief priests. 13 At midday,
O king, I saw on the way a light from
heaven, brighter than the sun, that shone
around me and those who journeyed with
me. 14 And when we had all fallen to the
ground, I heard a voice saying to me [l]in the
Hebrew language,[1] 'Saul, Saul, why are you
persecuting me? It is hard for you to kick
against the goads.' 15 And I said, 'Who are
you, Lord?' And the Lord said, 'I am Jesus
whom you are persecuting. 16 But rise and
[m]stand upon your feet, for I have appeared
to you for this purpose, [n]to appoint you as
a servant and witness to the things in
which you have seen me and to those in
which I will appear to you, 17 [o]delivering
you from your people and from the
Gentiles—[p]to whom I [q]am sending you
18 [r]to open their eyes, so that they may turn

21 [c]See ver. 11 [d]ver. 25
22 [e]See ch. 9:15
23 [f]ver. 13; ch. 26:30
24 [g]ver. 2, 7 [h]ch. 22:22
25 [i]See ch. 23:29 [j]ver. 11, 12 [k]ver. 21
Chapter 26
1 [l]See ch. 9:15
2 [m]ch. 25:7, 19; [ver. 7]
3 [n]See ch. 6:14 [o]See ch. 18:15
4 [p][Gal. 1:13] [q]ch. 24:17; 28:19
5 [r]ch. 22:3 [s]See ch. 24:5 [t]James 1:26, 27 [u]ch. 23:6
6 [v]See ch. 13:32
7 [w][ch. 2:33; Heb. 10:36; 11:13, 39] [x]Matt. 19:28; Luke 22:30; James 1:1; Rev. 21:12; [Ezra 6:17] [y]Phil. 3:11 [z]ver. 2
8 [a][ch. 17:33; 1 Cor. 15:12]
9 [b]1 Tim. 1:13; [John 16:2]; See ch. 3:17 [c]ch. 22:8
10 [d]See ch. 8:3 [e]ver. 12; ch. 9:1, 2, 14, 21; 22:4, 5 [f]See ch. 22:20
11 [g]ch. 22:19 [h]See ch. 13:45 [i]ch. 9:1 [j]ch. 22:5
12 [k]For ver. 12-18, see ch. 9:3-8; 22:6-11
14 [l]ch. 21:40; 22:2
16 [m]Ezek. 2:1; Dan. 10:11 [n]See ch. 22:14, 15
17 [o][ch. 12:11; 1 Chr. 16:35; Jer. 1:8, 19; 15:20] [p]See ch. 9:15 [q][Rom. 11:13; 1 Tim. 2:7]
18 [r]Isai. 35:5; 42:7

[1] Or *the Hebrew dialect* (that is, Aramaic)

26:3 familiar with all the customs and controversies of the Jews. As the great-grandson of Herod the Great and son of Herod Agrippa I, who had persecuted the church (12:1–23), Herod Agrippa II (A.D. 27–c. 100) had an intimate knowledge of Jewish matters. Although influential in Jewish religious affairs because he had political authority to appoint the high priest, Agrippa II was unpopular with the Jews because of his incestuous relationship with his sister Bernice (25:13 note).

26:5 strictest party . . . I have lived as a Pharisee. Knowing the background of Agrippa, Paul stressed his dependence on the God of his fathers (cf. 24:14) and his link with the Pharisees (Phil. 3:5, 6) to show the legitimacy of his Judaism. Paul argued that God had promised the resurrection of the body. Although this was the belief of Jews in general and the Pharisees in particular, it was being used as the basis of charges against him.

26:12–14 Paul's experience on the road to Damascus (9:1–19) was so important to him that he recounted it twice, once before the Jewish crowd in Jerusalem (22:6–16), and again before this mainly pagan audience in Caesarea.

from darkness to light and from [s]the power
of Satan to God, that they may receive [t]for-
giveness of sins and [u]a place among those
who are sanctified [v]by faith in me.’
19 “Therefore, O King Agrippa, I was not
disobedient to [w]the heavenly vision, **20** but
declared first [x]to those in Damascus, [y]then
in Jerusalem and throughout all the region
of Judea, and also [z]to the Gentiles, that
they should [a]repent and [b]turn to God, performing deeds [c]in keeping with their repentance. **21** For this reason [d]the Jews seized
me in the temple and tried to kill me. **22** [e]To
this day I have had the help that comes
from God, and so [f]I stand here testifying
both to small and great, saying nothing but
what [g]the prophets and Moses said would
come to pass: **23** [h]that the Christ [i]must suffer and that, [j]by being the first [k]to rise from
the dead, [l]he would proclaim [m]light both
to our people and to the Gentiles.”
24 And as he was saying these things in
his defense, Festus said with a loud voice,
“Paul, [n]you are out of your mind; your
great learning is driving you out of your
mind.” **25** But Paul said, “I am not out of my
mind, [o]most excellent Festus, but I am
speaking [p]true and [q]rational words. **26** For
[r]the king knows about these things, and to
him I speak boldly. For I am persuaded
that none of these things has escaped his
notice, for this has not been done in a corner. **27** King Agrippa, do you believe the

18 [s]See Luke 22:53; 1 Cor. 5:5 [t]See ch. 5:31 [u]See ch. 20:32 [v][ch. 15:9; 2 Thess. 2:13]
19 [w]ver. 13
20 [x]ch. 9:19, 20 [y]ch. 9:26-29; 22:17-20 [z]See ch. 13:46 [a]See ch. 2:38 [b]See ch. 14:15 [c]Matt. 3:8; Luke 3:8
21 [d]ch. 21:27, 30, 31; 24:18
22 [e]2 Cor. 1:10; [Heb. 13:5, 6] [f][Eph. 6:13] [g]See ch. 10:43; 24:14
23 [h][Luke 24:26; Heb. 2:10]; See ch. 3:18 [i][John 12:34] [j]1 Cor. 15:20, 23; Col. 1:18; Rev. 1:5 [k]Rom. 1:4 [l][Eph. 2:17] [m]ver. 18; See Luke 2:32
24 [n]ch. 12:15; [ver. 8; ch. 17:32; 2 Kin. 9:11; Jer. 29:26; Mark 3:21; John 10:20; 1 Cor. 1:23; 2:14; 4:10]
25 [o]See ch. 24:3 [p][2 Pet. 1:16] [q][2 Cor. 5:13]
26 [r][ver. 3]

Repentance

Repentance means changing one’s mind, so that one’s views, values, goals, and ways are changed, and one’s whole life is lived differently. Mind and judgment, will and affections, behavior and lifestyle, motives and plans: all are involved. Repenting means starting to live a new life.

The call to repent was the fundamental summons in the preaching of John the Baptist (Matt. 3:2), Jesus (Matt. 4:17), the Twelve (Mark 6:12), Peter at Pentecost (Acts 2:38), Paul to the Gentiles (Acts 17:30; 26:20), and the glorified Christ to five of the seven churches in Asia (Rev. 2:5, 16, 22; 3:3, 19). It was part of Jesus’ summary of the gospel that was to be taken to all the world (Luke 24:47). It corresponds to the constant summons of the Old Testament prophets to Israel to return to the God from whom they had strayed (e.g., Jer. 23:22; 25:4, 5; Zech. 1:3–6). Repentance is always set forth as the path to remission of sins and restoration to God’s favor, while impenitence is the road to ruin (e.g., Luke 13:1–8).

Faith and repentance are themselves fruits of regeneration. But as a practical matter, repentance is inseparable from faith. Turning towards Christ in faith is impossible without turning away from sin in repentance. The idea that there can be saving faith without repentance, and that one can be justified by embracing Christ as Savior while refusing Him as Lord, is a dangerous error. True faith acknowledges Christ as what He is, our God-appointed king as well as our God-given priest, and faith that trusts in Him as Savior will submit to Him as Lord also. To refuse this is to seek justification with an impenitent faith, which is no faith.

The *Westminster Confession* says that in repenting

> a sinner, out of the sight and sense, not only of the danger, but also the filthiness and odiousness of his sins, as contrary to the holy nature and righteous law of God, and upon the apprehension of His mercy in Christ to such as are penitent, so grieves for and hates his sins as to turn from them all unto God, purposing and endeavoring to walk with Him in all the ways of His commandments (*Westminster Confession,* 15.2).

Feelings of remorse, self-reproach, and sorrow for sin generated by fear of punishment, without any wish or resolve to forsake sinning should not be confused with repentance. David expresses true repentance in Ps. 51, having in his heart the serious purpose of sinning no more, and of living a righteous life (Luke 3:8; Acts 26:2).

26:20 See 2:38; 3:19 and note; 17:20; 20:21; theological note “Repentance.”

26:23 Christ must suffer . . . rise from the dead. The Jews had difficulty accepting the idea that the Messiah would suffer and die. Jesus and His apostles taught this doctrine from the Scriptures (17:2, 3; Luke 24:27; 1 Cor. 15:3, 4), yet the Jews rejected it, arrested Paul, and wanted to kill him.

26:27 do you believe the prophets. Agrippa faced a dilemma: if he said no, he would anger the Jews; if he said yes, he would lose face because Paul would ask him to believe the gospel.

prophets? I know that you believe." 28 And
Agrippa said to Paul, "In a short time
would you persuade me to be [s]a Christian?"[1] 29 And Paul said, "Whether short or
long, I would to God that not only you but
also all who hear me this day [t]might
become such as I am—except for [u]these
chains."
30 Then the king rose, and [v]the governor
and Bernice and those who were sitting
with them. 31 And when they had withdrawn, they said to one another, [w]"This
man is doing nothing to deserve death or
imprisonment." 32 And Agrippa said to
Festus, [x]"This man could have been set
[y]free if he had not appealed [z]to Caesar."

Paul Sails for Rome

27 And when it was decided [a]that [b]we
should sail for Italy, they delivered
Paul and some other prisoners to a centurion of the Augustan [c]Cohort named Julius.
2 And embarking in a ship of Adramyttium,
which was about to sail to the ports along
the coast of Asia, we put to sea, accompanied by [d]Aristarchus, a Macedonian from
Thessalonica. 3 The next day we put in at
Sidon. And [e]Julius [f]treated Paul kindly and
[g]gave him leave to go to his friends and be
cared for. 4 And putting out to sea from
there we sailed under the lee of Cyprus,
because the winds were against us. 5 And
when we had sailed across the open sea
along the coast of Cilicia and Pamphylia,
we came to Myra in Lycia. 6 There the centurion found [h]a ship of Alexandria sailing
for Italy and put us on board. 7 We sailed
slowly for a number of days and arrived
with difficulty off Cnidus, and as the wind
did not allow us to go farther, we sailed
under the lee of Crete off Salmone.
8 Coasting along it with difficulty, we came
to a place called Fair Havens, near which
was the city of Lasea.
9 Since much time had passed, and the
voyage was now dangerous because even
[i]the Fast[2] was already over, Paul advised
them, 10 saying, "Sirs, I perceive that the
voyage will be with [j]injury and much loss,
not only of the cargo and the ship, but also
of our lives." 11 But the centurion paid more
attention to [k]the pilot and to the owner of
the ship than to what Paul said. 12 And
because the harbor was not suitable to
spend the winter in, the majority decided
to put out to sea from there, on the chance
that somehow they could reach Phoenix, a
harbor of Crete, facing both southwest and
northwest, and spend the winter there.

The Storm at Sea

13 Now when the south wind blew gently,
supposing that they had obtained their
purpose, they weighed anchor and sailed
along Crete, close to the shore. 14 But soon
a tempestuous wind, called the northeast-
er, [l]struck down from the land. 15 And
when the ship was caught and could not
face the wind, we gave way to it and were
driven along. 16 Running under the lee of a
small island called Cauda,[3] we managed
with difficulty to secure the ship's boat.
17 After hoisting it up, they used supports to
undergird the ship. Then, fearing that they
would [m]run aground on the Syrtis, they
lowered the gear,[4] and thus they were driv-
en along. 18 Since we were violently storm-
tossed, they began the next day [n]to jettison
the cargo. 19 And on the third day they

28 [s]ch. 11:26; 1 Pet. 4:16
29 [t][1 Cor. 7:7] [u]See ch. 21:33
30 [v]See ch. 23:24
31 [w]See ch. 23:29
32 [x]ch. 28:18 [y]ch. 25:11; 28:19 [z]See ch. 9:15
Chapter 27
1 [a]ch. 25:12, 25 [b]See ch. 16:10 [c]See ch. 10:1
2 [d]See ch. 19:29
3 [e]ver. 43 [f]ch. 28:2 [g][ch. 24:23; 28:16, 30]
6 [h]ch. 28:11
9 [i]Lev. 16:29-31; 23:27-29; Num. 29:7
10 [j]ver. 21
11 [k]Rev. 18:17 (Gk.)
14 [l][Mark 4:37]
17 [m]ver. 26, 29
18 [n]Jonah 1:5; [ver. 38]

1 Or *In a short time you would persuade me to act like a Christian!*
2 That is, the Day of Atonement 3 Some manuscripts *Clauda* 4 That is, the sea-anchor (or possibly the mainsail)

26:28 would you persuade me to be a Christian. The king used a delaying tactic, arguing that a half-hour speech is insufficient time to become a Christian. In the first century, "Christian" (cf. 11:26) was probably a term of contempt (1 Pet. 4:16).

27:2 Adramyttium. On the coast between Troas and Pergamum.

we put to sea. This chapter is filled with nautical terms and directions, evidence that the author was an eyewitness.

we . . . Aristarchus. Paul had two companions with him: Luke as his physician (Col. 4:14) and Aristarchus (Col. 4:10; Philem. 24) from Thessalonica, probably his attendant.

27:3 put in at Sidon. An eastern Mediterranean port, today in Lebanon.

27:4 under the lee of Cyprus. That is, close under the eastern point of the island in order to be protected from the westerly winds of the summer and fall.

27:5 coast of Cilicia and Pamphylia. The ship went up the Syrian coast, past Antioch of Syria and then west to Myra. Myra was an important port of call for grain ships sailing between Alexandria and Rome.

27:11, 12 The captain and the owner wanted to reach the larger and safer harbor of Phoenix about forty miles to the west, but in going west past Cape Matala the ship would be exposed to winds from the northwest.

27:17 used supports. Because of the danger of violent storms on the Mediterranean, ancient vessels carried ropes to strengthen the hull by being tied around it sideways in an emergency.

lowered the gear. Fearing that they might be driven all the way to the Syrtis (a region of sands near modern Libya and Tunisia) the sailors lowered the sail. The description in Greek could also mean that they lowered a sea anchor to slow the ship down.

threw the ship's tackle overboard with
their own hands. **20** When neither sun nor
stars appeared for many days, and no small
tempest lay on us, all hope of our being
saved was at last abandoned.
21 Since they had been without food for a
long time, Paul stood up among them and
said, "Men, [o]you should have listened to
me and not have set sail from Crete and
incurred this [o]injury and loss. **22** Yet now I
urge you to [p]take heart, for there will be no
loss of life among you, but only of the ship.
23 For this very night [q]there [r]stood before
me [s]an angel of the God [t]to whom I belong
and [u]whom I worship, **24** and he said, 'Do
not be afraid, Paul; [v]you must stand before
Caesar. And behold, [w]God has granted you
all those who sail with you.' **25** So take
heart, men, for I have faith in God that it
will be exactly as I have been told. **26** But
[x]we must [y]run aground on some island."
27 When the fourteenth night had come,
as we were being driven across the Adriatic
Sea, about midnight the sailors suspected
that they were nearing land. **28** So they took
a sounding and found twenty fathoms.[1] A
little farther on they took a sounding again
and found fifteen fathoms.[2] **29** And fearing
that we might [z]run on the rocks, they let
down four anchors from the stern and
prayed for day to come. **30** And as the sailors
were seeking to escape from the ship, and
had lowered [a]the ship's boat into the sea
under pretense of laying out anchors from
the bow, **31** Paul said to the centurion and
the soldiers, "Unless these men stay in the
ship, you cannot be saved." **32** Then the soldiers cut away the ropes of the ship's boat
and let it go.
33 As day was about to dawn, Paul urged
them all to take some food, saying, "Today
is the fourteenth day that you have continued in suspense and without food, having
taken nothing. **34** Therefore I urge you to
take some food. It will give you strength,
for [b]not a hair is to perish from the head of
any of you." **35** And when he had said these
things, he took bread, and [c]giving thanks
to God in the presence of all he broke it
and began to eat. **36** Then they all [d]were
encouraged and ate some food themselves.
37 (We were in all 276[3] [e]persons in the
ship.) **38** And when they had eaten enough,

21 [o]ver. 10
22 [p]ver. 25, 36
23 [q]ch. 18:9; 23:11 [r]2 Tim. 4:17 [s]See ch. 8:26 [t]Ps. 119:94; Dan. 5:23 [u][Dan. 6:16]; See ch. 24:14
24 [v]ch. 23:11 [w][Gen. 18:26; 19:21, 29; Ezek. 14:14]
26 [x]ch. 28:1 [y]ver. 17, 29
29 [z]ver. 17, 26
30 [a]ver. 16
34 [b]1 Sam. 14:45; 2 Sam. 14:11; 1 Kin. 1:52; Luke 21:18; [Matt. 10:30]
35 [c]See Matt. 15:36
36 [d]ver. 22
37 [e]ch. 2:41; 7:14; Rom. 13:1; 1 Pet. 3:20

1 About 120 feet; a fathom (Greek *orguia*) was about 6 feet or 2 meters 2 About 90 feet (see previous note) 3 Some manuscripts *seventy-six*, or *about seventy-six*

27:24 granted you all . . . with you. In His kindness God saved everyone in the ship.

27:26 some island. The island of Malta, south of Sicily.

27:34 not a hair is to perish from . . . any. God is in control of the minute details of life (Luke 21:18).

27:37 276 persons in the ship. This number of passengers on an ancient seagoing vessel was not unusual. Some ships of the period could carry considerably more.

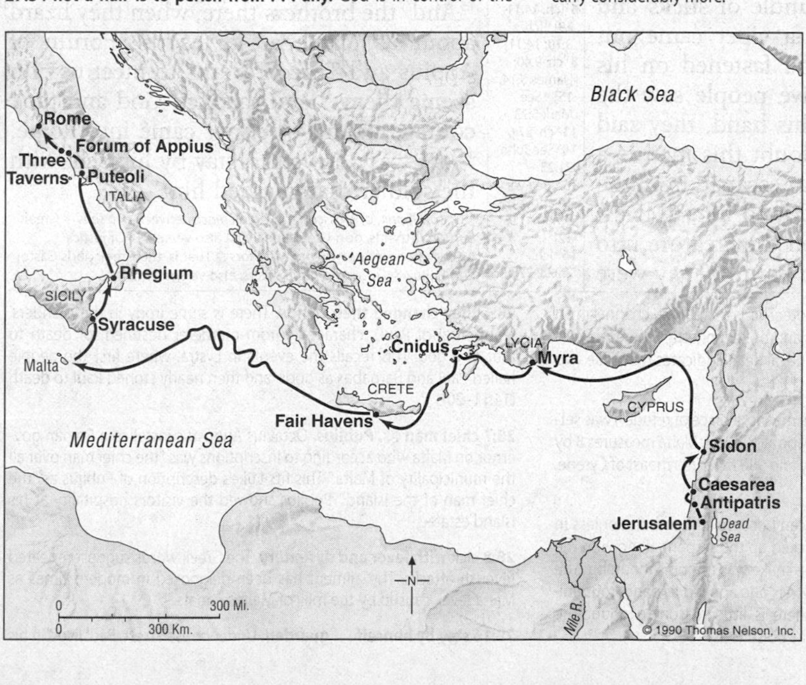

On to Rome (Paul's Fourth Journey)
In Jerusalem, following his third missionary journey, Paul struggled with Jews who accused him of profaning the temple (Acts 21:26-34). He was placed in Roman custody in Caesarea for two years, but after appealing to Caesar, was sent by ship to Rome. After departing the island of Crete, Paul's party was shipwrecked on Malta by a great storm. Three months later he finally arrived at the imperial city.

they lightened the ship, [f]throwing out the
wheat into the sea.

The Shipwreck

[39] Now when it was day, [g]they did not
recognize the land, but they noticed a bay
with a beach, on which they planned if
possible to run the ship ashore. [40] So they
cast off the anchors and left them in the
sea, at the same time loosening the ropes
that tied the rudders. Then hoisting the fore-
sail to the wind they made for the beach.
[41] But striking a reef,[1] [h]they ran the vessel
aground. The bow stuck and remained
immovable, and the stern was being broken up by the surf. [42] [i]The soldiers' plan
was to kill the prisoners, lest any should
swim away and escape. [43] But the centurion, [j]wishing to save Paul, kept them from
carrying out their plan. He ordered those
who could swim to jump overboard first
and make for the land, [44] and the rest on
planks or on pieces of the ship. And so it
was that [k]all were brought safely to land.

Paul on Malta

28 After we were brought safely
through, [l]we then learned that [m]the
island was called Malta. [2] [n]The native people[2] showed us unusual [o]kindness, for they
kindled a fire and welcomed us all, because
it had begun to rain and was cold. [3] When
Paul had gathered a bundle of sticks and
put them on the fire, a viper came out
because of the heat and fastened on his
hand. [4] When [p]the native people saw the
creature hanging from his hand, they said
to one another, [q]"No doubt this man is a
murderer. Though he has escaped from the
sea, [r]Justice[3] has not allowed him to live."
[5] He, however, [s]shook off the creature into
the fire and suffered no harm. [6] They were
waiting for him to swell up or suddenly fall
down dead. But when they had waited a
long time and saw no misfortune come to
him, [t]they changed their minds and [u]said
that he was a god.
[7] Now in the neighborhood of that place
were lands belonging to the chief man of
the island, named Publius, who received us
and entertained us hospitably for three
days. [8] It happened that the father of
Publius lay sick with fever and dysentery.
And Paul visited him and [v]prayed, and
[w]putting his hands on him healed him.
[9] And when this had taken place, the rest of
the people on the island who had diseases
also came and were cured. [10] They also honored us greatly,[4] and when we were about
to sail, they put on board whatever we
needed.

Paul Arrives at Rome

[11] After three months we set sail in [x]a
ship that had wintered in the island, a ship
of Alexandria, with the twin gods[5] as a fig-
urehead. [12] Putting in at Syracuse, we
stayed there for three days. [13] And from
there we made a circuit and arrived at
Rhegium. And after one day a south wind
sprang up, and on the second day we came
to Puteoli. [14] There we found [y]brothers[6]
and were invited to stay with them for
seven days. And so we came to Rome.
[15] And [y]the brothers there, when they heard
about us, came as far as the Forum of
Appius and Three Taverns to meet us. On
seeing them, [z]Paul thanked God and took
courage. [16] And when we came into Rome,
[a]Paul was allowed to stay by himself, with
the soldier that guarded him.

1 Or *sandbank*, or *crosscurrent*; Greek *place between two seas* 2 Greek *barbaroi* (that is, non-Greek speakers) also verse 4 3 Or *justice* 4 Greek *honored us with many honors* 5 That is, the Greek gods Castor and Pollux 6 Or *brothers and sisters*; also verses 15, 21

38 [f][ver. 18]
39 [g][ch. 28:1]
41 [h][2 Cor. 11:25]
42 [i][ch. 12:19]
43 [j]ver. 3
44 [k]ver. 22
Chapter 28
1 [l][ch. 27:39] [m]ch. 27:26
2 [n]ver. 4; Rom. 1:14; 1 Cor. 14:11; Col. 3:11 [o]ch. 27:3
4 [p]ver. 2 [q][Job 4:7; Luke 13:2, 4; John 9:2] [r][Num. 32:23; Amos 5:19; 9:3]
5 [s]Mark 16:18; Luke 10:19
6 [t][ch. 14:11, 19] [u][ch. 8:10; 14:11]
8 [v]ch. 9:40; [James 5:14, 15] [w]See Mark 5:23
11 [x]ch. 27:6
14 [y]See John 21:23
15 [y][See ver. 14 above] [z][Rom. 1:9-12]
16 [a][ch. 24:23; 27:3]

27:41 But striking a reef. See text note. This is the narrow channel in St. Paul's Bay between Malta and the island of Salmonetta, where the currents create sandbars. This sort of nautical detail indicates that Luke was an eyewitness of the event.

28:1 Malta. Ancient Melita (the name means "a place of refuge") was settled by Phoenicians who came there about 1000 B.C. Malta measures 8 by 18 miles and is 60 miles south of Sicily and 180 miles northeast of Cyrene, North Africa.

28:3–5 Being cold-blooded, snakes can become stiff and motionless in cold weather, and Paul must have picked up the serpent along with the brush. Some have suggested that the snake was nonpoisonous, but the Greek word translated "creature" in v. 4 is one applied to dangerous animals and poisonous snakes, and there is little reason to doubt the islanders' identification of the snake as poisonous.

28:6 they changed their minds. There is some irony in the islanders' reappraisal of Paul's character—from murderer destined for death to that of a god. This recalls the events in Lystra, where first the people hailed Paul and Barnabas as gods, and then nearly stoned Paul to death (14:11–20).

28:7 chief man . . . Publius. Octavius Augustus installed a Roman governor on Malta who according to inscriptions was "the chief man over all the municipality of Malta." This fits Luke's description of Publius as "the chief man of the island." Publius showed the visitors hospitality at his island estate.

28:8 sick with fever and dysentery. The Greek words suggest repeated feverish attacks. The ailment has been diagnosed in modern times as Malta fever, caused by the milk of Maltese goats.

28:16 stay by himself . . . guarded. Under house arrest, Paul lived in his

Paul in Rome

17 After three days he called together the
local leaders of the Jews, and when they
had gathered, he said to them, "Brothers,
[b] though I had done nothing against our
people or [c] the customs of our fathers, yet I
was delivered as a prisoner from Jerusalem
into the hands of the Romans. 18 When
they had examined me, they [d] wished to set
me at liberty, [e] because there was no reason
for the death penalty in my case. 19 But
because the Jews objected, I was compelled
[f] to appeal to Caesar—though I had no
charge to bring against [g] my nation. 20 For
this reason, therefore, I have asked to see
you and speak with you, since it is [h] because of [i] the hope of Israel that I am wearing [j] this [k] chain." 21 And they said to him,
"We have received no letters from Judea
about you, and none of [l] the brothers coming here has reported or spoken any evil
about you. 22 But we desire to hear from
you what your views are, for with regard to
this [m] sect we know that everywhere [n] it is
spoken against."
23 When they had appointed a day for
him, they came to him at his lodging in
greater numbers. From morning till
evening [o] he expounded to them, testifying
to [p] the kingdom of God and [q] trying to convince them about Jesus [r] both from the Law
of Moses and from the Prophets. 24 And
[s] some were convinced by what he said, but
others disbelieved. 25 And disagreeing
among themselves, they departed after
Paul had made one statement: [t] "The Holy
Spirit was right in saying to your fathers
through Isaiah the prophet:

26 [u] "'Go to this people, and say,
[v] You will indeed hear but never
understand,
and you will indeed see but never
perceive.
27 [w] For this people's heart has grown
dull,
and with their ears they can barely
hear,
and their eyes they have closed;
lest they should see with their
eyes
and hear with their ears
and understand with their heart
and [x] turn, and I would heal them.'

28 Therefore let it be known to you that [y] this
[z] salvation of God [a] has been sent to the
Gentiles; [b] they will listen." [1]
30 He lived there two whole years at his
own expense, [2] and [c] welcomed all who
came to him, 31 [d] proclaiming [e] the kingdom
of God and teaching about the Lord Jesus
Christ [f] with all boldness and [g] without hindrance.

17 [b] [ch. 25:8] [c] ch. 6:14; 15:1; 21:21 **18** [d] ch. 26:31, 32 [e] See 23:29 **19** [f] ch. 25:11; 26:32 [g] ch. 24:17; 26:4 **20** [h] See ch. 23:6 [i] [Luke 2:25] [j] ch. 26:29 [k] Eph. 6:20; 2 Tim. 1:16; See ch. 21:33; Phil. 1:7 **21** [l] ch. 22:5 **22** [m] See ch. 24:5 [n] Luke 2:34; [1 Pet. 2:12; 3:16; 4:14, 16] **23** [o] [ch. 17:2, 3] [p] ver. 31 [q] [ch. 19:8] [r] ch. 8:35; 24:14; 26:22 **24** [s] [ch. 14:4; 17:4, 5; 19:9; 23:7] **25** [t] Matt. 15:7 **26** [u] Cited from Isai. 6:9, 10 [v] Matt. 13:14, 15; Mark 4:12; [Luke 8:10] **27** [w] [John 12:40; Rom. 11:8] [x] See Luke 22:32 **28** [y] ch. 13:26 [z] Ps. 67:2; Isai. 40:5; Luke 2:30; 3:6; [Rom. 11:11] [a] See ch. 13:46 [b] John 10:16; [ch. 13:48; Matt. 8:11; 21:43] **30** [c] [Phil. 1:13] **31** [d] [ch. 8:12; 20:25] [e] ver. 23; See Matt. 12:28; 13:19 [f] See ch. 4:29 [g] [Phil. 1:12, 13; 2 Tim. 2:9]

1 Some manuscripts add verse 29: *And when he had said these words, the Jews departed, having much dispute among themselves* 2 Or *in his own hired dwelling*

own rented home. There he could entertain his friends and minister to groups such as the Roman Jews.

28:30, 31 From A.D. 60–62 Paul was under house arrest preaching and teaching to anyone who wanted to hear. His subject is summarized as the kingdom of God and Jesus Christ. At the end of Acts, Paul has not yet been tried before Nero, as the Lord said was going to happen (27:24). It appears that Paul expected to be acquitted and released (Phil. 1:25; 2:24; Philem. 22). This must have occurred before A.D. 64, when Nero set fire to Rome and accused Christians of that crime. When released, Paul seems to have taken up his ministry again, going as far as Greece (Nicopolis, Titus 3:12; Thessalonica, 2 Tim. 4:10), Crete (Titus 1:5), and Asia Minor (Ephesus, 2 Tim. 1:18; 4:12; Troas, 2 Tim. 4:13; Miletus, 2 Tim. 4:20). Possibly he went as far west as Spain (Rom. 15:23, 24, 28), as the first-century writing *1 Clement* may indicate. About A.D. 67, Paul was imprisoned again by Nero and executed. In 2 Tim. 4:6–8, Paul anticipates the end of his life.

28:31 with all boldness and without hindrance. For Paul, Luke, and those who followed, the message about Jesus and the glorious kingdom of God was to go on in triumph.

INTRODUCTION TO THE Epistles

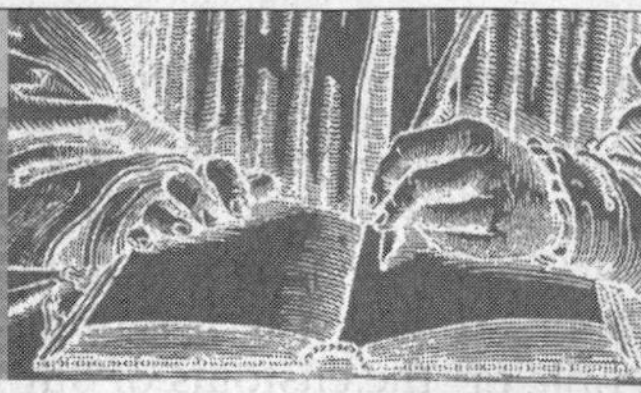

Of the twenty-seven books in the New Testament, twenty-one are letters written either to individual churches (Philippians, 2 John), groups of churches (Galatians, 1 Peter), or specific persons (Philemon, 3 John). Two other books contain letters within them (Acts 15:22–29; Rev. 1:4–3:22). Clearly this style of writing has a prominent place in the New Testament. However, beginning with the apostle Paul, Christians not only used but also modified the conventions of letter writing followed in Hellenistic culture. To better understand the epistles of the New Testament, it is helpful to consider the functions and conventions of letter writing in the Greco-Roman world, as well as how the apostles used and adapted that literary tradition.

GREEK AND ROMAN LETTER WRITING

Letter writing has a long history in the ancient Near East. It began as a means of official communication for military affairs and governmental administration, and examples of such letters may be found even in the Old Testament (2 Sam. 11:14, 15; Ezra 4:6–23; 7:11–26). With the development of paper made from papyrus, letter writing became a more common form of communication, but even then it was complicated by the restriction of the postal couriers to government correspondence. The rich could dispatch servants to deliver their letters, but most people had to rely on the travels of friends or even strangers to carry their mail.

Letter writing in the New Testament era was almost exclusively a product of previously existing relationships; people wrote to family members or others whom they had already met personally. Their letters were meant to fulfill three basic purposes: to provide basic or necessary information, to make requests of a social superior or give instructions to a subordinate, and to maintain and develop the personal relationship between the correspondents. The letter served as a substitute for the actual presence of the writer. Very often if the courier who delivered the letter was well known to the formal correspondents, he or she would expand or clarify the contents of the letter (cf. 1 Cor. 1:11; 7:1).

The form of Hellenistic letters had three major components: an opening, body, and conclusion. The opening and conclusion were primarily concerned with the personal relationship between the correspondents, and their language can reveal much about that relationship. When writing to a social equal or subordinate, it was customary to put the name of the sender first and then the recipient ("A to B, greetings"), followed by a health wish (cf. 3 John 1, 2). If the recipient was a superior, that name would be placed first ("To B, greetings from A"), and the health wish would be omitted. The body of a letter was concerned with providing information or instructions. Letters primarily intended to maintain or build a personal relationship usually had more lengthy openings and conclusions, and the body could be almost nonexistent.

THE LETTERS OF PAUL

Because Paul's missionary travels forced him to be separated from the churches he founded, it was natural that he would choose to write letters to maintain his relationship with the congregations. His letters were not, however, of the simple "staying in touch" variety; each of them was prompted by specific concerns or situations within the churches that required his instruction. The only exception to this pattern is possibly Romans, which appears to have been written to a church Paul did not know personally, and which does not seem to have raised specific matters prompting Paul to write. Paul's letters, then, served as a means of apostolic presence and instruction for the churches when the apostle himself could not be present.

Paul's apostolic office and function had significant influence on his use of letter-writing conventions. Rather than including a wish for health or prosperity in his openings, Paul called for God's grace upon the recipients and offered a prayer of thanksgiving on their behalf (but cf. Gal. 1:6–9, where Paul's strained relations with these churches led him to replace his usual thanksgiving with a rebuke). In this manner he adapted the traditional formulas for the physical health of the recipients to the religious function of concern for their spiritual well-being. Similarly he replaced the customary words of "farewell" in his closings with words of benediction and grace. Although his practice of giving his own name first in the opening salutation might be understood as assuming a position of greater social standing than his readers, Paul tempers this tone of authority by addressing them in the familial terms "brethren" and "beloved." His letters are a combination of the conventional features of family letters and the formal speeches of instruction found in contemporary philosophical epistles.

Like many writers of letters during this period, Paul seems generally to have used an amanuensis (a professional scribe) to write his letters. The scribe Tertius, who wrote Romans, inserted his own personal greetings in the conclusion (Rom. 16:22). Elsewhere Paul seems to call attention to portions of letters that he wrote in his own distinctive hand (1 Cor. 16:21; Gal. 6:11; cf. 1 Pet. 5:12). When Paul was responding to communications from the churches, he apparently had his letters carried back by the representatives from the congregation (Stephanas, Fortunatus, and Achaicus in 1 Cor. 16:17; cf. 7:1; Epaphroditus in Phil. 4:18). Otherwise the letters would be delivered by close associates (Titus in 2 Cor. 8:16, 17).

THE GENERAL EPISTLES

The General Epistles. The question of the degree of influence that Paul's letters had on the choice of this literary form by other apostles is currently being reexamined. This much at least is certain: the epistle became an important form of Christian writing not only for authors of the later New Testament books, but also for the "Apostolic Fathers," such as Ignatius of Antioch, Polycarp, and Clement of Rome.

The letters of James, Peter, John, and Jude, and the letter to the Hebrews all have significant differences from the Pauline letters. As a general rule, they do not follow the formal conventions of Hellenistic letters as closely as Paul. Hebrews and 1 John have no formal opening, nor do 1 John and James have a clear example of the usual closing greetings. Except for 2 and 3 John, it is difficult to determine what, if any, specific problems these letters were intended to address, nor is it clear whether they were written for particular recipients. For these reasons they are often called "General Epistles." In their form and content alike they are more like philosophical epistles than ordinary correspondence.

THE EPISTLE OF PAUL THE APOSTLE TO THE

Romans

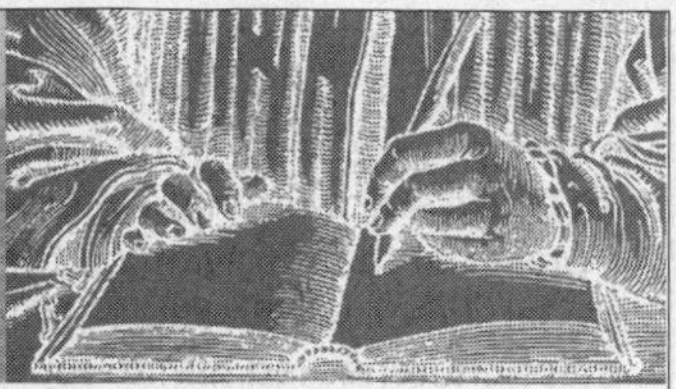

AUTHOR

The opening word of the letter (1:1), as well as the biographical details recorded in chs. 1, 15, and 16 show that Romans was written by the apostle Paul. The letter was already cited and listed as Paul's during the second century. Its authenticity has been disputed only rarely and never convincingly.

DATE AND OCCASION

Paul wrote Romans shortly before his visit to Jerusalem with the gift from the Gentile congregations (15:25; Acts 24:17). Internal indications suggesting that at this time he was a resident of Corinth include the reference to Phoebe, a member of the church at Cenchreae, the port of Corinth (16:1, 2), the references to Gaius as his host (1 Cor. 1:14), and to Erastus (Acts 19:22; 2 Tim. 4:20). The time of writing was probably during his three months in Greece, described in Acts 20:2, 3. While it is not possible to fix a date, it is known that Gallio (before whom Paul appeared in Acts 18:12) was proconsul (normally a one-year appointment) in Achaia in A.D. 52. Paul was in Corinth for "many days" (Acts 18:18), presumably during the period A.D. 51–53. He then sailed to Ephesus for a brief visit, and went to Caesarea and probably Jerusalem as well as Antioch (Acts 18:22). Returning through Galatia and Phrygia (Acts 18:23) to Ephesus, he was a resident there for about three years (Acts 19:8, 10) before deciding to go to Jerusalem via Macedonia and Achaia (Acts 19:21). The earliest possible date for the writing of Romans, therefore, is towards the end of A.D. 54; but a later date leaves more leeway for Paul's many activities, so the letter is best dated some time between the end of A.D. 55 and the early months of A.D. 57.

That the faith of the Roman Christians was well known (1:8), and that Paul had desired to visit them for some time (1:13), suggest that the Christian faith had been established in the capital of the empire for a considerable period. These facts are supported by the statement of the Roman historian Suetonius that Claudius had expelled the Jews (in A.D. 49) for rioting "at the instigation of Chrestus" (evidently a reference to Christ). Visitors from Rome were present on the Day of Pentecost (Acts 2:10, 11) and may have been the first to bring the good news to the city. Its strategic importance and the large number of Jews living there would have brought the gospel message to Rome as though attracted by a magnet. Despite tradition stretching back through Irenaeus, it is certain that the church was not founded by Peter or Paul. It is clear that Paul had never visited the church (1:8–13), and the absence of any reference to Peter or the other apostles suggests that the Roman church had not experienced direct apostolic ministry.

Both Jews and Gentiles were members of the church in Rome, and 1:13 indicates a predominance of Gentiles, as possibly does the warning to Gentile Christians not to be proud (11:13–24). The conflict between weak and strong in 14:1–15:13 may have arisen in a similar context. It is even possible that the several house churches in which the Christians met reflected these divisions (cf. 16:5, 14, 15).

Paul perceived his ministry to be at a turning point when Romans was written. He believed that he had fulfilled his ministry in the eastern Mediterranean (15:17–23) and that the time was ripe to move west and evangelize in Spain (15:24). He hoped to visit the Roman Christians on the way, fulfilling his long-time ambition, and perhaps gaining their assistance as a supporting church (15:24).

In light of this, it was essential for him to present his apostolic credentials (note "my gospel" in 2:16 and 16:25), so that they might recognize the authenticity of his ministry. Paul may also have thought it necessary to defend his ministry from the false insinuations of rumor-mongerers (3:8).

At the time of writing Romans, Paul was also

deeply concerned that the Christian church should be a fellowship of Jews and Gentiles together in the one body of Christ. This is clear from the importance he attaches to the Gentile love-gift to the Jerusalem church. It also surfaces throughout Romans in the theme of the unifying of Jew and Gentile—in sin because of Adam, and through grace in Christ. The saving righteousness of the gospel is needed by both, since all have sinned; it may be received by both, since it comes by grace through faith. The outworking of this saving righteousness in history is the clue to God's ultimate purposes for both; and this saving righteousness is to be expressed in the lives of both—personally, communally, and socially—in the body of Christ as the new people of God. The opportunity for writing while in Corinth, the pressing burden of his visit to Jerusalem, and the prospect of visiting Rome before preaching the gospel at the limits of the then-known world, all conspired to bring him to write this letter.

CHARACTERISTICS AND THEMES

Romans is Paul's fullest, grandest, most comprehensive statement of the gospel. Its compressed declarations of vast truths are like coiled springs—once loosed, they leap through mind and heart to fill one's horizon and shape one's life. John Chrysostom, the fifth century's greatest preacher, had Romans read aloud to him once a week. Augustine, Luther, and Wesley, three supremely significant contributors to the Christian heritage, all came to assured faith through the impact of Romans. All the Reformers saw Romans as the God-given key to understanding all Scripture, since here Paul brings together all the Bible's greatest themes—sin, law, judgment, human destiny, faith, works, grace, justification, sanctification, election, the plan of salvation, the work of Christ and of the Spirit, the Christian hope, the nature and life of the church, the place of Jew and non-Jew in the purposes of God, the philosophy of church and world history, the meaning and message of the Old Testament, the duties of Christian citizenship, and the principles of personal godliness and morality. From the vantage point given by Romans, the whole landscape of the Bible is open to view, and the relation of the parts to the whole becomes plain. The study of Romans is vitally necessary for the spiritual health and insight of the Christian.

OUTLINE OF ROMANS

I. Paul's Greetings and Personal Introduction (1:1–15)

II. Theme: The Righteousness of God for Jew and Gentile (1:16, 17)

III. Mankind's Universal Sinfulness (1:18–3:20)

- A. *Gentile Sinfulness (1:18–32)*
- B. *Jewish Sinfulness (2:1–3:8)*
- C. *Universal Sinfulness (3:9–20)*

IV. God's Righteousness for Justification (3:21–5:21)

- A. *Provided in Christ by Faith (3:21–31)*
- B. *Proved by the Example of Abraham (ch. 4)*
- C. *Guarantees Blessings for the Righteous (5:1–11)*
- D. *Rooted in the Obedience of Christ—the New Adam (5:12–21)*

V. Grace Reigns Through God's Righteousness (chs. 6–8)

- A. *Sin's Dominion Broken and Its Influence Resisted (ch. 6)*
- B. *Believers Dead to the Law's Condemnation Though Not Yet Made Sinless (ch. 7)*
- C. *Those Living by the Spirit Prove Victors over the Flesh (ch. 8)*

VI. God Demonstrates His Righteousness in Jew and Gentile (chs. 9–11)

- A. *God's Righteousness Established in History (ch. 9)*
- B. *God's Righteousness Received Only by Faith (ch. 10)*
- C. *God's Righteousness Revealed in Jew and Gentile (ch. 11)*

VII. God's Righteousness Grasped and Expressed in His People's Lives (12:1–15:13)

- A. *In the Response of Consecration (12:1, 2)*
- B. *In the Ministry of the Body of Christ (12:3–21)*
- C. *In the Realities of Political and Social Life (ch. 13)*
- D. *In the Fellowship of Weak and Strong (14:1–15:13)*

VIII. Paul's Plans and Concluding Greetings (15:14–16:27)

- A. *Paul's Vision for His Ministry (15:14–22)*
- B. *Paul's Plan to Visit Rome (15:23–33)*
- C. *Paul's Greetings to Christians in Rome (16:1–16)*
- D. *Paul's Warning Against Enemies and Assurance of Their Defeat (16:17–20)*
- E. *Paul's Companions Send Greetings (16:21–24)*
- F. *Paul's Apostolic Doxology (16:25–27)*

Greeting

1 Paul, [a]a servant[1] of Christ Jesus,
[b]called to be an apostle, [c]set apart for
the gospel of God, **2** which [d]he promised
beforehand [e]through his prophets in the
holy Scriptures, **3** concerning his Son, [f]who
was descended from David [g]according to
the flesh **4** and [h]was declared to be the Son
of God [i]in power according to the Spirit of
holiness by his resurrection from the dead,
Jesus Christ our Lord, **5** through whom [j]we
have received grace and [k]apostleship [l]to
bring about the obedience of faith for the
sake of his name [m]among all the nations,
6 including you who are [n]called to belong to
Jesus Christ,

7 To all those in Rome who are loved by
God and called to be saints:

[o]Grace to you and peace from God our
Father and the Lord Jesus Christ.

Longing to Go to Rome

8 First, [p]I thank my God through Jesus
Christ for all of you, [q]because your faith is
proclaimed in all the world. **9** [r]For God is
my witness, [s]whom I serve with my spirit
in the gospel of his Son, [t]that without ceasing I mention you **10** always in my prayers,
asking that somehow [u]by God's will I may
now at last succeed in coming to you. **11** For
[v]I long to see you, that I may impart to you
some spiritual gift to strengthen you—
12 that is, that we may be mutually encouraged [w]by each other's faith, both yours and
mine. **13** I want you to know, brothers,[2] that
[x]I have often intended to come to you (but
[y]thus far have been prevented), in order
that I may reap some [z]harvest among you
as well as among the rest of the Gentiles.
14 [a]I am under obligation both to Greeks
and to [b]barbarians,[3] both to the wise and
to the foolish. **15** So [c]I am eager to preach
the gospel to you also who are in Rome.

The Righteous Shall Live by Faith

16 For [d]I am not ashamed of the gospel,
for it is [e]the power of God for salvation to

Chapter 1
1 [a][Gal. 1:10] [b]1 Cor. 1:1; [1 Cor. 9:1; Heb. 5:4]; See 2 Cor. 1:1 [c]See Acts 13:2
2 [d]Tit. 1:2 [e]ch. 3:21; 16:26; Luke 1:70
3 [f]See Matt. 1:1 [g]Gal. 4:4
4 [h][Acts 13:33] [i]2 Cor. 13:4; Eph. 1:19, 20; Phil. 3:10; [Acts 10:38; 26:23]
5 [j]ch. 12:3; 15:15 [k]See Acts 1:25 [l]ch. 6:16; 16:26; 1 Pet. 1:2; [ch. 15:18; Acts 6:7] [m]See Acts 9:15
6 [n]Rev. 17:14; [ch. 8:28, 30]
7 [o]1 Cor. 1:3
8 [p]1 Cor. 1:4; Eph. 1:15, 16; Phil. 1:3; Col. 1:3, 4; [ch. 6:17; Phil. 4:6; 2 Tim. 1:3] [q]ch. 16:19; [1 Thess. 1:8]
9 [r]Phil. 1:8; 1 Thess. 2:5, 10; [ch. 9:1; 2 Cor. 1:23; 11:10, 31] [s]See Acts 24:14 [t]2 Tim. 1:3
10 [u]ch. 15:32; [1 Thess. 3:10] **11** [v]ch. 15:22, 23; [Acts 19:21] **12** [w]See 2 Pet. 1:1 **13** [x]ch. 15:22, 23; [Acts 19:21] [y]ch. 15:22; [1 Thess. 2:18] [z]Phil. 4:17; [John 4:36] **14** [a]1 Cor. 9:16 [b]See Acts 28:2 **15** [c][ch. 12:18] **16** [d][Ps. 40:9, 10]; See Mark 8:38 [e]1 Cor. 1:18, 24

[1] Or *slave*; Greek *bondservant* [2] Or *brothers and sisters*. The plural Greek word *adelphoi* (translated "brothers") refers to siblings in a family. In New Testament usage, depending on the context, *adelphoi* may refer either to men or to both men and women who are siblings (brothers and sisters) in God's family, the church [3] That is, non-Greeks

1:1 Paul. Ancient letters began with the general formula, "A to B sends greetings." Using his Roman name, Paul fills out this formula with Christian significance both in his self-description (vv. 1–6) and in the style of his greeting (vv. 7, 8).

servant. Someone totally at the disposal of a master (text note).

apostle. An official messenger of the gospel. See 2 Cor. 1:1 note.

gospel of God. God is both the source and the theme of the message; it is the message "of" God. Here and elsewhere, Paul's trinitarianism surfaces (1:3, 4; 5:1–5; 8:3, 4, 9–11, 16, 17; 14:17, 18; 15:16, 30).

1:2 which he promised beforehand. The gospel was announced in promise form in the biblically recorded preaching of the prophets, from which the apostolic presentation of the gospel is drawn (16:25–27).

1:3, 4 A description of the two stages of the Savior's ministry, rather than of His two natures. Although Son of God, He was "descended from David" in order to share our weakness, but was transformed by the "Spirit of holiness" at the Resurrection, and was brought into a new epoch of His personal human existence (1 Cor. 15:45; 2 Cor. 13:4).

1:5, 6 Paul sees Christ as the author of his salvation and also of his calling to be an evangelist to the Gentiles (11:13, 14; Acts 9:15; Eph. 3:8).

1:5 obedience of faith. Indicating both the obedience that flows from faith and the fact that faith implies obedient submission to the call of God (16:26).

1:7 Rome. Capital of the empire. We have no certain knowledge of the founding of the Roman church, although visitors from Rome were among those who heard the gospel preached on the day of Pentecost (Acts 2:10).

loved by God and called to be saints. The terms used in the greeting will prove to be keynotes of the letter itself, as God's calling, love, grace, and peace are explained at length.

1:8 I thank my God. Gratitude for God's work of grace in others was a constant feature of Paul's life (1 Cor. 11:4; Phil. 1:3; Col. 1:3; 1 Thess. 1:2; 2 Thess. 1:3; 2 Tim. 3:1; Philem. 4).

in all the world. News had spread to the entire empire of the presence of Christians in its capital city.

1:9 I mention you. Paul's constant prayerfulness is an expression of his wholehearted service and desire for spiritual usefulness. He prays in full submission to God's will (vv. 9–12; cf. Eph. 1:15; Phil. 1:9; Col. 1:9; 1 Thess. 1:3; 2 Thess. 1:11; 2 Tim. 1:3).

1:11 spiritual gift. Here the term is not used in the functional sense of 1 Cor. 12:1; Paul has in view rather the benefit that flows from exercising functional gifts in ministry to others.

1:12 mutually encouraged. Ministry is for the mutual strengthening of the whole body of Christ (Eph. 4:15, 16).

1:13 often intended. No record of these many occasions exists, but see Acts 19:21; 23:11 for Paul's sense of being driven by God towards Rome.

prevented. Probably by other, regular responsibilities. See Acts 16:6, 7 for interruptions in Paul's plans caused either by the inward counsel of the Holy Spirit or by prophetic utterance.

among the rest of the Gentiles. This suggests that Paul thought of the Roman church as predominantly Gentile.

1:14 under obligation. Paul's planning (v. 13) and his expectation (v. 14) are rooted in a sense of obligation. He has been given the gospel for the Gentiles (11:13, 14; cf. Eph. 3:1–8).

Greeks. The cultured Hellenistic world (the "wise").

barbarians. The uncultured, "foolish" of the ancient world (see text note).

1:16 I am not ashamed of the gospel. Although the gospel is folly to the cultured, Paul sees his message as divine wisdom (1 Cor. 1:22–25, 30), and is not embarrassed by God's way of salvation. See "Salvation" at 2 Cor. 6:5.

power. The regenerating, life-changing impact of the gospel word through the Holy Spirit is essential because of humanity's bondage to sin and Satan, and weakness and spiritual inability on account of sin (5:6; 8:5–9).

everyone who believes, to the Jew [f] first and
also to [g] the Greek. 17 For in it [h] the righteousness of God is revealed [i] from faith for
faith, [1] [j] as it is written, "The righteous shall
live by faith." [2]

God's Wrath on Unrighteousness

18 For [k] the wrath of God [l] is revealed from
heaven against all ungodliness and unrighteousness of men, who by their unrighteousness suppress the truth. 19 For what
can be [m] known about God is plain to
them, because God has shown it to them.
20 For his invisible attributes, namely, his
eternal power and divine nature, [n] have
been clearly perceived, ever since the creation of the world, in the things that have
been made. So they are without excuse.
21 For although they knew God, they did
not honor him as God or give thanks to

16 [f] ch. 2:9; See Acts 3:26 [g] [Mark 7:26]; See John 7:35 17 [h] ch. 3:21; [2 Cor. 5:21; Phil. 3:9] [i] See ch. 9:30 [j] Gal. 3:11; Heb. 10:38; Cited from Hab. 2:4 18 [k] Eph. 5:6; Col. 3:6; [ch. 5:9] [l] [ch. 2:5] 19 [m] ch. 2:14, 15; Acts 14:17; 17:24-27 20 [n] [Ps. 19:1-6; Jer. 5:21, 22]

[1] Or *beginning and ending in faith* [2] Or *The one who by faith is righteous shall live*

Mankind's Guilty Knowledge of God

All people are naturally inclined to some form of religion, yet they fail to worship their Creator, whose general revelation makes Him universally known. Sinful egoism and aversion to our Creator's claims have driven humanity into idolatry, the error of giving worship and homage to any power or object other than God (Is. 44:9–20; Rom. 1:21–23; Col. 3:5). In their idolatry, apostate humans "suppress the truth" and have "exchanged the glory of the immortal God for images resembling mortal man and birds and animals and reptiles" (Rom. 1:18, 23). They smother and quench, as far as they can, the awareness that general revelation provides of the transcendent Judge and Creator, and they transfer the ineradicable sense of deity to unworthy objects. This in turn leads to drastic moral decline and misery, as a first manifestation of God's wrath against apostasy (Rom. 1:18, 24–32).

God will not allow human beings to suppress entirely their sense of God and of His judgment. Some sense of right and wrong, as well as of accountability to God, always remains. Even in the fallen world everyone is endowed with a conscience that from time to time condemns them, telling them that they ought to suffer for wrongs they have done. When conscience speaks in these terms it speaks with the voice of God.

In one sense, fallen humanity does not know God, since what people believe about the objects of their worship falsifies and distorts the truth about God. In another sense all human beings do know God, but in guilt, with uncomfortable inklings of the judgment they cannot avoid. Only the gospel of Christ can speak peace to this aspect of the human condition.

believes. Salvation is unmerited, but it is not universally enjoyed; faith is required for it.

to the Jew first. While this was true in terms of the history of redemption (2:9, 10; John 4:22; cf. Mark 7:24–30), it was also the pattern of Paul's missionary outreach. Hence, in visiting the cities of the Roman world he began by expounding Scripture in the synagogues where possible, and he preached Christ as the fulfillment of the Old Testament promises (Acts 9:20; 13:5, 14; 14:1; 17:1, 17; 18:4, 19, 26; 19:8). Throughout Romans, Paul is careful not to deny the validity of the God-given privileges of His own people (3:11, 12; 9:4, 5).

1:17 righteousness of God. This is a key phrase in Romans (3:21; 5:19; 10:3), regularly explained in the letter as "righteousness . . . through (or of) faith" (3:22; cf. 9:30; 10:6). God's righteousness is shown in the righteousness of Christ that is imputed to, or considered by God to belong to, the one who believes. This imputation of righteousness to sinners who believe is fully consistent with the personal righteousness of God. As a just and righteous judge (2:5–16), God through the death of His Son justifies, or declares righteous, those sinners who come to true faith in Christ (3:21–26; 5:10). Luther's reading of this verse had a decisive impact on his understanding of justification.

from faith for faith. Paul emphasizes that at every point of its influence the gospel depends on faith, not works.

as it is written. Hab. 2:4 provides the biblical basis for and summary of what follows, indicating that the way of life by faith was already known in the Old Testament.

shall live. Life in contrast with spiritual death, and life in the sense of continuing in fellowship with God. From first to last, godly living means trusting in God and depending on His grace.

1:18 wrath. The divine Judge's righteous retribution and personal revulsion evoked by moral evil.

is revealed. God's judgment is not limited to the future; His antagonism to sin is already shown in the world. Its effects are visible even now.

ungodliness and unrighteousness. The order may be significant—since moral decay follows theological rebellion. Or Paul may be using the two words together to express one idea, wicked ungodliness.

suppress the truth. It is not that the truth is sought but cannot be found, but rather that, confronted with the truth (which is "clearly perceived," v. 20), fallen humanity seeks to hinder and obstruct its influence, and is therefore "without excuse" (v. 20). The "excuse" in view is an appeal to ignorance.

1:19 what can be known about God. Paul stresses the reality and universality of divine revelation, which is perpetual ("since the creation," v. 20) and perspicuous ("clearly perceived," v. 20). Divine invisibility, eternity, and power are all expressed in and through the created order (see "General Revelation" at Ps. 19:1). The invisible God is revealed through the visible medium of creation. This revelation is manifest; it is not obscured but clearly seen. See theological note "Mankind's Guilty Knowledge of God."

1:21 knew God. Here Paul stresses that humanity not only has the

him, but they [o]became futile in their thinking, and their foolish hearts were darkened.
22 [p]Claiming to be wise, they became fools,
23 and [q]exchanged the glory of [r]the immortal God for images resembling mortal man
and birds and animals and reptiles.
24 Therefore [s]God gave them up in the
lusts of their hearts to impurity, to [t]the dishonoring of their bodies among themselves, 25 because they exchanged the truth
about God for [u]a lie and worshiped and
served the creature rather than the Creator,
[v]who is blessed forever! Amen.
26 For this reason [w]God gave them up to
[x]dishonorable passions. For their women
exchanged natural relations for those that
are contrary to nature; 27 and the men likewise gave up natural relations with women
and were consumed with passion for one
another, [y]men committing shameless acts
with men and receiving in themselves the
due penalty for their error.
28 And since they did not see fit to acknowledge God, [z]God gave them up to [a]a
debased mind to do [b]what ought not to be
done. 29 They were filled with all manner
of unrighteousness, evil, covetousness,
malice. They are full of envy, murder, strife,
deceit, maliciousness. They are gossips,
30 slanderers, haters of God, insolent, haugh-

21 [o]2 Kin. 17:15; Jer. 2:5; Eph. 4:17, 18
22 [p]Jer. 10:14; 1 Cor. 1:20
23 [q]Ps. 106:20; Jer. 2:11; [Deut. 4:16-18; Acts 17:29] [r]1 Tim. 1:17
24 [s]ver. 26, 28; [Eph. 4:19] [t][1 Thess. 4:4]
25 [u]Isai. 28:15; 44:19, 20; Jer. 10:14; Amos 2:4; [2 Thess. 2:11] [v]ch. 9:5
26 [w]ver. 24, 28 [x][Col. 3:5; 1 Thess. 4:5]
27 [y]Lev. 18:22; 20:13
28 [z]ver. 24, 26 [a][Jer. 6:30] [b][Eph. 5:4]
32 [c]ch. 2:26; 8:4 [d]ch. 6:21 [e]Luke 11:48; Acts 8:1; 22:20; [1 Cor. 13:6; 2 Thess. 2:12]
Chapter 2
1 [f]ch. 1:20 [g]2 Sam. 12:5-7; [John 8:7]; See Matt. 7:2

ty, boastful, inventors of evil, disobedient
to parents, 31 foolish, faithless, heartless,
ruthless. 32 Though they know [c]God's
decree that those who practice such things
[d]deserve to die, they not only do them but
[e]give approval to those who practice them.

God's Righteous Judgment

2 Therefore you have [f]no excuse, O man,
every one of you who judges. For [g]in
passing judgment on another you condemn yourself, because you, the judge,
practice the very same things. 2 We know
that the judgment of God rightly falls on
those who do such things. 3 Do you suppose, O man—you who judge those who
do such things and yet do them yourself—
that you will escape the judgment of God?
4 Or do you presume on [h]the riches of his
kindness and [i]forbearance and [j]patience,
[k]not knowing that God's kindness is meant
to lead you to repentance? 5 But because
of your hard and impenitent heart you are
[l]storing up [m]wrath for yourself on the day
of wrath when God's righteous judgment
will be revealed.
6 [n]He will render to each one according
to his works: 7 to those who [o]by patience in

4 [h]ch. 9:23; 10:12 [i]ch. 3:25 [j]ch. 9:22; [Ex. 34:6] [k]Isai. 30:18; 2 Pet. 3:9, 15; Rev. 2:21 5 [l][Deut. 32:34]; See James 5:3 [m]Ps. 110:5 6 [n]Job 34:11; Ps. 62:12; Prov. 24:12; Jer. 17:10; 32:19; See Matt. 16:27 7 [o]See Luke 8:15

opportunity to know God through general revelation, but that the revelation yields real knowledge. Humanity's sin is the individual refusal to acknowledge what is already known to be true. While knowing God, people refuse to honor Him as God or give thanks to Him. The consequence of rejecting God was that their minds and hearts grew dark. A refusal to honor God leads all intellectual pursuits to frustration.

1:22, 23 Claiming to be wise, they became fools . . . exchanged the glory of the immortal God. Intellectual arrogance before God displays a reversed sense of values; the worship of God is exchanged for devotion to man-made and man-reflecting idols. The indelible instinct to worship is perverted by being centered on the wrong object (v. 25).

1:24 God gave them up. Judgment involves the removal of divine restraints, both on sinful actions and on their consequences (vv. 26, 28).

1:26, 27 The effect of perverting the instinct to worship God is the perversion of other instincts from their proper functions. Scripture views all homosexual actions in this light (Lev. 18:22; 21:13). The consequence is degradation of the body (v. 24), domination by lust, the disintegration of what is truly "natural" (v. 26), and bondage to uncontrollable passions (v. 27).

1:27 receiving in themselves the due penalty. Even in a morally fallen and therefore (to humanity) unpredictable world, the harvest reaped is related to the crop sown (Gal. 6:7, 8).

1:28 did not see fit . . . God gave them up. Sin brings a disdain for true values, and risks abandonment by God to a spirit of licentiousness (vv. 29–31).

1:32 know God's decree. Paul sees as evidence of the guilt and bondage of sin that the knowledge of divine judgment no longer acts as a restraint, but becomes a spur to further rebellion in the form of encouraging others to sin. This text confirms that part of God's revelation in nature communicates His moral character and a sense of moral duty in humanity.

2:1–16 In what follows, Paul turns to an imaginary representative of a real and identifiable group of people. Although he specifically mentions Jews only at v. 17, he probably has them in mind already. They agree with his statement about God's wrath, but assume they stand outside of it (hence his stern warning in v. 5). But the nature of this presumption, if not its specific form, is not limited to Jews. In this context Paul sets forth the principles of the divine judgment all must face. It is based on truth (v. 2) and marked by righteousness (v. 5). It is according to works (v. 6), impartial in nature (v. 11), and executed through Christ (v. 16). Such judgment will bring agonizing ruin to all sinners (vv. 8, 9).

2:1 no excuse. Paul unmasks those who will agree with his exposition of divine wrath on sin (1:18–32) but assume they are immune to it.

practice the very same things. Their judgment of others is also in effect a self-condemnation (v. 3).

2:2 rightly falls. A link with 1:18. God's judgment is based on the reality of the individual's response or non-response to Him, not on other considerations.

2:4 presume. They refuse to acknowledge that the kindness of God is intended to produce sorrow for sin and a turning away from it. They despise this purpose of divine generosity, and thereby show disdain for God Himself. See "God Is Love: Divine Goodness and Faithfulness" at Ps. 136:1.

2:5 storing up wrath. Religious presumption comes from a hard heart, since continued resistance to God's purposes in showing grace is a refusal of God's will, and increases guilt while protesting innocence. Wrath is stored up, pointing forward to proportionate punishment in hell.

2:6–10 The ground of judgment will be what people have been or done

well-doing seek for glory and honor and immortality, he will give eternal life; 8 but for those who are self-seeking[1] and [p]do not obey the truth, but obey unrighteousness, there will be wrath and fury. 9 There will be tribulation and distress [q]for every human being who does evil, the Jew [r]first and also the Greek, 10 but glory and honor and [s]peace for everyone who does good, [t]the Jew first and also the Greek. 11 For [u]God shows no partiality.

God's Judgment and the Law

12 For all who have sinned [v]without the law will also perish without the law, and all who have sinned under the law will be judged by the law. 13 For [w]it is not the hearers of the law who are righteous before God, but the doers of the law who will be justified. 14 For when Gentiles, who do not have the law, [x]by nature do what the law requires, they are a law to themselves, even though they do not have the law. 15 They show that the work of the law is [y]written on their hearts, while their conscience also bears witness, and their conflicting thoughts accuse or even excuse them 16 [z]on that day when, [a]according to my gospel, God judges [b]the secrets of men [c]by Christ Jesus.

17 But if you call yourself a Jew and [d]rely on the law and boast in God 18 and know his will and approve what is excellent, because you are instructed from the law; 19 and if you are sure that you yourself are [e]a guide to the blind, a light to those who are in darkness, 20 an instructor of the foolish, a teacher of children, having in the law [f]the embodiment of [g]knowledge and truth— 21 [h]you then who teach others, do you not teach yourself? While you preach against stealing, do you steal? 22 You who say that one must not commit adultery, do you commit adultery? You who abhor idols, do you [i]rob temples? 23 You who [j]boast in the law [k]dishonor God by breaking the law. 24 For, [l]as it is written, "The name of God is blasphemed [m]among the Gentiles because of you."

25 For circumcision indeed is of value [n]if you obey the law, but if you break the law, your circumcision becomes uncircumcision.

8 [p]2 Thess. 2:12
9 [q]Ezek. 18:20 [r]See 1 Pet. 4:17
10 [s]Isai. 57:19 [t]See ch. 1:16
11 [u]See Acts 10:34
12 [v]1 Cor. 9:21
13 [w]See James 1:22, 23
14 [x]See ch. 1:19
15 [y]Jer. 31:33
16 [z][ch. 3:6; 14:10; 1 Cor. 4:5]; See Acts 10:42; 17:31 [a]ch. 16:25; 2 Tim. 2:8; [Gal. 1:11; 1 Tim. 1:11] [b]Eccles. 12:14 [c]ch. 16:25; [1 Tim. 1:11; 2 Tim. 2:8]
17 [d]ver. 23; Mic. 3:11; [ch. 9:4; John 5:45]
19 [e][Job 29:15; Matt. 15:14; 23:16; John 9:39-41]
20 [f]2 Tim. 3:5; [Gal. 4:19; 2 Tim. 1:13] [g]Luke 11:52
21 [h]Matt. 23:3-28; [Ps. 50:16-21; Matt. 15:1-9] 22 [i]Acts 19:37; [Mal.3:8]
23 [j]See ver. 17; ch. 3:27 [k][Mal. 1:6] 24 [l]Cited from Isai. 52:5 [m][2 Sam. 12:14; Ezek. 36:20, 23; 2 Pet. 2:2] 25 [n]Gal. 5:3

1 Or *contentious*

(v. 6). Paul is not here denying what he elsewhere emphasizes: that salvation is a gift, not a reward (5:15, 17; 6:23). Divine judgment is based on every aspect of a person's relationship to God. Only those who receive grace do in fact seek "glory and honor and immortality" (v. 7). Others are "self-seeking" (v. 8), not God-honoring. Paul teaches that while salvation is by grace, judgment is according to works (2 Cor. 5:10). Apart from grace there is only one verdict possible to "the Jew first and also the Greek" (v. 10; cf. 1:16).

2:11 Right standing with God is not on the basis of ethnic background, nor any natural or self-generated distinctions among humanity (9:6–13; Gal. 6:15).

2:12–16 The Jews were ready to appeal to the Law of Moses, which they had and the Gentiles did not. The implication was that in this connection God does show "partiality" (v. 11). The role of the law is a major theme in Romans (3:27–31; 4:13–15; 5:13–15; 6:14, 15; 7:1–25; 13:8–10). Here in his first discussion of it, Paul shows that what pleases God is not knowledge of the law but obedience to God's will revealed in it. Therefore, "God shows no partiality" (v. 11).

2:12 all who have sinned. This category includes everyone, as is made clear in 3:19, 20, 23.

law. The law of Moses, crystallized in the Ten Commandments (Ex. 20:1–17; Deut. 5:1–22). The Mosaic law already reveals God's condemnation of sin, but the cause of sin lies in our hearts, that is, deeply rooted in our natures, and not in the law (7:13). The knowledge of "the work of the law" (v. 15) also resides in the heart, because mankind was created in the image of God (Gen. 1:26, 27). Since God judges people in accordance with standards known to them, a defense based on ignorance of the Mosaic law is irrelevant and illegitimate. It is not the degree of revelation received, but response to the revelation itself, however received, that will prove critical on the day when God will judge (v. 16).

2:14 by nature do what the law requires. No one can be justified on the basis of personal righteousness, but the universal presence of moral standards (although in various degrees of clarity), and the common sense of obligation to such standards, indicate a universal moral constitution and sense of accountability to God. This is evidenced by the fact that "their conscience also bears witness" (v. 15). See "Conscience and the Law" at 1 Sam. 24:5.

2:16 my gospel. The gospel Paul preaches. In this gospel, the bad news of judgment precedes the good news of grace.

by Christ Jesus. All judgment has been placed in His hand (Matt. 7:21–23; 25:31–33; John 5:22; 2 Cor. 5:10). Such judgment will be infallible, penetrating to "the thoughts and intentions of the heart"; nothing will be concealed from the Judge (Heb. 4:12, 13). Nor will anyone say that it is unfair for the human to be judged by the divine, since the agent of judgment will be the incarnate Christ, Himself a man. See "The Final Judgment" at Matt. 25:41.

2:17–29 Paul now turns directly to the Jewish claim to special privilege, dealing in more detail with the possession of the law (vv. 17–24) and circumcision (vv. 25–29). In connection with the law, he presses home the claim of v. 1 that the Jews were guilty of the sins for which they condemned others. In connection with circumcision, he argues that the sign without the reality is meaningless.

2:17–20 Paul lists the privileges of which the Jews boasted, thinking that these blessings gave them superiority over others.

2:21–23 The responsibilities that accompany privilege have not been fulfilled. Paul specifies the commandments against adultery, sacrilege, and theft (Ex. 20:4, 5, 14, 15).

2:25 circumcision . . . of value. Paul's argument in ch. 2 now moves to a climax. Condemnation results from failure to obey revelation of whatever kind. Jews have transgressed the Mosaic law in particular, emptying circumcision of its real significance. Paul recognizes the privilege of Jewishness (9:4, 5) and of circumcision in particular (3:1, 2; 4:11). But physical circumcision is a symbol of sanctification and renewal of life (v. 25; Deut. 30:6). The reality, not the sign, is the vital thing and may be possessed irrespective of Jewishness (vv. 26, 27).

26 So, if [o]a man who is uncircumcised keeps [p]the precepts of the law, will not his uncircumcision be regarded as circumcision? 27 Then he who is physically uncircumcised but keeps the law [q]will condemn you who have [r]the written code and circumcision but break the law. 28 For [s]no one is a Jew [t]who is merely one outwardly, nor is circumcision outward and physical. 29 But a Jew is one [u]inwardly, and [v]circumcision is a matter of the heart, by the Spirit, not by the letter. [w]His praise is not from man but from God.

God's Righteousness Upheld

3 Then what advantage has the Jew? Or what is the value of circumcision? 2 Much in every way. To begin with, [x]the Jews were entrusted with [y]the oracles of God. 3 [z]What if some were unfaithful? [a]Does their faithlessness nullify the faithfulness of God? 4 By no means! [b]Let God be true though [c]every one were a liar, as it is written,

[d]"That you may be justified in your words,
and prevail when you [e]are judged."

5 But if our unrighteousness serves to show the righteousness of God, what shall we say? That God is unrighteous to inflict [f]wrath on us? ([g]I speak in a human way.) 6 By no means! For then how could [h]God judge the world? 7 But if through my lie God's truth abounds to his glory, [i]why am I still being condemned as a sinner? 8 And why not [j]do evil that good may come?—as some people slanderously charge us with saying. Their condemnation is just.

No One Is Righteous

9 What then? Are we Jews[1] any better off?[2] No, not at all. For we have already charged that all, both Jews and Greeks, are under sin, 10 as it is written:

[n]"None is righteous, no, not one;
11 no one understands;
no one seeks for God.
12 All have turned aside; together they have become worthless;
no one does good,
not even one."
13 [o]"Their throat is [p]an open grave;
they use their tongues to deceive."
[q]"The venom of asps is under their lips."
14 [r]"Their mouth is full of curses and bitterness."
15 [s]"Their feet are swift to shed blood;
16 in their paths are ruin and misery,
17 and [t]the way of peace they have not known."
18 [u]"There is no fear of God before their eyes."

19 Now we know that whatever [v]the law says it speaks to those who are under the

26 [o]Eph. 2:11; [ch. 3:30] [p]ch. 1:32; 8:4
27 [q]See Matt. 12:41 [r]ver. 29; ch. 7:6; 2 Cor. 3:6
28 [s]ch. 9:6-8; [Gal. 6:15] [t][ver. 17]
29 [u]See 1 Pet. 3:4 [v][Deut. 10:16; 30:6; Jer. 4:4; Acts 7:51; Phil. 3:3; Col. 2:11] [w]2 Cor. 10:18; 1 Thess. 2:4; [Gal. 1:10]
Chapter 3
2 [x]Deut. 4:8; Ps. 147:19, 20; See John 4:22 [y]See Acts 7:38
3 [z]ch. 10:16; Heb. 4:2 [a][ch. 9:6; 2 Tim. 2:13]
4 [b]See John 8:26 [c]Ps. 62:9; 116:11; [ver. 7] [d]Cited from Ps. 51:4 (Gk.) [e][Job 9:32]
5 [f][ch. 2:5] [g]ch. 6:19; 1 Cor. 9:8; Gal. 3:15; [1 Cor. 15:32]
6 [h][Gen. 18:25; Job 8:3]; See ch. 2:16
7 [i][ch. 9:19]
8 [j][ch. 6:1, 15]
9 [k]ch. 2:1-29 [l]ch. 1:18-32 [m]Gal. 3:22; [ver. 19, 23; ch. 11:32; Prov. 20:9]

10 [n]ver. 10-12, cited from Ps. 14:1-3; 53:1-3 13 [o]Cited from Ps. 5:9 [p]Jer. 5:16 [q]Cited from Ps. 140:3 14 [r]Cited from Ps. 10:7 (Gk.) 15 [s]Cited from Prov. 1:16; ver. 15-17, cited from Isai. 59:7, 8 17 [t]Luke 1:79 18 [u]Cited from Ps. 36:1 19 [v]John 10:34; 15:25

1 Greek *Are we* 2 Or *at any disadvantage?*

2:29 a Jew is one. The work of the Spirit, issuing in a God-centered life, not the possession of "circumcision" (v. 28) and the "written code" (v. 27), makes one a member of God's covenant people. As Paul will show, his conclusion might shock the Jews he addresses, but it is rooted in the teaching of the Old Testament itself (cf. 9:6).

3:1 Paul's statement that there is no favoritism with God (2:11) does not mean that there is no "advantage" in being a Jew, only that disobedience nullifies that advantage.

3:2 the oracles of God. The phrase reveals the apostolic belief that the inspiration of the Old Testament extended to its words (Matt. 4:4).

3:3, 4 The response of unbelief does not nullify the faithfulness of God to the promises in His word. He keeps them (9:6, 7; 2 Tim. 2:13), as the Old Testament underlines.

3:5–8 Two related questions are presented here. The first is that if people's unrighteousness is an occasion for the righteousness of God to act, is it not unfair for God to execute His wrath upon unrighteousness? Paul's answer is brief. It is a "given" that God is going to judge the world and that His judgment will be fair. In the second step Paul reduces the objection to an absurd conclusion. If God somehow accepts the unrighteousness that is an occasion for His mercy, should He not welcome even more acts of unrighteousness from us? This conclusion is foolish (6:1, 2, 15). The ends do not justify the means.

3:5 I speak in a human way. Although it is only expressed as a possibility in a discussion, the suggestion that God could be unjust calls for an immediate correction.

3:6 The justice of God will be displayed in the Last Judgment. Obviously it will be no excuse for sins that they had a part in making judgment necessary. God's justification of sinners will not undo the elementary truth that He will judge the world in righteousness.

3:8 slanderously charge us. Foolish as the false conclusion is, it seems that Paul was accused of teaching it. A similar, but not identical issue, is discussed in 5:20–6:1.

3:10 as it is written. This is the common New Testament wording when appeal is made to the authority of Scripture (1:17; 3:3). The biblical texts, taken together, stress the universal reign of sin and the consequent depravity and condemnation of all mankind.

3:18 no fear of God. In the Old Testament, the essence of a proper attitude to God is "fear," the absence of which is practical atheism.

3:19 the law. Here "law" is a reference to the Old Testament Scriptures in general, since Paul's quotes come from Psalms, Ecclesiastes, and Isaiah.

says. A further indication that Paul sees Scripture as the living voice of God.

under the law. Not in the sense of 6:14, 15, but as in 2:12 (those who possess the Old Testament revelation, i.e., the Jews in particular).

law, [w]so that every mouth may be stopped, and [x]the whole world may be held accountable to God.
[20]For [y]by works of the law no human being[1] will be justified in his sight, since [z]through the law comes knowledge of sin.

The Righteousness of God Through Faith

[21]But now [a]the righteousness of God [b]has been manifested apart from the law, although [c]the Law and the Prophets bear witness to it—
[22]the righteousness of God [d]through faith in Jesus Christ for all who believe. [e]For there is no distinction:
[23]for [f]all have sinned and fall short of the glory

19 [w]Job 5:16; Ps. 63:11; 107:42; Ezek. 16:63; [ch. 1:20; 2:1] [x]See ver. 9 20 [y]Gal. 2:16; [Ps. 143:2; Acts 13:39] [z]ch. 7:7; [ch. 4:15; 5:13, 20] 21 [a]See ch. 1:17 [b]ch. 16:26; 2 Tim. 1:10 [c]Acts 10:43; [ch. 1:2; John 5:46] 22 [d]ch. 4:5; [2 Tim. 3:15] [e]ch. 10:12; [Gal. 3:28; Col. 3:11] 23 [f]See ver. 9

1 Greek *flesh*

The Atonement

An atonement is a reconciliation of alienated parties, the restoration of a broken relationship. Atonement is accomplished by making amends, blotting out offenses, and giving satisfaction for wrongs done.

According to Scripture every person sins and needs to make atonement, but lacks the power and resources for doing so. We have offended our Creator, whose nature it is to hate sin (Jer. 44:4; Hab. 1:13) and to punish it (Ps. 5:4–6; Rom. 1:18; 2:5–9). Those who have sinned cannot be accepted by and do not have fellowship with God unless atonement is made. Since there is sin in even the best actions of sinful creatures, anything we do in the hope of making amends can only increase our guilt or worsen our situation, for the "sacrifice of the wicked is an abomination to the Lord" (Prov. 15:8). There is no way to establish one's own righteousness before God (Job 15:14–16; Is. 64:6; Rom. 10:2, 3); it simply cannot be done.

But against this background of human hopelessness, Scripture reveals the grace and mercy of God, who Himself provides the atonement that sin has made necessary. God's amazing grace is the focus of Biblical faith; from Genesis to Revelation it shines out with breathtaking glory.

When God brought Israel out of Egypt, He set up as part of the covenant relationship a system of sacrifices that had at its heart the shedding of the blood of animals "to make atonement for your souls" (Lev. 17:11). These sacrifices were "typical"; that is, as "types" they pointed forward to something better. Sins were forgiven when sacrifices were faithfully offered, but it was not the blood of animals that blotted out sins (Heb. 10:4). It was the blood of the "antitype," Jesus Christ, whose death on the cross atoned for sins already committed, as well as sins that would be committed afterwards (Rom. 3:25, 26; 4:3–8; Heb. 9:11–15).

According to the New Testament, Christ's blood was shed as a sacrifice (Rom. 3:25; 5:9; Eph. 1:7; Rev. 1:5). Christ redeemed His people by means of a ransom; His death was the price that freed us from guilt and from enslavement to sin (Rom. 3:24; Gal. 4:4, 5; Col. 1:14). In Christ's death, God reconciled us to Himself, overcoming His own hostility that our sins provoked (Rom. 5:10; 2 Cor. 5:18, 19; Col. 1:20–22). The Cross propitiated God. That is to say, it quenched His wrath against us by expiating our sins, and so removing them from His sight (Rom. 3:25; Heb. 2:17; 1 John 2:2; 4:10). The Cross had this effect because in His suffering Christ assumed our identity and endured the retributive judgment due to us, that is, "the curse of the law" (Gal. 3:13). He suffered as our substitute, with the damning record of our transgressions nailed by God to His cross as the list of crimes for which He died (Col. 2:14; cf. Matt. 27:37; Is. 53:4–6; Luke 22:37).

every mouth . . . stopped . . . held accountable. No one, whether Jew or Gentile, has grounds for appeal; none can claim to be free from guilt before God. All are lost.

3:20 through the law comes knowledge of sin. See "The Three Purposes of the Law" at Deut. 13:10. While the Jews appeal to their possession of the law as proof of their privileged position before God, Paul has now demonstrated that any Jew's sin is unveiled and condemned, not hidden and condoned, by the law (note Paul's self-description in 7:7–11). At the Last Judgment, all argument with a perfectly just and omniscient Judge will be futile.

3:21–31 Having shown the need of both Jew and Gentile for the righteousness of God revealed in the gospel (1:16), Paul now explains how it is provided in Christ (vv. 21–26), and underlines two of the implications (vv. 27–31).

3:21 But now. The law of Moses, seen as demand, cannot save. Yet the gospel is not contrary to the law of Moses (1:2). The gospel was already proclaimed in both "the Law and the Prophets." But "now" (the time filled with redemptive significance because of the coming of Christ, v. 26) God's righteousness comes to historical realization through Christ and His work.

apart from the law. Righteousness with God is not achieved by our acts of obedience to the law. Nevertheless, Paul insists that the gospel is not lawless (v. 31; 6:15; 8:3, 4; 13:8, 10).

3:22 through faith in Jesus Christ for all who believe. The righteousness of God must be received now that it "has been manifested" (v. 21). To believe, for Paul, involves knowledge of the gospel's content, mental assent to its testimony about Christ (10:14), and obedient trust and reliance on Him as Savior and Lord (1:5). The righteousness of God is exclusively for those who have faith ("there is no distinction: for all have sinned"), whether Jew or Gentile (3:22–23).

3:23 fall short of the glory of God. See "Original Sin and Total Depravity" at Ps. 51:5. A poignant description of the consequence of sin.

of God, 24 [g]and are justified [h]by his grace as
a gift, [i]through the redemption that is in
Christ Jesus, 25 whom God [j]put forward as
[k]a propitiation [l]by his blood, to be received
by faith. This was to show God's righteousness, because in [m]his divine forbearance he had passed over [n]former sins. 26 It
was to show his righteousness at the present time, so that he might be just and the
justifier of the one who has faith in Jesus.

27 [o]Then what becomes of our boasting?
It is excluded. By what kind of law? By a
law of works? No, but by the law of faith.
28 For we hold that one is justified by faith
[p]apart from works of the law. 29 Or [q]is God
the God of Jews only? Is he not the God of
Gentiles also? Yes, of Gentiles also, 30 since
[r]God is one. He will justify the circumcised
by faith and [s]the uncircumcised through
faith. 31 Do we then overthrow the law by
this faith? By no means! On the contrary,
we uphold the law.

Abraham Justified by Faith

4 What then shall we say was gained by[1]
Abraham, [t]our forefather according to
the flesh? 2 For if Abraham was justified by
works, he has something to boast about,
but [u]not before God. 3 For what does the
Scripture say? [v]"Abraham believed God,
and it was counted to him as righteousness." 4 Now [w]to the one who works, his
wages are not counted as a gift but as his

24 [g]Tit. 3:7 [h]ch. 4:4, 5, 16; See Acts 15:11 [i]Eph. 1:7; Col. 1:14; Heb. 9:15; [1 Cor. 1:30] **25** [j]Eph. 1:9 [k]See 1 John 2:2 [l]ch. 5:9; Eph. 2:13 [m]ch. 2:4 [n][Acts 17:30] **27** [o]ch. 2:17, 23; 4:2; 1 Cor. 1:29-31; Eph. 2:9; 2 Tim. 1:9; See Acts 13:39 **28** [p]See James 2:18 **29** [q]ch. 9:24; 10:12; 15:9 **30** [r]Gal. 3:20; [ch. 10:12] [s]Gal. 3:8; [ch. 4:9]; See ch. 2:26

Chapter 4 1 [t]ver. 16 **2** [u][1 Cor. 1:31] **3** [v]ver. 9:22; Gal. 3:6; James 2:23; Cited from Gen. 15:6 (Gk.); [Tit. 3:8] **4** [w][ch. 11:6; Deut. 9:4, 5]

[1] Some manuscripts *say about*

Made in the image of the glorious God (Gen. 1:26, 27), humanity has exchanged God's glory for idolatry (1:23) and distorted the divine image. Now people are morally and spiritually ugly and depraved. Grace renews and restores humanity's lost glory in believers (5:2; 8:18; 1 Cor. 15:42–49; 2 Cor. 3:18; Eph. 4:24; Phil. 3:20, 21; Col. 3:10).

3:24 justified. In Scripture, justification is the opposite of condemnation (e.g., Prov. 17:15). It is the declaration of the believing sinner to be just, and it comes about by virtue of the imputed righteousness of Christ, the "gift of righteousness," as 5:17 terms it. Christ's righteousness is now legally considered to be the possession of the sinner. Justification is final and irreversible (8:1, 33, 34). It is grounded in Christ's lifelong obedience, in which He fulfilled the precepts of God's law for us, and in His death on the cross, bore the penalty of God's judgment against us. Believers now share the same righteous status as the risen Christ Himself, with whom they are united now and forever (2 Cor. 5:21).

by his grace as a gift. Paul's repetition of the same idea in different words emphasizes the divine initiative and mercy in freely granting our salvation.

redemption. Freedom gained through the payment of a price; here specifically, release from the former condition of bondage in sin. This is accomplished through Christ's death, the ransom price for our salvation (Mark 10:45; 1 Tim. 2:6; Heb. 9:15).

3:25 whom God put forward. See theological note "The Atonement." Christ died as a propitiatory sacrifice that satisfies the divine judgment against sinners, bringing about forgiveness and justification. But Paul is careful to indicate that the sacrifice does not cause God to love us. The opposite is true—God's love caused Him to offer His Son (5:8; 8:32; John 3:16).

by faith. The emphasis of v. 22 is repeated and thereby underscored. "By" indicates the means of our being linked to the righteousness of Christ. Faith is the instrumental cause, not the ultimate cause, of justification.

3:26 to show his righteousness. God's judicial righteousness is demonstrated in the gospel. Under the Mosaic sacrificial system, forgiveness was offered through (but not on the basis of) animal sacrifice. As the New Testament recognizes (Heb. 9:11–15; 10:1–4), such sacrifices cannot substitute for the sins of humans. The real significance of the Old Testament sacrifices lay in the way they pointed forward to Christ through whom God would deal with human sin in an appropriate and final way. In view of what He would later do, God could righteously pass over "former sins" (v. 25). The work of Christ reveals both the justice of God (He does punish sin in the Person of His own Son, 8:32), and the righteousness of God's way of salvation by "faith in Jesus" (v. 26). In dealing with Christ as sin-bearer and the human person as sinner, God does not compromise His own holiness, nor the necessity of sin's being atoned for. Yet He graciously provides a salvation that mankind was incapable of obtaining. In this respect, Paul sees the Cross as the manifestation of the glorious wisdom of God (1 Cor. 1:23, 24).

3:27 what becomes of our boasting. The point made in 2:17, 23 resurfaces. Since Jew and Gentile alike are under wrath for their sin, and since the law does not protect Jews, but rather reveals their condemnation, and since the gospel exposes a person's unrighteousness while revealing God's righteousness, no one, not even a Jew, has grounds for boasting (4:2, 3). Indeed, boasting "is excluded," since faith alone (vv. 27, 28, 30), not human achievement, brings salvation.

3:28 justified by faith. See "Justification and Merit" at Gal. 3:11.

3:30 God is one. Salvation does not come by the possession of the law. This implies that salvation is available to others as well as Jews. Paul confirms this truth in the face of Jewish opposition by appeal to the fundamental confession of Old Testament religion, that God is one (Deut. 6:4). This principle was implied already in the Old Testament prophets' composite lawsuits against the nations for their sins and against the Jews for theirs (e.g., Amos 1; 2). Paul stresses that justification comes to Jew ("the circumcised") and to Gentile ("the uncircumcised") in the same way—by faith alone.

3:31 Do we then overthrow the law by this faith. See "Antinomianism" at 1 John 3:7. Paul is rejecting the law as the way of salvation. But since the law as moral demand was not given to sinners in order to justify them (vv. 19, 20), the principle of salvation by grace through faith cannot be a contradiction of the law. As he later demonstrates, the gospel upholds and furthers the law's ultimate goal (8:3, 4; 13:8–10).

4:1–25 Paul confirms his argument that justification is by grace through faith in Christ (3:22–25) by an appeal to the life of Abraham. As spiritual father of the Jews (v. 1), Abraham provides a test case for Paul's doctrine. If he can show that Abraham was justified by faith, his earlier exposition becomes irrefutable in a Jewish context.

4:2, 3 Contrary to the view that Abraham was considered righteous and sustained in covenant with God on the basis of his obedience and faithfulness, Paul intends to demonstrate that the general statement in 3:27 is true of Abraham in particular. Abraham had nothing "to boast about," for Gen. 15:6 proves that it was by faith, not by law-keeping, that he was counted righteous. James also points to Abraham as an example of one who demonstrates true faith by his works (James 2:21). See "Justification and Merit" at Gal. 3:11.

4:4, 5 It is a general principle that wages are earned by work, not received "as a gift." But Gen. 15:6 makes no mention of works on Abraham's part, only of the trust he had in God. Although faith was Abraham's action, it contributed nothing to Abraham's resultant righteousness before God, which was God's own gift (v. 4). In this sense, while faith as the instrument of justification involves human activity, it is not a

due. 5 And to the one who does not work
but [x]trusts him who justifies the ungodly,
his faith is counted as righteousness, 6 just
as David also speaks of the blessing of the
one to whom God counts righteousness
apart from works:

7 [y]"Blessed are those whose lawless
deeds are forgiven,
and whose sins are covered;
8 blessed is the man against whom
the Lord will not [z]count
his sin."

9 Is this blessing then only for [a]the circumcised, or also for the uncircumcised?
[b]We say that faith was counted to Abraham
as righteousness. 10 How then was it counted to him? Was it before or after he had
been circumcised? It was not after, but
before he was circumcised. 11 [c]He received
the sign of circumcision as a seal of the
righteousness that he had by faith while he
was still uncircumcised. The purpose was
[d]to make him the father of all who believe
without being circumcised, so that righteousness would be counted to them as
well, 12 and to make him the father of the
circumcised who are not merely circumcised but who also walk in the footsteps of
the faith that our father Abraham had
before he was circumcised.

The Promise Realized Through Faith

13 For [e]the promise to Abraham and his
offspring [f]that he would be heir of the
world did not come through the law but
through the righteousness of faith. 14 [g]For if
it is the adherents of the law who are to be
the heirs, faith is null and the promise is
void. 15 For [h]the law brings wrath, but
[i]where there is no law [j]there is no transgression.

16 That is why it depends on faith, [k]in
order that the promise may rest on grace
and [l]be guaranteed to all his offspring—
not only to the adherent of the law but also
to the one who shares the faith of
Abraham, [m]who is the father of us all, 17 as
it is written, [n]"I have made you the father
of many nations"—in the presence of the
God in whom he believed, [o]who gives life
to the dead and calls into existence [p]the
things that do not exist. 18 In hope he
believed against hope, that he should
become the father of many nations, as he
had been told, [q]"So shall your offspring
be." 19 He did not weaken in faith when he
considered his own body, which was [r]as

5 [x]ch. 3:22; See John 6:29
7 [y]Cited from Ps. 32:1, 2
8 [z]2 Cor. 5:19
9 [a]ch. 3:30 [b]ver. 3
11 [c]Gen. 17:10, 11 [d]ver. 12, 16; [ch. 3:22]; See Luke 19:9
13 [e]Gal. 3:16; Heb. 6:15, 17; 7:6; 11:9, 17; [ch. 9:8]; See Acts 13:32 [f]Gen. 17:4-6
14 [g]Gal. 3:17, 18
15 [h]ch. 7:7, 10-25; 2 Cor. 3:7, 9; Gal. 3:10 [i][ch. 3:20] [j]Gal. 3:19
16 [k]See ch. 3:24 [l]Gal. 3:22; [ch. 15:8] [m][ch. 9:8]
17 [n]Cited from Gen. 17:5; [ver. 18] [o][Heb. 11:19]; See John 5:21 [p]1 Cor. 1:28; [Heb. 11:3]
18 [q]Cited from Gen. 15:5
19 [r]Heb. 11:12

"work" of merit. The righteousness of God was "counted" to Abraham (vv. 3, 9) and not earned by him. See "Faith and Works" at James 2:24.

4:6–8 That Paul's exegesis of Gen. 15:6 is correct is confirmed by an appeal to David's words in Ps. 32:1, 2. Blessedness, fellowship with God together with all its accompaniments, and salvation are not earned, but are the effect of the gift of forgiveness. It is by Christ's work, not ours, that we are justified. Human merit of any sort is excluded.

4:9–12 Paul now addresses a further criticism of his argument. Even if he has shown that righteousness comes by grace through faith in the case of Abraham, has he forgotten that Abraham was the father of the circumcised (and therefore not of the uncircumcised)? The apostle provides a devastating answer: Gen. 15:6 describes Abraham before he was circumcised (v. 10). The righteousness signified and sealed for him by circumcision had already been credited to him when he was still uncircumcised. He serves as the prototype for all believers, both Jew and Gentile. For the Jew, he serves as prototype because his circumcision pointed back to his justification; for the Gentile, because he received justification apart from circumcision.

4:13–15 The argument is now taken a stage further. The promise given to Abraham was that he would be the father of a multitude who would possess the land of Canaan, and he would also be the fountain of blessing for all nations (Gen. 12:2, 3, 7). Christ is the Seed of Abraham (Gal. 3:16) and has already begun to inherit the earth (Ps. 2:8; cf. Matt. 28:18, 19). This promise was received by Abraham through faith, "not . . . through the law" (v. 13). Paul assumes the truth of what he demonstrates in Gal. 3:17, that since the law came 430 years after the promise, the promises cannot be dependent on the law. If the inheritance were dependent on obedience to the law, faith would have no place in the divine scheme of things, and the promise would be void, since the law cannot bring about the obedience it requires for its fulfillment. Only "where there is no law" is there "no transgression"; where there is law, it "brings wrath" (v. 15). Given the established truth of the sinfulness of all people, it is impossible that the promise could be received on the basis of law-keeping.

4:16 That is why it depends on faith. Because the promise in all its elements is received by faith, it also rests "on grace." Had it been on the basis of works, the promise would have failed; had it been on the basis of circumcision, it could have been received only by Jews. Because it is by faith, and therefore by grace (by God's action, not man's), it is "guaranteed" to come to Abraham's true spiritual offspring, or all believers whether Jew or Gentile by birth.

4:17 as it is written. Again Paul appeals to Scripture (Gen. 17:5) for confirmation of his exposition. Rather than be father of Jews (the circumcised) only, it was already clear in Genesis that Abraham was to be the spiritual patriarch of all believers, Jew and Gentile alike. Nor is it unbelievable that the promise of God should be received by Gentiles also, for the one in whom Abraham believed "gives life to the dead." This is evidenced in the new life that came from the apparently dead womb of Sarah (v. 19), in the life given back to Isaac when he was under the sentence of death (Gen. 22), and ultimately in the life restored in the resurrection of Christ (4:24, 25).

calls into existence the things that do not exist. This may refer to God's creation of the world out of nothing (see Gen. 1; Is. 41:4; 48:13 for creation summoned into being by God's word), or to the birth of Isaac (in which a nation emerges from a barren womb). Perhaps this also alludes to the words of Hos. 1:10; 2:23 (9:25, 26).

4:18 In hope he believed. Trusting in God's power (v. 17), Abraham gained assurance that the promise would be fulfilled. Paul indicates that true faith is directed toward God and not humanity, toward the divine word and not toward the human situation.

against hope. In the natural course of events, believing that Sarah would bear his child (the first requirement for receiving what was promised) was utterly futile, for reasons given in v. 19.

good as dead ([s]since he was about a hundred years old), or when he considered [t]the
barrenness of Sarah's womb. [20]No distrust
made him waver concerning the promise of
God, but he grew strong in his faith as he
gave glory to God, [21]fully convinced that
[u]God was able to do what he had promised. [22]That is why his faith was "counted
to him as righteousness." [23]But [v]the words
"it was counted to him" were not written
for his sake alone, [24]but for ours also. It
will be counted to us [w]who believe in [x]him
who raised from the dead Jesus our Lord,
[25][y]who was delivered up for our trespasses
and raised [z]for our justification.

Peace with God Through Faith

5 [a]Therefore, since we have been justified
by faith, [b]we^1 have peace with God
through our Lord Jesus Christ. [2]Through
him we have also [c]obtained access by faith^2
into this grace [d]in which we stand, and [e]we^3
rejoice^4 in hope of the glory of God. [3]More
than that, we [f]rejoice in our sufferings,
knowing that suffering [g]produces endurance,
[4]and endurance produces character, and
character produces hope, [5]and [h]hope does
not put us to shame, because God's love
[i]has been poured into our hearts through
the Holy Spirit who has been given to us.
[6]For [j]while we were still weak, at the
right time [k]Christ died for the ungodly.
[7]For one will scarcely die for a righteous
person—though perhaps for a good person
one would dare even to die—[8]but [l]God
shows his love for us in that [m]while we
were still sinners, Christ died for us.
[9]Since, therefore, [n]we have now been justified by his blood, much more shall we be
saved by him from [o]the wrath of God. [10]For
if [p]while we were enemies [q]we were reconciled to God by the death of his Son, much
more, now that we are reconciled, shall we
be saved by [r]his life. [11]More than that, we
also rejoice in God through our Lord Jesus
Christ, through whom we have now received [s]reconciliation.

Death in Adam, Life in Christ

[12]Therefore, just as [t]sin came into the
world through one man, and [u]death

19 [s]Gen. 17:17 [t]Gen. 18:11 **21** [u]Gen. 18:14; [Heb. 11:19] **23** [v]ch. 15:4; 1 Cor. 9:9, 10; 10:6, 11; 2 Tim. 3:16, 17; [Ps. 102:18] **24** [w]ch. 10:9; 1 Pet. 1:21 [x]See Acts 2:24 **25** [y]ch. 5:6, 8; 8:32; Isai. 53:5, 6; Matt. 20:28; Gal. 1:4 [z]ch. 5:18; [1 Cor. 15:17]

Chapter 5

1 [a]ch. 3:28 [b][ch. 15:13; Heb. 12:28] **2** [c]Eph. 2:18; 3:12; [Heb. 10:19, 20; 1Pet. 3:18] [d]1 Cor. 15:1 [e]ver. 11; Heb. 3:6; [ch. 12:12] **3** [f]See Matt. 5:12 [g]See Luke 21:19; James 1:3 **5** [h]Ps. 119:116; Phil. 1:20 [i]Acts 2:17, 18, 33; Tit. 3:6; [Gal. 4:6]

6 [j]ver. 8, 10; [Hos. 13:9; Eph. 2:5] [k]See ch. 4:25 **8** [l]See John 3:16 [m]ver. 6, 10 **9** [n]See ch. 3:25 [o]1 Thess. 1:10; 2:16; See ch. 1:18 **10** [p]ver. 6, 8; Col. 1:21; [ch. 8:32] [q]2 Cor. 5:18-20; Eph. 2:16; Col. 1:20, 21 [r]2 Cor. 4:10, 11 **11** [s]ch. 11:15; 2 Cor. 5:18, 19 **12** [t]Gen. 2:17; 3:6; 1 Cor. 15:21, 22; [ver. 15-17; ch. 6:9; Ps. 51:5] [u]ch. 6:23; James 1:15

^1 Some manuscripts *let us* ^2 Some manuscripts omit *by faith* ^3 Or *let us*; also verse 3 ^4 Or *boast*; also verses 3, 11

4:19 about a hundred years old. See Gen. 17:1, 17.

4:20 he gave glory to God. Giving glory to God is a hallmark of faith, since it is dependence on God's power and trust in His word of promise (v. 21). Abraham's life of faith was one in which God's attributes formed the foundation (1:20), and therefore in which God's glory was displayed (cf. 1:21). It was through exercising this kind of faith that he was justified (v. 22).

4:25 The proof of justification by faith in Abraham's case leads Paul back to the foundation of justification in the work of Christ (3:24–26). Christ's death and resurrection are two aspects of one saving work. In the first part, Christ bore the legal penalty for our guilt. In the second, He rose from the dead, His resurrection confirming that His death was a sufficient and effective offering for sin, pleasing the Supreme Judge.

5:1–11 The implications of justification by grace through faith are now drawn out. The transition from wrath (1:18) to grace (3:21) transforms both the status and the experience of the believer. Instead of estrangement (3:10–17) there is now peace (5:1); in place of falling short of God's glory through sin (3:23), there is the hope of glory (5:2); instead of suffering as judgment (2:5, 6), there is joy in tribulation because of what God produces through it (5:3); instead of fearful uncertainty, there is assurance of God's love (vv. 6–8) and joy in Him (v. 11).

5:1 we have peace. See text note. Numerous manuscripts support "let us have" peace, but the flow of Paul's logic supports the first rendering. That "we have now received reconciliation" (v. 11) implies that we are at peace with God already. With peace established, we now have access to God's presence. The wall of partition has been removed. This peace is not a guarded truce subject to new warfare. It is a permanent peace.

5:2 hope. New Testament hope is the assurance of something not yet fully experienced, and quite different from uncertain, wishful thinking. That this hope will not be frustrated is guaranteed here and now by the love of God that the Holy Spirit pours into believers' hearts (vv. 4, 5).

5:4 character. It confirms our confidence that the glory we hope for will one day be ours (8:17–25).

5:6 Christ died. The nature of this outpoured love (v. 5) is seen in the Cross. There God acted "at the right time," both in the sense that the death of Christ took place according to the divine timetable (John 17:1; Acts 2:23; Gal. 4:4), and also because it meets us in the moment of our deepest need. This is Paul's point when he says "still weak" (v. 6), "still sinners" (v. 8), "while we were enemies" (v. 10).

5:8–11 Like 8:1–4, 32, this passage highlights the special purpose and effectiveness that Paul regularly ascribes to Christ's death. That is, Christ died specifically "for us" (v. 8) who now believe and are justified through our faith, and His death actually achieved for us the "reconciliation" that "we have now received" (v. 11). See "Definite Redemption" at John 10:15.

5:9 much more. Paul argues from the greater to the less. If God would do for us the work of reconciliation, at the cost of the suffering and death of His Son, He will not withhold the final salvation that is "by him," and by "his blood" as the ascendant Mediator. Keeping for final salvation those who have already been justified is simply God following through His initial purpose of love to them. The decisive, and more costly, expression of this loving purpose was Christ's actual reconciling death, which guarantees the justification and glorification of those for whom he died (8:32).

5:10 reconciled. Paul alone in the New Testament describes the sin-bearing work of Christ as reconciliation (11:15; 2 Cor. 5:18–20; Eph. 2:16; Col. 1:20, 22), although the idea is already present in the Old Testament, especially in Hosea. God's alienation from us is ended by removing the cause of alienation (our sin, guilt, and condemnation) by the death of Christ (cf. 2 Cor. 5:21). In this sense, reconciliation is objective (2 Cor. 5:18, 19). However, it must be "received" (v. 11; cf. 2 Cor. 5:20), by the laying aside of our own alienation and hostility, that is, by repentance and faith in Christ.

5:12–21 Paul's "Therefore" (v. 12) indicates that what follows is connected in Paul's mind with what has preceded, so that the comparison and contrast he draws between Adam and Christ is his theological elabora-

through sin, and [v]so death spread to all
men because [w]all sinned— [13]for sin indeed
was in the world before the law was given,
but [x]sin is not counted where there is no
law. [14]Yet death reigned from Adam to
Moses, even over those whose sinning was
not [y]like the transgression of Adam, [z]who
was a type of [a]the one who was to come.
[15]But the free gift is not like the trespass.
For if many died through one man's trespass, much more have the grace of God
and the free gift by the grace of that one
man Jesus Christ abounded for [b]many.
[16]And the free gift is not like the result
of that one man's sin. For [c]the judgment
following one trespass brought condemnation, but the free gift following many trespasses brought [d]justification. [17]If, because
of one man's trespass, death reigned
through that one man, much more will
those who receive the abundance of grace
and the free gift of righteousness [e]reign in
life through the one man Jesus Christ.

[18]Therefore, as one trespass[1] led to condemnation for all men, so one act of righteousness[2] leads to justification and life for
[f]all men. [19]For as by the one man's [g]dis-
obedience the many were made sinners, so
by the one man's [h]obedience the many will
be made righteous. [20]Now [i]the law came in
to increase the trespass, but where sin
increased, [j]grace abounded all the more,
[21]so that, [k]as sin reigned in death, [l]grace
also might reign through righteousness
leading to eternal life through Jesus Christ
our Lord.

Dead to Sin, Alive to God

6 What shall we say then? [m]Are we to
continue in sin that grace may abound?
[2]By no means! How can [n]we who died to
sin still live in it? [3]Do you not know that all
of us [o]who have been baptized [p]into Christ
Jesus were baptized into his death? [4]We
were [q]buried therefore with him by baptism

12 [v][ver. 14, 21; 1 Cor. 15:22] [w]Eph. 2:3
13 [x]See ch. 3:20
14 [y]Hos. 6:7 [z]1 Cor. 15:45 [a][Matt. 11:3]
15 [b]ver. 19; Isai. 53:11
16 [c]1 Cor. 11:32 [d]ver. 18
17 [e]Rev. 22:5
18 [f]See John 12:32
19 [g][2 Cor. 10:6] [h]Heb. 5:8; [Phil. 2:8]
20 [i]Gal. 3:19; See ch. 3:20 [j]1 Tim. 1:14
21 [k][ver. 12, 14] [l]See John 1:17
Chapter 6
1 [m]ver. 15; [ch. 3:8]
2 [n]ver. 11; ch. 7:4, 6; Gal. 2:19; Col. 2:20; 3:3; 1 Pet. 2:24
3 [o]Gal. 3:27 [p]See Matt. 28:19
4 [q]Col. 2:12

[1] Or *the trespass of one* [2] Or *the act of righteousness of one*

tion on what has already been said. Paul's stress on the "one man" throughout the passage (vv. 12, 15–17, 19) indicates that he viewed both Adam and Christ as historical individuals. In the case of Adam, the focus of attention is on his "one trespass" (vv. 16, 18, and text note) by which all "were made sinners" (v. 19). They had solidarity with Adam as their representative before God, and this constituted them sinners when Adam sinned.

5:12 just as sin came into. Paul here begins a comparison that is not concluded until vv. 18–21. The comparison is interrupted by a meditation extending through v. 17.

through one man. Death is not natural to humanity, but is the direct result of sin (Gen. 2:17).

because all sinned. The universal reign of death is the consequence of sin. Paul does not explain how all mankind was involved with Adam in his sinning, but simply asserts the fact. All sinned in the sin of Adam. See "Original Sin and Total Depravity" at Ps. 51:5.

5:14 death reigned. All people were subject to death before the law of Moses was given.

a type of the one who was to come. Adam, the first man, was the divinely appointed head of the whole of humanity, and his sin forfeited righteousness for all those he represented ("all men," vv. 12, 18; the "many," vv. 15, 19). In the same way, God made Christ the representative head of a new humanity so that His obedience to death might gain their justification. Inherent in this teaching is the thought that the restoration provided in salvation must follow the pattern, but reverse the content, of the original constitution of humanity before God (1 Cor. 15:45–49; Heb. 2:14–18).

5:15 But the free gift is not like the trespass. Paul spells out the contrast between Christ and Adam in vv. 15–17. Not only are the acts of the two men antithetical, but the grace of the work of Christ is seen to be greater than the sin, judgment, and condemnation of Adam in the way it brings justification, righteousness, and life to ruined souls ("much more," vv. 15, 17).

5:16 the judgment following one trespass. See "The Fall" at Gen. 3:6.

5:18, 19 Paul returns to the main thrust of his analogy, namely that there is a parallel between Adam and Christ in that condemnation and justification are the direct fruits of their actions. On the basis of the actions of "one," "many" are constituted either sinners or righteous. Adam is the representative head as well as the physical root of all, and all sinned and fell when he sinned. In contrast, "by the one man's obedience" those whom Christ represents are "made righteous" in Him (see "The Humble Obedience of Christ" at John 5:19). Christ is their representative Head, as well as the spiritual root of the new humanity, for through His resurrection they are given new birth and a living hope (1 Pet. 1:3; Eph. 2:1–7).

5:20 the law came. It was given as an additional (post-Fall) element in God's dealings with His people, so "to increase the trespass." While sin was in the world before the law was given (v. 13), the law reveals sin in its specific character as trespass, lapsing from a set standard. Such lapses "abound" because the law's demands stir up contrary cravings in sinners' hearts (7:5, 8). But in the face of this increase of sin, "grace abounded all the more," not only keeping pace with the offense, but outdoing it, in the great salvation accomplished through Christ.

6:1–14 Paul's insistence that the increase of sin is met by the increase of grace (5:20) leads to the question he now raises. So great was his emphasis on the freeness of God's grace in the face of sin that his preaching had been accused of antinomian tendencies, or ignoring the ethical requirements of the law (3:8). Now he makes the point that to continue in sin would involve a contradiction of the Christian's new identity in Christ. In view of this new identity (v. 11), Christians are to refuse to allow sin to usurp authority in their lives, and instead are to yield the whole of life to God (vv. 12, 13) in the assurance that since they are under grace, not law, as the means of their salvation, sin is no longer their master.

6:2 By no means. A frequently used expression of shocked recoil (3:31; 6:15; 7:7, 13; 9:14; 11:1, 11).

we who died to sin. Paul's point is that believers have been really united with Jesus Christ in both His death and His resurrection, and that this has so altered their condition that for them to continue sinning as before is not only inappropriate but actually impossible.

6:3, 4 Baptism, the sign and seal of initial union with Christ, is the burial service for the "old self" (v. 6) as well as the inauguration ceremony for the new person in Christ (v. 4). As such, it proclaims that those united to Christ have died to sin. From 5:20 to 8:4, sin is presented as the driving energy that produces sinful acts, and is personified as a tyrannical taskmaster, demanding dominion and needing to be resisted. See theological note "Baptism" on page 273.

into death, in order that, just as [r]Christ was
raised from the dead by [s]the glory of the
Father, we too might walk in [t]newness of
life.
5 For [u]if we have been united with him in
[v]a death like his, we shall certainly be united with him in a resurrection like his. **6** We
know that [w]our old self[1] [x]was crucified
with him in order that [y]the body of sin
might be brought to nothing, so that we
would no longer be enslaved to sin. **7** For
[z]one who has died [a]has been set free[2] from
sin. **8** Now [b]if we have died with Christ, we
believe that we will also live with him. **9** We
know that [c]Christ being raised from the
dead will never die again; [d]death no longer
has dominion over him. **10** For the death he
died he died to sin, [e]once for all, but the
life he lives he lives to God. **11** So you also
must consider yourselves [f]dead to sin and
alive to God in Christ Jesus.
12 Let not [g]sin therefore reign in your
mortal bodies, to make you obey their passions. **13** [h]Do not present your members to
sin as instruments for unrighteousness, but
[i]present yourselves to God as those who
have been brought from death to life, and
your members to God as instruments for
righteousness. **14** For [j]sin [k]will have no
dominion over you, since you are not
under law but under grace.

Slaves to Righteousness

15 What then? [l]Are we to sin [m]because we
are not under law but under grace? By no
means! **16** Do you not know that if you present yourselves [n]to anyone as obedient
slaves,[3] you are slaves of the one whom
you obey, either of sin, which leads to
death, or of obedience, which leads to
righteousness? **17** But [o]thanks be to God,
that you who were once slaves of sin have
become obedient from the heart to the
[p]standard of teaching to which you were
committed, **18** and, [q]having been set free
from sin, [r]have become slaves of righteousness. **19** [s]I am speaking in human terms,
because of your natural limitations. For
[t]just as you once presented your members
as slaves to impurity and to lawlessness
leading to more lawlessness, so now pre-

4 [r]ver. 9; ch. 8:11; See Acts 2:24 [s][John 11:40; 2 Cor. 13:4] [t]2 Cor. 5:17; Gal. 6:15; Eph. 4:23, 24; Col. 3:10; [ch. 7:6]
5 [u][2 Cor. 4:10] [v]Phil. 3:10, 11; [Col. 2:12; 3:1]
6 [w]Eph. 4:22; Col. 3:9 [x]Gal. 2:20; 5:24; 6:14 [y][ch. 7:24]
7 [z]1 Pet. 4:1 [a][ver. 18]
8 [b]2 Tim. 2:11; [2 Cor. 4:10; 13:4]
9 [c]Acts 13:34; Rev. 1:18 [d][ch. 5:14, 17]
10 [e]See Heb. 7:27
11 [f]See ver. 2
12 [g]ver. 14; Ps. 19:13; 119:133; Mic. 7:19; [2 Cor. 5:17]
13 [h]ch. 7:5; Col. 3:5 [i]ch. 12:1; 1 Pet. 2:24; 4:2
14 [j][ch. 8:2, 12] [k]See ver. 12
15 [l]ver. 1 [m][1 Cor. 9:21] **16** [n][ver. 20; Matt. 6:24]; See John 8:34 **17** [o]See ch. 1:8 [p][2 Tim. 1:13] **18** [q]ver. 22; ch. 8:2; [ver. 7]; See John 8:32 [r][ver. 22] **19** [s]See ch. 3:5 [t]See ver. 13

1 Greek *man* 2 Greek *has been justified* 3 Greek *bondservants*. Twice in this verse and verse 19; also once in verses 17, 20

6:6 our old self was crucified with him. While the "old self" includes pre-conversion life, it includes much more, and should be interpreted in the light of 5:12–21 to mean all that we were through our union with Adam. We are to think of all this as having been nailed to the cross to die.

body of sin. Perhaps in the sense of sin as a mass, or body, but probably the physical body seen as the sphere in which sin reigned (cf. "body of death" in 7:24).

might be brought to nothing. Union with Christ in His death does not destroy the body as such, but it does end the body's role as the inescapable tool of sin by destroying the reign of sin in the body. Christians' bodies are now dedicated to Christ and bear holy fruit in His service (6:13, 22; 7:4; 12:1). We are no longer "enslaved to sin," since bodily existence dominated by the cravings of sin has given way to bodily existence dominated by a passion for righteousness and holiness (v. 18).

6:7 free from sin. Lit. "justified." See text note. Here the language has an additional nuance of "delivered from," for Paul is discussing the reign of sin, and not merely its guilt (vv. 17–22). Paul personifies sin as a monarch (5:21); as a general who uses various parts of the body for weapons ("instruments," v. 13); and as an employer who pays wages (v. 23).

6:8 we will also live with him. This includes the idea of resurrection, but also implies present participation in the risen life of Christ as one who is "alive to God" (v. 11).

6:11 consider yourselves. Recognize that what has been said in vv. 1–10 is already the truth about yourself.

6:12 Let not sin therefore reign. Since the reign of sin has been broken, all attempts on sin's part to recover dominion can and must be resisted. The body (v. 13), once ruled by sinful desires, must no longer be yielded to them.

6:13 present yourselves to God. Paul sees the secret of sanctification to lie in giving the whole person to God, from which follows the offering of the various parts of the body to Him.

brought from death to life. All this is to be done in conscious awareness, and as a deliberate expression, of our new identity in Christ.

6:14 sin will have no dominion over you. This is an indicative statement, a promise, and not an imperative or exhortation.

not under law but under grace. The controlling principle in the life of the believer is the reign of grace that sets free from the reign of sin (5:21) and transforms into the likeness of Christ.

6:15–23 That the Christian is not under law but under grace might appear to provide license for moral carelessness. This Paul denies, since under the reign of grace Christians have become slaves of God. The freedom of grace is therefore freedom for obedience and service, not for license. See "The Freedom and Bondage of the Will" at Jer. 17:9.

6:17 thanks be to God. While Paul stresses the activity of the individual in conversion ("present yourselves," v. 16; "obedient," v. 17), he gratefully traces all right spiritual responses to the grace of God. While the individual is active in conversion, it is in a non-contributory and non-meritorious way, so that neither divine grace nor divine sovereignty is compromised.

the standard of teaching to which you were committed. The opposite of slavery to sin is commitment to the new life-style that grace produces. In view here are both the gospel itself and the kind of teaching given in chs. 12–16, perhaps with Christ Himself as the model (cf. Eph. 4:20, 21).

6:18 having been set free. See "Christian Liberty" at Gal. 5:1.

6:19 I am speaking in human terms, because of your natural limitations. The illustration of slavery is an inadequate representation of the Christian life, especially in the Roman context, because it could convey harsh connotations of human slavery and inadequately express the truth that the yoke of Christ is easy (Matt. 11:28–30). Nevertheless, Paul retains the metaphor, perhaps believing that the greater danger is of failing to fulfill personal moral responsibility to the Lord.

leading to more lawlessness. Sinfulness does not stand still, but grows worse.

sent your members [u]as slaves to righteousness leading to sanctification.
20 [v]When you were slaves of sin, you were
free in regard to righteousness. 21 [w]But what
fruit were you getting at that time from the
things [x]of which you are now ashamed?
[y]The end of those things is death. 22 But
now that you [z]have been set free from sin
and [a]have become slaves of God, [b]the fruit
you get leads to sanctification and [c]its end,
eternal life. 23 [d]For the wages of sin is death,
but the free gift of God is eternal life in
Christ Jesus our Lord.

Released from the Law

7 Or do you not know, brothers[1]—for I
am speaking to those who know the
law—that the law is binding on a person
only as long as he lives? 2 Thus [e]a married
woman is bound by law to her husband
while he lives, but if her husband dies she
is released from the law of marriage.[2]
3 Accordingly, [f]she will be called an adulteress if she lives with another man while
her husband is alive. But if her husband
dies, she is free from that law, and if she
marries another man she is not an adulteress.
4 Likewise, my brothers, [g]you also have
died [h]to the law [i]through the body of
Christ, so that you may belong to another,
to him who has been raised from the dead,
[j]in order that we may bear fruit for God.
5 For while we were living in the flesh, our
sinful passions, aroused by the law, were at
work [k]in our members [l]to bear fruit for
death. 6 But now we are released from the
law, having died to that which held us captive, so that we serve not under the old
written code but in [m]the new life of [n]the
Spirit.

19 [u][1 Cor. 9:27]
20 [v]See ver. 16
21 [w]ch. 7:5; [Jer. 12:13] [x][2 Cor. 4:2] [y]ch. 1:32; 8:6, 13; Prov. 14:12; Gal. 6:8
22 [z]See ver. 18 [a]1 Cor. 7:22; 1 Pet. 2:16 [b]ch. 7:4 [c]1 Pet. 1:9
23 [d][ch. 2:7]; See ch. 5:12
Chapter 7
2 [e]1 Cor. 7:39
3 [f]Matt. 5:32
4 [g]ver. 6; See ch. 6:2 [h]ch. 8:2; Gal. 2:19; 5:18; Eph. 2:15; Col. 2:14 [i][Eph. 2:16; Col. 1:22] [j]ch. 6:22; Gal. 5:22; Eph. 5:9
5 [k]ch. 6:13 [l]See ch. 6:21, 23
6 [m]See ch. 6:4 [n]ch. 2:27, 29; 2 Cor. 3:6

[1] Or *brothers and sisters;* also verse 4 [2] Greek *law concerning the husband*

Baptism

Christian baptism, which has the form of a ceremonial washing (like John's pre-Christian baptism), is a sign from God that signifies inward cleansing and remission of sins (Acts 22:16; 1 Cor. 6:11; Eph. 5:25–27), Spirit-wrought regeneration and new life (Titus 3:5), and the abiding presence of the Holy Spirit as God's seal testifying and guaranteeing that one will be kept safe in Christ forever (1 Cor. 12:13; Eph. 1:13, 14). Fundamentally, baptism signifies union with Christ in His death, burial, and resurrection (Rom. 6:3–7; Col. 2:11, 12), and this union with Christ is the source of every element in our salvation (1 John 5:11, 12). Receiving the sign of baptism in faith assures those baptized that God's gift of new life in Christ is freely given to them. At the same time, it commits them to live in a new way as disciples of Jesus.

Christ told His disciples to baptize in the name of the Father, the Son, and the Holy Spirit (Matt. 28:19). This formula means that the covenant relation which baptism formally confers is with all three Persons of the Godhead. When Paul says that the Israelites were "baptized into Moses" (1 Cor. 10:2), he means that they were put under Moses' control and direction. Baptism into the name of the triune God signifies control and direction by God.

The outward signs do not automatically or magically convey the inward blessings that they signify. No prescription of a particular mode of baptism can be found in the New Testament. The command to baptize may be fulfilled by immersion, dipping, or sprinkling; all three modes satisfy the meaning of the Greek verb *baptizo* and the symbolic requirement of passing under, and emerging from, cleansing water.

6:23 The triple contrast of wages, sin, and death, with gift, God, and eternal life, brings Paul's argument to a memorable focus.

7:1–12 Paul now expands on the theme of the believer's relationship to the law. Although the law is holy, just, and good (v. 12), the sinner's subjection to it resulted only in condemnation, because law in its justice uncovered every transgression and failure. In this section the relationship of the sinner to the law is compared with marriage. The point of the comparison is that death brings an end to these relationships, and the widowed partner is free to be in a new relationship. Because the "marriage" with the law was broken by death, the believer is not an adulteress and cannot be condemned by the law. The believer dies through being united with Christ in His death, breaking the chain of disobedience and death that bound the sinner together with Adam in his destiny (5:12–21). The other side of the illustration is that union with Christ in His resurrection gives the believer a new relationship, in which a true, if not yet perfect, obedience is offered to God in love and gratitude. In the new relationship with Christ, the energy of the Spirit ensures that there will be life and fruitfulness.

7:3 Paul assumes that remarriage after the death of a spouse is wholly consistent with the Christian gospel (1 Tim. 5:14).

7:4 body of Christ. Here referring to the physical death of Christ.

fruit. A metaphor meaning result or natural consequence.

7:6 held us captive. The complex of sin, condemnation, and death in Adam and under the law.

The Law and Sin

7 What then shall we say? That the law is
sin? By no means! Yet if it had not been for
the law, [o]I would not have known sin. I
would not have known what it is to covet if
[p]the law had not said, "You shall not
covet." 8 But sin, [q]seizing an opportunity
through the commandment, produced in
me all kinds of covetousness. [r]Apart from
the law, sin lies dead. 9 I was once alive
apart from the law, but when the commandment came, sin came alive and I died.
10 The very commandment [s]that promised
life proved to be death to me. 11 For sin,
[t]seizing an opportunity through the commandment, [u]deceived me and through it
killed me. 12 So [v]the law is holy, and the
commandment is holy and righteous and
good.

13 Did that which is good, then, bring
death to me? By no means! It was sin, producing death in me through what is good,
in order that sin might be shown to be sin,
and through the commandment might
become sinful beyond measure. 14 For we
know that the law is spiritual, but I am of
the flesh, [w]sold under sin. 15 I do not understand my own actions. For [x]I do not do
what I want, but I do the very thing I hate.
16 Now if I do what I do not want, I agree
with [y]the law, that it is good. 17 So now [z]it
is no longer I who do it, but sin that dwells
within me. 18 For I know that nothing good
dwells [a]in me, that is, in my flesh. For I
have the desire to do what is right, but not
the ability to carry it out. 19 [b]For I do not do
the good I want, but the evil I do not want

7 [o]See ch. 3:20 [p]ch. 13:9; Ex. 20:17; Deut. 5:21
8 [q]ver. 11; [Gal. 5:13] [r]1 Cor. 15:56
10 [s]See ch. 10:5
11 [t]ver. 8 [u][Gen. 3:13; Heb. 3:13]
12 [v]Ps. 19:8, 9; 119:137; 2 Pet. 2:21; [ver. 16]
14 [w]1 Kin. 21:20, 25; 2 Kin. 17:17; Isai. 50:1; 52:3
15 [x]ver. 18, 19; [Gal. 5:17]
16 [y]1 Tim. 1:8; [ver. 12]
17 [z]ver. 20
18 [a]Gen. 6:5; 8:21; Job 14:4; 15:14; Ps. 51:5 19 [b]ver. 15

7:7 That the law is sin? Paul's allusions to the law thus far have been negative in tone, especially his statement that the law arouses sinful passions (v. 5). Now he explains that recognizing the negative effect the law had on the life of fallen humanity is not a devaluation of the law itself (note the vehement language in 3:31). The God-ordained role of the law in a fallen world is to reveal the nature of human sin. The law not only defines sin, but acts as a catalyst, provoking the precise sinful reactions that it forbids and condemns (vv. 8–11). In itself the law, which brings us to know the reality of sin in our moral and spiritual system (3:20; 5:13, 20), is "holy and righteous and good" (v. 12). The law is a faithful revelation of what is right or wrong, and does not lose its validity to measure and direct our moral behavior.

7:8 sin lies dead. In the sense that either sin or its real offensiveness was not recognized.

7:9 I was once alive apart from the law . . . I died. He was alive, not in the sense of having spiritual life (6:11), but in his own estimation. Knowing the law, which promised life for obedience (v. 10), made Paul realize that law-keeping was required. Trying to obey it made him realize that inwardly, in the desires of his heart (especially coveting, v. 8, the sin forbidden in the tenth commandment), he was constantly breaking the law even before he knew it, and when he saw what he was doing he could not stop it. Thus, Paul writes that sin, the anti-God, anti-law driving force within him, "deceived me and . . . killed me" (v. 11). He became convinced that spiritually he was lifeless and lost. Paul offers his personal experience as an index of how sin and law relate in everyone.

7:10 promised life. See Lev. 18:5; Deut. 30:15, 19. In itself, the law marks out a path that guarantees God's favor and humanity's happiness. But where sin reigns, the law brings only misery and death.

7:11 sin . . . deceived me. Here, as elsewhere in Romans, the shadow of Eden emerges in Paul's language (Gen. 3:13; cf. 2 Cor. 11:3; 1 Tim. 2:14).

7:12 holy and righteous and good. The law reflects God's character ("holy"); it is the objective norm for humanity's covenantal response to God ("righteous"); and it is beneficial for each one of us personally, since we have been created in the image of God ("good").

7:13 Did that which is good, then, bring death to me. No, says Paul, it was sin in me that became the cause of my spiritual death by leading me to break God's good law. Sin is seen to be "sinful beyond measure."

7:14–25 The sudden change to the present tense in vv. 15–25, by contrast with the statements describing the past in vv. 7–13, raises the question whether Paul is now describing his present experience. A variety of interpretations exists, including the following: (a) Paul is describing the unregenerate person or perhaps the Jew in particular from the standpoint of the gospel; (b) Paul is describing a Christian in an unnatural and unhealthy spiritual condition, one failing to draw on the indwelling Spirit's resources; (c) Paul is describing the transitional experience, possibly his own, of one who has been awakened to his true spiritual need, but has not yet entered a full experience of justification by faith; (d) Paul is describing himself and Christians generally who, although in Christ and free from the condemnation of the law, do not yet perfectly fulfill the requirements of the law. The last view is the most probable interpretation. It accounts for Paul's shift to the present tense while his theme in vv. 7–25 (God's holy law stimulating and exposing sin) continues, and for the presence in Paul's self-analysis here of elements found only in persons who have been united with the risen Christ to new life in the Spirit (6:4–11; 7:6; 8:4–9). Paul is aware that God's law is "spiritual" (v. 14). He actually delights in God's law, desiring to fulfill it perfectly (vv. 15–23), and he is distressed that sin in him opposes that desire. He is grateful at the prospect of future deliverance from this frustration (v. 24; 8:23). He distinguishes between his "mind," which aims at obedience, and his "flesh," which continues to sin (v. 25). All of these observations show that Paul is describing his experience as a new man in Christ.

Paul is actually describing a profound conflict that every Christian finds inherent in his life in Christ: Christ dwells in him (Gal. 2:20), yet sin also dwells in him (vv. 17, 20). Perfect conformity to God's will is at present out of his reach. Salvation has "already" and "not yet" dimensions.

It is important to remember that Paul is still discussing the role of the law. He highlights the frustrations of the present Christian experience simply to show how, for Christians as for Jews, God's good law provokes, exposes, and condemns sin without either being tainted by it or bringing deliverance from it.

7:14 the law is spiritual. A further description of the law, in addition to v. 12. Far from repudiating the law (3:31), Paul declares that it sets forth the standard to which life governed by the Spirit should conform. By contrast, he calls himself "of the flesh" because he cannot fully reach this standard. As a moral ruin, now under reconstruction, he displays the marks of what he has been as a result of Adam as well as of what he will be as a result of Christ.

sold under sin. While not the whole truth about him (v. 25), Paul recognizes that from the viewpoint of God's holy law, this is the truth about his bodily existence and behavior (Christian though he is) and he proceeds to explain it.

7:15 I do not understand. Paul is able to analyze, but not to explain, the contrast between himself and the "sin that dwells within me" (vv. 17, 20). There is a real and bewildering conflict between the energies of sin and of grace in his life. He hints, however, that indwelling sin is a temporary lodger in him. While sin still accompanies his new identity in Christ in this life, the new identity will result in the final triumph over indwelling sin (6:2–14).

is what I keep on doing. 20 Now if I do what
I do not want, [c]it is no longer I who do it,
but sin that dwells within me.
21 So I find it to be a law that when I want
to do right, evil lies close at hand. 22 For [d]I
delight in the law of God, [e]in my inner
being, 23 but I see in my members [f]another
law waging war against the law of my mind
and making me captive to the law of sin
that dwells in my members. 24 Wretched
man that I am! Who will deliver me from
[g]this body of death? 25 Thanks be to God
through Jesus Christ our Lord! So then, I
myself serve the law of God with my mind,
but with my flesh I serve the law of sin.

Life in the Spirit

8 There is therefore now no condemnation for those who are in Christ Jesus.[1]
2 For the law of [h]the Spirit of life [i]has set
you[2] free in Christ Jesus from the law of sin
and death. 3 For [j]God has done what the
law, [k]weakened by the flesh, [l]could not do.
[m]By sending his own Son [n]in the likeness
of sinful flesh and [o]for sin,[3] he condemned
sin in the flesh, 4 in order that [p]the righteous requirement of the law might be fulfilled in us, [q]who walk not according to the
flesh but according to the Spirit. 5 For
[r]those who live according to the flesh set
their minds on [s]the things of the flesh, but
those who live according to the Spirit set
their minds on [t]the things of the Spirit. 6 To
set [u]the mind on the flesh is death, but to
set the mind on the Spirit is life and peace.
7 For the mind that is set on the flesh is
[v]hostile to God, for it does not submit to
God's law; [w]indeed, it cannot. 8 Those who
are in the flesh cannot please God.
9 You, however, are not in the flesh but in
the Spirit, if in fact [x]the Spirit of God
dwells in you. [y]Anyone who does not have
[z]the Spirit of Christ does not belong to
him. 10 But if Christ is in you, although the
body is dead because of sin, the Spirit is life

20 [c]ver. 17 **22** [d]Ps. 1:2; 112:1; 119:35 [e]2 Cor. 4:16; Eph. 3:16; [1 Pet. 3:4] **23** [f]Gal. 5:17; [James 4:1] **24** [g][ch. 6:6; 8:23]
Chapter 8
2 [h]1 Cor. 15:45; 2 Cor. 3:6 [i]ver. 12; See ch. 6:14, 18; 7:4 **3** [j]Heb. 10:1, 2, 10, 14; See Acts 13:39 [k]Gal. 4:9; Heb. 7:18 [l]Heb. 10:6, 8 [m]2 Cor. 5:21 [n]Phil. 2:7; See John 1:14 [o]Lev. 16:5; Heb. 10:6, 8; 13:11
4 [p]ch. 1:32; 2:26 [q]Gal. 5:16, 25 **5** [r][Gal. 6:8] [s]Gal. 5:19-21 [t]Gal. 5:22, 23, 25 **6** [u]ver. 13; [Col. 2:18]; See ch. 6:21
7 [v]James 4:4 [w]1 Cor. 2:14 **9** [x]ver. 11; 1 Cor. 3:16; 6:19; 2 Cor. 6:16; 2 Tim. 1:14 [y]Jude 19; [John 14:17] [z]See Acts 16:7

1 Some manuscripts add *who walk not according to the flesh (but according to the Spirit)* 2 Some manuscripts *me* 3 Or *and as a sin offering*

7:24 Who will deliver me. This is not a cry of despair, for Paul knows and provides the answer in v. 25.

body of death. The physical body, viewed as the means by which sin is expressed. Paul's desire here is not for death as such, but for the deliverance that will ultimately be consummated in resurrection (8:23; Phil. 3:20; 2 Cor. 5:2–4).

7:25 So then . . . sin. Paul here summarizes the state of frustration that he has been describing since v. 14.

I myself. This means "I, one and the same person." Paul totally approves God's good law, yet his "flesh" still serves sin. New life in the Spirit is experienced by individuals in mind, body, and spirit that continue to bear the marks of sin.

8:1–39 A vast rhapsodic expansion of the analysis of Christian assurance and hope contained in 5:1–11. Paul wants the glory of their salvation, rather than the depressing reminder just given of their continuing sinfulness, to fill his readers' minds and bring joy to their hearts.

8:1 therefore. The apostle's concern here is pastoral. Paul is telling his readers, in light of the foregoing reminder of their continuing sinfulness, they must now recall their acceptance, immunity, and security in Christ.

no condemnation. Probably in both senses—the judgment and the punishment.

8:2 the law of the Spirit of life . . . the law of sin and death. The law of the Spirit means His operative power (7:23). The law of sin is the operative power of sin, or else the divine law as used by sin to produce death (7:8–13).

8:3 what the law . . . could not do. Paul does not criticize the moral law, but notes once more that because of humanity's sinfulness it cannot bring salvation.

his own Son. The words are reminiscent of the binding of Isaac in Gen. 22:2, and point to the tremendous cost of our redemption (v. 32).

in the likeness of sinful flesh. The word "likeness" means similarity to a prototype; "sinful flesh" is human nature, which through the Fall came to be corrupted and controlled by sin. Christ's humanity was like ours in that He could be tempted, and lived His life as a part of a fallen world full of frailty and exposed to vast pressures. But He did not sin, and there was no moral and spiritual corruption in Him. Had Jesus been corrupted by sin in any way, He could not have fulfilled the Old Testament pattern, which required a sin offering to be "without blemish" (Lev. 4:3).

condemned sin in the flesh. Paul seems to mean that in the crucifixion of the incarnate Son of God sin was judged and condemned, so that now all its claims to have us condemned have become invalid. There is no condemnation remaining for those who are in Christ. See "Christian Liberty" at Gal. 5:1.

8:4–8 Paul's contrast between the old pattern of life and the new, between life in the flesh and in the Spirit (7:6), is now worked out in detail in terms of two settled attitudes or mind-sets: one under the influence of the "flesh," the other under the influence of Christ through the Spirit within believers.

8:7 hostile to God. Pure anti-God hostility, incapable of being anything else, is the real mind-set of everyone who is not yet renewed by the Spirit (3:9–18). The natural person regards God as an enemy.

8:9–11 Christians are not in Adam, dominated by "the flesh," but are under the rule of Christ, because the Spirit who dwells in them is the Spirit of Christ (see "The Holy Spirit" at John 14:26). Though the body is still subject to death, life prevails because those united with Christ live to God in the sphere of the Spirit. The duality in view here is not simply the distinction between the physical and spiritual sides of a believer's life, but between two spheres of existence—bodily life in a fallen world with its ever present physical death, and life in the Spirit, a participation in the resurrection of Christ (1:4).

8:10 the Spirit is life. This phrase could refer to the renewed spirit of the believer, but it probably means the Holy Spirit. The passage itself emphasizes the Holy Spirit, His work, and His close association with Christ. The indwelling "Spirit of God" is called the "Spirit of Christ" (v. 9), and His indwelling is the means whereby "Christ is in you" (v. 10). Paul views this relationship as so close that he can even say "the Lord is the Spirit" (2 Cor. 3:17; cf. 1 Cor. 15:45). These passages do not take away the distinction between Christ and the Spirit as separate Persons of the Trinity. Rather, Paul teaches that Christ and the Holy Spirit work together in applying the resurrected life of Christ to the believer. The Spirit's presence now is a guarantee of the future bodily resurrection of the believer (v. 11).

because of righteousness. 11 If the Spirit of
[a]him who raised Jesus from the dead
dwells in you, he who raised Christ Jesus
from the dead will also give life to your
mortal bodies [b]through his Spirit who
dwells in you.

Heirs with Christ

12 So then, brothers,[1] we are debtors, [c]not
to the flesh, to live according to the flesh.
13 For if you live according to the flesh you
will die, but if by the Spirit you [d]put to
death the deeds of the body, you will live.
14 For all who are [e]led by the Spirit of God
are [f]sons[2] of God. 15 For [g]you did not
receive [h]the spirit of slavery to fall back into
fear, but you have received the Spirit of
[i]adoption as sons, by whom we cry,
[j]"Abba! Father!" 16 [k]The Spirit himself bears
witness with our spirit that we are children
of God, 17 and if children, then [l]heirs—
heirs of God and fellow heirs with Christ,
[m]provided we suffer with him in order that
we may also be glorified with him.

Future Glory

18 For I consider that the sufferings of this
present time [n]are not worth comparing
with the glory that is to be revealed to us.
19 For the creation waits with eager longing
for [o]the revealing of the sons of God. 20 For
the creation [p]was subjected to futility, not
willingly, but [q]because of him who subjected it, in hope 21 that [r]the creation itself
will be set free from its bondage to decay
and obtain the freedom of the glory of the
children of God. 22 For we know that [s]the
whole creation [t]has been groaning together
in the pains of childbirth until now. 23 And
not only the creation, but we ourselves,
who have [u]the firstfruits of the Spirit,
[v]groan inwardly as [w]we wait eagerly for
adoption as sons, [x]the redemption of our
bodies. 24 For [y]in this hope we were saved.
Now [z]hope that is seen is not hope. For
who hopes for what he sees? 25 But if we
hope for what we do not see, we [a]wait for
it with patience.

26 Likewise the Spirit helps us in our
weakness. For [b]we do not know what to
pray for as we ought, but [c]the Spirit himself
intercedes for us with groanings too deep
for words. 27 And [d]he who searches hearts
knows what is [e]the mind of the Spirit,

11 [a]See Acts 2:24 [b][2 Cor. 3:6] **12** [c]See ver. 2 **13** [d]Col. 3:5 **14** [e]Gal. 5:18 [f]ver. 16, 19; ch. 9:8, 26; Deut. 14:1; Hos. 1:10; John 1:12 **15** [g]1 Cor. 2:12 [h]2 Tim. 1:7; [Gal. 2:4; Heb. 2:15; 1John 4:18] [i]ver. 23; Gal. 4:5; [ch. 9:4; Isai. 56:5; Jer. 31:9] [j]Gal. 4:6; [Mark 14:36] **16** [k]2 Cor. 1:22; 5:5; Eph. 1:13, 14; 1 John 3:24 **17** [l]Gal. 3:29; 4:7; Tit. 3:7 [m]2 Cor. 1:7; 2 Tim. 2:12; See Acts 14:22 **18** [n]2 Cor. 4:17; [1 Pet. 1:5, 6] **19** [o]1 Pet. 4:13; 5:1; 1 John 3:2; [ch. 2:7] **20** [p]Gen. 3:18, 19; Eccles. 1:2 [q]Gen. 3:17 **21** [r][Acts 3:21]

22 [s]Mark 16:15 [t]Jer. 12:4, 11 **23** [u][2 Cor. 5:5; James 1:18] [v]2 Cor. 5:2, 4 [w]ver. 19, 25; Isai. 25:9; Gal. 5:5 [x]See ch. 7:24; Luke 21:28 **24** [y][1 Thess. 1:3; 5:8] [z]2 Cor. 4:18; Heb. 11:1 **25** [a][1 Thess. 1:3; 5:8] **26** [b][Matt. 20:22; James 4:3] [c]Zech. 12:10; Eph. 6:18; See John 14:16 **27** [d]1 Sam. 16:7; 1Chr. 28:9; Prov. 15:11; 17:3; Jer. 11:20; 17:10; Luke 16:15; 1 Thess. 2:4 [e]See ver. 6

[1] Or *brothers and sisters*; also verse 29 [2] See discussion on "sons" in the preface

8:11 A Trinitarian account of the realization of salvation, presupposing the unity of Father, Son, and Holy Spirit in their essential being, just as they are united in the complex work of redemption.

8:12 From this point to the end of the chapter, Paul is generalizing about himself and all believers with him.

8:13 put to death the deeds of the body. See "Sanctification: The Spirit and the Flesh" at 1 Cor. 6:11. The body is not evil of itself. Sin originates in the heart, the spiritual center of our being, including the will (Mark 7:18–23). But since we live in physical bodies, sin finds expression through the body. Therefore, not only at the inner points of origin, but also in its bodily expressions, sin must be put to death, that is, terminated (6:12, 13; 12:1).

8:14 This way of holiness is now further described as the leading of the Spirit and is specified as the mark of God's sons. The language of "leading" is reminiscent of the "adoption" and leading of Israel in the Exodus and wilderness, which may be the background to Paul's thought here (9:4; Deut. 8:2, 15; 29:5). See "Adoption" at Gal. 4:5.

8:15 Spirit of adoption. In addition to justification and freedom from condemnation (v. 1), believers are taken into the family of God and are inwardly persuaded by the Spirit that they belong there. The cry of the believer, "Abba! Father!" (the Aramaic word *Abba* was used by Jesus Himself for God, Mark 14:36) indicates how vividly union with Christ was realized in the experience of the New Testament church. The cry is an expression of an assured awareness of sonship. The idea of adoption does not appear in the Old Testament legal system, and Paul seems to have borrowed this apt concept from Roman law, filling it out with the biblical theology of God's fatherhood over His people.

8:16 bears witness. This joint witness of our own spirit and the Holy Spirit surfaces in the cry "Abba! Father!" (Gal. 4:6).

8:17–21 As all the children in a human family are heirs of the father along with the oldest brother, so believers are God's heirs in and with Christ. But receiving the inheritance that comes to us in Christ involves sharing in His suffering, the pathway to sharing in His glory (2 Cor. 4:17). "Glorified," and "glory," in vv. 17–21 (cf. v. 30) mean the transforming, ennobling, joy-bringing manifestation of God in one's personal being. The glory to be revealed (v. 18) will appear as the sons of God are revealed in their new nature (v. 19), and the creation is liberated from its present state of imperfection and decay (vv. 20, 21). The revelation of this glory will more than wipe out all the harm and loss ("futility," v. 20) that the created order has suffered as a result of Adam's fall (Gen. 3:17). The regeneration of all things (Matt. 19:28; Acts 3:21; Rev. 21:1) in the created order corresponds to the freedom in glory (vv. 17, 18) enjoyed by the children of God.

8:22–25 The present condition of creation is not its final one; it is like a mother groaning in labor pains. The entire creation has a destiny planned by God, and longs to be fulfilled, much as believers do (vv. 23, 26). Our salvation has begun—we have the Holy Spirit as a down payment—but it will not be consummated until the resurrection (the full realization of adoption in Christ, v. 23). Inevitably, therefore, the Christian life involves patient waiting in hope.

8:24 in this hope we were saved. See "Hope" at Heb. 6:18. Travail (pain and grief because of how things are, 7:24, 25; 8:18, 36) is permeated with expectation, not disappointment and frustration (5:5), and with patience (v. 25) as well as eagerness (v. 23).

8:26 the Spirit helps. See "Prayer" at Luke 11:2. The Holy Spirit strengthens us in our state of weakness, of which we are constantly conscious. Perplexity as to how to pray for oneself is a universal Christian experience. Our inarticulate longings to pray properly are an indication to us that the indwelling Spirit is already helping us by interceding for us in our hearts, making requests that the Father will certainly answer.

because [1] the Spirit [f]intercedes for the
saints [g]according to the will of God. 28 And
we know that for those who love God all
things work together [h]for good,[2] for [i]those
who are called according to his purpose.
29 For those whom he [j]foreknew he also
[k]predestined [l]to be conformed to the image
of his Son, in order that he might be [m]the
firstborn among many brothers. 30 And
those whom he predestined he also called,
and those whom he called he also [n]justified, and those whom he justified he also
[o]glorified.

27 f[ver. 34] g[1 John 5:14] 28 h Ezra 8:22; [Eccles. 8:12] i ch. 9:24; 1 Cor. 1:9; 7:15, 17; Gal. 1:15; 5:8; Eph. 4:1, 4; 2 Tim. 1:9 29 j ch. 11:2; 1 Pet. 1:2

k 1 Cor. 2:7; Eph. 1:5, 11; [ch. 9:23] l Phil. 3:21; [1Cor. 15:49; Col. 3:10]; See 1 John 3:2 m Col. 1:15, 18; Heb. 1:6; Rev. 1:5 30 n 1 Cor. 6:11 o John 17:22; [Heb. 2:10]

1 Or *that* 2 Some manuscripts *God works all things together for good*, or *God works in all things for the good*

Perseverance of the Saints

In declaring the eternal security of God's people it is perhaps clearer to speak of their preservation than, as is usually done, of their perseverance. Perseverance means continued adherence to a belief despite discouragement and opposition. The reason that believers persevere in faith and obedience, however, is not the strength of their own commitment, but that Jesus Christ through the Holy Spirit preserves them.

John tells us that Jesus Christ is under promise to His Father (John 6:37–40) and to His people directly (John 10:28, 29) to keep them so that they never perish. In His prayer for the disciples at the close of the Last Supper, Jesus asked that those whom the Father had given Him (John 17:2, 6, 9, 24) would be preserved to glory. Christ continues to intercede for His people (Rom. 8:34; Heb. 7:25), and it is inconceivable that His prayer for them will go unanswered.

Paul celebrates the present and future security of the saints in the almighty love of God (Rom. 8:31–39). He rejoices in the certainty that God will complete the good work that He began in the lives of believers (Phil. 1:6; cf. 1 Cor. 1:8, 9; 1 Thess. 5:23, 24; 2 Thess. 3:3; 2 Tim. 1:12; 4:18).

The Westminster Confession says,

> They, whom God hath accepted in His Beloved, effectually called, and sanctified by His Spirit, can neither totally nor finally fall away from the state of grace, but shall certainly persevere therein to the end, and be eternally saved (17.1).

The regenerate are saved through persevering in faith and Christian living to the end (Heb. 3:6; 6:11; 10:35–39) as God preserves them.

This doctrine does not mean that all who ever professed to be Christians will be saved. Those who try to live a Christian life in their own abilities will fall away (Matt. 13:20–22). The false profession of many who say to Jesus, "Lord, Lord," will not be acknowledged (Matt. 7:21–23). Those who pursue holiness of heart and love of neighbor and so show themselves to have been regenerated by God are entitled to believe themselves secure in Christ. Belief in perseverance properly understood does not lead to careless living and arrogant presumption.

The regenerate may backslide and fall into sin. In so doing they oppose their own new nature, and the Holy Spirit convicts them of their sin (cf. John 16:8) and compels them to repent and be restored to righteousness. When regenerate believers manifest a humble, grateful desire to please the God who saved them, the knowledge that He has pledged to keep them safe forever increases that desire.

8:28 And we know. Christians assess the present in the light of their assurance about the future. As true Israelites, in whom the first and great commandment is fulfilled (Matt. 22:37, 38), our love for God is evoked by knowledge of His love for us (5:5–8).

called. Brought to faith (v. 30; cf. 1:6).

according to his purpose. The purpose of God guarantees "good" for His people. For them this is not necessarily ease and quiet, but being like Christ (vv. 17–23, 29). God's providence rules in such a way as to ensure everything that happens to us is working for our ultimate good.

8:29 foreknew . . . predestined. See "The Purpose of God: Predestination and Foreknowledge" at Mal. 1:2. Vv. 29, 30 explain God's "purpose" (v. 28). It is a plan of sovereign saving grace, entitling all who now believe to trace their faith and salvation back to an eternal decision by God to bring them to glory, and to look forward to that glory as a guaranteed certainty. The destiny appointed for believers (conformity to Christ and glorification with Him) flows from divine foreknowledge. Here it is persons, not facts or events, that God is said to foreknow. God does foresee events, but Paul's point is that God has of His own initiative chosen the objects of His active, saving love. "Know" implies intimate personal relationship, not merely awareness of facts and circumstances (Gen. 4:1; Amos 3:2; Matt. 1:25); it is virtually the equivalent of "elect."

8:30 Those predestined are, in due time, "called," or effectively summoned through the gospel into saving fellowship with Christ (1:6; cf. 1 Cor. 1:9). We note that all of those "called" are also "justified." The call cannot refer to the outward call of the gospel that many reject. It is an inward call of God that performs what He intends. All who are predestined are called in this way. Predestination includes God's determination that a person will receive such an effective call (that is, the "effectual call"). Predestination is not based on God's knowing beforehand how people will respond to the gospel. Just as the predestined are called, so the called are both justified and certain to be finally glorified. The past tense of "glorified" indicates that from God's standpoint the work is as good as done. He will complete it as planned. See theological note "The Perseverance of the Saints."

God's Everlasting Love

31 What then shall we say to these things?
[p]If God is for us, who can be[1] against us?
32 [q]He who did not spare his own Son but
[r]gave him up for us all, how will he not also
with him graciously give us all things?
33 Who shall bring any charge against God's
elect? [s]It is God who justifies. 34 [t]Who is to
condemn? Christ Jesus is the one who died—
more than that, who was raised—[u]who is
at the right hand of God, [v]who indeed is
interceding for us.[2] 35 Who shall separate
us from the love of Christ? Shall tribulation, or distress, or persecution, or famine,
or nakedness, or danger, or sword? 36 As it
is written,

> [w]"For your sake [x]we are being killed all
> the day long;
> we are regarded as sheep to be
> slaughtered."

37 No, in all these things we are more than
[y]conquerors through [z]him who loved us.
38 For I am sure that neither death nor life,
nor angels nor rulers, nor things present
nor things to come, nor powers, 39 nor
height nor depth, nor anything else in all
creation, will be able to separate us from
the love of God in Christ Jesus our Lord.

God's Sovereign Choice

9 [a]I am speaking the truth in Christ—I
am not lying; my conscience bears me
witness in the Holy Spirit—2 that I have
great sorrow and unceasing anguish in my
heart. 3 For [b]I could wish that I myself were
[c]accursed and cut off from Christ for the
sake of my brothers,[3] my kinsmen [d]accord-
ing to the flesh. 4 They are [e]Israelites, and to
them belong [f]the adoption, [g]the glory, [h]the
covenants, [i]the giving of the law, [j]the worship, and [k]the promises. 5 To them belong
[l]the patriarchs, and from their race, according to the flesh, is the Christ [m]who is God
over all, [n]blessed forever. Amen.
6 But it is not as though the word of God
has failed. For not all who are descended
from Israel belong to Israel, 7 and not all are
children of Abraham [o]because they are his

31 [p]Num. 14:9; 2 Kin. 6:16; Ps. 118:6; 1 John 4:4 **32** [q]John 3:16 [r]See ch. 4:25 **33** [s]Isai. 50:8, 9; [Rev. 12:10, 11] **34** [t]ver. 1 [u]See Mark 16:19 [v]Heb. 7:25; 1 John 2:1; [ver. 27] **36** [w]Cited from Ps. 44:22 [x]1 Cor. 4:9; 15:30, 31; 2 Cor. 4:10, 11; See Acts 20:24 **37** [y]1 Cor. 15:57; See John 16:33 [z]Gal. 2:20; Eph. 5:2; Rev. 1:5; 3:9

Chapter 9
1 [a]2 Cor. 11:10; 1 Tim. 2:7; [2 Cor. 12:19; Gal. 1:20]; See ch. 1:9 **3** [b][Ex. 32:32] [c]1 Cor. 12:3; 16:22; Gal. 1:8, 9 [d][ch. 11:14]

4 [e][ver. 6; ch. 2:28, 29; Gal. 6:16] [f][Ex. 4:22] See ch. 8:15 [g]Ex. 40:34; 1 Sam. 4:21; 1 Kin. 8:11 [h]Gen. 17:2; Deut. 29:14; Gal. 4:24; Eph. 2:12 [i]Deut. 4:14; [Ps. 147:19] [j]Heb. 9:1 (Gk.); [ch. 12:1] [k][Eph. 2:12]; See John 4:22; Acts 13:32 **5** [l]ch. 11:28 [m][Eph. 4:6; Col. 1:16-19] [n]ch. 1:25; John 1:1; 2 Cor. 11:31; Heb. 1:8 **7** [o][Gal. 4:23]; See John 8:33

[1] Or *who is* [2] Or *Is it Christ Jesus who died . . . for us?* [3] Or *brothers and sisters*

8:31–39 Paul now draws the entire argument of 1:16–8:39 to a triumphal conclusion in a series of challenges to every influence that might thwart the church's confident assurance of present preservation and future glory. The passage is reminiscent of the third Servant Song in Is. 50:4–9, on which it in part depends.

8:31 What then shall we say to these things. Vv. 28–30 may be primarily in view here, but they should not be separated from 1:16–8:27, and especially not from 8:1–27. "These things" embraces the whole display of free grace to lost sinners in the letter thus far.

who can be against us. There will certainly be opposition, but Paul's point is that it lacks the ability to destroy faith. Since "God is for us," victorious spiritual survival is assured. "For us" expresses the eternal commitment of almighty love that is spelled out in vv. 38, 39.

8:32 He who did not spare his own Son. Paul's words are an effective echo of the Septuagint (Greek translation) text of Gen. 22:12.

gave him up. The phrase is used elsewhere of active participation in the judicial condemnation of Christ (Matt. 20:19; 26:15, 16; 27:2, 18, 26; cf. Is. 53:6, 10).

for us all. Even for the worst of us who now believe (3:9–18; 5:6–8). Once more, as in 5:9, 10, Paul reasons from the greater to the less: for God to give His Son to die for us was the supreme gift, guaranteeing the subsequent gift of everything else that we need for our full and final glory (v. 30).

8:33 It is God who justifies. The Judge has already dealt with all charges against us in the death and resurrection of Christ (4:25). Self-justification is futile.

8:34 at the right hand of God. The position of honor and executive authority (cf. Ps. 110:1). There can be no condemnation for us (in either sense of the term, v. 1 note), if our enthroned sin-bearer intercedes for us in heaven (1 John 2:1) while the Holy Spirit intercedes in our hearts (v. 27).

8:35 the love of Christ. The ease with which Paul uses this phrase interchangeably with "the love of God in Christ" (v. 39) testifies to his underlying assumption of the identity of essence between the Father and the Son.

8:36 Paul's appeal to Old Testament Scripture indicates that suffering is not an unexpected novelty for God's people. But in Christ such sufferings become stepping stones on the pathway to glory (5:1–5; 8:17–23).

8:37 more than conquerors. The strength shown in enduring the hostility of persecutors and the pain of circumstances is astonishing.

8:38, 39 No aspect of the created order, nor any event or being within it, can end our enjoyment of the active love of God to us in Christ.

9:1–5 Paul himself now accounts for rejection of the gospel by most of his fellow Jews.

9:1 my conscience . . . witness. Scripture nowhere defines "conscience." Here as in 2:15 and 13:5, Paul clearly thinks of it as moral self-awareness informed by divine revelation. Paul is taking a lawful oath to swear to his sincerity.

9:3 I could wish that I myself were accursed. Although Paul is the apostle to the Gentiles, he echoes the sentiments of Moses in the face of the unbelief of the Jews (Ex. 32:30–32). They are his own countrymen and he agonizes over them (v. 2). To be willing to suffer God's curse for them is a strong statement of love.

9:4 to them . . . the adoption. The unbelief of Israel is magnified by the multiplied blessings they have experienced. In the eightfold privileges Paul lists in vv. 4, 5, he confirms his earlier statement in 3:1, 2.

9:5 Christ who is God over all. The text correctly translates Paul's words as directly ascribing deity to Christ. See "Jesus Christ, God and Man" at John 1:14.

9:6 word of God. His promise and plan to be the God of Abraham's seed (Gen. 17:7, 8). In the Old Testament era, natural descent did not automatically guarantee inheritance of the promise. God chose who should inherit it. This principle is evident in the families of Abraham and Isaac.

offspring, but [p]"Through Isaac shall your
offspring be named." 8 This means that it is
not the children of the flesh who are the
children of God, but [q]the children of the
promise are counted as offspring. 9 For this
is what the promise said: [r]"About this time
next year I will return and Sarah shall have
a son." 10 And not only so, but [s]also when
Rebecca had conceived children by one
man, our forefather Isaac, 11 though they
were not yet born and had done nothing
either good or bad—in order that God's
purpose of election might continue, not
because of works but because of [t]his call—
12 she was told, [u]"The older will serve the
younger." 13 As it is written, [v]"Jacob I loved,
but Esau I hated."

14 What shall we say then? [w]Is there injustice on God's part? By no means! 15 For he
says to Moses, [x]"I will have mercy on
whom I have mercy, and I will have compassion on whom I have compassion." 16 So
then it depends not on human will or exertion,[1] but on God, who has mercy. 17 For
the Scripture says to Pharaoh, [y]"For this
very purpose I have raised you up, that I
might show my power in you, and that my
name might be proclaimed in all the
earth." 18 So then he has mercy on whomever he wills, and he hardens whomever he
wills.

7 [p]Heb. 11:18; Cited from Gen. 21:12; [Gal. 3:29]
8 [q]Gal. 4:23, 28
9 [r]Cited from Gen. 18:10, 14; [Gen. 17:21]
10 [s]Gen. 25:21
11 [t][ch. 4:17]; See ch. 8:28
12 [u]Cited from Gen. 25:23
13 [v]Cited from Mal. 1:2, 3
14 [w]Deut. 32:4; 2 Chr. 19:7; Job 8:3; 34:10; Ps. 92:15
15 [x]Cited from Ex. 33:19
17 [y]Cited from Ex. 9:16
19 [z]2 Chr. 20:6; Job 9:12; Dan. 4:35
20 [a]Job 33:13 [b]Isai. 29:16; 45:9
21 [c]Isai. 64:8; Jer. 18:6 [d]2 Tim. 2:20
22 [e][ver. 21, 23; Acts 9:15] [f][Prov. 16:4; 1 Pet. 2:8]
23 [g]Eph. 3:16; See ch. 2:4 [h][ch. 8:29]

19 You will say to me then, "Why does he
still find fault? For [z]who can resist his
will?" 20 But who are you, O man, [a]to
answer back to God? [b]Will what is molded
say to its molder, "Why have you made me
like this?" 21 [c]Has the potter no right over
the clay, to make out of the same lump
[d]one vessel for honored use and another
for dishonorable use? 22 What if God, desiring to show his wrath and to make known
his power, has endured with much
patience [e]vessels of wrath [f]prepared for
destruction, 23 in order to make known [g]the
riches of his glory for vessels of mercy,
which he [h]has prepared beforehand for
glory— 24 even us whom he [i]has called, [j]not
from the Jews only but also from the
Gentiles? 25 As indeed he says in Hosea,

> [k]"Those who were not my people I will
> call 'my people,'
> and her who was not beloved I will
> call 'beloved.'"

26 > [l]"And in the very place where it was
> said to them, 'You are not my
> people,'
> there they will be called 'sons of
> the [m]living God.'"

24 [i]See ch. 8:28 [j]See ch. 3:29 25 [k]Cited from Hos. 2:23; [1 Pet. 2:10] 26 [l]Cited from Hos. 1:10 [m]See ch. 8:14; Matt. 16:16

1 Greek *not of him who wills or runs*

9:11 they were not yet born. The case of Jacob and Esau clinches the argument in three ways: (a) because they were twins, as nearly equal in nature as possible; (b) because the purpose of God reversed even the small distinction that did exist, by causing the older brother to serve the younger; (c) because the purpose of God was stated before they were born (and therefore was not dependent on their actions). Election is not based on foreseen actions, deeds, or faith. Rather, it is based on God's sovereign predestinating grace.

9:13 Jacob I loved, but Esau I hated. This distinguishing purpose of God in election (v. 11) is further confirmed by the words of Mal. 1:2, 3, which explain God's love to Israel as rooted in His free choice of Jacob rather than Esau. "Hated" here cannot be reduced to "loved less," as the context of Mal. 1:3, 4 makes clear. It must carry the sense of rejection and antipathy.

9:14 What shall we say then. Cf. 8:31. Paul recognizes that his previous statement cannot be allowed to pass without further comment. Could the distinguishing sovereign purpose of God throw into jeopardy His attribute of perfect righteousness? The idea is clearly unthinkable—"By no means!" (6:2, 15; 7:7). Paul explains why by citing two biblical texts (Ex. 33:19; 9:16) in vv. 15, 17, from which he concludes that God is righteous in showing mercy to some while He hardens the hearts of others. When God shows mercy it is not a person receiving a reward earned by one's own efforts, but God's sovereign free grace extended to persons who are morally incapable of any acceptable effort (1:18–3:20). God owes mercy to none, so there is no injustice when mercy is not shown. Mercy is a divine prerogative; it rests on God's good pleasure. When God "hardens" Pharaoh's heart (v. 18), He does not create fresh evil in it, but gives Pharaoh over to his already evil desires as an act of judgment, resulting eventually in God's display of "power" (v. 22) in the destruction of Pharaoh's army (Ex. 14:17, 18, 23–28).

9:17 the Scripture says to Pharaoh. It was God who thus spoke to Pharaoh through Moses (Ex. 9:16), but for Paul the words of Scripture and the voice and authority of God are one.

9:18 whomever he wills. See theological note "Election and Reprobation" on the next page.

9:19 Why does he still find fault. By what right can God lay the blame for their sins on those He has hardened against Himself? Paul answers partially in terms of human experience (vv. 20, 21). It is unreasonable and irreverent for anyone to question the rightness of God's ways. Potters have every right to do as they please with the clay (Is. 64:8). All belong to "the same lump" (cf. vv. 10–13) of fallen humanity in Adam (5:12–14); all actively sin even before God hardens them in sinning (1:18–28). That God should show mercy to any from the Adamic lump and create vessels of honor from it is the kindness of grace; that others should become vessels for lesser use is a matter of His sovereign prerogative and is itself a display of perfect justice towards them.

9:23 which he has prepared beforehand. See "The Purpose of God: Predestination and Foreknowledge" at Mal. 1:2. Paul does not elaborate on the preparation in view. The addition of "beforehand" in connection with the vessels of mercy may be pointing to the mercy that originates in God's good pleasure from eternity (8:29, 30), while the wrath in view is in direct response to existing ungodliness and unrighteousness (cf. 1:18–32). The distinction between elect and reprobate does not lie in anything in themselves (all deserve wrath), but exclusively in the will of God. Within that context, however, the objects prepared for destruction experience wrath that is the only possible and just reward for sin.

27 And Isaiah cries out concerning Israel:
[n]"Though the number of the sons of Israel[1]
be as the sand of the sea, [o]only a remnant
of them will be saved, 28 for the Lord will
carry out his sentence upon the earth fully
and without delay." 29 And as Isaiah predicted,

> [p,q]"If the Lord of hosts had not left us
> offspring,
> [r]we would have been like Sodom
> and become like Gomorrah."

Israel's Unbelief

30 What shall we say, then? [s]That Gentiles
who did not pursue righteousness have
attained it, that is, [t]a righteousness that is
by faith; 31 but that Israel [u]who pursued a
law that would lead to righteousness[2] [v]did
not succeed in reaching that law. 32 Why?
Because they did not pursue it by faith, but
as if it were based on works. They have
stumbled over the [w]stumbling stone, 33 as it
is written,

> [x]"Behold, I am laying in Zion [y]a stone
> of stumbling, and a rock of
> offense;
> [z]and whoever believes in him will
> not be [a]put to shame."

10 Brothers,[3] my heart's desire and
prayer to God for them is that they

27 [n]Cited from Isai. 10:22, 23; [Hos. 1:10] [o]ch. 11:5
29 [p]Cited from Isai. 1:9 [q]James 5:4 [r]Deut. 29:23; Isai. 13:19; Jer. 49:18; 50:40; Amos 4:11
30 [s][ch. 10:20] [t]ch. 1:17; 3:21, 22; 10:6; Gal. 2:16; 3:24; Phil. 3:9; Heb. 11:7
31 [u][ch. 10:2, 3; 11:7] [v][Gal. 5:4]
32 [w]See 1 Pet. 2:8
33 [x]1 Pet. 2:6, 7; Cited from Isai. 28:16; [Ps. 118:22] [y]Isai. 8:14 [z]ch. 10:11 [a]Isai. 49:23; Joel 2:26, 27

1 Or *children of Israel* 2 Greek *a law of righteousness* 3 Or *Brothers and sisters*

Election and Reprobation

To "elect" means to select or choose. According to the Bible, before creation God selected from the human race those whom He would redeem, justify, sanctify, and glorify in Jesus Christ (Rom. 8:28–39; Eph. 1:3–14; 2 Thess. 2:13, 14; 2 Tim. 1:9, 10). The divine choice is an expression of free and sovereign grace. It is not merited by anything in those who are chosen. God owes sinners no mercy of any kind, only condemnation; so it is a wonder that He should choose to save any of us.

Like every truth about God, the doctrine of election involves mystery, and it sometimes stirs controversy. But in Scripture it is a pastoral doctrine, helping Christians to see how great is the grace that saves them, and moving them to respond with humility, confidence, and praise. We do not know what others God has chosen among those who do not yet believe, nor why He chose us in particular. We do know that we believe now only because we were chosen, and we know that as believers we can rely on God to finish the good work He has begun (1 Cor. 1:8, 9; Phil. 1:6; 1 Thess. 5:23, 24; 2 Tim. 1:12; 4:18). For these reasons the knowledge of election is a source of gratitude and confidence.

Peter tells us we should be "diligent to make [our] calling and election sure" (2 Pet. 1:10)—that is, certain to us. Election is known by its fruits. Paul knew that the Thessalonians had been chosen because he saw their faith, hope, and love, the transformation of their lives brought about by the gospel (1 Thess. 1:3–6).

Reprobation is the name given to God's eternal decision regarding those sinners whom He has not chosen for life. In not choosing them for life, God has determined not to change them. They will continue in sin, and finally will be judged for what they have done. In some cases God may further remove the restraining influences that keep a person from extremes of disobedience. This abandonment, called "hardening," is itself a penalty for sins (Rom. 9:18; 11:25; cf. Ps. 81:12; Rom. 1:24, 26, 28).

Reprobation is taught in the Bible (Rom. 9:14–24; 1 Pet. 2:8), but as a doctrine its bearing on Christian behavior is indirect. God's decree of election is secret; which persons are elect and which are reprobate will not be revealed before the Judgment. Until that time, God's command is that the call to repent and believe be preached to everyone.

9:30 What shall we say, then. See v. 14. Having accounted for Jewish unbelief in terms of divine sovereignty, Paul now diagnoses it as due to a fatal prior commitment to a false way of righteousness. Divine sovereignty and the guilt of human willfulness are for Paul two aspects of reality. By God's grace and sovereignty, Gentiles who did not seek God's righteousness have now received it through faith in Christ, but Israel as a people have failed to receive it because they sought it by a legal means in which it could not be found. Christ has been to the Jews a stumbling stone (the image is from Is. 8:14; 28:16) over which they have fallen (vv. 32, 33; 1 Pet. 2:8).

9:31 a law that would lead to righteousness. Paul probably has the Mosaic law in view again. The mistake that the Jews have made lies not in what they pursued, but in the manner of pursuing it ("not . . . by faith, but . . . works," v. 32).

10:1 Brothers. A heartfelt appeal to the sympathy of his fellow Christians, the pathos of which is underlined by his recent reference to his relatives in the flesh (9:3, text note).

that they may be saved. Paul's concern in ch. 9 was with the salvation of the Jews, not merely with their role in redemptive history.

may be saved. 2 I bear them witness that
[b] they have a zeal for God, [c] but not according to knowledge. 3 For, being ignorant of
[d] the righteousness that comes from God,
and seeking to establish their own, they
did not submit to God's righteousness.
4 For [e] Christ is the end of the law for righteousness to everyone who believes. [1]

The Message of Salvation to All

5 For [f] Moses writes about the righteousness that is based on the law, that [g] the person who does the commandments shall
live by them. 6 But [h] the righteousness based
on faith says, [i] "Do not say in your heart,
'Who will ascend into heaven?'" (that is, to
bring Christ down) 7 or "'Who will descend
into the [j] abyss?'" (that is, [k] to bring Christ
up from the dead). 8 But what does it say?
[l] "The word is near you, in your mouth and
in your heart" (that is, the word of faith
that we proclaim); 9 because, if [m] you confess with your mouth that Jesus is Lord and
[n] believe in your heart [o] that God raised him
from the dead, you will be saved. 10 For
with the heart one believes and is justified,
and with the mouth one confesses and is
saved. 11 For the Scripture says, [p] "Everyone
who believes in him will not be put to
shame." 12 [q] For there is no distinction
between Jew and Greek; [r] the same Lord is
Lord of all, [s] bestowing his riches on all
who call on him. 13 For [t] "everyone who
calls on the name of the Lord will be
saved."

14 But how are they to call on him in
whom they have not believed? And how are
they to believe in him [u] of whom they have
never heard? [2] And how are they to hear
[v] without someone preaching? 15 And how
are they to preach unless they are sent? As
it is written, [w] "How beautiful are the feet of
those who preach the good news!" 16 But
[x] they have not all obeyed the gospel. For
Isaiah says, [y] "Lord, who has believed what
he has heard from us?" 17 So [z] faith comes
from hearing, and hearing through the
word of Christ.

18 But I ask, have they not heard? Indeed
they have, for

> [a] "Their voice has gone out [b] to all the
> earth,
> and their words to the ends of the
> world."

19 But I ask, did Israel not understand? First
Moses says,

Chapter 10
2 [b] See Acts 21:20 [c] [ch. 9:31]
3 [d] See ch. 1:17
4 [e] [Matt. 5:17; Gal. 3:24]
5 [f] Cited from Lev. 18:5
5 [g] Neh. 9:29; Ezek. 20:11, 13, 21; Matt. 19:17; Luke 10:28; Gal. 3:12; [ch. 7:10]
6 [h] See ch. 9:30 [i] [Deut. 30:12, 13]
7 [j] See Rev. 9:1 [k] Heb. 13:20
8 [l] Cited from Deut. 30:14
9 [m] Matt. 10:32; Luke 12:8; [1 Cor. 12:3; Phil. 2:11] [n] See Acts 16:31 [o] [1 Pet. 1:21]; See Acts 2:24
11 [p] See ch. 9:33
12 [q] See ch. 3:22, 29 [r] Acts 10:36 [s] See ch. 2:4
13 [t] Acts 2:21; Cited from Joel 2:32
14 [u] Eph. 4:21; [John 9:36; 17:20] [v] [Acts 8:31; Tit. 1:3]
15 [w] Cited from Isai. 52:7; [Nah. 1:15; Eph. 6:15] **16** [x] ch. 3:3; Heb. 4:2 [y] John 12:38; Cited from Isai. 53:1 **17** [z] Gal. 3:2, 5 **18** [a] Cited from Ps. 19:4; [1 Thess. 1:8] [b] [Mark 16:15]; See Matt. 24:14

1 Or *end of the law, that everyone who believes may be justified*
2 Or *him whom they have never heard*

10:2 zeal for God. Paul speaks here from personal experience, as to both the reality of the zeal and its wrong-headed and wrong-hearted character (Phil. 3:4–6).

10:3 being ignorant of the righteousness that comes from God. Paul contrasts the divinely established righteousness with a person's efforts to establish one's own. See "Faith and Works" at James 2:24.

establish. Covenant language (Gen. 6:18; 17:7). Even in the context of the covenant God had made with them, they perverted His grace by seeing it as dependent on their own law-keeping.

10:4 Christ is the end of the law. The interpretation followed here is that Christ is the goal or purpose of the law (Gal. 3:24). Another interpretation is that for believers Christ makes the law obsolete because they no longer strive to establish their own righteousness by it.

10:5 the righteousness that is based on the law. Paul's quotation from Lev. 18:5 is set originally in the context of God's redemptive grace requiring a person's responsive obedience (Lev. 18:2; cf. Ex. 20:1–17); it is not a statement about self-established righteousness.

10:6–8 Deuteronomy exhibits God's salvation as achieved not by humanity's strenuous efforts, but by divine grace bringing it near. In particular, Deut. 30 sets this in the context of an anticipated return from exile-judgment (Deut. 30:1–6). Paul sees this fulfilled in the new covenant in Christ (Jer. 31:31–34, cf. 2 Cor. 3:7–18). Thus Christ was the end (goal) of the Mosaic law. To seek a self-established righteousness now is the equivalent of attempting to do what God alone could do and has done, in Christ's incarnation and resurrection. By contrast with all human efforts, God has brought near the word of salvation, and with it salvation itself. See "The Word of God: Scripture as Revelation" at Ex. 32:16.

10:9, 10 confess . . . believe . . . believes . . . confesses. In the parallelism of v. 10 Paul reverses the order of verbs in v. 9 and thereby indicates that heart-belief and mouth-confession belong together for justification ("righteousness") and salvation.

10:12 there is no distinction. This is confirmed not only by the unity and universal kindness of God (v. 12), but specifically again by the teaching of the Old Testament in Joel 2:32, the statement fulfilled so dramatically at Pentecost (Acts 2:21).

10:14, 15 An analysis of what is involved when anyone calls on the name of the Lord in order to be saved.

10:14 him in whom. Lit. "Him whom," an indication that for Paul, Christ Himself is the one true preacher of the gospel (cf. Eph. 2:17; John 10:16). The ministry of preaching Christ is therefore one of great honor, hence the quotation from Is. 52:7 (2 Cor. 5:18–20).

10:18 Their voice has gone out to all the earth. The immediate context of the citation from Ps. 19:4 is that of God's general revelation (Ps. 19:1–3). Paul's use of it to prove from Scripture that Israel has heard the message of God implies that his quotation of this section of the psalm carries with it the teaching of the entire psalm, which speaks of both general revelation in nature and special revelation in His word. The latter takes place in the context of the former. The underlying logic may be: If those without special revelation have "heard" the message of God's glory in creation, how much more have those who received special revelation heard that message.

10:19–21 The failure of the Jews cannot be excused because they did not hear the message, or because they could not understand it. Moses and Isaiah contrast God's own people with those who lack understanding (Deut. 32:21), and with those who were not God-seekers but who were brought to know Him (Is. 65:1).

[c]"I will [d]make you jealous of those
who are not a nation;
with a [e]foolish nation I will make
you angry."

20 Then Isaiah is so bold as to say,

[f]"I have been found by those who did
not seek me;
I have shown myself to those who
did not ask for me."

21 But of Israel he says, [g]"All day long I have
held out my hands to a disobedient and
contrary people."

The Remnant of Israel

11 I ask, then, [h]has God rejected his
people? By no means! For [i]I myself
am an Israelite, a descendant of Abraham,
a member of the tribe of Benjamin. 2 [j]God
has not rejected his people whom he
[k]foreknew. Do you not know what the
Scripture says of Elijah, how he appeals to
God against Israel? 3 [l]"Lord, they have
killed your prophets, they have demolished
your altars, and I alone am left, and they
seek my life." 4 But what is God's reply to
him? [m]"I have kept for myself seven thousand men who have not bowed the knee to
Baal." 5 So too at the present time there is [n]a
remnant, chosen by grace. 6 [o]But if it is by
grace, it is no longer on the basis of works;

19 [c]Cited from Deut. 32:21 [d]ch. 11:11, 14 [e][Tit. 3:3]
20 [f]Cited from Isai. 65:1; [ch. 9:30]
21 [g]Cited from Isai. 65:2
Chapter 11
1 [h]1 Sam. 12:22; Jer. 31:37; 33:24 [i]2 Cor. 11:22; Phil. 3:5
2 [j]Ps. 94:14 [k]ch. 8:29
3 [l]Cited from 1 Kin. 19:10, 14
4 [m]Cited from 1 Kin. 19:18
5 [n]ch. 9:27; [Jer. 3:14; Zech. 13:8]
6 [o][ch. 4:4; Deut. 9:4, 5]
7 [p]See ch. 9:31 [q][ver. 25]
8 [r]Isai. 29:10 [s]Deut. 29:4; [Isai. 43:8; Jer. 5:21; Ezek. 12:2; Eph. 4:18]; See Matt. 13:14
9 [t]Cited from Ps. 69:22, 23
11 [u][Acts 28:28]
13 [v]ch. 15:16; [Acts 26:17]; See Acts 9:15

otherwise grace would no longer be grace.
7 What then? [p]Israel failed to obtain what
it was seeking. The elect obtained it, but
the rest [q]were hardened, 8 as it is written,

[r]"God gave them a spirit of stupor,
[s]eyes that would not see
and ears that would not hear,
down to this very day."

9 And David says,

[t]"Let their table become a snare and a
trap,
a stumbling block and a
retribution for them;
10 let their eyes be darkened so that
they cannot see,
and bend their backs forever."

Gentiles Grafted In

11 So I ask, did they stumble in order that
they might fall? By no means! Rather
through their trespass [u]salvation has come
to the Gentiles, so as to make Israel jealous. 12 Now if their trespass means riches
for the world, and if their failure means
riches for the Gentiles, how much more
will their full inclusion[1] mean!
13 Now I am speaking to you Gentiles.
Inasmuch then as [v]I am an apostle to the
Gentiles, I magnify my ministry 14 in order

[1] Greek *their fullness*

11:1–10 Paul now pointedly asks whether God has rejected His people. The apostle himself is evidence that God has not fully and finally rejected the people on whom He set His love. Just as a believing remnant could be found in Israel in Elijah's day, so there continues to be a remnant formed by God's grace. By grace the elect obtained the salvation they sought. The rest were hardened.

11:1 has God rejected. The verb conveys the sense of vigorous pushing away from Himself. The form of the question in Greek anticipates a negative answer.

I myself am an Israelite. See Phil. 3:5, 6. Paul's impeccable lineage is traced back to Abraham, the great patriarch, but also to Benjamin, the only son of Jacob to be born in Israel. It was the tribe in whose territory Jerusalem was and also the tribe of Saul, the first king.

11:2 whom he foreknew. Paul hints that God's special love and gracious choice of them makes it unthinkable that He should finally reject them as a people, even though they have now rejected Him by rejecting Christ.

11:5 a remnant, chosen by grace. In Elijah's time there was wholesale apostasy, and yet the presence of a remnant of the faithful indicated that God had not fully and finally rejected His people. Paul's thinking about the remnant is rooted in the teaching of Isaiah, whose son Shear-jashub's name means "a remnant shall return" (Is. 7:3 and text note; cf. 9:27; Is. 1:9; 6:13; 10:20–22; 11:11–16).

11:6 But if it is by grace, it is no longer on the basis of works. Again the way of grace is contrasted with works of the law (3:20, 27, 28; 4:2, 6; 9:12, 32).

11:8–10 The passages cited (Deut. 29:4; Is. 29:10; Ps. 69:22, 23) describe a biblical pattern of divine activity in the judicial hardening of hearts—a pattern Paul sees repeated in his own day.

11:11–24 The rejection of the Jewish people is neither total nor final. Just as the rejection of Christ among the Jews has led to the acceptance of the gospel among the Gentiles, so God means to use the Gentiles to provoke the Jews to envy the Gentiles' blessings, leading to their salvation and correspondingly greater riches.

11:11 did they stumble in order that they might fall. Once again the form of Paul's question anticipates (and receives) a negative answer. The Jews' rejection of Christ is not irreversible. Paul sees a divine pattern and purpose behind the unbelief of which the Jews are guilty. The pattern of his thought in v. 11, therefore, is as follows: (a) the transgression of the Jews has led to the justification of the Gentiles; (b) the salvation of the Gentiles will cause the Jews to envy; (c) the envy of the Jews will draw them to the same salvation as the Gentiles.

11:12 their full inclusion. In the context of Paul's argument, "full inclusion" here can only signify their reception of Christ and their restoration to God. The more difficult question is whether the term "full" points to a full restoration of the remnant or to the restoration of the full number of the nation in some sense. The second seems to fit better the general direction of the passage (vv. 25–32).

11:13 I am speaking to you Gentiles. Why he singles out the Gentiles in the Roman church is made clear in vv. 17–24.

apostle to the Gentiles. Paul here provides a unique insight into his thinking about his own ministry to the Gentiles: it too has his own Jewish people in view, in terms of 9:19 and 11:11 (Acts 9:15; Eph. 3:1; Gal. 2:8).

somehow to make my fellow Jews jealous,
and [w]thus save some of them. 15 For if their
rejection means [x]the reconciliation of the
world, what will their acceptance mean but
life from the dead? 16 [y]If the dough offered
as firstfruits is holy, so is the whole lump,
and if the root is holy, so are the branches.
17 But if [z]some of the branches were broken off, and you, [a]although a wild olive
shoot, were grafted in among the others
and now share in the nourishing root[1] of
the olive tree, 18 do not be arrogant toward
the branches. If you are, remember it is not
you who support the root, but the root that
supports you. 19 Then you will say,
"Branches were broken off so that I might
be grafted in." 20 That is true. They were
broken off because of their unbelief, but
you [b]stand fast through faith. So [c]do not
become proud, but [d]stand in awe. 21 For if
God did not spare the natural branches,
neither will he spare you. 22 Note then the
kindness and the severity of God: severity
toward those who have fallen, but God's
kindness to you, [e]provided you continue in
his kindness. Otherwise [f]you too will be cut
off. 23 And [g]even they, if they do not continue in their unbelief, will be grafted in, for
God has the power to graft them in again.
24 For if you were cut from what is by nature
a wild olive tree, and grafted, contrary to
nature, into a cultivated olive tree, how
much more will these, the natural branches, be grafted back into their own olive tree.

The Mystery of Israel's Salvation

25 [h]Lest you be wise in your own conceits,
I want you to understand this mystery,
brothers:[2] [i]a partial hardening has come
upon Israel, [j]until the fullness of the Gentiles has come in. 26 And in this way all
Israel will be saved, as it is written,

[k]"The Deliverer will come [l]from Zion,
he will banish ungodliness from
Jacob";
27 "and this will be my [m]covenant with
them
[n]when I take away their sins."

14 [w]1 Cor. 7:16; 9:22; 1 Tim. 4:16; James 5:20
15 [x]ch. 5:11
16 [y]Num. 15:18-21; Neh. 10:37; Ezek. 44:30
17 [z]Jer. 11:16; [Ps.52:8; John 15:2] [a][Eph. 2:12]
20 [b]1 Cor. 10:12; 2 Cor. 1:24 [c]ch. 12:3, 16; 1 Tim. 6:17 [d]Prov. 28:14; Isai. 66:2, 5; Jer. 44:10; Phil. 2:12
22 [e]1 Cor. 15:2; Heb. 3:6, 14 [f][John15:2]
23 [g]2 Cor. 3:16
25 [h]ch. 12:16 [i]2 Cor. 3:14; [ver. 7] [j][Rev. 7:9]; See Luke 21:24
26 [k]Cited from Isai. 59:20, 21; [John 4:22; Heb. 8:8-12] [l]Ps. 14:7; 53:6
27 [m]See ch. 9:4 [n]Isai. 27:9; [Heb. 8:12]

1 Greek *root of richness*; some manuscripts *richness* 2 Or *brothers and sisters*

11:15 life from the dead. This phrase may simply denote unprecedented blessing. Although the wording is slightly different from Paul's normal usage ("resurrection from the dead," 1:4; cf. 1 Cor. 15:12, 13, 21, 42), some take the phrase to refer to the general resurrection of the last day, understanding the conversion of the Jews to be an event of the end times, an immediate herald of the final resurrection.

11:16 so is the whole lump. Paul applies spiritually the principle that the firstfruits serve as the pledge of the final harvest (cf. Num. 15:17–21).

11:17 a wild olive shoot . . . grafted in. See Jer. 11:16; Hos. 14:6 for Israel as an olive tree. Wild olive shoots do seem to have been grafted into cultivated trees to bring fresh vitality to them. Paul's words, however, probably intentionally stretch beyond strict horticulture. Gentiles have been grafted into the people of God "contrary to nature" (v. 24).

11:18 do not be arrogant. Because their salvation is entirely by grace, they have no cause for boasting or despising Jewish believers. Such Gentile arrogance in relation to Jews would simply mirror the same spiritual pride that has led to the Jews' hardening (2:17).

11:20 While the rejoinder to Paul in v. 19 is formally true, the breaking off of the Jewish branches was an act of righteous judgment on unbelief, and the ingrafting of the Gentiles is a matter of grace and therefore of faith. Their ingrafting (v. 19) is not therefore based on any superior quality in the Gentiles.

awe. Tender-spirited awe, not arrogance, is the appropriate response to God's grace.

11:22 Note then the kindness and the severity of God. See "The Purpose of God: Predestination and Foreknowledge" at Mal. 1:2. Gentile believers are urged to take seriously the revelation of God's character in these events of providence. God's kindness bears fruit only when His people continue in it (2:4).

11:23, 24 The cutting off of Israel is because of unbelief, and not because the Gentiles were inherently better qualified for life in the olive tree. Moreover, Gentile believers should never forget that the gospel came to the Jew first (1:16, 17).

11:25–32 Paul's close reasoning here has been understood in three major ways: (a) He is showing how God saves all of His elect people ("all Israel" in v. 26 being taken as basically synonymous with the church, that is, spiritual Israel). (b) He is showing how God saves all the elect of Israel who are to be saved. (c) He is showing how God will, in the future, bring such widespread salvation to the Jewish people that, in an obvious general sense, it can be said that "all Israel will be saved" (v. 26). While not without difficulties, some form of this last view seems most likely for the following reasons. First, hints of it seem to appear already in vv. 11, 12, 15, 16, 24. Second, v. 25 suggests that an end to the partial hardening of Israel is in view. Third, "Israel" in v. 26 is not naturally interpreted as signifying a different entity from the Israel in view in vv. 1–24 and vv. 28–31, where national Israel (not spiritual Israel) is in view. Fourth, "mystery" in v. 25 would seem inappropriate and exaggerated if Paul's teaching were simply that all elect Jews will be saved. Finally, this view accords well with the quotations in vv. 26, 27 from Is. 59:20, 21; 27:9; Jer. 31:33, 34, which appear to speak of a comprehensive banishment of that sin that has been the cause of Israel's alienation from God.

11:25 mystery. In Paul, and Jewish thought generally, a divine secret that has now been revealed. Some interpreters conclude that what immediately follows constitutes the mystery (probably the widespread conversion of the Jews). Others hold that the mystery is the pattern of God's working in the Jew-Gentile interrelationship referred to in v. 11.

fullness. The term may be taken to have a specifically numerical connotation.

has come in. An expression used infrequently by Paul, but commonplace in the Gospels to describe entrance into life or the kingdom of God (e.g., Mark 9:47).

11:26 all Israel. A critical expression at this point in Paul's argument, and one whose meaning is much debated. It could mean "all (spiritual) Israel," that is, all elect persons both Jew and Gentile. Alternately, it may mean "all" Israel in the sense of "all Jews destined to be saved throughout history." Or, as suggested above, it may point to a time of mass conversion among Jewish people. See 11:25–32 note, points (a), (b), and (c). The exegesis of "all Israel" will depend on the interpretation and weighing of other factors in the passage.

The Deliverer will come from Zion. The quotation is from Ps. 14:7, Is. 27:9, and Is. 59:20, 21.

28 As regards the gospel, they are enemies of
God for your sake. But as regards election,
they are [o]beloved for the sake of their forefathers. 29 For the gifts and [p]the calling of
God are irrevocable. 30 Just as [q]you were at
one time disobedient to God but now have
received mercy because of their disobedience, 31 so they too have now been disobedient in order that by the mercy shown to
you they also may now[1] receive mercy.
32 For God [r]has consigned all to disobedience, that he may have mercy on all.

33 Oh, the depth of the riches and [s]wis-
dom and knowledge of God! [t]How unsearchable are his judgments and how
inscrutable his ways!

34 "For [u]who has known the mind of the
Lord,
or [v]who has been his counselor?"
35 "Or [w]who has given a gift to him
that he might be repaid?"

36 For [x]from him and through him and to
him are all things. [y]To him be glory forever.
Amen.

A Living Sacrifice

12 [z]I appeal to you therefore, brothers,[2] by the mercies of God, [a]to present your bodies [b]as a living sacrifice, holy
and acceptable to God, which is your spiritual worship.[3] 2 [c]Do not be conformed to
this world,[4] but be transformed by [d]the
renewal of your mind, that by testing you
may [e]discern what is the will of God, what
is good and acceptable and perfect.[5]

Gifts of Grace

3 For [f]by the grace given to me I say to
everyone among you [g]not to think of himself more highly than he ought to think,
but to think with sober judgment, [h]each
according to [i]the measure of faith that God
has assigned. 4 For [j]as in one body we have
many members,[6] and the members do not
all have the same function, 5 so we, [k]though
many, [l]are one body in Christ, and individually [m]members one of another. 6 [n]Hav-
ing gifts that differ according to the grace
given to us, let us use them: if [o]prophecy,
[p]in proportion to our faith; 7 if [q]service, in
our serving; the one who teaches, in his

28 [o]ch. 9:5; Deut. 7:8; 10:15 **29** [p]See ch. 8:28 **30** [q]Eph. 2:2, 3, 11, 13; Col. 1:21; 3:7; Tit. 3:3 **32** [r]See ch. 3:9 **33** [s]Col. 2:3; [Ps. 139:6; Eph. 3:10] [t]Deut. 29:29 **34** [u]Isai. 40:13; 1 Cor. 2:16; [Job 15:8] [v]Job 36:22, 23 **35** [w]Job 35:7; 41:11 **36** [x]1 Cor. 8:6; 11:12; Col. 1:16; [Heb. 2:10] [y]ch. 16:27; Eph. 3:21; Phil. 4:20; 1 Tim. 1:17; 1 Pet. 4:11; 2 Pet. 3:18; Jude 25; Rev. 1:6; 5:13
Chapter 12
1 [z]1 Cor. 1:10; 2 Cor. 10:1; Eph. 4:1 [a]ch. 6:13, 16, 19; [Ps. 50:13, 14; 1 Cor. 6:20]; See 1 Pet. 2:5 [b]Heb. 10:20

2 [c]1 Pet. 1:14; [1John 2:15] [d]Tit. 3:5; [Ps.51:10; 2 Cor. 4:16; Eph. 4:23; Col. 3:10] [e]Eph. 5:10; 1 Thess. 4:3 **3** [f]See ch. 1:5 [g]ver. 16; ch. 11:20 [h]1 Cor. 7:17 [i]Eph. 4:7 **4** [j]1 Cor. 12:12-14; Eph. 4:4, 16 **5** [k]1 Cor. 10:17, 33 [l]1 Cor. 12:20; Eph. 4:13; See John 17:11 [m]Eph. 4:25; [1 Cor. 6:15; 12:27] **6** [n]1 Cor. 12:4; 1 Pet. 4:10, 11; [1 Cor. 7:7; 12:7-11] [o]1 Cor. 12:10; See Acts 13:1 [p][2 Tim. 2:15] **7** [q]See Acts 6:1

1 Some manuscripts omit *now* 2 Or *brothers and sisters* 3 Or *your rational service* 4 Greek *age* 5 Or *what is the good and acceptable and perfect will of God* 6 Greek *parts*; also verse 5

11:29 the gifts . . . are irrevocable. See "Gifts and Ministries" at Eph. 4:7.

11:30 Paul's argument concludes in a manner parallel to 3:19–21, stressing that Jew and Gentile are united in two things: the disobedience of sin, and the offer to them of the mercy of God. The wisdom and sovereignty of God's grace are demonstrated in the way in which His purposes are fulfilled: the disobedience of the Jew leads to God's mercy reaching the Gentiles; the mercy of God to the Gentiles leads to the reception of mercy by the Jews. There is no difference—all (Jew and Gentile alike) have sinned (3:23), and God has mercy on both (1:16).

11:33–36 Having drawn together the various strands of his argument, Paul now responds in lyrical fashion with a song of praise that reaches heights that correspond to the depth of concern he had sounded in 9:2, 3. God's dealings with Jew and Gentile display a cross-section of His majesty in which His sovereign will ("from him"), His sovereign activity ("through him") and His sovereign glory ("to him") are richly displayed (v. 36).

12:1 The doxology at the end of ch. 11 and the nature of the opening verses of ch. 12 signal a new stage in Paul's exposition. From now until the conclusion of the letter he is concerned to apply his teaching.

mercies of God. Love for the poor and needy, and support for those who cannot support themselves in a sinful world (cf. Luke 10:36, 37). The doctrine of grace in chs. 3–11 leads to a life motivated by gratitude.

present your bodies as a living sacrifice. Jew and Gentile now belong together as the people of God for whom the final blood sacrifice has been made (3:25). The sacrifice that remains is that of thankful response (cf. 6:17). "Bodies" means whole persons as embodied individuals (6:12, 13, 19; 8:13).

spiritual worship. The worship that is appropriate for redeemed creatures to offer (see text note).

12:2 Do not be conformed . . . be transformed by the renewal of your mind. The Christian's mind-set is to be determined and reshaped by knowledge of the gospel, by the power of the Spirit, and by the concerns of the age to come (8:5–9; 13:11–14), rather than by the passing fashion of this age (2 Cor. 4:18; 1 John 2:17). Only by such sanctifying renewal is the Christian made sufficiently sensitive to "discern" the behavior that is God's will in each situation.

12:3 by the grace given to me. Paul's ministry exists only because of grace (1:5), as do spiritual gifts (Greek *charismata*, v. 6). Realistic assessment of one's gift ("think with sober judgment") is essential, and involves a recognition of one's "measure of faith," that is, knowing to what extent one has the faith suited for exercising particular gifts (v. 6). The faith by which we are justified is a separate question.

12:4–8 As in 1 Cor. 12, Paul makes use of the analogy of the body and its various parts to illustrate the nature of the church. He stresses its unity (v. 5), its diversity (v. 6), and the need to recognize one's gift and to use it appropriately (vv. 6–8).

12:6 Having gifts . . . let us use them. See "Gifts and Ministries" at Eph. 4:7.

prophecy. To prophesy is to speak the word of God, but the nature of New Testament prophecy is nowhere defined and is much debated. Prophecy is distinguished here and elsewhere from teaching (v. 7; Acts 13:1; 1 Cor. 12:29; Eph. 4:11), perhaps because of the greater sense of immediacy and spontaneity attached to it (Acts 13:1–3; 21:10, 11).

in proportion to our faith. Some interpreters see "faith" as the prophet's own faith (cf. vv. 3, 6). Others understand "faith" to mean the truth content of the gospel as the standard and measure of each prophetic utterance, testing whether the utterance conforms to "the pattern of the sound words" (2 Tim. 1:13).

12:7, 8 Paul recognizes the wide variety and practicality of these gifts

teaching; **8**the one who exhorts, in his
exhortation; the one who contributes, in
generosity; [r]the one who leads, [1] with zeal;
the one who does acts of mercy, with
[s]cheerfulness.

Marks of the True Christian

9[t]Let love be genuine. [u]Abhor what is
evil; hold fast to what is good. **10**[v]Love one
another with brotherly affection. [w]Outdo
one another in showing honor. **11**Do not be
slothful in zeal, [x]be fervent in spirit,[2] [y]serve
the Lord. **12**[z]Rejoice in hope, [a]be patient in
tribulation, [b]be constant in prayer. **13**[c]Con-
tribute to the needs of the saints and [d]seek
to show hospitality.
14[e]Bless those who persecute you; bless
and do not curse them. **15**[f]Rejoice with
those who rejoice, weep with those who
weep. **16**[g]Live in harmony with one
another. [h]Do not be haughty, but associate
with the lowly.[3] [i]Never be conceited.
17[j]Repay no one evil for evil, but [k]give
thought to do what is honorable in the
sight of all. **18**If possible, so far as it
depends on you, [l]live peaceably with all.
19Beloved, [m]never avenge yourselves, but
leave it[4] to the wrath of God, for it is written, [n]"Vengeance is mine, I will repay, says

8 [r]1 Tim. 5:17; [1 Cor. 12:28] [s]2 Cor. 9:7
9 [t]2 Cor. 6:6; 1 Tim. 1:5; 1 Pet. 1:22 [u]Ps. 97:10; 101:3; Amos 5:15; [1 Thess. 5:21, 22]
10 [v]See Heb. 13:1 [w]ch. 13:7; Phil. 2:3; 1 Pet. 2:17
11 [x]Acts 18:25 [y]Acts 20:19
12 [z]See ch. 5:2 [a]See Heb. 10:36 [b]See Acts 1:14
13 [c]ch. 15:25; 1 Cor. 16:1, 15; 2 Cor. 9:1, 12; Heb. 6:10; 13:16; [1 Tim. 6:18] [d]See Matt. 25:35
14 [e]See Matt. 5:44; 1 Pet. 3:9
15 [f]1 Cor. 12:26; [Job 30:25; Heb. 13:3]
16 [g]ch. 15:5; 2 Cor. 13:11; Phil. 2:2; 4:2; 1 Pet. 3:8 [h]ver. 3; Ps. 131:1; Jer. 45:5 [i]ch. 11:25; Prov. 3:7

the Lord." **20**To the contrary, [o]"if your
enemy is hungry, feed him; if he is thirsty,
give him something to drink; for by so
doing you will heap burning coals on his
head." **21**Do not be overcome by evil, but
overcome evil with good.

Submission to the Authorities

13 Let every person [p]be subject to the
governing authorities. For [q]there is
no authority except from God, and those
that exist have been instituted by God.
2Therefore whoever resists the authorities
resists what God has appointed, and those
who resist will incur judgment. **3**For rulers
are not a terror to good conduct, but to
bad. Would you have no fear of the one
who is in authority? Then do what is good,
and you [r]will receive his approval, **4**for [s]he
is God's servant for your good. But if you do
wrong, be afraid, for he does not bear the
sword in vain. For he is the servant of God,
[t]an avenger who carries out God's wrath on

17 [j]Prov. 20:22; Matt. 5:39; [ch. 14:19] [k]2 Cor. 8:21; [ch. 14:16] **18** [l]See Mark 9:50 **19** [m]Prov. 20:22; Matt. 5:39; [ch. 14:19] [n]Heb. 10:30; Cited from Deut. 32:35; [Ps. 94:1; 1 Thess. 4:6] **20** [o]Cited from Prov. 25:21, 22; [Ex. 23:4, 5; 2 Kin. 6:22; Luke 6:27]
Chapter 13 **1** [p]Tit. 3:1; 1 Pet. 2:13 [q][John 19:11]; See Dan. 2:21 **3** [r]1 Pet. 2:14 **4** [s]2 Chr. 19:6 [t]1 Thess. 4:6

[1] Or *gives aid* [2] Or *fervent in the Spirit* [3] Or *give yourselves to humble tasks* [4] Greek *give place*

(Greek *charismata*) and the intertwining of natural endowments with them. Throughout, it is clear that the blessing of those ministered to is the paramount consideration in using the gifts.

12:9–21 As in 1 Cor. 12–13, when discussing the church as the body of Christ, Paul stresses the importance of love. His series of rapid exhortations carries echoes of Jesus' teaching, and is expressed in vivid language.

12:9 be genuine. In classical Greek drama, the *hypokrites* (actor) wore a face-mask. The Christian's loving behavior should not be acting a part or wearing a mask, but an authentic expression of goodwill.

12:10 Love one another with brotherly affection. An unusual linguistic combination of brotherly love with the love of natural affection. The church is a family, the "household of God" (1 Tim. 3:15; cf. 1 Tim. 5:1, 2).

12:11 There must be no hesitation or sloth in Christian living. The Christian should be "fervent," living for Christ with enthusiasm and energy.

12:13 hospitality. Hospitality for visiting Christians was an important part of early Christian life (Heb. 13:2; 3 John 5–8).

12:14 See Luke 6:27, 28.

12:15 See Luke 6:31. The genuine unity of the body of Christ is especially evident in the empathy of its members in moments of high joy or deep sorrow.

12:16 Paul's language gives the idea of Christians sharing the same thoughts with respect to one another, another indication of the strategic role of the mind in sanctification (vv. 1, 2). One manifestation of this will be an absence of conceit and pride in worldly position (Phil. 2:1–8). Christians should be distinguished by their readiness to "associate with the lowly."

Never be conceited. See Prov. 3:7. A further focus on the thought-world. How we think determines how we live.

12:17 The unifying theme in vv. 17–21 is the way the Christian reacts to the non-Christian environment.

12:18 live peaceably with all. The Christian is a peacemaker by obligation and aim. Harmony is not always possible, since truth divides as well as unites. Paul's double qualification ("If . . . so far as") recognizes this, but the obligation to strive for peace in personal relations with others remains.

12:19–21 The Christian must be free from the desire to "get even." Such release from the instinct for revenge is possible because the believer knows that God will right all wrongs in His own perfect judgment (Deut. 32:35). Moreover, Scripture urges us, while God remains patient with the wrongdoer, to show grace to him (Prov. 25:21, 22).

12:20 heap burning coals on his head. This may lead to conversion, or at least to such a sense of shame that evil behavior is modified.

13:1 Christians have a distinct rationale for an appropriate submission to the governing authorities: the recognition that God Himself is the source of government in society (Prov. 8:15, 16; Dan. 2:21). See theological note "Christians and Civil Government" on the next page.

13:2, 3 Rebellion against the authority implies rebellion against God's ordinance.

13:4 God's servant for your good. The state's authority is for society's benefit; this is its normal function, and Paul assumes it may be realized in practical terms even when governments are professedly non-Christian.

the sword. The power of life and death. Capital punishment is undoubtedly in view. Elsewhere Paul accepts the principle of such punishment where appropriate (Acts 25:11).

wrath. What the individual must not do out of a motive of revenge (12:19), the state may legitimately do in the pursuit of justice.

the wrongdoer. 5 Therefore one must be in
subjection, not only to avoid God's wrath
but also [u]for the sake of conscience. 6 For
the same reason you also pay taxes, for the
authorities are ministers of God, attending
to this very thing. 7 [v]Pay to all what is owed
to them: taxes to whom taxes are owed,
revenue to whom revenue is owed, respect
to whom respect is owed, honor to whom
honor is owed.

Fulfilling the Law Through Love

8 [w]Owe no one anything, except to love
each other, for [x]the one who loves another
has fulfilled the law. 9 The commandments,
[y]"You shall not commit adultery, You shall
not murder, You shall not steal, You shall
not covet," and any other commandment,
are summed up in this word: [z]"You shall
love your neighbor as yourself." 10 Love
does no wrong to a neighbor; therefore
[a]love is the fulfilling of the law.

11 Besides this you know the time, that
the hour has come for you [b]to wake from
sleep. [c]For salvation is nearer to us now
than when we first believed. 12 [d]The night is

5 [u]1 Pet. 2:19; [Eccles. 8:2] 7 [v]Matt. 17:25; 22:21; Mark 12:17 8 [w][Lev. 19:13; Prov. 3:27, 28] [x]ver. 10; [Matt. 22:40; Col. 3:14] See John 13:34
9 [y]Matt. 19:18; Cited from Ex. 20:13-17; Deut. 5:17-21 [z]Cited from Lev. 19:18
10 [a][John 14:15]; See ver. 8 11 [b]1 Cor. 15:34; Eph. 5:14; 1 Thess. 5:6 [c][Isai. 56:1; Luke 21:28] 12 [d][John 9:4]

Christians and Civil Government

Civil government is a means ordained by God for ruling and maintaining order in communities. It is one of a number of such means, including ministers in the church and parents in the home. Each such means has its own sphere of authority under Christ, who now rules and sustains creation, and the limits of each sphere are set by reference to the others. In our fallen world these authorities are institutions of God's "common grace" (kindly providence), standing as a bulwark against anarchy and the dissolution of ordered society.

With reference to Rom. 13:1–7 and 1 Pet. 2:13–17, the *Westminster Confession* explains the sphere of civil government as follows:

> God, the supreme Lord and King of all the world, hath ordained civil magistrates, to be, under Him, over the people, for His own glory, and the public good; and, to this end, hath armed them with the power of the sword, for the defence and encouragement of them that are good, and for the punishment of evil doers . . . Civil magistrates may not assume to themselves the administration of the Word and sacraments; or the power of the keys of the kingdom of heaven (23.1, 3).

Because civil government exists for the welfare of the whole society, God gives it the "power of the sword," the lawful use of force to administer just laws (Rom. 13:4). Christians must acknowledge this as part of God's order (Rom. 13:1, 2). A government may collect taxes for the services it renders (Matt. 22:15–21; Rom. 13:6, 7). But if it forbids what God requires or requires what God forbids, Christians cannot submit, and some form of civil disobedience becomes inescapable (Acts 4:18–31; 5:17–29).

The church's sphere of authority relates to the civil government at the level of morality. The church has the responsibility to comment on the morality of governments and their policies on the basis of God's word, but should not appropriate to itself the power to set such policies. Whereas these assessments may foster political action among Christians, they should act in their capacity as citizens rather than as representatives of the church. In this way the gospel works through moral persuasion and the working of God's grace among citizens.

Christians should urge governments to fulfill their proper role. They are to pray for, obey, and yet watch over civil governments (1 Tim. 2:1–4; 1 Pet. 2:13, 14), reminding them that God ordained them to rule, protect, and keep order.

13:6 you also pay taxes. Christian submission is a response of the conscience instructed by divine revelation. Because the task of government is divinely ordained and requires financial support, the Christian can pay taxes with a distinctive motive and understanding, as an element of devotion to God.

13:7 Pay to all what is owed to them. See Matt. 22:21. Paul was evidently familiar with Jesus' statement, and here indicates how it is applied.

13:8–10 Paul now applies further his basic principle of Christian consecration. The connecting link between vv. 7 and 8 is found in the exhortation of v. 7, that the Christian has a financial obligation to the state. This is an application of a general principle now stated, that all obligations must be met. One obligation is permanent—to love others.

13:8 has fulfilled the law. See "Antinomianism" at 1 John 3:7.

13:9 love your neighbor as yourself. See Lev. 19:18; "Love" at 1 Cor. 13:13. Not an exhortation to self-love, but rather the concern assumed for oneself as created in the image of God (Gen. 1:26, 27) is to be exhibited to others (Luke 6:31).

13:11 know the time. Spiritual discernment is rooted in the apprehension of divine revelation. Paul's stress on the role of the mind is again evident.

salvation. Here in the sense of future, final redemption (8:23).

far gone; the day is at hand. So then let us
[e]cast off [f]the works of darkness and [g]put on
the armor of light. 13 [h]Let us walk properly
as in the daytime, [i]not in orgies and drunkenness, not in sexual immorality and sensuality, [j]not in quarreling and jealousy.
14 But [k]put on the Lord Jesus Christ, and
make no provision for the flesh, [l]to gratify
its desires.

Do Not Pass Judgment on One Another

14 As for [m]the one who is weak in
faith, welcome him, but not to
quarrel over opinions. 2 [n]One person
believes he may eat anything, while the
weak person eats only vegetables. 3 Let not
the one who eats despise the one who
abstains, and [o]let not the one who abstains
pass judgment on the one who eats, for
God has welcomed him. 4 [p]Who are you to
pass judgment on the servant of another? It
is before his own master[1] that he stands or
falls. And he will be upheld, for the Lord is
able to make him stand.

5 [q]One person esteems one day as better
than another, while another esteems all
days alike. [r]Each one should be fully convinced in his own mind. 6 The one who
observes the day, observes it in honor of
the Lord. The one who eats, eats in honor
of the Lord, since [s]he gives thanks to God,
while the one who abstains, abstains in
honor of the Lord and gives thanks to God.
7 For [t]none of us lives to himself, and none
of us dies to himself. 8 If we live, we live to
the Lord, and if we die, we die to the Lord.
So then, [u]whether we live or whether we
die, we are the Lord's. 9 For to this end
Christ [v]died and lived again, that he might
be Lord both [w]of the dead and of the living.

10 Why do you pass judgment on your
brother? Or you, why do you despise your
brother? For [w]we will all stand before [x]the
judgment seat of God; 11 for it is written,

> [y]"As I live, says the Lord, every knee
> shall bow to me,
> and every tongue shall confess[2]
> to God."

12 So then [z]each of us will give an account
of himself to God.

Do Not Cause Another to Stumble

13 [a]Therefore let us not pass judgment on
one another any longer, but rather decide
[b]never to put a stumbling block or hindrance in the way of a brother. 14 I know

12 [e]Col. 3:8 [f]Eph. 5:11; [John 3:20] [g]2 Cor. 6:7; Eph. 6:11, 13; 1 Thess. 5:8
13 [h]1 Thess. 4:12 [i]Luke 21:34; Gal. 5:21; 1 Pet. 4:3 [j]James 3:14, 16
14 [k]Gal. 3:27; [Job 29:14; Ps. 132:9; Luke 24:49; Eph. 4:24; Col. 3:10] [l]Gal. 5:16; 1 Pet. 2:11
Chapter 14
1 [m]ch. 15:1; 1 Cor. 8:9-11; 9:22
2 [n]ver. 14
3 [o]Col. 2:16
4 [p]James 4:12
5 [q]Gal. 4:10; [Zech. 7:5, 6] [r]ver. 23
6 [s]1 Cor. 10:30, 31; 1 Tim. 4:3, 4; See Matt. 15:36
7 [t]2 Cor. 5:15; Gal. 2:20; 1 Pet. 4:2; [1 Cor. 6:19; 1 Thess. 5:10]
8 [u]Phil. 1:20
9 [v]Rev. 1:18; 2:8 [w]See Acts 10:42; Rev. 20:12
10 [w][See ver. 9 above] [x]2 Cor. 5:10 11 [y]Phil. 2:10, 11; Cited from Isai. 45:23
12 [z]Matt. 12:36; 16:27; 1 Pet. 4:5; [Gal. 6:5] 13 [a]See Matt. 7:1 [b][1 Cor. 8:13]

1 Or *lord* 2 Or *shall give praise*

13:12 The night is far gone. Paul speaks here of the "night" of this present age. The "light of the world" has come (John 8:12), and we must prepare for the Second Advent of Christ and the age to come.

let us cast off . . . put on. The use of the metaphor "armor of light" stresses that developing positive spiritual graces, not merely rejecting vices, is essential to spiritual defense.

13:13 Let us walk properly. Paul's warning against a sinful life-style strikingly includes not only the traditional sins of the flesh ("orgies and drunkenness . . . . sexual immorality and sensuality") but also insidious vices that can be harbored or even paraded in the heart of the church ("quarreling and jealousy").

13:14 But put on the Lord Jesus Christ. A further exposition of what it means to "put on the armor of light" (v. 12), showing that those who are in Christ must live consistently with their new status (Eph. 4:1).

14:1 As for the one who is weak. The Christian's basic attitude to a fellow-Christian is one of welcome and acceptance based on God's attitude to us in Christ (v. 3; 15:7). There must be charity toward the "weak" person whose conscience is still bound by scruples from which the gospel normally sets us free (v. 2).

quarrel over opinions. In this instance, questions of food, drink, and the religious observation of days. While Paul does not regard these controversies as insoluble, he regards the unity of the church's fellowship as more important than resolving them (cf. 12:5, 10, 16). The issues in view here did not belong to the gospel, but to the relative strength or weakness of the individual's faith in the gospel. Where essentials of the gospel were at stake, Paul's response was very different (e.g., Gal. 1:6, 7; 3:1–5; Phil. 3:2, 18, 19).

14:2 eats only vegetables. Vegetarianism was not required by the Old Testament, though it appears there (e.g., Dan. 1:12).

14:3 despise . . . pass judgment. The tendency of those who better understand the gospel is to be impatient with the inhibitions of the "weak" as legalistic bondage. The temptation of the "weak" is to condemn the "strong" for behavior that seems to be lawless license. These mistaken responses should yield to the light of God's gracious acceptance of both "weak" and "strong." Furthermore, a fellow-believer is God's servant, not ours, and is answerable to Him, not to us. It must be understood that the issues in such possible disputes are not matters of real morality, but of morally indifferent things.

14:5 One person esteems one day as better than another. A pattern of holy days characterized the Jewish year, and it is probably to these that Paul refers, and not the Sabbath. If the Sabbath were in view it would have been more natural to say, "One man considers the Sabbath above the other days."

Each one should be fully convinced. See 4:21.

14:6, 7 An appeal to what is shared by both groups (v. 3), namely the desire to honor the same Lord. That both belong to Him puts minor divisions into perspective. See "The Kingdom of God" at Luke 17:20.

14:9–12 Christ alone is the Lord (v. 8) and Judge of His people (see "The Final Judgment" at Matt. 25:41). The cost to Him of this privilege was immense and exposes the inappropriateness of believers judging or despising their brothers. We must give an account of our own lives to the Lord, as those being judged, not as those who judge.

14:13–15:4 While Paul's own conscience has been liberated by the teaching of Christ (v. 14; cf. Mark 7:18, 19) he recognizes that not all believers have come to enjoy such freedom. Consideration for such brethren ("walking in love," v. 15) means avoiding behavior that might distress them. Two specific injunctions to this effect follow in vv. 15, 16.

and am persuaded in the Lord Jesus [c]that
nothing is unclean in itself, [d]but it is
unclean for anyone who thinks it unclean.
15 For if your brother is grieved by what you
eat, [e]you are no longer walking in love. [f]By
what you eat, do not destroy the one for
whom Christ died. 16 [g]So do not let what
you regard as good be spoken of as evil.
17 [h]For the kingdom of God is not a matter
of eating and drinking but [i]of righteousness and [j]peace and joy in the Holy Spirit.
18 Whoever thus serves Christ is [k]acceptable
to God and approved by men. 19 So then let
us [l]pursue what makes for peace and for
[m]mutual upbuilding.

20 [n]Do not, for the sake of food, destroy
the work of God. [o]Everything is indeed
clean, but [p]it is wrong for anyone to make
another stumble by what he eats. 21 [q]It is
good not to eat meat or drink wine or do
anything that causes your brother to stumble.[1] 22 The faith that you have, keep between yourself and God. [r]Blessed is the
one who has no reason to pass judgment
on himself for what he approves. 23 But
whoever has doubts is condemned if he
eats, because the eating is not from faith.
For whatever does not proceed from faith
is sin.[2]

The Example of Christ

15 [s]We who are strong [t]have an obligation to bear with the failings of
the weak, and not to please ourselves.
2 [u]Let each of us please his neighbor for his
good, to build him up. 3 For [v]Christ did not
please himself, but as it is written, [w]"The
reproaches of those who reproached you
fell on me." 4 For [x]whatever was written in
former days was written for our [y]instruc-
tion, that through endurance and through
[z]the encouragement of the Scriptures we
might have hope. 5 May the God of endurance and encouragement grant you [a]to live
in such harmony with one another, in
accord with Christ Jesus, 6 that together
you may with one voice glorify [b]the God
and Father of our Lord Jesus Christ.
7 Therefore welcome one another as Christ
has welcomed you, for the glory of God.

Christ the Hope of Jews and Gentiles

8 For I tell you that Christ [c]became a servant to the circumcised to show God's
truthfulness, in order [d]to confirm the
promises given to the patriarchs, 9 and in
order [e]that the Gentiles might glorify God
for his mercy. As it is written,

> [f]"Therefore I will praise you among the
> Gentiles,
> and sing to your name."

10 And again it is said,

> [g]"Rejoice, O Gentiles, with his people."

11 And again,

14 [c]ver. 2:20 See Acts 10:15 [d][1 Cor. 8:7, 10]
15 [e]Eph. 5:2 [f]1 Cor. 8:11; [ver. 20]
16 [g][ch. 12:17; 1 Cor. 10:29, 30]
17 [h]1 Cor. 8:8 [i][1 Cor. 6:9] [j]Gal. 5:22; [ch. 15:13]
18 [k][2 Cor. 8:21]
19 [l]Ps. 34:14; 1 Cor. 7:15; 2 Tim. 2:22 [m]ch. 15:2; 1 Cor. 14:12
20 [n]ver. 15 [o]Tit. 1:15; See ver. 14 [p]1 Cor. 8:9-12
21 [q]1 Cor. 8:13
22 [r]1 John 3:21
Chapter 15
1 [s][Gal. 6:1] [t]1 Thess. 5:14; See ch. 14:1
2 [u]1 Cor. 10:33; [1 Cor. 9:19, 22; 10:24; Phil. 2:4]
3 [v]Phil. 2:5, 8; [John 5:30; 6:38] [w]Cited from Ps. 69:9
4 [x]ch. 4:23 [y]2 Tim. 3:16 [z]Ps. 119:50
5 [a]See ch. 12:16
6 [b]2 Cor. 1:3; Eph. 1:3; 1 Pet. 1:3; [John 20:17; Eph. 1:17; Rev. 1:6]
8 [c]Matt. 15:24; John 1:11; [Heb. 3:1]; See Acts 3:26 [d][ch. 4:16; 2 Cor. 1:20]
9 [e]See ch. 3:29 [f]Cited from 2 Sam. 22:50; Ps. 18:49 10 [g]Cited from Deut. 32:43

1 Some manuscripts add *or be hindered or be weakened* 2 Some manuscripts insert here 16:25-27

14:15 By what you eat, do not destroy the one for whom Christ died. In the context of Jewish faith, "destroy" means to cut off from the covenant community (Deut. 28:21, 45, 48, 51, 61, 63). To encourage behavior that weak believers' consciences forbid is to encourage them to go against their conscience, a serious and dangerous act.

14:16–18 The strong are urged to weigh the importance of exercising their freedom against two considerations: (a) the use of their freedom may bring division and disrepute on the church; (b) God's kingdom (and therefore our freedom) is not a matter of food and drink, but of the blessings of grace (5:1, 2). Since freedom does not consist in these things, it cannot be lost by our refraining from them.

14:18 approved by men. See v. 16. While God alone is our Judge (v. 12), the impact of our actions on others plays a vital role in fellowship and evangelism.

14:19–21 The believer's responsibility is now stated positively: avoiding the destruction of others is complemented by promoting "peace" and the things that "upbuild" (v. 19). For the "strong," (15:1) this includes both maintaining fellowship with the "weak" and also encouraging them to understand the liberty that is theirs in Christ. When such aims are in view, freedom to eat and drink will be made subservient to them; the well-being of the brother will take precedence over the enjoyment of meat and wine.

14:22, 23 Paul further urges the "strong" (15:1) to enjoy the fact of their liberty of conscience in God's presence (while refraining from publicly exercising it). See "Conscience and the Law" at 1 Sam. 24:5.

15:1–4 We who are strong have an obligation to bear with the failings of the weak. Paul considers himself one of the "strong." He sees the misinformed conscience of the "weak" as real weakness, yet he emphasizes the responsibility of the "strong" to support the "weak." He does not encourage feelings of pride, or flaunting one's freedom in matters offensive to the weak.

15:2 See 14:19; 1 Cor. 8:1; 10:23.

15:3 Paul quotes from Ps. 69:9, one of the most frequently quoted psalms in the New Testament. The willingness of the Messiah to deny Himself and suffer for the benefit of others should serve as an example to the Christians in Rome.

15:4 written for our instruction. It is basic New Testament teaching that the Old Testament Scriptures were written by divine inspiration for the benefit of Christians (1 Cor. 10:11; 2 Tim. 3:15–17; 1 Pet. 1:10–12).

15:6 with one voice. See 10:9, 10. Unity in the church is essential if God is to be glorified. Paul has demonstrated that humanity, which has fallen short of God's glory, is restored to it in Christ's reconciling work (1:21, 23; 3:23; 5:2, 11; 8:17, 30).

15:8 Christ . . . a servant to the circumcised. The mutual acceptance of believers is rooted in Christ's humility (Mark 10:45).

> [h]"Praise the Lord, all you Gentiles,
> and let all the peoples extol him."

12 And again Isaiah says,

> [i,j]"The root of Jesse will come,
> even he who arises to rule the
> Gentiles;
> [k]in him will the Gentiles hope."

13 May the God of hope fill you with all [l]joy
and peace in believing, so that by the
power of the Holy Spirit you may abound
in hope.

Paul the Minister to the Gentiles

14 [m]I myself am satisfied about you, my
brothers,[1] that you yourselves are full of
goodness, filled with [n]all knowledge and
able to instruct one another. 15 But on some
points I have written to you very boldly by
way of reminder, [o]because of the grace
given me by God 16 to be [p]a minister of
Christ Jesus to the Gentiles [q]in the priestly
service of the gospel of God, so that [r]the
offering of the Gentiles may be acceptable,
sanctified by the Holy Spirit. 17 In Christ
Jesus, then, I have [s]reason to be proud of
[t]my work for God. 18 For I will not venture
to speak of anything except [u]what Christ
has accomplished through me [v]to bring the
Gentiles to obedience—by word and deed,
19 [w]by the power of signs and wonders, by
the power of the Spirit of God—so that
[x]from Jerusalem and all the way around [y]to
Illyricum I have fulfilled the ministry of the
gospel of Christ; 20 and thus I make it my
ambition to preach the gospel, not where
Christ has already been named, [z]lest I
build on someone else's foundation, 21 but
as it is written,

> [a]"Those who have never been told of
> him will see,
> and those who have never heard
> will understand."

Paul's Plan to Visit Rome

22 This is the reason why [b]I have so often
been hindered from coming to you. 23 But
now, since I no longer have any room for
work in these regions, and [c]since I have
longed for many years to come to you, 24 I
hope to see you in passing as I go [d]to
Spain, and [e]to be helped on my journey
there by you, once I have enjoyed your
company for a while. 25 At present, however, [f]I am going to Jerusalem bringing aid
to the saints. 26 For [g]Macedonia and Achaia
have been pleased to make some contribution for the poor among the saints at
Jerusalem. 27 They were pleased to do it,
and indeed [h]they owe it to them. For if the
Gentiles have come to share in their

11 [h]Cited from Ps.117:1 **12** [i]Cited from Isai. 11:10 [j]Isai. 11:1; [Rev. 5:5; 22:16] [k]Matt.12:21 **13** [l][ch. 5:1, 2; 14:17] **14** [m][2 Pet. 1:12; 3:1; 1 John 2:21] [n]1 Cor. 1:5; 13:2; [1 Cor. 8:1, 7, 10; 12:8] **15** [o]See ch. 1:5 **16** [p]See ch. 11:13 [q][Mal. 1:11] [r]Isai. 66:20; [Phil. 2:17] **17** [s]Phil. 3:3 [t]Heb. 2:17; 5:1 **18** [u]Acts 15:12; 21:19; Gal. 2:8 [v]See ch. 1:5 **19** [w]2 Cor. 12:12; [Acts 19:11] [x]Acts 22:17-21 [y][Acts 20:1, 2] **20** [z][2 Cor. 10:13, 15, 16] **21** [a]Cited from Isai. 52:15 **22** [b]ch. 1:13; [1 Thess. 2:18] **23** [c]ver. 29, 32; ch. 1:10, 11; Acts 19:21

24 [d]ver. 28 [e]See Acts 15:3 **25** [f]Acts 19:21; 20:22; 21:15; 24:17; [ver. 31] **26** [g]1 Cor. 16:1-4; 2 Cor. 8:1; 9:2, 13 **27** [h]1 Cor. 9:11; [Gal. 6:6]

[1] Or *brothers and sisters*; also verse 30

15:13 See "Hope" at Heb. 6:18. What was described as the effect of Scripture in v. 4 (having hope) is now attributed to the work of the Holy Spirit. Paul here follows a pattern evident throughout the New Testament in which God's saving acts are attributed to God's Word as well as to the work of the Holy Spirit (e.g., regeneration, 1 Pet. 1:23; sanctification, John 17:17; salvation, Rom. 1:16; searching the heart, Heb. 4:12).

15:14–22 Paul now begins to draw his letter to a close by returning to the theme of its introduction—his own ministry and his vision for the expansion of the influence of the gospel.

15:14 my brothers. A further indication of deeply felt emotion (1:13; 7:1, 4; 11:25; 12:1). Paul graciously assures the Romans that his lengthy exposition of the gospel is not intended to raise doubts about their spiritual understanding. Their knowledge of the gospel and ability to apply it practically in mutual admonition ("able to instruct one another"; cf. Col. 3:16) is not in question.

15:16 priestly service of the gospel of God. Paul sees the preaching of the gospel as the means by which the Gentiles will be brought to God as a sacrificial thank-offering (12:1).

15:17–20 Paul describes his ministry very naturally in Trinitarian terms (God the Father, vv. 17, 18; the Son, vv. 17–20; the Spirit, v. 19; cf. v. 16).

15:19 signs and wonders. See Ex. 7:3; Deut. 4:34; 6:22; 7:19; Is. 8:18; Dan. 6:27. A phrase rooted in the authentication of Moses' ministry at the time of the Exodus. God periodically gave such miracles at critical junctures of redemptive history, such as the Exodus, the prophetic ministries of Elijah and Elisha, the preserving of His people in the time of Daniel, and the ministry of Christ and the apostles. These events are unusual rather than normal and point to the successive stages of redemptive history and the new revelation that accompanies them.

from Jerusalem and all the way around to Illyricum. Paul's journeys, according to Acts, had stretched from the eastern Mediterranean as far west as Macedonia. There is no record of his personally entering Illyricum (northwest of Macedonia). While he may have done so, it seems more likely that he means he went as far as Macedonia. He established centers of mission, rather than preached personally in every village. From such centers, even Illyricum may have been reached with the gospel.

15:23, 24 Two things now make the visit to Rome possible: (a) the present phase of Paul's commission has been fulfilled; (b) the new phase involving outreach to Spain is imminent, and Paul seeks their fellowship in it.

15:24 Spain. The western extremity of the ancient world. Some suggest Paul thought of Spain as the Tarshish of Is. 66:19, and saw the extension of his preaching there as significant for the Christian mission (Matt. 24:14; Acts 1:8).

15:25–33 Paul now discloses his immediate plans to visit Jerusalem with the gifts the churches had raised for the Christians there. Jerusalem was an impoverished city in general; in addition, the Christians there would suffer particular hardship as a suspect minority. But Paul sees a significance deeper than charity in the gift. It is a duty (v. 27), a solemn obligation of the Gentiles in view of the privilege they have received in being grafted into God's olive tree (11:17). This conforms to the general principle that those who receive spiritual blessings should share their own material blessings (1 Cor. 9:3–14; Gal. 6:6).

spiritual blessings, they ought also to be of
service to them in material blessings.
28When therefore I have completed this
and have delivered to them what has been
collected,[1] I will leave [i]for Spain by way of
you. **29**I know that when I come to you I
will come in the fullness of the blessing[2] of
Christ.
30I appeal to you, brothers, by our Lord
Jesus Christ and by [j]the love of the Spirit,
[k]to strive together with me in your prayers
to God on my behalf, **31**[l]that I may be delivered from the unbelievers in Judea, and
that [m]my service for Jerusalem may be
acceptable to the saints, **32**so that by God's
will I may come to you with joy and [n]be
refreshed in your company. **33**May [o]the
God of peace be with you all. Amen.

Personal Greetings

16 I commend to you our sister
Phoebe, a servant of the church at
[p]Cenchreae, **2**that you [q]may welcome her
in the Lord in a way worthy of the saints,
and help her in whatever she may need
from you, for she has been a patron of
many and of myself as well.
3Greet [r]Prisca and Aquila, my fellow
workers in Christ Jesus, **4**who risked their
necks for my life, to whom not only I give
thanks but all the churches of the Gentiles
give thanks as well. **5**Greet also [s]the church
in their house. Greet my beloved
Epaenetus, who was [t]the first convert[3] to
Christ in Asia. **6**Greet Mary, who has
worked hard for you. **7**Greet Andronicus
and Junia,[4] my kinsmen and my [u]fellow
prisoners. They are well known to the
apostles,[5] and they were in Christ before
me. **8**Greet Ampliatus, my beloved in the
Lord. **9**Greet Urbanus, our fellow worker in
Christ, and my beloved Stachys. **10**Greet
Apelles, who is approved in Christ. Greet
those [v]who belong to the family of Aristobulus. **11**Greet my kinsman Herodion.
Greet those in the Lord who belong to the
family of Narcissus. **12**Greet those workers
in the Lord, Tryphaena and Tryphosa.
Greet the beloved Persis, who has worked
hard in the Lord. **13**Greet Rufus, chosen in
the Lord; also his mother, who has been a
mother to me as well. **14**Greet Asyncritus,
Phlegon, Hermes, Patrobas, Hermas, and
the brothers[6] who are with them. **15**Greet
Philologus, Julia, Nereus and his sister,
and Olympas, and all the saints who are
with them. **16**[w]Greet one another with a

28 [i]ver. 24
30 [j][Phil. 2:1; Col. 1:8] [k]Col. 4:12; [2 Cor. 1:11; Col. 2:1, 2; Heb. 13:18]
31 [l]2 Thess. 3:2; [2 Tim. 3:11; 4:17] [m]2 Cor. 8:4
32 [n][1 Cor. 16:18; 2 Cor. 7:13; Philem. 7, 20]
33 [o]ch. 16:20; 2 Cor. 13:11; Phil. 4:9; 1 Thess. 5:23; Heb. 13:20; [1 Cor. 14:33; 2 Thess. 3:16]
Chapter 16
1 [p]Acts 18:18
2 [q]Phil. 2:29
3 [r]See Acts 18:2
5 [s]1 Cor. 16:19; [Col. 4:15; Philem. 2] [t][1 Cor. 16:15]
7 [u]Col. 4:10; Philem. 23
10 [v]1 Cor. 1:11
16 [w]1 Cor. 16:20; 2 Cor. 13:12; 1 Thess. 5:26; [1 Pet. 5:14]

1 Greek *sealed to them this fruit* 2 Some manuscripts insert *of the gospel* 3 Greek *firstfruit* 4 Or *Junias* 5 Or *messengers* 6 Or *brothers and sisters*; also verse 17

15:29 fullness of the blessing of Christ. A striking comment in view of the manner in which Paul's aspirations were fulfilled (Acts 28:11–16).

15:31 Paul's concern is twofold: (a) that he may be protected from the hostility of the Jews that has marked the whole of his ministry; (b) that Jewish Christians in Jerusalem will respond to the Gentile gift, sealing the apostle's ministry (v. 32).

15:33 the God of peace. One of Paul's favorite designations for God (16:20; 2 Cor. 13:11; Phil. 4:9; 1 Thess. 5:23; 2 Thess. 3:16), but particularly appropriate here in regard to his present struggle (v. 30).

16:1–27 Paul's letters typically end with personal news and greetings. The closing chapter of Romans is remarkable for the large number of fellow believers mentioned. These verses give an insight into the warmth of the apostle's personal relationships as well as the fellowship of the early Christians.

16:1 Phoebe. Probably the bearer of Paul's letter. The name is common in Greek mythology and indicates a Gentile background.

a servant. Paul's word (Greek *diakonos*) is variously translated as "servant" (1 Tim. 4:6), or "deacon" (Phil. 1:1; 1 Tim. 3:8). It is uncertain whether Paul uses the term to refer to the specific church office of deacon, or describes Phoebe as a servant of the church in a more general sense.

Cenchreae. The port of Corinth on the Saronic Gulf, indicating Paul's location when Romans was sent.

16:3 Prisca and Aquila. The couple were tentmakers like Paul (Acts 18:3). He was with them in Corinth. They had left Rome following the decree of Claudius and accompanied Paul to Ephesus (Acts 18:18). They taught Apollos (Acts 18:24–26) and later returned to Rome.

16:5 Epaenetus. Evidently the first of a harvest of converts in Asia.

16:6 Mary, who has worked hard for you. Paul recognizes the devoted service of women (v. 12).

16:7 Andronicus and Junia. Early commentators understood these to be a husband and wife. They were fellow Jews, and had been converted ("in Christ") before Paul himself. They had apparently been in prison at some time with Paul (cf. 2 Cor. 11:23) and had served with distinction as special envoys ("apostles") of the churches. This use of "apostle" is broader than the strict sense of the Twelve plus Paul (see 2 Cor. 1:1 note).

16:8 Ampliatus. Probably a slave, whose name appears on a tomb in the Catacomb of Domitilla, niece of the Emperor Domitian.

16:9 Urbanus . . . Stachys. Common slave names, the former Roman, the latter Greek.

16:10 Apelles. A common Greek name, borne by one who had distinguished himself through trial and remained faithful (12:2).

Aristobulus. This may be the grandson of Herod the Great and friend of the Emperor Claudius.

16:11 Herodion. Perhaps a freedman of the household of Herod, since freedmen took the name of their patron.

Narcissus. Perhaps to be identified with Narcissus, the aide of Claudius, who was forced to commit suicide by Agrippina after Nero's accession.

16:12 Tryphaena and Tryphosa. Two women with names from a common root ("gentle," "delicate") and therefore possibly sisters.

16:13 Rufus, chosen in the Lord. One of the most intriguing of the names listed in view of Mark 15:21, a gospel possibly written from Rome. "Chosen" may reflect the unique circumstances that brought his family into contact with Christ. Paul's allusion to the mother as "his mother . . . to me as well" suggests deep affection for the family.

holy kiss. All the churches of Christ greet
you.

Final Instructions and Greetings

17 I appeal to you, brothers, to watch out
for those who cause divisions and create
obstacles [x] contrary to the doctrine that you
have been taught; [y] avoid them. 18 For such
persons do not serve our Lord Christ, but
[z] their own appetites,[1] and [a] by smooth talk
and flattery they deceive the hearts of the
naive. 19 For [b] your obedience is known to
all, so that I rejoice over you, but I want
you [c] to be wise as to what is good and
innocent as to what is evil. 20 [d] The God of
peace [e] will soon crush Satan under your
feet. [f] The grace of our Lord Jesus Christ be
with you.
21 [g] Timothy, my fellow worker, greets
you; so do Lucius and Jason and Sosipater,
my kinsmen.
22 I Tertius, [h] who wrote this letter, greet
you in the Lord.
23 [i] Gaius, who is host to me and to the
whole church, greets you. Erastus, the city
treasurer, and our brother Quartus, greet
you.[2]

Doxology

25 [j] Now to him who is able to strengthen
you [k] according to my gospel and the
preaching of Jesus Christ, [l] according to
the revelation of the mystery [m] that was
kept secret for [n] long ages 26 but [o] has now
been disclosed and through the prophetic
writings has been made known to all
nations, according to the command of the
eternal God, [p] to bring about the obedience of faith— 27 to [q] the only wise God [r] be
glory forevermore through Jesus Christ!
Amen.

17 [x] 1 Tim. 1:3; 6:3 [y] See 2 John 10 **18** [z] Phil. 3:19; [2 Tim. 3:4; Tit. 1:12] [a] Col. 2:4; 2 Pet. 2:3 **19** [b] ch. 1:8 [c] [Jer. 4:22]; See Matt. 10:16 **20** [d] See ch. 15:33 [e] Gen. 3:15; [Luke 10:17-19; Rev. 12:11] [f] 1 Cor. 16:23 **21** [g] See Acts 16:1 **22** [h] See 1 Cor. 16:21 **23** [i] 1 Cor. 1:14; [Acts 19:29; 20:4; 3 John 1] **25** [j] Eph. 3:20; Jude 24 [k] See ch. 2:16 [l] 1 Cor. 2:1; 4:1; Eph. 1:9; 3:3-5; 5:32; 6:19 [m] [1 Cor. 2:7] [n] 2 Tim. 1:9; Tit. 1:2 **26** [o] Col. 1:26; 2 Tim. 1:10; Tit. 1:3 [p] [Col. 1:6]; See ch. 1:5 **27** [q] 1 Tim. 1:17; 6:16 [r] See ch. 11:36

1 Greek *their own belly* 2 Some manuscripts insert verse 24: *The grace of our Lord Jesus Christ be with you all. Amen.*

16:16 holy kiss. The kiss is a common token of greeting in the East. Here Paul urges the believers to sanctify their greetings as symbols of fellowship.

16:17–20 Reflection on his knowledge of these believers, their problems in Rome (ch. 14), and the divisive activity of Satan (v. 20), evokes an urgent summons to guard their unity (Eph. 4:3). They are to avoid those "who cause divisions . . . contrary to the doctrine that you have been taught." Bluntly he indicates that their divisive spirit is sinful, a mark of life in the flesh, and a form of self-indulgence (Gal. 5:19, 20). Christians must learn not to be deceived by "smooth talk and flattery" (v. 18).

16:19 innocent. The Romans need spiritual wisdom and hearts without any alloy of evil.

16:20 Prior to the closing greetings and doxology, Paul includes a promise of a prophetic nature, rooted in the first biblical deliverance promise in Gen. 3:15. Satan is the source of all "evil" (v. 19; cf. Gen. 3:12; also see "Satan" at Job 1:6). "The God of peace" (wholeness and integrity as well as tranquillity) will act as the Divine Warrior to overcome him. This will take place "soon." Paul may be speaking here of matters in the near future, or about the last things, which by faith is always seen as near at hand.

The grace of our Lord Jesus Christ be with you. A characteristically Pauline ending (Gal. 6:18; 1 Thess. 5:28).

16:21 Along with Silas, Timothy was Paul's closest coworker following the disagreement with Barnabas (Acts 15:36–40), and is mentioned in ten of Paul's letters. Lucius (whom some identify with Luke), Jason (possibly Paul's host in Thessalonica, Acts 17:5–9) and Sosipater (Acts 20:4) were possibly church delegates accompanying Paul to deliver the collection in Jerusalem.

16:22 I Tertius. Paul regularly used a secretary, identifying his letters as his own by a brief greeting written in his own handwriting (1 Cor. 16:21; Gal. 6:11; Col. 4:18; 2 Thess. 3:17).

16:23 Paul may have been residing with Gaius at the time of writing. He is presumably to be identified with the Gaius of 1 Cor. 1:14, and may be the (Gaius?) Titius Justus of Acts 18:7. An Erastus is mentioned in Acts 19:22 and 2 Tim. 4:20. We do not know whether this is the same man. Of greater interest is that a Christian held such a responsible post in the local government of Corinth. Of Quartus nothing is known.

16:25–27 The authenticity of this closing doxology is questioned by some on the grounds of its length, its emphasis on mystery, and its textual history (it is found at different points in the letter, or even omitted altogether in various ancient manuscripts). There is, however, a certain appropriateness about its length, coming at the end of a letter like Romans. Its themes draw to a fitting conclusion much that has already been said. In particular, Paul draws attention to his own teaching of the gospel (2:16; cf. 1 Thess. 1:5; 2 Tim. 2:8) and its power to edify (1:11), to the revelation of God's mystery (11:25; cf. Eph. 3:2–6), to faith and obedience among the nations (1:5), and to the wisdom of God in redemption (11:33; cf. Eph. 3:10–12).

16:26 but has now . . . through the prophetic writings has been made known. Paul's "now" might suggest that he is referring to the New Testament Scriptures, but his emphasis is that it is only now, in the light of Christ's coming, that the message already enshrined in the Old Testament is spread to the nations.

THE FIRST EPISTLE OF PAUL THE APOSTLE TO THE

Corinthians

AUTHOR

This letter bears the name of Paul as the author. No one has seriously questioned that Paul was the author of the Corinthian letters. These epistles are acknowledged on all sides as fundamental for our understanding of the apostle Paul, his ministry, and his message.

DATE AND OCCASION

Paul makes it clear in 16:8 that he wrote this letter from Ephesus during the third missionary journey (A.D. 53–57). Since the apostle stayed in Ephesus well over two years (Acts 19:8, 10), 1 Corinthians was written about A.D. 55.

Although Luke says nothing about this correspondence in the Book of Acts, he does provide some important information about the founding of the church in Corinth during Paul's second missionary journey (A.D. 50–52; Acts 18:1–11). Paul arrived in Corinth after his visit to Athens (Acts 17:16–34), an experience that had impressed on his mind afresh the foolishness of worldly wisdom. Evidently, this incident with the Athenian philosophers had made Paul more determined than ever to preach the simple message of the cross, however offensive it might appear to some (2:1–5). Second, with the support of an influential Christian couple, Aquila and Priscilla (16:19), Paul preached in the synagogue until Jewish opposition forced him to focus his ministry on Gentiles. Third, the Christian congregation in Corinth, composed of both Jews and Gentiles, flourished dramatically (Acts 18:8–10). Finally, Paul's ministry in Corinth lasted a fairly long time (more than eighteen months according to Acts 18:11, 18). Paul had reason to expect some spiritual maturity from the Corinthian Christians.

This letter reveals that the Corinthian church, instead of maturing in the intervening period, had developed a remarkable number of serious problems, such as division, abuse of the sacraments, disorder during worship services, theological problems, and the extremes of moral laxity and unhealthy asceticism. What had happened? Corinth was one of the largest cities in the Roman world and one of the most corrupt (Acts 18:1 note). A strategic commercial center, the city sought to provide international pleasures. In that setting the Christians polarized, some insisting that association with sinners was permissible and necessary, others arguing that a measure of isolation was essential to preserve holiness. These opposing tendencies grew out of control in Corinth and endangered the future of the congregation.

We may infer from 5:9 that Paul had sent the church an earlier letter (which has not survived) exhorting the Corinthian believers to separate from immoral Christians. That letter must also have contained a request for an offering (16:1–4), and probably other instructions related to problems in the congregation. The troubles did not subside. Eventually, the apostle received reports that the church in Corinth was being torn apart by internal divisions, especially as a result of some in the congregation who viewed themselves as more spiritual and knowledgeable than their fellow-believers (1:11, 12; 3:1–4; 8:1–3). Paul also learned about other matters: criticisms hurled at him, gross immorality, and lawsuits between Christians (4:1–4; 5:1; 6:1–6). Moreover, the church itself had written to Paul requesting instruction about such matters as marriage and divorce, food offered to idols, spiritual gifts, and the method Paul was using for his collection (7:1, 25; 8:1; 12:1; 16:1). They also asked for a visit from Apollos (16:12). The apostle was confronted with a massive task, and this long letter to the Corinthians was an attempt to deal with the problem.

CHARACTERISTICS AND THEMES

The contents of the letter are determined by the kinds of problems that had surfaced in Corinth. Many scholars have suggested that the letter is roughly organized on the basis of a distinction between matters that had been reported to Paul (chs. 1–6) and problems that the Corinthians had raised in their letter (chs. 7–16). Such an outline does provide a valuable overview. Behind the great diversity of issues treated in this letter there lie some deep and recurring problems. Challenges to Paul's authority, pride in personal spirituality, and especially a lack of love were fundamental questions that the apostle needed to address. In the course of dealing with these issues, the apostle sets forth his teaching on important doctrines including God's sovereignty, the nature of the church, sanctification, and the bodily resurrection.

OUTLINE OF 1 CORINTHIANS

I. Introduction (1:1–9)

II. The Report from Chloe's Household (1:10–6:20)

- A. *Divisions in the Church (1:10–4:21)*
  1. The Report (1:10–17)
  2. The Gospel and True Wisdom (1:18–3:4)
  3. Ministry and Apostleship (3:5–4:21)
- B. *Moral and Ethical Problems (chs. 5; 6)*
  1. A Case of Incest (ch. 5)
  2. Lawsuits (6:1–11)
  3. Sexual Immorality (6:12–20)

III. Response to the Corinthians' Letter (7:1–16:12)

- A. *About Marriage and Divorce (ch. 7)*
  1. The Marriage Relationship (7:1–9)
  2. The Question of Divorce (7:10–24)
  3. The Special Problem of "Virgins" (7:25–40)
- B. *About Food Offered to Idols (8:1–11:1)*
  1. The Problem and Its Basic Solution (ch. 8)
  2. Paul's Authority to Deal with the Problem (ch. 9)
  3. The Israelites as Examples (10:1–22)
  4. Conclusions (10:23–11:1)
- C. *About the Worship Service (11:2–34)*
  1. Hair Covering (11:2–16)
  2. The Lord's Supper (11:17–34)
- D. *About Spiritual Gifts (chs. 12–14)*
  1. Unity and Diversity (ch. 12)
  2. The Greatness of Love (ch. 13)
  3. Prophecy and Tongues (14:1–25)
  4. The Principle of Order (14:26–40)
- E. *About the Resurrection (ch. 15)*
  1. Christ's Resurrection Is Essential (15:1–11)
  2. The Certainty of Resurrection (15:12–34)
  3. The Resurrection Body (15:35–49)
  4. Conclusion (15:50–58)
- F. *About the Collection and Other Matters (16:1–12)*

IV. Conclusion (16:13–24)

Greeting

1 Paul, [a]called [b]by the will of God to be
an apostle of Christ Jesus, and our
brother Sosthenes,
2 To the church of God that is in Corinth,
to those [c]sanctified in Christ Jesus, [d]called
to be saints together with all those who in
every place [e]call upon the name of our Lord
Jesus Christ, both their Lord and ours:
3 [d]Grace to you and peace from God our
Father and the Lord Jesus Christ.

Thanksgiving

4 I [f]give thanks to my God always for you
because of the grace of God that was given
you in Christ Jesus, 5 that in every way [g]you
were enriched in him in all [h]speech and
all knowledge— 6 even as [i]the testimony
about Christ was confirmed among you—
7 so that you are not lacking in any spiritual
gift, as you [j]wait for the revealing of our

Chapter 1
1 [a]See Rom. 1:1 [b]2 Cor. 1:1; Eph. 1:1; Col. 1:1; 2 Tim. 1:1
2 [c]ch. 6:11; [ver. 30]; See John 17:19 [d]See Rom. 1:7 [e]See Acts 9:14
3 [d][See ver. 2 above]
4 [f]See Rom. 1:8
5 [g]2 Cor. 9:11; [2 Cor. 6:10] [h]2 Cor. 8:7; [ch. 12:8]; See Rom. 15:14; 1 John 2:20
6 [i]2 Tim. 1:8; [2 Thess. 1:10; 1 Tim. 2:6; Rev. 1:2] 7 [j]Rom. 8:19; Phil. 3:20; Heb. 9:28; See Luke 17:30; 2 Pet. 3:12

1:1 apostle. Someone commissioned directly by Christ as His authoritative messenger (2 Cor. 1:1 note). Paul stresses the significance of this office elsewhere (ch. 9; 15:1–11; 2 Cor. 10–12; Gal. 1). Some of the problems in the Corinthian church involved challenges to Paul's authority.

Sosthenes. Perhaps the same person mentioned in Acts 18:17, ruler of the synagogue in Corinth at the time of Paul's first visit to the city.

1:2 sanctified . . . called to be saints. The word "saints" (lit. "holy ones") calls attention to the distinctive status of God's people. Paul often uses it to identify the Christians to whom he writes (e.g., Rom. 1:7). The description "sanctified" underlines this aspect of Christian life. The Corinthians were plagued by ethical problems and this letter touches repeatedly on the subject of sanctification. At the very beginning Paul calls special attention to it. Significantly, however, he encourages them in a pastoral way by reminding them that they *are* sanctified (6:11). The goal of holiness is realistic because God has already changed their hearts (Rom. 6:1–14; Gal. 5:24, 25).

1:5 in every way you were enriched. The Corinthians were tempted to become puffed up by their gifts of "knowledge" and of speaking "in tongues" (8:1; 14:23). Paul needs to rebuke them for their moral weakness and abuse of those gifts, but he does not deny or minimize the blessings they have received (v. 7).

Lord Jesus Christ, **8** [k]who will sustain you
to the end, [l]guiltless [m]in the day of our
Lord Jesus Christ. **9** [n]God is faithful, by
whom you were called into the [o]fellowship
of his Son, Jesus Christ our Lord.

Divisions in the Church

10 I appeal to you, brothers,[1] by the name
of our Lord Jesus Christ, that all of you
agree and that there be no [p]divisions
among you, but that you be united [q]in the
same mind and the same judgment. **11** For
it has been reported to me by Chloe's people that there is [r]quarreling among you, my
brothers. **12** What I mean is that [s]each one
of you says, "I follow Paul," or "I follow
[t]Apollos," or "I follow [u]Cephas," or "I follow Christ." **13** [v]Is Christ divided? Was Paul
crucified for you? Or were you [w]baptized
in the name of Paul? **14** I thank God that I
baptized none of you except [x]Crispus and
[y]Gaius, **15** so that no one may say that you
were baptized in my name. **16** (I did baptize also [z]the household of Stephanas.
Beyond that, I do not know whether I
baptized anyone else.) **17** For Christ did
not send me to baptize but to preach the
gospel, and [a]not with words of eloquent
wisdom, lest the cross of Christ be emptied
of its power.

Christ the Wisdom and Power of God

18 For the word of the cross is [b]folly to
[c]those who are perishing, but to us [d]who
are being saved it is [e]the power of God.
19 For it is written,

> [f]"I will destroy the wisdom of the wise,
> and the discernment of the
> discerning I will thwart."

20 [g]Where is the one who is wise? Where
is the scribe? Where is the debater of this
age? [h]Has not God made foolish the
wisdom of the world? **21** For since, in the
wisdom of God, the world did not know
God through wisdom, it pleased God
through the folly of what we preach to save
those who believe. **22** For [i]Jews demand
signs and Greeks seek wisdom, **23** but we
preach Christ [j]crucified, a stumbling block

8 [k][Phil. 1:6; 1 Thess. 3:13] [l]Col. 1:22 [m]ch. 5:5; 2 Cor. 1:14; Phil. 2:16; [Luke 17:24] **9** [n]ch. 10:13; Deut. 7:9; Isai. 49:7; 2 Cor. 1:18 [o]1 John 1:3 **10** [p]ch. 11:18 [q][Phil. 1:27] **11** [r]ch. 3:3 **12** [s]ch. 3:4; [Matt. 23:9, 10] [t]See Acts 18:24 [u]See John 1:42 **13** [v][ch. 12:5; 2 Cor. 11:4; Eph. 4:5] [w]See Acts 8:16 **14** [x]Acts 18:8 [y]See Rom. 16:23 **16** [z]ch. 16:15, 17 **17** [a]ch. 2:1, 4, 13; [2 Cor. 10:10; 11:6; 2 Pet. 1:16]

18 [b]ver. 21, 23, 25; ch. 2:14 [c]2 Cor. 2:15; 4:3; 2 Thess. 2:10 [d]ch. 15:2; [Acts 2:47] [e]Rom. 1:16; [ver. 24]

19 [f]Cited from Isai. 29:14; [Job 5:12, 13; Jer. 8:9; Matt. 11:25] **20** [g]Isai. 19:12 [h]ch. 2:6; 3:19; Isai. 44:25; Rom. 1:22; [ver. 26] **22** [i]See Matt. 12:38 **23** [j]Gal. 5:11; See 1 Pet. 2:8

[1] Or *brothers and sisters*. The plural Greek word *adelphoi* (translated "brothers") refers to siblings in a family. In New Testament usage, depending on the context, *adelphoi* may refer either to men or to both men and women who are siblings (brothers and sisters) in God's family, the church; also verses 11, 26

1:8 will sustain you. Paul encourages his readers by assuring them that God, who began a work of grace in them, can be trusted to complete it. Indeed, they will be presented "guiltless" at the time of Christ's return. Note the similarities between vv. 8, 9 and Phil. 1:6, 10 (cf. Eph. 5:26, 27; 1 Thess. 5:23, 24).

1:10 I appeal to you. This exhortation begins the body of the letter and announces Paul's primary concern. He has heard (vv. 11, 12) that the unity of the Corinthian church has broken down. Many of the problems addressed in this letter reflect the spirit of dissension that was in the community.

1:11 Chloe's people. Chloe must have been an influential Christian, perhaps a member of the Corinthian church, although she is not mentioned elsewhere.

1:12 Apollos. An effective preacher from Alexandria who had ministered in Ephesus and Corinth (Acts 18:24–19:1).

Cephas. Simon Peter's Aramaic name. He was obviously popular among some groups in Corinth (perhaps the Jewish Christians), but it is unclear whether he had actually visited the church.

1:13 Is Christ divided. With this question Paul anticipates one of his fundamental teachings about the church. Just as a physical body, though made up of many members, is one, so also the church, which is the body of Christ, cannot be divided (10:16, 17; 11:29; 12:12 note).

1:14 Crispus. The synagogue ruler whose conversion is recorded in Acts 18:8.

Gaius. A common name. Perhaps this is the Gaius described in Acts 19:29.

1:16 the household of Stephanas. Paul's first converts in Corinth, respected for their dedication. Stephanas himself was one of the representatives who brought a communication from the Corinthians to Paul (16:15–17). See "Infant Baptism" at Gen. 17:12.

1:17 words of eloquent wisdom. The Corinthian church had an unhealthy regard for rhetorical display. Paul will focus attention on what true wisdom is (1:18–2:16; 3:18–23). In this verse he reminds the Corinthians that the power of his own preaching did not depend on such skills (2:1–5).

cross of Christ. In the opinion of those who are wise according to this world, proclaiming the crucified Lord is foolishness. Paul therefore treats "wisdom" and "the cross" as opposites (v. 23 note).

1:18 perishing . . . being saved. According to the Bible there will be two types of response to the gospel arising from God's elective purpose (Is. 6:9, 10; Luke 2:34; Rom. 9:10–12; 2 Cor. 2:15, 16). This truth does not make God responsible for the perishing of unbelievers; they perish because of their own sin and stubborn impenitence. Those who believe and are saved, on the other hand, are "those who are called" (v. 24; Rom. 9:16).

1:20 wise . . . scribe . . . debater. It is not clear whether Paul intends a sharp distinction between these three categories. Possibly the first is general in character, while the other two are specifically Jewish scribes and Greek teachers.

this age . . . the world. Much of Paul's theology is built on the basic opposition between "the present evil age" (Gal. 1:4), or world, which is characterized by "the flesh," and the coming age, which has already dawned for those who have received the Spirit (10:11; Gal. 5:16, 17; Eph. 1:13, 14; 2:6; Phil. 3:20).

1:21 the folly of what we preach. This passage is filled with intense irony. Those who are wise according to the standards of the world think the gospel is foolish. But even the most "foolish" thing about God is wiser than human wisdom (vv. 25, 27). God can use the simplicity of the gospel to demonstrate that real foolishness belongs to those who oppose Him (v. 27). The arrogance of human wisdom blinds unbelievers to the truth. Jesus thanked the Father for His good pleasure in hiding these things from the wise and learned but revealing them to little children (Matt. 11:25, 26).

1:23 we preach Christ crucified. Paul identifies precisely what the

to Jews and folly to Gentiles, 24 but to those
who are called, both Jews and Greeks,
Christ [k]the power of God and [l]the wisdom
of God. 25 For the foolishness of God is
wiser than men, and the weakness of God
is stronger than men.

26 For consider your calling, brothers:
[m]not many of you were wise according to
worldly standards,[1] not many were powerful, not many were of noble birth. 27 But
[n]God chose what is foolish in the world to
shame the wise; [o]God chose what is weak
in the world to shame the strong; 28 God
chose what is low and despised in the
world, even [p]things that are not, to [q]bring
to nothing things that are, 29 so [r]that no
human being[2] might boast in the presence
of God. 30 He is the source of your life in
Christ Jesus, whom God made our [s]wis-
dom and our [t]righteousness and [u]sanctifi-
cation and [v]redemption. 31 Therefore, as it
is written, [w]"Let the one who boasts, boast
in the Lord."

Proclaiming Christ Crucified

2 And I, when I came to you, brothers,[3]
[x]did not come proclaiming to you [y]the
testimony[4] of God with lofty speech or
wisdom. 2 For I decided to know nothing
among you except [z]Jesus Christ and him
crucified. 3 And [a]I was with you [b]in weakness and in fear and much trembling, 4 and
my speech and my message were not in
plausible words of wisdom, but in demonstration of [c]the Spirit and of power, 5 that
your faith might not rest in the wisdom of
men but [d]in the power of God.

Wisdom from the Spirit

6 Yet among [e]the mature we do impart
wisdom, although it is not [f]a wisdom of
this age or of the rulers of this age, [g]who
are doomed to pass away. 7 But we impart a
secret and hidden wisdom of God, [h]which
God decreed before the ages for our glory.
8 None of [i]the rulers of this age understood
this, for [j]if they had, they would not have
crucified [k]the Lord of glory. 9 But, as it is
written,

> [l]"What no eye has seen, nor ear heard,
> nor the heart of man imagined,

24 [k][ver. 18] [l]ver. 30; Col. 2:3; [Luke 11:49] **26** [m]ch. 2:8; John 7:48; [ver. 20]; See Matt. 11:25 **27** [n]James 2:5 [o]Ps. 8:2 **28** [p]Rom. 4:17 [q]ch. 2:6; [Job 34; 19, 24] **29** [r]Eph. 2:9; [Judg. 7:2] **30** [s][ver. 24] [t]Jer. 23:5, 6; 33:16; 2 Cor. 5:21; Phil. 3:9 [u][ver. 2] [v]Eph. 1:7; Col. 1:14; [Rom. 3:24] **31** [w]2 Cor. 10:17; [Jer. 9:23, 24]

Chapter 2

1 [x]ver. 4, 13; [2 Cor. 1:12]; See ch. 1:17 [y]See Rom. 16:25 **2** [z]Gal. 6:14 **3** [a]Acts 18:1, 6, 12 [b]2 Cor. 11:30; 12:5, 9; 13:4, 9; Gal. 4:13 **4** [c]ch. 4:20; Rom. 15:13, 19; 1 Thess. 1:5; 2 Pet. 1:16

5 [d]2 Cor. 4:7; 6:7; [Zech. 4:6; 2 Cor. 10:4; 12:9] **6** [e]Phil. 3:15; [ch. 3:1] [f][James 3:15] [g]ch. 1:28 **7** [h]Rom. 16:25, 26; Eph. 3:5, 9; Col. 1:26; 2 Tim. 1:9 **8** [i]Acts 13:27; See Luke 24:20 [j]See Acts 3:17 [k]James 2:1; [Ps. 24:7-10; Acts 7:2] **9** [l][Isai. 64:4]

[1] Greek *according to the flesh* [2] Greek *no flesh* [3] Or *brothers and sisters* [4] Some manuscripts *mystery* (or *secret*)

world finds offensive about the gospel (cf. v. 17; 2:2). Possibly these words also reflect the reason for Paul's opposition to the gospel before his conversion. The thought that the Messiah (God's anointed) had been hanged on a tree and had come under the divine curse (Gal. 3:13; Deut. 21:23) was intolerable to many Jews.

1:24 Christ the power of God and the wisdom of God. God's wisdom and power are not abstract forces but personal qualities that manifest themselves fully in the life, teachings, death, and resurrection of Jesus Christ (v. 30; Rom. 1:4, 16; Col. 2:3).

1:26 consider your calling. Salvation, by its very nature, does not depend on human values. Even those in the Corinthian church who might have been justly admired could not have claimed that they were chosen because of their good qualities. Rather, God has mercy on all who acknowledge their sinfulness (Mark 2:17; John 9:39–41). See "Effectual Calling and Conversion" at 2 Thess. 2:14.

1:29 no human being might boast in the presence of God. This principle, which Paul underscores in v. 31 by quoting Jer. 9:24, provides the foundation for the biblical doctrine of salvation: it is a gracious gift from God that rules out human boasting (Eph. 2:8, 9).

1:30 whom God made our wisdom. See note on v. 24.

2:1 when I came to you. Paul must be referring to his first visit to Corinth, recorded in Acts 18:1–17 (Introduction: Date and Occasion).

with lofty speech or wisdom. Influenced by Greek culture, some of the Christians in Corinth may have been critical of Paul for not using the rhetorical techniques of their contemporaries (2 Cor. 11:5, 6). See notes 4:1, 8–13; 9:3, 19; 10:30; 16:3.

2:2 Jesus Christ and him crucified. See note 1:23.

2:3–5 Taken by themselves, these verses might suggest that Paul was timid, uneducated, and unable to speak with force and eloquence. Both the Book of Acts (e.g., 19:8) and Paul's own letters (ch. 13) prove otherwise. "Self-confidence," if it rests on arrogance concerning one's own strength, reflects a desire to be independent from God. Paul had learned that God can use human weakness to show forth His own glory (2 Cor. 12:7–10). Because he knew that men and women will be persuaded only "in demonstration of the Spirit and of power," Paul used his talents and training with full confidence.

2:6 mature. Lit. "perfect." The apostle does not have in mind a special category of elite Christians, an idea that may have been present among the Corinthians. The expression here is no doubt equivalent to "spiritual" (vv. 13, 15; 3:1), referring to the influence of the Holy Spirit. The mature or spiritual person is the person who has the Holy Spirit (cf. v. 14). Since every true believer has received the Spirit, every believer is spiritual and can understand God's wisdom, the gospel of Jesus Christ.

we do impart wisdom. The gospel, the proclamation of Christ crucified.

2:7 a secret and hidden wisdom of God. This passage should not be interpreted as a reference to mysteries accessible only to superior Christians. The riches of the gospel, though "hidden" during the Old Testament period, have now been revealed by the Spirit (v. 10). Eph. 3:2–6 makes plain that the word "mystery," used by Paul to emphasize the distinctiveness of his message to the Gentiles, has a strong temporal meaning. The "mystery" is a truth that "was not made known . . . in other generations" (Eph. 3:5); it was "kept secret for long ages" (Rom. 16:25). But now the truth has been clearly revealed to those who have the Spirit, who live in "the end of the ages" (10:11).

decreed. The word is used also in Rom. 8:29, 30 and Eph. 1:5 to express the certainty of God's goodwill for His people.

2:8 None of the rulers of this age understood. Unbelievers are still part of the old age and so have not received God's wisdom (v. 14). Paul emphasizes this point by focusing on the most influential members of society (1:20).

2:9 In contrast to the wise of this world (who cannot even conceive the greatness of divine salvation), those who love God know and partake of

what God has [m]prepared [n]for those
who love him"—
10 these things [o]God has revealed to us
through the Spirit. For the Spirit searches
everything, even [p]the depths of God. 11 For
who knows a person's thoughts [q]except
the spirit of that person, which is in him?
So also no one comprehends the thoughts
of God except the Spirit of God. 12 Now [r]we
have received not [s]the spirit of the world,
but the Spirit who is from God, that we
might understand the things freely given us
by God. 13 And we impart this [t]in words not
taught by human wisdom but taught by
the Spirit, [u]interpreting spiritual truths to
those who are spiritual.[1]
14 The natural person does not accept the
things of the Spirit of God, for they are [v]fol-
ly to him, and [w]he is not able to understand them because they are spiritually
discerned. 15 The [x]spiritual person judges
all things, but is himself to be judged by no

9 [m]See Matt. 25:34 [n]James 1:12
10 [o]Matt. 16:17; Gal. 1:12, 16; Eph. 3:3, 5; See John 14:26 [p][Rev. 2:24]
11 [q]Prov. 20:27
12 [r]Rom. 8:15 [s][1 John 4:4]
13 [t]ver. 1, 4; See ch. 1:17 [u]2 Cor. 10:12
14 [v]ch. 1:18 [w]Rom. 8:7
15 [x]ch. 3:1; 14:37; Gal. 6:1; [Prov. 28:5]

[1] Or *interpreting spiritual truths in spiritual language*, or *comparing spiritual things with spiritual*

Illumination and Conviction

Christians' knowledge of divine things is more than a knowledge of biblical words and theological ideas. It is an understanding of the reality and relevance of the works of God testified to by Scripture. The "natural person" (1 Cor. 2:14) who does not have the Spirit, even though familiar with Christian ideas, still lacks this deeper understanding, and is like the blind leaders of the blind (Matt. 15:14). Only the Holy Spirit, who searches "the depths of God" (1 Cor. 2:10), can bring this understanding to minds and hearts darkened by sin. It is called a "spiritual . . . understanding" because it is an understanding given by the Holy Spirit (Col. 1:9; cf. Luke 24:25; 1 John 5:20). Those who, along with correct instruction from the Scriptures, "have been anointed by the Holy One . . . have knowledge" (1 John 2:20).

The work of the Spirit in imparting this understanding is called "illumination," or enlightening. It is not a giving of new revelation, but a work within us that enables us to grasp and to affirm the revelation of the Bible, as it is read, preached, and taught. Sin clouds our minds and wills so that we miss and resist the force of Scripture. The Spirit, however, opens and unveils our minds and attunes our hearts so that we understand what God has revealed (2 Cor. 3:14–16; 4:6; Eph. 1:17, 18; 3:18, 19). Illumination is the application of God's revealed truth to our hearts, so that we grasp as reality for ourselves what the sacred text says.

Protestant theologians shortly after the Reformation spoke of illumination as an act of grace that proceeds in two stages. The first stage of illumination takes place when one encounters the ministry of the Word. This external illumination prepares a person for the second stage, the internal ministry of the Holy Spirit that leads to salvation. The Spirit speaks through the law, that convicts a person of sin, and the gospel, that conveys knowledge of God's grace and forgiveness (cf. Luke 1:79). It is through the illumination of the Spirit that the ministry of the Word conveys the effectual calling to salvation.

Although illumination by the Spirit begins the process, or order, of salvation (Heb. 6:4; 10:32), it continues throughout the life of the believer. The Holy Spirit leads us to a deeper understanding of God (John 16:13), prompting both repentance for the sins that we commit and assurance of God's grace and the certainty of our election. We receive this illumination through the ministry of the Word and through prayer, meditation on God and His revelation, and the struggle to live our lives in a manner consistent with revelation.

His blessings. The quotation is based on Is. 64:4, but includes other ideas found in the Old Testament.

2:10 revealed to us. See theological note "Illumination and Conviction."

searches everything. The idea of divine searching (cf. Ps. 139:1; Rom. 8:27) emphasizes God's omniscience, particularly His power to see what is invisible to humans (John 2:25). It does not imply that the Holy Spirit needs to seek knowledge of the Father that He otherwise lacks. The Spirit probes the depths of divine knowledge for our benefit.

2:11 the spirit . . . in him. This verse intends to make a common-sense observation, not to give an analysis of human personality. "Spirit" refers generally to the immaterial part of a human being, especially to the mental faculties (v. 16 note).

2:12 that we might understand. See "The Authentication of Scripture" at 2 Cor. 4:6.

2:13 interpreting spiritual truths to those who are spiritual. The precise meaning of this clause is disputed. Probably Paul had been criticized for not using human eloquence and wisdom (v. 1 note). In reply he says that the truths revealed by the Spirit must be explained in a way that is harmonious with the Spirit. See "The Authority of Scripture" at 2 Tim. 3:16.

2:14 natural. The "natural" (Greek *psychikos*) person, who still belongs to the old age, is contrasted with the one who is "spiritual" (*pneumatikos;* see 15:44, 45 and notes).

2:15 judges. The apostle may be responding to individuals who opposed him and passed negative judgments on him (v. 1 note).

one. 16 [y]"For who has understood the mind
of the Lord so as to instruct him?" But [z]we
have the mind of Christ.

Divisions in the Church

3 But I, brothers,[1] could not address you
as [a]spiritual people, but as [b]people of
the flesh, as [c]infants in Christ. 2 [d]I fed you
with milk, not solid food, for [e]you were not
ready for it. And even now you are not yet
ready, 3 for you are still of the flesh. For
while there is [f]jealousy and strife among
you, are you not of the flesh and behaving
only in a human way? 4 For [g]when one says,
"I follow Paul," and another, "I follow
Apollos," [h]are you not being merely
human?
5 What then is Apollos? What is Paul?
[i]Servants through whom you believed, [j]as
the Lord assigned to each. 6 [k]I planted,
[l]Apollos watered, [m]but God gave the
growth. 7 So [n]neither he who plants nor he
who waters is anything, but only God who
gives the growth. 8 He who plants and he
who waters are one, and each [o]will receive
his wages according to his labor. 9 For we
are [p]God's fellow workers. You are God's
field, [q]God's building.
10 [r]According to the grace of God given to
me, like a skilled master builder I laid a
[s]foundation, and [t]someone else is building
upon it. Let each one take care how he
builds upon it. 11 For no one can lay a
[u]foundation other [v]than that which is laid,
[w]which is Jesus Christ. 12 Now if anyone
builds on the foundation with gold, silver,
precious stones, wood, hay, straw—
13 [x]each one's work will become manifest,
for the Day will disclose it, because it will
be revealed [y]by fire, and [z]the fire will test
what sort of work each one has done. 14 If
the work that anyone has built on the foundation survives, [a]he will receive a reward.
15 If anyone's work is burned up, he will
suffer loss, though he himself will be saved,
[b]but only as through fire.
16 [c]Do you not know that you[2] are God's
temple and that God's Spirit dwells in you?
17 If anyone destroys God's temple, God
will destroy him. For [d]God's temple is
holy, and you are that temple.
18 [e]Let no one deceive himself. [f]If anyone
among you thinks that he is wise in this
age, let him become a fool that he may
become wise. 19 For [g]the wisdom of this
world is folly with God. For it is written,
[h]"He catches the wise in their craftiness,"
20 and again, [i]"The Lord knows the
thoughts of the wise, that they are futile."
21 So [j]let no one boast in men. For [k]all things

16 [y]Cited from Isai. 40:13; See Rom. 11:34 [z][John 15:15]
Chapter 3
1 [a]ch. 2:15; Rom. 7:14 [b][ch. 2:14] [c]Heb. 5:13; [ch. 2:6]
2 [d]Heb. 5:12, 13; 1 Pet. 2:2 [e]John 16:12
3 [f]Gal. 5:19, 20; [ch. 1:11; 11:18; Rom. 13:13]
4 [g]See ch. 1:12 [h][ver. 3]
5 [i]2 Cor. 6:4; Eph. 3:7; Col. 1:25; [2 Cor. 3:3] [j]See Rom. 12:6
6 [k]ch. 4:15; 9:1; 15:1; Acts 18:4-11; 2 Cor. 10:14, 15 [l]Acts 18:27 [m][ch. 15:10; Col. 1:18]
7 [n]2 Cor. 12:11; Gal. 6:3; [Gal. 2:6]
8 [o]ver. 14; ch. 15:58; 2 John 8; [ch. 4:5; Gal. 6:4, 5]; See Matt. 16:27; Rom. 2:6
9 [p]Mark 16:20; 2 Cor. 6:1 [q]Eph. 2:20-22; Col. 2:7; [ver. 16; Ps. 127:1]
10 [r][2 Pet. 3:15]; See Rom. 12:3 [s]ver. 11, 12; Rom. 15:20; [Rev. 21:14] [t][ch. 4:15]
11 [u]Isai. 28:16 [v][2 Cor. 11:4; Gal. 1:6, 7] [w][Eph. 2:20]
13 [x]ch. 4:5 [y]ver. 15; 2 Thess. 1:8 [z]1 Pet. 1:7
14 [a]See ver. 8
15 [b][Ps. 66:12; Isai. 43:2; Jude 23]
16 [c]ch. 6:19; 2 Cor. 6:16; Eph. 2:21
17 [d][2 Cor. 7:1]
18 [e][Isai. 5:21; Gal. 6:3] [f][ch. 8:2; Jer. 8:8, 9]
19 [g]See ch. 1:20 [h]Cited from Job 5:13
20 [i]Cited from Ps. 94:11
21 [j]ver. 4-6; ch. 1:12; 4:6 [k]Rom. 8:28

[1] Or *brothers and sisters* [2] The Greek for *you* is plural in verses 16 and 17

2:16 the mind of the Lord. See "Understanding the Word of God" at Ps. 119:34. Through the Spirit of the Lord, Paul has the mind of Christ, and therefore the mind of the Lord. Those opponents who do not see that the Spirit of Christ and the Spirit of the Lord are one and the same have no warrant to instruct or examine him. By implication, those who accept Paul's teaching have the blessing of the Spirit and understand the things of God.

3:1 spiritual. That is, belonging to the Holy Spirit (2:6 note).

people of the flesh. Paul's main word for describing the present evil age. Since the Corinthians had received the Holy Spirit, they were spiritual in the most fundamental sense, but their behavior was so inconsistent with that truth that Paul had to treat them as people who had little spiritual understanding.

3:3 jealousy and strife. See note 1:10.

3:6 I planted. Paul's aim was to preach the gospel in places where the message of Christ had not been heard (Rom. 15:20).

Apollos. See note 1:12.

3:9 God's fellow workers. Paul may mean either that Christian workers are co-laborers with God or that Christians who are co-laborers with one another belong to God. Paul's point is clear from the context: God alone is responsible for the success of Christian ministry.

3:10 skilled. A clear allusion to the previous discussion of true wisdom (1:17; 2:9, 10 notes).

foundation. As one called to proclaim the gospel where it was not known (v. 6 note), Paul had resolved to preach nothing but Christ crucified (2:2).

3:12–15 These verses address the evaluation of Christian ministry. Some who were seeking to build God's building in Corinth, but who depend on human wisdom, were using perishable materials ("wood, hay, straw") that will not survive the judgment of God's fire, while the builders themselves will barely escape destruction. Paul warns the church that they, like Solomon's temple (1 Chr. 22:14–16), should be built up with what is lasting. See "The Final Judgment" at Matt. 25:41.

3:16 God's temple. God signified His presence in the temple by filling it with the cloud of His glory (1 Kin. 8:10, 11). Now He lives in His people by filling them with the Holy Spirit. Paul's focus here is on God's people as a corporate whole; in 6:19 the emphasis shifts to the individual Christian's body.

3:17 God will destroy him. Paul leaves open the possibility that some of the Christian builders in Corinth are not only using perishable material but are actively destroying God's work. They will not be spared at the Judgment.

3:18–20 Here the apostle returns more directly to the contrast between human and divine wisdom (v. 10 note).

3:21 let no one boast. See note 1:29.

all things are yours. This principle demonstrates the pettiness and absurdity of the Corinthians' quarreling. If we belong to Christ, then because of Him all things belong to us (Rom. 8:17, 38, 39; Heb. 1:2), and

are yours, 22 whether Paul or Apollos or
Cephas or the world or life or death or the
present or the future—all are yours, 23 and
[l]you are Christ's, and [m]Christ is God's.

The Ministry of Apostles

4 This is how one should regard us, as
servants of Christ and [n]stewards of the
mysteries of God. 2 Moreover, it is required
of stewards that they be found trustworthy.
3 But with me it is a very small thing that I
should be judged by you or by any human
court. In fact, I do not even judge myself.
4 [o]I am not aware of anything against
myself, [p]but I am not thereby acquitted. It
is the Lord who judges me. 5 Therefore [q]do
not pronounce judgment before the time,
[r]before the Lord comes, [s]who will bring to
light the things now hidden in darkness
and will disclose the purposes of the heart.
[t]Then each one will receive his commendation from God.
6 I have applied all these things to myself
and Apollos for your benefit, brothers,[1]
that you may learn by us not to go beyond
what is written, that none of you may [u]be
puffed up in favor of one against another.
7 For who sees anything different in you?
[v]What do you have that you did not
receive? If then you received it, why do you
boast as if you did not receive it?
8 Already you have all you want! Already
you have become rich! Without us you
have become kings! And would that you
did reign, so that we might share the rule
with you! 9 For I think that God has exhibited us apostles as last of all, [w]like men sentenced to death, because we [x]have become
a spectacle to the world, to angels, and to
men. 10 [y]We are fools for Christ's sake, but
[z]you are wise in Christ. [a]We are weak,
but you are strong. You are held in honor,
but we in disrepute. 11 To the present hour
[b]we hunger and thirst, we are poorly
dressed and [c]buffeted and [d]homeless, 12 and
we [e]labor, working with our own hands.
[f]When reviled, we bless; [g]when persecuted,
we endure; 13 when slandered, we entreat.
[h]We have become, and are still, like the
scum of the world, [i]the refuse of all things.
14 I do not write these things [j]to make
you ashamed, but to admonish you [k]as my
beloved children. 15 For [l]though you have
countless guides in Christ, you do not have
many fathers. For [m]I became your father in
Christ Jesus through the gospel. 16 I urge
you, then, [n]be imitators of me. 17 That is
why [o]I sent[2] you Timothy, [p]my beloved
and faithful child in the Lord, to remind
you of my ways in Christ,[3] [q]as I teach them
everywhere in every church. 18 Some are [r]ar-
rogant, [s]as though I were not coming to
you. 19 But [t]I will come to you soon, if the
Lord wills, and I will find out not the talk
of these arrogant people but their power.
20 For [u]the kingdom of God does not consist in talk but in power. 21 What do you
wish? [v]Shall I come to you with a rod, or
with love in a spirit of gentleness?

Sexual Immorality Defiles the Church

5 It is actually reported that there is
[w]sexual immorality among you, and of

23 [l]2 Cor. 10:7; Gal. 3:29 [m][ch. 11:3]
Chapter 4
1 [n][ch. 9:17]; See 1 Pet. 4:10
4 [o]See Acts 23:1 [p]Job 9:2, 15; Ps. 130:3; 143:2; [1 John 3:21]
5 [q]Matt. 7:1; Rom. 2:1; [Matt. 13:29] [r]See John 21:22; Rom. 2:16 [s]ch. 3:13 [t]2 Cor. 10:18; See ch. 3:8
6 [u]ver. 18, 19; ch. 5:2; 13:4
7 [v]John 3:27; [1 Chr. 29:14; James 1:17; 1 Pet. 4:10]
9 [w]See Rom. 8:36 [x]Heb. 10:33 (Gk.); [Isai. 20:3]
10 [y][Acts 17:18]; See ch. 1:18; Acts 26:24 [z]2 Cor. 11:19 [a]ch. 2:3; 2 Cor. 13:9
11 [b]Rom. 8:35; 2 Cor. 11:27; Phil. 4:12 [c]2 Cor. 11:20, 23 [d][Matt. 8:20]
12 [e]See Acts 18:3 [f]See 1 Pet. 3:9 [g]See John 15:20
13 [h][Isai. 30:22; 64:6] [i]Lam. 3:45
14 [j][ch. 6:5; 15:34] [k]2 Cor. 6:13; 1 Thess. 2:11; 3 John 4
15 [l][ch. 3:10] [m]Philem. 10; [Gal. 4:19]
16 [n]ch. 11:1; Phil. 3:17; 1 Thess. 1:6; [Phil. 4:9; 2 Thess. 3:9] **17** [o]ch. 16:10 [p]1 Tim. 1:2; 2 Tim. 1:2 [q]ch. 7:17 **18** [r]See ver. 6 [s]ver. 21; [2 Cor. 10:2] **19** [t]ch. 11:34; 16:5, 6; Acts 19:21; 20:2; 2 Cor. 1:15, 16 **20** [u]See ch. 2:4 **21** [v]2 Cor. 1:23; 2:1, 3; 12:20; 13:2, 10
Chapter 5 **1** [w]2 Cor. 12:21

[1] Or *brothers and sisters* [2] Or *am sending* [3] Some manuscripts add *Jesus*

jealousy can have no place in our lives. How little the Corinthians appreciated their Christian privileges is pointed out again in 6:2.

4:1 regard us, as servants. These verses show that Paul was being judged and attacked by at least some of the Corinthians (2:1 note). **mysteries.** See note 2:7.

4:3 I do not even judge myself. Though Paul's conscience is clear (v. 5), ultimately only God determines whether one has proved faithful.

4:5 do not pronounce judgment. Not an absolute command (5:2; 6:2), but a reference to the misconceived criticisms raised against Paul.

bring to light the things now hidden. At the Judgment, nothing will escape God's searching light (Matt. 10:26 and parallels).

4:8–13 In this powerful passage the apostle makes use of biting irony to show the Corinthians how trivial are their concerns and how unfair their criticisms. The sufferings of Paul are comparable to the pain and public humiliation of captives condemned to die (2 Cor. 11:23–30). In contrast, some of the Corinthians think of themselves as notably successful, but only because they do not understand what it means to be "fools for Christ's sake" (v. 10).

4:14 not . . . make you ashamed. Paul's pastoral heart is revealed in these words. The harsh language of the previous passage was not intended to make them feel inferior but to raise their sensitivity to the truth.

4:15 countless guides. The Corinthians boasted of their allegiance to Apollos, Peter, and others, with the implication that they had no need for Paul. The apostle reminds them that his fatherly relationship to them is unique and they have no good reason to attack him.

4:17 I sent you Timothy. Timothy had left prior to the writing of this letter (16:10 note).

4:18 as though I were not coming to you. A group of Corinthians argued that Paul was bold only when absent and that he was afraid to meet them face to face (2 Cor. 10:1, 2). He has sent Timothy to them (v. 17), apparently to avoid an ugly confrontation, but he will not hesitate to come in person. It is up to them what will happen when that visit takes place (v. 21; 2 Cor. 13:1–10).

a kind that is not tolerated even among
pagans, [x]for a man has his father's wife.
2 And [y]you are arrogant! Ought you [z]not
rather to mourn? Let him who has done
this be removed from among you.
3 For though [a]absent in body, I am present in spirit; and as if present, I have
already pronounced judgment on the one
who did such a thing. 4 When you are
assembled [b]in the name of the Lord Jesus
and my spirit is present, with the power of
our Lord Jesus, 5 you are [c]to deliver this
man to Satan for the destruction of the
flesh, so [d]that his spirit may be saved [e]in
the day of the Lord.[1]
6 [f]Your boasting is not good. Do you not
know that [g]a little leaven leavens the whole
lump? 7 Cleanse out the old leaven that you
may be a new lump, as you really are
unleavened. For Christ, our Passover lamb,
has been sacrificed. 8 Let us therefore celebrate the festival, [h]not with the old leaven,
[i]the leaven of malice and evil, but with the
unleavened bread of sincerity and truth.
9 I wrote to you in my letter [j]not to associate with sexually immoral people—
10 [k]not at all meaning [l]the sexually immoral
of this world, or the greedy and swindlers,
or idolaters, [m]since then you would need to
go out of the world. 11 But now I am writing
to you not to associate with anyone [n]who
bears the name of brother if he is guilty of
sexual immorality or greed, or is an idolater, reviler, drunkard, or swindler—not
even to eat with such a one. 12 For what
have I to do with judging [o]outsiders? [p]Is it
not those inside the church whom you are
to judge? 13 God judges[2] those outside.
[q]"Purge the evil person from among you."

Lawsuits Against Believers

6 When one of you has a grievance
against another, does he dare go to law
before the unrighteous [r]instead of the saints?
2 Or do you not know that [s]the saints will
judge the world? And if the world is to be
judged by you, are you incompetent to try

1 [x]Lev. 18:8; Deut. 22:30; 27:20
2 [y]See ch. 4:6 [z][2 Cor. 7:7-10]
3 [a]Col. 2:5; [1 Thess. 2:17]
4 [b]2 Thess. 3:6; [Matt. 16:19; 18:18; John 20:23; 2 Cor. 13:3, 10; 1 Tim. 5:20]
5 [c]1 Tim. 1:20; [Job 2:6; Acts 26:18] [d][Prov. 23:14] [e]See ch. 1:8
6 [f]James 4:16; [ver. 2] [g]Gal. 5:9; [ch. 15:33]
8 [h]Ex. 12:15; Deut. 16:3 [i][Matt. 16:6, 12; Mark 8:15; Luke 12:1]
9 [j][2 Cor. 6:14; Eph. 5:11; 2 Thess. 3:6, 14]
10 [k][ch. 10:27] [l]Eph. 5:5; Col. 3:5; [ch. 6:9] [m][John 17:15]
11 [n]2 Thess. 3:6
12 [o]See Mark 4:11 [p][ch. 6:1-4]
13 [q][Deut. 13:5; 17:7, 12; 21:21; 22:21, 22, 24; Judg. 20:13]
Chapter 6 1 [r][Matt. 18:17] 2 [s]Dan. 7:22; [Matt. 19:28; Rev. 20:4]

1 Some manuscripts add *Jesus* 2 Or *will judge*

5:1 a man has his father's wife. The man's father may have died, or the woman may have been a stepmother. In any case, the sexual relationship in view is the incestuous union explicitly condemned in Lev. 18:8. Though the Greco-Roman culture of Paul's day tolerated a wide array of immoral activities, even Gentiles censured this kind of incest.

5:2 you are arrogant. This verse is the key to Paul's real concern. The fundamental problem here was not the sin of one individual, but the failure of the Corinthian church to deal with the sin—indeed, their sense of pride in tolerating it (v. 6). Possibly, the Corinthians had developed a theology that could accommodate such immorality. Instead, they had the responsibility of exercising discipline by excommunicating the offender ("removed from among you").

5:3–5 A very difficult passage. Though Paul is physically absent from the Corinthian community, he claims to pass a prophetic judgment in their midst. The apostle is commanding the church to expel the offender from their fellowship ("deliver this man to Satan"). The purpose of this judgment is the man's salvation, but that can be achieved only if his sinful tendencies are overcome ("the destruction of the flesh"). According to one interpretation of 2 Cor. 2:5–11, this man did repent of his sin. See "Church Discipline and Excommunication" at Matt. 18:15.

5:6 boasting. See notes on v. 2; 1:29.

leaven. Leaven was a common metaphor for a corrupting influence. During the annual Feast of Passover the Israelites removed all leaven from their houses (Ex. 12:15).

5:7 you really are. Paul makes this important qualification to encourage the Corinthians; in a fundamental sense, they are already purified (1:2 note).

Christ, our Passover. The apostle develops the imagery by suggesting that the Passover sacrifice, as a shadow of better things to come (Heb. 10:1), pointed forward to the death of Christ.

5:8 Let us therefore celebrate the festival. The final, and especially beautiful, step in Paul's argument is to draw a parallel between the Feast of Unleavened Bread and the life of purity that Christians should lead.

5:9–11 Prior to the writing of 1 Corinthians, Paul had sent a letter (no longer in existence) instructing the Corinthians to separate themselves from believers who practiced immorality. The Corinthians either misunderstood Paul, as if he were commanding complete separation from the world, or they tried to sidestep the issue by arguing that his request was unreasonable. The apostle explains that he had in mind anyone thought to be a Christian whose life openly contradicted the faith. The injunction to expel offenders ("not even to eat with such a one") has primary reference to community life within the church and probably does not mean that all personal contact must be avoided (2 Thess. 3:15, "warn him as a brother").

5:12, 13 By quoting the frequent command in Deuteronomy (e.g., Deut. 17:7) to purge or expel the wicked from Israel, Paul draws an important parallel between the Old Testament covenant community and the Christian church (10:1–11). The church has authority to exercise discipline within its own fellowship, not to regulate the behavior of non-Christians.

6:1 dare go to law before the unrighteous. With this verse, Paul appears to change the topic from the evils of immorality to the problem of lawsuits among Christians. It is important, however, to notice the connection. In the first place, the topic of immorality has not been abandoned, but will recur in v. 9. Secondly, the failings of the Corinthians with regard to lawsuits are an expression of the problem already discussed in ch. 5, namely, a weak doctrine of the church. Just as Christians are not responsible to regulate the lives of non-Christians, so non-Christians have no power to discipline in the church. If the Corinthians understood the relation between the Israelite community and the Christian fellowship (5:12, 13 note), they would realize it was absurd for believers to go outside the church to solve their disputes. Who could imagine a pagan Gentile settling disputes among Israelites in the wilderness? This text does not comment on the legitimate role of civil authorities to judge matters that God has put under them. See "Christians and Civil Government" at Rom. 13:1.

6:2–5 The absurdity of the situation in Corinth becomes clearer when one recognizes that, in the consummation of history (but not before; 5:12, 13), Christians will participate with Christ in judging not only unbelievers but angels. Even the least qualified among the Corinthians is in a better position than an unbeliever to arbitrate disputes in the church.

trivial cases? [3]Do you not know that we are
to judge angels? How much more, then,
matters pertaining to this life! [4]So if you
have such cases, [t]why do you lay them
before those who have no standing in the
church? [5][u]I say this to your shame. Can it
be that there is no one among you wise
enough to settle a dispute between the
brothers, [6]but brother goes to law against
brother, and that before unbelievers? [7]To
have lawsuits at all with one another is
already a defeat for you. [v]Why not rather
suffer wrong? Why not rather be defrauded? [8]But you yourselves wrong and
defraud—even [w]your own brothers![1]
[9]Do you not know that the unrighteous[2]
will not inherit the kingdom of God? Do

4 [t][ch. 5:12]
5 [u]ch. 15:34; [ch. 4:14]
7 [v][Matt. 5:39, 40]
8 [w]1 Thess. 4:6

[1] Or *brothers and sisters* [2] Or *wrongdoers*

Sanctification: The Spirit and the Flesh

According to the *Westminster Shorter Catechism* (Q. 35), sanctification is "the work of God's free grace, whereby we are renewed in the whole man after the image of God, and are enabled more and more to die unto sin, and live unto righteousness." It is a continuing change worked by God in us, freeing us from sinful habits and forming in us Christlike affections, dispositions, and virtues. It does not mean that sin is instantly eradicated, but it is also more than a counteraction, in which sin is merely restrained or repressed without being progressively destroyed. Sanctification is a real transformation, not just the appearance of one.

The basic meaning of "sanctify" is to set apart to God, for His use. But God works in those whom He claims as His own to conform them "to the image of his Son" (Rom. 8:29). This moral renovation, in which we are increasingly changed from what we once were, flows from the agency of the indwelling Holy Spirit (Rom. 8:13; 12:1, 2; 1 Cor. 6:11, 19, 20; 2 Cor. 3:18; Eph. 4:22–24; 1 Thess. 5:23; 2 Thess. 2:13; Heb. 13:20, 21). God calls His children to holiness, and graciously gives what He commands (1 Thess. 4:4; 5:23).

Regeneration is birth; sanctification is growth. In regeneration, God implants desires that were not there before: desire for God, for holiness, and for glorifying God's name in the world; desire to pray and worship; desire to love and bring benefit to others. In sanctification, the Holy Spirit "works in you, both to will and to work" according to God's purpose, enabling His people to fulfill their new, godly desires (Phil. 2:12, 13). Christians become increasingly Christlike, as the moral profile of Jesus (the "fruit of the Spirit") is progressively formed in them (2 Cor. 3:18; Gal. 4:19; 5:22–25).

Regeneration is a momentary act, bringing a person from spiritual death to life. It is exclusively God's work. Sanctification is an ongoing process, dependent on God's continuing action in the believer, and consisting of the believer's continuous struggle against sin. God's method of sanctification is neither activism (self-reliant activity) nor apathy (God-reliant passivity), but human effort dependent on God (2 Cor. 7:1; Phil. 3:10–14; Heb. 12:14). Knowing that without Christ's enabling we cannot do good works, but also that He is ready to strengthen us for all we have to do (Phil. 4:13), we "abide" in Christ, asking for His help constantly—and we receive it (Col. 1:11; 1 Tim. 1:12; 2 Tim. 1:7; 2:1).

The standard to which God's work of sanctifying His saints is directed is His own revealed moral law, expounded and modeled by Christ Himself. Christ's love, humility, and patience are a supreme standard for Christians (Rom. 13:10; Eph. 5:2; Phil. 2:5–11; 1 Pet. 2:21).

Believers find within themselves contrary urgings. The Spirit sustains their regenerate desires and purposes, but their fallen instincts (the "flesh") obstruct their path and drag them back. The conflict of these two is sharp. Paul says he is unable to do what is right, and unable to restrain himself from doing what is wrong (Rom. 7:14–25). This conflict and frustration will be with Christians as long as they are in the body. Yet by watching and praying against temptation, and cultivating opposite virtues, they may through the Spirit's help "put to death" particular bad habits (Rom. 8:13; Col. 3:5). They will experience many particular deliverances and victories in their battle with sin, while not being exposed to temptations that are impossible to resist (1 Cor. 10:13).

6:7 Why not rather suffer wrong. This remarkable question makes obvious how critical is the principle of community for the apostle. The point is certainly not that Christians should be encouraged to take abuse from others. After all, cheating and injustice should not even exist within the Christian community. That such injustices do exist, and are indeed performed by Christians against one another, demonstrates how far the Corinthians have fallen. Nevertheless, if the Corinthians understood the serious implications of all the improprieties in their church, and if they appreciated the qualities that should characterize believers (cf. 13:4–7), they would much sooner bear injustice than bring disgrace upon the Christian community by publicly exposing their misdeeds in the civil courts.

6:9 the unrighteous will not inherit the kingdom of God. See

not be deceived: [x]neither the sexually immoral, nor idolaters, nor adulterers, nor
men who practice homosexuality,[1] **10** nor
thieves, nor the greedy, nor drunkards, nor re-
vilers, nor swindlers will inherit the kingdom of God. **11** And [y]such were some of
you. But [z]you were washed, [a]you were sanctified, [b]you were justified in the name of
the Lord Jesus Christ and by the Spirit of
our God.

Flee Sexual Immorality

12 [c]"All things are lawful for me," but not
all things are helpful. "All things are lawful
for me," but I will not be enslaved by anything. **13** [d]"Food is meant for the stomach
and the stomach for food"—and God will
destroy both one [e]and the other. The body
is not meant for sexual immorality, but [f]for
the Lord, and [g]the Lord for the body. **14** And
[h]God raised the Lord and [i]will also raise us
up [j]by his power. **15** Do you not know that
[k]your bodies are members of Christ? Shall I
then take the members of Christ and make
them members of a prostitute? Never! **16** Or
do you not know that he who is joined[2] to
a prostitute becomes one body with her?
For, as it is written, [l]"The two will become
one flesh." **17** But he who is joined to the
Lord [m]becomes one spirit with him. **18** [n]Flee
from sexual immorality. Every other sin[3] a
person commits is outside the body, but
the sexually immoral person [o]sins against
his own body. **19** Or [p]do you not know that
your body is a temple of the Holy Spirit
within you, whom you have from God?
[q]You are not your own, **20** [r]for you were
bought with a price. [s]So glorify God in your
body.

Principles for Marriage

7 Now concerning the matters about
which you wrote: [t]"It is good for a
man not to have sexual relations with a

9 [x]ch. 15:50; Gal. 5:21; Eph. 5:5; 1 Tim. 1:9; Heb. 12:14; 13:4; Rev. 21:8; 22:15 **11** [y]ch. 12:2; Eph. 2:2, 3; 4:22; 5:8; Col. 3:7; Tit. 3:3 [z]Acts 22:16; Heb. 10:22; [Tit. 3:5] [a]See ch. 1:2 [b]Rom. 8:30 **12** [c]ch. 10:23 **13** [d][Matt. 15:17] [e]Col. 2:22 [f]ver. 15, 19 [g][Eph. 5:23] **14** [h]See Acts 2:24 [i]ch. 15:22, 23; [John 6:39, 40] [j]Matt. 22:29; [Eph. 1:19, 20] **15** [k]ver. 13; Eph. 5:30; [ch. 12:27; Rom. 12:5] **16** [l]Matt. 19:5; Mark 10:8; Eph. 5:31; Cited from Gen. 2:24

17 [m]Eph. 4:4; [John 17:21-23] **18** [n]2 Cor. 12:21; Eph. 5:3 [o][Prov. 5:11] **19** [p][John 2:21]; See ch. 3:16 [q]See Rom. 14:7 **20** [r]ch. 7:23; [Acts 20:28; Heb. 9:12, 14]; See 2 Pet. 2:1 [s][Phil. 1:20]
Chapter 7 **1** [t]ver. 8, 26

1 The two Greek terms translated by this phrase refer to the passive and active partners in consensual homosexual acts 2 Or *who holds fast* (compare Genesis 2:24 and Deuteronomy 10:20); also verse 17 3 Or *Every sin*

"Antinomianism" at 1 John 3:7. That the things of this world are incompatible with the kingdom of God is a recurring principle in Scripture (15:50; Gal. 5:21). The question arises whether anyone at all can be saved, since all are wicked. Paul's answer is twofold: on the one hand, God delights in justifying the wicked (Rom. 4:5); on the other hand, those whom God justifies (declares righteous because of Christ's death) He also sanctifies (leads into a holy way of life; Rom. 6:1–4). Paul is confident that the Corinthians are true believers, justified and sanctified (v. 11 note), and that their present misbehavior is an anomaly that can be corrected. But it must be corrected. Persistence in wickedness would be an indication that their faith is false and that they have no place in the kingdom.

6:11 But you were washed. See notes 1:2; 5:7; theological note "Sanctification: The Spirit and the Flesh."

6:12, 13 Paul may be quoting sayings, probably common in Corinth, that were used to excuse immoral behavior. The apostle's response suggests that, even if there is an element of truth in these slogans, the Corinthians have perverted it. Indeed, his qualifications have the effect of denying the very point of the sayings, and he ends by emphasizing the noble purpose for which God has given us a body.

6:14 will also raise us up. This reference to the Resurrection is unexpected here, and probably reflects the connection between inadequate doctrine and deficient life. Being exposed to Greek thought, many of the Corinthians appear to have had contempt for the body, even to the extent of denying the future bodily resurrection (ch. 15; 15:35 note). With such a weak doctrine, some of them may have regarded sexual relationships as inherently sinful because they take place through the body (7:1–5). A different group, influenced by the same false doctrine, apparently took the opposite view: since what one does with the body does not matter, even promiscuous sexual behavior is not wrong.

6:15 your bodies are members of Christ. The doctrine of the believer's union with Christ is one of the most fundamental teachings of the apostle. What is significant about this verse is that it represents that union as involving the whole person, not only the body (Rom. 12:1). The Corinthians are wrong in thinking that sexual union with a prostitute, just because it is physical, does not affect their relationship with Christ.

6:16, 17 one body with her . . . one spirit with him. The contrast is not that union with Christ is spiritual while union with a prostitute is physical; Paul has emphasized in v. 15 that union with Christ involves the body, a point developed in vv. 18–20. "One spirit" probably refers to the Holy Spirit (see 15:45 note). Through the Holy Spirit we (spirit and body) have become one with Christ, and this sublime union forbids giving our bodies to prostitutes. If what Paul condemns here had to do with the prostitutes who served at the temple of the goddess Aphrodite, the religious implications of the Corinthians' immorality would be even more obvious (10:20).

6:18 outside the body. The meaning of this passage is disputed. There seem to be many sins that are against the body. Nevertheless, in Paul's teaching the physical union involved in sexual immorality has special consequences because it interferes with our Christian identity as people who have been united with Christ through the Holy Spirit. It is perhaps significant that Paul's prohibition in this verse ("Flee from sexual immorality") is expressed in the same way as the command against idolatry (10:14).

6:19 a temple of the Holy Spirit. Here Paul applies to the individual the concept of the church as the new temple where God dwells (3:16 note). While we must be aware of this personal character of the Holy Spirit's indwelling, the emphasis in Scripture is on the corporate identity of God's people as a holy temple and a spiritual house (Eph. 2:19–22; 1 Pet. 2:4, 5).

7:1 Now concerning the matters about which you wrote. See Introduction: Date and Occasion.

It is good for a man not to have sexual relations with a woman. Very possibly this saying was used by an ascetic group among the Corinthian Christians who condemned sexual promiscuity and argued that Christians should avoid marriage and abstain from sexual relations even in marriage. The apostle had to be careful lest his teaching be distorted in one direction or another. Paul does not simply dismiss the slogan; he too opposes sexual immorality, and he recognizes a certain value in remaining unmarried (vv. 7, 8). He can give specific and valid reasons why a Christian may decide to stay single (vv. 29–35). But he must correct those who demand celibacy. In different contexts, Paul will speak of marriage in only positive terms (e.g., Eph. 5:22–33; 1 Tim. 3:2) and he condemns those who forbid marriage (1 Tim. 4:3).

woman." 2 But because of the temptation to
sexual immorality, each man should have
his own wife and each woman her own
husband. 3 [u]The husband should give to his
wife her conjugal rights, and likewise the
wife to her husband. 4 For the wife does not
have authority over her own body, but the
husband does. Likewise the husband does
not have authority over his own body, but
the wife does. 5 [v]Do not deprive one another, except perhaps by agreement for a limited time, that you may devote yourselves
to prayer; but then come together again,
[w]so that Satan may not tempt you because
of your lack of self-control.

6 Now as a concession, [x]not a command,
I say this.[1] 7 [y]I wish that all were [z]as I
myself am. But [a]each has his own gift from
God, [b]one of one kind and one of another.

8 To the unmarried and the widows I say
that [c]it is good for them to remain single
[d]as I am. 9 But if they cannot exercise
self-control, [e]they should marry. For it is
better to marry than to be aflame with
passion.

10 To the married [f]I give this charge (not
I, but the Lord): [g]the wife should not separate from her husband 11 (but if she does,
[h]she should remain unmarried or else be
reconciled to her husband), and [g]the husband should not divorce his wife.

12 To the rest I say (I, not the Lord) that if
any brother has a wife who is an unbeliever, and she consents to live with him, he
should not divorce her. 13 If any woman has
a husband who is an unbeliever, and he
consents to live with her, she should not
divorce him. 14 For the unbelieving husband is made holy because of his wife, and
the unbelieving wife is made holy because
of her husband. [i]Otherwise your children
would be unclean, but as it is, they are
holy. 15 But if the unbelieving partner separates, let it be so. In such cases the brother
or sister is not enslaved. God has called
you[2] [j]to peace. 16 Wife, how do you know
[k]whether you will save your husband?
Husband, how do you know whether you
will save your wife?

Live As You Are Called

17 Only let each person lead the life [l]that
the Lord has assigned to him, and to which
God has called him. [m]This is my rule in [n]all
the churches. 18 Was anyone at the time of
his call already circumcised? Let him not
seek to remove the marks of circumcision.

3 [u]Ex. 21:10
5 [v][Ex. 19:15; 1 Sam. 21:4; Eccles. 3:5; Zech. 12:12-14] [w]1 Thess. 3:5
6 [x]ver. 12, 25; 2 Cor. 8:8; [ver. 10, 40]
7 [y][Acts 26:29] [z]ver. 8; [ch. 9:5] [a]ch. 12:4, 11; 1 Pet. 4:10; [Rom. 12:6] [b]Matt. 19:11, 12
8 [c]ver. 1, 26 [d]ver. 7
9 [e][1 Tim. 5:14]
10 [f]See ver. 6 [g]Mal. 2:16; See Matt. 5:32
11 [h]Mark 10:12
[g][See ver. 10 above]
14 [i]Ezra; 9:2 Mal. 2:15
15 [j]Col. 3:15; See Rom. 14:19
16 [k]1 Pet. 3:1; See Rom. 11:14
17 [l]See Rom. 12:3 [m]ch. 4:17 [n]2 Cor. 8:18; 11:28

[1] Or *I say this:* [2] Some manuscripts *us*

7:3–5 These are remarkable verses in that they reveal viewpoints that appear to be far ahead of their time: a healthy perception of the woman's sexuality, and an understanding of the complete equality that exists between a man and a woman in the most intimate area of their relationship. The Scripture gives no support whatever to the notion that sexual relations are solely at the direction and for the enjoyment of the husband. The apostle allows for temporary abstention from sex (in a way similar to fasting; v. 5), but he does not allow protracted abstinence. God requires sexual union as part of marriage.

7:6–9 The "concession" probably refers to the brief periods of abstinence in v. 5: spouses may—but need not—deprive each other for a short period and for a specific reason. There are certain advantages for the work of the kingdom in remaining unmarried, and so Paul personally can wish that every believer would give his or her life exclusively to the advance of the gospel. But the apostle realizes that such a situation is not possible for everyone and would only lead many Christians into sexual temptation. Moreover, there are other reasons why one should marry that are not relevant to the present discussion (v. 1 note).

7:10 not I, but the Lord. In v. 12, Paul says, "I, not the Lord," but Paul is not suggesting that there is an opposition between what he says and what the Lord says. With regard to the problem treated in vv. 10, 11, there was a well-known instruction given by Jesus during His earthly ministry (Mark 10:1–12). In vv. 12–16, however, Paul discusses a difficult situation that had not been addressed by the Lord. His apostolic commands, however, come by inspiration and have divine authority, as 14:37 makes clear.

7:11 if she does. In spite of the Lord's command, it appears that some of the wives in Corinth, influenced by an ascetic viewpoint (v. 1), had in fact left their husbands. Because spouses are committed to each other until death (v. 39), even if they depart they may not remarry.

7:12 I, not the Lord. See note on v. 10.

who is an unbeliever. This is the special circumstance about which Jesus had left no direct instructions. If one spouse has been converted and the other not, should the marriage be dissolved, especially if the unbelieving spouse separates?

7:14 made holy. A striking affirmation of the special character of the home in which at least one parent is a believer (1:2 note). In Old Testament language, the whole family is regarded as being in covenant with God. Even the spouse who refuses to believe comes under the influence of God's work—much more so the children who are not old enough to profess their faith. Accordingly, Reformed theology has viewed this verse as providing part of the rationale for the baptism of children.

7:15 is not enslaved. Some interpret this statement to mean that if the unbelieving spouse deserts the marriage, the believing partner may remarry. The thrust of this passage, however, is simply that a Christian is not obligated to insist that the marriage remain intact. Such an insistence would prevent them from living in "peace."

7:16 whether you will save. Paul may be returning to the thought of v. 14 and giving a reason why Christians should not leave their unbelieving spouses: since they are in some sense "sanctified," there is a good possibility that they will be saved. Alternatively, v. 16 may explain v. 15: let the unbeliever go, because you have no assurance that he or she will be saved by being forced to stay married.

7:17 let each person lead the life . . . God has called him. The following verses make clear that the phrase "God has called him" is not a reference to a social position but to conversion itself. Note that vv. 17–24 set forth a principle that gives coherence to the whole chapter: becoming a believer does not require a change in status, whether marital, ethnic, or social (vv. 8, 20, 26). This verse has sometimes been misused as evidence that Christians should not attempt to improve their social or economic standing. On the contrary, Paul encourages slaves to obtain their freedom if the opportunity arises (v. 21).

Was anyone at the time of his call uncircumcised? [o]Let him not seek circumcision.
19 [p]For neither circumcision counts for anything nor uncircumcision, but [q]keeping the
commandments of God. 20 [r]Each one
should remain in the condition in which
he was called. 21 Were you a slave[1] when
called? Do not be concerned about it. But
if you can gain your freedom, avail yourself
of the opportunity. 22 For he who was called
in the Lord as a slave is [s]a freedman of the
Lord. Likewise he who was free when
called is [t]a slave of Christ. 23 [u]You were
bought with a price; [v]do not become slaves
of men. 24 So, brothers,[2] [w]in whatever condition each was called, there let him
remain with God.

The Unmarried and the Widowed

25 Now concerning[3] the betrothed,[4] [x]I
have no command from the Lord, but I give
my judgment as [y]one who by the Lord's
mercy is [z]trustworthy. 26 I think that in view
of the present[5] distress [a]it is good for a person to remain as he is. 27 Are you bound to
a wife? Do not seek to be free. Are you free
from a wife? Do not seek a wife. 28 But if
you do marry, you have not sinned, and if
a betrothed woman[6] marries, she has not
sinned. Yet those who marry will have
worldly troubles, and I would spare you
that. 29 This is what I mean, brothers: [b]the
appointed time has grown very short. From
now on, let those who have wives live as
though they had none, 30 and those who
mourn as though they were not mourning,
and those who rejoice as though they were
not rejoicing, and those who buy [c]as
though they had no goods, 31 and those
who deal with the world as though they
had no dealings with it. For [d]the present
form of this world is passing away.
32 I want you to be [e]free from anxieties.
[f]The unmarried man is anxious about the
things of the Lord, how to please the Lord.
33 But the married man is anxious about
worldly things, how to please his wife,
34 and his interests are divided. And the
unmarried or betrothed woman is anxious
about the things of the Lord, how to be
holy in body and spirit. But the married
woman is anxious about worldly things,
how to please her husband. 35 I say this for
your own benefit, [g]not to lay any restraint
upon you, but to promote good order and
to secure your undivided devotion to the
Lord.
36 If anyone thinks that he is not behaving properly toward his betrothed,[7] if his[8]
passions are strong, and it has to be, let
him do as he wishes: let them marry—it is
no sin. 37 But whoever is firmly established
in his heart, being under no necessity but
having his desire under control, and has
determined this in his heart, to keep her as
his betrothed, he will do well. 38 So then he
who marries his betrothed [h]does well, and
he who refrains from marriage will do even
better.
39 [i]A wife is bound to her husband as

18 [o]Acts 15:1, 5, 19, 24, 28; Gal. 5:2 **19** [p]Gal. 3:28; 5:6; 6:15; Col. 3:11 [q]See 1 John 2:3 **20** [r]ver. 24 **22** [s][Col. 3:24; Philem. 16]; See John 8:36 [t][ch. 9:21; 1 Pet. 2:16] **23** [u]See ch. 6:20 [v]Lev. 25:42, 55 **24** [w]ver. 20 **25** [x]See ver. 6 [y]2 Cor. 4:1; 1 Tim. 1:13, 16 [z]ch. 4:2 **26** [a]ver. 1, 8 **29** [b]See Rom. 13:11

30 [c]2 Cor. 6:10 **31** [d]Ps. 39:6; James 1:10; 1 Pet. 1:24; 4:7; 1 John 2:17 **32** [e]See Matt. 6:25; Luke 10:41 [f][1 Tim. 5:5] **35** [g][Prov. 22:25] **38** [h]Heb. 13:4 **39** [i]Rom. 7:2

1 Greek *bondservant*; also twice in verse 22 and once in verse 23 (plural) 2 Or *brothers and sisters*; also verse 29 3 The expression *Now concerning* introduces a reply to a question in the Corinthians' letter; see 7:1 4 Greek *virgins* 5 Or *impending* 6 Greek *virgin*; also verse 34 7 Greek *virgin*; also verses 37, 38 8 Or *her*

7:19 The first part of this verse is paralleled in Gal. 5:6 and 6:15. It would seem that the second part ("keeping the commandments of God") is another way of saying, "faith working through love" (Gal. 5:6), and that such working faith is what characterizes the "new creation" (Gal. 6:15).

7:21 Do not be concerned. The desire to attain a better condition is not wrong, as the rest of the verse makes clear. However, Paul does not want Christians troubling themselves about a situation that cannot be changed. Dissatisfaction and complaint can be fatal spiritually (10:10): they reflect lack of confidence in God.

7:23 bought with a price. This statement supports v. 22 (cf. 6:20). If we truly understood whose we are, we would realize that even slavery cannot damage our privileged position in Christ. Conversely, even the greatest human master is only a humble servant before Christ. Therefore, Christians need not, and must not, "become slaves of men."

7:25 Now concerning the betrothed. A new, but related topic that the Corinthians had raised in their letter to Paul (Introduction: Date and Occasion).

I have no command from the Lord. See note on v. 10.

I give my judgment. This language suggests that the comments Paul is about to make are not absolute commandments concerning right-or-wrong moral choices, but recommendations for a particular situation. This interpretation is confirmed by the statement in v. 28 and by the concluding words in v. 38.

7:26 the present distress. Lit. "the present necessity." Some believe that Paul is referring to a specific and unusual problem in Corinth. However, the language of v. 28 ("will have worldly troubles") suggests a more general idea: the predicament that faces all Christians as they seek to serve Christ in the present evil age (Gal. 1:4). We must consider this factor when making a decision about marriage, though other considerations should also be kept in mind (vv. 6–9 note).

7:29–31 the appointed time . . . very short . . . this world is passing away. The Christian life must be lived in the realization that there is no time to waste (Rom. 13:11, 12).

7:36–38 There are two different ways of understanding this passage. We simply do not know for certain whether Paul is addressing men who have deferred marriage to their fiancee ("betrothed") or fathers who have not permitted their daughters to marry. However, the main idea is clear: both married and unmarried status are good options, even though Paul sees a particular benefit in remaining unmarried.

7:39 is bound. Marriage is a life commitment.

long as he lives. But if her husband dies,
she is free to be married to whom she
wishes, only [j]in the Lord. 40 Yet [k]in my
judgment she is happier if she remains as
she is. And I think [l]that I too have the
Spirit of God.

Food Offered to Idols

8 Now concerning[1] [m]food offered to
idols: we know that [n]"all of us possess
knowledge." This "knowledge" [o]puffs up,
[p]but love builds up. 2 [q]If anyone imagines
that he knows something, [r]he does not yet
know as he ought to know. 3 But if anyone
loves God, [s]he is known by God.[2]

4 Therefore, as to the eating of food
offered to idols, we know that [t]"an idol has
no real existence," and that [u]"there is no
God but one." 5 For although there may be
[v]so-called gods in heaven or on earth—as
indeed there are many "gods" and many
"lords"— 6 yet [w]for us there is one God, the
Father, [x]from whom are all things and for
whom we exist, and [y]one Lord, Jesus
Christ, through whom are all things and
[z]through whom we exist.

7 However, not all possess this knowledge. But some, [a]through former association with idols, eat food as really offered to
an idol, and [b]their conscience, being weak,
is defiled. 8 [c]Food will not commend us to
God. We are no worse off if we do not eat,
and no better off if we do. 9 But take care
[d]that this right of yours does not somehow
become a stumbling block [e]to the weak.
10 For if anyone sees you who have knowledge eating[3] in an idol's temple, will he not
be encouraged,[4] if his conscience is weak,
to eat food offered to idols? 11 And so by
your knowledge this weak person is [f]de-
stroyed, the brother for whom Christ died.
12 Thus, sinning against your brothers[5] and
[g]wounding their conscience when it is
weak, [h]you sin against Christ. 13 Therefore,
[i]if food makes my brother stumble, I will
never eat meat, lest I make my brother
stumble.

Paul Surrenders His Rights

9 [j]Am I not free? [k]Am I not an apostle?
[l]Have I not seen Jesus our Lord? [m]Are
not you my workmanship in the Lord? 2 If
to others I am not an apostle, at least I am
to you, for you are [n]the seal of my apostleship in the Lord.

3 This is my defense to those who would

39 [j][2 Cor. 6:14] 40 [k]See ver. 6 [l][Acts 15:28]
Chapter 8 1 [m]ver. 4, 7, 10; See Acts 15:29 [n]See Rom. 15:14 [o]Rom. 14:3 [p]ch. 13:4-13 2 [q]Gal. 6:3 [ch. 3:18] [r][ch. 13:8, 9, 12; 1 Tim. 6:3, 4] 3 [s]Gal. 4:9; [Ex. 33:12, 17; Jer. 1:5; Nah. 1:7; 2 Tim. 2:19] 4 [t]ch. 10:19; Isai. 41:24; [Acts 14:15] [u]ver. 6; See Deut. 4:35, 39 5 [v]2 Thess. 2:4 6 [w]ver. 4; Mal. 2:10; Eph. 4:6 [x]See Rom. 11:36 [y]Eph. 4:5; [ch. 1:2; 1 Tim. 2:5]; See John 13:13 [z]John 1:3; Col. 1:16 7 [a][Rom. 14:14, 22, 23] [b]ch. 10:25, 28, 29 8 [c]Rom. 14:17 9 [d][ch. 10:23; Rom. 14:21; Gal. 5:13] [e]Rom. 14:1, 2

11 [f]Rom. 14:15, 20 12 [g][Zech. 2:8; Matt. 18:6] [h][Matt. 25:45] 13 [i]Rom. 14:13, 21; [2 Cor. 6:3; 11:29]
Chapter 9 1 [j]ver. 19 [k]Acts 14:14; 2 Cor. 12:12; 1 Thess. 2:6; [2 Cor. 10:7; Rev. 2:2] [l]ch. 15:8; Acts 9:3, 17; 18:9; 22:14, 18; 23:11 [m]See ch. 3:6 2 [n][2 Cor. 3:2]

[1] The expression *Now concerning* introduces a reply to a question in the Corinthians' letter; see 7:1 [2] Greek *him* [3] Greek *reclining at table* [4] Or *fortified*; Greek *built up* [5] Or *brothers and sisters*

free to be married. A widow, no less than the others treated in this chapter, has the choice to remain unmarried or to marry. The only consideration is that if she marries again the new spouse must be a Christian.

8:1 Now concerning food offered to idols. The Corinthians had raised the issue of idolatry dealt with in chs. 8–10, but the precise nature of their question is difficult to determine. According to some interpreters, the issues discussed in ch. 8 and in 10:25–30 are one and the same. Others, on the basis of 8:10, argue that ch. 8 deals with the serious problem that some Christians were attending pagan feasts and eating the food served there, while 10:25–30 concerns the lesser problem of meat purchased in the market.

all of us possess knowledge. Paul addresses the sin of arrogance as an introduction to the subject of idolatry (vv. 1–3). These comments reveal that behind the behavior of the Corinthians (or at least an important group among them) lay a serious problem of attitude. Their conduct was not guided by love (cf. ch. 13) but by pride.

8:3 known by God. The Corinthians should be less concerned about what they know than about who knows them (cf. 13:12).

8:4 an idol has no real existence. Apparently some of the Corinthians used the doctrine of monotheism as an argument supporting their practice: if there is only one God, who teaches us to mock idols (Is. 46:6, 7), why should we worry about eating food offered to them? Paul acknowledges this truth and affirms it (vv. 4–6), but goes on to point out an error in the Corinthians' use of this doctrine.

8:7 not all possess. Believers who have weak consciences are unable to dissociate various elements in pagan rituals from idolatry itself. When they eat food offered to idols, their conscience becomes "defiled." Such strong language (cf. "destroyed" in v. 11) suggests that these weak Christians are sinning not merely because they think they are doing something wrong, but because they have fallen back into their idolatrous ways.

8:10 eating in an idol's temple. See note on v. 1 (cf. 10:18–22).

8:11 by your knowledge. What was a source of pride for some of the Corinthians became the instrument that harmed others (v. 1 note).

destroyed. See note on v. 7.

8:12 wounding their conscience. Although the conscience is not infallible, it is a serious matter to violate it or tempt others to do so.

8:13 I will never eat meat. This concluding comment is intended to set forth the basic principle of love: seeking the good of others above one's own (10:24, 33; 13:5; Phil. 2:4).

9:1 Am I not free. Paul's willingness to forgo some of his rights is an illustration of the principle he stated in 8:9. The questions in v. 1 indicate that some of the Corinthians defended their conduct by questioning Paul's authority and criticizing his behavior.

9:3 those who would examine me. This statement makes explicit that Paul had indeed been criticized, though scholars debate the specific nature of the complaint (2:1 note). The next ten verses contain more than a dozen rhetorical questions that reflect Paul's deep emotion and provide clues about the historical situation. Paul defends his right to be supported by the churches, only to emphasize his choice not to receive support (vv. 15–18). Perhaps some of the Corinthians were upset because Paul refused their patronage, and concluded from this that he was not a legitimate apostle (2 Cor. 11:7–12). If not, why should they listen to his instruction?

examine me. 4 [o]Do we not have the right to
eat and drink? 5 [p]Do we not have the right
to take along a believing wife,[1] as do the
other apostles and [q]the brothers of the
Lord and [r]Cephas? 6 Or is it only Barnabas
and I who have no right to refrain from
working for a living? 7 [s]Who serves as a soldier at his own expense? [t]Who plants a
vineyard without eating any of its fruit? Or
who tends a flock without getting some of
the milk?

8 Do I say these things on human authority? Does not the Law say the same? 9 For it
is written in the Law of Moses, [u]"You shall
not muzzle an ox when it treads out the
grain." Is it for oxen that God is concerned? 10 Does he not speak entirely for
our sake? It was written [v]for our sake,
because [w]the plowman should plow in
hope and the thresher thresh in hope of
sharing in the crop. 11 [x]If we have sown
spiritual things among you, is it too much
if we reap material things from you? 12 If
others share this rightful claim on you, do
not we even more?

Nevertheless, [y]we have not made use of
this right, but we endure anything [z]rather
than put an obstacle in the way of the
gospel of Christ. 13 Do you not know that
[a]those who are employed in the temple
service get their food from the temple, and
those who serve at the altar share in the
sacrificial offerings? 14 In the same way, the
Lord commanded that [b]those who proclaim the gospel should get their living by
the gospel.

15 But [c]I have made no use of any of these
rights, nor am I writing these things to
secure any such provision. For I would
rather die than have anyone [d]deprive me of
my ground for boasting. 16 For if I preach
the gospel, that gives me no ground for
boasting. For [e]necessity is laid upon me.
Woe to me if I do not preach the gospel!
17 For if I do this of my own will, I have a
reward, but not of my own will, I am still
entrusted with [f]a stewardship. 18 What then
is my reward? That in my preaching [g]I may
present the gospel free of charge, so as not
to make full use of my right in the gospel.

19 For [h]though I am free from all, [i]I have
made myself a servant to all, that I might
[j]win more of them. 20 [k]To the Jews I became
as a Jew, in order to win Jews. To those
under the law I became as one under the
law (though not being myself under the
law) that I might win those under the law.
21 To [l]those outside the law I became [m]as
one outside the law (not being outside the
law of God but [n]under the law of Christ)
that I might win those outside the law.
22 [o]To the weak I became weak, that I might
win the weak. [p]I have become all things to
all people, that [q]by all means I might save
some. 23 I do it all for the sake of the gospel,
[r]that I may share with them in its blessings.

24 Do you not know that in a race all the
runners compete, but only one receives
[s]the prize? So [t]run that you may obtain it.

4 [o]ver. 14; 1 Thess. 2:6, 9; 2 Thess. 3:8, 9
5 [p][ch. 7:7] [q]See Matt. 12:46; [r]Matt. 8:14; See John 1:42
7 [s]2 Cor. 10:4; 1 Tim. 1:18; 2 Tim. 2:3, 4 [t][ch. 3:6-8; Deut. 20:6; Prov. 27:18; S. of S. 8:12]
9 [u]1 Tim. 5:18; Cited from Deut. 25:4
10 [v]See Rom. 4:24 [w]2 Tim. 2:6
11 [x][Rom. 15:27; Gal. 6:6]
12 [y]ver. 15, 18; See Acts 20:33 [z][2 Cor. 6:3; 11:12]
13 [a]Lev. 6:16, 26; 7:6; Num. 5:9, 10; 18:8-20; Deut. 18:1
14 [b]ver. 4; Matt. 10:10
15 [c]See Acts 18:3 [d]2 Cor. 11:10
16 [e][Acts 4:20; 9:6; Rom. 1:14]
17 [f]ch. 4:1; Gal. 2:7; [Phil. 1:16]
18 [g]2 Cor. 11:7; 12:13
19 [h]ver. 1; [ch. 10:29] [i][Gal. 5:13] [j]Matt. 18:15; 1 Pet. 3:1
20 [k]Acts 16:3; 21:23-26,
21 [l]Rom. 2:12, 14 [m][Gal. 2:3; 3:2] [n]See ch. 7:22
22 [o]2 Cor. 11:29 [p]ch. 10:33 [q]ch. 7:16; Rom. 11:14 **23** [r][ch. 10:24] **24** [s]Phil. 3:14; Col. 2:18 [t]Gal. 2:2; 5:7; Phil. 2:16; Heb. 12:1; [2 Tim. 4:7]

[1] Greek *a sister as wife*

9:5 a believing wife. The Corinthians themselves may have raised this issue, as though the lack of a wife discredited Paul and Barnabas, or it may be Paul's choice of an illustration to indicate the distinction between having a right and exercising it. Both Paul and Barnabas were unmarried at the time of their missionary work. Paul takes for granted that if he were to be married, it would be with a believer.

9:10 for our sake. It may appear that Paul denies the original meaning of Deut. 25:4, which commands Israelites to allow their oxen to eat as they work. We should remember that the whole complex of laws in Israel constantly reminded the community of religious principles. Some scholars have suggested that the command not to muzzle the ox was intended to reinforce the instructions about human relationships mentioned in the immediate context (Deut. 24:5–25:4).

9:12 we have not made use of this right. In spite of the strain caused by his secular work added to the heavy demands of his apostolic ministry, Paul was determined not to become a burden to the churches (1 Thess. 2:6–9). It appears from 2 Cor. 11:7–12 that the Corinthians misinterpreted Paul's motives. For reasons that are unclear, the apostle did make an exception in the case of the Philippian church in Macedonia (Phil. 4:15, 16).

9:14 get their living by the gospel. This principle is reflected not only in the Old Testament priesthood (v. 13) but also in several New Testament passages (e.g., Luke 10:7; Gal. 6:6; 1 Tim. 5:17, 18).

9:15, 16 no ground for boasting. As the rest of the passage makes clear, Paul considered that he could hardly boast about preaching since he was compelled by God's will to preach. So his ground for boasting (his "reward") is that he preaches free of charge (v. 18), and he will not allow anyone to take this away from him.

9:19 though I am free. Paul returns to the first question of v. 1. It appears that Paul must defend himself from the charge of inconsistency: he exercised freedom in his own behavior and therefore should not deprive others from doing the same. The apostle will return to this theme again in 10:23–33.

9:20 as one under the law. When ministering to Jews, Paul conformed to the Old Testament ceremonial regulations even though he knew that these matters were not essential. See "The Three Purposes of the Law" at Deut. 13:10.

9:21 as one outside the law. When ministering to Gentiles, Paul was willing to live like them, while recognizing that he was never free to disobey God.

9:22 weak. A restatement of the point made in 8:13.

9:24 run that you may obtain it. Paul elsewhere uses the illustration of

25 Every [u]athlete exercises self-control in all
things. They do it to receive a perishable
wreath, but we [v]an imperishable. 26 So I do
not run aimlessly; I [w]do not box as one
[x]beating the air. 27 But I discipline my body
and [y]keep it under control,[1] lest after
preaching to others [z]I myself should be
[a]disqualified.

Warning Against Idolatry

10 I want you to know, brothers,[2] that
our fathers were all under [b]the
cloud, and all [c]passed through the sea,
2 and all were baptized into Moses in the
cloud and in the sea, 3 and [d]all ate the same
[e]spiritual food, 4 and [f]all drank the same
spiritual drink. For they drank from the spiritual Rock that followed them, and the
Rock was Christ. 5 Nevertheless, with most
of them God was not pleased, for [g]they
were overthrown in the wilderness.

6 Now these things took place as examples for us, that we might not desire evil as
[h]they did. 7 [i]Do not be idolaters [j]as some of
them were; as it is written, [k]"The people
sat down to eat and drink and rose up to
play." 8 [l]We must not indulge in sexual
immorality [m]as some of them did, and
[n]twenty-three thousand fell in a single day.
9 We must not put Christ[3] to the test, [o]as
some of them did and [p]were destroyed by
serpents, 10 nor grumble, [q]as some of them
did and [r]were destroyed by [s]the Destroyer.
11 Now these things happened to them as
an example, but [t]they were written down
for our instruction, [u]on whom the end of
the ages has come. 12 Therefore [v]let anyone
who thinks that he stands take heed lest he
fall. 13 No temptation has overtaken you
that is not common to man. [w]God is faithful, and [x]he will not let you be tempted
beyond your ability, but with the temptation he will also provide the way of escape,
that you may be able to endure it.

14 Therefore, my beloved, [y]flee from idolatry. 15 I speak [z]as to sensible people; judge
for yourselves what I say. 16 [a]The cup of
blessing that we bless, is it not a participa-

25 [u]1 Tim. 6:12; 2 Tim. 2:5; 4:7; [Jude 3] [v]See James 1:12 **26** [w][Heb. 12:4] [x][ch. 14:9] **27** [y][Rom. 6:19] [z][S. of S. 1:6] [a][Jer. 6:30; Rom. 1:28; Heb. 6:8] **Chapter 10** **1** [b]See Ex. 13:21 [c]See Ex. 14:22 **3** [d]Ex. 16:15, 35; Deut. 8:3; Neh. 9:15, 20; Ps. 78:24 [e]Ps. 78:25; 105:40; John 6:31 **4** [f]See Ex. 17:6 **5** [g]Num. 14:29, 37; 26:64, 65; Ps. 106:26; Heb. 3:17; Jude 5 **6** [h]Num. 11:4, 33, 34; Ps. 78:18; 106:14 **7** [i]ver. 14 [j]Ex. 32:4 [k]Cited from Ex. 32:6 **8** [l]See ch. 6:18; Acts 15:20 [m]Num. 25:1

[n][Num. 25:9; Ps. 106:29] **9** [o]Num. 21:5; [Ex. 17:2, 7]; See Ps. 78:18 [p]See Num. 21:6 **10** [q]See Num. 14:2 [r]Num. 14:29-37 [s]Ex. 12:23; 2 Sam. 24:16; 1 Chr. 21:15; Ps. 78:49 **11** [t]See Rom. 4:23 [u]See Rom. 13:11 **12** [v]Rom. 11:20; [2 Pet. 3:17] **13** [w]See ch. 1:9 [x][Dan. 3:17]; See 2 Pet. 2:9 **14** [y]ver. 7 **15** [z][ch. 8:1] **16** [a]ch. 11:25; Matt. 26:27, 28

1 Greek *I pummel my body and make it a slave* 2 Or *brothers and sisters*
3 Some manuscripts *the Lord*

a race and its prize to emphasize the need for single-mindedness, determination, and perseverance (Phil. 3:12–14; 2 Tim. 4:7, 8).

9:27 I discipline my body. He continues the athletic metaphor by reminding his readers that fighters must discipline their bodies if they expect to win. Similarly, Christians must be willing to set aside their selfish interests for the sake of their primary goal.

lest . . . I myself should be disqualified. This statement has often been used as evidence that Christians can lose their salvation. The witness of the New Testament and of Paul in particular is that those whom God has brought to Himself are His forever (Rom. 8:28–30) because the life they have been given is eternal in character (John 5:24; Heb. 7:16). What God has begun He will bring to completion (Phil. 1:6). However, it would be wrong to dismiss or minimize Paul's concern (cf. 15:2; Phil. 3:11; Col. 1:23) by suggesting that it is merely hypothetical or relates only to rewards and not salvation. Paul was confident that absolutely nothing would be able to separate him from God's love (Rom. 8:38–39), but he never presumed that he was saved regardless of what he did. No Christian can afford to take lightly the warnings of Scripture (10:12).

10:2 all were baptized into Moses. Christian baptism stresses the union of the believer with Christ, and Paul uses the language of baptism in comparing the Israelites and the Corinthians (5:12, 13 note). All the Israelites went through the ordeal and deliverance of the Exodus by virtue of their identification with their leader, Moses. Note the repetition of "all" in vv. 1–3 (also 12:13). "All" the members of the Corinthian church have been baptized into Christ, and have therefore had a taste of God's deliverance, but that does not guarantee that God is pleased with each one without exception. This passage illustrates and explains the warning in 9:24–27.

10:3, 4 the same spiritual food . . . the same spiritual drink. Following the analogy with baptism, Paul warns the Corinthians not to find false comfort in their participation in the Lord's Supper (vv. 14–22). The Israelites also experienced divinely given food and drink. Here "spiritual" does not mean "immaterial"; nor does it merely suggest that the manna and the water had a deeper significance. Paul probably has in mind the activity of the Holy Spirit (2:6, 14; 3:1; 15:44–46; and notes). The Israelites had received a supernatural provision associated with the work of the Spirit.

the Rock was Christ. In the Old Testament, God is often compared with a rock, and Israel (called "Jeshurun") is described as having forsaken God, the "Rock of his salvation" (Deut. 32:15; cf. Ex. 17:6). The analogy between the Israelites and the Corinthians is not an arbitrary illustration; there is a theological connection. Without minimizing the privileges enjoyed by Christians (v. 11 note), Paul reminds us that the Deliverer of the Israelites was none other than our crucified and risen Savior.

10:6 examples. The Greek word is related to the English term "type" (so also in v. 11). Possibly the use of this word further indicates that the events of the wilderness have a divinely intended correspondence with the experiences of the Christian church.

10:11 the end of the ages has come. This statement reflects Paul's conviction that the coming of Christ inaugurated the "last days" (Heb. 1:2), the time when the great promises of the Old Testament come to pass (cf. 1:20 note). By pointing out this theme, Paul helps the Corinthians to realize that the Old Testament events looked forward and applied to them. Moreover, these facts suggest that, given their privileged position, the Corinthians ought to recognize their greater responsibility (cf. Heb. 11:39, 40).

10:12 take heed lest he fall. See note 9:27.

10:13 This well-known verse has provided great encouragement to Christians faced by temptations. At the same time, Paul's words contain an implicit rebuke. If God keeps us from temptations greater than we can withstand, we cannot plead our temptations as an excuse for sinning. Sin is never a necessity for a believer.

10:14 flee from idolatry. This command is related to Paul's previous remarks about eating food offered to idols (8:1 note). Specifically, Paul is grieved that some of the Corinthians are participating in pagan meals that had an inseparable element of idolatry.

10:16 The cup of blessing . . . The bread that we break. These state-

tion in the blood of Christ? [b]The bread that
we break, is it not a participation in the
body of Christ? 17 Because there is one
bread, we who are many are [c]one body, for
we all partake of the one bread. 18 Consider
[d]the people of Israel:[1] [e]are not those who
eat the sacrifices participants in the altar?
19 What do I imply then? That food offered
to idols is anything, or that [f]an idol is anything? 20 No, I imply that what pagans sacrifice [g]they offer to demons and not to
God. I do not want you to be participants
with demons. 21 [h]You cannot drink the cup
of the Lord and [i]the cup of demons. You
cannot partake of the table of the Lord
and [j]the table of demons. 22 [k]Shall we provoke the Lord to jealousy? [l]Are we stronger
than he?

Do All to the Glory of God

23 [m]"All things are lawful," but not all
things are helpful. "All things are lawful,"
but not all things build up. 24 [n]Let no one
seek his own good, but the good of his
neighbor. 25 [o]Eat whatever is sold in the
meat market without raising any question
on the ground of conscience. 26 For [p]"the
earth is the Lord's, and the fullness thereof." 27 If one of the unbelievers invites you
to dinner and you are disposed to go, [q]eat
whatever is set before you without raising
any question on the ground of conscience.
28 But if someone says to you, "This has
been offered in sacrifice," then do not eat
it, for the sake of the one who informed
you, and for the sake of conscience—29 I do
not mean [r]your conscience, but his. For
[s]why should my liberty be determined by
someone else's conscience? 30 If I partake
with thankfulness, why am I denounced
because of that [t]for which I give thanks?
31 So, whether you eat or drink, or [u]what-
ever you do, do all to the glory of God.
32 [v]Give no offense to Jews or to Greeks or
to [w]the church of God, 33 just as [x]I try to
please everyone in everything I do, [y]not
seeking my own advantage, but that of
many, that they may be saved.

11 [z]Be imitators of me, as I am of
Christ.

Head Coverings

2 Now I commend you [a]because you
remember me in everything and [b]maintain
the traditions [c]even as I delivered them to
you. 3 But I want you to understand that
[d]the head of every man is Christ, [e]the head
of a wife[2] is her husband, and [f]the head of
Christ is God. 4 Every man who prays or
prophesies with his head covered dishonors his head, 5 but every wife who prays or

16 [b]ch. 11:23, 24; Matt. 26:26; See Acts 2:42; 20:7
17 [c]ch. 12:12, 13, 20; Rom. 12:5; Eph. 4:4, 16; Col. 3:15
18 [d]Rom. 1:3; 4:1; 9:5; 2 Cor. 11:18 [e]Lev. 3:3; 7:15; [Heb. 13:10]
19 [f]See ch. 8:4
20 [g]Deut. 32:17
21 [h][2 Cor. 6:15, 16] [i][Deut. 32:38] [j][Isai. 65:11]
22 [k]Deut. 32:21 [l]Eccles. 6:10; Ezek. 22:14
23 [m]ch. 6:12; See ch. 8:9
24 [n]ver. 33; ch. 13:5; Phil. 2:21; [ch. 9:23; 2 Cor. 12:14]; See Rom. 15:1
25 [o]ch. 8:7
26 [p]Cited from Ps. 24:1; [Ex. 9:29; 19:5; Deut. 10:14; Job 41:11; Ps. 50:12]
27 [q]Luke 10:8
29 [r][ch. 8:9-12] [s][ch. 9:19; Rom. 14:16]
30 [t]Rom. 14:6; 1 Tim. 4:3, 4
31 [u]Col. 3:17; 1 Pet. 4:11 32 [v]ch. 8:13; Rom. 14:13; 2 Cor. 6:3 [w][ch. 11:16]; See Acts 20:28 33 [x]ch. 9:22; [Gal. 1:10] [y]See ver. 24
Chapter 11 1 [z]See ch. 4:16 2 [a][ch. 4:17; 1 Thess. 3:6] [b]2 Thess. 2:15; 3:6 [c][1 Thess. 4:1, 2] 3 [d]Eph. 1:22; 4:15; 5:23; Col. 1:18 [e]See Gen. 3:16 [f][ch. 3:23]

[1] Greek *Consider Israel according to the flesh* [2] Greek *gunē*. This term may refer to a *woman* or a *wife*, according to the context

ments about the Lord's Supper demonstrate the significance of taking part in a distinctively religious meal. Just as it would be impossible to take the Lord's Supper and claim that it had no religious significance, so it is naive for the Corinthians to think they can participate in temple feasts without being involved in idolatry. Another point is that the unity "in the body of Christ" symbolized by taking the bread and wine excludes union with idols. See "The Sacraments" at Matt. 28:19.

10:20 participants with demons. Although idols are nothing (v. 19), behind pagan rituals is the reality of Satan's work, and Christians should have nothing to do with that.

10:23 All things are lawful. See note 6:12, 13.

10:25 Eat whatever is sold in the meat market. In spite of his strong words against taking part in idolatrous feasts, Paul does not want the Corinthians to be overly scrupulous. The fact that food is offered to an idol does not change what the food is; it is still part of God's creation. Therefore, the Corinthian believers do not have to ask whether food in the market was brought from the temple, nor do they need to raise the question when invited to a meal (v. 27). They may freely eat what God has provided.

10:28 do not eat it. A different problem arises if someone announces that the meat comes from a pagan sacrifice. Presumably, such a comment indicates that the person has problems of conscience about it. In that case, it is right to abstain "for the sake of the one who informed you."

10:30 why am I denounced. This question makes plain that Paul had been accused of eating meat offered to idols, with the suggestion that he has no right forbidding the Corinthians to do the same (9:19 note).

10:31 do all to the glory of God. See "The Glory of God" at Ezek. 1:28.

10:33 not seeking my own advantage, but that of many. In combination with the desire to do everything for God's glory (v. 31), this principle provided Paul with his criterion of behavior. It is in fact the principle of Christian love, which "does not insist on its own way" (13:5).

11:1 The apostle does not set himself up as an absolute example; he is to be imitated to the extent that he imitates Christ.

11:3 the head. The significance of this metaphor has long been debated by scholars—it may indicate leadership and authority, or source and origin. The evidence from Greek literature is ambiguous, and the present context does not resolve the problem. The two ideas should probably not be regarded as excluding each other. In two other contexts where Paul speaks of Christ as head (Eph. 4:15; Col. 2:19), the notion of "source" may be present (cf. v. 8). Elsewhere Paul uses the metaphor with explicit reference to authority or submission (Eph. 1:22; 5:23, 24; Col. 1:18; 2:10). Here the stress probably falls on authority rather than source (cf. v. 10).

11:4 his head covered. What little evidence that exists seems to indicate that, with few exceptions, men in the first century left their heads uncovered while worshiping. The Jewish custom of men covering their heads at prayer probably does not go back to the New Testament period.

dishonors his head. Probably a reference to Christ as the head (v. 7). Neither the Bible nor other documents explain why such a practice would dishonor Christ (cf. v. 10 note).

[g]prophesies [h]with her head uncovered dishonors her head—it is the same [i]as if her
head were shaven. **6** For if a wife will not
cover her head, then she should cut her hair
short. But since it is disgraceful for a wife to
cut off her hair or shave her head, let her
cover her head. **7** For a man ought not to
cover his head, since [j]he is the image and
glory of God, but [k]woman is the glory of
man. **8** For [l]man was not made from woman,
but woman from man. **9** Neither was man
created for woman, but [m]woman for man.
10 That is why a wife ought to have a symbol
of authority on her head, because of the
angels.[1] **11** Nevertheless, [n]in the Lord woman
is not independent of man nor man of
woman; **12** for as woman was made from
man, so man is now born of woman. And
[o]all things are from God. **13** Judge for yourselves: is it proper for a wife to pray to God
with her head uncovered? **14** Does not nature
itself teach you that if a man wears long hair
it is a disgrace for him, **15** but if a woman
has long hair, it is her glory? For her hair
is given to her for a covering. **16** [p]If anyone is
inclined to be contentious, we have no such
practice, nor do [q]the churches of God.

The Lord's Supper

17 But in the following instructions I do
not commend you, because when you
come together it is not for the better but
for the worse. **18** For, in the first place,
when you come together as a church, [r]I
hear that there are divisions among you.
And I believe it in part,[2] **19** for [s]there must
be factions among you in order [t]that those
who are genuine among you may be recognized. **20** When you come together, it is
not the Lord's supper that you eat. **21** For
in eating, each one goes ahead with his
own meal. One goes hungry, [u]another gets
drunk. **22** What! Do you not have houses to
eat and drink in? Or do you despise [v]the
church of God and [w]humiliate those who
have nothing? What shall I say to you?
Shall I commend you in this? No, I will
not.

23 For [x]I received from the Lord what I
also delivered to you, that [y]the Lord Jesus
on the night when he was betrayed took
bread, **24** and when he had given thanks, he
broke it, and said, "This is my body which
is for[3] you. Do this in remembrance of
me."[4] **25** In the same way also he took the
cup, after supper, saying, "This cup is the
new covenant in my blood. Do this, as
often as you drink it, in remembrance of
me." **26** For as often as you eat this bread

5 [g]Luke 2:36; Acts 21:9; [ch. 14:34] [h][Num. 5:18] [i]Deut. 21:12
7 [j]See Gen. 1:26 [k][Prov. 12:4]
8 [l]Gen. 2:21-23; [1 Tim. 2:13]
9 [m]Gen. 2:18
11 [n]Gal. 3:28
12 [o]See Rom. 11:36
16 [p]1 Tim. 6:3, 4 [q]2 Thess. 1:4; [1 Thess. 2:14]; See ch. 7:17; 10:32
18 [r]ch. 1:10-12; [ch. 3:3]
19 [s][Matt. 18:7; Luke 17:1; Acts 20:30; 1 Tim. 4:1; 2 Pet. 2:1] [t]1 John 2:19; [Deut. 13:3]
21 [u][2 Pet. 2:13; Jude 12]
22 [v]See Acts 20:28 [w][Prov. 17:5; James 2:6]
23 [x]ch. 15:3; Gal. 1:12 [y]For ver. 23-25, see Matt. 26:26-28; Mark 14:22-24; Luke 22:19, 20

1 Or *messengers*, that is, people sent to observe and report 2 Or *I believe a certain report* 3 Some manuscripts *broken for* 4 Or *as my memorial*; also verse 25

11:5 with her head uncovered. Given the contrast with the previous verse, this comment suggests that women in the first century normally worshiped with a head covering. Some scholars think that Paul refers to a particular hairstyle (in Num. 5:18, loosening a woman's hair is part of the test for an unfaithful wife). See note on v. 15.

the same as if her head were shaven. In v. 6, shaving a woman's head is compared to having the hair cut short, presumably like a man's. It appears then that Paul is opposing a practice that tended to obliterate the distinction between the sexes. Possibly, the controversy reflects the idea of some Corinthians that they had achieved perfection and were no longer subject to the normal rules (Introduction: Date and Occasion).

11:7 woman is the glory of man. See "The Image of God" at Gen. 1:27.

11:9 woman for man. See "Body and Soul, Male and Female" at Gen. 2:7.

11:10 because of the angels. Many interpretations of this phrase have been suggested, but they are all speculative. Paul's argument is closely tied to a specific historical situation, and we should be cautious about applying all its details universally (vv. 4, 16 notes).

11:11, 12 These verses appear to be a qualification of the previous comments. With specific reference to our relationship "in the Lord," men and women are mutually dependent, since we are one in Him (Gal. 3:28).

11:14 nature. Interpreters differ about the meaning of this term. Some believe it refers to the created order. Others argue the apostle is here appealing to the common practices of his day.

11:15 for a covering. Paul may mean that since the woman's long hair serves as a covering, it is equally appropriate for her to wear a veil. Some argue that the hair is "in place of" a covering. This would support the view that Paul refers not to veils but a particular hairstyle (v. 5 note).

11:16 we have no such practice. Paul does not use exactly this kind of argument elsewhere in any of his letters. Such a conclusion to a difficult passage may give some support to the view that the apostle was not prescribing permanent forms of worship, but dealing with questions of cultural appropriateness. To be sure, such questions have theological implications (v. 5 note).

11:17 I do not commend you. The contrast between these words and v. 2 indicates the seriousness of the problem that Paul now addresses.

11:19 there must be factions among you. Paul recognizes that nothing occurs outside the divine will and that God may use human sin to further His own purposes. Or, Paul may be using irony, trying to make the Corinthians see that their infighting has the unworthy motive of seeing who can argue the best.

11:20 not the Lord's supper. Their mishandling of this observance has turned it into something quite different from what it should be.

11:21 One goes hungry, another gets drunk. Paul's concern here is not with drunkenness as such but with the humiliation of the poor. The Lord's Supper symbolizes, among other things, the unity of God's people (10:17). Those Corinthians who were well-off apparently did not share with the less fortunate among them at the feasts where the Lord's Supper was celebrated. This selfish behavior openly contradicted the meaning of the ceremony.

11:23–25 Paul's account of the institution of the Lord's Supper is in all essentials the same as what is in the Gospels (Matt. 26:26–29; Mark 14:22–25; Luke 22:17–20).

11:23 the Lord Jesus . . . took bread. See theological note "The Lord's Supper."

and drink the cup, you proclaim the Lord's
death [z]until he comes.
27 [a]Whoever, therefore, eats the bread or
drinks the cup of the Lord [b]in an unworthy
manner will be guilty of profaning [c]the
body and blood of the Lord. 28 [d]Let a person examine himself, then, and so eat of
the bread and drink of the cup. 29 For anyone who eats and drinks without discerning the body eats and drinks judgment on
himself. 30 That is why many of you are
weak and ill, and some [e]have died.[1] 31 [f]But
if we judged[2] ourselves truly, we would not
be judged. 32 But when we are judged by

26 [z]See John 21:22
27 [a][Num. 9:10, 13] [b][John 13:27] [c]John 6:51, 53-56
28 [d][2 Cor. 13:5; Gal. 6:4]
30 [e]See Matt. 27:52
31 [f]See 1 John 1:9

[1] Greek *have fallen asleep* (as in 15:6, 20) [2] Or *discerned*

The Lord's Supper

The Lord's Supper is an act of worship taking the form of a ceremonial meal, in which Christ's servants share bread and wine to commemorate Christ's death and to celebrate the new covenant relationship they enjoy with God.

> Our Lord Jesus, in the night wherein He was betrayed, instituted the sacrament of His body and blood, called the Lord's Supper, to be observed in His church, unto the end of the world, for the perpetual remembrance of the sacrifice of Himself in His death; the sealing of all benefits thereof unto true believers, their spiritual nourishment and growth in Him, their further engagement in and to all duties which they owe unto Him; and, to be a bond and pledge of their communion with Him, and with each other, as members of His mystical body (*Westminster Confession* 29.1).

The biblical passages dealing with the Supper, on which the above statement is based, are found in Matt. 26:26–29; Mark 14:22–25; Luke 22:17–20; and 1 Cor. 10:16–21; 11:17–34. Jesus' sermon (John 6:35–58) about Himself as the bread of life, and the need to feed on Him by eating His flesh and drinking His blood, was preached before the Supper was instituted, and is better understood as being about what the Supper signifies, communion with Christ by faith, than about the Supper itself.

At the time of the Reformation, questions about the nature of Christ's presence in the Supper and the relation of the Supper to His atoning death were centers of stormy controversy. The Roman Catholic church teaches that Christ is present by transubstantiation, as defined by the Fourth Lateran Council in 1215. "Transubstantiation" means that the substance of the bread and wine is miraculously transformed into Christ's body and blood. The bread and wine are no longer bread and wine, though they appear to be. Luther's doctrine, later called "consubstantiation," was that Christ's body and blood are present "in, with, and under" the form of the bread and wine, which in itself remains bread and wine. The Eastern Orthodox churches and some Anglicans have a similar belief. Zwingli denied that the glorified Christ, now in heaven, is present in any way that such words as "bodily," "physically," or "locally" might suggest. Calvin taught that while the bread and wine remained unchanged, the Spirit raises the believer through faith to enjoy the presence of Christ in a way that is glorious and real, though indescribable.

All the Reformers insisted that at the table we give thanks to Christ for a finished and accepted work of atonement. They denounced the Roman Catholic doctrine of the Mass because in it the sacrifice of the cross was said to be repeated, renewed, or presented again in a way that obscured its sufficiency.

The Lord's Supper has a past reference to Christ's death. It has a present reference to our corporate participation in Him through faith. It has a future reference in that it is a pledge of His return. It encourages the faithful in their daily walk and in their expectation. This service of worship in which Christians remember the suffering that Christ endured for them is a distinctive mark of the Christian religion all over the world.

11:26 you proclaim the Lord's death until he comes. Note the connection between preaching the gospel and celebrating the Lord's Supper. The Supper sets forth God's Word through visible rather than verbal means. Note also that celebrating the Supper gives expression to our sure hope of the Lord's return.

11:27–34 It is important to take this whole section together as a unit, and vv. 33, 34 make plain Paul still has in mind the abuses mentioned in vv. 21, 22. Phrases such as "in an unworthy manner" (v. 27) and "Let a person examine himself" (v. 28) can be extended and applied to many circumstances, but we should be careful not to wrench them from their context. In particular, it would be a misreading of v. 30 to think that God routinely brings illness and death to Christians who, in spite of their spiritual failings, partake of the Supper. The problem in Corinth was much more specific and serious. Some of the Corinthians were tearing apart the unity of the Christian body represented by the one loaf (10:17). The warning in v. 29 about "discerning the body" almost surely refers to this failure to maintain the unity of the church as the body of Christ (see 12:12 note). Because some of the believers in Corinth were celebrating the Supper in a way that destroyed the unity it represents, God had brought judgment upon the community. God's purpose in judging these believers, however, was to prevent them from being "condemned along with the world" (v. 32).

the Lord, [g]we are disciplined[1] so that we
may not be [h]condemned along with the
world.
33 So then, my brothers,[2] when you come
together to eat, wait for[3] one another— 34 [i]if
anyone is hungry, [j]let him eat at home—so
that when you come together it will not be
for judgment. About the other things [k]I will
give directions [l]when I come.

Spiritual Gifts

12 Now [m]concerning[4] spiritual gifts,[5]
brothers,[6] I do not want you to be
uninformed. 2 You know that [n]when you
were pagans [o]you were led astray to [p]mute
idols, however you were led. 3 Therefore I
want you to understand that [q]no one
speaking in the Spirit of God ever says
"Jesus is [r]accursed!" and [s]no one can say
"Jesus is Lord" except in the Holy Spirit.
4 Now [t]there are varieties of gifts, but [u]the
same Spirit; 5 and [v]there are varieties of
service, but [u]the same Lord; 6 and there are
varieties of activities, but it is [u]the same
God who empowers them all in everyone.
7 [w]To each is given the manifestation of the
Spirit for the common good. 8 To one is
given through the Spirit the utterance of
[x]wisdom, and to another the utterance of
[y]knowledge according to the same Spirit,
9 to another [z]faith by the same Spirit, to
another [a]gifts of healing by the one Spirit,
10 to another [b]the working of miracles, to
another [c]prophecy, to another [d]the ability
to distinguish between spirits, to another
[e]various kinds of tongues, to another [f]the
interpretation of tongues. 11 All these are
empowered by one and the same Spirit,
[g]who apportions to each one individually
[h]as he wills.

One Body with Many Members

12 For just as [i]the body is one and has
many members, and all the members of the
body, though many, are one body, [j]so it is
with Christ. 13 For [k]in one Spirit we were all
baptized into one body—[l]Jews or Greeks,

32 [g]See Prov. 3:11 [h]Rom. 5:16 **34** [i]ver. 21 [j]ver. 22 [k]ch. 7:17; Tit. 1:5 [l]See ch. 4:19 **Chapter 12** **1** [m]ch. 14:1 **2** [n]Eph. 2:11, 12; [1 Pet. 4:3]; See ch. 6:11 [o]1 Thess. 1:9 [p]Hab. 2:18, 19; [Ps. 115:5; Isai. 46:7; Jer. 10:5] **3** [q]1 John 4:2, 3 [r]See Rom. 9:3 [s]John 15:26; [Matt. 16:17]; See Rom. 10:9 **4** [t][Heb. 2:4]; See Rom. 12:6 [u]Eph. 4:4-6 **5** [v]Rom. 12:7; [Eph. 4:11] [u][See ver. 4 above] **6** [u][See ver. 4 above] **7** [w]Eph. 4:7; [ch. 14:26; Rom. 12:3] **8** [x]ch. 2:6, 7 [y]See ch. 1:5 **9** [z]ch. 13:2; 2 Cor. 4:13 [a]ver. 28, 30 **10** [b]ver. 28, 29; [Gal. 3:5] [c]ch. 13:2, 8; 14:1 [d][ch. 14:29; 1 John 4:1] [e]See Mark 16:17 [f]ver. 30; ch. 14:26 **11** [g][2 Cor. 10:13] [h]Heb. 2:4 **12** [i]See ch. 10:17 [j]ver. 27 **13** [k][Rom. 6:5; Eph. 2:18] [l]Gal. 3:28; Col. 3:11; [Eph. 2:13-17]

1 Or *when we are judged we are being disciplined by the Lord* 2 Or *brothers and sisters* 3 Or *share with* 4 The expression *Now concerning* introduces a reply to a question in the Corinthians' letter; see 7:1 5 Or *spiritual persons* 6 Or *brothers and sisters*

12:1 Now concerning spiritual gifts. See "Gifts and Ministries" at Eph. 4:7.

12:2, 3 As an introduction to the subject of spiritual gifts in Corinth, Paul reminds his readers of the contrast between their pagan and Christian experience. It is not clear whether anyone was actually uttering curses against Jesus (the statement may be only an illustration), but the focus of v. 3 is on the content of religious speech. In view of 14:6–19, we may infer that the apostle is anticipating his argument for understandable speech. Pagans too may have experienced miraculous speech, but what really matters is what is said.

12:4 varieties of gifts, but the same Spirit. Apparently, the Corinthians exaggerated the importance of the gift of tongues, so Paul must remind them that one and the same Spirit distributes a variety of gifts to His people. The added references to "the same Lord" (v. 5) and "the same God" (v. 6) reflect the importance of the doctrine of the Trinity for Paul; they also support his concern for unity within diversity.

12:7 for the common good. We completely misunderstand the purpose of the Spirit's gifts (here called a "manifestation") if we use them for selfish reasons. Because there are different needs in the Christian community, different gifts are required.

12:8–10 This list of gifts is not intended as a complete catalog (others are included in v. 28); possibly it reflects gifts that were especially evident in Corinth. We need not assume that all of the gifts were manifested in every church. The list in Rom. 12:6–8, for example, includes only two of the gifts mentioned here (prophesying and faith) and omits those that might be thought of as miraculous, such as healing and tongues. In determining the character of some of the gifts listed here, we are hindered by the absence of descriptions of them anywhere in the New Testament. "The utterance of wisdom" may have been an ability to resolve difficult spiritual problems and "the utterance of knowledge" a special revelation of some sort, but we cannot be certain. Similarly, it is not clear why Paul lists separately the gifts of "faith," "healing," and "working of miracles." The reference to "the ability to distinguish between spirits" perhaps should be understood in the light of 14:29. Our inability to determine the precise function of some of these gifts is not an obstacle to understanding the thrust of this passage, which aims not at giving detailed instruction about them but rather at emphasizing the variety of God's endowments to His church (v. 11).

12:10 various kinds of tongues. The proper description of this gift has generated much debate. According to one view, it refers to some kind of ecstatic speech, possibly related to "the tongues . . . of angels" mentioned in 13:1. On the other hand, the New Testament gives explicit and unequivocal evidence that the Holy Spirit granted to the early Christians the ability to speak in foreign, human languages (Acts 2:4–11). Though objections can be raised against this view as well (14:2 note), it can at least be supported by biblical precedent.

12:11 as he wills. This brief clause sets the preceding list of gifts in the proper perspective. Whether an individual or a church possesses a particular gift is not for us to decide. It is the Spirit who sovereignly provides for the people of God. That factor may explain why no New Testament passage gives a complete catalog of gifts or a precise definition of them, since they may vary significantly according to God's plans in changing situations. A church may appropriately pray for God to grant gifts to meet its needs, but such prayers must be offered in submission to His sovereign will and perfect wisdom.

12:12 the body is one. See "The Church" at Eph. 2:19. The description of Christ's church as a body is one of the most distinctive and significant teachings of Paul (1:13 note). Indeed, the apostle tells us that he was given a special revelation concerning this "mystery," which was hidden for many ages; namely, that God's people, both Jews and Gentiles, are now constituted one body by virtue of Christ's exaltation (Eph. 1:22, 23; 3:2–6). Both the existence and the growth of the church derive from this unity established by Christ through the Spirit (Eph. 4:3–6, 11–16; Col. 2:19; 3:14, 15).

12:13 all baptized . . . of one Spirit. The emphasis on the word "all" and the allusion to the sacraments recalls the similar description of the Israelites in 10:2–4 (notes). One of the truths signified and sealed by water baptism is the baptism of the Holy Spirit that incorporates believers into the one body of Christ. Baptism replaces circumcision as the sign of admission into God's covenant (Col. 2:11–14). Similarly, partaking of the Lord's Supper signifies our continued communion with Christ and His church (10:17; 11:29 note).

slaves[1] or free—and [m]all were made to
drink of one Spirit.
14 For the body does not consist of one
member but of many. **15** If the foot should
say, "Because I am not a hand, I do not
belong to the body," that would not make
it any less a part of the body. **16** And if the
ear should say, "Because I am not an eye, I
do not belong to the body," that would not
make it any less a part of the body. **17** If the
whole body were an eye, where would be
the sense of hearing? If the whole body
were an ear, where would be the sense of
smell? **18** But as it is, [n]God arranged the
members in the body, each one of them,
[o]as he chose. **19** If all were a single member,
where would the body be? **20** As it is, there
are many parts,[2] yet one body.
21 The eye cannot say to the hand, "I have
no need of you," nor again the head to the
feet, "I have no need of you." **22** On the contrary, the parts of the body that seem to be
weaker are indispensable, **23** and on those
parts of the body that we think less honorable we bestow the greater honor, and our
unpresentable parts are treated with
greater modesty, **24** which our more presentable parts do not require. But God has
so composed the body, giving greater
honor to the part that lacked it, **25** that there
may be no division in the body, but that
the members may have the same care for
one another. **26** If one member suffers, all
suffer together; if one member is honored,
[p]all rejoice together.
27 Now [q]you are the body of Christ and
individually [r]members of it. **28** And [s]God
has appointed in the church first [t]apostles,
second [u]prophets, third teachers, then
[v]miracles, then [w]gifts of healing, [x]helping,
[y]administrating, and [v]various kinds of
tongues. **29** Are all apostles? Are all prophets? Are all teachers? Do all work miracles?
30 Do all possess gifts of healing? Do all
speak with tongues? Do all interpret? **31** But
[z]earnestly desire the higher gifts.
And I will show you a still more excellent
way.

The Way of Love

13 If I speak in the tongues of men
and of angels, but have not love, I
am a noisy gong or a clanging cymbal.
2 And if I have [a]prophetic powers, and
understand all mysteries and all knowledge, and if I have all faith, [b]so as to
remove mountains, but have not love, I am
nothing. **3** [c]If I give away all I have, and [d]if I
deliver up my body to be burned,[3] but have
not love, I gain nothing.
4 [e]Love is patient and [f]kind; love [g]does
not envy or boast; it [h]is not arrogant **5** or

13 [m][John 7:37-39]
18 [n]ver. 28 [o]ver. 11; [ch. 3:5; Rom. 12:3]
26 [p]Rom. 12:15
27 [q][Eph. 1:23; 4:12; 5:30; Col. 1:24] [r]See Rom. 12:5
28 [s]ver. 18 [t]Eph. 4:11 [u]Eph. 2:20; 3:5 [v]ver. 10 [w]ver. 9 [x][Acts 20:35] [y][Rom. 12:8; 1 Tim. 5:17; Heb. 13:7, 17, 24]
31 [z]ch. 14:1, 39
Chapter 13
2 [a][ch. 14:1, 39; Matt. 7:22]; See Acts 2:18 [b]Matt. 17:20; Mark 11:23; [Luke 17:6]
3 [c][Matt. 6:2] [d]Dan. 3:28
4 [e][Prov. 10:12; 17:9; 1 Thess. 5:14; 2 Tim. 2:10; 1 Pet. 4:8] [f][2 Cor. 6:6; Gal. 5:22; Eph. 4:32; Col. 3:12] [g]Acts 7:9 [h]See ch. 4:6

1 Or *servants*; Greek *bondservants* 2 Or *members*; also verse 22
3 Some manuscripts *deliver up my body* [to death] *that I may boast*

12:14–20 Having established the unity of Christ's church, Paul sets forth its diversity. Some scholars have commented that the Corinthians' most fundamental problem was not their rejection of the church's unity, but rather their failure to acknowledge its diversity. Paul corrects their error through a comparison with the human body. He appeals to the sovereign will of God, who has "arranged the members in the body, each one of them, as he chose" (v. 18; cf. v. 11). If the Corinthians denied the validity of certain gifts, they were really questioning God's authority to distribute the gifts. Paul stresses unity, but not a uniformity that squelches valid forms of diversity.

12:22, 23 weaker . . . less honorable. This comparison manifests the problem that has occupied Paul throughout most of the letter, namely, a sense of spiritual superiority among some of the Corinthians and their consequent disdain for those who appear to be "weaker" and "less honorable." Their devaluing of certain gifts (possibly in favor of the gift of tongues) is Paul's concern here.

12:27 individually members. See "The Local Church" at Rev. 2:1.

12:28 See "Gifts and Ministries" at Eph. 4:7. The items in this verse are different from those in vv. 8–10—confirmation that Paul is not interested in giving a complete list. Here Paul begins with "apostles" and "prophets," whom he considers the foundation (Eph. 2:20), and adds as a third category "teachers," so that this listing is similar to that in Eph. 4:11. Though the Greek words for "helping" and "administrating" do not occur elsewhere in the New Testament, Paul probably has in mind the gifts of one who "does acts of mercy" or "leads" (Rom. 12:8).

12:29, 30 These rhetorical questions bring to a climax Paul's argument that we should not expect everyone to have the same gifts, since God has apportioned them as He wills (vv. 11, 18). Also see "The Apostles" at Acts 1:26.

12:31 desire the higher gifts. The meaning of this sentence is disputed. Some believe it refers to the more important gifts in v. 28 (especially prophecy, 14:1); others argue that it introduces the discussion of love in ch. 13. Most likely, Paul is anticipating what he will say later about gifts for "building up the church" (14:12), i.e., speaking "words with my mind in order to instruct others" (14:19).

more excellent way. Before explaining what the "higher gifts" are, as he will in ch. 14, Paul must point out what is the essential condition for the proper exercise of any gift—love.

13:1–3 Using intentional exaggeration, Paul emphasizes the uselessness of gifts exercised without love. The expression "tongues of men" probably refers to the gift of speaking in foreign languages (Acts 2:4–11), while the addition "and of angels" may be a deliberate exaggeration (similarly with "understand all mysteries" and "remove mountains"). Whether the Corinthians claimed to use angelic speech is impossible to determine (12:10 note). The expression "deliver up my body to be burned" may also be a dramatic overstatement.

13:4–7 Paul personifies love as a person who acts in the ways Christians should imitate. The total picture suggests a description of Christ Himself. Considering the kinds of problems this epistle addresses, these verses are a rebuke to the Corinthians, who were failing to conduct themselves with love.

rude. It [i]does not insist on its own way; it
[j]is not irritable or resentful; 6 it [k]does not
rejoice at wrongdoing, but [l]rejoices with
the truth. 7 [m]Love bears all things, believes
all things, hopes all things, [e]endures all
things.

8 Love never ends. As for prophecies,
they will pass away; as for tongues, they
will cease; as for knowledge, it will pass
away. 9 For [n]we know in part and we
prophesy in part, 10 but [o]when the perfect
comes, the partial will pass away. 11 When I
was a child, I spoke like a child, I thought
like a child, I reasoned like a child. When
I became a man, I gave up childish ways.
12 For [p]now we see in a mirror dimly, but
[q]then face to face. Now I know in part; then
I shall know fully, even as [r]I have been fully
known.

13 So now faith, hope, and love abide,
these three; but the greatest of these is
love.

Prophecy and Tongues

14 [s]Pursue love, and [t]earnestly desire
the [u]spiritual gifts, especially that
you may [v]prophesy. 2 For [w]one who speaks
in a tongue speaks not to men but to God;
for no one understands him, but he utters
mysteries in the Spirit. 3 On the other hand,
the one who prophesies speaks to people
for their upbuilding and encouragement
and consolation. 4 The one who speaks in a
tongue builds up himself, but the one who
prophesies builds up the church. 5 Now I
want you all to speak in tongues, but [x]even
more to prophesy. The one who prophesies
is greater than the one who speaks in
tongues, unless someone interprets, so
that the church may be built up.

6 Now, brothers,[1] if I come to you speaking in tongues, how will I benefit you
unless I bring you some [y]revelation or
knowledge or prophecy or [z]teaching? 7 If
even lifeless instruments, such as the flute
or the harp, do not give distinct notes, how
will anyone know what is played? 8 And [a]if
the bugle gives an indistinct sound, who
will get ready for battle? 9 So with yourselves, if with your tongue you utter speech
that is not intelligible, how will anyone
know what is said? For you will be [b]speak-

5 [i]See ch. 10:24 [j][Rom. 4:6; 2 Cor. 5:19]
6 [k][Rom. 1:32; 2 Thess. 2:12] [l][2 John 4; 3 John 3, 4]
7 [m]ch. 9:12 [e][See ver. 4 above]
9 [n][ch. 8:2]
10 [o][John 15:15]
12 [p]James 1:23; [Num. 12:8; Job 36:26; 2 Cor. 3:18; 5:7] [q]1 John 3:2; See Matt. 5:8 [r]See ch. 8:3
Chapter 14
1 [s]ch. 16:14 [t]ch. 12:31 [u]ch. 12:1 [v]See ch. 11:4; 13:2
2 [w]ver. 18-23, 27, 28
5 [x][Num. 11:29]
6 [y]ver. 26; Eph. 1:17 [z]ver. 26; Acts 2:42; Rom. 6:17
8 [a][Num. 10:9; Isai. 58:1; Jer. 4:19; Ezek. 33:3-6; Joel 2:1]
9 [b][ch. 9:26]

[1] Or *brothers and sisters*; also verses 20, 26, 39

13:5 resentful. Paul may mean that those who love do not devise evil against others. More likely he means that those who love do not focus their attention on the wrongs that others do to them.

13:7 all. Paul uses this word four times for rhetorical effect as he brings his description of love to a climax.

13:8 Love never ends. One could view this statement as a summary of the previous verse, especially in the light of the comment that love "bears all things." At the same time, the statement allows Paul to build a contrast between love, which always remains (v. 13), and the spiritual gifts, which will cease.

prophecies . . . tongues . . . knowledge. It is likely that Paul mentions these three items as representative of all the spiritual gifts, which have a temporary, earthly function until the end of the age. Others suggest that Paul mentions these three in particular because they have a revelatory function that came to an end with the completion of the New Testament canon (v. 10 note).

13:10 perfect. The context (especially v. 12) suggests strongly that Paul here is referring to the Second Coming of Christ as the final event in God's plan of redemption and revelation. In comparison with what we will receive then, the present blessings are only partial and thus imperfect. It is therefore a sign of immaturity for the Corinthians to treat the temporary, incomplete gifts of the Spirit as having ultimate significance. According to another view, Paul may be referring to the "complete" revelation contained in the New Testament Scriptures, which make prophecy and other revelatory gifts obsolete. Still other interpretations have been suggested, such as the maturity in love that the Corinthians should aim for, the maturing of the early church, or the death of the individual Christian.

13:12 I shall know fully, even as I have been fully known. Perhaps because the Corinthians liked to boast of their knowledge (8:1 note), Paul concludes by stressing the partial character of all present knowledge. The shift from the active ("know") to the passive ("have been") is found elsewhere in the apostle's letters and serves to emphasize dependence on God's grace (8:3; Gal. 4:9). Here the focus is on the intimacy and immediacy of God's knowing, which we will share someday.

13:13 the greatest . . . is love. See theological note "Love."

14:1 especially that you may prophesy. Having set the discussion within the proper framework of love, Paul now encourages the Corinthians to recognize the value of the spiritual gifts. Because the Corinthians have exaggerated the importance of the gift of tongues, however, the emphasis of ch. 14 is on the understandable gifts (v. 19)—primarily prophecy, but also the interpretation of tongues (vv. 27, 28).

14:2 speaks not to men but to God . . . utters mysteries. This verse (cf. v. 14) describes the gift of tongues in a way that seems inconsistent with the gift of speaking in foreign languages mentioned in Acts 2:4–11 (although some believe that the miracle on Pentecost was a miracle of hearing). Accordingly, many argue that Paul is dealing with something different—a kind of ecstatic speech used for intimate prayer (Rom. 8:26). However, the word translated "tongue" is the normal Greek term for "language." Secondly, Paul's use of the term "mysteries" is to indicate a divine truth not yet disclosed; it does not have the meaning of the English word "mysterious" (2:7 note). Thirdly, vv. 10, 11, as well as v. 21, support the idea that even here Paul is speaking of human languages (12:8–10 note).

in the Spirit. That is, as opposed to speaking with his mind (vv. 13–15); even the speaker does not understand what he is saying.

14:4 builds up himself. Those speaking in an uninterpreted language were encouraged and comforted, despite their not understanding the message.

14:6 how will I benefit you. This principle of benefiting others by edifying them becomes the key point of the passage. Paul is applying the teaching of 12:7 that God has granted a variety of gifts "for the common good."

14:7, 8 These verses illustrate the principle mentioned in v. 6. Musical instruments convey nothing to those who listen unless they are played with intelligent purpose.

ing into the air. 10 There are doubtless many
different languages in the world, and none
is without meaning, 11 but if I do not know
the meaning of the language, I will be [c]a
foreigner to the speaker and the speaker a
foreigner to me. 12 So with yourselves, since
you are eager for manifestations of the
Spirit, strive to excel in building up the
church.
13 Therefore, one who speaks in a tongue
should pray for the power to interpret.
14 For if I pray in a tongue, my spirit prays
but my mind is unfruitful. 15 What am I to
do? I will pray with my spirit, but I will
pray with my mind also; [d]I will sing praise
with my spirit, but I will sing [e]with my
mind also. 16 Otherwise, if you give thanks
with your spirit, how can anyone in the
position of an outsider[1] say [f]"Amen" to
[g]your thanksgiving when he does not know
what you are saying? 17 For you may be giving thanks well enough, but the other person is not being built up. 18 I thank God
that I speak in tongues more than all of
you. 19 Nevertheless, in church I would
rather speak five words with my mind in
order to instruct others, than ten thousand
words in a tongue.
20 Brothers, [h]do not be children in your
thinking. [i]Be infants in evil, but in your
thinking be [j]mature. 21 [k]In the Law it is
written, [l]"By people of strange tongues and
by the lips of foreigners will I speak to this
people, and even then they will not listen
to me, says the Lord." 22 Thus tongues are a
sign not for believers but for unbelievers,
while prophecy is a sign[2] not for unbelievers but for believers. 23 If, therefore, the
whole church comes together and all speak
in tongues, and outsiders or unbelievers
enter, [m]will they not say that you are out of

11 [c]See Acts 28:2
15 [d][Eph. 5:19; Col. 3:16; James 5:13] [e]Ps. 47:7
16 [f]1 Chr. 16:36; Neh. 5:13; 8:6; Ps. 106:48; Jer. 11:5; 28:6; Rev. 5:14; 7:12; 19:4; [2 Cor. 1:20] [g]ch. 11:24
20 [h]Eph. 4:14; Heb. 5:12, 13 [i][Ps. 131:2; Isai. 28:9; Rom. 16:19]; See Matt. 18:3 [j]ch. 2:6
21 [k]See John 10:34 [l]Cited from Isai. 28:11, 12; [Deut. 28:49]
23 [m][Acts 2:13]

1 Or *of him that is without gifts* 2 Greek lacks *a sign*

Love

New Testament Christianity is the human response to the revelation of the Creator as the God of love. Out of love for those who did not love, the Father gave the Son, the Son gave His life, and the Father and Son together have sent the Spirit, to save sinners from misery and lead them into glory. Believing in and being overwhelmed by this amazing reality of divine love sustains the love for God and neighbor that the two great commandments require (Matt. 22:35–40). Our love expresses our gratitude for God's gracious love to us, and imitates it as a model (Eph. 4:32–5:2; 1 John 3:16).

The indispensable mark of Christian life is Christian love. The measure and test of love to God is whole-hearted obedience (John 14:15, 21, 23; 1 John 5:3); the measure and test of love to our neighbors is laying down our lives for them (1 John 3:16; cf. John 15:12, 13). This sacrificial love involves giving, spending, and impoverishing ourselves for their well-being. Jesus' story of the Samaritan's kindness to a traditional enemy is His model definition of how to love one's neighbor (Luke 10:25–37).

Christian love is described in 1 Corinthians 13. Its total lack of self-concern is breathtaking. It seeks the neighbor's good, and its true measure is how much it gives to that end. Love is a principle of action rather than of emotion. It is a matter of doing things for people out of compassion for them, whether or not we feel personal affection for them. It is by their active love to one another that Jesus' disciples can be recognized (John 13:34, 35).

14:13 pray for the power to interpret. Without minimizing the significance of the gift of tongues, Paul encourages the Corinthians to use it in a way that makes it valuable for the congregation.

14:14 my spirit prays but my mind is unfruitful. Whatever spiritual benefit he might receive from the experience, his understanding is not built up. In the next verse, Paul emphasizes that he would rather have both benefits.

14:16 say "Amen" to your thanksgiving. The members of the congregation, if they are to participate in public worship, must be able to agree with the message of the hymns being sung and the prayers being offered. The custom of expressing their approval with an audible "Amen" ("So it is!") cannot be followed if no one understands what has been said.

14:18, 19 It may be that some of the Corinthians justified their emphasis on the gift of tongues by arguing that Paul himself exercised this gift. Without denying the fact, the apostle puts the gift in proper perspective by pointing out how much more valuable is doing something "in order to instruct others."

14:20–25 Up to this point, Paul has been discussing the use of tongues among believers. But what about unbelievers who hear the tongues? The Corinthians have ignored them, and Paul admonishes the church for this display of spiritual immaturity. He appeals to "the Law," (the Old Testament) to show that God uses unintelligible speech as a sign of judgment. Is. 28:11 explains how God judged the Israelites through Assyrians speaking a foreign language. If non-Christians come to the worship and hear an unintelligible language, they will be repelled (v. 23) and reject the gospel. In this situation uninterpreted tongues are a sign of judgment "for unbelievers" (v. 22). But the Corinthians should aim at bringing unbelievers to repentance and to the recognition that God is present (v. 25). Because God uses the understandable words of prophecy to accomplish this purpose, prophecy is a sign "for believers"; it is evidence of God's goodness to them (v. 22).

your minds? 24 But if all prophesy, and an
unbeliever or outsider enters, he is convicted by all, he is called to account by all,
25 [n]the secrets of his heart are disclosed,
and so, [o]falling on his face, he will worship
God and [p]declare that God is really among
you.

Orderly Worship

26 What then, brothers? When you come
together, each one has [q]a hymn, [r]a lesson,
[r]a revelation, [s]a tongue, or [t]an interpretation. [u]Let all things be done for building
up. 27 If any speak in [s]a tongue, let there be
only two or at most three, and each in turn,
and let someone interpret. 28 But if there is
no one to interpret, let each of them keep
silent in church and speak to himself and
to God. 29 Let two or three prophets speak,
and let the others [v]weigh what is said. 30 If
a revelation is made to another sitting
there, [w]let the first be silent. 31 For you can
all prophesy one by one, so that all may
learn and all be encouraged, 32 and the spirits of prophets are subject to prophets.
33 For God is not a God of [x]confusion but of
peace.

As in [y]all the churches of the saints,
34 [z]the women should keep silent in the
churches. For they are not permitted to
speak, but [a]should be in submission, as
[b]the Law also says. 35 If there is anything
they desire to learn, let them ask their husbands at home. For it is shameful for a
woman to speak in church.

36 Or was it from you that the word of
God came? Or are you the only ones it has
reached? 37 [c]If anyone thinks that he is a
prophet, or spiritual, he should acknowledge that the things I am writing to you are
a command of the Lord. 38 If anyone does
not recognize this, he is not recognized.
39 So, my brothers, [d]earnestly desire to
prophesy, and do not forbid speaking in
tongues. 40 [e]But all things should be done
decently and [f]in order.

The Resurrection of Christ

15 Now I would remind you, brothers,[1] of the gospel [g]I preached to
you, which you received, [h]in which you
stand, 2 and by which [i]you are being saved,
if you [j]hold fast to the word I preached to
you—[k]unless you believed in vain.

3 For [l]I delivered to you as of first importance what I also received: that Christ died
[m]for our sins [n]in accordance with the Scriptures, 4 that he was buried, that he was
raised [o]on the third day [p]in accordance
with the Scriptures, 5 and that [q]he appeared
to Cephas, then [r]to the twelve. 6 Then he
appeared to more than five hundred broth-

25 [n][Heb. 4:12] [o]Luke 17:16 [p]Isai. 45:14; Zech. 8:23 **26** [q]Eph. 5:19 [r]See ver. 6 [s]ver. 18 [t]ver. 5, 13, 27, 28; ch. 12:10, 30 [u]2 Cor. 12:19; 13:10; [ch. 12:7] **27** [s][See ver. 26 above] **29** [v][ch. 12:10; Job 12:11; 1 John 4:1] **30** [w][1 Thess. 5:19, 20] **33** [x][ver. 40] [y]See ch. 7:17 **34** [z][1 Tim. 2:11, 12] [a]See 1 Pet. 3:1 [b][ver. 21] **37** [c][2 Cor. 10:7; 1 John 4:6] **39** [d]ch. 12:31 **40** [e][ver. 31, 33] [f]Col. 2:5 **Chapter 15** **1** [g][2 Tim. 2:8]; See ch. 3:6 [h]Rom. 5:2; [2 Cor. 1:24; 1 Pet. 5:12] **2** [i]ch. 1:18 [j]ch. 11:2; [Heb. 3:6, 14] [k]Gal. 3:4 **3** [l]ch. 11:23; Gal. 1:12 [m]John 1:29; Gal. 1:4; Heb. 5:1, 3; 1 Pet. 2:24 [n]Isai. ch. 53; Dan. 9:26; Zech. 13:7; [1 Pet. 1:11] **4** [o][Hos. 6:2; Matt. 12:40; John 2:22] [p]Ps. 16:10; Isai. 53:10; [Acts 2:25-32; 13:33-35; 26:22, 23 **5** [q]Luke 24:34 [r]Mark 16:14; Luke 24:36; John 20:19, 26; Acts 10:41

[1] Or *brothers and sisters*; also verses 6, 31, 50, 58

14:26 for building up. See note on v. 6; "God's Pattern for Worship" at 1 Chr. 16:29.

14:27 let someone interpret. This concern for understanding has informed the whole discussion (v. 1 note). Paul's instructions in this verse and the following demonstrate that those who spoke in tongues controlled their utterance, although they may not have understood it.

14:29–33 Having given instructions for the proper exercise of the gift of tongues, Paul moves on to other directives that also affect the order of public worship. Since he had emphasized the importance of prophecy, he points out that even this gift should be exercised in an orderly fashion—"Let two or three prophets speak" (during the course of, or perhaps at various points in, the service), while "the others" who have the gift of prophecy should evaluate the message to ascertain that it is not false. Apparently the Corinthians were speaking in tongues and prophesying without regard for each other or for the content of the message (12:2, 3 note). Their disorder was a threat to the unity of the body and was incompatible with the God "of peace" (v. 33).

14:34, 35 These verses have created debate among Christians, at least partly because it is not known what problem exactly Paul was seeking to correct. It has even been proposed that these verses were not part of Paul's original letter. In view of 11:5 and other New Testament passages, it is certain that Paul is not absolutely forbidding women to speak in every church situation. Paul may have been addressing a particular problem in Corinth, such as women creating disorder during the worship service. He may have in mind a specific function, such as the evaluation of prophecy (vv. 29, 32), in which women should not participate. It has been suggested that vv. 34, 35 are a quotation from the Corinthians themselves that Paul rejects in v. 36.

14:36 These sarcastic questions show that Paul is not giving general instructions for worship. Rather, he is addressing serious problems arising out of the Corinthians' boastful arrogance.

14:38 does not recognize this, he is not recognized. See note 13:12 for the contrast between knowing and being known. The present verse may be a warning that those who are stubborn will be disciplined by Paul or by the church (2 Thess. 3:14), but the language suggests that they will come under direct divine judgment.

14:39, 40 These verses are a concise summary of ch. 14.

15:1 With this verse, Paul shifts to a new topic of great concern to him—the integrity of the gospel message as it focuses on the doctrine of the Resurrection.

15:2 if you hold fast. See note 9:27.

believed in vain. Denying the resurrection of Christ makes our faith useless (v. 14).

15:3–5 These verses give the essence not only of Paul's preaching but of the early church's teaching as a whole ("what I also received"): Christ's vicarious death and His resurrection as the fulfillment of the Old Testament message.

15:5–8 The fourfold repetition of "he appeared" indicates Paul's emphasis in this passage—the eyewitness proof that Christ was raised from the dead. Most of those who witnessed the resurrection appearances were

ers at one time, most of whom are still
alive, though some have fallen asleep.
7 Then he appeared to [s]James, then [t]to all
the apostles. 8 Last of all, as to one untimely born, [u]he appeared also to me. 9 For [v]I
am the least of the apostles, unworthy to
be called an apostle, because [w]I persecuted
the church of God. 10 But by the grace of
God I am what I am, and his grace toward
me was not in vain. On the contrary, [x]I
worked harder than any of them, [y]though it
was not I, but the grace of God that is with
me. 11 Whether then it was I or they, so we
preach and so you believed.

The Resurrection of the Dead

12 Now if Christ is proclaimed as raised
from the dead, [z]how can some of you say
that there is no resurrection of the dead?
13 But if there is no resurrection of the dead,
[a]then not even Christ has been raised.
14 And if Christ has not been raised, then
our preaching is in vain and your faith is in
vain. 15 We are even found to be misrepre-
senting God, because we testified about
God that [b]he raised Christ, whom he did
not raise if it is true that the dead are not
raised. 16 For if the dead are not raised, not
even Christ has been raised. 17 And if Christ
has not been raised, your faith is futile and
[c]you are still in your sins. 18 Then those also
who [d]have fallen asleep in Christ have perished. 19 If in this life only we have hoped in
Christ, [e]we are of all people most to be
pitied.

20 But in fact [f]Christ has been raised from
the dead, [g]the firstfruits of those who have
fallen asleep. 21 For as [h]by a man came
death, [i]by a man has come also the resurrection of the dead. 22 For [j]as in Adam all
die, so also in Christ shall all be made alive.
23 But each in his own order: Christ the
firstfruits, then [k]at his coming [l]those who
belong to Christ. 24 Then comes the end,
when he delivers [m]the kingdom to God the
Father after destroying [n]every rule and

7 [s]See Acts 12:17 [t]Luke 24:50; Acts 1:3, 4 **8** [u]See ch. 9:1 **9** [v]Eph. 3:7, 8; 2 Cor. 12:11; 1 Tim. 1:13-16 [w]See Acts 8:3 **10** [x]2 Cor. 11:23; 12:11; Col. 1:29 [y][ch. 3:6; 2 Cor. 3:5; Phil. 2:13]; See Matt. 10:20 **12** [z][Acts 23:8; 2 Tim. 2:18] **13** [a]1 Thess. 4:14 **15** [b]See Acts 2:24 **17** [c]See Rom. 4:25 **18** [d]1 Thess. 4:16; Rev. 14:13 **19** [e][ch. 4:9; 2 Tim. 3:12] **20** [f]2 Tim. 2:8; 1 Pet. 1:3 [g]ver. 23; See Acts 26:23

21 [h]See Rom. 5:12 [i]John 11:25; Rom. 6:23 **22** [j][Rom. 5:14-18] **23** [k]See 1 Thess. 2:19 [l]ver. 52; 1 Thess. 4:16; See Luke 14:14 **24** [m][Dan. 7:14, 27] [n]Eph. 1:21

still living at the time Paul wrote this letter, so it was possible for anyone to check the facts. Particularly significant is the reference to "more than five hundred brothers at one time," for it shows that the appearances cannot be explained away as mere personal hallucinations.

15:7 James. This is not John's brother, the apostle executed by Herod Agrippa (Acts 12:2), but the half brother of Jesus (John 7:5; Acts 12:17; 15:13; Gal. 1:19).

15:8 as to one untimely born. This self-deprecating remark may be an ironic criticism of the Corinthians who held Paul in low esteem (2:1 note). What the apostle means is suggested by the phrase "last of all." The appearances of the risen Lord had ceased, and Paul was a persecutor of the church when he received his calling to be an apostle (Gal. 1:13, 23; Phil. 3:6; 1 Tim. 1:13–16). Although Paul had not been with Jesus during His earthly ministry, he was granted the privilege of seeing Jesus risen from the dead, and was commissioned as an apostle with a special ministry to the Gentiles (Acts 9:3–5, 15; Gal. 1:15, 16). What Paul says strongly suggests that the apostolic office was a unique, foundational gift to the church (Eph. 2:20).

15:10 the grace of God. Having freely admitted the abnormal and undeserving character of his experience, Paul moves on to stress that his past life is no reason to reject his message. Where sin abounds, God's effectual grace abounds all the more (Rom. 5:20); where we are weak, God's grace is strong (2 Cor. 12:9, 10). Divine grace did not make Paul lazy, but caused him to labor "harder" than anyone else.

15:12 there is no resurrection. Paul finally addresses the problem that needs correction. Some of the Corinthians, perhaps without denying that Jesus had been raised, were questioning the doctrine of the resurrection because of their unbiblical understanding of the human body (v. 35 note). Paul needed to show them that the resurrection of Jesus cannot be separated from the resurrection of those who are His (vv. 20–23). If their resurrection is not true, neither is His. But to deny, even by implication, that Jesus' body was raised from the tomb destroys the message of the gospel.

15:14 our preaching is in vain and your faith is in vain. Cf. v. 17. The truth of the Christian message is tied to the historical reality of Christ's death and exaltation. The apostle cannot conceive of his message having any spiritual value if its historical foundation does not exist.

15:19 we are . . . most to be pitied. Though Paul would not deny that in the spiritual sense Christians enjoy a better present life than non-Christians, this verse emphasizes the greatness of what God has promised for the life to come. Our hope of salvation is so glorious that if we were still in our sins and lost (vv. 17, 18), we would have experienced the greatest and cruelest of all deceptions (vv. 31, 32).

15:20 the firstfruits. At harvesttime the Israelites were required to bring an offering from the first part of the crop (Lev. 23:10). This offering was a token of the whole harvest, that all belonged to God. Jesus is called the "firstfruits" because His resurrection and the resurrection of believers are closely related events. Jesus was "the first to rise from the dead" (Acts 26:23), rising as our representative. His resurrection caused us to be raised spiritually (Rom. 6:4; Eph. 2:6), and at the same time guarantees that we will be raised bodily. Another use of the metaphor is found in Rom. 8:23 (cf. also 2 Cor. 1:22; 5:5; Eph. 1:14).

15:21 This passage succinctly states one of Paul's most profound teachings—our twofold solidarity with the first man, Adam, and with the last man, Christ. By virtue of our humanity, we are united with Adam in our present natural existence, in sin, and in death; by virtue of our faith, we are united with Christ in spiritual existence, in righteousness, and in the life to come (vv. 45–49; Rom. 5:17–19). See theological note "Resurrection and Glorification" on the next page.

15:22 in Adam all die. See "The Fall" at Gen. 3:6.

15:24–28 See "Jesus' Heavenly Reign" at Acts 7:55. Although Paul's argument in this section is difficult in its details, its thrust is clear and powerful. The Corinthians must understand that the Resurrection is not an isolated event with limited repercussions. It is rather an integrating and culminating event in God's sovereign rule over history. Redemption is not complete "until he has put all his enemies under his feet" (v. 25, a clear reference to Ps. 110:1), and since death is "the last enemy" (v. 26), Christ's work is not done until death is destroyed. Paul's statement that the Son "will also be subjected" to the Father (v. 28) does not mean that the Son is inferior in dignity and being. Rather, in His messianic work the Son subjects Himself to the will of the Father "when he delivers the kingdom to God the Father" (v. 24). The climax of Christ's submissive, messianic work is this total conquest over His enemies, "that God may be all in all," when His absolute rule is universally acknowledged.

every authority and power. 25 For he must
reign [o]until he has put all his enemies
under his feet. 26 The last enemy to be [p]de-
stroyed is death. 27 For [q]“God[1] has put all
things in subjection under his feet.” But
when it says, “all things are put in subjection,” it is plain that he is excepted who
put all things in subjection under him.
28 When [r]all things are subjected to him,
then the Son himself will also be subjected
to him who put all things in subjection
under him, that [s]God may be all in all.
29 Otherwise, what do people mean by
being baptized on behalf of the dead? If the
dead are not raised at all, why are people
baptized on their behalf? 30 Why am [t]I in
danger every hour? 31 I protest, brothers, by
[u]my pride in you, which I have in Christ
Jesus our Lord, [v]I die every day! 32 What do
I gain if, humanly speaking, [w]I fought with
beasts at Ephesus? If the dead are not
raised, [x]“Let us eat and drink, for tomorrow we die.” 33 [y]Do not be deceived: [z]“Bad
company ruins good morals.”[2] 34 [a]Wake up
from your drunken stupor, as is right, and
do not go on sinning. For [b]some have no
knowledge of God. [c]I say this to your
shame.

The Resurrection Body

35 But someone will ask, [d]“How are the
dead raised? With what kind of body do

25 [o]See Ps. 110:1
26 [p]2 Tim. 1:10; [Rev. 20:14; 21:4]
27 [q]Eph. 1:22; Cited from Ps. 8:6; See Matt. 11:27; 28:18
28 [r]Phil. 3:21 [s][ch. 3:23; 11:3]
30 [t]2 Cor. 11:26
31 [u]1 Thess. 2:19 [v]Luke 9:23; See Rom. 8:36
32 [w][2 Cor. 1:8] [x]Cited from Isai. 22:13; [Isai. 56:12; Luke 12:19]
33 [y]James 1:16
[z][ch. 5:6] 34 [a]See Rom. 13:11 [b]1 Thess. 4:5 [c]ch. 6:5; [ch. 4:14] 35 [d][Ezek. 37:3]

1 Greek *he* 2 Probably from Menander's comedy *Thais*

Resurrection and Glorification

Jesus was the first to be raised from the dead to a glorified existence no longer subject to death as the punishment for sin (Acts 26:23). When He returns to this world He will raise His servants to a resurrection life like His own (1 Cor. 15:20–23; 2 Cor. 5:1–5; Phil. 3:20–21). He will, indeed, raise the whole human race from the dead; but those who are not His will be raised for condemnation (John 5:29) and subject to the “second death” for their sins (Rev. 2:11; 21:8). Christians alive at His coming will at that instant undergo a marvelous transformation (1 Cor. 15:50–54).

There is a continuity between the mortal and the immortal body. Jesus was raised in the same body in which He died. Paul compares the mortal body and the resurrection body to a seed and the plant that grows from it (1 Cor. 15:35–44). While there is continuity, there is discontinuity as well. Our present bodies, like Adam's, are natural and earthly, subject to weakness and death. The resurrection body, like Christ's, will be spiritual, created and sustained by the Holy Spirit, and will belong to the eternal, imperishable, heavenly order (1 Cor. 15:45–54).

After His resurrection, Jesus' disciples could recognize Him despite the differences in His new body. In the same way, Christians will recognize one another, and there will be joyful reunions when the separations caused by death are ended. This is apparent from 1 Thess. 4:13–18. In this passage Paul assured those who were grieving that they would see their Christian loved ones again.

Glorification is the work of transformation that removes all sin from us and makes us fit to be with God in perfect communion (1 Cor. 13:12). The saints will worship and serve God with a nature made whole and a heart set free. Our desire to be with God and enjoy His love will be fulfilled in the presence of the triune God (Job 19:26; Matt. 5:8; Rev. 22:3, 4).

Paul's description in Rom. 8:30 of the process whereby God saves His elect concludes with a striking past tense: “He also glorified” those who were saved. Literally, glorification is still in the future for everyone other than Jesus Himself. Paul's thought apparently is that our glorification has already been decided by God as part of His sovereign plan and can be spoken of as absolutely certain.

15:29 baptized on behalf of the dead. Apparently some in Corinth were being baptized on behalf of others who had already died. This practice is not mentioned elsewhere in the Bible or in other ancient writings. Numerous explanations of the practice have been proposed, all of them speculative and none persuasive. Paul mentions the rite only to show the logical inconsistency of his opponents' position.

15:32 beasts. Probably a reference to Paul's enemies in Ephesus (where this letter was written) who wanted to condemn him (cf. “the lion's mouth,” 2 Tim. 4:17 note). The hope of resurrection strengthens Paul to endure severe trials and persecutions (v. 19 note).

15:33 Bad company ruins good morals. Derived from a comedy written by the popular Greek author Menander (342–292 B.C.), this proverb was common in the ancient world (note the comparable Jewish saying in 5:6). Those Christians in Corinth with a defective view of the Resurrection not only had been influenced by the bad company they kept, but in their turn they were corrupting others in the congregation.

15:34 some have no knowledge of God. Probably a reference to members of the church who boasted of their knowledge (8:1 note) but whose denial of the Resurrection showed deep ignorance regarding the things of God.

15:35 With what kind of body do they come. In this verse Paul considers what was apparently the primary objection raised by some of the

they come?" 36 You foolish person! [e]What
you sow does not come to life unless it
dies. 37 And what you sow is not the body
that is to be, but a bare kernel, perhaps of
wheat or of some other grain. 38 But God
gives it a body as he has chosen, and to
each kind of seed its own body. 39 For not
all flesh is the same, but there is one kind
for humans, another for animals, another
for birds, and another for fish. 40 There are
heavenly bodies and earthly bodies, but the
glory of the heavenly is of one kind, and
the glory of the earthly is of another. 41 There
is one glory of the sun, and another glory of
the moon, and another glory of the stars;
for star differs from star in glory.

42 [f]So is it with the resurrection of the
dead. What is sown is perishable; what is
raised is imperishable. 43 It is sown in dishonor; [g]it is raised in glory. It is sown in
weakness; it is raised in power. 44 It is sown
a natural body; it is raised a spiritual body.
If there is a natural body, there is also a
spiritual body. 45 Thus it is written, [h]"The
first man Adam became a living being";[1]
[i]the last Adam became a [j]life-giving spirit.
46 But it is not the spiritual that is first but
the natural, and then the spiritual. 47 [k]The
first man was from the earth, [l]a man of
dust; [m]the second man is from heaven.
48 As was the man of dust, so also are those
who are of the dust, and as is the man of
heaven, [n]so also are those who are of
heaven. 49 Just [o]as we have borne the image
of the man of dust, [p]we shall[2] also bear the
image of the man of heaven.

Mystery and Victory

50 I tell you this, brothers: [q]flesh and
blood [r]cannot inherit the kingdom of God,
nor does the perishable inherit the imperishable. 51 Behold! I tell you a mystery. [s]We
shall not all sleep, [t]but we shall all be
changed, 52 in a moment, in the twinkling
of an eye, at the last trumpet. For [u]the
trumpet will sound, and [v]the dead will be
raised imperishable, and we shall be
changed. 53 For this perishable body must
put on the imperishable, and [w]this mortal
body must put on immortality. 54 When the
perishable puts on the imperishable, and

36 [e]John 12:24 **42** [f]Dan. 12:3; [Matt. 13:43] **43** [g]Phil. 3:21; Col. 3:4 **45** [h]Cited from Gen. 2:7 [i]Rom. 5:14 [j]John 5:21; [John 6:33, 39, 40, 54, 57; Rom. 8:2, 10]

47 [k]John 3:31 [l][Gen. 2:7; 3:19] [m]John 3:13, 31 **48** [n][Phil. 3:20] **49** [o]Gen. 5:3 [p]See Rom. 8:29 **50** [q]See Matt. 16:17 [r][John 3:3, 5] **51** [s]1 Thess. 4:15, 17; [t]Phil. 3:21 **52** [u]Matt. 24:31; 1 Thess. 4:16; [Isai. 27:13; Zech. 9:14] [v]John 5:25, 28; [Luke 20:36] **53** [w][2 Cor. 5:2-4]

1 Greek *a living soul* 2 Some manuscripts *let us*

Corinthians against a bodily resurrection. They were probably influenced by dualism, a pagan philosophy that contrasted the immaterial with the physical and argued that the immaterial was good but the material was evil. Along such lines some of the Christians had developed disdain for the human body, probably distorting their ideas about sexual relationships (6:14 note). They seem to have thought that since body was evil, the doctrine of the Resurrection meant that dishonorable bodies would be raised. Paul regards their position as foolish (v. 36) and gives an extensive discussion of the matter (vv. 36–49).

15:36 unless it dies. Because God is the creator of the world, the processes of nature reflect in various ways how He works. Nature provides useful metaphors and analogies of the divine work of salvation (Is. 55:10, 11). Jesus uses a seed ("if it dies, it bears much fruit") as an illustration of spiritual truth (John 12:24). Here Paul uses the same picture, but to illustrate the striking difference between what is planted and what eventually grows from the seed (v. 37). The same sort of analogy can be found in Plato's dialogue *Symposium*.

15:38 to each kind of seed its own body. At this point Paul shifts the illustration to emphasize the variations among different plants. He goes on to apply the idea to living creatures (v. 39) and heavenly bodies (vv. 40, 41).

15:42, 43 Finally the illustration is applied to the human body that dies and is buried, and is transformed in its resurrection. Paul does not suggest that the resurrection body is a different body altogether. Just as a plant arises directly from its seed, so the resurrection body is in essence the same as the body that "is sown." But the apostle's emphasis is on the astounding change that will take place: from "perishable," "dishonor," and "weakness," to "imperishable," "glory," and "power."

15:44 natural body . . . spiritual body. This last contrast is difficult to understand but of great importance. Paul does not have in mind a contrast between physical and nonphysical, material and immaterial. The resurrection body is a physical body, not an intangible ghost. The apostle has already used the words "natural" and "spiritual" to distinguish the individual who does not have the Holy Spirit from the one who does (2:6, 14 notes). The natural person belongs to the present age (1:20), while the spiritual person is a citizen of heaven (Phil. 3:20). Christians have received the Holy Spirit and are on that account "spiritual." They have not yet received the spiritual "body," the body that will be fully conformed to the life given by the Spirit. See Rom. 8:22–25 and note.

15:45 living being . . . life-giving spirit. Paul clarifies his meaning by continuing the contrast between the first and the last Adam (vv. 21, 22 note). The Greek word translated "being" (*psyche*) is related to the word translated "natural" in v. 44 (*psychikos*), while the word "spirit" (*pneuma*) corresponds to "spiritual" (*pneumatikos*). The words "life-giving spirit" are most probably a reference to the Holy Spirit. Jesus and the Holy Spirit are not the same Person, but He and the Spirit are identified in terms of their presence and activity in the church. This identity, known to us because Jesus too is life-giving, is the fulfillment of Jesus' role as Messiah and commenced with His resurrection and ascension. To be in Christ is to be in the Spirit also (6:11, 15, 19; 12:19). The association of Christ, the Holy Spirit, and life is apparent in Rom. 8:9–11 and 2 Cor. 3:6, 17, 18.

15:48 of dust . . . of heaven. Here is a final contrast, suggesting that vv. 42–44 refer to the distinction between earthly and heavenly human bodies. In this context the distinction, however, is not one of substance but of time; the present evil age is contrasted with the coming perfect age. Believers already enjoy some of the blessings of the coming age (10:11 note) but still await its consummation. God's work of redemption will not be complete until the bodily resurrection. We have borne the image of the first Adam, and since we belong to Christ, we are destined to bear the image of the last Adam (v. 49).

15:50 flesh and blood. This phrase alludes to the weakness of earthly, human existence and is an equivalent to "perishable." Paul is warning the Corinthians that without new "imperishable" bodies we "cannot inherit the kingdom of God." How then can some deny the doctrine of the Resurrection?

15:51 mystery. See note 2:7.

We shall not all sleep. Paul recognizes that many Christians will not die but will be alive at the time of Christ's return. Though these Christians will not be raised from death, they too will be transformed and receive imperishable and immortal bodies (1 Thess. 4:13–18 and notes).

the mortal puts on immortality, then shall
come to pass the saying that is written:

[x]"Death is swallowed up in victory."
55 [y]"O death, where is your victory?
O death, where is your sting?"

56 The sting of death is sin, and [z]the power
of sin is the law. 57 But thanks be to God,
[a]who gives us the victory through our Lord
Jesus Christ.
58 [b]Therefore, my beloved brothers, be
steadfast, immovable, always abounding in
[c]the work of the Lord, knowing that in the
Lord [d]your labor is not in vain.

The Collection for the Saints

16 Now concerning[1] [e]the collection
for the saints: as I directed the
churches of Galatia, so you also are to do.
2 On [f]the first day of every week, each of
you is to put something aside and store it
up, [g]as he may prosper, [h]so that there will
be no collecting when I come. 3 And when
I arrive, I will send [i]those whom you
accredit by letter to carry your gift to Jerusalem. 4 If it seems advisable that I should
go also, they will accompany me.

Plans for Travel

5 [j]I will visit you after passing through
[k]Macedonia, for [l]I intend to pass through
Macedonia, 6 and perhaps I will stay with
you or even spend the winter, so that you
may [m]help me on my journey, wherever I
go. 7 For I do not want to see you now [n]just
in passing. I hope to spend some time with
you, [o]if the Lord permits. 8 But I will stay in
Ephesus until [p]Pentecost, 9 for [q]a wide door
for effective work has opened to me, and
[r]there are many adversaries.
10 [s]When Timothy comes, see that you
put him at ease among you, for [t]he is doing
[u]the work of the Lord, as I am. 11 So [v]let no
one despise him. [w]Help him on his way [x]in
peace, that he may return to me, for I am
expecting him with the brothers.

Final Instructions

12 Now concerning [y]our brother Apollos,
I strongly urged him to visit you with the
other brothers, but it was not at all his will[2]
to come now. He will come when he has
opportunity.
13 [z]Be watchful, [a]stand firm in the faith,
[b]act like men, [c]be strong. 14 [d]Let all that you
do be done in love.
15 Now I urge you, brothers[3]—you know
that [e]the household[4] of Stephanas were

54 [x]Cited from Isai. 25:8; [Heb. 2:14, 15; Rev. 20:14; 21:4] 55 [y]Hos. 13:14 56 [z]Rom. 4:15; 5:13; 7:5, 8, 13 57 [a][Rom. 8:37; 1 John 5:4] 58 [b]2 Pet. 3:14 [c]ch. 16:10; Jer. 48:10; John 6:28 [d][Gal. 6:9]; See ch. 3:8
Chapter 16
1 [e]See Acts 24:17 2 [f]Acts 20:7; [Rev. 1:10] [g]2 Cor. 8:3, 11 [h]2 Cor. 9:3 3 [i][2 Cor. 8:18, 19] 5 [j]See ch. 4:19 [k]See Acts 16:9 [l]Acts 19:21 6 [m]ver. 11; See Acts 15:3 7 [n][2 Cor. 1:15, 16] [o]ch. 4:19; Acts 18:21; James 4:15 8 [p]See Acts 2:1 9 [q]See Acts 14:27 [r]Acts 19:9 10 [s]ch. 4:17; [2 Cor. 1:1]

[t]Rom. 16:21; 1 Thess. 3:2; [Phil. 2:20, 22] [u]See ch. 15:58 11 [v]1 Tim. 4:12; [Tit. 2:15] [w]ver. 6 [x]Acts 15:33 12 [y]See Acts 18:24 13 [z]See Matt. 24:42 [a]Gal. 5:1; Phil. 1:27; 4:1; 1 Thess. 3:8; 2 Thess. 2:15; See ch. 15:1 [b]1 Sam. 4:9; 2 Sam. 10:12; Isai. 46:8 [c]Eph. 3:16; [Eph. 6:10; Col. 1:11] 14 [d]ch. 14:1 15 [e]ch. 1:16

1 The expression *Now concerning* introduces a reply to a question in the Corinthians' letter; see 7:1; also verse 12 2 Or *God's will for him* 3 Or *brothers and sisters*; also verse 20 4 Greek *house*

15:54–57 This is one of the most eloquent and powerful passages in Scripture. With paraphrases of Isaiah and Hosea (based on the Septuagint, the Greek translation of the Old Testament), Paul alludes to his earlier argument in vv. 24–28 and vigorously assures us of the finality of death's destruction on the day of Resurrection. The Day will also mark the destruction of "sin" and "the law." In the letter to the Romans, Paul explains in detail how sin is the venom bringing death to all (Rom. 5:12), and how the law, though itself holy, becomes an instrument through which sin can deceive (Rom. 7:7–12).

15:58 be steadfast. In the face of false teaching and various temptations, the hope of the Resurrection should encourage the Corinthians to persevere in their faith. The exhortation to be "immovable," however, does not imply inactivity. On the contrary, the Corinthians must be fully active in "the work of the Lord." We can become easily discouraged by thinking that our labor may come to nothing (Gal. 2:2; Phil. 2:16; 1 Thess. 3:5), but we can remember the promise that when God creates the new heavens and new earth His people will enjoy the fruits of their toil, and see that their efforts are never "in vain" (Is. 65:17–25).

16:1 Now concerning the collection. From 2 Cor. 8:1–4 and Rom. 15:25–27 it appears that one of the purposes of Paul's third missionary journey was to raise an offering from the Gentiles for Jewish Christians in Judea who were in need, possibly as a result of persecution. Apparently, Paul had already told the Corinthians about this project in an earlier letter (5:9). They had asked for more information and perhaps expressed reservations about it (Introduction: Date and Occasion).

for the saints. See 1:2 note.

16:2 On the first day of every week. The reference is to Sunday, the day on which the resurrected Lord met with His disciples (John 20:19, 26; cf. also "the Lord's day" in Rev. 1:10). Acts 20:7 indicates that the early Christians met on Sunday "to break bread" (part of their worship), and it would have been appropriate to designate that day for collecting the offering.

16:3 those whom you accredit. This comment possibly reflects doubts on the part of some whether Paul should be given sole responsibility for the money (2:1 note).

16:5–9 These verses make clear that Paul wrote the letter from Ephesus and intended to visit Corinth by way of the northern land route around the Aegean Sea. Both Acts 20:1, 2 and 2 Cor. 2:12, 13 indicate that he carried out this plan. What Paul did not foresee at this time was the prior need to make a short and unpleasant visit to Corinth soon after writing 1 Corinthians (2 Cor. 1:23; 2:1; 13:2; Introduction to 2 Corinthians: Date and Occasion).

16:10 When Timothy comes. Earlier (4:17), Paul had mentioned that Timothy was coming as his representative (Acts 19:22). Paul wants them to treat his younger coworker with respect.

16:12 Now concerning our brother Apollos. Apparently, the Corinthians in their letter had asked for Apollos to return to them (Introduction: Date and Occasion; Acts 18:27–19:1). In spite of the improper attitude of the Corinthians (4:6; 4:15 note), Paul honored their request. It was not Apollos' "will" to go at this time, but he would come later.

16:15–18 This passage commends "Stephanas, Fortunatus, and Achaicus," who probably had carried the letter from the church in Corinth. Paul's emphasis (especially in the words "I urge you, brothers . . . be subject") suggests that these men, Stephanas in particular, were

[f]the first converts in Achaia, and that they
have devoted themselves [g]to the service of
the saints— 16 [h]be subject to such as these,
and to every fellow worker and laborer. 17 I
rejoice at the coming of Stephanas and
Fortunatus and Achaicus, because they
have made up for [i]your absence, 18 for they
[j]refreshed my spirit as well as yours. [k]Give
recognition to such men.

Greetings

19 The churches of Asia send you greetings. [l]Aquila and Prisca, together with [m]the
church in their house, send you hearty
greetings in the Lord. 20 All the brothers
send you greetings. [n]Greet one another
with a holy kiss.

21 I, Paul, write [o]this greeting with my
own hand. 22 If anyone has no love for the
Lord, let him be [p]accursed. Our Lord,
come![1] 23 [q]The grace of the Lord Jesus be
with you. 24 My love be with you all in
Christ Jesus. Amen.

15 [f][Rom. 16:5] [g]See Rom. 15:31 16 [h]1 Thess. 5:12; Heb. 13:17 17 [i]Phil. 2:30; [2 Cor. 11:9; Philem. 13] 18 [j]2 Cor. 7:13; [Rom. 15:32; Philem. 7, 20] [k]Phil. 2:29; 1 Thess. 5:12 19 [l]See Acts 18:2 [m]See Rom. 16:5 20 [n]See Rom. 16:16 21 [o]Col. 4:18; 2 Thess. 3:17; [Rom. 16:22; Gal. 6:11; Philem. 19] 22 [p]See Rom. 9:3 23 [q]Rom. 16:20

1 Greek *Maranatha*

appointed leaders but did not enjoy proper respect from the congregation. The phrase "for your absence" does not necessarily imply a criticism (the Greek at the end of Phil. 2:30 is almost identical), but here it may suggest that the church as a whole failed to refresh his spirit.

16:19 Asia. Ephesus, where 1 Corinthians was written, was the most important city in the Roman province of Asia, the southwestern part of the Anatolian peninsula, now part of modern Turkey (Acts 19:10).

Aquila and Prisca. This couple played an important role during Paul's initial visit to Corinth (Acts 18:1–3), so the congregation knew them well.

16:20 holy kiss. A normal greeting in the early church. Though this practice was not uncommon in Judaism and Roman culture, the word "holy" indicates the added significance such a greeting had among the saints, since it represented the special relationship of brothers and sisters in Christ.

16:21 with my own hand. The letter up to this point would have been written by a trained scribe (Rom. 16:22), but Paul's custom was to add a few words himself as a personal signature.

16:22 let him be accursed. These strong words, written in Paul's own hand, assert the apostolic authority behind the whole letter. This is not a curse on unbelievers in general but on those who reject the authority of the letter (Gal. 1:8, 9; 2 Thess. 3:14, 15).

Our Lord, come. Paul gives a transliteration of the Aramaic words *Marana tha* (or *Maran atha*, "Our Lord has come"), reflecting the worship of the early church in Palestine.

16:24 My love be with you all. After a long letter consisting primarily of severe rebukes, these affectionate words come as a surprise. Paul has not forgotten the pastoral needs of his congregation (1:2 note).

THE SECOND EPISTLE OF PAUL THE APOSTLE TO THE

Corinthians

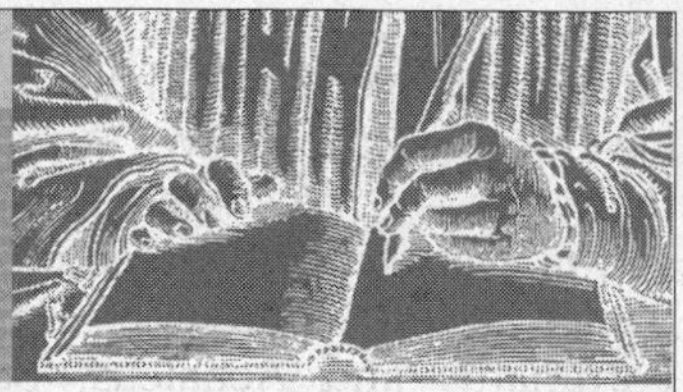

AUTHOR

That the apostle Paul was the author of this letter (1:1) is universally acknowledged. It is an intensely personal letter in which Paul gives many details of his movements and associations.

DATE AND OCCASION

The most likely date for the epistle is A.D. 55. Paul wrote it after he had left Ephesus (Acts 20:1) but before he arrived again in Corinth (Acts 20:2).

After founding the church at Corinth in A.D. 51–52 (Acts 18:1–18), Paul returned to Antioch, ending his second missionary journey (Acts 18:22). On his third missionary journey Paul traveled to Ephesus and stayed there three years (Acts 19:1–41; 20:31). During his stay at Ephesus, messengers had come from Corinth with questions Paul answered in 1 Corinthians (1 Cor. 16:17, 18). Sometime later, Paul apparently heard of difficulties at Corinth and made a quick voyage by sea from Ephesus to Corinth and back. This visit did not go well and Paul later referred to it as a visit made "in sorrow" (2:1). Though not recorded in Acts, this visit is indirectly attested when Paul writes in 2 Corinthians that he is coming to them for the "third time" (12:14; 13:1). We do not know many details about what made this visit sorrowful, but apparently someone at Corinth had opposed or seriously offended Paul (2:5, 10).

Most commentators think that after the sorrowful visit, Paul wrote the Corinthians a strong letter, commonly called the "severe letter," rebuking them and encouraging them to repent (2:3, 4; 7:8). It seems most likely that the letter referred to in these verses has not been preserved. But some hold that the letter referred to is 1 Corinthians. Others think that the originally separate letter has been preserved as 2 Corinthians 10–13. Paul sent Titus ahead by sea to Corinth, carrying the strong letter, while Paul took the longer land route around through Troas and Macedonia (2:12, 13; 7:5–9, 13–15; Acts 20:1, 2).

Paul did not know how the Corinthians would receive Titus and the strong letter. When he left Ephesus and traveled to Troas he experienced considerable anxiety because of his concern for the Corinthian church (2:13; 7:5). Though there was an opportunity for effective ministry when he reached Troas (2:12), Paul's spirit was still deeply troubled. He left Troas and went on to Philippi in Macedonia, hoping to meet Titus there. When Titus finally arrived (probably at Philippi but perhaps at Thessalonica) Paul was overwhelmed with joy as he heard about the genuine repentance of the Corinthians and their deep affection and loyalty to Paul (7:6–15).

Paul then wrote 2 Corinthians from Macedonia to express thanksgiving for the repentance and renewed obedience of the Corinthian church (7:5–16). He also wrote to encourage them to complete their collection for the poor Christians in Jerusalem (chs. 8; 9). Moreover, Paul shows concern throughout the epistle to defend his ministry against the accusations of "false apostles" (11:13) at Corinth who were challenging Paul's authority and the integrity of his ministry (chs. 10–13; also 3:1–6; 7:2).

Finally, Paul arrived in Corinth and stayed for three months (Acts 20:2, 3) before departing for Jerusalem with the collection that had been sent from many churches for the Christians there (Acts 20:3–21:17).

CHARACTERISTICS AND THEMES

Second Corinthians is a personal letter, filled with expressions of deep emotion. As such, it affords us extraordinary insight into the gospel ministry as carried out by Paul. Two chief themes reveal the nature of Paul's apostolic ministry. In chs. 1–7 it is a service of divine comfort and encouragement in the midst of suffering and troubles (1:3–7; 7:4, 7, 13), and in chs. 10–13 it is an experience of God's strength manifested in human weakness (12:9, 10).

Supporting themes include the blameless nature of Paul's conduct (1:12, 17, 18; 6:3–10; 7:2, 3), his frequent suffering for the sake of the church and for God's glory (1:5–11; 4:8–12; 6:4–10; 11:23–12:9), his strong love for all his churches, especially the Corinthian church (2:4; 11:2, 7–11; 12:14, 15), his apostolic authority to build them up and defeat any opposition (2:9; 10:8; 13:8–10), and the frequent emphasis that Paul judges not according to worldly standards but according to the invisible spiritual realm known to the eyes of faith (1:12). Other distinctive emphases are the glory of the ministry of the new covenant (ch. 3) and the principles of Christian stewardship (chs. 8; 9).

INTERPRETIVE DIFFICULTIES

Even though the authorship of 2 Corinthians is not disputed, many question the unity of the letter, most frequently proposing that chs. 10–13 should be considered a separate letter written on a different occasion and only later appended to chs. 1–9. The basic support for this argument is that Paul's tone and attitude toward the church at Corinth seems so positive and encouraging in chs. 1–9, but so severe and threatening in chs. 10–13. Could both sections have been written on the same occasion to the same church?

Certainly there is a change of tone at 10:1. But this can be accounted for by the change of subject matter. In the first part of the letter, Paul was primarily concerned to share his joy and thanksgiving at the repentance of the Corinthians. He also wanted to give an extensive and positive description of his own ministry. Having done that, he then appealed to them to complete the collection for the Jerusalem Christians (chs. 8; 9). Finally, leaving the most distasteful task until last, he took up the problem of the false apostles and their accusations against him (chs. 10–13). In light of the circumstances, a change in tone is understandable. From the earliest times in the history of the church there has been no indication of division in this letter, either in the manuscript tradition or in the early historical writings of the church. It has always been read and understood as one letter. This still seems the best solution.

OUTLINE OF 2 CORINTHIANS

I. Salutation (1:1, 2)

II. An Explanation of Paul's Ministry (1:3–7:16)

A. *Thanksgiving for God's Comfort (1:3–11)*
B. *Paul's Change of Plans Explained (1:12–2:4)*
C. *Paul's Forgiveness of a Penitent Sinner (2:5–11)*
D. *Paul's Journey to Troas and Macedonia (2:12, 13)*
E. *Excellence of the Gospel Ministry (2:14–7:4)*
   1. A Triumphal Procession and a Fragrant Aroma (2:14–17)
   2. A Living Letter of Recommendation (3:1–3)
   3. A New Covenant of Unfading Glory (3:4–4:6)
   4. A Glorious Ministry Carried in Earthen Vessels (4:7–5:10)
   5. A Ministry of Reconciliation (5:11–6:13)
   6. A Plea for Separation from Evil (6:14–7:4)
F. *Paul's Joy at the Coming of Titus (7:5–16)*

III. The Collection for Christians in Jerusalem (chs. 8; 9)

A. *The Example of Macedonia (8:1–7)*
B. *The Example of Jesus (8:8, 9)*
C. *A Reasonable and Fair Plea for Giving (8:10–9:15)*

IV. Defense Against the False Apostles (10:1–13:10)

A. *Paul's True Spiritual Power (10:1–12)*
B. *Paul's "Boasting" (10:13–12:21)*
   1. Definition of Proper Boasting (10:13–11:21)
   2. Boasting of Suffering and Weakness (11:22–33)
   3. Boasting of a Vision of Heaven (12:1–10)
   4. Paul's Care for the Corinthians (12:11–21)
C. *Warning: Paul Will Come with the Lord's Power (13:1–10)*

V. Final Greeting and Benediction (13:11–14)

Greeting

1 Paul, [a]an apostle of Christ Jesus [b]by
the will of God, and [c]Timothy our
brother,
To the church of God that is at Corinth,
[d]with all the saints who are in the whole of
Achaia:
2 [e]Grace to you and peace from God our
Father and the Lord Jesus Christ.

God of All Comfort

3 [f]Blessed be the [g]God and Father of our
Lord Jesus Christ, the Father of mercies
and [h]God of all comfort, **4** [i]who comforts us
in all our affliction, so that we may be able
to comfort those who are in any affliction,
with the comfort with which we ourselves
are comforted by God. **5** For as we share
abundantly in [j]Christ's sufferings, so
through Christ we share abundantly in
comfort too.[1] **6** [k]If we are afflicted, it is for
your comfort and salvation; and if we are
comforted, it is for your comfort, which
you experience when you patiently endure
the same sufferings that we suffer. **7** Our
hope for you is unshaken, for we know that
as you [l]share in our sufferings, you will also
share in our comfort.
8 For we do not want you to be ignorant,
brothers,[2] of [m]the affliction we experienced
in Asia. For we were so utterly burdened
beyond our strength that we despaired of
life itself. **9** Indeed, we felt that we had
received the sentence of death. But that
was to make us [n]rely not on ourselves [o]but
on God [p]who raises the dead. **10** [q]He delivered us from such a deadly peril, and he
will deliver us. [r]On him we have set our
hope that he will deliver us again. **11** [s]You
also must help us by prayer, so that many

Chapter 1
1 [a]Eph. 1:1; Col. 1:1; 1 Tim. 1:1; 2 Tim. 1:1; Tit. 1:1; [Rom. 1:1; Gal. 1:1] [b]See 1 Cor. 1:1 [c]See 1 Thess. 3:2 [d]Phil. 1:1; Col. 1:2
2 [e]See Rom. 1:7
3 [f]Eph. 1:3; 1 Pet. 1:3 [g]See Rom. 15:6 [h]Rom. 15:5
4 [i][Isai. 51:12; 66:13]
5 [j][ch. 4:10; Phil. 3:10; Col. 1:24]
6 [k]2 Tim. 2:10; [ch. 4:15; 12:15; Eph. 3:13]
7 [l]See Rom. 8:17
8 [m]Acts 19:23; 1 Cor. 15:32
9 [n]Luke 18:9 [o]Ps. 2:12; 25:2; 26:1
[p]ch. 4:14 **10** [q]See Rom.15:31 [r]1 Tim. 4:10 **11** [s][Acts 12:5; Rom. 15:30; Phil. 1:19; Philem. 22]

[1] Or *For as the sufferings of Christ abound for us, so also our comfort abounds through Christ* [2] Or *brothers and sisters*. The plural Greek word *adelphoi* (translated "brothers") refers to siblings in a family. In New Testament usage, depending on the context, *adelphoi* may refer either to men or to both men and women who are siblings (brothers and sisters) in God's family, the church

1:1 apostle. Paul describes himself as "apostle," but not his associate (also 1 Cor. 1:1; Col. 1:1). An apostle was an eyewitness of the Resurrection (Acts 1:22; 1 Cor. 15:8) who had been personally appointed by Christ (Matt. 10:1–7; Acts 1:24–26; Gal. 1:1) to govern the early church (1 Thess. 4:8; 2 Thess. 3:6, 14), and to teach or write with authority (1 Cor. 14:37; 1 Thess. 2:13; 4:15; 2 Pet. 3:15, 16). The term is used as a title of the twelve disciples and Paul. It is also used in a broader sense (Rom. 16:7), while in general or nontechnical use it means a "messenger" or "representative" (8:23; Phil. 2:25).

by the will of God. It is God's sovereign choice that ultimately places people in church offices and ministries. The apostolic office was extraordinary and temporary, and did not continue when there were no surviving eyewitnesses of the Resurrection, and when the canon of Scripture was complete. The ordinary offices continue to be necessary, and are filled by elders (Acts 20:28) and others whose gifts equip them for ministries (1 Cor. 12:7, 11, 28). Calls to the ordinary offices are confirmed by the people of God as the church discerns who has received the gifts and qualifications for the work (Eph. 4:11).

saints. A term commonly used by Paul to refer to all Christians (Rom. 15:25; Phil. 1:1).

in the whole of Achaia. Though the letter was intended primarily for the church at Corinth, Paul apparently realized that it would be read by neighboring churches in the region of Achaia, the southern part of modern Greece. On Corinth, see Acts 18:1 note.

1:2 Grace. Grace is God's undeserved favor—not just in initial forgiveness of sins, but in the ordinary events of everyday life as well.

peace. The outward blessing of social order and the inward blessing of a good relationship with God (Rom. 5:1; 1 Tim. 2:2).

God our Father and the Lord Jesus Christ. It is evidence of the deity of Christ that He with the Father should be mentioned equally as the origin of grace and peace for the Corinthian church.

1:3 Father of our Lord Jesus Christ. The three Persons of the Trinity are equally divine, yet they are one God, not three. As the names Father, Son, and Holy Spirit suggest, certain roles and activities correspond more closely to one Person than another. For example, the role of the Father is to initiate and direct.

Father of mercies and God of all comfort. A key theme of chs. 1–9. All consolation and encouragement in the world has its origin in God Himself.

1:4 that we may be able to comfort. God has a sovereign purpose both in our troubles and in the comfort that He gives us in them. If we have experienced God's comfort in suffering, we may be able to support others whose sufferings are like ours.

1:5 we share abundantly in Christ's sufferings. Not that we can add anything to Christ's suffering for us (Is. 53:11; John 19:30; Heb. 9:26–28), but God has called us to suffer for Christ and so to follow in Christ's steps (Rom. 8:17; Col. 1:24; Heb. 12:2, 3; 1 Pet. 2:21). Because believers are united to Christ and are spiritually part of His body, both our sufferings for the gospel and the comfort God provides in Christ are a result of our participation in Him (Phil. 3:10, 11). Here Paul hints at a persistent feature of his teaching. The key experiences of Christ, especially His suffering, death, and resurrection, are the pattern by which Christians can understand their own suffering and final triumph.

1:6 Paul sees God's sovereign hand and redemptive purpose in everything that happens to him, whether distress or comfort.

1:7 you share in our sufferings. Behind this verse lies Paul's teaching that all believers, as members of one body of Christ, are joined together so that every dimension of life in Christ is shared among them (1 Cor. 12:26). The more fully this reality influences the attitudes and actions of believers toward each other, the more fully they experience satisfying fellowship through Christ with one another.

1:8 the affliction we experienced in Asia. Apparently he refers to some hardship, persecution, illness, or injury that he suffered since he last saw his readers. These hardships would have occurred either in Ephesus or between Ephesus and Macedonia, although they are not mentioned in the summary statement of Acts 20:1.

our. In this letter Paul normally uses the editorial plural "we" or "our" to refer to himself alone.

1:9 we had received the sentence of death. Paul was convinced that God had decided it was time for him to die.

rely not on ourselves. God's purpose in our afflictions often is to drive us to this conclusion.

who raises the dead. The resurrection of the dead is a revelation of God's unsurpassable power (Eph. 1:20).

1:11 help us by prayer. Prayer has real results. God has ordained His relationship to the world in such a way that He will respond to our prayers, and even Paul needed the prayers of others.

will give thanks on our behalf [t]for the
blessing granted us through the prayers of
many.

Paul's Change of Plans

12 For our boast is this: [u]the testimony of
our conscience that we behaved in the
world with simplicity[1] and [v]godly sincerity,
[w]not by earthly wisdom but by the grace of
God, and supremely so toward you. 13 For
we are not writing to you anything other
than what you read and acknowledge[2] and
I hope you will fully acknowledge— 14 just
as you did [x]partially acknowledge us, that
[y]on the day of our Lord Jesus [z]you will
boast of us as [a]we will boast of you.
15 Because I was sure of this, [b]I wanted to
come to you first, so that you might have [c]a
second [d]experience of grace. 16 I wanted to
visit you [e]on my way to Macedonia, and to
come back to you from Macedonia and
have you send me on my way to Judea.
17 Was I vacillating when I wanted to do
this? Do I make my plans [f]according to the
flesh, ready to say "Yes, yes" and "No, no"
at the same time? 18 As surely as [g]God is
faithful, [h]our word to you has not been Yes
and No. 19 For [i]the Son of God, Jesus
Christ, whom we proclaimed among you,
[j]Silvanus and Timothy and I, was not Yes
and No, but [k]in him it is always Yes. 20 For
[l]all the promises of God find their Yes in
him. That is why it is through him that we
utter our [m]Amen to God for his glory.
21 And it is God who establishes us with
you in Christ, and [n]has anointed us, 22 and
who has also [o]put his seal on us and [p]giv-
en us his Spirit in our hearts as a guarantee.[3]
23 But [q]I call God to witness against me—
it was [r]to spare you that I refrained from
coming again to Corinth. 24 Not that we

11 [t][ch. 4:15; 9:11, 12] 12 [u][1 Thess. 2:10]; See Acts 23:1 [v]ch. 2:17; 4:2 [w]1 Cor. 2:4, 13 14 [x]ch. 2:5 [y]See 1 Cor. 1:8 [z][ch. 5:12; 9:3] [a]1 Cor. 9:15; Phil. 2:16; 4:1; 1 Thess. 2:19, 20 15 [b]See 1 Cor. 4:19 [c][Acts 18:1-18] [d][Rom. 1:11] 16 [e]Acts 19:21; [1 Cor. 16:5-7] 17 [f]ch. 10:2, 3 18 [g]See 1 Cor. 1:9 [h][ch. 2:17] 19 [i]See Matt. 14:33 [j]Acts 15:22 [k][Heb. 13:8] 20 [l][Rom. 15:8; Heb. 10:23] [m][Rev. 3:14]; See 1 Cor. 14:16 21 [n][1 John 2:20, 27] 22 [o]Eph. 1:13; 4:30 [p]ch. 5:5; Eph. 1:14; See Rom. 8:16 23 [q][Gal. 1:20]; See Rom. 1:9 [r]ch. 2:1, 3; See 1 Cor. 4:21

[1] Some manuscripts *holiness* [2] Or *understand*; twice in this verse; also verse 14 [3] Or *down payment*

many will give thanks. These thanks go to God because He delivered Paul from death (v. 10). One of God's purposes in answering prayer is that we will praise Him for it.

1:12 boast. Paul boasts not in his own ability, but in having a clear conscience and morally upright conduct. Paul's simplicity and godly sincerity are not the result of following the conventional wisdom of the world, but depend on "the grace of God." When Paul boasts he takes no credit for himself. It is the triumph of God's grace in him.

earthly wisdom. In this verse Paul introduces his denial of the charge that he had worldly motives for changing his plans to visit Corinth. Distinguishing divine wisdom (expressed in the cross of Christ) from "earthly" wisdom was a problem for some Corinthian believers. Worldly wisdom led to divisions in the church (1 Cor. 1:10–4:7), and by the standards of such wisdom Paul was not acceptable as an apostle (10:2–6).

1:13 Paul reminds the Corinthians that his writings, like his ministry, are not dishonest or tricky, full of hidden meanings and concealed aims, as perhaps some of his opponents at Corinth had claimed. Paul's writings were clear enough. In the same way all Scripture is written not mainly for scholars but for all believers. It is understandable to those who will read it, seeking God's help in understanding and being willing to obey it (Deut. 6:6, 7; Ps. 19:7; 119:130; Matt. 12:3, 5; 19:14; 21:42; Col. 4:16).

1:14 the day of our Lord Jesus. The day of Christ's return.

you will boast of us. They should be proud of what God has done for them in Paul.

1:15 a second experience of grace. Another translation is, "have double grace." Paul knows that his visits impart God's grace to churches.

1:17 according to the flesh. Such plans would be unreliable, vacillating, and unpredictable. Opponents were discrediting the apostle by charging that his change in plans showed weakness of character and lack of integrity. They did not have all the facts, however, and were using these circumstances to attack someone they had already condemned.

1:18 as God is faithful. Paul calls on God's faithfulness as the pattern and guarantee for his own faithfulness.

word. Paul reminds them that his gospel message was absolutely reliable and led to their salvation.

1:19 The absolute truthfulness and reliability of God's words in Christ are the standard that Paul follows in his own speech. This is consistent with Paul's general pattern of deriving moral absolutes from the moral character of God.

1:20 find their Yes in him. Christ fulfills all the promises of God to us, and all our confidence in God's promises must come from our trust in Jesus Christ as a person whom we know and can rely on.

1:21, 22 God . . . Christ . . . Spirit. This Trinitarian passage points to the roles of all three divine Persons in salvation.

1:21 God . . . establishes us. The ability to persevere, that is, to continue in the Christian life, is not from ourselves; it is a gift from God. God continues to give this ability to all who are born again (Phil. 1:6; 1 Pet. 1:5). Those who are guarded by God in this way continue to trust in Christ throughout their lives (13:5; Col. 1:23; Heb. 3:14), because God protects them through the faith He gives them (v. 24).

anointed. To "anoint" literally is to pour oil on the head, often as a sign of divine calling and empowerment (1 Sam. 2:10; 16:13 and notes). Paul reminds us that just as God anointed Jesus for a particular service and ministry, so He has anointed us for our ministries, not with oil, but with the power of the Holy Spirit (1 John 2:20, 27).

1:22 put his seal on us. An official seal indicated authority or ownership and guaranteed protection (Esth. 8:8; Dan. 6:17; Matt. 27:66; Rev. 7:3). God has sealed us, not with a physical seal of wax, but with the Holy Spirit in our hearts (Eph. 1:13; 4:30). This inward work takes place in a person once, at the time of first becoming a Christian.

guarantee. The Greek word means a deposit or down payment that is part of the total and that guarantees the whole payment will be made. The Holy Spirit is the guarantee of the complete salvation yet to be realized (5:5; Rom. 8:23; Eph. 1:14). We already have heavenly life within us, before we reach heaven (1 Cor. 3:16; Col. 1:27).

1:23 God to witness against me. Paul uses a solemn oath to persuade the Corinthians of his truthfulness. He says in effect, "If I am not telling the truth, I ask God to take my life."

to spare you. Paul would come with the Lord's authority and power on his next visit (10:3, 4; 13:2–4, 10), and he wanted to give them a chance to repent. This was the reason he changed his plans and did not come back to Corinth before going to Macedonia. It was not worldly vacillation or cowardice, as some were saying.

[s]lord it over your faith, but we work with
you for your joy, for you stand firm [t]in your
faith.

2 For I made up my mind [u]not to make
another painful visit to you. 2 For [v]if I
cause you pain, who is there to make me
glad but the one whom I have pained?
3 And I wrote as I did, so that when I came
I might not suffer pain from those who
should have made me rejoice, [w]for I felt
sure of all of you, that my joy would be the
joy of you all. 4 For [x]I wrote to you out of
much affliction and anguish of heart and
with many tears, not to cause you pain but
to let you know the abundant love that I
have for you.

Forgive the Sinner

5 Now [y]if anyone has caused pain, [z]he
has caused it not to me, but [a]in some
measure—not to put it too severely—to all
of you. 6 For such a one, [b]this punishment
by the majority is enough, 7 so [c]you should
rather turn to forgive and comfort him, or
he may be overwhelmed by excessive sorrow. 8 So I beg you to reaffirm your love for
him. 9 For this is why I wrote, that I might
[d]test you and know [e]whether you are obedient in everything. 10 Anyone whom you
forgive, I also forgive. What I have forgiven,
if I have forgiven anything, has been for
your sake in the presence of Christ, 11 so
that we would not be outwitted by Satan;
for [f]we are not ignorant of his designs.

Triumph in Christ

12 When [g]I came to Troas to preach the
gospel of Christ, even though [h]a door was
opened for me in the Lord, 13 my spirit [i]was
not at rest because I did not find my brother Titus there. So I took leave of them and
went on to Macedonia.

14 But [j]thanks be to God, who in Christ
always [k]leads us in triumphal procession,
and through us spreads [l]the fragrance of the
knowledge of him everywhere. 15 For we are
the aroma of Christ to God among [m]those
who are being saved and among [n]those who
are perishing, 16 [o]to one a fragrance from
death to death, [o]to the other a fragrance
from life to life. [p]Who is sufficient[1] for these

24 [s]1 Pet. 5:3; [ch. 4:5; Matt. 23:8-10] [t]Rom. 11:20; See 1 Cor. 15:1
Chapter 2
1 [u]ch. 1:23; [ch. 12:20, 21; 13:10]
2 [v][ch. 7:8]
3 [w]ch. 8:22; Gal. 5:10; 2 Thess. 3:4; [ch. 7:16]
4 [x]ch. 7:8, 12; See Acts 20:19
5 [y][1 Cor. 5:1, 2] [z][Gal. 4:12] [a]ch. 1:14
6 [b]1 Cor. 5:4, 5; [ch. 7:11]
7 [c]Gal. 6:1; [Eph. 4:32]
9 [d]Phil. 2:22 [e]ch. 7:15; 10:6
11 [f]See 1 Pet. 5:8
12 [g]Acts 16:8; 20:6 [h]See Acts 14:27
13 [i]ch. 7:5
14 [j]ch. 8:16; [ch. 9:15]; See Rom. 6:17 [k]Col. 2:15 (Gk.); [l]Eph. 5:2; Phil. 4:18; [S. of S. 1:3]
15 [m]See 1 Cor. 1:18 [n]ch. 4:3
16 [o][Luke 2:34; John 9:39; 1 Pet. 2:7, 8] [p]ch. 3:5, 6

[1] Or *competent*

2:1 painful. See Introduction: Date and Occasion.

2:3 I wrote as I did. After the painful visit (v. 1), Paul wrote a letter of rebuke to the Corinthian church, sending it by the hand of Titus (2:13; 7:6, 7, 13, 14).

2:4 not to cause you pain. Paul's purpose in writing the unpleasant letter was not simply to make the Corinthians sorrowful. He was seeking their best interests, even when that meant bringing pain both to them and to him.

2:5 if anyone has caused pain. This could be a reference to the man living with his father's wife (1 Cor. 5:1–8), but that is doubtful because the offense seems to be something directed against Paul himself (vv. 5, 10).

2:6 punishment by the majority. Apparently after Paul had left Corinth, or at least after Titus had come with the unpleasant letter, the Corinthians had exercised church discipline against the offender (cf. Matt. 18:15–20).

2:7 The purpose of church discipline is to restore, not to destroy or take revenge (10:8).

2:10 Paul will accept the judgment of the Corinthian congregation on this matter.

in the presence of Christ. A common theme in this epistle. All our actions are carried out not in secrecy but in the presence of Christ, the Lord of the church. If both Paul and Christ have forgiven the offender, the Corinthians should as well (cf. Matt. 16:19; John 20:23).

2:11 not be outwitted by Satan. Satan will win a victory if we either neglect church discipline entirely, or if we attend to it but remain harsh and unforgiving when there has been a change of heart.

2:12 Troas. A city in far northwest Asia Minor (now Turkey), across the Aegean Sea from Greece. Paul sailed from here to Philippi. It was in Troas that Paul had seen a vision of a man from Macedonia imploring him to come and help (Acts 16:8).

a door was opened for me. God provided opportunities for preaching the gospel.

2:13 my spirit was not at rest. Paul had hoped that Titus would meet him at Troas and report that the letter of rebuke had been well received. When Titus failed to appear, Paul was deeply troubled.

I took leave of them. A great opportunity for effective ministry did not make Paul turn aside from his prior commitment to care for the Corinthian church and straighten out its problems. Paul continued to feel a deep concern for all his churches (11:28, 29).

to Macedonia. Paul went first to Philippi, then perhaps to Thessalonica or Berea before Titus came. Acts 16:8–18:1 describes the previous journey of Paul along this route. At this point the narrative of his relationship with the Corinthian church is interrupted until 7:5, and Paul inserts an extensive digression on the nature of the new covenant ministry in which he is engaged.

2:14 always leads us in triumphal procession. Paul's narrative suddenly shifts from the visible reality of his anxiety for the Corinthians and his disappointment at not finding Titus in Troas, to the spiritual realm. Paul sees himself as part of God's triumphal procession into the heavenly city, much like a victory parade that an ancient general would lead upon returning to his own city with vanquished captives following behind the chariots. But here Paul—God's former enemy—is a joyful captive and one who participates in the blessings of the King's victory. We too have such a participation in the spiritual realm, marching in the victory procession of our great King, as the forces of the enemy crumble before His advance. Despite setbacks like Paul's at Troas, the eyes of faith can see the unrelenting progress of the kingdom of God.

2:15 we are the aroma of Christ to God. That we are a sweet aroma to God means that He delights in us and in our lives. This is the more real and final fulfillment of the Old Testament sacrifices that were a sweet aroma to God (Lev. 1:17).

2:16 Figuratively speaking there is a pleasant fragrance, spiritually perceived, about true Christians. On the other hand, this fragrance is a "fragrance from death" to unbelievers, for it warns them that they are unprepared for the day of judgment (Phil. 1:28).

sufficient for these things. Carrying a message of eternal life or death

things? 17 For we are not, like so many, ped-
dlers of God's word, but as men of sincerity, as commissioned by God, in the sight
of God we speak in Christ.

Ministers of the New Covenant

3 [q]Are we beginning to commend ourselves again? Or do we need, [r]as some
do, [s]letters of recommendation to you, or
from you? 2 [t]You yourselves are our letter of
recommendation, written on our[1] hearts,
to be known and read by all. 3 And you
show that you are a letter from Christ delivered by us, written not with ink but with
the Spirit of [u]the living God, not on [v]tablets
of stone but on [w]tablets of [x]human hearts.[2]
4 [y]Such is the confidence that we have
through Christ toward God. 5 [z]Not that we
are sufficient in ourselves to claim anything
as coming from us, but [a]our sufficiency is
from God, 6 who has made us competent[3]
to be [b]ministers of [c]a new covenant, not of
[d]the letter but of the Spirit. For the letter
kills, but [e]the Spirit gives life.
7 Now if [f]the ministry of death, carved in
letters on stone, came with such glory [g]that
the Israelites could not gaze at Moses' face
because of its glory, which was being
brought to an end, 8 will not the ministry
of the Spirit have even more glory? 9 For if
there was glory in [h]the ministry of condemnation, [i]the ministry of righteousness
must far exceed it in glory. 10 Indeed, in this
case, what once had glory has come to have
no glory at all, because of the glory that
surpasses it. 11 For if what was being
brought to an end came with glory, much
more will what is permanent have glory.
12 Since we have such a hope, [j]we are very
bold, 13 not like Moses, [k]who would put a

Chapter 3
1 [q]ch. 5:12; 10:12; 12:11 [r][ch. 11:4] [s][Acts 18:27; 1 Cor. 16:3]
2 [t][1 Cor. 9:2]
3 [u]See Matt. 16:16 [v]Ex. 24:12 [w]Prov. 3:3; 7:3; Jer. 17:1 [x]Ezek. 11:19; 36:26; [Jer. 31:33; Heb. 8:10]
4 [y]Eph. 3:12
5 [z][Eph 2:8] [a]See 1 Cor. 15:10
6 [b]Eph. 3:7; Col. 1:23, 25; [ch. 4:1; 5:18; 1 Tim. 1:12] [c]Jer. 31:31; Luke 22:20; 1 Cor. 11:25; Heb. 8:8, 13; [ver. 14; Heb. 9:15] [d]See Rom. 2:27 [e][John 6:63; Rom. 8:2]
7 [f]ver. 9; See Rom. 4:15 [g]ver. 13; Ex. 34:29–35 **9** [h]ver. 7; [Heb. 12:18-21] [i]ch. 11:15 **12** [j]ch. 7:4; Eph. 6:19 **13** [k]ver. 7

1 Some manuscripts *your* 2 Greek *fleshly hearts* 3 Or *sufficient*

is a sobering responsibility. No one is worthy of this solemn task, but God qualifies us for it nonetheless (3:6).

2:17 not, like so many. It is tragic that then and now many preach the gospel or teach Christianity as no more than a means of earning a living. Paul's goal was not personal benefit or financial reward, but the glory of God.

in the sight of God. All Paul's ministry was carried out in the sight of God, providing him a strong motive for keeping his conscience clear (1:12; Acts 23:1; 1 Tim. 1:5; 2 Tim. 1:3).

3:1 Both questions in this verse expect the answer "no." Paul does not reject letters of commendation generally (Acts 15:25, 26; 18:27; 1 Cor. 16:10, 11), but apparently Paul's opponents had brought some misleading letters of commendation to the church at Corinth, letters that the bearers were not worthy of. Paul shows that his letter is far better, because it consists of the lives of the Corinthian believers (v. 2).

3:2 written on our hearts. The Corinthians have a fixed place in his affections. Some manuscripts read "in your hearts." On this reading, Paul is telling the Corinthians that as a church they are an effective letter of recommendation for him (2:17; 1 Cor. 9:2).

3:3 letter from Christ delivered by us. The Corinthian church was a work of God's grace, but in this work Paul and his co-workers had been God's instruments.

tablets of stone. The Ten Commandments.

tablets of human hearts. Paul's point is twofold. First, the "letter," which the Corinthians are, is superior to the pen-and-ink letters of his opponents as well as the stone tablets of the law. Second, Paul presents the fruits of his apostleship as the fulfillment of Old Testament prophecy. As predicted in Jer. 31:33 and Ezek. 11:19; 36:26, in the new covenant God writes His laws on the hearts of His people, giving them a new desire and ability to obey Him. The law that is written in the heart is the unchanging and pure law of God, that is, His absolute moral standard.

3:4–6:13 After explaining his change of plans about visiting the Corinthians, Paul describes what true ministry is. It means being ministers of a glorious new covenant (3:4–4:6), trusting God in the midst of troubles (4:7–5:10), and speaking the message of reconciliation (5:11–6:13). Paul insists throughout the rest of the letter that faithfulness to these tasks—not eloquence, deep philosophical thought, or worldly standards of personal excellence—is the basis of a valid ministry.

3:4 Such is the confidence. Paul is confident before God that his ministry is authentic and that the Corinthians are "letters of recommendation" testifying to it. Paul's confidence is not in himself, but "through Christ."

3:5 sufficient. Paul answers the question of 2:16 ("Who is sufficient for these things?"). Earlier he had disavowed any dependence on merely human ability (1 Cor. 2:1–5). Unfortunately, Paul's opponents valued worldly ability more than the sufficiency that comes from God alone.

our sufficiency is from God. A major theme of 2 Corinthians. All ability and power in ministry comes from God, not from ourselves.

3:6 new covenant. The new legal relationship that God established with His people through Jesus Christ, His life, death, resurrection, and ascension.

the letter. The written law by itself, which demands perfect obedience but gives no power to obey.

the Spirit gives life. This is new life in Christ. In it the Holy Spirit writes God's law on our hearts (Jer. 31:31–34; Heb. 8:8–12; 9:13, 14), giving love for God's moral standards and power to obey them (Rom. 8:4; 1 Cor. 7:19). Saying that life is "not of the letter," Paul does not imply that there was no spiritual life whatever under the old covenant. He means that the written law, which was characteristic of the old covenant, did not by itself produce life in the believing community. The Holy Spirit, whose powerful, life-giving ministry is characteristic of the new covenant, does bring new life in much greater measure than under the old covenant.

3:7 the ministry of death. The written words of the Old Testament law by themselves condemned people who did not obey, without giving them life.

could not gaze at Moses' face. The old covenant was not without glory, even though it was written on stone (Ex. 34:29–35).

3:8 even more glory. The new covenant is more powerful, beautiful, and inward.

3:9 ministry of righteousness. Righteousness is given in justification, the gracious legal declaration that begins the Christian life. It continues in sanctification, the progressive growth of a believer in righteous thoughts, words, and deeds. Sanctification takes place by grace through faith, but it also requires study, prayer, and conscious effort.

3:11 what was being brought to an end. The old covenant (Heb. 8:13).

3:12 such a hope. The splendor of the new covenant, which will not fade or pass away, provides the apostle's hope and fuels his boldness.

very bold. Paul is not at all ashamed to stand before the world and pro-

veil over his face so that the Israelites might
not gaze at the outcome of what was being
brought to an end. 14 But [l]their minds were
[m]hardened. For to this day, [n]when they
read [o]the old covenant, that same veil
remains unlifted, because only through
Christ is it taken away. 15 Yes, to this day
whenever Moses is read a veil lies over their
hearts. 16 But when [p]one[1] turns to the Lord,
[q]the veil is removed. 17 Now the Lord[2] is the
Spirit, and where [r]the Spirit of the Lord is,
there is [s]freedom. 18 And we all, with
unveiled face, [t]beholding [u]the glory of the
Lord,[3] [v]are being transformed into the
same image [w]from one degree of glory to
another. For this comes from the Lord who
is the Spirit.

The Light of the Gospel

4 Therefore, having [x]this ministry [y]by
the mercy of God,[4] we do not lose
heart. 2 But we have renounced [z]disgrace-
ful, underhanded ways. We refuse to practice cunning or [a]to tamper with God's
word, but [b]by the open statement of the
truth [c]we would commend ourselves to
everyone's conscience in the sight of God.
3 And even [d]if our gospel is veiled, [e]it is
veiled only to [f]those who are perishing. 4 In
their case [g]the god of this world [d]has
blinded the minds of the unbelievers, to
keep them from seeing [h]the light of [i]the
gospel of the glory of Christ, [j]who is the
image of God. 5 For what [k]we proclaim is
not ourselves, but Jesus Christ as Lord,
with [l]ourselves as your servants[5] for Jesus'
sake. 6 For God, who said, [m]"Let light shine
out of darkness," [n]has shone in our hearts
to give [o]the light of the knowledge of the
glory of God in the face of Jesus Christ.

14 [l][ch. 4:4; Rom. 11:25] [m]See Mark 6:52 [n]Acts 13:15; 15:21 [o][ver. 6] **16** [p]Rom. 11:23; [Ex. 34:34] [q][Isai. 25:7] **17** [r]Isai. 61:1, 2; [Gal. 4:6] [s]Gal. 5:1, 13; See John 8:32 **18** [t]See 1 Cor. 13:12 [u]ch. 4:4, 6; 1 Tim. 1:11; See John 17:24 [v]Rom. 8:29; 1 Cor. 15:49 [w][Ps. 84:7]
Chapter 4
1 [x]See ch. 3:6 [y]1 Cor. 7:25; 1 Tim. 1:13 **2** [z]See Rom. 6:21 [a]ch. 2:17 [b]ch. 6:7; 7:14 [c]ch. 5:11, 12 **3** [d][ch. 3:14] [e][Matt. 13:15] [f]ch. 2:15; 1 Cor. 1:18; 2 Thess. 2:10 **4** [g]See John 12:31 [d][See ver. 3 above] [h]ver. 6; See Acts 26:18 [i]See ch. 3:18 [j]Col. 1:15; [Phil. 2:6; Heb. 1:3] **5** [k][1 Thess. 2:6] [l]1 Cor. 9:19; See ch. 1:24 **6** [m]Gen. 1:3 [n]2 Pet. 1:19 [o]ver. 4

[1] Greek *he* [2] Or *this Lord* [3] Or *reflecting the glory of the Lord* [4] Greek *as we have received mercy* [5] Greek *bondservants*

claim the excellent gospel. The reference to "boldness" links the discussion of vv. 7–11 with Paul's defense of his apostleship (10:1, 2). He is bold, not vacillating as his opponents accused him (1:17–2:4); and his boldness, taking the form of the fearless speech so evident in this epistle, is a great contrast to the deceitful selfishness of his opponents (2:17).

3:13 Some think that Moses' veil was to protect the Israelites from being harmed or frightened by the brightness. More likely, the veil was to keep them from seeing that the glory was fading away because of the temporary and inadequate character of the old covenant (Ex. 34:29–35). By contrast, Paul needs no veil, for the glory of the new covenant ministry does not fade away.

3:14 that same veil remains. Even today, Paul says, many Jewish people cannot see that the Mosaic covenant is temporary, and that its glory fades.

3:15 a veil lies over their hearts. The metaphor shifts somewhat, as it often does in Paul's writings. The veil is now not on Moses' face but on their hearts. The effect is the same—they cannot see that the old covenant fades.

3:16 the veil is removed. See "Understanding the Word of God" at Ps. 119:34.

3:17 the Lord is the Spirit. Here Paul stresses the close relationship between Christ and the Holy Spirit. By virtue of His resurrection and ascension, Christ and the life-giving Spirit are closely identified in function (1 Cor. 15:45). It is also possible to translate this phrase, "Now the Spirit is the Lord." The Holy Spirit is truly God; like the Father and the Son, He is the One who is known simply as "the Lord" in the Old Testament. Such a translation gives a natural sense to the word "is."

there is freedom. The bondage was to death, sin, and hopeless effort to obey the law by our own power.

3:18 we all. All Christians. A characteristic experience of new covenant believers is described here.

beholding. Unlike Moses (v. 13), who went before the people with a veil to hide the fading glory on his face, Paul stands before people "with unveiled face," knowing that the new covenant glory will never diminish. Likewise "we all" stand unashamedly before the world, reflecting in our own lives the glory of Christ. And far from a fading glory, our glory is ever-increasing, as we are changed more and more into the likeness of Christ. See "The Transfiguration of Jesus" at Mark 9:2.

into the same image. A reference to continual growth throughout life into increasing Christlikeness. This growth is moral and spiritual transformation "from one degree of glory to another." We are being progressively restored to greater and greater possession of the image of God which was corrupted at the fall of Adam.

4:1 Paul does not give up hope because the new covenant ministry in the power of the Holy Spirit is so excellent and powerful.

4:2 cunning . . . tamper with. This means "adulterate, falsify." Paul says he will never water down the Word of God or distort it to please the hearers. He implies that his opponents did practice such deception and distortion.

4:3 The veil imagery continues from 3:14–16. Those who are presently perishing (not believing in Christ) are blinded to the truth.

4:4 the god of this world. Satan (cf. 1 John 5:19) strongly influences this fallen, evil world that continues until the time Christ returns and brings in fully the age to come (cf. Gal. 1:4).

has blinded. The result is that unbelievers cannot appreciate or fully understand the claims of the gospel, unless God through the gospel enlightens them (4:6; John 3:3).

4:5 what we proclaim is not ourselves. The crucial issue is not whether people accept or reject Paul, but how they respond to Christ. Paul's opponents apparently focused on themselves, and veiled Christ's glory with their own pride.

4:6 For. One reason for not preaching ourselves is that only God gives new spiritual life.

Let light shine. God's sovereign initiative is necessary to enable us to embrace the gospel message. Just as God's original creative word made light where there was no light, so now God's creative word gives spiritual life and understanding of the gospel where previously there was none. See theological note "The Authentication of Scripture."

glory of God. In the Old Testament the glory of God was the bright light that surrounded the presence of God. It had led the people of Egypt as a pillar of cloud by day and a pillar of fire by night (Ex. 13:21–22). Later, it had filled the tabernacle under Moses (Ex. 33:8–13; 40:34–38), and had then filled Solomon's temple (1 Kin. 8:10, 11). But it departed from the temple in the time of Ezekiel because of the sins of the people (Ezek. 10:4, 18, 19; 11:23). It returned only in Jesus, who became flesh and dwelt

Treasures in Jars of Clay

7 But we have this treasure in [p]jars of
clay, [q]to show that the surpassing power
belongs to God and not to us. 8 We are
[r]afflicted in every way, but not crushed;
perplexed, but not driven to despair; 9 persecuted, but [s]not forsaken; [t]struck down,
but not destroyed; 10 [u]always carrying in the
body the death of Jesus, [v]so that the life of
Jesus may also be manifested in our bodies. 11 For we who live are always being
given over to death for Jesus' sake, so that
the life of Jesus also may be manifested in
our mortal flesh. 12 So [w]death is at work in
us, but life in you.
13 Since we have [x]the same spirit of faith

7 [p]2 Tim. 2:20; [ch. 5:1; Job 10:9; 13:12; Lam. 4:2; 1 Thess. 4:4; 1 Pet. 3:7] [q]1 Cor. 2:5; [Judg. 7:2] 8 [r]ch. 7:5; [Ps. 129:2] 9 [s]Heb. 13:5; [Deut. 4:31] [t]Ps. 37:24; Prov. 24:16; Mic. 7:8

10 [u]ch. 6:9; 1 Cor. 4:9; 15:31; [ch. 1:5, 9; Rom. 6:5; 8:36] [v]2 Tim. 2:11; [Rom. 5:10; 6:8] 12 [w][ch. 13:9] 13 [x]1 Cor. 12:9; 2 Pet. 1:1

The Authentication of Scripture

Why do Christians believe that the Bible is the Word of God, sixty-six books that together reveal God's redemption through Jesus Christ the Savior? The answer is that God Himself has confirmed this through what is called the "inward witness of the Holy Spirit." In the words of the *Westminster Confession* (1647):

> We may be moved and induced by the testimony of the Church to an high and reverent esteem of the holy Scripture; and the heavenliness of the matter, the efficacy of the doctrine, the majesty of the style, the consent of all the parts, the scope of the whole (which is to give all glory to God), the full discovery it makes of the only way of man's salvation, the many other incomparable excellencies, and the entire perfection thereof, are arguments whereby it doth abundantly evidence itself to be the Word of God; yet, notwithstanding, our full persuasion and assurance of the infallible truth, and divine authority thereof, is from the inward work of the Holy Spirit, bearing witness by and with the Word in our hearts (*Westminster Confession* 1.5).

The Spirit's witness to Scripture is like His witness to Jesus, which we find spoken of in John 15:26 and 1 John 5:7 (cf. 1 John 2:20, 27). It is not a matter of imparting new information, but of enlightening otherwise darkened minds to discern divinity through sensing its unique impact—the impact in the one case of the Jesus of the gospel, and in the other case of the words of Holy Scripture. The Spirit shines in our hearts to give us the light of the knowledge of the glory of God in the face of Jesus Christ (2 Cor. 4:6), but also the light of His glory in the teaching of Holy Scripture. The result of this witness is a state of mind in which both the Savior and the Scriptures have evidenced themselves to us as divine—Jesus, a divine person; Scripture, a divine word—in a way as direct and immediate as the way tastes and colors impress themselves on our senses. As a result, we no longer find it possible to doubt the divinity of Christ or the divine origin of the Bible.

God Himself authenticates Holy Scripture to us as His Word, going beyond human argument (strong as this may be), and the church's testimony (impressive as this is). God does it, rather, by opening our hearts and enlightening our minds to perceive the searching light and transforming power whereby Scripture evidences itself to be divine. This impact is itself the Spirit's witness "by and with the Word in our hearts." Argument, testimony from others, and our own particular experiences may support and clarify this witness, but the imparting of it, like the imparting of faith in Christ's divine Saviorhood, is the prerogative of the sovereign Holy Spirit alone.

among us. John says, "we have seen his glory, glory as of the only Son from the Father" (John 1:14). In contrast to the face of Moses, from which God's glory faded (3:13), God's glory forever shines brightly "in the face of Jesus Christ."

4:7 this treasure. The gospel ministry and the accompanying new covenant power of the Holy Spirit.

jars of clay. Our weak human natures, including but not limited to our physical bodies. They are a great contrast to the glory of the gospel, and Paul reminds us that God's way is to work through those who are weak or unimpressive in the world's eyes.

to God. A characteristic theme in the epistle. Paul's concern is always to give glory to God, not himself.

4:8 The great evangelist and theologian also faced great discouragements.

4:10 Paul's suffering and apparent defeats are evidence to all that he has no effective strength in himself and that, as Christ died, so also Paul knows he is "dead" in terms of his own ability to accomplish anything of eternal significance. Paul uses the key experiences of Christ (death and resurrection) as a pattern for understanding his own experiences as an apostle. Thus, Paul sees his own sufferings as an imitation of Christ's (1:5 and note).

that the life. In Paul's weakness Jesus' power is continually made known (cf. Gal. 2:20).

4:12 Though Paul suffers much hardship (as Jesus did), the result of his ministry is spiritual life and resurrection power in others. This is a paradox that the world will not understand. The recipients of a ministry may seem to fare much better in this world than the person who brings them the ministry, because the one who brings it may be suffering for the sake of the gospel (8:9).

4:13 Faith expresses itself in words that affirm confidence in what God has promised. Here Paul quotes the Septuagint (the Greek Old Testament translation) of Ps. 116:10.

according to what has been written, [y]"I
believed, and so I spoke," we also believe,
and so we also speak, 14 knowing that [z]he
who raised the Lord Jesus [a]will raise us
also with Jesus and [b]bring us with you into
his presence. 15 For [c]it is all for your sake,
so that as [d]grace extends to more and more
people it may increase thanksgiving, [e]to the
glory of God.
16 So we do not lose heart. [f]Though our
outer nature is wasting away, [g]our inner
nature [h]is being renewed day by day. 17 For
[i]this slight momentary affliction is preparing for us an eternal weight of glory beyond
all comparison, 18 [j]as we look not to the
things that are seen but to the things that
are unseen. For the things that are seen are
transient, but the things that are unseen
are eternal.

Our Heavenly Dwelling

5 For we know that if [k]the tent, which is
[l]our earthly home, is destroyed, we
have a building from God, [m]a house not
made with hands, eternal in the heavens.
2 For in this tent [n]we groan, longing to [o]put
on our heavenly dwelling, 3 if indeed by
putting it on[1] we may not be found naked.
4 For while we are still in this tent, we
groan, being burdened—not that we
would be unclothed, but that we would be
further clothed, so that what is mortal
[p]may be swallowed up by life. 5 He who has
prepared us for this very thing is God,
[q]who has given us the Spirit as a guarantee.
6 So we are always of good courage. We
know that [r]while we are at home in the
body we are away from the Lord, 7 for [s]we
walk by faith, not [t]by sight. 8 Yes, we are of
good courage, and we [u]would rather be
away from the body and at home with the
Lord. 9 So whether we are at home or away,
we make it our aim to [v]please him. 10 For
[w]we must all appear before the judgment
seat of Christ, [x]so that each one may
receive what is due for what he has done in
the body, whether good or evil.

The Ministry of Reconciliation

11 Therefore, knowing [y]the fear of the
Lord, we persuade others. But [z]what we are
is known to God, and I hope it is known

13 [y]Cited from Ps. 116:10 **14** [z]1 Thess. 4:14; See Acts 2:24 [a]ch. 1:9 [b][Jude 24] **15** [c][ch. 1:6]; See Rom. 8:28 [d][ch. 1:11; 9:11, 12] [e]ch. 8:19 **16** [f]See Acts 20:24 [g]See Rom. 7:22 [h][Isai. 40:30, 31]; See Rom. 12:2 **17** [i]Rom. 8:18; 1 Pet. 1:6; 5:10; [Ps. 30:5; Isai. 54:7] **18** [j]ch. 5:7; Rom. 8:24; Heb. 11:1, 13
Chapter 5
1 [k]2 Pet. 1:13, 14 [l]See ch. 4:7 [m]Mark 14:58 **2** [n]Rom. 8:23 [o][1 Cor. 15:53, 54] **4** [p]1 Cor. 15:54 **5** [q][Rom. 8:23]; See ch. 1:22 **6** [r][Heb. 11:13, 14] **7** [s][John 20:29]; See ch. 4:18

[t]1 Cor. 13:12 **8** [u][Phil. 1:23] **9** [v][Col. 1:10; 1 Thess. 4:1] **10** [w]Matt. 25:31, 32; [Rom. 14:10]; See Acts 10:42 [x]See Ps. 62:12 **11** [y][Job 31:23; Acts 9:31; Heb. 10:31; Jude 23] [z]ch. 4:2

[1] Some manuscripts *putting it off*

4:15 to the glory of God. God's ultimate goal in answering prayer and bringing us the blessings of salvation is for thanksgiving and glory to be offered to Him (Is. 43:7; Eph. 1:12; Rev. 4:11).

4:16 we do not lose heart. This phrase repeats v. 1. God brings glory to Himself even through the weaknesses and discouragements of Paul's ministry.

our outer nature is wasting away. The contrast between outward and inward is not simply between the body and the soul, but between the old fallen nature and the renewed humanity.

4:17 momentary affliction. An understatement. See the descriptions of these troubles in 4:8–12; 6:4–10; 11:23–33. These troubles are preparing a great reward for believers. Our faith and obedience in suffering pleases God, and He will not forget (Rom. 8:17, 18; 1 Pet. 1:6, 7).

eternal weight of glory. Troubles in this life are light and insignificant compared to the important and significant glory that we will enjoy for eternity.

4:18 things . . . unseen are eternal. A frequent theme in this book. The unseen world is what is most real and most important; the visible world is passing away.

5:1 tent. Our physical bodies. If Paul's sufferings must lead even to physical death, something far greater awaits him.

a house . . . in the heavens. This probably refers to our resurrection bodies, though some have argued that it signifies the heavenly place that God has prepared for us.

5:2 we groan. Sighing with frustration at the limitations of this present life, with its sin, weakness, and corruption (Rom. 8:22, 23).

5:3 naked. Without a body.

5:4 Paul longs for the resurrection body, free of the weaknesses and imperfections of this life.

what is mortal. Our present physical bodies.

swallowed up by life. The new, heavenly life to come will overtake our present existence. See "Resurrection and Glorification" at 1 Cor. 15:21.

5:5 guarantee. See note 1:22. The Holy Spirit's work in us now in daily renewal and spiritual strengthening (3:18; 4:16) is a foretaste and guarantee of future completion of that work in resurrection bodies and complete sanctification.

5:7 Again Paul specifies a contrast between the unseen spiritual realm of God's presence and activity and the present visible world.

5:8 The doctrine of the intermediate state between our death and Christ's return teaches that when Christians die they, that is, their spirits, go immediately into Christ's presence and are "at home with the Lord," while their bodies remain here and are buried in the grave (Luke 23:43; Phil. 1:23). When Christ returns, the bodies of believers will be raised from the dead and reunited with their spirits (1 Cor. 15:22, 23; 1 Thess. 4:14, 16). See "Death and the Intermediate State" at Phil. 1:23.

5:9 to please him. See "Pleasing God" at 1 Thess. 2:4.

5:10 Degrees of reward in heaven are taught in this verse. Though Christians have their sins forgiven and will never suffer the punishments of hell (Rom. 6:23; 8:1), they will all nonetheless stand before Christ at the Day of Judgment, to receive various degrees of reward for what they have done in this life (Matt. 6:20; Luke 19:11–27; 1 Cor. 3:12–15). This judgment will include a disclosure and evaluation of the motives of our hearts (1 Cor. 4:5).

5:11 the fear of the Lord. Not a terror of eternal condemnation, but a healthy, reverent fear of Christ's displeasure at the choices we have made, the things "done in the body" (v. 10). Such a fear would have been a healthy corrective for those Corinthians who were making trouble for Paul, and it could also have corrected the lives of many careless Christians throughout history.

known. Again, a spiritual viewpoint, not always evident to those in this world.

also to your conscience. 12 [a]We are not
commending ourselves to you again but
[b]giving you cause to boast about us, so that
you may be able to answer those who boast
about outward appearance and not about
what is in the heart. 13 For if we [c]are beside
ourselves, it is for God; if we are in our
right mind, it is for you. 14 For the love of
Christ [d]controls us, because we have concluded this: that [e]one has died for all,
therefore all have died; 15 and he died for
all, [f]that those who live might no longer
live for themselves but [g]for him who for
their sake died and was raised.
16 From now on, therefore, [h]we regard no
one according to the flesh. Even though we
once regarded Christ according to the
flesh, we regard him thus no longer.
17 Therefore, if anyone is [i]in Christ, he is [j]a
new creation.[1] [k]The old has passed away;
behold, the new has come. 18 All this is
from God, [l]who through Christ reconciled
us to himself and gave us [m]the ministry of
reconciliation; 19 that is, in Christ God was
reconciling[2] the world to himself, [n]not
counting their trespasses against them, and
entrusting to us [m]the message of reconciliation. 20 Therefore, [o]we are ambassadors for
Christ, [p]God making his appeal through
us. We implore you on behalf of Christ, be
reconciled to God. 21 [q]For our sake he made
him to be sin [r]who knew no sin, so that in
him we might become [s]the righteousness
of God.

6 [t]Working together with him, then, [u]we
appeal to you [v]not to receive the grace
of God in vain. 2 For he says,

[w]"In a favorable time I listened to you,
and in a day of salvation I have
helped you."

Behold, [x]now is the [y]favorable time; behold, now is the day of salvation. 3 We [z]put
no obstacle in anyone's way, so that no
fault may be found with our ministry, 4 but

12 [a]See ch. 3:1 [b][ch. 1:14] 13 [c]ch. 11:1, 16, 17; 12:6, 11 14 [d]Acts 18:5 [e]Rom. 5:15 15 [f][Rom. 6:11, 12]; See Rom. 14:7 [g][ch. 12:10] 16 [h][Gal. 2:6; Phil. 3:7, 8; Col. 2:11; 1 Tim. 5:21] 17 [i]ch. 12:2; Rom. 16:7; Gal. 1:22 [j][John 3:3]; See Rom. 6:4 [k]Isai. 43:18, 19; Rev. 21:5; [Isai. 65:17; Eph. 2:15; 4:24; Heb. 8:13] 18 [l]Col. 1:20; See Rom. 5:10; 1 John 2:2 [m]Rom. 5:11 19 [n]Ps. 32:2; Rom. 4:8; [1 Cor. 13:5] [m][See ver. 18 above] 20 [o]Eph. 6:20; [Mal. 2:7; Gal. 4:14] [p]ch. 6:1 21 [q]Rom. 8:3; Gal. 3:13; See Rom. 4:25 [r]See 1 Pet. 2:22 [s]See Rom. 1:17; 1 Cor. 1:30

Chapter 6 1 [t]Mark 16:20; 1 Cor. 3:9; [Acts 15:4] [u]ch. 5:20 [v][Heb. 12:15] 2 [w]Cited from Isai. 49:8 [x][Ps. 32:6; 69:13; Isai. 55:6; Heb. 3:13] [y][Luke 4:19] 3 [z]See 1 Cor. 8:13; 9:12

[1] Or *creature* [2] Or *God was in Christ, reconciling*

5:12 who boast about outward appearance. This is the world's method of evaluation, contrary to that of a true apostle, who endures troubles by focusing on the unseen and eternal (4:18). The false apostles at Corinth (11:13) were also typical representatives of the world, taking pride in their outward appearance, relying on the self, and loving money, power, and prestige. If the Corinthians understood Paul's self-defense in a spiritual way, they would have an answer for the false apostles and their superficial standards of judgment (1 Sam. 16:7).

5:13 beside ourselves. This probably refers to times of worship and prayer when Paul was caught up in intense awareness of the presence of God. Paul's language does not imply complete loss of awareness of one's surroundings, for the same Greek word is used of people who were "amazed" at Christ's miracles (Mark 5:42; cf. 6:51). The apostle's point is that whether engaged in private worship or in public ministry, he lives for God and for others, not for himself (v. 15). His opponents cannot make this claim.

5:14 the love of Christ. Grammatically this could be the love we have for Christ or the love Christ has for us. Since Paul is speaking of what Christ has done for him, he probably means the love that comes from Christ.

one has died for all. The ones He died for are the same as the "all" who "died" with Him as a result of His death, who are mentioned at the end of the verse.

5:16 Paul emphasizes spiritual judgment and spiritual insight into people's lives and situations. Our experience of Christ's love moves us to stop viewing others according to worldly standards and to learn how to view them from the standpoint of God's great act of salvation in Jesus Christ.

according to the flesh. When Christ was regarded from a worldly point of view, men rejected and crucified Him as a blasphemer and troublemaker. But from the divine viewpoint, Christ is the Messiah and Son of God, in whom the new creation and reconciliation with God is given.

5:17 in Christ. Union with Christ summarizes our experience of redemption. Believers are elected (Eph. 1:4, 11), justified (Rom. 8:1), sanctified (1 Cor. 1:2), and glorified (3:18) "in Christ." Here Paul focuses on the momentous significance of the believer's union with the Savior. Because Christ is the "last Adam," the One in whom humanity is recreated (1 Cor. 15:45; Eph. 2:10) and who inaugurates the new age of messianic blessing (Gal. 1:4; cf. Matt. 11:2–6), the believer's spiritual union with Christ is nothing less than participation in the "new creation." Translating "there is a new creation" instead of "he is a new creation" draws this conclusion more clearly, but the thought is there either way.

5:18 All this is from God. The whole plan of salvation and history of redemption is God-centered. Paul realizes that it is from Him, through Him, and for His glory (Rom. 11:36).

5:20 Paul may be appealing directly to the Corinthians to "be reconciled to God." But he is also summing up the appeal he gives to all the world. Reconciliation is the establishment or restoration of loving fellowship after estrangement. For Christians, reconciliation to God is renewed each day, in one sense (Matt. 6:12; 1 John 1:9).

5:21 An important summary of the gospel message. The verse explains how God imputed our sin to Christ. God as judge assigned the responsibility of our sin to Christ, making it possible for Him to be punished justly for that sin (Is. 53:6; 1 Pet. 2:24). The verse shows that Christ was our substitute, accepting the penalty of sin in our place. See "The Sinlessness of Jesus" at Heb. 4:15.

we might become the righteousness of God. Not only did God impute our sin to Christ, He also imputed Christ's perfect righteousness to us (that is, He counted it as belonging to us). This imputation is the basis for the progressive realization of God's righteousness in our moral character. Our thoughts and deeds are sanctified in increasing measure until we receive perfect righteousness in heaven.

6:1 in vain. If the Corinthians allow their church to be swept away by the "false apostles" (11:13), or if they refuse to purify themselves from "every defilement of body and spirit" (7:1), their lives will glorify God less and less, and the gospel they heard will bear little lasting fruit.

6:2 now is the day of salvation. When God offers deliverance, it is wise to respond immediately, before the offer is withdrawn. "Now" in a broad sense refers to the gospel age, while in a specific sense it refers to the time when an individual hears God's offer of salvation.

[a]as servants of God we commend ourselves
in every way: [b]by great endurance, [c]in afflictions, [d]hardships, calamities, **5** [e]beatings,
imprisonments, [f]riots, labors, sleepless
nights, hunger; **6** [g]by purity, [h]knowledge,
patience, kindness, [i]the Holy Spirit, [j]gen-
uine love; **7** by [k]truthful speech, and [l]the
power of God; with [m]the weapons of righteousness for the right hand and for the left;
8 through honor and dishonor, [n]through
slander and praise. We are treated as impostors, and yet are true; **9** as unknown, and
[o]yet well known; [p]as dying, and behold, we
live; [q]as punished, and yet not killed; **10** [r]as
sorrowful, yet always rejoicing; [s]as poor, yet
making many rich; [t]as having nothing, [u]yet
possessing everything.
11 We have spoken freely to you,[1] Corinthians; [v]our heart is wide open. **12** You are
not restricted by us, but [w]you are restricted
in your own affections. **13** [x]In return (I speak
[y]as to children) widen your hearts also.

The Temple of the Living God

14 [z]Do not be unequally yoked with unbelievers. For [a]what partnership has righ-

4 [a][1 Thess. 3:2; 2 Tim. 2:24, 25]; See ch. 3:6 [b]ch. 12:12; 2 Tim. 3:10 [c]Acts 9:16 [d]ch. 12:10 **5** [e]ch. 11:23-27; Acts 16:23 [f]Acts 17:5 **6** [g]1 Thess. 2:10 [h]ch. 11:6 [i]Rom. 15:19; 1 Thess. 1:5 [j]Rom. 12:9; [James 3:17] **7** [k]Eph. 1:13; Col. 1:5 [l]See 1 Cor. 2:5

[m]ch. 10:4; Eph. 6:11-17 **8** [n]Rom. 3:8 **9** [o][ch. 11:6] [p]See ch. 4:10 [q]Ps. 118:18 **10** [r]John 16:22; [ch. 7:4] [s][ch. 8:9; Prov. 13:7; 1 Cor. 1:5] [t]Acts 3:6 [u]1 Cor. 7:30 **11** [v]ch. 7:3; [ch. 11:11; 12:15; Ps. 119:32] **12** [w]ch. 7:2 **13** [x][Gal. 4:12] [y]1 Cor. 4:14 **14** [z]Deut. 7:3; Josh. 23:12; Ezra 9:2; Neh. 13:25; [1 Cor. 7:39] [a]Eph. 5:7, 11; 1 John 1:6

[1] Greek *Our mouth is open to you*

Salvation

The central theme of the Christian gospel is salvation. The gospel proclaims that as God saved Israel from Egypt and the psalmist from death (Ex. 15:2; Ps. 116:6), so He will save all who trust Christ from sin and its consequences. This salvation from sin and death is wholly God's work. "For by grace you have been saved through faith. And this is not your own doing; it is the gift of God" (Eph. 2:8). "Salvation belongs to the LORD" (Jon. 2:9). The Hebrew words that express the idea of salvation in the Old Testament have the general sense of deliverance from physical danger or moral distress (Ps. 85:8, 9; Is. 62:11). In such passages the Septuagint (the Greek translation of the Old Testament) uses Greek words that mean to save from death or dangers, as well as to preserve or to heal. New Testament passages that speak of salvation use all these ideas to explain the acts of God on behalf of the lost.

Salvation delivers the believer from the wrath of God, the dominion of sin, and the power of death (Rom. 1:18; 3:9; 5:21; 1 Thess. 5:9). God liberates sinners from the natural condition of being mastered by the world, the flesh, and the devil (John 8:23, 24; Rom. 8:7, 8; 1 John 5:19). He frees believers from the fears that a sinful life generates (Rom. 8:15; 2 Tim. 1:7; Heb. 2:14, 15), and from the vicious habits that enslaved them (Eph. 4:17–24; 1 Thess. 4:3–8; Titus 2:11–3:6). Salvation brings not only the promise of spiritual wholeness and peace, but also of physical healing (Matt. 9:21, 22; Mark 10:52; James 5:15). Although Christians have already received salvation, they will experience the benefits of salvation in their fullness only when Christ returns at the end of the age (Heb. 9:28; 1 Pet. 1:3–5).

Salvation is accomplished through what Christ did in history and by what He continues to do in believers by the Holy Spirit. The basis for our salvation is Jesus' death on the cross (see "The Atonement" at Rom. 3:25) and the righteousness He achieved for us in His active obedience. It is realized in our lives as Christ lives in us (John 15:4; 17:26; Col. 1:27) and we live in Christ, united with Him in His death and risen life (Rom. 6:3–10; Col. 2:12, 20; 3:1). This vital union, sustained by the Spirit through faith and formed in our new birth, presupposes our eternal election in Christ (Eph. 1:4–6). Jesus was foreordained to represent us and to bear our sins as our substitute (1 Pet. 1:18–20; cf. Matt. 1:21). We were chosen to be effectually called, conformed to His image, and glorified by the Spirit's power (Rom. 8:11, 29, 30).

6:6 A true minister of the gospel is known by pure speech, pure conduct, pure motives, and deep love for people.

the Holy Spirit. The power of the Holy Spirit was evident in Paul's ministry, whether bringing power to his preaching, convicting unbelievers of sin (cf. John 16:8–11), or giving spiritual gifts (1 Cor. 12:7–11). This work of the Holy Spirit was another way by which Paul's ministry was commended.

6:7 by truthful speech. Paul will not compromise the sanctity of truth or tell a lie to accomplish some desirable goal.

the power of God. Often to work miracles, bring healing, or silence enemies (cf. Acts 14:3, 9, 10; 19:11, 12; 20:10; 28:8, 9; Rom. 15:19).

the weapons of righteousness. That is, all the weaponry to be used against human or demonic opposition (10:5, 6; Acts 13:11; 16:18; Eph. 6:10–18).

6:8–10 A series of paradoxes again highlighting the contrast between the viewpoint of this world and the standpoint of the age to come, the standpoint invisible to the natural eye but seen by the eye of faith.

6:11 our heart is wide open. Paul reveals his inner feelings in this letter more than in any other. His "open heart" reveals his love for them.

6:14 yoked. Paul sees a deeper spiritual reality in the prohibition against unequal yoking found in Deut. 22:10.

with unbelievers. Note that the false apostles in Corinth claimed to be Christians but were in reality servants of Satan (11:14, 15). To join with

teousness with lawlessness? Or [b]what fellowship has light with darkness? 15 [c]What
accord has Christ with Belial?[1] Or what
portion does a believer share with an unbeliever? 16 What agreement has the temple
of God with idols? For [d]we are the temple
of the living God; as God said,

[e]"I will make my dwelling among them
and [f]walk among them,
and [g]I will be their God,
and they shall be my people.
17 Therefore [h]go out from their midst,
and be separate from them, says
the Lord,
and touch no unclean thing;
then I will welcome you,
18 [i]and I will be a father to you,
and you shall be sons and
daughters to me,
says the Lord Almighty."

7 Since we have these promises, beloved, [j]let us cleanse ourselves from
every defilement of body[2] and spirit, bringing holiness to completion in the fear of
God.

Paul's Joy

2 [k]Make room in your hearts[3] for us. [l]We
have wronged no one, we have corrupted
no one, we have taken advantage of no
one. 3 I do not say this to condemn you, for
I said before that [m]you are in our hearts, to
die together and to live together. 4 I am acting with [n]great boldness toward you; [o]I
have great pride in you; [p]I am filled with
comfort. In all our affliction, I am overflowing with joy.

5 For even [q]when we came into Macedonia, our bodies had no rest, but we were
afflicted at every turn—[r]fighting without
and fear within. 6 But [s]God, who comforts
the downcast, [t]comforted us by the coming
of Titus, 7 and not only by his coming but
also by the comfort with which he was comforted by you, as he told us of your longing,
your mourning, your zeal for me, so that I
rejoiced still more. 8 For [u]even if I made you
grieve with my letter, I do not regret it—
though [v]I did regret it, for I see that that
letter grieved you, though only for a while.
9 As it is, I rejoice, not because you were
grieved, but [w]because you were grieved
into repenting. For you felt a godly grief, so
that you suffered no loss through us.

10 For [x]godly grief produces a repentance that leads to salvation without regret,

14 [b]See Acts 26:18
15 [c][1 Cor. 10:21]
16 [d][Eph. 2:22]; See 1 Cor. 3:16 [e]Cited from Lev. 26:12; See Ex. 29:45 [f][Rev. 2:1; 21:3] [g]Ex. 6:7; Jer. 31:33; Ezek. 11:20
17 [h]Cited from Isai. 52:11; [ch. 7:1; Ezek. 20:34, 41; Zeph. 3:20; Rev. 18:4]
18 [i][Ex. 4:22; 2 Sam. 7:8, 14; Isai. 43:6; Jer. 31:9; Hos. 1:10; Rev. 21:7]
Chapter 7
1 [j]1 Pet. 2:11; 1 John 3:3
2 [k]ch. 6:12, 13; [l]Acts 20:33; [ch. 11:20]
3 [m][ch. 6:11-13]
4 [n]ch. 3:12 [o]ch. 1:12; 8:24; 9:2 [p]ch. 1:4; Phil. 2:17; Col. 1:24; [ch. 6:10]
5 [q]ch. 2:13 [r][Deut. 32:25; Lam. 1:20]
6 [s]ch. 1:4 [t]ver. 13; [1 Thess. 3:6, 7] 8 [u][ch. 2:2] [v]ch. 2:4 9 [w]Ps. 38:18; [1 Cor. 5:2]
10 [x][2 Sam. 12:13; Acts 11:18]

1 Greek *Beliar* 2 Greek *flesh* 3 Greek lacks *in your hearts*

them would distort all life and ministry in the church. The prohibition against being yoked together with unbelievers must be considered in situations where significant control over one's actions would be willingly yielded to an unbeliever through a voluntary partnership or association. Neither Paul nor the rest of the New Testament tells us to have no association at all with unbelievers (Mark 2:15–17; 1 Cor. 5:9, 10). But we are told not to be "yoked together" with them in such a way that they significantly influence the direction and outcome of our moral decisions and spiritual activities.

6:15 Belial. A name for Satan.

6:16 we are the temple of the living God. In the Old Testament God's dwelling place with His people was the tabernacle and later the temple built by Solomon. When Christ came, He was Himself the true temple or dwelling place of God (Matt. 1:23; John 2:21; Col. 2:9). Now God the Holy Spirit lives in us, and for this reason we are the new temple of God (1 Cor. 6:19; 1 Pet. 2:5).

as God said. The Old Testament promise that God would dwell among His people (Paul's quotation is from Lev. 26:11, 12) has become the new covenant promise that God would live in those who trust in Christ.

6:17 The quotation is mostly from Is. 52:11 and Ezek. 20:34, though the word order is changed. These commands to be separate all have to do with unbelievers (cf. v. 14; note that Is. 52:11 commands Israel to go out of unbelieving Babylon). The verses do not encourage separation from believers who hold different views on certain matters.

6:18 See 2 Sam. 7:14, 27. Paul has combined several Old Testament promises of God's presence and favor, but he makes their fulfillment depend clearly on Christians separating themselves from moral impurity. To give up moral defilement and gain the presence of the living God in return is a wise and desirable choice.

7:1 these promises. The Old Testament promises quoted in 6:16–18.

let us cleanse ourselves. We must play an active, vigorous role in sanctification (Phil. 2:12, 13).

every defilement Paul means all kinds of sin, however they come to expression in life. Physical cleanliness is not in view (Matt. 7:15; 1 Pet. 3:21).

7:2 We have wronged no one. Once again in defense against those who accuse him, Paul appeals to a blameless record in ministry.

7:3 Paul reveals how deeply he loves the church at Corinth; this is not deceitful speech, but an expression of his "genuine love" (6:6).

7:5 This verse resumes the narrative that broke off at 2:13. It shows Paul's turmoil of soul when a church he deeply loved strayed from obedience to the Lord.

Macedonia. Northern Greece, on the way to Corinth (2:12, 13 notes).

7:6 Titus had finally arrived in Macedonia with good news about the Corinthians and their response to Paul's "severe letter."

7:8 Paul's "severe letter" (no longer extant) was written to rebuke the Corinthians for their conduct during his earlier visit (2:3, 4 notes and Introduction: Date and Occasion). The problem was probably their failure as a church to defend Paul against the person who had wronged him. This verse shows clearly that a loving pastor must sometimes cause sorrow to those he cares for, if they fall into sin.

7:10 repentance. Turning from sin, a sincere decision to forsake a specific sin (or sins) and begin to obey God. Here, the term does not specifically refer to initial repentance that must accompany true saving faith (Mark 1:15; Acts 3:19; 17:30; 26:20), but to a turning from sin in the life of a Christian.

leads to salvation. "Salvation" here means not initial conversion, but

whereas [y]worldly grief produces death.
11 For see what earnestness this godly grief
has produced in you, but also what eagerness to clear yourselves, what indignation,
what fear, what longing, [z]what zeal, what
punishment! At every point you have
proved yourselves innocent in the matter.
12 So although I wrote to you, it was not for
the sake of the one [a]who did the wrong,
nor for the sake of the one who suffered the
wrong, but in order that your earnestness
for us might be revealed to you in the sight
of God. 13 Therefore [b]we are comforted.
And besides our own comfort, we rejoiced still more at the joy of Titus, because
his spirit [c]has been refreshed by you all.
14 For [d]whatever boasts I made to him
about you, I was not put to shame. But just
as everything we said to you [e]was true, so
also our boasting before Titus has proved
true. 15 And his affection for you is even
greater, as he remembers [f]the obedience of
you all, how you received him with fear
and trembling. 16 I rejoice, because I have
perfect [g]confidence in you.

Encouragement to Give Generously

8 We want you to know, brothers,[1]
about the grace of God that has been
[h]given among the churches of Macedonia,
2 for in a severe test of affliction, their abundance of joy and [i]their extreme poverty
have overflowed in a wealth of generosity
on their part. 3 For they gave [j]according to
their means, as I can testify, and beyond
their means, of their own free will, 4 beg-
ging us earnestly [k]for the favor of taking
part in [l]the relief of the saints— 5 and this,
not as we expected, but they [m]gave themselves first to the Lord and then by the will
of God to us. 6 Accordingly, [n]we urged
Titus that as he had started, so he should
complete among you [o]this act of grace.
7 But as [p]you excel in everything—in faith,
in speech, in knowledge, in all earnestness,
and in our love for you[2]—[q]see that you
excel in this act of grace also.
8 [r]I say this not as a command, but to
prove by the earnestness of others that
your love also is genuine. 9 For you know
the grace of our Lord Jesus Christ, that
[s]though he was rich, yet for your sake he
became poor, so that you by his poverty
might become rich. 10 And in this matter [t]I
give my judgment: [u]this benefits you, who
[v]a year ago started not only to do this work
but also to desire to do it. 11 So now finish
doing it as well, so that your readiness in
desiring it may be matched by your completing it out of what you have. 12 For if the
readiness is there, it is acceptable [w]accord-
ing to what a person has, not according to

10 [y][Prov. 17:22]
11 [z][ch. 2:6]
12 [a][1 Cor. 5:1, 2]
13 [b]ver. 6 [c]See Rom. 15:32
14 [d]ch. 8:24; 9:2; 10:8; [2 Thess. 1:4] [e]ch. 4:2; 6:7
15 [f]ch. 2:9; 10:6
16 [g]See ch. 2:3
Chapter 8
1 [h]ver. 5
2 [i][Mark 12:44]
3 [j]ver. 11; 1 Cor. 16:2
4 [k]ch. 9:2; Rom. 15:25, 26; See Acts 24:17 [l]See Rom 15:31
5 [m]ver. 1
6 [n]ver. 17; ch. 12:18 [o]ver. 19; [ver. 4]
7 [p]See 1 Cor. 1:5 [q]ch. 9:8
8 [r]1 Cor. 7:6
9 [s]Phil. 2:6, 7; [ch. 6:10; Matt. 20:28]
10 [t]1 Cor. 7:25 [u]Deut. 15:7, 8; Prov. 19:17; 28:27; 1 Tim. 6:18, 19; Heb. 13:16 [v]ch. 9:2
12 [w][ch. 9:7; Mark 12:43, 44; Luke 21:3]

1 Or *brothers and sisters* 2 Some manuscripts *in your love for us*

growth and progress in the Christian life. Ordinary Christian growth will include times of profound sorrow for remaining sin.

worldly grief. Regret and sorrow of different kinds that do not seek forgiveness in Christ.

7:11 The Corinthians responded as Paul had hoped when Titus brought the letter of rebuke.

7:12 the one who did the wrong. Probably not the man guilty of incest in 1 Cor. 5:1, though many have understood it this way (2:5 note).

in the sight of God. The Christian life is lived before the face of God.

7:13 his spirit has been refreshed. The personal contact of the Corinthians and Titus had encouraged Titus spiritually, making a noticeable change in him.

7:15 with fear and trembling. Apparently, even before Titus arrived with the letter of rebuke, the Holy Spirit had worked repentance in the Corinthian church.

8:1–9:15 This section concerns the collection of money for poor Christians in Jerusalem (cf. Acts 19:21, 22; Rom. 15:25–28; 1 Cor. 16:1–4).

8:1 grace. Giving money to help other Christians in need was itself the result of God's grace. He provided both the resources and the willingness to use them.

churches of Macedonia. Philippi, Thessalonica, Berea.

8:3 Paul tells the comparatively wealthy Corinthian church about the generosity of the impoverished churches in Macedonia, to the north.

8:5 not as we expected. They did much more than he expected.

gave themselves. They rededicated their lives to service for the Lord, and then to Paul as His servant.

8:7 you excel in everything. Despite its troubles, Corinth was a strong church in many ways. They had many spiritual gifts (1 Cor. 12–14), several of them listed here.

8:8 not as a command. Paul wants giving to be voluntary. In general, though Paul had great authority, he preferred to ask rather than command (Philem. 14 and note), a good pattern for those in authority (Matt. 20:25, 26).

8:9 though he was rich. In the glory and honor that was eternally His in heaven.

he became poor. He gave up His heavenly glory and came to earth to live as a man and to suffer and die. The Corinthians, like Christ, should give of themselves for the sake of others. See "The Humble Obedience of Christ" at John 5:19.

8:10 They had begun to give in accordance with Paul's instructions in 1 Cor. 16:1–3.

8:11 As in all of the Christian life, so it is in giving. Good motives are not enough, but must lead to good actions in accordance with our abilities.

8:12 As the widow's offering in Mark 12:41–44 teaches, willingness to give generously is pleasing to God, even though the gift may have to be small because the giver is poor.

not according to what he does not have. This is a warning against giving or promising to give an amount that you really do not have, hoping that God will repay it. Doing this forces a test on God (Luke 4:12). People

what he does not have. **13** I do not mean
that others should be eased and you burdened, but that as a matter of fairness **14** [x]your
abundance at the present time should
supply [x] their need, so that their abundance
may supply your need, that there may be
fairness. **15** As it is written, [y]"Whoever gathered much had nothing left over, and whoever gathered little had no lack."

Commendation of Titus

16 But [z]thanks be to God, [a]who put into
the heart of Titus the same earnest care I
have for you. **17** For [b]he not only accepted
our appeal, but being himself very earnest
he is going[1] to you of his own accord.
18 With him we are sending[2] [c]the brother
who is famous among [d]all the churches for
his preaching of the gospel. **19** And not only
that, but he has been [e]appointed by the
churches to travel with us as we carry out
this act of [f]grace that is being ministered by
us, [g]for the glory of the Lord himself and to
show our good will. **20** We take this course
so that no one should blame us about this
generous gift that is being administered by
us, **21** for [h]we aim at what is honorable [i]not
only in the Lord's sight but also in the sight
of man. **22** And with them we are sending
our brother whom we have often tested
and found earnest in many matters, but
who is now more earnest than ever because
of his great confidence in you. **23** As for
Titus, he is [j]my partner and fellow worker
for your benefit. And as for our brothers,
they are messengers[3] of the churches, the
glory of Christ. **24** So give proof before the
churches of your love and of [k]our boasting
about you to these men.

14 [x]ch. 9:12; [Acts 4:34] **15** [y]Cited from Ex. 16:18 **16** [z]See ch. 2:14 [a]Rev. 17:17 **17** [b]ver. 6 **18** [c]ch. 12:18 [d]See 1 Cor. 7:17 **19** [e][1 Cor. 16:3, 4] [f]ver. 6 [g]ch. 4:15 **21** [h]See Rom. 12:17 [i][Rom. 14:18; Phil. 4:8; 1 Pet. 2:12] **23** [j][Philem. 17] **24** [k]ch. 7:4, 14; 9:2, 3

Chapter 9
1 [l][1 Thess. 4:9] [m]See Rom. 15:25 **2** [n]ch. 8:24 [o]ch. 8:10 **3** [p]ch. 8:6, 17, 18, 22 [q]1 Cor. 16:2 **4** [r][Acts 20:4] **5** [s]Gen. 33:11; Judg. 1:15; 1 Sam. 25:27 [t][Phil. 4:17] [u][ch. 12:17, 18] **6** [v]Prov. 11:24, 25; 22:9; Gal. 6:7, 9; [Mal. 3:10; Luke 6:38] **7** [w]Deut. 15:10; See ch. 8:12 [x]See Ex. 25:2 **8** [y]Phil. 4:19; [Eph. 3:2] **9** [z]Cited from Ps. 112:9

The Collection for Christians in Jerusalem

9 Now [l]it is superfluous for me to write
to you about [m]the ministry for the
saints, **2** for I know your readiness, [n]of
which I boast about you to the people of
Macedonia, saying that Achaia has been
ready [o]since last year. And your zeal has
stirred up most of them. **3** But [p]I am sending[4] the brothers so that our boasting
about you may not prove vain in this matter, so that you may be ready, [q]as I said you
would be. **4** Otherwise, if some Macedo-
nians [r]come with me and find that you are
not ready, we would be humiliated—to say
nothing of you—for being so confident.
5 So I thought it necessary to urge the
brothers to go on ahead to you and arrange
in advance for the [s]gift you have promised,
so that it may be ready [t]as a willing gift,
[u]not as an exaction.[5]

The Cheerful Giver

6 The point is this: [v]whoever sows sparingly will also reap sparingly, and whoever
sows bountifully will also reap bountifully.
7 Each one must give as he has made up his
mind, [w]not reluctantly or under compulsion, for [x]God loves a cheerful giver. **8** And
[y]God is able to make all grace abound to
you, so that having all sufficiency[6] in all
things at all times, you may abound in
every good work. **9** As it is written,

[z]"He has distributed freely, he has
given to the poor;
his righteousness endures
forever."

[1] Or *he went* [2] Or *we sent*; also verse 22 [3] Greek *apostles* [4] Or *I have sent* [5] Or *a gift expecting something in return*; Greek *greed* [6] Or *all contentment*

should give as God causes them to prosper (1 Cor. 16:2). Even so, the more common offense is failing to give immediately and generously when God brings additional income.

8:14 fairness. Not that Paul wanted all Christians to have equal possessions or equal income, but that there might be a fair distribution of burdens. Paul calls for equity rather than strict equality.

8:15 When the people gathered manna in the wilderness, those who gathered more shared with those who had less, and here with respect to money, the rich should share with those in need.

8:17 Paul is sending Titus back to Corinth ahead of him.

8:18 the brother. No name is given. Luke is a frequent suggestion.

8:19 appointed by the churches. There was some congregational role in selecting representatives to accompany Paul.

for the glory of the Lord himself. Giving money and administering it well is not mundane or unspiritual, but in itself honors the Lord.

8:20, 21 Paul would not have misused any part of the gift sent to Jerusalem. He insisted that trusted representatives from several churches accompany him (Acts 20:4) so as to avoid even the suspicion of wrongdoing. On this passage Calvin comments that "nothing more certainly invites slanderous attacks than to be handling public money." Moreover, the representatives would have been a sort of bodyguard for someone carrying valuables.

8:22 our brother. Not identified.

9:2 Achaia. Southern Greece, where Corinth was located.

9:5 the gift. Paul wants to preserve the motive of willing, generous giving, and the actual amount he takes to Jerusalem is of secondary importance.

9:6 sows . . . reap. An agricultural metaphor—the farmer who plants much seed reaps a large crop, but a small planting yields a small harvest. This promise is also true in the spiritual realm. Those who give generously will reap abundantly for the kingdom. What is given is never lost; it is sown. While God may at times provide a generous harvest in the physical and material realm to those who give, this is not the New Testament promise or pattern (8:9; 11:27; Luke 6:20, 21, 24, 25; James 2:5).

9:7 God loves a cheerful giver. Giving can and should be joyful.

10 He who supplies [a]seed to the sower and
bread for food will supply and multiply
your seed for sowing and [b]increase the
harvest of your righteousness. 11 [c]You will
be enriched in every way for all your generosity, which [d]through us will produce
thanksgiving to God. 12 For the ministry of
this service is not only supplying [e]the
needs of the saints, but is also overflowing
in many thanksgivings to God. 13 By their
approval of this service, [f]they[1] will glorify
God because of your submission flowing
from your [g]confession of the gospel of
Christ, and the generosity of your contribution for them and for all others, 14 while
they long for you and pray for you, because
of the surpassing grace of God upon you.
15 [h]Thanks be to God for his inexpressible
gift!

Paul Defends His Ministry

10 [i]I, Paul, myself entreat you, by the
[j]meekness and gentleness of Christ—
I who am humble when face to face with
you, but bold toward you when I am
away!—2 I beg of you [k]that when I am present I may not have to show boldness with
such confidence as I count on showing
against [l]some who suspect us of walking
according to the flesh. 3 For though we
walk in the flesh, we are not waging war
according to the flesh. 4 For the [m]weapons
of [n]our warfare are not of the flesh but have
[o]divine power [p]to destroy strongholds. 5 We
destroy arguments and [q]every lofty opinion
raised against the knowledge of God, and
take every thought captive to [r]obey Christ,
6 [s]being ready to punish every disobedience, [t]when your obedience is complete.
7 [u]Look at what is before your eyes. [v]If
anyone is confident that he is Christ's, let
him remind himself that just as [w]he is
Christ's, [x]so also are we. 8 For even if I
boast a little too much of [y]our authority,
which the Lord gave for building you up
and not for destroying you, I will not be
ashamed. 9 I do not want to appear to be
frightening you with my letters. 10 For they
say, "His letters are weighty and strong, but
[z]his bodily presence is weak, and [a]his
speech of no account." 11 Let such a person
understand that what we say by letter when
absent, we do when present. 12 Not that we
dare to classify or [b]compare ourselves with
some of those who [c]are commending themselves. But when they measure themselves
by one another and compare themselves

10 [a]Isai. 55:10 [b][Hos. 10:12] **11** [c]1 Cor. 1:5 [d][ch. 1:11] **12** [e]ch. 8:14 **13** [f]See Matt. 5:16; 1 Pet. 2:12 [g]1 Tim. 6:12, 13; Heb. 3:1; 4:14; 10:23 **15** [h][John 3:16; Eph. 2:8]; See ch. 2:14 **Chapter 10** **1** [i]See Rom. 12:1 [j]Zech. 9:9; Matt. 11:29; Phil. 2:7, 8 **2** [k]ch. 13:2, 10; 1 Cor. 4:21; [ver. 6] [l][1 Cor. 4:18] **4** [m]ch. 6:7; [Eph. 6:11; 1 Thess. 5:8] [n]See 1 Cor. 9:7 [o]ch. 13:3, 4; See 1 Cor. 2:5 [p]Jer. 1:10 **5** [q][Isai. 2:11, 12] [r]ch. 9:13; [Rom. 5:19] **6** [s]See ver. 2 [t]ch. 2:9; 7:15 **7** [u][ch. 5:12; John 7:24] [v][1 Cor. 1:12; 14:37; 1 John 4:6] [w]1 Cor. 3:23 [x][ch. 11:23; 1 Cor. 9:1; Gal. 1:12] **8** [y]ch. 13:10 **10** [z]ch. 11:21; [ch. 12:7] [a]See 1 Cor. 1:17 **12** [b]1 Cor. 2:13 [c]ver. 18; ch. 3:1; 12:6; [Prov. 27:2

[1] Or *you*

9:14 Through such giving needs are met, and God is thanked. The recipients' prayers for the givers are no small reward.

9:15 Our giving is only a small imitation of God's own excellent generosity to us, especially in the "inexpressible gift" of His Son (John 3:16).

10:1–13:10 In these four chapters, Paul deals with the problem of false apostles (11:13) who had come to Corinth and who were opposing Paul's authority. Titus had brought good news about the previous problems at Corinth, but a new problem demanded Paul's attention. Paul was confident of the Corinthian church (7:16), but not all the Corinthians were equally confident of Paul. Between 9:12–15 and 10:1, the tone changes abruptly from something positive to exasperation as Paul defends the genuineness of his calling as an apostle. For a discussion of this shift in tone see Introduction: Interpretive Difficulties.

10:3 A repeated theme in this epistle is living not according to worldly standards or life-views but according to spiritual power and spiritual reality.

10:4 weapons. Prayer, the proclamation of the powerful Word of God, and the authority to drive away demonic opposition (Acts 16:18; Eph. 6:10–18). Also, there was a kind of powerful apostolic authority not often discussed, but apparent in the fate of Ananias and Sapphira (Acts 15:1–11) and Elymas (Acts 13:8–12).

strongholds. Paul is talking about spiritual strongholds, that is, centers of demonic opposition to the gospel (1 Pet. 5:8, 9; 1 John 5:19). Paul knew his opponents at Corinth were servants of Satan (11:14, 15), but that did not frighten him, for the power of the Holy Spirit within him was far greater.

10:5 every lofty opinion. False wisdom and sophisticated arguments were some of the weapons used by the servants of Satan in their attack against Paul. The apostle had earlier stressed the difference between the wisdom of the world and the spiritual wisdom of the cross, and he warned the Corinthians against being deluded by the wisdom of the world (1 Cor. 1:18–2:16). Now Paul sees that his opponents have made such inroads with their false wisdom that he must oppose it again in the strongest terms and, at the same time, regain the loyalty and obedience of the Corinthians.

every thought captive. If every thought, then the whole person—our every idea, motive, desire, and decision—belongs to Christ.

10:6 If the Corinthians join ranks in opposing the false apostles, Paul is ready to punish them for the harm they do.

10:8 Paul knows that he must now call upon the authority Christ has given him and warn the Corinthians that he is ready to use it (v. 4 note).

10:10 his speech of no account. Paul did not depend on the kind of trained oratory prized by the world and designed to get glory for the speaker. Those influenced by the opponents attacked Paul's ministry by saying he lacked this skill.

10:11 See note on v. 4.

10:12 classify or compare ourselves. Now the matter surfaces that caused Paul to defend his apostleship so vigorously. Encouraged by rival "apostles," some influential Corinthians had begun to compare these latecomers to Paul—with Paul coming out the loser. He was judged deficient as a speaker (v. 10; 11:5), weak in his relationship with the church (vacillating between boldness while absent and timidity when present, vv. 10, 11), unloving toward them (in refusing a monetary gift which, in their view, snubbed them as inferiors, 11:7–11; 12:14–18), and deficient in certain religious experiences of "power" (12:1–5 and notes). But Paul refuses to compare himself with his opponents on their shabby terms of self-boasting and self-promotion. When he yields and boasts to them (11:16–18), he does so ironically, using the form of comparison but always refusing their false values.

with one another, they are [d]without understanding.
13 But we will not boast [e]beyond limits,
but will [f]boast only with regard to the area
of influence God assigned to us, [g]to reach
even to you. 14 For we are not overextend-
ing ourselves, as though we did not reach
you. [h]We were the first to come all the way
to you with the gospel of Christ. 15 We do
not boast beyond limit in the labors of
others. But our hope is that [i]as your faith
increases, our area of influence among you
may be [j]greatly enlarged, 16 so that we may
preach the gospel in lands beyond you,
without boasting of work already done in
another's area of influence. 17 "Let [k]the one
who boasts, boast in the Lord." 18 For it is
[l]not the one who commends himself who
is approved, but the one [m]whom the Lord
commends.

Paul and the False Apostles

11 I wish you would bear with me in a
little foolishness. Do bear with me!
2 I feel a divine jealousy for you, for [n]I
betrothed you to one husband, [o]to present
you [p]as a pure virgin to Christ. 3 But I am
afraid that [q]as the serpent deceived Eve by
his cunning, your thoughts [r]will be led
astray from a [s]sincere and [t]pure devotion to
Christ. 4 For if someone comes and [u]pro-
claims another Jesus than the one we proclaimed, or if you receive a different spirit
from the one you received, or if you accept
[v]a different gospel from the one you accepted, you put up with it readily enough.
5 I consider that [w]I am not in the least inferior to these super-apostles. 6 [x]Even if I am
unskilled in speaking, [y]I am not so in
knowledge; indeed, in every way [z]we have
made this plain to you in all things.
7 Or [a]did I commit a sin in humbling
myself so that you might be exalted,
because [b]I preached God's gospel to you
free of charge? 8 I robbed other churches by
accepting support from them in order to
serve you. 9 And when I was with you and
was [c]in need, [d]I did not burden anyone, for
the brothers who came from Macedonia
[e]supplied my need. So I refrained and will
refrain [f]from burdening you in any way.
10 [g]As the truth of Christ is in me, this
boasting of mine [h]will not be silenced in
the regions of Achaia. 11 And why? [i]Because
I do not love you? [j]God knows I do!
12 And what I do I will continue to do, [k]in
order to undermine the claim of those who
would like to claim that in their boasted

12 [d][Prov. 26:12] 13 [e]ver. 15 [f]See Rom. 12:3 [g][Rom. 15:20] 14 [h]1 Cor. 3:5; 4:15; 9:1 15 [i]2 Thess. 1:3 [j][Acts 5:13] 17 [k]1 Cor. 1:31; [Jer. 9:23, 24] 18 [l]See ver. 12 [m]Rom. 2:29; 1 Cor. 4:5
Chapter 11
2 [n][Hos. 2:19, 20] [o]Col. 1:22, 28 [p]Eph. 5:27; Rev. 14:4 3 [q]Gen. 3:4; 1 Tim. 2:14; [John 8:44; 1 Thess. 3:5] [r]Col. 2:4, 8 [s][Eph. 6:5] [t]ch. 6:6
4 [u][1 Cor. 3:11] [v]Gal. 1:6 5 [w]ch. 12:11; Gal. 2:6 6 [x]See 1 Cor. 1:17 [y][Eph. 3:4] [z]ch. 4:2; 5:11; 12:12 7 [a][ch. 12:13] [b]See Acts 18:3 9 [c]Phil. 4:12 [d]ch. 12:13, 14
[e][1 Cor. 16:17; Phil. 4:15, 16] [f]ch. 12:16; 1 Thess. 2:6 10 [g]See Rom 1:9; 9:1 [h]1 Cor. 9:15 11 [i]See ch. 6:11 [j]ver. 31; ch.12:2, 3 12 [k][1 Cor. 9:12]

10:13 not boast beyond limits. Paul will take credit only for things that God has permitted him to do, but this includes having come to Corinth as their apostle. He implies that the opponents in Corinth with their boasting were intruding into his area of responsibility.

10:16 beyond you. Paul was hoping the Corinthians would prosper spiritually and become a base from which he could go on and evangelize beyond them, presumably to Rome and then to Spain (Acts 19:21; Rom. 15:22–29).

10:17 A quotation from Jer. 9:24. To "boast" in something means to declare how great something is. All of Paul's boasting in this letter ultimately ends up giving glory to God.

10:18 whom the Lord commends. The Lord's judgment is final, and will set aside every human judgment. Paul has been careful not to make any claim except what is based on God's purposes and on what God has done. He concludes the section with the very basic principle that a person should look for the approval of God and not man (Matt. 6:1–4; John 5:44; Rom. 2:29; Gal. 1:10).

11:2 I feel a divine jealousy. Paul longs for the Corinthians to remain loyal to Christ. He uses a metaphor of engagement and marriage. If the Corinthians follow the false apostles they will stray from Christ and be unfaithful to Him. Then they could no longer come to Him as a "pure virgin." It is assumed that God's ideal for marriage is no prior sexual relations—that a bride would come as a "pure virgin" to her husband, as her husband would also come to her.

11:3 Paul knows that the false apostles are a dangerous spiritual threat, comparable to the serpent (vv. 14, 15; Gal. 3:1).

11:4 another Jesus . . . different spirit . . . different gospel. The strongholds, arguments, and pretensions (10:4, 5) of Paul's opponents so distort the truth that their so-called "Jesus," "spirit," and "gospel" differ radically from what Paul has preached (1 Cor. 1:18–2:16; cf. Gal. 1:6–9). The "different gospel" of the opponents conforms to worldly ways of thinking so much that Paul and his apostolic ministry—a ministry manifesting the death of Jesus through adversity and suffering (4:7–18; 6:4–10; cf. 1 Cor. 4:8–13)—is despised and rejected in favor of ministries which satisfy the current taste for eloquence, philosophical wisdom, and spectacular displays of spiritual power (cf. 1 Cor. 1:22–25).

11:5 these super-apostles. There is a hint of mockery in Paul's use of this inflated title for his opponents in Corinth. It may even be a name they had applied to themselves. Some think that they used it to refer to the Jerusalem apostles.

11:6 unskilled in speaking. See note 10:10.

11:7 free of charge. When Paul was at Corinth he supported himself (Acts 18:3) and accepted help from other churches as well (v. 8). Some of the Corinthians seem to have been offended by Paul's refusal to accept their gift, probably offered to him in response to his preaching of the gospel to them. In ancient times, gift giving and receiving were often used to establish and maintain friendships among social equals. In this system Paul's refusal of a gift might be taken as an insult, a proud refusal to be involved with inferiors. But the apostle views his relationship with the Corinthians, not from the standpoint of worldly social convention (5:16), but from the standpoint of the new creation (5:17) in which he has been called to be an apostle and spiritual father. As a father, he may rightly give to his children without receiving anything in return (12:14, 15).

11:9 from Macedonia. Probably from Philippi (Phil. 4:15, 16).

11:10 this boasting. Paul had ministered to the Corinthians at great personal sacrifice and expense—unlike the false apostles who apparently were demanding support from the church (cf. vv. 7, 20).

the regions of Achaia. The area around Corinth.

mission they work on the same terms as we
do. 13 For such men are [l]false apostles, [m]de-
ceitful workmen, [n]disguising themselves as
apostles of Christ. 14 And no wonder, for
even Satan disguises himself as [o]an angel of
light. 15 So it is no surprise if his servants,
also, disguise themselves as [p]servants of
righteousness. [q]Their end will correspond
to their deeds.

Paul's Sufferings as an Apostle

16 I repeat, [r]let no one think me foolish.
But even if you do, accept me as a fool, so
that I too may boast a little. 17 What I am
saying [s]with this boastful confidence, [t]I say
not with the Lord's authority but as a fool.
18 Since [u]many boast according to the flesh,
I too will boast. 19 For you gladly bear with
fools, [v]being wise yourselves! 20 For you
bear it if someone [w]makes slaves of you, or
[x]devours you, or takes advantage of you, or
puts on airs, or [y]strikes you in the face.
21 To my shame, I must say, [z]we were too
weak for that!

But whatever anyone else dares to boast
of—I am speaking as a fool—I also dare to
boast of that. 22 Are they Hebrews? [a]So am
I. Are they Israelites? So am I. Are they offspring of Abraham? So am I. 23 Are they
[b]servants of Christ? [c]I am a better one—I
am talking like a madman—with far greater
labors, [d]far more imprisonments, [e]with
countless beatings, and [f]often near death.
24 Five times I received at the hands of the
Jews the [g]forty lashes less one. 25 Three
times I was [h]beaten with rods. [i]Once I was
stoned. Three times I [j]was shipwrecked; a
night and a day I was adrift at sea; 26 on frequent journeys, in danger from rivers, danger from robbers, [k]danger from my own
people, [l]danger from Gentiles, [m]danger in
the city, danger in the wilderness, danger
at sea, danger from false brothers; 27 [n]in toil
and hardship, through many a sleepless
night, [o]in hunger and thirst, often without
food, in cold and exposure. 28 And, apart
from other things, there is the daily pressure on me of my anxiety for [p]all the
churches. 29 [q]Who is weak, and I am not
weak? Who is made to fall, and I am not
indignant?

30 [r]If I must boast, I will boast of the
things that show my weakness. 31 [s]The God
and Father of the Lord Jesus, [t]he who is
blessed forever, [u]knows that I am not lying.
32 At Damascus, the governor under King
Aretas [v]was guarding the city of Damascus
in order to seize me, 33 [w]but I was let down
in a basket through a window in the wall
and escaped his hands.

13 [l]Rev. 2:2; [Gal. 1:7; 2:4; 6:12; Phil. 1:15; 3:18; Tit. 1:10, 12; 2 Pet. 2:1; 1 John 4:1] [m][Phil. 3:2] [n]ver. 14, 15
14 [o]Gal. 1:8
15 [p]ch. 3:9 [q]Phil. 3:19
16 [r]ch. 12:6
17 [s]ch. 9:4 [t][1 Cor. 7:12]
18 [u]Phil. 3:3, 4
19 [v]1 Cor. 4:10
20 [w]Gal. 2:4; [Gal. 4:3, 9; 5:1] [x][ch. 7:2] [y]1 Cor. 4:11
21 [z]ch. 10:10
22 [a]Rom. 11:1; Phil. 3:5
23 [b]See ch. 3:6; 10:7 [c]See 1 Cor. 15:10 [d]ch. 6:5 [e]Acts 16:23 [f]ch. 1:9, 10; 4:11; 6:9 Rom. 8:36; 1 Cor. 15:30-32
24 [g]Deut. 25:3
25 [h]Acts 16:22 [i]Acts 14:19 [j][Acts 27:41]
26 [k]Acts 9:23; 13:50; 14:5; 17:5; 1 Thess. 2:15; [Acts 18:12; 20:3, 19; 21:27; 23:10, 12; 25:3] [l]Acts 14:5; [Acts 19:23; 27:42] [m]Acts 21:31
27 [n]1 Thess. 2:9; 2 Thess. 3:8 [o]1 Cor. 4:11; Phil. 4:12
28 [p]See 1 Cor. 7:17
29 [q]See 1 Cor. 8:13; 9:22
30 [r]ch. 10:10; 12:5, 9; See 1 Cor. 2:3
31 [s]See Rom. 15:6 [t]See Rom. 9:5 [u]ver. 11
32 [v]Acts 9:24
33 [w]Acts 9:25

11:13 Paul's opponents at Corinth are not just fellow Christians who differ in certain non-essential matters; they are actual servants of Satan inside the church, competing for its leadership.

11:14 One of Satan's tricks is to claim to be doing good, and specifically to send to a church servants of his who purport to be Christians, but who bring only division, slander, immorality, and all kinds of destruction. Jesus told His disciples, "you will recognize them by their fruits" (Matt. 7:20; cf. Acts 20:29, 30; 2 Pet. 2).

11:15 Their end. Final judgment by God.

11:20 A description of some of the bold actions of the false apostles.

11:22–12:10 This part of the letter is known as the "Fool's Speech." In it Paul describes his ministry in terms that could not possibly be equaled by the false apostles. Yet he does not boast about his own knowledge or speaking skills or other abilities, but about how much he has suffered for the sake of Christ. Here Paul's boasting is ironic—he "boasts" of things normally considered shameful, signs of weakness and defeats. Thus, his boasts are an imitation or parody of the boasting of his opponents, who praised themselves to the Corinthians in extravagant speeches. The topics in this section progress to a climax where Paul deals with what may have been uppermost in the minds of his critics—unusual religious experiences (12:1–9).

11:22 Are they Hebrews. Paul's opponents were Jews, perhaps coming from Jerusalem and claiming to be endorsed by the Jerusalem apostles.

11:23–27 Paul, in recounting the marks of a true servant of Christ, points to suffering and humiliation, emphasizing again (as he did in 1 Cor. 1–4) Christ crucified.

11:23 Paul reveals his extreme hesitancy to speak at all in his own behalf.

11:24 forty lashes less one. Forty lashes was the maximum that could be inflicted on a person, according to Deut. 25:3. It was Jewish practice to set the limit a little lower as a safeguard against miscounting.

11:25 beaten with rods. One such occasion is reported in Acts 16:22.

Once I was stoned. In Lystra on Paul's first missionary journey (Acts 14:19), where the crowd thought they had killed Paul.

Three times I was shipwrecked. A shipwreck is found in Acts 27:39–44, but 2 Corinthians was written earlier, at the time described in Acts 20:2 (when Paul was in Macedonia). The three shipwrecks must have happened during his earlier missionary journeys.

11:26 Paul's goal was not his own personal comfort or safety. Many of the hardships he records in this larger section are not recorded at all in Acts. It is hard to imagine a more hazardous existence than Paul had, yet he was obedient to God and put his life in God's hands.

false brothers. People pretending to be Christians, who came into the church to stir up trouble.

11:28 Paul felt deeply the needs and suffering of his churches. His trust in God's sovereign care did not make him cold or unemotional.

11:32, 33 This incident is narrated from a different standpoint in Acts 9:24, 25. Apparently Paul's Jewish opponents in Damascus persuaded the governor to cooperate in their plot against Paul. Although these two verses may seem somewhat surprising in the context, they mention Paul's first—and rather humiliating—experience of being persecuted (rather than persecuting others) for the sake of the gospel. The apostle

Paul's Visions and His Thorn

12 I must go on boasting. Though
there is nothing to be gained by it,
I will go on to visions and [x]revelations of
the Lord. 2 I know a man [y]in Christ who
fourteen years ago was [z]caught up to [a]the
third heaven—whether in the body or out
of the body I do not know, [b]God knows.
3 And I know that this man was caught up
into [c]paradise—whether in the body or out
of the body I do not know, [b]God knows—
4 and he heard things that cannot be told,
which man may not utter. 5 On behalf of
this man I will boast, but on my own behalf
I will not boast, [d]except of my weaknesses.
6 Though if I should wish to boast, [e]I would
not be a fool, for I would be speaking the
truth. But I refrain from it, so that no one
may think more of me than he sees in me
or hears from me. 7 So [f]to keep me from
being too elated by the surpassing greatness of the revelations,[1] [g]a thorn was given
me in the flesh, [h]a messenger of Satan to
harass me, to keep me from being too
elated. 8 [i]Three times I pleaded with the
Lord about this, that it should leave me.
9 But he said to me, [j]"My grace is sufficient
for you, for [k]my power is made perfect in
weakness." Therefore I will boast all the
more gladly of my weaknesses, so that [l]the
power of Christ may rest upon me. 10 [m]For
the sake of Christ, then, [n]I am content with
weaknesses, insults, hardships, persecutions, and calamities. For [o]when I am weak,
then I am strong.

Concern for the Corinthian Church

11 [p]I have been a fool! You forced me to it,
for I ought to have been commended by
you. For I was [q]not at all inferior to these
super-apostles, [r]even though I am nothing.
12 [s]The signs of a true apostle were performed among you [t]with utmost patience,
with signs and wonders and mighty works.
13 For in what were you less favored than
the rest of the churches, except that [u]I
myself did not burden you? Forgive me this
wrong!
14 Here [v]for the third time I am ready to
come to you. And I will not be a burden,

Chapter 12
1 [x]Gal. 1:12; 2:2; Eph. 3:3
2 [y]See ch. 5:7 [z]ver. 4; 1 Thess. 14:17; Rev. 12:5; [Ezek. 8:3; Acts 8:39] [a]See Ps.148:4 [b]ch. 11:11
3 [c]Luke 23:43; Rev. 2:7; [Gen. 2:8] [b][See ver. 2 above]
5 [d]See 1 Cor. 2:3
6 [e]ch. 5:13; 11:16, 17; [ver. 11]
7 [f][ch. 10:10] [g][Num. 33:55; Ezek. 28:24] [h][Luke 13:16]; See 1 Cor. 5:5
8 [i][Matt. 26:44]
9 [j]Isai. 43:2 [k]Isai. 40:29-31; [Phil. 4:13] [l]See 1 Cor. 2:5
10 [m][ch. 5:15]; See Matt. 5:11, 12 [n]Rom. 5:3 [o][ch. 13:4]
11 [p][ver. 6] [q]See ch. 11:5; 1 Cor. 15:10 [r]See 1 Cor. 3:7; 15:9 12 [s]See Rom. 15:19; 1 Cor. 9:1 [t]ch. 6:4 13 [u]1 Cor. 9:12; See Acts 20:33 14 [v]ch. 13:1; [ch. 1:15; 13:2]

[1] Or . . . *hears from me, even because of the surpassing greatness of the revelations. So to keep me from being too elated*

makes a precarious escape from a relatively minor civil authority, like a common fugitive. He is not presenting himself as a hero.

12:1–6 In these verses Paul continues his "boasting" with the topic of a vision of heaven. His account contains some unexpected elements. Paul is not permitted to repeat the things he heard in the vision, and afterward he receives a painful "thorn" (v. 7 note) sent by God to keep him humble.

12:2 a man in Christ. Although he speaks indirectly, Paul clearly means himself.

third heaven. According to a common enumeration, the first heaven was the atmosphere of the birds and clouds, the second was the sky in which we see the stars, and the third would be heaven, the dwelling place of God. For fourteen years Paul had not made this experience a focus of his teaching, as some would have done. His focus was the message of Christ: "what we proclaim is not ourselves, but Jesus Christ as Lord" (4:5).

12:3 paradise. That is, the "third heaven" of v. 2. The Greek word for "paradise" is used with various meanings outside the New Testament, but in the New Testament all three occurrences refer to heaven, the place where the saints dwell with God (Luke 23:43; Rev. 2:7; and here).

12:6 I refrain. Paul wanted people to evaluate him on the basis of their firsthand knowledge of him.

12:7 a thorn. Many possibilities have been suggested for this "thorn," such as a physical ailment of some sort ("in the flesh"), a harassing demon ("a messenger of Satan"), or the constant harassment of Jewish persecutors. Throughout the history of the church no agreement has been reached among hundreds of commentators. As it stands, the "thorn" of Paul's experiences is readily applied to a variety of trials faced in this life. Few of God's servants have been free from at least some kind of hindrance, weakness, or opposition.

12:8 the Lord. Paul's usual expression to refer to Christ, not to God the Father. Although prayers in the New Testament are most often directed to God the Father, this is an example of prayer directed to Christ (others are in Acts 1:24; 7:59; 1 Cor. 16:22; Rev. 22:20). It is striking that in his "boasting" Paul testifies about a request God did not fulfill.

12:9 my power is made perfect in weakness. God will accomplish His purposes without taking from His servant the thorn that seems to hinder him. Despite human weaknesses, God's grace attains His purposes in a fallen world. This promise from God no doubt gave Paul strength and encouragement in subsequent sufferings. Paul shortly ties the general principle to its source—the cross of Christ (13:4). Paul's whole response to attacks on his apostolic authority has been patterned consciously on Christ, and Him crucified, and not on the so-called "Jesus" and the different "gospel" that his opponents have foisted on the erring Corinthians (11:4 note).

12:10 Paul's spiritual view was so clear that he could see his sufferings as reasons for rejoicing, because he knew that in them all of Christ's power was at work.

12:11 You forced me. Paul had to "boast" about his apostolic weakness because the Corinthians, who knew him well, had not defended him against the false apostles, but instead had been seduced (11:1–3) by inflated self-claims and untrue criticism of Paul.

12:12 signs of a true apostle. According to common understanding, the "signs of a true apostle" were simply miracles, "wonders and mighty works." Yet throughout this epistle Paul points to other marks that distinguish him from the false apostles: the changed lives of the Corinthians (3:2, 3), the blameless character of his ministry (6:3–10; 7:2; 8:20, 21), his genuine love for his churches (6:11, 12; 7:3; 11:7–11), and his sacrificial endurance of suffering (6:3–10; 11:23–33). In addition to these marks, Paul is ready to mention miraculous signs, but not to dwell on them. See 1 Cor. 13:2; "The Apostles" at Acts 1:26.

12:14 for the third time. See Introduction: Date and Occasion. The first visit was on Paul's second missionary journey (Acts 18:1–18). The second visit is not recorded but occurred sometime during Paul's stay at Ephesus (Acts 19:1–41).

for [w]I seek not what is yours but you. For
[x]children are not obligated to save up for
their parents, but [y]parents for their children. 15 [z]I will most gladly spend and be
spent for your souls. If [a]I love you more,
am I to be loved less? 16 But granting that [b]I
myself did not burden you, I was crafty,
you say, and got the better of you by deceit.
17 Did I take advantage of you [c]through any
of those whom I sent to you? 18 [d]I urged
Titus to go, and sent [e]the brother with him.
Did Titus take advantage of you? Did we
not act in the same spirit? Did we not take
the same steps?

19 Have you been thinking all along that
we have been defending ourselves to you?
It is [f]in the sight of God that we have been
speaking in Christ, and [g]all for your
upbuilding, beloved. 20 For I fear that perhaps [h]when I come I may find you not as I
wish, and that you may find me not as you
wish—that perhaps there may be quarreling, jealousy, anger, hostility, slander,
gossip, conceit, and disorder. 21 I fear that
when I come again my God may humble
me before you, and I may have to mourn
over many of those [i]who sinned earlier and
have not repented of the impurity, [j]sexual
immorality, and sensuality that they have
practiced.

Final Warnings

13 [k]This is the third time I am coming
to you. Every charge must be established [l]by the evidence of two or three witnesses. 2 [m]I warned [n]those who sinned
before and all the others, and I warn them
now while absent, as I did when present on
my second visit, that [o]if I come again I will
not spare them— 3 since you seek proof
that Christ [p]is speaking in me. He is not
weak in dealing with you, but [q]is powerful
among you. 4 For [r]he was crucified in
weakness, but [s]lives by the power of God.
For [t]we also are weak in him, but in dealing with you [u]we will live with him by the
power of God.

5 Examine yourselves, to see whether you
are in the faith. [v]Test yourselves. Or do you
not realize this about yourselves, that
[w]Jesus Christ is in you?—unless indeed
you fail to meet the test! 6 I hope you will
find out that we have not failed the test.
7 But we pray to God that you may not do
wrong—not that we may appear to have
met the test, but that you may do what is
right, though we may seem to have failed.
8 For we cannot do anything against the
truth, but only for the truth. 9 For we are
glad when [x]we are weak and you are
strong. Your [y]restoration is what we pray
for. 10 For this reason I write these things
while I am away from you, that when I
come [z]I may not have to be [a]severe in my
use of [b]the authority that the Lord has
given me for building up and not for tearing down.

Final Greetings

11 Finally, brothers,[1] rejoice. [c]Aim for restoration, comfort one another,[2] [d]agree with

14 [w]1 Cor. 10:24, 33 [x]1 Cor. 4:14, 15 [y][Prov. 19:14; Ezek. 34:2]
15 [z][ch. 1:6; Phil. 2:17; Col. 1:24; 1 Thess. 2:8; 2 Tim. 2:10] [a]See ch. 6:11
16 [b]ch. 11:9
17 [c][ch. 9:5]
18 [d]ch. 8:6 [e]ch. 8:18
19 [f]See Rom. 1:9; 9:1 [g]See 1 Cor. 14:26
20 [h][ch. 2:1-4]; See 1 Cor. 4:21
21 [i]ch. 13:2; [Rev. 2:21] [j]1 Cor. 5:1; See 1 Cor. 6:18
Chapter 13
1 [k]See ch. 12:14 [l]Cited from Deut. 19:15; See Num. 35:30
2 [m]ch. 10:2 [n]ch. 12:21 [o]ver. 10; See 1 Cor. 4:21
3 [p]See Matt. 10:20; 1 Cor. 5:4 [q]ch. 10:4
4 [r][Phil. 2:7, 8; 1 Pet. 3:18] [s]See Rom. 1:4; 6:4 [t][ch. 12:10] [u]See Rom. 6:8
5 [v][1 Cor. 11:28; Gal. 6:4] [w]Rom. 8:10; Gal. 4:19
9 [x]1 Cor. 4:10; [ch. 4:12; 12:5, 9, 10] [y]Eph. 4:12; 1 Thess. 3:10; [ver. 11]
10 [z][ch. 2:3] [a]Tit. 1:13 [b]ch. 10:8 11 [c]See Luke 6:40 [d]See Rom. 12:16

[1] Or *brothers and sisters* [2] Or *listen to my appeal*

I seek not what is yours but you. Unlike those preachers whose goal was their own financial reward.

12:16 got the better of you by deceit. Perhaps Paul's opponents were saying that his apparent selflessness was a trick to deceive them. Paul answers that he never exploited them through others (v. 17).

12:18 Titus was coming ahead of Paul (8:6, 16, 17).

12:19 Paul again emphasizes that he has not been speaking for his own reputation or glory but for the good of the church and for the glory of God. Again he reveals a strong awareness that all he writes and does is "in the sight of God."

12:21 Paul's fatherly ties with the Corinthian church are strong, and he knows that if he returns to find some of them (his "children," v. 14) still unruly, it will be humiliating for him, just as parents are humiliated by the misbehavior of their children.

many of those who sinned earlier and have not repented. False apostles were not the only problem in Corinth. There were some people still engaging in sin, and Paul warns them.

13:1 the third time. See note 12:14. Paul quotes Deut. 17:6 and 19:15. The "two or three witnesses" very likely does not mean Paul's two or three visits to Corinth (for Paul is still only one witness), but is rather a reminder that when he comes all charges will be considered fairly and dealt with in a just way.

13:3 Christ is speaking in me. A strong statement of Paul's apostolic authority. Christ Himself was speaking through Paul, and Christ's words through Paul would powerfully silence any offenders.

13:4 Paul's life (as that of all Christians) was united with Christ in His death and resurrection, and he continued to share in the resurrection power of Christ as long as he lived.

13:5 Examine . . . Test. See 1 Cor. 11:28; Gal. 6:4. Paul's words help clarify the doctrine of assurance of faith. Paul asks the Corinthians to examine their own lives for evidence of salvation. Such evidence would include trust in Christ (Heb. 3:6), obedience to God (Matt. 7:21), growth in holiness (Heb. 12:14; 1 John 3:3), the fruit of the Spirit (Gal. 5:22, 23), love for other Christians (1 John 3:14), positive influence on others (Matt. 5:16), adhering to the apostolic teaching (1 John 4:2), and the testimony of the Holy Spirit within them (Rom. 8:15, 16).

one another, [e]live in peace; and the God of
love and [f]peace will be with you. 12 [g]Greet
one another with a holy kiss. 13 [h]All the
saints greet you.

14 [i]The grace of the Lord Jesus Christ and
[j]the love of God and [k]the fellowship of the
Holy Spirit be with you all.

11 [e]See Mark 9:50 [f]See Rom. 15:33
12 [g]See Rom. 16:16
13 [h]Phil. 4:22 14 [i]Rom. 16:20 [j]Jude 21 [k]Phil. 2:1

13:13 All the saints. Christians in the church from which Paul was writing (Introduction: Date and Occasion).

13:14 A trinitarian benediction. See "One and Three: The Trinity" at Is. 44:6.

THE EPISTLE OF PAUL THE APOSTLE TO THE

Galatians

AUTHOR

The apostle Paul wrote Galatians (1:1). He mentions a group of his coworkers who had some role in sending the letter (1:2), but the letter's style and theology demonstrate that Paul was the immediate author. Since the eighteenth century, a few scholars have considered the letter pseudonymous (that is, that the name "Paul" was used by another, unknown author) but their arguments are generally regarded as having no foundation.

DATE AND OCCASION

The question of the letter's date is intertwined with the problem of its destination. Paul names his addressees as "Galatians" (3:1; cf. 1:2), but to which "Galatians" was he writing? He may have been writing specifically to the Celtic people who lived in northern Galatia and who were widely known as "Galatians," or he might have been addressing the people who lived in the entire province of Galatia. When we follow the course of Paul's first and second missionary journeys (Acts 13; 14; 15:36–18:22) we discover that this question has implications for the epistle's date and for its relationship to Paul's other letters. Paul visited Pisidian Antioch, Iconium, Lystra, and Derbe (all cities in south Galatia) on his first and second missionary journeys. If Paul wrote to southern Galatia, he probably wrote to those churches early in his career, shortly after the first missionary journey, or about the time of the Jerusalem Council (Acts 15; cf. Gal. 2:11–14). The date most often given by those who hold this view is A.D. 49. If this is correct, Galatians may be Paul's earliest epistle in existence today.

Many scholars think that Galatians was written to the ethnic Galatians in the north. If this view is correct, Paul probably wrote the letter after passing through "Galatia and Phrygia" (Acts 18:23) on his third missionary journey. Many who follow the "north Galatian theory" believe that Paul wrote the letter either during his two-year stay in Ephesus (Acts 19) or as he was traveling through Macedonia on his way to Greece at the end of his third missionary journey (Acts 20:1–6; cf. 2 Cor. 2:13). If this is correct, Galatians was probably written in A.D. 54 or 55. Theories that date the letter late in Paul's career have the merit of placing Galatians in the same period as 2 Corinthians, Romans, and perhaps Philippians—letters that share with Galatians some matters of common concern.

Galatians was written to answer specific problems in particular churches. In order to understand the epistle, some knowledge of the situation that provoked Paul to write is essential. Not long after the Galatians had accepted the gospel, agitators came among them who attacked Paul personally (4:17) and preached a distorted form of Christianity (1:6, 7). Their "gospel" required circumcision for salvation (6:12). Since the Galatians were uncircumcised Gentiles, the agitators insisted that the Galatians not only believe in Christ for salvation but also accept circumcision (2:3–5; 5:2, 6, 11; 6:12, 13, 15).

The zeal of these agitators likely reflects Jewish pressure as well as their own pride. Probably they were attempting to convert the Gentile Galatians to Judaism under pressure from nationalistic Jewish groups in Judea who, according to the Jewish historian Josephus, were becoming increasingly intolerant of contact between Jews and Gentiles during the last half of the first century.

The agitators were not content merely to preach their brand of the gospel. They also attempted to discredit Paul, who had founded the Galatian churches (4:17). Their attacks took three forms: First, they claimed that Paul was a renegade who had defied his superiors, the Jerusalem apostles. Paul responds to this attack in 1:11–2:10. Second, they said that Paul had recently argued with Peter over whether the gospel required Gentiles to become Jews in order to become Christians. Paul gives his account of the encounter with Peter in 2:11–14. Third, the agitators spread the notion that Paul had originally preached circumcision for salvation (5:11) but had recently changed his gospel so that he might more easily accommodate the Gentiles (1:10).

The Galatians, for their part, were showing interest both in the rumors about Paul and in the agitators' new form of the gospel. By the time Paul wrote, they were in the process of deserting the true gospel and, consequently, God Himself (1:6, 7). They now wanted to be "under the law" (4:21; cf. 5:1) and, specifically, to become circumcised (5:2). This transition to "a different gospel" (1:6) was not smooth. Dissension appears to have broken out within the community (5:15; 6:3–5).

Paul's purpose in writing was to persuade the Galatians that no Gentile needs to accept circumcision in order to belong to God's covenant people. The "truth of the gospel" (2:5, 14) is that entrance into communion with the people of God comes by faith in Jesus Christ. Anyone who seeks to violate that sacred sphere of faith by adding other requirements adulterates the gospel and must be resisted at all costs (1:8, 9). In order for his argument to be persuasive, Paul had to demonstrate that the rumors about him were false, and that both his gospel and his authority to preach it came from God Himself (1:11–2:14; cf. 5:11; 6:17).

CHARACTERISTICS AND THEMES

The Galatian letter stands like a sentinel over the truth that salvation is the gift of God's grace, unearned and undeserved, to be received by faith alone (2:15, 16). Indeed, faith itself is God's free gift (1:3, 6, 15; 2:19, 21; 6:18). Quite simply, this is "the truth of the gospel" (2:5, 14). Paul shows deep anger over the agitators' denial of it (3:1; 5:12), warning that those who reject it cannot expect to be saved (1:8; 5:4).

Faith alone is the key because Christ alone is the Savior. He bore the curse of the law in our place on the cross (3:13; 6:14). Made one with Him, we are clothed with His righteousness (3:26, 27), our sure hope (5:5). Because we are united to Christ, we receive the rights of His sonship (4:4, 5), and the Spirit of the Son becomes ours, enabling us to live in the Spirit, in fellowship with our Lord (2:20; 4:6, 7; 5:16–18, 25). The gift of the Spirit is the full blessing promised long ago to Abraham (3:6–9, 14). Against the proud imagination of sinners that they can earn their own salvation by keeping God's law, Paul boasts only in the cross, in faith receiving the promise of God (6:14).

OUTLINE OF GALATIANS

I. Salutation (1:1–5)

II. The Problem in Galatia: Another Gospel from False Teachers (1:6–9)

III. Defense of Paul's Apostleship (1:10–2:14)

- A. *Paul Seeks God's Approval Rather than Man's (1:10)*
- B. *Paul Not Dependent upon the Jerusalem Apostles for His Authority (1:11–2:14)*
  1. Called by God (1:11–16)
  2. Jerusalem Authorities Added Nothing to His Original Calling (1:17–2:10)
  3. Paul's Authority Demonstrated by His Challenge of Peter's Error (2:11–14)

IV. Paul's Defense of the Gospel (2:15–6:10)

- A. *Peace with God Comes Through Faith in Jesus Christ for Jew and Gentile Alike (2:15–21)*
- B. *Justification Through Faith Has Replaced Condemnation Under Law (3:1–5:12)*
  1. The Spirit's Presence Proves Faith's Effectiveness (3:1–5)
  2. Abraham's Faith Proves Faith's Effectiveness (3:6–9)
  3. Curse of the Law Proves the Ineffectiveness of Works (3:10–14)
  4. Promise to Abraham Has Priority Over Condemnation by the Law (3:15–4:7)
  5. First Personal Appeal Not to Abandon the Gospel (4:8–20)
  6. A Scriptural Proof (4:21–5:1)
  7. Second Personal Appeal Not to Abandon the Gospel (5:2–12)
- C. *Practical Effects of the Gospel (5:13–6:10)*
  1. Love Fulfills the Law (5:13–15)
  2. The Spirit Struggles with the Flesh (5:16–26)
  3. Church Works in Harmony (6:1–10)

V. Conclusion (6:11–18)

- A. *Third Personal Appeal Not to Abandon the Gospel (6:11–17)*
- B. *Benediction (6:18)*

Greeting

1 Paul, an [a]apostle—[b]not from men nor
through man, but [c]through Jesus
Christ and God the Father, [d]who raised
him from the dead— **2** and all [e]the brothers[1] who are with me,
To [f]the churches of Galatia:
3 [g]Grace to you and peace [h]from God our
Father and the Lord Jesus Christ, **4** [i]who
gave himself for our sins to deliver us from
the present [j]evil age, according to the will
of [k]our God and Father, **5** to whom be the
glory forever and ever. Amen.

No Other Gospel

6 I am astonished that you are [l]so quickly deserting [m]him who called you in the
grace of Christ and are turning to [n]a different gospel— **7** [o]not that there is another
one, but [p]there are some who trouble you
and want to distort the gospel of Christ.
8 But even if we or [q]an angel from heaven
should preach to you a gospel contrary to
the one we preached to you, [r]let him be
accursed. **9** As we have said before, so now
I say again: If anyone is preaching to you a
gospel contrary to the one you received,
[r]let him be accursed.
10 For am I now seeking the approval of
man, or of God? Or am I trying [s]to please
man? If I were still trying to please man, I
would not be a [t]servant[2] of Christ.

Paul Called by God

11 For [u]I would have you know, brothers,
that [v]the gospel that was preached by me is
not man's gospel.[3] **12** [w]For I did not receive
it from any man, nor was I taught it, but I
received it [x]through a revelation of Jesus
Christ. **13** For you have heard of [y]my former
life in Judaism, how [z]I persecuted the
church of God violently and tried to destroy
it. **14** And I was advancing in Judaism
beyond many of my own age among my
people, so extremely [a]zealous was I for [b]the
traditions of my fathers. **15** But when he
[c]who had set me apart [d]before I was born,[4]
and who [e]called me by his grace, **16** was

Chapter 1
1 [a]See 2 Cor. 1:1 [b]ver. 11, 12 [c]Acts 9:6; 20:24; 22:10, 15, 21; 26:16; [1 Tim. 1:1; Tit. 1:3] [d]See Acts 2:24
2 [e]Phil. 4:21 [f]Acts 16:6; 1 Cor. 16:1
3 [g]Rom. 1:7; 1 Cor. 1:3 [h]1 Tim. 1:2
4 [i]See Matt. 20:28; Rom. 4:25; 1 Cor. 15:3 [j][Eph. 2:2; 1 John 5:19]; See John 15:19 [k]Phil. 4:20; 1 Thess. 1:3; 3:11, 13
6 [l][ch. 4:13; Acts 16:6; 18:23] [m]ch. 5:8 [n]2 Cor. 11:4; [1 Tim. 1:3]
7 [o][Acts 4:12; 1 Cor. 3:11] [p]ch. 5:10; Acts 15:24; See 2 Cor. 11:13
8 [q]2 Cor. 11:14 [r]See Rom. 9:3
9 [r][See ver. 8 above]
10 [s]1 Thess. 2:4; [Rom. 2:29; 1 Cor. 10:33; Eph. 6:6; Col. 3:22] [t][Rom. 1:1] **11** [u]1 Cor. 15:1 [v]See Rom. 2:16 **12** [w]ver. 1; 1 Cor. 11:23; 15:3; [Acts 22:14] [x]ver. 16; See 1 Cor. 2:10; 2 Cor. 12:1 **13** [y][Acts 26:4] [z]See Acts 8:3 **14** [a]Phil. 3:6; See Acts 21:20 [b][Jer. 9:14; 2 Tim. 1:3]; See Matt. 15:2 **15** [c]Acts 13:2; Rom. 1:1 [d]Isai. 49:1, 5; Jer. 1:5; Luke 1:15 [e]ver. 6

1 Or *brothers and sisters*. The plural Greek word *adelphoi* (translated "brothers") refers to siblings in a family. In New Testament usage, depending on the context, *adelphoi* may refer either to men or to both men and women who are siblings (brothers and sisters) in God's family, the church; also verse 11 2 Or *slave;* Greek *bondservant* 3 Greek *not according to man* 4 Greek *set me apart from my mother's womb*

1:1 Paul. We know from fifteen references in Acts 7–13 that Paul was also called "Saul." In his letters, however, he always calls himself "Paul," a common Roman name.

apostle. The word means "messenger." Paul could on occasion use it to refer to an envoy such as Epaphroditus (Phil. 2:25), but he uses it here to denote the original apostles at Jerusalem (1:19; 1 Cor. 15:9). Paul claims the authority of an apostle to lay the foundation of the church (1 Cor. 3:10; 9:1; 14:37, 38; Eph. 2:20; 3:3–5). His apostleship and calling came from God Himself (1:11–2:10). See 2 Cor. 1:1 note.

1:3 Grace to you and peace. Each of Paul's letters begins with a reference to these two blessings from God. "Grace" translates the Greek *charis,* which means "an undeserved act of kindness." Paul uses this word more often than any other New Testament writer and gives it immense theological significance. It refers to all that God has given us in Christ, nothing of which we have earned or can repay. "Peace" refers to the relationship that Christ's death and resurrection (1:4) have established with God for those who believe the gospel. For Paul's own comments on the meaning of these two terms, see Rom. 5:1, 2.

1:6 called you in the grace. God's grace comes to us at His initiative, by His call, and not because of anything we have done to deserve it (1:15; Rom. 4:4–8; 8:30; 9:11–13).

1:7 some who trouble. Probably Jewish Christians from Jerusalem who insisted that Gentiles must not only believe in Jesus Christ but must also accept circumcision and thereby become Jews (2:3–5, 12; 6:12, 13). Various shades of this idea were widespread among early Jewish Christians (Acts 15:1; 21:20, 21; Phil. 3:2, 3).

1:8, 9 Those who add any additional requirements for salvation to faith in Jesus Christ, no matter how excellent their credentials, twist the gospel into another form. The preachers of the false gospel are under God's condemnation.

1:9 accursed. Paul's usual thanksgiving for his readers is here replaced by the threat of a curse, repeated for emphasis. The Greek word is *anathema* used also in Rom. 9:3.

1:10 seeking the approval of man. Paul's opponents in Galatia attacked not only the gospel but also its messenger, Paul. One of their charges was that Paul preached an easy form of the gospel, requiring neither circumcision nor obedience to the Sabbath laws and dietary restrictions (4:10; 5:11).

1:11 not man's. Paul defends himself against his opponents' charge that he is in rebellion against the Jerusalem apostles who gave him his authority in the first place. Paul contends that his authority comes from God alone, the Jerusalem apostles merely confirming it.

1:12 through a revelation. See Acts 9:3–5; 22:6–10; 26:13–18; 1 Cor. 15:8.

1:13 persecuted the church of God. Paul's persecution of the church before his call was well known to the early Christians (Acts 7:58; 8:3; 9:1, 2). Paul himself was profoundly ashamed of this part of his past (1 Cor. 15:9), although he looked on it as evidence that God's grace can overcome even the most rebellious sinners (Acts 22:4, 5; 26:9–11; 1 Cor. 15:10; Phil. 3:6; 1 Tim. 1:13, 14).

1:14 extremely zealous. Paul was fond of pointing out to opponents like those in Galatia that being a Jew, even a zealous Jew, is not sufficient for salvation. Paul considered his own experience proof that zeal for the law would not save (Rom. 9:30–10:4; 2 Cor. 11:22; Phil. 3:4–6).

1:15 before I was born. Paul consciously echoes the call of Jeremiah (Jer. 1:5) and, perhaps, the Servant spoken of by Isaiah (Is. 49:1, 5), who both like Paul were called to be God's messengers to Gentiles. Paul was conscious that his apostleship (v. 1 note) was in continuity with the Old Testament prophetic tradition.

called me by his grace. See note on v. 3; "Effectual Calling and Conversion" at 2 Thess. 2:14. Paul's call to be an apostle, like the faith of every believer, was the product of God's prior grace. Before our birth, and

pleased to reveal his Son to[1] me, in order
[f]that I might preach him among the
Gentiles, I did not immediately consult
with anyone;[2] 17 nor did I go up to Jerusalem to those who were apostles before
me, but I went away into Arabia, and returned again to Damascus.
18 Then [g]after three years I went up to
Jerusalem to visit Cephas and remained
with him fifteen days. 19 But I saw none of
the other apostles except James [h]the Lord's
brother. 20 (In what I am writing to you, [i]be-
fore God, I do not lie!) 21 [j]Then I went into
the regions of Syria and Cilicia. 22 And I was
still unknown in person to [k]the churches of
Judea that are in Christ. 23 They only were
hearing it said, "He who used to persecute
us is now preaching the faith he once tried
to destroy." 24 And they glorified God because of me.

Paul Accepted by the Apostles

2 Then after fourteen years I went up
again to Jerusalem with Barnabas, taking Titus along with me. 2 I went up
because of a revelation and set before them
(though privately before those [l]who
seemed influential) the gospel that [m]I proclaim among the Gentiles, [n]in order to
make sure I was not running or had not
[o]run in vain. 3 But even Titus, who was with
me, [p]was not forced to be circumcised,
though he was a Greek. 4 [q]Yet because of
false brothers secretly brought in—who
[r]slipped in to spy out [s]our freedom that we

16 [f]ch. 2:9; See Acts 9:15
18 [g][Acts 9:22, 23]
19 [h]See Matt. 12:46; Acts 12:17
20 [i]See Rom. 1:9; 9:1
21 [j][Acts 9:30; 11:25, 26; 13:1]
22 [k]1 Thess. 2:14

Chapter 2
2 [l]1 Tim. 3:16 [m]ver. 6, 9 [n]ch. 4:11; 1 Thess. 3:5 [o]Phil. 2:16
3 [p][Acts 16:3]
4 [q]Acts 15:24; 2 Cor. 11:26; [ch. 5:12] [r][2 Pet. 2:1; Jude 4] [s]See ch. 5:1

1 Greek *in* 2 Greek *with flesh and blood*

therefore before we could do anything good or bad, God chose to create faith in us (Rom. 9:10–13; Eph. 1:4–6). No one can earn God's call; it is a free gift.

1:16 Gentiles. Both "nations" and "Gentiles" are correct translations of the Greek word used here. Jewish writers used the term to refer to everyone that was not a Jew. Paul was called to preach to the Gentiles (2:9; Acts 9:15; 22:21; 26:17; Rom. 1:5; 15:16), but he did not regard this as a call to preach exclusively to Gentiles. In Acts 13–28 he frequently preaches to Jews, and such passages as Rom. 1:14–16; 9:1–5; 1 Cor. 9:20 show that he was ready to evangelize Jews.

consult with anyone. Paul did, of course, meet with Ananias three days after his conversion (Acts 9:10–19; 22:12–16). The word translated "consult," however, suggests laying something before someone or submitting it for comment and approval. Paul certainly did not consult Ananias in this sense. Ananias's role was to confirm Paul's calling to preach to the Gentiles and to baptize him.

1:17 Jerusalem . . . Arabia . . . Damascus. Paul's conversion and call took place near Damascus (Acts 9:3; 22:6; 26:12). He spent several days in the city after his conversion (Acts 9:19). This ancient city is on a fertile plain between two rivers, and the traveler from there must literally "go up" to Jerusalem in the Palestinian highlands. Jerusalem was the cultural and religious center of Palestine, and home to James, Peter, and John, who are prominent in Acts and Galatians as leaders of the early Christian community in Jerusalem (2:9). Paul stresses that his call to preach to the Gentiles came from God and not from the leaders of the Jerusalem church. Arabia was ruled by a Nabatean king, Aretas IV, who struggled with Rome for control of Damascus. When Paul was converted, Aretas's governor was in control of the city and apparently aided angry Jews in an effort to kill Paul (Acts 9:23–25; 2 Cor. 11:32, 33).

1:18 three years. The "many days" of Acts 9:23.

to Jerusalem. Paul's first trip to Jerusalem after his conversion (Acts 9:26–30).

visit. This translates a Greek word that means visiting someone for the purpose of getting information. Paul may have interviewed Peter about Jesus' life and teaching.

Cephas. Peter's Aramaic name was "Cephas." Both "Cephas" and "Peter" mean "rock."

1:19 James the Lord's brother. See Matt. 13:55 and Mark 6:3. This James is not the disciple James who is frequently coupled with Peter and John in the Gospels. Herod murdered that James in the church's earliest days (Acts 12:2). James, the Lord's brother, at first did not believe in Jesus (John 7:5) but later was converted, perhaps as a result of seeing the risen Lord (1 Cor. 15:7).

1:21 Syria and Cilicia. See Acts 9:30. Paul returned home to Tarsus (Acts 9:11; 21:39; 22:3), the most important city in Cilicia. This part of Cilicia was under the administration of the Roman province of Syria during the early first century. Paul's use of the two names is accurate.

1:22 Judea. Paul could be referring to the specific region of Old Testament Judah, or to the Roman province of Judea, which included ancient Judah, Samaria, and Galilee.

2:1 fourteen years. Either after his conversion or after his first visit to Jerusalem.

again to Jerusalem. This may refer to a second visit following his conversion, or to a third visit, recorded in Acts 15:2. The purpose of the visit mentioned here corresponds well with the purpose of the visit in Acts 15, but it is difficult, on this theory, to explain why Paul leaves the second visit (Acts 11:27–30) out of his narrative. If, as some scholars believe, Galatians was written after Paul's first missionary journey (Acts 13; 14) but before the Jerusalem Council (Acts 15), then the journey spoken of here is the Acts 11 journey, and the Acts 15 journey has not yet occurred.

Barnabas. A native of Cyprus and one of the earliest Christians (Acts 4:36). Barnabas's name means in Aramaic "Son of Encouragement," and his appearances in Acts demonstrate that he lived up to his name (Acts 4:36, 37; 11:22–24, 30).

Titus. Although not mentioned in Acts, Titus was one of Paul's trusted companions and messengers. See 2 Cor. 2:12, 13; 7:6; 8:6; Titus 1:4, 5.

2:2 a revelation. If this is the Acts 11 visit, the revelation may have been the prophecy of Agabus (11:28). If not, it was probably similar to other special revelations that Paul received from God (Acts 9:4–6; 16:9; 18:9, 10; 2 Cor. 12:1–6).

in vain. While the Jerusalem leaders were not the source of Paul's authority, his efforts to preach the gospel would have been hindered if these influential men had opposed him.

2:3 forced to be circumcised. See 5:12 and Acts 15:1. Circumcision was the distinguishing mark of the Jew, and the final step in the conversion of a male Gentile to the Jewish religion. Some Jewish Christians believed that Gentiles also had to accept circumcision and thus become Jews before they could be Christians and belong to God's chosen people. Paul was vehemently opposed to this teaching and maintains throughout Galatians that we are justified by faith in Christ alone.

2:4 false brothers. Paul considered the doctrine of salvation by grace through faith alone to be so important that he excluded from the church all who did not hold to it (1:8, 9; 5:2–4).

freedom. The freedom of the believer is not freedom to sin, but freedom from the curse the law pronounces on sin (3:10–14; 5:1, 13).

have in Christ Jesus, [t]so that they might
bring us into slavery— 5 to them we did not
yield in submission even for a moment, so
that [u]the truth of the gospel might be preserved for you. 6 And from those [v]who
seemed to be influential (what they were
makes no difference to me; [w]God shows no
partiality)—those, I say, who seemed influential [x]added nothing to me. 7 On the contrary, when they saw that I had been
[y]entrusted with [z]the gospel to the uncircumcised, just as Peter had been entrusted
with the gospel to the circumcised 8 (for he
who worked through Peter for his apostolic
ministry to the circumcised worked also
through me for mine to the Gentiles), 9 and
when James and Cephas and John, [v]who
seemed to be [a]pillars, perceived [b]the grace
that was given to me, they [c]gave the right
hand of fellowship to Barnabas and me,
that we should go to the Gentiles and they
to the circumcised. 10 Only, they asked us
to remember the poor, [d]the very thing I was
eager to do.

4 [t]ch. 4:3, 9, 24, 25; 2 Cor. 11:20; [Rom. 8:15]
5 [u]ver. 14; [ch. 4:16; 5:7; Tit. 1:14; 2 John 1]
6 [v]ver. 2, 9; [ch. 6:3; Acts 5:36]; See 1 Cor. 3:7 [w]See Deut. 10:17 [x][2 Cor. 11:5; 12:11]
7 [y]1 Thess. 2:4; 1 Tim. 1:11; See 1 Cor. 9:17 [z]ch. 1:16; See Acts 9:15
9 [v][See ver. 6 above] [a]Jer. 1:18; Rev. 3:12 [b]See Rom. 1:5 [c][2 Pet. 3:15]
10 [d]See Acts 24:17
11 [e][Acts 15:1, 35] [f]Job 21:31
12 [g]Acts 11:3; [ver. 14; Acts 10:28]; See Luke 15:2 [h]See Acts 11:2

Paul Opposes Peter

11 But [e]when Cephas came to Antioch, I
opposed him [f]to his face, because he
stood condemned. 12 For before certain
men came from James, [g]he was eating
with the Gentiles; but when they came he
drew back and separated himself, fearing
[h]the circumcision party. 13 And the rest of
the Jews acted hypocritically along with
him, so that even Barnabas was led astray
by their hypocrisy. 14 But when I saw that
their [i]conduct was not in step with [j]the
truth of the gospel, I said to Cephas
[k]before them all, "If you, though a Jew,
[l]live like a Gentile and not like a Jew, how
can you force the Gentiles to live like
Jews?"

Justified by Faith

15 We ourselves are Jews by birth and not
[m]Gentile sinners; 16 yet we know that [n]a per-

14 [i]Heb. 12:13 [j]See ver. 5 [k]1 Tim. 5:20 [l]See ver. 12 15 [m]ver. 17; [Eph. 2:3, 12
16 [n]ch. 3:11; See Acts 13:39

slavery. Probably bondage to sin (Rom. 6:15–23; 7:25) and to the curse that the law pronounces on those who sin (3:10).

2:5 truth of the gospel. See v. 14; 1:8, 9 and notes. Entrance into the community of God's covenant people (the church) comes only by faith that is graciously given to the believer by God (1:6, 15; Eph. 2:8). Any attempt to add entrance requirements, such as circumcision, is a denial of the sufficiency of faith in Christ's merits for satisfying God's justice, and therefore is a perversion of the gospel.

2:6 partiality. Just as the external mark of circumcision does not define the boundary of God's people, so worldly prestige is not important to God (1 Sam. 16:7; Rom. 2:25–29).

2:7 the uncircumcised. See note 1:16.

Peter . . . circumcised. Peter was apparently the chief spokesman of the early Jerusalem church (Acts 1–12). Only with great reluctance did he respond to God's command to associate with the Gentile Cornelius (Acts 10). Although Peter recognized the necessity of including Gentiles within God's people (Acts 10:34, 35; 11:17; 15:7–11), he evidently felt God's call to preach the gospel specifically to Jews.

2:9 James and Cephas and John. See notes on v. 7; 1:18, 19. These three men had special authority in the early Jerusalem church. Peter and John are frequently seen together (Acts 3; 4), and James was prominent in the Jerusalem church (Acts 12:17; 15:13; 21:18). "Pillars" was used as a metaphor in Greek as in English for persons in important leadership positions.

grace . . . given to me. Regarding Paul's conversion and call, see 1:15 and note. Paul frequently referred to his call as God's grace, given to him (Rom. 1:5; 12:3; 15:15, 16; 1 Cor. 3:10).

we should go to the Gentiles. Barnabas, like Paul, was chiefly a missionary to the Gentiles (Acts 13; 14; 15:36–41).

2:10 remember the poor. Some refer these words to the purpose of Paul's second visit to Jerusalem (Acts 11:27–30). On that visit, Paul and Barnabas were commissioned to take an offering from Antioch to the Christians in Judea who were suffering because of a famine. In this case, the poverty of which Paul speaks would be literal poverty. Others believe that these words refer to Paul's collection for the Jerusalem saints (Acts 24:17; Rom. 15:26; 1 Cor. 16:1–3; 2 Cor. 8; 9), to which the Galatians contributed (1 Cor. 16:1).

2:11 Antioch. The capital of the Roman province of Syria and the largest city of that province. Antioch was home to a large Jewish community and, not surprisingly, was the first place mentioned in Acts where Jewish Christians preached the gospel to Gentiles (Acts 11:19, 20). Not only was the church at Antioch the first church in our records to bring Jewish and Gentile Christians together in worship and fellowship, but, as far as we know, it was the first church to send missionaries to preach the gospel specifically to Gentiles (Acts 13:1–3).

2:12 drew back. Many Jewish Christians resisted God's commandment that Gentiles who believed in Christ should be received without having to follow the ceremonial law (Acts 10:28; 11:2, 3, 19; 15:1). Both Peter and Barnabas (v. 13) succumbed to pressure from a group that believed that to be circumcised, that is, to become a full Jewish proselyte, was necessary for becoming a Christian.

2:14 truth of the gospel. See note on v. 5.

live like a Gentile. Before the arrival of the "circumcision" group Peter had eaten freely with Gentiles (v. 12). Now, inconsistently, he was acting as if Gentiles must become Jews in order to become full members of God's people.

2:15, 16 These verses are central in Galatians. Paul's point is that everyone (circumcised Jew as well as uncircumcised Gentile) is placed in a right relationship with God through faith in Jesus Christ alone. The words "righteousness," "righteous," "justify," and "justification" in the New Testament are all from the same Greek root and have related meanings.

2:16 See "Faith and Works" at James 2:24. In the Old Testament, God rules and judges with perfect justice (1 Sam. 26:23), and pronounces His verdict of innocence or guilt. To "justify" is to declare to be right (Deut. 25:1). But if no one living is righteous before God (Ps. 143:2), how can there be hope of that verdict (Job 9:2)? As God is the Judge, whose verdict is final and just, so He is the Savior who can provide deliverance from His own judgment (Jon. 2:9). God's righteousness is revealed, not only as His requirement, but as His gift (Is. 45:24, 25; 54:14–17). That gift comes at last through the Messiah (Is. 53:8; Jer. 23:5, 6; 33:14–16). Paul proclaims the fulfillment of the Old Testament promise (Rom. 3:21–26). Faith receives the gift of Christ's righteousness as well as forgiveness through His atonement.

son is not justified[1] by works of the law
[o]but through faith in Jesus Christ,[2] so we
also have believed in Christ Jesus, in order
to be justified by faith in Christ and not by
works of the law, [p]because by works of the
law no one will be justified.
17 But if, in our endeavor to be justified in
Christ, we too were found [q]to be sinners, is
Christ then a servant of sin? Certainly not!
18 For if I rebuild what I tore down, I prove
myself to be a transgressor. 19 For through
the law I [r]died to the law, so that I might

16 [o]See Rom. 9:30 [p]Rom. 3:20; [Ps. 143:2]
17 [q]ver. 15
19 [r]See Rom. 6:2; 7:4

[1] Or *counted righteous* (three times in verse 16); also verse 17 [2] Or *through the faithfulness of Jesus Christ*

Justification and Merit

The doctrine of justification, the storm-center of the Reformation, was for Paul the heart of the gospel (Rom. 1:17; 3:21–5:21; Gal. 2:15–5:1), shaping his message (Acts 13:38, 39) and his devotion (2 Cor. 5:13–21; Phil. 3:4–14). Though other New Testament writers affirm the same doctrine in substance, the terms in which Protestants have affirmed and defended it for almost five centuries are drawn primarily from Paul.

Justification is God's act of pardoning sinners and accepting them as righteous for Christ's sake. In it, God puts permanently right their previously estranged relationship with Himself. This justifying sentence is God's bestowal of a status of acceptance for Jesus' sake (2 Cor. 5:21).

God's justifying judgment seems strange, for pronouncing sinners righteous may appear to be precisely the kind of unjust action by a judge that God's own law forbids (Deut. 25:1; Prov. 17:15). Yet it is a just judgment, for its basis is the righteousness of Jesus Christ. As "the last Adam" (1 Cor. 15:45), our representative head acting on our behalf, Christ obeyed the law that bound us and endured the punishment for lawlessness that we deserved, and so "merited" our justification. Our justification is on a just basis (Rom. 3:25, 26; 1 John 1:9), with Christ's righteousness reckoned to our account (Rom. 5:18, 19).

God's justifying decision is in effect the judgment of the Last Day regarding where we will spend eternity, brought forward into the present and pronounced here and now. It is a judgment on our eternal destiny; God will never go back on it, however much Satan may appeal against the verdict (Zech. 3:1; Rom. 8:33, 34; Rev. 12:10). To be justified is to be eternally secure (Rom. 5:1–5; 8:30).

The necessary means of justification is personal faith in Jesus Christ as crucified Savior and risen Lord (Rom. 4:23–25; 10:8–13). Faith is necessary because the meritorious ground of our justification is entirely in Christ. As we give ourselves in faith to Jesus, Jesus gives us His gift of righteousness, so that in the very act of "closing with Christ," as older Reformed teachers put it, we receive the divine pardon and acceptance we can find nowhere else (Gal. 2:15, 16; 3:24).

Historic Roman Catholic theology includes sanctification in the definition of justification, considered as a process rather than a single decisive event, and affirms that while faith contributes to our acceptance with God, our works of sanctification and merit must contribute too. Catholics see baptism as conveying the sanctifying grace that first justifies us. Afterward the sacrament of penance allows supplementary merit to be achieved through works, securing justification if the grace of God's initial acceptance is lost through mortal sin. This supplementary merit does not oblige God to be gracious although it is the normal context for receiving it. On the Roman Catholic view, believers effect their own salvation with the help of the grace that flows from Christ through the church's sacramental system. The Reformers pointed out that this view of salvation undercuts the sense of confidence that only free grace can provide to those who have no merits. Paul had already showed that all people, of whatever piety, are without merit, and need a free justification if they are to be saved. A justification that needs to be completed by the recipient is no resting place.

works of the law. Paul has been referring to the "works" that distinguish Jews from Gentiles (v. 15), such as circumcision, dietary restrictions, and Sabbath-keeping. His phrase, however, includes all the efforts of fallen humanity to keep God's law so as to merit His justifying verdict.

no one will be justified. A near quotation of Ps. 143:2. No one can keep the law fully, so legal observances such as circumcision cannot establish a right relationship with God. Something other than the law is needed for that, and God has provided it in the gift of Christ's righteousness and the blood of His atonement. Faith does not *merit* God's acceptance; it *accepts* Christ's merit before God (Phil. 3:9).

2:17 we . . . found to be sinners. The Galatian agitators and the "men . . . from James" (v. 12) considered Paul a "sinner" (like the Gentiles of v. 15) for breaking the Jewish dietary food laws. They had probably also accused Paul's gospel of promoting sin (Rom. 3:8).

2:18 tore down. The Greek word translated "tore down" is used in the New Testament to mean the tearing down of an edifice (Matt. 24:2; Mark 13:2; Luke 21:6; Rom. 14:20). Paul may be thinking of Peter's mistaken attempt to rebuild the wall between Jew and Gentile that was torn down by the gospel (v. 14; Eph. 2:14). To rebuild the wall of the law is to bring in again the condemnation of the law. The lawbreaker is not the one who turns from the law to Christ for justification; it is the one who turns back again from Christ to the law.

2:19 Paul died to the law in the death of Christ; he was crucified with Christ (v. 20), for he was united to Christ who died in his place (3:13; Rom.

[s]live to God. 20 I have been [t]crucified with
Christ. It is no longer I who live, but Christ
who lives [u]in me. And the life I now live in
the flesh I live by faith in the Son of God,
[v]who loved me and [w]gave himself for me.
21 I do not nullify the grace of God, for [x]if
justification[1] were through the law, [y]then
Christ died for no purpose.

By Faith, or by Works of the Law?

3 O foolish Galatians! Who has be-
witched you? [z]It was before your eyes
that Jesus Christ was publicly [a]portrayed as
crucified. 2 Let me ask you only this: [b]Did
you receive the Spirit by works of the law
or by [c]hearing with faith? 3 Are you so foolish? [d]Having begun by the Spirit, are you
now being perfected by[2] the flesh? 4 [e]Did
you suffer[3] so many things in vain—if
indeed it was in vain? 5 Does he who supplies the Spirit to you and [f]works miracles
among you do so [g]by works of the law, or
by hearing with faith—6 just as [h]Abraham
"believed God, and it was counted to him
as righteousness"?
7 Know then that it is [i]those of faith who
are [j]the sons of Abraham. 8 And the Scripture, foreseeing that [k]God would justify[4]
the Gentiles by faith, preached the gospel
beforehand to Abraham, saying, [l]"In you
shall all the nations be blessed." 9 So then,
those who are of faith are blessed along
with Abraham, the man of faith.

The Righteous Shall Live by Faith

10 For all who rely on works of the law are
[m]under a curse; for it is written, [n]"Cursed
be everyone who does not [o]abide by all
things written in the Book of the Law, and
do them." 11 Now it is evident that [p]no one
is justified before God by the law, for [q]"The
righteous shall live by faith."[5] 12 But the law
is not of faith, rather [r]"The one who does
them shall live by them." 13 Christ [s]re-
deemed us from the curse of the law by
becoming a curse for us—for it is written,
[t]"Cursed is everyone who is hanged [u]on a
tree"—14 so that in Christ Jesus the blessing of Abraham might [v]come to the Gentiles, so that [w]we might receive [x]the
promised Spirit through faith.

The Law and the Promise

15 [y]To give a human example, brothers:[6]
[z]even with a man-made covenant, no one
annuls it or adds to it once it has been rat-

19 [s]Luke 20:38; Rom. 6:11; 14:7, 8; 2 Cor. 5:15; 1 Thess. 5:10; Heb. 9:14; 1 Pet. 4:2 **20** [t]ch. 5:24; 6:14 [t]Rom. 6:6 [u]See John 17:23 [v]See Rom. 8:37 [w]See ch. 1:4 **21** [x][ch. 3:21; Heb. 7:11] [y][ch. 5:4]
Chapter 3
1 [z][Num. 21:9] [a][1 Cor. 1:23] **2** [b]ver. 14; Eph. 1:13; Heb. 6:4; See Acts 15:8 [c]Rom. 10:17 **3** [d]Phil. 1:6; [ch. 4:9] **4** [e]1 Cor. 15:2; [Heb. 10:35; 2 John 8] **5** [f][1 Cor. 12:10] [g]ver. 2 **6** [h]Cited from Gen. 15:6; [Rom. 4:9, 21, 22]; See Rom. 4:3 **7** [i]ver. 9 [j]See Luke 19:9 **8** [k]See Rom. 3:30 [l]Cited from Gen. 12:3 **10** [m][ch. 5:4]; See Rom. 4:15 [n]Cited from Deut. 27:26; [Jer. 11:3; Ezek. 18:4] [o][Matt. 5:19] **11** [p]See ch. 2:16 [q]Rom. 1:17; Heb. 10:38; Cited from Hab. 2:4 **12** [r]Cited from Lev. 18:5; See Rom. 10:5 **13** [s]ch. 4:5; [Rev. 22:3]; See 2 Pet. 2:1 [t]Cited from Deut. 21:23 [u]See Acts 5:30 **14** [v]Rom. 4:9, 16; [ver. 28] [w]ver. 2 [x]Acts 2:33; [Isai. 32:15; 44:3; Joel 2:28; John 7:39; Eph. 1:13] **15** [y]See Rom. 3:5 [z][Heb. 9:17]

1 Or *righteousness* 2 Or *now ending with* 3 Or *experience* 4 Or *count righteous*; also verses 11, 24 5 Or *The one who by faith is righteous will live* 6 Or *brothers and sisters*

4:25; 5:6). So too, he was raised with Christ and lived in relation to God (Col. 2:12; 3:1). Death to the law does not violate the law, for Christ met the law's demands. It is therefore "through the law" that believers are released from the bondage and condemnation of the law. See "The Three Purposes of the Law" at Deut. 13:10.

2:20 Union with Christ means that He represented us in His death and resurrection. But it means more, for it is a living union. Jesus is present with the believer; by the Spirit the Lord lives in inward fellowship with His own. Paul does not mean that the individuality of a person is suppressed or absorbed; he lives "in the flesh" by "faith." The union is a spiritual relationship of the utmost intimacy.

3:1 publicly portrayed. Perhaps in Paul's preaching.

3:2 Spirit. Paul appeals to the Galatians' own experience of the Holy Spirit to prove that becoming Jewish is not necessary for becoming a Christian (Acts 10:47; 11:17; 15:8).

3:3 by the flesh. Perhaps Paul has in mind not simply attempting to keep the law without the Spirit (Rom. 7:7–8:17) but also the attempting to gain favor with God by cutting the flesh in circumcision (Phil. 3:2, 3). In either case, Paul warns his readers against the attempt to win salvation by performing some work. Salvation comes only through God's grace by faith in Jesus Christ (2:16).

3:6 Abraham was the father of the Jews and the person with whom God first established circumcision as a covenantal sign (Gen. 17:10). Even this revered patriarch was placed in a right relationship with God by faith (Rom. 4:11). Paul reverses the charge that he is undercutting God's covenant with Abraham. The true children of Abraham share his faith, whether they are physically descended from him or not. The promise to Abraham is also a promise of blessing to the Gentiles, a blessing that must be received with faith like Abraham's.

3:10 Paul's point is that no one can keep the law in its entirety, and he supports his point by quoting Deut. 27:26. Following the passage from which Paul quotes, Deuteronomy lists the curses that will fall upon Israel for disobedience. Most Jews of Paul's day realized that Israel had broken the law and had received the curses that were predicted (Deut. 28:15–30:20).

3:11 See theological note "Justification and Merit" on previous page.

3:12 the law is not of faith. Here Paul speaks of the law as God's requirement, apart from the promise of God's covenant. Leviticus (18:5) states the requirement and predicts the failure and curse that followed (26:14–38). The promise is also repeated (26:40–45), for it is not voided (3:15–22).

3:13 a curse for us. Since we broke God's covenant by violating the law, we deserve to receive the law's curse and God's condemnation. But Christ bore the law's curse in our place, giving us peace with God (Rom. 3:21–26; 4:25; 5:1–8; 2 Cor. 5:21; Col. 2:13–15; cf. Mark 10:45; John 1:29; 1 Pet. 2:24). See "The Atonement" at Rom. 3:25.

3:14 the blessing of Abraham. See v. 8; Gen 12:3; "Christ the Mediator" at 1 Tim. 2:5. Believing Gentiles, whose lives are marked by the indwelling Spirit, fulfill the promise that through Abraham all nations will be blessed. The Spirit is the blessing promised to Abraham.

3:15–18 God promised saving blessing to the nations through Abraham "and his offspring"—Christ, descended from Abraham in His human nature. That covenant promise was not cancelled by the later giving of the law through Moses. The law does not oppose the promises (v. 21), but assumes them. Its requirements show the hopelessness of earning salvation and point God's people to faith in Christ (v. 24).

ified. 16 Now [a]the promises were made [b]to
Abraham and to his offspring. It does not
say, "And to offsprings," referring to many,
but referring to one, [c]"And to your offspring," who is Christ. 17 This is what I
mean: the law, which came [d]430 years
afterward, does not annul a covenant previously ratified by God, so as [e]to make the
promise void. 18 For if the inheritance
comes by the law, it no longer comes by
promise; but [f]God gave it to Abraham by a
promise.

19 Why then the law? [g]It was added
because of transgressions, [h]until the offspring should come to whom the promise
had been made, and it was [i]put in place
through angels [j]by an intermediary. 20 Now
[k]an intermediary implies more than one,
but [l]God is one.

21 Is the law then contrary to the promises of God? Certainly not! For [m]if a law had
been given that could give life, then righteousness would indeed be by the law.
22 But the Scripture [n]imprisoned everything
under sin, so that [o]the promise by faith in
Jesus Christ might be given [p]to those who
believe.

23 Now before faith came, we were held
captive under the law, [q]imprisoned until
the coming faith would be revealed. 24 So
then, [r]the law was our [s]guardian until
Christ came, [t]in order that we might be justified by faith. 25 But now that faith has
come, we are no longer under a guardian,
26 for in Christ Jesus [u]you are all sons of
God, through faith. 27 For as many of you as
[v]were baptized [w]into Christ have [x]put on
Christ. 28 [y]There is neither Jew nor Greek,
there is neither slave[1] nor free, [z]there is
neither male nor female, for you are all one
in Christ Jesus. 29 And [a]if you are Christ's,
then you are Abraham's offspring, [b]heirs
according to promise.

Sons and Heirs

4 I mean that the heir, as long as he is a
child, is no different from a slave,[2]
though he is the owner of everything, 2 but
he is under guardians and managers until

16 [a]Rom. 4:13, 16; See Luke 1:55 [b]Acts 13:32 [c]Acts 3:25 **17** [d]Ex. 12:40, 41; [Gen. 15:13; Acts 7:6] [e]Rom. 4:14 **18** [f][Heb. 6:13, 14] **19** [g][Rom. 4:15] [h]ver. 16 [i]Acts 7:53; Heb. 2:2 [j]Ex. 20:19, 21, 22; Deut. 5:5, 22, 23, 27, 31; Acts 7:38 **20** [k]1 Tim. 2:5; Heb. 8:6; 9:15; 12:24; [Heb. 6:17] [l]Rom. 3:30 **21** [m]See ch. 2:21 **22** [n]Rom. 11:32; See Rom. 3:9 [o]Rom. 4:16 [p]See Acts 10:43 **23** [q][1 Pet. 1:5] **24** [r][Matt. 5:17; Rom. 10:4; Col. 2:17; Heb. 9:9, 10] [s]1 Cor. 4:15 (Gk.) [t]ver. 11; See ch. 2:16

26 [u]ch. 4:5, 6; [John 1:12]; See Rom. 8:14-16 **27** [v]Rom. 6:3 [w]See Acts 8:16 [x]See Rom. 13:14 **28** [y][ver. 14; ch. 5:6; 6:15]; See Rom. 3:30; 1 Cor. 12:13 [z]1 Cor. 11:11 **29** [a]See Rom. 9:7; 1 Cor. 3:23 [b]ch. 4:1, 7; Rom. 8:17; Eph. 3:6; [ch. 4:28; 2 Tim. 1:1; Tit. 1:2; Heb. 9:15]

1 Greek *bondservant* 2 Greek *bondservant*; also verse 7

3:16 offspring. Paul is aware that the noun "offspring" in the singular may be collective as well as individual (v. 29; Rom. 4:18). He is affirming that Christ is the Seed (descendant) to whom the promise finally refers. See "God's Covenant of Grace" at Gen. 12:1.

3:17 430 years. In Ex. 12:40 this figure is given for the length of Israel's stay in Egypt. In the Greek Old Testament (Septuagint) version of Exodus, the time of the patriarchs' stay in Canaan is included in the 430 years. But Paul is not necessarily following the Septuagint in alluding to the passage. It is enough for his purpose to show that centuries passed before the law was given at Sinai (cf. Gen. 15:13; Acts 7:6).

3:19 because of transgressions. Probably in order to define sin specifically as sin against God's explicitly stated will, and so to make sin that much worse (Rom. 5:13, 20).

offspring. In Gen. 17:19 God promises Abraham a son, Isaac, and says that He will establish a covenant with Isaac and his "offspring." Paul regards this use of a singular noun as a pointer to Jesus who healed the broken covenant between God and His chosen people.

through angels. See Deut. 33:2; Acts 7:53; Heb. 2:2.

3:20 intermediary. Moses mediated between God and Israel when God made His covenant with Israel at Mount Sinai (Ex. 19–34). The promise given to Abraham, however, required no mediator and therefore takes precedence over the covenant at Sinai.

God is one. See Deut. 6:4. God's covenant with Abraham, because it did not involve a mediator, demonstrated God's unity and sovereignty more perfectly than the covenant at Sinai. The fulfillment of God's covenant with Abraham by the inclusion of the Gentiles in the people of God also demonstrates the unity of God more clearly than the Sinai covenant because it shows His sovereignty over all creation (Rom. 3:29, 30).

3:21 Humanity's inability to keep the law, not the law itself, is the source of humanity's broken relationship with God.

contrary to the promises of God. Paul strongly denies this mistaken conclusion from his argument. The law could be in competition with the gospel only if it could impart life by delivering sinners from its own condemnation. Although the law is good and shows what is pleasing to God (Lev. 18:5; Rom. 7:10), it was not able to give life to lawbreakers (2 Cor. 3:6). The Jews, possessing the law, were condemned by it. Scripture takes full account of this, showing that all are condemned sinners and pointing to the need for the promised Savior.

3:24 guardian. A "guardian" was a slave responsible for a child's training, especially for pointing out and punishing misbehavior. Like a guardian, the law pointed out sin and punished it. Another important function of guardians was to separate and protect the child from the influence of outsiders. The law functioned in a similar way to separate Israel from the Gentiles. That function of the ceremonial law has also ended. See "The Law of God" at Ex. 20:1.

3:26 you are all sons of God. We are adopted "sons" because we are united to the true Son, Jesus Christ. Baptism seals that union with Christ. It is a vital union; Christ lives in us (2:20). It is also a representative union; Christ died and lives for us (Rom. 6:5–11). To be clothed with Christ implies both, in that His righteousness is our covering, and we are a new creation in Christ (Rom. 13:14; Eph. 4:24; Col. 3:10).

3:28 you are all one in Christ Jesus. The wall of separation between Jew and Gentile is removed for those united to Christ: all in Christ are Abraham's seed (Eph. 2:14–16; Col. 3:11). Indeed, no human distinctions avail as advantages in the matter of salvation. Paul does not obliterate these distinctions, such as those between the sexes, but indicates they give no preferential status in terms of our union with Christ. Until Christ returns, the created order remains and order in the church takes account of it (1 Cor. 11:3; 14:34; 1 Tim. 2:11–14). See "The Church" at Eph. 2:19.

4:1–7 Paul has compared the law to a prison warden (3:23) and a guardian (3:24 note). Now he compares its preparatory role to that of guardians or trustees of a minor. The full right reserved for one who has grown up is adoption as a son and receiving the inheritance.

the date set by his father. **3** In the same way
we also, when we were children, [c]were
enslaved to the elementary principles[1] of
the world. **4** But [d]when the fullness of time
had come, God sent forth his Son, [e]born [f]of
woman, born [g]under the law, **5** [h]to redeem
those who were under the law, so that we
might receive [i]adoption as sons. **6** And
because you are sons, God has sent [j]the
Spirit of his Son into our hearts, crying,
"Abba! Father!" **7** So you are no longer a
slave, but a son, and if a son, then [k]an heir
through God.

Paul's Concern for the Galatians

8 Formerly, when you [l]did not know
God, you [m]were enslaved to those that by
nature [n]are not gods. **9** But now that you
have come to know God, or rather [o]to be
known by God, [p]how can you turn back
again to [q]the weak and worthless elementary principles of the world, whose slaves
you want to be once more? **10** [r]You observe

Chapter 4
3 [c]See ch. 2:4
4 [d][1 Tim. 2:6]; See Mark 1:15 [e]Phil. 2:7; See John 1:14 [f][1 Tim. 2:15]; See Gen. 3:15 [g][Luke 2:21, 22, 27]
5 [h]See ch. 3:13 [i]ch. 3:26; See Rom. 8:15
6 [j][Rom. 5:5; 2 Cor. 3:17]; See Acts 16:7
7 [k]See ch. 3:29

8 [l]1 Cor. 1:21; 1 Thess. 4:5; 2 Thess. 1:8; 1 John 4:8 [m][Eph. 2:11, 12; 1 Thess. 1:9] [n]2 Chr. 13:9; Isai. 37:19; Jer. 2:11; 5:7; 16:20; [1 Cor. 8:4] **9** [o]See 1 Cor. 8:3 [p][ch. 3:3] [q]Rom. 8:3; Heb. 7:18 **10** [r]Rom. 14:5; Col. 2:16

1 Or *elemental spirits*; also verse 9

Adoption

The gift of justification (that is, of present acceptance by God, the world's Judge) is accompanied by the gift of adoption, that is, of becoming a child of the heavenly Father (Gal. 3:26; 4:4–7). In Paul's world, adoption was ordinarily of young adult males of good character to become heirs and maintain the family name for rich people who otherwise had no children. Paul, however, proclaims God's gracious adoption of persons of bad character to become "heirs of God and fellow heirs with Christ" (Rom. 8:17).

Justification is the basic blessing on which adoption is founded; adoption is the crowning blessing for which justification clears the way. Adopted status belongs to all who receive Christ (John 1:12). In and through Christ God loves His adopted children as He loves His only begotten Son, and will share with them the glory that is Christ's now (Rom. 8:17, 38, 39). Believers are under God's fatherly care and discipline (Matt. 6:26; Heb. 12:5–11). They are to pray to God as their own Father in heaven (Matt. 6:5–13), imitate His virtues (Matt. 5:44–48; 6:12, 14, 15; 18:21–35; Eph. 4:32–5:2), and trust His fatherly love (Matt. 6:25–34), thus expressing the filial instinct that the Holy Spirit has implanted in them (Rom. 8:15–17; Gal. 4:6).

Adoption and regeneration accompany each other as two aspects of the salvation that Christ brings (John 1:12, 13) but they should be distinguished. Adoption results in a new relationship, while regeneration is a change of our moral nature. Yet the connection is clear. God wants His children, whom He loves, to have His character, and He takes action accordingly.

4:3 enslaved to the elementary principles. The Greek phrase refers to the basic elements that make up the world; in ancient thought, these were earth, wind, water, and fire. Sometimes these elements were revered as deities governing the universe. Here Paul may be thinking especially of the sacred calendar of the law, its seasons determined by the heavenly bodies (cf. Col. 2:8, 20–22). Legalism subjected life to the control of the structures of the world.

4:4 the fullness of time. The time set by the Father (v. 2), "the end of the ages" (1 Cor. 10:11), when the promises of God are realized.

God sent forth his Son. His eternal Son, sent to be born of a woman.

under the law. Although Christ was without sin (2 Cor. 5:21), He was born under the law, not only as One obligated to fulfill it, but also as One identified with sinners who are under the curse of the law. His death freed us from that curse (3:10–14).

4:5 to redeem. The concept of redemption comes from the institution of slavery. In both the Jewish and Greco-Roman worlds, a slave could buy his freedom (or someone else could buy it for him) by paying a redemption price to his owners. The price of our redemption was paid by the Father in the blood of His Son (1 Pet. 1:17, 18), and by the Son in giving His life a ransom for many (Matt. 20:28).

those . . . under the law. Not only Jews, circumcised under the law of Moses, but also Gentiles, for both are under the curse of the law (3:13, 14).

adoption as sons. Paul has been speaking of God's people under the law as children (Ex. 4:23; Is. 1:2). He now describes the only way in which the children become full members of the household, no longer minors. God seals our adoption by giving us the Spirit of His Son (Rom. 8:9–17). See theological note "Adoption."

4:6 Abba. The Aramaic word for "Father," used by Jesus (Mark 14:36). It was natural for Jesus, God's Son in a unique sense, to use this term. Now the Spirit puts the same word on the lips of men and women who are adopted in Christ.

4:9 known by God. Their knowledge of God was not the result of their own inquiry, but the sovereign work of the One who opened their understanding. See "True Knowledge of God" at Jer. 9:24.

turn back again. Amazingly, Paul likens the bondage of ceremonial legalism to the bondage of pagan superstition. To accept circumcision as necessary for salvation is to turn back from the liberty of grace to the bondage of the world with its times and seasons (v. 10; Col. 2:8, 20–22), whether these times be Jewish or Gentile.

weak . . . principles. Before their conversion, the Galatians were subject to the "principles" of a pagan world: its false gods, its astrology, its seasonal rituals (v. 3 note).

4:10 Paul may be referring to the observance of Jewish festivals. The Jewish agitators among the Galatians probably required not only circumcision for salvation but also adoption of the whole law, including the food laws and religious festivals.

days and months and seasons and years!
11 I am afraid [s]I may have labored over you
in vain.
12 Brothers,[1] [t]I entreat you, become as I
am, for I also have become as you are. [u]You
did me no wrong. 13 You know it was [v]be-
cause of a bodily ailment that I preached
the gospel to you [w]at first, 14 and though my
condition was a trial to you, you did not
scorn or despise me, but received me [x]as
an angel of God, [y]as Christ Jesus. 15 What
then has become of the blessing you felt?
For I testify to you that, if possible, you
would have gouged out your eyes and
given them to me. 16 Have I then become
your enemy by [z]telling you the truth?[2]
17 They make much of you, but for no good
purpose. They want to shut you out, that
you may make much of them. 18 It is always
good to be made much of for a good purpose, and [a]not only when I am present
with you, 19 [b]my little children, [c]for whom I
am again in the anguish of childbirth until
Christ [d]is formed in you! 20 I wish I could
be present with you now and change my
tone, for I am perplexed about you.

Example of Hagar and Sarah

21 Tell me, you who desire to be under
the law, do you not listen to the law? 22 For
it is written that Abraham had two sons,
[e]one by a slave woman and [f]one by a free
woman. 23 But [g]the son of the slave was
born according to the flesh, while [h]the son
of the free woman was born through promise. 24 Now this may be interpreted allegorically: these women are two [i]covenants.
[j]One is from Mount Sinai, bearing children
for slavery; she is Hagar. 25 Now Hagar is
Mount Sinai in Arabia;[3] she corresponds to
the present Jerusalem, for she is in slavery
with her children. 26 But [k]the Jerusalem
above is free, and she is our mother. 27 For
it is written,

> [l]"Rejoice, O barren one who does not
> bear;
> break forth and cry aloud, you
> who are not in labor!
> For the children of the desolate one
> will be more
> than those of the one who has a
> husband."

28 Now you,[4] brothers, [m]like Isaac, [n]are children of promise. 29 But just as at that time
he who was born according to the flesh
[o]persecuted him who was born according
to the Spirit, [p]so also it is now. 30 But what
does the Scripture say? [q]"Cast out the slave
woman and her son, for the son of the
slave woman shall not inherit with the son
of the free woman." 31 So, brothers, we are
not children of the slave but [r]of the free
woman.

1 Or *brothers and sisters*; also verses 28, 31 2 Or *by dealing truthfully with you* 3 Some manuscripts *For Sinai is a mountain in Arabia* 4 Some manuscripts *we*

11 [s]ch. 2:2; 5:2, 4; 1 Thess. 3:5
12 [t][2 Cor. 6:13] [u][2 Cor. 2:5]
13 [v]See 1 Cor. 2:3 [w][ch. 1:6]
14 [x]1 Sam. 29:9; [Mal. 2:7 (Gk.); 2 Cor. 5:20] [y]See Matt. 10:40
16 [z]See ch. 2:5
18 [a][ver. 13]
19 [b][1 Cor. 4:15; Philem. 10] [c][James 1:18] [d]Rom. 8:10
22 [e]Gen. 16:5 [f]Gen. 21:2
23 [g]ver. 29; [Rom. 9:7] [h]ver. 28; Gen. 17:16-19; 18:10, 14; 21:1, 2; Heb. 11:11
24 [i]See Rom. 9:4 [j]Deut. 33:2
26 [k][Heb. 12:22; Rev. 3:12; 21:2, 10]
27 [l]Cited from Isai. 54:1
28 [m]See ver. 23 [n]Rom. 9:8; See ch. 3:29
29 [o]Gen. 21:9 [p]See ch. 5:11
30 [q]Cited from Gen. 21:10; [John 8:35]
31 [r][1 Pet. 3:6]

4:12 become as I am, for I also have become as you are. In order to bring the gospel to the Gentile Galatians, Paul had to leave behind the legal restrictions of the Mosaic ceremonial law that forbade Jewish interaction with Gentiles (1 Cor. 9:19–23). Paul became like the Galatians in freedom from the law, and he now encourages them to be like him in freedom from legalistic bondage.

You did me no wrong. Paul's positive characterization of his previous relationship with the Galatian Christians (developed further in vv. 13–16) contains an implicit plea for good relations to continue. Paul's depth of concern for the Galatians is evident throughout this section.

4:13 because of a bodily ailment. It is not known what Paul suffered from. Eye difficulties (v. 15; 6:11), as well as malaria and epilepsy, have been suggested. There may or may not be a connection with Paul's "thorn . . . in the flesh" (2 Cor. 12:7). Paul's illness apparently made him stay longer in Galatia, where he had continuing opportunities to minister.

4:17 make much of you. See 6:12. The source of their zeal may have been a desire to avoid persecution, perhaps by Jewish nationalists who were not Christians and who saw the inclusiveness of the Christian movement as a threat to their cause.

4:19, 20 A touching witness to the depth of Paul's feeling for those whom he brought to faith in Christ. Paul's anger in this epistle (1:6, 9; 3:1; 5:12) reflects not only the seriousness with which he regards the task of preserving the truth of the gospel, but also the love which he had for his "children" in Christ.

4:22 two sons. The older son Ishmael was born to Hagar (Gen. 16); the younger son Isaac to Sarah (Gen. 21:1–6). Hagar was Sarah's slave.

4:23 Ishmael, the son of Abraham and Hagar, was born after Abraham and Sarah despaired of having the son God had promised. Isaac was born to Sarah by a miracle long after her child-bearing years had ended. God showed that none of His promises are empty (Gen. 18:14; Luke 1:37).

4:24 allegorically. Their historical occurrence has a deeper significance.

4:25 Mount Sinai. The place where God established His covenant with Israel (Ex. 19–34).

corresponds to the present Jerusalem. In both Paul's day and our own, most Jews remain, like all unbelievers, in slavery to sin and under the curse that the covenant of Sinai pronounces upon all who disobey its conditions.

4:26 Jerusalem above. Jerusalem was the city where God had set His name, the place of His dwelling in the midst of His people (Ps. 78:68, 69). The reality of God's dwelling with us was accomplished in Christ, the true temple (John 2:19). The true Jerusalem is in heaven where He is (Heb. 12:22; Rev. 21:2).

4:30 the free woman. We are not slaves to sin or under the curse of the law (Rom. 6:1–7:6).

Christ Has Set Us Free

5 For [s]freedom Christ has [t]set us free;
[u]stand firm therefore, and do not submit again to [v]a yoke of [w]slavery.
2 Look: I, Paul, say to you that [x]if you
accept circumcision, [y]Christ will be of no
advantage to you. 3 I testify again to every
man who accepts circumcision that [z]he is
obligated to keep the whole law. 4 You are
[a]severed from Christ, [b]you who would be
justified[1] by the law; [c]you have fallen away
from grace. 5 For through the Spirit, by
faith, we ourselves eagerly [d]wait for the
hope of righteousness. 6 For in Christ Jesus
[e]neither circumcision nor uncircumcision
counts for anything, but [f]only faith working through love.

Chapter 5
1 [s]ch. 2:4; 5:13; See James 1:25 [t]See John 8:32 [u]See 1 Cor. 16:13 [v]Acts 15:10 [w]See ch. 2:42
2 [x]ver. 3, 11; Acts 15:1; 1 Cor. 7:18 [y]See ch. 4:11
3 [z]Rom. 2:25
4 [a]Rom. 7:6 (Gk.) [b][ch. 2:21; 3:10; Rom. 9:31, 32] [c][Heb. 12:15; 2 Pet. 3:17]
5 [d]See Rom. 8:23, 25
6 [e]ch. 6:15; 1 Cor. 7:19; Col. 3:11; See ch. 3:28 [f][Eph. 6:23; 1 Thess. 1:3; James 2:18, 20, 22]

1 Or *counted righteous*

Christian Liberty

Salvation in Christ is liberation, and the Christian life is one of liberty—Christ has set us free (Gal. 5:1; cf. John 8:32, 36). Christ's liberating action is not basically social, political, or economic improvement, as is sometimes suggested today; it is liberation from the law as a means to salvation, from the power of sin, and from superstition.

First, Christians have been set free from the law as a system of salvation. Being justified by faith in Christ, they are no longer under God's law, but under His grace (Rom. 3:19; 6:14, 15; Gal. 3:23–25). Their standing with God (the "peace" and "access" of Rom. 5:1, 2) is assured because they have been accepted and adopted in Christ. It does not, nor ever will, depend on what they do, nor will it ever be imperiled by what they fail to do. They live, not by being perfect, but by being forgiven.

Although they are fallen, human beings think they can gain a right relationship with God through disciplines of obedience, ritual, and asceticism. Without God's righteousness, they go about "seeking to establish their own" righteousness—as Paul describes the Jews (Rom. 10:3). Paul knew that this is a hopeless enterprise. No human performance is ever good enough, and there are always wrong desires in the heart, no matter how correct the outward actions are (Rom. 7:7–11; cf. Phil. 3:6). God looks at the heart first.

Far from opening the way of life, the law's work is to arouse, expose, and condemn the sin that permeates our moral lives, making us aware of its reality and consequences (Rom. 3:19; 1 Cor. 15:56; Gal. 3:10). The futility of treating the law as a system of salvation, and seeking righteousness by it, is plain (Gal. 3:10–12; 4:21–31). This futility is the bondage to the law from which Christ sets us free.

Second, Christians have been set free from sin's dominion (John 8:34–36; Rom. 6:14–23). They have been supernaturally regenerated and made alive to God through union with Christ in His death and risen life (Rom. 6:3–11). The desire of their heart now is to serve God in righteousness (Rom. 6:18, 22). Sin's dominion involves not only constant acts of disobedience, but also a constant disregard for God's moral law, rising sometimes to resentment or even hatred towards the law. Now, however, being changed in heart, motivated by thankfulness for the gift of grace, and energized by the Holy Spirit, Christians are "not under the old written code but in the new life of the Spirit" (Rom. 7:6).

Third, Christians have been set free from superstitions, including the idea that matter and physical pleasure are intrinsically evil. Against this idea, Paul insists that Christians are free to enjoy as God's good gifts all created things (1 Tim. 4:1–5), provided we do not transgress the moral law, nor hinder our own spiritual well-being or that of others (1 Cor. 6:12, 13; 8:7–13).

5:1 yoke. Jewish literature of the time compares the law to a yoke to which the obedient submit. Paul does not want his Gentile readers to let the law take the place of Christ in their lives (Matt. 11:29; Acts 15:10). See theological note "Christian Liberty."

5:2 Regarding Christ and circumcision as necessary for salvation is the same as denying the sufficiency of Christ's death for salvation. For those set free in Christ, to be circumcised for salvation is to undertake to do what they can never do (2:21), and to reject what Christ has done for them. It is to return again to the dominion of sin and the law's curse.

5:4 fallen away from grace. That is, they would be renouncing God's grace by no longer relying on it. Those who are chosen in Christ will be kept from such a renunciation of the gospel, and Paul continues to have confidence that his warning will be heeded (v. 10). There may be those, however, who appear to us to be true members of Christ who will abandon the gospel (Rom. 11:22; 1 John 2:19). Scripture admonishes us, therefore, to be "diligent to make your calling and election sure" (2 Pet. 1:10) by living in a way that demonstrates the reality of the Spirit's presence within us (5:16–6:10; Heb. 10:26, 27; 2 Pet. 1:5–11).

5:5 by faith . . . the hope of righteousness. The sure hope of righteousness by faith is in contrast to the vain hope of righteousness by legal works. The Holy Spirit gives eager anticipation of justification on the last Day because we have already been justified in Christ (Rom. 5:1–5, 9, 10). That same Spirit, imparting to us the saving benefits of our risen Savior, is our foretaste of the fulfilled heritage in glory (2 Cor. 5:5; Eph. 1:13).

5:6 Paul is not arguing against circumcision itself (6:15; 1 Cor. 7:19; cf. Acts 16:3) but against the attempt to make the rite a requirement for salvation. The one who believes in Jesus Christ, and demonstrates the reality of his belief through a sanctified life, is saved. See "Faith and Works" at James 2:24.

7 [g]You were running well. Who hindered
you from obeying [h]the truth? 8 This persuasion is not from [i]him who calls you. 9 [j]A little leaven leavens the whole lump. 10 [k]I
have confidence in the Lord that you will
[l]take no other view than mine, and [m]the
one who is troubling you will bear the
penalty, whoever he is. 11 But if I, brothers,[1]
still preach[2] circumcision, [n]why am I still
being persecuted? In that case [o]the offense
of the cross has been removed. 12 I wish
[p]those who unsettle you would emasculate
themselves!

13 For you were called to freedom, brothers. [q]Only do not use your freedom as an
opportunity for the flesh, but through love
[r]serve one another. 14 For [s]the whole law is
fulfilled in one word: [t]"You shall love your
neighbor as yourself." 15 But if you [u]bite
and devour one another, watch out that
you are not consumed by one another.

Walk by the Spirit

16 But I say, [v]walk by the Spirit, and you
will not gratify [w]the desires of the flesh.
17 For [x]the desires of the flesh are against
the Spirit, and the desires of the Spirit are
against the flesh, for these are opposed to
each other, [y]to keep you from doing the
things you want to do. 18 But if you are [z]led
by the Spirit, [a]you are not under the law.

19 Now [b]the works of the flesh are evident:
sexual immorality, impurity, sensuality,
20 idolatry, sorcery, enmity, strife, jealousy,
fits of anger, rivalries, dissensions, [c]divi-
sions, 21 envy,[3] drunkenness, orgies, and
things like these. I warn you, as I warned
you before, that [d]those who do such things
will not inherit the kingdom of God. 22 But
[e]the fruit of the Spirit is [f]love, joy, peace,
patience, [g]kindness, goodness, faithfulness, 23 [h]gentleness, [i]self-control; [j]against
such things there is no law. 24 And those
who belong to Christ Jesus [k]have crucified
the flesh with its [l]passions and desires.

25 If we live by the Spirit, [m]let us also walk
by the Spirit. 26 [n]Let us not become conceited, provoking one another, envying one
another.

Bear One Another's Burdens

6 Brothers,[4] [o]if anyone is caught in any
transgression, [p]you who are spiritual
should restore him in [q]a spirit of gentleness. Keep watch on yourself, lest you too
be tempted. 2 [r]Bear one another's burdens,

7 [g]See 1 Cor. 9:24 [h]See ch. 2:5
8 [i]ch. 1:6
9 [j]1 Cor. 5:6; [1 Cor. 15:33; Heb. 12:15]
10 [k]See 2 Cor. 2:3 [l][Phil. 3:15] [m]ch. 1:7; [ver. 12]
11 [n]ch. 4:29; 6:12 [o]1 Cor. 1:23; See 1 Pet. 2:8
12 [p][ver. 10]; See ch. 2:4
13 [q]1 Pet. 2:16; Jude 4; [1 Cor. 8:9; 2 Pet. 2:19] [r]1 Cor. 9:19
14 [s][Matt. 7:12; 22:40] [t]Cited from Lev. 19:18; [ver. 22; ch. 6:2]; See Matt. 19:19; John 13:34
15 [u][Phil. 3:2]
16 [v]ver. 24, 25; Rom. 8:4; See Rom. 13:14 [w]Eph. 2:3
17 [x]Rom. 7:23; 8:5-7 [y]Rom. 7:15, 18, 19
18 [z]Rom. 8:14 [a]See Rom. 7:4
19 [b]1 Cor. 3:3; Eph. 5:3; Col. 3:5; James 3:14, 15; [Matt. 15:18-20]
20 [c]1 Cor. 11:19

21 [d][Col. 3:6]; See 1 Cor. 6:9 22 [e][Rom. 7:4; 8:5; Eph. 5:9] [f]See Rom. 5:1-5; Col. 3:12-17 [g]2 Cor. 6:6 23 [h]Eph. 4:2 [i]Acts 24:25 [j]1 Tim. 1:9 24 [k][ver. 16]; See Rom. 6:6 [l]Rom. 7:5 25 [m][ver. 16] 26 [n]Phil. 2:3
Chapter 6 1 [o][Ps. 141:5; 2 Cor. 2:7; Heb. 12:13; James 5:19] [p][Rom. 15:1; 1 Cor. 10:15]; See 1 Cor. 2:15 [q]1 Cor. 4:21; [2 Tim. 2:25] 2 [r]Rom. 15:1; 1 Thess. 5:14

1 Or *brothers and sisters*; also verse 13 2 Greek *proclaim* 3 Some manuscripts add *murder* 4 Or *brothers and sisters*; also verse 18

5:11 still preach circumcision. Paul may be referring to his life before his conversion, or he may be refuting a false charge from his opponents that he preaches the necessity of circumcision for salvation when the Jerusalem apostles are present but leaves out that requirement when in the company of Gentiles (1:10).

offense of the cross. See 1 Cor. 1:18–2:5.

5:12 emasculate themselves. Paul's anger is a result of seeing young believers led astray. Jesus had some equally strong words of warning for those who dared to lead others into error (Luke 17:1, 2).

5:13 freedom. Christian liberty is freedom *from* sin, not liberty *to* sin (Rom. 6:1–7:6). See "The Freedom and Bondage of the Will" at Jer. 17:9.

5:14 the whole law. Paul's letter to the Galatians does not nullify the law. Christ fulfilled the law; He did not abolish it (Matt. 5:17). Certain provisions of the law such as its dietary requirements are no longer applicable in the new covenant, but the ethical commands of the law remain as declarations of God's will for Christian behavior (Rom. 8:2–8; 13:8–10).

love. See Rom. 13:10; 1 Cor. 13; cf. Matt. 19:19.

5:16 walk by the Spirit. The Holy Spirit's dwelling within the believer is a sign that the believer is part of God's people and an heir of the covenant promises given to Abraham (3:14; 4:6; 5:5). The Spirit's presence is also a sign that in the final day God will declare the believer righteous (5:5; 2 Cor. 1:22; 5:5).

5:17 the flesh. See "Sanctification: The Spirit and the Flesh" at 1 Cor. 6:11. Paul says in 6:13 that the agitators in Galatia want to circumcise the Galatians in order to glory in their "flesh." The word "flesh" is used at least three ways by Paul. The broadest use is a simple reference to humanness. Another use is for the physical body. The narrowest use, especially when placed in contrast to "spirit," is to refer to the sinful human nature, which includes the mind and soul. If the Galatians abandon Christ and place their confidence in the law, they will be turning back to reliance on the flesh, and thus to existence under the law's curse. There is hope as well as warning in Paul's words. Although the desires of the flesh oppose the Spirit, the desires given by the Holy Spirit deliver us from the flesh and the law.

5:20 idolatry . . . divisions. Paul lists gross sins that the legalists would condemn, but follows them with the very sins they were guilty of (v. 15).

5:21 will not inherit the kingdom of God. One of four occurrences of this phrase in the Pauline letters (1 Cor. 6:9, 10; 15:50; cf. Eph. 5:5). Paul's point is that those who do not exhibit the graces of the Spirit (v. 22) in their lives will not take part in God's eternal kingdom.

5:22 fruit of the Spirit. Paul uses the metaphor of fruit to describe the conduct of the believer in Rom. 6:22; Eph. 5:9; and Phil. 1:11. John the Baptist likewise claimed that true repentance would produce the "fruit" of concrete ethical behavior (Matt. 3:8; Luke 3:8). The love produced by the Spirit is like the love of Christ. It goes far beyond the performance of legalistic self-righteousness (Luke 10:25–37).

5:24 have crucified the flesh. See 2:20; 6:14; Rom. 6:6. For the people of Christ, the Cross broke the grip of the law (2:19) and also the grip of the flesh. By faith they recognize the reality of their union with Christ in His death. So, too, they have been raised to new life in the Spirit of Christ and therefore walk in the Spirit (Col. 3:1, 3, 5).

6:1 you . . . spiritual. Those who are in step with the Spirit (5:25) should reach out to the believer whom sin has ensnared, but should be cautious lest sin also ensnare them in the process.

and [s]so fulfill [t]the law of Christ. 3For [u]if
anyone thinks he is something, [v]when he is
nothing, he deceives himself. 4But let each
one [w]test his own work, and then his reason to boast will be in himself alone and
not in his neighbor. 5For [x]each will have to
bear his own load.
6[y]One who is taught the word must
share all good things with the one who
teaches. 7[z]Do not be deceived: God is not
mocked, for [a]whatever one sows, that will
he also reap. 8For [b]the one who sows to his
own flesh [c]will from the flesh reap corruption, but [d]the one who sows to the Spirit
will from the Spirit reap eternal life. 9And
[e]let us not grow weary of doing good, for in
due season we will reap, [f]if we do not give
up. 10So then, [g]as we have opportunity, let
us [h]do good to everyone, and especially to
those who are [i]of the household of faith.

Final Warning and Benediction

11See with what large letters I am writing
to you [j]with my own hand. 12[k]It is those
who want to make a good showing in the
flesh [l]who would force you to be circumcised, and only [m]in order that they may not
be persecuted for the cross of Christ. 13For
even those who are circumcised do not
themselves keep the law, but they desire to
have you circumcised that they may boast
in your flesh. 14But far be it from me to
boast [n]except in the cross of our Lord Jesus
Christ, by which[1] the world [o]has been
crucified to me, and I to the world. 15For
[p]neither circumcision counts for anything,
nor uncircumcision, but [q]a new creation.
16And as for all who walk by this rule,
[r]peace and mercy be upon them, and upon
[s]the Israel of God.
17From now on let no one cause me trouble, for I bear on my body the marks of
Jesus.
18[t]The grace of our Lord Jesus Christ be
[u]with your spirit, brothers. Amen.

2 [s][ch. 5:14] [t]1 John 4:21; See John 13:34
3 [u][ch. 2:6]; See 1 Cor. 3:7, 18 [v]2 Cor. 12:11
4 [w][1 Cor. 11:28; 2 Cor. 13:5]
5 [x][Rom. 14:12]
6 [y][Rom. 15:27; 1 Cor. 9:11]
7 [z]1 Cor. 6:9; 15:33; James 1:16 [a]See 2 Cor. 9:6
8 [b][Hos. 8:7]; See Job 4:8 [c]See Rom. 6:21 [d]See James 3:18
9 [e]2 Thess. 3:13; [1 Cor. 15:58] [f]Heb. 12:3, 5; [Heb. 10:36]; See Matt. 10:22
10 [g]Prov. 3:27; John 9:4; 12:35 [h]Eph. 4:28; 1 Tim. 6:18; [1 Thess. 5:15] [i][Eph. 2:19; 1 Tim. 5:8; Heb. 3:6]
11 [j]See 1 Cor. 16:21
12 [k]See 2 Cor. 11:13 [l]ch. 2:3 [m]ch. 5:11
14 [n]1 Cor. 2:2; [Phil. 3:3, 7, 8] [o]See Rom. 6:6
15 [p][Rom. 2:28]; See ch. 5:6 [q][John 3:5, 7]; See Rom. 6:4
16 [r]Ps. 125:5; 128:6 [s]ch. 3:7, 9, 29; Rom. 2:29; 4:12; 9:6-8; Phil. 3:3
18 [t]Philem. 25; See Rom. 16:20 [u]2 Tim. 4:22

1 Or *through whom*

6:2 the law of Christ. This includes loving, not only one's neighbor (5:14; Matt. 22:39), but one's enemy as well (Matt. 5:43), with God's love as the model.

6:4 test his own work. Paul urges the Galatian Christians to examine themselves as individuals before God, rather than drawing false confidence from relative comparisons with others (cf. 2 Cor. 13:5, 6).

reason to boast will be in himself. Lit. "have reason to boast in himself." As Paul subsequently makes clear, reason for "boasting" is not to be found in one's obedience to the law. While the Judaizers "boasted" of their success in encouraging legalism (v. 13), Paul "boasts" in the cross of Christ alone (v. 14; cf. 2 Cor. 11:16–12:10).

6:5 load. This is a different Greek word from the "burden" of v. 2, signaling a shift in the metaphor. Paul encouraged Christians to help others with the "burden" of overcoming temptation (v. 2). Here Paul means that we should not take pride in how much better we are than others, for God alone is our Judge.

6:10 The church has a responsibility to help relieve the suffering of those outside its fellowship, but it has a special responsibility to help brothers and sisters in Christ who are in need (1 Thess. 3:12).

6:11 Paul sometimes dictated his letters to a secretary (Rom. 16:22) but customarily wrote the conclusion himself (1 Cor. 16:21; Col. 4:18; 2 Thess. 3:17). His "large letters" may mean that his eyesight was poor (cf. 4:15).

6:12 circumcised. See note 2:3.

may not be persecuted. It is possible that those advocating circumcision in Galatia were doing so under pressure from extremely zealous Jewish nationalists in Judea (4:17 note).

6:14 boast . . . in the cross. For a more detailed outworking of this concept, see 1 Cor. 1:18–2:5.

6:15 circumcision. See note 5:6.

a new creation. The Holy Spirit's activity in the believers' lives reverses the effects of the Fall and produces a renewed people (2 Cor. 5:17) who will eventually take their place in the new heavens and the new earth (Rev. 21:1).

6:16 Israel of God. This phrase may refer to the newly constituted people of God, whose identifying mark is the Holy Spirit and not circumcision. Such people would include both Gentiles and Jews. But it could also refer to the "fullness" of Israel, the elect of the Jewish nation for whose salvation Paul was deeply concerned (cf. Rom. 9:1–5; 11:12, 26, 31).

6:17 marks. The Greek word denotes the brands used to mark a slave as the property of a certain master. The word was also used to refer to the mark that pagan priests carried to identify the god they served. Paul uses the word to refer to the scars he received during his missionary activity (2 Cor. 11:23–25). These scars branded him as a slave of Christ (Rom. 1:1; Phil. 1:1; Titus 1:1).

6:18 A fitting conclusion to the letter in which Paul is most intensely concerned with God's grace. The benediction summarizes Paul's hope that among the Galatians the gospel of God's grace will triumph.

THE EPISTLE OF PAUL THE APOSTLE TO THE

Ephesians

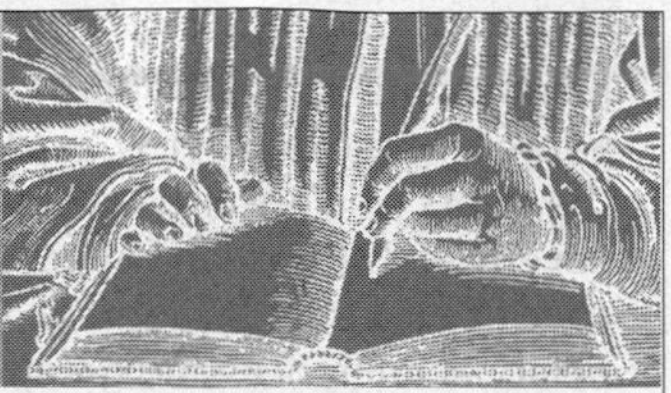

AUTHOR

In a straightforward way this letter claims to be by Paul (1:1; 3:1). Themes and language common in his earlier letters are frequently encountered in Ephesians. The verbal similarities with Colossians are especially striking.

In the modern era, however, the question has been raised whether Paul was the author. For some, Ephesians appears to be too dependent on Colossians. Although the letter sounds like Paul, phrases tend to build and multiply more than in the earlier letters. The letter is less instructional and more prayerful. Doctrine has given way to doxology, reasoned argument to awe. Ideas that are only implicit in his earlier letters (e.g., that beyond local churches there is one worldwide church) become explicit here. Such considerations lead many to say that Ephesians was written by one of Paul's students who was attempting to develop some of Paul's ideas, especially those in Colossians.

The language and style of Ephesians certainly differ in some respects from Paul's other letters. Still, they are so like Paul that even if the letter did not bear his name, it is difficult to imagine the church ever crediting it to anyone else. Ephesians and Colossians are very similar. But those who doubt Pauline authorship do not sufficiently appreciate how awkward it is to imagine a person so anxious to imitate his teacher that he transcribes some verses from Colossians word-for-word, yet so creative that he transforms Paul's style from one of doctrine and persuasion into one of doxology and prayer, and so daring as to move dramatically beyond Paul's theology of the exalted and reigning Christ to one of a universal church.

The verbal similarities with Colossians are most easily explained by assuming that Paul wrote Ephesians shortly after completing Colossians. Paul adopted a devotional and prayerful approach as he contemplated the eternal and universal significance of Christ's church, thus continuing his reflections on the subject that dominated his correspondence with the Colossians—the eternal and universal significance of Christ Himself.

DATE AND OCCASION

The imprisonment mentioned in 3:1 and 6:20 is the same as that referred to in Col. 4:3, 10, 18, and is probably Paul's two-year house arrest in Rome (A.D. 60–62) recounted in Acts 28.

Ephesus was the capital of the Roman province of Asia on the west coast of Asia Minor. It lay between the eastern and western halves of the Roman Empire and was among the top five cities of the empire in the first century. It was important to the spread of Christianity. During Paul's unusually long stay in Ephesus, it became the center for evangelizing the western part of Asia Minor (Acts 19:10). Paul's affectionate ties with this church are revealed in his farewell speech to its elders (Acts 20:16–38).

Ephesus' most prominent civic monument was one of the seven wonders of the ancient world, the temple of the goddess Diana. In one inscription, the city describes itself as the "nurturer" of the goddess, and the goddess in turn makes Ephesus the "most glorious" of the Asian cities. People from the area would appreciate the irony of Paul's words about Christ nourishing His own body, the church (5:29). They would appreciate the point of contrast when Paul describes Christ's church as a glorious or radiant bride (5:27). It is also in Ephesus that Paul's preaching of Christ comes into dramatic conflict with an important trade dependent on pagan worship (Acts 19:23–41), and that the gospel inspires a great turning away from the occult (Acts 19:17–20). Paul's call to expose the deeds of darkness (5:8–14) and prepare for war against "the spiritual forces of evil in the heavenly places" (6:12) would strike the original readers with special force.

The letter probably had a broader audience than Ephesus alone. Some of the oldest Greek manuscripts do not include "in Ephesus" in the address of the letter (1:1), reading instead: "to the saints who are also faithful in Christ Jesus." Several early Christian writers seem unaware of a specifically Ephesian address. The letter lacks the personal references and greetings Paul almost always includes in his correspondence. At the same time, no manuscripts name any other city as the address of the epistle. Many scholars believe Ephesians was written as a general letter to a number of churches in the region. This would be in keeping with the sweeping contents of the letter as a whole.

It is likely that Paul originally sent the letter to Ephesus, but as the letter was sent from church to church the address was omitted because the contents had little to do with Ephesus in particular. Or it may be that the letter was originally in two forms, one for the Ephesians and one for general circulation.

CHARACTERISTICS AND THEMES

Like the letter to the Romans, Ephesians provides a special view into Paul's thought, since he had the luxury of addressing an important issue without the distraction of having to settle a local controversy. The focus of Ephesians is the mystery of the church.

The church is God's new humanity, a colony where the Lord of history has established a foretaste of the renewed unity and dignity of the human race (1:10–14; 2:11–22; 3:6, 9–11; 4:1–6:9). The church is a community where God's power to reconcile people to Himself is experienced and shared in transformed relationships (2:1–10; 4:1–16; 4:32–5:2; 5:22–6:9). It is a new temple, a building of people, grounded in the sure revelation of what God has done in history (2:19–22; 3:17–19). The church is an organism where power and authority are exercised after the pattern of Christ (1:22; 5:25–27), and its stewardship is a means of serving Him (4:11–16; 5:22–6:9). The church is an outpost in a dark world (5:3–17), looking for the day of final redemption. Above all, the church is the bride preparing for the approach of her lover and husband (5:22–32).

OUTLINE OF EPHESIANS

I. Salutation (1:1, 2)

II. Praise to God for Blessings in Christ (1:3–14)

- A. *Elected by the Father (1:3–6)*
- B. *Redeemed by the Son (1:7–10)*
- C. *Sealed by the Spirit (1:11–14)*

III. Prayer for the Church (1:15–23)

IV. Our Position in Christ (2:1–3:13)

- A. *Reconciled with God and Seated with Christ (2:1–10)*
- B. *Reconciled with God's People and Growing into God's Temple (2:11–22)*
- C. *Recipients and Revealers of God's Mystery (3:1–13)*

V. Prayer for the Church and Doxology (3:14–21)

VI. Our Walk in Christ: Toward Unity and Purity (4:1–6:9)

- A. *Unity and Diversity (4:1–16)*
- B. *A New Mind (4:17–24)*
- C. *A New Walk: In Unity, Love, Purity, Light, and Wisdom (4:25–5:17)*
- D. *The Filling of the Spirit (5:18–6:9)*
  1. In Worship and Submission to One Another (5:18–21)
  2. Mutual Submission in Specific Relationships (5:22–6:9)
     - a. *Husbands and Wives (5:22–33)*
     - b. *Parents and Children (6:1–4)*
     - c. *Masters and Slaves (6:5–9)*

VII. Our Stand Against the Spiritual Forces of Darkness (6:10–20)

- A. *Call to Arms Against Our Real Enemy (6:10–12)*
- B. *Our Armor, Weaponry and Strategy (6:13–20)*

VIII. Final Greetings (6:21–24)

Greeting

1 Paul, [a]an apostle of Christ Jesus [b]by
the will of God,
To the saints who are in Ephesus, and
[c]are faithful[1] in Christ Jesus:
2 [d]Grace to you and peace from God our
Father and the Lord Jesus Christ.

Spiritual Blessings in Christ

3 [e]Blessed be [f]the God and Father of our
Lord Jesus Christ, who has blessed us in
Christ with every spiritual blessing [g]in the
heavenly places, 4 [h]even as he [i]chose us in
him [j]before the foundation of the world,
that we should be [k]holy and blameless
before him. In love 5 [l]he predestined us[2] for
[m]adoption through Jesus Christ, [n]accord-
ing to the purpose of his will, 6 [o]to the
praise of his glorious grace, with which he
has blessed us in [p]the Beloved. 7 [q]In him we
have [r]redemption [s]through his blood, [t]the
forgiveness of our trespasses, [u]according to
the riches of his grace, 8 which he lavished
upon us, in all wisdom and insight 9 [v]mak-
ing known[3] to us the mystery of his will,
[n]according to his purpose, which he [w]set
forth in Christ 10 as a plan for [x]the fullness
of time, [y]to unite all things in him, things
in heaven and things on earth.
11 In him we have obtained [z]an inheritance, [a]having been predestined [b]according
to the purpose of him who works all things
according to [c]the counsel of his will, 12 so
that we who were the first to hope in Christ
might be [d]to the praise of his glory. 13 In
him you also, when you heard [e]the word of
truth, the gospel of your salvation, and believed in him, [f]were sealed with the [g]prom-
ised Holy Spirit, 14 who is [h]the guarantee[4]

Chapter 1
1 [a]See 2 Cor. 1:1 [b]See 1 Cor. 1:1 [c]Col. 1:2 **2** [d]See Rom. 1:7 **3** [e]2 Cor. 1:3; 1 Pet. 1:3 [f]See Rom. 15:6 [g]ver. 20; ch. 2:6; 3:10; 6:12 **4** [h][ch. 2:10; 2 Thess. 2:13; 1 Pet. 1:2] [i]James 2:5; [Deut. 7:6; 26:18] [j][2 Tim. 1:9]; See Matt. 13:35 [k]ch. 5:27; Col. 1:22; 1 Thess. 4:7 **5** [l]ver. 11; Rom. 8:29, 30 [m]See Rom. 8:15 [n]ver. 9; [Luke 2:14; Heb. 2:4]; See Luke 12:32 **6** [o]ver. 12, 14 [p][John 3:35; 10:17; Col. 1:13]; See Matt. 3:17

7 [q]Col. 1:14 [r]Rom. 3:24; 1 Cor. 1:30; [ch. 4:30] [s]See Acts 20:28 [t]See Acts 2:38 [u][ch. 3:8, 16; Col. 1:27]; See Rom. 2:4 **9** [v]See Rom. 16:25 [n][See ver. 5 above] [w][ver. 11; Rom. 8:28; 9:11] **10** [x]See Mark 1:15 [y]Col. 1:16, 20; [ch. 3:15; Phil. 2:9, 10] **11** [z]Deut. 4:20; 32:9; See ver. 14 [a]ver. 5 [b]ch. 3:11 [Rev. 4:11]; See Rom. 8:28 [c][Acts 20:27] **12** [d]ver. 6, 14; [Phil. 1:11] **13** [e]2 Cor. 6:7; Col. 1:5; 2 Tim. 2:15 [Acts 13:26; 15:7] [f]ch. 4:30 [g]See Acts 1:4 **14** [h]2 Cor. 1:22

1 Some manuscripts *saints who are also faithful* 2 Or *before him in love, having predestined us* 3 Or *he lavished upon us in all wisdom and insight, making known . . .* 4 Or *down payment*

1:3–14 One long sentence in Greek, this is an expansion of the condensed praise of God's purpose in Rom. 8:28–30. Praise goes to the Father who elects (vv. 4–6), the Son who redeems (vv. 7–12), and the Spirit who seals (vv. 13, 14). Paul reflects on believers' election from eternity, their forgiveness in the present, and their inheritance in the future. Key throughout is the repetition of the phrases "in Christ" or "in Him," referring to the intimate union God has established between Christ and His people.

1:3 in the heavenly places. Two of the other five instances where this phrase appears in Ephesians have a bearing on its meaning here. Christ was raised from the dead and seated at the right hand of the Father "in the heavenly places," from where He governs "all things to [for the sake of] the church" (v. 22). Moreover, believers have also been raised up and seated with Him "in the heavenly places" (2:6). Christ's victory over death has won believers a series of benefits for which Paul blesses the Father.

1:4 he chose us in him. See "Election and Reprobation" at Rom. 9:18. Paul rejoices that God chooses people for a relationship with Himself (Rom. 8:29–33; 9:6–26; 11:5, 7, 28; 16:13; Col. 3:12; 1 Thess. 1:4; 2 Thess. 2:13; Titus 1:1). Some suggest "in him" means God foresaw who would have faith in Christ and elected them. Not only does this add a thought that is not in the text, but elsewhere Paul teaches that the very state of being "in Christ" is something to which one is chosen (1 Cor. 1:26–31). Paul says explicitly that the ground of God's predestinating love is His own good pleasure (vv. 5, 10; cf. Deut. 7:7, 8), not anything we have done or will do (Rom. 9:11, 16). "In him" means that God's choice always had in view a fallen people in union with their Redeemer (2 Tim. 1:9). See also 1 Pet. 1:18–21; Rev. 13:8.

holy and blameless. See 5:27; Col. 1:22. God intends to bring His elect all the way from spiritual death in sin (2:1–5) to the forgiveness of sins in Christ (1:7), and finally to the elimination of all sin from their experience (Rom. 8:29, 30).

In love. If "in love" belongs with the preceding phrase, it helps explain the nature of the holiness and blamelessness to which believers are called; this is consistent with the use of the phrase elsewhere in Ephesians (3:17; 4:2, 15, 16; 5:2). If it belongs with v. 5, the phrase explains predestination not simply as a matter of God's decision, but as an act of His love (Hos. 11:1). This understanding is probably better. It is consistent with 2:4, 5.

1:5 adoption. See Rom. 8:14–17, 29; Gal. 3:26, 27; "Adoption" at Gal. 4:5.

1:6 The thought of God's almighty love leads to an extravagant outpouring of praise (vv. 12, 14) to God, who has not only the power but the will to overcome all obstacles in bringing the spiritually dead into a living relationship with Himself (expanded in 2:1–10).

grace . . . blessed us in the Beloved. This recalls the language of Col. 1:13, but also brings into view the Redeemer as Himself an object of God's electing love (1 Pet. 1:18–21; Rev. 13:8). The language of grace dominates vv. 6–8.

1:7 See notes Col. 1:14; 2:13.

redemption. This means deliverance, as from slavery or captivity, by paying a price or ransom. For the redemption that is yet to come, see v. 1.

1:9 mystery. See 3:3, 5, 6, 10, and notes; Col. 1:27.

1:10 the fullness of time. This does not refer simply to the future. Christ has already come to bring redemption and adoption (Gal. 4:4). By virtue of His death and resurrection, He has already assumed headship over the church, and, though behind the scenes, He already rules the universe (Acts 2:32–36; Col. 1:15–20). Still, a future emphasis dominates. The visible unity of the church is a foretaste of Christ's eventual visible rule over all things. This is why Paul stresses the unity of Jew and Gentile in the church (vv. 11–14; 2:11–22), and the practice of love among Christians (4:2, 15; 4:32–5:2, 21–23). The theme introduced here in vv. 9–12 is expanded in 3:2–12.

1:11–14 Paul anticipates what he will say in 3:6 about Jews and Gentiles being "fellow heirs" of the promise in Christ. Believing Jews of Paul's day, "who were the first to hope in Christ" (v. 12), have become heirs by the will of God. Gentiles who have now received the same promise that was made to Israel—the gift of the Holy Spirit—have likewise become heirs to the praise of God's glory.

1:11 all things . . . his will. A sweeping statement on the extent of God's will.

1:13 sealed. Like the indelible impression made by a king's signet ring, the Holy Spirit is an inward mark of God's ownership of His people. See "Salvation" at 2 Cor. 6:5.

the promised Holy Spirit. As Jesus says in Luke 24:49, the Holy Spirit is the promise of the Father. Remarkably, this promise is extended to Gentiles, as well as Jews, on the basis of their trusting Christ (Ezek. 36:26, 27; Joel 2:28; John 14–16; Acts 1:4, 5; 2:33, 38, 39; Gal. 3:14; 4:6).

1:14 guarantee. The Spirit is not only a fulfillment of God's promise to

of our [i]inheritance until [j]we acquire [k]pos-
session of it,[1] [l]to the praise of his glory.

Thanksgiving and Prayer

15 For this reason, [m]because I have heard
of your faith in the Lord Jesus and your
love[2] toward all the saints, 16 I [n]do not cease
to give thanks for you, [o]remembering you
in my prayers, 17 that [p]the God of our Lord
Jesus Christ, the Father of glory, [q]may give
you a spirit of wisdom and of revelation in
the knowledge of him, 18 [r]having the eyes of
your hearts enlightened, that you may
know what is [s]the hope to which he has
called you, what are [t]the riches of his glorious inheritance in the saints, 19 and what is
the immeasurable greatness of his power
toward us who believe, [u]according to the
working of [v]his great might 20 that he
worked in Christ [w]when he raised him
from the dead and [x]seated him at his right
hand [y]in the heavenly places, 21 [z]far above
[a]all rule and authority and power and
dominion, and above [b]every name that is
named, not only in [c]this age but also in the
one to come. 22 And [d]he put all things
under his feet and gave him as [e]head over
all things to the church, 23 [f]which is his
body, [g]the fullness of him [h]who fills [i]all in
all.

By Grace Through Faith

2 [j]And you were [k]dead in the trespasses
and sins 2 [l]in which you once walked,
following the course of this world, following [m]the prince of the power of the air, the
spirit that is now at work in [n]the sons of
disobedience— 3 among whom we all once
lived in [o]the passions of our flesh, carrying
out the desires of the body[3] and the mind,
and [p]were by nature [q]children of wrath,
like the rest of mankind. 4 But[4] God, being
[r]rich in mercy, [s]because of the great love
with which he loved us, 5 even [t]when we
were dead in our trespasses, [u]made us alive
together with Christ—[v]by grace you have
been saved— 6 and raised us up with him

14 [i]Acts 20:32; [ver. 18] [j]Tit. 2:14; See ver. 7 [k]See 1 Pet. 2:9 [l]ver. 6, 12
15 [m]Col. 1:4; Philem. 5; See Rom. 1:8
16 [n]Col. 1:9 [o]Rom. 1:9; 2 Tim. 1:3
17 [p]See Rom. 15:6 [q][Col. 1:9]
18 [r][Heb. 6:4; 10:32; Rev. 3:17, 18]; See Acts 26:18 [s]ch. 4:4; [ch. 2:12] [t]ch. 3:8, 16; Col. 1:27; See ver. 7
19 [u]ch. 3:7; Phil. 3:21; Col. 1:29; 2:12 [v]ch. 6:10; [Dan. 4:30]
20 [w]See Acts 2:24 [x]See Mark 16:19; Acts 2:33; 1 Pet. 3:22 [y]See ver. 3
21 [z]ch. 4:10; Col. 2:10; See John 3:31 [a]1 Cor. 15:24 [b]ch. 3:15; Phil. 2:9; [Heb. 1:4] [c][Matt. 12:32]

22 [d]Cited from Ps. 8:6; See 1 Cor. 15:27 [e]ch. 4:15; 5:23; Col. 1:18; 2:19; [1 Cor. 11:3; Col. 2:10] 23 [f]ch. 4:12, 16; 5:30; Col. 1:18, 24; [ch. 5:23; 1 Cor. 12:27] [g]ch. 3:19; See John 1:16 [h]ch. 4:10 [i][Jer. 23:24; Col. 3:11]
Chapter 2 1 [j]Col. 2:13; [Col. 1:21] [k]ver. 5; [ch. 4:18]; See Luke 15:24 2 [l]ch. 4:17, 22; 5:8; Col. 3:7; See Rom. 11:30; 1 Cor. 6:11 [m][ch. 6:12; Rev. 9:11]; See John 12:31 [n]ch. 5:6; [1 Pet. 1:14] 3 [o]Gal. 5:16 [p]See Ps. 51:5; Rom. 5:12 [q][2 Pet. 2:14] 4 [r]ver. 7; Tit. 3:5; See Rom. 2:4 [s]See John 3:16 5 [t]ver. 1; [Rom. 5:6, 8, 10] [u]Col. 2:12, 13; [John 14:19; Rev. 20:4] [v]ver. 8; See Acts 15:11

[1] Or *until God redeems his possession* [2] Some manuscripts omit *your love* [3] Greek *flesh* [4] Or *And*

indwell His people, but also is a guarantee that He will bring them to their final inheritance. As a down payment or first installment on their full redemption, the Spirit is a foretaste of the glory of the age to come (Rom. 8:18–23).

possession. The Old Testament teaches that God chose a people as His inheritance (Deut. 32:9; Ps. 33:12) and purchased them out of bondage to become a prized possession (Ex. 19:5; Deut. 7:6). Peter agrees with Paul's striking application of this idea to Gentiles as well as to Jews (1 Pet. 2:9).

1:15 because I have heard. See Introduction: Date and Occasion. Paul had ministered in Ephesus for over two years, but the time of writing may be as much as five years later. The church had grown considerably since then. It may be that Paul mentions people whose faith and love he knows only by report because Ephesians was a circular letter for several churches.

1:17 wisdom and of revelation. See "Illumination and Conviction" at 1 Cor. 2:10.

1:18 that you may know. See "True Knowledge of God" at Jer. 9:24.

1:19–23 These verses distill the New Testament's teaching on the resurrection and enthronement of Jesus (Col. 1:18 note). They also make two vital contributions to understanding Jesus' resurrection and the status of believers. First, the same power that raised Jesus from the dead is at work in believers (2:4, 5; 3:16, 17). Second, Christ enjoys His position as head over everything for the sake of the church. Not only is Christ at the most exalted position in the universe, He is there representing believers (2:6; Col. 3:3) and governing the universe for their sake. The principles of conduct in Ephesians emphasize that authority exists for the sake of service. Jesus' majestic use of power and authority in the interest of His people is the Christian's model (4:1, 2, 7–13; 4:32–5:2, 22–33). Paul reminds his Gentile readers of two specific ways Christ's power has blessed them: He brought them from death to life (2:1–10), and from alienation from God's people to inclusion with them (2:11–22).

1:20 seated him . . . in the heavenly places. See "The Ascension of Jesus" at Luke 24:51.

1:21 above all rule and authority. See note 3:10.

this age . . . the one to come. See 1 Cor. 15:24.

2:1–3 The natural state of all human beings is a kind of spiritual death. This spiritual condition is universal: both Gentiles (v. 2) and Jews (v. 3) are "by nature children of wrath" (v. 3; on Paul's view of "nature" see Rom. 1). Second, they are in active rebellion against God; note the use of "walked" in regard to Gentiles in v. 2 and "lived" in reference to Jews in v. 3. Third, they are subject to the evil rule of Satan (called in v. 2 "the prince of the power of the air"; cf. Gal. 4:3; Col. 1:13). Fourth, they are totally unable to change themselves from rebellion against God (John 3:3). Fifth, they are exposed to the just anger of God (v. 3; 5:6; Rom. 1:18–20).

2:1 you were dead. See "Regeneration: The New Birth" at John 3:3.

2:4 But God. Paul paints this bleak portrait of the human situation to throw into relief God's gracious and merciful response to it.

because of the great love. God loves His people of His own will. Paul excludes any consideration of merit, effort, or ability on the part of those who come to life (cf. Deut. 7:7, 8). The hopeless condition of sinners apart from Christ that Paul has described in vv. 1–3 is the basis for understanding his teaching on God's election in 1:4–6, and on His gift of life here in vv. 4–10. Note the summary in Rom. 8:29, 30.

2:5, 6 made us alive . . . raised us up . . . seated us. These are historical events in the life of Christ: His resurrection from the dead and enthronement at the right hand of God. But Paul also applies them to what has happened to believers. Paul teaches a union between Christ and those who come to trust Him (1:3; Col. 3:1–4), so that what is said of the Redeemer can also be said of the redeemed. What once happened to Jesus will one day happen to believers as well (2 Cor. 4:16): they will be resurrected to glory at His return (Rom. 8:11; 1 Cor. 15). For the present, there is a new mind (4:23, 24; Rom. 12:1, 2), a new identity as God's children (Rom. 8:14–17), and a new ability to live free from the control of Satan (Rom. 8:1–4; 2 Cor. 5:17).

and [w]seated us with him in the heavenly
places in Christ Jesus, **7** so that in the coming ages he might show the immeasurable
[x]riches of his grace in [y]kindness toward us
in Christ Jesus. **8** For [z]by grace you have
been saved [a]through faith. And this is [b]not
your own doing; [c]it is the gift of God, **9** [d]not
a result of works, [e]so that no one may
boast. **10** For [f]we are his workmanship, [g]cre-
ated in Christ Jesus [h]for good works,
[i]which God prepared beforehand, [j]that we
should walk in them.

One in Christ

11 Therefore remember that at one time
you Gentiles in the flesh, called "the uncircumcision" by what is called [k]the circumcision, which is made in the flesh by
hands— **12** remember [l]that you were at that
time separated from Christ, [m]alienated
from the commonwealth of Israel and
strangers to [n]the covenants of promise,
[o]having no hope and without God in the
world. **13** But now in Christ Jesus you who
once were [p]far off have been brought near
[q]by the blood of Christ. **14** For [r]he himself is
our peace, [s]who has made us both one and
has broken down [t]in his flesh the dividing
wall of hostility **15** by abolishing the law of
commandments and [u]ordinances, that he
might create in himself one [v]new man in
place of the two, so making peace, **16** and
might [w]reconcile us both to God in one
body through the cross, thereby killing the
hostility. **17** And he came and [x]preached
peace to you who were [y]far off and peace
to those who were [z]near. **18** For [a]through
him we both have [b]access in [c]one Spirit to
the Father. **19** So then you are no longer
[d]strangers and aliens,[1] but you are [e]fellow
citizens with the saints and [f]members of
the household of God, **20** [g]built on the foundation of the [h]apostles and prophets,
[i]Christ Jesus himself being [j]the cornerstone, **21** [k]in whom the whole structure,
being joined together, grows into [l]a holy
temple in the Lord. **22** In him [m]you also are

6 [w]See ch. 1:20 **7** [x]ver. 4 [y]Tit. 3:4 **8** [z]ver. 5 [a]1 Pet. 1:5; [Rom. 4:16] [b][2 Cor. 3:5] [c][John 4:10; Heb. 6:4] **9** [d]2 Tim. 1:9; Tit. 3:5; See Rom. 3:20, 28 [e]1 Cor. 1:29; [Judg. 7:2] **10** [f]Deut. 32:6, 15; Ps. 100:3 [g][ch. 3:9; 4:24; Col. 3:10] [h]ch. 4:24 [i][ch. 1:4] [j]Col. 1:10 **11** [k]Rom. 2:26, 28; [Col. 2:11, 13] **12** [l]1 Cor. 12:2; [ch. 5:8; Col. 3:7] [m]ch. 4:18; Col. 1:21; [Ezek. 14:5; Gal. 2:15; 4:8] [n]See Rom. 9:4 [o]1 Thess. 4:13; See ch. 1:18 **13** [p]ver. 17; Acts 2:39 [q][Col. 1:20]; See Rom. 3:25

14 [r]Ps. 72:7; Mic. 5:5; Zech. 9:10; [Col. 3:15]; See Luke 2:14 [s]See Gal. 3:28 [t]Col.1:21, 22; [Rom. 7:4] **15** [u]Col. 2:14, 20 [v]See Rom. 6:4 **16** [w]Col. 1:20-22; [1 Cor. 12:13] **17** [x]Isai. 57:19 [y]ver. 13 [z]Deut. 4:7; Ps. 148:14 **18** [a][John 14:6] [b]ch. 3:12; [John 10:7, 9]; See Rom. 5:2 [c]ch. 4:4; 1 Cor. 12:13; [John 4:23] **19** [d]ver. 12; [Heb. 11:13; 13:14] [e]Phil. 3:20; [Heb. 12:22, 23] [f]See Gal. 6:10 **20** [g][Jer. 12:16]; See 1 Cor. 3:9 [h]Matt. 16:18; Rev. 21:14 [i][1 Cor. 3:11] [j]Ps. 118:22; Isai. 28:16 **21** [k]ch. 4:15, 16 [l]See 1 Cor. 3:16, 17 **22** [m]1 Pet. 2:5

[1] Or *sojourners*

2:7 The ground of our salvation is God's love and mercy, and its goal is the promotion of His grace and kindness (3:6 note).

2:8 you have been saved. Salvation is a completed action that has a present effect. In his earlier letters Paul usually refers to salvation either as a future event (Rom. 5:9, 10) or as a present process (1 Cor. 1:18; 2 Cor. 2:15). One exception is Rom. 8:24, where Paul puts salvation in the past, but qualifies it as needing completion at Christ's return: "in this hope we were saved."

And this is not your own doing; it is the gift of God. This parenthesis is thought by many to refer to the whole complex of salvation by grace through faith as a gift of God. Others, however, take "this" as referring specifically to "faith." Sinners are dependent on God's gracious gift for their believing response to Christ from the moment of conversion. Paul makes explicit here what is implicit elsewhere in the New Testament about the ultimate source of saving faith (Acts 13:48; Phil. 1:29).

2:9 works. Only faith, not works, can bring us acceptance with God. But good works are the vital consequence and evidence of life with God (Titus 2:14; 3:8, 14; James 2:14–26). God chose us to make us holy sons and daughters (1:4, 5), and He has now fashioned us to be new bearers of His image (4:24), designed for the kind of life that conforms to God's character (4:1–6:20). Also see "Antinomianism" at 1 John 3:7.

2:10 that we should walk in them. See 4:1; 5:2, 8, 15; note the ironic comparison with 2:2; 4:17.

2:11 made in the flesh by hands. The opposite of this circumcision is the spiritual circumcision of the heart (Deut. 10:16; Jer. 4:4), applied to Gentiles as well as Jews (Rom. 2:28, 29; Phil. 3:3; Col. 2:11–13).

2:12 at that time. Contrast with "But now" in v. 13; see also 5:8. In Rom. 9:3–5, Paul lists the privileges of Jews. Here he lists five disadvantages of Gentiles.

alienated . . . strangers to the covenants of promise. They were not citizens of the nation with whom God was in covenant relation. Though God's relationship with Israel included a promise to bless the nations (Gen. 12:3), Gentiles had no awareness of that hope.

without God in the world. God had revealed Himself to all humanity in nature and in the conscience. But Gentiles had suppressed what truth they did know, turning instead to idolatry (Acts 17:22–31; Rom. 1:18–2:16).

2:13 in Christ Jesus . . . by the blood of Christ. There are two dimensions to Gentiles' being brought near to God. The first is their experience of spiritual union with Christ (vv. 4–10); the second is the historical basis of that experience in Christ's sacrificial death (vv. 14–16; 1:7).

far off . . . near. See v. 17.

2:14–16 See 4:22–24; Col. 3:9–12 and notes.

2:14 the dividing wall of hostility. This refers to the courts of the temple in Jerusalem. A wall separated Gentiles and Jews, and signs were posted excluding Gentiles from the inner courts where sacrifices for sin were performed.

2:15 abolishing the law of commandments. Christ offered in His own body the final sacrifice to which the temple's sacrifices merely pointed. The ceremonial laws of the Old Testament that separated Jews and Gentiles are no longer appropriate after their fulfillment in Christ.

2:17, 18 Isaiah had prophesied a day when God's peace would be proclaimed to those "far" and "near" (Is. 57:19). Through the gospel of Christ the Spirit brings Gentiles ("you who were far off") and Jews ("those who were near") together before the Father, in fulfillment of Isaiah's promise.

2:19–22 These verses describe the reversal of the Gentile disadvantages outlined in vv. 11, 12 (cf. 3:6). The building of a new spiritual temple replaces the outmoded one in Jerusalem.

2:19 no longer strangers. The kingdom of God is now international. See theological note "The Church" on page 359.

2:20 The foundation of God's house was laid once for all by the New Testament apostles and prophets. The cornerstone is Christ (1 Cor. 3:10, 11).

2:21, 22 grows . . . being built. God's house grows through the continued addition and integration of people as "living stones" (1 Pet. 2:5). The

being built together [n]into a dwelling place
for God by[1] the Spirit.

The Mystery of the Gospel Revealed

3 For this reason I, Paul, [o]a prisoner
for Christ Jesus [p]on behalf of you
Gentiles— 2 assuming that you have heard
of [q]the stewardship of [r]God's grace that
was given to me for you, 3 [s]how the mystery
was made known to me [t]by revelation, [u]as
I have written briefly. 4 [v]When you read
this, you can perceive my insight into [w]the
mystery of Christ, 5 which was not made
known to the sons of men in other generations as it has now been revealed to his
holy apostles and prophets by the Spirit.
6 This mystery is[2] that the Gentiles are [x]fel-
low heirs, [y]members of the same body, and
[z]partakers of the promise in Christ Jesus
through the gospel.
7 [a]Of this gospel I was made [b]a minister
according to the gift of [c]God's grace, which
was given me [d]by the working of his power.
8 To me, [e]though I am the very least of all
the saints, this grace was given, [f]to preach
to the Gentiles the [g]unsearchable [h]riches of
Christ, 9 and [i]to bring to light for everyone
what is the plan of the mystery [j]hidden for
ages in[3] God [k]who created all things, 10 so
that through the church the manifold [l]wis-
dom of God [m]might now be made known
to [n]the rulers and authorities [o]in the heavenly places. 11 This was [p]according to the
eternal purpose that he has realized in
Christ Jesus our Lord, 12 in whom we have
[q]boldness and [r]access with [s]confidence
through our [t]faith in him. 13 So I ask you
not to lose heart over what I am suffering
[u]for you, [v]which is your glory.

Prayer for Spiritual Strength

14 For this reason I bow my knees before
the Father, 15 from whom [w]every family[4] in
heaven and on earth is named, 16 that
according to [x]the riches of his glory [y]he
may grant you to be strengthened with
power through his Spirit [z]in your inner
being, 17 [a]so that Christ may dwell in your
hearts through faith—that you, being
[b]rooted and [c]grounded in love, 18 may have
strength to [d]comprehend with all the saints
what is the breadth and length and [e]height

22 [n][ch. 3:17; 2 Cor. 6:16; 1 Tim. 3:15]
Chapter 3
1 [o]ch. 4:1; Acts 23:18; Phil. 1:7 [ch. 6:20] [p]ver. 13; Col. 1:24 **2** [q]ch. 1:10; Col. 1:25; 1 Tim. 1:4 [r]ver. 7; ch. 4:7; See Acts 11:23; Rom. 1:5 **3** [s]Acts 22:17, 21; 26:16-18 [t][Dan. 2:29]; See Rom 16:25; 2 Cor. 12:1 [u][ch. 1:9, 10] **4** [v][2 Cor. 11:6] [w]Col. 4:3 **6** [x]See Gal. 3:29 [y]ch. 2:16 [z]ch. 5:7 **7** [a]Col. 1:23, 25 [b]See 2 Cor. 3:6 [c]See ver. 2 [d][ver. 20]; See ch. 1:19 **8** [e]See 1 Cor. 15:9 [f]See Acts 9:15 [g][Job 5:9; Rom. 11:33] [h]See ch. 1:18; Rom. 2:4 **9** [i]See ver. 2, 3 [j]Col. 1:26 [k]Rev. 4:11; [ch. 2:10]

10 [l]Rom. 11:33 [m][1 Pet. 1:12] [n]ch. 1:21; [ch. 6:12] [o]See ch. 1:3 **11** [p]See ch. 1:11 **12** [q]Heb. 4:16; 10:19 [r]See ch. 2:18 [s]2 Cor. 3:4 [t]Mark 11:22; Phil. 3:9 **13** [u]ver. 1 [v][2 Cor. 1:6] **15** [w]See ch. 1:10, 21 **16** [x]See ver. 8 [y]1 Cor. 16:13; [ch. 6:10; Phil. 4:13; Col. 1:11] [z]See Rom. 7:22 **17** [a][ch. 2:22] [b]Col. 2:7 [c]Col. 1:23 **18** [d][John 1:5] [e]Rom. 8:39; [Job 11:8, 9]

1 Or *in* 2 The words *This mystery is* are inferred from verse 4 3 Or *by* 4 Or *fatherhood*; the Greek word *patria* is closely related to the word for *Father* in verse 14

house is also a temple because God Himself lives in this new building of people.

3:1 Paul begins a prayer that his Gentile readers will be filled with the presence of Christ and be able to grasp the truth about their Redeemer's love and power (vv. 14–21). Paul interrupts himself to explain the nature of his own ministry and insight into the union of Jew and Gentile in Christ (vv. 2–13).

prisoner. Paul is under house arrest in Rome (Acts 28:16, 30).

3:3 as I have written briefly. See 1:9, 10.

3:5 as it has now been revealed. The Old Testament's silence about Paul's mystery—the union of Jews and Gentiles in the church (v. 6)—was relative, not absolute. It was anticipated by the prophets ("Blessed be Egypt my people, and Assyria the work of my hands, and Israel my inheritance," Is. 19:25). If the idea had been altogether absent from the Old Testament, Paul could not have said, as he did in Rom. 4, that the Abrahamic covenant included all who were of a like faith with Abraham, including Gentiles. Paul told Agrippa that his proclamation of light to both Jews and Gentiles did not go beyond what had been promised by Moses and the prophets (Acts 26:22, 23).

3:6 Gentiles are fellow heirs. Although the Old Testament gives occasional glimpses of a unified human race, only in the light of Christ's sacrifice does God's plan become clear: in one magnificent act He removed the enmity between Himself and humanity and also took away the divisions that fracture humanity (2:14–18). Paul had reflected before on the unusual way God included Gentiles among His people: contrary to the rules of agriculture, the Gentiles were a wild branch grafted into a cultivated tree (Rom. 11:11–24).

3:8 Compare the progression of Paul's self-description from 1 Cor. 15:9 to Eph. 3:8 to 1 Tim. 1:15, 16.

3:10 the rulers . . . in the heavenly places. Paul has already mentioned "the prince of the power of the air" (2:2), and will return to the Christians' battle against their spiritual enemies in the universe (6:10–17). It is helpful here to recall Paul's recent controversy with the false teachers in Colossae. He had argued in his letter to that church that Jesus is Lord of all things, including the spirit world, and further that it is only in Jesus that heaven and earth are reconciled (Col. 1:15–20; 2:8–23). Accordingly, the establishment of peace between Jews and Gentiles in the church is a signal to all powers in the universe. For Paul, there is no deeper division in the human race than that between Jew and Gentile. That they could be united with each other in Christ displays the profound wisdom of God (Is. 55:8, 9; 1 Cor. 2:6–10), and proves even to supernatural powers that Jesus is Lord of the universe (1:20–23).

3:14 bow my knees. Jews normally prayed standing (Matt. 6:5; Luke 18:11, 13). Kneeling appears to have been an expression of humility and urgency (Ezra 9:5; Luke 22:41; Acts 7:59, 60). This verse returns to the prayer Paul had begun introducing in v. 1 (note).

3:15 every family in heaven. Jewish intertestamental and rabbinic literature refers to families of angels.

3:16 in your inner being. This is some of Paul's most pointed language about the work of the Holy Spirit within individuals (2 Cor. 5:17). Much of Ephesians addresses believers' corporate identity (e.g., 4:3–6, 12–16). But Christ also dwells in individual hearts. Christianity is neither a common confession to the exclusion of individual experience, nor a private piety without corporate vision.

3:18 breadth and length and height and depth. These measures of space recall the temple image of 2:21. As the "living stones" (1 Pet. 2:5) are linked in love, God's dwelling grows and is filled with Christ Himself. God uses the love among "all the saints"—Jew and Gentile alike—to build a whole that is greater than any of its individual parts. The spatial language exalts Christ's love for His people—a love that is inclusive, inexhaustible, and self-sacrificing.

and depth, 19 and to know the love of
Christ [f] that surpasses knowledge, that [g] you
may be filled with all [h] the fullness of God.
20 [i] Now to [j] him who is able to do far
more abundantly than all that we ask or
think, [k] according to the power at work
within us, 21 [l] to him be glory in the church

19 [f] [Phil. 4:7] [g] Col. 2:10 [h] ch. 1:23 20 [i] Rom. 16:25; Jude 24 [j] [2 Cor. 9:8] [k] [ver. 7] 21 [l] See Rom. 11:36

The Church

The church exists in and through Jesus Christ, and so is a distinctive New Testament reality. At the same time it is continuous with Israel, the seed of Abraham and God's covenant people. The new covenant under which the church lives (1 Cor. 11:25; Heb. 8:7–13) is a new form of the relationship in which God says to His chosen community, "I will be your God, and you shall be my people" (Jer. 7:23; 31:33; cf. Ex. 6:7).

Under the new covenant, the Old Testament priests, sacrifices, and sanctuary have been superseded by the mediation of Jesus (Heb. 1–10). Believers in Christ are the seed of Abraham and the people of God (Gal. 3:29; 1 Pet. 2:4–10). Second, the limitation of the old covenant to one nation (Deut. 7:6; Ps. 147:19, 20) is replaced by the inclusion in Christ on equal terms of believers from every nation (Eph. 2; 3; Rev. 5:9, 10). Third, the Spirit is poured out on the church, so that fellowship with Christ (1 John 1:3), ministry from Christ (John 14:18; Eph. 2:17), and foretastes of heaven (2 Cor. 1:22; Eph. 1:14) become realities in the experience of the church.

The unbelief of most Jews (Rom. 9–11) and the majority of Gentiles in the church is depicted by Paul as God's breaking off the natural branches of His olive tree (the historical covenant community) and replacing them with wild olive shoots (Rom. 11:17–24). The new covenant does not exclude Jews, and Paul taught that their general rejection of it will one day be reversed (Rom. 11:15, 23–31).

The New Testament teaches that the church is the fulfillment of the Old Testament hopes and patterns, brought about by Jesus Christ. The church is the family and flock of God (John 10:16; Eph. 2:18; 3:15; 4:6; 1 Pet. 5:2–4), His Israel (Gal. 6:16), the body and bride of Christ (Eph. 1:22, 23; 5:23–32; Rev. 19:7; 21:2, 9–27), and the temple of the Holy Spirit (1 Cor. 3:16; cf. Eph. 2:19–22).

The church is a single worshiping community, permanently gathered in the true sanctuary, the heavenly Jerusalem (Gal. 4:26; Heb. 12:22–24) and the place of God's presence. The church is one, although the worshiping community consists of the church militant—those who are still on earth—and the church triumphant—those who have died and entered glory. On earth, the church appears in its local congregations, each one a microcosm of the church as a whole. According to Paul the one church universal is the body of Christ (1 Cor. 12:12–26; Eph. 1:22, 23; 3:6; 4:4), but so is each local congregation (1 Cor. 12:27; "The Local Church" at Rev. 2:1).

The church on earth is one in Christ despite the great number of local congregations and denominations (Eph. 4:3–6). It is holy because it is consecrated to God corporately, as each Christian is individually (Eph. 2:21). It is catholic (meaning "universal") because it is worldwide. Finally, it is apostolic because it is founded on apostolic teaching (Eph. 2:20). All four qualities may be seen in Eph. 2:19–22.

There is a distinction to be drawn between the church as people see it and as God alone sees it. This difference is the historic distinction between the "visible church" and the "invisible church." "Invisible" does not mean that no part of it can be seen, but that its exact boundary is not known to us. Only God knows (2 Tim. 2:19) which members of the earthly congregations are inwardly born again, and so belong to the church as an eternal and spiritual fellowship. Jesus taught that in the organized church there would always be people who seemed to be Christians, not excluding leaders, who were nevertheless not renewed in heart and would be exposed and rejected at the Judgment (Matt. 7:15–23; 13:24–30, 36–43, 47–50; 25:1–46). There are not two churches, one visible and another hidden in heaven, but one church only, known perfectly to God and known imperfectly on earth.

The New Testament assumes that all Christians will share in the life of a local congregation, worshiping in the body, accepting its nurture and discipline (Matt. 18:15–20; Gal. 6:1), and sharing its ministry and witness. Christians who refuse to join other believers disobey God and spiritually impoverish themselves (Heb. 10:25).

3:20 the power at work within us. See 1:19–23; 2:5, 6. The first half of the letter climaxes as Paul considers the overwhelming power of God, who carries out His gracious (2:7) and all-wise (v. 10) plan for the reconciliation of the human race.

3:21 glory. Because of the power that God has given to the church, Paul gives glory to Him.

in the church and in Christ Jesus. In this letter Paul uses a variety of images to describe the mutual relationship between the church and Christ: the body and the head (1:22, 23), the reconciled and the reconciler (2:14–18; 4:3), and the bride and her groom (5:22, 33).

and in Christ Jesus throughout all generations, forever and ever. Amen.

Unity in the Body of Christ

4 I therefore, [m]a prisoner for the Lord,
urge you to [n]walk in a manner worthy
of [o]the calling to which you have been
called, 2 with all [p]humility and [q]gentleness,
with [r]patience, [s]bearing with one another
in love, 3 eager to maintain the unity of the
Spirit in [t]the bond of peace. 4 There is [u]one
body and [v]one Spirit—just as you were
called to the one [w]hope that belongs to
your call— 5 [x]one Lord, [y]one faith, [z]one
baptism, 6 [a]one God and Father of all, [b]who
is over all and through all and in all. 7 But
[c]grace was given [d]to each one of us [e]ac-
cording to the measure of Christ's gift.
8 Therefore it says,

> [f]"When he ascended on high [g]he led a
> host of captives,
> and he gave gifts to men."

9 ([h]In saying, "He ascended," what does it
mean but that he had also descended into
[i]the lower parts of the earth? 10 He who
descended is the one who also [j]ascended
[k]far above all the heavens, that he might
[l]fill all things.) 11 And [m]he gave the [n]apos-
tles, the prophets, the [o]evangelists, the

Chapter 4
1 [m]See ch. 3:1 [n]Col. 1:10; 2:6; 1 Thess. 2:12; [Phil. 1:27] [o]See Rom. 8:28
2 [p]Acts 20:19; Phil. 2:3; Col. 3:12; 1 Pet. 3:8; 5:5; [Col. 2:18, 23] [q]Gal. 5:23 [r]Col. 1:11 [s]Col. 3:13
3 [t]Col. 3:14; [Acts 8:23]
4 [u]ch. 2:16 [v]See ch. 2:18 [w]ch. 1:18
5 [x]Zech. 14:9; See 1 Cor. 1:13; 8:6 [y][ver. 13; Jude 3] [z]See Gal. 3:27, 28
6 [a]1 Cor. 12:5, 6 [b]Rom. 9:5
7 [c]See ch. 3:2 [d][Matt. 25:15; 1 Cor. 12:7] [e]Rom. 12:3; [ver. 16]
8 [f]Cited from Ps. 68:18 [g]Judg. 5:12; [Col. 2:15]
9 [h]See John 3:13 [i]Ps. 63:9; Isai. 44:23
10 [j]See Mark 16:19 [k]Heb. 4:14; 7:26; 9:24 [l]ch. 1:23
11 [m][1 Cor. 12:5, 6]

[p]pastors and teachers,[1] 12 [q]to equip the
saints for the work of ministry, for [r]build-
ing up [s]the body of Christ, 13 until we all
attain to [t]the unity of the faith and of the
knowledge of the Son of God, [u]to mature
manhood,[2] to the measure of the stature of
[v]the fullness of Christ, 14 so that we may no
longer be children, [w]tossed to and fro by
the waves and carried about by every wind
of doctrine, by human cunning, by craftiness in [x]deceitful schemes. 15 Rather,
[y]speaking the truth in love, we are to [z]grow
up in every way into him who is [a]the head,
into Christ, 16 [b]from whom the whole body,
joined and held together by every joint
with which it is equipped, [c]when each part
is working properly, makes the body grow
so that it builds itself up in love.

The New Life

17 Now this I say and [d]testify in the Lord,
[e]that you must no longer walk as the
Gentiles do, [f]in the futility of their minds.
18 They [g]are darkened in their understanding, [h]alienated from the life of God because

[n]See 1 Cor. 12:28 [o]Acts 21:8; 2 Tim. 4:5 [p]Jer. 3:15; [Acts 20:28] **12** [q]See 2 Cor. 13:9 [r]ver. 16, 29 [s]See 1 Cor. 12:27 **13** [t][ver. 5] [u]Heb. 5:14 [v]ch. 1:23 **14** [w][Matt. 11:7; Heb. 13:9; James 1:6; Jude 12] [x]ch. 6:11 **15** [y]1 John 3:18; [ver. 25] [z]ch. 2:21 [a]See ch. 1:22 **16** [b]Col. 2:19 [c][ver. 7] **17** [d]1 Thess. 2:11 [e]ver. 22; ch. 2:1-3; Col. 3:7; 1 Pet. 4:3 [f]Rom. 1:21; 1 Pet. 1:18; [Col. 2:18; 2 Pet. 2:18] **18** [g][Rom. 11:10] [h]See ch. 2:12

[1] Or *the pastor-teachers* [2] Greek *to a full-grown man*

4:1 walk. Throughout the second half of this letter, Paul unfolds the "walk," or life of good works, first mentioned in 2:10. This figure of speech for moral conduct is common in Scripture.

calling. Paul earlier spoke of a hope to which believers are called (1:18; 4:4); now he focuses on the life to which they are called. He has already provided strong indications of its shape and significance (1:4; 2:10).

4:4–6 one. This word is repeated seven times in vv. 4–6—three times for Persons of the Godhead, and four times for aspects of His salvation.

4:7 But grace was given to each one of us. All Christians share the grace of salvation through faith (2:5, 8). Each Christian is also given some particular gift of grace to benefit the church (Paul speaks of his own in 3:2, 8). See theological note "Gifts and Ministries."

4:8 Ps. 68 celebrates God's triumphant march from Mount Sinai in the wilderness to Mount Zion in Jerusalem and His enthronement there. Paul regards this as prefiguring Christ's victorious ascent into heaven.

captives. The spiritual forces of darkness were defeated at the Cross (Col. 2:15 and note). While Ps. 68:18 describes the victorious Lord receiving gifts from men, Paul pictures Christ as sharing His tribute with men. Paul may have thought of this psalm because it was associated with Pentecost. This was the day the ascended Christ poured out the Spirit on the church (Acts 2:32, 33).

4:9 Christ came to the exalted position He now enjoys through humiliation. His incarnation was His taking on a human nature here in "the lower parts of the earth"; cf. 1:20–23; Phil. 2:1–11. This pattern of service is to be imitated by believers.

4:11 apostles. In a restricted sense, those who had been with Jesus and witnessed His resurrection (or received a special revelation of the risen Jesus) and who had been commissioned by Jesus to be founders of the church (Acts 1:21, 22; 1 Cor. 15:1–9). The word was also used in a broader sense of people sent out as delegates of particular churches (2 Cor. 8:23; Phil. 2:25), though these do not appear to be the ones Paul has in mind in this passage. See 2 Cor. 1:1 note.

prophets. The New Testament prophets conveyed special revelation to the early church. Their functions included prediction, exhortation, encouragement, warning, and explanation (Acts 15:32; 21:9–11; 1 Cor. 14:3). The teaching of the New Testament prophets and apostles laid the foundation of the church (2:20), and certain aspects of their work related to that unique task have been discontinued.

evangelists. People especially gifted to proclaim the gospel (Acts 21:8; 1 Cor. 1:17).

pastors and teachers. The two words go together to refer to a single set of individuals who both shepherd and instruct God's flock. See "Pastors and Pastoral Care" at 1 Pet. 5:2.

4:12, 13 It is not primarily those mentioned in v. 11 who do the work of the ministry; it is the people they equip. Effective teachers help each believer to find their own way of benefiting the rest of the church.

4:16 body. Paul uses the analogy of the human body. Believers are not given gifts for their own private benefit, and no one can grow to maturity in isolation. Paul himself strives for a knowledge of the Son of God that comes to maturity only when all believers attain it as well.

4:17–19 This passage closely resembles the critique of Gentile culture in Rom. 1. While the letter to the Romans shows God as giving Gentiles over to a reckless and wanton life (Rom. 1:24–31), Ephesians presents the same progression from the human side: those who have turned aside "have given themselves up" (v. 19). Similarly in Exodus God is said to harden Pharaoh's heart (e.g., Ex. 4:21; 7:3), but Pharaoh also hardens his own heart (Ex. 8:15, 32; 9:34).

of the ignorance that is in them, due to
[i]their hardness of heart. 19 They [j]have
become callous and [k]have given themselves
up to sensuality, greedy to practice every
kind of impurity. 20 But that is not the way
you [l]learned Christ!— 21 assuming that
[m]you have heard about him and [n]were
taught in him, as the truth is in Jesus, 22 to
[o]put off [p]your old self,[1] which belongs to
your former manner of life and is corrupt
through [q]deceitful desires, 23 and [r]to be
renewed in the spirit of your minds, 24 and
to put on [s]the new self, [t]created after the
likeness of God in true righteousness and
holiness.

18 [i]See Mark 3:5 **19** [j][Prov. 23:35]; 1 Tim. 4:2 [k][1 Kin. 21:25; Rom. 1:24, 26, 28] **20** [l]See Matt. 11:29 **21** [m]ch. 1:13 [n]Col. 2:7 **22** [o]Col. 3:8; Heb. 12:1; James 1:21; 1 Pet. 2:1 [p]Rom. 6:6; Col. 3:9 [q][Heb. 3:13] **23** [r]See Rom. 12:2 **24** [s]See Rom. 6:4 [t]See ch. 2:10

25 Therefore, having put away falsehood,
let each one of you [u]speak the truth with
his neighbor, for [v]we are members one of
another. 26 [w]Be angry and do not sin; do not
let the sun go down on your anger, 27 and
[x]give no opportunity to the devil. 28 Let the
thief no longer steal, but rather [y]let him
labor, [z]doing honest work with his own
hands, so [a]that he may have something to
share with anyone in need. 29 [b]Let no corrupting talk come out of your mouths, but

25 [u]Zech. 8:16; Col. 3:9; [ver. 15] [v]Rom. 12:5 **26** [w][Ps. 37:8] **27** [x]See James 4:7 **28** [y]Acts 20:35; Gal. 6:10 [z]1 Thess. 4:11; 2 Thess. 3:8, 11, 12 [a][Prov. 21:26] **29** [b]ch. 5:4; Col. 3:8; [Matt. 12:34]

[1] Greek *man*; also verse 24

Gifts and Ministries

The New Testament depicts two broad types of ministry within local churches. While all Christians fulfill informal ministering roles, some held formal and official ministerial offices. Paul addressed these official ministers as "overseers and deacons" (Phil. 1:1), and sometimes referred to the "bishops" (lit. "overseers") as "elders" (Titus 1:5, 7 and notes). The "bishops" or "elders" bore primary responsibility for ruling and teaching the church (1 Tim. 5:17 note), and the "deacons" were apparently especially charged with ministering to the material needs of the believers (Acts 6:1–6; 1 Tim. 3:8 note; cf. James 2:15, 16).

It is clear, however, that these officers who oversee local churches should not restrict the informal ministries, but rather should facilitate them (Eph. 4:11–13). Conversely those who minister informally should not be defiant or disruptive, but should allow the elders to direct their ministries in ways that are orderly and edifying (i.e., strengthening and upbuilding, 1 Cor. 14:3–5, 12, 26, 40; Heb. 13:17). The body of Christ grows to maturity in faith and love as "each part is working properly" (Eph. 4:16) and fulfills its particular form of service as granted by God's grace (Eph. 4:7, 12).

The word "gift" (lit. "donation") appears in connection with spiritual service only in Eph. 4:7, 8. Paul explains the phrase "he gave gifts to men" (Eph. 4:8 note) as the ascended Christ giving to His church persons called to and equipped for the ministries of apostle, prophet, evangelist, pastor, and teacher (Eph. 4:11 note). Also, through the enabling ministry of these persons, Christ bestows a ministry role on every Christian. Elsewhere (Rom. 12:4–8; 1 Cor. 12–14) Paul calls the divinely given abilities to serve *charismata* (specific manifestations of *charis*, "grace," 1 Cor. 12:4) and *pneumatika* (specific demonstrations of the ministry of the Holy Spirit, God's pneuma, 1 Cor. 12:1).

Amid many debated questions regarding spiritual gifts in the New Testament, three certainties stand out. First, a spiritual gift is an ability to express, celebrate, display, and so communicate Christ in a way that builds up and strengthens the faith of other Christians and enlarges the church. Second, spiritual gifts may be broadly classified as either abilities of speech or of loving, practical helpfulness. In Rom. 12:6–8, Paul's list of gifts alternates between the categories: prophecy, teaching, and exhorting are gifts of speech; serving, giving, leading, and showing mercy are gifts of helpfulness. However much they differ as forms of human activity, all are of equal dignity when one properly uses the gift one has (1 Pet. 4:10, 11). Third, no Christian is without some gift of ministry (1 Cor. 12:7; Eph. 4:7). It is every believer's responsibility to find, develop, and fully use whatever capacities for service God has given.

4:21 heard about him. That is, in the message proclaimed about Him.

as the truth is in Jesus. God has broken the cycle of death by giving them an understanding of His Son and His work on their behalf (1:13, 15).

4:22–24 put off . . . be renewed . . . put on. Belonging to Christ involves repudiating an old life and embracing a new one. The image is that of taking off fraying clothes and putting on new ones.

4:25–5:5 Paul outlines six concrete ways that Christians "put off" their old lives and "put on" life in Christ: they must turn from lying to telling the truth (4:25, 26); from uncontrolled anger to self-control (4:26, 27); from stealing to useful labor (4:28); from harmful to helpful speech (4:29, 30); from bitterness to love (4:31–5:2); and from unrestrained sexual desires to a thankful acknowledgement of God's good gifts (5:3–5). In each case, Paul offers a reason for the change from old to new.

4:27 Because practical unity among believers displays God's reconciling power (vv. 1–10; 2:14–16), the devil especially prizes its disruption (2:2; 6:11).

only such as is good for building up, as fits
the occasion, that it may give [c]grace to
those who hear. 30 And [d]do not grieve the
Holy Spirit of God, [e]by whom you were
sealed for the day of [f]redemption. 31 [g]Let all
bitterness and wrath and anger and clamor
and slander be put away from you, along
with all malice. 32 [h]Be kind to one another,
tenderhearted, [i]forgiving one another, as
God in Christ forgave you.

Walk in Love

5 [j]Therefore be imitators of God, as beloved children. 2 And [k]walk in love, [l]as
Christ loved us and [m]gave himself up for us,
a [n]fragrant [o]offering and sacrifice to God.
3 But [p]sexual immorality and all impurity
or covetousness [q]must not even be named
among you, as is proper among saints. 4 Let
there be [r]no filthiness nor foolish talk nor
crude joking, [s]which are out of place, but
instead [t]let there be thanksgiving. 5 For you
may be sure of this, that [u]everyone who is
sexually immoral or impure, or who is covetous ([v]that is, an idolater), has no inheritance in the kingdom of Christ and God.
6 [w]Let no one [x]deceive you with empty
words, for because of these things [y]the
wrath of God comes upon [z]the sons of disobedience. 7 Therefore [a]do not associate

29 [c]Col. 4:6; [Eccles. 10:12]
30 [d]Isai. 63:10; [1 Thess. 5:19] [e]ch. 1:13 [f]See ch. 1:7
31 [g]Col. 3:8, 19
32 [h]Col. 3:12, 13; 1 Pet. 3:8 [i][2 Cor. 2:7, 10]; See Matt. 6:14
Chapter 5
1 [j][ch. 4:32; Matt. 5:7, 48; Luke 6:36]
2 [k]Rom. 14:15; [Col. 3:14]; See John 13:34 [l]See Rom. 8:37 [m]See Rom. 4:25 [n]See Gen. 8:21 [o]Heb. 7:27; 9:14; 10:10, 12
3 [p]1 Cor. 6:18; See Gal. 5:19 [q][ver. 12; Ps. 16:4]
4 [r]ch. 4:29; [Eccles. 10:13] [s][Rom. 1:28] [t]ver. 20
5 [u]See 1 Cor. 6:9 [v]Col. 3:5
6 [w]See Matt. 24:4 [x]Col. 2:8 [y]Rom. 1:18; Col. 3:6 [z]ch. 2:2; [1 Pet. 1:14]
7 [a]ch. 3:6
8 [b]See ch. 2:1, 2

with them; 8 for [b]at one time you were
[c]darkness, but now you are light in the
Lord. [d]Walk as children of light 9 (for [e]the
fruit of light is found in all that is good and
right and true), 10 and [f]try to discern what is
pleasing to the Lord. 11 [g]Take no part in the
[h]unfruitful [i]works of darkness, but instead
[j]expose them. 12 For [k]it is shameful even to
speak of the things that they do in secret.
13 But when [l]anything is exposed by the
light, it becomes visible, 14 for anything that
becomes visible is light. Therefore it says,

[m]"Awake, O sleeper,
and [n]arise from the dead,
and [o]Christ will shine on you."

15 [p]Look carefully then how you walk, not
as unwise but as wise, 16 [p]making the best
use of the time, because [q]the days are evil.
17 Therefore do not be foolish, but understand what [r]the will of the Lord is. 18 And
[s]do not get drunk with wine, for that is [t]de-
bauchery, but [u]be filled with the Spirit,
19 addressing one another in [v]psalms and
hymns and spiritual songs, singing and

[c]See Acts 26:18 [d]Isai. 2:5; See Luke 16:8; John 12:35, 36 **9** [e][Gal. 5:22]; See Rom. 7:4 **10** [f]1 Thess. 2:4; 5:21 **11** [g]See 1 Cor. 5:9 [h]Rom. 6:21 [i]Rom. 13:12 [j]Lev. 19:17; 1 Tim. 5:20 **12** [k][ver. 3] **13** [l]John 3:20, 21; [ver. 9] **14** [m][Isai. 51:17; 52:1; 60:1; Mal. 4:2]; See Rom. 13:11 [n]Isai. 26:19 [o]Luke 1:78, 79 **15** [p]Col. 4:5; [Prov. 15:21] **16** [p][See ver. 15 above] [q]ch. 6:13; Eccles. 12:1; Amos 5:13; Gal. 1:4 **17** [r]Rom. 12:2; 1 Thess. 4:3; 5:18 **18** [s]Prov. 20:1; 23:20, 31; 1 Cor. 5:11 [t]Tit. 1:6; 1 Pet. 4:4 [u][Luke 1:15] **19** [v]Acts 16:25; 1 Cor. 14:26; Col. 3:16; James 5:13

4:30 do not grieve. That is, by the destructive use of speech described in v. 29. That the Holy Spirit can be saddened is an indication of His being a Person and not an impersonal force. The idea is not new to the New Testament, as is clear from Paul's quotation of the prophet Isaiah (Is. 63:10).

4:32–5:2 as God . . . as Christ. Believers must extend to others the forgiveness and love God has extended to them. In the same way, because Israel was purchased from slavery in Egypt, they were to have a special regard for aliens, slaves, and the dispossessed in their own midst (Ex. 22:21; 23:9; Lev. 19:33, 34; Deut. 5:15). The same logic is found in Jesus' new commandment: "as I have loved you, you also are to love one another" (John 13:34).

5:1 as beloved children. See note Col. 3:12. A firm knowledge of God's love and of one's place in His family (1:5) motivates the self-sacrifice necessary for Christian life (cf. v. 2).

5:3, 4 proper . . . out of place. To trivialize the sexual relationship ("crude joking"), or on the other hand to idolize it, is out of step with our identity as "saints." As those called out of the human race (1:4–6) to bear God's restored image (4:24), we can accept God's gifts, including sexuality, with thanksgiving, and restore them to their proper use (Prov. 5:18, 19; 1 Tim. 4:1–5; Heb. 13:4).

5:6 Although the day of reckoning may be denied with "empty words" (cf. 2 Pet. 3:3, 4), God's judgment will make a final separation between "the sons of disobedience" (2:2; cf. 5:5) and God's beloved children (1:4, 5; 5:1).

5:7 associate with them. Christians must consider the fearful destiny of non-believers and refuse to join them in their folly. Instead, they should remember their status as partakers with the Jews in the promise of God in Christ (3:6).

5:8 one time . . . but now. See 2:11, 13. Paul wants believers to do more than abstain from the things that bring God's wrath. They should live as "children of light" (cf. Col. 1:13 note). A result of the believers' union with Christ is that He who is "the light of the world" (John 8:12; 9:5) has made them also "the light of the world" (Matt. 5:14).

5:13 it becomes visible. Paul assumes that certain sins are so shameful that bringing them to light will shame some non-believers into repentance. The Christians' presence alone may expose sins through contrast or they may openly denounce them. Paul quotes what may be an early Christian hymn reminiscent of a number of Old Testament passages (e.g., Is. 60:1) and calling upon the spiritually dead to rise up and receive the light of Christ (cf. 2:1–10).

5:18 drunk with wine. This is more than a prohibition of simple drunkenness. Paul probably refers to an orgiastic form of worship such as was practiced by the cult of Dionysus (Bacchus), the god of wine. Worship of Dionysus involved drunken states in which the god was thought to enter the bodies of worshipers, inspiring prophecy and frenzied dancing and music. Such worship is "debauchery."

be filled with the Spirit. While the sealing of the Spirit (1:13, 14; 4:30) is a once-for-all initiation into the Christian life, the filling of the Spirit applies to all the Christian life. This filling is not only repeatable, but is to be sought again and again. In the parallel passage in Colossians, Paul tells Christians to let the "peace of Christ" govern their hearts and to allow the "word of Christ" to dwell in them richly (Col. 3:15, 16). The one who is filled with the Spirit is filled with Christ and His word (John 14:16, 26; 16:12–15; 17:17).

5:19 one another . . . to the Lord. Worship is offered to God alone. At the same time, in corporate worship there is a human audience as well since people worship together and address each other for their mutual benefit (1 Cor. 14; Heb. 10:24).

psalms and hymns and spiritual songs. See "Music in the Church" at Col. 3:16.

making melody to the Lord with all your
heart, 20 [w]giving thanks always and for
everything to God the Father [x]in the name
of our Lord Jesus Christ, 21 [y]submitting to
one another out of reverence for Christ.

Wives and Husbands

22 [z]Wives, [a]submit to your own husbands, [b]as to the Lord. 23 For [c]the husband
is the head of the wife even as [d]Christ is the
head of the church, his body, and is [e]him-
self its Savior. 24 Now as the church submits
to Christ, so also wives should submit [f]in
everything to their husbands.
25 [g]Husbands, love your wives, as Christ
loved the church and [h]gave himself up for
her, 26 that he might sanctify her, having
cleansed her by [i]the washing of water [j]with
the word, 27 so [k]that he might present the
church to himself in splendor, [l]without
spot or wrinkle or any such thing, that she
might be holy and without blemish.[1] 28 In
the same way [m]husbands should love their
wives as their own bodies. He who loves
his wife loves himself. 29 For no one ever
hated his own flesh, but nourishes and
cherishes it, just as Christ does the church,
30 because [n]we are members of his body.
31 [o]"Therefore a man shall leave his father
and mother and hold fast to his wife, and
[p]the two shall become one flesh." 32 This
mystery is profound, and I am saying that
it refers to Christ and the church.
33 However, [q]let each one of you love his
wife as himself, and let the wife see that
she [r]respects her husband.

Children and Parents

6 [s]Children, obey your parents in the
Lord, for this is right. 2 [t]"Honor your
father and mother" (this is the first commandment with a promise), 3 "that it may
go well with you and that you may live long
in the land." 4 Fathers, do not provoke your

20 [w]Col. 3:17; 1 Thess. 1:2; 2 Thess. 1:3 [x]Heb. 13:15; [John 14:13] **21** [y][Phil. 2:3] **22** [z]For ver. 22–ch. 6:9, see Col. 3:18–4:1 [a]See Gen. 3:16 [b][ch. 6:5] **23** [c]1 Cor. 11:3 [d]See ch. 1:22, 23 [e][1 Cor. 6:13] **24** [f][Col. 3:20, 22; Tit. 2:9] **25** [g]ver. 28, 33; [1 Pet. 3:7] [h]ver. 2 **26** [i]Tit. 3:5; [Rev. 7:14] [j]ch. 6:17; Heb. 6:5; See John 15:3 **27** [k]2 Cor. 11:2; See ch. 1:4 [l]S. of S. 4:7 **28** [m]ver. 25, 33 **30** [n][Gen. 2:23]; See 1 Cor. 6:15 **31** [o]Matt. 19:5; Mark 16:7, 8; Cited from Gen. 2:24 [p]1 Cor. 6:16 **33** [q]ver. 25, 28 [r]1 Pet. 3:2, 6
Chapter 6 **1** [s]Prov. 1:8; 6:20; 23:22 **2** [t]Cited from Ex. 20:12

1 Or *holy and blameless*

5:21 This transitional verse is last in a series of expressions explaining the effects of being filled with the Spirit (vv. 19–21 note). Regardless of their social rank, all Christians should pattern their social behavior on the humility and kindness of Christ (4:32–5:2; cf. Luke 22:24–27; John 13:14–16). This submission "to one another" is the basis for the forms of authority in specific relationships discussed in 5:22–6:9.

5:22–6:9 At least as far back as Aristotle (fourth century B.C.), Greek ethics had addressed relationships within the household in a familiar pattern: husbands and wives, parents and children, masters and slaves. Consistently, the interest was to help the male head of household learn to govern his family and slaves. In their treatment of such rules, Paul and Peter transform the question from how husbands, fathers, and masters dominate to how they can imitate the love of Christ they know in their own lives by nurturing those in their care. Simultaneously, as wives, children, and slaves define their roles in terms of service to Christ, they turn from being passive objects in a social world that devalues them, and become instead active partners with God in His plan to bring unity to a race divided by gender, age, and economics.

5:22–32 Jesus gives life to a new community of love—the church, His own body. His love also defines the marriage relationship for His people. Paul teaches that the genders are complementary, and a man and a woman are equal before God. Yet in marriage the husband has leadership. This leadership is not absolute but gives the husband the initiative in marriage, to which the wife responds. Paul's understanding is grounded in the creation order (1 Cor. 11:8, 9; 1 Tim. 2:13), and he takes account of the lingering effects, even among Christians, of the Fall (1 Tim. 2:14). Redemption in Christ restores the intimacy men and women were created to enjoy in marriage.

5:22 submit. A Christian wife is called to grateful acceptance of her husband's care and leadership. See theological note "The Christian Family" on the next page.

as to the Lord. See v. 24.

5:23 head of the wife . . . head of the church. In other passages on Christ's headship in this letter, Paul speaks of the way Christ governs the universe and the church (1:22), and serves as the source of the body's health and growth to maturity (4:14–16).

his body. That is, the church as His body—Christ Himself indwells the church (vv. 28–30).

Savior. It is especially in His role as Savior that Christ serves as the husband's model (vv. 25–27 and notes).

5:24 as the church . . . so also wives. The church's subjection to Christ is a revealed and heavenly order, not a natural order. Christ's disciples were His friends, not just His servants, and He died for them (John 15:12–15; cf. Luke 22:25–27).

5:25 Husbands, love. The emphasis in the passage is not the husband's authority to govern, but his responsibility to love.

as Christ loved the church and gave himself up for her. Nowhere in the New Testament is Christ's self-sacrificing love applied more directly to a specific relationship as a pattern to be emulated (cf. v. 2).

5:26, 27 Paul outlines in these verses the entire process to which Christ has committed Himself in His relationship with the church: He has washed her from sin and is preparing her for a glorious destiny with Himself (see text note, v. 27). Husbands are called in like manner to adapt their lives to their wives' needs, and to provide for their growth and development.

5:28–32 A person's union with his or her own body is intimate and permanent, and marriage creates a similiar union (Gen. 2:24). Christ has joined the church to Himself through the bonds of the covenant He fulfilled, and this intimate union forms an analogy for Christian marriage (see 2:6 and note).

6:1–3 Children have responsibility for carrying out part of Christ's plan to bring unity to the human race—this time, unity between generations. For Paul, part of what characterizes Gentile culture as standing under God's judgment is that it is marked by children's disobedience to their parents (Rom. 1:30; 2 Tim. 3:2).

6:2 the first commandment with a promise. The law of God has lost its power to condemn those who are in Christ (Col. 2:13, 14), and the observance of the ceremonial law is inappropriate following their fulfillment in Christ (2:15; Col. 2:16, 17). However the "weightier matters of the law" (Matt. 23:23) are revelations of God's character, and establish permanent ethical principles. One of these is that children must honor their parents.

6:4 Fathers. Conversely, to parents Paul stresses the responsibility of those in authority.

children to anger, [u]but bring them up in
the discipline and instruction of the Lord.

Slaves and Masters

5 [v]Slaves,[1] obey your earthly masters[2]
with fear and trembling, [w]with a sincere
heart, [x]as you would Christ, 6 not by the
way of eye-service, as [y]people-pleasers, but
as servants[3] of Christ, doing the will of God
from the heart, 7 rendering service with a
good will as to the Lord and not to man,
8 [z]knowing that whatever good anyone
does, this he will receive back from the
Lord, [a]whether he is a slave or free.
9 Masters, do the same to them, [b]and stop
your threatening, knowing that [c]he who is
both their Master[4] and yours is in heaven,
and that [d]there is no partiality with him.

The Whole Armor of God

10 Finally, [e]be strong in the Lord and in
[f]the strength of his might. 11 [g]Put on [h]the

4 [u]Gen. 18:19; Deut. 4:9; 6:7; 11:19; Ps. 78:4; Prov. 19:18; 22:6; 29:17; [2 Tim. 3:15] 5 [v]See 1 Pet. 2:18 [w][2 Cor. 11:3] [x][ch. 5:22] 6 [y]See Gal. 1:10 8 [z]See Ps. 62:12 [a]Gal. 3:28; Col. 3:11 9 [b]Lev. 25:43 [c]John 13:13; [Job 31:13-15] [d]See Deut. 10:17 10 [e]Rom. 4:20 (Gk.); 2 Tim. 2:1; [1 John 2:14]; See ch. 3:16 [f]ch. 1:19 11 [g]ver. 14; Job 29:14; See Rom. 13:12 [h]ver. 13; [2 Cor. 10:4]

1 Or *servants*; Greek *bondservants*; similarly verse 8 2 Or *your masters according to the flesh* 3 Or *slaves*; Greek *bondservants* 4 Greek *Lord*

The Christian Family

The family is the oldest and most basic of human institutions. In both the Israelite culture of the Old Testament and the Hellenistic culture of the New Testament, the household might consist of parents and children, relatives from several generations, servants, and even friends, depending on the economic resources of the head of the family. The Bible stresses its importance as a spiritual unit and a training ground for mature adult character.

The Bible pictures a clear authority structure within the family, whereby the husband is to lead the wife and the parents are to lead the children. But just as all leadership should be a form of ministry rather than tyranny, so these domestic leadership roles must be fulfilled in love (Eph. 5:22–6:4; Col. 3:18–21; 1 Pet. 3:1–7). The fourth commandment requires the head of the household to lead his whole family in sabbath observance; the fifth requires children to respect and submit to their parents (Ex. 20:8–12; Eph. 6:1–3). Jesus Himself set an example in this as a child (Luke 2:51). Later, He fiercely opposed supposed gestures of piety that were really evasions of responsibility toward parents (Mark 7:6–13), and His own last act before death was to provide for His mother's future (John 19:25–27).

The family is to be a community of teaching and learning about God and godliness. Children must be instructed (Gen. 18:18, 19; Deut. 4:9; 6:6–8; 11:18–21; Prov. 22:6; Eph. 6:4) and encouraged to use that instruction as a basis for their lives (Prov. 1:8; 6:20). Discipline should be used as a means of corrective training to lead children beyond childish folly to self-controlled wisdom (Prov. 13:24; 19:18; 22:15; 23:13, 14; 29:15, 17). Just as there is purposeful, loving discipline in God's family (Prov. 3:11, 12; Heb. 12:5–11), so there must be in the human family.

The family is meant to function as a spiritual unit. The Old Testament Passover was a family observance (Ex. 12:3). Joshua set an example when he said, "as for me and my house, we will serve the LORD" (Josh. 24:15). Households became the units of Christian commitment in New Testament times (Acts 11:14; 16:15, 31–33; 1 Cor. 1:16). The fitness of candidates for church office was assessed by observing whether they had led their own family well (1 Tim. 3:4, 5, 12; Titus 1:6).

Building strong family life is always a priority in serving God.

bring them up. The Greek suggests the idea of nurturing and helping to flourish (cf. 5:29). Parents are entrusted with the minds, feelings, and bodies of tender bearers of the divine image. Accordingly, children do not exist for parents, but parents for children—to help them come into their own personhood before God.

discipline. The shaping of the will through training.

instruction. The shaping of the mind through teaching.

6:5–8 Slaves follow the example of Christ through obedient submission (Phil. 2:1–11). All believers are called to share Christ's humiliation and sufferings in this age, in order to be exalted and glorified with Him in the next (Rom. 8:17). Paul is not interested in making anyone's share of suffering greater than it has to be (1 Cor. 7:21). He also does not pretend there is an easy route around it. As slaves serve the exalted Christ, and not merely an earthly master, they do so in the new reality inaugurated by Christ (2 Cor. 5:17). Paul would insist that being owned by Christ makes all other definitions of our personhood irrelevant: "You were bought with a price; do not become slaves of men" (1 Cor. 7:23). By rendering ungrudging service to their true heavenly owner, slaves can work not for their value in the marketplace, but for their value to the One who poured out His own life for them.

6:9 do the same. If masters can expect their Christian slaves to serve them willingly, slaves can expect from Christian masters to be treated the way Christ treats His own.

6:10–17 The Christian duty of unity and purity is complicated by the presence of hostile spiritual powers. Christ's cross and resurrection are the devil's undoing (Col. 2:15 note), and at Christ's Second Coming, Satan's defeat will be completed (Rom. 16:20). But the peace of the Cross is experienced in the meantime in the midst of spiritual struggle. The forces of darkness are defeated, but not yet harmless.

6:10 be strong . . . the strength of his might. Paul uses similar terms in 1:19 to describe the power that raised Jesus from the dead. We are not encouraged to face the evil hosts of darkness in our own strength,

whole armor of God, that you may be able
to stand against [i]the schemes of the devil.
12 For [j]we do not wrestle against flesh and
blood, but against [k]the rulers, against the
authorities, against [l]the cosmic powers
over [m]this present darkness, against [n]the
spiritual forces of evil [o]in the heavenly
places. 13 Therefore [p]take up the whole
armor of God, that you may be able to
withstand in [q]the evil day, and having done
all, to stand firm. 14 Stand therefore, [r]having
fastened on the belt of truth, and [s]having
put on the breastplate of righteousness,
15 and, [t]as shoes for your feet, having put
on the readiness given by the gospel of
peace. 16 In all circumstances take up [u]the
shield of faith, with which you can extinguish all [v]the flaming darts of [w]the evil one;
17 and take [s]the helmet of salvation, and
[x]the sword of the Spirit, which is the word
of God, 18 praying [y]at all times [z]in the Spirit,
[a]with all prayer and supplication. To that
end [b]keep alert with all perseverance, making [c]supplication for all the saints, 19 and
[d]also for me, that words may be given to
me in opening my mouth [e]boldly to proclaim [f]the mystery of the gospel, 20 for
which I [g]am an ambassador [h]in chains, that
I may declare it boldly, as I ought to speak.

Final Greetings

21 [i]So that you also may know how I am
and what I am doing, [j]Tychicus the
beloved brother and faithful minister in the
Lord will tell you everything. 22 I have sent
him to you for this very purpose, that you
may know how we are, and that he may
[k]encourage your hearts.
23 [l]Peace be to the brothers,[1] and [m]love
with faith, from God the Father and the
Lord Jesus Christ. 24 Grace be with all who
[n]love our Lord Jesus Christ with love incor-
ruptible.

11 [i]ch. 4:14 12 [j]See 1 Cor. 9:25 [k]ch. 1:21 [l]See ch. 2:2 [m]Luke 22:53; Col. 1:13 [n][ch. 3:10] [o]See ch. 1:3 13 [p][1 Pet. 4:1] [q]ch. 5:16 14 [r]1 Pet. 1:13; [Isai. 11:5]; See Luke 12:35 [s]Isai. 59:17; 1 Thess. 5:8; [Isai. 61:10; 2 Cor. 6:7] 15 [t]Isai. 52:7; Rom. 10:15; [Ex. 12:11] 16 [u][1 John 5:4] [v][Ps. 120:4] [w]See Matt. 13:19 17 [s][See ver. 14 above] [x]Heb. 4:12; [Isai. 49:2; Hos. 6:5; 2 Cor. 6:7] 18 [y]Luke 18:1 [z]Jude 20; See Rom. 8:26 [a]Col. 4:2-4 [b]See Mark 13:33

[c]1 Tim. 2:1 19 [d]Col. 4:3; 1 Thess. 5:25; 2 Thess. 3:1; [Isai. 50:4] [e]See Acts 4:29 [f]ch. 3:3 20 [g]See 2 Cor. 5:20 [h]See Acts 28:20 21 [i]Col. 4:7-9 [j]Acts 20:4; 2 Tim. 4:12; Tit. 3:12 22 [k]Col. 2:2 23 [l]Gal. 6:16; 2 Thess. 3:16; 1 Pet. 5:14 [m][Gal. 5:6; 1 Thess. 5:8] 24 [n][1 Cor. 16:22]

1 Or *brothers and sisters*

but in the strength that raised Jesus and believers with Him (2:4–6; 3:16–19).

6:11 Put on the whole armor of God. The new set of clothes (4:22–24 note) now becomes a warrior's battle gear (Col. 3:10, 12 notes).

stand. Repeated three times in vv. 11, 13, 14 (the related term "withstand" in v. 13 has the same meaning). The "walking" image of chs. 4 and 5 (4:1 note) gives way to the picture of a soldier standing firm in battle.

6:12 See 1:21; 2:2; 3:10.

rulers . . . spiritual forces. These terms all refer to powerful spiritual beings that make up the "power of the air" (2:2) ruled by Satan.

darkness. See 5:8–14.

6:13 the whole armor of God. Paul combines the weapons of a Roman foot soldier with a number of Old Testament images of God, or the Messiah, as a warrior. Strikingly, what is said of God and the Messiah in the Old Testament is applied to believers.

6:14 fastened . . . truth. The Roman soldier's leather belt supported and protected his lower abdomen, gathered his tunic together, and held his sword. Paul seems to have in mind the confidence that comes from certainty about the truthfulness of God's Word.

breastplate of righteousness. Believers are protected by the righteousness of Christ imputed to them (Rom. 4:6–11; Phil. 3:9), and they can stand up to the accusations of the devil; *devil* in Greek means "slanderer" (Rom. 8:31–34). Simultaneously, Paul sees believers taking on the righteous character of Christ (4:25; 5:9), while their growing conformity to His image gives them confidence in resisting temptation.

6:15 shoes for your feet. Despite a clear allusion to Is. 52:7, Paul does not have in mind the barefooted messenger who takes the gospel to others. The image here is of the Roman soldier's sturdy sandals, which gave him stability and protection in battle. Ironically, the peace that comes from the gospel readies one for war against evil (2:14, 15, 17).

6:16 shield of faith. The Roman shield was large enough to cover the whole body; it was made of wood, covered with hide, and bound with iron at the top and bottom. When dipped in water before a battle, it could extinguish fire arrows that had been dipped in pitch and set ablaze.

6:17 helmet of salvation. For Paul, salvation is a present experience (2:8 and note) as well as a future hope (1 Thess. 5:8). The believer's final ground of confidence is the faithfulness of God to complete the salvation He has begun (Phil. 1:6).

sword of the Spirit, which is the word of God. The one offensive weapon in the believer's arsenal is compared to the Roman sword, short and designed for hand-to-hand combat. See Jesus' use of Scripture in Matt. 4:1–11; Luke 4:1–13.

6:18–20 The battle theme in this passage ends with an urgent call to militant prayer on behalf of all believers and on behalf of Paul's ministry. See 1:15–23 for Paul's dependence on prayer.

6:21–24 Tychicus. See note Col. 4:7, 8. The absence of personal greetings in this letter may be an indication that it was intended for circulation to more than one church. See Introduction: Date and Occasion.

THE EPISTLE OF PAUL THE APOSTLE TO THE

Philippians

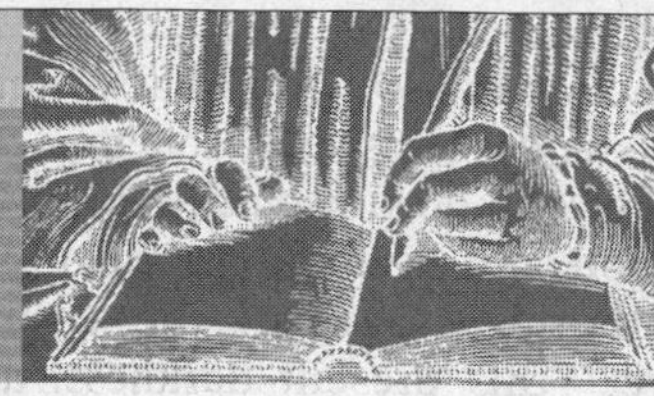

AUTHOR

The author identifies himself as Paul (1:1), and the early church unanimously attributed this letter to him. It has many personal references, and is similar to the other Pauline writings. These facts together leave no doubt that Paul is the author.

The beginning of Paul's involvement with the church at Philippi is recorded in Acts 16. Prompted by a vision (Acts 16:6–10), Paul and his colleagues traveled to Philippi (Acts 16:12). During their brief visit, God did mighty works and a church was established (Acts 16:40), Paul's first on European soil. Paul himself returned on at least two more occasions to strengthen the believers (Acts 20:1–6; 2 Cor. 2:13).

DATE AND OCCASION

Paul writes from prison (1:12–30), but the location of the imprisonment is a matter of discussion. Some think he wrote from Ephesus, though Acts 19 says nothing of his being imprisoned during his lengthy Ephesian ministry. A stronger case can be made for his having written the letter during his imprisonment in Caesarea (Acts 23:23–26:32). But it is probable, in accord with long-standing tradition, that Paul wrote Philippians during the Roman imprisonment described in Acts 28 and that he did so toward the end of this period, around A.D. 61. His references to the "imperial guard" (1:13) and "Caesar's household" (4:22) accord best with a Roman setting, and the language of 1:7–26 suggests legal proceedings at the highest level. Finally, the continuing success of Paul's ministry during his imprisonment (1:12–14) is in keeping with his freedom to preach during his confinement in Rome (Acts 28:16–31).

The city of Philippi was named for Philip of Macedon, father of Alexander the Great. One reason for its importance is that it lay on the main road between the eastern provinces and Rome. A Roman colony populated in part by retired Roman soldiers, its inhabitants enjoyed the privileges of Roman citizenship. The absence of Old Testament quotations and Jewish names in the letter indicates that the church of Philippi was largely Gentile.

Philippians rings with joy and gratitude for the way God is carrying forward His saving work among the Philippians and for the special bond that exists between Paul and his readers. At the same time, there is a gravity to the letter. The Philippians face persecution (1:27–30) and feel the pressures exerted on them by false teachings (3:2–21). Conflicts in the church jeopardize the believers' witness to the world and their ability to withstand its assaults (1:27–2:18; 4:2, 3).

CHARACTERISTICS AND THEMES

1. Paul's Affection for His Readers. This epistle amply attests to the special bond of love Paul felt for the Philippians (1:3–8; 4:10–19). The church at Philippi had faithfully supported Paul's ministry, and their willingness to suffer with him for Christ was a source of encouragement for Paul.

2. Joy. Even though he was in jail, Paul's letter resounds with the theme of joy. Forms of the word "joy" occur sixteen times in the letter. Paul's joy is grounded in the peace of God, the antidote to all anxiety (4:4–7).

3. The Triune God. Paul uses the word "God" to refer to the Father (1:2; 2:11; 4:20). Paul's favorite designation for Jesus Christ is "the Lord" (*kyrios* in Greek; see 1:2; 2:11, 19; 3:8, 20; 4:23). On the one hand, Paul affirms in this letter that the Father and the Son are identical in being. Both are divine and worship is due to both (2:6–11). In calling Jesus Christ "the Lord," Paul identifies Him with Yahweh, the God of Israel. Yet by calling the Father "God" and Jesus "the Lord," Paul shows that there is a distinction of Persons within the Godhead. Finally, the Holy Spirit is united with God the Father (3:3) and with Jesus Christ (1:19). Paul's theology is Trinitarian, confessing one God in three Persons. See "One and Three: The Trinity" at Is. 44:6.

4. The Example of Christ's Humility. The majestic "hymn to Christ" (2:6–11) offers a model for believers. Before He was incarnated ("became flesh," John 1:14), Christ Jesus was truly God. Nevertheless, He emptied Himself and took the form of a slave by abandoning His divine privileges and taking on human nature. Yet in relinquishing these privileges He did not cease to be God. Rather, Christ manifested His divine character by becoming a human being.

5. Justification by Grace Through Faith. Against those who require obedience to the Old Testament law as a way of meriting salvation, Paul stresses God's will that His people should be saved by receiving His righteousness as a gift and not by striving to establish their own. Although Paul had been scrupulous in his obedience to the law, he came to realize that his confidence in such obedience was a great sin, for it kept him from trusting God. Paul views his former boasting with disgust (3:7, 8) and Christ alone is now his confidence (3:3, 9).

6. The Christian Life. The letter is filled with instruction on practical Christianity. Just as Christ became a slave, so also the Christian becomes the slave of Christ (1:1). Only the person enslaved to Christ is free to love and serve others (2:3–5).

Paul stresses the importance of identification with Christ in His death and resurrection. As it was for Christ, suffering for the believer is the prelude to resurrection (3:10, 11). For the present, it is in the midst of ongoing struggle that the Christian experiences joy and power (3:10; 4:13).

The importance of striving toward the goal of full salvation is highlighted. Confident of God's calling, Paul pushes forward toward the heavenly prize (3:13, 14). As Christians work they realize that God is working in them (2:12, 13). Human effort is precisely the area where the power of God is manifested.

OUTLINE OF PHILIPPIANS

I. Salutation (1:1, 2)

II. Opening Message: Thanksgiving and Prayer (1:3–11)

III. The Truth of the Gospel (1:12–2:30)

- A. *The Gospel and Paul (1:12–26)*
  1. Paul's Imprisonment (1:12–14)
  2. Rival Messengers (1:15–18)
  3. Paul's Prospects (1:19–26)
- B. *The Gospel and the Philippians (1:27–2:18)*
  1. A Call to Unity (1:27–2:4)
  2. The Example of Christ (2:5–11)
  3. A Further Call to Unity (2:12–18)
- C. *Two of Paul's Coworkers in the Gospel (2:19–30)*

IV. Truth Against Error (3:1–4:1)

- A. *The Gospel Against Legalists (3:1–11)*
- B. *The Already and the Not Yet (3:12–16)*
- C. *The Gospel Against Libertines (3:17–4:1)*

V. Exhortations (4:2–9)

VI. Thanksgiving (4:10–20)

- A. *Contentment (4:10–13)*
- B. *Partnership (4:14–20)*

VII. Final Greeting and Benediction (4:21–23)

Greeting

1 Paul and Timothy, servants[1] of Christ
Jesus,
To all the [a]saints in Christ Jesus who are
at Philippi, with the [b]overseers[2] and [c]dea-
cons:[3]
2 [d]Grace to you and peace from God our
Father and the Lord Jesus Christ.

Thanksgiving and Prayer

3 [e]I thank my God [f]in all my remembrance of you, 4 always in every prayer of
mine for you all making my prayer with
joy, 5 [g]because of your partnership in the
gospel from the first day until now. 6 And I
am sure of this, that he who began [h]a good
work in you [i]will bring it to completion at
[j]the day of Jesus Christ. 7 It is right for me
to feel this way about you all, because I
hold you [k]in my heart, for you are all [l]par-
takers with me of grace, both [m]in my
imprisonment and in [n]the defense and
confirmation of the gospel. 8 For [o]God is
my witness, [p]how I yearn for you all with
the affection of Christ Jesus. 9 And it is my
prayer that [q]your love may abound more
and more, [r]with knowledge and all discernment, 10 so that you may approve what
is excellent, [s]and so be pure and blameless
[t]for the day of Christ, 11 filled [u]with the fruit
of righteousness that comes [v]through Jesus
Christ, [w]to the glory and praise of God.

The Advance of the Gospel

12 I want you to know, brothers,[4] that
what has happened to me has really [x]served
to advance the gospel, 13 so that it has
become known throughout the whole
imperial guard[5] and [y]to all the rest that [z]my
imprisonment is for Christ. 14 And most of
the brothers, having become confident in
the Lord by my imprisonment, are much
more bold [a]to speak the word[6] without fear.
15 [b]Some indeed preach Christ from envy
and rivalry, but others from good will.

Chapter 1
1 [a]2 Cor. 1:1; Col. 1:2 [b]See Acts 20:28 [c]1 Tim. 3:8, 12
2 [d]Rom. 1:7; 1 Cor. 1:3
3 [e]See Rom. 1:8 [f]Rom. 1:9; Eph. 1:16; 2 Tim. 1:3
5 [g][ch. 2:12; 4:15; Acts 16:12-40]
6 [h][1 Thess. 1:3] [i]Ps. 57:2 (Heb.); 138:8; [1 Thess. 5:24] [j]See 1 Cor. 1:8
7 [k]2 Cor. 7:3 [l][ch. 4:14] [m]Acts 20:23; 26:29; Col. 4:18; 2 Tim. 2:9; Philem. 10, 13; See Eph. 3:1 [n]ver. 16
8 [o]See Rom. 1:9; 9:1 [p][ch. 4:1; Rom. 1:11; 15:23; 1 Thess. 3:6; 2 Tim. 1:4]
9 [q]1 Thess. 3:12; 2 Thess. 1:3 [r]Col. 1:9; 3:10; Philem. 6
10 [s]Acts 24:16; 1 Thess. 3:13; 5:23 [t]ver. 6 11 [u][Col. 1:6, 10]; See James 3:18 [v][John 15:4, 5] [w]See Eph. 1:12, 14 12 [x]ver. 25; 1 Tim. 4:15 13 [y][Acts 28:30, 31; 2 Tim. 2:9] [z][Luke 21:13]; See ver. 7 14 [a][Acts 4:31] 15 [b]See 2 Cor. 11:13

[1] Or *slaves*; Greek *bondservants* [2] Or *bishops*; Greek *episkopoi* [3] Or *servants*, or *ministers*; Greek *diakonoi* [4] Or *brothers and sisters*. The plural Greek word *adelphoi* (translated "brothers") refers to siblings in a family. In New Testament usage, depending on the context, *adelphoi* may refer either to men or to both men and women who are siblings (brothers and sisters) in God's family, the church; also verse 14 [5] Greek *in the whole praetorium* [6] Some manuscripts add *of God*

1:1 Paul and Timothy. Timothy, present at the founding of the Philippian church (Acts 16), is known to the readers (2:22). Elsewhere Paul calls himself "an apostle" and Timothy "our brother" (2 Cor. 1:1; Col. 1:1).

servants. A "servant" is a slave (text note). Timothy is like a son to Paul (2:22), but both are under Christ the Lord.

in Christ Jesus. One of Paul's favorite ways of describing the believer's union with Christ. This phrase occurs ten times in Philippians.

overseers and deacons. These terms designate the twofold leadership in the church at Philippi (1 Tim. 3:1–13).

1:2 Grace . . . and peace. These two words, a concise expression of the effect of Christ's saving work, appear together in all thirteen of Paul's salutations. The common source of grace and peace is "God our Father and the Lord Jesus Christ."

1:3, 4 Paul's memory of the Philippians prompts him to pray for them frequently ("in every prayer of mine") and gratefully ("I thank my God").

1:4 with joy. Joy is a dominant theme in Philippians (vv. 18, 26; 3:1; 4:4, 10). See Introduction.

1:5 your partnership. The Philippians' financial support is especially in view (4:10–20).

in the gospel. The word "gospel," Paul's favorite term for his message, occurs nine times in Philippians (more, proportionately, than in any other letter). Paul and the Philippians are bound together by their common commitment to the gospel (v. 7).

from the first day. That is, since the gospel first came to Philippi (4:15; Acts 16:12–40).

1:6 he . . . will bring it to completion. The perseverance of the saints depends upon God's preserving them by grace. See "Perseverance of the Saints" at Rom. 8:30. God's saving purpose will be fulfilled on "the day of Christ" (v. 10; 2:16), when He returns in glory to raise His people from the dead (3:11, 20, 21) and to receive universal homage (2:9–11).

1:7 hold you in my heart. The Greek words could be rendered, "you have me in your heart." The Philippians are "partakers . . . of grace" with Paul through supporting his ministry (cf. v. 5).

defense and confirmation. The terms suggest apostolic witness during a trial (cf. v. 16; Mark 13:9–11).

1:8 affection. The Greek noun, like the related verb used often of Jesus in the Gospels (e.g., Matt. 9:36; 14:14), indicates deep emotion.

1:9, 10 Paul tells the Philippians not only that he prays for them (v. 4), but also the content of that prayer. Christian belief ("knowledge and all discernment") comes to expression in Christian love and in behavior that is "pure and blameless" (cf. Col. 1:9–11). The absence of love shows that supposed knowledge is worthless (1 Cor. 13:1–3), and love is itself knowledge of the deepest kind (1 Cor. 8:1–3). The seriousness of Paul's prayer that "love may abound" among the Philippians will become more apparent in 2:1–18.

1:11 Not only is the sinner justified through faith in Christ (3:9), but "the fruit of righteousness," or the righteous life that ensues, is also "through Jesus Christ" through the work of His Spirit (Gal. 5:22, 23), "to the glory and praise of God" the Father. All three Persons of the Godhead are active in the sanctification of believers.

1:12 to advance the gospel. Because of Paul's imprisonment, the gospel has moved irresistibly through the palace guard and beyond.

1:13 all the rest. Paul's imprisonment for Christ had become known not only to the soldiers assigned to the emperor, but also to the imperial household (cf. 4:22) and perhaps to the Roman populace beyond.

1:14 brothers. Paul uses this term to address both men and women.

in the Lord. This important Pauline phrase points to the believer's union with Christ and to the divine resources available through Christ to those united with Him (4:13). The phrase occurs nine times in Philippians (counting 2:19). By means of Paul's imprisonment, the Lord strengthens and encourages the Christians to proclaim the gospel fearlessly.

1:15–18 There are not rival messages, since both parties preach Christ, but opposing motives and attitudes. The motive of one group is goodwill and love for Christ, and Paul's defense of the gospel explains why

16 The latter do it out of love, [c]knowing that
I am put here for [d]the defense of the
gospel. 17 The former proclaim Christ [e]out
of rivalry, not sincerely but thinking to
afflict me in my imprisonment. 18 What
then? Only that in every way, whether in
pretense or in truth, Christ is proclaimed,
and in that I rejoice.

To Live Is Christ

Yes, and I will rejoice, 19 for I know that
[f]through your prayers and [g]the help of [h]the
Spirit of Jesus Christ this will turn out for
my deliverance, 20 as it is my eager expectation and hope [i]that I will not be at all
ashamed, but that with full [j]courage now
as always Christ [k]will be honored in my
body, [l]whether by life or by death. 21 For to
me [m]to live is Christ, and to die is gain. 22 If
I am to live in the flesh, that means fruitful
labor for me. Yet which I shall choose I cannot tell. 23 [n]I am hard pressed between the
two. My desire is [o]to depart and [p]be with

16 [c][1 Cor. 9:17] [d]ver. 7
17 [e]ch. 2:3; See James 3:14
19 [f]See 2 Cor. 1:11 [g]Gal. 3:5 [h]See Acts 16:7
20 [i]Rom. 5:5; [Joel. 2:27; 2 Tim. 2:15] [j]See Acts 4:13 [k][1 Cor. 6:20] [l]Rom. 14:8
21 [m][Gal. 2:20]
23 [n][2 Cor. 5:8] [o]2 Tim. 4:6 [p]See John 12:26

Death and the Intermediate State

We do not know how humans would have left this world had there been no Fall; some doubt whether they ever would have done so. But as it is, the fruit of sin and God's judgment on it brings about the separation of body and soul through bodily death (Gen. 2:17; 3:19, 22; Rom. 5:12; 8:10; 1 Cor. 15:21), making it a certainty for everyone. This separation of soul and body is a consequence of the spiritual separation from God that first brought about physical death (Gen. 2:17; 5:5) and that will be deepened after death for those who leave this world without Christ. In itself death is an enemy (1 Cor. 15:26) and a terror (Heb. 2:15).

For Christians the final terror of physical death is abolished. Jesus, the risen Savior, Himself passed through a terrible death, enduring the anger of God. He takes from us God's anger, and He lives to help us as we leave this world for the place He has prepared in the next (John 14:2, 3). Christians know that their own forthcoming death is an appointment to meet their Savior that He will faithfully keep. Paul could say, "For to me to live is Christ, and to die is gain." He longed "to depart and be with Christ, for that is far better" (Phil. 1:21, 23), knowing that to be "away from the body" is to be "at home with the Lord" (2 Cor. 5:8).

At death the souls of believers are made perfect in holiness and enter into the worshiping life of heaven (Heb. 12:22–24). In a word, they are glorified. Some have not accepted this, but teach instead that there is a purgatorial discipline after death amounting to a further stage of sanctification. In this purgatory the soul is prepared over a period of time, to be purified for the vision of God. This doctrine is not found in the Bible. The saints living on earth at Christ's coming will be perfected morally to be with Him in the moment when their body is transformed (1 Cor. 15:51–54), and it seems that Paul, and the thief on the cross, expected the same admission to God's presence. Others say that believers pass into a soul-sleep and are unconscious between death and resurrection. The Bible, however, consistently represents the departed as conscious (Luke 16:22; 23:43; Phil. 1:23; 2 Cor. 5:8; Rev. 6:9–11; 14:13).

In itself to be without the body is a disadvantage; we live through our bodies, and to be without a body is to be limited and impoverished. Paul longs to be "clothed" with the resurrection body, and wants not at all to be "unclothed" (2 Cor. 5:4). The resurrection of the body is a distinctive Christian hope confessed by every branch of the church on earth.

Death is decisive for destiny. The Bible does not teach that after death there is another possibility of salvation for the lost (Luke 16:26; Heb. 9:27). After death, both the godly and the ungodly reap what they sowed in this world (Gal. 6:7, 8).

they love the apostle (vv. 15, 17). The dominant motive of the other group is "rivalry" (v. 17), the very attitude against which Paul warns the Philippians (2:1–5). They preach Christ so that they themselves can seem important, an attitude quite different from Paul's (vv. 20, 21), and they respond to Paul's success by seeking to increase his suffering (v. 16).

1:19 Spirit of Jesus Christ. Paul identifies the third Person of the Trinity as the Spirit of God and as the Spirit of Christ (Rom. 8:9; Gal. 4:6).

deliverance. Paul expects to be released from prison, but he cannot be certain of it (vv. 20–27; 2:24). God will deliver him (v. 28) through His appointed agencies, both human and divine ("your prayers" and "the Spirit of Jesus Christ").

1:20 Paul's passion is neither to live nor to die, but to see Christ magnified whatever happens (2:17; cf. Rom. 12:1, 2).

1:21 to live is Christ. Christ is Paul's reason for being.

to die is gain. Far from severing Paul's union with Christ, death will bring Paul into a deeper experience of that union.

1:23 hard pressed. Paul wants to be with Christ but also to remain on earth for the sake of the church. This is his dilemma. However, the outcome is in God's hands, and Paul is confident that God has further work for him to do among the Philippians (vv. 24, 25).

be with Christ. Paul's language here sheds light on the character of the intermediate state (i.e., the condition of a person between the times of physical death and the resurrection). See theological note "Death and the Intermediate State."

Christ, for that is far better. 24 But to remain
in the flesh is more necessary on your
account. 25 [q]Convinced of this, [r]I know that
I will remain and continue with you all, for
your [s]progress and [t]joy in the faith, 26 so
that in me [u]you may have ample cause to
glory in Christ Jesus, because of my coming
to you again.
27 Only [v]let your manner of life be [w]wor-
thy[1] of the gospel of Christ, so that whether
I come and see you or am absent, I may
hear of you [x]that you are standing firm in
one spirit, with [y]one mind [z]striving side by
side for the faith of the gospel, 28 and not
frightened in anything by your opponents.
This is [a]a clear sign to them of their destruction, but [b]of your salvation, and that from
God. 29 For [c]it has been granted to you that
for the sake of Christ you should not only
believe in him but also [b]suffer for his sake,
30 engaged in the same [d]conflict that [e]you
saw I had and now hear that I still have.

Christ's Example of Humility

2 So if there is any encouragement in
Christ, any comfort from [f]love, any
[g]participation in the Spirit, any [h]affection
and sympathy, 2 [i]complete my joy by being
[j]of the same mind, having the same love,
being in full accord and of one mind. 3 Do
nothing from [k]rivalry or [l]conceit, but in
[m]humility count others more significant
than yourselves. 4 Let each of you [n]look not
only to his own interests, but also to the
interests of others. 5 [o]Have this mind
among yourselves, which is yours in Christ
Jesus,[2] 6 [p]who, though he was in [q]the form
of God, did not count equality with God [r]a
thing to be grasped, 7 but [s]made himself
nothing, taking the form of a [t]servant,[3] [u]be-
ing born in the likeness of men. 8 And being
found in human form, he humbled himself
by [v]becoming obedient to the point of
death, [w]even death on a cross. 9 [x]Therefore
[y]God has [z]highly exalted him and be-

25 [q][ch. 2:24] [r][Acts 20:25] [s]ver. 12 [t]Rom. 15:13 **26** [u]See 2 Cor. 1:14 **27** [v][ch. 3:20] [w]See Eph. 4:1 [x]See 1 Cor. 16:13 [y][ch. 2:2; 1 Cor. 1:10] [z]Jude 3 **28** [a][2 Thess. 1:5] [b]See Acts 14:22 **29** [c]See Matt. 5:12 [b][See ver. 28 above] **30** [d]Col. 1:29; 2:1; 1 Tim. 6:12; 2 Tim. 4:7; [Heb. 10:32] [e]Acts 16:19-40; 1 Thess. 2:2
Chapter 2
1 [f][Rom. 15:30; 2 Thess. 2:16] [g]2 Cor. 13:14 [h]Col. 3:12 **2** [i]John 3:29; 15:11 [j]See Rom. 12:16

3 [k]ch. 1:17 [l]Gal. 5:26 [m][Eph. 5:21]; See Rom. 12:10; Eph. 4:2 **4** [n]See Rom. 15:2 **5** [o]Rom. 15:3; See Matt. 11:29 **6** [p]See John 1:1 [q]See 2 Cor. 4:4 [r]John 5:18; 10:33; [John 14:28] **7** [s]2 Cor. 8:9; 13:4; See Mark 9:12 [t]See Isai. 42:1; Matt. 20:28 [u]Rom. 8:3; Gal. 4:4; See John 1:14 **8** [v]Heb. 5:8; [Matt. 26:39; John 10:18; Rom. 5:19] [w]Heb. 12:2 **9** [x]John 10:17; [Isai. 52:13; 53:12; Heb. 2:9] [y]See Matt. 28:18 [z]Acts 2:33

[1] Greek *Only behave as citizens worthy* [2] Or *which was also in Christ Jesus* [3] Greek *bondservant*

1:27 one spirit . . . one mind. Paul is appealing for unity among the believers.

striving. Paul urges readers not to break under the pressure of opposition, but instead to exert pressure of their own. This means proclaiming the gospel they have believed (Eph. 1:13), and living worthy of it.

1:28–30 Paul offers the Philippian believers four assurances. (a) Their courage in the face of opposition is a sign of the divine judgment facing the persecutors (2 Thess. 1:5–10). (b) Their courage is also a sign of the believers' own salvation in the full, redemptive sense (Rom. 1:16; 13:11). (c) Suffering for Christ is an honor given by God (3:10). (d) Paul shares in their struggle (vv. 7–26; Acts 16:19–24; 1 Thess. 2:2), and his example can encourage them just as it does "the brothers" (v. 14).

2:1–4 The poetic quality of these verses makes Paul's words especially forceful. The fourfold appeal of v. 1 (note the repeated phrase ". . . any") is the basis for the exhortations of vv. 2–4.

2:1 encouragement in Christ. In their union with the Savior they find encouragement to pursue unity with each other. To follow Christ's example, they must first be in Christ (cf. v. 5).

comfort from love. Believers are encouraged because Christ loves them (Gal. 2:20), and because they love Christ and one another (v. 2).

participation in the Spirit. This phrase may also be rendered "fellowship produced by the Spirit."

2:2 of the same mind . . . same love . . . full accord . . . one mind. The accent on unity is strong (cf. 1:27).

2:3 rivalry. Pride is competitive by nature and tries to lift a person above others, so promoting conflicts rather than harmony (vv. 2, 14; 1:27). By contrast, humility accepts a place of service, with concern for the needs and interests of others (v. 4). Love (v. 2) is essential for humility (1:9; 1 Cor. 13:4, 5).

2:5 This verse connects the exhortations (vv. 1–4) to the hymn (vv. 6–11). Addressing the pride that lies at the root of the Philippians' discord (1:27–2:4), Paul points to Christ as the supreme example of humility. But Christ is not only an example (Rom. 15:1–3; 2 Cor. 10:1); He is first of all Lord and Savior (v. 11; 3:20).

2:6–11 This "hymn to Christ" may be divided into six stanzas. The first three (vv. 6–8) celebrate Christ's humiliation, the last three (vv. 9–11) His exaltation.

2:6 in the form of God. The word "form" refers to the underlying reality and not to appearance only. Jesus' being in "the form of God" means that He is divine.

not . . . grasped. This figure of speech means that something desirable was already possessed. Jesus was not trying to become God, and did not cling to the privileges that were always His.

2:7 made himself nothing. Lit. "emptied Himself." Christ is not said to have removed from Himself His identity as God. The phrase means that He humbled Himself, relinquishing His heavenly status, not His divine being. The nature of His self-emptying is defined in three phrases that follow ("taking . . . being born . . . being found"). See "The Humanity of Jesus" at 2 John 7.

a servant. That is, a slave. This language vividly expresses Christ's willingness to deprive Himself of His exalted status (v. 6 note).

the likeness of men. Christ is truly human. "Likeness" means more than similarity. In order to die (v. 8), He had to be completely human. At the same time, Paul makes a distinction between Christ and other human beings. Unlike them, He has no sin (2 Cor. 5:21). And regarding His divine nature He remains transcendent over created reality; He cannot cease to be a heavenly being even in His humiliation.

2:8 human form. Christ's appearance as a man was not an illusion. He revealed Himself through a complete and genuine human nature united with His divine nature in one Person, who is both human and divine.

he humbled himself. The language here is parallel to the phrase "made himself nothing" in v. 7. Each act occurs by the free exercise of Christ's own will.

obedient. Submission to the Father's will (Heb. 10:5–9) is more significant for the One who is equal with the Father (v. 6) than for anyone else. Paul's words embrace Christ's whole lifetime of obedience, while emphasizing that the supreme expression of obedience was His death.

a cross. The accent is on Christ's willingness to suffer the most shameful

stowed on him [a]the name that is above
every name, 10 so that at the name of Jesus
[b]every knee should bow, [c]in heaven and on
earth and under the earth, 11 and [d]every
tongue confess that Jesus Christ is [e]Lord,
to the glory of God the Father.

Lights in the World

12 Therefore, my beloved, [f]as you have
always [g]obeyed, so now, not only as in my
presence but much more in my absence,
work out your own salvation with fear and
trembling, 13 for [h]it is God who works in
you, both to will and to work for [i]his good
pleasure.

14 Do all things [j]without grumbling or
[k]questioning, 15 that you may be blameless
and innocent, [l]children of God [m]without
blemish [n]in the midst of [o]a crooked and
twisted generation, among whom you
shine [p]as lights in the world, 16 holding fast
to [q]the word of life, so that in [r]the day of
Christ [s]I may be proud that [t]I did not run
in vain or labor in vain. 17 Even if I am to be
[u]poured out as a drink offering upon [v]the
sacrificial offering of your faith, I am glad
and rejoice with you all. 18 Likewise you
also should be glad and rejoice with me.

Timothy and Epaphroditus

19 I hope in the Lord Jesus [w]to send
Timothy to you soon, so that I too may be
cheered by news of you. 20 For I have no
one [x]like him, who will be genuinely concerned for your welfare. 21 They all [y]seek
their own interests, not those of Jesus
Christ. 22 But you know Timothy's[1] [z]proven
worth, how [a]as a son[2] with a father [b]he has
served with me in the gospel. 23 I hope
therefore to send him just as soon as I see
how it will go with me, 24 and [c]I trust in the
Lord that shortly I myself will come also.

9 [a]Eph. 1:21; Heb. 1:4; [Acts :5:41] **10** [b]Isai. 45:23; Rom. 14:11 [c][Rev. 5:3, 13]; See Eph. 1:10 **11** [d][Rom. 10:9; 1 Cor. 12:3] [e][Rom. 14:9]; See John 13:13 **12** [f][ch. 1:5; 4:15] [g]Heb. 5:9; [2 Cor. 10:5; 1 Pet. 1:2] **13** [h]1 Cor. 12:6; [Heb. 13:21]; See 1 Cor. 15:10 [i][1 Tim. 2:4] **14** [j]1 Pet. 4:9 [k]1 Tim. 2:8 **15** [l][Matt. 5:45; Eph. 5:1] [m]Jude 24 [n]1 Pet. 2:12 [o]See Deut. 32:5 [p]Matt. 5:14, 16; [Tit. 2:10] **16** [q][Acts 5:20] [r]See 1 Cor. 1:8 [s]See 2 Cor. 1:14 [t]Gal. 2:2; 1 Thess. 3:5; [Gal. 4:11] **17** [u][1 John 3:16]; See 2 Cor. 12:15 [v][Rom. 15:16] **19** [w][1 Cor. 4:17; 1 Thess. 3:2] **20** [x][1 Cor. 16:10] **21** [y][2 Tim. 3:2]; See 1 Cor. 10:24 **22** [z]2 Cor. 2:9 [a]1 Cor. 4:17; 1 Tim. 1:2; 2 Tim. 1:2 [b][2 Tim. 3:10] **24** [c][ch. 1:25; Philem. 22]

[1] Greek *his* [2] Greek *child*

and painful of deaths, rather than on the atoning significance of the event (cf. Rom. 3:21–26).

2:9 Therefore God. The Father's act is a direct response to Christ's obedience.

highly exalted him. Christ is restored to the glorious status He had at the beginning but voluntarily relinquished for a time in order to become a human being (John 16:28; Heb. 2:9, 14).

2:10 at the name of Jesus. This may mean "the name belonging to Jesus," i.e., "Lord" (v. 11). Paul more likely means that the utterance of the name "Jesus" is the signal that "every knee should bow" to offer Him worship and acclaim Him Lord.

2:11 Lord. Christ's humility is His glory (cf. Matt. 23:12). The "name that is above every name" (v. 9) is "Lord." In the Septuagint (the Greek translation of the Old Testament), God's name is represented by the title "Lord" (Greek *kyrios*). Christ is now acclaimed to be what He has always been, the true God (1 John 5:20). The ascription of praise embraces both the humanity ("Jesus") and the deity ("Lord") of Christ; He is worshiped as the God-Man. See "Jesus Christ, God and Man" at John 1:14.

God the Father. Jesus Christ is the Son of the Father. So united are the Persons of the Godhead that the act of worshiping the Son glorifies the Father. Although he does so elsewhere (Rom. 8:3; Gal. 4:4), Paul does not refer to Jesus as the Son of God in Philippians.

2:12 Therefore. On the basis of Christ's supreme example, Paul resumes his appeal. The apostle's presence encourages the Philippians to obey, but the basic motivation is from "God who works" in them (v. 13), and their obedience will flourish in Paul's absence as well (1:27).

your own salvation. As in 1:28, this is salvation in the full, redemptive sense with particular stress on the sanctification of the believer. The sanctifying process calls for obedience to the exhortation of vv. 1–5. See "Sanctification: The Spirit and the Flesh" at 1 Cor. 6:11.

fear and trembling. This is awe and reverence rather than panic and alarm. The right emotions are stirred by the presence of God (v. 13), and not by questions or doubts about eternal security.

2:13 God who works in you. The use of human effort (v. 12), far from violating God's will, is just what He commands for achieving His saving purpose (Eph. 2:8–10). Having invoked the example of Christ, Paul reassures the Philippians that they do not will and work on their own, but their wills and their actions are the very arenas where God's own power is working (4:13; 1 Thess. 2:13).

2:14 without grumbling or questioning. The Philippians must not imitate the ancient Israelites (Ex. 15:24; 16:7–9; 1 Cor. 10:10). Note also the allusion in v. 15 to Deut. 32:5. The Philippians may well have been guilty of grumbling against church leaders, as the Israelites did against Moses (v. 29; 1 Thess. 5:12, 13).

2:15 that you may be. The corporate witness of a united church is in view.

blameless and innocent . . . without blemish. The meanings of these terms overlap considerably. Paul describes the quality of life required of "children of God." Such persons will "shine as lights in the world," in marked contrast to their "crooked and twisted" contemporaries, but offering hope to them at the same time (cf. Matt. 5:14–16; Acts 2:40).

2:16 holding fast. Paul is concerned with the Philippians' own fidelity to the gospel of Jesus Christ (1:27; 2:1–5).

the word of life. This refers to both the gospel and the ethical teachings founded on it (1:27; 4:8, 9).

I may be proud. Paul's pride on the "day of Christ" (1:10; cf. 1:6) will be the Philippians' spiritual growth rather than his own (1:9–11).

2:17 if I am to be poured out. Paul here refers not to his present suffering, but to the possibility that he will die as a martyr.

drink offering. A libation normally of wine, not blood, that accompanied sacrifices.

sacrificial offering of your faith. The Philippians' gifts to Paul (4:10–20).

I am glad and rejoice. For Paul, suffering can cause joy to flourish. It is to be the same for the Philippians (v. 18).

2:21 their own. This verse echoes the same thought as v. 4. Timothy's life is a model of the humility to which Paul calls his readers, and an image of Christ's own humility (vv. 5–11).

2:22 as a son with a father. Timothy worked closely with Paul for Christ; both are His servants (1:1). As Christ's servant, Timothy "will be genuinely concerned" for the welfare of others (v. 20).

2:23 to send him. Amid difficult circumstances (1:29, 30), perhaps including a forthcoming trial, Paul needs a person of Timothy's character. In vv. 23, 24 Paul echoes the confidence expressed in 1:19–26.

2:24 in the Lord. The plans concerning both Timothy and Paul are submitted to the divine will (v. 19).

25 I have thought it necessary to send to
you [d]Epaphroditus my brother and fellow
worker and [e]fellow soldier, and your messenger and [f]minister to my need, 26 for he
has been longing for you all and has been
distressed because you heard that he was
ill. 27 Indeed he was ill, near to death. But
God had mercy on him, and not only on
him but on me also, lest I should have sorrow upon sorrow. 28 I am the more eager to
send him, therefore, that you may rejoice at
seeing him again, and that I may be less
anxious. 29 So [g]receive him in the Lord with
all joy, and [h]honor such men, 30 for he nearly died [i]for the work of Christ, risking his
life [j]to complete what was lacking in your
service to me.

Righteousness Through Faith in Christ

3 Finally, my brothers,[1] [k]rejoice in the
Lord. [l]To write the same things to you
is no trouble to me and is safe for you.
2 Look out for [m]the dogs, look out for
[n]the evildoers, look out for those who
mutilate the flesh. 3 For [o]we are the real circumcision, [p]who worship [q]by the Spirit of
God[2] and [r]glory in Christ Jesus and put no
confidence in the flesh— 4 [s]though I myself
have reason for confidence in the flesh
also. If anyone else thinks he has reason for
confidence in the flesh, I have more: 5 [t]cir-
cumcised on the eighth day, [u]of the people
of Israel, [v]of the tribe of Benjamin, [u]a
Hebrew of Hebrews; as to the law, [w]a
Pharisee; 6 [x]as to zeal, [y]a persecutor of the
church; [z]as to righteousness, under the
law[3] blameless. 7 But [a]whatever gain I had,
[b]I counted as loss for the sake of Christ.
8 Indeed, I count everything as loss because
of [c]the surpassing worth of [d]knowing
Christ Jesus my Lord. For his sake I [e]have
suffered the loss of all things and count
them as rubbish, in order that I may gain
Christ 9 and be found in him, not having [f]a
righteousness of my own that comes from
the law, but [g]that which comes through
faith in Christ, the righteousness from God
that depends on faith— 10 [h]that I may know

25 [d]ch. 4:18 [e]Philem. 2 [f][ch. 4:18] 29 [g]Rom. 16:2 [h]1 Cor. 16:18; 1 Thess. 5:12:13; 1 Tim. 5:17 30 [i][Acts 20:24] [j][ch. 4:10]; See 1 Cor. 16:17 **Chapter 3** 1 [k]ch. 4:4; 1 Thess. 5:16 [l][2 Pet. 1:12] 2 [m]Ps. 22:16, 20; Isai. 56:10, 11; Rev. 22:15; [Gal. 5:15] [n][2 Cor. 11:13] 3 [o]See Rom. 2:29 [p][John 4:23] [q][Gal. 5:25; Jude 20] [r]Rom. 15:17; [Gal. 6:14] 4 [s]2 Cor. 11:18 5 [t]See Gen. 17:12 [u]2 Cor. 11:22 [v]Rom. 11:1 [w]Acts 23:6; 26:5 6 [x]Acts 22:3, 4; Gal. 1:13, 14 [y]See Acts 8:3 [z][ver. 9]

7 [a][Luke 14:33] [b][Heb. 11:26] 8 [c][2 Cor. 5:15] [d]Isai. 53:11; Jer. 9:23, 24; John 17:3; 2 Pet. 1:3 [e]Luke 9:25 (Gk.) 9 [f]Rom. 10:5; [ver. 6] [g]See Rom. 9:30; 1 Cor. 1:30 10 [h][Eph. 4:13]

1 Or *brothers and sisters*; also verses 13, 17 2 Some manuscripts *God in spirit* 3 Greek *in the law*

2:25 Epaphroditus. This fellow worker of Paul, like Timothy, is worthy of honor. Like Timothy and like Jesus Himself, he is a man for others. He obeys Christ by enlisting as a servant to other believers, both the Philippians (4:18) and Paul, for whose sake he risks his life (vv. 26, 27, 30).

2:26 distressed. Such is the attitude of Epaphroditus that he is less concerned about his sickness than about the effect of this news on the Philippians.

3:1 Finally, my brothers. This anticipates the letter's closing exhortations (4:2–9).

rejoice in the Lord. This appeal is repeated in 4:4.

the same things. This refers to what Paul is about to say in vv. 2–21 (cf. v. 18). Here Paul repeats material he had previously communicated, either personally or by letter, that the Philippians might be "safe" against false teaching in the church.

3:2 dogs . . . those who mutilate. Paul's opponents here may be either Christians (as in Galatians) or non-Christians who champion the law of Moses and insist on circumcision as the badge of salvation (cf. Acts 15:1).

3:3 we are the real circumcision. In response to the Judaizers and their mistaken emphasis upon the external physical rite of circumcision, Paul asserts that Christians are the true circumcision, i.e., the spiritual Israel (Gal. 3:6–4:7).

glory in Christ Jesus. This stands in stark contrast to "confidence in the flesh."

flesh. As used by Paul, this term often embraces all that is natural and human. In this verse, however, the physical act of circumcision is probably in view (v. 5; Gal. 6:12–15).

3:4–6 These verses list Paul's sevenfold pedigree under the law.

3:5 the eighth day. Paul was circumcised in accordance with Gen. 17:12.

of Israel. See Rom. 9:3, 4; 11:1.

of the tribe of Benjamin. Paul, formerly Saul of Tarsus, may have been named for King Saul, also from Benjamin (1 Sam. 9:1, 2).

a Pharisee. Paul's life was one of scrupulous obedience to the law, both the Torah and associated Jewish traditions (Acts 22:3; 26:5; Gal. 1:14).

3:6 persecutor of the church. See Acts 9:13, 14; 22:4, 5; 26:9–11; 1 Cor. 15:9; Gal. 1:13, 14.

blameless. This is not a claim of sinlessness (Rom. 7:7–13), but of fidelity to the Old Testament's prescribed way of life. Paul's obedience to the law was honorable, but his resulting "confidence" (the word is repeated three times in vv. 3 and 4) was the worst of sins.

3:7 whatever gain. Paul is obviously not thinking of his transgressions of the law but of his scrupulous obedience to its commands (v. 6).

I counted as loss. This decision is the more meaningful, because it is (at least in part) a virtue that he renounces, perhaps even harder than renouncing vice. Yet as Paul now grasps, the nobler one's lineage and the higher one's attainments, the greater the temptation to pride and self-confidence (Luke 18:9–14; Eph. 2:8, 9). Paul freely discards all sources of self-confidence and personal profit for Christ.

3:8 rubbish. The Greek word is graphic; it means "refuse" and was once translated "dung." Paul flings away in disgust whatever interferes with "the surpassing worth of knowing Christ Jesus my Lord."

3:9–11 Verse 9 speaks of justification, v. 10 of sanctification, and v. 11 of glorification. The sequence of privilege-death-exaltation suggests a connection with 2:6–11.

3:9 not having a righteousness of my own. Paul now recognizes that salvation is based not upon human attainments of obedience to the law, but entirely and exclusively upon "the righteousness from God," given to those united with Christ (Rom. 1:16, 17; 3:21–26).

faith in Christ. Christ is the object of faith (Gal. 2:16), and now that he trusts Christ alone, Paul abandons all reliance on his own credentials (vv. 7, 8). Faith is the instrument, not the ground, of salvation, and Paul declares that we are saved "through faith," never that we are saved "on account of faith." The ground of salvation is the merit of Christ. Faith as the instrument does not provide value of its own but links us to Christ and His merit.

depends on faith. Faith receives God's gift of righteousness (Rom. 3:22;

him and [i]the power of his resurrection, and
[j]may share his sufferings, becoming like
him in his death, 11 that by any means possible I may [k]attain the resurrection from
the dead.

Straining Toward the Goal

12 Not that I have already [l]obtained this
or [m]am already perfect, but I press on to
make it my own, because Christ Jesus has
made me his own. 13 Brothers, I do not consider that I have made it my own. But one
thing I do: [n]forgetting what lies behind and
straining forward to what lies ahead, 14 I
press on toward the goal for [o]the prize of
the upward [p]call of God in Christ Jesus.
15 Let those of us who are [q]mature think
this way, and if in anything [r]you think otherwise, [s]God will reveal that also to you.
16 Only [t]let us hold true to what we have
attained.

17 Brothers, [u]join in imitating me, and
keep your eyes on those who walk [v]accord-
ing to the example you have in us. 18 For
[w]many, of whom I have often told you and
now tell you [x]even with tears, walk as enemies of the cross of Christ. 19 [y]Their end is
destruction, [z]their god is their belly, and
[a]they glory in their shame, with [b]minds set
on earthly things. 20 But [c]our citizenship is
in heaven, and [d]from it we [e]await a Savior,
the Lord Jesus Christ, 21 who will transform
[f]our lowly body [g]to be like his glorious
body, [h]by the power that enables him even
[i]to subject all things to himself.

4 Therefore, my brothers,[1] whom I love
and [j]long for, [k]my joy and [l]crown,
[m]stand firm thus in the Lord, my beloved.

10 [i][Rom. 1:4; 6:5] [j]1 Pet. 4:13; See 2 Cor. 1:5 **11** [k]Acts 26:7 **12** [l][1 Tim. 6:12, 19] [m]Heb. 11:40; 12:23; [Heb. 5:9] **13** [n][Ps. 45:10; Luke 9:62; Heb. 6:1] **14** [o]1 Cor. 9:24 [p][Heb. 3:1; 1 Pet. 5:10]; See Rom. 8:28 **15** [q]1 Cor. 2:6; See Matt. 5:48 [r][Gal. 5:10] [s][John 7:17] **16** [t]Gal. 6:16 **17** [u][ch. 4:9]; See 1 Cor. 4:16 [v]1 Pet. 5:3 **18** [w]See 2 Cor. 11:13 [x][Acts 20:31] **19** [y]2 Cor. 11:15; [2 Thess. 1:9; 2 Pet. 2:1, 3] [z]See Rom. 16:18 [a][Hos. 4:7; 2 Cor. 11:12; Gal. 6:13; Jude 13] [b]Rom. 8:5; Col. 3:2 **20** [c]See Eph. 2:19 [d]Acts 1:11 [e]See 1 Cor. 1:7 **21** [f][1 Cor. 15:43-53] [g][ver. 10; Col. 3:4]; See Rom. 8:29 [h]See Eph. 1:19 [i]1 Cor. 15:28
Chapter 4 1 [j]See ch. 1:8 [k]ch. 1:4; 2:16; See 2 Cor. 1:14 [l]Prov. 16:31; 17:6 [m]ch. 1:27

[1] Or *brothers and sisters*; also verses 8, 21

5:17), and on the ground of this righteousness the verdict of justification is given when a person believes (Rom. 4:3; 5:1; Gal. 3:6). In this way faith and justification occur at the same time, although faith is logically first.

3:10 I may know him. This is Paul's most passionate longing (1:20–23); he speaks not merely of greater mental awareness, but of deepened personal union. The following two clauses explain how knowing Christ is presently experienced.

his resurrection. For Paul, identification with the crucified and risen Christ is fundamental to Christian living. Elsewhere (2 Cor. 4:7, 10, 11), Paul teaches that it is through participation in the sufferings of Christ that the power of Christ's resurrection is manifested in the life of the Christian. This identification with the sufferings of Christ is not exclusively in martyrdom (2:17) but for all of life.

3:11 by any means. Paul recognizes that the believer's perseverance depends on the will and the working of the sovereign God (1:6; 2:13; 3:12–14, 21; cf. Heb. 6:3).

the resurrection. Sharing in Christ's suffering prepares for sharing in His glory at the resurrection from the dead (vv. 20, 21; Rom. 8:17).

3:12 Not that I have already obtained. The prize of salvation in its fullness has not yet been won, a point Paul emphasizes against ideas of perfectionism (cf. 1 Cor. 4:8; 2 Tim. 2:18; 1 John 1:8). Yet the saving process that will be consummated on the day of Christ (1:6, 10) and the resurrection from the dead (3:11) has already begun.

3:14 the goal. The objective of Paul's striving promises a splendid trophy—salvation in all its fullness (cf. 1:28; Rom. 13:11).

the upward call of God. God has already called Paul (Rom. 8:30; Gal. 1:15). It is because "Christ Jesus has made [Paul] his own" (v. 12) that he presses forward toward the goal of life in glory (v. 13).

3:15 those of us who are mature. These words may be a tribute to persons who in fact think and live maturely. Another possibility is that here Paul is speaking ironically to people who consider themselves already "perfect" (v. 12), and whose thinking Paul needs to correct.

think this way. This refers to the teaching of vv. 12–14.

if . . . you think otherwise. These words may reinforce the preceding appeal to agree with Paul, but the repeated phrases ("think this way . . . think") recall 2:1–5 and suggest that the apostle is also concerned that the Philippians agree among themselves.

God will reveal. Whether spiritual discernment and understanding or agreement among believers is in view, the grace of God is necessary (1:9–11). In the meantime, believers' conduct should accord with the degree of insight which God has already granted (v. 16).

3:17 the example. Paul's example is the opposite of what follows in vv. 18, 19. Paul is faithful to the Cross (Gal. 6:14), Christ is his glory (v. 21; cf. v. 3), and his mind is set on heavenly things (vv. 20, 21).

3:18, 19 These verses could describe all sorts of opponents (1 Cor. 1:23), including the Judaizers (vv. 2–6; Gal. 2:15–21). Paul may be thinking especially of persons who conceive of Christ as pure spirit, and who scorn the idea of His bringing salvation by means of the Incarnation and a body of flesh that could die (Col. 1:22). Such persons consider themselves to be living on an exalted spiritual plane, which frees them to enjoy sensual pleasures, whether food ("their god is their belly") or sex ("they glory in their shame"; cf. 1 Cor. 6:9, 10).

3:18 with tears. Paul weeps, not because he fears someone can undo what Christ has done, but because of the destruction in store for opponents of the gospel. This destiny (v. 19) completes the destructive process initiated by their own sin (Rom. 1:18–32; Gal. 6:7, 8).

3:20 our citizenship. Just as Philippi was a Roman colony (Acts 16:12), the church is a colony of heaven.

we await. This anticipation is a counterpart to the longing of 1:23. All other instances of this verb in Paul's epistles have a similar focus (Rom. 8:19, 23, 25; 1 Cor. 1:7; Gal. 5:5).

3:21 transform our lowly body. In the face of a contempt for the physical (vv. 18, 19 note), Paul celebrates Christ's transformation of our bodies (cf. 1 Cor. 15:50–53). See "Resurrection and Glorification" at 1 Cor. 15:21.

like his glorious body. Christ Himself rose bodily from the grave, the "firstfruits" of a great harvest (1 Cor. 15:20–23). As the Father vindicated Christ's obedience (2:6–11), so too the believers' faithfulness in affliction will end in the glorious resurrection prepared for them.

subject all things. See 1 Cor. 15:20–28.

4:1 stand firm. Paul may be anticipating the exhortations that follow, especially the difficult ones of vv. 2 and 3. This helps to explain the presence of so many terms of affection in v. 1. The challenge to "stand firm" harks back to 1:27 (where the same command occurs), and rests immediately upon the declaration of hope in 3:20, 21. Paul is thinking of Christ's return when he calls his readers a "joy" and "crown" (1 Thess. 2:19, 20).

Exhortation, Encouragement, and Prayer

2 I entreat Euodia and I entreat Syntyche
to [n]agree in the Lord. 3 Yes, I ask you also,
true companion,[1] help these women, who
have labored side by side with me in the
gospel together with Clement and the rest
of my fellow workers, [o]whose names are in
the book of life.
4 [p]Rejoice in the Lord always; again I will
say, Rejoice. 5 Let your reasonableness be
known to everyone. [q]The Lord is at hand;
6 [r]do not be anxious about anything, [s]but in
everything by prayer and supplication [t]with
thanksgiving let your requests be made
known to God. 7 And [u]the peace of God,
[v]which surpasses all understanding, will
guard your hearts and your minds in Christ
Jesus.
8 Finally, brothers, whatever is true,
whatever is honorable, whatever is just,
whatever is pure, whatever is lovely, whatever is commendable, if there is any excellence, if there is anything worthy of praise,
think about these things. 9 What you have
learned and [w]received and heard and seen
[x]in me—practice these things, and [y]the
God of peace will be with you.

God's Provision

10 I rejoiced in the Lord greatly that now
at length [z]you have revived your concern
for me. You were indeed concerned for me,
but you had no opportunity. 11 Not that I
am speaking of being in need, for I have
learned in whatever situation I am to be
[a]content. 12 I know how to be brought low,
and I know how to abound. In any and
every circumstance, I have learned the
secret of facing plenty and [b]hunger, abundance and [c]need. 13 I can do all things
[d]through him who strengthens me.
14 Yet it was kind of you [e]to share my
trouble. 15 And you Philippians yourselves
know that [f]in the beginning of the gospel,
when I left Macedonia, [g]no church entered

2 [n]ch. 2:2
3 [o]See Luke 10:20
4 [p]ch. 3:1
5 [q]See James 5:8
6 [r]See Matt. 6:25 [s][Prov. 16:3] [t]See Rom. 1:8
7 [u][ver. 9; Isai. 26:3; Col. 3:15]; See John 14:27 [v][Eph. 3:19]
9 [w]1 Thess. 4:1 [x][ch. 3:17] [y][ver. 7]; See Rom. 15:33
10 [z][2 Cor. 11:9; ch. 2:30]
11 [a]1 Tim. 6:6, 8; [2 Cor. 9:8; Heb. 13:5]
12 [b]1 Cor. 4:11; 2 Cor. 11:27 [c]2 Cor. 11:9
13 [d][2 Cor. 12:9]; See Eph. 3:16; 1 Tim. 1:12
14 [e][ch. 1:7; Rev. 1:9]
15 [f]ch. 1:5 [g]2 Cor. 11:8, 9

[1] Or *loyal Syzygus*; Greek *true yokefellow*

4:2 I entreat. Paul pleads rather than commands, and by addressing each woman in turn strengthens the appeal.

Euodia . . . Syntyche. These women are mentioned only here in the New Testament. They are courageous fellow workers of Paul and apparently persons of influence in the church.

agree. Paul's main concern is not that they should agree with each other, as is sometimes suggested, but that they should both have the attitude commended in 2:2.

4:3 companion. The Greek word (*syzygos*) may be a proper name.

with Clement. The name occurs only here in the New Testament.

book of life. The names of all God's elect are inscribed in this book (Rev. 3:5; 20:15).

4:4 Rejoice. The theme of joy is prominent in Philippians. The command to rejoice can always be obeyed, even in the midst of conflict, adversity, and deprivation, because joy rests not on favorable circumstances, but "in the Lord." Paul uses repetition to emphasize this truth.

4:5 reasonableness. The Greek word denotes the generous spirit that rises above offenses, or a forbearing spirit, of which Jesus provides the supreme example (2 Cor. 10:1). Such a person does not insist on his rights (2:1–4). Only such persons learn the secret of joy.

The Lord is at hand. This may be understood temporally, looking to Christ's coming as a future event (3:20, 21), and taking hope from this. Or Paul may also be speaking of Christ's abiding presence with those united to Him (1:1).

4:6 do not be anxious about anything. Although the same word is used in 2:20 of a loving concern for others, here it denotes an anxiety that is incompatible with trust in God.

in everything. Paul's language is deliberately all-inclusive; there are no restrictions on applying it.

prayer and supplication with thanksgiving . . . requests. The four terms used here make up two couplets. Paul is not defining separate types of prayers. Rather, the cluster of words shows what importance he attaches to the practice of prayer. Presenting requests in prayer provides an outlet for anxiety (1 Pet. 5:7). Doing so "with thanksgiving" is itself an antidote to worry.

4:7 peace of God. This is the direct answer to the prayer of anxiety. Things that cannot be fully comprehended can nonetheless be peacefully experienced by those who are "in Christ" (1:1; cf. Eph. 3:18, 19).

4:8 Concluding these exhortations, Paul calls his readers to a life of obedience, the right response to the peace of God. The virtues listed are not exhaustive but representative, and they come to expression in countless ways (note the repeated "whatever"). Thinking on such things is not an end in itself, but preparation for purposeful action (v. 9).

true. See Eph. 4:24, 25.

honorable. The Greek word means "worthy of respect."

just. See Titus 1:8.

pure. See 1 Tim. 5:22.

lovely . . . commendable. Terms used only here in the New Testament.

4:9 The Philippians are to be guided both by Paul's teaching and by his example, especially his love for the Philippians (v. 1; 1:3–8; 2:12).

the God of peace. An even richer promise than "the peace of God" (v. 7). Its fulfillment depends on obedience.

4:10–20 Paul returns to a theme of ch. 1—the Philippians' partnership in the gospel (1:5), especially their financial support.

4:10 you had no opportunity. Paul adds a qualification, lest they think he is rebuking them.

4:11–13 These verses do not deny the reality of Paul's need, but rather testify that he is content to live both in plenty and in want.

4:13 I can do all things. Relying on Christ's power and following His example (2:5; 3:10), Paul is able to face all circumstances with contentment. He wants to impress the same lesson on his readers (vv. 6, 7, 19).

4:14 The qualifications of vv. 10–13 call for the restatement of Paul's gratitude for their assistance to him in his time of real need (1:17).

4:15, 16 Even before Paul left Macedonia, the Philippians were repeatedly generous to him.

4:15 in the beginning of the gospel. That is, upon the arrival of the gospel in Philippi (1:5).

when I left. Paul left Macedonia to go to Achaia during his second missionary journey (Acts 16:40–18:18).

into partnership with me in giving and
receiving, except you only. **16** Even in
Thessalonica you sent me help for my
needs once and again. **17** [h]Not that I seek
the gift, but I seek [i]the fruit that increases
to your credit.[1] **18** I have received full payment, and more. I am well supplied, [j]hav-
ing received from Epaphroditus the gifts
you sent, [k]a fragrant offering, [l]a sacrifice
acceptable and pleasing to God. **19** And my
God [m]will supply every need of yours [n]ac-
cording to his riches in glory in Christ
Jesus. **20** To [o]our God and Father be [p]glory
forever and ever. Amen.

Final Greetings

21 Greet every saint in Christ Jesus. [q]The
brothers who are with me greet you. **22** [r]All
the saints greet you, especially those of
Caesar's household.

23 [s]The grace of the Lord Jesus Christ be
with your spirit.

17 [h][2 Cor. 9:5] [i]Rom. 1:13; [Tit. 3:14] **18** [j]ch. 2:25 [k]See Gen. 8:21 [l]Heb. 13:16 **19** [m]Ps. 23:1; 2 Cor. 9:8 [n]See Rom. 2:4 **20** [o]Gal. 1:4; 1 Thess. 1:3; 3:11, 13 [p]Gal. 1:5; See Rom. 11:36 **21** [q]Gal. 1:2 **22** [r]2 Cor. 13:13 **23** [s]See Rom. 16:20

1 Or *I seek the profit that accrues to your account*

4:17, 18 As is made emphatically clear in v. 18, Paul is amply supplied and wants to place no further strain on the church's resources. Yet the main cause of Paul's rejoicing (v. 10) is not that his needs have been fully met. Rather he perceives that the Philippians' gifts are an act of worship pleasing to God (Heb. 13:15, 16), and he knows that God will richly bless them in return (2 Cor. 9:6). See "Pleasing God" at 1 Thess. 2:4.

4:19 every need of yours. This refers to material and spiritual needs (vv. 6, 7). The promise is for those who are in Christ Jesus (v. 21; 1:1).

4:21 every saint. This recalls 1:1.

brothers. Here, as elsewhere, fellow-believers of both sexes. Paul frequently addresses the Philippians with this term (1:12; 3:1).

who are with me. See 1:1, 14.

4:22 All the saints greet you. This points to the corporate unity of believers, within a single congregation and among local churches, like Philippi and Rome.

Caesar's household. Not members of the royal family, but servants in the palace, the Roman believers with whom Paul has most contact (1:13).

THE EPISTLE OF PAUL THE APOSTLE TO THE

Colossians

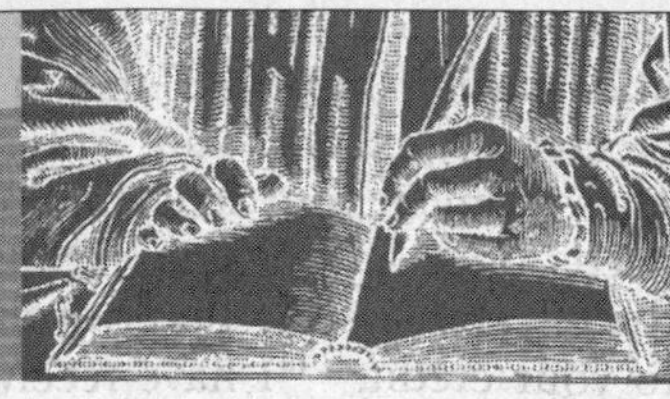

AUTHOR

Colossians was written by Paul the apostle (1:1; 4:18). Though many modern scholars have doubts about Paul's authorship of this letter, compelling grounds for questioning its authenticity are lacking. The language and style are well within the range Paul displays elsewhere and, while aspects of the vocabulary of Colossians are distinctive (e.g., terms such as "fullness," "mystery," "elemental spirits," and "asceticism"), these stem largely from Paul's use of the language of his opponents in order to refute them.

That no hierarchical church order is in evidence, nor any reference to any formal authority in the church, points tellingly to the period when Paul and his associates were themselves at work in the churches they founded.

DATE AND OCCASION

Paul never visited Colossae (2:1). The church there was founded by a Colossian named Epaphras, apparently in the wake of Paul's ministry in Ephesus (A.D. 53–55), from where "all the residents of Asia heard the word of the Lord, both Jews and Greeks" (Acts 19:10). Some five to seven years later, the founder of the Colossian church joined Paul in prison at Rome (Acts 28; Col. 4:12, 13) to tell the apostle of a strange teaching threatening the health of his home church and to remain with Paul to pray for the churches of the Lycus Valley.

In earlier days, Colossae, a city on the Lycus River in southeastern Asia Minor, had been a prosperous and large city, enjoying a thriving wool industry and a strategic location on a main overland trade route between Ephesus one hundred miles to the west and the Euphrates some four hundred miles to the east. In Roman times, however, Colossae had declined in the face of the growth of two sister cities in the Lycus Valley: Laodicea, the district capital ten miles to the west, and Hierapolis, famous for its healing springs some twelve miles to the northwest. In Paul's day, Colossae was a fairly unimportant market town, easily the least significant city to which any of Paul's surviving letters were addressed.

CHARACTERISTICS AND THEMES

The Christians Paul addresses in this letter were struggling with a Greek-influenced form of Jewish philosophy that viewed Christians as still vulnerable to spiritual forces. It was thought that these forces needed to be placated through veneration, through some sort of asceticism of food and drink, and by honoring certain days prescribed in Old Testament ceremonial law. The epistle is designed to help Christians understand that in order for them to gain acceptance before God, they need *Christ only*. God has already accepted them by virtue of their union with Christ in His death and resurrection. While there is a perfection, or maturity, that still stands before them as a goal (1:22, 23, 28), they are already "filled in him," the perfect One (2:10).

INTERPRETIVE DIFFICULTIES

Paul addresses the false teaching at Colossae. Phrygia, the region in south central Asia Minor where Colossae was located, is an area with a peculiar religious history. In ancient times, the region had given birth to the worship of the goddess Cybele, whose cult (renewed during the Roman era) was characterized by ritual cleansing in the blood of a bull, ecstatic states, prophetic rapture, and inspired dancing. In the latter half of the second century A.D., Phrygia became the center of a distorted version of Christianity known as Montanism, a teaching that prized ecstatic and apocalyptic prophecy, freedom from the responsibilities of daily life, and rigorous fasts and penances for ritual purity.

Within a few years of the inception of Christianity among these Phrygians, Epaphras and Paul found that an appetite had emerged for something more than the crucified and risen Christ. It is notoriously difficult to reconstruct the false teaching to which Paul was responding because the letter is less a critique of error than a positive statement of the sufficiency of the person and work of Christ. However, certain features of the false teaching do surface.

It claimed to be a "philosophy" (2:8), a term that often in the Hellenistic age referred not to rational inquiry, but to occult speculations and practices based on a body of tradition.

The teaching appears to have been largely Jewish, as evidenced by the value placed on legal ordinances, food regulations, Sabbath and New Moon observance, and other prescriptions of the Jewish calendar (2:16). Though circumcision is mentioned, it was not necessarily seen as one of the legal requirements (2:11).

The role of angelic spirits was also an important element in this teaching. Three key factors point to this. There is stress on Christ's superiority to and victory over "rulers" and "authorities" (1:16; 2:10, 15).

The phrase "elemental spirits of the world" (2:8, 20; cf. Gal. 4:3) also points to angelic beings. An old and popular line of interpretation views Paul arguing against the basic principle that life with God comes through works-righteousness. However, the letter's implied competition between Christ and spirit-beings suggests a more transcendent and sinister background. The Greek word translated "elemental spirits" was used in this time period to refer to gods of stars and planets, and even to the physical elements (earth, wind, fire, and water) that were thought to control the destiny of men and women. The Phrygian god Cybele and her lover Attis were transformed at some time by popular pagan piety into astral and cosmic powers.

Along this line, even some Jewish thinking merged the angels with astral powers who protect the planets. Moreover, intertestamental Jewish literature envisioned Israel caught between two kingdoms, one good and one evil, that both claimed allegiance. The victory of the good and the overthrow of the evil power was understood to be promised if Israel repented, obeyed fully, and kept the Sabbath perfectly. The Colossians appear to have come under the influence of a combination of Jewish and pagan piety presenting itself as a philosophical system and encouraging submission to these occult astral or cosmic powers.

The role of angels in the Colossian error is evident in the phrase "worship of angels" (2:18). Early Christians knew that there were angels who had been agents at creation and in the giving of the law (Acts 7:53; Gal. 3:19; Heb. 2:2). The false teaching in Colossae had confused the limited and legitimate role of angels as "ministering spirits" (Heb. 1:14), with the larger role attributed to angels in some parts of Judaism, not to mention the astral powers of the Gentiles. As a means of overcoming fear of these astral or cosmic powers, and under the guise of revelations which so-called "philosophers" received in ecstatic states, the Colossians were being urged to become ascetics and to worship angels.

OUTLINE OF COLOSSIANS

I. Introduction (1:1–14)

- A. *Salutation (1:1, 2)*
- B. *Thanksgiving for the Colossians (1:3–8)*
- C. *Intercession for the Colossians (1:9–14)*

II. In Praise of the Son (1:15–23)

- A. *Head over Creation and the Cosmic Powers (1:15–17)*
- B. *Head over Re-creation and Reconciliation (1:18–20)*
- C. *The Purpose and Effect of Reconciliation (1:21–23)*

III. The Purpose of Paul's Ministry and His Interest in the Colossians (1:24–2:7)

IV. The Sufficiency of Christ (2:8–23)

- A. *Not the Emptiness of Human Tradition but Fullness in Christ (2:8–10)*
- B. *Renewal and Victory in Christ (2:11–15)*
- C. *Freedom from the Law and Asceticism (2:16–23)*

V. Life in Christ (3:1–4:6)

- A. *Putting off the Old Humanity, Putting on the New (3:1–17)*
  1. The Basis for Obedience: Union with Christ in His Death and Life (3:1–4)
  2. Death to the Old Humanity (3:5–8)

OUTLINE OF COLOSSIANS (Cont.)

3. New Life in Christ (3:9–14)
4. The Peace, the Word, and the Worship of Christ (3:15–17)

B. Instructions for Christian Living (3:18–4:6)

1. In Social Relationships (3:18–4:1)
2. In Prayer (4:2–4)
3. Among Outsiders to the Faith (4:5, 6)

VI. Final Greetings (4:7–18)

Greeting

1 Paul, [a]an apostle of Christ Jesus [b]by
the will of God, and Timothy [c]our
brother,
2To the [d]saints and faithful brothers[1] in
Christ at Colossae:
[e]Grace to you and peace from God our
Father.

Thanksgiving and Prayer

3[f]We always thank God, the Father of
our Lord Jesus Christ, when we pray for
you, **4**since we heard of [g]your faith in
Christ Jesus and of [g]the love that you have
for all the saints, **5**because of [h]the hope
[i]laid up for you in heaven. Of this you have
heard before in [j]the word of the truth, the
gospel, **6**which has come to you, as indeed
[k]in the whole world it is [l]bearing fruit and
growing—as it also does among you, since
the day you [m]heard it and understood [n]the
grace of God in truth, **7**just as you learned
it from [o]Epaphras our beloved [p]fellow servant.[2] He is [p]a faithful minister of Christ on
your[3] behalf **8**and has made known to us
your [q]love in the Spirit.

9And so, [r]from the day we heard, [s]we
have not ceased to pray for you, asking that
[t]you may be filled with the knowledge of
his will in all [u]spiritual wisdom and understanding, **10**so as [v]to walk in a manner worthy of the Lord, [w]fully pleasing to him,
[x]bearing fruit in every good work and
increasing in the knowledge of God.
11[y]May you be strengthened with all power,
according to his glorious might, for [z]all
endurance and patience [a]with joy, **12**[b]giving
thanks[4] to the Father, who has qualified
you[5] to share in [c]the inheritance of the
saints in light. **13**He [d]has delivered us from
[e]the domain of darkness and transferred us
to [f]the kingdom of [g]his beloved Son, **14**[h]in
whom we have redemption, the forgiveness
of sins.

Chapter 1
1 [a]See 2 Cor. 1:1 [b]See 1 Cor. 1:1 [c]See 1 Thess. 3:2
2 [d]Eph. 1:1; See Phil. 1:1 [e]Rom. 1:7
3 [f]Eph. 1:15, 16; Philem. 4:5
4 [g]See 1 Thess. 1:3
5 [h]ver. 23; See Acts 23:6; Tit. 1:2; Heb. 3:6 [i]2 Tim. 4:8; 1 Pet. 1:4 [j]See Eph. 1:13
6 [k][ver. 23; Ps. 98:3]; See Matt. 24:14 [l]John 15:5, 16; [Phil. 1:11] [m][Rom. 16:26; Eph. 4:21] [n]See Acts 11:23
7 [o]ch. 4:12; Philem. 23 [p]ch. 4:7
8 [q][Rom. 15:30]
9 [r]ver. 4 [s]2 Thess. 1:11 [t][Eph. 1:17] [u]ch. 4:5; Eph. 1:8; [1 Cor. 12:8]
10 [v][Ps. 1:1, 3]; See Eph. 4:1 [w][2 Cor. 5:9; Eph. 5:10; 1 Thess. 4:1] [x]ver. 6 **11** [y]See Eph. 3:16 [z]Eph. 4:2 [a]See Matt. 5:12 **12** [b]ch. 3:15; Eph. 5:20 [c]See Acts 26:18 **13** [d]1 Thess. 1:10 [e]Luke 22:53; Eph. 6:12 [f]2 Pet. 1:11 [g][Eph. 1:6] **14** [h]See Eph. 1:7

[1] Or *brothers and sisters*. The plural Greek word *adelphoi* (translated "brothers") refers to siblings in a family. In New Testament usage, depending on the context, *adelphoi* may refer either to men or to both men and women who are siblings (brothers and sisters) in God's family, the church [2] Greek *fellow bondservant* [3] Some manuscripts *our* [4] Or *patience, with joy giving thanks* [5] Some manuscripts *us*

1:1, 2 Regarding Paul's salutations, see note Rom. 1:1.

1:1 Timothy. See Introduction to 1 Timothy: Date and Occasion.

1:4 faith in Christ Jesus. In the face of a teaching circulating in Colossae that questioned whether Christ alone could be sufficient, Paul reminds the readers through his prayer of thanksgiving that what they already have "in Christ" is enough.

1:5 because of the hope. Faith, hope, and love, are central to Paul's understanding of the Christian life (Rom. 5:2–5; 1 Cor. 13:13; Gal. 5:5, 6; 1 Thess. 1:3; 5:8; cf. Heb. 10:22–24). He treats them as gifts of God rather than as virtues produced by the believers themselves. Paul emphasizes the sovereignty of God in salvation and the believers' security in their relationship with Christ (Eph. 1:4; 2:8).

1:6 in the whole world. See note on v. 23.

1:7 Epaphras. See Introduction: Date and Occasion.

1:10 fully pleasing to him. See "Pleasing God" at 1 Thess. 2:4.

1:12–14 Paul expresses his gratitude for the Colossians' good beginning (vv. 3–8) and encourages them to recognize that their heavenly Father has decisively rescued them from the powers of darkness. They can therefore be thankful for the redemption they enjoy (2:7; 3:17; 4:2).

1:12 qualified you. The false teaching in Colossae resulted in cowardice before the pagan supernatural beings thought to have the power to disqualify even believers from life with God (2:16, 18, 20–23). This accounts for Paul's use of "qualified" here—no power in the universe can question the credentials of those who are "in Christ" (vv. 2, 4).

1:13 delivered us. This language recalls God's rescue of Israel first from slavery in Egypt and then from captivity in Babylon. Paul envisions humanity outside of Christ as being helplessly under the "domain of darkness," the evil rule of Satan (cf. Eph. 2:1–3; 6:11). Believers are rescued from this world order (Gal. 1:4) and brought under the dominion and protection of God's Son. The image of light is appropriate here, for elsewhere Paul speaks of the light of the gospel shining in the darkness and penetrating the blindness of those who are perishing (2 Cor. 3:15; 4:4–6; 6:14; Eph. 5:8–14; Phil. 2:15; 1 Thess. 5:5).

his beloved Son. Note the portrayal of Jesus in the Synoptic Gospels as God's beloved son (Matt. 3:17; 17:5; Mark 1:11; 9:7; Luke 3:22), and the rich Old Testament background out of which the designation arises (Deut. 18:15; Ps. 2:7; Is. 42:1).

1:14 redemption. In Rom. 8:23 Paul speaks of a bodily redemption still to be anticipated. Here redemption is understood as the forgiveness of sins and is something that has already been given (note the "once . . . now" pattern of vv. 21, 22; cf. 2:13, 17, 20; 3:9, 10). Compare Paul's approach to the Corinthians, who overemphasized the "already" of salvation and neglected what is yet to come (1 Cor. 4:8–13; ch. 15).

the forgiveness of sins. See 2:13 and note.

The Preeminence of Christ

15 [i]He is the image of [j]the invisible God,
[k]the firstborn of all creation. 16 For by[1] him
all things were created, [l]in heaven and on
earth, visible and invisible, whether
[m]thrones or [n]dominions or rulers or authorities—all things were created [o]through
him and for him. 17 And [p]he is before all
things, and in him all things [q]hold together. 18 And [r]he is the head of the body, the
church. He is [s]the beginning, [t]the firstborn
from the dead, that in everything he might
be preeminent. 19 For [u]in him all the [v]full-
ness of God was pleased to dwell, 20 and
[w]through him to reconcile to himself all
things, whether on earth or in heaven,
[x]making peace [y]by the blood of his cross.
21 [z]And you, who once were alienated
and hostile in mind, [a]doing evil deeds, 22 he
has now reconciled [b]in his body of flesh by
his death, [c]in order to present you holy and
blameless and [d]above reproach before him,
23 [e]if indeed you continue in the faith,
[f]stable and steadfast, not shifting from [g]the
hope of the gospel that you heard, which
has been proclaimed [h]in all creation[2] under
heaven, [i]and of which I, Paul, became a
minister.

Paul's Ministry to the Church

24 Now [j]I rejoice in my sufferings for your
sake, and in my flesh [k]I am filling up [l]what
is lacking in Christ's afflictions [m]for the

15 [i]See 2 Cor. 4:4 [j]See 1 Tim. 1:17 [k][Ps. 89:27]; See Rom. 8:29 **16** [l]Eph. 1:10 [m][Ezek. 10:1] [n]Eph. 1:21 [o]Rom. 11:36; 1 Cor. 8:6 **17** [p][John 8:58]; See John 1:1 [q][Heb. 1:3] **18** [r]See Eph. 1:22, 23 [s]Rev. 3:14 [t]Acts 26:23; 1 Cor. 15:20; Rev. 1:5 **19** [u]ch. 2:9 [v]See John 1:16 **20** [w]See 2 Cor. 5:18; Eph. 1:10 [x]See Eph. 2:14 [y][Eph. 2:13]

21 [z]See Eph. 2:1, 2, 12 [a][Tit. 1:16] **22** [b][Rom. 7:4] [c]Jude 24; See Eph. 1:4; 5:27 [d]1 Cor. 1:8 **23** [e]See John 15:4 [f]ch. 2:7; Eph. 3:17 [g]ver. 5, 6 [h]Mark 16:15; [Acts 2:5] [i]See 2 Cor. 3:6 **24** [j]See 2 Cor. 7:4 [k][2 Tim. 1:8; 2:10] [l]See 2 Cor. 1:5 [m][Eph. 4:12]

1 That is, by means of; or *in* 2 Or *to every creature*

1:15–20 Paul breaks into a doxology to the grandeur and glory of Jesus Christ. Many believe Paul is appropriating an early Christian hymn. By pointing to the supremacy of Christ both in creation (vv. 15–17) and in redemption (vv. 18–20), he points out what was missing in the false teaching at Colossae—an adequate view of the person of Christ. By doing this in a kind of hymn, he invites the readers to worship the Son of God.

1:15 image of the invisible God. For Paul, belief in the deity of Christ (Rom. 9:5; Phil. 2:6; Titus 2:13) is practical. Since He is by nature God, Christ reveals the God who is otherwise invisible (1 Tim. 1:17; 6:16). The thought is also found in John 1:1–18 and Heb. 1:3. Calvin observes that "we must be careful not to look for Him anywhere else, for apart from Christ whatever offers itself to us in the name of God will turn out to be an idol" (*Commentary* on Col. 1:15).

the firstborn of all creation. Paul is not saying that the Son was the first created being (v. 17 note). In the Old Testament, a firstborn son would be the principal heir of an estate (Deut. 21:17; cf. Ex. 4:22; Ps. 89:27). Used of Christ, the term "firstborn" means that He has such honor and dignity, not that He was the oldest child in a family. Christ is especially loved by His Father (v. 13), and all things were created in Him, by Him, and for Him (vv. 16, 17).

1:16 all things were created through him and for him. Because He is both agent and goal of creation, Christ is Lord of all that is, even of the angelic hierarchy which the Colossians think they must placate or revere.

1:17 A strong restatement of the temporal priority and universal significance of Christ, this verse makes explicit what was implicit in v. 16: Christ existed before *all* creation. He is Himself not created. Nor can it be said, as followers of Arius (c. A.D. 250–336) later maintained, that "there was a time when he was not." The thought that Jesus is the moment-by-moment sustainer and unifying power of the universe is echoed in Heb. 1:2, 3.

1:18 head of the body, the church. Using this theme of the second section of the hymn, Paul explains the image in Eph. 1:21–23, and works out its implications in Eph. 4:15 and 5:23.

the beginning, the firstborn from the dead. Jesus' resurrection marks the beginning of a new creation (3:10 note; 2 Cor. 5:17). As the first to rise from the dead, Christ inaugurates the new age anticipated by the Old Testament prophets (Acts 2:29–36; 13:32–35) and founds a new humanity in Himself to replace the old humanity in Adam. His own resurrection is an anticipation and a guarantee of the resurrection that all His brothers and sisters will enjoy (Rom. 8:29; 1 Cor. 15:20–28; Heb. 1:6; 12:23).

that . . . preeminent. Without detracting from the glory the pre-existent Son already had with the Father, the New Testament teaches that Christ's resurrection marks out for Him a new and higher standing, and wins for Him an even greater name (Acts 13:33, 34; Rom. 1:4; Eph. 1:20–23; Phil. 2:1–11; Heb. 1:4, 5). By virtue of His resurrection from the dead, Jesus Christ is Lord of the universe that was created by Him, that He has always sustained, and which now He has redeemed.

1:19 See 2:9.

1:20 The high point of the hymn. Humankind's fall into sin brought with it the corruption of all creation, seen and unseen (Gen. 3; Rom. 5:12; 8:20; Eph. 2:2; 6:12). Through Christ's incarnation and atoning death, God's righteousness is satisfied (Rom. 3:21–26), peace between God and humankind is restored (2 Cor. 5:17–21), the eventual glorification of the created order is assured (Rom. 8:18–21), and the rebellious spirit beings have their powers limited (2:15 note).

1:21–23 Having considered Christ's majestic role in creation and in the reconciliation and pacification of the universe, Paul returns to the Colossians themselves. Once God's enemies and alienated from His life, they have now been given peace with God (Rom. 5:1, 2).

1:21 alienated . . . evil deeds. The text may be taken as indicating either that mental alienation from God has a behavioral root or that mental alienation is expressed behaviorally. Paul's point is that mind and will cooperate in their rebellion against God.

1:22 Christ's death in the flesh means that the reconciliation God has accomplished is not merely a matter of the universal pacification of the hostile powers; it brings with it the personal renewal and purification of those who grasp and adhere to the gospel (2:13; Rom. 5:6–11; Eph. 2:4–10).

1:23 continue in the faith . . . not shifting from the hope. Saving faith is persevering and enduring faith (v. 11), anchored in hope (v. 5). But contrary to the opponents' teaching, true faith and hope are nowhere else than in Christ. This relationship with Christ is confirmed by faith and hope, rather than by rigorous ascetic disciplines.

proclaimed in all creation. Paul can speak of one of the conditions of the consummation of the ages, the worldwide proclamation of the gospel (v. 6; Matt. 24:14; Mark 13:10), as already having been completed. Paul here is using hyperbole (literary exaggeration for emphasis). Still, by aiming his ministry at the urban centers of the Roman Empire, he understood himself to be reaching the civilized world (Acts 19:10; Rom. 15:18–25).

1:24–2:5 Paul has reminded the Colossians of the cosmic scope of Christ's lordship (1:15–20) and the way Christ's redemptive work has come to bear on their lives (1:21, 23). Now he turns to his own role in God's redemptive plan and the relationship he hopes to establish between himself and the Colossians, most of whom he has not met, in order to woo them from the captivity of the so-called "philosophy" in their midst (2:8).

1:24 filling up what is lacking. Given the context of this passage, which stresses the total sufficiency of Christ, as well as what he says elsewhere

sake of his body, that is, the church, 25 [n]of
which I became a minister according to
[o]the stewardship from God that was given
to me for you, to make the word of God
fully known, 26 [p]the mystery hidden for ages
and generations but now revealed to his
saints. 27 [q]To them God chose to make
known how great among the Gentiles are
[r]the riches of the glory of [p]this mystery,
which is Christ in you, [s]the hope of glory.
28 Him we proclaim, warning everyone and
teaching everyone with all wisdom, that
[t]we may present everyone [u]mature in
Christ. 29 For this [v]I toil, [w]struggling [x]with
all his energy that he powerfully works
within me.

2 For I want you to know [y]how great a
[w]struggle I have for you and for those
at Laodicea and for all who have not seen
me face to face, 2 that [z]their hearts may
be encouraged, being [a]knit together in
love, to reach all the riches of full assurance
of understanding and the knowledge of
[b]God's mystery, which is Christ, 3 [c]in
whom are hidden all the treasures of wisdom and knowledge. 4 I say this in order
[d]that no one may delude you with plausible arguments. 5 For [e]though I am absent in
body, yet I am with you in spirit, rejoicing
to see your [f]good order and [g]the firmness
of your faith in Christ.

Alive in Christ

6 [h]Therefore, as you received Christ Jesus
the Lord, so walk in him, 7 [i]rooted and
[j]built up in him and [k]established in the
faith, just [l]as you were taught, abounding
[m]in thanksgiving.

8 See to it that no one takes you captive
by [n]philosophy and [o]empty deceit, according to [p]human tradition, according to the
[q]elemental spirits[1] of the world, and not
according to Christ. 9 For [r]in him the whole
fullness of deity dwells [s]bodily, 10 and [t]you
have been filled in him, who is [u]the head of
all rule and authority. 11 In him also [v]you
were circumcised with a circumcision
made without hands, by [w]putting off the

25 [n]ver. 23 [o]See Eph. 3:2
26 [p]Eph. 3:9; See Rom. 16:25, 26
27 [q][ch. 2:2] [r]Eph. 1:18; 3:16 [p][See ver. 26 above] [s]1 Tim 1:1
28 [t]See ver. 22-23 [u]See Matt. 5:48
29 [v]1 Tim. 4:10; 1 Cor. 15:10 [w]ch. 4:12; [ch. 2:1] [x]See Eph. 1:19
Chapter 2
1 [y]Phil. 1:30 [w][See ch. 1:29 above]
2 [z]ch. 4:8; Eph. 6:22 [a][ch. 3:14] [b]See ch. 1:27
3 [c]Isai. 11:2; 45:3; 1 Cor. 1:24, 30; 2:6, 7; [Luke 11:49; Eph. 1:8]
4 [d]Rom. 16:18; [Eph. 5:6; 2 Pet. 2:3]
5 [e]1 Cor. 5:3 [f]1 Cor. 14:40 [g]1 Pet. 5:9

6 [h]ch. 1:10; 1 Thess. 4:1 **7** [i]Eph. 3:17 [j]Acts 20:32; Eph. 2:20; See 1 Cor. 3:9 [k]Heb. 13:9 [l]Eph. 4:21 [m]ch. 4:2; Eph. 5:20 **8** [n][1 Tim.6:20] [o]Eph. 5:6 [p]See Matt. 15:2 [q]ver. 20 **9** [r]ch. 1:19; John 1:14 [s][ver. 17] **10** [t]Eph. 3:19 [u]See Eph. 1:21, 22 **11** [v][Eph. 2:11]; See Rom. 2:29 [w]ver. 15; ch. 3:9

[1] Or *elementary principles*; also verse 20

(e.g., Rom. 3:21–26; 2 Cor. 5:17–21), Paul does not mean that Christ's saving work on the cross is deficient in some respect. Rather, because the church is called to suffer for Christ (2 Cor. 4:7–12; 1 Thess. 3:2–4), there is a divinely appointed requisite of suffering to be endured by Christians. Paul may also have in view here the sufferings which will accompany the endtimes (Matt. 24:21, 22), a period ushered in by the death and resurrection of Christ (Rom. 13:11–14; 1 Cor. 7:29). This also explains the reference to Paul's suffering for the sake of the church (Eph. 3:13; 2 Tim. 2:10). As a servant of the gospel, Paul rejoices in his opportunity to participate in the sufferings of God's people. The passage does not mean that the church is a continuing incarnation of Christ whose members by suffering add saving merit beyond what Christ achieved.

1:26 mystery. In contemporary pagan religion the "mysteries" were secret insights given (usually for a fee) to a select, initiated few. With some irony Paul uses the term for the revelation God has made available freely to the nations (v. 27; 2:2; 4:3; Eph. 1:9; 3:3, 4, 9; 5:32; 6:19). In Paul's use, "mystery" refers to what once was hidden, but is now being revealed.

hidden. God's saving purpose for Gentiles was largely hidden from them prior to the coming of Christ. Previous generations were allowed to "walk in their own ways" (Acts 14:16; cf. Rom. 1:24–32; Eph. 2:12). The Old Testament revealed in shadows, signs, and hints that God would personally take up residence in His people (v. 27; Ezek. 36:25–27), and that He would create a new humanity uniting Gentiles and Jews through the Messiah (Gen. 12:3; Zech. 9:9, 10; Eph. 3:5, 6 notes).

2:1 Laodicea. See Introduction: Date and Occasion. Though Paul had not visited this church either, he expected this letter to be read there (4:16).

2:6, 7 A good example of Paul's pastoral style, in which the "ought" of the Christian life builds upon the "is" of having received the gift of life in Christ. Although Paul sometimes describes the good news of Jesus Christ as a tradition that can be received, his use of "tradition" does not refer to human custom or historical opinion but to the handing over of a divine message from God (1 Cor. 11:2; 2 Thess. 3:6). Because the Colossians will continue on the basis of what they have already come to know of Christ, their further obedience will be grounded in thankfulness (3:17) rather than in frustrated, anxious guilt (3:1 note).

2:8 the elemental spirits of the world. See Introduction: Interpretive Difficulties.

2:9, 10 A stunning rebuttal of the false teachers who encourage submission to the "elemental spirits" (v. 8) as a means of overcoming fears of not being acceptable before God. As outlined in the following verses, the "fullness" of God that the false teachers pretend to offer resides in Christ and is obtained only through Him (1:19, 20). See "Jesus Christ, God and Man" at John 1:14.

2:11 circumcision. It is often thought that Paul mentions circumcision at this point because the false teachers in Colossae were commending it, much as those in Galatia were. However, in this letter there is no direct argument made against circumcision, as there is in Galatians. It is better to think of Paul as introducing the topic to show that something of what the Colossians are promised by the false teachers—power over the flesh (v. 23)—is already theirs in their relationship with Christ.

As the initiating rite of the old covenant, circumcision had signified cutting away sin, undergoing a change of heart, and being included in the household of faith (Deut. 10:16; 30:6; Jer. 4:4; 9:25, 26; Ezek. 44:7, 9). Dramatically, Paul says that in their baptism into Christ and into His body, these Gentiles have already been circumcised. Baptism is "the circumcision of Christ," and it signifies the washing away of sin, personal renewal by the Spirit of God, and membership in the body of Christ (cf. v. 13; Acts 2:38; Rom. 6:4; 1 Cor. 12:13; Titus 3:5; 1 Pet. 3:21). The passage makes an important point about the unity of the covenant of grace in both the Old and New Testament era: Gentile believers are not expected to follow the old covenant *mode* of identification with God and His people (Acts 15). But their faith in Christ has nevertheless made them as much children of Abraham as if they were ethnic Jewish believers (Rom. 2:28, 29; Gal. 3:26–29; Phil. 3:3). Baptism is not identical to circumcision, but it corresponds to it in essence (Rom. 4:11) and has replaced it as the sign of the covenant.

body of the flesh, by the circumcision of Christ, 12 [x]having been buried with him in baptism, in which [y]you were also raised with him through faith in [z]the powerful working of God, [z]who raised him from the dead. 13 [a]And you, who were dead in your trespasses and the uncircumcision of your flesh, God [b]made alive together with him, having forgiven us all our trespasses, 14 by [c]canceling [d]the record of debt that stood against us with its legal demands. This he set aside, nailing it to the cross. 15 [w]He disarmed the rulers and authorities[1] and [e]put them to open shame, by [f]triumphing over them in him.[2]

Let No One Disqualify You

16 Therefore let no one [g]pass judgment on you [h]in questions of food and drink, or with regard to [i]a festival or [j]a new moon or a Sabbath. 17 [k]These are a shadow of the things to come, but [l]the substance belongs to Christ. 18 Let no one [m]disqualify you, [n]insisting on asceticism and worship of angels, [o]going on in detail about visions,[3] [p]puffed up without reason by [q]his sensuous mind, 19 and [r]not [s]holding fast to the Head, from whom the whole body, nourished and knit together through its joints and ligaments, grows with a growth that is from God.

20 If with Christ [t]you died to the [u]elemental spirits of the world, [v]why, as if you were still alive in the world, do you submit to regulations— 21 [w]"Do not handle, Do not taste, Do not touch" 22 ([x]referring to things that all perish as they are used)—according to [y]human precepts and teachings? 23 These have indeed an appearance of wisdom in [z]promoting self-made religion and asceticism and severity to the body, but they are [a]of no value in stopping the indulgence of the flesh.

Put on the New Self

3 [b]If then you have been raised with Christ, seek [c]the things that are above,

12 [x]Rom. 6:4 [y]ch. 3:1; [Rom. 6:5] [z][1 Cor. 6:14]; See Acts 2:24; Eph. 1:19 **13** [a]See Eph. 2:1 [b]See Eph. 2:5 **14** [c]See Acts 3:19 [d]See Rom. 7:4 **15** [w][See ver. 11 above] [e][Gen. 3:15; Ps. 68:18; Isai. 53:12; Matt. 12:29; Luke 10:18; John 12:31; 16:11; Eph. 4:8; Heb. 2:14] [f]Eph. 2:16 **16** [g]Rom. 14:3, 10, 13 [h]Rom. 14:17; Heb. 9:10; See Lev. 11:2 [i]Lev. 23:2; Rom. 14:5 [j][Mark 2:28]; See Num. 28:11 **17** [k]Heb. 8:5; 10:1 [l][ver. 2] **18** [m]1 Cor. 9:24 [n]ver. 28 [o][Ezek. 13:7; 1 Tim. 1:7] [p][Eph. 4:17]

[q][Rom. 8:7] **19** [r]See Eph. 4:15, 16 [s]Rev. 2:13; 3:11 **20** [t]See Rom. 6:2 [u]ver. 8 [v][Gal. 4:9] **21** [w]ver. 16; 1 Tim. 4:3 **22** [x]1 Cor. 6:13 [y]Isai. 29:13; Matt. 15:9; [Tit. 1:14] **23** [z]ver. 18 [a][1 Tim. 4:8]
Chapter 3 **1** [b]ch 2:12 [c][Phil. 3:14]

1 Probably demonic rulers and authorities 2 Or *in it* (that is, the cross) 3 Or *about the things he has seen*

2:13 forgiven us all our trespasses. It is more characteristic of Paul to speak of justification than of forgiveness, and of sin in the singular than of sins in the plural (Rom. 5:12–21). His purpose here may be to emphasize that God has not only overcome sin as a general power, but He has also put away the guilt that stems from particular acts. See "Regeneration: The New Birth" at John 3:3.

2:14 canceling the record of debt. The law is compared to a certificate of indebtedness written in the debtor's own hand. Jesus was born "under the law," subject to its demands and curses (Gal. 4:4). On the cross He was "made . . . to be sin" (2 Cor. 5:21) and endured the law's curse against unrighteousness (Gal. 3:13). In the execution of the death sentence on Jesus when He was nailed to the cross, Paul sees the cancellation of the death warrant that stood against transgressors of the law. The believer is no longer subject to the threat of the law's condemnation.

2:15 put them to open shame. The image is of a conquering Roman general parading his vanquished and humiliated enemies behind his chariot. An invisible cosmic struggle took place at the cross, and the prince of this age was "cast out" (John 12:31), "thrown down to the earth" (Rev. 12:9), and "bound" (Rev. 20:2; see also Matt. 12:29; Luke 10:18). Through Jesus' death for sinners, Satan was robbed of his power to intimidate and control people through the threat of death and eternal separation from God (Ezek. 18; Rom. 5:12; 6:23; Heb. 2:14, 15). The struggle with Satan and his legions will not see its conclusion until the Lord's return in glory (2 Cor. 4:4; Eph. 6:10–18; 1 Pet. 5:8), but the devil's power is broken. As Luther sang, "Lo, his doom is sure." With the ground of their constant accusations taken away, the hostile powers of Satan have lost their advantage forever. See "Demons" at Deut. 32:17.

2:16, 17 In Colossae, the Sabbath was kept and festivals observed in order to placate supernatural powers or angels thought to direct the course of the stars, regulate the calendar, and determine human destiny. This, Paul says, is a form of bondage from which Christ came to liberate men and women.

2:18 worship of angels. This can be taken as a reference to practices found among some Jewish mystics, whose goal was to participate in angelic worship before the throne of God and to attain to ecstatic prayer through asceticism and strict observance of the Torah. In this case, "worship of angels" would mean "worship along with angels." This line of interpretation assumes that the false teachers actually practiced a more-or-less orthodox Judaism and wanted to worship God. But the appearance given by Colossians is that the church was being tempted to worship not God but spirits intermediate between God and humans (Introduction: Interpretive Difficulties).

2:19 To seek the favor of angelic beings is to fail to honor Christ for what He is as the fullness of deity (v. 9; 1:19); and secondly, not to enjoy the totality of the redemption that has been won in His death and resurrection (vv. 10–15; 1:20–22).

Head . . . body. This language looks back at 1:18, and ahead to the way Paul develops the idea of the Christian life under Christ's headship in the context of membership in the church in 3:1–4:6.

2:20 elemental spirits. See Introduction: Interpretive Difficulties; theological note "Christians in the World" on the next page.

2:23 self-made religion. God accepts worship offered according to His will revealed in Scripture, not religious exercises done at the dictate of presumptuous human whim (Matt. 15:9). The idea that God must be worshiped only in the way He has instituted has had a profound influence in Reformed churches.

of no value. The Greek of this verse is very difficult. It apparently means not only that the ascetic disciplines Paul is opposing are worthless, but that they are actively harmful, exciting their own sort of "indulgence of the flesh." This is precisely what the Reformers—preeminently Luther—saw themselves up against in the extra-biblical rituals that had emerged in the medieval church.

3:1–4:6 The route to maturity is not the path of secret revelations, or of self-punishing disciplines. It consists in understanding and living on the basis of the believer's death and resurrection "with Christ" (3:1). The Colossians have a false notion of heavenly reality, which ironically leads them to fruitless efforts on the earthly plane.

3:1 If then you have been raised with Christ. Note the parallel statements of fact in this section: believers have died with Christ (v. 3; 2:11, 12, 20); they have been raised with Him (v. 1; 2:12, 13); they are with Christ in

where Christ is, [d]seated at the right hand of
God. 2 [e]Set your minds on things that are
above, not on things that are on earth. 3 For
[f]you have died, and your life is hidden with
Christ in God. 4 When Christ [g]who is your[1]
life [h]appears, then you also will appear
with him [i]in glory.

5 [j]Put to death therefore [k]what is earthly
in you:[2] [l]sexual immorality, impurity,
[m]passion, evil desire, and covetousness,

Chapter 3 [d]See Eph. 1:20 **2** [e]See Matt. 16:23 **3** [f]ch. 2:20; See Rom. 6:2 **4** [g]See John 11:25 [h][Phil. 3:21; 1 Pet. 1:1, 7, 13; 1 John 2:28; 3:2] [i]1 Cor. 15:43 **5** [j]Rom. 8:13; [Gal. 5:24] [k]Rom. 6:13 [l]See Eph. 5:3, 5 [m]Rom. 1:26

1 Some manuscripts *our* 2 Greek *therefore your members that are on the earth*

Christians in the World

The word "world" in the New Testament is sometimes used as in the Old Testament to mean this earth, the good natural order that God created. Usually, however, it designates humanity as a whole, now fallen into sin and moral disorder, radically opposed to God. People in the world incur guilt and shame by their misuse of created things. Paul can even speak of creation itself yearning for deliverance from the evil occasioned by the fall of Adam and Eve (Rom. 8:20–23).

Christians are sent into the world of fallen humanity by their Lord (John 17:18) to witness to it about God's Christ and His kingdom (Matt. 24:14; cf. Rom. 10:18; Col. 1:6, 23) and to serve its needs. But they are to do so without falling victim to its materialism (Matt. 6:19–24, 32), its lack of concern about God and eternity (Luke 12:13–21), and its pursuit of pleasure and status above all else (1 John 2:15–17). The outlook and mindset of human societies reflect more of the pride seen in Satan, who for now continues to influence them (John 14:30; 2 Cor. 4:4; 1 John 5:19; cf. Luke 4:5–7), than the humility seen in Christ. Christians, like Christ Himself, are to empathize with people's anxieties and needs in order to serve them and communicate God's love for them effectively.

Christians are to consider themselves pilgrims in this fallen world, through which they momentarily pass as they travel home to God (1 Pet. 2:11). The Bible sanctions neither monastic withdrawal from this world (John 17:15) nor worldliness (Titus 2:12). Jesus encourages His disciples to match the ingenuity of the unredeemed who use their resources to further their goals, but specifies that the disciples' proper goals have to do, not with earthly security, but with heavenly glory (Luke 16:9). Christians are to be different from those around them, observing God's moral absolutes, practicing love, and not losing their dignity as bearers of God's image (Rom. 12:2; Eph. 4:17–24; Col. 3:5–11). Separation from fallen humanity's values and lifestyles is a prerequisite for practicing Christlikeness in positive terms (Eph. 4:25–5:17).

The Christian's appointed task, therefore, is threefold. The church's main mandate is evangelism (Matt. 28:19, 20; Luke 24:46–48), and every Christian must seek to further the conversion of unbelievers, not least by the example of one's own changed life (1 Pet. 2:12). Also, love of neighbor should constantly lead the Christian into deeds of mercy for all people, believers and unbelievers alike. Finally, Christians are called to fulfill the "cultural mandate" that God gave to mankind at creation (Gen. 1:28–30; Ps. 8:6–8). Humanity was created to manage God's world, and this stewardship is part of the human vocation in Christ, with God's honor and the good of others as its goal. The Protestant "work ethic" is essentially a religious discipline, the fulfillment of a divine "calling" to be stewards of God's creation.

Knowing that God in providential kindness and forbearance continues, in the face of human sin, to preserve and enrich His erring world (Acts 14:16, 17), Christians are to involve themselves in all forms of lawful human activity. By acting in accord with Christian values they will become salt (a preservative agent) and light (an illumination that shows the way) in the human community (Matt. 5:13–16). As Christians thus fulfill their vocation, they will transform the cultures around them.

heaven (v. 3; Eph. 2:6); they will be with Him at His return (v. 4); they have "put off the old self" (v. 9), and "put on the new self" (v. 10). Paul's instructions for behavior come only after his description of the redemption God has richly bestowed on His people (2:6, 7 note). Obedience is a response to God's favor, and not a means of gaining it.

seated at the right hand of God. A pivotal, exultant theme in the New Testament (Acts 2:33–35; 5:31; 7:55, 56; Rom. 8:34; Eph. 1:20; Heb. 1:3, 13; 8:1; 10:12; 12:2; 1 Pet. 3:22; Rev. 3:21).

3:3 hidden with Christ in God. Some understand this to mean that the new life of the Christian is not obvious to others and is "hidden" or concealed in that sense. However, comparison with 2:3 indicates that more is in view. The believer is inseparably united with Christ (John 6:51–58 note; cf. Gal. 2:20). The full reality of the new life is not yet fully revealed, but to be "hidden with Christ in God" means that the new life is secure in Christ. What God has freely given neither man nor angel can take away (John 10:29).

3:4 When Christ . . . appears. The hope of Christ's return is central to the ethics of this section (vv. 5–11).

3:5 Put to death. The first of a series of behavioral imperatives that continue through 4:6. Although Paul rejects legalistic asceticism, he calls upon believers to become in practice what they are in principle: dead to sin and alive to God (Rom. 6:1–14). There is a way of living incompatible

[n]which is idolatry. 6 [o]On account of these
the wrath of God is coming.[1] 7 [p]In these
you too once walked, when you were living
in them. 8 But now [q]you must put them all
away: [r]anger, wrath, malice, [s]slander, and
obscene talk from your mouth. 9 [t]Do not lie
to one another, seeing that [u]you have put
off [v]the old self[2] with its practices 10 and
[w]have put on [x]the new self, [y]which is being
renewed in knowledge [z]after the image of
[a]its creator. 11 [b]Here there is not Greek and
Jew, circumcised and uncircumcised, barbarian, Scythian, slave,[3] free; but Christ is
[c]all, and in all.

12 [d]Put on then, as [e]God's chosen ones,
holy and beloved, [f]compassion, [g]kindness,
[h]humility, meekness, and patience, 13 [h]bear-
ing with one another and, [i]if one has a
complaint against another, [g]forgiving each
other; [g]as the Lord has forgiven you, so you

5 [n][Job 31:25, 26] 6 [o]See Eph. 5:6 7 [p]See Eph. 2:2, 11 8 [q]See Eph. 4:22 [r]Eph. 4:31 [s]See Eph. 4:29 9 [t]Lev. 19:11; See Eph. 4:25 [u]ch. 2:11 [v]Rom. 6:6; Eph. 4:22 10 [w]Eph. 4:24 [x]See Rom. 6:4 [y]See Rom. 12:2 [z]See Rom. 8:29 [a][Eph. 2:10] 11 [b][Rom. 10:12]; See 1 Cor.12:13; Gal. 5:6 [c]Eph. 1:23 12 [d]ver. 10 [e]Rom. 8:33; [f]Phil. 2:1 [g]Eph. 4:32 [h]See Eph. 4:2

also must forgive. 14 And above all these put
on [j]love, which [k]binds everything together
in [l]perfect harmony. 15 And let [m]the peace
of Christ rule in your hearts, to which
indeed you were called [n]in one body. And
[o]be thankful. 16 Let [p]the word of Christ
dwell in you richly, teaching and admonishing one another in all wisdom, [q]singing
psalms and hymns and spiritual songs,
[r]with thankfulness in your hearts to God.
17 And [s]whatever you do, in word or deed,
do everything in the name of the Lord
Jesus, [t]giving thanks to God the Father
through him.

13 [h][See ver. 12 above] [i]Mark 11:25 [g][See ver. 12 above] 14 [j][1 Thess. 5:8]; See Eph. 5:2 [k]Eph. 4:3 [l]Heb. 6:1; [John 17:23] 15 [m]See Phil. 4:7 [n]Eph. 2:16 [o]ver. 17 16 [p]John 15:3 [q]See Eph. 5:19 [r]ch. 4:6 17 [s]ver. 23; 1 Cor. 10:31 [t]ch. 1:12; 4:2; See Eph. 5:20

1 Some manuscripts add *upon the sons of disobedience* 2 Greek *man*; also as supplied in verse 10 3 Greek *bondservant*

with life in Christ, and Paul calls for a rigorous departure from that old life. In v. 5 he lists five vices; four have to do with sex, the fifth is covetousness; in v. 8 he lists five more vices, all having to do with anger and abusive speech.

3:7 In these you too once walked. That is, before they were brought "to the kingdom of his beloved Son" (1:13).

3:10 new self. In Christ, God's second Adam (1 Cor. 15:20–28, 45–49), the human race is reconstituted. Each of the attributes Paul lists in v. 12 can be traced to the character of God generally, or to Christ specifically. This demonstrates how literally Paul understood the idea of believers taking on the "image" of their Creator. See "The Image of God" at Gen. 1:27.

3:11 This verse was probably written with an eye to the exclusiveness of the Colossian false teachers. However, the cross-cultural unity of all those who belong to Christ is an idea that comes readily enough to Paul's mind (Gal. 3:28; 1 Cor. 7:17–24).

barbarian. Those who did not speak Greek were considered uncivilized by Greeks.

Scythian. By reputation, an uncultured slave class drawn from tribes around the Black Sea. Scythians were lampooned in Greek comedy because of their uncouth ways and speech, and Josephus called them "little better than wild beasts."

slave, free. In the body of Christ, distinctions of social position are irrelevant (1 Cor. 7:17–24). Simultaneously, as Paul's separate instructions to slaves and slaveholders in 3:22–4:1 make clear, unity in Christ does not imply or mandate a uniformity of function or capacity. What is important is to recognize that "Christ is all, and in all." In the Pauline churches, diverse social positions continued to exist and were not subject to a uniform leveling process. Rather, they become opportunities for expressing Christ's love across traditional social boundaries.

3:12–14 These verses outline the obligations all Christians have toward one another; 3:18–4:2 will focus on opportunities for service within specified relationships.

3:12 Put on. Paul envisions believers taking on the character of the Lord Himself. The "new self" of v. 10 is not something believers must construct by their own power. Their new identities take shape as they come to know Christ better, since He is the image of the invisible God and the One in whom all the treasures of wisdom and knowledge are hidden (1:15; 2:3).

as God's chosen ones, holy and beloved. In contrast to the Colossians' fear of cosmic powers, believers are entitled to a clear sense that God guarantees their relationship with Him (John 6:37, 44, 65; 15:16; Eph. 1:4, 5; Phil. 1:6). They can know that they have been declared holy on the basis of a righteousness that is not their own (Rom. 3:21–26; 1 Cor. 1:2, 30), and that God genuinely, even passionately, loves them (John 3:16; Rom. 8:32; Gal. 2:20; Titus 3:4; 1 John 4:9, 10).

compassion. An emotional, caring relationship with those whose lives are hurt and broken (Matt. 9:36; 14:14; Rom. 12:1).

kindness. Readiness to do good, even when it may be undeserved (Rom. 2:4; Titus 3:4).

humility. A posture of lowliness and servanthood (Mark 10:45; Phil. 2:1–11).

meekness. Or, "gentleness" in offering help, a non-coercive approach to encouraging change in others' lives (Matt. 11:29; 2 Cor. 10:1; Gal. 6:1; 2 Tim. 2:25).

patience. Willingness to take the long view in the face of human frailty (Rom. 2:4; 1 Tim. 1:16).

3:13, 14 See Eph. 4:32–5:2, where Paul grounds Christian forbearance, forgiveness, and love explicitly in the example provided by the redemptive pattern of Christ's work.

3:15 the peace of Christ. In its practice of love, forgiveness, and graciousness, the Christian community is to be a showcase of the reconciliation and peace Christ has brought between heaven and earth (1:20–22; 2:14, 15), and within a fractured humanity (vv. 11, 13). Many manuscripts read "the peace of God" in this verse.

3:16 dwell in you richly. Because the believer is united with Christ (3:3 note), not only the "word of Christ," but Christ Himself lives in the hearts of the faithful (Gal. 2:20; Eph. 3:17; cf. Rom. 8:9). With God's wisdom present in this way (3:3; cf. 1 Cor. 1:30), the ethical demands of Christian love can be lived out in every part of life, including the everyday responsibilities that are reviewed in 3:18–4:6).

teaching and admonishing. The first half of this verse is strongly reminiscent of 1:28. In the ministry of the Colossians to one another, the word of Christ will be as effective as the presence of the apostle himself.

psalms and hymns and spiritual songs. In the Greek translation of the Old Testament, the three nouns used in this phrase are often synonymous. It is not likely that in Colossians they designate three separate types of song (Eph. 5:19). See theological note "Music in the Church" on the next page.

3:17 do everything in the name of the Lord Jesus. See "God's Pattern for Worship" at 1 Chr. 16:29.

Rules for Christian Households

18 [u]Wives, submit to your husbands, as
[v]is fitting in the Lord. 19 Husbands, love
your wives, and [w]do not be harsh with
them. 20 Children, obey your parents [x]in
everything, for this pleases the Lord.
21 Fathers, do not provoke your children,
lest they become discouraged. 22 Slaves,[1]
obey [x]in everything those who are your
earthly masters,[2] not by way of eye-service,
as people-pleasers, but with sincerity of
heart, fearing the Lord. 23 [y]Whatever you
do, work heartily, [z]as for the Lord and not
for men, 24 knowing that from the Lord
[a]you will receive the inheritance as your
reward. [b]You are serving the Lord Christ.
25 For the wrongdoer will be paid back for
the wrong he has done, and there is no partiality.

4 Masters, treat your slaves[3] justly and
fairly, knowing that you also have a
Master in heaven.

18 [u]For ver. 18–ch. 4:1, see Eph. 5:22–6:9 [v]Eph. 5:4; Philem. 8
19 [w]Eph. 4:31
20 [x][Eph. 5:24; Tit. 2:9]
22 [x][See ver. 20 above]
23 [y]ver. 17 [z][Philem. 16]
24 [a][Eph. 6:8] [b][1 Cor. 7:22]

Chapter 4
2 [c]For ver. 2-4, see Eph. 6:18-20 [d]ch. 2:7
3 [e]See Acts 14:27 [f]See Rom. 16:27 [g]ver. 18; Eph. 6:20; See Phil. 1:7
5 [h]See Eph. 5:15-17 [i]See Mark 4:11
6 [j]ch. 3:16 [k]See Mark 9:50 [l]1 Pet. 3:15

Further Instructions

2 [c]Continue steadfastly in prayer, being
watchful in it [d]with thanksgiving. 3 At the
same time, pray also for us, that God may
[e]open to us a door for the word, [f]to declare
the mystery of Christ, [g]on account of which
I am in prison— 4 that I may make it clear,
which is how I ought to speak.
5 [h]Conduct yourselves wisely[4] toward
[i]outsiders, making the best use of the time.
6 Let your speech always [j]be gracious, [k]sea-
soned with salt, [l]so that you may know
how you ought to answer each person.

Final Greetings

7 Tychicus will tell you [m]all about my
activities. He is a beloved brother and faithful minister and fellow servant[5] in the Lord.

7 [m]For ver. 7-9, see Eph. 6:21, 22

1 Or *Servants*; Greek *Bondservants* 2 Or *your masters according to the flesh* 3 Or *servants*; Greek *bondservants* 4 Greek *Walk in wisdom*
5 Greek *fellow bondservant*; also verse 12

Music in the Church

Some branches of the Reformed faith, eager to protect the church from the addition of human tradition, impressed by the continuity between Israel and the church, and noticing that the terms "psalms," "hymns," and "songs" are used in the Book of Psalms, believe that Paul envisioned only the singing of the psalms from the Old Testament in public worship. This restriction appears, however, to miss his point. He piles up the terms to highlight the wide range of musical expression that grateful and heartfelt praise to God calls forth from the body of Christ.

The word "psalms" refers at least to the use of the Old Testament psalter (Luke 20:42; 24:44; Acts 1:20; 13:33), but may also refer to fresh compositions for worship (1 Cor. 14:26). The word "spiritual" (Greek *pneumatikos*) qualifies the potentially secular term "songs" as being taught or led by the Spirit (cf. 1 Cor. 2:6; 15:44, 45 notes).

Christ's redemptive work brought an outpouring of hymns of praise from His people, often patterned after the songs of the Old Testament (e.g., Luke 1:46–53, 67–79; 2:14, 29–32). Paul personally employed music within his own worship (Acts 16:25), and it has long been observed that his letters contain portions of early Christian hymns (Eph. 5:14; Phil. 2:6–11; Col. 1:15–20; 1 Tim. 3:16 and notes). Early Christian songs of praise appear also to underlie John 1:1–14; Heb. 1:3; 1 Pet. 1:18–21; 2:21–25; 3:18–22. The "new songs" of the Book of Revelation are themselves a study in the vibrancy of early Christian worship (Rev. 4:8, 11; 5:9, 10, 12, 13; 7:10, 12; 11:15, 17, 18; 12:10–12; 15:3, 4; 19:1–8; 21:3, 4).

3:18, 19 See note Eph. 5:22–32; "The Christian Family" at Eph. 5:22.

3:20, 21 See notes Eph. 6:1–3, 4.

3:22–4:1 This treatment of slave and free in Colossians is probably related to the subject matter of the letter to Philemon. Onesimus was a runaway slave whom Paul was returning with a letter to his owner Philemon. Onesimus was accompanying Tychicus with the letter to the Colossians (4:7–9), and they were probably carrying the letter to Philemon as well (Introduction to Philemon).

4:2–6 Two other ways in which believers can set their "minds on things that are above" (3:2) are praying (Eph. 6:18–20 note) and telling their faith wisely and persuasively to outsiders so that they may be drawn to the fullness of life in Christ.

4:7–17 The letter ends with a brief look at the complex and fluid network of leaders that tied Paul's churches together. Some of the same names occur in Philem. 23, 24.

4:7 Tychicus. The primary carrier of the letters to the Colossians, Philemon, and the Ephesians (Eph. 6:21, 22). First mentioned as part of Paul's entourage in Acts 20:4, Tychicus was from the Roman province of Asia (in modern Turkey), and appears to have been one of Paul's more trusted emissaries toward the end of his ministry (2 Tim. 4:12; Titus 3:12).

8 I have sent him to you for this very purpose, that you may know how we are and
that he may encourage your hearts, 9 and
with him [n]Onesimus, our faithful and [o]be-
loved brother, who is one of you. They will
tell you of everything that has taken place
here.
10 [p]Aristarchus my fellow prisoner greets
you, and Mark [q]the cousin of Barnabas
(concerning whom you have received
instructions—[r]if he comes to you, welcome him), 11 and Jesus who is called
[s]Justus. [t]These are the only men of the circumcision among my fellow workers for
the kingdom of God, and [u]they have been
a comfort to me. 12 [v]Epaphras, who is one
of you, a servant of Christ Jesus, greets you,
always [w]struggling on your behalf in his
prayers, that you may stand [x]mature and
fully assured in all the will of God. 13 For I
bear him witness that he has worked hard
for you and for those in Laodicea and in
Hierapolis. 14 [y]Luke the beloved physician
greets you, as does [z]Demas. 15 Give my
greetings to the brothers[1] at Laodicea, and
to Nympha and [a]the church in her house.
16 And when [b]this letter has been read
among you, have it also read in the church
of the Laodiceans; and see that you also
read the letter from Laodicea. 17 And say to
[c]Archippus, "See that you fulfill [d]the ministry that you have received in the Lord."
18 I, Paul, [e]write this greeting with my
own hand. [f]Remember [g]my chains. [h]Grace
be with you.

9 [n]Philem. 10 [o]Philem. 16 **10** [p]Acts 19:29; 20:4; 27:2; Philem. 24; [Rom. 16:7] [q]See Acts 15:37, 39] [r][2 Tim. 4:11] **11** [s][Acts 1:23; 18:7] [t]See Acts 11:2 [u][Philem. 7] **12** [v]ch. 1:7; Philem. 23 [w]See Rom. 15:30 [x]See Matt. 5:48 **14** [y]2 Tim. 4:11; See Acts 16:10 [z]2 Tim. 4:10; Philem. 24 **15** [a]See Rom. 16:5 **16** [b]1 Thess. 5:27 **17** [c]Philem. 2 [d]2 Tim. 4:5 **18** [e]See 1 Cor. 16:21 [f][Heb. 13:3] [g]ver. 3; See Phil. 1:7 [h]1 Tim. 6:21; 2 Tim. 4:22; [Tit. 3:15]

1 Or *brothers and sisters*

4:9 Onesimus. See Introduction to Philemon.

4:10 Aristarchus. This Jew from Thessalonica had been publicly associated with Paul's tumultuous ministry in Ephesus (Acts 19:29). He had traveled with Paul's company through Greece (Acts 20:4) and on to Jerusalem and Rome (Acts 27:2), where he now shared the apostle's imprisonment.

Mark. The rift that had emerged more than a decade earlier between Paul and the cousins Barnabas and John Mark (author of the Gospel of Mark, Acts 13:13; 15:37–40) had healed (2 Tim. 4:11; Philem. 24). Paul's special mention of Mark testifies to the power of the reconciling work of Christ (1:20–22) and to the peace that is to rule within Christ's body (3:15).

4:11 Jesus who is called Justus. Otherwise unknown.

4:12 Epaphras. See 1:7; Introduction: Date and Occasion.

4:13 Hierapolis. See Introduction: Date and Occasion.

4:14 Luke. This traveling companion of Paul in Acts was with Paul on what may have been the eve of his death (2 Tim. 4:11). As author of the Gospel of Luke and Acts, he was also Paul's chronicler. Though his writing shows him to be exceptionally literate, the mention of his occupation does not necessarily mark him as a man of high social standing, since physicians were often slaves.

Demas. Demas abandoned Paul during his second imprisonment in Rome (2 Tim. 4:10). He is mentioned one other time (Philem. 24).

4:15 Nympha. Some manuscripts identify this person, who hosted the Laodicean house church, as a woman. There are several references to women (whose marital status is not mentioned) as patrons or hosts of churches, or as workers in ministry (Acts 12:12; 16:13–15; Rom. 16:1, 2, 6, 7, 12, 13; Phil. 4:2, 3; 2 John 1, 5). The standard of relationships between men and women, particularly husbands and wives, set out in 3:18 and parallels (1 Cor. 14:33–35; Eph. 5:22–33; 1 Tim. 2:11–15) was not inconsistent with the partnership in ministry that existed between men and women in the early church.

church in her house. There is no evidence of churches owning separate property for worship until the middle of the third century. Until then, house churches were the norm. Those who exercised a ministry of hospitality by having churches in their homes were important benefactors of the early church (Acts 12:12; Rom. 16:5; 1 Cor. 16:19; Philem. 2). On hospitality, see Rom. 12:13; 1 Tim. 3:2; Titus 1:8; Heb. 13:2; 1 Pet. 4:9.

4:16 letter from Laodicea. Some suggest that Paul is referring to the letter to the Ephesians, which in some ancient manuscripts lacks a destination, and which may have gone out as a circular letter (Introduction to Ephesians: Date and Occasion). Since Tychicus is the bearer of Ephesians as well (Eph. 6:21, 22), the conclusion that the Ephesian and Laodicean letters were one and the same would imply that Colossians and Ephesians were written at about the same time, and that Tychicus traveled first to Laodicea and then to Colossae. However, it may be more natural to assume, on the basis of the more reflective style of Ephesians, that it was written some time after Colossians, and that Tychicus brought the Ephesian letter around to the churches on a subsequent trip (if, indeed, it was a circular letter). The best proposal for the identity of the letter from Laodicea is that it was a separate letter that has not survived.

4:17 Archippus. If Philemon was host of the house church in Colossae, which had seen the Onesimus incident, this verse may well suggest that Archippus was its spiritual leader.

4:18 with my own hand. Paul's general practice was to dictate his letters, but to write the closing sentences himself. These concluding sections would vary, depending on the circumstances. Sometimes they include personal greetings to strengthen the bond between himself, his workers, and his churches (vv. 7–17; Rom. 16); sometimes they include a summary of the contents of the letter (e.g., Gal. 6:11–17); and sometimes they had a signature that guaranteed the authenticity of the letter (1 Cor. 16:21; Philem. 19).

THE FIRST EPISTLE OF PAUL THE APOSTLE TO THE

Thessalonians

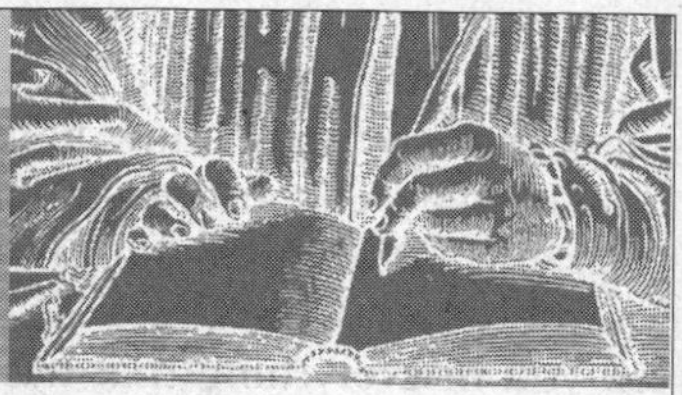

AUTHOR

The author of this epistle identifies himself as the apostle Paul (1:1; 2:18). The authenticity of 1 Thessalonians has occasionally been challenged but with notable lack of success.

The contributions of Silas and Timothy to the substance of the Thessalonian letters cannot be detected with any certainty. It remains possible that certain peculiarities of these letters, in comparison with the rest of Paul's writings, are due to the influence of either of these close associates of Paul.

DATE AND OCCASION

Paul wrote the first letter to the Thessalonians almost certainly from Corinth, where Silas and Timothy, senders with him of the letters, were reunited with him (Acts 18:5; 2 Cor. 1:19). The letter was most likely written in A.D. 50 or 51, with 2 Thessalonians following shortly. Therefore, 1 and 2 Thessalonians are among the earliest letters we have from the hand of Paul, with only Galatians having any reasonable claim to be earlier (Introduction to Galatians).

Paul wrote 1 Thessalonians after receiving a report from Timothy regarding the state of the Thessalonian congregation (3:6, 7). Paul writes with joy and relief that the Thessalonians were continuing firm in the faith despite the premature departure of Paul and his coworkers, and despite the harassment they still suffered from hostile factions.

The city of Thessalonica was named for Alexander the Great's half sister. It was founded about 315 B.C. by her husband, King Cassander of Macedonia. In Roman times Thessalonica was a provincial capital with over 200,000 inhabitants.

On his second missionary tour, Paul and his companions Silas and Timothy had come to Thessalonica by road from Philippi, where they had been "shamefully treated" (2:2). Acts 17:2 records that Paul preached and debated in the synagogues for three successive Sabbaths.

The congregation was predominantly Gentile. This indicates that a successful ministry among Gentiles continued after Paul's access to the synagogue was cut off. During their stay in Thessalonica, which cannot have lasted more than a few months, the missionaries apparently received more than one contribution for their support from the congregation at Philippi (Phil. 4:15, 16). This, combined with earnings from their own labors (2:9; 2 Thess. 3:7, 8), meant that they were able to support themselves without depending on the Thessalonians. Their example of humble, industrious behavior was a rebuke to the minority in the church who wanted to refrain from working for a living.

Eventually, members of the Jewish community enlisted unscrupulous men to stir up animosity against the Christians. A riot ensued, and a number of Christians including a Jewish convert named Jason were dragged before the authorities. Jason and the others were forced to post security money to guarantee that the church would not cause trouble. Paul, Silas, and Timothy were whisked away by the believers under cover of night and soon found themselves in Berea to the west (Acts 17:5–10).

CHARACTERISTICS AND THEMES

A rich vein of teaching about the last days runs through the Thessalonian letters. Paul's preaching at Athens, recorded in Acts 17, confirms that his strategy among non-Jewish audiences at this time was to stress the coming judgment (4:6) that God has placed in the hands of the risen Christ.

The return of Christ would occur on what

Paul calls the "day of the Lord," (5:2; 2 Thess. 2:1 note). On this day there will be a resurrection of the just to inherit salvation in the Lord's presence (4:16; 5:10), and of the unjust (presupposed by Paul though never explicitly stated) to be eternally separated from Christ (2 Thess. 1:9). The end will be preceded by a widespread apostasy and the appearance of a diabolical "man of lawlessness" (2 Thess. 2:3). Since this person had not yet appeared, those in the congregation who were saying that the "day of the Lord" had already arrived were wrong and should be silenced.

Another notable characteristic of the letters is Paul's affirmation that Christ is divine, the more striking because of the early date of the letters and the spontaneous and unguarded nature of the references. Several times Christ and God the Father are linked together as the common source of divine blessings and as the object of prayer (1:1; 3:11; 2 Thess. 1:1, 2, 12; 2:16; 3:5). In Paul's use of the Old Testament expression "day of the Lord," in which "the Lord" is now revealed to be the Lord Jesus Christ (5:2; 2 Thess. 2:2), there is a similar assignment of the prerogatives of deity to Jesus Christ (5:2 note). The united work of the three Persons of the Trinity is mentioned in 2 Thess. 2:13, 14.

OUTLINE OF 1 THESSALONIANS

I. Salutation (1:1)

II. History (1:2–3:13)

- A. *Paul's Grounds for Thanksgiving (1:2–2:16)*
  1. Their Election Shown in Faith, Love, and Hope (1:2–10)
  2. The Missionaries' Fruitful Ministry Among Them (2:1–12)
  3. Their Reception of the Gospel as the Word of God (2:13–16)
- B. *Paul's Absence Explained (2:17–3:10)*
- C. *Paul's Prayer (3:11–13)*

III. Instruction (4:1–5:22)

- A. *Ethics (4:1–12)*
  1. Sexual Morality (4:1–8)
  2. Brotherly Love and Witness (4:9–12)
- B. *Eschatology (4:13–5:11)*
  1. The Dead (4:13–18)
  2. The Day of the Lord (5:1–11)
- C. *Congregational Life (5:12–22)*

IV. Concluding Prayer, Charges, and Benediction (5:23–28)

Greeting

1 Paul, [a]Silvanus, and Timothy,
To the church of the [b]Thessalonians
in God the Father and the Lord Jesus
Christ:
[c]Grace to you and peace.

The Thessalonians' Faith and Example

2 [d]We give thanks to God always for all of
you, constantly[1] [e]mentioning you in our
prayers, 3 remembering before [f]our God
and Father [g]your work of faith and labor of
[h]love and [i]steadfastness of hope in our
Lord Jesus Christ. 4 For we know, [j]broth-
ers[2] loved by God, [k]that he has chosen you,
5 because [l]our gospel came to you not only
in word, but also in power and [m]in the
Holy Spirit and with full [n]conviction. You

Chapter 1
1 [a]Acts 15:22; 2 Cor. 1:19; 2 Thess. 1:1; 1 Pet. 5:12 [b]See Acts 17:1 [c]Rom. 1:7
2 [d]ch. 2:13; See Rom. 1:8; Eph. 5:20 [e]Rom. 1:9; 2 Tim. 1:3
3 [f]See Gal. 1:4 [g]2 Thess. 1:11; [John 6:29; Gal. 5:6; Heb. 6:10; James 2:22] [h]2 Thess. 1:3, 4; [Col. 1:4; 1 Tim. 1:14; Rev. 2:19] [i]Rom. 8:25; 15:4
4 [j]2 Thess. 2:13 [k]2 Pet. 1:10
5 [l]2 Thess. 2:14 [m]2 Cor. 6:6; See 1 Cor. 2:4 [n]Col. 2:2; [Heb. 2:3]

[1] Or *without ceasing* [2] Or *brothers and sisters*. The plural Greek word *adelphoi* (translated "brothers") refers to siblings in a family. In New Testament usage, depending on the context, *adelphoi* may refer either to men or to both men and women who are siblings (brothers and sisters) in God's family, the church

1:1 Silvanus. The Latin name of Silas, a prophet of the Jerusalem church delegated to accompany Paul and Barnabas to Antioch to deliver the decision of the Jerusalem council (Acts 15:22, 27, 32, 40). Silas was chosen by Paul to be his associate on this second missionary journey.

Timothy. The son of a Greek father and a devout Jewish mother, he was at the time of writing a relative newcomer to the Christian mission. Paul and Silas had drafted this young but highly regarded disciple to join in their ministry roughly a year earlier in Lystra (Acts 16:1).

in God the Father and the Lord Jesus Christ. This points to the unique intimacy between the Father and the Son, because the church is said to be "in" both (Introduction: Characteristics and Themes).

1:3 work of faith. The faith of the Thessalonians, obviously a chief concern for Paul, is referred to again in v. 8; 3:2, 5–7, 10; 5:8.

labor of love. Their love was shown especially in the welcome they gave to the travelers (v. 9). Paul commends their love again in 4:9, 10, where he says they are "taught by God" in their love for one another.

steadfastness of hope. Their eschatological hope is their assurance that the Lord Jesus will return to deliver them from their present troubles and from God's coming wrath. For the triad of "faith," "hope," and "love," see 5:8; Rom. 5:2–5; 1 Cor. 13:13; Gal. 5:5, 6; Col. 1:4, 5; Heb. 6:10–12; 10:22–24; 1 Pet. 1:3–8, 21, 22.

1:4 chosen you. Divine election is a theme of both Thessalonian epistles (5:9; 2 Thess. 2:13). Paul is not afraid to assure this young, predominantly Gentile congregation that they were elected by God. Paul sees in them the fruit of God's electing grace, manifested in their response to the preaching of the gospel and their early progress in sanctification (2 Thess. 2:13 note).

know [o]what kind of men we proved to be
among you for your sake. **6** And [p]you
became imitators of us [q]and of the Lord,
for [r]you received the word in much affliction, [s]with the [t]joy of the Holy Spirit, **7** so
that you became an example to all the
believers in Macedonia and in Achaia. **8** For
not only has the word of the Lord [u]sound-
ed forth from you in Macedonia and
Achaia, but your faith in God has gone
forth [v]everywhere, so that we need not say
anything. **9** For they themselves report concerning us the kind of [w]reception we had
among you, and how [x]you turned to God
[y]from idols to serve the living and [z]true
God, **10** and [a]to wait for his Son [b]from heav-
en, [c]whom he raised from the dead, Jesus
[d]who delivers us from [e]the wrath to come.

Paul's Ministry to the Thessalonians

2 For you yourselves know, brothers,[1]
that our [f]coming to you [g]was not in
vain. **2** But though we had already suffered
and been shamefully treated [h]at Philippi, as
you know, [i]we had boldness in our God [j]to
declare to you the gospel of God in the
midst of much [k]conflict. **3** For [l]our appeal
does not spring from [m]error or [n]impurity or
[o]any attempt to deceive, **4** but just as we
have been approved by God [p]to be entrusted with the gospel, so we speak, not [q]to
please man, but to please God [r]who tests
our hearts. **5** [s]For we never came with
words of flattery,[2] as you know, nor with a
pretext for greed—[t]God is witness. **6** [u]Nor
did we seek glory from people, whether
from you or from others, [v]though we could
have made [w]demands as [x]apostles of
Christ. **7** But we were [y]gentle[3] among you,
[z]like a nursing mother taking care of her
own children. **8** So, being affectionately
desirous of you, we were ready to share
with you not only the gospel of God [a]but
also our own selves, because you had
become very dear to us.
9 For you remember, brothers, [b]our labor
and toil: we [c]worked night and day, that
we might not be a burden to any of you,
while we proclaimed to you the gospel of
God. **10** You are witnesses, and [d]God also,
[e]how holy and righteous and blameless
was our conduct toward you believers.
11 For you know how, [f]like a father with his
children, **12** we exhorted each one of you
and encouraged you and [g]charged [h]you to
walk in a manner worthy of God, [i]who calls
you into his own kingdom and glory.
13 And [j]we also thank God constantly[4] for
this, that when you received [k]the word of
God, which you heard from us, you
accepted it [l]not as the word of men but as
what it really is, the word of God, [m]which

4 [o][ch. 2:10; Acts 20:18; 2 Thess. 3:7] **6** [p][ch. 2:14; 2 Thess. 3:7, 9]; See 1 Cor. 4:16 [q]1 Cor. 11:1 [r]Acts 17:5-10 [s]See Matt. 5:12 [t]Acts 13:52; Gal. 5:22 **8** [u][Rom. 10:18; 2 Thess. 3:1] [v][Rom. 1:8; 16:19; 2 Thess. 1:4] **9** [w]ch. 2:1 [x]See Acts 14:15 [y]1 Cor. 12:2; [Gal. 4:8] [z]See John 17:3 **10** [a]See 1 Cor. 1:7 [b]ch. 4:16; [2 Thess. 1:10]; See Acts 1:11 [c]See Acts 2:24 [d]Col. 1:13 [e]ch. 2:16; 5:9; Matt. 3:7; Rom. 5:9 **Chapter 2** **1** [f]ch. 1:9 [g][2 Thess. 1:10] **2** [h]Acts 16:22-24 [i]See Acts 4:13 [j]Acts 17:2-9 [k]Phil. 1:30 **3** [l][2 Cor. 2:17] [m]2 Thess. 2:11 [n]ch. 4:7 [o]2 Cor. 4:2 **4** [p]See Gal. 2:7 [q]See Gal. 1:10 [r]Ps. 17:3; See Rom. 8:27 **5** [s]See Acts 20:33

[t]ver. 10; See Rom. 1:9 **6** [u][2 Cor. 4:5]; See John 5:41 [v]1 Cor. 9:4; 2 Thess. 3:9; [Philem. 8, 9] [w][ver. 9; 2 Cor. 11:9] [x]See 1 Cor. 9:1 **7** [y]2 Tim. 2:24; [1 Cor. 14:20] [z][ver. 11; Isai. 49:23; 60:16] **8** [a]See 2 Cor. 12:15 **9** [b]2 Thess. 3:8; [Phil. 4:16] [c]See Acts 18:3 **10** [d]ver. 5 [e]See ch. 1:5 **11** [f][ver. 7]; See 1 Cor. 4:14 **12** [g]Eph. 4:17 [h]See Eph. 4:1 [i]ch. 5:24; 2 Thess. 2:14; 1 Pet. 5:10; See Rom. 8:28 **13** [j]See ch. 1:2, 3 [k][Rom. 10:17] [l][Gal. 4:14]; See Matt. 10:20 [m]Heb. 4:12

[1] Or *brothers and sisters*; also verses 9, 14, 17 [2] Or *with a flattering speech* [3] Some manuscripts *infants* [4] Or *without ceasing*

1:6 imitators. The Spirit plays an especially prominent role in sustaining the believer who undergoes persecution for Christ (Matt. 10:19, 20; 1 Pet. 4:12–14).

1:7, 8 Paul is writing from Achaia, having traversed Macedonia and come through Athens to Corinth. Along the way he has found that the Christians already know of his work in Thessalonica and have learned of the faith of the Thessalonians. The Thessalonian Christians, beginners in Christ though they were, are examples to others of faith, love, and hope.

1:9, 10 These verses parallel the preaching of Paul at Athens (Acts 17:22–31). In preaching to the Jews, Paul could presuppose knowledge of the existence of the true God and the authority of the Old Testament Scriptures, and go on to proclaim the advent of God's promised Messiah. To those uninstructed in the faith of Israel, Paul stresses two things: first, acknowledging the true and living God and forsaking dead idols; second, preparing for God's coming universal judgment to be executed by Jesus Christ, the God-Man, who died and rose from the dead (4:6; Acts 17:29–31).

1:10 from heaven. See 4:16; 2 Thess. 1:7; cf. Acts 1:11; Phil. 3:20.

Jesus who delivers us from the wrath to come. Jesus' death turned away God's wrath long ago, but the full import of this saving work will not be displayed until Judgment Day. Then, through Christ's intervention, believers will be spared the condemnation and punishment their sins would otherwise deserve.

2:1–12 Paul seems to respond to certain doubts or criticisms of his ministry. He implicitly defends his ministry of the gospel, and at the same time, by recalling the work he and his companions have done, he gives the Thessalonians a pattern of loving service to follow.

2:2 we had boldness in our God. Despite being called by God to enter Macedonia (Acts 16:9, 10), Paul and Silas had been severely beaten and chained in a Macedonian prison (at Philippi). The missionaries had to be courageous and selflessly devoted to God's purpose.

the gospel of God. Paul stresses the pure, and indeed divine, source of his message and ministry. Note the repetition of the phrase in vv. 8 and 9. The gospel is always carried as a trust from God Himself.

2:4 See theological note "Pleasing God."

2:8 Apparent throughout this section (vv. 17–20; 3:6–12) is Paul's deep affection for his spiritual children, who but months before were complete strangers to him, alienated by race, culture, and religion.

2:12 This verse summarizes Paul's exhortation and charge during his initial visit in Thessalonica. In contrast to the idols the Thessalonians had forsaken (1:9), the true and living God has a "kingdom and glory," and in His fathomless mercy He chooses to share this kingdom with those who worship Him through Jesus Christ. Called to enter this kingdom, believers know its power and enjoy its life here and now (Rom. 14:17; 1 Cor. 4:20; Col. 1:13, 14) while they long for the day they will enter its fullness.

2:13 at work in you. The Word of God, though it comes through human agency, is a divine message that works in believers through the Holy Spirit (Is. 55:11; Acts 20:32; 2 Tim. 2:15–17; Heb. 4:12).

is at work in you believers. 14 For you,
brothers, [n]became imitators of [o]the churches of God in Christ Jesus that are in Judea.
For [p]you suffered the same things from
your own countrymen [q]as they did from
the Jews, 15 [r]who killed both the Lord Jesus
and [s]the prophets, and drove us out, and
displease God and [t]oppose all mankind
16 [u]by hindering us from speaking to the
Gentiles that they might be saved—so as
always [v]to fill up the measure of their sins.
But [w]God's wrath has come upon them at
last![1]

Paul's Longing to See Them Again

17 But since we were torn away from you,
brothers, for a short time, [x]in person not in
heart, we endeavored the more eagerly and
with great desire [y]to see you face to face,
18 because we wanted to come to you—I,
Paul, again and again—but Satan [z]hin-
dered us. 19 For what is our hope or [a]joy or
crown of boasting [b]before our Lord Jesus at
his [c]coming? Is it not you? 20 For you are
our glory and joy.

3 Therefore when we could bear it no
longer, we were willing [d]to be left
behind at Athens alone, 2 and we [e]sent
Timothy, [f]our brother and God's coworker[2] in the gospel of Christ, to establish

14 [n]See ch. 1:6 [o]See 1 Cor. 7:17 [p]ch. 3:4; Acts 17:5; 2 Thess. 1:4, 5 [q][Heb. 10:33, 34] **15** [r]See Luke 24:20 [s]Jer. 2:30; Matt. 23:29-34; See Matt. 5:12 [t][Esth. 3:8] **16** [u]Acts 13:45, 50; 14:2, 19; 17:5, 13; 18:12; 22:21, 22 [v]See Gen. 15:16 [w]See ch. 1:10 **17** [x]1 Cor. 5:3; Col. 2:5 [y]ch. 8:10 **18** [z]Rom. 15:22; [Rom. 1:13]

19 [a]See Phil. 4:1 [b]1 Cor. 15:31; [2 Thess. 1:4]; See 2 Cor. 1:14 [c]ch. 3:13; 4:15; 5:23; Matt. 24:3; 1 Cor. 15:23; 2 Thess. 2:1, 8; James 5:7, 8; 2 Pet. 1:16; 3:4, 12; 1 John 2:28
Chapter 3 1 [d]Acts 17:15, 16 **2** [e]See Phil. 2:19 [f]2 Cor. 1:1; Col. 1:1; Philem. 1; Heb. 13:23

1 Or *completely*, or *forever* 2 Some manuscripts *servant*

Pleasing God

It is a familiar truth that every Christian's overriding purpose must be to glorify God. Everything we say and do, our relationships with others, the use we make of the gifts and opportunities God gives us, and even our enduring of adverse situations and human hostility, must be managed so as to give God honor and praise for His wisdom and goodness (1 Cor. 10:31; cf. Matt. 5:16; Eph. 3:10; Col. 3:17).

Equally important is the truth that every Christian has a personal calling to please God. Jesus did not live to please Himself, nor may we (John 8:29; Rom. 15:1–3). Faith (Heb. 11:5, 6), praise (Ps. 69:30, 31), generosity (Phil. 4:18; Heb. 13:16), obedience to divinely instituted authority (Col. 3:20), and single-mindedness in Christian service (2 Tim. 2:4), are all ways of pleasing our Creator. God enables us to live according to the Bible and takes pleasure in us as we serve Him. In His sovereign grace He gives what He commands and delights in the result (Heb. 13:21; cf. Phil. 2:12, 13).

We please God through our relationship with Him. Abraham was called God's friend (2 Chr. 20:7; Is. 41:8; James 2:23), and Christ called His disciples His friends (Luke 12:4; John 15:14). Under divine inspiration, Paul compares the church to the Bride of Christ (Eph. 5:32; cf. Rev. 21:2). Like friends and family members, God and His people have pleasure in each other.

We also please God through imitating His deeds. His love in us is living and active, compelling His people to use their talents and energies in all kinds of activities. But Christians are especially called to works of mercy, because God is merciful (Deut. 10:17–19; Luke 6:35, 36).

2:14 suffered . . . from your own countrymen. The power of God's word in them was proved as they faced fierce persecution from their kinsmen and, like the churches in Judea, endured it with faith and joy (Acts 17:5–9).

2:15 Just as Jesus noted the continuity of those who persecuted the prophets with those who persecuted Him (Matt. 23:29–32), so Paul (also Stephen, Acts 7:52) sees the same continuity extending to those Jews (with whom he formerly worked) who persecute Christ by opposing the gospel (Acts 9:4). Paul's fullest elaboration of his approach to this problem of Jewish opposition to the gospel is found in Rom. 9–11.

2:16 wrath has come upon them at last. See text note. These last two words may also be translated "the end" (Matt. 10:22; 1 Cor. 1:8; 15:24). This may be a prophecy of the catastrophe which overtook Jerusalem in A.D. 70, within twenty years of Paul's writing, or it may refer to the sequence of calamities that had already begun and were to reach their culmination in that momentous disaster. Or it may refer to the punitive hardening of a large segment of Israel in their culpable rejection of Christ, a hardening that Jesus saw as the fulfillment of Isaiah's dire prophecy (Is. 6:9, 10; Matt. 13:14, 15). Compare a similar outworking of God's wrath upon Gentiles outlined in Rom. 1:18–32. As Paul would later write (Rom. 11:25), a "partial hardening" has befallen Israel and will remain until the full number of Gentiles are brought in (i.e., until the end). The part of Israel not subject to hardening is the remnant (Is. 6:13) that in the gospel era continues as the object of God's mercy, finding salvation in Jesus the Messiah.

2:17 torn away. The Greek word means "orphaned," a word used for parents as well as children who have been separated. Paul continues to use the family imagery of vv. 7 and 11 in depicting his relationship with the Thessalonian congregation.

2:19 at his coming. The Greek word *parousia* ("coming") is used for the Second Coming of Christ six times in the Thessalonian correspondence (see also 3:13; 4:15; 5:23; 2 Thess. 2:1, 8). Paul's only other use of the term in this sense is in 1 Cor. 15:23. Christ's coming is presented as the time when the outcome of our works of faith is disclosed. Paul's joy and crown at that day will be his beloved spiritual children, those converted under his ministry (2 Cor. 1:14; Phil. 2:16).

and exhort you in your faith, **3** that no
one be moved by these afflictions. For
you yourselves know that [g]we are destined for this. **4** For when we were with
you, we kept telling you beforehand that
we were to suffer affliction, [h]just as it has
come to pass, and just as you know. **5** For
this reason, [i]when I could bear it no
longer, [i]I sent to learn about your faith,
[j]for fear that somehow [k]the tempter had
tempted you and [l]our labor would be in
vain.

Timothy's Encouraging Report

6 But [m]now that Timothy has come to us
from you, and has brought us the good
news of [n]your faith and love and reported
[o]that you always remember us kindly and
[p]long to see us, as we long to see you—
7 for this reason, brothers,[1] in all our distress and affliction [q]we have been comforted about you through your faith. **8** For
now we live, if you [r]are standing fast in
the Lord. **9** For [s]what thanksgiving can
we return to God for you, for all the joy
that we feel for your sake before our God,
10 as we pray most earnestly [t]night and day
[u]that we may see you face to face and [v]sup-
ply what is lacking in your faith?
11 Now may [w]our God and Father himself, and our Lord Jesus, [x]direct our way to
you, **12** and may the Lord [y]make you
increase and abound in love [z]for one
another and for all, as we do for you, **13** so
that he may [a]establish your hearts blameless in holiness before [w]our God and

3 [g]See Acts 9:16; 14:22 **4** [h]See ch. 2:14 **5** [i]ver. 1, 2 [j][1 Cor. 7:5; 2 Cor. 11:3] [k]Matt. 4:3 [l]See Phil. 2:16 **6** [m]Acts 18:5; [2 Cor. 7:6, 9] [n]See ch. 1:3 [o][1 Cor. 11:2] [p]See Phil. 1:8 **7** [q]2 Cor. 1:4 **8** [r]See 1 Cor. 16:13 **9** [s][ch. 1:2] **10** [t]2 Tim. 1:3 [u]ch. 2:17; [Rom. 1:10] [v]See 2 Cor. 13:9 **11** [w]See Gal. 1:4 [x]2 Thess. 3:5 **12** [y]ch. 4:1, 10; Phil. 1:9; 2 Thess. 1:3 [z]ch. 4:9; 5:15 **13** [a]James 5:8 [w][See ver. 11 above]

[b]See ch. 2:19 [c]Zech. 14:5; Jude 14
Chapter 4
1 [d]Phil. 4:9; Col. 2:6 [e]See Eph. 4:1 [f]See Col. 1:10 [g]See ch. 3:12 **2** [h][1 Cor. 11:2] **3** [i]Rom. 6:19, 22; 1 Cor. 1:30; 2 Thess. 2:13; 1 Tim. 2:15; Heb. 12:14; 1 Pet. 1:2 [j]See 1 Cor. 6:18 **4** [k]1 Pet. 3:7; [2 Cor. 4:7] [l][Rom. 1:24] **5** [m]See Rom. 1:26

Father, at [b]the coming of our Lord Jesus
[c]with all his saints.

A Life Pleasing to God

4 Finally, then, brothers,[2] we ask and
urge you in the Lord Jesus, that as you
[d]received from us [e]how you ought to live[3]
and [f]to please God, just as you are doing,
that you [g]do so more and more. **2** For [h]you
know what instructions we gave you
through the Lord Jesus. **3** For this is the will
of God, [i]your sanctification:[4] [j]that you
abstain from sexual immorality; **4** that each
one of you know how to control his own
[k]body[5] in holiness and [l]honor, **5** not in [m]the
passion of lust [n]like the Gentiles [o]who do
not know God; **6** that no one transgress and
[p]wrong his brother in this matter, because
the Lord is [q]an avenger in all these things,
as we told you beforehand and solemnly
warned you. **7** For [r]God has not called us
for [s]impurity, but in holiness. **8** Therefore
[t]whoever disregards this, disregards not
man but God, [u]who gives his Holy Spirit to
you.
9 Now concerning [v]brotherly love [w]you
have no need for anyone to write to you,
for you yourselves have been [x]taught by
God [y]to love one another, **10** for that indeed
is what [z]you are doing to all the brothers

[n]Eph. 4:17 [o]Ps. 79:6; Jer. 9:3; 10:25; See Gal. 4:8 **6** [p]1 Cor. 6:8 [q]Rom. 13:4; [Rom. 12:19; Heb. 13:4] **7** [r]ver. 3; See 1 Pet. 1:15 [s]ch. 2:3 **8** [t][ch. 2:13]; See Luke 10:16 [u]1 John 3:24; 4:13 **9** [v]See Heb. 13:1 [w]ch. 5:1 [x]John 6:45; [1 John 2:27] [y]See John 13:34 **10** [z]ch. 1:7

1 Or *brothers and sisters* 2 Or *brothers and sisters*; also verses 10, 13
3 Greek *walk* 4 Or *your holiness* 5 Or *how to take a wife for himself*; Greek *how to possess his own vessel*

3:3, 4 Paul did not promise the followers of Jesus a life of ease or public approval, nor did Jesus (Mark 8:34; John 15:18–21).

3:11 Paul addresses God the Father and the Lord Jesus jointly in prayer (Introduction: Characteristics and Themes). The answer to this prayer for reunion came several years later (Acts 20:1).

3:13 at the coming of our Lord Jesus. The work of sanctification already begun in believers is brought to glorious completion at the Second Coming of the Lord (5:23; cf. 1 Cor. 1:8; Phil. 1:6; 2 Thess. 3:3; Jude 24).

his saints. Lit. "holy ones." Either the angels who will accompany Christ at His return (2 Thess. 1:7; cf. Matt. 13:39, 48, 49; 16:27) or human saints (2 Thess. 1:10; Rev. 19:14) or both.

4:1 Paul praises the Thessalonians for their progress in learning how to please God, but challenges them to excel further. Paul recognized the constant need for growth and for "straining forward" (Phil. 3:13). Spiritual complacency contradicts a believer's confession.

4:2 Again Paul stresses that the authority for his instructions was not his own and not of human origin, but from the risen Lord (2:13).

4:3 the will of God, your sanctification. Scripture generally conceives of the will of God in one of two senses. Sometimes, as in Eph. 1:11, what is meant is the eternal purpose of God that determines history, and that we cannot know except by observing the outworking of history or through a special revelation (prophecy). This is often called by theologians the "decretive," "hidden," or "secret" will of God. Elsewhere, as here and in 5:18, what is meant is the *duty* God has announced through revelation, the "preceptive" or "revealed" will of God (Deut. 29:29).

4:5 like the Gentiles. Pagan society in Paul's day provided little inducement to sexual purity. Marital infidelity, at least for men, was the norm, and some of the pagan religions from which the Thessalonians had been freed sanctioned gross sexual misconduct in their rituals. The Christian gospel brings a moral awakening and a fresh revelation of God's righteous standards.

4:6 wrong his brother. Illicit sexual involvement affects not only the consenting parties. Spouses are wronged and families, friends, and fellow Christians shamed. Ultimately, these sins like all others are sins against God.

4:8 Paul claims divine authority, not merely for his spoken proclamation, but for his written instructions as well (see also 5:27).

gives his Holy Spirit. Paul pointedly reminds them of their renewed capacities for holiness resulting from God's continual endowment of the Holy Spirit who dwells within them (1 Cor. 6:19; Gal. 3:5). The construction in Greek emphasizes the term "Holy," which is especially fitting in this context.

throughout Macedonia. But we urge you,
brothers, to [a]do this more and more, 11 and
to aspire [b]to live quietly, and [c]to mind your
own affairs, and [d]to work with your hands,
as we instructed you, 12 so that you may
[e]live[1] properly before [f]outsiders and be
dependent on no one.

The Coming of the Lord

13 But we do not want you to be uninformed, brothers, about those who are
asleep, [g]that you may not grieve as others
do [h]who have no hope. 14 For [i]since we
believe that Jesus died and rose again, even
so, through Jesus, God will bring with him
[j]those who have fallen asleep. 15 For this we
declare to you [k]by a word from the Lord,[2]
that [l]we who are alive, who are left until
[m]the coming of the Lord, will not precede
those who have fallen asleep. 16 For [n]the

10 [a]See ch. 3:12
11 [b]Prov. 17:14; 20:3; 25:8; 2 Thess. 3:12 [c]2 Thess. 3:11; 1 Pet. 4:15 [d][Acts 18:3]; See Eph. 4:28
12 [e]Rom. 13:13; [Col. 4:5] [f]See Mark 4:11

13 [g][Lev. 19:28; Deut. 14:1; 2 Sam. 12:20-23; Mark 5:39] [h]Eph. 2:12 14 [i]1 Cor. 15:13; [2 Cor. 4:14; Rev. 1:18] [j]1 Cor. 15:18 15 [k]See 1 Kin. 13:17 [l]1 Cor. 15:51 [m]See ch. 2:19 16 [n]See Matt. 16:27

1 Greek *walk* 2 Or *by the word of the Lord*

The Return of Jesus Christ

The New Testament repeatedly announces that Jesus Christ will one day return. His second "coming" or "presence" (Greek *parousia*) will be a royal visit. Christ's return will be personal and physical (Matt. 24:44; Acts 1:11; Col. 3:4; 2 Tim. 4:8; Heb. 9:28), visible and triumphant (Mark 8:38; 2 Thess. 1:10; Rev. 1:7).

At the Second Coming, Jesus will bring an end to history. He will raise the dead and judge the world (John 5:28, 29), and impart to God's children their final glory (Rom. 8:17, 18; Col. 3:4). Paul says that Christ will then deliver the kingdom and become subject to the Father (1 Cor. 15:24–28 note). In saying this, Paul does not mean that Christ is reduced in honor, but that He will have completed the plan God assigned to Him for redeeming the elect. In heaven, the elect will honor the Lamb who opened the book of God's salvation (Rev. 5).

According to 1 Thess. 4:16, 17, Christ's coming will be a descent from the sky, heralded by a trumpet, a shout, and the voice of the archangel. Those who have died in Christ will be raised, and Christians living on earth will be caught up to meet Christ. This event will mark the end of life in this world as we have known it, and the beginning of life in unbroken communion with God. The idea that Christians will be taken out of this world for a period after which Christ will appear still a third time for the "Second Coming" has been widely held, but lacks scriptural support.

The New Testament specifies much that will take place between Christ's two comings. However, apart from the fall of Jerusalem in A.D. 70 (Luke 21:20, 24), these predictions are of ongoing processes rather than single events, and do not yield even an approximate date for Jesus' reappearance. The Gentile world will be summoned to faith (Matt. 24:14), and Jews will be brought into the kingdom (Rom. 11:25–29, a passage that may or may not anticipate a national conversion). There will be false prophets and false christs (Matt. 24:5, 24; 1 John 2:18, 22; 4:3). There will be apostasy from the faith and tribulation for the faithful (2 Thess. 2:3; 1 Tim. 4:1; 2 Tim. 3:1–5; Rev. 7:13, 14; cf. 3:10). A "man of lawlessness" must appear (2 Thess. 2:3–12). No dates can be deduced from these predictions; the time of Jesus' return remains completely unknown (Matt. 24:36).

Christ teaches that it will be a tragic disaster for anyone who is not ready when He returns (Matt. 24:36–51). The thought of His return should be constantly in our minds, encouraging us in our present Christian service (1 Cor. 15:58) and teaching us to live ready to meet Christ at any time (Matt. 25:1–13).

4:11 aspire. The Greek word for this term often denoted the attempt to garner civic honor and recognition through outward displays of generosity by the wealthy. Paul's use of the term turns it on its head: the Thessalonians should be zealous for the honor that comes not through self-assertion or an ostentatious show of personal greatness, but through humble, industrious, and unimpeachable behavior. This exhortation, pertinent to all Christians, had a particular urgency in Thessalonica where the Christians had already been falsely accused of sedition (Acts 17:6–9). By living lives that were respectable and unpretentious, the Christians were to allay any lingering suspicions.

4:13 asleep. This was a standard metaphor for death among pagans as well as Jews and Christians. The term has no particular reference to the state of the soul or consciousness of the deceased, since it is used freely by groups with widely diverging beliefs on this subject. For the New Testament understanding of a conscious and blessed existence between death and the resurrection, see Luke 16:19–31; 23:42, 43; John 14:1–3; 2 Cor. 5:6–8; Phil. 1:23; Rev. 6:9–11; 7:9–17; 20:4–6. See "Death and the Intermediate State" at Phil. 1:23.

grieve. Christ's resurrection affords Christians a deeply seated hope and assurance of never-ending fellowship with Him. Therefore their grief over departed brethren is softened, and they are upheld in hope.

4:14 God will bring with him. Probably this is to be understood as a "bringing" into God's presence (3:13) and kingdom by resurrection (1 Cor. 6:14; 2 Cor. 4:14), though some believe it signifies a bringing of the saints to earth when Christ returns.

4:15 will not precede. According to 2 Esdras, a Jewish work of the second century A.D., those who survive until the coming of the glorious

Lord himself will descend [o]from heaven
[p]with a cry of command, with the voice of
[q]an archangel, and [r]with the sound of the
trumpet of God. And [s]the dead in Christ
will rise first. 17 Then we who are alive, who
are left, will be [t]caught up together with
them [u]in the clouds to meet the Lord in the
air, and so [v]we will always be with the
Lord. 18 Therefore encourage one another
with these words.

The Day of the Lord

5 Now concerning [w]the times and the
seasons, brothers,[1] [x]you have no need
to have anything written to you. 2 For you
yourselves are fully aware that [y]the day of
the Lord will come like a thief in the night.
3 While people are saying, "There is peace
and security," then [z]sudden destruction
will come upon them [a]as labor pains come
upon a pregnant woman, and they will not
escape. 4 But you [b]are not in darkness,
brothers, for that day to surprise you like a
thief. 5 For you are all [c]children[2] of light,
children of the day. We are not of the night
or of the darkness. 6 So then [d]let us not
sleep, as others do, but let us [e]keep awake
and [f]be sober. 7 For those who sleep, sleep
at night, and those who get drunk, [g]are
drunk at night. 8 But since we belong to the
day, let us be sober, [h]having put on the
breastplate of [i]faith and love, and for a helmet the hope of salvation. 9 For God has
not destined us for [j]wrath, but [k]to obtain
salvation through our Lord Jesus Christ,
10 [l]who died for us so that whether we are
awake or asleep we might live with him.
11 Therefore encourage one another and
build one another up, just as you are
doing.

Final Instructions and Benediction

12 We ask you, brothers, [m]to respect
those who labor among you and [n]are over
you in the Lord and admonish you, 13 and
to esteem them very highly in love because
of their work. [o]Be at peace among yourselves. 14 And we urge you, brothers,
admonish [p]the idle,[3] [q]encourage the faint-

16 [o]2 Thess. 1:7 [p][Joel 2:11] [q]Jude 9 [r]Matt. 24:31; 1 Cor. 15:52 [s]1 Cor. 15:23; [2 Thess. 2:1; Rev. 14:13] **17** [t]See 2 Cor. 12:2 [u][Dan. 7:13; Acts 1:9; Rev. 11:12] [v]See John 12:26
Chapter 5
1 [w]Dan. 2:21; Acts 1:7 [x]ch. 4:9 **2** [y][2 Thess. 2:2]; See Matt. 24:43; Luke 17:24 **3** [z]Luke 21:34; [Ps. 35:8; Luke 17:26-30; 2 Thess. 1:9] [a]See Isai. 13:8 **4** [b]1 John 2:8 **5** [c]See Luke 16:8 **6** [d][Mark 13:36]; See Rom. 13:11-13 [e]See Matt. 24:42 [f]See 1 Pet. 1:13 **7** [g][Acts 2:15; 2 Pet. 2:13] **8** [h]Isai. 59:17; Eph. 6:14, 17 [i][Eph. 6:23]
9 [j]See ch. 1:10 [k]2 Thess. 2:13, 14; [Heb. 10:39] **10** [l]Rom. 14:9; [2 Tim. 2:11] **12** [m]1 Cor. 16:18; Phil. 2:29 [n]1 Cor. 16:16; Heb. 13:17 **13** [o]See Mark 9:50 **14** [p]2 Thess. 3:6, 7, 11 [q]Isai. 35:4; [Heb. 12:12]

1 Or *brothers and sisters*; also verses 4, 12, 14, 25, 26, 27 2 Or *sons*; twice in this verse 3 Or *disorderly*, or *undisciplined*

Messiah are more blessed than those who have died before (2 Esdras 13:14–24). Some of the Thessalonians may have caught wind of a similar misconception. Paul to the contrary assures the Thessalonians that both groups will be on equal footing (1 Cor. 15:52), that both will enter the fullness of the kingdom together.

4:16 the dead in Christ will rise first. For Paul, those "in Christ" constitute a subcategory of those "in Adam" (the whole human race), and comprise all who participate in the salvation of Christ (1 Cor. 15:22, 23), whether they lived before or after Christ. Therefore, this rising of the "dead in Christ" is a resurrection of all the righteous dead, and not merely of New Testament believers, at the time of Christ's return (as in 1 Cor. 15:23; cf. John 5:28, 29). The resurrection of the unrighteous is mentioned explicitly by Paul only in Acts 24:15, though he also presupposes it in his warnings of a universal judgment of individuals at the time of Christ's return (Acts 17:31; Rom. 2:5–16). See theological note "The Return of Jesus Christ" on previous page.

4:17 caught up. This description of the catching-up or "rapture" of the church is not presented so as to satisfy all our cravings for detailed knowledge of end-time chronology. For instance, we are not told whether the assembled company will descend to earth or return to heaven. The presentation is pastoral, to comfort those grieved and confused by the death of beloved Christians. The assurance that all the righteous without distinction will be with the Lord forever, and united at the coming of Christ, is the burden of this passage (v. 18). The "cry," "voice," and "trumpet" of v. 16 give the distinct impression that the rapture will be public and not secret (Luke 17:24; 21:35; Rev. 1:7). See note 5:1–11.

5:1–11 The Thessalonians are told to prepare for the same thing that will come unexpectedly upon the ungodly—the day of the Lord (vv. 2, 4). Paul assumes that Christians and non-Christians alike will be alive and present when the Day arrives, Christians watchful and ready, non-Christians surprised as by a thief who comes at night. In other words, the rapture of Christians spoken of in 4:17 will not occur before the arrival of the Day that will also bring sudden and inescapable destruction to the wicked (2 Thess. 2:1, 2 notes). See "The Return of Jesus Christ" at 4:16.

5:2 day of the Lord. A prominent designation of the day on which Christ returns. It is well known from the Old Testament (e.g., Joel 2:1, 31; Amos 5:18; Zeph. 1:7, 14; Mal. 4:5), where it is used of God's drawing near in judgment. This prominent association of the day of the Lord with judgment is carried on in the New Testament, where the last judgment and final rewards and punishments are in view (Acts 17:31; Rom. 2:5, 16; 2 Cor. 1:14). According to 2 Pet. 3:10–13, the heavens, the earth, and the elements will be destroyed to make way for a new heaven and new earth.

like a thief in the night. See Matt. 24:43, 44; 2 Pet. 3:10; Rev. 3:3; 16:15. Paul seems to be familiar with at least some of Jesus' "Olivet Discourse" (Matt. 24:3–25:46; Mark 13:3–37; Luke 21:5–36).

5:9 God has not destined us for wrath. God has appointed His people to obtain salvation and glory in Jesus Christ (1:10; 2 Thess. 2:14). Yet the Thessalonians and many other Christians have been appointed by God to undergo and withstand tribulation of every kind (3:2–4; 2 Thess. 1:4; James 1:2–4; 1 Pet. 4:12–14; Rev. 1:9). The "wrath" in this context is evidently the condemnation and punishment that will fall in "the day of wrath" (Rom. 2:5) upon the impenitent (Eph. 5:6; Col. 3:6; Rev. 6:16, 17; 11:18).

5:12 Even at this early stage in the life of the congregation there were leaders who had spiritual care and oversight. Paul endorses a proper esteem for church workers and leaders, asking love and respect for them. Some Thessalonians named elsewhere who may have been in Paul's mind here are Jason (Acts 17:6–9), Aristarchus (Acts 20:4; 27:2; Col. 4:10; Philem. 24), Secundus (Acts 20:4), and possibly Gaius (Acts 19:29).

5:14 brothers. This address (also v. 12) indicates that the exhortations that follow assign the responsibility for ministry to all the congregation, not just to acknowledged leaders.

the idle. The contexts here and in 2 Thess. 3:6, 7, 11 show that the form of idleness in view is an irresponsible refusal to work for a living (text note). Many think this behavior was fed by an overripe expectancy of Christ's Second Coming (Introduction to 2 Thessalonians).

hearted, [r]help the weak, [s]be patient with
them all. 15 See that [t]no one repays anyone
evil for evil, but always [u]seek to do good to
one another and to everyone. 16 [v]Rejoice
always, 17 [w]pray without ceasing, 18 [x]give
thanks in all circumstances; for this is the
will of God in Christ Jesus for you. 19 [y]Do
not quench the Spirit. 20 Do not despise
[z]prophecies, 21 but [a]test everything; hold
fast what is good. 22 Abstain from every
form of evil.

23 Now may [b]the God of peace himself
[c]sanctify you completely, and may your
[d]whole [e]spirit and soul and body be kept
blameless at [f]the coming of our Lord Jesus
Christ. 24 [g]He who calls you is faithful; [h]he
will surely do it.

25 [i]Brothers, pray for us.

26 [j]Greet all the brothers with a holy kiss.

27 I put you under oath before the Lord to
have [k]this letter read to all the brothers.

28 [l]The grace of our Lord Jesus Christ be
with you.

14 [r]Acts 20:35; See Rom. 15:1 [s]See 1 Cor. 13:4 **15** [t][1 Pet. 3:9; See Rom. 12:17 [u][Rom. 12:9]; See Gal. 6:10 **16** [v]Phil. 4:4 **17** [w]See Luke 18:1 **18** [x]See Eph. 5:20 **19** [y][1 Cor. 14:30; Eph. 4:30; 1 Tim. 4:14; 2 Tim. 1:6] **20** [z]See 1 Cor. 11:4

21 [a]1 John 4:1; [Job 34:4]; See Eph. 5:10 **23** [b]See Rom. 15:33 [c]Ex. 31:13; John 17:17 [d]2 Pet. 3:14; Jude 1 [e]Luke 1:46, 47; Heb. 4:12; [1 Cor. 14:14] [f]See ch. 2:19 **24** [g]See 1 Cor. 1:9 [h][Phil. 1:6] **25** [i]2 Thess. 3:1; Heb. 13:18 **26** [j]See Rom. 16:16 **27** [k]Col. 4:16 **28** [l]See Rom. 16:20

5:15 A Christian must seek justice for others (Is. 56:1; 58:6–8). It is a remarkable part of Christian morality that the Christian, following the example of Christ (1 Pet. 2:21–23), should refuse to seek personal retaliation (Matt. 5:38–42; Rom. 12:17–21; 1 Cor. 6:7; 1 Pet. 3:9).

5:19–21 Paul admonishes the Thessalonians not to despise legitimate prophecy; both Silas and Paul were "prophets" (Acts 13:1; 15:32). Nevertheless, claims to divine prophecy must be tested and not accepted uncritically (2 Thess. 2:2; cf. 1 Cor. 14:29).

5:23 sanctify. The complete mending of all human imperfection is not only possible but certain. God is faithful and will accomplish it (v. 24). The time element must be remembered. Ultimate perfection, to include a glorified body as well, will be accomplished at the Second Coming of Jesus Christ (Phil. 1:6). See "Sanctification: The Spirit and the Flesh" at 1 Cor. 6:11.

your whole spirit and soul and body. Three words are used to emphasize the wholeness of the perfection. "Spirit" and "soul" are used as virtual synonyms in the Bible for the spiritual component of a person. When the terms occur together (as here and in Heb. 4:12) it is difficult to find any significant difference in meaning. Compare the fourfold representation of "heart," "soul," "mind," and "strength" in Mark 12:30.

5:27 put you under oath. The Greek verb is unusually strong. Paul is laying a solemn weight upon them that the whole congregation must learn the contents of this epistle—so important did he consider his apostolic teaching for their spiritual good (2:13; 4:2 notes).

THE SECOND EPISTLE OF PAUL THE APOSTLE TO THE

Thessalonians

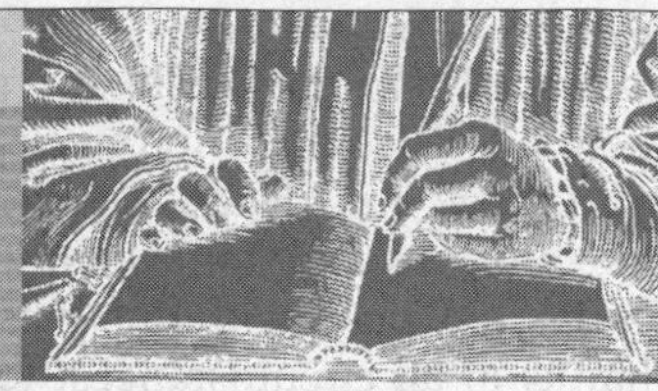

AUTHOR

The author of 2 Thessalonians claims to be Paul (1:1; 3:17), and in the first half of the second century the epistle was apparently known to Ignatius of Antioch, Polycarp, and Justin Martyr. Despite this early attestation, 2 Thessalonians has suffered more frequent and more influential attacks on its authenticity than has 1 Thessalonians. The close similarities in subject matter and even in phrasing between the two letters have been seen by some scholars as an indication of imitation. But this evidence can be read the other way. Who is more capable of echoing Paul's thought than Paul himself?

Some have said that the two letters teach contradictory eschatologies (doctrines of the end time and eternal future) and therefore cannot be from one author. The first letter is thought to teach an imminent return of Christ, whereas 2 Thessalonians insists that certain intervening events must occur before Christ returns. But the conflict is illusory. Nothing definite about the imminence of the Second Coming of Christ is stated in 1 Thessalonians, which stresses only the suddenness and unexpectedness with which the day of the Lord will overtake the unwary. The second letter specifies an order of events so as to counteract a new misunderstanding at Thessalonica that the day of the Lord had already arrived.

In 2:5 and 3:10 Paul reminds the Thessalonians of what he had taught while he was with them. If these statements were written by someone else using Paul's name and were not by Paul, they could have been exposed without difficulty at any time during the first generation after the events reported. Also, it is difficult to explain why anyone using Paul's name falsely as a means of gaining influence would include such a sharp attack on some of the readers as is found in 3:10, 11. On such counts the proposal that the letter is not by Paul creates more difficulties than it solves.

DATE AND OCCASION

Second Thessalonians 2:15 mentions an earlier letter from Paul. Very probably 1 Thessalonians was this earlier letter, and 2 Thessalonians is to be dated shortly after it, about A.D. 51. Both letters were written from Corinth.

CHARACTERISTICS AND THEMES

1. Eschatology. Since sending the first letter, Paul had received further reports concerning the congregation. There was cause for rejoicing in their continued growth in faith, love, and patience (1:3, 4), as well as cause for concern in certain doctrinal and behavioral matters. Second Thessalonians was written mainly to supplement Paul's earlier teaching by correcting a premature and unsettling announcement that the day of the Lord had already arrived (2:1–11). This misguided claim may have been due in part to wrong inferences drawn from Paul's own teaching, coupled with the congregation's painful experience of persecutions thought to be indicative of end-time disturbances.

2. The Importance of Work. A second motive for writing was to deal with the chronic idleness of some members (3:6–15). Their behavior had continued uncorrected since the last letter (1 Thess. 4:11, 12; 5:14) and, indeed, ever since the missionaries had been present (3:10, 11). Exhortations were made even then in an attempt to rectify the situation but, according to fresh reports (3:11), matters had only grown worse. Many scholars believe the cause of idleness was the erroneous expectation that the Lord's return might happen so soon (2:1–3) that working for a living amounted to a denial of faith. Some connection between a faulty eschatology and faulty conduct of this sort is likely in the Thessalonian context. Yet it must be said that Paul never draws the connection himself. Since 3:10 shows that the problem had surfaced while the missionaries were still in Thessalonica, it is unlikely that eschatological errors gave birth to the problem, though they may have provided a convenient excuse for continuing in it.

OUTLINE OF 2 THESSALONIANS

I. Salutation (1:1, 2)

II. Paul's Cause for Boasting (1:3–12)

- A. *Endurance During Persecution (1:3, 4)*
- B. *Glorified at Christ's Return (1:5–10)*
- C. *Prayer for the Work of Faith (1:11, 12)*

III. Instruction (2:1–3:15)

- A. *The Day of the Lord (2:1–12)*
- B. *Prayer and Exhortation (2:13–3:5)*
- C. *Labor (3:6–15)*

IV. Concluding Benediction (3:16–18)

Greeting

1 [a]Paul, Silvanus, and Timothy,
To the church of the Thessalonians in
God our Father and the Lord Jesus Christ:
2 Grace to you and peace from God our
Father and the Lord Jesus Christ.

Thanksgiving

3 [b]We ought always to give thanks to God
for you, brothers,[1] as is right, because your
faith is growing abundantly, and the love of
every one of you for one another is increasing. 4 Therefore [c]we ourselves boast about
you [d]in the churches of God for your steadfastness and faith [e]in all your persecutions
and in the afflictions that you are enduring.

The Judgment at Christ's Coming

5 This is [f]evidence of the righteous judgment of God, that you may be [g]considered
worthy of the kingdom of God, for which
you are also suffering— 6 since indeed God
considers it [h]just [i]to repay with affliction
those who afflict you, 7 and to grant [j]relief
to you who are afflicted as well as to us,
when [k]the Lord Jesus is revealed from
heaven [l]with his mighty angels 8 [m]in flaming fire, inflicting vengeance on those [n]who
do not know God and on those who [o]do
not obey the gospel of our Lord Jesus.
9 They will suffer the punishment of [p]eter-
nal destruction, [q]away from[2] the presence
of the Lord and from the glory of his might,
10 [r]when he comes on [s]that day [t]to be glorified in his saints, and to be marveled at
among all who have believed, because our
[u]testimony to you [v]was believed. 11 To this
end we [w]always pray for you, that our God
may [x]make you worthy of his calling and

Chapter 1
1 [a]For ver. 1, 2, see 1 Thess. 1:1
3 [b]ch. 2:13; See Eph. 5:20; 1 Thess. 1:2, 3
4 [c][2 Cor. 7:14]; See 1 Thess. 2:19 [d][1 Thess. 1:8]; See 1 Cor. 7:17 [e][Mark 10:30]; See 1 Thess. 2:14
5 [f][Phil. 1:28] [g][Acts 14:22]; See Luke 20:35
6 [h][Rev. 6:10] [i][Ex. 23:22; Joel 3:4, 7]
7 [j][Rev. 6:11; 11:18; 14:13] [k]See Luke 17:30 [l]See Jude 14

8 [m]Isai. 66:15, 16; Matt. 25:41; 1 Cor. 3:13; Heb. 10:27; 12:29; 2 Pet. 3:7; [Mal. 4:1] [n]See Gal. 4:8 [o]Rom. 2:8 9 [p][Phil. 3:19; 1 Thess. 5:3] [q]Isai. 2:10, 19, 21; [ch. 2:8] 10 [r]See 1 Thess. 1:10 [s]See 1 Cor. 3:13 [t]Ps. 89:7 (Gk.); Isai. 49:3; John 17:10 [u][1 Cor. 1:6] [v][1 Thess. 2:1, 13; 1 Tim. 3:16] 11 [w]Col. 1:9 [x][ver. 5]

[1] Or *brothers and sisters*. The plural Greek word *adelphoi* (translated "brothers") refers to siblings in a family. In New Testament usage, depending on the context, *adelphoi* may refer either to men or to both men and women who are siblings (brothers and sisters) in God's family, the church [2] Or *destruction that comes from*

1:1 See note 1 Thess. 1:1.

1:4 persecutions and in the afflictions. One instance of persecution is recounted in Acts 17:5–9, and the Thessalonian correspondence reveals that antagonism had not disappeared (1 Thess. 1:6; 2:14; 3:3).

1:5 considered worthy. A life worthy of God (1 Thess. 2:12), of God's calling (1:11; Eph. 4:1), of the Lord (Col. 1:10), of the gospel (Phil. 1:27, 28), or of the kingdom (v. 5) is a life of patient, joyful discipleship even in the face of life-threatening abuse from those hostile to the faith. Such lives are sure evidence that God's judgment is right.

for which you are also suffering. Even while enjoying the benefits of citizenship in the heavenly kingdom (1 Thess. 2:12 note), Christians still must suffer for its sake (Acts 14:22), since the kingdom will inevitably confront diabolical opposition.

1:6 repay with affliction. In Rom. 2:9 the same Greek word for "tribulation" (trouble) is used for the woe brought upon evildoers at the Last Judgment. Paul appears to be speaking of the same judgment here, as the next verses are concerned with ultimate bliss and woe.

1:8 obey the gospel. The gospel must be accepted, believed, and obeyed (1 Pet. 4:17). Its divine command is for absolute surrender to God through the peace made by Jesus Christ.

1:9 eternal destruction. The fearful doctrine of eternal punishment (Is. 66:24; Matt. 25:42, 46; Mark 9:43, 48), staggering as it is, assured the hounded Thessalonian Christians of final and perfect justice. They were to refrain from taking personal revenge (1 Thess. 5:15; cf. Rom. 12:17–21) for the atrocities they suffered (v. 4), entrusting themselves instead to the God "who judges justly" (1 Pet. 2:23; cf. Jer. 17:10; Acts 17:31; Rom. 2:6, 11, 16; Rev. 22:12).

1:10 on that day. The "day of the Lord" (1 Thess. 5:2). Although we have no way of knowing how long the Day will last, the impression given is that the final judgment of the ungodly closely accompanies the coming of Christ for His saints.

1:11 his calling. Such "calling" should be related to 1 Thess. 2:12, where God is the One who calls; what we are called to is God's own kingdom and glory (2:14).

may fulfill every resolve for good and every
[y]work of faith by his power, 12 so that the
name of our Lord Jesus [z]may be glorified in
you, and you in him, according to the grace
of our God and the Lord Jesus Christ.

The Man of Lawlessness

2 Now concerning [a]the coming of our
Lord Jesus Christ and our [b]being gathered together to him, we ask you, brothers,[1] 2 not to be quickly shaken in mind or
[c]alarmed, either [d]by a spirit or a [e]spoken
word, or [e]a letter seeming to be from us, to
the effect that [f]the day of the Lord has
come. 3 [g]Let no one deceive you in any way.
For that day will not come, [h]unless the
rebellion comes first, and [i]the man of lawlessness[2] is revealed, [j]the son of destruction,[3] 4 who opposes and exalts himself
against every so-called god or object of
worship, so that he takes his seat in the
temple of God, [k]proclaiming himself to be
God. 5 Do you not remember that when I
was still with you I told you these things?
6 And you know what is restraining him
now so that he may be revealed in his time.
7 For [l]the mystery of lawlessness [m]is already
at work. Only he who now restrains it will
do so until he is out of the way. 8 And then
[n]the lawless one will be revealed, whom
the Lord Jesus [o]will kill with [p]the breath of
his mouth and bring to nothing by [q]the
appearance of his coming. 9 The coming of
the lawless one is by the activity of Satan
[r]with all power and false signs and wonders, 10 and with all wicked deception for
[s]those who are perishing, because they
refused to love the truth and so be saved.
11 Therefore [t]God sends them a strong delusion, so that they may believe [u]what is
false, 12 in order that all may be condemned
[v]who did not believe the truth but [w]had
pleasure in unrighteousness.

11 [y]1 Thess. 1:3 **12** [z][Isai. 66:5; Acts 13:48] **Chapter 2** **1** [a]See 1 Thess. 2:19 [b][Matt. 24:31; 1 Thess. 4:15-17] **2** [c]Matt. 24:6; Mark 13:7 [d][1 John 4:1] [e]ver. 15; [1 Thess. 5:2] [f]See 1 Cor. 1:8 **3** [g]Eph. 5:6 [h]1 Tim. 4:1 [i][ver. 8; Dan. 7:25; 8:25; 11:36; Rev. 13:5, 6] [j]John 17:12; [Matt. 23:15] **4** [k][Isai. 14:14; Ezek. 28:2] **7** [l]Rev. 17:5, 7 [m]1 John 2:18; 4:3 **8** [n]See ver. 3 [o][Dan. 7:10, 11] [p]Isai. 11:4 [q][1 Tim. 6:14; 2 Tim. 1:10; 4:1, 8; Tit. 2:13] **9** [r][Rev. 13:14]; See Matt. 24:24 **10** [s]See 1 Cor. 1:18 **11** [t][1 Kin. 22:22; Ezek. 14:9; Rev. 17:17] [u][1 Thess. 2:3; 1 Tim. 4:2]; See Rom. 1:25 **12** [v]Rom. 2:8 [w]See Rom. 1:32

[1] Or *brothers and sisters*; also verses 13, 15 [2] Some manuscripts *sin* [3] Greek *the son of perdition* (a Hebrew idiom)

1:12 our God and the Lord Jesus Christ. As it stands the Greek can also be translated, "our God and Lord, Jesus Christ." This would be a distinct use of the term "God" in reference to Jesus Christ. Arguing against such a translation is the infrequent application of this term to Christ in the New Testament (Rom. 9:5; Titus 2:13; 2 Pet. 1:1). On the other hand, Paul often brings Christ and God the Father together into close unity in other phrases in these letters (e.g., vv. 1, 2; 2:16; 1 Thess. 1:1; 3:11), and he clearly ascribes attributes of deity to Christ. In either translation the joint dignity of the Father and the Son is clear.

2:1 concerning the coming . . . and our being gathered together to him. This is the rapture of the saints spoken of in 1 Thess. 4:17 (note). Paul appears to equate the time of Christ's coming and the rapture with the "day of the Lord" (1 Thess. 5:2; cf. 1 Cor. 1:7, 8; Phil. 2:16). In this scene all believers are gathered before the Lord "at his coming" (1 Thess. 2:19) and "on the day of our Lord Jesus" (2 Cor. 1:14). The "rebellion" must come and the "man of lawlessness" (v. 3) must be revealed before the day of the Lord arrives, and therefore they must also occur before the rapture of the saints. If the false teachers were saying that the day of the Lord had arrived (v. 2) and were anticipating the rapture at any moment, they could be proved wrong by the absence of these prior signs.

2:2 letter. This reference does not prove there was a forged letter bearing Paul's name already in existence, but only that Paul saw this as a possibility. Word may have reached him that the new teaching was circulating with some pretense of having his authority. Paul's injunction is meant to ensure that no vehicle of instruction—even one supposed to have come from him—should be heeded if it asserts that the day of the Lord has already come (cf. Gal. 1:8).

2:3 the rebellion. This might refer to a falling away of many within the church (1 Tim. 4:1; 2 Tim. 3:1–9; Jude 17–19), to an apostasy of the Jewish people, or to a worldwide rebellion against God.

man of lawlessness. This is an individual embodiment of wickedness, whose arrogant blasphemies Paul lists (cf. 1 John 2:22). He will draw away by deception those already inclined against the true God (v. 10) and will ultimately commit the sacrilege of thrusting himself upon humanity as its object of worship (v. 4). He comes by the power of Satan, as Christ came by the power of God, and he works fraudulent wonders as Christ worked true ones (v. 9; cf. Acts 2:22). Paul depicts this imposter as a parody or antithesis of the true Christ. Paul himself does not use the term "antichrist" (1 John 2:18, 22; 4:3), but it is a fitting designation. His fate is sealed; he will be destroyed by the coming of Christ. See "The Return of Christ" at 1 Thess. 4:16.

2:4 exalts himself against every so-called god. This description of the man of lawlessness echoes that of Daniel's little "horn" (Dan. 7:8, 20, 21; 8:9–12; cf. 11:31, 36) and foreshadows John's description of the beast from the sea (Rev. 13:1–8).

takes his seat in the temple of God. Some conclude from this verse that the temple in Jerusalem, still standing when Paul wrote but destroyed in A.D. 70, must be rebuilt for the use of "the man of lawlessness." Others understand "temple" in another of its New Testament meanings, as the church (Eph. 2:19–22; 1 Pet. 2:5). The reference may be an intentionally exaggerated way of talking about the imposter's aspirations to heavenly power. Just as another prototype of sin, the king of Babylon wanted to set his throne in heaven (Is. 14:13, 14; cf. the king of Tyre in Ezek. 28:2), so the man of lawlessness will boast of himself as the possessor of God's heavenly sanctuary (Rev. 13:6).

2:6 The identity of what is "restraining" the man of lawlessness (vv. 6, 7; cf. Rev. 20:1–3) is no longer self-evident to readers of 2 Thessalonians. Interpreters have proposed numerous alternatives. The restraining power seems to be both impersonal (v. 6, "what is restraining") and personal (v. 7, "he who now restrains"). Hence it may be an institution that can also be represented by a single person, such as the Roman state with its emperor, the Jewish state with its leader, or the universal ministry of the gospel with Paul as its chief minister. Whatever the precise reference, it is clear that behind the restraining power is the will of God.

2:7 already at work. Though the man of lawlessness has not yet appeared, Paul will not allow his readers to let down their guard. The same satanic power that will ultimately spawn this unholy deceiver was already at work in Paul's day (1 John 2:18) and is at work in ours. Because it is now restrained, the church has a strong encouragement to carry out its mission.

2:8 with the breath of his mouth. The description is from Is. 11:4. It reappears in Rev. 19:15, 21 where the beast and his false prophet meet their final end.

2:9 The coming of Christ is to be preceded by the "coming of the lawless one."

Stand Firm

13 But [x]we ought always to give thanks to
God for you, [y]brothers beloved by the
Lord, because God chose you [z]as the firstfruits[1] [a]to be saved, [b]through sanctification
by the Spirit and belief in the truth. 14 To
this he called you through [c]our gospel, [a]so
that you may obtain the glory of our Lord
Jesus Christ. 15 So then, brothers, [d]stand
firm and hold to [e]the traditions that you
were taught by us, either [f]by our spoken
word or by [f]our letter.
16 Now may our Lord Jesus Christ himself, and God our Father, [g]who loved us
and gave us eternal comfort and good
[h]hope through grace, 17 comfort your hearts
and [i]establish them in every good work
and word.

Pray for Us

3 Finally, brothers,[2] [j]pray for us, that
[k]the word of the Lord may speed
ahead and be honored,[3] as happened

13 [x]ch. 1:3 [y]1 Thess. 1:4; [Deut. 33:12] [z]Eph. 1:4 [a]1 Thess. 5:9; [2 Tim. 1:9] [b]See 1 Thess. 4:3
14 [c]1 Thess. 1:5 [a][See ver. 13 above]
15 [d]See 1 Cor. 16:13 [e]ch. 3:6; 1 Cor. 11:2 [f]ver. 2
16 [g]John 3:16; 1 John 4:10; Rev. 1:5 [h]1 Pet. 1:3
17 [i]ch. 3:3; 1 Thess. 3:13
Chapter 3 1 [j]See 1 Thess. 5:25 [k]Ps. 147:15; [1 Thess. 1:8]

1 Some manuscripts *chose you from the beginning* 2 Or *brothers and sisters*; also verses 6, 13 3 Or *glorified*

Effectual Calling and Conversion

"Effectual calling" is the title of ch. 10 of the *Westminster Confession* (1647). The chapter begins:

> All those whom God hath predestinated unto life, and those only, He is pleased, in His appointed and accepted time, effectually to call, by His Word and Spirit, out of that state of sin and death, in which they are by nature, to grace and salvation, by Jesus Christ; enlightening their minds spiritually and savingly to understand the things of God, taking away their heart of stone, and giving unto them a heart of flesh; renewing their wills, and, by His almighty power, determining them to that which is good, and effectually drawing them to Jesus Christ: yet so, as they come most freely, being made willing by His grace.

What is described here is the process of Christian conversion, involving illumination, regeneration, and the transformation of the will. It is a sovereign work of God, "effectually" (that is, effectively) performed by the power of the Holy Spirit. The doctrine corresponds to Paul's use of the word "call" in the sense of "to bring to faith," and his use of "called" to mean "converted" (Rom. 1:6; 8:28, 30; 9:24; 1 Cor. 1:9, 24, 26; 7:18, 21; Gal. 1:15; Eph. 4:1, 4; 2 Thess. 2:14). This calling is different from the general invitation, as described in Jesus' explanation of the parable of the wedding feast (Matt. 22:14). The general, external invitation can fail to be answered, but the effectual calling is a particular act of God resulting in regeneration. It cannot be refused (John 10:3, 4).

Original sin means that all human beings are by nature "dead," or unresponsive to God. Through the effectual calling, God gives life to the dead. The outward call of God to faith in Christ is communicated everywhere through reading, preaching, and explaining the gospel. In the inner, effectual call the Holy Spirit enlightens the mind and renews the heart of those God has chosen so that the gospel is accepted as the truth of God, and God in Christ becomes the object of love and affection. When once regenerated and having the will set free to choose God and the good, a sinner turns away from the former pattern of living and receives Jesus Christ as Lord and Savior, to start a new life with Him.

2:13, 14 There is a wealth of instruction in these two verses. Major elements in the biblical doctrine of salvation—election, calling, faith, sanctification, and glorification—are presented in their mutual relations. There is a harmonious working of all three Persons of the Trinity: God the Father choosing and calling, God the Son sharing His glory with His people, and God the Holy Spirit imparting His sanctifying grace (1 Pet. 1:2).

2:13 But. With this word Paul begins to assure his readers that he does not include them with those he has just mentioned in vv. 11 and 12, who refuse to love the truth and will fall prey to deception.

God chose you. See note 1 Thess. 1:4. From the beginning (Eph. 1:4), God chose them "through" sanctification and believing the truth, not "because of" these actions. According to Paul, the elect cannot continue to live in a godless fashion after they are converted.

2:14 To this. That is, to salvation.

he called you. On God's calling see 1:11; 1 Thess. 2:12; 1 Tim. 6:12; theological note "Effectual Calling and Conversion."

through our gospel. The gospel, which concerns God's Son (Rom. 1:3), is the means employed by God to call sinners to glory.

obtain the glory of our Lord Jesus Christ. This is another way of speaking about the salvation to which God has called us (Rom. 8:30; 1 Thess. 2:12; 1 Pet. 5:10).

2:15 hold to the traditions. Paul passed on authoritative practical and doctrinal traditions, by word and by letter (Rom. 6:17; 1 Cor. 11:2, 23; 15:3; 2 Tim. 1:13).

letter. Probably 1 Thessalonians.

3:1, 2 Paul requests prayer for the success of the gospel and for the protection of those who bring it. Paul faced almost constant physical danger during his years of ministry. This text, along with Rom. 15:30, 31; 2 Cor. 1:11; Phil. 1:19, shows how much he relied on the prayers of God's people for the continuation of his ministry, if not for his own survival.

among you, 2 and [l]that we may be delivered
from wicked and evil men. For [m]not all
have faith. 3 But [n]the Lord is faithful. He
will establish you and [o]guard you against
[p]the evil one.[1] 4 And [q]we have confidence in
the Lord about you, that you are doing and
will do the things that we command. 5 May
the Lord [r]direct your hearts to the love of
God and to the steadfastness of Christ.

Warning Against Idleness

6 Now we command you, brothers, [s]in
the name of our Lord Jesus Christ, [t]that
you keep away from any [u]brother [v]who is
walking in idleness and not in accord with
the tradition that you received from us.
7 For you yourselves know [w]how you ought
to imitate us, because [x]we were not idle
when we were with you, 8 nor did we eat
anyone's bread without paying for it, but
[y]with toil and labor we worked night and
day, that we might not be a burden to any
of you. 9 It was [z]not because we do not have
that right, but to give you in ourselves [a]an
example to imitate. 10 For even when we
were with you, we would give you this
command: [b]If anyone is not willing to
work, let him not eat. 11 For we hear that
some among you [c]walk in idleness, not
busy at work, but [d]busybodies. 12 Now such
persons we command and encourage in
the Lord Jesus Christ to do their work quietly and to earn their own living.[2]
13 As for you, brothers, [e]do not grow
weary in doing good. 14 If anyone does not
obey what we say in this letter, take note of
that person, and [f]have nothing to do with
him, that he may be ashamed. 15 [g]Do not
regard him as an enemy, but [h]warn him as
a brother.

Benediction

16 Now may [i]the Lord of peace himself
[j]give you peace at all times in every way.
[k]The Lord be with you all.
17 I, Paul, write [l]this greeting with my
own hand. This is the sign of genuineness
in every letter of mine; it is the way I write.
18 [m]The grace of our Lord Jesus Christ be
with you all.

2 [l]Rom. 15:31 [m][Deut. 32:20]
3 [n]See 1 Cor. 1:9 [o]Matt. 6:13; John 17:15 [p]See Matt. 13:19
4 [q]See 2 Cor. 2:3
5 [r]1 Thess. 3:11
6 [s]1 Cor. 5:4 [t]ver. 14; [Matt. 18:17; 2 Tim. 3:5]; See 1 Cor. 5:9; 2 John 10 [u]1 Cor. 5:11 [v]ver. 11; 1 Thess. 5:14
7 [w][Acts 20:35]; See 1 Thess. 1:6 [x]1 Thess. 1:5
8 [y]See 1 Thess. 2:9
9 [z]1 Cor. 9:4; 1 Thess. 2:6 [a]ver. 7; 1 Pet. 5:3
10 [b][Gen. 3:19]; See 1 Thess. 4:11
11 [c]ver. 6 [d]1 Tim. 5:13; 1 Pet. 4:15
13 [e]Gal. 6:9; [1 Cor. 15:58]
14 [f]See ver. 6 **15** [g]See Lev. 19:17; Matt. 18:15 [h]1 Thess. 5:12, 14; [Tit. 3:10]
16 [i]See Rom. 15:33; Eph. 6:23 [j]Num. 6:26 [k]Ruth 2:4 **17** [l]See 1 Cor. 16:21
18 [m]See Rom. 16:20

1 Or *evil* 2 Greek *eat their own bread*

3:3 faithful. Contrasting with the faithlessness mentioned in the previous verse is the steadfast faithfulness of our unchanging God (Mal. 3:6; 1 Cor. 1:9; 10:13; 2 Cor. 1:18; James 1:17).

3:5 love of God . . . steadfastness of Christ. Our hearts should journey to these safe spiritual harbors of meditation; it is a journey directed by the Lord.

3:6–15 See Introduction: Characteristics and Themes. Paul takes firm measures against an ongoing problem of idleness and its consequences (v. 10; cf. 1 Thess. 4:11). Paul obviously regards the offense as serious, but he treats the offenders as fellow believers.

3:6 keep away. Paul may have had in mind Jesus' instructions on church discipline recorded in Matt. 18:15–17. He gives similar charges in vv. 14, 15; Rom. 16:17; 1 Cor. 5:9–13; 2 Tim. 3:1–5; Titus 3:10, 11.

3:9 have that right. Paul consistently teaches that those who labor in the gospel deserve their wages (1 Cor. 9:6–18). Paul normally accepted support for his ministry, but when he feared his motives would be called into question, or when (as in Thessalonica) a strong example was needed for those who refused to work, Paul forsook his rights and would not accept compensation.

3:10 Apparently the problem of idleness had surfaced before Paul and his companions left the city. Even then they had felt it necessary to urge the "idle" to work (vv. 6, 11).

3:11 not busy at work, but busybodies. Without any business of their own, these idlers attended to the business of others.

3:14 have nothing to do with him. See note on vv. 6–15; "Church Discipline and Excommunication" at Matt. 18:15.

be ashamed. This is not retribution, but an attempt to elicit repentance and, ultimately, restoration to fellowship in the church.

3:17 Though Paul had the help of secretaries in writing his letters, he customarily penned the final greeting or benediction in his own hand. He calls attention to this practice, as a mark of the letter's authenticity, here and in 1 Cor. 16:21; Col. 4:18. From Gal. 6:11 and Philem. 19, it appears that Paul wrote more than just the concluding phrases of those two letters.

THE FIRST EPISTLE OF PAUL THE APOSTLE TO

Timothy

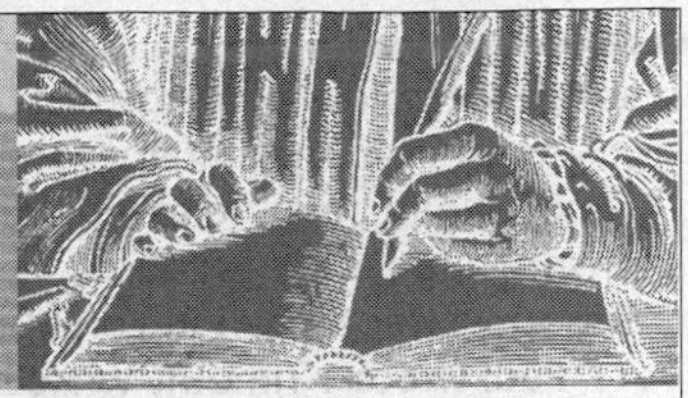

AUTHOR

According to the salutations of the letters, the author of the three Pastoral Letters (1 and 2 Timothy, Titus) was the apostle Paul. The tradition of the early church is in agreement. Nevertheless, some New Testament scholars have questioned the Pauline authorship of these letters, citing alleged differences in vocabulary, style, and theology. Such arguments fail to carry conviction, and there is no persuasive reason to deny that Paul wrote these letters.

DATE AND OCCASION

The apparent inconsistencies between Paul's travels as reflected in the Pastoral Letters and his three missionary journeys as recorded in Acts have led to the suggestion that the Pastorals were written during what might be called Paul's "fourth" missionary journey. Acts ends not with Paul's death but with his house arrest in Rome (Acts 28:16, 30, 31). While the late first-century writing *1 Clement* suggests that Paul was martyred in Rome, it does not link his martyrdom with the imprisonment recorded in Acts 28. The fourth-century church historian Eusebius preserves a tradition that Paul was released from that imprisonment, continued his missionary labors, and was martyred by Nero on his second visit to Rome. This tradition is supported not only by the Pastoral Letters but by Philippians and Philemon as well, which, if they were written during the Roman imprisonment recorded in Acts 28, provide evidence that Paul expected to be released (Phil. 1:25, 26; Philem. 22). A fourth missionary journey and a second imprisonment, after the imprisonment recorded in Acts 28, is the most probable setting for the Pastorals.

If there were two imprisonments, Paul was released from his first around A.D. 62. According to later tradition, he was martyred by Nero, who died in A.D. 68. Paul composed 1 Timothy while the apostle was still in the midst of his fourth missionary journey, probably during the earlier part of this period, between A.D. 62 and 64.

Timothy was a native of Lystra, a Roman colony in the province of Galatia. The son of a mixed marriage, his father was a Gentile and his mother was a Jew (Acts 16:1). Little is known about his father, who seems not to have become a Christian, but his mother and grandmother must have been converted as a result of Paul's visit to Lystra on his first missionary journey (2 Tim. 1:5). From his childhood, they had instructed Timothy in the Jewish Scriptures (2 Tim. 3:14, 15), and they were undoubtedly influential in Timothy's own conversion to Christianity.

When Paul returned to Lystra on his second missionary journey, some of the Christians called his attention to this young believer and Paul decided to take him along on his journey (Acts 16:2, 3). Two specific actions seem to have taken place at this time. First, since Paul would be evangelizing Jews, he circumcised Timothy according to Jewish custom (Acts 16:3). Second, Paul and the elders of the church laid their hands upon Timothy to set him apart and equip him for ministry (1:18; 4:14; 2 Tim. 1:6; 2:2).

Timothy traveled with Paul throughout most of his second and third missionary journeys (Acts 17:14, 15; 18:5; 19:22; 20:4), and for part of the fourth. He seems to have become Paul's protégé, and Paul speaks figuratively of himself as Timothy's "father" (Phil. 2:22) and of Timothy as his "son" (1:2, 18; 1 Cor. 4:17; 2 Tim. 1:2; 2:1). As Paul's coworker, Timothy served as Paul's representative in the churches of Thessalonica (1 Thess. 3:2, 6), Corinth (1 Cor. 4:17; 16:10), Philippi (Phil. 2:19, 23), and Ephesus (1:3).

Paul himself seems to characterize Timothy as having a "spirit . . . of fear" (2 Tim. 1:7). Paul felt it necessary to ask the church at Corinth to receive Timothy in a manner which would set him at ease (1 Cor. 16:10, 11). In the Pastorals he had to exhort Timothy not to let anyone despise him on account of his youth (4:12), not to neglect the spiritual gift which he had received (4:14), and not to be ashamed to speak out boldly for the gospel (2 Tim. 1:8).

Apart from the statement in Heb. 13:23 that Timothy had been "released" (presumably from prison), little is known about what happened to Timothy after the writing of 2 Timothy.

Paul wrote 1 Timothy while he was in Macedonia (1:3). He thought it necessary to leave Timothy behind in Ephesus because of the presence of false teachers in that city (1:3). Paul had established the Ephesian church early on his third missionary journey, spending about three years there (Acts 19; 20:31). At the close of that journey he had warned the Ephesian elders that false teachers, some coming from the leadership itself, would plague the church (Acts 20:29, 30), and this letter indicates that his prediction apparently came true (1:6, 19; 4:1, 2; 6:3–5, 10, 21). There is evidence that some of the false teachers either came from or moved into positions of leadership in the church (1:7, 20; 2:12; 3:6; 5:19, 20; 6:3–5, 10), and the false teachers seem especially to have made inroads among some of the women in the church (2:9–15; 3:11; 5:11–15).

CHARACTERISTICS AND THEMES

The letter is noteworthy for its interest in church organization. It provides the longest description in the New Testament on the qualifications for "overseer" or elder (3:2–7), along with evidence for two kinds of elders, ruling and teaching (5:17); comments about supporting and rebuking elders (5:17–20); and the only explicit description in the New Testament of the qualifications for deacons (3:8–10, 12, 13). Paul's specific directives to Timothy also contain much practical advice on how a church leader is to function.

This letter is also noteworthy for its emphasis on sound doctrine (1:10; 3:9; 4:6; 6:3) and contains two theological meditations on the salvation God extends in Jesus Christ (1:13–16; 2:3–6). These include affirmations of salvation by grace (1:13–16), Christ as the one Mediator between God and humanity (2:5), and the substitutionary atonement of Christ (2:6). First Timothy also includes a poetic meditation on the work of Christ which affirms His incarnation, resurrection, and ascension (3:16); an anticipation of the Second Coming of Christ (6:14); a marvelous doxology (6:15, 16); and evidence of the expansion of the concept of "Scripture" beyond the Old Testament to include elements of the New Testament revelation (5:18, where the words of Christ as recorded in Luke 10:7 are cited).

Also distinctive about 1 Timothy are its comments about women (2:9–15), which include a lengthy section on proper care for widows in the church (5:3–16), and the background information that the book provides about Timothy, including probable references to both his baptism (6:12) and his ordination (1:18; 4:14).

INTERPRETIVE DIFFICULTIES

The details of Paul's fourth missionary journey are sketchy, since the journey must be reconstructed largely from hints in the Pastoral Letters. There is some evidence that Paul fulfilled his earlier wish to go to Spain (Rom. 15:24, 28). Either on his return from Spain or, if the contemplated journey to Spain never took place, upon his departure from Rome, he seems to have returned to the east, probably first sailing to Crete (Titus 1:5). He then traveled north to Ephesus (1:3), perhaps making a side excursion to Colossae (cf. Philem. 22), and then on to Macedonia (1:3; cf. Phil. 1:25, 26). From that point on things become less clear. Paul seems to have planned (possibly at two different times) to leave Macedonia for both Ephesus (3:14, 15; 4:13) and Nicopolis (Titus 3:12). The last we hear is that he is back in Rome awaiting execution (2 Tim. 1:8, 12; 2:9; 4:6, 7, 16), having visited Troas (2 Tim. 4:13), Miletus, and perhaps Corinth (2 Tim. 4:20).

On the false teaching at Ephesus, see "Introduction to 2 Timothy: Interpretive Difficulties."

OUTLINE OF 1 TIMOTHY

I. Salutation (1:1, 2)

II. Dealing with False Teachers of the Law (1:3–11)

A. *False Teachers and Their Doctrines (1:3–7)*

B. *The Purpose of the Law (1:8–11)*

OUTLINE OF 1 TIMOTHY (Cont.)

III. Paul's Testimony and Charge (1:12–20)
- A. *Paul's Call to Ministry (1:12–17)*
- B. *Exhortation to Faithfulness (1:18–20)*

IV. Instructions for the Life of the Church (2:1–3:13)
- A. *Instructions for Prayer and Worship (2:1–15)*
  1. On Prayer for All (2:1–7)
  2. Instructions for Men (2:8)
  3. Instructions for Women (2:9–15)
- B. *Instructions on Church Leadership (3:1–13)*
  1. Overseers (3:1–7)
  2. Deacons (3:8–13)

V. The Problem of False Doctrines (3:14–4:5)
- A. *Paul's Purpose in Writing the Letter (3:14–16)*
- B. *Errors of the False Teachers (4:1–5)*

VI. Guidelines for a Young Pastor (4:6–6:19)
- A. *Admonitions to Timothy Regarding His Ministry (4:6–5:2)*
- B. *Instructions Regarding Specific Groups (5:3–6:2)*
  1. Widows (5:3–16)
  2. Elders (5:17–25)
  3. Slaves (6:1, 2)
- C. *Dealing with False Teachers (6:3–10)*
- D. *Admonitions to Timothy Regarding His Ministry (6:11–16)*
- E. *Exhortations to the Rich (6:17–19)*

VII. Conclusion (6:20, 21)

Greeting

1 Paul, [a]an apostle of Christ Jesus [b]by
command of [c]God our Savior and of
Christ Jesus [d]our hope,
2 To Timothy, [e]my true child in the faith:
[f]Grace, mercy, and peace from God the
Father and Christ Jesus our Lord.

Warning Against False Teachers

3 [g]As I urged you when I was going to
Macedonia, remain at Ephesus that you
may charge certain persons not [h]to teach
any different doctrine, **4** nor [i]to devote
themselves to myths and endless [j]genealo-
gies, which promote [k]speculations rather
than the stewardship[1] from God that is by
faith. **5** The aim of our charge is love [l]that
issues from a pure heart and [m]a good conscience and [n]a sincere faith. **6** Certain persons, by [o]swerving from these, have wandered away into [p]vain discussion, **7** desiring
to be teachers of the law, [q]without understanding either what they are saying or the
things about which they make confident
assertions.
8 Now we know that [r]the law is good, if
one uses it lawfully, **9** understanding this,
that the [s]law is not laid down for the just
but for the lawless and disobedient, for the
ungodly and sinners, for the unholy and
profane, for those who strike their fathers
and mothers, for murderers, **10** the sexually
immoral, men who practice homosexuality, enslavers,[2] liars, perjurers, and whatever else is contrary to [t]sound[3] doctrine,

Chapter 1
1 [a]See 2 Cor. 1:1 [b]Tit. 1:3; [Rom. 16:26] [c]See Luke 1:47 [d]Col. 1:27
2 [e]Tit. 1:4 [f]2 Tim. 1:2; 2 John 3; [Jude 2]
3 [g][Tit. 1:5] [h]ch. 6:3; [Gal. 1:6, 7]
4 [i]ch. 4:7; 2 Tim. 4:4; Tit. 1:14; 2 Pet. 1:16; [j]Tit. 3:9 [k]ch. 6:4
5 [l]2 Tim. 2:22 [m]1 Pet. 3:16, 21 [n]Rom. 12:9; 2 Tim. 1:5
6 [o]ch. 6:21 [p]Tit. 1:10
7 [q][ch. 6:4; Col. 2:18]
8 [r]Rom. 7:16
9 [s]Gal. 5:23
10 [t]2 Tim. 4:3; [ch. 6:3; 2 Tim. 1:13; Tit. 1:13; 2:2]

[1] Or *good order* [2] That is, those who take someone captive in order to sell him into slavery [3] Or *healthy*

1:1, 2 Opening salutation, including sender, recipient, and benediction.

1:1 apostle of Christ Jesus. One sent out as an official representative of Christ. This phrase is commonly used by Paul as a self-designation in the openings of his letters.

God our Savior. As Author of the covenant of grace, God is Savior (2:3; 4:10; Titus 1:3; 2:10; 3:4).

Christ Jesus our hope. Jesus is the basis for Christian hope, because He is the Mediator of the covenant of grace (2:5; 4:10; 5:5; 6:17). See "Hope" at Heb. 6:18.

1:2 true child. Cf. Titus 1:4. Paul views Timothy as his spiritual son (v. 18; 1 Cor. 4:17; Phil. 2:22; 2 Tim. 1:2; 2:1; Introduction: Date and Occasion).

Grace, mercy, and peace. Paul commonly substitutes "grace" for the more standard salutation "greetings" (e.g., James 1:1). He typically adds the Jewish greeting "peace," meaning "health, wholeness of life." Here and in 2 Tim. 1:2 he also adds "mercy."

1:3–7 Paul moves into the body of the letter. His intention is to instruct Timothy in how to act as Paul's representative at Ephesus (Introduction: Date and Occasion). He begins with the problem of false teaching at Ephesus (Introduction to 2 Timothy: Interpretive Difficulties).

1:3 teach any different doctrine. The conflict in Ephesus centers on proper teaching (v. 10; 4:1, 2; 6:3; 2 Tim. 2:18).

1:4 myths. See 4:7; 2 Tim. 4:4. In Titus 1:14 Paul speaks of "Jewish myths," perhaps referring to the kinds of legends about Old Testament figures that are found in many of the apocryphal Jewish writings.

endless genealogies. Perhaps a reference to an early form of the detailed speculations (often combined with Jewish myths) that developed in Gnosticism concerning the origins of the world and the innumerable spiritual beings supposedly involved in creation (cf. Titus 3:9).

1:5 love. Paul's command highlights the close connection between Christian belief and practice (cf. Gal. 5:6).

1:7 the law. The law of Moses.

1:8–11 Paul's comments about the false teachers lead him into a digression on the purpose of the law.

1:8 the law is good. See Rom. 7:7–12; Gal. 3:19–25.

1:10 sound doctrine. Or "sound teaching," a running theme throughout the Pastoral Letters (3:9; 4:6; 6:3; 2 Tim. 1:13, 14; 2:2; 4:3; Titus 1:9, 13; 2:1, 2).

11 in accordance with [u]the glorious gospel
of [v]the blessed God [w]with which I have
been entrusted.

Christ Jesus Came to Save Sinners

12 I thank him [x]who has given me
strength, Christ Jesus our Lord, because he
judged me faithful, [y]appointing me to his
service, 13 though formerly I was a blasphemer, [z]persecutor, and insolent opponent. But [a]I received mercy [b]because I had
acted ignorantly in unbelief, 14 and [c]the
grace of our Lord overflowed for me with
the [d]faith and love that are in Christ Jesus.
15 The saying is [e]trustworthy and deserving
of full acceptance, that Christ Jesus [f]came
into the world to save sinners, [g]of whom I
am the foremost. 16 But I received mercy for
this reason, that in me, as the foremost,
Jesus Christ might display his perfect
patience as an example to those who were
to believe in him for eternal life. 17 To [h]the
King of ages, [i]immortal, [j]invisible, [k]the
only God, [l]be honor and glory forever and
ever.[1] Amen.
18 This charge [m]I entrust to you, Timothy,
my child, in accordance with [n]the prophecies previously made about you, that by
them you may [o]wage the good warfare,
19 [p]holding faith and a good conscience. By
rejecting this, some have [q]made shipwreck
of their faith, 20 among whom are [r]Hyme-
naeus and [s]Alexander, whom I [t]have handed over to Satan that they may learn not to
[u]blaspheme.

Pray for All People

2 First of all, then, I urge that supplications, prayers, intercessions, and
thanksgivings be made for all people, 2 [v]for
kings and all who are in high positions,
that we may lead a peaceful and quiet life,
godly and [w]dignified in every way. 3 This is
good, and [x]it is pleasing in the sight of
[y]God our Savior, 4 who desires [z]all people
to be saved and [a]to come to [b]the knowledge of the truth. 5 For [c]there is one God,
and there is one mediator between God
and men, the man[2] Christ Jesus, 6 [d]who

11 [u][2 Cor. 4:4] [v]ch. 6:15 [w]Tit. 1:3; See Rom. 2:16; Gal. 2:7
12 [x]Acts 9:22; Phil. 4:13 [y]See 2 Cor. 3:6
13 [z]See Acts 8:3 [a]1 Cor. 7:25; 2 Cor. 4:1 [b]See Acts 3:17
14 [c]Rom. 5:20 [d][Luke 7:47, 50]; See 1 Thess. 1:3
15 [e]ch. 3:1; 4:9; 2 Tim. 2:11; Tit. 3:8; [Rev. 22:6] [f]Matt. 9:13; See John 3:17; Rom. 4:25 [g][1 Cor. 15:9]
17 [h][Ps. 10:16; Rev. 4:9, 10] [i]ch. 6:15, 16; Rom. 1:23 [j]John 1:18; Col. 1:15; Heb. 11:27; 1 John 4:12 [k]Jude 25 [l]1 Chr. 29:11
18 [m]2 Tim. 2:2 [n]ch. 4:14 [o]1 Cor. 9:7; 2 Cor. 10:4; 2 Tim. 2:3, 4; [ch. 6:12]

19 [p][ch. 3:9] [q][ch. 6:9] 20 [r]2 Tim. 2:17 [s]2 Tim. 4:14 [t]See 1 Cor. 5:5 [u]Acts 13:45
Chapter 2 2 [v]Ezra 6:10 [w]ch. 3:4 3 [x]ch. 5:4 [y]ch. 1:1 4 [z]ch. 4:10; Ezek. 18:23, 32 [a]2 Tim. 3:7 [b]2 Tim. 2:25; Tit. 1:1; Heb. 10:26 5 [c]See Gal. 3:20 6 [d]See Matt. 20:28

[1] Greek *to the ages of ages* [2] *men* and *man* render the same Greek word that is translated *people* in verses 1 and 4

1:11 in accordance with the glorious gospel. The good news of what God has done in Christ is the standard by which doctrine, as well as one's understanding of the law, is judged to be sound.

1:12–17 From his comments about the law Paul turns to his call by Christ and provides an exposition of the gospel as the grace God pours out upon sinners in Jesus Christ.

1:13 a blasphemer, persecutor, and insolent opponent. Before his conversion Paul persecuted the church (Acts 8:3; 9:1–5; 22:4, 5; 26:9, 11; Gal. 1:13; Phil. 3:6).

because I had acted ignorantly in unbelief. God did not grant Paul what he deserved, but what he needed (cf. Acts 3:17–20).

1:15 The saying is trustworthy and deserving of full acceptance. This expression calls attention to an important point. In the New Testament it is found only in the Pastoral Letters (3:1; 4:9; 2 Tim. 2:11; Titus 3:8).

I am the foremost. Lit. "I am the first." This is not a characterization of himself prior to his conversion. Rather, as Paul has grown in Christ he has become increasingly aware of his own sinfulness.

1:16 eternal life. God grants to all who believe in Christ not just "eternal" life, but life in all its fullness (cf. 4:8; 6:12, 19; 2 Tim. 1:1, 10; Titus 1:2; 3:7).

1:18–20 Paul returns to the theme of vv. 3–7, focusing less on Timothy's potential for success as Paul's representative than on Timothy's continued faithfulness to Christ, especially in contrast to two members (perhaps leaders) of the church at Ephesus who "made shipwreck of their faith" (v. 19).

1:18 prophecies previously made about you. This refers to an event, mentioned also in 4:14 and in 2 Tim. 1:6 (cf. 2 Tim. 2:2), in which a group of elders, along with Paul, laid hands on Timothy (perhaps when Timothy was set apart for ministry). At that time Timothy received a spiritual gift, along with a word of prophecy appointing him for service (cf. Acts 13:1–3).

1:19 a good conscience. See "Conscience and the Law" at 1 Sam. 24:5.

1:20 Hymenaeus and Alexander. Singling out these two individuals raises the question whether they were leaders in the church. Hymenaeus is mentioned again in 2 Tim. 2:17, 18 as one who has "swerved from the truth." It is unclear whether the name "Alexander" here and in Acts 19:33, 34 and 2 Tim. 4:14, 15 all refer to the same person.

I have handed over to Satan. This is probably a reference to putting these two individuals outside the fellowship of the church and, hence, back into the world—the domain of Satan (John 12:31; 14:30; 16:11; 2 Cor. 4:4; Eph. 2:2). Paul uses a similar expression in 1 Cor. 5:5 (cf. Matt. 18:17).

may learn not to blaspheme. The purpose of this excommunication is disciplinary—that the two would recognize their errors and repent (2 Tim. 2:25, 26; Titus 3:10).

2:1–15 Paul moves to a series of instructions on prayer and worship, probably in response to abuses caused by the false teachers (see Introduction to 2 Timothy: Interpretive Difficulties).

2:1 all people. As can be seen from the next expression ("for kings and all who are in high positions"), this does not mean "every human being," but rather "all types of people," whatever their station in life.

2:4 who desires all people to be saved. This does not mean that God sovereignly wills every human being to be saved (i.e., that God saves everyone). It may refer to God's general benevolence in taking no delight in the death of the wicked, or to God's desire that all types of people (v. 1 note) be saved (i.e., God does not choose His elect from any single group).

2:5 there is one God. This is the fundamental affirmation of the Jewish religion (Deut. 6:4; cf. Rom. 3:30; 1 Cor. 8:6; Gal. 3:20; Eph. 4:6).

one mediator between God and men. There is One who arbitrates between God and humanity and reconciles them. See theological note "Christ the Mediator."

the man Christ Jesus. Paul's focus is on Christ's humanity, perhaps because the false teachers had denied that Christ was truly human. The

gave himself as a ransom for all, which is [e]the testimony given [f]at the proper time.
7 [g]For this I was appointed a preacher and an apostle ([h]I am telling the truth, I am not lying), [i]a teacher of the Gentiles in faith and truth.
8 I desire then that [j]in every place the

6 [e]See 1 Cor. 1:6 [f]ch. 6:15; Tit. 1:3; [Gal. 4:4]
7 [g]ch. 1:11; Eph. 3:7, 8; 2 Tim. 1:11 [h]See Rom. 9:1 [i]See Acts 9:15 8 [j][John 4:21]

Christ the Mediator

The saving ministry of Jesus Christ is summed up in the statement that He is the "mediator between God and men" (1 Tim. 2:5). A mediator is one who brings together parties who are out of communication and who may be alienated, estranged, or at war with each other. The mediator must have links with both sides so as to identify with and maintain the interests of both, and represent each to the other on a basis of goodwill. Thus Moses was mediator between God and Israel (Gal. 3:19), speaking to Israel on God's behalf when God gave the law (Ex. 20:18–21) and speaking to God on Israel's behalf when Israel had sinned (Ex. 32:9–33:17).

Every member of our fallen and rebellious race is by nature "hostile to God" (Rom. 8:7), standing under God's wrath, the punitive rejection whereby as Judge He expresses active anger at our sins (Rom. 1:18; 2:5–9; 3:5, 6). Reconciliation of the alienated parties is needed, but can only occur if God's wrath is quenched and the human heart, that opposes God and motivates a life against God, is changed. In mercy, God sent His Son into the world to bring about the needed reconciliation. It was not that the kindly Son acted to placate the harsh Father; the initiative was the Father's own. In Augustine's words, "in a wonderful and divine way even when He hated us, He loved us" (*Commentary on John* 110.6; cf. John 3:16; Rom. 5:5–8; 1 John 4:8–10). In all His mediatorial ministry the Son was doing His Father's will (see "The Humble Obedience of Christ" at John 5:19).

Objectively and once for all, Christ achieved reconciliation for His people through penal substitution. On the cross He took our place, carried our identity as it were, bore the curse due to us (Gal. 3:13), and by His sacrificial shedding of blood made peace for us (Eph. 2:16–18; Col. 1:20). Peace here means an end to hostility, guilt, and exposure to the retributive punishment that was otherwise unavoidable—in other words, forgiveness for all the past, and eternal, personal acceptance for the future. Those who have received reconciliation through faith in Christ are justified and have peace with God (Rom. 5:1, 10). The Mediator's present work, which He carries forward through human messengers, is to persuade those for whom He achieved reconciliation actually to receive it (John 12:32; Rom. 15:18; 2 Cor. 5:18–21; Eph. 2:17).

Jesus is "the mediator of a new covenant" (Heb. 9:15; 12:24), the initiator of a new relationship of conscious peace with God, going beyond what was known under the Old Testament arrangements for dealing with the guilt of sin (Heb. 9:11–10:18).

One of Calvin's great contributions to Christian understanding was his observation that the New Testament writers expound Jesus' mediatorial ministry in terms of the three "offices" (defined roles) of prophet, priest, and king. These three aspects of Christ's work are found together in the letter to the Hebrews, where Jesus is both the messianic King, exalted to His throne (1:3, 13; 4:16; 2:9), as well as the great High Priest (2:17; 4:14–5:10; chs. 7–10), who offered Himself to God as a sacrifice for our sins. In addition, Christ is the messenger ("apostle," 3:1), who preached the message concerning Himself (2:3). In Acts 3:22 Jesus is called a "prophet" for the same reason that Hebrews calls Him "apostle," namely, because He instructed people by declaring to them the word of God.

While in the Old Testament the mediating roles of prophet, priest, and king were fulfilled by separate individuals, all three offices now coalesce in the one person of Jesus. It is His glory, given Him by the Father, to be in this way the all-sufficient Savior. We who believe are called to understand this, and to show ourselves His people by obeying Him as our king, trusting Him as our priest, and learning from Him as our prophet and teacher. To center on Jesus Christ in this way is the hallmark of authentic Christianity.

full humanity of Christ is essential to His serving as Mediator of the covenant of grace.

2:6 who gave himself as a ransom. By His death on the cross, Christ paid the price necessary to free people from their sins (Matt. 20:28; Mark 10:45; Titus 2:14; 1 Pet. 1:18, 19). Thus, He is the "one mediator" (v. 5).

all. In keeping with vv. 1 and 4, this is probably a reference to all *types* of people. Alternately, it expresses Paul's conviction that Christ's death was sufficient to ransom all humanity, yet by sovereign design and effect not all are redeemed. See "Definite Redemption" at John 10:15.

2:7 I am telling the truth . . . not lying. An odd statement to make to a close friend, but Paul may have intended for the letter to be read to the whole church (6:21 note). Presumably the false teachers had questioned Paul's call and mission.

2:8–15 Paul moves to the problem of the divisive spirit of the false teachers, with specific admonitions for men and women (note on vv. 1–15).

men should pray, [k]lifting [l]holy hands without anger or quarreling; 9 likewise also
[m]that women should adorn themselves in
respectable apparel, with modesty and self-
control, not with braided hair and gold or
pearls or costly attire, 10 [n]but with what is
proper for women who profess godliness—
with good works. 11 Let a woman learn quietly [o]with all submissiveness. 12 [p]I do not
permit a woman to teach or to exercise
authority over a man; rather, she is to remain quiet. 13 [q]For Adam was formed first,
[r]then Eve; 14 and Adam was not deceived,
but [s]the woman was deceived and became
a transgressor. 15 Yet she will be saved
through [t]childbearing—if they continue
in [u]faith and love and holiness, with self-
control.

8 [k]Ps. 63:4; 119:48; [Isai. 1:15] [l]Job 17:9; Ps. 24:4
9 [m]1 Pet. 3:3; [Isai. 3:18-23]
10 [n][1 Pet. 3:4]
11 [o]Tit. 2:5
12 [p][1 Cor. 14:34]
13 [q]Gen. 1:27; 2:8 [r]Gen. 2:18, 22
14 [s]Gen. 3:6, 13
15 [t][Gal. 4:4] [u]ch. 1:14

Chapter 3
1 [v]See ch. 1:15 [w]See Acts 20:28
2 [x]Tit. 1:6-9 [y][ch. 5:9] [z]ver. 11; Tit. 2:2 [a]1 Pet. 4:9 [b]2 Tim. 2:24

Qualifications for Overseers

3 The saying is [v]trustworthy: If anyone
aspires to [w]the office of overseer, he
desires a noble task. 2 Therefore [x]an overseer[1] must be above reproach, [y]the
husband of one wife,[2] [z]sober-minded, self-
controlled, respectable, [a]hospitable, [b]able
to teach, 3 not a drunkard, not violent but
[c]gentle, not quarrelsome, [d]not a lover of
money. 4 He must manage his own household well, with all dignity [e]keeping his children submissive, 5 for if someone does not
know how to manage his own household,
how will he care for [w]God's church? 6 He
must not be a recent convert, or he may

3 [c]Tit. 3:2 [d]Heb. 13:5; [ch. 6:10] 4 [e][ver. 12] 5 [w][See ver. 1 above]

[1] Or *bishop*; Greek *episkopos*; a similar term occurs in verse 1 [2] Or *a man of one woman;* also verse 12

2:8 every place. This probably refers to corporate worship.

men. Paul assumes in 1 Cor. 11:5 that women, too, will pray when the church meets for worship. Here he is addressing a specific problem at Ephesus.

lifting holy hands. On this posture in prayer, see Ps. 63:4; 141:2.

without anger or quarreling. Paul is not concerned to mandate a particular posture, but to encourage a proper attitude (1:5).

2:9 respectable apparel . . . costly attire. Paul is not concerned with clothing and jewelry as such, but with the attitude of the one wearing them (1 Pet. 3:3, 4). Greco-Roman society was characterized by extravagance in dress.

2:11 quietly. As 1 Cor. 11:5 indicates, Paul does not forbid all vocal participation by women in the worship service. Rather, Paul enjoins silence of a particular sort—a silence that respects the authoritative teaching and governing role assigned to the leaders of the church (v. 12).

all submissiveness. Submission does not necessarily indicate a lower status. Elsewhere Paul applies the concept to wives (Eph. 5:22; Col. 3:18; Titus 2:5; cf. 1 Cor. 14:34), husbands and wives (Eph. 5:21), children (3:4), slaves (Titus 2:9), prophets (1 Cor. 14:32), Christians (Rom. 13:1, 5; 1 Cor. 16:16; Titus 3:1), the church (Eph. 5:24), and even Christ Himself (1 Cor. 15:28).

2:12 I do not permit. Here Paul exercises his apostolic authority in restricting women from exercising a certain kind of authority and teaching.

to exercise authority over. This Greek word appears only here in the New Testament and is probably used by Paul to refer to some level of judicial or governing authority. Under the influence of the false teachers, certain women have apparently moved into positions of governing authority within the church, which Paul prohibited (1 Cor. 14:34).

quiet. See note on v. 11.

2:13 Paul appeals to creation (Gen. 2:7, 21, 22). He uses a similar argument, though with some qualification, in 1 Cor. 11:8–12.

2:14 Again Paul alludes to Genesis, this time to the account of the Fall (Gen. 3:1–6). The argument might seem unfair, since both Adam and Eve sinned. But Paul's point is correct: Eve was the one who was "deceived" by the serpent. Paul's argument here, with its emphasis on who was deceived, is probably a reflection of the relative success that the false teachers at Ephesus have had in leading women astray (5:11–15; 2 Tim. 3:6, 7). Elsewhere Paul has no qualms about blaming the Fall on Adam (Rom. 5:12–19; 1 Cor. 15:21, 22).

2:15 she. This probably refers to any woman who has been deceived.

will be saved. Probably not "brought safely," as some hold. Paul uses his normal word meaning "redemption from sin," thereby contrasting being deceived into sin (v. 14) with being saved from it. Alternately, the term "saved" may indicate the reception of some important, though unspecified, benefit from God.

through childbearing. The interpretation "through the birth of the Child" (Jesus), however attractive it might be theologically, is doubtful. Clearly Paul intends another allusion to Genesis, this time to God's statement to Eve after the Fall concerning her role in childbearing (Gen. 3:16).

if they continue in faith and love and holiness, with self-control. This qualification shows that Paul is not suggesting that childbearing is an act that merits salvation, which would contradict his doctrine of justification by faith. Rather, his point seems to be that those women at Ephesus who have been deceived by the false teachers need to focus on their proper role, and especially their attitudes (vv. 8–10; 1:5, 19). Given his use of Gen 2; 3 in his argument and the false teachers' disparagement of marriage (4:3), Paul finds "childbearing" to be a convenient symbol for that role (5:14).

3:1–13 Paul now turns to the subject of leadership in the church. He discusses first overseers (vv. 1–7; text notes, v. 1), then deacons (vv. 8–10, 12, 13, with a digression on women in v. 11). Paul's focus on the personal qualities of those who would serve in these positions, rather than their duties, indicates his concern to install the right people, perhaps because some of the false teachers have come from, or are seeking, positions of leadership.

3:1 The saying is trustworthy. See note 1:15. The use of this expression here reflects the importance Paul attaches to the task of the overseer.

overseer. One of a group of individuals charged with the general care of the church (v. 5; Phil. 1:1). The word is used interchangeably with "elder" (Acts 20:17, 28; Titus 1:5–7). See "Pastors and Pastoral Care" at 1 Pet. 5:2.

3:2 above reproach. A general heading to the qualifications for overseer or elder. This expression does not mean "without sin," which would disqualify everyone, but "above scandalous reproach." Paul's overriding concern is that overseers (elders) have a good standing among non-Christians (v. 7). On the qualifications for overseers (elders), see Titus 1:6–9.

the husband of one wife. This difficult expression (v. 12; Titus 1:6; cf. 5:9) has been understood to prohibit polygamy, remarriage after a divorce, or marital infidelity. Given the widespread immorality in the Greco-Roman world, the last would seem to fit Paul's focus the best.

able to teach. To mention the teaching aspect of the overseer's (elder's) task is important, given the problem at Ephesus (5:17).

3:5 care for God's church. A general statement of the overseer's (elder's) responsibility.

3:6 not be a recent convert, or he may become puffed up with

[f]become puffed up with conceit and fall into the condemnation of the devil. 7 Moreover, he must be well thought of by [g]outsiders, so that he may not fall into disgrace, into [h]a snare of the devil.

Qualifications for Deacons

8 [i]Deacons likewise must be dignified, not double-tongued,[1] [j]not addicted to much wine, [k]not greedy for dishonest gain. 9 They must [l]hold the mystery of the faith with [m]a clear conscience. 10 And [n]let them also be tested first; then let them serve as deacons if they prove themselves blameless. 11 [o]Their wives[2] likewise must be dignified, not slanderers, but sober-minded, [p]faithful in all things. 12 Let deacons each be [q]the husband of one wife, [q]managing their children and their own households well. 13 For [r]those who serve well as deacons gain a good standing for themselves and also great confidence in the faith that is in Christ Jesus.

The Mystery of Godliness

14 I hope to come to you soon, but I am writing these things to you so that, 15 if I delay, you may know how one ought to behave in the household of God, which is the church of the living God, a pillar and buttress of truth. 16 Great indeed, we confess, is the mystery of godliness:

[s]He[3] was manifested in the flesh,
vindicated[4] by the Spirit,[5]
[t]seen by angels,
[u]proclaimed among the nations,
[v]believed on in the world,
[w]taken up in glory.

Some Will Depart from the Faith

4 Now [x]the Spirit expressly says that [y]in later times some will depart from the faith by devoting themselves to [z]deceitful spirits and teachings of demons, 2 through the insincerity of [a]liars whose consciences are seared, 3 [b]who forbid marriage and [c]require abstinence from foods [d]that God created [e]to be received with thanksgiving by those who believe and know the truth. 4 For [f]everything created by God is good,

6 [f]ch. 6:4; 2 Tim. 3:4 7 [g]See Mark 4:11 [h]2 Tim. 2:26; [ch. 6:9] 8 [i]Phil. 1:1 [j][ch. 5:23; Tit. 2:3] [k]Tit. 1:7; 1 Pet. 5:2 9 [l][ch. 1:19] [m]See Acts 23:1 10 [n][ch. 5:22] 11 [o]Tit. 2:3 [p][Tit. 2:10] 12 [q]ver. 2, 4 13 [r]See Matt. 25:21

16 [s]John 1:14; 1 Pet. 1:20 [t]Luke 2:13; 24:4 [u]Gal. 2:2 [v]2 Thess. 1:10 [w]See Acts 1:2
Chapter 4
1 [x]See John 14:17 [y][2 Thess. 2:3-9; 2 Tim. 3:1]; See 1 Cor. 11:19 [z]1 John 4:6 (Gk.); See Matt. 7:15 2 [a][1 Thess. 2:3; 2 Thess. 2:11] 3 [b][Dan. 11:37; Heb. 13:4] [c]See Col. 2:16 [d]Gen. 1:29; 9:3 [e]See Rom. 14:6 4 [f]Gen. 1:31

[1] Or *devious in speech* [2] Or *Wives*, or *Women* [3] Greek *Who*; some manuscripts *God*; others *Which* [4] Or *justified* [5] Or *vindicated in spirit*

conceit. For a Christian to move too quickly into this position could be an occasion for pride.

fall into the condemnation of the devil. Paul does not view lightly the fall of those holding this office, perhaps because some overseers had become involved in the false teaching (v. 1).

3:8 Deacons. Deacons are officers in the church alongside overseers or elders (cf. Phil. 1:1). The precise tasks of the deacon are not spelled out in this passage. The church has usually viewed the ministry in terms of the role of the seven chosen to help the apostles in Acts 6:1–6, although "deacon" is not used in regard to the seven in that passage.

3:9 the mystery. A term used elsewhere by Paul to refer to the revealed truth of the gospel (v. 16; Rom. 16:25, 26; 1 Cor. 2:7; 4:1; Eph. 1:9; 3:3–9; 6:19; Col. 1:26, 27; 2:2; 4:3). Perhaps some of the deacons at Ephesus had been taken in by the false teaching.

3:10 be tested first. This is probably not a reference to a specific testing period, but rather a careful examination of their conduct and their commitment to sound teaching.

prove themselves blameless. Paul uses the same Greek word in regard to overseers in Titus 1:6, 7; his requirement that overseers be "above reproach" in v. 2 (note) uses a Greek synonym.

3:11 Their wives. Lit. "women." This verse abruptly interrupts the section on deacons. Its meaning is contested. The "women" are probably either the wives of the deacons or themselves deacons. The abruptness of the insertion probably reflects Paul's concern that women, in particular, have not fared well at the hands of the false teachers (2:14; 5:15).

3:12 the husband of one wife. See note on v. 2.

3:14–16 Having provided Timothy with specific instructions on prayer, worship, and church offices, Paul now states his reason for writing the letter (Introduction: Date and Occasion). He discusses the nature of the church and offers a poetic meditation on the work of Christ.

3:15 pillar and buttress. Both terms have the connotation of providing support. Paul's intent is to emphasize, over against the false teachers, that the truth of the gospel is found in and sustained by God's church (2 Tim. 2:19).

3:16 mystery of godliness. See note on v. 9. What follows may be a fragment of an early Christian hymn.

He was manifested in the flesh. A reference to the Incarnation, with a hint at Christ's preexistence.

vindicated by the Spirit. A reference to Christ's resurrection (Rom. 1:4).

seen by angels. A reference to the Ascension (Acts 1:10, 11).

proclaimed among the nations. See "The Authentication of Scripture" at 2 Cor. 4:6.

taken up in glory. A reference to Christ's exaltation to the right hand of God (Acts 7:56).

4:1–5 Returning to his main theme again (1:3–20), Paul continues his attack on the false teachers and their teachings.

4:1 the Spirit expressly says. Presumably a specific revelation the Holy Spirit granted to someone, perhaps Paul himself (Acts 20:22–31; cf. 21:11).

in later times. This is not a period just prior to the Second Coming of Christ. Rather, in keeping with the overall New Testament perspective, it is the era inaugurated by Christ's First Advent and completed at His second (Acts 2:17; Heb. 1:2; 1 Pet. 1:20; 1 John 2:18; cf. 2 Tim. 3:1).

some will . . . demons. A reference to the false teachers, who have arisen within the church.

4:3 forbid marriage and require abstinence from foods. The false teachers promote a rigorous lifestyle (cf. Col. 2:20–23). Some Gnostics argued that since the material world was evil, the spiritual individual should avoid it.

that. The following argument focuses on foods. Paul has already affirmed marriage in 3:2, 12.

4:4 everything created by God is good. Contrary to the false teachers, the Christian affirms the essential goodness of God's creation (Gen. 1).

and [g]nothing is to be rejected if it is [e]re-
ceived with thanksgiving, 5 for it is made
holy [h]by the word of God and prayer.

A Good Servant of Christ Jesus

6 [i]If you put these things before the
brothers,[1] you will be a good servant of
Christ Jesus, being trained in the words of
the faith and of the good doctrine that you
have [j]followed. 7 Have nothing to do with
irreverent, [k]silly myths. Rather [l]train yourself for godliness; 8 for while [m]bodily training is of some value, godliness [n]is of value
in every way, as [o]it holds promise for the
present life and also for the life to come.
9 The saying is [p]trustworthy and deserving
of full acceptance. 10 For to this end we toil
and strive,[2] because we have our hope set
on the living God, [q]who is the Savior of all
people, especially of those who believe.
11 Command and teach [r]these things.
12 [s]Let no one despise you for your youth,
but set the believers [t]an example in speech,
in conduct, in love, in faith, in purity.
13 Until I come, devote yourself to the public reading of Scripture, to exhortation, to
teaching. 14 [u]Do not neglect the gift you
have, which was given you [v]by prophecy
when the council of elders [w]laid their
hands on you. 15 Practice these things,
devote yourself to them, so that [x]all may
see your progress. 16 [y]Keep a close watch on
yourself and on the teaching. Persist in
this, for by so doing you will save [z]both
yourself and [a]your hearers.

Instructions for the Church

5 [b]Do not rebuke an older man but
encourage him as you would a father.
[c]Treat younger men like brothers, 2 older
women like mothers, younger women like
sisters, in all purity.
3 Honor widows [d]who are truly widows.
4 But if a widow has children or grandchildren, let them first learn [e]to show godliness
to their own household and to make some
return to their parents, for [f]this is pleasing
in the sight of God. 5 She [g]who is truly a

4 [g]See Acts 10:15 [e][See ver. 3 above] 5 [h]Gen. 1:25, 31 6 [i][2 Tim. 3:14, 15] [j]2 Tim. 3:10 7 [k]See ch. 1:4 [l]Heb. 5:14 8 [m][Col. 2:23] [n][ch. 6:6] [o]Ps. 37:4, 9, 11; 84:11; 112:2; 145:19; Prov. 19:23; 22:4; Matt. 6:33; Mark 10:30; 1 Pet. 3:9 9 [p]See ch. 1:15 10 [q]See ch. 2:4; John 4:42 11 [r]ch. 5:7; 6:2 12 [s]1 Cor. 16:11; [2 Tim. 2:22; Tit. 2:15] [t]Tit. 2:7; 1 Pet. 5:3 14 [u]See 1 Thess. 5:19 [v]ch. 1:18 [w]See Acts 6:6 15 [x]Phil. 1:12 16 [y][Acts 20:28] [z]Ezek. 33:9 [a]See Rom. 11:14

Chapter 5 1 [b][Lev. 19:32] [c]Tit. 2:6 3 [d]ver. 5, 16 4 [e]Matt. 15:4-6; Mark 7:10-13; Eph. 6:1, 2; [Gen. 45:9-11] [f]ch. 2:3 5 [g]ver. 3, 16

1 Or *brothers and sisters*. The plural Greek word *adelphoi* (translated "brothers") refers to siblings in a family. In New Testament usage, depending on the context, *adelphoi* may refer either to men or to both men and women who are siblings (brothers and sisters) in God's family, the church 2 Some manuscripts *and suffer reproach*

4:6–5:2 Having exposed the false teachers for what they are, Paul continues with a series of personal admonitions to Timothy regarding his ministry.

4:6 trained. The "good servant" must be continually nourished by true doctrine.

4:7 irreverent, silly myths. See note 1:4.

train yourself for godliness. Throughout this section, Paul intertwines spiritual discipline with official duties.

4:9 See note 1:15.

4:10 Savior of all people. The general call to repentance and salvation is extended to all people (Matt. 11:28). See "Definite Redemption" at John 10:15.

especially of those who believe. Salvation is God's gift, in particular to those who trust in His provision in Christ (Matt. 22:14; Rom. 8:30).

4:12 Let no one despise you for your youth. The negative commands here and in v. 14 may indicate that Timothy had a tendency towards shyness or timidity. Furthermore, some in the church at Ephesus may not have accepted his authority (Introduction: Date and Occasion). Timothy was probably in his thirties, and therefore was younger than many of the Christians (and elders) at Ephesus.

example . . . in purity. Timothy is to establish his authority, not by flaunting it but by setting an example of godly living (Titus 2:7).

4:13 Until I come. See 3:14, 15 and Introduction: Date and Occasion.

devote yourself . . . to teaching. These are positive methods for exposing the false teaching and neutralizing its impact (cf. 1:3, 4).

4:14 the gift. See note 1:18.

4:15 your progress. A reference to the advancement of Timothy's spiritual life, his ministry, or perhaps both. Noteworthy is the fact that it is "progress," not arrival.

4:16 on yourself and on the teaching. That Paul summarizes his instructions to Timothy in this manner is an indication of where the false teachers have gone astray, and, hence, where Christians in general can go astray.

you will save. God alone grants salvation (v. 10; 1:1; 2:3), but He is pleased to use His people as instruments in bringing salvation to others. Salvation is not completed when one comes to faith. To be sure, faith brings justification and the assurance of salvation. But faith also begins the lifelong process of sanctification that continues until the Christian's final glorification in heaven.

yourself. Sanctification is a work of God which demands the cooperative activity of the Christian (Phil. 2:12).

5:1 Do not rebuke an older man. A command that balances that in 4:12. Timothy is not to abuse the authority he possesses.

encourage. The good minister appeals to other believers with the respect deserved by members of one's family.

5:3–6:2 Paul now turns his attention to three groups in which problems had apparently arisen in the church at Ephesus: widows, elders, and slaves.

5:3–16 Paul's concern to identify needy widows and provide for their proper care forms the backdrop for a discussion of the problems of younger widows, some of whom have apparently become influenced by the false teaching at Ephesus (Introduction: Date and Occasion).

5:3 Honor. That is, care for.

who are truly widows. The care of widows, who frequently had great material needs, is a major theme in the Old Testament (Deut. 24:19–21; Is. 1:17; Jer. 22:3; Zech. 7:9, 10; Mal. 3:5) and was a special concern of the early church (v. 16; Acts 6:1; James 1:27).

5:4 But if a widow has children or grandchildren. The truly needy widow had no family from which to receive support (vv. 8, 16).

widow, left all alone, has set her hope on
God and [h]continues in supplications and
prayers night and day, 6 but [i]she who is
self-indulgent is [j]dead even while she lives.
7 [k]Command these things as well, so that
they may be without reproach. 8 But if anyone does not provide for his relatives, and
especially for [l]members of his household,
he has [m]denied the faith and is worse than
an unbeliever.
9 Let a widow be enrolled if she is not less
than sixty years of age, having been [n]the
wife of one husband,[1] 10 and having a reputation for good works: if she has brought
up children, has [n]shown hospitality, [o]has
washed the feet of the saints, has [p]cared for
the afflicted, and has [q]devoted herself to
every good work. 11 But refuse to enroll
younger widows, for when [r]their passions
draw them away from Christ, they desire to
marry 12 and so incur condemnation for
having abandoned their former faith.
13 Besides that, they learn to be idlers, going
about from house to house, and not only
idlers, but also [s]gossips and [t]busybodies,
saying what they should not. 14 So I would
have [u]younger widows marry, bear children, [v]manage their households, and [w]give
the adversary no occasion for slander.
15 [x]For some have already strayed after
Satan. 16 If any believing woman has relatives who are widows, let her care for them.
Let the church not be burdened, so that it
may care for those [y]who are really widows.
17 Let the elders [z]who rule well be considered worthy of [a]double honor, especially those who labor in preaching and
teaching. 18 For the Scripture says, [b]"You
shall not muzzle an ox when it treads out
the grain," and, [c]"The laborer deserves his
wages." 19 Do not admit a charge against an
elder except [d]on the evidence of two or
three witnesses. 20 As for those who persist
in sin, [e]rebuke them in the presence of all,
[f]so that the rest may stand in fear. 21 In the
presence of God and of Christ Jesus and of
the elect angels [g]I charge you to keep these
rules without prejudging, [h]doing nothing
from partiality. 22 [i]Do not be hasty in the
[j]laying on of hands, nor [k]take part in the
sins of others; keep yourself pure. 23 (No
longer drink only water, but [l]use a little
wine [m]for the sake of your stomach and

5 [h][Luke 2:37; 18:1-5]
6 [i]James 5:5; [Ezek. 16:49] [j]Rev. 3:1
7 [k]ch. 4:11; 6:2
8 [l]See Gal. 6:10 [m]Rev. 2:13; [2 Tim. 3:5; Tit. 1:16; 2 Pet. 2:1; Rev. 3:8]
9 [n][ch. 3:2]
10 [n][See ver. 9 above] [o]See Gen. 18:4 [p]ver. 16 [q][ch. 6:18]
11 [r][Rev. 18:3, 7, 9]
13 [s]3 John 10 (Gk.) [t]2 Thess. 3:11; 1 Pet. 4:15
14 [u][1 Cor. 7:9] [v][Tit. 2:5] [w]ch. 6:1; Tit. 2:5, 8
15 [x][ch. 1:20]
16 [y]ver. 3, 5
17 [z]Rom. 12:8; 1 Thess. 5:12; [1 Cor. 12:28] [a]Deut. 21:17
18 [b]1 Cor. 9:9; Cited from Deut. 25:4 [c]Matt. 10:10; [Lev. 19:13; Deut. 24:15; 1 Cor. 9:4, 7-14]
19 [d]See Deut. 19:15 20 [e]Tit. 1:13; 2:15 [f]Deut. 13:11 21 [g]ch. 6:13; 2 Tim. 2:14; 4:1 [h]See 2 Cor. 5:16 22 [i][ch. 3:10] [j]See Acts 6:6 [k][2 John 11] 23 [l][ch. 3:8] [m]Ps. 104:15

[1] Or *a woman of one man*

5:5 hope on God. Genuine poverty often drove widows to exemplary lives of prayer and faithful dependence upon God. For such widows, the church is to be the visible hand of God in providing for needs.

5:6 dead. Spiritually dead.

5:7 Command . . . that they may be without reproach. Perhaps a reference not to the whole church, but just to the widows.

5:9 a widow be enrolled. Some have seen here an official order of widows with duties to perform (vv. 5, 10); others have seen an agreement whereby some widows provide certain services for the church in exchange for material support. More likely the list is simply of widows who are to receive support from the church (v. 16). This list constitutes a portion of the larger group of widows dealt with in vv. 3–5.

less than sixty years of age. A round number reflecting the expectation in that culture of the age under which remarriage would still be possible (cf. vv. 11–14).

the wife of one husband. See note 3:2.

5:10 has brought up children. The verbs in this verse are in the past tense. Paul's concern is not with what the widow might still do for the church but with what she has accomplished in her life.

washed the feet of the saints. A conventional expression of hospitality in a culture where people wore sandals and walked dusty roads (cf. John 13:4, 5). Jesus commanded His disciples to wash each others' feet (John 13:14, 15).

5:11 passions draw them away. Lit. "when they live sensually."

5:12 having abandoned their former faith. This probably does not refer to a vow of celibacy or of devotion to the church, but to their basic commitment to Christ (vv. 11, 15).

5:13 gossips. Lit. "those who talk nonsense." This is probably a reference to the false teachings (v. 15; 1:3; 4:7).

5:14 bear children. See note 2:15.

5:15 Paul gives much attention to widows because some of the younger widows had come under the influence of the false teachers (2 Tim. 3:6, 7).

5:17–25 As with widows, Paul addresses the twin issues of proper honor for elders and how to deal with those who sin.

5:17 elders. See note 3:1; "Pastors and Pastoral Care" at 1 Pet. 5:2.

double honor. The honor of the position as well as financial remuneration (v. 18).

especially . . . teaching. This is a reference to two kinds of elders: those who govern the church and those who, in addition, carry out the more specialized ministry of preaching and teaching.

5:18 For the Scripture says. That Paul cites both Deut. 25:4 and a saying of Jesus recorded in Luke 10:7 as "Scripture" is an indication of how soon Christian writings were being placed on the same level of authority as the Old Testament (2 Pet. 3:15, 16).

5:20 those who persist in sin. Elders who sin (some had apparently become involved in the false teaching).

5:21 the elect angels. Those who will presumably serve as witnesses at the Judgment (cf. Matt. 25:31; Rev. 14:10).

5:22 Do not be hasty . . . hands. To participate in the ordination of an elder known to be unqualified is to approve of his sins and to risk sharing the guilt for them.

keep yourself pure. See 4:12, 16.

5:23 No longer . . . only water. The practice of abstaining from wine as a matter of principle perhaps reflects the influence of the false teachers' concept of purity (4:3).

use a little wine . . . ailments. Paul recognizes a medicinal value of wine.

your frequent ailments.) **24** The sins of some
men are conspicuous, going before them to
judgment, but the sins of others appear
later. **25** So also good works are conspicuous, and [n]even those that are not cannot
remain hidden.

6 [o]Let all who are under a yoke as slaves[1]
regard their own masters as worthy of
all honor, [p]so that the name of God and the
teaching may not be reviled. **2** Those who
have believing masters must not be disrespectful on the ground that they are [q]broth-
ers; rather they must serve all the better
since those who benefit by their good service are believers and beloved.

False Teachers and True Contentment

[r]Teach and urge these things. **3** If anyone
[s]teaches a different doctrine and does not
agree with [t]the sound[2] words of our Lord
Jesus Christ and the teaching [u]that accords
with godliness, **4** [v]he is puffed up with conceit and [w]understands nothing. He has an
unhealthy craving for [x]controversy and for
[y]quarrels about words, which produce
envy, dissension, slander, evil suspicions,
5 and constant friction among people [z]who
are depraved in mind and deprived of the
truth, [a]imagining that godliness is a means
of gain. **6** Now there is great gain in [b]godli-
ness [c]with contentment, **7** for [d]we brought
nothing into the world, and[3] we cannot
take anything out of the world. **8** But [e]if we
have food and clothing, with these we will
be content. **9** But [f]those who desire to be
rich fall into temptation, [g]into a snare, into
many senseless and harmful desires that
[h]plunge people into ruin and destruction.
10 For the love of money is a root of [i]all
kinds of evils. It is through this craving that
some have wandered away from the faith
and pierced themselves with many pangs.

Fight the Good Fight of Faith

11 But as for you, [j]O man of God, [k]flee
these things. [l]Pursue righteousness, godliness, faith, love, steadfastness, gentleness.
12 [m]Fight the good fight of the faith. [n]Take
hold of the eternal life [o]to which you were
called and about which you made [p]the
good confession in the presence of many
witnesses. **13** [q]I charge you in the presence
of God, who gives life to all things, and of
Christ Jesus, [r]who in his testimony before[4]
Pontius Pilate made [p]the good confession,
14 to keep the commandment unstained
and free from reproach until [s]the appearing
of our Lord Jesus Christ, **15** which he will
display [t]at the proper time—he who is [u]the
blessed and only Sovereign, [v]the King of
kings and Lord of lords, **16** [w]who alone has
immortality, [x]who dwells in [y]unapproach-
able light, [z]whom no one has ever seen or
can see. To him be honor and eternal
dominion. Amen.

25 [n][Ps. 37:6; Prov. 10:9]
Chapter 6
1 [o]See 1 Pet. 2:18 [p]Isai. 52:5; Rom. 2:24; Tit. 2:5
2 [q]See Philem. 16 [r]ch. 4:11, 13; 5:7
3 [s]ch. 1:3 [t]See ch. 1:10 [u]Tit. 1:1
4 [v]ch. 3:6; 2 Tim. 3:4 [w]1 Cor. 8:2; [ch. 1:7] [x]ch. 1:4; 2 Tim. 2:23; Tit. 3:9 [y]2 Tim. 2:14; [Acts 18:15]
5 [z]2 Tim. 3:8; [Eph. 4:22; Tit. 1:15] [a]Tit. 1:11; 2 Pet. 2:3
6 [b][ch. 4:8] [c]Ps. 37:16; Prov. 15:16; 16:8; Phil. 4:11; Heb. 13:5
7 [d]Job 1:21; Ps. 49:17; Eccles. 5:15
8 [e]Gen. 28:20; Prov. 30:8
9 [f]Prov. 15:27; 23:4; 28:20; Matt. 13:22 [g][ch. 3:7] [h][ch. 1:19]
10 [i][Ex. 23:8; Deut. 16:19]
11 [j]2 Tim. 3:17 [k]2 Tim. 2:22 [l]See Prov. 15:9
12 [m][ch. 1:18]; See 1 Cor. 9:25 [n][Phil. 3:12] [o]1 Pet. 5:10 [p]See 2 Cor. 9:13
13 [q]See ch. 5:21 [r][Matt. 27:11; John 18:37; Rev. 1:5; 3:14] [p][See ver. 12 above]
14 [s]See 2 Thess. 2:8 **15** [t]See ch. 2:6 [u]ch. 1:11 [v]See Rev. 17:14 **16** [w]See ch. 1:17 [x][Ps. 104:2] [y]Job 37:23 [z]See John 1:18

[1] Greek *bondservants* [2] Or *healthy* [3] Greek *for*; some manuscripts insert [it is] *certain* [that] [4] Or *in the time of*

5:24 The sins of some men . . . judgment. Another reference to the importance of care in screening candidates for ordination.

6:1, 2 Finally, Paul addresses the problem of slaves who have not been showing proper respect for their Christian masters.

6:1 under a yoke. Paul gives instructions to slaves in Eph. 6:5–8; Col. 3:22–25; and Titus 2:9, 10.

the teaching. Presumably this is in contrast to the false teaching, which may have encouraged insubordination among some of the Christian slaves.

6:3–10 Paul returns one last time to the problem of the false teachers, noting especially their divisiveness and their greed. This leads him to reflect upon the proper perspective one should have on material possessions.

6:4 controversy and for quarrels about words. Contentiousness was one of the prominent characteristics of the false teachers (1:4; 2 Tim. 2:14, 23; Titus 3:9).

6:5 a means of gain. Perhaps some of the false teachers were seeking the position of elder out of greed (v. 10; Titus 1:11).

6:6 contentment. Christians can be content because their needs are met by Christ (2 Cor. 12:9, 10; Phil. 4:11, 13).

6:10 some have wandered away from the faith. See note on v. 5.

6:11–16 As he has done previously, Paul follows his comments about the false teachers with personal exhortations to Timothy, concluding with a marvelous doxology.

6:12 Fight the good fight of the faith. A metaphor for the Christian life viewed in terms of faithfulness to Christ (2 Tim. 4:7).

Take hold of the eternal life. That is, do not become complacent. While faith in Christ begins new life (4:8), the goal of the Christian life is always future (v. 19; 1:16 note; Phil. 3:12; 2 Tim. 4:8).

to which you were called. Eternal life is not something we naturally choose, but something to which God supernaturally calls us (Rom. 8:30).

good confession in the presence of many witnesses. This probably refers to Timothy's baptism. The "good confession" that one has come to faith in Christ leads naturally into the "good fight" of seeking to live in faithfulness to Him.

6:13 before Pontius Pilate made the good confession. This may refer to Jesus' trial before Pilate (Matt. 27:11; Mark 15:2; Luke 23:3; John 18:33–37; 19:8–11), but is more likely an allusion to His death.

6:14 the commandment. Probably a reference to all that Paul has charged concerning Timothy's personal discipline and official duties.

appearing. The Second Coming of Christ (2 Tim. 4:1, 8; Titus 2:13).

6:15 King of kings and Lord of lords. This expression is applied to Christ in Rev. 19:16; cf. 17:14.

17 As for the rich in [a]this present age, charge them [b]not to be haughty, nor [c]to set their hopes on [d]the uncertainty of riches, but on God, [e]who richly provides us with everything to enjoy. 18 They are to do good, [f]to be rich in good works, to be generous and [g]ready to share, 19 thus [h]storing up treasure for themselves as a good foundation for the future, so that they may [i]take hold of [j]that which is truly life.

20 O Timothy, guard the deposit entrusted to you. [k]Avoid the [l]irreverent babble and contradictions of what is falsely called "knowledge," 21 for by professing it some have swerved from the faith.

[m]Grace be with you.[1]

17 [a]2 Tim. 4:10; Tit. 2:12 [b]Rom. 11:20; 12:3, 16 [c]See Mark 10:24 [d]Prov. 23:5; [Matt. 13:22] [e]See Acts 14:17 18 [f]Luke 12:21; Tit. 3:8, 14 [g]See Rom. 12:13 19 [h]See Matt. 6:19, 20 [i]ver. 12 [j][2 Tim. 1:1] 20 [k]2 Tim. 3:5; [Col. 2:8; 2 Tim. 4:4; Tit. 1:14] [l]2 Tim. 2:16 21 [m]See Col. 4:18

1 The Greek for *you* is plural

6:17–19 Having condemned the love of money and affirmed the future orientation of Christian hope, Paul provides an exhortation for those who do find themselves rich in this world (presumably not from greed).

6:17 to enjoy. See note 4:4.

6:19 storing up . . . a good foundation. See Matt. 6:20.

take hold of that which is truly life. See note on v. 12.

6:20, 21 Paul brings the letter to a close with one final charge to Timothy, once again set within the context of dealing with the false teachers.

6:20 the deposit entrusted to you. That is, the sound doctrine of the gospel (1:10, 11; cf. 2 Tim. 1:14).

what is falsely called "knowledge." The false teachers emphasize "knowledge" (Greek *gnosis*, from which the word *Gnosticism* is derived; see Introduction to 2 Timothy: Interpretive Difficulties).

6:21 Grace be with you. This abrupt conclusion, lacking Paul's usual personal greetings, suggests that Paul saw the situation he was addressing to be quite serious. Some of the earliest Greek manuscripts have the plural form of "you" (as in 2 Tim. 4:22; Titus 3:15) in this benediction, suggesting that Paul intended for the letter to be read to the entire church.

THE SECOND EPISTLE OF PAUL THE APOSTLE TO

Timothy

AUTHOR

The second letter to Timothy was written by Paul. See "Introduction to 1 Timothy: Author."

DATE AND OCCASION

Although it does not appear last in the section of Paul's letters in the New Testament, 2 Timothy is the last letter written by Paul. He prepared it after his fourth missionary journey, probably between A.D. 64 and 68. See "Introduction to 1 Timothy: Date and Occasion."

Paul wrote 2 Timothy during his second Roman imprisonment (1:8; 2:9). Why he was under arrest, or even where he was arrested, is unknown. Paul had received no support at his preliminary hearing (4:16). His trial still awaited him, but he knew that it would end in his execution (4:6). Most of his friends found it convenient to be elsewhere (4:10, 11). He had been troubled by the actions of Phygelus and Hermogenes (1:15, 16) and Alexander the coppersmith (4:14), although a Christian named Onesiphorus had been an encouragement to him (1:16, 17).

Timothy was still in Ephesus (4:19), where Paul had left him previously (1 Tim. 1:3), and where the false teaching that Paul had addressed in his first letter to Timothy continued to be a problem (2:17, 18; 3:1–8). Remembering their longstanding friendship, Paul desired to see Timothy one last time before his death (1:4).

Paul seems to have written 2 Timothy with two purposes in mind. First, he directs Timothy to come to Rome (4:9, 21), providing instructions on who and what (4:11–13) to bring with him. Second, he wants to provide Timothy with a final letter of personal encouragement in his ministry (1:5–14; 2:1–16, 22–26; 3:10–4:5).

CHARACTERISTICS AND THEMES

Both of Paul's letters to Timothy provide important background information about the apostle's young protégé. This second letter names his mother (Eunice) and his grandmother (Lois), identifying them both as Christians (1:5). It speaks of Timothy's early training in the Scriptures (3:15) and includes a probable reference to his ordination (1:6; cf. 2:2).

Also like the earlier letter, 2 Timothy exhibits a strong concern for sound doctrine (1:13, 14; 2:2; 4:3) and contains marvelous meditations on the grace of God (1:9–11), the faithfulness of Christ (2:11–13), and the nature and function of Scripture (3:15–17). There are affirmations of salvation by grace (1:9), election (1:9; 2:10, 19), and the divine inspiration of Scripture (3:16). Second Timothy also affirms the resurrection (2:8) and the Second Coming (4:1, 8) of Christ.

As the last of Paul's letters, 2 Timothy provides an important final picture of Paul. His situation was bleak. No longer could he look forward to fruitful ministry (cf. Phil. 1:22–26), and most of his friends had left him (4:10, 11). Yet Paul remained confident. He was not ashamed to suffer for the gospel (1:12) and he was willing to endure everything for the sake of the elect (2:10). He knew that he had been faithful to Christ (4:7) and that Christ Himself is faithful (1:12; 2:13). Paul had confidence that the One who in the past had rescued him *from* death (3:11; 4:17) would rescue him *through* death for eternal life (4:8, 18).

INTERPRETIVE DIFFICULTIES

There was false teaching at Ephesus that Paul describes as coming from within the church (2 Tim. 2:18; 4:4; 1 Tim. 1:6, 19; 4:1; 6:10, 21). It was characterized by a concern with fables or myths (4:4; 1 Tim. 1:4; 4:7), genealogies (1 Tim. 1:4), quarrels about words (2:14, 23; 1 Tim. 6:4), controversies (1 Tim. 1:4; 6:4), knowledge (1 Tim. 6:20), meaningless talk (1 Tim. 1:6), and godless chatter (2:16; 1 Tim. 6:20). The false doctrines included the prohibition of marriage and of certain foods (1 Tim. 4:3) and the belief that the resurrection had already taken place (2:18). Those who taught these false doctrines also sought to interpret the Jewish law (1 Tim. 1:7) and accordingly placed restrictions on prayer (1 Tim. 2:1–7).

Specific leaders of the movement included Hymenaeus (2:17; 1 Tim. 1:20), Alexander (1 Tim. 1:20), and Philetus (2:17). Some who sought leadership positions in the movement did so for financial gain (1 Tim. 6:5, 10). The false teachers had been divisive (1 Tim. 6:4, 5) and seem to have been particularly effective in deceiving the female members of the church (3:6, 7; 1 Tim. 2:14; 5:11–15), perhaps by offering them positions of leadership (1 Tim. 2:11, 12).

A number of these features—the specific doctrinal teachings, the interest in myths and genealogies, and the concern for "knowledge" (Greek *gnosis*)—suggest that the false teaching at Ephesus might have been an early form of Gnosticism, a heretical movement that became a strong competitor to the developing church in the second and third centuries. However, some of the more characteristic aspects of later Gnosticism are lacking, and some assert that the movement can be explained in terms of Jewish and Hellenistic influences. These two suggestions need not be seen as contradictory, for Gnosticism itself was a product of both Jewish and Hellenistic ideas. But the precise nature of the false teaching at Ephesus remains elusive.

OUTLINE OF 2 TIMOTHY

I. Salutation and Thanksgiving (1:1–5)

II. Exhortations to Boldness and Faithfulness (1:6–2:13)

- A. *Do Not Be Ashamed of Paul's Imprisonment (1:6–14)*
- B. *Examples of Unfaithfulness and of Faithfulness (1:15–18)*
- C. *Be Strong and Endure in Grace (2:1–13)*

III. The Problem of False Teachers (2:14–4:5)

- A. *Faithfulness in the Face of False Teachers (2:14–26)*
- B. *The Impact of False Teachers (3:1–9)*
- C. *Continue in the Things You Have Learned (3:10–17)*
- D. *Final Charge for Ministry (4:1–5)*

IV. Paul's Personal Relationship with Timothy (4:6–18)

- A. *Paul's Impending Death (4:6–8)*
- B. *Final Instructions to Timothy (4:9–18)*
  1. Request for Timothy to Come to Rome (4:9–13)
  2. Warning Against Alexander the Coppersmith (4:14, 15)
  3. Paul's Legal Situation and Confidence (4:16–18)

V. Conclusion (4:19–22)

- A. *Final Greetings and Information (4:19–21)*
- B. *Benediction (4:22)*

Greeting

1 Paul, [a]an apostle of Christ Jesus [b]by
the will of God according to [c]the promise of the life that is in Christ Jesus,
2 To Timothy, [d]my beloved child:
[e]Grace, mercy, and peace from God the
Father and Christ Jesus our Lord.

Guard the Deposit Entrusted to You

3 [f]I thank God [g]whom I serve, as did my
ancestors, [h]with a clear conscience, as I
remember you [i]constantly in my prayers
night and day. 4 [j]As I remember your tears,
[k]I long to see you, that I may be filled
with joy. 5 I am reminded of [l]your sincere
faith, a faith that dwelt first in your grandmother Lois and [m]your mother Eunice
and now, I am sure, dwells in you as well.

Chapter 1
1 [a]See 2 Cor. 1:1 [b]See 1 Cor. 1:1 [c]Tit. 1:2; Heb. 9:15
2 [d]1 Cor. 4:17; [ch. 2:1]; See 3 John 4 [e]See 1 Tim. 1:2
3 [f]See Rom. 1:8 [g]See Acts 22:3; 24:14 [h]1 Tim. 3:9; See Acts 23:1 [i]Rom. 1:9
4 [j][Acts 20:37] [k]Phil. 1:8; [ch. 4:9, 21]
5 [l]Rom. 12:9; 1 Tim. 1:5 [m]Acts 16:1; [ch. 3:15; Ps. 86:16; 116:16]

1:1, 2 Opening salutation, including sender, recipient, and benediction.

1:1 apostle of Christ Jesus. One sent out as an official representative of Christ (2 Cor. 1:1 note).

by the will of God. Paul identifies the One who commissioned him (1 Cor. 1:1; 2 Cor. 1:1; Eph. 1:1; Col. 1:1).

according to the promise of the life that is in Christ Jesus. The role of the apostle is to proclaim the life that is in Christ (1 Tim. 1:16 note).

1:2 beloved child. See Introduction to 1 Timothy: Date and Occasion; 1 Cor. 4:17 (cf. 1 Tim. 1:2).

Grace . . . our Lord. See note 1 Tim. 1:2.

1:3–5 As in most of his letters (the exceptions are Galatians, 1 Timothy, and Titus), Paul follows his salutation with a section giving thanks to God for the recipients of the letter. Here he focuses on his relationship with Timothy and his confidence in Timothy's faith.

1:4 I remember your tears. Probably the tears Timothy shed the last time Paul left him.

I long to see you. Paul anticipates his request in 4:9, 21.

1:5 Lois . . . Eunice. These women are named only here in the New

6 For this reason I remind you [n]to fan into
flame the gift of God, which is in you
through the laying on of my hands, 7 for
God gave us [o]a spirit not of fear but [p]of
power and love and self-control.
8 Therefore [q]do not be ashamed of [r]the
testimony about our Lord, nor of [s]me his
prisoner, but [t]share in suffering for the
gospel by the power of God, 9 [u]who saved
us and [v]called us to[1] a holy calling, [w]not
because of our works but because of [v]his
own purpose and grace, which he gave us
in Christ Jesus [x]before the ages began,[2]
10 and which now has [y]been manifested
through [z]the appearing of our Savior Christ
Jesus, [a]who abolished death and [b]brought
life and [c]immortality to light through the
gospel, 11 [d]for which I was appointed a
preacher and apostle and teacher, 12 [e]which
is why I suffer as I do. But [f]I am not
ashamed, for [g]I know whom I have
believed, and I am convinced that he is
able to guard until [h]that Day [i]what has
been entrusted to me.[3] 13 [j]Follow [k]the pattern of [l]the sound[4] words [m]that you have
heard from me, in [n]the faith and love that
are in Christ Jesus. 14 By the Holy Spirit
[o]who dwells within us, guard [i]the good
deposit entrusted to you.
15 You are aware that [p]all who are in Asia
turned away from me, among whom are
Phygelus and Hermogenes. 16 May the Lord
grant mercy to [q]the household of Onesiphorus, for he often [r]refreshed me and was
not ashamed of [s]my chains, 17 but when he
arrived in Rome [t]he searched for me
earnestly and found me— 18 may the Lord
grant him to find mercy from the Lord on
[u]that Day!—and you well know all the
service he [v]rendered at Ephesus.

A Good Soldier of Christ Jesus

2 You then, [w]my child, [x]be strengthened
by the grace that is in Christ Jesus,
2 and [y]what you have heard from me in the
presence of many witnesses [z]entrust to
faithful men [a]who will be able to teach
others also. 3 [b]Share in suffering as [c]a good

6 [n]1 Tim. 4:14; [1 Thess. 5:19]
7 [o]Rom. 8:15; [John 14:27; Rev. 21:8] [p]Luke 24:49; Acts 1:8
8 [q]See Mark 8:38 [r]See 1 Cor. 1:6 [s][ver. 16]; See Eph. 3:1 [t]ch. 2:3, 9; 4:5
9 [u]1 Tim. 1:1; Tit. 3:4 [v][Heb. 3:1]; See Rom. 8:28 [w]Tit. 3:5; See Rom. 3:27 [x]Tit. 1:2; [Rom. 16:25]; See Eph. 1:4
10 [y]See Rom. 16:26 [z]See 2 Thess. 2:8 [a]1 Cor. 15:26; [1 Cor. 15:54, 55; Heb. 2:14, 15] [b][Job 33:30] [c]Rom. 2:7
11 [d]See 1 Tim. 2:7
12 [e]ch. 2:9 [f]ver. 8 [g][Ps. 10:14; 1 Pet. 4:19] [h]ver. 18; ch. 4:8; See 1 Cor. 3:13 [i]1 Tim. 6:20
13 [j][ch. 3:14; Tit. 1:9; Rev. 3:3] [k][Rom. 2:20; 6:17] [l]See 1 Tim. 1:10 [m]ch. 2:2 [n]1 Tim. 1:14 **14** [o]See Rom. 8:9 [i][See ver. 12 above] **15** [p]Acts 19:10; [ch. 4:10, 11, 16] **16** [q]ch. 4:19 [r]Philem. 7, 20 [s][ver. 8]; See Acts 28:20 **17** [t]Matt. 25:36-40 **18** [u]ver. 12 [v]Heb. 6:10
Chapter 2 **1** [w]See ch. 1:2 [x]See Eph. 6:10 **2** [y]ch. 1:13 [z]1 Tim. 1:18 [a][Tit. 1:5] **3** [b]ch. 1:8; 4:5 [c]1 Tim. 1:18

[1] Or *with* [2] Greek *before times eternal* [3] Or *what I have entrusted to him*; Greek *my deposit* [4] Or *healthy*

Testament. See Introduction to 1 Timothy: Date and Occasion.

1:6–14 Paul moves into the body of letter. As he exhorts Timothy to boldness and faithfulness, Paul discusses the gospel and his own role in proclaiming it.

1:6 fan into flame the gift of God. This strong expression suggests that Timothy was being less forceful than he should have been in using the spiritual gift God had given him.

laying on of my hands. See note 1 Tim. 1:18.

1:7 fear. Or, "cowardice." This strong expression was necessary, given Timothy's natural timidity and the gravity of his situation.

1:8 me his prisoner. Paul is in prison in Rome (2:9; Introduction: Date and Occasion).

1:9 to a holy calling. The goal of God's election and calling is the sanctification of His people (Eph. 1:4).

not . . . grace. This is a marvelous affirmation that salvation is by grace, not by human merit (Eph. 2:8, 9).

because of his own purpose. God's decree of redemption is based solely on His own purpose and good pleasure. Elsewhere, this divine purpose is identified as mercy (Titus 3:5) and love (Eph. 1:4, 5).

before the ages began. An affirmation that the divine decree of redemption through Christ is from eternity (Eph. 1:4; Titus 1:2; 1 Pet. 1:20; Rev. 13:8).

1:10 our Savior Christ Jesus. Christ is the Mediator of the covenant of grace (Titus 1:4; 2:13; 3:6).

who abolished death and brought life and immortality to light. That is, through His death and resurrection (Heb. 2:14, 15; Rev. 1:18).

1:11 preacher. See 1 Tim. 2:7.

1:12 I suffer. Paul is in prison (v. 8; 2:9).

I am not ashamed. Having exhorted Timothy not to be ashamed to speak out for Christ (v. 8), Paul presents himself as a model of boldness in the face of suffering (2:8–10; 3:10, 11).

that Day. Judgment Day (v. 18; 4:8).

1:13 sound words. This theme runs throughout the Pastoral Letters (1 Tim. 1:10 note).

1:14 the good deposit entrusted to you. See note 1 Tim. 6:20.

1:15–18 Paul's concern that Timothy be faithful leads him to set forth specific examples of unfaithfulness and faithfulness.

1:15 all. Paul is probably writing with intentional exaggeration to make sure his readers see the extent of the disloyalty.

Asia. A Roman province across the Aegean Sea from Greece and today part of western Turkey. Ephesus, where Timothy was serving as Paul's representative, was the leading city of this province.

Phygelus and Hermogenes. Not mentioned elsewhere in the New Testament. Probably Paul mentions them because he had counted on their support.

1:16 Onesiphorus. A member of the church at Ephesus who distinguished himself through his loyalty to Paul (v. 18; cf. 4:19).

1:17 when he arrived in Rome. Onesiphorus may have come to Rome to aid Paul.

1:18 that Day. The Day of Judgment (v. 12; 4:8).

2:1–13 Paul again exhorts Timothy to be faithful, beginning with three analogies from everyday life that emphasize wholehearted devotion to a task.

2:1 my child. See note 1:2.

2:2 many witnesses. This may refer to Timothy's ordination (1:6; 1 Tim. 1:18; 4:14).

faithful men who will be able to teach others. Presumably bishops or elders (1 Tim. 3:2; 5:17; cf. Titus 1:7 note).

soldier of Christ Jesus. 4 No soldier [d]gets
entangled in civilian pursuits, since his aim
is to please the one who enlisted him. 5 [e]An
athlete is not [f]crowned unless he competes
according to the rules. 6 It is [g]the hardworking farmer who ought to have the first
share of the crops. 7 Think over what I say,
for the Lord will give you understanding in
everything.

8 Remember Jesus Christ, [h]risen from the
dead, the [i]offspring of David, [j]as preached
in my gospel, 9 [k]for which I am suffering,
[l]bound with chains as a criminal. But [m]the
word of God is not bound! 10 Therefore [n]I
endure everything for the sake of the elect,
that they also may obtain [o]the salvation
that is in Christ Jesus with [p]eternal glory.
11 The saying is [q]trustworthy, for:

[r]If we have died with him, we will
also [s]live with him;
12 [t]if we endure, we will also reign with
him;
[u]if we deny him, he also will deny us;
13 [v]if we are faithless, [w]he remains
faithful—
for [x]he cannot deny himself.

4 [d]2 Pet. 2:20 **5** [e]See 1 Cor. 9:25 [f][ch. 4:8] **6** [g]1 Cor. 9:10; [Heb. 6:7] **8** [h]1 Cor. 15:20 [i]See Matt. 1:1 [j]See Rom. 2:16 **9** [k]ch. 1:8, 12 [l]See Phil. 1:7 [m][ch. 4:17]; See Phil. 1:13 **10** [n]Eph. 3:13; Col. 1:24; [1 Cor. 13:7] [o]2 Cor. 1:6 [p]1 Pet. 5:10 **11** [q]See 1 Tim. 1:15 [r][1 Thess. 5:10]; See Rom. 6:8 [s]Rev. 20:4 **12** [t][2 Thess. 1:4, 5]; See Rom. 8:17; Heb. 10:36; Rev. 20:4 [u]See Matt. 10:33 **13** [v]See Rom. 3:3 [w]See 1 Cor. 1:9 [x]Num. 23:19; Tit. 1:2

14 [y]1 Tim. 5:21; 6:13 [z]1 Tim. 6:4; [ver. 23] [a]Tit. 3:9

A Worker Approved by God

14 Remind them of these things, and
[y]charge them before God[1] [z]not to quarrel
about words, [a]which does no good, but
only ruins the hearers. 15 Do your best to
present yourself to God as one approved,[2]
a worker [b]who has no need to be ashamed,
rightly handling the word of truth. 16 But
[c]avoid [d]irreverent babble, for it will lead
people into more and more ungodliness,
17 and their talk will spread like gangrene.
Among them are [e]Hymenaeus and Philetus, 18 who have swerved from the truth,
[f]saying that the resurrection has already
happened. They are upsetting the faith of
some. 19 But God's firm foundation stands,
bearing this seal: [g]"The Lord knows those
who are his," and, "Let everyone [h]who
names the name of the Lord depart from
iniquity."

20 Now in [i]a great house there are not
only vessels of gold and silver but also of

15 [b][Phil. 1:20] **16** [c]Tit. 3:9 [d]1 Tim. 6:20 **17** [e]1 Tim. 1:20 **18** [f][1 Cor. 15:12] **19** [g]Num. 16:5; Nah. 1:7; John 10:14, 27; [Luke 13:27]; See 1 Cor. 8:3 [h]Isai. 26:13 **20** [i]See 1 Tim. 3:15

1 Some manuscripts *the Lord* 2 That is, one approved after being tested

2:5, 6 crowned . . . crops. These two analogies add a promise of future reward (vv. 10–12).

2:8 risen from the dead. The resurrection of Christ is at the center of Paul's theology (Rom. 6:4–10; 1 Cor. 15:12–22). It is the basis for the hope expressed in vv. 11, 12.

the offspring of David. Jesus fulfills God's promise to grant to one of David's descendants an eternal kingship (2 Sam. 7:12–16; Matt. 1:1; Mark 12:35; Luke 1:32, 33; John 7:42; Acts 2:30–36; Rev. 5:5). For the association of Christ's resurrection and His descent from David, see Rom. 1:3, 4.

2:9 I am suffering. See note 1:8.

2:10 the elect. Those whom God has chosen to be saved (Titus 1:1).

the salvation that is in Christ Jesus. The salvation that comes through faith in Christ (3:15). See "Salvation" at 2 Cor. 6:5.

eternal glory. This glory is the final, complete salvation of the elect in the new order of God. The saints will have resurrection bodies and transformed human natures (1 Cor. 15:42–49). They will experience the triumph of Christ over sin and death, and know fullness of joy in a life secured for them by Christ's death, resurrection, and ascension (v. 11; Matt. 13:43; 1 Tim. 1:16 note; cf. Ps. 16:11).

2:11 The saying is trustworthy. See note 1 Tim. 1:15. What follows may be part of an early Christian hymn.

If we have died with him. A reference to the believer's union with Christ in His death on the cross (Rom. 6:3–11).

2:12 if we endure. This refers to perseverance in the face of hardship (v. 10).

we will also reign with him. A New Testament image for the eternal glory that Christians receive through Christ (Matt. 19:28; Rom. 5:17; Rev. 3:21; 5:10; 20:4, 6; 22:5).

if we deny him, he also will deny us. A sober warning against apostasy (Matt. 10:33).

2:13 if we are faithless, he remains faithful. This is a wonderful affirmation of assurance that although we are called to endure and be faithful, salvation does not rest ultimately on our faithfulness, but upon that of Christ (v. 19).

he cannot deny himself. Christian hope is rooted firmly in the unchanging character of God (Num. 23:19; Titus 1:2).

2:14 quarrel about words. One of the characteristics of the false teachers (v. 23; 1 Tim. 1:4; 6:4; Titus 3:9).

2:15 the word of truth. The gospel (2:8, 9; 4:2).

2:17 Hymenaeus. Mentioned also in 1 Tim. 1:19, 20 as one who has made "shipwreck" of his faith.

Philetus. Mentioned nowhere else in the New Testament.

2:18 the resurrection has already happened. This Gnostic belief denied the future bodily resurrection of Christians and affirmed instead a spiritual resurrection at conversion; it resulted in an overemphasis on present experience (1 Cor. 15:12–14).

They are upsetting the faith of some. The doctrines of the false teachers are incompatible with the gospel. Timothy must warn the church against them (v. 14).

2:19 God's firm foundation. The church (cf. 1 Tim. 3:15), which is God's elect.

stands. In contrast to those who wander away (v. 18).

seal. An expression of ownership and security.

The Lord knows those who are his. A quotation of Num. 16:5 (according to the Septuagint translation). Inscribed on the people of God is His eternal decree of election (v. 11), which ensures the security of the body of Christ (John 10:29).

Let everyone . . . depart. Also inscribed on the membership of God's church is His call to holiness (v. 21), including the repudiation of false teaching.

2:20, 21 These verses provide an example from everyday life of the importance of holiness—being set apart for a noble (godly) task.

wood and clay, [j]some for honorable use,
some for dishonorable. 21 Therefore, [k]if anyone cleanses himself from what is dishonorable,[1] he will be a vessel for honorable
use, set apart as holy, useful to the master
of the house, [l]ready for every good work.
22 So [m]flee [n]youthful passions and pursue
righteousness, faith, love, and peace, along
with [o]those who call on the Lord [p]from a
pure heart. 23 Have nothing to do with foolish, ignorant [q]controversies; you know that
they breed quarrels. 24 And [r]the Lord's servant[2] must not be quarrelsome but [s]kind to
everyone, [t]able to teach, patiently enduring
evil, 25 correcting his opponents [u]with gentleness. God [v]may perhaps grant them
repentance [w]leading to a knowledge of the
truth, 26 and they may escape from [x]the
snare of the devil, after being captured by
him to do his will.

Godlessness in the Last Days

3 But understand this, that [y]in the last
days there will come times of difficulty. 2 For people will be [z]lovers of self,
[a]lovers of money, [b]proud, [b]arrogant, abusive, [b]disobedient to their parents, ungrateful, unholy, 3 [c]heartless, unappeasable,
slanderous, without self-control, brutal,
[d]not loving good, 4 treacherous, reckless,
[e]swollen with conceit, [f]lovers of pleasure
rather than lovers of God, 5 having the
appearance of godliness, but [g]denying its
power. [h]Avoid such people. 6 For among
them are [i]those who creep into households
and capture weak women, burdened with
sins and led astray by various passions, 7 always learning and never able to [j]arrive at a
knowledge of the truth. 8 Just as [k]Jannes
and Jambres [l]opposed Moses, so these
men also oppose the truth, [m]men corrupted in mind and [n]disqualified regarding the
faith. 9 But they will not get very far, for
their folly will be plain to all, [o]as was that
of those two men.

All Scripture Is Breathed Out by God

10 [p]You, however, have followed my
teaching, my conduct, my aim in life, my
faith, my patience, my love, my steadfastness, 11 my persecutions and sufferings that
happened to me [q]at Antioch, [r]at Iconium,
and [s]at Lystra—which persecutions I
endured; yet [t]from them all [u]the Lord rescued me. 12 Indeed, all who desire to [v]live a
godly life in Christ Jesus [w]will be persecuted, 13 while [x]evil people and impostors will
go on from bad to worse, deceiving and
[y]being deceived. 14 But as for you, [z]contin-
ue in what you have learned and have firmly believed, knowing from whom[3] you
learned it 15 and how [a]from childhood you
have been acquainted with [b]the sacred

20 [j]Rom. 9:21 **21** [k][Prov. 25:4; Isai. 52:11] [l]ch. 3:17; Tit. 3:1; [1 Tim. 5:10] **22** [m]1 Tim. 6:11 [n][1 Tim. 4:12] [o]Acts 7:59; 9:14 [p]1 Tim. 1:5 **23** [q]See 1 Tim. 6:4 **24** [r][1 Tim. 3:3] [s]1 Thess. 2:7 [t]1 Tim. 3:2 **25** [u]Gal. 6:1; Tit. 3:2; [1 Tim. 6:11; 1 Pet. 3:15] [v]Dan. 4:27; Acts 8:22; See Acts 5:31 [w]See 1 Tim. 2:4 **26** [x]1 Tim. 3:7
Chapter 3
1 [y]See 1 Tim. 4:1 **2** [z][Phil. 2:21] [a]Luke 16:14; [1 Tim. 6:10] [b]Rom. 1:30 **3** [c]Rom. 1:31 [d][Tit. 1:8] **4** [e]1 Tim. 3:6; 6:4 [f]Phil. 3:19 **5** [g]See 1 Tim. 5:8 [h]1 Tim. 6:20; [Tit. 1:14]

6 [i][Tit. 1:11] **7** [j]1 Tim. 2:4 **8** [k]Ex. 7:11 [l][Acts 13:8] [m]See 1 Tim. 6:5 [n]Tit. 1:16 **9** [o]Ex. 7:12; 8:18; 9:11 **10** [p][Phil. 2:22]

11 [q]Acts 13:14, 45, 50 [r]Acts 14:1, 2, 5 [s]Acts 14:6, 19 [t]Ps. 34:19 [u]ch. 4:17; [2 Cor. 1:10] **12** [v]Tit. 2:12 [w]See Acts 14:22 **13** [x][Rev. 22:11] [y]Tit. 3:3 **14** [z][1 Tim. 4:6] **15** [a][Eph. 6:4]; See ch. 1:5 [b][John 5:39]

1 Greek *from these things* 2 Greek *bondservant* 3 The Greek for *whom* is plural

2:23 controversies . . . quarrels. See note 2:14.

2:25, 26 The Christian must never assume that those who are ensnared by the devil's false teaching are irretrievably lost. The gospel must be proclaimed to all.

3:1–9 Paul continues on the theme of false teaching by turning to an attack on the false teachers themselves, noting their impact upon the church at Ephesus, but concluding with the affirmation that they will not succeed in the end.

3:1 the last days. The era inaugurated by Christ's First Advent and completed by His second (1 Tim. 4:1 note).

3:5 having the appearance of godliness, but denying its power. What makes the false teachers so dangerous is that they appear to be Christians (Matt. 7:15, 21–23).

3:6 weak women. Paul's point is not that all women are this way, but that some have been especially vulnerable to deception. The false teachers at Ephesus had been especially successful in deceiving women (1 Tim. 2:14; 5:13–15).

3:8 Jannes and Jambres. In Jewish tradition, these names were given to two Egyptian magicians who opposed Moses before Pharaoh (Ex. 7; 8).

3:10–17 With the problem of the false teachers fully in view, Paul once more turns to exhorting Timothy to faithfulness, first in terms of the example which Paul has set, and then as obedience to Scripture.

3:10, 11 Once again Paul appeals to his own life as an example for Timothy (1:11–13; 2:8–10).

3:11 Antioch . . . Iconium . . . Lystra. Three cities in the Roman province of Galatia where Paul preached the gospel on his first missionary journey (Acts 13:14–14:20). Against significant opposition, Paul succeeded in establishing a church in each city (Acts 14:21–23). Paul mentions these cities, including Timothy's home of Lystra, in order to appeal to the roots of Timothy's faith (vv. 14, 15; 1:5).

the Lord rescued me. See 4:18 and note.

3:12 all who desire to live a godly life . . . will be persecuted. The New Testament teaches that Christians should expect persecution (Matt. 10:17, 18; John 15:20; 1 Pet. 4:12; 5:9).

3:14 from whom you learned it. A reference to Timothy's mother and grandmother (1:5), as well as to Paul himself.

3:15 from childhood. According to custom, the Jewish parent was to begin instructing a child in the law when the child reached five years of age.

you have been acquainted with the sacred writings. The false teachers have been misinterpreting the Old Testament (1 Tim. 1:7; Titus 3:9). Timothy needs to remember the proper instruction he received at the hands of his mother and grandmother. The "sacred writings" here are the books of the Old Testament. The New Testament did not yet exist as a collection. Indeed, some of the New Testament books had probably not yet been written.

writings, [c]which are able to make you wise
for salvation through faith in Christ Jesus.
16 [d]All Scripture is breathed out by God and
profitable for teaching, for reproof, for correction, and for training in righteousness,
17 that [e]the man of God[1] may be competent,
[f]equipped [g]for every good work.

Preach the Word

4 [h]I charge you in the presence of God
and of Christ Jesus, [i]who is to judge
the living and the dead, and by [j]his appearing and his kingdom: 2 preach the word; be
ready in season and out of season; [k]re-
prove, rebuke, and [l]exhort, with complete
patience and teaching. 3 [m]For the time is
coming when people will not endure
[n]sound[2] teaching, but having itching ears
they will accumulate for themselves teachers to suit their own passions, 4 and [o]will
turn away from listening to the truth and
[p]wander off into myths. 5 As for you, [q]always

15 [c]Ps. 119:99 16 [d]Rom. 15:4; 2 Pet. 1:20, 21 17 [e]See 1 Tim. 6:11 [f][Luke 6:40] [g]See ch. 2:21
Chapter 4
1 [h]ch. 2:14; 1 Tim. 5:21; 6:13 [i]See Acts 10:42 [j]ver. 8; See 2 Thess. 2:8
2 [k]1 Tim. 5:20; Tit. 1:13; 2:15 [l]1 Tim. 4:13 3 [m]ch. 3:1 [n]See 1 Tim. 1:10 4 [o]See 1 Tim. 6:20 [p]See 1 Tim. 1; 4, 6 5 [q]1 Pet. 1:13

1 That is, a messenger of God (the phrase echoes a common Old Testament expression) 2 Or *healthy*

The Authority of Scripture

The Christian principle of biblical authority means that God is the author of the Bible, and has given it to direct the belief and behavior of His people. Our ideas about God and our conduct should be measured, tested, and where necessary corrected and enlarged, by reference to the Bible. Authority is also the right to command. God's written Word in its truth and wisdom is the way God has chosen to exercise His rule over us, and Scripture is the instrument of Christ's lordship over the church. The work of the Scripture in the church is illustrated by the seven letters of Revelation (Rev. 2; 3).

The Roman Catholic view of the Bible has compromised its unique authority by combining it with the tradition of the church. Roman Catholics accept the Bible as God-given truth, but insist that it is incomplete without the official interpretation of the church as it is led by the Spirit. In the past, giving the church authority over the Bible has led to discouraging or prohibiting ordinary Christians from reading it. At the present time, the Roman Catholic church encourages all Christians to read the Bible.

Many Protestants regard the Bible as having its unique authority in its subject matter, or in the experience and insights of the human authors. The central assumption is that the Bible remains fundamentally a human book and not a divine revelation. The Bible is a guide for their religious experience, but it is not clearly distinguished from other sources, such as political movements and social forces. All too often, the Bible is displaced by voices that oppose it.

Historic Protestantism accepts the Scripture as the only written revelation of God. It is inspired, or "breathed out by God" (2 Tim. 3:16), distinguishing it from all other words. As a result, the Scriptures are infallible and true in all that they affirm. They are sufficient, containing everything that is necessary to know for salvation and eternal life. They are clear, so that a person without special preparation can understand what God requires without the intervention of an official interpreter.

The canonical Scripture is the voice of God in the world. It has an authority, or right to command, corresponding to its divine Author. For this reason, we submit our thoughts and moral standards to the Bible. It was through the recognition that the Bible cannot be subject to any person or group, however exalted, that the Reformers freed their consciences from human traditions and authorities.

salvation . . . in Christ Jesus. The Old Testament, interpreted properly, leads one to understand the central role of Jesus Christ in God's overall plan for His Creation.

3:16 All Scripture. The Old Testament (v. 15 note).

breathed out by God. This is one of the most important expressions in the New Testament of the doctrine of the divine inspiration of Scripture. The Bible has been breathed out by the Spirit of God (2 Pet. 1:21). God is the source and ultimate Author of Scripture. Though written by human authors, Scripture nevertheless has the full weight of His authority. See theological note "The Authority of Scripture."

4:1–5 Paul brings to a conclusion the appeal to Timothy begun in 1:6.

4:1 in the presence of God. Paul mentions witnesses to impress on Timothy the utmost seriousness of the charge.

Christ Jesus, who is to judge. For Christ as Judge, see v. 8; Matt. 25:31–46; John 5:22, 27; Acts 10:42.

his appearing. Christ's Second Coming (cf. v. 8; 1 Tim. 6:14; Titus 2:13).

4:2 the word. The gospel (cf. 2:15).

in season and out of season. In every situation, whether good or bad, the Word is to be proclaimed.

4:3 sound teaching. See note 1:13.

they. Presumably a reference to some who are associated with the church.

itching ears. Some people have an endless fascination with everything but the truth.

4:4 myths. See note 1 Tim. 1:4.

4:5 A final exhortation to faithfulness, even though others may be turning away.

be sober-minded, [r]endure suffering, do the
work of [s]an evangelist, [t]fulfill your ministry.
6 For [u]I am already being poured out as a
drink offering, and the time of my [v]depar-
ture has come. 7 [w]I have fought the good
fight, [x]I have finished the race, I have kept
the faith. 8 Henceforth there is [y]laid up for
me [z]the crown of righteousness, which the
Lord, [a]the righteous judge, will award to
me on [b]that Day, and not only to me but
also to all [c]who have loved his appearing.

Personal Instructions

9 [d]Do your best to come to me soon.
10 For [e]Demas, [f]in love with [g]this present
world, [h]has deserted me and gone to Thessalonica. Crescens has gone to Galatia,[1]
[i]Titus to Dalmatia. 11 [h]Luke alone is with
me. Get [j]Mark and bring him with you, for
he is very useful to me for ministry.
12 [k]Tychicus I have sent to Ephesus.
13 When you come, bring the cloak that I
left with Carpus at Troas, also the books,
and above all the parchments. 14 [l]Alexander
the coppersmith did me great harm; [m]the
Lord will repay him according to his deeds.
15 Beware of him yourself, for he strongly
opposed our message. 16 At my first defense
no one came to stand by me, but all deserted me. [n]May it not be charged against
them! 17 But [o]the Lord stood by me and
[p]strengthened me, so that through me the

5 [r]ch. 1:8; 2:3, 9 [s]Acts 21:8; Eph. 4:11 [t]Col. 4:17 6 [u]Phil. 2:17 [v]Phil. 1:23; [2 Pet. 1:14] 7 [w]See 1 Tim. 6:12 [x]Acts 20:24 8 [y]Col. 1:5; 1 Pet. 1:4 [z]See James 1:12 [a]Ps. 7:11 [b]ch. 1:12 [c][Rev. 22:20] 9 [d]ch. 1:4 10 [e]Col. 4:14; Philem. 24 [f]See 1 John 2:15 [g]1 Tim. 6:17; Tit. 2:12 [h][ch. 1:15] [i][Tit. 3:12] 11 [h][See ver. 10 above] [j]See Acts 12:12

12 [k]Acts 20:4; Eph. 6:21; Col. 4:7; Tit. 3:12 14 [l]See 1 Tim. 1:20 [m]Ps. 62:12; Prov. 24:12; [Neh. 6:14; 13:29; Ps. 28:4; Rev. 18:6] 16 [n][Acts 7:60] 17 [o]Acts 23:11; 27:23; [Matt. 10:19] [p]See 1 Tim. 1:12

[1] Some manuscripts *Gaul*

4:6–8 Paul's impending death provides the reason for his extended appeal to Timothy (Introduction: Date and Occasion).

4:6 already. Paul accepts the inevitability of his death, even if it may still be several months away.

poured out as a drink offering. This metaphor for death (cf. Phil. 2:17) is taken from the language of the Old Testament sacrificial system. A drink offering of wine was poured out in the sanctuary as an offering to God (Num. 15:5, 7, 10; 28:7). Paul understands his impending death as an offering to Christ.

my departure. Another metaphor for death (Phil. 1:23). Paul held steadfastly to the hope and assurance of a destination beyond the grave (v. 18).

4:7 With these three metaphors Paul signifies the end of his ministry. His concern is not that he has been a success, but rather that he has been faithful to his Lord.

4:8 the crown of righteousness. Perhaps the crown awarded for the faithful life of one who has received the righteousness of Christ through faith (Rom. 3:22). More likely, this is the crown consisting of perfect righteousness—eternal life that is given the believer as the climax of the process of sanctification (2:10; James 1:12; 1 Pet. 5:4; Rev. 2:10).

the righteous judge. Christ in His role as the Judge who brings to completion the work He has begun in His elect.

that Day. The Judgment Day (1:12, 18).

his appearing. Christ's Second Coming (v. 1).

4:9–18 Paul now turns to his primary reason for writing the letter: he wants to see Timothy one last time. Paul gives Timothy various instructions regarding his journey to Rome, informs Timothy of his present status, and concludes with a profound expression of trust in his Lord.

4:9 Do your best to come to me. Paul had hinted at his desire to see Timothy in 1:4.

soon. See note on v. 21.

4:10 Demas. A coworker present with Paul during his first Roman imprisonment (Col. 4:14; Philem. 24).

Thessalonica. A city in the Roman province of Macedonia where Paul had established a church on his second missionary journey (Acts 17:1–10).

Crescens. Mentioned nowhere else in the New Testament, he was apparently another of Paul's coworkers.

Galatia. A Roman province Paul visited on his first missionary journey (3:11 note).

Titus. Another of Paul's coworkers. See Introduction to Titus: Date and Occasion.

Dalmatia. Another name for the Roman province of Illyricum, the westernmost province reached by Paul on his first three missionary journeys (Rom. 15:19).

4:11 Luke. The "beloved physician," mentioned in Col. 4:14 and Philem. 24, who traveled with Paul throughout much of his second and third missionary journeys (Introduction to Luke: Author).

Get Mark and bring him with you. A beautiful example of Christian forgiveness. John Mark's desertion of Paul and Barnabas during their first missionary journey (Acts 13:13) had resulted in the dissolution of the partnership between Paul and Barnabas (Acts 15:37–39). Later Mark regained Paul's favor (Col. 4:10; Philem. 24). Now, at the end of his life, Paul wants to see him, "for he is very useful."

4:12 Tychicus. A coworker of Paul mentioned in Acts 20:4; Eph. 6:21; Col. 4:7; Titus 3:12.

to Ephesus. Tychicus is to take this letter to Timothy and serve as his replacement.

4:13 cloak. A heavy woolen garment used for protection against dampness and cold. Paul is anticipating the arrival of winter (v. 21).

Carpus. Mentioned nowhere else in the New Testament.

Troas. A port linking the Roman province of Asia with Macedonia across the Aegean Sea (Acts 16:7, 8 note). Paul had traveled through Troas on his second and third missionary journeys (Acts 16:8, 11; 20:5, 6). When Paul was in Troas on this fourth and final journey is not clear.

parchments. Parchment is a writing material made from the skins of animals, especially sheep or goats. Probably Paul was asking for parts of the Old Testament.

4:14 Alexander the coppersmith. See note 1 Tim. 1:20.

did me great harm. This incident is mentioned nowhere else in the New Testament.

the Lord will repay him according to his deeds. That is, on the day of final judgment (Matt. 16:27; Rom. 2:6; Rev. 22:12).

4:16 first defense. A preliminary hearing prior to Paul's actual trial, which he now awaits (Introduction: Date and Occasion).

May it not be charged against them. An expression of forgiveness in the face of death reminiscent of Christ (Luke 23:34) and of Stephen (Acts 7:60).

4:17 But the Lord stood by me. Paul had learned long ago that he could always depend upon the One who had commissioned him (2 Cor. 12:9, 10; Phil. 4:11–13).

message might be fully proclaimed and [q] all the Gentiles might hear it. So [r] I was rescued [s] from the lion's mouth. 18 The Lord will rescue me from every evil deed and bring me safely into his heavenly kingdom. [t] To him be the glory forever and ever. Amen.

Final Greetings

19 Greet [u] Prisca and Aquila, and [v] the household of Onesiphorus. 20 Erastus remained at Corinth, and I left [w] Trophimus, who was ill, at Miletus. 21 [x] Do your best to come before winter. Eubulus sends greetings to you, as do Pudens and Linus and Claudia and all the brothers.[1]

22 The Lord be [y] with your spirit. [z] Grace be with you.[2]

16 [q] See Acts 9:15 [r] ch. 3:11 [s] Ps. 22:21; [1 Sam. 17:37] 18 [t] See Rom. 11:36 19 [u] See Acts 18:2 [v] ch. 1:16 20 [w] Acts 20:4; 21:29 21 [x] ver. 9 22 [y] Gal. 6:18; Philem. 25 [z] See Col. 4:18

1 Or *brothers and sisters*. The plural Greek word *adelphoi* (translated "brothers") refers to siblings in a family. In New Testament usage, depending on the context, *adelphoi* may refer either to men or to both men and women who are siblings (brothers and sisters) in God's family, the church 2 The Greek for *you* is plural

the message might be fully proclaimed. This probably refers to Paul's proclamation of the gospel at his preliminary hearing.

all the Gentiles might hear. Paul had preached the gospel in a public forum at the center of the Roman Empire.

rescued from the lion's mouth. A metaphor for a narrow escape from death. Paul's preliminary hearing has resulted in a temporary reprieve.

4:18 will rescue me from every evil deed. Paul does not believe that Christ will prevent his physical death (v. 6), but is expressing his absolute trust in Christ (2:13).

bring me safely into his heavenly kingdom. This is the ultimate hope of all who trust in Christ.

4:19–21 As is his custom, Paul closes the letter with personal greetings and a benediction.

4:19 Prisca and Aquila. "Prisca" is a shortened form of "Priscilla," as it is spelled elsewhere in Acts and Paul's letters. She and her husband Aquila had been friends of Paul from the time he first visited Corinth on his second missionary journey. They were Jews, and like Paul were tentmakers (Acts 18:2, 3). They had come to Corinth from Rome. Later they accompanied Paul to Ephesus (Acts 18:18, 19) and hosted a house church there for several years before returning to Rome (Rom. 16:3, 4; 1 Cor. 16:19). They had now apparently returned to Ephesus where Timothy was (1 Tim. 1:3).

the household of Onesiphorus. See note 1:16. This greeting indicates that Timothy was still in Ephesus (1:18).

4:20 Erastus. Presumably the same person as Corinth's treasurer mentioned in Rom. 16:23.

Corinth. The provincial capital of the Roman province of Achaia, it was visited by Paul on his second and third missionary journeys. Corinth is fifty miles west of Athens.

Trophimus. A member of the church at Ephesus who accompanied Paul to Jerusalem at the close of his third missionary journey (Acts 20:4; 21:29).

Miletus. A seaport just south of Ephesus, which Paul had visited at the end of his third missionary journey (Acts 20:15, 17). When Paul visited Miletus on his fourth and final journey is not clear.

4:21 before winter. Winter weather would prevent travel by ship. Paul may have felt that if Timothy waited too long, he would not arrive before Paul's execution (v. 9). In any event, he needed his cloak before winter (v. 13).

Eubulus . . . Pudens and Linus and Claudia. These would be Christians in Rome, although none is mentioned elsewhere in the New Testament. According to Roman Catholic tradition Linus succeeded Peter as bishop of Rome.

4:22 Grace be with you. Here, the Greek word for "you" is plural (text note). Presumably Paul intended the letter to be read to the entire church (1 Tim. 6:21 note; Titus 3:15).

THE EPISTLE OF PAUL THE APOSTLE TO

Titus

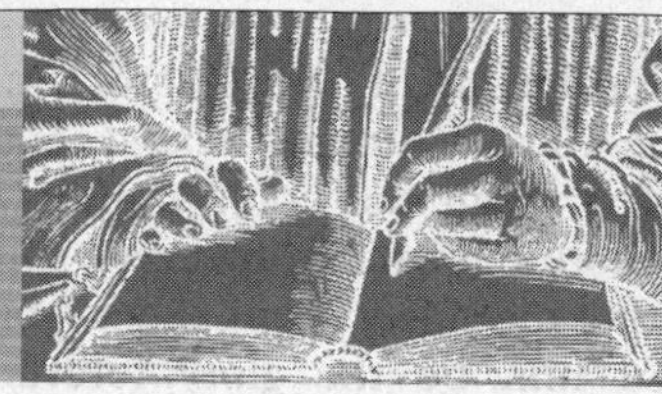

AUTHOR

Titus was written by Paul. See "Introduction to 1 Timothy: Author."

DATE AND OCCASION

Titus, like 1 Timothy, was composed while Paul was still in the midst of his fourth missionary journey and probably dates to between A.D. 62 and 64. See "Introduction to 1 Timothy: Date and Occasion."

Titus was a Gentile Christian who was probably converted by Paul (1:4). The New Testament provides little information about him, and he is not mentioned in Acts. Paul took him to Jerusalem early in his missionary labors, where he refused to have Titus circumcised (Gal. 2:1–3), and Titus apparently traveled with Paul on his second and third missionary journeys and for part of the fourth. He was a trusted associate of Paul, upon whom Paul could count in delicate situations, such as that at Corinth (2 Cor. 2:13; 7:6, 13, 14; 8:6, 16, 23; 12:18). Titus later served as Paul's representative on the island of Crete (1:5) and in the province of Dalmatia (2 Tim. 4:10).

Paul wrote to Titus from Macedonia (3:12). On an earlier leg of his journey he and Titus had been involved in missionary activity on the island of Crete. When Paul departed, he left Titus behind to continue the work (1:5). In this letter Paul wrote to Titus to encourage him to bring his ministry on the island to a close. Specifically, Paul wanted Titus to complete the organization of the churches (1:5–9), to deal with the false teachers who were present (1:10–14; 3:9–11), and to give instructions to the churches on proper conduct (2:1–3:8). When a replacement arrived, Titus was to meet Paul in Nicopolis (3:12).

CHARACTERISTICS AND THEMES

Like 1 Timothy, Titus is noteworthy for its information on church organization. It provides a lengthy description of the qualifications for the office of overseer and elder (1:6–9), as well as important evidence that the terms "overseer" and "elder" refer to one rather than two distinct offices (1:7).

Also like 1 Timothy, Titus exhibits a strong concern for sound doctrine (1:9, 13; 2:1, 2) and contains two marvelous theological meditations on the grace that God has extended in Jesus Christ (2:11–14; 3:4–7). These include affirmations of the Second Coming of Christ (2:13), the substitutionary atonement of Christ (2:14), regeneration by the Holy Spirit (3:5), and justification by grace (3:5, 7). Titus also affirms the deity of Christ in a striking manner—the title "Savior" is applied freely, and in the same contexts, to both God (1:3; 2:10; 3:4) and Christ (1:4; 2:13; 3:6), and 2:13 speaks of "our great God and Savior Jesus Christ."

Paul's concern in this letter for sound doctrine is balanced by an emphasis on proper Christian conduct. For Paul, the two clearly go hand in hand. In particular, he stresses the quality of sober-mindedness (in the Greek, 1:8; 2:2, 4–6, 12) and the importance of doing what is good (2:7, 14; 3:1, 8, 14).

CHARACTERISTICS AND THEMES

Paul describes the false teaching on Crete as something that had come from within the church (1:10, 16). It was characterized by a concern with Jewish myths (1:14), genealogies and quarrels about the law (3:9), and human commandments (1:14). The false teachers came from a narrowly Jewish-Christian perspective (1:10) and sought leadership positions for financial gain (1:11). They had been effective in leading people astray and were divisive (1:10; 3:10).

Virtually everything that Paul says in Titus about the false teaching on Crete has parallels with what he says in 1 and 2 Timothy about that in Ephesus (Introduction to 2 Timothy: Interpretive Difficulties). It is not clear why this should be the case. There is no reason to believe that there was some sort of direct link between the two false teachings, or that everything being taught in one place was being taught in the other. On the other hand, the false teachings in the two areas may have been similar manifestations of a more general syncretistic movement in the Roman Empire at this time (compare the problems which Paul addresses in his letters to the Colossians and Ephesians).

On the evidence for a "fourth" missionary journey by Paul, see "Introduction to 1 Timothy: Interpretive Difficulties."

OUTLINE OF TITUS

I. Salutation (1:1–4)

II. Organizing the Churches on Crete (1:5–16)

- A. *Why Paul Left Titus on Crete (1:5)*
- B. *Qualifications for Elders (1:6–9)*
- C. *Dealing with False Teachers (1:10–16)*

III. Instructing Various Groups (ch. 2)

- A. *Instructions for Titus and Those Under His Care (2:1–10)*
- B. *The Theological Basis for Christian Living (2:11–14)*
- C. *Concluding Charge to Titus (2:15)*

IV. Instructing on Doing What Is Good (3:1–11)

- A. *Initial Charge (3:1, 2)*
- B. *Human Depravity Without Christ (3:3)*
- C. *The Sinner's Experience of the Grace of God (3:4–7)*
- D. *Final Charge (3:8–11)*

V. Conclusion (3:12–15)

Greeting

1 Paul, a servant[1] of God and [a]an apostle of Jesus Christ, for the sake of the
faith of God's elect and [b]their knowledge of
the truth, [c]which accords with godliness,
2 [d]in hope of eternal life, which God, [e]who
never lies, [f]promised [g]before the ages began[2] 3 and [h]at the proper time manifested
in his word [i]through the preaching [j]with
which I have been entrusted [k]by the command of God our Savior;
4 To Titus, [l]my true child in [m]a common
faith:
[n]Grace and peace from God the Father
and Christ Jesus our Savior.

Qualifications for Elders

5 [o]This is why I left you in Crete, so that
you might put what remained into order,
and [p]appoint elders in every town as I
directed you— 6 [q]if anyone is above
reproach, the husband of one wife,[3] and

Chapter 1
1 [a]See 2 Cor. 1:1 [b]See 1 Tim. 2:4 [c]1 Tim. 6:3
2 [d]2 Tim. 1:1; Heb. 9:15; [ch. 2:13; 3:7] [e]Num. 23:19; 2 Tim. 2:13; Heb. 6:18 [f]Rom. 1:2 [g]See 2 Tim. 1:9
3 [h]See 1 Tim. 2:6 [i][Rom. 10:14] [j]See 1 Tim. 1:11 [k]1 Tim. 1:1
4 [l]See 3 John 4 [m]Jude 3; See 2 Pet. 1:1 [n]See 1 Tim. 1:2
5 [o][1 Tim. 1:3] [p][Acts 14:23; 2 Tim. 2:2]
6 [q]For ver. 6-8, see 1 Tim. 3:2-4

[1] Or *slave*; Greek *bondservant* [2] Greek *before times eternal* [3] Or *a man of one woman*

1:1–4 Opening salutation, including sender, recipient, and benediction.

1:1 servant of God. Or "slave of God," one who is owned by and who serves God (Rom. 1:1; Phil. 1:1).

apostle of Jesus Christ. One sent out as an official representative of Christ (1 Tim. 1:1 note).

for the sake of the faith . . . godliness. The goals of Paul's apostleship.

God's elect. Those whom God has chosen to believe in Christ (2 Tim. 2:10).

1:2 in hope of eternal life. The blessings secured by Christ (1 Tim. 1:1, 16 note; 2 Tim. 1:1).

who never lies. An affirmation of the complete trustworthiness of God (Num. 23:19).

promised before the ages began. Affirmation of the eternal nature of the divine decree of redemption through Christ (2 Tim. 1:9).

1:3 God our Savior. As author of the covenant of grace, God is Savior (2:10; 3:4; 1 Tim. 1:1; 2:3; 4:10).

1:4 true child. Lit. "legitimate son" (1 Tim. 1:2). This probably indicates that Titus was one of Paul's converts.

Grace and peace. See note 1 Tim. 1:2.

Christ Jesus our Savior. As mediator of the covenant of grace, Christ is Savior (2:13; 3:6; 2 Tim. 1:10). Paul uses the title "Savior" interchangeably for both God and Christ throughout this letter (v. 3 note), thereby reflecting his belief in the deity of Christ (2:13).

1:5–9 Paul moves into the body of the letter. His intention is to instruct Titus regarding how to act as Paul's representative on Crete (Introduction: Date and Occasion). He begins by discussing church organization.

1:5 put what remained into order. As the rest of the verse makes clear, what was left unfinished was the organization of the newly formed churches.

elders. A group of individuals charged with the general care of a local church (Acts 14:23; 20:17; 1 Tim. 5:17). As v. 7 makes clear, Paul used the term interchangeably with "overseer." Paul discusses the qualifications for overseers in similar terms, yet with some differences, in 1 Tim. 3:2–7. Paul intends neither list to be complete, but simply to indicate the personal qualities of those who would serve as church leaders.

1:6 the husband of one wife. Probably a reference to marital fidelity, (1 Tim. 3:2 note).

his children are believers and not open to
the charge of [r]debauchery or insubordination. **7** For an overseer,[1] [s]as God's steward,
must be above reproach. He must not [t]be
arrogant or quick-tempered or a drunkard
or violent [u]or greedy for gain, **8** but hospitable, a lover of good, self-controlled,
upright, holy, [v]and disciplined. **9** He must
[w]hold firm to the trustworthy word as
taught, so that he may be able to give
instruction in [x]sound[2] doctrine and also to
rebuke those who contradict it.

10 For there are many who are insubordi-
nate, [y]empty talkers and deceivers, especially those of [z]the circumcision party.
11 They must be silenced, since [a]they are
upsetting whole families by teaching [b]for
shameful gain what they ought not to
teach. **12** [c]One of the Cretans,[3] a prophet of
their own, said, "Cretans are always liars,
evil beasts, lazy gluttons."[4] **13** This testimony is true. Therefore [d]rebuke them
[e]sharply, that they [f]may be sound in the
faith, **14** [g]not devoting themselves to Jewish
myths and [h]the commands of people [i]who
turn away from the truth. **15** [j]To the pure, all
things are pure, but to the defiled and [k]un-
believing, nothing is pure; but both [l]their
minds and their consciences are defiled.
16 [m]They profess to know God, but they
[n]deny him by their works. They are
detestable, disobedient, [o]unfit for any good
work.

6 [r]See Eph. 5:18 **7** [s]Luke 12:42; 1 Cor. 4:1; 1 Pet. 4:10 [t]2 Pet. 2:10 [u]1 Tim. 3:8; 1 Pet. 5:2 **8** [v][1 Cor. 9:25] **9** [w][2 Thess. 2:13, 15]; See 1 Tim. 1:15; 2 Tim. 1:13 [x]See 1 Tim. 1:10 **10** [y]1 Tim. 1:6 [z]See Acts 11:2 **11** [a][2 Tim. 3:6] [b]1 Tim. 6:5; 2 Pet. 2:3 **12** [c][Acts 17:28] **13** [d]ch. 2:15; 1 Tim. 5:20 [e]2 Cor. 13:10 [f]ch. 2:1, 2 **14** [g]See 1 Tim. 1:4 [h]See Col. 2:22 [i]See 1 Tim. 6:20 **15** [j][Luke 11:41; 1 Tim. 4:3]; See Acts 10:15 [k][Rom. 14:23] [l]See 1 Tim. 6:5

Teach Sound Doctrine

2 But as for you, teach what accords
with [p]sound[5] doctrine. **2** Older men
are to be sober-minded, dignified, self-
controlled, [p]sound in faith, in love, and in
steadfastness. **3** [q]Older women likewise are
to be reverent in behavior, [r]not slanderers
[s]or slaves to much wine. They are to teach
what is good, **4** and so train the young
women to love their husbands and chil-
dren, **5** to be self-controlled, [t]pure, [u]work-

16 [m][1 John 2:4] [n]See 1 Tim. 5:8 [o]2 Tim. 3:8
Chapter 2 **1** [p]See 1 Tim. 1:10 **2** [p][See ver. 1 above] **3** [q][1 Tim. 2:9] [r]1 Tim. 3:11 [s][1 Tim. 3:8; 5:23] **5** [t]1 Pet. 3:2 [u][1 Tim. 5:14]

[1] Or *bishop*; Greek *episkopos* [2] Or *healthy*; also verse 13 [3] Greek *One of them* [4] Probably from Epimenides of Crete [5] Or *healthy*; also verses 2, 8

1:7 For an overseer. Paul's casual shift from "elder" to "overseer" shows that he understands the two terms as referring to the same office: "elder" suggesting one's character (spiritually mature) and "overseer" suggesting one's task (Acts 20:17, 28).

greedy for gain. One should not view church leadership as an opportunity for making money (v. 11; 1 Tim. 6:5, 10). Paul does support the concept of remuneration for certain church leaders (1 Tim. 5:17).

1:8 self-controlled. Or, sensible. A major emphasis in this letter (2:2, 4–6, 12).

1:9 the trustworthy word as taught. As in his letters to Timothy, Paul is concerned with the transmission of and commitment to sound doctrine in accordance with the gospel (1 Tim. 1:10 note).

rebuke those who contradict. Two tasks of the elder that are especially relevant in view of the false teachers on Crete are teaching sound doctrine and refuting that which is false. See "Pastors and Pastoral Care" at 1 Pet. 5:2.

1:10–16 Paul's mention of the necessity to refute false teaching leads him into a discussion of the false teachers and how Titus is to deal with them.

1:10 those of the circumcision. Those who come from a narrowly Jewish-Christian perspective are in view (Acts 15:1, 5; Gal. 6:12, 13). See Introduction: Interpretive Difficulties.

1:11 upsetting whole families. This may refer to the false teachers' activity in local house churches, thus the necessity for better organization (v. 5).

shameful gain. See note on v. 7.

what they ought not to teach. Their teaching was not in accord with "sound doctrine" (v. 9).

1:12 a prophet of their own. Paul quotes Epimenides, a sixth century B.C. poet and religious reformer from Knossos on Crete, who was known for his predictions and wisdom. Paul is not placing Epimenides on the same level as the Old Testament prophets; he is simply appealing to the esteem in which Epimenides was held in the ancient world.

1:13 them . . . they. He means the false teachers (2 Tim. 2:25, 26), and probably also their followers.

1:14 Jewish myths. Perhaps a reference to the kinds of legends about Old Testament figures that are found in many of the apocryphal Jewish writings (1 Tim. 1:4; 4:7; 2 Tim. 4:4).

commands. These are probably related to the false teachers' distinctive interpretations of the Jewish law (3:9; 1 Tim. 1:7; 4:3).

1:15 To the pure, all things are pure. The false teachers have apparently prohibited the use of certain things (1 Tim. 4:3 note). For Paul's response, see 1 Tim. 4:3–5.

1:16 they deny him. The New Testament teaches that the lack of actions consistent with a changed life renders one's faith in Christ suspect (Matt. 7:16–20; James 2:14–16; 1 John 3:17).

by their works. Paul condemns not only the doctrine of the false teachers, but also their actions (2 Tim. 3:2–5). Both sound doctrine and actions in accordance with a changed life are necessary for Christians.

2:1–15 Paul now turns to the kinds of things which Titus, in contrast with the false teachers, ought to teach and concludes with a meditation on the grace of God.

2:1 sound doctrine. See note 1:9.

2:2–6 See 1 Tim. 5:1, 2.

2:2 sober-minded. The quality of sober-mindedness dominates Paul's advice in this section (vv. 4–6, 12; 1:8 and note).

2:3 teach what is good. Probably, as the next verse suggests, in the sense of their manner in the home.

2:4 train. That is, "bring them to their senses." This is a verbal form of the adjective translated "sober-minded" (v. 2) and "self-controlled" (v. 5) throughout this section. Paul probably has in mind the problems that some of the younger widows encountered at Ephesus (1 Tim. 5:11–13).

2:5 self-controlled. Lit. "sober-minded" (vv. 2, 4, 6, 12; 1:8 note).

working at home. Or, "busy at home." Contrast the behavior of some of the younger widows at Ephesus (1 Tim. 5:13).

ing at home, kind, and [v]submissive to their
own husbands, [w]that the word of God may
not be reviled. 6 Likewise, urge [x]the
younger men to be self-controlled. 7 Show
yourself in all respects to be [y]a model of
good works, and in your teaching [z]show
integrity, [a]dignity, 8 and [b]sound speech that
cannot be condemned, [c]so that an opponent may be put to shame, having nothing
evil to say about us. 9 [d]Slaves[1] are to be submissive to their own masters [e]in everything; they are to be well-pleasing, not
argumentative, 10 not pilfering, [f]but showing all good faith, [g]so that in everything
they may adorn the doctrine of God our
Savior.

11 For [h]the grace of God [i]has appeared,
bringing salvation [j]for all people, 12 training
us to renounce ungodliness and [k]worldly
passions, and [l]to live self-controlled,
upright, and godly lives in [m]the present
age, 13 [n]waiting for our blessed [o]hope, the
[p]appearing of the glory of our great [q]God
and Savior Jesus Christ, 14 [r]who gave himself for us to [s]redeem us from all lawlessness and [t]to purify for himself [t]a people for
his own possession who are [u]zealous for
good works.

15 Declare these things; exhort and [v]re-
buke with all authority. [w]Let no one disregard you.

Be Ready for Every Good Work

3 Remind them [x]to be submissive to
rulers and authorities, [y]to be obedient,
to be ready for every good work, 2 [z]to speak
evil of no one, [a]to avoid quarreling, to be
gentle, and [b]to show perfect courtesy toward
all people. 3 For [c]we ourselves were once
foolish, disobedient, led astray, slaves to
various passions and pleasures, passing
our days in malice and envy, hated by others and hating one another. 4 But when [d]the
goodness and loving kindness of God our
Savior appeared, 5 he saved us, [e]not because of works done by us in righteousness, but [f]according to his own mercy, by
[g]the washing of regeneration and [h]renewal

5 [v]See Gen. 3:16 [w]See 1 Tim. 6:1
6 [x]1 Tim. 5:1
7 [y]1 Tim. 4:12; 1 Pet. 5:3 [z][2 Cor. 11:3] [a]1 Tim. 2:2
8 [b][1 Tim. 6:3] [c]Neh. 5:9; 1 Tim. 5:14; 1 Pet. 2:12; 3:16
9 [d]See 1 Pet. 2:18 [e][Col. 3:22]
10 [f][1 Tim. 3:11] [g]Matt. 5:16; Phil. 2:15
11 [h]ch. 3:7; See Acts 11:23 [i]ch. 3:4 [j][Ps. 67:2]; See 1 Tim. 2:4
12 [k]1 Pet. 4:2; 1 John 2:16 [l]2 Tim. 3:12; [Acts 24:25] [m]1 Tim. 6:17; 2 Tim. 4:10
13 [n]See 1 Cor. 1:7; 2 Pet. 3:12 [o]See ch. 1:2 [p]See 2 Thess. 2:8 [q]2 Pet. 1:1
14 [r]See Matt. 20:28 [s]Ps. 130:8; See 1 Pet. 1:18 [t]Ezek. 37:23; See Ex. 19:5 [u]ch. 3:8; Eph. 2:10
15 [v]ch. 1:13; 1 Tim. 5:20 [w]See 1 Tim. 4:12

Chapter 3 1 [x]Rom. 13:1; 1 Pet. 2:13 [y]See 2 Tim. 2:21 2 [z]Eph. 4:31 [a]1 Tim. 3:3 [b]See 2 Tim. 2:25 3 [c]See 1 Cor. 6:11 4 [d]See Rom. 2:4 5 [e]See Rom. 3:27 [f]Eph. 2:4; 1 Pet. 1:3 5 [g]See John 3:5; 1 Cor. 6:11; 1 Pet. 3:21 [h]See Rom. 12:2

1 Or *servants*; Greek *bondservants*

submissive. See note 1 Tim. 2:11.

that the word of God may not be reviled. Paul's overriding concern throughout this section is that the behavior of Christians reflect positively on the gospel (vv. 8, 10).

2:7 be a model. Paul gives similar counsel to Timothy (1 Tim. 4:12 note).

good works. One of Paul's main themes in this letter from here on (v. 14; 3:1, 8, 14).

2:9 Slaves. Paul gives instructions to slaves in Eph. 6:5–8; Col. 3:22–25; and 1 Tim. 6:1, 2.

2:10 adorn the doctrine of God. See note on v. 5.

2:11–14 These verses provide the theological basis for the practical instructions given in vv. 2–10.

2:11 the grace of God. The unmerited compassion of God.

has appeared. That is, in Jesus Christ (3:4, 6; 2 Tim. 1:10).

bringing salvation. God's purpose in extending grace to sinners is their salvation (3:4–7; 2 Tim. 1:9).

all people. All types of people, regardless of gender, age, or social class are in view (vv. 2–10; 1 Tim. 2:1–6).

2:13 our blessed hope, the appearing of the glory. The Second Coming (1 Tim. 6:14; 2 Tim. 4:1, 8). See "Hope" at Heb. 6:18.

our great God and Savior Jesus Christ. This is one of the clearest affirmations in the New Testament of the deity of Christ.

2:14 who gave himself for us. That is, on the cross. Paul follows with two aspects of the work of Christ.

redeem us from all lawlessness. Paul's first point focuses on the individual: Christ paid the price necessary to free people from their sins (Matt. 20:28; Mark 10:45; 1 Tim. 2:6; 1 Pet. 1:18, 19).

purify for himself a people for his own possession. Paul's second point focuses on the church: Christ purifies individuals from their sins (Heb. 9:14; 1 John 1:7, 9) so that together they might constitute a people special to Him (Ezek. 37:23). On Christ purifying the church, see Eph. 5:25–27.

zealous for good works. See note on v. 7.

2:15 exhort and rebuke. An appropriate summation of the contrasting aspects of Paul's charge to Titus in vv. 2–10 and 1:10–16.

with all authority. That is, as Paul's representative.

Let no one disregard you. See v. 8; 1 Tim. 4:12.

3:1–8 Having provided instructions for specific groups, Paul now gives Titus general counsel, sandwiched around another meditation on the grace of God, on encouraging the people to do "every good work" (v. 1).

3:1 rulers and authorities. On Christian submission to governing authorities, see Rom. 13:1–7; 1 Pet. 2:13–17; cf. 1 Tim. 2:2.

every good work. The theme for this section is doing good (v. 8; 2:7 note).

3:3 This verse presents a graphic description of human depravity apart from Christ (Eph. 2:1–3).

3:4 But when the goodness and loving kindness of God our Savior appeared. In keeping with v. 3, Paul's primary concern here is with the sinner's experience of God's grace, rather than the First Advent of Christ (2 Tim. 1:10).

3:5 he saved us. See 2 Tim. 1:9.

not because of works . . . but according to his own mercy. Salvation is by grace, not works (v. 6; Eph. 2:8, 9; 2 Tim. 1:9).

washing. Spiritual cleansing, of which baptism is the sign and seal (1 Cor. 6:11; Eph. 5:26).

of regeneration and renewal. Both words characterize the "washing." "Regeneration" is the new life that begins when a person comes to faith in Christ (John 3:3, 5; 1 Pet. 1:3, 23). Renewal is closely related to rebirth; it signifies the complete transformation of a person's life that begins when one is regenerated (Rom. 12:2; 2 Cor. 5:17). See "Regeneration: The New Birth." at John 3:3.

of the Holy Spirit, 6 whom he [i]poured out on
us richly through Jesus Christ our Savior,
7 so that [j]being justified by his grace we
might become [k]heirs [l]according to the hope
of eternal life. 8 The saying is [m]trustworthy,
and I want you to insist on these things, so
that those who have believed in God may be
careful [n]to devote themselves to good
works. These things are excellent and profitable for people. 9 But [o]avoid foolish [p]con-
troversies, [q]genealogies, dissensions, and
quarrels about the law, for [r]they are unprofitable and worthless. 10 As for a person who
stirs up division, [s]after warning him once
and then twice, [t]have nothing more to do
with him, 11 knowing that such a person is
warped and sinful; he is self-condemned.

6 [i]Joel 2:28; Acts 2:33; 10:45; Rom. 5:5
7 [j]ch. 2:11 [k]Rom. 8:17 [l]See ch. 1:2
8 [m]See 1 Tim. 1:15 [n]ver. 14; ch. 2:14
9 [o]2 Tim. 2:16 [p]See 1 Tim. 6:4 [q]1 Tim. 1:4 [r]2 Tim. 2:14
10 [s]See Matt. 18:15 [t]See 2 John 10
12 [u]See 2 Tim. 4:12 [v][2 Tim. 4:10]
13 [w]See Acts 18:24

Final Instructions and Greetings

12 When I send Artemas or [u]Tychicus to
you, do your best to come to me [v]at
Nicopolis, for I have decided to spend the
winter there. 13 Do your best to speed Zenas
the lawyer and [w]Apollos on their way; see
that they lack nothing. 14 And let our people learn [x]to devote themselves to good
works, so as to help cases of urgent need,
and not [y]be unfruitful.
15 All who are with me send greetings
to you. Greet those who love us in the
faith.
[z]Grace be with you all.

14 [x]ver. 8 [y]2 Pet. 1:8; [Phil. 1:11; 4:17; Col. 1:10] 15 [z]See Col. 4:18

of the Holy Spirit. The Spirit applies to individuals the grace of God that is extended in Christ (John 3:5, 6). Note the trinitarianism of vv. 4–6.

3:7 justified. Declared righteous before God.

by his grace. Left to ourselves (vv. 3, 4), we could never stand righteous before God. The point of vv. 3–7 is that righteousness comes through God's grace alone (Rom. 3:21–25).

heirs. God's purpose in extending His grace to sinners is not only to save them from eternal judgment, but to make them part of His family through adoption and thus heirs of His promises (Rom. 8:17; Gal. 3:29; 4:7).

3:8 The saying is trustworthy. See note 1 Tim. 1:15. The expression points back to vv. 4–7.

good works. See note on v. 1.

3:9–11 By way of contrast with the instructions that he has just given, Paul returns one last time to the problem of the false teachers.

3:9 controversies. A prominent characteristic of the false teachers was their contentiousness (1 Tim. 1:4; 6:4).

about the law. The law of Moses (1:10 note; cf. 1 Tim. 1:7).

unprofitable. To be contrasted with doing what is good, which is "profitable" (v. 8).

3:10 Church discipline is to be based on a series of warnings (Matt. 18:15–17).

division. The false teachers had caused division in the churches (1 Tim. 6:4, 5).

3:12–15 Paul closes the letter with personal instructions to Titus, final greetings, and a benediction.

3:12 Artemas. Mentioned nowhere else in the New Testament, he is apparently one of Paul's coworkers.

Tychicus. A coworker of Paul mentioned in Acts 20:4; Eph. 6:21; Col. 4:7; 2 Tim. 4:12.

come to me. Titus's ministry on Crete is nearing its end (Introduction: Date and Occasion).

Nicopolis. A city on the west coast of the Roman province of Epirus (modern Albania).

I have decided to . . . winter there. Paul is probably in Macedonia.

3:13 Zenas . . . Apollos. Probably the bearers of this letter. Zenas is mentioned nowhere else in the New Testament; he is apparently one of Paul's coworkers. Apollos was a native of Alexandria and noted for his eloquence (Acts 18:24–26). He is best known for his ministry at Corinth (Acts 18:27–19:1; 1 Cor. 1:12; 3:4–22; 16:12).

3:14 good works. See note 2:7.

3:15 you all. Presumably Paul intended the letter to be read to the entire church (1 Tim. 6:21; 2 Tim. 4:22).

THE EPISTLE OF PAUL THE APOSTLE TO

Philemon

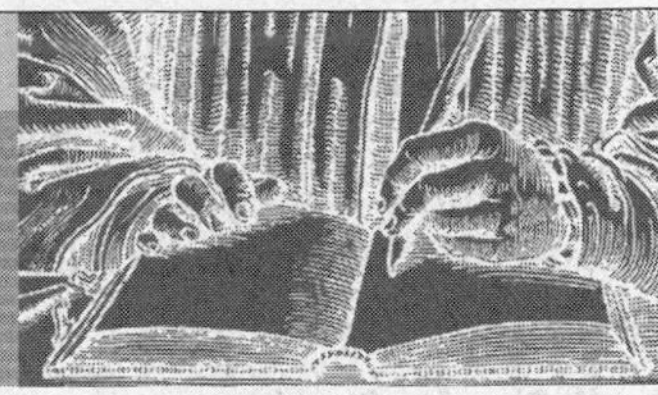

AUTHOR

The letter to Philemon was written by the apostle Paul, and its authenticity has not been seriously challenged.

DATE AND OCCASION

The letter was written while Paul was in prison in Rome (c. A.D. 60), and was probably sent to Philemon together with the letter to the Colossians. Philemon was a Christian brother and slaveholder in Colossae. His slave Onesimus had run away and had somehow met Paul in Rome. Through Paul's teaching, Onesimus had become a Christian.

Paul's purpose in writing was to ask Philemon to receive Onesimus back not as a slave but as a Christian brother. In pursuit of this goal, Paul barely restrains himself from demanding the favor. He writes as powerful an appeal as he can.

CHARACTERISTICS AND THEMES

Philemon shows us the apostle using all his personal force to bring about a Christian answer to a very serious problem. Paul's judgment appears to be that Philemon should free the offending slave, for the sake of Christian love toward a fellow Christian. Paul's letter is passionate but carefully composed to achieve the desired end. The document was written in his own hand, and is much more than an example of rhetoric. It brings us close to Paul's ministry, so that we can practically feel his profound desire to make Christian love the first rule of human action.

OUTLINE OF PHILEMON

I. Introductory Greetings (vv. 1–3)

II. Thanksgiving (vv. 4–7)

III. Paul's Request for Onesimus (vv. 8–21)

IV. Intended Visit (vv. 21, 22)

V. Closing Greetings and Blessing (v. 25)

Greeting

1 Paul, [a]a prisoner for Christ Jesus, and
[b]Timothy our brother,
To Philemon our beloved fellow worker
2 and Apphia our sister and [c]Archippus our
[d]fellow soldier, and [e]the church in your
house:
3 [f]Grace to you and peace from God our
Father and the Lord Jesus Christ.

Philemon's Love and Faith

4 [g]I thank my God always when I remember you in my prayers, 5 because I [h]hear of
your love and [i]of the faith that you have
toward the Lord Jesus and all the saints,
6 and I pray that the sharing of your faith
may become effective for the full [j]knowledge

1 [a]ver. 9; See Eph. 3:1 [b]See 1 Thess. 3:2
2 [c]Col. 4:17 [d]Phil. 2:25 [e]See Rom. 16:5
3 [f]See Rom. 1:7
4 [g]See Rom. 1:8, 9
5 [h]Col. 1:4 [i]Eph. 1:15
6 [j]Phil. 1:9; Col. 1:9

1 prisoner. Paul knows that he belongs to Christ, and if he is in prison it is by Christ's permission (Phil. 1:7).

2 Apphia . . . Archippus. These are probably members of Philemon's household, since they are mentioned in addition to the church.

in your house. The early Christians met in believers' homes (1 Cor. 16:19; Col. 4:15).

6 may become effective. Paul is going to suggest a good work that will call on Philemon's generosity in an important and visible way.

of every good thing that is in us for the sake
of Christ.[1] 7 For I have derived much joy
and [k]comfort from your love, my brother,
because the hearts of the saints [l]have been
refreshed through you.

Paul's Plea for Onesimus

8 Accordingly, [m]though I am bold enough
in Christ to command you to do [n]what is
required, 9 yet for love's sake I prefer to
appeal to you—I, Paul, an old man and
now [o]a prisoner also for Christ Jesus— 10 I
appeal to you for [p]my child, [q]Onesimus,[2]
[r]whose father I became in my imprisonment. 11 (Formerly he was useless to you,
but now he is indeed useful to you and to
me.) 12 I am sending him back to you, sending my very heart. 13 I would have been glad
to keep him with me, in order that he
might serve me [s]on your behalf [t]during my
imprisonment for the gospel, 14 but I preferred to do nothing without your consent
in order that your goodness might not be
[u]by compulsion but of your own free will.
15 For this perhaps is why [v]he was parted
from you for a while, that you might have
him back forever, 16 [w]no longer as a slave[3]
but more than a slave, as [x]a beloved brother—especially to me, but how much more
to you, [y]both in the flesh and in the Lord.
17 So if you consider me [z]your partner,
receive him as you would receive me. 18 If
he has wronged you at all, or owes you anything, charge that to my account. 19 [a]I, Paul,
write this with my own hand: I will repay
it—to say nothing of your owing me even
your own self. 20 Yes, brother, I want some
benefit from you in the Lord. [b]Refresh my
heart in Christ.
21 [c]Confident of your obedience, I write
to you, knowing that you will do even more
than I say. 22 At the same time, prepare a
guest room for me, for [d]I am hoping that
[e]through your prayers [f]I will be graciously
given to you.

Final Greetings

23 [g]Epaphras, my [h]fellow prisoner in
Christ Jesus, sends greetings to you, 24 and
so do [i]Mark, [i]Aristarchus, [j]Demas, and
[j]Luke, my fellow workers.
25 [k]The grace of the Lord Jesus Christ be
with your spirit.

7 [k][2 Cor. 7:4, 13; Col. 4:11] [l]ver. 20; 2 Tim. 1:16; [Rom. 15:32; 2 Cor. 7:13]
8 [m][1 Thess. 2:6] [n]Eph. 5:4
9 [o]ver. 1
10 [p]See 3 John 4 [q]Col. 4:9 [r]ver. 13; 1 Cor. 4:15; [Gal. 4:19]
13 [s]See 1 Cor. 16:17 [t]ver. 10; See Phil. 1:7
14 [u][2 Cor. 9:7; 1 Pet. 5:2]
15 [v][Gen. 45:5, 8]
16 [w]See 1 Cor. 7:22 [x]Matt. 23:8; Col. 4:9; 1 Tim. 6:2 [y]Col. 3:22, 23; [Eph. 6:5]
17 [z]2 Cor. 8:23
19 [a]See 1 Cor. 16:21
20 [b]See ver. 7
21 [c]See 2 Cor. 2:3
22 [d]Phil. 1:25; 2:24 [e]See 2 Cor. 1:11 [f][Heb. 13:19]
23 [g]See Col. 1:7 [h]Rom. 16:7
24 [i]See Col. 4:10 [j]See Col. 4:14; 2 Tim. 4:10, 11
25 [k]See Gal. 6:18

[1] Or *for Christ's service* [2] *Onesimus* means *useful* (see verse 11) or *beneficial* (see verse 20) [3] Greek *bondservant*; twice in this verse

7 hearts. The word translated "hearts" is used also in vv. 12 and 20. It emphasizes the emotions more than the usual Greek word for "heart."

9 an old man. Paul appeals for mercy by describing himself as old and in prison. He does this "for love's sake," not for his own sake.

10 my child, Onesimus. Onesimus is Paul's spiritual son because he was converted through Paul's ministry.

11 useless . . . useful. Paul makes a play on words—Onesimus's name means "useful" or "beneficial" (text note). The pun softens the effect on Philemon of having to hear about someone who had injured him. Onesimus had run away and had probably been stealing (v. 18).

14 of your own free will. In his letters Paul appeals more than once to the principle that a free and voluntary action is of more value than one that is compulsory (1 Cor. 9:16, 17; 2 Cor. 9:7).

16 more than a slave. Paul seems to be asking Philemon to set Onesimus free. It is implied that the Christians' common freedom in Christ is incompatible with the state of slavery, marked as it is by compulsion (v. 14 note), not to mention chains (v. 10, 13, 14; see 1 Pet. 2:18 note).

17 as you would receive me. Paul is willing to throw his friendship with Philemon into the balance to make sure that Philemon will not refuse his request for Onesimus. Paul's offer to pay Onesimus's debts (v. 18) is real, but secondary by comparison.

19 even your own self. This means that Philemon, like Onesimus, owed his Christian faith to the ministry of Paul.

22 a guest room. Paul anticipates being released, which apparently happened. Whether he reached Colosse is not known.

THE EPISTLE TO THE

Hebrews

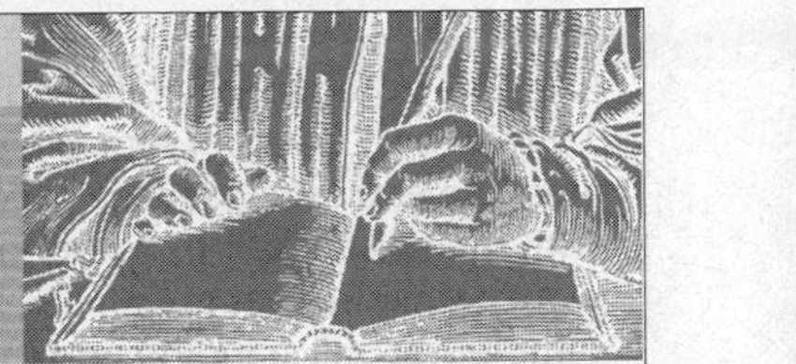

AUTHOR

The author of Hebrews was skilled in Greek and Hellenistic literary style, immersed in the Old Testament (in the Greek translation, the Septuagint), sensitive to the history of redemption culminating in Jesus, and pastorally concerned for the original readers, who knew him personally (13:22, 23) and whose background he knows (10:32–34). Like his readers, he came to faith not through direct contact with Jesus, but through the apostles' preaching (2:3, 4). In addition, he was acquainted with Timothy (13:23).

But the epistle does not tell us his name, leaving a tantalizing mystery. In the Eastern church by the time of Clement of Alexandria (c. A.D. 150–215) and Origen (A.D. 185–253) the epistle was attributed to Paul, although both of these theologians recognized the stylistic differences between Hebrews and the Pauline epistles. In the West, Tertullian (c. A.D. 155–220) proposed Barnabas, a Levite of the Jewish Dispersion who was noted for his encouragement of others (Acts 4:36). Other early suggestions were Luke and Clement of Rome (c. A.D. 95). From the fifth to the sixteenth centuries Paul's authorship was accepted in East and West. During the Reformation Luther proposed Apollos, a Jewish Christian from Alexandria who was skilled in speech and powerful in the Scriptures (Acts 18:24). Suggestions in the modern period have included Priscilla (but cf. 11:32, where the author refers to himself with a masculine gender participle), Epaphras (Col. 1:7), and Silas (Acts 15:22, 32, 40; 1 Pet. 5:12). While it is difficult to rule out many of these candidates, it is equally hard to make a convincing case for any one of them. From the standpoint of early tradition, Paul has the strongest claim, but as Calvin observed, Hebrews differs from Paul in style, teaching method, and in the author's inclusion of himself among the disciples of the apostles (2:3)—a statement at odds with Paul's characteristic claim to have received his appointment and revelation of the gospel directly from Christ (Gal. 1:1, 11, 12).

If the author is not Paul (or someone such as Luke whose other writings we have), knowing the author's name would add little to our understanding of the epistle in any case. The epistle does have theological affinities with Paul. On the other hand, John's lofty doctrine of Christ as the divine "Word" is detectable. But these combined characteristics, along with the portrayal of Jesus' suffering as described in the first three (Synoptic) Gospels, are to be expected in view of the Holy Spirit's unifying authorship of all of Scripture. While the human author of this book remains unknown, the important thing is that this writing, like the Old Testament before it, is what "the Holy Spirit says" (3:7).

DATE AND OCCASION

Hebrews offers a fair amount of information about the original recipients and their situation, while leaving questions of date and destination without certain answers. The original readers spoke Greek and used the Greek translation of the Old Testament. They could follow arguments drawn from the Old Testament and were interested in the Old Testament sanctuary, sacrificial system, and priesthood. They had not heard the gospel directly from Jesus, but from apostles (2:3), had faced previous persecution (10:32–34) and were facing present persecution, including expulsion from Jewish institutions (13:12, 13). They were in danger of falling away, perhaps fearing death (2:14–18), although their faith had not yet led to martyrdom (12:4). In addition, they may have been undergoing a transition in church leadership (13:7, 17), and were therefore concerned about security and permanence (6:19; 11:10; 13:8, 14). Finally, they receive greeting through the author "from Italy" (13:24).

Drawing these features together, we conclude that the recipients were Jewish Christians of the Dispersion (the scattering of Jews outside

Palestine), probably in Italy. This would take 13:24 to be a greeting sent "home" by expatriates. The earliest evidence of acquaintance with the epistle is from Rome, in *1 Clement*, a work dating from about A.D. 96. Apparently the temple was still standing and its sacrificial rituals were being performed (10:2, 3, 11). Perhaps the situation is that of the persecutions under Nero (c. A.D. 64). In that case, the suffering mentioned in 10:32–34 could have been caused by the edict of Claudius, which expelled Jews from Rome in A.D. 49 (Acts 18:2).

Subject to suffering and shame for their confession of Jesus, stripped of the familiar and visible institutions of organized Jewish religion, and confused by the hidden character of Jesus' glory (veiled in suffering when He was on earth and now hidden in heaven), the readers are tempted to turn away from the faith (10:38, 39), to fall into unbelief and so to give up their pilgrimage toward God's rest and God's city (4:1, 2, 11; 11:10, 14–16; 13:14).

CHARACTERISTICS AND THEMES

Hebrews' high literary style and special focus on Christ's high priesthood set it apart from other New Testament books. Its unique contribution to the New Testament revelation of Jesus Christ is the disclosure of Jesus' fulfillment of the sanctuary, sacrifices, and priesthood established in the law of Moses.

The author refers to his work as a "word of exhortation" (13:22). Since the same Greek expression in Acts 13:15 refers to a synagogue speech, the term may identify this "epistle" as an expository sermon in written form. Hebrews is aptly described as a "word of exhortation," for exhortation or encouragement is the heart of the book's purpose (3:13; 6:18; 10:25; 12:5). The author repeatedly calls his readers to an active and courageous response (4:11, 14, 16; 6:1; 10:19–25).

The exhortation to persevere in the pilgrimage of faith is grounded in the author's proof that the Old Testament itself testified to the imperfection of the covenant at Sinai and its sacrificial system, thereby pointing ahead to a new High Priest—Jesus Christ. Jesus is better than the mediators, sanctuary, and sacrifices of the old order. He is worthy of "more glory" than Moses (3:3). The arguments from lesser to greater of 2:2, 3; 9:13, 14; 10:28, 29; and 12:25 ("if . . . much less") underscore the greater grace and glory, and the greater accountability, which have now arrived in the new covenant mediated by Jesus. Unlike the earthly and external aspects of the Old Testament sanctuary, Jesus sanctifies us for the true worship of God, so that we draw near to heaven itself with clean consciences. He is the guarantee of this better covenant bond, for He links us inseparably with the God of grace.

OUTLINE OF HEBREWS

I. Christ Is Superior to the Angels (chs. 1; 2)

- A. *Prologue: God's Last and Best Word Is Spoken in His Son (1:1–4)*
- B. *Scripture Testifies to the Son's Greater Honor (1:5–14)*
- C. *Exhortation Not to Neglect the Salvation Revealed Through the Son (2:1–4)*
- D. *The Son Became Like His Brothers as Our High Priest (2:5–18)*

II. Christ Is Superior to Moses (3:1–4:13)

- A. *The Son Has Greater Honor Than the Servant (3:1–6)*
- B. *Exhortation Not to Imitate Those Who Disbelieved in the Wilderness (3:7–4:13)*

III. Christ Is Superior to Aaron (4:14–7:28)

- A. *Christ the Eternal High Priest (4:14–5:11)*
- B. *Exhortation to Perseverance and Spiritual Maturity (5:12–6:12)*
- C. *A Priest Forever by Divine Oath (6:13–20)*
- D. *A Priest Forever After the Order of Melchizedek (ch. 7)*

IV. The Superior Priestly Ministry of Christ (8:1–10:18)

- A. *A Superior Covenant (ch. 8)*
- B. *A Superior Tabernacle (9:1–10)*
- C. *A Superior Sacrifice That Cleanses the Conscience (9:11–28)*
- D. *Christ's Sacrifice Once for All (10:1–18)*

V. Call to Persevere in Faith (10:19–12:29)

- A. *A Superior Covenant Implies Greater Responsibility (10:19–39)*
- B. *Examples of the Life of Faith (ch. 11)*
- C. *True Children of God (12:1–17)*
- D. *The Heavenly Jerusalem (12:18–29)*

VI. Conclusion (ch. 13)

- A. *Final Exhortations (13:1–19)*
- B. *Benediction and Greetings (13:20–25)*

The Supremacy of God's Son

1 Long ago, at many times and [a]in many
ways, God spoke to our fathers by the
prophets, 2but [b]in these last days [c]he has
spoken to us by [d]his Son, whom he
appointed [e]the heir of all things, [f]through
whom also he created [g]the world. 3He is
the radiance of the glory of God and [h]the
exact imprint of his nature, and he upholds
the universe by the word of his power.
[i]After making purification for sins, [j]he sat
down [k]at the right hand of the Majesty on
high, 4having become as much superior to
angels as the name [l]he has inherited is
more excellent than theirs.
5For to which of the angels did God ever
say,

[m]"You are my Son,
today I have begotten you"?

Or again,

[n]"I will be to him a father,
and he shall be to me a son"?

6And again, when he brings [o]the firstborn
into the world, he says,

[p]"Let all God's angels worship him."

7Of the angels he says,

[q]"He makes his angels winds,
and his ministers a flame of fire."

8But of the Son he says,

Chapter 1
1 [a][Num. 12:6, 8; Joel 2:28]
2 [b]1 Pet. 1:20; [ch. 9:26; Acts 2:17] [c]ch. 2:3 [d]See Matt. 14:33 [e]Ps. 2:8; Matt. 21:38; See Matt. 28:18 [f][ch. 3:3]; See John 1:3 [g]ch. 11:3
3 [h]See 2 Cor. 4:4 [i]See ch. 9:14 [j]See Mark 16:19 [k][Luke 22:69]
4 [l]Eph. 1:21; Phil. 2:9
5 [m]ch. 5:5; Acts 13:33; Cited from Ps. 2:7 [n]Cited from 2 Sam. 7:14; [Ps. 89:26, 27]
6 [o]See Rom. 8:29 [p]Cited from Deut. 32:43 (Gk.); [Ps. 97:7]
7 [q]Cited from Ps. 104:4

1:1–4 The prologue introduces the two time periods in God's speaking to His people: "Long ago" (v. 1) and "these last days" (v. 2). The Son's coming marks our time period as the "latter days" of salvation promised through the prophets (Jer. 23:20; Hos. 3:5; Mic. 4:1; cf. 1 Cor. 10:11).

1:1 at many times. The piecemeal character of prophetic revelation showed its incompleteness, just as the repetition of animal sacrifices showed that they could not remove guilt (10:1).

in many ways. These ways included visions, dreams, and dark sayings (Num. 12:6–8, alluded to later in 3:5).

God spoke. An important theme in Hebrews (2:2, 3; 4:12; 6:5; 11:3; 12:25).

1:2 his Son. This revelation is qualitatively superior to that given through the prophets. Moses, the greatest prophet, was only a servant in God's house; Christ is "over God's house as a son" (3:6). The Son speaks, as the prophets did, but speaks as the Son whose revelation is final.

heir of all things. The Son's supremacy will be displayed at the end of history, for "all things were created . . . for him" (Col. 1:16). He is the firstborn (v. 6), the preeminent heir, whose enemies will be put under His feet (v. 13, citing Ps. 110:1). As God's adopted sons through Jesus, we too are heirs (v. 14; 6:12, 17; Gal. 4:6, 7; Rom. 8:14–17).

through whom . . . he created the world. The Son's supremacy was displayed at the dawn of history, for "by him all things were created" (Col. 1:16; cf. John 1:3). The Greek word rendered "world" is lit. "ages" (also "universe" in 11:3), highlighting the successive periods of history in the created order. Vv. 10–12 quote Ps. 102:25–27 as testimony to the Son's role in creation and His eternal permanence, in contrast to the created universe.

1:3 radiance of the glory. The Greek word rendered "radiance" describes divine wisdom personified in the Jewish intertestamental book Wisdom of Solomon (Wis. 7:25–28). But Hebrews speaks not merely of a personified divine attribute, but of a divine Person who entered history to purify sinners.

exact imprint of his nature. This verse expresses both the Son's oneness with the Father and the distinction of divine persons. As One whose being corresponds exactly to the Father, the Son accurately reveals the Father. Christ is "the image of the invisible God" (Col. 1:15), through whom we see the Father (John 14:9; 2 Cor. 4:4–6).

upholds the universe by the word of his power. In the midst of history the Son's command holds the created order in existence (Col. 1:17; 2 Pet. 3:4–7), preserving it from destruction until that day when His voice will remove all but the unshakable kingdom of God and its heirs (12:26–28).

purification for sins. A change of verb tense focuses attention on the Son's atoning death in history, the priestly act that cleanses us to worship in God's presence (9:14).

sat down at the right hand . . . on high. The Son's enthronement at God's "right hand" in heaven, promised in Ps. 110:1 (1:13), reveals His superiority in two ways. At the "right hand" of the Majesty Christ is ministering in the true, heavenly sanctuary and not an earthly copy (8:1, 2, 5). Secondly, He "sat down" because His sacrificial work (unlike that of Levitical priests) was finished once for all (10:11, 12).

1:4 superior to angels. This is proved by the series of Old Testament quotations that follow (vv. 5–14).

inherited . . . more excellent. The eternal Son took on a human nature to rescue us from sin and death (2:14, 15). Now, having for a time voluntarily taken a position "lower than the angels" (2:7), as the resurrected and ascended Messiah He is "declared to be the Son of God in power" (Rom. 1:4) to save His people (v. 5 note). Christ's exaltation thus inaugurates a new phase of His messianic and redemptive Sonship, and gives Him a dignity far above that of angels.

1:5, 6 The series of quotations begins with examples from the Psalms (v. 5, from Ps. 2:7), the Prophets (v. 5, from 2 Sam. 7:14; in the Hebrew Bible the books of Samuel are counted with the Prophets), and the Law (v. 6, from Deut. 32:43). Verse 6 is probably from the Greek translation (Septuagint) of Deut. 32:43, although it also recalls Ps. 97:7.

1:5 You are my Son. The Father's decree declaring the Messiah to be His Son is identified with Christ's exaltation (v. 4 note; 5:5; Acts 13:32–35; Rom. 1:4). Though Jesus is the eternal and divine Son of God (Mark 1:11; John 3:16), the declaration of redemptive Sonship prophesied in Ps. 2:7 was conferred on Him in time, when He completed His messianic work. Believers cannot become divine and share in Christ's eternal divine Sonship, but their adoption as sons of God means that they participate in Christ's redemptive Sonship through union with the "founder of their salvation" (2:10; cf. 3:14 note; Rom. 8:29).

1:6 brings . . . into the world. As the Son condescends to assume our human nature, angels worship Him (Luke 2:13, 14).

firstborn. As in Ps. 89:27, the term means "of the highest rank," above the kings of the earth, and not "first in order of birth." In Ex. 4:22 it means "chosen" or "most desired" (Col. 1:15 note).

1:7 The storm clouds of Ps. 104 adorn the Lord's heavenly court. "Winds" and "flame" associate angels with the created world's mutability in contrast to the Son's eternal permanence (vv. 10–12).

ministers. In contrast to the Son's royal enthronement (vv. 8, 9), the angels are merely "ministers," or "servants."

1:8, 9 From Ps. 45:6, 7. The one who addresses the Son with the words "O God" is Himself "God, your God." The Son is God, and yet distinct from the Father (John 1:1).

[r]"Your throne, O God, is forever and
ever,
the scepter of uprightness is the
scepter of your kingdom.
9 You have loved righteousness and
hated wickedness;
therefore God, your God, [s]has
anointed you
with [t]the oil of gladness beyond
your companions."

10 And,

[u]"You, Lord, laid the foundation of the
earth in the beginning,
and the heavens are the work of
your hands;
11 they will perish, but you remain;
they will all wear out like a
garment,
12 like a robe you will roll them up,
like a garment they will be
changed.[1]
But you are [v]the same,
and your years will have no end."

13 And to which of the angels has he ever
said,

[w]"Sit at my right hand
[x]until I make your enemies a
footstool for your feet"?

14 Are they not all ministering spirits [y]sent
out to serve for the sake of those who are
to [z]inherit salvation?

8 [r]Cited from Ps. 45:6, 7
9 [s]Isai. 61:1 [t]Isai. 61:3
10 [u]Cited from Ps. 102:25-27
12 [v]ch. 13:8
13 [w]Cited from Ps. 110:1 [x]ch. 10:13
14 [y]Gen. 19:16; 28:12; 32:1, 2; Judg. 6:11; 13:3; Ps. 34:7; 91:11; 103:20, 21; Dan. 3:28; 6:22; 10:11; Matt. 18:10 [z]See Matt. 25:34

Chapter 2
2 [a]See Acts 7:53 [b][ch. 10:28; Num. 15:30, 31; Deut. 4:3; 17:2, 5, 12; 27:26] [c]ch. 10:35; 11:26
3 [d][ch. 10:28, 29; 12:25] [e]Matt. 22:5 (Gk.) [f]ch. 1:2 [g]Mark 16:20; [Acts 5:32] [h][Luke 1:2]
4 [g][See ver. 3 above] [i]Acts 2:22, 43 [j][1 Cor. 12:4, 11] [k][Eph. 1:5]
5 [l]ch. 6:5
6 [m]Cited from Ps. 8:4-6

Warning Against Neglecting Salvation

2 Therefore we must pay much closer
attention to what we have heard, lest
we drift away from it. 2 For since [a]the
message declared by angels proved to be
reliable and [b]every transgression or disobedience received a just [c]retribution, 3 [d]how
shall we escape if we [e]neglect such a great
salvation? It was [f]declared at first by the
Lord, and it was [g]attested to us [h]by those
who heard, 4 [g]while God also bore witness
[i]by signs and wonders and various miracles
and by [j]gifts of the Holy Spirit [k]distributed
according to his will.

The Founder of Salvation

5 Now it was not to angels that God subjected the world [l]to come, of which we are
speaking. 6 It has been testified somewhere,

[m]"What is man, that you are mindful of
him,
or the son of man, that you care
for him?
7 You made him for a little while lower
than the angels;
you have crowned him with glory
and honor,[2]
8 putting everything in subjection
under his feet."

Now in putting everything in subjection to
him, he left nothing outside his control. At

1 Some manuscripts omit *like a garment* 2 Some manuscripts insert *and set him over the works of your hands*

1:9 loved righteousness. On the Son's obedience and righteousness, see 4:15; 5:8; 7:26.

1:10 On the Son as Creator, see v. 2 and note.

1:11 you remain. The Son's unchanging eternity as God is essential to His high priesthood (7:3, 23, 24). Through Him the inheritance of believers remains forever (10:34; 12:27, 28; 13:14).

1:13, 14 The Son's position of heavenly authority (v. 3; 8:1) is contrasted to the angels' role as servants to "those who are to inherit salvation" (that is, who share as co-heirs in the Son's rights as heir, vv. 2, 5; 2:10; 6:12; cf. Rom. 8:17, 29). The angels are servants to Christ, but also to His people, who inherit salvation through union with Him. In this His people are favored above the angels (cf. 2:16; 1 Cor. 6:3).

2:1 Compare similar exhortations in 3:12–14; 4:1, 11; 6:11, 12; 10:22–25; 12:1–13; and especially 12:25–29, another reminder of Sinai.

2:2, 3 The argument is from the lesser to the greater. If what the angels said was "reliable," then what comes from One superior to angels must be more so. The Greek word for "reliable" is legal terminology, as is "witness" in v. 4.

2:2 declared by angels. The role of the angels in the giving of the law is suggested in Deut. 33:2 and became a standard element of Jewish and Christian (Acts 7:53; Gal. 3:19) descriptions of Sinai.

just retribution. Illustrated in 10:28, 29 (cf. 6:6). Violators of the Lord's covenant were purged from the covenant community through death.

2:3 salvation. First mentioned in 1:14, this salvation includes inheritance of the world to come (v. 5; 11:16), entry into glory as God's adopted sons (v. 10), purification from sins (1:3; 2:11, 17), freedom from the fear of death (vv. 14, 15), and the privilege of drawing near to God (4:16; 10:22) to offer worship that pleases Him (12:28; 13:15, 16).

those who heard. The apostles were witnesses of what Jesus said and did in His ministry, death, and resurrection (Acts 1:21, 22; 10:39–41; 1 Pet. 5:1; 2 Pet. 1:15). The writer and his readers have heard the gospel through them (Introduction: Author).

2:4 signs and wonders . . . various miracles. These terms are used in the New Testament for the special miracles that God used to demonstrate the authority of the Savior (Acts 2:22), as well as to certify the ministries of the apostles and Stephen (Acts 6:8; 14:3; Rom. 15:19; 2 Cor. 12:12).

2:5–9 The author uses the contrast between angels and human beings in v. 5 to point to the way that the Son, in assuming a full and complete humanity (vv. 14, 17), restores man's dignity and divinely-intended place in creation.

2:6 testified somewhere. Such vagueness in scriptural references is characteristic of the author of Hebrews, who stresses the divine authorship of Scripture rather than the human authors (e.g., 1:5, 7, 8; 2:12; 3:7; 4:3; 5:5, 6). This way of citing a well-known Old Testament proof text about man in creation is evidence for the Jewish background of the recipients.

present, [n]"we do not yet see everything in
subjection to him. 9 But we see him [o]who
for a little while was made lower than the
angels, namely Jesus, [p]crowned with glory
and honor [q]because of the suffering of
death, so that by the grace of God he might
[r]taste death [s]for everyone.
10 For it [t]was fitting that he, [u]for whom
and by whom all things exist, in bringing
many sons [v]to glory, should make the
[w]founder of their salvation [x]perfect through
suffering. 11 For [y]he who sanctifies and
[z]those who are sanctified [a]all have one origin. That is why he is not ashamed to call
them [b]brothers,[1] 12 saying,

> [c]"I will tell of your name to my
> brothers;
> in the midst of the [d]congregation I
> will sing your praise."

13 And again,

> [e]"I will put my trust in him."

And again,

> [f]"Behold, I and the children [g]God has
> given me."

14 Since therefore the children share in
flesh and blood, he himself likewise [h]par-
took of the same things, that [i]through
death he might [j]destroy [k]the one who has
the power of death, that is, the devil, 15 and
deliver all those who [l]through fear of death
were subject to lifelong slavery. 16 For surely it is not angels that he helps, but he
[m]helps the offspring of Abraham. 17 Therefore he had [n]to be made like his brothers in

8 [n][1 Cor. 15:25] **9** [o]ver. 7 [p]Acts 3:13; 1 Pet. 1:21; See Acts 2:33 [q]Phil. 2:7-9; See John 10:17 [r]Matt. 16:28; John 8:52 [s]See John 12:32 **10** [t][Luke 24:26] [u]Rom. 11:36 [v][ch. 3:1; Rom. 8:30] [w][ch. 5:9] [x]ch. 5:9; 7:28; Luke 13:32; [Phil. 3:12] **11** [y]ch. 13:12 [z]ch. 10:10, 14, 29 [a]Acts 17:28 [b]Matt. 25:40 **12** [c]Cited from Ps. 22:22 [d]ch. 12:23 **13** [e][Ps. 18:2; Isai. 8:17; 12:2] [f]Cited from Isai. 8:18 [g]See John 17:2 **14** [h]See John 1:14 [i]See 1 Cor. 15:54-56 [j][Col. 2:15; 2 Tim. 1:10] [k]1 John 3:8; [John 16:11] **15** [l]See Rom. 8:15 **16** [m]Isai. 41:8, 9; [ch. 8:9] **17** [n]Phil. 2:7

[1] Or *brothers and sisters*. The plural Greek word *adelphoi* (translated "brothers") refers to siblings in a family. In New Testament usage, depending on the context, *adelphoi* may refer either to men or to both men and women who are siblings (brothers and sisters) in God's family, the church; also verse 12

2:8 we do not yet. Ps. 8 describes the glorious status of man as the head of all creation. But it is obvious that man is far from enjoying any such status and some explanation is required.

2:9 we see him. Jesus has the crown of glory and honor. It must now be shown that He received it as a man, and so can satisfy the words of the psalm quoted.

made lower. The expression can refer to status or to time (that is, "a little later," Luke 22:58; Acts 5:34). If it refers to time, it indicates the temporary character of Jesus' humiliation.

taste death for everyone. Here, "everyone" must be understood in the light of the context and of the results of Jesus' death described elsewhere in Hebrews. It refers to the "many sons" whom God brings to glory (v. 10), whom Jesus calls "brothers" (v. 11). Those for whom Jesus tasted death were made holy and perfect once for all by His sacrifice (10:10, 14), their consciences cleansed from acts that lead to death (9:14), so they are freed from the fear of death (2:14, 15). By contrast, there are those (even within Christian congregations) who do not trust the Son but subject Him to ridicule (6:6). For them, "there no longer remains a sacrifice for sins, but a fearful expectation of judgment" (10:26, 27). Thus "everyone" here includes all those (but only those) who persevere in trusting Jesus (3:6, 14).

2:10–18 For God's adopted sons to reach the glory promised in Ps. 8, the unique Son had to suffer death on their behalf, destroying their enemy, freeing them from slavery, and atoning for their sins. Bonds of kinship in the eternal plan of God unite the redeemed to the "founder of their salvation" (vv. 10, 11).

2:10 founder. The Greek term can also be translated "Author" or "Leader" (12:2; Acts 3:15; 5:31). Jesus went first on the path of suffering, and He guides us as our captain to the glory that He achieved.

make . . . perfect. See note 5:9.

2:11 he who sanctifies. See "The Atonement" at Rom. 3:25.

all have one origin. Or, "have the same origin," that is, God. Another interpretation is, "are of one nature," that is, human nature.

not ashamed. In view of the Son's glory portrayed in ch. 1, we might expect Him to recoil from identification with fallible human beings, but He willingly calls us brothers and sisters. Such a family relationship is essential to His compassionate, priestly ministry (v. 17; 5:1; 7:5).

2:12 Introduced here primarily because of the words "my brothers," Ps. 22:22 is the turning point in a psalm of the Anointed One's passage through suffering to deliverance. The context of the words quoted corresponds to their use in Hebrews.

2:13 I will put my trust in him. This confession of faith appears in 2 Sam. 22:3; Is. 8:17; 12:2—in all three a servant of God expresses trust in the face of danger. For the Son—"the founder and perfecter of our faith" (12:2)—to take these words on His lips implies His condescension, in regard to His human nature, to live by faith as we must.

I and the children God has given me. As Isaiah and his children were signs of God's faithfulness to their generation (Is. 8:18), so the Son who is greater than the prophets (1:1, 2; 3:3–6) now has His circle of "children," given to Him by the Father (John 17:6).

2:14–18 Christ is presented first as our Redeemer and Warrior who defeats our oppressor and sets us free, then as our merciful High Priest who helps us in our trials.

2:14 flesh and blood. This is an idiomatic way of saying "human." The same Greek phrase is seen at Matt. 16:17; 1 Cor. 15:50; Gal. 1:16; Eph. 6:12; it may emphasize the limitations of the human condition.

partook of the same things. That is, the same humanity, a phrase stressing the completeness of the Son's incarnation. In order for Christ to triumph over death and the devil by enduring God's judgment upon sinners, it was necessary for Him to share their "flesh and blood" nature.

the one who has the power of death. Having tempted humanity to sin, the devil then acts as an accuser (Rev. 12:10), demanding that a just punishment be exacted; and "the wages of sin is death" (Rom. 6:23; cf. 1 Cor. 15:56). The devil's power to kill is destroyed only when our sin has been punished—in Christ's death. Then his accusations have no ground (Col. 2:14, 15).

2:16 This verse resumes the contrast of v. 5. The background is Is. 41:8–14, where Israel is called "offspring of Abraham," whom the Lord will "hold" and whom He "helps" (Is. 41:13; cf. Heb. 2:18), so they need not "fear" (Is. 41:10; Heb. 2:15; cf. 13:5, 6). On Abraham and his descendants, see 6:15–17; 11:9; Rom. 4:11–18; 9:7, 8; Gal. 3:29.

helps. Another translation is "takes on" or "lays hold of," as of "taking on" human nature in the Incarnation. Either way, the point is that the sort of incarnation described in v. 14 is determined by the sort of creatures whom God wills to save. These are human beings, and the eternal Word must be incarnated as a human being: "the Word became flesh" (John 1:14).

2:17 he had to be made like his brothers. Only the One who had been tested in every way as we are could be the merciful High Priest (4:15; 5:2).

every respect, [o]so that he might become a
merciful and faithful high priest [p]in the
service of God, to make propitiation for the
sins of the people. **18**For because he himself has suffered [q]when tempted, he is able
to help those who are being tempted.

Jesus Greater Than Moses

3 Therefore, holy brothers,[1] you who
share in [r]a heavenly calling, consider
Jesus, [s]the apostle and high priest of our
confession, **2**who was faithful to him who
appointed him, [t]just as Moses also was
faithful in all God's[2] house. **3**For Jesus has
been counted worthy of more glory than
Moses—as much more glory as the builder
of a house has more honor than the house
itself. **4**(For every house is built by someone, but [u]the builder of all things is God.)
5[v]Now Moses was faithful in all God's
house [w]as a servant, [x]to testify to the things
that were to be spoken later, **6**but Christ is
faithful over God's house as [y]a son. And
[z]we are his house if indeed we [a]hold fast
our confidence and our boasting in our
hope.[3]

A Rest for the People of God

7Therefore, as the Holy Spirit says,

[b]"Today, if you hear his voice,
8 do not harden your hearts as in the rebellion,
on the day of testing in the wilderness,
9 where your fathers put me to the test
and saw my works **10**for [c]forty years.
Therefore I was provoked with that generation,
and said, 'They always go astray in their heart;
they have not known my ways.'
11 [d]As I swore in my wrath,
'They shall not enter my rest.'"

12Take care, brothers, lest there be in any of

17[o]ch. 4:15, 16; [ch. 5:2, 7, 8] [p]ch. 5:1; Rom. 15:17 **18**[q]ch. 4:15; Luke 22:28 **Chapter 3** **1**[r]Eph. 4:1; Phil. 3:14 [s][John 20:21; Rom. 15:8] **2**[t]ver. 5 **4**[u]Eph. 2:10; 3:9 **5**[v]ver. 2; Cited from Num. 12:7 [w]Ex. 14:31; Deut. 34:5; Josh. 1:2; 8:31; Ps. 105:26; Rev. 15:3 [x]Deut. 18:15, 18, 19 **6**[y]See ch. 1:2 [z]1 Cor. 3:16; 6:19; 2 Cor. 6:16; Eph. 2:21; 1 Tim. 3:15; 1 Pet. 2:5 [a]ver. 14; ch. 6:11; Ps. 119:33, 112; Matt. 10:22; Rev. 2:26

7[b]ver. 15; ch. 4:7; Cited from Ps. 95:7-11 **10**[c]See Acts 7:36 **11**[d]ch. 4:3, 5

[1] Or *brothers and sisters*; also verse 12 [2] Greek *his*; also verses 5, 6
[3] Some manuscripts insert *firm to the end*

Only the One who had responded to every test in perfect obedience could be the faithful High Priest, without sin (4:15; 7:26) and worthy to offer Himself as the unblemished sacrifice (9:14).

merciful and faithful high priest. This echoes the prophecy that pronounced judgment on Eli's house, of Aaron's family, and the coming of a faithful High Priest who would minister forever (1 Sam. 2:35). The faithfulness (3:6) and mercy of Christ (5:2) are explained in what follows.

make propitiation for. This term means that He bore God's wrath and curse that rested on "the people" who sinned (Rom. 3:25, 26). See "Christ the Mediator" at 1 Tim. 2:5.

2:18 he himself has suffered. See "The Humanity of Jesus" at 2 John 7.

3:1 holy brothers. This typical Christian title of address (3:12; 10:19; Acts 1:16; 1 Cor. 3:1) has special significance here, since Jesus has made us His "brothers" and "sanctified" us (2:11).

heavenly calling. The Lord calls from heaven, summoning us to enduring faith (12:25). He also calls us to heaven, the better country (11:16) and the eternal inheritance of those who are called (9:15).

consider. Since Christ is able to deal with the most important problems we face, the reader should be eager to give close attention to what will now be said about Him.

apostle. This title is applied to Jesus only here in the New Testament. It stresses His faithful accomplishment of the mission on which the Father sent Him (v. 2; cf. 10:5–10; John 6:38; 20:21).

3:2–6 With reference to Num. 12:7, Moses and Christ are compared as to faithfulness and contrasted as to honor. Though privileged to speak to God face to face and to see His form (Num. 12:8), Moses was still only "a servant" in the house of God (v. 5). Christ, as agent of creation (1:2, 10), deserves honor as divine builder of all things and as Son "over God's house" (v. 6).

3:3 builder of a house. The necessary implication is that Jesus is the builder of the house, and therefore that He is divine (v. 4). This passage points both to Christ's identity as God ("the builder") and to His personal distinction from the Father (v. 6).

3:5 faithful in all God's house. Since the writer alludes to Num. 12:7, the emphasis is on the dignity of Moses' service. Moses is the unique minister of the law, but Jesus' ministry is higher still.

to testify . . . spoken later. Moses' ministry was to testify to Christ's coming (John 5:46, 47). The Mosaic law by its shadows pointed toward the coming good things brought by Christ (9:11; 10:1), for in its regulations the Holy Spirit showed that access into God's presence would come only when the earthly tabernacle was replaced by something better (9:8).

3:6 over God's house. Note the prepositions: Moses was "in" the house, but Christ is "over" the house (10:21).

we are his house. God's house consists of His people (1 Sam. 2:35; 2 Sam. 7:16; Eph. 2:19–22; 1 Tim. 3:15; 1 Pet. 2:5), an important theme throughout Scripture.

if indeed we hold fast. This condition tells the readers how they can know that they belong to God—their faith must prove itself by persevering (v. 14; 6:11; 10:23). The note of warning is a fitting introduction to the quotation from Ps. 95 that follows.

3:7–4:13 The writer quotes Ps. 95:7–11, and then uses numerous brief quotations and echoes of it to keep his exposition to the point. Important key words in this section are "today" (3:13, 15; 4:7) and "rest" (4:3, 5, 6, 8–11); the treatment of "rest" is developed from the Sabbath teaching of Gen. 2:2. Corresponding to this teaching is the exhortation to "enter that rest" (4:11) and the warning not to "harden your hearts" (3:15; 4:7).

3:8 day of testing. A significant occasion of testing occurred at Rephidim (Ex. 17:1–7), where the people grumbled and Moses struck the rock to give them water. The entire forty-year period of disobedience and resistance while wandering in the wilderness may also be in view (vv. 9, 10; Ps. 78:40).

3:11 swore. Num. 14:21–30 records God's promise not to allow that generation to enter the Promised Land. Hebrews understands this oath to point also to a divine, eternal Sabbath rest (4:1–11).

my rest. See note 4:8.

3:12, 13 The author addresses his readers in terms of their confession of faith (v. 1) as "brothers," yet also recognizes that some within the Christian fellowship may have an "evil, unbelieving heart" (cf. 12:15–17). Christ saves completely those who come to God through Him (7:25), but Christians must guard their own and each other's endurance by

you an evil, unbelieving heart, leading you
to fall away from [e]the living God. 13 But [f]ex-
hort one another every day, as long as it is
called "today," that none of you may be
hardened by [g]the deceitfulness of sin. 14 For
we share in Christ, [h]if indeed we hold our
original confidence firm to the end. 15 As it
is said,

> [b]"Today, if you hear his voice,
> do not harden your hearts as in the
> rebellion."

16 For [i]who were those who heard and yet
rebelled? Was it not [j]all those who left
Egypt led by Moses? 17 And with whom was
he provoked for forty years? Was it not
with those who sinned, [k]whose bodies fell
in the wilderness? 18 And to whom did he
swear that [l]they would not enter his rest,
but to those who were disobedient? 19 So
we see that [m]they were unable to enter
because of unbelief.

4 Therefore, while the promise of entering his rest still stands, let us fear lest
any of you should seem [n]to have failed to
reach it. 2 For good news came to us just as
to them, but the message they heard did
not benefit them, because [o]they were not
united by faith with those who listened.[1]
3 For we who have believed enter that rest,
as he has said,

> [p]"As I swore in my wrath,
> 'They shall not enter my rest,'"

although his works were finished from the
foundation of the world. 4 For he has somewhere spoken of the seventh day in this
way: [q]"And God rested on the seventh day
from all his works." 5 And again in this passage he said,

> [r]"They shall not enter my rest."

6 Since therefore it remains for some to
enter it, and those who formerly received
the good news [s]failed to enter because of
disobedience, 7 again he appoints a certain day, "Today," saying through David
so long afterward, in the words already
quoted,

> [t]"Today, if you hear his voice,
> do not harden your hearts."

8 For if Joshua had given them rest, God[2]
would not have spoken of another day later
on. 9 So then, there remains a Sabbath rest
for the people of God, 10 for whoever has
entered God's rest has also [u]rested from his
works as God did from his.
11 Let us therefore strive to enter that rest,
so [v]that no one may fall by the same sort of
disobedience. 12 For [w]the word of God is

1 Some manuscripts *it did not meet with faith in the hearers* 2 Greek *he*

12 [e]See Matt. 16:16
13 [f][ch. 10:24, 25] [g][Isai. 44:20; Rom. 7:11; Eph. 4:22]
14 [h]ver. 6; ch. 10:23; 1 Cor. 15:2
15 [b][See ver. 7 above]
16 [i]Num. 14:2; Deut. 1:34, 35 [j][Num. 14:24, 30; Deut. 1:36, 38]
17 [k]Num. 14:29; See Jude 5
18 [l]Deut. 1:34, 35; [ch. 4:2]
19 [m]ch. 4:6; Ps. 78:22; 106:24
Chapter 4
1 [n]ch. 12:15
2 [o]Rom. 3:3
3 [p]ch. 3:11; Cited from Ps. 95:11
4 [q]Cited from Gen. 2:2; [Ex. 20:11; 31:17]
5 [r]ver. 3
6 [s]See ch. 3:19
7 [t]See ch. 3:7, 8
10 [u][Rev. 14:13]
11 [v][ch. 3:12]
12 [w]1 Pet. 1:23

encouraging one another (10:24, 25), as the author does throughout this letter (13:22).

3:12 unbelieving heart. That is, a heart like that of "your fathers" (v. 9), which kept them from entering God's rest (v. 19).

3:13 today. See note 4:7.

deceitfulness of sin. Sin promotes the illusion that disobedience is more secure (Ex. 17:3) or pleasurable (11:25, 26; Ex. 16:3) than the pilgrimage of faith.

3:14 we share in Christ. The Greek can be taken to mean that we are partakers with Christ, His companions (1:9), sharing new life with Him. It is also possible to translate "share in Christ," indicating that He is the benefit we share in, through our intimate union with Him.

3:16–19 Neither the blessing of the Exodus from Egypt nor the privilege of hearing God's voice guaranteed to the generation that was in the wilderness that they would enter God's rest, the rest that is the goal of our pilgrimage (4:8 note). Their rebellion (v. 16), sin (v. 17), and disobedience (v. 18; 4:6) was rooted in unbelief, in their failure to cling permanently to God's promise (v. 19; 4:2, 3).

4:1 let us fear. The divine judgment inspires fear (10:27, 31; 12:21), but we should not fear what men may do (11:27; 13:6).

4:2 good news came to us. The good news of deliverance and God's love that Israel heard at Sinai was not as clear as the salvation spoken now through the Lord (2:3), but it would have been of value to the hearers, ushering them into God's rest, if they had combined it with faith.

4:3–5 The basic theme of these verses is that a "rest" of God has existed from the seventh day of Creation (v. 4; Gen. 2:2), even though the disobedient generation could not enter it. The writer understands the promises about the physical land to point ultimately to the divine rest (3:11 note), which only those who believe may enter (v. 3).

4:7 Today. The readers have already learned that they live in the time called "today" (3:13); therefore they must heed the promises and the warnings. Through David the offer of entry (and a warning against failure to enter) is continued to a new generation, who "today" must respond to God's voice.

4:8 Another indication (cf. vv. 3–5) that the physical land of Canaan did not fulfill the promise of God's rest. When David wrote, Israel long ago had entered Canaan under Joshua. If the land they entered under Joshua had fulfilled the promise of divine rest, the psalm's warning to David's generation would have been pointless. The patriarchs' hope was fixed on a better, heavenly country (11:16). There are similar arguments from the Old Testament in 7:11; 8:7.

4:9 there remains a Sabbath rest. The final Sabbath celebration awaits God's people in the future.

4:10 rested from his works. The reference is probably not to conversion, in which we transfer trust from our works to Christ, but to our final deliverance from suffering, testing, and effort (v. 11). Those who die in the Lord "rest from their labors" (Rev. 14:13).

4:12, 13 The preceding argument (3:7–4:11) has illustrated how the word of God's power exposed the faithlessness of the wilderness generation and how Scripture (e.g., Ps. 95) penetrates and judges those whom it invites today, as it warns about the deceitfulness of sin (3:13) and the possibility of falling short (v. 1).

living and [x]active, [y]sharper than any [z]two-
edged sword, piercing to the division of
soul and of spirit, of joints and of marrow,
and [a]discerning the thoughts and intentions of the heart. 13 And [b]no creature is
hidden from his sight, but all are [c]naked
and exposed to the eyes of him to whom
we must give account.

Jesus the Great High Priest

14 Since then we have [d]a great high priest
[e]who has passed through the heavens,
Jesus, the Son of God, [f]let us hold fast our
confession. 15 For we do not have a high
priest [g]who is unable to sympathize with
our weaknesses, but one who in every
respect has been [d]tempted as we are, [h]yet
without sin. 16 [i]Let us then with confidence
draw near to the throne of grace, that we
may receive mercy and find grace to help in
time of need.

5 For every high priest chosen from
among men [j]is appointed to act on
behalf of men [k]in relation to God, [l]to offer
gifts and sacrifices for sins. 2 [m]He can deal

12 [x][Jer. 23:29; 1 Thess. 2:13] [y]Isai. 49:2; Eph. 6:17 [z]Prov. 5:4; Rev. 1:16; 2:12 [a][1 Cor. 14:24, 25] **13** [b]2 Chr. 16:9; Job 34:21; Ps. 33:13-15 [c]Job 26:6 **14** [d]ch. 2:17, 18; [ch. 10:21] [e]Eph. 4:10 [f]ch. 10:23 **15** [g][ch. 5:2; Isai. 53:3]

[d][See ver. 14 above] [h]ch. 9:28; 1 Pet. 2:22; 1 John 3:5; [ch. 7:26; John 8:46; 14:30] **16** [i]ch. 10:19; Eph. 3:12; [ch. 7:19, 25]
Chapter 5 **1** [j]ch. 8:3 [k]ch. 2:17 [l]ch. 8:3, 4; 9:9; 10:11; 11:4 **2** [m]ch. 2:18; 4:15

The Sinlessness of Jesus

The New Testament teaches that Jesus was entirely free from sin (John 8:46; 2 Cor. 5:21; Heb. 4:15; 7:26; 1 Pet. 2:22; 1 John 3:5). This assertion means not only that He never disobeyed His Father, but that He loved God's law and found whole-hearted joy in keeping it. In fallen human beings there is always some reluctance to obey God, and sometimes resentment amounting to hatred at the claims He makes on us (Rom. 8:7). But Jesus' moral nature was unfallen, as was Adam's prior to his sin, and in Jesus there was no prior inclination away from God for Satan to exploit, as there is in us. Jesus loved His Father and His Father's will with all His heart, mind, soul, and strength.

Heb. 4:15 says that Jesus was "in every respect . . . tempted as we are," though without sinning. The temptations we face—temptations to wrongfully indulge natural desires, to evade moral and spiritual issues, to cut moral corners and take easy ways out, to be less than loving and sympathetic to others, to be self-centered and lost in self-pity—all these came upon Jesus, but He yielded to none of them (see "The Humanity of Jesus" at 2 John 7). In Gethsemane and on the Cross He fought temptation and resisted sin to the point of death. Christians must learn from Him to do likewise (Luke 14:25–33; Heb. 12:3–13).

For our salvation it was necessary that Jesus be free from sin. He was "a lamb without blemish or spot," able to offer His "precious" blood for us (1 Pet. 1:19). If He had been sinful He would have needed a savior Himself, and His death would not have helped us. Christ obeyed on our behalf the moral commandments applying to all humanity. He also fulfilled all the will of God applying to Him in particular, as the One called to be the Messiah. His perfect obedience qualifies Him to be our all-sufficient Savior.

4:12 division of soul and of spirit, of joints and of marrow. Though some find support here for the view that a human being is basically a trichotomy consisting of body, soul, and spirit, the context is against it. It stresses the power of God's word to enter the deepest recesses of a person's being, and not a sort of division into constituent parts. Also, if the idea of division were intended, we would expect the author to say "bone and marrow" instead of "joints and of marrow."

4:14–16 The sobering thought of our complete exposure before God draws us to the merciful High Priest who, having been tempted, can help us in our weakness (themes announced in 2:17, 18). An exhortation to "hold fast our confession" (v. 14) caps the preceding section, and an invitation to approach God's throne introduces the discussion of Christ as the merciful High Priest.

4:14 passed through the heavens. Christ was raised, ascended, and sits at God's right hand (8:1), where He ministers as our great and eternal High Priest (7:26; 9:11, 24).

the Son of God. See note 1:5 (cf. 5:5).

4:15 in every respect has been tempted. This is a vivid restatement of 2:17, 18. As temptation is again mentioned, the author is careful to add that Christ was "without sin" despite His knowledge of our weakness. See theological note "The Sinlessness of Jesus."

4:16 Let us then with confidence draw near. Confident access to God is a priestly privilege reserved for those who have been purified from sin's pollution by Jesus' sacrifice (7:19; 10:19, 22), and so can offer sacrifices of thanksgiving pleasing to God (12:28; 13:15, 16). On the priestly privilege of Christian believers see Rom. 5:1, 2; Eph. 2:13–22; 1 Pet. 2:4–10.

mercy . . . grace to help. Mercy addresses our need for forgiveness when we have succumbed to temptation, and grace brings timely support to sustain us in the midst of temptation (2:18).

5:1–10 As the Old Testament priests were identified with the weak and erring people whom they represented (vv. 1–3) and served at God's appointment (v. 4), so also Christ became High Priest by the Father's appointment (vv. 5, 6) and was identified with His people through suffering (vv. 7–10).

5:1 offer gifts and sacrifices for sins. The phrase "gifts and sacrifices" covers offerings of several different kinds called for in the work of Old Testament priests (8:3; Lev. 1–7). But the main interest here is in those offered for sins.

5:2 can deal gently. The weakness of the Old Testament high priest in the face of his own temptations compelled him to moderate his indignation over others' sins and "deal gently" with them. Jesus' sympathy

gently with the ignorant and wayward,
since he himself [n]is beset with weakness.
3 Because of this he is obligated to offer sacrifice for his own sins [o]just as he does for
those of the people. 4 And [p]no one takes
this honor for himself, but only when
called by God, [q]just as Aaron was.
5 So also Christ [r]did not exalt himself to
be made a high priest, but was appointed
by him who said to him,

[s]"You are my Son,
today I have begotten you";

6 as he says also in another place,

[t]"You are a priest forever,
after the order of Melchizedek."

7 In the days of his flesh, [u]Jesus[1] offered
up prayers and supplications, [v]with loud
cries and tears, to him [w]who was able to
save him from death, and [x]he was heard
because of his reverence. 8 Although [y]he
was a son, [z]he learned obedience through
what he suffered. 9 And [a]being made perfect, he became the source of eternal salvation to all who obey him, 10 being designated by God a high priest [b]after the order of
Melchizedek.

Warning Against Apostasy

11 About this we have much to say, and it
is [c]hard to explain, since you have become
dull of hearing. 12 For though by this time
you ought to be teachers, you need someone to teach you again [d]the basic principles
of the oracles of God. You need [e]milk, not
solid food, 13 for everyone who lives on milk
is unskilled in the word of righteousness,
since he is [f]a child. 14 But solid food is for
[g]the mature, for those who have their powers [h]of discernment trained by constant
practice to distinguish good from evil.

6 Therefore [i]let us leave [j]the elementary
doctrine of Christ and go on to maturity, not laying again a foundation of repentance [k]from dead works and of faith toward
God, 2 and of [l]instruction about washings,[2]

2 [n][ch. 7:28]
3 [o]ch. 7:27; 9:7; Lev. 4:3; 9:7; 16:6
4 [p]Num. 16:5, 40; 18:7; 2 Chr. 26:18 [q]Ex. 28:1; 1 Chr. 23:13
5 [r]John 8:54 [s]See ch. 1:5
6 [t]ch. 7:17, 21; Cited from Ps. 110:4 [q][See ver. 4 above]
7 [u]Matt. 26:39, 44; Mark 14:36, 39; Luke 22:41, 44 [v]Ps. 22:1, 2; [Matt. 27:46, 50; Mark 15:34, 37; Luke 23:46] [w]Mark 14:36 [x]Ps. 22:24
8 [y]See ch. 1:2 [z]Phil. 2:8
9 [a]See ch. 2:10
10 [b]ver. 6; ch. 6:20
11 [c][2 Pet. 3:16]
12 [d]ch. 6:1 [e]1 Cor. 3:2
13 [f]1 Cor. 3:1; [1 Pet. 2:2]
14 [g]Eph. 4:13 [h]Gen. 3:22; 1 Kin. 3:9; Isai. 7:15
Chapter 6 1 [i][Phil. 3:12-14] [j]ch. 5:12 [k]ch. 9:14 2 [l]Acts 19:4, 5

1 Greek *he* 2 Or *baptisms* (that is, cleansing rites)

also is strongly motivated, since He fully identifies with the struggles of His people. Yet Jesus never succumbed to temptation (4:15).

ignorant and wayward. The law (Num. 15:27–31) distinguished between sins committed out of weakness or ignorance, and sins committed in defiance of the Lord's authority (10:26, 27).

5:3 The Old Testament high priest was himself in need of atonement and forgiveness (7:27; 9:7; Lev. 16:11), unlike our sinless High Priest (4:15; 7:26).

5:4 called by God, just as Aaron was. The initial call of Aaron (Ex. 28:1) was confirmed in response to the challenge of Korah, Dathan, and Abiram (Num. 16) through the budding of Aaron's staff (9:4; Num. 17:1–10). The priestly privilege of approach to God is by invitation only—mediated through physical descent for the Old Testament Levitical priests, but finally established through the divine oath to Jesus the Son (7:11–28).

5:5 You are my Son. Ps. 2:7 is quoted twice in Hebrews (1:5), both times in a leading position. Here it is the opening step of a long and detailed discussion of Melchizedek.

5:6 Melchizedek. This mysterious figure is mentioned only twice in the Old Testament (Gen. 14:18; Ps. 110:4). But the association here of the title "priest forever, after the order of Melchizedek" with the words "my Son" (v. 5) shows the exalted character of this priesthood, and justifies the author's fuller explanation in ch. 7.

5:7 loud cries and tears. Jesus' anguish at the prospect of the Cross (Mark 14:33–36; John 12:27) shows that He is not aloof from the weakness and fears that threaten us.

was heard. The psalmists praised God that He heard their cries of distress (Ps. 22:24; 30:23; 116:1). Jesus' plea for salvation from death was answered not through escape from the ordeal of the Cross, but through His Resurrection from death.

5:8 he learned obedience. Though entirely free from sin (4:15), Jesus' struggle against temptation was real (2:18). As One who came into the world to do the Father's will (10:7), Christ successfully met each increasingly difficult challenge to His integrity, climaxing in the shameful and painful death on the cross (Phil. 2:8). This life of learned obedience offsets the disobedience of Adam (Rom. 5:19) and qualifies Christ to serve as the eternal High Priest (2:17, 18; 4:15).

5:9 being made perfect. This does not mean that Jesus finally became sinless, since He was always without sin (4:15), but that He finished the course of suffering that was set before Him, including the sacrificial death. Having done this, He was "made perfect," or completely qualified to serve as the uniquely effective High Priest. The language here may allude to the concept of priestly consecration.

eternal salvation. Jesus lives forever to intercede as our High Priest (7:24, 25).

5:10 Melchizedek. See ch. 7.

5:11–6:12 Christ's priestly ministry after the order of Melchizedek is "hard to explain" (5:11) because of the readers' immaturity. The exhortation in this section focuses on the dangers posed by a failure to "go on to maturity" (6:1 text note).

5:11 dull of hearing. The Greek word translated "dull" reappears in 6:12 (translated "sluggish"), suggesting that the danger of spiritual laziness is in view throughout this section.

5:12 basic principles of the oracles of God. Such truths are listed in 6:1, 2.

5:13 milk. Although milk is nourishing for infants (1 Pet. 2:2), the author desires that his readers become mature Christians, for whom solid food is appropriate (1 Cor. 3:1, 2).

5:14 The maturity needed to grasp Christ's priestly ministry is not intellectual sophistication, but spiritual discernment arising from consistent obedience to God's will (Phil. 1:9–11).

6:1 the elementary doctrine of Christ. These are the ABC's of Christian doctrine, which are now briefly enumerated (vv. 1, 2). All these doctrines can be found in the Book of Acts.

repentance . . . and of faith. See Mark 1:15; Acts 20:21.

6:2 washings. (Lit. "baptisms"). The plural is unexpected; there is only one Christian baptism (Eph. 4:5). Yet even today when Christian baptism

[m]the laying on of hands, [n]the resurrection
of the dead, and [o]eternal judgment. 3 And
this we will do [p]if God permits. 4 For it is
impossible to restore again to repentance
those [q]who have once been enlightened,
who have tasted [r]the heavenly gift, and
[s]have shared in the Holy Spirit, 5 and [t]have
tasted the goodness of the word of God and
the powers of the age to come, 6 if they
[u]then fall away, since [v]they are crucifying
once again the Son of God to their own
harm and holding him up to contempt. 7 For
[w]land that has drunk the rain that often falls
on it, and produces a crop useful to those
for whose sake it is cultivated, receives a
blessing from God. 8 But [x]if it bears thorns
and thistles, it is worthless and near to
being cursed, [y]and its end is to be burned.

9 Though we speak in this way, yet in
your case, beloved, we feel sure of better
things—things that belong to salvation.
10 For [z]God is not so unjust as to overlook
[a]your work and the love that you showed
for his sake in [b]serving the saints, as you
still do. 11 And we desire each one of you to
show the same earnestness to have the full
assurance [c]of hope until the end, 12 so that
you may not be sluggish, but [d]imitators of
those who through faith and patience
inherit the promises.

The Certainty of God's Promise

13 For when God made a promise to
Abraham, since he had no one greater by

2 [m]Acts 8:17; 19:6 [n]Acts 17:31, 32 [o]See Acts 10:42 **3** [p]See 1 Cor. 16:7 [q]ch. 10:32 [r][John 4:10; Eph. 2:8] [s]ch. 2:4, 5; Gal. 3:2, 5 **5** [t]Ps. 34:8 **6** [u][Matt. 19:26]; See 1 John 5:16 [v][ch. 10:29] **7** [w]Ps. 65:10 **8** [x]Isai. 5:1-7; [Gen. 3:17-18; Deut. 29:22, 23; Jer. 44:22; Luke 13:6-9] [y][Mal. 4:1; John 15:6]

10 [z]Prov. 19:17; Matt. 10:42; 25:40; Mark 9:41 [a]1 Thess. 1:3 [b]Rom. 15:31; 2 Cor. 8:4; 9:1, 12; 2 Tim. 1:18; Rev. 2:19 **11** [c]Rom. 5:2-5 **12** [d]ch. 13:7; [ch. 10:36]

is discussed, other baptisms, at least John the Baptist's, must be mentioned. This was certainly true in New Testament times (9:10; Matt. 3:11; 28:19; Mark 1:4; John 4:1; Acts 1:5). Another possibility is that the word refers specifically to Old Testament ceremonial washings (see 9:10) as part of the essential background for Christ's work.

laying on of hands. This action accompanied blessing, healing the sick, ordination of church officers, and especially the gift of the Spirit, which was also associated with baptism (Matt. 19:13–15; Luke 4:40; Acts 6:6; 8:17; 9:17; 28:8; 1 Tim. 4:14). Alternatively, as is possible with "washings," the writer may be referring to the Old Testament foundations of Christ's work.

6:3 if God permits. This conventional phrase acknowledges the need for God's help in learning and teaching Christian doctrine. Its use suggests that the material to follow is difficult, as indeed it is.

6:4–12 This sober warning has been variously interpreted. Some understand the author to refer to genuine Christians who lose their salvation, but such a reading conflicts with passages that teach that those whom God has truly saved will persevere in faith to the end (John 10:28, 29; Rom. 8:28–30; "Perseverance of the Saints" at Rom. 8:30). Others interpret the warning as an argument directed against a Judaizing heretical sect, followers of a heresy serious enough that embracing it would lead to the loss of all hope of salvation. Another interpretation holds that the author is describing the apostates of vv. 4–8 in terms of their profession and the blessings they appeared to share with genuine believers up to the moment of their apostasy. Although Jesus saves completely (7:25) and has made perfect forever (10:13) those who hear His word with faith, the author exhorts the readers to prove the faith they profess by their perseverance. Without faith, proximity to God in the fellowship of His covenant people is no blessing; rather, it subjects apostates to more severe judgment.

6:4 once been enlightened. That is, had the knowledge of God disclosed in the gospel message (10:26; John 1:9; 2 Cor. 4:4–6) and publicly confessed in baptism. In early Christian writings, conversion and baptism were sometimes termed "enlightenment." The Greek word for "once" is prominent in Hebrews. It is used in connection with the once-for-all sacrifice of Christ in 10:2, 10.

tasted the heavenly gift. Some see here a reference to participation in the sacrament of the Lord's Supper. Or the phrase could be paired with "enlightened" as a broad description of apparent conversion.

shared in the Holy Spirit. They had some experience with the gifts of the Holy Spirit, but it is not necessary to conclude that regeneration is specifically intended.

6:5 powers of the age to come. Most obviously, the signs and wonders that accompanied the introduction of the gospel (2:4 note).

6:6 if they then fall away. There is a kind of falling away that is irreversible (1 John 5:16). Christian salvation is final (10:4), and the decision to reject it, if made at a certain level, cannot be reversed. According to 1 John 2:19, anyone who makes such a decision was not really a member of the household of faith, although they may have seemed to be. Judas Iscariot is the clearest example of someone who participated in the coming of the kingdom, but did not enter it (Matt. 26:47–49; cf. Matt. 7:21–23). This warning is not to encourage speculation about whether others are irretrievably lost, but urges us to cling closely to the Savior ourselves. See "The Unpardonable Sin" at Mark 3:29.

crucifying once again the Son of God. By renouncing their faith in Christ they declare that Christ's cross is not a holy sacrifice for others' sins, but the deserved execution of a guilty criminal (10:29). Such apostates have returned to a point where the Cross does nothing but condemn them as accomplices in murder (Acts 18:5, 6).

There is an analogy between the once-for-all character of Christ's sacrifice for sin and the believer's symbolic participation in that crucifixion through baptism (v. 4 note). Christ's sacrificial death cannot be repeated. In the same way, the believer's participation in His death, sealed by baptism (Rom. 6:3, 4; Col. 2:12), cannot be withdrawn and then repeated.

contempt. The apostasy described in ch. 6 is not a matter of private, internal doubt. It is the forceful, complete, and public rejection of a faith once confessed. As such, it has bad effects for others as well as for the apostate (12:15).

6:7, 8 According to the prophetic imagery of the Old Testament, the ground is God's people (Is. 5:1–7), and the rain falling on it is the Word (Is. 55:10, 11) or the Spirit of God (Is. 44:3, 4). The unproductive field is destroyed (Is. 5:4–6). See also Matt. 13:7, 8, 22, 23.

6:9–12 By bearing firstfruits of a useful crop, the readers give reason for confidence that they will prove to be the land that receives God's blessing of salvation. Still, they must shake off their present sluggishness to receive the inheritance promised to patient believers. The severity of the previous warning should not lead to despair.

6:10 serving . . . still do. For example, through standing with those ridiculed or imprisoned for their faith (10:32–34).

6:11 hope. Because the goal of faith is in the future, the faithful must hold on "until the end" (cf. 3:14; 6:18, 19; 11:1).

6:12 sluggish. This term (translated "dull" in 5:11) marks the beginning and end of the exhortation.

through faith and patience inherit the promises. Abraham is the preeminent example (vv. 15, 17; 11:8–19); but biblical history is full of witnesses who have run the course of patient faith ahead of us (11:4–38), and have now received the promised inheritance through Christ's perfecting work (11:13, 39, 40).

6:13–20 Faith can endure patiently because God's oath secures His

whom to swear, [e]he swore by himself,
14 saying, [f]"Surely I will bless you and multiply you." 15 And thus Abraham,[1] [g]having
patiently waited, obtained the promise.
16 For people swear by something greater
than themselves, and in all their disputes
[h]an oath is final for confirmation. 17 So
when God desired to show more convincingly to [i]the heirs of the promise [j]the
unchangeable character of his purpose, [k]he
guaranteed it with an oath, 18 so that by two
unchangeable things, in which [l]it is impossible for God to lie, we who have fled for
refuge might have strong encouragement to
hold fast to the hope [m]set before us. 19 We
have this as a sure and steadfast anchor of
the soul, a hope that enters into [n]the inner
place behind the curtain, 20 where Jesus has
gone [o]as a forerunner on our behalf, [p]hav-
ing become a high priest forever after the
order of Melchizedek.

13 [e]Gen. 22:16 14 [f]Cited from Gen. 22:17 15 [g]ver. 12, 17; [ch. 7:6]; See Rom. 4:13 16 [h]Ex. 22:11 17 [i]ch. 11:9 [j]ver. 18; [Ps. 110:4; Prov. 19:21] [k][Gal. 3:20] 18 [l]See Tit. 1:2 [m]ch. 12:1, 2 19 [n]ch. 9:7; Lev. 16:15 20 [o]ch. 4:14; 8:1; 9:24 [p]ch. 3:1; 5:6, 10; 7:17, 21

The Priestly Order of Melchizedek

7 For this [q]Melchizedek, king of [r]Salem,
priest of [s]the Most High God, met
Abraham returning from the slaughter of
the kings and blessed him, 2 and to him
Abraham apportioned a tenth part of everything. He is first, by translation of his
name, king of righteousness, and then he is
also king of Salem, that is, king of peace. 3 He

Chapter 7 1 [q]Gen. 14:18-20 [r]Ps. 76:2 [s]Num. 24:16; Deut. 32:8

1 Greek *he*

Hope

Christians look forward with hope to the joy of being with Christ in glory forever. Faith is defined as "the assurance of things hoped for" (Heb. 11:1) because the invisible things hoped for in the future are grasped through faith. Hope is certain; it is "a sure and steadfast anchor of the soul" (Heb. 6:18, 19). According to the Bible, Christ is "our hope" (1 Tim. 1:1), and our God is called "the God of hope" (Rom. 15:13).

An ethic of hope pervades the New Testament. It is an ethic of pilgrimage for strangers on their way home (Heb. 11:13; 1 Pet. 2:11). It is an ethic of purity, as the one who hopes to be like Jesus when He appears "purifies himself as he is pure" (1 John 3:3). It is an ethic of preparedness, since we should be ready to leave this world at any time (2 Cor. 5:6–8; Phil. 1:21–24; cf. Luke 12:15–21). Hope calls us to be patient (Rom. 8:25; cf. 5:1–5). Hope gives strength and confidence for running the race, fighting the good fight, and enduring the tribulations that continue in this life (John 16:33; Acts 14:22; Rom. 8:18; 2 Tim. 4:7, 8).

Though the Christian life is marked more by suffering than by triumph (Acts 14:22; 1 Cor. 4:8–13; 2 Cor. 4:7–18), our hope is sure and our mood should be free from despair (1 John 4:18).

promise to us, as it did to Abraham. Our confidence rests in the eternal high priesthood of Jesus after the order of Melchizedek, a priesthood secured by divine promise and oath (7:20–22, 28).

6:13 he swore by himself. That God, whose "word is truth" (John 17:17; cf. Titus 1:2), should reinforce the surety of that infallible promise through an oath underscores the permanence and seriousness of the divine promise (Gen. 15:8–21; 22:17). While sinful and fallible human beings "swear by something greater" than themselves (v. 16), God, the highest authority, "swore by himself" (v. 13).

6:15 having patiently waited, obtained. The divine promise and oath (Gen. 22:17) was God's response to Abraham's attempted sacrifice of Isaac, the child of divine promise (Gen. 12:2; 15:4–6), in obedience to divine direction (Gen. 22:2). In the birth and then the rescue of Isaac (Gen. 21:1–3; 22:11, 12), Abraham did receive the promised blessing of offspring. Nevertheless, he did not see the complete fulfillment of those covenantal promises (11:39, 40; cf. Rom. 4:13, 16, 17).

6:17 the heirs of the promise. God's oath-bound promise was not only for Abraham but for all who follow his footsteps of faith (1:14; 6:12; 10:36; Rom. 4:23, 24).

his purpose. God's unchanging purpose was to bless the world through the seed of Abraham (Gen. 12:3); the meaning of this was revealed in the gospel (Gal. 3:6–9).

6:18 two unchangeable things. The unchanging promise God conveyed to Abraham and the oath that confirmed it, raising it above all uncertainty or distrust (vv. 13, 14 note). The oath confirms that the promise was indeed the purpose of God.

the hope set before us. See theological note "Hope."

6:19 the inner place behind the curtain. Our life's anchor is secured in the innermost section of the heavenly tabernacle, the original from which the earthly sanctuary was modeled (8:2; 9:11, 12, 24, 25; 10:19, 20).

6:20 has gone as a forerunner. Entrance to the inner sanctuary is not possible without Jesus. He went in first, so that His people could follow. But His entrance, and how His people have a part in it, requires a lengthy explanation. This verse begins the discussion of Christ's priesthood "after the order of Melchizedek," announced in 5:6 but delayed until now.

7:1–28 The central point of this chapter is that the solemn promise of Ps. 110:4 was fulfilled only in Jesus Christ. Jesus' eternal priesthood is explained in terms of the two Old Testament texts that mention Melchizedek: Gen. 14:17–20 and Ps. 110:4.

7:1 king of Salem. The introduction of Melchizedek emphasizes that he was a king as well as a priest. As such he is a type of Christ, who is our prophet, priest, and king. "Salem" was apparently an ancient name for Jerusalem (Ps. 76:2).

7:2 king of righteousness. "Melchizedek" is interpreted by the Hebrew words *melek*, "king," and *zedek*, "righteousness."

7:3 Some believe that Melchizedek is a preincarnate appearance of

is without father or mother [t]or genealogy,
having neither beginning of days nor end of
life, but resembling the Son of God he continues a priest forever.
4 See how great this man was to whom
Abraham [u]the patriarch gave a tenth of the
spoils! 5 And [v]those descendants of Levi
who receive the priestly office have a commandment in the law to take tithes from
the people, that is, from their brothers,[1]
though these also are descended from
Abraham. 6 But this man [w]who does not
have his descent from them received tithes
from Abraham and blessed [x]him who had
the promises. 7 It is beyond dispute that the
inferior is blessed by the superior. 8 In the
one case tithes are received by mortal men,
but in the other case, by one [y]of whom it is
testified that [z]he lives. 9 One might even say
that Levi himself, who receives tithes, paid
tithes through Abraham, 10 for he was still
in the loins of his ancestor when
Melchizedek met him.

Jesus Compared to Melchizedek

11 [a]Now if perfection had been attainable
through the Levitical priesthood (for under
it the people received the law), what
further need would there have been for
another priest to arise after the order of
Melchizedek, rather than one named after
the order of Aaron? 12 For when there is a
change in the priesthood, there is necessarily a change in the law as well. 13 For the
one of whom these things are spoken
belonged to another tribe, from which no
one has ever served at the altar. 14 For it is
evident that our Lord was descended [b]from
Judah, and in connection with that tribe
Moses said nothing about priests.
15 This becomes even more evident when
another priest arises in the likeness of
Melchizedek, 16 who has become a priest,
not on the basis of a legal requirement concerning bodily descent, but by the power of
an indestructible life. 17 For it is witnessed
of him,

> [c]"You are a priest forever,
> after the order of Melchizedek."

18 On the one hand, a former commandment is set aside [d]because of its weakness
and uselessness 19 (for [e]the law made nothing perfect); but on the other hand, [f]a better hope is introduced, through which [g]we
draw near to God.
20 And it was not without an oath. For
those who formerly became priests were

3 [t][ver. 6]
4 [u][Acts 2:29; 7:8, 9]
5 [v]Num. 18:21, 26; 2 Chr. 31:4, 5
6 [w][ver. 3] [x]See Rom. 4:13
8 [y][ch. 5:6; 6:20] [z][John 6:57; Rev. 1:17, 18]
11 [a]ver. 18, 19; ch. 8:7; [Gal. 2:21]
14 [b]Isai. 11:1; Mic. 5:2; Matt. 1:3; Luke 3:33; Rev. 5:5
17 [c]ver. 21; ch. 5:6; 6:20; Cited from Ps. 110:4
18 [d]Rom. 8:3; Gal. 4:9
19 [e]ch. 9:9; 10:1; Lev. 16:16; See Acts 13:39 [f]ch. 6:18 [g][ver. 25; Lev. 10:3]; See ch. 4:16

1 Or *brothers and sisters*

Christ, but this is unlikely since terms of comparison and analogy are used: (a) he "resembles the Son of God" (a comparison of the Son with Himself would be odd); (b) the Son became High Priest "after the order of Melchizedek" (6:20) later, through His incarnation, atoning death, and exaltation. In addition, in Gen. 14 Melchizedek is presented as one who has a recognized political position (king of Salem), whereas Old Testament theophanies are brief and exceptional.

without father . . . mother . . . beginning of days nor end of life. While most figures in Genesis are located in a genealogical line, Melchizedek appears without ancestors or progeny, and without notice of his birth or death. The Holy Spirit has described him in a way that is prophetic of Christ.

genealogy. The appointment of priests in the line of Melchizedek is without regard to ancestry, since no genealogy is recorded for this line.

7:4–10 Two actions show Melchizedek's priestly superiority to Abraham's Levite descendants: Abraham gave a tithe to Melchizedek (vv. 4–6, 8–10), and Melchizedek blessed Abraham (vv. 6, 7).

7:5 descendants of Levi. The Levitical priests inherited a right to tax even persons descended from Abraham (Num. 18:21–29).

7:7 the superior. Giving the blessing, like receiving the tenth, clearly demonstrates superiority, in this case the superiority of Melchizedek over Abraham.

7:8 mortal men . . . it is testified that he lives. The "mortal men" are the Levites, whose office and authority is transmitted through descent and inheritance, in association with the provisions of the law (v. 5). Melchizedek, however, "lives." The declaration that he is living is found in Ps. 110:4, quoted in 5:6, and returned to the foreground with the allusions in 6:20 and 7:3. In the next section (vv. 11–28), the importance of this declaration or "oath" is explained (vv. 20–22).

7:9 paid tithes through Abraham. The argument depends on Abraham's representative status as the progenitor of a priestly system based on physical descent; those priests cannot rise above Abraham. The argument does not mean that every person who descended from Abraham participated in whatever Abraham did, simply by reason of physical descent. The text does not imply any preexistence of Levi.

7:11 if perfection had been attainable through the Levitical priesthood. That is, if the Levitical priests had been able to give the people permanent, free access to God. As in 4:8 and 8:7, the author argues that certain promises in the Old Testament itself indicate that the law was imperfect and would be replaced in the "last days" (1:2). The rhetorical question announces that the effectiveness of the Levitical system will be compared with that of "another priest."

under it the people received the law. Because of sin and the need for a ministry of reconciliation, the Levitical priesthood was instituted, together with the Mosaic law that provided for it. The law and the priesthood are being considered together, as one system of religious life. If defective, they will both be changed (v. 12).

7:13–28 The differences between Jesus and the Levites are now quickly reviewed. His descent is from Judah, not Levi (v. 14); He lives eternally (v. 16); His priesthood is founded on the divine oath (v. 20).

7:16 power of an indestructible life. Christ's eternal priesthood (Ps. 110:4) is grounded in the indomitable power of His resurrection (Rom. 6:9, 10).

7:19 See note on v. 11.

a better hope. This hope, together with the divine promise and oath, was mentioned in 6:17, 18. Vv. 20–28 continue the emphasis on the connection between our hope and the certainty of God's promise and oath.

made such without an oath, [21]but this one was made a priest with an oath by the one who said to him:

[h]"The Lord has sworn
and will not change his mind,
'You are a priest forever.'"

[22]This makes Jesus the guarantor of [i]a better covenant.

[23]The former priests were many in number, because they were prevented by death from continuing in office, [24]but he holds his priesthood permanently, because he continues [j]forever. [25]Consequently, he is able to save to the uttermost[1] [k]those who draw near to God [l]through him, since he always lives [m]to make intercession for them.

[26]For it was indeed fitting that we should have such a high priest, [n]holy, innocent, unstained, [o]separated from sinners, and [p]exalted above the heavens. [27]He has no need, like those high priests, to offer sacrifices daily, [q]first for his own sins and then for those of the people, since he did this [r]once for all when he offered up himself. [28]For the law appoints men [s]in their weakness as high priests, but the word of the oath, which came later than the law, appoints a Son who has been made [t]perfect forever.

Jesus, High Priest of a Better Covenant

8 Now the point in what we are saying is this: we have such a high priest, [u]one who is seated at the right hand of the throne of the Majesty in heaven, [2]a minister in the holy places, in [v]the true tent[2] that the Lord [w]set up, not man. [3]For [x]every high priest is appointed to offer gifts and sacrifices; thus [y]it is necessary for this priest also to have something to offer. [4]Now if he were on earth, he would not be a priest at all, since there are priests who offer gifts according to the law. [5]They serve [z]a copy and [a]shadow of the heavenly things. For when Moses was about to erect the tent, he was instructed by God, saying, [b]"See that you make everything according to the pattern that was shown you on the mountain." [6]But as it is, Christ[3] has obtained a ministry that is [c]as much more excellent

1 Or *at all times* (that is, completely) 2 Or *tabernacle*; also verse 5
3 Greek *he*

21 [h]See ver. 17
22 [i]ch. 8:6
24 [j]ver. 21, 28
25 [k][ver. 19] [l][John 14:6] [m]ch. 9:24; See Rom. 8:34
26 [n]Ps. 16:10; Rev. 15:4; 16:5; [Mark 1:24] [o]See ch. 4:15 [p][ch. 8:1]; See ch. 4:14
27 [q]See ch. 5:3 [r]ch. 9:12; 10:10; [ch. 9:28]
28 [s][ch. 5:2] [t]ch. 2:10; 5:9
Chapter 8
1 [u]See Mark 16:19
2 [v]ch. 9:24; [ch. 9:11] [w]Ex. 33:7
3 [x]See ch. 5:1 [y]ch. 9:12-14; 10:9-12; Eph. 5:2
5 [z]ch. 9:23 [a]ch. 10:1; Col. 2:17 [b]Cited from Ex. 25:40
6 [c]ch. 1:4; 2 Cor. 3:6-11

7:21 oath. The divine oath expressed in Ps. 110:4 ("The LORD has sworn") demonstrates the unchangeable permanence of the new priesthood of Jesus (6:17, 18).

7:22 guarantor. This renders a Greek word found only here in the New Testament. Jesus Himself, as the substance of what was promised and the possessor of indestructible resurrection life (v. 16), is the guarantee of a new and better covenant.

covenant. The first of seventeen occurrences of this important word (Greek *diatheke*) in Hebrews. It is the usual translation of the Old Testament word for "covenant" (Hebrew *berith*) in the Greek Old Testament. A "new covenant" was promised in Jer. 31:31–34, which will be cited in 8:8–12 and 10:16, 17.

7:23 priests were many. The reference is to the many high priests who succeeded one another in office. The law of priestly succession (Ex. 29:29, 30) presupposed the eventual death of the priest. This lack of permanence, together with the repetition of the Old Testament sacrifices (10:11), shows the inadequacy of the old order.

7:25 Jesus' eternal life and priesthood make possible His eternal intercession for worshipers who "draw near to God through him," leading to their complete and eternal salvation. "Uttermost" may refer to comprehensive salvation (meeting our every need) or to eternal salvation (especially as it is grounded in Jesus' always living to pray for us).

7:26 holy, innocent, unstained, separated from sinners. In 2:18 and 4:15–5:3, the author showed the importance of Jesus' identification with us in undergoing temptation. But it is also imperative that He be "without sin" (4:15) to be qualified to enter the heavenly sanctuary on our behalf (8:1, 2; 9:11, 12, 24, 25). See "The Sinlessness of Jesus" at 4:15.

7:27 The contrast between the Levitical priests' repeated daily (and yearly) sacrifices and Jesus' once-for-all offering of Himself is developed in 9:25–10:18.

7:28 This verse summarizes the contrast between the old and new covenant priesthood. First, the old covenant priesthood was appointed by law without a divine oath (v. 20), while the eternal priesthood of Christ was appointed by an oath (v. 21). Second, the temporary appointment of weak and sinful (v. 27) men is contrasted with the eternal appointment of the sinless "Son . . . perfect forever."

8:1–6 The discussion of Jesus' qualifications and appointment as the ultimate High Priest now leads to a description of His ministry in the heavenly sanctuary.

8:1 the point. The writer pauses to summarize what has been said thus far. He has explained how Jesus is the new High Priest in the order of Melchizedek—One who "was indeed fitting" (7:26). Now he will tell what Jesus does in this role. The pause reminds us that the writer knows his argument is difficult but that he has a clear purpose in what he says.

8:2 the true tent. See text note. The heavenly temple of God is the original after which the earthly tent and temple were copied (v. 5).

not man. See 9:11, 24. God appointed an earthly sanctuary as a means of His presence among His people, but "the Most High does not dwell in houses made by hands" (Acts 7:48, 49; cf. 1 Kin. 8:27).

8:3 something to offer. Jesus' offering was Himself (7:27), His own blood (9:12) and body (10:10).

8:4 he would not be a priest. Under the provisions of the Mosaic law, Jesus could not be a priest (7:13). Jesus' priestly service is of a different order; it is not a mere supplement to the old system.

8:5 copy and shadow. The tabernacle made by Moses provided for worship modeled after the spiritual realm in which Christ ministers. That tabernacle and its worship pointed forward to God's plan of salvation that would be revealed in Christ.

8:6 The new covenant was better because it was made with an oath (7:22), and now it is seen to rest on "better promises" as well (cited in vv. 8–12). On both counts, the ministry that serves the new covenant is "more excellent."

than the old as [d]the covenant [e]he mediates
is better, since it is enacted on better promises. 7 [f]For if that first covenant had been
faultless, there would have been no occasion to look for a second.
8 For he finds fault with them when he
says:[1]

[g]"Behold, the days are coming,
declares the Lord,
when I will establish a new
covenant with the house of
Israel
and with the house of Judah,
9 not like the covenant that I made
with their fathers
on the day when I took them by
the hand to bring them out of
the land of Egypt.
For they did not continue in my
covenant,
and so I showed no concern for
them, declares the Lord.
10 [h]For this is the covenant that I will
make with the house of Israel
after those days, declares the
Lord:
I will put my laws into their minds,
and [i]write them on their hearts,
and I will be their God,
and they shall be my people.
11 And they shall not teach, each one
his neighbor
and each one his brother, saying,
'Know the Lord,'
for they shall [j]all know me,
from the least of them to the
greatest.
12 For I will be merciful toward their
iniquities,
[k]and I will remember their sins no
more."

13 In speaking of a new covenant, he makes the first one obsolete. And [l]what is becoming obsolete and growing old is ready to vanish away.

The Earthly Holy Place

9 Now even the first covenant had regulations for worship and [m]an earthly place of holiness. 2 For [n]a tent[2] was prepared, the first section, in which were [o]the lampstand and [p]the table and [q]the bread of the Presence.[3] It is called the Holy Place. 3 Behind [r]the second curtain was a second section[4] called the Most Holy Place, 4 having the golden [s]altar of incense and [t]the ark of the covenant covered on all sides with gold, in which was [u]a golden urn holding the manna, and [v]Aaron's staff that budded, and [w]the tablets of the covenant. 5 Above it were [x]the cherubim of glory overshadowing

6 [d]ch. 7:22 [e]ch. 9:15; 12:24; [Gal. 3:19]
7 [f]See ch. 7:11
8 [g]Cited from Jer. 31:31-34
10 [h]ch. 10:16; Rom. 11:27 [i][2 Cor. 3:3]
11 [j]Isai. 54:13; John 6:45; 1 John 2:27
12 [k]ch. 10:17; Rom. 11:27
13 [l][2 Cor. 5:17]
Chapter 9
1 [m]Ex. 25:8
2 [n]Ex. 26:1 [o]Ex. 25:31-39; 26:35; 40:4 [p]Ex. 25:23-29 [q]Ex. 25:30; Lev. 24:5-8
3 [r]Ex. 26:31-33; 40:3, 21
4 [s]Lev. 16:12, 13 [t]Ex. 25:10; 26:33; 40:3, 21; Rev. 11:19 [u]Ex. 16:33, 34 [v]Num. 17:10 [w]Ex. 25:16; 40:20; Deut. 10:2, 5; 1 Kin. 8:9, 21; 2 Chr. 5:10
5 [x]Ex. 25:18-22; [1 Kin. 8:6, 7]

1 Some manuscripts *For finding fault with it he says to them* 2 Or *tabernacle*; also verses 11, 21 3 Greek *the presentation of the loaves* 4 Greek *tent*; also verses 6, 8

he mediates. A legal intermediary who represents two parties and through whose work a new relationship is established. Moses is described as the mediator of the law (Gal. 3:19, 20). Crucial to Christ's mediatorial work was His offering of Himself as an atoning sacrifice for sin (9:14, 15; 12:24; 1 Tim. 2:5, 6).

8:7–13 The promise of a new covenant in Jer. 31:31–34 is a unifying theme of 8:7–10:18, where the word translated "covenant" occurs fourteen times. In addition, it occurs three other places in Hebrews (7:22; 12:24; 13:20) and sixteen times elsewhere in the New Testament.

8:7 God's promise of a new covenant through Jeremiah implied that the first covenant with Israel at Sinai was not faultless. As in 4:8 and 7:11, an Old Testament promise is shown to imply the insufficiency of the old covenant order.

8:8 finds fault with them when he says. While the law was "holy and righteous and good" (Rom. 7:12), it could not in itself empower obedience (7:18, 19), as the quotation from Jer. 31:31–34 makes clear. The result was that the people "did not continue" in that covenant.

8:10 put my laws into their minds. Unlike the law's sacrifices, Christ's death cleanses the conscience (9:9–14), so that we do the will of God (10:36; 13:21).

8:11 shall all know me. Under the law, access to God's presence was restricted (9:7, 8). But now all who come to God through Jesus Christ may enter the true sanctuary (10:19–22).

8:12 I will remember their sins no more. Unlike the repeated sacrifices of the law, which were an annual reminder of sins (10:3), Jesus' offering of Himself has brought forgiveness, holiness, and perfection once for all (10:10, 13, 18).

8:13 obsolete . . . ready to vanish away. The author advances a definition of "obsolete" in order to say that the first covenant was as good as dead from the moment Jeremiah announced the new.

9:1 worship . . . holiness. This verse begins a lengthy comparison of Old Testament sacrifice and the sacrifice of Christ, that continues into ch. 10. The first part is a summary of the Old Testament sanctuary and its activities.

9:3 curtain. This curtain, or veil closed off the Most Holy Place, where God's presence among His people was most intensely revealed (6:19). With Jesus' death, this curtain was torn in two (10:20; Matt. 27:51).

9:4 golden altar of incense. Although this incense altar, was just outside the curtain (Ex. 40:26), its function was so closely associated with the inner chamber and the ark therein (Ex. 30:6) that it was considered to belong there (1 Kin. 6:22). When the high priest entered the Most Holy Place, he burned incense, producing smoke to hide the mercy seat on top of the ark of the Testimony, shielding himself from the Lord's burning purity (Lev. 16:12, 13).

Aaron's staff. The staff that budded to show that priestly privilege comes only by God's appointment (Num. 17:10), as taught in 5:4, 5.

9:5 cherubim of glory. The "mercy seat," comprising the lid of the ark, had on it two figures of cherubim facing each other, representative of God's heavenly courtiers, who serve constantly in His presence.

[y]the mercy seat. Of these things we cannot
now speak in detail.
6 These preparations having thus been
made, [z]the priests go regularly into the first
section, performing their ritual duties, 7 but
into the second only [a]the high priest goes,
and he but [a]once a year, and not without
taking blood, [b]which he offers for himself
and for the unintentional sins of the people. 8 By this the Holy Spirit indicates that
[c]the way into the holy places is not yet
opened as long as the first section is still
standing 9 (which is symbolic for the present age).[1] According to this arrangement,
gifts and sacrifices are offered [d]that cannot
perfect the conscience of the worshiper,
10 but deal only with [e]food and drink and
[f]various washings, regulations for the body
imposed until the time of reformation.

Redemption Through the Blood of Christ

11 But when Christ appeared as a high
priest [g]of the good things that have come,[2]
then through [h]the greater and more perfect
tent ([i]not made with hands, that is, not of
this creation) 12 he [j]entered [k]once for all
into the holy places, not by means of [l]the
blood of goats and calves but [m]by means of
his own blood, [n]thus securing an eternal
redemption. 13 For if the sprinkling of
defiled persons with [o]the blood of goats
and bulls and with [p]the ashes of a heifer
sanctifies[3] for the purification of the flesh,
14 how much more will [q]the blood of Christ,
who through the eternal Spirit [r]offered
himself without blemish to God, [s]purify
our[4] conscience [t]from dead works [u]to serve
the living God.
15 Therefore he is [v]the mediator of a new
covenant, so that [w]those who are called
may [x]receive the promised eternal inheritance, [y]since a death has occurred that
redeems them from the transgressions
committed under the first covenant.[5] 16 For
where a will is involved, the death of the
one who made it must be established.

5 [y]Lev. 16:2
6 [z][Num. 28:3]
7 [a]Lev. 16:15, 34; [ch. 10:3; Ex. 30:10] [b]See ch. 5:3
8 [c]ch. 10:20; [John 14:6]
9 [d]See ch. 7:19
10 [e]See Lev. 11:2 [f]Mark 7:4, 8; See Lev. 11:25
11 [g]ch. 10:1 [h][ver. 24; ch. 8:2] [i]See Mark 14:58
12 [j]ver. 24 [k]ch. 7:27; 10:10 [l]ch. 10:4 [m]See Acts 20:28 [n]Job 33:24; [Dan. 9:24; 1 Cor. 6:20]
13 [o]Lev. 16:14-16 [p]Num. 19:2, 17, 18
14 [q]ver. 12; 1 John 1:7; Rev. 7:14 [r]ch. 7:27; 8:3 [s]ch. 1:3; 10:22 [t]ch. 6:1 [u]Rom. 6:13; 1 Pet. 4:2
15 [v]ch. 8:6; 12:24 [w][ch. 3:1]; See Rom. 8:28 [x][ch. 10:36; Ex. 32:13] [y]Rom. 3:24, 25; 5:6

1 Or *which is symbolic for the age then present* 2 Some manuscripts *good things to come* 3 Or *For if the blood of goats and bulls, and the sprinkling of defiled persons with the ashes of a heifer, sanctifies* 4 Some manuscripts *your* 5 The Greek word means both *covenant* and *will*; also verses 16, 17

Of these things . . . cannot now speak in detail. First-century Jewish writers such as Philo gave great attention to the symbolism of the sanctuary furniture. The author of Hebrews, however, desires to address what took place in the tabernacle, and he says no more about the furniture, whatever symbolic value it might have.

9:6 priests go regularly into the first section. Their task was to replace the showbread (Ex. 25:30; Lev. 24:5–9), to keep the lampstand burning (Ex. 27:20, 21; Lev. 24:1–4), and to burn fragrant incense twice daily, symbolizing the people's prayers (Ex. 30:7–9; Luke 1:8–10; Rev. 8:3).

9:7, 8 That only one person, once a year, and only with special preparation, could enter the Most Holy Place, was the Holy Spirit's revelation through the law that the earthly sanctuary could not be the means of open, confident approach to God. The new covenant promise, "they shall all know me" (8:11), could not be fulfilled in the earthly tent.

9:7 for himself. Levitical priests were themselves in need of atonement, unlike our High Priest, Jesus (5:3; 7:26, 27).

unintentional. See note 5:2.

9:9 symbolic for the present age. The writer interprets the tabernacle ceremonies as prophetic of the time of the gospel (8:5 note). In this case, the ritual requirements display the weakness that the gospel would overcome.

9:11 good things that have come. See text note. Cleansing of conscience and confidence to draw near to God were still to come while the first covenant's sanctuary and sacrifices were in force (10:1), but they have arrived through Christ. The author of Hebrews views the benefits of the age to come as already experienced (in part) by the church (6:5; 12:22–24).

greater and more perfect tent. The heavenly reality behind the law's earthly copy (8:5; 9:24).

9:12 once for all. In contrast to the repetition of sacrifices by the Levitical priests (10:2, 3, 10–14). This emphatic word anticipates the climactic statement in vv. 26–28.

blood of goats and calves. This was used by the high priest on the yearly Day of Atonement to cleanse the Most Holy Place (Lev. 16:11–16).

eternal redemption. A redemption is a purchase by payment of a price or ransom. The effect of Christ's redemption is permanent because it was by His own blood.

9:13 ashes of a heifer. This residue was used with water to purify persons who had touched a corpse (Num. 19:9, 17, 18). Their uncleanness was not moral but ceremonial.

purification of the flesh. They became eligible again for their duties of worship.

9:14 how much more. As in 2:2, 3, the writer uses an argument from the lesser to the greater. The lesser is the blood of animals offered by the high priest on earth; the greater is the blood shed by Christ. The lesser had ceremonial power; the greater can take away guilt from the conscience.

without blemish. A sacrifice must be without defect in order to be an atoning substitute for sinners (Num. 6:14; 1 Pet. 1:19).

dead works. Not works of the law that are useless for justification (Gal. 3:1–14), but sinful deeds that deserve the covenant curse of death (6:1). See "Conscience and the Law" at 1 Sam. 24:5.

to serve the living God. The goal of forgiveness is ultimately God-centered—not merely to free us from the fear of judgment, but to qualify us to worship before God in a way that brings Him pleasure (12:28; 13:15, 16, 21).

9:15 Christ's death inaugurates the new covenant, even as it brings redemption from the curse that rested on violators of the first covenant. See "Christ the Mediator" at 1 Tim. 2:5.

redeems. A payment to release someone from captivity (cf. v. 12). Violation of God's covenant creates a liability to condemnation that can only be satisfied through the violator's death, or by redemption through a substitute.

9:16 where a will is involved. The Greek word for "will" (*diatheke*) is the same word translated "covenant" in this passage and elsewhere. The point being made is that a death is required in order to secure what God

17 For [z]a will takes effect only at death,
since it is not in force as long as the one
who made it is alive. **18** Therefore not even
the first covenant was inaugurated [a]with-
out blood. **19** For when every commandment of the law had been declared by
Moses to all the people, he took [b]the blood
of calves and goats, [c]with water and scarlet
wool and hyssop, and sprinkled both the
book itself and all the people, **20** saying,
[d]"This is the blood of the covenant that
God commanded for you." **21** And in the
same way he sprinkled with the blood both
[e]the tent and all the vessels used in worship. **22** Indeed, under the law almost everything is purified with blood, and [f]without
the shedding of blood there is no forgiveness of sins.

23 Thus it was necessary for [g]the copies of
the heavenly things to be purified with
these rites, but the heavenly things themselves with better sacrifices than these.
24 For Christ has entered, not into holy
places [h]made with hands, which are copies
of the true things, but into heaven itself,
now to appear in the presence of God [i]on
our behalf. **25** Nor was it to offer himself
repeatedly, as [j]the high priest enters [k]the
holy places every year with blood not his
own, **26** for then he would have had to suffer repeatedly since the foundation of the
world. But as it is, [l]he has appeared [m]once
for all [n]at the end of the ages to put away
sin by the sacrifice of himself. **27** And just as
[o]it is appointed for man to die once, and
[p]after that comes judgment, **28** so Christ,
having been offered once [q]to bear the sins
of [r]many, will appear [s]a second time, [t]not
to deal with sin but to save those who are
eagerly [u]waiting for him.

Christ's Sacrifice Once for All

10 For since the law has but [v]a shadow
[w]of the good things to come instead
of the true form of these realities, [x]it can
never, by the same sacrifices that are continually offered every year, make perfect
those who draw near. **2** Otherwise, would
they not have ceased to be offered, since
the worshipers, having once been cleansed,
would no longer have any consciousness of
sin? **3** But [y]in these sacrifices [z]there is a
reminder of sin every year. **4** For [a]it is

17 [z][Gal. 3:15] **18** [a]Ex. 24:6, 8 **19** [b]ver. 12 [c][Lev. 14:4, 7; Num. 19:6, 17 **20** [d]Cited from Ex. 24:8; [Matt. 26:28] **21** [e][Ex. 29:12, 36; Lev. 8:15, 19; 16:14, 16; 2 Chr. 29:22] **22** [f]Lev. 17:11 **23** [g]ch. 8:5 **24** [h]ch. 8:2; [ver. 11] [i]ch. 7:25; See Rom. 8:34 **25** [j]See ver. 7 [k]ch. 10:19 **26** [l]1 John 3:5 [m]ver. 12; ch. 7:27; 10:10; 1 Pet. 3:18 [n][ch. 1:2; 1 Cor. 10:11] **27** [o]See Gen. 3:19 [p]See Matt. 16:27 **28** [q]Isai. 53:12; 1 Pet. 2:24; 3:18 [r]Matt. 20:28; 26:28; Mark 10:45; Rev. 5:9 [s]Acts 1:11 [t]See ch. 4:15 [u]Tit. 2:13; [Isai. 25:9]

Chapter 10 **1** [v]ch. 8:5; Col. 2:17 [w]ch. 9:11 [x][ch. 9:9] **3** [y]See ch. 9:7 [z]Lev. 16:21 **4** [a]ver. 11

promised to do. If the writer is not speaking of a last will, he is probably referring to the ratification of a covenant by means of a representative sacrifice such as is found in Gen. 15.

9:19 Moses . . . took the blood. The immediate reference is to Ex. 24:4–8. In this ceremony God, the author of the scroll, and the people of the congregation were sworn to the covenant with its penalties.

9:20 This is the blood. The covenant was written down on the scroll, but it had to be ratified with the offering of blood. This blood was not shed by those who might have broken the covenant, but by animals that substituted for them (cf. Gen. 15:9–18; Jer. 34:18–20). All this was a vivid demonstration that the ultimate sanction, or penalty, of the covenant was death.

9:21–24 The sanctuary, the meeting place of the holy God with sinful people, must itself be purified through sacrificial blood, the only means of forgiveness. This is true not only of the earthly tent of the old covenant (vv. 21, 22) but also of the heavenly reality (vv. 23, 24), which was purified by Christ's sacrifice on the cross (v. 23 note).

9:22 almost everything. The tent and its furniture were so closely identified with the worshipers who met God there that the sacrificial blood needed for the worshipers to be forgiven (10:18) was also required to cleanse the instruments and environment of their worship (Lev. 16:16).

without the shedding of blood there is no forgiveness. This is the fundamental principle (Lev. 17:11), now restated after being introduced in vv. 16–18. Having established it, the writer turns his attention from the earthly sanctuary to the heavenly.

9:23 the heavenly things themselves with better sacrifices. The heavenly sanctuary itself does not need to be purified from defilement by human sin. However, just as the earthly sanctuary was purified by sacrificial blood and set apart as the place where sinful humans could approach God, so also the true, heavenly sanctuary has now been set apart by the sacrifice of Christ as a meeting place for sinful people to enter, drawing near to God through the blood of Jesus (10:19–22; 12:24).

9:24 appear in the presence of God on our behalf. Just as the high priest appeared for Israel on the Day of Atonement (Lev. 16:32, 33).

9:25 repeatedly. The same Greek word is in v. 26 and in 10:11. The repetition of sacrifices was evidence that they were not effective to remove guilt (10:2), and it was a recurring reminder of sins (10:3). The author earlier stressed that the Day of Atonement ceremonies took place only once a year (v. 7); here the emphasis is that they are repeated again and again (10:1).

blood not his own. The high priest's offering contrasts with Christ's offering of Himself. As one who himself needed atonement (v. 7), no Levitical high priest could offer himself as an unblemished substitute for others (v. 14).

9:26 foundation of the world . . . end of the ages. These phrases set forth a vast span of time, during all of which Christ had to offer Himself only once. The "end of the ages" is the same as the "last days" (1:2), a period ushered in by the death, resurrection, and ascension of Christ.

9:27 to die once, and after that comes judgment. Thus both reincarnation and the belief that physical death is the end of personal existence are excluded. Christ suffered the common human destiny of death and judgment (v. 28), but for Him the judgment consisted in resurrection and vindication (1 Tim. 3:16). This vindication will be fully manifested when He comes again (1 Thess. 1:10). See "Death and the Intermediate State" at Phil. 1:23.

9:28 to bear the sins of many. An intentional reference to the Suffering Servant in Is. 53:12.

10:1 a shadow of the good things to come. The "good things" were future with respect to the law, which foreshadowed them; with Christ's coming they are present (9:11 note).

make perfect. The worshipers could not be "cleansed" for all time (v. 2). The law could not remove guilt from them and give them permanent access to God (7:11, 19; 9:9).

10:2 The sacrifices were repeated again and again, showing that they provided no lasting solution to the problem of sin.

10:3 reminder of sin. The Old Testament sacrifices were a public notice,

impossible for the blood of bulls and goats
to take away sins.
5 Consequently, [b]when Christ[1] came into
the world, he said,

[c]"Sacrifices and offerings you have not
desired,
but a body have you prepared
for me;
6 in burnt offerings and sin offerings
you have taken no pleasure.
7 Then I said, 'Behold, I have come to
do your will, O God,
as it is written of me in the scroll
of the book.'"

8 When he said above, "You have neither
desired nor taken pleasure in [c]sacrifices
and offerings and burnt offerings and sin
offerings" (these are offered according to
the law), 9 then he added, [d]"Behold, I have
come to do your will." He abolishes the
first in order to establish the second. 10 And
by that will [e]we have been sanctified
through the offering of [f]the body of Jesus
Christ [g]once for all.
11 And every priest stands [h]daily at his
service, [i]offering repeatedly the same sacrifices, [j]which can never take away sins.
12 But when Christ[2] had offered for all time
a single sacrifice for sins, he [k]sat down at
the right hand of God, 13 waiting from that
time [l]until his enemies should be made a
footstool for his feet. 14 For by a single offering [m]he has perfected for all time those
who are being sanctified.
15 And the Holy Spirit also bears witness
to us; for after saying,

16 [n]"This is the covenant that I will make
with them
after those days, declares the Lord:
I will put my laws on their hearts,
and write them on their minds,"

17 then he adds,

[o]"I will remember their sins and their
lawless deeds no more."

18 Where there is forgiveness of these, there
is no longer any offering for sin.

The Full Assurance of Faith

19 [p]Therefore, brothers,[3] since we have
confidence to enter [q]the holy places by the
blood of Jesus, 20 by [r]the new and living
way that he opened for us through [s]the

5 [b][ch. 1:6] [c]Cited from Ps. 40:6-8
8 [c][See ver. 5 above]
9 [d]ver. 7
10 [e]ch. 2:11; 13:12 [f]Matt. 26:26; Mark. 14:22; Luke 22:19; 1 Cor. 11:24; [ver. 5] [g]ch. 7:27; 9:12
11 [h][Num. 28:3] [i]See ch. 5:1 [j]ver. 1, 4; [ch. 9:9]
12 [k]ch. 1:3; See Mark. 16:19
13 [l]ch. 1:13; [1 Cor. 15:25-28]
14 [m]ver. 1
16 [n]ch. 8:10; Rom. 11:27; Cited from Jer. 31:33
17 [o]ch. 8:12; Cited from Jer. 31:34
19 [p]See ch. 4:16 [q]ch. 9:25
20 [r]ch. 9:8; [John 10:9; 14:6] [s]ch. 9:3

[1] Greek *he* [2] Greek *this one* [3] Or *brothers and sisters*

before God and humanity, that the people were still sinners (Num. 5:15). In the new covenant, God will "remember" their sins "no more" (8:12; 10:17).

10:4 The inadequacy of the Old Testament sacrifices is sharply expressed in such passages as 1 Sam. 15:22; Is. 1:10–17; Amos 5:21–24; Mic. 6:6–8. The law was frustrated by the sin of the people (8:8–12; Rom. 8:3, 4).

10:5–10 Ps. 40:6–8 is here interpreted to point to the replacement of the Old Testament system of animal sacrifice by the obedience and atoning death of Christ.

10:5 a body have you prepared for me. The Hebrew text of Ps. 40:6 reads, "God has opened my ear" (cf. Is. 50:5). Hebrews follows the Septuagint (Greek Old Testament) translation of the verse, speaking of the readiness of the whole person ("the body") and not only a representative part (the ears). The "body . . . prepared for me" is the humanity assumed by Christ in the course of His full obedience to the Father (2:14; 5:8).

10:7 the book. Ultimately the Old Testament as a whole, which points to Christ (Luke 24:27, 45–47).

10:8 sacrifices and offerings and burnt offerings and sin offerings. These terms sum up the whole Levitical sacrificial system. Over against all this (called "the first" in v. 9) Christ has another sacrifice ("the second"). Although instituted by God in the Law (2:2; 8:9; 12:18–21, 25), the Levitical system was not the means willed by God to remove His people's sin permanently.

10:9 to do your will. He will be obedient through suffering (2:10; 5:8), atoning for sin through the sacrifice of His body (v. 10).

abolishes the first. That is, the Levitical sacrificial system of the Old Testament (8:13).

10:10 by that will. The unchanging purpose of God, which Jesus Christ willingly accomplished, brought salvation to us (vv. 7, 9 and notes).

we have been sanctified. Here and in v. 14 the topic is not the process of sanctification (as in 12:14), but the once-for-all change in our status when we are united with Christ by faith, and in this way are separated from sin's pollution and qualified for the worship of God. Being "cleansed," "sanctified," and "made perfect" are virtually synonymous in Hebrews.

10:11 every priest stands daily at his service. The daily morning and evening sacrifices, no less than the yearly Day of Atonement offerings, announce by their repetition that they cannot take sin's guilt away. A further contrast (standing versus sitting) emblematic of the difference between the Levitical priesthood and the priesthood of Christ is introduced.

10:12 sat down. In contrast to the Levitical priests who stand and whose work is never done, Jesus "sat down at the right hand of God," as Ps. 110:1 announces (1:3; cf. 1:13; 8:1).

10:15 the Holy Spirit also bears witness. With other New Testament books, Hebrews affirms that the Spirit is the primary author of Scripture (3:7; 9:8; Acts 4:25). The two quotations following from Jer. 31 mark the beginning (8:8) and the end of the important argument developed from that passage.

10:16, 17 The two quotations from Jer. 31 demonstrate that Christ's once-for-all sacrifice results in both the inner transformation or sanctification of the believer (v. 16), and in the forgiveness of sins or justification (v. 17).

10:19 Therefore, brothers. The writer includes himself with the readers in a renewed appeal for confidence, or boldness, in approaching God. This confidence is grounded, not in any merits we possess, but in the person and work of our great High Priest who is able to "sympathize with our weaknesses" (4:15).

to enter . . . by the blood of Jesus. Not only Jesus on our behalf (9:24), but also we ourselves enter into God's heavenly sanctuary through dependence on Jesus' sacrifice.

curtain, that is, through his flesh, 21 and
since we have [t]a great priest over the house
of God, 22 let us draw near with a true heart
in full assurance of faith, with our hearts
[u]sprinkled clean [v]from an evil conscience
and our bodies [w]washed with pure water.
23 [x]Let us hold fast the confession of our
hope without wavering, for [y]he who promised is faithful. 24 And [z]let us consider how
to stir up one another to love and good
works, 25 [a]not neglecting to meet together,
as is the habit of some, but encouraging
one another, and [b]all the more as you see
[c]the Day drawing near.

26 For [d]if we go on sinning deliberately
[e]after receiving the knowledge of the truth,
[f]there no longer remains a sacrifice for sins,
27 [g]but a fearful expectation of judgment,
and [h]a fury of fire that will consume the
adversaries. 28 [i]Anyone who has set aside
the law of Moses dies without mercy [j]on
the evidence of two or three witnesses.
29 How much worse punishment, do you
think, will be deserved by the one [k]who has
spurned the Son of God, and has profaned
[l]the blood of the covenant [m]by which he
was sanctified, and has [n]outraged the Spirit
of grace? 30 For we know him who said,
[o]"Vengeance is mine; I will repay." And
again, [p]"The Lord will judge his people."
31 [q]It is a fearful thing to fall into the hands
of the living God.

32 But recall the former days when, after
[r]you were enlightened, you endured [s]a
hard struggle with sufferings, 33 sometimes
being [t]publicly exposed to reproach and
affliction, and sometimes being partners
with those so treated. 34 For [u]you had compassion on those in prison, and [v]you joyfully accepted the plundering of your
property, since you knew that you yourselves had [w]a better possession and an

21 [t]Zech. 6:11-13; [ch. 4:14]; See ch. 2:17 **22** [u]Ezek. 36:25; [ch. 12:24; 2 Cor. 7:1; 1 Pet. 1:2] [v]ch. 9:14 [w][1 Cor. 6:11] **23** [x]ch. 4:14 [y]ch. 11:11; See 1 Cor. 1:9 **24** [z][ch. 3:13] **25** [a][Acts 2:42] [b]Rom. 13:11-13 [c]See 1 Cor. 3:13 **26** [d]Num. 15:30; Deut. 17:12 [e]ch. 6:4; 2 Pet. 2:20, 21 [f][ch. 6:6; 1 John 5:16] **27** [g]ch. 2:3; 12:25 [h]Ps. 79:5; Isai. 26:11; Zeph. 1:18; 3:8; [Ezek. 36:5; Zech. 8:2]; See 2 Thess. 1:8 **28** [i]Deut. 17:2-6

[j]See Num. 35:30 **29** [k][ch. 6:6] [l]ch. 13:20; Zech. 9:11 [m]ch. 9:13, 14 [n][Matt. 12:31; 32; Eph. 4:30 **30** [o]Rom. 12:19; Cited from Deut. 32:35 [p]Ps. 50:4; 135:14; Cited from Deut. 32:36 **31** [q]Isai. 33:14; Luke 12:5 **32** [r]ch. 6:4 [s]See Phil. 1:30 **33** [t]1 Cor. 4:9 (Gk.) **34** [u][ch. 13:3; Matt. 25:36; 2 Tim. 1:16] [v]See Matt. 5:12 [w]1 Pet. 1:4

10:20 the curtain, that is, through his flesh. In a surprising figure of speech, the author identifies the veil of the temple as Jesus' body. The analogy lies in that just as the veil of the temple was torn to open the way into the Most Holy Place (6:19; 9:3; Matt. 27:51), so also Christ's body was torn so that His blood might be shed to open the way into the heavenly sanctuary (v. 19). The parallel is figurative and is not to be pressed.

10:21 over the house of God. See note 3:6.

10:22 draw near. See note 4:16.

full assurance of faith. The call for faith hints at the subject of ch. 11.

our hearts sprinkled . . . and our bodies washed. The inner cleansing of conscience that makes Jesus' death superior to the sacrifices under the law (9:13, 14) is visibly symbolized in baptism (Eph. 5:26). As the high priest washed his body with water in preparation for entering the Most Holy Place (Lev. 16:4; Ex. 29:4), so we may enter now as priests into God's presence.

10:23 hold fast the confession of our hope. In another Hebrews passage mentioning "the house of God" (v. 21; cf. 3:1–14), there is a similar exhortation to be "firm" (3:14), and a similar assurance that Christ "is faithful" (cf. 3:5, 6). Probably "our original confidence" (3:14), like the "confession of our hope" (v. 23), refers to the time of baptism (note the term "water" in v. 22) and entrance into the church (v. 32).

10:24 consider how to stir up one another. The duty of encouraging one another can find expression in the church meetings (v. 25). "Love" completes a familiar triad with "faith" (v. 22) and "hope" (v. 23). This triad seems to have played a prominent role in the teaching of the early church (1 Cor. 13:13; Col. 1:4, 5; 1 Thess. 1:3).

10:25 not neglecting to meet together. The believers had been severely persecuted (vv. 32–34). Assembling with other believers is an important part of Christian life. See "The Local Church" at Rev. 2:1.

the Day drawing near. The day of Jesus' appearance a second time to bring salvation to those who wait for Him (9:28; 12:26, 27).

10:26 sinning deliberately. Christians who claim to be sinless are self-deluded (1 John 1:8), and those who sin should not despair of grace (4:16; 1 John 2:1, 2). The willful sin here is abandoning one's confession altogether, trampling the Son underfoot, treating His sacrificial blood as unclean, and insulting God's gracious Spirit (6:6 note; 10:29). The seriousness of the charge is indicated by its willfulness (cf. Num. 15:30) and the measure of knowledge or enlightenment it refuses (cf. Heb. 6:4; 10:32).

no longer remains a sacrifice for sins. Since God has set aside the Levitical system of animal sacrifices (v. 9), those who abandon their confession of trust in Christ have nowhere to turn for forgiveness.

10:28 set aside the law of Moses. That is, turned from God to idols (Deut. 17:2–7).

10:29 This argument, from the law as the lesser to the gospel as the greater, is also found in 2:2, 3. If contemptuous violation of the law given through Moses the servant (3:5) warranted the punishment of death, then scorn for the Son of God (1:2, 3; 3:6; 6:6; 2 Pet. 2:1), His sacrificial blood (9:20; cf. Ex. 24:8; Mark 14:24), and the Spirit of grace through whom He offered Himself (9:14) deserves nothing less than "a fury of fire that will consume the adversaries" (v. 27).

10:30 The Lord will judge his people. The two quotations from the Song of Moses (Deut. 32:35, 36) show that God is ready to judge according to His covenant, discriminating those who are truly His own from apostates (cf. 1 Pet. 4:17).

10:31 A fitting conclusion to the grave warning of this passage.

10:32–39 As in 6:9–12, the writer now balances his severe warning with an encouraging reminder that his readers have exhibited the fruits of grace, especially by their mutual support in the face of earlier suffering.

10:32 endured a hard struggle. Even when they were new in the faith, these Christians suffered persecution.

10:33 Public insult, imprisonment, and the seizure of property (but not martyrdom, 12:4) were among the forms of persecution that the recipients previously suffered. These may reflect conditions after the edict of Claudius (A.D. 49) evicted Jews from Rome (Introduction: Date and Occasion).

10:34 you had compassion . . . joyfully accepted. It would encourage the readers to remember the solidarity and joy they shared, despite persecution.

better possession. The heavenly city and country of God (11:10, 16; 12:22), that cannot be shaken by the cataclysm that will destroy the present created order (12:27, 28). In comparison to this eternal inheritance (9:15), property lost for Christ's sake is of no value.

abiding one. 35 Therefore do not throw
away your confidence, which has [x]a great
reward. 36 For [y]you have need of endurance,
so that [z]when you have done the will of
God you may [a]receive what is promised.
37 For,

[b]"Yet a little while,
and [c]the coming one will come and
will not delay;
38 [d]but my righteous one shall live by
faith,
and if he shrinks back,
my soul has no pleasure in him."

39 But we are not of those who shrink back
and are destroyed, but of those who have
faith and preserve their souls.

By Faith

11 Now faith is the assurance of things
hoped for, the conviction of [e]things
not seen. 2 For by it the people of old
received their commendation. 3 By faith we
understand that the universe was created
by [f]the word of God, so that what is seen
was not made out of [g]things that are visible.
4 By faith [h]Abel offered to God [i]a more
acceptable sacrifice than Cain, through
which he was commended as righteous,
God commending him by accepting his
gifts. And [j]through his faith, though he
died, he [k]still speaks. 5 By faith [l]Enoch was
taken up so that he should not see death,
and he was not found, because God had
taken him. Now before he was taken he
was commended as having pleased God.
6 And without faith it is impossible to
please him, for whoever would draw near
to God [m]must believe that he exists and
[m]that he rewards those who seek him. 7 By
faith [n]Noah, being warned by God concerning [o]events as yet unseen, in reverent
fear constructed an ark for the saving of his
household. By this he condemned the
world and became an heir of [p]the righteousness that comes by faith.
8 By faith [q]Abraham obeyed when he was
called to go out to a place [r]that he was to
receive as an inheritance. And he went out,
not knowing where he was going. 9 By faith
he went to live in [s]the land of promise, as
in a foreign land, [t]living in tents [u]with Isaac
and Jacob, heirs with him of the same
promise. 10 For he was looking forward to
[v]the city that has [w]foundations, [x]whose

35 [x]ch. 2:2; 11:26 **36** [y]ch. 12:1-7; Luke 21:19; Rom. 2:7; 12:12; See Matt. 10:22 [z]ch. 13:21; [1 John 2:17] [a]ch. 11:39 **37** [b]Isai. 26:20; Hag. 2:6; Luke 18:8 [c]Cited from Hab. 2:3, 4 **38** [d]Rom. 1:17; Gal. 3:11
Chapter 11
1 [e]Rom. 8:24; 2 Cor. 4:18; 5:7; 1 Pet. 1:8 **3** [f]See Gen. 1:1 [g][Rom. 4:17] **4** [h]Gen. 4:4-8; 1 John 3:12 [i]Prov. 15:8 [j]Gen. 4:10 [k]ch. 12:24 **5** [l]Gen. 5:22-24; [2 Kin. 2:11] **6** [m]1 Chr. 28:9; Jer. 29:12-14; [John 4:24] **7** [n]Gen. 6:13-22; Luke 17:26; 1 Pet. 3:20 [o]ver. 1 [p]Rom. 4:13; [Gen. 6:9; Ezek. 14:14, 20]
8 [q]Gen. 12:1-4; Acts 7:2-4 [r]Gen. 12:7 **9** [s]Acts 7:5 [t]Gen. 12:8; 13:3, 18; 18:1, 9 [u]Gen. 35:27 **10** [v]ch. 12:22; [ch. 13:14] [w]Ps. 87:1; Rev. 21:14 [x]Rev. 21:2, 10

10:35 great reward. Like Moses, we must fix our eyes on the future reward (11:26).

10:36 done the will of God. His laws are written in their hearts (8:10; 10:16), so they follow in the footsteps of Jesus, who came to do God's will (vv. 9, 10; 13:21).

receive what is promised. See note 6:12.

10:37, 38 Three elements from Hab. 2:3, 4 will be illustrated in the lives of Old Testament people of faith: (a) faith fixes its sights on the One who is coming, hoping in His future appearing (11:1, 7, 10, 13, 20, 22, 27); (b) faith receives God's verdict of righteousness (11:4, 7; 12:23); (c) faith does not draw back in the face of suffering (11:24–26, 35–38).

10:39 The substance of this encouragement is like that of 6:9, 10. Here the writer has included himself, saying "we" instead of "you."

11:1–40 This famous discourse on faithful men and women of the Old Testament begins and ends with commentary that alerts the reader to the specific aspect of Old Testament faith highlighted here—the certainty of receiving what God has promised but not yet given (vv. 1, 2, 39, 40).

11:1 things hoped for . . . things not seen. For the time being, only faith can see the future, as it receives the promises of God.

11:2 received their commendation. God declared that they were righteous by faith (v. 4 note), as is explicitly stated regarding Abel and Enoch (vv. 4, 5; cf. v. 39).

11:3 Although no human witnessed the creation, we know from Scripture that God brought the world into being through His Word (Ps. 33:6, 9). We discern that "what is seen" is not ultimate, self-existent reality.

11:4 a more acceptable sacrifice. The principle that sacrifices were worthless without faith was true from the beginning (cf. 10:4 note). It was for Christ alone to offer not only a better but a perfect sacrifice.

commended . . . commending. The Greek word used twice in this verse is also found in vv. 2, 5, and 39. Abel is the first example of one who received this divine commendation as a righteous one who lived by faith (cf. 10:38; Rom. 1:17). The entire chapter offers such examples.

still speaks. As one of the "cloud of witnesses" (12:1).

11:5 As one who did "not see death" (cf. Gen. 5:18–24), Enoch prefigured the deliverance from death into which Jesus leads the faithful.

pleased God. Pleasing God is the criterion of appropriate worship (12:28; 13:16, 21; Rom. 12:1; Phil. 4:18).

11:6 Faith is an absolute necessity, whether to perceive the things for which we should hope (v. 1), to understand that God is the Creator of all (v. 3), or to offer acceptable worship (v. 4). See "Pleasing God" at 1 Thess. 2:4.

11:7 events as yet unseen. Although faith perceives things that are invisible because they transcend the physical universe (11:3, 27), in this section the emphasis is on faith concerning things that are future but nevertheless certain because God has promised them. The coming flood of judgment was not yet visible when God's word of warning came to Noah. Noah built the ark in reverent response to God's warning, and through his active faith his family received salvation. The unbelieving world was condemned for its preoccupation with the present, and Noah inherited the righteousness that comes by faith (10:38; Rom. 4:13).

11:8–10 Abraham's faith regarding the promise of a homeland was demonstrated: (a) when he obeyed God's voice, leaving Ur for a future inheritance, the location of which he did not know (v. 8); (b) when he lived as a stranger in the land promised to him (vv. 9, 13); and (c) when he looked beyond Canaan to a lasting, heavenly country and city, designed and built by God Himself (vv. 10, 14–16; 13:14).

designer and builder is God. 11 By faith
[y]Sarah herself received power to conceive,
even when she was past the age, since she
considered [z]him faithful who had promised. 12 Therefore from one man, and [a]him
as good as dead, were born descendants
[b]as many as the stars of heaven and as
many as the innumerable grains of sand by
the seashore.
13 These all died in faith, [c]not having
received the things promised, but [d]having
seen them and greeted them from afar, and
[e]having acknowledged that they were
[f]strangers and exiles on the earth. 14 For
people who speak thus make it clear that
they are seeking a homeland. 15 If they had
been thinking of that land from which they
had gone out, [g]they would have had
opportunity to return. 16 But as it is, they
desire a better country, that is, a heavenly
one. Therefore God is not ashamed [h]to be
called their God, for [i]he has prepared for
them a city.
17 By faith [j]Abraham, when he was tested,
offered up Isaac, and he who had received
the promises was in the act of offering
up his only son, 18 of whom it was said,
[k]"Through Isaac shall your offspring be
named." 19 [l]He considered that God was
able even to raise him from the dead, from
which, figuratively speaking, he did receive
him back. 20 By faith [m]Isaac invoked future
blessings on Jacob and Esau. 21 By faith
[n]Jacob, when dying, blessed each of the
sons of Joseph, [o]bowing in worship over
the head of his staff. 22 By faith [p]Joseph, at
the end of his life, made mention of the
exodus of the Israelites and gave directions
concerning his bones.
23 By faith [q]Moses, when he was born,
was hidden for three months by his parents, because they saw that the child was
beautiful, and they were not afraid of [r]the
king's edict. 24 By faith Moses, when he was
grown up, [s]refused to be called the son of
Pharaoh's daughter, 25 [t]choosing rather to
be mistreated with the people of God than
to enjoy [u]the fleeting pleasures of sin. 26 [v]He
considered the reproach of Christ greater
wealth than the treasures of Egypt, for he
was looking to [w]the reward. 27 By faith he
[x]left Egypt, [y]not being afraid of the anger of
the king, for he endured [z]as seeing him

11 [y]Gen. 17:19; 18:11-14; 21:2 [z]ch. 10:23 **12** [a]Rom. 4:19 [b]Gen. 22:17; 32:12; See Gen. 15:5 **13** [c]ver. 39 [d]ver. 27; John 8:56; [Matt. 13:17] [e]Gen. 23:4; 47:9; [1 Chr. 29:15; Ps. 39:12] [f]Eph. 2:19 **15** [g][Gen. 24:6-8 **16** [h]Gen. 26:24; 28:13; Ex. 3:6; 4:5; [ch. 2:11] [i][ver. 10; Matt. 25:34; John 14:2] **17** [j]Gen. 22:1-10; James 2:21 **18** [k]Rom. 9:7; Cited from Gen. 21:12 **19** [l]Rom. 4:17-21 **20** [m]Gen. 27:27-29, 39, 40 **21** [n]Gen. 48:16, 20 [o][Gen. 47:31] **22** [p]Gen. 50:24, 25; Ex. 18:19 **23** [q]Ex. 2:2, 3; Acts 7:20 [r]Ex. 1:16, 22 **24** [s]Ex. 2:10, 11 **25** [t][Job 36:21; Ps. 84:10] [u]1 John 2:17 **26** [v]ch. 13:13; [Ps. 89:50, 51; Phil. 3:7, 8; 1 Pet. 4:14] [w]ch. 2:2; 10:35 **27** [x]Ex. 12:37; 13:17, 18 [y]Ex. 10:28, 29 [z]ver. 13; See 1 Tim. 1:17

11:11, 12 Abraham's faith regarding the promise of descendants was rewarded with the conception of Isaac, which was miraculous, since Sarah was barren and Abraham was (with respect to the possibility of reproduction) "as good as dead" (Rom. 4:19). Despite misguided alternatives (Gen. 16:1–4) and questioning doubts (Gen. 17:17, 18), in the end Abraham and Sarah "considered him faithful who had promised" (v. 11).

11:13–16 The inheritance on which the patriarchs' faith was fixed was invisible for two reasons: it was heavenly, not earthly; and future, not present. See notes on vv. 8–10, 20, 21, 22.

11:13 having seen them . . . afar. Abraham saw from afar the day that Jesus the Messiah would come, and rejoiced (John 8:56).

strangers and exiles on the earth. All the heirs of salvation are homeless refugees on the earth (v. 38) because, until Christ's return, we are in exile from the home we are waiting to inherit (1 Pet. 1:1, 4, 5, 17; 2:11).

11:16 a better country. The Old Testament believers themselves realized that the hope and promises to which they looked forward in faith were heavenly, and not merely physical.

11:17–19 The ultimate test of Abraham's faith was the sacrifice of Isaac. Isaac was the "only son" (cf. John 3:16) so far as the promises were concerned (v. 19)—neither Abraham's servant Eliezer (Gen. 15:2) nor his other son Ishmael (Gen. 17:20, 21) would do. If Isaac were to perish without offspring, the promises of God would fail. Abraham's readiness to slay the son of promise at God's command could arise from nothing less than the conviction that "God was able even to raise . . . the dead" (v. 19). Isaac's "resurrection" was only figurative, but believers who have died for their faith look forward to a literal resurrection (cf. v. 35), in which Jesus has led the way (13:20).

11:20 future blessings. That Jacob would possess a fruitful land, and have dominion over nations, including the descendants of Esau (Gen. 27:27–29).

11:21 In his blessing, Jacob foresaw that the descendants of Joseph's younger son would surpass those of Joseph's older son, in numbers and influence (Gen. 48:13–20). Jacob himself was a younger brother who had been elevated over an older one.

11:22 Joseph remembered the promise of the Exodus that had first been spoken to Abraham long before Isaac's birth (Gen. 15:13, 14) and that would await fulfillment through four more centuries of oppression. Joseph's instructions to take his bones to the Promised Land expressed faith in things not yet seen (Ex. 13:19).

11:23–28 Prominent aspects of the faith associated with Moses are fearlessness (vv. 23, 27), and willingness to suffer disgrace instead of enjoying sin's temporary pleasure (vv. 24–26).

11:23 the child was beautiful. The description is quoted from Ex. 2:2 (cf. Acts 7:20). Moses' parents understood upon seeing him that the child would have a special role in God's redemptive plan.

11:25, 26 Moses' decision to forfeit "the treasures of Egypt" and to suffer "the reproach of Christ" should encourage those who have lost possessions and suffered insult for their faith (10:33, 34). In their present trials, in which identification with Christ means expulsion from the camp of Israel, they must be willing to bear His disgrace (13:13). Moses' choice exemplifies certainty of what he hoped for (v. 1), since he was looking ahead to his reward (10:35; 11:6, 13).

11:27 left Egypt, not being afraid. This is often taken to refer to the first time Moses left Egypt. Moses, having chosen to identify himself with his own people against the Egyptians (vv. 24, 25), had killed an Egyptian and had to flee. About this departure, Ex. 2:14 says that he "was afraid." If this verse does refer to the flight to Midian, the phrase "not being afraid" probably refers to Moses' unshakable faith in God's redemptive plan. Although Moses experienced the quite natural apprehension that Pharaoh would do him personal harm if he stayed in Egypt, he did not fear that his divine commission to rescue God's people was in jeopardy. With this hope in God's purposes he left and "endured" in Midian.

who is invisible. 28 By faith [a]he kept the
Passover and sprinkled the blood, so that
the Destroyer of the firstborn might not
touch them.
29 By faith [b]the people crossed the Red
Sea as if on dry land, but the Egyptians,
when they attempted to do the same, were
drowned. 30 By faith [c]the walls of Jericho fell
down after they had been encircled for
seven days. 31 By faith [d]Rahab the prostitute
did not perish with those who were disobedient, because she [e]had given a friendly welcome to the spies.
32 And what more shall I say? For time
would fail me to tell of [f]Gideon, [g]Barak,
[h]Samson, [i]Jephthah, of [j]David and [k]Samuel
and the prophets—33 who through faith
conquered kingdoms, enforced justice,
obtained promises, [l]stopped the mouths
of lions, 34 [m]quenched the power of fire,
escaped the edge of the sword, were made
strong out of weakness, [n]became mighty
in war, [n]put foreign armies to flight.
35 [o]Women received back their dead by resurrection. Some were tortured, refusing to
accept release, so that they might rise again
to a better life. 36 Others suffered mocking
and flogging, and even [p]chains and imprisonment. 37 [q]They were stoned, they were
sawn in two,[1] [r]they were killed with the
sword. [s]They went about in skins of sheep
and goats, destitute, afflicted, mistreated—
38 of whom the world was not worthy—
[t]wandering about in deserts and mountains, and in dens and caves of the earth.
39 And all these, [u]though commended
through their faith, [u]did not receive what
was promised, 40 since God had provided
something better for us, [v]that apart from us
they should not be made perfect.

Jesus, Founder and Perfecter of Our Faith

12 Therefore, since we are surrounded
by so great a cloud of witnesses, let
us also lay aside every weight, and [w]sin
which clings so closely, and [x]let us run
[y]with endurance the race that is [z]set before
us, 2 looking to Jesus, the founder and

28 [a]Ex. 12:21-30 29 [b]Ex. 14:21-30 30 [c]Josh. 6:15, 16, 20 31 [d]Josh. 6:25; James 2:25 [e]Josh. 2:1, 8-13 32 [f]Judg. 6:11 [g]Judg. 4:6 [h]Judg. 13:24 [i]Judg. 11:1 [j]1 Sam. 16:1, 13 [k]1 Sam. 1:20 33 [l]Judg. 14:6; 1 Sam. 17:35; Dan. 6:22 34 [m]Dan. 3:25 [n]Judg. 7:21; 1 Sam. 17:51; 2 Sam. 12:29 35 [o]1 Kin. 17:22; 2 Kin. 4:35 36 [p]Gen. 39:20; Jer. 20:2; 37:15 37 [q]1 Kin. 21:13; 2 Chr. 24:21 [r]1 Kin. 19:10; Jer. 26:23 [s]2 Kin. 1:8

38 [t]1 Sam. 22:1; 1 Kin. 18:4; 19:9 39 [u]ver. 2, 13; [1 Pet. 1:12] 40 [v][Rev. 6:11]
Chapter 12 1 [w]See Eph. 4:22 [x]See 1 Cor. 9:24 [y]See ch. 10:36 [z]ch. 6:18

1 Some manuscripts add *they were tempted*

It is possible, however, that this verse refers to the Exodus; here Moses clearly was without fear. If so, v. 27 mentions the Exodus in a general way, with details such as the Passover and the parting of the Red Sea following in vv. 28, 29.

11:28 sprinkled the blood. Moses directed that blood be sprinkled on the doorframes of Israelite homes in expectation of the coming destruction of firstborn children in the land, and of the deliverance of Israelite households from this awful event (Ex. 12:7, 12, 13). This was yet another act of confidence in what was not yet seen.

11:30 The Israelites marched around Jericho seven times in obedience to the Lord's command. Their only knowledge that this would defeat the city was provided by God's promise, "I have given Jericho into your hand" (Josh. 6:2).

11:31 Rahab proved her allegiance to God when she protected the Israelite spies. She was justified (James 2:25) and became an ancestor of Jesus Christ (Matt. 1:5), even though she had been a prostitute.

11:32 what more shall I say. The question is rhetorical. The author proceeds to mention in passing many more names and acts of heroism to show the power of faith (vv. 32–38).

11:32–38 The list of accomplishments through faith moves from those in which faith's victory was manifest in history (vv. 33–35) to those in which faith entailed suffering and apparent defeat (vv. 35–38). For the specific events in view, see cross references.

11:33 obtained promises. That is, they saw answers to particular promises along the way. For the promise of Christ's coming they still waited in faith (v. 39). The promises made to Abraham were partly fulfilled in this world, as his descendants multiplied (v. 12) and lived in the Promised Land (vv. 9, 33). But to the extent that these promises referred to the heavenly reality, "his rest" (4:10), they could not be fulfilled until Christ came.

11:35 Women received back their dead. A reference to events recorded in 1 Kin. 17:22, 23; 2 Kin. 4:36, 37.

Some were tortured. An apparent reference to events during the Maccabean revolt (c. 167–157 B.C.), which occurred after the close of the Old Testament, but which are recorded in 2 Maccabees 6; 7 in the Apocrypha.

11:37 sawn in two. According to tradition, the prophet Isaiah died in this way.

11:39 commended. See note on v. 4.

did not receive what was promised. Although some Old Testament promises were fulfilled, their true hope (the promise of the coming Messiah) was yet to come (v. 33 and note). This verse summarizes the message of vv. 13–16 and applies it to the second half of the chapter.

11:40 something better . . . apart from us. This verse asserts both the redemptive-historical difference between the Old Testament and New Testament periods, and the unity of the people of God in both eras. Though the Old Testament believers lived by faith (10:38), they were not privileged to witness on earth the fulfillment of the great promise of God. Nevertheless, they too participate in the benefits of Christ's high-priestly work, and, along with new covenant saints, they are "made perfect." Those of the old and new eras together await the perfection that will appear only at the Second Coming (12:26; 13:14; Rom. 8:18; Eph. 1:9, 10).

12:1 cloud of witnesses. The readers are in effect running a race before a great crowd of people who have already finished the race with honors. Their example encourages the readers, and admonishes them if they should stumble.

every weight, and sin which clings so closely. Among the burdens to be thrown off are fear that shrinks back in the face of suffering (10:38, 39), bitter discouragement that defiles others through doubt (v. 15), and sensuality that seeks immediate gratification (v. 16).

run . . . the race. The athletic competitions of the Greeks provided a common New Testament analogy for the Christian life (1 Cor. 9:24–27; Phil. 2:16; 2 Tim. 2:5; 4:7, 8). Like a runner, the Christian must be in constant motion toward the goal despite opposition. This demands strenuous effort and endurance, which is learned from constant discipline.

12:2 looking to Jesus. The cloud of Old Testament witnesses inspires us, but our principal encouragement is found in the person and work of Christ, who has gone before us as the "founder and perfecter of our faith," and is the supreme example of faith in the race (v. 3).

founder. See note 2:10.

perfecter of our faith, [a]who for the joy that
was set before him endured the cross,
despising [b]the shame, and [c]is seated at the
right hand of the throne of God.

Do Not Grow Weary

3 [d]Consider him who endured from sinners such hostility against himself, so that
you may not grow weary or [e]fainthearted.
4 In your struggle against sin you have not
yet resisted to the point of shedding your
blood. 5 And have you forgotten the exhortation that addresses you as sons?

[f]"My son, [g]do not regard lightly the
discipline of the Lord,
nor be weary when reproved by
him.
6 For [h]the Lord disciplines the one he
loves,
and chastises every son whom he
receives."

7 It is for discipline that you have to endure.
[i]God is treating you as sons. For what son
is there whom his father does not discipline? 8 If you are left without discipline, [j]in
which all have participated, then you are
illegitimate children and not sons. 9 Besides
this, we have had earthly fathers who disciplined us and we respected them. Shall we
not much more be subject to [k]the Father of
spirits [l]and live? 10 For they disciplined us
for a short time as it seemed best to them,
but he disciplines us for our good, [m]that we
may share his holiness. 11 [n]For the moment
all discipline seems painful rather than
pleasant, but later it yields [o]the peaceful
fruit of righteousness to those who have
been trained by it.

12 Therefore [p]lift your drooping hands
and strengthen your weak knees, 13 and
[q]make straight paths for your feet, so that
what is lame may not be put out of joint
[r]but rather be healed. 14 [s]Strive for peace
with everyone, and for the [t]holiness [u]with-
out which no one will see the Lord. 15 See
to it that no one [v]fails to obtain the grace of
God; that no [w]"root of bitterness" springs

2 [a]Luke 24:26; Phil. 2:8; [Isai. 53:11] [b]Ps. 22:6, 7; 69:19; Isai. 53:3 [c]ch. 1:3
3 [d][Matt. 10:24; Rev. 2:3] [e]Gal. 6:9
5 [f]Cited from Prov. 3:11, 12 [g]Job 5:17
6 [h]Ps. 94:12; 119:67, 75; Rev. 3:19
7 [i]Deut. 8:5; 2 Sam. 7:14; [Prov. 13:24; 19:18; 23:13]
8 [j][1 Pet. 5:9]
9 [k]See Num. 16:22 [l][Isai. 38:16]
10 [m][2 Pet. 1:4]; See Lev. 11:44
11 [n][1 Pet. 1:6] [o]James 3:17, 18
12 [p]Cited from Isai. 35:3; [Job 4:3, 4]
13 [q]Prov. 4:26, 27 [r]James 5:16; [Gal. 6:1]
14 [s]See Rom. 14:19 [t]1 Thess. 4:7 [u]Matt. 5:8; [2 Cor. 7:1; Eph. 5:5; Rev. 21:27; 22:4]
15 [v]ch. 4:1; [2 Cor. 6:1; Gal. 5:4] [w]Deut. 29:18

perfecter of our faith. As "perfecter" Jesus has brought the faith of all who approach God through Him to its intended goal: thankful worship acceptable to God, presented in His presence (10:14; 11:40; 12:28).

for the joy that was set before him. Jesus endured the cross in anticipation of the joy of being Savior of His people when the necessary suffering was over. As Moses looked to his reward (11:26), so Jesus was aware of His own reward.

A less probable, though possible, interpretation is to translate "in place of the joy set before Him." On this reading, Jesus chose suffering instead of the joy that would have been His if He had refused to die, and instead remained in heaven (Phil. 2:6), or at least avoided the Cross on earth (John 10:17, 18; 12:27).

despising the shame. Crucifixion was so shameful a form of execution that it was forbidden to be inflicted on Roman citizens; in addition, the Jews believed that "everyone who is hanged on a tree" is cursed by God (Gal. 3:13; cf. Deut. 21:23).

12:3 hostility. Like Jesus, the readers had also experienced the hostility of sinners (10:33).

fainthearted. A warning from Prov. 3:11, 12, quoted in vv. 5, 6.

12:4 shedding your blood. The readers have known persecution, but nothing as serious as what Jesus suffered, or indeed, what has been cataloged in 11:35–38. It is not time for them to think of giving up.

12:5 sons. God's plan to lead many sons to glory meant that the author of their salvation was to be perfected through suffering (2:10), even though He was the Son who deserved no suffering (5:8). It is not surprising, then, that the adopted sons who follow Him should be prepared for their inheritance through painful discipline.

12:8 Many Roman nobles had illegitimate sons, who were financially supported but left virtually without discipline. On the other hand, the son of a nobleman's legal wife, who would carry the father's name and inherit the estate, was subjected to a training regimen comparable to slavery (Gal. 4:1, 2).

12:9 earthly fathers. Lit. "fathers of our flesh," in direct contrast to "Father of spirits." This argument from the lesser to the greater—from the lesser of the human parental relationship to the greater of divine fatherhood—is completed in v. 10.

12:10 The discipline of our earthly fathers is limited by time and by their fallible wisdom. The heavenly Father's discipline is planned by His infinite wisdom for "our good," and it makes us holy, as He is holy (v. 14; 1 Pet. 1:15, 16).

12:11 peaceful fruit of righteousness. This gives some idea what holiness involves (vv. 10, 14).

trained. The writer returns to the athletic analogy of v. 1.

12:12, 13 The race will be completed successfully only if action is taken to heal spiritual injuries of the past (v. 12) and avoid pitfalls in the future (v. 13). The context of Is. 35:3, 4 (from which Hebrews has taken "lift your drooping hands . . . your weak knees") is one of encouraging the fearful. Compare Hebrews' calls for mutual encouragement (e.g., 3:13), including that which follows in 12:15, and the warning against losing heart (vv. 3, 5). The context of Prov. 4:25–27 (source of "make straight paths for your feet") is a call to single-minded adherence to the path of righteousness. The metaphor of strengthening and healing injured limbs to run the race is explained in specific commands (vv. 14–17).

12:14 Strive for peace with everyone. Despite being tempted in persecution to repay evil for evil, believers should live at peace with everyone "so far as it depends on you" (Rom. 12:18), just as our Lord Jesus did not retaliate with insults or threats (1 Pet. 2:23).

holiness. Hebrews has declared how Jesus' sacrifice makes us holy once for all in status (10:10) giving us confident access to God. In this verse "holiness" is purity of life. It is provided by God (13:21) and guided by His discipline (v. 10), but we must "strive for" it.

see the Lord. That is, be with God, the goal of salvation (Rev. 22:4). Those who now by grace through faith pursue and receive the holiness of Christ will indeed see the Lord, and become like Him (2 Cor. 3:18; 1 John 3:2).

12:15 The readers are responsible to each other, to watch out for one another so "no one fails to obtain" God's grace (cf. 4:1).

root of bitterness. In Deut. 29:18, the "root bearing . . . bitter fruit" is a

up and causes trouble, and by it many
become defiled; **16** that no one is [x]sexually
immoral or unholy like Esau, who sold his
birthright for a single meal. **17** For you know
that [y]afterward, when he desired to inherit
the blessing, he was rejected, for he found
no chance to repent, though he sought it
with tears.

A Kingdom That Cannot Be Shaken

18 For you have not come to [z]what may
be touched, a blazing fire and darkness and
gloom and a tempest **19** and [a]the sound of a
trumpet and a voice whose words [b]made
the hearers beg that no further messages be
spoken to them. **20** For they could not
endure the order that was given, [c]"If even
a beast touches the mountain, it shall be
stoned." **21** Indeed, [d]so terrifying was the
sight that Moses said, "I tremble with fear."
22 But you have come to [e]Mount Zion and
to the city of the living God, [f]the heavenly
Jerusalem, and to [g]innumerable angels in
festal gathering, **23** and to [h]the assembly[1] of
the firstborn who are [i]enrolled in heaven,
and to [j]God, the judge of all, and to the
spirits of the righteous made perfect, **24** and
to Jesus, [k]the mediator of a new covenant,
and to [l]the sprinkled blood [m]that speaks a
better word than the blood of Abel.

25 See that you do not refuse him who is
speaking. For [n]if they did not escape when
they refused him who warned them on
earth, much less will we escape if we reject
him who warns from heaven. **26** At that time
[o]his voice shook the earth, but now he has
promised, [p]"Yet once more I will shake not
only the earth but also the heavens." **27** This
phrase, "Yet once more," indicates [q]the
removal of things that are shaken—that is,
things that have been made—in order that
the things that cannot be shaken may

16 [x]ch. 13:4; Gen. 25:33
17 [y]Gen. 27:34, 36, 38
18 [z]Ex. 19:18; 20:18; Deut. 4:11; 5:22; [2 Cor. 3:9]
19 [a]Ex. 19:16, 19 [b]Ex. 20:19; Deut. 5:5; 18:16
20 [c]Cited from Ex. 19:12, 13
21 [d][Ex. 19:16; Deut. 9:19]
22 [e]Rev. 14:1 [f]See Gal. 4:26 [g]Jude 14
23 [h][Ex. 4:22] [i]Luke 10:20 [j]Gen. 18:25
24 [k]ch. 8:6; 9:15 [l]See ch. 10:22 [m]ch. 11:4; Gen. 4:10
25 [n]See ch. 2:3
26 [o]Ex. 19:18 [p]Cited from Hag. 2:6; [Hag. 2:21]
27 [q]See Ps. 102:26

[1] Or *church*

person who spreads doubt and disloyalty toward the Lord among the covenant people. Here, too, this "root of bitterness" is a person who "causes trouble" and causes others to be "defiled." To sustain each other's faith, we must encourage the weak, but also oppose apostates, who may influence others.

12:16 Esau is presented as an example of one who despised the promises of God (in contrast to the people of faith in ch. 11), and whose loss was irrevocable (v. 17). Moses traded Egypt's treasures for the disgrace of Christ because he saw the reward (11:26); Esau traded his birthright for a bowl of food because lentil stew was all he could see (Gen. 25:29–34).

sold his birthright. As firstborn son, Esau had a special "birthright" (Gen. 25:31–34; 27:36). Later, under the Mosaic law, the right was to a double share of property (Deut. 21:17). In actuality, Esau despised his place in the line of covenant promises, and not property alone.

12:17 you know that afterward. The readers will remember the second stage of Esau's loss, when his brother Jacob took his place as their father Isaac gave the solemn blessing (Gen. 27). This blessing included the substance of the promise made to Abraham (Gen. 12:2, 3; 27:29).

no chance to repent. Though Esau mourned his loss with tears (Gen. 27:38; cf. 2 Cor. 7:10), he did not actually repent of the sin of despising God's promises. Another view is that the repentance he sought was a change in his father's mind.

12:18–24 The old and new covenants are compared in terms of the mountains (Sinai and Zion) associated with each. Fear was the dominant theme at Sinai, a touchable (and thus earthly and mutable) mountain on which the law was given (vv. 18–21). Joy and confidence characterize the heavenly (and thus eternal) Zion, because the Savior is there with the blood of forgiveness (vv. 22–24).

12:18 what may be touched. Like the sanctuary established by the first covenant (9:1, 11, 24), the mountain on which the law was given was part of the "things that have been made," that are destined to be "shaken" and removed by God's voice from heaven (v. 27). As something that can be "touched," Sinai testifies to the impermanence of the first covenant (8:13).

12:19 beg that no further messages be spoken to them. Afraid that direct contact with the Lord's awesome holiness would destroy them (Ex. 20:19), the Israelites pleaded with Moses to mediate God's words to them.

12:21 The giving of the law took place with an awesome demonstration of God's power. Fear was a proper reaction (cf. Is. 6:4, 5; Matt. 17:6; Rev. 1:17).

12:22 you have come. We are still in our earthly pilgrimage, and like the patriarchs (11:13), still look for the "city . . . to come" (13:14). Nevertheless, because of Jesus our forerunner, we have arrived by faith at the heavenly Jerusalem and may enter into the Most Holy Place in worship (10:19–22). See "Heaven" at Rev. 21:1.

innumerable angels. They always serve God's majesty (Deut. 33:2; Ps. 68:17; Dan. 7:10). Here they are assembled as for a festival, or holiday celebration.

12:23 assembly of the firstborn. All the firstborn in Israel were sanctified at the time of the Passover and consecrated to service in God's presence, but the Levites served the sanctuary in the place of the firstborn (Num. 3:11–13). In the heavenly assembly all believers, redeemed from destruction, are "firstborn," consecrated to God, and enrolled as His priests. Unlike Esau, who scorned his right as the firstborn (v. 16), believers share gratefully in the inheritance of Jesus, the firstborn (1:6, 14; 2:11, 12). In the heavenly assembly all believers may worship, in heaven and on earth (10:22, 25). See "The Church" at Eph. 2:19.

righteous made perfect. These are the spirits of those who have died in the Lord (2 Cor. 5:8; Rev. 14:13). Particularly in view are the Old Testament and intertestamental saints to whose righteousness by faith God Himself testified (11:2, 4, 5, 39), and who are now perfected (11:40) through the sacrifice of Jesus.

12:24 Jesus' presence in the heavenly Zion explains its atmosphere of joy and confidence. The blood of Abel cried for vengeance from the ground (Gen. 4:10), but the blood of Jesus, to use the same figure, "speaks a better word" (that is, cries out for forgiveness for the children of God, 9:12–15; 10:19–22).

12:25–27 God's voice speaking the gospel must be listened to with even greater attention and faith than the law spoken at Sinai (2:1–4; 3:1–5; 10:28, 29).

12:25 The contrast between the Old Testament message and the message through the Son from heaven goes back to 1:1–4. By closing the circle, the writer is bringing his argument toward conclusion.

12:27 the removal . . . shaken. Christ will roll up the heavens and the earth "like a garment," but He will remain (1:12). The passing of the first covenant, which is "obsolete and growing old" (8:13), with its sanctuary (9:8) and sacrifices (10:9), is the foretaste of this final shaking.

remain. 28 Therefore let us be grateful for
receiving [r]a kingdom that cannot be
shaken, and thus [s]let us offer to God
acceptable worship, with reverence and
awe, 29 for our [t]God is a consuming fire.

Sacrifices Pleasing to God

13 Let [u]brotherly love continue. 2 [v]Do
not neglect to show hospitality to
strangers, for thereby [w]some have entertained angels unawares. 3 [x]Remember those
who are in prison, as though in prison with
them, and those who are mistreated, since
you also are in the body. 4 [y]Let marriage be
held in honor among all, and let the marriage bed be undefiled, for God will judge
[z]the sexually immoral and adulterous.
5 Keep your life [a]free from love of money,
and [b]be content with what you have, for he
has said, [c]"I will never leave you nor forsake you." 6 So we can confidently say,

[d]"The Lord is my helper;
[e]I will not fear;
what can man do to me?"

7 Remember [f]your leaders, those who
spoke to you the word of God. Consider
the outcome of their way of life, and [g]imi-
tate their faith. 8 Jesus Christ is [h]the same
yesterday and today and forever. 9 Do not
be [i]led away by diverse and strange teachings, for it is good for the heart to be
strengthened by grace, [j]not by foods,
which have not benefited those devoted to
them. 10 We have an altar [k]from which
those who serve the tent have no right to
eat. 11 For [l]the bodies of those animals
whose blood is brought into the holy
places by the high priest as a sacrifice for
sin are burned [m]outside the camp. 12 So
Jesus also [n]suffered [o]outside the gate in
order to sanctify the people [p]through his
own blood. 13 Therefore let us go to him
outside the camp and bear [q]the reproach
he endured. 14 For [r]here we have no lasting

28 [r]Dan. 2:44 [s]ch. 13:15 29 [t]Cited from Deut. 4:24; See 2 Thess. 1:8
Chapter 13
1 [u]Rom. 12:10; 1 Thess. 4:9; 1 Pet. 1:22; 2 Pet. 1:7; [1 Pet. 2:17; 3:8; 1 John 3:10; 4:7, 20, 21]
2 [v]See Matt. 25:35; 1 Pet. 4:9 [w]Gen. 18:3; 19:2
3 [x]ch. 10:34; Matt. 25:36
4 [y]1 Cor. 7:38; [1 Tim. 4:3] [z]See 1 Cor. 6:9
5 [a]1 Tim. 3:3 [b]1 Tim. 6:7, 8; [Phil. 4:11]; See Matt. 6:25 [c]Cited from Josh. 1:5; [Ps. 37:25; 2 Cor. 4:9]
6 [d]Cited from Ps. 118:6; [Ps. 27:1] [e]Ps. 56:4, 11

7 [f]ver. 17, 24 [g][ch. 6:12] 8 [h]ch. 1:12; John 8:58; Rev. 1:4, 8; [2 Cor. 1:19] 9 [i]Jude 12; See Eph. 4:14 [j]See Col. 2:16 10 [k][1 Cor. 9:13; 10:18] 11 [l]See Ex. 29:14 [m]ver. 13 12 [n]ch. 9:12 [o]Matt. 21:39; 27:32; John 19:17, 20; [Acts 7:58] [p][Rev. 14:20] 13 [q]ch. 11:26; 1 Pet. 4:14 14 [r][ch. 11:10, 16; 12:28; Mic. 2:10]; See Eph. 2:19

12:28 offer to God acceptable worship. Gratitude derives from knowing that our names are written in heaven (Luke 10:20) and from our experience of God's "inexpressible gift"—Jesus Christ (2 Cor. 9:15). Reverence and awe come from an appreciation of who God is (v. 29). Acceptable worship combines these motives.

12:29 a consuming fire. This solemn quotation from Deut. 4:24 provides a fitting conclusion to an exhortation that stresses the holiness of God and the finality of His judgment on apostates (10:27).

13:1–3 Here the readers' responsibility to guard and encourage each other's perseverance in faith takes tangible forms: brotherly love to all fellow-believers (Rom. 12:10; 1 Pet. 1:22), hospitality to those needing shelter or food (11:38), identification with prisoners (10:34), and compassionate support for those mistreated because of their confession (10:33; 11:25; cf. Matt. 25:35–37).

13:2 Do not neglect. The pressure of suffering can drive fundamental responsibilities of love from our minds (vv. 3, 7, 16).

entertained angels unawares. Abraham, himself a stranger (11:13), showed hospitality to "three men" (Gen. 18:2) who proved to be the Lord Himself with two of His supernatural messengers (Gen. 18:1–19:22).

13:3 Remember those who are in prison. Paul's commendation of Onesiphorus, who "was not ashamed of my chains," shows the importance of this encouragement even for an apostle (2 Tim. 1:16–18).

13:4 A second hint that sexual immorality may tempt the readers (12:16). The antidote to immorality is not ascetic self-denial, but a proper appreciation of the honor God has bestowed on the marriage relationship (Eph. 5:22–33; 1 Cor. 7:3–5).

13:5, 6 Those tempted by the love of money and discontent are particularly people who seek their security in financial resources (Matt. 6:19–21, 24–34). But God's promise to stay with Joshua gives greater confidence: "I will not leave you or forsake you" (Josh. 1:5). Our confident response reaffirms that the Lord our helper (2:18; 4:16) sets us free from all kinds of fear (2:15; 11:23, 27).

13:7 your leaders. The ministry of the congregation's first generation of teachers (2:3) has been completed, and the author will later exhort his readers to submit to the new leaders, as their leaders' pastoral role requires (v. 17).

imitate their faith. We must imitate those who inherit the promises through enduring faith (6:12).

13:8 Though human leaders pass from the scene, Jesus Christ is "the same" (1:12) "yesterday" (in which God spoke through prophets, 1:1), "today" (as God summons us to enter His rest through faith, 3:7, 13; 4:7), and "forever" (1:8; 7:17, 21, 24, 28). He is the strong anchor amid sufferings and uncertainties (6:19).

13:9 strange teachings. These doctrines, or teachings, apparently maintained that because the readers were not taking part in the ritual life of the temple (v. 13), including the sacrificial feasts, they had no access to God. The author responds that grace, not ceremonial food, strengthens our hearts, for by grace we participate in the worship at the heavenly altar where Jesus ministers.

which have not benefited. Just as the sin offering could not secure cleansing of the conscience (9:9), so also the peace offering could not guarantee that the worshiper had peace and communion with God (Lev. 7:11–18; 1 Cor. 10:18).

13:10 The Levitical priests had the right to a portion of every animal sacrificed as a peace offering at the Old Testament tabernacle (Lev. 6:18, 29; 7:6, 28–36). As long as those priests and others depend on the old system of animal sacrifices for atonement and peace with God, they cannot benefit from Christ's heavenly high priestly ministry.

13:11, 12 The symbolism of the Day of Atonement expressed two important aspects of Christ's atoning work. First, the blood brought into the Most Holy Place declared that only through the death of a blameless substitute could anyone approach the holy God. Second, the bodies of the animals burned outside the camp indicated that the substitute became unclean as the bearer of the people's sins.

13:13 go to him outside the camp. Jesus' suffering outside the city gate symbolized not only the curse He bore as our sin-bearer, but also His rejection by the Jewish religious establishment and its leaders. The readers are now summoned to accept with courage their own expulsion from Jewish institutions (synagogue and temple, and perhaps family as well), in the confident expectation of the city that is to come (v. 14).

bear the reproach. See 11:25, 26 and note; Ps. 69:7–9; Rom. 15:3.

city, but we seek the city that is to come.
15 [s]Through him then let us continually
offer up [t]a sacrifice of praise to God, that is,
[u]the fruit of lips that acknowledge his
name. 16 Do not neglect to do good and [v]to
share what you have, for such [w]sacrifices
are pleasing to God.

17 Obey [x]your leaders and submit to
them, [y]for they are keeping watch over
your souls, as those who will have to [z]give
an account. [a]Let them do this with joy and
not with groaning, for that would be of no
advantage to you.

18 [b]Pray for us, for we are sure that we
have a clear conscience, desiring to act
honorably in all things. 19 I urge you the
more earnestly to do this in order [c]that I
may be restored to you the sooner.

Benediction

20 Now [d]may the God of peace [e]who
brought again from the dead our Lord
Jesus, [f]the great shepherd of the sheep,
by [g]the blood of the eternal covenant,
21 [h]equip you with everything good that you
may do his will, [i]working in us[1] that which
is pleasing in his sight, through Jesus
Christ, [j]to whom be glory forever and ever.
Amen.

Final Greetings

22 I appeal to you, brothers,[2] bear with
my word of exhortation, for [k]I have written
to you briefly. 23 You should know that [l]our
brother Timothy has been released, with
whom I shall see you if he comes soon.
24 Greet all [m]your leaders and all the saints.
Those who come from Italy send you greetings. 25 [n]Grace be with all of you.

15 [s]Eph. 5:20 [t]Lev. 7:12; Ps. 107:22; 116:17 [u]Isai. 57:19; Hos. 14:2; [Ps. 119:108] 16 [v]See Rom. 12:13 [w]Mic. 6:7, 8; Phil. 4:18 17 [x]ver. 7, 24 [y]See Ezek. 3:17 [z]Jer. 13:20; Ezek. 34:10 [a][Acts 20:24, 31] 18 [b]1 Thess. 5:25; 2 Thess. 3:1 19 [c][Philem. 22] 20 [d]See Rom. 15:33 [e]See Acts 2:24 [f]Isai. 63:11; See John 10:11 [g]ch. 10:29; Zech. 9:11; [Isai. 54:10]

21 [h]2 Thess. 2:17; 1 Pet. 5:10 [i]ch. 10:36; [Phil. 2:13] [j]See Rom. 11:36 22 [k][1 Pet. 5:12] 23 [l]See 1 Thess. 3:2 24 [m]ver. 7, 17 25 [n]See Col. 4:18

1 Some manuscripts *you* 2 Or *brothers and sisters*

13:15 continually offer. The time of animal sacrifice is past, but the servants of God, like all priests, still have gifts and offerings for Him. These spiritual sacrifices (1 Pet. 2:5) include praises toward God (v. 15) and acts of love toward other people (v. 16).

sacrifice of praise. In the Greek translation of Lev. 7:11–21, this phrase refers to a kind of "peace offering," which was an animal sacrifice. But the meaning here is closer to Ps. 50:14, 23 where the Lord calls for "thanksgiving" instead of animal sacrifices.

the fruit of lips that acknowledge his name. In Hos. 14:12 this attractive figure of speech is used for the words that one offers to God when one's sins are forgiven. This is "the sacrifice of praise."

13:16 Do not neglect. Sacrifices of words must be accompanied by deeds of love toward others (James 1:27). Paul calls material gifts a "fragrant offering, a sacrifice acceptable" to God in Phil. 4:18. See note on v. 2.

13:17 Obey . . . submit. The new generation of leaders (13:7) was apparently not receiving the respectful submission that their task warranted.

they are keeping watch. Faithful church leaders are like faithful shepherds (Jer. 23:4; Acts 20:28; 1 Pet. 5:2–4) or watchmen who call out danger alarms to the city (Ezek. 33:6). The leaders' care is deep and genuine because they were appointed by God and will give their account to Him (cf. 4:13). Everyone will suffer if their ministry is resisted.

13:18 Pray for us. Believers have the privilege of acting as priests by praying for each other, in reliance upon their open access to the throne of grace (4:16).

we have a clear conscience. Perhaps the author wants to reassure his readers that he is exercising his own leadership in a careful way, according to the guidelines he has just given (v. 17; cf. 2 Cor. 1:12).

13:19 restored to you the sooner. The precise circumstances of the author are unknown. He has previously been with the group he addresses, and is anxious to see them again.

13:20, 21 This benediction gathers together the letter's prominent themes, as well as introducing new ones.

13:20 the great shepherd of the sheep. The Good Shepherd leads and protects His sheep (Ps. 23; Ezek. 34:11–16, 31), and He has laid down His life for them (John 10:11; 1 Pet. 2:24, 25).

by the blood of the eternal covenant. The sacrifice of Christ defeated death (2:14) and inaugurated the new and eternal covenant (9:12–15). After being raised, "Christ . . . will never die again" (Rom. 6:9); the effects of His sacrifice are eternal.

13:21 do his will. God has made full provision for our growth in godliness (2 Pet. 1:3), and He is always ready to help in time of need or temptation (2:18; 4:16).

working in us that which is pleasing in his sight. God will help us to love Him and our neighbor, the sacrifices that delight Him (vv. 15, 16; Phil. 2:13).

through Jesus Christ. All of salvation, forgiveness of sins and renewal of life, is through Jesus Christ.

13:22 my word of exhortation. This sermon, in the form of a letter, would take an hour or so to read aloud. The writer could have expanded certain sections if he had wished (9:5).

13:24 Greet all your leaders. The author goes out of his way to ensure appropriate recognition of the congregation's leaders (cf. v. 17).

from Italy. See Introduction: Date and Occasion.

THE EPISTLE OF

James

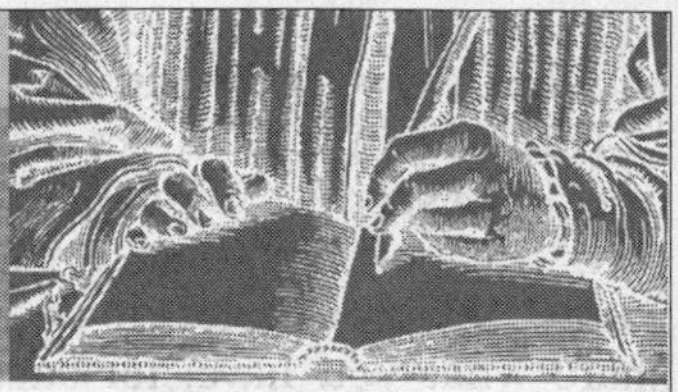

AUTHOR

The author of this letter identifies himself as James. Though several different persons named "James" are mentioned in the New Testament church, it is almost certain that the author of this book is James the brother of Jesus. The author assumes a position of authority in the church, which certainly was accorded James, the Lord's brother. The James who was a leader of the Jerusalem church and who presided at the council of Jerusalem (Acts 15) is identified in Gal. 1:19 as "the Lord's brother." He was considered one of the pillars of the church along with Peter and John (Gal. 2:9). The New Testament lists James as one of the sons of Mary, Jesus' mother (Matt. 13:55; Mark 6:3). James, along with his brothers, was skeptical of Jesus during His earthly ministry (John 7:5), but was converted when he became an eyewitness of the Resurrection (1 Cor. 15:7). The early church historian Hegesippus identified him as "James the Just," testifying to his extraordinary godliness, his zeal for obedience to the law of God, and his singular devotion to prayer. It was said that James's knees became so calloused from prayer that they resembled the knees of camels. Josephus records that James was martyred in A.D. 62. Eusebius says he was beaten to death with a club after being thrown from the temple parapet; Hegesippus also records that he was thrown from the pinnacle of the temple.

DATE AND OCCASION

James was written between A.D. 44, the beginning of the persecution that spread to the Diaspora (Acts 12), and A.D. 62, the year of James's death. Since no mention is made of the controversy leading to the council of Jerusalem (Acts 15), it is probable that James was written before A.D. 49. James is possibly the earliest New Testament writing.

CHARACTERISTICS AND THEMES

James has been variously considered an epistle, a sermon (to be read aloud in the churches), a form of wisdom literature, a diatribe, and a moral exhortation. These categories are not mutually exclusive, and there are elements of all these forms in James.

The epistle has a markedly Jewish flavor and refers frequently to the Old Testament. The literary structure of parallelism is used (1:9, 10), along with aphorisms, concrete images drawn from nature, and groups of sayings that have a clear similarity to the style of Jesus. The epistle teaches a high Christology and stresses the importance of dealing with affliction from the standpoint of faith. The crucial relationship between faith and active works of obedience receives special attention (2:14–26).

OUTLINE OF JAMES

I. Perseverance (ch. 1)

- A. *Salutation (1:1)*
- B. *Trials (1:2–11)*
- C. *Tests of Faith (1:12–18)*
- D. *Obeying the Word of God (1:19–27)*

II. Faith (ch. 2)

- A. *Faith and Law (2:1–13)*
- B. *Faith and Works (2:14–26)*

III. The Tongue (3:1–12)

IV. Heavenly and Earthly Wisdom (3:13–18)

V. Submission to God's Will (ch. 4)

- A. *Source of Quarrels in Evil Desires (4:1–6)*
- B. *Drawing Near to God (4:7–10)*

OUTLINE OF JAMES (Cont.)

C. *Slander (4:11, 12)*

D. *Submission to Divine Providence (4:13–17)*

VI. Patience (ch. 5)

A. *Judgment on the Rich (5:1–6)*

B. *Teaching and Examples of Patience (5:7–11)*

C. *Oaths and Vows (5:12)*

D. *Effective Prayer (5:13–18)*

E. *Rescuing Erring Brothers (5:19, 20)*

Greeting

1 [a]James, a servant[1] of God and [b]of the
Lord Jesus Christ,
To [c]the twelve tribes in [d]the Dispersion:
Greetings.

Testing of Your Faith

2 [e]Count it all joy, my brothers,[2] when
you meet trials [f]of various kinds, 3 for you
know that [g]the testing of your faith [h]pro-
duces steadfastness. 4 And let steadfastness
have its full effect, that you may be [i]perfect
and complete, lacking in nothing.
5 [j]If any of you lacks wisdom, [k]let him ask
God, [l]who gives generously to all without
reproach, and it will be given him. 6 But
[m]let him ask in faith, [n]with no doubting,
for the one who doubts is like [o]a wave of
the sea that is driven and tossed by the
wind. 7 For that person must not suppose
that he will receive anything from the Lord;
8 [p]he is a double-minded man, [q]unstable in
all his ways.
9 Let the lowly brother boast in his exaltation, 10 and [r]the rich in his humiliation,
because [s]like a flower of the grass[3] he will
pass away. 11 For the sun rises with its
scorching heat and [t]withers the grass; its
flower falls, and its beauty perishes. So also
will the rich man fade away in the midst of
his pursuits.
12 [u]Blessed is the man who remains
steadfast under trial, for when he has stood
the test he will receive [v]the crown of life,
[w]which God has promised to those who
love him. 13 Let no one say when he is
tempted, "I am being tempted by God," for
God cannot be tempted with evil, and he
himself tempts no one. 14 But each person
is tempted when he is lured and enticed by
his own desire. 15 Then desire [x]when it has
conceived gives birth to sin, and [y]sin when
it is fully grown brings forth death.
16 Do not be deceived, my beloved brothers. 17 [z]Every good gift and every perfect gift

Chapter 1
1 [a]See Acts 12:17 [b]Rom. 1:1; 2 Pet. 1:1; Jude 1 [c]Luke 22:30; Acts 26:7 [d]1 Pet. 1:1; [Acts 2:9-11]; See John 7:35
2 [e]See Matt. 5:12 [f]1 Pet. 1:6
3 [g]1 Pet. 1:7 [h]Rom. 5:3; [ch. 5:11; Heb. 10:36; 2 Pet. 1:6]
4 [i]1 Thess. 5:23; See Matt. 5:48
5 [j]1 Kin. 3:9-12; Prov. 2:3-6 [k]See Matt. 7:7 [l]Prov. 28:5
6 [m]Mark 11:24 [n]Matt. 21:21 [o][Isai. 57:20; Eph. 4:14]
8 [p]ch. 4:8 [q][2 Pet. 2:14; 3:16]
10 [r]Jer. 9:23 [s][Ps. 102:4, 11; 1 Cor. 7:31; 1 Pet. 1:24]
11 [t]Isai. 40:7
12 [u]ch. 5:11; Matt. 10:22; 1 Pet. 3:14; [Dan. 12:12] [v]Rev. 2:10; 3:11; [1 Cor. 9:25; 2 Tim. 4:8; 1 Pet. 5:4] [w]ch. 2:5 **15** [x]Job 15:35; Ps. 7:14; Isai. 59:4 [y]Rom. 5:12; 6:23 **17** [z]Ps. 85:12; John 3:27; 1 Cor. 4:7

[1] Or *slave*; Greek *bondservant* [2] Or *brothers and sisters*. The plural Greek word *adelphoi* (translated "brothers") refers to siblings in a family. In New Testament usage, depending on the context, *adelphoi* may refer either to men or to both men and women who are siblings (brothers and sisters) in God's family, the church; also verses 16, 19 [3] Or *a wild flower*

1:1 James, a servant. James identifies himself as a slave of God and of Christ. A bondservant (text note) is one purchased and owned by a master or "lord." This indicates not only humility on the part of the writer but a profound testimony to his conversion to faith in his earthly half brother as his Redeemer (1 Cor. 15:3). James is a servant to both God and Jesus, a crucial theological bracketing.

1:2 Count it all joy. This is a call to understand suffering from the vantage point of confidence in God's sovereignty. What follows requires careful thinking from a theological perspective.

brothers. Fellow believers are addressed in familial terms befitting those who have God as Father.

trials. Various kinds of trying circumstances, often related to persecution such as the early Christians endured.

1:3 testing. Trials can be considered pure joy only when there is knowledge that they are designed by God for a purpose. They are tests of faith given in order to develop perseverance. In turn, perseverance produces mature Christian character (Rom. 5:3).

1:5 wisdom. To be wise in biblical terms is to know and understand godliness, to do what is pleasing to God (Heb. 5:14). Ch. 3 elaborates this theme.

ask God. God is the source of wisdom. He grants it to those who sincerely seek it from Him.

1:8 double-minded man. This rare expression was possibly coined by James. It suggests a man who has two souls; he is as unstable as a person with a split personality.

1:9, 10 boast. Both the poor and the rich are exhorted to take pride in their positions. The poor brother is wealthy in spiritual treasure. He has high status in the kingdom of God. If the term "rich" refers to wealthy Christians, James means they can rejoice that they have learned where true treasure is found. If "rich" refers to the ungodly, the reference to their "boast" is ironic.

1:11 See Job 14:2; Ps. 103; Is. 40:6, 7.

1:12 Blessed. This echoes the prophetic oracles of salvation used by Old Testament prophets and by Jesus (Matt. 5:3–11).

1:13 tempted. There is an important difference between the concepts "test" and "tempt." God tests people, but never tempts them in the sense of enticing them to sin. Jesus, in the wilderness, was tested by God and tempted by Satan. There is also a difference between temptations that arise from our own sinful inclinations (internal) and those coming from without (external). Jesus, being free of original sin, was tempted externally but not internally. The testing of our faith may be the occasion for temptations to come, both internal and external, yet the temptations never have God as their author.

is from above, coming down from [a]the
Father of lights [b]with whom there is no
variation or shadow due to change.[1] 18 [c]Of
his own will he [d]brought us forth by the
word of truth, [e]that we should be a kind of
[f]firstfruits of his creatures.

Hearing and Doing the Word

19 [g]Know this, my beloved brothers: let
every person [h]be quick to hear, [i]slow to
speak, [j]slow to anger; 20 for the anger of
man does not produce the righteousness
that God requires.[2] 21 Therefore [k]put away
all filthiness and rampant wickedness and
receive with [l]meekness the implanted
word, [m]which is able to save your souls.
22 But be [n]doers of the word, and not
hearers only, deceiving yourselves. 23 For if
anyone is a hearer of the word and not a
doer, he is like a man who looks intently at
his natural face in a mirror. 24 For he looks
at himself and goes away and at once forgets what he was like. 25 But the one who
looks into the perfect law, [o]the law of liberty, and perseveres, being no hearer who
forgets but a doer who acts, [p]he will be
blessed in his doing.
26 If anyone thinks he is religious [q]and
does not bridle his tongue but deceives his
heart, this person's [r]religion is worthless.
27 Religion that is pure and undefiled before
God, the Father, is this: [s]to visit [t]orphans
and widows in their affliction, and [u]to keep
oneself [v]unstained from the world.

The Sin of Partiality

2 My brothers,[3] [w]show no partiality as
you hold the faith in our Lord Jesus
Christ, [x]the Lord of glory. 2 For if a man
wearing a gold ring and fine clothing comes
into your assembly, and a poor man in
shabby clothing also comes in, 3 and if you
pay attention to the one who wears the fine
clothing and say, "You sit here in a good
place," [y]while you say to the poor man,
"You stand over there," or, "Sit down at my
feet," 4 have you not then made distinctions
among yourselves and become [z]judges
with evil thoughts? 5 Listen, my beloved
brothers, [a]has not God chosen those who
are poor in the world to be [b]rich in faith
and heirs of [c]the kingdom, [d]which he has
promised to those who love him? 6 But you
[e]have dishonored the poor man. Are not
the rich the ones who oppress you, and the
ones who [f]drag you [g]into court? 7 Are they
not the ones who blaspheme the honorable
[h]name by which you were called?
8 If you really fulfill the royal law according to the Scripture, [i]"You shall love your

17 [a]1 John 1:5 [b]Mal. 3:6 **18** [c]John 1:13 [d][Gal. 4:19; 1 Pet. 1:3, 23] [e][Eph. 1:12] [f]Jer. 2:3; Rev. 14:4; [Rom. 8:19-23] **19** [g]1 John 2:21 [h][Eccles. 5:1, 2] [i]Prov. 10:19; 17:27 [j]See Prov. 14:29 **21** [k]Col. 3:8 [l]ch. 3:13 [m]1 Cor. 15:2; Eph. 1:13 **22** [n]Rom. 2:13; [ch. 2:14-20; Matt. 7:21, 24-27; Luke 8:21; John 13:17] **25** [o]ch. 2:12; [Gal. 2:4; 5:1, 13; 1 Pet. 2:16; 2 Pet. 2:19]; See John 8:32 [p]Ps. 1:1, 2; Luke 11:28 **26** [q]ch. 3:2, 3; Ps. 39:1; [ch. 3:6; Ps. 34:13; 141:3] [r]Acts 26:5 **27** [s]Matt. 25:36 [t]Job 31:17, 18; Isai. 1:17, 23 [u]1 Tim. 5:22; 1 John 5:18 [v]2 Pet. 3:14
Chapter 2
1 [w]1 Cor. 2:8; [Acts 7:2] [x]ver. 9; Lev. 19:15; Deut. 1:17; 16:19; Prov. 24:23; Rom. 2:11; Eph. 6:9

3 [y][Prov. 18:23] **4** [z]John 7:24 **5** [a]1 Cor. 1:27, 28; [Job 34:19] [b]2 Cor. 8:9; Rev. 2:9; See Luke 12:21 [c]Matt. 5:3; Luke 6:20; 12:32 [d]See ch. 1:12 **6** [e][1 Cor. 11:22] [f]Acts 16:19 [g]Acts 8:3; 17:6; 18:12; [ch. 5:6] **7** [h][Isai. 63:19; 65:1; Amos 9:12; Acts 15:17] **8** [i]Cited from Lev. 19:18

[1] Some manuscripts *variation due to a shadow of turning* [2] Greek *the righteousness of God* [3] Or *brothers and sisters*; also verses 5, 14

1:17 Father of lights. Nature's luminaries vary in magnitude and are subject to phases, eclipses, and shadows. God is the ultimate Author of light. In Him there are no changes of brightness or clarity. There is no fluctuation in His character.

1:18 he brought us forth. Lit. "gave birth to us." This refers to the grace of regeneration by which we are adopted into God's family (1 Pet. 1:23).

1:19 quick to hear, slow to speak. Though the Christian community places high regard on the talent of eloquent speech, James places the accent on listening. It is the person who listens intently to the Word of truth who progresses in godliness.

1:22 be doers. True hearing of the Word must lead to godly action.

1:23 mirror. In the ancient world mirrors were made of polished metal, not glass. Scripture is a mirror of the soul's need for grace. It reveals our true character to us.

1:25 perfect law. James uses this phrase as a synonym for sacred Scripture (Ps. 19).

liberty. The law of God sets us free (John 8:36; Rom. 8:2, 15; Gal. 5:13).

1:26 tongue. See ch. 3.

1:27 Religion that is pure and undefiled. James stresses concern for widows and orphans as a true measure of obedience that is pleasing to God. It reflects the concerns of God Himself (Deut. 10:18; Ps. 9:18 note; 68:5; 146:9). Israel was given this responsibility in the Old Testament (Deut. 14:29; Ezek. 22:7).

2:1 partiality. The expression is similar to that found in Gal. 2:6. James forbids having a respect for persons based purely on externals. It is contrary to the behavior of God who is no respecter of persons (Rom. 2:11; Eph. 6:9; Col. 3:25). In the light of Christ's divine glory it is foolish to show favoritism based on inferior levels of human glory.

Lord Jesus Christ, the Lord of glory. This may be rendered, "our Lord Jesus Christ, the glory." Here Jesus may be identified with the glory of God. He is Immanuel, "God with us," the dwelling of God with man.

2:4 made distinctions. Though God calls us to discern and to discriminate between good and evil, discrimination based on mere externals such as economic status, racial or ethnic differences, and the like is considered an evil form of judgment.

2:5 has not God chosen. Inheritance in the kingdom is based on God's sovereign election. He chooses not according to merit or worldly status. The standards of this world have no influence on God's gracious election (1 Cor. 1:28, 29; Eph. 1:4). The text does not warrant any form of "poverty mysticism" by which poverty in itself renders a person good (Ps. 9:18 note).

2:6 oppress. The verb is a strong word and is used to refer to the oppressive work of Satan (Acts 10:38). The rich used political and judicial power to exploit the poor and needy of the nation. As a group, the rich have a strong tendency to rely upon wealth and power rather than to find their redemption in Christ.

2:8 royal law. The supreme law of God.

love your neighbor. James regards the sin of favoritism as a violation of the great commandment (Lev. 19:18; Deut. 6:5; Matt. 22:36–39), making the perpetrator a lawbreaker.

neighbor as yourself," you are doing well.
9 But if you [j]show partiality, you are committing sin and are convicted by the law as
transgressors. 10 For whoever keeps the
whole law but fails in one point [k]has
become accountable for all of it. 11 For he
who said, [l]"Do not commit adultery," also
said, [l]"Do not murder." If you do not commit adultery but do murder, you have
become a transgressor of the law. 12 So
speak and so act as those who are to be
judged under [m]the law of liberty. 13 For
[n]judgment is without mercy to one who
has shown no mercy. Mercy triumphs over
judgment.

Faith Without Works Is Dead

14 What good is it, my brothers, if someone says he has faith [o]but does not have
works? Can that faith save him? 15 [p]If a
brother or sister is poorly clothed and lacking in daily food, 16 [q]and one of you says to
them, "Go in peace, be warmed and filled,"
without giving them the things needed for
the body, what good[1] is that? 17 So also
faith by itself, if it does not have works, is
dead.

18 But someone will say, "You have faith
and I have works." Show me your faith
[r]apart from your works, and I will show
you my faith [s]by my works. 19 [t]You believe
that God is one; you do well. Even [u]the
demons believe—and shudder! 20 Do you
want to be shown, you foolish person, that
faith apart from works is useless? 21 [v]Was
not Abraham our father justified by works
when he offered up his son Isaac on the
altar? 22 You see that [w]faith was active along
with his works, and faith was completed
[x]by his works; 23 and the Scripture was fulfilled that says, [y]"Abraham believed God,
and it was counted to him as righteousness"—and he was called a [z]friend of God.
24 You see that a person is justified by
works and not by faith alone. 25 And in the
same way was not also [a]Rahab the prostitute justified by works [b]when she received
the messengers and sent them out by
another way? 26 For as the body apart from
the spirit is dead, so also faith apart from
works is dead.

9 [j]ver. 1 10 [k]Matt. 5:19; Gal. 3:10 11 [l]Cited from Ex. 20:14, 13 12 [m]See ch. 1:25 13 [n]Job 22:6-11; Ps. 18:25, 26; Prov. 21:13; Ezek. 25:11-14; Matt. 6:15; 18:32-35; Luke 6:38 14 [o][ch. 1:22] 15 [p][Job 31:19, 20]; See Luke 3:11 16 [q]1 John 3:17, 18

18 [r][Rom. 3:28; 4:6; Heb. 11:33] [s]Matt. 7:16, 17; Gal. 5:6 19 [t]Deut. 6:4; [Rom. 2:17-25] [u]Matt. 8:29; Mark 1:24; 5:7; Luke 4:33, 34; Acts 16:17; 19:15 21 [v]Gen. 22:9, 12, 16-18 22 [w]Heb. 11:17 [x]See 1 Thess. 1:3

23 [y]Rom. 4:3; Gal. 3:6; Cited from Gen. 15:6 [z]2 Chr. 20:7; Isai. 41:8 25 [a]Heb. 11:31 [b]Josh. 2:1-22; 6:23

[1] Or *benefit*

2:10 whole law . . . one point. This text does not negate the biblical concept of gradation of evil. Some sins are more heinous than others. However, even in the smallest sin a serious offense is made against God. To sin at one point is to sin against the law and therefore against the Lawgiver. James, like Jesus, warns against a superficial understanding of the law of God (Matt. 5:17–20).

2:13 See Zech. 7:9; Matt. 5:7; 18:21–35. Though God is never obligated to show mercy, He freely chooses to do so in abundance. He reserves the divine prerogative to show mercy upon whom He wills (Rom. 9). By His law, however, we are commanded to temper justice with mercy. He warns that if we refuse to show mercy we will not receive mercy from Him.

2:14 Can that faith save. This introduces the crucial issue of the relationship between faith and works. The question under scrutiny is, What kind of faith is saving faith? James's question is rhetorical; the obvious answer is that faith without works cannot save. Faith that yields no deeds is not saving faith. The New Testament does not teach justification by the profession of faith or the claim to faith; it teaches justification by the possession of true faith.

2:15, 16 Describes a "faith" of words without actions.

2:17 faith by itself . . . is dead. When Luther and the Reformers insisted on the formula "Justification by faith alone," they meant to insist that justification rests upon reliance on the merit of Christ alone. The "alone" does not mean that the faith exists alone without any subsequent fruit of obedience. Luther insisted that saving faith is a living faith. "Dead" faith does not mean a faith that has perished. Rather, the image suggests a faith that never had any true life in it. A dead faith cannot make one alive, cannot "save your souls" (1:21), and is therefore false and useless.

2:18 Show me your faith. James challenges anyone who claims to have faith to demonstrate it, to make it visible. The only evidence visible to human eyes is the deeds of obedience. Though God can read the heart, our only view of the heart is by the sight of outward fruit.

2:19 You believe that God is one. To believe that God is one can be a mere intellectual assertion. To believe "in" God requires personal trust. To believe that He is, is to assent to a proposition even the demons acknowledge. Saving faith includes cognitive knowledge but goes beyond it to personal trust and submission.

2:20 foolish person. This is a strong rebuke. It is a moral judgment more than an intellectual judgment, recalling the judgment that falls upon "the fool" in the wisdom literature of the Old Testament.

useless. Barren of fruit.

2:21 justified. James appeals to Abraham as his chief exhibit of one who is justified by his works. This involves no conflict with Paul who also appeals to Abraham as the chief exhibit of one justified by faith. Note that James appeals to Gen. 22, while Paul appeals to Gen. 15. In the sight of God Abraham is justified in Gen. 15, long before he offers Isaac on the altar. God knew Abraham's faith to be genuine. Abraham is justified to us, to human eyes, in Gen. 22 when he shows his faith through his obedience. Jesus used the same verb in Luke 7:35 when he declared "wisdom is justified by all her children" (i.e., shown to be genuine wisdom by its results). Here, to "justify" does not mean to be reconciled to God but to demonstrate the truth of a prior claim. Just as true wisdom is demonstrated by its fruit, Abraham's claim to faith is justified by his outward obedience. Yet his works were not the meritorious cause of his salvation; they added no merit to the perfect and sufficient merit of Christ.

2:22 faith was completed. The full outworking of faith is seen in works. True faith always produces fruit. Faith and works may be distinguished, but never separated or divorced.

2:24 not by faith alone. A person is not shown to be just by the mere profession of faith or by having a faith that remains alone. A person is only shown to be just by what he or she does. None of our deeds are worthy of ultimate justification in the sight of God. Only the merit of Christ avails for that kind of justification. Only by trusting in Christ alone can we be made righteous in the sight of God. Here James attacks all forms of antinomianism that seek to have Jesus as Savior without embracing Him as Lord. Just as Paul demonstrated that trusting in one's own works is deadly, so James teaches that resting on empty or dead faith is deadly. See theological note "Faith and Works" on next page.

Taming the Tongue

3 [c]Not many of you should become
teachers, my brothers, for you know
that we who teach will be judged with
greater strictness. 2 For [d]we all stumble in
many ways, and if anyone does not stumble in what he says, [e]he is a perfect man,
[f]able also to bridle his whole body. 3 If we
put [g]bits into the mouths of horses so that
they obey us, we guide their whole bodies
as well. 4 Look at the ships also: though
they are so large and are driven by strong
winds, they are guided by a very small rud-
der wherever the will of the pilot directs.
5 So also the tongue is a small member, yet
[h]it boasts of great things.

How great a forest is set ablaze by such a
small fire! 6 And [i]the tongue is a fire, a
world of unrighteousness. The tongue is
set among our members, [j]staining the

Chapter 3
1 [c]Matt. 23:8; [Rom. 2:20, 21; 1 Tim. 1:7]
2 [d]1 Kin. 8:46; Prov. 20:9; Eccles. 7:20; 1 John 1:8 [e][Matt. 12:37] [f]See ch. 1:26
3 [g]Ps. 32:9
5 [h][Ps. 12:3, 4; 73:8, 9]
6 [i]Ps. 120:2-4; Prov. 16:27 [j]Matt. 15:18

Faith and Works

Faith is the means or instrument by which a person is saved. Christians are justified before God by faith (Rom. 3:26; 4:1–5; Gal. 2:16), and by faith they live their lives (2 Cor. 5:7) and sustain their hope (Heb. 10:35–12:3).

Faith cannot be defined in subjective terms, as a feeling or optimistic decision. Neither is it a passive orthodoxy. Faith is a response, directed toward an object and defined by what is believed. Christian faith is trust in the eternal God and His promises secured by Jesus Christ. It is called forth by the gospel as the gospel is made understandable through the gracious work of the Holy Spirit. Christian faith is a personal act, involving the mind, heart, and will, just as it is directed to a personal God, and not an idol or an idea.

It is usual to analyze faith as involving three steps: knowledge, agreement, and trust. First is knowledge, or acquaintance with the content of the gospel; second is agreement, or recognition that the gospel is true; and third is trust, the essential step of committing the self to God. These steps go together in the sense that there can be Christian faith only when the gospel is known and its truth is accepted (Rom. 10:14). Calvin defined faith as "a firm and sure knowledge of the divine favor towards us, founded on the truth of a free promise in Christ, and revealed to our minds and sealed on our hearts by the Holy Spirit" (Calvin, *Institutes* III.2.7).

Through faith we receive Christ, who satisfied the law on our behalf. In this way we are justified through faith alone, without doing the works of the law. But since faith unites us with Christ, it cannot be lifeless. Directed toward God and resting in Him, it is active, "working through love" (Gal. 5:6), seeking to do all the "good works, which God prepared beforehand" for us (Eph. 2:10). Justification is by faith alone, but justifying faith can never be alone.

When James says that faith without works is dead, he is describing a faith that knows the gospel and even agrees with it, but has fallen short of trust in God. Failure to grow, develop, and bear the fruits of righteousness shows that the free gift of God in Christ has never been received. The answer for those with such a faith is not to save themselves by establishing a righteousness of their own, as if they could create faith by their own efforts, but to call on the name of the Lord (Rom. 10:13). God alone can save those for whom it is otherwise impossible (Mark 10:27). Paul shows that good works cannot break this impossibility; James shows that the faith required is faith that rests in the living God.

Even when we have believed, the good works we do are never perfect. They are acceptable to God only because of the mercy of Christ (Rom. 7:13–20; Gal. 5:17). We express our love for God through doing what pleases Him, and He in His kindness promises to reward us for what we do (Phil. 3:12–14; 2 Tim. 4:7, 8). In this we are not making God our debtor, any more than when we first believed in Him. As Augustine noted, God in rewarding us is graciously crowning His own gracious gifts.

3:1–12 James echoes Jesus' emphasis on the crucial importance of the use of words in daily life (Matt. 12:36; Mark 7:20–23).

3:1 judged with greater strictness. James gives a sober warning concerning the responsibility of teachers. Teachers exert influence over trusting students, a relationship that makes the students vulnerable to serious error. The teacher is held in strict account for what he or she teaches. This strict judgment should restrain teachers from careless words. The tongue of the teacher can be a devastating peril. The early church gave high esteem to the office of the teacher (Matt. 5:19; 18:6; cf. Rom. 14:10–12).

3:3–5 James uses metaphors from common experience to illustrate his cardinal point that great results can be achieved by small means. The tongue is a small part of the body that is capable of creating great disasters.

3:6 tongue is a fire. An uncontrolled tongue is likened to a fire that rages out of control (Ps. 120:3, 4; Prov. 16:27).

staining. Evil speech (including blasphemy, gossip, slander, lying, false vows, and the like) has the power to spoil, stain, and corrupt the entire moral character of a person.

whole body, setting on fire the entire
course of life,[1] and set on fire by hell.[2] 7 For
every kind of beast and bird, of reptile and
sea creature, can be tamed and has been
tamed by mankind, 8 but no human being
can tame the tongue. It is a restless evil,
[k]full of deadly poison. 9 With it we bless
our Lord and Father, and with it we curse
people [l]who are made in the likeness of
God. 10 From the same mouth come blessing and cursing. My brothers,[3] these things
ought not to be so. 11 Does a spring pour
forth from the same opening both fresh
and salt water? 12 Can a fig tree, my brothers, bear olives, or a grapevine produce
figs? Neither can a salt pond yield fresh
water.

Wisdom from Above

13 Who is wise and understanding among
you? [m]By his good conduct let him show
his works [n]in the meekness of wisdom.
14 But if you have bitter [o]jealousy and selfish ambition in your hearts, do not boast
and be false to the truth. 15 This is not [p]the
wisdom that comes down from above, but
is earthly, unspiritual, [q]demonic. 16 For
where jealousy and selfish ambition exist,
there will be disorder and every vile practice. 17 But [r]the wisdom from above is first
pure, then [s]peaceable, gentle, open to
reason, [t]full of mercy and good fruits, [u]im-
partial and [v]sincere. 18 And [w]a harvest of
righteousness [x]is sown in peace by those
who make peace.

Warning Against Worldliness

4 What causes quarrels and what causes
fights among you? Is it not this, that
your passions[4] are [y]at war within you?[5]
2 You desire and do not have, so you murder. You covet and cannot obtain, so you
fight and quarrel. You do not have, because
you do not ask. 3 You ask and do not
receive, because you ask [z]wrongly, to
spend it on your passions. 4 [a]You adulterous people! Do you not know that friendship with the world is enmity with God?
[b]Therefore whoever wishes to be a friend of
the world makes himself an enemy of God.
5 Or do you suppose it is to no purpose that
the Scripture says, "He yearns jealously
over the spirit [c]that he has made to dwell in
us"? 6 But [d]he gives more grace. Therefore it
says, [e]"God opposes the proud, but [d]gives
grace to the humble." 7 Submit yourselves

8 [k]Ps. 140:3; Eccles. 10:11; Rom. 3:13
9 [l]See Gen. 1:26
13 [m]ch. 2:18 [n]ch. 1:21
14 [o]ver. 16; Acts 5:17; Rom. 2:8; 2 Cor. 12:20; Gal. 5:20; Phil. 1:17; 2:3; [Rom. 13:13]
15 [p]ch. 1:17 [q][1 Kin. 22:22; 2 Thess. 2:9, 10; 1 Tim. 4:1; Rev. 2:24]
17 [r][1 Cor. 2:6, 7] [s]Heb. 12:11 [t][Luke 6:36] [u]ch. 2:4 (Gk.) [v]Rom. 12:9
18 [w]Prov. 11:18; Isai. 32:17; Hos. 10:12; Amos 6:12; Phil. 1:11 [x]Matt. 5:9; Gal. 6:7, 8
Chapter 4
1 [y]Rom. 7:23; 1 Pet. 2:11
3 [z][1 John 5:14]
4 [a]Isai. 54:5; Jer. 2:2 [b]John 15:19; 1 John 2:15; [Matt. 6:24]
5 [c]1 Cor. 6:19; 2 Cor. 6:16
6 [d]Isai. 54:7, 8; See Matt. 13:12 [e]1 Pet. 5:5; Cited from Prov. 3:34 (Gk.)

1 Or *wheel of birth* 2 Greek *Gehenna* 3 Or *brothers and sisters*; also verse 12 4 Greek *pleasures*; also verse 3 5 Greek *in your members*

3:8 no human being can tame the tongue. The tongue is harder to tame than wild beasts. It is filled with poison more venomous than a viper's (Ps. 58:4; 140:3; Rom. 3:13, 14).

3:9 bless . . . curse. The tongue is capable of use for both virtue and vice. The same mouth uses the tongue for these contradictory purposes.

made in the likeness of God. See "The Image of God" at Gen. 1:27.

3:11, 12 Note the similarity here between James's metaphors and those used by Jesus in Matt. 7:16.

3:13 wise . . . show. Just as James exhorts believers to demonstrate their faith through works, so he also calls for the demonstration of wisdom by godly living.

meekness. The sign of wisdom is a gentle and humble spirit. As arrogance and foolishness go together, so do humility and wisdom.

3:14 bitter jealousy and selfish ambition. Envy and covetousness poison the spirit. They are linked to self-centered and self-serving ambition. These vices blind one from true understanding and are contrary to the love of neighbor.

3:15 earthly, unspiritual, demonic. Divine wisdom is set in bold contrast with the wisdom of this world. The wisdom of the flesh reflects the deception of Satan and is foolishness in the sight of God.

3:16 every vile practice. As James earlier showed that the tongue is capable of creating disastrous evil, so here he emphasizes the destructive power of envy and selfish ambition. From them flow all kinds of evil, including vandalism, murder, adultery, warfare, theft, slander, and other sins that violate people and provoke chaos in the community.

3:17 wisdom from above. Wisdom that is a gift of God (1:5) reflects the purity of God Himself. Again wisdom is linked to godliness as God Himself is the source and fountainhead of true wisdom.

peaceable. This is authentic peace, free of a quarrelsome attitude.

gentle. Thoughtful and respectful of other people's feelings.

open to reason. Willing to listen to and obey others.

full of mercy. The wise person is not stingy in mercy but demonstrates charity in broad measure.

impartial and sincere. The wise person is fair and without deception, deceit, or fraud.

3:18 harvest of righteousness. The fruit reaped by the planting of wisdom is a bountiful crop of righteousness.

4:1 fights. James probes the root cause of divisions among the saints. They are caused by evil desires. Envy is still in view as an evil desire that is destructive.

4:2 you do not ask. That is, "you do not ask" from "God, who gives generously to all" (1:5). Envy is a sin against God. It flows from a lack of gratitude toward God who bestows gifts upon His people. It also results from a failure to seek one's own gifts from God rather than from the world.

4:3 wrongly. God refuses to grant our petitions when they proceed from evil desires. To pray from wrong motives is not to pray in faith (Rom. 14:23; Heb. 11:6).

4:4 adulterous people. Spiritual infidelity is in view here.

4:5 Scripture says. James probably did not have one specific text in mind, a problem similar to that found in Matt. 2:23. The idea may derive partly from Ex. 20:5; Deut. 4:24. If the verse is understood as speaking of the human spirit, James is thinking of texts like Gen. 6:3; 8:21, about the consequences of original sin.

4:6 See Prov. 3:34.

4:7 Submit. This requires a willing act of accepting the authority of God.

therefore to God. [f]Resist the devil, and he will flee from you. **8** [g]Draw near to God, and he will draw near to you. [h]Cleanse your hands, you sinners, and [i]purify your hearts, [j]you double-minded. **9** [k]Be wretched and mourn and weep. Let your laughter be turned to mourning and your joy to gloom. **10** [l]Humble yourselves before the Lord, and he will exalt you.

11 [m]Do not speak evil against one another, brothers.[1] The one who speaks against a brother or [n]judges his brother, speaks evil against the law and judges the law. But if you judge the law, you are not a doer of the law but a judge. **12** There is only [o]one lawgiver and [p]judge, he who is able to save and [q]to destroy. But [r]who are you to judge your neighbor?

Boasting About Tomorrow

13 Come now, you who say, [s]"Today or tomorrow we will go into such and such a town and spend a year there and trade and make a profit"—**14** yet you do not know what tomorrow will bring. What is your life? For [t]you are a mist that appears for a little time and then vanishes. **15** Instead you ought to say, [u]"If the Lord wills, we will live and do this or that." **16** As it is, you boast in your arrogance. [v]All such boasting is evil. **17** [w]So whoever knows the right thing to do and fails to do it, for him it is sin.

Warning to the Rich

5 Come now, [x]you rich, weep and howl for the [y]miseries that are coming upon you. **2** [z]Your riches have rotted and [z]your garments are moth-eaten. **3** Your gold and silver have corroded, and their corrosion will be evidence against you and will eat your flesh like fire. [a]You have laid up treasure [b]in the last days. **4** Behold, [c]the wages of the laborers who mowed your fields, which you kept back by fraud, are crying out against you, and [d]the cries of the harvesters have reached the ears of [e]the Lord of hosts. **5** [f]You have lived on the earth in luxury and [g]in self-indulgence. You have fattened your hearts in [h]a day of slaughter. **6** You have condemned; [i]you have murdered [j]the righteous person. He does not resist you.

Patience in Suffering

7 Be patient, therefore, brothers,[2] until the coming of the Lord. See how the farmer waits for the precious fruit of the earth, being patient about it, until it receives [k]the early and the late rains. **8** You also, be patient. [l]Establish your hearts, for the coming of the Lord [m]is at hand. **9** Do not grumble against one another, brothers, [n]so that you may not be judged; behold, [o]the Judge is standing [p]at the door. **10** As an example of suffering and patience, brothers, take [q]the prophets who spoke in the name of the Lord. **11** Behold, we consider those blessed

7 [f]1 Pet. 5:8, 9; [Eph. 4:27; 6:11]
8 [g]2 Chr. 15:2; Lam. 3:57; Zech. 1:3; Mal. 3:7; [Luke 15:20] [h]Isai. 1:16 [i]Jer. 4:14 [j]ch. 1:8
9 [k][Matt. 5:4]
10 [l]ver. 6; Isai. 57:15; [Luke 1:52]; See Matt. 23:12
11 [m]2 Cor. 12:20; 1 Pet. 2:1; [ch. 5:9] [n]See Matt. 7:1
12 [o]Isai. 33:22 [p]ch. 5:9 [q]Matt. 10:28 [r]Rom. 14:4
13 [s]Prov. 27:1; Luke 12:18-20
14 [t]Ps. 102:3; [Job 7:7]
15 [u]See Acts 18:21
16 [v][1 Cor. 5:6]
17 [w][Luke 12:47, 48; 2 Pet. 2:21]; See John 9:41
Chapter 5
1 [x]Luke 6:24; [Prov. 11:28; Amos 6:1; 1 Tim. 6:9] [y]Rom. 3:16
2 [z]Job 13:28; Isai. 50:9; Matt. 6:19, 20
3 [a]Matt. 6:19; Luke 12:21; Rom. 2:5 [b][ver. 8, 9]
4 [c]Job 24:10; See Lev. 19:13 [d]Deut. 24:15 [e]Rom. 9:29 **5** [f][Job 21:13; Luke 16:19; 2 Pet. 2:13] [g]1 Tim. 5:6 [h]Jer. 12:3 **6** [i]ch. 4:2 [j][Acts 3:14] **7** [k]See Deut. 11:14 **8** [l]1 Thess. 3:13 [m]1 Pet. 4:7; [Rom. 13:11, 12; Phil. 4:5; Heb. 10:25, 37] **9** [n]Matt. 7:1 [o][1 Pet. 4:5; Rev. 22:12] [p]Matt. 24:33; Mark 13:29; [1 Cor. 4:5] **10** [q]Matt. 5:12; 23:34; Acts 7:52; Heb. 11:32-38

[1] Or *brothers and sisters* [2] Or *brothers and sisters*; also verses 9, 10, 12, 19

We are under His authority whether we submit to it or not. Here "submit" means "to obey."

Resist the devil, and he will flee. Satan is not equal in power or authority to God. Though Satan is powerful, he is not invincible. He flees from saints wearing the armor of God who resist him.

4:9 Be wretched and mourn and weep. This is a call to genuine repentance by which we mourn for our sins.

4:11 speak evil. A sin of speech, slander flows out of envy and reflects the work of Satan. The Greek word for "devil" means "slanderer." Slandering other Christians destroys fellowship and breaks the royal law. When we speak falsely against a fellow believer, we speak not only against the person but against the law of God. The slanderer sets himself above the law.

4:14 know what tomorrow will bring. James rebukes the person who lives life and makes future plans without any regard for the providence of God. Such a person lives without regard for divine sovereignty.

4:15 If the Lord wills. The word "if" refers to future events that are conditional. Here the primary consideration in all future planning is the will of the sovereign God.

4:16 boast. Boasting of one's own power and accomplishments is evil. The Christian is to boast only of the Lord (2 Cor. 11:30; 12:5, 9).

4:17 sin. The sins of neglect and of omission are in view here.

5:1 rich. The Bible nowhere condemns wealth itself. It is often viewed as the blessing of God (Prov. 10:22). However, the rich, as a social class, are often guilty of exploiting and oppressing the poor. God reserves severe judgment for this (Luke 6:24).

5:2, 3 rotted . . . moth-eaten . . . corroded. Earthly treasures are subject to decay and eventually perish. James echoes the teaching of Jesus (Matt. 6:20).

5:4 wages . . . you kept back. This is a violation of the law of God. Wages are not only to be paid, they are to be paid on time (Lev. 19:13; Deut. 24:14, 15).

5:5 fattened your hearts. Like animals fattened for slaughter, the rich are unaware of the disaster awaiting them.

5:6 condemned . . . murdered. The unjust use of power often causes the death of innocent people. The verse could also be understood figuratively, since to rob people of their wages and livelihood is to commit a kind of murder against them.

5:7 patient. The saints require patience as they await God's promised vindication of His people. God promises justice to correct prevailing forms of injustice in this world (Luke 18:1–8).

5:9 Judge is standing at the door. This verse reflects the urgent sense

who remained steadfast. You have heard of
[r]the steadfastness of Job, and you have
seen [s]the purpose of the Lord, how [t]the
Lord is compassionate and merciful.
12 But above all, my brothers, [u]do not
swear, either by heaven or by earth or by
any other oath, but let your "yes" be yes
and your "no" be no, so that you may not
fall under condemnation.

The Prayer of Faith

13 Is anyone among you suffering? Let
him pray. Is anyone cheerful? Let him [v]sing
praise. 14 Is anyone among you sick? Let
him call for the elders of the church, and
let them pray over him, [w]anointing him
with oil in the name of the Lord. 15 And the
prayer of faith will save the one who is sick,
and the Lord will raise him up. And [x]if he
has committed sins, he will be forgiven.
16 Therefore, [y]confess your sins to one
another and pray for one another, [z]that you
may be healed. [a]The prayer of a righteous
person has great power as it is working.[1]
17 Elijah was a man [b]with a nature like ours,
and [c]he prayed fervently that it might not
rain, and for [d]three years and six months it
did not rain on the earth. 18 [e]Then he
prayed again, and heaven gave rain, and
the earth bore its fruit.
19 My brothers, [f]if anyone among you
wanders from the truth and someone
[g]brings him back, 20 let him know that whoever brings back a sinner from his wandering [h]will save his soul from death and [i]will
cover a multitude of sins.

11 [r]Job 1:21, 22; 2:10 [s]Job 42:10, 12 [t]See Ex. 34:6 12 [u]Matt. 5:34 13 [v][Col. 3:16] 14 [w]Mark 6:13; [Mark 16:18] 15 [x]Isai. 33:24; Matt. 9:2; Mark 2:5; Luke 5:20 16 [y]Acts 19:18 [z]Heb. 12:13 [a]Gen. 18:23-32; 20:17; Num. 11:2; 1 Kin. 13:6; 17:22; 2 Kin. 4:33; 19:15-20; 20:2-5; Job 42:8; Prov. 15:29 17 [b]Acts 14:15 [c]1 Kin. 17:1; 18:1 [d]Luke 4:25 18 [e]1 Kin. 18:42, 45 19 [f][Matt. 18:15; Gal. 6:1] [g]Ps. 51:13; Dan. 12:3; Mal. 2:6; [Luke 1:16] 20 [h]See Rom. 11:14 [i]1 Pet. 4:8; [Neh. 4:5; Ps. 32:1; 85:2; Prov. 10:12]

[1] Or *The effective prayer of a righteous person has great power*

of the nearness of Christ's coming. James is echoing the New Testament hope of the return of Jesus who comes at the end of the age. James may also be thinking of the radical nearness of judgment facing every person whose life will soon be over and who will stand before the judgment of God. See v. 3 where James mentions the "last days."

5:12 above all. This emphatic exhortation signals a weighty priority for godliness. To exalt refraining from false oaths and vows to a high level of priority may seem strange to some, but is consistent with the biblical concern for covenant-keeping and the sanctity of the faith.

do not swear. This is not a prohibition against cursing or the use of vulgarity. It concerns taking oaths by appealing to objects as witnesses (which in biblical terms is a form of idolatry). Only God has the power to be an omnipresent, omniscient witness to oaths and vows. Just and godly vows are not prohibited because they form a vital part of all covenants.

"yes" be yes. The Christian is expected to be a person whose word can be trusted. James's teaching here echoes that of Jesus in the Sermon on the Mount (Matt. 5:34–37).

5:13 Let him sing praise. See "Music in the Church" at Col. 3:16.

5:14 elders. See Acts 14:23; Titus 1:5.

anointing him with oil. Olive oil was commonly used in medicine in the ancient world (Mark 6:13; Luke 10:34). The oil may also have a symbolic reference to the healing power of God.

5:15 prayer of faith. There is no special "prayer of faith" that has healing power. The power of trusting and faithful prayer is accented here; the Christian community should be devoutly engaged in intercessory prayer for the sick. This verse is the classic proof text for the institution of the Roman Catholic sacrament of extreme unction. Extreme unction is a healing rite that has come to be thought of primarily as the "last rites" in preparation for death.

committed sins. Sin and illness are not unrelated. Forgiveness is therapeutic to the body as well as to the soul.

5:16 confess your sins. Though confession to a priest is not required by Scripture, confession to God and to one another is. Overreaction against the Roman Catholic sacrament of penance may lead to a neglect of authentic godly confession.

righteous person. A godly person who prays in faith is a just or righteous person.

5:17 Elijah. Though Elijah held the special office of Old Testament prophet, he shares a common humanity with all believers. His effectual prayer life is a model for the saints.

5:19 wanders from the truth. To stray into sinful patterns.

5:20 brings back a sinner. The care of the souls of the community is a matter of concern for every member, not only church officers or the clergy. Mutual help and encouragement are required.

cover. Refers to God's covering of sins with forgiveness (Ps. 32:1; 85:2).

THE FIRST EPISTLE OF

Peter

AUTHOR

The author identifies himself as "Peter, an apostle of Jesus Christ" (1:1). That he is the well-known apostle of the Gospels and Acts is confirmed by both internal and external evidence. The author describes himself as "a witness of the sufferings of Christ" (5:1), and there are numerous echoes of Jesus' teaching and deeds in the epistle (e.g., 5:2, 3; John 21:15–17). Parallels of thought and phrase between 1 Peter and Peter's speeches in Acts lend further support to Peter's authorship (e.g., 2:7, 8; Acts 4:10, 11).

The external attestation of 1 Peter as a genuine epistle of Peter is widespread, early, and clear; there is no evidence that it was ever attributed to anyone else. Apart from the possible witness of 2 Pet. 3:1 (note), Irenaeus (c. A.D. 185; *Against Heresies* 4.9.2), Tertullian (c. A.D. 160–225), Clement of Alexandria (c. A.D. 150–215), and Origen (c. A.D. 185–253) all attributed the epistle to Peter. By the time of Eusebius (c. A.D. 265–339) there was no question of its authenticity (*Ecclesiastical History* 3.3.1).

Although the case for Peter's authorship is strong, linguistic and historical objections have been raised in the last two centuries. The Greek of 1 Peter is said to be too polished and too influenced by the Septuagint (the Greek translation of the Old Testament) to have come from an uneducated Galilean fisherman like Peter (Acts 4:13). The persecutions alluded to in the epistle (4:12–19; 5:6–9) are alleged to reflect a situation later than Peter's lifetime.

None of these objections is decisive against Peter's authorship. In response to the linguistic objection, several points can be made. First-century Galilee was bilingual (Aramaic and Greek), and it is not unlikely that a commercial fisherman would have known the language of commerce. The description of Peter and John as "uneducated, common men" in Acts 4:13 may refer only to their lack of formal training in the Scriptures. The thirty years that elapsed between Peter's days as a fisherman and the time the epistle was written would have provided ample opportunity for him to improve his proficiency in Greek. Finally, Silvanus' possible role as secretary (5:12) could account for the smoother style of 1 Peter as compared to 2 Peter.

With regard to the historical objections, the sufferings alluded to by Peter can just as well be accounted for by local, sporadic harassment, which was the routine experience of early Christians from the days of the apostles on, as by official persecution in the days of Domitian (c. A.D. 95) or Trajan (c. A.D. 111).

DATE AND OCCASION

According to 5:13, Peter was in "Babylon" when he wrote the epistle. Various identifications of the location have been suggested, among them (a) a military outpost in Egypt, (b) the ancient Mesopotamian city itself, and (c) Rome. Several lines of evidence favor the latter. Mark, who was with Peter when he wrote (5:13), is known to have been with Paul in Rome (Col. 4:10; Philem. 24). Rome is often seen as the "Babylon" of Revelation (Rev. 17:5, 9). This interpretation has been generally accepted since the second century. The uniform testimony of early church history is that Peter was in Rome at the end of his life.

If Rome is the place of origin, the epistle must have been composed between A.D. 60 and 68. The first limit is established by Peter's familiarity with Ephesians and Colossians (cf. 2:18 with Col. 3:22; and 3:1–6 with Eph. 5:22–24), the second limit by the tradition that Peter was crucified upside down in Rome in A.D. 68 at the latest.

While the introduction ("the dispersion," 1:1 and note) and the frequent Old Testament quotations and allusions in the epistle might imply Jewish Christian recipients (so Calvin), there are stronger indications that most were from a pagan background. The reference in 1:18, for example, to "the futile ways inherited from your forefathers" hardly seems fitting for Jews. Furthermore, the sins listed in 4:3 are typically pagan.

It is apparent from the letter that the readers were suffering persecution for their faith (1:6, 7; 3:13–17; 4:12–19; 5:8, 9). But nothing in the letter indicates official, legislative persecution or requires a date of composition later than the 60s. Their sufferings were the trials common to first-century Christians, and included insults (4:4, 14) and slanderous accusations of wrongdoing (2:12; 3:16). Beatings (2:20), social ostracism, sporadic mob violence, and local police action may have been involved as well.

CHARACTERISTICS AND THEMES

Peter writes to encourage persecuted and bewildered Christians and to exhort them to stand fast in their faith (5:12). To that end he repeatedly turns their thoughts to the joys and glories of their eternal inheritance (1:3–13; 4:13; 5:1, 4) and instructs them about proper Christian behavior in the midst of unjust suffering (4:1, 19). While addressed primarily to persecuted Christians, the principles Peter teaches apply to all suffering, regardless of the cause, provided it is not occasioned by one's own sin. On the basis of this epistle, Peter has with justice been called "the apostle of hope" (cf. 1:3, 13, 21; 3:15). The central exhortation of the entire epistle can be summed up in the phrase "trust and obey" (cf. 4:19).

OUTLINE OF 1 PETER

I. Salutation (1:1, 2)

II. The Christian's Sure Salvation (1:3–12)

III. The Implications of Salvation (1:13–3:12)

A. *Personal Holiness (1:13–16)*

B. *Reverent Fear (1:17–21)*

C. *Mutual Love (1:22–2:3)*

D. *Membership in a Spiritual Community (2:4–10)*

E. *The Christian and Social Relationships (2:11–3:12)*

1. The World in General (2:11, 12)
2. The State (2:13–17)
3. The Household (2:18–3:7)
4. Summary (3:8–12)

IV. Christian Suffering and Service (3:13–5:11)

A. *The Blessing of Suffering for Righteousness' Sake (3:13–22)*

B. *Living for God's Glory (4:1–11)*

C. *Suffering as a Christian (4:12–19)*

D. *Humility and Alertness in Suffering (5:1–11)*

1. Faithful and Humble Leadership (5:1–4)
2. Humility and Alertness (5:5–9)
3. Promise of Strength and Vindication (5:10, 11)

V. Final Greetings (5:12–14)

Greeting

1 Peter, an apostle of Jesus Christ, To
those who are elect exiles of [a]the dispersion in Pontus, Galatia, Cappadocia,
Asia, and Bithynia, 2 according to [b]the foreknowledge of God the Father, [c]in the sanctification of the Spirit, for obedience to
Jesus Christ and [d]for sprinkling with his
blood:
May [e]grace and [f]peace be multiplied to
you.

Born Again to a Living Hope

3 [g]Blessed be the God and Father of our
Lord Jesus Christ! [h]According to his great
mercy, [i]he has caused us to be born again
to a living hope [j]through the resurrection
of Jesus Christ from the dead, 4 to [k]an inheritance that is imperishable, undefiled,
and [l]unfading, [m]kept in heaven for you,
5 who by God's power are being guarded
[n]through faith for a salvation [o]ready to be
revealed in the last time. 6 In this you
rejoice, though now for a little while, if
necessary, you have been grieved by [p]vari-
ous trials, 7 so that [q]the tested genuineness
of your faith—more precious than gold
that perishes [r]though it is tested by [s]fire—
may be found to result in [t]praise and glory
and honor at the revelation of Jesus Christ.
8 [u]Though you have not seen him, you love
him. [v]Though you do not now see him,
you believe in him and rejoice with joy
that is inexpressible and filled with glory,

Chapter 1
1 [a]See James 1:1
2 [b]Acts 2:23; [Rom. 8:29; 11:2] [c]See 1 Thess. 4:3 [d]Heb. 10:22; 12:24 [e]2 Pet. 1:2 [f]Dan. 4:1; Jude 2
3 [g]2 Cor. 1:3; Eph. 1:3 [h]Tit. 3:5 [i]ver. 23 [j]ch. 3:21; [1 Cor. 15:20]
4 [k]Rom. 8:17 [l][ch. 5:4] [m][Col. 1:5; 2 Tim. 4:8]
5 [n]Eph. 2:8 [o][ch. 5:10; Rom. 8:18; 2 Cor. 4:17; Heb. 12:11]
6 [p]James 1:2; [ch. 4:12]
7 [q]James 1:3 [r]Job 23:10; Ps. 66:10; Prov. 17:3; Isai. 48:10 [s]1 Cor. 3:13 [t]Rom. 2:7, 10; 1 Cor. 4:5; [2 Thess. 1:7-12] 8 [u][1 John 4:20] [v][Heb. 11:27]; See John 20:29

1:1 Peter. The name (which means "rock") was given by Jesus (Matt. 16:18; John 1:42) in anticipation of the disciple's role in the early church. His given Hebrew name was probably "Simeon," or "Simon" in Greek. "Cephas" (John 1:42; 1 Cor. 1:12) is the transliteration of the Aramaic word for "rock."

apostle. See note 2 Cor. 1:1.

elect. Peter reminds his readers of their privileged and secure position as the objects of God's sovereign, gracious, eternal choice to be His people in and through Jesus Christ (2:9, 10).

exiles. This word (seen again in 2:11) emphasizes the temporary nature of a sojourner's stay in a place. As exiles, Christians live in the world, but their real homeland is in heaven (Phil. 3:20; Heb. 11:13–16) and their hope is anchored there.

the dispersion. This word (Greek *diaspora*) was a technical term among Greek-speaking Jews for the Jews living outside Palestine (John 7:35). Here it is probably used figuratively to describe Christians as people who are away from their true homeland.

Pontus. Although 1 Peter has the character of a general letter (like James, 2 Peter, 1 John, Jude), it differs from the other General Epistles in that it specifies the areas in which the readers lived.

1:2 foreknowledge. Includes God's sovereign, loving, effective choice and purpose (Rom. 8:29 note). The corresponding verb ("foreknown") is used of Christ in v. 20.

in the sanctification of the Spirit. Note the close connection of the Father's electing love with the Spirit's work of applying redemption to the elect (2 Thess. 2:13). This "sanctification" includes all the Spirit's operations in setting sinners apart from sin (including regeneration and faith) and purifying them for God's service (sanctification in the progressive sense).

obedience. The initial act of obedience is faith in Christ (John 6:28, 29) and the fundamental element of all obedience is continued faith. To suggest that election is on the basis of God's foreknowledge (that is, mere foresight) of faith would introduce a contradiction into this verse, since election is "for" or with the goal of faith (obedience), and not because of it (Eph. 1:3, 4; 2 Tim. 1:9).

his blood. Sprinkling of blood was part of the Old Testament ritual service. In general, the appearance of blood advertises the death of a victim. Abel's blood cried for vengeance (Gen. 4:10), and Jesus' blood cries for forgiveness (Luke 23:34; Heb. 12:24). In the worship of the Old Testament, the death of the victim establishes a covenant, and the sprinkling incorporates the worshipers as participants, making them publicly liable for the covenant's benefits and responsibilities (Ex. 24:8).

grace and peace. This greeting is also a blessing, and would have special relevance for suffering Christians. Grace is God's loving favor to sinners in Christ, while peace is the objective condition of being right with God through Christ (Rom. 5:1, 2), together with all that flows from that relationship. This verse proclaims all three persons of the one God who blesses. See "One and Three: The Trinity" at Is. 44:6.

1:3 According to his great mercy. This emphasizes that salvation is based entirely on God's loving initiative.

caused us to be born again. Although the verb used here and in 1:23 occurs nowhere else in the New Testament, the thought is found frequently (John 1:12, 13; 3:3–8; Titus 3:5; James 1:18).

living hope. A key word in this epistle is "hope" (1:13, 21; 3:15). In the Bible, hope is not uncertainty or wishful thinking, but a confident expectation of future blessing based on facts and promises. "Living" indicates the undying and permanent character of this hope.

1:4 inheritance. As God's children by the New Birth, Christians are heirs of God and co-heirs with Christ (Rom. 8:16, 17). Their inheritance is called "salvation" (v. 5; Heb. 1:14).

1:5 who by God's power are being guarded through faith. This verse stresses both the priority of divine grace and the importance of the human action that results from grace. Faith is the gift of God, but believers are still responsible for exercising that faith, or steadfast trust, in spiritual battle (5:8, 9; Eph. 6:16; Phil. 2:12, 13). The strength of God's protection is conveyed by means of a military term, here translated "guarded," signifying vigilant defense of a fortress.

salvation. Here the word means complete and final future deliverance from sin and full enjoyment of eternal glory (v. 9; 4:13, 14; 5:1, 4).

the last time. Christ's return and the final manifestation of His power and glory.

1:6 if necessary. Although God never tempts anyone to sin (James 1:13), He allows or sends trials when necessary and in the right measure for strengthening faith (v. 7).

1:7 This explains why trials might be necessary (v. 6; cf. Rom. 5:3, 4; James 1:2–4).

tested by fire. As men use fire to refine precious metals, so God uses trials to distinguish genuine faith from superficial profession, and at the same time to strengthen faith (Job 23:10).

be found to result in praise and glory and honor. The ultimate goal of trials is the reward of glorification (5:1, 4).

at the revelation of Jesus Christ. This is the Second Coming (v. 5; 4:13; 5:1; 1 Cor. 4:3–5).

9 obtaining [w] the outcome of your faith, the
salvation of your souls.
10 Concerning this salvation, [x] the prophets who prophesied about the grace that
was to be yours searched and inquired
carefully, 11 inquiring [y] what person or time
[z] the Spirit of Christ in them was indicating
[a] when he predicted [b] the sufferings of
Christ and the subsequent glories. 12 [c] It was
revealed to them that [d] they were serving
not themselves but you, in the things that
have now been announced to you through
those who preached the good news to you
[e] by the Holy Spirit sent from heaven,
[f] things into which angels long to look.

Called to Be Holy

13 Therefore, [g] preparing your minds for
action,[1] and [h] being sober-minded, set your
hope fully on the grace that will be brought
to you at the revelation of Jesus Christ. 14 As
obedient children, [i] do not be conformed to
the passions [j] of your former ignorance,
15 but [k] as he who called you is holy, you
also be holy [l] in all your conduct, 16 since it
is written, [m] "You shall be holy, for I am
holy." 17 And if you [n] call on him as Father
who [o] judges [p] impartially according to each
one's deeds, conduct yourselves [q] with fear
throughout the time of your exile, 18 knowing that you [r] were ransomed from [s] the
futile ways inherited from your forefathers,
not with perishable things such as silver or
gold, 19 but [t] with the precious blood of
Christ, like that of [u] a lamb [v] without blemish or spot. 20 He was foreknown before the
foundation of the world but [w] was made
manifest [x] in the last times for your sake,
21 [y] who through him are believers in God,
[z] who raised him from the dead and [a] gave
him glory, so that your faith and hope are
in God.
22 Having purified your souls by your
obedience to the truth for [b] a sincere brotherly love, [c] love one another earnestly from

9 [w] Rom. 6:22 **10** [x] 2 Pet. 1:19; [Dan. 8:15; Matt. 13:17; Luke 10:24] **11** [y] Dan. 9:24-26 [z] Rom. 8:9; [2 Pet. 1:21]; See Acts 16:7 [a] See Matt. 26:24 [b] Isai. 52:13–53:12; Luke 24:26; Acts 3:18 **12** [c] Dan. 12:4, 9, 13 [d] [Matt. 13:17; Heb. 11:39, 40] [e] Acts 2:2-4 [f] [Dan. 8:13; 12:5-7; Eph. 3:10] **13** [g] See Luke 12:35 [h] ch. 4:7; 5:8; 1 Thess. 5:6, 8; 2 Tim. 4:5 **14** [i] ch. 4:2, 3; Rom. 12:2; Tit. 3:3 [j] Acts 17:30 **15** [k] 1 John 3:3; [2 Cor. 7:1; 1 Thess. 4:7; Heb. 12:14] [l] James 3:13 **16** [m] Cited from Lev. 11:44

17 [n] Jer. 3:19; Mal. 1:6; 2 Cor. 6:18; [Matt. 6:9] [o] See Ps. 62:12 [p] See James 2:1 [q] ch. 3:15; 2 Cor. 7:1; [Rom. 11:20] **18** [r] [Ps. 49:8; 130:8; 1 Cor. 6:20; Tit. 2:14; 2 Pet. 2:1] [s] See Eph. 4:17 **19** [t] See Acts 20:28 [u] See John 1:29 [v] Heb. 9:14; [Ex. 12:5] **20** [w] See Rom. 16:26 [x] Heb. 1:2 **21** [y] John 12:44 [z] [Rom. 10:9]; See Acts 2:24 [a] Acts 3:13; Heb. 2:9; [ch. 3:22]; See John 7:39 **22** [b] Rom. 12:9; See Heb. 13:1 [c] 1 Tim. 1:5

[1] Greek *girding up the loins of your mind*

1:9 obtaining. Believers already enjoy certain essential elements of salvation (e.g., peace and fellowship with God), but full possession awaits the return of Christ (v. 5).

souls. Used here to mean "self" or "person"; compare the same usage in 3:20.

1:11 what . . . time. The prophets knew the Messiah would come (Is. 7:14; 9:6; 11:1), but they did not know when or how (cf. Dan. 12:6, 9).

the Spirit of Christ. This exact phrase appears only here and in Rom. 8:9 (cf. Acts 16:6, 7; Gal. 4:6; Phil. 1:19). The Holy Spirit is called this because He is sent by Christ (John 15:26) and because after the Resurrection, Christ and the Spirit act as one in applying redemption to the believer. See notes Rom. 8:10; 1 Cor. 15:45.

1:12 It was revealed to them. Peter does not say how or when the prophets learned that they were actually serving future generations.

things . . . announced. The sufferings and glories of Christ (v. 11) are the content of the gospel (Luke 24:25–27, 45–47). The events predicted by the prophets are the events fulfilled in Christ and told to the church by the gospel messengers.

Holy Spirit sent from heaven. The origin of the gospel message is God. The same Spirit who inspired the prophets directed the gospel messengers. The Old and New Testaments are a unity centering on Christ and His salvation.

angels long to look. Celestial beings are intensely interested in redemption, but their knowledge and experience of it are limited. God's plan is made known to them through the church (Eph. 3:10).

1:13 preparing your minds for action. As we would say, "fasten your belt" or "roll up your sleeves." Peter asks us to prepare for vigorous and sustained spiritual exertion.

1:15 called you. God's gracious initiative effectually calls us into the new life in Christ.

be holy. Just as Old Testament Israel was set apart by God from the surrounding nations to be holy, so also the church is to be set apart from sin to the service of God (2:9; Lev. 19:2). The Christian's standard of and motivation for holiness is the absolute moral perfection of God Himself (v. 16; Matt. 5:48; Eph. 5:1).

1:17 Father who judges impartially. Though Christians will not be condemned for their sins (2:24; Is. 53:4, 5), they will be judged for their deeds as Christians and rewarded accordingly (Rom. 14:10–12; 1 Cor. 3:12–15). The reward promised, however, is not based strictly on merit; though it is bestowed according to works, the reward is still gracious. Augustine called it God's crowning His own gifts.

with fear. God is both Father and Judge, and believers must approach Him with humble reverence and awe (Ps. 34:11).

throughout the time of your exile. The Greek word for "exile" suggests those who live in a place as unnaturalized aliens, and emphasizes the Christian's temporary, pilgrim status in the world.

1:18 ransomed. Freed from the bondage of sin by the payment of a price (Rom. 8:2; Gal. 3:13; Eph. 1:7). The price of redemption is the blood of Christ (v. 19).

futile ways inherited. The emptiness and worthlessness of pagan worship is a frequent theme of scriptural writers (Jer. 2:5; Acts 14:15). Although the New Testament condemns certain Jewish traditions that added to the demands of the Old Testament law (Mark 7:8–13), Peter here seems to have Gentile paganism in view (1:14; 4:3).

1:19 lamb. The lamb is from the Old Testament sacrificial system, especially the Passover (Ex. 12:3; Is. 53:7; John 1:29).

without blemish or spot. In order to be acceptable, a sacrifice had to be free from all defect (Lev. 22:20–25). Christ's sinless life qualified Him to die for the sins of others (Heb. 4:15; 7:26, 27).

1:20 before the foundation of the world. Christ was chosen as Redeemer of the elect in eternity past (John 17:24; Eph. 1:4).

the last times. Includes the entire period between the first and second comings of Jesus (Acts 2:17; Heb. 1:2).

1:21 through him are believers in God. As the Mediator between God and humanity, Christ provides the only access to God (John 14:6). In Christ the Father is revealed (John 1:18), and Christ's redeeming death has opened the path of access to God (3:18).

a pure heart, 23 [d]since you have been born
again, [e]not of perishable seed but of imperishable, through [f]the living and abiding
word of God; 24 for

[g]"All flesh is like grass
and all its glory like the flower of
grass.
The grass withers,
and the flower falls,
25 [h]but the word of the Lord remains
forever."

And this word [i]is the good news that was
preached to you.

A Living Stone and a Holy People

2 [j]So put away all malice and all deceit
and hypocrisy and envy and all slander. 2 [k]Like newborn infants, long for the
pure spiritual [l]milk, that by it you may
grow up to salvation— 3 if indeed you have
[m]tasted that the Lord is good.
4 As you come to him, a living stone [n]re-
jected by men but in the sight of God chosen and precious, 5 [o]you yourselves like
living stones are being built up as [p]a spiritual house, to be [q]a holy priesthood, [r]to
offer spiritual sacrifices [s]acceptable to God
through Jesus Christ. 6 For it stands in
Scripture:

[t]"Behold, I am laying in Zion a stone,
a cornerstone chosen and
precious,
[u]and whoever believes in him will not
be put to shame."

7 So the honor is for you who [v]believe, but
for those who [v]do not believe,

[w]"The stone that the builders rejected
has become the cornerstone,"[1]

8 and

[x]"A stone of stumbling,
and a rock of offense."

They stumble because they disobey the
word, [y]as they were destined to do.
9 But you are [z]a chosen race, [a]a royal
[b]priesthood, [c]a holy nation, [d]a people for
his own possession, that you may proclaim

23 [d]ver. 3; [John 3:3; James 1:18] [e]John 1:13 [f]Heb. 4:12 24 [g]James 1:10, 11; Cited from Isai. 40:6, 8 25 [h][Matt. 24:35] [i]Isai. 40:9 **Chapter 2** 1 [j]Eph. 4:22, 25, 31; Col. 3:8 2 [k]See Matt. 18:3 [l]1 Cor. 3:2; Heb. 5:12, 13 3 [m]Ps. 34:8; Heb. 6:5 4 [n]ver. 6, 7 5 [o]Eph. 2:20-22; [1 Cor. 3:9] [p]Heb. 3:4, 6 [q]ver. 9 [r]Isai. 56:7; Mal. 1:11; Rom. 12:1; Heb. 13:15 [s]Rom. 15:16; Phil. 4:18 6 [t]Cited from Isai. 28:16 [u]Rom. 9:33; 10:11 7 [v][2 Cor. 2:16] [w]Cited from Ps. 118:22 8 [x]Rom. 9:33; Cited from Isai. 8:14

[y][Rom. 9:22; Jude 4] 9 [z]Deut. 10:15; Isai. 43:20 [a]Ex. 19:6; Rev. 1:6; 5:10 [b]Isai. 61:6; 66:21 [c]Deut. 7:6 [d]Ex. 19:5; Deut. 7:6; Isai. 43:21; Mal. 3:17

[1] Greek *the head of the corner*

1:23 Genuine and enduring love for others (v. 22) is possible only because of the love God has first shown to us in giving us the new birth in Christ (John 13:35; 1 John 4:7–11).

born again. See note 1:3; "Regeneration: The New Birth" at John 3:3.

perishable . . . imperishable. Peter compares and contrasts human procreation with the life-giving power of God's Word (Luke 8:11).

through the . . . word of God. God's Word is used by the Holy Spirit as an instrument to bring sinners to a knowledge of God's grace in Jesus Christ (Heb. 4:12; James 1:18).

2:2 newborn infants. Peter continues the imagery of new birth (1:23). Believers should have the same yearning for spiritual food that a healthy infant has for its mother's milk.

pure . . . milk. Although the churches to which Peter writes no doubt included many recent converts, the emphasis at this point is not that teaching should be elementary, like the "milk" of 1 Cor. 3:1–3, but that it should be pure. If it is founded on God's Word, teaching will be pure and nourishing (1:22–25).

2:4 come to him. "Coming" to Christ includes initial repentance and faith, but the Greek tense implies a continual drawing near as well.

living stone. Christ is this stone (1 Cor. 10:4). The image of "rock" and "stone" is common in the Old Testament (Ps. 118:22; Is. 8:14; 28:16) and is applied by Jesus to Himself (Matt. 21:42). "Living" indicates that Christ is the source and giver of life (John 1:4; 1 Cor. 15:45). Jesus often uses imagery drawn from stonemasonry, a trade He was intimately acquainted with. Carpenters in antiquity worked with stones as well as wood.

2:5 living stones. A phrase emphasizing both Christians' union with and resemblance to Christ, the "living stone" (v. 4).

spiritual house. The background of the symbolism is the Old Testament temple as the house or dwelling place of God. The church, indwelt by the Holy Spirit, is the true temple of God (2 Cor. 6:16; Eph. 2:19–22; Heb. 3:6).

holy priesthood. Every true believer is a priest (v. 9) in the sense of having equal and immediate access to God and serving Him personally.

spiritual sacrifices. While Christ's once-for-all sacrifice of propitiation on the cross has fulfilled the Old Testament sacrificial system and rendered it obsolete (Heb. 8:13; 10:9, 10, 18), the appropriateness of "sacrifice" (understood as the grateful response of a redeemed people) remains. These sacrifices are "spiritual" in contrast to all the material sacrifices prescribed in the Old Testament sacrificial system. Such sacrifice is seen both in the Christian's worship and pattern of living (Rom. 12:1; Phil. 4:18; Heb. 13:5; Rev. 8:3, 4; cf. Ps. 51:16, 17).

acceptable to God through Jesus Christ. The priesthood of all believers depends on the eternal high priesthood of Christ, through whose once-for-all sacrifice and continual intercession both Christians personally and their sacrifices are acceptable to God (Heb. 13:15, 16).

2:6 cornerstone. The great stone laid for the foundation at the place where two walls come together and of special importance for the stability of the entire building. The church is established on the prophets and apostles, who are held together by the chief cornerstone—Christ (Eph. 2:20).

2:7 the cornerstone. Lit. "the head of the corner."

2:8 they were destined. This verse teaches both divine sovereignty and human responsibility. People are condemned ("stumble") because they "disobey" but this disobedience does not occur apart from the sovereign will of God (Rom. 9:14–24).

2:9, 10 Peter's language in these verses, applying the Old Testament terms for Israel to the church, asserts the continuity between Old Testament Israel and the New Testament church, representing them as the one people of God.

2:9 But you. This marks a sharp contrast between the destiny of unbelievers (v. 8) and the status of the elect. The theme of God's sovereign choice of both Christ and the church is prominent in this passage (vv. 6, 9).

that you may proclaim. The election and calling of God's people is not only for salvation but for service as well. All believers are called to bear joyful witness to the saving acts of God.

the excellencies of him who called you [e]out
of darkness into [f]his marvelous light.
10 [g]Once you were not a people, but now you
are God's people; once you had not received
mercy, but now you have received mercy.
11 Beloved, I urge you [h]as sojourners and
exiles [i]to abstain from the passions of the
flesh, [j]which wage war against your soul.
12 [k]Keep your conduct among the Gentiles
honorable, so that when they speak against
you as evildoers, [l]they may see your good
deeds and glorify God on [m]the day of visitation.

Submission to Authority

13 [n]Be subject for the Lord's sake to every
human institution,[1] whether it be to the
emperor[2] as supreme, 14 or to governors as
sent by him [o]to punish those who do evil
and [p]to praise those who do good. 15 For
this is the will of God, [q]that by doing good
you should put to silence the ignorance of
foolish people. 16 [r]Live as people who are
free, not using your freedom as a cover-up
for evil, but [s]living as servants[3] of God.
17 [t]Honor everyone. [u]Love the brotherhood.
[v]Fear God. Honor the emperor.

18 [w]Servants, be subject to your masters
with all respect, not only to the good and
gentle but also to the unjust. 19 For this is a
gracious thing, when, [x]mindful of God, one
endures sorrows while suffering unjustly.
20 For what credit is it if, when you sin and
are beaten for it, you endure? But [y]if when
you do good and suffer for it you endure,
this is a gracious thing in the sight of God.
21 For [z]to this you have been called, [y]be-
cause Christ also suffered for you, [a]leaving
you an example, so that you might follow
in his steps. 22 [b]He committed no sin, neither was deceit found in his mouth.
23 [c]When he was reviled, he did not revile in
return; when he suffered, he did not
threaten, [d]but continued entrusting himself to him who judges justly. 24 [e]He himself
bore our sins in his body on the tree, that
we [f]might die to sin and [g]live to righteousness. [h]By his wounds you have been
healed. 25 For [i]you were straying like sheep,

9 [e][Isai. 42:16]; See Acts 26:18 [f]Ps. 36:9 **10** [g]Hos. 1:6, 9, 10; 2:23; Rom. 9:25, 26; 10:19 **11** [h]See Lev. 25:23 [i]Rom. 13:14; Gal. 5:24 [j]James 4:1 **12** [k][ch. 3:16; 2 Cor. 8:21; Phil. 2:15; Tit. 2:8] [l]Matt. 5:16; 2 Cor. 9:13; Gal. 1:24 [m]Isai. 10:3; Luke 19:44 **13** [n]Rom. 13:1; Tit. 3:1 **14** [o]Rom. 13:4 [p]Rom. 13:3 **15** [q]ver. 12 **16** [r]See James 1:25 [s]1 Cor. 7:22; [Rom. 6:22] **17** [t]Rom. 12:10; 13:7 [u]See Heb. 13:1 [v]Prov. 24:21

18 [w]Eph. 6:5; Col. 3:22; 1 Tim. 6:1; Tit. 2:9 **19** [x]ch. 3:14, 17; [ch. 4:16]

20 [y]ch. 3:17, 18; 4:13, 16 **21** [z]ch. 3:9; See Acts 14:22 [y][See ver. 20 above] [a]See Matt. 11:29 **22** [b]Isai. 53:9; [2 Cor. 5:21; Heb. 4:15; 1 John 3:5] **23** [c]ch. 3:9; Isai. 53:7; Heb. 12:3 [d]Luke 23:46 **24** [e]Isai. 53:4, 11; Matt. 8:17; Heb. 9:28 [f]Rom. 6:2, 11; 7:4, 6; Col. 2:20; 3:3 [g]Rom. 6:13 [h]Isai. 53:5 **25** [i]Isai. 53:6; [Ps. 119:176; Ezek. 34:6; Luke 15:4]

[1] Or *every institution ordained for people* [2] Or *king*; also verse 17
[3] Greek *bondservants*

2:10 not a people, but now you are God's people. The Greek word translated "people" (*laos*) is used in the Septuagint, the Greek translation of the Old Testament, primarily for Israel. Continuing to apply to the church Old Testament texts dealing with Israel, Peter draws on the Septuagint of Hos. 1:6, 9, 10; and 2:23. In its original context, this is a prophecy about God's embracing Israel after He had rejected her. Peter, like Paul (Rom. 9:25, 26), interprets the Hosea passages to include the reception of Gentiles into the people of God. God's mercy extends to undeserving Jews and Gentiles alike, and there is essential continuity between Old Testament Israel and the New Testament church.

2:11 passions of the flesh. Bodily desires are not wrong in themselves, but are perverted by man's sinful nature. The expression includes not just sins of the body, but other desires of our fallen nature (Gal. 5:19–21).

2:12 speak against you as evildoers. Among the charges against Christians in Peter's time were disloyalty to the emperor (John 19:12), propagation of unlawful customs (Acts 16:20, 21), defamation of the gods (Acts 19:23–27), and general troublemaking (Acts 17:6, 7).

glorify God on the day of visitation. God's "visitation" is His drawing near either for judgment or mercy.

2:13 Be subject . . . to every human institution. This introduces the theme of voluntary submission and obedience to those in authority developed in 2:13–3:6.

for the Lord's sake. A person should submit to ordinances because this will commend Christ to others and keep reproach from His name. Submission to others also in itself is a service to Christ (Col. 3:23, 24).

the emperor as supreme. Chiefly the Roman emperor, at this time Nero (A.D. 54–68). The king is supreme, relative to governors and other rulers. Though Peter does not discuss the origin of kingly authority (cf. Rom. 13:1–7), Scripture teaches elsewhere that submission is required as long as it does not involve violation of the law of God (Matt. 22:21; Acts 4:19; 5:29).

2:16 free. Submission does not mean a denial of Christian freedom, but is the act of God's truly free people.

not . . . as a cover-up for evil. Christian freedom must not be used as a pretext for rebellion (1 Cor. 7:20–24) or a license to sin (Gal. 5:13; 2 Pet. 2:19, 20).

as servants of God. Christian freedom rests not on escape from service but on a change of masters (Rom. 6:22).

2:17 Honor everyone. The exhortation is either to recognize the value of every person as a bearer of the image of God, or what is more likely in this context, to respect all those in positions of authority.

Fear God. See note 1:17.

2:18 Servants. The vast majority of such servants were slaves and were treated as property. To a large extent the economy of the ancient world depended on slavery. Like other New Testament writers, Peter does not condemn slavery, and slaves are commanded to obey their masters. Nevertheless, the New Testament requires that slaves be treated with respect, and masters are not to mistreat their slaves (Eph. 6:9; Col. 4:1). Furthermore, the spiritual equality of slave and free in the church community is strongly emphasized (Gal. 3:28; cf. 1 Cor. 12:13; Col. 3:11), and slaves are encouraged to seek their freedom by lawful means (1 Cor. 7:21–24). In the late 1700's, when slavery came under attack, these teachings helped to undermine the institution of slavery.

2:21 to this you have been called . . . leaving you an example. Suffering is a part of the Christian's calling (2 Tim. 3:12) because it was first part of Christ's (John 15:18–20). Christians are united with Christ in His sufferings as well as His resurrection (2 Cor. 1:5; 4:10; Phil. 3:10, 11), and the example of Christ provides a pattern by which Christians are to understand their own lives.

2:22 See "The Sinlessness of Jesus" at Heb. 4:15.

2:24 bore our sins. See Is. 53:12. Christ is more than an example; He is the sin-bearer. As the perfect sacrifice (1:19; 2:24), Christ suffered the curse of sin, accepting the punishment our sins deserved and providing forgiveness and freedom.

tree. The cross (Acts 10:39). This Old Testament idiom emphasizes that Christ died bearing a curse (Deut. 21:22–23; Gal. 3:13).

but have now returned to [j]the Shepherd
and Overseer of your souls.

Wives and Husbands

3 Likewise, wives, [k]be subject to your
own husbands, so that [l]even if some
do not obey the word, [m]they may be won
without a word by the conduct of their
wives—2 when they see your [n]respectful
and pure conduct. 3 [o]Do not let your adorning be external—the braiding of hair, the
wearing of gold, or the putting on of clothing—4 but let your adorning be [p]the hidden
person of the heart with the imperishable
beauty of a gentle and quiet spirit, which in
God's sight is very precious. 5 For this is
how the holy women who hoped in God
used to adorn themselves, by submitting to
their husbands, 6 as Sarah obeyed Abraham, [q]calling him lord. And you are her
children, if you do good and [r]do not fear
anything that is frightening.
7 Likewise, [s]husbands, live with your
wives in an understanding way, showing
honor to the woman as the weaker [t]vessel,
since they are heirs with you[1] of the grace
of life, so that your prayers may not be
hindered.

25 [j]See John 10:11
Chapter 3
1 [k]See Gen. 3:16 [l]1 Cor. 7:16 [m]Matt. 18:15; 1 Cor. 9:19-22
2 [n]Tit. 2:5
3 [o]1 Tim. 2:9; [Isai. 3:18-23]
4 [p]Rom. 2:29; [Rom. 7:22; 2 Cor. 4:16; Eph. 3:16]
6 [q]Gen. 18:12 [r]Prov. 3:25
7 [s]Eph. 5:25; Col. 3:19 [t]See 1 Thess. 4:4
8 [u]See Rom. 12:16 [v]See Heb. 13:1 [w]Eph. 4:32 [x]See Eph. 4:2
9 [y]ch. 2:23; See Rom. 12:17 [z]Luke 6:28; Rom. 12:14; 1 Cor. 4:12 [a]ch. 2:21
10 [b]Cited from Ps. 34:12-16
13 [c][Prov. 16:7]
14 [d]ch. 2:19, 20; 4:14, 16; Matt. 5:10

Suffering for Righteousness' Sake

8 Finally, all of you, [u]have unity of mind,
sympathy, [v]brotherly love, [w]a tender heart,
and [x]a humble mind. 9 [y]Do not repay evil
for evil or reviling for reviling, but on the
contrary, [z]bless, for [a]to this you were
called, that you may obtain a blessing.
10 For

[b]"Whoever desires to love life
and see good days,
let him keep his tongue from evil
and his lips from speaking
deceit;
11 let him turn away from evil and do
good;
let him seek peace and
pursue it.
12 For the eyes of the Lord are on the
righteous,
and his ears are open to their
prayer.
But the face of the Lord is against
those who do evil."

13 Now [c]who is there to harm you if you
are zealous for what is good? 14 [d]But even if
you should suffer for righteousness' sake,

[1] Some manuscripts *since you are joint heirs*

2:25 but have now returned. This refers to the readers' initial conversion to Christ and suggests redirection of life and new personal attachment.

Shepherd. Familiar Old Testament imagery for God's care of His covenant people (Ps. 23:1; Ezek. 34; 37:24) is applied to Christ (5:4; John 10:11; Heb. 13:20; Rev. 7:17).

3:1 Likewise, wives, be subject. The word "likewise" refers back to the general principle of submission in 2:13 and is not intended to equate the wife's submission to the husband with that of a slave to a master. The word "likewise" recurs in v. 7, establishing that just as the wife submits to her husband, so also the husband must give understanding and honor to the wife (cf. Eph. 5:25). The relationship of men and women involves both spiritual equality ("heirs with you," v. 7; cf. Gal. 3:28) and some differentiation of roles and functions in the home and church (Eph. 5:22–33; 1 Tim. 2:8–15).

without a word. In ancient Roman culture the wife was expected to adopt the religion of her husband, and some of the Christian women in the Asian churches apparently had unbelieving spouses. Peter urges these Christian wives not to rely on argument, which might be seen as insubordination by the already suspicious husbands. Rather, the wives' gentle responsiveness will recommend the gospel to their unbelieving spouses. The enduring principle involved in this statement is not silence (v. 15), but a sensitivity to the concerns of the unbelieving husband so that the gospel may be presented in the best light.

3:3 hair . . . gold . . . clothing. Not a blanket prohibition of modest adornment, but a warning against preoccupation with outward appearances (1 Tim. 2:9, 10). Excess in this area is well attested in the pagan literature and art of the first century. The principle enjoined is modesty.

3:6 calling him lord. A conventional Eastern expression of respect and submission (Gen. 18:12).

children. That is, those who resemble Sarah in her submissive attitude.

do good. Here submission to husbands is primarily in view (cf. 2:15), but this probably includes continued allegiance to Christ as well.

do not fear. In dealing with unbelieving husbands (v. 1 note), the Christian wives were to maintain their commitment to Christ while at the same time showing proper deference to their husbands. The difficulties involved could lead to displeasure and intimidation on the husband's part and thus to "fear" on the wife's part.

3:7 the weaker vessel. "Weaker" refers to physical strength, not to the moral, spiritual, or mental ability of the wife. The discrepancy in physical strength provides one reason for the special consideration the husband is to show his wife.

heirs with you of the grace of life. Fellowship in the faith adds another reason for showing respect. Here Peter assumes that both husband and wife in this situation are Christians (cf. v. 1). Women enjoy full spiritual equality with men (Gal. 3:28).

your prayers . . . hindered. Estrangement from others often affects our relationship with God (Matt. 5:23, 24). In particular, the failure to observe God's will for the marriage relationship can disrupt our spiritual relationship with God. The importance of healthy family relationships is apparent from the typological comparison of Christ and church with husband and wife (Eph. 5:23, 24), and by the persistent New Testament characterization of the church as the family of God (1:14–17; Rom. 8:14–17; 1 Tim. 3:14, 15; 5:1, 2).

3:8, 9 Note the parallel teaching in Rom. 12:9–21.

3:9 Do not repay . . . blessing. Christians are not to retaliate in response to persecution, but instead are to "bless" their enemies (1 Cor. 4:12; cf. 1 Thess. 5:15). Such blessing may take the form of prayer (Matt. 5:44).

3:13 who is there to harm you. Peter is not denying that the Asian

you will be blessed. [e]Have no fear of them,
[f]nor be troubled, **15**but [g]in your hearts
regard Christ the Lord as holy, [h]always
being prepared to make a defense to anyone who asks you for a reason for the hope
that is in you; **16**yet do it with gentleness
and [i]respect, [j]having a good conscience, so
that, [k]when you are slandered, those who
revile your good behavior in Christ may be
put to shame. **17**For [l]it is better to suffer for
doing good, if that should be God's will,
than for doing evil.
18For Christ also [m]suffered[1] [n]once for
sins, the righteous for the unrighteous,
[o]that he might bring us to God, being put
to death [p]in the flesh but made alive [q]in the
spirit, **19**in which[2] he went and [q]pro-
claimed to the spirits in prison, **20**because[3]
they formerly did not obey, [r]when God's
patience waited in the days of Noah, [s]while
the ark was being prepared, in which a few,
that is, [t]eight persons, were brought safely
through water. **21**Baptism, which corresponds to this, [u]now saves you, not as a
removal of dirt from the body but [v]as an
appeal to God for a good conscience,
[w]through the resurrection of Jesus Christ,
22who has gone into heaven and [x]is at the
right hand of God, [y]with angels, authorities, and powers having been subjected to
him.

14[e]Isai. 8:12, 13; [ver. 6; Matt. 10:28] [f]John 14:1, 27 **15**[g][Isai. 29:23; Matt. 6:9] [h]Col. 4:6; [2 Tim. 2:25] **16**[i]See ch. 1:17 [j]Heb. 13:18 [k]ch. 2:12 **17**[l]ch. 2:20; [ch. 4:15, 16] **18**[m]ch. 2:21; 4:1; See Rom. 4:25 [n]Heb. 9:26, 28 [o]Rom. 5:2 [p]ch. 4:1; Col. 1:22; [2 Cor. 13:4] [q]ch. 4:6 **19**[q][See ver. 18 above] **20**[r]Gen. 6:3, 5, 13, 14 [s]Heb. 11:7 [t]Gen. 7:1, 7, 23; 8:18; 2 Pet. 2:5 **21**[u]Mark 16:16; Acts 16:33; Rom. 6:3-6; Tit. 3:5 [v][Rom. 10:10] [w]ch. 1:3

Stewards of God's Grace

4 Since therefore [z]Christ suffered in the
flesh,[4] [a]arm yourselves with the same
way of thinking, for [b]whoever has suffered
in the flesh [c]has ceased from sin, **2**[d]so as to
live for [e]the rest of the time in the flesh [f]no
longer for human passions but [g]for the will
of God. **3**The time that is past [h]suffices [i]for
doing what the Gentiles want to do, living
in sensuality, passions, drunkenness,
orgies, drinking parties, and lawless idolatry. **4**With respect to this they are surprised

22[x]Acts 2:33, 34; Rom. 8:34; Eph. 1:20; Col. 3:1; Heb. 1:3 [y]Rom. 8:38; 1 Cor. 15:24; Eph. 1:21
Chapter 4 1[z]ch. 3:18 [a][Eph. 6:13] [b]Rom. 6:2, 7; Gal. 5:24; Col. 3:3, 5 [c][2 Pet. 2:14] **2**[d]Rom. 6:14; 14:7; 2 Cor. 5:15 [e]ch. 1:14 [f]Tit. 2:12; 1 John 2:16 [g]Rom. 6:11 **3**[h]Ezek. 44:6; 45:9; Acts 17:30 [i]Eph. 4:17-19; 1 Thess. 4:5; [1 Cor. 12:2]

[1] Some manuscripts *died* [2] Or *the Spirit, in whom* [3] Or *when*
[4] Some manuscripts add *for us*; some *for you*

Christians (Introduction: Date and Occasion) may suffer for their faith (4:12). This statement may be interpreted either as a truism teaching that mistreatment is less likely if one's behavior is exemplary, or, more likely, as a statement that, whatever happens to the Christian, no external force can cause spiritual harm (Ps. 56:4; Luke 12:4, 5).

3:14 blessed. Recalls Matt. 5:10–12. Christians who suffer for the truth are blessed by God, even if their reward is delayed.

3:15 always being prepared. Readiness to confess Christ is an important aspect of setting apart Christ as Lord.

defense. The word may suggest response to abusive or derisive inquiries from hostile people. Such a response includes an explanation of the main points of Christianity.

3:16 revile your good behavior. By their conduct Christians show that accusations against them are unfounded (2:12, 15).

3:17 if that should be God's will. Unjust suffering is within the providence of God and is for the good of His children and His own glory (1:6, 7; 4:19).

3:18 once. Christ's substitutionary death is sufficient, and no further sacrifices are necessary (Heb. 9:12, 26–28).

made alive in the spirit. See Rom. 1:4; 8:11.

3:19 proclaimed to the spirits in prison. Four main interpretations of vv. 19, 20 may be mentioned: (a) Christ as preincarnate and preaching through Noah (2 Pet. 2:5) to the people before the Flood (Gen. 6–8). Noah called them to repentance, but they disobeyed and are now imprisoned. The point of Peter's argument would then be that as God vindicated Noah then, He would vindicate Christians now. (b) Christ's preaching in the short interval between His death and Resurrection, during a "descent into hell." It is said that Christ announced His victory to the spirits of Noah's wicked contemporaries confined in the realm of the dead. (c) A similar idea is that Christ proclaimed His victory to fallen angels, often identified with the "sons of God" of Gen. 6:2, 4 (cf. Job 1:6; 2:1), in their place of confinement. (d) Christ proclaiming His victory to fallen angels after the Resurrection, at the time of His Ascension into heaven. The point of the last three interpretations is that just as Jesus was vindicated, so too Christians will be vindicated.

3:21 Baptism, which corresponds to this, now saves you. Baptism is a sign and seal of God's grace in Jesus Christ. The startling statement that baptism "saves you" shows how close is the relationship between the sign and the reality it signifies. Noah's physical salvation through the waters of the Flood prefigured the waters of baptism and the salvation they signify. Baptism symbolizes judgment on sin in the death of Christ and then also renewal of life (Rom. 6:4). The floodwaters were judgment to the wicked, and at the same time physical salvation for the just, Noah and his family.

not as a removal of dirt from the body. Lest his readers mistakenly attribute a magical or mechanical power to the sacrament, Peter states that the means of salvation is not performance of the external rite, but what it symbolizes—union with Christ in His death and Resurrection.

3:22 at the right hand of God. The place of supreme privilege and sovereignty in the universe (Eph. 1:20–23; Heb. 1:3).

4:1 has ceased from sin. Some interpret this to refer to the character-building effects of suffering. But the preceding reference to baptism (3:21; cf. Rom. 6:1–10) indicates that Peter is thinking of the union of believers with Christ in His suffering and death, a union particularly symbolized by baptism (Rom. 6:4). Though Christ was always sinless (2:22; 2 Cor. 5:21; Heb. 4:15), He nevertheless fully identified with sinful humanity by coming "in the likeness of sinful flesh" (Rom. 8:3) and becoming subject to temptation, suffering, and death (Mark 1:12, 13; Heb. 2:10; 4:15). Christ "died to sin" (Rom. 6:10) in the sense that after His death and Resurrection He was no longer subject to the power of sin and death.

4:3 This catalog of sins closely resembles Rom. 13:13 and Gal. 5:19–21, and is strong evidence for the pagan background of most of Peter's audience (1:14, 18; Introduction: Date and Occasion).

sensuality. Unrestrained indulgence of one's desires, especially for sensual pleasure (Rom.13:13; 2 Cor. 12:21; Eph. 4:19).

passions. The usual word for evil desire, often relating to sexual immorality.

orgies. Excessive feasting, often in honor of a pagan god.

drinking parties. The excessive use of alcohol is frequently condemned in Scripture (Rom. 13:13; Gal. 5:21).

when you do not join them in the same
flood of [j]debauchery, and [k]they malign
you; 5 but they will give account to him
who is ready [l]to judge the living and the
dead. 6 For this is why [m]the gospel was
preached even to those who are dead, that
though judged in the flesh the way people
are, they might live in the spirit the way
God does.

7 [n]The end of all things is at hand; therefore [o]be self-controlled and sober-minded
[p]for the sake of your prayers. 8 Above all,
keep loving one another earnestly, since
[q]love covers a multitude of sins. 9 [r]Show
hospitality to one another without grumbling. 10 [s]As each has received a gift, use it
to serve one another, [t]as good stewards of
God's varied grace: 11 whoever speaks, as
one who speaks [u]oracles of God; whoever
serves, as one who serves [v]by the strength
that God supplies—in order that in everything [w]God may be glorified through Jesus
Christ. [x]To him belong glory and [y]domin-
ion forever and ever. Amen.

Suffering As a Christian

12 Beloved, do not be surprised at [z]the
fiery trial when it comes upon you to test
you, as though something strange were
happening to you. 13 But rejoice [a]insofar as

4 [j]See Eph. 5:18 [k]ch. 2:12; 3:16
5 [l][James 5:9]; See Acts 10:42
6 [m]ch. 3:19
7 [n]See James 5:8 [o]See ch. 1:13 [p]Matt. 26:41; Luke 21:36
8 [q][1 Cor. 13:5, 6]; See James 5:20
9 [r]Heb. 13:2; [1 Tim. 3:2; Tit. 1:8]
10 [s]Rom. 12:6, 7; 1 Cor. 4:7; [Matt. 25:15] [t]Luke 12:42; 1 Cor. 4:1, 2; Tit. 1:7
11 [u]Acts 7:38; Rom. 3:2; Heb. 5:12 [v]Rom. 12:3 [w]1 Cor. 10:31 [x]See Rom. 11:36 [y]ch. 5:11; Jude 25; Rev. 1:6; 5:13
12 [z]ch. 1:7
13 [a]Phil. 3:10, 11; See Acts 5:41

Pastors and Pastoral Care

The apostles told all Christians to watch over each other with loving care and prayer (Gal. 6:1, 2; Heb. 12:15, 16; 1 John 3:16–18; 5:16), but they also appointed in each congregation guardians, called "elders" (Acts 14:23; Titus 1:5), who would look after the people as shepherds look after sheep (Acts 20:28–31; 1 Pet. 5:1–4), leading them by example (1 Pet. 5:3) away from all that is harmful into all that is good. By virtue of their role, the elders (presbyters) are also called "shepherds" ("pastors," Eph. 4:11) and "overseers" (Acts 20:28, cf. v. 17; Titus 1:7, cf. v. 5), and are spoken of in other terms that express leadership (1 Thess. 5:12; Heb. 13:7, 17, 24). The congregation, for its part, is to acknowledge the God-given authority of its leaders and to follow their lead (Heb. 13:17).

This pattern is already present in the Old Testament, where God is the shepherd of Israel (Ps. 80:1) and kings, prophets, priests, and elders (local rulers) are called to act as His agents in an under-shepherd role (Num. 11:24–30; Deut. 27:1; Ezra 5:5; 6:14; 10:8; Ps. 77:20; Jer. 23:1–4; Ezek. 34; Zech. 11:16, 17). In the New Testament, Jesus the Good Shepherd (John 10:11–30) is also the Chief Shepherd (1 Pet. 5:4), and the elders are His subordinates. The apostle Peter calls himself an "elder" under Christ (1 Pet. 5:1), remembering perhaps that shepherding was the specific task Jesus gave him when restoring him to ministry (John 21:15–17).

Some but not all elders teach (1 Tim. 5:17; Titus 1:9; Heb. 13:7), and Eph. 4:11–16 says that Christ gave the church "pastors and teachers" to equip everyone for service through the discovery and development of each person's spiritual gifts (vv. 12–16). In the congregational leadership envisaged by the apostles, there may have been teachers who were not elders, as well as elders who did not teach, and also those who both ruled and taught.

The pastoral role of elders demands mature and stable Christian character, and a well-ordered personal life (1 Tim. 3:1–7; Titus 1:5–9). The elder who serves faithfully will be rewarded (Heb. 13:17; 1 Pet. 5:4; cf. 1 Tim. 4:7, 8).

4:6 For this is why. This verse follows on the idea of a universal divine judgment just stated, but the reason or purpose of the preaching is not given until the end of the verse.

was preached even to those who are dead. Although some connect this preaching with 3:19, 20, it is more likely unrelated. These people may have been Christians who had heard Peter preach, but who had died by the time of the letter.

judged in the flesh. Probably a reference to the physical death of the hearers. Although Christ has triumphed over physical death in His death and Resurrection (Rom. 6:9), the full extent of that victory has not yet been manifested in the lives of God's people, and physical death is a reality Christians still face. Nevertheless, we now enjoy spiritual resurrection through union with Christ, and we have full assurance that Christ's victory will be extended to our physical bodies (1 Cor. 15:25, 26; cf. Rom. 8:11).

4:7 is at hand. The "end of all things" may refer to the destruction of Jerusalem in A.D. 70 or, more comprehensively, to the final consummation of Christ's kingdom at His return. The call to vigilance is frequent in the New Testament. The entire period between the Resurrection of Christ and His Second Coming is seen as the "last times" (1:20 note; Acts 2:17; 1 Tim. 4:1 note).

4:8 love covers . . . sins. Love keeps no record of wrongs but forgives in response to God's forgiveness (Prov. 10:12; Matt. 18:21, 22; 1 Cor. 13:4–7; James 5:20). See "Love" at 1 Cor. 13:13.

4:9 hospitality. One of the fruits of love (v. 8). Situations necessitating hospitality would include homelessness due to persecution, Christians traveling on business, and itinerant missionaries (Rom. 12:13; 3 John 5–8).

4:10 each . . . serve. See Rom. 12:3–8.

4:13 But rejoice. The same paradox of exultation in suffering is found in 1:6, 7.

you share Christ's sufferings, that you may
also rejoice and be glad [b]when his glory is
revealed. 14 [c]If you are insulted [d]for the
name of Christ, you are blessed, because
the Spirit of glory[1] and of God rests upon
you. 15 But [e]let none of you suffer as a murderer or a thief or an evildoer or [f]as a med-
dler. 16 Yet [e]if anyone suffers as a [g]Christian,
let him not be ashamed, but let him glorify
God [d]in that name. 17 For it is time for judgment [h]to begin at the household of God;
and [i]if it begins with us, what will be the
outcome for those who [j]do not obey the
gospel of God? 18 And

[k]"If the righteous is scarcely saved,
what will become of the ungodly
and the sinner?"[2]

19 Therefore let those who suffer according
to God's will [l]entrust their souls to a faithful Creator while doing good.

Shepherd the Flock of God

5 So I exhort the elders among you, [m]as
a fellow elder and [n]a witness of the sufferings of Christ, as well as a partaker in the
glory that is going to be revealed: 2 [o]shep-
herd the flock of God that is among you,
exercising oversight,[3] [p]not under compulsion, but willingly, as God would have
you;[4] [q]not for shameful gain, but eagerly;
3 not [r]domineering over those in your
charge, but [s]being examples to the flock.
4 And when [t]the chief Shepherd appears,
you will receive the [u]unfading [v]crown of
glory. 5 Likewise, you who are younger, be
subject to the elders. [w]Clothe yourselves,
all of you, with humility toward one another, for [x]"God opposes the proud but gives
grace to the humble."
6 Humble yourselves, therefore, under
the mighty hand of God so that at the
proper time he may exalt you, 7 [y]casting all
your anxieties on him, because [z]he cares
for you. 8 [a]Be sober-minded; [b]be watchful.
Your [c]adversary the devil [d]prowls around
[e]like a roaring lion, seeking someone to
devour. 9 [f]Resist him, [g]firm in your faith,
knowing that [h]the same kinds of suffering
are being experienced by your brotherhood
throughout the world. 10 And [i]after you
have suffered a little while, the God of all
grace, [j]who has called you to his [k]eternal
glory in Christ, will himself [l]restore, confirm, strengthen, and [m]establish you. 11 [n]To
him be the dominion forever and ever.
Amen.

13 [b][ch. 1:5-7; 5:1; Rom. 8:17, 18; Jude 24] 14 [c]Ps. 89:51; Matt. 5:11 [d]John 15:21; [Heb. 11:26] 15 [e]ch. 2:19, 20; 3:14, 17 [f]1 Thess. 4:11; 2 Thess. 3:11; 1 Tim. 5:13 16 [e][See ver. 15 above] [g]See Acts 26:28 [d][See ver. 14 above] 17 [h]Jer. 25:29; Ezek. 9:6; Amos 3:2; Rom. 2:9 [i][Luke 23:31] [j][2 Thess. 1:8] 18 [k]Prov. 11:31 19 [l]Ps. 31:5; Luke 23:46; [Ps. 10:14; 2 Tim. 1:12]
Chapter 5
1 [m][2 John 1; 3 John 1] [n]See Luke 24:48 2 [o][Jude 12]; See John 21:16 [p][Philem. 14] [q]1 Tim. 3:8; Tit. 1:7 3 [r]Ezek. 34:4; Matt. 20:25; Mark 10:42; 2 Cor. 1:24 [s]Phil. 3:17; 2 Thess. 3:9; 1 Tim. 4:12; Tit. 2:7

4 [t]Heb. 13:20 [u][ch. 1:4] [v]1 Cor. 9:25; See James 1:12 5 [w][Matt. 20:26, 27; John 13:4, 5, 14] [x]See James 4:6, 10 7 [y][Ps. 37:5; 55:22]; See Matt. 6:25 [z]Ps. 40:17 8 [a]See ch. 1:13 [b]See Matt. 24:42 [c]Eph. 4:27; 6:11; Rev. 12:9, 12; [Job 1:9-12; Luke 22:31; 2 Cor. 2:11] [d]Job 1:7; 2:2 [e][Ps. 22:21] 9 [f]James 4:7 [g]Col. 2:5 [h]Acts 14:22; 1 Thess. 3:3; 2 Tim. 3:12 10 [i]ch. 1:6 [j]1 Cor. 1:9; 1 Thess. 2:12; 1 Tim. 6:12 [k]2 Tim. 2:10 [l]Heb. 13:21 [m]Luke 22:32; Rom. 16:25 11 [n]See ch. 4:11

[1] Some manuscripts insert *and of power* [2] Greek *where will the ungodly and sinner appear?* [3] Some manuscripts omit *exercising oversight* [4] Some manuscripts omit *as God would have you*

share Christ's sufferings. Christians share in Christ's sufferings, not by contributing to Christ's finished work of atonement for sin, but by experiencing similar mistreatment because they are identified and united with Christ (vv. 14, 16; Rom. 8:17; 2 Cor. 1:5 and note; Phil. 1:29; Col. 1:24 and note).

4:17 judgment . . . at the household of God. Peter returns to the theme of divine sovereignty over the suffering of God's people. This judgment may have the purpose of purification (Mal. 3:2–4; Heb. 12:9–11), or of strengthening faith (1:6, 7).

4:18 righteous is scarcely saved. It is not that final salvation is uncertain, but that the way to it is through hard discipline (Matt. 7:14; Acts 14:22).

5:1 a fellow elder. Although Peter has already mentioned his office as an apostle (1:1), here he stresses his solidarity and shared eldership with the leaders of the Asian churches so as to encourage them.

5:2 shepherd the flock of God. This phrase broadly describes the functions of elders. The shepherd imagery suggests care, protection, discipline, and guidance (2:25 note). Jesus portrayed His own care for the church (John 10:1–18) and God's gracious interest in sinners (Luke 15:3–7) as works of shepherding. The use of the word by Peter recalls his own recommissioning (John 21:15–17). See theological note "Pastors and Pastoral Care."

not for shameful gain. Peter condemns not fair compensation, but love of gain and the abuse of trust (1 Cor. 9:14; 1 Tim. 5:17, 18).

5:3 not domineering . . . but being examples. Peter warns against haughty abuse of power and exhorts his audience to be like Jesus (Mark 10:42–45; John 13:1–17; Phil. 2:5–11).

5:4 chief Shepherd. Christ (2:25). The title brings out the relationship of Christ's pastoral care and work to that of church leaders, who serve as undershepherds responsible to the chief Shepherd.

5:5 elders. In v. 1 the Greek word is used in the technical sense of a church office holder, but here there is probably a more general reference to older people (cf. 1 Tim. 5:1).

5:8 adversary the devil. The Greek word translated "adversary" was in common use for an opponent in a lawsuit, and "devil" (Greek *diabolos*) is the usual translation of the Hebrew *Satan,* which means "slanderer" or "accuser" and also serves as a proper name for the devil (Job 1:6; Zech. 3:1, 2; cf. Rev. 12:9, 10). The phrase reveals the ultimate source behind all persecution.

lion. The imagery is perhaps borrowed from the Book of Psalms where the psalmist's enemies and the wicked are compared to lions (Ps. 7:2; 10:9, 10). The metaphor conveys the strength and destructiveness of the devil and accentuates the need for alertness on the part of believers.

5:10 God of all grace. God bestows help and strength sufficient for every occasion and need.

called you to his eternal glory. God's eternal plan for believers will bring them to glory (John 17:22–24; Rom. 8:28–30; 2 Cor. 4:17; 2 Tim. 2:10).

in Christ. All the blessings of God's grace in this life and the next come through the believer's union with Christ. See note 2 Cor. 5:17.

Final Greetings

12 By [o]Silvanus, a faithful brother as I
regard him, [p]I have written briefly to you,
exhorting and declaring that this is [q]the
true grace of God. [r]Stand firm in it. 13 She
who is at Babylon, who is likewise chosen,
sends you greetings, and so does [s]Mark,
my son. 14 [t]Greet one another with the kiss
of love.

[u]Peace to all of you who are in Christ.

12 [o]Acts 15:22; 2 Cor. 1:19; 1 Thess. 1:1; 2 Thess. 1:1 [p][Heb. 13:22] [q]See Acts 11:23 [r]See 1 Cor. 15:1

13 [s]See Acts 12:12 14 [t]See Rom. 16:16 [u]Eph. 6:23

5:12 By Silvanus. Probably this is Silas, Paul's companion on the second missionary journey (Acts 15:40). Silvanus may simply have carried the epistle, or he may have acted as a secretary, perhaps even helping Peter draft the letter.

5:13 She . . . at Babylon. Probably a reference to the church in Rome (Introduction: Date and Occasion).

Mark, my son. John Mark (Acts 12:12, 25; 13:5, 13; 15:37–39). According to Papias (c. A.D. 60–130), Mark worked closely with Peter and derived much of the information for the Gospel of Mark from the apostle.

5:14 kiss of love. The kiss was and is a common form of greeting in the Near East (Matt. 26:48, 49; Luke 15:20), corresponding to today's handshake. For the Christians, the cultural form became an outward sign of their love and unity (a "holy kiss," Rom. 16:16; 1 Thess. 5:26).

THE SECOND EPISTLE OF

Peter

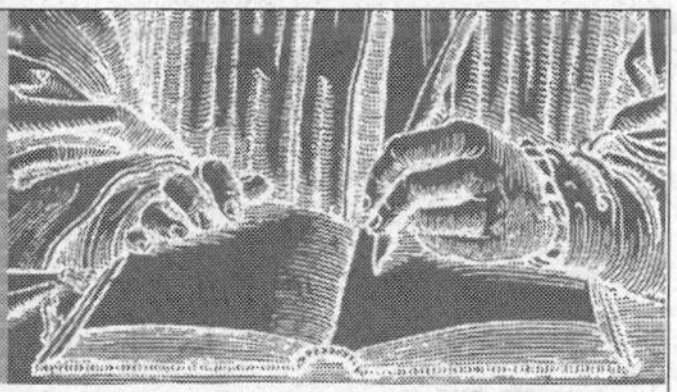

AUTHOR

This epistle claims to have been written by Simon Peter (1:1), and several things in the epistle support the claim. The author refers to his own imminent death in terms that recall Jesus' words to Peter (1:14; cf. John 21:18, 19); he claims to have been an eyewitness of the Transfiguration (1:16–18; cf. Matt. 17:1–8 and parallels); and he seems to imply a connection between this epistle and 1 Peter (3:1).

Although there are possible allusions to 2 Peter in Christian literature of the late first and early second centuries, it is not as well attested as 1 Peter or other New Testament books. Origen (c. 185–254) was the first to attribute the epistle explicitly to Peter, but he recorded that others doubted Peter's authorship. Eusebius (c. 265–339) listed it among the disputed books, and Jerome (c. 342–420), while noting some disagreement regarding its authenticity, suggested that stylistic differences with 1 Peter were due to Peter's use of different secretaries. The epistle was accepted as authentic and canonical by influential fourth-century church fathers such as Athanasius, Cyril of Jerusalem, Ambrose, and Augustine, as well as by the late fourth-century church councils of Hippo and Carthage, and its subsequent place in the New Testament canon was assured.

Notwithstanding the epistle's own claims, a number of objections have been raised to Peter's authorship. Among the more common ones are the lack of early attestation, slow recognition by the church, stylistic differences with 1 Peter, and the apparent use of Hellenistic religious and philosophical language. The usual alternative to Peter's authorship is pseudonymity, i.e., that 2 Peter was written by a later unknown author who attributed the work to a well-known writer as a literary device to commend his message. While several of the objections must be taken seriously (especially attestation and style), their force should not be exaggerated, and none is conclusive against Peter's authorship.

There is great stylistic diversity between 1 and 2 Peter. Many of the favorite words and expressions of 1 Peter, for example, are absent in 2 Peter. The differences are not absolute, however, and several striking similarities do exist between the two epistles. There are also a number of parallels between 2 Peter and Peter's speeches in Acts (e.g., the use of the Greek word *eusebeia*, "godliness," in 1:3, 6, 7; 3:11, a word occurring elsewhere in the New Testament only in the Pastoral Epistles).

The claim that 2 Peter is pseudonymous is weak. Genuine examples of pseudepigraphy (writings by authors pretending to be someone else of greater authority) in early Christian literature are almost all heretical, an indication that the device was used to commend works whose content was suspect. There is strong evidence that the church did not tolerate the practice, but in fact strictly rejected pseudepigrapha.

The case against Peter's authorship is, in conclusion, not proved, and the epistle's own claim to have been written by Peter can be taken at face value.

DATE AND OCCASION

Assuming Peter's authorship, 2 Peter must have been written before the apostle's death in A.D. 67–68. The reference to his imminent death in 1:14 suggests a time near the end of his life. If 3:1 refers to 1 Peter, the date of composition must be sometime after 63–64 (Introduction to 1 Peter: Date and Occasion). A date between 65–67 is therefore plausible.

The place of origin of 2 Peter is uncertain. Rome is a likely suggestion, given Peter's location there in 1 Peter (1 Pet. 5:13 note) and the tradition that he was martyred there under Nero.

Unlike 1 Peter, there is little information in this epistle about its recipients. If 3:1 refers to 1 Peter, the recipients, Christians in Asia Minor, are the same in both epistles. If 3:1 is not a reference to 1 Peter, but to a lost epistle instead, there are no firm data to determine the recipients.

CHARACTERISTICS AND THEMES

Second Peter is written to Christians being threatened by false teaching from within (2:1). As an antidote, Peter stresses the truth and ethical implications of the gospel against the false teachers.

Although the false teaching is difficult to define precisely, it appears to be an early precursor of Gnosticism. This term designates any of a variety of heretical movements in the early Christian centuries (especially the second century) that combined ideas from Greek philosophy, oriental mysticism, and Christianity, and emphasized salvation through intuitive, esoteric knowledge (the Greek word for "knowledge" is *gnosis*) rather than through faith in Christ.

Because in the gnostic system the physical body was regarded as evil, second-century Gnostics were usually characterized by either blatant immorality or rigorous asceticism. Asceticism is not addressed as a problem in 2 Peter, but immorality is (2:13–19). The false teachers seem to be using Christian liberty as a license to sin, especially to commit sexual immorality (2:14). In addition, they are guilty of denying the Lord (2:1), despising authority and slandering celestial beings (2:10), and scoffing at the Second Coming of Christ (3:3, 4).

INTERPRETIVE DIFFICULTIES

Some relationship between 2 Peter and Jude is virtually certain. Although verbatim agreement is rare (2:17; cf. Jude 13), they have similar ideas, words, Old Testament illustrations, and order of text (2:1–18; cf. Jude 4–16). Several explanations are possible. Either 2 Peter used Jude (the scholarly consensus), or Jude used 2 Peter, or there was a common source unknown to us.

OUTLINE OF 2 PETER

I. Salutation (1:1)

II. The Truth of the Gospel (1:2–21)

- A. *Spiritual Growth as Confirmation of Election (1:2–11)*
  1. Christian Privileges (1:2–4)
  2. Christian Responsibility (1:5–11)
- B. *The Truth of the Gospel Attested by Apostolic and Prophetic Testimony (1:12–21)*
  1. Peter's Purpose (1:12–15)
  2. Apostolic Testimony (1:16–18)
  3. Prophetic Testimony (1:19–21)

III. False Teachers (ch. 2)

- A. *Their Coming and Conduct Described (2:1–3)*
- B. *Their Certain Judgment Pronounced (2:4–11)*
- C. *Their Immoral Ways Denounced (2:12–22)*

IV. The Second Coming of Christ (3:1–16)

- A. *Peter's Purpose Reiterated (3:1, 2)*
- B. *The Certainty of Judgment (3:3–10)*
- C. *The Ethical Implications of Christ's Coming (3:11–16)*

V. Concluding Exhortation (3:17, 18)

Greeting

1 Simeon[1] Peter, a servant[2] and apostle of Jesus Christ,
To those who have obtained [a]a faith of equal standing with ours [b]by the righteousness of our [c]God and Savior Jesus Christ:
2 [d]May grace and peace be multiplied to you [e]in the knowledge of God and of Jesus our Lord.

Chapter 1
1 [a]Rom. 1:12; 2 Cor. 4:13; Tit. 1:4 [b]Rom. 3:21-26 [c]Tit. 2:13
2 [d]1 Pet. 1:2; Jude 2 [e]ver. 3, 8; ch. 2:20; [John 17:3; Phil. 3:8]

1 Some manuscripts *Simon* 2 Or *slave*; Greek *bondservant*

1:1 Simeon. Greek *Symeon*, which is closer to the Hebrew form of the name. See note 1 Pet. 1:1.

apostle. See note 2 Cor. 1:1.

a faith of equal standing. Though some interpret this to refer to "the faith" as a body of belief (Jude 3), it more likely refers to the subjective experience of the believer. As an apostle writing to those who will live on after his death (vv. 13–15), Peter assures his readers that they do not have a second-class Christianity, inferior to Peter's and the other apostles' (cf. John 20:29).

by the righteousness. This probably refers to God's fairness and impartiality in bestowing the gift of faith upon all types of people, rather than to the vicarious righteousness of Christ by which Christians are justified (Rom. 3:22; 4:6). The word "righteousness" is generally used in an ethical sense in Peter's letters (2:5, 21; 3:13; 1 Pet. 2:24; 4:18).

our God and Savior Jesus Christ. Since one definite article governs both nouns in the Greek (lit. "the God of us and Savior"), this phrase ascribes deity to Jesus.

1:2 knowledge of God and of Jesus. "Knowledge" is an important theme in 2 Peter (related words occur eleven times); here it is likely a subtle attack on false teachers and their preoccupation with esoteric knowledge. Peter seems to reserve the particular Greek word used here (*epignosis*) for the fundamental saving knowledge of God gained in con-

Make Your Calling and Election Sure

3 His divine power has granted to us all
things that pertain to life and godliness,
through the knowledge of him [f]who called
us to[1] his own glory and excellence,[2] 4 by
which he has granted to us his precious
and very great promises, so that through
them you may become [g]partakers of the
divine nature, [h]having escaped from the
corruption that is in the world because of
sinful desire. 5 For this very reason, make
every effort to supplement your faith [i]with
virtue,[3] and virtue [j]with knowledge, 6 and
knowledge with self-control, and self-
control [k]with steadfastness, and steadfastness with godliness, 7 and godliness [l]with
brotherly affection, and brotherly affection
[m]with love. 8 For if these qualities[4] are
yours and are increasing, they keep you
from being ineffective or [n]unfruitful in the
knowledge of our Lord Jesus Christ. 9 For
whoever lacks these qualities is so nearsighted that he [o]is blind, having forgotten
that he was [p]cleansed from his former sins.
10 Therefore, brothers,[5] be all the more diligent to make your calling and [q]election
sure, for if you practice these qualities [r]you
will never fall. 11 For in this way there will
be richly provided for you [s]an entrance into
the eternal kingdom of our Lord and Savior
Jesus Christ.
12 Therefore I intend [t]always to remind
you of these qualities, though you know
them and are established in [u]the truth that
you have. 13 I think it right, as long as I am
in this [v]body,[6] [w]to stir you up by way of
reminder, 14 [x]since I know that the putting
off of my body will be soon, [y]as our Lord
Jesus Christ made clear to me. 15 And I will
make every effort so that after my departure
you may be able at any time to recall these
things.

Christ's Glory and the Prophetic Word

16 For we did not follow [z]cleverly devised
[a]myths when we made known to you [b]the
power and [c]coming of our Lord Jesus
Christ, but [d]we were eyewitnesses of his
majesty. 17 For when he received honor and
glory from God the Father, and the voice
was borne to him by the Majestic Glory,

3 [f][1 Thess. 2:12; 2 Thess. 2:14; 2 Tim. 1:9; 1 Pet. 5:10]
4 [g][Eph. 4:24; Heb. 12:10; 1 John 3:2] [h]ch. 2:18, 20
5 [i]Phil. 4:8 [j]1 Pet. 3:7
6 [k]See Heb. 10:36; James 1:3
7 [l]See Heb. 13:1 [m]1 Cor. ch. 13; 1 John 4:16
8 [n]See John 15:2; Tit. 3:14
9 [o]Job 5:14; 12:25; Isai. 59:10; Zeph. 1:17; [1 John 2:9-11] [p]Eph. 5:26; Tit. 2:14; Heb. 9:14; 1 John 1:7; Rev. 7:14
10 [q]1 Thess. 1:4 [r][ch. 3:17; 1 John 2:10]
11 [s]Col. 1:13; [Acts 14:22]
12 [t]Jude 5; [Rom. 15:14, 15; Phil. 3:1; 1 John 2:21] [u]2 John 2
13 [v]2 Cor. 5:1, 4 [w]ch. 3:1
14 [x][Deut. 4:21, 22; 31:14; 2 Tim. 4:6]
[y]John 21:18, 19 16 [z]See 1 Cor. 1:17 [a]See 1 Tim. 1:4 [b]1 Cor. 2:4 [c]See 1 Thess. 2:19 [d]Matt. 17:1, 2, 6; Mark 9:2; Luke 9:28, 29; John 1:14

1 Or *by* 2 Or *virtue* 3 Or *excellence*; twice in this verse 4 Greek *these things*; also verses 9, 10, 12 5 Or *brothers and sisters*. The plural Greek word *adelphoi* (translated "brothers") refers to siblings in a family. In New Testament usage, depending on the context, *adelphoi* may refer either to men or to both men and women who are siblings (brothers and sisters) in God's family, the church 6 Greek *tent*; also verse 14

version (1:2, 3, 8; 2:20). Knowledge of God and of Jesus are connected because God is known savingly only in and through Jesus Christ (Matt. 11:27).

1:4 partakers of the divine nature. Believers are not absorbed into deity, nor do they become divine. Rather, they have received the Holy Spirit and are sons of God (John 1:12; Rom. 8:9–21). As such they are being conformed to the likeness of Christ (Rom. 8:29) and the image of God in them is being renewed in true righteousness.

1:5–7 The order of virtues here ("faith . . . love") is not a sequence in time, as if stages of the Christian life were being described (vv. 8, 9). Peter is using a rhetorical figure that builds a series of elements to a climax. The beginning and conclusion of the series are significant, however. Early Christian virtue lists often begin with "faith," the starting point of the Christian life, and end with "love" (Rom. 5:1–5; 1 Cor. 13), the preeminent fruit of the Christian life.

1:7 brotherly affection. Greek *philadelphia,* the family affection among believers as brothers and sisters in God's family (Rom. 12:10; Heb. 13:1; 1 Pet. 1:22).

1:9 nearsighted . . . blind. Lit. "blind, being nearsighted." The combination of terms here is strange, since the two physical conditions are mutually exclusive. Some suggest on the basis of the etymology of the Greek word for "nearsighted" that Peter is alluding to the squinting or narrowing of the eyes, and that a deliberate rejection of the truth is in view. However, because the nearsighted person squints in order to see *better,* it is possible that Peter is simply multiplying related terms for effect.

1:10 make your calling and election sure. While God's choice of the elect is firm and certain in God (2 Tim. 2:19), it may not always be obvious to the individual Christian. Assurance of God's call comes through the evidence of the Holy Spirit's work in our lives (1 John 3:10, 14) as well as through the internal testimony of the Spirit in our hearts (Gal. 4:6).

if you practice these qualities. God's promise of salvation is to those with a genuine, persevering faith (Matt. 10:22; 24:12, 13; Heb. 3:6). True faith perseveres to the end and will inevitably bear fruit (Gal. 5:6, 22, 23).

1:13 in this body. This phrase emphasizes the transitory nature of human life this side of Christ's return (2 Cor. 5:1, 4).

1:15 make every effort. Again, Peter's purpose in writing this epistle is to establish his readers firmly in the truth of the gospel (v. 12).

departure. Lit. "exodus." Death is a "going out" or "departure" from this life (Luke 9:31 note).

1:16 we. Peter links his message with that of the other apostles to affirm that they all preach the same message.

myths. This word is always used in the New Testament in a negative sense and in contrast to the truth of the gospel (1 Tim. 1:4; 2 Tim. 4:4).

the power and coming of . . . Christ. The Greek word translated "coming" is *parousia,* the usual New Testament term for Christ's Second Coming in glory (3:4, 12; Matt. 24:27; 1 Thess. 3:13). "Power" is elsewhere associated with Christ's coming (Matt. 24:30).

eyewitnesses of his majesty. Peter was present at Christ's transfiguration (Matt. 17:1–8 and parallels). The eyewitness testimony of the apostles to the Transfiguration establishes the truth of Peter's message in general, and in particular provides the historical basis for the apostolic expectation of the Second Coming. The Transfiguration was understood by the apostles to have been a brief anticipation of the divine glory with which Christ will return to earth (Matt. 16:27–17:8).

1:17 Majestic Glory. An indirect way, typical of Jewish speech, of referring to God Himself. The reason for speaking indirectly was to avoid any possible misuse of the sacred name of God.

[e]"This is my beloved Son,[1] with whom I am
well pleased," 18 we ourselves heard this
very voice borne from heaven, for we were
with him on [f]the holy mountain. 19 And [g]we
have something more sure, the prophetic
word, to which you will do well to pay
attention [h]as to a lamp shining in a dark
place, until [i]the day [j]dawns and the morning star rises in your hearts, 20 knowing this
first of all, that no prophecy of Scripture
comes from someone's own interpretation.
21 For [k]no prophecy was ever produced by
the will of man, but men spoke from God
[l]as they were carried along by the Holy
Spirit.

False Prophets and Teachers

2 But [m]false prophets also arose among
the people, [n]just as there will be false
teachers among you, who will [o]secretly
bring in destructive heresies, [o]even denying
the Master [p]who bought them, bringing
upon themselves swift destruction. 2 And
many will follow their sensuality, and
because of them the way of truth [q]will be
blasphemed. 3 And [r]in their greed they will
exploit you [s]with false words. [t]Their condemnation from long ago is not idle, and
their destruction is not asleep.
4 For if God did not spare [u]angels when
they sinned, but [v]cast them into hell[2] and
committed them to chains[3] of gloomy
darkness [w]to be kept until the judgment;
5 if he did not spare the ancient world, but
[x]preserved Noah, a herald of righteousness, with seven others, when he brought
[y]a flood upon the world of the ungodly; 6 if
by [z]turning the cities of Sodom and
Gomorrah to ashes he condemned them to
extinction, [a]making them an example of
[b]what is going to happen to the ungodly;[4]
7 and [c]if he rescued righteous Lot, greatly
distressed by the sensual conduct of the
wicked 8 (for as that righteous man lived
among them day after day, [d]he was tor-

17 [e]Matt. 17:5; Mark 9:7; Luke 9:35; [Matt. 3:17] **18** [f][Ex. 3:5; Josh. 5:15] **19** [g]See 1 Pet. 1:10 [h]Ps. 119:105; John 5:35 [i]Rev. 2:28; 22:16; [Mal. 4:2] [j]2 Cor. 4:6 **21** [k]2 Tim. 3:16 [l]1 Pet. 1:11; [2 Sam. 23:2; Luke 1:70; Acts 1:16; 3:18]
Chapter 2
1 [m]Deut. 13:1; See Matt. 7:15 [n]Acts 20:30; 2 Cor. 11:13; 1 Tim. 4:1; [Matt. 24:11] [o]Jude 4; [Matt. 10:33; Gal. 2:4] [p]1 Cor. 6:20; 7:23; Gal. 3:13; 4:5; Rev. 5:9; [Ex. 15:16; 1 Pet. 1:18; Rev. 14:3, 4] **2** [q]Rom. 2:24

3 [r][2 Cor. 12:17, 18; 1 Tim. 6:5; Tit. 1:11] [s]Rom. 16:18; Col. 2:4 [t][Deut. 32:35; Phil. 3:19] **4** [u]Jude 6 [v][Rev. 20:2, 3, 10] [w]Matt. 25:41 **5** [x]See 1 Pet. 3:20 [y]ch. 3:6; Job 22:16 **6** [z]See Gen. 19:24 [a][Num. 26:10] [b]Jude 15 **7** [c]Gen. 19:16 **8** [d]Ps. 119:136, 158; [Ezek. 9:4]

1 Or *my Son, my* (or *the*) *Beloved* 2 Greek *Tartarus* 3 Some manuscripts *pits* 4 Some manuscripts *an example to those who were to be ungodly*

1:19 we have something more sure, the prophetic word. The prophetic word of Scripture is a more solid proof than even the spectacular experience of witnessing the Transfiguration.

the morning star. This probably alludes to Num. 24:17, a passage that is interpreted messianically (Rev. 2:28; 22:16). If so, the symbol refers to Christ in His Second Coming.

rises in your hearts. A difficult phrase, since "day dawns" and "morning star" apparently refer to the Second Coming of Christ, an external event. Peter probably refers to the effect on believers of the full revelation that will accompany Christ's return. His readers must pay attention to the sure "prophetic word" until the day when that word will be superseded by the full revelation to come.

1:20 someone's own interpretation. Some take this verse to be about the interpretation of prophecy, to the effect that no one is allowed to interpret Scripture on their own, privately. But Peter's concern here is the reliability of Scripture itself, and not the authority of those who interpret it. That point comes up later (3:16). In the present context, Peter is arguing that the prophetic testimony in Scripture comes altogether from God, including not only visions but also words used to describe and interpret them (Dan. 8:15–19; Zech. 1:9).

1:21 carried along by the Holy Spirit. The Holy Spirit is the source of prophecy, enabling the prophets to speak and write as God's representatives (2 Tim. 3:16; 1 Pet. 1:10–12).

2:1 heresies. The Greek term at one time referred to groups or sects in a neutral sense (cf. "sect," Acts 24:5). It was used by Paul of divisive groups (1 Cor. 11:19; Gal. 5:20), and it came to denote the specific teachings of such groups. Here, teachings regarding Christian conduct are probably in view—conduct that placed the teachers under judgment (v. 3; 3:7).

denying the Master who bought them. Peter is not saying Christians can lose their salvation (John 10:28, 29; Rom. 8:28–30), but is describing the false teachers in terms of their own profession of faith (vv. 20, 21). By teaching and practicing immorality they despise the lordship of Christ and prove their profession to be false (1 John 2:3, 4, 19).

Though the phrase "the Master who bought them" is taken by some to mean that Christ's substitutionary death applies to all rather than to the elect only (see "Definite Redemption" at John 10:15), Peter's concern here is to highlight the responsibility of the false teachers rather than to advance a theory of the Atonement. With their claim to be redeemed by Christ, their "sensuality" (v. 2) brings particular dishonor on Christ and His sacrifice for sin.

2:2 sensuality. Incorrigible and reckless sensual indulgence, especially in sexual immorality (1 Pet. 4:3).

blasphemed. Immoral behavior by those who claim to be Christians gives Christianity a bad name among unbelievers. Christians are often urged to exemplary behavior so that the cause of the gospel will not be hindered (1 Tim. 6:1; Titus 2:5, 9, 10).

2:3 in their greed. See 2 Cor. 9:14, 15; 12:17, 18; 1 Tim. 6:5; 1 Pet. 5:2 and note.

2:4 angels when they sinned. The meaning of this phrase is disputed. Many view this as an allusion to the sin of the "sons of God" in Gen. 6:1–4 (cf. Jude 6). On this reading, Peter may be assuming for illustrative purposes the elaboration of the Gen. 6 narrative in the apocryphal book of *1 Enoch* (Jude 14 note). While "sons of God" can refer to angels (e.g., Job 1:6; 2:1), this interpretation is not without difficulties (Gen. 6:2 note). Others speculate that the "angels" are the evil angels who sinned before the Fall of humanity in Gen. 3. Either way, the point is that if God judged evil angels, He will certainly judge ungodly people as well.

cast them into hell. The verb means "to cast into Tartarus." In Greek mythology Tartarus was the place of punishment for departed spirits. Just as Paul can quote an apt verse from a pagan writer for his own purposes (cf. Acts 17:28; Titus 1:12), so Peter here uses Homeric imagery to convey the idea of a special place of confinement until final judgment.

2:5 herald of righteousness. This description of Noah is unique in Scripture, but is well-known in Jewish tradition. It refers either to exhortations that were not recorded in the Old Testament, or to Noah's lifestyle, that condemned sin and recommended righteous living to his contemporaries (Gen. 6:9).

2:7 righteous Lot. A surprising description in view of the portrait of Lot in Genesis (Gen. 19). Lot's righteousness may have been inferred (either by Peter or extrabiblical tradition) from Abraham's intercession for the righteous of Sodom and Lot's subsequent deliverance.

menting his righteous soul over their lawless deeds that he saw and heard); 9 then
[e]the Lord knows how to rescue the godly
from trials,[1] and to keep the unrighteous
under punishment until the day of judgment, 10 and especially [f]those who indulge
in the lust of defiling passion and [g]despise
authority.

Bold and willful, they do not tremble [g]as
they blaspheme the glorious ones, 11 [h]where-
as angels, though greater in might and
power, do not pronounce a blasphemous
judgment against them before the Lord.
12 [i]But these, like irrational animals, [j]crea-
tures of instinct, born to be caught and
destroyed, blaspheming about matters of
which they are ignorant, will also be
destroyed in their destruction, 13 suffering
wrong as [k]the wage for their wrongdoing.
They count it pleasure [l]to revel in the daytime. They are blots and blemishes, revel-
ing in their deceptions,[2] while [m]they feast
with you. 14 They have eyes full of adultery,
[n]insatiable for sin. They entice unsteady
souls. They have hearts [o]trained in greed.
[p]Accursed children! 15 Forsaking the right
way, [q]they have gone astray. They have followed [r]the way of Balaam, the son of Beor,
who loved [s]gain from wrongdoing, 16 but
was rebuked for his own transgression; [t]a
speechless donkey spoke with human voice
and restrained the prophet's madness.

17 [u]These are waterless springs and mists
driven by a storm. [v]For them the gloom of
utter darkness has been reserved. 18 For,
[w]speaking loud boasts of folly, they entice
by sensual passions of the flesh those who
are barely [x]escaping from those who live in
error. 19 They promise them [y]freedom, [z]but
they themselves are slaves[3] of corruption.
For whatever overcomes a person, to that
he is enslaved. 20 For if, [a]after they have
escaped the defilements of the world
[b]through the knowledge of our Lord and
Savior Jesus Christ, they are again entangled in them and overcome, [c]the last state
has become worse for them than the first.
21 For [d]it would have been better for them
never to have known the way of righteousness than after knowing it to turn back

9 [e]1 Cor. 10:13; Rev. 3:10 **10** [f]Jude 16, 18 [g]Jude 8; [Ex. 22:28] **11** [h]Jude 9 **12** [i]Jude 10 [j][Jer. 12:3; Phil. 3:19] **13** [k]ver. 15 [l][Rom. 13:13; 1 Thess. 5:7]; See James 5:5 [m][1 Cor. 11:21] **14** [n][1 Pet. 4:1] [o]ver. 3; [1 Tim. 4:7] [p][Eph. 2:3] **15** [q]Ezek. 14:11 [r]Num. 22:5, 7; Deut. 23:4; Neh. 13:2; Jude 11; Rev. 2:14 [s]ver. 13 **16** [t]Num. 22:21, 23, 28 **17** [u]Jude 12 [v]Jude 13 **18** [w]Jude 16 [x]ver. 20; ch. 1:4 **19** [y]Gal. 5:13; See James 1:25 [z]John 8:34; Rom. 6:16 **20** [a]ver. 18 [b]See ch. 1:2 [c]Matt. 12:45 **21** [d][Ezek. 18:24; Luke 12:47; Heb. 6:4-6; 10:26, 27; James 4:17]

[1] Or *temptations* [2] Some manuscripts *love feasts* [3] Greek *bondservants*

2:9 then the Lord. The implication of the three examples in vv. 4–8 is clear: God will surely judge the wicked and deliver the righteous.

keep . . . under punishment. Some commentators and most English translations see here a reference to preliminary punishment before the final judgment. This is the most natural reading of the Greek, although some commentators including Calvin understand it as a reference to future punishment on Judgment Day ("reserve the unjust for punishment on the day of judgment"). Because Peter's concern in this passage is the certainty of final judgment, the latter seems more appropriate to the argument than the former.

2:10 blaspheme the glorious ones. Probably a reference to angels. The statement in v. 11 that "whereas angels . . . do not pronounce a blasphemous judgment against them" (cf. Jude 10, 11) indicates that evil angels are in view. When warned of the danger of falling into the power of the spiritual forces of evil (cf. 1 Cor. 5:5; 1 Tim. 1:20), the false teachers apparently mocked the power of the devil and his demons. Even today, a flippant attitude toward Satan and his power can lead to spiritual danger.

2:13 their deceptions, while they feast with you. The false teachers were not promoting love at their feasts (Jude 12), but harmful lies. Peter uses a Greek word for "deceptions" which sounds similar to the Greek for "love."

2:14 eyes full of adultery. Lit. "eyes full of an adulterous woman," a vivid portrayal of their insatiable sensuality (v. 2 note).

entice unsteady souls. In contrast to the "established" believers of 1:12, the "unsteady" lack a firm foundation in the Christian faith, and are easy prey to the enticements of false teachers.

trained in greed. An athletic metaphor. At least part of their purpose in making disciples was to profit financially from them (vv. 3, 15).

2:15 way of Balaam. Jewish exegetical tradition had made Balaam proverbial for his greed, so the false teachers with their desire for gain are compared with him (Jude 11). According to Num. 31:16 he was also guilty of leading others into sin.

2:16 speechless donkey. Peter probably intends an ironic contrast with v. 12. While the false teachers resembled "irrational animals" in their slavery to greed, their prototype Balaam was himself rebuked by a beast.

2:17 waterless springs. Just as water sustains physical life, so true spiritual teaching nourishes spiritual life (Prov. 13:14; John 4:13–15)—a vivid image in a culture where water was a treasured resource. Like the dry well that only disappoints the thirsty (Jer. 14:3), the false teachers can only deceive and disappoint.

mists driven by a storm. Like hazy clouds that provide no refreshing rain (Jude 12), the false teaching cannot provide spiritual sustenance.

2:18 entice . . . those who are barely escaping. New converts or those not yet well grounded in the faith fall prey to the false teachers (v. 14 and note).

2:19 They promise them freedom. The false teachers may have used Paul's declaration that the Christian is not under law as the basis for their mistaken teaching that the Christian is free from the restraint of God's moral law (cf. Rom. 6:15; 1 Cor. 9:21; Gal. 5:18).

slaves of corruption. A profound irony of sin is evident here: the quest for freedom from God leads only to slavery to sin and self. True freedom from sin involves joyful "slavery" to God (cf. Rom. 6:18).

2:20–22 The false teachers rather than those who "are barely escaping" (v. 18) are probably in view. These false teachers apparently professed to be Christians, but their return to their old sinful way of life showed that their knowledge of Christ and the way of righteousness was only superficial (v. 1 note).

2:21 better . . . never to have known the way of righteousness. Deliberate rejection of the truth increases one's responsibility before God (Luke 12:47, 48). The phrase "to have known the way" refers to an intellectual knowledge of the ethical teachings and mode of life characteristic of Christians (note the phrase "holy commandment"). Their conversion was illusory. Scripture elsewhere teaches that those who are truly regenerate will persevere in the faith (John 10:26–30; cf. 1 John 2:19).

from [e]the holy commandment delivered to
them. **22**What the true proverb says has
happened to them: "The [f]dog returns to its
own vomit, and the sow, after washing herself, returns to wallow in the mire."

The Day of the Lord Will Come

3 This is now the second letter that I am
writing to you, beloved. In both of
them [g]I am stirring up your sincere mind
by way of reminder, **2**[h]that you should
remember the predictions of [i]the holy
prophets and the commandment of the
Lord and Savior through your apostles,
3knowing this first of all, that scoffers will
come [j]in the last days with scoffing, [k]fol-
lowing their own sinful desires. **4**[l]They will
say, "Where is the promise of [m]his coming?
For ever since the fathers fell asleep, all
things are continuing as they were from the
beginning of creation." **5**For they deliberately overlook this fact, that the heavens
existed long ago, and the earth [n]was
formed out of water and through water [o]by
the word of God, **6**and that by means of
these the world that then existed [p]was del-
uged with water and [q]perished. **7**But by the
same word [r]the heavens and earth that
now exist are stored up for fire, being kept
until the day of judgment and [s]destruction
of the ungodly.

8But do not overlook this one fact,
beloved, that with the Lord one day is as a
thousand years, and [t]a thousand years as
one day. **9**[u]The Lord is not slow to fulfill his
promise [v]as some count slowness, but [w]is
patient toward you,[1] [x]not wishing that any
should perish, but [y]that all should reach
repentance. **10**But [z]the day of the Lord will
come like a thief, and then [a]the heavens
will pass away with a roar, and [b]the heavenly bodies[2] will be burned up and dissolved, and the earth and the works that
are done on it will be exposed.[3]

21 [e]Rom. 7:12
22 [f]Prov. 26:11
Chapter 3
1 [g]ch. 1:13
2 [h]Jude 17 [i]Luke 1:70; Acts 3:21
3 [j]Jude 18 [k]ch. 2:10
4 [l]Isai. 5:19; Jer. 17:15; Ezek. 11:3; 12:22, 27; Mal. 2:17 [m]See 1 Thess. 2:19
5 [n]Ps. 24:2; 136:6 [o]Gen. 1:6, 9; Ps. 33:6; [Heb. 11:3]
6 [p]ch. 2:5 [q]Gen. 7:11, 21
7 [r]ver. 10, 12 [s][2 Thess. 1:9]
8 [t]Ps. 90:4
9 [u]Hab. 2:3; Heb. 10:37 [v][Eccles. 8:11; Rev. 2:21] [w]Isai. 30:18; Luke 18:7 [x]Ezek. 18:23, 32; 33:11 [y]1 Tim. 2:4
10 [z]See Matt. 24:43 [a][Rev. 6:14; 20:11; 21:1]; See Matt. 24:35 [b]Isai. 34:4; [Isai. 24:19; Mic. 1:4; Nah. 1:5]

1 Some manuscripts *on your account* 2 Or *elements*; also verse 12
3 Greek *found*; some manuscripts *will be burned up*

2:22 The dog . . . the sow. In contrast to the modern view of dogs as "man's best friend," the ancient Jews despised them (Ex. 22:31; Prov. 26:11; Rev. 22:15). Swine were avoided as unclean (Lev. 11:7; Is. 65:4). Peter's point is that mere religious profession or even outward change does not change a person's heart. The apostasy of the false teachers reveals their true nature.

3:1 second letter. The first letter may well be 1 Peter, and, if so, the recipients of the two letters are the same.

stirring up . . . by way of reminder. If 1 Peter is in view, the reminder is probably Peter's general concern, quite evident in both epistles, that his readers should live holy lives worthy of the gospel.

3:3 the last days. See note 1 Pet. 1:20.

3:4 the promise of his coming. From the delay in Christ's return, the false teachers wrongly concluded that He would never return to judge them. Peter portrays their scoffing as ironic evidence that the last days are indeed present.

since the fathers fell asleep. Perhaps a reference to Old Testament forefathers (John 6:31; Acts 3:13), though many interpret this as a reference to the deaths of people belonging to the first Christian generation, especially Christian leaders such as Stephen (Heb. 13:7).

3:5, 6 Against the false teacher's denial that God would intervene in history, Peter cites creation and the Flood as prime examples of God's intimate involvement and intervention in the process of history.

3:5 out of water and through water. God created the earth by separating and gathering the waters (Gen. 1:2, 6–10).

the word of God. His creative command (Gen. 1:3–30; Ps. 33:6; Heb. 11:3). God preceded history; the heavens and earth came into existence only at His command. He created all things out of nothing, by the word of God.

3:6 world . . . perished. God also intervened, in judgment, with the Flood (2:5; Gen. 6–8).

3:7 by the same word. The same divine word that created the world and brought judgment at the Flood. Whether manifested by water or fire, the role of God's all-powerful word in creation, in the Flood, and in final judgment is stressed.

stored up for fire. Sodom and Gomorrah serve for Peter as a paradigm of final fiery judgment (2:6). Although this picture of a universal inferno at the last judgment is unique to Peter, the idea of divine judgment by fire is common in the Old Testament (e.g., Deut. 32:22; Is. 66:15, 16; Mal. 4:1) and is found in the New Testament as well (e.g., Matt. 3:12; 1 Cor. 3:13; 2 Thess. 1:7, 8).

3:8 one day . . . a thousand years. Though this passage—and Ps. 90:4 upon which it is based—is sometimes implausibly cited in support of the theory that when a "day" is mentioned in biblical prophecy a literal thousand years is meant, Peter's point is to assert that God is sovereign over time and that His perspective on time differs radically from ours.

3:9 as some count slowness. See v. 4.

patient . . . all should reach repentance. Peter's Christian readers must realize that the apparent delay of divine judgment is a sign of God's forbearance and mercy toward them, particularly toward the believers in their midst who have been confused and misled by the false teachers. The repentance in view, for the sake of which God delays judgment, is that of God's people rather than the world at large. God is not willing that any of His elect should perish (John 6:39).

3:10 day of the Lord. The time of divine intervention and judgment (Is. 13:9–13; Joel 1:15; 3:14; 1 Thess. 5:2), synonymous with the Second Coming of Christ (v. 12).

like a thief. Jesus used this metaphor to convey how unexpected the event would be (Luke 12:39, 40).

the heavens . . . with a roar. The language is reminiscent of the Old Testament and of Jesus Himself (Is. 34:4; 64:1–4; Matt. 24:29–31).

heavenly bodies. Greek *stoicheia,* a term used for (a) the elements making up the world (according to the philosophers these were earth, air, fire, and water); (b) heavenly bodies such as the sun, moon, and stars; (c) angelic beings with power over nature (Introduction to Colossians: Interpretive Difficulties). Most interpreters favor (b) or a combination of (b) and (c).

will be exposed. Or "found." The Greek text of this phrase is disputed (text note). Some manuscripts say "will be burned up," presumably to mean that the earth will undergo a catastrophic judgment.

11 Since all these things are thus to be dissolved, [c]what sort of people ought you to
be in lives of holiness and godliness,
12 [d]waiting for and hastening the coming of
the day of God, because of which the heavens will be set on fire and dissolved, and
[e]the heavenly bodies will melt as they
burn! 13 But according to his promise we
are waiting for [f]new heavens and a new
earth [g]in which righteousness dwells.

Final Words

14 [h]Therefore, beloved, since you are waiting for these, be diligent to be found by
him [i]without spot or [j]blemish, and [k]at
peace. 15 And count [l]the patience of our
Lord as salvation, just as [m]our beloved
brother Paul also wrote to you [n]according
to the wisdom given him, 16 as he does in
all his letters when he speaks in them of
these matters. [o]There are some things in
them that are hard to understand, which
the ignorant and unstable twist to their
own destruction, [p]as they do the other
Scriptures. 17 You therefore, beloved,
[q]knowing this beforehand, [r]take care that
you are not carried away with the error of
lawless people and lose your own stability.
18 But [s]grow in the grace and knowledge of
our Lord and Savior Jesus Christ. [t]To him
be the glory both now and to the day of
[u]eternity. Amen.

11 [c]1 Pet. 1:15
12 [d][Luke 12:36; 1 Cor. 1:7; 1 Thess. 1:10; Tit. 2:13; Jude 21] [e]See ver. 10
13 [f]Isai. 65:17; 66:22; Rev. 21:1 [g]Isai. 60:21; Rev. 21:27
14 [h]1 Cor. 15:58 [i]James 1:27 [j]Phil. 2:15 [k][Phil. 1:10; 1 Thess. 3:13; 5:23]
15 [l]See ver. 9 [m][Acts 15:25] [n]1 Cor. 3:10
16 [o][Heb. 5:11] [p][Isai. 28:13] 17 [q]ch. 1:12; [Mark 13:23] [r]ch. 1:10; 1 Cor. 10:12
18 [s]ch. 1:5; Eph. 4:15; Col. 1:10; 2:19; 1 Pet. 2:2 [t]See Rom. 11:36 [u][ver. 8]

3:12 hastening the coming. Though sometimes translated "eagerly awaiting," the Greek word usually means "hasten." The time of Christ's coming is determined by the sovereign counsel of God, but it does not take place without reference to other events (these too are ordained by God). That God's delay is merciful (v. 9 and note) indicates that the evangelization of the elect is one relevant factor (Mark 13:10). Other factors include prayer (Luke 11:2) and obedience (v. 11). Such a teaching should profoundly encourage Christians. Our actions do matter.

the day of God. An unusual expression (Rev. 16:14), equivalent to "the day of the Lord" (v. 10). The use of the phrases "day of the Lord" and "day of God" for Christ's Second Coming indicates Peter's high Christology: the coming One is none other than God Himself.

3:13 new heavens and a new earth. See "Heaven" and note at Rev. 21:1.

3:15 patience . . . as salvation. See notes on vv. 9 and 12.

wisdom given him. Tantamount to a claim of divine inspiration for Paul's letters (v. 16 note; cf. Eph. 3:2–7).

3:16 the other Scriptures. Peter views Paul's letters in the same category as the inspired, authoritative writings of the Old Testament (v. 15; 1:20, 21), and in harmony with Paul's own claims to unique apostolic authority (Rom. 1:1; 1 Cor. 2:13; Gal. 1:1).

3:17 lawless people. The false teachers, characterized as people who ignore all moral restraints.

lose your own stability. Not that true believers can lose their salvation (2:21 note), but a warning to them of their own weakness and the dangers that surround them, to motivate them to watchfulness and growth in godly living.

3:18 grow in . . . knowledge. This knowledge is the ever-deepening experience of Christ and understanding of His truth that should characterize the entire course of the believer's life, as opposed to the pretentious, esoteric "knowledge" of the false teachers.

To him be the glory. This statement presupposes the deity of Christ (v. 12; 1:1 notes). It ascribes glory directly to Him (Rev. 1:5, 6).

to the day of eternity. Glory belongs to Christ both now and throughout the endless day that will dawn when He comes again (1:19; Is. 60: 19, 20).

THE FIRST EPISTLE OF

John

AUTHOR

In style, diction, and content, 1 John follows the fourth Gospel closely. It is almost certainly by the same author (Introduction to John: Author). While both writings are anonymous, their traditional assignment to John, son of Zebedee, cannot be disproved. It rests on firmer evidence than more speculative proposals, such as John the Elder or John Mark. The emphasis in the opening verse on authoritative proclamation and eyewitness testimony is most naturally seen as a reflection of John's apostolic calling (John 19:35; 20:3–8; 21:24).

DATE AND OCCASION

First John was written to warn and instruct the readers about a kind of false teaching that denied Jesus Christ had come in the flesh (4:2, 3). The teaching was that Christ only appeared to be human, so that there was no real incarnation, and no divine Savior who was able to die for sinners. Christ only seemed to die. Such teaching is known from early Christian history and is called "docetism" (from Greek *dokeo*, "to seem").

Some scholars think that the false teaching was a variety of Gnosticism, a religious movement that connected salvation with an experience of individual, esoteric revelation (*gnosis* is the Greek word for "knowledge"). An example would be the teaching of the late first-century teacher Cerinthus. Later writers did regard Cerinthus as both Gnostic and docetic, but there is little in 1 John to connect the false teaching opposed there with the specific ideas attributed to Cerinthus, or even to Gnosticism more generally.

Several considerations indicate that 1 John was written after the Gospel of John. First, it refers very briefly to ideas that the Gospel unfolds much more clearly and fully. Apparently the readers are presumed to have knowledge of the Gospel. Second, the conflict with docetism is absent from the Gospel and appears to be a later development. Third, there is no hint in 1 John of the ideological conflict with "the Jews" that pervades the first half of the Gospel. The Gospel shows the Christian community painfully distinguishing itself from the Jewish people, while 1 John reflects a later time, when Christian self-identification was well-established and could be presupposed.

Another indication for the date of 1 John comes from comparison with the letters of Ignatius (about A.D. 110) and Polycarp. These writings criticize false teachings similar to but more developed than those addressed in 1 John. To accommodate this development, 1 John should be dated some years earlier than 110.

CHARACTERISTICS AND THEMES

Although 1 John has traditionally been regarded as a letter, it lacks key distinguishing features of a letter (salutation, introductory greeting, final greeting). On the other hand, John addresses the readers as "My little children" (2:1). He seems to be writing to a specific group of people with whom he has a close relationship. In its basic purposes of admonition and instruction, 1 John is similar to most of the New Testament letters.

It is notoriously difficult to outline this brief letter. Its themes seem to be linked loosely together. The language is not difficult or technical, but the ideas are profound. John says that God has been revealed in Christ in order to communicate eternal life to those who believe. God is light, truth, and love—each of these characteristics is the subject of some meditation, but always in connection with the development of corresponding virtues in the believers.

The ideals of purity and love that are held out to the reader are gifts of God, communicated from His self-revelation. At the same time, they are real only in action. This reality is possible through being born again and through the forgiveness of sins.

The enemy of the gospel attacks at every point. He impugns the self-revelation of God by trying to deny that Jesus Christ was incarnated. With this he threatens to undermine the believer's confidence before God. Moreover, the adversary tries to make the case that someone can believe in God without taking part in the love and kindness that is God's nature. This would make salvation also a mere appearance. To the light and truth of the gospel, the antichrist opposes darkness and lies, or the rule of hatred and mental confusion.

Unlike those of Paul, John's ideas are not reasoned logically from point to point. The final statements, that God is light, and that Jesus Christ cleanses us from all sin, are already stated in the first few verses. These he elaborates in a spiritual way throughout what follows.

OUTLINE OF 1 JOHN

I. Introduction: Eternal Life Has Appeared (1:1–4)

II. Light and Darkness (1:5–2:27)

- A. *Walk in the Light (1:5–2:11)*
  1. Forgiveness of Sin (1:5–10)
  2. Keeping the Commandments (2:1–6)
  3. Loving the Brother (2:7–11)
- B. *Escaping from Sin (2:12–17)*
  1. Overcoming the Wicked One (2:12–14)
  2. Overcoming the World (2:15–17)
- C. *Counsel for the Last Hour (2:18–27)*
  1. Apostasy (2:18–21)
  2. Denial of Christ (2:22–24)
  3. Reminder About the Anointing (2:25–27)

III. The Life of Righteousness (2:28–4:6)

- A. *The Righteousness of God's Children (2:28–3:3)*
- B. *The Practice of Sin and the Devil (3:4–10)*
- C. *Love Against Hate (3:11–15)*
- D. *Love and Generosity (3:16–18)*
- E. *Assurance (3:19–24)*
- F. *The Spirit of God and the Antichrist (4:1–6)*

IV. Love Is Perfected in Us (4:7–5:12)

- A. *God Is Love (4:7–21)*
- B. *Belief and Obedience (5:1–12)*

V. Conclusion (5:13–21)

- A. *Prayer for the Sinner (5:13–17)*
- B. *Life in God (5:18–21)*

The Word of Life

1 [a]That which was [b]from the beginning,
[c]which we have heard, [d]which we have
seen with our eyes, [e]which we looked upon
and [f]have touched with our hands, concerning the word of life— **2** [g]the life [h]was
made manifest, and we have seen it, and
[i]testify to it and proclaim to you the eternal
life, [a]which was with the Father and [h]was
made manifest to us— **3** [c]that which we
have seen and heard we proclaim also to
you, so that you too may have fellowship
with us; and indeed [j]our fellowship is with
the Father and with his Son Jesus Christ.
4 And we are writing these things so [k]that
our[1] joy may be complete.

Walking in the Light

5 [l]This is the message we have heard
from him and proclaim to you, that [m]God

Chapter 1 1 [a]See John 1:1 [b][ch. 2:13, 14] [c]Acts 4:20 [d]John 19:35 [e]ch. 4:14; John 1:14; 2 Pet. 1:16 [f]Luke 24:39; John 20:27 **2** [g]John 1:4; 11:25; 14:6 [h]ch. 3:5, 8; Rom. 16:26; 1 Tim. 3:16 [i]See John 15:27 [a][See ver. 1 above] **3** [c][See ver. 1 above] [j]John 17:21; 1 Cor. 1:9; [ch. 2:24] **4** [k]John 15:11; 16:24 **5** [l]ch. 3:11 [m]James 1:17; [ch. 4:8; John 4:24]

[1] Some manuscripts *your*

1:1–4 The central event of history is the appearance of eternal life in Jesus Christ. John is one of the chosen witnesses who saw, heard, and touched One who had existed from the beginning—the Son of God, whose eternal fellowship with the Father is now extended to others. This extension takes place through the apostolic proclamation, including the writing of 1 John itself.

1:1 the beginning. This verse echoes John 1:1, as that verse in turn echoes Gen. 1:1. The two New Testament verses highlight the Incarnation as an event as significant as creation itself.

heard . . . seen . . . looked upon . . . touched. These vivid verbs defend the reality of the human nature of Christ against the docetic speculation that is later rejected explicitly (2:22; 4:2, 3; Introduction: Date and Occasion).

the word of life. The subject of John's proclamation is Jesus, the incarnate Word (John 1:1–14).

1:5–10 Like John's Gospel, 1 John begins with a contrast between light and darkness. In the Gospel, the incarnate Christ is the light that continues to shine in the darkness of a world that tries to exclude Him. Believers are faced with a choice: either to "walk in the light," coming to Him and opening their hearts to Him in confession of sin, or to "walk in

is light, and in him is no darkness at all.
6 [n]If we say we have fellowship with him
while we walk in darkness, we lie and [o]do
not practice the truth. **7** But [p]if we walk in
the light, [q]as he is in the light, we have fellowship with one another, and [r]the blood
of Jesus his Son cleanses us from all sin.
8 [s]If we say we have no sin, we deceive ourselves, and [t]the truth is not in us. **9** [u]If we
confess our sins, he is [v]faithful and just to
forgive us our sins and [r]to cleanse us from
all unrighteousness. **10** If we say we have
not sinned, [w]we make him a liar, and [x]his
word is not in us.

Christ Our Advocate

2 My little children, I am writing these
things to you so that you may not sin.
But if anyone does sin, [y]we have an advocate with the Father, Jesus Christ the righteous. **2** [z]He is the propitiation for our sins,
and not for ours only but [a]also for the sins
of the whole world. **3** And by this we know
that we have come to know him, if we
[b]keep his commandments. **4** Whoever says
"I know him" but does not keep his commandments [c]is a liar, and [c]the truth is not
in him, **5** but whoever [d]keeps his word, in
him truly [e]the love of God is perfected. [f]By
this we may be sure that we are in him:
6 whoever says he [g]abides in him [h]ought to
walk in the same way in which he walked.

The New Commandment

7 Beloved, I am writing you [i]no new commandment, but [j]an old commandment
[k]that you had from the beginning. The old
commandment is the word that you have
heard. **8** At the same time, it is [l]a new commandment that I am writing to you, which
is true in him and in you, because[1] [m]the
darkness is passing away and [n]the true
light is already shining. **9** Whoever says he

6 [n]ch. 2:11; John 12:35; 2 Cor. 6:14 [o]John 3:21 **7** [p][Isai. 2:5] [q][Ps. 104:2; 1 Tim. 6:16] [r]Eph. 1:7; Heb. 9:14; 1 Pet. 1:19; Rev. 5:9; 7:14; 12:11 **8** [s][Job 15:14; Jer. 2:35]; See James 3:2 [t]ch. 2:4 **9** [u]Ps. 32:5; 51:3; Prov. 28:13 [v][Ps. 143:1; Rom. 3:26] [r][See ver. 7 above] **10** [w]ch. 5:10 [x]John 5:38; 8:37
Chapter 2
1 [y]Rom. 8:34; 1 Tim. 2:5; Heb. 7:25 **2** [z]ch. 4:10; Rom. 3:25; [2 Cor. 5:18, 19; Col. 1:20] [a]ch. 4:14; John 1:29; 4:42; 11:51, 52; 12:32

3 [b]John 14:15; 15:10 **4** [c]ch. 1:8; John 8:44 **5** [d]ch. 5:3; John 14:23 [e]ch. 4:12 [f]ch. 3:24; 4:13; 5:2 **6** [g]John 15:4, 5, 7 [h]See Matt. 11:29 **7** [i]2 John 5 [j]Lev. 19:18 [k][ver. 24; ch. 3:11; 2 John 5, 6] **8** [l]See John 13:34 [m]Rom. 13:12; Eph. 5:8; 1 Thess. 5:4, 5 [n]John 1:9; 8:12

1 Or *that*

darkness," denying that they are sinners. The contrast between light and darkness is inseparably linked to a contrast between those who "practice the truth" and agree with God, and those who make God "a liar." It is an inescapable reality that believers sin; the remedy for sin—confession, and cleansing by the blood of Jesus—is God's continuing irrevocable gift to believers. Because Jesus' death has paid in full the penalty for sin, and because God has recognized Jesus as His true Son by raising Him from the dead, God grants forgiveness and cleansing as a matter of faithfulness and justice. He will not and cannot refuse.

1:5 God is light. This description of God emphasizes His attributes of moral purity and omniscience, reinforcing John's focus on our need to confess sin.

1:7 the blood of Jesus his Son. As Heb. 9:22 indicates, "without the shedding of blood there is no forgiveness." The shedding of the blood of Christ was a voluntary substitutionary sacrifice of infinite value for the elect; it paid in full God's penalty for sin (Heb. 9:27, 28).

1:9 If we confess our sins. God's forgiveness is given as soon as we admit our need of it, not on the basis of any acts we have done to earn it, but solely because of His grace. The free gift of forgiveness carries with it purification from unrighteousness. God accepts us as righteous because He imputes to us the righteousness of Christ. That is, the very righteousness of Christ our sin-bearer is reckoned to our account.

1:10 If we say we have not sinned. Perhaps the sin that "leads to death" mentioned in 5:16 is a stubborn refusal to accept God's diagnosis of our need and His offer of forgiveness.

2:1–6 Forgiveness does not remove the moral obligation to obey the commands of God. Some readers may take the promise of 1:9 as a license to sin, but John makes clear that this would be to abuse and misapply the promise (v. 1). "Jesus Christ the righteous" is presented as sacrifice, advocate, and example. His atonement is effective for the elect of Israel and of the whole world.

In the Bible, to "know" someone includes close communion and love. To know Christ means to "keep his commandments." This knowledge of Christ is called a "perfected" love of God (v. 5), not because it makes us personally sinless, but because it is irrevocably established in those who live by it. Anyone who presumes to have received forgiveness from God but who spurns the gift of obedient love as unnecessary is a "liar." Instead of receiving "Jesus Christ the righteous" as Savior, such a person manufactures a false christ, a savior who is indifferent to righteousness.

2:1 that you may not sin. John wants his readers to respond to God's mercy with a life of obedience. This is an expression of concern for those among whom he has served (2 John 4–6; 3 John 3, 4). 1 John does not give details about the sins of the readers or of their heretical opponents (unlike, e.g., 1 Corinthians).

advocate. The Greek word is *parakletos*, a "helper," such as an attorney in a legal matter. In the Gospel of John it is used of the Holy Spirit (John 14:16, 26; 15:26; 16:7). The word is not found elsewhere in the New Testament, although it is common in other literature.

2:2 propitiation. A propitiation is a sacrifice to God meant to take away the enmity brought by sin between God and the worshiper. Only Christ can be an effective propitiation.

of the whole world. Christ's sacrifice is sufficient not only for John and his immediate community, but is valid anywhere in the world. It is a sacrifice that requires no addition or supplement.

2:6 walk in the same way in which he walked. John assumes that his readers have the kind of knowledge about Jesus' life and purposes that is found in the Gospel.

2:7–11 The commandment of God in Christ is both "old" and "new." It is old, because it dates to the dawn of the Christian era; believers had this command "from the beginning," when Jesus Christ began to teach. It is new because it is continually reapplied in new acts of love, with their source in Him and their outworking "in you." Love belongs to the realm of light, as over against darkness, where hatred still has sway. John speaks of love for the "brother," which Jesus gave as a commandment to His disciples just before His death. John draws sharply the contrast between a Christian community ruled by love, and the hatred that rules outside (John 15:18, 19).

2:7 from the beginning. While John sometimes uses this word to refer to the beginning of all things (vv. 13, 14; 1:1), here he refers to the beginning of the Christian movement in the life and teaching of Jesus (v. 24; 3:11). As the next verse shows, the coming of Jesus was the critical turning point ushering in a new epoch, the dawning of a new day.

is in the light and [o]hates his brother is still
in darkness. 10 Whoever loves his brother
abides in the light, and in him[1] there is no
[p]cause for stumbling. 11 But whoever hates
his brother is in the darkness and [q]walks in
the darkness, and does not know where he
is going, because the darkness has blinded
his eyes.

12 I am writing to you, little children,
because [r]your sins are forgiven for
his name's sake.
13 I am writing to you, fathers,
because you know [s]him who is
from the beginning.
I am writing to you, young men,
because [t]you have overcome the
evil one.
I write to you, children,
because [u]you know the Father.
14 I write to you, fathers,
because you know [s]him who is
from the beginning.
I write to you, young men,
because [t]you are strong,
and the word of God abides in
you,
and you have overcome the evil
one.

Do Not Love the World

15 [v]Do not love the world or the things in
the world. [w]If anyone loves the world, the
love of the Father is not in him. 16 For all
that is in the world—[x]the desires of the
flesh and [y]the desires of the eyes and pride
in possessions—is not from the Father but
is from the world. 17 And [z]the world is passing away along with its desires, but whoever does the will of God abides forever.

Warning Concerning Antichrists

18 Children, [a]it is the last hour, and as
you have heard that [b]antichrist is coming,
so now [c]many antichrists have come.
[d]Therefore we know that it is the last hour.
19 [e]They went out from us, but they were

9 [o]ch. 4:20; [ch. 3:14, 15; Tit. 3:3] **10** [p]John 11:10; [Prov. 4:19; 2 Pet. 1:10] **11** [q]See ch. 1:6 **12** [r]Luke 24:47 Acts 10:43; 13:38 **13** [s][ch. 1:1] [t]Eph. 6:10; [ch. 5:4, 5] [u]John 14:7 **14** [s][See ver. 13 above] [t][See ver. 13 above] **15** [v][Rom. 12:2; 2 Tim. 4:10] [w]See James 4:4 **16** [x]Rom. 13:14; Eph. 2:3; 1 Pet. 4:2; 2 Pet. 2:18 [y]Eccles. 4:8; 5:11 **17** [z]See 1 Cor. 7:31 **18** [a][2 Tim. 3:1; James 5:3; 2 Pet. 3:3; Jude 18] [b]ver. 22; ch. 4:3 2 John 7; [Matt. 24:5, 24] [c][ch. 4:1; Matt. 24:5] [d]1 Tim. 4:1 **19** [e]Deut. 13:13; Acts 20:30

[1] Or *it*

2:12–14 The three groups addressed in these verses are actually one group, the recipients of the letter, characterized in different ways. They are "children" because with the forgiveness of sins they have been welcomed into the family of God their Father. They are "fathers" because their knowledge of God in Jesus Christ qualifies them to hand this knowledge down to future generations. They are called "young men" because their decisive rejection of the evil one is a victory like that of Jesus, who fought with Satan in the wilderness and won (Matt. 4:1–11).

2:12 for his name's sake. The power of the name of Jesus is central to early Christian proclamation (Acts 2:38; 3:6; 4:12). John 17:11, 12 indicates that God has given His own name to Jesus to protect His disciples and keep them safe. God's name would come to dishonor if His forgiveness should fail.

2:13 you have overcome the evil one. The theme of overcoming is picked up again in 5:4, 5; there the victory is over "the world" that opposes God. The victory John describes is resisting temptation and keeping faithful to God's word. It contrasts with the defeat of the human race at the Fall (Gen. 3). For John, victory in the battle against temptation has in effect already been won, since our union with God cannot be broken (John 10:27–30).

2:15–17 The moral admonition not to love the world is also practical advice, for it is already clear that the world is passing away (v. 17). As in John's Gospel, the "world" is the system of rebellion and pride that seeks to displace God and His rule. It is this system rather than the created order itself which is "not from the Father" and which has already been marked for judgment and destruction (John 12:31). Those who are not of the world receive the word of the Father from Jesus (John 17:14) and show by their response to it that they are chosen for salvation and eternal life.

2:16 desires . . . pride. Those who love this world (v. 15) are shortsighted; they want to be satisfied and honored now (Luke 6:24–26). In contrast, those who love the Father have a long-term perspective and wait for God's reward (Luke 6:20–23).

2:17 whoever does the will of God abides forever. John is not teaching that our obedience merits eternal life. Only the obedience of Jesus could satisfy God's demands. Believers receive eternal life as a gift (5:11), and the gift of love transforms them so that they do God's will in gratitude (3:16).

2:18–28 From the time that Jesus pronounced judgment on this world, "the last hour" has been upon it, a final intensification of opposition to God that ends with the final Judgment. The prediction of "the antichrist" is not from the Old Testament but from Jesus (Matt. 24:5, 24). This prediction began to be fulfilled in the New Testament era with those who denied the Father and the Son (v. 22) and left the church to propagate their false teaching (v. 19). Their denial of the Son was a rejection of the Father who sent Him (2:23; John 15:23). In contrast to the antichrists, believers have an anointing from the Holy Spirit (vv. 20, 27) that opens their hearts and minds to know the saving truth. The Spirit Himself is the best teacher; He will remain with us always and protect us from falsehoods that could lead us away from Christ. The Spirit abides wherever the message of the gospel is received, and wherever the Spirit abides, the Son and the Father are present as well (v. 24).

2:18 it is the last hour. John will not satisfy the desire to "know times or seasons that the Father has fixed by his own authority" (Acts 1:7); he characterizes the whole time between the first and the second comings of Christ as "the last hour" (cf. Acts 2:17; 1 Cor. 10:11). No matter how long this "hour" may extend in terms of calendar time, it remains true that "the time is near" (Rev. 1:3; cf. Rev. 1:1; 22:20) for all of God's promises to be fulfilled.

antichrist is coming . . . many antichrists have come. This is commonly seen as a distinct prediction of many antichrists through the course of history, followed by a final Antichrist at the end (2 Thess. 2:3–10; Rev. 13:11–18). John, however, may be referring only to the sort of false teachers who already trouble the church (v. 22; 4:3).

2:19 They went out from us. Paul too warns against false teachers who will arise from among the believers (Acts 20:29–31). As in the case of Simon the sorcerer (Acts 8:9–24), visible membership in the church does not guarantee salvation. Inward apathy or hostility to the gospel may be masked by outward conformity. The false teachers revealed their hostility not just by leaving, but by the way they left. Because they went out to oppose the word of the gospel, their departure was as much a renunciation of the church and its message as was Judas's departure from the Last Supper (John 13:30).

not of us; for [f]if they had been of us, they
would have continued with us. But they
went out, [g]that it might become plain that
they all are not of us. 20 But you have been
[h]anointed by [i]the Holy One, and [j]you all
have knowledge.[1] 21 I write to you, not
because you do not know the truth, but
because you know it, and because no lie is
of the truth. 22 Who is the liar but [k]he who
denies that Jesus is the Christ? This is [b]the
antichrist, he who denies the Father and
the Son. 23 [l]No one who denies the Son has
the Father. Whoever confesses the Son
has the Father also. 24 Let [m]what you heard
from the beginning abide in you. If what
you heard from the beginning abides in
you, then [n]you too will abide in the Son
and in the Father. 25 And this is the promise that he made to us[2]—[o]eternal life.

26 I write these things to you about [p]those
who are trying to deceive you. 27 But [q]the
anointing that you received from him
abides in you, and [r]you have no need that
anyone should teach you. But as his
anointing teaches you about everything—
and [s]is true and is no lie, just as it has
taught you—abide in him.

Children of God

28 And now, little children, abide in him,
so that [t]when he appears [u]we may have
confidence and not shrink from him in
shame at his [v]coming. 29 If you know that
[w]he is righteous, you may be sure that
[x]everyone who practices righteousness has
been born of him.

3 See [y]what kind of love the Father has
given to us, that we should be called
[z]children of God; and so we are. The reason why [a]the world does not know us is
that [b]it did not know him. 2 Beloved, we are
[z]God's children [c]now, and what we will be
[d]has not yet appeared; but we know that
[e]when he appears[3] [f]we shall be like him,
because [g]we shall see him as he is. 3 And
everyone who [h]thus hopes in him [i]purifies
himself as he is pure.

4 Everyone who makes a practice of sinning also practices lawlessness; [j]sin is lawlessness. 5 You know that [k]he appeared to
[l]take away sins, and [m]in him there is no
sin. 6 No one who abides in him keeps on
sinning; [n]no one who keeps on sinning has
either seen him or known him. 7 Little children, [o]let no one deceive you. [p]Whoever
practices righteousness is righteous, as he
is righteous. 8 [q]Whoever makes a practice of

19 [f]See John 17:12 [g]1 Cor. 11:19 **20** [h]ver. 27; [2 Cor. 1:21] [i]See Mark 1:24 [j]ver. 27; See John 14:26 **22** [k]ch. 4:3; 2 John 7 [b][See ver. 18 above] **23** [l]ch. 4:15; 5:1; 2 John 9 **24** [m]ch. 3:11; 2 John 6 [n][John 14:23]; See ch. 1:3 **25** [o]John 17:2 **26** [p]ch. 3:7; 2 John 7 **27** [q]ver. 20 [r]Jer. 31:34; Heb. 8:11 [s]John 14:17 **28** [t]ch. 3:2; [Col. 3:4] [u]ch. 3:21; 4:17; 5:14 [v]See 1 Thess. 2:19 **29** [w]ch. 3:7 [x]ch. 3:9; 4:7; 5:1, 4, 18; 3 John 11

Chapter 3
1 [y]ch. 4:10; John 3:16 [z]John 1:12 [a][ch. 4:17] [b]John 16:3; 17:25 **2** [z][See ver. 1 above] [c]Rom. 8:15; Gal. 3:26; Eph. 1:5 [d][Rom. 8:18; 2 Cor. 4:17] [e]ch. 2:28 [f]Rom. 8:29; 2 Cor. 3:18; 4:11; Phil. 3:21; 2 Pet. 1:4 [g]John 17:24; 1 Cor. 13:12; Rev. 22:4 **3** [h]Rom. 15:12 [i]2 Cor. 7:1 **4** [j][ch. 5:17; Rom. 4:15] **5** [k]Heb. 9:26; See ch. 1:2 [l][Isai. 53:11, 12] [m]See 1 Pet. 2:22 **6** [n]ch. 2:4; 4:8; 3 John 11 **7** [o]ch. 2:26 [p]ch. 2:29 **8** [q]Matt. 13:38; John 8:44

[1] Some manuscripts *you know everything* [2] Some manuscripts *you*
[3] Or *when it appears*

2:20 anointed by the Holy One. "Christ" means "Anointed," referring to the unique office of Jesus as God's Savior. God anointed Jesus directly with the Holy Spirit to be the consummate Prophet, Priest, and King (Acts 10:38; Heb. 1:1–9). Believers also have prophetic, priestly, and kingly responsibilities and are anointed with the Holy Spirit (2 Cor. 1:21, 22) for these duties (1 Cor. 12).

2:22 denies that Jesus is the Christ. To separate Christ the Savior from Jesus the man was a hallmark of docetism, the heresy that Christ only appeared to be a human being (Introduction: Date and Occasion).

2:25 eternal life. This is the supreme gift of God, mediated by Jesus Christ (John 5:24–27) and given freely to the redeemed through faith in Christ (5:11, 13; John 3:16).

2:27 you have no need that anyone should teach you. Believers have an illumination from God through the ministry of the Holy Spirit, who accompanies the Word and keeps us in the truth of the gospel. It is no contradiction that we should listen receptively to other believers, especially when they admonish and instruct us. They also have the Spirit, and the confusion generated by false teaching is a real danger (Matt. 24:24).

2:28 at his coming. John refers to the visible and final return of Christ at the end of the age. At that time Christ will come as the Judge, but those who "abide in" Him by continuing to trust in the gospel message (v. 24) need have no fear of condemnation (John 3:17, 18). See "The Return of Jesus Christ" at 1 Thess. 4:16.

2:29–3:3 As those taught by the Spirit, believers know an entire system of truth and life that remains hidden to those who are in the world. Essential to this is knowing that although for the time being it may not be outwardly recognized, we can still be sure that we are "children of God" and "born of him." The public revelation of this truth waits for the public revelation of God Himself "when he appears," at the Second Coming. True children of God will bear the family likeness, both now, as our hope lends our lives a focused purity resembling His, and at the end, when "we shall be like him." Only then will our knowledge of Him be complete, but even now our knowledge that "he is righteous" will bring increasing righteousness to our own lives.

3:3 thus hopes. The promise of His appearing fills believers, not with apprehension, but with confidence (1 Thess. 5:4).

3:4–10 The basic contrast between light and darkness, between the children of God and of the world, is now explained as a contrast between those who sin and those who do not. Jesus was sinless, and what is more He came to take away sin (v. 5; John 1:29). The New Birth sets a person irrevocably against sin, and because the seed of new life "abides" in that person (v. 9; cf. John 10:28, 29), the defeat of corruption and death for him is inevitable. In this sense sin will be impossible (Rom. 6:8, 9). John addresses this absolute aspect of being born again and speaks accordingly. He is not denying that sin and death have influence until the very end (1 Cor. 15:26; Rev. 20:14). He says clearly that in this life no one can be without sin (1:8).

3:4 lawlessness. Though the Old Testament is not quoted explicitly in 1 John, its authority is presupposed. In particular, the moral law, summed up in the law of love, is still the norm for God's people (Rom. 13:8–10). "Lawlessness" is disobedience to that law.

3:6 keeps on sinning; no one who keeps on sinning. The present tense of the Greek suggests behavior that is characteristic or usual. In this way John acknowledges, but does not excuse, the possibility of occasional sin. Another possibility is that John has in mind the specific sin of apostasy, mentioned in 2:19 (cf. also 5:16–18). If so, John means that true believers will not totally abandon their faith.

3:7 practices righteousness. See theological note "Antinomianism."

sinning is of the devil, for the devil has
been sinning from the beginning. The reason the Son of God appeared was [r]to
destroy the works of the devil. 9 [s]No one
born of God makes a practice of sinning,
for God's[1] seed abides in him, and he cannot keep on sinning because he has been
born of God. 10 By this it is evident who are
the children of God, and who are the children of the devil: whoever does not practice righteousness is not of God, [t]nor is the
one who [u]does not love his brother.

Love One Another

11 For [v]this is the message that you have
heard from the beginning, [w]that we should
love one another. 12 We should not be like
[x]Cain, who was of the evil one and murdered his brother. And why did he murder
him? [y]Because his own deeds were evil and
his brother's righteous. 13 Do not be surprised, brothers,[2] [z]that the world hates
you. 14 We know that [a]we have passed out
of death into life, because we love the
brothers. Whoever does not love abides in
death. 15 [b]Everyone who hates his brother is
a murderer, and you know that [c]no murderer has eternal life abiding in him.

8 [r]Heb. 2:14; [Gen. 3:15; Luke 10:18; John 16:11] **9** [s]ch. 5:18 **10** [t]ch. 4:8 [u]ch. 4:20, 21 **11** [v]ch. 1:5; 2:24 [w]See John 13:34 **12** [x]Gen. 4:4, 8; Heb. 11:4; Jude 11 [y]Ps. 38:20; Prov. 29:10 **13** [z]John 15:18; 17:14 **14** [a]John 5:24 **15** [b]Matt. 5:21, 22 [c]Gal. 5:21; Rev. 21:8

[1] Greek *his* [2] Or *brothers and sisters.* The plural Greek word *adelphoi* (translated "brothers") refers to siblings in a family. In New Testament usage, depending on the context, *adelphoi* may refer either to men or to both men and women who are siblings (brothers and sisters) in God's family, the church; also verses 14, 16

Antinomianism

Antinomianism means "opposed to law." Antinomian views are those denying that God's law in Scripture should directly control the Christian's life.

Dualistic antinomianism appeared early in the Gnostic heresies, like those opposed by Peter and Jude (2 Pet. 2; Jude 4–19). The Gnostics taught that salvation was for the soul only, making bodily behavior irrelevant both to God's interest and to the soul's health. The conclusion was that one may behave riotously and it will not matter.

A "spiritual" antinomianism puts such trust in the Holy Spirit's inward prompting as to deny any need to be taught by the law how to live. Freedom from the law as a way of salvation is assumed to bring with it freedom from the law as a guide to conduct. In the first 150 years of the Reformation era this kind of antinomianism was common. The Corinthian church may have been in the grip of this error, since Paul warns them that a truly spiritual person acknowledges the authority of God's Word (1 Cor. 14:37; cf. 7:40).

Another kind of antinomianism begins from the point that God does not see the sin in believers, because they are in Christ, who kept the law for them. From this they draw the false conclusion that their behavior makes no difference, provided they keep on believing. But 1 John 1:8–2:1 and 3:4–10 point in a different direction. It is not possible to be in Christ and at the same time to embrace sin as a way of life.

Some dispensationalists have held that since Christians live under a dispensation of grace, not law, keeping the moral law is at no stage necessary for them. Rom. 3:31 and 1 Cor. 6:9–11 clearly show, however, that keeping the law is a continuing obligation for Christians.

It is sometimes said that the motive and intention of "love" is the only law God requires of Christians. The commands of the Decalogue and other ethical parts of Scripture, although they are ascribed to God directly, are regarded as no more than guidelines that love may at any time disregard. But Rom. 13:8–10 teaches that specific commands reveal what true love is. The law of God exposes the counterfeit love that will not accept its responsibilities toward God and neighbor.

The moral law revealed in the Decalogue and expounded in other parts of the Bible is an expression of God's righteousness, given to be a code of practice for God's people in every age. The law is not opposed to the love and goodness of God, but shows what it is in action. The Spirit gives Christians the power to observe the law, making us more and more like Christ, the archetypal observer of the law (Matt. 5:17).

3:8 destroy the works of the devil. The opposition between Christ and Satan was foretold as early as Gen. 3:15. Satan used the righteous law of God as a tool to hold sinners captive to the fear of death and condemnation. By accepting in His own Person the penalty due to sinners under the law, Christ took away the foundation of Satan's plan (Heb. 2:14, 15).

3:11–15 The history of the world is the story of hatred, right back to the archetypal conflict between Cain and Abel. John traces Cain's hatred to the radical difference of his motivations from those of Abel (John 3:19; 8:37), a difference that will always exist between the world and the people of God (v. 13). When the fellowship of believers is free from animosity, as John expects it will be, we know that we "have passed out of death into life" (v. 14). But if such animosity invades the fellowship, it does so only by rejection of "the message that you have heard from the beginning" (v. 11).

3:11 love one another. The command of Christ, founded on His own gift of love (v. 16; John 13:34, 35).

3:12 Cain. Gen. 4:5 explains that Cain envied Abel because Abel's offering was accepted by God.

[16]By this we know love, that [d]he laid
down his life for us, and [e]we ought to lay
down our lives for the brothers. [17]But [f]if
anyone has the world's goods and sees his
brother in need, yet [g]closes his heart
against him, [h]how does God's love abide in
him? [18]Little children, let us not [i]love in
word or talk but in deed and [j]in truth.
[19]By this we shall know that we are of the
truth and reassure our heart before him;
[20]for whenever our heart condemns us,
God is greater than our heart, and he
knows everything. [21]Beloved, [k]if our heart
does not condemn us, [l]we have confidence
before God; [22]and [m]whatever we ask we
receive from him, because we keep his
commandments and [n]do what pleases him.
[23]And this is his commandment, [o]that we
believe in the name of his Son Jesus Christ
and [p]love one another, [q]just as he has commanded us. [24][r]Whoever keeps his commandments abides in him, and he in them.
And [s]by this we know that he abides in us,
by the Spirit whom he has given us.

Test the Spirits

4 Beloved, [t]do not believe every spirit,
but [u]test the spirits to see whether they
are from God, for [v]many [w]false prophets
[x]have gone out into the world. [2]By this you
know the Spirit of God: [y]every spirit that
confesses that [z]Jesus Christ has come in
the flesh is from God, [3]and every spirit
[a]that does not confess Jesus is not from
God. This is the spirit of the antichrist,
which you heard was coming and [b]now is
in the world already. [4]Little children, you
are from God and have overcome them, for
[c]he who is in you is greater than [d]he who is
in the world. [5][e]They are from the world;
therefore they speak from the world, and
[f]the world listens to them. [6]We are from
God. [g]Whoever knows God listens to us;
whoever is not from God does not listen to
us. By this we know [h]the Spirit of truth and
[i]the spirit of error.

God Is Love

[7]Beloved, [j]let us love one another, for
love is from God, and [k]whoever loves has
been born of God and knows God.
[8][l]Anyone who does not love does not know
God, because [m]God is love. [9]In this the
love of God was made manifest among us,
that [n]God sent his only Son into the world,
so that we might live through him. [10]In this
is love, [o]not that we have loved God [n]but
that he loved us and sent his Son to be [p]the
propitiation for our sins. [11]Beloved, if God

16 [d]See John 15:13 [e][Phil. 2:17]
17 [f]James 2:15, 16 [g]Deut. 15:7 [h][ch. 4:20]
18 [i]Ezek. 33:31; Eph. 4:15 [j]2 John 1; 3 John 1
21 [k][1 Cor. 4:4] [l]ch. 5:14; [Job 11:15; 22:26; Rom. 14:22]
22 [m]See Matt. 7:7 [n]John 8:29
23 [o]John 6:29; [Acts 18:8] [p]ver. 11 [q][ch. 2:8]
24 [r][John 6:56; 14:20; 15:4, 5; 17:21] [s]ch. 4:13 Rom. 8:9
Chapter 4
1 [t]Jer. 29:8 [u]1 Thess. 5:21; [1 Cor. 12:10; 14:29; Rev. 2:2] [v]See ch. 2:18 [w]2 Pet. 2:1 [x]2 John 7
2 [y][1 Cor. 12:3] [z]2 John 7
3 [a]ch. 2:22; 2 John 7 [b]ch. 2:18; [2 Thess. 2:3-7]
4 [c]See Rom. 8:31 [d][1 Cor. 2:12]; See John 12:31 5 [e]John 3:31; 8:23 [f]John 15:19
6 [g][John 8:47; 10:16; 18:37; 1 Cor. 14:37] [h]John 14:17; 15:26; 16:13 [i][1 Cor. 2:12; 1 Tim. 4:1] 7 [j]ch. 3:11 [k]ch. 2:29 8 [l]ch. 3:10 [m]ver. 16; 2 Cor. 13:11; [ch. 1:5; John 4:24] 9 [n]See John 3:16 10 [o]Rom. 5:8, 10 [n][See ver. 9 above] [p]See ch. 2:2

3:16–24 Mutual love in the fellowship is evidence of new life. It is based on the love of Jesus Christ, who "laid down his life" in our place. Measuring ourselves against such an example, our heart "condemns us" (v. 20), and our confidence can only be restored by someone greater than our hearts—God Himself. God, who "knows everything," has proved His love for sinners by the gift of His Son (4:10; Rom. 5:8). Confidence founded on this reality carries with it the assurance that our deeds are also accepted by God (v. 22), and when guilt is dealt with we are released to pray unhindered (v. 22). Confident prayer is a hallmark of the children of God (John 15:7; Rom. 8:15, 16).

3:16 laid down his life. Christ accepted the painful death of the Cross so that we might be saved from eternal punishment (John 10:11). Our love for one another may not require such a costly decision as this, but there must be some decision and action. John mentions material assistance as one example (v. 17; James 1:27).

3:20 God is greater than our heart. The Word of God which acquits us must prevail over the word of our hearts that condemns us.

3:22 whatever we ask. Jesus expressed such confidence in the Father (John 11:41, 42) and encouraged His disciples to have similar confidence (John 14:13, 14). This confidence depends on the awareness that our desires are attuned to God's (5:14, 15).

3:23 this is his commandment. The two parts of this commandment parallel the two parts of the Ten Commandments, reminding us that our relationship with God takes precedence over our relationship with our neighbor. Faith in Christ relates us rightly to God, and His renewing grace enables us to love one another.

4:1–6 God's gift of His one Holy Spirit stands in contrast to the many lying spirits that drive false prophets into the world to spread opposition to Christ (2:18). Like Paul in 1 Cor. 12:3, John shows how to distinguish the Spirit of Truth from spirits of error: those who confess Jesus as the Messiah are from God, while those who will not confess Jesus are not. This confession is the great divide between those "from God" and those who are "from the world."

4:1 gone out into the world. See note 2:19.

4:2 Jesus Christ has come in the flesh. John distinguishes the gospel from the error of the docetists who said that Jesus Christ was not truly human (Introduction: Date and Occasion). The humanity of Christ was essential if He was to die for our sins.

4:3 the antichrist. See note 2:18.

4:4 he who is in the world. In its hostility to God, the world is pervaded by the purposes of the devil, who has captured the human race through temptation (5:19).

4:6 from God. The Holy Spirit unites believers. See "The Local Church" at Rev. 2:1.

4:7–12 The love of God the Father for "his only Son" (v. 9) is the source of the love that binds the fellowship of believers together as a family. By giving us His Son, the Father introduced us to the perfect love and eternal life that the Father and the Son have always enjoyed.

4:9 only Son. This means that Jesus is God's Son in eternity, as the Second Person of the Trinity. The Greek can also be translated "one and only Son," referring to Christ's uniqueness rather than to His eternal generation.

4:10 propitiation for our sins. See note 2:2. Christ turned away the righteous anger of God and satisfied the demands of His justice on our behalf. It was to fulfill God's love that He did this.

so loved us, we also ought to love one
another. 12 [q]No one has ever seen God; if
we love one another, God abides in us and
[r]his love is perfected in us.
13 [s]By this we know that we abide in him
and he in us, because he has given us of his
Spirit. 14 And [t]we have seen and testify that
[u]the Father has sent his Son to be the
Savior of [v]the world. 15 [w]Whoever confesses
that Jesus is the Son of God, God abides in
him, and he in God. 16 So [x]we have come to
know and to believe the love that God has
for us. [y]God is love, and [z]whoever abides in
love abides in God, and God abides in him.
17 By this [a]is love perfected with us, so that
[b]we may have confidence for the day of
judgment, because [c]as he is so also are we
in this world. 18 There is no fear in love, but
[d]perfect love casts out fear. For fear has to
do with punishment, and whoever fears
has not [a]been perfected in love. 19 [e]We love
because he first loved us. 20 [f]If anyone says,
"I love God," and [g]hates his brother, he is
a liar; for he who does not love his brother
whom he has seen cannot[1] love God
[h]whom he has not seen. 21 And [i]this commandment we have from him: [j]whoever
loves God must also love his brother.

Overcoming the World

5 [k]Everyone who believes that [l]Jesus is
the Christ has been born of God, and
[m]everyone who loves the Father loves whoever has been born of him. 2 [n]By this we
know that we love the children of God,
when we love God and obey his commandments. 3 For [o]this is the love of God,
that we [p]keep his commandments. And
[q]his commandments are not burdensome.
4 For [r]everyone who has been born of God
overcomes the world. And this is the victory that has overcome the world—[s]our faith.
5 Who is it that overcomes the world except
the one who believes [t]that Jesus is the Son
of God?

Testimony Concerning the Son of God

6 This is he who came [u]by water and
blood—Jesus Christ; not by the water only
but by the water and the blood. And [v]the
Spirit is the one who testifies, because [w]the
Spirit is the truth. 7 For there are three that
testify: 8 the Spirit and the water and the
blood; and these three agree. 9 [x]If we
receive the testimony of men, the testimony of God is greater, for this is the testimony of God [y]that he has borne
concerning his Son. 10 Whoever believes in
the Son of God [z]has the testimony in himself. Whoever does not believe God [a]has
made him a liar, [b]because he has not
believed in the testimony that God has
borne concerning his Son. 11 And this is the
testimony, that God gave us [c]eternal life,
and [d]this life is in his Son. 12 [e]Whoever has
the Son has life; whoever does not have the
Son of God does not have life.

That You May Know

13 I write [f]these things to you who [g]be-
lieve in the name of the Son of God that
you may know that you have eternal life.
14 And this is [h]the confidence that we have
toward him, that [i]if we ask anything according to his will he hears us. 15 And if we

12 [q]ver. 20; John 1:18; 1 Tim. 6:16 [r]ch. 2:5 **13** [s]ch. 3:24 **14** [t]ch. 1:1, 2 [u]See John 3:17 [v]See ch. 2:2 **15** [w]ch. 5:5; [Rom. 10:9]; See Matt. 14:33 **16** [x]John 6:69 [y]See ver. 8 [z]ver. 12; ch. 3:24 **17** [a][ch. 2:5] [b]ch. 2:28; 3:21 [c][ch. 3:1] **18** [d][John 3:18; Rom. 8:15] [a][See ver. 17 above] **19** [e]ver. 10 **20** [f]ch. 2:4; 3:17 [g]ch. 2:9, 11 [h]ver. 12; [1 Pet. 1:8] **21** [i]Gal. 6:2 [j]ver. 7; ch. 3:11
Chapter 5
1 [k]John 1:12 [l]ch. 2:22 [m]John 8:42 **2** [n]ch. 2:5; 3:24; 4:13 **3** [o]2 John 6; See John 14:15 [p]See ch. 2:3 [q]Matt. 11:30
4 [r]ch. 3:9; 4:4; John 16:33 [s][1 Cor. 15:57; Eph. 6:16] **5** [t]ch. 4:15 **6** [u][ver. 8] [v]John 15:26; [Acts 5:32] [w]John 14:17; 15:26; 16:13 **9** [x]John 5:34, 36, 37; 8:17, 18 [y]See Matt. 3:17

10 [z][Rom. 8:16; Gal. 4:6; Rev. 12:17; 19:10] [a]ch. 1:10; [John 3:33] [b][John 5:38]
11 [c]ch. 2:25; [ch. 4:9] [d]See John 1:4 **12** [e][John 3:15, 36; 5:24; 6:40, 47]
13 [f]John 20:31 [g]John 1:12 **14** [h]ch. 2:28; 3:21; 4:17 [i]ch. 3:22; [Prov. 10:24]

1 Some manuscripts *how can he*

4:14 Savior of the world. See note 2:2.

4:16 God is love. God's love is shown in His covenant faithfulness and in His relentless pursuit of sinners in spite of their rebellion or indifference (v. 8; Ex. 34:5–7).

4:17 so also are we. Though not like Christ in the completeness of our obedience, we are like Him in our basic orientation, and stand out as He did by contrast with the world at large (John 17:16).

4:18 not been perfected in love. God's love is perfect in itself, and it brings to us the sure promise of perfection as soon as we receive it (vv. 12, 17; 2:5). But because we are being made perfect in His love over time (3:2), the remnants of fear may temporarily coexist with love. "Perfected love" from God "casts out fear" progressively rather than instantaneously.

5:4 overcomes the world. See note 2:13.

5:6 by water and blood. Some suggest that the water refers to the baptism of Jesus and the blood to the Crucifixion. This is unlikely, since John in his Gospel does not directly recount the baptism of Jesus. Others suggest that "water and blood" refers to the two sacraments, baptism and the Lord's Supper. This is also unlikely, since John does not recount the institution of the sacraments in his Gospel. The difficult saying of this verse probably reflects John 19:34. In John's Gospel, the testimony God bears to Jesus His Son is a key theme. The blood and water that flowed from Jesus after His death attested to the reality of His death; the wound in Jesus' side later confirmed the reality of His bodily resurrection (John 20:20, 25–27). Both the death and the resurrection were denied by the docetists, who denied the humanity of Christ (4:2).

5:7 three that testify. See "One and Three: The Trinity" at Is. 44:6.

5:9 the testimony of God is greater. By appealing directly to God as witness, John, like Jesus, overrules all human dispute (John 5:31–39).

5:11 eternal life . . . in his Son. This is the cardinal truth of the Christian message.

5:13 John's Gospel was written to move readers to faith in Jesus that they might receive eternal life (John 20:31). This letter was written to assure those who have believed that they actually possess the priceless gift.

know that he hears us in whatever we ask,
we know that we have the requests that we
have asked of him.
16 If anyone sees his brother committing a
sin not leading to death, he shall ask, and
[j]God[1] will give him life—to those who
commit sins that do not lead to death.
[k]There is sin that leads to death; [l]I do not
say that one should pray for that. 17 [m]All
wrongdoing is sin, but there is sin that
does not lead to death.
18 We know that [n]everyone who has been
born of God does not keep on sinning, but
[o]he who was born of God [p]protects him,
and the evil one does not touch him.
19 We know that we are from God, and
[q]the whole world lies in the power of the
evil one.
20 And we know that the Son of God has
come and [r]has given us understanding, so
that we may know [s]him who is true; and
we are in him who is true, in his Son Jesus
Christ. He is the true God and [t]eternal life.
21 Little children, [u]keep yourselves from idols.

16 [j][Job 42:8; James 5:15] [k]Matt. 12:31, 32; Mark 3:29; Luke 12:10; Heb. 6:4-6; 10:26 [l][Jer. 7:16; 14:11] **17** [m][ch. 3:4] **18** [n]ch. 3:9 [o]John 1:18 [p]John 17:12 **19** [q][Luke 4:6; Gal. 1:4] **20** [r][Luke 24:45] [s]See John 17:3; Rev. 3:7 [t]ver. 11-13 **21** [u]1 Cor. 10:7, 14

[1] Greek *he*

5:16 sin that leads to death. Some connect this sin with the unforgivable sin mentioned in Matt. 12:31, 32; Mark 3:28–30; Luke 12:8–10. More likely, John is referring to a stubborn refusal to accept the message of the gospel (1:10 note; John 8:24). See "The Unpardonable Sin" at Mark 3:29.

5:18 does not keep on sinning. See note 3:6.

5:19 the power of the evil one. No one can escape the devil's net of temptation, sin, and condemnation without divine help. But neither can people escape their responsibility by trying to blame another agent, even the devil, for their own condition (Gen. 3:12, 13). Paradoxically, enslavement to sin is voluntary (James 1:13–15). Only the Son of God can break this bondage and replace it with a life of forgiveness, gratitude, and obedience (3:8).

5:20 him who is true. Being in God who is true and being in His Son Jesus Christ go together inseparably. The grammar of this verse is difficult, but it is most reasonable to understand that "the true God and eternal life" is Jesus Christ. If the phrase refers back to the Father the verse becomes needlessly repetitive. Moreover, the phrase "eternal life" is applied to Christ in 1:2 as well.

THE SECOND EPISTLE OF

John

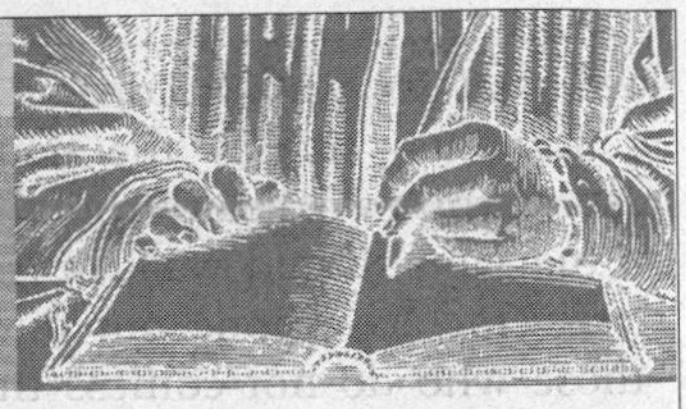

AUTHOR

The style, diction, and content of 2 John mark it as written by the same author as 1 John and the Gospel of John. This author has been traditionally identified as the apostle John, son of Zebedee, and no more plausible ascription has been proposed.

DATE AND OCCASION

Second John was written to warn against the same strain of false teaching that 1 John opposes, namely "docetism" (see "Introduction to 1 John: Date and Occasion"). It must have been written at about the same time, in the last two decades of the first century. While it repeats ideas from 1 John, it does not presuppose knowledge of 1 John on the part of the reader.

CHARACTERISTICS AND THEMES

Second John is a letter, with salutation, introductory greeting, and final greeting. It is written to a Christian lady and her family, either her natural family or the fellowship of believers associated with her. Like the early letters of Paul, it is a letter of encouragement and warning written to a specific fellowship for which the author has pastoral responsibility.

OUTLINE OF 2 JOHN

I. Salutation and Greeting (vv. 1–3)

II. Love and Obedience (vv. 4–6)

III. The Danger of False Teaching (vv. 7–11)

IV. Conclusion and Farewell (vv. 12, 13)

Greeting

1 [a]The elder to the elect lady and her children, [b]whom I love in truth, and not only
I, but also all who [c]know [d]the truth, 2 [e]be-
cause of the truth that abides in us and will
be with us forever:

3 [f]Grace, mercy, and peace will be with
us, from God the Father and from Jesus
Christ the Father's Son, in truth and love.

Walking in Truth and Love

4 [g]I rejoiced greatly to find some of your
children walking in the truth, just as we
were commanded by the Father. 5 And now
I ask you, dear lady—[h]not as though I were
writing you a new commandment, but the
one we have had from the beginning—
[i]that we love one another. 6 And [j]this is

1 [a]3 John 1; [1 Pet. 5:1] [b]1 John 3:18; 3 John 1 [c]John 8:32; [1 Tim. 2:4; Heb. 10:26] [d]John 1:17; 14:6; See Gal. 2:5
2 [e][1 Cor. 13:6]
3 [f]1 Tim. 1:2; 2 Tim. 1:2; [Jude 2]
4 [g]3 John 3, 4
5 [h]1 John 2:7 [i]See 1 John 3:11 6 [j]1 John 5:3; [1 John 2:5]; See John 14:15

1–3 The author identifies himself only as "The elder" and the addressee only as "the elect lady." These terms are appropriate for a relationship of mutual love and respect in which the author has had pastoral responsibility for the addressee. John's concern for her depends on the truth all Christians share and is an example of the love that binds all Christians together.

1 The elder. There is no real difficulty with an apostle identifying himself as an elder, since the responsibilities of an apostle toward each individual congregation were the same as the responsibilities of an elder (1 Pet. 5:1–4).

the elect lady. Some consider this expression and the similar expression in v. 13 as a metaphor for a church, but such usage is otherwise unknown.

3 Grace, mercy, and peace. Like the apostle Paul, John begins his greeting with mention of the rich Christian blessings of grace and peace (Gal. 1:3 note), but adds "mercy." The source of this blessed "grace, mercy, and peace" is none other than God Himself, who is truth (John 14:6; 1 John 5:6) and love (1 John 4:8).

4–6 The elder and the lady share the joy of seeing members of her household continue to be faithful to the truth. The mark of Christian faithfulness is love for one another, the central command given to Christians by Jesus Himself (John 13:34). That love is defined by all the commands Christ gave His followers.

5 not . . . a new commandment. See note 1 John 2:7–11.

love, that we walk according to his commandments; this is the commandment,
just [k]as you have heard from the beginning,
so that you should walk in it. 7 For [l]many
deceivers [m]have gone out into the world,
[n]those who do not confess the coming of
Jesus Christ in the flesh. Such a one is the
deceiver and the antichrist. 8 Watch yourselves, [o]so that you may not lose what we[1]
have worked for, but [p]may win a full
reward. 9 Everyone who goes on ahead and
does not abide in the teaching of Christ,
[q]does not have God. Whoever abides in the
teaching [q]has both the Father and the Son.
10 If anyone comes to you and does not
bring this teaching, [r]do not receive him
into your house or give him any greeting,
11 for whoever greets him [s]takes part in his
wicked works.

Final Greetings

12 [t]Though I have much to write to you, I
would rather not use paper and ink.
[u]Instead I hope to come to you and talk face
to face, [v]so that our joy may be complete.
13 The children of your elect sister greet
you.

6 [k]1 John 2:24
7 [l]See 1 John 2:18, 26
[m]1 John 4:1
[n]1 John 2:22; 4:2, 3
8 [o][Gal. 3:4; Heb. 10:35]
[p]See 1 Cor. 3:8
9 [q]See 1 John 2:23
10 [r][Rom. 16:17; Gal. 1:8, 9; 2 Thess. 3:6, 14; Tit. 3:10]
11 [s][1 Tim. 5:22]
12 [t]3 John 13
[u]3 John 14
[v]John 15:11; 17:13

1 Some manuscripts *you*

The Humanity of Jesus

Jesus was a man who convinced those closest to Him that He was also God; His humanness is not in doubt. John's condemnation of those who denied that "Jesus Christ has come in the flesh" (1 John 4:2, 3; 2 John 7) was aimed at teachers who replaced the Incarnation with the idea that Jesus was a supernatural being (not God) who seemed human but was really only so in appearance, a messenger who could not die for sins.

The Gospels show Jesus experiencing human limitations (hunger, Matt. 4:2; fatigue, John 4:6; ignorance of fact, Luke 8:45–47) and sorrow (John 11:35, 38). Hebrews stresses that if Christ had not shared all these facets of human experience—weakness, temptation, pain—He would not be qualified to help us as we face such trials (Heb. 2:17, 18; 4:15, 16; 5:2, 7–9). As it is, His full human experience guarantees that in every moment of our relationship with God we may go to Him, confident that He has been there before us, and is the helper we need.

Christians, focusing on Jesus' deity, have sometimes thought that it honors Jesus to minimize His humanness. For example, it is sometimes suggested that Jesus was always consciously omniscient, and only pretended to be ignorant of facts. Or it might be thought that He only pretended to be hungry and weary, because as a kind of superman He was above the needs of daily existence. But the Incarnation means that the Son of God has only one Person, existing in two natures, and there is nothing lacking from His human nature, sin only excepted. The idea that Jesus' two natures were like alternating electrical circuits, so that sometimes He acted in His humanity and sometimes in His divinity, is also mistaken.

Jesus could not sin, but he was able to be tempted. Satan tempted Him to disobey the Father through self-gratification, self-display, and self-aggrandizement (Matt. 4:1–11), and the temptation to retreat from the Cross was constant (Luke 22:28; cf. Matt. 16:23; and Jesus' prayer in Gethsemane). Being human, Jesus could not conquer temptation without a struggle, but being divine it was His nature to do His Father's will (John 5:19, 30), and therefore to resist and fight temptation until He had overcome it. Since His human nature was conformed to His divine nature, it was impossible that He should fail in the course of His resistance. It was inevitable that He would endure temptations to the end, feeling their entire force, and emerge victorious for His people. From Gethsemane we know how acute and agonizing His struggles were. The happy result for us is that because "he himself has suffered when tempted, he is able to help those who are being tempted" (Heb. 2:18).

7–11 False teachers had been troubling some of the Christian communities by attacking the central truth of the gospel—that Jesus is the Anointed One, the eternal Son of God who took on human nature to accomplish salvation (1 John 2:22; 4:2, 3). To reject this truth is to reject all hope of reconciliation with God, while to receive it is to receive God Himself. John warns the lady and her household that the work of false teachers threatens their spiritual progress and even their hope of eternal reward. In the face of such dangers, the only safe course is to avoid all involvement with the false teachers.

7 gone out. See note 1 John 2:19.

do not confess the coming of Jesus Christ in the flesh. The deceivers were docetists, who denied the reality of the human nature of Christ (1 John 4:2 note). See theological note "The Humanity of Jesus."

the antichrist. See note 1 John 2:18.

10 do not receive him into your house or give him any greeting. This stern measure contrasts sharply with the exhortation given in 3 John 5–8 to welcome believers who proclaim the truth.

12, 13 A letter is no substitute for personal fellowship. John hopes to share with his readers the mutual encouragement that can only take place in person. He closes by bringing greetings from one Christian community to another, a common practice in apostolic letters and a reminder of Christian unity.

THE THIRD EPISTLE OF

John

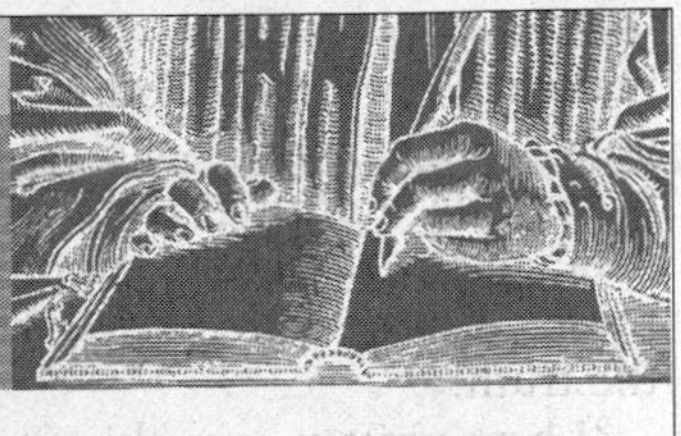

AUTHOR

The third letter of John is by the author of 2 John, as indicated by key similarities of style and structure. Like the Gospel of John and 1 and 2 John, the traditional ascription to the apostle John cannot be disproved and is more likely than any alternative.

DATE AND OCCASION

While 1 and 2 John celebrate truths that unite all Christians, 3 John laments the petty rivalry that sets Christians against one another. In particular, the letter was occasioned by a sharp conflict between Diotrephes (apparently an elder in a congregation under John's care) and others in the congregation over hospitality shown to traveling missionaries. It is likely that Demetrius, who is commended to Gaius by the letter, was himself such a traveling missionary in need of temporary lodging.

There is no trace in 3 John of the Christological conflict that looms large in 1 and 2 John, and it may be that 3 John was written earlier than either 1 or 2 John, possibly in the eighties of the first century.

CHARACTERISTICS AND THEMES

Third John is marked by its salutation, introductory greeting, and final greeting as a letter. More specifically, it is a letter of commendation introducing Demetrius to the recipient, Gaius.

OUTLINE OF 3 JOHN

I. Salutation and Greeting (vv. 1, 2)

II. Faithfulness to the Truth (vv. 3, 4)

III. The Importance of Hospitality (vv. 5–11)

- A. *Positive Encouragement (vv. 5–8)*
- B. *Negative Example (vv. 9, 10)*
- C. *Summary: Good Versus Evil (v. 11)*

IV. Commendation of Demetrius (v. 12)

V. Conclusion and Farewell (vv. 13, 14)

Greeting

1 [a]The elder to the beloved Gaius, [b]whom
I love in truth.
2 Beloved, I pray that all may go well with
you and that you may be in good health, as
it goes well with your soul. **3** For [c]I rejoiced
greatly when the brothers[1] came and testified to your truth, as indeed you are walking in the truth. **4** I have no greater joy than
to hear that [d]my children are walking in the
truth.

1[a]2 John 1 [b]1 John 3:18; 2 John 1
3[c]2 John 4
4[d][1 Cor. 4:14, 15; Gal. 4:19; 1 Tim. 1:2; 2 Tim. 1:2; Tit. 1:4; Philem. 10]
5[e][Gal. 6:10; Heb. 13:1] [f]See Matt. 25:35

Support and Opposition

5 Beloved, it is a faithful thing you do
in all your efforts for [e]these brothers,
[f]strangers as they are, **6** who testified to
your love before the church. You will do
well to send them on their journey in a

[1] Or *brothers and sisters*. The plural Greek word *adelphoi* (translated "brothers") refers to siblings in a family. In New Testament usage, depending on the context, *adelphoi* may refer either to men or to both men and women who are siblings (brothers and sisters) in God's family, the church; also verses 5, 10

1, 2 The author identifies himself as "The elder," as in 2 John. He writes to his beloved friend Gaius to commend him for his hospitality and to discuss with him the situation in the congregation of which Gaius is a part. John begins with a prayer for well-being, a common way of opening a personal letter.

3, 4 See the similar expression of joy in 2 John 4.

5–8 John commends Gaius for receiving traveling Christian teachers with hospitality. The obligation to welcome and encourage those who proclaim the true gospel from place to place, and the joy that comes from this, stand in contrast to the need to avoid those who proclaim a false gospel (1 John 4:1–3; 2 John 10, 11). Those who proclaim the message and those who encourage and support them work together in serving the truth.

manner [g]worthy of God. [7]For they have
gone out for the sake of [h]the name,
[i]accepting nothing from the Gentiles.
[8]Therefore we ought to support people like
these, that we may be fellow workers for
the truth.

[9]I have written something to the church,
but Diotrephes, who likes to put himself
first, does not acknowledge our authority.
[10]So if I come, I will bring up what he is
doing, talking wicked nonsense against us.
And not content with that, he refuses to
welcome the brothers, and also stops those
who want to and puts them out of the
church.

[11]Beloved, [j]do not imitate evil but imitate
good. [k]Whoever does good is from God;
[l]whoever does evil has not seen God. [12]De-
metrius [m]has received a good testimony
from everyone, and from the truth itself.
We also add our testimony, and [n]you know
that our testimony is true.

Final Greetings

[13] [o]I had much to write to you, but I
would rather not write with pen and ink.
[14]I hope to see you soon, and we will talk
face to face.

[15]Peace be to you. The friends greet you.
Greet the friends, [p]every one of them.

6 [g]1 Thess. 2:12; [Col. 1:10]
7 [h]See Acts 5:41 [i]1 Cor. 9:12, 15
11 [j][Ps. 34:14; 37:27; Isai. 1:16, 17] [k]1 John 2:29 [l]See 1 John 3:6
12 [m][1 Tim. 3:7] [n]John 21:24
13 [o]2 John 12
15 [p]John 10:3

7 Gentiles. Those who are not God's people. Such usage indicates that the Christian community (made up of ethnic Jews and Gentiles) had come to see itself as the new Israel.

9, 10 The cooperation and love that should be normal among Christians had been broken by the behavior of Diotrephes, who abused his position of leadership in the congregation by attacking other Christian workers. Evidently Diotrephes regarded other Christian teachers as threats rather than as coworkers. Proud and selfish, he turned away traveling evangelists and punished with excommunication those who welcomed them.

9 I have written something to the church. A previous letter that has not survived.

10 if I come, I will bring up what he is doing. The author's understated response to Diotrephes's severe provocation indicates his pastoral sensitivity, but also leaves no doubt that his visit will put a decisive stop to Diotrephes's behavior. The apostle's personal presence was an extension of the authoritative presence of Christ, both for encouragement and for warning (2 Cor. 13:1–3, 10).

11 Tyranny like that of Diotrephes reflects the opposite of the love of God; the temptation to respond in kind must be resisted.

12 The body of the letter closes with a commendation of Demetrius, the bearer of the letter, as a faithful Christian. Such commendation by name, like the naming of the addressee of the letter, was necessary to ensure that the letter was neither suppressed nor misused by those who, like Diotrephes, would disrupt the unity of the congregation (v. 9). Demetrius may have been a traveling teacher himself; if so, John's letter would encourage Gaius to show hospitality.

13, 14 The letter concludes in a way similar to 2 John 12, 13, with some difference of wording but the same personal touch.

THE EPISTLE OF

Jude

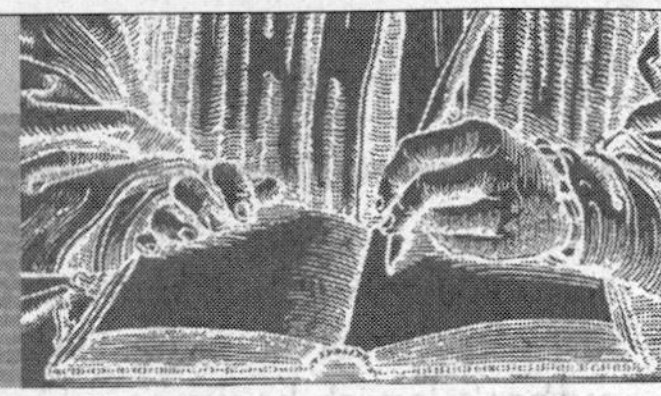

AUTHOR

The author of this epistle identifies himself as "Jude, a servant of Jesus Christ and brother of James" (v. 1). The name "Judah" (Greek *Judas*; English "Jude") was common among first-century Jews, and at least eight different persons of that name are mentioned in the New Testament, including two of Jesus' disciples (Luke 6:16). The author cannot, therefore, be identified on the basis of name alone.

The best clue to his identity is the description "brother of James" (v. 1). The only James known well enough in the early church to be referred to in this unqualified way is James, the prominent church leader (Acts 12:17; 15:13), author of the epistle that bears his name, and half brother of Jesus (Matt. 13:55; Mark 6:3; Gal. 1:19). If this identification of James is correct, the author of the present epistle is Jude, the half brother of Jesus (Matt. 13:55; Mark 6:3), who along with his other brothers did not believe in Jesus until after the Resurrection (Mark 3:21, 31; John 7:5; Acts 1:14).

Jude might be one of those referred to at another point in the New Testament, in Paul's reference to the itinerant ministry of the Lord's brothers and their wives (1 Cor. 9:5). Probably it is Jude's humility that explains why he does not mention that he was related to Jesus (note the similar reserve in James 1:1).

Several objections to the authenticity of Jude have been raised, but all rest on questionable assumptions or exegesis. Most are linked with proposing a date too late for Jude's lifetime ("Date and Occasion" below). Some argue that the quality of the Greek used in this epistle is better than one could expect of a Galilean, but Galilee was bilingual (Greek and Aramaic) in the first century, and too little is known about Jude's Greek to conclude that he could not have written this letter. We can accept that the author is Jude, the brother of Jesus.

Despite its brevity, the epistle was widely used in the early church because of its obvious orthodoxy and value. Questions about its canonical status arose largely because of its use of apocryphal literature (vv. 9, 14, 15 and notes; "Interpretive Difficulties" below). In addition to possible allusions in the so-called "Apostolic Fathers" (e.g., Clement of Rome; the Shepherd of Hermas; the Epistle of Barnabas; all prior to 150), Jude is listed in the Muratorian Canon (c. 200) and was accepted as authentic by Clement of Alexandria (c. 150–c. 215), Tertullian (c. 160–c. 225), Origen (c. 185–c. 253), and Athanasius (c. 296–373).

DATE AND OCCASION

Practically the only evidence for the date of Jude is what can be inferred about the time of its author and of the heresy he combats. If Jude was younger than Jesus and James, as his position in the lists of brothers in Matt. 13:55 and Mark 6:3 suggests, he could have survived well into the last quarter of the first century. Assuming that Peter wrote 2 Peter, and with most scholars that 2 Peter uses Jude (Introduction to 2 Peter: Interpretive Difficulties), Jude would have been written before A.D. 65–67, the likely date for 2 Peter.

Some argue for a second-century date on the grounds that Jude is combatting Gnosticism. While the teachings Jude opposes may have been precursors of Gnosticism, they cannot be identified with the fully-developed Gnostic heresies of the second century (Introduction to 2 Peter: Characteristics and Themes).

There is no indication in the letter of its place of writing or its destination. While some believe Jude's use of the Old Testament and Jewish apocryphal literature points to a Jewish Christian audience, this material reveals more about his own background than that of his readers. Perhaps Jude wrote the letter as a circular letter to a number of churches whose conditions he knows from having conducted an itinerant ministry among them (cf. 1 Cor. 9:5).

CHARACTERISTICS AND THEMES

1. The Jewish Christian Character of the Epistle. This letter strongly reflects the milieu of first-century Jewish Christianity, as one would expect from an author like Jude. Evidence for the author's Jewish background includes his many allusions to the Old Testament (though he does not quote directly), his familiarity with Jewish apocryphal tradition, and his strong ethical concern.

2. Denunciation of False Teachers. Jude confronts a threat similar to that opposed in 2 Peter—false teachers who were using Christian liberty and the free grace of God as a license for immorality (v. 4; cf. 2 Pet. 2:1–3). Most of the epistle (vv. 4–19) is devoted to stern denunciation of the false teachers in order to impress the readers with the seriousness of the threat. But Jude's strategy is more than mere negative opposition. He urges his readers to grow in their knowledge of Christian truth (v. 20), to bear a firm witness for the truth (v. 3), and to seek to reclaim those whose faith was wavering (vv. 22, 23). This prescription for confronting spiritual error is as effective today as when it was first written.

INTERPRETIVE DIFFICULTIES

1. The Relationship of Jude to 2 Peter. See "Introduction to 2 Peter: Interpretive Difficulties."

2. The Use of Nonbiblical and Apocryphal Materials. As noted above, Jude's use of apocryphal Jewish materials was the chief obstacle to the epistle's acceptance in the New Testament canon.

Allusion to or citation of extrabiblical materials is rare in the New Testament. But given the currency of apocryphal religious works during the period, and the desire of the New Testament writers to communicate the gospel in terms familiar to their readers, it is not surprising to find some occasional use. Examples include 2 Tim. 3:8, which uses Jewish traditions about Ex. 7:11; and the quotation of pagan poets in Acts 17:28; 1 Cor. 15:33; and Titus 1:12.

The inclusion of such quotations in the inspired canon, for illustrative purposes or as an appeal to conventional wisdom, does not imply that the apocryphal and nonbiblical documents were themselves inspired, nor that everything in them is being endorsed by the Bible. It is the use of the particular reference that is inspired, not the source of that reference.

OUTLINE OF JUDE

I. Salutation (vv. 1, 2)

II. Purpose of the Letter (vv. 3, 4)

III. Denunciation of False Teachers (vv. 5–19)

- A. *Three Examples of Divine Judgment on the Ungodly (vv. 5–7)*
- B. *Arrogance of the False Teachers (vv. 8–10)*
- C. *Three Examples of Those Who Led Others into Sin (v. 11)*
- D. *Depravity and Danger of the False Teachers (vv. 12, 13)*
- E. *Enoch's Prophecy of Judgment (vv. 14, 15)*
- F. *Proud Words of the False Teachers (v. 16)*
- G. *Apostolic Prophecies of Mockers (vv. 17–19)*

IV. Positive Exhortations (vv. 20–23)

V. Concluding Doxology (vv. 24, 25)

Greeting

1 Jude, a servant[1] of Jesus Christ and
brother of James,
[a]To those who are called, [b]beloved in
God the Father and [c]kept for[2] Jesus Christ:
2 May [d]mercy, [e]peace, and love be multiplied to you.

Judgment on False Teachers

3 Beloved, although I was very eager to
write to you about our [f]common salvation,
I found it necessary to write appealing to
you [g]to contend for the faith that was once
for all delivered to the saints. 4 For [h]certain
people [i]have crept in unnoticed [j]who long
ago were designated for this condemnation, ungodly people, who pervert [k]the
grace of our God into sensuality and [l]deny
our only Master and Lord, Jesus Christ.
5 Now I want [m]to remind you, although
you once fully knew it, that [n]Jesus, who
saved[3] a people out of the land of Egypt,
[o]afterward destroyed those who did not
believe. 6 And [p]the angels who did not stay
within their own position of authority, but
left their proper dwelling, he has kept in
eternal chains under gloomy darkness until
the judgment of the great day—7 just as
[q]Sodom and Gomorrah and [r]the surrounding cities, which likewise indulged in sexual immorality and [s]pursued unnatural
desire,[4] serve as an example by undergoing
a punishment of eternal fire.
8 Yet in like manner these people also,
relying on their dreams, defile the flesh,
reject authority, and [t]blaspheme the glorious ones. 9 But when [u]the archangel [v]Mi-
chael, contending with the devil, was

1 [a]Rom. 1:7; 1 Cor. 1:24 [b]1 Thess. 1:4; 2 Thess. 2:13 [c]John 17:11, 15; 1 Thess. 5:23 **2** [d][2 John 3] [e]1 Pet. 1:2; 2 Pet. 1:2 **3** [f]Tit. 1:4 [g]1 Tim. 6:12; 2 Tim. 4:7; [Luke 13:24; 1 Cor. 9:25; Phil. 1:27] **4** [h]2 Pet. 2:1 [i][Gal. 2:4] [j]1 Pet. 2:8 [k]See Acts 11:23 [l]Tit. 1:16; 2 Pet. 2:1; 1 John 2:22 **5** [m]2 Pet. 1:12; 3:17 [n][1 Cor. 10:4, 5, 9] [o]Num. 14:29, 37; 26:64, 65; Ps. 106: 26; Heb. 3:17-19

6 [p]2 Pet. 2:4; [Rev. 20:2] **7** [q]See Gen. 19:24 [r]Deut. 29:23; Hos. 11:8 [s]2 Pet. 2:10
8 [t]2 Pet. 2:10 **9** [u]Dan. 10:13; 12:1; Rev. 12:7 [v]1 Thess. 4:16; [2 Pet. 2:11]

1 Or *slave*; Greek *bondservant* 2 Or *by* 3 Some manuscripts *although you fully knew it, that the Lord who once saved* 4 Greek *other flesh*

1 Jude . . . brother of James. See Introduction: Author.

called. The expression of God's sovereign and gracious initiative in effectually summoning to salvation those whom He has chosen.

beloved. That is, God has "set apart" for His special care and use those whom He has called.

kept for Jesus Christ. See text note. The elect will persevere in faith because God preserves them (v. 24; John 10:27–30; 1 Pet. 1:5).

2 mercy, peace, and love. Jude fills a traditional Jewish greeting ("mercy and peace") with profound Christian meaning by adding "love." God's mercy to undeserving sinners and the peace that results are grounded in His love manifested in Jesus Christ (John 3:16).

3 I found it necessary. Instead of the doctrinal treatise he had intended to write, Jude feels compelled to address the problem of false teachers (v. 4). We do not know whether his original intention was fulfilled at some other time.

contend for the faith. Here "faith" indicates the content of the message taught by the apostles and held in common by all Christians, rather than the personal exercise of trust by a believer. Christianity includes an authoritative body of belief given by God to the church through the apostles (1 Cor. 15:3–8). Together with the Old Testament (Eph. 2:20), this apostolic witness, as found in the New Testament, is the standard for the church (2 John 9, 10).

4 certain people . . . crept in unnoticed. The troublemakers apparently have come from outside the particular church Jude addresses, perhaps posing as itinerant prophets or teachers (2 John 10, 11).

designated for this condemnation. This difficult phrase probably refers to various prophecies about the coming and condemnation of ungodly men like the false teachers, perhaps including the prophecy of Enoch in vv. 14, 15 and the apostolic prophecies in vv. 17, 18. Or less likely, it may refer to the fate of the wicked being written in heavenly books (Jer. 22:30; Rev. 17:8).

pervert the grace of our God into sensuality. Jude's opponents were guilty of antinomianism—the belief that Christians are under no obligation to follow the moral law as a rule of life. Such teaching was a persistent problem in the early church (Rom. 3:8; 6:15; 1 Cor. 6:12–15; Gal. 5:13), especially where Paul's emphasis upon justification by grace through faith was misunderstood and perverted.

deny . . . Master . . . Lord, Jesus Christ. By their godless and immoral behavior the false teachers deny Christ. The designation of Christ as "Lord" recognizes Christ's deity.

5 destroyed those who did not believe. God judged Israel with forty years of wandering in the wilderness for unbelief when they refused to enter Canaan following the report of the spies (Num. 14:27–34; Heb. 3:16–19). Just as judgment fell on the apostate Israelites after their deliverance from Egypt, so also it will fall on apostate church members (Heb. 4:1, 2).

6 angels. See note 2 Pet. 2:4.

not stay within their own position . . . left their proper dwelling. The angels in question rebelled against their God-given responsibilities and abandoned their areas of ministry or residence. Some take this to mean they left heaven and came to the earth.

the great day. The day of judgment at the Second Coming of Christ.

7 likewise. Sodom, Gomorrah, and the other cities resemble the angels of v. 6 in the immorality and perversity of their sexual transgression. The comparison could also point to the flagrancy and pride with which they deserted their proper place.

sexual immorality and . . . unnatural desire. The "unnatural desire" in view is the homosexuality described in Gen. 19:4, 5.

an example . . . punishment of eternal fire. The fiery destruction of Sodom and Gomorrah and the surrounding towns in Gen. 19 serves throughout Scripture as a model of God's judgment on sin (Deut. 29:23; Is. 1:9; Jer. 49:17, 18; Rom. 9:29).

8 dreams. Probably a reference to the false teachers' claims to divine revelation through visionary experiences, claims they might use to justify the three actions that follow.

defile the flesh. Sexual immorality (v. 4 and note), perhaps even homosexuality (v. 7; Rom. 1:26, 27).

reject authority. Though some take this to be human or angelic authority, a reference to the lordship and authority of Jesus Christ is more likely (v. 4).

blaspheme the glorious ones. See note 2 Pet. 2:10.

9 the archangel Michael. According to Dan. 10:13, 21; 12:1, Michael is one of the chief angels and the special guardian of Israel. In Rev. 12:7, Michael leads the angelic host in war against the devil and his angels. See "Angels" at Zech. 1:9.

9 Evidence indicates that this incident is based on *The Assumption of Moses*, an apocryphal Jewish work (of which only fragments have survived), which expands on the narrative of the burial of Moses in Deut. 34:5, 6 (Introduction: Interpretive Difficulties). The story concerns a confrontation between the archangel Michael and the devil over possession

disputing [w]about the body of Moses, he did
not presume to pronounce a blasphemous
judgment, but said, [x]"The Lord rebuke
you." 10 But these people blaspheme all that
they do not understand, and they are
destroyed by all that they, like unreasoning
animals, understand instinctively. 11 Woe
to them! For they walked in [z]the way of
Cain and abandoned themselves for the
sake of gain [a]to Balaam's error and [b]per-
ished in Korah's rebellion. 12 These are
blemishes[1] [c]on your love feasts, as they
feast with you without fear, [d]looking after
themselves; [e]waterless clouds, [f]swept along
by winds; fruitless trees in late autumn,
twice dead, [g]uprooted; 13 [h]wild waves of the
sea, casting up the foam of [i]their own
shame; [j]wandering stars, [k]for whom the
gloom of utter darkness has been reserved
forever.

14 It was also about these that Enoch, [l]the
seventh from Adam, prophesied, saying,
[m]"Behold, the Lord came with ten thousands of his holy ones, 15 [n]to execute judgment on all and to convict all the ungodly
of all their deeds of ungodliness that they
have [o]committed in such an ungodly way,
and of all [p]the harsh things that ungodly
sinners have spoken against him." 16 These
are grumblers, malcontents, [q]following
their own sinful desires; [r]they are loud-
mouthed boasters, [s]showing favoritism to
gain advantage.

A Call to Persevere

17 But you must [t]remember, beloved, the
predictions of the apostles of our Lord
Jesus Christ. 18 They[2] said to you, [u]"In the
last time there will be scoffers, following
their own ungodly passions." 19 It is these
who cause divisions, worldly people, [v]de-
void of the Spirit. 20 But you, beloved,

9 [w][Deut. 34:6] [x]Zech. 3:2
10 [y]2 Pet. 2:12
11 [z]See Gen. 4:5-8 [a]See 2 Pet. 2:15 [b]Num. 16:1-3, 31-35
12 [c]2 Pet. 2:13 [d]Ezek. 34:2, 8, 10 [e]Prov. 25:14; 2 Pet. 2:17 [f]Heb. 13:9 [g]Matt. 15:13
13 [h]Isai. 57:20 [i][2 Cor. 4:2; Phil. 3:19] [j][Isai. 14:12] [k]2 Pet. 2:17
14 [l]Gen. 5:18 [m]See Deut. 33:2; [Dan. 7:10; Mark 8:38; 1 Thess. 3:13; 2 Thess. 1:7]
15 [n][2 Pet. 2:5] [o]2 Pet. 2:6 [p]1 Sam. 2:3; Ps. 94:4; John 6:60
16 [q]2 Pet. 2:10 [r]2 Pet. 2:18 [s]Lev. 19:15; Deut. 10:17 17 [t]2 Pet. 3:2
18 [u]2 Pet. 3:3 19 [v][Rom. 8:9; Phil. 3:3]

1 Or *reefs* 2 Or *Christ, because they*

of the body of Moses. As usually interpreted, Jude's point is that the rash talk of the false teachers contrasts with the temperate speech of Michael (2 Pet. 2:10 and note). Others interpret Jude as contrasting Michael's appeal to God's authority with the false teachers' claim to having their own spiritual authority.

11 way of Cain. See Gen. 4:1–15; Heb. 11:4; 1 John 3:12. According to Jewish tradition, to which Jude may be referring, Cain was the archetypal sinner and the instructor of others in sin.

Balaam's error. See note 2 Pet. 2:15.

Korah's rebellion. Korah, along with Dathan and Abiram, led 250 men in rebellion against the authority of Moses and Aaron (Num. 16). Korah's rebellion and the resulting divine judgment provide an apt parallel to the defiance of the false teachers against church authority and the false teachers' dangerous ability to lead others astray, as well as a graphic illustration of the divine judgment awaiting the false teachers (Num. 16:31–33).

12 blemishes. The Greek word translated "blemishes" usually means "rocks" or "hidden reefs," which are a danger to ships. If Jude is making a play on words, it is to the effect that teachers are "dangerous, rocky blemishes" in what should be calm waters.

love feasts. See note 2 Pet. 2:13; cf. 1 Cor. 11:20–34.

feast with you without fear. The false teachers may have made the love feasts occasions for blatant immorality. Even apart from this their presence at the meals would have been a concern to Jude. Because teaching took place at the love feasts (Acts 20:7, 11), there was opportunity for the false teachers to advance their ideas.

waterless clouds. A metaphor for a form of hypocrisy that fails to produce what is promised (2 Pet. 2:17 note).

fruitless trees . . . twice dead, uprooted. Like trees failing to bear fruit at harvesttime, the lives of these people are barren and fall under God's judgment (Matt. 7:16–20; Luke 13:6–9).

13 wandering stars. Shooting stars, comets, or most probably, planets. Either the opponents' teaching is short-lived (like the light of a shooting star) or untrustworthy and useless (as when an unpredictable heavenly body is used for navigation).

14 Enoch, the seventh from Adam. The Enoch of Gen. 5:24 is seventh from Adam if Adam is counted as first. In vv. 14, 15, Jude quotes almost verbatim from a popular apocryphal work, the *Book of Enoch* or *1 Enoch.* In doing so Jude does not imply that *1 Enoch* is divinely inspired or that it was written by Enoch himself (Gen. 5:24). The source he uses was familiar to his readers and would be useful for confirming his theme of coming divine judgment on the ungodly (Introduction: Interpretive Difficulties).

prophesied. In saying that Enoch "prophesied" about these men, Jude neither confirms nor denies the popular attribution of this apocryphal text to the biblical Enoch. The quotation from *1 Enoch,* in agreement with a host of Old Testament prophecies (e.g., Dan. 7:9, 10; Zech. 14:3–5), teaches that God will come with His heavenly hosts to judge the wicked, and Jude is justified in applying this biblical idea to his specific situation.

holy ones. Probably a reference to the angelic host that will accompany the Lord's return (Zech. 14:5; Matt. 25:31).

15 ungodly . . . ungodly. The repetition of this term is important; the same Greek word is used in vv. 4 and 18. Rebellion by the false teachers is first and foremost against God and His authority, and it will meet with God's certain judgment (v. 4 note).

16 grumblers, malcontents. Like Israel in the wilderness (v. 5; 1 Cor. 10:10), the false teachers resist God's will, perhaps by complaining about the law's restrictions on their behavior.

loud-mouthed boasters. These may have been claims to having visionary experiences (v. 8), freedom from the law (vv. 4, 8), or possession of the Holy Spirit (vv. 18, 19).

showing favoritism to gain advantage. They show partiality to the rich members of the church (James 2:1–4), and perhaps go on to adapt their teaching to please the influential in their audience.

18 last time. See note 1 Pet. 1:20.

scoffers. They mock especially the moral law of God and the certainty of divine punishment on the disobedient (Ps. 1:1; 35:16; Prov. 14:9; 2 Pet. 3:3, 4).

19 cause divisions. Division in the church was an inevitable result of the false teachers' arrogance (v. 16) and their claim, against the church leadership and ordinary Christians, to possess the Spirit. The false teachers may have been classifying people as the later Gnostics did into the "spiritual" (themselves) and the "natural" (ordinary Christians).

worldly people, devoid of the Spirit. Against his opponents' claims, Jude argues that the false teachers themselves are the ones who live entirely at the level of natural, earthly life (v. 10).

[w]build yourselves up in your most holy
faith; [x]pray in the Holy Spirit; 21 [y]keep yourselves in the love of God, [z]waiting for the
mercy of our Lord Jesus Christ that leads to
eternal life. 22 And have mercy on those
who doubt; 23 save others by [a]snatching
them out of [b]the fire; to others show mercy
[c]with fear, hating even [d]the garment[1]
stained by the flesh.

Doxology

24 [e]Now to him who is able [f]to keep you
from stumbling and [g]to present you
[h]blameless before the presence of his glory
with great joy, 25 to [i]the only God, our
Savior, through Jesus Christ our Lord, [j]be
glory, majesty, dominion, and authority,
before all time and now and forever.
Amen.

20 [w]See Col. 2:7 [x]Eph. 6:18; [Rom. 8:26]
21 [y]2 Cor. 13:14; [Acts 13:43] [z]Tit. 2:13; 2 Pet. 3:12
23 [a]Amos 4:11; Zech. 3:2 [b]See 1 Cor. 3:15 [c][2 Cor. 5:11] [d]Rev. 3:4; [Zech. 3:4]
24 [e]Rom. 16:25; Eph. 3:20 [f]John 17:12 [g]Col. 1:22; [1 Pet. 4:13] [h]Eph. 1:4; 5:27; Phil. 2:15; Rev. 14:5
25 [i]John 5:44; 1 Tim. 1:17 [j]See Rom. 11:36

1 Greek *chiton*, a long garment worn under the cloak next to the skin

20–23 Jude now turns from denunciation of the false teachers to positive exhortation of his readers. To contend for the faith when it is under attack means more than opposing false teachers with words. It involves a positive life faithful to the gospel. The Trinitarian form of Jude's exhortation should be noted ("Holy Spirit . . . God . . . Lord Jesus Christ").

20 build . . . holy faith. Jude, like Peter (1 Pet. 2:5) and Paul (1 Cor. 3:16, 17), compares the church to a building. As in v. 3, "faith" refers to the foundational message of the prophets and apostles (Eph. 2:20–22).

pray in the Holy Spirit. In contrast to the false teachers, the prayers of Jude's readers are controlled by the Spirit, as indeed their whole lives should be (Gal. 5:16–18; Eph. 6:18).

22, 23 The exact Greek text of these verses is disputed, and it is hard to tell whether two or three groups of sinners are in view. Whatever the textual solution, Jude clearly recognizes that different pastoral strategies are to be employed with different people. Some can profit from gentle counseling (Gal. 6:1). Others will require confrontation or action of some sort, to pull them "out of the fire."

23 mercy with fear. See Gal. 6:1.

garment stained by the flesh. A vivid metaphor for the contaminating influence of the false teachers, this phrase underscores the care that Jude's readers must exercise in their contact with the false teachers and those under their influence (1 Cor. 5:11; 2 John 10, 11). On the metaphor, see Is. 64:6; Zech. 3:1–5; Matt. 22:12; Rev. 3:4, 5, 18; 19:8.

24, 25 Like Rom. 16:25–27, Jude's conclusion is a doxology expressing confidence in God's power to preserve His people to the end, and acknowledging God's eternal greatness in His "glory, majesty, dominion, and authority."

THE REVELATION OF JESUS CHRIST

Revelation

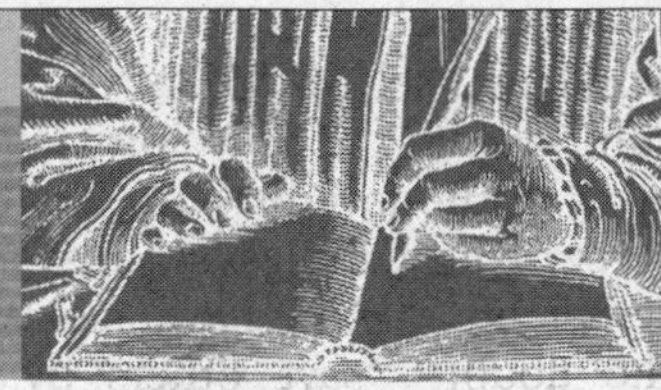

AUTHOR

The writer identifies himself as John (1:1, 4, 9; 22:8). He was well known to the churches in Asia Minor (1:9; "Date and Occasion" below). As early as the second century A.D., Justin Martyr, Irenaeus, and others identified the author as the apostle John. In the third century however, Dionysius, bishop of Alexandria, compared the style and themes of Revelation with the Gospel of John and concluded that the two must have different authors. On balance it is still probable that the apostle John was the author. Revelation stresses that its message and content derive ultimately from Jesus Christ and from God the Father (1:1, 10, 11; 22:16, 20). It possesses full divine authority (22:18, 19).

DATE AND OCCASION

Revelation was written during a time of persecution, probably near the end of the reign of the Roman Emperor Nero (A.D. 54–68) or during the reign of Domitian (A.D. 81–96). Most scholars favor a date about A.D. 95.

Revelation is addressed to seven churches in Asia Minor (1:4, 11), in an area now part of western Turkey. Each church receives rebukes and encouragement in accord with its condition (2:1–3:22). Persecution had fallen on some Christians (1:9; 2:9, 13) and more was coming (2:10; 13:7–10). Roman officials would try to force Christians to worship the emperor. Heretical teachings and declining fervor tempted Christians to compromise with pagan society (2:2, 4, 14, 15, 20–24; 3:1, 2, 15, 17). Revelation assures Christians that Christ knows their condition and that He calls them to stand fast against all temptation. Their victory has been secured through the blood of the Lamb (5:9, 10; 12:11). Christ will come soon to defeat Satan and all his agents (19:11–20:10), and Christ's people will enjoy everlasting peace in His presence (7:15–17; 21:3, 4).

INTERPRETIVE DIFFICULTIES

1. Approaches to the Book. Interpreters disagree concerning the period of time and the manner in which the visions of 6:1–18:24 are fulfilled. "Preterists" think fulfillment occurred in the fall of Jerusalem (if Revelation was written in A.D. 67–68), the fall of the Roman Empire, or both. "Futurists" think fulfillment will occur in a period of final crisis just before the Second Coming. "Historicists" think that 6:1–18:24 offers a basically chronological outline of the course of church history from the first century (6:1) until the Second Coming (19:11). "Idealists" think that the scenes of Revelation depict not specific events but principles of spiritual war. The principles are operative throughout the church age and may have repeated embodiments.

A combination of these views is probably closest to the truth. The imagery in Revelation is multifaceted and is in principle capable of multiple embodiments. Idealists maintain that general principles are expressed. If so, those principles had a particular relevance to the seven churches and their struggles in the first century (1:4; "Date and Occasion" above), but the principles will also come to climactic expression in the final crisis of the Second Coming (22:20; cf. 2 Thess. 2:1–12). Christians throughout history are involved in the same spiritual war and so must apply the principles to themselves and their own time (1:3 note). Hence, many passages have at least three main applications: to the first century, to the final crisis, and to whatever time in which Christians live.

On the other hand, suppose that the preterists are basically correct in thinking that Revelation refers mainly to the events of the early church period. They can easily acknowledge that the underlying principles of conflict have wider bearing. Then the practical results will be similar to the idealist approach. Patience and humility are needed when one confronts disagreements on these matters. In the meantime, Revelation has broad lessons from which all can profit.

2. The Millennium. The thousand-year period of Christ's rule described in 20:1–10, commonly called the "millennium," is variously understood by interpreters. "Premillennialists" believe that the thousand years follow the Second Coming that is described in 19:11–21. After the Second Coming, Satan is bound and Christ ushers in a long period of earthly peace and prosperity. Some think of this as a literal thousand years and others consider the number to mean a very long period of time. Christians receive resurrection bodies at the beginning of the millennium, but the final judgment for all others takes place at the end, after a rebellion led by Satan. In the second century, Justin Martyr and Papias were among those holding a premillennial view.

"Amillennialists" understand the millennium to be a picture of the present reign of Christ and of the saints in heaven (analogous to 6:9, 10). The "first resurrection" (20:5) is either the life of Christians who have died and are with Christ in heaven, or life in Christ that starts with spiritual new birth (Rom. 6:8–11; Eph. 2:6; Col. 3:1–4). Satan has been bound through the triumph of Christ in His crucifixion and resurrection (John 12:31; Col. 2:15).

"Postmillennialists" believe that the kingdom of Christ and the church will experience much more expansion on earth before the Second Coming. The thousand years are understood by some as a final period of earthly Christian triumph following the spread of the gospel (19:11–21 note). Others agree with amillennialists in identifying 20:1–6 with the entire period that begins with the resurrection of Christ.

The dispute partly concerns the chronological relation of 20:1–10 to 19:11–21. Premillennialists believe that the events described in 20:1–10 simply follow the Second Coming, which is depicted in 19:11–21. But 20:1–15 might also represent a seventh cycle of judgments leading up to the Second Coming (see "Characteristics and Themes: Literary Form"). The final battle in 20:7–10 seems to be the same as the final battle in 16:14, 16; 17:14; 19:11–21. Similar language from Ezek. 38; 39 is used in the various descriptions. The judgment of Satan in 20:10 parallels the judgments against Babylon (chs. 17; 18) and against the Beast and the False Prophet (19:11–21). These enemies of God are consigned to everlasting punishment, and the visions depicting their judgment may be parallel descriptions rather than different events in a sequence. Certain features in 20:11–15 correspond to earlier descriptions of the Second Coming (6:14; 11:18). Most important, all of Christ's enemies have been judged in 19:11–21. If 20:1–6 represents later events, there would be no one left for Satan to deceive in 20:3.

Caution is needed because the different millennial positions depend on the interpretation of Old Testament prophetic texts as well as these verses in Revelation. Moreover, like most of Revelation, 20:1–10 uses language that in principle may legitimately be capable of multiple fulfillments. These facts make precise interpretation difficult (it is God's prerogative to reveal only as much about the order of future events as is good for us to know—Acts 1:7). The major point is that Satan will finally be defeated, and that even before that time God takes care of His saints and blesses them through His triumphant rule. This assurance ought to comfort Christians, whatever their millennial position.

CHARACTERISTICS AND THEMES

1. Content. In the opening vision Christ appears as the majestic King and Judge of the universe and Ruler of the churches (1:12–20). In 2:1–3:22 Christ addresses specific needs of each church. His powerful promises also remind the churches of the scope and profundity of their calling (2:7, 10, 11, 17, 26–28; 3:5, 12, 21). The selection of exactly seven churches suggests the wider relevance of the message (1:4 note).

In 4:1–22:5 Christ's rebukes and encouragement take a new form. Through Christ and His angels (22:8, 9, 16) John receives a series of visions intended to open Christians' eyes to the kingship and majesty of God, the nature of spiritual warfare, God's judgments on evil, and the outcome of the conflict. God and His army must win the battle (17:14; 19:1, 2), but His forces are opposed by Satan, the "great . . . dragon" (12:3), who leads the whole world astray (12:9). Satan has two agents, the "beast" and the "false prophet," who together with him make up a counterfeit trinity (ch. 13; 16:13; see

"Characteristics and Themes: Other Features" below). In opposition to these threats the saints must maintain a true and faithful witness, even to the point of martyrdom (12:11), and must maintain true spiritual purity (14:4; 19:8). In the new heaven and new earth, their witness finds its fulfillment in the final light of God's truth (21:22–27), and their purity takes perfect form in the spotless bride of the Lamb (21:9).

The principal theme of Revelation is that God rules history and will bring it to a triumphal climax in Christ. At the center are the visions of Christ (1:12–16) and of God (4:1–5:14). God displays His majesty, authority, and righteousness as the Ruler and Judge of the universe (1:12–20 note). These central visions already foreshadow the consummation of history, when God's glory will fill all things (21:22, 23; 22:5; 4:1–5:14 note). Detailed elements in the visions flesh out these truths, and are to be seen as part of a larger picture. Revelation is thus a picture book, a dramatic presentation to enable Christians to have a God-centered view of history. It is not a puzzle book to serve as a source of mysterious calculations.

2. Literary Form. The Greek title of Revelation is *Apokalypsis*, meaning "revelation" or "disclosure." Hence, the book is an "apocalypse," a revelation concerning the ultimate goal of history. The Book of Revelation is apocalyptic literature; like portions of Ezekiel, Daniel, and Zechariah, it contains visions with many symbolic elements. Using visual imagery as well as verbal promises and warnings, it weaves together into a poetic tapestry the themes of the whole of Scripture. Its depths are displayed through its multiple allusions. Yet as a revelation, or disclosure, it is intended to nourish all who are servants of Christ (1:1).

The Prologue of Revelation (1:1–3) explains its basic purpose. Rev. 1:4–22:21 is a letter with a greeting (1:4, 5), body (1:5–22:20), and farewell (22:21). The formal features of this common arrangement are also found in Paul's letters.

The main portion of the book (4:1–22:5) consists of seven cycles of judgments, each of which leads to a description of the Second Coming (4:1–8:1; 8:2–11:19; 12:1–14:20; 15:1–16:21; 17:1–19:10; 19:11–21; 20:1–15). A final, eighth portion presents the supreme vision of the New Jerusalem (21:1–22:5). Each cycle is best understood as depicting the same spiritual war, but from a fresh vantage point. Later cycles concentrate more and more on the most intense phases of conflict and on the Second Coming itself.

Symbolic personages are introduced into the drama one by one, and their destinies are revealed in the reverse order, as follows:

A. The People of God Depicted with the Imagery of Light and Creation (12:1, 2)
  B. The Dragon—Satan (12:3–6)
    C. The Beast and the False Prophet (13:1–18)
      D. The Bride: The People of God in the Imagery of Sexual Purity (14:1–5)
        E. Babylon the Harlot (17:1–6)
        E. Babylon Destroyed (17:15–18:24)
      D. The Bride Is Blessed with Marriage (19:1–10)
    C. The Beast and the False Prophet Are Destroyed (19:11–21)
  B. The Dragon Is Destroyed (20:1–10)
A. The People of God in the Imagery of Light and Creation (21:1–22:5)

3. Other Features. Many thematic features unify the book. Repeated use of the number seven signifies completeness. God's plan and power determine the outcomes. Praise to God rises from the angels and saints (1:6 note). The present struggles of the church (2:1–3:22) contrast with its final rest. The church must maintain its witness and purity. Everything moves forward to the victory of Christ at His coming.

One of the most prominent features of the book is the presentation of Satanic counterfeits that oppose God in a spiritual war of cosmic proportions. The beast introduced in 13:1–10 is a counterfeit of Christ. Note the following parallels: (a) The beast is an image of Satan, whom Satan brought forth (13:1), just as Christ is the exact image of God, begotten by the Father (Ps. 2:7; Col. 1:15; Heb. 1:3); (b) the beast has ten crowns and blasphemous names (13:1), while Christ has many crowns and worthy names (19:12); (c) the dragon gave the beast his power, throne, and great authority (13:2), just as Christ has power (5:12, 13), throne (3:21), and authority (12:10) from the Father (John 5:21–23); (d) the beast has a seemingly fatal wound from which he has recovered (13:3), counterfeiting Christ's resurrection, and the beast's recovery is one of the principal features that attracts followers (13:4), just as the resurrection of Christ is one of the principal points of evangelistic proclamation; (e) worship is directed both to the dragon and the beast (13:4), just as Christians worship both the Father and the Son (John 5:23); (f) the beast attracts the worship of the whole world (13:7), just as Christ will be worshiped universally; (g) the beast utters blasphemies (13:5), while Christ utters the praises of God (Heb. 2:12); (h) the beast makes war against the saints (13:7), while Christ makes war against the beast (19:11–21). The song of praise to the beast in 13:4 counterfeits the song to God in Ex. 15:11. The striking juxtaposition of Christ and the beast in 19:11–21 shows that these are the two main warriors in the battle: Christ is the divine warrior, fulfilling the imagery of Ex. 15:3; Is. 59:16–18; 63:1–6; Hab. 3:3–15; Zech. 9:13–15; 14:1–5; and the beast is the unholy, counterfeit warrior, fulfilling the imagery of Dan. 7:1–8.

Satan himself attempts to counterfeit God the Father. He engages in a mock creation, in which he brings forth his image out of chaotic waters (13:1; parallel to Gen. 1:2). Similarly, the false prophet, or beast from the earth (13:11–18), counterfeits the work of the Holy Spirit. He desires that people worship not himself, but the beast, just as the Holy Spirit glorifies Christ (John 16:14). He works false miraculous signs (13:13, 14), counterfeiting the miracles of the Holy Spirit. He forces a mark on his subjects (13:16), just as Christians are sealed with the Holy Spirit (Eph. 1:13).

Together—Satan, the beast, and the false prophet—form an unholy trio (16:13), counterfeiting the Holy Trinity. Satan as a deceiver is always trying to make his ways look attractive (2 Cor. 11:14, 15). When divine revelation opens our eyes, there is a world of difference between his horrors and God's beauties. Satan is an imitator, not a creator, and his productions are always bestial and degenerate like himself. Beasts must give way before Christ the King (19:11–21).

One final counterfeit figure exists, namely Babylon the harlot, the counterfeit of the bride of Christ (17:1–19:10). Her corruptions are contrasted with the purity of the bride of the Lamb (19:7–9). Babylon sums up in herself the worship of the godless world. By contrast the bride, the church, represents the worshipers of the true God. Satan attacks the saints in two main ways. The beast attacks with power and persecution, endeavoring to destroy the witness of the saints and force them to worship the beast. Babylon attacks with seduction, endeavoring to destroy the purity of the saints.

OUTLINE OF REVELATION

I. Introduction (ch. 1)

- A. *Prologue (1:1–3)*
- B. *Greeting and Praise (1:4–8)*
- C. *Vision of Christ the Judge (1:9–20)*

II. Exhortations to the Seven Churches (chs. 2; 3)

- A. *Ephesus (2:1–7)*
- B. *Smyrna (2:8–11)*
- C. *Pergamum (2:12–17)*
- D. *Thyatira (2:18–29)*
- E. *Sardis (3:1–6)*
- F. *Philadelphia (3:7–13)*
- G. *Laodicea (3:14–22)*

III. Heavenly Visions (4:1–22:5)

- A. *Cycle One: The Scroll and Its Seven Seals (4:1–8:1)*
  1. God the King, and Christ the Worthy One (chs. 4; 5)
  2. Opening Six Seals (ch. 6)
  3. Care for the Saints (ch. 7)
  4. Opening the Seventh Seal (8:1)
- B. *Cycle Two: Seven Angels with Seven Trumpets (8:2–11:19)*
  1. Seven Angels Before God (8:2–6)
  2. Six Angels Blow Their Trumpets (8:7–9:21)
  3. Care for John and the Two Witnesses (10:1–11:14)
  4. The Seventh Angel Blows His Trumpet (11:15–19)
- C. *Cycle Three: Seven Symbolic Histories (chs. 12–14)*
  1. Principal Personages: the People of God versus Satan (12:1–6)
  2. Six Symbolic Histories Unfold (12:7–14:11)
     - a. *History of the Dragon (12:7–12)*
     - b. *History of the Woman (12:13–17)*
     - c. *History of the Beast from the Sea (13:1–10)*
     - d. *History of the Beast from the Earth—the False Prophet (13:11–18)*
     - e. *The 144,000 (14:1–5)*
     - f. *Three Angelic Messengers (14:6–11)*
  3. Care for the Saints (14:12, 13)
  4. The Seventh Symbolic History (One Like the Son of Man) Unfolds (14:14–20)
- D. *Cycle Four: Seven Bowls of God's Wrath from the Temple (chs. 15; 16)*
- E. *Cycle Five: Judgment on Babylon and Vindication of the Church (17:1–19:10)*
- F. *Cycle Six: The Final Battle (19:11–21)*
- G. *Cycle Seven: The Reign of the Saints and the Last Judgment (20:1–21:8)*
- H. *The New Jerusalem (21:9–22:5)*

IV. Final Exhortations (22:6–20)

V. Closing Blessing (22:21)

Prologue

1 The revelation of Jesus Christ, which
God [a]gave him [b]to show to his servants[1] the things that must soon take
place. [c]He made it known by sending his
angel to his servant[2] John, 2 [d]who bore witness to the word of God and to [e]the testimony of Jesus Christ, even [f]to all that he
saw. 3 [g]Blessed is the one who reads aloud
the words of this prophecy, and blessed are
those who hear, and who keep what is
written in it, [h]for the time is near.

Greeting to the Seven Churches

4 John to the seven churches that are in
Asia:

Grace to you and peace from [i]him [j]who
is and [k]who was and who is to come, and
from [l]the seven spirits who are before his
throne, 5 and from Jesus Christ [m]the faithful
witness, [n]the firstborn of the dead, and
[o]the ruler of kings on earth.

To [p]him who loves us and [q]has freed us
from our sins by his blood 6 and made us [r]a
kingdom, [r]priests to [s]his God and Father,
to him be [t]glory and [u]dominion forever and
ever. Amen. 7 Behold, [v]he is coming with
the clouds, and [w]every eye will see him,
even those who pierced him, and all tribes
of the earth will wail[3] on account of him.
Even so. Amen.

8 [x]"I am the Alpha and the Omega," says
the Lord God, [y]"who is and who was and
who is to come, the Almighty."

Vision of the Son of Man

9 I, John, your brother and [z]partner in
[a]the tribulation and [b]the kingdom and [c]the
patient endurance that are in Jesus, was on

Chapter 1
1 [a]John 17:7, 8; [John 8:26; 14:10] [b]ch. 22:6 [c]ch. 22:16 **2** [d]John 19:35 [e]ch. 6:9; 12:17; 19:10; See 1 Cor. 1:6 [f]ver. 11, 19 **3** [g]ch. 22:7; [Luke 11:28; John 8:51; 1 John 2:3] [h]ch. 22:10; [1 John 2:18]; See Rom. 13:11 **4** [i]ver. 8; ch. 4:8; Heb. 13:8 [j]Ex. 3:14 (Gk.) [k]John 1:1 [l]ch. 3:1; 4:5; 5:6 **5** [m]ch. 3:14; John 18:37; 1 Tim. 6:13; [ch. 2:13; Ps. 89:37; Isai. 55:4] [n]Col. 1:18; [Ps. 89:27; Acts 26:23; 1 Cor. 15:20] [o]ch. 17:14; 19:16; [Ps. 89:27] [p]John 13:34; 15:9 [q]1 Pet. 1:18, 19 **6** [r]ch. 5:10; 20:6; 1 Pet. 2:9 [s]See Rom. 15:6 [t]See Rom. 11:36 [u]1 Pet. 4:11 **7** [v]Dan. 7:13; See Matt. 16:27 [w]Zech. 12:10; John 19:37 **8** [x]ch. 21:6; 22:13; [Isai. 41:4; 43:10; 44:6] [y]ver. 4 **9** [z][Phil. 4:14] [a]John 16:33 [b]2 Tim. 2:12 [c]ch. 3:10

1 Greek *bondservants* 2 Greek *bondservant* 3 Or *mourn*

1:1–3 The main portion of Revelation (1:4–22:21) has the form of a letter, with greetings, body, and farewell. This Prologue helps orient readers to the content they may expect. Stress is placed on the divine authority of the message (from God and Jesus Christ), its certainty (note the word "must" in v. 1), and its crucial relevance (v. 3). God makes thorough provision for the communication process: the message originates with God the Father, is given to Jesus Christ, and is made known to John through an angel (v. 1). John testifies by writing it (v. 2), and all are encouraged to read and hear (v. 3).

Revelation stresses that though it comes in symbolic form, it is understandable. It is "revelation," disclosing rather than hiding truth (v. 1). It is for "his servants," not a special elite (v. 1). God expects Christians to "keep what is written," to profit spiritually (v. 3). A blessing encourages people to read and hear (v. 3).

1:1 soon. See 22:6, 7, 10, 12, 20. Spiritual war takes place throughout the church age, and the seven churches will soon experience all dimensions of the conflict. Moreover, the "last days" spoken of by Old Testament prophecy have been inaugurated by Christ's resurrection (Acts 2:16, 17). The time of waiting is over, and God is conducting the final phase of His victorious warfare against evil. By such reckoning, today is "the last hour" (1 John 2:18).

1:2 testimony of Jesus Christ. Because of the imminence of persecution threatening to suppress Christian witness (17:6), Revelation is full of the theme of witness. Jesus Christ is the preeminent witness (v. 5; 3:14; 19:11). Imitation of Him may include martyrdom (12:11). Revelation itself is a testimony intended to strengthen the testimony of its readers. Its message carries full divine authority and authenticity (19:10; 22:6, 16, 20).

1:3 Blessed. Revelation not only pronounces judgment on the faithless, but blessing on the faithful (14:13; 16:15; 19:9; 20:6; 22:7, 14).

prophecy. See 22:7–10, 18, 19. Like Old Testament prophecy, Revelation combines visions of God's future with exhortation to faithfulness. This prophecy is a distinctive and inspired form of the witness that all Christians are to give (v. 2 note).

keep. Revelation is not intended to tickle our fancy but to strengthen our hearts (Introduction: Characteristics and Themes: Content).

1:4 to the seven churches. See v. 11; 2:1–3:22. Revelation is organized in sevens, the biblical number symbolic of completeness (Gen. 2:2, 3). The choice of seven churches expresses this theme and hints at the wider relevance of the message to all churches (vv. 1, 3; 2:7, 11, 17, 29; 3:6, 13, 22; 22:7, 11–14, 16, 18–21).

Asia. The Roman province of Asia lies in what is now western Turkey.

him who is and who was and who is to come. Similar to the divine name in Ex. 3:14, 15. See note on v. 8.

seven spirits. The Holy Spirit is described in sevenfold fullness (4:5; Zech. 4:2, 6). Note the origin of grace and peace from the Trinity: God the Father ("him who is"), the Son (1:5), and the Spirit (cf. 2 Cor. 13:14; 1 Pet. 1:1, 2).

1:5–8 John praises God, in a way similar to the beginning of most Pauline letters. The themes of God's sovereignty, redemption, and the Second Coming of Christ recur throughout Revelation.

1:5 The key role of Jesus Christ in the whole of Revelation is already anticipated in this description.

faithful witness. See note on v. 2.

the firstborn. See note on v. 18.

ruler. See note 4:1–5:14.

freed us. See note 5:1–14.

1:6 The theme of worship and praise of God extends throughout Revelation. Note the praises in 4:8, 11; 5:9, 13; 7:12; 11:15; 12:10–12; 15:3, 4; 19:1–8. Utterances of praise are an integral part of the spiritual war.

kingdom, priests. Saints enjoy God's rule and as priests have intimate access to Him (Heb. 10:19–22; 1 Pet. 2:5–9). In the future, they will reign with Him (2:26, 27; 3:21; 5:10; 20:4, 6). All nations now share in the priestly privileges given to Israel in Ex. 19:6. The purposes of redemption that are seen in the Exodus from Egypt, and the purposes of dominion given to humanity at creation, are both fulfilled through Christ (5:9, 10). The theme of priestly worship and access to God is complementary to the temple theme in Revelation (4:1–5:14 note).

1:8 the Alpha and the Omega. The first and last letters of the Greek alphabet. God is Alpha (Creator) and Omega (the One who ushers in the new heaven and new earth). He is Lord of all—past, present, and future—as suggested by "who is . . . is to come" (cf. 4:1–5:14 note). His sovereignty in creation guarantees the fulfillment of His purposes in re-creation (Rom. 8:18–25).

who is to come. In the future God will come to fulfill all His purposes (21:1–22:5).

1:9–11 An identification of John and his circumstances (in which he represents the whole church) prepares the way for the first main vision in 1:12–3:22.

1:9 patient endurance. The exhortation to endure and remain faithful

the island called Patmos [d]on account of the
word of God and the testimony of Jesus.
10 [e]I was in the Spirit [f]on the Lord's day,
and I heard behind me a loud voice [g]like a
trumpet 11 saying, [h]"Write what you see in
a book and send it to the seven churches,
to Ephesus and to Smyrna and to Pergamum and to Thyatira and to Sardis and to
Philadelphia and to Laodicea."

12 Then I turned to see the voice that was
speaking to me, and on turning I saw [i]sev-
en golden lampstands, 13 and in the midst
of the lampstands [j]one like [k]a son of man,
[l]clothed with a long robe and [m]with a gold-
en sash around his chest. 14 [n]The hairs of
his head were white like wool, as white as
snow. [o]His eyes were like a flame of fire,
15 [p]his feet were like burnished bronze,
refined in a furnace, and [q]his voice was like
the roar of many waters. 16 [r]In his right
hand he held seven stars, [s]from his mouth
came a sharp two-edged sword, and [t]his
face was like the sun shining [u]in full
strength.

17 [v]When I saw him, I fell at his feet as
though dead. But [v]he laid his right hand on
me, [w]saying, "Fear not, [x]I am the first and
the last, 18 and the living one. [y]I died, and
behold I am alive forevermore, and [z]I have
the keys of Death and Hades. 19 [a]Write
therefore [b]the things that you have seen,
those that are and those that are to take
place after this. 20 As for the mystery of the
seven stars that you saw in my right hand,
and [c]the seven golden lampstands, the
seven stars are the angels of the seven
churches, and [d]the seven lampstands are
the seven churches.

To the Church in Ephesus

2 "To the angel of the church in Ephesus
write: 'The words of [e]him who holds
the seven stars in his right hand, [f]who
walks among the seven golden lampstands.

2 [g]"'I know your works, your toil and
your patient endurance, and how you cannot bear with those who are evil, but [h]have
tested those [i]who call themselves apostles
and are not, and found them to be false. 3 I
know you are enduring patiently and bearing up [j]for my name's sake, and you [k]have

9 [d]See ver. 2 **10** [e]ch. 4:2; [ch. 17:3; 21:10; Matt. 22:43; 1 Kin. 18:12; Ezek. 3:12; 2 Cor. 12:2] [f]Acts 20:7; 1 Cor. 16:2 [g]ch. 4:1 **11** [h]ver. 2, 19 **12** [i]ver. 20; ch. 2:1; Ex. 25:37; 2 Chr. 4:20; Zech. 4:2; [ch. 11:4] **13** [j]Dan. 7:13 [k]ch. 14:14; Dan. 10:16 [l]Dan. 10:5 [m]ch. 15:6 **14** [n]Dan. 7:9 [o]ch. 2:18; 19:12; [Dan. 10:6] **15** [p]Ezek. 1:7; Dan. 10:6 [q]ch. 14:2; 19:6; Ezek. 43:2 **16** [r]ver. 20; ch. 2:1; 3:1 [s]ch. 19:15; [ch. 2:12, 16; Isai. 49:2; Eph. 6:17; Heb. 4:12] [t]Matt. 17:2 [u]Judg. 5:31 **17** [v]Dan. 8:17, 18; 10:9, 10, 15; [Luke 24:37; John 21:12] [w]Matt. 17:7 [x]ch. 2:8; 22:13; Isai. 41:4; 44:6; 48:12 **18** [y]Rom. 6:9; 14:9 [z][ch. 9:1; 20:1] **19** [a]ver. 2, 11 [b]ver. 12-16 **20** [c]See ver. 12 [d][Matt. 5:14, 15]
Chapter 2 **1** [e]ch. 1:16, 20 [f]ch. 1:13 **2** [g]ver. 19; ch. 3:1, 8, 15 [h]See 1 John 4:1 [i]See 2 Cor. 11:13 **3** [j]John 15:21 [k][Heb. 12:3, 5]

runs through Revelation (2:2, 3, 13, 19; 3:10; 6:11; 13:10; 14:12; 16:15; 18:4; 20:4; 22:7, 11, 14). Here is practical exhortation in the midst of persecution and temptation (Introduction: Date and Occasion).

Patmos. A small island off the west coast of Asia Minor. Patmos had a Roman penal settlement used for persons considered dangerous to good order.

1:10 in the Spirit. The Spirit provides John with the special visions and transports him to vantage points to view them (4:2; 17:3; 21:10).

the Lord's day. Sunday, the Christian day of worship celebrating Christ's resurrection. The Sunday celebration anticipates the celebration of God's final victory (19:1–10).

loud voice. The voice of Christ. Loud voices and noises indicate the power and universal relevance of the messages and events (1:15; 4:1, 5; 5:2, 12; 6:1; 7:2, 10; 8:5, 13; 10:3; 11:12, 15, 19; 12:10; 14:7, 9, 15, 18; 19:1, 3, 6, 17).

1:11 seven churches. See note on v. 4.

1:12–20 Christ appears in overwhelming glory (cf. 21:22–24). "Like a son of man" alludes to Dan. 7:13. The features of vv. 12–16 are reminiscent of Dan. 7:9, 10; 10:5, 6; and Ezek. 1:25–28, but include more distant similarities to many Old Testament appearances of God. The vision shows Christ as Judge and Ruler—first of all over the churches (1:20–3:22), but also over the whole universe (2:27; 3:21). His deity, authority, and conquest of death guarantee final victory (vv. 17, 18; 17:14; 19:11–16). This vision of God's sovereignty exercised through Christ is a fundamental point of the message of Revelation (Introduction: Interpretive Difficulties). Christ's war-like appearance (v. 16) anticipates His role in the final battle (19:11–21) and looks backward to God's battles in the Old Testament (Ex. 15:3; Deut. 32:41, 42; Is. 59:17, 18; Zech. 14:3). Christ presents the pattern in which the destiny of the whole universe is summed up (Eph. 1:10; Col. 1:16, 17). Because all things hold together in Christ (Col. 1:17), the trinitarian imagery of vv. 12–20 and chs. 4; 5 forms a foundation for the whole of Revelation. Because the Trinity is deeply mysterious, the imagery of Revelation has inexhaustible profundity.

1:12 seven golden lampstands. The lampstands symbolize the churches in their light-bearing or witness-bearing function (1:20; Matt. 5:14–16). Christ walks among the churches as Lord and Shepherd (v. 13), just as God's cloud of glory descended to dwell in the tabernacle and the temple, which had their lampstands (Ex. 25:31–40; 1 Kin. 7:49). God's character as light (1 John 1:5) is supremely manifested in Christ (John 1:4, 5; 8:12; 9:5; Acts 26:13), but is also reflected in various ways in His creation: in fiery angels (10:1; Ezek. 1:13), in natural light (21:23; Gen. 1:3), in the temple lampstands, in the churches, and in each individual person (Matt. 5:14–16).

1:15 roar of many waters. See note on v. 10.

1:16 sword. See 19:15; Is. 11:4; Heb. 4:12.

the sun. See 21:22–25; Is. 60:1–3, 19, 20.

1:17 the first and the last. Essentially the same as the Alpha and the Omega (v. 8 note; 2:8; 22:13; Is. 41:4; 44:6; 48:12).

1:18 the living one. Christ's resurrection and new life provide for the new life of His people (2:8; 5:9, 10; 20:4, 5) and the renewal of the world itself (22:1).

keys of Death. This phrase anticipates 20:14.

1:19 This verse probably suggests a threefold division of Revelation into past (vv. 12–16), present (chs. 2; 3), and future (4:1–22:5). But the division is only a rough one, since each portion contains some references to all three periods.

1:20 the angels. The Greek word means "messengers." It may refer to human messengers, specifically the pastors of the churches, or to angels. The prominence of angels in Revelation would support the latter meaning here (22:6; Dan. 10:10–21).

2:1–3:22 See theological note "The Local Church" on next page. Christ shows care for the churches by addressing each according to its needs, with encouragement, rebuke, exhortation, and promise. He shows detailed knowledge of them ("I know"). In all the letters there are allusions to circumstances or traditions of the particular city, probably

not grown weary. 4But I have this against
you, that you have abandoned [l]the love
you had at first. 5Remember therefore from
where you have fallen; repent, and do [m]the
works you did at first. If not, [n]I will come
to you and remove your lampstand from its
place, unless you repent. 6Yet this you
have: you hate the works of [o]the Nicolaitans, which I also hate. 7[p]He who has an
ear, let him hear what the Spirit says to the
churches. [q]To the one who conquers I will
grant to eat of [r]the tree of life, which is in
[s]the paradise of God.'

4 [l]Jer. 2:2 5 [m]ver. 2; [Heb. 10:32] [n]ch. 3:3, 19 6 [o]ver. 15 7 [p]ver. 11, 17, 29; ch. 3:6, 13, 22; 13:9 [q]ch. 3:5; 21:7 [r]See Gen. 2:9 [s]Ezek. 28:13; 31:8 (Gk.)

8 [t]See ch. 1:17 [u]ch. 1:18 9 [v]James 2:5; [1 Tim. 6:18; Heb. 10:34; 11:26]

To the Church in Smyrna

8"And to the angel of the church in
Smyrna write: 'The words of [t]the first and
the last, [u]who died and came to life.
9"'I know your tribulation and [v]your
poverty ([v]but you are rich) and the slander[1]
of [w]those who say that they are Jews and
are not, but are a synagogue of Satan. 10Do
not fear what you are about to suffer.
Behold, the devil is about to throw some of
you into prison, [w]that you may be tested,

[w]ch. 3:9, 10 10 [w][See ver. 9 above]

1 Greek *blasphemy*

The Local Church

Each local church is a manifestation of the one universal church, and will embody the nature of that church as the Father's regenerate family, Christ's ministering body, and a fellowship sustained by the Holy Spirit. In the course of separating from the Roman Catholic church, the Reformers needed to be sure about what were the marks of the true church. From Scripture, they found the answer in terms of two criteria.

1. The faithful preaching of the Word of God: This means that the church teaches the Christian gospel according to the Scripture. Any group that denies the Trinity, the deity of Christ, the sin-bearing Atonement, or justification by faith alone, is like the separatists of earlier times whose denials of the Incarnation (1 John 4:1–3) caused John to say, "they were not of us" (1 John 2:19).

2. The right use of the sacraments: This criterion means that baptism and the Lord's Supper are used and explained as setting forth the gospel of faith in Christ. Turning these sacraments into superstitions that take away the sufficiency of faith in Christ undercuts the identity of the church, like anything else that obstructs faith in Christ. One purpose of baptism is to mark those who are received into the visible church. The Lord's Supper confirms for the faithful their membership in the church and their community with each other and with Christ.

Christians have found other marks of identity alongside these minimal two. Luther specified the keys of discipline (Matt. 16:19), an authorized ministry (Acts 14:23; 20:28), public worship (Heb. 10:25), and suffering under the cross (Acts 14:22; 20:29). The Reformed churches specified a functioning system of discipline, often calling discipline the third mark of the visible church (Titus 1:13; 2:15; 3:10). Charismatics point to the active ministry of every member as a mark of the true church (Eph. 4:7–16).

These additional marks are not, however, essential in the way that the first two are. A church that lacks the additional marks is seriously deficient, but it would not be true to say that it is no church at all.

including some that are no longer recognized. At the same time, all the churches are included in a universal calling to faithfulness and endurance until the promises reach their fulfillment in the heavenly Jerusalem. Their struggles contrast with the peace and satisfaction pictured in 21:1–22:5. The exhortations are reinforced by an opening allusion to some element of the majestic vision of 1:12–20, and therefore have universal bearing (1:4 note).

Each message has the same basic form:

1. Addressee: "to the angel of the church . . . write."
2. Identification of Christ, alluding back to His majesty displayed in 1:12–20: "The words of him."
3. Claim of knowledge: "I know."
4. Evaluation: rebukes or commendations.
5. Promise or threat: usually "I will."
6. Promise to "the one who conquers."
7. Exhortation to listen: "He who has an ear."

Note that (6) and (7) can occur in reverse order, and (5) can be included with (4).

2:5 remove your lampstand. The city of Ephesus had been relocated because of the gradual silting up of its river, the Cayster, and had been "removed" from earlier sites. By analogy, Christ threatens to remove the church unless its people repent.

2:6 Nicolaitans. A heretical group, probably holding views similar to the teaching of Balaam and Jezebel (vv. 14, 20 notes).

2:7 one who conquers. In this and parallel verses to the other churches, faithful saints are promised participation in all aspects of the new Jerusalem (2:11, 17, 26; 3:5, 12, 21; 21:1–22:5).

tree of life. See note 22:2.

2:9 synagogue of Satan. The Jewish synagogue in Smyrna was composed of Jews who had refused the message concerning the coming of the Messiah. Though they professed to worship God, their opposition to Christians showed that they were in fact under the power of satanic darkness (2 Cor. 4:4).

and for [x]ten days [y]you will have tribulation.
[z]Be faithful [a]unto death, and I will give you
[b]the crown of life. 11 [c]He who has an ear, let
him hear what the Spirit says to the
churches. [c]The one who conquers will not
be hurt by [d]the second death.'

To the Church in Pergamum

12 "And to the angel of the church in
Pergamum write: 'The words of him who
has [e]the sharp two-edged sword.
13 " 'I know where you dwell, [f]where
Satan's throne is. Yet you hold fast my
name, and you did not [g]deny my faith[1]
even in the days of Antipas [h]my faithful
witness, who was killed among you, where
Satan dwells. 14 But I have a few things
against you: you have some there who hold
the teaching of [i]Balaam, who taught Balak
to put a stumbling block before the sons of
Israel, so that they might [j]eat food sacrificed to idols and [k]practice sexual immorality. 15 So also you have some who hold the
teaching of [l]the Nicolaitans. 16 Therefore
repent. If not, [m]I will come to you soon and
[n]war against them with [e]the sword of my
mouth. 17 [c]He who has an ear, let him hear
what the Spirit says to the churches. [c]To
the one who conquers I will give some of
[o]the hidden manna, and I will give him a
white stone, with [p]a new name written on
the stone [q]that no one knows except the
one who receives it.'

To the Church in Thyatira

18 "And to the angel of the church in
Thyatira write: 'The words of the Son of
God, [r]who has eyes like a flame of fire, and
whose feet are like burnished bronze.
19 [s] " 'I know your works, your love and
faith and service and patient endurance,
and that your latter works exceed the first.
20 But I have this against you, that you tolerate that woman [t]Jezebel, who calls herself a prophetess and is teaching and
seducing my servants[2] [u]to practice sexual
immorality and [u]to eat food sacrificed to
idols. 21 I gave her time to repent, but [v]she
refuses to repent of her sexual immorality.
22 Behold, I will throw her onto a sickbed,
and those who commit adultery with her I
will throw into great tribulation, unless
they repent of her works, 23 and I will strike
her children dead. And all the churches
will know that I am he [w]who searches mind
and heart, and [x]I will give to each of you as
your works deserve. 24 But to the rest of you
in Thyatira, who do not hold this teaching,
who have not learned what some call [y]the
deep things of Satan, to you I say, I [z]do not
lay on you any other burden. 25 Only hold
fast [a]what you have until I come. 26 [b]The
one who conquers and who keeps my
works [c]until the end, [d]to him I will give
authority over the nations, 27 and [e]he will
[f]rule them with a rod of iron, [g]as when
earthen pots are broken in pieces, even as I
myself have received authority from my
Father. 28 And I will give him [h]the morning
star. 29 [t]He who has an ear, let him hear
what the Spirit says to the churches.'

To the Church in Sardis

3 "And to the angel of the church in
Sardis write: 'The words of him [i]who
has the seven spirits of God and the seven
stars.
" 'I know your works. You have the reputation [j]of being alive, [k]but you are dead.
2 Wake up, and strengthen what remains
and is about to die, for I have not found
your works [l]complete in the sight of my
God. 3 [m]Remember, then, what you
received and heard. Keep it, and repent. If

10 [x]Matt. 24:9 [y][Gen. 24:55; Dan. 1:12, 14] [z]See Matt. 10:22; Heb. 3:6 [a]ch. 12:11 [b]See James 1:12 **11** [c]See ver. 7 [d]ch. 20:6, 14; 21:8 **12** [e]ver. 16; ch. 1:16 **13** [f]ver. 9 [g]See 1 Tim. 5:8 [h]Acts 22:20 **14** [i]See 2 Pet. 2:15 [j]ver. 20; Acts 15:29; 1 Cor. 8:10; 10:19 [k]Num. 25:1; 31:16; 1 Cor. 10:8 **15** [l]ver. 6 **16** [m][ch. 22:7] [n]See 2 Thess. 2:8 [e][See ver. 12 above] **17** [c][See ver. 11 above] [o][John 6:48-50] [p]ch. 3:12; Isai. 62:2; 65:15 [q]ch. 19:12; [ch. 14:3] **18** [r]ch. 1:14, 15 **19** [s]ver. 2 **20** [t]1 Kin. 16:31; 21:25; 2 Kin. 9:7 [u]See ver. 14 **21** [v][ch. 9:20, 21; 16:9, 11]; See Rom. 2:4 **23** [w]Ps. 7:9; 26:2; Jer. 20:12; See Rom. 8:27 [x]See Matt. 16:27 **24** [y][1 Cor. 2:10] [z][Acts 15:28] **25** [a]ch. 3:11 **26** [b]See ver. 7 [c]See Heb. 3:6 [d]Ps. 2:8; [ch. 3:21; 20:4] **27** [e]Ps. 2:9 [f]ch. 12:5; 19:15 [g]Isai. 30:14; Jer. 19:11 **28** [h][2 Pet. 1:19]; See ch. 22:16

29 [t][See ver. 20 above]
Chapter 3 **1** [i]See ch. 1:4, 16 [j]1 Tim. 5:6 [k]See Luke 15:24 **2** [l]Acts 14:26 **3** [m][2 Tim. 1:13]

1 Or *your faith in me* 2 Greek *bondservants*

2:10 Be faithful. The city of Smyrna prided itself on faithfulness to Rome.

crown of life. Smyrna's goddess Cybele is pictured in coins with a crown patterned after a city battlement. The buildings on Smyrna's Mt. Pagos were said to look like a crown. Over against these claims, Jesus offers to give the true crown.

2:13 where Satan's throne is. Pergamum possessed the oldest temple in Asia Minor devoted to emperor worship.

2:14 Balaam. Balaam (Num. 22:5) gave Balak advice leading to Israel's harlotry in Moab (Num. 25:1–4). Jezebel (v. 20) and other professing Christians in the seven churches were indulging in pleasures offered by their pagan environment (17:1–19:10 note).

2:15 Nicolaitans. See note on v. 6.

2:17 hidden manna. Perhaps an allusion to the manna preserved in the Most Holy Place of the tabernacle (Ex. 16:33–35; Heb. 9:4). Christ promises to nourish the faithful with an unfailing supply of heavenly, spiritual food (John 6:32–58).

2:18 burnished bronze. Thyatira had a famous guild of bronze workers.

2:20 Jezebel. See 1 Kin. 16:31; 19:1, 2; 21:5–26; 2 Kin. 9:30–37. The woman at Thyatira is called Jezebel because, like the Old Testament figure, she seduced people to sexual immorality and idolatry, two major forms of indulgence in pagan Asia Minor. See notes 14:8 and 17:1–19:10.

you will not wake up, [n]I will come [o]like a thief, and you will not know at what hour I will come against you. **4** Yet you have still a few names in Sardis, people who have not [p]soiled their garments, and they will walk with me [q]in white, for they are [r]worthy. **5** [s]The one who conquers will be clothed thus in white garments, and I will never [t]blot his name out of [u]the book of life. [v]I will confess his name before my Father and before his angels. **6** [s]He who has an ear, let him hear what the Spirit says to the churches.'

To the Church in Philadelphia

7 "And to the angel of the church in Philadelphia write: 'The words of [w]the holy one, [x]the true one, [y]who has the key of David, [z]who opens and no one will shut, who shuts and no one opens.

8 " 'I know your works. Behold, I have set before you [a]an open door, which no one is able to shut. I know that you have but little power, and yet you have kept my word and have not denied my name. **9** Behold, I will make those of [b]the synagogue of Satan who say that they are Jews and are not, but lie—behold, [c]I will make them come and bow down before your feet and they will learn that [d]I have loved you. **10** [e]Because you have kept my word about patient endurance, I will keep you from the hour of trial that is coming on the whole world, to try [f]those who dwell on the earth. **11** [g]I am coming soon. [h]Hold fast what you have, so that no one may seize [i]your crown. **12** [j]The one who conquers, I will make him [k]a pillar in the temple of my God. Never shall he go out of it, and I will write on him [l]the name of my God, and [m]the name of the city of my God, [m]the new Jerusalem, [n]which comes down from my God out of heaven, and my own [o]new name. **13** [j]He who has an ear, let him hear what the Spirit says to the churches.'

To the Church in Laodicea

14 "And to the angel of the church in Laodicea write: 'The words of the [p]Amen, [q]the faithful and true witness, [r]the beginning of God's creation.

15 " 'I know your works: you are neither cold nor hot. [s]Would that you were either cold or hot! **16** So, because you are lukewarm, and neither hot nor cold, I will spit you out of my mouth. **17** [t]For you say, I am rich, I have prospered, and I need nothing, not realizing that you are wretched, pitiable, poor, [u]blind, and naked. **18** I counsel you [v]to buy from me gold refined by fire, so that you may be rich, and [w]white garments so that you may clothe yourself and [x]the shame of your nakedness may not be seen, and salve to anoint your eyes, [u]so that you may see. **19** [y]Those whom I love, I reprove and discipline, so be zealous and repent. **20** Behold, I stand at the door and [z]knock. [a]If anyone hears my voice and opens the door, [b]I will come in to him and eat with him, and he with me. **21** [c]The one who conquers, [d]I will grant him to sit with me on my throne, as [e]I also conquered and sat down with my Father on his throne. **22** [c]He who has an ear, let him hear what the Spirit says to the churches.' "

The Throne in Heaven

4 After this I looked, and behold, a door standing open in heaven! And the first voice, which I had heard speaking to me

3 [n]ch. 2:5 [o]ch. 16:15; Matt. 24:43; 1 Thess. 5:2, 4; 2 Pet. 3:10 **4** [p]Jude 23 [q]ch. 6:11; 7:9; [Eccles. 9:8] [r][Luke 20:35] **5** [s]See ch. 2:7 [t]See Ex. 32:32 [u]ch. 13:8; 17:8; 20:12, 15; 21:27; Phil. 4:3 [v]Matt. 10:32; Luke12:8 **6** [s][See ver. 5 above] **7** [w]ch. 6:10 [x]ver. 14; ch. 19:11; 1 John 5:20 [y]Isai. 22:22; [Luke 1:32] [z]Job 12:14; [Matt. 16:19] **8** [a]Acts 14:27; 1 Cor. 16:9; 2 Cor. 2:12; Col. 4:3 **9** [b]ch. 2:9 [c][Isai. 45:14; 49:23; 60:14] [d]Isai. 43:4 **10** [e]ch. 1:9; 2 Pet. 2:9 [f]ch. 6:10; 8:13; 11:10; 13:8, 14; 17:8 **11** [g]ch. 22:7, 12, 20 [h]ch. 2:25 [i]ch. 2:10 **12** [j]See ch. 2:7 [k]1 Kin. 7:21; 2 Chr. 3:17; Jer. 1:18; Gal. 2:9; [Ps. 23:6; 27:4] [l]ch. 14:1; 22:4 [m]ch. 21:2; Ezek. 48:35; [Gal. 4:26; Heb. 12:22] [n]ch. 21:10 [o]ch. 2:17 **13** [j][See ver. 1 above] **14** [p]2 Cor. 1:20 [q]ver. 7; ch. 1:5; 19:11; 22:6 [r]Col. 1:15, 18; [ch. 21:6; 22:13; Prov. 8:22] **15** [s][2 Pet. 2:21]

17 [t]Hos. 12:8; Zech. 11:5; 1 Cor. 4:8 [u]John 9:39-41; Eph. 1:18 **18** [v]Isai. 55:1; Matt. 13:44; 25:9 [Prov. 8:19] [w][ch. 19:8]; See ver. 4 [x]ch. 16:15 [u][See ver. 17 above] **19** [y]See Heb. 12:6 **20** [z][S. of S. 5:2] [a]Luke 12:36 [b]John 14:23; [Luke 24:29, 30] **21** [c]See ch. 2:7 [d]ch. 20:4; [ch. 2:26; John 12:26; 2 Tim. 2:12]; See Matt. 19:28 [e]ch. 5:5; 6:2; 17:14; John 16:33 **22** [c][See ver. 21 above]

3:3 I will come like a thief. The seemingly impregnable fortress of Sardis had in wartime been captured twice by surprise, probably at night. Christ warns that a similar experience will befall the church, unless its people wake up.

3:5 book of life. The heavenly roster of those destined to new life (13:8 note).

3:9 synagogue of Satan. See note 2:9.

3:12 a pillar in the temple. Philadelphia had suffered from earthquakes, making the promise of security and stability particularly pointed.

3:15 neither cold nor hot. Laodicea's water supply had to be provided from a distant source through pipes. The resulting water was lukewarm and barely drinkable. By contrast, the neighboring town of Hierapolis had medicinal hot springs, and neighboring Colossae was supplied by a cold mountain stream. Christ urges the church to be refreshing (cold) or medicinally healing (hot), rather than like the Laodicean water supply.

4:1–5:14 God appears in a beautiful scene of worship as the King of heaven and earth. He is surrounded by angelic courtiers (1 Kin. 22:19; Job 1:6; 2:1; Ps. 89:6, 7; Ezek. 1; Dan. 7:9, 10). His rule was established in creation (4:11), is exercised in the panorama of history (6:1–22:5), is brought to fulfillment through the Lamb (ch. 5; 22:1) and is celebrated in songs of praise (1:6 note). Revelation is preeminently a book about God and His greatness. The secrets of history and of spiritual conflict center on God Himself. The whole universe is destined to be filled with the glory (21:22, 23) and goodness of God (22:1–5), and with His praise (5:13). Hence the pattern for the outcome of history is revealed in miniature here (Matt. 6:10).

When God's people are beset by temptation or persecution, a revela-

[f]like a trumpet, said, [g]"Come up here, and
[h]I will show you what must take place after
this." **2**At once [i]I was in the Spirit, and
behold, [j]a throne stood in heaven, with
one seated on the throne. **3**And he who sat
there had the appearance of [k]jasper and
carnelian, and around the throne was [l]a
rainbow that had the appearance of an
emerald. **4**Around the throne were [m]twen-
ty-four thrones, and seated on the thrones
were twenty-four elders, [n]clothed in white
garments, with [o]golden crowns on their
heads. **5**From the throne came [p]flashes of
lightning, and rumblings[1] and peals of
thunder, and before the throne were burning [q]seven torches of fire, [r]which are the
seven spirits of God, **6**and before the
throne there was [s]as it were a sea of glass,
like crystal.

And around the throne, on each side of
the throne, are [t]four living creatures, [u]full
of eyes in front and behind: **7**[v]the first living creature like a lion, the second living
creature like an ox, the third living creature
with the face of a man, and the fourth living creature like an eagle in flight. **8**And the
four living creatures, [w]each of them with
six wings, are [x]full of eyes all around and
within, and [y]day and night they never cease
to say,

> [z]"Holy, holy, holy, is the Lord God
> Almighty,
> [a]who was and is and is to come!"

9And whenever the living creatures give
glory and honor and thanks to him who is
seated on the throne, [b]who lives forever
and ever, **10**the twenty-four elders [c]fall
down before him who is seated on the
throne and worship him who lives forever
and ever. They cast [d]their crowns before
the throne, saying,

> **11** [e]"Worthy are you, our Lord and God,
> to receive glory and honor and
> power,
> for [f]you created all things,
> and [g]by your will they existed and
> were created."

The Scroll and the Lamb

5 Then I saw in the right hand of him
who was seated on the throne [h]a

Chapter 4 **1** [f]ch. 1:10; [Ex. 19:19, 20] [g]ch. 11:12 [h]ch. 1:1, 19; 22:6 **2** [i]See ch. 1:10 [j]Ps. 11:4; 103:19; Isai. 66:1; Matt. 5:34; 23:22; See 1 Kin. 22:19 **3** [k]ch. 21:11 [l]Ezek. 1:28; [ch. 10:1; Gen. 9:13-17] **4** [m]ch. 11:16 [n]See ch. 3:4 [o]ver. 10; See James 1:12 **5** [p]ch. 8:5; 11:19; 16:18; [Ex. 19:16] [q][Zech. 4:2] [r]See ch. 1:4 **6** [s]ch. 15:2; [ch. 21:18, 21; Ps. 77:19] [t]Ezek. 1:5 [u]Ezek. 10:12 **7** [v][Ezek. 1:10; 10:14] **8** [w]Isai. 6:2 [x]ver. 6 [y]ch. 14:11 [z]Isai. 6:3 [a]See ch. 1:4 **9** [b]ch. 1:18; 5:13; 15:7; Dan. 4:34; 12:7 **10** [c]ch. 5:8, 14; 7:11; 11:16; 19:4 [d]ver. 4 **11** [e]ch. 5:12 [f]ch. 10:6; 14:7; Gen. 1:1; Acts 14:15 [g]Ps. 33:9-11; [Eph. 1:11]
Chapter 5 **1** [h]Ezek. 2:9, 10

1 Or *voices*, or *sounds*

tion of God's character and glory is the best remedy. His power guarantees the final victory, His justice guarantees vindication of the right, His goodness and magnificence guarantee blessing and comfort. The blood of the Lamb demonstrates that redemption has already been accomplished.

4:1 Come up here. Moses went up to Mount Sinai (Ex. 19:3, 20) and Paul was caught up to heaven (2 Cor. 12:2) to receive special revelations.

what must take place after this. See note 1:19.

4:2 in the Spirit. See note 1:10.

a throne stood in heaven. God's kingly rule is a fundamental theme of the book. In the Old Testament, the tabernacle (Ex. 25–40) and temple (1 Kin. 5–7; 2 Chr. 2–4) were shadows of God's throne room in heaven (Ex. 25:40; Heb. 8:5, 6; 9:1–14). John sees the heavenly original rather than an earthly copy. Revelation fittingly contains many allusions to the temple (3:12; 7:15; 11:19; 14:15, 17; 15:5–16:1; 16:17; 21:22) and to elements within it. For example, there are the lamps (1:12; 4:5), the living creatures like cherubim (4:6–9), incense and prayer (5:8), songs of praise like those offered by the Levitical singers in the Old Testament (4:8, 11; 5:9–13; 1 Chr. 16), a sacrifice (5:6, 9), the ark of the covenant (11:19), the altar (11:1), and the outer court (11:2).

one seated on the throne. The details of God's appearance are not described, reminding us that His greatness and glory always exceed human comprehension. See note 1:12–20.

4:4 twenty-four elders. These angelic ministers (7:13) are here called "elders" because of their wisdom. As God's cabinet officers, they must reflect His own wisdom, which is symbolized by age (Dan. 7:9). The term "elder" also suggests an analogy with the church's elders who serve on earth; hence, some have suggested the elders here are simply a representation of the church.

4:5 lightning. God exhibits His power in a manner analogous to His self-revelation at Mount Sinai (Ex. 19:16–19) and other divine appearances (8:5; 11:19; 16:18; Ps. 18:11–15; Ezek. 1:4). He reminds the church of the power of His voice (1:10, 15 and notes) and the final shaking of creation still to come (11:19; 21:1; Heb. 12:25–27).

seven torches. See note 1:12; cf. Zech. 4:2, 6. The sevenfold light of the Holy Spirit is the original light of which the seven-branched lampstand of Ex. 25:31–40 was a copy. The similarities with 1:12 suggest that the seven churches, as a true temple of God, are to give out light reflecting the very presence of God through His Spirit.

seven spirits of God. The Holy Spirit (1:4 note).

4:6 sea of glass. See 15:2; Ex. 24:10. This imagery might suggest a number of associations. The parallel verse in 15:2 calls to mind the waters of the Red Sea. The defeat of Pharaoh and the pushing back of the waters foreshadowed God's final victory over evil (Is. 51:9–11). If so, the sea of glass pictures waters subdued under God's power. Moreover, the extent and beauty of the crystal-like sea, when taken together with the precious stones in v. 3 and 21:18–21, suggest the magnificence and preciousness of God's throne. The numerous parallels elsewhere with the temple (4:2 note) might suggest that this sea is the heavenly counterpart of the sea in Solomon's temple (1 Kin. 7:23–25). Finally, the picture of heavenly water might suggest that God faithfully supplies water from heaven (Deut. 11:11). It is consistent with the style of Revelation to weave together a number of Old Testament images.

four living creatures. These angelic ministers of God are reminiscent of the living creatures or cherubim of Ezek. 1 and 10 and the seraphim of Is. 6. They are guardians and bearers of the throne of God, as in Gen. 3:24; Ex. 25:17–22; Ps. 18:10; 1 Chr. 28:18.

4:11 God's servants bring songs of praise as a fitting response to His glory and deeds (1:6 note; Ex. 15:11; Is. 6:3).

you created. The praise and imagery of ch. 4 focus on creation, asserting God's sovereignty over the universe (1:8 note).

5:1–14 John recounts two parts of a single magnificent vision of God's

scroll written within and on the back,
[i]sealed with seven seals. 2 And [j]I saw a
strong angel proclaiming with a loud voice,
"Who is worthy to open the scroll and
break its seals?" 3 And no one in heaven or
on earth or under the earth was able to
open the scroll or to look into it, 4 and I
began to weep loudly because no one was
found worthy to open the scroll or to look
into it. 5 And one of the elders said to me,
"Weep no more; behold, [k]the Lion [l]of the
tribe of Judah, [m]the Root of David, has conquered, so that he can open the scroll and
its seven seals."

6 And between the throne and the four
living creatures and among the elders I saw
[n]a Lamb standing, as though it had been
slain, with seven horns and with [o]seven
eyes, which are [p]the seven spirits of God
sent out into all the earth. 7 And he went
and took the scroll from the right hand of
him who was seated on the throne. 8 And
when he had taken the scroll, the four living creatures and the twenty-four elders
[q]fell down before the Lamb, [r]each holding
a harp, and [s]golden bowls full of incense,
[t]which are the prayers of the saints. 9 And
they sang [u]a new song, saying,

"Worthy are you to take the scroll
and to open its seals,
for [v]you were slain, and by your
blood [w]you ransomed people
for God
from [x]every tribe and language and
people and nation,
10 and you have made them [y]a kingdom
and priests to our God,
and they shall reign on the earth."

11 Then I looked, and I heard around the
throne and the living creatures and the elders the voice of many angels, numbering
[z]myriads of myriads and thousands of
thousands, 12 saying with a loud voice,
[a]"Worthy is the Lamb who was slain, to
receive power and wealth and wisdom and
might and honor and glory and blessing!"
13 And I heard [b]every creature in heaven
and on earth and under the earth and in
the sea, and all that is in them, saying, "To
him who sits on the throne and to the
Lamb be blessing and honor and glory and
might forever and ever!" 14 And the four living creatures [c]said, "Amen!" and the elders
[d]fell down and worshiped.

The Seven Seals

6 Now I watched when the Lamb
opened one of [e]the seven seals, and I
heard [f]one of the four living creatures say
[g]with a voice like thunder, [h]"Come!" 2 And

1 [i]Isai. 29:11; Dan. 12:4
2 [j][ch. 10:1; 18:21]
5 [k]Gen. 49:9 [l]Heb. 7:14 [m]ch. 22:16; Isai. 11:1, 10; Rom. 15:12
6 [n]ver. 9, 12; ch. 13:8; Isai. 53:7; John 1:29, 36; 1 Pet. 1:19 [o]Zech. 3:9; 4:10 [p]See ch. 1:4
8 [q]See ch. 4:10 [r]ch. 14:2; 15:2 [s][ch. 15:7] [t]ch. 8:3, 4; Ps. 141:2
9 [u]ch. 14:3; See Ps. 33:3
[v]ver. 6 [w]ch. 14:3, 4; See 2 Pet. 2:1 [x]ch. 7:9; 11:9; 14:6; See Dan. 3:4
10 [y]See ch. 1:6
11 [z]Dan. 7:10; [Heb. 12:22]
12 [a]ch. 4:11
13 [b]Ps. 145:21; 150:6
14 [c]ch. 7:12; 19:4 [d]ver. 8; See ch. 4:10
Chapter 6
1 [e]ch. 5:1, 5-7 [f]ch. 4:7 [g]ch. 14:2; 19:6 [h]ch. 22:20

glory in chs. 4 and 5 (4:1–5:14 note). A second dramatic act within the vision is introduced in 5:1. From creation in 4:11, the action shifts to a focus on redemption and re-creation. God's purposes of redemption and rule can be accomplished only through One who is uniquely worthy—Jesus Christ. He is simultaneously the fierce Lion of the tribe of Judah, warring against God's enemies (17:14; 19:11–21), and the gentle Lamb that has been slain, who purchased His people with the blood of His atoning sacrifice (vv. 9, 10). Only God in His trinitarian fullness can accomplish these magnificent purposes. Note the presence of the Father ("him who was seated on the throne," vv. 1, 7), the Son ("Lamb," vv. 6, 7), and the Spirit of God (v. 6; 1:4 note), who is the horns and eyes of the Lamb.

This chapter constitutes the opening scene for the first cycle of judgments that lead up to the Second Coming of Christ (Introduction: Outline). The Lamb and the sealed scroll are introduced. The opening of the seals in 6:1–8:1 sets in motion a series of judgments that have their origin in God's throne and purpose, and that issue in His final manifestation as Judge. See notes 6:12–17 and 8:1.

5:1 scroll. The scroll might represent a number of things—God's covenant, His law, His promises, His plans, or perhaps a legal will. The close parallel with Dan. 12:4 makes it likely that the scroll is a heavenly book containing God's plan and the destiny of the world. The unsealing of the book implies the accomplishment of the things God has purposed. John weeps (v. 4) because he longs for God's purposes to be accomplished (Matt. 6:10), and it is hard to see how that can happen. However, through Christ's decisive sacrifice a whole host is redeemed (v. 9), and the purposes of the Exodus and of man's original dominion are finally fulfilled (v. 10).

5:6 as though it had been slain. "As though" is used because the Lamb was slain, but is now alive "forevermore" (1:18). Only on the basis of Christ's death and resurrection can God's purposes for history be accomplished.

seven horns. Horns frequently represent power (Ps. 89:17; 92:10; Dan. 7:8; 8:3), in this case the power of Christ's Spirit-filled eternal life (John 3:34; Rom. 8:11; 1 Cor. 15:45).

seven spirits of God. See note 1:4.

5:9 every tribe and language and people and nation. In spiritual battle, both God and Satan claim allegiances on a universal scale (7:9; 10:11; 11:9; 12:5; 13:7; 14:6, 8; 15:4; 17:15; 18:3; 19:15; 20:3). Through the merit and power of Christ's sacrifice, God's purposes will be accomplished, fulfilling the Abrahamic promise of blessing to all nations (7:9–17; 21:24–27; Gen. 12:3; 22:18; Is. 60:1–5).

5:10 kingdom and priests. See note 1:6.

5:11–14 Praises that started in the inner circles of worship around the throne now extend outwards until they fill the universe.

6:1–8:1 Judgments from God's throne unfold as the seven seals are opened one by one. The participation of the Lamb reminds us that such judgments are based on His unique qualifications and accomplishments (ch. 5). In formal structure, 5:1–8:1 runs parallel to 8:2–11:19. Each has an opening scene introducing the origin of the judgments (ch. 5; 8:2–6). Six judgments follow (ch. 6; 8:7–9:21). A dramatic interlude promises care for God's people (ch. 7; 10:1–11:14). The seventh and climactic judgment follows the interlude (8:1; 11:15–19; Introduction: Outline). The seven judgments move forward toward the Second Coming, which occurs in 6:12–17 and 11:15–19. The first four of the seven judgments have an inner unity. The four living creatures of 4:6 and the four horsemen of Zech. 1:8 are reflected in 6:1–8. The four major regions of the world (dry land, sea, fresh water, and sky) are considered in 8:7–12.

6:1–8 The four horsemen represent conquest, war, famine, and death.

I looked, and behold, [i]a white horse! And
[j]its rider had a bow, and [k]a crown was
given to him, and he came out [l]conquer-
ing, and to conquer.
3When he opened the second seal, I
heard [m]the second living creature say,
"Come!" **4**And out came another horse,
[n]bright red. Its rider was permitted [o]to take
peace from the earth, so that men should
slay one another, and he was given a great
sword.
5When he opened the third seal, I heard
the [m]third living creature say, "Come!" And
I looked, and behold, [p]a black horse! And
its rider had a pair of scales in his hand.
6And I heard what seemed to be a voice in
the midst of the four living creatures, saying, [q]"A quart[1] of wheat for a denarius,[2]
and three quarts of barley for a denarius,
and [r]do not harm the oil and wine!"
7When he opened the fourth seal, I
heard the voice of [m]the fourth living creature say, "Come!" **8**And I looked, and
behold, [s]a pale horse! And its rider's name
was Death, and Hades followed him. And
they were given authority over a fourth of
the earth, to kill [t]with sword and with
famine and with pestilence and [u]by wild
beasts of the earth.
9When he opened the fifth seal, I saw
under [v]the altar [w]the souls of those who
had been slain [x]for the word of God and for
[y]the witness they had borne. **10**They cried
out with a loud voice, "O Sovereign Lord,
[z]holy and true, [a]how long [b]before you will
judge and [c]avenge our blood on [d]those
who dwell on the earth?" **11**Then they were
each given [e]a white robe and [f]told to rest a
little longer, [g]until the number of their fellow servants[3] and their brothers[4] [h]should
be complete, who were to be killed as they
themselves had been.
12When he opened the sixth seal, I
looked, and behold, [i]there was a great
earthquake, and [j]the sun became black as
[k]sackcloth, the full moon became like
blood, **13**and [l]the stars of the sky fell to the
earth [m]as the fig tree sheds its winter fruit
when shaken by a gale. **14**[n]The sky vanished [m]like a scroll that is being rolled up,
and [o]every mountain and island was
removed from its place. **15**Then the kings of
the earth and the great ones and the generals and the rich and the powerful, and
everyone, slave[5] and free, [p]hid themselves
in the caves and among the rocks of the
mountains, **16**[q]calling to the mountains and
rocks, "Fall on us and hide us from the face
of [r]him who is seated on the throne, and
from the wrath of the Lamb, **17**for [s]the great
day of their wrath has come, and [t]who can
stand?"

The 144,000 of Israel Sealed

7 After this I saw four angels standing at
the four corners of the earth, holding

2 [i]Zech. 6:3; [ch. 19:11, 19, 21] [j][Ps. 45:4, 5; Hab. 3:8, 9; Zech. 9:13, 14] [k]ch. 14:14; [Zech. 6:11] [l]See ch. 3:21
3 [m]ch. 4:7
4 [n]Zech. 1:8; 6:2 [o][Matt. 10:34; 24:6, 7]
5 [m][See ver. 3 above] [p]Zech. 6:2
6 [q][Ezek. 4:10, 11; 5:10, 16] [r]ch. 7:3; 9:4
7 [m][See ver. 3 above]
8 [s][Zech. 6:3] [t]Ezek. 14:21 [u]Lev. 26:22; Deut. 32:24
9 [v]ch. 14:18; 16:7 [w]ch. 20:4 [x]ch. 1:9 [y]See ch. 1:2
10 [z][Ps. 94:3; Zech. 1:12] [a]ch. 3:7 [b]ch. 11:18; 19:2 [c]Ps. 79:10; 119:84; Luke 18:7, 8 [d]See ch. 3:10
11 [e]ch. 3:4; 7:9 [f]ch. 14:13 [g][Heb. 11:40] [h][Gen. 15:16]
12 [i]ch. 11:13; 16:18; [Heb. 12:26] [j]See Matt. 24:29 [k]Isai. 50:3
13 [l][ch. 8:10; 9:1] [m]Isai. 34:4
14 [n][ch. 20:11; 21:1] [m][See ver. 13 above] [o]ch. 16:20; [Isai. 54:10; Jer. 4:24; Ezek. 38:20; Nah. 1:5]
15 [p]Isai. 2:19, 21 **16** [q]Hos. 10:8; Luke 23:30 [r]ch. 4:2 **17** [s]Jer. 30:7; Joel 2:11, 31 [t]Ezra 9:15; Ps. 76:7; Mal. 3:2; Luke 21:36

1 Greek *choinix*, a dry measure equal to about a quart 2 A *denarius* was a day's wage for a laborer 3 Greek *fellow bondservants* 4 Or *brothers and sisters.* The plural Greek word *adelphoi* (translated "brothers") refers to siblings in a family. In New Testament usage, depending on the context, *adelphoi* may refer either to men or to both men and women who are siblings (brothers and sisters) in God's family, the church 5 Or *servant*; Greek *bondservant*

These calamities characterize an indefinite period before the Second Coming (Mark 13:6–8). Such things occurred in the tumults of the Roman Empire, and may be expected to occur now and before the Second Coming. The imagery is capable of multiple applications throughout the history of the church (Introduction: Interpretive Difficulties). The seven churches were exhorted to put their confidence, not in the peace and prosperity supposedly achieved by Roman rule, but in God and His promises of a new world (2:17; 3:12; 21:4). When tumults occurred, they were assured that the Lamb was still in control—in fact, the tumults issued from His worthiness to break the seals and from the voice of the living creatures. Such judgments represented the chastening hand of God on a rebellious world (9:20, 21). The saints would be cared for in the midst of such trials (ch. 7). They were sealed as a mark of ownership and protection (7:1–10; 9:4) and given perfect rest in the end (7:15–17). Such promises hold for saints throughout the church age, no less than for the seven churches.

6:2 white horse. On the basis of similarities with 19:11, some think that Christ appears here, conquering through the gospel. More probably, the white horse symbolizes conquest as one form of earthly calamity. Thus the calamity of vv. 1, 2 is parallel to the calamities of vv. 3–8 (6:1–8:1 note).

6:6 A quart of wheat. Famine will come, so severe that a laborer's entire wages will go merely for food. Families will have to buy barley, a lower quality of grain. Oil and wine are spared, perhaps an indication that the rich will still be able to indulge themselves.

6:9–11 Martyred saints cry out for justice, not because of selfish desires, but in tune with the justice of God's throne (v. 10). They desire to see God's justice fully manifested.

6:10 those . . . on the earth. Revelation shows that humanity consists of two groups: the people of God, whose citizenship is in heaven (Phil. 3:20), and, in opposition to them, the rebellious earth-dwellers (v. 15; 8:13; 11:10; 13:3, 8, 12, 14; 17:2, 8).

6:12–17 All dwellers on earth and in the created universe itself experience God's judgment. These verses give the first of seven descriptions in Revelation of events associated with the Second Coming (Introduction: Characteristics and Themes: Literary Form). In Luke 21:25–27 and Mark 13:24–26 the coming of the Son of Man immediately follows unusual phenomena involving the sun, moon, and stars. The mention of seven types of people (v. 15) suggests complete judgment, as does the characterization of "the great day of . . . wrath" (vv. 16, 17). Since this world is to be so thoroughly shaken, saints must place their hope in God (Luke 12:32–34; 1 Cor. 7:29–31; Heb. 12:25–29).

7:1–17 The announcement of the seventh seal is dramatically delayed

back [u]the four winds of the earth, [v]that no
wind might blow on earth or sea or against
any tree. 2 Then I saw another angel ascending [w]from the rising of the sun, with [x]the
seal of the living God, and he called with a
loud voice to the four angels who had been
given power to harm earth and sea, 3 saying, [y]"Do not harm the earth or the sea or
the trees, until we have sealed the servants[1]
of our God [z]on their foreheads." 4 And [a]I
heard the number of the sealed, 144,000,
sealed from every tribe of the sons of Israel:

5 12,000 from the tribe of Judah were
sealed,
12,000 from the tribe of Reuben,
12,000 from the tribe of Gad,
6 12,000 from the tribe of Asher,
12,000 from the tribe of Naphtali,
12,000 from the tribe of Manasseh,
7 12,000 from the tribe of Simeon,
12,000 from the tribe of Levi,
12,000 from the tribe of Issachar,
8 12,000 from the tribe of Zebulun,
12,000 from the tribe of Joseph,
12,000 from the tribe of Benjamin
were sealed.

A Great Multitude from Every Nation

9 After this I looked, and behold, [b]a great
multitude that no one could number,
[c]from every nation, from all tribes and peoples and languages, standing before the
throne and before the Lamb, [d]clothed in
white robes, with [e]palm branches in their
hands, 10 and crying out with a loud voice,
[f]"Salvation belongs to our God who sits on
the throne, and to the Lamb!" 11 And all the
angels were standing around the throne
and around the elders and [g]the four living
creatures, and they [h]fell on their faces
before the throne and worshiped God,
12 [i]saying, "Amen! Blessing and glory and
wisdom and thanksgiving and honor and
power and might be to our God forever
and ever! Amen."
13 Then one of the elders addressed me,
saying, "Who are these, [d]clothed in white
robes, and from where have they come?"
14 I said to him, "Sir, you know." And he
said to me, "These are the ones coming out
of [j]the great tribulation. [k]They have washed
their robes and [l]made them white [m]in the
blood of the Lamb.

15 "Therefore they are before the throne
of God,
and [n]serve him day and night in
his temple;
and he who sits on the throne [o]will
shelter them with his presence.
16 [p]They shall hunger no more, neither
thirst anymore;
[q]the sun shall not strike them,
nor any scorching heat.
17 For the Lamb in the midst of the
throne [r]will be their shepherd,
and he will guide them to springs
of [s]living water,
and [t]God will wipe away every tear
from their eyes."

The Seventh Seal and the Golden Censer

8 When the Lamb opened [u]the seventh
seal, there was silence in heaven for
about half an hour. 2 Then I saw the seven
angels [v]who stand before God, and seven

Chapter 7
1 [u]Jer. 49:36; Dan. 7:2 [v][ver. 3]
2 [w]ch. 16:12 [x]ch. 9:4
3 [y]ch. 6:6; 9:4 [z]ch. 14:1; 22:4; Ezek. 9:4; [ch. 13:16; Ezek. 3:8, 9]
4 [a]ch. 9:16
9 [b][Rom. 11:25] [c]ch. 5:9 [d]ver. 14; See ch. 3:4 [e][Lev. 23:40; John 12:13]
10 [f]ch. 12:10; 19:1; See Ps. 3:8
11 [g]ch. 4:6 [h]See ch. 4:10
12 [i]ch. 5:14; 19:4; [1 Chr. 29:10, 11]
13 [d][See ver. 4 above]
14 [j]See Matt. 24:21 [k]ch. 22:14; [Isai. 1:18; Zech. 3:3-5] [l][Dan. 12:10; 1 John 1:7] [m]ch. 1:5
15 [n]ch. 22:3 [o]ch. 21:3; [Isai. 4:5, 6]
16 [p]Isai. 49:10 [q]Ps. 121:6
17 [r]Ps. 23:1, 2; [Matt. 2:6]; See John 10:11 [s]ch. 22:1; [Ps. 36:8, 9; John 4:14] [t]ch. 21:4; Isai. 25:8
Chapter 8
1 [u]ch. 5:1; 6:1
2 [v]Luke 1:19

1 Greek *bondservants*

while the saints receive assurance that God knows them and protects them in the midst of the calamities depicted in ch. 6.

7:3 sealed. The faithful are sealed as a sign of protection and ownership (9:4; 14:1; Ezek. 9:4).

7:4–8 The balanced numbering suggests that "twelve" is a symbolic number for the fullness of the people of God. The early association of the tribe of Dan with idolatry (Judg. 18) may explain its omission from this list (21:8; 22:15). Some think that the 144,000 here includes only Jewish believers. But the "servants of our God" in v. 3 must include Gentile saints as well. The equal status of Gentiles and Jews in the seven churches (Eph. 2:11–22) and the promises associated only with the 144,000 (9:4; 14:1–5) confirm this. According to vv. 1–8, the saints are known by God individually, and none slips by His care (Matt. 10:30); according to vv. 9–17, no human can count their number.

7:14 great tribulation. Many identify the "great tribulation" with a final period of persecution shortly before the Second Coming. But tribulations for Christians occur throughout the church age, so that the whole age can also be characterized as a time of tribulation (2 Thess. 1:5, 6; 2 Tim. 3:1, 12). The passage was intended to comfort first-century Christians as well as those in the final crisis. See note 11:2.

8:1 silence in heaven. The next event after 6:12–17 would most naturally be the appearing of Christ Himself as the final Warrior and Judge (Mark 13:24–26). The silence may indicate that heaven stands in awe at His presence (Hab. 2:20; Zeph. 1:7). At this early point, the seer is not given a fuller picture disclosing the events of final judgment and re-creation. This reserve maintains the reader's interest for later cycles of judgment.

8:2–11:19 Seven angels blow seven trumpets. The trumpets set in motion seven judgments leading up to the Second Coming. The trumpets form the second cycle out of several that depict God's rule over history from various angles. On the structure of these judgments, see note 6:1–8:1. Like the trumpets used in the battle of Jericho (Josh. 6), these trumpets lead up to the fall of the worldly city (11:8 note, 11:13), and in the seventh trumpet the complete victory of God arrives. The trumpet plagues are reminiscent of the plagues on Egypt, signifying God's judgments on idolatrous power.

The seven seals began with announcements of riders commissioned to bring calamities (6:1–8 note). The seven trumpets, by contrast, contain

trumpets were given to them. 3 And another angel came and stood [w]at the altar with
a golden censer, and he was given much
incense to offer with [x]the prayers of all the
saints on [y]the golden altar before the
throne, 4 and [z]the smoke of the incense,
with the prayers of the saints, rose before
God from the hand of the angel. 5 Then the
angel took the censer and [a]filled it with fire
from the altar and threw it on the earth,
and [b]there were peals of [c]thunder, rumblings,[1] flashes of lightning, and an earthquake.

The Seven Trumpets

6 Now the seven angels who had the
seven trumpets prepared to blow them.
7 The first angel blew his trumpet, and
there followed [d]hail and [e]fire, mixed with
blood, and these were thrown upon the
earth. And a [f]third of the earth was burned
up, and a third of [g]the trees were burned
up, and all green grass was burned up.
8 The second angel blew his trumpet, and
something like [h]a great mountain, burning
with fire, was thrown into the sea, and a
third of the sea [i]became blood. 9 A third of
the living creatures in the sea died, and a
third of [j]the ships were destroyed.
10 The third angel blew his trumpet, and
[k]a great star fell from heaven, blazing like a
torch, and it fell on a third of the rivers and
on [l]the springs of water. 11 The name of the
star is Wormwood.[2] A third of the waters
[m]became wormwood, and many people
died from the water, [n]because it had been
made bitter.
12 The fourth angel blew his trumpet, and
a third of [o]the sun was struck, and a third
of the moon, and a third of the stars, so
that a third of their light might be darkened, and a third of the day might be kept
from shining, and likewise a third of the
night.
13 Then I looked, and I heard an eagle
crying with a loud voice as it flew directly
overhead, [p]"Woe, woe, woe to those who
dwell on the earth, at the blasts of the other
trumpets that the three angels are about to
blow!"

9 And the fifth angel blew his trumpet,
and [q]I saw a star fallen from heaven to
earth, and he was given [r]the key to the
shaft of [s]the bottomless pit.[3] 2 He opened
the shaft of the bottomless pit, and from
the shaft [t]rose smoke like the smoke of a
great furnace, and [u]the sun and the air
were darkened with the smoke from the
shaft. 3 Then from the smoke came [v]locusts
on the earth, and they were given power
like the power of scorpions of the earth.
4 They were told [w]not to harm [x]the grass of
the earth or any green plant or any tree, but
only those people who do not have [y]the
seal of God on their foreheads. 5 They were

3 [w]Amos 9:1 [x]ch. 5:8 [y]ch. 9:13; Ex. 30:1, 3
4 [z][Ps. 141:2]
5 [a]Lev. 16:12 [b][Ps. 18:7, 8] [c]See ch. 4:5
7 [d]Ex. 9:23, 24; Ps. 18:13; Ezek. 38:22 [e]Joel 2:30 [f]ver. 8-12; ch. 9:15, 18; 12:4; [Zech. 13:8, 9] [g]ch. 9:4; Isai. 2:13
8 [h]Jer. 51:25; [Mark 11:23] [i]ch. 11:6; [Ex. 7:17, 19]
9 [j]Isai. 2:16
10 [k]ch. 9:1; [Isai. 14:12] [l]ch. 14:7; 16:4
11 [m]Deut. 29:18; Jer. 9:15; 23:15 [n][Ex. 15:23]
12 [o][Ex. 10:21-23; Isai. 13:10; 30:26]
13 [p][ch. 9:12; 11:14]
Chapter 9
1 [q]ch. 8:10; [ch. 12:9; Luke 10:18] [r]See ch. 1:18 [s]ver. 2, 11; ch. 11:7; 17:8; 20:1, 3; Luke 8:31; Rom. 10:7
2 [t][Gen. 19:28; Isai. 34:10] [u][Joel 2:10]
3 [v]See Ex. 10:4
4 [w]ch. 6:6; 7:3 [x]ch. 8:7 [y]See ch. 7:2, 3

[1] Or *voices*, or *sounds* [2] *Wormwood* is the name of a plant and of the bitter-tasting extract derived from it [3] Greek *the abyss*; also verses 2, 11

descriptions of the calamities themselves. The intensity of judgment has increased. Yet still some things are spared: most of the trumpet plagues fall on a third of the people or the land, not on all; the locust plague of 9:1–12 is over after five months; some people survive the collapse of the city in 11:13. By contrast, the later judgments with the bowls (15:1–16:21) are thoroughly devastating.

8:2–6 The trumpet judgments issue from God's angels, who stand before His throne (v. 2). The vision of chs. 4; 5 remains an anchor point for this new cycle of visions. Like the seal judgments of 6:1–8:1, these judgments are executed according to God's plan and in accord with His orders. The prayers of the saints play a notable part in originating the judgments (vv. 3, 4).

8:7–12 The first four trumpet plagues strike the four major regions of creation: land, sea, fresh water, and sky. The first four bowls affect the same four regions (16:1–9). Within the period of the early church, these visions were fulfilled both through natural calamities and through analogous spiritual calamities afflicting the souls of the wicked. In such apocalyptic imagery, the one type of calamity can represent the other. The general principles can be applied more broadly. Both human beings and the natural world undergo stress until the time of final renewal (Rom. 8:18–25). Final destruction of the natural universe, as well as the judgment of human beings, accompanies the Second Coming (2 Pet. 3:10, 12).

8:7 hail and fire. Parallel to Ex. 9:23, 24.

8:8 blood. Parallel to Ex. 7:14–24.

8:12 darkened. Parallel to Ex. 10:21–23.

8:13 Woe. A typical beginning to a prophetic oracle (e.g., Amos 5:18; 6:1). The three last trumpets are grouped together as three woes (9:12; 11:14). These plagues explicitly differentiate between the righteous and the wicked, as did the earlier Egyptian plagues.

9:1–12 The trumpet blast sets in motion a horrific army of locusts, energized by demonic sources (vv. 1, 2). The imagery derives from Ex. 10:13–15 and Joel 2:1–11, where a literal locust plague foreshadows even more devastating judgment coming from a divinely commissioned army (Joel 2:11). Their terrorizing powers compare only to those of the beast (13:1–10). These infernal monsters attack only the wicked, not the saints (v. 4).

The wicked sometimes suffer even in this life as a preview of their final punishment (20:11–15). According to idealist interpreters (Introduction: Interpretive Difficulties), the vision depicts the self-defeating and tormenting nature of wickedness in the human soul. Powers from the abyss attack not the saints but only the wicked. Historicists have generally seen the vision as a depiction of Islamic conquest of a degenerate Western Europe (A.D. 612–762), but such an application would be only one embodiment of the principle, and an imperfect one at that. Futurists understand the vision as a supernatural plague of demonic spirits, to be loosed on the earth shortly before the Second Coming. The fundamental principle is the same in all these interpretations, and multiple applications of the principle are possible.

allowed to torment them [z]for five months,
but not to kill them, and their torment was
like the torment of a scorpion when it
stings someone. 6 And in those days [a]peo-
ple will seek death and will not find it.
They will long to die, but death will flee
from them.
7 [b]In appearance the locusts were like
horses prepared for battle: [c]on their heads
were what looked like crowns of gold; their
faces were [d]like human faces, 8 their hair
like women's hair, and [e]their teeth like
lions' teeth; 9 they had breastplates like
breastplates of iron, and the noise of their
wings was [f]like the noise of many chariots
with [g]horses rushing into battle. 10 They
have tails and stings like scorpions, and
their power to hurt people [h]for five months
is in their tails. 11 They have [i]as king over
them the angel of the bottomless pit. His
name in Hebrew is [j]Abaddon, and in Greek
he is called Apollyon.[1]
12 [k]The first woe has passed; behold, two
woes are still to come.
13 Then the sixth angel blew his trumpet,
and I heard a voice from [l]the four horns of
the golden altar before God, 14 saying to the
sixth angel who had the trumpet, "Release
[m]the four angels who are bound at [n]the
great river Euphrates." 15 So the four angels,
who had been prepared for the hour, the
day, the month, and the year, were released
[o]to kill a third of mankind. 16 The number
of [p]mounted troops was [q]twice ten thousand times ten thousand; [r]I heard their
number. 17 And this is how I saw the horses in my vision and those who rode them:
they wore breastplates the color of fire and
of sapphire[2] and of sulfur, and the heads of
the horses were [s]like lions' heads, and fire
and smoke and sulfur came out of their
mouths. 18 By these three plagues a third of
mankind was killed, by the fire and smoke
and sulfur coming out of their mouths.
19 For the power of the horses is in their
mouths and in their tails, for their tails are
like serpents with heads, and by means of
them they wound.
20 The rest of mankind, who were not
killed by these plagues, [t]did not repent of
[u]the works of their hands nor give up worshiping [v]demons [w]and idols of gold and silver and bronze and stone and wood, which
cannot see or hear or walk, 21 nor did they
repent of their murders or their [x]sorceries
or their sexual immorality or their thefts.

The Angel and the Little Scroll

10 Then I saw another mighty angel
coming down from heaven,
wrapped in a cloud, with [y]a rainbow over
his head, and [z]his face was like the sun,
and [a]his legs like pillars of fire. 2 [b]He had a
little scroll open in his hand. And he set his
right foot on the sea, and his left foot on
the land, 3 and called out with a loud voice,
[c]like a lion roaring. When he called out,
the seven thunders sounded. 4 And when
the seven thunders had sounded, I was
about to write, but I heard a voice from
heaven saying, [d]"Seal up what the seven
thunders have said, and do not write it
down." 5 And the angel whom I saw standing on the sea and on the land [e]raised his
right hand to heaven 6 and swore by [f]him
who lives forever and ever, [g]who created
heaven and what is in it, the earth and
what is in it, and the sea and what is in it,
that there would be no more delay, 7 but
that [h]in the days of the trumpet call to be

5 [z]ver. 10
6 [a]Job 3:21; 7:15, 16; Jer. 8:3
7 [b]Joel 2:4 [c][Nah. 3:17] [d]Dan. 7:8
8 [e]Joel 1:6
9 [f]Joel 2:5 [g]Jer. 8:6; [Job 39:21-25]
10 [h]ver. 5
11 [i][Job 18:14; Prov. 30:27; Eph. 2:2] [j]See Job 26:6
12 [k][ch. 8:13; 11:14]
13 [l]Ex. 30:3
14 [m][ch. 7:1] [n]ch. 16:12
15 [o]See ch. 8:7
16 [p]Ezek. 38:4 [q][Ps. 68:17; Dan. 7:10] [r]ch. 7:4
17 [s][1 Chr. 12:8; Isai. 5:28, 29]
20 [t]See ch. 2:21 [u]Deut. 31:29; Jer. 1:16; 25:14 [v]See 1 Cor. 10:20 [w]Ps. 115:4-7; 135:15-17; Dan. 5:23
21 [x]ch. 21:8; 22:15; Gal. 5:20

Chapter 10
1 [y]Ezek. 1:28 [z]ch. 1:16; Matt. 17:2 [a]ch. 1:15
2 [b]ver. 8-10
3 [c]Joel 3:16; Amos 1:2
4 [d]Dan. 8:26; 12:4, 9; [ch. 22:10]
5 [e]See Gen. 14:22
6 [f]See ch. 4:9 [g]See ch. 4:11
7 [h]ch. 11:15

[1] *Abaddon* means *destruction*; *Apollyon* means *destroyer* [2] Greek *hyacinth*

9:5 five months. A normal locust swarm would move on after a few days. This demonic swarm stays for the whole period during which locusts might be seen.

9:11 Apollyon. See text note. There may be an ironic allusion to Nero or Domitian, both of whom saw themselves as similar to the Greek god Apollo.

9:13–21 The Roman Empire feared an attack of the Parthians from beyond the Euphrates (v. 14), the eastern border of the empire. But all such fears are dwarfed by what Revelation pictures. Outside threats experienced by the Roman Empire presage the final day of cosmic battle (16:14). The events of these verses are similar to those of 16:14, but the consequences are less severe, leaving time for repentance (vv. 18–21).

10:1–11:14 Between the sixth and seventh trumpet there is an interlude with two scenes (ch. 10 and 11:1–14). Both scenes concern the role of God's people and their prophetic witness during the time of trial. In the first scene John receives prophetic messages and is commissioned to proclaim them. The second depicts the history of the two witnesses and their larger environment.

10:1–11 Dan. 10:5, 6 and the call of Ezekiel (Ezek. 2:1–3:11) are paralleled in this chapter. John receives the prophetic messages of a "little scroll." Some have thought that the scroll contains the contents of 12:1–22:5, and that 12:1 begins a new major division in the structure of Revelation. More likely, the vision of this chapter speaks in a general fashion of John's receiving power to continue to prophesy. Though John's role is unique, he is still in many ways an example and pattern for the church's witness (1:2 note). The church must take to heart the message of the book (1:3), live by it, and be ready to communicate its implications to "peoples and nations and languages and kings" (v. 11).

10:1, 2 A mighty angel appears, reflecting the very glory of God and His throne room (cf. 1:14–16; Ezek. 1:27, 28; Dan. 10:5, 6). The angel's majesty reinforces the authority and divine source of the message.

sounded by the seventh angel, the mystery
of God would be fulfilled, [i]just as he
announced to his servants[1] the prophets.
8 Then the voice that I had heard from
heaven spoke to me again, saying, "Go,
take the scroll that is open in the hand of
the angel who is standing on the sea and
on the land." 9 So I went to the angel and
told him to give me the little scroll. And he
said to me, [j]"Take and [k]eat it; it will make
your stomach bitter, but in your mouth it
will be sweet as honey." 10 And I took the
little scroll from the hand of the angel and
ate it. It was sweet as honey in my mouth,
but when I had eaten it my stomach was
made bitter. 11 And I was told, [l]"You must
again prophesy about many peoples and
nations and languages and kings."

The Two Witnesses

11 Then I was given [m]a measuring rod
like a staff, and I was told, "Rise
and measure the temple of God and the
altar and those who worship there, 2 but do
not measure [n]the court outside the temple;
leave that out, for [o]it is given over to the
nations, and they will trample the holy city
for [p]forty-two months. 3 And I will grant
authority to my two witnesses, and they
will prophesy for [p]1,260 days, [q]clothed in
sackcloth."
4 These are [r]the two olive trees and the
two lampstands that stand before the Lord
of the earth. 5 And if anyone would harm
them, [s]fire pours from their mouth and
consumes their foes. If anyone would harm
them, [t]this is how he is doomed to be
killed. 6 They have the power [u]to shut the
sky, that no rain may fall during the days of
their prophesying, and they have power
over the waters to turn them into blood
and [v]to strike the earth with every kind of
plague, as often as they desire. 7 And when
they have finished their testimony, [w]the
beast that rises from [x]the bottomless pit[2]
[y]will make war on them and conquer them
and kill them, 8 and their dead bodies will
lie in the street of the great city that symbolically[3] is called [z]Sodom and [a]Egypt,
where their Lord was crucified. 9 For three
and a half days some from the peoples and
tribes and languages and nations will gaze
at their dead bodies and [b]refuse to let them
be placed in a tomb, 10 and [c]those who

7 [i][Amos 3:7] 9 [j]Ezek. 2:8; 3:1-3 [k][Jer. 15:16] 11 [l][Ezek. 37:4] **Chapter 11** 1 [m]ch. 21:15, 16; Ezek. 40:3; Zech. 2:1 2 [n]Ezek. 40:17, 20 [o]See Luke 21:24 [p]ch. 12:6; 13:5 3 [p][See ver. 2 above] [q]Isai. 20:2 4 [r]Zech. 4:3, 11, 14; [Ps. 52:8; Jer. 11:16] 5 [s][2 Kin. 1:10, 12; Jer. 5:14] [t][Num. 16:29, 35] 6 [u][1 Kin. 17:1; Luke 4:25; James 5:17] [v][Ex. ch. 7–10; 1 Sam. 4:8] 7 [w]ch. 17:8; [ch. 13:1] [x]See ch. 9:1 [y]Dan. 7:21 8 [z]Isai. 1:10; 3:9 [a][Ezek. 23:3, 8, 19, 27] 9 [b]Ps. 79:2, 3 10 [c][John 16:20]; See ch. 3:10

[1] Greek *bondservants* [2] Or *the abyss* [3] Greek *spiritually*

10:9 make your stomach bitter. The contents of the book contain news of suffering.

sweet as honey. See Ps. 19:10; 119:103; Ezek. 2:3. The Word of God provides communion with God and His goodness; hence, sweetness accompanies even the message of woe.

10:11 many peoples. See note 5:9.

11:1–14 This second part of the interlude concentrates on the story of the two witnesses. Like Moses and Elijah, these witnesses perform striking miracles (vv. 5, 6). Other Old Testament backgrounds are woven into the vision. The mention of two olive trees and lampstands (v. 4) likens the witnesses to the vision of Zech. 4, in which the trees probably symbolize the ruling and priestly offices of Zerubbabel and Joshua. Thus the witnesses are prominent representatives of God. The witnesses' stand against "the beast" (vv. 7–10) reminds us of the conflicts against bestial kingdoms in Daniel. There is a reminder of wicked, oppressive cities and powers in v. 8: Sodom, Egypt, and the Jerusalem that crucified Jesus. The resurrection in vv. 11, 12 recalls the resurrection of Christ, but also the language of Ezek. 37 and the rapture of Elijah. The two witnesses, along with John (ch. 10), are models for the saints. All are to be faithful to the testimony of Jesus, even in the face of violent persecution from the beast. They must be willing to face martyrdom, God guaranteeing their vindication (vv. 11, 12).

11:1, 2 The description is reminiscent of the fall of Jerusalem in A.D. 70. Assuming that Revelation was written before A.D. 70, some interpreters see chs. 6–11 or even larger portions of Revelation as prophecy concerning the fall of Jerusalem. But these verses may just as easily be a figure of the preservation of God's people in the midst of attacks. The temple represents the presence of God on earth, especially through His people (4:1–5:14 note). Measurement signifies God's knowledge and care (Ezek. 40; 41). The altar and those who worship there represent the true worshipers of God, who are sealed and protected (ch. 7). The destruction of the outer court represents the attack of outsiders on God's people.

11:2 forty-two months. A time of distress and intense conflict between God's people and their opponents (13:5). It is also described as 1,260 days (v. 3; 12:6) or "a time, and times, and half a time" (i.e., three and a half years, 12:14). It is half of seven years, which from a symbolic point of view suggests a complete period of suffering, cut short by half. The main background is found in Dan. 7:25, which in turn is related to other passages (Dan. 9:27; 12:7, 11, 12). Some futurist interpreters look for a period of time of this length shortly before the Second Coming. But like other numbers in Revelation, this one may be symbolic in character, relating to the three and a half days in vv. 9, 11. It would then designate a persecution of limited length.

11:3 two witnesses. Possibly two literal individual human beings are in view: either two Christian prophets who were martyred shortly before the fall of Jerusalem, or two prophets who will appear shortly before the Second Coming. But their identification with two lampstands (v. 4) suggests they might be symbolic figures standing for the witness of the lampstand churches of 1:20. If this is the case, they would symbolize churches rather than specific individuals. Two lampstands, rather than seven, are mentioned to imitate the pattern of Zech. 4 and of Moses and Elijah (11:1–14 note; cf. Deut. 17:6; Matt. 17:3, 4; Luke 10:1).

11:7 the beast. See note 13:2 and Introduction: Characteristics and Themes: Other Features.

11:8 the great city. This verse suggests to many that ancient Jerusalem is in view throughout this chapter (11:1, 2 note). But the symbolism has many potential applications. The city is the worldly city, representing humanity and human civilization in its rebellion against God. Babel, Sodom, Egypt, Jerusalem, ancient Rome, modern cities, and a final apostasy before the Second Coming are all examples. See Introduction: Interpretive Difficulties and note on 17:1–19:10.

11:9 three and a half days. See note on v. 2.

peoples and tribes and languages and nations. See note 5:9.

11:10 those who dwell on the earth. See note 6:10.

dwell on the earth will rejoice over them
and make merry and [d]exchange presents,
because these two prophets [e]had been a
torment to those who dwell on the earth.
11 But after the three and a half days [f]a
breath of life from God entered them, and
they stood up on their feet, and great fear
fell on those who saw them. 12 Then they
heard a loud voice from heaven saying to
them, [g]"Come up here!" And [h]they went
up to heaven [i]in a cloud, and their enemies
watched them. 13 And at that hour there
was [j]a great earthquake, and [k]a tenth of the
city fell. Seven thousand people were killed
in the earthquake, and the rest were terrified and [l]gave glory to [m]the God of heaven.
14 [n]The second woe has passed; behold,
the third woe is soon to come.

The Seventh Trumpet

15 Then [o]the seventh angel blew his trumpet, and [p]there were loud voices in heaven,
saying, [q]"The kingdom of the world has
become the kingdom of our Lord and of
[r]his Christ, and [s]he shall reign forever and
ever." 16 And the twenty-four elders [t]who sit
on their thrones before God [u]fell on their
faces and worshiped God, 17 saying,

"We give thanks to you, Lord God
Almighty,
[v]who is and who was,
for you have taken your great power
and [w]begun to reign.
18 The nations raged,
but [x]your wrath came,
and [y]the time for the dead to be
judged,
and for rewarding your servants,[1] the
prophets and saints,
and [z]those who fear your name,
both small and great,
and [a]for destroying the destroyers of
the earth."

19 Then [b]God's temple in heaven was
opened, and [c]the ark of his covenant was
seen within his temple. There were flashes
of lightning, rumblings,[2] peals of thunder,
an earthquake, and [d]heavy hail.

The Woman and the Dragon

12 And a great sign appeared in heav-
en: a woman [e]clothed with [f]the
sun, with [f]the moon under her feet, and on
her head a crown of twelve stars. 2 She was
pregnant and [g]was crying out in birth pains
and the agony of giving birth. 3 And another sign appeared in heaven: behold, a great
[h]red dragon, [i]with seven heads and [j]ten
horns, and on his heads [k]seven diadems.
4 His tail swept down [l]a third of the stars of
heaven and [m]cast them to the earth. And
the dragon stood before the woman who
was about to give birth, so that when she

10 [d]Neh. 8:10, 12; Esth. 9:19, 22 [e][1 Kin. 18:17]
11 [f]Gen. 2:7; Ezek. 37:5, 9, 10, 14
12 [g]ch. 4:1 [h][ch. 12:5; 2 Kin. 2:11] [i][Acts 1:9]
13 [j]ch. 6:12 [k][ch. 16:19] [l]ch. 14:7; 16:9; 19:7; Josh. 7:19 [m]2 Chr. 36:23
14 [n][ch. 8:13; 9:12]
15 [o]ch. 10:7 [p]ch. 16:17; 19:1; [Isai. 27:13] [q]ch. 12:10 [r]Ps. 2:2 (Gk.); Luke 9:29 [s]See Luke 1:33
16 [t]ch. 4:4 [u]See ch. 4:10
17 [v]ch. 16:5; [ch. 1:4, 8; 4:8] [w]ch. 19:6; Ps. 97:1
18 [x]Ps. 2:5; 110:5 [y]ch. 6:10; 20:12; [Dan. 7:10; 2 Thess. 1:6, 7] [z]ch. 19:5 [a][ch. 13:10]
19 [b]ch. 15:5 [c]See Heb. 9:4 [d]ch. 16:21
Chapter 12
1 [e][Ps. 104:2] [f][S. of S. 6:10]
2 [g][Isai. 66:7-10; Mic. 4:10]
3 [h][ch. 17:3; Isai. 27:1] [i]ch. 13:1; 17:9, 12 [j]Dan. 7:7 [k][ch. 19:12] 4 [l]See ch. 8:7 [m]Dan. 8:10

[1] Greek *bondservants* [2] Or *voices*, or *sounds*

11:11, 12 If the two witnesses are individuals, their resurrection should presumably be interpreted literally. If the witnesses are symbolic of the churches, their resurrection symbolizes the victory of Christian witness after a time of intense persecution (6:9, 10; 20:1–6). See note on v. 3.

11:15–19 The second cycle of judgments (8:2–11:19) closes with a second description of the Second Coming by focusing on the last judgment (v. 18) and the triumph of God's kingly rule (vv. 15, 17).

11:19 God's temple. See note 4:2.

ark. The ark of the covenant was the most holy object in the tabernacle (Ex. 25:10–22). It was normally concealed from sight behind the tabernacle curtains. The revealing of this innermost object signifies that God has revealed His glory, both the glory of His law (the covenant words) and of His mercy (as signified by the atonement cover).

12:1–14:20 This third cycle of visions consists primarily of histories of key symbolic characters: the dragon, the woman, the beast, the false prophet, the 144,000, angelic announcers, and the Son of Man (Introduction: Outline). Unlike the cycles of seven seals (5:1–8:1) and seven trumpets (8:2–11:19), these visions have no explicit numbering. But, like the preceding cycles, they lead to a vision of the Second Coming (14:14–20). The two preceding cycles focused on the judgments issuing from God's throne. This cycle depicts in depth the nature of the spiritual conflict. Characters appear in symbolic form to represent the forces on the two sides of a cosmic spiritual war.

God Himself has already been revealed in chs. 4; 5. Opposing God are Satan (the dragon) and his agents, the beast (13:1–10) and the false prophet (13:11–18; 16:13). On God's side are His people, portrayed as a light-bearing woman (12:1–6, 13–17) and as a chaste, numbered, and protected multitude (14:1–5). These two complementary pictures show the saints in their capacity as witnesses of God's light and as separated from the corruptions of the world. Thus the saints are exhorted to remain faithful to Christ in response to the persecution by the beast, and to remain pure by resisting the seduction by the harlot (Introduction: Characteristics and Themes: Content). The symbolic pictures show the two sides stripped of all inconsistency and confusion to clearly express the nature of spiritual warfare (Eph. 6:10–20). The present conflicts will be followed by the peace of 21:1–22:5 when the fulfillment of God's plans takes effect.

12:1 a woman. The imagery calls to mind Joseph's dream (Gen. 37:9, 10) and the picture of Jerusalem bringing forth the Messiah and His remnant (Is. 54:1–4; 66:7–13; Mic. 5:3). The Old Testament saints collectively are in view. Mary the mother of Jesus is included in this group, but only as an outstanding member of the whole. The later history shows that the New Testament saints also are included (vv. 13–17). The light-bearing character of the woman foreshadows the glory of the new Jerusalem (21:11, 22–27). In her privileges the church now already partakes in the blessings to come. But she is still buffeted by Satan (chs. 12–14 note).

12:3 a great red dragon. This figure is identified as Satan, the devil, in v. 9. The image of a dragon depicts Satan in his monstrous power and hideous enmity against God. Satan has constantly opposed the plans of God and has been repeatedly defeated in the great acts of God's saving power (Gen. 3:1, 15; Ps. 74:13, 14; Is. 27:1; 51:9, 10; Ezek. 29:3; Luke 10:18;

bore her child [n]he might devour it. 5 She
gave birth to a male child, [o]one who is to
rule all the nations with a rod of iron, but
her child was [p]caught up to God and to his
throne, 6 and the woman fled into the
wilderness, where she has a place prepared
by God, in which she is to be nourished for
[q]1,260 days.

Satan Thrown Down to Earth

7 Now war arose in heaven, [r]Michael and
[s]his angels fighting against the dragon. And
the dragon and his angels fought back,
8 but he was defeated and there was no
longer any place for them in heaven. 9 And
[t]the great dragon was thrown down, [u]that
ancient serpent, who is called the devil and
Satan, [v]the deceiver of the whole world—
[w]he was thrown down to the earth, and his
angels were thrown down with him. 10 And
I heard a loud voice in heaven, saying,
"Now [x]the salvation and the power and the
kingdom of our God and the authority of
his Christ have come, for the accuser of our
brothers[1] has been thrown down, [y]who
accuses them day and night before our
God. 11 And [z]they have conquered him by
the blood of the Lamb and by the word of
their testimony, for [a]they loved not their
lives [b]even unto death. 12 Therefore, [c]re-
joice, O heavens and you who dwell in
them! But [d]woe to you, O earth and sea, for
the devil has come down to you in great
wrath, because [e]he knows that his time is
short!"
13 And when the dragon saw that he had
been thrown down to the earth, he pursued [f]the woman who had given birth to
the male child. 14 But the woman was given
the two [g]wings of the great eagle so that
she might fly from the serpent [h]into the
wilderness, to the place where she is to be
nourished [i]for a time, and times, and half a
time. 15 The serpent poured water [j]like a
river out of his mouth after the woman, to
sweep her away with a flood. 16 But the
earth came to the help of the woman, and
the earth opened its mouth and swallowed
the river that the dragon had poured from
his mouth. 17 Then the dragon became furious with the woman and went off [k]to make
war on the rest of [l]her offspring, [m]on those
who keep the commandments of God and
hold to [n]the testimony of Jesus. And he
stood[2] on the sand of the sea.

The First Beast

13 And I saw a beast rising out of the
sea, [o]with ten horns and seven
heads, with ten diadems on its horns and
[p]blasphemous names on its heads. 2 And
the beast that I saw was [q]like a leopard; its
feet were like [r]a bear's, and its mouth was
like [s]a lion's mouth. And to it [t]the dragon
gave his power and [u]his throne and great
authority. 3 One of its heads seemed to
have a mortal wound, but its mortal wound
was healed, and [v]the whole earth marveled
as they followed the beast. 4 And they worshiped the dragon, for he had given his
authority to the beast, and they worshiped
the beast, saying, [w]"Who is like the beast,
and who can fight against it?"

4 [n][Matt. 2:16]
5 [o]Matt. 2:6; See ch. 2:27 [p]See 2 Cor. 12:2
6 [q]ch. 11:2; 13:5
7 [r]See Jude 9 [s]See Matt. 25:41
9 [t]Luke 10:18; John 12:31 [u]ch. 20:2; Gen. 3:1 [v]ch. 20:3, 10; [ch. 13:14; John 8:44] [w]See ch. 9:1
10 [x]ch. 7:10; 19:1 [y]Job 1:9; 2:5; Zech. 3:1
11 [z]ch. 15:2; [Rom. 16:20]; See John 16:33 [a]Luke 14:26; John 12:25 [b]ch. 2:10
12 [c]ch. 18:20; Ps. 96:11; Isai. 44:23; 49:13 [d]ch. 8:13 [e][Matt. 8:29]; See ch. 10:6
13 [f]ver. 5
14 [g]See Ex. 19:4 [h]ver. 6 [i]Dan. 7:25; 12:7; See ver. 6
15 [j][Isai. 59:19]
17 [k]ch. 11:7; 13:7 [l]Gen. 3:15 [m]ch. 14:12; See 1 John 2:3 [n]ch. 1:2; 6:9; 19:10
Chapter 13
1 [o]Dan. 7:3; See ch. 12:3 [p]ch. 17:3
2 [q]Dan. 7:6 [r]Dan. 7:5 [s]Dan. 7:4
[t]ver. 4, 11; [Luke 4:6] [u]ch. 16:10 3 [v][ch. 17:8] 4 [w][ch. 18:18]

1 Or *brothers and sisters* 2 Some manuscripts *And I stood*, connecting the sentence with 13:1

11:14–23; John 12:31; Col. 2:15). He rises against the Messiah (vv. 4, 5) and His servants (v. 17) but will finally be consigned to everlasting punishment (20:10).

12:5 a male child. In fulfillment of Mic. 5:3, Christ is born and His triumphant rule over the nations will be established, as certified by His resurrection and ascension.

12:6 God promises protection for a persecuted church. On the 1,260 days, see note 11:2.

12:7–12 The victory of Christ (v. 5) results in sweeping consequences, beginning with the expulsion of Satan by Michael, who is functioning as an agent of Christ. The passage does not speak of the fall of Satan at the time of creation but of the defeat of Satan in the crucifixion and resurrection of Christ (v. 12; John 12:31; Col. 2:15).

12:13–17 Having failed to destroy Christ (vv. 4, 5), the Dragon tries to destroy the people of Christ. He uses his mouth, representing deceit (vv. 15, 9; 2 Thess. 2:9, 10). When deceit fails, he tries persecuting power (12:17–13:10).

12:14 a time, and times, and half a time. See note 11:2.

13:1–10 A beast rising out of the sea represents persecuting power, especially the power of a demonized state. See Introduction: Characteristics and Themes: Other Features.

13:2 leopard . . . bear's . . . lion's. This beast combines features from the four beasts of Dan. 7:1–8, 17–27, which represent idolatrous kingdoms. This beast in Revelation must be a worldly kingdom summing up all of them. In this way the state persecutions of Daniel and his friends suggest the nature of the persecution that the seven churches must face from the Roman state—and possibly persecutions of later ages. Interpreters disagree about which particular persecution the beast most directly represents (Introduction: Interpretive Difficulties). In Asia Minor, local officials threatened to kill Christians if they refused to worship the Roman Emperor. A similar opposition to godly worship will crop up just before the Second Coming (2 Thess. 2:4). Persecutions come sporadically in the period between these two times (Matt. 24:9; 2 Tim. 3:12, 13; 1 Pet. 4:12–19). Both a repeated pattern of Satanic opposition and a final, climactic outbreak are apparently suggested in 2 Thess. 2:7, 8. Christians must not be surprised by these pressures. They must face martyrdom, if necessary, knowing that God is in control and that His triumph is certain.

5 And the beast was given [x] a mouth uttering haughty and blasphemous words, and
it was allowed to exercise authority for
[y] forty-two months. **6** It opened its mouth to
utter blasphemies against God, blaspheming his name and his dwelling,[1] that is,
those who dwell in heaven. **7** Also it was
allowed [z] to make war on the saints and to
conquer them.[2] And authority was given it
over every tribe and people and language
and nation, **8** and all [a] who dwell on earth
will worship it, everyone whose name has
not been written before the foundation of
the world in [b] the book of life of [c] the Lamb
[d] that was slain. **9** [e] If anyone has an ear, let
him hear:

10 [f] If anyone is to be taken captive,
to captivity he goes;
[g] if anyone is to be slain with the
sword,
with the sword must he be slain.

[h] Here is a call for the endurance and faith
of the saints.

The Second Beast

11 Then [i] I saw another beast rising out of
the earth. It had two horns like a lamb and
it spoke like a dragon. **12** It exercises all the
authority of the first beast in its presence,[3]
and makes the earth and its inhabitants
worship the first beast, [j] whose mortal
wound was healed. **13** [k] It performs great
signs, even [l] making fire come down from
heaven to earth in front of people, **14** and by
the signs that it is allowed to work in the
presence of[4] the beast [m] it deceives those
who dwell on earth, telling them to make
an image for the beast [n] that was wounded
by the sword and yet lived. **15** And it was
allowed to give breath to the image of the
beast, so that the image of the beast might
even speak and might cause those who
would not [o] worship the image of the beast
[p] to be slain. **16** Also it causes all, both small
and great, both rich and poor, both free
and slave,[5] [q] to be marked on the right
hand or the forehead, **17** so that no one can
buy or sell unless he has the mark, that is,
[r] the name of the beast or [s] the number of its
name. **18** [t] This calls for wisdom: let the one
who has understanding calculate the number of the beast, for it is the number [u] of a
man, and his number is 666.[6]

The Lamb and the 144,000

14 Then I looked, and behold, on
[v] Mount Zion [w] stood the Lamb, and
with him [x] 144,000 who [y] had his name and
his Father's name written [z] on their foreheads. **2** And I heard a voice from heaven
[a] like the roar of many waters and [b] like the
sound of loud thunder. The voice I heard
was like the sound of [c] harpists playing on
their harps, **3** and they were singing [d] a new
song before the throne and before the four

5 [x] Dan. 7:8, 11, 20; 11:36; [2 Thess. 2:4] [y] ch. 11:2; 12:6 **7** [z] ch. 11:7; 12:17; Dan. 7:21 **8** [a] See ch. 3:10 [b] See ch. 3:5 [c] See ch. 5:6 [d] [Acts 2:23; 1 Pet. 1:19, 20] **9** [e] See ch. 2:7 **10** [f] [Isai. 33:1; Jer. 15:2; 43:11] [g] See Gen. 9:6 [h] ch. 14:12 **11** [i] [ver. 1, 14; ch. 16:13] **12** [j] ver. 3 **13** [k] ch. 16:14; 19:20; Deut. 13:1-3; Matt. 24:24; 2 Thess. 2:9-11 [l] ch. 20:9; 1 Kin. 18:38; 2 Kin. 1:10, 12; Luke 9:54 **14** [m] [ch. 12:9] [n] ver. 3, 12 **15** [o] ch. 14:9, 11; 16:2; 19:20; 20:4 [p] [ch. 16:6] **16** [q] [ch. 7:3]; See Gal. 6:17 **17** [r] ch. 14:11 [s] ch. 15:2 **18** [t] [ch. 17:9] [u] [ch. 21:17]
Chapter 14
1 [v] See ch. 5:6 [w] Ps. 2:6; Heb. 12:22 [x] ch. 7:4 [y] ch. 3:12 [z] ch. 7:3 **2** [a] See ch. 1:15 [b] ch. 6:1; 19:6 [c] ch. 5:8; 15:2 **3** [d] ch. 5:9

[1] Or *tabernacle* [2] Some manuscripts omit this sentence [3] Or *on its behalf* [4] Or *on behalf of* [5] Greek *bondservant* [6] Some manuscripts *616*

13:5 forty-two months. See note 11:2.

13:7 war on the saints. The beast compels worship (v. 8), and when the saints refuse to submit, they are martyred. But despite their apparent defeat, martyrs enjoy victory with Christ both immediately (6:9–11) and when their prayers for the final defeat of the beast are answered (19:11–21).

tribe and people and language and nation. See note 5:9.

13:8 book of life. The Greek may also be rendered "written in the slain Lamb's Book of Life from the foundation of the world" (cf. 17:8). The book is the heavenly roster of those destined to new life through the purchase of Christ's blood (3:5; 5:9). In the midst of persecution and the immense power of the beast, the saints may find security in God's guarantee of their heavenly citizenship (17:8; 20:12, 15; 21:27). A similar guarantee is found in ch. 7.

13:10 endurance. See note 1:9.

13:11–18 The beast from the earth, also called the false prophet (16:13; 19:20; 20:10), functions as a propagandist for the beast. His actions counterfeit the witness of the Holy Spirit (see Introduction: Characteristics and Themes: Other Features). In first-century Asia Minor, the main propagandists would have been priests of the emperor cult and the "Commune of Asia," a council of distinguished city representatives promoting loyalty to the emperor. In modern times as well, totalitarianism enlists propagandists. Just before the Second Coming, counterfeit miracles will accompany the appearance of the "man of lawlessness" (2 Thess. 2:3, 9). The false prophet embodies a repeatable pattern (Introduction: Interpretive Difficulties).

13:16 marked. The mark of the beast is a counterfeit for the seal of God's name on the saints (7:2–8; 14:1; Ezek. 9). The beast owns those who are marked, and they are his slaves (14:9; 19:20; 20:4). Speculations about a visible mark miss the main point of the spiritual distinction between the two groups.

13:18 666. By the time of Domitian, the earlier emperor Nero had become a traditional antichrist figure, and 666 was probably already known to be the numerical value associated with the name Nero Caesar in Hebrew. The number then designates either Nero himself (who was to rise from the dead and lead an invasion against Rome according to a widespread belief during Domitian's reign) or a later figure imitating Nero's godlessness. Many have tried to identify the final Antichrist on the basis of the number, but its connections with Nero may well be its only significance (see text note). We need to be always watchful for Christ's coming, without falling into trying to set dates (Matt. 24:36–51).

14:1–5 The 144,000 represent the saints in their complete number (7:4–8 note). They form a priestly company (5:10) consecrated to offer praise to God on the holy mount.

living creatures and before the elders. [e]No
one could learn that song except the
144,000 who had been redeemed from the
earth. 4 It is these who have not defiled
themselves with women, for [f]they are virgins. It is these [g]who follow the Lamb
wherever he goes. These have been redeemed from mankind as [h]firstfruits for
God and the Lamb, 5 and [i]in their mouth
no lie was found, for they are [j]blameless.

The Messages of the Three Angels

6 Then I saw another angel [k]flying directly overhead, with an eternal gospel to proclaim to [l]those who dwell on earth, to every
nation and tribe and language and people.
7 And he said with a loud voice, [m]"Fear God
and [n]give him glory, because the hour of
his judgment has come, and [o]worship him
who made heaven and earth, the sea and
the [p]springs of water."
8 Another angel, a second, followed, saying, [q]"Fallen, fallen is [r]Babylon the great,
[s]she who made all nations drink [t]the wine
of the passion[1] of her sexual immorality."
9 And another angel, a third, followed
them, saying with a loud voice, "If anyone
[u]worships the beast and its image and
receives [v]a mark on his forehead or on his
hand, 10 he also will drink [w]the wine of
God's wrath, [x]poured full strength into the
cup of his anger, and [y]he will be tormented
with fire and sulfur in the presence of the
holy angels and in the presence of the
Lamb. 11 And [z]the smoke of their torment
goes up forever and ever, and [a]they have no
rest, day or night, these [u]worshipers of the
beast and its image, and whoever receives
the mark of its name."
12 [b]Here is a call for the endurance of the
saints, those who [c]keep the commandments of God and their faith in Jesus.[2]

13 And I heard a voice from heaven saying, "Write this: [d]Blessed are the dead
[e]who die in the Lord from now on."
"Blessed indeed," says the Spirit, [f]"that
they may rest from their labors, for their
deeds follow them!"

The Harvest of the Earth

14 Then I looked, and behold, a white
cloud, and seated on the cloud one [g]like a
son of man, [h]with a golden crown on his
head, and a sharp sickle in his hand. 15 And
another angel [i]came out of the temple, calling with a loud voice to him who sat on the
cloud, [j]"Put in your sickle, and reap, for
the hour to reap has come, for [k]the harvest
of the earth is fully ripe." 16 So he who sat
on the cloud swung his sickle across the
earth, and the earth was reaped.
17 Then another angel came out of the
temple in heaven, and he too had a sharp
sickle. 18 And another angel came out from
the altar, [l]the angel who has authority over
the fire, and he called with a loud voice
to the one who had the sharp sickle, "Put
in your sickle and gather the clusters from
the vine of the earth, [m]for its grapes are
ripe." 19 So the angel swung his sickle across
the earth and gathered the grape harvest of
the earth and threw it into the great [n]wine-
press of the wrath of God. 20 And [o]the winepress was trodden [p]outside the city, and
blood flowed from the winepress, as high
as [q]a horse's bridle, for 1,600 stadia.[3]

The Seven Angels with Seven Plagues

15 Then [r]I saw another sign in heaven,
great and amazing, [s]seven angels
with seven plagues, which are the last, for
with them the wrath of God is finished.

3 [e][ch. 2:17; 19:12] 4 [f]2 Cor. 11:2 [g][ch. 3:4; 17:14] [h]James 1:18 5 [i]Zeph. 3:13; [Ps. 32:2; Isai. 63:8; John 1:47] [j]See Jude 24 6 [k]ch. 8:13 [l][ch. 3:10] 7 [m]ch. 15:4 [n]See ch. 11:13 [o]Neh. 9:6; See ch. 4:11 [p]ch. 8:10; 16:4 8 [q]ch. 18:2; Isai. 21:9; Jer. 51:8 [r]ch. 16:19; 17:5; 18:10; [Dan. 4:30] [s]Jer. 51:7 [t]ch. 18:3 9 [u]See ch. 13:15 [v]ch. 13:16 10 [w]ch. 16:19; See Job 21:20 [x][ch. 18:6; Isai. 1:22] [y]ch. 20:10 11 [z]Isai. 34:10; [ch. 18:18; 19:3; Gen. 19:28] [a]ch. 4:8 [u][See ver. 9 above] 12 [b]ch. 13:10 [c]ch. 12:17

13 [d]ch. 20:6; [Eccles. 4:2] [e]1 Cor. 15:18; 1 Thess. 4:16 [f]ch. 6:11 14 [g]See ch. 1:13 [h]ch. 6:2 15 [i][ch. 15:6; 16:17] [j]ver. 18; Joel 3:13; Mark 4:29; [Matt. 13:39] [k]Jer. 51:33 18 [l][ch. 16:8] [m]Joel 3:13 19 [n]ch. 19:15 20 [o]Isai. 63:3; Lam. 1:15 [p][Heb. 13:12] [q][ch. 19:14]

Chapter 15 1 [r][ch. 12:1, 3] [s]ch. 16:1; 17:1; 21:9

1 Or *wrath* 2 Greek *and the faith of Jesus* 3 About 184 miles; a *stadion* was about 607 feet or 185 meters

14:4 virgins. Sexual imagery is used to denote spiritual purity. Christ's faithful followers keep away from Babylon the harlot (v. 8; 17:1–6) and are loyal to Him exclusively, as His pure bride (19:7, 8; Eph. 5:26, 27). Purity in sexual behavior is included as one element in this comprehensive purity (1 Cor. 6:15–20).

14:6 every nation and tribe and language and people. See note 5:9.

14:8 Babylon the great. See note 17:1–19:10.

wine . . . of her sexual immorality. Sexual immorality, as well as idolatry (which is spiritual adultery), were major temptations for the seven churches (2:20 note). But the effect, like that of drunkenness, is shame, foolishness, and disgrace (17:2, 4; 18:3; 19:2; Prov. 9:13–18; Jer. 51:7).

14:9 the beast. See note 13:2 and Introduction: Characteristics and Themes: Other Features.

a mark. See note 13:16.

14:12 endurance of the saints. See note 1:9.

14:14–20 A description of the Second Coming as the harvest over which Christ presides (Matt. 13:36–43; cf. Joel 3:12–16)—the "one like a son of man" (1:13; Dan. 7:13, 14). Two harvests are described, grain (vv. 14–16) and grapes (vv. 17–20). These are perhaps two aspects of the same events of judgment. However, the grain harvest may symbolize the harvest of the righteous (Luke 3:17), followed by the harvest of the wicked (grapes).

15:1–16:21 The cycle of seven bowls of God's wrath composes the fourth cycle of visions leading up to the Second Coming (Introduction: Characteristics and Themes: Literary Form). The opening scene of worship (15:1–16:1) calls to mind the worship around God's throne in chs. 4; 5. The overcomers rejoice in God's presence (15:3, 4). Seven resplendent

2 And I saw [t]what appeared to be a sea of
glass mingled with fire—and also those
[u]who had conquered the beast and its
image and [v]the number of its name, standing beside the sea of glass [w]with harps of
God in their hands. 3 And they sing the
song of Moses, [y]the servant[1] of God, and
the song of the Lamb, saying,

[z]"Great and amazing are your deeds,
O Lord God the Almighty!
[a]Just and true are your ways,
O King of the nations![2]
4 [b]Who will not fear, O Lord,
and glorify your name?
For you alone are [c]holy.
[d]All nations will come
and worship you,
for your righteous acts have been
revealed."

5 After this I looked, and [e]the sanctuary of
[f]the tent[3] of witness in heaven was opened,
6 and out of the sanctuary came [g]the seven
angels with the seven plagues, clothed in
[h]pure, bright [i]linen, [j]with golden sashes
around their chests. 7 And one of [k]the four
living creatures gave to the seven angels
seven [l]golden bowls full of the wrath of God
[m]who lives forever and ever, 8 and [n]the sanctuary was filled with smoke from the glory
of God and from his power, and [o]no one
could enter the sanctuary until the seven
plagues of the seven angels were finished.

The Seven Bowls of God's Wrath

16 Then I heard a loud voice from the
temple telling [p]the seven angels,
"Go and [q]pour out on the earth [r]the seven
bowls of the wrath of God."
2 So the first angel went and poured out
his bowl on the earth, and harmful and
painful [s]sores came upon the people who
bore [t]the mark of the beast and worshiped
its image.
3 The second angel poured out his bowl
into the sea, and [u]it became like the blood
of a corpse, and [v]every living thing died
that was in the sea.
4 The third angel poured out his bowl
into [w]the rivers and the springs of water,
and [x]they became blood. 5 And I heard the
angel in charge of the waters[4] say,

[y]"Just are you, [z]O Holy One, [a]who is
and who was,
for you brought these judgments.
6 For [b]they have shed the blood of
[c]saints and prophets,
and [d]you have given them blood to
drink.
It is what they deserve!"

7 And I heard [e]the altar saying,

"Yes, Lord God the Almighty,
[f]true and just are your judgments!"

8 The fourth angel poured out his bowl
on the sun, and it was allowed to scorch
people [g]with fire. 9 They were scorched by
the fierce heat, and [h]they cursed[5] the name
of God who had power over these plagues.

2 [t]ch. 4:6; 21:18, 21 [u]ch. 12:11 [v]ch. 13:17 [w]ch. 5:8; 14:2
3 [x]Ex. 15:1; Deut. 31:30 [y]See Heb. 3:5 [z]Deut. 32:3, 4; [Job 37:5; Ps. 111:2; 139:14; 145:17] [a]ch. 16:7; Hos. 14:9
4 [b]ch. 14:7; Mal. 2:2 [c]ch. 16:5; Heb. 7:26 [d]See Ps. 86:9
5 [e]ch. 11:19 [f]Ex. 38:21; Num. 1:50; Acts 7:44
6 [g]See ver. 1 [h]Ezek. 28:13 [i]ch. 19:8 [j]ch. 1:13
7 [k]ch. 4:6 [l][ch. 5:8] [m]ch. 1:18; 4:9; 5:13
8 [n]Ex. 40:34; Isai. 6:4; Hag. 2:7; [1 Kin. 8:10, 11; 2 Chr. 5:13, 14] [o]Ex. 40:35; 1 Kin. 8:11

Chapter 16
1 [p]See ch. 15:1 [q]Ps. 79:6; Jer. 10:25; Zeph. 3:8 [r]ch. 15:7
2 [s]ver. 11; Ex. 9:9-11 [t]ch. 13:16
3 [u]ch. 8:8 [v]ch. 8:9
4 [w]ch. 8:10 [x]Ex. 7:17-20
5 [y]Jer. 12:1; John 17:25 [z]ch. 11:17; [ch. 1:4, 8; 4:8] [a]ch. 15:4
6 [b]ch. 18:24; [ch. 13:15] [c]ch. 11:18 [d][Isai. 49:26; Luke 11:49, 50] 7 [e]ch. 6:9 [f]ch. 15:3; 19:2; [Ps. 119:137] 8 [g]ch. 9:17; [ch. 14:18] 9 [h]ver. 11, 21

[1] Greek *bondservant* [2] Some manuscripts *the ages* [3] Or *tabernacle*
[4] Greek *angel of the waters* [5] Greek *blasphemed*; also verses 11, 21

angels receive bowls from the presence of God in the temple. The bowls symbolize the cup of God's wrath, which makes the nations drunk (14:10; 16:19; Is. 51:17, 20, 22; Jer. 25:15–29; Lam. 4:21; Ezek. 23:31–34; Hab. 2:16). The bowls are poured out at God's command (16:1), resulting in seven last plagues. The plagues lead up to the Second Coming, since "with them the wrath of God is finished" (15:1).

The seven bowls show notable similarities with the seven trumpets. The first four bowls, like the first four trumpets, result in devastation on the four major regions of creation: land, sea, fresh water, and sky. Like the trumpets, the bowls are reminiscent of the plagues against Egypt. But the bowls result in more severe judgments than did the trumpets. The trumpet judgments typically affected a third of the total, but the bowls affect the whole.

These bowls symbolize the judgments of God against evildoers. The general pattern may include both the judgments against the godless Roman Empire and the final crisis leading up to the Second Coming (Introduction: Interpretive Difficulties).

15:2 sea of glass. See note 4:6.

those who had conquered. The saints through their prayers have a role to play in the judgments of God (6:9–11). As in ch. 7, they are protected from the judgments that fall on the earth.

15:3 song of Moses. An allusion to Ex. 15. Like the Israelites, the saints are delivered from idolatrous oppression through plagues sent from God.

Just. God's acts of judgment are never arbitrary or spiteful, but just payment for evil deeds (v. 4; 16:5, 7; 19:2, 11).

15:5 the sanctuary. The inner area of God's heavenly dwelling has already been pictured in chs. 4; 5 (4:1–5:14 note).

15:6 pure, bright linen. Linen was an Old Testament priestly clothing (Ex. 28:42; Lev. 16:4). The holiness of God's judgments is thereby emphasized (v. 3 note).

15:7 four living creatures. See note 4:6.

15:8 smoke. Smoke or thick cloud frequently accompanies God's presence, especially when He is angry. The associations include Mount Sinai (Ex. 19:9, 16, 18; 20:18) and the visions of Isaiah and Ezekiel (Is. 6:4; Ezek. 1:4; cf. Num. 12:5; Ps. 18:8, 11; 74:1).

16:2 sores. Like the Egyptian plague of boils (Ex. 9:8–12).

16:3, 4 blood. Like the Egyptian plague of blood (Ex. 7:14–24).

16:5 Just. See note 15:3.

[i]They did not repent [j]and give him glory.
10 The fifth angel poured out his bowl on
[k]the throne of the beast, and [l]its kingdom
was plunged into darkness. People gnawed
their tongues in anguish 11 and cursed [m]the
God of heaven for their pain and [n]sores.
[o]They did not repent of their deeds.
12 The sixth angel poured out his bowl on
[p]the great river Euphrates, and [q]its water
was dried up, [r]to prepare the way for the
kings [s]from the east. 13 And I saw, coming out
of the mouth of [t]the dragon and out of the
mouth of [u]the beast and out of the mouth of
[v]the false prophet, three [w]unclean spirits like
[x]frogs. 14 For they are [y]demonic spirits, [z]per-
forming signs, who go abroad to the kings
of the whole world, [a]to assemble them for
battle on [b]the great day of God the
Almighty. 15 ("Behold, [c]I am coming like a
thief! [d]Blessed is the one who stays awake,
keeping his garments on, [e]that he may not
go about naked and be seen exposed!")
16 And [f]they assembled them at the place
that in Hebrew is called [g]Armageddon.

The Seventh Bowl

17 The seventh angel poured out his bowl
into [h]the air, and a loud voice came out of
the temple, from the throne, saying, [i]"It is
done!" 18 And there were [j]flashes of lightning, rumblings,[1] peals of thunder, and [k]a
great earthquake [l]such as there had never
been since man was on the earth, so great
was that earthquake. 19 [m]The great city [n]was
split into three parts, and the cities of the
nations fell, and God [o]remembered
[p]Babylon the great, [q]to make her drain the
cup of the wine of the fury of his wrath.
20 And [r]every island fled away, and no
mountains were to be found. 21 And [s]great
hailstones, about one hundred pounds[2]
each, fell from heaven on people; and [t]they
cursed God for [u]the plague of the hail,
because the plague was so severe.

The Great Prostitute and the Beast

17 Then [v]one of the seven angels who
had [w]the seven bowls came and
said to me, "Come, I will show you the
judgment of [x]the great prostitute [y]who is
seated on many waters, 2 [z]with whom the
kings of the earth have committed sexual
immorality, and [a]with the wine of whose
sexual immorality [b]the dwellers on earth
have become drunk." 3 And [c]he carried me

9 [i][Dan. 5:22]; See ch. 2:21 [j][Dan. 5:23]; See ch. 11:13 10 [k]ch. 13:2 [l]ch. 9:2; Ex. 10:21 11 [m]ch. 11:13 [n]ver. 2 [o]See ch. 2:21 12 [p]ch. 9:14 [q]Isai. 11:15; 44:27; Jer. 50:38; 51:32, 36 [r][Isai. 41:2, 25; 46:11] [s]ch. 7:2 13 [t]ch. 12:3, 9 [u]ch. 13:1 [v]ch. 19:20; 20:10; [ch. 13:11, 14] [w]ch. 18:2 [x][Ex. 8:6] 14 [y][1 Tim. 4:1] [z]See ch. 13:13 [a]ch. 20:8; [ch. 17:14; 19:19; 1 Kin. 22:20] [b]See ch. 6:17 15 [c]See ch. 3:3 [d]ch. 3:2, 3; See Matt. 24:42 [e]ch. 3:18 16 [f]ch. 19:19 [g]Zech. 12:11; See Judg. 5:19 17 [h][Eph. 2:2] [i]See ch. 10:6 18 [j]ch. 4:5; 8:5; 11:19 [k]ch. 6:12; 11:13

[l]Dan. 12:1; Joel 2:2; Matt. 24:21 19 [m]ch. 11:8 [n][ch. 11:13] [o]See ch. 14:8 [p]ch. 18:5; [Ps. 74:18] [q]See ch. 14:10 20 [r]See ch. 6:14 21 [s]ch. 11:19 [t]ver. 9, 11 [u]Ex. 9:23-25

Chapter 17 1 [v]ch. 21:9 [w]ch. 15:7 [x]ch. 19:2; Nah. 3:4; [Isai. 1:21; Jer. 2:20] [y]ver. 15; [Jer. 51:13] 2 [z]ch. 18:3, 9; [Isai. 23:17] [a]See ch. 3:10 [b]ch. 14:8; Jer. 51:7 3 [c]ch. 21:10

1 Or *voices, or sounds* 2 Greek *a talent in weight*

16:10 darkness. Like the Egyptian plague of darkness (Ex. 10:21–23).

16:14 to assemble them for battle. In the climactic battle all the forces of wickedness are assembled to make war against the warrior Lamb (17:14). The imagery alludes to the battle between God and Pharaoh in Ex. 15:2, but the panorama is universal in scope. Several passages in Revelation describe the battle with increasing detail and precision (17:13, 14; 19:11–21; 20:7–10; cf. 6:12–17), all based on the eschatological battle of Gog and Magog in Ezek. 38; 39. Throughout the church age there are times of intense confrontation between God and the forces of Satan (2:10, 13), but the most intense takes place at the Second Coming (19:11–21).

16:16 Armageddon. A transliteration of the Hebrew for "mount of Megiddo." In ancient Israel, Megiddo was a key city overlooking a major travel route between the great kingdoms of Mesopotamia and Egypt. Huge armies could assemble in the neighboring Plain of Esdraelon. Thus it is a fitting name for the location of the climactic battle.

16:17–21 The seventh bowl brings the cycle of judgments to an end. Like the other cycles, this one ends with the Second Coming (Introduction: Characteristics and Themes: Literary Form), though the symbols of the Second Coming are not as obvious as in some other cases. Note the following features: the readers have been told that the end of the wrath of God would come with the seventh bowl (15:1); the removal of all islands and mountains in v. 20 corresponds to the final shaking of the earth in 6:14 and 20:11 (Heb. 12:26, 27); elsewhere the fall of Babylon is immediately followed by the marriage supper of the Lamb (19:1–10); in 17:14–17 the fall of Babylon is associated with the last battle, which takes place at the Second Coming (19:11–21). Moreover, that final battle was imminent in v. 16. The judgment of the seventh bowl continues the practice of drawing the imagery of the final battle from the conflict with Gog and Magog (v. 14 note) by grouping together an earthquake, the overturning of the mountains, and hail, as in Ezek. 38:19–23. Hence it describes the divine plague-judgments accompanying the battle; a description of other aspects of the battle is delayed until 19:11–21 in keeping with the dramatic plan of Revelation.

17:1–19:10 Babylon the prostitute appears, representing the seductions of the world (17:4; 18:3; see Introduction: Characteristics and Themes: Other Features). "Babylon" is probably a symbol for the city of Rome (17:9 note, 17:18) with its immorality. Paganism made each of the cities of Asia Minor into a small manifestation of this Babylon. Full economic and social participation (13:17) involved attendance at pagan religious feasts and celebrations. Worship of the emperor was an expected expression of political allegiance. Pagans called Christians atheists because they did not worship the many gods, and called them haters of humankind because they withdrew from compromised forms of social life (1 Pet. 2:12; 4:3, 4). In reaction to this pressure, some professing Christians argued that participation in idolatrous feasts and sexual immorality were acceptable (2:12, 20; 1 Cor. 6:12–20). The woman Jezebel in 2:20–23 was a key seducer whose work is generalized and more deeply symbolized in Babylon the prostitute (2:21, 22; cf. 17:2).

A few interpreters favor identifying Babylon, "the great prostitute," with Jerusalem. In refusing to accept the Messiah, she became a prostitute in the imagery of the Old Testament (Is. 1:21; Ezek. 16; 23; Hos. 2; cf. Luke 11:47–51; 21:9–18). But Jerusalem was only one instance of a society seducing people away from true worship. Ancient Babylon was another, and accordingly Revelation takes up the language of the prophetic condemnations of Babylon and Tyre (Jer. 50; 51; Ezek. 27). Modern cities with their false religions and sexual exploitation are also forms of Babylon. Thus the symbolism of Babylon is capable of many historical embodiments, including the final, climactic manifestation of this "Babylon" just before the Second Coming.

When the destruction of false worship is complete (17:1–18:24), the true worshipers, the bride of the Lamb, stand out in their splendor and joy (19:1–10).

away in the Spirit [d]into a wilderness, and I
saw a woman sitting on [e]a scarlet beast that
was full of [f]blasphemous names, and [g]it
had seven heads and ten horns. **4**The
woman [h]was arrayed in purple and scarlet,
and adorned [i]with gold and jewels and
pearls, holding in her hand [j]a golden cup
full of abominations and the impurities of
her sexual immorality. **5**And on her forehead was written a name of [k]mystery:
[l]"Babylon the great, mother of prostitutes
and of earth's abominations." **6**And I saw
the woman, drunk [m]with the blood of the
saints, the blood of [n]the martyrs of Jesus.[1]

When I saw her, I marveled greatly. **7**But
the angel said to me, "Why do you marvel?
I will tell you [o]the mystery of the woman,
and of the beast with seven heads and ten
horns that carries her. **8**The beast that you
saw [p]was, and is not, and [p]is about to rise
from [q]the bottomless pit[2] and [r]go to
destruction. And [s]the dwellers on earth
whose names have not been written in [t]the
book of life from the foundation of the
world will marvel to see the beast, because
[u]it was and is not and is to come. **9**[v]This
calls for a mind with wisdom: the seven
heads are seven mountains on which the
woman is seated; **10**they are also seven
kings, five of whom have fallen, one is, the
other has not yet come, and when he does
come he must remain only a little while.
11As for the beast [w]that was and is not, it is
an eighth but it belongs to the seven, and
it goes to destruction. **12**And [x]the ten horns
that you saw are ten kings who have not yet
received royal power, but they are to
receive authority as kings [y]for one hour,
together with the beast. **13**These are of one
mind and hand over their power and
authority to the beast. **14**They [z]will make
war on the Lamb, and [a]the Lamb will conquer them, for he is [b]Lord of lords and
[b]King of kings, and those with him are
[c]called and chosen and faithful."

15And the angel[3] said to me, [d]"The
waters that you saw, where the prostitute is
seated, are peoples and multitudes and
nations and languages. **16**And [e]the ten
horns that you saw, they and the beast [f]will
hate the prostitute. They will make her
[g]desolate and [h]naked, and [i]devour her
flesh and [j]burn her up with fire, **17**for [k]God
has put it into their hearts to carry out his
purpose by being of one mind and [l]hand-
ing over their royal power to the beast,
until the words of God are fulfilled. **18**And
the woman that you saw is [m]the great city
that has dominion over the kings of the
earth."

The Fall of Babylon

18 After this I saw [n]another angel coming down from heaven, having great
authority, and [o]the earth was made bright

3[d]ch. 12:6, 14 [e][ch. 12:3] [f]ch. 13:1 [g]ver. 7, 9, 12 **4**[h]ch. 18:16 [i]Dan. 11:38 [j]Jer. 51:7; [ch. 18:6] **5**[k]ver. 7; 2 Thess. 2:7 [l]See ch. 14:8 **6**[m]ch. 16:6; [ch. 13:15] [n]ch. 2:13 **7**[o]ver. 5 **8**[p]ver. 11; [ch. 1:4; 13:3] [q]ch. 11:7 [r]See ch. 9:1 [s]ch. 13:10 [t]See ch. 3:10 [u]See ch. 3:5 **9**[v][ch. 13:18] **11**[w]ver. 8; [ch. 11:17] **12**[x]ver. 16; Dan. 7:24; [ch. 13:1; Zech. 1:18-21] [y][ch. 18:10, 17, 19] **14**[z]See ch. 16:14 [a]See ch. 3:21 [b]ch. 19:16; Deut. 10:17; Ps. 136:3; Dan. 2:47; 1 Tim. 6:15; [ch. 1:5; Matt. 28:18; Acts 10:36] [c]See ch. 2:10; Luke 18:7 (Gk.); Rom. 1:6 **15**[d]ver. 1; [Isai. 8:7] **16**[e]See ver. 12 [f][Jer. 50:41, 42] [g]ch. 18:17, 19 [h]Ezek. 16:37, 39 [i][ch. 19:18] [j]ch. 18:8; [Lev. 21:9] **17**[k]2 Cor. 8:16 [l][2 Thess. 2:11] **18**[m]ch. 16:19
Chapter 18 **1**[n]ch. 17:1, 7 [o]Ezek. 43:2

1 Greek *the witnesses to Jesus* 2 Greek *the abyss* 3 Greek *he*

17:3 in the Spirit. See note 1:10.

scarlet beast. This prostitute rides upon a hideous beast, evidently the same beast as in 13:1–10. The beast, representing the Roman Empire, supports the city of Rome in its luxurious idolatry. It also spreads the practices of Rome throughout the empire. Eventually, however, the beast turns against the prostitute and destroys her (vv. 16, 17). The rapacious powers of Roman government and the Roman legions destroy prosperity, and eventually the military powers of surrounding tribes destroy the city of Rome completely. The lesson from Roman times can be generalized: idolatrous states end up destroying the very powers, riches, privileges, and people that they originally supported. False worship is self-destructive.

17:4 sexual immorality. See note 2:20.

17:7–18:24 Seven messages of judgment on Babylon are arranged into larger groups: three angelic messages of doom (17:7–18; 18:1–3; 18:4–8), three laments by those committed to Babylon (18:9–10, 11–17a, 17b-19), and a climactic pronouncement of the permanence of her fall (18:21–24). Note also the many allusions to Jer. 50; 51 and Ezek. 27.

17:8 was, and is not, and is about to rise. The description is a counterfeit of the sovereignty of God, which is proclaimed in 1:4, 8; 4:8. "And is not" indicates that persecution is at an ebb but will rise with renewed intensity in the future. The beast represents a repeated pattern of persecution, as did the four successive beasts of Dan. 7 (13:2 note).

book of life. See note 13:8.

17:9 seven mountains. Rome was built on seven mountains, or hills.

17:10 five of whom have fallen. If Revelation was written about A.D. 67, these five may be the first five Roman emperors, beginning with Julius Caesar. The sixth is Nero, the currently reigning emperor. But it might also be the case that five simply represents an indefinite number of previous persecuting states (such as the beasts of Dan. 7). The presence of the sixth indicates in symbolic fashion that Christians are near the end, but not quite there.

17:12 ten horns. The number "ten" goes back through v. 7 and 13:1 to Dan. 7:7, 24. But the beast of Revelation cannot simply be identified with the fourth beast of Daniel; rather, he is a combination of the characteristics of all four of Daniel's beasts. In Revelation, the ten horns are kingly confederates of the beast. In view of 16:12, 14, 16; 19:19; 20:8, the political powers beyond the borders of the Roman Empire are most directly in mind. Rome was eventually overrun by barbarian tribes. But the picture rises beyond the limitations of Rome and opens up a picture of the final battle in which the beast will enlist large-scale assistance.

17:15 peoples and multitudes and nations and languages. See note 5:9.

17:16 will hate the prostitute. See note 17:1–19:10.

17:17 God has put it into their hearts. In the midst of trials, the saints are assured that God is in control even of this appalling conflict.

with his glory. **2** And he called out with a
mighty voice,

[p]"Fallen, fallen is Babylon the great!
She has become [q]a dwelling place
for demons,
a haunt [r]for every unclean spirit,
a haunt [s]for every unclean bird,
a haunt for every unclean and
detestable beast.
3 For all nations have drunk[1]
[t]the wine of the passion of her
sexual immorality,
and [u]the kings of the earth have
committed immorality with
her,
and [v]the merchants of the earth
have grown rich from the
power of her luxurious living."

4 Then I heard another voice from heaven
saying,

[w]"Come out of her, my people,
lest you take part in her sins,
lest you share in her plagues;
5 for [x]her sins are heaped high as
heaven,
and [y]God has remembered her
iniquities.
6 [z]Pay her back as she herself has paid
back others,
and repay her [a]double for her
deeds;
mix a double portion for her [b]in
the cup she mixed.
7 [c]As she glorified herself and lived in
luxury,
so give her a like measure of
torment and mourning,
since in her heart she says,
[d]'I sit as a queen,
I am no widow,
and mourning I shall never see.'
8 For this reason her plagues will come
[e]in a single day,
death and mourning and famine,
and [f]she will be burned up with fire;
for [g]mighty is the Lord God who
has judged her."

9 And [h]the kings of the earth, who committed sexual immorality and lived in luxury with her, [i]will weep and wail over her
[j]when they see the smoke of her burning.
10 [k]They will stand far off, in fear of her torment, and say,

"Alas! Alas! [l]You great city,
you mighty city, Babylon!
For [m]in a single hour your judgment
has come."

11 And [n]the merchants of the earth weep
and mourn for her, since no one buys their
cargo anymore, **12** cargo of gold, silver, jewels, pearls, fine linen, purple cloth, silk,
scarlet cloth, all kinds of scented wood, all
kinds of articles of ivory, all kinds of articles of costly wood, bronze, iron and marble, **13** cinnamon, spice, incense, myrrh,
frankincense, wine, oil, fine flour, wheat,
cattle and sheep, horses and chariots, and
slaves, that is, human souls.[2]

14 "The fruit for which your soul
longed
has gone from you,
and all your delicacies and your
splendors
are lost to you,
never to be found again!"

15 [o]The merchants of these wares, who
gained wealth from her, [p]will stand far off,
in fear of her torment, weeping and mourning aloud,

16 "Alas, alas, for the great city
[q]that was clothed in fine linen,
in purple and scarlet,
adorned with gold,
with jewels, and with pearls!
17 For [r]in a single hour all this wealth
[s]has been laid waste."

2 [p]See ch. 14:8 [q]Isai. 13:21; 34:14; Jer. 50:39; 51:37; [Zeph. 2:14, 15] [r]ch. 16:13 [s]Isai. 14:23; 34:11
3 [t]ch. 14:8 [u]ver. 9; ch. 17:2 [v]ver. 11, 15; Ezek. 27:33
4 [w][2 Cor. 6:17]; See Isai. 48:20
5 [x]Jer. 51:9; [Gen. 18:20, 21; Ezra 9:6; Jonah 1:2] [y]ch. 16:19
6 [z]Ps. 137:8; Jer. 50:15, 29; 51:24, 49 [a]Jer. 16:18 [b][ch. 14:10; 16:19; 17:4]
7 [c][Ezek. 28:2-8] [d]Isai. 47:7, 8; Zeph. 2:15; [ch. 3:17]
8 [e]Isai. 47:9; [ver. 10] [f]ch. 17:16
[g]Jer. 50:34
9 [h]ver. 3; ch. 17:2; [Ezek. 26:16, 17] [i][Jer. 50:46] [j]ver. 18; ch. 19:3
10 [k]ver. 15, 17 [l]See ch. 14:8 [m]ver. 17, 19; [ver. 8]
11 [n]ver. 3, 15; [Ezek. 27:36]
15 [o]ver. 3, 11 [p]ver. 10
16 [q]ch. 17:4
17 [r]ver. 10, 19 [s]ch. 17:16

[1] Some manuscripts *fallen by* [2] Or *and slaves, and human lives*

18:1 his glory. Because of his exalted commission, the angel's splendor reflects that of God Himself (10:1, 2 note).

18:2 dwelling place. See Jer. 50:39.

18:3 wine of . . . her sexual immorality. See note 2:20.

18:4 Come out. See Is. 48:20; 52:11; Jer. 50:8; 51:6, 45; 2 Cor. 6:17.

18:5 heaped high as heaven. An ironic reminiscence of Gen. 11:4; Jer. 51:9.

18:6 Pay her back. Judgment fits the nature of the offense (Ex. 21:23–25).

18:8 burned up with fire. See Jer. 50:32.

18:11 buys their cargo. Kings, merchants, and sailors have been seduced to worship luxury.

And [t]all shipmasters and seafaring men,
sailors and all whose trade is on the sea,
stood far off [18]and [u]cried out [v]as they saw
the smoke of her burning,

[w]"What city was like the great city?"

[19]And they threw [x]dust on their heads as
they wept and mourned, crying out,

"Alas, alas, for the great city
[y]where all who had ships at sea
grew rich by her wealth!
For [z]in a single hour she has been
laid waste.

[20] [a]Rejoice over her, O heaven,
and you saints and [b]apostles and
prophets,
for [c]God has given judgment for you
against her!"

[21]Then [d]a mighty angel [e]took up a stone
like a great millstone and threw it into the
sea, saying,

"So will Babylon [f]the great city be
thrown down with
violence,
and will be found no more;
[22] and [g]the sound of harpists and
musicians, of flute players and
trumpeters,
will be heard in you no more,
and a craftsman of any craft
will be found in you no more,
and [h]the sound of the mill
will be heard in you no more,
[23] and the light of a lamp
will shine in you no more,
and [i]the voice of bridegroom and
bride
will be heard in you no more,
for [j]your merchants were the great
ones of the earth,
and all nations were deceived [k]by
your sorcery.
[24] And [l]in her was found the blood of
prophets and of saints,
and of [m]all who have been slain on
earth."

17 [t]Ezek. 27:28, 29
18 [u]Ezek. 27:30 [v]ver. 9 [w]Ezek. 27:32; [ch. 13:4]
19 [x]See Josh. 7:6; Job 2:12 [y]ver. 3, 15 [z]ver. 10, 17
20 [a]Deut. 32:43; Jer. 51:48; See ch. 12:12 [b]Luke 11:49, 50 [c]ch. 19:2
21 [d]ch. 5:2; 10:1 [e][Jer. 51:63, 64] [f]ver. 10
22 [g]Isai. 14:11; 24:8; Ezek. 26:13 [h]Eccles. 12:4; Jer. 25:10
23 [i]Jer. 7:34; 16:9; 33:11 [j]Isai. 23:8 [k]Nah. 3:4
24 [l]ch. 17:6; [Matt. 23:35, 36] [m][Jer. 51:49]

Chapter 19
1 [n]See ch. 11:15 [o]ch. 4:11; 7:10; 12:10
2 [p]ch. 15:3; 16:7 [q]See ch. 17:1 [r]Deut. 32:43; 2 Kin. 9:7; [ch. 16:6]; See ch. 6:10
3 [s]ch. 18:9, 18; Isai. 34:10; [ch. 14:11]
4 [t]ch. 4:4, 6, 10; 5:14
5 [u]Ps. 22:23; 113:1; 134:1; 135:1 [v]ch. 11:18
6 [w]Dan. 10:6; [ver. 1] [x]See ch. 1:15 [y]ch. 6:1; 14:2 [z]ch. 11:15, 17; Ps. 97:1
7 [a]Matt. 22:2; 25:10; Luke 12:36; 14:8; John 2:1; [Eph. 5:22-32] [b]ch. 21:2, 9; [Isai. 54:5; Hos. 2:19, 20]

Rejoicing in Heaven

19 After this I heard [n]what seemed to
be the loud voice of a great multitude in heaven, crying out,

"Hallelujah!
[o]Salvation and glory and power belong
to our God,
[2] for [p]his judgments are true and
just;
for he has judged [q]the great
prostitute
who corrupted the earth with her
immorality,
and [r]has avenged on her the blood of
his servants."[1]

[3]Once more they cried out,

"Hallelujah!
[s]The smoke from her goes up forever
and ever."

[4]And [t]the twenty-four elders and the four
living creatures fell down and worshiped
God who was seated on the throne, saying,
"Amen. Hallelujah!" [5]And from the throne
came a voice saying,

[u]"Praise our God,
all you his servants,
[v]you who fear him,
small and great."

The Marriage Supper of the Lamb

[6]Then I heard what seemed to be [w]the
voice of a great multitude, like [x]the roar of
many waters and [y]like the sound of mighty
peals of thunder, crying out,

"Hallelujah!
For the Lord our God
the Almighty [z]reigns.
[7] Let us rejoice and exult
and give him the glory,
for [a]the marriage of the Lamb has
come,
and [b]his Bride has made herself
ready;

[1] Greek *bondservants*; also verse 5

18:21 The finality of Babylon's fall is depicted by the irreversible act of throwing a large stone into the sea (Jer. 51:63, 64).

19:1–10 The triumph of the pure bride is contrasted with the destruction of the corrupt false church (Babylon). Note the repeated "Hallelujah!" (vv. 1, 3–6).

19:2 just. See note 15:3.

19:4 twenty-four elders . . . four living creatures. See notes 4:4, 6. The final celebration of God's victory fittingly takes place before His presence in the company of the heavenly host (Heb. 12:22–24).

19:7 marriage of the Lamb. The wedding imagery expresses the intimacy, love, and joy between Christ and His people. It fulfills the commitments expressed earlier in Scripture (Is. 54:5–8; Hos. 2:19, 20; Eph. 5:26, 27).

8 [c]it was granted her to clothe herself
with fine linen, bright and pure"—
for the fine linen is [d]the righteous deeds of
the saints.
9 And the angel said[1] to me, "Write this:
[e]Blessed are those who are invited to the
marriage supper of the Lamb." And he said
to me, [f]"These are the true words of God."
10 Then [g]I fell down at his feet to worship
him, [h]but he said to me, "You must not do
that! I am a fellow servant[2] with you and
your brothers who hold to [i]the testimony
of Jesus. Worship God." For the testimony
of Jesus is the spirit of prophecy.

The Rider on a White Horse

11 Then I saw [j]heaven opened, and
behold, [k]a white horse! The one sitting on
it is called [l]Faithful and True, and [m]in
righteousness he judges and makes war.
12 [n]His eyes are like a flame of fire, and on
his head are [o]many diadems, and he has [p]a
name written that no one knows but himself. 13 He is clothed in [q]a robe dipped in[3]
blood, and the name by which he is called
is [r]The Word of God. 14 And the armies of
heaven, [s]arrayed in fine linen, white and
pure, [t]were following him on white horses.
15 [u]From his mouth comes a sharp sword
[v]with which to strike down the nations,
and [w]he will rule them with a rod of iron.
[x]He will tread the winepress of the fury of
the wrath of God the Almighty. 16 On his
robe and on his thigh [y]he has a name written, [z]King of kings and Lord of lords.

17 Then I saw an angel standing in the
sun, and with a loud voice he called to [a]all
the birds that fly directly overhead,
[b]"Come, gather for [c]the great supper of
God, 18 [d]to eat the flesh of kings, the flesh
of captains, the flesh of mighty men, the
flesh of horses and their riders, and the
flesh of all men, both free and slave,[4] both
small and great." 19 And I saw [e]the beast
and the kings of the earth with their armies
[f]gathered to make war against him who
was sitting on the horse and against his
army. 20 And the beast was captured, and
with it [g]the false prophet [h]who in its presence[5] had done the signs by which he
deceived those who had received the mark
of the beast and those who [i]worshiped its
image. These two were [j]thrown alive into
the lake of [k]fire that burns with sulfur.
21 And the rest were slain by the sword [l]that
came from the mouth of him who was sitting on the horse, and [m]all the birds were
gorged with their flesh.

The Thousand Years

20 Then I saw an angel coming down
from heaven, [n]holding in his hand
the key to [o]the bottomless pit[6] and a great
chain. 2 And he seized [p]the dragon, that
ancient serpent, who is the devil and Satan,
and [q]bound him for a thousand years, 3 and

8 [c][Ps. 45:13-15; Ezek. 16:10] [d][Ps. 132:9; Isai. 61:10]
9 [e]Luke 14:15; See ver. 7 [f][ch. 21:5; 22:6]
10 [g]ch. 22:8 [h]ch. 22:9; See Acts 10:26 [i]ch. 1:2; 6:9; 12:17
11 [j]See Ezek. 1:1 [k]See ch. 6:2 [l]See ch. 3:7, 14 [m][Ps. 96:13; Isai. 11:4]
12 [n]ch. 1:14; 2:18 [o][ch. 12:3] [p]ver. 16; ch. 2:17; [Prov. 30:4]
13 [q]Isai. 63:2, 3 [r]See John 1:1
14 [s]ch. 3:4; 7:9 [t][ch. 14:20]
15 [u]ver. 21; See ch. 1:16 [v][Isai. 11:4; 2 Thess. 2:8] [w]ch. 2:27; 12:5 [x]ch. 14:20; Isai. 63:3
16 [y]ver. 12 [z]See ch. 17:14
17 [a]ver. 21 [b]Jer. 12:9; Ezek. 39:17 [c][Isai. 34:6; Jer. 46:10; Ezek. 39:19]
18 [d]Ezek. 39:18, 20
19 [e]ch. 11:7; 13:1 [f]ch. 16:16
20 [g]ch. 16:13; 20:10 [h]ch. 13:11-14 [i]See ch. 13:15 [j]ch. 20:10, 14, 15; [Dan. 7:11] [k]ch. 14:10; 21:8; See 2 Thess. 1:8
21 [l]ver. 15 [m]ver. 17
Chapter 20 1 [n]See ch. 1:18 [o]See ch. 9:1 2 [p]See ch. 12:9 [q][2 Pet. 2:4; Jude 6]

1 Greek *he said* 2 Greek *fellow bondservant* 3 Some manuscripts *sprinkled with* 4 Greek *bondservant* 5 Or *on its behalf* 6 Greek *the abyss*; also verse 3

19:9 marriage supper. Note the contrasts between this blessed feast and the horrific feast of vv. 17, 18.

19:10 the testimony of Jesus is the spirit of prophecy. The angel is a fellow servant of the prophets (22:9). John has the spirit of prophecy (22:6); he receives the testimony (witness) that Jesus gives and presents it to the church (1:2; 6:9). John's ministry compares to that of the angels.

19:11–21 The sixth cycle of judgments leading to the Second Coming (Introduction: Characteristics and Themes: Literary Form) is presented in these verses. In the latter cycles the imagery concentrates more and more intensively on the Second Coming and the events that immediately precede it. In this cycle, all the events are actually part of the Second Coming. But, as is typical of Revelation, they reveal principles of spiritual war that have been operative throughout the church age (Eph. 6:10–20; 1 John 5:4, 5). At the end, Jesus Christ is revealed (22:13; Heb. 13:8).

Christ appears to wage final battle against all the enemies of God, led by the beast and the false prophet. Christ's holy attributes contrast markedly with the unholy counterfeit attributes of the beast (13:1–10 note). This final war brings to a climax all the wars that God has waged on behalf of His people (Ex. 15:2; Deut. 20; Is. 59:16–18; Ezek. 38; 39; Hab. 3:8–15; Zech. 12:1–9; 14:3–5) and consummates the triumph achieved by Christ on the cross (5:9, 10; 12:10, 11; John 12:31; Col. 2:15). Some have interpreted the imagery as a reference to the spread of Christ's rule through submission to the gospel, but the parallels with other visions show that the final battle is primarily in view (16:14, 16–21 and notes; 17:14; 20:7–10).

19:11 heaven opened. In contrast to 4:1, the heavenly presence of God is now revealed not merely to John the seer but to the whole of humanity. The appearance of Christ in His majesty must mean the end of the battle and the destruction of all enemies before Him.

19:17 the great supper. See Ezek. 39:4, 17–20.

19:19 beast. See note 13:1–10.

armies gathered. See note 16:14.

19:20 lake of fire. Hell, the place of everlasting torment for the wicked (14:9, 10; 20:10, 14, 15; 21:8; Is. 66:24). Fire is frequently associated with all-consuming judgment (Is. 66:15, 16; Joel 2:3). See "Hell" at Mark 9:43.

20:1–10 An angel descending from heaven binds Satan for a thousand years (see Introduction: Interpretive Difficulties: The Millennium). The faithful martyrs (v. 4) come to life and reign with Christ. After the thousand years, Satan is released, gathers the nations for battle, and is finally rendered powerless (v. 10).

20:2 a thousand years. See note on vv. 1–10.

bound him. Satan's power to influence the nations is suppressed. Premillennialists and some postmillennialists associate this event with

threw him into [o]the pit, and shut it and
[r]sealed it over him, so that [s]he might not
deceive the nations any longer, until the
thousand years were ended. After that he
must be released for a little while.
4 Then I saw [t]thrones, and [u]seated on
them were those to whom the authority to
judge was committed. Also I saw [v]the souls
of those who had been beheaded for the
testimony of Jesus and for the word of
God, and [w]who had not worshiped the
beast or its image and had not received its
mark on their foreheads or their hands.
[x]They came to life and [y]reigned with Christ
for a thousand years. 5 The rest of the dead
did not come to life until the thousand
years were ended. This is the first resurrection. 6 [z]Blessed and holy is the one who
shares in the first resurrection! Over such
[a]the second death has no power, but they
will be [b]priests of God and of Christ, and
they [c]will reign with him for a thousand
years.

The Defeat of Satan

7 And when the thousand years are
ended, [d]Satan will be released from his
prison 8 and will come out [e]to deceive the
nations that are at the four corners of the
earth, [f]Gog and Magog, [g]to gather them for
battle; their number is like the sand of the
sea. 9 And [h]they marched up over the broad
plain of the earth and surrounded [i]the
camp of the saints and [j]the beloved city,
but [k]fire came down from heaven[1] and
consumed them, 10 and the devil [l]who had
deceived them was [m]thrown into the lake
of fire and sulfur where [n]the beast and the
false prophet were, and they will be tormented day and night forever and ever.

The Great White Throne Judgment

11 Then I saw a great white throne and
him who was seated on it. From his presence [o]earth and sky fled away, and [p]no
place was found for them. 12 And I saw the
dead, great and small, standing before the
throne, and [q]books were opened. Then
another book was opened, which is [r]the
book of life. And [s]the dead were judged by
what was written in the books, [t]according
to what they had done. 13 And the sea gave
up the dead who were in it, [u]Death and
Hades gave up the dead who were in them,
and they were judged, each one of them,
[t]according to what they had done. 14 Then
[u]Death and Hades [v]were thrown into the
lake of fire. This is [w]the second death, the

3 [o][See ver. 1 above] [r]Dan. 6:17; [Matt. 27:66] [s]ver. 8, 10 **4** [t]Dan. 7:9; Matt. 19:28 [u]ch. 3:21; Dan. 7:22 [v]ch. 6:9 [w]ch. 13:12, 14-16 [x][John 14:19; 2 Tim. 2:11] [y]ver. 6; ch. 5:10; 22:5; Dan. 7:18; Matt. 20:21, 27; 2 Tim. 2:12; [Ps. 45:16] **6** [z]ch. 14:13 [a]ver. 14; ch. 2:11; 21:8 [b]See ch. 1:6 [c]ver. 4 **7** [d]ver. 2 **8** [e]ver. 3, 10 [f]Ezek. 38:2; 39:1 [g]See ch. 16:14 **9** [h][Isai. 8:8; Ezek. 38:9, 16; Hab. 1:6] [i]Heb. 13:11, 13 [j][Ps. 132:13] [k]See ch. 13:13 **10** [l]ver. 3, 8 [m]See ch. 19:20 [n]See ch. 16:13 **11** [o]See Ps. 102:26 [p]ch. 12:8; Dan. 2:35 **12** [q]Dan. 7:10 [r]See ch. 3:5 [s]Rom. 14:10; 2 Cor. 5:10; See ch. 11:18 [t]See Matt. 16:27 **13** [u]ch. 6:8 [t][See ver. 12 above] **14** [u][See ver. 13 above] [v][ch. 21:4; Luke 20:36; 1 Cor. 15:26] [w]ver. 6

1 Some manuscripts *from God, out of heaven*, or *out of heaven from God*

the beginning of an extraordinary future era of peace and prosperity, contrasting with the present (1 Thess. 2:18; 1 Pet. 5:8). Amillennialists think that the binding of Satan has already taken place through Christ's death and resurrection (12:9; Matt. 12:29; John 12:31; Col. 2:15). The present spread of the gospel to the nations, as initiated in Acts, is the result of a restriction on Satan's power to deceive. Possibly this restriction on Satan's power is closely associated with the present temporary demise of the beast (17:8).

20:3 deceive the nations. See vv. 8, 10; 13:14; 16:14; 19:20.

20:4 souls. See 6:9, 10. Martyrs are singled out as the most notable group of faithful witnesses. But other saints are not excluded from the privileges mentioned.

the beast. See note 13:1–10.

reigned. See 2:26, 27; 3:21.

20:5, 6 the first resurrection. If this resurrection means bodily resurrection, it coincides with the Second Coming (1 Cor. 15:51–57; 1 Thess. 4:13–18) and the premillennialists are correct (vv. 1–10 note). On the other hand, the language concerning the second death in vv. 6, 14 and 21:8 suggests a contrast between the first death and the second. The first death is bodily death, but it is only preliminary, not ultimate. The second death is ultimate and spiritual in character. Likewise, the first and second resurrections may be preliminary and ultimate, respectively. The first is spiritual, the second is of the body. The first resurrection is then to be understood as coinciding either with spiritual new birth (John 5:24, 25) or with going to be with Christ at the time of bodily death (6:9, 10; 2 Cor. 5:8; Phil. 1:23).

20:6 priests. See note 1:6.

20:8 Gog and Magog. These names, taken from Ezek. 38; 39, represent the final enemies of God.

gather them for battle. See 16:14.

20:11–15 God appears in a scene of final judgment. God's authority to judge has already been anticipated in chs. 4; 5. Now He executes the judgment that befits His character and power over the created universe. The vision shares features with Ps. 7:6–8; 47:8, 9; Dan. 7:9, 10 and other Old Testament judgment scenes (cf. Matt. 25:31–46).

Injustices and sufferings in history never escape God's eye. Those who persecute and practice injustice cannot ultimately win. God will judge every deed, all wrongs will be righted, and all attempts to dethrone God and enthrone anything or anyone else will be turned around to frustrate God's enemies completely. The prospect of final judgment ought to be a terror to God's enemies but a foundation of assurance to the saints.

This judgment follows the thousand years of vv. 2, 7. Premillennialists believe that the Second Coming precedes the thousand years, and hence must include a distinct judgment of its own. At the Second Coming Christians receive their reward, and this later judgment is for the wicked and those living in untransformed bodies during the thousand years. Amillennialists and postmillennialists, on the other hand, have generally understood this passage as one among many references to a universal final judgment at the Second Coming (vv. 1–10 note).

20:11 throne. See 4:2 note.

earth and sky fled away. See 6:14.

20:12 book of life. See note 13:8.

20:14 lake of fire . . . the second death. The final state of eternal torment, to which all who impenitently rebel against God's sovereign rule are consigned. See note 19:20; "Hell" at Mark 9:43.

lake of fire. 15 And if anyone's name was not
found written in the book of life, [x]he was
thrown into the lake of fire.

The New Heaven and the New Earth

21 Then I saw [y]a new heaven and a
new earth, for [z]the first heaven and
the first earth had passed away, and the sea
was no more. 2 And I saw [a]the holy city,
[b]new Jerusalem, [c]coming down out of
heaven from God, [d]prepared [e]as a bride
adorned for her husband. 3 And I heard a
loud voice from the throne saying,
"Behold, [f]the dwelling place[1] of God is
with man. He will [g]dwell with them, and
they will be his people,[2] and God himself
will be with them as their God.[3] 4 [h]He will
wipe away every tear from their eyes, and
[i]death shall be no more, [j]neither shall there
be mourning nor crying nor pain anymore,
for the former things have passed away."

15 [x]Matt. 13:42, 50
Chapter 21
1 [y]Isai. 65:17; 66:22; 2 Pet. 3:13 [z]ch. 20:11
2 [a]ch. 11:2; 22:19; Isai. 52:1 [b]See ch. 3:12 [c][Heb. 11:10] [d]ch. 19:7; [John 14:3] [e]Isai. 61:10
3 [f]See Lev. 26:11, 12 [g][ch. 7:15]
4 [h]See ch. 7:17 [i][ch. 20:14; 1 Cor. 15:26] [j]Isai. 35:10; 51:11; 65:19

1 Or *tabernacle* 2 Some manuscripts *peoples* 3 Some manuscripts omit *as their God*

Heaven

"Heaven" is the biblical term for God's dwelling place (Ps. 33:13, 14; Matt. 6:9), the place of His presence to where the glorified Christ has returned (Acts 1:11). The church militant and triumphant unites there for worship (Heb. 12:22–25), and one day Christ's people will be there with Christ forever (John 17:5, 24; 1 Thess. 4:16, 17). Heaven is the place of God's rest (John 14:2). It is described as a city (Heb. 11:10) and a country (Heb. 11:16).

To think of heaven as a "place" is more right than wrong, though the word could mislead. Scripture describes heaven as a spatial reality that touches and interpenetrates created space. According to Ephesians, the throne of Christ at the Father's right hand (Eph. 1:20), and the life of Christians in Christ, are both in "heavenly places" (Eph. 1:3, 20; 2:6). Paul alludes to his experience in the "third heaven" or "paradise" (2 Cor. 12:2, 3). A resurrection body, adapted to heaven's life, awaits us (2 Cor. 5:1–8). While we are in our present bodies the realities of heaven are unseen, and we know them only by faith (2 Cor. 4:18; 5:7). The hope founded on what faith sees gives us the courage to endure (Rom. 8:25; cf. Gal. 5:5; 1 John 3:3).

We can form an idea of the perfect life of heaven from what we know imperfectly now (1 Cor. 13:12). Our communion with God and with other Christians will be unbroken (Ps. 23:6). According to Revelation, there will be no tears, sorrow, or death (Rev. 21:4). According to Romans, the earth itself together with life on it has been "subjected to futility" on account of sin (Rom. 8:20). Through the Spirit, we know that this "corruption" will be undone, and the possibilities dimly perceived in the fallen creation will be fulfilled in "the freedom of the glory of the children of God" (Rom. 8:21).

According to the *Shorter Catechism,* we were created "to glorify God, and enjoy Him forever." The crowns, feasts, and celebrations of victory described in the Scripture bring one aspect of this joy before our eyes. The triumph of the Lamb that was slain and His saints with Him (Rev. 5:6; 14:1) is another. At the center is the union of God with His people (Rev. 22:4). This was held out as the promise of the covenant (Jer. 30:22), and it is destined to be realized in a way beyond imagination (Eph. 2:7; 3:9; cf. 1 Cor. 2:9).

21:1–8 The voice of God announces the descent of the New Jerusalem against the backdrop of total renovation—a new heaven and a new earth. God is the Alpha (1:8 note), the Creator whose purposes were expressed from the beginning, and the Omega, the Consummator who brings His purposes to final realization. God's glory, power, and beauty within the sphere of heaven (ch. 4) now extend to all His people (v. 3). Evil and pain are abolished in the new creation, in contrast to the pain, suffering, and struggles running through the earlier parts of Revelation. The promises made to overcomers are now fulfilled (2:7 note).

The final visions of Revelation weave into a beautiful unity a host of biblical themes. Note the themes of creation (v. 1), the holy city of Jerusalem, communion with God expressed through marriage imagery (v. 2), the dwelling of God, including the tabernacle and temple (4:1–5:14 note), saints as God's own people (v. 3), the end of suffering and death (v. 4), new deeds of salvation, trustworthiness of God's Word (v. 5), living water (v. 6), becoming a son of God (v. 7), warnings to the faithless, and judgment (v. 8).

These verses are usually grouped with 21:9–22:5. The two passages present two aspects of the final vision of the New Jerusalem. Many realities are introduced in vv. 1–8 that appear with greater elaboration and in more visionary description in 21:9–22:5. But vv. 1–8 also have close relations to 20:11–15. The final judgment of God, in fact, has two sides: the negative side (the judgment of the wicked) is expressed in 20:11–15, while the positive side (the reward for the righteous) is expressed here. Within the negative message of 20:11–15 there is a positive note, the Book of Life (20:15). Similarly, within the positive message of vv. 1–8 there is one negative note, the lake of fire (v. 8). These verses and 20:11–15 are symmetric scenes depicting judgment both negatively and positively.

21:1 a new heaven and a new earth. Some have thought that the new universe will be an entirely new world with no connection with the old. But Is. 65:17–25 and Rom. 8:21–23 indicate that a transfiguration of the old world is in view, like the way in which our new bodies will be transfigurations of the old (1 Cor. 15:35–57). Everything is new (v. 5), which indicates the thoroughness of transfiguration, but the result is redemption and not simply abolition of the old. See theological note "Heaven."

5 And [k]he who was seated on the throne
said, "Behold, I [l]am making all things
new." Also he said, "Write this down, for
[m]these words are trustworthy and true."
6 And he said to me, [n]"It is done! [o]I am the
Alpha and the Omega, the beginning and
the end. [p]To the thirsty I will give from the
spring of the water of life without payment.
7 [q]The one who conquers will have this heritage, and [r]I will be his God and [s]he will be
my son. 8 [t]But as for the cowardly, the faithless, the detestable, as for murderers, the
sexually immoral, sorcerers, idolaters, and
all liars, [u]their portion will be in [v]the lake
that burns with fire and sulfur, which is
[w]the second death."

The New Jerusalem

9 Then came [x]one of the seven angels
who had the seven bowls full of [y]the seven
last plagues and spoke to me, saying,
"Come, I will show you [z]the Bride, the wife
of the Lamb." 10 And [a]he carried me away
in the Spirit to [b]a great, high mountain,
and showed me the holy city Jerusalem
coming down out of heaven from God,
11 [c]having the glory of God, [d]its radiance
[e]like a most rare jewel, like a jasper, clear as
crystal. 12 It had a great, high wall, [f]with
twelve gates, and at the gates twelve angels,
and on the gates the names of the twelve
tribes of the sons of Israel were inscribed—
13 on the east three gates, on the north three
gates, on the south three gates, and on the
west three gates. 14 And the wall of the city
had twelve [g]foundations, and [h]on them
were the twelve names of the twelve apostles of the Lamb.
15 And the one who spoke with me [i]had a
measuring rod of gold to measure the city
and its gates and walls. 16 The city lies
foursquare; its length the same as its
width. And he measured the city with his
rod, 12,000 stadia.[1] Its length and width
and height are equal. 17 He also measured
its wall, 144 cubits[2] by [j]human measurement, which is also [k]an angel's measurement. 18 The wall was built of [l]jasper, while
the city was pure gold, [l]clear as glass.
19 [m]The foundations of the wall of the city
were adorned with every kind of jewel. The
first was jasper, the second sapphire, the
third agate, the fourth emerald, 20 the fifth
onyx, the sixth carnelian, the seventh
chrysolite, the eighth beryl, the ninth
topaz, the tenth chrysoprase, the eleventh
jacinth, the twelfth amethyst. 21 And the
twelve gates were twelve pearls, each of the
gates made of a single pearl, and [n]the street
of the city was pure gold, transparent as
glass.
22 And [o]I saw no temple in the city, for its
temple is the Lord God the Almighty and
the Lamb. 23 And the city [p]has no need of
sun or moon to shine on it, for [q]the glory
of God gives it light, and its lamp is the
Lamb. 24 By its light [r]will the nations walk,

5 [k]ch. 4:2, 9; 5:1; 20:11 [l]See 2 Cor. 5:17 [m]ch. 22:6; [ch. 3:14; 19:11; 1 Tim. 1:15]
6 [n]See ch. 10:6 [o]ch. 1:8; 22:13 [p]ch. 22:17; See John 4:10; 7:37
7 [q]ch. 2:7 [r]ver. 3 [s]See 2 Cor. 6:18
8 [t]ch. 22:15; 1 Cor. 6:9, 10; Gal. 5:19-21; Eph. 5:5; 1 Tim. 1:9; Heb. 12:14 [u]Luke 12:46 [v]ch. 19:20 [w]ch. 2:11; 20:6, 14
9 [x]ch. 17:1 [y]ch. 15:1 [z]ver. 2
10 [a]ch. 17:3; [Ezek. 43:5] [b]Ps. 87:1; Ezek. 40:2
11 [c]ver. 23; [ch. 22:5; Ps. 84:11; Ezek. 43:2, 4] [d][Matt. 5:14; Phil. 2:15] [e]ch. 4:3, 6
12 [f]Ezek. 48:31-34
14 [g]Heb. 11:10; [1 Cor. 3:11] [h]Matt. 16:18; Eph.2:20
15 [i]See ch. 11:1
17 [j]Deut. 3:11; [ch.13:18] [k]ver. 9
18 [l]ver. 11
19 [m][Isai. 54:11, 12]
21 [n]ch. 22:2
22 [o][John 4:23]
23 [p]ch. 22:5; Isai. 60:19, 20; [ver. 25] [q]ver. 11 24 [r]Isai. 60:3; [ch. 22:2]

1 About 1,380 miles; a *stadion* was about 607 feet or 185 meters
2 A *cubit* was about 18 inches or 45 centimeters

21:6 water of life. See note 22:1.

21:8 second death. See note 20:14.

21:9–22:5 The picture of the New Jerusalem now unfolds in detail. The final dwelling place of the saints is simultaneously the fulfillment of earlier revelations of God appearing in glory and reigning in His heavenly court (21:22, 23; 22:1, 3; cf. ch. 4), the holy city Jerusalem (21:10), the Garden of Eden (22:1–3), the bride, the marriage partner of the Lord (21:9), and the temple as the dwelling place of God (21:22, 23). The central figure and the central blessing of the city is God Himself and the Lamb (21:22, 23; 22:1–5). The final revelation of God necessarily brings to a climax all earlier revelations. It completes God's purpose of bringing all things under one Head—Christ (11:15; Eph. 1:10). It harmonizes with the creation of all things by Christ at the beginning (1:17; 4:11; Col. 1:15–17) and the redemption of all things through Christ in the middle (5:9–14; Rom. 11:36; Col. 1:18–20). Because of the fluid character of the imagery, it is wise not to distinguish rigidly between the inhabitants of the city (the saints) and the city itself (saints together with the glorified creation).

21:9 Bride. See note 19:1–10.

21:10 in the Spirit. See note 1:10.

mountain. The mountain as God's special meeting place with human beings, alluding to 14:1; Ex. 15:17; 19:1–25; Ps. 48:1, 2; 68:15, 16; Ezek. 28:14; Mic. 4:1, 2; and other passages.

21:11 glory of God. Closely associated with the imagery of light, glory represents the majesty, awesomeness, and beauty of God. Glory, a prominent theme in 21:9–22:5, is associated with the temple and the appearing of God in the Old Testament (vv. 22, 23; 15:8; 22:5; Ex. 16:10; 24:16, 17; 40:34, 35; Is. 6:3; 40:3; 60:1, 2, 19, 20; Hab. 2:14; Zech. 2:5; John 1:14). God's heavenly splendor as seen in ch. 4 now fills the new world.

21:16 length and width and height. The city is a perfect cube, the same shape as the Most Holy Place in the tabernacle and the temple. The whole city is architecturally perfect, and has become the most intimate dwelling place of God (vv. 22, 23; 22:4).

21:17 144 cubits. That is, twelve times twelve cubits. All the dimensions of the city reveal its associations with the twelve tribes of Israel and the twelve apostles (vv. 12, 14). "Twelve" symbolically designates the people of God.

21:19 every kind of jewel. The list of precious stones shows the beauty and magnificence of the city and the way it reflects the beauty of God, who fills it with His glory (4:3). The list also corresponds roughly to the twelve precious stones of Aaron's breastplate (Ex. 28:15–21). The prerogatives once reserved for the high priest now belong to the entire city.

21:22 temple. See note on 4:1–5:14.

21:23 sun or moon. Fulfillment of Is. 60:19, 20.

21:24 the nations. Redeemed humanity in all its cultural diversity (5:9 note; Is. 60:3–12).

and the kings of the earth [s]will bring their
glory into it, 25 and [t]its gates will never be
shut by day—and [u]there will be no night
there. 26 They will bring into it the glory and
the honor of the nations. 27 But [v]nothing
unclean will ever enter it, nor anyone who
does what is detestable or false, but only
those who are written in the Lamb's [w]book
of life.

The River of Life

22 Then the angel[1] showed me [x]the
river of [y]the water of life, bright as
crystal, flowing from the throne of God and
of the Lamb 2 through the middle of [z]the
street of the city; [a]also, on either side of the
river, [b]the tree of life[2] with its twelve kinds
of fruit, yielding its fruit each month. The
leaves of the tree were [c]for the healing of
the nations. 3 [d]No longer will there be anything accursed, but [e]the throne of God and
of the Lamb will be in it, and [f]his servants[3]
will worship him. 4 [g]They will see his face,
and [h]his name will be on their foreheads.
5 And [i]night will be no more. They will
need no light of lamp [j]or sun, for [k]the Lord
God will be their light, and [l]they will reign
forever and ever.

Jesus Is Coming

6 And he said to me, [m]"These words are
trustworthy and true. And the Lord, the
God of [n]the spirits of the prophets, [o]has
sent his angel to show his servants what
must soon take place."

7 "And behold, [p]I am coming soon.
[q]Blessed is the one who keeps the words of
the prophecy of this book."
8 I, [r]John, am the one who heard and saw
these things. And when I heard and saw
them, [s]I fell down to worship at the feet of
the angel who showed them to me, 9 [s]but
he said to me, "You must not do that! I am
a fellow servant[4] with you and your brothers the prophets, and with those [m]who
keep the words of this book. Worship
God."
10 And he said to me, [t]"Do not seal up the
words of the prophecy of this book, for the
time is near. 11 [u]Let the evildoer still do evil,
and the filthy still be filthy, and the righteous still do right, and the holy still be
holy."
12 "Behold, [v]I am coming soon, [w]bringing
my recompense with me, [x]to repay everyone for what he has done. 13 [y]I am the
Alpha and the Omega, [z]the first and the
last, [a]the beginning and the end."
14 Blessed are those who [b]wash their
robes,[5] so that they may have the right to
[c]the tree of life and that [d]they may enter the
city by the gates. 15 [e]Outside are [f]the dogs
[g]and sorcerers and the sexually immoral

24 [s]ver. 26; [Isai. 60:5, 16] 25 [t]Isai. 60:11 [u]See ver. 23 27 [v][ch. 22:14, 15; Isai. 35:8; 52:1; Ezek. 44:9; Joel 3:17; Zech. 14:21] [w]See ch. 3:5
Chapter 22
1 [x]Ezek. 47:1; Zech. 14:8; [Ps. 46:4] [y]See ch. 21:6 2 [z]ch. 21:21 [a]Ezek. 47:12 [b]ver. 14, 19; ch. 2:7; Gen. 2:9 [c][ch. 21:24] 3 [d]Zech. 14:11; [Gen. 3:17] [e]ch. 21:3, 23; Ezek. 48:35 [f]ch. 7:15 4 [g]Matt. 5:8; 1 Cor. 13:12; 1 John 3:2 [h]ch. 3:12; 7:3; 14:1 5 [i]ch. 21:25 [j]See ch. 21:23 [k]Ps. 36:9; See ch. 21:11 [l]Dan. 7:18, 27; Rom. 5:17; 2 Tim. 2:12; See ch. 20:4 6 [m]See ch. 21:5 [n]1 Cor. 14:32 [o]ch. 1:1
7 [p]ver. 12, 20; ch. 3:11 [q]ch. 1:3 8 [r]ch. 1:1, 4, 9 [s]ch. 19:10 9 [s][See ver. 8 above] [m][See ver. 6 above] 10 [t][ch. 10:4]
11 [u]Ezek. 3:27; [Dan. 12:10; 2 Tim. 3:13] 12 [v]ver. 7, 20 [w]Isai. 40:10; 62:11 [x]See Matt. 16:27 13 [y]See ch. 1:8 [z]See ch. 1:17 [a]ch. 21:6 14 [b]See ch. 7:14 [c]ver. 2, 19 [d]Ps. 118:20; See ch. 21:27 15 [e][Gal. 5:19-21]; See Matt. 8:12 [f]See Phil. 3:2 [g]See ch. 21:8

[1] Greek *he* [2] Or *the Lamb. In the midst of the street of the city, and on either side of the river, was the tree of life* [3] Greek *bondservants*; also verse 6 [4] Greek *fellow bondservant* [5] Some manuscripts *do his commandments*

glory. See Is. 60:3–5; Hag. 2:7–9.

21:25 gates will never be shut. Ancient city gates needed to be shut in case of attack. Here is fulfillment of Is. 60:11.

21:27 book of life. See note 13:8.

22:1–5 The final description of paradise contains elements alluding to the Garden of Eden. The intimacy of God with His people (vv. 3, 4) and the abundance of His blessing (vv. 1, 2, 5) are stressed even more than in the preceding verses. The final state restores the unbroken, idyllic communion between God and human beings. But the apex of history is more magnificent than the beginning. The garden is now also a city, and the light has driven out all night.

Revelation is designed not only to inform and assure Christians about God's final purposes, but to increase their longing for God and the realization of His purpose. The certainty of that consummation comforts saints during times of temptation and persecution.

22:1 river of the water of life. Abundant supply of life-giving water comes from God. Revelation weaves together allusions to Gen. 2:10–14; Ps. 46:4; Ezek. 47:1–12; Joel 3:18; John 4:10–14; 7:37–39.

22:2 tree of life. Access to God's life-giving blessings, barred after the Fall, is here renewed (vv. 14, 19; 2:7; Gen. 2:9; 3:22–24; Ezek. 47:12).

22:6–21 The central visionary part of Revelation ends with v. 5. The book now concludes with promise, exhortation, and confirmation in order to drive home the message of the visions and to stir up hope for the coming of the Lord Jesus (v. 20). Its major themes continue to be woven into this concluding section. There are many allusions to ch. 1.

22:6 trustworthy and true. See note 1:2.

22:7 soon. See note 1:1.

22:8 worship. See 19:10.

22:10 Do not seal. Daniel's scroll was sealed because the time of fulfillment was distant (Dan. 12:4).

the time is near. See note 1:1.

22:11 See Ezek. 3:27; Dan. 12:10; 2 Cor. 2:15, 16. If people do not repent when they hear the word of God, it increases their hardness. If hearing Revelation does not change the course of people's lives, it sets them more firmly in their present course, whichever side of the battle that may be.

22:12 for what he has done. See 20:12.

22:13 the Alpha and the Omega. See note 1:8.

22:14 Blessed. See note 1:3.

tree of life. See note on v. 2.

22:15 Outside. See 20:15; 21:8, 27. All evil doers are banished from the holy city, not only to punish them for their evil, but to protect the city

and murderers and idolaters, and everyone
who loves and practices falsehood.
16 [h] "I, Jesus, have sent my angel to testify
to you about these things [i] for the churches. I am [j] the root and [k] the descendant of
David, [l] the bright morning star."
17 The Spirit and [m] the Bride say, "Come."
And let the one who hears say, "Come."
And [n] let the one who is thirsty come; let
the one who desires take the [o] water of life
without price.
18 I warn everyone who hears the words
of the prophecy of this book: [p] if anyone
adds to them, God will add to him the
plagues described in this book, 19 and if
anyone takes away from the words of the
book of this prophecy, God will take away
his share in [q] the tree of life and in [r] the holy
city, which are described in this book.
20 He who testifies to these things says,
"Surely [s] I am coming soon." Amen. [t] Come,
Lord Jesus!
21 The grace of the Lord Jesus be with
all.[1] Amen.

16 [h] ch. 1:1 [i] ch. 1:4 [j] See ch. 5:5 [k] See Matt. 1:1 [l] [ch. 2:28; Num. 24:17; Isai. 60:3; Matt. 2:2]
17 [m] ch. 21:2, 9 [n] ch. 21:6; Isai. 55:1; John 7:37 [o] See ch. 21:6
18 [p] Deut. 4:2; 12:32; [Prov. 30:6]
19 [q] ver. 2, 14 [r] See ch. 21:2
20 [s] ver. 7, 12 [t] [2 Tim. 4:8]

1 Some manuscripts *all the saints*

from their contamination. The firmness of God's commitment to exclude evil from the final kingdom is a blessing and an encouragement to the saints.

22:17 water of life. See note on v. 1.

22:18, 19 This warning against adding or subtracting puts the Book of Revelation on the same level as Old Testament words of God (Deut. 4:2; 12:32). The Word of God is to be protected from corruption, and distinguished from mere human words.

22:20 soon. See note 1:1.

Come, Lord Jesus. The whole of Revelation is meant to stir Christians' longing and prayers for the realization of God's purposes accompanying the Second Coming. Revelation ends on this note (1 Cor. 16:22).

CONCORDANCE

AARON
The Lord said to **A**, "Go into Ex 4:27
Lord spoke to Moses and **A** Ex 6:13
A also and his sons I will Ex 29:44
the names of the sons of **A**: Nm 3:2
congregation saw that **A** Nm 20:29
called by God, just as **A** was. Heb 5:4

ABADDON
His name in Hebrew is **A**, Rv 9:11

ABANDON
For you will not **a** my soul to Ps 16:10
The Lord will not **a** him to Ps 37:33
he will not **a** his heritage; Ps 94:14
For you will not **a** my soul to Acts 2:27

ABANDONED
And they **a** the Lord, the God Jgs 2:12
'Because they **a** the Lord 1 Kgs 9:9
that he was not **a** to Hades, Acts 2:31
that you have **a** the love you Rv 2:4

ABBA
"**A**, Father, all things are Mk 14:36
whom we cry, "**A**! Father!" Rom 8:15
crying, "**A**! Father!" Gal 4:6

ABEDNEGO
and Azariah he called **A**. Dn 1:7
and **A** over the affairs of the Dn 2:49
and **A**, and to cast them into Dn 3:20

ABEL
she bore his brother **A**. Now Gn 4:2
rose up against his brother **A** Gn 4:8
the tribes of Israel to **A** 2 Sm 20:14
By faith **A** offered to God a Heb 11:4
word than the blood of **A**. Heb 12:24

ABHOR
and my soul will **a** you. Lv 26:30
You shall utterly detest and **a** Dt 7:26
I hate and **a** falsehood, but Ps 119:163
You who **a** idols, do you rob Rom 2:22
A what is evil; hold fast to Rom 12:9

ABHORS
the Lord **a** the bloodthirsty and Ps 5:6

ABIATHAR
named **A**, escaped and fled 1 Sm 22:20
son of Zeruiah and with **A** 1 Kgs 1:7
the priests Zadok and **A**, 1 Chr 15:11

ABIDE
"My spirit shall not **a** in man Gn 6:3
of the Most High will **a** Ps 91:1
A in me, and I in you. As the Jn 15:4
If anyone does not **a** in me he Jn 15:6
and love **a**, these three; 1 Cor 13:13
heard from the beginning **a** 1 Jn 2:24
a in him, so that when he 1 Jn 2:28
By this we know that we **a** 1 Jn 4:13
on ahead and does not **a** 2 Jn 1:9

ABIDES
be moved, but **a** forever. Ps 125:1
flesh and drinks my blood **a** Jn 6:56
Whoever **a** in me and I in Jn 15:5
No one who **a** in him keeps 1 Jn 3:6
keeps his commandments **a** 1 Jn 3:24
God **a** in us and his love is 1 Jn 4:12
and whoever **a** in love 1 Jn 4:16
Whoever **a** in the teaching 2 Jn 1:9

ABIDING
shadow, and there is no **a**. 1 Chr 29:15
do not have his word **a** in you Jn 5:38
better possession and an **a** Heb 10:34
through the living and **a** word 1 Pt 1:23
murderer has eternal life **a** in 1 Jn 3:15

ABIGAIL
When **A** saw David, she 1 Sm 25:23
sent and spoke to **A**, 1 Sm 25:39

ABILITY
have given to all able men **a**, Ex 31:6
to each according to his **a**. Mt 25:15
according to his **a**, Acts 11:29
but not the **a** to carry it out. Rom 7:18
tempted beyond your **a**, 1 Cor 10:13
to another the **a** to 1 Cor 12:10

ABIMELECH
And **A** king of Gerar sent and Gn 20:2
At that time **A** and Phicol Gn 21:22
Isaac went to Gerar to **A** Gn 26:1
Now **A** the son of Jerubbaal Jgs 9:1
God returned the evil of **A**, Jgs 9:56

ABISHAI
and to Joab's brother **A** 1 Sm 26:6
So Joab and **A** his brother 2 Sm 3:30
And David said to **A**, "Now 2 Sm 20:6

ABIJAH
and **A** his son reigned in 2 Chr 12:16
And **A** pursued Jeroboam 2 Chr 13:19
A slept with his fathers, 2 Chr 14:1

ABLE
if you are **a** to number them." Gn 15:5
Moses chose **a** men out of all Ex 18:25
I am not **a** to carry all this Nm 11:14
because the Lord was not **a** Nm 14:16
man shall give as he is **a**, Dt 16:17
that we should be **a** thus 1 Chr 29:14
But who is **a** to build him a 2 Chr 2:6
silver and gold are not **a** Ez 7:19
our God whom we serve is **a** Dn 3:17
who walk in pride he is **a** Dn 4:37
"Do you believe that I am **a** Mt 9:28
Are you **a** to drink the cup Mt 20:22
of God, you will not be **a** to Acts 5:39
will be **a** to separate us from Rom 8:39
Now to him who is **a** to Rom 16:25
that you may be **a** to 1 Cor 10:13
Now to him who is **a** to do Eph 3:20
a to teach, patiently 2 Tm 2:24
he is **a** to help those who are Heb 2:18
which is **a** to save your souls. Jas 1:21
Now to him who is **a** to keep Jude 1:24

ABNER
of his army was **A** 1 Sm 14:50
and **A** sat by Saul's side, 1 Sm 20:25
A was making himself strong 2 Sm 3:6
But **A** was not with David 2 Sm 3:22
the king lamented for **A**, 2 Sm 3:33

ABODE
strength to your holy **a**. Ex 15:13
His **a** has been established in Ps 76:2
From your lofty **a** you water Ps 104:13

ABOLISH
think that I have come to **a** Mt 5:17
I have not come to **a** them but Mt 5:17

ABOLISHED
who **a** death and brought 2 Tm 1:10

ABOLISHES
He **a** the first in order to Heb 10:9

ABOLISHING
by **a** the law of commandments Eph 2:15

ABOMINABLE
to practice any of these **a** Lv 18:30
And you shall not bring an **a** Dt 7:26
doing **a** iniquity; there is none Ps 53:1
and they made their **a** images Ez 7:20

ABOMINATION
as with a woman; it is an **a**. Lv 18:22
does these things is an **a** Dt 18:12
seven that are an **a** to him: Prv 6:16
are both alike an **a** Prv 17:15
the scoffer is an **a** to mankind. Prv 24:9
when they committed **a**? Jer 6:15
And they shall set up the **a** Dn 11:31
is taken away and the **a** Dn 12:11
"So when you see the **a** Mt 24:15
"But when you see the **a** Mk 13:14

ABOUND
the Lord will make you **a** Dt 28:11
in sin that grace may **a**? Rom 6:1
you may **a** in every good work. 2 Cor 9:8
prayer that your love may **a** Phil 1:9
make you increase and **a** 1 Thes 3:12

ABOUNDED
grace **a** all the more, Rom 5:20

ABOUNDING
a in steadfast love and faithfulness Ex 34:6
Lord is slow to anger and **a** Nm 14:18
slow to anger and **a** in Neh 9:17
a in steadfast love to all who Ps 86:5
slow to anger and **a** in Ps 86:15
and **a** in steadfast love; and he Jl 2:13
slow to anger and **a** in Jon 4:2
taught, **a** in thanksgiving. Col 2:7

ABRAHAM
but your name shall be **A**, Gn 17:5
Then **A** took Ishmael his Gn 17:23
these things God tested **A** Gn 22:1
Now **A** was old, well Gn 24:1
A breathed his last and died Gn 25:8
"I am the God of **A** your Gn 26:24
the son of David, the son of **A**. Mt 1:1
'I am the God of **A**, and the Mt 22:32
"**A** believed God, and it was Rom 4:3
just as **A** "believed God, and it Gal 3:6
By faith **A** obeyed when he Heb 11:8

ABRAM
he fathered **A**, Nahor, and Haran Gn 11:26
And **A** and Nahor took wives. Gn 11:29
Now the Lord said to **A**, "Go Gn 12:1
A, I am your shield; your Gn 15:1
shall your name be called **A**, Gn 17:5

ABSALOM
A the son of Maacah the 2 Sm 3:3
Now **A**, David's son, had a 2 Sm 13:1
"**A** has struck down all the 2 Sm 13:30
So **A** lived apart in his 2 Sm 14:24
surrounded **A** and struck 2 Sm 18:15
"O my son **A**, O **A**, my son, 2 Sm 19:4

ABSTAIN
you **a** from sexual immorality; 1 Thes 4:3
A from every form of evil. 1 Thes 5:22
sojourners and exiles to **a** 1 Pt 2:11

ABSTAINS
eats despise the one who **a**, Rom 14:3
God, while the one who **a**, Rom 14:6

ABUNDANCE
bread from heaven in **a**. Ps 105:40
a of salvation, wisdom, and Is 33:6
according to the **a** Lam 3:32
he will have an **a**, Mt 13:12
contributed out of their **a**, Mk 12:44
for out of the **a** of the heart Lk 6:45
those who receive the **a** Rom 5:17

ABUNDANT
according to your **a** mercy blot Ps 51:1
Lord, and **a** in power; his Ps 147:5
but to let you know the **a** 2 Cor 2:4

ABUNDANTLY
God, for he will **a** pardon. Is 55:7
may have life and have it **a**. Jn 10:10
For as we share **a** in 2 Cor 1:5
who is able to do far more **a** Eph 3:20
your faith is growing **a**, 2 Thes 1:3

ABUSE
a scoffer gets himself **a**, Prv 9:7
and quarreling and **a** will cease. Prv 22:10
pray for those who **a** you. Lk 6:28

ABYSS
them to depart into the **a**. Lk 8:31
into the **a**?" (that is, to bring Rom 10:7

ACCEPTABLE
meditation of my heart be **a** Ps 19:14
no prophet is **a** in his hometown. Lk 4:24
holy and **a** to God, which is Rom 12:1
what is good and **a** and perfect. Rom 12:2
thus let us offer to God **a** Heb 12:28
to offer spiritual sacrifices **a** 1 Pt 2:5

ACCEPTANCE
but the upright enjoy **a**. Prv 14:9
what will their **a** mean but Rom 11:15
and deserving of full **a**, 1 Tm 1:15

ACCEPTED
they may be **a** before the Lord. Ex 28:38
to be **a** it must be perfect; Lv 22:21
and the Lord **a** Job's prayer. Jb 42:9

and their sacrifices will be **a** Is 56:7
gospel from the one you **a**, 2 Cor 11:4

ACCESS
him we have also obtained **a** Rom 5:2
him we both have **a** Eph 2:18
we have boldness and **a** Eph 3:12

ACCOMPLISH
and I will **a** all my purpose,' Is 46:10
but it shall **a** that which I Is 55:11
of him who sent me and to **a** Jn 4:34
the Father has given me to **a**, Jn 5:36

ACCOMPLISHED
from the law until all is **a**. Mt 5:18
things are about to be **a**?" Mk 13:4
having **a** the work that you Jn 17:4
except what Christ has **a** Rom 15:18

ACCORD
the prophets with one **a** 1 Kgs 22:13
and serve him with one **a**. Zep 3:9
I have not come of my own **a**. Jn 7:28
I lay it down of my own **a**. Jn 10:18
All these with one **a** were Acts 1:14
being in full **a** and of one mind. Phil 2:2

ACCORDANCE
died for our sins in **a** 1 Cor 15:3
in **a** with the glorious gospel 1 Tm 1:11

ACCORDS
and the teaching that **a** 1 Tm 6:3
truth, which **a** with godliness, Ti 1:1
teach what **a** with healthy doctrine. Ti 2:1

ACCOUNT
"You will not call to **a**"? Ps 10:13
against you falsely on my **a**. Mt 5:11
judgment people will give **a** Mt 12:36
or persecution arises on **a** Mt 13:21
to write an orderly **a** for you, Lk 1:3
but on **a** of the crowd he could Lk 19:3
But I do not **a** my life of Acts 20:24
each of us will give an **a** Rom 14:12
On **a** of these the wrath of God Col 3:6
will have to give an **a**. Heb 13:17
but they will give **a** to him 1 Pt 4:5

ACCOUNTABLE
whole world may be held **a** Rom 3:19
in one point has become **a** Jas 2:10

ACCURSED
wish that I myself were **a** Rom 9:3
God ever says "Jesus is **a**!" 1 Cor 12:3
let him be **a**. Our Lord, come! 1 Cor 16:22
to you, let him be **a**. Gal 1:8
will there be anything **a**, Rv 22:3

ACCUSATION
"What **a** do you bring against Jn 18:29
you and to make an **a**, Acts 24:19

ACCUSATIONS
today against all the **a** Acts 26:2

ACCUSE
In return for my love they **a** Ps 109:4
so that they might **a** him. Mt 12:10
And they began to **a** him, Lk 23:2
their conflicting thoughts **a** Rom 2:15

ACCUSER
appeal for mercy to my **a**. Jb 9:15
lest your **a** hand you over to Mt 5:25
for the **a** of our brothers has Rv 12:10

ACHAIA
Gallio was proconsul of **A**, Acts 18:12
the first converts in **A**, 1 Cor 16:15
who are in the whole of **A**: 2 Cor 1:1

ACKNOWLEDGE
turn again to you and **a** 1 Kgs 8:33
In all your ways **a** him, and he Prv 3:6
Only **a** your guilt, that you Jer 3:13
I also will **a** before my Mt 10:32
the Son of Man also will **a** Lk 12:8
they did not see fit to **a** Rom 1:28
the fruit of lips that **a** his name. Heb 13:15

ACQUIRE
Do not toil to **a** wealth; be Prv 23:4
our inheritance until we **a** Eph 1:14

ACQUIT
for I will not **a** the wicked. Ex 23:7
who **a** the guilty for a bribe, Is 5:23
Shall I **a** the man with wicked Mi 6:11

ACQUITTED
and I would be **a** forever by Jb 23:7
but I am not thereby **a**. 1 Cor 4:4

ACT
place and forgive and **a** 1 Kgs 8:39
trust in him, and he will **a**. Ps 37:5
is time for the Lord to **a**, Ps 119:126
has been caught in the **a** Jn 8:4
so one **a** of righteousness Rom 5:18
So speak and so **a** as those Jas 2:12

ACTED
they on their part **a** with Jos 9:4
We have **a** very corruptly Neh 1:7
I know that you **a** in ignorance, Acts 3:17

ACTS
of the land of Egypt by great **a** Ex 7:4
Now the rest of all the **a** 1 Kgs 15:23
repays the one who **a** in pride Ps 31:23

ADAM
But for **A** there was not Gn 2:20
the Lord God made for **A** Gn 3:21
Thus all the days that **A** lived Gn 5:5
Yet death reigned from **A** Rom 5:14
For as in **A** all die, so also 1 Cor 15:22

ADD
You shall not **a** to the word that Dt 4:2
You shall not **a** to it or take Dt 12:32
Do not **a** to his words, lest he Prv 30:6
you by being anxious can **a** Mt 6:27
them, God will **a** to him the Rv 22:18

ADDED
nothing can be **a** to it, nor Eccl 3:14
and all these things will be **a** Mt 6:33
and there were **a** that day Acts 2:41
And the Lord **a** to their Acts 2:47
law? It was **a** because of Gal 3:19

ADMINISTERED
he **a** justice and equity 1 Chr 18:14
gift that is being **a** by us 2 Cor 8:20

ADMINISTRATING
a, and various kinds of 1 Cor 12:28

ADMONISH
while I **a** you! O Israel, if you Ps 81:8
but to **a** you as my beloved 1 Cor 4:14
a the idle, encourage the 1 Thes 5:14

ADMONISHING
teaching and **a** one another Col 3:16

ADONIJAH
Now **A** the son of Haggith 1 Kgs 1:5
A is king, although you, my 1 Kgs 1:18
And **A** feared Solomon. So 1 Kgs 1:50

ADOPTION
received the Spirit of **a** Rom 8:15
we wait eagerly for **a** as sons, Rom 8:23
and to them belong the **a**, Rom 9:4
that we might receive **a** as sons. Gal 4:5
he predestined us for **a** Eph 1:5

ADORN
women should **a** themselves 1 Tm 2:9
that in everything they may **a** Ti 2:10
who hoped in God used to **a** 1 Pt 3:5

ADORNED
she painted her eyes and **a** 2 Kgs 9:30
He **a** the house with 2 Chr 3:6
as a bride **a** for her husband. Rv 21:2

ADORNING
Do not let your **a** be external 1 Pt 3:3
but let your **a** be the hidden 1 Pt 3:4

ADULLAM
escaped to the cave of **A**. 1 Sm 22:1

of Israel shall come to **A**. Mi 1:15

ADULTERERS
For the land is full of **a**; Jer 23:10
They are all **a**; they are like a Hos 7:4
a, or even like this tax collector. Lk 18:11
nor **a**, nor men who practice 1 Cor 6:9

ADULTERESS
both the adulterer and the **a** Lv 20:10
This is the way of an **a**: Prv 30:20
by another man and is an **a**, Hos 3:1
another man she is not an **a**, Rom 7:3

ADULTEROUS
me and of my words in this **a** Mk 8:38
the sexually immoral and **a**. Heb 13:4
You **a** people! Do you not know Jas 4:4

ADULTERY
"You shall not commit **a**. Ex 20:14
"And you shall not commit **a**. Dt 5:18
He who commits **a** lacks Prv 6:32
already committed **a** with her Mt 5:28
a divorced woman commits **a**. Mt 5:32
marries another, commits **a**." Mt 19:9
immorality, theft, murder, **a**, Mk 7:21
marries another commits **a** Mk 10:11
marries another commits **a**, Lk 16:18
been caught in the act of **a**. Jn 8:4
"You shall not commit **a**, Rom 13:9

ADVANCE
a against a nation at ease, Jer 49:31
to me has really served to **a** Phil 1:12

ADVANCED
old, **a** in years. The way of Gn 18:11
King David was old and **a** 1 Kgs 1:1
and how he had **a** him above Est 5:11
and both were **a** in years. Lk 1:7

ADVANTAGE
'What **a** have I? How am I Jb 35:3
and man has no **a** over the Eccl 3:19
it is to your **a** that I go away, Jn 16:7
Christ will be of no **a** to you. Gal 5:2
for that would be of no **a** Heb 13:17
favoritism to gain **a**. Jude 1:16

ADVERSARIES
you for us, or for our **a**?" Jos 5:13
you will destroy all the **a** Ps 143:12
Lord takes vengeance on his **a** Na 1:2

ADVERSARY
Who is my **a**? Let him come Is 50:8
and give the **a** no occasion 1 Tm 5:14
Your **a** the devil prowls 1 Pt 5:8

ADVERSITY
and opens their ear by **a**. Jb 36:15
and a brother is born for **a**. Prv 17:17
and in the day of **a** consider: Eccl 7:14
Lord give you the bread of **a** Is 30:20

ADVICE
but a wise man listens to **a**. Prv 12:15
but with those who take **a** Prv 13:10
Listen to **a** and accept Prv 19:20

ADVOCATE
sin, we have an **a** with the 1 Jn 2:1

AFFAIRS
who conducts his **a** with justice. Ps 112:5
and to mind your own **a**, 1 Thes 4:11

AFFECTION
another with brotherly **a**. Rom 12:10
Spirit, any **a** and sympathy, Phil 2:1
and brotherly **a** with love. 2 Pt 1:7

AFFECTIONS
restricted in your own **a**. 2 Cor 6:12

AFFLICT
taskmasters over them to **a** Ex 1:11
and you shall **a** yourselves. Lv 23:32
And I will **a** the offspring 1 Kgs 11:39

AFFLICTED
He delivers the **a** by their Jb 36:15
your hand; forget not the **a**. Ps 10:12
smitten by God, and **a**. Is 53:4

and he was **a**, yet he opened Is 53:7
those **a** with various diseases Mt 4:24
If we are **a**, it is for your 2 Cor 1:6

AFFLICTION
Lord has listened to your **a**. Gn 16:11
tried you in the furnace of **a**. Is 48:10
every disease and every **a** Mt 4:23
momentary **a** is preparing 2 Cor 4:17

AFFLICTIONS
Many are the **a** of the Ps 34:19
what is lacking in Christ's **a** Col 1:24

AFLAME
better to marry than to be **a** 1 Cor 7:9

AFRAID
and I was **a**, because I was Gn 3:10
for he was **a** to look at God. Ex 3:6
Do not be **a** and do not be 1 Chr 28:20
it is I. Do not be **a**." Mt 14:27
"Why are you so **a**? Have you Mk 4:40
to anyone, for they were **a**. Mk 16:8
"Do not be **a**, Mary, for you Lk 1:30
"Do not be **a**, but go on Acts 18:9

AGABUS
a prophet named **A** came Acts 21:10

AGAG
and the people spared **A** 1 Sm 15:9
And Samuel hacked **A** 1 Sm 15:33

AGE
be buried in a good old **a**. Gn 15:15
So even to old **a** and gray Ps 71:18
either in this **a** or in the age Mt 12:32
and of the close of the **a**?" Mt 24:3
he is of **a**. He will speak for Jn 9:21
it is not a wisdom of this **a** 1 Cor 2:6
us from the present evil **a**, Gal 1:4

AGES
O Lord, throughout all **a**. Ps 135:13
God decreed before the **a** 1 Cor 2:7
the mystery hidden for **a** in God Eph 3:9
for all at the end of the **a** Heb 9:26

AGONY
pangs and **a** will seize them; Is 13:8
And being in an **a** he prayed Lk 22:44

AGREE
if two of you **a** on earth Mt 18:19
their testimony did not **a**. Mk 14:56
that all of you **a** and that 1 Cor 1:10
a with one another, live 2 Cor 13:11
doctrine and does not **a** 1 Tm 6:3
the blood; and these three **a**. 1 Jn 5:8

AGREEMENT
and your **a** with Sheol will Is 28:18
except perhaps by **a** for a 1 Cor 7:5
What **a** has the temple of 2 Cor 6:16

AGRIPPA
A the king and Bernice Acts 25:13
And **A** said to Paul, "In a Acts 26:28

AHAB
went to show himself to **A**. 1 Kgs 18:2
A rode and went to Jezreel. 1 Kgs 18:45
And after this **A** said to 1 Kgs 21:2
go down to meet **A** king of 1 Kgs 21:18

AHAZ
A the son of Jotham, king 2 Kgs 16:1
So **A** sent messengers to 2 Kgs 16:7
Again the Lord spoke to **A**, Is 7:10

AHINOAM
of Saul's wife was **A** 1 Sm 14:50
David also took **A** of 1 Sm 25:43

AHITHOPHEL
days the counsel that **A** 2 Sm 16:23
A was the king's counselor, 1 Chr 27:33

AI
sent men from Jericho to **A**, Jos 7:2
The men of Bethel and **A**, Ezr 2:28
for **A** is laid waste! Cry, O Jer 49:3

AIJALON
moon, in the valley of **A**." Jos 10:12

AIM
who **a** bitter words like arrows, Ps 64:3
for we **a** at what is 2 Cor 8:21
A for restoration, comfort 2 Cor 13:11
The **a** of our charge is love 1 Tm 1:5
my **a** in life, my faith, my 2 Tm 3:10

AIR
so near to another that no **a** can Jb 41:16
Look at the birds of the **a**: Mt 6:26
box as one beating the **a**. 1 Cor 9:26
prince of the power of the **a**, Eph 2:2
to meet the Lord in the **a**, 1 Thes 4:17

ALARM
When you blow an **a**, the Nm 10:5
I had said in my **a**, "I am cut Ps 31:22
Let not your thoughts **a** you Dn 5:10

ALARMED
and the visions of my head **a** Dn 4:5
See that you are not **a**, for this Mt 24:6
"Do not be **a**. You seek Jesus Mk 16:6

ALERT
Therefore be **a**, remembering Acts 20:31
To that end keep **a** with all Eph 6:18

ALEXANDER
of the crowd prompted **A**, Acts 19:33

ALIEN
or violence to the resident **a**, Jer 22:3

ALIENATED
a from the commonwealth of Eph 2:12
a from the life of God Eph 4:18
who once were **a** and hostile Col 1:21

ALIENS
no longer strangers and **a**, Eph 2:19

ALIVE
into the ark to keep them **a** Gn 6:19
"Joseph is still **a**, and he is Gn 45:26
I kill and I make **a**; I wound Dt 32:39
'This is my son that is **a**, 1 Kgs 3:23
is **a**; he was lost, and is found.'" Lk 15:32
dead to sin and **a** Rom 6:11
came, sin came **a** and I died. Rom 7:9
shall all be made **a**. 1 Cor 15:22
made us **a** together with Eph 2:5
God made **a** together with Col 2:13
Then we who are **a**, who 1 Thes 4:17
in the flesh but made **a** 1 Pt 3:18

ALLEGIANCE
of Canaan and swear **a** Is 19:18
every tongue shall swear **a**.' Is 45:23

ALLOW
over the door and will not **a** Ex 12:23
enter yourselves nor **a** those Mt 23:13
would not **a** them to speak, Lk 4:41
the Spirit of Jesus did not **a** Acts 16:7

ALLOWED
no evil shall be **a** to befall Ps 91:10
hardness of heart Moses **a** Mt 19:8
Am I not **a** to do what I Mt 20:15
"Moses **a** a man to write a Mk 10:4
Also it was **a** to make war on Rv 13:7

ALMIGHTY
"I am God **A**; walk before me, Gn 17:1
"I am God **A**: be fruitful and Gn 35:11
not the discipline of the **A**. Jb 5:17
For the arrows of the **A** are in Jb 6:4
contend with the **A**? Jb 40:2
abide in the shadow of the **A**. Ps 91:1
and who is to come, the **A**." Rv 1:8
is the Lord God the **A** Rv 21:22

ALMS
But give as **a** those things Lk 11:41
the Beautiful Gate to ask **a** Acts 3:2

ALONE
that the man should be **a**; Gn 2:18
other than the Lord **a**, shall Ex 22:20
O Lord, are God **a**." 2 Kgs 19:19
Lord, you **a**. You have made Neh 9:6
things; you **a** are God. Ps 86:10
one is good except God **a**. Mk 10:18
shall not live by bread **a**.'" Lk 4:4
can forgive sins but God **a**?" Lk 5:21
one is good except God **a**. Lk 18:19
Yet I am not **a**, for the Father Jn 16:32
by works and not by faith **a**. Jas 2:24

ALOUD
I cried **a** to the Lord, and he Ps 3:4
I cry **a** to God, **a** to God, Ps 77:1
crying **a**, "Have mercy on us, Mt 9:27

ALPHA
"I am the **A** and the Omega," Rv 1:8
I am the **A** and the Omega, Rv 21:6
I am the **A** and the Omega, Rv 22:13

ALPHAEUS
James the son of **A**, and Thaddaeus; Mt 10:3
he saw Levi the son of **A** Mk 2:14

ALTAR
Then Noah built an **a** to the Gn 8:20
So he built there an **a** to the Gn 12:7
Abraham built the **a** there Gn 22:9
So he built an **a** there and Gn 26:25
There he erected an **a** and Gn 33:20
Make an **a** there to the God Gn 35:1
And Moses built an **a** and Ex 17:15
An **a** of earth you shall make Ex 20:24
"You shall make the **a** of Ex 27:1
make atonement for the **a** Ex 29:37
the tabernacle and the **a**, Ex 40:33
blood against the sides of the **a** Lv 1:5
on the **a** of the Lord your Dt 12:27
that time Joshua built an **a** Jos 8:30
Manasseh built there an **a** Jos 22:10
Then Gideon built an **a** there Jgs 6:24
early and built there an **a** Jgs 21:4
And Saul built an **a** to the 1 Sm 14:35
David built there an **a** 2 Sm 24:25
He erected an **a** for Baal 1 Kgs 16:32
And he repaired the **a** 1 Kgs 18:30
David built there an **a** 1 Chr 21:26
He also restored the **a** 2 Chr 33:16
and they built the **a** of the God Ezr 3:2
are offering your gift at the **a** Mt 5:23
I found also an **a** with this Acts 17:23
up his son Isaac on the **a**? Jas 2:21
And I heard the **a** saying, Rv 16:7

ALTARS
You shall tear down their **a** Ex 34:13
cut down your incense **a** Lv 26:30
You shall tear down their **a** Dt 12:3
And he built **a** in the house 2 Kgs 21:4
he whose high places and **a** Is 36:7
will break down their **a** Hos 10:2

ALWAYS
and his commandments **a**. Dt 11:1
I have set the Lord **a** before Ps 16:8
I am with you **a**, to the end Mt 28:20
For you **a** have the poor with Mk 14:7
giving thanks **a** and for Eph 5:20
Rejoice in the Lord **a**; again I Phil 4:4
Rejoice **a**, 1 Thes 5:16
a being prepared to make a 1 Pt 3:15

AMAZED
And all the people were **a**, Mt 12:23
And the disciples were **a** Mk 10:24
so that Pilate was **a**. Mk 15:5
come with Peter were **a**, Acts 10:45

AMAZIAH
and **A** his son reigned in 2 Kgs 12:21
king of Israel captured **A** 2 Kgs 14:13
Then **A** the priest of Bethel Am 7:10

AMBASSADOR
for which I am an **a** in Eph 6:20

AMBASSADORS
we are **a** for Christ, God 2 Cor 5:20

AMBITION
and thus I make it my **a** Rom 15:20
bitter jealousy and selfish **a** Jas 3:14

AMBUSH
Lay an **a** against the city, Jos 8:2

a highway from Egypt to **A**, Is 19:23
A shall not save us; we will Hos 14:3

ASTONISHED
passing by it will be **a** 1 Kgs 9:8
the crowds were **a** at his teaching, Mt 7:28
they were amazed and **a**, Acts 2:7
they were **a**. And they Acts 4:13

ASTRAY
they go **a** from birth, speaking lies. Ps 58:3
and whoever is led **a** by it is Prv 20:1
we like sheep have gone **a**; Is 53:6
that never went **a**. Mt 18:13
to lead **a**, if possible, the elect. Mk 13:22
"See that you are not led **a**. Lk 21:8

ATE
she took of its fruit and **a**, Gn 3:6
and he **a**; and he brought Gn 27:25
do." So Mephibosheth **a** at 2 Sm 9:11
Man **a** of the bread of the Ps 78:25
and I **a** them, and your Jer 15:16
Then I **a** it, and it was in my Ez 3:3
And they all **a** and were Mt 14:20
And they all **a** and were Mt 15:37
And they all **a** and were satisfied. Mk 6:42
And they all **a** and were Lk 9:17

ATHENS
"Men of **A**, I perceive that Acts 17:22
to be left behind at **A** alone 1 Thes 3:1

ATHLETE
Every **a** exercises self-control 1 Cor 9:25
An **a** is not crowned unless 2 Tm 2:5

ATONE
you **a** for our transgressions. Ps 65:3
and **a** for our sins, for your Ps 79:9
you will not be able to **a**; Is 47:11
when I **a** for you for all that Ez 16:63
and to **a** for iniquity, to bring Dn 9:24

ATONED
so that their blood guilt be **a** Dt 21:8
Eli's house shall not be **a** 1 Sm 3:14
a for their iniquity and did Ps 78:38
and faithfulness iniquity is **a** Prv 16:6
away, and your sin **a** for. Is 6:7
this iniquity will not be **a** for you Is 22:14
the guilt of Jacob will be **a** Is 27:9

ATONEMENT
a bull as a sin offering for **a**. Ex 29:36
Aaron shall make **a** on its Ex 30:10
And the priest shall make **a** Lv 4:20
the tent of meeting to make **a** Lv 6:30
you on the altar to make **a** Lv 17:11
month is the day of **a**. Lv 23:27
for his God and made **a** Nm 25:13
Accept **a**, O Lord, for your Dt 21:8
days shall they make **a** Ez 43:26

ATONING
he has made an end of **a** Lv 16:20

ATTAIN
until we all **a** to the unity of Eph 4:13
any means possible I may **a** Phil 3:11

ATTAINED
righteousness have **a** Rom 9:30
true to what we have **a**. Phil 3:16

ATTEND
a to my cry! Give ear to my Ps 17:1
will **a** and listen for the time Is 42:23

ATTENTIVE
be open and your ears **a** 2 Chr 6:40
ears of all the people were **a** Neh 8:3
Let your ears be **a** to the Ps 130:2
be **a** to the words of my mouth. Prv 7:24

ATTRIBUTES
For his invisible **a**, namely, Rom 1:20

AUGUSTUS
a decree went out from Caesar **A** Lk 2:1

AUTHOR
and you killed the **A** of life, Acts 3:15

AUTHORITIES
many even of the **a** believed Jn 12:42
subject to the governing **a**. Rom 13:1
against the **a**, against the Eph 6:12
be submissive to rulers and **a**, Ti 3:1
a, and powers having been 1 Pt 3:22

AUTHORITY
them as one who had **a**, Mt 7:29
that the Son of Man has **a** Mt 9:6
"All **a** in heaven and on Mt 28:18
A new teaching with **a**! He Mk 1:27
"Tell us by what **a** you do Lk 20:2
I do not speak on my own **a**, Jn 14:10
For there is no **a** except Rom 13:1
the wife does not have **a** 1 Cor 7:4
to have a symbol of **a** 1 Cor 11:10
far above all rule and **a** Eph 1:21
to teach or to exercise **a** over 1 Tm 2:12
exhort and rebuke with all **a**. Ti 2:15
their own position of **a**, Jude 1:6
him I will give **a** over the nations, Rv 2:26
were those to whom the **a** Rv 20:4

AVENGE
may the Lord **a** me against 1 Sm 24:12
and shall I not **a** myself on a Jer 5:9
I will **a** their blood, blood that Jl 3:21
never **a** yourselves, but Rom 12:19

AVENGED
I swear I will be **a** on you, Jgs 15:7

AVENGER
for you a refuge from the **a**, Nm 35:12
to still the enemy and the **a**. Ps 8:2
an **a** who carries out God's Rom 13:4
because the Lord is an **a** 1 Thes 4:6

AVOID
A it; do not go on it; turn Prv 4:15
not only to **a** God's wrath Rom 13:5
have been taught; **a** them. Rom 16:17
A the irreverent babble and 1 Tm 6:20
But **a** irreverent babble, for 2 Tm 2:16
its power. **A** such people. 2 Tm 3:5
to **a** quarreling, to be gentle, Ti 3:2
But **a** foolish controversies, Ti 3:9

AWAKE
a and sing for joy! For your Is 26:19
stay **a**, for you do not know Mt 24:42
Therefore stay **a** — for you Mk 13:35
"**A**, O sleeper, and arise from Eph 5:14

AWARD
will **a** to me on that Day, and 2 Tm 4:8

AWE
the ends of the earth are in **a** Ps 65:8
of Jacob and will stand in **a** Is 29:23
they were filled with **a** and Mt 27:54
with reverence and **a**, Heb 12:28

AWESOME
"How **a** is this place! This is Gn 28:17
for it is an **a** thing that I will Ex 34:10
the great and **a** God who Neh 1:5
"How **a** are your deeds! So Ps 66:3
them praise your great and **a** Ps 99:3
Holy and **a** is his name! Ps 111:9
before the great and **a** Mal 4:5

AXE
his **a** head fell into the 2 Kgs 6:5
Even now the **a** is laid to the Lk 3:9

AZAZEL
Lord and the other lot for **A**. Lv 16:8

BAAL
So Israel yoked himself to **B** Nm 25:3
said to the prophets of **B**, 1 Kgs 18:25
Thus Jehu wiped out **B** 2 Kgs 10:28
they prophesied by **B** and led Jer 23:13

BABEL
of his kingdom was **B**, Gn 10:10
Therefore its name was called **B**, Gn 11:9

BABES
Out of the mouth of **b** and Ps 8:2

BABY
the **b** leaped in her womb. Lk 1:41
you will find a **b** wrapped in Lk 2:12
she has delivered the **b**, Jn 16:21

BABYLON
Nebuchadnezzar the king of **B** Ezr 2:1
fallen is **B**; and all the carved Is 21:9
To **B** you shall go, and there Jer 20:6
carried into exile to **B** the rest Jer 39:9
Do not fear the king of **B**, Jer 42:11
"Flee from the midst of **B**, Jer 50:8
"I will repay **B** and all the Jer 51:24
'Thus shall **B** sink, to rise no Jer 51:64
"Is not this great **B**, which I Dn 4:30
fallen is **B** the great, she who Rv 14:8
"**B** the great, mother of Rv 17:5
fallen is **B** the great! She has Rv 18:2

BAD
good for **b**, or bad for good; Lv 27:10
"**B**, Bad," says the buyer, but Prv 20:14
"For no good tree bears **b** Lk 6:43
nothing either good or **b** Rom 9:11
"**B** company ruins good 1 Cor 15:33

BAG
would be sealed up in a **b**, Jb 14:17
he took a **b** of money with Prv 7:20

BAKER
cupbearer and the chief **b**, Gn 40:2
like a heated oven whose **b** Hos 7:4

BAKERS
perfumers and cooks and **b**. 1 Sm 8:13

BALAAM
And God came to **B** at night Nm 22:20
And **B** said to the donkey, Nm 22:29
"The oracle of **B** the son of Nm 24:3

BALAK
"**B** the son of Zippor, king of Nm 22:10

BALANCE
me be weighed in a just **b**, Jb 31:6
A false **b** is an abomination to Prv 11:1

BALANCES
You shall have just **b**, just Lv 19:36
have been weighed in the **b** Dn 5:27

BALD
They shall not make **b** patches Lv 21:5
they make themselves **b** Ez 27:31
make yourselves as **b** as the Mi 1:16

BALDNESS
cut yourselves or make any **b** Dt 14:1
and **b** on all their heads. Ez 7:18

BALM
a little **b** and a little honey, Gn 43:11
Is there no **b** in Gilead? Is Jer 8:22
Take **b** for her pain; perhaps Jer 51:8

BAND
I pursue after this **b**? 1 Sm 30:8
leader of a marauding **b**, 1 Kgs 11:24
They **b** together against the Ps 94:21

BANDS
with the **b** of love, and I Hos 11:4

BANK
by the other cows on the **b** Gn 41:3
Stand on the **b** of the Nile to Ex 7:15
not put my money in the **b**, Lk 19:23

BANNER
of it, The Lord is my **b**, Ex 17:15
You have set up a **b** for those Ps 60:4
and his **b** over me was love. Sg 2:4

BANQUETING
He brought me to the **b** house, Sg 2:4

BAPTISM
The **b** of John, from where Mt 21:25
and proclaiming a **b** Mk 1:4
and with the **b** with which I Mk 10:39
proclaiming a **b** of repentance Lk 3:3
been baptized with the **b** Lk 7:29
I have a **b** to be baptized Lk 12:50

John had proclaimed a **b** Acts 13:24
he knew only the **b** Acts 18:25
They said, "Into John's **b**." Acts 19:3
therefore with him by **b** Rom 6:4
one Lord, one faith, one **b**, Eph 4:5
been buried with him in **b**, Col 2:12
B, which corresponds to this, 1 Pt 3:21

BAPTIST
In those days John the **B** came Mt 3:1
"Some say John the **B**, others Mt 16:14
"John the **B** has been raised Mk 6:14
"The head of John the **B**." Mk 6:24
once the head of John the **B** Mk 6:25
"For John the **B** has come Lk 7:33

BAPTIZE
"I **b** you with water for Mt 3:11
He will **b** you with the Holy Mt 3:11
but he will **b** you with the Mk 1:8
He will **b** you with the Holy Lk 3:16
"I **b** with water, but among Jn 1:26
but he who sent me to **b** with Jn 1:33
Jesus himself did not **b**, Jn 4:2
did **b** also the household of 1 Cor 1:16
did not send me to **b** 1 Cor 1:17

BAPTIZED
and they were **b** by him in the Mt 3:6
to John, to be **b** by him. Mt 3:13
when all the people were **b**, Lk 3:21
just, having been **b** with the Lk 7:29
were coming and being **b** Jn 3:23
for John **b** with water, but Acts 1:5
"Repent and be **b** every one Acts 2:38
received his word were **b**, Acts 2:41
were **b**, both men and women. Acts 8:12
prevents me from being **b**?" Acts 8:36
Then he rose and was **b**; Acts 9:18
commanded them to be **b** Acts 10:48
'John **b** with water, but you Acts 11:16
And after she was **b**, and Acts 16:15
Paul believed and were **b**. Acts 18:8
Rise and be **b** and wash Acts 22:16
into Christ Jesus were **b** Rom 6:3
Or were you **b** in the name 1 Cor 1:13
and all were **b** into Moses 1 Cor 10:2
one Spirit we were all **b** 1 Cor 12:13
people mean by being **b** 1 Cor 15:29
as many of you as were **b** Gal 3:27

BAPTIZES
is he who **b** with the Holy Spirit.' Jn 1:33

BAPTIZING
b them in the name of the Mt 28:19
but for this purpose I came **b** Jn 1:31
that Jesus was making and **b** Jn 4:1
withhold water for **b** Acts 10:47

BARABBAS
notorious prisoner called **B**. Mt 27:16
he released for them **B**, Mt 27:26

BARAK
She sent and summoned **B** Jgs 4:6
B, Samson, Jephthah, of Heb 11:32

BARE
of the world were laid **b**, 2 Sm 22:16
of the world were laid **b** Ps 18:15
and the Lord will lay **b** their Is 3:17

BARLEY
a cake of **b** bread tumbled into Jgs 7:13
at the beginning of **b** harvest. Ru 1:22
is a boy here who has five **b** Jn 6:9

BARN
gather his wheat into the **b**, Mt 3:12
the wheat into my **b**.'" Mt 13:30
neither storehouse nor **b**, Lk 12:24

BARNABAS
who was also called **B** by the Acts 4:36
And Paul and **B** spoke out Acts 13:46

BARNS
the blessing on you in your **b** Dt 28:8
then your **b** will be filled Prv 3:10
nor reap nor gather into **b**, Mt 6:26

BARRACKS
to be brought into the **b**. Acts 21:34

BARREN
Sarai was **b**; she had no child. Gn 11:30
because she was **b**. And the Gn 25:21
He gives the **b** woman a Ps 113:9
O **b** one, who did not bear; Is 54:1
because Elizabeth was **b**, and Lk 1:7
with her who was called **b**. Lk 1:36
'Blessed are the **b** and the Lk 23:29
O **b** one who does not bear; Gal 4:27

BARTHOLOMEW
Philip and **B**; Thomas and Mt 10:3

BARTIMAEUS
B, a blind beggar, the son of Mk 10:46

BARUCH
And **B** the son of Neriah did Jer 36:8
the prophet spoke to **B** Jer 45:1

BASHAN
had given a possession in **B**, Jos 22:7
you cows of **B**, who are on the Am 4:1

BASIC
to teach you again the **b** Heb 5:12

BASKET
she took for him a **b** made of Ex 2:3
One **b** had very good figs, like Jer 24:2
a lamp and put it under a **b**, Mt 5:15
wall, lowering him in a **b** Acts 9:25
but I was let down in a **b** 2 Cor 11:33

BASKETS
And they took up twelve **b** Mt 14:20

BATHE
of Pharaoh came down to **b** Ex 2:5
shave off all his hair and **b** Lv 14:8

BATHED
"The one who has **b** does not Jn 13:10

BATHING
from the roof a woman **b**; 2 Sm 11:2

BATHSHEBA
B, and went in to her and 2 Sm 12:24
"Call **B** to me." So she came 1 Kgs 1:28

BATTLE
the **b** is not yours but God's. 2 Chr 20:15
me with strength for the **b**; Ps 18:39
the Lord, mighty in **b**! Ps 24:8
made ready for the day of **b**, Prv 21:31
nor the **b** to the strong, nor Eccl 9:11
who will get ready for **b**? 1 Cor 14:8

BEELZEBUL
the master of the house **B**, Mt 10:25
if I cast out demons by **B**, Mt 12:27

BEAM
was like a weaver's **b**, 1 Sm 17:7
a **b** shall be pulled out of his Ezr 6:11
b from the woodwork respond. Hb 2:11

BEAMS
He lays the **b** of his chambers Ps 104:3

BEAR
who made the **B** and Orion, the Jb 9:9
roaring lion or a charging **b** Prv 28:15
the virgin shall conceive and **b** Is 7:14
The cow and the **b** shall graze; Is 11:7
He is a **b** lying in wait for Lam 3:10
like a **b**. It was raised up on Dn 7:5
will fall upon them like a **b** Hos 13:8
She will **b** a son, and you Mt 1:21
to **b** witness about the light, Jn 1:7
in order that we may **b** fruit Rom 7:4
have an obligation to **b** Rom 15:1
we shall also **b** the image 1 Cor 15:49
B one another's burdens, and Gal 6:2
for I **b** on my body the marks Gal 6:17

BEARD
hair from my head and **b** Ezr 9:3
to those who pull out the **b**; Is 50:6

BEARING
and fruit trees **b** fruit in Gn 1:11
b with one another and, if Col 3:13
are enduring patiently and **b** Rv 2:3

BEARS
every healthy tree **b** good Mt 7:17
but if it dies, it **b** much fruit. Jn 12:24
he it is that **b** much fruit, for Jn 15:5
their conscience also **b** Rom 2:15
The Spirit himself **b** witness Rom 8:16
Love **b** all things, believes 1 Cor 13:7
And the Holy Spirit also **b** Heb 10:15

BEAST
the Lord God formed every **b** Gn 2:19
For every **b** of the forest is Ps 50:10
the foal of a **b** of burden.'" Mt 21:5
For every kind of **b** and bird, of Jas 3:7
the number of the **b**, Rv 13:18
received the mark of the **b** Rv 19:20

BEASTS
And God made the **b** of the Gn 1:25
I fought with **b** at Ephesus? 1 Cor 15:32

BEAT
were mocking him as they **b** Lk 22:63
they **b** them and charged Acts 5:40

BEATING
and **b** for the backs of fools. Prv 19:29
they stopped **b** Paul. Acts 21:32
I do not box as one **b** the air. 1 Cor 9:26

BEAUTIFUL
that you are a woman **b** Gn 12:11
I have a **b** inheritance. Ps 16:6
He has made everything **b** Eccl 3:11
You are altogether **b**, my love; Sg 4:7
How **b** upon the mountains are Is 52:7
She has done a **b** thing to me. Mk 14:6
temple that is called the **B** Acts 3:2
"How **b** are the feet of Rom 10:15

BEAUTY
the king will desire your **b**. Ps 45:11
and **b** is vain, but a woman Prv 31:30
no **b** that we should desire him. Is 53:2
and its **b** perishes. So also Jas 1:11
with the imperishable **b** 1 Pt 3:4

BED
every night I flood my **b** with Ps 6:6
so does a sluggard on his **b**. Prv 26:14
take up your **b**, and walk." Jn 5:8
and let the marriage **b** be Heb 13:4

BEDS
they rest in their **b** who walk Is 57:2

BEERSHEBA
they made a covenant at **B**. Gn 21:32
that he had and came to **B**, Gn 46:1
Judah, from Dan to **B**." 2 Sm 3:10

BEFALL
and no plague will **b** you to Ex 12:13
no evil shall be allowed to **b** Ps 91:10

BEFITS
Praise **b** the upright. Ps 33:1
holiness **b** your house, O Lord, Ps 93:5

BEG
I **b** you to look at my son, for Lk 9:38
So I **b** you to reaffirm your 2 Cor 2:8

BEGAN
At that time people **b** to call Gn 4:26
When man **b** to multiply on Gn 6:1
with the Holy Spirit and **b** Acts 2:4
that he who **b** a good work in Phil 1:6

BEGGAR
a blind **b**, the son of Mk 10:46
had seen him before as a **b** Jn 9:8

BEGIN
it is time for judgment to **b** 1 Pt 4:17

BEGINNING
In the **b**, God created the heavens Gn 1:1
The fear of the Lord is the **b** Prv 1:7
the end of a thing than its **b**, Eccl 7:8
In the **b** was the Word, and the Jn 1:1
He was in the **b** with God. Jn 1:2
He is the **b**, the firstborn from Col 1:18
having neither **b** of days nor Heb 7:3

That which was from the **b**, 1 Jn 1:1
the **b** of God's creation. Rv 3:14
the **b** and the end. To the Rv 21:6
the last, the **b** and the end." Rv 22:13

BEGOTTEN
my Son; today I have **b** you. Ps 2:7
Son, today I have **b** you.' Acts 13:33
today I have **b** you"? Or Heb 1:5
Son, today I have **b** you"; Heb 5:5

BEGS
Give to everyone who **b** from Lk 6:30

BEHALF
sought God on **b** of the child. 2 Sm 12:16
ask the Father on your **b**; Jn 16:26
always struggling on your **b** Col 4:12
as a forerunner on our **b**, Heb 6:20
presence of God on our **b**. Heb 9:24

BEHAVE
know how one ought to **b** 1 Tm 3:15

BEHAVED
our conscience that we **b** 2 Cor 1:12

BEHAVING
thinks that he is not **b** 1 Cor 7:36

BEHAVIOR
So he changed his **b** before 1 Sm 21:13
are to be reverent in **b**, Ti 2:3
who revile your good **b** 1 Pt 3:16

BEHEADED
He sent and had John **b** Mt 14:10
of those who had been **b** Rv 20:4

BEHELD
they **b** God, and ate and drank. Ex 24:11
He has not **b** misfortune in Nm 23:21

BEHOLD
and **b**, it was very good. And Gn 1:31
that I may **b** wondrous Ps 119:18
"**B**, a virgin shall conceive and Mt 1:23
"**B**, the Lamb of God, who Jn 1:29
said to them, "**B** the man!" Jn 19:5
"Woman, **b**, your son!" Jn 19:26

BEINGS
lower than the heavenly **b** Ps 8:5
O heavenly **b**, ascribe to the Ps 29:1
Who among the heavenly **b** Ps 89:6

BEL
B bows down; Nebo stoops; Is 46:1
And I will punish **B** in Jer 51:44

BELIAL
accord has Christ with **B**? 2 Cor 6:15

BELIEF
Spirit and **b** in the truth 2 Thes 2:13

BELIEVE
"that they may **b** that the Lord, Ex 4:5
and may also **b** you forever." Ex 19:9
how long will they not **b** Nm 14:11
of this word you did not **b** Dt 1:32
B in the Lord your God, 2 Chr 20:20
I **b** that I shall look upon the Ps 27:13
because they did not **b** in God Ps 78:22
for I **b** in your commandments. Ps 119:66
that you may know and **b** Is 43:10
days that you would not **b** Hb 1:5
"Do you **b** that I am able to do Mt 9:28
one of these little ones who **b** Mt 18:6
cross, and we will **b** in him. Mt 27:42
repent and **b** in the gospel." Mk 1:15
"Do not fear, only **b**." Mk 5:36
that all might **b** through him. Jn 1:7
for unless you **b** that I am he Jn 8:24
b the works, that you may Jn 10:38
I **b** that you are the Christ, Jn 11:27
b in the light, that you may Jn 12:36
B in God; **b** also in me. Jn 14:1
so that the world may **b** Jn 17:21
Do not disbelieve, but **b**." Jn 20:27
written so that you may **b** Jn 20:31
word of the gospel and **b**. Acts 15:7
"**B** in the Lord Jesus, and Acts 16:31
Jesus Christ for all who **b**. Rom 3:22
him the father of all who **b** Rom 4:11
will be counted to us who **b** Rom 4:24
we **b** that we will also live Rom 6:8
that Jesus is Lord and **b** Rom 10:9
And how are they to **b** Rom 10:14
to save those who **b**. 1 Cor 1:21
be given to those who **b**. Gal 3:22
his power toward us who **b**, Eph 1:19
For since we **b** that Jesus 1 Thes 4:14
especially of those who **b**. 1 Tm 4:10
draw near to God must **b** Heb 11:6
You **b** that God is one; you do Jas 2:19
the honor is for you who **b**, 1 Pt 2:7
that we **b** in the name of his 1 Jn 3:23
do not **b** every spirit, but test 1 Jn 4:1
Whoever does not **b** God has 1 Jn 5:10
those who did not **b**. Jude 1:5

BELIEVED
And he **b** the Lord, and he Gn 15:6
and they **b** in the Lord and Ex 14:31
And the people of Nineveh **b** Jon 3:5
And blessed is she who **b** Lk 1:45
who **b** in his name, he gave Jn 1:12
many **b** in his name when Jn 2:23
The man **b** the word that Jn 4:50
he himself **b**, and all his household Jn 4:53
Yet many of the people **b** in Jn 7:31
And many **b** in him there. Jn 10:42
and they have **b** that you sent me. Jn 17:8
not seen and yet have **b**." Jn 20:29
And all who **b** were together Acts 2:44
who had heard the word **b**, Acts 4:4
full number of those who **b** Acts 4:32
appointed to eternal life **b**. Acts 13:48
Many of them therefore **b**, Acts 17:12
who through grace had **b**, Acts 18:27
Holy Spirit when you **b**?" Acts 19:2
"Abraham **b** God, and it was Rom 4:3
of the God in whom he **b**, Rom 4:17
who has **b** what he has Rom 10:16
now than when we first **b**. Rom 13:11
— unless you **b** in vain. 1 Cor 15:2
so we also have **b** in Christ Gal 2:16
just as Abraham "**b** God, and it Gal 3:6
and **b** in him, were sealed Eph 1:13
b on in the world, taken up 1 Tm 3:16
I know whom I have **b**, 2 Tm 1:12
learned and have firmly **b**, 2 Tm 3:14
so that those who have **b** in God Ti 3:8
For we who have **b** enter that Heb 4:3
"Abraham **b** God, and it was Jas 2:23
because he has not **b** in the 1 Jn 5:10

BELIEVER
woman who was a **b**, Acts 16:1
Or what portion does a **b** 2 Cor 6:15

BELIEVERS
And more than ever **b** were Acts 5:14
are a sign not for **b** 1 Cor 14:22
an example to all the **b** 1 Thes 1:7
but set the **b** an example in 1 Tm 4:12
by their good service are **b** 1 Tm 6:2
and his children are **b** and not Ti 1:6
who through him are **b** 1 Pt 1:21

BELIEVES
'Whoever **b** will not be in haste.' Is 28:16
but **b** that what he says will Mk 11:23
that whoever **b** in him may Jn 3:15
that whoever **b** in him should Jn 3:16
Whoever **b** in him is not Jn 3:18
Whoever **b** in the Son has Jn 3:36
hears my word and **b** Jn 5:24
and whoever **b** in me shall Jn 6:35
who looks on the Son and **b** Jn 6:40
whoever **b** has eternal life. Jn 6:47
Whoever **b** in me, as the Jn 7:38
everyone who lives and **b** Jn 11:26
"Whoever **b** in me, **b** not in me Jn 12:44
so that whoever **b** in me may Jn 12:46
whoever **b** in me will also do Jn 14:12
that everyone who **b** Acts 10:43
to everyone who **b**, Rom 1:16
and whoever **b** in him will Rom 9:33
to everyone who **b**. Rom 10:4
"Everyone who **b** in him Rom 10:11
b all things, hopes all 1 Cor 13:7
and whoever **b** in him will 1 Pt 2:6
Everyone who **b** that Jesus is 1 Jn 5:1
Whoever **b** in the Son of God 1 Jn 5:10

BELIEVING
and that by **b** you may have Jn 20:31
the right to take along a **b** 1 Cor 9:5

BELLY
on your **b** you shall go, and Gn 3:14
And Jonah was in the **b** Jon 1:17
and three nights in the **b** Mt 12:40
their god is their **b**, and they Phil 3:19

BELONG
to the Lord your God **b** Dt 10:14
"The secret things **b** to the Dt 29:29
The plans of the heart **b** Prv 16:1
It shall **b** to those who walk Is 35:8
Spirit of Christ does not **b** Rom 8:9
I do not **b** to the body," 1 Cor 12:15
his coming those who **b** 1 Cor 15:23
And those who **b** to Christ Gal 5:24
But since we **b** to the day, 1 Thes 5:8
things that **b** to salvation. Heb 6:9
To him **b** glory and dominion 1 Pt 4:11
and glory and power **b** Rv 19:1

BELONGS
Salvation **b** to the Lord; your Ps 3:8
this: that power **b** to God, Ps 62:11
b steadfast love. For you will Ps 62:12
For our shield **b** to the Lord, Ps 89:18
but the victory **b** to the Lord. Prv 21:31
pay. Salvation **b** to the Lord!" Jon 2:9
to such **b** the kingdom of God. Mk 10:14
called to the one hope that **b** Eph 4:4
but the substance **b** to Christ. Col 2:17
"Salvation **b** to our God who Rv 7:10

BELOVED
"The **b** of the Lord dwells in Dt 33:12
That your **b** ones may be Ps 60:5
You have caused my **b** and Ps 88:18
That your **b** ones may be Ps 108:6
for he gives to his **b** sleep. Ps 127:2
My **b** is mine, and I am his; he Sg 2:16
Let me sing for my **b** my love Is 5:1
"This is my **b** Son, with whom Mt 3:17
"This is my **b** Son, with whom Mt 17:5
not beloved I will call '**b**.'" Rom 9:25
they are **b** for the sake of Rom 11:28
he has blessed us in the **B**. Eph 1:6
"This is my **b** Son, with 2 Pt 1:17
B, let us love one another, for 1 Jn 4:7

BELSHAZZAR
King **B** made a great feast for a Dn 5:1
In the first year of **B** king of Dn 7:1

BELT
Righteousness shall be the **b** Is 11:5
and faithfulness the **b** of his loins. Is 11:5
of camel's hair and a leather **b** Mt 3:4
having fastened on the **b** Eph 6:14

BENEFIT
what **b** is that to you? For Lk 6:32
how will I **b** you unless I 1 Cor 14:6

BENEFITS
and forget not all his **b**, Ps 103:2
A man who is kind **b** Prv 11:17

BENJAMIN
but his father called him **B**. Gn 35:18
Of the people of **B**, their Nm 1:36

BEREFT
Why should I be **b** of you Gn 27:45
evil for good; my soul is **b**. Ps 35:12
my soul is **b** of peace; I have Lam 3:17

BESET
he himself is **b** with weakness. Heb 5:2

BEST
making the **b** use of the time, Eph 5:16
Do your **b** to present 2 Tm 2:15

BESTOW
splendor and majesty you **b** Ps 21:5
less honorable we **b** 1 Cor 12:23

BESTOWED
sight of all Israel and **b** 1 Chr 29:25
many that were blind he **b** Lk 7:21
highly exalted him and **b** Phil 2:9

BESTOWING
b his riches on all who call Rom 10:12

BESTOWS
the Lord **b** favor and honor. Ps 84:11

BETHANY
Now when Jesus was at **B** Mt 26:6
Jesus therefore came to **B**, Jn 12:1

BETHEL
the name of that place **B**, Gn 28:19

BETHLEHEM
O **B** Ephrathah, who are too Mi 5:2
"In **B** of Judea, for so it is Mt 2:5
which is called **B**, because he Lk 2:4
and comes from **B**, the village Jn 7:42

BETRAY
many will fall away and **b** Mt 24:10
sought an opportunity to **b** Mt 26:16
would you **b** the Son of Man Lk 22:48
For he knew who was to **b** him; Jn 13:11
who is it that is going to **b** you?" Jn 21:20

BETRAYED
Judas Iscariot, who **b** him. Mt 10:4
The Son of Man is **b** into the Mk 14:41
the night when he was **b** 1 Cor 11:23

BETRAYER
see, my **b** is at hand." Mt 26:46
his **b**, saw that Jesus was Mt 27:3
Now the **b** had given them a Mk 14:44

BETROTHED
is there any man who has **b** Dt 20:7
his mother Mary had been **b** Mt 1:18
Now concerning the **b**, 1 Cor 7:25
and if a **b** woman marries, 1 Cor 7:28
to keep her as his **b**, he will 1 Cor 7:37
for I **b** you to one husband, 2 Cor 11:2

BETTER
your steadfast love is **b** Ps 63:3
A good name is **b** than Eccl 7:1
For it is **b** that you lose one of Mt 5:29
For it is **b** to marry than to 1 Cor 7:9
Christ, for that is far **b**. Phil 1:23
Jesus the guarantor of a **b** Heb 7:22
they desire a **b** country, that Heb 11:16
had provided something **b** Heb 11:40
blood that speaks a **b** Heb 12:24
For it is **b** to suffer for doing 1 Pt 3:17
For it would have been **b** 2 Pt 2:21

BEWARE
B lest you say in your heart, Dt 8:17
"**B** of false prophets, who come Mt 7:15
B of the leaven of the Mt 16:11

BILDAD
B the Shuhite, and Zophar the Jb 2:11

BILHAH
And **B** conceived and bore Gn 30:5

BIND
You shall **b** them as a sign on Dt 6:8
b them around your neck; Prv 3:3
and whatever you **b** on earth Mt 16:19
'**B** him hand and foot and Mt 22:13

BINDS
unless he first **b** the strong Mk 3:27
which **b** everything together Col 3:14

BIRD
and every winged **b** according Gn 1:21
of the earth and upon every **b** Gn 9:2
"Flee like a **b** to your mountain, Ps 11:1

BIRDS
the **b** of the heavens, and the Ps 8:8
Look at the **b** of the air: they Mt 6:26

BIRTH
go astray from **b**, speaking lies. Ps 58:3
Now the **b** of Jesus Christ took Mt 1:18
but the beginning of the **b** Mt 24:8
And she gave **b** to her firstborn Lk 2:7
And a man lame from **b** was Acts 3:2
not many were of noble **b**. 1 Cor 1:26
it has conceived gives **b** Jas 1:15

BIRTHRIGHT
said, "Sell me your **b** now." Gn 25:31
Thus Esau despised his **b**. Gn 25:34
firstborn according to his **b** Gn 43:33
who sold his **b** for a single meal. Heb 12:16

BITTER
who put **b** for sweet and sweet Is 5:20

BITTERLY
She weeps **b** in the night, Lam 1:2
he went out and wept **b**. Mt 26:75

BITTERNESS
The heart knows its own **b**, Prv 14:10
Let all **b** and wrath and Eph 4:31
that no "root of **b**" springs Heb 12:15

BLACK
and the day shall be **b** over them; Mi 3:6
the sun became **b** as sackcloth, Rv 6:12

BLACKSMITH
Now there was no **b** to be 1 Sm 13:19

BLAMELESS
walk before me, and be **b**, Gn 17:1
You shall be **b** before the Dt 18:13
me! Then I shall be **b**, and Ps 19:13
justified in your words and **b** Ps 51:4
May my heart be **b** in your Ps 119:80
guards him whose way is **b**, Prv 13:6
that we should be holy and **b** Eph 1:4
and so be pure and **b** for the Phil 1:10
that you may be **b** and innocent, Phil 2:15
to present you holy and **b** Col 1:22
holy and righteous and **b** 1 Thes 2:10
soul and body be kept **b** 1 Thes 5:23
and to present you **b** before Jude 1:24

BLAMELESSLY
He who walks **b** and does Ps 15:2
God, walking **b** in all the Lk 1:6

BLASPHEME
and **b** the glorious ones. Jude 1:8

BLASPHEMED
"The name of God is **b** Rom 2:24
the way of truth will be **b**. 2 Pt 2:2

BLASPHEMES
Whoever **b** the name of the Lv 24:16
but whoever **b** against the Mk 3:29
but the one who **b** against Lk 12:10

BLASPHEMING
He is **b**! Who can forgive sins Mk 2:7

BLASPHEMY
every sin and **b** will be Mt 12:31
but the **b** against the Spirit Mt 12:31

BLEMISH
lamb shall be without **b**, Ex 12:5
youths without **b**, of good Dn 1:4
be holy and without **b**. Eph 5:27
offered himself without **b** Heb 9:14
like that of a lamb without **b** 1 Pt 1:19

BLESS
and I will **b** you and make Gn 12:2
I will **b** those who **b** you, Gn 12:3
I will surely **b** you, and I Gn 22:17
The Lord **b** you and keep you; Nm 6:24
b you, and multiply you. He Dt 7:13
I **b** the Lord who gives me Ps 16:7
I will **b** the Lord at all times; Ps 34:1
Lord, **b** his name; tell of his Ps 96:2
B the Lord, O my soul, and all Ps 103:1
him, that I might **b** him and Is 51:2
b those who curse you, pray Lk 6:28
B those who persecute you; Rom 12:14
we **b**; when persecuted, we 1 Cor 4:12
"Surely I will **b** you and Heb 6:14
b, for to this you were called, 1 Pt 3:9

BLESSED
And God **b** them, saying, "Be Gn 1:22
of the earth shall be **b**." Gn 12:3
nations of the earth be **b**, Gn 22:18
For the Lord your God has **b** Dt 2:7
b be the name of the Lord." Jb 1:21
B is the man who walks not in Ps 1:1
B be the Lord forever! Amen Ps 89:52
B be the name of the Lord Ps 113:2
B is he who comes in the Ps 118:26
"**B** are the poor in spirit, for Mt 5:3
"**B** are those who mourn, for Mt 5:4
"**B** are the meek, for they shall Mt 5:5
"**B** are those who hunger and Mt 5:6
"**B** are the merciful, for they Mt 5:7
"**B** are the pure in heart, for Mt 5:8
"**B** are the peacemakers, for Mt 5:9
"**B** are those who are Mt 5:10
"**B** are you when others revile Mt 5:11
And **b** is the one who is not Mt 11:6
"**B** are you among women, Lk 1:42
'**B** is he who comes in the Lk 13:35
B are those who have not Jn 20:29
families of the earth be **b**.' Acts 3:25
more **b** to give than to receive. Acts 20:35
b is the man against whom Rom 4:8
shall all the nations be **b**." Gal 3:8
who has **b** us in Christ with Eph 1:3
waiting for our **b** hope, the Ti 2:13
B is the man who remains Jas 1:12
you will be **b**. Have no fear 1 Pt 3:14
B are those who wash their Rv 22:14

BLESSING
so that you will be a **b**. Gn 12:2
turned the curse into a **b**. Neh 13:2
and after **b** it broke it and Mt 26:26
Christ with every spiritual **b** Eph 1:3
that you may obtain a **b**. 1 Pt 3:9

BLESSINGS
who will bless you with **b** Gn 49:25
And all these **b** shall come Dt 28:2
share with them in its **b**. 1 Cor 9:23

BLIND
Lord opens the eyes of the **b**. Ps 146:8
Then the eyes of the **b** shall be Is 35:5
the **b** receive their sight and Mt 11:5
You **b** fools! For which is Mt 23:17
"Can a **b** man lead a **b** man? Lk 6:39
that though I was **b**, now I see." Jn 9:25
are a guide to the **b**, Rom 2:19

BLOOD
Whoever sheds the **b** of man, Gn 9:6
in the Nile turned into **b**. Ex 7:20
I do not delight in the **b** of Is 1:11
For flesh and **b** has not Mt 16:17
not of **b** nor of the will of the Jn 1:13
on my flesh and drinks my **b** Jn 6:54
as a propitiation by his **b**, Rom 3:25
now been justified by his **b**, Rom 5:9
new covenant in my **b**. 1 Cor 11:25
redemption through his **b**, Eph 1:7
been brought near by the **b** Eph 2:13
wrestle against flesh and **b**, Eph 6:12
peace by the **b** of his cross. Col 1:20
much more will the **b** of Christ, Heb 9:14
people through his own **b**. Heb 13:12
and for sprinkling with his **b**: 1 Pt 1:2
and the **b** of Jesus his Son 1 Jn 1:7
freed us from our sins by his **b** Rv 1:5

BLOODGUILT
has restrained you from **b** 1 Sm 25:26
so his Lord will leave his **b** Hos 12:14

BLOODGUILTINESS
Deliver me from **b**, O God, O Ps 51:14

BLOODSHED
because you did not hate **b**, Ez 35:6
and **b** follows bloodshed. Hos 4:2

BLOSSOM
and may people **b** in the Ps 72:16
Israel shall **b** and put forth Is 27:6
the fig tree should not **b**, Hb 3:17

BLOT
"I will **b** out man whom I Gn 6:7
that I have made I will **b** Gn 7:4
I will **b** out of my book. Ex 32:33
to your abundant mercy **b** Ps 51:1
and **b** out all my iniquities. Ps 51:9
and I will never **b** his name Rv 3:5

BLOTS
I am he who **b** out your Is 43:25

BLOW
And God made a wind **b** over Gn 8:1
the priests shall **b** the trumpets. Jos 6:4
He caused the east wind to **b** Ps 78:26

BLOWS
the breath of the Lord **b** Is 40:7
The wind **b** where it wishes, Jn 3:8

BOANERGES
whom he gave the name **B**, Mk 3:17

BOAST
Do not **b** about tomorrow, for Prv 27:1
but let him who boasts **b** Jer 9:24
he has something to **b** about, Rom 4:2
boasts, **b** in the Lord." 1 Cor 1:31
love does not envy or **b**; 1 Cor 13:4
For our **b** is this: the 2 Cor 1:12
boasts, **b** in the Lord." 2 Cor 10:17
If I must **b**, I will **b** of 2 Cor 11:30
Therefore I will **b** all the 2 Cor 12:9
But far be it from me to **b** Gal 6:14
works, so that no one may **b**. Eph 2:9

BOASTING
gives me no ground for **b**. 1 Cor 9:16
without **b** of work already 2 Cor 10:16
arrogance. All such **b** is evil. Jas 4:16

BOASTS
rain is a man who **b** of a gift Prv 25:14
"Let the one who **b**, boast 1 Cor 1:31
"Let the one who **b**, boast 2 Cor 10:17
yet it **b** of great things. How Jas 3:5
speaking loud **b** of folly, they 2 Pt 2:18

BOAZ
So **B** took Ruth, and she Ru 4:13

BODIES
the dishonoring of their **b** Rom 1:24
reign in your mortal **b**, Rom 6:12
give life to your mortal **b** Rom 8:11
the redemption of our **b**. Rom 8:23
to present your **b** as a living Rom 12:1
you not know that your **b** 1 Cor 6:15
There are heavenly **b** 1 Cor 15:40
be manifested in our **b**. 2 Cor 4:10

BODILY
Spirit descended on him in **b** Lk 3:22
fullness of deity dwells **b**, Col 2:9
for while **b** training is of 1 Tm 4:8

BODY
"The eye is the lamp of the **b**. Mt 6:22
with him in order that the **b** Rom 6:6
will deliver me from this **b** Rom 7:24
For as in one **b** we have Rom 12:4
So glorify God in your **b**. 1 Cor 6:20
But I discipline my **b** and 1 Cor 9:27
For just as the **b** is one 1 Cor 12:12
many parts, yet one **b**. 1 Cor 12:20
Now you are the **b** of 1 Cor 12:27
With what kind of **b** do 1 Cor 15:35
there is also a spiritual **b**. 1 Cor 15:44
which is his **b**, the fullness of Eph 1:23
members of the same **b**, and Eph 3:6
There is one **b** and one Spirit Eph 4:4
for building up the **b** of Christ, Eph 4:12
his **b**, and is himself its Savior. Eph 5:23
we are members of his **b**. Eph 5:30
will transform our lowly **b** Phil 3:21
has now reconciled in his **b** Col 1:22
by putting off the **b** of the Col 2:11
you were called in one **b**. Col 3:15
the offering of the **b** of Jesus Heb 10:10
For as the **b** apart from the Jas 2:26
bore our sins in his **b** 1 Pt 2:24

BOLD
but the righteous are **b** as a lion. Prv 28:1
a hope, we are very **b**, 2 Cor 3:12
though I am **b** enough in Phlm 1:8

BOLDLY
He began to speak **b** in the Acts 18:26
that I may declare it **b**, as I Eph 6:20

BOLDNESS
the word of God with **b**. Acts 4:31
in whom we have **b** and Eph 3:12

BOND
I will bring you into the **b** Ez 20:37
unity of the Spirit in the **b** Eph 4:3

BONDAGE
out of the house of **b**, saying, Jer 34:13
will be set free from its **b** Rom 8:21

BONE
"This at last is '**b** of my bones Gn 2:23
"Surely you are my **b** and Gn 29:14
also that I am your **b** Jgs 9:2

BONES
He keeps all his **b**; not one of Ps 34:20
the **b** that you have broken rejoice Ps 51:8
dry **b**, hear the word of the Lord. Ez 37:4
Not one of his **b** will be broken. Jn 19:36

BOOK
"Take this **B** of the Law and Dt 31:26
This **B** of the Law shall not Jos 1:8
whose names are in the **b** Phil 4:3
blot his name out of the **b** Rv 3:5
not found written in the **b** Rv 20:15

BORN
For to us a child is **b**, to us a son Is 9:6
unless one is **b** again he cannot Jn 3:3
set me apart before I was **b**, Gal 1:15
he has caused us to be **b** 1 Pt 1:3
because he has been **b** 1 Jn 3:9

BORNE
Surely he has **b** our griefs and Is 53:4
And I have seen and have **b** Jn 1:34

BOUGHT
for you were **b** with a price. 1 Cor 6:20

BOW
You shall not **b** down to them Dt 5:9
let us worship and **b** down; let Ps 95:6
every knee shall **b** to me, Rom 14:11
Jesus every knee should **b**, Phil 2:10

BRANCH
In that day the **b** of the Lord Is 4:2
up for David a righteous **B**, Jer 23:5
and every **b** that does bear Jn 15:2

BREAD
king of Salem brought out **b** Gn 14:18
I am about to rain **b** from Ex 16:4
and the **b** of the Presence; Ex 35:13
that man does not live by **b** Dt 8:3
Man ate of the **b** of the Ps 78:25
and gave them **b** from Ps 105:40
"'Man shall not live by **b** alone, Mt 4:4
'Man shall not live by **b** alone.'" Lk 4:4
Give us each day our daily **b**, Lk 11:3
"I am the **b** of life; whoever Jn 6:35
breaking of **b** and the prayers. Acts 2:42
The **b** that we break, is it 1 Cor 10:16
as often as you eat this **b** 1 Cor 11:26

BREAKING
sins that people commit by **b** Nm 5:6
the **b** of bread and the prayers. Acts 2:42
the law dishonor God by **b** Rom 2:23

BREASTPLATE
put on righteousness as a **b**, Is 59:17
and having put on the **b** Eph 6:14
having put on the **b** of faith 1 Thes 5:8

BREATH
everything that has the **b** Gn 1:30
into his nostrils the **b** Gn 2:7
"Remember that my life is a **b**; Jb 7:7
mankind stands as a mere **b**! Ps 39:5
Man is like a **b**; his days are Ps 144:4
Let everything that has **b** Ps 150:6
who gives **b** to the people on it Is 42:5
and put **b** in you, and you Ez 37:6

BREATHED
of dust from the ground and **b** Gn 2:7
All Scripture is **b** out by God 2 Tm 3:16

BRIBE
And you shall take no **b**, Ex 23:8
The wicked accepts a **b** Prv 17:23
and a **b** corrupts the heart. Eccl 7:7

BRIDE
and as a **b** adorns herself with Is 61:10
I will show you the **B**, the Rv 21:9

BRIGHTER
which shines brighter and **b** Prv 4:18
b than the sun, that shone Acts 26:13

BROKE
because you **b** faith with me Dt 32:51
and the high places and **b** 2 Chr 14:3
and after blessing it **b** it and Mk 14:22
he **b** it, and said, "This is 1 Cor 11:24

BROKEN
sacrifices of God are a **b** spirit Ps 51:17
and Scripture cannot be **b** Jn 10:35
made us both one and has **b** Eph 2:14

BROKENHEARTED
The Lord is near to the **b** Ps 34:18
poor and needy and the **b**, Ps 109:16
He heals the **b** and binds up Ps 147:3
has sent me to bind up the **b**, Is 61:1

BROTHER
and a **b** is born for adversity. Prv 17:17
who sticks closer than a **b**. Prv 18:24
who is near than a **b** Prv 27:10
First be reconciled to your **b**, Mt 5:24
"If your **b** sins against you, Mt 18:15
If your **b** sins, rebuke him, Lk 17:3
pass judgment on your **b**? Rom 14:10
if food makes my **b** stumble, 1 Cor 8:13
Whoever loves his **b** abides 1 Jn 2:10
God must also love his **b**. 1 Jn 4:21

BROTHERHOOD
Love the **b**. Fear God. Honor 1 Pt 2:17
being experienced by your **b** 1 Pt 5:9

BROTHERLY
Love one another with **b** Rom 12:10
Now concerning **b** love you 1 Thes 4:9
Let **b** love continue. Heb 13:1
to the truth for a sincere **b** 1 Pt 1:22
b love, a tender heart, and a 1 Pt 3:8
and godliness with **b** 2 Pt 1:7

BROTHERS
and pleasant it is when **b** Ps 133:1
who sows discord among **b**. Prv 6:19
and who are my **b**?" Mt 12:48
of the least of these my **b**, Mt 25:40
For not even his **b** believed in him. Jn 7:5
firstborn among many **b**. Rom 8:29
not ashamed to call them **b**, Heb 2:11

BROTHER'S
know; am I my **b** keeper?" Gn 4:9
the speck that is in your **b** Lk 6:41

BUILD
let us **b** ourselves a city and a Gn 11:4
and on this rock I will **b** Mt 16:18
and in three days I will **b** Mk 14:58
which is able to **b** you up Acts 20:32
one another and **b** 1 Thes 5:11

BUILDER
like a skilled master **b** 1 Cor 3:10
as much more as the **b** of a Heb 3:3
whose designer and **b** is God. Heb 11:10

BUILDING
he is like a man **b** a house, Lk 6:48
and someone else is **b** 1 Cor 3:10
to excel in **b** up the church. 1 Cor 14:12
for **b** up the body of Christ, Eph 4:12
only such as is good for **b** Eph 4:29

BUILDS
Unless the Lord **b** the house, Ps 127:1
"Woe to him who **b** his Jer 22:13
one take care how he **b** 1 Cor 3:10
puffs up, but love **b** up. 1 Cor 8:1
the body grow so that it **b** Eph 4:16

BUILT
By wisdom a house is **b**, Prv 24:3
be like a wise man who **b** Mt 7:24
that the church may be **b** 1 Cor 14:5
b on the foundation of the Eph 2:20
like living stones are being **b** 1 Pt 2:5

BURDEN
Cast your **b** on the Lord, and Ps 55:22
is easy, and my **b** is light." Mt 11:30

BURDENS
Bear one another's **b**, and so Gal 6:2

BURDENSOME
his commandments are not **b**. 1 Jn 5:3

BURIED
We were **b** therefore with Rom 6:4
having been **b** with him in Col 2:12

BURNED
thrown into the fire, and **b**. Jn 15:6
deliver up my body to be **b**, 1 Cor 13:3
heavenly bodies will be **b** up 2 Pt 3:10

BURNING
bush was **b**, yet it was not consumed Ex 3:2
and keep your lamps **b**, Lk 12:35
so doing you will heap **b** Rom 12:20

BUSINESS
It is an unhappy **b** that God Eccl 1:13
and went about the king's **b**, Dn 8:27
'Engage in **b** until I come.' Lk 19:13

BUSY
folly, and his heart is **b** with Is 32:6
not **b** at work, but busybodies 2 Thes 3:11

BYWORD
and a **b** among all the peoples Dt 28:37
You have made us a **b** among Ps 44:14
And as you have been a **b** Zec 8:13

CAESAR
it lawful to pay taxes to **C**, Mk 12:14
to them. I appeal to **C**." Acts 25:11

CAESAREA
came into the district of **C** Mt 16:13
towns until he came to **C**. Acts 8:40

CAIAPHAS
priest, whose name was **C**, Mt 26:3

CAIN
C spoke to Abel his brother. Gn 4:8
acceptable sacrifice than **C**, Heb 11:4

CALEB
But **C** quieted the people Nm 13:30

CALF
tool and made a golden **c**. Ex 32:4
made yourselves a golden **c**. Dt 9:16
And bring the fattened **c** Lk 15:23

CALL
that time people began to **c** Gn 4:26
I **c** upon the Lord, who is Ps 18:3
all nations **c** him blessed! Ps 72:17
to all who **c** on him in truth. Ps 145:18
c upon him while he is near; Is 55:6
Then all nations will **c** you Mal 3:12
and you shall **c** his name Mt 1:21
I have not come to **c** the Lk 5:32
No longer do I **c** you Jn 15:15
works but because of his **c** Rom 9:11
But how are they to **c** on Rom 10:14
hope that belongs to your **c** Eph 4:4
the prize of the upward **c** Phil 3:14
And if you **c** on him as 1 Pt 1:17

CALLED
God **c** the light Day, and the Gn 1:5
And whatever the man **c** Gn 2:19
if my people who are **c** 2 Chr 7:14
good, for those who are **c** Rom 8:28
and those whom he **c** he Rom 8:30
For you were **c** to freedom, Gal 5:13
the hope to which he has **c** Eph 1:18
to which you have been **c**, Eph 4:1
just as you were **c** to the one Eph 4:4
To this he **c** you through 2 Thes 2:14
life to which you were **c** 1 Tm 6:12
who saved us and **c** us to a 2 Tm 1:9
so that those who are **c** may Heb 9:15
For to this you have been **c**, 1 Pt 2:21

CALLING
your sins, **c** on his name.' Acts 22:16
For the gifts and the **c** Rom 11:29
For consider your **c**, 1 Cor 1:26
in a manner worthy of the **c** Eph 4:1
us and called us to a holy **c**, 2 Tm 1:9
make your **c** and election sure, 2 Pt 1:10

CALLS
and he **c** his own sheep by Jn 10:3
to pass that everyone who **c** Acts 2:21
For "everyone who **c** on the Rom 10:13
He who **c** you is faithful; 1 Thes 5:24

CAMEL
a gnat and swallowing a **c**! Mt 23:24
It is easier for a **c** to go Mk 10:25

CANA
day there was a wedding at **C** Jn 2:1
So he came again to **C** in Jn 4:46

CANAAN
settled in the land of **C**, Gn 13:12
famine was in the land of **C**. Gn 42:5
I will give the land of **C**, 1 Chr 16:18
sacrificed to the idols of **C**, Ps 106:38
throughout all Egypt and **C**, Acts 7:11

CANCELING
by **c** the record of debt that Col 2:14

CAPTIVE
died to that which held us **c**, Rom 7:6
and take every thought **c** 2 Cor 10:5
we were held **c** under the Gal 3:23

CAPTIVES
leading a host of **c** in your Ps 68:18
to proclaim liberty to the **c**, Is 61:1
to proclaim liberty to the **c** Lk 4:18
on high he led a host of **c**, Eph 4:8

CARE
and the son of man that you **c** Ps 8:4
of man, that you **c** for him? Heb 2:6

CAREFUL
and be **c** to do them, that it may Dt 6:3
being **c** to do according to all Jos 1:7
and be **c** to obey my rules, Ez 20:19

CAREFULLY
Look **c** then how you walk, Eph 5:15
searched and inquired **c**, 1 Pt 1:10

CARES
When the **c** of my heart are Ps 94:19
for the Lord of hosts **c** for his Zec 10:3
but the **c** of the world and Mt 13:22
him, because he **c** for you. 1 Pt 5:7

CARMEL
together at Mount **C**. 1 Kgs 18:20
man of God at Mount **C**. 2 Kgs 4:25
Your head crowns you like **C**, Sg 7:5
and the top of **C** withers." Am 1:2

CARRIED
he has borne our griefs and **c** Is 53:4
and fro by the waves and **c** Eph 4:14
not **c** away with the error 2 Pt 3:17

CAST
Why are you **c** down, O my Ps 42:11
by the Spirit of God that I **c** Mt 12:28
comes to me I will never **c** Jn 6:37
So then let us **c** off the Rom 13:12
of the stars of heaven and **c** Rv 12:4

CASTING
c all your anxieties on him, 1 Pt 5:7

CATTLE
the **c** on a thousand hills. Ps 50:10

CAUGHT
if anyone is **c** in any Gal 6:1
will be **c** up together with 1 Thes 4:17

CAUSE
and defend my **c** against an Ps 43:1
I will **c** your name to be Ps 45:17
divorce one's wife for any **c**?" Mt 19:3

CAUSES
If your right eye **c** you to sin, Mt 5:29
but whoever **c** one of these Mt 18:6

CEASE
before my eyes; **c** to do evil, Is 1:16
they will **c**; as for knowledge, 1 Cor 13:8

CEASES
love of the Lord never **c**; Lam 3:22

CENTURION
And when the **c**, who stood Mk 15:39
When the **c** heard about Jesus, Lk 7:3
a **c** of what was known as Acts 10:1

CEPHAS
You shall be called **C**" Jn 1:42

CHAFF
but are like **c** that the wind Ps 1:4
but the **c** he will burn with Mt 3:12

CHAINS
I am an ambassador in **c**, Eph 6:20
Remember my **c**. Grace be Col 4:18
bound with **c** as a criminal. 2 Tm 2:9

CHANGE
that he should **c** his mind. Nm 23:19
"For I the Lord do not **c**; Mal 3:6
has sworn and will not **c** Heb 7:21
variation or shadow due to **c**. Jas 1:17

CHANGED
but we shall all be **c**, 1 Cor 15:51

CHARACTER
he speaks out of his own **c**, Jn 8:44
and endurance produces **c**, Rom 5:4
and **c** produces hope, Rom 5:4
promise the unchangeable **c** Heb 6:17

CHARGE
you, that every **c** may be Mt 18:16
Who shall bring any **c** Rom 8:33
present the gospel free of **c**, 1 Cor 9:18
Every **c** must be established 2 Cor 13:1
I **c** you in the presence of 1 Tm 6:13

CHARIOTS
returned and covered the **c** Ex 14:28
c of fire and horses of fire 2 Kgs 2:11

CHASTISEMENT
upon him was the **c** that Is 53:5

CHEEK
strike all my enemies on the **c**; Ps 3:7
slaps you on the right **c**, Mt 5:39
one who strikes you on the **c**, Lk 6:29

CHEER
sad face, and be of good **c**,' Jb 9:27
your consolations **c** my soul. Ps 94:19
and let your heart **c** you in Eccl 11:9

CHEERFUL
A glad heart makes a **c** face, Prv 15:13
but the **c** of heart has a Prv 15:15
for God loves a **c** giver. 2 Cor 9:7
Is anyone **c**? Let him sing praise. Jas 5:13

CHERUB
Make one **c** on the one end, Ex 25:19
He rode on a **c** and flew; 2 Sm 22:11

CHERUBIM
of Eden he placed the **c** Gn 3:24
The **c** spread out their wings 2 Chr 5:8
He sits enthroned upon the **c**; Ps 99:1
Above it were the **c** of glory Heb 9:5

CHILD
Train up a **c** in the way he Prv 22:6
but a **c** left to himself brings Prv 29:15
For to us a **c** is born, to us a son Is 9:6
humbles himself like this **c** Mt 18:4
When I was a **c**, I spoke 1 Cor 13:11

CHILDISH
man, I gave up **c** ways. 1 Cor 13:11

CHILDREN
pain you shall bring forth **c**. Gn 3:16
teach them diligently to your **c**, Dt 6:7
c are a heritage from the Ps 127:3
hand of a warrior are the **c** Ps 127:4
blessed are his **c** after him! Prv 20:7
he gave the right to become **c** Jn 1:12
our spirit that we are **c** Rom 8:16
of God, as beloved **c**. Eph 5:1
do not provoke your **c** to Eph 6:4
C, obey your parents in Col 3:20
For you are all **c** of light, 1 Thes 5:5
As obedient **c**, do not be 1 Pt 1:14

CHOOSE
Therefore **c** life, that you and Dt 30:19
c this day whom you will Jos 24:15
You did not **c** me, but I chose Jn 15:16

CHOSE
So Lot **c** for himself all the Gn 13:11
Moses **c** able men out of all Ex 18:25
he **c**, he shortened the days. Mk 13:20
But God **c** what is foolish in 1 Cor 1:27
one of them, as he **c**. 1 Cor 12:18
even as he **c** us in him before Eph 1:4
because God **c** you as the 2 Thes 2:13

CHOSEN
The Lord your God has **c** you to Dt 7:6
made a covenant with my **c** Ps 89:3
A good name is to be **c** rather Prv 22:1
and Israel my **c**, I call you by Is 45:4
Mary has **c** the good portion, Lk 10:42
I know whom I have **c**. Jn 13:18
is a remnant, **c** by grace. Rom 11:5
as God's **c** ones, holy and Col 3:12
God, that he has **c** you, 1 Thes 1:4
has not God **c** those who are Jas 2:5
men but in the sight of God **c** 1 Pt 2:4
But you are a **c** race, a royal 1 Pt 2:9

CHRIST
was born, who is called **C**. Mt 1:16
"You are the **C**, the Son of Mt 16:16
or Jesus who is called **C**?" Mt 27:17
of the gospel of Jesus **C**, Mk 1:1
a Savior, who is **C** the Lord. Lk 2:11
that the **C** should suffer and Lk 24:46
truth came through Jesus **C**. Jn 1:17
I believe that you are the **C**, Jn 11:27
believe that Jesus is the **C**, Jn 20:31
you in the name of Jesus **C** Acts 2:38
that by the name of Jesus **C** Acts 4:10
of peace through Jesus **C** Acts 10:36
through faith in Jesus **C** Rom 3:22
through our Lord Jesus **C**. Rom 5:1
still sinners, **C** died for us. Rom 5:8
have been baptized into **C** Rom 6:3
for those who are in **C** Rom 8:1
from the love of God in **C** Rom 8:39
but we preach **C** crucified 1 Cor 1:23
bodies are members of **C**? 1 Cor 6:15
and the Rock was **C**. 1 Cor 10:4
that **C** died for our sins in 1 Cor 15:3
But in fact **C** has been 1 Cor 15:20
For we are the aroma of **C** 2 Cor 2:15
For the love of **C** controls 2 Cor 5:14
if anyone is in **C**, he is a 2 Cor 5:17
but through faith in Jesus **C**, Gal 2:16
C redeemed us from the Gal 3:13
For freedom **C** has set us free; Gal 5:1
that he worked in **C** when Eph 1:20
created in **C** Jesus for good Eph 2:10
insight into the mystery of **C**, Eph 3:4
so that **C** may dwell in your Eph 3:17
For to me to live is **C**, and to Phil 1:21
as loss for the sake of **C**. Phil 3:7
comes through faith in **C**, Phil 3:9
When **C** who is your life Col 3:4
Let the word of **C** dwell in Col 3:16
And the dead in **C** will 1 Thes 4:16
that **C** Jesus came into the 1 Tm 1:15
the salvation that is in **C** 2 Tm 2:10
more will the blood of **C**, Heb 9:14
Jesus **C** is the same Heb 13:8
for obedience to Jesus **C** and 1 Pt 1:2
For **C** also suffered once for 1 Pt 3:18
denies that Jesus is the **C**? 1 Jn 2:22
believes that Jesus is the **C** 1 Jn 5:1
The revelation of Jesus **C**, Rv 1:1

CHRISTIAN
persuade me to be a **C**?" Acts 26:28
Yet if anyone suffers as a **C**, 1 Pt 4:16

CHRISTIANS
were first called **C**. Acts 11:26

CHRISTS
For false **c** and false prophets Mt 24:24
False **c** and false prophets Mk 13:22

CHRIST'S
We are fools for **C** sake, but 1 Cor 4:10
we share abundantly in **C** 2 Cor 1:5
And if you are **C**, then you Gal 3:29
to the measure of **C** Eph 4:7
up what is lacking in **C** Col 1:24
insofar as you share **C** 1 Pt 4:13

CHURCH
this rock I will build my **c**, Mt 16:18
tell it to the **c**. And if he Mt 18:17
fear came upon the whole **c** Acts 5:11
elders for them in every **c**, Acts 14:23
to care for the **c** of God, Acts 20:28
Is it not those inside the **c** 1 Cor 5:12
has appointed in the **c** 1 Cor 12:28
prophesies builds up the **c**. 1 Cor 14:4
in building up the **c**. 1 Cor 14:12
head over all things to the **c**, Eph 1:22
so that through the **c** the Eph 3:10
to him be glory in the **c** Eph 3:21
Christ is the head of the **c**, Eph 5:23
as Christ loved the **c** and Eph 5:25
that he might present the **c** Eph 5:27
no **c** entered into partnership Phil 4:15
the **c**. He is the beginning, Col 1:18
sake of his body, that is, the **c**, Col 1:24
will he care for God's **c**? 1 Tm 3:5
Let the **c** not be burdened, 1 Tm 5:16

CHURCHES
So the **c** were strengthened Acts 16:5
As in all the **c** of the saints, 1 Cor 14:33
So give proof before the **c** 2 Cor 8:24
became imitators of the **c** 1 Thes 2:14
John to the seven **c** that are in Rv 1:4
what the Spirit says to the **c**. Rv 2:7
about these things for the **c**. Rv 22:16

CIRCUMCISED
male among you shall be **c**. Gn 17:10
He will justify the **c** by faith Rom 3:30
believe without being **c**, Rom 4:11
For even those who are **c** Gal 6:13
In him also you were **c** with Col 2:11

CIRCUMCISION
He received the sign of **c** Rom 4:11
For neither **c** counts for Gal 6:15
For we are the real **c**, who Phil 3:3
the flesh, by the **c** of Christ, Col 2:11

CITIZENS
but you are fellow **c** with the Eph 2:19

CITIZENSHIP
But our **c** is in heaven, and Phil 3:20

CITY
When he built a **c**, he called Gn 4:17
let us build ourselves a **c** Gn 11:4
A **c** set on a hill cannot be hidden. Mt 5:14
we seek the **c** that is to come. Heb 13:14
And I saw the holy **c**, new Rv 21:2

CLAP
C your hands, all peoples! Ps 47:1
Let the rivers **c** their hands; let Ps 98:8
the trees of the field shall **c** Is 55:12

CLAY
Does the **c** say to him who Is 45:9
we are the **c**, and you are our Is 64:8
like the **c** in the potter's hand, Jer 18:6
potter no right over the **c**, Rom 9:21
this treasure in jars of **c**, 2 Cor 4:7
but also of wood and **c**, 2 Tm 2:20

CLEAN
Create in me a **c** heart, O Ps 51:10
make yourselves **c**; remove the Is 1:16
For you **c** the outside of the Mt 23:25
be **c**." And immediately the Lk 5:13
"What God has made **c**, Acts 10:15
with our hearts sprinkled **c** Heb 10:22

CLEANSE
and **c** me from my sin! Ps 51:2
let us **c** ourselves from every 2 Cor 7:1
C your hands, you sinners, and Jas 4:8
forgive us our sins and to **c** 1 Jn 1:9

CLEANSED
having **c** their hearts by faith. Acts 15:9
having **c** her by the washing Eph 5:26
having once been **c**, would Heb 10:2
forgotten that he was **c** 2 Pt 1:9

CLEANSES
if anyone **c** himself from 2 Tm 2:21
the blood of Jesus his Son **c** 1 Jn 1:7

CLEOPAS
named **C**, answered him, Lk 24:18

CLINGS
My soul **c** to you; your right Ps 63:8
and sin which **c** so closely, Heb 12:1

CLOAK
you take your neighbor's **c** Ex 22:26
let him have your **c** as well. Mt 5:40
stripped him of the purple **c** Mk 15:20

CLOSE
right, evil lies **c** at hand. Rom 7:21
Keep a **c** watch on yourself 1 Tm 4:16

CLOSER
is a friend who sticks **c** Prv 18:24
we must pay much **c** attention Heb 2:1

CLOTHE
how much more will he **c** Lk 12:28
C yourselves, all of you, with 1 Pt 5:5

CLOTHED
wife garments of skins and **c** Gn 3:21
I was naked and you **c** me, I Mt 25:36
in the city until you are **c** Lk 24:49

CLOTHING
and for my **c** they cast lots. Ps 22:18
are you anxious about **c**? Mt 6:28
who come to you in sheep's **c** Mt 7:15
But if we have food and **c**, 1 Tm 6:8

CLOUD
them by day in a pillar of **c** Ex 13:21
Moses entered the **c** and Ex 24:18
the Lord is riding on a swift **c** Is 19:1
and a voice came out of the **c**, Mk 9:7
Son of Man coming in a **c** Lk 21:27
a **c** took him out of their sight. Acts 1:9
surrounded by so great a **c** Heb 12:1

CLOUDS
he makes the **c** his chariot; he Ps 104:3
coming with the **c** of heaven." Mk 14:62
with them in the **c** to meet 1 Thes 4:17
he is coming with the **c**, and Rv 1:7

COALS
for you will heap burning **c** Prv 25:22
you will heap burning **c** Rom 12:20

COINS
put in two small copper **c**, Mk 12:42
having ten silver **c**, if she loses Lk 15:8
And he poured out the **c** of the Jn 2:15

COLD
little ones even a cup of **c** water Mt 10:42
love of many will grow **c**. Mt 24:12
Would that you were either **c** Rv 3:15

COLT
on a **c**, the foal of a donkey. Zec 9:9
sitting on a donkey's **c**!" Jn 12:15

COMFORT
rod and your staff, they **c** me. Ps 23:4
Let your steadfast love **c** Ps 119:76
C, **c** my people, says Is 40:1
so I will **c** you; you shall be Is 66:13

and treated others with **c**: Lk 18:9
and holding him up to **c**. Heb 6:6

CONTEND
write appealing to you to **c** Jude 1:3

CONTENT
situation I am to be **c**. Phil 4:11
with these we will be **c**. 1 Tm 6:8
and be **c** with what you Heb 13:5

CONTENTMENT
gain in godliness with **c**, 1 Tm 6:6

CONTINUAL
cheerful of heart has a **c** Prv 15:15

CONTINUE
but **c** in the fear of the Lord Prv 23:17
C steadfastly in prayer, being Col 4:2
c in what you have learned 2 Tm 3:14
Let brotherly love **c**. Heb 13:1

CONTRARY
To the **c**, "if your enemy is Rom 12:20
preach to you a gospel **c** Gal 1:8
but on the **c**, bless, for to this 1 Pt 3:9

CONTRITE
a broken and **c** heart, O God, Ps 51:17
also with him who is of a **c** Is 57:15
to revive the heart of the **c**. Is 57:15
he who is humble and **c** in Is 66:2

CONTROL
having his desire under **c**, 1 Cor 7:37
body and keep it under **c**, 1 Cor 9:27
know how to **c** his own body 1 Thes 4:4

CONTROLS
For the love of Christ **c** 2 Cor 5:14

CONTROVERSIES
ignorant **c**; you know that 2 Tm 2:23
But avoid foolish **c**, genealogies, Ti 3:9

CONVERT
He must not be a recent **c**, 1 Tm 3:6

CONVICT
he will **c** the world concerning Jn 16:8
judgment on all and to **c** Jude 1:15

CONVICTION
Holy Spirit and with full **c**. 1 Thes 1:5
the **c** of things not seen. Heb 11:1

CONVINCED
And some were **c** by what Acts 28:24
fully **c** that God was able to Rom 4:21
C of this, I know that I will Phil 1:25
and I am **c** that he is able 2 Tm 1:12

COPY
They serve a **c** and shadow of Heb 8:5

CORINTH
left Athens and went to **C**. Acts 18:1
while Apollos was at **C**, Acts 19:1

CORNELIUS
there was a man named **C**, Acts 10:1
"**C**, a centurion, an upright Acts 10:22

CORNERSTONE
rejected has become the **c**. Ps 118:22
stone, a precious **c**, of a sure Is 28:16
rejected has become the **c**; Mt 21:42
which has become the **c**. Acts 4:11
Jesus himself being the **c**, Eph 2:20
a **c** chosen and precious, and 1 Pt 2:6
rejected has become the **c**," 1 Pt 2:7

CORRECTION
for **c**, and for training in 2 Tm 3:16

CORRUPT
Now the earth was **c** in God's Gn 6:11
manner of life and is **c** Eph 4:22

CORRUPTION
or let your holy one see **c**. Ps 16:10
or let your Holy One see **c**. Acts 2:27
having escaped from the **c** 2 Pt 1:4

COSMIC
against the **c** powers over Eph 6:12

COST
sit down and count the **c**, Lk 14:28

COUNSEL
man who walks not in the **c** Ps 1:1
You guide me with your **c**, Ps 73:24
Without **c** plans fail, but Prv 15:22

COUNSELOR
shall be called Wonderful **C**, Is 9:6

COUNT
does not first sit down and **c** Lk 14:28
whom the Lord will not **c** Rom 4:8
but in humility **c** others more Phil 2:3
did not **c** equality with God a Phil 2:6
I **c** everything as loss because Phil 3:8
the loss of all things and **c** Phil 3:8
C it all joy, my brothers, when Jas 1:2

COUNTED
he **c** it to him as righteousness. Gn 15:6
is why his faith was "**c** Rom 4:22
it was **c** to him as righteousness"? Gal 3:6
I **c** as loss for the sake of Christ. Phil 3:7
For Jesus has been **c** worthy Heb 3:3

COUNTENANCE
The Lord lift up his **c** upon Nm 6:26

COUNTING
not **c** their trespasses against 2 Cor 5:19

COUNTS
man against whom the Lord **c** Ps 32:2
of the one to whom God **c** Rom 4:6
For neither circumcision **c** Gal 6:15

COURAGE
and let your heart take **c**, Ps 31:24
"Take **c**, for as you have Acts 23:11
we are of good **c**, and we 2 Cor 5:8
but that with full **c** now as Phil 1:20

COURAGEOUS
Be strong and **c**. Do not fear or Dt 31:6
Be strong and **c**, for you shall Jos 1:6

COURTS
For a day in your **c** is better Ps 84:10
and his **c** with praise! Give Ps 100:4

COVENANT
But I will establish my **c** Gn 6:18
I establish my **c** with you and Gn 9:9
that day the Lord made a **c** Gn 15:18
And I will establish my **c** Gn 17:7
So shall my **c** be in your Gn 17:13
obey my voice and keep my **c**, Ex 19:5
generations, as a **c** forever. Ex 31:16
due. It is a **c** of salt forever Nm 18:19
your word and kept your **c**. Dt 33:9
with me an everlasting **c**, 2 Sm 23:5
The Lord made a **c** with 2 Kgs 17:35
Remember his **c** forever, 1 Chr 16:15
And they entered into a **c** 2 Chr 15:12
Therefore let us make a **c** Ezr 10:3
for those who keep his **c** Ps 25:10
"I have made a **c** with my Ps 89:3
He remembers his **c** forever, Ps 105:8
he remembers his **c** forever. Ps 111:5
with you an everlasting **c**, Is 55:3
But this is the **c** that I will Jer 31:33
with them an everlasting **c**, Jer 32:40
I will make a **c** of peace with Ez 37:26
and your wife by **c**. Mal 2:14
for this is my blood of the **c**, Mt 26:28
and to remember his holy **c**, Lk 1:72
"and this will be my **c** Rom 11:27
"This cup is the new **c** 1 Cor 11:25
to be ministers of a new **c**, 2 Cor 3:6
when they read the old **c**, 2 Cor 3:14
the guarantor of a better **c**. Heb 7:22
For if that first **c** had been Heb 8:7
I will establish a new **c** Heb 8:8
For this is the **c** that I will Heb 8:10
is the mediator of a new **c**, Heb 9:15
the mediator of a new **c**, Heb 12:24
the blood of the eternal **c**, Heb 13:20

COVENANTS
the **c**, the giving of the law, Rom 9:4
these women are two **c**. Gal 4:24
Israel and strangers to the **c** Eph 2:12

COVER
and I did not **c** my iniquity; I Ps 32:5
soul from death and will **c** Jas 5:20

COVER-UP
using your freedom as a **c** 1 Pt 2:16

COVERED
is forgiven, whose sin is **c**. Ps 32:1
His splendor **c** the heavens, and Hb 3:3
and whose sins are **c**; Rom 4:7
prophesies with his head **c** 1 Cor 11:4

COVERS
but love **c** all offenses. Prv 10:12
Whoever **c** an offense seeks Prv 17:9
since love **c** a multitude of sins. 1 Pt 4:8

COVET
"You shall not **c** your Ex 20:17
You shall not **c**," and any Rom 13:9
You **c** and cannot obtain, so Jas 4:2

COVETOUSNESS
on your guard against all **c**, Lk 12:15
produced in me all kinds of **c**. Rom 7:8
and all impurity or **c** Eph 5:3

CRAFTINESS
the wise in their own **c**, Jb 5:13
the wise in their **c**," 1 Cor 3:19
by **c** in deceitful schemes. Eph 4:14

CRAFTY
Now the serpent was more **c** Gn 3:1
I was **c**, you say, and got 2 Cor 12:16

CREATE
C in me a clean heart, O God, Ps 51:10
that he might **c** in himself Eph 2:15

CREATED
God **c** the heavens and the earth. Gn 1:1
So God **c** the great sea Gn 1:21
So God **c** man in his own Gn 1:27
he commanded and they were **c**. Ps 148:5
Lord, who **c** the heavens and Is 42:5
c in Christ Jesus for good Eph 2:10
For everything **c** by God is 1 Tm 4:4
through whom also he **c** Heb 1:2
who **c** heaven and what is in Rv 10:6

CREATION
work that he had done in **c**. Gn 2:3
But from the beginning of **c**, Mk 10:6
from the beginning of the **c** Mk 13:19
ever since the **c** of the world, Rom 1:20
For the **c** waits with eager Rom 8:19
we know that the whole **c** Rom 8:22
he is a new **c**. The old has 2 Cor 5:17
uncircumcision, but a new **c**. Gal 6:15
God, the firstborn of all **c**. Col 1:15
has been proclaimed in all **c** Col 1:23
a kind of firstfruits of his **c**. Jas 1:18
from the beginning of **c**." 2 Pt 3:4
the beginning of God's **c**. Rv 3:14

CREATOR
Remember also your **C** in the Eccl 12:1
the **C** of the ends of the earth. Is 40:28
creature rather than the **C**, Rom 1:25
after the image of its **c**. Col 3:10
their souls to a faithful **C** 1 Pt 4:19

CREATURE
"For the life of every **c** is its Lv 17:14

CREATURES
the earth is full of your **c**. Ps 104:24
c of instinct, born to be 2 Pt 2:12

CRIED
I **c** to you for help, and you Ps 30:2

CRIMSON
though they are red like **c**, Is 1:18

CRIPPLED
better for you to enter life **c** Mt 18:8

CROOKED
The way of the guilty is **c**, Prv 21:8
and the **c** shall become straight, Lk 3:5
blemish in the midst of a **c** Phil 2:15

CROSS
whoever does not take his **c** Mt 10:38
himself and take up his **c** Lk 9:23
lest the **c** of Christ be 1 Cor 1:17
that case the offense of the **c** Gal 5:11
boast except in the **c** of our Lord Gal 6:14
in one body through the **c**, Eph 2:16
of death, even death on a **c**. Phil 2:8
peace by the blood of his **c**. Col 1:20
set aside, nailing it to the **c**. Col 2:14
before him endured the **c**, Heb 12:2

CROWN
An excellent wife is the **c** Prv 12:4
Grandchildren are the **c** Prv 17:6
wearing the **c** of thorns and Jn 19:5
there is laid up for me the **c** 2 Tm 4:8
the test he will receive the **c** Jas 1:12
receive the unfading **c** of glory. 1 Pt 5:4
and I will give you the **c** of life. Rv 2:10

CROWNED
the heavenly beings and **c** Ps 8:5
An athlete is not **c** unless he 2 Tm 2:5
you have **c** him with glory Heb 2:7

CRUCIFIED
mocked and flogged and **c**, Mt 20:19
There they **c** him, and with Jn 19:18
this Jesus whom you **c**." Acts 2:36
know that our old self was **c** Rom 6:6
but we preach Christ **c** 1 Cor 1:23
Jesus Christ and him **c**. 1 Cor 2:2
they would not have **c** the 1 Cor 2:8
For he was **c** in weakness, 2 Cor 13:4
I have been **c** with Christ. Gal 2:20
was publicly portrayed as **c**. Gal 3:1
to Christ Jesus have **c** Gal 5:24
which the world has been **c** Gal 6:14

CRUCIFY
of whom you will kill and **c**, Mt 23:34
him and led him away to **c** Mt 27:31
they kept shouting, "**C**, **c** him!" Lk 23:21
"Shall I **c** your King?" The Jn 19:15

CRUCIFYING
since they are **c** once again Heb 6:6

CRUSHED
and saves the **c** in spirit. Ps 34:18
he was **c** for our iniquities; Is 53:5
but not **c**; perplexed, but not 2 Cor 4:8

CRY
and his ears toward their **c**. Ps 34:15
to me and heard my **c**. Ps 40:1
the very stones would **c** out." Lk 19:40
heaven with a **c** of command, 1 Thes 4:16

CUNNING
deceived Eve by his **c**, 2 Cor 11:3
by human **c**, by craftiness in Eph 4:14

CUP
with oil; my **c** overflows. Ps 23:5
clean the outside of the **c** Mt 23:25
let this **c** pass from me; Mt 26:39
The **c** of blessing that we 1 Cor 10:16
"This **c** is the new covenant 1 Cor 11:25

CURSE
"I will never again **c** the Gn 8:21
you today a blessing and a **c**: Dt 11:26
bless those who **c** you, pray Lk 6:28
bless and do not **c** them. Rom 12:14
of the law by becoming a **c** Gal 3:13

CURSED
c is the ground because of Gn 3:17
"'**C** be the man who makes a Dt 27:15
"'**C** be anyone who dishonors Dt 27:16
"'**C** be anyone who moves his Dt 27:17
"'**C** be anyone who misleads Dt 27:18
"'**C** be anyone who perverts Dt 27:19
"'**C** be anyone who lies with Dt 27:20
"'**C** be anyone who strikes Dt 27:24
"'**C** be anyone who takes a Dt 27:25
"'**C** be anyone who does not Dt 27:26
"**C** is everyone who is hanged Gal 3:13

CURTAIN
out the heavens like a **c**, Is 40:22
the **c** of the temple was torn Mt 27:51
inner place behind the **c**, Heb 6:19
for us through the **c**, Heb 10:20

CYMBAL
noisy gong or a clanging **c**. 1 Cor 13:1

CYPRUS
From the land of **C** it is Is 23:1
of pines from the coasts of **C**, Ez 27:6
we had come in sight of **C**, Acts 21:3
sailed under the lee of **C**, Acts 27:4

CYRENE
they seized one Simon of **C**, Lk 23:26

CYRUS
"Thus says **C** king of Persia, 2 Chr 36:23
who says of **C**, 'He is my Is 44:28

DAGON
offer a great sacrifice to **D** Jgs 16:23
it into the house of **D** 1 Sm 5:2

DAILY
Give us this day our **d** bread, Mt 6:11
and take up his cross **d** Lk 9:23
Give us each day our **d** bread, Lk 11:3
examining the Scriptures **d** Acts 17:11
there is the **d** pressure on 2 Cor 11:28

DAMASCUS
And when the Syrians of **D** 2 Sm 8:5
King Ahaz went to **D** 2 Kgs 16:10
For the head of Syria is **D**, Is 7:8
An oracle concerning **D**. Is 17:1
three transgressions of **D**, Am 1:3
to the synagogues at **D**, Acts 9:2
and I journeyed toward **D** Acts 22:5
declared first to those in **D**, Acts 26:20
At **D**, the governor under 2 Cor 11:32
and returned again to **D**. Gal 1:17

DAN
she called his name **D**. Gn 30:6
D shall judge his people as Gn 49:16
out, from **D** to Beersheba, Jgs 20:1
the other he put in **D**. 1 Kgs 12:29

DANCE
to mourn, and a time to **d**; Eccl 3:4
and you did not **d**; we sang a Mt 11:17

DANCING
for me my mourning into **d**; Ps 30:11
praise his name with **d**, Ps 149:3

DANGER
The prudent sees **d** and Prv 27:12
nakedness, or **d**, or sword? Rom 8:35

DANIEL
D, and Job were in it, as I Ez 14:20
And God gave **D** favor and Dn 1:9
Then this **D** became Dn 6:3
and **D** was brought and cast Dn 6:16

DARIUS
even until the reign of **D** Ezr 4:5
Then **D** the king made a Ezr 6:1

DARK
you have said in the **d** Lk 12:3
as to a lamp shining in a **d** 2 Pt 1:19

DARKENED
their foolish hearts were **d**. Rom 1:21
They are **d** in their Eph 4:18

DARKNESS
and **d** was over the face of the Gn 1:2
separated the light from the **d**. Gn 1:4
my God lightens my **d**. 2 Sm 22:29
Lord my God lightens my **d**. Ps 18:28
follows me will not walk in **d**, Jn 8:12
fellowship has light with **d**? 2 Cor 6:14
for at one time you were **d**, Eph 5:8
and in him is no **d** at all. 1 Jn 1:5
hates his brother is still in **d**. 1 Jn 2:9
hates his brother is in the **d** 1 Jn 2:11
chains under gloomy **d** Jude 1:6
kingdom was plunged into **d**. Rv 16:10

DAUGHTERS
your sons and your **d** shall Jl 2:28
and your sons and your **d** Acts 2:17
you shall be sons and **d** 2 Cor 6:18

DAVID
D took the lyre and played 1 Sm 16:23
Now **D** was the son of an 1 Sm 17:12
was knit to the soul of **D**, 1 Sm 18:1
and there they anointed **D** 2 Sm 2:4
And sons were born to **D** 2 Sm 3:2
And it was told King **D**, 2 Sm 6:12
D said to Nathan, "I have 2 Sm 12:13
And **D** built there an altar 2 Sm 24:25
D said to Solomon, "My 1 Chr 22:7
the son of **D**, the son of Abraham. Mt 1:1
mercy on us, Son of **D**." Mt 9:27
to the city of **D**, which is called Lk 2:4
Son of **D**, have mercy on me!" Lk 18:38
comes from the offspring of **D**, Jn 7:42
For **D** says concerning him, Acts 2:25
of **D** and Samuel and the Heb 11:32
the Root of **D**, has conquered, Rv 5:5

DAWN
righteous is like the light of **d**, Prv 4:18
at early **d**, they went to the Lk 24:1

DAY
God called the light **D**, and the Gn 1:5
in the **d** that the Lord God Gn 2:4
"Remember the Sabbath **d**, Ex 20:8
for it is a **d** of atonement, to Lv 23:28
in a pillar of cloud by **d** Nm 14:14
but you shall meditate on it **d** Jos 1:8
There has been no **d** like it Jos 10:14
This is the **d** that the Lord Ps 118:24
you do not know what a **d** Prv 27:1
For the **d** of the Lord is near Ob 1:15
Give us this **d** our daily bread, Mt 6:11
you do not know on what **d** Mt 24:42
Give us each **d** our daily bread, Lk 11:3
the **d** is at hand. So then let Rom 13:12
spirit may be saved in the **d** 1 Cor 5:5
that on the **d** of our Lord 2 Cor 1:14
you were sealed for the **d** Eph 4:30
to withstand in the evil **d**, Eph 6:13
it to completion at the **d** Phil 1:6
since we belong to the **d**, 1 Thes 5:8
when he comes on that **d** 2 Thes 1:10
exhort one another every **d**, Heb 3:13
and glorify God on the **d** 1 Pt 2:12
that with the Lord one **d** 2 Pt 3:8

DAYS
his **d** shall be 120 years." Gn 6:3
he shall read in it all the **d** Dt 17:19
shall follow me all the **d** Ps 23:6
So teach us to number our **d** Ps 90:12
also your Creator in the **d** Eccl 12:1
and female servants in those **d** Jl 2:29
is from of old, from ancient **d**. Mi 5:2
because the **d** are evil. Eph 5:16
but in these last **d** he has Heb 1:2

DEACONS
with the overseers and **d**: Phil 1:1
D likewise must be dignified, 1 Tm 3:8
then let them serve as **d** 1 Tm 3:10
Let **d** each be the husband 1 Tm 3:12
those who serve well as **d** 1 Tm 3:13

DEAD
that he has risen from the **d**, Mt 28:7
him who raised from the **d** Rom 4:24
must consider yourselves **d** Rom 6:11
God raised him from the **d**, Rom 10:9
For if the **d** are not raised, 1 Cor 15:16
And you were **d** in the Eph 2:1
even when we were **d** in our Eph 2:5
the resurrection from the **d**. Phil 3:11
who raised him from the **d**. Col 2:12
And the **d** in Christ will 1 Thes 4:16
risen from the **d**, the 2 Tm 2:8
judge the living and the **d**, 2 Tm 4:1
the resurrection of the **d**, Heb 6:2
and him as good as **d**, were Heb 11:12
faith apart from works is **d**. Jas 2:26
of Jesus Christ from the **d**, 1 Pt 1:3
to judge the living and the **d**. 1 Pt 4:5

DEATH
murderer shall be put to **d**. Nm 35:16
the valley of the shadow of **d**, Ps 23:4
delivered my soul from **d**, Ps 116:8
He will swallow up **d** forever Is 25:8
he poured out his soul to **d** Is 53:12
but has passed from **d** to life. Jn 5:24
reconciled to God by the **d** Rom 5:10
For the wages of sin is **d**, Rom 6:23
from the law of sin and **d**. Rom 8:2
I am sure that neither **d** Rom 8:38
you proclaim the Lord's **d** 1 Cor 11:26
"O **d**, where is your 1 Cor 15:55
The sting of **d** is sin, and 1 Cor 15:56
point of **d**, even **d** on a cross. Phil 2:8
becoming like him in his **d**, Phil 3:10
Put to **d** therefore what is Col 3:5
that through **d** he might Heb 2:14
is fully grown brings forth **d**. Jas 1:15
we have passed out of **d** 1 Jn 3:14
There is sin that leads to **d**; 1 Jn 5:16
And its rider's name was **D**, Rv 6:8
Over such the second **d** has no Rv 20:6
This is the second **d**, the lake Rv 20:14
which is the second **d**." Rv 21:8

DEBAUCHERY
for that is **d**, but be filled Eph 5:18
and not open to the charge of **d** Ti 1:6
them in the same flood of **d**, 1 Pt 4:4

DEBORAH
Now **D**, a prophetess, the wife Jgs 4:4
Then sang **D** and Barak the Jgs 5:1

DEBT
I forgave you all that **d** Mt 18:32
by canceling the record of **d** Col 2:14

DEBTORS
we also have forgiven our **d**. Mt 6:12
we are **d**, not to the flesh, to Rom 8:12

DEBTS
and forgive us our **d**, as we Mt 6:12

DECEIT
No one who practices **d** shall Ps 101:7
D is in the heart of those Prv 12:20
d, sensuality, envy, slander, Mk 7:22
d, maliciousness. They are Rom 1:29
put away all malice and all **d** 1 Pt 2:1
was **d** found in his mouth. 1 Pt 2:22

DECEITFUL
The heart is **d** above all Jer 17:9
d workmen, disguising 2 Cor 11:13

DECEITFULNESS
cares of the world and the **d** Mt 13:22
cares of the world and the **d** Mk 4:19
may be hardened by the **d** Heb 3:13

DECEIVE
Let no one **d** himself. If 1 Cor 3:18
Let no one **d** you with empty Eph 5:6
we **d** ourselves, and the truth 1 Jn 1:8
let no one **d** you. Whoever 1 Jn 3:7

DECEIVED
"The serpent **d** me, and I ate." Gn 3:13
care lest your heart be **d**, Dt 11:16
d me and through it killed me. Rom 7:11
Do not be **d**: God is not mocked, Gal 6:7
Do not be **d**, my beloved brothers. Jas 1:16

DECEIVER
a one is the **d** and the antichrist. 2 Jn 1:7
the **d** of the whole world — Rv 12:9

DECEIVERS
empty talkers and **d**, especially Ti 1:10
For many **d** have gone out 2 Jn 1:7

DECEIVES
he is nothing, he **d** himself. Gal 6:3
not bridle his tongue but **d** Jas 1:26

DECIDED
For I **d** to know nothing 1 Cor 2:2

DECLARE
The heavens **d** the glory of Ps 19:1
The heavens **d** his righteousness, Ps 50:6
my mouth will **d** your praise. Ps 51:15
With my lips I **d** all the Ps 119:13
and new things I now **d**; Is 42:9
that I may **d** it boldly, as I Eph 6:20
D these things; exhort and Ti 2:15

DEED
For God will bring every **d** Eccl 12:14
what good **d** must I do to Mt 19:16
was a prophet mighty in **d** Lk 24:19
"I did one **d**, and you all Jn 7:21
obedience — by word and **d**, Rom 15:18
in word or **d**, do everything Col 3:17
me from every evil **d** 2 Tm 4:18
in word or talk but in **d** 1 Jn 3:18

DEEDS
in glorious **d**, doing wonders? Ex 15:11
known his **d** among the peoples! Ps 105:1
They do all their **d** to be seen Mt 23:5
the due reward of our **d**; Lk 23:41
than the light because their **d** Jn 3:19
may be clearly seen that his **d** Jn 3:21
performing **d** in keeping Acts 26:20
are those whose lawless **d** Rom 4:7
you put to death the **d** of Rom 8:13
in mind, doing evil **d**, Col 1:21
sins and their lawless **d** Heb 10:17
according to each one's **d**, 1 Pt 1:17
they may see your good **d** 1 Pt 2:12

DEER
As a **d** pants for flowing streams, Ps 42:1

DEFEND
d your cause; remember how Ps 74:22
d the rights of the poor and Prv 31:9
and they do not **d** the rights Jer 5:28

DEFENSE
This is my **d** to those who 1 Cor 9:3
that I am put here for the **d** Phil 1:16
being prepared to make a **d** 1 Pt 3:15

DEFERRED
Hope **d** makes the heart sick, Prv 13:12

DEFILE
resolved that he would not **d** Dn 1:8
These are what **d** a person. Mt 15:20

DEFRAUD
Do not **d**, Honor your father Mk 10:19
yourselves wrong and **d** 1 Cor 6:8

DEITY
him the whole fullness of **d** Col 2:9

DELAY
I hasten and do not **d** to Ps 119:60
will surely come; it will not **d**. Hb 2:3
Will he **d** long over them? Lk 18:7
earth fully and without **d**." Rom 9:28
will come and will not **d**; Heb 10:37
there would be no more **d**, Rv 10:6

DELIGHT
but his **d** is in the law of the Ps 1:2
D yourself in the Lord, and he Ps 37:4
you **d** in truth in the inward Ps 51:6
For you will not **d** in Ps 51:16
then will you **d** in right Ps 51:19
commandments, for I **d** in it. Ps 119:35
to me a joy and the **d** Jer 15:16
For I **d** in the law of God, in Rom 7:22

DELIGHTS
rescue him, for he **d** in him!" Ps 22:8
d in the welfare of his servant!" Ps 35:27
drink from the river of your **d**. Ps 36:8
when he **d** in his way; Ps 37:23
the son in whom he **d**. Prv 3:12
because he **d** in steadfast love. Mi 7:18

DELILAH
So **D** said to Samson, "Please Jgs 16:6
So **D** took new ropes and Jgs 16:12

DELIVER
In your righteousness **d** me Ps 71:2
d us, and atone for our sins, Ps 79:9
but **d** us from evil. Mt 6:13
set our hope that he will **d** 2 Cor 1:10
gave himself for our sins to **d** Gal 1:4

DELIVERED
who was **d** up for our Rom 4:25
He **d** us from such a deadly 2 Cor 1:10
He has **d** us from the domain Col 1:13
and that we may be **d** from 2 Thes 3:2
faith that was once for all **d** Jude 1:3

DELIVERER
the Lord raised up a **d** for the Jgs 3:9
and my fortress and my **d**, Ps 18:2
You are my help and my **d**; Ps 40:17
You are my help and my **d**; Ps 70:5
my stronghold and my **d**, Ps 144:2
"The **D** will come from Rom 11:26

DELIVERS
the Lord hears and **d** them Ps 34:17
he **d** them from the wicked Ps 37:40
but righteousness **d** from death. Prv 10:2
when he **d** the kingdom to 1 Cor 15:24
Jesus who **d** us from the 1 Thes 1:10

DEMETRIUS
a man named **D**, a silversmith Acts 19:24

DEMON
And when the **d** had been cast Mt 9:33
the spirit of an unclean **d**, Lk 4:33
Now he was casting out a **d** Lk 11:14
"I do not have a **d**, but I honor Jn 8:49
one who is oppressed by a **d**. Jn 10:21

DEMON-OPPRESSED
a **d** man who was mute was Mt 9:32
Then a **d** man who was blind Mt 12:22

DEMON-POSSESSED
two **d** men met him, coming Mt 8:28
what had happened to the **d** Mt 8:33
came to Jesus and saw the **d** Mk 5:15
seen it told them how the **d** Lk 8:36

DEMONIC
but is earthly, unspiritual, **d**. Jas 3:15
For they are **d** spirits, Rv 16:14

DEMONS
And the **d** begged him, saying, Mt 8:31
And if I cast out **d** by Mt 12:27
And they cast out many **d** Mk 6:13
power and authority over all **d** Lk 9:1
Beelzebul, the prince of **d**," Lk 11:15
sacrifice they offer to **d** 1 Cor 10:20
spirits and teachings of **d**, 1 Tm 4:1
the **d** believe — and shudder! Jas 2:19

DEN
become a **d** of robbers in your Jer 7:11
brought and cast into the **d** Dn 6:16
but you make it a **d** of robbers." Mt 21:13

DENARIUS
Bring me a **d** and let me look Mk 12:15

DENIED
Peter again **d** it, and at once a Jn 18:27
he has **d** the faith and is 1 Tm 5:8

DENIES
but whoever **d** me before Mt 10:33
No one who **d** the Son has 1 Jn 2:23

DENY
I also will **d** before my Mt 10:33
let him **d** himself and take up Lk 9:23
you will **d** me three times." Lk 22:61
him, he also will **d** us; 2 Tm 2:12
and you did not **d** my faith Rv 2:13

DENYING
and **d** the Lord, and turning Is 59:13
d its power. Avoid such people. 2 Tm 3:5
even **d** the Master who bought 2 Pt 2:1

DEPART
The scepter shall not **d** from Gn 49:10
and lest they **d** from your heart Dt 4:9
Book of the Law shall not **d** Jos 1:8
when he is old he will not **d** Prv 22:6
'**D** from me, you cursed, into Mt 25:41
My desire is to **d** and be with Phil 1:23

DEPARTED
"The glory has **d** from Israel, 1 Sm 4:22

nor have our steps **d** from Ps 44:18

DEPENDS
So then it **d** not on human Rom 9:16
so far as it **d** on you, live Rom 12:18
from God that **d** on faith Phil 3:9

DEPOSIT
guard the **d** entrusted to 1 Tm 6:20
guard the good **d** entrusted 2 Tm 1:14

DEPRIVE
partial to the wicked or to **d** Prv 18:5
and **d** the innocent of his right! Is 5:23
and to **d** the thirsty of drink. Is 32:6
Do not **d** one another, 1 Cor 7:5
die than have anyone **d** 1 Cor 9:15

DEPTH
nor height nor **d**, nor Rom 8:39
Oh the **d** of the riches and Rom 11:33
length and height and **d**, Eph 3:18

DEPTHS
from the **d** of the earth you Ps 71:20
delivered my soul from the **d** Ps 86:13
Lord, from the **d** of the pit; Lam 3:55
cast all our sins into the **d** Mi 7:19
even the **d** of God. 1 Cor 2:10

DESCEND
"I saw the Spirit **d** from Jn 1:32
the Lord himself will **d** 1 Thes 4:16

DESCENDED
because the Lord had **d** Ex 19:18
for an angel of the Lord **d** Mt 28:2
and the Holy Spirit **d** on him Lk 3:22
For not all who are **d** from Rom 9:6
He who **d** is the one who Eph 4:10

DESERT
He turns a **d** into pools of Ps 107:35
make straight in the **d** a Is 40:3

DESERVE
to the proud what they **d**! Ps 94:2
practice such things **d** to die, Rom 1:32
each of you as your works **d**. Rv 2:23

DESERVED
us less than our iniquities **d** Ezr 9:13

DESERVES
of you less than your guilt **d**. Jb 11:6
for the laborer **d** his wages. Do Lk 10:7
"The laborer **d** his wages." 1 Tm 5:18

DESIGNER
whose **d** and builder is God. Heb 11:10

DESIRE
Your **d** shall be for your Gn 3:16
Its **d** is for you, but you must Gn 4:7
him with their whole **d**, 2 Chr 15:15
Lord, you hear the **d** of the Ps 10:17
I **d** to do your will, O my God; Ps 40:8
He fulfills the **d** of those Ps 145:19
and nothing you **d** can Prv 3:15
A **d** fulfilled is sweet to the Prv 13:19
no beauty that we should **d** Is 53:2
the hungry and satisfy the **d** Is 58:10
For I **d** steadfast love and not Hos 6:6
'I **d** mercy, and not sacrifice.' Mt 9:13
For I have the **d** to do what Rom 7:18
necessity but having his **d** 1 Cor 7:37
But earnestly **d** the higher 1 Cor 12:31
My **d** is to depart and be with Phil 1:23
all who **d** to live a godly life 2 Tm 3:12
they **d** a better country, that Heb 11:16
and enticed by his own **d**. Jas 1:14
the world because of sinful **d**. 2 Pt 1:4

DESIRED
More to be **d** are they than Ps 19:10
What is **d** in a man is Prv 19:22
And whatever my eyes **d** Eccl 2:10
many prophets and kings **d** Lk 10:24

DESIRES
and he will give you the **d** Ps 37:4
will is to do your father's **d**. Jn 8:44
you will not gratify the **d** Gal 5:16
For the **d** of the flesh are Gal 5:17
flesh with its passions and **d**. Gal 5:24
who **d** all people to be saved 1 Tm 2:4
following their own sinful **d**. 2 Pt 3:3
the **d** of the flesh and the 1 Jn 2:16
away along with its **d**, 1 Jn 2:17
their own sinful **d**; Jude 1:16

DESOLATE
For the children of the **d** one Is 54:1
went away in the boat to a **d** Mk 6:32

DESOLATION
see the abomination of **d** Mt 24:15
see the abomination of **d** Mk 13:14
then know that its **d** has Lk 21:20

DESPAIR
but not driven to **d**; 2 Cor 4:8

DESPISE
therefore I **d** myself, and Jb 42:6
O God, you will not **d**. Ps 51:17
do not **d** the Lord's discipline Prv 3:11
be devoted to the one and **d** Lk 16:13
Let not the one who eats **d** Rom 14:3
Let no one **d** you for your 1 Tm 4:12

DESPISED
Thus Esau **d** his birthright. Gn 25:34
scorned by mankind and **d** Ps 22:6
He was **d** and rejected by men; Is 53:3
chose what is low and **d** 1 Cor 1:28

DESPISES
Whoever **d** the word brings Prv 13:13
Whoever **d** his neighbor is a Prv 14:21
A fool **d** his father's Prv 15:5
but a foolish man **d** his mother. Prv 15:20
ignores instruction **d** Prv 15:32

DESTINED
know that we are **d** 1 Thes 3:3
For God has not **d** us for 1 Thes 5:9
word, as they were **d** to do. 1 Pt 2:8

DESTITUTE
regards the prayer of the **d** Ps 102:17
the rights of all who are **d**. Prv 31:8
d, afflicted, mistreated — Heb 11:37

DESTROY
fear him who can **d** both soul Mt 10:28
only to steal and kill and **d**. Jn 10:10
through death he might **d** Heb 2:14

DESTROYED
my skin has been thus **d**, Jb 19:26
My people are **d** for lack of Hos 4:6
is **d**, we have a building 2 Cor 5:1
who shrink back and are **d**, Heb 10:39

DESTROYS
the complacency of fools **d** Prv 1:32
he who does it **d** himself. Prv 6:32
but one sinner **d** much good. Eccl 9:18
approaches and no moth **d**. Lk 12:33
If anyone **d** God's temple, 1 Cor 3:17

DESTRUCTION
Pride goes before **d**, and a Prv 16:18
way is easy that leads to **d**, Mt 7:13
of wrath prepared for **d**, Rom 9:22
people into ruin and **d**. 1 Tm 6:9
upon themselves swift **d**. 2 Pt 2:1

DETERMINED
Since his days are **d**, and the Jb 14:5
you not heard that I **d** Is 37:26
having **d** allotted periods Acts 17:26

DETERMINES
He **d** the number of the stars; Ps 147:4

DEVIL
to be tempted by the **d**. Mt 4:1
who sowed them is the **d**. Mt 13:39
fire prepared for the **d** and his Mt 25:41
And yet one of you is a **d**." Jn 6:70
give no opportunity to the **d**. Eph 4:27
the schemes of the **d**. Eph 6:11
into a snare of the **d**. 1 Tm 3:7
Your adversary the **d** prowls 1 Pt 5:8
of sinning is of the **d**, 1 Jn 3:8
and the **d** who had deceived Rv 20:10

DEVOTE
But we will **d** ourselves to Acts 6:4
that you may **d** yourselves to 1 Cor 7:5
d yourself to the public 1 Tm 4:13
And let our people learn to **d** Ti 3:14

DEVOTED
or he will be **d** to the one and Mt 6:24
And they **d** themselves to the Acts 2:42
and that they have **d** 1 Cor 16:15

DEVOUR
"Shall the sword **d** forever? 2 Sm 2:26
who **d** widows' houses and Mk 12:40
But if you bite and **d** one Gal 5:15
lion, seeking someone to **d**. 1 Pt 5:8

DEVOUT
d men are taken away, while Is 57:1
man was righteous and **d**, Lk 2:25

DIBON
and to **D**, to the high places to Is 15:2
O inhabitant of **D**! For the Jer 48:18

DIE
eat of it you shall surely **d**." Gn 2:17
integrity? Curse God and **d**." Jb 2:9
but fools **d** for lack of sense. Prv 10:21
and a time to **d**; a time to Eccl 3:2
believes in me shall never **d**. Jn 11:26
one would dare even to **d** Rom 5:7
and if we **d**, we **d** to the Lord. Rom 14:8
For as in Adam all **d**, 1 Cor 15:22
is Christ, and to **d** is gain. Phil 1:21
it is appointed for man to **d** Heb 9:27
that we might **d** to sin and 1 Pt 2:24

DIED
at the right time Christ **d** Rom 5:6
How can we who **d** to sin still Rom 6:2
For the death he **d** he **d** Rom 6:10
that Christ **d** for our sins in 1 Cor 15:3
and he **d** for all, that those 2 Cor 5:15
If with Christ you **d** to the Col 2:20
we believe that Jesus **d** 1 Thes 4:14
If we have **d** with him, we 2 Tm 2:11
last, who **d** and came to life. Rv 2:8

DIES
When the wicked **d**, his hope Prv 11:7
but if it **d**, it bears much fruit. Jn 12:24
and none of us **d** to himself. Rom 14:7
come to life unless it **d**. 1 Cor 15:36

DIFFERENT
because he has a **d** spirit Nm 14:24
Christ and are turning to a **d** Gal 1:6
If anyone teaches a **d** 1 Tm 6:3

DIFFICULT
"How **d** it is for those who Lk 18:24

DIGNITY
Strength and **d** are her Prv 31:25
teaching show integrity, **d**, Ti 2:7

DIGS
He who **d** a pit will fall into Eccl 10:8

DILIGENT
The plans of the **d** lead surely Prv 21:5
be all the more **d** to make 2 Pt 1:10
be **d** to be found by him 2 Pt 3:14

DIMLY
we see in a mirror **d**, 1 Cor 13:12

DIRECT
God will **d** you, you will be Ex 18:23
and **d** your heart in the way. Prv 23:19
May the Lord **d** your hearts 2 Thes 3:5

DIRGE
sang a **d**, and you did not weep.' Lk 7:32

DISASTER
D pursues sinners, but the Prv 13:21
D after **d**! Behold, it comes. Ez 7:5
love, and relenting from **d**. Jon 4:2

DISBELIEVE
side. Do not **d**, but believe." Jn 20:27

DISBELIEVED
he said, but others **d**. Acts 28:24

DISCERN
Who can **d** his errors? Ps 19:12
you **d** my thoughts from afar. Ps 139:2
that by testing you may **d** Rom 12:2
and try to **d** what is pleasing Eph 5:10

DISCERNING
The **d** sets his face toward Prv 17:24
be **d** enough to desist. Prv 23:4
whoever is **d**, let him know Hos 14:9
eats and drinks without **d** 1 Cor 11:29
and **d** the thoughts and Heb 4:12

DISCERNMENT
who have their powers of **d** Heb 5:14

DISCIPLE
"A **d** is not above his teacher, Mt 10:24
cold water because he is a **d**, Mt 10:42
A **d** is not above his teacher, Lk 6:40
life, he cannot be my **d**. Lk 14:26
after me cannot be my **d**. Lk 14:27
that he has cannot be my **d**. Lk 14:33

DISCIPLES
Go therefore and make **d** Mt 28:19
my word, you are truly my **d**, Jn 8:31
know that you are my **d**, Jn 13:35
And in Antioch the **d** were Acts 11:26

DISCIPLINE
therefore despise not the **d** Jb 5:17
is the man whom you **d**, Ps 94:12
do not despise the Lord's **d** Prv 3:11
He dies for lack of **d**, and Prv 5:23
Whoever loves **d** loves Prv 12:1
loves him is diligent to **d** Prv 13:24
but the rod of **d** drives it far Prv 22:15
Do not withhold **d** from a Prv 23:13
D your son, and he will give Prv 29:17
But I **d** my body and keep it 1 Cor 9:27
but bring them up in the **d** Eph 6:4
do not regard lightly the **d** Heb 12:5
For the moment all **d** seems Heb 12:11
I reprove and **d**, so be zealous Rv 3:19

DISCIPLINED
The Lord has **d** me severely, Ps 118:18
we are **d** so that we may 1 Cor 11:32
upright, holy, and **d**. Ti 1:8
had earthly fathers who **d** Heb 12:9

DISCIPLINES
son, the Lord your God **d** you. Dt 8:5
For the Lord **d** the one he Heb 12:6
but he **d** us for our good, Heb 12:10

DISCLOSED
but has now been **d** and Rom 16:26
secrets of his heart are **d**, 1 Cor 14:25

DISCOURAGED
He will not grow faint or be **d** Is 42:4
lest they become **d**. Col 3:21

DISCRETION
may the Lord grant you **d** 1 Chr 22:12
knowledge and **d** to the youth — Prv 1:4
d will watch over you, Prv 2:11
that you may keep **d**, and your Prv 5:2
and I find knowledge and **d**. Prv 8:12
beautiful woman without **d**. Prv 11:22

DISGRACE
honor, but fools get **d**. Prv 3:35
then comes **d**, but with the Prv 11:2
and with dishonor comes **d**. Prv 18:3
that he may not fall into **d**, 1 Tm 3:7

DISGUISES
for even Satan **d** himself 2 Cor 11:14

DISHONEST
and one with a **d** tongue Prv 17:20
and one who is **d** in a very Lk 16:10
wine, not greedy for **d** gain. 1 Tm 3:8

DISHONOR
counted worthy to suffer **d** Acts 5:41
You who boast in the law **d** Rom 2:23
It is sown in **d**; it is raised 1 Cor 15:43

DISHONORABLE
God gave them up to **d** Rom 1:26
use and another for **d** Rom 9:21
honorable use, some for **d**. 2 Tm 2:20
himself from what is **d**, 2 Tm 2:21

DISHONORS
and him who **d** you I will Gn 12:3
"'Cursed be anyone who **d** Dt 27:16

DISMAYED
be not **d**, for I am your God; I Is 41:10
righteousness will never be **d**. Is 51:6

DISOBEDIENCE
by the one man's **d** the many Rom 5:19
God has consigned all to **d**, Rom 11:32
ready to punish every **d**, 2 Cor 10:6
now at work in the sons of **d** Eph 2:2
comes upon the sons of **d**. Eph 5:6
every transgression or **d** received Heb 2:2
fall by the same sort of **d**. Heb 4:11

DISOBEDIENT
as you were at one time **d** Rom 11:30
d to their parents, ungrateful, 2 Tm 3:2
d, unfit for any good work. Ti 1:16

DISOBEY
They stumble because they **d** 1 Pt 2:8

DISORDER
gossip, conceit, and **d**. 2 Cor 12:20
will be **d** and every vile practice. Jas 3:16

DISPERSED
of the whole earth were **d**. Gn 9:19
So the Lord **d** them from Gn 11:8

DISPERSION
of your slaughter and **d** Jer 25:34
Does he intend to go to the **D** Jn 7:35
To the twelve tribes in the **D**: Jas 1:1
who are elect exiles of the **d** 1 Pt 1:1

DISPLAY
Jesus Christ might **d** his 1 Tm 1:16
which he will **d** at the 1 Tm 6:15

DISQUALIFIED
I myself should be **d**. 1 Cor 9:27
corrupted in mind and **d** 2 Tm 3:8

DISQUALIFY
Let no one **d** you, insisting on Col 2:18

DISRESPECTFUL
masters must not be **d** 1 Tm 6:2

DISTINCTION
making no **d**. These six Acts 11:12
and he made no **d** between Acts 15:9
believe. For there is no **d**: Rom 3:22
For there is no **d** between Rom 10:12

DISTINGUISH
You are to **d** between the Lv 10:10
to another the ability to **d** 1 Cor 12:10
by constant practice to **d** Heb 5:14

DISTRESS
In my **d** I called upon the Ps 18:6
out of my **d**, and he answered Jon 2:2
or **d**, or persecution, or Rom 8:35

DISTRIBUTED
He has **d** freely; he has given Ps 112:9
and it was **d** to each as any Acts 4:35
"He has **d** freely, he has 2 Cor 9:9
by gifts of the Holy Spirit **d** Heb 2:4

DIVIDE
they **d** my garments among Ps 22:18
they cast lots to **d** his garments. Lk 23:34

DIVIDED
and a **d** household falls. Lk 11:17
And **d** tongues as of fire Acts 2:3
Is Christ **d**? Was Paul crucified 1 Cor 1:13

DIVINE
his eternal power and **d** Rom 1:20
because in his **d** forbearance Rom 3:25
not of the flesh but have **d** 2 Cor 10:4
become partakers of the **d** 2 Pt 1:4

DIVISION
I tell you, but rather **d**. Lk 12:51
that there may be no **d** 1 Cor 12:25
piercing to the **d** of soul and Heb 4:12

DIVISIONS
out for those who cause **d** Rom 16:17
and that there be no **d** 1 Cor 1:10
It is these who cause **d**, Jude 1:19

DIVORCE
He may not **d** her all his days. Dt 22:19
he writes her a certificate of **d** Dt 24:1
resolved to **d** her quietly. Mt 1:19
give her a certificate of **d**.' Mt 5:31
"Is it lawful to **d** one's wife for Mt 19:3
heart Moses allowed you to **d** Mt 19:8
the husband should not **d** 1 Cor 7:11
him, he should not **d** her. 1 Cor 7:12
her, she should not **d** him. 1 Cor 7:13

DIVORCED
And whoever marries a **d** Mt 5:32
he who marries a woman **d** Lk 16:18

DIVORCES
the man who hates and **d**, Mal 2:16
to you that everyone who **d** Mt 5:32
whoever **d** his wife, except for Mt 19:9
"Everyone who **d** his wife Lk 16:18

DOCTRINE
'My **d** is pure, and I am clean Jb 11:4
obstacles contrary to the **d** Rom 16:17
about by every wind of **d**, Eph 4:14
not to teach any different **d**, 1 Tm 1:3
is contrary to healthy **d**, 1 Tm 1:10
and of the good **d** that you have 1 Tm 4:6
anyone teaches a different **d** 1 Tm 6:3
to give instruction in sound **d** Ti 1:9
what accords with sound **d**. Ti 2:1
they may adorn the **d** of God Ti 2:10
let us leave the elementary **d** Heb 6:1

DOERS
but the **d** of the law who Rom 2:13
But be **d** of the word, and not Jas 1:22

DOMINION
and subdue it and have **d** Gn 1:28
You have given him **d** over the Ps 8:6
in all places of his **d**. Bless Ps 103:22
his **d** is an everlasting **d**, Dn 4:34
death no longer has **d** over him. Rom 6:9
To him belong glory and **d** 1 Pt 4:11

DOOR
sin is crouching at the **d**. Its Gn 4:7
I am the **d**. If anyone enters Jn 10:9
the Judge is standing at the **d**. Jas 5:9
I stand at the **d** and knock. If Rv 3:20

DOUBLE-MINDED
I hate the **d**, but I love Ps 119:113
he is a **d** man, unstable in all Jas 1:8
purify your hearts, you **d**. Jas 4:8

DOUBT
little faith, why did you **d**?" Mt 14:31
and does not **d** in his heart, Mk 11:23
mercy on those who **d**; Jude 1:22

DOUBTING
with no **d**, for the one who Jas 1:6

DOVE
And the **d** came back to him Gn 8:11
of God descending like a **d** Mt 3:16

DOWNCAST
"Why are your faces **d** today?" Gn 40:7
God, who comforts the **d**, 2 Cor 7:6

DRAGON
and he will slay the **d** that is Is 27:1
a great red **d**, with seven Rv 12:3
And they worshiped the **d**, Rv 13:4

DRAW
will **d** all people to myself." Jn 12:32
us then with confidence **d** Heb 4:16
let us **d** near with a true Heb 10:22
D near to God, and he will Jas 4:8

DREAD
d and great darkness fell Gn 15:12
they shall turn in **d** to the Mi 7:17

DREAM
Now Joseph had a **d**, and Gn 37:5
Therefore show me the **d** Dn 2:6
your old men shall **d** dreams, Jl 2:28
appeared to Joseph in a **d** Mt 2:13
and your old men shall **d** Acts 2:17

DRINK
D water from your own Prv 5:15
will eat or what you will **d**, Mt 6:25
let him come to me and **d**. Jn 7:37
you eat this bread and **d** 1 Cor 11:26
and all were made to **d** 1 Cor 12:13
being poured out as a **d** offering 2 Tm 4:6

DRUNK
Be **d**, but not with wine; Is 29:9
For these men are not **d**, Acts 2:15
And do not get **d** with wine, Eph 5:18

DRUNKARD
for the **d** and the glutton Prv 23:21
d, or swindler — not even 1 Cor 5:11
not a **d**, not violent but 1 Tm 3:3
or quick-tempered or a **d** Ti 1:7

DRUNKENNESS
down with dissipation and **d** Lk 21:34
not in orgies and **d**, not in Rom 13:13
d, orgies, and things like Gal 5:21
d, orgies, drinking parties, and 1 Pt 4:3

DRY
God called the **d** land Earth, Gn 1:10
plant, and like a root out of **d** Is 53:2
O **d** bones, hear the word of Ez 37:4

DUE
in themselves the **d** Rom 1:27
one may receive what is **d** 2 Cor 5:10
d to their hardness of heart. Eph 4:18
is no variation or shadow **d** Jas 1:17

DUST
Lord God formed the man of **d** Gn 2:7
and to **d** you shall return." Gn 3:19
remembers that we are **d**. Ps 103:14
All are from the **d**, and to Eccl 3:20

DUTY
for this is the whole **d** Eccl 12:13

DWELL
"But will God indeed **d** 2 Chr 6:18
and I shall **d** in the house of Ps 23:6
so that Christ may **d** in your Eph 3:17
of God was pleased to **d**, Col 1:19

DWELLING
"I will make my **d** among 2 Cor 6:16
being built together into a **d** Eph 2:22
the **d** place of God is with Rv 21:3

DWELLS
I know that nothing good **d** Rom 7:18
if in fact the Spirit of God **d** Rom 8:9
God's Spirit **d** in you? 1 Cor 3:16
the whole fullness of deity **d** Col 2:9
Holy Spirit who **d** within us, 2 Tm 1:14

DWELT
The glory of the Lord **d** on Ex 24:16
Zion, where you have **d**. Ps 74:2
the Word became flesh and **d** Jn 1:14

EAGER
So I am **e** to preach the gospel Rom 1:15
the creation waits with **e** Rom 8:19
since you are **e** for 1 Cor 14:12

EAGERLY
inwardly as we wait **e** Rom 8:23
by faith, we ourselves **e** wait Gal 5:5
but to save those who are **e** Heb 9:28

EAGLES
mount up with wings like **e**; Is 40:31

EAGLE'S
youth is renewed like the **e**. Ps 103:5

EAR
Incline your **e**, and hear Prv 22:17
no eye has seen, nor **e** 1 Cor 2:9
And if the **e** should say, 1 Cor 12:16
He who has an **e**, let him hear Rv 2:7

EARNESTLY
Therefore pray **e** to the Lord Lk 10:2
But **e** desire the higher 1 Cor 12:31
Pursue love, and **e** desire 1 Cor 14:1
love, love one another **e** 1 Pt 1:22
keep loving one another **e**, 1 Pt 4:8

EARS
but having itching **e** they 2 Tm 4:3
on the righteous, and his **e** 1 Pt 3:12

EARTH
God created the heavens and the **e**. Gn 1:1
God called the dry land **E**, Gn 1:10
that the Lord God made the **e** Gn 2:4
is your name in all the **e**! Ps 8:1
The **e** is the Lord's and the Ps 24:1
the whole **e** is full of his glory!" Is 6:3
Creator of the ends of the **e**. Is 40:28
I made the **e** and created Is 45:12
the heavens and the **e** Jer 32:17
heavens and founded the **e** Zec 12:1
for they shall inherit the **e**. Mt 5:5
"You are the salt of the **e**, Mt 5:13
come, your will be done, on **e** Mt 6:10
Heaven and **e** will pass Mt 24:35
authority in heaven and on **e** Mt 28:18
Lord of heaven and **e**, yes, Lk 10:21
I am lifted up from the **e**, Jn 12:32
I glorified you on **e**, having Jn 17:4
and to the end of the **e**." Acts 1:8
For "the **e** is the Lord's, 1 Cor 10:26
into the lower parts of the **e**? Eph 4:9
heaven and on **e** and under the **e** Phil 2:10
new heavens and a new **e** 2 Pt 3:13
a new heaven and a new **e**, Rv 21:1

EARTHLY
heavenly bodies and **e** 1 Cor 15:40
if the tent, which is our **e** 2 Cor 5:1
shame, with minds set on **e** Phil 3:19
to death therefore what is **e** Col 3:5

EASIER
For which is **e**, to say, 'Your Mt 9:5
Again I tell you, it is **e** for a Mt 19:24

EAST
a garden in Eden, in the **e**, Gn 2:8
as far as the **e** is from the Ps 103:12
behold, wise men from the **e** Mt 2:1
lightning comes from the **e** Mt 24:27

EASY
gate is wide and the way is **e** Mt 7:13
For my yoke is **e**, and my Mt 11:30

EAT
for in the day that you **e** Gn 2:17
give him bread to **e**, and if he Prv 25:21
your life, what you will **e** Mt 6:25
disciples, and said, "Take, **e**; Mt 26:26
stumble, I will never **e** 1 Cor 8:13
as often as you **e** this bread 1 Cor 11:26
I will come in to him and **e** Rv 3:20

EATING
of God is not a matter of **e** Rom 14:17

EATS
If anyone **e** of this bread, he Jn 6:51
For anyone who **e** and 1 Cor 11:29

EBENEZER
and called its name **E**; 1 Sm 7:12

EDEN
God planted a garden in **E**, Gn 2:8
in the land of Nod, east of **E**. Gn 4:16
makes her wilderness like **E**, Is 51:3
You were in **E**, the garden Ez 28:13

EFFECT
And the **e** of righteousness Is 32:17
For a will takes **e** only at Heb 9:17
steadfastness have its full **e**, Jas 1:4

EFFORT
very reason, make every **e** 2 Pt 1:5

EGYPT
When Abram entered **E**, Gn 12:14
They took Joseph to **E**. Gn 37:28
of Canaan, and came into **E**, Gn 46:6
children of Israel, out of **E**." Ex 3:10
a people has come out of **E**, Nm 22:11
You brought a vine out of **E**; Ps 80:8
An oracle concerning **E**. Is 19:1
will be a highway from **E** Is 19:23
"A beautiful heifer is **E**, Jer 46:20
They played the whore in **E**; Ez 23:3
bring to ruin the pride of **E**, Ez 32:12
and his mother, and flee to **E**, Mt 2:13
By faith he left **E**, not being Heb 11:27
is called Sodom and **E**, Rv 11:8

ELDER
a charge against an **e** 1 Tm 5:19
among you, as a fellow **e** 1 Pt 5:1
The **e** to the elect lady and 2 Jn 1:1
The **e** to the beloved Gaius, 3 Jn 1:1

ELDERS
when the council of **e** 1 Tm 4:14
Let the **e** who rule well be 1 Tm 5:17
into order, and appoint **e** in Ti 1:5
Let him call for the **e** of the Jas 5:14
So I exhort the **e** among you, 1 Pt 5:1
younger, be subject to the **e**. 1 Pt 5:5

ELEAZAR
And **E** the son of Aaron the Nm 3:32
Then Moses and **E** came Nm 20:28

ELECT
But for the sake of the **e** Mt 24:22
if possible, even the **e**. Mt 24:24
and they will gather his **e** Mt 24:31
not God give justice to his **e**, Lk 18:7
any charge against God's **e**? Rom 8:33
The **e** obtained it, but the Rom 11:7
Christ Jesus and of the **e** 1 Tm 5:21
for the sake of the **e**, 2 Tm 2:10
the sake of the faith of God's **e** Ti 1:1
Christ, To those who are **e** 1 Pt 1:1
The elder to the **e** lady and 2 Jn 1:1
The children of your **e** sister 2 Jn 1:13

ELECTION
that God's purpose of **e** Rom 9:11
But as regards **e**, they are Rom 11:28
to make your calling and **e** sure, 2 Pt 1:10

ELI
Now **E** the priest was sitting 1 Sm 1:9
the ark of God, **E** fell over 1 Sm 4:18

ELIHU
Now **E** had waited to speak to Jb 32:4

ELIJAH
Now **E** the Tishbite, of 1 Kgs 17:1
And **E** went up by a 2 Kgs 2:11
"Behold, I will send you **E** Mal 4:5
But I tell you that **E** has Mt 17:12
Are you **E**?" He said, "I am Jn 1:21
E was a man with a nature Jas 5:17

ELISHA
spirit of Elijah rests on **E**." 2 Kgs 2:15
all the great things that **E** 2 Kgs 8:4
So **E** died, and they buried 2 Kgs 13:20

ELIZABETH
Aaron, and her name was **E**. Lk 1:5
And when **E** heard the Lk 1:41

ELOQUENT
"Oh, my Lord, I am not **e**, Ex 4:10
He was an **e** man, Acts 18:24
and not with words of **e** 1 Cor 1:17

EMBRACE
a time to **e**, and a time to Eccl 3:5

EMMAUS
going to a village named **E**, Lk 24:13

EMPOWERED
All these are **e** by one and 1 Cor 12:11

attributes, namely, his **e** Rom 1:20
righteousness leading to **e** Rom 5:21
but the free gift of God is **e** Rom 6:23
is preparing for us an **e** weight 2 Cor 4:17
not made with hands, **e** in the 2 Cor 5:1
will from the Spirit reap **e** life. Gal 6:8
This was according to the **e** Eph 3:11
loved us and gave us **e** 2 Thes 2:16
Take hold of the **e** life to 1 Tm 6:12
in hope of **e** life, which God, Ti 1:2
blood, thus securing an **e** Heb 9:12
may receive the promised **e** Heb 9:15
who has called you to his **e** 1 Pt 5:10
you an entrance into the **e** 2 Pt 1:11
he made to us — **e** life. 1 Jn 2:25
that God gave us **e** life, and 1 Jn 5:11
may know that you have **e** 1 Jn 5:13
He is the true God and **e** life. 1 Jn 5:20
Jesus Christ that leads to **e** Jude 1:21

ETERNITY
Also, he has put **e** into man's Eccl 3:11
or confounded to all **e**. Is 45:17
lifted up, who inhabits **e**, Is 57:15
now and to the day of **e**. 2 Pt 3:18

EUNUCHS
have made themselves **e** Mt 19:12

EUPHRATES
And the fourth river is the **E**. Gn 2:14

EUTYCHUS
And a young man named **E**, Acts 20:9

EVANGELIST
the house of Philip the **e**, Acts 21:8
do the work of an **e**, 2 Tm 4:5

EVANGELISTS
apostles, the prophets, the **e**, Eph 4:11

EVE
called his wife's name **E**, Gn 3:20
as the serpent deceived **E** 2 Cor 11:3
was formed first, then **E**; 1 Tm 2:13

EVER
will reign forever and **e**." Ex 15:18
let them **e** sing for joy, and Ps 5:11
and your faithfulness will **e** Ps 40:11
and my sin is **e** before me. Ps 51:3
And more than **e** believers Acts 5:14
No one has **e** seen God; if 1 Jn 4:12
they will reign forever and **e**. Rv 22:5

EVERLASTING
see it and remember the **e** Gn 9:16
be in your flesh an **e** Gn 17:13
earth and the world, from **e** Ps 90:2
from **e** to **e**! And let all Ps 106:48
Counselor, Mighty God, **E** Is 9:6
I will make with you an **e** Is 55:3
I will make with them an **e** Jer 32:40
ourselves to the Lord in an **e** Jer 50:5
It shall be an **e** covenant Ez 37:26
His kingdom is an **e** kingdom, Dn 4:3
him; his dominion is an **e** Dn 7:14

EVIDENCE
to death on the **e** of witnesses. Nm 35:30
the truth gives honest **e**, Prv 12:17
established by the **e** of two or Mt 18:16
be established by the **e** 2 Cor 13:1
elder except on the **e** of two 1 Tm 5:19

EVIL
the knowledge of good and **e**. Gn 2:9
God, knowing good and **e**." Gn 3:5
intention of man's heart is **e** Gn 8:21
God and turned away from **e**. Jb 1:1
of death, I will fear no **e**, Ps 23:4
Turn away from **e** and do Ps 34:14
I sinned and done what is **e** Ps 51:4
who love the Lord, hate **e**! Ps 97:10
Lord, and turn away from **e**. Prv 3:7
of the Lord is hatred of **e**. Prv 8:13
Be assured, an **e** person will Prv 11:21
thing, whether good or **e**. Eccl 12:14
Woe to those who call **e** good Is 5:20
Hate **e**, and love good, and Am 5:15
"Woe to him who gets **e** gain Hb 2:9
but deliver us from **e**. Mt 6:13
If you then, who are **e**, know Mt 7:11
the good I want, but the **e** Rom 7:19
Abhor what is **e**; hold fast to Rom 12:9
but overcome **e** with good. Rom 12:21
as good be spoken of as **e**. Rom 14:16
"Purge the **e** person from 1 Cor 5:13
deliver us from the present **e** Gal 1:4
because the days are **e**. Eph 5:16
all the flaming darts of the **e** Eph 6:16
impurity, passion, **e** desire, and Col 3:5
no one repays anyone **e** 1 Thes 5:15
from every form of **e**. 1 Thes 5:22
guard you against the **e** 2 Thes 3:3
patiently enduring **e**, 2 Tm 2:24
to speak **e** of no one, to avoid Ti 3:2
there be in any of you an **e**, Heb 3:12
to distinguish good from **e**. Heb 5:14
cannot be tempted with **e**, Jas 1:13
Do not speak **e** against one Jas 4:11
to punish those who do **e** 1 Pt 2:14
freedom as a cover-up for **e**, 1 Pt 2:16
Do not repay **e** for **e** or 1 Pt 3:9
let him turn away from **e** 1 Pt 3:11
you have overcome the **e** 1 Jn 2:13
God protects him, and the **e** 1 Jn 5:18
Beloved, do not imitate **e** 3 Jn 1:11

EXACT
of the glory of God and the **e** Heb 1:3

EXALT
Lord with me, and let us **e** Ps 34:3
keep his way, and he will **e** Ps 37:34
E the Lord our God, and Ps 99:9
I will **e** you; I will praise your Is 25:1
So also Christ did not **e** Heb 5:5
the Lord, and he will **e** you. Jas 4:10
at the proper time he may **e** 1 Pt 5:6

EXALTED
blessed be my rock, and **e** 2 Sm 22:47
blessed be my rock, and **e** Ps 18:46
you are **e** far above all gods. Ps 97:9
Be **e**, O God, above the Ps 108:5
and the Lord alone will be **e** Is 2:11
The Lord is **e**, for he dwells Is 33:5
and lifted up, and shall be **e**. Is 52:13
humbles himself will be **e**. Mt 23:12
God **e** him at his right hand Acts 5:31
Therefore God has highly **e** Phil 2:9

EXALTS
Righteousness **e** a nation, Prv 14:34
to you, and therefore he **e** Is 30:18
Whoever **e** himself will be Mt 23:12
who opposes and **e** himself 2 Thes 2:4

EXAMINE
Let us test and **e** our ways, Lam 3:40
Let a person **e** himself, 1 Cor 11:28
E yourselves, to see 2 Cor 13:5

EXAMPLE
For I have given you an **e**, Jn 13:15
happened to them as an **e**, 1 Cor 10:11
walk according to the **e** Phil 3:17
give you in ourselves an **e** 2 Thes 3:9
his perfect patience as an **e** 1 Tm 1:16
but set the believers an **e** 1 Tm 4:12
for you, leaving you an **e**, 1 Pt 2:21

EXAMPLES
things took place as **e** 1 Cor 10:6
in your charge, but being **e** 1 Pt 5:3

EXCEL
of the Spirit, strive to **e** 1 Cor 14:12
But as you **e** in everything 2 Cor 8:7

EXCELLENCE
if there is any **e**, think about Phil 4:8
us to his own glory and **e**, 2 Pt 1:3

EXCELLENT
praise him according to his **e** Ps 150:2
will and approve what is **e**, Rom 2:18
show you a still more **e** way. 1 Cor 12:31
you may approve what is **e**, Phil 1:10
These things are **e** and profitable Ti 3:8
he has inherited is more **e** Heb 1:4
as much more **e** than the old Heb 8:6

EXCHANGED
and **e** the glory of the Rom 1:23
because they **e** the truth Rom 1:25

EXCUSE
but now they have no **e** Jn 15:22
So they are without **e**. Rom 1:20

EXERCISES
Every athlete **e** self-control 1 Cor 9:25

EXHORT
reprove, rebuke, and **e**, with 2 Tm 4:2
things; **e** and rebuke with all Ti 2:15
But **e** one another every day, Heb 3:13

EXHORTATION
if you have any word of **e** Acts 13:15
one who exhorts, in his **e**; Rom 12:8
Scripture, to **e**, to teaching. 1 Tm 4:13

EXIST
things and for whom we **e**, 1 Cor 8:6
and by whom all things **e**, Heb 2:10

EXPECT
at an hour you do not **e**. Mt 24:44

EXPECTATION
as it is my eager **e** and hope Phil 1:20
but a fearful **e** of judgment, Heb 10:27

EXPOSE
of darkness, but instead **e** Eph 5:11

EXPOSED
lest his deeds should be **e**. Jn 3:20
But when anything is **e** Eph 5:13

EXTINGUISH
faith, with which you can **e** Eph 6:16

EXTOL
"Remember to **e** his work, of Jb 36:24
I will **e** you, O Lord, for you Ps 30:1
I will **e** you, my God and Ps 145:1
and let all the peoples **e** Rom 15:11

EXTORT
he said to them, "Do not **e** Lk 3:14

EXULT
I will be glad and **e** in you; I Ps 9:2
is the Lord; **e** before him! Ps 68:4
My inmost being will **e** Prv 23:16
and **e**, O earth; break forth, Is 49:13
Let us rejoice and **e** and give Rv 19:7

EYE
e for **e**, tooth for tooth, Ex 21:24
He who formed the **e**, does he Ps 94:9
heard that it was said, 'An **e** Mt 5:38
And if your **e** causes you to Mt 18:9
that is in your brother's **e**, Lk 6:41
Your **e** is the lamp of your Lk 11:34
a camel to go through the **e** Lk 18:25
as it is written, "What no **e** 1 Cor 2:9
in the twinkling of an **e**, 1 Cor 15:52

EYE-SERVICE
not by the way of **e**, as Eph 6:6
masters, not by way of **e**, Col 3:22

EYES
that when you eat of it your **e** Gn 3:5
Open my **e**, that I may Ps 119:18
I lift up my **e** to the hills. Ps 121:1
But my **e** are toward you, O Ps 141:8
for my **e** have seen your salvation Lk 2:30
having the **e** of your hearts Eph 1:18
For the **e** of the Lord are on 1 Pt 3:12
every tear from their **e**." Rv 7:17
away every tear from their **e**, Rv 21:4

EYEWITNESSES
from the beginning were **e** Lk 1:2
Jesus Christ, but we were **e** 2 Pt 1:16

EZEKIEL
word of the Lord came to **E** Ez 1:3
Thus shall **E** be to you a sign; Ez 24:24

EZRA
king of Persia, **E** the son of Ezr 7:1
king of kings, to **E** the priest, Ezr 7:12
And they told **E** the scribe to Neh 8:1

FACE
God was hovering over the **f** Gn 1:2

"For I have seen God **f** Gn 32:30
said, "you cannot see my **f**, Ex 33:20
The Lord make his **f** to shine Nm 6:25
and pray and seek my **f** 2 Chr 7:14
Lift up the light of your **f** upon Ps 4:6
Hide your **f** from my sins, and Ps 51:9
therefore I have set my **f** Is 50:7
angels always see the **f** Mt 18:10
mirror dimly, but then **f** to **f**. 1 Cor 13:12
of the glory of God in the **f** 2 Cor 4:6
But the **f** of the Lord is 1 Pt 3:12
two-edged sword, and his **f** Rv 1:16
They will see his **f**, and his Rv 22:4

FACTIONS
for there must be **f** among 1 Cor 11:19

FAIL
flesh and my heart may **f**, Ps 73:26
Without counsel plans **f**, Prv 15:22
that your faith may not **f**. Lk 22:32
unless indeed you **f** to meet 2 Cor 13:5

FAILED
the word of God has **f**. Rom 9:6
Israel **f** to obtain what it Rom 11:7
find out that we have not **f** 2 Cor 13:6
received the good news **f** Heb 4:6

FAILINGS
to bear with the **f** of the weak, Rom 15:1

FAILS
See to it that no one **f** to Heb 12:15
keeps the whole law but **f** Jas 2:10
right thing to do and **f** to do it, Jas 4:17

FAINT
they shall walk and not **f**. Is 40:31

FAINTHEARTED
the idle, encourage the **f**, 1 Thes 5:14
may not grow weary or **f**. Heb 12:3

FAITH
If you are not firm in **f**, you Is 7:9
righteous shall live by his **f**. Hb 2:4
you afraid, O you of little **f**?" Mt 8:26
saying, "According to your **f** Mt 9:29
I say to you, if you have **f** Mt 17:20
answered them, "Have **f** in God Mk 11:22
in Israel have I found such **f**." Lk 7:9
to the Lord, "Increase our **f**!" Lk 17:5
of Man comes, will he find **f** Lk 18:8
cleansed their hearts by **f**. Acts 15:9
who are sanctified by **f** Acts 26:18
righteous shall live by **f**." Rom 1:17
of God through **f** in Jesus Rom 3:22
blood, to be received by **f**. Rom 3:25
that one is justified by **f** apart Rom 3:28
justify the circumcised by **f** Rom 3:30
justifies the ungodly, his **f** Rom 4:5
That is why it depends on **f**, Rom 4:16
we have been justified by **f**, Rom 5:1
righteousness that is by **f**; Rom 9:30
righteousness based on **f** says, Rom 10:6
So **f** comes from hearing, Rom 10:17
the one who is weak in **f**, Rom 14:1
that your **f** might not rest in 1 Cor 2:5
and if I have all **f**, but have 1 Cor 13:2
So now **f**, hope, and love 1 Cor 13:13
is in vain and your **f** 1 Cor 15:14
stand firm in the **f**, be strong. 1 Cor 16:13
you stand firm in your **f**. 2 Cor 1:24
for we walk by **f**, not by 2 Cor 5:7
whether you are in the **f**. 2 Cor 13:5
of the law but through **f** in Jesus Gal 2:16
to be justified by **f** in Christ Gal 2:16
live in the flesh I live by **f** Gal 2:20
justify the Gentiles by **f**, Gal 3:8
righteous shall live by **f**." Gal 3:11
we might be justified by **f**. Gal 3:24
For through the Spirit, by **f**, Gal 5:5
I have heard of your **f** Eph 1:15
have been saved through **f**. Eph 2:8
in your hearts through **f** Eph 3:17
one Lord, one **f**, one baptism, Eph 4:5
attain to the unity of the **f** Eph 4:13
take up the shield of **f**, Eph 6:16
that which comes through **f** Phil 3:9
you continue in the **f**, Col 1:23
him and established in the **f**, Col 2:7
about you through your **f**. 1 Thes 3:7
put on the breastplate of **f** 1 Thes 5:8
made shipwreck of their **f**, 1 Tm 1:19
if they continue in **f** and 1 Tm 2:15
some will depart from the **f** 1 Tm 4:1
in love, in **f**, in purity. 1 Tm 4:12
the good fight of the **f**. 1 Tm 6:12
f, love, and peace, 2 Tm 2:22
disqualified regarding the **f**. 2 Tm 3:8
for salvation through **f** 2 Tm 3:15
the race, I have kept the **f**. 2 Tm 4:7
healthy in **f**, in love, Ti 2:2
that the sharing of your **f** Phlm 1:6
one shall live by **f**, Heb 10:38
Now **f** is the assurance of Heb 11:1
By **f** we understand that the Heb 11:3
And without **f** it is impossible Heb 11:6
By **f** Abraham obeyed when Heb 11:8
By **f** Moses, when he was Heb 11:23
and perfecter of our **f**, Heb 12:2
that the testing of your **f** Jas 1:3
But let him ask in **f**, with no Jas 1:6
if someone says he has **f** Jas 2:14
So also **f** by itself, if it does Jas 2:17
and I will show you my **f** Jas 2:18
along with his works, and **f** Jas 2:22
the spirit is dead, so also **f** Jas 2:26
And the prayer of **f** will save Jas 5:15
are being guarded through **f** 1 Pt 1:5
tested genuineness of your **f** 1 Pt 1:7
the outcome of your **f**, 1 Pt 1:9
him glory, so that your **f** 1 Pt 1:21
Resist him, firm in your **f**, 1 Pt 5:9
those who have obtained a **f** 2 Pt 1:1
the world — our **f**. 1 Jn 5:4
to you to contend for the **f** Jude 1:3

FAITHFUL
the Lord your God is God, the **f** Dt 7:9
will raise up for myself a **f** 1 Sm 2:35
have redeemed me, O Lord, **f** Ps 31:5
The Lord preserves the **f** Ps 31:23
The works of his hands are **f** Ps 111:7
The Lord is **f** in all his Ps 145:13
own steadfast love, but a **f** Prv 20:6
A **f** man will abound with Prv 28:20
because of the Lord, who is **f**, Is 49:7
him, 'Well done, good and **f** Mt 25:21
"One who is **f** in a very little Lk 16:10
Because you have been **f** Lk 19:17
God is **f**, by whom you were 1 Cor 1:9
God is **f**, and he will not 1 Cor 10:13
He who calls you is **f**; 1 Thes 5:24
But the Lord is **f**. He will 2 Thes 3:3
sober-minded, **f** in all things. 1 Tm 3:11
are faithless, he remains **f** 2 Tm 2:13
but Christ is **f** over God's Heb 3:6
for he who promised is **f**. Heb 10:23
we confess our sins, he is **f** 1 Jn 1:9
Be **f** unto death, and I will Rv 2:10
one sitting on it is called **F** Rv 19:11

FAITHFULLY
"And if you **f** obey the voice of Dt 28:1
the Lord and serve him **f** 1 Sm 12:24
Lord, but those who act **f** Prv 12:22
my word speak my word **f**. Jer 23:28

FAITHFULNESS
A God of **f** and without Dt 32:4
Lord are steadfast love and **f**, Ps 25:10
in steadfast love and **f**. Ps 86:15
I will make known your **f** Ps 89:1
his **f** is a shield and buckler. Ps 91:4
endures forever, and his **f** Ps 100:5
love toward us, and the **f** Ps 117:2
Let not steadfast love and **f** Prv 3:3
be the belt of his waist, and **f** Is 11:5
morning; great is your **f**. Lam 3:23
faithlessness nullify the **f** Rom 3:3
kindness, goodness, **f**, Gal 5:22

FAITHLESS
I look at the **f** with disgust, Ps 119:158
Return, O **f** children, declares Jer 3:14
foolish, **f**, heartless, Rom 1:31
if we are **f**, he remains 2 Tm 2:13

FAITHLESSNESS
Does their **f** nullify the Rom 3:3

FALL
though he **f**, he shall not be Ps 37:24
a haughty spirit before a **f**. Prv 16:18
For if they **f**, one will lift up Eccl 4:10
And not one of them will **f** Mt 10:29
for all have sinned and **f** Rom 3:23
take heed lest he **f**. 1 Cor 10:12
puffed up with conceit and **f** 1 Tm 3:6
heart, leading you to **f** away Heb 3:12
if they then **f** away, since Heb 6:6
It is a fearful thing to **f** Heb 10:31
be no, so that you may not **f** Jas 5:12
qualities you will never **f**. 2 Pt 1:10

FALLEN
How the mighty have **f**! 2 Sm 1:19
"How you are **f** from heaven, Is 14:12
of those who have **f** 1 Cor 15:20
you have **f** away from grace. Gal 5:4
him those who have **f** 1 Thes 4:14

FALLING
Lord upholds all who are **f** Ps 145:14
to you to keep you from **f** Jn 16:1

FALLS
rejoice when your enemy **f**, Prv 24:17
and a divided household **f**. Lk 11:17
unless a grain of wheat **f** Jn 12:24
the judgment of God rightly **f** Rom 2:2

FALSE
"You shall not bear **f** witness Ex 20:16
"You shall not spread a **f** Ex 23:1
therefore I hate every **f** Ps 119:104
A **f** witness will not go Prv 19:5
"Beware of **f** prophets, who Mt 7:15
And many **f** prophets will Mt 24:11
Do not steal, Do not bear **f** Mk 10:19
hearts, do not boast and be **f** Jas 3:14
are from God, for many **f** 1 Jn 4:1
does what is detestable or **f**, Rv 21:27

FALSEHOOD
I hate and abhor **f**, but I Ps 119:163
Remove far from me **f** and Prv 30:8
true, and in him there is no **f**. Jn 7:18
having put away **f**, for we are Eph 4:25

FALSELY
you shall not deal **f**; you Lv 19:11
all kinds of evil against you **f** Mt 5:11
contradictions of what is **f** 1 Tm 6:20

FAMILIES
curse, and in you all the **f** Gn 12:3
to the Lord, and all the **f** Ps 22:27

FAMILY
from whom every **f** in Eph 3:15

FAMINE
will arise seven years of **f**, Gn 41:30
not a **f** of bread, nor a thirst Am 8:11
or **f**, or nakedness, or sword? Rom 8:35

FAN
I remind you to **f** into flame 2 Tm 1:6

FAR
their lips, but their heart is **f** Mt 15:8
If possible, so **f** as it Rom 12:18
Jesus you who once were **f** Eph 2:13
be with Christ, for that is **f** Phil 1:23

FASHIONED
hands have made and **f** Ps 119:73

FAST
shall serve him and hold **f** Dt 13:4
"And when you **f**, do not look Mt 6:16
unbelief, but you stand **f** Rom 11:20
evil; hold **f** to what is good. Rom 12:9
being saved, if you hold **f** 1 Cor 15:2
holding **f** to the word of life, Phil 2:16
hold **f** what is good. 1 Thes 5:21
Let us hold **f** the confession Heb 10:23

FASTING
And after **f** forty days and forty Mt 4:2
church, with prayer and **f** Acts 14:23

FATHER
a man shall leave his **f** Gn 2:24
you, and you shall be the **f** Gn 17:4
"Honor your **f** and your Ex 20:12
revere his mother and his **f**, Lv 19:3

"'Honor your **f** and your Dt 5:16
anyone who dishonors his **f** Dt 27:16
For my **f** and my mother Ps 27:10
F of the fatherless and Ps 68:5
As a **f** shows compassion to Ps 103:13
him whom he loves, as a **f** Prv 3:12
A wise son makes a glad **f**, Prv 10:1
Listen to your **f** who gave Prv 23:22
loves wisdom makes his **f** Prv 29:3
Everlasting **F**, Prince of Peace. Is 9:6
Our **F** in heaven, hallowed be Mt 6:9
acknowledge before my **F** Mt 10:32
Whoever loves **f** or mother Mt 10:37
commanded, 'Honor your **f** Mt 15:4
a man shall leave his **f** Mt 19:5
And call no man your **f** on Mt 23:9
What **f** among you, if his son Lk 11:11
They will be divided, **f** Lk 12:53
And Jesus said, "**F**, forgive Lk 23:34
The **F** loves the Son and has Jn 3:35
can come to me unless the **F** Jn 6:44
from God; he has seen the **F**. Jn 6:46
I and the **F** are one." Jn 10:30
No one comes to the **F** except Jn 14:6
know that I am in my **F**, Jn 14:20
keep my word, and my **F** Jn 14:23
to the **F**, for the **F** is greater Jn 14:28
As the **F** has sent me, even Jn 20:21
was to make him the **f** Rom 4:11
For I became your **f** in 1 Cor 4:15
and I will be a **f** to you, 2 Cor 6:18
our hearts, crying, "Abba! **F**!" Gal 4:6
access in one Spirit to the **F**. Eph 2:18
"Honor your **f** and mother" Eph 6:2
son is there whom his **f** Heb 12:7
coming down from the **F** Jas 1:17
See what kind of love the **F** 1 Jn 3:1
confess his name before my **F** Rv 3:5

FATHERLESS
He executes justice for the **f** Dt 10:18
get it. the **f**, and the widow, Dt 24:19
Father of the **f** and protector of Ps 68:5
the widow and the **f**, Ps 146:9

FATHERS
visiting the iniquity of the **f** Ex 20:5
glory of children is their **f**. Prv 17:6
he who **f** a wise son will be Prv 23:24
F, do not provoke your Eph 6:4
F, do not provoke your Col 3:21

FATHER'S
A wise son hears his **f** Prv 13:1
A fool despises his **f** Prv 15:5
know that I must be in my **F** Lk 2:49
do not make my **F** house a Jn 2:16
to snatch them out of the **F** Jn 10:29
In my **F** house are many Jn 14:2

FAULT
you, go and tell him his **f**, Mt 18:15

FAULTS
me innocent from hidden **f**. Ps 19:12

FAVOR
But Noah found **f** in the eyes of Gn 6:8
the Lord bestows **f** and Ps 84:11
A good man obtains **f** from Prv 12:2
And the **f** of God was upon him. Lk 2:40
and in stature and in **f** Lk 2:52

FEAR
the Lord your God you shall **f**. Dt 6:13
God require of you, but to **f** Dt 10:12
they may hear and learn to **f** Dt 31:12
"Now therefore **f** the Lord Jos 24:14
Serve the Lord with **f**, and Ps 2:11
the **f** of the Lord is clean, Ps 19:9
the shadow of death, I will **f** Ps 23:4
whom shall I **f**? The Lord is Ps 27:1
The **f** of the Lord is the Ps 111:10
The **f** of the Lord is the Prv 1:7
The **f** of the Lord prolongs Prv 10:27
The **f** of the Lord is Prv 15:33
The **f** of the Lord leads to Prv 19:23
heard. **F** God and keep his Eccl 12:13
his delight shall be in the **f** Is 11:3
f not, for I am with you; be Is 41:10
And do not **f** those who kill Mt 10:28
I will warn you whom to **f**: Lk 12:5
to completion in the **f** 2 Cor 7:1
your own salvation with **f** Phil 2:12
God gave us a spirit not of **f** 2 Tm 1:7
F God. Honor the emperor. 1 Pt 2:17
no **f** of them, nor be troubled, 1 Pt 3:14
There is no **f** in love, but 1 Jn 4:18
but perfect love casts out **f**. 1 Jn 4:18
Do not **f** what you are about to Rv 2:10

FEARFULLY
I praise you, for I am **f** Ps 139:14

FEARS
and upright man, who **f** God Jb 1:8
delivered me from all my **f**. Ps 34:4
Blessed is the man who **f** Ps 112:1
Blessed is the one who **f** Prv 28:14
punishment, and whoever **f** 1 Jn 4:18

FEED
f them and be their shepherd. Ez 34:23
He said to him, "**F** my lambs." Jn 21:15
Jesus said to him, "**F** my sheep. Jn 21:17
your enemy is hungry, **f** Rom 12:20

FEEDS
Whoever **f** on my flesh and Jn 6:54
Whoever **f** on this bread will Jn 6:58

FEET
have put all things under his **f**, Ps 8:6
He made my **f** like the **f** Ps 18:33
have pierced my hands and **f** Ps 22:16
of the miry bog, and set my **f** Ps 40:2
word is a lamp to my **f** Ps 119:105
upon the mountains are the **f** Is 52:7
your enemies under your **f**'? Mt 22:44
"How beautiful are the **f** Rom 10:15
subjection under his **f**." 1 Cor 15:27
he put all things under his **f** Eph 1:22
straight paths for your **f**, Heb 12:13

FELLOW
fall, one will lift up his **f**. Eccl 4:10
heirs of God and **f** heirs with Rom 8:17
For we are God's **f** workers. 1 Cor 3:9

FELLOWSHIP
the apostles' teaching and **f**, Acts 2:42
you were called into the **f** 1 Cor 1:9
what **f** has light with darkness? 2 Cor 6:14
the love of God and the **f** 2 Cor 13:14
they gave the right hand of **f** Gal 2:9
so that you too may have **f** 1 Jn 1:3
and indeed our **f** is with the 1 Jn 1:3
If we say we have **f** with him 1 Jn 1:6
he is in the light, we have **f** 1 Jn 1:7

FEMALE
male and **f** he created them. Gn 1:27
Male and **f** he created them, Gn 5:2
'God made them male and **f**.' Mk 10:6
there is neither male nor **f**, Gal 3:28

FERVENT
be slothful in zeal, be **f** Rom 12:11

FEW
let your words be **f**. Eccl 5:2
called, but **f** are chosen. Mt 22:14
but the laborers are **f**. Lk 10:2

FIELD
Consider the lilies of the **f**, Mt 6:28
The **f** is the world, and the Mt 13:38
You are God's **f**, God's 1 Cor 3:9

FIELDS
your eyes, and see that the **f** Jn 4:35

FIG
And they sewed **f** leaves Gn 3:7
And seeing a **f** tree by the Mt 21:19

FIGHT
The Lord will **f** for you, and Ex 14:14
goes before you will himself **f** Dt 1:30
Our God will **f** for us." Neh 4:20
f against those who **f** against me! Ps 35:1
F the good **f** of the faith. 1 Tm 6:12
I have fought the good **f**, 2 Tm 4:7

FILL
fruitful and multiply and **f** Gn 1:28
"Be fruitful and multiply and **f** Gn 9:1
May the God of hope **f** Rom 15:13
the heavens, that he might **f** Eph 4:10

FILLED
may the whole earth be **f** Ps 72:19
the glory of the Lord **f** the temple. Ez 43:5
For the earth will be **f** with Hb 2:14
strong drink, and he will be **f** Lk 1:15
And Elizabeth was **f** with the Lk 1:41
And they were all **f** with the Acts 2:4
Then Peter, **f** with the Holy Acts 4:8
regain your sight and be **f** Acts 9:17
And the disciples were **f** Acts 13:52
are full of goodness, **f** with Rom 15:14
that you may be **f** with all Eph 3:19
that is debauchery, but be **f** Eph 5:18
f with the fruit of righteousness Phil 1:11
to see you, that I may be **f** 2 Tm 1:4
that is inexpressible and **f** 1 Pt 1:8

FILLS
hungry soul he **f** with good Ps 107:9
Blessed is the man who **f** Ps 127:5
fullness of him who **f** all in all. Eph 1:23

FILTHINESS
Let there be no **f** nor foolish Eph 5:4
Therefore put away all **f** Jas 1:21

FIND
and be sure your sin will **f** Nm 32:23
Lord your God and you will **f** Dt 4:29
for I **f** my delight in your Ps 119:47
who seek me diligently **f** Prv 8:17
excellent wife who can **f**? Prv 31:10
seek, and you will **f**; knock, and Mt 7:7
his life for my sake will **f** Mt 16:25
Son of Man comes, will he **f** Lk 18:8
and will go in and out and **f** Jn 10:9
all the promises of God **f** 2 Cor 1:20

FINDS
Blessed is the one who **f** Prv 3:13
For whoever **f** me finds life Prv 8:35
He who **f** a wife finds a good Prv 18:22
and the one who seeks **f**, Mt 7:8
Whoever **f** his life will lose Mt 10:39
the one that is lost, until he **f** Lk 15:4

FINGER
down and wrote with his **f** Jn 8:6
said to Thomas, "Put your **f** Jn 20:27

FINISH
build and was not able to **f**.' Lk 14:30
to myself, if only I may **f** Acts 20:24
So now **f** doing it as well, 2 Cor 8:11

FINISHED
And on the seventh day God **f** Gn 2:2
"It is **f**," and he bowed his Jn 19:30
the good fight, I have **f** the 2 Tm 4:7
although his works were **f** Heb 4:3

FIRE
dark, behold, a smoking **f** pot Gn 15:17
appeared to him in a flame of **f** Ex 3:2
and by night in a pillar of **f** Ex 13:21
your God is a consuming **f**, Dt 4:24
dwell with the consuming **f**? Is 33:14
Is not my word like **f**, and Jer 23:29
walking in the midst of the **f**, Dn 3:25
the Holy Spirit and with **f**. Mt 3:11
be thrown into the hell of **f**. Mt 18:9
cursed, into the eternal **f** Mt 25:41
hell, to the unquenchable **f**. Mk 9:43
And divided tongues as of **f** Acts 2:3
revealed by **f**, and the **f** will test 1 Cor 3:13
our God is a consuming **f**. Heb 12:29
though it is tested by **f** 1 Pt 1:7
now exist are stored up for **f**, 2 Pt 3:7
snatching them out of the **f**; Jude 1:23
second death, the lake of **f**. Rv 20:14

FIRM
people, "Fear not, stand **f**, Ex 14:13
Stand **f**, hold your position 2 Chr 20:17
my covenant will stand **f** Ps 89:28
his heart is **f**, trusting in the Ps 112:7
when he made **f** the skies Prv 8:28
Be watchful, stand **f** in the 1 Cor 16:13
your joy, for you stand **f** 2 Cor 1:24
stand **f** therefore, and do not Gal 5:1

Your throne, O God, is **f** and Ps 45:6
his steadfast love endures **f**, Ps 100:5
You are a priest **f** after the order Ps 110:4
of this bread, he will live **f**. Jn 6:51
Helper, to be with you **f**, Jn 14:16
place, "You are a priest **f**, Heb 5:6
yesterday and today and **f**. Heb 13:8
word of the Lord remains **f**." 1 Pt 1:25
the will of God abides **f**. 1 Jn 2:17
in us and will be with us **f**: 2 Jn 1:2
they will reign **f** and ever. Rv 22:5

FORFEIT
gain the whole world and **f** Mk 8:36

FORGAVE
to the Lord," and you **f** the Ps 32:5
You **f** the iniquity of your Ps 85:2
servant released him and **f** Mt 18:27
I **f** you all that debt because Mt 18:32
another, as God in Christ **f** Eph 4:32

FORGET
then take care lest you **f** the Dt 6:12
does not **f** the cry of the afflicted. Ps 9:12
the Lord, O my soul, and **f** Ps 103:2
I will never **f** your precepts, Ps 119:93
do not **f**, and do not turn Prv 4:5

FORGETS
and goes away and at once **f** Jas 1:24

FORGETTING
do: **f** what lies behind and Phil 3:13

FORGIVE
from heaven and will **f** 2 Chr 7:14
my trouble, and **f** all my sins. Ps 25:18
For I will **f** their iniquity, Jer 31:34
and **f** us our debts, as we also Mt 6:12
For if you **f** others their Mt 6:14
sin against me, and I **f** him? Mt 18:21
Who can **f** sins but God alone?" Mk 2:7
who is in heaven may **f** Mk 11:25
f, and you will be forgiven; Lk 6:37
and **f** us our sins, for we Lk 11:4
And Jesus said, "Father, **f** Lk 23:34
you, so you also must **f**. Col 3:13
he is faithful and just to **f** 1 Jn 1:9

FORGIVEN
one whose transgression is **f**, Ps 32:1
our debts, as we also have **f** Mt 6:12
'Your sins are **f**,' or to say, Mt 9:5
sins, which are many, are **f** Lk 7:47
whose lawless deeds are **f**, Rom 4:7
together with him, having **f** Col 2:13
as the Lord has **f** you, so you Col 3:13
committed sins, he will be **f**. Jas 5:15
because your sins are **f** 1 Jn 2:12

FORGIVENESS
But with you there is **f**, that Ps 130:4
out for many for the **f** Mt 26:28
of repentance for the **f** Mk 1:4
of Jesus Christ for the **f** Acts 2:38
believes in him receives **f** Acts 10:43
through his blood, the **f** of our Eph 1:7
we have redemption, the **f** Col 1:14
of blood there is no **f** Heb 9:22
Where there is **f** of these, Heb 10:18

FORGIVING
you, O Lord, are good and **f**, Ps 86:5
another, tenderhearted, **f** Eph 4:32
complaint against another, **f** Col 3:13

FORM
The earth was without **f** and Gn 1:2
himself nothing, taking the **f** Phil 2:7
Abstain from every **f** 1 Thes 5:22

FORMED
then the Lord God **f** the man of Gn 2:7
For you **f** my inward parts; Ps 139:13
did not create it empty, he **f** Is 45:18
"Before I **f** you in the womb Jer 1:5
of childbirth until Christ is **f** Gal 4:19
For Adam was **f** first, then Eve; 1 Tm 2:13

FORMER
which belongs to your **f** manner Eph 4:22
passions of your **f** ignorance 1 Pt 1:14

FORSAKE
He will not leave you or **f** Dt 31:6
I will not leave you or **f** you. Jos 1:5
if you **f** him, he will **f** you. 2 Chr 15:2
For the Lord will not **f** his Ps 94:14
let the wicked **f** his way, and Is 55:7
will never leave you nor **f** Heb 13:5

FORSAKEN
my God, why have you **f** me? Ps 22:1
not seen the righteous **f** Ps 37:25
my God, why have you **f** me? Mt 27:46
my God, why have you **f** me? Mk 15:34

FORTRESS
The Lord is my rock and my **f** Ps 18:2
For you are my rock and my **f**; Ps 31:3

FOUGHT
I have **f** the good fight, 2 Tm 4:7

FOUND
you seek him, he will be **f** 2 Chr 15:2
at a time when you may be **f**; Ps 32:6
the Lord while he may be **f**; Is 55:6
in the balances and **f** wanting; Dn 5:27
he was lost, and is **f**.'" Lk 15:32

FOUNDATION
cornerstone, of a sure **f**: Is 28:16
you loved me before the **f** Jn 17:24
For no one can lay a **f** 1 Cor 3:11
chose us in him before the **f** Eph 1:4
built on the **f** of the apostles Eph 2:20
was foreknown before the **f** 1 Pt 1:20

FOUNDER
to glory, should make the **f** Heb 2:10
looking to Jesus, the **f** and Heb 12:2

FOXES
And Jesus said to him, "**F** Mt 8:20

FRAGRANCE
to death, to the other a **f** 2 Cor 2:16

FRAGRANT
gave himself up for us, a **f** Eph 5:2

FREE
Lord sets the prisoners **f**; Ps 146:7
and the truth will set you **f**." Jn 8:32
sets you **f**, you will be **f** indeed. Jn 8:36
But the **f** gift is not like the Rom 5:15
who has died has been set **f** Rom 6:7
that you have been set **f** Rom 6:22
the Spirit of life has set you **f** Rom 8:2
there is neither slave nor **f**, Gal 3:28
freedom Christ has set us **f**; Gal 5:1
Live as people who are **f**, 1 Pt 2:16

FREED
everyone who believes is **f** Acts 13:38
To him who loves us and has **f** Rv 1:5

FREEDOM
to decay and obtain the **f** Rom 8:21
of the Lord is, there is **f**. 2 Cor 3:17
For **f** Christ has set us free; Gal 5:1
For you were called to **f**, Gal 5:13
Only do not use your **f** as an Gal 5:13
are free, not using your **f** 1 Pt 2:16

FRIEND
as a man speaks to his **f**. Ex 33:11
A **f** loves at all times, and a Prv 17:17
to ruin, but there is a **f** Prv 18:24
are the wounds of a **f**; Prv 27:6
Do not forsake your **f** and Prv 27:10
whoever wishes to be a **f** Jas 4:4

FRIENDS
whisperer separates close **f**. Prv 16:28
in the house of my **f**.' Zec 13:6
lays down his life for his **f**. Jn 15:13
You are my **f** if you do what Jn 15:14
but I have called you **f**, for Jn 15:15

FRIENDSHIP
The **f** of the Lord is for those Ps 25:14
Make no **f** with a man given Prv 22:24
Do you not know that **f** with Jas 4:4

FRUIT
and **f** trees bearing **f** in Gn 1:11
one wise, she took of its **f** Gn 3:6
of water that yields its **f** Ps 1:3
heritage from the Lord, the **f** Ps 127:3
The **f** of the righteous is a Prv 11:30
Bear **f** in keeping with repentance. Mt 3:8
healthy tree bears good **f**, Mt 7:17
you should go and bear **f** Jn 15:16
in order that we may bear **f** Rom 7:4
But the **f** of the Spirit is love, Gal 5:22
(for the **f** of light is found in Eph 5:9
filled with the **f** of Phil 1:11
kinds of **f**, yielding its **f** each Rv 22:2

FRUITFUL
And God said to them, "Be **f** Gn 1:28
sons and said to them, "Be **f** Gn 9:1
will make you exceedingly **f**, Gn 17:6
be **f** and multiply. A nation Gn 35:11
Your wife will be like a **f** Ps 128:3
they shall multiply and be **f**. Ez 36:11

FRUITS
recognize them by their **f**. Mt 7:16

FULFILL
The Lord will **f** his purpose Ps 138:8
come to abolish them but to **f** Mt 5:17
the work of an evangelist, **f** 2 Tm 4:5
The Lord is not slow to **f** 2 Pt 3:9

FULFILLED
A desire **f** is sweet to the Prv 13:19
who loves another has **f** Rom 13:8
For the whole law is **f** in one Gal 5:14

FULFILLING
love is the **f** of the law. Rom 13:10

FULL
the whole earth is **f** of his glory!" Is 6:3
for the earth shall be **f** of the Is 11:9
seven men of good repute, **f** Acts 6:3
near with a true heart in **f** Heb 10:22

FULLNESS
earth is the Lord's and the **f** Ps 24:1
But when the **f** of time had Gal 4:4
which is his body, the **f** of Eph 1:23
may be filled with all the **f** Eph 3:19
For in him all the **f** of God Col 1:19
For in him the whole **f** of deity Col 2:9

FULLY
then I shall know **f**, 1 Cor 13:12
set your hope **f** on the grace 1 Pt 1:13

FUTILE
to him, but they became **f** Rom 1:21
the wise, that they are **f**." 1 Cor 3:20
raised, your faith is **f** 1 Cor 15:17
were ransomed from the **f** 1 Pt 1:18

FUTURE
the upright, for there is a **f** Ps 37:37
Surely there is a **f**, and Prv 23:18
a good foundation for the **f**, 1 Tm 6:19

GABRIEL
answered him, "I am **G**, and I Lk 1:19

GAIN
and not to selfish **g**! Ps 119:36
What does man **g** by all the Eccl 1:3
does it profit a man to **g** Mk 8:36
but have not love, I **g** nothing. 1 Cor 13:3
What do I **g** if, humanly 1 Cor 15:32
is Christ, and to die is **g**. Phil 1:21
in order that I may **g** Christ Phil 3:8
Now there is great **g** in 1 Tm 6:6

GALILEE
Then Jesus came from **G** to the Mt 3:13
And he went about all **G**, Mt 4:23
I will go before you to **G**." Mt 26:32
and the leading men of **G**. Mk 6:21
Judea, beginning from **G** Acts 10:37

GALL
to drink, mixed with **g**, he Mt 27:34

GARDEN
And the Lord God planted a **g** Gn 2:8

at the east of the **g** of Eden Gn 3:24
You were in Eden, the **g** Ez 28:13
valley, where there was a **g**, Jn 18:1
was crucified there was a **g**, Jn 19:41

GARMENT
Shem and Japheth took a **g**, Gn 9:23
or take a widow's **g** in pledge, Dt 24:17
will all wear out like a **g**. Ps 102:26
of mourning, the **g** of praise Is 61:3
I spread the corner of my **g** Ez 16:8
unshrunk cloth on an old **g**, Mt 9:16
touched the fringe of his **g**, Lk 8:44

GARMENTS
for Adam and for his wife **g** Gn 3:21
These are the **g** that they Ex 28:4
these are the holy **g**. He shall Lv 16:4
they divide my **g** among Ps 22:18
he has clothed me with the **g** Is 61:10
from Edom, in crimsoned **g** Is 63:1
your hearts and not your **g**." Jl 2:13
angel, clothed with filthy **g**. Zec 3:3
Jesus, they took his **g** and Jn 19:23

GATE
This is the **g** of the Lord; the Ps 118:20
"Enter by the narrow **g**. For Mt 7:13
they laid daily at the **g** Acts 3:2

GATEKEEPER
To him the **g** opens. The sheep Jn 10:3

GATES
Enter his **g** with thanksgiving, Ps 100:4
build my church, and the **g** Mt 16:18
high wall, with twelve **g**, Rv 21:12

GATHER
us, O Lord our God, and **g** Ps 106:47
Lord, and all nations shall **g** Jer 3:17
G together, yes, gather, O Zep 2:1
and whoever does not **g** Mt 12:30
trumpet call, and they will **g** Mt 24:31

GATHERED
where two or three are **g** Mt 18:20
How often would I have **g** Mt 23:37
Before him will be **g** all the Mt 25:32

GATHERS
he **g** the outcasts of Israel. Ps 147:2

GAVE
to their ability they **g** Ezr 2:69
The Lord **g**, and the Lord has Jb 1:21
so loved the world, that he **g** Jn 3:16
"Of those whom you **g** me I Jn 18:9
he bowed his head and **g** Jn 19:30
spare his own Son but **g** Rom 8:32
as we expected, but they **g** 2 Cor 8:5
who **g** himself for our sins to Gal 1:4
of God, who loved me and **g** Gal 2:20
as Christ loved us and **g** Eph 5:2
who **g** himself as a ransom 1 Tm 2:6
who **g** himself for us to redeem Ti 2:14

GAZA
Samson went to **G**, and Jgs 16:1
Baldness has come upon **G**; Jer 47:5
three transgressions of **G**, Am 1:6

GAZE
all the days of my life, to **g** Ps 27:4
directly forward, and your **g** Prv 4:25

GENEALOGIES
to myths and endless **g**, 1 Tm 1:4

GENEALOGY
people to be enrolled by **g**. Neh 7:5
The book of the **g** of Jesus Mt 1:1

GENERATION
of the Lord to the coming **g**; Ps 22:30
and their children to another **g**. Jl 1:3
An evil and adulterous **g** Mt 16:4

GENERATIONS
throughout all **g**. Ps 102:12
endures throughout all **g**. Ps 145:13
So all the **g** from Abraham to Mt 1:17
behold, from now on all **g** Lk 1:48
to the sons of men in other **g** Eph 3:5

GENEROUS
rich in good works, to be **g** 1 Tm 6:18

GENEROUSLY
with the man who deals **g** Ps 112:5

GENTILE
let him be to you as a **G** Mt 18:17
though a Jew, live like a **G** Gal 2:14

GENTILES
Do not even the **G** do the same? Mt 5:47
up empty phrases as the **G** Mt 6:7
"Go nowhere among the **G** Mt 10:5
Spirit, "'Why did the **G** rage, Acts 4:25
poured out even on the **G**. Acts 10:45
a door of faith to the **G**. Acts 14:27
God first visited the **G**, Acts 15:14
For when **G**, who do not Rom 2:14
Is he not the God of **G** also? Rom 3:29
has come to the **G**, so as to Rom 11:11
I am speaking to you **G**. Rom 11:13
to Jews and folly to **G**, 1 Cor 1:23
preach him among the **G**, Gal 1:16
that God would justify the **G** Gal 3:8
how great among the **G** are Col 1:27
your conduct among the **G** 1 Pt 2:12

GENTLE
learn from me, for I am **g** Mt 11:29
imperishable beauty of a **g** 1 Pt 3:4

GENTLENESS
supported me, and your **g** Ps 18:35
by the meekness and **g** 2 Cor 10:1
g, self-control; against such Gal 5:23
restore him in a spirit of **g**. Gal 6:1
with all humility and **g**, with Eph 4:2
faith, love, steadfastness, **g**. 1 Tm 6:11
yet do it with **g** and respect, 1 Pt 3:16

GENUINE
Let love be **g**. Abhor what is Rom 12:9
that your love also is **g**. 2 Cor 8:8

GENUINENESS
so that the tested **g** of your 1 Pt 1:7

GETHSEMANE
them to a place called **G**, Mt 26:36

GHOST
and said, "It is a **g**!" and they Mt 14:26

GIBEAH
them before the Lord at **G** 2 Sm 21:6
Blow the horn in **G**, the Hos 5:8

GIBEON
when the inhabitants of **G** Jos 9:3
he feared greatly, because **G** Jos 10:2
stand still at **G**, and moon, Jos 10:12

GIDEON
Then **G** built an altar there to Jgs 6:24
would fail me to tell of **G**, Heb 11:32

GIFT
So if you are offering your **g** Mt 5:23
receive the **g** of the Holy Spirit. Acts 2:38
then God gave the same **g** Acts 11:17
justified by his grace as a **g**, Rom 3:24
But the free **g** is not like the Rom 5:15
of grace and the free **g** Rom 5:17
sin is death, but the free **g** Rom 6:23
But each has his own **g** 1 Cor 7:7
for his inexpressible **g**! 2 Cor 9:15
doing; it is the **g** of God, Eph 2:8
Do not neglect the **g** you 1 Tm 4:14
you to fan into flame the **g** 2 Tm 1:6
have tasted the heavenly **g**, Heb 6:4
Every good **g** and every perfect Jas 1:17

GIFTS
your train and receiving **g** Ps 68:18
know how to give good **g** Mt 7:11
For the **g** and the calling of Rom 11:29
Having **g** that differ Rom 12:6
concerning spiritual **g**, 1 Cor 12:1
there are varieties of **g**, 1 Cor 12:4
same Spirit, to another **g** 1 Cor 12:9
miracles, then **g** of healing, 1 Cor 12:28
Do all possess **g** of healing? 1 Cor 12:30
earnestly desire the higher **g**. 1 Cor 12:31

desire the spiritual **g**, 1 Cor 14:1
of captives, and he gave **g** Eph 4:8

GILEAD
Is there no balm in **G**? Is Jer 8:22
If there is iniquity in **G**, Hos 12:11

GILGAL
and they encamped at **G** Jos 4:19
with him, to the camp at **G**. Jos 10:15
"Come, let us go to **G** 1 Sm 11:14

GIVE
"To your offspring I will **g** Gn 12:7
upon you and **g** you peace. Nm 6:26
I will **g** to the Lord the thanks Ps 7:17
My son, **g** me your heart, Prv 23:26
If your enemy is hungry, **g** Prv 25:21
my glory I **g** to no other, nor Is 42:8
And I will **g** you a new Ez 36:26
"Thus, when you **g** to the Mt 6:2
G us this day our daily bread, Mt 6:11
"Do not **g** dogs what is holy, Mt 7:6
Father who is in heaven **g** Mt 7:11
heavy laden, and I will **g** Mt 11:28
served but to serve, and to **g** Mt 20:28
For what can a man **g** in Mk 8:37
g, and it will be given to you. Lk 6:38
will the heavenly Father **g** Lk 11:13
Jesus said to her, "**G** me a drink." Jn 4:7
I **g** them eternal life, and Jn 10:28
A new commandment I **g** Jn 13:34
the Father, and he will **g** Jn 14:16
'It is more blessed to **g** Acts 20:35
from the dead will also **g** Rom 8:11
So then each of us will **g** Rom 14:12
If I **g** away all I have, and 1 Cor 13:3
Each one must **g** as he has 2 Cor 9:7
of him to whom we must **g** Heb 4:13
a loud voice, "Fear God and **g** Rv 14:7
To the thirsty I will **g** from Rv 21:6

GIVEN
God said, "Behold, I have **g** Gn 1:29
For they are wholly **g** to me Nm 8:16
but the earth he has **g** to the Ps 115:16
a child is born, to us a son is **g**; Is 9:6
"Ask, and it will be **g** to you; Mt 7:7
"This is my body, which is **g** Lk 22:19
even one thing unless it is **g** Jn 3:27
Holy Spirit who has been **g** Rom 5:5
the things freely **g** us by God. 1 Cor 2:12
To each is **g** the manifestation 1 Cor 12:7
But grace was **g** to each one Eph 4:7

GIVER
for God loves a cheerful **g**. 2 Cor 9:7

GIVES
unfolding of your words **g** Ps 119:130
craves, but the righteous **g** Prv 21:26
Whoever **g** to the poor will Prv 28:27
He **g** power to the faint, and Is 40:29
And whoever **g** one of these Mt 10:42
from heaven, but my Father **g** Jn 6:32
It is the Spirit who **g** life; the Jn 6:63
thanks be to God, who **g** 1 Cor 15:57
letter kills, but the Spirit **g** 2 Cor 3:6
the presence of God, who **g** 1 Tm 6:13

GIVING
so that your **g** may be in secret. Mt 6:4
bore witness to them, by **g** Acts 15:8

GLAD
Therefore my heart is **g**, and Ps 16:9
I will rejoice and be **g** in your Ps 31:7
Be **g** in the Lord, and rejoice, Ps 32:11
For our heart is **g** in him, Ps 33:21
a river whose streams make **g** Ps 46:4
let the many coastlands be **g**! Ps 97:1
father and mother be **g**; Prv 23:25
Rejoice and be **g**, for your Mt 5:12
of your faith, I am **g** and Phil 2:17

GLADNESS
anointed you with the oil of **g** Ps 45:7
With joy and **g** they are led Ps 45:15
Let me hear joy and **g**; let the Ps 51:8
Serve the Lord with **g**! Come Ps 100:2
give them **g** for sorrow. Jer 31:13
you with the oil of **g** Heb 1:9

GLOOMY
when you fast, do not look **g** Mt 6:16

GLORIFIED
"Now is the Son of Man **g**, Jn 13:31
he justified he also **g**. Rom 8:30
that day to be **g** in his saints, 2 Thes 1:10
in everything God may be **g** 1 Pt 4:11

GLORIFIES
It is my Father who **g** me, of Jn 8:54

GLORIFY
heart, and I will **g** your name Ps 86:12
in him, God will also **g** him Jn 13:32
g your Son that the Son may Jn 17:1
see your good deeds and **g** God 1 Pt 2:12

GLORIOUS
in holiness, awesome in **g** Ex 15:11
On the **g** splendor of your Ps 145:5
Lord shall be beautiful and **g**, Is 4:2
his law and make it **g**. Is 42:21
Son of Man will sit on his **g** Mt 19:28
lowly body to be like his **g** Phil 3:21
all power, according to his **g** Col 1:11
accordance with the **g** gospel 1 Tm 1:11

GLORIOUSLY
the Lord, for he has done **g**; Is 12:5

GLORY
The **g** of the Lord dwelt on Ex 24:16
"Please show me your **g**." Ex 33:18
But the **g** of the Lord Nm 14:10
Ichabod, saying, "The **g** 1 Sm 4:21
Declare his **g** among the 1 Chr 16:24
and crowned him with **g** Ps 8:5
The heavens declare the **g** Ps 19:1
doors, that the King of **g** may Ps 24:7
beings, ascribe to the Lord **g** Ps 29:1
earth be filled with his **g**! Ps 72:19
Declare his **g** among the Ps 96:3
Let your **g** be over all the earth! Ps 108:5
to anger, and it is his **g** Prv 19:11
It is the **g** of God to conceal Prv 25:2
whole earth is full of his **g**!" Is 6:3
My **g** I will not give to another. Is 48:11
And behold, the **g** of the God Ez 43:2
house of David and the **g** Zec 12:7
with power and great **g**. Mt 24:30
Son of Man comes in his **g**, Mt 25:31
when he comes in the **g** Mk 8:38
with great power and **g**. Mk 13:26
appeared to them, and the **g** Lk 2:9
"**G** to God in the highest, and Lk 2:14
We have seen his **g**, **g** as of Jn 1:14
your own presence with the **g** Jn 17:5
The God of **g** appeared to our Acts 7:2
and exchanged the **g** of the Rom 1:23
and fall short of the **g** of God, Rom 3:23
comparing with the **g** Rom 8:18
the **g**, the covenants, the Rom 9:4
you do, do all to the **g** 1 Cor 10:31
he is the image and **g** 1 Cor 11:7
is of one kind, and the **g** 1 Cor 15:40
it is raised in **g**. It is sown 1 Cor 15:43
this case, what once had **g** 2 Cor 3:10
one degree of **g** to another. 2 Cor 3:18
us an eternal weight of **g** 2 Cor 4:17
be to the praise of his **g**. Eph 1:12
to the riches of his **g** Eph 3:16
according to his riches in **g** Phil 4:19
are the riches of the **g** Col 1:27
will appear with him in **g**. Col 3:4
the world, taken up in **g**. 1 Tm 3:16
He is the radiance of the **g** Heb 1:3
have crowned him with **g** Heb 2:7
is like grass and all its **g** like 1 Pt 1:24
Lord and God, to receive **g** Rv 4:11
to shine on it, for the **g** of God Rv 21:23

GLUTTONOUS
drunkards or among **g** Prv 23:20

GNASHING
will be weeping and **g** of teeth. Mt 8:12
will be weeping and **g** of teeth. Mt 13:42
will be weeping and **g** of teeth. Mt 24:51

GNATS
so that it may become **g** in all Ex 8:16
came swarms of flies, and **g** Ps 105:31

GO
G therefore and make Mt 28:19
is to your advantage that I **g** Jn 16:7
But if I **g**, I will send him to Jn 16:7

GOAL
I press on toward the **g** Phil 3:14

GOAT
one male **g** for a sin offering; Nm 7:16
lie down with the young **g**, Is 11:6

GOATS
oxen, five rams, five male **g**, Nm 7:17
the sheep from the **g**. Mt 25:32
by means of the blood of **g** Heb 9:12

GOD
In the beginning, **G** created the Gn 1:1
deep. And the Spirit of **G** was Gn 1:2
Then **G** said, "Let us make Gn 1:26
So **G** created man in his own Gn 1:27
And **G** saw everything that he Gn 1:31
So **G** blessed the seventh day Gn 2:3
And the rib that the Lord **G** Gn 2:22
And the Lord **G** made for Gn 3:21
therefore the Lord **G** sent him Gn 3:23
Enoch walked with **G** after he Gn 5:22
the sons of **G** saw that the Gn 6:2
covenant between **G** and every Gn 9:16
and said to him, "I am **G** Gn 17:1
swear to me here by **G** Gn 21:23
Abraham said, "**G** will provide Gn 22:8
And behold, the angels of **G** Gn 28:12
for you have striven with **G** Gn 32:28
saying, "For I have seen **G** Gn 32:30
And **G** said to him, "Your Gn 35:10
"For," he said, "**G** has made Gn 41:51
evil against me, but **G** meant Gn 50:20
And **G** heard their groaning, Ex 2:24
And he said, "I am the **G** of Ex 3:6
people, and I will be your **G**, Ex 6:7
no one like the Lord our **G**. Ex 8:10
But **G** led the people around Ex 13:18
this is my **G**, and I will Ex 15:2
of the hill with the staff of **G** Ex 17:9
while Moses went up to **G**. Ex 19:3
"I am the Lord your **G**, who Ex 20:2
them, for I the Lord your **G** Ex 20:5
but do not let **G** speak to us, Ex 20:19
"You shall not revile **G**, Ex 22:28
written with the finger of **G**. Ex 31:18
"The Lord, the Lord, a **G** Ex 34:6
shall worship no other **g**, Ex 34:14
profane the name of your **G**: Lv 18:21
holy, for I the Lord your **G** Lv 19:2
you and will be your **G**, Lv 26:12
The word that **G** puts in my Nm 22:38
G is not man, that he should Nm 23:19
May the Lord, the **G** of your Dt 1:11
them, for it is the Lord your **G** Dt 3:22
'O Lord **G**, you have only Dt 3:24
Lord your **G** is a consuming fire, Dt 4:24
Lord your **G** is a merciful **G**. Dt 4:31
your heart, that the Lord is **G** Dt 4:39
the name of the Lord your **G** Dt 5:11
a Sabbath to the Lord your **G**. Dt 5:14
the voice of the living **G** Dt 5:26
The Lord our **G**, the Lord is one. Dt 6:4
You shall love the Lord your **G** Dt 6:5
It is the Lord your **G** you shall Dt 6:13
shall not put the Lord your **G** Dt 6:16
therefore that the Lord your **G** Dt 7:9
and do them, the Lord your **G** Dt 7:12
of them, for the Lord your **G** Dt 7:21
his son, the Lord your **G** Dt 8:5
what does the Lord your **G** Dt 10:12
Behold, to the Lord your **G** Dt 10:14
For the Lord your **G** is **G** of Dt 10:17
to love the Lord your **G**, Dt 11:13
For the Lord your **G** is testing Dt 13:3
walk after the Lord your **G** Dt 13:4
For the Lord your **G** will bless Dt 15:6
by loving the Lord your **G** Dt 19:9
to the Lord your **G**. Dt 25:16
belong to the Lord our **G**, Dt 29:29
return to the Lord your **G**, Dt 30:2
of the Lord your **G** Dt 30:16
loving the Lord your **G**, for Dt 30:20
them, for it is the Lord your **G** Dt 31:6
ascribe greatness to our **G**! Dt 32:3
A **G** of faithfulness and Dt 32:4
eternal **G** is your dwelling place, Dt 33:27
dismayed, for the Lord your **G** Jos 1:9
followed the Lord my **G**. Jos 14:8
you, to love the Lord your **G**, Jos 22:5
us that the Lord is **G**." Jos 22:34
to love the Lord your **G**. Jos 23:11
things that the Lord your **G** Jos 23:14
Lord and said, "O Lord **G**, Jgs 16:28
be my people, and your **G** Ru 1:16
there is no rock like our **G**. 1 Sm 2:2
the Lord is a **G** of knowledge, 1 Sm 2:3
sins against a man, **G** will 1 Sm 2:25
of valor whose hearts **G** 1 Sm 10:26
when the Lord your **G** 1 Sm 12:12
armies of the living **G**?" 1 Sm 17:26
know that there is a **G** 1 Sm 17:46
himself in the Lord his **G**. 1 Sm 30:6
But **G** will not take away 2 Sm 14:14
my **G**, my rock, in whom I 2 Sm 22:3
This **G** — his way is 2 Sm 22:31
And **G** gave Solomon 1 Kgs 4:29
of Israel, there is no **G** 1 Kgs 8:23
"But will **G** indeed dwell 1 Kgs 8:27
true to the Lord our **G**, 1 Kgs 8:61
If the Lord is **G**, follow 1 Kgs 18:21
that you, O Lord, are **G**, 1 Kgs 18:37
And a man of **G** came 1 Kgs 20:28
be that the Lord your **G** 2 Kgs 19:4
"O Lord the **G** of Israel, 2 Kgs 19:15
So now, O Lord our **G**, 2 Kgs 19:19
Jabez called upon the **G** 1 Chr 4:10
broke faith with the **G** 1 Chr 5:25
again inquired of **G**, 1 Chr 14:14
brought in the ark of **G** 1 Chr 16:1
He is the Lord our **G**; 1 Chr 16:14
for the footstool of our **G**, 1 Chr 28:2
in the hearing of our **G**, 1 Chr 28:8
my son, know the **G** of your 1 Chr 28:9
dismayed, for the Lord **G**, 1 Chr 28:20
my son, whom alone **G** 1 Chr 29:1
to the house of my **G** 1 Chr 29:3
I know, my **G**, that you 1 Chr 29:17
"Bless the Lord your **G**." 1 Chr 29:20
the name of the Lord my **G** 2 Chr 2:4
Lord filled the house of **G**. 2 Chr 5:14
and said, "O Lord, **G** of 2 Chr 6:14
"And now arise, O Lord **G**, 2 Chr 6:41
Blessed be the Lord your **G**, 2 Chr 9:8
hearts to seek the Lord **G** 2 Chr 11:16
Behold, **G** is with us at 2 Chr 13:12
cried to the Lord his **G**, 2 Chr 14:11
Lord lives, what my **G** 2 Chr 18:13
and said, "O Lord, **G** of our 2 Chr 20:6
Then the Spirit of **G** 2 Chr 24:20
should you suppose that **G** 2 Chr 25:8
He set himself to seek **G** 2 Chr 26:5
vessels of the house of **G** 2 Chr 28:24
For the Lord your **G** is 2 Chr 30:9
sets his heart to seek **G**, 2 Chr 30:19
service of the house of **G** 2 Chr 31:21
not believe him, for no **g** 2 Chr 32:15
he set in the house of **G**, 2 Chr 33:7
favor of the Lord his **G** 2 Chr 33:12
He prayed to him, and **G** 2 Chr 33:13
and his prayer to his **G**, 2 Chr 33:18
to the covenant of **G**, 2 Chr 34:32
serve the Lord their **G**. 2 Chr 34:33
And **G** has commanded 2 Chr 35:21
king, "The hand of our **G** Ezr 8:22
to lift my face to you, my **G**, Ezr 9:6
guilt, seeing that you, our **G**, Ezr 9:13
And I said, "O Lord **G** of Neh 1:5
from the law of **G**, clearly, Neh 8:8
But you are a **G** ready to Neh 9:17
"Now, therefore, our **G**, Neh 9:32
and upright, one who feared **G** Jb 1:1
Shall we receive good from **G**, Jb 2:10
man be in the right before **G**? Jb 4:17
blessed is the one whom **G** Jb 5:17
find out the deep things of **G**? Jb 11:7
yet in my flesh I shall see **G**, Jb 19:26
But you say, 'What does **G** Jb 22:13
man be in the right before **G**? Jb 25:4
For **G** speaks in one way, and Jb 33:14
Of a truth, **G** will not do Jb 34:12
Behold, **G** is exalted in his Jb 36:22
Behold, **G** is great, and we Jb 36:26
G is clothed with awesome Jb 37:22
my deliverer, my **G**, my rock, Ps 18:2
Lord my **G** lightens my darkness. Ps 18:28
heavens declare the glory of **G**, Ps 19:1
My **G**, my **G**, why have you Ps 22:1

the **G** of glory thunders, the Ps 29:3
I say, "You are my **G**." Ps 31:14
a song of praise to our **G**. Ps 40:3
to do your will, O my **G**; your Ps 40:8
My soul thirsts for **G**, for the Ps 42:2
Hope in **G**; for I shall again Ps 42:11
I will go to the altar of **G**, Ps 43:4
Hope in **G**; for I shall again Ps 43:5
Your throne, O **G**, is forever Ps 45:6
G is our refuge and strength, a Ps 46:1
still, and know that I am **G**. Ps 46:10
For **G** is the King of all the Ps 47:7
Our **G** comes; he does not keep Ps 50:3
Have mercy on me, O **G**, Ps 51:1
in me a clean heart, O **G**, Ps 51:10
The sacrifices of **G** are a Ps 51:17
On **G** rests my salvation and Ps 62:7
us with righteousness, O **G** Ps 65:5
Shout for joy to **G**, all the Ps 66:1
hear, all you who fear **G**, Ps 66:16
G settles the solitary in a Ps 68:6
O **G**, from my youth you Ps 71:17
Your righteousness, O **G**, Ps 71:19
your faithfulness, O my **G**; Ps 71:22
my heart may fail, but **G** Ps 73:26
Your way, O **G**, is holy. Ps 77:13
should set their hope in **G** Ps 78:7
They spoke against **G**, "Can Ps 78:19
Sing aloud to **G** our strength; Ps 81:1
O **G**, do not keep silence; do Ps 83:1
sing for joy to the living **G**. Ps 84:2
in the house of my **G** Ps 84:10
thanks to you, O Lord my **G**, Ps 86:12
a **G** greatly to be feared in the Ps 89:7
to everlasting you are **G**. Ps 90:2
my **G**, in whom I trust." Ps 91:2
For he is our **G**, and we are Ps 95:7
Know that the Lord, he is **G**! Ps 100:3
My heart is steadfast, O **G**! Ps 108:1
Who is like the Lord our **G**, Ps 113:5
Search me, O **G**, and know Ps 139:23
good success in the sight of **G** Prv 3:4
It is the glory of **G** to conceal Prv 25:2
Every word of **G** proves true; Prv 30:5
he cannot find out what **G** Eccl 3:11
do not know the work of **G** Eccl 11:5
Fear **G** and keep his Eccl 12:13
Mighty **G**, Everlasting Father, Is 9:6
"O Lord of hosts, **G** of Israel, Is 37:16
desert a highway for our **G**. Is 40:3
fades, but the word of our **G** Is 40:8
Lord is the everlasting **G**, Is 40:28
dismayed, for I am your **G**; Is 41:10
last; besides me there is no **g**. Is 44:6
who says to Zion, "Your **G** Is 52:7
on him, and to our **G**, Is 55:7
says my **G**, "for the wicked." Is 57:21
between you and your **G**, Is 59:2
my soul shall exult in my **G**, Is 61:10
the bride, so shall your **G** Is 62:5
"Am I a **G** at hand, declares Jer 23:23
And I will be their **G**, and Jer 31:33
I am the Lord, the **G** of all Jer 32:27
in Eden, the garden of **G**; Ez 28:13
If this be so, our **G** whom we Dn 3:17
I prayed to the Lord my **G** Dn 9:4
you, by the help of your **G**, Hos 12:6
Return to the Lord, your **G**, Jl 2:13
The Lord **G** has sworn by his Am 4:2
Thus says the Lord **G** Ob 1:1
to walk humbly with your **G**? Mi 6:8
is a jealous and avenging **G**; Na 1:2
Then the Lord my **G** will Zec 14:5
Will man rob **G**? Yet you are Mal 3:8
Immanuel" (which means, **G** Mt 1:23
in heart, for they shall see **G**. Mt 5:8
You cannot serve **G** and money. Mt 6:24
What therefore **G** has joined Mt 19:6
is impossible, but with **G** Mt 19:26
that are Caesar's, and to **G** Mt 22:21
'I am the **G** of Abraham, and Mt 22:32
shall love the Lord your **G** Mt 22:37
that is, "My **G**, my **G**, why Mt 27:46
The Lord our **G**, the Lord is Mk 12:29
at the right hand of **G**. Mk 16:19
will be impossible with **G**." Lk 1:37
and my spirit rejoices in **G** Lk 1:47
to them, 'The kingdom of **G** Lk 10:9
shall love the Lord your **G** Lk 10:27
But if it is by the finger of **G** Lk 11:20
No one is good except **G** Lk 18:19
and the Word was with **G**, Jn 1:1
right to become children of **G**, Jn 1:12
No one has ever seen **G**; the Jn 1:18
"For **G** so loved the world, that Jn 3:16
G is spirit, and those who Jn 4:24
Believe in **G**; believe also in me. Jn 14:1
him, "My Lord and my **G**!" Jn 20:28
is the Christ, the Son of **G**, Jn 20:31
G raised him up, loosing the Acts 2:24
at the right hand of **G**, Acts 2:33
not lied to men but to **G**." Acts 5:4
The **G** of our fathers raised Acts 5:30
and saw the glory of **G**, Acts 7:55
'To the unknown **g**.' What Acts 17:23
the whole counsel of **G**. Acts 20:27
now I commend you to **G** Acts 20:32
for it is the power of **G** Rom 1:16
in it the righteousness of **G** Rom 1:17
For **G** shows no partiality. Rom 2:11
Let **G** be true though every Rom 3:4
fall short of the glory of **G**, Rom 3:23
the promise of **G**, Rom 4:20
but **G** shows his love for us in Rom 5:8
more have the grace of **G** Rom 5:15
that for those who love **G** Rom 8:28
If **G** is for us, who can be Rom 8:31
us from the love of **G** Rom 8:39
and the severity of **G**: Rom 11:22
no authority except from **G**, Rom 13:1
an account of himself to **G**. Rom 14:12
Has not **G** made foolish the 1 Cor 1:20
of man imagined, what **G** 1 Cor 2:9
Apollos watered, but **G** 1 Cor 3:6
So glorify **G** in your body. 1 Cor 6:20
let him remain with **G**. 1 Cor 7:24
will not commend us to **G**. 1 Cor 8:8
G is faithful, and he will 1 Cor 10:13
do all to the glory of **G**. 1 Cor 10:31
G is not a **G** of confusion 1 Cor 14:33
For "**G** has put all things 1 Cor 15:27
are comforted by **G**. 2 Cor 1:4
not on ourselves but on **G** 2 Cor 1:9
For all the promises of **G** 2 Cor 1:20
But thanks be to **G**, who 2 Cor 2:14
Our sufficiency is from **G**, 2 Cor 3:5
power belongs to **G** 2 Cor 4:7
that is, in Christ **G** was 2 Cor 5:19
the righteousness of **G**. 2 Cor 5:21
has the temple of **G** 2 Cor 6:16
or under compulsion, for **G** 2 Cor 9:7
lives by the power of **G**. 2 Cor 13:4
G shows no partiality) — Gal 2:6
to the promises of **G**? Gal 3:21
G is not mocked, for whatever Gal 6:7
for good works, which **G** Eph 2:10
one **G** and Father of all, who Eph 4:6
Therefore be imitators of **G**, Eph 5:1
on the whole armor of **G**, Eph 6:11
he was in the form of **G**, Phil 2:6
And the peace of **G**, which Phil 4:7
And my **G** will supply every Phil 4:19
in the knowledge of **G**. Col 1:10
the image of the invisible **G**, Col 1:15
have been approved by **G** 1 Thes 2:4
received the word of **G**, 1 Thes 2:13
For **G** has not called us for 1 Thes 4:7
have been taught by **G** 1 Thes 4:9
For **G** has not destined us 1 Thes 5:9
righteous judgment of **G**, 2 Thes 1:5
hearts to the love of **G** 2 Thes 3:5
For there is one **G**, and the 1 Tm 2:5
For everything created by **G** 1 Tm 4:4
is pleasing in the sight of **G**. 1 Tm 5:4
fan into flame the gift of **G**, 2 Tm 1:6
Scripture is breathed out by **G** 2 Tm 3:16
of the glory of our great **G** Ti 2:13
times and in many ways, **G** Heb 1:1
while **G** also bore witness by Heb 2:4
For the word of **G** is living Heb 4:12
For **G** is not so unjust as to Heb 6:10
the hands of the living **G**. Heb 10:31
would draw near to **G** Heb 11:6
for our **G** is a consuming fire. Heb 12:29
a sacrifice of praise to **G**, Heb 13:15
lacks wisdom, let him ask **G**, Jas 1:5
"I am being tempted by **G**," Jas 1:13
You believe that **G** is one; you Jas 2:19
says, "Abraham believed **G**, Jas 2:23
the world is enmity with **G**? Jas 4:4
Draw near to **G**, and he will Jas 4:8
to the foreknowledge of **G** 1 Pt 1:2
For this is the will of **G**, 1 Pt 2:15
who speaks oracles of **G**; 1 Pt 4:11
suffered a little while, the **G** 1 Pt 5:10
man, but men spoke from **G** 2 Pt 1:21
and proclaim to you, that **G** 1 Jn 1:5
our heart condemns us, **G** 1 Jn 3:20
you know the Spirit of **G**: 1 Jn 4:2
We are from **G**. Whoever 1 Jn 4:6
No one has ever seen **G**; 1 Jn 4:12
G is love, and whoever 1 Jn 4:16
If anyone says, "I love **G**," 1 Jn 4:20
For this is the love of **G**, 1 Jn 5:3
He is the true **G** and eternal life. 1 Jn 5:20
holy, holy, is the Lord **G** Rv 4:8
springs of living water, and **G** Rv 7:17
For the Lord our **G** the Rv 19:6

GODLINESS

Rather train yourself for **g**; 1 Tm 4:7
value, **g** is of value in every way, 1 Tm 4:8
teaching that accords with **g**, 1 Tm 6:3
Now there is great gain in **g** 1 Tm 6:6
Pursue righteousness, **g**, 1 Tm 6:11
having the appearance of **g**, 2 Tm 3:5
truth, which accords with **g**, Ti 1:1
that pertain to life and **g**, 2 Pt 1:3
and steadfastness with **g**, 2 Pt 1:6
be in lives of holiness and **g**, 2 Pt 3:11

GODLY

the Lord has set apart the **g** Ps 4:3
For you felt a **g** grief, so that 2 Cor 7:9
For **g** grief produces a 2 Cor 7:10
a peaceful and quiet life, **g** 1 Tm 2:2
all who desire to live a **g** 2 Tm 3:12
self-controlled, upright, and **g** Ti 2:12
knows how to rescue the **g** 2 Pt 2:9

GODS

you, O Lord, among the **g**? Ex 15:11
shall have no other **g** before me. Ex 20:3
You shall not make **g** of silver Ex 20:23
not bow down to their **g** Ex 23:24
they said to me, 'Make us **g** Ex 32:23
many people, saying that **g** Acts 19:26

GOLD

be desired are they than **g**, Ps 19:10
above **g**, above fine **g**. Ps 119:127
is better than silver or **g**. Prv 22:1
they offered him gifts, **g** and Mt 2:11
For which is greater, the **g** Mt 23:17
said, "I have no silver and **g**, Acts 3:6
Your **g** and silver have Jas 5:3
more precious than **g** that 1 Pt 1:7

GOLGOTHA

came to a place called **G** Mt 27:33
in Aramaic is called **G**. Jn 19:17

GOLIATH

a champion named **G** of Gath, 1 Sm 17:4
gave him the sword of **G** 1 Sm 22:10
Lahmi the brother of **G** 1 Chr 20:5

GOMER

G, Magog, Madai, Javan, Gn 10:2
So he went and took **G**, the Hos 1:3

GOMORRAH

destroyed Sodom and **G**. Gn 13:10
like Sodom, and become like **G**. Is 1:9
for the land of Sodom and **G** Mt 10:15

GOOD

God saw that the light was **g**. Gn 1:4
and behold, it was very **g**. Gn 1:31
Lord God said, "It is not **g** Gn 2:18
me, but God meant it for **g**, Gn 50:20
there is none that does **g**. Ps 14:1
taste and see that the Lord is **g**! Ps 34:8
Trust in the Lord, and do **g**; Ps 37:3
No **g** thing does he withhold Ps 84:11
For you, O Lord, are **g** and Ps 86:5
You are **g** and do **g**; teach Ps 119:68
Behold, how **g** and pleasant it Ps 133:1
Praise the Lord! For it is **g** Ps 147:1
Do not withhold **g** from those Prv 3:27
Whoever diligently seeks **g** Prv 11:27
A joyful heart is **g** medicine, Prv 17:22
She does him **g**, and not Prv 31:12
Woe to those who call evil **g** Is 5:20
the feet of him who brings **g** Is 52:7
who shall hear of all the **g** Jer 33:9
told you, O man, what is **g**; Mi 6:8

The Lord is **g**, a stronghold in Na 1:7
feet of him who brings **g** news, Na 1:15
rise on the evil and on the **g**, Mt 5:45
are evil, know how to give **g** Mt 7:11
every healthy tree bears **g** fruit, Mt 7:17
you ask me about what is **g**? Mt 19:17
said to him, 'Well done, **g** Mt 25:21
lawful on the Sabbath to do **g** Mk 3:4
"Why do you call me **g**? Mk 10:18
Love your enemies, do **g** to Lk 6:27
The **g** person out of the good Lk 6:45
are evil, know how to give **g** Lk 11:13
I am the **g** shepherd. Jn 10:11
things work together for **g**, Rom 8:28
of those who preach the **g** Rom 10:15
is the will of God, what is **g** Rom 12:2
evil; hold fast to what is **g**. Rom 12:9
but overcome evil with **g**. Rom 12:21
no one seek his own **g**, 1 Cor 10:24
us not grow weary of doing **g**, Gal 6:9
created in Christ Jesus for **g** Eph 2:10
he who began a **g** work in you Phil 1:6
hold fast what is **g**. 1 Thes 5:21
created by God is **g**, 1 Tm 4:4
Fight the **g** fight of the faith. 1 Tm 6:12
They are to do **g**, to be rich 1 Tm 6:18
I have fought the **g** fight, 2 Tm 4:7
he disciplines us for our **g**, Heb 12:10
tasted that the Lord is **g**. 1 Pt 2:3
they may see your **g** deeds 1 Pt 2:12
will of God, that by doing **g** 1 Pt 2:15
better to suffer for doing **g**, 1 Pt 3:17

GOODNESS

Surely **g** and mercy shall Ps 23:6
Oh, how abundant is your **g**, Ps 31:19
For how great is his **g**, and Zec 9:17
kindness, **g**, faithfulness, Gal 5:22
in order that your **g** Phlm 1:14
and have tasted the **g** of the Heb 6:5

GOSPEL

and proclaiming the **g** Mt 4:23
And this **g** of the kingdom Mt 24:14
The beginning of the **g** of Jesus Mk 1:1
the **g** must first be proclaimed Mk 13:10
continued to preach the **g**. Acts 14:7
an apostle, set apart for the **g** Rom 1:1
I am eager to preach the **g** Rom 1:15
I am not ashamed of the **g**, Rom 1:16
priestly service of the **g** Rom 15:16
but to preach the **g**, 1 Cor 1:17
For if I preach the **g**, that 1 Cor 9:16
it all for the sake of the **g**, 1 Cor 9:23
you, brothers, of the **g** 1 Cor 15:1
And even if our **g** is veiled, 2 Cor 4:3
for his preaching of the **g**. 2 Cor 8:18
that we may preach the **g** 2 Cor 10:16
if you accept a different **g** 2 Cor 11:4
is preaching to you a **g** contrary Gal 1:9
the word of truth, the **g** Eph 1:13
Christ Jesus through the **g**. Eph 3:6
the readiness given by the **g** Eph 6:15
the mystery of the **g**, Eph 6:19
of life be worthy of the **g** Phil 1:27
the word of the truth, the **g**, Col 1:5
from the hope of the **g** Col 1:23
to be entrusted with the **g**, 1 Thes 2:4
who do not obey the **g** 2 Thes 1:8
share in suffering for the **g** 2 Tm 1:8
this is why the **g** was preached 1 Pt 4:6
those who do not obey the **g** 1 Pt 4:17
overhead, with an eternal **g** Rv 14:6

GOSPEL'S

his life for my sake and the **g** Mk 8:35

GOSSIP

g, conceit, and disorder. 2 Cor 12:20

GOSSIPS

maliciousness. They are **g**, Rom 1:29
not only idlers, but also **g** 1 Tm 5:13

GOVERNMENT

and the **g** shall be upon his Is 9:6
Of the increase of his **g** and of Is 9:7

GRACE

g is poured upon your lips; Ps 45:2
and dwelt among us, full of **g** Jn 1:14
g and truth came through Jn 1:17
be saved through the **g** Acts 15:11
to the gospel of the **g** Acts 20:24
and to the word of his **g**, Acts 20:32
and are justified by his **g** Rom 3:24
access by faith into this **g** Rom 5:2
much more have the **g** of Rom 5:15
receive the abundance of **g** Rom 5:17
but where sin increased, **g** Rom 5:20
as sin reigned in death, **g** Rom 5:21
not under law but under **g**. Rom 6:14
But if it is by **g**, it is no Rom 11:6
differ according to the **g** Rom 12:6
But by the **g** of God I am 1 Cor 15:10
for your sake, so that as **g** 2 Cor 4:15
to you not to receive the **g** 2 Cor 6:1
For you know the **g** of our 2 Cor 8:9
But he said to me, "My **g** 2 Cor 12:9
and who called me by his **g**, Gal 1:15
I do not nullify the **g** of God, Gal 2:21
you have fallen away from **g**. Gal 5:4
the praise of his glorious **g**, Eph 1:6
to the riches of his **g**, Eph 1:7
by **g** you have been saved — Eph 2:5
immeasurable riches of his **g** Eph 2:7
For by **g** you have been saved Eph 2:8
to the gift of God's **g**, Eph 3:7
But **g** was given to each one Eph 4:7
all partakers with me of **g**, Phil 1:7
and good hope through **g**, 2 Thes 2:16
The **g** of our Lord Jesus 2 Thes 3:18
be strengthened by the **g** 2 Tm 2:1
For the **g** of God has appeared, Ti 2:11
so that being justified by his **g** Ti 3:7
of death, so that by the **g** Heb 2:9
near to the throne of **g**, Heb 4:16
receive mercy and find **g** Heb 4:16
no one fails to obtain the **g** Heb 12:15
to be strengthened by **g**, Heb 13:9
opposes the proud, but gives **g** Jas 4:6
set your hope fully on the **g** 1 Pt 1:13
are heirs with you of the **g** 1 Pt 3:7
stewards of God's varied **g**: 1 Pt 4:10
opposes the proud but gives **g** 1 Pt 5:5
little while, the God of all **g**, 1 Pt 5:10
that this is the true **g** 1 Pt 5:12
But grow in the **g** and 2 Pt 3:18

GRACIOUS

And I will be **g** to whom I Ex 33:19
to shine upon you and be **g** Nm 6:25
But the Lord was **g** to 2 Kgs 13:23
are a God merciful and **g**, Ps 86:15
The Lord is merciful and **g**, Ps 103:8
G is the Lord, and righteous; Ps 116:5
The Lord is **g** and merciful, Ps 145:8
G words are like a honeycomb, Prv 16:24
the Lord waits to be **g** Is 30:18
the God of hosts, will be **g** Am 5:15
Let your speech always be **g**, Col 4:6
For this is a **g** thing, when, 1 Pt 2:19

GRAFT

for God has the power to **g** Rom 11:23

GRAIN

brothers went down to buy **g** Gn 42:3
"When anyone brings a **g** Lv 2:1
"And this is the law of the **g** Lv 6:14
And the **g** offering with it Lv 23:13
The firstfruits of your **g**, of Dt 18:4
your neighbor's standing **g**, Dt 23:25
you provide their **g**, for so Ps 65:9
began to pluck heads of **g** Mt 12:1
on good soil and produced **g**, Mt 13:8
choked it, and it yielded no **g**. Mk 4:7
I say to you, unless a **g** of Jn 12:24

GRANT

May he **g** you your heart's Ps 20:4
and encouragement **g** Rom 15:5
riches of his glory he may **g** Eph 3:16

GRANTED

For it has been **g** to you that Phil 1:29
His divine power has **g** to us 2 Pt 1:3

GRASS

for man, his days are like **g**; Ps 103:15
But if God so clothes the **g**, Lk 12:28
for "All flesh is like **g** and all 1 Pt 1:24

GRAVE

their throat is an open **g**; they Ps 5:9
And they made his **g** with the Is 53:9
"Their throat is an open **g**; Rom 3:13

GREAT

And I will make of you a **g** Gn 12:2
of lords, the **g**, the mighty, Dt 10:17
gentleness made me **g**. 2 Sm 22:36
in keeping them there is **g** Ps 19:11
king is not saved by his **g** Ps 33:16
For you are **g** and do Ps 86:10
How **g** are your works, O Lord! Ps 92:5
are above the earth, so **g** Ps 103:11
For your steadfast love is **g** Ps 108:4
G are the works of the Lord, Ps 111:2
G peace have those who Ps 119:165
G is the Lord, and greatly to Ps 145:3
g is your faithfulness. Lam 3:23
is the **g** and first commandment. Mt 22:38
But whoever would be **g** Mk 10:43
you all is the one who is **g**." Lk 9:48
in a cloud with power and **g** Lk 21:27
G indeed, we confess, is the 1 Tm 3:16
Now there is **g** gain in 1 Tm 6:6
escape if we neglect such a **g** Heb 2:3

GREATER

is no other commandment **g** Mk 12:31
You will see **g** things than these." Jn 1:50
G love has no one than this, Jn 15:13
the reproach of Christ **g** Heb 11:26
condemns us, God is **g** than 1 Jn 3:20
for he who is in you is **g** 1 Jn 4:4
I have no **g** joy than to hear 3 Jn 1:4

GREATEST

himself like this child is the **g** Mt 18:4
to which of them was the **g**. Lk 9:46
but the **g** of these is love. 1 Cor 13:13

GREATNESS

and I will declare your **g**. Ps 145:6
according to his excellent **g**! Ps 150:2
apparel, marching in the **g** Is 63:1
immeasurable **g** of his power Eph 1:19

GREED

but inside they are full of **g** Mt 23:25
of sexual immorality or **g**, 1 Cor 5:11
nor with a pretext for **g** 1 Thes 2:5
And in their **g** they will 2 Pt 2:3
have hearts trained in **g**. 2 Pt 2:14

GREEDY

Whoever is **g** for unjust Prv 15:27
nor thieves, nor the **g**, 1 Cor 6:10
up to sensuality, **g** to practice Eph 4:19

GREEK

Aramaic, in Latin, and in **G**. Jn 19:20
Jew first and also to the **G**. Rom 1:16
between Jew and **G**; Rom 10:12
There is neither Jew nor **G**, Gal 3:28
Here there is not **G** and Jew, Col 3:11
Hebrew is Abaddon, and in **G** Rv 9:11

GREEN

of life, I have given every **g** Gn 1:30
He makes me lie down in **g** Ps 23:2
But I am like a **g** olive tree in Ps 52:8
will flourish like a **g** Prv 11:28

GREW

And the child **g** and became Lk 2:40
fell on the rock, and as it **g** Lk 8:6
in the faith, and they **g** Acts 16:5
promise of God, but he **g** Rom 4:20

GRIEF

my eye is wasted from **g**; my Ps 31:9
the end of joy may be **g**. Prv 14:13
g is upon me; my heart is sick Jer 8:18
but, though he cause **g**, Lam 3:32
For you felt a godly **g**, so 2 Cor 7:9

GRIEFS

Surely he has borne our **g** Is 53:4

GRIEVANCE

When one of you has a **g** 1 Cor 6:1

GRIEVE

And do not **g** the Holy Spirit Eph 4:30
that you may not **g** as 1 Thes 4:13

GRIEVED
man on the earth, and it **g** Gn 6:6
Peter was **g** because he said Jn 21:17
you have been **g** by various trials, 1 Pt 1:6

GROAN
because the needy **g**, says the Ps 12:5
I **g** because of the tumult of Ps 38:8
land the wounded shall **g**. Jer 51:52
"As for you, son of man, **g**; Ez 21:6
to you, 'Why do you **g**?' you Ez 21:7
firstfruits of the Spirit, **g** Rom 8:23
For in this tent we **g**, 2 Cor 5:2

GROANING
And God heard their **g**, and Ex 2:24
was moved to pity by their **g** Jgs 2:18
me, from the words of my **g**? Ps 22:1
creation has been **g** together Rom 8:22
with joy and not with **g**, Heb 13:17

GROANINGS
intercedes for us with **g** Rom 8:26

GROUND
the man of dust from the **g** Gn 2:7
not eat of it,' cursed is the **g** Gn 3:17
till you return to the **g**, for Gn 3:19
will never again curse the **g** Gn 8:21
you are standing is holy **g**." Ex 3:5
of water into thirsty **g**, Ps 107:33
farther, he fell on the **g** Mk 14:35
wrote with his finger on the **g**. Jn 8:6
you are standing is holy **g**. Acts 7:33

GROW
You cause the grass to **g** Ps 104:14
Let both **g** together until the Mt 13:30
And let us not **g** weary of Gal 6:9
truth in love, we are to **g** Eph 4:15
so that you may not **g** weary Heb 12:3
milk, that by it you may **g** 1 Pt 2:2
But **g** in the grace and 2 Pt 3:18

GROWTH
but God gave the **g**. 1 Cor 3:6
ligaments, grows with a **g** Col 2:19

GRUMBLE
nor **g**, as some of them 1 Cor 10:10
Do not **g** against one another, Jas 5:9

GRUMBLED
And the people **g** against Ex 15:24
all the people of Israel **g** Nm 14:2
Pharisees and their scribes **g** Lk 5:30
So the Jews **g** about him, Jn 6:41

GRUMBLING
because he has heard your **g** Ex 16:7
that his disciples were **g** Jn 6:61
Do all things without **g** Phil 2:14
to one another without **g**. 1 Pt 4:9

GUARANTEE
Spirit in our hearts as a **g**. 2 Cor 1:22
given us the Spirit as a **g**. 2 Cor 5:5
who is the **g** of our inheritance Eph 1:14

GUARANTEED
may rest on grace and be **g** Rom 4:16
of his purpose, he **g** it with Heb 6:17

GUARANTOR
This makes Jesus the **g** of a Heb 7:22

GUARD
Oh, **g** my soul, and deliver Ps 25:20
of Israel will be your rear **g**. Is 52:12
So **g** yourselves in your Mal 2:15
But be on **g**; I have told you Mk 13:23
angels concerning you, to **g** Lk 4:10
all understanding, will **g** Phil 4:7
O Timothy, **g** the deposit 1 Tm 6:20
that he is able to **g** 2 Tm 1:12
who dwells within us, **g** 2 Tm 1:14

GUARDS
Whoever **g** his mouth Prv 13:3
whoever **g** his soul will keep Prv 22:5

GUIDANCE
He did not seek **g** from the 1 Chr 10:14
who understands obtain **g**, Prv 1:5
Where there is no **g**, a people Prv 11:14

GUIDE
the peoples with equity and **g** Ps 67:4
You **g** me with your counsel, Ps 73:24
One who is righteous is a **g** Prv 12:26
And the Lord will **g** you Is 58:11
in the shadow of death, to **g** Lk 1:79
of truth comes, he will **g** Jn 16:13

GUIDED
you have **g** them by your Ex 15:13
his people like sheep and **g** Ps 78:52

GUILT
and Aaron shall bear any **g** Ex 28:38
who sins, thus bringing **g** on Lv 4:3
lambs and offer it for a **g** Lv 14:12
pardon my **g**, for it is great. Ps 25:11
Fools mock at the **g** offering, Prv 14:9
your **g** is taken away, and your Is 6:7
they acknowledge their **g** Hos 5:15
I have found in him no **g** Lk 23:22
and told them, "I find no **g** Jn 18:38
they found in him no **g** Acts 13:28

GUILTY
will by no means clear the **g**, Ex 34:7
name of brother if he is **g** 1 Cor 5:11
manner will be **g** of profaning 1 Cor 11:27

HABAKKUK
The oracle that **H** the prophet saw. Hb 1:1
A prayer of **H** the prophet, Hb 3:1

HABIT
meet together, as is the **h** Heb 10:25

HADES
will be brought down to **H**. Mt 11:23
and in **H**, being in torment, Lk 16:23
not abandon my soul to **H**, Acts 2:27
the keys of Death and **H**. Rv 1:18
Then Death and **H** were Rv 20:14

HAGAR
servant whose name was **H**. Gn 16:1
And **H** bore Abram a son, Gn 16:15
her, "What troubles you, **H**? Gn 21:17

HAGGAI
Now the prophets, **H** and Ezr 5:1
Lord came by the hand of **H** Hg 1:1

HAIR
not a **h** of your head will perish. Lk 21:18
wiped his feet with her **h**, Jn 11:2

HAIRS
But even the **h** of your head Mt 10:30

HALLELUJAH
in heaven, crying out, "**H**! Rv 19:1
Once more they cried out, "**H**! Rv 19:3
"Amen. **H**!" Rv 19:4
of thunder, crying out, "**H**! Rv 19:6

HALLOWED
Our Father in heaven, **h** be Mt 6:9
"Father, **h** be your name. Your Lk 11:2

HAND
because he is at my right **h**, Ps 16:8
for the Lord upholds his **h**. Ps 37:24
"Sit at my right **h**, until I Ps 110:1
lead me, and your right **h** Ps 139:10
Whatever your **h** finds to do, Eccl 9:10
needy, do not let your left **h** Mt 6:3
snatch them out of my **h**. Jn 10:28
"Because I am not a **h**, 1 Cor 12:15
seated him at his right **h** Eph 1:20
who is seated at the right **h** Heb 8:1

HANDIWORK
the sky above proclaims his **h**. Ps 19:1

HANDLING
to be ashamed, rightly **h** 2 Tm 2:15

HANDS
they have pierced my **h** and Ps 22:16
He who has clean **h** and a pure Ps 24:4
Clap your **h**, all peoples! Ps 47:1
Lift up your **h** to the holy Ps 134:2
a little folding of the **h** to rest, Prv 6:10
poor and reaches out her **h** Prv 31:20
of the field shall clap their **h**. Is 55:12
I spread out my **h** all the day Is 65:2
said, "Father, into your **h** Lk 23:46
they prayed and laid their **h** Acts 6:6
and to work with your **h**, 1 Thes 4:11
should pray, lifting holy **h** 1 Tm 2:8
washings, the laying on of **h**, Heb 6:2
thing to fall into the **h** Heb 10:31

HANNAH
The name of the one was **H**, 1 Sm 1:2
And in due time **H** 1 Sm 1:20
And **H** prayed and said, "My 1 Sm 2:1

HAPPINESS
who brings good news of **h**, Is 52:7

HARD
Is anything too **h** for the Lord? Gn 18:14
is narrow and the way is **h** Mt 7:14
they said, "This is a **h** saying; Jn 6:60
things in them that are **h** 2 Pt 3:16

HARDEN
it was the Lord's doing to **h** Jos 11:20
do not **h** your hearts, as at Ps 95:8
from your ways and **h** Is 63:17
do not **h** your hearts as in the Heb 3:8

HARDENED
has blinded their eyes and **h** Jn 12:40
it, but the rest were **h**, Rom 11:7
But their minds were **h**. 2 Cor 3:14
that none of you may be **h** by Heb 3:13

HARDENS
always, but whoever **h** Prv 28:14
he wills, and he **h** Rom 9:18

HARDNESS
to them, "Because of your **h** Mt 19:8
with anger, grieved at their **h** Mk 3:5
to them, "Because of your **h** Mk 10:5
their unbelief and **h** of heart, Mk 16:14
in them, due to their **h** of heart. Eph 4:18

HARM
does him good, and not **h**, Prv 31:12
Son of God to their own **h** Heb 6:6
Now who is there to **h** you if 1 Pt 3:13

HARMONY
Live in **h** with one Rom 12:16
grant you to live in such **h** Rom 15:5
together in perfect **h**. Col 3:14

HARSH
turns away wrath, but a **h** Prv 15:1
your wives, and do not be **h** Col 3:19

HARVEST
And he said to them, "The **h** Lk 10:2
that the fields are white for **h**. Jn 4:35
And a **h** of righteousness is Jas 3:18

HASTY
but he who has a **h** temper Prv 14:29
but everyone who is **h** comes Prv 21:5
Do you see a man who is **h** Prv 29:20
nor let your heart be **h** to Eccl 5:2
Do not be **h** in the laying 1 Tm 5:22

HATE
"You shall not **h** your Lv 19:17
your eyes; you **h** all evildoers. Ps 5:5
O you who love the Lord, **h** Ps 97:10
Do I not **h** those who **h** you, Ps 139:21
all who **h** me love death." Prv 8:36
H evil, and love good, and Am 5:15
love your neighbor and **h** Mt 5:43
betray one another and **h** Mt 24:10
are you when people **h** Lk 6:22
do good to those who **h** you, Lk 6:27
but I do the very thing I **h**. Rom 7:15

HATED
it has hated me before it **h** Jn 15:18
I loved, but Esau I **h**." Rom 9:13
For no one ever **h** his own Eph 5:29
our days in malice and envy, **h** Ti 3:3
loved righteousness and **h** Heb 1:9

HATES
six things that the Lord **h**, Prv 6:16
Whoever spares the rod **h** Prv 13:24
who does wicked things **h** Jn 3:20
Whoever **h** me **h** my Father Jn 15:23
says he is in the light and **h** 1 Jn 2:9
But whoever **h** his brother is 1 Jn 2:11
says, "I love God," and **h** 1 Jn 4:20

HATRED
The fear of the Lord is **h** Prv 8:13
H stirs up strife, but love Prv 10:12

HAUGHTY
before destruction, and a **h** Prv 16:18
Do not be **h**, but associate Rom 12:16

HEAD
he shall bruise your **h**, and Gn 3:15
you anoint my **h** with oil; my Ps 23:5
burning coals on his **h**, Prv 25:22
helmet of salvation on his **h**; Is 59:17
has nowhere to lay his **h**." Mt 8:20
burning coals on his **h**." Rom 12:20
to understand that the **h** 1 Cor 11:3
his feet and gave him as **h** Eph 1:22
For the husband is the **h** Eph 5:23
And he is the **h** of the body, Col 1:18
a flame of fire, and on his **h** Rv 19:12

HEAL
forgive their sin and **h** 2 Chr 7:14
me; **h** me, for I have sinned Ps 41:4
H the sick, raise the dead, Mt 10:8
me this proverb, 'Physician, **h** Lk 4:23
and turn, and I would **h** Acts 28:26

HEALED
you for help, and you have **h** Ps 30:2
and with his stripes we are **h**. Is 53:5
compassion on them and **h** Mt 14:14
And he **h** many who were Mk 1:34
another, that you may be **h**. Jas 5:16
his wounds you have been **h**. 1 Pt 2:24

HEALING
shall rise with **h** in its wings. Mal 4:2
gospel of the kingdom and **h** Mt 4:23
Spirit, to another gifts of **h** 1 Cor 12:9
then gifts of **h**, helping, 1 Cor 12:28
Do all possess gifts of **h**? 1 Cor 12:30
of the tree were for the **h** Rv 22:2

HEALS
all your iniquity, who **h** Ps 103:3
He **h** the brokenhearted and Ps 147:3

HEALTH
you restore him to full **h**. Ps 41:3
sweetness to the soul and **h** Prv 16:24
Oh restore me to **h** and make Is 38:16

HEALTHY
A **h** tree cannot bear bad fruit, Mt 7:18

HEAR
"**H**, O Israel: The Lord our Dt 6:4
ways, then I will **h** from 2 Chr 7:14
Let me **h** joy and gladness; let Ps 51:8
Incline your ear, and **h** Prv 22:17
In that day the deaf shall **h** Is 29:18
are yet speaking I will **h**. Is 65:24
has ears to **h**, let him **h**. Mt 11:15
The reason why you do not **h** Jn 8:47
And how are they to **h** Rom 10:14
He who has an ear, let him **h** Rv 2:7

HEARD
And they **h** the sound of the Gn 3:8
I had **h** of you by the hearing Jb 42:5
Who has **h** such a thing? Who Is 66:8
"You have **h** that it was said to Mt 5:21
no eye has seen, nor ear **h**, 1 Cor 2:9
him you also, when you **h** Eph 1:13
of God, which you **h** from 1 Thes 2:13
and what you have **h** from 2 Tm 2:2
message that you have **h** 1 Jn 3:11

HEARING
So faith comes from **h**, Rom 10:17

HEARS
"Everyone then who **h** these Mt 7:24
truly, I say to you, whoever **h** Jn 5:24

according to his will he **h** 1 Jn 5:14
If anyone **h** my voice and Rv 3:20

HEART
thoughts of his **h** was only evil Gn 6:5
for the intention of man's **h** Gn 8:21
every man whose **h** moves him Ex 25:2
hate your brother in your **h**, Lv 19:17
after him with all your **h** Dt 4:29
Lord your God with all your **h** Dt 6:5
your God with all your **h** Dt 10:12
to him freely, and your **h** Dt 15:10
your God with all your **h** Dt 30:6
your God with all your **h** Dt 30:10
to serve him with all your **h** Jos 22:5
a man after his own **h**, 1 Sm 13:14
the Lord looks on the **h**." 1 Sm 16:7
his statutes with all his **h** 2 Kgs 23:3
serve him with a whole **h** 1 Chr 28:9
My eyes and my **h** will be 2 Chr 7:16
lay up his words in your **h**. Jb 22:22
who saves the upright in **h**. Ps 7:10
The fool says in his **h**, "There Ps 14:1
and the meditation of my **h** Ps 19:14
give you the desires of your **h**. Ps 37:4
My **h** overflows with a Ps 45:1
Create in me a clean **h**, O God, Ps 51:10
a broken and contrite **h**, Ps 51:17
cherished iniquity in my **h**, Ps 66:18
up your word in my **h**, Ps 119:11
O God, and know my **h**! Ps 139:23
in the Lord with all your **h**, Prv 3:5
keep them within your **h**. Prv 4:21
Bind them on your **h** always; Prv 6:21
them on the tablet of your **h**. Prv 7:3
Anxiety in a man's **h** Prv 12:25
Hope deferred makes the **h** Prv 13:12
A joyful **h** is good medicine, Prv 17:22
face reflects face, so the **h** Prv 27:19
A wise man's **h** inclines him Eccl 10:2
lowly, and to revive the **h** Is 57:15
The **h** is deceitful above all Jer 17:9
seek me with all your **h**, Jer 29:13
And I will give them one **h**, Ez 11:19
I will give you a new **h**, Ez 36:26
"Blessed are the pure in **h**, Mt 5:8
treasure is, there your **h** will be Mt 6:21
of the abundance of the **h** Mt 12:34
your God with all your **h** Mt 22:37
this they were cut to the **h**, Acts 2:37
And God, who knows the **h**, Acts 15:8
a matter of the **h**, by the Spirit Rom 2:29
Lord and believe in your **h** Rom 10:9
the purposes of the **h**. 1 Cor 4:5
not about what is in the **h**. 2 Cor 5:12
to the Lord with all your **h**, Eph 5:19
the will of God from the **h**, Eph 6:6
on the Lord from a pure **h**. 2 Tm 2:22
and intentions of the **h**. Heb 4:12
draw near with a true **h** Heb 10:22
earnestly from a pure **h**, 1 Pt 1:22
brotherly love, a tender **h**, 1 Pt 3:8
he who searches mind and **h**, Rv 2:23

HEARTS
that he may incline our **h** 1 Kgs 8:58
let the **h** of those who 1 Chr 16:10
for the Lord searches all **h** 1 Chr 28:9
I will write it on their **h**. Jer 31:33
men, but God knows your **h**. Lk 16:15
each other, "Did not our **h** Lk 24:32
"Let not your **h** be troubled. Jn 14:1
having cleansed their **h** Acts 15:9
law is written on their **h**, Rom 2:15
And he who searches **h** Rom 8:27
but on tablets of human **h**. 2 Cor 3:3
has shone in our **h** to give 2 Cor 4:6
Christ may dwell in your **h** Eph 3:17
will guard your **h** and your Phil 4:7
do not harden your **h** as in Heb 3:8
put my laws on their **h**, Heb 10:16
but in your **h** sanctify Christ 1 Pt 3:15

HEAVEN
God called the expanse **H**. Gn 1:8
heaven and the highest **h** 1 Kgs 8:27
about to take Elijah up to **h** 2 Kgs 2:1
then I will hear from **h** 2 Chr 7:14
"How you are fallen from **h**, Is 14:12
"**H** is my throne, and the earth Is 66:1
behold, with the clouds of **h** Dn 7:13
Our Father in **h**, hallowed be Mt 6:9

for yourselves treasures in **h**, Mt 6:20
earth shall be bound in **h**, Mt 16:19
enter the kingdom of **h**. Mt 19:23
H and earth will pass away, Mt 24:35
coming on the clouds of **h**." Mt 26:64
to them, "All authority in **h** Mt 28:18
there will be more joy in **h** Lk 15:7
But it is easier for **h** and Lk 16:17
you will have treasure in **h**; Lk 18:22
of God is revealed from **h** Rom 1:18
caught up to the third **h** 2 Cor 12:2
But our citizenship is in **h**, Phil 3:20
the hope laid up for you in **h**. Col 1:5
will descend from **h** 1 Thes 4:16
the true things, but into **h** Heb 9:24
and unfading, kept in **h** for you, 1 Pt 1:4
Then I saw a new **h** and a Rv 21:1

HEAVENLY
him a little lower than the **h** beings Ps 8:5
can you believe if I tell you **h** Jn 3:12
to put on our **h** dwelling, 2 Cor 5:2
spiritual blessing in the **h** places, Eph 1:3
seated us with him in the **h** Eph 2:6
bring me safely into his **h** 2 Tm 4:18
better country, that is, a **h** Heb 11:16

HEAVENS
God created the **h** and the earth. Gn 1:1
When I look at your **h**, the Ps 8:3
The **h** declare the glory of God, Ps 19:1
The **h** declare his righteousness Ps 50:6
of the earth, and the **h** are Ps 102:25
love is great above the **h**; Ps 108:4
Our God is in the **h**; he does Ps 115:3
is firmly fixed in the **h**. Ps 119:89
Lift up your eyes to the **h**, Is 51:6
For as the **h** are higher than Is 55:9
"For behold, I create new **h** Is 65:17
I will show wonders in the **h** Jl 2:30
ascended far above all the **h**, Eph 4:10
we are waiting for new **h** 2 Pt 3:13

HEAVY
and night your hand was **h** Ps 32:4
like a **h** burden, they are too Ps 38:4
all who labor and are **h** Mt 11:28

HEBREW
came and told Abram the **H**, Gn 14:13
he said to them, "I am a **H**, Jon 1:9

HEED
that he stands take **h** 1 Cor 10:12

HEEDS
Whoever **h** instruction is on Prv 10:17
instruction, but whoever **h** Prv 13:18
instruction, but whoever **h** Prv 15:5

HEEL
and you shall bruise his **h**." Gn 3:15

HEIR
own son shall be your **h**." Gn 15:4
that he would be **h** Rom 4:13
a son, and if a son, then an **h** Gal 4:7
whom he appointed the **h** Heb 1:2
the world and became an **h** Heb 11:7

HEIRS
h of God and fellow **h** Rom 8:17
are Abraham's offspring, **h** Gal 3:29
the Gentiles are fellow **h**, Eph 3:6
his grace we might become **h** Ti 3:7
vessel, since they are **h** with 1 Pt 3:7

HELL
will be liable to the **h** of fire. Mt 5:22
both soul and body in **h**. Mt 10:28
of life, and set on fire by **h**. Jas 3:6
sinned, but cast them into **h** 2 Pt 2:4

HELMET
as a breastplate, and a **h** Is 59:17
and take the **h** of salvation, Eph 6:17
faith and love, and for a **h** 1 Thes 5:8

HELP
is none like you to **h**, 2 Chr 14:11
to my God I cried for **h**. From Ps 18:6
my God, I cried to you for **h**, Ps 30:2
strength, a very present **h** Ps 46:1
H us, O God of our salvation, Ps 79:9

From where does my **h** come? Ps 121:1
will strengthen you, I will **h** Is 41:10
"I believe; **h** my unbelief!" Mk 9:24
the fainthearted, **h** the 1 Thes 5:14
tempted, he is able to **h** those Heb 2:18
mercy and find grace to **h** Heb 4:16

HELPED
because you, Lord, have **h** Ps 86:17
in a day of salvation I have **h** Is 49:8
in a day of salvation I have **h** 2 Cor 6:2

HELPER
I will make him a **h** fit for him." Gn 2:18
have been the **h** of the fatherless. Ps 10:14
say, "The Lord is my **h**; I will Heb 13:6

HELPING
healing, **h**, administrating, 1 Cor 12:28

HELPS
not, I am the one who **h** Is 41:13
Likewise the Spirit **h** us in Rom 8:26

HERITAGE
Behold, children are a **h** Ps 127:3

HERMON
Tabor and **H** joyously praise Ps 89:12
It is like the dew of **H**, which Ps 133:3

HEROD
of Judea in the days of **H** Mt 2:1
governor of Judea, and **H** being Lk 3:1

HERODIAS
in prison for the sake of **H**, Mt 14:3
came, the daughter of **H** Mt 14:6

HEZEKIAH
year of King **H**, Sennacherib 2 Kgs 18:13
As soon as King **H** heard it, 2 Kgs 19:1
came in the days of **H**, 1 Chr 4:41
"Did **H** king of Judah and all Jer 26:19

HID
and the man and his wife **h** Gn 3:8
And Moses **h** his face, for he Ex 3:6
shall live, because she **h** Jos 6:17

HIDDEN
Declare me innocent from **h** Ps 19:12
and search for it as for **h** Prv 2:4
to you new things, **h** things Is 48:6
God, and your sins have **h** Is 59:2
city set on a hill cannot be **h**. Mt 5:14
of heaven is like treasure **h** Mt 13:44
the mystery **h** for ages and Col 1:26
have died, and your life is **h** Col 3:3
are not cannot remain **h**. 1 Tm 5:25

HIDE
h me in the shadow of your wings, Ps 17:8
H your face from my sins, and Ps 51:9
H not your face from me, lest Ps 143:7
And I will not **h** my face any Ez 39:29

HIDING
You are a **h** place for me; you Ps 32:7
You are my **h** place and my Ps 119:114

HIGH
name of the Lord, the Most **H**. Ps 7:17
he will lift me **h** upon a rock. Ps 27:5
he shall be **h** and lifted up, Is 52:13
he makes me tread on my **h** Hb 3:19
called the Son of the Most **H**. Lk 1:32
For we do not have a **h** Heb 4:15

HIGHER
For as the heavens are **h** Is 55:9
earnestly desire the **h** gifts. 1 Cor 12:31

HILL
shall dwell on your holy **h**? Ps 15:1
city set on a **h** cannot be hidden. Mt 5:14

HILLS
the cattle on a thousand **h**. Ps 50:10
I lift up my eyes to the **h**. Ps 121:1

HINDER
for us, for nothing can **h** 1 Sm 14:6
come to me and do not **h** Mt 19:14

HINDERED
h you from obeying the truth? Gal 5:7
your prayers may not be **h**. 1 Pt 3:7

HOLD
vain, for the Lord will not **h** Ex 20:7
H me up, that I may be Ps 119:117
and your right hand shall **h** Ps 139:10
Keep **h** of instruction; do not Prv 4:13
For I, the Lord your God, **h** Is 41:13
who, hearing the word, **h** Lk 8:15
For we **h** that one is Rom 3:28
evil; **h** fast to what is good. Rom 12:9
and in him all things **h** together. Col 1:17
Take **h** of the eternal life to 1 Tm 6:12
Let us **h** fast the confession Heb 10:23
H fast what you have, so that Rv 3:11

HOLDING
h fast to the word of life, so Phil 2:16
and not **h** fast to the Head, Col 2:19
h faith and a good 1 Tm 1:19

HOLINESS
is like you, majestic in **h**, Ex 15:11
the Lord in the splendor of **h**. Ps 29:2
the Lord in the splendor of **h**; Ps 96:9
bringing **h** to completion 2 Cor 7:1
in true righteousness and **h**. Eph 4:24
hearts blameless in **h** 1 Thes 3:13
control his own body in **h** 1 Thes 4:4
us for impurity, but in **h**. 1 Thes 4:7
in faith and love and **h**, 1 Tm 2:15
that we may share his **h**. Heb 12:10
and for the **h** without which Heb 12:14
ought you to be in lives of **h** 2 Pt 3:11

HOLY
seventh day and made it **h**, Gn 2:3
which you are standing is **h** Ex 3:5
a kingdom of priests and a **h** Ex 19:6
the Sabbath day, to keep it **h**. Ex 20:8
to make atonement in the **h** Lv 6:30
and be **h**, for I am **h**. Lv 11:44
therefore, and be **h**, Lv 20:7
You shall be **h** to me, for I Lv 20:26
you shall not profane my **h** Lv 22:32
the Sabbath day, to keep it **h**, Dt 5:12
The Lord is in his **h** temple; Ps 11:4
soul to Sheol, or let your **h** Ps 16:10
And who shall stand in his **h** Ps 24:3
and take not your **H** Spirit Ps 51:11
Your way, O God, is **h**. What Ps 77:13
and give thanks to his **h** Ps 97:12
and awesome name! **H** is he! Ps 99:3
is within me, bless his **h** Ps 103:1
H and awesome is his name! Ps 111:9
"**H**, **h**, **h** is the Lord of Is 6:3
like him? says the **H** One. Is 40:25
and the **H** One of Israel is Is 54:5
but keep the Sabbath day **h**, Jer 17:22
"And my **h** name I will make Ez 39:7
in whom is the spirit of the **h** Dn 4:8
But the Lord is in his **h** Hb 2:20
will baptize you with the **H** Mt 3:11
are — the **H** One of God." Mk 1:24
to know, that you are the **H** Jn 6:69
receive power when the **H** Acts 1:8
were all filled with the **H** Acts 2:4
soul to Hades, or let your **H** Acts 2:27
So the law is **h**, and the Rom 7:12
as a living sacrifice, **h** and Rom 12:1
For God's temple is **h**, and 1 Cor 3:17
body is a temple of the **H** 1 Cor 6:19
world, that we should be **h** Eph 1:4
thing, that she might be **h** Eph 5:27
in order to present you **h** Col 1:22
as God's chosen ones, **h** and Col 3:12
men should pray, lifting **h** 1 Tm 2:8
us and called us to a **h** 2 Tm 1:9
use, set apart as **h**, ready for 2 Tm 2:21
upright, **h**, and disciplined. Ti 1:8
and renewal of the **H** Ti 3:5
h, innocent, unstained, and Heb 7:26
confidence to enter the **h** Heb 10:19
as he who called you is **h**, 1 Pt 1:15
be **h** in all your conduct 1 Pt 1:15
a spiritual house, to be a **h** 1 Pt 2:5
race, a royal priesthood, a **h** 1 Pt 2:9
h, is the Lord God Almighty, Rv 4:8
For you alone are **h**. All Rv 15:4

HOME
Even the sparrow finds a **h**, Ps 84:3
He came to his own **h**, and Jn 1:11
come to him and make our **h** Jn 14:23
that while we are at **h** 2 Cor 5:6
pure, working at **h**, kind, that Ti 2:5

HOMES
"See, we have left our **h** Lk 18:28
breaking bread in their **h**, Acts 2:46

HOMOSEXUALITY
nor men who practice **h**, 1 Cor 6:9
men who practice **h**, liars, 1 Tm 1:10

HONEST
speaks the truth gives **h** Prv 12:17
Whoever gives an **h** answer Prv 24:26
rather let him labor, doing **h** Eph 4:28

HONEY
land flowing with milk and **h**, Ex 3:8
sweeter also than **h** and Ps 19:10
my taste, sweeter than **h** Ps 119:103
is not good to eat much **h**, Prv 25:27

HONOR
"**H** your father and your Ex 20:12
"'**H** your father and your Dt 5:16
those who **h** me I will **h**, 1 Sm 2:30
crowned him with glory and **h**. Ps 8:5
H the Lord with your wealth Prv 3:9
humility comes before **h**. Prv 15:33
It is an **h** for a man to keep Prv 20:3
For God commanded, '**H** your Mt 15:4
that a prophet has no **h** Jn 4:44
knew God, they did not **h** Rom 1:21
is owed, **h** to whom **h** Rom 13:7
"**H** your father and mother" Eph 6:2
worthy of double **h**, 1 Tm 5:17
Let marriage be held in **h** Heb 13:4
H everyone. Love the 1 Pt 2:17
creatures give glory and **h** Rv 4:9

HONORABLE
is true, whatever is **h**, Phil 4:8
wood and clay, some for **h** 2 Tm 2:20

HONORABLY
desiring to act **h** in all things. Heb 13:18

HONORED
if one member is **h**, all 1 Cor 12:26
as always Christ will be **h** Phil 1:20

HONORS
person is despised, but who **h** Ps 15:4
is generous to the needy **h** Prv 14:31

HOPE
Though he slay me, I will **h** Jb 13:15
do I wait? My **h** is in you. Ps 39:7
H in God; for I shall again Ps 42:5
Let not those who **h** in you be Ps 69:6
But I will **h** continually and Ps 71:14
I **h** in your word. Ps 119:81
H deferred makes the heart Prv 13:12
is a future, and your **h** will Prv 23:18
We set our **h** on you, for you Jer 14:22
flesh also will dwell in **h**. Acts 2:26
stand, and we rejoice in **h** Rom 5:2
and character produces **h**, Rom 5:4
For in this **h** we were saved. Rom 8:24
Now **h** that is seen is not Rom 8:24
Rejoice in **h**, be patient in Rom 12:12
So now faith, **h**, and love 1 Cor 13:13
On him we have set our **h** 2 Cor 1:10
Since we have such a **h**, 2 Cor 3:12
eagerly wait for the **h** Gal 5:5
may know what is the **h** Eph 1:18
you were called to the one **h** Eph 4:4
because of the **h** laid up for Col 1:5
not shifting from the **h** of the Col 1:23
is Christ in you, the **h** of glory. Col 1:27
For what is our **h** or joy 1 Thes 2:19
and for a helmet the **h** 1 Thes 5:8
because we have our **h** 1 Tm 4:10
in **h** of eternal life, which God, Ti 1:2
waiting for our blessed **h**, Ti 2:13
heirs according to the **h** Ti 3:7
and our boasting in our **h**. Heb 3:6
have the full assurance of **h** Heb 6:11
to hold fast to the **h** Heb 6:18

anchor of the soul, a **h** that Heb 6:19
the other hand, a better **h** Heb 7:19
fast the confession of our **h** Heb 10:23
to be born again to a living **h** 1 Pt 1:3
sober-minded, set your **h** 1 Pt 1:13
so that your faith and **h** 1 Pt 1:21
you for a reason for the **h** 1 Pt 3:15

HOPED
is the assurance of things **h** for, Heb 11:1

HOPES
For who **h** for what he sees? Rom 8:24
believes all things, **h** all 1 Cor 13:7
And everyone who thus **h** 1 Jn 3:3

HOREB
the wilderness and came to **H**, Ex 3:1
made a covenant with us in **H**. Dt 5:2

HORSE
the **h** and his rider he has Ex 15:1
not in the strength of the **h**, Ps 147:10
A whip for the **h**, a bridle Prv 26:3
a man riding on a red **h**! He Zec 1:8
looked, and behold, a white **h**! Rv 6:2
And out came another **h**, Its Rv 6:4
looked, and behold, a black **h**! Rv 6:5
I looked, and behold, a pale **h**! Rv 6:8
and behold, a white **h**! The Rv 19:11

HOSANNA
the Lord! **H** in the highest!" Mt 21:9

HOSPITABLE
respectable, **h**, able to teach, 1 Tm 3:2
but **h**, a lover of good, upright, Ti 1:8

HOSPITALITY
saints and seek to show **h**. Rom 12:13
up children, has shown **h**, 1 Tm 5:10
Do not neglect to show **h** Heb 13:2
Show **h** to one another 1 Pt 4:9

HOST
were finished, and all the **h** Gn 2:1
As the **h** of heaven cannot Jer 33:22
multitude of the heavenly **h** Lk 2:13
ascended on high he led a **h** Eph 4:8

HOSTILE
that is set on the flesh is **h** Rom 8:7
once were alienated and **h** Col 1:21

HOSTILITY
flesh the dividing wall of **h** Eph 2:14
from sinners such **h** Heb 12:3

HOT
you are neither cold nor **h**. Rv 3:15

HOT-TEMPERED
A **h** man stirs up strife, but Prv 15:18

HOUR
anxious can add a single **h** Mt 6:27
of Man is coming at an **h** Mt 24:44
But the **h** is coming, and is Jn 4:23
answered them, "The **h** has Jn 12:23
I have come to this **h**. Jn 12:27

HOUSE
not covet your neighbor's **h**; Ex 20:17
But as for me and my **h**, Jos 24:15
and I shall dwell in the **h** Ps 23:6
that I may dwell in the **h** Ps 27:4
For zeal for your **h** has Ps 69:9
of heart within my **h**; Ps 101:2
the Lord builds the **h**, Ps 127:1
The Lord tears down the **h** Prv 15:25
By wisdom a **h** is built, and by Prv 24:3
h shall be called a **h** of prayer Is 56:7
a wise man who built his **h** Mt 7:24
enter a strong man's **h** Mt 12:29
h shall be called a **h** of prayer, Mt 21:13
divided against itself, that **h** Mk 3:25
make my Father's **h** a **h** of trade. Jn 2:16
In my Father's **h** are many Jn 14:2
more as the builder of a **h** Heb 3:3
built up as a spiritual **h**, 1 Pt 2:5

HOUSEHOLD
will be those of his own **h**. Mt 10:36
to those who are of the **h** Gal 6:10
He must manage his own **h** 1 Tm 3:4
for members of his **h**, 1 Tm 5:8
judgment to begin at the **h** 1 Pt 4:17

HUMAN
"Whoever takes a **h** life shall Lv 24:17
a stone was cut out by no **h** Dn 2:34
So then it depends not on **h** Rom 9:16
And being found in **h** form, Phil 2:7
the Lord's sake to every **h** 1 Pt 2:13

HUMBLE
are called by my name **h** 2 Chr 7:14
He leads the **h** in what is Ps 25:9
he adorns the **h** with salvation. Ps 149:4
he is scornful, but to the **h** Prv 3:34
he who is **h** and contrite in Is 66:2
walk in pride he is able to **h**. Dn 4:37
but gives grace to the **h**." Jas 4:6
H yourselves before the Lord, Jas 4:10
H yourselves, therefore, 1 Pt 5:6

HUMBLED
exalts himself will be **h**, Mt 23:12
he **h** himself by becoming Phil 2:8

HUMBLES
Whoever **h** himself like this Mt 18:4
be humbled, and whoever **h** Mt 23:12

HUMBLY
love kindness, and to walk **h** Mi 6:8

HUMILITY
in wisdom, and **h** comes Prv 15:33
heart is haughty, but **h** Prv 18:12
with all **h** and gentleness, Eph 4:2
rivalry or conceit, but in **h** Phil 2:3
h, meekness, and patience, Col 3:12
yourselves, all of you, with **h** 1 Pt 5:5

HUNGER
they shall not **h** or thirst, Is 49:10
"Blessed are those who **h** and Mt 5:6
comes to me shall not **h**, Jn 6:35
They shall **h** no more, neither Rv 7:16

HUNGRY
the longing soul, and the **h** Ps 107:9
who gives food to the **h**. Ps 146:7
If your enemy is **h**, give Prv 25:21
gives his bread to the **h** and Ez 18:7
and forty nights, he was **h**. Mt 4:2
For I was **h** and you gave Mt 25:35
"Blessed are you who are **h** Lk 6:21
"if your enemy is **h**, if he is Rom 12:20

HURT
the fire, and they are not **h**; Dn 3:25
who conquers will not be **h** Rv 2:11

HUSBAND
desire shall be for your **h**, Gn 3:16
wife is the crown of her **h**, Prv 12:4
The **h** should give to his 1 Cor 7:3
not separate from her **h** 1 Cor 7:10
and the **h** should not 1 Cor 7:11
If any woman has a **h** 1 Cor 7:13
A wife is bound to her **h** 1 Cor 7:39
I betrothed you to one **h**, 2 Cor 11:2
For the **h** is the head of the Eph 5:23
see that she respects her **h**. Eph 5:33
be above reproach, the **h** 1 Tm 3:2

HUSBANDS
submit to your own **h**, Eph 5:22
H, love your wives, as Eph 5:25
young women to love their **h** Ti 2:4
be subject to your own **h**, 1 Pt 3:1
Likewise, **h**, live with your 1 Pt 3:7

HYMN
when they had sung a **h**, Mt 26:30
when they had sung a **h**, Mk 14:26
each one has a **h**, a lesson, 1 Cor 14:26

HYMNS
praying and singing **h** Acts 16:25
another in psalms and **h** Eph 5:19
singing psalms and **h** and Col 3:16

HYPOCRISY
but within you are full of **h** Mt 23:28
But, knowing their **h**, he Mk 12:15
of the Pharisees, which is **h**. Lk 12:1
was led astray by their **h**. Gal 2:13
malice and all deceit and **h** 1 Pt 2:1

HYPOCRITE
You **h**, first take the log out of Mt 7:5
You **h**, first take the log out Lk 6:42

HYPOCRITES
nor do I consort with **h**. Ps 26:4
you must not be like the **h**. Mt 6:5
put me to the test, you **h**? Mt 22:18

HYSSOP
Purge me with **h**, and I shall Ps 51:7

IDLE
an **i** person will suffer hunger. Prv 19:15
brothers, admonish the **i**, 1 Thes 5:14
because we were not **i** 2 Thes 3:7
from long ago is not **i**, 2 Pt 2:3

IDLENESS
does not eat the bread of **i**. Prv 31:27
who is walking in **i** 2 Thes 3:6
among you walk in **i**, 2 Thes 3:11

IDOL
it he makes into a god, his **i**, Is 44:17
"an **i** has no real existence," 1 Cor 8:4
is anything, or that an **i** 1 Cor 10:19

IDOLATER
or greed, or is an **i**, reviler, 1 Cor 5:11
an **i**), has no inheritance in Eph 5:5

IDOLATERS
greedy and swindlers, or **i**, 1 Cor 5:10
nor **i**, nor adulterers, 1 Cor 6:9
Do not be **i** as some of them 1 Cor 10:7

IDOLATRY
my beloved, flee from **i**. 1 Cor 10:14
i, sorcery, enmity, strife, Gal 5:20
and covetousness, which is **i**. Col 3:5
parties, and lawless **i**. 1 Pt 4:3

IDOLS
Do not turn to **i** or make for Lv 19:4
concerning food offered to **i**: 1 Cor 8:1
That food offered to **i** 1 Cor 10:19
you turned to God from **i** 1 Thes 1:9
keep yourselves from **i**. 1 Jn 5:21

IGNORANCE
life of God because of the **i** Eph 4:18
passions of your former **i**, 1 Pt 1:14
should put to silence the **i** 1 Pt 2:15

IGNORANT
being **i** of the righteousness Rom 10:3
we do not want you to be **i**, 2 Cor 1:8
with foolish, **i** controversies; 2 Tm 2:23
to understand, which the **i** 2 Pt 3:16

IGNORES
at once, but the prudent **i** Prv 12:16
disgrace come to him who **i** Prv 13:18
Whoever **i** instruction Prv 15:32

IMAGE
"Let us make man in our **i**, Gn 1:26
created man in his own **i**, Gn 1:27
in the **i** of God he created him Gn 1:27
his own likeness, after his **i**, Gn 5:3
God made man in his own **i**. Gn 9:6
make for yourself a carved **i**, Ex 20:4
the glory of God for the **i** Ps 106:20
conformed to the **i** of his Son, Rom 8:29
we shall also bear the **i** 1 Cor 15:49
glory of Christ, who is the **i** 2 Cor 4:4
He is the **i** of the invisible Col 1:15
in knowledge after the **i** Col 3:10

IMAGES
of the immortal God for **i** Rom 1:23

IMITATE
ourselves an example to **i**. 2 Thes 3:9
of their way of life, and **i** Heb 13:7
do not imitate evil but **i** 3 Jn 1:11

IMITATORS
I urge you, then, be **i** of me. 1 Cor 4:16
Be **i** of me, as I am of Christ. 1 Cor 11:1

INVITED
Blessed are those who are **i** Rv 19:9

INVITES
one of the unbelievers **i** 1 Cor 10:27

INWARD
you delight in truth in the **i** Ps 51:6
For you formed my **i** parts; Ps 139:13

IRON
I sharpens **i**, and one man Prv 27:17
rule them with a rod of **i**. Rv 19:15

IRREVERENT
Have nothing to do with **i**, 1 Tm 4:7
But avoid **i** babble, for it 2 Tm 2:16

IRREVOCABLE
the calling of God are **i**. Rom 11:29

ISAAC
she tells you, for through **I** Gn 21:12
wood in order and bound **I** Gn 22:9
God of Abraham, the God of **I**, Ex 3:6
one man, our forefather **I**, Rom 9:10
he was tested, offered up **I**, Heb 11:17

ISAIAH
sackcloth, to the prophet **I** 2 Kgs 19:2
And the Lord said to **I**, "Go out Is 7:3

ISCARIOT
the Cananaean, and Judas **I**, Mt 10:4

ISHMAEL
You shall call his name **I**, Gn 16:11
Then Abraham took **I** his Gn 17:23
Isaac and **I** his sons buried Gn 25:9

ISRAEL
spoke thus to the people of **I**, Ex 6:9
Then Moses made **I** set out Ex 15:22
Give ear, O Shepherd of **I**, Ps 80:1
And he will redeem **I** from Ps 130:8
I was holy to the Lord, the Jer 2:3
Like a stubborn heifer, **I** Hos 4:16
For **I** has forgotten his Hos 8:14
in an unclean land, and **I** Am 7:17
lost sheep of the house of **I**. Mt 10:6
restore the kingdom to **I**?" Acts 1:6
God has brought to **I** Acts 13:23
I failed to obtain what it Rom 11:7

ITCHING
teaching, but having **i** ears 2 Tm 4:3

JABBOK
crossed the ford of the **J**. Gn 32:22

JACOB
so his name was called **J**. Gn 25:26
J said to his father, "I am Gn 27:19
Then **J** kissed Rachel and Gn 29:11
And **J** was left alone. And a Gn 32:24
Now the sons of **J** were twelve. Gn 35:22

JAMES
J the son of Zebedee and John Mt 4:21
And are not his brothers **J** Mt 13:55
took with him Peter and **J**, Mt 17:1
"Tell these things to **J** Acts 12:17
the other apostles except **J** Gal 1:19

JAPHETH
Noah fathered Shem, Ham, and **J**. Gn 5:32

JARS
have this treasure in **j** of clay, 2 Cor 4:7

JEALOUS
I the Lord your God am a **j** Ex 20:5
name is **J**, is a **j** God), Ex 34:14
is a consuming fire, a **j** God. Dt 4:24
Then the Lord became **j** for his Jl 2:18
I am exceedingly **j** for Jerusalem Zec 1:14
to make my fellow Jews **j**, Rom 11:14

JEALOUSY
For while there is **j** and 1 Cor 3:3
I feel a divine **j** for you, for 2 Cor 11:2
j, fits of anger, rivalries, Gal 5:20

JEHOSHAPHAT
J made ships of Tarshish 1 Kgs 22:48

JEPHTHAH
Now **J** the Gileadite was a Jgs 11:1

JEREMIAH
Lord by the mouth of **J**, 2 Chr 36:21
The words of **J**, the son of Jer 1:1
word of the Lord came to **J** Jer 37:6

JERICHO
When Joshua was by **J**, he Jos 5:13
"Remain at **J** until your 2 Sm 10:5
By faith the walls of **J** fell Heb 11:30

JERUSALEM
the ark of God back to **J**, 2 Sm 15:29
desired to build in **J**, 1 Kgs 9:19
"In **J** will I put my name." 2 Kgs 21:4
And I will stretch over **J** 2 Kgs 21:13
He carried away all **J** 2 Kgs 24:14
the house of the Lord in **J**, 1 Chr 6:32
So I went to **J** and was Neh 2:11
Speak tenderly to **J**, and cry to Is 40:2
O **J**, the holy city; for there Is 52:1
I create **J** to be a joy, and her Is 65:18
J has become a filthy thing Lam 1:17
and will again choose **J**." Zec 2:12
troubled, and all **J** with him; Mt 2:3
we are going up to **J**. And the Mt 20:18
"O **J**, **J**, the city that Mt 23:37
when they drew near to **J**, Mk 11:1
for the redemption of **J**. Lk 2:38
boy Jesus stayed behind in **J**. Lk 2:43
but you say that in **J** is the Jn 4:20
will be my witnesses in **J** Acts 1:8
and elders who were in **J**. Acts 16:4
so that from **J** and all the Rom 15:19
the heavenly **J**, and to Heb 12:22
the new **J**, which comes down Rv 3:12
showed me the holy city **J** Rv 21:10

JESSE
And **J** said to David his 1 Sm 17:17
a shoot from the stump of **J**, Is 11:1
"The root of **J** will come, Rom 15:12

JESUS
The book of the genealogy of **J** Mt 1:1
and you shall call his name **J**, Mt 1:21
Then **J** was led up by the Spirit Mt 4:1
These twelve **J** sent out, Mt 10:5
heard about the fame of **J**, Mt 14:1
And after six days **J** took with Mt 17:1
together in order to arrest **J** Mt 26:4
false testimony against **J** Mt 26:59
But **J** remained silent. And Mt 26:63
"This man was with **J** of Mt 26:71
or **J** who is called Christ?" Mt 27:17
"This is **J**, the King of the Jews." Mt 27:37
And **J** cried out again with a Mt 27:50
And **J** came and said to them, Mt 28:18
beginning of the gospel of **J** Mk 1:1
"**J**, Son of David, have mercy Mk 10:47
And at the ninth hour **J** Mk 15:34
And **J** increased in wisdom Lk 2:52
He drew near to **J** to kiss him, Lk 22:47
and truth came through **J** Jn 1:17
J wept. Jn 11:35
the soldiers had crucified **J**, Jn 19:23
I have dealt with all that **J** Acts 1:1
This **J** God raised up, and of Acts 2:32
"I am **J**, whom you are persecuting. Acts 9:5
the grace of the Lord **J**, Acts 15:11
"Believe in the Lord **J**, Acts 16:31
"This **J**, whom I proclaim to Acts 17:3
"**J** I know, and Paul Acts 19:15
'I am **J** of Nazareth, whom Acts 22:8
that is in Christ **J**, Rom 3:24
life through the one man **J** Rom 5:17
those who are in Christ **J**. Rom 8:1
with your mouth that **J** Rom 10:9
among you except **J** 1 Cor 2:2
J Christ, through whom are 1 Cor 8:6
and no one can say "**J** 1 Cor 12:3
but **J** Christ as Lord, with 2 Cor 4:5
so that the life of **J** also may 2 Cor 4:11
law but through faith in **J** Gal 2:16
you are all one in Christ **J**. Gal 3:28
For in Christ **J** neither Gal 5:6
created in Christ **J** for good Eph 2:10
J himself being the cornerstone, Eph 2:20
to completion at the day of **J** Phil 1:6
which is yours in Christ **J**, Phil 2:5
so that at the name of **J** Phil 2:10
in the name of the Lord **J**, Col 3:17
the coming of our Lord **J** 2 Thes 2:1
that Christ **J** came into the 1 Tm 1:15
live a godly life in Christ **J** 2 Tm 3:12
of our great God and Savior **J** Ti 2:13
namely **J**, crowned with glory Heb 2:9
consider **J**, the apostle and Heb 3:1
J, the Son of God, let us hold Heb 4:14
This makes **J** the guarantor Heb 7:22
looking to **J**, the founder and Heb 12:2
through the resurrection of **J** 1 Pt 1:3
and coming of our Lord **J** 2 Pt 1:16
and the blood of **J** his Son 1 Jn 1:7
J Christ the righteous. 1 Jn 2:1
Whoever confesses that **J** 1 Jn 4:15
The revelation of **J** Christ, Rv 1:1
quickly," Amen. Come, Lord **J**! Rv 22:20

JETHRO
J, the priest of Midian, and he Ex 3:1
Moses went back to **J** his Ex 4:18

JEW
take hold of the robe of a **J**, Zec 8:23
the **J** first and also to the Greek. Rom 1:16
is no distinction between **J** Rom 10:12
the Jews I became as a **J**, 1 Cor 9:20
There is neither **J** nor Greek, Gal 3:28
there is not Greek and **J**, Col 3:11

JEWELS
She is more precious than **j**, Prv 3:15
adorns herself with her **j**. Is 61:10
for like the **j** of a crown they Zec 9:16

JEWS
has been born king of the **J**? Mt 2:2
"Are you the King of the **J**?" Mt 27:11
for salvation is from the **J**. Jn 4:22
Or is God the God of **J** only? Rom 3:29
For **J** demand signs and 1 Cor 1:22
To the **J** I became as a Jew, 1 Cor 9:20
J or Greeks, slaves or free 1 Cor 12:13
the Gentiles to live like **J**?" Gal 2:14
Satan who say that they are **J** Rv 3:9

JEZEBEL
Ahab told **J** all that Elijah 1 Kgs 19:1
whom **J** his wife incited. 1 Kgs 21:25

JOB
land of Uz whose name was **J**, Jb 1:1
and **J**, were in it, they would Ez 14:14
of the steadfastness of **J**, Jas 5:11

JOEL
of his firstborn son was **J**, 1 Sm 8:2
J the son of Zichri was their Neh 11:9
word of the Lord that came to **J**, Jl 1:1

JOHN
In those days **J** the Baptist Mt 3:1
Now when he heard that **J** Mt 4:12
Zebedee, and **J** his brother; Mt 10:2
"Go and tell **J** what you hear Mt 11:4
He sent and had **J** beheaded Mt 14:10
"Some say **J** the Baptist, Mt 16:14
from God, whose name was **J**. Jn 1:6
Now Peter and **J** were going Acts 3:1
to take with them **J** Acts 15:37
James and Cephas and **J**, Gal 2:9
I **J** am the one who heard and Rv 22:8

JOIN
and do not **j** with those who Prv 24:21
And I will **j** with it the stick Ez 37:19
And many nations shall **j** Zec 2:11
j in imitating me, and keep Phil 3:17
surprised when you do not **j** 1 Pt 4:4

JOINED
What therefore God has **j** Mt 19:6
But he who is **j** to the Lord 1 Cor 6:17
being **j** together, grows into a Eph 2:21
j and held together by every Eph 4:16
father and mother and be **j** Eph 5:31

JOINTS
knit together through its **j** Col 2:19
of **j** and of marrow, and Heb 4:12

JOKING
nor foolish talk nor crude **j**, Eph 5:4

JONAH
But **J** rose to flee to Tarshish — Jon 1:3
a great fish to swallow up **J**. — Jon 1:17
the sign of the prophet **J**. — Mt 12:39

JONATHAN
And Saul and **J** his son — 1 Sm 13:16
"Shall **J** die, who has — 1 Sm 14:45
Then **J** made a covenant — 1 Sm 18:3
And **J** spoke well of David — 1 Sm 19:4
"**J** lies slain on your high places. — 2 Sm 1:25

JORDAN
of you will pass over the **J** — Nm 32:21
gave you beyond the **J**, — Jos 1:14
them that the waters of the **J** — Jos 4:7
"Go and wash in the **J** — 2 Kgs 5:10
and fled; **J** turned back. — Ps 114:3
baptized by him in the river **J**, — Mt 3:6
place in Bethany across the **J**, — Jn 1:28

JOSEPH
of Rachel: **J** and Benjamin. — Gn 35:24
Now Israel loved **J** more than — Gn 37:3
So when **J** came to his — Gn 37:23
Now **J** was handsome in form — Gn 39:6
And **J** stored up grain in — Gn 41:49
So **J** went up to bury his — Gn 50:7
and Jacob the father of **J** the — Mt 1:16
Mary had been betrothed to **J**, — Mt 1:18
And **J** took the body and — Mt 27:59

JOSHUA
So Moses said to **J**, "Choose — Ex 17:9
And **J** the son of Nun, the — Nm 11:28
J the son of Nun, who stands — Dt 1:38
the Lord said to **J** the son of — Jos 1:1

JOSIAH
J by name, and he shall — 1 Kgs 13:2
J put away the mediums — 2 Kgs 23:24
people of the land made **J** — 2 Chr 33:25
the Lord came in the days of **J** — Jer 1:2

JOY
and rejoicing with great **j**, — 1 Kgs 1:40
strength and **j** are in his place. — 1 Chr 16:27
the **j** of the Lord is your strength — Neh 8:10
the sons of God shouted for **j**? — Jb 38:7
You have put more **j** in my — Ps 4:7
you make him glad with the **j** — Ps 21:6
but **j** comes with the morning. — Ps 30:5
to God my exceeding **j**, and I — Ps 43:4
Restore to me the **j** of your — Ps 51:12
Shout for **j** to God, all the earth; — Ps 66:1
of your hands I sing for **j**. — Ps 92:4
for they are the **j** of my heart. — Ps 119:111
of the righteous brings **j**, — Prv 10:28
who plan peace have **j**. — Prv 12:20
everlasting **j** shall be upon — Is 35:10
j and gladness will be found in — Is 51:3
"For you shall go out in **j** — Is 55:12
take **j** in the God of my salvation. — Hb 3:18
in my womb leaped for **j**. — Lk 1:44
you good news of a great **j** — Lk 2:10
and that your **j** may be full. — Jn 15:11
and no one will take your **j** — Jn 16:22
j, peace, patience, kindness, — Gal 5:22
complete my **j** by being of the — Phil 2:2
my **j** and crown, stand firm — Phil 4:1
with the **j** of the Holy Spirit, — 1 Thes 1:6
Let them do this with **j** — Heb 13:17
Count it all **j**, my brothers, — Jas 1:2
in him and rejoice with **j** — 1 Pt 1:8
these things so that our **j** — 1 Jn 1:4

JOYFUL
let us make a **j** noise to the — Ps 95:1
Make a **j** noise to the Lord, all — Ps 98:4
Make a **j** noise to the Lord, — Ps 100:1
A **j** heart is good medicine, — Prv 17:22

JUDAH
she called his name **J**. — Gn 29:35
And **J** said to Israel his — Gn 43:8

JUDAS
and **J** Iscariot, who betrayed him. — Mt 10:4
After him **J** the Galilean rose — Acts 5:37

JUDE
J, a servant of Jesus Christ — Jude 1:1

JUDEA
was born in Bethlehem of **J** — Mt 2:1
king of **J**, there was a priest — Lk 1:5
in Jerusalem and in all **J** — Acts 1:8
from the unbelievers in **J**, — Rom 15:31
Christ Jesus that are in **J**. — 1 Thes 2:14

JUDGE
Shall not the **J** of all the — Gn 18:25
for he comes to **j** the earth. — 1 Chr 16:33
God is a righteous **j**, and a God — Ps 7:11
he will **j** the peoples with equity — Ps 96:10
for there I will sit to **j** all the — Jl 3:12
"**J** not, that you be not judged. — Mt 7:1
for I did not come to **j** the — Jn 12:47
a day on which he will **j** — Acts 17:31
j, practice the very same things. — Rom 2:1
fact, I do not even **j** myself. — 1 Cor 4:3
know that the saints will **j** — 1 Cor 6:2
who is to **j** the living and the — 2 Tm 4:1
the righteous **j**, will award to — 2 Tm 4:8
is only one lawgiver and **j**, — Jas 4:12
to him who is ready to **j** — 1 Pt 4:5
to whom the authority to **j** — Rv 20:4

JUDGED
"Judge not, that you be not **j**. — Mt 7:1
under the law will be **j** — Rom 2:12
But if we **j** ourselves — 1 Cor 11:31
that we who teach will be **j** — Jas 3:1
And the dead were **j** by what — Rv 20:12

JUDGES
Then the Lord raised up **j**, — Jgs 2:16
surely there is a God who **j** — Ps 58:11
God **j** the secrets of men by — Rom 2:16
It is the Lord who **j** me. — 1 Cor 4:4
call on him as Father who **j** — 1 Pt 1:17
and in righteousness he **j** — Rv 19:11

JUDGMENT
for the **j** is God's. And the case — Dt 1:17
wicked will not stand in the **j**, — Ps 1:5
but it is God who executes **j**, — Ps 75:7
Teach me good **j** and — Ps 119:66
bring every deed into **j**, — Eccl 12:14
will the Lord enter into **j**, — Is 66:16
murders will be liable to **j**.' — Mt 5:21
bearable on the day of **j** — Mt 10:15
on the day of **j** people will — Mt 12:36
but has given all **j** to the Son, — Jn 5:22
but judge with right **j**." — Jn 7:24
sin and righteousness and **j**: — Jn 16:8
We know that the **j** of God — Rom 2:2
God's righteous **j** will be revealed — Rom 2:5
who resist will incur **j**. — Rom 13:2
will all stand before the **j** seat — Rom 14:10
Therefore let us not pass **j** — Rom 14:13
body eats and drinks **j** — 1 Cor 11:29
all appear before the **j** seat — 2 Cor 5:10
Therefore let no one pass **j** — Col 2:16
and after that comes **j**, — Heb 9:27
a fearful expectation of **j**, — Heb 10:27
Mercy triumphs over **j**. — Jas 2:13
For it is time for **j** to begin at — 1 Pt 4:17
until the day of **j**, — 2 Pt 2:9
gloomy darkness until the **j** — Jude 1:6

JUST
iniquity, **j** and upright is he. — Dt 32:4
his hands are faithful and **j**; — Ps 111:7
of the righteous are **j**; — Prv 12:5
and does what is **j** — Ez 18:27
are right and his ways are **j**; — Dn 4:37
so that he might be **j** and — Rom 3:26
whatever is **j**, whatever is — Phil 4:8
or disobedience received a **j** — Heb 2:2
he is faithful and **j** to forgive — 1 Jn 1:9
his judgments are true and **j**; — Rv 19:2

JUSTICE
He executes **j** for the — Dt 10:18
You shall not pervert **j**. You — Dt 16:19
j and abundant righteousness — Jb 37:23
He loves righteousness and **j**; — Ps 33:5
For the Lord loves **j**; he will — Ps 37:28
sing of steadfast love and **j**; — Ps 101:1
are they who observe **j**, — Ps 106:3
When **j** is done, it is a joy to — Prv 21:15
men do not understand **j**, — Prv 28:5
seek **j**, correct oppression; — Is 1:17
And I will make **j** the line, — Is 28:17
For the Lord is a God of **j**; — Is 30:18
he will bring forth **j** to the nations. — Is 42:1
and I will set my **j** for a light — Is 51:4
For I the Lord love **j**; I hate — Is 61:8
I will feed them in **j**. — Ez 34:16
and establish **j** in the gate; it — Am 5:15
But let **j** roll down like — Am 5:24
Lord require of you but to do **j**, — Mi 6:8
j and mercy and faithfulness. — Mt 23:23
and neglect **j** and the love of — Lk 11:42
enforced **j**, obtained — Heb 11:33

JUSTIFICATION
and raised for our **j**. — Rom 4:25
many trespasses brought **j**. — Rom 5:16
of righteousness leads to **j** — Rom 5:18
for if **j** were through the law, — Gal 2:21

JUSTIFIED
so that you may be **j** in your — Ps 51:4
of the law who will be **j**. — Rom 2:13
no human being will be **j** — Rom 3:20
and are **j** by his grace as a — Rom 3:24
For we hold that one is **j** — Rom 3:28
For if Abraham was **j** by — Rom 4:2
since we have been **j** by faith, — Rom 5:1
we have now been **j** by his — Rom 5:9
whom he called he also **j**, — Rom 8:30
whom he **j** he also glorified. — Rom 8:30
heart one believes and is **j**, — Rom 10:10
you were **j** in the name of — 1 Cor 6:11
know that a person is not **j** — Gal 2:16
in order to be **j** by faith in — Gal 2:16
of the law no one will be **j**. — Gal 2:16
in our endeavor to be **j** in — Gal 2:17
it is evident that no one is **j** — Gal 3:11
in order that we might be **j** — Gal 3:24
you who would be **j** by the — Gal 5:4
so that being **j** by his grace we — Ti 3:7
not Abraham our father **j** — Jas 2:21
You see that a person is **j** — Jas 2:24
also Rahab the prostitute **j** — Jas 2:25

JUSTIFIER
he might be just and the **j** — Rom 3:26

JUSTIFIES
He who **j** the wicked and he — Prv 17:15
work but trusts him who **j** — Rom 4:5
elect? It is God who **j**. — Rom 8:33

JUSTIFY
He will **j** the circumcised by — Rom 3:30
foreseeing that God would **j** — Gal 3:8

JUSTLY
himself to him who judges **j**. — 1 Pt 2:23

KEEP
of Eden to work it and **k** it. — Gn 2:15
you shall **k** my covenant, — Gn 17:9
me and **k** my commandments. — Ex 20:6
the Sabbath day, to **k** it holy. — Ex 20:8
The Lord bless you and **k** — Nm 6:24
you may **k** the commandments — Dt 4:2
to fear me and to **k** all my — Dt 5:29
K back your servant also — Ps 19:13
Blessed are those who **k** his — Ps 119:2
all evil; he will **k** your life. — Ps 121:7
k watch over the door of my — Ps 141:3
You **k** him in perfect peace — Is 26:3
life, **k** the commandments." — Mt 19:17
and **k** your lamps burning, — Lk 12:35
"If you love me, you will **k** — Jn 14:15
K watch on yourself, lest you — Gal 6:1
but let us **k** awake and be — 1 Thes 5:6
of others; **k** yourself pure. — 1 Tm 5:22
K your life free from love of — Heb 13:5
K your conduct among the — 1 Pt 2:12
that we **k** his commandments. — 1 Jn 5:3
to **k** you from stumbling — Jude 1:24

KEEPER
know; am I my brother's **k**?" — Gn 4:9

KEEPING
k steadfast love for — Ex 34:7
by **k** all his statutes and his — Dt 6:2
in **k** them there is great — Ps 19:11
Bear fruit in **k** with — Mt 3:8
k watch over their flock by — Lk 2:8
but **k** the commandments — 1 Cor 7:19
for they are **k** watch over — Heb 13:17

KEEPS
the faithful God who **k** Dt 7:9
He **k** all his bones; not one Ps 34:20
Even a fool who **k** silent is Prv 17:28
but blessed is he who **k** the Prv 29:18
commandments and **k** them, Jn 14:21
For whoever **k** the whole Jas 2:10
No one who abides in him **k** 1 Jn 3:6

KEPT
For when I **k** silent, my Ps 32:3
the race, I have **k** the faith. 2 Tm 4:7
k in heaven for you, 1 Pt 1:4

KEYS
I will give you the **k** of the Mt 16:19
and I have the **k** of Death Rv 1:18

KILL
a time to **k**, and a time to Eccl 3:3
and they will **k** him, and he Mt 17:23

KILLED
and you **k** the Author of Acts 3:15
me and through it **k** me. Rom 7:11
we are being **k** all the day Rom 8:36

KILLS
and whoever **k** a person Lv 24:21
For the letter **k**, but the 2 Cor 3:6

KIND
his words and **k** in all his Ps 145:13
A man who is **k** benefits Prv 11:17
for he is **k** to the ungrateful Lk 6:35
Love is patient and **k**; love 1 Cor 13:4
Be **k** to one another, Eph 4:32
but **k** to everyone, 2 Tm 2:24
pure, working at home, **k**, that Ti 2:5

KINDNESS
"He who withholds **k** from a Jb 6:14
and **k** will find life, Prv 21:21
and the teaching of **k** is on Prv 31:26
I led them with cords of **k**, Hos 11:4
but to do justice, and to love **k**, Mi 6:8
show **k** and mercy to one Zec 7:9
of his **k** and forbearance and Rom 2:4
fallen, but God's **k** to you, Rom 11:22
patience, **k**, the Holy Spirit, 2 Cor 6:6
k, goodness, faithfulness, Gal 5:22
of his grace in **k** toward us in Eph 2:7
k, humility, meekness, Col 3:12
and loving **k** of God our Ti 3:4

KINDS
according to their own **k**, Gn 1:12
produced in me all **k** of Rom 7:8
to another various **k** of 1 Cor 12:10
is a root of all **k** of evils. 1 Tm 6:10
you meet trials of various **k**, Jas 1:2
knowing that the same **k** of 1 Pt 5:9

KING
In those days there was no **k** Jgs 17:6
your God was your **k**. 1 Sm 12:12
that the **K** of glory may come Ps 24:7
the Lord sits enthroned as **k** Ps 29:10
For God is the **K** of all the Ps 47:7
Behold, a **k** will reign in Is 32:1
your **k** is coming to you; Zec 9:9
has been born **k** of the Jews? Mt 2:2
it is the city of the great **K**. Mt 5:35
your **k** is coming to you, and Mt 21:5
"Are you the **K** of the Mt 27:11
is Jesus, the **K** of the Jews." Mt 27:37
saying, "Blessed is the **K** Lk 19:38
he himself is Christ, a **k**." Lk 23:2
You are the **K** of Israel!" Jn 1:49
"You say that I am a **k**. For Jn 18:37
"We have no **k** but Caesar." Jn 19:15
To the **K** of ages, immortal, 1 Tm 1:17
the **K** of kings and Lord of 1 Tm 6:15
K of kings and Lord of lords. Rv 19:16

KINGDOM
and you shall be to me a **k** of Ex 19:6
Yours is the **k**, O Lord, 1 Chr 29:11
The scepter of your **k** is a Ps 45:6
Your **k** is an everlasting Ps 145:13
His **k** is an everlasting Dn 4:3
"Repent, for the **k** of heaven is Mt 3:2
for theirs is the **k** of heaven. Mt 5:3
Your **k** come, your will be Mt 6:10
But seek first the **k** of God Mt 6:33
will enter the **k** of heaven, Mt 7:21
is least in the **k** of heaven is Mt 11:11
"The **k** of heaven may be Mt 13:23
"The **k** of heaven is like a grain Mt 13:31
"The **k** of heaven is like leaven Mt 13:33
"The **k** of heaven is like treasure Mt 13:44
"Again, the **k** of heaven is Mt 13:45
"Again, the **k** of heaven is Mt 13:47
the keys of the **k** of heaven, Mt 16:19
"Therefore the **k** of heaven Mt 18:23
to enter the **k** of God." Mt 19:24
"For the **k** of heaven is like a Mt 20:1
and **k** against kingdom, Mt 24:7
And this gospel of the **k** Mt 24:14
inherit the **k** prepared for Mt 25:34
to enter the **k** of God with Mk 9:47
for to such belongs the **k** of Mk 10:14
'The **k** of God has come near Lk 10:9
Instead, seek his **k**, and Lk 12:31
for behold, the **k** of God is Lk 17:21
he cannot enter the **k** of God. Jn 3:5
"My **k** is not of this world. Jn 18:36
For the **k** of God is not a Rom 14:17
For the **k** of God does not 1 Cor 4:20
inherit the **k** of God, 1 Cor 15:50
is the scepter of your **k**. Heb 1:8
a **k** that cannot be shaken, Heb 12:28
and made us a **k**, priests to his Rv 1:6
"The **k** of the world has Rv 11:15

KINGS
The **k** of the earth set Ps 2:2
May all **k** fall down before Ps 72:11
and all the **k** of the earth Ps 102:15
is God of gods and Lord of **k**, Dn 2:47
for **k** and all who are in 1 Tm 2:2
the King of **k** and Lord of 1 Tm 6:15
and the ruler of **k** on earth. Rv 1:5

KINGSHIP
For **k** belongs to the Lord, Ps 22:28

KISS
K the Son, lest he be angry, Ps 2:12
righteousness and peace **k** Ps 85:10
the Son of Man with a **k**?" Lk 22:48

KNEE
'To me every **k** shall bow, Is 45:23
not bowed the **k** to Baal." Rom 11:4
every **k** shall bow to me, Rom 14:11
Jesus every **k** should bow, Phil 2:10

KNEES
and make firm the feeble **k**. Is 35:3
For this reason I bow my **k** Eph 3:14
strengthen your weak **k**, Heb 12:12

KNEW
Now Adam **k** Eve his wife, Gn 4:1
you in the womb I **k** you, Jer 1:5
for I **k** that you are a Jon 4:2
to them, 'I never **k** you; you Mt 7:23
For although they **k** God, Rom 1:21
to be sin who **k** no sin, 2 Cor 5:21

KNOCK
seek, and you will find; **k**, and it Mt 7:7
I stand at the door and **k**. Rv 3:20

KNOW
"**K** for certain that your Gn 15:13
K then in your heart that, Dt 8:5
For I **k** that my Redeemer Jb 19:25
"I **k** that you can do all Jb 42:2
Make me to **k** your ways, O Ps 25:4
still, and **k** that I am God. Ps 46:10
For I **k** my transgressions, Ps 51:3
me, O God, and **k** my heart! Ps 139:23
for you do not **k** what a day Prv 27:1
And I applied my heart to **k** Eccl 1:17
I will give them a heart to **k** Jer 24:7
saying, '**K** the Lord,' from the Jer 31:34
do not let your left hand **k** Mt 6:3
for you do not **k** on what Mt 24:42
yet the world did not **k** him. Jn 1:10
you, we speak of what we **k**, Jn 3:11
we worship what we **k**, Jn 4:22
One thing I do **k**, that though Jn 9:25
my own and my own **k** me, Jn 10:14
that they **k** you the only true Jn 17:3
and we **k** that his testimony Jn 21:24
"It is not for you to **k** times Acts 1:7
therefore **k** for certain that Acts 2:36
We **k** that our old self was Rom 6:6
For I **k** that nothing good Rom 7:18
And we **k** that for those Rom 8:28
For I decided to **k** nothing 1 Cor 2:2
Do you not **k** that your 1 Cor 6:15
Or do you not **k** that your 1 Cor 6:19
part; then I shall **k** fully, 1 Cor 13:12
yet we **k** that a person is not Gal 2:16
that you may **k** what is the Eph 1:18
and to **k** the love of Christ Eph 3:19
that I may **k** him and the Phil 3:10
for I **k** whom I have 2 Tm 1:12
yet you do not **k** what Jas 4:14
And by this we **k** that we 1 Jn 2:3
Whoever says "I **k** him" but 1 Jn 2:4
We **k** that we have passed 1 Jn 3:14
By this we **k** love, that he 1 Jn 3:16
And by this we **k** that he 1 Jn 3:24
By this we **k** that we abide 1 Jn 4:13
By this we **k** that we love 1 Jn 5:2
you may **k** that you have 1 Jn 5:13
we **k** that we have the 1 Jn 5:15
We **k** that we are from God, 1 Jn 5:19

KNOWING
be like God, **k** good and evil." Gn 3:5
k that suffering produces Rom 5:3
worth of **k** Christ Jesus my Phil 3:8

KNOWLEDGE
and the tree of the **k** of good Gn 2:9
counsel by words without **k**? Jb 38:2
and night to night reveals **k**. Ps 19:2
Is there **k** in the Most Ps 73:11
Such **k** is too wonderful for Ps 139:6
Lord is the beginning of **k**; Prv 1:7
The wise lay up **k**, but the Prv 10:14
loves discipline loves **k**, Prv 12:1
the prudent acts with **k**, Prv 13:16
has understanding seeks **k**, Prv 15:14
restrains his words has **k**, Prv 17:27
Desire without **k** is not good, Prv 19:2
be full of the **k** of the Lord Is 11:9
filled with the **k** of the glory Hb 2:14
and wisdom and **k** of God! Rom 11:33
This "**k**" puffs up, but love 1 Cor 8:1
And so by your **k** this 1 Cor 8:11
all mysteries and all **k**, 1 Cor 13:2
the **k** of him everywhere. 2 Cor 2:14
of Christ that surpasses **k**, Eph 3:19
treasures of wisdom and **k**. Col 2:3
what is falsely called "**k**," 1 Tm 6:20
But grow in the grace and **k** 2 Pt 3:18

KNOWN
Make them **k** to your children Dt 4:9
You make **k** to me the path Ps 16:11
The Lord has made **k** his Ps 98:2
make **k** his deeds among the Ps 105:1
make **k** his deeds among the Is 12:4
I will make **k** in the midst Ez 39:7
or hidden that will not be **k**. Mt 10:26
side, he has made him **k**. Jn 1:18
For what can be **k** about Rom 1:19
I would not have **k** what it Rom 7:7
"For who has **k** the mind Rom 11:34
loves God, he is **k** by God. 1 Cor 8:3
to be **k** and read by all. 2 Cor 3:2
God, or rather to be **k** by God, Gal 4:9
requests be made **k** to God. Phil 4:6
never to have **k** the way of 2 Pt 2:21

KNOWS
But he **k** the way that I take; Jb 23:10
for the Lord **k** the way of the Ps 1:6
For he **k** the secrets of the Ps 44:21
k the thoughts of man, that Ps 94:11
he **k** what is in the darkness, Dn 2:22
he **k** those who take refuge in Na 1:7
for your Father **k** what you Mt 6:8
that day and hour no one **k**, Mt 24:36
hearts **k** what is the mind Rom 8:27
imagines that he **k** something, 1 Cor 8:2
"The Lord **k** those who are 2 Tm 2:19
So whoever **k** the right Jas 4:17
been born of God and **k** God. 1 Jn 4:7

KORAH
and he said to **K** and all his Nm 16:5
from the dwelling of **K**, Nm 16:24

Aaron in the company of **K**, Nm 26:9

LABAN

brother whose name was **L**. Gn 24:29

LABOR

Six days you shall **l**, and do Ex 20:9
fruit of the **l** of your hands; Ps 128:2
and your **l** for that which Is 55:2
Come to me, all who **l** and Mt 11:28
wages according to his **l**. 1 Cor 3:8
the Lord your **l** is not in 1 Cor 15:58
not run in vain or **l** in vain. Phil 2:16

LABORER

Sweet is the sleep of a **l**, Eccl 5:12
"The **l** deserves his wages." 1 Tm 5:18

LACK

the Lord **l** no good thing. Ps 34:10
but fools die for **l** of sense. Prv 10:21
of your **l** of self-control. 1 Cor 7:5

LACKING

and complete, **l** in nothing. Jas 1:4

LACKS

He who commits adultery **l** Prv 6:32
worthless pursuits **l** sense. Prv 12:11
If any of you **l** wisdom, let Jas 1:5

LAID

and the Lord has **l** on him Is 53:6
other than that which is **l**, 1 Cor 3:11
that he **l** down his life for 1 Jn 3:16

LAKE

alive into the **l** of fire that Rv 19:20
thrown into the **l** of fire. Rv 20:14

LAMB

for himself the **l** for a burnt Gn 22:8
and kill the Passover **l**. Ex 12:21
wolf shall dwell with the **l**, Is 11:6
like a **l** that is led to the Is 53:7
said, "Behold, the **L** of God, Jn 1:29
like a **l** before its shearer Acts 8:32
For Christ, our Passover **l**, 1 Cor 5:7
like that of a **l** without 1 Pt 1:19
the elders I saw a **L** standing, Rv 5:6
"Worthy is the **L** who was Rv 5:12
It is these who follow the **L** Rv 14:4

LAMBS

I am sending you out as **l** in Lk 10:3
He said to him, "Feed my **l**." Jn 21:15

LAMB'S

written in the **L** book of life. Rv 21:27

LAME

their sight and the **l** walk, Mt 11:5
to enter life **l** than with two Mk 9:45
so that what is **l** may not Heb 12:13

LAMP

For you are my **l**, O Lord, 2 Sm 22:29
For it is you who light my **l**; Ps 18:28
Your word is a **l** to my Ps 119:105
For the commandment is a **l** Prv 6:23
Nor do people light a **l** and Mt 5:15
"The eye is the **l** of the body. Mt 6:22
was a burning and shining **l**, Jn 5:35
as to a **l** shining in a 2 Pt 1:19
light, and its **l** is the Lamb. Rv 21:23

LAMPS

who took their **l** and went to Mt 25:1
and keep your **l** burning, Lk 12:35

LAND

and let the dry **l** appear." And Gn 1:9
God called the dry **l** Earth, Gn 1:10
offspring I will give this **l**." Gn 12:7
a **l** flowing with milk and Ex 3:8
You shall not pollute the **l** Nm 35:33
that you may do them in the **l** Dt 6:1
Lord showed him all the **l**, Dt 34:1
their sin and heal their **l**. 2 Chr 7:14
Lord in the **l** of the living. Ps 116:9
upright will inhabit the **l**, Prv 2:21
off out of the **l** of the living, Is 53:8
bring you into your own **l**. Ez 36:24
you may live long in the **l**." Eph 6:3

LANGUAGE

had one **l** and the same Gn 11:1
Lord confused the **l** of all the Gn 11:9
them speak in his own **l**. Acts 2:6
the meaning of the **l**, 1 Cor 14:11
tribe and **l** and people and Rv 5:9

LAODICEA

and for those at **L** and for all Col 2:1
also read the letter from **L**. Col 4:16

LAST

first, and with the **l**; I am he. Is 41:4
"I am the first and I am the **l**; Is 44:6
many who are first will be **l**, Mt 19:30
he must be **l** of all and Mk 9:35
raise him up on the **l** day." Jn 6:40
will judge him on the **l** day. Jn 12:48
the **l** Adam became a 1 Cor 15:45
that in the **l** days there will 2 Tm 3:1
but in these **l** days he has Heb 1:2
laid up treasure in the **l** days. Jas 5:3
to be revealed in the **l** time. 1 Pt 1:5
Children, it is the **l** hour, 1 Jn 2:18
They said to you, "In the **l** Jude 1:18
not, I am the first and the **l**, Rv 1:17
Omega, the first and the **l**, Rv 22:13

LATTER

It shall come to pass in the **l** Is 2:2
to his goodness in the **l** days. Hos 3:5
It shall come to pass in the **l** Mi 4:1

LAUGH

time to weep, and a time to **l**; Eccl 3:4
weep now, for you shall **l**. Lk 6:21

LAUGHS

He who sits in the heavens **l**; Ps 2:4
but the Lord **l** at the wicked, Ps 37:13

LAUGHTER

said, "God has made **l** for me; Gn 21:6
our mouth was filled with **l**, Ps 126:2
Let your **l** be turned to Jas 4:9

LAVISHED

which he **l** upon us, in all Eph 1:8

LAW

do all the words of this **l**. Dt 29:29
you shall read this **l** before Dt 31:11
to do all the words of this **l**, Dt 31:12
This Book of the **L** shall not Jos 1:8
from the **l** of God, clearly, Neh 8:8
but his delight is in the **l** of Ps 1:2
The **l** of the Lord is perfect, Ps 19:7
your **l** is within my heart." Ps 40:8
who walk in the **l** of the Ps 119:1
Oh how I love your **l**! It is Ps 119:97
for I do not forget your **l**. Ps 119:153
The one who keeps the **l** is Prv 28:7
for a **l** will go out from me, Is 51:4
I will put my **l** within them, Jer 31:33
abolish the **L** or the Prophets; Mt 5:17
for this is the **L** and the Mt 7:12
all the **L** and the Prophets." Mt 22:40
dot of the **L** to become void. Lk 16:17
For the **l** was given through Jn 1:17
the **l** will also perish Rom 2:12
by nature do what the **l** Rom 2:14
work of the **l** is written on Rom 2:15
For by works of the **l** no Rom 3:20
manifested apart from the **l**, Rom 3:21
apart from works of the **l**. Rom 3:28
For the **l** brings wrath, Rom 4:15
Now the **l** came in to Rom 5:20
passions, aroused by the **l**, Rom 7:5
Apart from the **l**, sin lies Rom 7:8
So the **l** is holy, and the Rom 7:12
For I delight in the **l** of Rom 7:22
flesh I serve the **l** of sin. Rom 7:25
For God has done what the **l**, Rom 8:3
of the **l** for righteousness to Rom 10:4
is the fulfilling of the **l**. Rom 13:10
To those under the **l** I 1 Cor 9:20
the power of sin is the **l**. 1 Cor 15:56
of the **l** but through faith Gal 2:16
For through the **l** I died to Gal 2:19
curse of the **l** by becoming a Gal 3:13
held captive under the **l**, Gal 3:23
So then, the **l** was our Gal 3:24
obligated to keep the whole **l**. Gal 5:3
would be justified by the **l**; Gal 5:4
For the whole **l** is fulfilled Gal 5:14
you are not under the **l**. Gal 5:18
such things there is no **l**. Gal 5:23
by abolishing the **l** of Eph 2:15
own that comes from the **l**, Phil 3:9
(for the **l** made nothing Heb 7:19
who looks into the perfect **l**, Jas 1:25
keeps the whole **l** but fails in Jas 2:10

LAWLESSNESS

leading to more **l**, Rom 6:19
and the man of **l** is 2 Thes 2:3
For the mystery of **l** is 2 Thes 2:7
us from all **l** and to purify Ti 2:14
of sinning also practices **l**; 1 Jn 3:4

LAWS

I will put my **l** into their minds, Heb 8:10
I will put my **l** on their hearts, Heb 10:16

LAY

"You shall therefore **l** up Dt 11:18
and **l** up his words in your Jb 22:22
has nowhere to **l** his head." Mt 8:20
and I **l** down my life for the Jn 10:15
For no one can **l** a foundation 1 Cor 3:11
let us also **l** aside every weight, Heb 12:1
and we ought to **l** down our 1 Jn 3:16

LAYING

I am **l** in Zion a stone of Rom 9:33
Do not be hasty in the **l** 1 Tm 5:22
not **l** again a foundation of Heb 6:1
I am **l** in Zion a stone, and 1 Pt 2:6

LAZARUS

laid a poor man named **L**, Lk 16:20
when he called **L** out of the Jn 12:17

LAZY

liars, evil beasts, **l** gluttons." Ti 1:12

LEAD

of cloud to **l** them along the Ex 13:21
L me, O Lord, in your Ps 5:8
L me in your truth and teach Ps 25:5
and **l** me on a level path Ps 27:11
sake you **l** me and guide Ps 31:3
L me in the path of your Ps 119:35
Let not your mouth **l** you Eccl 5:6
and a little child shall **l** them. Is 11:6
and gently **l** those that are Is 40:11
And **l** us not into temptation, Mt 6:13
And if the blind **l** the blind, Mt 15:14
Only let each person **l** the 1 Cor 7:17
that we may **l** a peaceful 1 Tm 2:2

LEADERS

Remember your **l**, those Heb 13:7
Obey your **l** and submit to Heb 13:17

LEADS

He **l** me beside still waters. Ps 23:2
The fear of the Lord **l** to Prv 19:23
the way is hard that **l** to life, Mt 7:14
by name and **l** them out. Jn 10:3
repentance that **l** to life." Acts 11:18
l to justification and Rom 5:18
of sin, which **l** to death, Rom 6:16
There is sin that **l** to death; 1 Jn 5:16

LEAH

name of the older was **L**, Gn 29:16
loved Rachel more than **L**, Gn 29:30
L went out to meet him Gn 30:16

LEAN

and do not **l** on your own Prv 3:5

LEARN

l to do good; seek justice, bring Is 1:17
upon you, and **l** from me, Mt 11:29

LEARNED

What you have **l** and Phil 4:9
for I have **l** in whatever Phil 4:11
you have **l** and have firmly 2 Tm 3:14

LEARNING

wise hear and increase in **l**, Prv 1:5
always **l** and never able to 2 Tm 3:7

LEAST
Yet the one who is l in the Mt 11:11
For I am the l of the 1 Cor 15:9
though I am the very l of all Eph 3:8
from the l of them to the Heb 8:11

LEAVE
Therefore a man shall l his Gn 2:24
'For this reason a man shall l Mt 19:5
Peace I l with you; my peace Jn 14:27
a man shall l his father and Eph 5:31
"I will never l you nor Heb 13:5

LED
I have l you in the paths of Prv 4:11
like a lamb that is l to the Is 53:7
lamb l to the slaughter. Jer 11:19
I l them with cords of Hos 11:4
For all who are l by the Rom 8:14
But if you are l by the Spirit, Gal 5:18
on high he l a host of Eph 4:8

LEFT
it to the right hand or to the l, Jos 1:7
to the right or to the l; Prv 4:27
do not let your l hand know Mt 6:3
right, but the goats on the l. Mt 25:33

LEGION
He replied, "My name is L, Mk 5:9

LEND
to him and l him sufficient for Dt 15:8
And if you l to those from Lk 6:34

LENDS
to the poor l to the Lord, Prv 19:17

LENGTH
l of days forever and ever. Ps 21:4
for l of days and years of life Prv 3:2
and l and height and Eph 3:18

LESSON
a hymn, a l, a revelation, 1 Cor 14:26

LETTER
by the Spirit, not by the l. Rom 2:29
You yourselves are our l of 2 Cor 3:2
For the l kills, but the 2 Cor 3:6
what we say in this l, 2 Thes 3:14

LETTERS
death, carved in l on stone, 2 Cor 3:7
For they say, "His l are 2 Cor 10:10
as he does in all his l when 2 Pt 3:16

LEVEL
My foot stands on l ground; Ps 26:12
and lead me on a l path Ps 27:11
the upright is a l highway. Prv 15:19
The path of the righteous is l; Is 26:7
places shall become l ways, Lk 3:5

LEVI
his name was called L. Gn 29:34
Simeon and L are brothers; Gn 49:5
sons of L according to their Ex 6:16
To the tribe of L alone Jos 13:14
he saw L the son of Mk 2:14

LIAR
poor man is better than a l. Prv 19:22
for he is a l and the father of Jn 8:44
sinned, we make him a l, 1 Jn 1:10
hates his brother, he is a l; 1 Jn 4:20

LIBERTY
to proclaim l to the captives, Is 61:1
For why should my l be 1 Cor 10:29
the law of l, and perseveres, Jas 1:25
be judged under the law of l. Jas 2:12

LIE
you shall not l to one Lv 19:11
not man, that he should l, Nm 23:19
way, and when you l down, Dt 6:7
He makes me l down in Ps 23:2
A faithful witness does not l, Prv 14:5
and the leopard shall l down Is 11:6
There they shall l down in Ez 34:14
for a l and worshiped and Rom 1:25
Do not l to one another, Col 3:9
it is impossible for God to l, Heb 6:18

LIES
no one who utters l shall Ps 101:7
he is a liar and the father of l. Jn 8:44

LIFE
his nostrils the breath of l, Gn 2:7
the way to the tree of l. Gn 3:24
a reckoning for the l of man. Gn 9:5
then you shall pay l for l, Ex 21:23
For the l of the flesh is in Lv 17:11
shall make it good, l for l. Lv 24:18
Therefore choose l, that you Dt 30:19
"Remember that my l is a Jb 7:7
known to me the path of l; Ps 16:11
follow me all the days of my l, Ps 23:6
desires l and loves many Ps 34:12
the blessing, l forevermore. Ps 133:3
discipline are the way of l, Prv 6:23
that it will cost him his l. Prv 7:23
me finds l and obtains favor Prv 8:35
the righteous is a tree of l, Prv 11:30
and kindness will find l, Prv 21:21
delivered my l from the pit Is 38:17
awake, some to everlasting l, Dn 12:2
not be anxious about your l, Mt 6:25
way is hard that leads to l, Mt 7:14
and whoever loses his l for Mt 10:39
I do to have eternal l?" Mt 19:16
and to give his l as a Mt 20:28
It is better for you to enter l Mk 9:43
for one's l does not consist Lk 12:15
not be anxious about your l, Lk 12:22
and the l was the light of men. Jn 1:4
not perish but have eternal l. Jn 3:16
in the Son has eternal l; Jn 3:36
welling up to eternal l." Jn 4:14
who sent me has eternal l. Jn 5:24
to them, "I am the bread of l; Jn 6:35
believes has eternal l. Jn 6:47
have the words of eternal l, Jn 6:68
I came that they may have l Jn 10:10
down his l for the sheep. Jn 10:11
I give them eternal l, and Jn 10:28
way, and the truth, and the l. Jn 14:6
And this is eternal l, that Jn 17:3
you may have l in his name. Jn 20:31
to eternal l believed. Acts 13:48
who gives l to the dead Rom 4:17
shall we be saved by his l. Rom 5:10
l through Jesus Christ Rom 5:21
brought from death to l, Rom 6:13
is eternal l in Christ Jesus Rom 6:23
that neither death nor l, Rom 8:38
lead the l that the Lord 1 Cor 7:17
kills, but the Spirit gives l. 2 Cor 3:6
And the l I now live in the Gal 2:20
manner of l and is corrupt Eph 4:22
whether by l or by death. Phil 1:20
names are in the book of l. Phil 4:3
When Christ who is your l Col 3:4
Take hold of the eternal l 1 Tm 6:12
in hope of eternal l, which Ti 1:2
Keep your l free from love Heb 13:5
will receive the crown of l, Jas 1:12
to love l and see good 1 Pt 3:10
pertain to l and godliness, 2 Pt 1:3
passed out of death into l, 1 Jn 3:14
that he laid down his l for 1 Jn 3:16
Whoever has the Son has l; 1 Jn 5:12
grant to eat of the tree of l, Rv 2:7
in the book of l of the Lamb Rv 13:8
in the Lamb's book of l. Rv 21:27
the tree of l with its twelve Rv 22:2

LIFT
The Lord l up his Nm 6:26
I l up my eyes to the hills. Ps 121:1
L up your hands to the holy Ps 134:2
Let us l up our hearts and Lam 3:41
I tell you, l up your eyes, Jn 4:35

LIFTED
he shall be high and l up, Is 52:13
And I, when I am l up from Jn 12:32

LIGHT
And God said, "Let there be l," Gn 1:3
God called the l Day, and the Gn 1:5
and when I waited for l, Jb 30:26
Lift up the l of your face upon Ps 4:6
The Lord is my l and my Ps 27:1
before God in the l of life. Ps 56:13
feet and a l to my path. Ps 119:105
let us walk in the l of the Lord. Is 2:5
darkness have seen a great l; Is 9:2
I form l and create darkness, Is 45:7
I will make you as a l for the Is 49:6
on them a l has dawned." Mt 4:16
"You are the l of the world. Mt 5:14
is easy, and my burden is l." Mt 11:30
The l shines in the darkness, Jn 1:5
the l has come into the world, Jn 3:19
"I am the l of the world. Jn 8:12
have the l, believe in the l, Jn 12:36
"'I have made you a l for Acts 13:47
and put on the armor of l. Rom 13:12
give the l of the knowledge 2 Cor 4:6
Or what fellowship has l 2 Cor 6:14
himself as an angel of l. 2 Cor 11:14
that becomes visible is l. Eph 5:14
in unapproachable l, 1 Tm 6:16
into his marvelous l. 1 Pt 2:9
proclaim to you, that God is l, 1 Jn 1:5
But if we walk in the l, as 1 Jn 1:7
his brother abides in the l, 1 Jn 2:10
By its l will the nations Rv 21:24
the Lord God will be their l, Rv 22:5

LIGHTNING
face like the appearance of l, Dn 10:6
For as the l comes from the Mt 24:27
His appearance was like l, Mt 28:3
"I saw Satan fall like l from Lk 10:18

LIKENESS
in our image, after our l. Gn 1:26
he made him in the l of God. Gn 5:1
or any l of anything that is Ex 20:4
be satisfied with your l. Ps 17:15
Son in the l of sinful flesh Rom 8:3
created after the l of God in Eph 4:24
being born in the l of men. Phil 2:7
who are made in the l of God. Jas 3:9

LILIES
Consider the l of the field, Mt 6:28

LION
and the l shall eat straw like Is 11:7
around like a roaring l, 1 Pt 5:8
the L of the tribe of Judah, Rv 5:5

LIPS
grace is poured upon your l; Ps 45:2
My l will shout for joy, my Ps 71:23
My l will pour forth praise, Ps 119:171
he who opens wide his l Prv 13:3
for I am a man of unclean l, Is 6:5
honors me with their l, Mt 15:8
the fruit of l that acknowledge Heb 13:15

LISTEN
"If you will diligently l to Ex 15:26
L to advice and accept Prv 19:20
I am well pleased; l to him." Mt 17:5
and they will l to my voice. Jn 10:16
the Gentiles; they will l." Acts 28:28

LISTENS
but a wise man l to advice. Prv 12:15
is of the truth l to my voice." Jn 18:37
Whoever knows God l to us; 1 Jn 4:6

LIVE
life and eat, and l forever — Gn 3:22
man shall not see me and l." Ex 33:20
man does not l by bread alone, Dt 8:3
a man dies, shall he l again? Jb 14:14
that I may l and keep your Ps 119:17
my commandments, and l. Prv 4:4
hear, that your soul may l; Is 55:3
of man, can these bones l?" Ez 37:3
but the righteous shall l by Hb 2:4
"'Man shall not l by bread Mt 4:4
though he dies, yet shall he l, Jn 11:25
does not l in temples Acts 17:24
for "'In him we l and Acts 17:28
"The righteous shall l by Rom 1:17
If we l, we l to the Lord, Rom 14:8
that those who l might no 2 Cor 5:15
It is no longer I who l, but Gal 2:20
in the flesh I l by faith in Gal 2:20
for "The righteous shall l by Gal 3:11
If we l by the Spirit, let us Gal 5:25
For to me to l is Christ, Phil 1:21

Indeed, all who desire to **l** 2 Tm 3:12
one shall **l** by faith, Heb 10:38
L as people who are free, 1 Pt 2:16
so that we might **l** through 1 Jn 4:9

LIVES
but man **l** by every word that Dt 8:3
I know that my Redeemer **l**, Jb 19:25
The Lord **l**, and blessed be Ps 18:46
and everyone who **l** and Jn 11:26
but the life he **l** he **l** to Rom 6:10
live, but Christ who **l** in me. Gal 2:20
since he always **l** to make Heb 7:25
down our **l** for the brothers. 1 Jn 3:16

LIVING
and the man became a **l** Gn 2:7
of the **l** God speaking out Dt 5:26
thirsts for God, for the **l** God. Ps 42:2
the fountain of **l** waters, Jer 2:13
I am the **l** bread that came Jn 6:51
will flow rivers of **l** water.'" Jn 7:38
your bodies as a **l** sacrifice, Rom 12:1
our hope set on the **l** God, 1 Tm 4:10
For the word of God is **l** Heb 4:12
the hands of the **l** God. Heb 10:31
again to a **l** hope through the 1 Pt 1:3
you yourselves like **l** stones 1 Pt 2:5
and the **l** one. I died, and Rv 1:18

LOAD
will have to bear his own **l**. Gal 6:5

LOCUSTS
The **l** came up over all the Ex 10:14
and his food was **l** and wild Mt 3:4

LOFTY
stars, how **l** they are! Jb 22:12
From your **l** abode you Ps 104:13

LONG
and that your days may be **l**. Dt 6:2
"How **l** will you go 1 Kgs 18:21
O Lord — how **l**? Ps 6:3
we are killed all the day **l**; Ps 44:22
As **l** as I am in the world, I Jn 9:5
being killed all the day **l**; Rom 8:36
as **l** as it is called "today," Heb 3:13
things into which angels **l** 1 Pt 1:12
that the heavens existed **l** 2 Pt 3:5

LONGED
people **l** to see what Mt 13:17

LONGING
O Lord, all my **l** is before you; Ps 38:9
For he satisfies the **l** soul, Ps 107:9
eager **l** for the revealing Rom 8:19
For in this tent we groan, **l** 2 Cor 5:2

LONGS
My soul **l**, yes, faints Ps 84:2
My soul **l** for your salvation; Ps 119:81

LOOK
Those who **l** to him are Ps 34:5
Let your eyes **l** directly Prv 4:25
that we should **l** at him, Is 53:2
evil and cannot **l** at wrong, Hb 1:13
so that, when they **l** on me, Zec 12:10
you, '**L**, here is the Christ!' Mk 13:21
L, I tell you, lift up your eyes, Jn 4:35
as we **l** not to the things 2 Cor 4:18
L carefully then how you Eph 5:15
Let each of you **l** not only to Phil 2:4
into which angels long to **l**. 1 Pt 1:12

LOOKING
Turn my eyes from **l** at Ps 119:37
For he was **l** forward to Heb 11:10
l to Jesus, the founder and Heb 12:2

LOOKS
but the Lord **l** on the 1 Sm 16:7
everyone who **l** at a woman Mt 5:28
to the plow and **l** back is fit Lk 9:62
that everyone who **l** on the Jn 6:40
he is like a man who **l** Jas 1:23
But the one who **l** into the Jas 1:25

LORD (LORD; Heb., *Yahweh*)
in the day that the **L** God Gn 2:4
And he believed the **L**, and Gn 15:6
too hard for the **L**? Gn 18:14
"The **L** watch between you Gn 31:49
And the angel of the **L** Ex 3:2
But the **L** hardened the Ex 9:12
"I am the **L** your God, who Ex 20:2
The **L** passed before him and Ex 34:6
and the glory of the **L** filled Ex 40:34
for I the **L** your God am holy. Lv 19:2
with the glory of the **L**, Nm 14:21
might know that the **L** is God; Dt 4:35
for I the **L** your God am a Dt 5:9
L our God, the **L** is one. Dt 6:4
You shall love the **L** your God Dt 6:5
love the **L** your God and Dt 11:1
for it is the **L** your God who Dt 31:6
you, to love the **L** your God, Jos 22:5
house, we will serve the **L**." Jos 24:15
He said, "The **L** is my rock 2 Sm 22:2
for the glory of the **L** 1 Kgs 8:11
If the **L** is God, follow 1 Kgs 18:21
But the **L** was gracious 2 Kgs 13:23
Oh give thanks to the **L**; 1 Chr 16:8
For the **L** your God is 2 Chr 30:9
"You are the **L**, you alone. Neh 9:6
The **L** gave, and the Lord has Jb 1:21
delight is in the law of the **L**, Ps 1:2
I have set the **L** always Ps 16:8
For who is God, but the **L**? Ps 18:31
The law of the **L** is perfect, Ps 19:7
in your sight, O **L**, Ps 19:14
The **L** is my shepherd; I shall Ps 23:1
The **L** is my light and my Ps 27:1
the **L** counts no iniquity, Ps 32:2
Oh, taste and see that the **L** Ps 34:8
Delight yourself in the **L**, Ps 37:4
For the **L**, the Most High, is to Ps 47:2
Cast your burden on the **L**, Ps 55:22
Oh sing to the **L** a new song; Ps 96:1
Make a joyful noise to the **L**, Ps 100:1
Bless the **L**, O my soul, and Ps 103:1
This is the day that the **L** Ps 118:24
Unless the **L** builds the Ps 127:1
O **L**, what is man that you Ps 144:3
that has breath praise the **L**! Ps 150:6
The fear of the **L** is the Prv 1:7
Trust in the **L** with all your Prv 3:5
The name of the **L** is a Prv 18:10
holy, holy is the **L** of hosts; Is 6:3
for the **L** God is my strength Is 12:2
and the **L** has laid on him the Is 53:6
"Seek the **L** while he may be Is 55:6
L, whose trust is the **L**. Jer 17:7
I prayed to the **L** my God and Dn 9:4
For the day of the **L** is great Jl 2:11
who desire the day of the **L**! Am 5:18
and what does the **L** require Mi 6:8
The **L** is slow to anger and Na 1:3
glory of the **L** as the waters Hb 2:14
But the **L** is in his holy Hb 2:20
The **L** your God is in your Zep 3:17
awesome day of the **L** comes. Mal 4:5

LORD (Lord; Heb., *Adonai*)
Remember the **L**, who is Neh 4:14
'Behold, the fear of the **L**, Jb 28:28
the **L** is the upholder of my Ps 54:4
and that to you, O **L**. For you Ps 62:12
For you, O **L**, are good and Ps 86:5
The Lord says to my **L**: "Sit Ps 110:1
Great is our **L**, and his Ps 147:5
died I saw the **L** sitting upon a Is 6:1

LORD (Lord; Gk., *Kyrios*)
Prepare the way of the **L**; Mt 3:3
'You shall not put the **L** your Mt 4:7
L,' will enter the kingdom of Mt 7:21
"You shall love the **L** your Mt 22:37
"'The **L** said to my **L**, Mt 22:44
O Israel: The **L** our God, Mk 12:29
and the glory of the **L** shone Lk 2:9
"Why do you call me '**L**, Lk 6:46
"You shall love the **L** your Lk 10:27
him, "We have seen the **L**." Jn 20:25
of the **L** shall be saved.' Acts 2:21
him both **L** and Christ, Acts 2:36
"Believe in the **L** Jesus, Acts 16:31
Jesus is **L** and believe in Rom 10:9
of the **L** will be saved." Rom 10:13
in spirit, serve the **L**. Rom 12:11
If we live, we live to the **L**, Rom 14:8
boasts, boast in the **L**." 1 Cor 1:31
crucified the **L** of glory. 1 Cor 2:8
as the **L** assigned to each. 1 Cor 3:5
about the things of the **L**, 1 Cor 7:34
that the **L** Jesus on the 1 Cor 11:23
"Jesus is **L**" except in the 1 Cor 12:3
our **L** Jesus Christ. 1 Cor 15:57
has no love for the **L**, 1 Cor 16:22
the Spirit of the **L** is, 2 Cor 3:17
first to the **L** and then by 2 Cor 8:5
boasts, boast in the **L**." 2 Cor 10:17
cross of our **L** Jesus Christ, Gal 6:14
one **L**, one faith, one baptism, Eph 4:5
what is pleasing to the **L**. Eph 5:10
to the **L** with all your Eph 5:19
that Jesus Christ is **L**, Phil 2:11
brothers, rejoice in the **L**. Phil 3:1
Rejoice in the **L** always; Rejoice. Phil 4:4
received Christ Jesus the **L**, Col 2:6
in the name of the **L** Jesus, Col 3:17
as for the **L** and not for men, Col 3:23
have received in the **L**." Col 4:17
and may the **L** make you 1 Thes 3:12
day of the **L** will come like 1 Thes 5:2
of our **L** Jesus Christ. 1 Thes 5:23
of our **L** Jesus Christ and 2 Thes 2:1
"The **L** knows those who 2 Tm 2:19
no one will see the **L**. Heb 12:14
say, "The **L** is my helper; Heb 13:6
yourselves before the **L**, Jas 4:10
but the word of the **L** 1 Pt 1:25
tasted that the **L** is good. 1 Pt 2:3
hearts sanctify Christ as **L**, 1 Pt 3:15
of our **L** Jesus Christ, 2 Pt 1:16
The **L** is not slow to fulfill 2 Pt 3:9
the **L** came with ten Jude 1:14
holy, is the **L** God Almighty, Rv 4:8
are you, our **L** and God, for Rv 4:11
for he is **L** of lords and King Rv 17:14
King of kings and **L** of lords. Rv 19:16
Amen. Come, **L** Jesus! Rv 22:20

LORD'S (LORD'S; Heb., *Yahweh*)
But the **L** portion is his Dt 32:9
The earth is the **L** and the Ps 24:1
the **L** discipline or be weary Prv 3:11

LORD'S (Lord's; Gk., *Kyrios*)
whether we die, we are the **L**. Rom 14:8
For "the earth is the **L**, 1 Cor 10:26
you proclaim the **L** death 1 Cor 11:26
And the **L** servant must 2 Tm 2:24
Be subject for the **L** sake to 1 Pt 2:13

LOSE
time to seek, and a time to **l**; Eccl 3:6
For it is better that you **l** one Mt 5:29
Whoever finds his life will **l** Mt 10:39
that I should **l** nothing of all Jn 6:39
so that you may not **l** what 2 Jn 1:8

LOSES
and whoever **l** his life for Mt 10:39
silver coins, if she **l** one coin, Lk 15:8
Whoever loves his life **l** it, Jn 12:25

LOSS
up, he will suffer **l**, but 1 Cor 3:15
I count everything as **l** Phil 3:8

LOST
For I am **l**; for I am a man of Is 6:5
I will seek the **l**, and I will Ez 34:16
but if salt has **l** its taste, It is Mt 5:13
"I was sent only to the **l** Mt 15:24
if he has **l** one of them, and go Lk 15:4
he was **l**, and is found.'" Lk 15:32
to seek and to save the **l**." Lk 19:10
gave me I have **l** not one." Jn 18:9

LOT
And **L**, who went with Abram Gn 13:5
and **L** was sitting in the gate Gn 19:1

LOTS
for my clothing they cast **l**. Ps 22:18
among them by casting **l**. Mt 27:35
And they cast **l** for them, Acts 1:26

LOVE
only son Isaac, whom you **l**, Gn 22:2
but showing steadfast **l** to Ex 20:6
and abounding in steadfast **l** Ex 34:6
but you shall **l** your Lv 19:18
abounding in steadfast **l**, Nm 14:18

but showing steadfast **l** to Dt 5:10
You shall **l** the Lord your God Dt 6:5
you, to **l** the Lord your God, Jos 22:5
for his steadfast **l** endures 2 Chr 5:13
save me in your steadfast **l**! Ps 31:16
L the Lord, all you his saints Ps 31:23
Your steadfast **l**, O Lord, your Ps 36:5
according to your steadfast **l**; Ps 51:1
his steadfast **l** endures Ps 100:5
and abounding in steadfast **l**. Ps 103:8
for his steadfast **l** endures Ps 136:1
and abounding in steadfast **l**. Ps 145:8
wise man, and he will **l** you. Prv 9:8
but **l** covers all offenses. Prv 10:12
and by steadfast **l** his Prv 20:28
with the wife whom you **l**, Eccl 9:9
and his banner over me was **l**. Sg 2:4
Many waters cannot quench **l**, Sg 8:7
but my steadfast **l** shall not Is 54:10
For I the Lord **l** justice; I Is 61:8
in his **l** and in his pity he Is 63:9
you with an everlasting **l**; Jer 31:3
for his steadfast **l** endures Jer 33:11
steadfast **l** with those who Dn 9:4
with the bands of **l**, and I Hos 11:4
hold fast to **l** and justice, Hos 12:6
Hate evil, and **l** good, and Am 5:15
you who hate the good and **l** Mi 3:2
to do justice, and to **l** kindness, Mi 6:8
But I say to you, **L** your Mt 5:44
"You shall **l** the Lord your Mt 22:37
For even sinners **l** those Lk 6:32
"Lord, he whom you **l** is ill." Jn 11:3
you, that you **l** one another: Jn 13:34
"If you **l** me, you will keep Jn 14:15
I loved you. Abide in my **l**. Jn 15:9
Greater **l** has no one than Jn 15:13
so that you will **l** one Jn 15:17
do you **l** me more than Jn 21:15
because God's **l** has been Rom 5:5
but God shows his **l** for us Rom 5:8
those who **l** God all things Rom 8:28
us from the **l** of Christ? Rom 8:35
Let **l** be genuine. Abhor Rom 12:9
L one another with Rom 12:10
L does no wrong to a Rom 13:10
and by the **l** of the Spirit, Rom 15:30
for those who **l** him"— 1 Cor 2:9
puffs up, but **l** builds up. 1 Cor 8:1
of angels, but have not **l**, 1 Cor 13:1
L is patient and kind; 1 Cor 13:4
l does not envy or boast; 1 Cor 13:4
L bears all things, hopes all 1 Cor 13:7
L never ends. As for 1 Cor 13:8
and **l** abide, these three; 1 Cor 13:13
the greatest of these is **l**. 1 Cor 13:13
that you do be done in **l**. 1 Cor 16:14
For the **l** of Christ controls 2 Cor 5:14
only faith working through **l**. Gal 5:6
the fruit of the Spirit is **l**, Gal 5:22
blameless before him. In **l** Eph 1:4
because of the great **l** with Eph 2:4
rooted and grounded in **l**, Eph 3:17
speaking the truth in **l** Eph 4:15
And walk in **l**, as Christ Eph 5:2
Husbands, **l** your wives, Eph 5:25
should **l** their wives as Eph 5:28
that your **l** may abound more Phil 1:9
in Christ, any comfort from **l**, Phil 2:1
whom I **l** and long for, Phil 4:1
And above all these put on **l**, Col 3:14
by God to **l** one another, 1 Thes 4:9
breastplate of faith and **l**, 1 Thes 5:8
hearts to the **l** of God and 2 Thes 3:5
in **l**, in faith, in purity. 1 Tm 4:12
For the **l** of money is a 1 Tm 6:10
l, steadfastness, gentleness. 1 Tm 6:11
power and **l** and self-control. 2 Tm 1:7
faith, **l**, and peace, 2 Tm 2:22
my **l**, my steadfastness, 2 Tm 3:10
to **l** and good works, Heb 10:24
Let brotherly **l** continue. Heb 13:1
promised to those who **l** him. Jas 1:12
"You shall **l** your neighbor as Jas 2:8
for a sincere brotherly **l**, 1 Pt 1:22
l one another earnestly 1 Pt 1:22
L the brotherhood. Fear God. 1 Pt 2:17
since **l** covers a multitude of 1 Pt 4:8
brotherly affection with **l**. 2 Pt 1:7
in him truly the **l** of God is 1 Jn 2:5
Do not **l** the world or the 1 Jn 2:15
See what kind of **l** the 1 Jn 3:1
who does not **l** his brother. 1 Jn 3:10
that we should **l** one 1 Jn 3:11
because we **l** the brothers. 1 Jn 3:14
By this we know **l**, that he 1 Jn 3:16
Little children, let us not **l** 1 Jn 3:18
Christ and **l** one another, 1 Jn 3:23
Beloved, let us **l** one another, 1 Jn 4:7
know God, because God is **l**. 1 Jn 4:8
In this the **l** of God was 1 Jn 4:9
In this is **l**, not that we 1 Jn 4:10
we also ought to **l** one 1 Jn 4:11
God is **l**, and whoever 1 Jn 4:16
but perfect **l** casts out fear. 1 Jn 4:18
We **l** because he first loved 1 Jn 4:19
God must also **l** his brother. 1 Jn 4:21
By this we know that we **l** 1 Jn 5:2
For this is the **l** of God, that 1 Jn 5:3
— that we **l** one another. 2 Jn 1:5
And this is **l**, that we walk 2 Jn 1:6
blemishes on your **l** feasts, Jude 1:12
keep yourselves in the **l** of Jude 1:21
that you have abandoned the **l** Rv 2:4
Those whom I **l**, I reprove Rv 3:19

LOVED

because the Lord your God **l** Dt 23:5
you have **l** righteousness and Ps 45:7
I have **l** you with an Jer 31:3
"For God so **l** the world, that Jn 3:16
just as I have **l** you, Jn 13:34
has **l** me, so have I **l** you. Jn 15:9
because you have **l** me and Jn 16:27
through him who **l** us. Rom 8:37
who **l** me and gave himself Gal 2:20
love with which he **l** us, Eph 2:4
And walk in love, as Christ **l** Eph 5:2
as Christ **l** the church and Eph 5:25
who **l** us and gave us 2 Thes 2:16
not that we have **l** God but 1 Jn 4:10
We love because he first **l** 1 Jn 4:19

LOVELY

How **l** is your dwelling place, Ps 84:1
is sweet, and your face is **l**. Sg 2:14
is pure, whatever is **l**, if there Phil 4:8

LOVER

hear this, you **l** of pleasures, Is 47:8
not a **l** of money. 1 Tm 3:3
but hospitable, a **l** of good, Ti 1:8

LOVERS

For people will be **l** of self, 2 Tm 3:2
l of pleasure rather than 2 Tm 3:4

LOVES

He **l** righteousness and Ps 33:5
For the Lord **l** justice; he Ps 37:28
reproves him whom he **l**, Prv 3:12
Whoever **l** discipline **l** knowledge Prv 12:1
A friend **l** at all times, and Prv 17:17
He who **l** money will not be Eccl 5:10
Whoever **l** father or mother Mt 10:37
who is forgiven little, **l** little." Lk 7:47
And he who **l** me will be Jn 14:21
for the one who **l** another Rom 13:8
But if anyone **l** God, he is 1 Cor 8:3
for God **l** a cheerful giver. 2 Cor 9:7
He who **l** his wife **l** himself. Eph 5:28
disciplines the one he **l**, Heb 12:6
Whoever **l** his brother 1 Jn 2:10
If anyone **l** the world, the 1 Jn 2:15
and whoever **l** has been 1 Jn 4:7
whoever **l** God must also 1 Jn 4:21
and everyone who **l** the 1 Jn 5:1
To him who **l** us and has Rv 1:5

LOVING

to do, **l** the Lord your God, Dt 11:22
by **l** the Lord your God, and Dt 30:16
l the Lord your God, for he is Dt 30:20
self-control, brutal, not **l** good, 2 Tm 3:3
But when the goodness and **l** Ti 3:4
keep **l** one another earnestly, 1 Pt 4:8

LOW

God chose what is **l** and 1 Cor 1:28
know how to be brought **l**, Phil 4:12

LOWLY

sets on high those who are **l**, Jb 5:11
of pride'; but he saves the **l**. Jb 22:29
is high, he regards the **l**, Ps 138:6
Better to be **l** and have a Prv 12:9
but he who is **l** in spirit Prv 29:23
to revive the spirit of the **l**, Is 57:15
for I am gentle and **l** in Mt 11:29
but associate with the **l**. Rom 12:16
who will transform our **l** Phil 3:21
Let the **l** brother boast in his Jas 1:9

LUKE

L the beloved physician Col 4:14
L alone is with me. Get 2 Tm 4:11
and **L**, my fellow workers. Phlm 1:24

LUKEWARM

So, because you are **l**, and Rv 3:16

LUST

those who **l** after tribute; Ps 68:30
are taken captive by their **l**. Prv 11:6
not in the passion of **l** like 1 Thes 4:5
in the **l** of defiling passion 2 Pt 2:10

LUSTFUL

with **l** intent has already Mt 5:28

LYDIA

us was a woman named **L**, Acts 16:14

LYING

haughty eyes, a **l** tongue, Prv 6:17
but a **l** tongue is but for a Prv 12:19
A **l** tongue hates its victims, Prv 26:28

MACEDONIA

a man of **M** was standing Acts 16:9
to return through **M**. Acts 20:3
when we came into **M**, 2 Cor 7:5

MAGDALENE

among whom were Mary **M** Mt 27:56
infirmities: Mary, called **M**, Lk 8:2
Mary **M** went and Jn 20:18

MAGOG

I will send fire on **M** and on Ez 39:6
of the earth, Gog and **M**, their Rv 20:8

MAJESTIC

is like you, **m** in holiness, Ex 15:11
O Lord, our Lord, how **m** is Ps 8:1
Glorious are you, more **m** Ps 76:4
to him by the **M** Glory, 2 Pt 1:17

MAJESTY

In the greatness of your **m** Ex 15:7
through the skies in his **m**. Dt 33:26
Splendor and **m** are 1 Chr 16:27
is clothed with awesome **m**. Jb 37:22
"Adorn yourself with **m** and Jb 40:10
one, in your splendor and **m**! Ps 45:3
Lord reigns; he is robed in **m**; Ps 93:1
glorious splendor of your **m**, Ps 145:5
from the splendor of his **m**. Is 2:10
he had no form or **m** that we Is 53:2
astonished at the **m** of God. Lk 9:43
right hand of the **M** on high, Heb 1:3
throne of the **M** in heaven, Heb 8:1
were eyewitnesses of his **m**. 2 Pt 1:16
m, dominion, and authority, Jude 1:25

MAKE

"Let us **m** man in our image, Gn 1:26
will **m** him a helper fit for him." Gn 2:18
was to be desired to **m** one wise, Gn 3:6
"I have determined to **m** an end Gn 6:13
M yourself an ark of gopher Gn 6:14
the sign of the covenant that I **m** Gn 9:12
and let us **m** a name for ourselves, Gn 11:4
will **m** of you a great nation, and Gn 12:2
I will **m** your offspring as the Gn 13:16
I will **m** you exceedingly fruitful, Gn 17:6
blessed him and will **m** him Gn 17:20
let us **m** our father drink wine, Gn 19:32
let us **m** a covenant with you, Gn 26:28
Almighty bless you and **m** you Gn 28:3
M an altar there to the God who Gn 35:1
"**M** everyone go out from me." Gn 45:1
I will **m** you into a great nation. Gn 46:3
I will **m** you fruitful and multiply Gn 48:4
'God **m** you as Ephraim and as Gn 48:20
and **m** frogs come up on the land Ex 8:5
and I **m** them know the statutes Ex 18:16
not **m** for yourself a carved Ex 20:4
not **m** gods of silver to be with Ex 20:23

If you **m** me an altar of stone, Ex 20:25
its furniture, so you shall **m** it. Ex 25:9
You shall **m** a mercy seat of pure Ex 25:17
"You shall **m** a table of acacia Ex 25:23
see that you **m** them after the Ex 25:40
Aaron's sons you shall **m** coats Ex 28:40
days you shall **m** atonement Ex 29:37
"Up, **m** us gods who shall go Ex 32:1
I can **m** atonement for your sin." Ex 32:30
Take care, lest you **m** a covenant Ex 34:12
who could **m** a contribution of Ex 35:24
and **m** atonement for him, Nm 6:11
I the Lord **m** myself known Nm 12:6
that I would **m** you dwell, Nm 14:30
"**M** a fiery serpent and set it Nm 21:8
to **m** atonement for you. Nm 28:22
shall not **m** for yourself a carved Dt 5:8
shall **m** no covenant with them Dt 7:2
shall **m** yourself tassels on the Dt 22:12
I kill and I **m** alive; I wound Dt 32:39
Come now, **m** a covenant Jos 9:11
not rebel against the Lord or **m** Jos 22:19
but do not **m** yourself known Ru 3:3
May the Lord **m** the woman Ru 4:11
voice and **m** them a king." 1 Sm 8:22
Hebrews **m** themselves swords 1 Sm 13:19
Saul thought to **m** David fall 1 Sm 18:25
I will **m** myself yet more 2 Sm 6:22
'I will **m** this dry streambed 2 Kgs 3:16
I God, to kill and to **m** alive, 2 Kgs 5:7
I Darius **m** a decree; let it be Ezr 6:12
Tobiah sent letters to **m** me Neh 6:19
her not to **m** it known. Est 2:10
and you **m** it known to me.' Jb 42:4
O Lord, **m** me dwell in safety. Ps 4:8
M them bear their guilt, O God Ps 5:10
"O Lord, **m** me know my end Ps 39:4
not **m** me the scorn of the fool! Ps 39:8
river whose streams **m** glad Ps 46:4
man who would not **m** God his Ps 52:7
You **m** the going out of the Ps 65:8
distress; **m** haste to answer me. Ps 69:17
M your vows to the Lord Ps 76:11
You **m** us an object of contention Ps 80:6
And I will **m** him the firstborn, Ps 89:27
M a joyful noise to the Lord, all Ps 98:4
M a joyful noise to the Lord, all Ps 100:1
he might **m** known his mighty Ps 106:8
I **m** your enemies your footstool. Ps 110:1
M me understand the way of Ps 119:27
M your face shine upon your Ps 119:135
nothing can **m** them stumble. Ps 119:165
and he will **m** straight your paths. Prv 3:6
To **m** an apt answer is a joy to Prv 15:23
to **m** you know what is right Prv 22:21
M no friendship with a man Prv 22:24
and perfume **m** the heart glad, Prv 27:9
my son, and **m** my heart glad, Prv 27:11
the work of God: who can **m** Eccl 7:13
M haste, my beloved, and be like Sg 8:14
I will **m** boys their princes, and Is 3:4
m known his deeds among the Is 12:4
its maker, "He did not **m** me"; 29:16
m straight in the desert a highway Is 40:3
I **m** of you a threshing sledge, Is 41:15
m the wilderness a pool of water, Is 41:18
I will **m** a way in the wilderness Is 43:19
I **m** well-being and create calamity, Is 45:7
will you liken me and **m** me equal, Is 46:5
m you as a light for the nations, Is 49:6
up the sea, I **m** the rivers a desert; Is 50:2
I will **m** with you an everlasting Is 55:3
I will **m** an everlasting covenant Is 61:8
I will **m** Jerusalem a heap of ruins Jer 9:11
gods who did not **m** the heavens Jer 10:11
the covenant that I will **m** Jer 31:33
I will **m** with them an everlasting Jer 32:40
m offerings to the queen of Jer 44:17
I will **m** Pathros a desolation Ez 30:14
I will **m** you a perpetual Ez 35:9
my holy name I will **m** known in Ez 39:7
days shall they **m** atonement Ez 43:26
I will **m** it like the mourning for Am 8:10
not labor, nor did you **m** it grow, Jon 4:10
"Write the vision; **m** it plain on Hb 2:2
will **m** them strong in the Lord, Zec 10:12
day I will **m** Jerusalem a heavy Zec 12:3
and I will **m** you fishers of men." Mt 4:19
cannot **m** one hair white or black Mt 5:36
if you will, you can **m** me clean." Mt 8:2
them not to **m** him known. Mt 12:16
"Either **m** the tree good and its Mt 12:33
I will **m** three tents here, Mt 17:4
but you **m** it a den of robbers." Mt 21:13
For they **m** their phylacteries Mt 23:5
Go therefore and **m** disciples Mt 28:19
of the Lord, **m** his paths straight. Mk 1:3
how will you **m** it salty again? Mk 9:50
"Have you no answer to **m**? Mk 14:60
the outside **m** the inside also? Lk 11:40
all alike began to **m** excuses. Lk 14:18
tell you, **m** friends for yourselves Lk 16:9
day the things that **m** for peace! Lk 19:42
for a pretense **m** long prayers. Lk 20:47
take him by force to **m** him king, Jn 6:15
'**M** for us gods who will go Act 7:40
to Moses directed him to **m** it, Act 7:44
not my hand **m** all these things? Act 7:50
defense that I now **m** before you. Act 22:1
and tried to **m** them blaspheme, Act 26:11
was to **m** him the father Rom 4:11
over the clay, to **m** out of the Rom 9:21
to show his wrath and to **m** Rom 9:22
in order to **m** known the Rom 9:23
"I will **m** you jealous of Rom 10:19
I **m** it my ambition to preach Rom 15:20
to **m** some contribution for Rom 15:26
Do I **m** my plans according to 2 Cor 1:17
m up my mind not to **m** 2 Cor 2:1
to **m** sure I was not running or Gal 2:2
They **m** much of you, but for Gal 4:17
may the Lord **m** you increase 1 Thes 3:12
God may **m** you worthy 2 Thes 1:11
they **m** confident assertions. 1 Tm 1:7
my right hand until I **m** your Heb 1:13
to **m** propitiation for the sins Heb 2:17
the covenant that I will **m** with Heb 10:16
not sinned, we **m** him a liar, 1 Jn 1:10
one who conquers, I will **m** him Rv 3:12
pit will **m** war on them Rv 11:7

MAKER

a man be pure before his **M**? Jb 4:17
righteousness to my **M**. Jb 36:3
kneel before the Lord, our **M**! Ps 95:6
Let Israel be glad in his **M**; Ps 149:2
the Lord is the **m** of them Prv 22:2
forgotten the Lord, your **M**, Is 51:13
his **M** and built palaces, Hos 8:14

MAKES

for it is the blood that **m** Lv 17:11
The Lord **m** poor and makes 1 Sm 2:7
He **m** nations great, and he Jb 12:23
He **m** me lie down in green Ps 23:2
and he **m** known to them Ps 25:14
Hope deferred **m** the heart Prv 13:12
A glad heart **m** a cheerful Prv 15:13
Good sense **m** one slow to Prv 19:11
and **m** intercession for the Is 53:12
For he **m** his sun rise on the Mt 5:45
world **m** himself an enemy Jas 4:4
No one born of God **m** a 1 Jn 3:9

MAKING

"Behold, I am **m** a covenant. Ex 34:10
is sure, **m** wise the simple; Ps 19:7
a rock, **m** my steps secure. Ps 40:2
Of **m** many books there is Eccl 12:12
m himself equal with God. Jn 5:18
God **m** his appeal through 2 Cor 5:20
place of the two, so **m** peace, Eph 2:15
m the best use of the time, Eph 5:16
After **m** purification for sins, Heb 1:3

MALE

m and female he created Gn 1:27
M and female he created Gn 5:2
made them **m** and female, Mt 19:4
'God made them **m** and Mk 10:6
there is neither **m** nor Gal 3:28

MALICE

evil, covetousness, **m**. They Rom 1:29
from you, along with all **m**. Eph 4:31
anger, wrath, **m**, slander, Col 3:8
So put away all **m** and all 1 Pt 2:1

MAN

"Let us make **m** in our Gn 1:26
formed the **m** of dust from Gn 2:7
"It is not good that the **m** Gn 2:18
she was taken out of **M**." Gn 2:23
sheds the blood of **m**, Gn 9:6
you know that **m** does not live Dt 8:3
out a **m** after his own 1 Sm 13:14
But how can a **m** be in the Jb 9:2
what is **m** that you are Ps 8:4
Blessed is the **m** who makes Ps 40:4
Blessed is the **m** who fears Ps 112:1
Blessed is the **m** who fills Ps 127:5
O Lord, what is **m** that you Ps 144:3
that seems right to a **m**, Prv 14:12
Do you see a **m** who is Prv 26:12
and one **m** sharpens Prv 27:17
is the whole duty of **m**. Eccl 12:13
by men; a **m** of sorrows, and as Is 53:3
came one like a son of **m**, Dn 7:13
and said, 'Therefore a **m** Mt 19:5
for the Son of **M** is coming Mt 24:44
For what does it profit a **m** Mk 8:36
'**M** shall not live by bread Lk 4:4
descending on the Son of **M**." Jn 1:51
said to them, "Behold the **m**!" Jn 19:5
the world through one **m**, Rom 5:12
each **m** should have his 1 Cor 7:2
head of every **m** is Christ, 1 Cor 11:3
woman is the glory of **m**. 1 Cor 11:7
When I became a **m**, 1 Cor 13:11
"The first **m** Adam 1 Cor 15:45
"For this reason a **m** shall Eph 5:31
men, the **m** Christ Jesus, 1 Tm 2:5
authority over a **m**; 1 Tm 2:12
that the **m** of God may be 2 Tm 3:17
appointed for **m** to die once, Heb 9:27
Blessed is the **m** who Jas 1:12
one like a son of **m**, Rv 1:13

MANAGE

He must **m** his own 1 Tm 3:4
to **m** his own household, 1 Tm 3:5
m their households, 1 Tm 5:14

MANASSEH

the name of the firstborn **M**. Gn 41:51
These are the clans of **M**, Nm 26:34

MANGER

cloths and laid him in a **m**, Lk 2:7

MANIFEST

that will not be made **m**, Lk 8:17
but was made **m** in the last 1 Pt 1:20
the life was made **m**, and 1 Jn 1:2
God was made **m** among us, 1 Jn 4:9

MANIFESTATION

To each is given the **m** of 1 Cor 12:7

MANIFESTED

has been **m** apart from the Rom 3:21
also be **m** in our bodies. 2 Cor 4:10
He was **m** in the flesh, 1 Tm 3:16
m through the appearing 2 Tm 1:10
and at the proper time **m** in Ti 1:3

MANKIND

scorned by **m** and despised by Ps 22:6
Surely all **m** stands as a mere Ps 39:5
that the remnant of **m** Acts 15:17
of wrath, like the rest of **m**. Eph 2:3

MANNA

of Israel called its name **m**. Ex 16:31
with **m** that your fathers Dt 8:16
Our fathers ate the **m** in the Jn 6:31
give some of the hidden **m**, Rv 2:17

MANNER

m will be guilty 1 Cor 11:27
urge you to walk in a **m** Eph 4:1
Only let your **m** of life be Phil 1:27
so as to walk in a **m** worthy Col 1:10

MAN'S

for the intention of **m** heart Gn 8:21
For a **m** ways are before the Prv 5:21
because of one **m** trespass, Rom 5:17
so by the one **m** obedience Rom 5:19
by me is not **m** gospel Gal 1:11

MARK

And the Lord put a **m** on Gn 4:15
whose other name was **M**, Acts 12:12
Barnabas took **M** with him Acts 15:39
and so does **M**, my son. 1 Pt 5:13
its **m** on their foreheads Rv 20:4

MARKS
for I bear on my body the **m** Gal 6:17

MARRED
his appearance was so **m**, Is 52:14

MARRIAGE
marry nor are given in **m**, Mt 22:30
marrying and giving in **m**, Mt 24:38
released from the law of **m**. Rom 7:2
from **m** will do even 1 Cor 7:38
Let **m** be held in honor Heb 13:4

MARRIED
Thus a **m** woman is bound Rom 7:2
To the **m** I give this 1 Cor 7:10
But the **m** man is anxious 1 Cor 7:33
she is free to be **m** to 1 Cor 7:39

MARRIES
And whoever **m** a divorced Mt 5:32
immorality, and **m** another, Mt 19:9
m another commits adultery, Lk 16:18
So then he who **m** his 1 Cor 7:38

MARRY
neither **m** nor are given Mt 22:30
self-control, they should **m**. 1 Cor 7:9
Yet those who **m** will 1 Cor 7:28
have younger widows **m**, 1 Tm 5:14

MARTHA
But **M** was distracted with Lk 10:40
Now Jesus loved **M** and her Jn 11:5
M served, and Lazarus was Jn 12:2

MARVELOUS
doing; it is **m** in our eyes. Ps 118:23
and it is **m** in our eyes'? Mt 21:42
of darkness into his **m** light. 1 Pt 2:9

MARY
of Joseph the husband of **M**, Mt 1:16
the child with **M** his mother, Mt 2:11
among whom were **M** Mt 27:56
M Magdalene and the other Mt 27:61
M Magdalene and the other Mt 28:1
the virgin's name was **M**. Lk 1:27
But **M** treasured up all these Lk 2:19
M has chosen the good Lk 10:42
But **M** stood weeping Jn 20:11
and **M** the mother of Acts 1:14

MASTER
is not greater than his **m**.' If Jn 15:20
It is before his own **m** that Rom 14:4
like a skilled **m** builder I 1 Cor 3:10
is both their **M** and yours is Eph 6:9
you also have a **M** in heaven. Col 4:1
useful to the **m** of the 2 Tm 2:21

MASTERS
"No one can serve two **m**, Mt 6:24
Slaves, obey your earthly **m** Eph 6:5
M, do the same to them, and Eph 6:9
to their own **m** in everything; Ti 2:9
be subject to your **m** with 1 Pt 2:18

MATTHEW
he saw a man called **M** sitting Mt 9:9

MATTHIAS
them, and the lot fell on **M**, Acts 1:26

MATURE
Yet among the **m** we do 1 Cor 2:6
in your thinking be **m**. 1 Cor 14:20
Son of God, to **m** manhood, Eph 4:13
Let those of us who are **m** Phil 3:15
everyone **m** in Christ. Col 1:28
that you may stand **m** and Col 4:12
But solid food is for the **m**, Heb 5:14

MATURITY
of Christ and go on to **m**, Heb 6:1

MEANS
that by all **m** I might save 1 Cor 9:22
gave according to their **m**, 2 Cor 8:3
that by any **m** possible I Phil 3:11
that godliness is a **m** of gain. 1 Tm 6:5

MEASURE
and what is the **m** of my days; Ps 39:4
and with the **m** you use it Mt 7:2

he gives the Spirit without **m**. Jn 3:34
to the **m** of Christ's gift. Eph 4:7

MEAT
I ate no delicacies, no **m** or Dn 10:3
It is good not to eat **m** or Rom 14:21
I will never eat **m**, 1 Cor 8:13

MEDIATES
the covenant he **m** is better, Heb 8:6

MEDIATOR
and there is one **m** between 1 Tm 2:5
Therefore he is the **m** of a Heb 9:15
the **m** of a new covenant, Heb 12:24

MEDICINE
A joyful heart is good **m**, Prv 17:22

MEDITATE
but you shall **m** on it day and Jos 1:8
I will **m** on your precepts Ps 119:15
and I will **m** on your Ps 119:48
I **m** on all that you have Ps 143:5

MEDITATES
and on his law he **m** day and Ps 1:2

MEDITATION
and the **m** of my heart Ps 19:14
the **m** of my heart shall be Ps 49:3
May my **m** be pleasing to Ps 104:34

MEDIUM
who is a **m** or a wizard Lv 20:27
there is a **m** at Endor." 1 Sm 28:7

MEEK
But the **m** shall inherit the Ps 37:11
equity for the **m** of the earth; Is 11:4
The **m** shall obtain fresh joy Is 29:19
"Blessed are the **m**, for they Mt 5:5

MEEKNESS
by the **m** and gentleness 2 Cor 10:1
with **m** the implanted word, Jas 1:21

MEET
love and faithfulness **m**; Ps 85:10
you, prepare to **m** your God, Am 4:12
clouds to **m** the Lord in 1 Thes 4:17
not neglecting to **m** Heb 10:25

MEGIDDO
one; the king of **M**, one; Jos 12:21
in the plain of **M**. Zec 12:11

MELCHIZEDEK
And **M** king of Salem Gn 14:18
forever after the order of **M**." Ps 110:4
For this **M**, king of Salem, Heb 7:1
after the order of **M**." Heb 7:17

MELODY
I will sing and make **m** to the Ps 27:6
I will sing and make **m** Ps 108:1
singing and making **m** to Eph 5:19

MELT
bodies will **m** as they burn! 2 Pt 3:12

MEMBERS
one of your **m** than that your Mt 5:29
Do not present your **m** to Rom 6:13
were at work in our **m** to Rom 7:5
one body we have many **m**, Rom 12:4
bodies are **m** of Christ? 1 Cor 6:15
God arranged the **m** in 1 Cor 12:18
heirs, **m** of the same body, Eph 3:6
for we are **m** one of Eph 4:25

MEN
the mighty **m** that were of old, Gn 6:4
know that they are but **m**! Ps 9:20
despised and rejected by **m**; Is 53:3
will make you fishers of **m**." Mt 4:19
and the life was the light of **m**. Jn 1:4
obey God rather than **m**. Acts 5:29
and the **m** likewise gave up Rom 1:27
to all **m** because all sinned Rom 5:12
of God is wiser than **m**, 1 Cor 1:25
between God and **m**, 1 Tm 2:5
to faithful **m** who will be 2 Tm 2:2
but **m** spoke from God as 2 Pt 1:21

MERCIES
brothers, by the **m** of God, Rom 12:1
the Father of **m** and God of 2 Cor 1:3

MERCIFUL
Lord, a God **m** and gracious, Ex 34:6
For the Lord your God is a **m** Dt 4:31
are a gracious and **m** God. Neh 9:31
The Lord is **m** and gracious, Ps 103:8
"Blessed are the **m**, for they Mt 5:7
Be **m**, even as your Father is Lk 6:36
For I will be **m** toward Heb 8:12
Lord is compassionate and **m**. Jas 5:11

MERCY
"You shall make a **m** seat of Ex 25:17
Surely goodness and **m** shall Ps 23:6
you will not restrain your **m** Ps 40:11
Have **m** on me, O God, Ps 51:1
according to your abundant **m** Ps 51:1
Have **m** upon us, O Lord, Ps 123:3
known; in wrath remember **m**. Hb 3:2
for they shall receive **m**. Mt 5:7
'I desire **m**, and not sacrifice.' Mt 9:13
'I desire **m**, and not sacrifice,' Mt 12:7
justice and **m** and Mt 23:23
"I will have **m** on whom I Rom 9:15
the one who does acts of **m**, Rom 12:8
Lord's **m** is trustworthy. 1 Cor 7:25
ministry by the **m** of God, 2 Cor 4:1
But God, being rich in **m**, Eph 2:4
overshadowing the **m** seat. Heb 9:5
M triumphs over judgment. Jas 2:13
According to his great **m**, 1 Pt 1:3
now you have received **m**. 1 Pt 2:10

MERIBAH
These are the waters of **M**, Nm 20:13
quarreled at the waters of **M**; Dt 33:8
him at the waters of **M**, Ps 106:32

MERRY
your wine with a **m** heart, Eccl 9:7
relax, eat, drink, be **m**.' Lk 12:19

MESHACH
Mishael he called **M**, Dn 1:7
Shadrach, **M**, and Abednego, Dn 3:28

MESSAGE
and entrusting to us the **m** 2 Cor 5:19
so that through me the **m** 2 Tm 4:17
For since the **m** declared by Heb 2:2
This is the **m** we have heard 1 Jn 1:5

MESSIAH
"We have found the **M**" Jn 1:41
"I know that **M** is coming (he Jn 4:25

METHUSELAH
Thus all the days of **M** were Gn 5:27

MICHAEL
"At that time shall arise **M**, Dn 12:1
But when the archangel **M**, Jude 1:9
Now war arose in heaven, **M** Rv 12:7

MIGHTY
These were the **m** men that Gn 6:4
with a **m** hand and redeemed Dt 7:8
How the **m** have fallen! 2 Sm 1:19
The Lord, strong and **m**, the Ps 24:8
The **M** One, God the Lord, Ps 50:1
who is **m** as you are, O Lord, Ps 89:8
Praise him for his **m** deeds; Ps 150:2
M God, Everlasting Father, Is 9:6
a **m** one who will save; he Zep 3:17
under the **m** hand of God so 1 Pt 5:6

MILE
forces you to go one **m**, Mt 5:41

MILK
a land flowing with **m** and Ex 3:8
Come, buy wine and **m** Is 55:1
I fed you with **m**, not solid 1 Cor 3:2
You need **m**, not solid food, Heb 5:12
lives on **m** is unskilled in Heb 5:13
long for the pure spiritual **m**, 1 Pt 2:2

MILLSTONE
great **m** fastened around his Mt 18:6

MIND
he should change his **m**. Nm 23:19
and with a willing **m**, 1 Chr 28:9
me; test my heart and my **m**. Ps 26:2
and will not change his **m**, Ps 110:4
peace whose **m** is stayed on Is 26:3
soul and with all your **m**. Mt 22:37
the law of God with my **m**, Rom 7:25
For the **m** that is set on the Rom 8:7
by the renewal of your **m**, Rom 12:2
my spirit prays but my **m** 1 Cor 14:14
Have this **m** among Phil 2:5
and to **m** your own 1 Thes 4:11
and will not change his **m**, Heb 7:21
have unity of **m**, sympathy, 1 Pt 3:8

MINDFUL
what is man that you are **m** of Ps 8:4
man, that you are **m** of him, Heb 2:6

MINDS
you who test the **m** and hearts, Ps 7:9
set their **m** on the things Rom 8:5
with **m** set on earthly Phil 3:19
and your **m** in Christ Jesus. Phil 4:7
Set your **m** on things that are Col 3:2
put my laws into their **m**, Heb 8:10
preparing your **m** for action, 1 Pt 1:13

MINISTERING
and the angels were **m** to Mk 1:13
Are they not all **m** spirits Heb 1:14

MINISTRY
and to the **m** of the word." Acts 6:4
us the **m** of reconciliation; 2 Cor 5:18
the saints for the work of **m**, Eph 4:12
an evangelist, fulfill your **m**. 2 Tm 4:5
Christ has obtained a **m** that Heb 8:6

MIRACLES
his **m** and the judgments 1 Chr 16:12
that he has done, his **m**, Ps 105:5
the working of **m**, 1 Cor 12:10
third teachers, then **m**, 1 Cor 12:28
Do all work **m**? 1 Cor 12:29
and works **m** among you do Gal 3:5
and various **m** and by gifts Heb 2:4

MIRACULOUS
that is why these **m** powers Mt 14:2
That is why these **m** powers Mk 6:14

MIRIAM
And **M** sang to them: "Sing Ex 15:21
M and Aaron spoke against Nm 12:1

MIRROR
For now we see in a **m** 1 Cor 13:12
at his natural face in a **m**. Jas 1:23

MIRY
destruction, out of the **m** bog, Ps 40:2

MISERIES
weep and howl for the **m** that Jas 5:1

MISERY
over the **m** of Israel. Jgs 10:16
remember their **m** no more. Prv 31:7
their paths are ruin and **m**, Rom 3:16

MISLEADS
"'Cursed be anyone who **m** Dt 27:18
Whoever **m** the upright Prv 28:10

MISSES
with his feet **m** his way. Prv 19:2

MIST
and a **m** was going up from Gn 2:6
a cloud and your sins like **m**; Is 44:22
For you are a **m** that Jas 4:14

MOCK
All who see me **m** me; they Ps 22:7
Fools **m** at the guilt offering, Prv 14:9
And they will **m** him and Mk 10:34

MOCKED
And at noon Elijah **m** 1 Kgs 18:27
they **m** him, saying, "Hail, Mt 27:29
and elders, **m** him, saying, Mt 27:41
not be deceived: God is not **m**, Gal 6:7

MOCKER
Wine is a **m**, strong drink a Prv 20:1

MODEL
to be a **m** of good works, Ti 2:7

MODESTY
treated with greater **m**, 1 Cor 12:23
with **m** and self-control, 1 Tm 2:9

MOMENT
joy of the godless but for a **m**? Jb 20:5
For his anger is but for a **m**, Ps 30:5
be brought forth in one **m**? Is 66:8
in a **m**, in the twinkling 1 Cor 15:52
in submission even for a **m**, Gal 2:5

MOMENTARY
For this slight **m** affliction 2 Cor 4:17

MONEY
He who loves **m** will not be Eccl 5:10
be redeemed without **m**." Is 52:3
and he who has no **m**, come, Is 55:1
You cannot serve God and **m**. Mt 6:24
nor bag, nor bread, nor **m**; Lk 9:3
the gift of God with **m**! Acts 8:20
not a lover of **m**. 1 Tm 3:3
For the love of **m** is a root 1 Tm 6:10
lovers of **m**, proud, arrogant, 2 Tm 3:2
life free from love of **m**, Heb 13:5

MOON
of the full **m** and spreads over Jb 26:9
fingers, the **m** and the stars, Ps 8:3
darkness, and the **m** to blood, Jl 2:31
and the **m** will not give its Mt 24:29
and the **m** to blood, Acts 2:20
another glory of the **m**, 1 Cor 15:41

MORALS
company ruins good **m**." 1 Cor 15:33

MORDECAI
citadel whose name was **M**, Est 2:5

MORNING
evening and there was **m**, Gn 1:5
In the **m** you shall say, 'If Dt 28:67
in the **m** you hear my voice; Ps 5:3
they are new every **m**; Lam 3:23
and the **m** star rises in 2 Pt 1:19
of David, the bright **m** star." Rv 22:16

MORTAL
'Can **m** man be in the right Jb 4:17
reign in your **m** bodies, Rom 6:12
and the **m** puts on 1 Cor 15:54

MOSES
She named him **M**, she said, Ex 2:10
of it, he sought to kill **M**. Ex 2:15
Now **M** was keeping the flock Ex 3:1
God said to **M**, "I am who I Ex 3:14
So **M** and Aaron went to Ex 7:10
Then **M** stretched out his Ex 9:23
Then **M** made Israel set out Ex 15:22
while **M** went up to God. Ex 19:3
M entered the cloud and Ex 24:18
M erected the tabernacle. Ex 40:18
M and Aaron were among Ps 99:6
the law of my servant **M**, Mal 4:4
there appeared to them **M** Mt 17:3
the law was given through **M**; Jn 1:17
reigned from Adam to **M**, Rom 5:14
into **M** in the cloud 1 Cor 10:2
just as **M** also was faithful in Heb 3:2
Now **M** was faithful in all Heb 3:5
And they sing the song of **M**, Rv 15:3

MOTH
where **m** and rust destroy Mt 6:19

MOTHER
and his **m** and hold fast Gn 2:24
because she was the **m** of all Gn 3:20
your father and your **m**, Ex 20:12
cursed his father or his **m**; Lv 20:9
your father and your **m**, Dt 5:16
and in sin did my **m** conceive Ps 51:5
making her the joyous **m** of Ps 113:9
son is a sorrow to his **m**. Prv 10:1
foolish man despises his **m**. Prv 15:20
brings shame to his **m**. Prv 29:15
As one whom his **m** comforts, Is 66:13
When his **m** Mary had been Mt 1:18
Whoever loves father or **m** Mt 10:37
told him, "Who is my **m**, Mt 12:48
'Whoever reviles father or **m** Mt 15:4
father and **m** and be joined Mt 19:5
Honor your father and **m**, Mt 19:19
disciple, "Behold, your **m**!" Jn 19:27
father and **m** and be joined Eph 5:31
"Honor your father and **m**" Eph 6:2

MOTHER'S
my **m** womb, and naked shall Jb 1:21
forsake not your **m** teaching, Prv 1:8
his **m** womb he shall go Eccl 5:15

MOUNTAIN
came to Horeb, the **m** of God. Ex 3:1
city of our God! His holy **m**, Ps 48:1
very high **m** and showed him Mt 4:8
crowds, he went up on the **m**, Mt 5:1
seed, you will say to this **m**, Mt 17:20
the Spirit to a great, high **m**, Rv 21:10

MOUNTAINS
How beautiful upon the **m** Is 52:7
the **m** and the hills before Is 55:12
faith, so as to remove **m**, 1 Cor 13:2

MOURN
and those who **m** are lifted to Jb 5:11
a time to laugh; a time to **m**, Eccl 3:4
God; to comfort all who **m**; Is 61:2
"Blessed are those who **m**, Mt 5:4

MOURNING
and your days of **m** shall be Is 60:20
I will turn their **m** into joy; Jer 31:13
neither shall there be **m** nor Rv 21:4

MOUTH
comes from the **m** of the Lord. Dt 8:3
shall not depart from your **m**, Jos 1:8
Out of the **m** of babes and Ps 8:2
Let the words of my **m** and Ps 19:14
He put a new song in my **m**, Ps 40:3
My **m** is filled with your Ps 71:8
Whoever guards his **m** Prv 13:3
A fool's **m** is his ruin, and Prv 18:7
in your **m** and covered you Is 51:16
yet he opened not his **m**; and Is 53:7
there was no deceit in his **m**. Is 53:9
comes from the **m** of God.'" Mt 4:4
of the heart the **m** speaks. Mt 12:34
what comes out of the **m**; Mt 15:11
if you confess with your **m** Rom 10:9
I will spit you out of my **m**. Rv 3:16

MULTIPLY
"Be fruitful and **m** and fill Gn 1:22
"Be fruitful and **m** and fill the Gn 9:1
they shall be fruitful and **m**. Jer 23:3
I will bless you and **m** you." Heb 6:14

MULTITUDE
and will cover a **m** of sins. Jas 5:20
since love covers a **m** of sins. 1 Pt 4:8
a great **m** that no one could Rv 7:9

MULTITUDES
M, multitudes, in the valley of Jl 3:14

MURDER
"You shall not **m**. Ex 20:13
"'You shall not **m**. Dt 5:17
those of old, 'You shall not **m**; Mt 5:21
adultery, You shall not **m**, Rom 13:9
also said, "Do not **m**." If you Jas 2:11

MURDERER
The **m** shall be put to death. Nm 35:16
He was a **m** from the Jn 8:44
you suffer as a **m** or a thief 1 Pt 4:15
hates his brother is a **m**, 1 Jn 3:15

MURDERERS
fathers and mothers, for **m**, 1 Tm 1:9
the detestable, as for **m**, Rv 21:8

MUSIC
you, O Lord, I will make **m**. Ps 101:1
and we will play my **m** on Is 38:20

and have put on the **n** self, Col 3:10
when I will establish a **n** Heb 8:8
mediator of a **n** covenant, Heb 9:15
and a **n** earth in which 2 Pt 3:13

NEWBORN
Like **n** infants, long for the 1 Pt 2:2

NEWNESS
we too might walk in **n** of life. Rom 6:4

NEWS
of him who brings good **n**, Is 52:7
and the poor have good **n** Mt 11:5
and to bring you this good **n**. Lk 1:19
I bring you good **n** of a great Lk 2:10
preaching good **n** of peace Acts 10:36
who preach the good **n**!" Rom 10:15
us the good **n** of your faith 1 Thes 3:6
And this word is the good **n** 1 Pt 1:25

NICODEMUS
of the Pharisees named **N**, Jn 3:1

NIGHT
and the darkness he called **N**. Gn 1:5
But the **n** is long, and I am Jb 7:4
law he meditates day and **n**. Ps 1:2
lamp does not go out at **n**. Prv 31:18
Watchman, what time of the **n**? Is 21:11
my covenant with the **n**, Jer 33:20
mother by **n** and departed to Mt 2:14
I tell you, this very **n**, you Mt 26:34
This **n** your soul is required Lk 12:20
This man came to Jesus by **n** Jn 3:2
come like a thief in the **n**. 1 Thes 5:2
We are not of the **n** or of 1 Thes 5:5
And **n** will be no more. They Rv 22:5

NINEVEH
"Arise, go to **N**, that great city, Jon 1:2
An oracle concerning **N**. The Na 1:1
The men of **N** will rise up Mt 12:41

NOAH
and called his name **N**, "Out Gn 5:29
But **N** found favor in the eyes Gn 6:8
Then the Lord said to **N**, "Go Gn 7:1
went into the ark with **N**, Gn 7:15
When **N** awoke from his Gn 9:24
"This is like the days of **N** to Is 54:9
As were the days of **N**, so Mt 24:37
until the day when **N** Mt 24:38
By faith **N**, being warned by Heb 11:7
waited in the days of **N**, 1 Pt 3:20
world, but preserved **N**, with 2 Pt 2:5

NOBLE
for I will speak **n** things, Prv 8:6
But he who is **n** plans **n** things, Is 32:8
not many were of **n** birth. 1 Cor 1:26
he desires a **n** task. 1 Tm 3:1

NOISE
let us make a joyful **n** to the Ps 95:1
Make a joyful **n** to the Lord, Ps 100:1

NOTHING
And **n** that they propose to do Gn 11:6
Only do **n** to these men, for Gn 19:8
fish we ate in Egypt that cost **n**, Nm 11:5
strong drink, and eat **n** unclean, Jgs 13:4
my father does **n** either great or 1 Sm 20:2
Lord my God that cost me **n**." 2 Sm 24:24
speak to me **n** but the truth 1 Kgs 22:16
N shall be left, says the Lord. 2 Kgs 20:17
"**N** has been done for him." Est 6:3
tested me, and you will find **n**; Ps 17:3
there is **n** hidden from its heat. Ps 19:6
the counsel of the nations to **n**; Ps 33:10
there is **n** on earth that I desire Ps 73:25
from me; I will know **n** of evil Ps 101:4
n can make them stumble Ps 119:165
is **n** twisted or crooked in them. Prv 8:8
of the sluggard craves and gets **n** Prv 13:4
pretends to be rich, yet has **n**; Prv 13:7
will seek at harvest and have **n**. Prv 20:4
there is **n** new under the sun. Eccl 1:9
There is **n** better for a person Eccl 2:24
perceived that there is **n** better Eccl 3:12
shall take **n** for his toil that he Eccl 5:15
brings princes to **n**, and makes Is 40:23
All who fashion idols are **n**, Is 44:9

my people are taken away for **n**? Is 52:5
arm! **N** is too hard for you. Jer 32:17
who puts **n** into their mouths. Mi 3:5
for **n** is covered that will not be Mt 10:26
said **n** to them without a parable Mt 13:34
three days and have **n** to eat. Mt 15:32
n will be impossible for you." Mt 17:20
swears by the temple, it is **n**, Mt 23:16
with **n** but a linen cloth about Mk 14:51
n will be impossible with God. Lk 1:37
"Take **n** for your journey, no staff, Lk 9:3
enemy, and **n** shall hurt you. Lk 10:19
lack anything?" They said, "**N**." Lk 22:35
n deserving death has been done Lk 23:15
you have **n** to draw water with, Jn 4:11
that **n** worse may happen to you." Jn 5:14
"I can do **n** on my own. As I Jn 5:30
fragments, that **n** may be lost." Jn 6:12
"If I glorify myself, my glory is **n**. Jn 8:54
not from God, he could do **n**." Jn 9:33
for apart from me you can do **n**. Jn 15:5
you have asked **n** in my name. Jn 16:24
but that night they caught **n**. Jn 21:3
Artemis may be counted as **n**, Acts 19:27
there is **n** to their charges Acts 25:11
But I have **n** definite to write Acts 25:26
of sin might be brought to **n**, Rom 6:6
know that **n** good dwells in me, Rom 7:18
and had done **n** either good Rom 9:11
Lord Jesus that **n** is unclean in Rom 14:14
For I decided to know **n** among 1 Cor 2:2
but have not love, I am **n**. 1 Cor 13:2
but have not love, I gain **n**. 1 Cor 13:3
when he is **n**, he deceives himself. Gal 6:3
Do **n** from rivalry or conceit, but Phil 2:3
made himself **n**, taking the form Phil 2:7
n is to be rejected if it is received 1 Tm 4:4
Have **n** to do with irreverent, 1 Tm 4:7
doing **n** from partiality. 1 Tm 5:21
with conceit and understands **n**. 1 Tm 6:4
we brought **n** into the world, 1 Tm 6:7
Have **n** to do with foolish, 2 Tm 2:23
defiled and unbelieving, **n** is pure; Ti 1:15
have **n** more to do with him, Ti 3:10
to say **n** of your owing me even Phlm 1:19
I have prospered, and I need **n**, Rv 3:17
But **n** unclean will ever enter it, Rv 21:27

NULLIFY
Does their faithlessness **n** Rom 3:3
I do not **n** the grace of God, Gal 2:21

NUMBER
if you are able to **n** them." Gn 15:5
So teach us to **n** our days Ps 90:12
He determines the **n** of the Ps 147:4
brings out their host by **n**, Is 40:26
"Though the **n** of the sons Rom 9:27
multitude that no one could **n**, Rv 7:9
of a man, and his **n** is 666. Rv 13:18

OATH
is keeping the **o** that he swore Dt 7:8
you, Do not take an **o** at all, Mt 5:34
by earth or by any other **o**, Jas 5:12

OBADIAH
O took a hundred 1 Kgs 18:4
And **O** recognized him 1 Kgs 18:7
The vision of **O**. Thus says the Ob 1:1

OBEDIENCE
and to him shall be the **o** of Gn 49:10
bring about the **o** of faith for Rom 1:5
so by the one man's **o** the Rom 5:19
leads to death, or of **o**, Rom 6:16
bring the Gentiles to **o**— Rom 15:18
when your **o** is complete. 2 Cor 10:6
he learned **o** through what Heb 5:8
for **o** to Jesus Christ and for 1 Pt 1:2
souls by your **o** to the truth 1 Pt 1:22

OBEDIENT
priests became **o** to the faith. Acts 6:7
become **o** from the heart Rom 6:17
you are **o** in everything. 2 Cor 2:9
by becoming **o** to the point Phil 2:8
rulers and authorities, to be **o**, Ti 3:1
As **o** children, do not be 1 Pt 1:14

OBEY
"But if you carefully **o** his Ex 23:22
"And if you will indeed **o** Dt 11:13

Be careful to **o** all these Dt 12:28
commandments and **o** his voice, Dt 13:4
who will not **o** the voice of Dt 21:18
and **o** his voice in all that I Dt 30:2
If you **o** the commandments Dt 30:16
all things, so we will **o** you. Jos 1:17
Behold, to **o** is better than 1 Sm 15:22
be careful to **o** my statutes. Ez 37:24
whoever does not **o** the Son Jn 3:36
"We must **o** God rather Acts 5:29
and do not **o** the truth, Rom 2:8
of the one whom you **o**, Rom 6:16
o your parents in the Lord, Eph 6:1
Slaves, **o** your earthly Eph 6:5
Children, **o** your parents in Col 3:20
who do not **o** the gospel of 2 Thes 1:8
salvation to all who **o** him, Heb 5:9
O your leaders and submit Heb 13:17
who do not **o** the gospel of 1 Pt 4:17
when we love God and **o** 1 Jn 5:2

OBEYED
because you have **o** my Gn 22:18
But they have not all **o** Rom 10:16
as you have always **o**, not Phil 2:12
By faith Abraham **o** when Heb 11:8

OBLIGATION
I am under **o** both to Rom 1:14
have an **o** to bear with Rom 15:1

OBSERVE
Blessed are they who **o** Ps 106:3
your law and **o** it with my Ps 119:34
and let your eyes **o** my Prv 23:26
teaching them to **o** all that I Mt 28:20

OBSOLETE
he makes the first one **o**. Heb 8:13

OBSTACLE
than put an **o** in the way 1 Cor 9:12
We put no **o** in anyone's 2 Cor 6:3

OBTAIN
who understands **o** guidance, Prv 1:5
lowly in spirit will **o** honor. Prv 29:23
The meek shall **o** fresh joy Is 29:19
you could **o** the gift of Acts 8:20
Israel failed to **o** what it Rom 11:7
So run that you may **o** it. 1 Cor 9:24
but to **o** salvation through 1 Thes 5:9
so that you may **o** the 2 Thes 2:14
that they also may **o** the 2 Tm 2:10
one fails to **o** the grace of Heb 12:15
that you may **o** a blessing. 1 Pt 3:9

OBTAINED
Through him we have also **o** Rom 5:2
The elect **o** it, but the rest Rom 11:7
In him we have **o** an Eph 1:11
Not that I have already **o** Phil 3:12
But as it is, Christ has **o** a Heb 8:6

OBTAINING
o the outcome of your faith, 1 Pt 1:9

OFFENDED
A brother **o** is more Prv 18:19
the one who is not **o** by me." Mt 11:6

OFFENSE
Whoever covers an **o** seeks Prv 17:9
his glory to overlook an **o**. Prv 19:11
and a stone of **o** and a rock Is 8:14
stumbling, and a rock of **o**; Rom 9:33
In that case the **o** of the cross Gal 5:11
stumbling, and a rock of **o**." 1 Pt 2:8

OFFER
and thus let us **o** to God Heb 12:28
continually **o** up a sacrifice Heb 13:15
to **o** spiritual sacrifices 1 Pt 2:5

OFFERED
o himself without blemish Heb 9:14
so Christ, having been **o** Heb 9:28
But when Christ had **o** for Heb 10:12

OFFERING
the lamb for a burnt **o**, Gn 22:8
Sacrifice and **o** you have not Ps 40:6
be pleased with a burnt **o**. Ps 51:16
when his soul makes an **o** Is 53:10

So if you are **o** your gift at Mt 5:23
a fragrant **o** and sacrifice to Eph 5:2
through the **o** of the body Heb 10:10
For by a single **o** he has Heb 10:14

OFFERINGS
burnt **o** and sacrifices." Mk 12:33
"Sacrifices and **o** you have Heb 10:5

OFFSPRING
and between your **o** and her Gn 3:15
"To your **o** I will give this Gn 12:7
I will make your **o** as the Gn 13:16
His **o** shall endure forever, Ps 89:36
for sin, he shall see his **o**; Is 53:10
the promise are counted as **o**. Rom 9:8
then you are Abraham's **o**, Gal 3:29

OIL
you anoint my head with **o**; Ps 23:5
the **o** of gladness instead of Is 61:3
has anointed you with the **o** Heb 1:9
anointing him with **o** in the Jas 5:14

OLD
The **o** has passed away; 2 Cor 5:17
to put off your **o** self, which Eph 4:22
have put off the **o** self with its Col 3:9
than the **o** as the covenant Heb 8:6

OLIVE
And there are two **o** trees by Zec 4:3
although a wild **o** shoot, Rom 11:17
These are the two **o** trees Rv 11:4

OLIVES
Jesus went to the Mount of **O**. Jn 8:1
fig tree, my brothers, bear **o**, Jas 3:12

OLIVET
on the mount called **O**. Lk 21:37
from the mount called **O**, Acts 1:12

OMEGA
"I am the Alpha and the **O**," Rv 1:8
I am the Alpha and the **O**, Rv 21:6
I am the Alpha and the **O**, Rv 22:13

OMRI
O overcame the people 1 Kgs 16:22
O did what was evil in 1 Kgs 16:25

ONESIMUS
and with him **O**, our faithful Col 4:9
to you for my child, **O**, Phlm 1:10

OPEN
and his ears are **o** to their 1 Pt 3:12
I have set before you an **o** Rv 3:8
"Who is worthy to **o** the scroll Rv 5:2

OPENED
eat of it your eyes will be **o**, Gn 3:5
yet he **o** not his mouth; and Is 53:7
that anyone **o** the eyes of Jn 9:32
I see the heavens **o**, Acts 7:56
that he **o** for us through Heb 10:20

OPENS
the Lord **o** the eyes of the Ps 146:8
To him the gatekeeper **o**. The Jn 10:3
so he **o** not his mouth. Acts 8:32
my voice and **o** the door, Rv 3:20

OPINIONS
between two different **o**? 1 Kgs 18:21
but not to quarrel over **o**. Rom 14:1

OPPORTUNITY
But sin, seizing an **o** Rom 7:8
as an **o** for the flesh, Gal 5:13
So then, as we have **o**, let us Gal 6:10
and give no **o** to the devil. Eph 4:27
for me, but you had no **o**. Phil 4:10

OPPOSES
it says, "God **o** the proud, Jas 4:6
for "God **o** the proud but 1 Pt 5:5

OPPRESS
wrong a sojourner or **o** him, Ex 22:21
"You shall not **o** your Lv 19:13
do not **o** the widow, the Zec 7:10

OPPRESSED
Lord is a stronghold for the **o**, Ps 9:9
executes justice for the **o**, Ps 146:7
He was **o**, and he was Is 53:7

ORDERLY
to write an **o** account for you, Lk 1:3

ORGIES
the **o** on the mountains. Truly Jer 3:23
not in **o** and drunkenness, Rom 13:13
envy, drunkenness, **o**, and Gal 5:21
drunkenness, **o**, drinking parties, 1 Pt 4:3

ORPHANS
"I will not leave you as **o**; Jn 14:18
to visit **o** and widows in Jas 1:27

OUTCOME
Consider the **o** of their way Heb 13:7
obtaining the **o** of your faith, 1 Pt 1:9
what will be the **o** for those 1 Pt 4:17

OUTSIDERS
I to do with judging **o**? 1 Cor 5:12
and **o** or unbelievers 1 Cor 14:23
yourselves wisely toward **o**, Col 4:5
o and be dependent 1 Thes 4:12
be well thought of by **o**, 1 Tm 3:7

OUTSTRETCHED
you with an **o** arm and with Ex 6:6
strong hand and an **o** arm, Ps 136:12
and my **o** arm have made Jer 27:5
and an **o** arm and with Ez 20:33

OUTWARD
man looks on the **o** appearance 1 Sm 16:7
who boast about **o** appearance 2 Cor 5:12

OVERCOME
and the darkness has not **o** it. Jn 1:5
— I have **o** the world." Jn 16:33
Do not be **o** by evil, but Rom 12:21
and you have **o** the evil 1 Jn 2:14
you are from God and have **o** 1 Jn 4:4

OVERCOMES
For whatever **o** a person, 2 Pt 2:19
born of God **o** the world. 1 Jn 5:4
Who is it that **o** the world 1 Jn 5:5

OVERFLOWS
my head with oil; my cup **o**. Ps 23:5
My heart **o** with a pleasing Ps 45:1

OVERSEER
aspires to the office of **o**, 1 Tm 3:1
Therefore an **o** must be 1 Tm 3:2
For an **o**, as God's steward, Ti 1:7
and **O** of your souls. 1 Pt 2:25

OVERSEERS
Spirit has made you **o**, Acts 20:28
with the **o** and deacons: Phil 1:1

OVERTAKEN
my iniquities have **o** me, Ps 40:12
No temptation has **o** you 1 Cor 10:13

OWE
O no one anything, except Rom 13:8

OX
"You shall not muzzle an **o** Dt 25:4
lion shall eat straw like the **o**. Is 11:7
"You shall not muzzle an **o** 1 Cor 9:9

PAGANS
not tolerated even among **p**, 1 Cor 5:1
No, I imply that what **p** 1 Cor 10:20
you were **p** you were led 1 Cor 12:2

PAIN
in **p** you shall bring forth Gn 3:16
"Man is also rebuked with **p** Jb 33:19
nor crying nor **p** anymore, Rv 21:4

PAINFUL
and from the **p** toil of our Gn 5:29
p rather than pleasant, Heb 12:11

PALMS
you on the **p** of my hands; Is 49:16

PARABLE
I will open my mouth in a **p**; Ps 78:2
to them without a **p**. Mt 13:34

PARADISE
you will be with me in **P**." Lk 23:43
life, which is in the **p** of God.' Rv 2:7

PARALYTIC
bringing to him a **p** carried by Mk 2:3

PARDON
and **p** our iniquity and our Ex 34:9
Please **p** the iniquity of Nm 14:19
p my guilt, for it is great. Ps 25:11
God, for he will abundantly **p**. Is 55:7

PARDONING
Who is a God like you, **p** Mi 7:18

PARENTS
or brothers or **p** or children, Lk 18:29
even by **p** and brothers and Lk 21:16
of evil, disobedient to **p**, Rom 1:30
to save up for their **p**, 2 Cor 12:14
obey your **p** in the Lord, Eph 6:1
obey your **p** in everything, Col 3:20
disobedient to their **p**, unholy, 2 Tm 3:2

PARTAKE
for we all **p** of the one 1 Cor 10:17

PARTAKERS
and **p** of the promise in Eph 3:6
for you are all **p** with me of Phil 1:7
may become **p** of the divine 2 Pt 1:4

PARTIAL
who is not **p** and takes no Dt 10:17
the **p** will pass away. 1 Cor 13:10

PARTIALITY
You shall not show **p**, and Dt 16:19
or **p** or taking bribes." 2 Chr 19:7
P in judging is not good. Prv 24:23
But if you show **p**, you are Jas 2:9

PARTICIPATION
is it not a **p** in the blood 1 Cor 10:16
love, any **p** in the Spirit, Phil 2:1

PARTNERSHIP
For what **p** has righteousness 2 Cor 6:14
because of your **p** in the Phil 1:5
no church entered into **p** Phil 4:15

PARTS
you formed my inward **p**; Ps 139:13
it is, there are many **p**, 1 Cor 12:20
into the lower **p** of the earth? Eph 4:9

PASS
the blood, I will **p** over you, Ex 12:13
and it shall not **p** away. Ps 148:6
to you, all you who **p** by? Lam 1:12
Heaven and earth will **p** Lk 21:33
the partial will **p** away. 1 Cor 13:10
and then the heavens will **p** 2 Pt 3:10

PASSED
p between these pieces. Gn 15:17
The Lord **p** before him and Ex 34:6
but has **p** from death to life. Jn 5:24
he had **p** over former sins. Rom 3:25
The old has **p** away; the 2 Cor 5:17
We know that we have **p** 1 Jn 3:14

PASSION
than to be aflame with **p**. 1 Cor 7:9
not in the **p** of lust like 1 Thes 4:5

PASSIONS
in the flesh, our sinful **p**, Rom 7:5
flesh with its **p** and desires. Gal 5:24
ungodliness and worldly **p**, Ti 2:12
do not be conformed to the **p** 1 Pt 1:14

PASSOVER
in haste. It is the Lord's **P**. Ex 12:11
and keep the **P** to the Lord Dt 16:1
So they slaughtered the **P** Ezr 6:20
and they prepared the **P**. Mt 26:19
intending after the **P** to Acts 12:4
For Christ, our **P** lamb, 1 Cor 5:7

By faith he kept the **P** and Heb 11:28

PASTORS

evangelists, the **p** and teachers, Eph 4:11

PASTURE

we are the people of his **p**, Ps 95:7
people, and the sheep of his **p**. Ps 100:3
and on rich **p** they shall Ez 34:14
will go in and out and find **p**. Jn 10:9

PASTURES

He makes me lie down in green **p**. Ps 23:2

PATCH

for the **p** tears away from the Mt 9:16

PATH

known to me the **p** of life; Ps 16:11
Lead me in the **p** of your Ps 119:35
feet and a light to my **p**. Ps 119:105
But the **p** of the righteous is Prv 4:18
is on the **p** to life, Prv 10:17
The **p** of the righteous is Is 26:7
some seeds fell along the **p**, Mt 13:4

PATHS

He leads me in **p** of Ps 23:3
O Lord; teach me your **p**. Ps 25:4
he will make straight your **p**. Prv 3:6
the Lord; make his **p** straight." Mt 3:3
known to me the **p** of life; Acts 2:28
and make straight **p** for Heb 12:13

PATIENCE

to those who by **p** in Rom 2:7
has endured with much **p** Rom 9:22
peace, **p**, kindness, goodness, Gal 5:22
and gentleness, with **p**, Eph 4:2
perfect **p** as an example 1 Tm 1:16
and **p** inherit the promises. Heb 6:12
when God's **p** waited in the 1 Pt 3:20
And count the **p** of our Lord 2 Pt 3:15

PATIENT

hope, be **p** in tribulation, Rom 12:12
Love is **p** and kind; love 1 Cor 13:4
weak, be **p** with them all. 1 Thes 5:14
Be **p**, therefore, brothers, until Jas 5:7
but is **p** toward you, 2 Pt 3:9

PATIENTLY

I waited **p** for the Lord; he Ps 40:1
you **p** endure the same 2 Cor 1:6
to teach, **p** enduring evil, 2 Tm 2:24

PATTERN

Follow the **p** of the 2 Tm 1:13

PAUL

who was also called **P**, Acts 13:9
they stoned **P** and dragged Acts 14:19
Felix left **P** in prison. Acts 24:27
What is **P**? Servants 1 Cor 3:5
I, **P**, an old man and now a Phlm 1:9

PAY

wrath will **p** the penalty, Prv 19:19
Is it lawful to **p** taxes to Mt 22:17
P to all what is owed to Rom 13:7
Therefore we must **p** much Heb 2:1
do well to **p** attention as to 2 Pt 1:19

PEACE

said to Moses, "Go in **p**." Ex 4:18
upon you and give you **p**. Nm 6:26
greet him: '**P** be to you, 1 Sm 25:6
with God, and be at **p**; Jb 22:21
who speak **p** with their Ps 28:3
good; seek **p** and pursue it. Ps 34:14
for he will speak **p** to his Ps 85:8
Pray for the **p** of Jerusalem! Ps 122:6
for war, and a time for **p**. Eccl 3:8
Everlasting Father, Prince of **P**. Is 9:6
You keep him in perfect **p** Is 26:3
"There is no **p**," says the Is 48:22
lightly, saying, '**P**, **p**,' Jer 6:14
We looked for **p**, but no good Jer 8:15
and he shall speak **p** to the Zec 9:10
come to bring **p** to the earth. Mt 10:34
our feet into the way of **p**." Lk 1:79
and on earth **p** among those Lk 2:14
first say, '**P** be to this house!' Lk 10:5
P I leave with you; my **p** Jn 14:27
that in me you may have **p**. Jn 16:33
and said, "**P** be with you." Jn 20:26
preaching good news of **p** Acts 10:36
we have **p** with God Rom 5:1
on the Spirit is life and **p**. Rom 8:6
God has called you to **p**. 1 Cor 7:15
God of confusion but of **p**. 1 Cor 14:33
joy, **p**, patience, kindness, Gal 5:22
For he himself is our **p**, Eph 2:14
of the two, so making **p**, Eph 2:15
and preached **p** to you who Eph 2:17
far off and **p** to those who Eph 2:17
of the Spirit in the bond of **p**. Eph 4:3
given by the gospel of **p**. Eph 6:15
And the **p** of God, which Phil 4:7
making **p** by the blood of his Col 1:20
And let the **p** of Christ rule Col 3:15
"There is **p** and security," 1 Thes 5:3
Now may the Lord of **p** 2 Thes 3:16
faith, love, and **p**, 2 Tm 2:22
Strive for **p** with everyone, Heb 12:14
is sown in **p** by those who Jas 3:18
let him seek **p** and pursue it. 1 Pt 3:11
spot or blemish, and at **p**. 2 Pt 3:14

PEACEMAKERS

"Blessed are the **p**, for they Mt 5:9

PEARL

who, on finding one **p** of Mt 13:46
the gates made of a single **p**, Rv 21:21

PEARLS

and do not throw your **p** Mt 7:6
in search of fine **p**, Mt 13:45
and gold or **p** or costly attire, 1 Tm 2:9
twelve gates were twelve **p**, Rv 21:21

PENALTY

great wrath will pay the **p**, Prv 19:19
for the death **p** in my case. Acts 28:18
the due **p** for their error. Rom 1:27

PENTECOST

When the day of **P** arrived, Acts 2:1

PEOPLE-PLEASERS

the way of eye-service, as **p**, Eph 6:6
by way of eye-service, as **p**, Col 3:22

PEOPLE

At that time **p** began to call upon Gn 4:26
these the **p** of the whole earth Gn 9:19
"Behold, they are one **p**, Gn 11:6
will you kill an innocent **p**? Gn 20:4
Egyptians were in dread of the **p** Ex 1:12
beating a Hebrew, one of his **p**. Ex 2:11
surely seen the affliction of my **p** Ex 3:7
the God of Israel, 'Let my **p** go, Ex 5:1
shall no longer give the **p** straw to Ex 5:7
why have you done evil to this **p**? Ex 5:22
take you to be my **p**, and I will be Ex 6:7
will put a division between my **p** Ex 8:23
you refuse to let my **p** go, behold, Ex 10:4
the womb among the **p** of Israel, Ex 13:2
Pharaoh let the **p** go, God Ex 13:17
Moses said to the **p**, "Fear not, Ex 14:13
Moses and the **p** of Israel sang Ex 15:1
p rested on the seventh day. Ex 16:30
was no water for the **p** to drink. Ex 17:1
do you sit alone, and all the **p** Ex 18:14
"Go down and warn the **p**, Ex 19:21
when all the **p** saw the thunder Ex 20:18
and told the **p** all the words Ex 24:3
the **p** saw that Moses delayed to Ex 32:1
and behold, it is a stiff-necked **p**. Ex 32:9
Israel, 'You are a stiff-necked **p**; Ex 33:5
person shall be cut off from his **p** Lv 7:21
the iniquities of the **p** of Israel Lv 16:21
for himself and for the **p**, Lv 16:24
possession among the **p** of Israel Lv 25:33
p complained in the hearing of Nm 11:1
the burden of all this **p** on me? Nm 11:11
pardon the iniquity of this **p**, Nm 14:19
holy contributions that the **p** of Nm 18:19
statute for the **p** of Israel, Nm 19:10
now, curse this **p** for me, since Nm 22:6
did not consume the **p** of Israel Nm 25:11
to be a **p** of his own inheritance, Dt 4:20
"For you are a **p** holy to the Dt 7:6
destroy not your **p** and your Dt 9:26
And all the **p** shall say, 'Amen.' Dt 27:17
this Jordan, you and all this **p** Jos 1:2
The **p** came up out of the Jordan Jos 4:19
But the **p** of Benjamin did not Jgs 1:21
"Because this **p** have transgressed Jgs 2:20
the **p** of Israel did what was evil Jgs 3:7
will return with you to your **p**." Ru 1:10
Your **p** shall be my people, and Ru 1:16
shall be shepherd of my **p** Israel, 2 Sm 5:2
all the Jews, the **p** of Mordecai, Est 3:6
Lord restores the fortunes of his **p** Ps 14:7
The Lord is the strength of his **p**; Ps 28:8
God restores the fortunes of his **p**, Ps 53:6
my **p** did not listen to my voice; Ps 81:11
the Lord will not forsake his **p**; Ps 94:14
and we are the **p** of his pasture, Ps 95:7
and we are his; we are his **p**, Ps 100:3
there is no guidance, a **p** falls, Prv 11:14
p is the glory of a king, Prv 14:28
Preacher also taught the **p** Eccl 12:9
know, my **p** do not understand." Is 1:3
Comfort, comfort my **p**, says Is 40:1
blows on it; surely the **p** are grass. Is 40:7
my **p** shall know my name. Is 52:6
But my **p** have forgotten me; Jer 18:15
weeks are decreed about your **p** Dn 9:24
My **P**, for you are not my **p**, Hos 1:9
"You are not my **p**," it shall be Hos 1:10
And my **p** shall never again be Jl 2:26
the **p** of Syria shall go into exile Am 1:5
remnant of my **p** shall plunder Zep 2:9
with all the remnant of the **p**, Hg 1:12
he will save his **p** from their sins Mt 1:21
who will shepherd my **p** Israel.'" Mt 2:6
prophets and righteous **p** longed Mt 13:17
p say that the Son of Man is?" Mt 16:13
proclaimed that **p** should repent. Mk 6:12
p honors me with their lips, Mk 7:6
can one feed these **p** with bread Mk 8:4
and for glory to your **p** Israel." Lk 2:32
when all the **p** were baptized, Lk 3:21
what then shall I compare the **p** Lk 7:31
Jesus went, the **p** pressed around Lk 8:42
the **p** rejoiced at all the glorious Lk 13:17
And the **p** stood by, watching, Lk 23:35
Father is seeking such **p** to Jn 4:23
I do not receive glory from **p**. Jn 5:41
one man should die for the **p**, Jn 11:50
earth, will draw all **p** to myself." Jn 12:32
and having favor with all the **p**. Acts 2:47
great many **p** were added to the Acts 11:24
many in this city who are my **p** Acts 18:10
The native **p** showed us unusual Acts 28:2
then, has God rejected his **p**? Rom 11:1
God has not rejected his **p** Rom 11:2
with sexually immoral **p** 1 Cor 5:9
who prophesies speaks to **p** for 1 Cor 14:3
are of all **p** most to be pitied. 1 Cor 15:19
Nor did we seek glory from **p**, 1 Thes 2:6
thanksgivings be made for all **p**, 1 Tm 2:1
desires all **p** to be saved and to 1 Tm 2:4
God, who is the Savior of all **p**, 1 Tm 4:10
desires that plunge **p** into ruin 1 Tm 6:9
For **p** will be lovers of self, 2 Tm 3:2
purify for himself a **p** for his own Ti 2:14
our **p** learn to devote themselves Ti 3:14
propitiation for the sins of the **p**. Heb 2:17
Sabbath rest for the **p** of God, Heb 4:9
a **p** for his own possession 1 Pt 2:9
you were not a **p**, but now you 1 Pt 2:10
Live as **p** who are free, not using 1 Pt 2:16
p who have not soiled their Rv 3:4
with them, and they will be his **p** Rv 21:3

PEOPLES

Clap your hands, all **p**! Shout Ps 47:1
he is exalted over all the **p**. Ps 99:2
all nations! Extol him, all **p**! Ps 117:1
kingdom, that all **p**, nations, Dn 7:14
the hills; and **p** shall flow to it, Mi 4:1
and let all the **p** extol Rom 15:11
from all tribes and **p** and Rv 7:9

PERFECT

My dove, my **p** one, is the only Sg 6:9
You keep him in **p** peace Is 26:3
You therefore must be **p**, as Mt 5:48
good and acceptable and **p**. Rom 12:2
but when the **p** comes, 1 Cor 13:10
for my power is made **p** in 2 Cor 12:9
this or am already **p**, Phil 3:12
together in **p** harmony. Col 3:14
his **p** patience as an 1 Tm 1:16
salvation **p** through suffering. Heb 2:10

And being made **p**, he — Heb 5:9
has been made **p** forever. — Heb 7:28
make **p** those who draw — Heb 10:1
they should not be made **p**. — Heb 11:40
of the righteous made **p**, — Heb 12:23
that you may be **p** and — Jas 1:4
Every good gift and every **p** — Jas 1:17
who looks into the **p** law, — Jas 1:25
but **p** love casts out fear. — 1 Jn 4:18

PERFECTER
the founder and **p** of our — Heb 12:2

PERFECTION
I have seen a limit to all **p**, — Ps 119:96
Now if **p** had been attainable — Heb 7:11

PERISH
the way of the wicked will **p**. — Ps 1:6
so the wicked shall **p** before — Ps 68:2
They will **p**, but you will — Ps 102:26
sword will **p** by the sword. — Mt 26:52
you will all likewise **p**. — Lk 13:3
should not **p** but have eternal — Jn 3:16
life, and they will never **p**, — Jn 10:28
they will **p**, but you remain; — Heb 1:11
wishing that any should **p**, — 2 Pt 3:9

PERISHABLE
For this **p** body must put — 1 Cor 15:53
not with **p** things such as — 1 Pt 1:18

PERJURERS
enslavers, liars, **p**, and — 1 Tm 1:10

PERMIT
I do not **p** a woman to teach — 1 Tm 2:12

PERSECUTE
you and **p** you and utter — Mt 5:11
pray for those who **p** you, — Mt 5:44
me, they will also **p** you. — Jn 15:20
Bless those who **p** you; — Rom 12:14

PERSECUTED
bless; when **p**, we endure; — 1 Cor 4:12
in Christ Jesus will be **p**, — 2 Tm 3:12

PERSECUTION
or distress, or **p**, or famine, — Rom 8:35

PERSEVERANCE
end keep alert with all **p**, — Eph 6:18

PERSEVERES
the law of liberty, and **p**, — Jas 1:25

PERSIA
of the kingdom of **P**, — 2 Chr 36:20
first year of Cyrus king of **P**, — Ezr 1:1
The army of **P** and Media and — Est 1:3
are the kings of Media and **P**. — Dn 8:20

PERSIST
P in this, for by so doing — 1 Tm 4:16
As for those who **p** in sin, — 1 Tm 5:20

PERSUADE
of the Lord, we **p** others. — 2 Cor 5:11

PERVERT
in secret to **p** the ways of — Prv 17:23
who **p** the grace of our God — Jude 1:4

PERVERTS
"'Cursed be anyone who **p** — Dt 27:19

PESTILENCE
nor the **p** that stalks in — Ps 91:6

PETER
Simon (who is called **P**) and — Mt 4:18
And I tell you, you are **P**, — Mt 16:18
Now **P** was sitting outside — Mt 26:69
Cephas" (which means **P**). — Jn 1:42
Jesus said to Simon **P**, son of — Jn 21:15
Then **P**, filled with the Holy — Acts 4:8
P was sleeping between — Acts 12:6
through **P** for his apostolic — Gal 2:8

PHARAOH
But the Lord afflicted **P** and — Gn 12:17
Then Joseph said to **P**, "The — Gn 41:25
Then **P** said to Joseph, "Your — Gn 47:5
"Go in, tell **P** king of Egypt to — Ex 6:11
When **P** let the people go, — Ex 13:17

PHARISEE
You blind **P**! First clean the — Mt 23:26
"Brothers, I am a **P**, a son — Acts 23:6
Hebrews; as to the law, a **P**; — Phil 3:5

PHARISEES
that of the scribes and **P**, — Mt 5:20

PHILADELPHIA
angel of the church in **P** write: — Rv 3:7

PHILIP
P and Bartholomew; Thomas — Mt 10:3

PHILOSOPHERS
p conversed with him. — Acts 17:18

PHILOSOPHY
captive by **p** and empty deceit, — Col 2:8

PHOEBE
to you our sister **P**, — Rom 16:1

PHYLACTERIES
For they make their **p** broad — Mt 23:5

PHYSICIAN
are well have no need of a **p**, — Mt 9:12
Luke the beloved **p** greets — Col 4:14

PIECES
passed between these **p**. — Gn 15:17
And they paid him thirty **p** — Mt 26:15

PIERCED
they have **p** my hands and — Ps 22:16
on him whom they have **p**, — Zec 12:10
But one of the soldiers **p** his — Jn 19:34
on him whom they have **p**." — Jn 19:37

PIGS
throw your pearls before **p**, — Mt 7:6

PILATE
him over to **P** the governor. — Mt 27:2
P answered, "What I have — Jn 19:22
denied in the presence of **P**, — Acts 3:13
Pontius **P** made the good — 1 Tm 6:13

PILLAR
and she became a **p** of salt. — Gn 19:26
by day in a **p** of cloud to — Ex 13:21
In the **p** of the cloud he — Ps 99:7
a **p** and buttress of truth — 1 Tm 3:15

PIT
He drew me up from the **p** of — Ps 40:2
your life from the **p**, — Ps 103:4
both will fall into a **p**." — Mt 15:14
and threw him into the **p**, — Rv 20:3

PITIED
of all people most to be **p**. — 1 Cor 15:19

PLACES
blessing in the heavenly **p**, — Eph 1:3
once for all into the holy **p**, — Heb 9:12

PLAGUE
"Yet one **p** more I will bring — Ex 11:1
at their gates, whatever **p**, — 2 Chr 6:28
earth with every kind of **p**, — Rv 11:6

PLAN
Do not **p** evil against your — Prv 3:29
but those who **p** peace — Prv 12:20
p and foreknowledge of — Acts 2:23
as a **p** for the fullness of — Eph 1:10

PLANNED
I **p** from days of old — 2 Kgs 19:25
"As I have **p**, so shall it be, — Is 14:24

PLANS
desire and fulfill all your **p**! — Ps 20:4
the **p** of his heart to all — Ps 33:11
Without counsel **p** fail, — Prv 15:22
P are established by — Prv 20:18
But he who is noble **p** noble — Is 32:8

PLANTED
And the Lord God **p** a garden — Gn 2:8
He is like a tree **p** by streams — Ps 1:3
has not **p** will be rooted — Mt 15:13
I **p**, Apollos watered, but — 1 Cor 3:6

PLANTS
vegetation, **p** yielding seed, — Gn 1:11
So neither he who **p** nor — 1 Cor 3:7
Who **p** a vineyard without — 1 Cor 9:7

PLAY
is upon you, he will **p** it, — 1 Sm 16:16
p skillfully on the strings, — Ps 33:3

PLAYED
"'We **p** the flute for you, we — Lk 7:32
anyone know what is **p**? — 1 Cor 14:7

PLEAD
If you will seek God and **p** — Jb 8:5
and to the Lord I **p** for mercy: — Ps 30:8
P my cause and redeem — Ps 119:154
for the Lord will **p** their — Prv 22:23

PLEADED
Three times I **p** with the — 2 Cor 12:8

PLEASANT
tree that is **p** to the sight — Gn 2:9
have fallen for me in **p** places; — Ps 16:6
Behold, how good and **p** it is — Ps 133:1
to our God; for it is **p**, — Ps 147:1
Light is sweet, and it is **p** — Eccl 11:7
How beautiful and **p** you are, — Sg 7:6
painful rather than **p**, — Heb 12:11

PLEASE
This will **p** the Lord more — Ps 69:31
When a man's ways **p** the — Prv 16:7
in the flesh cannot **p** God. — Rom 8:8
Let each of us **p** his — Rom 15:2
Lord, how to **p** the Lord. — 1 Cor 7:32
just as I try to **p** — 1 Cor 10:33
we make it our aim to **p** — 2 Cor 5:9
but to **p** God who tests our — 1 Thes 2:4
ought to live and to **p** God, — 1 Thes 4:1
since his aim is to **p** the one — 2 Tm 2:4
it is impossible to **p** him, — Heb 11:6

PLEASED
you will not be **p** with a — Ps 51:16
with whom I am well **p**." — Mt 3:17
it **p** God through the folly — 1 Cor 1:21
was **p** to reveal his Son to — Gal 1:16
of God was **p** to dwell, — Col 1:19
commended as having **p** God. — Heb 11:5
with whom I am well **p**," — 2 Pt 1:17

PLEASES
he does all that he **p**. — Ps 115:3
Whatever the Lord **p**, he does, — Ps 135:6
for this **p** the Lord. — Col 3:20
and do what **p** him. — 1 Jn 3:22

PLEASING
May my meditation be **p** to — Ps 104:34
the things that are **p** to him." — Jn 8:29
a sacrifice acceptable and **p** — Phil 4:18
of the Lord, fully **p** to him, — Col 1:10
for such sacrifices are **p** to — Heb 13:16

PLEASURE
but the Lord takes **p** in — Ps 147:11
Whoever loves **p** will be a — Prv 21:17
for it is your Father's good **p** — Lk 12:32
and to work for his good **p**. — Phil 2:13
lovers of **p** rather than — 2 Tm 3:4
nor taken **p** in sacrifices and — Heb 10:8

PLEASURES
at your right hand are **p** — Ps 16:11
cares and riches and **p** of life, — Lk 8:14
enjoy the fleeting **p** of sin. — Heb 11:25

PLENTIFUL
disciples, "The harvest is **p**, — Mt 9:37

PLOW
hand to the **p** and looks back — Lk 9:62

PLOWSHARES
shall beat their swords into **p**, — Is 2:4
Beat your **p** into swords, and — Jl 3:10
shall beat their swords into **p**, — Mi 4:3

PLUNDER
So you shall **p** the Egyptians — Ex 3:22

house and **p** his goods, Mt 12:29

POINT
obedient to the **p** of death, Phil 2:8
p has become accountable Jas 2:10

POISON
a restless evil, full of deadly **p**. Jas 3:8

POLLUTE
You shall not **p** the land in Nm 35:33

POLLUTED
And they **p** the house of 2 Chr 36:14
and the land was **p** with Ps 106:38
spring or a **p** fountain is a Prv 25:26
from the things **p** by idols, Acts 15:20

PONDER
Be angry, and do not sin; **p** in Ps 4:4
about and **p** what he has Ps 64:9
I will **p** the way that is Ps 101:2

POOR
But there will be no **p** among Dt 15:4
cease to be **p** in the land. Dt 15:11
The Lord makes **p** and 1 Sm 2:7
and the hope of the **p** shall Ps 9:18
delivering the **p** from him Ps 35:10
freely; he has given to the **p**; Ps 112:9
who is generous to the **p**. Prv 14:21
Better is a **p** person who Prv 19:1
The rich and the **p** meet Prv 22:2
defend the rights of the **p** Prv 31:9
to bring good news to the **p**; Is 61:1
"Blessed are the **p** in spirit, Mt 5:3
and the **p** have good news Mt 11:5
possess and give to the **p**, Mt 19:21
For you always have the **p** Mt 26:11
and he saw a **p** widow put in Lk 21:2
for your sake he became **p**, 2 Cor 8:9
those who are **p** in the world Jas 2:5

PORTION
But the Lord's **p** is his people, Dt 32:9
be a double **p** of your spirit 2 Kgs 2:9
my heart and my **p** forever. Ps 73:26
The Lord is my **p**; Ps 119:57
they shall possess a double **p**; Is 61:7
"The Lord is my **p**," says Lam 3:24

POSSESS
to give you this land to **p**." Gn 15:7
And your offspring shall **p** Gn 22:17
the land to you to **p** it. Nm 33:53
they shall **p** a double portion; Is 61:7
and **p** the kingdom forever, Dn 7:18
Do all **p** gifts of healing? 1 Cor 12:30

POSSESSING
nothing, yet **p** everything. 2 Cor 6:10

POSSESSION
Canaan, for an everlasting **p**, Gn 17:8
I will give it to you for a **p**. Ex 6:8
until we acquire **p** of it, Eph 1:14
a better **p** and an abiding Heb 10:34
a people for his own **p**, 1 Pt 2:9

POSSESSIONS
in the abundance of his **p**." Lk 12:15
his own **p** who are zealous Ti 2:14
the eyes and pride in **p** — 1 Jn 2:16

POSSIBLE
with God all things are **p**." Mt 19:26
astray, if **p**, even the elect. Mt 24:24
with men is **p** with God." Lk 18:27
If **p**, so far as it depends Rom 12:18
that by any means **p** I may Phil 3:11

POT
a smoking fire **p** and a Gn 15:17
there is death in the **p**!" 2 Kgs 4:40

POTIPHAR
had sold him in Egypt to **P**, Gn 37:36
and **P**, an officer of Pharaoh, Gn 39:1

POTTER
Shall the **p** be regarded as Is 29:16
the clay, and you are our **p**; Is 64:8
as it seemed good to the **p** to Jer 18:4
Has the **p** no right over the Rom 9:21

POUR
p out your heart before him; Ps 62:8
My lips will **p** forth praise, Ps 119:171
that I will **p** out my Spirit on Jl 2:28
for you and **p** down for you Mal 3:10
that I will **p** out my Spirit Acts 2:17

POURED
Spirit was **p** out even on Acts 10:45
has been **p** into our hearts Rom 5:5
For I am already being **p** 2 Tm 4:6

POVERTY
mere talk tends only to **p**. Prv 14:23
sleep, lest you come to **p**; Prv 20:13
is hasty comes only to **p**. Prv 21:5
give me neither **p** nor riches; Prv 30:8
but she out of her **p** has put Mk 12:44
p have overflowed in 2 Cor 8:2
so that you by his **p** might 2 Cor 8:9

POWER
'My **p** and the might of my Dt 8:17
and the **p** and the glory 1 Chr 29:11
God is exalted in his **p**; Jb 36:22
beholding your **p** and glory. Ps 63:2
Ascribe **p** to God, whose Ps 68:34
our Lord, and abundant in **p**; Ps 147:5
He gives **p** to the faint, and Is 40:29
by your great **p** and by your Jer 32:17
made the earth by his **p**, Jer 51:15
the **p**, and the might, Dn 2:37
nor by **p**, but by my Spirit, Zec 4:6
Scriptures nor the **p** of God. Mt 22:29
with **p** and great glory. Mt 24:30
hand of **P** and coming on Mt 26:64
God after it has come with **p**." Mk 9:1
and the **p** of the Most High Lk 1:35
And the **p** of the Lord was Lk 5:17
right hand of the **p** of God." Lk 22:69
But you will receive **p** when Acts 1:8
"By what **p** or by what name Acts 4:7
Stephen, full of grace and **p**, Acts 6:8
saying, "Give me this **p** too, Acts 8:19
the Holy Spirit and with **p**. Acts 10:38
for it is the **p** of God for Rom 1:16
so that by the **p** of the Rom 15:13
Christ be emptied of its **p**. 1 Cor 1:17
saved it is the **p** of God. 1 Cor 1:18
also raise us up by his **p**. 1 Cor 6:14
and the **p** of sin is the 1 Cor 15:56
surpassing **p** belongs to God 2 Cor 4:7
of his **p** toward us who Eph 1:19
with **p** through his Spirit Eph 3:16
the **p** of his resurrection, Phil 3:10
be strengthened with all **p**, Col 1:11
of fear but of **p** and love and 2 Tm 1:7
godliness, but denying its **p**. 2 Tm 3:5
by the word of his **p**. Heb 1:3
glory and honor and **p**, Rv 4:11
Salvation and glory and **p** Rv 19:1
the second death has no **p**, Rv 20:6

POWERFUL
The voice of the Lord is **p**; Ps 29:4
not many were **p**, 1 Cor 1:26
you, but is **p** among you. 2 Cor 13:3
in the **p** working of God, Col 2:12

POWERS
nor things to come, nor **p**, Rom 8:38
against the cosmic **p** over Eph 6:12
of God and the **p** of the age Heb 6:5
and **p** having been subjected 1 Pt 3:22

PRACTICE
For they preach, but do not **p**. Mt 23:3
p these things, and the God Phil 4:9
P these things, devote 1 Tm 4:15
for if you **p** these qualities 2 Pt 1:10
of God makes a **p** of sinning, 1 Jn 3:9

PRAISE
is my God, and I will **p** him, Ex 15:2
Lord and **p** him in holy 2 Chr 20:21
P befits the upright. Ps 33:1
his **p** shall continually be in Ps 34:1
a song of **p** to our God. Many Ps 40:3
mouth will declare your **p**. Ps 51:15
Let the peoples **p** you, O God; Ps 67:3
My **p** is continually of you. Ps 71:6
Let the heavens **p** your Ps 89:5
and his courts with **p**! Give Ps 100:4
P the Lord! Oh give thanks Ps 106:1
His **p** endures forever! Ps 111:10
Let my soul live and **p** Ps 119:175
I **p** you, for I am fearfully Ps 139:14
My mouth will speak the **p** Ps 145:21
P the Lord! **P** the Lord, Ps 146:1
P him for his mighty deeds; Ps 150:2
that has breath **p** the Lord! Ps 150:6
Let another **p** you, and not Prv 27:2
a man is tested by his **p**. Prv 27:21
and let her works **p** her in Prv 31:31
and **p** the name of the Lord Jl 2:26
you have prepared **p**'?" Mt 21:16
I will sing **p** with my 1 Cor 14:15
to the **p** of his glorious grace, Eph 1:6
be to the **p** of his glory. Eph 1:12
of it, to the **p** of his glory. Eph 1:14
is anything worthy of **p**, Phil 4:8
I will sing your **p**." Heb 2:12
up a sacrifice of **p** to God, Heb 13:15
cheerful? Let him sing **p**. Jas 5:13
may be found to result in **p** 1 Pt 1:7

PRAISED
Lord, who is worthy to be **p**, Ps 18:3
and greatly to be **p** in the city Ps 48:1
the Lord, and greatly to be **p**; Ps 96:4

PRAISES
and sing **p** to your name. 2 Sm 22:50
Sing **p** to our King, sing Ps 47:6
joy, when I sing **p** to you; Ps 71:23
I will sing **p** to my God Ps 146:2
of the Lord, the **p** of the Lord, Is 63:7

PRAISING
p and giving thanks to the Ezr 3:11
glorifying and **p** God for all Lk 2:20
p God and having favor Acts 2:47

PRAY
by ceasing to **p** for you, 1 Sm 12:23
and **p** and seek my face 2 Chr 7:14
and my God, for to you do I **p**. Ps 5:2
P for the peace of Jerusalem! Ps 122:6
Love your enemies and **p** for Mt 5:44
"And when you **p**, you must Mt 6:5
But when you **p**, go into your Mt 6:6
P then like this: Our Father Mt 6:9
therefore **p** earnestly to the Mt 9:38
Watch and **p** that you may Mt 26:41
p for those who abuse you. Lk 6:28
to him, "Lord, teach us to **p**, Lk 11:1
know what to **p** for as we Rom 8:26
should **p** for the power 1 Cor 14:13
For if I **p** in a tongue, 1 Cor 14:14
I will **p** with my spirit, 1 Cor 14:15
but I will **p** with my 1 Cor 14:15
we have not ceased to **p** for Col 1:9
p without ceasing, 1 Thes 5:17
Let him **p**. Is anyone Jas 5:13
and let them **p** over him, Jas 5:14
and **p** for one another, Jas 5:16
faith; **p** in the Holy Spirit; Jude 1:20

PRAYER
plea; the Lord accepts my **p**. Ps 6:9
O God, hear my **p**; give ear to Ps 54:2
Hear my **p**, O Lord; let my Ps 102:1
but the **p** of the upright is Prv 15:8
a house of **p** for all peoples." Is 56:7
house of **p**,' but you make it Mt 21:13
And whatever you ask in **p**, Mt 21:22
devoting themselves to **p**, Acts 1:14
be constant in **p**. Rom 12:12
may devote yourselves to **p**; 1 Cor 7:5
also must help us by **p**, 2 Cor 1:11
with all **p** and supplication. Eph 6:18
but in everything by **p** and Phil 4:6
Continue steadfastly in **p**, Col 4:2
by the word of God and **p**. 1 Tm 4:5
And the **p** of faith will save Jas 5:15
The **p** of a righteous person Jas 5:16
his ears are open to their **p**. 1 Pt 3:12

PRAYERS
for a pretense make long **p**. Mk 12:40
breaking of bread and the **p**. Acts 2:42
us through the **p** of many. 2 Cor 1:11
remembering you in my **p**, Eph 1:16
your **p** and the help Phil 1:19
supplications, **p**, intercessions, 1 Tm 2:1

so that your **p** may not be 1 Pt 3:7
which are the **p** of the saints. Rv 5:8

PRAYING
And whenever you stand **p**, Mk 11:25
I am **p** for them. I am not Jn 17:9
Then after fasting and **p** Acts 13:3
were **p** and singing hymns Acts 16:25
p at all times in the Spirit, Eph 6:18

PREACH
that time Jesus began to **p**, Mt 4:17
For they **p**, but do not practice Mt 23:3
us to **p** to the people Acts 10:42
continued to **p** the gospel. Acts 14:7
So I am eager to **p** the Rom 1:15
And how are they to **p** Rom 10:15
who **p** the good news!" Rom 10:15
ambition to **p** the gospel, Rom 15:20
baptize but to **p** the gospel, 1 Cor 1:17
of what we **p** to save those 1 Cor 1:21
but we **p** Christ crucified, 1 Cor 1:23
For if I **p** the gospel, that 1 Cor 9:16
Woe to me if I do not **p** 1 Cor 9:16
so we **p** and so you 1 Cor 15:11
so that we may **p** the 2 Cor 10:16
heaven should **p** to you a Gal 1:8
in order that I might **p** him Gal 1:16
to **p** to the Gentiles the Eph 3:8
Some indeed **p** Christ from Phil 1:15
p the word; be ready in 2 Tm 4:2

PREACHED
have good news **p** to them. Mt 11:5
he **p** good news to the people Lk 3:18
of the gospel I **p** to you, 1 Cor 15:1
to the one we **p** to you, Gal 1:8
that the gospel that was **p** Gal 1:11
p the gospel beforehand to Gal 3:8
And he came and **p** peace to Eph 2:17
those who **p** the good news 1 Pt 1:12
news that was **p** to you. 1 Pt 1:25

PREACHING
came **p** in the wilderness Mt 3:1
And he was **p** the word to Mk 2:2
teaching and **p** Jesus as the Acts 5:42
teaching and **p** the word Acts 15:35
hear without someone **p**? Rom 10:14
That in my **p** I may 1 Cor 9:18
lest after **p** to others I 1 Cor 9:27
then our **p** is in vain and 1 Cor 15:14
If anyone is **p** to you a gospel Gal 1:9
us is now **p** the faith he Gal 1:23
labor in **p** and teaching. 1 Tm 5:17
through the **p** with which I Ti 1:3

PRECEPTS
the **p** of the Lord are right, Ps 19:8
all his **p** are trustworthy; Ps 111:7
I will meditate on your **p** Ps 119:15
I will meditate on your **p**. Ps 119:78
how I love your **p**! Ps 119:159
for I have chosen your **p**. Ps 119:173
for I give you good **p**; do not Prv 4:2

PRECIOUS
How **p** is your steadfast love, Ps 36:7
P in the sight of the Lord is Ps 116:15
She is more **p** than jewels, Prv 3:15
She is far more **p** than Prv 31:10
tested stone, a **p** cornerstone, Is 28:16
more **p** than gold that 1 Pt 1:7
but with the **p** blood of 1 Pt 1:19
a cornerstone chosen and **p**, 1 Pt 2:6
to us his **p** and very great 2 Pt 1:4

PREDESTINED
plan had **p** to take place. Acts 4:28
he also **p** to be conformed Rom 8:29
And those whom he **p** he Rom 8:30
he **p** us for adoption through Eph 1:5
having been **p** according to Eph 1:11

PREDICTIONS
remember the **p** of the holy 2 Pt 3:2
the **p** of the apostles of our Jude 1:17

PREPARE
You **p** a table before me in Ps 23:5
P the way of the Lord; Mt 3:3
And if I go and **p** a place for Jn 14:3

PREPARED
inherit the kingdom **p** for Mt 25:34
which he has **p** beforehand Rom 9:23
what God has **p** for those 1 Cor 2:9
He who has **p** us for this 2 Cor 5:5
which God **p** beforehand, Eph 2:10
always being **p** to make a 1 Pt 3:15
p as a bride adorned for her Rv 21:2

PREPARING
affliction is **p** for us an 2 Cor 4:17
p your minds for action, 1 Pt 1:13

PRESENCE
from the **p** of the Lord Gn 3:8
bread of the **P** on the table Ex 25:30
me not away from your **p**, Ps 51:11
Let us come into his **p** with Ps 95:2
Come into his **p** with Ps 100:2
shall dwell in your **p**. Ps 140:13
Leave the **p** of a fool, for Prv 14:7
glorify me in your own **p** Jn 17:5
us with you into his **p**. 2 Cor 4:14
now to appear in the **p** of Heb 9:24

PRESENT
in body, I am **p** in spirit; 1 Cor 5:3
so that he might **p** the Eph 5:27
powers over this **p** darkness, Eph 6:12
in order to **p** you holy and Col 1:22
that we may **p** everyone Col 1:28
Do your best to **p** yourself 2 Tm 2:15
to **p** you blameless before Jude 1:24

PRESERVES
The Lord **p** the faithful but Ps 31:23
The Lord **p** all who love Ps 145:20
is that wisdom **p** the life of Eccl 7:12

PRESS
I **p** on toward the goal for Phil 3:14

PRESSURE
my **p** will not be heavy upon Jb 33:7
there is the daily **p** on 2 Cor 11:28

PREVAIL
not by might shall a man **p**. 1 Sm 2:9
When iniquities **p** against me, Ps 65:3
but they shall not **p** over Jer 15:20
of hell shall not **p** against it. Mt 16:18

PRICE
the **p** of wisdom is above Jb 28:18
you were bought with a **p**. 1 Cor 6:20
You were bought with a **p**; 1 Cor 7:23
the water of life without **p**. Rv 22:17

PRIDE
P and arrogance and the Prv 8:13
P goes before destruction, Prv 16:18
One's **p** will bring him low, Prv 29:23
envy, slander, **p**, foolishness. Mk 7:22
and **p** in possessions — 1 Jn 2:16

PRIEST
"You are a **p** forever after Ps 110:4
the apostle and high **p** of our Heb 3:1
For we do not have a high **p** Heb 4:15
place, "You are a **p** forever, Heb 5:6
should have such a high **p**, Heb 7:26
this: we have such a high **p**, Heb 8:1

PRIESTHOOD
but he holds his **p** permanently Heb 7:24
house, to be a holy **p**, 1 Pt 2:5
race, a royal **p**, a holy nation, 1 Pt 2:9

PRIESTS
a kingdom of **p** and a holy Ex 19:6
a kingdom and **p** to our God, Rv 5:10
but they will be **p** of God and Rv 20:6

PRINCE
Everlasting Father, **P** of Peace. Is 9:6
demons by the **p** of demons." Mt 9:34
following the **p** of the power Eph 2:2

PRISCILLA
from Italy with his wife **P**, Acts 18:2
but when **P** and Aquila Acts 18:26

PRISON
from the **p** those who sit in Is 42:7
I was in **p** and you came to Mt 25:36
those who are in **p**, Heb 13:3
to the spirits in **p**, 1 Pt 3:19
will be released from his **p** Rv 20:7

PRISONER
For this reason I, Paul, a **p** Eph 3:1

PRIZE
only one receives the **p**? 1 Cor 9:24
goal for the **p** of the upward Phil 3:14

PROCLAIM
they shall come and **p** his Ps 22:31
I will **p** and tell of them, yet Ps 40:5
The heavens **p** his Ps 97:6
p on the housetops. Mt 10:27
"Go into all the world and **p** Mk 16:15
word of faith that we **p**); Rom 10:8
who **p** the gospel should 1 Cor 9:14
you **p** the Lord's death 1 Cor 11:26
Him we **p**, warning Col 1:28

PROCLAIMED
and **p** the name of the Lord. Ex 34:5
name might be **p** in all the Rom 9:17
which has been **p** in all Col 1:23
p among the nations, taken 1 Tm 3:16

PROCLAIMING
p thanksgiving aloud, and Ps 26:7
did not come **p** to you the 1 Cor 2:1

PRODUCED
p in me all kinds of Rom 7:8
For no prophecy was ever **p** 2 Pt 1:21

PRODUCES
and pressing anger **p** strife. Prv 30:33
knowing that suffering **p** Rom 5:3
For godly grief **p** a 2 Cor 7:10
and **p** a crop useful to those Heb 6:7
of your faith **p** steadfastness. Jas 1:3

PROFANE
God and not **p** the name of Lv 21:6

PROFESS
women who **p** godliness — 1 Tm 2:10
They **p** to know God, but they Ti 1:16

PROFIT
and her **p** better than gold. Prv 3:14
Riches do not **p** in the day of Prv 11:4
For what will it **p** a man if Mt 16:26

PROFITABLE
by God and **p** for teaching, 2 Tm 3:16
are excellent and **p** for people. Ti 3:8

PROMISE
his **p** that he made. 1 Kgs 8:20
to me according to your **p**. Ps 119:58
I am sending the **p** of my Lk 24:49
but to wait for the **p** of the Acts 1:4
For the **p** is for you and for Acts 2:39
so that the **p** by faith in Gal 3:22
and partakers of the **p** in Eph 3:6
first commandment with a **p**), Eph 6:2
according to the **p** of the life 2 Tm 1:1
Therefore, while the **p** of Heb 4:1
to fulfill his **p** as some count 2 Pt 3:9
But according to his **p** we 2 Pt 3:13
And this is the **p** that he 1 Jn 2:25

PROMISED
will bless you, as he **p** you, Dt 15:6
do this thing that he has **p**: Is 38:7
able to do what he had **p**. Rom 4:21
the **p** Spirit through faith. Gal 3:14
were sealed with the **p** Eph 1:13
for he who **p** is faithful. Heb 10:23
which God has **p** to those Jas 1:12

PROMISES
all the good **p** that the Lord Jos 21:45
law, the worship, and the **p**. Rom 9:4
For all the **p** of God find 2 Cor 1:20
Since we have these **p**, 2 Cor 7:1
and patience inherit the **p**. Heb 6:12
his precious and very great **p**, 2 Pt 1:4

PROPERLY
Let us walk **p** as in the Rom 13:13

behaving **p** toward his 1 Cor 7:36
each part is working **p**, Eph 4:16
so that you may live **p** 1 Thes 4:12

PROPHECIES
As for **p**, they will pass 1 Cor 13:8
Do not despise **p**, 1 Thes 5:20
in accordance with the **p** 1 Tm 1:18

PROPHECY
to us, let us use them: if **p**, Rom 12:6
of miracles, to another **p**, 1 Cor 12:10
or **p** or teaching? 1 Cor 14:6
while **p** is a sign not for 1 Cor 14:22
that no **p** of Scripture comes 2 Pt 1:20
For no **p** was ever produced 2 Pt 1:21

PROPHESY
and you will **p** with them 1 Sm 10:6
to me, "**P** over these bones, Ez 37:4
and your daughters shall **p**, Jl 2:28
did we not **p** in your name, Mt 7:22
and your daughters shall **p**, Acts 2:17
my Spirit, and they shall **p**. Acts 2:18
in part and we **p** in part, 1 Cor 13:9
But if all **p**, and an 1 Cor 14:24
earnestly desire to **p**, 1 Cor 14:39

PROPHET
I will raise up for them a **p** Dt 18:18
The one who receives a **p** Mt 10:41
"A **p** is not without honor, Mk 6:4
no **p** is acceptable in his Lk 4:24
thinks that he is a **p**, 1 Cor 14:37

PROPHETIC
Where there is no **p** vision Prv 29:18
the **p** writings has been Rom 16:26
And if I have **p** powers, 1 Cor 13:2
more sure, the **p** word, 2 Pt 1:19

PROPHETS
ones, do my **p** no harm!" Ps 105:15
to abolish the Law or the **P**; Mt 5:17
for this is the Law and the **P**. Mt 7:12
"Beware of false **p**, who come Mt 7:15
False christs and false **p** Mk 13:22
all that the **p** have spoken! Lk 24:25
To him all the **p** bear Acts 10:43
second **p**, third teachers, 1 Cor 12:28
Are all **p**? Are all teachers? 1 Cor 12:29
and the spirits of **p** are 1 Cor 14:32
of the apostles and **p**, Eph 2:20
the **p**, the evangelists, Eph 4:11
spoke to our fathers by the **p**, Heb 1:1
the **p** who prophesied about 1 Pt 1:10
for many false **p** have gone 1 Jn 4:1

PROPITIATION
forward as a **p** by his blood, Rom 3:25
to make **p** for the sins of the Heb 2:17
He is the **p** for our sins, and 1 Jn 2:2
Son to be the **p** for our sins. 1 Jn 4:10

PROSPER
His ways **p** at all times; your Ps 10:5
the will of the Lord shall **p** Is 53:10

PROSPERITY
I saw the **p** of the wicked. Ps 73:3
In the day of **p** be joyful, Eccl 7:14

PROSPERS
In all that he does, he **p**. Ps 1:3

PROSTITUTE
them members of a **p**? 1 Cor 6:15
the **p** justified by works Jas 2:25

PROSTITUTES
but a companion of **p** Prv 29:3
the tax collectors and the **p** Mt 21:31
your property with **p**, Lk 15:30

PROSTRATE
Then I lay **p** before the Lord Dt 9:18
utterly bowed down and **p**; Ps 38:6
and they shall **p** themselves; Is 49:7

PROTECT
deliver him; I will **p** him, Ps 91:14

PROTECTS
the Lord **p** him and keeps Ps 41:2

was born of God **p** him, 1 Jn 5:18

PROUD
of the **p** but maintains the Prv 15:25
Haughty eyes and a **p** heart, Prv 21:4
is better than the **p** in spirit. Eccl 7:8
money, **p**, arrogant, abusive, 2 Tm 3:2
it says, "God opposes the **p**, Jas 4:6
for "God opposes the **p** but 1 Pt 5:5

PROVE
P me, O Lord, and try me; test Ps 26:2
but to **p** by the earnestness 2 Cor 8:8
p themselves blameless. 1 Tm 3:10

PROVERB
I will incline my ear to a **p**; Ps 49:4
to understand a **p** and a Prv 1:6
What the true **p** says has 2 Pt 2:22

PROVES
the word of the Lord **p** true; Ps 18:30
Every word of God **p** true; Prv 30:5

PROVIDE
Abraham said, "God will **p** Gn 22:8
he will also **p** the way of 1 Cor 10:13
And God is able to **p** you 2 Cor 9:8
But if anyone does not **p** for 1 Tm 5:8

PROVIDED
of the Lord it shall be **p**." Gn 22:14
O God, you **p** for the needy. Ps 68:10
will be richly **p** for you an 2 Pt 1:11

PROVIDES
He **p** food for those who fear Ps 111:5
yet night and **p** food for her Prv 31:15
who richly **p** us with 1 Tm 6:17

PROVOKE
God, so as to **p** him to anger, Dt 4:25
Shall we **p** the Lord to 1 Cor 10:22
Fathers, do not **p** your Eph 6:4
do not **p** your children, Col 3:21

PROVOKED
how you **p** the Lord your Dt 9:7
again and **p** the Holy One Ps 78:41

PROWLS
Your adversary the devil **p** 1 Pt 5:8

PRUDENT
restrains his lips is **p**. Prv 10:19
A **p** man conceals knowledge, Prv 12:23
but the **p** gives thought to Prv 14:15
but a **p** wife is from the Prv 19:14
Therefore he who is **p** will Am 5:13

PRUNES
that does bear fruit he **p**, Jn 15:2

PSALMS
addressing one another in **p** Eph 5:19
singing **p** and hymns and Col 3:16

PUBLIC
devote yourself to the **p** 1 Tm 4:13

PUFFS
This "knowledge" **p** up, 1 Cor 8:1

PUNISH
then I will **p** their Ps 89:32
I will **p** the world for its evil, Is 13:11
being ready to **p** every 2 Cor 10:6
by him to **p** those who do 1 Pt 2:14

PUNISHMENT
Cain said to the Lord, "My **p** Gn 4:13
will you do on the day of **p**, Is 10:3
will go away into eternal **p**, Mt 25:46
They will suffer the **p** of 2 Thes 1:9
How much worse **p**, do Heb 10:29
under **p** until the day 2 Pt 2:9
For fear has to do with **p**, 1 Jn 4:18
a **p** of eternal fire. Jude 1:7

PURE
Can a man be **p** before his Jb 4:17
is man, that he can be **p**? Jb 15:14
The words of the Lord are **p** Ps 12:6
you show yourself **p**; Ps 18:26
clean hands and a **p** heart, Ps 24:4

young man keep his way **p**? Ps 119:9
"I have made my heart **p**; Prv 20:9
"Blessed are the **p** in heart, Mt 5:8
to present you as a **p** 2 Cor 11:2
is just, whatever is **p**, Phil 4:8
of others; keep yourself **p**. 1 Tm 5:22
on the Lord from a **p** heart. 2 Tm 2:22
To the **p**, all things are pure, Ti 1:15
earnestly from a **p** heart, 1 Pt 1:22
purifies himself as he is **p**. 1 Jn 3:3

PURGE
P me with hyssop, and I shall Ps 51:7
"**P** the evil person from 1 Cor 5:13

PURIFICATION
sprinkle the water of **p** upon Nm 8:7
After making **p** for sins, he Heb 1:3
for the **p** of the flesh, Heb 9:13

PURIFIED
with the **p** you show Ps 18:26
Having **p** your souls by your 1 Pt 1:22

PURIFIES
hopes in him **p** himself as he 1 Jn 3:3

PURIFY
and to **p** for himself a Ti 2:14
p our conscience from dead Heb 9:14
sinners, and **p** your hearts, Jas 4:8

PURITY
He who loves **p** of heart, Prv 22:11
by **p**, knowledge, patience, 2 Cor 6:6
in love, in faith, in **p**. 1 Tm 4:12
women like sisters, in all **p**. 1 Tm 5:2

PURPOSE
and that no **p** of yours can be Jb 42:2
to God who fulfills his **p** for Ps 57:2
The Lord will fulfill his **p** Ps 138:8
made everything for its **p**, Prv 16:4
but it is the **p** of the Lord Prv 19:21
I will accomplish all my **p**,' Is 46:10
accomplish that which I **p**, Is 55:11
But for this **p** I have come Jn 12:27
For this **p** I was born and Jn 18:37
and for this **p** I have come Jn 18:37
The **p** was to make him the Rom 4:11
called according to his **p**. Rom 8:28
according to the **p** of his will, Eph 1:5
of his will, according to his **p**, Eph 1:9
to the **p** of him who Eph 1:11
to the eternal **p** that he has Eph 3:11
of his own **p** and grace, 2 Tm 1:9
unchangeable character of his **p**, Heb 6:17
and you have seen the **p** of Jas 5:11

PURSUE
do good; seek peace and **p** it. Ps 34:14
So then let us **p** what Rom 14:19
P love, and earnestly 1 Cor 14:1
P righteousness, godliness, 1 Tm 6:11
and **p** righteousness, 2 Tm 2:22
let him seek peace and **p** it. 1 Pt 3:11

QUALITIES
For if these **q** are yours and 2 Pt 1:8

QUARREL
so quit before the **q** breaks Prv 17:14
but not to **q** over opinions. Rom 14:1
God not to **q** about words, 2 Tm 2:14
obtain, so you fight and **q**. Jas 4:2

QUARRELING
not in **q** and jealousy. Rom 13:13
hands without anger or **q**; 1 Tm 2:8
no one, to avoid **q**, to be gentle, Ti 3:2

QUARRELSOME
house shared with a **q** wife. Prv 21:9
not **q**, not a lover of money. 1 Tm 3:3

QUEEN
made her **q** instead of Vashti. Est 2:17
hand stands the **q** in gold of Ps 45:9
The **q** of the South will rise Mt 12:42

QUENCH
Do not **q** the Spirit. 1 Thes 5:19

QUICK
A man of **q** temper acts Prv 14:17
let every person be **q** to hear, Jas 1:19

QUICK-TEMPERED
He must not be arrogant or **q** Ti 1:7

QUIET
and in **q** resting places. Is 32:18
he will **q** you by his love; Zep 3:17
lead a peaceful and **q** life, 1 Tm 2:2
of a gentle and **q** spirit, 1 Pt 3:4

QUIETLY
wait **q** for the salvation Lam 3:26
and to aspire to live **q**, 1 Thes 4:11
Let a woman learn **q** with 1 Tm 2:11

QUIVER
who fills his **q** with them! Ps 127:5

RABBI
But you are not to be called **r**, Mt 23:8
"**R**" (which means Teacher), Jn 1:38

RACE
under the sun the **r** is not to Eccl 9:11
that in a **r** all the runners 1 Cor 9:24
fight, I have finished the **r**, 2 Tm 4:7
endurance the **r** that is set Heb 12:1
But you are a chosen **r**, a 1 Pt 2:9

RACHEL
R his daughter is coming Gn 29:6
served seven years for **R**, Gn 29:20
Then God remembered **R**, Gn 30:22

RADIANCE
He is the **r** of the glory of Heb 1:3

RADIANT
Those who look to him are **r**, Ps 34:5
My beloved is **r** and ruddy, Sg 5:10
Then you shall see and be **r**; Is 60:5
and his clothes became **r**, as no Mk 9:3

RAHAB
name was **R** and lodged there. Jos 2:1
the father of Boaz by **R**, Mt 1:5
By faith **R** the prostitute Heb 11:31
also **R** the prostitute justified Jas 2:25

RAIN
not caused it to **r** on the land, Gn 2:5
I will send **r** on the earth Gn 7:4
and sends **r** on the just and Mt 5:45

RAISE
and I will **r** him up on the Jn 6:40
and will also **r** us up by 1 Cor 6:14
whom he did not **r** if it is 1 Cor 15:15
Jesus will **r** us also with 2 Cor 4:14
even to **r** him from the Heb 11:19
and the Lord will **r** him up. Jas 5:15

RAISED
and **r** for our justification. Rom 4:25
he who **r** Christ Jesus from Rom 8:11
that God **r** him from the Rom 10:9
that he was **r** on the third 1 Cor 15:4
what is **r** is imperishable. 1 Cor 15:42
and **r** us up with him and Eph 2:6
who **r** him from the dead 1 Pt 1:21

RAN
and **r** and embraced him Lk 15:20

RANSOM
Truly no man can **r** another, Ps 49:7
But God will **r** my soul from Ps 49:15
and to give his life as a **r** Mt 20:28
who gave himself as a **r** for 1 Tm 2:6

RANSOMED
knowing that you were **r** 1 Pt 1:18
and by your blood you **r** Rv 5:9

RAVENS
And the **r** brought him 1 Kgs 17:6
Consider the **r**: they neither Lk 12:24

REACH
to **r** all the riches of full Col 2:2
seem to have failed to **r** it. Heb 4:1
but that all should **r** 2 Pt 3:9

READ
the Covenant and **r** it in the Ex 24:7
And afterward he **r** all the Jos 8:34
They **r** from the book, from Neh 8:8
to be known and **r** by all. 2 Cor 3:2

READINESS
so that your **r** in desiring 2 Cor 8:11
having put on the **r** given Eph 6:15

READING
to the public **r** of Scripture, 1 Tm 4:13

READY
preach the word; be **r** in 2 Tm 4:2
a salvation **r** to be revealed 1 Pt 1:5

REAP
and sow trouble **r** the same. Jb 4:8
will also **r** bountifully. 2 Cor 9:6
one sows, that will he also **r**. Gal 6:7

REAPS
'One sows and another **r**.' Jn 4:37

REASON
"Come now, let us **r** together, Is 1:18
peaceable, gentle, open to **r**, Jas 3:17
asks you for a **r** for the hope 1 Pt 3:15

REBEKAH
R had a brother whose Gn 24:29
And **R** lifted up her eyes, Gn 24:64
But Jacob said to **R** his Gn 27:11

REBELLION
An evil man seeks only **r**, Prv 17:11
your hearts as in the **r**, Heb 3:8

REBUKE
Lord, **r** me not in your anger, Ps 6:1
Better is open **r** than hidden Prv 27:5
man to hear the **r** of the wise Eccl 7:5
If your brother sins, **r** him, Lk 17:3
r them in the presence of 1 Tm 5:20
reprove, **r**, and exhort, 2 Tm 4:2
exhort and **r** with all Ti 2:15

RECEIVE
But to all who did **r** him, who Jn 1:12
But you will **r** power when Acts 1:8
blessed to give than to **r**.'" Acts 20:35
so that we might **r** the Gal 3:14
you will **r** the inheritance as Col 3:24
that we may **r** mercy and Heb 4:16
You ask and do not **r**, because Jas 4:3
to **r** glory and honor and Rv 4:11

RECEIVED
you, they have **r** their reward. Mt 6:2
You **r** without paying; give Mt 10:8
believe that you have **r** it, Mk 11:24
his blood, to be **r** by faith. Rom 3:25
but you have **r** the Spirit of Rom 8:15
For I **r** from the Lord 1 Cor 11:23
Therefore, as you **r** Christ Col 2:6
As each has **r** a gift, use it 1 Pt 4:10

RECEIVES
For everyone who asks **r**, and Mt 7:8
"Whoever **r** you **r** me, and Mt 10:40
him **r** forgiveness of sins Acts 10:43

RECEIVING
train and **r** gifts among men, Ps 68:18
for we are **r** the due reward Lk 23:41
and **r** in themselves the Rom 1:27

RECKONING
I will require a **r** for the life Gn 9:5

RECOGNIZE
You will **r** them by their Mt 7:16

RECOMPENSE
him, and his **r** before him. Is 40:10
for the Lord is a God of **r**; Jer 51:56

RECONCILE
and might **r** us both to God Eph 2:16
and through him to **r** to Col 1:20

RECONCILED
First be **r** to your brother, Mt 5:24
we were **r** to God by Rom 5:10
more, now that we are **r**, Rom 5:10
else be **r** to her husband), 1 Cor 7:11
who through Christ **r** us 2 Cor 5:18
of Christ, be **r** to God. 2 Cor 5:20
he has now **r** in his body of Col 1:22

RECONCILIATION
we have now received **r**. Rom 5:11
means the **r** of the world, Rom 11:15
gave us the ministry of **r**; 2 Cor 5:18
to us the message of **r**. 2 Cor 5:19

RECONCILING
God was **r** the world to 2 Cor 5:19

RECORD
by canceling the **r** of debt Col 2:14

RED
set out from the **R** Sea, Ex 15:22
your God did to the **R** Sea, Jos 4:23
to him who divided the **R** Ps 136:13
though they are **r** like Is 1:18
crossed the **R** Sea as if Heb 11:29

REDEEM
and I will **r** you with an Ex 6:6
God went to **r** to be his 2 Sm 7:23
R us for the sake of your Ps 44:26
Draw near to my soul, **r** me; Ps 69:18
R me from man's Ps 119:134
shortened, that it cannot **r**? Is 50:2
there the Lord will **r** you Mi 4:10
to **r** those who were under Gal 4:5
who gave himself for us to **r** Ti 2:14

REDEEMED
people whom you have **r**; Ex 15:13
Let the **r** of the Lord say so, Ps 107:2
and you shall be **r** without Is 52:3
people; he has **r** Jerusalem. Is 52:9
and has **r** him from hands Jer 31:11
O Lord; you have **r** my life. Lam 3:58
for he has visited and **r** his Lk 1:68
Christ **r** us from the curse of Gal 3:13

REDEEMER
For I know that my **R** lives, Jb 19:25
O Lord, my rock and my **r**. Ps 19:14
Our **R** — the Lord of hosts is Is 47:4
Holy One of Israel is your **R**, Is 54:5

REDEEMS
The Lord **r** the life of his Ps 34:22
He **r** my soul in safety from Ps 55:18
and violence he **r** their life, Ps 72:14
who **r** your life from the pit, Ps 103:4
that **r** them from the Heb 9:15

REDEMPTION
then he shall give for the **r** Ex 21:30
Take my right of **r** yourself, Ru 4:6
He sent **r** to his people; he Ps 111:9
for the **r** of Jerusalem. Lk 2:38
because your **r** is drawing Lk 21:28
through the **r** that is in Rom 3:24
as sons, the **r** of our bodies. Rom 8:23
and sanctification and **r**. 1 Cor 1:30
In him we have **r** through Eph 1:7
were sealed for the day of **r**. Eph 4:30
in whom we have **r**, the Col 1:14
thus securing an eternal **r**. Heb 9:12

REFINER'S
For he is like a **r** fire and Mal 3:2

REFUGE
to be cities of **r** for you, Nm 35:11
my rock, in whom I take **r**, 2 Sm 22:3
Blessed are all who take **r** in Ps 2:12
God is our **r** and strength, Ps 46:1
my God the rock of my **r**. Ps 94:22
But the Lord is a **r** to his Jl 3:16

REGARD
So do not let what you **r** Rom 14:16
we **r** no one according to 2 Cor 5:16
"My son, do not **r** lightly the Heb 12:5

REGENERATION
by the washing of **r** and Ti 3:5

REHOBOAM
And **R** his son reigned in 1 Kgs 11:43

Then King **R** took counsel 1 Kgs 12:6
And **R** slept with his 1 Kgs 14:31

REIGN
The Lord will **r** forever and Ex 15:18
The Lord will **r** forever, Ps 146:10
Let not sin therefore **r** in Rom 6:12
For he must **r** until he 1 Cor 15:25
we will also **r** with him; 2 Tm 2:12
and they will **r** with him for Rv 20:6

REIGNS
The Lord **r**, let the earth Ps 97:1
says to Zion, "Your God **r**." Is 52:7
Lord our God the Almighty **r**. Rv 19:6

REJECTED
builders **r** has become the Ps 118:22
He was despised and **r** by Is 53:3
builders **r** has become the Mt 21:42
the stone that was **r** by you, Acts 4:11
God has not **r** his people Rom 11:2
and nothing is to be **r** if it is 1 Tm 4:4
a living stone **r** by men but 1 Pt 2:4
builders **r** has become the 1 Pt 2:7

REJECTS
one who **r** me **r** him who sent Lk 10:16
The one who **r** me and does Jn 12:48

REJOICE
fear, and **r** with trembling. Ps 2:11
Be glad in the Lord, and **r**, Ps 32:11
bones that you have broken **r**. Ps 51:8
let us **r** and be glad in it. Ps 118:24
and **r** in the wife of your Prv 5:18
but **r** that your names are Lk 10:20
R with those who **r**, Rom 12:15
R in the Lord always; again Phil 4:4
R always, 1 Thes 5:16
In this you **r**, though now 1 Pt 1:6

REJOICES
is glad, and my whole being **r**; Ps 16:9
and my spirit **r** in God my Lk 1:47
but **r** with the truth. 1 Cor 13:6

REJOICING
r that they were counted Acts 5:41
as though they were not **r**, 1 Cor 7:30
as sorrowful, yet always **r**; 2 Cor 6:10

RELEASED
But now we are **r** from the Rom 7:6

RELIGION
r and asceticism and Col 2:23
R that is pure and undefiled Jas 1:27

RELY
our God, for we **r** on you, 2 Chr 14:11
But that was to make us **r** 2 Cor 1:9
For all who **r** on works of Gal 3:10

REMAIN
But to **r** in the flesh is Phil 1:24
are not cannot **r** hidden. 1 Tm 5:25
they will perish, but you **r**; Heb 1:11

REMAINS
Blessed is the man who **r** Jas 1:12
but the word of the Lord **r** 1 Pt 1:25

REMEMBER
I will see it and **r** the Gn 9:16
"**R** the Sabbath day, to keep Ex 20:8
You shall **r** the Lord your Dt 8:18
R the wonderful works 1 Chr 16:12
R also your Creator in the Eccl 12:1
and I will not **r** your sins. Is 43:25
and I will **r** their sin no Jer 31:34
they asked us to **r** the poor, Gal 2:10
r that you were at that time Eph 2:12
and I will **r** their sins no Heb 8:12

REMEMBERS
he **r** that we are dust. Ps 103:14
He **r** his covenant forever, Ps 105:8

REMEMBRANCE
for you. Do this in **r** of me." Lk 22:19
you. Do this in **r** of me." 1 Cor 11:24

REMNANT
for you a **r** on earth, Gn 45:7
for we are left a **r** that has Ezr 9:15
A **r** will return, the Is 10:21
I will gather the **r** of Israel; Mi 2:12
that the **r** of mankind may Acts 15:17
present time there is a **r**, Rom 11:5

REMOVED
prayer or **r** his steadfast love Ps 66:20
righteous will never be **r**, Prv 10:30
to the Lord, the veil is **r**. 2 Cor 3:16

RENEW
and **r** a right spirit within Ps 51:10
Lord shall **r** their strength; Is 40:31

RENEWAL
wait, till my **r** should come. Jb 14:14
but be transformed by the **r** Rom 12:2
regeneration and **r** of the Holy Ti 3:5

RENEWED
youth is **r** like the eagle's. Ps 103:5
is being **r** day by day. 2 Cor 4:16
and to be **r** in the spirit of Eph 4:23
which is being **r** in knowledge Col 3:10

RENOUNCE
who does not **r** all that he Lk 14:33
training us to **r** ungodliness Ti 2:12

REPAID
If the righteous is **r** on Prv 11:31
You will be **r** at the resurrection Lk 14:14

REPAY
The Lord **r** you for what you Ru 2:12
nor **r** us according to our Ps 103:10
R no one evil for evil, but Rom 12:17
is mine; I will **r**." And Heb 10:30
Do not **r** evil for evil or 1 Pt 3:9

REPENT
and **r** in dust and ashes." Jb 42:6
If a man does not **r**, God will Ps 7:12
"**R**, for the kingdom of heaven Mt 3:2
I tell you; but unless you **r**, Lk 13:3
And Peter said to them, "**R** Acts 2:38
R therefore, and turn again, Acts 3:19
R, therefore, of this and pray Acts 8:22
all people everywhere to **r**, Acts 17:30
that they should **r** and Acts 26:20
where you have fallen; **r** Rv 2:5

REPENTANCE
Bear fruit in keeping with **r**. Mt 3:8
baptize you with water for **r**, Mt 3:11
of **r** for the forgiveness Mk 1:4
righteous but sinners to **r**." Lk 5:32
and that **r** and forgiveness Lk 24:47
to give **r** to Israel and Acts 5:31
a baptism of **r** to all the Acts 13:24
of **r** toward God and Acts 20:21
is meant to lead you to **r**? Rom 2:4
produces a **r** that leads to 2 Cor 7:10
grant them **r** leading to a 2 Tm 2:25
of **r** from dead works Heb 6:1
again to **r** those who have Heb 6:4
but that all should reach **r**. 2 Pt 3:9

REPENTS
who **r** than over ninety-nine Lk 15:7
God over one sinner who **r**." Lk 15:10
him, and if he **r**, forgive him, Lk 17:3

REPROACH
and above **r** before him, Col 1:22
overseer must be above **r**, 1 Tm 3:2
and bear the **r** he endured. Heb 13:13

REPUTATION
and having a **r** for good 1 Tm 5:10

REPUTE
you seven men of good **r**, Acts 6:3

REQUESTS
let your **r** be made known Phil 4:6
we have the **r** that we have 1 Jn 5:15

REQUIRE
the Lord your God **r** of you, Dt 10:12
and what does the Lord **r** of Mi 6:8

REQUIREMENT
in order that the righteous **r** Rom 8:4

RESCUE
deliver me and **r** me; Ps 71:2
who is able to **r** in this way." Dn 3:29
The Lord will **r** me from 2 Tm 4:18
how to **r** the godly from 2 Pt 2:9

RESCUES
He delivers and **r**; he works Dn 6:27

RESIST
R the devil, and he will flee Jas 4:7
R him, firm in your faith, 1 Pt 5:9

RESPECT
r to whom **r** is owed, Rom 13:7
brothers, to **r** those who labor 1 Thes 5:12
to your masters with all **r**, 1 Pt 2:18
do it with gentleness and **r**, 1 Pt 3:16

RESPECTABLE
themselves in **r** apparel, 1 Tm 2:9
r, hospitable, able to teach, 1 Tm 3:2

REST
is a Sabbath of solemn **r**, Ex 31:15
and find **r** for your souls. Jer 6:16
laden, and I will give you **r**. Mt 11:28
have believed enter that **r**, Heb 4:3
there remains a Sabbath **r** Heb 4:9

RESTORATION
Aim for **r**, comfort one 2 Cor 13:11

RESTORE
R to me the joy of your Ps 51:12
spiritual should **r** him in a Gal 6:1
For it is impossible to **r** Heb 6:4

RESTORES
He **r** my soul. He leads me in Ps 23:3

RESURRECTION
For in the **r** they neither Mt 22:30
You will be repaid at the **r** Lk 14:14
I am the **r** and the life. Jn 11:25
that there will be a **r** of Acts 24:15
with him in a **r** like his. Rom 6:5
So is it with the **r** of the 1 Cor 15:42
him and the power of his **r**, Phil 3:10
attain the **r** from the dead. Phil 3:11
through the **r** of Jesus Christ 1 Pt 1:3
through the **r** of Jesus 1 Pt 3:21
ended. This is the first **r**. Rv 20:5

RETRIBUTION
a stumbling block and a **r** Rom 11:9
received a just **r**, Heb 2:2

RETURN
and to dust you shall **r**." Gn 3:19
For if you **r** to the Lord, 2 Chr 30:9
but if you **r** to me and keep Neh 1:9
it shall not **r** to me empty, Is 55:11
"**r** to me with all your heart, Jl 2:12
the Lord of hosts: **R** to me, Zec 1:3
R to me, and I will **r** to you, Mal 3:7

REUBEN
and she called his name **R**, Gn 29:32
And **R** said to them, "Shed Gn 37:22
R, you are my firstborn, my Gn 49:3

REVEALED
but the things that are **r** Dt 29:29
he has **r** his righteousness in Ps 98:2
glory of the Lord shall be **r**, Is 40:5
and **r** them to little Mt 11:25
of God is **r** from faith for Rom 1:17
glory that is to be **r** to us. Rom 8:18
the coming faith would be **r**. Gal 3:23
it has now been **r** to his holy Eph 3:5
ready to be **r** in the last 1 Pt 1:5

REVELATION
according to the **r** of the Rom 16:25
but I received it through a **r** Gal 1:12
was made known to me by **r**, Eph 3:3
at the **r** of Jesus Christ. 1 Pt 1:7
you at the **r** of Jesus Christ. 1 Pt 1:13
The **r** of Jesus Christ, which Rv 1:1

REVERE
Every one of you shall **r** his Lv 19:3

REVERENCE
and **r** my sanctuary: Lv 19:30
another out of **r** for Christ. Eph 5:21
worship, with **r** and awe, Heb 12:28

REVIVE
seek God, let your hearts **r**. Ps 69:32
Will you not **r** us again, that Ps 85:6
and to **r** the heart of the Is 57:15

REVIVING
the Lord is perfect, **r** the soul; Ps 19:7

REWARD
your **r** shall be very great." Gn 15:1
them there is great **r**. Ps 19:11
the fruit of the womb a **r**. Ps 127:3
and the Lord will **r** you. Prv 25:22
for your **r** is great in heaven, Mt 5:12
they have received their **r**. Mt 6:5
the due **r** of our deeds; Lk 23:41
the inheritance as your **r**. Col 3:24
which has a great **r**. Heb 10:35
for he was looking to the **r**. Heb 11:26
for, but may win a full **r**. 2 Jn 1:8

REWARDED
So the Lord has **r** me Ps 18:24
commandment will be **r**. Prv 13:13
but the righteous are **r** Prv 13:21

RICH
hand of the diligent makes **r**. Prv 10:4
The **r** and the poor meet Prv 22:2
let not the **r** man boast in Jer 9:23
only with difficulty will a **r** Mt 19:23
poor, yet making many **r**; 2 Cor 6:10
his poverty might become **r**. 2 Cor 8:9
But God, being **r** in mercy, Eph 2:4
As for the **r** in this present 1 Tm 6:17

RICHES
delight as much as in all **r**. Ps 119:14
Whoever trusts in his **r** Prv 11:28
are never satisfied with **r**, Eccl 4:8
of **r** choke the word, Mt 13:22
known the **r** of his glory Rom 9:23
bestowing his **r** on all Rom 10:12
Oh the depth of the **r** and Rom 11:33
immeasurable **r** of his grace Eph 2:7
that according to the **r** of Eph 3:16
are the **r** of the glory Col 1:27

RIGHT
and do that which is **r** in Ex 15:26
And you shall do what is **r** Dt 6:18
because he is at my **r** hand, Ps 16:8
the precepts of the Lord are **r**, Ps 19:8
and renew a **r** spirit within Ps 51:10
you; your **r** hand upholds me. Ps 63:8
my Lord: "Sit at my **r** hand, Ps 110:1
Do not swerve to the **r** or to Prv 4:27
There is a way that seems **r** Prv 14:12
the ways of the Lord are **r**, Hos 14:9
what your **r** hand is doing, Mt 6:3
he gave the **r** to become Jn 1:12
Has the potter no **r** over Rom 9:21
But take care that this **r** of 1 Cor 8:9
him at his **r** hand in the Eph 1:20
that is good and **r** and true), Eph 5:9
in the Lord, for this is **r**. Eph 6:1
seated at the **r** hand of God. Col 3:1
"Sit at my **r** hand until I Heb 1:13
and is seated at the **r** hand Heb 12:2
So whoever knows the **r** Jas 4:17

RIGHTEOUS
Noah was a **r** man, blameless Gn 6:9
"You are more **r** than I, 1 Sm 24:17
Lord knows the way of the **r**, Ps 1:6
For the Lord is **r**; he loves Ps 11:7
are true, and **r** altogether. Ps 19:9
toward the **r** and his ears Ps 34:15
yet I have not seen the **r** Ps 37:25
The salvation of the **r** is Ps 37:39
Let the **r** one rejoice in the Ps 64:10
Your testimonies are **r** Ps 119:144
Surely the **r** shall give Ps 140:13
keep to the paths of the **r**. Prv 2:20
blesses the dwelling of the **r**. Prv 3:33
but the desire of the **r** will Prv 10:24
The **r** is delivered from Prv 11:8
The fruit of the **r** is a tree Prv 11:30
but the house of the **r** will Prv 12:7
hears the prayer of the **r**. Prv 15:29
When the **r** increase, the Prv 29:2
Surely there is not a **r** man Eccl 7:20
by his knowledge shall the **r** Is 53:11
and all our **r** deeds are like a Is 64:6
but the **r** shall live by his faith. Hb 2:4
For I came not to call the **r**, Mt 9:13
separate the evil from the **r** Mt 13:49
Then the **r** will answer him, Mt 25:37
but the **r** into eternal life." Mt 25:46
"The **r** shall live by faith." Rom 1:17
God's **r** judgment will be Rom 2:5
as it is written: "None is **r**, Rom 3:10
scarcely die for a **r** person — Rom 5:7
the many will be made **r**. Rom 5:19
is holy and **r** and good. Rom 7:12
in order that the **r** Rom 8:4
for "The **r** shall live by Gal 3:11
how holy and **r** and 1 Thes 2:10
This is evidence of the **r** 2 Thes 1:5
which the Lord, the **r** judge, 2 Tm 4:8
but my **r** one shall live by Heb 10:38
The prayer of a **r** person has Jas 5:16
of the Lord are on the **r**, 1 Pt 3:12
the **r** for the unrighteous, 1 Pt 3:18
for your **r** acts have been Rv 15:4
for the fine linen is the **r** Rv 19:8

RIGHTEOUSNESS
he counted it to him as **r**. Gn 15:6
but in **r** shall you judge Lv 19:15
his **r** and his faithfulness, 1 Sm 26:23
I hold fast my **r** and will not Jb 27:6
he judges the world with **r**; Ps 9:8
with me according to my **r**; Ps 18:20
He leads me in paths of **r** for Ps 23:3
r and peace kiss each other. Ps 85:10
R and justice are the Ps 89:14
and his **r** endures forever. Ps 111:3
I walk in the way of **r**, in Prv 8:20
R exalts a nation, but sin is Prv 14:34
Whoever pursues **r** and Prv 21:21
God shows himself holy in **r**. Is 5:16
R shall be the belt of his Is 11:5
He put on **r** as a breastplate, Is 59:17
be called: 'The Lord is our **r**.' Jer 23:6
to bring in everlasting **r**, Dn 9:24
Sow for yourselves **r**; reap Hos 10:12
seek **r**; seek humility; Zep 2:3
the sun of **r** shall rise with Mal 4:2
who hunger and thirst for **r**, Mt 5:6
the kingdom of God and his **r**, Mt 6:33
For in it the **r** of God is Rom 1:17
But now the **r** of God has Rom 3:21
the **r** of God through faith Rom 3:22
It was to show his **r** at the Rom 3:26
it was counted to him as **r**. Rom 4:3
counted to Abraham as **r**. Rom 4:9
so one act of **r** leads to Rom 5:18
r leading to eternal Rom 5:21
to God as instruments for **r**. Rom 6:13
But the **r** based on faith Rom 10:6
might become the **r** of God. 2 Cor 5:21
his **r** endures forever." 2 Cor 9:9
it was counted to him as **r**"? Gal 3:6
eagerly wait for the hope of **r**. Gal 5:5
God in true **r** and holiness. Eph 4:24
put on the breastplate of **r**, Eph 6:14
not having a **r** of my own Phil 3:9
Pursue **r**, godliness, faith, 1 Tm 6:11
passions and pursue **r**, 2 Tm 2:22
up for me the crown of **r**, 2 Tm 4:8
You have loved **r** and hated Heb 1:9
heir of the **r** that comes by Heb 11:7
the **r** that God requires. Jas 1:20
die to sin and live to **r**. 1 Pt 2:24
way of **r** than after knowing 2 Pt 2:21
earth in which **r** dwells. 2 Pt 3:13
whoever does not practice **r** 1 Jn 3:10

RISE
live; their bodies shall **r**. Is 26:19
For he makes his sun **r** on Mt 5:45
'After three days I will **r**.' Mt 27:63
dead in Christ will **r** first. 1 Thes 4:16
so that they might **r** again Heb 11:35

RISEN
'He has **r** from the dead,' Mt 27:64
He has **r**; he is not here. See Mk 16:6
"The Lord has **r** indeed, Lk 24:34
Christ, **r** from the dead, as 2 Tm 2:8

ROBBERS
become a den of **r** in your Jer 7:11
him they crucified two **r**, Mk 15:27
have made it a den of **r**." Lk 19:46
before me are thieves and **r**, Jn 10:8

ROCK
The Lord is my **r** and my Ps 18:2
bog, and set my feet upon a **r**, Ps 40:2
who built his house on the **r**. Mt 7:24
and on this **r** I will build Mt 16:18
and a **r** of offense; Rom 9:33
and the **R** was Christ. 1 Cor 10:4
and a **r** of offense." They 1 Pt 2:8

ROD
me; your **r** and your staff, Ps 23:4
Whoever spares the **r** Prv 13:24
if you strike him with a **r**, Prv 23:13
I come to you with a **r**, 1 Cor 4:21

ROOM
go into your **r** and shut the Mt 6:6
went up to the upper **r**, Acts 1:13
Make **r** in your hearts for 2 Cor 7:2

ROOMS
Father's house are many **r**. Jn 14:2

ROOT
In that day the **r** of Jesse, Is 11:10
and like a **r** out of dry ground; Is 53:2
"The **r** of Jesse will come, Rom 15:12
of money is a **r** of all kinds 1 Tm 6:10

ROYAL
If you really fulfill the **r** law Jas 2:8
a **r** priesthood, a holy nation, 1 Pt 2:9

RUBBISH
things and count them as **r**, Phil 3:8

RUDE
or **r**. It does not insist on its 1 Cor 13:5

RUIN
companions may come to **r**, Prv 18:24
a **r**, without inhabitant. Jer 46:19
A **r**, ruin, ruin I will make Ez 21:27
and the **r** of that house was Lk 6:49
in their paths are **r** and Rom 3:16
into **r** and destruction. 1 Tm 6:9

RUINS
And your ancient **r** shall be Is 58:12
make Jerusalem a heap of **r**, Jer 9:11
fallen; I will rebuild its **r**, Acts 15:16
"Bad company **r** good 1 Cor 15:33
but only **r** the hearers. 2 Tm 2:14

RULE
to **r** over the day and over Gn 1:18
but when the wicked **r**, Prv 29:2
his **r** shall be from sea to Zec 9:10
even he who arises to **r** Rom 15:12
far above all **r** and authority Eph 1:21
who is the head of all **r** and Col 2:10
And let the peace of Christ **r** Col 3:15
Let the elders who **r** well 1 Tm 5:17
and he will **r** them with a Rv 2:27

RULER
nor curse a **r** of your people. Ex 22:28
A **r** who lacks understanding Prv 28:16
Many seek the face of a **r**, Prv 29:26
land, and **r** is against **r**. Jer 51:46
a **r** came in and knelt before Mt 9:18
now will the **r** of this world Jn 12:31
'Who made you a **r** and a Acts 7:27

RULERS
and the **r** take counsel Ps 2:2
but the **r** scoffed at him, Lk 23:35
and the **r** were gathered Acts 4:26
None of the **r** of this age 1 Cor 2:8
and blood, but against the **r**, Eph 6:12
or **r** or authorities — Col 1:16
submissive to **r** and authorities, Ti 3:1

RULES
and his kingdom **r** over all. Ps 103:19
r without prejudging, 1 Tm 5:21
competes according to the **r**. 2 Tm 2:5

RUMORS
hear of wars and **r** of wars. Mt 24:6

RUN
they shall **r** and not be Is 40:31
So **r** that you may obtain 1 Cor 9:24
So I do not **r** aimlessly; 1 Cor 9:26
running or had not **r** in vain. Gal 2:2
that I did not **r** in vain or Phil 2:16
and let us **r** with endurance Heb 12:1

RUNNERS
in a race all the **r** compete, 1 Cor 9:24

RUNNING
You were **r** well. Who hindered Gal 5:7

RUST
where moth and **r** destroy Mt 6:19

RUTH
and the name of the other **R**. Ru 1:4
Also **R** the Moabite, the Ru 4:10

SABBATH
rest, a holy **S** to the Lord; Ex 16:23
"Remember the **S** day, to Ex 20:8
"'Observe the **S** day, to keep it Dt 5:12
but keep the **S** day holy Jer 17:24
Son of Man is lord of the **S**." Mt 12:8
or a new moon or a **S**. Col 2:16

SACKCLOTH
long ago in **s** and ashes. Mt 11:21

SACRED
and of the **s** stone that fell Acts 19:35
with the **s** writings, 2 Tm 3:15

SACRIFICE
and Jacob offered a **s** in the Gn 31:54
you shall say, 'It is the **s** of Ex 12:27
"When you offer a **s** of peace Lv 19:5
ram as a **s** of peace offering Nm 6:17
to obey is better than **s**, 1 Sm 15:22
in the morning I prepare a **s** Ps 5:3
S and offering you have not Ps 40:6
Offer to God a **s** of Ps 50:14
steadfast love and not **s**, Hos 6:6
desire mercy, and not **s**.' For Mt 9:13
from offering **s** to them. Acts 14:18
your bodies as a living **s**, Rom 12:1
a fragrant offering and **s** to Eph 5:2
a **s** acceptable and pleasing Phil 4:18
to offer **s** for his own Heb 5:3
away sin by the **s** of himself. Heb 9:26
offer up a **s** of praise to Heb 13:15

SACRIFICED
what has been **s** to idols, Acts 15:29
Passover lamb, has been **s**. 1 Cor 5:7

SACRIFICES
Offer right **s**, and put your Ps 4:5
The **s** of God are a broken Ps 51:17
and ate **s** offered to the Ps 106:28
and to make **s** forever." Jer 33:18
to offer gifts and **s** for sins. Heb 5:1
to offer spiritual **s** acceptable 1 Pt 2:5

SADDUCEES
of the Pharisees and **S**." Mt 16:6
The same day **S** came to Mt 22:23

SAFE
that I may be **s** and have Ps 119:117
man runs into it and is **s**. Prv 18:10
trusts in the Lord is **s**. Prv 29:25

SAFETY
O Lord, make me dwell in **s**. Ps 4:8
He redeems my soul in **s** Ps 55:18
of counselors there is **s**. Prv 11:14

SAINTS
As for the **s** in the land, they Ps 16:3
preserves the lives of his **s**; Ps 97:10
Lord is the death of his **s**. Ps 116:15
But the **s** of the Most High Dn 7:18
And many bodies of the **s** Mt 27:52
done to your **s** at Jerusalem. Acts 9:13
of the **s** in prison after Acts 26:10
by God and called to be **s**: Rom 1:7
for the **s** according to the Rom 8:27
needs of the **s** and seek to Rom 12:13
in a way worthy of the **s**, Rom 16:2
that the **s** will judge the 1 Cor 6:2
the needs of the **s**, 2 Cor 9:12
inheritance in the **s**, Eph 1:18
am the very least of all the **s**, Eph 3:8
but now revealed to his **s**. Col 1:26
Lord Jesus with all his **s**. 1 Thes 3:13
washed the feet of the **s**, 1 Tm 5:10
for all delivered to the **s**. Jude 1:3
which are the prayers of the **s**. Rv 5:8
the righteous deeds of the **s**. Rv 19:8

SAKE
Yet for your **s** we are killed Ps 44:22
We are fools for Christ's **s**, 1 Cor 4:10
I counted as loss for the **s** of Phil 3:7
suffer for righteousness' **s**, 1 Pt 3:14

SALT
she became a pillar of **s**. Gn 19:26
"You are the **s** of the earth, Mt 5:13
be gracious, seasoned with **s**, Col 4:6

SALVATION
I wait for your **s**, O Lord. Gn 49:18
and see the **s** of the Lord, Ex 14:13
and he has become my **s**; Ex 15:2
scoffed at the Rock of his **s**. Dt 32:15
because I rejoice in your **s**. 1 Sm 2:1
and the horn of my **s**, my 2 Sm 22:3
my God, the rock of my **s**, 2 Sm 22:47
Tell of his **s** from day to 1 Chr 16:23
S belongs to the Lord; your Ps 3:8
heart shall rejoice in your **s**. Ps 13:5
be the God of my **s** — Ps 18:46
Lord is my light and my **s**; Ps 27:1
The **s** of the righteous is Ps 37:39
your faithfulness and your **s**; Ps 40:10
to me the joy of your **s**, Ps 51:12
O God, O God of my **s**, Ps 51:14
He only is my rock and my **s**, Ps 62:2
righteousness, O God of our **s**, Ps 65:5
Our God is a God of **s**, and Ps 68:20
Surely his **s** is near to those Ps 85:9
noise to the rock of our **s**! Ps 95:1
tell of his **s** from day to day. Ps 96:2
I will lift up the cup of **s** Ps 116:13
song; he has become my **s**. Ps 118:14
My soul longs for your **s**; Ps 119:81
S is far from the wicked, Ps 119:155
I long for your **s**, O Lord, Ps 119:174
Lord, the strength of my **s**, Ps 140:7
water from the wells of **s**. Is 12:3
that my **s** may reach to the Is 49:6
near, my **s** has gone out, the Is 51:5
happiness, who publishes **s**, Is 52:7
and a helmet of **s** on his Is 59:17
you shall call your walls **S**, Is 60:18
me with the garments of **s**; Is 61:10
for the **s** of the Lord. Lam 3:26
pay. **S** belongs to the Lord!" Jon 2:9
will wait for the God of my **s**; Mi 7:7
righteous and having **s** is he, Zec 9:9
and has raised up a horn of **s** Lk 1:69
for my eyes have seen your **s** Lk 2:30
"Today **s** has come to this Lk 19:9
know, for **s** is from the Jews. Jn 4:22
And there is **s** in no one Acts 4:12
that you may bring **s** to Acts 13:47
you that this **s** of God has Acts 28:28
God for **s** to everyone who Rom 1:16
trespass **s** has come to Rom 11:11
For **s** is nearer to us now Rom 13:11
behold, now is the day of **s**. 2 Cor 6:2
leads to **s** without regret, 2 Cor 7:10
truth, the gospel of your **s**, Eph 1:13
and take the helmet of **s**, Eph 6:17
work out your own **s** with Phil 2:12
for a helmet the hope of **s**. 1 Thes 5:8
but to obtain **s** through 1 Thes 5:9
may obtain the **s** that is in 2 Tm 2:10
wise for **s** through faith in 2 Tm 3:15
bringing **s** for all people, Ti 2:11
those who are to inherit **s**? Heb 1:14
if we neglect such a great **s**? Heb 2:3
s perfect through suffering. Heb 2:10
source of eternal **s** to all who Heb 5:9
— things that belong to **s**. Heb 6:9
faith for a **s** ready to be 1 Pt 1:5
faith, the **s** of your souls. 1 Pt 1:9
Concerning this **s**, the 1 Pt 1:10
it you may grow up to **s** — 1 Pt 2:2
patience of our Lord as **s**, 2 Pt 3:15
to you about our common **s**, Jude 1:3
"**S** belongs to our God who Rv 7:10

SAMARIA
And he had to pass through **S**. Jn 4:4
and in all Judea and **S**, Acts 1:8

SAMARITAN
But a **S**, as he journeyed, Lk 10:33
The **S** woman said to him, Jn 4:9

SAME
not all have the **s** function, Rom 12:4
of gifts, but the **s** Spirit; 1 Cor 12:4
of service, but the **s** Lord; 1 Cor 12:5
but it is the **s** God who 1 Cor 12:6
joy by being of the **s** mind, Phil 2:2
arm yourselves with the **s** 1 Pt 4:1

SAMSON
son and called his name **S**. Jgs 13:24
And **S** said, "With the heaps Jgs 15:16

SAMUEL
and she called his name **S**, 1 Sm 1:20
Therefore Eli said to **S**, "Go, 1 Sm 3:9
When **S** became old, he 1 Sm 8:1
the Lord had revealed to **S**: 1 Sm 9:15
because of the words of **S**. 1 Sm 28:20
S also was among those who Ps 99:6
of David and **S** and the Heb 11:32

SANCTIFICATION
righteousness leading to **s**. Rom 6:19
the fruit you get leads to **s** Rom 6:22
and **s** and redemption. 1 Cor 1:30
is the will of God, your **s**: 1 Thes 4:3
through **s** by the Spirit 2 Thes 2:13
Father, in the **s** of the Spirit, 1 Pt 1:2

SANCTIFIED
that they also may be **s** in Jn 17:19
among all those who are **s**. Acts 20:32
those who are **s** by faith in Acts 26:18
s by the Holy Spirit. Rom 15:16
to those **s** in Christ Jesus, 1 Cor 1:2
were washed, you were **s**, 1 Cor 6:11
who are **s** all have one Heb 2:11
s through the offering Heb 10:10
those who are being **s**. Heb 10:14
by which he was **s**, Heb 10:29

SANCTIFIES
I am the Lord who **s** you. Lv 20:8
I am the Lord who **s** them. Ez 20:12
For he who **s** and those Heb 2:11

SANCTIFY
know that I, the Lord, **s** you. Ex 31:13
the Lord, who **s** you, am holy. Lv 21:8
S them in the truth; your Jn 17:17
that he might **s** her, having Eph 5:26
himself **s** you completely, 1 Thes 5:23
to **s** the people through Heb 13:12

SANCTUARY
your abode, the **s**, O Lord, Ex 15:17
And let them make me a **s**, Ex 25:8
the Lord! Praise God in his **s**; Ps 150:1
yet I have been a **s** to them Ez 11:16
and will set my **s** in their Ez 37:26

SAND
and as the **s** that is on Gn 22:17
shall be like the **s** of the sea, Hos 1:10
who built his house on the **s**. Mt 7:26

SANDALS
near; take your **s** off your feet, Ex 3:5
"Take off your **s** from your Jos 5:15
whose **s** I am not worthy to Mt 3:11

SANG
when the morning stars **s** Jb 38:7
And they **s** a new song, Rv 5:9

SARAH
but **S** shall be her name. Gn 17:15
S, who is ninety years old Gn 17:17
Now Abraham and **S** were Gn 18:11

SATAN
Then **S** stood against 1 Chr 21:1
and **S** also came among them. Jb 1:6
And the Lord said to **S**, "The Zec 3:2
said to him, "Be gone, **S**! for it Mt 4:10
to Peter, "Get behind me, **S**! Mt 16:23
crush **S** under your feet. Rom 16:20
so that **S** may not tempt 1 Cor 7:5
for even **S** disguises 2 Cor 11:14
a messenger of **S** to harass 2 Cor 12:7
is called the devil and **S**, Rv 12:9
who is the devil and **S**, Rv 20:2
S will be released from his Rv 20:7

SATISFIED
yet his appetite is not **s**. Eccl 6:7
soul he shall see and be **s**; Is 53:11
for they shall be **s**. Mt 5:6

SATISFIES
who **s** you with good so that Ps 103:5
For he **s** the longing soul, Ps 107:9

SATISFY
S us in the morning with Ps 90:14
for that which does not **s**? Is 55:2

SAUL
a son whose name was **S**, 1 Sm 9:2
and there **S** and all the 1 Sm 11:15
that I have made **S** king, 1 Sm 15:11
"**S** has struck down his 1 Sm 18:7
Thus it is said, "Is **S** also 1 Sm 19:24
And there lay **S** sleeping 1 Sm 26:7
Then **S** said to his 1 Sm 31:4
And **S** approved of his Acts 8:1
voice saying to him, "Saul, **S**, Acts 9:4
But **S**, who was also called Acts 13:9

SAVE
"How can this man **s** us?" 1 Sm 10:27
our God, **s** us, please, 2 Kgs 19:19
deliver my life; **s** me Ps 6:4
For you **s** a humble people, Ps 18:27
s me in your steadfast love! Ps 31:16
For God will **s** Zion and Ps 69:35
S me according to your Ps 109:26
I am yours; **s** me, for I Ps 119:94
warrior who cannot **s**? Jer 14:9
I will **s** you from far away Jer 30:10
to **s** you in all your cities? Hos 13:10
a mighty one who will **s**; Zep 3:17
for he will **s** his people from Mt 1:21
he cried out, "Lord, **s** me." Mt 14:30
For whoever would **s** his Mt 16:25
it in three days, **s** yourself! Mt 27:40
to do harm, to **s** life or to kill?" Mk 3:4
to seek and to **s** the lost." Lk 19:10
Christ? **S** yourself and us!" Lk 23:39
the world but to **s** the world. Jn 12:47
and thus **s** some of them. Rom 11:14
to **s** those who believe. 1 Cor 1:21
all means I might **s** some. 1 Cor 9:22
into the world to **s** sinners, 1 Tm 1:15
for by so doing you will **s** 1 Tm 4:16
to him who was able to **s** Heb 5:7
is able to **s** to the uttermost Heb 7:25
not to deal with sin but to **s** Heb 9:28
which is able to **s** your souls. Jas 1:21
Can that faith **s** him? Jas 2:14
he who is able to **s** and to Jas 4:12
And the prayer of faith will **s** Jas 5:15
will **s** his soul from Jas 5:20
s others by snatching them Jude 1:23

SAVED
you, a people **s** by the Lord, Dt 33:29
who **s** them out of the hand Jgs 2:16
and I am **s** from my enemies. Ps 18:3
Yet he **s** them for his name's Ps 106:8
I was brought low, he **s** me. Ps 116:6
"Turn to me and be **s**, all the Is 45:22
name of the Lord shall be **s**. Jl 2:32
endures to the end will be **s**. Mt 10:22
"Who then can be **s**?" Mt 19:25
"He **s** others; he cannot save Mt 27:42
human being would be **s**. Mk 13:20
"Your faith has **s** you; Lk 7:50
will those who are **s** be Lk 13:23
might be **s** through him. Jn 3:17
things so that you may be **s**. Jn 5:34
those who were being **s**. Acts 2:47
by which we must be **s**." Acts 4:12
what must I do to be **s**?" Acts 16:30
much more shall we be **s** by Rom 5:9
For in this hope we were **s**. Rom 8:24
remnant of them will be **s**, Rom 9:27
the dead, you will be **s**. Rom 10:9
one confesses and is **s**. Rom 10:10
of the Lord will be **s**." Rom 10:13
way all Israel will be **s**, Rom 11:26
but to us who are being **s** 1 Cor 1:18
he himself will be **s**, 1 Cor 3:15
so that his spirit may be **s** 1 Cor 5:5
that they may be **s**. 1 Cor 10:33
by which you are being **s**, 1 Cor 15:2
being **s** and among those 2 Cor 2:15
by grace you have been **s** — Eph 2:5
For by grace you have been **s** Eph 2:8
that they might be **s** — 1 Thes 2:16
the truth and so be **s**. 2 Thes 2:10
as the firstfruits to be **s**, 2 Thes 2:13
people to be **s** and to come 1 Tm 2:4
Yet she will be **s** through 1 Tm 2:15
who **s** us and called us to a 2 Tm 1:9
he **s** us, not because of works Ti 3:5
the righteous is scarcely **s**, 1 Pt 4:18
who **s** a people out of the Jude 1:5

SAVES
the Lord **s** not with sword 1 Sm 17:47
But he **s** the needy from the Jb 5:15
of pride'; but he **s** the lowly. Jb 22:29
who **s** the upright in heart. Ps 7:10
Now I know that the Lord **s** Ps 20:6
and **s** the crushed in Ps 34:18
from the wicked and **s** them, Ps 37:40
and **s** the lives of the needy. Ps 72:13
hears their cry and **s** them. Ps 145:19
A truthful witness **s** lives, Prv 14:25
to this, now **s** you, not as 1 Pt 3:21

SAVING
your **s** power among all Ps 67:2
me in your **s** faithfulness. Ps 69:13
did not trust his **s** power. Ps 78:22
that you may know the **s** acts Mi 6:5

SAVIOR
and my refuge, my **s**; 2 Sm 22:3
the Lord gave Israel a **s**, 2 Kgs 13:5
O **S** of those who seek refuge Ps 17:7
They forgot God, their **S**, Ps 106:21
he will send them a **s** and Is 19:20
Holy One of Israel, your **S**. Is 43:3
and besides me there is no **s**. Is 43:11
O God of Israel, the **S**. Is 45:15
a righteous God and a **S**; Is 45:21
that I am the Lord your **S**, Is 49:26
am your **S** and your Is 60:16
And he became their **S**. Is 63:8
its **s** in time of trouble, like a Jer 14:8
besides me there is no **s**. Hos 13:4
spirit rejoices in God my **S**, Lk 1:47
day in the city of David a **S**, Lk 2:11
is indeed the **S** of the world." Jn 4:42
right hand as Leader and **S**, Acts 5:31
has brought to Israel a **S**, Acts 13:23
body, and is himself its **S**. Eph 5:23
and from it we await a **S**, Phil 3:20
of God our **S** and of Christ 1 Tm 1:1
in the sight of God our **S**, 1 Tm 2:3
who is the **S** of all people, 1 Tm 4:10
of our **S** Christ Jesus, 2 Tm 1:10
by the command of God our **S**; Ti 1:3
the doctrine of God our **S**. Ti 2:10
great God and **S** Jesus Christ, Ti 2:13
of God our **S** appeared, Ti 3:4
and **S** through your apostles, 2 Pt 3:2
to be the **S** of the world. 1 Jn 4:14
to the only God, our **S**, be Jude 1:25

SCALES
and false **s** are not good. Prv 20:23
like **s** fell from his eyes, Acts 9:18
And its rider had a pair of **s** Rv 6:5

SCARLET
and tied a **s** thread on his Gn 38:28
though your sins are like **s**, Is 1:18

SCATTERED
'He who **s** Israel will Jer 31:10
of God who are **s** abroad. Jn 11:52
Now those who were **s** Acts 8:4

SCEPTER
The **s** shall not depart from Gn 49:10
is the **s** of your kingdom. Heb 1:8

SCHEMES
and the **s** of the wily are Jb 5:13
by craftiness in deceitful **s**. Eph 4:14
against the **s** of the devil. Eph 6:11

SCOFFERS
nor sits in the seat of **s**; Ps 1:1
How long will **s** delight in Prv 1:22
first of all, that **s** will come in 2 Pt 3:3
last time there will be **s**, Jude 1:18

SCORPION
an egg, will give him a **s**? Lk 11:12
torment of a **s** when it stings Rv 9:5

SCRIPTURE
"Today this **S** has been Lk 4:21
and **S** cannot be broken — Jn 10:35
And the **S**, foreseeing that Gal 3:8
But the **S** imprisoned Gal 3:22
to the public reading of **S**, 1 Tm 4:13
All **S** is breathed out by 2 Tm 3:16
royal law according to the **S**, Jas 2:8
that no prophecy of **S** 2 Pt 1:20

SCRIPTURES
neither the **S** nor the power Mt 22:29
But how then should the **S** Mt 26:54
that the **S** of the prophets Mt 26:56
the **S** the things concerning Lk 24:27
he opened to us the **S**?" Lk 24:32
You search the **S** because you Jn 5:39
with them from the **S**, Acts 17:2
examining the **S** daily to Acts 17:11
man, competent in the **S**. Acts 18:24
showing by the **S** that Acts 18:28
his prophets in the holy **S** Rom 1:2
of the **S** we might have Rom 15:4
in accordance with the **S**, 1 Cor 15:3
as they do the other **S**. 2 Pt 3:16

SCROLL
Eat this **s**, and go, speak to the Ez 3:1
And he rolled up the **s** and Lk 4:20
"Who is worthy to open the **s** Rv 5:2

SEA
and the Lord drove the **s** Ex 14:21
By his power he stilled the **s**; Jb 26:12
May he have dominion from **s** Ps 72:8
The **s** is his, for he made it, Ps 95:5
sins into the depths of the **s**. Mi 7:19
a wave of the **s** that is driven Jas 1:6
a beast rising out of the **s**, Rv 13:1

SEAL
God the Father has set his **s**." Jn 6:27
and who has also put his **s** 2 Cor 1:22
Lamb opened the seventh **s**, Rv 8:1

SEALED
were **s** with the promised Eph 1:13
by whom you were **s** for the Eph 4:30

SEALS
the scroll and break its **s**?" Rv 5:2
opened one of the seven **s**, Rv 6:1

SEARCH
if you **s** after him with all Dt 4:29
S me, O God, and know my Ps 139:23
if you seek it like silver and **s** Prv 2:4
"I the Lord **s** the heart and Jer 17:10
You **s** the Scriptures because Jn 5:39

SEARCHED
O Lord, you have **s** me and Ps 139:1
s and inquired carefully, 1 Pt 1:10

SEARCHES
for the Lord **s** all hearts 1 Chr 28:9
And he who **s** hearts Rom 8:27
For the Spirit **s** everything, 1 Cor 2:10
am he who **s** mind and heart, Rv 2:23

SEARED
whose consciences are **s**, 1 Tm 4:2

SEAS
gathered together he called **S**. Gn 1:10

SEASON
For everything there is a **s**, Eccl 3:1
for in due **s** we will reap, Gal 6:9
be ready in **s** and out of 2 Tm 4:2

SEAT
You shall make a mercy **s** of Ex 25:17
nor sits in the **s** of scoffers; Ps 1:1
was ancient of days took his **s**; Dn 7:9
the judgment **s** of God; Rom 14:10
the judgment **s** of Christ, 2 Cor 5:10
overshadowing the mercy **s**. Heb 9:5

SEATED
our God, who is **s** on high, Ps 113:5
Son of Man **s** at the right Mt 26:64
with him and **s** us with him Eph 2:6
s at the right hand of God. Col 3:1
one who is **s** at the right Heb 8:1

SECRET
"The **s** things belong to the Dt 29:29
me wisdom in the **s** heart. Ps 51:6
our **s** sins in the light of your Ps 90:8
that your giving may be in **s**. Mt 6:4
was kept **s** for long ages Rom 16:25
But we impart a **s** and 1 Cor 2:7
I have learned the **s** of Phil 4:12

SECRETS
For he knows the **s** of the Ps 44:21
to know the **s** of the kingdom Lk 8:10
God judges the **s** of men by Rom 2:16
the **s** of his heart are 1 Cor 14:25

SECURE
and set me **s** on the heights. Ps 18:33
a rock, making my steps **s**. Ps 40:2

SECURITY
and **s** within your towers!" Ps 122:7
"There is peace and **s**," 1 Thes 5:3

SEED
sowed good **s** in his field, Mt 13:23
like a grain of mustard **s**, Mt 17:20
He who supplies **s** to the 2 Cor 9:10
not of perishable **s** but of 1 Pt 1:23
for God's **s** abides in him, 1 Jn 3:9

SEEING
keep on **s**, but do not perceive.' Is 6:9
because **s** they do not see, Mt 13:13
to keep them from **s** the 2 Cor 4:4

SEEK
But from there you will **s** the Dt 4:29
If you **s** him, he will be 1 Chr 28:9
and pray and **s** my face 2 Chr 7:14
those who **s** him shall Ps 22:26
With my whole heart I **s** Ps 119:10
"**S** the Lord while he may be Is 55:6
When you **s** me with all Jer 29:13
I will **s** the lost, and I will Ez 34:16
But **s** first the kingdom of Mt 6:33
s, and you will find; knock, Mt 7:7
Man came to **s** and to save Lk 19:10
by those who did not **s** me; Rom 10:20
a wife? Do not **s** a wife. 1 Cor 7:27
s the things that are above, Col 3:1
rewards those who **s** him. Heb 11:6

SEEKS
understanding **s** knowledge, Prv 15:14
As a shepherd **s** out his Ez 34:12
no one **s** for God. Rom 3:11

SEES
For the Lord **s** not as man 1 Sm 16:7
And whoever **s** me sees him Jn 12:45
who hopes for what he **s**? Rom 8:24

SELF
We know that our old **s** was Rom 6:6
and to put on the new **s**, Eph 4:24
off the old **s** with its practices Col 3:9
and have put on the new **s**, Col 3:10
people will be lovers of **s**, 2 Tm 3:2

SELF-CONTROL
A man without **s** is like a Prv 25:28
because of your lack of **s**. 1 Cor 7:5
if they cannot exercise **s**, 1 Cor 7:9
Every athlete exercises **s** 1 Cor 9:25
gentleness, **s**; against such Gal 5:23
apparel, with modesty and **s**, 1 Tm 2:9
love and holiness, with **s**. 1 Tm 2:15
but of power and love and **s**. 2 Tm 1:7
without **s**, brutal, 2 Tm 3:3
and knowledge with **s**, and 2 Pt 1:6
and **s** with steadfastness, 2 Pt 1:6

SELF-CONTROLLED
s, respectable, hospitable, 1 Tm 3:2
a lover of good, **s**, upright, holy, Ti 1:8
s, healthy in faith, in love, Ti 2:2
to be **s**, pure, working at home, Ti 2:5
urge the younger men to be **s**. Ti 2:6
and to live **s**, upright, Ti 2:12
therefore be **s** and 1 Pt 4:7

SELF-INDULGENCE
they are full of greed and **s**. Mt 23:25
the earth in luxury and in **s**. Jas 5:5

SELF-INDULGENT
but she who is **s** is dead 1 Tm 5:6

SELF-MADE
s religion and asceticism Col 2:23

SELF-SEEKING
but for those who are **s** and Rom 2:8

SELFISH
and not to **s** gain! Ps 119:36
and **s** ambition in your Jas 3:14
For where jealousy and **s** Jas 3:16

SEND
"Here am I! **S** me." Is 6:8
harvest to **s** out laborers into Mt 9:38
For God did not **s** his Son Jn 3:17
if I go, I will **s** him to you. Jn 16:7
For Christ did not **s** me to 1 Cor 1:17

SENDING
"Behold, I am **s** you out as Mt 10:16
me, even so I am **s** you." Jn 20:21
By **s** his own Son in the Rom 8:3

SENSUAL
greatly distressed by the **s** 2 Pt 2:7
they entice by **s** passions of 2 Pt 2:18

SENT
in the thing for which I **s** it. Is 55:11
will of him who **s** me and to Jn 4:34
in me but in him who **s** me. Jn 12:44
preach unless they are **s**? Rom 10:15
come, God **s** forth his Son, Gal 4:4
God has **s** the Spirit of his Gal 4:6
Holy Spirit **s** from heaven, 1 Pt 1:12
loved us and **s** his Son to 1 Jn 4:10

SEPARATE
and let it **s** the waters from Gn 1:6
together, let not man **s**." Mt 19:6
Who shall **s** us from the Rom 8:35
the wife should not **s** from 1 Cor 7:10
midst, and be **s** from them, 2 Cor 6:17

SEPARATED
at that time **s** from Christ, Eph 2:12
unstained, **s** from sinners, Heb 7:26

SEPARATES
and a whisperer **s** close Prv 16:28
a shepherd **s** the sheep from Mt 25:32
the unbelieving partner **s**, 1 Cor 7:15

SERPENT
Now the **s** was more crafty Gn 3:1
So Moses made a bronze **s** Nm 21:9
And as Moses lifted up the **s** Jn 3:14
the dragon, that ancient **s**, Rv 20:2

SERVANT
"Speak, for your **s** hears." 1 Sm 3:10
the righteous one, my **s**, and Is 53:11
among you must be your **s**, Mt 20:26
done, good and faithful **s**. Mt 25:21
No **s** can serve two masters, Lk 16:13
I have made myself a **s** to 1 Cor 9:19
taking the form of a **s**, Phil 2:7
you will be a good **s** of 1 Tm 4:6
And the Lord's **s** must not 2 Tm 2:24

SERVANTS
say, 'We are unworthy **s**; Lk 17:10
No longer do I call you **s**, Jn 15:15
as **s** of Christ and stewards 1 Cor 4:1
but as **s** of God we commend 2 Cor 6:4
but as **s** of Christ, doing Eph 6:6
evil, but living as **s** of God. 1 Pt 2:16
S, be subject to your masters 1 Pt 2:18

SERVE
the older shall **s** the younger Gn 25:23
to **s** the Lord your God with Dt 10:12
to him and to **s** him with all Jos 22:5
this day whom you will **s**, Jos 24:15
and him only shall you **s**.'" Mt 4:10
not to be served but to **s**, Mt 20:28
No servant can **s** two Lk 16:13
so that we **s** not under the Rom 7:6
but with my flesh I **s** the Rom 7:25
The older will **s** the younger Rom 9:12
in spirit, **s** the Lord. Rom 12:11
but through love **s** one Gal 5:13
then let them **s** as deacons 1 Tm 3:10
rather they must **s** all the 1 Tm 6:2
works to **s** the living God. Heb 9:14
gift, use it to **s** one another, 1 Pt 4:10
s as an example by Jude 1:7

SERVICE
if **s**, in our serving; the one Rom 12:7
there are varieties of **s**, 1 Cor 12:5

SETH
a son and called his name **S**, Gn 4:25
his image, and named him **S**. Gn 5:3

SEVEN
Take with you **s** pairs of all Gn 7:2
march around the city **s** times, Jos 6:4
Yet I will leave **s** 1 Kgs 19:18
S times a day I praise Ps 119:164
s that are an abomination to Prv 6:16
And **s** women shall take hold Is 4:1
there shall be **s** weeks. Then Dn 9:25
him? As many as **s** times?" Mt 18:21
Then it goes and brings **s** Lk 11:26
"I have kept for myself **s** Rom 11:4
John to the **s** churches that Rv 1:4
who holds the **s** stars in his Rv 2:1
opened one of the **s** seals, Rv 6:1
and **s** trumpets were given to Rv 8:2
And when the **s** thunders Rv 10:4
angels **s** golden bowls full Rv 15:7

SEVENTH
And on the **s** day God Gn 2:2
but on the **s** day you shall Ex 23:12

SEXUAL
except on the ground of **s** Mt 5:32
not in **s** immorality and Rom 13:13
Flee from **s** immorality. 1 Cor 6:18
We must not indulge in **s** 1 Cor 10:8
But **s** immorality and all Eph 5:3
that you abstain from **s** 1 Thes 4:3

SEXUALLY
And you shall not lie **s** with Lv 18:20
with **s** immoral people — 1 Cor 5:9
neither the **s** immoral, nor 1 Cor 6:9
that everyone who is **s** Eph 5:5
the **s** immoral, men who 1 Tm 1:10
for God will judge the **s** Heb 13:4

SHADOW
the valley of the **s** of death, Ps 23:4
refuge in the **s** of your wings. Ps 36:7
These are a **s** of the things Col 2:17
law has but a **s** of the good Heb 10:1

SHADRACH
Hananiah he called **S**, and Dn 1:7
"Blessed be the God of **S**, Dn 3:28

SHAME
Then I shall not be put to **s**, Ps 119:6
but the wicked brings **s** and Prv 13:5
hope does not put us to **s**, Rom 5:5
him will not be put to **s**." Rom 10:11

in the world to **s** the wise; 1 Cor 1:27
the cross, despising the **s**, Heb 12:2

SHARE
tunics is to **s** with him who Lk 3:11
now **s** in the nourishing Rom 11:17
word must **s** all good things Gal 6:6
to **s** with anyone in Eph 4:28
and may **s** his sufferings, Phil 3:10
you who **s** in a heavenly call, Heb 3:1
that we may **s** his holiness. Heb 12:10
and to **s** what you have, Heb 13:16
But rejoice insofar as you **s** 1 Pt 4:13

SHARED
and have **s** in the Holy Spirit, Heb 6:4

SHARON
I am a rose of **S**, a lily of the Sg 2:1
the majesty of Carmel and **S**. Is 35:2

SHARPER
s than any two-edged sword, Heb 4:12

SHEBA
Now when the queen of **S** 1 Kgs 10:1

SHED
by man shall his blood be **s**, Gn 9:6
and they make haste to **s** Prv 1:16
"Their feet are swift to **s** Rom 3:15

SHEEP
we are regarded as **s** to be Ps 44:22
and the **s** of his pasture. Ps 100:3
gone astray like a lost **s**; Ps 119:176
All we like **s** have gone Is 53:6
and like a **s** that before its Is 53:7
"My people have been lost **s**. Jer 50:6
for my **s** and will seek Ez 34:11
like **s** without a shepherd. Mt 9:36
I am sending you out as **s** Mt 10:16
The **s** hear his voice, and he Jn 10:3
to you, I am the door of the **s**. Jn 10:7
I lay down my life for the **s**. Jn 10:15
My **s** hear my voice, and I Jn 10:27
He said to him, "Tend my **s**." Jn 21:16
said to him, "Feed my **s**. Jn 21:17
we are regarded as **s** to be Rom 8:36
great shepherd of the **s**, Heb 13:20
you were straying like **s**, 1 Pt 2:25

SHELTER
under the **s** of your wings! Ps 61:4
He who dwells in the **s** of the Ps 91:1

SHEM
old, Noah fathered **S**, Ham, Gn 5:32

SHEOL
I shall go down to **S** to my Gn 37:35
they go down alive into **S**, Nm 16:30
he brings down to **S** and 1 Sm 2:6
so he who goes down to **S** Jb 7:9
not abandon my soul to **S**, Ps 16:10
soul from the power of **S**, Ps 49:15
her steps follow the path to **S**; Prv 5:5
let it be deep as **S** or high as Is 7:11
to the gates of **S** for the rest Is 38:10
when I cast it down to **S** Ez 31:16
them from the power of **S**? Hos 13:14
His greed is as wide as **S**; like Hb 2:5

SHEPHERD
the God who has been my **s** Gn 48:15
as sheep that have no **s**. 1 Kgs 22:17
'You shall be **s** of my 1 Chr 11:2
The Lord is my **s**; I shall not Ps 23:1
they are given by one **S**. Eccl 12:11
will tend his flock like a **s**; Is 40:11
and will keep him as a **s** Jer 31:10
As a **s** seeks out his flock Ez 34:12
And he shall stand and **s** his Mi 5:4
are afflicted for lack of a **s**. Zec 10:2
like sheep without a **s**. Mt 9:36
I am the good **s**. The good Jn 10:11
The good **s** lays down his Jn 10:11
I am the good **s**. I know my Jn 10:14
the great **s** of the sheep, Heb 13:20
to the **S** and Overseer of 1 Pt 2:25
s the flock of God that is 1 Pt 5:2
And when the chief **S** 1 Pt 5:4
of the throne will be their **s**, Rv 7:17

SHEPHERDS
"And I will give you **s** after Jer 3:15
"Woe to the **s** who destroy Jer 23:1
Should not **s** feed the sheep? Ez 34:2
region there were **s** out in the Lk 2:8

SHIELD
"Fear not, Abram, I am your **s**; Gn 15:1
Lord is my strength and my **s**; Ps 28:7
my hiding place and my **s**; Ps 119:114
take up the **s** of faith, Eph 6:16

SHINE
The Lord make his face to **s** Nm 6:25
make his face to **s** upon us, Ps 67:1
Arise, **s**, for your light has Is 60:1
let your light **s** before others, Mt 5:16
Then the righteous will **s** Mt 13:43
"Let light **s** out of 2 Cor 4:6
and Christ will **s** on you." Eph 5:14

SHINES
of beauty, God **s** forth. Ps 50:2
which **s** brighter and Prv 4:18
from the east and **s** as far as Mt 24:27
The light **s** in the darkness, Jn 1:5

SHIPWRECK
some have made **s** of their 1 Tm 1:19

SHONE
of his face **s** because he had Ex 34:29
and his face **s** like the sun, Mt 17:2
and the glory of the Lord **s** Lk 2:9
has **s** in our hearts to give 2 Cor 4:6

SHORT
those days will be cut **s**. Mt 24:22
and fall **s** of the glory of God, Rom 3:23

SHOULDER
government shall be upon his **s**, Is 9:6

SHOUT
May we **s** for joy over your Ps 20:5
S for joy in the Lord, O you Ps 33:1

SHOW
to the land that I will **s** you. Gn 12:1
And I will **s** you a still 1 Cor 12:31
s the immeasurable riches Eph 2:7
S me your faith apart from Jas 2:18
S hospitality to one another 1 Pt 4:9

SHREWD
are more **s** in dealing with Lk 16:8

SHROUD
wrapped it in a clean linen **s** Mt 27:59

SICK
deferred makes the heart **s**, Prv 13:12
but those who are **s**. Mt 9:12
s and in prison and you did Mt 25:43
Is anyone among you **s**? Jas 5:14

SICKLE
Put in the **s**, for the harvest is Jl 3:13
"Put in your **s**, and reap, Rv 14:15

SIDE
The Lord is on my **s**; I will Ps 118:6
God, who is at the Father's **s**, Jn 1:18
striving **s** by **s** for the faith Phil 1:27

SIGHT
done what is evil in your **s**, Ps 51:4
Precious in the **s** of the Ps 116:15
the blind receive their **s** and Mt 11:5
we walk by faith, not by **s**. 2 Cor 5:7
and it is pleasing in the **s** of 1 Tm 2:3
which is pleasing in his **s**, Heb 13:21
but in the **s** of God chosen 1 Pt 2:4
which in God's **s** is very 1 Pt 3:4

SIGN
And God said, "This is the **s** Gn 9:12
and it shall be a **s** of the Gn 17:11
The blood shall be a **s** for Ex 12:13
You shall bind them as a **s** on Dt 6:8
himself will give you a **s**. Is 7:14
generation seeks for a **s**, Mt 12:39
generation seeks for a **s**, Mt 16:4
but no **s** will be given to it Mt 16:4
and what will be the **s** of Mt 24:3
in heaven the **s** of the Son Mt 24:30
betrayer had given them a **s**, Mt 26:48
He received the **s** of Rom 4:11
Thus tongues are a **s** not 1 Cor 14:22
This is a clear **s** to them of Phil 1:28
This is the **s** of genuineness 2 Thes 3:17
And a great **s** appeared in Rv 12:1
And another **s** appeared in Rv 12:3
Then I saw another **s** in Rv 15:1

SIGNS
Now Jesus did many other **s** Jn 20:30
above and **s** on the earth Acts 2:19
by **s** and wonders and Heb 2:4

SILAS
called Barsabbas, and **S**, Acts 15:22
and **S** were praying and Acts 16:25
When **S** and Timothy Acts 18:5

SILENCE
time to sew; a time to keep **s**, Eccl 3:7
let all the earth keep **s** Hb 2:20
put to **s** the ignorance of 1 Pt 2:15
there was **s** in heaven for Rv 8:1

SILENT
For when I kept **s**, my bones Ps 32:3
done, and I have been **s**; Ps 50:21
Even a fool who keeps **s** is Prv 17:28
that before its shearers is **s**, Is 53:7
Be **s** before the Lord GOD! Zep 1:7
lamb before its shearer is **s**, Acts 8:32
let each of them keep **s** 1 Cor 14:28

SILOAM
the tower in **S** fell and killed Lk 13:4
wash in the pool of **S**" (which Jn 9:7

SILVANUS
you, **S** and Timothy and I, 2 Cor 1:19
Paul, **S**, and Timothy, To 1 Thes 1:1
By **S**, a faithful brother as I 1 Pt 5:12

SILVER
if you seek it like **s** and Prv 2:4
of gold in a setting of **s**. Prv 25:11
The **s** is mine, and the gold is Hg 2:8
paid him thirty pieces of **s**. Mt 26:15
said, "I have no **s** and gold, Acts 3:6
s, precious stones, wood, 1 Cor 3:12
things such as **s** or gold, 1 Pt 1:18

SIMEON
And she called his name **S**. Gn 29:33
Reuben, **S**, Levi, and Judah, Ex 1:2
And **S** blessed them and said Lk 2:34

SIMON
are you, **S** Bar-Jona! For Mt 16:17
S, whom he named Peter, Lk 6:14
"So you are **S** the son of Jn 1:42
Judas, the son of **S** Iscariot. Jn 13:26
So **S** Peter went aboard and Jn 21:11
and **S** the Zealot and Acts 1:13
there was a man named **S**, Acts 8:9

SIN
s is crouching at the door. Gn 4:7
"You have sinned a great **s**. Ex 32:30
he shall confess his **s** that he Nm 5:7
and be sure your **s** will find Nm 32:23
put to death for his own **s**. Dt 24:16
please pardon my **s** and 1 Sm 15:25
their **s** and heal their 2 Chr 7:14
Be angry, and do not **s**; ponder Ps 4:4
forgiven, whose **s** is covered. Ps 32:1
I acknowledged my **s** to you, Ps 32:5
in my bones because of my **s**. Ps 38:3
I am sorry for my **s**. Ps 38:18
and cleanse me from my **s**! Ps 51:2
and my **s** is ever before me. Ps 51:3
and in **s** did my mother Ps 51:5
you covered all their **s**. Selah Ps 85:2
that I might not **s** against Ps 119:11
away, and your **s** atoned for. Is 6:7
yet he bore the **s** of many, Is 53:12
right eye causes you to **s**, Mt 5:29
Therefore I tell you, every **s** Mt 12:31
ones who believe in me to **s**, Mt 18:6
"Temptations to **s** are sure to Lk 17:1
who takes away the **s** of the Jn 1:29

“Let him who is without **s** Jn 8:7
who commits **s** is a slave to **s**. Jn 8:34
and Greeks are under **s**, Rom 3:9
law comes knowledge of **s**. Rom 3:20
Lord will not count his **s**.” Rom 4:8
Therefore, just as **s** came Rom 5:12
but where **s** increased, Rom 5:20
Are we to continue in **s** that Rom 6:1
dead to **s** and alive to Rom 6:11
Are we to **s** because we Rom 6:15
For the wages of **s** is death, Rom 6:23
That the law is **s**? By no Rom 7:7
For **s**, seizing an opportunity Rom 7:11
but **s** that dwells within me. Rom 7:17
he condemned **s** in the flesh, Rom 8:3
body is dead because of **s**, Rom 8:10
not proceed from faith is **s**. Rom 14:23
you **s** against Christ. 1 Cor 8:12
The sting of death is **s**, 1 Cor 15:56
and the power of **s** is the 1 Cor 15:56
him to be **s** who knew no 2 Cor 5:21
Be angry and do not **s**; do Eph 4:26
for those who persist in **s**, 1 Tm 5:20
by the deceitfulness of **s**. Heb 3:13
put away **s** by the sacrifice Heb 9:26
the fleeting pleasures of **s**. Heb 11:25
and **s** which clings so Heb 12:1
In your struggle against **s** Heb 12:4
conceived gives birth to **s**, Jas 1:15
and **s** when it is fully grown Jas 1:15
fails to do it, for him it is **s**. Jas 4:17
He committed no **s**, neither 1 Pt 2:22
that we might die to **s** and 1 Pt 2:24
Son cleanses us from all **s**. 1 Jn 1:7
If we say we have no **s**, we 1 Jn 1:8
to you so that you may not **s**. 1 Jn 2:1
lawlessness; **s** is lawlessness. 1 Jn 3:4
and in him there is no **s**. 1 Jn 3:5
a **s** not leading to death, 1 Jn 5:16

SINAI
Now Mount **S** was wrapped Ex 19:18
the Lord dwelt on Mount **S**, Ex 24:16
spoke to Moses on Mount **S**, Lv 25:1

SINCERE
trembling, with a **s** heart, Eph 6:5
conscience and a **s** faith. 1 Tm 1:5
good fruits, impartial and **s**. Jas 3:17
truth for a **s** brotherly love, 1 Pt 1:22

SINFUL
in the flesh, our **s** passions, Rom 7:5
likeness of **s** flesh and for sin, Rom 8:3
the world because of **s** desire. 2 Pt 1:4
following their own **s** desires. 2 Pt 3:3
following their own **s** desires; Jude 1:16

SING
saying, “I will **s** to the Lord, Ex 15:1
I will **s** and make melody to Ps 27:6
S to him a new song; play Ps 33:3
Let the nations be glad and **s** Ps 67:4
I will **s** of the steadfast love Ps 89:1
S to the Lord with thanksgiving; Ps 147:7
cheerful? Let him **s** praise. Jas 5:13

SINGING
into his presence with **s**! Ps 100:2
s and making melody to the Eph 5:19
s psalms and hymns and Col 3:16

SINGLE
them to remain **s** as I am. 1 Cor 7:8

SINNED
“I have **s** against the 2 Sm 12:13
be that my children have **s**, Jb 1:5
for I have **s** against you!” Ps 41:4
have I **s** and done what is Ps 51:4
we have **s** and done wrong Dn 9:5
because I have **s** against him, Mi 7:9
I have **s** against heaven Lk 15:18
For all who have **s** without Rom 2:12
for all have **s** and fall short Rom 3:23
do marry, you have not **s**, 1 Cor 7:28
who **s** earlier and have 2 Cor 12:21
spare angels when they **s**, 2 Pt 2:4
If we say we have not **s**, 1 Jn 1:10

SINNER
but one **s** destroys much Eccl 9:18
over one **s** who repents.” Lk 15:10
‘God, be merciful to me, a **s**!’ Lk 18:13
back a **s** from his wandering Jas 5:20
of the ungodly and the **s**?” 1 Pt 4:18

SINNERS
nor stands in the way of **s**, Ps 1:1
therefore he instructs **s** in the Ps 25:8
and **s** will return to you. Ps 51:13
Let not your heart envy **s**, Prv 23:17
to call the righteous, but **s**.” Mt 9:13
in that while we were still **s**, Rom 5:8
we too were found to be **s**, Gal 2:17
for the ungodly and **s**, for 1 Tm 1:9
into the world to save **s**, 1 Tm 1:15
Cleanse your hands, you **s**, Jas 4:8

SINNING
Thus, **s** against your 1 Cor 8:12
right, and do not go on **s**. 1 Cor 15:34
For if we go on **s** Heb 10:26
s also practices lawlessness; 1 Jn 3:4
abides in him keeps on **s**; 1 Jn 3:6
makes a practice of **s** is of the 1 Jn 3:8
of God makes a practice of **s**, 1 Jn 3:9
of God does not keep on **s**, 1 Jn 5:18

SINS
If anyone **s** unintentionally Lv 4:2
of the **s** that people commit Nm 5:6
are my iniquities and my **s**? Jb 13:23
also from presumptuous **s**; Ps 19:13
Remember not the **s** of my Ps 25:7
trouble, and forgive all my **s**. Ps 25:18
Hide your face from my **s**, Ps 51:9
us, and atone for our **s**, Ps 79:9
our secret **s** in the light of Ps 90:8
with us according to our **s**, Ps 103:10
who does good and never **s**. Eccl 7:20
though your **s** are like scarlet, Is 1:18
for you have cast all my **s** Is 38:17
I will not remember your **s**. Is 43:25
and your **s** have hidden his Is 59:2
he will uncover your **s**. Lam 4:22
the soul that **s** shall die. Ez 18:4
None of the **s** that he has Ez 33:16
save his people from their **s**.” Mt 1:21
my son; your **s** are forgiven.” Mt 9:2
“If your brother **s** against Mt 18:15
for the forgiveness of **s**. Mt 26:28
for the forgiveness of **s**. Mk 1:4
and forgive us our **s**, for we Lk 11:4
If your brother **s**, rebuke Lk 17:3
that you would die in your **s**, Jn 8:24
If you forgive the **s** of Jn 20:23
the forgiveness of your **s**, Acts 2:38
Israel and forgiveness of **s**. Acts 5:31
of **s** through his name.” Acts 10:43
and wash away your **s**, Acts 22:16
had passed over former **s**. Rom 3:25
and whose **s** are covered; Rom 4:7
when I take away their **s**.” Rom 11:27
that Christ died for our **s** 1 Cor 15:3
you are still in your **s**. 1 Cor 15:17
who gave himself for our **s** to Gal 1:4
dead in the trespasses and **s** Eph 2:1
the forgiveness of **s**. Col 1:14
nor take part in the **s** of 1 Tm 5:22
making purification for **s**, Heb 1:3
and I will remember their **s** Heb 8:12
once to bear the **s** of many, Heb 9:28
Therefore, confess your **s** to Jas 5:16
will cover a multitude of **s**. Jas 5:20
He himself bore our **s** in his 1 Pt 2:24
also suffered once for **s**, 1 Pt 3:18
love covers a multitude of **s**. 1 Pt 4:8
cleansed from his former **s**. 2 Pt 1:9
If we confess our **s**, he is 1 Jn 1:9
us our **s** and to cleanse 1 Jn 1:9
is the propitiation for our **s**, 1 Jn 2:2
because your **s** are forgiven 1 Jn 2:12
he appeared to take away **s**, 1 Jn 3:5
be the propitiation for our **s**. 1 Jn 4:10
to those who commit **s** that 1 Jn 5:16
us from our **s** by his blood Rv 1:5

SIT
when you **s** in your house, Dt 6:7
Lord: “**S** at my right hand, Ps 110:1
to give light to those who **s** Lk 1:79
Lord, **S** at my right hand, Acts 2:34
“**S** at my right hand until I Heb 1:13

SITS
nor **s** in the seat of scoffers; Ps 1:1
But the Lord **s** enthroned Ps 9:7
“To him who **s** on the throne Rv 5:13

SKIN
and I have escaped by the **s** Jb 19:20
change his **s** or the leopard Jer 13:23
and **s** had covered them. But Ez 37:8

SKULL
(which means Place of a **S**), Mt 27:33

SKY
and the **s** above proclaims his Ps 19:1

SLAIN
is the Lamb who was **s**, Rv 5:12

SLANDER
who does not **s** with his Ps 15:3
and whoever utters **s** is a Prv 10:18
— **s**, gossip, conceit, 2 Cor 12:20
clamor and **s** be put away Eph 4:31
hypocrisy and envy and all **s**. 1 Pt 2:1

SLANDERED
when **s**, we entreat. We 1 Cor 4:13
so that, when you are **s**, 1 Pt 3:16

SLANDERERS
s, haters of God, insolent, Rom 1:30
not **s**, but sober-minded, 1 Tm 3:11
not **s** or slaves to much wine. Ti 2:3

SLAUGHTER
like a lamb that is led to the **s**, Is 53:7
was led to the **s** and like a Acts 8:32

SLAVE
among you must be your **s**, Mt 20:27
who commits sin is a **s** to sin. Jn 8:34
there is neither **s** nor free, Gal 3:28
whether he is a **s** or free. Eph 6:8
s, free; but Christ is all, Col 3:11

SLAVERY
the spirit of **s** to fall back Rom 8:15
submit again to a yoke of **s**. Gal 5:1
were subject to lifelong **s**. Heb 2:15

SLAVES
you are **s** of the one whom Rom 6:16
and have become **s** of God, Rom 6:22
not slanderers or **s** to much Ti 2:3
s to various passions and Ti 3:3
but they themselves are **s** of 2 Pt 2:19

SLAY
Though he **s** me, I will hope Jb 13:15

SLEEP
caused a deep **s** to fall upon Gn 2:21
will neither slumber nor **s**. Ps 121:4
A little **s**, a little slumber, a Prv 6:10
Love not **s**, lest you come Prv 20:13
Sweet is the **s** of a laborer, Eccl 5:12
We shall not all **s**, but 1 Cor 15:51

SLOW
and gracious, **s** to anger, Ex 34:6
‘The Lord is **s** to anger and Nm 14:18
s to anger and abounding in Neh 9:17
s to anger and abounding in Ps 86:15
s to anger and abounding in Ps 103:8
s to anger and abounding in Ps 145:8
Whoever is **s** to anger has Prv 14:29
but he who is **s** to anger Prv 15:18
The Lord is **s** to anger and Na 1:3
If it seems **s**, wait for it; it will Hb 2:3
s to speak, **s** to anger; Jas 1:19
The Lord is not **s** to fulfill 2 Pt 3:9

SLOWNESS
his promise as some count **s**, 2 Pt 3:9

SLUGGARD
Go to the ant, O **s**; consider Prv 6:6
The desire of the **s** kills Prv 21:25
so does a **s** on his bed. Prv 26:14

SLUMBER
he who keeps you will not **s**. Ps 121:3
A little sleep, a little **s**, a Prv 6:10

SMITH
and the **s** has material for a — Prv 25:4
Behold, I have created the **s** — Is 54:16

SNARE
which became a **s** to them. — Ps 106:36
into a **s** of the devil. — 1 Tm 3:7
fall into temptation, into a **s**, — 1 Tm 6:9
from the **s** of the devil, — 2 Tm 2:26

SNATCH
and no one will **s** them out — Jn 10:28

SNOW
and I shall be whiter than **s**. — Ps 51:7
they shall be as white as **s**; — Is 1:18
and his clothing white as **s**. — Mt 28:3

SOBER
but to think with **s** — Rom 12:3
us keep awake and be **s**. — 1 Thes 5:6
to the day, let us be **s**, and — 1 Thes 5:8

SOBER-MINDED
one wife, **s**, self-controlled, — 1 Tm 3:2
but **s**, faithful in all things. — 1 Tm 3:11
As for you, always be **s**, — 2 Tm 4:5
Older men are to be **s**, — Ti 2:2
for action, and being **s**, — 1 Pt 1:13
and **s** for the sake — 1 Pt 4:7
Be **s**; be watchful. Your — 1 Pt 5:8

SODOM
Now the men of **S** were — Gn 13:13
"If I find at **S** fifty — Gn 18:26
Then the Lord rained on **S** — Gn 19:24
As when God overthrew **S** — Jer 50:40
in you had been done in **S**, — Mt 11:23
when Lot went out from **S**, — Lk 17:29
is called **S** and Egypt, — Rv 11:8

SOLDIER
Who serves as a **s** at his — 1 Cor 9:7
fellow worker and fellow **s**, — Phil 2:25
as a good **s** of Christ Jesus. — 2 Tm 2:3
No **s** gets entangled in — 2 Tm 2:4

SOLE
place for the **s** of your foot, — Dt 28:65
From the **s** of the foot even to — Is 1:6

SOLID
you with milk, not **s** food, — 1 Cor 3:2
You need milk, not **s** food, — Heb 5:12
But **s** food is for the mature, — Heb 5:14

SOLOMON
"**S** your son shall reign — 1 Kgs 1:13
David has made **S** king, — 1 Kgs 1:43
S loved the Lord, walking — 1 Kgs 3:3
As soon as **S** had finished — 1 Kgs 9:1
The proverbs of **S**, son of king — Prv 1:1
yet I tell you, even **S** in all — Mt 6:29
to hear the wisdom of **S**, — Mt 12:42
But it was **S** who built a — Acts 7:47

SON
He said, "Take your **s**, your — Gn 22:2
said to me, "You are my **S**; — Ps 2:7
and the **s** of man that you care — Ps 8:4
as a father the **s** in whom — Prv 3:12
A wise **s** hears his father's — Prv 13:1
shall conceive and bear a **s**, — Is 7:14
child is born, to us a **s** is given; — Is 9:6
out of Egypt I called my **s**. — Hos 11:1
prophet, nor a prophet's **s**, — Am 7:14
said, "This is my beloved **S**, — Mt 3:17
but the **S** of Man has — Mt 8:20
and no one knows the **S** — Mt 11:27
Is not this the carpenter's **s**? — Mt 13:55
the **S** of the living God." — Mt 16:16
said, "This is my beloved **S**, — Mt 17:5
and they will see the **S** of — Mt 24:30
for the **S** of Man is coming — Mt 24:44
"Truly this was the **S** of — Mt 27:54
and of the **S** and of the — Mt 28:19
firstborn **s** and wrapped him — Lk 2:7
divided, father against **s** and — Lk 12:53
when the **S** of Man comes, — Lk 18:8
For the **S** of Man came to — Lk 19:10
glory as of the only **S** from — Jn 1:14
that he gave his only **S**, — Jn 3:16
glorify your **S** that the **S** may — Jn 17:1
"Woman, behold, your **s**!" — Jn 19:26
By sending his own **S** in the — Rom 8:3
his own **S** but gave him — Rom 8:32
then the **S** himself will — 1 Cor 15:28
a slave, but a **s**, and if a **s**, — Gal 4:7
how as a **s** with a father he — Phil 2:22
and to wait for his **S** — 1 Thes 1:10
he has spoken to us by his **S**, — Heb 1:2
over God's house as a **s**. — Heb 3:6
and the blood of Jesus his **S** — 1 Jn 1:7
that God sent his only **S** into — 1 Jn 4:9
that Jesus is the **S** of God? — 1 Jn 5:5
and this life is in his **S**. — 1 Jn 5:11
Whoever has the **S** has life; — 1 Jn 5:12

SONG
is my strength and my **s**, — Ex 15:2
Sing to him a new **s**; play — Ps 33:3
He put a new **s** in my mouth, — Ps 40:3
to the Lord a new **s**, — Ps 149:1
God is my strength and my **s**, — Is 12:2
Sing to the Lord a new **s**, — Is 42:10
And they sang a new **s**, — Rv 5:9
God, and the **s** of the Lamb, — Rv 15:3

SONGS
who gives **s** in the night, — Jb 35:10
Shout to God with loud **s** of — Ps 47:1
and hymns and spiritual **s**, — Eph 5:19
and hymns and spiritual **s**, — Col 3:16

SONS
your **s** and your daughters — Jl 2:28
for they shall be called **s** of — Mt 5:9
to him, "Then the **s** are free. — Mt 17:26
A man had two **s**. And he — Mt 21:28
that is, **S** of Thunder); — Mk 3:17
"The **s** of this age marry — Lk 20:34
that you may become **s** of — Jn 12:36
Spirit of God are **s** of God. — Rom 8:14
eagerly for adoption as **s**, — Rom 8:23
and you shall be **s** and — 2 Cor 6:18
Jesus you are all **s** of God, — Gal 3:26
might receive adoption as **s**. — Gal 4:5
in the **s** of disobedience — — Eph 2:2
God is treating you as **s**. — Heb 12:7

SOON
The God of peace will **s** — Rom 16:20
things that must **s** take place. — Rv 1:1
"Surely I am coming **s**." — Rv 22:20

SORROW
knowledge increases **s**. — Eccl 1:18
give them gladness for **s**. — Jer 31:13
but your **s** will turn into joy. — Jn 16:20
that I have great **s** and — Rom 9:2

SORROWS
rejected by men; a man of **s**, — Is 53:3
our griefs and carried our **s**; — Is 53:4
one endures **s** while suffering — 1 Pt 2:19

SOUL
with all your **s** and with all — Dt 6:5
heart and with all your **s**, — Dt 10:12
heart and with all your **s**." — Jos 22:5
He restores my **s**. He leads me — Ps 23:3
so pants my **s** for you, O God. — Ps 42:1
are you cast down, O my **s**, — Ps 42:11
Bless the Lord, O my **s**, and — Ps 103:1
fulfilled is sweet to the **s**, — Prv 13:19
Out of the anguish of his **s** — Is 53:11
hear, that your **s** may live; — Is 55:3
The **s** that sins shall die. — Ez 18:20
body but cannot kill the **s**. — Mt 10:28
with all your **s** and with all — Mt 22:37
not abandon my **s** to Hades, — Acts 2:27
piercing to the division of **s** — Heb 4:12
wage war against your **s**. — 1 Pt 2:11

SOULS
and whoever captures **s** is — Prv 11:30
in it, and find rest for your **s**. — Jer 6:16
you will find rest for your **s**. — Mt 11:29
which is able to save your **s**. — Jas 1:21
faith, the salvation of your **s**. — 1 Pt 1:9

SOUND
let the **s** of his praise be — Ps 66:8
heaven a **s** like a mighty — Acts 2:2
bugle gives an indistinct **s**, — 1 Cor 14:8
For the trumpet will **s**, — 1 Cor 15:52
and with the **s** of the — 1 Thes 4:16
does not agree with the **s** — 1 Tm 6:3
be able to give instruction in **s** — Ti 1:9
you, teach what accords with **s** — Ti 2:1

SOURCE
He is the **s** of your life in — 1 Cor 1:30
he became the **s** of eternal — Heb 5:9

SOVEREIGN
to God and said, "**S** Lord, — Acts 4:24
is the blessed and only **S**, — 1 Tm 6:15
"O **S** Lord, holy and true, — Rv 6:10

SOW
those who plow iniquity and **s** — Jb 4:8
Those who **s** in tears shall — Ps 126:5
they neither **s** nor reap nor — Mt 6:26
"A sower went out to **s**. — Mt 13:3
and the **s**, after washing herself, — 2 Pt 2:22

SOWS
but one who **s** righteousness — Prv 11:18
Whoever **s** injustice will — Prv 22:8
'One **s** and another reaps.' — Jn 4:37
The point is this: whoever **s** — 2 Cor 9:6
mocked, for whatever one **s**, — Gal 6:7

SPARE
He who did not **s** his own — Rom 8:32
For if God did not **s** the — Rom 11:21
For if God did not **s** angels — 2 Pt 2:4

SPARES
Whoever **s** the rod hates — Prv 13:24

SPECK
Why do you see the **s** that is — Mt 7:3

SPEECH
understand one another's **s**." — Gn 11:7
Day to day pours out **s**, and — Ps 19:2
Fine **s** is not becoming to a — Prv 17:7
God with lofty **s** or wisdom. — 1 Cor 2:1
in faith, in **s**, in knowledge, — 2 Cor 8:7
Let your **s** always be gracious, — Col 4:6
believers an example in **s**, — 1 Tm 4:12
and healthy **s** that cannot be — Ti 2:8

SPIRIT
And the **S** of God was — Gn 1:2
Then the Lord said, "My **S** — Gn 6:3
filled him with the **S** of God, — Ex 31:3
filled him with the **S** of God, — Ex 35:31
And the **S** of God came — Nm 24:2
a man in whom is the **s**, — Nm 27:18
The **S** of the Lord was upon — Jgs 3:10
Then the **S** of the Lord — Jgs 15:14
Now the **S** of the Lord — 1 Sm 16:14
an evil **s** from God is — 1 Sm 16:15
"The **S** of the Lord speaks — 2 Sm 23:2
portion of your **s** on me." — 2 Kgs 2:9
You gave your good **S** to — Neh 9:20
and the **s** of God is in my — Jb 27:3
The **S** of God has made me, — Jb 33:4
your hand I commit my **s**; — Ps 31:5
and renew a right **s** within — Ps 51:10
and take not your Holy **S** — Ps 51:11
uphold me with a willing **s**. — Ps 51:12
of God are a broken **s**; — Ps 51:17
you send forth your **S**, — Ps 104:30
shall I go from your **S**? — Ps 139:7
Let your good **S** lead me on — Ps 143:10
but the Lord weighs the **s**. — Prv 16:2
The **s** of man is the lamp of — Prv 20:27
and the **s** returns to God — Eccl 12:7
until the **S** is poured upon — Is 32:15
all these is the life of my **s**. — Is 38:16
Who has measured the **S** of — Is 40:13
I have put my **S** upon him; — Is 42:1
I will pour my **S** upon your — Is 44:3
is of a contrite and lowly **s**, — Is 57:15
and grieved his Holy **S**; — Is 63:10
the **S** of the Lord gave them — Is 63:14
Then the **S** lifted me up, and — Ez 3:12
and a new **s** I will put — Ez 11:19
and a new **s** I will put — Ez 36:26
because an excellent **s** was in — Dn 6:3
that I will pour out my **S** on — Jl 2:28
My **S** remains in your midst. — Hg 2:5
with child from the Holy **S**. — Mt 1:18
and he saw the **S** of God — Mt 3:16
by the **S** into the wilderness — Mt 4:1

"Blessed are the poor in **s**, Mt 5:3
I will put my **S** upon him, Mt 12:18
But if it is by the **S** of God Mt 12:28
against the **S** will not be Mt 12:31
The **s** indeed is willing, Mt 26:41
voice and yielded up his **s**. Mt 27:50
the Son and of the Holy **S**, Mt 28:19
grew and became strong in **s**, Lk 1:80
and the Holy **S** was upon Lk 2:25
And Jesus, full of the Holy **S**, Lk 4:1
"The **S** of the Lord is upon Lk 4:18
for the Holy **S** will teach Lk 12:12
your hands I commit my **s**!" Lk 23:46
"I saw the **S** descend from Jn 1:32
one is born of water and the **S**, Jn 3:5
God is **s**, and those who Jn 4:24
It is the **S** who gives life; Jn 6:63
Now this he said about the **S**, Jn 7:39
even the **S** of truth, whom Jn 14:17
But the Helper, the Holy **S**, Jn 14:26
When the **S** of truth comes, Jn 16:13
his head and gave up his **s**. Jn 19:30
them, "Receive the Holy **S**. Jn 20:22
be baptized with the Holy **S**." Acts 1:5
the Holy **S** has come upon Acts 1:8
the Holy **S** and began to Acts 2:4
that I will pour out my **S** Acts 2:17
the gift of the Holy **S**. Acts 2:38
Peter, filled with the Holy **S**, Acts 4:8
full of the **S** and of wisdom, Acts 6:3
might receive the Holy **S**, Acts 8:15
be filled with the Holy **S**." Acts 9:17
the Holy **S** fell on all who Acts 10:44
the Holy **S** fell on them Acts 11:15
by giving them the Holy **S** Acts 15:8
"Did you receive the Holy **S** Acts 19:2
the Holy **S** came on them, Acts 19:6
the Holy **S** who has been Rom 5:5
but in the new life of the **S**. Rom 7:6
flesh but according to the **S**. Rom 8:4
minds on the things of the **S**. Rom 8:5
if in fact the **S** of God dwells Rom 8:9
If the **S** of him who raised Rom 8:11
but if by the **S** you put to Rom 8:13
The **S** himself bears Rom 8:16
Likewise the **S** helps us in Rom 8:26
because the **S** intercedes Rom 8:27
in zeal, be fervent in **s**, Rom 12:11
and joy in the Holy **S**. Rom 14:17
sanctified by the Holy **S**. Rom 15:16
For the **S** searches 1 Cor 2:10
the things of the **S** of God, 1 Cor 2:14
God's **S** dwells in you? 1 Cor 3:16
becomes one **s** with him. 1 Cor 6:17
of the Holy **S** within you, 1 Cor 6:19
in the **S** of God ever 1 Cor 12:3
of gifts, but the same **S**; 1 Cor 12:4
For in one **S** we were all 1 Cor 12:13
my **s** prays but my mind 1 Cor 14:14
us his **S** in our hearts 2 Cor 1:22
kills, but the **S** gives life. 2 Cor 3:6
Now the Lord is the **S**, 2 Cor 3:17
who has given us the **S** as 2 Cor 5:5
a different **s** from the one 2 Cor 11:4
Did you receive the **S** by Gal 3:2
promised **S** through faith. Gal 3:14
God has sent the **S** of his Son Gal 4:6
For through the **S**, by faith, Gal 5:5
But I say, walk by the **S**, Gal 5:16
But if you are led by the **S**, Gal 5:18
But the fruit of the **S** is love, Gal 5:22
let us also walk by the **S**. Gal 5:25
sows to the **S** will from the Gal 6:8
with the promised Holy **S**, Eph 1:13
may give you a **s** of wisdom Eph 1:17
through his **S** in your inner Eph 3:16
There is one body and one **S** Eph 4:4
grieve the Holy **S** of God, Eph 4:30
but be filled with the **S**, Eph 5:18
and the sword of the **S**, Eph 6:17
praying at all times in the **S**, Eph 6:18
any participation in the **S**, Phil 2:1
with the joy of the Holy **S**, 1 Thes 1:6
who gives his Holy **S** to 1 Thes 4:8
Do not quench the **S**. 1 Thes 5:19
by the **S** and belief in 2 Thes 2:13
Now the **S** expressly says 1 Tm 4:1
By the Holy **S** who dwells 2 Tm 1:14
and renewal of the Holy **S**, Ti 3:5
S distributed according to Heb 2:4
the division of soul and of **s**, Heb 4:12
who through the eternal **S** Heb 9:14
And the Holy **S** also bears Heb 10:15
body apart from the **s** is dead, Jas 2:26
in the sanctification of the **S**, 1 Pt 1:2
or time the **S** of Christ in 1 Pt 1:11
of a gentle and quiet **s**, 1 Pt 3:4
but made alive in the **s**, 1 Pt 3:18
they might live in the **s** the 1 Pt 4:6
carried along by the Holy **S**. 2 Pt 1:21
do not believe every **s**, for 1 Jn 4:1
By this you know the **S** of 1 Jn 4:2
This is the **s** of the antichrist, 1 Jn 4:3
he has given us of his **S**. 1 Jn 4:13
And the **S** is the one who 1 Jn 5:6
faith; pray in the Holy **S**; Jude 1:20
I was in the **S** on the Lord's Rv 1:10
let him hear what the **S** says Rv 2:7
The **S** and the Bride say, Rv 22:17

SPIRITS
the God of the **s** of all flesh, Nm 16:22
and he cast out the **s** with a Mt 8:16
that the **s** are subject to you, Lk 10:20
and the evil **s** came out of Acts 19:12
to distinguish between **s**, 1 Cor 12:10
and the **s** of prophets are 1 Cor 14:32
according to the elemental **s** Col 2:8
the elemental **s** of the world, Col 2:20
deceitful **s** and teachings of 1 Tm 4:1
all ministering **s** sent out to Heb 1:14
to the Father of **s** and live? Heb 12:9
and to the **s** of the righteous Heb 12:23
proclaimed to the **s** in prison, 1 Pt 3:19
but test the **s** to see whether 1 Jn 4:1
and from the seven **s** who are Rv 1:4
God of the **s** of the prophets, Rv 22:6

SPIRITUAL
some **s** gift to strengthen Rom 1:11
we know that the law is **s**, Rom 7:14
which is your **s** worship. Rom 12:1
share in their **s** blessings, Rom 15:27
not lacking in any **s** gift, 1 Cor 1:7
interpreting **s** truths to 1 Cor 2:13
truths to those who are **s**. 1 Cor 2:13
The **s** person judges all 1 Cor 2:15
could not address you as **s** 1 Cor 3:1
If we have sown **s** things 1 Cor 9:11
and all drank the same **s** 1 Cor 10:4
Now concerning **s** gifts, 1 Cor 12:1
and earnestly desire the **s** 1 Cor 14:1
that he is a prophet, or **s**, 1 Cor 14:37
body; it is raised a **s** body. 1 Cor 15:44
there is also a **s** body. 1 Cor 15:44
But it is not the **s** that is 1 Cor 15:46
natural, and then the **s**. 1 Cor 15:46
you who are **s** should restore Gal 6:1
with every **s** blessing in the Eph 1:3
and hymns and **s** songs, Eph 5:19
against the **s** forces of evil Eph 6:12
s wisdom and understanding, Col 1:9
and hymns and **s** songs, Col 3:16
long for the pure **s** milk, 1 Pt 2:2
being built up as a **s** house, 1 Pt 2:5
to offer **s** sacrifices acceptable 1 Pt 2:5

SPIRITUALLY
they are **s** discerned. 1 Cor 2:14

SPLENDOR
S and majesty are before 1 Chr 16:27
worship the Lord in the **s** of Ps 29:2
Worship the Lord in the **s** of Ps 96:9
You are clothed with **s** and Ps 104:1
On the glorious **s** of your Ps 145:5
the church to himself in **s**, Eph 5:27

SPOT
without **s** or wrinkle or any Eph 5:27
a lamb without blemish or **s**. 1 Pt 1:19
him without **s** or blemish, 2 Pt 3:14

SPRING
Branch to **s** up for David, Jer 33:15
in him a **s** of water welling Jn 4:14
give from the **s** of the water Rv 21:6

STAFF
And Moses took the **s** of God Ex 4:20
with me; your rod and your **s**, Ps 23:4

STAND
the people, "Fear not, **s** firm, Ex 14:13
S firm, hold your position 2 Chr 20:17
will not **s** in the judgment, Ps 1:5
him, and **s** in awe of him, Ps 22:23
of the righteous will **s**. Prv 12:7
the wall and **s** in the breach Ez 22:30
ones who **s** by the Lord Zec 4:14
divided against itself will **s**. Mt 12:25
this grace in which we **s**, Rom 5:2
For we will all **s** before Rom 14:10
received, in which you **s**, 1 Cor 15:1
s firm in the faith, be strong. 1 Cor 16:13
set us free; **s** firm therefore, Gal 5:1
that you may be able to **s** Eph 6:11
S therefore, having fastened Eph 6:14
So then, brothers, **s** firm 2 Thes 2:15
grace of God. **S** firm in it. 1 Pt 5:12
I **s** at the door and knock. Rv 3:20

STANDING
you are **s** is holy ground." Ex 3:5
where you are **s** is holy." Jos 5:15
if you are **s** fast in the 1 Thes 3:8

STANDS
nor **s** in the way of sinners, Ps 1:1
The counsel of the Lord **s** Ps 33:11
the earth, and it **s** fast. Ps 119:90
that he **s** take heed lest 1 Cor 10:12
God's firm foundation **s**, 2 Tm 2:19

STAR
a **s** shall come out of Jacob, Nm 24:17
O Day **S**, son of Dawn! Is 14:12
When they saw the **s**, they Mt 2:10
and I saw a **s** fallen from Rv 9:1
the bright morning **s**." Rv 22:16

STARS
rule the night — and the **s**. Gn 1:16
as the **s** of heaven and Gn 22:17
like the **s** forever and ever. Dn 12:3
as the **s** of heaven and Heb 11:12

STATUTES
and keep all his **s**, Ex 15:26
the **s** and the rules that the Dt 6:1
and his **s** I did not put away Ps 18:22
steadfast in keeping your **s**! Ps 119:5
walk in my **s** and be careful Ez 36:27

STEADFAST
but showing **s** love to Dt 5:10
For your **s** love is before my Ps 26:3
God, according to your **s** love; Ps 51:1
For great is your **s** love Ps 86:13
his **s** love endures forever, Ps 100:5
The **s** love of the Lord Lam 3:22
be **s**, immovable, knowing 1 Cor 15:58
in the faith, stable and **s**, Col 1:23
who remains **s** under trial, Jas 1:12

STEADFASTNESS
faith, love, **s**, gentleness. 1 Tm 6:11
of your faith produces **s**. Jas 1:3
and self-control with **s**, 2 Pt 1:6

STEAL
"You shall not **s**. Ex 20:15
adultery, You shall not **s**, Mt 19:18
The thief comes only to **s** Jn 10:10
against stealing, do you **s**? Rom 2:21
not murder, You shall not **s**, Rom 13:9
Let the thief no longer **s**, Eph 4:28

STEPHEN
gathering, and they chose **S**, Acts 6:5
as they were stoning **S**, Acts 7:59

STEPS
a rock, making my **s** secure. Ps 40:2
Keep steady my **s** Ps 119:133
the Lord establishes his **s**. Prv 16:9
you might follow in his **s**. 1 Pt 2:21

STEWARD
For an overseer, as God's **s**, Ti 1:7

STEWARDS
as servants of Christ and **s** 1 Cor 4:1
Moreover, it is required of **s** 1 Cor 4:2
as good **s** of God's varied 1 Pt 4:10

STEWARDSHIP
am still entrusted with a **s**. 1 Cor 9:17
heard of the **s** of God's grace Eph 3:2

to the **s** from God that Col 1:25
than the **s** from God that 1 Tm 1:4

STIFF-NECKED
and behold, it is a **s** people. Ex 32:9
Do not now be **s** as your 2 Chr 30:8
"You **s** people, you always Acts 7:51

STILL
"Sun, stand **s** at Gibeon, Jos 10:12
"Be **s**, and know that I am Ps 46:10
The sun and moon stood **s** in Hb 3:11
while we were **s** sinners, Rom 5:8

STING
O Sheol, where is your **s**? Hos 13:14
death, where is your **s**?" 1 Cor 15:55
The **s** of death is sin, 1 Cor 15:56

STIRS
Hatred **s** up strife, but love Prv 10:12
but a harsh word **s** up anger. Prv 15:1
A greedy man **s** up strife, Prv 28:25
As for a person who **s** up Ti 3:10

STONE
this **s** shall be a witness Jos 24:27
with a sling and with a **s**, 1 Sm 17:50
strike your foot against a **s**. Ps 91:12
The **s** that the builders Ps 118:22
and its **s** wall was broken Prv 24:31
and a **s** of offense and Is 8:14
in Zion, a **s**, a tested **s**, Is 28:16
I will remove the heart of **s** Ez 11:19
"'The **s** that the builders Mt 21:42
strike your foot against a **s**.'" Lk 4:11
I am laying in Zion a **s** of Rom 9:33
to him, a living **s** rejected by men 1 Pt 2:4
and "A **s** of stumbling, and a 1 Pt 2:8

STONES
God is able from these **s** to Mt 3:9
the very **s** would cry out." Lk 19:40
you yourselves like living **s** 1 Pt 2:5

STOREHOUSE
the full tithes into the **s**, Mal 3:10

STORM
He made the **s** be still, and Ps 107:29
a shelter from the **s** and a Is 25:4
there arose a great **s** on the Mt 8:24

STRAIGHT
make your way **s** before me. Ps 5:8
and he will make **s** your Prv 3:6
blameless keeps his way **s**, Prv 11:5
who can make **s** what he Eccl 7:13
make **s** in the desert a Is 40:3
of the Lord; make his paths **s**." Mt 3:3
and make **s** paths for your Heb 12:13

STRAINING
You blind guides, **s** out a Mt 23:24
s forward to what lies ahead, Phil 3:13

STRANGE
For by people of **s** lips and Is 28:11
For you bring some **s** Acts 17:20
"By people of **s** tongues 1 Cor 14:21
by diverse and **s** teachings, Heb 13:9
as though something **s** 1 Pt 4:12

STRANGER
I was a **s** and you welcomed Mt 25:35
A **s** they will not follow, but Jn 10:5

STRANGERS
and **s** to the covenants Eph 2:12
So then you are no longer **s** Eph 2:19
they were **s** and exiles on Heb 11:13
to show hospitality to **s**, Heb 13:2

STREAMS
He is like a tree planted by **s** Ps 1:3
As a deer pants for flowing **s**, Ps 42:1
All **s** run to the sea, but the Eccl 1:7
like **s** of water in a dry place, Is 32:2

STRENGTH
The Lord is my **s** and my Ex 15:2
me with **s** for the battle; 2 Sm 22:40
Seek the Lord and his **s**; 1 Chr 16:11
joy of the Lord is your **s**." Neh 8:10
you have established **s** Ps 8:2
The Lord is my **s** and my Ps 28:7
God is our refuge and **s**, a Ps 46:1
but God is the **s** of my heart Ps 73:26
Blessed are those whose **s** is Ps 84:5
Seek the Lord and his **s**; Ps 105:4
Lord, the **s** of my salvation, Ps 140:7
A wise man is full of **s**, and Prv 24:5
the Lord shall renew their **s**; Is 40:31
mind and with all your **s**.' Mk 12:30
may have **s** to comprehend Eph 3:18
and in the **s** of his might. Eph 6:10
as one who serves by the **s** 1 Pt 4:11

STRENGTHEN
s me according to your Ps 119:28
S the weak hands, and make Is 35:3
I will **s** you, I will help you, Is 41:10
spiritual gift to **s** you — Rom 1:11
able to **s** you according to Rom 16:25
and **s** your weak knees, Heb 12:12
s, and establish you. 1 Pt 5:10

STRENGTHENED
to be **s** with power through Eph 3:16
May you be **s** with all Col 1:11
You then, my child, be **s** by 2 Tm 2:1
Lord stood by me and **s** me, 2 Tm 4:17
the heart to be **s** by grace, Heb 13:9

STRENGTHENS
through him who **s** me. Phil 4:13

STRIFE
Hatred stirs up **s**, but love Prv 10:12
A man of wrath stirs up **s**, Prv 29:22
s, deceit, maliciousness. Rom 1:29

STRIKE
lest you **s** your foot against Ps 91:12
"**S** the shepherd, and the Zec 13:7
'I will **s** the shepherd, Mt 26:31
lest you **s** your foot against a Lk 4:11

STRIKES
To one who **s** you on the Lk 6:29
airs, or **s** you in the face. 2 Cor 11:20

STRIPES
and with his **s** we are healed. Is 53:5

STRIVING
all is vanity and a **s** after Eccl 1:14

STRONG
Be **s** and courageous. Do not Dt 31:6
Be **s** and courageous, for you Jos 1:6
This God is my **s** refuge 2 Sm 22:33
Be **s**, and show yourself a 1 Kgs 2:2
Be **s** and courageous. 1 Chr 22:13
"Be **s** and courageous. 2 Chr 32:7
Wait for the Lord; be **s**, and Ps 27:14
a **s** tower against the enemy. Ps 61:3
but you are my **s** refuge. Ps 71:7
The name of the Lord is a **s** Prv 18:10
arm, for love is **s** as death, Sg 8:6
the child grew and became **s**, Lk 2:40
We who are **s** have an Rom 15:1
are weak, but you are **s**. 1 Cor 4:10
faith, act like men, be **s**. 1 Cor 16:13
are weak and you are **s**. 2 Cor 13:9
Finally, be **s** in the Lord Eph 6:10

STRONGHOLD
The Lord is a **s** for the Ps 9:9
horn of my salvation, my **s**. Ps 18:2
Lord, my strength and my **s**, Jer 16:19

STRUGGLE
how great a **s** I have for Col 2:1
you endured a hard **s** with Heb 10:32
In your **s** against sin you Heb 12:4

STUDY
set his heart to **s** the law of Ezr 7:10
in order to **s** the words of Neh 8:13
and much **s** is a weariness Eccl 12:12

STUMBLE
foes, it is they who **s** and fall. Ps 27:2
nothing can make them **s**. Ps 119:165
And many shall **s** on it. They Is 8:15
in which they shall not **s**, Jer 31:9
causes your brother to **s**. Rom 14:21
lest I make my brother **s**. 1 Cor 8:13
They **s** because they disobey 1 Pt 2:8

STUMBLING
and a rock of **s** to both houses Is 8:14
stumbled over the **s** stone, Rom 9:32
put a **s** block or hindrance Rom 14:13
a **s** block to Jews and folly 1 Cor 1:23
become a **s** block to the 1 Cor 8:9
and "A stone of **s**, and a rock 1 Pt 2:8
him there is no cause for **s**. 1 Jn 2:10
you from **s** and to present Jude 1:24

SUBDUE
the earth and **s** it and have Gn 1:28

SUBJECT
Let every person be **s** to Rom 13:1
be **s** to such as these, 1 Cor 16:16
him even to **s** all things to Phil 3:21
more be **s** to the Father Heb 12:9
Be **s** for the Lord's sake to 1 Pt 2:13
Servants, be **s** to your 1 Pt 2:18
be **s** to your own husbands, 1 Pt 3:1
younger, be **s** to the elders. 1 Pt 5:5

SUBJECTED
For the creation was **s** to Rom 8:20
When all things are **s** to 1 Cor 15:28
that God **s** the world to Heb 2:5
and powers having been **s** 1 Pt 3:22

SUBJECTION
Therefore one must be in **s**, Rom 13:5
in **s** under his feet." 1 Cor 15:27
putting everything in **s** Heb 2:8

SUBMISSION
speak, but should be in **s**, 1 Cor 14:34
your **s** flowing from your 2 Cor 9:13
to them we did not yield in **s** Gal 2:5

SUBMISSIVE
Nazareth and was **s** to them. Lk 2:51
keeping his children **s**, 1 Tm 3:4
and **s** to their own husbands, Ti 2:5
Slaves are to be **s** to their own Ti 2:9
Remind them to be **s** to rulers Ti 3:1

SUBMIT
for it does not **s** to God's law; Rom 8:7
they did not **s** to God's Rom 10:3
and do not **s** again to a yoke Gal 5:1
s to your own husbands, Eph 5:22
so also wives should **s** in Eph 5:24
Wives, **s** to your husbands, Col 3:18
Obey your leaders and **s** to Heb 13:17
S yourselves therefore to God. Jas 4:7

SUBMITS
Now as the church **s** to Christ, Eph 5:24

SUBMITTING
s to one another out of Eph 5:21
by **s** to their husbands, 1 Pt 3:5

SUCCESS
that you may have good **s** Jos 1:7
And David had **s** in all 1 Sm 18:14
favor and good **s** in the sight Prv 3:4

SUFFER
and **s** many things from Mt 16:21
certainly **s** at their hands." Mt 17:12
Man must **s** many things and Mk 8:31
worthy to **s** dishonor for the Acts 5:41
provided we **s** with him in Rom 8:17
suffers, all **s** together; 1 Cor 12:26
same sufferings that we **s**. 2 Cor 1:6
him but also **s** for his sake, Phil 1:29
we were to **s** affliction, 1 Thes 3:4
you do good and **s** for it you 1 Pt 2:20
But even if you should **s** for 1 Pt 3:14
For it is better to **s** for doing 1 Pt 3:17
But let none of you **s** as a 1 Pt 4:15
Therefore let those who **s** 1 Pt 4:19
fear what you are about to **s**. Rv 2:10

SUFFERED
himself has **s** when tempted, Heb 2:18
because Christ also **s** for 1 Pt 2:21
For Christ also **s** once for 1 Pt 3:18
for whoever has **s** in the 1 Pt 4:1
And after you have **s** a little 1 Pt 5:10

SUFFERING
knowing that **s** produces — Rom 5:3
but share in **s** for the gospel — 2 Tm 1:8
salvation perfect through **s**. — Heb 2:10

SUFFERINGS
that, we rejoice in our **s**, — Rom 5:3
For I consider that the **s** of — Rom 8:18
abundantly in Christ's **s**, — 2 Cor 1:5
the same **s** that we suffer. — 2 Cor 1:6
and may share his **s**, — Phil 3:10
Now I rejoice in my **s** for — Col 1:24
my persecutions and **s** that — 2 Tm 3:11
as you share Christ's **s**, — 1 Pt 4:13

SUFFERS
If one member **s**, all suffer — 1 Cor 12:26
Yet if anyone **s** as a Christian, — 1 Pt 4:16

SUFFICIENT
"My grace is **s** for you, — 2 Cor 12:9

SUN
And the **s** stood still, and — Jos 10:13
he has set a tent for the **s**, — Ps 19:4
rising of the **s** to its setting. — Ps 50:1
From the rising of the **s** to — Ps 113:3
is nothing new under the **s**. — Eccl 1:9
the **s** of righteousness shall — Mal 4:2
For he makes his **s** rise on — Mt 5:45
and his face shone like the **s**, — Mt 17:2
the **s** shall be turned to — Acts 2:20
and his face was like the **s** — Rv 1:16
need no light of lamp or **s**, — Rv 22:5

SUPERIOR
having become as much **s** to — Heb 1:4
inferior is blessed by the **s**. — Heb 7:7

SUPPER
During **s**, when the devil had — Jn 13:2
rose from **s**. He laid aside his — Jn 13:4
it is not the Lord's **s** that — 1 Cor 11:20
the cup, after **s**, saying, — 1 Cor 11:25
the marriage **s** of the Lamb." — Rv 19:9

SUPPLICATION
Spirit, with all prayer and **s**. — Eph 6:18
making **s** for all the saints, — Eph 6:18
and **s** with thanksgiving let — Phil 4:6

SUPPLICATIONS
then, I urge that **s**, prayers, — 1 Tm 2:1
in **s** and prayers night — 1 Tm 5:5
Jesus offered up prayers and **s**, — Heb 5:7

SUPPLY
And my God will **s** every — Phil 4:19

SUPREME
For the word of the king is **s**, — Eccl 8:4
it be to the emperor as **s**, — 1 Pt 2:13

SURE
and be **s** your sin will find — Nm 32:23
the testimony of the Lord is **s**, — Ps 19:7
your commandments are **s**; — Ps 119:86
of a **s** foundation: — Is 28:16
For I am **s** that neither — Rom 8:38
your calling and election **s**, — 2 Pt 1:10

SURELY
S goodness and mercy shall — Ps 23:6
says, "**S** I am coming soon." — Rv 22:20

SURPASSES
because of the glory that **s** — 2 Cor 3:10
of Christ that **s** knowledge, — Eph 3:19
which **s** all understanding, — Phil 4:7

SURPASSING
to show that the **s** power — 2 Cor 4:7
because of the **s** grace of — 2 Cor 9:14
by the **s** greatness of the — 2 Cor 12:7
of the **s** worth of knowing — Phil 3:8

SURROUNDED
Therefore, since we are **s** — Heb 12:1

SUSTAIN
the Lord, and he will **s** you; — Ps 55:22
who will **s** you to the end, — 1 Cor 1:8

SWALLOWED
"Death is **s** up in victory." — 1 Cor 15:54
mortal may be **s** up by life. — 2 Cor 5:4

SWALLOWING
straining out a gnat and **s** a — Mt 23:24

SWEAR
and does not **s** deceitfully. — Ps 24:4
every tongue shall **s** — Is 45:23
of old, 'You shall not **s** falsely, — Mt 5:33
all, my brothers, do not **s**, — Jas 5:12

SWEAT
By the **s** of your face you — Gn 3:19
and his **s** became like great — Lk 22:44

SWERVE
but I do not **s** from your — Ps 119:157
Do not **s** to the right or to — Prv 4:27
they do not **s** from their paths. — Jl 2:7

SWORD
a flaming **s** that turned every — Gn 3:24
Gird your **s** on your thigh, — Ps 45:3
words are like **s** thrusts, — Prv 12:18
come to bring peace, but a **s**. — Mt 10:34
For all who take the **s** will — Mt 26:52
nakedness, or danger, or **s**? — Rom 8:35
for he does not bear the **s** — Rom 13:4
and the **s** of the Spirit, — Eph 6:17
than any two-edged **s**, — Heb 4:12
came a sharp two-edged **s**, — Rv 1:16

SWORDS
Beat your plowshares into **s**, — Jl 3:10
and they shall beat their **s** — Mi 4:3

SYMBOL
have a **s** of authority on — 1 Cor 11:10

SYMPATHIZE
to **s** with our weaknesses, — Heb 4:15

SYMPATHY
show him **s** and comfort him. — Jb 2:11
Spirit, any affection and **s**, — Phil 2:1
of mind, **s**, brotherly love, — 1 Pt 3:8

SYRIA
the Ashtaroth, the gods of **S**, — Jgs 10:6
and the kings of **S**. — 1 Kgs 10:29
the army of the king of **S**, — 2 Kgs 5:1
in **S** of Damascus, — 1 Chr 18:6

TABERNACLE
the pattern of the **t**, — Ex 25:9
glory of the Lord filled the **t**. — Ex 40:34

TABITHA
in Joppa a disciple named **T**, — Acts 9:36
the body he said, "**T**, arise." — Acts 9:40

TABLE
You prepare a **t** before me in — Ps 23:5
of the **t** of the Lord — 1 Cor 10:21

TABLET
write them on the **t** of your — Prv 3:3
write them on the **t** of your — Prv 7:3
on the **t** of their heart, — Jer 17:1

TABLETS
that I may give you the **t** of — Ex 24:12
and put the **t** in the ark — Dt 10:5
not on **t** of stone but on — 2 Cor 3:3

TABOR
gather your men at Mount **T**, — Jgs 4:6
and come to the oak of **T**. — 1 Sm 10:3
T and Hermon joyously — Ps 89:12

TAKE
lest he reach out his hand and **t** — Gn 3:22
I will **t** nothing but what the — Gn 14:24
"**T** your son, your only son — Gn 22:2
shall not **t** a wife for my son — Gn 24:37
Rebekah is before you; **t** her — Gn 24:51
Would you **t** away my son's — Gn 30:15
us **t** their daughters as wives, — Gn 34:21
t some of the choice fruits of — Gn 43:11
t your father and your — Gn 45:18
t your sandals off your feet, — Ex 3:5
And **t** in your hand this staff, — Ex 4:17
'**T** your staff and cast it down — Ex 7:9
with the Lord to **t** away the frogs — Ex 8:8
man shall **t** a lamb according — Ex 12:3
T a bunch of hyssop and dip it — Ex 12:22
'**T** care not to go up into the — Ex 19:12
shall not **t** the name of the Lord — Ex 20:7
you shall **t** no bribe, for a bribe — Ex 23:8
you shall **t** all the fat that covers — Ex 29:13
shall **t** the atonement money — Ex 30:16
Then I will **t** away my hand, — Ex 33:23
will **t** seven days to ordain you. — Lv 8:33
shall not **t** a woman as a rival — Lv 18:18
"**T** a census of all the congregation — Nm 1:2
And the priest shall **t** holy water — Nm 5:17
Do not **t** us across the Jordan." — Nm 32:5
t up arms, ready to go before — Nm 32:17
"Only **t** care, and keep your soul — Dt 4:9
shall not **t** the name of the Lord — Dt 5:11
t possession of the land — Dt 9:23
shall not add to it or **t** from it. — Dt 12:32
man shall not **t** his father's wife, — Dt 22:30
"**T** this Book of the Law and put — Dt 31:26
t vengeance on my adversaries — Dt 32:41
t up each of you a stone upon — Jos 4:5
"**T** off your sandals from your — Jos 5:15
some days he returned to **t** her. — Jgs 14:8
that you should **t** notice of me, — Ru 2:10
T my right of redemption yourself, — Ru 4:6
he will **t** your sons and appoint — 1 Sm 8:11
Lord **t** vengeance on David's — 1 Sm 20:16
has sent us to you to **t** you — 1 Sm 25:40
me go over and **t** off his head." — 2 Sm 16:9
my rock, in whom I **t** refuge, — 2 Sm 22:3
not **t** my steadfast love from — 1 Chr 17:13
land or **t** their daughters for — Neh 10:30
But he knows the way that I **t**; — Jb 23:10
Can one **t** him by his eyes, — Jb 40:24
Blessed are all who **t** refuge — Ps 2:12
let all who **t** refuge in you rejoice; — Ps 5:11
my God, in you do I **t** refuge; — Ps 7:1
O God, for in you I **t** refuge. — Ps 16:1
for all those who **t** refuge in him. — Ps 18:30
to shame, for I **t** refuge in you. — Ps 25:20
and let your heart **t** courage; — Ps 27:14
and let your heart **t** courage, — Ps 31:24
t not your Holy Spirit from me. — Ps 51:11
to **t** sweet counsel together; — Ps 55:14
In you, O Lord, do I **t** refuge; — Ps 71:1
It is better to **t** refuge in the Lord — Ps 118:8
t not the word of truth utterly — Ps 119:43
If I **t** the wings of the morning — Ps 139:9
T my instruction instead of silver, — Prv 8:10
shield to those who **t** refuge — Prv 30:5
lizard you can **t** in your hands, — Prv 30:28
eat and drink and **t** pleasure — Eccl 3:13
no longer knew how to **t** advice. — Eccl 4:13
that you should **t** hold of this, — Eccl 7:18
Do not **t** to heart all the things — Eccl 7:21
not **t** your stand in an evil cause, — Eccl 8:3
even women shall **t** hold of one — Is 4:1
I will **t** you by the hand — Is 42:6
I will **t** vengeance, and I will — Is 47:3
iniquities, like the wind, **t** us away. — Is 64:6
T my yoke upon you, and learn — Mt 11:29
"**T**, eat; this is my body." — Mt 26:26
deny himself and **t** up his cross — Mk 8:34
we cannot **t** anything out of the — 1 Tm 6:7
T hold of the eternal life to — 1 Tm 6:12
"Worthy are you to **t** the scroll — Rv 5:9
God will **t** away his share — Rv 22:19

TAKES
Blessed is the man who **t** — Ps 34:8
who **t** away the sin of the — Jn 1:29
and if anyone **t** away from — Rv 22:19

TAKING
t the form of a servant. And — Phil 2:7

TALENTS
To one he gave five **t**, to — Mt 25:15

TALK
consist in **t** but in power. — 1 Cor 4:20
Let no corrupting **t** come — Eph 4:29
foolish **t** nor crude joking, — Eph 5:4
and obscene **t** from your — Col 3:8
let us not love in word or **t** — 1 Jn 3:18

TAMAR
and her name was **T**. — Gn 38:6
whom **T** bore to Judah, — Ru 4:12
sister, whose name was **T**. — 2 Sm 13:1
So **T** lived, a desolate — 2 Sm 13:20

His daughter-in-law **T** also 1 Chr 2:4
of Perez and Zerah by **T**, Mt 1:3

TAME
but no human being can **t** the Jas 3:8

TASTE
Oh, **t** and see that the Lord is Ps 34:8
"Do not handle, Do not **t**, Col 2:21
might **t** death for everyone. Heb 2:9

TASTED
who have **t** the heavenly gift, Heb 6:4
if indeed you have **t** that the 1 Pt 2:3

TAUGHT
for he **t** them as one who Mk 1:22
not **t** by human wisdom 1 Cor 2:13
One who is **t** the word must Gal 6:6
him and were **t** in him, Eph 4:21
the faith, just as you were **t**, Col 2:7
have been **t** by God to 1 Thes 4:9

TAXES
Is it lawful to pay **t** to Mt 22:17
t to whom taxes are owed, Rom 13:7

TEACH
mouth and **t** you what you Ex 4:12
You shall **t** them diligently to Dt 6:7
You shall **t** them to your Dt 11:19
T me your way, O Lord, and Ps 27:11
and you **t** me wisdom in the Ps 51:6
Then I will **t** transgressors Ps 51:13
So **t** us to number our days Ps 90:12
T me to do your will, for Ps 143:10
each one **t** his neighbor and Jer 31:34
to him, "Lord, **t** us to pray, Lk 11:1
he will **t** you all things and Jn 14:26
woman to **t** or to exercise 1 Tm 2:12
hospitable, able to **t**, 1 Tm 3:2
Command and **t** these 1 Tm 4:11
T and urge these things. 1 Tm 6:2
But as for you, **t** what accords Ti 2:1
And they shall not **t**, each Heb 8:11
for you know that we who **t** Jas 3:1

TEACHER
disciple is not above his **t**, Mt 10:24
If I then, your Lord and **T**, Jn 13:14
preacher and apostle and **t**, 2 Tm 1:11

TEACHERS
third **t**, then miracles, 1 Cor 12:28
Are all **t**? Do all work 1 Cor 12:29
evangelists, the pastors and **t**, Eph 4:11
for themselves **t** to suit their 2 Tm 4:3
this time you ought to be **t**, Heb 5:12
many of you should become **t**, Jas 3:1

TEACHES
our serving; the one who **t**, Rom 12:7
If anyone **t** a different 1 Tm 6:3

TEACHING
forsake not your mother's **t**, Prv 1:8
is a lamp and the **t** a light, Prv 6:23
t them to observe all that I Mt 28:20
he will know whether the **t** Jn 7:17
apostles' **t** and fellowship, Acts 2:42
one who teaches, in his **t**; Rom 12:7
warning everyone and **t** Col 1:28
t and admonishing one Col 3:16
to exhortation, to **t**. 1 Tm 4:13
labor in preaching and **t**. 1 Tm 5:17
and the **t** that accords with 1 Tm 6:3
by God and profitable for **t**, 2 Tm 3:16
and in your **t** show integrity, Ti 2:7
Whoever abides in the **t** has 2 Jn 1:9

TEACHINGS
to human precepts and **t**? Col 2:22
spirits and **t** of demons, 1 Tm 4:1
by diverse and strange **t**, Heb 13:9

TEAR
a time to **t**, and a time to Eccl 3:7
He will wipe away every **t** Rv 21:4

TEARS
Those who sow in **t** shall Ps 126:5
wipe away **t** from all faces, Is 25:8
now tell you even with **t**, Phil 3:18

TEETH
he gnashes his **t** and melts Ps 112:10
weeping and gnashing of **t**." Mt 8:12

TEMPER
A man of quick **t** acts Prv 14:17
but he who has a hasty **t** Prv 14:29

TEMPEST
from the raging wind and **t**." Ps 55:8
and no small **t** lay on us, Acts 27:20

TEMPLE
to build a **t** for the name 2 Chr 2:1
of the Lord filled the **t**. 2 Chr 7:1
The Lord is in his holy **t**; the Ps 11:4
But the Lord is in his holy **t**; Hb 2:20
them, "Destroy this **t**, Jn 2:19
about the **t** of his body. Jn 2:21
are God's **t** and that God's 1 Cor 3:16
is holy, and you are that **t**. 1 Cor 3:17
body is a **t** of the Holy 1 Cor 6:19
grows into a holy **t** in the Eph 2:21
his seat in the **t** of God, 2 Thes 2:4
for its **t** is the Lord God the Rv 21:22

TEMPLES
does not live in **t** made by Acts 17:24

TEMPT
so that Satan may not **t** 1 Cor 7:5

TEMPTATION
And lead us not into **t**, but Mt 6:13
one by whom the **t** comes! Mt 18:7
you may not enter into **t**. Mt 26:41
But because of the **t** to 1 Cor 7:2
No **t** has overtaken you 1 Cor 10:13
desire to be rich fall into **t**, 1 Tm 6:9

TEMPTATIONS
"Woe to the world for **t** to sin! Mt 18:7
For it is necessary that **t** Mt 18:7
"**T** to sin are sure to come, Lk 17:1

TEMPTED
wilderness to be **t** by the devil. Mt 4:1
on yourself, lest you too be **t**. Gal 6:1
tempter had **t** you and our 1 Thes 3:5
help those who are being **t**. Heb 2:18
Let no one say when he is **t**, Jas 1:13
But each person is **t** when Jas 1:14

TEMPTER
And the **t** came and said to Mt 4:3
the **t** had tempted you 1 Thes 3:5

TEMPTS
and he himself **t** no one. Jas 1:13

TEN
covenant, the **T** Commandments Ex 34:28
that is, the **T** Commandments, Dt 4:13

TEND
He will **t** his flock like a Is 40:11
said to him, "**T** my sheep." Jn 21:16

TENDER
because of the **t** mercy of our Lk 1:78
brotherly love, a **t** heart, 1 Pt 3:8

TENDERHEARTED
Be kind to one another, **t**, Eph 4:32

TENT
about in a **t** for my dwelling. 2 Sm 7:6
Let me dwell in your **t** Ps 61:4
the **t** where he dwelt Ps 78:60
For we know that if the **t**, 2 Cor 5:1
while we are still in this **t**, 2 Cor 5:4
perfect **t** (not made with Heb 9:11
and the sanctuary of the **t** of Rv 15:5

TENTMAKERS
for they were **t** by trade. Acts 18:3

TERROR
You will not fear the **t** of the Ps 91:5
For rulers are not a **t** to Rom 13:3

TEST
the Lord your God to the **t**, Dt 6:16
me; **t** my heart and my mind. Ps 26:2
Let us **t** and examine our Lam 3:40
the Lord your God to the **t**.'" Mt 4:7
and the fire will **t** what 1 Cor 3:13
not put Christ to the **t**, 1 Cor 10:9
T yourselves. Or do you not 2 Cor 13:5
But let each one **t** his own Gal 6:4
but **t** everything; hold 1 Thes 5:21
for when he has stood the **t** Jas 1:12
it comes upon you to **t** you, 1 Pt 4:12
but **t** the spirits to see 1 Jn 4:1

TESTED
After these things God **t** Gn 22:1
For you, O God, have **t** us; Ps 66:10
and a man is **t** by his praise. Prv 27:21
And let them also be **t** first; 1 Tm 3:10
so that the **t** genuineness of 1 Pt 1:7

TESTIFY
And we have seen and **t** 1 Jn 4:14

TESTIMONY
world as a **t** to all nations, Mt 24:14
of the **t** about our Lord, 2 Tm 1:8
And this is the **t**, that God 1 Jn 5:11

TESTING
For the Lord your God is **t** Dt 13:3
that by **t** you may discern Rom 12:2
for you know that the **t** of Jas 1:3

TESTS
The Lord **t** the righteous, Ps 11:5
gold, and the Lord **t** hearts. Prv 17:3
but to please God who **t** 1 Thes 2:4

THANK
I will render **t** offerings to Ps 56:12
Let them **t** the Lord for his Ps 107:8
declared, "I **t** you, Father, Mt 11:25
I **t** you that I am not like Lk 18:11
First, I **t** my God through Rom 1:8
I **t** my God in all my Phil 1:3
We always **t** God, the Father Col 1:3

THANKFUL
in one body. And be **t**. Col 3:15

THANKFULNESS
If I partake with **t**, why 1 Cor 10:30
with **t** in your hearts to God. Col 3:16

THANKING
t and praising the Lord, 1 Chr 23:30

THANKS
Oh give **t** to the Lord; call 1 Chr 16:8
praising and giving **t** to the Ezr 3:11
and give **t** to his holy name. Ps 30:4
I will give **t** to your name, Ps 54:6
will give **t** to you forever; Ps 79:13
Give **t** to him; bless his Ps 100:4
Oh give **t** to the Lord, for he Ps 118:1
to give **t** to the name of the Ps 122:4
I give you **t**, O Lord, with Ps 138:1
All your works shall give **t** Ps 145:10
But **t** be to God, that you Rom 6:17
I give **t** to my God always 1 Cor 1:4
But **t** be to God, who 1 Cor 15:57
But **t** be to God, who in 2 Cor 2:14
T be to God for his 2 Cor 9:15
I do not cease to give **t** for Eph 1:16
giving **t** always and for Eph 5:20
give **t** in all circumstances 1 Thes 5:18
to give **t** to God for 2 Thes 2:13

THANKSGIVING
a sacrifice of **t** to the Lord, Lv 22:29
Offer to God a sacrifice of **t**, Ps 50:14
I will magnify him with **t**. Ps 69:30
Enter his gates with **t**, and Ps 100:4
Sing to the Lord with **t**; Ps 147:7
But I with the voice of **t** will Jon 2:9
us will produce **t** to God. 2 Cor 9:11
but instead let there be **t**. Eph 5:4
with **t** let your requests Phil 4:6
were taught, abounding in **t**. Col 2:7
with **t** by those who 1 Tm 4:3
wisdom and **t** and honor and Rv 7:12

THIEF
The **t** comes only to steal Jn 10:10
come like a **t** in the night. 1 Thes 5:2
the Lord will come like a **t**, 2 Pt 3:10
I am coming like a **t**! Blessed Rv 16:15

THIEVES
and where **t** do not break — Mt 6:20
nor **t**, nor the greedy, nor — 1 Cor 6:10

THINK
you not to **t** of himself more — Rom 12:3
praise, **t** about these things. — Phil 4:8
T over what I say, for the — 2 Tm 2:7

THINKING
became futile in their **t**, — Rom 1:21
not be children in your **t**. — 1 Cor 14:20
with the same way of **t**, — 1 Pt 4:1

THINKS
If anyone among you **t** — 1 Cor 3:18
who **t** that he stands — 1 Cor 10:12
For if anyone **t** he is something, — Gal 6:3
If anyone else **t** he has reason — Phil 3:4
If anyone **t** he is religious — Jas 1:26

THIRST
and for my **t** they gave me — Ps 69:21
and **t** for righteousness, — Mt 5:6
believes in me shall never **t**. — Jn 6:35

THIRSTS
My soul **t** for God, for the — Ps 42:2
I seek you; my soul **t** for you; — Ps 63:1
my soul **t** for you like a — Ps 143:6
"Come, everyone who **t**, come — Is 55:1
up and cried out, "If anyone **t**, — Jn 7:37

THIRSTY
hungry and **t**, their soul — Ps 107:5
bread to eat, and if he is **t**, — Prv 25:21
I was **t** and you gave me — Mt 25:35
of this water will be **t** again, — Jn 4:13
feed him; if he is **t**, give — Rom 12:20
And let the one who is **t** — Rv 22:17

THORN
a **t** was given me in the flesh, — 2 Cor 12:7

THORNS
together a crown of **t**, — Mt 27:29
But if it bears **t** and thistles, — Heb 6:8

THOUGHT
but the prudent gives **t** to — Prv 14:15
a child, I **t** like a child, — 1 Cor 13:11
and take every **t** captive to — 2 Cor 10:5

THOUGHTS
intention of the **t** of his heart — Gn 6:5
knows the **t** of man, that — Ps 94:11
Try me and know my **t**! — Ps 139:23
For my **t** are not your — Is 55:8
person's **t** except the spirit — 1 Cor 2:11
and discerning the **t** and — Heb 4:12

THREE
For just as Jonah was **t** — Mt 12:40
For where two or **t** are — Mt 18:20
'After **t** days I will rise.' — Mt 27:63
and love abide, these **t**; — 1 Cor 13:13
be only two or at most **t**, — 1 Cor 14:27
of two or **t** witnesses. — 2 Cor 13:1
For there are **t** that testify: — 1 Jn 5:7

THRONE
Your **t** shall be established — 2 Sm 7:16
Your **t**, O God, is forever and — Ps 45:6
nations; God sits on his holy **t**. — Ps 47:8
Your **t** is established from of — Ps 93:2
I saw the Lord sitting upon a **t**, — Is 6:1
then a **t** will be established in — Is 16:5
the Lord: "Heaven is my **t**, — Is 66:1
will sit on his glorious **t**, — Mt 19:28
draw near to the **t** of grace, — Heb 4:16
right hand of the **t** of God. — Heb 12:2
cast their crowns before the **t**, — Rv 4:10
Then I saw a great white **t** — Rv 20:11
but the **t** of God and of the — Rv 22:3

THROW
Son of God, **t** yourself down, — Mt 4:6
you be the first to **t** a stone at — Jn 8:7
Therefore do not **t** away — Heb 10:35

TIME
for such a **t** as this?" — Est 4:14
to you at a **t** when you may — Ps 32:6
this **t** forth and forevermore. — Ps 121:8
and a **t** for every matter — Eccl 3:1
everything beautiful in its **t**. — Eccl 3:11
for it is the **t** to seek the — Hos 10:12
at the right **t** Christ died for — Rom 5:6
But when the fullness of **t** — Gal 4:4
making the best use of the **t**, — Eph 5:16
will appear a second **t**, — Heb 9:28
for all **t** a single sacrifice — Heb 10:12
For it is **t** for judgment to — 1 Pt 4:17

TIMES
a stronghold in **t** of trouble. — Ps 9:9
I will bless the Lord at all **t**; — Ps 34:1
A friend loves at all **t**, and — Prv 17:17
him? As many as seven **t**?" — Mt 18:21
"It is not for you to know **t** — Acts 1:7
praying at all **t** in the Spirit, — Eph 6:18
Now concerning the **t** and — 1 Thes 5:1
will come **t** of difficulty. — 2 Tm 3:1

TIMOTHY
was there, named **T**, — Acts 16:1
T, my fellow worker, — Rom 16:21
entrust to you, **T**, my child, — 1 Tm 1:18
T has been released, — Heb 13:23

TITHE
"Every **t** of the land, is the — Lv 27:30
towns the **t** of your grain — Dt 12:17
the **t** of everything. — 2 Chr 31:5

TITHES
to the Lord from all your **t**, — Nm 18:28
In your **t** and contributions. — Mal 3:8
Bring the full **t** into the — Mal 3:10

TITUS
find my brother **T** there. — 2 Cor 2:13
As for **T**, he is my partner — 2 Cor 8:23

TODAY
my Son; **t** I have begotten you. — Ps 2:7
t you will be with me in — Lk 23:43
as long as it is called "**t**," — Heb 3:13
yesterday and **t** and forever. — Heb 13:8
Come now, you who say, "**T** — Jas 4:13

TOIL
grow: they neither **t** nor spin, — Mt 6:28
For to this end we **t** and — 1 Tm 4:10

TOMB
Therefore order the **t** to be — Mt 27:64
stone rolled away from the **t**, — Lk 24:2
and his **t** is with us to this — Acts 2:29

TOMORROW
Do not boast about **t**, for you — Prv 27:1
eat and drink, for **t** we die." — Is 22:13
do not be anxious about **t**, — Mt 6:34
yet you do not know what **t** — Jas 4:14

TONGUE
Keep your **t** from evil and — Ps 34:13
that I may not sin with my **t**; — Ps 39:1
and my **t** will sing aloud of — Ps 51:14
My **t** will sing of your — Ps 119:172
but the **t** of the wise brings — Prv 12:18
of kindness is on her **t**. — Prv 31:26
For one who speaks in a **t** — 1 Cor 14:2
The one who speaks in a **t** — 1 Cor 14:4
one who speaks in a **t** — 1 Cor 14:13
thousand words in a **t**. — 1 Cor 14:19
and every **t** confess that — Phil 2:11
bridle his **t** but deceives his — Jas 1:26
human being can tame the **t**. — Jas 3:8
let him keep his **t** from evil — 1 Pt 3:10

TONGUES
to gather all nations and **t**. — Is 66:18
And divided **t** as of fire — Acts 2:3
speak in other **t** as the Spirit — Acts 2:4
in **t** and extolling God. — Acts 10:46
in **t** and prophesying. — Acts 19:6
various kinds of **t**, — 1 Cor 12:10
Do all speak with **t**? Do all — 1 Cor 12:30
want you all to speak in **t**, — 1 Cor 14:5
come to you speaking in **t**, — 1 Cor 14:6
speak in **t** more than all — 1 Cor 14:18
not forbid speaking in **t**. — 1 Cor 14:39

TOOTH
eye for eye, **t** for **t**, foot — Ex 21:24
'An eye for an eye and a **t** — Mt 5:38

TORN
of the temple was **t** in two, — Mt 27:51

TORTURED
Some were **t**, refusing to — Heb 11:35

TOUCH
"**T** not my anointed ones, — Ps 105:15
T me, and see. For a spirit — Lk 24:39
and **t** no unclean thing; — 2 Cor 6:17
Do not taste, Do not **t**" — Col 2:21
and the evil one does not **t** — 1 Jn 5:18

TOUCHED
whose hearts God had **t**. — 1 Sm 10:26
And as many as **t** it were — Mt 14:36

TOWER
a city and a **t** with its top — Gn 11:4
a strong **t** against the enemy. — Ps 61:3
of the Lord is a strong **t**; — Prv 18:10

TRADITION
So for the sake of your **t** you — Mt 15:6
deceit, according to human **t**, — Col 2:8
the **t** that you received — 2 Thes 3:6

TRADITIONS
maintain the **t** even as I — 1 Cor 11:2
to the **t** that you were — 2 Thes 2:15

TRAIN
T up a child in the way he — Prv 22:6
Rather **t** yourself for — 1 Tm 4:7

TRAINED
being **t** in the words of the — 1 Tm 4:6
t by constant practice — Heb 5:14
who have been **t** by it. — Heb 12:11

TRAINING
for while bodily **t** is of some — 1 Tm 4:8
and for **t** in righteousness, — 2 Tm 3:16
t us to renounce ungodliness — Ti 2:12

TRANCE
and in a **t** I saw a vision, — Acts 11:5
the temple, I fell into a **t** — Acts 22:17

TRANSFERRED
of darkness and **t** us to the — Col 1:13

TRANSFIGURED
And he was **t** before them, — Mt 17:2

TRANSFORM
who will **t** our lowly body — Phil 3:21

TRANSFORMED
but be **t** by the renewal of — Rom 12:2
are being **t** into the same — 2 Cor 3:18

TRANSGRESSION
forgiving iniquity and **t** and — Ex 34:7
Blessed is the one whose **t** is — Ps 32:1
stricken for the **t** of my — Is 53:8
is no law there is no **t**. — Rom 4:15
if anyone is caught in any **t**, — Gal 6:1

TRANSGRESSIONS
Deliver me from all my **t**. — Ps 39:8
abundant mercy blot out my **t**. — Ps 51:1
For I know my **t**, and my sin — Ps 51:3
so far does he remove our **t** — Ps 103:12
he was wounded for our **t**; — Is 53:5
It was added because of **t**, — Gal 3:19
the **t** committed under the — Heb 9:15

TRANSGRESSORS
Then I will teach **t** your — Ps 51:13
was numbered with the **t**; — Is 53:12
makes intercession for the **t**. — Is 53:12

TREADING
ox when it is **t** out the grain. — Dt 25:4

TREADS
ox when it **t** out the grain." — 1 Cor 9:9
when it **t** out the grain," — 1 Tm 5:18

TREASURE
For where your **t** is, there — Mt 6:21
and you will have **t** in — Mt 19:21
But we have this **t** in jars — 2 Cor 4:7
thus storing up **t** for — 1 Tm 6:19

TREASURED
a people for his **t** possession, Dt 7:6
But Mary **t** up all these Lk 2:19

TREASURES
but lay up for yourselves **t** in Mt 6:20
in whom are hidden all the **t** Col 2:3

TREAT
You shall **t** the stranger Lv 19:34
T younger men like 1 Tm 5:1

TREE
The **t** of life was in the midst Gn 2:9
but of the **t** of the knowledge Gn 2:17
remain all night on the **t**, Dt 21:23
He is like a **t** planted by Ps 1:3
the righteous is a **t** of life, Prv 11:30
Every **t** therefore that does Mt 3:10
for the **t** is known by its Mt 12:33
who is hanged on a **t**" — Gal 3:13
sins in his body on the **t**, 1 Pt 2:24
the right to the **t** of life and Rv 22:14

TREMBLE
t before him, all the earth; 1 Chr 16:30
Lord reigns; let the peoples **t**! Ps 99:1

TREMBLING
with fear, and rejoice with **t**. Ps 2:11
him with fear and **t**. 2 Cor 7:15
salvation with fear and **t**, Phil 2:12

TRESPASS
If, because of one man's **t**, Rom 5:17
Rather through their **t** Rom 11:11

TRESPASSES
if you forgive others their **t**, Mt 6:14
t brought justification. Rom 5:16
the forgiveness of our **t**, Eph 1:7
And you were dead in the **t** Eph 2:1
when we were dead in our **t**, Eph 2:5
having forgiven us all our **t**, Col 2:13

TRIAL
remains steadfast under **t**, Jas 1:12
at the fiery **t** when it comes 1 Pt 4:12
the hour of **t** that is coming Rv 3:10

TRIALS
when you meet **t** of various Jas 1:2
been grieved by various **t**, 1 Pt 1:6
to rescue the godly from **t**, 2 Pt 2:9

TRIBES
All these are the twelve **t** Gn 49:28
from all **t** and peoples and Rv 7:9

TRIBULATION
then there will be great **t**, Mt 24:21
the world you will have **t**. Jn 16:33
Shall **t**, or distress, or Rom 8:35
in hope, be patient in **t**, Rom 12:12
coming out of the great **t**. Rv 7:14

TRIUMPHAL
leads us in **t** procession, 2 Cor 2:14

TRIUMPHING
by **t** over them in him. Col 2:15

TROUBLE
is few of days and full of **t**. Jb 14:1
a stronghold in times of **t**. Ps 9:9
a very present help in **t**. Ps 46:1
righteous is delivered from **t**, Prv 11:8
although man's **t** lies heavy Eccl 8:6
our salvation in the time of **t**. Is 33:2
a stronghold in the day of **t**; Na 1:7
for the day is its own **t**. Mt 6:34

TROUBLED
"Let not your hearts be **t**. Jn 14:1
Let not your hearts be **t**, Jn 14:27
no fear of them, nor be **t**, 1 Pt 3:14

TRUE
not come to pass or come **t**, Dt 18:22
all that he says comes **t**. 1 Sm 9:6
word of the Lord proves **t**; 2 Sm 22:31
your commandments are **t**. Ps 119:151
The **t** light, which enlightens Jn 1:9
"I am the **t** vine, and my Jn 15:1
that they know you the only **t** Jn 17:3
Let God be **t** though every Rom 3:4
brothers, whatever is **t**, Phil 4:8
serve the living and **t** God, 1 Thes 1:9
let us draw near with a **t** Heb 10:22
this is the **t** grace of God. 1 Pt 5:12
He is the **t** God and eternal 1 Jn 5:20
it is called Faithful and **T**, Rv 19:11
words are trustworthy and **t**." Rv 21:5

TRUMPET
For the **t** will sound, 1 Cor 15:52
the sound of the **t** of God. 1 Thes 4:16

TRUST
and put your **t** in the Lord. Ps 4:5
O my God, in you I **t**; let me Ps 25:2
and put their **t** in the Lord. Ps 40:3
am afraid, I put my **t** in you. Ps 56:3
me, for I **t** in your word. Ps 119:42
T in the Lord with all your Prv 3:5
T in the Lord forever, for the Is 26:4
Lord, whose **t** is the Lord. Jer 17:7
"I will put my **t** in him." Heb 2:13

TRUSTED
But I have **t** in your steadfast Ps 13:5
and I have **t** in the Lord Ps 26:1
his servants, who **t** in him, Dn 3:28

TRUSTS
"He **t** in the Lord; let him Ps 22:8
the one who **t** in the Lord. Ps 32:10
blessed is the one who **t** in Ps 84:12
Whoever **t** in his riches Prv 11:28
and blessed is he who **t** in Prv 16:20
but the one who **t** in the Prv 28:25
but whoever **t** in the Lord Prv 29:25
"Blessed is the man who **t** Jer 17:7
work but **t** him who justifies Rom 4:5

TRUSTWORTHY
Your decrees are very **t**; O Ps 93:5
just; all his precepts are **t**; Ps 111:7
"These words are **t** and true. Rv 22:6

TRUTH
Lead me in your **t** and teach Ps 25:5
Behold, you delight in **t** in Ps 51:6
that I may walk in your **t**; Ps 86:11
The sum of your word is **t**, Ps 119:160
I the Lord speak the **t**; I Is 45:19
Speak the **t** to one another; Zec 8:16
among us, full of grace and **t**. Jn 1:14
the Father in spirit and **t**, Jn 4:23
and the **t** will set you free." Jn 8:32
way, and the **t**, and the life. Jn 14:6
the Father, the Spirit of **t**, Jn 15:26
When the Spirit of **t** comes, Jn 16:13
in the truth; your word is **t**. Jn 17:17
said to him, "What is **t**?" Jn 18:38
unrighteousness suppress the **t** Rom 1:18
the **t** about God for Rom 1:25
but rejoices with the **t**. 1 Cor 13:6
do anything against the **t**, 2 Cor 13:8
so that the **t** of the gospel Gal 2:5
you from obeying the **t**? Gal 5:7
the **t** in love, we are to Eph 4:15
the **t** with his neighbor, Eph 4:25
fastened on the belt of **t**, Eph 6:14
to love the **t** and so be 2 Thes 2:10
Spirit and belief in the **t**. 2 Thes 2:13
to the knowledge of the **t**. 1 Tm 2:4
handling the word of **t**. 2 Tm 2:15
at a knowledge of the **t**. 2 Tm 3:7
the knowledge of the **t**, Heb 10:26
obedience to the **t** for a sincere 1 Pt 1:22
lie and do not practice the **t**. 1 Jn 1:6
and the **t** is not in us. 1 Jn 1:8
or talk but in deed and in **t**. 1 Jn 3:18
because the Spirit is the **t**. 1 Jn 5:6

TRUTHFUL
T lips endure forever, but a Prv 12:19
A **t** witness saves lives, Prv 14:25
by **t** speech, and the power 2 Cor 6:7

TRUTHFULNESS
circumcised to show God's **t**, Rom 15:8

TRUTHS
interpreting spiritual **t** to 1 Cor 2:13

TRY
Prove me, O Lord, and **t** me; Ps 26:2
T me and know my thoughts! Ps 139:23
and **t** to discern what is Eph 5:10

TUNIC
sue you and take your **t**, Mt 5:40

TURN
T from your burning anger Ex 32:12
You shall not **t** aside to the Dt 5:32
and if you do not **t** aside Dt 28:14
Do not **t** from it to the right Jos 1:7
and **t** from their wicked 2 Chr 7:14
will not **t** away his face 2 Chr 30:9
remember and **t** to the Lord, Ps 22:27
I do not **t** aside from your Ps 119:102
Lord, and **t** away from evil. Prv 3:7
You **t** things upside down! Is 29:16
when you **t** to the right or Is 30:21
"**T** to me and be saved, all Is 45:22
but that the wicked **t** from Ez 33:11
And he will **t** the hearts of Mal 4:6
cheek, **t** to him the other also. Mt 5:39
unless you **t** and become like Mt 18:3
therefore, and **t** again, Acts 3:19
that they may **t** from darkness Acts 26:18
and will **t** away from listening 2 Tm 4:4
let him **t** away from evil 1 Pt 3:11

TURNED
one who feared God and **t** Jb 1:1
we have **t** every one to his Is 53:6
Ephraim is a cake not **t**. Hos 7:8
The sun shall be **t** to darkness, Jl 2:31
the sun shall be **t** to Acts 2:20
who believed **t** to the Lord. Acts 11:21
All have **t** aside; together Rom 3:12

TWELVE
All these are the **t** tribes of Gn 49:28
And he called to him his **t** Mt 10:1

TWINKLING
in the **t** of an eye, at the 1 Cor 15:52

TWO-EDGED
sharper than any **t** sword, Heb 4:12
mouth came a sharp **t** sword, Rv 1:16

TYPE
who was a **t** of the one Rom 5:14

UNAPPROACHABLE
who dwells in **u** light, 1 Tm 6:16

UNAWARES
have entertained angels **u**. Heb 13:2

UNBELIEF
there, because of their **u**. Mt 13:58
marveled because of their **u**. Mk 6:6
said, "I believe; help my **u**!" Mk 9:24
and continued in **u**, Acts 19:9
off because of their **u**, Rom 11:20
do not continue in their **u**, Rom 11:23
had acted ignorantly in **u**, 1 Tm 1:13
to enter because of **u**. Heb 3:19

UNBELIEVER
has a wife who is an **u**, 1 Cor 7:12
a husband who is an **u**, 1 Cor 7:13
and an **u** or outsider 1 Cor 14:24
believer share with an **u**? 2 Cor 6:15
and is worse than an **u**. 1 Tm 5:8

UNBELIEVERS
brother, and that before **u**? 1 Cor 6:6
for **u** but for believers. 1 Cor 14:22
blinded the minds of the **u**, 2 Cor 4:4
unequally yoked with **u**. 2 Cor 6:14

UNBELIEVING
For the **u** husband is 1 Cor 7:14
pure, but to the defiled and **u**, Ti 1:15
any of you an evil, **u** heart, Heb 3:12

UNBORN
to a people yet **u**, Ps 22:31
them, the children yet **u**, Ps 78:6

UNCERTAINTY
hopes on the **u** of riches, 1 Tm 6:17

UNCHANGEABLE
But he is **u**, and who can Jb 23:13
the **u** character of his Heb 6:17
so that by two **u** things, Heb 6:18

UNCIRCUMCISED
with the gospel to the **u**, Gal 2:7
and Jew, circumcised and **u**, Col 3:11

UNCIRCUMCISION
counts for anything nor **u**, 1 Cor 7:19
nor **u** counts for anything, Gal 5:6

UNCLEAN
lost; for I am a man of **u** lips, Is 6:5
that nothing is **u** in itself, Rom 14:14
and touch no **u** thing; 2 Cor 6:17

UNDEFILED
let the marriage bed be **u**, Heb 13:4
Religion that is pure and **u** Jas 1:27
u, and unfading, 1 Pt 1:4

UNDERSTAND
uttered what I did not **u**, Jb 42:3
to see if there are any that **u**, Ps 14:2
Make me **u** the way of your Ps 119:27
minds to **u** the Scriptures, Lk 24:45
"Do you **u** what you are Acts 8:30
I do not **u** my own actions. Rom 7:15
and he is not able to **u** 1 Cor 2:14
but **u** what the will of the Eph 5:17
By faith we **u** that the Heb 11:3
in them that are hard to **u**, 2 Pt 3:16

UNDERSTANDING
Give me **u**, that I may keep Ps 119:34
do not lean on your own **u**. Prv 3:5
slow to anger has great **u**, Prv 14:29
To get **u** is to be chosen Prv 16:16
he who keeps **u** will Prv 19:8
wisdom, instruction, and **u**. Prv 23:23
and **u** to interpret dreams, Dn 5:12
God, which surpasses all **u**, Phil 4:7
Who is wise and **u** among Jas 3:13
come and has given us **u**, 1 Jn 5:20

UNDERSTANDS
and **u** every plan and 1 Chr 28:9
no one **u**; no one seeks for Rom 3:11
to God; for no one **u** him, 1 Cor 14:2
with conceit and **u** nothing. 1 Tm 6:4

UNDIVIDED
your **u** devotion to the 1 Cor 7:35

UNEQUALLY
Do not be **u** yoked with 2 Cor 6:14

UNFADING
undefiled, and **u**, kept in heaven 1 Pt 1:4
you will receive the **u** crown 1 Pt 5:4

UNFOLDING
The **u** of your words gives Ps 119:130

UNFRUITFUL
prays but my mind is **u**. 1 Cor 14:14
Take no part in the **u** Eph 5:11
of urgent need, and not be **u**. Ti 3:14

UNGODLINESS
u and unrighteousness of Rom 1:18
he will banish **u** from Rom 11:26
into more and more **u**, 2 Tm 2:16
training us to renounce **u** Ti 2:12

UNGODLY
him who justifies the **u**, Rom 4:5
time Christ died for the **u**. Rom 5:6
for the **u** and sinners, for 1 Tm 1:9
what will become of the **u** 1 Pt 4:18

UNITE
u my heart to fear your Ps 86:11
time, to **u** all things in him, Eph 1:10

UNITED
For if we have been **u** with Rom 6:5
but that you be **u** in the 1 Cor 1:10
because they were not **u** by Heb 4:2

UNITY
is when brothers dwell in **u**! Ps 133:1
eager to maintain the **u** of Eph 4:3
until we all attain to the **u** Eph 4:13
have **u** of mind, sympathy, 1 Pt 3:8

UNIVERSE
and he upholds the **u** by the Heb 1:3
that the **u** was created by Heb 11:3

UNJUST
rain on the just and on the **u**. Mt 5:45
of both the just and the **u**. Acts 24:15
For God is not so **u** as to Heb 6:10

UNLEAVENED
observe the feast of **u** bread, Ex 12:17

UNPROFITABLE
for they are **u** and worthless. Ti 3:9

UNPUNISHED
evil person will not go **u**, Prv 11:21
false witness will not go **u**, Prv 19:5

UNRIGHTEOUS
sins, the righteous for the **u**, 1 Pt 3:18
and to keep the **u** under 2 Pt 2:9

UNRIGHTEOUSNESS
who by their **u** suppress Rom 1:18
obey the truth, but obey **u**, Rom 2:8
But if our **u** serves to show Rom 3:5
but had pleasure in **u**. 2 Thes 2:12
tongue is a fire, a world of **u**. Jas 3:6
and to cleanse us from all **u**. 1 Jn 1:9

UNSEARCHABLE
and his greatness is **u**. Ps 145:3
his understanding is **u**. Is 40:28
How **u** are his judgments Rom 11:33
the **u** riches of Christ, Eph 3:8

UNSEEN
to the things that are **u**. 2 Cor 4:18
things that are **u** are eternal. 2 Cor 4:18

UNSTABLE
man, **u** in all his ways. Jas 1:8
which the ignorant and **u** 2 Pt 3:16

UNVEILED
And we all, with **u** face, 2 Cor 3:18

UNWISE
walk, not as **u** but as wise, Eph 5:15

UNWORTHY
say, 'We are **u** servants; Lk 17:10
in an **u** manner will be 1 Cor 11:27

UPHOLD
and **u** me with a willing Ps 51:12
U me according to your Ps 119:116
the contrary, we **u** the law. Rom 3:31

UPHOLDS
but the Lord **u** the Ps 37:17
The Lord **u** all who are Ps 145:14
and he **u** the universe by the Heb 1:3

UPRIGHT
that man was blameless and **u**, Jb 1:1
For the word of the Lord is **u**, Ps 33:4
up sound wisdom for the **u**; Prv 2:7
but the prayer of the **u** is Prv 15:8
u, holy, and disciplined. Ti 1:8
and to live self-controlled, **u**, Ti 2:12

UR
in **U** of the Chaldeans. Gn 11:28

URGE
u you to walk in a manner Eph 4:1
Teach and **u** these things. 1 Tm 6:2
Beloved, I **u** you as 1 Pt 2:11

URIAH
U said to David, "The ark 2 Sm 11:11
he assigned **U** to the 2 Sm 11:16
and they took **U** from Egypt Jer 26:23
of Solomon by the wife of **U**, Mt 1:6

USEFUL
u to the master of the 2 Tm 2:21

USELESS
faith apart from works is **u**? Jas 2:20

UTTER
I will **u** dark sayings from of Ps 78:2

UTTERANCE
as the Spirit gave them **u**. Acts 2:4
the Spirit the **u** of wisdom, 1 Cor 12:8

VAIN
of the Lord your God in **v**, Ex 20:7
rage, and the peoples plot in **v**? Ps 2:1
who build it labor in **v**. Ps 127:1
They shall not labor in **v** or Is 65:23
unless you believed in **v**. 1 Cor 15:2
your labor is not in **v**. 1 Cor 15:58
the grace of God in **v**. 2 Cor 6:1
did not run in **v** or labor in Phil 2:16

VALLEY
through the **v** of the shadow Ps 23:4
Every **v** shall be lifted up, Is 40:4
is near in the **v** of decision. Jl 3:14
Every **v** shall be filled, and Lk 3:5

VALUE
Are you not of more **v** than Mt 6:26
godliness is of **v** in every 1 Tm 4:8

VANITY
V of vanities, says the Preacher, Eccl 1:2

VARIETIES
Now there are **v** of gifts, 1 Cor 12:4

VARIOUS
to another **v** kinds of 1 Cor 12:10
when you meet trials of **v** Jas 1:2
you have been grieved by **v** 1 Pt 1:6

VEIL
And the **v** shall separate for Ex 26:33
he put a **v** over his face. Ex 34:33
that same **v** remains 2 Cor 3:14

VENGEANCE
For the Lord has a day of **v**, Is 34:8
"**V** is mine, I will repay, Rom 12:19
"**V** is mine; I will repay." Heb 10:30

VESSEL
lump one **v** for honored use Rom 9:21
he will be a **v** for honorable 2 Tm 2:21

VICTORY
until he brings justice to **v**; Mt 12:20
is swallowed up in **v**." 1 Cor 15:54
And this is the **v** that has 1 Jn 5:4

VINDICATED
the flesh, **v** by the Spirit, 1 Tm 3:16

VINE
"I am the true **v**, and my Jn 15:1

VIOLENCE
V shall no more be heard in Is 60:18
Put away **v** and oppression, Ez 45:9

VIOLENT
drunkard, not **v** but gentle, 1 Tm 3:3

VIRGIN
Behold, the **v** shall conceive Is 7:14
"Behold, the **v** shall conceive Mt 1:23
to a **v** betrothed to a man Lk 1:27
to present you as a pure **v** 2 Cor 11:2

VIRTUE
to supplement your faith with **v**, 2 Pt 1:5

VISIONS
your young men shall see **v**. Jl 2:28
young men shall see **v**, Acts 2:17

VISITATION
know the time of your **v**." Lk 19:44
glorify God on the day of **v**. 1 Pt 2:12

VOICE
Today, if you hear his **v**, Ps 95:7
lift up your **v** with strength, Is 40:9
in the tombs will hear his **v** Jn 5:28
The sheep hear his **v**, and he Jn 10:3

“Today, if you hear his **v**, Heb 3:7
If anyone hears my **v** and Rv 3:20

VOW
If a man vows a **v** to the Nm 30:2
When you **v** a **v** to God, Eccl 5:4

WAGES
the laborer deserves his **w**. Lk 10:7
his **w** are not counted as a Rom 4:4
For the **w** of sin is death, Rom 6:23
laborer deserves his **w**.” 1 Tm 5:18

WAIT
I **w** for your salvation, O Gn 49:18
W for the Lord; be strong, Ps 27:14
Be still before the Lord and **w** Ps 37:7
I **w** for the Lord, my soul Ps 130:5
but they who **w** for the Lord Is 40:31
but to **w** for the promise of Acts 1:4
groan inwardly as we **w** Rom 8:23
to eat, **w** for one another. 1 Cor 11:33
and to **w** for his Son 1 Thes 1:10

WAITED
I **w** patiently for the Lord; Ps 40:1
when God’s patience **w** in 1 Pt 3:20

WAITS
For the creation **w** with Rom 8:19

WALK
You shall **w** in all the way Dt 5:33
God, to **w** in all his ways, Dt 10:12
Even though I **w** through the Ps 23:4
from those who **w** uprightly. Ps 84:11
I will **w** before the Lord in Ps 116:9
Jacob, come, let us **w** in the light Is 2:5
“This is the way, **w** in it,” Is 30:21
they shall **w** and not faint. Is 40:31
the good way is; and **w** in it, Jer 6:16
and those who **w** in pride he Dn 4:37
“Do two **w** together, unless Am 3:3
and to **w** humbly with your Mi 6:8
me will not **w** in darkness, Jn 8:12
who **w** not according to the Rom 8:4
Let us **w** properly as in Rom 13:13
But I say, **w** by the Spirit, Gal 5:16
And **w** in love, as Christ Eph 5:2
carefully then how you **w**, Eph 5:15
so as to **w** in a manner Col 1:10
But if we **w** in the light, 1 Jn 1:7
And this is love, that we **w** 2 Jn 1:6

WALKED
Enoch **w** with God, and he Gn 5:24
Noah **w** with God. Gn 6:9
the boat and **w** on the water Mt 14:29
in which you once **w**, Eph 2:2

WALKING
the Lord God **w** in the garden Gn 3:8
w blamelessly in all the Lk 1:6
you are no longer **w** in Rom 14:15

WALKS
your God **w** in the midst Dt 23:14
Blessed is the man who **w** not Ps 1:1
Whoever **w** in uprightness Prv 14:2
Let him who **w** in darkness Is 50:10
The one who **w** in the Jn 12:35
and **w** in the darkness, 1 Jn 2:11

WALL
and the **w** fell down flat, Jos 6:20
Come, let us build the **w** of Neh 2:17
the dividing **w** of hostility Eph 2:14
It had a great, high **w**, with Rv 21:12

WANT
is my shepherd; I shall not **w**. Ps 23:1
For I do not do what I **w**, Rom 7:15

WANTING
in the balances and found **w**; Dn 5:27

WAR
a time to hate; a time for **w**, Eccl 3:8
neither shall they learn **w** Is 2:4
to the end there shall be **w**. Dn 9:26
waging **w** against the law Rom 7:23
we are not waging **w** 2 Cor 10:3
which wage **w** against your 1 Pt 2:11

WARFARE
For the weapons of our **w** 2 Cor 10:4
you may wage the good **w**, 1 Tm 1:18

WARN
But if you **w** the wicked, and Ez 3:19
But if you **w** the wicked to Ez 33:9
I **w** you, as I warned you Gal 5:21
but **w** him as a brother. 2 Thes 3:15

WARNED
by them is your servant **w**; Ps 19:11
him who **w** them on earth, Heb 12:25

WARS
He makes **w** cease to the end Ps 46:9
And you will hear of **w** and Mt 24:6

WASH
W me thoroughly from my Ps 51:2
and I shall be clean; **w** me, Ps 51:7
w your heart from evil, Jer 4:14
began to **w** the disciples’ feet Jn 13:5
and **w** away your sins, Acts 22:16
Blessed are those who **w** Rv 22:14

WASHED
But you were **w**, you were 1 Cor 6:11
bodies **w** with pure water. Heb 10:22
They have **w** their robes and Rv 7:14

WASHING
her by the **w** of water with Eph 5:26
by the **w** of regeneration and Ti 3:5

WATCH
“The Lord **w** between you Gn 31:49
keeping **w** on the evil and Prv 15:3
W therefore, for you know Mt 25:13
W and pray that you may Mt 26:41
keeping **w** over their flock by Lk 2:8
Keep **w** on yourself, lest you Gal 6:1
Keep a close **w** on yourself 1 Tm 4:16

WATCHFUL
Be **w**, stand firm in the 1 Cor 16:13
being **w** in it with Col 4:2
Be sober-minded; be **w**. Your 1 Pt 5:8

WATER
by streams of **w** that yields its Ps 1:3
I am poured out like **w**, Ps 22:14
Drink **w** from your own Prv 5:15
give him **w** to drink, Prv 25:21
and by springs of **w** will Is 49:10
is like a tree planted by **w**, Jer 17:8
“I baptize you with **w** for Mt 3:11
cup of cold **w** because he is Mt 10:42
unless one is born of **w** and Jn 3:5
have given you living **w**.” Jn 4:10
will flow rivers of living **w**.’” Jn 7:38
of **w** with the word, Eph 5:26
washed with pure **w**. Heb 10:22
formed out of **w** and through **w** 2 Pt 3:5
them to springs of living **w**, Rv 7:17

WATERED
waters will himself be **w**. Prv 11:25
I planted, Apollos **w**, but 1 Cor 3:6

WATERS
over the face of the **w**. Gn 1:2
He leads me beside still **w**. Ps 23:2
water, whose **w** do not fail. Is 58:11
the fountain of living **w**, Jer 2:13
nor he who **w** is anything, 1 Cor 3:7

WAVE
doubts is like a **w** of the sea Jas 1:6

WAVES
tossed to and fro by the **w** Eph 4:14

WAY
in the good and the right **w**. 1 Sm 12:23
his **w** is perfect; the word of 2 Sm 22:31
nor stands in the **w** of sinners, Ps 1:1
the **w** of the wicked will perish. Ps 1:6
his **w** is perfect; the word of the Ps 18:30
he instructs sinners in the **w**. Ps 25:8
Teach me your **w**, O Lord, Ps 27:11
Commit your **w** to the Lord; trust Ps 37:5
Teach me your **w**, O Lord, that I Ps 86:11
are those whose **w** is blameless, Ps 119:1
young man keep his **w** pure? Ps 119:9
me understand the **w** of your Ps 119:27
O Lord, the **w** of your statutes; Ps 119:33
there be any grievous **w** in me, Ps 139:24
will walk in the **w** of the good Prv 2:20
taught you the **w** of wisdom; Prv 4:11
do not walk in the **w** of the evil. Prv 4:14
The **w** of the wicked is like deep Prv 4:19
Keep your **w** far from her, Prv 5:8
arrogance and the **w** of evil Prv 8:13
I walk in the **w** of righteousness, Prv 8:20
w of the Lord is a stronghold Prv 10:29
w of a fool is right in his own, Prv 12:15
the **w** of the wicked leads them Prv 12:26
a **w** that seems right to a man, Prv 14:12
The **w** of the wicked is an Prv 15:9
w of a sluggard is like a hedge Prv 15:19
There is a **w** that seems right Prv 16:25
Every **w** of a man is right in his Prv 21:2
Train up a child in the **w** he Prv 22:6
This is the **w** of an adulteress: Prv 30:20
do not know the **w** the spirit Eccl 11:5
shall be called the **W** of Holiness; Is 35:8
“My **w** is hidden from the Lord, Is 40:27
leads you in the **w** you should go. Is 48:17
turned every one to his own **w**; Is 53:6
he will prepare the **w** before me. Mal 3:1
Jesus Christ took place in this **w**. Mt 1:18
‘Prepare the **w** of the Lord; Mt 3:3
the same **w**, let your light shine Mt 5:16
the gate is wide and the **w** is easy Mt 7:13
gate is narrow and the **w** is hard Mt 7:14
settle with him on the **w**, Lk 12:58
I must go on my **w** today Lk 13:33
while he was still a long **w** off, Lk 15:20
but truly teach the **w** of God. Lk 20:21
you know the **w** to where I am Jn 14:4
Jesus said to him, “I am the **w**, Jn 14:6
in the same **w** as you saw him Acts 1:11
found any belonging to the **W**, Acts 9:2
been instructed in the **w** of the Acts 18:25
persecuted this **W** to the death, Acts 22:4
you, that according to the **W**, Acts 24:14
(I speak in a human **w**.) Rom 3:5
hindrance in the **w** of a brother. Rom 14:13
also provide the **w** of escape, 1 Cor 10:13
same **w** also he took the cup, 1 Cor 11:25
you a still more excellent **w**. 1 Cor 12:31
does not insist on its own **w**; 1 Cor 13:5
We are afflicted in every **w**, 2 Cor 4:8
put no obstacle in anyone’s **w**, 2 Cor 6:3
is not the **w** you learned Christ! Eph 4:20
peace at all times in every **w**. 2 Thes 3:16
of mine; it is the **w** I write. 2 Thes 3:17
godliness is of value in every **w**, 1 Tm 4:8
they walked in the **w** of Cain Jude 1:11

WAYS
show me now your **w**, Ex 33:13
God, to walk in all his **w**, Dt 10:12
God, by walking in his **w**, Dt 30:16
For I have kept the **w** of 2 Sm 22:22
Make me to know your **w**, Ps 25:4
teach transgressors your **w**, Ps 51:13
In all your **w** acknowledge Prv 3:6
neither are your **w** my **w**, Is 55:8
for the **w** of the Lord are Hos 14:9
how inscrutable his **w**! Rom 11:33
we all stumble in many **w**, Jas 3:2

WEAK
willing, but the flesh is **w**.” Mt 26:41
For while we were still **w**, Rom 5:6
God chose what is **w** in 1 Cor 1:27
a stumbling block to the **w**. 1 Cor 8:9
To the **w** I became **w**, 1 Cor 9:22
For when I am **w**, then 2 Cor 12:10
strengthen your **w** knees, Heb 12:12

WEAKER
be **w** are indispensable, 1 Cor 12:22
the woman as the **w** vessel, 1 Pt 3:7

WEAKNESS
Spirit helps us in our **w**. Rom 8:26
and the **w** of God is stronger 1 Cor 1:25
power is made perfect in **w**.” 2 Cor 12:9
he himself is beset with **w**. Heb 5:2

WEAKNESSES
not boast, except of my **w**. 2 Cor 12:5
to sympathize with our **w**, Heb 4:15

WEALTH
Honor the Lord with your **w** Prv 3:9
who have **w** to enter the Mk 10:23

WEAPONS
with the **w** of righteousness 2 Cor 6:7
For the **w** of our warfare 2 Cor 10:4

WEARY
they shall run and not be **w**; Is 40:31
And let us not grow **w** of Gal 6:9
do not grow **w** in doing 2 Thes 3:13

WEDDING
who had no **w** garment. Mt 22:11
Jesus also was invited to the **w** Jn 2:2

WEEP
a time to **w**, and a time to Eccl 3:4
"Blessed are you who **w** now, Lk 6:21
w with those who **w**. Rom 12:15

WEEPING
W may tarry for the night, Ps 30:5
He who goes out **w**, bearing Ps 126:6
In that place there will be **w** Mt 8:12

WEPT
When I **w** and humbled my Ps 69:10
Jesus **w**. Jn 11:35

WEST
as the east is from the **w**, Ps 103:12

WHIRLWIND
Elijah up to heaven by a **w**, 2 Kgs 2:1
Job out of the **w** and said: Jb 38:1
and they shall reap the **w**. Hos 8:7
His way is in **w** and storm, Na 1:3

WHITE
they shall be as **w** as snow; Is 1:18
his clothing was **w** as snow, Dn 7:9
The hairs of his head were **w** Rv 1:14
they will walk with me in **w**, Rv 3:4
Then I saw a great **w** throne Rv 20:11

WHITER
and I shall be **w** than snow. Ps 51:7

WHOLE
to the Lord with my **w** heart; Ps 9:1
who seek him with their **w** Ps 119:2
for this is the **w** duty of Eccl 12:13
the **w** world and forfeits Mt 16:26
the **w** world as a testimony Mt 24:14
you the **w** counsel of God. Acts 20:27
and the **w** world may be Rom 3:19
For we know that the **w** Rom 8:22
obligated to keep the **w** law. Gal 5:3
Put on the **w** armor of God, Eph 6:11
For whoever keeps the **w** Jas 2:10
for the sins of the **w** world. 1 Jn 2:2

WICKED
not in the counsel of the **w**, Ps 1:1
Therefore the **w** will not stand Ps 1:5
the **w** will be no more; he Ps 37:10
but all the **w** he will Ps 145:20
the heart of the **w** is of Prv 10:20
but the lamp of the **w** will Prv 13:9
grave with the **w** and with a Is 53:9
let the **w** forsake his way, Is 55:7
But the **w** are like the Is 57:20
nor speak to warn the **w** Ez 3:18
in the death of the **w**, Ez 18:23
though I say to the **w**, Ez 33:14
For everyone who does **w** Jn 3:20

WIDE
For the gate is **w** and the Mt 7:13

WIDOW
for the fatherless and the **w**, Dt 10:18
and he saw a poor **w** put in Lk 21:2

WIDOWS
Honor **w** who are truly 1 Tm 5:3
to visit orphans and **w** in Jas 1:27

WIFE
and hold fast to his **w**, Gn 2:24
not covet your neighbor's **w**, Ex 20:17
and rejoice in the **w** of your Prv 5:18
An excellent **w** is the crown Prv 12:4
but a prudent **w** is from Prv 19:14
a quarrelsome **w** are alike; Prv 27:15
An excellent **w** who can Prv 31:10
everyone who divorces his **w**, Mt 5:32
own **w** and each woman 1 Cor 7:2
should not divorce his **w**. 1 Cor 7:11
of the **w** even as Christ Eph 5:23
of you love his **w** as himself, Eph 5:33
the husband of one **w**, 1 Tm 3:2
Bride, the **w** of the Lamb." Rv 21:9

WILLING
and uphold me with a **w** Ps 51:12
The spirit indeed is **w**, but Mt 26:41

WILLINGLY
subjected to futility, not **w**, Rom 8:20
not under compulsion, but **w**, 1 Pt 5:2

WILL
I **w** make him a helper fit for Gn 2:18
the woman, "You **w** not surely die. Gn 3:4
I **w** put enmity between you and Gn 3:15
whoever finds me **w** kill me." Gn 4:14
Lord said, "I **w** blot out man Gn 6:7
I **w** destroy them with the earth. Gn 6:13
"I **w** never again curse the Gn 8:21
I **w** make of you a great nation, Gn 12:2
w bless you and make your name Gn 12:2
I **w** bless those who bless you, Gn 12:3
w surely multiply your offspring Gn 16:10
And I **w** establish my covenant Gn 17:7
I **w** give you a son by her. Gn 17:16
w make him into a great nation. Gn 17:20
I **w** spare the whole place for Gn 18:26
w you kill an innocent people? Gn 20:4
I **w** make a nation of the son Gn 21:13
Abraham said, "God **w** provide Gn 22:8
"I **w** draw water for your camels Gn 24:19
w multiply your offspring as the Gn 26:4
"If God **w** be with me and **w** Gn 28:20
"I **w** serve you seven years Gn 29:18
Then we **w** say that a fierce Gn 37:20
w come seven years of great Gn 41:29
boy is not with us, he **w** die, Gn 44:31
I **w** make you fruitful and Gn 48:4
I **w** send you to Pharaoh that you Ex 3:10
go, and I **w** be with your Ex 4:12
But I **w** harden his heart, so that Ex 4:21
No straw **w** be given you, but Ex 5:18
Thus I **w** put a division between Ex 8:23
long **w** you refuse to humble Ex 10:3
and I **w** strike all the firstborn Ex 12:12
And I **w** harden Pharaoh's heart, Ex 14:4
I **w** send an angel before you, Ex 33:2
"I **w** make all my goodness Ex 33:19
on whom I **w** show mercy. Ex 33:19
w write on the tablets the words Ex 34:1
I **w** drive out before you the Ex 34:11
I **w** make my dwelling among Lv 26:11
And I **w** lay your cities waste Lv 26:31
I **w** remember my covenant Lv 26:42
the Lord **w** give you meat, Nm 11:18
We **w** not turn aside into field Nm 21:22
there you **w** serve gods of wood Dt 4:28
He **w** love you, bless you, Dt 7:13
I **w** raise up for them a prophet Dt 18:18
with Moses, so I **w** be with you. Jos 1:5
I myself **w** drive them out from Jos 13:6
my house, we **w** serve the Lord." Jos 24:15
For where you go I **w** go, Ru 1:16
I **w** give him to the Lord all the 1 Sm 1:11
Spirit of the Lord **w** rush upon 1 Sm 10:6
w not cast away his people, 1 Sm 12:22
I **w** make for you a great name, 2 Sm 7:9
David said, "I **w** deal loyally 2 Sm 10:2
lion, **w** utterly melt with fear, 2 Sm 17:10
I **w** surely tear the kingdom 1 Kgs 11:11
Whoever **w** not obey the law Ezr 7:26
Our God **w** fight for us." Neh 4:20
"We **w** not give our daughters Neh 10:30
man has he **w** give for his life. Jb 2:4
I **w** not restrain my mouth; Jb 7:11
I **w** complain in the bitterness Jb 7:11
'Hear, and I **w** speak; I **w** Jb 42:4
the way of the wicked **w** perish. Ps 1:6
How long **w** you love vain words Ps 4:2
In peace I **w** both lie down Ps 4:8
in Sheol who **w** give you praise? Ps 6:5
W you forget me forever? Ps 13:1
yourself in the Lord, and he **w** Ps 37:4
"I **w** guard my ways, that I may Ps 39:1
I desire to do your **w**, O my God; Ps 40:8
Man in his pomp **w** not remain; Ps 49:12
w teach transgressors your ways, Ps 51:13
you **w** not delight in sacrifice, Ps 51:16
I **w** sing praises to you among Ps 57:9
w render to a man according Ps 62:12
I **w** not set before my eyes Ps 101:3
Teach me to do your **w**, for you Ps 143:10
highly, and she **w** exalt you; Prv 4:8
Do not say, "I **w** repay evil"; Prv 20:22
lamp of the wicked **w** be put Prv 24:20
He who digs a pit **w** fall into it, Eccl 10:8
Ahaz said, "I **w** not ask, and I Is 7:12
zeal of the Lord of hosts **w** do this. Is 9:7
word of our God **w** stand forever. Is 40:8
w gather the lambs in his arms; Is 40:11
To whom then **w** you liken God, Is 40:18
I **w** make all his ways level; Is 45:13
"To whom **w** you liken me Is 46:5
Israel, in whom I **w** be glorified." Is 49:3
I **w** make you as a light for the Is 49:6
the **w** of the Lord to crush him; Is 53:10
I **w** make a new covenant with Jer 31:31
I **w** put my law within them, Jer 31:33
w pour out my Spirit on all flesh; Jl 2:28
he **w** turn the hearts of fathers Mal 4:6
She **w** bear a son, and you shall Mt 1:21
you **w** fall down and worship me." Mt 4:9
who sees in secret **w** reward you. Mt 6:4
kingdom come, your **w** be done, Mt 6:10
"Ask, and it **w** be given to you; Mt 7:7
the one who does the **w** of my Mt 7:21
that place there **w** be weeping Mt 8:12
I also **w** acknowledge before my Mt 10:32
you that it **w** be more tolerable Mt 11:24
does the **w** of my Father Mt 12:50
would save his life **w** lose it, Mt 16:25
last **w** be first, and the first last." Mt 20:16
not as I **w**, but as you **w**." Mt 26:39
I drink it, your **w** be done." Mt 26:42
"The Holy Spirit **w** come upon Lk 1:35
not to do my own **w** but the **w** Jn 6:38
this is the **w** of him who sent me, Jn 6:39
any one's **w** is to do God's **w**, Jn 7:17
you free, you **w** be free indeed. Jn 8:36
one of his bones **w** be broken." Jn 19:36
w pour out my Spirit on all flesh, Acts 2:17
w raise up for you a prophet Acts 7:37
discern what is the **w** of God, Rom 12:2
what the **w** of the Lord Eph 5:17
who works in you, both to **w** Phil 2:13
For this is the **w** of God, your 1 Thes 4:3
the **w** of God in Christ Jesus 1 Thes 5:18
Yet she **w** be saved through 1 Tm 2:15
captured by him to do his **w**. 2 Tm 2:26
distributed according to his **w**. Heb 2:4
For where a **w** is involved, Heb 9:16
a **w** takes effect only at death, Heb 9:17
come to do your **w**, O God,' Heb 10:7
good that you may do his **w**, Heb 13:21
"Today or tomorrow we **w** go Jas 4:13
we **w** live and do this or that." Jas 4:15
good, if that should be God's **w**, 1 Pt 3:17
passions but for the **w** of God. 1 Pt 4:2
ever produced by the **w** of man, 2 Pt 1:21
according to his **w** he hears us. 1 Jn 5:14
and by your **w** they existed Rv 4:11
They **w** need no light of lamp Rv 22:5

WILLS
mercy on whomever he **w**, Rom 9:18
to you soon, if the Lord **w**, 1 Cor 4:19
one individually as he **w**. 1 Cor 12:11
ought to say, "If the Lord **w**, Jas 4:15

WIN
that I might **w** more of 1 Cor 9:19
that I might **w** the weak. 1 Cor 9:22
but may **w** a full reward. 2 Jn 1:8

WIND
like a mighty rushing **w**, Acts 2:2
by every **w** of doctrine, Eph 4:14
is driven and tossed by the **w**. Jas 1:6

WINE
W is a mocker, strong drink Prv 20:1
For your love is better than **w**; Sg 1:2
Come, buy **w** and milk Is 55:1
Neither is new **w** put into Mt 9:17
the water now become **w**, Jn 2:9
are filled with new **w**." Acts 2:13

or drink **w** or do anything Rom 14:21
do not get drunk with **w**, Eph 5:18
not addicted to much **w**, 1 Tm 3:8
but use a little **w** for the 1 Tm 5:23

WINESKINS
is new wine put into old **w**. Mt 9:17

WINGS
under whose **w** you have Ru 2:12
me in the shadow of your **w**, Ps 17:8
they shall mount up with **w** Is 40:31
rise with healing in its **w**. Mal 4:2
her brood under her **w**, Lk 13:34

WIPE
and the Lord God will **w** Is 25:8
He will **w** away every tear Rv 21:4

WISDOM
for that will be your **w** and Dt 4:6
And God gave Solomon **w** 1 Kgs 4:29
and you teach me **w** in the Ps 51:6
Lord is the beginning of **w**; Ps 111:10
For the Lord gives **w**; from Prv 2:6
Lord is the beginning of **w**, Prv 9:10
opens her mouth with **w**, Prv 31:26
the world by his **w**, Jer 10:12
Yet **w** is justified by her Mt 11:19
And Jesus increased in **w** Lk 2:52
and **w** and knowledge of Rom 11:33
For the **w** of this world is 1 Cor 3:19
may give you a spirit of **w** Eph 1:17
If any of you lacks **w**, let him Jas 1:5
But the **w** from above is first Jas 3:17

WISE
Behold, I give you a **w** 1 Kgs 3:12
is sure, making **w** the simple; Ps 19:7
Be not **w** in your own eyes; Prv 3:7
hate you; reprove a **w** man, Prv 9:8
A **w** son makes a glad father, Prv 10:1
captures souls is **w**. Prv 11:30
Whoever walks with the **w** Prv 13:20
silent is considered **w**; Prv 17:28
but they are exceedingly **w**: Prv 30:24
And those who are **w** shall Dn 12:3
w men from the east came to Mt 2:1
w and understanding and Mt 11:25
Claiming to be **w**, they Rom 1:22
Lest you be **w** in your Rom 11:25
the world to shame the **w**; 1 Cor 1:27
that he is **w** in this age, 1 Cor 3:18
but you are **w** in Christ. 1 Cor 4:10
w for salvation through 2 Tm 3:15

WISER
of God is **w** than men, 1 Cor 1:25

WITHER
season, and its leaf does not **w**. Ps 1:3

WITHERS
The grass **w**, the flower fades Is 40:7
The grass **w**, and the flower 1 Pt 1:24

WITHHOLD
No good thing does he **w** Ps 84:11
Do not **w** discipline from a Prv 23:13
"Can anyone **w** water for Acts 10:47

WITNESS
"You shall not bear false **w** Ex 20:16
A truthful **w** saves lives, Prv 14:25
You shall not bear false **w**, Mt 19:18
but came to bear **w** about the Jn 1:8
conscience also bears **w**, Rom 2:15
The Spirit himself bears **w** Rom 8:16
Spirit also bears **w** to us; Heb 10:15
Jesus Christ the faithful **w**, Rv 1:5

WITNESSES
of two **w** or of three Dt 19:15
and you will be my **w** in Acts 1:8
of two or three **w**. 1 Tm 5:19
in the presence of many **w**. 1 Tm 6:12
by so great a cloud of **w**, Heb 12:1

WIVES
W, submit to your own Eph 5:22
Husbands, love your **w**, as Eph 5:25
love their **w** as their own Eph 5:28
Their **w** likewise must be 1 Tm 3:11
Likewise, **w**, be subject to 1 Pt 3:1

WOLF
The **w** shall dwell with the Is 11:6
The **w** and the lamb shall Is 65:25
sees the **w** coming and Jn 10:12

WOMAN
into a **w** and brought her Gn 2:22
between you and the **w**, Gn 3:15
"A **w** shall not wear a man's Dt 22:5
that you are a worthy **w**. Ru 3:11
but a **w** who fears the Lord Prv 31:30
at a **w** with lustful intent Mt 5:28
brought a **w** who had been Jn 8:3
Thus a married **w** is bound Rom 7:2
but **w** is the glory of man. 1 Cor 11:7
in the Lord **w** is not 1 Cor 11:11
sent forth his Son, born of **w**, Gal 4:4
Let a **w** learn quietly with 1 Tm 2:11
showing honor to the **w** as 1 Pt 3:7

WOMB
I came from my mother's **w**, Jb 1:21
and from my mother's **w** Ps 22:10
took me from my mother's **w**. Ps 71:6
together in my mother's **w**. Ps 139:13
his mother's **w** he shall go Eccl 5:15
"Before I formed you in the **w** Jer 1:5
even from his mother's **w**. Lk 1:15
his mother's **w** and be born?" Jn 3:4

WOMEN
"Blessed are you among **w**, Lk 1:42
the **w** should keep silent 1 Cor 14:34
likewise also that **w** should 1 Tm 2:9
Older **w** likewise are to be Ti 2:3
For this is how the holy **w** 1 Pt 3:5

WONDERFUL
things too **w** for me, Jb 42:3
I will recount all of your **w** Ps 9:1
Your testimonies are **w**; Ps 119:129
Such knowledge is too **w** Ps 139:6
W are your works; my soul Ps 139:14
Three things are too **w** for Prv 30:18
and his name shall be called **W** Is 9:6
for you have done **w** things, Is 25:1

WONDERFULLY
for I am fearfully and **w** Ps 139:14

WONDERS
I will remember your **w** of Ps 77:11
who alone does great **w**, Ps 136:4
his signs, how mighty his **w**! Dn 4:3
"And I will show **w** in the Jl 2:30
And I will show **w** in the Acts 2:19
and **w** and various miracles Heb 2:4

WOOD
down before a block of **w**?" Is 44:19
stones, **w**, hay, straw — 1 Cor 3:12

WORD
After these things the **w** of Gn 15:1
but man lives by every **w** that Dt 8:3
For it is no empty **w** for you, Dt 32:47
his way is perfect; the **w** 2 Sm 22:31
For the **w** of the Lord is Ps 33:4
mighty ones who do his **w**, Ps 103:20
I have stored up your **w** in Ps 119:11
salvation; I hope in your **w**. Ps 119:81
Your **w** is a lamp to my Ps 119:105
but a good **w** makes him Prv 12:25
Every **w** of God proves true; Prv 30:5
so shall my **w** be that goes Is 55:11
but by every **w** that comes Mt 4:4
And he was preaching the **w** Mk 2:2
In the beginning was the **W**, Jn 1:1
And the **W** became flesh and Jn 1:14
whoever hears my **w** and Jn 5:24
in the truth; your **w** is truth. Jn 17:17
his **w** were baptized, Acts 2:41
to the ministry of the **w**." Acts 6:4
through the **w** of Christ. Rom 10:17
For the **w** of the cross is 1 Cor 1:18
if you hold fast to the **w** I 1 Cor 15:2
law is fulfilled in one **w**: Gal 5:14
One who is taught the **w** Gal 6:6
when you heard the **w** of Eph 1:13
washing of water with the **w**, Eph 5:26
which is the **w** of God, Eph 6:17
to speak the **w** without fear. Phil 1:14
holding fast to the **w** of life, Phil 2:16
Let the **w** of Christ dwell in Col 3:16
you do, in **w** or deed, giving Col 3:17
rightly handling the **w** of 2 Tm 2:15
preach the **w**; be ready in 2 Tm 4:2
For the **w** of God is living Heb 4:12
created by the **w** of God, Heb 11:3
But be doers of the **w**, and Jas 1:22
living and abiding **w** of God; 1 Pt 1:23
And this **w** is the good 1 Pt 1:25
because they disobey the **w**, 1 Pt 2:8
more sure, the prophetic **w**, 2 Pt 1:19
concerning the **w** of life — 1 Jn 1:1
and the **w** of God abides in 1 Jn 2:14
who bore witness to the **w** of Rv 1:2

WORDS
shall therefore lay up these **w** Dt 11:18
Give ear to my **w**, O Lord; Ps 5:1
words of the Lord are pure **w**, Ps 12:6
your ear to me; hear my **w**. Ps 17:6
is no speech, nor are there **w**, Ps 19:3
Let the **w** of my mouth and the Ps 19:14
sweet are your **w** to my taste, Ps 119:103
Lord is faithful in all his **w** Ps 145:13
My son, if you receive my **w** Prv 2:1
My son, be attentive to my **w**; Prv 4:20
but my **w** will not pass away. Mt 24:35
disciples were amazed at his **w**. Mk 10:24
You have the **w** of eternal life, Jn 6:68
in me, and my **w** abide in you, Jn 15:7
with **w** of eloquent wisdom, 1 Cor 1:17
impart this in **w** not taught by 1 Cor 2:13
I would rather speak five **w** 1 Cor 14:19
never came with **w** of flattery, 1 Thes 2:5
with the healthy **w** of our Lord 1 Tm 6:3
the pattern of the healthy **w** 2 Tm 1:13
the one who reads aloud the **w** Rv 1:3
the one who keeps the **w** of Rv 22:7
anyone takes away from the **w** Rv 22:19

WORK
finished his **w** that he had Gn 2:2
days you shall do your **w**, Ex 23:12
you in all the **w** of your hands. Dt 2:7
On it you shall not do any **w**, Dt 5:14
who does the **w** of the Lord Jer 48:10
them, "This is the **w** of God, Jn 6:29
We must **w** the works of him Jn 9:4
each one's **w** will become 1 Cor 3:13
according to the power at **w** Eph 3:20
that he who began a good **w** Phil 1:6
w out your own salvation Phil 2:12
you do, **w** heartily, Col 3:23
which is at **w** in you 1 Thes 2:13
every good **w** and word. 2 Thes 2:17
equipped for every good **w**. 2 Tm 3:17
your **w** and the love Heb 6:10

WORKER
What gain has the **w** from Eccl 3:9
give to this last **w** as I give Mt 20:14
a **w** who has no need to 2 Tm 2:15

WORKERS
For we are God's fellow **w**. 1 Cor 3:9

WORKING
but only faith **w** through love. Gal 5:6
according to the **w** of his Eph 1:19
me by the **w** of his power. Eph 3:7
w in us that which is Heb 13:21

WORKMANSHIP
For we are his **w**, created in Eph 2:10

WORKS
over the **w** of your hands; Ps 8:6
The Lord **w** righteousness Ps 103:6
Remember the wondrous **w** Ps 105:5
and let her **w** praise her in Prv 31:31
not because of **w** but Rom 9:11
no longer on the basis of **w**; Rom 11:6
not justified by **w** of the law Gal 2:16
the Spirit by **w** of the law Gal 3:2
not a result of **w**, so that no Eph 2:9
in Christ Jesus for good **w**, Eph 2:10
for it is God who **w** in you, Phil 2:13
So also good **w** are 1 Tm 5:25
good, to be rich in good **w**, 1 Tm 6:18
not because of our **w** but 2 Tm 1:9
to be a model of good **w**, Ti 2:7
he saved us, not because of **w** Ti 3:5
to love and good **w**, Heb 10:24

your faith apart from your **w**, Jas 2:18
so also faith apart from **w** is Jas 2:26

WORLD
the foundations of the **w** 2 Sm 22:16
yes, the **w** is established; 1 Chr 16:30
and he judges the **w** with Ps 9:8
for the **w** and its fullness Ps 50:12
He will judge the **w** with Ps 98:9
I will punish the **w** for its Is 13:11
"You are the light of the **w**. Mt 5:14
but the cares of the **w** and Mt 13:22
the whole **w** and forfeits his Mt 16:26
the whole **w** as a testimony Mt 24:14
the foundation of the **w**, Lk 11:50
was coming into the **w**. Jn 1:9
takes away the sin of the **w**! Jn 1:29
"For God so loved the **w**, that Jn 3:16
into the **w** to condemn the Jn 3:17
indeed the Savior of the **w**." Jn 4:42
"I am the light of the **w**. Jn 8:12
I have come into the **w** as Jn 12:46
you are not of the **w**, Jn 15:19
In the **w** you will have Jn 16:33
I have sent them into the **w**. Jn 17:18
is proclaimed in all the **w**. Rom 1:8
and the whole **w** may be Rom 3:19
not be conformed to this **w**, Rom 12:2
the **w** did not know God 1 Cor 1:21
For the wisdom of this **w** 1 Cor 3:19
reconciling the **w** to himself, 2 Cor 5:19
by which the **w** has been Gal 6:14
the foundation of the **w**, Eph 1:4
and without God in the **w**. Eph 2:12
into the **w** to save sinners, 1 Tm 1:15
whom also he created the **w**. Heb 1:2
from the foundation of the **w**. Heb 4:3
with the **w** is enmity with Jas 4:4
of the **w** but was made 1 Pt 1:20
for the sins of the whole **w**. 1 Jn 2:2
Do not love the **w** or the 1 Jn 2:15
than he who is in the **w**. 1 Jn 4:4
of the **w** in the book Rv 13:8

WORLDLY
ungodliness and **w** passions, Ti 2:12

WORSHIP
there and **w** and come again Gn 22:5
W the Lord in the splendor 1 Chr 16:29
nations shall **w** before you. Ps 22:27
w the Lord in the splendor of Ps 29:2
come, let us **w** and bow down; Ps 95:6
W the Lord in the splendor Ps 96:9
serve and **w** any god except Dn 3:28
rose and have come to **w** him." Mt 2:2
"'You shall **w** the Lord your Lk 4:8
him must **w** in spirit and Jn 4:24
which is your spiritual **w**. Rom 12:1
offer to God acceptable **w**, Heb 12:28
throne and **w** him who lives Rv 4:10
All nations will come and **w** Rv 15:4
words of this book. **W** God." Rv 22:9

WORTH
Man does not know its **w**, Jb 28:13
of the wicked is of little **w**. Prv 10:20
not **w** comparing with the Rom 8:18
w of knowing Christ Phil 3:8

WORTHLESS
A **w** man plots evil, and his Prv 16:27
they have become **w**; Rom 3:12
they are unprofitable and **w**. Ti 3:9
this person's religion is **w**. Jas 1:26

WORTHY
who is **w** to be praised, 2 Sm 22:4
Lord, who is **w** to be praised, Ps 18:3
in a manner **w** of the calling Eph 4:1
of life be **w** of the gospel Phil 1:27
if there is anything **w** of Phil 4:8
so as to walk in a manner **w** Col 1:10
make you **w** of his calling 2 Thes 1:11
considered **w** of double honor, 1 Tm 5:17
journey in a manner **w** of God. 3 Jn 1:6
"**W** are you, our Lord and Rv 4:11
saying with a loud voice, "**W** Rv 5:12

WOUNDS
Faithful are the **w** of a Prv 27:6
'What are these **w** on your Zec 13:6
By his **w** you have been 1 Pt 2:24

WRATH
until the **w** of the Lord 2 Chr 36:16
he will speak to them in his **w**, Ps 2:5
Surely the **w** of man shall Ps 76:10
kings on the day of his **w**. Ps 110:5
A soft answer turns away **w**, Prv 15:1
this cup of the wine of **w**, Jer 25:15
For the **w** of God is Rom 1:18
by him from the **w** of God. Rom 5:9
by nature children of **w**, Eph 2:3
things the **w** of God comes Eph 5:6
On account of these the **w** of Col 3:6
has not destined us for **w**, 1 Thes 5:9

WRESTLE
For we do not **w** against Eph 6:12

WRESTLED
And a man **w** with him Gn 32:24

WRETCHED
W man that I am! Who will Rom 7:24

WRITE
You shall **w** them on the Dt 6:9
w them on the tablet of your Prv 3:3
and **w** them on their hearts, Heb 8:10

WRITINGS
if you do not believe his **w**, Jn 5:47
w has been made Rom 16:26
with the sacred **w**, 2 Tm 3:15

WRITTEN
w with the finger of God. Ex 31:18
according to all that is **w** in it. Jos 1:8
shall be found **w** in the book. Dn 12:1
names are **w** in heaven." Lk 10:20
but these are **w** so that you Jn 20:31
not to go beyond what is **w**, 1 Cor 4:6
w not with ink but with 2 Cor 3:3
and who keep what is **w** in it, Rv 1:3
not found **w** in the book Rv 20:15
but only those who are **w** Rv 21:27

WRONG
Love does no **w** to a Rom 13:10
back for the **w** he has done, Col 3:25

WRONGDOING
it does not rejoice at **w**, 1 Cor 13:6
All **w** is sin, but there is 1 Jn 5:17

YEAR
Three times in the **y** shall Ex 34:23
once in the **y** because of all Lv 16:34
but in the seventh **y** there Lv 25:4
That fiftieth **y** shall be a Lv 25:11
every **y** at the feast Lk 2:41
For a whole **y** they met Acts 11:26
continually offered every **y**, Heb 10:1

YEARNS
My soul **y** for you in the Is 26:9
Therefore my heart **y** for Jer 31:20

YES
but let your "**y**" be **y** and Jas 5:12

YESTERDAY
Jesus Christ is the same **y** Heb 13:8

YIELDS
of water that **y** its fruit in Ps 1:3
He indeed bears fruit and **y**, Mt 13:23
but later it **y** the peaceful Heb 12:11

YOKE
Take my **y** upon you, and Mt 11:29
For my **y** is easy, and my Mt 11:30
submit again to a **y** of slavery. Gal 5:1
Let all who are under a **y** 1 Tm 6:1

YOKED
Do not be unequally **y** 2 Cor 6:14

YOUNG
How can a **y** man keep his Ps 119:9
The glory of **y** men is their Prv 20:29
and your **y** men shall see Jl 2:28
and your **y** men shall see Acts 2:17
and so train the **y** women to Ti 2:4

YOUTH
heart is evil from his **y**. Gn 8:21
that your **y** is renewed like Ps 103:5
May our sons in their **y** be Ps 144:12
and discretion to the **y** — Prv 1:4
rejoice in the wife of your **y**, Prv 5:18
in the days of your **y**, Eccl 12:1
to the wife of your **y**. Mal 2:15
one despise you for your **y**, 1 Tm 4:12

YOUTHFUL
So flee **y** passions and 2 Tm 2:22

ZACCHAEUS
there was a man named **Z**. Lk 19:2

ZEAL
and see my **z** for the 2 Kgs 10:16
For **z** for your house has Ps 69:9
My **z** consumes me, Ps 119:139
The **z** of the Lord of hosts will Is 9:7
"**Z** for your house will Jn 2:17
that they have a **z** for God, Rom 10:2
the one who leads, with **z**; Rom 12:8
Do not be slothful in **z**, Rom 12:11
as to **z**, a persecutor of the Phil 3:6

ZEALOT
Simon who was called the **Z**, Lk 6:15

ZEALOUS
being **z** for God as all of Acts 22:3
who are **z** for good works. Ti 2:14
you if you are **z** for what is 1 Pt 3:13
discipline, so be **z** and repent. Rv 3:19

ZEBEDEE
in the boat with **Z** their Mt 4:21
of the sons of **Z** came up to Mt 20:20

ZEBULUN
So she called his name **Z**. Gn 30:20
Z shall dwell at the shore Gn 49:13

ZECHARIAH
and **Z** his son reigned in 2 Kgs 14:29
Uriah the priest and **Z** the son Is 8:2
Lord came to the prophet **Z**, Zec 1:7
there was a priest named **Z**, Lk 1:5
And his father **Z** was filled Lk 1:67

ZEDEKIAH
changed his name to **Z**. 2 Kgs 24:17
sons of **Z** before his eyes, 2 Kgs 25:7

ZEPHANIAH
Z the priest read this letter Jer 29:29

ZERUBBABEL
is the word of the Lord to **Z**: Zec 4:6

ZEUS
Barnabas they called **Z**, Acts 14:12
And the priest of **Z**, whose Acts 14:13

ZION
city of David, which is **Z**. 1 Kgs 8:1
and out of Mount **Z** a 2 Kgs 19:31
city of David, which is **Z**. 2 Chr 5:2
The Lord is great in **Z**; he is Ps 99:2
us one of the songs of **Z**!" Ps 137:3
For out of **Z** shall go the law, Is 2:3
and come to **Z** with singing; Is 35:10
O **Z**, herald of good news; Is 40:9
I will put salvation in **Z**, Is 46:13
a Redeemer will come to **Z**, Is 59:20
Say to the daughter of **Z**, Is 62:11
land: "Is the Lord not in **Z**? Jer 8:19
Blow a trumpet in **Z**; Jl 2:1
The Lord roars from **Z**, and Jl 3:16
Sing aloud, O daughter of **Z**; Zep 3:14
I have returned to **Z** and will Zec 8:3
"Say to the daughter of **Z**, Mt 21:5
I am laying in **Z** a stone of Rom 9:33
to Mount **Z** and to the Heb 12:22
on Mount **Z** stood the Lamb, Rv 14:1

ZIPPORAH
gave Moses his daughter **Z**. Ex 2:21

ZOAR
Now Lot went up out of **Z** Gn 19:30
Moab; her fugitives flee to **Z**, Is 15:5
from **Z** to Horonaim and Jer 48:34